The Middle East
and
North Africa
2014

The Middle East and North Africa 2014

60th Edition

Routledge
Taylor & Francis Group
LONDON AND NEW YORK

60th edition published 2013
by Routledge
2 Park Square, Milton Park, Abingdon, Oxon, OX14 4RN

and by Routledge
711 Third Avenue, New York, NY 10017

Routledge is an imprint of the Taylor & Francis Group, an Informa business

First published 1948

ISBN: 978-1-85743-697-6
ISSN: 0076-8502

Typeset in New Century Schoolbook
by Data Standards Limited, Frome, Somerset
Printed and bound by Polestar Wheatons Limited, Exeter, Devon

FSC
www.fsc.org
MIX
Paper from responsible sources
FSC® C020872

FOREWORD

This edition of THE MIDDLE EAST AND NORTH AFRICA, the 60th in print, provides comprehensive coverage of political and economic life at the regional, sub-regional and national levels. The volume is divided into three separate, though complementary, sections. In Part One a collection of introductory essays addresses the most pertinent issues affecting the region, including the growing influence of political Islam and its intellectual origins, and concerns over nuclear proliferation. In Part Two specialist authors, researchers and commentators examine in detail the main political and economic events in each of the countries and territories in the region. In addition, all statistical and directory material has been thoroughly updated. Extensive coverage of international organizations and research bodies active in the Middle East and North Africa is included in a section of Regional Information, together with bibliographies of essential books and journals. A calendar of the key political events of 2012–13 enables rapid reference to the year's main developments.

The year under review was marked by the escalation of the civil conflict between government forces and armed opposition groups in Syria, and by political change across the region. In early August 2013 the Office of the UN High Commissioner for Refugees reported that more than 2m. people had fled Syria since the outbreak of conflict in February 2011. Moreover, later in August 2013 more than 1,400 people were reported to have been killed in missile attacks on areas surrounding the capital, Damascus. It was later confirmed by UN inspectors that the nerve agent sarin had been used in the attack, prompting vehement international criticism and a UN Security Council Resolution in September binding Syria to disclose and destroy its chemical weapons arsenal.

Meanwhile, Egyptian President Muhammad Mursi, who had been elected just one year earlier in the country's first freely contested presidential election, was deposed and detained by the armed forces in July 2013, following mass protests in the capital, Cairo, by groups opposed to his rule. An interim President, Adli Mahmoud Mansour, was appointed and hundreds of supporters of Mursi's Muslim Brotherhood movement were killed or detained by the authorities. In Tunisia, similar protests against that country's Islamist-led Government persisted into late September, prompting talks over the formation of an interim, non-partisan administration to oversee early legislative elections. Elsewhere in the region, Hassan Rouhani secured an overwhelming victory at the Iranian presidential election in May 2013, while in June Sheikh Tamim bin Hamad Al Thani became Amir of Qatar, following his father's abdication. There were also changes of government in Algeria, Cyprus, Israel, Jordan, Kuwait, Libya, Morocco and the Palestinian Territories.

The entire content of the print edition of THE MIDDLE EAST AND NORTH AFRICA is available online at www.europaworld.com. This prestigious resource incorporates sophisticated search and browse functions as well as specially commissioned visual and statistical content. An ongoing programme of updates of key areas of information ensures currency of content, and enhances the richness of the coverage.

The Editors are grateful to all the contributors for their articles and advice, and to the numerous governments and organizations that provided statistical and other information.

September 2013

ACKNOWLEDGEMENTS

The Editors gratefully acknowledge the interest and co-operation of all the contributors to this volume, and of numerous national statistical and information offices, and government departments, as well as embassies in London and throughout the region, whose kind assistance in updating the material contained in THE MIDDLE EAST AND NORTH AFRICA is greatly appreciated.

We acknowledge particular indebtedness for permission to reproduce material from the following publications: the United Nations' statistical databases and *Demographic Yearbook, Statistical Yearbook, Monthly Bulletin of Statistics, Industrial Commodity Statistics Yearbook* and *International Trade Statistics Yearbook*; the United Nations Educational, Scientific and Cultural Organization's *Statistical Yearbook* and Institute for Statistics database; the Human Development Report of the United Nations Development Programme; the Food and Agriculture Organization of the United Nations' statistical database; the statistical databases of the UNCTAD/WTO International Trade Centre; the statistical databases of the World Health Organization; the International Labour Office's statistical database and *Yearbook of Labour Statistics*; the World Bank's *World Bank Atlas, Global Development Finance, World Development Report* and *World Development Indicators* database; the International Monetary Fund's statistical database, *International Financial Statistics* and *Government Finance Statistics Yearbook*; the World Tourism Organization's *Compendium* and *Yearbook of Tourism Statistics*; the US Geological Survey; the International Telecommunication Union; the United Nations Economic and Social Commission for Western Asia's *National Accounts Studies of the ESCWA Region*; Lloyd's List; and *The Military Balance 2013*, a publication of the International Institute for Strategic Studies, Arundel House, 13–15 Arundel Street, London WC2R 3DX, United Kingdom. We are also grateful to the Israeli embassy, London, for the use of two maps illustrating the disengagement agreements between Israel and Egypt, and Israel and Syria (both 1974).

The following publications have been of special value in providing regular coverage of the affairs of the Middle East and North Africa region: *Middle East Economic Digest*; and *Keesing's Record of World Events*.

HEALTH AND WELFARE STATISTICS: SOURCES AND DEFINITIONS

Total fertility rate Source: WHO Statistical Information System. The number of children that would be born per woman, assuming no female mortality at child-bearing ages and the age-specific fertility rates of a specified country and reference period.

Under-5 mortality rate Source: WHO Statistical Information System. Defined by WHO as the probability of a child born in a specific year or period dying before reaching the age of five, if subject to the age-specific mortality rates of the year or period.

HIV/AIDS Source: UNAIDS. Estimated percentage of adults aged 15 to 49 years living with HIV/AIDS. < indicates 'fewer than'.

Health expenditure Source: WHO Statistical Information System.

US $ per head (PPP)

International dollar estimates, derived by dividing local currency units by an estimate of their purchasing-power parity (PPP) compared with the US dollar. PPPs are the rates of currency conversion that equalize the purchasing power of different currencies by eliminating the differences in price levels between countries.

% of GDP

GDP levels for OECD countries follow the most recent UN System of National Accounts. For non-OECD countries a value was estimated by utilizing existing UN, IMF and World Bank data.

Public expenditure

Government health-related outlays plus expenditure by social schemes compulsorily affiliated with a sizeable share of the population, and extrabudgetary funds allocated to health services. Figures include grants or loans provided by international agencies, other national authorities, and sometimes commercial banks.

Access to water and sanitation Source: WHO/UNICEF Joint Monitoring Programme on Water Supply and Sanitation (JMP) (Progress on Drinking Water and Sanitation, 2012 update). Defined in terms of the percentage of the population using improved facilities in terms of the type of technology and levels of service afforded. For water, this includes house connections, public standpipes, boreholes with handpumps, protected dug wells, protected spring and rainwater collection; allowance is also made for other locally defined technologies. Sanitation is defined to include connection to a sewer or septic tank system, pour-flush latrine, simple pit or ventilated improved pit latrine, again with allowance for acceptable local technologies. Access to water and sanitation does not imply that the level of service or quality of water is 'adequate' or 'safe'.

Carbon dioxide emissions Source: World Bank, World Development Indicators database, citing the Carbon Dioxide Information Analysis Center (sponsored by the US Department of Energy). Emissions comprise those resulting from the burning of fossil fuels (including those produced during consumption of solid, liquid and gas fuels and from gas flaring) and from the manufacture of cement.

Human Development Index (HDI) Source: UNDP, *Human Development Report* (2012). A summary of human development measured by three basic dimensions: prospects for a long and healthy life, measured by life expectancy at birth; knowledge, measured by adult literacy rate (two-thirds' weight) and the combined gross enrolment ratio in primary, secondary and tertiary education (one-third weight); and standard of living, measured by GDP per head (PPP US $). The index value obtained lies between zero and one. A value above 0.796 indicates very high human development, between 0.710 and 0.796 high human development, between 0.534 and 0.710 medium human development, and below 0.534 low human development. A centralized data source for all three dimensions was not available for all countries. In some cases other data sources were used to calculate a substitute value; however, this was excluded from the ranking. Other countries, including non-UNDP members, were excluded from the HDI altogether. In total, 186 countries were ranked for 2012.

CONTENTS

PART THREE

Regional Information

REGIONAL ORGANIZATIONS

THE CONTRIBUTORS

Ahmed Aghrout. Research Fellow, School of Humanities, Languages and Social Sciences, University of Salford, United Kingdom.

Khalid Almezaini. Lecturer in Politics and International Relations of the Gulf States, Qatar University, Doha, Qatar, and Visiting Research Fellow, London School of Economics, United Kingdom.

Liam Anderson. Professor of Political Science, Wright State University, Dayton, Ohio, USA.

Sara Bazoobandi. Lecturer in International Political Economy, Regent's University, London, United Kingdom, and Associate Fellow, Royal Institute of International Affairs (Chatham House), London, United Kingdom.

Dana Blander. Research Fellow, The Israel Democracy Institute, Jerusalem, Israel.

Simon Chapman. Editor of *The Middle East and North Africa*, 1989–97.

Charles Charalambous. Independent communications consultant and journalist; formerly Financial Correspondent for the *Cyprus Mail*.

Jill Crystal. Professor, Department of Political Science, Auburn University, Auburn, Alabama, USA.

Richard German. Writer and researcher on international political and economic affairs.

Gareth Jenkins. Non-resident Senior Fellow with the Silk Road Studies Program, based in İstanbul, Turkey.

George Joffé. Lecturer on the Middle East and North Africa, Department of Politics and International Studies, University of Cambridge, United Kingdom, and former deputy director of the Royal Institute of International Affairs (Chatham House), London, United Kingdom.

Kimberly Jones. Lecturer in International Affairs, and Faculty Associate, Middle East Center for Peace, Culture and Development, Northeastern University, Boston, Massachusetts, USA.

Nur Masalha. Professor of Religion and Politics, and Director of the Centre for Religion and History, School of Theology, Philosophy and History, St Mary's University College, Twickenham, United Kingdom.

Philip McCrum. Analyst of the political and economic affairs of the Middle East, and Editorial Director, Continental Europe, Middle East and Africa, The Economist Group, Dubai, United Arab Emirates.

Gerd Nonneman. Dean and Professor of International Politics and Gulf Studies, Georgetown University School of Foreign Service in Qatar, and Associate Editor of *The Journal of Arabian Studies* (Routledge).

Nigel Parsons. Senior Lecturer, Politics Programme, Massey University, Palmerston North, New Zealand.

Neil Partrick. Writer and consultant on the Gulf and wider Middle East.

J. E. Peterson. Historian and political analyst specializing in the contemporary Arabian Peninsula and Gulf, and former historian of the Sultan's Armed Forces of Oman.

Christopher Phillips. Lecturer in the International Relations of the Middle East, Queen Mary, University of London, United Kingdom.

David Roberts. Lecturer, King's College London, United Kingdom, and former Director of the Qatar office of the Royal United Services Institute for Defence and Security Studies.

Jalil Roshandel. Associate Professor, Political Science and Security Studies, East Carolina University, Greenville, North Carolina, USA.

Adham Saouli. Lecturer in Politics and International Relations, University of Edinburgh, United Kingdom.

Moin Siddiqi. Independent economist specializing in macroeconomic developments and the banking sector in the Middle East and Africa; also advises on trends in petroleum markets.

Aurora Sottimano. Lecturer, Department of Political Studies, British University in Egypt, Cairo, Egypt, and Fellow of the Centre for Syrian Studies, University of St Andrews, United Kingdom.

Richard Spencer. A retired senior officer with extensive battlefield and legal experience of low intensity conflict. He writes particularly on the evolving nature of Law of Armed Conflict.

Ronald Bruce St John. Independent scholar specializing in the political economy of developing states, including Libya.

Denis J. Sullivan. Professor of Political Science, and Director of Middle East Center for Peace, Culture and Development, Northeastern University, Boston, Massachusetts, USA.

Elizabeth Taylor. Writer and researcher on international political and economic affairs.

Mehmet Uğur. Professor of Economics and Institutions, University of Greenwich Business School, London, United Kingdom.

Marc Valeri. Senior Lecturer in Political Economy of the Middle East and Director of the Centre for Gulf Studies, University of Exeter, United Kingdom.

James H. Wyllie. Visiting Scholar, Alfred von Oppenheim Center for European Policy Studies, Deutsche Gesellschaft für Auswärtige Politik e.V. (German Council on Foreign Relations), Berlin, Germany, and Reader in International Relations, School of Social Science, King's College, University of Aberdeen, United Kingdom.

Yahia Zoubir. Professor of International Relations and International Management, KEDGE Business School, France.

ABBREVIATIONS

AAHO	Afro-Asian Housing Organization
AAPSO	Afro-Asian People's Solidarity Organization
Acad.	Academy
AD	Algerian dinars
AD	anno Domini
ADC	Aide-de-camp
Adm.	Admiral
AED	UAE dirhams
Admin.	Administrative, Administration, Administrator
Admin.-Gen	Administrator-General
AfDB	African Development Bank
Agric.	Agriculture
AH	anno Hegirae (year of the Hegira)
a.i.	ad interim
AIDS	acquired immunodeficiency syndrome
AIWO	Agudath Israel World Organization
ALF	Arab Liberation Front
AM	Amplitude Modulation
a.m.	ante meridiem (before noon)
Apdo	Apartado (Post Box)
API	American Petroleum Institute
approx.	approximately
apptd	appointed
ARE	Arab Republic of Egypt
AŞ	Anonim Şirketi (Joint-Stock Company)
Ass.	Assembly
asscn	association
Assoc.	Associate
Asst	Assistant
AU	African Union
auth.	authorized
Ave	Avenue
Avda	Avenida
BADEA	Banque arabe pour le développement economique en Afrique (Arab Bank for Economic Development in Africa)
BC	before Christ
b/d	barrels per day
BD	Bahrain dinars
Bd	Board
Bde	Brigade
Bldg	Building
Blvd	Boulevard
BP	Boîte Postale (Post Box)
br.(s)	branch(es)
Brig.	Brigadier
BST	British Standard Time
Bul.	Bulvar (Boulevard)
C	Centigrade
c.	circa
Cad.	Caddesi (Street)
CAFRAD	Centre africain de formation et de recherches administratives pour le développement
cap.	capital
Capt.	Captain
CARE	Co-operative for American Relief Everywhere
Cdre	Commodore
CE	Common era
cen.	central
CEN-SAD	Community of Sahel-Saharan States
CEO	Chief Executive Officer
cf.	confer (compare)
Chair.	Chairman/person/woman
Cie	Compagnie (Company)
c.i.f.	cost, insurance and freight
C-in-C	Commander-in-Chief
circ.	circulation
CIS	Commonwealth of Independent States
cm	centimetre(s)
CMEA	Council for Mutual Economic Assistance
CNG	compressed natural gas
cnr	corner
c/o	care of
Co	Company
Col	Colonel
Comm.	Commission
Commdr	Commander
Commdt	Commandant
Commr	Commissioner
Conf.	Conference
Confed.	Confederation
Cons.-Gen.	Consul-General
COO	Chief Operating Officer
Corpn	Corporation
Cttee	Committee
cu	cubic
cwt	hundredweight
Del.	Delegate, Delegation
Dep.	Deputy
dep.	deposits
Dept	Department
Devt	Development
DFLP	Democratic Front for the Liberation of Palestine
Dir	Director
Div.	Division
DPA	Deutsche Presse-Agentur
Dr	Doctor
dcha	derecha (right)
DU	depleted uranium
dwt	dead weight tons
E	East, Eastern
EC	European Community
ECOSOC	Economic and Social Council (UN)
ECU	European Currency Unit(s)
Ed.(s)	Editor(s)
edn	edition
EFTA	European Free Trade Association
e.g.	exempli gratia (for example)
ELA	emergency liquidity assistance
Eng.	Engineer
est.	established; estimate(d)
excl.	excluding
EU	European Union
Exec.	Executive
F	Fahrenheit
f.	founded
FAO	Food and Agriculture Organization
FAPS	Framework Agreement on Permanent Status
FDI	foreign direct investment
Fed.	Federal, Federation
Flt	Flight
FM	Frequency Modulation
fmr(ly)	former(ly)
f.o.b.	free on board
Fr.	Franc
ft	foot (feet)
g	gram(s)
GAFTA	Greater Arab Free Trade Agreement
GATT	General Agreements on Tariffs and Trade
GCC	Gulf Cooperation Council
GDP	gross domestic product
GEF	Gobal Environment Facility
Gen.	General
GHQ	General Headquarters
GMT	Greenwich Mean Time
GNP	gross national product
Gov.	Governor
Govt	Government
GRE	Government-related entity
grt	gross registered ton(s)
GSM	Global System for Mobile Communications
GW	gigawatt(s)
GWh	gigawatt hour(s)
ha	hectare(s)
HE	His (or Her) Excellency, His Eminence
HIV	human immunodeficiency virus
hl	hectolitre(s)
HLTF	High Level Task Force
HM	His (or Her) Majesty
Hon.	Honorary; Honourable
HQ	Headquarters
HRH	His (or Her) Royal Highness
IAEA	International Atomic Energy Agency

IATA	International Air Transport Association
ibid	ibidem (from the same source)
IBRD	International Bank for Reconstruction and Development
ICAO	International Civil Aviation Organization
ICATU	International Conference of Arab Trade Unions
ICT	Information and Communication Technologies
ID	new Iraqi dinars
IDA	International Development Association
IDF	Israel(i) Defence Forces
i.e.	id est (that is to say)
IFC	International Finance Corporation
IISS	International Institute of Strategic Studies
ILO	International Labour Office/Organization
IMF	International Monetary Fund
in(s)	inch(es)
Inc	Incorporated
incl.	include, including
Ind.	Independent
Insp.	Inspector
Inst.	Institute; Institution
Int.	International
IPO	initial public offering
IR	Iranian rials
IRF	International Road Federation
Is	Islands
ISIC	International Standard Industrial Classification
IT	information technology
ITU	International Telecommunication Union
ITUC	International Trade Union Confederation
IUU	illegal, unreported and unregulated
izqda	izquierda (left)
JD	Jordanian dinars
Jr	Junior
Jt	Joint
KD	Kuwaiti dinars
kg	kilogram(s)
KFAED	Kuwait Fund for Arab Economic Development
km	kilometre(s)
kV	kilovolt(s)
kW	kilowatt(s)
kWh	kilowatt hour(s)
lb	pound(s)
LD	Libyan dinars
Legis.	Legislative
LNG	liquefied natural gas
Lot	Lotissement
LPG	liquefied petroleum gas
Lt	Lieutenant
Ltd	Limited
m	metre(s)
m.	million
MAFTA	Mediterranean Arab Free Trade Area
Mah.	Mahallesi (district)
Maj.	Major
Man.	Manager, Managing
MB	Bachelor of Medicine
MD	Doctor of Medicine
mem.(s)	member(s)
Mfg	Manufacturing
Mgr	Monseigneur, Monsignor
Mil.	Military
MINURSO	United Nations Mission for the Referendum in Western Sahara
mm	millimetre(s)
MOC	memorandum of co-operation
MOU	memorandum of understanding
MP	Member of Parliament
MSS	Manuscripts
Mt	Mount
MTBE	methyl tertiary butyl ether
MW	megawatt(s); medium wave
MWh	megawatt hour(s)
N	North, Northern
n.a.	not available
Nat.	National
NATO	North Atlantic Treaty Organization
NE	North-East
NEPAD	New Partnership for Africa's Development
n.e.s.	not elsewhere specified
NGLs	natural gas liquids
NGO(s)	non-governmental organization(s)
n.i.e.	not included elsewhere
NIS	new Israeli shekels
no.	number
NPT	Non-Proliferation Treaty
nr	near
nrt	net registered ton(s)
NTC	National Transitional Council
NW	North-West
OAPEC	Organization of Arab Petroleum Exporting Countries
OAU	Organization of African Unity
OECD	Organisation for Economic Co-operation and Development
OIC	Organization of Islamic Cooperation (previously Organization of the Islamic Conference)
OPEC	Organization of the Petroleum Exporting Countries
Org.(s)	Organization(s)
oz	ounce(s)
p.	page
PA	Palestinian Authority
p.a.	per annum
Parl.	Parliament(ary)
PCC	Palestinian Central Council
Perm.	Permanent
Perm. Rep.	Permanent Representative
PFLP	Popular Front for the Liberation of Palestine
PhD	Doctor of Philosophy
PLC	Palestinian Legislative Council; Public Limited Company
PLO	Palestine Liberation Organization
p.m.	post meridiem (after noon)
PNC	Palestine National Council
POB	Post Office Box
PPP	purchasing-power parity
PRSP	Poverty Reduction Strategy Paper
Pres.	President
Prof.	Professor
Propr	Proprietor
Pty	Proprietary
p.u.	paid up
publ.(s)	publication(s), published, publishes
Publr	Publisher
QE	Qatar Exchange
QIA	Qatar Investment Authority
QR	Qatari riyals
q.v.	quod vide (to which refer)
RCC	Revolutionary Command Council (Iraq, Libya)
RCD	Regional Co-operation for Development
Rd	Road
RDA	Rassemblement démocratique africain
REC	regional economic communities
regd	registered
Rep.	Representative
Repub.	Republic
res	reserves
retd	retired
Rev.	Reverend
RO	rial Omani
ro-ro	roll-on roll-off
S	South, Southern
SBA(s)	Sovereign Base Area(s)
SDR(s)	special drawing right(s)
SE	South-East
Sec.	Secretary
Secr.	Secretariat
SITC	Standard International Trade Classification
Soc.	Society; Société
Sok.	Sokak (Street)
SpA	Società per Azioni (Limited Company)
sq	square (in measurements)
Sq.	Square
SR	Saudi riyals
Sr	Senior
St	Saint; Street
STL	Special Tribunal for Lebanon
Stn	Station
subs.	subscribed
Supt	Superintendent
SW	South-West
Tapline	Trans-Arabian Pipeline Company
TAŞ	Türk Anonim Şirketi (Turkish Joint-Stock Company)
TD	Tunisian dinars
tel.	telephone
TEU	20-ft equivalent unit
TL	Turkish lira

trans.	translated; translation
Treas.	Treasurer
TV	Television
UA	Unit(s) of Account
UAE	United Arab Emirates
UAR	United Arab Republic
UBAF	Union des banques arabes et françaises
UHF	Ultra High Frequency
UK	United Kingdom
UN	United Nations
UNAIDS	United Nations Joint Programme on HIV/AIDS
UNCTAD	United Nations Conference on Trade and Development
UNDOF	United Nations Disengagement Observer Force
UNDP	United Nations Development Programme
UNEF	United Nations Emergency Force
UNEP	United Nations Environment Programme
UNESCO	United Nations Educational, Scientific and Cultural Organization
UNFICYP	United Nations Peace-keeping Force in Cyprus
UNFPA	United Nations Population Fund
UNICEF	United Nations Children's Fund
UNIDO	United Nations Industrial Development Organization
UNIFIL	United Nations Interim Force in Lebanon
Univ.	University
UNMEM	United Nations Middle East Mission
UNMOVIC	United Nations Monitoring, Verification and Inspection Commission
UNRWA	United Nations Relief and Works Agency for Palestine Refugees in the Near East
UNSCOM	United Nations Special Commission
UNTSO	United Nations Truce Supervision Organization
UNWTO	World Tourism Organization
UPAF	Union Postale Africaine (African Postal Union)
UP	University Press
UPI	United Press International
USA (US)	United States of America (United States)
USAID	US Agency for International Development
USIS	United States Information Services
USSR	Union of Soviet Socialist Republics
UTA	Union de Transports Aériens
VAT	value-added tax
VHF	Very High Frequency
vol.(s)	volume(s)
W	West, Western
WFTU	World Federation of Trade Unions
WHO	World Health Organization
WSSD	World Summit on Sustainable Development
WTI	West Texas Intermediate
WTO	World Tourism Organization; World Trade Organization
YR	Yemeni riyals
yr	year

INTERNATIONAL TELEPHONE CODES

To make international calls to telephone and fax numbers listed in THE MIDDLE EAST AND NORTH AFRICA, dial the international code of the country from which you are calling, followed by the appropriate country code for the organization you wish to call (listed below), followed by the area code (if applicable) and telephone or fax number listed in the entry.

	Country code	+ GMT*
Algeria	213	+1
Bahrain	973	+3
Cyprus	357	+2
'Turkish Republic of Northern Cyprus'	90 392	+2
Egypt	20	+2
Iran	98	+3½
Iraq	964	+3
Israel	972	+2
Jordan	962	+2
Kuwait	965	+3
Lebanon	961	+2
Libya	218	+1
Morocco	212	0
Oman	968	+4
Palestinian Territories	970 or 972	+2

	Country code	+ GMT*
Qatar	974	+3
Saudi Arabia	966	+3
Spain (for Spanish North Africa)	34	+1
Syria	963	+2
Tunisia	216	+1
Turkey	90	+2
United Arab Emirates	971	+4
Yemen	967	+3

* Time difference in hours + Greenwich Mean Time (GMT). The times listed compare the standard (winter) times. Some countries adopt Summer (Daylight Saving) Times—i.e. + 1 hour—for part of the year.

Note: Telephone and fax numbers using the Inmarsat ocean region code 870 are listed in full. No country or area code is required, but it is necessary to precede the number with the international access code of the country from which the call is made.

EXPLANATORY NOTE ON THE DIRECTORY SECTION

The Directory section of each chapter is arranged under the following headings, where they apply:

THE CONSTITUTION

THE GOVERNMENT
- HEAD OF STATE
- CABINET/COUNCIL OF MINISTERS
- MINISTRIES

LEGISLATURE

ELECTION COMMISSION

POLITICAL ORGANIZATIONS

DIPLOMATIC REPRESENTATION

JUDICIAL SYSTEM

RELIGION

THE PRESS

PUBLISHERS

BROADCASTING AND COMMUNICATIONS
- TELECOMMUNICATIONS
- RADIO
- TELEVISION

FINANCE
- CENTRAL BANK
- STATE BANKS
- COMMERCIAL BANKS
- DEVELOPMENT BANKS
- INVESTMENT BANKS
- SAVINGS BANKS
- ISLAMIC BANKS
- FOREIGN BANKS
- SOVEREIGN WEALTH FUNDS
- STOCK EXCHANGE
- INSURANCE

TRADE AND INDUSTRY
- GOVERNMENT AGENCIES
- DEVELOPMENT ORGANIZATIONS
- CHAMBERS OF COMMERCE AND INDUSTRY
- INDUSTRIAL AND TRADE ASSOCIATIONS
- EMPLOYERS' ASSOCIATIONS
- HYDROCARBONS
- UTILITIES
- HOLDING COMPANIES
- MAJOR COMPANIES
- CO-OPERATIVES
- TRADE UNIONS

TRANSPORT
- RAILWAYS
- ROADS
- INLAND WATERWAYS
- SHIPPING
- CIVIL AVIATION

TOURISM

DEFENCE

EDUCATION

TRANSCRIPTION OF ARABIC NAMES

The Arabic language is used over a vast area. Though the written language and the script are standard throughout the Middle East, the spoken language and also the pronunciation of the written signs exhibit wide variation from place to place. This is reflected, and even exaggerated, in the different transcriptions in use in different countries. The same words, names and even letters will be pronounced differently by an Egyptian, a Lebanese or an Iraqi—they will be heard and transcribed differently by an Englishman, a Frenchman or an Italian. There are several more or less scientific systems of transliteration in use, sponsored by learned societies and Middle Eastern governments, most of them requiring diacritical marks to indicate Arabic letters for which there are no Latin equivalents.

Arabic names occurring in the historical and geographical sections of this book have been rendered in the system most commonly used by British and American Orientalists, but with the omission of the diacritical signs. For the convenience of the reader, these are explained and annotated below. The system used is a transliteration—i.e. it is based on the writing, which is standard throughout the Arab world, and not on the pronunciation, which varies from place to place. In a few cases consistency has been sacrificed in order to avoid replacing a familiar and accepted form by another which, although more accurate, would be unrecognizable.

Consonants

d represents two Arabic letters. The second, or emphatic *d*, is transliterated *ḍ*. It may also be represented, for some dialects, by *dh* and by *z*, e.g. Qāḍī, qadhi, qazi.

dh in literary Arabic and some dialects, pronounced like English *th* in *this*. In many dialects pronounced *z* or *d*.

gh A strongly guttural *g*—sometimes written *g*, e.g. Baghdād, Bagdad.

h represents two Arabic letters. The second, more guttural *h*, is transliterated *ḥ*, e.g. Ḥusain, Husein.

j as English *j* in *John*, also represented by *dj* and *g*. In Egypt this letter is pronounced as a hard *g*, and may be thus transcribed (with *u* before *e* and *i*), e.g. Najib, Nadjib, Nagib, Naguib, Neguib.

kh as *ch* in Scottish *loch*, also sometimes represented by *ch* and *h*, e.g. Khalīl, Chalil, Halil.

q A guttural *k*, pronounced farther back in the throat. Also transcribed *ḳ*, *k*, and, for some dialects, *g*, e.g. Waqf, Waḳf, Wakf, wagf.

s represents two Arabic letters. The second, emphatic *s*, is transliterated *ṣ*. It may also be represented by ç , e.g. Sāliḥ, Saleh, Çaleh.

sh as in English *ship*. The French transcription *ch* is found in Algeria, Lebanon, Morocco, Syria and Tunisia, e.g. Shaikh, Sheikh, Cheikh.

t represents two Arabic letters. The second, emphatic *t*, is transliterated *ṭ*.

th in literary Arabic and some dialects, pronounced as English *th* in *through*. In many dialects pronounced *t* or *s*, e.g. Thābit, Tabit, Sabit.

w as in English, but often represented by *ou* or *v*, e.g. Wādā, Vadi, Oued.

z represents two Arabic letters. The second, or emphatic *z*, is transliterated *ẓ*. It may also be represented, for some dialects, by *dh* or *d*, e.g. Ḥāfiẓ, Hafidh, Hafid.

ʻ A glottal stop, as in Cockney *ʻliʻl boʻls'*.

Vowels

The Arabic script only indicates three short vowels, three long vowels, and two diphthongs, as follows:

a as in English *hat*, and often rendered *e*, e.g. balad, beled, emir, amir; with emphatics or gutturals usually pronounced as *u* in *but*, e.g. Khalīfa, Baghdād.

i as in English *bit*. Sometimes rendered *e*, e.g. jihād, jehād.

u as in English *good*. Often pronounced and written *o*, e.g. Muhammad, Mohammad.

In some Arabic dialects, particularly those of North Africa, unaccented short vowels are often omitted altogether, and long vowels shortened, e.g. Oued for Wādī, bled for balad, etc.

ā Long *a*, variously pronounced as in *sand, dart* and *hall*.

ī As *ee* in *feet*. In early books often rendered *ee*.

ū As *oo* in *boot*. The French transcription *ou* is often met in English books, e.g. Maḥmūd, Mahmood, Mahmoud.

ai Pronounced in classical Arabic as English *i* in *hide*, in colloquial Arabic as *a* in *take*. Variously transcribed as *ai, ay, ei, ey* and *â* , e.g. sheikh, shaikh, shaykh, etc.

aw Pronounced in classical Arabic as English *ow* in *town*, in colloquial Arabic as in *grow*. Variously rendered *aw, ew, au, ô, av, ev*, e.g. Tawfīq, Taufiq, Tevfik, etc.

Sun- and Moon-Letters

In Arabic pronunciation, when the word to which the definite article, *al*, is attached begins with one of certain letters called 'Sun-letters', the *l* of the article changes to the initial letter in question, e.g. *al-shams* (the sun) is pronounced *ash-shams*; *al-rajul* (the man) is pronounced *ar-rajul*.

There are 14 Sun-letters in the Arabic alphabet, which are transcribed as: d, dh, n, r, s, sh, t, th, z, zh (d, s, t and z, and their emphatic forms, ḍ, ṣ, ṭ and ẓ, are not differentiated in this book). The remaining 15 letters in the Arabic alphabet are known as 'Moon-letters'.

TURKISH ORTHOGRAPHY AND PRONUNCIATION

Turkish has been written in Roman characters since 1928. The following pronunciations are invariable:

c hard *j*, as in *majority, jam*.

ç *ch*, as in *church*.

g hard *g*, as in *go, big*.

ğ not voiced, or pronounced *y*; Ereğli is pronounced *erayly*.

ı short vowel, as the second vowel of *'centre'*, or French *'le'*.

i *i* sound of *Indic, bitter* (NOT as in *bite*, might).

o *o*, as in *hot, boss*.

ö *i* sound of *'birth'*, or French *'oeuvre'*.

ş *sh*, as in *cash*.

u as in *do, too*, German *'um'*.

ü as in *burette*, German *'Hütte'*.

CALENDAR OF POLITICAL EVENTS IN THE MIDDLE EAST AND NORTH AFRICA, OCTOBER 2012–SEPTEMBER 2013

OCTOBER 2012

4 **Jordan**: King Abdullah ibn al-Hussein dissolved the House of Representatives. On 10 October the Prime Minister, Fayez al-Tarawneh, submitted the resignation of his Government and on the following day the King appointed a new, interim Cabinet under the premiership of a member of the Senate, Abdullah Ensour. Early legislative elections were subsequently scheduled for 23 January 2013.

7 **Kuwait**: The Amir, Sheikh Sabah al-Ahmad al-Jaber al-Sabah issued a decree dissolving the National Assembly. It was later announced that elections would take place on 1 December.

Libya: Mustafa Abu Shagur was dismissed as Prime Minister-designate by the General National Congress (GNC), following a vote of no confidence. Earlier that day the GNC had rejected a 10-member 'emergency' cabinet presented for approval by Abu Shagur. On 14 October Ali Zidan was elected as Prime Minister-designate in Abu Shagur's place.

23 **Palestinian Territories/Qatar**: The Amir of Qatar, Sheikh Hamad bin Khalifa Al Thani, conducted a one-day official visit to the Gaza Strip, becoming the first head of state to do so since Hamas seized power in the territory in 2007.

NOVEMBER 2012

5 **Saudi Arabia**: Prince Muhammad ibn Nayef ibn Abd al-Aziz Al Sa'ud was appointed as Minister of the Interior by King Abdullah ibn Abd al-Aziz Al Sa'ud.

14 **Libya**: A Cabinet comprising 20 ministers, including Prime Minister Zidan, was sworn in to office by the GNC President, Muhammad Yousuf Magariaf. The previous day four of the intended nominees—including the prospective Minister of the Interior, Ashour Shuwail—had been deemed unfit to take office by the country's Transparency and Integrity Commission (TIC), owing to alleged links with former Libyan leader Muammar al-Qaddafi. A further two nominees remained under investigation by the Commission, while another had withdrawn his candidacy earlier that month for separate reasons. Muhammad al-Barghati was appointed as Minister of Defence and Al-Kilani al-Jazi as Minister of Finance. However, Shuwail was subsequently cleared of any wrongdoing, following an appeal to the TIC. He was duly appointed as Minister of the Interior on 11 December.

DECEMBER 2012

1 **Kuwait**: Elections to the National Assembly duly took place. Shi'a Islamist candidates secured 17 seats (compared with just seven at the previous election in February 2012), while Sunni Islamists won just four seats (compared with 23 in February). It was reported that 30 new deputies had been elected to parliament, including three women. As a result of an electoral boycott by Islamist, liberal and nationalist opposition movements, the majority of those elected were reported to be supportive of the Government. According to the Ministry of Information, turn-out was recorded at 38.8%.

22 **Egypt**: At a national referendum—the first round of which had taken place on 15 December—a draft Constitution was approved by 63.8% of participating voters, according to official results. The total rate of participation was recorded at 32.9%. The new Constitution entered into effect on 26 December.

JANUARY 2013

6 **Egypt**: A total of 10 new ministers were sworn into office by President Muhammad Mursi in a partial reorganization of the Cabinet. Most notable among the appointments were those of Al-Mursi al-Sayid Hegazi as Minister of Finance and Maj.-Gen. Muhammad Ibrahim as Minister of the Interior. Hatem Abd al-Latif became Minister of Transport, while Ahmad Emam took the post of Minister of Electricity and Energy.

22 **Israel**: At legislative elections, Likud—in alliance with Israel Beytenu—secured the largest representation in the Knesset, winning 31 of the chamber's 120 seats. A newly formed centrist party, Yesh Atid, won 19 seats, while the right-wing Jewish Home party took 12 seats. Labour and Shas each won 11 seats. Some seven other parties also won representation, among which, most notably, the Hatnua party of former deputy prime minister Tzipi Livni won six seats and Kadima (which had been the leading party in the governing coalition between 2006–09) just two. The rate of voter participation was recorded at 67.8%. On 2 February President Shimon Peres instructed incumbent Prime Minister, Likud Chairman Binyamin Netanyahu, to form a new government.

23 **Jordan**: Elections to an expanded, 150-seat House of Representatives were conducted. Independents and tribal representatives loyal to King Abdullah were reported to have secured around three-quarters of the seats available, with moderate Islamist and other candidates critical of the Government winning the remaining seats. Some 37 of the newly elected deputies were thought to be aligned with the opposition. According to the IEC, the rate of voter participation was 56.5%.

FEBRUARY 2013

1 **Saudi Arabia**: Prince Muqrin ibn Abd al-Aziz Al Sa'ud was appointed as Second Deputy Prime Minister.

5 **Egypt/Iran**: President Mahmoud Ahmadinejad began a two-day visit to Egypt, becoming the first Iranian President to visit that country since 1979.

9 **Syria**: President Bashar al-Assad issued a decree reorganizing the Council of Ministers. Most notably, Ismael Ismael was nominated as Minister of Finance and Suleiman al-Abbas as Minister of Petroleum and Mineral Resources. Hussein Farzat was assigned the role of Minister of Housing and Urban Development, and Hussein Arnous that of Minister of Public Works. Ahmad al-Qadri was appointed as Minister of Agriculture and Agrarian Reform. The responsibilities of

the former Ministry of Labour and Social Affairs were divided: Hassan Hijazi became Minister of Labour, and Kinda al-Shammat Minister of Social Affairs.

28 **Cyprus**: Nikos Anastasiades was inaugurated as President by the speaker of the House of Representatives. Anastasiades had defeated Stavros Malas to win the presidential election at a run-off ballot held on 24 February, with 57.5% of the valid votes cast. On 1 March a new Council of Ministers, comprising members of the President's Democratic Rally (DISY), the Democratic Party (DIKO), the European Party (Evro.Ko) and independents, took office. Ioannis Kasoulides of DISY was appointed as Minister of Foreign Affairs, which role he had held in 1997–2003, while Michalis Sarris, a former banker, regained the finance portfolio, having previously served in the role in 2005–08. Other notable appointees included DIKO's Fotis Fotiou as Minister of Defence, DISY's Socrates Hasikos as Minister of the Interior, and Nikos Kouyalis of Evro.Ko as Minister of Agriculture, Natural Resources and the Environment.

MARCH 2013

14 **Tunisia**: A revised Council of Ministers, comprising members of Hizb al-Nahdah, the Congrès pour la République (CPR), the Forum Démocratique pour le Travail et les Libertés (Ettakatol) and independents, took office, having received the approval of the National Constituent Assembly at a vote of confidence. Ali Laârayedh of Hizb al-Nahdah, who had served as Minister of the Interior in the outgoing administration of Hamadi Jebali, was appointed as Prime Minister. The four main portfolios (justice, the interior, foreign affairs and defence) were allocated to independents. The reorganization was prompted by Jebali's resignation on 19 February. In the weeks prior to that his resignation, Jebali had attempted to form a non-aligned, technocratic Government, These attempts were prompted by civil unrest in the capital, Tunis, and other cities in the aftermath of the assassination of an influential opposition politician.

17 **United Arab Emirates**: A reorganization of the Council of Ministers was effected. Most notable among the new appointees were Abd al-Rahman Muhammad al-Owais, who became Minister of Health, Suhail bin Muhammad al-Mazroui, who was appointed as Minister of Energy, and Abdullah bin Muhammad al-Nuaimi, the new Minister of Public Works.

18 **Israel**: A new coalition Government, comprising members of Likud, Israel Beytenu, Yesh Atid, Jewish Home and Hatnua, took office. Netanyahu was reappointed as Prime Minister, while also assuming the post of Minister of Foreign Affairs. Yair Lapid of Yesh Atid became Minister of Finance and Livni Minister of Justice. The leader of Jewish Home, Naftali Bennett, was assigned the role of Minister of Industry, Trade and Labour, along with the religious services and Jerusalem and diaspora affairs portfolios. Likud's Moshe Ya'alon and Gideon Sa'ar were appointed as Minister of Defence and Minister of Interior, respectively.

22 **Lebanon**: The Prime Minister, Najib Miqati, tendered the resignation of his Council of Ministers, citing disagreement among its constituent parties. The resignation followed the failure of the Government to agree the composition of a committee to supervise the conduct of legislative elections scheduled for June. President Michel Suleiman requested that Miqati remain in office until a new Cabinet could be formed. On 6 April Tammam Salam was appointed as Prime Minister-designate, having won a vote of confidence at the National Assembly the previous day.

25 **Cyprus**: An agreement was reached between the Government of Cyprus and the so-called 'troika' of international organizations—comprising the European Commission, the European Central Bank and the IMF—permitting the provision to Cyprus of financial assistance to the value of €10,000m. Under the terms of the agreement, deposits of less than €100,000 were to remain exempt from any losses, but deposits above that level held in the country's two largest banks, the Bank of Cyprus and the Cyprus Popular Bank (Laiki Bank), were to be frozen and subject to deductions of up to 40%. Certain of Laiki Bank's assets were to be merged into the Bank of Cyprus, while the remainder of Laiki Bank was to be liquidated. Bank branches throughout the country, which had been closed since 15 March, reopened on 28 March, after the imposition by the Cypriot Government of strict capital controls, amid fears of significant withdrawals of deposits.

31 **Jordan**: A new Cabinet, under Ensour as Prime Minister, took office. Most notably, Umayya Touqan, the former Governor of the Central Bank, was appointed as Minister of Finance, and a former Director of the Public Security Department, Hussein Hazaa Majali, as Minister of the Interior and Municipal Affairs. The number of ministers was reduced to just 18.

APRIL 2013

2 **Cyprus**: Michalis Sarris resigned as Minister of Finance, following the conclusion of discussions over the bail-out and amid criticism of his tenure as chairman of Laiki Bank prior to rejoining the Government. The recently appointed Minister of Labour and Social Insurance, Haris Georgiades, assumed the finance portfolio in place of Sarris, while Zeta Emilianidou, a former civil servant, joined the Government in Georgiades' former post. The terms of the bail-out agreement were narrowly approved by the legislature on 30 April 2013.

13 **Palestinian Territories**: Salam Fayyad resigned as Prime Minister. Relations between Fayyad and Executive President Mahmud Abbas had become strained through disagreement on issues of economic policy, and had deteriorated markedly in March when Fayyad accepted the resignation of Nabil Qassis—a close associate of the President—as Minister of Finance.

MAY 2013

7 **Egypt**: Prime Minister Hisham Qandil announced a reorganization of his Cabinet. New Ministers of Finance, Justice and Planning were among the nine new appointees. The number of ministers affiliated to the Muslim Brotherhood reportedly increased from eight to 10.

27 **Saudi Arabia**: Prince Mitab ibn Abdullah Al Sa'ud was appointed to the newly created role of Minister of the National Guard. Prince Mitab, a son of King Abdullah, had previously held the title of Minister of State.

31 **Lebanon**: Members of the National Assembly voted to extend the current legislative term until 20 November 2014, delaying the legislative elections that had been due to take place in June 2013. The precarious security

situation in the country caused by the ongoing conflict in neighbouring Syria was cited as the principal reason for the extension, although the Assembly had also been unable to agree on the adoption of an electoral law to govern the conduct of the June elections.

JUNE 2013

1 **Turkey**: Violent clashes erupted between protesters and police, following attempts by the the police forcibly to remove demonstrators from a park in the centre of İstanbul. The protests had begun the previous day in an attempt to oppose Government plans for the redevelopment of the park. In the aftermath of the violence, anti-Government protests took place in the park and in other cities across Turkey, including the capital, Ankara. A total of three people were reported to have died as a result of the ensuing clashes.

6 **Palestinian Territories**: A new Administration was sworn into office by President Abbas. Rami Hamdallah, hitherto the Chairman of the Palestinian Central Elections Commission, was appointed as Prime Minister. Most notably, Muhammad Mustafa became Deputy Prime Minister for Economic Affairs, while Ziad Abu Amr was also appointed as Deputy Prime Minister. Shukri Bishara took the finance portfolio. However, on 20 June Hamdallah tendered his resignation, citing strained relations with his two deputies. Despite subsequent reports that Hamdallah had decided to remain in office, his resignation was accepted by President Abbas on 23 June. Hamdallah was to remain in post on an interim basis, pending the appointment of a new premier.

11 **'Turkish Republic of Northern Cyprus' (TRNC)**: President Derviş Eroğlu appointed Sibel Siber, of the Republican Turkish Party (CTP), as Prime Minister at the head of an interim Council of Ministers. The appointment of Siber followed the resignation of İrsen Küçük and his administration earlier that month. Küçük had been defeated at a vote of no confidence by the Legislative Assembly, which had been prompted by the decision of eight deputies from his National Unity Party (UBP) to join the opposition Democrat Party (DP). Siber's Council of Ministers was approved by the legislature on 23 June and was expected to remain in office until after early legislative elections, scheduled for 28 July.

14 **Iran**: Hassan Rouhani was elected as President at the first round of voting. According to official results published by the Ministry of the Interior, Rouhani—whose candidacy had been endorsed by former Presidents Ali Akbar Hashemi Rafsanjani and Muhammad Khatami—secured 50.7% of the total votes cast. His closest rival, Muhammad Baqir Qalibaf, won 16.6% of the vote, while Saeed Jalili took 11.4%. Three other candidates also contested the election: Mohsen Rezai won 10.6% of the vote, Ali Akbar Velayati 6.2% and Muhammad Gharazi 1.2%. Voter turn-out was recorded at 72.2%.

25 **Libya**: Nuri Ali Abu Sahmain was elected as President of the GNC, becoming the de facto head of state. Abu Sahmain, an independent deputy whose candidacy was endorsed by the Justice and Construction Party, secured the support of 96 of the GNC's 200 deputies at the second round of voting. The election followed the resignation on 28 May of Magariaf, who had sought to comply with legislation approved by the GNC earlier that month that barred those who had served in senior government posts during the rule of Muammar al-Qaddafi from holding offices of state. (Magariaf had been Libya's ambassador to India in 1978–80, before becoming a leading opponent of Qaddafi.)

Qatar: Sheikh Tamim bin Hamad Al Thani became Amir, following the abdication of his father, Sheikh Hamad. A revised Council of Ministers was sworn into office by the new Amir on 26 June. Sheikh Abdullah bin Nasser bin Khalifa Al Thani became Prime Minister, in place of Sheikh Hamad bin Jasim bin Jaber Al Thani; Sheikh Abdullah also assumed responsibility for the interior portfolio. Khalid bin Muhammad al-Attiya was appointed as Minister of Foreign Affairs, which post had previously been held by the outgoing Prime Minister. Other notable appointees included the former CEO of Qatar National Bank, Ali Sharif al-Emadi, as Minister of Finance and the former Director-General of the Al Jazeera television network, Sheikh Ahmad bin Jasim bin Muhammad Al Thani, as Minister of Economy and Trade.

JULY 2013

3 **Egypt**: Muhammad Mursi was deposed as President by the armed forces, following popular protests prompted by concerns over his perceived authoritarianism and failure to address social and economic issues. The Constitution was suspended and Adli Mahmoud Mansour, the President of the Supreme Constitutional Court, was appointed as Interim President, taking office on 4 July. Following his removal from office, Mursi and other senior members of the Muslim Brotherhood were detained, and on 8 July at least 51 people were killed in clashes between supporters of Mursi and the security forces outside the headquarters of the Republican Guard in Cairo. On 10 July Hazem al-Biblawi, who had served as Deputy Prime Minister for Economic Affairs and Minister of Finance in July–December 2011, was appointed as Prime Minister, and on 14 July a former head of the International Atomic Energy Agency, Mohammed el-Baradei, was sworn into office as Vice-President for International Relations.

9 **Morocco**: The Secretary-General of Istiqlal, Hamid Chabat, announced his party's intention to withdraw from the governing coalition, citing its disagreement with the economic policies pursued by the leading party in the coalition, the Parti de la Justice et du Développement (PJD). Five of Istiqlal's six ministers duly submitted their resignations to King Muhammad VI the following day, and the King's formal acceptance was granted on 22 July. It was reported, however, that the Minister of National Education, Muhammad el-Ouafa, intended to remain in the Government, contrary to his party's instructions.

27 **Kuwait**: Early elections took place to the National Assembly, following a decision by the Constitutional Court in June upholding amendments to the electoral law first decreed by the Amir in October 2012. According to the final results of these latest elections, candidates representing tribal areas secured 24 of the Assembly's 50 seats. Shi'a Islamist candidates won just eight seats, while Sunni Islamists took seven seats. Liberals and their allies were reported to have won five seats, while the remainder went to independent candidates, some of whom represented the *bidoun* ('stateless' Arabs). Turn-out was recorded at 52.5%.

30 **Israel/Palestinian Territories**: Preliminary discussions regarding a peace accord between Israel

and the Palestinian (National) Authority (PA) took place in Washington, DC, USA. The talks were led by Minister of Justice Livni for Israel and Saeb Erakat for the PA, under the auspices of the US Secretary of State, John F. Kerry. Further talks between Israeli and PA representatives were held in Jerusalem and Jericho in August and September.

AUGUST 2013

3 **Iran**: Rouhani received the official endorsement of the Supreme Guide, Ayatollah Sayed Ali Khamenei, and duly assumed the presidency. A swearing-in ceremony took place in the legislature the following day.

4 **Kuwait**: A new Council of Ministers was announced in an Amiri decree. Sheikh Jaber Mubarak al-Hamad al-Sabah remained as Prime Minister, although several of the key portfolios were reallocated. Sheikh Muhammad Khalid al-Ahmad al-Sabah became Deputy Prime Minister and Minister of the Interior, while Lt-Gen. Sheikh Khalid al-Jarrah al-Sabah was appointed as Deputy Prime Minister and Minister of Defence. Mustafa al-Shimali, hitherto the Minister of Finance, was appointed as Deputy Prime Minister and Minister of Oil. Al-Shimali was replaced as Minister of Finance by Sheikh Salim Abd al-Aziz al-Saud al-Sabah, who also assumed the title of Deputy Prime Minister.

14 **Egypt**: The interim Government declared a month-long national state of emergency and imposed curfews in the capital, Cairo, and other major cities, following violent clashes between security forces and demonstrators demanding the reinstatement of Mursi as President. According to official sources, some 525 people were killed in the clashes, which erupted after security forces intervened to remove protesters from an encampment set up in Cairo by supporters of Mursi and the Muslim Brotherhood. Meanwhile, el-Baradei resigned the vice-presidency, citing his disagreement with the Government's decision forcibly to remove the protesters. El-Baradei, who had left the country following his resignation, was subsequently charged with 'breaching national trust', while Muhammad Badie, the Spiritual Guide and leader of the Brotherhood was detained and charged with 'incitement to murder'.

17 **Iran**: President Rouhani's Council of Ministers took office. On 15 August some 15 of the President's 18 nominees had been approved at separate votes of confidence in the legislature. The successful nominees included, most notably, Muhammad Javad Zarif as Minister of Foreign Affairs, Mostafa Pour-Muhammadi as Minister of Justice and Bijan Namdar Zanganeh as Minister of Petroleum. The nominees for the posts of Minister of Education, Minister of Science, Research and Technology, and Minister of Sports and Youth were rejected. Further nominations for those posts were expected to be presented to the legislature by November.

21 **Syria**: Around 1,400 people were reported to have been killed following missile attacks on the Ghouta area to the east of the capital, Damascus. The attacks prompted international condemnation, led by the USA, the United Kingdom and France, following reports that the missiles had contained chemical agents. A report published by the UN on 16 September on the results of an inspection of the sites affected by the missile strikes confirmed that UN experts had found 'clear and convincing evidence that surface-to-surface rockets containing the nerve agent sarin' had indeed been deployed. The Syrian Government denied that it had been responsible for the attacks.

SEPTEMBER 2013

2 **'TRNC'**: A new coalition Government, formed by the CTP and the DP, took office. The Leader of the CTP, Özkan Yorgancıoğlu, was appointed as Prime Minister, while his DP counterpart, Serdar Denktaş, became Deputy Prime Minister and Minister of Economy and Tourism. Among the other notable appointments were those of the CTP's Özdil Nami as Minister of Foreign Affairs and the DP's Mustafa Arabacıoğlu as Minister of Education, Sports and Youth. Zeren Mungan, also of the CTP, retained the post of Minister of Finance he had held in the outgoing interim administration.

11 **Algeria**: President Abdelaziz Bouteflika effected a reorganization of the Council of Ministers. Abdelmalek Sellal remained as Prime Minister, although several of the major portfolios were reallocated. The chief of staff of the armed forces, Lt-Gen. Ahmed Gaid Salah, joined the Government as Vice-Minister of National Defence. (Bouteflika himself was nominally the minister in charge of the department, but it was expected that Salah would take over the functions of that role.) Tayeb Belaïz was appointed as Minister of State and Minister of the Interior and Local Authorities, and Ramtane Lamamra as Minister of Foreign Affairs. Tayeb Louh became Minister of Justice and Attorney-General.

19 **Palestinian Territories**: A new Council of Ministers was confirmed in office, following the reappointment of Rami Hamdallah as Prime Minister in mid-August. The composition of the new administration was identical to that originally appointed in June.

27 **Syria**: The UN Security Council adopted unanimously a binding resolution (No. 2118), which demanded the destruction of Syria's chemical weapons capability. The resolution effectively endorsed a plan agreed earlier that month by representatives of the USA and Russia, under the terms of which Syria was bound to disclose full details of chemical weapons in its possession to UN-appointed inspectors and to facilitate the destruction of those weapons by mid-2014.

28 **Tunisia**: It was announced that the coalition Government, led by al-Nahdah, had agreed to resign and to begin talks with opposition parties over the formation of a non-partisan, interim administration, in advance of early elections to the National Constituent Assembly. The announcement followed months of protests in Tunis and other cities across the country by campaigners opposed to the Islamist party's conduct in office, prompted in part by the assassinations of two well-known opposition politicians in February and July.

PART ONE

General Survey

ARAB–ISRAELI RELATIONS 1967–2013

PAUL COSSALI

Revised for this edition by the editorial staff

Israel's decisive victory in the June war of 1967 had resulted in the capture of considerable territory from its Arab neighbours. In addition to the Egyptian Sinai and the Syrian Golan Heights, Israel also occupied the last remaining areas of historic Palestine: the West Bank of the Jordan river (including Arab East Jerusalem) and the Gaza Strip. The conflict had created a further 380,000 refugees and brought 1m. Arabs under Israeli occupation. The overwhelming majority of these were Palestinian. The speed with which Israel's armed forces had routed their Arab adversaries dramatically underlined its military superiority. With its acquisition of Arab land, Israel now possessed valuable bargaining chips for any future negotiations towards a settlement of the Middle East conflict. Israeli euphoria was mirrored by deep depression in the Arab world. The sense of national humiliation that had accompanied the 'loss' of Palestine in 1948 was now painfully revisited. For the Palestinians the June war had exposed the emptiness of Egyptian President Gamal Abd al-Nasir (Nasser)'s rhetoric when he had promised that Arab might would erase the Zionist entity and recover Palestinian rights.

RESOLUTION 242

In August 1967 Arab leaders met for a summit conference in Khartoum, Sudan. The conference reiterated the opposition of the assembled states to recognition or direct negotiations with Israel. Israel's Prime Minister, meanwhile, affirmed that Israel would refuse to withdraw from any of the Arab territories occupied in June without negotiations. The gulf between the two parties bedevilled early attempts by the UN Security Council to agree on a resolution to address the crisis. While the Arab world, backed by the USSR, was adamant that the UN should demand the withdrawal of Israeli forces from occupied Arab territory, Israel and the USA were opposed to draft resolutions that did not provide adequate guarantees of Israel's security. A formula meeting the minimum demands of both sides eventually found expression in UN Resolution 242 (Documents on Palestine, see p. 64). Adopted unanimously by the Security Council on 22 November 1967, the resolution emphasized the 'inadmissibility' of the acquisition of territory by war, and called 'for a just and lasting peace in which every state in the area can live in security' and for a settlement of the 'refugee problem'. Resolution 242 called on Israel to withdraw from 'territories occupied in the recent conflict', but crucially did not specify the extent of the withdrawal. Arguments generated by the ambiguities and omissions of Resolution 242 were to be a theme of the Arab–Israeli debate for years to come.

Israel's Prime Minister, Levi Eshkol, did not reject Resolution 242, but stated his preference for direct negotiations leading to agreements between Israel and its neighbours. In late 1968 Israel presented a nine-point plan for a Middle East peace to the UN General Assembly, which did not offer an Israeli withdrawal but proposed mutually agreeable 'boundary settlements'. The proposal elicited no response from an Arab world that remained highly suspicious of Israeli intentions. Speculation that Israel planned to remain in control of conquered lands had been aroused by Israel's de facto annexation of Arab East Jerusalem in mid-1967 and the establishment of Jewish settlements on the West Bank in September of that year. Despite the existence of a formal cease-fire, there were frequent artillery duels across the Suez Canal, and in Gaza Palestinian fighters fought an increasingly desperate campaign against the occupying army. Raids by Palestinian irregulars across the Jordanian border were met with heavy Israeli reprisals, as were the increasing incidences of the hijacking of Israeli airliners by Palestinian radicals. In response to one of these attacks, Israeli commandos raided Beirut airport in late 1968, destroying 13 aircraft. Despite international condemnation of Israel, the newly installed Administration under Richard Nixon in the USA went ahead with the earlier decision of Lyndon B. Johnson's Administration to supply the Israelis with 50 *Phantom* aircraft, a decision that confirmed the region as a major arena of US–Soviet rivalry. In July 1969, after continued fighting along both the Suez and Jordan fronts, President Nasser publicly gave up hope of a peaceful settlement and predicted that 'a war of attrition' would be necessary to dislodge Israel from the territories occupied in 1967.

Attempts by the USSR, the USA, France and the United Kingdom to obtain agreement on the implementation of Resolution 242 made little initial progress. The major obstacles remained Arab insistence that the resolution should be implemented *in toto* and did not require negotiation, and Israel's demand for direct negotiation to decide on new international boundaries. In December 1969 the US Secretary of State, William Rogers, produced a set of proposals designed to steer a middle course between the conflicting viewpoints. Known as the Rogers Plan, its most important aspect was to clarify the US opinion that there should be only minor modifications to the pre-June 1967 boundaries. Although Israel's Minister of Foreign Affairs, Abba Eban, had assured the international community that 'everything was negotiable', Israel's initial response to Rogers was antagonistic, apparently revealing serious divisions within the Israeli Cabinet over the extent of compliance with Resolution 242. In January 1970 the Israeli air force launched a series of strikes on Egyptian targets, prompting Egypt to appeal for greater assistance from the USSR and for the USA to intensify diplomatic initiatives in the region. Israeli requests for more *Phantoms* were turned down by Nixon, and behind the scenes considerable pressure was placed on Israel to renew its cease-fire with Egypt and to promise a withdrawal from most of the territory occupied after the June war. No such undertaking on the latter issue was given publicly, but sufficient understanding was achieved in private for Rogers to relaunch his proposals with the backing of the four major powers. In July 1970 Nasser signalled Egyptian acceptance of US appeals for a renewal of the cease-fire, to be followed by UN-mediated negotiations on the implementation of Resolution 242. A week later, after receiving assurances on the future supply of arms, the Israeli Government also agreed to the US proposals. However, it added the provisos that Israel would never return to the pre-war borders and that none of its troops would be withdrawn from the cease-fire line until a binding peace agreement had been signed. The renewed cease-fire along the Suez Canal came into effect on 8 August and was to last for 90 days. During this time the two sides were to engage in indirect negotiations through the UN Special Representative, Dr Gunnar Jarring. However, these negotiations were suspended after a single meeting when Israel recalled its diplomats in protest against the movement of Soviet missiles behind the Egyptian lines.

'BLACK SEPTEMBER'

In September 1970 the focus of attention in the Middle East shifted to Jordan. In the years since the radicalizing experience of the Six-Day War, thousands of Palestinians had flocked to the various guerrilla organizations that made up the nascent Palestine Liberation Organization (PLO). Mindful of the sensitivity of the Palestinian cause to the mass of their citizens, many Arab leaders had allowed Palestinian groups an unprecedented degree of freedom to organize and agitate. In Jordan, where perhaps one-half of the population was of Palestinian origin, Palestinian groups had taken advantage of their freedom of movement to mount attacks against Israeli targets. Retaliation in the form of ground and air raids followed Palestinian infiltration. These had resulted in heavy casualties and served to depopulate parts of the East Bank of the Jordan. Ideological differences strained further the relations between Jordan's King Hussein and the Palestinian organizations. The latter's blend of revolutionary Marxism and radical Arab nationalism sat uneasily with a pro-Western monarchy. Moreover, while the Palestinian resistance movement had committed itself in 1968 in the Palestinian National Charter or PLO Covenant (Documents on Palestine, see p. 65) to the dismantling of the 'Zionist' state and its replacement with a 'secular democratic Palestine', the Jordanian monarch had been swift to follow Egypt in signing up to the Rogers Plan, with its implicit acceptance of the State of Israel. By mid-1970 it became difficult to see how the uneasy state of coexistence could last. Matters came to a head at the beginning of September when militants of the Popular Front for the Liberation of Palestine (PFLP), one of the more radical groupings of the PLO, hijacked and then blew up three airliners on an airfield in Jordan. Soon afterwards King Hussein appointed a military Government in Jordan, which mobilized against PLO bases in the kingdom. After 10 days of heavy fighting the Palestinian resistance movement in Jordan had been crushed. A cease-fire, ending what would be referred to by Palestinians as 'Black September', was signed in Cairo, Egypt, on 27 September. President Nasser suffered a heart attack the following day and died soon after.

SADAT ASSUMES THE EGYPTIAN PRESIDENCY

Egypt's new President, Anwar Sadat, agreed to the 90-day cease-fire renewal along the Suez front. After receiving the promise of US credits to the value of US $500m., the Israeli Government also agreed to return to the talks under Jarring's auspices. On 8 February 1971 Jarring wrote to the Governments of Israel and Egypt, inviting each to give firm commitments to resolve the deadlock. He suggested that Israel should withdraw to the international boundary as of 4 June 1967, and that Egypt should give a parallel undertaking to conclude a peace agreement explicitly ending the state of war with Israel and recognizing Israel's right to exist in peace and security. In effect, both parties were being asked formally to accept their principal obligations under Resolution 242. Egypt replied that it would be prepared to meet the requirements stipulated by Jarring as long as Israel agreed to withdraw its forces to the international boundary. Israel responded that, while it was prepared to withdraw to 'secure, recognized and agreed boundaries to be established in the peace agreement', it would not retreat to the pre-war border. This embarrassed the US Administration, which had first withheld and then granted military and economic assistance to Israel in an attempt to persuade the Israeli Government to accept only 'minor rectification' of the armistice line. In December 1971 the UN General Assembly, in a resolution reaffirming the principles of Resolution 242, urged Israel to respond favourably to Jarring's proposals. Only seven states, one of them being Israel, voted against the resolution. In a gesture of frustration with Israeli intransigence, the USA abstained. Nevertheless, the sale of US military aircraft to Israel continued during 1972, eliciting fierce criticism from the Egyptians. Sadat's failure to deliver the political settlement he had promised his people at the beginning of 1971 had left him frustrated and politically exposed. In July 1972 the Egyptian President unexpectedly requested the withdrawal from Egypt of Soviet military advisers. This was interpreted by observers as a final appeal to the Nixon Administration to bring pressure on Israel to accede to a settlement involving a withdrawal from the occupied Sinai.

Although the cease-fire along the Suez Canal was maintained during 1972, the absence of political progress sustained regular incidences of violent conflict elsewhere. In February Israeli forces launched a major incursion into southern Lebanon, in an attempt to destroy PLO guerrilla bases there; four months later Israeli air raids on Lebanese territory left more than 70 civilians killed or wounded. The war of terror and counter-terror between Israel and the Palestinians continued to escalate. In mid-1972 several Palestinian leaders were killed or maimed by letter bombs in Beirut, Lebanon. In September Palestinian gunmen took several Israeli athletes hostage during the Olympic games in Munich, West Germany, in a declared attempt to win the freedom of Arab prisoners in Israeli gaols. The athletes were later killed by their captors during an abortive rescue operation at Fürstenfeldbruck airport. Israel responded to the Munich events with a series of attacks on Palestinian targets in Lebanon and the assassination in various European capitals of those PLO personnel it believed to have been responsible for masterminding the operation.

THE OCTOBER WAR

The beginning of 1973 saw further Israeli air-strikes on guerrilla bases in Lebanon and the shooting down of a Libyan airliner that had strayed over occupied Sinai. These two incidents caused a storm of protest in the Arab world and thwarted all expectations of progress at a US-hosted series of talks with Egyptian, Jordanian and Israeli leaders in Washington, DC. Instead, a resolution of the Arab–Israeli conflict appeared more remote than ever. Israel had ceded none of the land it had occupied in 1967, and had established some 50 civilian and paramilitary settlements in these territories. Although the Jordanian and Egyptian Governments had signalled that they would be prepared to recognize Israel in return for an Israeli withdrawal from Arab lands, Israel remained in defiance of those UN resolutions calling upon it to return to its pre-1967 borders. The USA, meanwhile, found itself isolated in its support for Israel. In Europe, where the Jewish state had long benefited from a groundswell of popular sympathy, an increasing dependence on Arab petroleum and a frustration with what was regarded as the overly partisan support for Israel in the USA saw members of the European Community (EC, now the European Union—EU) becoming more critical of perceived Israeli intransigence. However, as long as the political support of the USA was forthcoming and its military superiority unchallenged, the Israeli Government appeared unconcerned either by the regional stalemate or by Israel's creeping political isolation.

This complacency was dramatically challenged on 6 October 1973, when Egyptian and Syrian forces launched a full-scale assault on Israeli positions in the Golan Heights and along the Suez Canal. The timing of the assault was not accidental. With public services in Israel effectively suspended because of observation of Yom Kippur (the Day of Atonement—the holiest day in the Jewish calendar), Israel's army found it difficult to mobilize its forces rapidly. By midnight on the first day of the war 400 Egyptian tanks had crossed the Suez Canal, outflanking the supposedly impregnable Israeli fortifications on the eastern bank known as the Bar Lev line. Meanwhile, the Israeli army and air force were struggling to contain a massive assault by Syrian tanks beyond the Golan Heights. Over the next three weeks Israel suffered heavy casualties, but was able to reverse the early territorial losses. Counter-attacking forces pushed the Egyptians back across the Suez Canal and succeeded in isolating Egyptian armed forces on the western side of the canal around the city of Suez. In the north, Israel's troops had occupied further Syrian territory and had advanced towards the capital, Damascus. The UN Security Council, adopting Resolution 338 on 22 October, urged a cease-fire and reaffirmed the principles defined in Resolution 242.

By the time a disengagement had been agreed at the end of October 1973, the military advantage lay clearly with the Israelis. It was the Arab world, however, that was considered to have gained the most politically from the conflict. Not only had the war demonstrated that the gap in military strength compared with Israel had narrowed, but it had also added a new dimension to the conflict. Soon after the outbreak of the war, there were demands from within the Arab world to deny oil to Israel's supporters. In mid-October Arab oil exporters, meeting in Kuwait, agreed to cut production, while Abu Dhabi, United Arab Emirates (UAE), took the lead in halting the export of oil to the USA. Western nations were soon experiencing rising fuel prices and growing shortages, underlining the extent of their dependency on oil produced in the Arab world. In early November the member states of the EC endorsed a statement demanding an Israeli withdrawal from the territories occupied in 1967 and asserting the need for any Middle East settlement to meet the legitimate rights of the Palestinians. Meanwhile, President Nixon dispatched his Secretary of State, Dr Henry Kissinger, on a series of visits to Middle East capitals. His diplomacy led to disengagement agreements between Egypt and Israel (18 January 1974) and between

Syria and Israel (31 May 1974). In June 1974 Nixon embarked on his own tour of the region; he reassured Israel of continuing US support, but also forecast a new era of co-operation with the Arab world. Arab leaders broadly welcomed Nixon's overtures, believing that at last US influence would be used to promote a settlement based on Israel's withdrawal. The embargo on the export of Arab oil to the USA was revoked, and diplomatic relations between Syria and the USA were re-established.

THE PALESTINIAN PROFILE RAISED

Israel's international position had been weakened by the revelation of the extent to which the world was dependent upon Arab goodwill. Israel's Prime Minister Golda Meir was criticized for her Government's failure to anticipate the Arab attack, and while her Labour Party won a narrow victory at the end of 1973, she was unable to rebuild her coalition in April 1974. Meir was succeeded by Itzhak Rabin as Labour leader and Prime Minister. Within the Arab world the effect of the war was to strengthen the position of the regimes in Egypt and Syria and to give new authority to King Faisal of Saudi Arabia—whose control of the greatest share of Middle Eastern oil reserves made him a dominant figure in Arab politics. Satisfaction greeted Israel's relinquishing of small areas of Arab territory under the US-brokered disengagement agreements, but the central problem of the future of the Palestinians had been made no clearer by the October conflict. Nevertheless, the PLO and the Palestinians saw their international profile raised in the wake of the new Arab confidence. In November 1973 the Arab governments had recognized the PLO as 'the sole, legitimate representative of the Palestinian people', and the centrality of the Palestinians to the Middle East conflict was strikingly endorsed in September 1974 when the UN General Assembly voted for the first time since Israel's establishment to include 'the Palestine question' on its agenda. In the following month the PLO Chairman, Yasser Arafat, addressed the General Assembly, speaking of his vision of a unitary and secular Palestine for both Arabs and Jews. Also in October Arab heads of state, meeting in Rabat, Morocco, had formally affirmed the status of the PLO as the 'sole legitimate representative of the Palestinian people' (Documents on Palestine, see p. 68).

The elevation of the PLO to the status of a principal player on the Middle East stage was welcomed by the Arab people, but served only to deepen the impasse with regard to a settlement. The Israeli Government refused to have any dealings with the PLO, dismissing it as a terrorist organization. The PLO's position was in itself complicated by internal divisions over political objectives. Although committed through its Charter to the replacement of Israel with a 'secular democratic' Palestine, by the end of 1974 majority opinion within the PLO had reluctantly accepted the idea of a Palestinian state in the West Bank and Gaza with East Jerusalem as its capital. While this was also the preferred option of the 'conservative', Western-aligned Arab states headed by Egypt and Jordan, the Governments of Libya and Iraq continued to give their backing to the significant minority of 'rejectionists' within the Palestinian national movement who were bitterly opposed to any formula involving a compromise with 'Zionism' and 'imperialism'. These radical factions viewed the Arab-US rapprochement with disdain, and violently underscored their opposition to compromise with Israel through bloody assaults on targets inside Israel.

Arab hopes that the diplomatic initiative unleashed by the October war would lead to a breakthrough in the regional stalemate were frustrated through the latter part of 1974. The disengagement agreements had been honoured by both sides, but attempts by Kissinger to further the process of disengagement on the Egyptian–Israeli front by securing a partial Israeli withdrawal in Sinai foundered on Israel's insistence that such an agreement be accompanied by a non-aggression pact with Egypt. Unwilling to risk the opprobrium of the Arab world by pursuing a separate peace treaty with Israel, Sadat rejected the Israeli conditions. The US Secretary of State blamed Israeli obstinacy for the failure of his shuttle diplomacy to build upon the initial disengagements, while President Gerald Ford intimated that the granting of increased military and economic aid to Israel would be dependent upon a more flexible response to US initiatives. In mid-1975 Kissinger returned to Israel to promote a second disengagement agreement between Israel and Egypt. This time his efforts bore fruit: on 4 September both states signed an agreement in Geneva, Switzerland, that provided for an Israeli withdrawal from the Mitla and Gidi passes in Sinai and a return of the Abu Rudeis oilfields (on which Israel had depended for some 50% of its oil supplies). A UN buffer zone would be established between the two forces, along with five 'listening posts' to monitor troop movements on either side. Non-military cargoes sailing to and from Israel would be allowed to pass through the newly reopened Suez Canal. In addition, both sides agreed to respect the cease-fire and to resolve their conflict by peaceful means. Although greeted in the West as a triumph of US diplomacy, the agreement was viewed in most of the Arab world—and particularly by the Syrians and the PLO—as a dangerous capitulation to US and Israeli interests. The united Arab front presented during the October war was undermined, and Egypt had clearly aligned itself with the USA. Relations between Egypt and Russia, strained for some years, deteriorated further as Sadat repeatedly criticized Egypt's former ally. In March 1975 Sadat abrogated the 1971 Soviet-Egyptian Treaty of Friendship. Syria now assumed leadership of the Arab cause. In October 1975 Syria's President Hafiz al-Assad visited the Russian capital, Moscow, securing the promise of increased arms supplies to match the deliveries made by the USA to Israel.

In late 1975 and early 1976 the international position of the PLO was further enhanced through a series of debates at the UN. In November 1975 the General Assembly adopted three resolutions: the first concerned the establishment of a 20-nation committee to devise plans for the implementation of Palestinian 'self-determination and national independence'; the second extended an invitation to the PLO to take part in future debates on the Middle East; and, most controversially, the third condemned Zionism as 'a form of racism and racial discrimination'. However, the USA blocked a resolution in January 1976 affirming the Palestinians' right to establish their own state, and again sided with Israel in March to defeat a resolution condemning Israel's actions in the Occupied Territories. However, the US delegate did issue a statement strongly critical of Israeli settlement policy. This policy continued to exacerbate tensions in Palestinian areas under Israeli control, prompting sustained rioting throughout the West Bank and Gaza in the following months. Israeli attempts to defuse unrest by allowing Palestinians on the West Bank to hold municipal elections only confirmed the weight of nationalist sentiment when the electorate voted overwhelmingly for candidates closely identified with the PLO.

CIVIL WAR IN LEBANON

Palestinian militancy in the Occupied Territories had been intensified by the outbreak in April 1975 of full-scale civil war in Lebanon. This increasingly bloody conflict saw Palestinians allied with the forces of the Lebanese left against the conservative Christian establishment. Attempts by the USA, France and various Arab leaders to broker an end to the hostilities failed to produce anything more than temporary cease-fires in a cycle of violence where the civilian population, and particularly the Palestinians, were the principal victims. By May 1976 the leftist-Palestinian alliance was on the brink of a military victory. Fearing that such an outcome would prompt an Israeli intervention, Syria's President Assad won tacit US approval to send his troops across the border to prevent a Christian defeat. Following intensive lobbying by Kuwait and Saudi Arabia, a limited Arab summit was convened in Riyadh, Saudi Arabia, in October, at which the leaders of Egypt, Syria, Lebanon and the PLO agreed to a cease-fire that would see the reform of the Lebanese political system and the stationing of an Arab peacekeeping force in the country. By the end of 1976 this force had established some semblance of order throughout most of the country.

Although the Arab focus on the civil war in Lebanon was welcomed in Israel, the Labour Government of Itzhak Rabin was beset by its own internal pressures. A weak economy and a series of scandals involving senior Labour politicians had combined to undermine the governing coalition. Street protests in the West Bank and Gaza in 1976 were met by increasingly repressive measures by the Israeli security forces. On 20 December, following the publication of a UN report critical of Israel, the General Assembly once again censured the Israeli Government for its treatment of the Palestinians. Settlement policy served to fuel Palestinian protests and lay at the core of international concern. The Rabin administration was itself divided over the issue of whether it should be controlling or facilitating Jewish settlement in the territories occupied in 1967. No such dilemma exercised the nationalist Likud opposition led by Menachem Begin. In the approach to the 1977 election Begin campaigned hard for the expansion of Jewish settlement and permanent Israeli control over the West Bank. However, on the issue of relations with the Palestinians and the PLO there was broad agreement between the major political blocs in Israel. Both were opposed to negotiation with a 'terrorist' organization and refused to accept the notion of an independent Palestinian state. The PLO, meanwhile, remained publicly committed to the replacement of Israel with a unitary secular democracy. The entrenched position of the conflict's two principal protagonists confirmed that the possibility of an overall settlement remained as remote as ever. Nevertheless, the ending of the Lebanese civil war and the election of Jimmy Carter to the US presidency gave new impetus to the search for a way out of the regional deadlock.

NEW DIPLOMATIC INITIATIVES

With the Lebanese situation no longer consuming the political energies of the Arab world, attention once again turned to Israel. The common position of the Arab states was that an overall settlement should be predicated upon the withdrawal of Israeli forces from all lands occupied in 1967 and the establishment of a Palestinian state in the West Bank and Gaza. It would be necessary to enlist the support of the USA to exert pressure on Israel to achieve these goals. Early indications certainly gave grounds for optimism in that the new US Administration had identified the Middle East conflict as a primary foreign policy concern and had promised more direct involvement in the region. In February 1977 President Carter sent his Secretary of State, Cyrus Vance, on a tour of the Middle East and invited Israeli and Arab leaders to visit him in Washington, DC. Carter also stated that a 'homeland' for the Palestinians should be a goal of regional peace efforts, while US officials were reported to be in contact with the PLO with the aim of persuading them to modify their position on Israel. In apparent response to both US and Arab lobbying, PLO representatives indicated their willingness to establish a state 'on any part of Palestine' vacated by Israel.

US attempts to foster better relations between Israel and the Arab world faced an immediate challenge with the victory of the right-wing Likud coalition in Israel's May 1977 elections. President Carter issued an early invitation to the new Israeli Prime Minister, Menachem Begin, to visit Washington, DC. Prior to the Israeli leader's arrival in July, the US Department of State reiterated the USA's support for UN Resolution 242 and reaffirmed Carter's belief in 'the need for a homeland for the Palestinians, whose exact nature should be negotiated between the parties'. (These sentiments were echoed in a declaration published by a meeting of EC heads of government at the end of June, which also urged that representatives of the Palestinian people be included in any peace negotiations.) Begin's visit to the USA failed to generate an understanding on which to base a peace settlement. A tour of the Middle East by Vance in August produced a brief sense of optimism when the Saudi Arabian Government reported that the PLO might accept Resolution 242 if it were amended to include provision for Palestinian self-determination. President Carter subsequently raised the possibility of the PLO's being represented in a reconvened Geneva Conference if the movement accepted Resolution 242. However, following the Begin Government's categorical rejection of either dialogue with the PLO or the notion of Palestinian self-determination, the PLO refused to amend its stance over Resolution 242. Within days of Vance's departure from the region, the Begin Government announced that it would be extending health, education and welfare services to the Palestinian populations of the West Bank and Gaza. Arab fears that this was in fact the precursor to Israeli annexation of the two territories were deepened by the announcement that three new Jewish settlements were to be built on the West Bank, and by the unveiling of a draft Israeli proposal for a territorial settlement that envisaged the maintenance of the occupation throughout the West Bank and Gaza. The USA sought to mollify Arab anger with an appeal for Palestinian representatives to be included in an Arab delegation to a future peace conference. This proposal was reluctantly accepted by the Israeli Government. On 1 October the USA and the USSR issued a joint statement urging a Middle East settlement that would ensure 'the legitimate rights of the Palestinians'. The inclusion of such a phrase signalled an important shift in the official US attitude to the Arab–Israeli conflict and clearly troubled the Begin Government. The PLO gave qualified acceptance of the US-Soviet statement as the basis for a reconvened peace summit.

SADAT VISITS ISRAEL

The course of the Arab–Israeli conflict underwent fundamental change at the end of 1977. In a speech to the Egyptian parliament on 9 November, President Sadat expressed his frustration with the lack of progress towards a peace settlement and announced that he would be prepared to go to Jerusalem to negotiate directly with Israel. His offer was immediately taken up by Israel, and on 19 November Sadat flew to Tel-Aviv. His initiative was warmly welcomed in the West, where it was regarded as a bold attempt to break with the sterile attitudes of the past. Within the Arab world, however, Sadat's visit was viewed with a mix of scepticism and hostility. This reaction was centred on a conviction that the Egyptian leader was prepared fatally to undermine the cause of Arab unity for an initiative that was self-serving and unlikely to achieve its minimum expectations. Egypt's Minister of Foreign Affairs resigned in protest against the visit. Arab fears were undimmed by the international euphoria that accompanied the Sadat trip, and appeared to be confirmed when it emerged that Israeli leaders had stated a readiness to withdraw from most Egyptian territory but were unprepared to cede all Arab lands captured in 1967. When negotiations between the two states resumed on 25 December 1977 in Egypt, at Ismailia, Menachem Begin produced a set of proposals for the West Bank and Gaza that offered the Palestinian population a modest degree of self-rule under the auspices of Israeli 'security and public order' control. Sadat's embarrassment at the limited scope of Israeli proposals on issues of territory and Palestinian self-determination was matched by a deepening Arab cynicism towards the motives of Egypt's ruler. Israeli-Egyptian talks on military and political issues affecting a settlement resumed in Cairo on 16 January 1978, but were suspended almost immediately because of Egyptian anger with Israel's insistence on retaining settlements in occupied Sinai.

ISRAEL INVADES SOUTHERN LEBANON

The Palestinians had been among the most vociferous in denouncing Sadat's overtures to Israel. In March 1978 PLO gunmen launched a sea-borne raid north of Tel-Aviv, killing 36 Israelis. Israel responded with a major land and air assault on Palestinian bases in southern Lebanon. The USA hurriedly introduced a resolution at the UN Security Council: Resolution 425, adopted on 19 March, demanded that Israel withdraw its troops, under UN supervision, and respect Lebanese territorial integrity, sovereignty and independence. Israel agreed to a cease-fire the following day, but by this time its forces were in occupation of nearly all Lebanese territory up to the Litani river. Israel's invasion was condemned internationally for its high human cost: an estimated 1,000 Lebanese and Palestinian civilians had been killed in the Israeli bombardments, and more than 200,000 had fled their homes. Friction soon developed over the role of the UN Interim Force in Lebanon (UNIFIL), the body mandated to supervise an Israeli withdrawal. The Israel Defence Forces (IDF) undertook a partial withdrawal at the end of April, but Israeli leaders insisted that they would maintain an armed presence in the country until the UN force could ensure the security of northern Israel against Palestinian incursions. Although determined not to relinquish its presence in southern Lebanon, the PLO promised to co-operate with UNIFIL. Israeli forces eventually withdrew from Lebanese territory on 13 June, but handed over their positions to their right-wing Lebanese militia allies, rather than to UNIFIL. Alarmed at the instability caused by Israel's invasion of Lebanon and the prospect of the Sadat peace initiative unravelling, President Carter persuaded the Israeli and Egyptian ministers responsible for foreign affairs to attend talks in the United Kingdom in July. When this meeting ended with the Egyptians announcing that they would not take part in further negotiations unless Israel changed its positions, Carter invited Begin and Sadat to a final attempt to break the deadlock at the US presidential retreat at Camp David, Maryland, in September.

THE CAMP DAVID ACCORDS

The Camp David talks lasted for 12 days. At their conclusion on 17 September 1978 President Carter announced that the Egyptian and Israeli leaders had signed two documents providing a framework for peace in the Middle East (Documents on Palestine, see p. 69). The first committed Israel and Egypt to conclude a peace treaty that would provide for an Israeli withdrawal from Sinai and the establishment of normal relations. The second concerned the future of the West Bank and Gaza and proposed the election of a self-governing Palestinian authority to replace the existing military administration. Palestinian autonomy would last for a period of five years, during which time there would be negotiations to determine the final status of the territories and to conclude a peace treaty between Israel and Jordan. The agreements were greeted in the West as a triumph of US politics and diplomacy. They were also given cautious approval in Israel, where there was satisfaction that a peace treaty could be completed with Egypt without substantive concessions on the issues of Israeli settlements and continued territorial control over the other lands conquered in 1967.

Jordan and Saudi Arabia, both key players in shaping regional opinion, declared strong reservations about the terms of the Camp David accords. The more radical Arab states, led by Syria, joined the PLO in declaring their outright rejection. In November 1978 representatives of the League of Arab States (Arab League) convened in Baghdad, Iraq, to discuss action to be taken against Egypt—which was not invited to the session. After heated debate over measures to isolate the Sadat Government, it was agreed that formal sanctions would be postponed until such time as a peace treaty with Israel was actually signed. It was argued that this would allow Sadat to reconsider a political course that would lead to total dependence on the USA. Accelerated settlement construction in the Occupied Territories, coupled with Israel's reluctance to comply with Egyptian requests for a timetable for the implementation of autonomy proposals on the West Bank, led to increasingly bitter recriminations and the missing of the deadline, of 18 December, for the bilateral treaty to be signed. Ministerial meetings in Washington, DC, failed to break the deadlock, and on 7 March 1979 the US President flew to the Middle East. After intensive discussions Carter announced on his return to the USA that 'we have now defined the major components of a peace treaty'. On 26 March, and despite reports of a serious rift on the issue of Israeli settlement on the West Bank, the Israeli-Egyptian peace treaty was signed in Washington, DC, by Anwar Sadat and Menachem Begin (Documents on Palestine, see p. 71). The optimism in the West that was generated by the symbolism of an Arab and an Israeli leader shaking hands on the White House lawn was swiftly dispelled by the decision of the rest of the Arab world to impose an immediate political and economic boycott of Egypt, and to transfer the Arab League headquarters from Cairo to the Tunisian capital, Tunis. Sadat maintained that his treaty with Israel was the first step towards a comprehensive regional settlement that would restore the rights of the Palestinians. To the rest of the Arab world it appeared that Egypt had entered into a separate understanding that would see the return of Sinai to Egypt, but would leave the rest of occupied Arab land under Israeli control. This perception was reinforced by a broadcast made by Begin in which he asserted that no border would ever be drawn 'through the land of Israel' and that 'we shall never withdraw from the Golan Heights'.

Early agreements were reached between Israel and Egypt on the issue of border controls, oil sales and the return of Sinai's St Catherine's monastery to Egypt. However, discussion on the implementation of Palestinian autonomy continued to be soured by the Likud Government's settlement policy. In May 1979 Israel disclosed plans for an ambitious programme of settlement construction in the West Bank and Gaza, and in September the ban on Israeli citizens purchasing Arab land in the Occupied Territories was ended. Although the left-wing opposition in Israel, loosely organized under the banner of the Peace Now movement, was able to mount legal challenges to the proposed construction of certain settlements, the process of expropriation, land clearance and large-scale construction was leaving an ever larger imprint on the physical landscape of the West Bank and Gaza.

Western European governments became more vocal in their opposition to Israeli policy in the Occupied Territories, recognizing the centrality of the Palestinians, and the PLO, to the Arab–Israeli issue. In July 1979 the EC representative at the UN appealed for a role for the PLO in the efforts to bring peace to the Middle East, while strongly criticizing Israeli policy. In November the PLO was awarded political recognition by the Italian Government. PLO leaders also held talks with government representatives in Portugal, Belgium, Italy and Greece. Speculation that the USA was itself engaging in dialogue with the PLO was repeatedly denied by President Carter. In September, however, the US ambassador to the UN, Andrew Young, met with the PLO observer, Labib Terzi. Protests from the Israeli Government forced Young to resign; the departing ambassador described the USA's refusal to talk to the PLO as 'ridiculous'. The influence of the Jewish lobby on US policy was again demonstrated in March 1980 when President Carter retracted an affirmative US vote on UN Security Council Resolution 465 (Documents on Palestine, see p. 72), which sought the dismantling of 'existing settlements' in the Occupied Territories. The EC states continued, meanwhile, to develop links with the PLO and to lend support to the idea of Palestinian self-determination. In June an EC summit meeting in Venice, Italy, issued a statement declaring collectively for the first time support for full Palestinian self-determination and a role for the PLO in the search for a comprehensive peace. The statement also repeated opposition to Israeli settlements and any change to the status of Jerusalem.

Ronald Reagan was elected US President at the end of 1980. Viewed as strongly sympathetic to the Jewish state, his appointment of a team of pro-Israeli foreign affairs advisers caused consternation in the Arab world. Concerns were heightened when the new President appeared to reverse existing US policy by declaring that Israeli settlements were 'not illegal'. The Reagan Administration faced an early test of its attitudes to the Arab–Israeli conflict following the shooting down of two Syrian helicopters by Israeli military aircraft over Lebanon. In response Syria deployed batteries of anti-aircraft missiles in the Beqa'a valley. Israel demanded the withdrawal of the missiles, while the US Special Envoy to the Middle East, Philip Habib, urged Saudi Arabia to persuade Syria to withdraw the missiles. The Saudi Government, however, joined the rest of the Arab world in strongly supporting the Syrian position. In June 1981 Begin warned that if the USA failed to arrange the withdrawal of the missiles through diplomacy, then Israel would remove them by force. In the same month the Israeli Government dramatically underlined its willingness to resort to military measures by bombing and destroying an Iraqi nuclear installation near Baghdad. Israel justified the raid on the grounds of self-defence, although most experts, including the International Atomic Energy Agency (IAEA), concurred that Iraq would not have the means to produce nuclear weapons for many years. President Reagan indicated his Administration's displeasure by suspending the sale of four *F-16* fighter aircraft to Israel. He commented, none the less, that Israel had 'reason for concern' about Iraq's nuclear programme.

Begin's Likud coalition was returned to power in the June 1981 election. Ariel Sharon, one of the nation's foremost 'hawks', was appointed as Minister of Defence. Ten days after the election Israel launched air-strikes against Palestinian targets in Lebanon, causing many deaths. The PLO retaliated with rocket fire against Israel's northern townships. Pressure from the USA on Israel, and from Saudi Arabia on the Palestinians, eventually brought about a cease-fire, which came into effect on 24 July.

ASSASSINATION OF SADAT

In October 1981 President Anwar Sadat was killed by Islamist extremists during a military parade in Cairo. The assassination followed months of tension in Egypt as intercommunal fighting was followed by a clampdown on the media and the detention of hundreds of Sadat's political opponents. The death of the Egyptian President marked the final chapter of the Camp David process. Sadat's successor, Hosni Mubarak, made it clear that, although he would refrain from any political initiatives that could jeopardize the scheduled return of Sinai to Egypt, his principal strategic goal would be to mend fences with the rest of the Arab world. Sadat's funeral brought an impressive array of Western dignitaries to Cairo, but was largely ignored by the local population. The absence of public grief contrasted sharply with the scenes that had accompanied Nasser's funeral, and was interpreted as a telling symbol of Egyptian and Arab disaffection with Sadat's pro-Western foreign policy.

Saudi Arabia had already attempted to fill the vacuum created by the failures of Camp David by launching its own peace initiative in August 1981. Known as the Fahd Plan, after its author the Saudi Crown Prince, it promised recognition of Israel in return for the establishment of a Palestinian state in the Occupied Territories (Documents on Palestine, see p. 73). The EC states responded positively to the proposal, noting its similarities to their own Venice Declaration of the previous year, the USA less so. Prime Minister Begin dismissed the Plan as a recipe for Israel's destruction, while the Arab world, with the exception of Libya, accorded it varied levels of approval. However, the tentative prospect of agreement on a joint Arab-European framework for a regional settlement quickly receded. Following a visit to Israel, the French Minister of Foreign Affairs distanced his Government from the European initiative. In November Syria led several Arab states in opposition to the timing—rather than the substance—of the Fahd Plan. The regional political climate became even less receptive to peace initiatives at the end of 1981 when the Israeli Knesset (parliament) endorsed government legislation extending Israeli laws, jurisdiction and administration over the occupied Golan Heights. The UN Security Council, in Resolution 497, unanimously condemned the annexation of the Syrian territory and gave Israel two weeks to rescind its decision. Despite the regional disquiet over the Golan annexation, Israel proceeded with its scheduled withdrawal from Sinai on 25 April 1982. Prior to the evacuation Israeli troops had forcibly removed settlers who had occupied the Yamit settlement in the north of the peninsula.

ISRAEL'S REINVASION OF LEBANON

The dismissal of elected pro-PLO mayors in the West Bank in early 1982 precipitated sustained street protests there and in Gaza against Israeli occupation, in which several Palestinians were killed. In May the Israeli air force broke the cease-fire that had held along its northern border, launching strikes on Palestinian targets inside Lebanon. The attempted assassination of Israel's ambassador to the United Kingdom by radical Palestinians opposed to the PLO was followed by further Israeli air raids on targets in Lebanon, to which the PLO retaliated with rocket attacks on northern Israel. Although the Palestinian counter-attack did not result in any casualties, it became the official pretext for a full-scale Israeli invasion of Lebanon, designated Operation Peace for Galilee. By 10 June, four days after 30,000 troops of the IDF had crossed into Lebanese territory, the main coastal cities had been captured and Israeli tanks had taken up positions on the outskirts of Beirut. Syrian ground forces stationed in Lebanon put up some resistance to the Israeli advance, while the Syrian air force suffered heavy losses as the Israelis demonstrated their overwhelming superiority in the air.

A cease-fire between the two sides was brokered by the USA on 11 June 1982, but fighting with Palestinian forces intensified as the Israeli army tightened its siege of west Beirut: water, electricity, food and medical supplies were cut, while Israeli artillery and aircraft maintained a relentless bombardment. Ariel Sharon announced that the siege would be lifted only if PLO combatants surrendered or left the city. This the PLO finally agreed to do on 21 August, as part of an arrangement that also provided for the deployment of a multinational force (MNF) to supervise the withdrawal and protect the civilians of west Beirut. By the end of the month the PLO had evacuated its forces from the city. A second Israeli objective was also achieved on 23 August, when the Lebanese National Assembly was persuaded to elect the pro-Israeli Phalangist commander, Bashir Gemayel, as the new Lebanese President. On 14 September Gemayel was assassinated in a bomb explosion at his party headquarters. Two days later the IDF command apparently allowed right-wing Christian militias into the Palestinian refugee camps of Sabra and Chatila to 'mop up' remaining resistance. Over a 48-hour period the militias killed an estimated 1,500 civilians. International outrage at the massacre forced the Israeli Government to launch an inquiry into the circumstances surrounding the events in the Palestinian camps. A report published in February 1983 considered Minister of Defence Sharon as principally responsible for the Sabra and Chatila operation. He resigned his post, but remained in the Government as a Minister without Portfolio.

THE REAGAN PLAN

In September 1982 US President Ronald Reagan formulated new proposals to settle the Arab–Israeli conflict. The Reagan Plan envisaged the restoration of the Occupied Territories to their Arab populations, but ruled out the creation of a Palestinian state. Instead, it proposed Palestinian self-government in association with Jordan. The position of Jordan's King Hussein was crucial to the success of the US proposal. Visiting Washington, DC, in December, Hussein made it clear that he would only be prepared to explore the Reagan proposals if he received a mandate to that effect from the Palestinians. Although it emerged that Arafat and Palestinian moderates were not fundamentally opposed to the Reagan Plan, there was strong opposition from PLO factions backed by Syria.

On 17 May 1983 the Lebanese administration of President Amin Gemayel (brother of Bashir) and the Israeli Government signed a US-brokered agreement providing for the withdrawal of Israeli troops from Lebanon and the establishment of joint Israeli-Lebanese patrols along their common border. However, the Begin Government stressed that any withdrawal from southern Lebanon would be conditional upon a simultaneous withdrawal of Syrian troops from the Beqa'a valley. The agreement was roundly condemned by President Assad of Syria, who was committed to ensuring that the Israelis would gain no influence over Lebanese affairs as a result of their 1982 invasion. To underline his regime's opposition to a softening of the Arab approach towards Israel, Assad subsequently gave his backing to a revolt by dissidents within Arafat's own Fatah movement. Under the command of Abu Musa, and supported by units of the Syrian army, the Fatah rebels captured loyalist positions in the Beqa'a valley. In June 1983 Assad expelled Arafat from Syria. Meanwhile, Palestinian and Lebanese guerrilla attacks on the Israeli army had persuaded Israel's Cabinet to order a unilateral pull-back of Israeli forces behind the more easily defensible line of the Awali river. The withdrawal not only confirmed that the agreement of 17 May would not be implemented; it also exposed the weakness of the Gemayel regime. Shortly after the 4 September retreat of the IDF to the Awali, the pro-Syrian Druze militia, led by Walid Joumblatt, launched a full-scale assault on the Christian forces allied to the Lebanese President. The Druze made rapid and significant gains, prompting the US offshore fleet to shell Druze- and Syrian-controlled territory in the hills above Beirut. Saudi Arabia succeeded in mediating a cease-fire between the warring factions, which came into effect on

25 September. The terms of the cease-fire provided for a dialogue of national reconciliation with Syrian participation, effectively awarding Syria a power of veto over political developments in Lebanon. Syria also continued its military support for Fatah rebels laying siege to Arafat's last remaining stronghold around the northern Lebanese port of Tripoli. The increasingly isolated PLO leader was only able to gain the neutrality of other opposition groups within the PLO by bowing to demands to submit to the Palestinian Central Council (PCC)'s denunciation of the Reagan Plan.

The growth of Syrian influence in Lebanese affairs, and the delivery to Damascus of Soviet long-range surface-to-surface missiles in October 1983, alarmed the US Administration and encouraged the Department of State to view the Lebanese situation increasingly in the context of the Cold War. US intervention on the side of the Gemayel Government had concomitantly strengthened Lebanese Muslim, and wider Arab, perceptions that the USA lacked the credibility to be an honest regional broker. Deepening anger at the Western role in Lebanon found violent expression in simultaneous suicide bombings of the headquarters of the US and French contingents of the MNF in Beirut, in which 241 US Marines and 58 French soldiers were killed. Two extremist Shi'ite groups linked to Iran claimed responsibility for the attacks, although US officials also ascribed a degree of culpability to Syria and the USSR (both of which denied any involvement). Shortly afterwards a bomb attack on Israel's military headquarters in Tyre caused 60 deaths. Israeli military aircraft bombed Palestinian and Druze positions in retaliation for the attack, and the Israeli authorities appealed for closer military co-ordination with the USA. The announcement of a policy of 'strategic co-operation' between the USA and Israel was denounced by Syria, which ordered a general mobilization of its forces on 7 November. Continued faith in military support from the USA and Israel allowed Gemayel's Government to resist demands from Syria and its Lebanese allies for the abrogation of the 17 May agreement and for constitutional changes. Israeli air raids on Syrian-controlled territory continued through the latter part of 1983, and on 4 December two US aircraft were shot down in a direct clash with Syrian forces.

ARAFAT'S DEPARTURE FROM LEBANON

Although the Assad Government saw its prestige in the Arab world enhanced by its confrontational stance towards the USA and Israel, its military involvement in the bloody conflict between Arafat loyalists and Abu Musa's forces proved deeply unpopular. As the siege of Arafat's fighters in Tripoli became more desperate, residual sympathy for the initial aims of the dissidents—to challenge the autocratic and unprincipled style of Arafat's leadership—was replaced by the perception that Abu Musa had become little more than a Syrian 'puppet' and that the struggle had become one for PLO independence from external control. This was felt particularly strongly in the Occupied Territories. Arafat's standing was further enhanced when on 24 November he was able to exchange six Israeli prisoners for 4,800 Lebanese and Palestinians held by the Israelis. Lobbying by the USSR and by the states of the Persian (Arabian) Gulf achieved Syrian agreement to end the Tripoli siege through the evacuation of Arafat and some 4,000 loyalists by sea. Their departure was, however, delayed until 20 December by an Israeli naval bombardment of Tripoli and refusal to guarantee the UN evacuation fleet safe passage.

Renewed attacks on the US contingent of the MNF in Lebanon, and further US bombardments of anti-Gemayel forces around Beirut, caused increasing disquiet among the USA's European partners in the MNF. At the beginning of February 1984 further heavy fighting in Lebanon prompted the resignation of the Lebanese Government and the disintegration of the Lebanese army along sectarian lines. With Druze and Shi'ite militiamen co-operating effectively against the embattled Gemayel, the role of the MNF became increasingly untenable. By the end of February US, Italian and the token British force had withdrawn from Beirut. French troops followed in March, leaving west Beirut, as in the days before the Israeli invasion, under the control of left-wing and Muslim militias. On 5 March Gemayel abrogated the 17 May Lebanese-Israel agreement in return for guarantees of internal security from Syria. At the end of April a new Government of national unity was installed in Lebanon. Gemayel retained the presidency, but the new Lebanese Cabinet reflected Syrian influence and the growing importance of the Shi'a community. The new Government resolved to secure the complete and unconditional removal of Israeli forces from the country, and awarded responsibility for the southern region to the leader of the Shi'a Amal militia, Nabih Berri, whose fighters had been at the forefront of resistance to the IDF.

Menachem Begin unexpectedly resigned the Israeli premiership on 30 August 1983. He was succeeded by the equally hawkish Minister of Foreign Affairs, Itzhak Shamir. The new Israeli Prime Minister was faced by a series of pressing challenges. Spiralling inflation and massive debt had brought the country to the verge of bankruptcy, and forced the imposition of austerity measures including huge reductions in public spending, cuts in subsidies on basic commodities and the devaluation of the national currency. Defence and settlement were not immune from the cuts, causing a backlash from Shamir's right-wing coalition partners who were eager to sustain the rapid colonization of the Occupied Territories initiated by his predecessor. The publication in February 1984 of a long-suppressed report by the Ministry of Justice into Jewish terrorism against Palestinians in the Occupied Territories also served to embarrass the Likud leader, detailing as it did the consistent failures of the Israeli Government to apprehend the perpetrators. In April the security forces finally acted, arresting some 30 people suspected of planting bombs on Arab buses. At their trial the leaders of the so-called Jewish Underground confessed to attacks including an armed assault on Hebron University in July 1983 that had left three students dead. Their stated aim was to force a mass Palestinian exodus from the West Bank. Statements from right-wing political leaders effectively condoning the actions of the extremists caused consternation among liberal Israeli opinion.

Abroad, Shamir was also having to come to terms with the scale of the failure of the Lebanese war. Far from securing a 'client regime' in Beirut, it had brought about the defeat of Israel's Christian allies and served to entrench Syrian influence. Despite the reverses suffered by the PLO, the Israeli army and its militia allies of the self-styled South Lebanon Army (SLA) were now confronted by a Shi'a guerrilla foe which was proving to be a dedicated adversary. The human cost of the invasion and occupation—600 deaths and 3,000 wounded by June 1984—had led to domestic agitation for withdrawal, as well as deeper questioning of the wisdom of Israel's military adventure.

PLO-JORDANIAN INITIATIVES

On leaving Tripoli in late 1983, Arafat travelled to Egypt for a meeting with President Mubarak. This was the first time a prominent Arab leader had set foot on Egyptian territory since the Camp David accords. The Palestinian leader's de facto ending of the Arab boycott of Egypt was followed by the signing of an Egyptian-Jordanian protocol in January 1984, raising expectations of the emergence of a moderate Arab alignment comprising Egypt, Jordan and the PLO. Syria and the left-wing PLO factions denounced the rapprochement with Egypt and the developing relationship between the PLO and Jordan. The Israeli Prime Minister also criticized the Arafat-Mubarak meeting as a 'severe blow to the peace process', but the US Administration welcomed the dialogue as a boost for the Reagan Plan. In a move that was interpreted as preparing the constitutional ground for a joint Palestinian-Jordanian initiative, King Hussein decided on 5 January to reconvene the Jordanian parliament (its representation theoretically divided the East and West Banks of the Jordan), which had been suspended since the 1974 Rabat summit decision to accord the PLO the status of sole representative of the Palestinian people.

In 1984 early elections were forced on the Shamir Government by the defection of a minor party from the ruling coalition. The precarious state of the economy became a principal election issue. With the occupation of Lebanon costing an estimated US $1m. per day, the pledge of the Labour leader, Shimon Peres, to bring Israeli troops home within 'three to six months' proved to be popular with the electorate. At the election, held on 23 July, Likud and the Labour Party each secured one-third of Knesset seats, with the balance being held by several small left- and right-wing parties. The ensuing political deadlock was broken when Peres and Shamir agreed to form a government of national unity with a two-year rotation of the posts of Prime Minister and Minister of Foreign Affairs.

After securing the endorsement, in November 1984, of the 17th session of the Palestine National Council (PNC—the supreme organ of the PLO) for further negotiations with Jordan on a common approach to a Middle East settlement, Yasser Arafat and King Hussein signed an accord in the Jordanian capital in February 1985. This provided for Palestinian self-determination within the framework of a Jordanian-Palestinian federation. It also appealed for peace negotiations involving all parties to the conflict and the five permanent members of the UN Security Council. The Amman agreement was opposed by Syria and Arafat's Damascus-based opposition. The USA viewed the raising of the Jordanian profile positively, but still refused to deal directly with the PLO. Visits to the Middle East by the US Secretary of State, George Shultz, in early 1985 failed to resolve the central dilemma of Palestinian representation in future peace talks. In the Occupied Territories Israel responded to violence and civil unrest with deportations of activists and lengthy closures of Palestinian universities. In October, in response to the PLO's killing of three Israelis in Cyprus, Israel's air force bombed the PLO headquarters in Tunis, killing 75 people. In the same month gunmen belonging to a pro-Arafat faction of the PLO hijacked an Italian cruise-liner, murdering an elderly Jewish American passenger. Arafat's condemnation of the incident did not persuade the US Administration to compromise the official position that the PLO and personalities close to it should be excluded from the peace process. Moreover, the reluctance of the PLO to meet US preconditions for a dialogue, namely that it accept Resolution 242 in its entirety and recognize the State of Israel, had begun to frustrate King Hussein. Mindful also of a general lack of enthusiasm in the Arab world for the Jordanian-Palestinian accord, the King moved to ease the traditionally frosty relations with his northern neighbour. On 21 October Jordan signalled its intention to move away from further collaboration with Yasser Arafat by signing an agreement with Syria that included a pledge not to seek a separate peace with Israel. In February 1986 King Hussein announced the end of political co-ordination with the PLO leadership, citing his disappointment at the organization's preoccupation with self-determination at the expense of the 'liberation of the land', and at its refusal to accept Resolution 242.

ISRAELI WITHDRAWAL TO THE SOUTHERN LEBANESE 'SECURITY ZONE'

At the beginning of 1985, after failing to reach agreement in UN-brokered talks on a withdrawal from Lebanon, the Israeli Cabinet announced plans for a unilateral departure in three phases. By 10 June the Israelis had evacuated most of the territory they held, leaving in their wake fresh outbreaks of fighting between Christian and Muslim forces. Shi'ite militias harried the retreating IDF, their anger exacerbated by the revelation that the departing Israelis had secretly transferred more than 1,000 Lebanese Shi'ite prisoners to Israel. Israel retained a strip of Lebanese territory, 8 km–10 km wide, along its northern border as a self-declared 'security zone'. Responsibility for policing the zone would fall to the IDF and their allies in the SLA.

THE 'WAR OF THE CAMPS'

Syria was determined that Arafat's PLO should not re-establish itself in Lebanon after the Israeli withdrawal. In 1985 the pro-Syrian Amal militia began a bombardment of the Palestinian refugee camps in Beirut, besieging the inhabitants and causing hundreds of casualties. During 1986 the fighting spread to the southern cities of Tyre and Sidon, where PLO forces—many of them loyal to Arafat—had once again developed a power base. The extended assault on the Palestinians would prove to be a political mistake for Assad. Confronted by a common enemy, the erstwhile pro-Syrian factions of the PLO joined forces with the Arafat loyalists to defend their Palestinian constituency. Crucially, none of the other leftist or Muslim militias shared Amal's enthusiasm for siding with Syria against the PLO. Several of the militias gave active support to the Palestinians, prompting a series of clashes with Amal at the beginning of 1987. With Western media attention arousing widespread international sympathy for the plight of the Palestinians, Syria acted to end the sieges in February.

The 'war of the camps' paved the way for the reunification of the PLO. The 18th session of the PNC, held in Algiers, Algeria, in April 1987, was attended by all principal factions of the organization. In return for factional fealty to his leadership, Arafat agreed to abrogate the Amman accord with Jordan and to downgrade co-operation with Egypt until Cairo formally renounced the Camp David agreements. The unification was greeted with great enthusiasm among a Palestinian population tired of resistance to Israel being compromised by factional wrangling. The outcome of the 18th PNC was less welcome among the neighbouring Arab states, each of which saw its future ability to manipulate the PLO as being seriously undermined.

THE PALESTINIAN UPRISING

During 1987 demonstrations against Israeli policy grew in frequency in the Occupied Territories, as did incidences of armed attacks against Israel's security forces. Israel responded with widespread administrative detentions, house demolitions and other retaliatory measures. On 8 December four workers in Gaza were killed in a road traffic accident involving an Israeli military vehicle. Their funerals precipitated huge demonstrations in Gaza and prolonged assaults on Israeli security forces, whose increasing use of live ammunition in counter-operations caused a number of fatalities. The rioting quickly spread to the West Bank. As the number of Palestinian deaths mounted and the street protests intensified, the populations of the Occupied Territories began to refer to their revolt as the *intifada* (uprising). Initially spontaneous, the *intifada* soon became co-ordinated under the leadership of the clandestine Unified National Leadership of the Uprising (UNLU), an umbrella organization composed of the different PLO factions and the militant Islamic Jihad. Broadly loyal to the PLO, UNLU issued regular communiqués co-ordinating strikes and demonstrations and encouraging civil disobedience. That Israel was clearly caught off guard by the scale and the ferocity of the revolt was apparently reflected in its initial response. Shootings and beatings of unarmed demonstrators caused an international outcry, and mass arrests of activists and continued deportations of suspected ringleaders only appeared to fuel the rebellion.

Amid mounting international concern at events in the Occupied Territories, US Secretary of State George Shultz formulated proposals to end the conflict. His plan (Documents on Palestine, see p. 73) appealed for negotiations between Israel and a Jordanian-Palestinian delegation, based on Resolutions 242 and 338, to determine an interim form of autonomy for the Occupied Territories. Such a transitional arrangement would last for three years and would provide for an Israeli military withdrawal on the West Bank and for municipal elections of Palestinian officials. Negotiations on a final settlement would begin within the year and be paralleled by an international conference involving the five permanent members of the UN Security Council and all other parties to the conflict. This latter conference would have no power to veto any agreements reached in the separate Israeli-Jordanian-Palestinian talks. Israeli Prime Minister Shamir pronounced that the Shultz Plan had 'no prospect of implementation'. Jordan announced itself opposed to 'partial or interim solutions', although welcoming US acknowledgement of the legitimate rights of the Palestinians. However, Egypt and Syria gave no indication that they would support the Plan's implementation, while the PLO rejected it outright on the grounds that it failed to make provision for a Palestinian state or for the organization's own participation in the process. The PLO position won the backing of the Arab League, convened in an emergency summit meeting in Algiers in June, which promised financial support to sustain the 'heroic' Palestinian uprising.

By early 1988 the *intifada* was firmly entrenched in the Occupied Territories. Suspension of fuel supplies, the cutting of telephone links with the outside world, the closure of media outlets and a daily round of arrests and shootings had failed to curb the protests. After reports of initial friction between UNLU and the external leadership over the co-ordination of the uprising, it had become clear that a good working relationship existed—with the PLO abroad taking responsibility for ensuring the passage of funds to the Occupied Territories and for overall political strategy. Arafat's deputy, Khalil al-Wazir (alias 'Abu Jihad'), who had been accorded responsibility for co-ordinating strategy with cadres in the West Bank and Gaza, was killed by an Israeli assassination squad in Tunis on 16 April. His death led to furious protests in the Occupied Territories, to which the Israeli security forces' response was severe: 16 Palestinians were shot dead in a single day. By the end of July 1988 more than 290 people had been killed in the *intifada*.

DECLARATION OF PALESTINIAN INDEPENDENCE

King Hussein announced in July 1988 that he was severing Jordan's legal and administrative links with the West Bank. He explained his decision in terms of complying with the wishes of the PLO and the Arab League. In the short term the King's decision dealt a blow to US peace plans, and also undermined the Israeli Labour Party's advocacy of a Jordanian-Palestinian federation. UNLU issued a statement applauding the Jordanian decision as the 'greatest accomplishment' of the *intifada*, while for the PLO it presented a serious challenge. The Occupied Territories (with the exception of Arab Jerusalem) were now claimed by no sovereign state as their territory, providing the PLO with an historic opportunity to assert sovereignty over a specific area. Arafat immediately began canvassing international support for a new peace strategy. Addressing the European Parliament in September 1988, he asserted the PLO's willingness to recognize Israel's right to security in return for Israeli recognition of an independent Palestinian state. He also declared his movement's opposition to armed action outside the Occupied Territories. In Algiers on 15 November, at the close of the 19th session of the PNC, an independent State of Palestine was unilaterally declared (Documents on Palestine, see p. 74), with the PLO's Executive Committee functioning as an ad hoc government. Addressing the UN General Assembly in December, Arafat went further, explicitly recognizing Israel and renouncing 'terrorism'. He also appealed for an international peace conference to be held on the basis of Resolutions 242 and 338. Shamir (who had been returned to power in the previous month's Israeli general election) dismissed Arafat's address as a 'public relations exercise'. After concerted mediation by the Swedish Government, the outgoing Reagan Administration acknowledged the PLO's concessions by holding the USA's first official talks with representatives of the movement. Despite reservations that too much had been conceded with too few firm guarantees, the declaration of Palestinian independence and the opening of a dialogue with the USA were regarded in the Occupied Territories as vindication of the sacrifices of the *intifada*.

Under pressure to respond to Arafat's diplomatic offensive with ideas of its own, the Shamir Government (a Likud-Labour coalition) produced its own initiative for a negotiated end to the conflict. Formally announced in April 1989, the Shamir proposals provided for elections in the West Bank and Gaza in return for an end to the *intifada*. The elections would produce a Palestinian delegation to conduct negotiations on a final settlement. As further details of the plan emerged in May, it became clear that Shamir was offering little more than a reworking of the Camp David proposals. The declared opposition to a Palestinian state, and the proposed Israeli veto over any future changes to the status of the Occupied Territories, effectively ensured that the Shamir Plan would be unacceptable to the PLO and to the wider Arab world. Attempts by Egypt's President Mubarak and by the US Secretary of State, James Baker, to make the proposals more acceptable to Arab opinion failed to produce an outcome that would meet minimum Palestinian demands.

Among the population of the Occupied Territories, there were signs of exhaustion with the efforts necessary to sustain the uprising. The mass character of the *intifada* had been gradually undermined by the lengthening lists of dead and injured and by the weight of punitive Israeli reprisals. The failure of Arafat's 'historic' concessions to achieve substantive political gains had come as a bitter disappointment and had led to fierce debate as to the wisdom of the PLO's peace strategy. This, in turn, had created a steady growth in factional tension and an alarming increase in killings of Palestinians suspected of 'collaboration' with the Israeli authorities. Disillusion within the territories, and political impasse without, had strengthened the hand of the radical resistance; foremost among these movements was the Islamic Resistance Movement (Hamas), a radical offshoot of the Muslim Brotherhood opposed to any accommodation with Israel. Palestinian despondency was further deepened by the relaxation of emigration controls in the USSR and the prediction of a huge increase in Soviet Jewish migration to Israel. Shamir had welcomed the prospect of new arrivals, while Israeli officials stated that they would not dissuade the estimated 150,000 new immigrants from settling in the Occupied Territories. This brought protest from the Arab League, but also a less predictable warning from the new US Administration of George Bush that it was opposed not only to the settling of new immigrants in Gaza and the West Bank but also in East Jerusalem.

THE GULF CONFLICT

In August 1990 Iraqi troops invaded Kuwait. A proposal by Iraq's President, Saddam Hussain, to link Iraq's withdrawal from Kuwait with an Israeli withdrawal from the Occupied Territories was greeted with great enthusiasm by Palestinians. After early attempts to co-ordinate a pan-Arab response to the Iraqi invasion had led to confused acrimony, Yasser Arafat joined the small number of Arab states—principally Jordan, Yemen and Sudan—aligned with Iraq against the deployment of a US-led multinational force in Saudi Arabia. Willing the opprobrium of the West and the 'conservative' Arab states through such close identification with Iraq was regarded by many observers as a grave political error. Palestinian commentators rejoined that such was the groundswell of popular support for an Arab leader portrayed as confronting Western hypocrisy and interference that Arafat had no other option. For Israel, the crisis in the Gulf region could be argued to have created a welcome diversion of international attention from its suppression of the *intifada*. It was crucial to Western strategy to avoid scenarios that might involve the intervention of an explicit 'Israeli factor' in the impending conflict, as this would almost certainly signal the end of the uneasy Arab alliance against Saddam Hussain. Ensuring that Israel was not drawn into the conflict thus became an unswerving priority of the USA. There was a similar realization that those Arab states giving their reluctant support to the military build-up in Saudi Arabia would expect political reward for their loyalty in the form of movement towards a resolution of their conflict with Israel. The killing of 17 Palestinians by Israeli troops in Jerusalem's Old City in October provided the Bush Administration with an early test, and in supporting Resolution 672 the USA voted for the first time in the UN Security Council to censure Israel.

On 19 January 1991, three days after the multinational force had begun its aerial bombardment of Iraq, Saddam Hussain carried out his threat to launch *Scud* missiles against Israel. Armed with conventional warheads, the strikes caused widespread panic and damage to buildings but only minor casualties. The attacks drew immediate demands for retaliation from senior Israeli political and military figures. The USA and the European members of the multinational force urged restraint, as Egypt and Syria made it clear they would not remain aligned against Saddam Hussain if Iraq were attacked by Israel. The USA reinforced its appeal for restraint with an airlift of *Patriot* anti-missile batteries to Israel and the concerted targeting of *Scud* missile launchers inside Iraq. The Bush Administration also assured Shamir that it would provide funding for the development of Israel's own anti-ballistic missile project.

The decisive defeat of Iraq by the multinational force left the PLO demoralized and isolated. The members of the Cooperation Council for the Arab States of the Gulf (Gulf Cooperation Council—GCC) punished the PLO for its support of Iraq by cutting off funds, and openly canvassed for a change in its leadership. Israel drew comfort from the PLO's vulnerability, and had attracted considerable international sympathy through its restraint following the *Scud* attacks. Shamir was, none the less, wary of the political pressures that might accompany the post-war search for a resolution of the Arab–Israeli conflict. As expected, US Secretary of State James Baker made several tours of the Middle East in the weeks following the end of the war. However, his attempts to procure support for a regional peace conference, to be sponsored jointly by the USA and USSR, failed to win the firm endorsement of either Israel or the front-line Arab states. Israel indicated that it would only support such a conference if it led directly to bilateral talks. Shamir also ruled out goodwill gestures to the populations of the Occupied Territories as long as the *intifada* continued. After lengthy talks in Damascus, President Assad reaffirmed that Syria would only attend a peace conference held under UN auspices and based on Resolutions 242 and 338. Jordan and the PLO indicated that they were in full agreement with Syria.

THE MADRID PEACE CONFERENCE

In May 1991 Syria and Lebanon signed a treaty of 'fraternity, co-operation and friendship', confirming Syria's dominant role in the affairs of its neighbour. Two months later the Lebanese army forced the PLO to surrender its heavy weaponry and positions around Sidon in a series of brief but decisive battles. This prompted speculation that, deprived of its Soviet sponsor, Syria had reached an understanding with the USA whereby the latter would tolerate Syrian control in Lebanon in return for President Assad's backing for the Bush Administration's Middle East peace plans. Both Syria and the USA, it was suggested, wanted to ensure that the PLO remained militarily weakened and diplomatically isolated. In July it was announced that President Assad had abandoned his opposition to US conditions for the convening of a peace conference. Syria's volte-face was swiftly followed by Jordanian, Egyptian and Lebanese acceptance of the USA's proposals. Saudi Arabia also lent its support to the proposed conference, and to an Egyptian suggestion that the Arab states should end their trade boycott of Israel in return for a moratorium on settlement in the Occupied Territories. Shamir rejected the offer. Indeed, despite the de facto capitulation of the Arab world to Israeli conditions for an international conference, Shamir's Cabinet would only endorse the Prime Minister's acceptance on the understanding that Israel must hold a power of veto regarding the composition of any Palestinian representation. Yasser Arafat was placed in a difficult position by the proposed conference. It was clear that the PLO would not be represented officially. Yet such was the pressure from the USA and the Arab states to support the Baker proposals that by September Arafat had authorized Palestinian representation through a Jordanian-Palestinian delegation approved, but not nominated, by the PLO.

The peace conference was convened in Madrid, Spain, on 30 October 1991, but ended after three days with little sign of agreement. Baker subsequently issued invitations to all parties to attend follow-up talks in Washington, DC, in December. This attempt to sustain momentum was broadly welcomed by the Arabs but brought a protest from the Israelis, who complained of 'American compulsion' and announced that they would not be going to Washington, DC, until five days after the official start of the talks. The Israeli decision was held up in the Arab world as evidence of Shamir's contempt for the peace process. Palestinian and Arab scepticism deepened at the conclusion of the Washington, DC, talks, with little progress having been made in any of the negotiations. Israeli talks with the Lebanese and Syrian delegations stalled on Israel's refusal to accept that Resolution 242 compelled it to withdraw from all occupied Arab territory, and by a Lebanese insistence that Resolution 425 was not negotiable. Appeals by the Arab delegations for some sort of US intervention to break the deadlock were met with Baker's assertion that the USA would be adopting a 'hands off' approach. By now it had become an article of faith in the Arab world that there would be no breakthrough in the peace process without US intervention. This perception became further entrenched after the third round of bilateral talks in January 1992, which once again broke up without any obvious signs of progress.

Palestinian support for participation in the peace process was also being eroded by a dramatic rise in settlement construction in the West Bank and Gaza. Work had begun on 13,500 housing units during 1991—a 65% increase over all the units established in the previous 23 years, boosting the Israeli population of the territories to an estimated 200,000. The US Administration signalled its displeasure at the scale of settlement building by informing Congress that Israel's request for US $10,000m. in loan guarantees would not be granted until there was a halt to settlement activity.

ITZHAK RABIN BECOMES ISRAEL'S PRIME MINISTER

The Israeli general election of 23 June 1992 produced unexpectedly large gains for the opposition Labour Party headed by Itzhak Rabin. The inauguration of a Rabin-led Government in Israel was warmly welcomed in the USA and Europe, where it was widely considered that Shamir's stonewalling in the post-Madrid talks had become the chief obstacle in the peace process. However, Rabin's refusal to heed demands for a moratorium on settlement construction was greeted with disappointment by the international community, and the sixth and seventh rounds of bilateral talks finished without a breakthrough. Yasser Arafat encountered mounting pressure from his Palestinian constituency over the lack of progress in the peace process. In the West Bank and Gaza the radical Hamas and Islamic Jihad movements had demonstrated their contempt for the political process sanctioned by the PLO leader with a series of armed attacks on Israeli forces. Six Israeli soldiers were killed during the first two weeks of December 1992, prompting the Israeli Prime Minister to order the arrest of 1,600 alleged Islamist activists on 16–17 December; 413 of these were subsequently expelled via the security zone into southern Lebanon. The mass deportation elicited strong international condemnation and the unanimous adoption of UN Security Council Resolution 799, demanding the immediate return of those expelled. Several Palestinians were killed in Gaza in demonstrations that flared up in response to the expulsions. Concerted diplomatic activity by the USA helped to defuse support in the UN Security Council for the imposition of sanctions on Israel for its non-compliance with Resolution 799. The Palestinians and most Arab states condemned the US moves as a further example of its complicity in safeguarding Israel from international law.

Newly elected US President Bill Clinton's Secretary of State, Warren Christopher, toured the Middle East in February 1993, in an attempt to revive the peace process following the deportations. Syria and Lebanon stated that they could separate the deportations issue from the peace process, but emphasized that regional peace would be impossible without a resolution of the Palestinian issue. King Hussein proved less amenable to Christopher's urgings, indicating that it would be impossible for Jordan to attend the next round of talks in the absence of the Palestinians. The Palestinian team clearly wanted concessions from the USA in return for their continued attendance at the peace talks. During meetings with the US Secretary of State they were reported to have sought, and gained, assurances including the Clinton Administration's reaffirmation of its commitment to Resolutions 242 and 338, and its acknowledgement of East Jerusalem as occupied territory. However, when Israel failed to confirm that deportation would no longer be employed against the Palestinian population of the West Bank and Gaza, the PLO ordered the Palestinian delegates not to attend the next round of negotiations. Palestinian opposition to the Madrid peace process was counterpoised by pressure from the USA, the EC and moderate Arab states to resume the dialogue. To a chorus of domestic protests, Arafat finally consented to Palestinian representation at the ninth round of talks. Disarray in the Palestinian ranks appeared to harden Israeli resolve against concessions on any of the contentious issues. The talks ended with Palestinian complaints that no progress had been made. The 10th round of negotiations, which opened in June, also ended in mutual recrimination and deep pessimism. Several Palestinian delegates demonstrated their lack of faith in the process by refusing to make the journey to Washington, DC.

OPERATION ACCOUNTABILITY

Lack of progress at the negotiating tables was reflected in volatility elsewhere. In July 1993, following the killing of seven Israeli soldiers by Hezbollah fighters in southern Lebanon, the IDF launched Operation Accountability. In the most severe Israeli bombardment of Lebanese territory since 1982, scores were killed and 300,000 fled their homes. Coercing the Lebanese and Syrians to rein in Hezbollah militants by means of the deliberate targeting of civilians and the creation of a refugee crisis provoked international condemnation, and led Syria and the USA to mediate an 'understanding' between Israel and Hezbollah whereby the IDF would refrain from attacking civilian targets as long as Hezbollah confined its operations to Lebanese territory. Although Israel declared its attack on southern Lebanon a success, nine of its soldiers were killed in ambushes in the three weeks after their bombardment.

THE OSLO ACCORDS

In August 1993, with the peace process begun in Madrid seemingly on the point of collapse, there came the dramatic revelation that Israel and the PLO had been engaged in parallel but secret negotiations in the Norwegian capital, Oslo. The two sides were reported to have reached agreement on mutual recognition and on staged Palestinian autonomy in the West Bank and Gaza. The precise details of these Oslo accords were kept deliberately vague, but were said to include an early withdrawal of Israeli forces from Gaza and the Jericho area of the West Bank; the redeployment of Israeli troops in other areas of the West Bank; the gradual transfer of civic power to a Palestinian authority; the creation of a Palestinian police force; and the election of a Palestinian council. Negotiations on what were termed 'permanent status' issues would begin within two years of the Gaza and Jericho withdrawals and be concluded within five years. Palestinian reaction to the Oslo agreements was mixed. Refugees in Lebanon decked their camps with the black flags of mourning, while one prominent Palestinian intellectual scorned Oslo for transforming the PLO from a liberation movement to a municipal council. Within the West Bank and Gaza, where the attrition of the five years of the *intifada* had left a collective exhaustion, many Palestinians expressed guarded approval. Egypt and Jordan were quick to give their backing to the PLO Chairman's gambit, followed by cautious approval from the GCC states. However, Arafat failed to secure the endorsement of the Syrian leader during lengthy talks in Damascus. President Assad complained that the Israeli-PLO deal had made an Israeli withdrawal from the Golan Heights and Lebanon more difficult to achieve.

The Israeli Cabinet unanimously approved the Oslo accords. The opposition Likud accused the Government of laying the cornerstone of a Palestinian state, and representatives of the settler movement vowed to obstruct the implementation of the agreements. However, opinion polls suggested that a significant majority of Israelis supported their Government on Oslo. The emergence of the militant Hamas movement had made recognition of the PLO politically inevitable and psychologically acceptable, and few could justify the continued exposure of Israeli soldiers to the lethal and immutable hostility of Gaza's crowded slums and refugee camps. Agreement with the Palestinians also offered the prospect of an end to the Arab economic boycott of Israel and of normalized relations with the Arab states.

THE DECLARATION OF PRINCIPLES

The formal signing of the Israeli-PLO Declaration of Principles on Palestinian Self-Rule (Documents on Palestine, see p. 76) took place in Washington, DC, on 13 September 1993 and concluded with a brief but symbolic handshake between Itzhak Rabin and Yasser Arafat. The following day Rabin was received in Morocco by King Hassan, on the first official visit by an Israeli Prime Minister to any Arab country other than Egypt. The same day Jordanian and Israeli government representatives agreed an agenda for forthcoming negotiations between the two states. The PLO leader also benefited from the approval with which the international community greeted the Oslo accords. Israeli-Palestinian negotiations on the implementation of the first stages outlined in the Declaration of Principles began in Egypt on 13 October 1993. However, it swiftly became evident that there were serious differences between the two sides over the interpretation of key articles. An Israeli proposal for the troops withdrawn from the Palestinian areas in Gaza to be redeployed around the Strip's Jewish settlements elicited strong protest from the Palestinians. Similar disagreements arose over the size of the proposed Jericho enclave and the future of the estimated 17,000 Palestinians held in Israeli gaols.

Hopes that the Oslo agreements would end the violence in the Occupied Territories also proved to be unfounded. On the eve of the Washington, DC, signings Hamas gunmen had killed three Israeli soldiers on the outskirts of Gaza City, and attacks by Palestinian militants on soldiers and settlers in the Occupied Territories persisted throughout late 1993. Several Palestinians were killed in reprisal attacks by settlers. Meanwhile, Israel's security forces pursued their controversial policy of 'targeted killings' of Palestinians suspected of involvement in military operations. The continued instability made the prospect of a withdrawal from Gaza and Jericho by the 13 December deadline increasingly unlikely. Rabin appeared unperturbed by the delay, pointing out that the timetable laid out in the Declaration of Principles was not a rigid one. However, the failure to meet the deadline caused further erosion of Palestinian support for Arafat and his agreements with Israel. The initial enthusiasm that had greeted the prospect of an end to the occupation had now given way to a deepening concern that the PLO Chairman had overplayed his hand. The Rabin Government had demonstrated that it would be resolute in exploiting the ambiguities that underlay so much of the Declaration. The failure of the PLO to establish the principle of the illegality of the settlements, or even a moratorium on further construction, was regarded as a particularly grave error.

While the PLO's negotiations with Israel faltered, Jordanian and Israeli representatives, meeting in Washington, DC, were reported to have laid the foundations for a formal peace treaty. In Syria, where official commentaries had been severe in their criticism of Arafat's deal with Israel, the news of the rapidly warming relations between the Jordanian regime and Israel was greeted with a similarly harsh response. In an attempt to draw Syria more fully into the peace process, President Clinton met with President Assad in Geneva in January 1994. Assad reaffirmed that Syria would not countenance any normalization of relations with Israel until Israel had committed itself to a full withdrawal from the Golan Heights.

After a series of meetings in early February 1994, Israel and the PLO agreed the security and territorial arrangements for the Gaza Strip that would follow an Israeli redeployment. Under the terms of the agreement, Israel would maintain control of the settlement blocs and the border area with Egypt while the rest of the Strip would be transferred to the new Palestinian (National) Authority (PA). The perimeter area of the settlements and their access roads would be patrolled jointly by the IDF and the new Palestinian security force.

Arab–Israeli relations were plunged into further crisis on 25 February 1994, with the deaths of 29 Palestinians in an attack on the Ibrahimi mosque in Hebron by an extremist Jewish settler. A further 33 Palestinians were killed in demonstrations that erupted in the Occupied Territories in the eight days following the massacre. The PLO, Jordan, Syria and Lebanon declared the suspension of their participation in the peace process. The PLO initially demanded the removal of the 400 militant settlers living in central Hebron and the dispatch of an international protection force to the Occupied Territories as the price for a resumption of talks with Israel. After intense

US lobbying, however, the Syrian and Jordanian Governments signalled a willingness to return to the negotiating tables. Nevertheless, by the beginning of April Arafat had agreed to resume negotiations with Israel, with the PLO following suit shortly afterwards. Arafat's failure to extract any significant concessions from Israel on the settlement issue in the aftermath of the Hebron killings was viewed with dismay in the Occupied Territories.

THE CAIRO AGREEMENT

Israeli and Palestinian officials finally signed their agreement on autonomy proposals for the Gaza Strip and Jericho in Cairo on 4 May 1994 (Documents on Palestine, see p. 79). Contingents of the Palestinian police force began arriving soon afterwards and, by 17 May, amid Palestinian celebrations, the IDF had completed its scheduled withdrawals from Jericho and Gaza. In Gaza the PA inherited administrative and economic chaos. On 1 July Arafat finally made the journey to Gaza. In his first public address he acknowledged the lack of enthusiasm for the Oslo accords, but reassured his audiences that Gaza and Jericho were the stepping stones to an independent Palestinian state with Jerusalem as its capital.

JORDAN'S PEACE WITH ISRAEL

King Hussein confirmed the extent to which Jordan had travelled in peace talks with Israel by announcing on 9 July 1994 his readiness to meet Israeli Prime Minister Itzhak Rabin. The decision followed a US undertaking to work towards waiving Jordan's US $900m. debt to the USA and to persuade Saudi Arabia and the Gulf states to end their political and economic boycott of Jordan. On 25 July, at a ceremony in Washington, DC, the leaders of Jordan and Israel formally ended the state of war between the two countries. The overwhelming majority of Israelis welcomed the development. Jordanians were less sanguine, conceding that the agreement with Israel was the price that would have to be paid if Jordan was to resolve the problems it had created by its stance following Iraq's invasion of Kuwait. Palestinians condemned the Israeli-Jordanian agreement as premature, with Arafat reserving especially strong criticism for a paragraph of the document signed by Rabin and King Hussein that acknowledged Jordan's 'special role' as guardian of Muslim holy sites in Jerusalem. The rest of the Arab world responded to the Israeli-Jordanian agreement and the PLO's quarrel with Jordan with a large measure of indifference. Although the Syrian leadership echoed the PLO's dissatisfaction with Jordan's action, other Arab states indicated a readiness to develop links with Israel. Morocco established ties in September, and Tunisia announced the opening of a special interest section at the Belgian embassy in Tel-Aviv. Also in September the six member states of the GCC announced an end to the 'secondary' economic boycott of Israel. On 26 October Israel and Jordan sealed their agreement with the signing of a peace treaty.

By late 1994 Palestinian-Israeli negotiations on the implementation of the Declaration of Principles had become deadlocked. It became evident that Israel would not accede to further troop redeployments on the West Bank or the release of gaoled Palestinians until the PA had proved itself willing and able to halt the 'anti-Oslo' violence of Islamist militants and PLO 'rejectionists'. Palestinians accused Israel of using the 'security agenda' to ensure that the PA played the role of Israel's gendarme, while at the same time exploiting delays in agreed land transfers to pursue the infrastructural development—road building and settlement expansion—that would create the necessary 'facts' to prejudice the course and outcome of the 'final status' talks. Nevertheless, a series of killings and suicide bombings by Hamas and Islamic Jihad—most notoriously the killing of 22 Israelis in the bombing of a Tel-Aviv bus in October—bolstered Israeli demands that the PA must curb the violence before progress could be made on the implementation of the Oslo agreements. Under mounting Israeli and US pressure, Arafat ordered the detention of scores of activists connected to the Islamist movement. The arrests precipitated a serious crisis in the PA's relations with the Islamist opposition, which deepened dramatically on 18 November when Palestinian police opened fire on an Islamist demonstration in Gaza City, killing 12 protesters. Israel relaxed its closure of the West Bank and Gaza in March 1995, granting permits for work in Israel to some 20,000 Palestinians. In the course of meetings with Arafat, however, the Israeli Minister of Foreign Affairs, Shimon Peres, insisted that further troop redeployments and the holding of scheduled elections for a Palestinian legislative assembly would be conditional on a cessation of Palestinian violence. Arafat continued his crackdown on opposition groups in Gaza, attracting condemnation from human rights organizations for what was perceived as increasing authoritarianism.

PROGRESS ON THE ISRAELI-SYRIAN TRACK

After a period of deadlock in Israel's negotiations with Syria and the intensification of Hezbollah attacks on IDF and SLA targets in southern Lebanon, it was reported that Israel and Syria had succeeded in narrowing their differences over future arrangements on the Golan Heights. Emboldened by references made by Peres to the Golan as Syrian territory, President Assad hinted that he would be prepared to share the territory's water resources with Israel in the event of the latter's evacuation. In June 1995 Syria also conceded that a future demilitarized zone on either side of a new border would not have to be equal in size: Syria had hitherto insisted on 'symmetry' in all security arrangements. An attempt in Israel by opponents of a withdrawal to derail the negotiations, by introducing legislation requiring a withdrawal from the Golan to be subject to a referendum, was narrowly defeated in the Knesset.

OSLO II

Throughout mid-1995 Israeli and Palestinian negotiators attempted to forge an agreement on implementing the long-overdue second phase of Palestinian autonomy. Meeting in Washington, DC, on 28 September, Israeli Minister of Foreign Affairs Peres and PLO leader Arafat put their signatures to a document detailing the interim stage of the Declaration of Principles. The Interim Agreement on the West Bank and Gaza Strip (Documents on Palestine, see p. 86), or Oslo II, committed Israel to redeploying its forces from the 440 villages of the West Bank and six of the seven cities (there was no agreement on redeployment from Hebron). Oslo II was greeted with a mixture of indifference and resignation by the Israeli public. Among Palestinians there was anger at acceptance of a continued settler and IDF presence in the heart of Hebron, and at failure to secure guarantees on Palestinian detainees. IDF redeployment on the West Bank began in mid-October; Jenin, on 25 October, was the first city to be evacuated by Israeli troops. However, Palestinian relief at the removal of the Israeli military presence was tempered by the realization that the IDF often withdrew not much further than municipal boundaries, leading to comments that this was not so much an ending of an occupation but its reorganization.

ASSASSINATION OF ITZHAK RABIN

On 4 November 1995 the Israeli Prime Minister, Itzhak Rabin, was assassinated by a Jewish nationalist extremist while leaving a peace rally in Tel-Aviv. The manner and circumstances of Rabin's death completed his metamorphosis from warrior to peacemaker, and prompted an outpouring of popular grief in Israel. For the right-wing Likud leader, Binyamin Netanyahu, the assassination was a major embarrassment. Netanyahu came under fierce attack from the liberal establishment for not having distanced himself from the increasingly rancorous verbal attacks on Rabin by the settler lobby, while Rabin's widow accused Netanyahu of bearing moral responsibility for her husband's death. Rabin's funeral was attended by several Arab representatives, including high-ranking government ministers from Oman and Qatar.

The IDF's redeployment in the West Bank was completed by the end of 1995, paving the way for elections to the Palestinian Legislative Council (PLC). The left-wing factions of the PLO urged a boycott of the process and, after some prevarication, Hamas also stated that it would not take part. Following talks between Hamas and the PA leadership in Cairo, none the less, a joint communiqué stressed the importance of national unity.

The Islamists also reportedly undertook to refrain from attacks on Israeli targets until after the elections. The assassination—attributed to Israeli agents—in early January 1996 of Yahya Ayyash, a senior Hamas operative believed to have co-ordinated recent suicide bombings in Israel, indicated an early end to the de facto cease-fire, which had lasted for several months. As predicted, Arafat's official Fatah candidates put up a strong showing at the elections to the PLC held on 20 January, winning a comfortable majority of the seats. It was unclear what the relationship would be between the PLC and the PNC, theoretically the Palestinians' supreme decision-making body. Arafat secured a resounding victory in the concurrent election for Palestinian Executive President. Hamas carried out its threat to avenge the killing of Ayyash with several suicide attacks in Israeli cities in February and March that left 57 people dead. The scale of the bloodshed led Peres to demand that Arafat dismantle Hamas's institutional base. The PLO leader was reluctant to risk full-scale internecine conflict by acceding to this demand, but the success of the Oslo process had become so tied to the fortunes of the Israeli Labour Party that Arafat would inevitably need to take some action against the Islamists to bolster Peres's chances of electoral success. Hundreds of supporters of Hamas and Islamic Jihad were rounded up, and on 3 March five Palestinian militias were officially outlawed by the PA.

OPERATION GRAPES OF WRATH

The resumption of talks between Israel and Syria in December 1995 had failed to achieve progress on the issue of the Golan Heights, despite Peres's assertions that peace with Syria would be a priority of his premiership. With talks again deadlocked, the two states' proxy war in Lebanon intensified. In April 1996, following the killing of two Lebanese children by Israeli tank-fire and retaliatory rocket assaults on northern Israel by Hezbollah, Peres authorized intense aerial and artillery strikes, not only against suspected Hezbollah targets but also against power stations near Beirut and the main north–south arterial highway. Several Lebanese and Syrian troops were killed when Beirut's international airport was struck. However, continued rocket attacks on northern Israel confirmed that Hezbollah's operational abilities remained largely unaffected by the Israeli onslaught. Peres's sense of unease at the palpable failure of Operation Grapes of Wrath to achieve its objectives was magnified by strong criticism from abroad. This condemnation became even more forceful after Israeli shells landed on a UNIFIL base at Qana in southern Lebanon, killing 105 civilian refugees who had been sheltering there and wounding Fijian soldiers serving with the peace-keeping force. The deaths at Qana galvanized efforts to bring about a cease-fire. Mediation efforts by the USA and then France eventually brought an end to the hostilities and a reaffirmation of earlier 'understandings' on the non-targeting of civilians in the zone of conflict.

NETANYAHU WINS POWER

With US Middle East policy so firmly linked to the victory of the Labour Party in the forthcoming Israeli general election, the Clinton Administration attempted to lend support to the embattled Peres. Promises of military and technological aid and the establishment of a formal defence treaty were made during a prime ministerial visit to Washington, DC. Arafat also again answered appeals to aid the Peres campaign, presiding over the 21st session of the PNC at which, on 24 April 1996, the articles in the Palestinian National Charter denying Israel's right to exist were formally abrogated. Peres expressed delight at the PNC decision, but neither this development nor the clear preference of the international community for his re-election was able to save him from a narrow defeat in the polls on 19 May.

Early statements by the new Israeli Prime Minister, Binyamin Netanyahu, confirmed that his Likud-led coalition would compromise less than its predecessor in the peace process. In Washington, DC, in July 1996, he dismissed the 'land-for-peace' formula and confirmed that progress on the interim Oslo arrangements depended upon the PA ceasing political activity in Jerusalem and controlling its Islamist opposition. At a meeting of Arab ministers responsible for foreign affairs in Cairo, Arafat assessed that Netanyahu was not interested in peace and that the Oslo process had reached a critical juncture. The sense of crisis was heightened a few days later when the Israeli Prime Minister announced the reopening of the ancient Hasmonean tunnel that ran under the Muslim quarter of Jerusalem's Old City and alongside the al-Aqsa mosque. Arafat denounced the reopening of the Hasmonean as a 'crime against our holy places', while Fatah-led demonstrations on 25 September soon became armed clashes between Palestinian and Israeli security personnel. The three days that followed witnessed the most serious violence in the Occupied Territories since June 1967: some 55 Palestinians and 14 Israeli soldiers were killed before a cease-fire was mediated.

AGREEMENT ON HEBRON

Several months of faltering negotiations between Israel and the PA eventually produced agreement on arrangements for the city of Hebron. Under the terms of the protocol, signed on 15 January 1997, Israel undertook to withdraw from 80% of the city but to remain in control of the settler enclave for a period of at least two years. The Israelis also agreed to begin immediate discussion of the outstanding interim issues of Oslo II: Palestinian detainees in Israeli gaols; the opening of a West Bank–Gaza 'corridor'; and the inauguration of Gaza airport.

HAR HOMA

Hopes that the peace process was back on track proved to be short-lived. In February 1997 Israel's Ministerial Committee on Jerusalem announced the construction of the 6,500-unit settlement of Har Homa, south-east of Jerusalem at Jabal Abu Ghunaim. The decision attracted strong condemnation from President Clinton, who had recently lauded the Hebron agreements. US attempts to persuade Israel and the PA to restart negotiations continued to founder on Israel's rejection of Palestinian demands for an end to construction at Har Homa. In May the USA undermined the principal Israeli justification for continued settlement on occupied territory—namely that it was needed to relieve Israel's chronic housing shortage—by leaking an intelligence report claiming that many of the houses in Israeli settlements were standing empty. In July it was finally announced that Israel and the PA would be resuming talks on the Oslo accords. The breakthrough had reportedly been achieved following an Israeli promise to suspend construction at Har Homa for a period of three to six months, and indications from the USA that it would be assuming a more active part in the peace process. A sense of relief that the peace process might yet be salvaged was swiftly undermined when on 30 July Hamas bombers struck again in West Jerusalem, killing 14 and wounding more than 150 in the city's central market. Netanyahu accused Arafat of responsibility for the atrocity because of his failure to deal with Islamist extremism.

Israel's relations with Jordan were further strained in September 1997 following the attempted assassination by Israeli agents of Khalid Meshaal, a Jordanian citizen and the chief of the Hamas political bureau in Amman. The two Israelis apprehended by the Jordanian security forces following the attack were subsequently returned to Israel—but not before King Hussein had unleashed a stinging attack on Netanyahu's handling of the peace process, and Israel had announced that it would be releasing the Hamas spiritual leader, Sheikh Ahmad Yassin, from a long prison sentence. Netanyahu's troubles were increased by Israeli reverses in Lebanon. Some 17 Israeli soldiers were killed in action in Lebanon during September, prompting public debate as to the wisdom of maintaining the 'security zone'.

THE WYE RIVER MEMORANDUM

Increasingly concerned by the lack of progress in the peace process, President Clinton hosted a bilateral summit meeting attended by Netanyahu and Arafat at the Wye Plantation, Maryland, USA. Convened on 15 October 1998, with the expressed aim of reaching agreement on all the outstanding provisions of the interim phase of the Oslo accords, as defined in the Interim Agreement of September 1995, the negotiations between the Israeli and Palestinian teams concluded on 23 October with the signing of the Wye River Memorandum (Documents on Palestine, see p. 92). This committed Israel to withdraw from 13.1% of the West Bank, but to do so in three phases, each being contingent on the PA's meeting 'concrete and verifiable' security arrangements. The terms of the Wye Memorandum were viewed as more favourable to Israel than to the Palestinians, and opinion polls in Israel revealed 75% support for the agreements. Despite the positive interpretation of Arafat's spokesmen, Palestinians were concerned that Wye had committed them to entering the crucial 'final status' talks with Israel in absolute control of 60% of the West Bank and in security control of a further 22%. Given the linkage of redeployment with security issues, there was also a fear that the authoritarian character of the PA would become more pronounced.

Although the first redeployment agreed at Wye—the evacuation of territory around the town of Jenin—took place without significant delay, events precipitated by the agreement ensured no lessening in the climate of mistrust and suspicion. Hamas and Islamic Jihad militants demonstrated their rejection of the agreements with bomb attacks on Israeli targets in Israel and Gaza. In the West Bank there were several incidences of militant settlers seizing land in areas thought likely to be subject to negotiation in the 'final status' talks. The IDF did little to restrain the encroachments, and peace groups in Israel accused the Government of political and legal collusion with the land seizures. Disagreement over the release of detainees led to an upsurge in street protests that left a number of Palestinians dead. In December 1998 Israel's Minister of Foreign Affairs informed US Secretary of State Madeleine Albright that the second Israeli withdrawal, scheduled for that month, would be suspended because of Palestinian incitement. The Israeli premier was also having to face domestic difficulties. Having failed to secure Knesset approval for the 1999 budget or to entice the opposition Labour Party into a national unity government, Netanyahu bowed to the inevitable and voted for early Knesset and prime ministerial elections.

The end of 1998 witnessed another escalation in the conflict in Lebanon, with seven Israeli soldiers killed in Hezbollah offensives in the occupied zone in November. In the following month Israel conducted air-strikes against the Beqa'a valley, and shelled power and water facilities in the south. One assault caused the deaths of eight civilians, to which Hezbollah fighters responded with rocket attacks on targets in northern Israel, causing widespread damage and a number of casualties. Four Israeli soldiers were killed in early 1999, ensuring that the issue of the Israeli presence in Lebanon became a principal focus of the Labour and Likud electoral campaigns. Labour's candidate for the premiership, Ehud Barak, promised to effect an Israeli withdrawal from the Lebanese arena within a year of being elected.

EHUD BARAK ELECTED

Israel's elections held on 17 May 1999 produced a convincing victory for Ehud Barak and the One Israel alliance over Binyamin Netanyahu and Likud (with the Labour leader taking some 56% of the votes cast in the election for Prime Minister). Netanyahu immediately resigned as Likud leader, leaving the veteran hardliner, Ariel Sharon, as caretaker leader. Barak's Cabinet was sworn in on 6 July. At a joint press conference with Egypt's President Mubarak in Alexandria on 9 July, Barak vowed 'to turn every stone in order to find a way to go forward without risking our vital security interests'.

WYE TWO

Early discussions between Israeli and Palestinian negotiators, encouraged by delegations from EU countries and by an official visit by US Secretary of State Madeleine Albright, culminated in an agreement in the Egyptian resort of Sharm el-Sheikh to revise the timetable for the outstanding provisions of the 1998 Wye Memorandum. The Sharm el-Sheikh Memorandum or Wye Two (Documents on Palestine, see p. 94), signed on 4 September 1999, included a commitment to achieve a framework agreement on permanent status issues by February 2000 and for the phased 13% Israeli redeployment in the West Bank to be completed by 20 January 2000. 'Final status' negotiations were scheduled to be completed by September 2000, although Barak commented that these might result in a series of long-term interim arrangements rather than a permanent settlement. The transfer to the PA of 400 sq km (7%) of West Bank territory was initiated on 10 September 1999, and the southern 'safe passage' between Gaza and the West Bank was opened on 5 October.

While Barak was more circumspect in his promises to the settler lobby than had been his Likud predecessor, the new Government did not delay in underlining that there would be no radical revision of settlement policy in the West Bank. Commitment to the concept of 'natural growth' saw the Ministry of Construction and Housing issue tenders for 2,600 units in the first three months of Barak's administration. Moreover, in October 1999 the Cabinet decided that the overwhelming majority of the 42 outpost settlements established in the final months of the Netanyahu administration would be allowed to remain *in situ*. Barak's settlement policy was condemned by the PA, which on 6 December announced that it was suspending involvement in the 'final status' talks.

ISRAELI-SYRIAN TALKS REVIVED

Barak's pre-election commitment to effect an Israeli withdrawal from Lebanon, and his declared intention to achieve a peace treaty with Syria, had prompted speculation that there would be a swift resumption of the bilateral talks broken off in 1996. US intermediaries were informed that Syria's President Assad would only resume negotiations on the basis of the understandings purportedly reached with the Rabin Government (i.e. that Israel was committed to a withdrawal from the occupied Golan Heights). Irritated by this precondition but aware of Assad's desire to secure a deal with Israel on the Golan, Barak's administration attempted to pressure Syria by conferring 'national priority' status on the Golan—enabling settlers there to benefit from extra government aid and tax benefits. Syria responded by accusing Israel of trying to sabotage the peace process. In December 1999 a meeting with Israeli and Syrian leaders by US Secretary of State Albright was followed by an announcement that the Israeli Prime Minister and the Syrian Minister of Foreign Affairs, Farouk al-Shara', would be resuming negotiations 'from the point where they left off' in February 1996. President Clinton met with President Assad in Geneva on 26 March 2000. The US President reportedly brought a proposal from Barak that Israel retain sovereignty over the shores of Lake Tiberias (the Sea of Galilee) and the waters of the Jordan river following a withdrawal. However, this had already been rejected by Syria, and the meeting ended with Syrian officials angrily claiming that the meeting had been designed to fail so that Barak could avoid the territorial concessions on the Golan that might precipitate the fall of his Government. Both Jordan and Oman postponed scheduled negotiations on economic initiatives with Israel in response to the breakdown on the Israeli-Syrian track.

ISRAELI DEPARTURE FROM SOUTHERN LEBANON

On 6 March 2000 the Israeli Cabinet ratified its decision to effect a withdrawal of Israeli forces from Lebanon by early July. In mid-May the IDF began redeploying in preparation for the final evacuation. Fortified positions were handed over to the SLA, but many of these were swiftly abandoned as Israel's proxy militia began to disintegrate. Hezbollah and its supporters quickly overran villages and military outposts in the occupation zone. Realizing that an orderly retreat was now impossible, Israeli commanders ordered an immediate withdrawal. By 24 May the last Israeli soldier had left Lebanese territory. There followed a largely peaceful takeover of the south by Lebanese security forces and various militia groups. Some 6,000 SLA fighters and their families were given refuge in Israel, while 1,500 surrendered to Hezbollah and the Lebanese police. Hezbollah's Secretary-General, Sheikh Hasan Nasrallah, urged restraint in dealing with collaborators, but insisted that the conflict would continue until the Lebanese prisoners held in Israeli detention were released and violations of Lebanese waters and airspace ended. Israeli claims to have withdrawn from all Lebanese territory were disputed by Lebanon's President Emile Lahoud, who asserted that Israel still controlled three parcels of land belonging to Lebanon, including the 25-sq-km enclave of Shebaa Farms. (The UN and most independent experts agreed that Shebaa Farms was Syrian rather than Lebanese territory.)

DEATH OF PRESIDENT HAFIZ AL-ASSAD

President Assad of Syria died on 10 June 2000. He was succeeded by his eldest surviving son, Bashar. There were hopes in Europe and Washington, DC, that the new leader would liberalize the governing regime and open Syria up to the West. However, there seemed little immediate prospect that the accession of Bashar al-Assad to the Syrian presidency would facilitate a revival of negotiations on the Israeli-Syrian track of the peace process.

CAMP DAVID II

In mid-May 2000 it was disclosed that the PA and the Israeli Government had been involved in a secret dialogue in the Swedish capital, Stockholm. The negotiations had been facilitated by a US Administration apparently anxious to see an Israeli-Palestinian agreement on a future settlement before November's US presidential election. On 5 July Bill Clinton invited Barak and Arafat to an open-ended summit meeting at Camp David to forge the all-important framework agreement on 'final status' issues. Talks opened at Camp David on 11 July, but after 15 days of exhaustive negotiations the summit broke up in acrimony, with the Israelis and the Palestinians each accusing the other of responsibility for the failure. Although it was reported that Barak had verbally made a number of significant concessions—including a proposal to transfer part of the Negev desert to the PA in exchange for annexation of settlement blocs in the West Bank—serious disagreements remained on the issues of refugees and the status of Jerusalem. An Israeli offer of PA control over some Arab districts of Jerusalem was turned down by the Palestinians, who insisted on sovereignty over all of East Jerusalem, with each religious denomination having control over its holy places. President Clinton made it clear that he believed Barak to have been the more flexible in the negotiations, and that Arafat bore the greater responsibility for the collapse of the talks. However, the PA President was warmly commended in the Arab world for having resisted US and Israeli pressure to conclude a 'dishonourable peace'. PA officials were also adamant that the concessions offered by Barak were neither as transparent nor as generous as reported in the international media.

THE AL-AQSA UPRISING

On 28 September 2000 the leader of Israel's Likud opposition, Ariel Sharon, staged a tour of the al-Aqsa compound at Temple Mount/Haram al-Sharif in Jerusalem's Old City. The visit was viewed as provocative by Palestinians and led to scuffles and stone-throwing. The following day Palestinians in the al-Aqsa compound demonstrated at the conclusion of Friday's prayers and were fired on by Israeli security forces, leaving seven Palestinians dead and more than 200 wounded. Demonstrations quickly spread to other parts of the Occupied Territories, and in a number of locations Palestinian security forces engaged Israeli troops in prolonged gun battles. Palestinian casualties mounted, with each death fanning the flames of a revolt that was soon being referred to as the al-Aqsa *intifada*. By 9 October 90 Palestinians, 18 of them children, had been shot dead in clashes with Israeli security forces, and more than 2,500 wounded; 13 of those killed were Arab citizens of Israel, as protests in support of Palestinians in the Occupied Territories were quelled with unprecedented force. Although mass street protests reminiscent of the early months of the previous *intifada* remained an important characteristic of this new rebellion, the uprising swiftly came under the leadership and direction of militias affiliated to Arafat's Fatah movement.

SHARM EL-SHEIKH SUMMIT FAILURE

Following the mob killing on 12 October 2000 of two Israeli soldiers being held in a police station in Ramallah, on the West Bank, Israel launched heavy air and naval attacks on PA buildings and installations in the major cities of Gaza and the West Bank. Polarization widened with these events and their aftermath, confirming convictions that neither the Israeli nor the Palestinian leader was in a mood to make a success of the Sharm el-Sheikh summit—which both had agreed to attend following intense diplomacy by UN Secretary-General Kofi Annan—when it convened on 16 October. Barak refused to revoke the military sieges in the West Bank and Gaza (which had been sealed off since 6 October), and only reluctantly agreed to an international investigation—by an inquiry panel to be appointed by the US President—into the causes of the violence. The meeting ended on 17 October with an unsigned statement committing the two parties to take steps to return to the situation that had existed before 28 September. This 'compromise' was immediately rejected by militia leaders in the Occupied Territories for not meeting the 'minimal expectations' of the Palestinian people.

THE ARAB LEAGUE SUMMIT

On 7 October 2000 the UN Security Council had adopted Resolution 1322, which condemned Israel's 'excessive use of force' against the Palestinians following 28 September. (The US ambassador to the UN abstained in the vote, which was carried by 14 votes to none.) Popular Arab anger at the bloodshed in the West Bank and Gaza also persuaded Arab heads of state to bring forward the date of their scheduled summit from January 2001 to 21–22 October 2000. However, although Libya's Muammar al-Qaddafi and the more radical Arab leaders assembled in Cairo had urged the severing of all ties with Israel and the use of the oil 'weapon' to counterbalance US support for Israel, the summit's final communiqué reflected the determination of most Arab governments not to antagonize the US Administration. As expected, the document professed strong support for the Palestinians, but little in the way of tangible action. Avoiding appeals for the closure of diplomatic missions, Arab leaders asked instead for a halt to the establishment of new ties with Israel. Oman and Tunisia had closed their trade offices in Tel-Aviv prior to the Cairo meeting, and Morocco followed suit the day after the Arab declaration. In November Qatar also formally succumbed to pressure to shut an Israeli mission in the capital, Doha.

THE CLINTON PLAN

In December 2000, against a backdrop of rising casualties in Israel and the Occupied Territories, the outgoing US President Bill Clinton invited Israeli and Palestinian officials to Washington, DC, to present a parting bid by his Administration to secure a lasting peace settlement between Israel and the Palestinians. The Clinton Plan was essentially a reworking of the Camp David proposals and envisaged the creation of a non-militarized Palestinian state in Gaza and the West Bank, with provision for Israel to annex the larger settlement blocs near its borders and the Palestinians being compensated with lands inside Israel's 1967 borders. The Arab parts of East Jerusalem were to be placed under Palestinian sovereignty, while there would be 'shared functional sovereignty under' the al-Aqsa compound and 'behind' the Western Wall. The exiled Palestinian population would be given the opportunity to settle in the West Bank-Gaza state or offered compensation. They would not, however, be entitled to return to their lands in what was now Israel. At talks in the Egyptian resort of Taba in January 2001 the Palestinian side refused to endorse the Clinton proposals, citing their reluctance to forswear the right of return of Palestinian refugees or the 'cantonization' of the West Bank that would follow from Israeli annexation of its major West Bank settlement blocs.

ARIEL SHARON WINS THE ISRAELI PREMIERSHIP

Unable to sustain his fractious coalition, Ehud Barak resigned the Israeli premiership in November 2000, paving the way for a prime ministerial election early the following year. Likud leader Ariel Sharon won a handsome victory against Barak in the 6 February 2001 polls. Sharon's electioneering slogan 'Let the IDF win' struck a chord with an electorate disenchanted with the Labour leader's failure to deliver on peace with the Palestinians and more widely convinced than ever that Arafat was not to be trusted. Having stated during his election campaign that his reference was for a government of national unity, Sharon offered key portfolios in his Cabinet—which included representatives of far-right parties—to senior Labour figures. The veteran Shimon Peres accepted the post of Deputy Prime Minister and Minister of Foreign Affairs.

In the Arab world and in Europe there was a general consensus that the policies of the new US Administration of George W. Bush would be critical in determining the parameters of the crisis in the Middle East. During his election campaign Bush had promised a less partisan approach to the Arab–Israeli conflict, but had also indicated that he did not advocate direct US involvement in negotiations between the Arabs and the Israelis.

In a rare address to the PLC in March 2001, Yasser Arafat acknowledged that peace remained the 'strategic option' of the Palestinians but cautioned the new Israeli Prime Minister that he demanded a settlement based on 'international legitimacy'. In an interview with a Saudi newspaper shortly afterwards the PA President asserted that the '*intifada* would continue', and that future negotiations must resume from the point at which they had stalled under the Barak Government. Ariel Sharon reiterated that he would not entertain negotiations while violence persisted in the Occupied Territories, and scorned the notion that his administration would be bound by any promises made by his Labour predecessor. Arafat's public demands for an end to attacks on civilians were ignored by the different militia groups operating with apparent autonomy in large parts of Gaza and the West Bank. Proposals by the Jordanian and Egyptian Governments to end the violence and restart the peace process won the backing of the EU and the USA, but failed to win the unqualified support of either the PA or the Sharon Government.

TENSIONS IN LEBANON

Meanwhile, Hezbollah guerrillas maintained their sporadic military campaign against the disputed Shebaa Farms region. On 16 February 2001 an attack on an Israeli patrol in the area resulted in a number of Israeli casualties. Two months later another Israeli soldier was killed in a Hezbollah rocket attack against an Israeli tank. Israel responded with the bombing of a Syrian radar station at Dahr al-Baydar, east of Beirut, killing and wounding an undisclosed number of Syrian military personnel. The attack was roundly condemned in Beirut and Damascus, with the Syrian Minister of Foreign Affairs promising a response 'at an appropriate time'. Israel denied that the attack represented an escalation of the situation, but a spokesman warned that the new Government would not follow the 'policy of restraint' exercised by Barak's administration.

THE MITCHELL REPORT

In May 2001 the international fact-finding commission chaired by former US Senator George Mitchell and established by the previous October's Sharm el-Sheikh summit to investigate the causes of the al-Aqsa *intifada* produced its report. The Mitchell Report trod a finely balanced line between Israeli and Palestinian narratives of the recent conflict, criticizing both Israel's excessive use of lethal force and the indiscriminate actions of Palestinian gunmen. More pertinently, Mitchell placed responsibility on both sides to work towards an end to the violence by instituting 'confidence-building measures'. These included a call on the PA 'to prevent terrorist operations and punish perpetrators' and for Israel to freeze all settlement activity in the West Bank and Gaza. Sharon and his Minister of Foreign Affairs, Shimon Peres, categorically rejected the link between a freeze on settlement and an end to violence as a 'reward' for 'terrorism'. In an apparent departure from the international community's interpretation of the Mitchell recommendations, Secretary of State Colin Powell advised that there was no link between the call for an immediate cessation of violence and the need for subsequent confidence-building measures, which might well include a moratorium on settlement construction. Having earlier expressed his 'reservations' over this key element of Mitchell's findings, Sharon now declared his readiness to accept 'in principle' all the report's recommendations.

CEASE-FIRE PROPOSALS FALTER

Arafat's own attempts to mobilize international opinion around a moratorium on settlements were derailed almost immediately by a Hamas suicide bombing outside a Tel-Aviv nightclub on 1 June 2001, in which some 21 people were killed. The PA came under intense pressure from EU states and the USA to call an early cease-fire, with the US Secretary of State reportedly warning Arafat that without such a declaration the USA would sever relations with the PLO and do nothing to moderate Israeli reprisals. On 2 June Arafat duly abandoned his earlier conditions for a cessation of violence and announced that the PA would 'do all that is necessary to achieve an immediate, unconditional, real and effective cease-fire'. Islamist groups rejected the PA President's appeal for a cease-fire, reasserting their right to carry out 'resistance' activities anywhere.

TENET'S 'CEASE-FIRE'

President Bush moved swiftly to consolidate the cease-fire declaration by sending the Director of the US Central Intelligence Agency (CIA), George Tenet, to the Middle East to mediate its terms. In essence Tenet's proposals, presented on 12 June 2001, confirmed the Israeli position that there would need to be a cessation of violence for a significant period (six weeks, according to the Israelis) before other confidence-building measures could be considered. The cease-fire proved to be stillborn. With the IDF continuing to target Islamist militants and Palestinian groups determined to retaliate, it was only a matter of weeks before the region was witnessing the same levels of violence that were occurring prior to 2 June. Meeting in Genoa, Italy, in July, the Group of Eight (G8) industrialized nations announced that acceptable 'third party monitoring' might be the most effective way of implementing the Mitchell and Tenet recommendations. The Israeli Prime Minister reluctantly noted that he might be prepared to see more CIA personnel involved in the dormant Israeli-Palestinian security committees, but otherwise was strongly opposed to any measure that could be interpreted as 'internationalizing' the conflict. Yet Sharon appeared to be unmoved by continuing concern over Israel's conduct in the West Bank and Gaza, stepping up its policy of assassination of Palestinian militants during mid-2001 and inviting the inevitable revenge attacks.

GLOBAL INSECURITY

The terrorist attacks on New York and Washington, DC, of 11 September 2001, and the US Administration's subsequent decision to prosecute a 'war on terror', presented President Bush with a foreign policy challenge not dissimilar to that which had arisen during his father's presidency 11 years earlier as a result of Iraq's invasion of Kuwait. In order to secure legitimacy for a military campaign to dismantle the al-Qa'ida network of the Saudi Arabian-born militant Islamist Osama bin Laden, held responsible for the attacks on the USA, Washington was again required to manage the differing agendas of the Arabs and the Israelis. (Bin Laden was killed by US forces in mid-2011.) However, while it was evident that the Arab states did not wish to incur Bush's displeasure by opposing his initiative on global terrorism, there were two issues on which they sought assurances: the scale and legal framework of any military action and the nature of future US engagement with the Arab–Israeli conflict, which the Arab nations had hitherto perceived as insufficient and favourable to Israel.

For Arafat, the new political realities offered an exit strategy from the *intifada*. In the days following the attacks the PA made every effort to demonstrate Palestinian readiness to accommodate US sensitivities, and on 17 September 2001 Arafat declared that he had 'issued strong and clear instructions for a full commitment to a cease-fire'. Predictions that US-Israeli relations would be strained by the countries' competing priorities following the attacks on New York and Washington, DC, appeared to be supported by both Governments' actions. Sharon's public comparison of Arafat with the al-Qa'ida leader, and his demand that the nascent 'coalition against terror' should target the 'terrorist organization led by Arafat' annoyed and embarrassed the US Administration. Israel's escalating assaults on the West Bank and Gaza—28 Palestinians were killed in Israeli raids in the week after 11 September—further discomfited Bush.

US POLICY DEFINED

In early November 2001 President Bush outlined US policy on the Middle East in a speech to the UN General Assembly in New York. Citing the applicability of UN Security Council Resolutions 242 and 338 to any settlement, Bush also proclaimed that he was 'working towards a day when two states, Israel and Palestine, live peacefully within secure and recognized borders'. On 19 November Secretary of State Powell confirmed the US Administration's commitment to a 'just and lasting peace between Israel and its Arab neighbours' based on relevant Security Council resolutions. Although stating that Israel's occupation of the West Bank, Gaza and East Jerusalem 'must end', he made it clear that the first stage in achieving this goal would necessarily be an end to violence in Israel and the Occupied Territories. He announced the appointment of Gen. (retd) Anthony Zinni as a new US envoy to the region. Zinni's 'immediate mission' would be the achievement of a cease-fire between Israelis and Palestinians. Primary responsibility for the success or failure of the Zinni mission, Powell confirmed, lay with Arafat's PA. The Palestinian leadership, he contended, 'must make a 100% effort to end violence and to end terror'. This emphasis by the US Administration on Arafat imposing authority over his fractured domain obviously worked in Israel's favour. Moreover, the sudden collapse of the Taliban regime in Afghanistan was perceived to have made the US need for Arab support in the 'war on terror' less urgent and thus ease Israel's recently strained relations with the USA.

ISRAEL DESCRIBES ARAFAT AS 'IRRELEVANT'

A period of comparative calm in the Occupied Territories came to an end on 22 November 2001 with the deaths of five Palestinian minors in Khan Younis, and Israel's killing of a senior Hamas military leader, Mahmoud Abu Hanoud, and two of his bodyguards on the West Bank. Hamas fulfilled its threat of retribution for the death of Abu Hanoud with two devastating suicide bombings in West Jerusalem and Haifa on 1 and 2 December, respectively; a total of 25 Israelis were killed in the attacks. On 3 December the widely anticipated retaliatory actions against the PA were initiated by Israeli forces. *F-16* fighter jets and helicopter gunships struck against numerous PA targets throughout the West Bank and Gaza. Israeli helicopters subsequently fired on Arafat's presidential compound in Ramallah before encircling it with tanks. The PA's rounding up of more than 100 Islamist militants failed to mollify the Israeli Government and, following the ambush by suspected Fatah gunmen of a settler bus on the West Bank in which 10 people died, Sharon stepped up the military assault on PA targets in the West Bank and the rhetorical attacks on the Palestinian President. In December he declared that Arafat was now 'irrelevant' to the peace process.

On 16 December 2001 Arafat acceded to international opinion and reiterated his demand 'for a complete cessation of military activities, especially suicide attacks, which we have always condemned'. He asserted that the PA would locate and punish 'planners', 'executors' and 'violators' of the cease-fire. The PA did arrest some wanted militants, but refrained from more substantial actions to dismantle 'the terrorist infrastructure', as demanded by the USA. It was clear that, in the context of continuing Israeli military actions in Gaza and the West Bank, the PLO leader was not willing to risk the prospect of civil war by moving against forces being lauded as 'heroes of the resistance' by large sections of the Palestinian community.

THE SAUDI INITIATIVE

In February 2002 substance was given to rumours of a new Middle East peace plan, with the announcement by Saudi Arabia's Crown Prince Abdullah of an initiative for a comprehensive resolution of the Arab–Israeli conflict. The central tenet of the Saudi proposals was for the Arab states collectively to normalize relations with Israel within its pre-June 1967 borders, in return for the establishment of a Palestinian state in the West Bank and Gaza with East Jerusalem as its capital. Abdullah stated that the plan would be officially launched at the summit meeting of Arab League heads of state to be held in Beirut in March. EU ministers responsible for foreign affairs praised the Saudi proposals as making a 'significant contribution' to the search for a regional peace. With the exception of Syria and Libya, Arab responses were also largely positive. Seeing Crown Prince Abdullah's plan as a chance to isolate Sharon internationally and exacerbate tensions within the Likud-led coalition, PA officials expressed full support for the Saudi formula.

However, encouraged by the lukewarm reception extended to the Saudi plan in Washington, DC, and in particular the emphasis placed by spokesmen for the Bush Administration on the need for a cessation of violence to precede political dialogue, the Israeli Government appeared unwilling to engage with the Saudi offer.

RESOLUTION 1397

The ferocity of Israel's continuing attacks on the Palestinian territories caused alarm in the USA, not least because of the imperatives flowing from the Bush Administration's renewed focus on achieving 'regime change' in Iraq. With Vice-President Dick Cheney already scheduled to tour Middle East capitals to garner Arab acquiescence in, if not support for, military action against Baghdad, Sharon's adventurism was seen to be undermining his principal foreign policy objective. Even Bush was moved to direct rare criticism at his ally. The EU condemned Israel's excessive use of force, and warned that there was 'no military solution to the conflict'. The UN Secretary-General, Kofi Annan, was also unusually forthright in attributing responsibility to Israel for the deepening of the conflict. On 12 March 2002 the UN Security Council adopted Resolution 1397 (Documents on Palestine, see p. 104). This was the first UN resolution to affirm the 'vision' of a Palestinian state. It was also noteworthy for being the first resolution on the Middle East to be sponsored by the USA for 25 years. The resolution welcomed the recent Saudi peace initiative, demanded 'immediate cessation of all acts of violence', and called on the Israelis and Palestinians to co-operate in implementing the Tenet and Mitchell proposals with a view to resuming negotiations on a political settlement.

THE BEIRUT DECLARATION

Vice-President Cheney's tour of Arab states failed to elicit support for military action against Iraq. He also encountered unanimity in Arab insistence that it was the issue of Palestine, not Iraq, that was the major cause of instability in the region. These priorities were forcibly restated at the 14th Arab League summit in Beirut on 27–28 March 2002. Arab leaders assented to a text demanding Israel's full withdrawal from lands occupied in 1967, and what were termed 'territories still occupied in southern Lebanon', the creation of a Palestinian state in the West Bank and Gaza Strip with East Jerusalem as its capital, and a 'just solution' to the refugee issue, based on the principles of repatriation or compensation in accordance with UN General Assembly Resolution 194 (Documents on Palestine, see p. 63). In return, the Arab world would 'consider the Arab–Israeli conflict at an end and enter into a peace agreement with Israel'.

OPERATION DEFENSIVE SHIELD

Undoubtedly mindful of the impending summit in Beirut, militant Islamist and nationalist organizations sought to heighten tension in the region with a series of deadly suicide attacks. In the week preceding the Beirut summit 23 Israelis were killed in attacks blamed on Hamas and the Fatah-affiliated al-Aqsa Martyrs Brigades. While the summit was in session, Hamas launched its bloodiest attack of the second *intifada*, killing 29 mainly elderly Israelis gathered for a Passover celebration. At a crisis meeting of the Cabinet following the bombing, Sharon responded to the growing sense of panic and outrage in Israel by authorizing a major assault on PA-controlled areas of the West Bank. Code-named Operation Defensive Shield, the Israeli operation began with the destruction of much of Arafat's Ramallah compound (trapping the PLO leader with his advisers and security coterie in a couple of rooms) but soon extended into a reoccupation of all the major population centres on the West Bank. Scores of Palestinians and more than 30 Israeli soldiers were killed in the fighting. The scenes of devastation provoked massive protests throughout the Arab world and sharp rebukes to Israel from the Governments of Egypt and Jordan. By contrast, the response from Washington, DC, was initially muted, confirming in the view of some analysts that the Bush Administration had given a green light to the Israeli assault.

Nevertheless, with anti-US sentiment rising in the Arab world as the human and material costs of Israel's offensive spiralled, the Bush Administration signalled a volte-face in its support for Sharon's West Bank campaign. On 4 April 2002 the US President publicly urged Israeli forces to withdraw from Palestinian areas 'without delay'. Although once again castigating Yasser Arafat for lack of leadership and for betraying 'the hopes of his people', he also appealed for Israeli settlement activity to cease and for an end to the Israeli occupation in accordance with UN Resolutions 242 and 338. Recognizing, moreover, EU and Arab appeals for the USA to 're-engage' with the Middle East conflict, Bush announced that he would be dispatching Secretary of State Powell to the region with a brief to secure a cease-fire and restart the political process.

By the time Powell arrived in Israel on 11 April 2002, the IDF had withdrawn from several areas of the West Bank. The Secretary of State travelled to Arafat's shattered compound in Ramallah for talks with the PA President, but Arafat refused to countenance a cease-fire as long as Israeli forces remained in occupation of 'Area A' Palestinian territories. In response to Powell's insistence that the PA crack down on Palestinian militants, the PA's chief negotiator, Saeb Erakat, informed his guest that 'the Palestinian Authority has ceased to exist'. Meanwhile, international attention focused on the Palestinian refugee camp of Jenin, the centre of which had been destroyed in the fiercest fighting of the Israeli campaign. Palestinian residents claimed that the IDF had perpetrated a massacre in the camp, an allegation vigorously denied in Israel. At the request of Israel, the US Administration blocked a formal UN investigation into the events in Jenin. However, a report commissioned by the UN Secretary-General into the events subsequently declared that there was no independent evidence to support the massacre allegations.

The limitations of Israel's offensive in delivering security to its citizens were rudely exposed in June 2002 with a succession of suicide bombings in Israeli cities, which claimed the lives of a number of soldiers and civilians. The Israeli Government responded by declaring that the IDF would now be free to reoccupy any PA territory deemed necessary to meet its security needs. Within days most of the West Bank had been reoccupied with little Palestinian resistance. In a separate development the Government confirmed that it had completed the first stage in the construction of a 'security fence' intended to follow the entire length of the West Bank in order to prevent Palestinian militants from penetrating Israeli cities.

BUSH OUTLINES US POLICY

On 24 June 2002 the US President made a major policy statement on the Middle East. Bush declared that he would offer US support for a 'provisional' Palestinian state once 'Palestinians embrace democracy, confront corruption and firmly reject terror'. It was made clear that this could not be achieved under Arafat's stewardship. Only after the Palestinians had effected progress on security issues would Israel be required to stop its settlement activity and begin working towards a 'final status' agreement. At the end of this process Israel's occupation would be 'ended through a settlement negotiated between the parties, based on UN Resolutions 242 and 338, with Israeli withdrawal to secure and recognized borders'. The address was not well received in the Arab world. There was disappointment that Bush had not referred to the Arab initiative elaborated in Beirut in March, and that the Palestinians had not been given a timetable for independence, but rather the prospect of open-ended negotiations on the establishment of an entity with powers and borders that were undefined.

ARAFAT UNDER RENEWED PRESSURE

Arafat's domestic position was generally regarded as having been strengthened by the US Administration's apparent attempts to sideline him. Earlier speculation that the PA leader would face a serious challenge in forthcoming elections was now ended, with all potential candidates—including those personalities favoured by the USA—declaring that they would not be seen to be doing the Bush Administration's bidding by standing against the PLO veteran. Arafat continued the tentative reform process within his administration, dismissing his head of security in the West Bank and Gaza's unpopular police chief.

The PLC met in Arafat's Ramallah compound on 9 September 2002. The PA leader used his address to condemn not only Israeli policies in the West Bank and Gaza, but also suicide attacks against civilians in Israel. The latter tactic, he admonished, had given the Sharon Government the pretext to reoccupy Palestinian territories and maintain its stranglehold over civil and economic affairs. However, the PLO Chairman refused to be drawn on the creation of the post of prime minister, claiming privately that such a development was part of an Israeli-US plot to remove him as Palestinian leader. His woes were heightened following two suicide bombings in Tel-Aviv on 18 and 19 September. Claimed by Hamas and Islamic Jihad, respectively, the attacks ended six weeks of relative calm within Israel and left seven people dead and more than 60 injured. The Israeli Cabinet immediately authorized an assault on Arafat's Muqata'a compound in Ramallah, besieging the PA leader and 250 others in an inner sanctum. On 24 September the UN Security Council adopted Resolution 1435, which demanded that Israel 'immediately cease measures in and around Ramallah' and expedite a swift withdrawal from Palestinian cities. The USA abstained on the resolution. However, in a meeting with a senior Sharon aide in Washington, DC, the US National Security Advisor, Condoleezza Rice, voiced the Bush Administration's firm opposition to the Israeli operation against Arafat's headquarters. Under US pressure Israeli troops withdrew from the Muqata'a.

The US stance over the Ramallah siege was not predicated upon any residual belief in Arafat's political leadership. As the USA escalated its war of words against Saddam Hussain's regime in Baghdad during mid-2002, it was evident that attempts to win Arab acquiescence for a US-led military campaign in Iraq were being jeopardized by the scenes of destruction from the occupied Palestinian territories and rumours that the Israeli Cabinet had drawn up plans for Arafat's deportation.

The violence in Israel and the Palestinian territories continued unabated during late 2002, with major suicide bombings being carried out by Palestinian groups in Hadera on 21 October and in Jerusalem a month later. Palestinian fighters also killed the IDF's commander in Hebron in November during an ambush that claimed the lives of 12 Israeli security personnel. Raids by the IDF in Gaza and the West Bank continued to exact a heavy toll on Palestinian militants and civilians alike. In December the PLO General Secretary, Mahmud Abbas, delivered his own withering critique of the *intifada*, condemning its slide into militarism and accusing the gunmen of distorting the initial popular character of the uprising. By relying on armed struggle, Abbas opined, the *intifada* had played to Israel's strongest suit and had brought about 'the total destruction of all we have built'. He argued that the way forward lay in ending armed actions and exposing Sharon's intransigence through a return to the negotiating table.

The Israelis went to the polls on 28 January 2003, re-electing Ariel Sharon's Likud, who went on to form a ruling coalition with the 15 members of the Knesset (MKs) representing the centrist Shinui party and the 13 MKs of the far-right National Union (Haichud Haleumi) and the NRP.

ABBAS APPOINTED AS PA PRIME MINISTER

Sharon's buoyant political standing in Israel stood in sharp relief to the travails faced by the PA leader. Heavy lobbying from the so-called Quartet group (comprising the UN, the USA, the EU and Russia) had forced Arafat to abandon his opposition to the creation of a prime ministerial post within the PA. The PCC subsequently approved the appointment of Arafat nominee Mahmud Abbas to the new position. Under the new division of powers ratified by the PLC on 10 March 2003, Arafat would retain control over foreign policy (including negotiations with Israel) and the PLO's 'national security' forces. Abbas would be responsible for internal government and policing in the self-rule areas.

THE 'ROADMAP' PLAN

The invasion of Iraq by US and British forces in March 2003, and the subsequent collapse of Saddam Hussain's regime, shifted the international spotlight onto the Israeli–Palestinian conflict and paved the way for the launch of the 'roadmap' plan for an Israel-Palestinian peace. Drafted by the Quartet group over the previous few months, its main provisions had been widely circulated. However, the USA and Israel had resisted its formal presentation at various stages during 2002 and 2003, on the grounds that the regional climate was unfavourable. Anxious to demonstrate to the Arab world that the British Government at least was sensitive to their concerns over Western policy in their region, the British Secretary of State for Foreign and Commonwealth Affairs, Jack Straw, acknowledged 'double standards' in relation to the implementation of UN resolutions pertaining to Iraq and Israel and the Palestinian territories.

The roadmap proposals (Documents on Palestine, see p. 104) were formally presented to the Israeli and Palestinian Prime Ministers on 30 April 2003. They laid out three main stages for the achievement of a 'final and comprehensive settlement'. The first phase would see 'restructured and reformed' Palestinian security forces ending 'violence, terrorism and incitement' emanating from the PA areas. This would be coupled with political and constitutional reform to prepare the way for Palestinian statehood and 'free, fair and open elections'. For its part, the Israeli Government would 'withdraw from Palestinian areas occupied from September 28th 2000' and 'freeze all settlement activity, consistent with the Mitchell Report'. This final phase was due to be completed by the end of 2005.

Privately, the Palestinian leadership entertained grave reservations over the new peace proposal. Objections centred on the vagueness of the language and the emphasis on conditionality rather than reciprocity. Palestinians feared that the Israeli Government would once again be able to exploit the inherent ambiguities in the text to ensure that negotiations would be subject to obfuscation and delay. Despite these concerns, the Palestinians judged that in the prevailing geopolitical climate they had no option other than to accept the roadmap. The Israeli Prime Minister, however, declared that his Government could not accept the roadmap as it currently stood. Paradoxically, the absence of guarantees on conditionality were chief among his objections. Without the PA disarming and uprooting the Palestinian militias, stated the Israeli Ministry of Foreign Affairs, they would not be prepared to engage with the process, including the demands for a settlement freeze.

ROADMAP UNDER FIRE

On 18 May 2003 Mahmud Abbas met with the Israeli Prime Minister for the first time, in an attempt to win his public backing for the roadmap. This was not forthcoming. However, on 23 May the US Administration stated that it would 'fully and seriously' address the Israeli Government's reservations over the roadmap. The Israeli Cabinet subsequently voted narrowly to accept the new peace initiative. For the Arab world, the US assurances to Sharon fed the old belief that Washington was an unsuitable guardian of the peace process, being either unable or unwilling to apply the levels of pressure on Israel that would make the roadmap viable.

The US President chose to formally celebrate Israeli and Palestinian acceptance of the roadmap with back-to-back summits in Egypt and Jordan at the beginning of June 2003. In an address that appeared to have been scripted in part at least by the USA, Mahmud Abbas declared that he would bring about the end to the armed *intifada*, while denouncing 'terrorism against Israelis wherever they might be'. Although this formulation won the Palestinian Prime Minister plaudits from the international community, the implicit characterization of all Palestinian military operations—including those directed against soldiers and armed settlers—as 'terrorism' caused a tide of anger in the West Bank and Gaza, where such actions were universally accepted as the legitimate response of an occupied population to the agents of occupation. Palestinians were similarly alarmed by Abbas's assertion that the destination of the roadmap was an ending to 'the occupation and suffering of Palestinians and Israelis' rather than to secure, in accordance with UN resolutions, a full Israeli withdrawal from the territories it occupied in 1967 (including East Jerusalem), and a just resolution to the issue of Palestinian refugees. In his own speech Ariel Sharon declared that he understood 'the importance of territorial contiguity in the West Bank for a viable Palestinian state', promised to resume 'direct negotiations according to the steps in the roadmap' and to dismantle 'unauthorized' settler outposts. He did not mention any commitment to the settlement freeze demanded under the terms of the roadmap.

On 7 June 2003 Islamist and leftist PLO factions issued a statement harshly criticizing 'the results of Aqaba and Sharm el-Sheikh' and reaffirming their commitment to 'national unity, the *intifada* and resistance'. Calling the roadmap 'a security arrangement' rather than a peace plan, Hamas announced that it was ending its cease-fire negotiations with the PA. Palestinian militants underlined their rejection of Aqaba with separate ambushes in Gaza and Hebron on 8 June, which left five Israeli soldiers dead. Two days later Hamas's senior political leader in Gaza, Abd-al-Aziz al-Rantisi, was wounded in an attempted assassination strike by Israeli helicopter gunships. The next day a Hamas suicide bomber killed 16 people in a devastating attack on a bus in West Jerusalem. Over the following week a series of tit-for-tat attacks left more than a score of people dead (the overwhelming majority Palestinian) and threatened to leave the new peace process stillborn. It took the dispatch of Secretary of State Powell to the region on 19 June to achieve a lessening of the violence. Powell urged Sharon to scale down his offensives against the Palestinian groups in order to give the Palestinian Prime Minister political breathing space and a chance to reconstitute the Palestinian security forces. At the end of June Hamas, Islamic Jihad and the Fatah dissidents of the al-Aqsa Martyrs Brigades acceded to Abbas's plea for a cease-fire, announcing that they would suspend all attacks on Israeli targets for a period of three months. Although Israeli leaders complained that this would allow the Palestinian factions to rearm and reorganize after the reversals of the previous months, the USA persuaded Israel not to undermine the cease-fire.

Abbas and Sharon journeyed separately to Washington, DC, in July 2003 to meet with President Bush. Despite a significant downturn in violent incidents in Israel and the Palestinian territories, both men delivered downbeat assessments of the roadmap's progress. Throughout August the cease-fire came under increasing strain as Israeli forces resumed the targeting of Palestinian militants and both Hamas and Islamic Jihad warned that their organizations would seek retaliation. This came on 19 August with a suicide bombing in Jerusalem that killed 20 Israelis. Israel exacted its own revenge on 21 August with the assassination in Gaza of prominent Hamas leader, Ismail Abu Shanab, and two of his bodyguards. Predictably, both Hamas and Islamic Jihad responded to the killing of Abu Shanab by officially declaring their cease-fire at an end.

ABBAS RESIGNS

Amid the IDF's sustained targeting of suspected Hamas militants, the Sharon Cabinet announced on 1 September 2003 that it was suspending all contacts with PA officials. The Israeli move sealed the fate of the PA Prime Minister. Since Abbas had staked his political credibility on his ability to deliver and sustain a Palestinian cease-fire, it was difficult to see how his fragile authority would survive the collapse of the 40-day truce he had brokered. On 6 September he resigned as Prime Minister. His closest political ally, Minister of State for Security Muhammad Dahlan, followed suit the next day. Abbas claimed to the PLC in Ramallah that it was the impasse created by Israel's refusal to implement the roadmap and the USA's reluctance to exert pressure that 'fundamentally' lay behind his decision to resign. However, his additional references to the problem of 'domestic incitement' hinted that Arafat's blocking of his internal reform programme had been a more significant factor in his decision to step down. For the USA and Israel, Abbas's resignation was further evidence of Arafat's role in undermining the peace process. Meanwhile, there was no respite in Israel's pursuit of Hamas activists, with 12 of its senior figures being killed in Gaza alone in the three weeks following the Jerusalem bus bombing.

Abbas's nominated successor to the position of PA premier was Ahmad Quray, identified with the Fatah mainstream and considered more of an Arafat loyalist than his predecessor. On the core issues of a cease-fire and the roadmap, Quray stuck to formulations that had the imprimatur of the Palestinian President. A Palestinian cease-fire and implementation of the PA's responsibilities under the terms of the roadmap could only be brought about through US and international pressure on Israel to cease their assassinations of Palestinian militants, ease the blockade of Palestinian areas and show a commitment to end settlement activity. Both the USA and Israel reacted coolly to Quray's nomination, observing that he would be judged on his willingness to challenge the PA President's monopoly on power and disarm the Palestinian armed groups. However, on 4 October 2003 19 people were killed and tens injured in a suicide bombing carried out by Islamic Jihad in Israel's third largest city of Haifa. Although the Prime Minister-designate joined Arafat in strong condemnation of the bombing, Quray insisted that he would not risk a Palestinian civil war by targeting Islamist factions. Israeli officials rejoined that there could be no meeting with a new Palestinian administration as long as it refused to tackle the extremists.

ISRAEL TARGETS SYRIA

Israeli retaliation for the Haifa bombing was anticipated, but the chosen target was not. In the early hours of 5 October 2003 Israeli jets bombed a military training facility north of the Syrian capital, Damascus, causing widespread damage but no fatalities. Israeli spokesmen justified the raid on the grounds that the camp was being used by members of Islamic Jihad. The authenticity of Syrian denials of the Israeli claim were difficult to verify, although independent reports from Damascus did suggest that the radical Palestinian organizations were far less visible in Syria following the USA's earlier insistence to President Assad that he close their offices and withdraw other facilities.

ISRAEL'S SECURITY BARRIER

Israel continued to court international controversy during late 2003 with the ongoing construction of its West Bank separation wall. In early October John Dugard, Special Rapporteur for the UN Commission on Human Rights to the Occupied Territories, published a report in which he estimated that the new barrier had brought about de facto Israeli annexation of large parts of the West Bank and would incorporate one-half of the combined settler population of the West Bank and East Jerusalem. While acknowledging the legitimacy of Israeli security fears, he condemned the wall as 'an unlawful act of annexation'. The Israeli Government denounced the report as 'biased and one-sided'. EU leaders meeting in Brussels, Belgium, on 17 October also charged that the proposed route for the wall could 'make the two-state solution physically impossible to implement'. Two days previously the USA had vetoed a draft Security Council resolution condemning the security barrier as illegal and calling for it to be dismantled. The US ambassador stated that the resolution had 'failed to address terrorism'. Despite the use of its veto, US policy was officially against the barrier in so far as the new structure deviated from the 'Green Line' demarcating Israel from the West Bank.

THE DISENGAGEMENT PLAN

On 18 December 2003 the Israeli Prime Minister warned that the PA's failure to live up to its obligations under the terms of the roadmap would result in a 'unilateral step of disengagement from the Palestinians'. According to Sharon, the PA had 'a few months' to demonstrate its compliance before Israel imposed its own solution to the conflict. Although the Israeli premier insisted that his disengagement plan would be 'fully co-ordinated with the United States', the White House Press Secretary stated that the Bush Administration opposed 'unilateral steps that block the road towards negotiations under the roadmap' and 'any effort, any Israeli effort, to impose a settlement'. Egyptian attempts to revive the commitment of all Palestinian factions to a cease-fire once again foundered on the Islamist groups' insistence that such a move could not be considered without a guarantee of Israeli reciprocity. At the beginning of 2004 the prospect of the Sharon Government suspending offensive operations against the Palestinian territories appeared as remote as ever. IDF attacks in Gaza and Nablus in December 2003 and January 2004 left many Palestinians dead, and on 14 January a female Hamas suicide bomber killed four Israeli security personnel at the Erez border crossing into Israel. Two weeks later 11 Israelis were killed in a Hamas bombing of a bus in Jerusalem. This followed a major incursion into Gaza that had left 13 Palestinians dead.

SHARON DETAILS WITHDRAWAL FROM GAZA

Details of the Israeli Prime Minister's plans for unilateral disengagement from the Palestinians were made public at the beginning of February 2004. Confirming that his Government would no longer adhere to the pretence that the PA might be a negotiating partner, Sharon revealed that he intended to withdraw the IDF from Gaza and evacuate its Jewish settlements. The implicit *quid pro quo* in the Sharon design was the consolidation of Israeli rule over the major settlement blocs on the West Bank. Although the decision to abandon Israeli settlements drew predictable fire from the territorial maximalists of the nationalist right, few Israelis were prepared to justify the human and financial cost of maintaining control over more than 1m. Palestinians in Gaza, for the sake of some 8,500 settlers. Opinion polls suggested that an overwhelming majority of the Israeli public favoured a Gaza pull-out, including a majority of Likud voters.

On 12 February 2004 Colin Powell intimated that the USA would reserve judgement on the Israeli plan for Gaza until it was clear how it would be seen in the context of the overall pattern of Jewish settlement in the Occupied Territories. Nevertheless, the following day the White House spokesman opined that the evacuation of settlements would serve to 'reduce friction' between Israelis and Palestinians. Such a move, he added, was consistent with 'Israel's responsibilities in moving ahead towards the vision the President described on 24 June 2002'. However, the Arab world in general and the Palestinians in particular were deeply distrustful of Sharon's motives in wanting to disengage from Gaza. While publicly welcoming a withdrawal from any part of the Occupied Territories, PA officials castigated the Israeli premier for his failure to consult them over the Gaza plan and his studied refusal, despite US pressure, to meet with the PA Prime Minister. Instead, Sharon signalled that the Egyptians would be his preferred Arab interlocutors over the Gaza evacuation. The Israeli Minister of Foreign Affairs was dispatched to Cairo on 11 March to discuss the security implications of such a withdrawal. Although Egypt's President Mubarak was anxious to avoid the creation of a Hamas-controlled entity in the Strip, government officials had firmly rejected any idea that Egypt might fill the security vacuum left by the departing Israelis.

ISRAEL TARGETS HAMAS LEADERS

On 22 March 2004 Sheikh Ahmad Yassin, the founder and spiritual leader of Hamas, was killed in an Israeli missile strike, along with several of his followers. The IDF Chief of Staff, Lt-Gen. Moshe Ya'alon, tacitly acknowledged that their actions might inflame Gaza's security situation in the short term, but claimed that it would forestall the creation of a Hamas fiefdom in the Strip. On 24 March the USA vetoed a draft resolution in the UN Security Council condemning the assassination because it was not balanced by a statement deploring Hamas's terrorist activities. Chief spokesman and noted hardliner Abd al-Aziz al-Rantisi was subsequently announced as the Islamist organization's new head in Gaza. However, less than five weeks later he too was killed by a rocket fired from an Israeli helicopter. Having suffered the loss of so many of its leading figures in the previous few months, Hamas declared that it would not announce the name of al-Rantisi's successor. The effective decapitation of the organization in Gaza and the West Bank and the forcing of its leaders into a clandestine existence was perceived in Israeli government circles as vindication of their controversial policy of assassination.

ARAB ANGER AT MAJOR US POLICY CHANGE

The Israeli Prime Minister met with President Bush in Washington, DC, on 14 April 2004 to seek backing for his Government's plans to redraw lines of control in Gaza and the West Bank. The level of support that the US President was prepared to declare for the Sharon initiatives surpassed expectations. In a dramatic departure from the formal policy positions of all previous administrations (and from UN Resolution 242), President Bush presented a letter of assurances to the Israeli leader that effectively recognized Israeli retention of some of the settlement blocs in the West Bank (described as 'currently existing population centres') and declared US opposition to the right of Palestinian refugees to return to land in Israel. In return for the USA's disengagement from the international consensus on the legal framework that should underpin a solution to the Middle East conflict, the Israeli Prime Minster promised to withdraw from the Gaza Strip and evacuate its settlements. In Israel, as in the rest of the world, Sharon's visit was regarded as a diplomatic triumph. Washington's key Arab allies in the region were unusually vocal in their reaction to Bush's endorsement of the Israeli premier's ambitions with regard to the West Bank. After King Abdullah cancelled a scheduled meeting with the US leader, a spokesman for the Jordanian monarch declared that the meeting would be delayed until the US Administration 'clarify their position on the peace process and the final status of the Palestinian territories'.

On 4 May 2004 the Quartet group met at the UN headquarters in New York to express support not only for the Gaza withdrawal but also to reaffirm that the Middle East peace process would need to be based on Resolutions 242 and 338 and to be guided by the principles of multilateralism and negotiation. Two days later King Abdullah held his rescheduled meeting with President Bush in Washington, DC, and emerged with his own letter of assurances on the US position towards a resolution of the Israeli–Palestinian conflict. The letter affirmed US support for the creation of a 'Palestinian state that is viable, contiguous, sovereign and independent'. It also stated that the USA would not prejudge the outcome of any 'final status' negotiations, which 'must still emerge from the parties in accordance with Resolutions 242 and 338'. The 'clarification' delivered to the Jordanian monarch on the assurances given to Sharon failed to allay suspicion in the Arab world that the USA under President Bush had sought to strengthen Israel's hand in future negotiations with the Palestinians. Meanwhile, on 6 May the UN General Assembly gave overwhelming backing to Resolution 58/292, which reaffirmed the status of the Palestinian territories, including East Jerusalem, as one of military occupation where Israel had only the duties and responsibilities of an occupying power. The USA voted against the resolution, which was supported by the EU states. The EU had already distanced itself from the Bush Administration's apparent concessions to Sharon, reiterating its opposition to any changes to Israel's 1967 borders that were not achieved through agreement between the parties.

ISRAELI OFFENSIVE IN GAZA

Violence in the Gaza Strip continued in May 2004. Following the deaths of 11 soldiers and a settler family in Palestinian militant attacks, Sharon ordered a force of 1,000 men and 100 tanks into Rafah on 18 May. The stated purpose behind the invasion, code-named Operation Rainbow in the Cloud, was to uncover the tunnels running under the border with Egypt, which Israel claimed were used to smuggle arms and ammunition to Gaza's gunmen. Over the following seven days scores of Palestinian homes were demolished and up to 1,000 people made homeless as Israeli forces implemented plans to widen the 'free-fire zone' along the Egyptian border. Forty-three Palestinians were also reported to have been killed during the invasion, more than one-half of them civilians. The UN Security Council unanimously adopted Resolution 1544 condemning Israeli actions in Rafah. In a telling display of its own displeasure with the negative fallout from Rafah on the wider Arab world, the USA chose to abstain on the resolution. This was the first time for two years that the USA had failed to veto a Security Council resolution that was critical of Israel. It was a message that was not lost on Sharon, who subsequently ordered an IDF withdrawal from the parts of Rafah that had been occupied.

ICJ DECLARES ISRAEL'S SECURITY BARRIER ILLEGAL

In July 2004 the International Court of Justice (ICJ), based in The Hague, Netherlands, published its findings on the legality of Israel's West Bank security barrier following its referral by the UN. Citing other precedents, it prefaced its main judgments by determining, contrary to arguments put forward by the USA and Israel, that the UN General Assembly did have the right to request from the ICJ an advisory opinion on the wall's status under international law. The opinion of 14 of the 15 judges (the US judge being the dissenting voice) held that Israel's security barrier violated international law and should be dismantled forthwith, with reparations to be made to those Palestinians who had been adversely affected. They also advised that, 'The United Nations, and especially the General Assembly and the Security Council, should consider what further action is required to bring an end to the illegal situation resulting from the construction of the wall and the associated regime, taking due account of the present advisory opinion'. The Arab world was heartened by the outcome of the ICJ's deliberations. Particularly welcome to the Palestinians was the explicit reaffirmation that the Palestinian territories were indeed occupied, that the Fourth Geneva Convention applied to all the territories seized by Israel in 1967, and that the Israeli settlements were illegal. Israel and the USA dismissed the ICJ ruling, having already stated that the issue of the barrier was essentially political and needed to be resolved within the context of a negotiated peace settlement.

FURTHER VIOLENCE IN GAZA

In September 2004 two children in Sderot were killed after Hamas fighters fired a volley of crude *Qassam* rockets from sites in Gaza. Having publicly committed themselves to severe retaliation in the event of fatalities from such an attack and determined to avoid the drawing of parallels with their evacuation from Lebanon, on 30 September Israeli troops and tanks invaded northern areas of the Gaza Strip, including the Jabalia refugee camp. During 16 days of fighting, code-named Operation Days of Penitence Israeli forces killed 116 Palestinians, 50 of them civilians. Additionally, IDF bulldozers destroyed large numbers of homes and razed hundreds of hectares of agricultural land. One Israeli soldier was killed in the fighting. Israeli analysts believed that the Gaza assault was designed to demonstrate the heavy price that would be visited on the local populace if militants continued to operate in their midst. Hamas leaders, for their part, declared that they would continue to fire mortars at Israel until 'Israel's aggression stops'. Although President Bush failed to criticize the Israeli actions in Gaza, the EU issued a statement expressing member states' concerns over 'the disproportionate nature' of Israel's assault in Gaza.

DEATH OF ARAFAT

In November 2004 Yasser Arafat died in Paris, France, after a long illness. Within hours of Arafat's death, Mahmud Abbas was made Chairman of the PLO's Executive Committee, and the Speaker of the PLC, Rawhi Fattouh, was appointed acting President, with the sole remit of organizing a presidential election by 9 January 2005. The rise of Abbas to the key position in the PLO represented a victory for the moderate, pragmatic trend in the Palestinian nationalist movement. Both Abbas and Prime Minster Quray shared a commitment to end the armed *intifada* and to pursue peace negotiations with Israel based on the principles of the roadmap. However, Abbas's political position was far from secure. The veteran personality faced powerful dissenting voices from within Fatah, as well as from traditional opponents in the Islamist movement. Both the home-grown young reformists that had come to political prominence during the first *intifada* and the armed militants that had evolved during the second were wary of Abbas. Distrust centred on his perceived closeness to the USA and a fear that he would not be as resolute on the core issues of refugees and Jerusalem as Arafat had been. The so-called 'old guard' also feared losing status and privilege as a result of any crackdown on incompetence and cronyism.

BUSH STRESSES NEED FOR PA REFORM

For the Sharon Government, Abbas's expected rise to the apex of the Palestinian political movement elicited a mixed response. Having derided Arafat as the reason for the stalled peace process, the cautious public welcome extended to a man known to be a favourite of the USA was expected. Nevertheless, it was also clear that Arafat's demise had also removed an alibi for Sharon's reluctance to meet Israel's own responsibilities under the roadmap, particularly a freeze on settlement in the West Bank. Moreover, the unilateralist approach to the Gaza withdrawal could no longer be so easily justified now that there was an obvious partner in the PA. As before, the extent of the Israeli premier's concern with the situation created by the death of his old foe would largely be dictated by the response in Washington, DC. Speaking in Canada shortly after his re-election as US President, Bush confirmed the new outlook, stating that the real issue in the search for an Israeli-Palestinian peace was not so much about the 'shape of a border or the site of a settlement' but the 'need for Palestinian democracy'. The President's comments were warmly received in Israel.

MAHMUD ABBAS BECOMES PALESTINIAN PRESIDENT

Fatah endorsed Mahmud Abbas as its sole presidential candidate for the 9 January 2005 poll after the acknowledged West Bank leader of the Palestinian 'young guard', the imprisoned Marwan Barghouthi, withdrew his challenge under domestic and international pressure. Hamas leaders also urged their supporters to boycott the election in protest against the lack of progress towards setting a firm date for legislative elections. The turn-out in the presidential poll was only marginally more than 50%. This was a reflection of the absence of a serious challenger to Fatah's Abbas, the boycott call by the Islamist groups and the fact that campaigning took place amid continuing violence in Gaza and the West Bank. Abbas campaigned on a platform of reforming the PA and ending the 'militarized' *intifada*, and succeeded in winning 62% of the votes cast, easily beating off the challenge of assorted independent and minor faction candidates. The new President moved swiftly to assert his authority in Gaza, chasing militiamen off the streets and deploying PA security forces around the Strip's borders to forestall further rocket attacks against Israeli targets.

PALESTINIAN FACTIONS MOVE TOWARDS CEASE-FIRE

Mahmud Abbas and Ariel Sharon held a summit meeting in the Egyptian resort of Sharm el-Sheikh on 8 February 2005. Jordan's King Abdullah and Egypt's President Mubarak were also present. The summit brought a number of agreements, most significantly the announcement of a cease-fire under the terms of which, according to the Israeli Prime Minister, 'all Palestinians will stop all acts of violence against all Israelis everywhere and, at the same time, Israel will cease all its military activity against all Palestinians anywhere'. Additionally, it was announced that the IDF would move towards a withdrawal from some of the quieter urban centres on the West Bank, with the possibility of further redeployments at a later date. The key regional leaders had given tacit consent to the Gaza withdrawal being a unilateralist step and for any further moves in the peace process to be delayed until after the withdrawal had been completed. Jordan and Egypt also announced that they would be returning their ambassadors to Israel. Both Arab states had withdrawn their representatives four years earlier in protest against Israel's response to the outbreak of the second *intifada*.

On 25 February 2005 the embryonic truce came under strain with a Palestinian suicide bombing in Tel-Aviv in which five Israelis were killed. Responsibility appeared to lie with a rogue cell loyal to Islamic Jihad. The Israeli Government was quick to criticize the PA for its 'inadequate' policies vis-à-vis the armed Palestinian factions. However, a government spokesman insisted that the Syrian regime had been the patron of the attack. The claim was denied vigorously in Damascus, where the Tel-Aviv bombing was officially condemned and the press office serving Islamic Jihad closed down. Despite the Israeli intelligence services presenting evidence of Syrian complicity, there were many observers who believed that the accusations dovetailed too neatly with mounting international pressure on the Assad Government (intensified by the assassination of former Lebanese Prime Minister Rafiq Hariri) to remove its forces from Lebanese territory. The subsequent decision in Damascus to accede to the demands of UN Security Council Resolution 1559 and withdraw its troops and security personnel from its Lebanese neighbour was greeted with considerable satisfaction in Israel.

The intra-Palestinian dialogue facilitated by Egypt over the previous two years finally produced an agreement on 17 March 2005. Under the terms of the Cairo Declaration, the 13 Palestinian groups represented agreed to observe a cease-fire as long as Israel refrained from 'all forms of aggression' and released Palestinian detainees. The price paid by Abbas for the 'fruitful success' of national unity was a resurrection of the old principles of the Palestinian movement. Clause 1 of the Declaration reaffirmed the Palestinian right of resistance to Israeli occupation and the right of return of Palestinian refugees. Notwithstanding the upbeat response of Abbas to the document, it appeared as confirmation of the ascendancy of the Islamist power bloc.

RIGHT-WING PROTESTS AT GAZA WITHDRAWAL

Although opinion polls revealed that a majority of Israelis backed the Gaza evacuation plans, its opponents were able to mobilize tens of thousands of supporters to rallies protesting against withdrawal. There were also several instances of nationalist hardliners blockading the main arterial route between Tel-Aviv and Jerusalem to demonstrate their opposition. A sizeable core of Sharon's ruling Likud party continued to view the impending evacuations with undisguised distaste. The rebels had the tacit backing of several Likud ministers, most prominently Minister of Finance Binyamin Netanyahu.

ABBAS RECEIVES US BACKING

The middle of May 2005 witnessed another serious breach of the cease-fire in Gaza involving the firing of scores of mortars at Israeli settlements, in retaliation for the killing of a Hamas fighter and other alleged infringements by the IDF. The Sharon Government warned that unless the PA restored calm it would resume its policy of assassination of Hamas leaders. It was in the context of this volatility that Mahmud Abbas journeyed to Washington, DC, to hold his first meeting with the US President on 26 May. Having complained bitterly that Sharon was actively seeking to undermine his authority, both domestically and internationally, the Palestinian President's political investment in a positive outcome from his US visit was considerable. Fortunately for Abbas, the Bush Administration had been shaken by Hamas's recent successes in municipal elections and viewed the Israeli Prime Minister's studied churlishness towards the PA leader as irresponsible at a time when Abbas was in need of political buttressing. As a result Bush delivered several assurances on US attitudes towards the shape of a final settlement of the Israeli–Palestinian conflict that redressed some of the more starkly pro-Israeli statements of recent years. He repeated his Government's opposition to Israel's settlement expansion and other action that 'contravenes Israel's roadmap obligations or prejudices final status negotiations with regard to Gaza, the West Bank and Jerusalem'. He also declared that 'a state of scattered territories' on the West Bank was unacceptable and that he remained wedded to the idea of 'contiguity' of Palestinian territory on the West Bank. Most critically for a Palestinian audience, the US President noted that any final solution to the dispute with Israel would have to be mutually agreed, including any adjustments to the 1949 armistice lines. There were also disappointments for the PA President. Israel's Gaza and West Bank withdrawals would remain unilateral initiatives, there would be no pressure on Israel with regard to settlement construction until after those withdrawals, and future progress on implementation of the roadmap would need to be conditional on an end to all forms of Palestinian armed resistance.

PA–HAMAS TENSIONS

On 3 June 2005 Abbas formally bowed under the weight of internal and international pressure demanding a postponement of the July elections. Relief in Washington, DC, Tel-Aviv and among the Fatah leadership in Gaza and the West Bank was not shared by the opposition Palestinian factions or indeed by the majority of Palestinians.

Five Israelis were killed in a suicide bombing in the coastal town of Netanya on 12 July 2005. The attack was claimed by Islamic Jihad, the faction that had demonstrated the least discipline in observing the cease-fire declared in Cairo. Israel retaliated with a reoccupation of the town of Tulkarm and the arrest and killing of a number of militants, most of whom were from Islamic Jihad. Hamas, in turn, responded with sustained rocket fire at Israeli communities, killing one woman. Keen to demonstrate a willingness to restore order in Gaza, PA security forces fired on a car carrying Hamas gunmen, wounding five. Hamas militiamen subsequently swept onto the streets of Gaza, occupying two police stations, establishing roadblocks and engaging PA forces in prolonged gun battles; two died in the fighting. While PA spokesmen declared that Hamas was attempting to wrest control of the PA through force of arms and the Islamists conceded, privately at least, that they had made a political blunder, Egyptian mediators arrived in Gaza to secure an end to the fighting and a restoration of the cease-fire.

ISRAELI WITHDRAWAL FROM GAZA

Settler supporters and other opponents of the Gaza disengagement stepped up their demonstrations ahead of the 17 August 2005 deadline for evacuation of the settlements. Amid rising tensions over the impending withdrawal, Minister of Finance Binyamin Netanyahu resigned from the Government in protest. His resignation was applauded by some personalities on the Israeli right, but many others saw it as an act of political opportunism designed to position Netanyahu more favourably with Likud's nationalist core in any forthcoming leadership bid. By the eve of the timetabled evacuation from Gaza it was evident that many of the estimated 8,500 settlers had accepted the compensation packages on offer and left their homes voluntarily.

Despite the dark warnings from nationalist hardliners that the removal of settlers could prompt a slide into civil war, the evacuation took place without the anticipated violence. In some of the more populous settlements residents and their supporters publicly committed to active resistance against the evictions, but the deployment of tens of thousands of Israeli security personnel ensured that the high emotions generated little more than shouting and scuffles. On 23 August the Israeli Government announced that all the Gaza settlers had been evacuated, three weeks earlier than had originally been scheduled, and by the early morning of 12 September the last Israeli forces had left the Strip. Arab euphoria was, nevertheless, restrained by the conviction that Israeli withdrawal in Gaza was Israel's token sacrifice for realizing the strategic goal of annexation of significant parts of the West Bank. Ambivalence towards the Gaza withdrawal was also the predominant mood within the PA, where anger centred on the failure to agree arrangements with Israel on the Strip's border crossing into Egypt, the re-establishment of the Gaza–West Bank 'corridor' and the removal of settlement debris.

FACTIONAL TENSIONS IN GAZA

Hopes that the Gaza withdrawal would lead to a marked reduction in Palestinian–Israeli violence proved to be illusory, but fears that inter-factional tensions in Gaza would be exacerbated by the Israeli departure were quickly realized. In early September 2005 Musa Arafat, the PA's former Chief of Military Intelligence and a nephew of Yasser Arafat, was seized from his home and executed by a large force of gunmen reportedly aligned to the cross-factional Popular Resistance Committees (PRCs). On 23 September an explosion at a rally organized by Hamas in the Jabalia refugee camp left more than 20 Palestinians dead and scores injured. The Islamist organization was swift to accuse the Israelis of launching a missile strike—a claim denied both by Israel and the PA, with eyewitness accounts suggesting that it was the mishandling of rockets during the parade which had caused the devastation. Yet, having formally blamed Israel for the explosion, Hamas was tied to its own internal logic of retaliation, firing more than 20 mortars towards the border town of Sderot.

Over subsequent days the Israeli air force struck at targets inside Gaza, killing several Hamas and Islamic Jihad activists as well as bombing buildings that it claimed were used in the manufacture and storage of munitions. The IDF also employed artillery to lay down deterrent fire at those areas of the Strip recognized as potential sites for firing mortars into Israel. On the West Bank Israeli forces arrested several hundred Palestinians, most of them Hamas political activists. The PA were pointedly unsympathetic to Hamas's predicament, reflecting private anger at the unnecessary provocation of the initial mortar attacks and the damage perceived to have been inflicted on a revival of dialogue with Israel. On 27 September 2005 the Palestinian Minister of the Interior instructed the PA's security forces to arrest armed militants, sparking widespread clashes.

Meanwhile, the Israeli authorities announced that Palestinian vehicles would be barred from travelling on the major arterial highway through the West Bank. The Israeli daily *Ma'ariv* reported that this was the latest step in a government plan to realize what the newspaper dubbed 'road apartheid' in the West Bank. It opined that the ongoing development of the transport infrastructure in the West Bank, with its ambitious construction of new roads and tunnels, had been designed to produce a dual usage road network—one for Arabs and one for Jews. This prefigured, according to many analysts, the planned territorial separation inherent in the Israeli Prime Minister's recent pronouncements on the need for the Jewish state to pursue the unilateralist path towards a settlement of the conflict.

On 26 October 2005 five Israelis were killed in a suicide bomb attack in Hadera. Islamic Jihad claimed responsibility for the attack, stating that it was in revenge for the killing a few days previously of Luay Saadi, its military leader on the West Bank. Ariel Sharon immediately announced 'a broad and continuous offensive' against the PA and confirmed that he would not meet the Palestinian President until Abbas had taken concrete steps to end the 'terror'. Over the next few days Israeli forces killed several militants in air-strikes on Gaza, as well as carrying out further arrests on the West Bank, bringing the total number of

Palestinians detained since the Gaza withdrawal to nearly 800.

SHARON FORMS NEW POLITICAL MOVEMENT

The Israeli Prime Minister declared on 21 November 2005 that he was leaving Likud to form a new party, Kadima (Forward), to contest the general election scheduled for March 2006. He stated that Kadima would remain committed to the roadmap and promised that there would be no 'unilateral withdrawals from Palestinian territory in the near future'. However, he made no commitment to resume negotiations with the PA, confirming Palestinian and Arab suspicions that however momentous the political upheaval in Israel, it would not result in a significant change in policy vis-à-vis the West Bank and Gaza. At the end of November Shimon Peres resigned from the Labour Party and signalled that he too would be joining the new party.

OLMERT REPLACES SHARON

Ariel Sharon suffered a stroke on 18 December 2005, highlighting concerns over the health of the 77-year-old premier. These fears were realized on 4 January 2006, when Sharon suffered a massive haemorrhage that left him in a coma. His medical team quickly announced that he would never recover sufficiently to return to political life. The removal of such a dominant figure from the Israeli scene was a particularly bitter blow to his fledgling party, since it had been widely predicted that Sharon's personal popularity would guarantee Kadima a landslide victory in Israel's March general election. Sharon had intended Kadima to appeal to the growing constituency in Israel that distrusted the Palestinians but viewed territorial compromise as the only way to preserve the Jewish character of the state. However, in line with his reputation for notorious political secrecy, it was evident that even Sharon's immediate colleagues were unclear as to the extent of withdrawals from Palestinian lands that their stricken leader had envisaged. Ehud Olmert, Sharon's deputy and acting Prime Minister, was formally chosen to lead Kadima into the 2006 elections on 16 January. A former mayor of Jerusalem, Olmert was considered to be more amenable to territorial concession than Sharon, but his lack of obvious charisma, and more importantly a military pedigree, meant that many doubted he possessed the political muscle to face down the nationalist camp and stage a pull-out from parts of the West Bank.

HAMAS SECURES CONTROL OF THE PALESTINIAN LEGISLATURE

Hamas's buoyant showing in opinion polls, and the prospect of a major share of power in a new administration, persuaded the movement's local leadership that the need to rehabilitate their highly negative international image should inform campaign priorities and policy presentation. The demand for the destruction of the Israeli state was dropped from its manifesto, confirming, according to a leading member, that the movement was prepared to accept the interim solution of a state based on the Palestinian territories occupied in 1967. Hamas activists also emphasized their discipline in maintaining their truce with Israel and their new focus on the political process rather than 'armed struggle'. Nevertheless, a senior leader in Gaza confirmed that there could be no revival of negotiations with Israel based on a moribund Oslo process and that, should Hamas come to power, its priority would be to develop links with the Arab world and not 'the enemy' Israel.

Hamas's subsequent capture of 73 seats in the 132-seat PLC was greeted locally and internationally with a mixture of surprise and trepidation. Ismail Haniya, the first candidate on the Hamas list, attributed his party's success to their platform of 'resistance' and the desire for a 'new political system based on partnership'. Other Hamas leaders insisted that they had no desire to monopolize political power and would actively be seeking to bring members of Fatah and independents into a broad-based coalition.

The difficulties experienced by Hamas in translating electoral success into the exercise of effective government only illuminated the challenge faced by the rest of the world in coming to a *modus vivendi* with the PLC's major political force. For acting Israeli Prime Minister Olmert, it was clear that the international community should have no dealings with 'a PA part or all of which is composed of an armed organization that calls for the destruction of the state of Israel'. For the USA, the Hamas victory presented its own dilemmas. The overwhelming consensus of the US political establishment was that Hamas was unacceptable as an interlocutor of Palestinian national aspirations. Yet, having argued so fiercely for the spread of democracy through the Arab world in general and the Palestinian territories in particular, rejection of the democratic choice in an election unanimously declared as free and fair seemed destined to inflict even further damage on the USA's already battered image in the region. There was also a keen realization that, while loyalty to Israel and rhetoric of the 'war on terror' ruled out accommodation with Hamas for as long as the latter refused to renounce violence and recognize Israel, the implosion of the PA through the withholding of foreign aid would also not serve US interests in the Middle East.

Thus, while the Bush Administration gave notice at the end of January 2006 of the US Government's intention to cut aid to an authority controlled by Hamas, its officials also urged Arab states to make up any shortfall in humanitarian funding. The EU countries, the largest donors to the PA, also raised the spectre of a cut in funding if a newly formed administration failed to meet the conditions laid out by the USA and Israel. Meeting in Brussels on 30 January, EU ministers responsible for foreign affairs postponed any decision on the aid issue. They released a more nuanced statement on the Palestinian obligation towards the achievement of a peace settlement than the pronouncements emanating from the US Administration. According to observers, this was designed to strengthen the hand of the more moderate elements in Hamas. However, the movement's external leader, the Damascus-based Khalid Meshaal, declared that the attempts by the USA and the EU to modify Hamas policy through a threat to funding represented 'bribery, intimidation and blackmail', to which his movement would remain immune. He also urged the Arab and Islamic world 'to compensate the Palestinian people for any loss of aid'.

Hamas delivered a statement of principles to Abbas on 12 March 2006, in which it declared that it reserved the right to 'reassess' peace accords with Israel on the basis of international law and in accordance with the rights of the Palestinian people. The document also stated that it would address the question of recognition of the Jewish state 'in consultation with Palestinian organizations and institutions, and the Palestinian people its entirety'. These formulations were reportedly dismissed by the PA President as being too vague, and effectively ended negotiations on a power-sharing arrangement with Fatah.

ISRAELI GENERAL ELECTION

Hamas's accession to power strengthened the unilateralist approach to a settlement within the ranks of Olmert's Kadima party in the run-up to Israel's own general election. In an interview with *The Jerusalem Post* on 9 March 2006, the acting Prime Minister cautioned that if Hamas failed within a 'reasonable' period of time to recognize Israel and renounce violence, a Kadima-led Government would act to establish Israel's permanent borders 'whereby we will completely separate from the majority of the Palestinian population and preserve a large and stable Jewish majority in Israel'. Olmert confirmed the intention to annex the main West Bank settlement blocs in the West Bank as well as the Jordan valley in the east of the territory. The Israeli premier had previously announced that Kadima would evacuate 17 of the more isolated West Bank settlements should it win the 28 March elections. This would involve the removal of some 60,000 settlers who would be offered resettlement in the major blocs (housing some 350,000 Israelis) slated for annexation. The PA's outgoing chief negotiator, Saeb Erakat, condemned the proposals, warning that 'the road to peace and security in the region is not through unilateralism'.

Only 63% of Israel's electorate voted in the 28 March 2006 general election, the lowest ever turn-out in Israeli history.

Kadima were confirmed as the largest party, with 29 representatives in the 120-seat Knesset. Likud performed disastrously, capturing only 12 seats and tying in a distant third place with the ultra-Orthodox Shas party. The far-right nationalists of Israel Beytenu secured 12 seats. In his victory speech Olmert reiterated his plans to separate from the Palestinians; the US Secretary of State, Condoleezza Rice, commented that the Bush Administration would prefer Israel to negotiate under the auspices of the roadmap but recognized that this was not possible while an unreformed Hamas controlled the PA. Israeli officials said that they interpreted Rice's comments as support for continued unilateral actions. In Gaza, meanwhile, the new PA administration was finally inaugurated, with every cabinet post going to Hamas supporters. As expected, Ismail Haniya was sworn in as Prime Minister. In one of his first statements to a Western audience, the new Palestinian Prime Minister argued that Olmert's plan for unilateral withdrawals was 'a recipe for conflict' and that there could be no end to hostilities without a full Israeli withdrawal to the 1967 borders, the release of prisoners and a recognition of the refugees' right to return. The USA responded to the creation of a Hamas-led administration by ordering its officials to sever all ties with the PA.

TENSIONS INCREASE FOLLOWING FORMATION OF HAMAS-LED ADMINISTRATION

In April 2006 the EU followed the US lead and froze aid to the PA. Although EU officials gave assurances that they would not allow the collapse of essential services, it was expected to take some time before they had developed a funding model that bypassed the Hamas-controlled ministries. Widespread bread rationing had already been instituted in Gaza during March as a result of Israel's frequent closure of the Karni crossing into Israel. UN representatives in the region also warned that one in four Palestinians in the West Bank and Gaza relied on PA salaries, and that failure to pay the 72,000 members of the various PA security services would bring about a further deterioration in the already volatile security situation. The first days of the new administration had already witnessed several clashes between Fatah and Hamas gunmen.

Militants of the PRC and Islamic Jihad resumed their sporadic launching of mortars and rockets from Gaza at the end of March 2006, prompting the IDF to step up artillery and air attacks on suspected launch sites. By mid-April it was reported that as many as 300 shells per day were being fired by the IDF into northern areas of Gaza and that an estimated 30 Palestinians were killed during the first three weeks of April. Despite international concern that the IDF's bombardment of Gaza was disproportionate and in potential violation of international law, the US Administration blocked a draft resolution critical of Israeli actions. On 17 April Islamic Jihad once again demonstrated its ability to penetrate Israel's security cordons by dispatching another suicide bomber to the heart of Tel-Aviv. Nine Israelis died and many more were injured in the deadliest attack of its kind for nearly two years. The Palestinian President condemned the bombing, while Hamas described it as a 'legitimate response' to Israel's 'policy of occupation and brutal aggression'. A spokesman for the Israeli Prime Minister decried the comments of the Hamas leadership, claiming that the PA 'had defined itself as a terrorist entity'.

Ehud Olmert concluded negotiations on the formation of a ruling coalition by the end of April 2006, buttressing his principal partnership with the Labour Party by securing the support of the 12 Shas MKs and the seven elected for the Pensioner's Party. In a 4 May speech to the Knesset ahead of a vote of confidence in his new coalition, Olmert returned to the theme of withdrawal from parts of the occupied West Bank. He paid fulsome tribute to the 'achievements' of the settler movement, and reaffirmed his own deeply held belief 'in the people of Israel's eternal historic right to the entire land of Israel'. Nevertheless, he warned that Israel's retention of isolated settlements beyond the route of the security barrier 'creates an inseparable mixture of populations which will endanger the existence of the state of Israel as a Jewish state'. Government aides intimated that the process of redefining borders would begin at some point towards the end of 2007.

At the beginning of May 2006 the Association of International Development Agencies estimated that 78% of the population of Gaza was living under the poverty line of US $2 per day. It was also reported that hospitals in the Strip had run out of essential medicines and that the salaries of many PA employees had gone unpaid. Attempts by the international community to devise a mechanism for the delivery of aid which bypassed the structures of the PA continued to be thwarted over the failure of the EU and the USA to achieve a consensus. A British-originated proposal to set up a trust fund managed by the World Bank or the UN to distribute donor cash in the West Bank and Gaza was opposed by the Bush Administration, on the grounds that it involved the payment of PA salaries and would entail a degree of technical co-ordination with the PA itself. US opposition to the proposals served to highlight claims that the Bush Administration was intent on 'regime change' within the PA. After EU officials indicated that they would act without US support if a meeting of the Quartet group on 9 May failed to break the impasse, an interim agreement was reached on a three-month emergency aid package. The Quartet agreed to further discussions on a funding programme that would be acceptable to all members.

The prospect of a slight easing of the humanitarian crisis in the PA territories, particularly in Gaza, brought some comfort to a beleaguered Palestinian populace which continued to face the twin threat of Israeli military action and domestic insecurity. In the aftermath of the Tel-Aviv suicide bombing the Israeli security forces mounted a series of air-strikes on suspected militants in Gaza and the West Bank, and mounted several incursions deep into the heart of the West Bank. Hundreds were reported to have been arrested in the raids, with suspected members of Islamic Jihad being the principal targets. Israel's new Minister of Defence, Amir Peretz, also ordered the shelling of northern areas of Gaza to continue. In mid-May 2006 it was reported that more than 5,000 shells had been fired into Gaza in the previous six weeks; 45 Palestinians were also reported to have been killed as a result of Israeli military action in the first two weeks of May.

NATIONAL RECONCILIATION DOCUMENT ISSUED BY PALESTINIAN PRISONERS

Hopes that tensions would be eased and that a way could be found to end the stand-off between the PA and the international community were raised on 11 May 2006, with the release of a document drawn up by prisoners linked to Fatah and Hamas and officially termed the National Reconciliation Document. Trading on their elevated status within the Palestinian political community, the prisoners appealed for the formation of a national unity government and for the Palestinian President to lead negotiations with Israel on the creation of a Palestinian state in Gaza, the West Bank and East Jerusalem. Although the document stopped short of explicit recognition of Israel, it was warmly welcomed by Abbas as a mandate for bypassing the Hamas administration and reviving peace talks with Israel. A Hamas spokesman in Gaza expressed approval for 'national dialogue', but stated that the proposals needed 'more discussion'. Indeed, the potential for reconciliation receded less than a week later with Hamas's decision to deploy some 3,000 of its fighters on the streets of Gaza. The PA's Minister of the Interior, Said Siyam, stated that the decision was designed to combat 'a state of chaos and anarchy', but many observers saw the deployment of a private army as a direct challenge to the Palestinian President's authority. The attempted assassination of the Palestinian chief of intelligence and the uncovering of a bomb plot against Abbas's security commander, Rashid Abu Shbak, heightened tensions even further. A Jordanian diplomat was also killed in crossfire between Hamas and Fatah gunmen on 22 May. Leaders of both factions appealed for calm, while stating that the Palestinian people could not countenance a slide into civil war.

The Israeli Prime Minister held talks in Washington, DC, with President Bush on 23 May 2006. Prior to the meeting Olmert had restated his Government's belief that he did not have a credible Palestinian negotiating partner and that he considered Mahmud Abbas to be both weak and ineffectual. The latter's desperation to force a way out of the Palestinians' crippling political and economic isolation resulted in the issuing of an ultimatum to Hamas. Abbas gave notice to the movement's leadership that unless it recognized Israel and a two-state solution he would put the issue to a national referendum. The chance of Hamas offering formal recognition of Israel subsided with the killing, on 9 June, of a Palestinian family of seven, after Israeli gunboats shelled a section of a beach in Gaza where they were picnicking. The Islamists responded by declaring their cease-fire with Israel to be at an end and launching a volley of rockets into Israel, including the town of Sderot. Retaliatory air-strikes in subsequent days left several militants and as many as 14 Palestinian civilians dead. The upsurge in violence cast a shadow over a tour of European capitals by the Israeli Prime Minister, in what proved to be a largely fruitless attempt to win backing for his Government's plans to annex settlement blocks and draw final borders. It also nudged Hamas to announce on 11 June that it would be boycotting the proposed 26 July referendum. The movement's leaders again claimed the referendum idea as a coup attempt against their Government, while analysts predicted that a large majority vote in favour of negotiation and recognition would either force a change in Hamas policy or new elections. A 'no' vote would almost certainly lead to Abbas's resignation.

On 18 June 2006 the Quartet group announced backing for an EU proposal to release a further US $126m. in emergency aid to Gaza and the West Bank. US pressure on Arab banks not to transfer funds from sympathetic donors to the PA had deepened the financial crisis and forced Hamas officials to deal in cash; on 14 June Minister of Foreign Affairs al-Zahhar returned to Gaza from an international fundraising mission with a reported $20m. in 12 suitcases. The Palestinian President called the EU aid package a step in the right direction, but declared it 'inadequate' to meet the scale of need. On 21 June there were strong indications that Hamas's resolve on the 'prisoners' document' had weakened. Yasser Abd al-Rabbuh, a senior member of the PLO executive, announced that Hamas had agreed to sections of the proposals relating to recognition and negotiations with Israel. Amid rumours of a deepening rift in the Islamist organization, he also opined that it would only be a matter of days before agreement was achieved on the creation of a national unity government. This was achieved on 27 June, with Hamas agreeing to surrender control of the PA to a power-sharing administration and the signing of a document recognizing Israel and its agreements with the PLO. A spokesman for the Palestinian President stated that there was an understanding that a new PA administration would include all the main Palestinian parties. While the agreement on the prisoners' document was a clear victory for the Palestinian President, it was also evident that it would not bring about immediate change. Hamas's military wing and its external leadership were opposed to the deal and there were concerns that they might thwart its implementation. Israel also declared itself unimpressed. Government spokesmen announced that they were still waiting for an explicit recognition from Hamas and stated that the prisoners' document itself was unacceptable since it enshrined the right of violent resistance in the territories occupied in 1967.

HAMAS ABDUCTION OF ISRAELI SOLDIER

In an operation that overshadowed the PLO-Hamas agreement and may well have been designed to scupper it, militants from Hamas and the PRC attacked an IDF outpost on the southern edge of Gaza in the early morning of 25 June 2006. Two soldiers were killed in the raid and a third, Corporal Gilad Shalit, was captured and taken back into Gaza. The Israeli Government immediately informed the Palestinian President that they held him responsible for the safe return of their soldier and warned Hamas that it would pay a deadly price for the raid. The movement's political leadership denied any prior knowledge of the attack or of the captured soldier's whereabouts, while the PA President slated the raid as violating the 'national consensus'. Notwithstanding the threat of severe Israeli reprisals, the kidnapping of Shalit offered the opportunity of the release of some of the 9,000 Palestinians held in Israeli gaols and was generally welcomed on the Palestinian street. Shortly after Israel's 48-hour deadline for the release of their soldier had expired, Israeli jets struck at bridges on the Strip's main north–south highway and fired on the Strip's only power station, cutting electricity to most of the population. Israeli tanks also crossed the border into southern Gaza and assumed positions near the disused airport, while the deployment of heavy armour in the north of Gaza was accompanied by the leafleting of border towns warning residents to stay indoors. On 29 June Israel conducted large-scale raids on the West Bank, arresting more than 60 Hamas officials, including 20 legislators and eight cabinet ministers. Defending the move, Israel's Minister of Defence, Amir Peretz, stated that the detained men could be put on trial for 'acts of terror'.

International appeals for restraint had little impact on events on the ground. Ruling out any possibility of a prisoner exchange deal to secure Shalit's release, Israeli forces carried out their Government's threat to 'compromise the Hamas government's ability to rule' with an air-strike that destroyed the office of the Palestinian Prime Minister. Palestinian militants responded with the launch of further rockets into Israel, reaching the centre of Ashkelon for the first time. Olmert called the strike a 'major escalation' and vowed retaliation. On 5 July Israeli forces rolled into the northern areas of Gaza, where they met fierce resistance from Palestinian militants. Three days of heavy fighting left 30 Palestinians and one Israeli soldier dead, as well as resulting in widespread destruction to farmland and residential areas.

CONFLICT ERUPTS BETWEEN ISRAEL AND HEZBOLLAH IN SOUTHERN LEBANON

Regional tensions increased dramatically on 12 July 2006, when Hezbollah guerrillas snatched two Israeli soldiers and killed three others in a cross-border raid. A further five Israeli soldiers were killed when troops mounting an attempted rescue raid were caught in a Hezbollah ambush. The radical Shi'a movement claimed that the kidnappings were part of a strategy to win the release of Lebanese and other Arab prisoners held in Israeli gaols. Commentators variously ascribed the Hezbollah action as being motivated by a desire to open up a 'second front' in solidarity with Hamas and as an attempt by the movement's Syrian and Iranian backers to deflect attention from the former's embarrassment over the inquiry into the assassination of Rafiq Hariri and the latter's nuclear enrichment programme. The Israeli Prime Minister also saw the hand of Syria and Iran behind the raid and called it an 'act of war'. Hezbollah came under thinly veiled criticism from the Saudi leadership for provoking a regional crisis, a viewpoint that was echoed by Jordan and, to a lesser extent, Egypt.

The Lebanese Government, which contained two Hezbollah cabinet ministers and which had been engaged in a fitful campaign to build a national consensus over the disarming of Hezbollah, claimed that it had no prior knowledge of the soldiers' abductions and demanded their immediate release. Yet, despite Lebanese protestations of their lack of culpability, the Israeli Cabinet gave Olmert the authorization to conduct an extensive military campaign against Israel's northern neighbour. On 13 July Israeli warplanes forced the closure of Beirut's international airport, bombed key road bridges and destroyed power plants. A blockade of the Lebanese coast was also announced, while the Israeli air force and IDF artillery bombarded suspected Hezbollah positions in the south of the country. Israel defended itself from accusations that its targeting of civilian infrastructure amounted to collective punishment by declaring that it needed to ensure Hezbollah could not reorganize or resupply. It was evident in comments from President Bush and his senior aides that the USA was giving its full backing to Israel in a battle perceived in Washington, DC, as a proxy conflict with the detested regimes in Damascus and Tehran (Iran). The British Government under Tony Blair also broke ranks with majority opinion in the EU, and his own Labour Party, by expressing support for Israel to prosecute a war of self-defence against Hezbollah.

Israel widened its air assaults during July 2006, destroying residential areas of the Hezbollah-controlled suburbs of south Beirut as well as roads, bridges and power plants throughout the country. The towns and villages of southern Lebanon were subjected to relentless artillery air attack, causing an increasing number of civilian casualties and the creation of hundreds of thousands of refugees. Hezbollah gave credence to its claim that Israel's bombing had failed to have a significant impact on its military capabilities by firing hundreds of *Katyusha* and longer-range missiles into northern Israel, reaching as far south as the port city of Haifa. The rocket barrage forced many residents to seek permanent refuge in bomb shelters, while thousands more left their homes for safer areas further south. By the end of the first week of the conflict the Israeli Prime Minister had defined his country's war aims as securing the release of his captured servicemen, the disarmament of Hezbollah and the deployment of the Lebanese army in the south. However, it rapidly became evident that the overwhelming majority of Lebanese from all confessional groups would not turn against Hezbollah as some commentators had predicted, and as Israel's leaders had hoped.

Attempts by the international community to bring an end to the hostilities continued to be defeated by Israeli Prime Minister Olmert's insistence that there could be no let-up in army operations and the USA's tacit backing for such a stance. Instead, the call-up of Israeli reservists and the massing of IDF troops and tanks on Israel's northern border appeared to confirm speculation that key figures in the political and military establishment were dissatisfied with the concentration on aerial bombardment and wished to expand incursions by ground troops. Leaders of the G8 nations meeting in St Petersburg, Russia, on 16 July 2006 were unable to agree on a appeal for an immediate cease-fire, but suggested that the UN Security Council should consider the positioning of an international security presence along the Israeli–Lebanese border. During a tour of regional capitals on 24–25 July, including a surprise visit to the Lebanese Prime Minister in Beirut, US Secretary of State Rice affirmed Washington's conviction that a durable cease-fire agreement was of greater importance than the 'false promise' of an immediate truce, and that arrangements for a truce would need to include the removal of Hezbollah forces from Lebanon's border with Israel. Her stance was judged by many commentators in the Arab world as US stalling on the diplomatic peace initiative to allow Israeli forces further time to degrade Hezbollah's military capabilities.

As expected, the IDF committed growing numbers of ground forces to the battle in southern Lebanon, meeting determined resistance from Hezbollah. Several villages regarded as strongholds of the militia were captured briefly by Israeli troops but at the cost of mounting casualties and domestic unease. The Israeli raids also palpably failed to reduce the number of missiles which Hezbollah continued to fire indiscriminately across the Lebanese border. Israel's huge bombardments by land, sea and air courted even greater controversy. Four UN observers were killed in an Israeli air assault on their position on 25 July 2006, leading UN Secretary-General Kofi Annan formally to accuse Israel of deliberately targeting UNIFIL. Five days later Israel's bombing of an apartment building in the town of Qana killed at least 40 civilians, most of them women and children. Israeli government spokesmen said that the loss of life in Qana was regrettable, but insisted that the village had been used as a launch site for Hezbollah rocket fire. News of the deaths caused outrage in the Arab world and anti-US rioting in Beirut, and contributed to appeals from the EU, the People's Republic of China, Jordan, Egypt, Saudi Arabia and Kuwait for an immediate cease-fire.

The events in Qana, and the warning from pro-Western Arab leaders that Israel's war with Hezbollah was further radicalizing Arab opinion, helped to intensify international efforts to end the fighting. On 5 August 2006 it was announced in Beirut that the USA and France were close to finalizing an agreement on a draft resolution that would involve an immediate cease-fire, to be followed by the disarming of Hezbollah, the withdrawal of Israeli forces from Lebanese territory and the deployment of an international monitoring presence. Both the Israeli and Lebanese Governments stated that they were dissatisfied with elements of the text. Israeli officials expressed concern that the proposals did not appeal for the deployment of an international force prior to an end to hostilities, while the Lebanese Government protested against the resolution's appeal for Israel to stop 'offensive military action' rather than military action per se. They argued that, since Israel had couched its entire operation against Lebanon as 'defensive', this would provide a pretext for continued attacks by Israeli forces. Hezbollah's Nasrallah also vowed that his movement could not be held to a truce as long as Israeli forces remained in occupation of any Lebanese territory. At an emergency summit meeting of the Arab League in Beirut on 7 August, delegates agreed to send a negotiating team to the UN to press Lebanese demands for a rewording of the draft. Meanwhile, Israeli forces continued to sustain heavy losses in the south of Lebanon and on their northern border.

The UN Security Council unanimously adopted Resolution 1701 on 11 August 2006 calling for a full cessation of hostilities between Israel and Hezbollah to begin on the morning of 14 August. The resolution also mandated a UN Interim Force of 15,000 troops to monitor the cease-fire and to 'take all necessary action' needed to perform its duties. Under its terms the Lebanese army was to move into the south of the country and to cut off arms supplies to Hezbollah. Member states were also to undertake not to supply military equipment to 'any entity or individual' in Lebanon, with the exception of Lebanese army and UN troops. Israeli forces would withdraw fully from Lebanon as UNIFIL and Lebanese army forces deployed. The Governments of Lebanon and Israel both voted to accept the resolution, but fighting continued to rage as Israel sought to inflict further damage on Hezbollah and apparently seize as much strategic territory as possible in the brief window of opportunity before the cease-fire came into effect. To underline its claim that it was unbowed after a month of Israeli bombardments, Hezbollah fired 250 rockets into Israel, the highest single daily total of the war. According to Lebanese and Israeli government sources, more than 1,000 Lebanese and 40 Israeli civilians had been killed during the conflict. Some 96 Israeli soldiers were also killed, with an unknown number of casualties suffered by Hezbollah fighters.

AFTERMATH OF THE ISRAEL–HEZBOLLAH CONFLICT

Transforming the tense truce in southern Lebanon into a more stable cease-fire presented an immediate challenge to the key regional and international players. EU states, particularly France, showed reluctance to commit troops to a UN peacekeeping force as long as aspects of its mandate were unclear. Olmert commented on 22 August 2006 that there could be no lifting of Israel's air and sea blockade until UN troops had been deployed along the Syrian–Lebanese border; government officials also insisted that the brief of an international force would need to include the disarming of Hezbollah. President Assad of Syria rejoined that such a deployment would be 'an infringement on Lebanese sovereignty', and his Minister of Foreign Affairs warned that it would lead to the closure of his country's border with Lebanon. With thousands of Israeli troops *in situ* in southern Lebanon, the UN's Special Envoy for the implementation of Resolution 1559, Terje Rød-Larsen, advised that there was a real possibility of a renewal of violence 'which might escalate and spin out of control'. Meeting in Brussels on 25 August, EU ministers responsible for foreign affairs responded to US and UN urgings to defuse the precarious security situation in southern Lebanon by agreeing to commit 7,000 ground troops to police the cease-fire. The bulk of these were to be provided by Italy (3,000) and France (2,000), with the remainder comprising Spanish, Belgian, Polish and Finnish contingents. Ministers promised that the deployment, the largest in the EU's history, would begin within days. The Governments of Turkey, China, Nepal and New Zealand also expressed a willingness to contribute to the 15,000-strong UN detachment called for by Resolution 1701.

Anxieties over the vulnerability of the cease-fire eased further with the steady deployment of UN forces in Lebanon. By mid-September 2006 there were an estimated 4,600 soldiers operating under the UN flag in the south of the country. These were joined by the first units of the Lebanese army to patrol the villages and towns bordering Israel for almost 30 years. The IDF made concomitant withdrawals from Lebanese territory, and by 23 September it was reported that all Israeli forces had been pulled back over the border. Hezbollah's leader, Sheikh Nasrallah, made a rare and defiant public appearance in front of a huge crowd of supporters in Beirut on 22 September to celebrate a 'divine' victory over Israel. He pledged that his movement would retain its military capability, including a claimed 20,000 rockets, until a time that 'we build a strong and just state that is capable of protecting the nation and the citizens'. He also used his address to confirm that captured Israeli servicemen would only be released in exchange for Hezbollah prisoners held in Israel.

Hezbollah's triumphalism contrasted sharply with the gloomy introspection that accompanied Israel's own reflections on the 34-day conflict. While few would lend credence to the Shi'a organization's claim that it had scored a victory over the IDF, Israel's own failure to achieve either of its stated war aims—the release of abducted soldiers and the destruction of Hezbollah as a fighting force—sat uncomfortably with a national psyche unused to such palpable exposure of military shortcomings. Recriminations centred on poor decision-making by IDF chiefs and the quality of political leadership provided by Olmert and the Minister of Defence, Peretz. More significantly, the experiences of Lebanon and Gaza had forced a fundamental rethink of Ariel Sharon's and Kadima's promotion of unilateral disengagement as the most effective way of realizing Israel's territorial claims in the West Bank and defining future borders. The Vice-Premier and Minister for the Development of the Negev and Galilee, Kadima's Shimon Peres, argued that neither the Lebanese Government nor the PA exercised full authority or military control over their territories. As a result, he asserted, the unilateral withdrawals from Lebanon in 2000 and Gaza in 2005 had not led to the peace that had followed the negotiated settlements achieved with Egypt and then Jordan.

INSECURITY IN THE WEST BANK AND GAZA

The performance of Hezbollah in its conflict with the IDF had inflated the Islamist movement's popularity throughout the Arab world, particularly in the West Bank and Gaza. For a significant number of Palestinians, the perceived successes of Hezbollah entrenched the conviction that in the absence of political dialogue, military resistance to Israel was the only feasible alternative. Nevertheless, the financial crisis within the PA and the worsening humanitarian situation in the Gaza Strip continued to provide the impetus for Fatah and Hamas negotiators to reach an agreement on a national unity administration in accordance with the provisions of the so-called prisoners' document. It appeared that a power-sharing agreement had been reached in mid-September 2006. According to press reports, the two sides had engineered a formula to address the Quartet group's insistence that Hamas renounce violence, recognize Israel and abide by previous peace agreements. Hamas spokesmen said that they would not renege on their charter advocating for the establishment of an Islamic state in all of historic Palestine, but had agreed with Fatah that they would delegate all negotiating power to Mahmud Abbas as head of the PLO. They also conceded that the new administration—to be headed by Haniya but with a majority of Fatah and non-Hamas ministers—would recognize past peace deals with Israel and would commit itself to the notion of *hudna*, a long-term truce with Israel in exchange for a Palestinian state in the territories occupied in 1967.

It was unlikely that these outcomes would be sufficiently explicit to satisfy either the Israeli or US Governments, but EU leaders, including visiting British Prime Minister Tony Blair, gave a cautious welcome to the principle of a cabinet of national unity in the PA-administered areas. However, Palestinian hopes for an end to the crisis of governance and, with it, the burden of sanctions quickly receded. During a visit to New York at the end of September 2006, the Palestinian President assured the UN General Assembly that a new Palestinian administration would abide by the Oslo accords, in which the PLO and Israel recognized each other. Nevertheless, the Quartet group refused to accept a Palestinian unity administration that included Hamas, without the Islamist party's unambiguous recognition of the Jewish state. Abbas failed to secure a compromise from Haniya on his return to Ramallah.

The breakdown of talks on the formation of a national unity administration in the PA was followed by an intensification of the simmering rivalry between security forces loyal to Fatah and the militias led by Hamas. Several people were killed in clashes in Gaza in early October 2006, in what was described as the most serious bout of factional violence since the Hamas election victory in January. Fighting also spread to cities in the West Bank, forcing Hamas to close its government offices. The failure of a Qatari mission to broker another Fatah-Hamas power-sharing agreement only served to exacerbate tensions between the two groups.

The crisis in Gaza and the West Bank coincided with a visit to the region by US Secretary of State Condoleezza Rice, in what she portrayed as an opportunity to 'rally moderate forces and moderate voices' after the recent conflict between Israel and Hezbollah and in light of continuing tensions with Iran. In meetings with Abbas, she expressed the USA's ongoing concern with the humanitarian plight of the Palestinian populations in the West Bank and Gaza and reiterated the Bush Administration's commitment to a two-state solution. However, Rice confirmed that there could be no easing of the international boycott of a Hamas-led PA and offered no new steps to restart the peace process. A similar message was conveyed by the Secretary of State to a meeting of Arab ministers responsible for foreign affairs in Cairo. While the Saudi Minister of Foreign Affairs, Prince Sa'ud al-Faisal Al Sa'ud, appealed to the USA directly to address the region's 'core problem' of Israel and the Palestinian territories, the settlement of which would provide the key to other disputes, Rice would only restate that Washington's strategic priority remained the battle against extremists and their sponsors.

Dismay at the Bush Administration's passive stance towards the Arab–Israeli question was not confined to the Arab world. A former senior aide to the Clinton Administration decried Bush's hands-off approach as counter-productive and 'utterly incomprehensible', while a group of 135 former world presidents and government ministers issued a statement in which they described the Middle East as being in its 'worst crisis for years'. They added that there was now a 'desperate need for fresh thinking and the injection of new political will' and pointed to the importance of convening a new Middle East peace conference. Hamas leaders reacted negatively to the Rice visit and its central message. Ismail Haniya accused the US Secretary of State of seeking to rearrange the regional and Palestinian political scene 'in a way that serves the American and Israeli agenda'. The Islamist movement's growing distrust of the US role deepened after it was revealed that the US Administration had earmarked US $42m. to fund its opponents ahead of possible early Palestinian elections. Reports in Israel suggested that these funds were being channelled into military training projects for security forces loyal to President Abbas and his Fatah faction. Hamas was, meanwhile, reported to be expanding its own so-called Executive Force from 3,000 to 7,500 men and to be importing arms through Egypt.

In November 2006 the IDF intensified its operations in the northern Gaza Strip in a stated attempt to thwart rocket fire into Israel. According to an IDF spokeswoman, during the previous 10 months some 800 rockets had been fired into Israel from Gaza, 300 of which were claimed to have emanated from the town of Beit Hanoun, the main target of the Israeli strikes. During an incursion into the town in the first weeks of November Israeli forces killed at least 70 Palestinians—both civilians and militants—for the loss of one of soldier. Destruction to residential areas and the civilian infrastructure was widespread. The IDF deemed its actions in Beit Hanoun, dubbed Operation Autumn Clouds, an unqualified success and claimed to have seized large quantities of rockets and other weapons as well as having killed many gunmen. Scores of *Qassam* rockets were fired by Hamas and Islamic Jihad militants in retaliation for the deaths in Beit Hanoun. Less crude than previously, the rockets claimed the lives of two Israelis in Sderot (the first such deaths since 2005), wounded several others and created widespread panic. Israel responded with the targeted killing of senior Islamists and a further incursion into Beit Hanoun and nearby Jabalia.

In late November 2006 the Palestinian President declared that he had achieved the agreement of all the Palestinian factions to abide by a cease-fire if Israel were to end its targeted killings and withdraw its troops from all parts of Gaza. Olmert responded positively to the offer, stating that he would instruct the withdrawal of his forces from Gaza if the rocket fire ceased. Two days later, as a shaky cease-fire took hold, the Israeli Prime Minister delivered a major policy speech in which he offered the prospect of a return to the roadmap negotiations and the creation of an 'independent and viable Palestinian state' if the PA was able to form an administration that satisfied the criteria of the Quartet group. In the mean time, he said, his Government would be prepared to release 'many Palestinian prisoners' if the abducted Corporal Gilad Shalit was returned alive and well. As a number of commentators pointed out, the Olmert speech represented a significant departure from the Sharon legacy of bold unilateralism in dealings with the PA. It also dovetailed with assertions, most recently and forcefully articulated by British Prime Minister Blair, of the importance of undermining the forces of anti-Western radicalism in the Middle East by moves towards a resolution of the Palestinian issue.

PALESTINIAN FACTIONAL DIVIDE WIDENS

The cease-fire between Israeli forces and Palestinian militias in Gaza continued to hold, but the repeated failure of Fatah-Hamas negotiations to deliver agreement on the formation of a national unity cabinet continued to stoke factional tensions. Although the UN warned in December 2006 that the humanitarian situation in the Palestinian territories had reached crisis point, Hamas persisted with its refusal to join a power-sharing administration if this meant recognition of Israel. In his first trip outside the Palestinian territories since being appointed PA Prime Minister in March, Ismail Haniya confirmed in Tehran that Hamas would never recognize 'the usurper Zionist government and will continue our *jihad*-like movement until the liberation of Jerusalem'. It was also reported that Hamas officials were increasingly confident that they would be able to make up a substantial part of the funding shortage created by the US and EU sanctions policy. Iran, Qatar and Sudan promised the Haniya Cabinet up to US $350m. in aid.

Also in December 2006 PA President Abbas announced that he planned to dissolve the Hamas administration and order new presidential and legislative elections. Hamas condemned the announcement as 'a coup' and a recipe for civil war, a charge rejected by Abbas, who insisted that he had the constitutional authority to call new elections at any time. Hamas's Prime Minister subsequently renewed his movement's assertion that the USA was orchestrating the campaign to bring about the collapse of his Cabinet. Islamist suspicions were further aroused by a surprise meeting between Abbas and Israel's Prime Minister in Jerusalem on 23 December. According to an Israeli spokesman, the first such meeting between Israeli and Palestinian leaders for nearly two years focused on the crisis within the PA, the release of Corporal Shalit and the continuation of the cease-fire in Gaza. It was later reported that Olmert had agreed to allow the transfer of a large consignment of guns and ammunition from Egypt to Abbas's presidential guard in Gaza. A senior source in the Israeli Government confided that the arms transfer was designed to bolster Abbas against 'the other forces' in Gaza. The absence of real initiatives to restart the peace process continued to be a source of frustration for European and moderate Arab leaders alike, with much of the negative emotion directed at a passive Bush Administration. A further visit to the region by the US Secretary of State in mid-January 2007 also failed to inspire regional optimism. Sharing a platform with Mahmud Abbas in Ramallah, Rice said that she would accelerate progress on the roadmap, a message that was repeated in talks with Jordan's King Abdullah. In discussions with Israel's Prime Minister, she was also said to have appealed for further concessions to be made to the PA President in an effort to strengthen his hand in his ongoing power struggle with Hamas. US officials subsequently announced that Rice would be hosting a three-way summit with Abbas and Olmert in the near future.

The apparent willingness of the USA to increase its involvement in the Israeli-Palestinian peace process was broadly welcomed in Europe. Anxious to maintain momentum, Germany's Chancellor, Angela Merkel, who held the Presidency of the Council of the EU, successfully lobbied for a meeting of the Quartet group to be held prior to the Israeli-Palestinian talks. The Arab world was more circumspect in its view of the USA's new diplomatic efforts. The Palestinian President was an immediate beneficiary of Rice's trip, as the Israeli Government announced shortly after the Secretary of State's departure from the region that it would be releasing a further US $100m. in frozen tax revenues to the PA. Nevertheless, Abbas had serious objections to a key element in a revived roadmap, namely the plan's vision for the creation of a Palestinian state with provisional borders. Such transitional arrangements, Abbas had informed Rice, were not viewed by the Palestinians as 'a realistic option'. Arab commentators also questioned the motivations underpinning the USA's new-found interest in the Middle East peace process. Scepticism centred on the poor record of the Bush Administration in sustaining past initiatives on the Arab-Israeli track and a widely held belief that the USA's latest expression of concern was subservient to the twin regional ambitions of winning support for new initiatives in Iraq and rallying Arab Sunni opinion for a potential confrontation with Iran.

Shortly after his meetings with the US Secretary of State, the Palestinian President travelled to Damascus for talks with President Assad and Khalid Meshaal, chief of Hamas's political bureau and the acknowledged power broker of the movement. Abbas had described his proposed meeting with Meshaal as 'the last chance' to achieve an agreement on a national unity administration. The precursors to the talks had not been positive, with the Palestinian territories, and especially Gaza, still in the grip of violent Fatah–Hamas rivalries. Nevertheless, the Hamas leadership was acutely aware of the economic and political damage being suffered as a result of the sanctions regime. Despite a growing unease with President Abbas's willingness to be recruited to the camp of moderates within the new ideological fault lines being drawn by the Bush Administration, a power-sharing arrangement with Fatah appeared to be the only viable solution to end the PA's crippling isolation and to ease a growing dependence on Iran. Abbas left Damascus commenting that progress had been made during the talks, but that the two organizations were still some way short of an agreement. The main area of dispute was reported to be the allocation of ministerial positions in any new administration, and in particular which faction would hold the interior portfolio and, with it, control of the PA's security forces. Both men expressed their rejection of violence to settle political differences and committed themselves to a continuation of their dialogue. The ritual denunciation of internecine conflict had little immediate impact on the street. In the week after the Abbas-Meshaal meeting more than 30 Palestinians were killed in factional clashes in Gaza. A further cease-fire was hastily brokered at the end of January 2007, bringing another lull in the fighting. The day before it came into effect a suicide bomber from Gaza belonging to Islamic Jihad killed three people in Eilat. It was the first such incident inside Israel for nine months. Islamic Jihad claimed that it had carried out the attack because of the failure to bring about a unity administration. Fatah condemned the bombing, while a spokesman for Hamas deemed it a 'natural response' to Israeli policies.

MECCA AGREEMENT FAILS TO END PA CRISIS

Responding to the growing distaste in the Arab world at the scenes of inter-Palestinian fighting in the Occupied Territories and a fear of the destabilizing effect this was having on an already troubled Middle East, the Saudi Government invited representatives of Fatah and Hamas to reconciliation talks in Mecca, Saudi Arabia, at the beginning of 2007. Within two days it was announced that the Fatah and Hamas leaders had agreed on the formation of a national unity cabinet. Under the terms of the agreement, Hamas's representation would be reduced, with several key portfolios going to independents selected by Hamas and approved by Fatah. Ismail Haniya would remain as Prime Minister. Critically, nowhere in the Mecca document did Hamas commit itself to recognition of Israel or renunciation of violence. There was, however, an agreement to 'respect' past peace deals and to be guided by the terms of the prisoners' document worked out between representatives of the two factions the previous year. This, according to a Palestinian spokesman, contained implicit recognition of Israel by all parties. While Palestinians in the West Bank and Gaza swept onto the streets in noisy celebration of the Mecca agreement, a senior aide to Mahmud Abbas conceded that it might not satisfy all the requirements for the ending of the PA's siege. The hope remained that, in the interest of the wider peace process and in recognition of the downgrading of the Hamas role in a new administration, the international community would adopt a pragmatic line towards the constructive ambiguities of the new situation. These slim hopes receded the following day when a senior Hamas official in Gaza informed the United Kingdom-based news service, Reuters, that his organization would never recognize Israel. Moreover, while the EU states extended a guarded welcome to the outcome at Mecca, US officials reportedly told the Palestinian President on 15 February that they would not engage with any of the ministers in a new Palestinian cabinet, including those belonging to Fatah, unless the administration as a whole met international conditions.

The US warning was followed by a statement from the Israeli Prime Minister saying that his Government had agreed with the USA that they would withhold recognition from a Palestinian coalition administration. Later Rice clarified the US position on a cabinet of Palestinian national unity. Officially, the USA would suspend judgement on the coalition agreement until it was properly finalized. However, the Secretary of State expressed doubts that the cabinet would 'meet the Quartet's principles'.

The new Palestinian administration was sworn in on 17 March 2007. Hamas remained the senior partner in the coalition, but several key portfolios, including those of finance, foreign affairs and the all-important interior, were allocated to independents. EU leaders broadly welcomed the new Cabinet, in particular the appointment of Dr Salam Fayyad as Minister of Finance. The United Kingdom indicated that it would work with non-Hamas members of the coalition, a position that was shared by France and Germany. However, on the issue of broadening contacts and ending the economic boycott of the PA, a spokeswoman for the European Commission summed up the developing consensus by saying that 'we will not be taking any decisions before we have been able to judge the programme and actions of the new administration'. The USA also softened its previously uncompromising stance. There would be no lifting of the ban on direct funding, but a spokeswoman for the US consulate in East Jerusalem confirmed that there would not be a suspension of contacts with individuals 'who are not members of foreign terrorist organizations . . . solely based on their participation in the unity government'. The US position represented a rare policy divergence from that of its Israeli ally. At his weekly cabinet meeting on 18 March, Ehud Olmert confirmed that his Government would not engage with the new PA administration and would continue to withhold hundreds of millions of dollars of Palestinian tax revenues. He stated that he would continue to meet with the Palestinian President but would limit discussions to 'quality of life' issues. In a further visit to the Middle East at the end of March, the US Secretary of State sought to persuade the Israeli Prime Minister to be more flexible in his dealings with Mahmud Abbas. Rice was able to secure a commitment from both men to fortnightly meetings, in which both 'day to day' issues and the broader 'political horizon' would form the agenda.

ATTEMPTS TO RELAUNCH THE SAUDI PEACE PLAN

As expected, Arab leaders meeting in the Saudi capital on 28–29 March 2007 formally approved the relaunch of the peace plan that had first been adopted at the Beirut summit in 2002. Under the terms of the Riyadh communiqué, the Arab states would formally extend recognition to Israel and normalize relations in return for a withdrawal from all the territories occupied in 1967, the establishment of a Palestinian state, with East Jerusalem as its capital, and a 'just solution' to the Palestinian refugee issue. The Saudis had applied their full political weight in securing complete Arab backing for the Riyadh communiqué, in particular ensuring that neither Hamas nor Syria jeopardized the deal. Arab leaders emphasized that, for Israel, this was a 'take it or leave it' opportunity. 'If Israel refuses that means it doesn't want peace', opined the Saudi Minister of Foreign Affairs, 'then the conflict goes back into the hands of the lords of war'. This warning was echoed by Jordan's King Abdullah, who insisted that Israel must now choose between 'peace and co-existence' and a 'cycle of constant war and increasing hatred'.

The Arab initiative was greeted enthusiastically in Europe, and the Arab world's choice of peace as 'a strategic option' was described as 'very positive' by the Bush Administration. The Olmert Government was predictably more nuanced in its response. The Vice-Premier, Shimon Peres, while welcoming the prospect of dialogue with the Arab world, voiced his opposition to any negotiations based on predetermined outcomes. The Israeli Prime Minister stated that he applauded 'the revolutionary change in outlook' that had inspired the Arab 'land-for-peace' proposal, but that he was troubled by certain aspects of the plan. He remained adamant that a 'just solution' for the refugee problem could never encompass a return to the pre-1967 borders of Israel. Furthermore, while observing that he could envisage a comprehensive peace agreement being achieved within the coming five years, Olmert remained highly critical of the Palestinian leadership's ability to reform their administration, defeat terrorism and fulfil their other commitments. Speaking with the visiting German Chancellor, Angela Merkel, shortly afterwards, he also extended an invitation to all Arab heads of state to take part in a dialogue without preconditions.

Crisis soon enveloped the new Palestinian unity administration after only the briefest periods of calm between competing factions in Gaza. On 23 April 2007 the new independent Minister of the Interior, Hani Talab al-Qawasmi, tendered his resignation in protest against the failure of either Hamas or Fatah to co-operate with a new 'security plan', which envisaged the reform of the myriad security forces operating in the PA. He was persuaded to stay on in his post by Prime Minister Haniya, but few observers believed that al-Qawasmi, largely unknown prior to his appointment, possessed the political authority to counter the entrenched positions of the dominant parties. In addition to the creeping lawlessness, cross-border mortar and rocket fire threatened to end the five-month cease-fire with Israel. After a period of relative restraint, Israeli forces struck at militants in Gaza and conducted a raid in Ramallah on 21–22 April. Nine Palestinians were killed in the attacks. Hamas's military wing responded by declaring that its cease-fire with Israel was over. Several rockets were directed at the Israeli town of Sderot on the morning of 24 April.

Al-Qawasmi formally resigned from the Cabinet on 14 May 2007, citing his main reason as his refusal 'to be a minister without authority', a scarcely veiled reference to his failure to wrest control of the security services from their Fatah chiefs. Prime Minister Haniya took temporary control of the interior portfolio. Al-Qawasmi's departure came at a time of intensifying factional clashes and abductions in Gaza, apparently sparked by Mahmud Abbas's decision to deploy 3,000 members of his security forces in the Strip as police officers. After four days of fighting more than 30 Palestinians were reported to have been killed, with many more injured. In the midst of their clashes with Fatah, Hamas militants fired rockets into Israel in a move interpreted by some observers as an attempt to provoke Israel and thus unite Palestinians. Israeli officials had previously warned that they would abandon their policy of restraint should attacks from Gaza persist. On 16 May Israel launched a series of aerial attacks against mainly Hamas targets in Gaza. Eight people died on 20 May in a strike on the home of a prominent Hamas politician. This came as senior Israeli politicians warned that they were considering a revival of their assassination policy against Hamas's political leadership, including Haniya and Meshaal. The Palestinian President urged the US Secretary of State to intervene with Israel to prevent a further military escalation. The UN's new Special Co-ordinator for the Middle East Peace Process, Michael Williams, also warned that the upsurge in fighting threatened to wreck any hopes of a revitalized peace process.

However, international calls for both sides to demonstrate restraint went unheeded. Two Israelis were killed in Sderot in separate rocket attacks during the last week of May 2007, stimulating an exodus of thousands of the town's residents. The reiteration of the threat to assassinate Hamas politicians was accompanied by further strikes on targets in Gaza, including a missile attack on the compound of the Hamas Prime Minister, while 33 Hamas politicians were also rounded up in raids across the West Bank (nearly all of the 40 Hamas figures arrested following the abduction of Corporal Shalit the previous year remained in detention). The Israeli Government rejected a Hamas offer for a broad cease-fire to encompass the West Bank. Tzipi Livni, Israel's Deputy Prime Minister and Minister of Foreign Affairs, accused Hamas of having used previous cease-fires simply to regroup and rearm. However, despite the deaths of more than 50 Palestinians in the last fortnight of May, the Hamas leader in Damascus remained optimistic about the abilities of his movement to continue 'resistance'. In an interview with the British press, Meshaal also commented that the intra-Palestinian conflict in Gaza was being stoked by US financial and military support for Fatah.

ISRAEL AND THE USA CRITICIZED IN LEAKED UN REPORT

An internal UN report by Alvaro de Soto, outgoing Special Co-ordinator for the Middle East Peace Process, was leaked to the international press in June 2007. It contained harsh criticism of all the major players in the Israeli–Palestinian conflict. According to de Soto, Israel had adopted an 'essentially rejectionist stance' towards the Palestinians and set unachievable conditions for dialogue, while the Palestinians had a 'patchy at best, reprehensible at worst' record of preventing violence against Israelis. The Peruvian diplomat was especially critical of the Quartet-led boycott of the Palestinian administration. He condemned the crippling impact of this policy on ordinary Palestinians and the effective transformation of the Quartet group from a 'negotiation-promoting foursome' into a vehicle for 'imposing sanctions on a freely elected government of a people under occupation'. The Bush Administration was castigated for having 'pummelled into submission' the UN's role as an impartial Middle East negotiator and, claimed de Soto, bore prime responsibility for the reorientation of the Quartet group's founding brief to satisfy what was in essence an Israeli-US agenda. The continued focus on the shortcomings of Hamas had also lifted pressure from Israel, according to de Soto, with the consequence that 'the Israeli settlement enterprise and barrier construction has continued unabated'. Equally controversially, de Soto argued that the USA had actively attempted to derail the creation of a Palestinian unity administration and that its officials had been pushing for a confrontation between Fatah and Hamas.

HAMAS OUSTS FATAH IN GAZA

After a brief lull, the power struggle between Hamas and Fatah resumed in June 2007, leading the Palestinian President to claim in a televised address on 5 June that Palestinians were 'on the brink of civil war'. Less than a week later fighting between the two factions was raging throughout Gaza. It quickly became evident that Hamas forces were now intent on scoring a decisive victory over their erstwhile partners in the national unity administration. Pleas by Mahmud Abbas to Khalid Meshaal for Hamas to agree to a cease-fire were ignored. Instead, Hamas's radio station broadcast a statement on 13 June in which the organization urged its Fatah-allied rivals to relinquish their weapons and announced its intention to seize the presidential compound. Over the following 48 hours Hamas fighters carried out a total rout of their Fatah rivals throughout the Gaza Strip at the cost of scores of dead and hundreds of wounded. Hundreds of Fatah fighters were reported to have escaped to Egypt by sea, while Israeli border guards allowed senior members of the organization to transit to the West Bank. Hamas was accused of perpetrating summary killings of captured Fatah fighters and admitted to the execution of Fatah's most senior military commander in the Strip, Samih al-Madhoun.

Many reporters were surprised by the ease and speed with which Hamas fighters were able to defeat an enemy that was far larger numerically. According to observers, the Hamas victory came as a result of many Fatah units simply refusing to participate in the fighting and because the Hamas fighters were better armed, disciplined and motivated. On 14 June 2007 the Palestinian President responded to the Hamas takeover in Gaza by dismissing the national unity administration. On the West Bank forces loyal to Fatah also moved swiftly against the Islamist movement, arresting leading figures and shutting down party headquarters and media outlets. On 17 June in Ramallah Abbas swore in a new Palestinian Emergency Cabinet, composed almost exclusively of independent technocrats and headed by Dr Salam Fayyad as Prime Minister. Haniya characterized the appointment of a new administration and Abbas's proposals for early elections as 'illegal'. However, the general tone of the Hamas leadership's comments on the new situation tended to be conciliatory. Spokesmen for the movement insisted that their campaign in Gaza had not been directed against Fatah as a whole, but against sections of the organization that they claimed were acting in furtherance of US and Israeli interests. The former Fatah 'strongman' in Gaza, Muhammad Dahlan, was alleged to have been plotting his own coup against Hamas (a claim that was confirmed in 2008 by a senior aide to the US Vice-President, Dick Cheney). Haniya also told reporters that Hamas remained committed to a two-state solution with Israel and wanted to establish an immediate dialogue with Fatah to heal their divisions. He also promised that the immediate priority of his movement would be to end the lawlessness that had reigned in Gaza for so long and to confiscate illegally held weapons. Hamas's studied moderation reflected the pyrrhic nature of its victory in Gaza. The Islamists had demonstrated that they were the pre-eminent military force in Gaza, but their political isolation had only deepened.

Privately, Jordan and Egypt were said to be furious with the Israeli and US Governments for their failure to give Abbas sufficient political and military support prior to the Gaza debacle. However, it also became rapidly evident that the Gaza–West Bank divisions could, and would, be exploited by the USA and Israel to ensure that the Islamists' political gains in Gaza, whether real or imagined, would be reversed. The USA now saw an opportunity to demonstrate to the Palestinians and the wider Arab world that rewards flowed from moderation. This lesson would most effectively be understood if a successful Fatah-led administration in the West Bank could be contrasted with a failing and isolated Hamas fiefdom in Gaza. Ways of bolstering the Palestinian President and the newly installed Emergency Cabinet became the focus of discussions between the US Administration and Ehud Olmert during the Israeli Prime Minister's visit to the USA on 19 June 2007. The US Secretary of State subsequently promised to resume economic assistance to the new Palestinian administration. On 24 June the Israeli Cabinet approved the transfer, in stages, of the estimated US $600m. in withheld tax revenues. At a summit meeting with Abbas, President Mubarak of Egypt and Jordan's King Abdullah in Sharm el-Sheikh on 25 June, Olmert also agreed to the release of 250 Palestinians held in Israeli prisons. However, he remained firm on Israel's reluctance to be drawn on discussions pertaining to final borders, Jerusalem or refugees.

The continued Israeli blockade of Gaza was criticized in a report published by an Israeli human rights organization, Gisha, on 4 July 2007. The report's authors concluded that dependency and poverty, exacerbated by Gaza's closure, were fostering extremism. Gisha estimated that 75% of Gaza's factories had closed because of an inability to import raw materials or export produce. The UN Relief and Works Agency for Palestine Refugees in the Near East and the UN Development Programme announced on 9 July that they were suspending all construction projects in the Strip because Israel would not allow the import of cement. Anxious to avoid the charge of causing hunger in Gaza, Israel relaxed its closure of border crossings to allow the entry of UN distributed foodstuffs; nevertheless, an Israeli official overseeing policy towards Gaza described the Israeli priorities as 'no development, no progress, no humanitarian crisis'. On the West Bank, meanwhile, it was reported that large numbers of militants belonging to the Fatah-aligned al-Aqsa Martyrs Brigades had signed pledges renouncing violence and that some had surrendered weapons at Palestinian security compounds. Israel had given an undertaking to stop targeting Fatah militants who had forsworn attacks against Israel.

BUSH ADMINISTRATION TO SPONSOR PEACE CONFERENCE

On 16 July 2007 the US President announced that his Administration would be sponsoring a Middle East peace conference to take place before the end of 2007. The conference would be chaired by his Secretary of State and would encompass negotiations on all areas of the Israeli–Arab dispute, including 'final status' issues. The invitees included the members of the Quartet group, Israel, Arab states and Palestinian representatives who 'recognized Israel and renounced violence'. The belated push by the Bush presidency to address the core of the Palestinian–Israeli dispute was broadly welcomed internationally, even though the ongoing desire to contain Iran's regional influence was viewed as being the context in which the conference initiative could be best understood. The response in Israel and the Arab states was more muted. Syria indicated that it would only attend if the return of the occupied Golan were to be an agreed outcome. Chief Palestinian negotiator Saeb Erakat welcomed the emphasis on addressing final settlement issues and Bush's promise of further aid to the PA in the West Bank, but stressed that Palestinians needed to 'start seeing deeds not words'. The Israeli Government was less than lukewarm in its reception of the Bush proposals, declaring that there could be no negotiations at this stage on borders, Jerusalem or refugees.

It was expected that the Quartet group's newly appointed envoy to the Middle East, former British Prime Minister Tony Blair, would play a key role in the diplomatic efforts leading up to the conference. Blair had been appointed to the position of Quartet envoy in June 2007, with a brief to support Palestinian governance and economic development. The Israeli Government broadly welcomed his appointment as long as his energies were focused on Palestinian institution building. However, many in the Arab world considered Blair to be too close to the Bush Administration to serve as an honest broker. For their part, the Palestinians acknowledged the opportunities that came with Blair's status and had requested the expansion of his role to include the policing of Israeli commitments to the mired peace process, most specifically a settlement freeze and the removal of West Bank checkpoints. Privately, it was known that Tony Blair saw his mission as having far wider responsibilities than the Quartet envoy's declared mandate suggested. Blair made his first visit to the region on 23 July. After talks with Shimon Peres, Israel's newly elected President, in Jerusalem and with Mahmud Abbas and Dr Salam Fayyad in Ramallah, Blair shared with reporters his belief that there was not going to be a quick breakthrough in the latest attempts to revive the peace process.

At the end of July 2007 Arab League ministers responsible for foreign affairs met to discuss the US President's proposal for a regional peace conference. The plan was given qualified support, with the main issue of contention being the League's insistence that the conference should be open to all relevant parties, including Hamas and Syria.

Following US pressure, Olmert became the first Israeli leader to hold talks in the West Bank for seven years when he met Mahmud Abbas in Jericho on 6 August 2007. Prior to the meeting Olmert had stated that he intended to discuss 'fundamental issues'. The two leaders emerged after three hours of discussions with the talks characterized by both sides as positive and constructive. However, Israeli officials said that discussions had not touched on the 'final status' issues, while the chief Palestinian negotiator expressed a degree of frustration with the absence of concrete progress. According to press reports, it was agreed that the Israelis and the West Bank PA would address such issues as checkpoints via joint security committees. In Gaza Hamas responded to the Olmert-Abbas talks with the same disdain it had expressed following the Bush announcement of a regional conference. Smarting from the recent US promise of US $80m. to provide training for security forces loyal to Abbas on the West Bank, a Hamas spokesman derided the meetings with Israeli leaders as offering 'no benefit to the Palestinian people'. Rice had also announced at the end of July that Israel and Egypt were to receive military aid worth $30,000m. and $13,000m., respectively, over a 10-year period. The USA also concluded agreements on arms sales to Saudi Arabia worth $20,000m.

ISRAELI PLANES BOMB 'NUCLEAR FACILITY' IN SYRIA

On 6 September 2007 the Syrian Arab News Agency reported that air defences had opened fire on Israeli aircraft that had entered Syrian airspace. According to a military spokesman, the Syrian defensive action had forced the warplanes to 'drop ammunition', harmlessly, over an unpopulated area in the north of the country. Israeli officials refused to comment on the reports of a raid over Syria, but leaks to the international media suggested that the Israeli air force had indeed targeted a nuclear facility, which was in the early stages of construction with assistance from the Democratic People's Republic of Korea (North Korea). The Syrian Government remained largely silent about these reports. President Bashar al-Assad told the BBC in October that Israeli planes had struck at an uncommissioned military base. He denied that it was a nuclear facility, but refused to elaborate further. The absence of an outcry in the Arab world gave credence to suggestions that Syria's neighbours had been uneasy with whatever was being developed on the site. It was unclear whether the US Administration had given the green light for the raid. The US Secretary of Defense, Robert Gates, offered no comment other than to confirm that his Government was 'closely watching' both Syria and North Korea. The fact that both Israel and Syria minimized the incident prompted speculation that both Governments wanted to avoid escalating regional tensions in the approach to November's Annapolis peace summit in Maryland.

LITTLE OPTIMISM PRIOR TO ANNAPOLIS

The ongoing violence in and around the Gaza Strip served as a stark reminder of the complexities and challenges facing the revived peace process. Negotiations between Israel and the West Bank leadership of the PA took place against a background of low-intensity warfare between the IDF and the various Palestinian factions in Gaza. On 11 September 2007 a rocket struck an army base just north of the Strip, wounding 69 soldiers, 11 of them seriously. The Government of Ehud Olmert responded by declaring the Gaza Strip a 'hostile entity' and promised to intensify its economic blockade, including further reductions in electricity and fuel supplies. The US Secretary of State, Condoleezza Rice, gave tacit US backing to the Israeli decision. The PA leader, Mahmud Abbas, joined Hamas in denouncing the Israeli threats as a form of collective punishment. The UN Secretary-General, Ban Ki-Moon, also urged Israel to reconsider its decision, adding his concern that the general population of Gaza 'should not be punished for the unacceptable actions of militants and extremists'.

The weeks prior to the US-hosted peace summit in Annapolis witnessed increased political and diplomatic activity in the region. Having so publicly and belatedly invested the US Administration's authority in the achievement of an Israeli-Palestinian peace, securing the attendance in Annapolis of the key regional players and ensuring positive outcomes from the Olmert-Abbas negotiations were the twin imperatives handed by President Bush to his Secretary of State. The challenges were considerable, not least because of the obvious political weakness of the main protagonists. The Israeli Prime Minister had failed to recover his political authority following criticism of his handling of the July 2006 war against Hezbollah. Adding to his vulnerability were persistent allegations of personal corruption and financial impropriety. The domestic standing of his Palestinian interlocutor was even less secure. Abbas's Fatah party had long been tainted with charges of corruption and gangsterism and, following June's debacle in Gaza, it was clearly not credible for him to claim that his regime enjoyed a democratic mandate. More damaging for Abbas was his opponents' charge that he was operating 'under licence' from the Israeli and US Governments.

A growing weight of Palestinian and Arab opinion held that a Fatah-Hamas rapprochement should be the strategic priority of the Palestinian leadership. Nevertheless, the Israeli Prime Minister had made it very clear to Abbas that the Israeli Government would cease to deal with the PA should it include representatives of Hamas. The emphasis, therefore, of PA diplomacy in the run-up to the Annapolis meeting was to gain short-term domestic support by winning concessions from the Israelis and, secondly, to restore nationalist—as opposed to Islamist—stewardship of the Palestinian future by securing Israeli commitment to a timetable for the creation of a Palestinian state together with an acceptable resolution of the so-called 'core' issues. Predictably, Israel resisted the PA push. Instead, Israeli negotiators declared that they were seeking no more than a vague declaration of principles to be drafted prior to Annapolis.

By the end of October 2007 both the US Secretary of State and Israel's Prime Minister were lowering international expectations of what might be achieved in Maryland. US officials began referring to the event as a meeting rather than a conference, while Olmert ruled out the possibility of Annapolis being the venue for 'the declaration of peace'. The modest package of concessions that Israel was prepared to offer in advance of Annapolis also frustrated the PA leadership. Eighty-six predominantly Fatah prisoners had been released by the beginning of October, with the promise in November of the release of a further 500 at an unspecified date in the future. This would still leave an estimated 8,000 Palestinian security prisoners in Israeli gaols. Nor was Israel prepared to accede to the PA request for a reduction in the hundreds of roadblocks and checkpoints on the West Bank. On the issue of settlements, the 'biggest hurdle' to the achievement of peace according to Abbas, there was also to be disappointment for the Palestinians. Despite pressure from the USA for Israel to compensate for its pre-conference reluctance to address the detail of the 'core issues' by agreeing to a moratorium on settlement construction, Olmert asserted that Israel would not stop building work in the major settlement blocs on the West Bank (or in East Jerusalem).

The diminishing prospects of a breakthrough in Annapolis ensured a wariness among Arab states (with the exception of Jordan and Egypt) about accepting the US Government's informal invitation to attend. Following Israel's refusal to engage with the Saudi peace initiative of March, earlier in 2007, and against the backdrop of a worsening humanitarian situation in Gaza, many voices in the Arab world were raised against the usefulness of an event that had failed to achieve prior Israeli commitment to evacuate the Occupied Territories in line with UN Resolution 242. Senior figures in the Saudi Arabian Government had already signalled that the kingdom would not send a representative to Maryland if nothing more substantive would be achieved than a 'photo-opportunity'. There was greater uncertainty over Syrian representation given the Assad Government's sponsorship of Hamas and other Palestinian groupings opposed to Abbas and the Annapolis event. Nevertheless, by mid-November, and despite significant reservations, it was being reported that both Syria and Saudi Arabia would accept a US invitation to attend the summit. The Saudi decision came after intensive lobbying by the US Secretary of State, supported by the conviction that a failure to send representation to the event would provide Israel's leaders with an alibi for their own intransigence in the search for peace. Syrian acceptance reportedly came after assurances from the USA that the Golan Heights would be on the summit agenda, and amid a reluctance by the Syrian leadership to risk a further deterioration of relations with the USA. The shifting viewpoint in Damascus was emphasized by the cancellation of an 'anti-Annapolis' meeting suggested by Hamas and its regional allies, which Syria had earlier agreed to host.

On 19 November 2007 the Quartet's special envoy to the Middle East, Tony Blair, announced plans to boost the Palestinian economy and generate tens of thousands of jobs in the West Bank and Gaza through an array of development initiatives. These included the creation of a Turkish-sponsored industrial park near Jericho, a road construction project on the West Bank and a sewerage treatment plant in Gaza. The Israeli Deputy Prime Minister and Minister of Defence, Ehud Barak, chose the occasion of the Blair announcement to confirm that his Government was prepared to remove 24 roadblocks and one checkpoint in the West Bank. Meanwhile, the Israeli Prime Minister shuttled to Cairo for talks with Egypt's President, Hosni Mubarak. For Abbas's part, the PA leader urged the Arab states, which were due to deliberate on a unified response to the question of attendance in Annapolis at an Arab League summit on 23 November, not to miss the opportunities presented by the Annapolis conference. The USA also sought to secure a positive response from the Arab world by reinforcing the Administration's commitment to a 'serious effort' that would serve 'as a launching point for negotiations leading to the establishment of a Palestinian state and the realization of Israeli-Palestinian peace'. As expected, Arab ministers meeting in Cairo endorsed attendance at the summit. It was argued that, given that League members had made the pursuit of peace with Israel a 'strategic' objective, it would not be prudent to boycott the event and to miss an opportunity to internationalize the conflict, or to run the risk of the Arab world being blamed for failure. On the eve of the summit Palestinians in Gaza and Israelis in Jerusalem held rallies protesting against the Maryland meeting. The Hamas leader, Mahmoud Zahar, warned Abbas that he would be considered a 'traitor' if he made any concessions to Israel, while Binyamin Netanyahu of Likud berated Olmert for contemplating a peace deal with a Palestinian leadership that was 'not lifting a finger to halt terror'.

THE ANNAPOLIS CONFERENCE

US President Bush opened the Annapolis meeting on 27 November 2007 by reading the text of the Joint Understanding on Negotiations (Documents on Palestine, see p. 109) reached by Israel and the Abbas PA. He stated that the purpose of the meeting was 'not to conclude an agreement', but 'to launch negotiations between Israelis and Palestinians'. To this end, he announced that Israeli and Palestinian leaders would meet on a bi-weekly basis, with the aim of concluding a permanent peace deal by the end of 2008, which would see two states, Israel and Palestine, 'living side by side in peace and security'. Both Israel and the Palestinians were also committed to ongoing implementation of their obligations under the 2003 roadmap. This would be a necessary condition of a future peace treaty. The US President added that his Administration would be the judge of respective compliance. No mention was made of the core issues. In Abbas's speech, the PA leader disavowed 'terrorism', but stated that the removal of settlements, the dismantling of the security barrier and the release of Palestinian prisoners were prerequisites for a peace agreement. He also restated that a future Palestinian state would have East Jerusalem as its capital. Israeli Prime Minister Olmert's address was noteworthy only insofar that he included a passage that acknowledged the suffering of the Palestinian people and recognized 'this pain and deprivation is one of the deepest foundations which fermented the ethos of hatred towards us'. George Bush concluded by promising that the USA would put its weight behind the achievement of a peace deal according to the specified time frame.

Having been perceived as showing little interest in resolution of the Arab–Israeli dispute in his previous seven years in office, this new-found commitment of the US President was met with some scepticism. Despite the main protagonists' upbeat assessments on the discussions that had taken place during the closed session, the Annapolis summit did little to dispel fears that the US hosts would not be prepared to sustain the levels of engagement and pressure necessary to achieve the stated outcomes. The failure of recent initiatives to address the Gaza–West Bank divide was cited as a further reason for pessimism. Polls in Israel revealed that fewer than 20% of respondents believed that Annapolis had been a success, although 53% of Israelis were also said to support a deal that would involve the creation of a Palestinian state alongside Israel. It was unclear what progress had been made in revitalizing the Israeli-Syrian track. Many analysts believed that the West and the moderate Sunni Arab world would be the beneficiaries if the prospect of a deal on the Golan Heights would entice Syria away from its alliance with Iran and its backing of Hezbollah in Lebanon and of Hamas in Gaza.

The difficulties for the USA in brokering an agreement were thrown into focus in the days preceding the first set of Palestinian-Israeli talks that had been agreed at Annapolis. At the beginning of December 2007 Israel's Ministry of Construction and Housing announced plans to add a further 300 homes to the controversial Har Homa settlement to the south-east of Jerusalem. On 11 December, the day before Israeli and Palestinian negotiators were due to meet in Jerusalem, Israeli tanks entered the southern district of Gaza, killing at least six militants. Palestinians stated that the Israeli actions threatened to undermine the revived peace process. Meanwhile, the fortunes of Abbas's shaky administration received a welcome boost with pledges of US $7,000m. in aid from an international donor conference in Paris. However, officials from the World Bank warned that, without an easing of the restrictions on the movement of goods and people in the Occupied Territories, the aid package would not deliver the regeneration intended.

BUSH VISITS ISRAEL AND THE WEST BANK

Rocket fire from Gaza and Israeli reprisals prefaced President George Bush's first ever visit to Israel and the West Bank in January 2008. Thirteen Palestinian militants, including two senior commanders of Islamic Jihad, were killed in Israeli air-strikes in mid-December 2007. A further nine Palestinians were killed at the beginning of January 2008, after it was reported that the port city of Ashkelon had been hit by a *Katyusha* rocket launched from Gaza. However, while strongly condemning Hamas for the rocket salvoes from Gaza, the Israeli Prime Minister was also unusually blunt in his assessment of Israel's own failures to meet its roadmap commitments. In an interview with *The Jerusalem Post*, he acknowledged that Israel was acting against the spirit of the peace process with the continued expansion of its West Bank settlements. A spokesman for the Prime Minister later confirmed that he would be assuring the US President on his forthcoming visit that Israel would prioritize the dismantling of unauthorized settlement outposts on the West Bank. International concern over the pace of Israeli settlement was broached with the Israeli Prime Minister during the US President's three-day visit beginning on 9 January. Bush stated that a Palestinian state would not be viable if it was 'a Swiss cheese' of disconnected cantons. These comments, plus a general plea for Israel to end its occupation of Palestinian territory, were not seen as marking any kind of departure from accepted US policy towards conflict resolution in the Middle East.

Although Bush did not go so far as to repeat explicitly his 2004 comments that the new 'realities' represented by Israeli settlement would inform the content of a future peace deal, he suggested that UN resolutions should not dictate outcomes. Bush also singled out the Palestinian President for praise, contrasting the improved fortunes of West Bank Palestinians with the 'misery' that the Hamas takeover had delivered to Gaza. The US President followed his Israeli visit with tours of key regional allies, including a stop-over in the Saudi Arabian capital, Riyadh, for talks with King Abdullah. While Saudi Arabia's backing for the new peace process was viewed as critical in Washington, DC, to winning wider Arab support, it was clear that the kingdom's rulers would be unwilling to play an active role in promotion of the Annapolis initiative without Israel having first demonstrated its own seriousness by halting settlement construction in the Occupied Territories.

GAZA BLOCKADE FAILS TO STEM ROCKET FIRE

Fighting in Gaza worsened in January 2008, with 40 Palestinians killed in a series of mid-month strikes by the IDF. The attacks, which claimed at least 10 civilian deaths, were justified by Israel's Ministry of Defence as a response to the continued firing of makeshift rockets and mortars into southern Israel. The military action was accompanied by the halting of fuel shipments to the Strip, leading to the closure of the territory's only power plant and accusations from human rights organizations that Israel was engaged in collective punishment. Israel's Supreme Court upheld the blockade of fuel and electricity supplies, judging that the flow was 'sufficient to answer the vital humanitarian needs of the Strip for the time being'. The ruling was welcomed by the Olmert Government, which claimed that Hamas had stockpiles of fuel and that shortages were being exaggerated by the Islamists. A Ministry of Foreign Affairs spokesman nevertheless confirmed that normal supplies would be resumed if the rocket fire ended. On 28 January militiamen in Gaza used explosives and bulldozers to demolish several sections of the border wall separating Gaza and Egypt. Tens of thousands of Palestinians from Gaza subsequently flooded into Egypt, many of them seizing the opportunity to stock up on foodstuffs and other supplies that seven months of the Israeli blockade had made either impossible to obtain or prohibitively expensive. After several days of largely unfettered movement across the border, pressure from Israel and a fear of being sucked into a de facto security responsibility in Gaza led to a concerted effort by Egyptian troops to reseal the border. Hamas's flagging fortunes in Gaza and its standing in the Arab world had been given a considerable boost by its orchestration of the break-out. Nevertheless, strong opposition from Israel, the Quartet and Abbas's Fatah ensured that attempts by Hamas officials to persuade Egypt to allow its forces a future role in border security were rebuffed.

At the end of February 2008 Hamas claimed responsibility for a rocket attack near Sderot that killed one Israeli and injured another. The following day several crude but longer-range missiles hit the centre of Ashkelon, more than 10 km north of Gaza. Israel responded by sending tanks into northern Gaza and carrying out a series of air and artillery strikes at suspected militant targets. Israel's deputy defence minister, Matan Vilnai, controversially warned the militants responsible for firing rockets into southern Israel that the IDF would deploy all means deemed appropriate to end the attacks and that the Palestinians would bring a 'holocaust' on themselves if they continued. Five days of intensified assault centred on the Jabalia refugee camp left 107 Palestinians dead, more than one-half of them non-combatants. Two Israeli soldiers were also killed in the fighting. The Israeli actions against Gaza were criticized by both the EU and the UN. Following an emergency session of the UN Security Council, advocated by Libya, the Secretary-General, Ban Ki-Moon, commented that, while he recognized Israel's right to defend itself, he condemned 'the disproportionate and excessive use of force that has killed and injured so many civilians'. He also characterized Palestinian rocket fire as 'acts of terrorism', which should cease immediately. Israeli troops withdrew from Gaza on 3 March, ahead of a visit by the US Secretary of State. However, the Israeli Prime Minister pledged that the IDF campaign to reduce rocket fire and weaken Hamas was part of an ongoing combat operation. He stated that the military attacks on Gaza would end if there was no *Qassam* fire on Israel.

LITTLE PROGRESS REPORTED ON ISRAEL-PA TALKS

By the end of March 2008 both Israeli and Palestinian negotiators were expressing strong reservations over the possibility of reaching a deal by the end of that year. In mid-March the Quartet envoy, Tony Blair, had also warned that, without 'change on the ground', it was unlikely that negotiations would succeed. Veteran Palestinian negotiator Saeb Erakat took up this theme at a press conference on 19 March. According to Erakat, 358 Palestinians had been killed since the Maryland summit and more than 2,000 had been arrested. He also claimed that 5,378 housing units were under current construction in the West Bank. In this context it was almost impossible, Erakat protested, to convince ordinary Palestinians to support the peace process. He added that leaders on both sides knew what the parameters of a peace deal would be and implied that they lacked the political courage to see them through.

Likewise, respected policy research body the International Crisis Group issued a report in March in which it argued that efforts led by Israel and the USA to isolate Hamas had backfired, weakening Abbas's authority and failing to prevent consolidation of Hamas control over the Strip. Gaza witnessed another spike in fighting in mid-April, when Palestinian gunmen attacked a fuel depot at the border crossing of Nahal Oz. Two Israeli workers and two of the attackers were killed. On 16 April three Israeli soldiers and 15 Palestinian militants were killed in separate incidents in Gaza.

Following a meeting in London, United Kingdom, at the beginning of May 2008, the Quartet group issued a guarded statement on the state of the negotiations between Israel and the PA. According to the Quartet, 'much remained to be done' to improve the quality of Palestinians' life on the West Bank and to keep the political process on track. The statement singled out Israel's continuing settlement activity, as well as the worsening humanitarian situation in Gaza, as a source of 'deep concern'. The actions of Palestinian militants in Gaza, in particular the indiscriminate rocket attacks on civilian targets in Israel, were also condemned. The official communiqué was reported to disguise a far bleaker mood expressed about the state of the peace process during the private sessions. Leaks from the meeting revealed that the Saudi Minister of Foreign Affairs, Prince al-Faisal Al Sa'ud, was especially scathing over the lack of progress since Annapolis. He also expressed the opinion that one of the major obstacles to be overcome in reaching a lasting peace was the fact that the Israeli–Palestinian problem had become 'part and parcel of internal domestic issues in Europe and the United States', with the result that 'any action taken by Israel, no matter how illegal or outrageous' was justified. Al-Faisal Al Sa'ud criticized Israel for its demand of 'absolute security' when this could only be achieved via the 'absolute insecurity' of the Palestinians.

TURKEY MEDIATES ISRAELI-SYRIAN DIALOGUE

On 24 April 2008 Syria's President, Bashar al-Assad, confirmed in an interview with the Qatari *Al-Watan* newspaper that Turkey had been mediating between Syria and Israel for the past year. According to Assad, the 'communications' had recently yielded an offer from the Israeli Prime Minister to return the Golan Heights, a commitment that Olmert had never made publicly. Assad implied that a situation had now been reached where it would be appropriate for the contacts with Israel to be upgraded to more formal negotiations, with Turkey continuing to play the role of mediator. He appeared to rule out the possibility of face-to-face talks with Israel until after a new US President was elected. The Israeli Government refused to comment on the Syrian leader's claims regarding the Golan. However, four weeks later Israel confirmed that it was about to embark on Turkish-brokered peace negotiations with Syria. The timing of the announcement puzzled many observers. Although, historically, Israel was more disposed to achieving peace via bilateral agreements as opposed to comprehensive initiatives, neither the local nor the regional climates were viewed as particularly conducive to the achievement of an Israeli-Syrian deal. Commentators continued to emphasize the domestic weakness of the Israeli Prime Minister and doubted whether he possessed the political or moral authority to carry support at home for a peace that would inevitably involve the return of the Golan Heights. Moreover, there was little on the political horizon to suggest that Syria was going to end support for Hamas and Hezbollah, or to readdress its close ties with Iran. Without guarantees on such realignments, it was considered inconceivable that Israel would relinquish such a valuable bargaining chip as the Golan Heights. Syria's motivation in resuming negotiations with Israel, albeit indirectly, was thought to be influenced to no small degree by a desire to improve strained relations with the USA.

CEASE-FIRE IN GAZA

By mid-May 2008 the economic and humanitarian crisis in Gaza had persuaded Hamas and the other militant groups to agree to an Egyptian mediated cease-fire. Essentially, the Egyptian proposals committed Israel and Palestinian factions to end military operations in and around Gaza for a period of six months. This would be accompanied by an easing of the restrictions on the passage of goods and fuel into the Strip. An end to the daily missile attacks on Israeli communities in southern Israel was a welcome prospect for the Government. However, the question of whether the rockets should be silenced via agreement with Hamas or through military action was the subject of fierce debate within the Olmert Cabinet. Some argued that the human and political cost of a ground war to depose Hamas would be too great. The less compromising members of the Government, including the Vice-Premier, Haim Ramon, asserted that, since a military confrontation with Hamas and the other militant factions in Gaza was an inevitability, it would be counter-productive to ease the military pressure. A six-month cease-fire, it was believed, would simply give the militants a breathing space in which to develop their offensive capabilities. This viewpoint was strengthened by a June report authored by Israel's internal intelligence service, Shin Bet, which stated that Hamas had significantly extended its military power in the year since the group had taken over the Strip. By mid-June the Prime Minister had persuaded his colleagues to back the cease-fire deal, while confirming that the military option would remain prominently on the table. Barak lent his support to Olmert, primarily on the grounds that legitimacy for Israel's eventual assault on the Islamists of Gaza would be stronger if other options for dealing with Palestinian militancy had demonstrably been exhausted.

The cease-fire came into effect on 19 June 2008 and was restricted to Gaza, despite an earlier demand by Hamas that it should include the West Bank. Under the somewhat ambivalent terms of the agreement, Israel would begin to ease its blockade if there was calm for three days and would further ease the movement of goods at cargo crossings one week after this. Negotiations would then begin on the opening of the Rafah crossing, with Israel making it clear that it would only assent to such a development if there was clear progress in achieving the freedom of captured Israeli soldier Corporal Shalit. Hours before the cease-fire was due to come into effect six Palestinian militants were killed in air-strikes in Gaza and tens of mortars and rockets were reportedly fired out of the Strip. In the week following the agreement the fragility of the cease-fire was underlined by accusations from both sides of violations. On 25 June Israel temporarily closed all border crossings after Islamic Jihad fired four rockets into Israel. The militant group claimed that the rockets were a response to the killing of one of its commanders by the IDF on the West Bank.

ISRAELI-HEZBOLLAH PRISONER EXCHANGE

In mid-July 2008 the Israeli Government concluded a deal with Lebanon's Hezbollah, which saw the return of five Lebanese held by Israel in exchange for the transfer to Israel of the bodies of the two IDF soldiers whose seizure in 2006 had ignited the war with Hezbollah. The remains of a number of Arab fighters killed in conflict with Israel over the years were also handed over. The exchange of prisoners and war dead was believed to have been a consequence of the resumed Israeli-Syrian peace negotiations and, more indirectly, of the cease-fire with Hamas. The grim relief in Israel at having recovered the bodies of their slain soldiers contrasted sharply with the wild celebrations that accompanied the return of the prisoners to Lebanon, where they were fêted not only by Hezbollah, but also by President Michel Suleiman and Prime Minister Fouad Siniora. Several commentators argued that Israel's readiness to engage in such unequal transfers would make operations to seize Israeli soldiers a priority for all Israel's enemies. It also allowed advocates of an uncompromising approach to the Jewish state to argue that it was militancy and militarism rather than accommodation and diplomacy that brought concessions from Israel.

OLMERT ANNOUNCES RESIGNATION

The Israeli Prime Minister announced on 30 July 2008 that he would be stepping down in September in order to fight the various corruption charges being laid against him. Olmert's personal relationship with the PA President, Mahmoud Abbas, was widely reported to be warm. However, their positive personal chemistry could not mask the near universal assessment that the Palestinian-Israeli talks would not deliver agreement before the end of the year, as had been pledged at Annapolis. The political weakness of Olmert (and of Abbas) remained a critical reason for the absence of progress.

PA PESSIMISM

At the end of August 2008 US Secretary of State Condoleezza Rice concluded her seventh visit to Israel and the Palestinian territories since the Annapolis conference. Israel released 198 Palestinian detainees as a goodwill gesture to coincide with the visit. Although the granting of freedom to the predominantly Fatah detainees was welcomed by the PA on the West Bank, Palestinian leaders remained resolutely downbeat over the status of the peace process. Angered by reports that the rate of settlement construction in the first half of 2008 was nearly double that of the same period in the previous year, PA Prime Minister Salam Fayyad expressed his concern that the prospect of an independent Palestinian state was receding. Addressing the Israeli Council on Foreign Relations in Jerusalem on 3 September, the PA's Minister of Foreign Affairs, Riyad al-Maliki, stated that, despite an exchange of positions and ideas, Israeli and Palestinian negotiators had made no progress in the 10 months following Annapolis. In a September report to international donor governments, the World Bank delivered an assessment of the Palestinian economy that contrasted sharply with the optimistic forecasts for development in the West Bank that had been predicted in the months following the Maryland conference. Acknowledging that Israel had eased some of the travel restrictions on the West Bank during 2008, the report's authors argued that piecemeal removal of checkpoints had had little impact. Instead, economic activity continued to be stifled by the Israeli occupation, leaving the Palestinian economy stagnant and dependent on international aid. The report also rejected the argument that Israeli security concerns legitimized the scale of the control over Palestinian movement, stating that: 'Overwhelming evidence suggests that the current restrictions correlate to settlement locations and expansions.'

LIVNI SUCCEEDS OLMERT AS KADIMA LEADER

Livni defeated the challenge of former army chief Shaul Mofaz, to win the leadership of the ruling Kadima party in September 2008. Once regarded as having a distinctly hawkish attitude to relations with Israel's Arab neighbours, Livni had followed Ehud Olmert to occupy a more centrist position. Like Olmert, she believed that continued Israeli rule over a hostile Palestinian Arab population was eroding Israel's standing in the international community and inflating the demographic challenge to the Jewish character of the Israeli state. Unsurprisingly, the new Kadima leader refused to be drawn on the details of any concessions she might need to make to achieve a Palestinian state. The outgoing party leader (and caretaker Prime Minister) proved to be less reticent in his own assessment of the steps Israel would have to take to achieve peace with the Arab world. In an interview in the Israeli daily *Yedioth Ahronoth* published at the end of September, Olmert argued that, in order to reach agreement with the Palestinians, 'we will need to withdraw from almost all the territories, if not all the territories'. This would include, he added, parts of East Jerusalem. He also conceded that the Palestinians would need to receive territorial compromise from within the 1948 borders of Israel for any land occupied in 1967 that Israel might retain as a result of a peace settlement. To achieve peace with Damascus and neutralize Syrian support for Hezbollah and Hamas, an Israeli withdrawal from the Golan Heights was, he conceded, unavoidable. Commentators argued that Olmert's candour, particularly on the issue of East Jerusalem, would make Livni's attempts to build a new coalition government more problematic.

The new Kadima leader warned in her first foreign policy speech on 5 October 2008 that the failure to achieve a peace agreement with the Palestinians was strengthening the hand of extremists; indeed, the political mood in Israel appeared to be hardening. Opinion polls pointed to strong support for Binyamin Netanyahu's Likud party, while on the West Bank there was a rise in violent incidents connected to militant nationalists. Speaking against a backdrop of settler raids on Palestinian communities and a bombing directed against a prominent Israeli opponent of the settlements, the army chief responsible for security in the West Bank, Maj.-Gen. Gadi Shamni, criticized the political and religious leaders in Israel whose rhetoric afforded legitimacy to the violence of the ultranationalists. Meanwhile, within the ranks of Israel's defence establishment powerful voices were being raised in favour of the IDF adopting a doctrine of 'disproportionate force' in the event of a conflict similar to the one fought against Hezbollah in 2006. The IDF's chief of its northern command, Gen. Gadi Eisenkot, warned in early October that the Israeli 'plan' in any repeat conflict with the Shi'a militia would be to destroy those communities identified as being the origin of rocket fire.

By the end of October 2008 Livni admitted failure in her attempt to build a new coalition government after her efforts to win the support of the ultra-orthodox Shas party faltered. The question of Jerusalem and Shas's demands for guarantees over its future status appeared to be the main stumbling blocks. In response, Israeli President Shimon Peres confirmed that a general election would take place in early 2009, with Ehud Olmert remaining as caretaker Prime Minister in the intervening period. Livni's inability to put together a Kadima-led coalition provided final confirmation that the Annapolis chapter in the tortuous history of Israel-Palestinian peacemaking would not lead to any kind of breakthrough. It did, however, offer the prospect of an electoral contest in which the ideological fault lines vis-à-vis engagement or disengagement with the Palestinians would be more clearly drawn than they had been for some time. Palestinian protestations that they would expect to open peace talks with any future Israeli leader, regardless of political hue, failed to conceal the strong preference within the PA and the wider Arab world for an Israeli Government led by Livni rather than Netanyahu. In November the PA took out Hebrew-language adverts in the three main Israeli dailies in which they raised once again the offer made in the 2002 Arab peace plan. They promised 'normal relations' between Israel and '57 Arab Islamic countries', in exchange for 'a full peace agreement and an end to the occupation'. Both Livni and Olmert responded positively to the adverts, Netanyahu less so. The Likud leader reiterated that facilitating economic development in the West Bank would be his focus as premier rather than the creation of an independent Palestinian state. Barack Obama, the newly elected US President, gave his own backing to the renewed peace offer, stating that 'the Israelis would be crazy not to accept this initiative'.

ISRAEL LAUNCHES MAJOR ASSAULT ON GAZA

The four-month-old cease-fire between Israel and the Palestinian militias in Gaza was severely shaken on 5 November 2008, after air-strikes and an IDF incursion into Gaza left six Hamas members dead. The attack came after the IDF reported that a unit sent to destroy a tunnel inside Gaza had been fired on by Palestinian militants. Hamas responded to the deaths of their members by firing volleys of rockets into southern Israel, causing panic but no injuries or damage.

In the first week of December 2008 Israeli riot police forcibly evacuated an apartment building in Hebron, which they said had been illegally seized and occupied by militant settlers in the Arab part of the city. Shortly afterwards Israel announced an easing of travel restrictions around the West Bank city of Nablus, allowing the city's Palestinian residents the first opportunity in six years to leave the municipality in their cars without having to receive prior permission from the Israeli authorities. Nevertheless, such measures did little to contain the groundswell of Palestinian anger over continuing settlement activity. Speaking during a visit to London in mid-December, the PA Prime Minister, Salam Fayyad, made the issue of Israeli settlements on the West Bank a core theme, criticizing the EU for failing to pressure the Olmert Government to halt settlement building on the West Bank. He also expressed his dismay that the settlement issue was not a focus of proper debate in the Israeli election campaign, and added that the actions of the incoming Obama Administration with regard to Israeli settlement would be a considered by the Arab world as a 'litmus test' of the USA's seriousness in brokering a peace deal between Israelis and Palestinians.

Throughout December 2008 tensions rose along the Gaza Strip's border with Israel. In the week prior to the formal end of the six-month cease-fire, Israeli artillery and air-strikes on the Strip were met with the firing of more than 50 rockets at the Israeli towns of Sderot and Ashkelon. On 18 December, 24 hours before the formal end of the truce, a Hamas spokesman declared that the 'calm ... is finished'. He defended Hamas's decision not to extend the cease-fire by claiming that Israel 'did not abide by its obligations'. This was a reference not just to the violence of 5 November, but also to the Islamists' anger that their cease-fire had not led to an easing of Israel's blockade of the Strip. Hamas leaders had always stated that a relaxation of sanctions against Gaza was a part of the cease-fire agreement brokered by Egypt in June; however, an Israeli spokesman denied this. Olmert's initial response to the Hamas announcement and the resumption of regular rocket and mortar fire from Gaza was to order the closure of all crossings into the Strip. A military response was also widely predicted, but when it came on 27 December its scale and extent took most observers by surprise. In a series of raids beginning in mid-morning, Israeli fighter jets struck at a number of Hamas bases and other targets in the Strip, killing at least 200 people, including more than 50 civilians. Hundreds were also reported to have been wounded in the attacks, which Israel said were directed against the 'terrorist infrastructure' in the Strip. The Israeli Minister of Defence, Ehud Barak, warned that the Israeli attacks against Gaza would 'widen as necessary' as his country sought to put an end to the rocket fire that had made life intolerable for nearly 1m. citizens in southern Israel.

Amid further air-strikes and mounting loss of life, there were appeals from EU leaders and the UN Secretary-General, Ban Ki-Moon, for an immediate end to all hostilities and a restoration of the cease-fire. In Washington, DC, senior figures in the outgoing Bush Administration refused to condemn the Israeli strikes, instead acknowledging Israel's right to defend its citizens and asserting, in the words of Secretary of State Rice, that Hamas was 'responsible for breaking the cease-fire and for the renewal of violence in Gaza'. President-elect Obama refused to comment on Israel's offensive, stating that it would be inappropriate for him to speak on policy matters before his inauguration in January 2009. (During a brief visit to Sderot earlier in 2008 Obama had stated that he would expect Israel to do anything in its power to stop rockets threatening its citizens.) Across the Arab world the images of suffering and destruction from Gaza provoked street protests, with much of the demonstrators' anger—particularly in Cairo and Amman—being directed against their own Governments for their perceived collusion with US and Israeli efforts to weaken the Hamas regime in Gaza. The most strident official criticism of the attacks on Gaza came from Damascus. President Bashar al-Assad announced that he was cancelling his indirect negotiations with Israel (which had been effectively on hold since Olmert announced his intention to resign as Israeli Prime Minister) and urged other Arab states to cut their ties with Israel. In a further sign of deteriorating relations with Egypt, Syrian officials heaped scorn on the Mubarak Government's refusal to fully open their border with Gaza for humanitarian aid and medical emergencies. The response of the pro-Western leaders in the Arab world was more obviously nuanced, with condemnation of the Israeli assault being accompanied by strong criticism of Hamas both for provoking Israel and for its failure properly to commit to national unity talks with Fatah.

At an emergency meeting of Arab League ministers responsible for foreign affairs in Cairo on 31 December 2008, Saudi Arabia's Minister of Foreign Affairs, Prince Sa'ud al-Faisal Al Sa'ud, warned Palestinian leaders that the Arab world could not 'extend ... the hand of real help, if you do not extend the hand of affection for each other'. Hamas officials decried the Arab League's inaction as 'pathetic', while their spokesman in Gaza, Fawzi Bahroum, accused PA President Mahmud Abbas of ordering Fatah members in Gaza to provide intelligence on the movement of Hamas leaders to the Israelis. This accusation followed Abbas's assertion that Hamas was culpable for the Israeli assault on Gaza and claims that Fatah security forces in the West Bank had routinely beaten Hamas supporters during protests against the raids. Indeed, the fact that there were more demonstrations against the war within Arab communities in Israel than there were on the West Bank illustrated for many the breadth of the divisions that existed between Hamas-ruled Gaza and Fatah-controlled West Bank.

There was a strong conviction that Israel's assault on Gaza, known as Operation Cast Lead, had been planned many months in advance and that the targets attacked on 27 December 2008 had been chosen after lengthy intelligence gathering. The 'shock and awe' element of the initial strikes was viewed not just as a product of tactical military thinking but also as a reassertion of deterrent capability via an application of disproportionate force. Freeing Israeli communities from the rocket and mortar fire coming from the Strip was the minimum outcome required by Israel's political leaders. It was equally clear, however, that there was no appetite in Israel for the reoccupation of Gaza—the only guaranteed way to topple the de facto Hamas administration. Rather, Israeli leaders calculated that a sustained offensive against the Palestinian militias and the Islamists' political infrastructure would force a weakened Hamas to accept a cease-fire on Israeli terms and damage its standing in the eyes of its Palestinian constituency. According to Palestinian observers, the forcing of a dependent political entity on the PA, as opposed to a fully sovereign state, was central to Israel's war agenda. The timing of the attack on Gaza was also linked to the forthcoming Israeli elections and to the change of administration in Washington, DC. With Binyamin Netanyahu's Likud commanding a clear lead in the opinion polls, tough action against Hamas, especially if this involved minimal Israeli casualties, was predicted to boost the electoral fortunes of Kadima and Labour. There was also uncertainty within the Israeli Government over how accommodating an Administration led by Barack Obama might be towards Israel in the face of the inevitable international appeals for restraint and a cessation of hostilities. Although Obama's first act after securing the Democratic party nomination the previous year was to assert his loyalty to Israel in an address to the lobbyists of the influential American Israel Public Affairs Committee (AIPAC), promises by his officials of a more inclusive and less narrowly assertive approach to foreign policy suggested that an Obama-led White House would not be quite as unabashedly pro-Israel in its outlook.

By the fourth day of the bombardment the number of Palestinians killed in Gaza had risen to more than 370. It was unclear how many of the dead were non-combatants. Although Israel refused to allow journalists into the Strip, reports from residents and local journalists indicated that hundreds of buildings had been destroyed and that hospitals were struggling to cope with the wounded. As well as targeting Hamas's political and military facilities, Israel's air force concentrated attacks on the estimated 200 tunnels straddling the Egypt–Gaza border which were used to smuggle foodstuffs, fuel and weapons into the Strip. However, despite the intensity of the aerial bombardment, fighters from Hamas and other militias continued to launch mortars and rockets into Israel, killing three civilians and one soldier. For the first time Hamas deployed modified *Katyusha* rockets, presumably smuggled into the territory via Egypt, hitting the city of Beersheva, some 40 km from Gaza, on 30 December 2008. By January 2009 the failure of the Israeli air campaign to suppress the rocket fire made a ground campaign inevitable. Israeli troops and tanks, supported by heavy artillery fire, entered Gaza on 3 January. The invasion was strongly condemned by Egypt and Jordan as an unacceptable escalation of the conflict. Mauritania, the only Arab country other than Egypt and Jordan to have diplomatic relations with Israel, recalled its representative to Israel in protest.

INTERNATIONAL EFFORTS TO END GAZA CONFLICT

The ground offensive concentrated diplomatic efforts to achieve a cease-fire. On 5 January 2009 French President Nicolas Sarkozy flew to the Middle East to lead international efforts to bring about a truce. The outcome of his talks with

Egyptian, Palestinian and Israeli leaders was a Franco-Egyptian peace initiative. This proposed an immediate cease-fire, a withdrawal of Israeli forces from Gaza and a 'lasting halt' to the rocket fire from Gaza. It also acknowledged Israel's requirement for an end to rocket smuggling from Egypt to Gaza and the Palestinian demand for an end to the economic blockade and the reopening of the border with Israel. The Franco-Egyptian initiative was generally welcomed by the international community; the reception in Israel and from Hamas was more cautious. An Israeli spokesman stated that the Israeli Government accepted the principles of the proposals, but that the real challenge was 'to get the details to match the principles'. Foremost among Israeli concerns was that the international community should be seen to be imposing cease-fire conditions on Hamas rather than seeking its assent. Olmert and Livni were equally adamant that Hamas should not be able to claim that its 'resistance' had forced an opening of the crossings into Gaza. According to the Hamas representative in Lebanon, any plan that did not involve the opening of border crossings would be 'unacceptable'.

Prior to the Sarkozy visit the USA had blocked a Libyan proposal at the UN, which appealed for an immediate cease-fire in the conflict. The US Deputy Permanent Representative to the UN, Alejandro Wolff, defended the US position, stating that while Washington was committed to achieving a cease-fire as early as possible it rejected the idea of a 'return to the *status quo ante*'. The sustainable cease-fire required, he commented, would need to ensure 'no more rocket attacks ... no more smuggling of arms'. On 8 January 2009 the UN Security Council passed Resolution 1860 (Documents on Palestine, see p. 110), which called for 'an immediate, durable and fully respected cease-fire, leading to a full withdrawal of Israeli forces from Gaza'. The vote was passed by 14 votes to none, with the USA abstaining. The US decision not to block the resolution was seen as an attempt by the Bush Administration to avoid negative publicity in its final days in office, rather than a substantive reappraisal of policy towards a cease-fire. US Secretary of State Rice said that the USA broadly accepted the goals of the resolution, but wanted to see the details of the Franco-Egyptian peace proposals (to which the resolution referred) before giving its backing. Israeli Prime Minister Olmert rejected the resolution, insisting that it was 'not practical' and that it gave no guarantee against further rocket attacks. Buoyed by overwhelming public domestic support for the war in Gaza, he promised that the Israeli offensive would continue. Hamas also dismissed the cease-fire proposal on the grounds that it was not consulted in its preparation.

ISRAEL AND HAMAS ACCUSED OVER CONDUCT OF GAZA WAR

The Israeli ground offensive in Gaza succeeded in slowing the rate of rocket fire from Gaza, but at a human cost that provoked increasing international alarm. Scores of Palestinian civilians were killed in two separate incidents in Gaza during the first week of the invasion: the first after Israeli troops shelled a building they had allegedly previously told civilians to take shelter in, and the second when artillery fire hit a UN school where local Palestinians had sought refuge. Elsewhere, Palestinian medical personnel reported that nearly all the casualties they had dealt with since the ground invasion began were non-combatants. Of particular concern was the high proportion of young people and children among the dead and wounded. Human rights organizations, including the UN, charged both Hamas and Israel with committing war crimes in Gaza. In a report on the conduct of the war the human rights organization Amnesty International later accused Israel of 'reckless attacks', 'wanton destruction', the withholding of medical treatment, and of using Palestinians as human shields during its ground offensive. It also stated that the high number of civilians killed either at close range or as a result of precision-guided ordnance made Israeli claims that they had done everything possible to avoid non-combatant casualties simply not credible. Israeli officials denied that any systematic abuse had taken place in Gaza, a position that was undermined by the testimony of a group of soldiers who served during the campaign, 'Breaking the Silence'. The group charged that the IDF had adopted a policy of avoiding military casualties at all costs during the war. This had resulted in the killing of civilians and destruction of property. Amnesty International also asserted that Hamas's rocket fire was 'indiscriminate and therefore illegal under international law', and that Palestinian militias had endangered civilian life by firing and storing weapons in or from residential areas. They did not, however, find any evidence to support the Israeli claim that Hamas militants had forced civilians to stay behind in buildings used for military purposes. None the less, there were credible media reports linking Hamas to the killing and torture of Fatah members.

ISRAEL CALLS OFF GAZA ASSAULT BEFORE OBAMA'S INAUGURATION

Arab disunity over the Gaza conflict was once again underlined by the decisions of eight Arab states, including Egypt, Saudi Arabia and Jordan, not to attend an emergency Arab summit in Qatar on 16 January 2009. Spokesmen for those nations boycotting the summit claimed that, given the atmosphere of mistrust among Arab leaders and in the absence of any emerging consensus on the way forward, the meeting could only be counter-productive. Attendees at the Qatari meeting heard Syria's President Assad declare that the 2002 Arab peace offer to Israel was 'dead', and reiterate his appeal for Egypt and Jordan to cut their ties with Israel.

On 17 January 2009 Olmert declared that Israel had achieved its goals in the war against Hamas and would be observing a unilateral cease-fire. He said that Israeli troops would remain in Gaza 'for the time being'. The significance of the timing of the announcement, just three days before the inauguration of Barack Obama as US President, was not lost. The following day Hamas leaders in Gaza also declared a cease-fire, conditional upon Israel withdrawing its forces from Gaza. (Some 17 rockets were fired at Israel the day after Israel called a halt to hostilities, three of them after the Hamas announcement.) Israel subsequently began what was to be a swift withdrawal of its tanks and troops behind its borders. Meanwhile, at the invitation of President Mubarak, world leaders gathered at a summit in the Red Sea resort of Sharm el-Sheikh to discuss how to secure a durable peace in Gaza. Prime Minister Olmert declined to attend and Hamas was not invited. Backing the idea of a full Middle East peace conference along the lines of the 1991 Madrid Conference, Jordan's King Abdullah said that the EU must co-ordinate with the incoming Obama Administration to find an immediate solution to the Israeli–Palestinian conflict.

Some 1,400 Palestinians were killed during the three-week conflict in Gaza. Amnesty International reported that 900 of these were civilians, including 300 children and 115 women. Some 21,000 Palestinian homes were wholly or partially destroyed in the conflict, as well as 80 government buildings. Around 400,000 residents of the Strip were reportedly left without running water. The UN estimated that Gaza had suffered US $2,000m. worth of damage. A total of 13 Israelis also died during the conflict; 10 were soldiers—four of whom, according to the IDF, were killed during so-called friendly fire incidents. Prime Minister Olmert expressed his 'deep remorse' for the loss of civilian life in Gaza, but claimed that the campaign had been successful and had 'proven Israel's power and strengthened its deterrence'. Possibly as a result of the relatively small number of casualties sustained during the fighting, the war remained popular in Israel, achieving 90% backing at the beginning and at its end. It boosted the popularity of the ruling Kadima party, narrowing the lead that Netanyahu had enjoyed over Tzipi Livni at its outbreak. According to many analysts, Hamas had suffered significant military damage during the war but had not been fatally weakened. Judging their political standing was more difficult. They faced severe criticism both domestically and regionally for their ill-advised and ill-timed goading of the Israeli military machine. They failed to end their diplomatic isolation, or more significantly, gain any concessions on the reopening of borders or an easing of the blockade. Instead, Israeli officials were adamant that there could be no possibility of a relaxation of the blockade as long as Gilad Shalit continued to be held hostage by Hamas. Tellingly, the 'victory' rallies that Hamas organized after the cease-fire were more muted affairs than their organizers had hoped for. Of the five highest ranking Hamas political leaders in Gaza, two were killed in Israeli air-strikes during the fighting. The fortunes of President Abbas declined through the course of the conflict; at a time of national crisis for the Palestinian people, he was uniformly criticized for being an ineffectual and compromised bystander. Palestinian sources commented that many ordinary Palestinians had been alienated from their political leaders by the war.

PRESIDENT OBAMA COMMITS ADMINISTRATION TO ACHIEVING PEACE IN MIDDLE EAST

President Obama appointed George Mitchell as his Special Envoy for Middle East Peace, while Hillary Clinton was appointed Secretary of State. A week after Obama's inauguration Mitchell made his first trip to the region as Special Envoy, visiting Cairo and Jerusalem. In an interview with the Arab television channel Al Arabiya, Obama stated that the appointment of Mitchell was aimed at 'fulfilling [the] campaign promise that we're not going to wait until the end of my Administration to deal with Palestinian and Israeli peace. We're going to start now.' The difficulties facing the new Administration were underlined by a series of truce violations along the Gaza–Israel border. An Israeli soldier was killed by a remote-controlled explosive device while patrolling the border fence. Israel retaliated with air-strikes on tunnels into Egypt and suspected weapons storage sites. A number of Palestinians were wounded in the strikes, which were followed by the firing of several rockets into southern Israel, one of which reached the southern city of Ashkelon. In Jerusalem Mitchell defined his immediate priorities as supporting Egyptian efforts to achieve a more durable cease-fire and addressing the humanitarian needs of Gaza's 1.5m. inhabitants. The latter challenge was potentially more complex than the former given Israel's refusal to allow anything other than emergency aid into Gaza, and the international community's ongoing insistence that reconstruction and relief funds should be channelled via the PA in Ramallah rather than Gaza's Hamas rulers. At the end of January 2009 the Quartet group's Middle East envoy, Tony Blair, commented in an interview with the British daily *The Times* that Hamas needed to be brought into the peace process as the continued isolation of Gaza was a source of dangerous instability.

NETANYAHU HEADS RIGHT-WING GOVERNMENT AFTER ISRAELI POLL

The resumption of rocket fire from Gaza so soon after the cease-fire prompted further debate in the Israeli media over whether the war had been the success trumpeted by Olmert and Livni. A significant minority of Israeli voters believed that the conflict had ended too early and that the IDF should have inflicted greater punishment on Hamas. This was the position of the front-runner, Binyamin Netanyahu, who fought his campaign on a platform that was resolutely uncompromising in its offer to Israel's Arab neighbours. The Likud leader ruled out the ceding of any territory to the Palestinians, arguing that it would 'be grabbed by extremists', and insisted that there would be no evacuation of West Bank settlements. He refused to endorse the idea of an independent Palestinian state, instead repeating his belief that economic development (and presumably some form of administrative autonomy) would be the most that would be offered to the Palestinians. Unlike the Labour and Kadima parties, Likud also opposed the return of the Golan Heights to Syria.

The results of the 10 February 2009 election confirmed the rightward shift in Israel. Although Kadima emerged as the largest party in the Knesset with 28 seats, Likud came a close second with 27 seats, and parties of the religious and nationalist right appeared to command a clear majority in the legislature. Foremost among these was Israel Beytenu, led by the controversial Avigdor Lieberman, which won 15 seats, beating Ehud Barak's Labour Party (13 seats) into third place. Having ruled out the formation of a 'unity government' with Likud, Livni quickly conceded that she would be unable to form a ruling coalition and opted to take Kadima into opposition. Netanyahu was asked by President Peres on 20 February to put together a new government, having secured Lieberman's support. No doubt mindful of the negative international reception to the prospect of a hard-line nationalist government in Israel, both party leaders expressed a preference for a broader-based coalition. After many days of intense negotiations Netanyahu persuaded Barak's Labour Party to join him in government. Barak's decision to take Labour into a right-wing coalition caused deep divisions within his parliamentary party and was only ratified by a small majority in a meeting of the party's central committee. Barak was accused of political opportunism and of betraying Labour's core values. Netanyahu presented his new Cabinet, which also included the Shas and Jewish Home parties, on 30 March. Barak retained his position as Minister of Defence, while Lieberman was appointed Minister of Foreign Affairs.

US ENGAGEMENT UNSETTLES ISRAEL

US Secretary of State Hillary Clinton made her first visit to the Middle East at the beginning of March 2009. She attended an international donors conference for the PA in Sharm el-Sheikh, where she pledged US $900m. in aid, subject to congressional approval and guarantees that it would not end up in 'the wrong hands'. She also insisted that the USA would pursue peace 'on many fronts'. This apparent reference to a thawing of relations with Syria appeared to be confirmed shortly afterwards with Clinton's announcement that two senior US diplomats would be sent to Damascus for 'preliminary conversations'. During meetings with Palestinian and Israel leaders in Jerusalem and Ramallah, Clinton stressed again the Obama Administration's commitment to a two-state solution. She condemned extremism and the ongoing rocket fire from Gaza, and reaffirmed the friendship between Israel and the USA. Visiting at a time when coalition talks were ongoing in Israel, the Secretary of State avoided any direct criticism of Israel. In a press conference with Abbas, she did, however, characterize Israel's proposed demolition of tens of Arab homes in East Jerusalem as 'unhelpful and not in keeping with the obligations entered into under the roadmap'. It was reported that Abbas had also pressed Clinton for help on the easing of the blockade of Gaza. Although the Sharm el-Sheikh conference had provided the PA with pledges totalling $4.4m. in aid, plans for addressing the massive reconstruction need continued to be thwarted by Israel's refusal to allow building materials into the Strip.

The USA's promise to be proactive in restarting the peace process, the objective of which would be the creation of an independent Palestinian state, appeared destined to strain relations with the Netanyahu Government in Israel. Although the new Israeli Prime Minister insisted that peace was 'a common and enduring goal' for all Israeli Governments and that he would 'negotiate with the PA for peace', he maintained his opposition to the idea of a Palestinian state. Netanyahu's ideological loyalty to Israel's settler movement was an even more potent ingredient for tension with the Obama Administration, given the USA's view that continued settlement on the West Bank was a major stumbling block to any progress in the peace process. Without progress on the Palestinian-Israeli track, US Administration aides would argue, the prospect for regional peace and a diminution of the global threat posed by Islamist extremism would be undermined. The first speech by Minister of Foreign Affairs Lieberman only served to deepen the concern of the international community for the future of the peace process under the new Israeli Government. In contrast to the more conciliatory comments made by Prime Minister Netanyahu, Lieberman stated that he favoured an aggressive policy towards the Palestinians. Israel, he argued, had given up territory 'three times the size of Israel' since 1967 and had 'showed willingness' to its neighbours, but had achieved nothing in return. He also commented that Israel had not ratified and would not be bound by the Annapolis agreements. The EU signalled its own displeasure at Netanyahu's reversal of the Olmert Government's position on a Palestinian state by suspending negotiations on a proposal to award Israel preferential political, diplomatic and trading links. Israel rejoined that unless it opted for a more 'discreet dialogue' with Israel, the EU would be excluded from 'the diplomatic process'.

In April 2009 Obama signalled the next stage of his Middle East engagement by inviting the Israeli, Palestinian and Egyptian leaders to the White House. While meeting Jordan's King Abdullah in Washington, DC, Obama acknowledged that both within and outside the Middle East there was 'a profound cynicism about the possibility of any progress being made whatsoever' towards peace. He argued that this mood needed to be countered with 'gestures of good faith' and 'some hard choices'. He also hinted that should the two main parties to the conflict fail to move the process on, his Administration would not refrain from applying pressure of its own. His National Security Adviser, Gen. James Jones, Jr, was also reported, in a memo leaked to the Israeli newspaper *Ha'aretz*, to have informed a European minister responsible for foreign affairs that Obama was planning to be 'forceful' with Israel, reportedly commenting that 'the new administration will convince Israel to compromise on the Palestinian question'. Such sentiment created sufficient alarm among supporters of Israel in the USA for AIPAC and US congressional leaders to petition President Obama to allow Israel to set the pace of negotiations and to require any territorial withdrawals to be preceded by Palestinian institution building. In the event Netanyahu's visit to the White House was marked by a restating of known positions: a shared concern over Iran's nuclear ambitions, Obama's backing of a Palestinian state and a freeze on settlement building, as well as Netanyahu's refusal to mention either as desired outcomes. At the end of May Mahmud Abbas also met with the US President. In the unfamiliar position of not being the player in the conflict being asked to make concessions by a US leader, Abbas felt confident enough to strike a less compromising tone with reporters, insisting that the PA would not engage in dialogue with the Israeli Government until it halted settlement activity on the West Bank and in East Jerusalem and publicly announced its backing for the creation of a Palestinian state. Abbas suggested that the USA should use its considerable influence to force Israel 'to comply with the conditions'. Although the international spotlight was now shining most directly on Obama's attempts to cajole a recalcitrant Netanyahu, divisions among the Palestinians and Abbas's own political vulnerability continued to cast doubt over the peace process. There was no sign of an end to a rift that was bitterly resented by the majority of the Palestinian population. Egyptian reconciliation efforts progressed fitfully and apparently fruitlessly; three Hamas members and three Fatah security police were killed in Qalqilya at the end of May in the most serious outbreak of inter-factional fighting on the West Bank for nearly two years.

On his return to Israel, Netanyahu confirmed that settlement would continue on the West Bank to accommodate what he termed 'natural growth'. In an attempt to deflect some of the criticism that would come from this clear snub to the USA, the Likud leader did announce that his Government intended to remove 22 small and unauthorized settlements from the West Bank, although some commentators noted that promises by previous Israeli Governments to remove West Bank settlements had been quietly shelved. Hillary Clinton reacted sharply to Israel's stance, declaring that the US President 'wants to see a stop to settlements—not some settlements, not outposts, not natural growth exceptions,' and that she intended 'to press that point'. Meanwhile, a report by the World Bank on water resources in the West Bank stated that Israel was using 80% of the water from a critical aquifer shared with the PA.

OBAMA'S OVERTURE TO THE ARAB WORLD; NETANYAHU UNBOWED ON SETTLEMENTS

At the beginning of June 2009 President Obama began a short tour of the Middle East, stopping first in Riyadh and then Cairo, where he made a much anticipated speech at Cairo University. In the parts of his address relating to the Arab–Israeli conflict, Obama returned to the now common theme of the inadmissibility of settlement building on land claimed by Palestinians, and affirmed that 'just as Israel's right to exist cannot be denied, neither can Palestine's'. He also condemned the use of violence against Israelis by Palestinian militants. The Arab world was largely positive in its response to the speech. A Hamas spokesman welcomed the change in tone and substance from the Bush Administration, but criticized the absence of any concrete proposals. The Director of Israel's Government press office described the speech as 'not bad', noting that his country was not against reconciliation with the Palestinians but wanted the process to be managed in a way that denied its hijacking by extremists.

Speaking on 14 June 2009, Netanyahu declared that he would accept the idea of a Palestinian state subject to it having no army or military agreement with any other state and conditional upon the Palestinians recognizing Israel as a Jewish state. He also declared that the Palestinians who were expelled or fled in 1948 would never be allowed to return to the territory that had become Israel. Jerusalem would remain the undivided capital of the Israeli state. He did not specify from which parts of the territories occupied in 1967 Israel might withdraw to allow for the creation of the 'Palestinian state', but echoed Lieberman's comments that Israeli withdrawal from occupied territory had not brought peace. Referring to the settlers as 'our brothers and sisters', he stated that their lives could not be compromised by refusing to allow their communities to grow normally. PA officials were swift and unanimous in their rejection of a speech that proposed a vision of the future that fell so dramatically short of the Palestinians' minimum national aspirations.

The USA chose to respond favourably to the Netanyahu speech. The fact that the Israeli Prime Minister had for the first time accepted the idea of a Palestinian state was lauded as 'an important step'. The conditions and caveats attached by Netanyahu to Palestinian statehood which had so exercised the media reporting of the speech, were quietly glossed over by US Administration officials. However, having conceded the idea of a Palestinian state and having come under attack from coalition partners for doing so, Netanyahu showed no sign of relinquishing ground on the settlement issue. The same week Israel's Ministry of Defence put forward proposals calling for the legalization of 60 existing homes at a Jewish settlement north of Ramallah, and the construction of a further 240 homes on the same site. According to Israeli peace activists, the intended construction would effectively bar Palestinians in the village of al-Jania from working their lands and could not by any reasonable definition be classified as 'natural growth'. The announcement was a direct challenge to the Obama Administration and drew a sharp response. At the end of June 2009 Netanyahu sent Ehud Barak to Washington, DC, in an attempt to defuse the diplomatic spat. In a four-hour meeting with George Mitchell, Barak proposed that Israel would cease building any new homes on the West Bank for a three-month period, but that houses currently under construction should be completed. This partial and temporary freeze would not apply to East Jerusalem. However, Mitchell refused to compromise, reiterating the US demand of a total halt to Israeli settlement construction. The USA also expressed its dissatisfaction over approval granted by the municipal authorities in Jerusalem for the construction of Jewish-only apartments in the Palestinian Sheikh Jarrah district of Jerusalem.

The extent to which the new Israeli Government had underestimated President Obama's resolve over the settlement issue was uncertain. Nevertheless, it was clear that Israel was no longer facing a situation where the USA's publicly stated displeasure over settlement was accompanied by de facto acquiescence. Several Israeli commentators predicted that Netanyahu would find it difficult to weather a sustained period of stormy relations with the USA and that some significant concessions would be needed to mollify the Obama Administration. These would need to be more substantive than the recent relaxations of the checkpoint regime. On 21 July 2009 *Ha'aretz* reported that Netanyahu had authorized the removal of 23 'illegal' settlement outposts on the West Bank. A date for the evacuations was not set, however, and Israeli army chiefs denied that they had been given orders to carry out such an operation. Settler groups declared that they would resist any attempt to remove their outposts and set up a further 11 encampments on a single night at the end of July, apparently without interference from the IDF. The land grab was coordinated to coincide with a further visit to the region by Mitchell and several other senior US officials, including the

Secretary of Defense, Robert Gates. The Israeli press reported that Mitchell's talks centred on an Israeli-proposed deal to bridge the settlement impasse. Their proposals envisaged the completion of 2,500 new homes currently under construction in settlements close to the 'Green Line', to be followed by the complete freeze demanded by the USA. There was no official response from Washington to the Israeli offer.

ARAB WORLD REMAINS CAUTIOUS ABOUT CONCESSIONS TO ISRAEL

The Arab world watched the unfolding US–Israeli dispute from the diplomatic sidelines. In a speech in mid-July 2009 Secretary of State Hillary Clinton reminded the Arab world that peacemaking was not the prerogative of the USA or Israel alone, and that she expected action 'to support the PA with words and deeds, to take steps to improve relations with Israel, and to embrace peace and accept Israel's place in the region'. It was thought that the kind of normalization measures sought by Clinton included allowing Israeli airlines to overfly the Persian (Arabian) Gulf, the opening of Israeli interest sections in Arab capitals and ending the ban on visitors entering Arab countries with Israeli stamps in their passports. However, it was widely held that the Arab world would wait to see how far Obama was prepared to squeeze Netanyahu on the settlement issue before being seen to offer any concessions. Meanwhile, the USA announced that it would be restoring its ambassador to Syria (withdrawn in 2005, following the assassination of former Lebanese premier Rafiq Hariri). At the end of July Mitchell held talks with Syrian President Bashar al-Assad in Damascus, which were described by US officials as 'candid and positive'.

In mid-August 2009 Egyptian President Hosni Mubarak made his first trip to the White House in more than five years. Both he and President Obama were upbeat over the progress that had been made to resume the Israeli-Palestinian dialogue. Amid media reports that Israel had suspended issuing permits for new construction in the West Bank settlements, Obama stated he was pleased that Israel was taking 'discussions with us very seriously'. Mubarak's own assessment was that the process 'was moving in the right direction', and that the Arab world was 'ready to help if Israelis and Palestinians returned to peace talks'.

US ATTEMPTS TO RESTART TALKS STALL

At the end of August 2009 Binyamin Netanyahu travelled to Europe to meet Mitchell, the British Prime Minister, Gordon Brown, and Germany's Chancellor, Angela Merkel, in order to discuss the resumption of peace talks with the Palestinians. On the whole, US officials were positive that a formula for facilitating a return to peace talks could be reached. At the core of the agreement would be an Israeli commitment to freezing settlement construction on the West Bank for a period of nine to 12 months. Critically, however, Israeli government spokesmen were explicit in their exclusion of East Jerusalem from such a freeze. In return for action on settlement construction, Israel would be seeking US resolve for a tougher stance against Iran and its nuclear programme, as well as the previously mooted 'normalization' measures with the Arab world. These would include overflight rights for the Israeli national carrier, El Al, Israeli diplomatic and trade representation in Arab capitals, and a lifting on the ban on travellers entering Arab countries with Israeli stamps in their passports. Morocco, the UAE, Bahrain and Qatar were said to be receptive to the proposals; Saudi Arabia remained opposed on the grounds that Israel had not yet committed itself to sufficiently significant concessions. Nevertheless, it was reported that the Saudis had maintained secret contact with Israel in order to share concerns over the perceived common threat posed by the Ahmadinejad Government in Tehran.

PA officials were far more downbeat in their responses to the latest diplomatic moves. Mahmud Abbas had been adamant that the Palestinians would not return to the negotiating table without a complete settlement freeze in all of the Occupied Territories. It was difficult to see how this supposed 'red line' could be reconciled with Israel's insistence that it would not include the expanded municipal boundaries of Jerusalem in the moratorium under discussion with the Obama Administration. Palestinian scepticism was fuelled by the dialogue taking place between the Israeli Prime Minister and the right-wing and religious nationalist parties in his governing coalition. The outcome of Netanyahu's attempts to preserve his Government in the face of US pressure on the settlement issue was cabinet endorsement of a position and an attitude that fell short of the USA's expectations. Israel would agree to a suspension of building on the West Bank, but this would exclude not only East Jerusalem, as expected, but also 2,500 housing units which the Israeli Government claimed were currently under construction in West Bank settlements. Israel's Ministry of Defence also indicated that it would approve the construction of a further 500 new homes prior to any freeze in settlement construction. Eli Yashol, leader of the ultra-orthodox Shas party and a Deputy Prime Minister in the coalition Government, stressed the temporary and 'strategic' nature of the proposals.

The Obama Administration was swift to respond to Israel's announcements, emphasizing once again that the USA did not 'accept the legitimacy of continued settlement expansion' and that such actions hindered US efforts to restart peace negotiations. Disappointment in Washington, DC, with Israel's stance was magnified in the Arab world. Intensive efforts by George Mitchell during September 2009 failed to bridge what appeared to an ever deepening divide on settlement expansion. The Obama Administration had hoped that a planned meeting at the UN in New York would provide the occasion for an announcement of a formal resumption of peace negotiations between Israel and the PA. Instead, the tripartite meeting on 22 September produced little more than a hesitant handshake between Abbas and Netanyahu and the frustrated acknowledgement from the US President that his first serious attempt at brokering progress in the Middle East peace process had effectively stalled. Israeli and Palestinian officials blamed each other's intransigence for the failure to restart talks. The PA President reiterated the need for Israel to accede to a full settlement-building freeze in all of the Occupied Territories before face-to-face talks could begin. For his part, Israel's Minister of Foreign Affairs, Avigdor Lieberman, declared that Israel was ready to sit down at the negotiating table with the Palestinians and that it was the latter's insistence on preconditions that were responsible for the continuation of the impasse. President Obama urged both sides to demonstrate 'the flexibility, common sense and compromise which is necessary to achieve our goals'.

THE GOLDSTONE REPORT

In mid-September 2009 the UN Human Rights Council (UNHRC) investigation into the Gaza war, chaired by former South African judge, Richard Goldstone, released its findings. The 575-page Goldstone Report accused both Israel and Gaza's Palestinian militias of war crimes and possible crimes against humanity. However, the most serious criticism was levelled against Israel for the manner in which the war was conducted and for Israel's continued occupation of Palestinian territory. Especially damning for Israel was the rejection of its claim that the war had been fought in self-defence. Goldstone concluded that Israel's assault on Gaza 'was a deliberately disproportionate attack designed to punish, humiliate and terrorize a civilian population'. Among its recommendations was a requirement that Israel launch a credible investigation into the report findings. Failure to do so within six months would result in the report's findings being formally handed over to the ICJ, and would thus open the possibility of key figures in Israel's political and military establishment being arraigned for war crimes. Hamas was castigated for indiscriminate rocket fire against Israeli population centres and for extra-judicial execution, mistreatment and imprisonment of its political opponents.

Israel had refused to co-operate with Goldstone during his inquiry and had denied him entry to the country. Predictably, the Israeli Government dismissed the report, claiming that the UNHRC was biased against Israel. The Israeli position received strong backing in Washington, DC, where a Department of State spokesman said that the US Administration had 'very serious concerns' with Goldstone's conclusions. The PA initially welcomed the Goldstone Report and played a key role in the drafting of a UNHRC resolution endorsing its findings. However, following intense diplomatic pressure from the US, Mahmud Abbas controversially withdrew his support for a UNHRC resolution, effectively delaying any further action until March 2010. A presidential aide to Obama claimed that the change in the Palestinian position had come about through the realization that in the context of efforts to restart the peace process 'this was not the best time to go forward with this'.

Attempts by the PA to defend the volte-face and to claim that the withdrawal of support for Goldstone had only delayed the UN debate, failed to silence the chorus of condemnation in the Palestinian territories and around the Arab world for what was scorned as unprincipled capitulation to US pressure. By the first week in October 2009 PA officials were admitting that the withdrawal of their endorsement for Goldstone had been a political blunder. Abbas sought to limit further damage to his credibility by lending his support for a new UNHRC resolution to be brought before a special council session. The resolution adopting the Goldstone findings and condemning Israeli policies in East Jerusalem was approved in Geneva on 16 October by 25 votes to six, with 11 abstentions. The US representative voted against the resolution. Israel vehemently rejected the outcome.

At the end of January 2010 Israel published its own 47-page report to the UN on the actions of its armed forces during the Gaza conflict. It admitted that there had been some 'operational lapses and errors in the exercise of discretion', but insisted that the IDF had not violated international law and that there were no grounds for the holding of an independent inquiry as demanded by Goldstone. The report revealed that, to date, 36 incidents had been referred for criminal investigation and that one—the theft by a soldier of a credit card to withdraw cash—had resulted in a criminal conviction.

PALESTINIANS PESSIMISTIC ABOUT PEACE OVERTURES

Although Hamas had denied the charges of war crimes levelled against it by Goldstone, its leaders were sharply critical of the PA's failure to exploit the report's publication to embarrass Israel. According to the Islamist group, the episode demonstrated once again how the Abbas leadership had been compromised by such close identification with the USA's policy agenda. At a meeting in Damascus in October 2009, Hamas and several other Palestinian opposition parties signalled that they would be suspending involvement in talks brokered by Egypt on the subject of Palestinian reconciliation. It had been reported that these negotiations had made substantial progress in preceding months. A healing of the rift between the Gaza and West Bank leaderships would have been enormously popular among ordinary Palestinians, and for many commentators the achievement of Palestinian unity was an essential prerequisite in the search for peace in the Middle East, despite the challenges that such a development would present to the US Administration and its allies. Disaffection with the impasse in the peace process among all echelons of the PA's dominant Fatah movement became increasingly evident in the latter months of 2009. In October a 'leaked' internal party memo revealed that faith in the Obama Administration to deliver on the promise of bringing peace to the Middle East had 'evaporated'. It accused the USA of retreating from its earlier commitments on halting settlement construction and defining the framework for peace negotiations, blaming Obama's inability to 'stand the pressure of the Zionist lobby'.

Palestinian disillusionment deepened at the beginning of November 2009, when US Secretary of State Hillary Clinton visited Israel and the Palestinian territories. Speaking at a press conference alongside Israel's Prime Minister, Clinton signalled a climbdown from Washington's earlier insistence that Israel halt all settlement activity in the West Bank and East Jerusalem. Praising Netanyahu's commitment to exercise 'restraint' in building new settlements as an 'unprecedented' concession, Clinton confirmed that the Obama Administration no longer maintained that a halt to Israeli settlement building in the Occupied Territories should be a condition to a resumption of peace talks with the PA. Her comments brought formal protests from the PA as well as several Arab states, including Jordan and Egypt. In a meeting with Arab ministers responsible for foreign affairs in Marrakesh, Morocco, shortly afterwards, Clinton attempted to defuse some of the fury in the Arab world by insisting that the Israeli proposals did indeed fall short of US hopes, but would have a 'significant and meaningful' impact on settlement building in Palestinian territory. However, the Secretary-General of the Arab League, Amr Moussa, expressed the Arab world's 'deep disappointment' with the USA's permissive response to the 'illegal' policies of its Israeli ally.

A spokesman for the PA President was uncharacteristically blunt in concluding that the peace process had been paralysed by a combination of Israel's 'intransigence' and the USA's 'back-pedalling'. Within days the PA President announced that he would not be standing in the Palestinian presidential elections expected to take place in 2010, citing his frustration with the lack of progress in the peace process. Yet, since significant obstacles would need to be overcome before a presidential election could be convened in the Palestinian territories, Abbas was expected to remain in his current role for several months at least. His statement was therefore viewed as a gambit designed to persuade the Obama Administration to exert more pressure on Israel. Nevertheless, it also underscored the Palestinian view that after nearly 20 years of the Oslo process and five years of subservience to the US agenda, the prospects of statehood in the Occupied Territories were as distant as ever. In a speech on 11 November to mark the fifth anniversary of the death of Yasser Arafat, Abbas maintained his new defiant stance, saying that he would not return to negotiations unless the Israeli Government agreed to a settlement freeze, which included East Jerusalem and excluded 'natural growth' in existing West Bank settlements.

The new pessimism regarding the peace process stemmed not just from the failure of the Obama Administration to persuade Israelis and Palestinians to return to the negotiating table, but also from a realization that public opinion in Israel and the Palestinian territories had not been so sharply differentiated for a generation. While the Palestinians bemoaned the futility of the diplomatic path and warned of the need for a 'third *intifada*', majority Israeli opinion appeared locked in an ever more uncompromising mindset. During a low-key visit to the USA at the beginning of November 2009 the Israeli Prime Minister told a convention of American Jewish leaders that he was committed to the short-term goal of peace between Israel and its Palestinian neighbours. However, it appeared that a significant number of Israelis subscribed to the viewpoint of Netanyahu's maverick Minister of Foreign Affairs, Avigdor Lieberman, who had recently commented that Israel's dispute with the Arab world was probably intractable and that Israelis should resign themselves to a low-intensity conflict with the Palestinians for the foreseeable future. How these emerging realities would inform the future approaches of the Obama Administration to resolve the conflict remained unclear. Several analysts predicted a move away from the language and processes of the comprehensive settlement in favour of the pursuit of incremental gains, which would, in turn, serve as staging posts for further agreements. Such an approach corresponded with the focus of Quartet envoy Tony Blair on the development of the West Bank economy and, indeed, the consensus within the governing Likud party that the conflict could be managed via improved living standards for the Palestinians and the transfer of up to 60% of the West Bank to the PA.

CONCERNS MOUNT OVER ISRAELI SETTLEMENT PLANS

In November 2009 Netanyahu outlined the details of his Government's proposed 'restraint' on settlement. He announced that Israel would refrain from issuing new residential construction permits in 'Judea and Samaria' for a period of 10 months. East Jerusalem would be exempt from the new restrictions (a few days earlier the Jerusalem municipal planning committee had approved 900 new homes in the

Gilo settlement) and construction would continue on the estimated 3,000 homes on the West Bank where work had already begun or permits for construction had been issued. Some public buildings in existing settlements would also continue to be built. Netanyahu called his proposal a 'far reaching and painful step' that was being taken 'out of a deep desire to move forward towards peace'. The Palestinians condemned the proposals for excluding Jerusalem and insisted that they could not return to the negotiating table unless there was a complete halt to settlement activity in all of the territories occupied in 1967.

Meanwhile, in October 2009 Israel released 20 female Palestinian prisoners in exchange for a video of Corporal Gilad Shalit, who had been captured in 2006 and was still being held by Hamas in Gaza, in a deal mediated by the German military intelligence service. At the end of November 2009 the Israeli Government announced that it would be prepared to release up to 1,000 Palestinians held in Israeli gaols in exchange for Shalit's safe return. The negotiations on the releases were once again mediated by German intelligence officers, but the exchange faltered on an Israeli insistence that some of the detainees should be deported from Palestinian territory once freed, and Hamas's refusal to agree to such terms.

At the end of December 2009 the Egyptian authorities began the US-financed construction of an underground metal wall along its border with Gaza, designed to prevent arms-smuggling. In January 2010 a report commissioned by 80 humanitarian agencies operating in Gaza, including the World Health Organization, warned that the Israeli (and Egyptian) blockade of Gaza was putting the health and lives of its 1.5m. residents at risk.

ASSASSINATION OF MAHMOUD AL-MABHOUH

Three Palestinian members of the Fatah-aligned al-Aqsa Martyrs Brigades were shot dead in the Palestinian city of Nablus at the end of December 2009. The Israeli military claimed that the men had been implicated in the fatal shooting of a settler two days earlier. On the same day an Israeli air-strike in Gaza killed three unarmed Palestinians who, according to the IDF, were scouting for infiltration points near the border fence with Israel. In January 2010 it was reported in Dubai, UAE, that a senior Hamas operative reported to be involved in arms procurement, Mahmoud al-Mabhouh, had been killed at a hotel in the emirate. Video footage quickly emerged which suggested that al-Mabhouh had been assassinated by an 11-strong team that had travelled to the UAE on forged European and Australian passports. The assassination bore all the hallmarks of an Israeli intelligence operation, and both Hamas and media commentators were swift to implicate the Israeli external intelligence agency, Mossad. Israel adhered to its normal practice of refusing to confirm or deny the allegations. In Dubai the chief of police in charge of the investigation called on Interpol to help apprehend the head of Mossad if it was established that Israel had been behind the killing. It was also revealed that two Palestinians had been arrested in Amman and deported to Dubai on suspicion of involvement in the al-Mabhouh plot. Both men were identified as former Fatah security officials, leading to charges by Hamas of Fatah complicity with Israel in the murder; the subsequent arrest in Damascus of a member of Hamas provoked a similar counter-charge. Meanwhile, the British Government ordered the expulsion of an Israeli diplomat from its London embassy, following a statement to the House of Commons by the British Secretary of State for Foreign and Commonwealth Affairs, David Miliband, in which he stated that there were 'compelling reasons to believe Israel was responsible for the misuse of the British passports' by the alleged perpetrators of the killing.

THE 'PROXIMITY TALKS'

At the beginning of March 2010 the PA President was given approval by the Arab League (and later the PLO) to accept an invitation from the Obama Administration to take part in indirect peace negotiations with the Israeli Government. The so-called 'proximity talks' would be facilitated by US officials shuttling between Ramallah and Jerusalem, and would be the first formal negotiations between Israel and the PA for more than a year. The Netanyahu Government was upbeat about the resumption of a dialogue, the Palestinians far less so. Anxious that the PA should not to be dragged into an open-ended negotiating process that failed to deliver substantive outcomes, the Arab governments had set a time limit of four months for the peace talks. There existed a deep scepticism within the PA that any concrete developments could be achieved within such a time frame, given the right-wing hue of the Israeli Government and the USA's seeming inability to wrest the kind of concessions from Israel that might reassure the Arab world that the peace process could be moved forward. A spokesman for Abbas confirmed that the Palestinians were participating more out of a desire to expose Israel's lack of commitment to peace than out of any real conviction in the possibility of progress.

As Obama's Special Envoy, George Mitchell, arrived in Israel in early March 2010 to finalize arrangements for the talks, Abbas delivered a speech in Ramallah in which he declared the peace process almost at 'a dead end' and accused Israel of using procrastination to strengthen its control of the Occupied Territories and 'prevent any realistic possibility of establishing an independent, viable state of Palestine'. Shortly afterwards US Vice-President Joseph Biden flew to Israel to lend his support to Mitchell. His visit was soon embroiled in controversy. Following an initial meeting with Netanyahu, during which Biden affirmed the Obama Administration's full commitment to Israel's security, the Israeli Ministry of the Interior announced its approval for a plan to build 1,600 new homes in the Ramat Shlomo settlement established in an area of the West Bank that had been annexed to Jerusalem. Biden issued an unusually strong condemnation of the Israeli decision. Despite protestations from Israel's Ministry of the Interior that the timing of the announcement was coincidental and that final approval for the settlement expansion had yet to be granted, the decision to build in Ramat Shlomo was viewed by much of the international community as a crass and even calculated snub to US peacemaking efforts. The PA responded with predictable outrage. Speaking on behalf of the Secretary-General of the Arab League, Amr Moussa, Abbas confirmed that the Palestinians would be withdrawing from the proximity talks before they had formally started. They would not return, he stated, unless Israel gave an undertaking not to expand its settlements. A 'day of rage' called by Palestinian factions to protest against settlement expansion in Jerusalem led to violent clashes between Palestinian demonstrators and Israeli forces in Arab neighbourhoods of the city.

In mid-March 2010 David Axelrod, Senior Advisor to President Obama, expressed the US Administration's concern regarding the Netanyahu Government, calling Israel's announcement on the proposed Ramat Shlomo development 'very destructive' and an 'affront' and an 'insult' to the latest US peacemaking initiatives. Meanwhile, Secretary of State Clinton continued to pressurize Netanyahu into backing down on the Jerusalem settlement issue prior to the latter's forthcoming visit to the USA. Israel's ambassador to the USA, Michael Oren, who had himself been summoned to the Department of State to hear of the Obama Administration's disapproval, described Israel-US relations as being at their lowest point for more than 30 years. In Israel Netanyahu's Government was rebuked by Kadima and other opposition groups for eroding what they regarded as a strategic priority of all Israeli governments: namely, a positive working relationship with the incumbent US President. Hillary Clinton made it clear that while the bond with Israel remained unshakeable, the Obama Administration had resolved to advance the cause for peace in the Middle East and that she expected Israel's leaders to take the necessary actions to 'demonstrate the requisite commitment to the process'.

The US view that responsibility for rescuing the peace process from its current impasse lay with Israel was shared by the Quartet group in a strongly worded statement issued following its meeting in Moscow in March 2010. The statement demanded a halt to all Israeli settlement activity in the territories occupied by Israel in 1967 and urged the international community to support talks between Israel and the Palestinians that would lead to an independent, 'viable' Palestinian state within 24 months. There were conflicting reports in the international media over the 'confidence-building measures' that Clinton had been able to extract from the Israeli Government in the run-up to Netanyahu's visit to the USA on 21 March 2010. It was widely believed that Netanyahu had given private assurances to the US Secretary of State on a further easing of the roadblock regime, the withdrawal of IDF forces from some areas of the West Bank and the release of some Palestinian prisoners. However, additional speculation that the Israeli Prime Minister had promised Clinton that Israel would observe a de facto, if unannounced, freeze on new settlement construction in Jerusalem for a four-month period, was contradicted by Netanyahu in an address to AIPAC prior to his meeting with President Obama. He dismissed the notion that the construction of Jewish homes in East Jerusalem was an obstacle to peace, and gave no indication that his Government would sanction a moratorium. Talks between the Israeli and US leaders on 23 March were subject to a media blackout and were not accorded the usual photo opportunity for the waiting press corps. US officials denied that this departure from protocol was intended as a slight to Obama's Israeli guest. Nevertheless, it was revealed that their 90-minute exchange had failed to bridge their divergent views on the legitimacy of settlement construction in Jerusalem and on the need to extend the freezing of Israel's building programme on the West Bank. Netanyahu's aides complained that Obama and Clinton 'had adopted a patently Palestinian line'. The sense of crisis developed the following day when it was reported in Israel that final approval had been granted for the construction of a apartment block for Jewish settlers on the site of the historic Shepherd Hotel in the Sheikh Jarrah district of Jerusalem.

ARMAMENTS SEIZURE

There was no thaw in Israel's relations with Syria during the first half of 2010, with Syrian support for Hezbollah and Hamas being cited by the Netanyahu Government as the main obstacle to rapprochement. In November 2009 the Israeli Navy intercepted the German-owned cargo ship MV *Francop* in the eastern Mediterranean Sea and diverted it to the Israeli port of Ashdod, where several hundred tons of arms and ammunition stored in crates labelled as bulldozer parts were discovered. Israeli officials claimed that the shipment had originated in Iran and was destined for Hezbollah militants in Lebanon via the Syrian port of Latakia. Neither the Syrian Government's nor Hezbollah's denials of knowledge of the shipment were regarded as credible by many international observers. In April 2010 Israeli President Shimon Peres stated that the Assad Government had supplied Hezbollah with *Scud* missiles, with an effective range of 600 km, which would bring all of Israel's major cities and its nuclear reactor in Dimona within striking reach. US CIA officials were said to have substantiated Peres's claims, although once again the allegations were denied by Damascus. Syria countered that Israel was attempting to divert attention from its international isolation over the settlement issue. The US Secretary of State warned both Syria and Iran at the end of April that the Obama Administration was committed to Israel's security and that there would be 'consequences' for any state or group threatening the country's ally. At the same time, Israeli Minister of Defence Ehud Barak served notice that his Government would hold both the Lebanese and Syrian Governments accountable for allowing Hezbollah to deploy any weapons to the region he defined as 'balance breaking'. In the same month Netanyahu announced that he would not be attending a 47-nation nuclear weapons proliferation conference in Washington, DC, amid fears that Arab and Islamic nations would exploit the gathering to focus attention on Israel's own nuclear weapons capability. In September 2009 Israel had rejected a resolution from the Geneva Conference of the IAEA to open its nuclear facilities to inspection.

US ATTEMPTS TO RESTART TALKS

Throughout April 2010 Hillary Clinton and Special Envoy George Mitchell maintained efforts to convene indirect talks between Israel and the PA. The considerable but familiar challenge lay in finding a formula that would accommodate Israel's ongoing refusal to accept a curb on settlement in East Jerusalem and a Palestinian reluctance to engage in any process that did not come with specific US guarantees. The first of these was that the Obama Administration would need to secure a face-saving (for the PA) concession from Israel on the ongoing expansion of Jewish communities in parts of the city captured in 1967; the second was that should the talks resume, they would need to address the substantive issues of the conflict, most notably borders, Jerusalem and refugees. The task facing the US Administration was made more urgent by warnings from Jordan and Egypt that the current impasse in the peace process was once again fuelling anti-US sentiment. On 23 April 2010 Mitchell returned to the Middle East for talks with Israeli and Palestinian leaders, amid speculation that a deal for restarting indirect negotiations was imminent. Although Netanyahu publicly stated that his Government would never agree to halt the construction of Jewish homes in 'the capital of Israel', it was reported that government officials had promised Mitchell that Israel would not approve any large settlement projects in Jerusalem while talks were ongoing and that the proposed expansion of Ramat Shlomo would be subject to delay for an unspecified period.

The Palestinians also appeared to be prepared for some gentle back-pedalling on preconditions for participation in proximity talks. Chief PA negotiator Saeb Erakat was highly sceptical about the Israeli Government's commitment to a meaningful peace process, but commented that the PA 'should give the proximity talks the chance they deserve'. This new-found willingness followed assurances reportedly given to the PA President that the Obama Administration was supportive of the Palestinian position on Israeli settlements, and that in the event of the subject of further provocative Israeli settlement-building activity being raised at the UN, the USA would not employ its veto. At the beginning of May 2010 the Arab League endorsed PA participation in four months of proximity negotiations, after which the Arab states would refer the matter to the UN Security Council. The PLO gave its own backing to the process a week later, and on 9 May the US-mediated talks between Israel and the PA finally started. Prior to the commencement of the dialogue the Israeli Prime Minister expressed his belief that for real progress to be made the two parties would need to sit in the same room, a step that the Palestinians said they were not prepared to take without a full settlement freeze. Even under the most optimistic of scenarios, the gap between the minimum demands of Abbas's PA and the maximum likely to be conceded by a Netanyahu-led Government appeared unbridgeable.

GAZA FLOTILLA RAID

On 31 May 2010 Israeli naval commandos raided a flotilla of ships attempting to break the Israeli blockade on Gaza and deliver some 10,000 tons of humanitarian aid to the Strip's population. The six vessels in the flotilla had sailed from Turkey and Cyprus and were carrying 650 pro-Palestinian activists of varying nationalities. The interceptions took place approximately 60 miles off the Gaza coast in international waters. Five of the six ships in the convoy were boarded without major incident and diverted to the Israeli port of Ashdod. However, violent confrontations broke out on the largest vessel, the Turkish-registered MV *Mavi Marmara*, leaving nine Turkish activists dead and several others seriously wounded. A number of Israeli soldiers were also injured in the attack. A spokeswoman for the IDF claimed that the Israeli commandos had been forced to open fire in self-defence after coming under attack with knives and clubs. The ship's passengers alleged that the Israeli soldiers had begun firing before landing on the ship's deck and that they had resisted an unprovoked attack with the few means at their disposal. Those detained as a result of the raid were subsequently deported from Israel. The seizure of the flotilla was decried by Palestinian leaders, while the fiercest response came from Turkey, hitherto Israel's closest ally in the Arab world. Israel's assertion that it needed to prevent any challenge to its sea blockade of Gaza to prevent arms-smuggling to Hamas did, however, find a sympathetic response in Washington, DC, where US Vice-President Biden expressed support for Israel's right to take actions to defend its security interests. The UN Security

Council later issued a statement regretting and condemning 'the acts' which led to the loss of life, while also calling for an impartial investigation into the incident. Several rockets were fired from Gaza in purported response to the killing of the Turkish activists, and five Palestinian militants were killed after they had fired rockets or attempted to infiltrate Israeli territory. A week later at least four Palestinians who, it was claimed, were wearing diving suits in preparation for an attack on targets in Israel, were killed following a raid by Israeli naval forces.

Despite a well-rehearsed public relations campaign, Israel's image was undoubtedly damaged by the deaths of those on board the MV *Mavi Marmara*. The incident also focused attention, as indeed was the intention of the flotilla's organizers, on the ongoing blockade of Gaza and the growing humanitarian crisis there. Nor was all the criticism directed at Israel. Responding to the clamour in the Arab world for action to end the siege, President Mubarak of Egypt announced on 1 June 2010 that Egypt would allow the opening of the Rafah crossing for an indefinite period. Egypt's participation in the Gaza blockade had long been a source of controversy in the Arab world and had laid Cairo open to accusations of 'collaboration' with Israel. Egyptian officials had always retorted that their decision to close the border with Gaza, for all but the briefest of 'windows' since the Hamas takeover, was a consequence of wishing not to dilute Israel's responsibility in international law for the occupation of the Strip and the welfare of its population. Critics of Egypt's policy commented on the willingness of the Mubarak Government to be 'complicit' in Israel's siege, owing to its own antipathy towards Hamas and a desire not to jeopardize the US $2,000m. in aid it received each year from the USA. Although thousands of Palestinians flocked to the Rafah crossing following its opening, reporters claimed that only a small number were processed by Egyptian border police. UN officials responsible for Gaza's predominantly Palestinian refugee population dampened speculation that the limited Egyptian measure would provide any kind of solution to the humanitarian crisis in the short term, let alone the mid- to long term.

GAZA BLOCKADE CONDEMNED

Israeli Prime Minister Netanyahu was initially defiant in the face of calls for an easing of the Gaza blockade. These appeals came not just from the Arab world and EU leaders, but also from Washington, DC, where Hillary Clinton was unusually forthright in declaring Israel's siege 'unsustainable and unacceptable'. However, on 7 June 2010 Israel's Minister of Defence, Barak, announced in the Knesset that, in addition to a domestic inquiry into the storming of the aid flotilla, the Government would seek to review the blockade of Gaza and establish whether it was consistent with the standards of international law. EU leaders had already indicated that they would work with Israel to address concerns over the smuggling of arms into the Strip in the event of a loosening of restrictions. The Quartet group's Special Envoy, Blair, also pressed Israel for greater transparency on the goods and materials Israel would allow into Gaza, urging a move away from a list of permitted items to a defined and limited list of prohibited items. On 17 June the Israeli Government announced a partial easing of the blockade that would allow some previously banned food and consumer items into Gaza, but would still prohibit cross-border trade and construction materials for private building purposes. Hamas decried the proposals as inadequate, while EU leaders and non-governmental organizations working in Gaza expressed disappointment with the limited nature of the Israeli measures. A few days later Israel agreed to a more substantial easing of the blockade, declaring that it would begin permitting the passage of 'civilian products for a civilian population'. Under the terms of a new ruling, a Netanyahu spokesman stated that all goods except so-called 'dual use items', such as chemicals, lathes and ball bearings, would be allowed to enter the territory. Building materials for PA- and UN-approved projects would also be permitted. Additionally, Israel agreed to expand capacity at crossing points and to 'streamline' the policy on the movement of people in and out of Gaza. The revisions received a warm welcome in Washington, DC, where Israel was commended for responding to the international community and offering the hope of 'significantly improve[d] conditions for Palestinians in Gaza'. International aid agencies, however, reserved judgement on the extent to which the relaxation of the goods inward regime would improve the quality of life in Gaza and repeated that Gazan dependency on international charity would persist as long as it could not import the produce it required, and the air, land and naval siege persisted.

DIRECT NEGOTIATIONS RESUME

On 31 August 2010 Binyamin Netanyahu travelled to Washington, DC, to begin direct talks with Mahmud Abbas. On the same day Hamas gunmen on the West Bank killed four Israelis outside a settlement near the city of Hebron. The killings were condemned by the Obama Administration and by PA Prime Minister Salam Fayyad, who stated that the attack went 'against Palestinian interests'. The deaths and the pledge by Hamas's military wing that it would be joining forces with other militant Palestinian factions to launch further attacks against Israelis added to the already high level of scepticism over the prospects for progress in the first face-to-face talks for 20 months. Although the first day of negotiations concluded with a statement from the US President to the effect that a peace deal could be secured 'within a year', the absence of any indication that Israel would cede to requests to extend its moratorium on settlement building meant that such optimism appeared without foundation. The new insistence by Israel's Prime Minster that the PA extend recognition of Israel as 'the nation state of the Jewish people' was also regarded by many as unnecessarily provocative and indicative of an outlook that was combative rather than compromising. The second round of talks commenced in Egypt's Red Sea resort of Sharm el-Sheikh in mid-September. They were prefaced by ongoing requests from US Special Envoy George Mitchell that Israel extend its settlement freeze and the PA's assertion that it regarded Israel's compliance as the litmus test of its commitment to the peace process. The meetings in Egypt, and later Jerusalem, concluded with no sign of a breakthrough and against the backdrop of renewed hostilities along the Gaza–Israel border. Israeli air force jets bombed targets in the Strip after Palestinian militants fired several mortars and rockets into Israel.

ISRAEL ENDS SETTLEMENT FREEZE

With the deadline for the end of the settlement freeze rapidly approaching, Barack Obama used the forum of the UN General Assembly to address Israel directly on the settlement issue. He stated that 'Israel's settlement moratorium has made a difference on the ground, and improved the atmosphere for talks. We believe it should be extended.' Behind the scenes US and EU officials were also intensively lobbying their Israeli counterparts for a renewal of the freeze. US Secretary of State Hillary Clinton met with Syria's Minister of Foreign Affairs Walid al-Mouallem, the highest-level such meeting for three years, in an attempt to persuade Syria to re-engage in negotiations with Israel and thus provide an extra incentive for Netanyahu to demonstrate goodwill on settlement. However, as widely anticipated, a combination of the Israeli Prime Minister's own ideological convictions and his desire not to alienate the hard-line nationalists in his ruling coalition led to the announcement on 26 September 2010 that the ban on settlement activity would be lifted, with the proviso that 'restraint' should be exercised in the scale of construction. The decision was greeted with general dismay in Washington, DC, and in European capitals. French President Nicolas Sarkozy, hosting a visit to Paris by the Palestinian President, said that he 'deplored' the Israeli decision at a time when 'talks were finally and concretely under way'. For his part, Abbas said he would consult with fellow Palestinians and the Arab League before announcing the PA's formal response. With all shades of Palestinian opinion resolutely opposed to continuing direct talks with Israel if building resumed, the PA leader's pause was intended to facilitate a last-ditch attempt by Washington to persuade Israel to reconsider its decision.

At the end of September 2010 the Israeli press reported that the USA was offering a number of incentives to the Netanyahu

Government in return for renewing the settlement freeze for a further 60–90 day period. These were said to include guarantees on vetoing any UN resolutions perceived as being hostile to Israel while talks were progressing, substantial upgrades to Israel's military capabilities, and a promise to support a continued Israeli military presence in the Jordan valley as part of any future peace deal. Israeli officials refused to be drawn on the accuracy of the reports. On 2 October the Executive Committee of the PLO met in Ramallah. At the conclusion of the meeting, the PLO's Yasser Abd al-Rabbuh confirmed that the Palestinians would not return to the negotiating table without a freeze on settlement. The Israeli Prime Minister subsequently accused the Palestinians of sabotaging the peace process through their insistence on unreasonable preconditions for their participation. He alluded to the fact that the PA had negotiated for 17 years while settlement activity had been taking place and that the 'measured and restrained building in Judea and Samaria in the coming year will have no influence on the peace map'. At its summit in the Libyan city of Sirte on 8 October, the Arab League endorsed the Palestinian decision to withdraw from direct talks with Israel and called on the USA to pressurize Israel to halt settlement activity.

THE USA FAILS TO PERSUADE ISRAEL TO EXTEND SETTLEMENT MORATORIUM

Although US officials attempted to project an upbeat message following the breakdown of a process in which they had expended considerable political energy and capital, the prospects of finding a sustainable formula to rescue their initiative appeared limited. Palestinian negotiators asserted that while failure to agree a settlement freeze had precipitated their walkout, US Special Envoy Mitchell's claims that progress had been made on other issues during the negotiations of September 2010 were simply untrue. The Israeli daily *Ha'aretz* quoted Arab and Western diplomats as saying that core problems had not been addressed and also the complaint from Mahmud Abbas that Netanyahu had resisted meaningful discussion of any issue other than security. The task faced by the Obama Administration was made even more difficult during late 2010 following announcements by the Israeli authorities of plans to build 800 housing units in the West Bank settlement of Ariel and a further 1,300 homes in the settlement blocs in East Jerusalem. Chief Palestinian negotiator Saeb Erakat denounced the decision as evidence of Israel choosing 'settlements over peace', while the EU High Representative for Foreign Affairs and Security Policy, Catherine Ashton, UN Secretary-General Ban Ki-Moon and US Department of State Spokesman Philip Crowley led the international condemnation.

However, the announcement of further settlement expansion was warmly received by Netanyahu's right-wing religious and nationalist coalition partners and by their allies in the settler movement. Indeed, it was increasingly evident in the bad-tempered exchanges with the US Administration over a renewal of the settlement moratorium that the Israeli Prime Minister was far more attentive to the mood of the pro-settlement lobby than he was to Labour Party threats to abandon his Government over the stalled peace process. In November 2010 Netanyahu's Likud party pushed a bill through the Knesset which would require a national referendum to ratify any proposed withdrawals from territories formally annexed after 1967 (East Jerusalem and the Golan Heights) if these had not initially secured the approval of a two-thirds' parliamentary majority. Any land to be ceded to the Palestinians in exchange for Israel's retention of settlement blocs in the West Bank would also be subject to a national vote. The new law was attacked by the PA for making the requirements of international law conditional 'on the whims of Israeli public opinion'. Objections were also raised by Israeli opposition parties and peace groups over the new legislation's undermining of Knesset authority and for erecting a further barrier to a 'land-for-peace' deal.

Hopes that the USA would persuade Israel to sign up to a new settlement deal had receded by the beginning of December 2010. Notwithstanding the generous military package—including the promise of 20 *F-35* advanced jet fighters (worth US $3,000m.)—and various political inducements offered in return for a 90-day construction freeze, there was strong resistance to acceptance within the Netanyahu Cabinet. The most vocal opposition came from the Minister of Foreign Affairs, Avigdor Lieberman, who commented that his constituency would not countenance a freeze for 'a single day'. There were reports in Israel's media that the Shas party would be prepared to abstain on the deal, on condition that the USA gave a written commitment that construction in East Jerusalem would be exempt from the settlement ban. The Shas leader also demanded an acceleration in West Bank settlement construction, particularly in the environs of Jerusalem, once the moratorium had ended. It was always unlikely that Washington would provide written guarantees on Jerusalem, but the fact that the USA had given its tacit acceptance that occupied East Jerusalem would not be part of a future moratorium continued to anger the Palestinians.

On 7 December 2010 the USA announced that it was abandoning attempts to persuade Israel to agree to a 90-day settlement freeze. Administration insiders claimed that the decision was taken for three principal reasons. First, because there was no prospect of Israel agreeing to include East Jerusalem in the moratorium, a key demand of the PA; second, there was limited optimism that meaningful progress could be made during the 90-day negotiating opportunity that the freeze would provide; and third, that there had been disagreements over the package of incentives being offered to Israel as part of the deal. Department of State spokesman Crowley told reporters in a press briefing, 'we have been pursuing a moratorium as a means to create conditions for a return to meaningful and sustained negotiations. After a considerable effort, we have concluded that this does not create a firm basis to work towards our shared goal of a framework agreement.' Speaking on behalf of the Quartet group, Tony Blair opined that the US decision was appropriate 'in the light of the impasse that we have reached'. Predictably, Israeli and PA officials blamed each other for the latest development. Israel's Cabinet Secretary stated that the failures stemmed from PA and the US Administration's attempt to impose preconditions on negotiations.

What was indisputable was that the US announcement represented a significant blow to US credibility in the Middle East, and provided further ammunition to those in the Arab world who claimed that Washington was incapable of dealing with Israeli intransigence, even when the consequences resulted in long-term damage to its own interests, both regionally and globally. It was now expected that the US Administration would seek to advance the peace process via indirect talks in which the focus would shift away from securing agreement on the more contentious issues of Jerusalem and settlement to narrowing the gap on those core issues where it was perceived that progress could be made: namely borders and security. There was little optimism that such an approach would yield results as long as Israel's Government was so effectively dominated by hard-line nationalists.

The PA also faced some difficult choices. The failure of the USA to persuade Israel to halt settlement construction in either East Jerusalem or the West Bank bolstered the growing consensus within Palestinian society of a damaging over-reliance on Washington to achieve strategic outcomes. An enduring aspect of this narrative remained the conviction that the PA's security co-operation with Israel and the EU's generous funding of its para-state institutions had allowed Israel to sustain 'occupation on the cheap'. Healing the rift between Fatah and Hamas should be a national priority with concomitant consideration given to the usefulness of the continued existence of the PA as currently constituted.

In the immediate aftermath of the US retreat on the settlement freeze, PA officials suggested that diplomatic efforts would now be focused on taking unilateral action to win UN recognition of an independent Palestinian state within the territories occupied in 1967. While such a move would be met with implacable opposition from Israel and scarcely more approval in Washington, DC, there were signs that European frustration with the absence of traction in the peace process might lead to EU nations lending their backing to the Palestinian bid. In response to the impasse of the US-led process, 26 former leaders of the EU, including nine heads of state, sent a letter to all EU member governments (as well as EU President Herman van Rompuy and Catherine Ashton) stating that the situation in the Middle East had now reached a point where a peaceful resolution could not be achieved without a 'rapid and dramatic move' towards a two-state solution. It also called on EU leaders to block imports of all goods produced in the settlements and for any future upgrade to Israeli ties with the EU to be tied to a settlement freeze. A spokesman for Israel's Ministry of Foreign Affairs stated that the letter would only 'reinforce those who are suspicious of Europe's intentions and continue to marginalize the EU's role in peacemaking in this region'. Meanwhile, Lieberman informed a group of Israeli diplomats that a comprehensive peace deal with the Palestinians was both 'impossible' and 'forbidden'. He suggested instead that Israel should work towards finalizing long-term agreements with the Palestinians on economic and security concerns. Netanyahu's office rejoined by stating that these were the personal opinions of the Minister of Foreign Affairs and not government policy.

BARAK LEAVES THE LABOUR PARTY

Thirteen Palestinians were killed in Gaza during December 2010, as Israeli forces responded with air-strikes to increased rocket fire from militants. Tensions remained high along the border during the first half of January 2011. Israel's Ministry of Defence reported that 25 mortars and rockets had been fired from the Strip in a 10-day period and that they had retaliated against facilities belonging to both Hamas and Islamic Jihad. Three foreign workers were reported to have been injured in the fire from Gaza, while a militant from Islamic Jihad was killed in a targeted air attack; a Palestinian farmer was also shot dead by the IDF near the border fence. Comparative calm was restored after Hamas leaders warned other militant factions that violation of the cease-fire agreement would risk an escalated Israeli response.

On 17 January 2011 Israel's Labour leader and Minister of Defence, Ehud Barak, responded to increasing criticism of his role in supporting the hawkish policies of the Netanyahu Government by announcing his decision to resign from the party, but to stay in government. He stated that he was setting up a new party, Ha'atzmaut (Independence). Four Labour MKs joined Barak in the new party, while the remaining Labour cabinet ministers immediately resigned their posts. The realignment reduced Netanyahu's majority in the 120-seat Knesset from 74 to 66 seats. The Israeli Prime Minister welcomed Barak's decision and stated that departure of the Labour MKs had made his Government stronger.

THE 'PALESTINE PAPERS'

In January 2011 the Qatar-based satellite broadcaster Al Jazeera reported that it had acquired more than 1,600 confidential files documenting the Israel-Palestinian peace process during the period 1999–2009. The so-called Palestine Papers were said to have been leaked from the Ramallah-based offices of the PA's Negotiation Support Unit. Al Jazeera shared the documents with the British daily *The Guardian*. Many of the documents—which included minutes of meetings, maps, e-mails and draft agreements—covered the post-Annapolis period of 2008–09 and provided important, if not always surprising, evidence of the priorities and negotiating positions of the three principal players in the peace process, the Israeli Government, the PA and the US Administration. They revealed that the Israeli side adopted a consistent and tough negotiating position, which enjoyed default backing from Washington's officials. The picture of the PA sketched through the documents suggested a far less confident approach and a private willingness to consider compromises on core issues that were dramatically removed from their public stance or the national consensus. This was particularly evident with the future status of Jerusalem. The Palestinians' chief negotiator, Saeb Erakat, suggested to Ehud Olmert that the PA would agree to Israeli annexation of the Jewish and Armenian quarters of the Old City and all the major settlement blocs built in East Jerusalem with the exception of Har Homa. This was rejected by Israel's then Minister of Foreign Affairs, Tzipi Livni.

The Palestine Papers revealed that the PA also agreed to Israel's annexation of the West Bank settlements close to or straddling the 1967 border, in exchange for land of equivalent size within Israel. Again the PA proposal was rejected by the Israeli side, which demanded that the major settlement blocs within the West Bank, Gush Etzion, Ma'aleh Adumim, Giv'at Ze'ev and Ariel, must also be ceded to Israel, with 50% compensation of lands inside Israel. The PA responded that Israel's annexation of the land would not allow territorial contiguity, and would deprive the Palestinians of important aquifers and undermine the viability of a Palestinian state. On the highly sensitive issue of refugees, the PA apparently conceded to an Israeli demand that only 10,000 of the estimated 5m. Palestinians and their descendants displaced as a result of the creation of the State of Israel in 1948 would be allowed to return. The Israelis offered to resettle Palestinian refugees in South America. The leaked documents also exposed the depth of security co-ordination between Israel and the PA and their shared desire, encouraged by the USA, to neutralize Hamas as a political, as well as a military, force.

The political fallout from the publication of the documents was considerable. The PA initially denied their authenticity and then blamed the Qatari Government for engaging in a conspiracy against the Palestinian authorities; protests were also organized by Fatah against the Al Jazeera offices in Ramallah. However, as it became clear that the Palestine Papers were indeed genuine and the cries of betrayal on the Palestinian street became louder, PA officials reverted to damage limitation, claiming that the documents were selective and presented out of context. Hamas leaders were not alone among Palestinians in denouncing the PA for collusion with the Israeli occupation and for attempting to strike a deal for which no mandate existed. The only solace for Mahmud Abbas to emerge from the publication of the papers was that they demonstrated that Palestinian desperation to find compromises was met with an inflexible Israeli response. As many commentators observed, the lament by Israeli politicians that there had been no partner in peace on the Palestinian side would cease to have any meaningful resonance. In mid-February 2011 the PA's chief negotiator, Saeb Erakat, who had been heavily criticized following the release of the documents, tendered his resignation to President Abbas on the grounds that the leak had come from his office. However, his offer was rejected.

ISRAELI ANXIETY OVER EVENTS IN EGYPT

Israel's political establishment, unruffled by the revelations of the Palestine Papers, was alarmed by the popular protests which led to Egypt's President, Hosni Mubarak, being deposed in February 2011. For nearly three decades the Egyptian President had proved himself to be a reliable guardian of Cairo's peace treaty with Israel. This role had guaranteed the steady flow on US dollars into Egypt's coffers, but had proved increasingly unpopular among ordinary Egyptians in the absence of progress towards the establishment of a Palestinian state and a wider accord with the Arab world. For Israel, peace with Egypt had been of enormous benefit. With the country's southern border no longer seen as vulnerable, Israel had gained 'strategic depth' and had been able massively to reduce the proportion of its gross national product that was spent on defence. The Mubarak regime, sharing Israel's antipathy towards political Islamism, had also been an important ally in countering the influence of Hamas. It came as no surprise, therefore, that muted public comment on the Egyptian uprising by the Israeli Government masked private anxieties, chief among which were fears that free elections in Egypt would bring to power a government dominated by the Muslim Brotherhood and with it the very real possibility of an abrogation of their peace treaty. Even if the Islamists failed to achieve a majority stake in a democratically elected government, it was a palpable truth that the other emerging political forces in Egypt, whether secularist, nationalist or leftist, shared differing degrees of hostility towards Israel. In the immediate term, Israel's military leaders were alarmed by evidence that Hamas and its Egyptian allies were exploiting the breakdown of law and order in the Sinai to smuggle more sophisticated weaponry into Gaza. There was relief in Israel, however, when the military council which assumed power in Egypt after Mubarak's overthrow affirmed that it would respect the country's peace agreement with Israel.

Events in Egypt and the civil strife which engulfed much of the Arab world during the early part of 2011 inspired more modest protests in the Palestinian territories. Hamas had organized demonstrations in Gaza in support of the anti-Mubarak protests in Egypt, but were quick to break up rallies calling for more democratic openings in Gaza itself. Fatah forces took similar action on the streets of the West Bank.

USA VETOES SETTLEMENT RESOLUTION

On 18 February 2011 the USA used its veto to defeat a UN Security Council Resolution condemning Israeli settlements in the Occupied Territories. The resolution had been worded to complement official US policy on the status of the settlements and had been supported by all other Security Council members, including the United Kingdom and France. The US ambassador to the UN, Susan Rice, commented that the exercise of Washington's veto did not equate to US acceptance of the legitimacy of the settlements, but rather stemmed from a belief that the passing of the draft resolution risked 'hardening the positions of both sides and could encourage the parties to stay out of negotiations'. The Israeli Prime Minister stated that he 'deeply appreciated' the US Administration's actions. Both PA and Hamas leaders issued strong condemnation of the US decision and called for a 'day of rage' in response. The British, French and German Governments also expressed disappointment with the US veto, issuing a joint statement in which they reaffirmed their view that all Israeli settlements were illegal and threatened the possibility of a two-state solution.

RENEWED VIOLENCE IN THE WEST BANK AND GAZA

The UN vote coincided with moves by the Israeli Government to regularize the status of the various outpost settlements on the West Bank which were deemed to be 'unauthorized'. In line with promises given to the Obama Administration, Israeli troops were sent to dismantle the settlement outpost of Havat Gilad, sparking violent confrontations with residents and their supporters. Militant settler groups later carried out their threat to attack Palestinian communities in response to Israeli government measures against the outposts; homes and property were damaged in two Palestinian villages. In conscious adoption of the tactics and language of Palestinian protest, nationalist hardliners also blocked streets with burning tyres in Jerusalem, stoned cars belonging to Palestinians on the West Bank and issued calls for their own 'day of rage' to combat evacuation plans. Meanwhile, other outposts which were deemed to have been constructed on state-owned, rather than privately owned West Bank Palestinian land (as was the case with Havat Gilad), were reportedly going to be granted official status by the Israeli Government. On 11 March 2011 five members of the same family in the Jewish settlement of Itamar, near Nablus, were stabbed to death by Palestinian assailants. The dead included an infant and two young children. The killings were claimed by the al-Aqsa Martyrs Brigades and were condemned by the PA as 'inhuman and immoral'. The day after the attack Israel's Cabinet announced that a further 500 homes were to be built in West Bank settlements. The Knesset Speaker, Likud's Reuven Rivlin, said that 'more building ... more hanging on to the land' should be 'the answer to the murderers'.

The simmering violence across the Israel–Gaza border also intensified in March 2011. Several Palestinians were killed, at least four of them civilians, and tens wounded as mortar and rocket attacks from Gaza were met by an escalating Israeli response involving air-strikes and tankfire. For the first time since the end of Operation Cast Lead in January 2009, Hamas claimed that its cadres had been responsible for some of the rocket fire. Israeli spokesmen reported that dozens of rockets had landed in Israel during the flare-up and that two had reached the cities of Beersheva and Ashdod, more than 20 miles from Gaza's borders. Islamic Jihad also said that it had fired *Grad*-type rockets from Gaza. A calm of sorts was restored by the end of March, but the lull proved to be shortlived. On 7 April an anti-tank missile fired from Gaza by Hamas militants struck an Israeli school bus travelling along the border, fatally wounding a teenage boy. Nineteen Palestinians were killed, at least six of them civilians, and many more injured in Israeli retaliatory attacks on targets in the Strip. Militant groups in Gaza also fired at least 100 mortars and rockets into Israel. The IDF declared that several of the projectiles had been intercepted by a newly deployed missile defence system dubbed 'Iron Dome'. Both the Israeli Government and the Hamas leadership in Gaza sought to prevent further fighting, issuing calls for calm while reserving the right to respond to the perceived provocations of the other side.

HAMAS AND FATAH IN UNITY DEAL

After years of fitful Egyptian-mediated unity talks, Hamas and Fatah leaders announced at the end of April 2011 that they had agreed a formula to heal their long-standing rift. Impetus for the deal had come most fundamentally from the 'Arab spring' uprisings across the Middle East and North Africa region, and their inspiration within the Palestinian context of a priority grass-roots demand for national unity. The release of the Palestine Papers had already amplified voices questioning the legitimacy of PA rule in the West Bank while Hamas was itself facing mounting criticism for its repressive governance in Gaza. Mubarak's overthrow in Egypt had also presented the country's interim military council with the opportunity to plough a more neutral furrow in their brokerage of a deal, and in so doing to demonstrate the new regime's break with the pro-US and pro-Israeli policies of its predecessor. Few observers had placed much faith in the sincerity of the Mubarak Government's attempts to achieve reconciliation of the Palestinian factions when neither Washington nor Tel-Aviv would welcome such an outcome. Moreover, neither Fatah, nor more particularly Hamas, wished to upset the new rulers in Egypt by being seen to resist a more genuine attempt to facilitate a unity deal.

On 4 May 2011 Fatah and Hamas leaders met in Cairo to sign an accord designed to heal their divisions. Representatives of the Arab League were also in attendance at the ceremony. Under the terms of the deal, it was agreed that a caretaker national unity administration would be established in the West Bank and Gaza, with full parliamentary and presidential elections being held within a year. The signing of the pact was warmly welcomed on the Palestinian street, although there were few illusions over the size of the obstacles preventing its implementation. These were almost immediately demonstrated by the failure of the two sides to agree on who should hold the office of Prime Minister in the new administration. The PA in Ramallah insisted that Salam Fayyad should continue in the role. Fayyad was viewed as a competent technocrat and credited with having overseen a revival in the West Bank's economy. It was also argued that his continued stewardship of the PA would soften US opposition to the new unity deal. However, Fayyad's candidature was strongly opposed by Hamas because of the perceived closeness of his ties to Israel, especially on the question of security co-oper-ation. Notwithstanding the tensions which militated against the formation of a new Palestinian cabinet, Washington responded frostily to the Cairo accord. US Department of State spokesman Mark Toner stated that the Obama Administration would reserve judgement on its relations with a new Palestinian administration, and any future aid, until its composition was known. He warned that Hamas involvement would not be welcome as long as the movement failed to abide by the Quartet principles for resolution of the conflict with Israel. The reaction of the Netanyahu Government to the Fatah-Hamas reconciliation was unambiguous. Declaring that Mahmud Abbas must choose between 'peace with Israel or peace with Hamas', he announced that his Government was withholding the transfer of tax revenues to the PA. UN Secretary-General Ban Ki-Moon criticized the Israeli decision and urged the release of an estimated US $80m. in taxes owed to the Palestinians. The

EU announced that it would release extra funds to make up the shortfall and ensure the payment of salaries to PA employees.

International pessimism over the moribund peace process was underlined in May 2011 by George Mitchell's resignation as US President Obama's Middle East peace envoy. Mitchell was succeeded by his deputy, David Hale. Although the former US Senate leader cited the expiry of his agreed two-year term in the position as the reason for his departure, it was widely accepted that Mitchell had resigned out of conviction that his mission to secure a regional peace had been an unmitigated failure.

AL-NAKBA PROTESTERS KILLED ON ISRAEL'S NORTHERN BORDERS

At least 13 protesters, most of them Palestinian, were shot dead and scores more wounded by Israeli troops in demonstrations and marches called on 15 May 2011 to mark *al-Nakba* ('the Catastrophe'), the anniversary of the creation of the State of Israel in 1948. The worst violence took place on Israel's northern borders as predominantly Palestinian demonstrators attempted to cross from Lebanese and Syrian territory into northern Israel and the occupied Golan Heights, respectively. Although recent events in other parts of the Arab world had heightened expectations in Israel that the *al-Nakba* protests might be more widespread than in previous years, the authorities were unprepared for the scale of the demonstrations organized from Lebanon and Syria. Israeli troops used tear gas, rubber bullets and live ammunition to force back the crowds who succeeded in breaching sections of the border fencing to make the symbolic crossing into Israel. Marches towards crossing points into Israel were also made in the Gaza Strip and were met with live fire, injuring an estimated 19 protesters. At the traditional flashpoints on the West Bank and in East Jerusalem there were sustained clashes between rock-throwing youths and Israel's security forces. The Israeli Government claimed that its actions to defend its borders against 'violent rioters' were legitimate. Responding to international concern over its use of lethal force to repel the demonstrators, Israeli officials rejoined that President Assad had cynically engineered the confrontations to divert attention from his brutal suppression of pro-democracy protests in Syria (where more than 2,000 anti-Government protesters had reportedly been killed by security forces). Meanwhile, in Cairo demonstrations were held outside the Israeli embassy, culminating in the reported deaths of at least two people in clashes between Egyptian security forces and protesters who had broken into the embassy in early September.

OBAMA AND NETANYAHU SPEECHES OFFER DIFFERING VISIONS

President Obama delivered a much anticipated speech on the situation in the Middle East at the US Department of State on 19 May 2011. Much of the address was taken up with the US response to the new realities created by the protests taking place across the Arab world; however, it concluded with a review of the current state of the Arab–Israeli dispute. The US President reiterated his 'unshakeable' commitment to Israel's security and his opposition to attempts to isolate Israel in 'international forums', including the Palestinian bid to win UN backing for a declaration of independence in September. He also warned that peace and prosperity for the Palestinians could not be achieved as long as Hamas followed 'a path of terror and rejection' and that the inclusion of the unreformed Islamists in a Palestinian administration posed fundamental questions to which the Palestinians needed to provide 'credible answers'. Acknowledging the current logjam in negotiations and global frustration with 'an endless process that never produces an outcome', Obama stated that his friendship with Israel compelled him 'to tell the truth: the status quo is unsustainable, and Israel must act boldly to advance a lasting peace'. The parameters of the peace deal were known, namely the creation of a sovereign and 'contiguous' Palestinian state alongside Israel. The borders of this state would be based on the 1967 lines, with mutually agreed land swaps. The US President argued that provision for Israeli security needs and agreement on the borders of the Palestinian state should be the immediate focus of peacemaking efforts and that this would provide a secure basis from which to address the more emotive issues of Jerusalem and Palestinian refugees.

There was no indication in the Obama address that the USA had any plans for how to navigate out of the existing impasse, a reflection of the fact that the Administration had already concluded that there was simply no chance of any progress on an Israeli-Palestinian peace under the Netanyahu Government. The response to the President's speech in the Arab world and from Israel was broadly predictable. Palestinian officials criticized Obama's failure to mention settlements and the implicit rejection of a unity government, but welcomed the explicit reference to the 1967 borders delineating a future Palestinian state. Israel's Prime Minister was uncompromising in his rejection of the Obama vision, dismissing a withdrawal to the 1967 lines as 'unrealistic' and 'indefensible'. A meeting between Netanyahu and Obama on the day after the latter's speech failed to narrow the gap. The Israeli premier maintained this hard-line approach in major speech to a joint session of the US Congress on 24 May 2011. He told a largely sympathetic audience that the main obstacle to peace was the Palestinians' refusal to accept 'a state if it meant accepting a Jewish state alongside it'. Moreover, while agreeing to give up 'parts of the Jewish homeland' to facilitate its establishment, Netanyahu confirmed that Israel's self-defined security needs would be the ultimate arbiter of final border arrangements. The speech also emphasized the ongoing threats to the region posed by 'genocidal' Iran and its sponsorship of militant Islamist groups, especially Hamas and Hezbollah. In this context Netanyahu warned that the world must guard against the possibility of the uprisings in the Arab world producing new tyrannies. The PA claimed that the Netanyahu vision made any further negotiations with the Israeli Government 'pointless'.

EGYPT OPENS BORDER CROSSING TO GAZA

Egypt's new rulers fulfilled their promises to ease the plight of Gaza's Palestinians by opening their border crossing with the Strip on 28 May 2011. Under the terms of the unity accord agreed between Hamas and the PA, freedom of movement was to be granted to women, children and men over the age of 40. Travel for males between 18 and 40 years of age would be subject to a successful visa application. The border would additionally remain closed to commercial traffic and the times of opening limited to eight hours per day, six days a week. Hamas officials warmly welcomed the development and promised full co-operation with the Egyptian authorities in management of the crossing. However, Israel's authorities expressed concern that the relaxation of border controls would make weapons-smuggling easier. On 5 June, in scenes reminiscent of the *al-Nakba* day incidents, 12 Arab demonstrators were reportedly killed as they attempted to cross from Syria into the occupied Golan Heights. The protests had ostensibly been organized by Damascus to mark the anniversary of the June war of 1967. Israel disputed the casualty figures, while observers claimed that at least some of the deaths had occurred as a result of an ill-fated attempt by the protesters to cross a minefield. Reports that those taking part in the march had been paid by to do so by Hezbollah (and possibly pro-Syrian Palestinian factions) gave weight to claims in Israel and elsewhere that this was another attempt by the Assad regime to deflect attention from the worsening internal situation in Syria.

ISRAEL ATTEMPTS TO HEAD OFF PALESTINIAN UN BID

Meanwhile, classified cables leaked to the Israeli daily *Ha'aretz* revealed the growing alarm within Israel at the Palestinian bid to gain UN recognition of a Palestinian state. The documents reported that Israel's Ministry of Foreign Affairs had issued instructions to its overseas missions to draw up plans for a diplomatic and media campaign aimed at persuading as many countries as possible to withhold support for the Palestinian initiative. Purportedly issued by the

Director-General of the Ministry, the document was reported to have stated that 'the Palestinian effort must be referred to as a process that erodes the legitimacy of the State of Israel. The primary argument is that by pursuing this process in the UN, the Palestinians are trying to achieve their aims in a manner other than in negotiations with Israel, and this violates the principle that the only route to resolving the conflict is through bilateral negotiations.' Israel's Minister of Foreign Affairs, Avigdor Lieberman, later asserted in talks with the EU High Representative for Foreign Affairs and Security Policy, Catherine Ashton, that if the PA persisted with the UN move, Israel would no longer be committed to the agreements it had signed with the Palestinians over the previous 18 years. Lieberman added that the PA's tactic had reduced the potential for renewed dialogue to 'zero'. PA negotiator, Muhammad Shtayeh, said that the Authority would continue to pursue the independence declaration option and that he viewed the Palestinian bid as 'complementary' to negotiations. At a meeting of the Arab League on 14 July 2011 in Doha, ministers responsible for foreign affairs pledged to give their full support to the PA in its attempt to win international support for UN recognition of an independent Palestinian state.

ISRAELIS KILLED IN ATTACK FROM SINAI

On 18 September 2011 a large group of heavily armed Palestinian fighters carried out co-ordinated attacks on Israeli military and passenger vehicles travelling along the highway north of the Red Sea port of Eilat. Eight Israelis, including six civilians, were killed and several more were injured in the assaults. The insurgents were pursued by Israeli forces over the border into the Egyptian Sinai, and in a series of clashes lasting many hours at least eight were killed, along with two Israeli soldiers. Five members of an Egyptian border force, presumably targeted in error by an IDF helicopter, also lost their lives, prompting a fierce rebuke from the Egyptian authorities and several days of violent protests outside Israel's embassy in Cairo. Demonstrators demanded the abrogation of the Camp David accords and the expulsion of the Israeli ambassador. Official Egyptian anger was exacerbated by accusations from Israel's Minister of Defence that Egypt's new military rulers were losing control of the Sinai and that 'terrorist' groups were flourishing. Barak's comments reflected Israel's growing unease at the apparent erosion of central government authority in the peninsula—typified by recent attacks on the pipeline transporting gas from Egypt to Israel—and the concomitant fear that the security of its porous southern border would be increasingly difficult to maintain. Concerns that the diplomatic dispute with Egypt was in danger of serious escalation forced Barak to issue a statement of regret for the killing of the Egyptian soldiers and a promise that Israel would launch a joint investigation with the Egyptian military into the circumstances surrounding their deaths. Israel also permitted the Egyptian army to deploy thousands of troops and heavy weaponry in the Sinai in an attempt to address the deteriorating security situation. This represented a significant revision of the 1979 peace treaty, which limited Egypt's military presence in the territory. Meanwhile, Israeli defence officials appealed for the construction of a newly initiated border fence with Egypt to be accelerated.

Although none of the established Palestinian factions claimed responsibility for the attacks, the Israeli Government was swift to blame the Gaza-based PRC. Israeli officials claimed that fighters from the organization had used tunnels to cross from Gaza into Egypt before making their way to the ambush sites. Israel ordered air-strikes against targets connected with the group, killing several militants, including the PRC's commander. Hamas's military wing responded by announcing that it was no longer abiding by its cease-fire. Over the following week Israel launched at least 45 air raids on Gaza, while Palestinian groups fired rockets into southern Israel; 26 Palestinians, the majority of whom were militants, and one Israeli were killed in the exchanges.

There was speculation in the Israeli media that senior IDF officials were considering a major assault on Gaza in response to the attacks. However, it appeared that Prime Minister Netanyahu wished to avoid engendering sympathy for the Palestinians prior to their UN membership bid and further inflaming strident anti-Israeli feeling in Egypt. The strength of this sentiment was underlined on 9 September 2011, when the Israeli embassy in Cairo was broken into by a group of protesters in full view, and without the early intervention, of the sizeable police force deployed to protect it. The Israeli ambassador and other embassy staff were immediately evacuated back to Israel for their own protection.

US UNEASY WITH PALESTINIAN UN BID

Throughout September 2011 the Obama Administration intensified its efforts to obstruct the Palestinian UN membership bid. However, the USA was concerned that its reputation within the Arab and Islamic world would be damaged if it had to employ its veto in the Security Council to block the PA's move. US officials were acutely aware of the implicit contradictions in endorsing the 'Arab spring' but denying the Palestinians recognition of statehood. Nevertheless, the USA continued to express its opposition, arguing that unilateral measures were counter-productive and could not be a substitute for negotiated agreements. The US Department of State's resolve in blocking the PA's bid was inevitably stiffened by the outright opposition of a strongly pro-Israel Congress and threats by senior figures in the Netanyahu Government to annex swaths of the West Bank should the Palestinians secure UN membership. Obama tried to balance warnings directed against the PA with a stated commitment to finding a framework for fresh talks. Quartet envoy Tony Blair was instructed in early September to meet with Israeli and Palestinian leaders to try to secure the outline agreements that could serve as the basis for a revival of negotiations. As universally predicted, his efforts failed to convince the Palestinians to waver from their insistence that a settlement freeze was a precondition for their participation. Moreover, it was unlikely that the PA President would survive politically if he abandoned his UN mission because of pressure from the Obama Administration. With the EU nations unwilling to lend unconditional support to Abbas (but reluctant to join the US opposition), it was Turkish President Erdoğan who became the main proponent of the Palestinian cause. Still angered by Israel's refusal to apologize for the *Mavi Marmara* incident and keen to project Turkish influence into the emerging Arab democracies of North Africa, Erdoğan made a high-profile visit to the region in mid-September. Addressing a meeting of the Arab League in Cairo, he declared that 'The Palestinian cause is the cause of human dignity. It's time to raise the Palestinian flag at the United Nations.' The Turkish President also warned that 'Israel will break away from solitude only when it acts as a reasonable, responsible, serious and normal state'.

The diplomatic manoeuvring around the PA's UN bid was viewed negatively by increasing sections of the Palestinian population, who questioned the relevance and legitimacy of the PA and suspected that the UN vote would be of symbolic import only. PA Prime Minister Fayyad had earlier indicated that he held similar concerns, while Hamas had made clear its opposition to the plan.

QUARTET SECURES COMPROMISE

The UN General Assembly meeting opened on 21 September 2011. Intense lobbying by the Quartet group in the interim had produced a last-minute agreement to prevent the diplomatic confrontation feared by the USA. Under the terms of the deal, Abbas would formally submit the request for UN membership, but the vote would be deferred by the Security Council until scrutiny of the bid had been completed, a process that could last months. In return, the Quartet had promised that the Security Council's deliberations would run in parallel with a renewed attempt to restart negotiations on a peace settlement. The latter proposed the convening of a preparatory meeting between the two sides within one month, the submission of concrete proposals on security and borders within three months, and the conclusion of a final agreement within 12 months. However, in the statement subsequently issued by the Quartet, there was no mention of the need for a settlement freeze nor acknowledgement of the principle that the 1967 borders would be the basis for territorial arrangements. The fact that Abbas accepted a compromise that appeared to offer very little in terms of revitalizing the peace process was a reflection not only of the pressure he had been subjected to by the USA and key EU states, but also of the realization that the PA bid might not achieve the backing of the nine members of the 15-seat Security Council necessary to gain recognition and thus force the USA to employ its veto. The indications remained that, despite their declared support for Palestinian statehood, both France and the United Kingdom would probably abstain in a Security Council vote.

ISRAEL ANNOUNCES NEW SETTLEMENT CONSTRUCTION

The PA President was fêted by Fatah supporters on his return to Ramallah. However, the mood of celebration was short lived. On 27 September 2011 Israel announced that it would begin constructing a further 1,100 homes, public buildings and an industrial unit in the settlement of Gilo, which had originally been built on West Bank land that was later annexed to Israel by the Greater Jerusalem municipality. Palestinians saw a clear connection between the timing of the announcement on Gilo's expansion and the PA's UN bid, indicating the Netanyahu Government's desire to punish the PA President. The decision elicited the usual expressions of displeasure from US Secretary of State Hillary Clinton and EU High Representative for Foreign Affairs and Security Policy Catherine Ashton. Two weeks later plans were submitted to Israel's Ministry of Construction and Housing for the establishment of a new settlement, Givat Hamatos, on the southern fringe of Jerusalem, comprising 2,600 housing units. This would be the first new settlement built in the Occupied Territories since Har Homa in 1997. More critically, its construction would effectively fill the last remaining gap in the arc of settlements surrounding Arab East Jerusalem. Israeli planners claimed that they would reserve one-third of the units for an extension of the adjoining Palestinian suburb of Beit Safafa. The UN Secretary-General condemned the Givat Hamatos plans as 'contrary to international law'.

PRISONER EXCHANGE BENEFITS HAMAS

In mid-October 2011 it was reported that Israel and Hamas had reached an agreement for the release of Gilad Shalit, the Israeli soldier captured on the Gaza border in 2006. The deal had been mediated by Egyptian officials and a German intermediary. Under the terms of the agreement, Shalit was to be exchanged for more than 1,000 Palestinians held in Israeli gaols. The latter were to be released in stages and included many who had been convicted of killing Israeli soldiers and civilians. Significantly, the two highest-profile prisoners, Fatah militia leader Marwan Barghouthi and PFLP Secretary-General Ahmad Saadat, were excluded from the list. The majority of the released Palestinians were allowed to return to either the West Bank or Gaza, but some 200 agreed to deportation as a condition of their freedom. The timing of the announcement on the exchange deal evoked considerable comment given that it had been widely rumoured that an outline agreement on the conditions for Shalit's release had been concluded several months previously. Many analysts believed that Netanyahu had approved the prisoner exchange arrangement at that time as a further rebuke to the PA President. While Abbas welcomed the Shalit deal, it was clear that his rivals in Hamas would be the main beneficiaries of the prisoner releases. The exchanges were also a reminder that, despite the uncertainties of the political transition in Cairo, Egypt remained the principal broker in Israel's relations with the rest of the Arab world.

Violence once again flared along the Gaza–Israel border at the end of October 2011 following an Israeli air-strike that killed five Islamic Jihad militants. An IDF spokesman said the men had been targeted as they prepared to launch a *Grad* missile into Israel. Rocket fire from Gaza killed an Israeli civilian in Ashkelon, and a further five Islamic Jihad fighters were killed in retaliatory air-strikes. A cease-fire was eventually established.

MIXED UN FORTUNES FOR THE PA

On 31 October 2011 UNESCO voted by 107 votes to 14 to accept the 'State of Palestine' as a full member state. The vote had undoubted symbolic and political significance for the Palestinians and also conferred on the PA the right to seek World Heritage status for historical sites in East Jerusalem and the West Bank. The exercise of this right would raise further questions about the legality of the Israeli claim of sovereignty over East Jerusalem. Israel and the USA strongly criticized the decision, which US Department of State spokeswoman Victoria Nuland described as 'regrettable and premature'. Nuland further stated that the US Administration would immediately halt payments to UNESCO (amounting to 22% of the organization's annual budget), citing a law adopted in the early 1990s that allowed the USA to terminate funding to any UN body that admitted 'Palestine' as a member. The Israeli Ministry of Foreign Affairs condemned the UN bid as a 'unilateral Palestinian manoeuvre, which ... further removes the possibility of a peace agreement'. On the following day Israel's Cabinet agreed to accelerate the construction of 2,000 new homes in East Jerusalem and the West Bank settlements of Efrat and Ma'aleh Adumim, ban UNESCO missions to Israel, and suspend the transfer of tax revenues to the PA. Meanwhile, the UN admissions committee responsible for considering the Palestinian membership bid failed, as expected, to arrive at a consensus position. Having calculated that they could only secure the support of eight of the Security Council members, the Palestinians decided not to request a vote. The decision was taken after the Sarkozy administration, which had supported the Palestinians in the UNESCO vote, indicated that France, like the United Kingdom, would abstain in a Security Council vote. Nevertheless, if it won a simple majority in a General Assembly vote, the PA could upgrade its status at the UN from observer to non-member state.

Notwithstanding the USA's unwavering support for Israel at the UN, relations between the Obama Administration and the Israeli Government continued to be characterized by mutual mistrust. Obama was overheard at the November 2011 Group of Twenty (G20) summit meeting of leading industrial nations in Cannes, France, apparently agreeing with Sarkozy's assessment of the Israeli Prime Minister as dislikeable and a 'liar'. Shortly afterwards, both US Secretary of State Clinton and US Secretary of Defense Leon Panetta expressed their exasperation with aspects of Israeli policy. Panetta criticized Israel for its increasingly bellicose rhetoric towards Iran, its failure to improve relations with Egypt and Turkey, and its lack of commitment to negotiations with the PA.

ISRAELI AND PALESTINIAN REACTIONS TO THE 'ARAB SPRING'

Netanyahu delivered his assessment of the 'Arab spring' in a speech to the Knesset in November 2011. He contended that US and European support for the popular uprisings that had shaken autocratic Arab regimes across the Middle East and North Africa was 'naive' and that the 'Arab spring' had become an 'Islamic, anti-Western, anti-liberal, anti-Israeli, undemocratic wave'. He expressed regret that the Mubarak regime had been overthrown in Egypt and concern that the ruling Hashemite dynasty in Jordan was also vulnerable. Within this context of current unrest and future uncertainty, Netanyahu argued that it would be foolish to make concessions or pursue agreements with the Palestinians. Several days later Barak described the initial results of Egypt's first democratic parliamentary elections, which suggested a big majority for the Muslim Brotherhood and their Islamist rivals, as 'very, very disturbing'. Despite statements from the moderate leadership of Egypt's largest Islamist grouping pledging to respect Egypt's international commitments, the fear remained in Israel that relations with an Islamist government in Cairo would be tense. Of particular concern were the close historical and ideological ties between Egypt's Muslim Brotherhood and Hamas, and the impetus that this might give to the hitherto fitful attempts to consolidate a Palestinian rapprochement. However, many observers also noted that the electoral successes of the Egyptian Islamists and the new realities created by the 'Arab spring' were exerting a moderating influence on the Palestinian group.

Following renewed negotiations in Cairo aimed at breaking the impasse in efforts to form a unified Palestinian administration, a Hamas spokesman confirmed to British newspaper *The Guardian* in December that his organization was no longer wedded to a purely militaristic response to Israel and would seek in future to emphasize non-violent forms of resistance. Such a development would be welcomed in Gaza, where the deprivations of the blockade and the autocratic nature of Hamas rule were breeding dissent and disaffection. Events in Syria were also informing the strategic reassessment. Whereas the Shi'a-dominated Hezbollah in Lebanon voiced mainly unambiguous support for the Assad regime in its battle against a largely Sunni insurgency, Hamas struggled to maintain an official neutrality. The Syrian Government had long been the movement's most important source of support in the Arab world, but ideologically Hamas was far closer to the forces of the Syrian opposition. Under pressure from Iran to follow Hezbollah and adopt a more unequivocal position on the conflict, Hamas's external leadership judged that it was no longer tenable to base itself in the Syrian capital. Although Hamas made no official announcement of an intention to close down its office, by the end of December most of the movement's senior leaders, including Khalid Meshaal, had effectively left Syria to assume temporary residence in Jordan, Qatar and Tunisia. The Damascus exiles refrained from overt criticism of the Syrian Government, but the Gaza-based leaders were less circumspect. In a speech in Cairo in February 2012, Ismail Haniyeh paid tribute to 'the heroic people of Syria who are striving for freedom, democracy and reform'. Dissatisfaction with Hamas over its position on the Syrian conflict reportedly led Iran to end its financial support for the Hamas administration in Gaza (totalling US $23m. per month). Shortly afterwards a Hamas chief in Gaza, Salah Bardawil, confirmed that his organization would not get involved in any future conflict between Iran and Israel, declaring that 'Hamas is not part of military alliances in the region. Our strategy is to defend our rights.'

The Palestinian Islamists' rift with Iran and Syria (and to a lesser extent with Hezbollah) contributed in part to the announcement in February 2012 that Fatah and Hamas had agreed in principle to the formation of a transitional unity government, headed by Abbas and composed largely of technocrats. The new administration would exercise authority until new elections could be arranged. The Netanyahu administration responded to the news by reiterating that Abbas would have to choose between peace with Israel and peace with Hamas. The USA and EU states similarly repeated their opposition to Hamas's involvement in Palestinian governance as long as the Islamists refused to renounce violence or confer explicit recognition on Israel. Nevertheless, the West's censure of Abbas for reconciling with Hamas failed to carry the same political weight that it had previously. Whereas there had earlier been some residual belief within the PA leadership that Obama-sponsored negotiations with Israel might yield progress towards a settlement freeze and an agreement on the creation of a Palestinian state, it was now uniformly held that there was neither the will nor the framework to deliver on either front. PA negotiators had met with their Israeli counterparts at the beginning of 2012 as part of the Quartet plan formulated to dissuade the PA from pursuing UN membership. Although both sides were tasked with presenting proposals on future borders and security guarantees, the low-key meeting ended with no agreements and no expectations of future progress. Ostensibly, Abbas had sacrificed very little by re-establishing ties with Hamas.

The extent to which the Israeli–Palestinian conflict had slipped down the regional and international agenda was underscored during the visit of Israel's Prime Minster to the USA in March 2012. Netanyahu made no reference to peace with the Palestinians during his opening address at the White House, concentrating instead on the threat posed by Iran and Israel's right to prevent Tehran from acquiring a nuclear weapons capability. President Obama only devoted brief comments to the Israeli–Palestinian conflict. Indeed, there was an acknowledgement that the prospects for meaningful progress on the Middle East's core conflict were probably as remote as they had been at any time since the beginning of the Oslo process.

The IDF and Palestinian factions once again exchanged airstrikes and rockets following the targeted killing of the PRC's Secretary-General in Gaza on 9 March 2012. Over several days 25 Palestinians were killed and many more were injured; one Israeli was seriously injured during the rocket attacks, which reached as far as Ashdod and Beersheva. Israel's Ministry of Defence claimed that more than 150 rockets had been fired by Palestinian groups during the latest bout of cross-border violence but that many of them had been intercepted by the IDF's 'Iron Dome' anti-missile system.

ISRAELI SETTLEMENT ACTIVITY

EU states continued to voice deep unease with the ongoing expansion of Israeli settlements in East Jerusalem and the West Bank. In April 2012 the British Secretary of State for Foreign and Commonwealth Affairs, William Hague, castigated settlement activity as 'the most significant and live threat to the viability of the two-state solution'. His comments came after the release of leaked reports from EU mission heads in Jerusalem and Ramallah that warned of a sharp rise in the number of attacks by militant settlers on Palestinians and their property. According to the reports, there were 411 recorded attacks leading to injury or property damage in 2011 compared with 132 in 2009. In more than 90% of cases passed to the Israeli authorities, no charges were laid against the perpetrators, which the reports suggested had given rise to the perception that settler violence was condoned by the Israeli Government. Israel denied colluding with militant settler leaders and continued to reject any linkage between settlement growth and conflict resolution.

With many senior positions in the dominant Likud party occupied by leaders from settler councils committed to consolidating control over the West Bank, the pressure remained on Netanyahu to demonstrate his pro-settlement credentials. In April 2012 the Israeli Prime Minister blocked an order by the Minister of Defence to evacuate hard-line settlers from a house that they had occupied in Hebron. Netanyahu subsequently withdrew his opposition to the evacuation, stating that the rule of law must prevail, but soon afterwards announced his intention to prevent the demolition of four West Bank settler outposts ordered by the Supreme Court on the grounds that they had been established without proper authorization. By the end of the month a special ministerial committee had granted retrospective approval to three of the outposts, effectively creating the first new settlements on the West Bank since 1999. The Supreme Court rejected the Government's attempt to save the fourth outpost, Ulpana, which had been built on private Palestinian land, ordering that it should be evacuated by July 2012. Following fierce lobbying by settler organizations, Netanyahu announced in June that Ulpana would be dismantled and re-sited within the nearby settlement of Beit El. In a further move to placate hard-line settlers, Netanyahu authorized the construction of an additional 300 homes in Beit El. The Prime Minister claimed that there was no contradiction between 'preserving the law and preserving the settlements'.

PALESTINIAN PRISONERS WIN CONCESSIONS

In April 2012 Palestinian prisoners in Israeli gaols began a hunger strike in protest against poor conditions and the use of administrative detention. Some 2,000 prisoners joined the protest, which, following a deal brokered by representatives of the Jordanian and Egyptian Governments, finally ended in mid-May, when several of the hunger strikers were reported to be close to death. Under the agreement, the Israeli Government pledged to examine gaol conditions, to end solitary confinement, to allow Gaza prisoners family visits and not to extend administrative detention terms without new evidence. For their part, Palestinian prisoner groups confirmed that they would end what Israeli officials termed the 'planning and direction of terrorist activity'.

An attack from Sinai on Israelis constructing the border fence with Egypt left a civilian worker and two of the assailants dead. The attack was reportedly carried out by an Egyptian and a Saudi belonging to an al-Qa'ida-affiliated organization, reinforcing Israel's concerns about the security situation in the Sinai. Several hours later an Israeli air-strike killed a member of Islamic Jihad in northern Gaza. The IDF claimed that the attack was unrelated to the Sinai incident. It did, however, provoke immediate retaliation in the form of rocket fire from Gaza. For the first time in many months Hamas's military wing claimed responsibility for some of the estimated 100 rockets fired from Gaza. At least seven Palestinians were killed in further air-strikes, including three non-combatants. Four Israeli border guards were also lightly injured before another Egyptian-mediated cease-fire led to the restoration of relative calm.

MURSI ELECTED IN EGYPT

Although Israeli leaders would have preferred a victory for former Prime Minister Ahmad Shafiq in Egypt's presidential election in June 2012, the eventual success of Muhammad Mursi, the candidate of the Muslim Brotherhood's Freedom and Justice Party, was not greeted with undue alarm in Israel. While the Brotherhood's ties with Hamas troubled the Israeli intelligence community, there was an acknowledgement that Mursi was unlikely to risk antagonizing the USA (which provided significant financial and military aid to Egypt) through any radical shift in policy towards Israel or the Palestinians. However, the sensitivities in the relationship were exposed with the publication in Israel in late July of a letter, purportedly sent by the new Egyptian President to his Israeli counterpart, in which Mursi expressed his support for a regional peace and the security of the Israeli people. An Egyptian government spokesman insisted that Mursi had not written the letter, although Israeli officials remained adamant that the communication had been sent from Egypt's embassy in Tel-Aviv.

Publicly, the Israeli Government expressed greater concern about the growing instability in Syria and in particular the security of that country's substantial chemical weapons arsenal. In July 2012 Netanyahu warned that Israel would be forced to act to prevent Hezbollah or other militant groups from acquiring these chemical weapons in the event of the Assad regime collapsing. He also blamed Hezbollah for a suicide bombing against a tourist bus in Bulgaria that left five Israelis dead and many more injured.

OPERATION PILLAR OF DEFENCE

There was a major escalation in tensions between Israel and Hamas in November 2012, following renewed exchanges between the Israeli military and Hamas militants in July. In response to protracted rocket fire from the Gaza Strip into southern Israel, Israeli forces began an intensive series of strikes from the air and sea against Hamas, Islamic Jihad and other militant groups, and their missile capabilities and weapons storage facilities. Among the targets of Operation Pillar of Defence was the head of Hamas's military wing, Ahmad Said Khalil al-Jabari, who, together with another Hamas official, was killed in an air-strike on 14 November. As the confrontation deepened, Hillary Clinton travelled to Israel for talks with Netanyahu and other government officials, and subsequently to Ramallah for discussions with Abbas, before proceeding to Cairo to meet with President Muhammad Mursi. It was reported that Israel had come under intense international pressure not to begin a ground offensive in Gaza. After eight days of confrontation, a cease-fire took effect on 21 November. Under its terms, Israel was to cease hostilities and targeted killings, enter discussions on the reopening of border crossings with Gaza, and ease restrictions on the movement of goods and people, while the Palestinian militant organizations were required to halt rocket attacks and border assaults. At the conclusion of hostilities, according to initial reporting by the UN Office for the Co-ordination of Humanitarian Affairs, some 103 civilians were killed and 153 people in total. Six Israelis were killed, four of whom were civilians.

On 29 November 2012 the UN General Assembly voted (by 138 votes to nine, with 41 abstentions) to award Palestine the status of Non-Member Observer State. Netanyahu denounced the decision, and reiterated that there could be no establishment of a Palestinian state in the absence of a settlement guaranteeing Israel's security. In early December the Israeli Ministry of Finance announced its intention to appropriate some NIS 460m. in tax and customs revenues due to the PA, in partial payment for debts owed for power supply. Also in early December Israel confirmed that it would proceed with its project to construct 3,000 settlement homes on land effectively separating East Jerusalem from the West Bank.

REGIONAL INSTABILITY

There was an escalation in tension in February 2013, when President Assad stated that Israel was attempting to destabilize Syria. In January Syria had accused Israel of carrying out an air-strike on Syrian territory. It was reported that the attack had targeted a weapons convoy bound for Lebanon, and presumed to be intended for use by Hezbollah. For its part, Syria claimed that a military research facility had been hit. Israel declined to comment on the allegations, although Israeli politicians continued to demonstrate their concern over the proliferation of arms and the increasing prominence of militant Islamist groups among the opposition forces in Syria, and the potential for the conflict to spill over into Lebanon. In early September the Israeli Government expressed its support for efforts by the interim, military-backed administration in Egypt to combat the growing presence of Islamist militants in the Sinai Peninsula, and the restrictions imposed by the Egyptian authorities on the transit of goods across the border into the Gaza Strip. Following the removal from power of President Mursi in July, the interim administration had sought to reduce Egypt's ties with Hamas and to curtail the activities of the Muslim Brotherhood (see the chapter on Egypt).

NEW ISRAELI GOVERNMENT

Meanwhile, at the Israeli general election of January 2013 Likud—in alliance with Israel Beytenu—remained the largest group in the Knesset, although the total number of seats held by those parties was reduced, compared with 2009. The centrist Yesh Atid party, which was predominantly focused on domestic issues, and the pro-settlement Jewish Home party both performed strongly and joined a new coalition Government formed by Netanyahu in early March. Despite the designation of Tzipi Livni as chief negotiator with a mandate to pursue talks with the PA, the allocation of the Jerusalem affairs and housing portfolios to members of Jewish Home was taken as a more significant indicator of the Government's priorities. Following the appointment of the new Israeli Government, President Obama visited the region, holding talks with Netanyahu in Israel and Abbas in Ramallah, and urged Israel to resume negotiations. Following subsequent 'shuttle' visits by the new US Secretary of State, John F. Kerry, Livni and Saeb Erakat travelled to Washington, DC, for preliminary talks at the end of July. All parties reportedly agreed an aim of reaching a limited accord within nine months. Amid much scepticism in the region and the wider international community, discussions continued in Jerusalem and Jericho in August and September, attended by Obama's Special Envoy for Israeli-Palestinian Negotiations, Martin Indyk.

DOCUMENTS ON PALESTINE

Note: The inclusion of a document does not imply the Editor's endorsement of its content.

DECLARATION OF FIRST WORLD ZIONIST CONGRESS

*The Congress, convened in Basle by Dr Theodor Herzl in August 1897, adopted the following programme.**

The aim of Zionism is to create for the Jewish people a home in Palestine secured by public law.

The Congress contemplates the following means to the attainment of this end:

1. The promotion on suitable lines, of the settlement of Palestine by Jewish agriculturists, artisans and tradesmen.
2. The organization and binding together of the whole of Jewry by means of appropriate institutions, local and general, in accordance with the laws of each country.
3. The strengthening of Jewish sentiment and national consciousness.
4. Preparatory steps towards obtaining government consent as are necessary, for the attainment of the aim of Zionism.

* Text supplied by courtesy of Josef Fraenkel.

MCMAHON CORRESPONDENCE*

Ten letters passed between Sir Henry McMahon, British High Commissioner in Cairo, and Sherif Husain of Mecca from July 1915 to March 1916. Husain offered Arab help in the war against the Turks if Britain would support the principle of an independent Arab state. The most important letter is that of 24 October 1915, from McMahon to Husain:

...I regret that you should have received from my last letter the impression that I regarded the question of limits and boundaries with coldness and hesitation; such was not the case, but it appeared to me that the time had not yet come when that question could be discussed in a conclusive manner.

I have realized, however, from your last letter that you regard this question as one of vital and urgent importance. I have, therefore, lost no time in informing the Government of Great Britain of the contents of your letter, and it is with great pleasure that I communicate to you on their behalf the following statement, which I am confident you will receive with satisfaction:

The two districts of Mersina and Alexandretta and portions of Syria lying to the west of the districts of Damascus, Homs, Hama and Aleppo cannot be said to be purely Arab, and should be excluded from the limits demanded.

With the above modification, and without prejudice to our existing treaties with Arab chiefs, we accept those limits.

As for those regions lying within those frontiers wherein Great Britain is free to act without detriment to the interest of her ally, France, I am empowered in the name of the Government of Great Britain to give the following assurances and make the following reply to your letter:

(1) Subject to the above modifications, Great Britain is prepared to recognize and support the independence of the Arabs in all the regions within the limits demanded by the Sherif of Mecca

(2) Great Britain will guarantee the Holy Places against all external aggression and will recognize their inviolability

(3) When the situation admits, Great Britain will give to the Arabs her advice and will assist them to establish what may appear to be the most suitable forms of government in those various territories

(4) On the other hand, it is understood that the Arabs have decided to seek the advice and guidance of Great Britain only, and that such European advisers and officials as may be required for the formation of a sound form of administration will be British

(5) With regard to the *vilayets* of Baghdad and Basra, the Arabs will recognize that the established position and interests of Great Britain necessitate special administrative arrangements in order to secure these territories from foreign aggression, to promote the welfare of the local populations and to safeguard our mutual economic interests

I am convinced that this declaration will assure you beyond all possible doubt of the sympathy of Great Britain towards the aspirations of her friends the Arabs and will result in a firm and lasting alliance, the immediate results of which will be the expulsion of the Turks from the Arab countries and the freeing of the Arab peoples from the Turkish yoke, which for so many years has pressed heavily upon them...

* British White Paper, Cmd. 5957, 1939.

ANGLO-FRANCO-RUSSIAN AGREEMENT (SYKES—PICOT AGREEMENT)

(April–May 1916)

*The allocation of portions of the Ottoman empire by the three powers was decided between them in an exchange of diplomatic notes. The Anglo-French agreement*dealing with Arab territories became known to Sherif Husain only after publication by the new Bolshevik Government of Russia in 1917:*

1. That France and Great Britain are prepared to recognize and protect an independent Arab State or a Confederation of Arab States in the areas (A) and (B) marked on the annexed map (*not reproduced here—Ed.*), under suzerainty of an Arab Chief. That in area (A) France, and in area (B) Great Britain shall have priority of right of enterprises and local loans. France in area (A) and Great Britain in area (B) shall alone supply foreign advisers or officials on the request of the Arab State or the Confederation of Arab States.

2. France in the Blue area and Great Britain in the Red area shall be at liberty to establish direct or indirect administration or control as they may desire or as they may deem fit to establish after agreement with the Arab State or Confederation of Arab States.

3. In the Brown area there shall be established an international administration of which the form will be decided upon after consultation with Russia, and after subsequent agreement with the other Allies and the representatives of the Sherif of Mecca.

4. That Great Britain be accorded

(*a*) The ports of Haifa and Acre

(*b*) Guarantee of a given supply of water from the Tigris and the Euphrates in area (A) for area (B)

His Majesty's Government, on their part, undertake that they will at no time enter into negotiations for the cession of Cyprus to any third Power without the previous consent of the French Government.

5. Alexandretta shall be a free port as regards the trade of the British Empire and there shall be no discrimination in treatment with regard to port dues or the extension of special privileges affecting British shipping and commerce; there shall be freedom of transit for British goods through Alexandretta and over railways through the Blue area, whether such goods are going to or coming from the Red area, area (A) or area (B); and there shall be no differentiation in treatment, direct or indirect, at the expense of British goods on any railway or of British goods and shipping in any port serving the areas in question.

Haifa shall be a free port as regards the trade of France, her colonies and protectorates, and there shall be no differentiation in treatment or privilege with regard to port dues against French shipping and commerce. There shall be freedom of transit through Haifa and over British railways through the Brown area, whether such goods are coming from or going to the Blue area, area (A) or area (B), and there shall be no differentiation in treatment, direct or indirect, at the expense of French goods on any railway or of French goods and shipping in any port serving the areas in question.

6. In area (A), the Baghdad Railway shall not be extended southwards beyond Mosul, and in area (B), it shall not be extended northwards beyond Samarra, until a railway connecting Baghdad with Aleppo along the basin of the Euphrates will have been completed, and then only with the concurrence of the two Governments.

7. Great Britain shall have the right to build, administer and be the sole owner of the railway connecting Haifa with area (B). She shall have, in addition, the right in perpetuity and at all times of carrying troops on that line. It is understood by both Governments that this railway is intended to facilitate communication between Baghdad and Haifa, and it is further understood that, in the event of technical difficulties and expenditure incurred in the maintenance of this line in the Brown area rendering the execution of the project impracticable, the French Government will be prepared to consider plans for enabling the line in question to traverse the polygon formed by Banias-Umm Qais-Salkhad-Tall 'Osda-Mismieh before reaching area (B).

(*Clause 8 referred to customs tariffs.*)

9. It is understood that the French Government will at no time initiate any negotiations for the cession of their rights and will not cede their prospective rights in the Blue area to any third Power other than the Arab State or Confederation of Arab States, without the previous consent of His Majesty's Government who, on their part, give the French Government a similar undertaking in respect of the Red area.

10. The British and French Governments shall agree to abstain from acquiring and to withhold their consent to a third Power acquiring territorial possessions in the Arabian Peninsula; nor shall they consent to the construction by a third Power of a naval base in the islands on the eastern seaboard of the Red Sea. This, however, will not prevent such rectification of the Aden boundary as might be found necessary in view of the recent Turkish attack.

11. The negotiations with the Arabs concerning the frontiers of the Arab State or Confederation of Arab States shall be pursued through the same channel as heretofore in the name of the two Powers.

12. It is understood, moreover, that measures for controlling the importation of arms into the Arab territory will be considered by the two Governments.

* E. L. Woodward and Rohan Butler (Eds). *Documents on British Foreign Policy 1919–1939.* First Series, Vol. IV, 1919. London, HMSO, 1952.

BALFOUR DECLARATION

(2 November 1917)

Balfour was British Secretary of State for Foreign Affairs, Rothschild the British Zionist leader.

Dear Lord Rothschild,

I have much pleasure in conveying to you on behalf of His Majesty's Government the following declaration of sympathy with Jewish Zionist aspirations, which has been submitted to and approved by the Cabinet.

'His Majesty's Government view with favour the establishment in Palestine of a national home for the Jewish people, and will use their best endeavours to facilitate the achievement of this object, it being clearly understood that nothing shall be done which may prejudice the civil and religious rights of existing non-Jewish communities in Palestine, or the rights and political status enjoyed by Jews in any other country.'

I should be grateful if you would bring this declaration to the knowledge of the Zionist Federation.

Yours sincerely, Arthur James Balfour

HOGARTH MESSAGE*

(4 January 1918)

The following is the text of a message which Commander D. G. Hogarth, CMG, RNVR, of the Arab Bureau in Cairo, was instructed on 4 January 1918 to deliver to King Husain of the Hedjaz at Jeddah:

1. The *Entente* Powers are determined that the Arab race shall be given full opportunity of once again forming a nation in the world. This can only be achieved by the Arabs themselves uniting, and Great Britain and her Allies will pursue a policy with this ultimate unity in view.

2. So far as Palestine is concerned, we are determined that no people shall be subject to another, but—

(*a*) In view of the fact that there are in Palestine shrines, Wakfs and Holy places, sacred in some cases to Moslems alone, to Jews alone, to Christians alone, and in others to two or all three, and inasmuch as these places are of interest to vast masses of people outside Palestine and Arabia, there must be a special régime to deal with these places approved of by the world.

(*b*) As regards the Mosque of Omar, it shall be considered as a Moslem concern alone and shall not be subjected directly or indirectly to any non-Moslem authority.

3. Since the Jewish opinion of the world is in favour of a return of Jews to Palestine, and inasmuch as this opinion must remain a constant factor, and, further, as His Majesty's Government view with favour the realization of this aspiration, His Majesty's Government are determined that in so far as is compatible with the freedom of the existing population, both economic and political, no obstacle should be put in the way of the realization of this ideal.

In this connection the friendship of world Jewry to the Arab cause is equivalent to support in all States where Jews have political influence. The leaders of the movement are determined to bring about the success of Zionism by friendship and co-operation with the Arabs, and such an offer is not one to be lightly thrown aside.

* British White Paper, Cmd. 5964, 1939.

ANGLO-FRENCH DECLARATION*

(7 November 1918)

The object aimed at by France and Great Britain in prosecuting in the East the war let loose by the ambition of Germany is the complete and definite emancipation of the peoples so long oppressed by the Turks and the establishment of national Governments and Administrations deriving their authority from the initiative and free choice of the indigenous populations.

In order to carry out these intentions France and Great Britain are at one in encouraging and assisting the establishments of indigenous Governments and Administrations in Syria and Mesopotamia, now liberated by the Allies, and in the territories the liberation of which they are engaged in securing and recognizing these as soon as they are actually established.

Far from wishing to impose on the populations of these regions any particular institutions they are only concerned to ensure by their support and by adequate assistance the regular working of Governments and Administrations freely chosen by the populations themselves. To secure impartial and equal justice for all, to facilitate the economic development of the country by inspiring and encouraging local initiative, to favour the diffusion of education, to put an end to dissensions that have too long been taken advantage of by Turkish policy which the two Allied Governments uphold in the liberated territories.

* Report of a Committee set up to consider Certain Correspondence between Sir Henry McMahon and the Sherif of Mecca in 1915 and 1916, 16 March 1939 (British White Paper, Cmd. 5974).

RECOMMENDATIONS OF THE KING-CRANE COMMISSION*

(28 August 1919)

The Commission was set up by President Wilson of the USA to determine which power should receive the Mandate for Palestine. The following are extracts from their recommendations on Syria:

1. We recommend, as most important of all, and in strict harmony with our Instructions, that whatever foreign administration (whether of one or more Powers) is brought into Syria, should come in, not at all as a colonising Power in the old sense of that term, but as a Mandatory under the League of Nations with the clear consciousness that 'the well-being and development' of the Syrian people form for it a 'sacred trust'.

2. We recommend, in the second place, that the unity of Syria be preserved, in accordance with the earnest petition of the great majority of the people of Syria.

3. We recommend, in the third place, that Syria be placed under one mandatory Power, as the natural way to secure real and efficient unity.

4. We recommend, in the fourth place, that Amir Faisal be made the head of the new united Syrian State.

5. We recommend, in the fifth place, serious modification of the extreme Zionist program for Palestine of unlimited immigration of Jews, looking finally to making Palestine distinctly a Jewish State.

(1) The Commissioners began their study of Zionism with minds predisposed in its favor, but the actual facts in Palestine, coupled with the force of the general principles proclaimed by the Allies and accepted by the Syrians have driven them to the recommendation here made.

(2) The Commission was abundantly supplied with literature on the Zionist program by the Zionist Commission to Palestine; heard in conferences much concerning the Zionist colonies and their claims; and personally saw something of what had been accomplished. They found much to approve in the aspirations and plans of the Zionists, and had warm appreciation for the devotion of many of the colonists, and for their success, by modern methods in overcoming great, natural obstacles.

(3) The Commission recognised also that definite encouragement had been given to the Zionists by the Allies in Mr Balfour's often-quoted statement, in its approval by other representatives of the Allies. If, however, the strict terms of the Balfour Statement are adhered to—favoring 'the establishment in Palestine of a national home for the Jewish people', 'it being clearly understood that nothing shall be done which may prejudice the civil and religious rights of existing non-Jewish communities in Palestine'—it can hardly be doubted that the extreme Zionist program must be greatly modified. For 'a national home for the Jewish people' is not equivalent to making Palestine into a Jewish State; nor can the erection of such a Jewish State be accomplished without the gravest trespass upon the 'civil and religious rights of existing non-Jewish communities in Palestine'. The fact came out repeatedly in the Commission's conference with Jewish representatives, that the Zionists looked forward to a practically complete dispossession of the present non-Jewish inhabitants of Palestine, by various forms of purchase.

In his address of 4 July 1918, President Wilson laid down the following principle as one of the four great 'ends for which the associated peoples of the world were fighting': 'The settlement of every question, whether of territory, of sovereignty, of economic arrangement, or of political relationship upon the basis of the free acceptance of that settlement by the people immediately concerned, and not upon the basis of the material interest or advantage of any other nation or people which may desire a different settlement for the sake of its own exterior influence or mastery.' If that principle is to rule, and so the wishes of Palestine's population are to be decisive as to what is to be done with Palestine, then it is to be remembered that the non-Jewish population of Palestine—nearly nine-tenths of the whole—are emphatically against the entire Zionist program. The tables show that there was no one thing upon which the population of Palestine were more agreed than upon this. To subject a people so minded to unlimited Jewish immigration, and to steady financial and social pressure to surrender the land, would be a gross violation of the principle just quoted, and of the people's rights, though it kept within the forms of law.

It is to be noted also that the feeling against the Zionist program is not confined to Palestine, but shared very generally by the people throughout Syria, as our conferences clearly showed. More then 72%—1,350 in all—of all the petitions in the whole of Syria were directed against the Zionist program. Only two requests—those for a united Syria and for independence—had a larger support. This general feeling was duly voiced by the General Syrian Congress in the seventh, eighth and tenth resolutions of their statement.

The Peace Conference should not shut its eyes to the fact that the anti-Zionist feeling in Palestine and Syria is intense and not lightly to be flouted. No British officer, consulted by the Commissioners, believed that the Zionist program could be carried out except by force of arms. The officers generally thought that a force of not less than 50,000 soldiers would be required even to initiate the program. That of itself is evidence of a strong sense of the injustice of the Zionist program, on the part of the non-Jewish populations of Palestine and Syria. Decisions requiring armies to carry out are sometimes necessary, but they are surely not gratuitously to be taken in the interests of serious injustice. For the initial claim, often submitted by Zionist representatives, that they have a 'right' to Palestine, based on an occupation of 2,000 years ago, can hardly be seriously considered.

There is a further consideration that cannot justly be ignored, if the world is to look forward to Palestine becoming a definitely Jewish State, however gradually that may take place. That consideration grows out of the fact that Palestine is the Holy Land for Jews, Christians, and Moslems alike. Millions of Christians and Moslems all over the world are quite as much concerned as the Jews with conditions in Palestine, especially with those conditions which touch upon religious feelings and rights. The relations in these matters in Palestine are most delicate and difficult. With the best possible intentions, it may be doubted whether the Jews could possibly seem to either Christians or Moslems proper guardians of the holy places, or custodians of the Holy Land as a whole.

The reason is this: The places which are most sacred to Christians—those having to do with Jesus—and which are also sacred to Moslems, are not only not sacred to Jews, but abhorrent to them. It is simply impossible, under those circumstances, for Moslems and Christians to feel satisfied to have these places in Jewish hands, or under the custody of Jews. There are still other places about which Moslems must have the same feeling. In fact, from this point of view, the Moslems, just because the sacred places of all three religions are sacred to them, have made very naturally much more satisfactory custodians of the holy places than the Jews could be. It must be believed that the precise meaning in this respect of the complete Jewish occupation of Palestine has not been fully sensed by those who urge the extreme Zionist program. For it would intensify, with a certainty like fate, the anti-Jewish feeling both in Palestine and in all other portions of the world which look to Palestine as the Holy Land.

In view of all these considerations, and with a deep sense of sympathy for the Jewish cause, the Commissioners feel bound to recommend that only a greatly reduced Zionist program be attempted by the Peace Conference, and even that, only very gradually initiated. This would have to mean that Jewish immigration should be definitely limited, and that the project for making Palestine distinctly a Jewish commonwealth should be given up.

There would then be no reason why Palestine could not be included in a united Syrian State, just as other portions of the country, the holy places being cared for by an international and inter-religious commission, somewhat as at present, under the oversight and approval of the Mandatory and of the League of Nations. The Jews, of course, would have representation upon this commission.

* US Department of State. *Papers Relating to the Foreign Relations of the United States. The Paris Peace Conference 1919.* Vol. XII. Washington, 1947.

ARTICLE 22 OF THE COVENANT OF THE LEAGUE OF NATIONS

(28 April 1919)

To those colonies and territories which as a consequence of the late War have ceased to be under the sovereignty of the States which formerly governed them and which are inhabited by peoples not yet able to stand by themselves under the strenuous conditions of the modern world, there should be applied the principle that the well-being and development of such peoples form a sacred trust of civilization and that securities for the performance of this trust should be embodied in this Covenant.

The best method of giving practical effect to this principle is that the tutelage of such peoples should be entrusted to advanced nations who by reason of their resources, their experience or their geographical position can best undertake this responsibility, and who are willing to accept it, and that this tutelage should be exercised by them as Mandatories on behalf of the League.

The character of the Mandate must differ according to the stage of the development of the people, the geographical situation of the territory, its economic conditions and other similar circumstances.

Certain communities formerly belonging to the Turkish Empire have reached a stage of development where their existence as independent nations can be provisionally recognized subject to the rendering of administrative advice and assistance by a Mandatory until such time as they are able to stand alone. The wishes of these communities must be a principal consideration in the selection of the Mandatory. [...]

In every case of Mandate, the Mandatory shall render to the Council an annual report in reference to the territory committed to its charge.

The degree of authority, control, or administration to be exercised by the Mandatory shall, if not previously agreed upon by the Members of the League, be explicitly defined in each case by the Council.

A permanent Commission shall be constituted to receive and examine the annual reports of the Mandatories and to advise the Council on all matters relating to the observance of the Mandates.

CHURCHILL MEMORANDUM*

(3 June 1922)

The Secretary of State for the Colonies has given renewed consideration to the existing political situation in Palestine, with a very earnest desire to arrive at a settlement of the outstanding questions which have given rise to uncertainty and unrest among certain sections of the population. After consultation with the High Commissioner for Palestine the following statement has been drawn up. It summarizes the essential parts of the correspondence that has already taken place between the Secretary of State and a Delegation from the Moslem Christian Society of Palestine, which has been for some time in England, and it states the further conclusions which have since been reached.

The tension which has prevailed from time to time in Palestine is mainly due to apprehensions, which are entertained both by sections of the Arab and by sections of the Jewish population. These apprehensions, so far as the Arabs are concerned, are partly based upon exaggerated interpretations of the meaning of the Declaration favouring the establishment of a Jewish National Home in Palestine, made on behalf of His Majesty's Government on 2 November 1917. Unauthorized statements have been made to the effect that the purpose in view is to create a wholly Jewish Palestine. Phrases have been used such as that Palestine is to become 'as Jewish as England is English'. His Majesty's Government regard any such expectation as impracticable and have no such aim in view. Nor have they at any time contemplated, as appears to be feared by the Arab Delegation, the disappearance or the subordination of the Arabic population, language or culture in Palestine. They would draw attention to the fact that the terms of the Declaration referred to do not contemplate that Palestine as a whole should be converted into a Jewish National Home, but that such a Home should be founded *in Palestine*. In this connection it has been observed with satisfaction that at the meeting of the Zionist Congress, the supreme governing body of the Zionist Organization, held at Carlsbad in September 1921, a resolution was passed expressing as the official statement of Zionist aims 'the determination of the Jewish people to live with the Arab people on terms of unity and mutual respect, and together with them to make the common home into a flourishing community, the upbuilding of which may assure to each of its peoples an undisturbed national development'.

It is also necessary to point out that the Zionist Commission in Palestine, now termed the Palestine Zionist Executive, has not desired to possess, and does not possess, any share in the general administration of the country. Nor does the special position assigned to the Zionist Organization in Article IV of the Draft Mandate for Palestine imply any such functions. That special position relates to the measures to be taken in Palestine affecting the Jewish population, and contemplates that the Organization may assist in the general development of the country, but does not entitle it to share in any degree in its Government.

Further, it is contemplated that the status of all citizens of Palestine in the eyes of the law shall be Palestinian, and it has never been intended that they, or any section of them, should possess any other juridical status.

So far as the Jewish population of Palestine are concerned, it appears that some among them are apprehensive that His Majesty's Government may depart from the policy embodied in the Declaration of 1917. It is necessary, therefore, once more to affirm that these fears are unfounded, and that the Declaration, re-affirmed by the Conference of the Principal Allied Powers at San Remo and again in the Treaty of Sèvres, is not susceptible of change.

During the last two or three generations the Jews have recreated in Palestine a community, now numbering 80,000, of whom about one-fourth are farmers or workers upon the land. This community has its own political organs; an elected assembly for the direction of its domestic concerns; elected councils in the towns; and an organization for the control of its schools. It has its elected Chief Rabbinate and Rabbinical Council for the direction of its religious affairs. Its business is conducted in Hebrew as a vernacular language, and a Hebrew Press serves its needs. It has its distinctive intellectual life and displays considerable economic activity. This community, then, with its town and country population, its political, religious and social organizations, its own language, its own customs, its own life, has in fact 'national' characteristics. When it is asked what is meant by the development of the Jewish National Home in Palestine, it may be answered that it is not the imposition of a Jewish nationality upon the inhabitants of Palestine as a whole, but the further development of the existing Jewish community, with the assistance of Jews in other parts of the world, in order that it may become a centre in which the Jewish people as a whole may take, on grounds of religion and race, an interest and a pride. But in order that this community should have the best prospect of free development and provide a full opportunity for the Jewish people to display its capacities, it is essential that it should know that it is in Palestine as of right and not on sufferance. That is the reason why it is necessary that the existence of a Jewish National Home in Palestine should be internationally guaranteed, and that it should be formally recognized to rest upon ancient historic connection.

This, then, is the interpretation which His Majesty's Government place upon the Declaration of 1917, and, so understood, the Secretary of State is of opinion that it does not contain or imply anything which need cause either alarm to the Arab population of Palestine or disappointment to the Jews.

For the fulfilment of this policy it is necessary that the Jewish community in Palestine should be able to increase its numbers by immigration. This immigration cannot be so great in volume as to exceed whatever may be the economic capacity of the country at the time to absorb new arrivals. It is essential to ensure that the immigrants should not be a burden upon the people of Palestine as a whole, and that they should not deprive any section of the present population of their employment. Hitherto the immigration has fulfilled these conditions. The number of immigrants since the British occupation has been about 25,000...

* Palestine, Correspondence with the Palestine Arab Delegation and the Zionist Organization (British White Paper, Cmd. 1700), pp. 17–21.

MANDATE FOR PALESTINE*

(24 July 1922)

The Council of the League of Nations:

Whereas the Principal Allied Powers have agreed, for the purpose of giving effect to the provisions of Article 22 of the Covenant of the League of Nations to entrust to a Mandatory selected by the said Powers the administration of the territory of Palestine, which formerly belonged to the Turkish Empire, within such boundaries as may be fixed by them; and

Whereas the Principal Allied Powers have also agreed that the Mandatory should be responsible for putting into effect the declaration originally made on 2 November 1917 by the Government of His Britannic Majesty, and adopted by the said Powers, in favour of the establishment in Palestine of a National Home for the Jewish people, it being clearly understood that nothing should be done which might prejudice the civil and religious rights of existing non-Jewish communities in Palestine, or the rights and political status enjoyed by Jews in any other country; and

Whereas recognition has thereby been given to the historical connection of the Jewish people with Palestine and to the grounds for reconstituting their National Home in that country; and

Whereas the Principal Allied Powers have selected His Britannic Majesty as the Mandatory for Palestine; and

Whereas the Mandate in respect of Palestine has been formulated in the following terms and submitted to the Council of the League for approval; and

Whereas His Britannic Majesty has accepted the Mandate in respect of Palestine and undertaken to exercise it on behalf of the League of Nations in conformity with the following provisions; and

Whereas by the aforementioned Article 22 (paragraph 8), it is provided that the degree of authority, control or administration to be exercised by the Mandatory, not having been previously agreed upon by the Members of the League, shall be explicitly defined by the Council of the League of Nations;

Confirming the said Mandate, defines its terms as follows:

ARTICLE 1. The Mandatory shall have full powers of legislation and of administration, save as they may be limited by the terms of this Mandate.

ARTICLE 2. The Mandatory shall be responsible for placing the country under such political, administrative and economic conditions as will secure the establishment of the Jewish National Home, as laid down in the preamble, and the development of self-governing institutions, and also for safeguarding the civil and religious rights of all the inhabitants of Palestine, irrespective of race and religion.

ARTICLE 3. The Mandatory shall, so far as circumstances permit, encourage local autonomy.

ARTICLE 4. An appropriate Jewish Agency shall be recognized as a public body for the purpose of advising and co-operating with the Administration of Palestine in such economic, social and other matters as may affect the establishment of the Jewish National Home and the interests of the Jewish population in Palestine, and, subject always to the control of the Administration, to assist and take part in the development of the country.

The Zionist organization, so long as its organization and constitution are in the opinion of the Mandatory appropriate, shall be recognized as such agency. It shall take steps in consultation with His Britannic Majesty's Government to secure the co-operation of all Jews who are willing to assist in the establishment of the Jewish National Home.

ARTICLE 5. The Mandatory shall be responsible for seeing that no Palestine territory shall be ceded or leased to, or in any way placed under the control of, the Government of any foreign Power.

ARTICLE 6. The Administration of Palestine, while ensuring that the rights and position of other sections of the population are not prejudiced, shall facilitate Jewish immigration under suitable conditions and shall encourage, in co-operation with the Jewish Agency referred to in Article 4, close settlement by Jews on the land, including State lands and waste lands not required for public purposes.

ARTICLE 7. The Administration of Palestine shall be responsible for enacting a nationality law. There shall be included in this law provisions framed so as to facilitate the acquisition of Palestinian citizenship by Jews who take up their permanent residence in Palestine.

ARTICLE 13. All responsibility in connection with the Holy Places and religious buildings or sites in Palestine, including that of preserving existing rights and of securing free access to the Holy Places, religious buildings and sites and the free exercise of worship, while ensuring the requirements of public order and decorum, is assumed by the Mandatory, who shall be responsible solely to the League of Nations in all matters connected herewith, provided that nothing in this Article shall prevent the Mandatory from entering into such arrangements as he may deem reasonable with the Administration for the purpose of carrying the provisions of this Article into effect; and provided also that nothing in this Mandate shall be construed as conferring upon the Mandatory authority to interfere with the fabric of the management of purely Moslem sacred shrines, the immunities of which are guaranteed.

ARTICLE 14. A special Commission shall be appointed by the Mandatory to study, define and determine the rights and claims in connection with the Holy Places and the rights and claims relating to the different religious communities in Palestine. The method of nomination, the composition and the functions of this Commission shall be submitted to the Council of the League for its approval, and the Commission shall not be appointed or enter upon its functions without the approval of the Council.

ARTICLE 28. In the event of the termination of the Mandate hereby conferred upon the Mandatory, the Council of the League of Nations shall make such arrangements as may be deemed necessary for safe-guarding in perpetuity, under guarantee of the League, the rights secured by Articles 13 and 14, and shall use its influence for securing, under the guarantee of the League, that the Government of Palestine will fully honour the financial obligations legitimately incurred by the Administration of Palestine during the period of the Mandate, including the rights of public servants to pensions or gratuities.

* British White Paper, Cmd. 1785.

REPORT OF PALESTINE ROYAL COMMISSION (PEEL COMMISSION)*

(July 1937)

The Commission under Lord Peel was appointed in 1936. The following are extracts from recommendations made in Ch. XXII:

Having reached the conclusion that there is no possibility of solving the Palestine problem under the existing Mandate (or even under a scheme of cantonization), the Commission recommend the termination of the present Mandate on the basis of Partition and put forward a definite scheme which they consider to be practicable, honourable and just. The scheme is as follows:

The Mandate for Palestine should terminate and be replaced by a Treaty System in accordance with the precedent set in Iraq and Syria.

Under Treaties to be negotiated by the Mandatory with the Government of Transjordan and representatives of the Arabs of Palestine on the one hand, and with the Zionist Organization on the other, it would be declared that two sovereign independent States would shortly be established—(1) an Arab State consisting of Transjordan united with that part of Palestine allotted to the Arabs, (2) a Jewish State consisting of that part of Palestine allotted to the Jews. The Mandatory would undertake to support any requests for admission to the League of Nations made by the Governments of the Arab and Jewish States. The Treaties would include strict guarantees for the protection of minorities. Military Conventions would be attached to the Treaties.

A new Mandate should be instituted to execute the trust of maintaining the sanctity of Jerusalem and Bethlehem and ensuring free and safe access to them for all the world. An enclave should be demarcated to which this Mandate should apply, extending from a point north of Jerusalem to a point south of Bethlehem, and access to the sea should be provided by a corridor extending from Jerusalem to Jaffa. The policy of the Balfour Declaration would not apply to the Mandated Area.

The Jewish State should pay a subvention to the Arab State. A Finance Commission should be appointed to advise as to its amount and as to the division of the public debt of Palestine and other financial questions.

In view of the backwardness of Transjordan, Parliament should be asked to make a grant of £2,000,000 to the Arab State.

* *Palestine Royal Commission: Report*, 1937 (British Blue Book, Cmd. 5479).

WHITE PAPER*

(May 1939)

The main recommendations are extracted below:

10....His Majesty's Government make the following declaration of their intentions regarding the future government of Palestine:

(i) The objective of His Majesty's Government is the establishment within ten years of an independent Palestine State in such treaty relations with the United Kingdom as will provide satisfactorily for the commercial and strategic requirements of both countries in the future. This proposal for the establishment of the independent State would involve consultation with the Council of the League of Nations with a view to the termination of the Mandate.

(ii) The independent State should be one in which Arabs and Jews share in government in such a way as to ensure that the essential interests of each community are safeguarded.

(iii) The establishment of the independent State will be preceded by a transitional period throughout which His Majesty's Government will retain responsibility for the government of the country. During the transitional period the people of Palestine will be given an increasing part in the government of their country. Both sections of the population will have an opportunity to participate in the machinery of government, and the process will be carried on whether or not they both avail themselves of it.

(iv) As soon as peace and order have been sufficiently restored in Palestine steps will be taken to carry out this policy of giving the people of Palestine an increasing part in the government of their country, the objective being to place Palestinians in charge of all the Departments of Government, with the assistance of British advisers and subject to the control of the High Commissioner. With this object in view His Majesty's Government will be prepared immediately to arrange that Palestinians shall be placed in charge of certain Departments, with British advisers. The Palestinian heads of Departments will sit on the Executive Council, which advises the High Commissioner. Arab and Jewish representatives will be invited to serve as heads of Departments approximately in proportion to their respective populations. The number of Palestinians in charge of Departments will be increased as circumstances permit until all heads of Departments are Palestinians, exercising the administrative and advisory functions which are at present performed by British officials. When that stage is reached consideration will be given to the question of converting the Executive Council into a Council of Ministers with a consequential change in the status and functions of the Palestinian heads of Departments.

(v) His Majesty's Government make no proposals at this stage regarding the establishment of an elective legislature. Nevertheless they would regard this as an appropriate constitutional development, and, should public opinion in Palestine hereafter show itself in favour of such a development, they will be prepared, provided that local conditions permit, to establish the necessary machinery.

(vi) At the end of five years from the restoration of peace and order, an appropriate body representative of the people of Palestine and of His Majesty's Government will be set up to review the working of the constitutional arrangements during the transitional period and to consider and make recommendations regarding the Constitution of the independent Palestine State.

(vii) His Majesty's Government will require to be satisfied that in the treaty contemplated by sub-paragraph (i) or in the Constitution contemplated by sub-paragraph (vi) adequate provision has been made for:

(*a*) the security of, and freedom of access to, the Holy Places, and the protection of the interests and property of the various religious bodies

(*b*) the protection of the different communities in Palestine in accordance with the obligations of His Majesty's Government to both Arabs and Jews and for the special position in Palestine of the Jewish National Home

(*c*) such requirements to meet the strategic situation as may be regarded as necessary by His Majesty's Government in the light of the circumstances then existing

His Majesty's Government will also require to be satisfied that the interests of certain foreign countries in Palestine, for the preservation of which they are presently responsible, are adequately safeguarded.

(viii) His Majesty's Government will do everything in their power to create conditions which will enable the independent Palestine State to come into being within ten years. If, at the end of ten years, it appears to His Majesty's Government that, contrary to their hope, circumstances require the postponement of the establishment of the independent State, they will consult with representatives of the people of Palestine, the Council of the League of Nations and the neighbouring Arab States before deciding on such a postponement. If His Majesty's Government come to the conclusion that postponement is unavoidable, they will invite the co-operation of these parties in framing plans for the future with a view to achieving the desired objective at the earliest possible date.

14....they believe that they will be acting consistently with their Mandatory obligations to both Arabs and Jews, and in the manner best calculated to serve the interests of the whole people of Palestine by adopting the following proposals regarding immigration:

(i) Jewish immigration during the next five years will be at a rate which, if economic absorptive capacity permits, will bring the Jewish population up to approximately one-third of the total population of the country. Taking into account the expected natural increase of the Arab and Jewish populations, and the number of illegal Jewish immigrants now in the country, this would allow for the admission, as from the beginning of April this year, of some 75,000 immigrants over the next five years. These immigrants would, subject to the criterion of economic absorptive capacity, be admitted as follows:

(*a*) For each of the next five years a quota of 10,000 Jewish immigrants will be allowed, on the understanding that a shortage in any one year may be added to the quotas for subsequent years, within the five-year period, if economic absorptive capacity permits

(*b*) In addition, as a contribution towards the solution of the Jewish refugee problem, 25,000 refugees will be admitted as soon as the High Commissioner is satisfied that adequate provision for their maintenance is ensured, special consideration being given to refugee children and dependants

(ii) The existing machinery for ascertaining economic absorptive capacity will be retained, and the High Commissioner will have the ultimate responsibility for deciding the limits of economic capacity. Before each periodic decision is taken, Jewish and Arab representatives will be consulted.

(iii) After the period of five years no further Jewish immigration will be permitted unless the Arabs of Palestine are prepared to acquiesce in it.

(iv) His Majesty's Government are determined to check illegal immigration, and further preventive measures are being adopted. The numbers of any Jewish illegal immigrants who, despite these measures, may succeed in coming into the country and cannot be deported will be deducted from the yearly quotas.

15. His Majesty's Government are satisfied that, when the immigration over five years which is now contemplated has taken place they will not be justified in facilitating, nor will they be under any obligation to facilitate, the further development of the Jewish National Home by immigration regardless of the wishes of the Arab population.

16. The Administration of Palestine is required, under Article 6 of the Mandate, 'while ensuring that the rights and position of other sections of the population are not prejudiced', to encourage 'close settlement by Jews on the land', and no restriction has been imposed hitherto on the transfer of land from Arabs to Jews. The Reports of several expert Commissions have indicated that, owing to the natural growth of the Arab population and the steady sale in recent years of Arab land to Jews, there is now in certain areas no room for further transfers of Arab land, whilst in some other areas such transfers of land must be restricted if Arab cultivators are to maintain their existing standard of life and a considerable landless Arab population is not soon to be created. In these circumstances, the High Commissioner will be given general powers to prohibit and regulate transfers of land. These powers will date from the publication of this statement of Policy and the High Commissioner will retain them throughout the transitional period.

17. The policy of the Government will be directed towards the development of the land and the improvement, where possible, of methods of cultivation. In the light of such development it

will be open to the High Commissioner, should he be satisfied that the 'rights and position' of the Arab population will be duly preserved, to review and modify any orders passed relating to the prohibition or restriction of the transfer of land.

* British White Paper, Cmd. 6019.

BILTMORE PROGRAMME*

(11 May 1942)

Representatives of Zionist organizations, including the World Zionist Organization and the Jewish Agency, attended a six-day Extraordinary Zionist Conference, held at the Biltmore Hotel in New York, USA.

The following programme was approved by a Zionist Conference held in the Biltmore Hotel, New York City:

1. American Zionists assembled in this Extraordinary Conference reaffirm their unequivocal devotion to the cause of democratic freedom and international justice to which the people of the United States, allied with the other United Nations, have dedicated themselves, and give expression to their faith in the ultimate victory of humanity and justice over lawlessness and brute force.

2. This Conference offers a message of hope and encouragement to their fellow Jews in the Ghettos and concentration camps of Hitler-dominated Europe and prays that their hour of liberation may not be far distant.

3. The Conference sends its warmest greetings to the Jewish Agency Executive in Jerusalem, to the Va'ad Leumi, and to the whole Yishuv in Palestine, and expresses its profound admiration for their steadfastness and achievements in the face of peril and great difficulties...

4. In our generation, and in particular in the course of the past twenty years, the Jewish people have awakened and transformed their ancient homeland; from 50,000 at the end of the last war their numbers have increased to more than 500,000. They have made the waste places to bear fruit and the desert to blossom. Their pioneering achievements in agriculture and in industry, embodying new patterns of co-operative endeavour, have written a notable page in the history of colonization.

5. In the new values thus created, their Arab neighbours in Palestine have shared. The Jewish people in its own work of national redemption welcomes the economic, agricultural and national development of the Arab peoples and states. The Conference reaffirms the stand previously adopted at Congresses of the World Zionist Organization, expressing the readiness and the desire of the Jewish people for full co-operation with their Arab neighbours.

6. The Conference calls for the fulfilment of the original purpose of the Balfour Declaration and the Mandate which *'recognizing the historical connection of the Jewish people with Palestine'* was to afford them the opportunity, as stated by President Wilson, to found there a Jewish Commonwealth.

The Conference affirms its unalterable rejection of the White Paper of May 1939 and denies its moral or legal validity. The White Paper seeks to limit, and in fact to nullify Jewish rights to immigration and settlement in Palestine, and, as stated by Mr Winston Churchill in the House of Commons in May 1939, constitutes 'a breach and repudiation of the Balfour Declaration'. The policy of the White Paper is cruel and indefensible in its denial of sanctuary to Jews fleeing from Nazi persecution; and at a time when Palestine has become a focal point in the war front of the United Nations, and Palestine Jewry must provide all available manpower for farm and factory and camp, it is in direct conflict with the interests of the allied war effort.

7. In the struggle against the forces of aggression and tyranny, of which Jews were the earliest victims, and which now menace the Jewish National Home, recognition must be given to the right of the Jews of Palestine to play their full part in the war effort and in the defence of their country, through a Jewish military force fighting under its own flag and under the high command of the United Nations.

8. The Conference declares that the new world order that will follow victory cannot be established on foundations of peace, justice and equality, unless the problem of Jewish homelessness is finally solved.

The Conference urges that the gates of Palestine be opened; that the Jewish Agency be vested with control of immigration into Palestine and with the necessary authority for upbuilding the country, including the development of its unoccupied and uncultivated lands; and that Palestine be established as a Jewish Commonwealth integrated in the structure of the new democratic world.

Then and only then will the age-old wrong to the Jewish people be righted.

* Text supplied by courtesy of Josef Fraenkel.

UN GENERAL ASSEMBLY RESOLUTION ON THE FUTURE GOVERNMENT OF PALESTINE (PARTITION RESOLUTION)

(29 November 1947)

The General Assembly,

Having met in special session at the request of the mandatory Power to constitute and instruct a special committee to prepare for the consideration of the question of the future government of Palestine at the second regular session;

Having constituted a Special Committee and instructed it to investigate all questions and issues relevant to the problem of Palestine, and to prepare proposals for the solution of the problem, and

Having received and examined the report of the Special Committee (document A/364) including a number of unanimous recommendations and a plan of partition with economic union approved by the majority of the Special Committee,

Considers that the present situation in Palestine is one which is likely to impair the general welfare and friendly relations among nations;

Takes note of the declaration by the mandatory Power that it plans to complete its evacuation of Palestine by 1 August 1948;

Recommends to the United Kingdom, as the mandatory Power for Palestine, and to all other Members of the United Nations the adoption and implementation, with regard to the future government of Palestine, of the Plan of Partition with Economic Union set out below;

Requests that

(*a*) The Security Council take the necessary measures as provided for in the plan for its implementation;

(*b*) The Security Council consider, if circumstances during the transitional period require such consideration, whether the situation in Palestine constitutes a threat to the peace. If it decides that such a threat exists, and in order to maintain international peace and security, the Security Council should supplement the authorization of the General Assembly by taking measures, under Articles 39 and 41 of the Charter, to empower the United Nations Commission, as provided in this resolution, to exercise in Palestine the functions which are assigned to it by this resolution;

(*c*) The Security Council determine as a threat to the peace, breach of the peace or act of aggression, in accordance with Article 39 of the Charter, any attempt to alter by force the settlement envisaged by this resolution;

(*d*) The Trusteeship Council be informed of the responsibilities envisaged for it in this plan;

Calls upon the inhabitants of Palestine to take such steps as may be necessary on their part to put this plan into effect;

Appeals to all Governments and all peoples to refrain from taking any action which might hamper or delay the carrying out of these recommendations...

Official Records of the second session of the General Assembly, Resolutions, p. 131.

THE DECLARATION OF THE ESTABLISHMENT OF THE STATE OF ISRAEL

(14 May 1948)

The Declaration was approved and signed by the 33 members of the Va'ad Leumi (National Council) at a meeting held in Tel-Aviv on 14 May 1948, prior to the expiry of the Mandate for Palestine.

The Land of Israel was the birthplace of the Jewish people. Here their spiritual, religious and political identity was shaped. Here they first attained to statehood, created cultural values of national and universal significance and gave to the world the eternal Book of Books.

After being forcibly exiled from their land, the people kept faith with it throughout their Dispersion and never ceased to pray and hope for their return to it and for the restoration in it of their political freedom.

Impelled by this historic and traditional attachment, Jews strove in every successive generation to re-establish themselves in their ancient homeland. In recent decades they returned in their masses. Pioneers, defiant returnees, and defenders, they made deserts bloom, revived the Hebrew language, built villages and towns, and created a thriving community controlling its own economy and culture, loving peace but knowing how to defend itself, bringing the blessings of progress to all the country's inhabitants, and aspiring towards independent nationhood.

In the year 5657 (1897), at the summons of the spiritual father of the Jewish State, Theodor Herzl, the First Zionist Congress convened and proclaimed the right of the Jewish people to national rebirth in its own country.

This right was recognized in the Balfour Declaration of the 2nd November, 1917, and reaffirmed in the Mandate of the League of Nations which, in particular, gave international sanction to the historic connection between the Jewish people and Eretz-Israel and to the right of the Jewish people to rebuild its National Home.

The catastrophe which recently befell the Jewish people—the massacre of millions of Jews in Europe—was another clear demonstration of the urgency of solving the problem of its homelessness by re-establishing in Eretz-Israel the Jewish State, which would open the gates of the homeland wide to every Jew and confer upon the Jewish people the status of a fully privileged member of the community of nations.

Survivors of the Nazi holocaust in Europe, as well as Jews from other parts of the world, continued to migrate to Eretz-Israel, undaunted by difficulties, restrictions and dangers, and never ceased to assert their right to a life of dignity, freedom and honest toil in their national homeland.

In the Second World War the Jewish community of this country contributed its full share to the struggle of the freedom- and peace-loving nations against the forces of Nazi wickedness and, by the blood of its soldiers and its war effort, gained the right to be reckoned among the peoples who founded the United Nations.

On the 29th November, 1947, the United Nations General Assembly passed a resolution calling for the establishment of a Jewish State in Eretz-Israel; the General Assembly required the inhabitants of Eretz-Israel to take such steps as were necessary on their part for the implementation of that resolution. This recognition by the United Nations of the right of the Jewish people to establish their State is irrevocable.

This right is the natural right of the Jewish people to be masters of their own fate, like all other nations, in their own sovereign State.

Accordingly we, members of the National Council, representatives of the Jewish Community of Eretz-Israel and of the Zionist Movement, are here assembled on the day of the termination of the British Mandate over Eretz-Israel and, by virtue of our natural and historic right and on the strength of the resolution of the United Nations General Assembly, hereby declare the establishment of a Jewish state in Eretz-Israel, to be known as the State of Israel.

We declare that, with effect from the moment of the termination of the Mandate being tonight, the eve of Sabbath, the 6th Iyar, 5708 (15th May, 1948), until the establishment of the elected, regular authorities of the State in accordance with the Constitution which shall be adopted by the Elected Constituent Assembly not later than the 1st October 1948, the People's Council shall act as a Provisional Council of State, and its executive organ, the People's Administration, shall be the Provisional Government of the Jewish State, to be called 'Israel'.

The State of Israel will be open for Jewish immigration and for the Ingathering of the Exiles; it will foster the development of the country for the benefit of all its inhabitants; it will be based on freedom, justice and peace as envisaged by the prophets of Israel; it will ensure complete equality of social and political rights to all its inhabitants irrespective of religion, race or sex; it will guarantee freedom of religion, conscience, language, education and culture; it will safeguard the Holy Places of all religions; and it will be faithful to the principles of the Charter of the United Nations.

The State of Israel is prepared to co-operate with the agencies and representatives of the United Nations in implementing the resolution of the General Assembly of the 29th November, 1947, and will take steps to bring about the economic union of the whole of Eretz-Israel.

We appeal to the United Nations to assist the Jewish people in the building-up of its State and to receive the State of Israel into the community of nations.

We appeal—in the very midst of the onslaught launched against us now for months—to the Arab inhabitants of the State of Israel to preserve peace and participate in the upbuilding of the State on the basis of full and equal citizenship and due representation in all its provisional and permanent institutions.

We extend our hand to all neighbouring states and their peoples in an offer of peace and good neighbourliness, and appeal to them to establish bonds of co-operation and mutual help with the sovereign Jewish people settled in its own land. The State of Israel is prepared to do its share in a common effort for the advancement of the entire Middle East.

We appeal to the Jewish people throughout the Diaspora to rally round the Jews of Eretz-Israel in the tasks of immigration and upbuilding and to stand by them in the great struggle for the realization of the age-old dream—the redemption of Israel.

Placing our trust in the Almighty, we affix our signatures to this proclamation at this session of the provisional Council of State, on the soil of the Homeland, in the city of Tel-Aviv, on this Sabbath eve, the 5th day of Iyar, 5708 (14th May, 1948).

English rendition as published on the website of the Knesset (www.knesset.gov.il/docs/eng/megilat_eng.htm).

UN GENERAL ASSEMBLY RESOLUTION 194 (III)

(11 December 1948)

The resolution's terms have been reaffirmed every year since 1948.

11. *Resolves* that the refugees wishing to return to their homes and live at peace with their neighbours should be permitted to do so at the earliest practicable date, and that compensation should be paid for the property of those choosing not to return and for the loss of or damage to property which, under principles of international law or in equity, should be made good by the Governments or authorities responsible; ...

Official Records of the third session of the General Assembly, Part I, Resolutions, p. 21.

UN GENERAL ASSEMBLY ON THE ADMISSION OF ISRAEL TO MEMBERSHIP IN THE UNITED NATIONS

(11 May 1949)

Having received the report of the Security Council on the application of Israel for membership of the United Nations,

Noting that, in the judgement of the Security Council, Israel is a peace-loving State and is able and willing to carry out the obligations contained in the Charter,

Noting that the Security Council has recommended to the General Assembly that it admit Israel to membership in the United Nations,

Noting furthermore the declaration by the State of Israel that it 'unreservedly accepts the obligations of the United Nations Charter and undertakes to honour them for the day when it becomes a Member of the United Nations',

Recalling its resolutions of 29 November 1947 and 11 December 1948 and taking note of the declarations and explanations made by the representative of the Government of Israel before the *ad hoc* Political Committee in respect of the implementation of the said resolutions,

The General Assembly,

Acting in discharge of its functions under Article 4 of the Charter and rule 125 of its rules of procedure,

1. *Decides* that Israel is a peace-loving State which accepts the obligations contained in the Charter and is able and willing to carry out those obligations;

2. *Decides* to admit Israel to membership in the United Nations.

Official Records of the third session of the General Assembly, Resolutions, p. 18.

UN GENERAL ASSEMBLY RESOLUTION ON THE INTERNATIONALIZATION OF JERUSALEM

(9 December 1949)

The General Assembly,

Having regard to its resolution 181 (II) of 29 November 1947 and 194 (III) of 11 December 1948,

Having studied the reports of the United Nations Conciliation Commission for Palestine set up under the latter resolution,

I. Decides

In relation to Jerusalem,

Believing that the principles underlying its previous resolutions concerning this matter, and in particular its resolution of 29 November 1947, represent a just and equitable settlement of the question,

1. To restate, therefore, its intention that Jerusalem should be placed under a permanent international regime, which should envisage appropriate guarantees for the protection of the Holy Places, both within and outside Jerusalem, and to confirm specifically the following provisions of General Assembly resolution 181 (II): (1) The City of Jerusalem shall be established as a *corpus separatum* under a special international regime and shall be administered by the United Nations; (2) The Trusteeship Council shall be designated to discharge the responsibilities of the Administering Authority...; and (3) The City of Jerusalem shall include the present municipality of Jerusalem plus the surrounding villages and towns, the most eastern of which shall be Abu Dis; the most southern, Bethlehem; the most western, Ein Karim (including also the built-up area of Motsa); and the most northern, Shu'fat, as indicated on the attached sketchmap;... [*Map not reproduced–Ed.*]

Official Records of the fourth session of the General Assembly, Resolutions, p. 25.

LAW OF RETURN 5710-1950

(5 July 1950)

Legislation guaranteeing the right of immigration into Israel for all Jews was approved by the Knesset on 5 July 1950. [Subsequent amendments are not reproduced here.]

1. Every Jew has the right to come to this country as an oleh.

2. (a) Aliyah shall be by oleh's visa; (b) An oleh's visa shall be granted to every Jew who has expressed his desire to settle in Israel, unless the Minister of Immigration is satisfied that the applicant

(1) is engaged in an activity directed against the Jewish people; or

(2) is likely to endanger public health or the security of the State.

3.

(a) A Jew who has come to Israel and subsequent to his arrival has expressed his desire to settle in Israel may, while still in Israel, receive an oleh's certificate.

(b) The restrictions specified in section 2 (b) shall apply also to the grant of an oleh's certificate, but a person shall not be regarded as endangering public health on account of an illness contracted after his arrival in Israel.

4. Every Jew who has immigrated into this country before the coming into force of this Law, and every Jew who was born in this country, whether before or after the coming into force of this Law, shall be deemed to be a person who has come to this country as an oleh under this Law.

5. The Minister of Immigration is charged with the implementation of this Law and may make regulations as to any matter relating to such implementation and also as to the grant of oleh's visas and oleh's certificates to minors up to the age of 18 years.

UN SECURITY COUNCIL RESOLUTION 242

(22 November 1967)

The Security Council,

Expressing its continued concern with the grave situation in the Middle East,

Emphasizing the inadmissibility of the acquisition of territory by war and the need to work for a just and lasting peace in which every state in the area can live in security,

Emphasizing further that all Member States in their acceptance of the Charter of the United Nations have undertaken a commitment to act in accordance with Article 2 of the Charter,

1. *Affirms* that the fulfilment of Charter principles requires the establishment of a just and lasting peace in the Middle East which should include the application of both the following principles:

(i) Withdrawal of Israeli armed forces from territories occupied in the recent conflict;

(ii) Termination of all claims or states of belligerency and respect for the acknowledgement of the sovereignty, territorial integrity and political independence of every State in the area and their right to live in peace within secure and recognized boundaries free from threats or acts of force;

2. *Affirms further* the necessity

(*a*) For guaranteeing freedom of navigation through international waterways in the area;

(*b*) For achieving a just settlement of the refugee problem;

(*c*) For guaranteeing the territorial inviolability and political independence of every State in the area, through measures including the establishment of demilitarized zones;

3. *Requests* the Secretary-General to designate a Special Representative to proceed to the Middle East to establish and maintain contacts with the States concerned in order to promote agreement and assist efforts to achieve a peaceful and accepted settlement in accordance with the provisions and principles in this resolution;

4. *Requests* the Secretary-General to report to the Security Council on the progress of the efforts of the Special Representative as soon as possible.

UN Document S/RES/242 (1967).

UN SECURITY COUNCIL RESOLUTION 252

(21 May 1968)

Resolution 252 was the first Security Council resolution dealing specifically with the issue of Jerusalem. It was adopted by 13 votes to none; the USA and Canada abstained in the vote. [The two General Assembly resolutions, the Jordanian Permanent Representative's letter and the report of the Secretary-General, to which the introductory section refers, are not reproduced here.]

The Security Council,

Recalling General Assembly resolutions 2253 (ES-V) of 4 July 1967 and 2254 (ES-V) of 14 July 1967,

Having considered the letter of the Permanent Representative of Jordan on the situation in Jerusalem (S/8560) and the report of the Secretary-General (S/8146),

Having heard the statements made before the Council,

Noting that since the adoption of the above-mentioned resolutions Israel has taken further measures and actions in contravention of those resolutions,

Bearing in mind the need to work for a just and lasting peace,

Reaffirming that acquisition of territory by military conquest is inadmissible,

1. *Deplores* the failure of Israel to comply with the General Assembly resolutions mentioned above;

2. *Considers* that all legislative and administrative measures and actions taken by Israel, including expropriation of land and properties thereon, which tend to change the legal status of Jerusalem are invalid and cannot change that status;

3. *Urgently calls upon* Israel to rescind all such measures already taken and to desist forthwith from taking any further action which tends to change the status of Jerusalem;

4. *Requests* the Secretary-General to report to the Security Council on the implementation of the present resolution.

UN Document S/RES/252 (1968)

PALESTINIAN NATIONAL CHARTER (PLO COVENANT)

Resolutions of the Palestine National Council, July 1–17, 1968.

In September 1993 the Chairman of the Palestine Liberation Organization (PLO), Yasser Arafat, declared those articles of the PLO Covenant which deny Israel's right to exist or are inconsistent with the PLO's commitments to Israel under the terms of subsequent accords to be invalid. Revision of those articles, presented here in italics, was to be undertaken as part of the ongoing peace process. In April 1996 the Palestine National Council (PNC) voted to amend the PLO Covenant, thereby removing all clauses demanding the destruction of Israel. In December 1998, at a meeting of the PNC attended by US President Bill Clinton, the removal from the Covenant of all such clauses was reaffirmed.

The following is the complete and unabridged text of the Palestinian National Covenant, as published officially in English by the PLO.

Article I

Palestine is the homeland of the Arab Palestinian people; it is an indivisible part of the Arab homeland, and the Palestinian people are an integral part of the Arab nation.

Article II

Palestine, with the boundaries it had during the British Mandate, is an indivisible territorial unit.

Article III

The Palestinian Arab people possess the legal right to their homeland and have the right to determine their destiny after achieving the liberation of their country in accordance with their wishes and entirely of their own accord and will.

Article IV

The Palestinian identity is a genuine, essential, and inherent characteristic; it is transmitted from parents to children. The Zionist occupation and the dispersal of the Palestinian Arab people, through the disasters which befell them, do not make them lose their Palestinian identity and their membership in the Palestinian community, nor do they negate them.

Article V

The Palestinians are those Arab nationals who, until 1947, normally resided in Palestine regardless of whether they were evicted from it or have stayed there. Anyone born, after that date, of a Palestinian father—whether inside Palestine or outside it—is also a Palestinian.

Article VI

The Jews who had normally resided in Palestine until the beginning of the Zionist invasion will be considered Palestinians.

Article VII

That there is a Palestinian community and that it has material, spiritual, and historical connection with Palestine are indisputable facts. It is a national duty to bring up individual Palestinians in an Arab revolutionary manner. All means of information and education must be adopted in order to acquaint the Palestinian with his country in the most profound manner, both spiritual and material, that is possible. He must be prepared for the armed struggle and ready to sacrifice his wealth and his life in order to win back his homeland and bring about its liberation.

Article VIII

The phase in their history, through which the Palestinian people are now living, is that of national (watani) struggle for the liberation of Palestine. Thus the conflicts among the Palestinian national forces are secondary, and should be ended for the sake of the basic conflict that exists between the forces of Zionism and of imperialism on the one hand, and the Palestinian Arab people on the other. On this basis the Palestinian masses, regardless of whether they are residing in the national homeland or in diaspora (mahajir) constitute—both their organizations and the individuals—one national front working for the retrieval of Palestine and its liberation through armed struggle.

Article IX

Armed struggle is the only way to liberate Palestine. This is the overall strategy, not merely a tactical phase. The Palestinian Arab people assert their absolute determination and firm resolution to continue their armed struggle and to work for an armed popular revolution for the liberation of their country and their return to it. They also assert their right to normal life in Palestine and to exercise their right to self-determination and sovereignty over it.

Article X

Commando action constitutes the nucleus of the Palestinian popular liberation war. This requires its escalation, comprehensiveness, and the mobilization of all the Palestinian popular and educational efforts and their organization and involvement in the armed Palestinian revolution. It also requires the achieving of unity for the national (watani) struggle among the different groupings of the Palestinian people, and between the Palestinian people and the Arab masses, so as to secure the continuation of the revolution, its escalation, and victory.

Article XI

The Palestinians will have three mottoes: national (wataniyya) unity, national (qawmiyya) mobilization, and liberation.

Article XII

The Palestinian people believe in Arab unity. In order to contribute their share toward the attainment of that objective, however, they must, at the present stage of their struggle, safeguard their Palestinian identity and develop their consciousness of that identity, and oppose any plan that may dissolve or impair it.

Article XIII

Arab unity and the liberation of Palestine are two complementary objectives, the attainment of either of which facilitates the attainment of the other. Thus, Arab unity leads to the liberation of Palestine, the liberation of Palestine leads to Arab unity; and work towards the realization of one objective proceeds side by side with work towards the realization of the other.

Article XIV

The destiny of the Arab nation, and indeed Arab existence itself, depend upon the destiny of the Palestine cause. From this interdependence springs the Arab nation's pursuit of, and striving for, the liberation of Palestine. The people of Palestine play the role of the vanguard in the realization of this sacred (qawmi) goal.

Article XV

The liberation of Palestine, from an Arab viewpoint, is a national (qawmi) duty and it attempts to repel the Zionist and imperialist aggression against the Arab homeland, and aims at the elimination of Zionism in Palestine. Absolute responsibility for this falls upon the Arab nation—peoples and governments—with the Arab people of Palestine in the vanguard. Accordingly, the Arab nation must mobilize all its military, human, moral, and spiritual capabilities to participate actively with the Palestinian people in the liberation of Palestine. It must, particularly in the phase of the armed Palestinian revolution, offer and furnish the Palestinian people with all possible help, and material and human support, and make available to them the means and opportunities that will enable them to continue to carry out their leading role in the armed revolution, until they liberate their homeland.

Article XVI

The liberation of Palestine, from a spiritual point of view, will provide the Holy Land with an atmosphere of safety and tranquility, which in turn will safeguard the country's religious sanctuaries and guarantee freedom of worship and of visit to all, without discrimination of race, color, language, or religion. Accordingly, the people of Palestine look to all spiritual forces in the world for support.

Article XVII

The liberation of Palestine, from a human point of view, will restore to the Palestinian individual his dignity, pride, and freedom. Accordingly the Palestinian Arab people look forward to the support of all those who believe in the dignity of man and his freedom in the world.

Article XVIII

The liberation of Palestine, from an international point of view, is a defensive action necessitated by the demands of self-defense. Accordingly the Palestinian people, desirous as they are of the friendship of all people, look to freedom-loving, and peace-loving states for support in order to restore their legitimate rights in Palestine, to re-establish peace and security in the country, and to enable its people to exercise national sovereignty and freedom.

Article XIX

The partition of Palestine in 1947 and the establishment of the state of Israel are entirely illegal, regardless of the passage of time, because they were contrary to the will of the Palestinian people and to their natural right in their homeland, and inconsistent with the principles embodied in the Charter of the United Nations, particularly the right to self-determination.

Article XX

The Balfour Declaration, the Mandate for Palestine, and everything that has been based upon them, are deemed null and void. Claims of historical or religious ties of Jews with Palestine are incompatible with the facts of history and the true conception of what constitutes statehood. Judaism, being a religion, is not an independent nationality. Nor do Jews constitute a single nation with an identity of its own; they are citizens of the states to which they belong.

Article XXI

The Arab Palestinian people, expressing themselves by the armed Palestinian revolution, reject all solutions which are substitutes for the total liberation of Palestine and reject all proposals aiming at the liquidation of the Palestinian problem, or its internationalization.

Article XXII

Zionism is a political movement organically associated with international imperialism and antagonistic to all action for liberation and to progressive movements in the world. It is racist and fanatic in its nature, aggressive, expansionist, and colonial in its aims, and fascist in its methods. Israel is the instrument of Zionist movement, and geographical base for world imperialism placed strategically in the midst of the Arab homeland to combat the hopes of the Arab nation for liberation, unity, and progress. Israel is a constant source of threat vis-à-vis peace in the Middle East and the whole world. Since the liberation of Palestine will destroy the Zionist and imperialist presence and will contribute to the establishment of peace in the Middle East, the Palestinian people look for the support of all the progressive and peaceful forces and urge them all, irrespective of their affiliations and beliefs, to offer the Palestinian people all aid and support in their just struggle for the liberation of their homeland.

Article XXIII

The demand of security and peace, as well as the demand of right and justice, require all states to consider Zionism an illegitimate movement, to outlaw its existence, and to ban its operations, in order that friendly relations among peoples may be preserved, and the loyalty of citizens to their respective homelands safeguarded.

Article XXIV

The Palestinian people believe in the principles of justice, freedom, sovereignty, self-determination, human dignity, and in the right of all peoples to exercise them.

Article XXV

For the realization of the goals of this Charter and its principles, the Palestine Liberation Organization will perform its role in the liberation of Palestine in accordance with the Constitution of this Organization.

Article XXVI

The Palestine Liberation Organization, representative of the Palestinian revolutionary forces, is responsible for the Palestinian Arab people's movement in its struggle—to retrieve its homeland, liberate and return to it and exercise the right to self-determination in it—in all military, political, and financial fields and also for whatever may be required by the Palestine case on the inter-Arab and international levels.

Article XXVII

The Palestine Liberation Organization shall co-operate with all Arab states, each according to its potentialities; and will adopt a neutral policy among them in the light of the requirements of the war of liberation; and on this basis it shall not interfere in the internal affairs of any Arab state.

Article XXVIII

The Palestinian Arab people assert the genuineness and independence of their national (wataniyya) revolution and reject all forms of intervention, trusteeship, and subordination.

Article XXIX

The Palestinian people possess the fundamental and genuine legal right to liberate and retrieve their homeland. The Palestinian people determine their attitude toward all states and forces on the basis of the stands they adopt vis-à-vis to the Palestinian revolution to fulfil the aims of the Palestinian people.

Article XXX

Fighters and carriers of arms in the war of liberation are the nucleus of the popular army which will be the protective force for the gains of the Palestinian Arab people.

Article XXXI

The Organization shall have a flag, an oath of allegiance, and an anthem. All this shall be decided upon in accordance with a special regulation.

Article XXXII

Regulations, which shall be known as the Constitution of the Palestinian [sic] Liberation Organization, shall be annexed to this Charter. It will lay down the manner in which the Organization, and its organs and institutions, shall be constituted; the respective competence of each; and the requirements of its obligation under the Charter.

Article XXXIII

This Charter shall not be amended save by [vote of] a majority of two-thirds of the total membership of the National Congress of the Palestine Liberation Organization [taken] at a special session convened for that purpose.

English rendition as published in Basic Political Documents of the Armed Palestinian Resistance Movement*; Leila S. Kadi (Ed.), Palestine Research Centre, Beirut, December 1969, pp. 137–141.*

UN SECURITY COUNCIL RESOLUTION ON JERUSALEM

(25 September 1971)

The resolution, No. 298 (1971), was passed nemine contradicente, *with the abstention of Syria.*

The Security Council,

Recalling its resolutions 252 (1968) of 21 May 1968, and 267 (1969) of 3 July 1969, and the earlier General Assembly resolution 2253 (ES-V) and 2254 (ES-V) of 4 and 14 July 1967, concerning measures and actions by Israel designed to change the status of the Israeli-occupied section of Jerusalem,

Having considered the letter of the Permanent Representative of Jordan on this situation in Jerusalem and the reports of the Secretary-General, and having heard the statements of the parties concerned in the question,

Recalling the principle that acquisition of territory by military conquest is inadmissible,

Noting with concern the non-compliance by Israel with the above-mentioned resolutions,

Noting with concern also that since the adoption of the above-mentioned resolutions Israel has taken further measures designed to change the status and character of the occupied section of Jerusalem,

1. *Reaffirms* its resolutions 252 (1968) and 267 (1969);

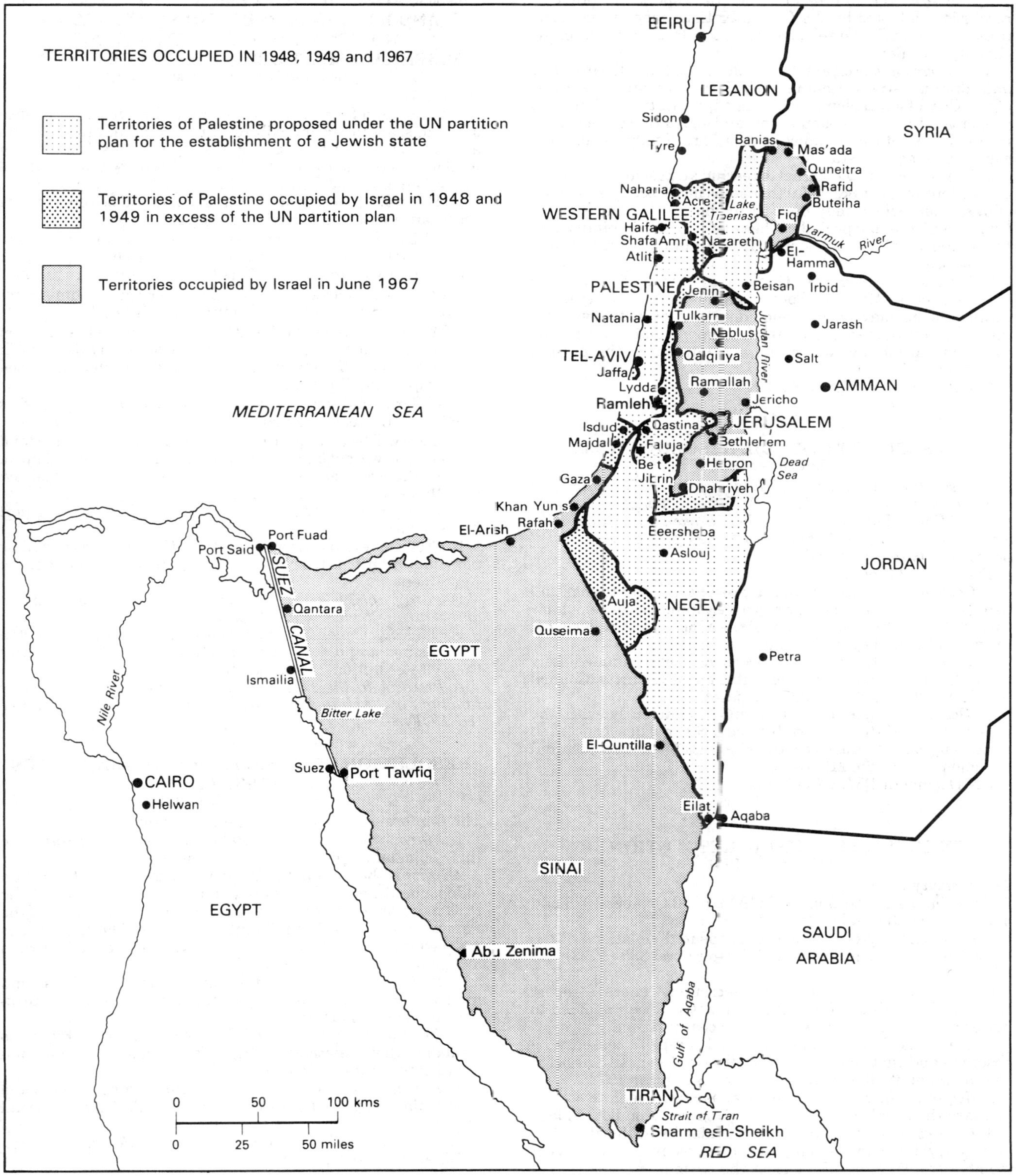
TERRITORIES OCCUPIED IN 1948, 1949 and 1967
Territories of Palestine proposed under the UN partition plan for the establishment of a Jewish state
Territories of Palestine occupied by Israel in 1948 and 1949 in excess of the UN partition plan
Territories occupied by Israel in June 1967
BEIRUT
LEBANON
SYRIA
Sidon
Tyre
Banias
Mas'ada
Quneitra
Rafid
Buteiha
Naharia
Acre
Lake Tiberias
WESTERN GALILEE
Fiq
Haifa
Shafa Amr
Nazareth
Yarmuk River
Atlit
El-Hamma
PALESTINE
Jenin
Beisan
Irbid
Natania
Tulkarm
Jarash
Nablus
Jordan River
TEL-AVIV
Qalqiliya
Salt
Jaffa
Lydda
Ramallah
AMMAN
Ramleh
Jericho
MEDITERRANEAN SEA
Isdud
Qastina
JERUSALEM
Majdal
Faluja
Bethlehem
Beit Jibrin
Hebron
Dead Sea
Gaza
Dhahriyeh
Khan Yunis
Rafah
El-Arish
Beersheba
Port Fuad
Port Said
Aslouj
JORDAN
SUEZ CANAL
Auja
NEGEV
Qantara
Quseima
EGYPT
Petra
Ismailia
Nile River
Bitter Lake
El-Quntilla
Suez
Port Tawfiq
CAIRO
Helwan
Eilat
Aqaba
SINAI
EGYPT
SAUDI ARABIA
Abu Zenima
Gulf of Aqaba
0 50 100 kms
0 25 50 miles
TIRAN
Strait of Tiran
Sharm esh-Sheikh
RED SEA

2. *Deplores* the failure of Israel to respect the previous resolutions adopted by the United Nations concerning measures and actions by Israel purporting to affect the status of the City of Jerusalem;

3. *Confirms* in the clearest possible terms that all legislative and administrative actions taken by Israel to change the status of the City of Jerusalem, including expropriation of land and properties, transfer of populations and legislation aimed at the incorporation of the occupied section, are totally invalid and cannot change that status;

4. *Urgently calls upon* Israel to rescind all previous measures and actions and to take no further steps in the occupied section of Jerusalem which may purport to change the status of the City, or which would prejudice the rights of the inhabitants and the interests of the international community, or a just and lasting peace;

5. *Requests* the Secretary-General, in consultation with the President of the Security Council and using such instrumentalities as he may choose, including a representative or a mission, to report to the Council as appropriate and in any event within 60 days on the implementation of the present resolution.

UN Document S/RES/298 (1971).

UN SECURITY COUNCIL RESOLUTION 338

(22 October 1973)

UN Resolutions between 1967 and October 1973 reaffirmed Security Council Resolution 242. In an attempt to end the fourth Middle East war, which had broken out between the Arabs and Israel on 6 October 1973, the UN Security Council passed the following Resolution:

The Security Council,

1. *Calls upon* all parties to the present fighting to cease all firing and terminate all military activity immediately, not later than 12 hours after the moment of the adoption of the decision, in the positions they now occupy;

2. *Calls upon* the parties concerned to start immediately after the ceasefire the implementation of Security Council Resolution 242 (1967) in all of its parts;

3. *Decides that*, immediately and concurrently with the ceasefire negotiations start between the parties concerned under appropriate auspices aimed at establishing a just and durable peace in the Middle East.

UN Document PR/73/29 (1973).

UN SECURITY COUNCIL RESOLUTION 340

(25 October 1973)

The Security Council,

Recalling its Resolutions 338 (1973) of 22 October 1973 and 339 (1973) of 23 October 1973,

Noting with regret the reported repeated violations of the ceasefire in non-compliance with Resolutions 338 (1973) and 339 (1973),

Noting with concern from the Secretary-General's report that the UN military observers have not yet been enabled to place themselves on both sides of the ceasefire line,

1. *Demands* that an immediate and complete ceasefire be observed and that the parties withdraw to the positions occupied by them at 16.50 hours GMT on 22 October 1973;

2. *Requests* the Secretary-General as an immediate step to increase the number of UN military observers on both sides;

3. *Decides* to set up immediately under its authority a UN emergency force to be composed of personnel drawn from member states of the UN, except the permanent members of the Security Council, and requests the Secretary-General to report within 24 hours on the steps taken to this effect;

4. *Requests* the Secretary-General to report to the Council on an urgent and continuing basis on the state of implementation of this Resolution, as well as Resolutions 338 (1973) and 339 (1973);

5. *Requests* all member states to extend their full co-operation to the UN in the implementation of this Resolution, as well as Resolutions 338 (1973) and 339 (1973).

UN Document PR/73/31 (1973).

DISENGAGEMENT AGREEMENT BETWEEN SYRIAN AND ISRAELI FORCES AND PROTOCOL TO AGREEMENT ON UNITED NATIONS DISENGAGEMENT OBSERVER FORCE (UNDOF)

(signed in Geneva, 31 May 1974)

(Annex A)

A. Israel and Syria will scrupulously observe the cease-fire on land, sea and air and will refrain from all military actions against each other, from the time of signing this document in implementation of the United Nations Security Council Resolution 338 dated 22 October 1973.

B. The military forces of Israel and Syria will be separated in accordance with the following principles:

1. All Israeli military forces will be west of a line designated line A on the map attached hereto (*reproduced below*), except in Quneitra (Kuneitra) area, where they will be west of a line A-1.

2. All territory east of line A will be under Syrian administration and Syrian civilians will return to this territory.

3. The area between line A and the line designated as line B on the attached map will be an area of separation. In this area will be stationed UNDOF established in accordance with the accompanying Protocol.

4. All Syrian military forces will be east of a line designated as line B on the attached map.

5. There will be two equal areas of limitation in armament and forces, one west of line A and one east of line B as agreed upon.

C. In the area between line A and line A-1 on the attached map there shall be no military forces.

D. *Paragraph D deals with practical details of signing and implementation.*

E. Provisions of paragraphs A, B and C shall be inspected by personnel of the United Nations comprising UNDOF under the Agreement.

F. *Paragraphs F and G deal with repatriation of prisoners and return of bodies of dead soldiers.*

H. This Agreement is not a peace agreement. It is a step towards a just and durable peace on the basis of the Security Council Resolution 338 dated 22 October 1973.

A Protocol to the Disengagement Agreement outlined the functions of the United Nations Disengagement Observer Force (UNDOF).

RESOLUTION OF CONFERENCE OF ARAB HEADS OF STATE

(Rabat, 28 October 1974)

The Conference of the Arab Heads of State:

1. *Affirms* the right of the Palestinian people to return to their homeland and to self-determination.

2. *Affirms* the right of the Palestinian people to establish an independent national authority, under the leadership of the PLO in its capacity as the sole legitimate representative of the Palestine people, over all liberated territory. The Arab States are pledged to uphold this authority, when it is established, in all spheres and at all levels.

3. *Supports* the PLO in the exercise of its national and international responsibilities, within the context of the principle of Arab solidarity.

4. *Invites* the kingdom of Jordan, Syria and Egypt to formalize their relations in the light of these decisions and in order that they be implemented.

5. *Affirms* the obligation of all Arab States to preserve Palestinian unity and not to interfere in Palestinian internal affairs.

Sources: *Le Monde: Problèmes Politiques et Sociaux*, 7 March 1975; *Arab Report and Record*.

UN GENERAL ASSEMBLY RESOLUTION 3236 (XXIX)

(22 November 1974)

The General Assembly,

Having considered the question of Palestine,

Having heard the statement of the Palestinian Liberation Organization, the representative of the Palestinian people,

Having also heard other statements made during the debate,

Deeply concerned that no just solution to the problem of Palestine has yet been achieved and recognizing that the

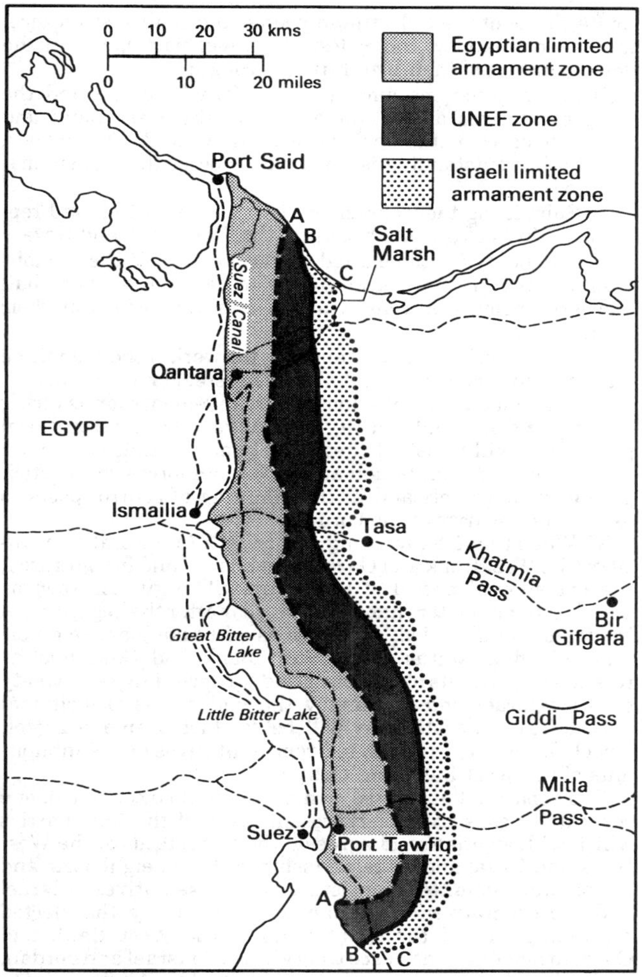

Disengagement Agreement of 18 January 1974 between Israel and Egypt

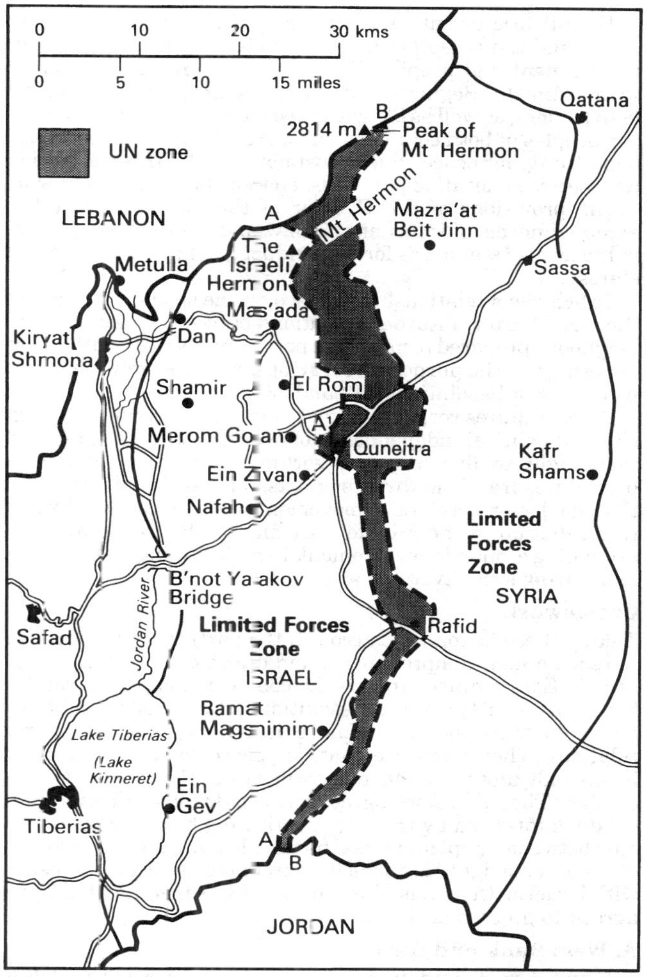

Disengagement Agreement of 31 May 1974 between Israel and Syria

problem of Palestine continues to endanger international peace and security,

Recognizing that the Palestinian people is entitled to self-determination in accordance with the Charter of the United Nations,

Expressing its grave concern that the Palestinian people has been prevented from enjoying its inalienable rights, in particular its right to self-determination,

Guided by the purposes and principles of the Charter,

Recalling its relevant resolutions which affirm the right of the Palestinian people to self-determination,

1. *Reaffirms* the inalienable rights of Palestinian people in Palestine, including:

(*a*) The right to self-determination without external interference

(*b*) The right to national independence and sovereignty

2. *Reaffirms also* the inalienable right of the Palestinians to return to their homes and property from which they have been displaced and uprooted, and calls for their return;

3. *Emphasizes* that full respect for and the realization of these inalienable rights of the Palestinian people are indispensable for the solution of the question of Palestine;

4. *Recognizes* that the Palestinian people is a principal party in the establishment of a just and durable peace in the Middle East;

5. *Further Recognizes* the right of the Palestinian people to regain its rights by all means in accordance with the purposes and principles of the Charter of the United Nations;

6. *Appeals* to all States and international organizations to extend their support to the Palestinian people in its struggle to restore its rights, in accordance with the Charter;

7. *Requests* the Secretary-General to establish contacts with the Palestinian Liberation Organization on all matters concerning the question of Palestine;

8. *Requests* the Secretary-General to report to the General Assembly at its thirtieth session on the implementation of the present resolution;

9. *Decides* to include the item 'Question of Palestine' in the provisional agenda of its thirtieth session.

UN Document BR/74/55 (1974).

CAMP DAVID: THE FRAMEWORK FOR PEACE IN THE MIDDLE EAST

Muhammad Anwar al-Sadat, President of the Arab Republic of Egypt, and Menachem Begin, Prime Minister of Israel, met with President Jimmy Carter of the USA at Camp David from 5 September to 17 September 1978, and agreed on the following framework for peace in the Middle East. They invited other parties to the Arab–Israeli conflict to adhere to it.

Preamble

The search for peace in the Middle East must be guided by the following:

The agreed basis for a peaceful settlement of the conflict between Israel and its neighbours in UN Security Council Resolution 242 in all its parts.

The historic initiative by President Sadat in visiting Jerusalem and the reception accorded to him by the Parliament, Government and people of Israel, and the reciprocal visit of Prime Minister Begin to Ismailia, the peace proposals made by both leaders, as well as the warm reception of these missions by the peoples of both countries, have created an unprecedented opportunity for peace which must not be lost if this generation and future generations are to be spared the tragedies of war.

The provisions of the Charter of the UN and the other accepted norms of international law and legitimacy now provide accepted standards for the conduct of relations between all states.

To achieve a relationship of peace, in the spirit of article 2 of the UN Charter, future negotiations between Israel and any neighbour prepared to negotiate peace and security with it, are necessary for the purpose of carrying out all the provisions and principles of Resolutions 242 and 338.

Peace requires respect for the sovereignty, territorial integrity and political independence of every state in the area and their right to live in peace within secure and recognized boundaries free from threats or acts of force. Progress toward that goal can accelerate movement towards a new era of reconciliation in the Middle East marked by co-operation in promoting economic development, in maintaining stability and in assuring security...

Framework

Taking these factors into account, the parties are determined to reach a just, comprehensive and durable settlement of the Middle East conflict through the conclusion of peace treaties based on Security Council Resolutions 242 and 338 in all their parts. Their purpose is to achieve peace and good neighbourly relations. They recognize that, for peace to endure, it must involve all those who have been most deeply affected by the conflict. They therefore agree that this framework as appropriate is intended by them to constitute a basis for peace not only between Egypt and Israel but also between Israel and each of its other neighbours which is prepared to negotiate peace with Israel on this basis. With that objective in mind, they have agreed to proceed as follows:

A. West Bank and Gaza

1. Egypt, Israel, Jordan and the representatives of the Palestinian people should participate in negotiations on the resolution of the Palestinian problem in all its aspects to achieve that objective, negotiations relating to the West Bank and Gaza should proceed in three stages.

(A) Egypt and Israel agree that, in order to ensure a peaceful and orderly transfer of authority, and taking into account the security concerns of all the parties, there should be transitional arrangements for the West Bank and Gaza for a period not exceeding five years. In order to provide full autonomy to the inhabitants, under these arrangements the Israeli military government and its civilian administration will be withdrawn as soon as a self-governing authority has been freely elected by the inhabitants of these areas to replace the existing military government.

To negotiate the details of transitional arrangement, the Government of Jordan will be invited to join the negotiations on the basis of this framework. These new arrangements should give due consideration to both the principle of self-government by the inhabitants of these territories and to the legitimate security concerns of the parties involved.

(B) Egypt, Israel and Jordan will agree on the modalities for establishing the elected self-governing authority in the West Bank and Gaza. The delegations of Egypt and Jordan may include Palestinians from the West Bank and Gaza or other Palestinians as mutually agreed. The parties will negotiate an agreement which will define the powers and responsibilities of the self-governing authority to be exercised in the West Bank and Gaza. A withdrawal of Israeli armed forces will take place and there will be a redeployment of the remaining Israeli forces into specified security locations.

The negotiations shall be based on all the provisions and principles of UN Security Council Resolution 242. The negotiations will resolve, among other matters, the location of the boundaries and the nature of the security arrangements. The solution from the negotiations must also recognize the legitimate rights of the Palestinian people and their just requirements. In this way, the Palestinians will participate in the determination of their own future through:

(i) The negotiations among Egypt, Israel, Jordan and the representatives of the inhabitants of the West Bank and Gaza to agree on the final status of the West Bank and Gaza and other outstanding issues by the end of the transitional period.

(ii) Submitting their agreement to a vote by the elected representatives of the inhabitants of the West Bank and Gaza.

(iii) Providing for the elected representatives of the inhabitants of the West Bank and Gaza to decide how they shall govern themselves consistent with the provisions of their agreement.

(iv) Participating as stated above in the work of the committee negotiating the peace treaty between Israel and Jordan.

The agreement will also include arrangements for assuring internal and external security and public order. A strong local police force will be established, which may include Jordanian citizens. In addition, Israeli and Jordanian forces will participate in joint patrols and in the manning of control posts to assure the security of the borders.

(C) When the self-governing authority (administrative council) in the West Bank and Gaza is established and inaugurated, the transitional period of five years will begin. As soon as possible, but not later than the third year after the beginning of the transitional period, negotiations will take place to determine the final status of the West Bank and Gaza and its relationship with its neighbours, and to conclude a peace treaty between Israel and Jordan by the end of the transitional period. These negotiations will be conducted among Egypt, Israel, Jordan and the elected representatives of the inhabitants of the West Bank and Gaza.

Two separate but related committees will be convened; one committee, consisting of representatives of the four parties which will negotiate and agree on the final status of the West Bank and Gaza, and its relationship with its neighbours, and the second committee, consisting of representatives of Israel and representatives of Jordan to be joined by the elected representatives of the inhabitants of the West Bank and Gaza, to negotiate the peace treaty between Israel and Jordan, taking into account the agreement reached on the final status of the West Bank and Gaza.

2. All necessary measures will be taken and provisions made to assure the security of Israel and its neighbours during the transitional period and beyond. To assist in providing such security, a strong local police force will be constituted by the self-governing authority. It will be composed of inhabitants of the West Bank and Gaza. The police will maintain continuing liaison on internal security matters with the designated Israeli, Jordanian and Egyptian officers.

3. During the transitional period, the representatives of Egypt, Israel, Jordan and the self-governing authority will constitute a continuing committee to decide by agreement on the modalities of admission of persons displaced from the West Bank and Gaza in 1967, together with necessary measures to prevent disruption and disorder. Other matters of common concern may also be dealt with by this committee.

4. Egypt and Israel will work with each other and with other interested parties to establish agreed procedures for a prompt, just and permanent implementation of the resolution of the refugee problem.

B. Egypt-Israel

1. Egypt and Israel undertake not to resort to the threat or the use of force to settle disputes. Any disputes shall be settled by peaceful means in accordance with the provisions of article 33 of the Charter of the UN.

2. In order to achieve peace between them, the parties agree to negotiate in good faith with a goal of concluding within three months from the signing of this framework a peace treaty between them, while inviting the other parties to the conflict to proceed simultaneously to negotiate and conclude similar peace treaties with a view to achieving a comprehensive peace in the area. The framework for the conclusion of a peace treaty between Egypt and Israel will govern the peace negotiations between them. The parties will agree on the modalities and the

timetable for the implementation of their obligations under the treaty.

Associated principles

1. Egypt and Israel state that the principles and provisions described below should apply to peace treaties between Israel and each of its neighbours—Egypt, Jordan, Syria and Lebanon.

2. Signatories shall establish among themselves relationships normal to states at peace with one another. To this end, they should undertake to abide by all the provisions of the Charter of the UN. Steps to be taken in this respect include:

(a) Full recognition;

(b) Abolishing economic boycotts;

(c) Guaranteeing that under their jurisdiction the citizens of the other parties shall enjoy the protection of the due process of law.

3. Signatories should explore possibilities for economic development in the context of final peace treaties, with the objective of contributing to the atmosphere of peace, co-operation, and friendship which is their common goal.

4. Claims commissions may be established for the mutual settlement of all financial claims.

5. The United States shall be invited to participate in the talks on matters related to the modalities of the implementation of the agreements and working out the time-table for the carrying out of the obligation of the parties.

6. The UN Security Council shall be requested to endorse the peace treaties and ensure that their provisions shall not be violated. The permanent members of the Security Council shall be requested to underwrite the peace treaties and ensure respect for their provisions. They shall also be requested to conform their policies and actions with the undertakings contained in this framework.

The second agreement signed at Camp David was a framework for the conclusion of a peace treaty between Egypt and Israel. The actual Treaty was signed on 26 March 1979, and is reproduced below.

THE PEACE TREATY BETWEEN EGYPT AND ISRAEL SIGNED IN WASHINGTON ON 26 MARCH 1979

The Government of the Arab Republic of Egypt and the Government of the State of Israel:

Preamble

Convinced of the urgent necessity of the establishment of a just, comprehensive and lasting peace in the Middle East in accordance with Security Council Resolutions 242 and 338;

Reaffirming their adherence to the 'Framework for Peace in the Middle East agreed at Camp David', dated 17 September 1978;

Noting that the aforementioned framework as appropriate is intended to constitute a basis for peace not only between Egypt and Israel but also between Israel and each of the other Arab neighbours which is prepared to negotiate peace with it on this basis;

Desiring to bring to an end the state of war between them and to establish a peace in which every state in the area can live in security;

Convinced that the conclusion of a treaty of peace between Egypt and Israel is an important step in the search for comprehensive peace in the area and for the attainment of the settlement of the Arab–Israeli conflict in all its aspects;

Inviting the other Arab parties to this dispute to join the peace process with Israel guided by and based on the principles of the aforementioned framework;

Desiring as well to develop friendly relations and co-operation between themselves in accordance with the UN Charter and the principles of international law governing international relations in times of peace;

Agree to the following provisions in the free exercise of their sovereignty, in order to implement the 'framework for the conclusion of a peace treaty between Egypt and Israel'.

Article I

1. The state of war between the parties will be terminated and peace will be established between them upon the exchange of instruments of ratification of this treaty.

2. Israel will withdraw all its armed forces and civilians from the Sinai behind the international boundary between Egypt and Mandated Palestine, as provided in the annexed protocol (annexed), and Egypt will resume the exercise of its full sovereignty over the Sinai.

3. Upon completion of the interim withdrawal provided for in Annex 1, the parties will establish normal and friendly relations, in accordance with Article III (3).

Article II

The permanent boundary between Egypt and Israel is the recognized international boundary between Egypt and the former Mandated Territory of Palestine, as shown on the map at Annex 2 (*not reproduced here—Ed.*), without prejudice to the issue of the status of the Gaza Strip. The parties recognize this boundary as inviolable. Each will respect the territorial integrity of the other, including their territorial waters and airspace.

Article III

1. The parties will apply between them the provisions of the Charter of the UN and the principles of international law governing relations among states in times of peace.

In particular:

A. They recognize and will respect each other's sovereignty, territorial integrity and political independence.

B. They recognize and will respect each other's right to live in peace within their secure and recognized boundaries.

C. They will refrain from the threat of use of force, directly or indirectly, against each other and will settle all disputes between them by peaceful means.

2. Each party undertakes to ensure that acts or threats of belligerency, hostility, or violence do not originate from and are not committed from within its territory, or by any forces subject to its control or by any other forces stationed on its territory, against the population, citizens or property of the other party. Each party also undertakes to refrain from organizing, instigating, inciting, assisting or participating in acts or threats of belligerency, hostility, subversion or violence against the other party, anywhere, and undertakes to ensure that perpetrators of such acts are brought to justice.

3. The parties agree that the normal relationship established between them will include full recognition, diplomatic, economic and cultural relations, termination of economic boycotts and discriminatory barriers to the free movement of people and goods, and will guarantee the mutual enjoyment by citizens of the due process of law. The process by which they undertake to achieve such a relationship parallel to the implementation of other provisions of this treaty is set out in the annexed protocol (Annex 3).

Article IV

1. In order to provide maximum security for both parties on the basis of reciprocity, agreed security arrangements will be established including limited force zones in Egyptian and Israeli territory, and UN forces and observers, described in detail as to nature and timing in Annex 1, and other security arrangements the parties may agree upon.

2. The parties agree to the stationing of UN personnel in areas described in Annex 1, the parties agree not to request withdrawal of the UN personnel and that these personnel will not be removed unless such removal is approved by the Security Council of the UN, with the affirmative vote of the five members, unless the parties otherwise agree.

3. A joint commission will be established to facilitate the implementation of the treaty, as provided for in Annex 1.

4. The security arrangements provided for in paragraphs 1 and 2 of this article may at the request of either party be reviewed and amended by mutual agreement of the parties.

Article V

Article V deals with rights of passage of shipping through the Suez Canal, the Strait of Tiran and the Gulf of Aqaba.

Article VI

1. This treaty does not affect and shall not be interpreted as affecting in any way the rights and obligations of the parties under the Charter of the UN.

2. The parties undertake to fulfil in good faith their obligations under this treaty, without regard to action or inaction of any other party and independently of any instrument external to this treaty.

3. They further undertake to take all the necessary measures for the application in their relations of the provisions of the multilateral conventions to which they are parties. Including the submission of appropriate notification to the Secretary-General of the UN and other depositories of such conventions.

4. The parties undertake not to enter into any obligation in conflict with this treaty.

5. Subject to Article 103 of the UN Charter, in the event of a conflict between the obligations of the parties under the present treaty and any of their other obligations, the obligations under this treaty will be binding and implemented.

Article VII

1. Disputes arising out of the application or interpretation of this treaty shall be resolved by negotiations.

2. Any such disputes which cannot be settled by negotiations shall be resolved by conciliation or submitted to arbitration.

Article VIII

The parties agree to establish a claims commission for the mutual settlement of all financial claims.

Article IX

1. This treaty shall enter into force upon exchange of instruments of ratification.

2. This treaty supersedes the agreement between Egypt and Israel of September 1975.

3. All protocols, annexes, and maps attached to this treaty shall be regarded as an integral part hereof.

4. The treaty shall be communicated to the Secretary-General of the UN for registration in accordance with the provisions of Article 102 of the Charter of the UN.

Annex 1—military and withdrawal arrangements

Israel will complete withdrawal of all its armed forces and civilians from Sinai within three years of the date of exchange of instruments of ratification of the treaty. The withdrawal will be accomplished in two phases, the first, within nine months, to a line east of Al Arish and Ras Muhammad; the second to behind the international boundary. During the three-year period, Egypt and Israel will maintain a specified military presence in four delineated security zones (see map—*not reproduced here—Ed.*), and the UN will continue its observation and supervisory functions. Egypt will exercise full sovereignty over evacuated territories in Sinai upon Israeli withdrawal. A joint commission will supervise the withdrawal, and security arrangements can be reviewed when either side asks but any change must be by mutual agreement.

Annex 2—maps (*not reproduced here*)

Annex 3—normalization of relations

Ambassadors will be exchanged upon completion of the interim withdrawal. All discriminatory barriers and economic boycotts will be lifted and, not later than six months after the completion of the interim withdrawal, negotiations for a trade and commerce agreement will begin. Free movement of each other's nationals and transport will be allowed and both sides agree to promote 'good neighbourly relations'. Egypt will use the airfields left by Israel near Al Arish, Rafah, Ras al-Naqb and Sharm al-Shaikh, only for civilian aircraft. Road, rail, postal, telephone, wireless and other forms of communications will be opened between the two countries on completion of interim withdrawal.

Exchange of letters

Negotiations on the West Bank and Gaza—Negotiations on autonomy for the West Bank and Gaza will begin within one month of the exchange of the instruments of ratification. Jordan will be invited to participate and the Egyptian and Jordanian delegations may include Palestinians from the West Bank and Gaza, or other Palestinians as mutually agreed. If Jordan decides not to take part, the negotiations will be held by Egypt and Israel. The objective of the negotiations is the establishment of a self-governing authority in the West Bank and Gaza 'in order to provide full autonomy to the inhabitants'.

Egypt and Israel hope to complete negotiations within one year so that elections can be held as soon as possible. The self-governing authority elected will be inaugurated within one month of the elections at which point the five year transitional period will begin. The Israeli military Government and its civilian administration will be withdrawn, Israeli armed forces withdrawn and the remaining forces redeployed 'into specified security locations'.

UN SECURITY COUNCIL RESOLUTION ON ISRAELI SETTLEMENTS

(1 March 1980)

The resolution, No. 465, was adopted unanimously by the 15 members of the Council. The USA repudiated its vote in favour of the resolution on 3 March 1980.

The Security Council, taking note of the reports of the Commission of the Security Council established under resolution 446 (1979) to examine the situation relating to the settlements in the Arab territories occupied since 1967, including Jerusalem, contained in documents S/13450 and S/13679,

—Taking note also of letters from the permanent representative of Jordan (S/13801) and the permanent representative of Morocco, Chairman of the Islamic Group (S/13802),

—Strongly deploring the refusal by Israel to co-operate with the Commission and regretting its formal rejection of resolutions 446 (1979) and 452 (1979),

—Affirming once more that the fourth Geneva Convention relative to the protection of civilian persons in time of war of 12 August 1949 is applicable to the Arab territories occupied by Israel since 1967, including Jerusalem,

—Deploring the decision of the Government of Israel to officially support Israeli settlement in the Palestinian and other Arab territories occupied since 1967,

—Deeply concerned over the practices of the Israeli authorities in implementing that settlement policy in the occupied Arab territories, including Jerusalem, and its consequences for the local Arab and Palestinian population,

—Taking into account the need to consider measures for the impartial protection of private and public land and property, and water resources,

—Bearing in mind the specific status of Jerusalem and, in particular, the need for protection and preservation of the unique spiritual and religious dimension of the holy places in the city,

—Drawing attention to the grave consequences which the settlement policy is bound to have on any attempt to reach a comprehensive, just and lasting peace in the Middle East,

—Recalling pertinent Security Council resolutions, specifically resolutions 237 (1967) of 14 June 1967, 252 (1968) of 21 May 1968, 267 (1969) of 3 July 1969, 271 (1969) of 15 September 1969 and 298 (1971) of 25 September 1971, as well as the consensus statement made by the President of the Security Council on 11 November 1976,

—Having invited Mr Fahd Qawasmah, Mayor of Al-Khalil (Hebron), in the occupied territories, to supply it with information pursuant to rule 39 of provisional rules of procedure,

1. Commends the work done by the Commission in preparing the report contained in document S/13679,

2. Accepts the conclusions and recommendations contained in the above-mentioned report of the Commission,

3. Calls upon all parties, particularly the Government of Israel, to co-operate with the Commission,

4. Strongly deplores the decision of Israel to prohibit the free travel of Mayor Fahd Qawasmah in order to appear before the Security Council, and requests Israel to permit his free travel to the United Nations headquarters for that purpose,

5. Determines that all measures taken by Israel to change the physical character, demographic composition, institutional structure or status of the Palestinian and other Arab territories occupied since 1967, including Jerusalem, or any part thereof, have no legal validity and that Israel's policy and practices of settling parts of its population and new immigrants in those

territories constitute a flagrant violation of the Fourth Geneva Convention relative to the protection of civilian persons in time of war and also constitute a serious obstruction to achieving a comprehensive, just and lasting peace in the Middle East,

6. Strongly deplores the continuation and persistence of Israel in pursuing those policies and practices and calls upon the Government and people of Israel to rescind those measures, to dismantle the existing settlements and in particular to cease, on an urgent basis, the establishment, construction and planning of settlements in the Arab territories occupied since 1967, including Jerusalem,

7. Calls upon all states not to provide Israel with any assistance to be used specifically in connection with settlements in the occupied territories,

8. Requests the Commission to continue to examine the situation relating to settlements in the Arab territories occupied since 1967 including Jerusalem, to investigate the reported serious depletion of natural resources, particularly the water resources, with a view of ensuring the protection of those important natural resources of the territories under occupation, and to keep under close scrutiny the implementation of the present resolution,

9. Requests the Commission to report to the Security Council before 1 September 1980, and decides to convene at the earliest possible date thereafter in order to consider the report and the full implementation of the present resolution.

PRESIDENT CARTER'S STATEMENT REPUDIATING US VOTE IN SUPPORT OF UN SECURITY COUNCIL RESOLUTION 465

(3 March 1980)

I want to make it clear that the vote of the US in the Security Council of the UN does not represent a change in our position regarding the Israeli settlements in the occupied areas nor regarding the status of Jerusalem.

While our opposition to the establishment of the Israeli settlements is long-standing and well-known, we made strenuous efforts to eliminate the language with reference to the dismantling of settlements in the resolution. This call for dismantling was neither proper nor practical. We believe that the future disposition of the existing settlements must be determined during the current autonomy negotiations.

As to Jerusalem, we strongly believe that Jerusalem should be undivided with free access to the holy places for all faiths, and that its status should be determined in the negotiations for a comprehensive peace settlement.

The US vote in the UN was approved with the understanding that all references to Jerusalem would be deleted. The failure to communicate this clearly resulted in a vote in favour of the resolution rather than abstention.

THE FAHD PLAN

In August 1981 Crown Prince Fahd of Saudi Arabia launched an eight-point peace plan for the Middle East. During the remainder of 1981 some Arab states showed their support, but failure to agree on the 'Fahd Plan' caused the break-up of the Fez Arab Summit in November only a few hours after it had opened. The plan is as follows:

1. Israel to withdraw from all Arab territory occupied in 1967, including Arab Jerusalem.
2. Israeli settlements built on Arab land after 1967 to be dismantled.
3. A guarantee of freedom of worship for all religions in holy places.
4. An affirmation of the right of the Palestinian Arab people to return to their homes, and compensation for those who do not wish to return.
5. The West Bank and Gaza Strip to have a transitional period under the auspices of the United Nations for a period not exceeding several months.
6. An independent Palestinian state should be set up with Jerusalem as its capital.
7. All states in the region should be able to live in peace.
8. The UN or member-states of the UN to guarantee carrying-out of these principles.

THE SHULTZ PLAN

At the beginning of February 1988 the Government of the USA announced a new plan for the resolution of the Palestine issue, which came to be known as the 'Shultz Plan', after the US Secretary of State, George Shultz. The presentation of the plan followed more than a year of diplomatic activity during which the idea of an international peace conference under the auspices of the UN, which had been agreed in principle by Shimon Peres, the Israeli Minister of Foreign Affairs, and King Hussein of Jordan, had won increasing support. The main provisions of the plan, as they were subsequently clarified, were for a six-month period of negotiations between Israel and a joint Jordanian/Palestinian delegation, to determine the details of a transitional autonomy arrangement for the West Bank and the Gaza Strip, which would last for three years; during the transitional period a permanent settlement would be negotiated by the Israeli and Jordanian/Palestinian delegations; both sets of negotiations would run concurrently with and, if necessary, with reference to, an international peace conference, involving the five permanent members of the UN Security Council and all the interested parties (including the Palestinians in a joint Jordanian/Palestinian delegation), which, like the separate Israeli-Jordanian/Palestinian negotiations, would be conducted on the basis of all the participants' acceptance of UN Security Council Resolutions 242 and 338, but would have no power to impose a settlement.

On 6 March 1988 the Israeli newspaper, Yedioth Aharonoth, *published a photocopy of a letter from George Shultz to the Israeli Prime Minister, Itzhak Shamir, containing details of his peace proposals. The contents of the letter, identical versions of which were believed to have been delivered to the Governments of Egypt, Jordan and Syria, were as follows:*

Dear Mr Prime Minister,

I set forth below the statement of understandings which I am convinced is necessary to achieve the prompt opening of negotiations on a comprehensive peace. This statement of understandings emerges from discussions held with you and other regional leaders. I look forward to the letter of reply of the government of Israel in confirmation of this statement.

The agreed objective is a comprehensive peace providing for the security of all the States in the region and for the legitimate rights of the Palestinian people.

Negotiations will start on an early date certain between Israel and each of its neighbors which is willing to do so. Those negotiations could begin by May 1, 1988. Each of these negotiations will be based on United Nations Security Council Resolutions 242 and 338, in all their parts. The parties to each bilateral negotiation will determine the procedure and agenda of their negotiation. All participants in the negotiations must state their willingness to negotiate with one another.

As concerns negotiations between the Israeli delegation and Jordanian-Palestinian delegation, negotiations will begin on arrangements for a transitional period, with the objective of completing them within six months. Seven months after transitional negotiations begin, final status negotiations will begin, with the objective of completing them within one year. These negotiations will be based on all the provisions and principles of the United Nations Security Council Resolution 242. Final status talks will start before the transitional period begins. The transitional period will begin three months after the conclusion of the transitional agreement and will last for three years. The United States will participate in both negotiations and will promote their rapid conclusion. In particular, the United States will submit a draft agreement for the parties' consideration at the outset of the negotiations on transitional arrangements.

Two weeks before the opening of negotiations, an international conference will be held. The Secretary-General of the United Nations will be asked to issue invitations to the parties involved in the Arab–Israeli conflict and the five permanent members of the United Nations Security Council. All participants in the conference must accept United Nations Security Council Resolutions 242 and 338, and renounce violence and terrorism. The parties to each bilateral negotiations may refer reports on the status of their negotiations to the conference, in a manner to be agreed. The conference will not be able to impose solutions or veto agreements reached.

Palestinian representation will be within the Jordanian-Palestinian delegation. The Palestinian issue will be addressed in the negotiations between the Jordanian-Palestinian and Israeli delegations. Negotiations between the Israeli delegation and the Jordanian-Palestinian delegation will proceed independently of any other negotiations.

This statement of understandings is an integral whole. The United States understands that your acceptance is dependent on the implementation of each element in good faith.

Sincerely yours,
George P. Shultz.

DECLARATION OF PALESTINIAN INDEPENDENCE

In November 1988 the 19th session of the PNC culminated in the declaration 'in the name of God and the Palestinian Arab people' of the independent State of Palestine, with the Holy City of Jerusalem as its capital. The opportunity for the PLO to assert sovereignty over a specific area arose through the decision of King Hussein of Jordan, in July 1988, to sever Jordan's 'administrative and legal links' with the West Bank. The Declaration of Independence cited UN General Assembly Resolution 181 of 1947, which partitioned Palestine into two states, one Arab and one Jewish, as providing the legal basis for the right of the Palestinian Arab people to national sovereignty and independence. At the end of the session, the PNC issued a political statement. Details of the Declaration of Independence, and of the political statement, set out below, are taken from an unofficial English-language translation of the proceedings, distributed by the PLO.

'The National Council proclaims, in the name of God and the Palestinian Arab people, the establishment of the State of Palestine on our Palestinian land, with the Holy City of Jerusalem as its capital.

The State of Palestine is the state of Palestinians wherever they may be. In it they shall develop their national and cultural identity and enjoy full equality in rights. Their religious and political beliefs and their human dignity shall be safeguarded under a democratic parliamentary system of government built on the freedom of opinion; and on the freedom to form parties; and on the protection of the rights of the minority by the majority and respect of the decisions of the majority by the minority; and on social justice and equal rights, free of ethnic, religious, racial or sexual discrimination; and on a constitution that guarantees the rule of law and the independence of the judiciary; and on the basis of total allegiance to the centuries-old spiritual and civilizational Palestinian heritage of religious tolerance and coexistence.

The State of Palestine is an Arab state, an integral part of the Arab nation and of that nation's heritage, its civilization and its aspiration to attain its goals of liberation, development, democracy and unity. Affirming its commitment to the Charter of the League of Arab states and its insistence on the reinforcement of joint Arab action, the State of Palestine calls on the people of its nation to assist in the completion of its birth by mobilizing their resources and augmenting their efforts to end the Israeli occupation.

The State of Palestine declares its commitment to the principles and objectives of the United Nations, and to the Universal Declaration of Human Rights, and to the principles and policy of non-alignment.

The State of Palestine, declaring itself a peace-loving state committed to the principles of peaceful coexistence, shall strive with all states and peoples to attain a permanent peace built on justice and respect of rights, in which humanity's constructive talents can prosper, and creative competition can flourish, and fear of tomorrow can be abolished, for tomorrow brings nothing but security for the just and those who regain their sense of justice.

As it struggles to establish peace in the land of love and peace, the State of Palestine exhorts the United Nations to take upon itself a special responsibility for the Palestinian Arab people and their homeland; and exhorts the peace-loving, freedom-cherishing peoples and states of the world to help it attain its objectives and put an end to the tragedy its people are suffering by providing them with security and endeavouring to end the Israeli occupation of the Palestinian territories.

The State of Palestine declares its belief in the settlement of international and regional disputes by peaceful means in accordance with the Charter and resolutions of the United Nations; and its rejection of threats of force or violence or terrorism and the use of these against its territorial integrity and political independence or the territorial integrity of any other state, without prejudice to its natural right to defend its territory and independence.

The Palestine National Council resolves:

First: On the escalation and continuity of the *intifada*

A. To provide all the means and capabilities needed to escalate our people's *intifada* in various ways and on various levels to guarantee its continuation and intensification.

B. To support the popular institutions and organizations in the occupied Palestinian territories.

C. To bolster and develop the Popular Committees and other specialized popular and trade union bodies, including the attack group and the popular army, with a view to expanding their role and increasing their effectiveness.

D. To consolidate the national unity that emerged and developed during the *intifada*.

E. To intensify efforts on the international level for the release of the detainees, the repatriation of the deportees, and the termination of the organized, official acts of repression and terrorism against our children, our women, our men, and our institutions.

F. To call on the United Nations to place the occupied Palestinian land under international supervision for the protection of our people and the termination of the Israeli occupation.

G. To call on the Palestinian people outside our homeland to intensify and increase their support, and to expand the family-assistance program.

H. To call on the Arab nation, its people, forces, institutions and governments, to increase their political, material and informational support of the *intifada*.

I. To call on all free and honorable people worldwide to stand by our people, our revolution, our *intifada* against the Israeli occupation, the repression, and the organized, fascist official terrorism to which the occupation forces and the armed fanatic settlers are subjecting our people, our universities, our institutions, our national economy, and our Islamic and Christian holy places.

Second: In the political field

Proceeding from the above, the Palestine National Council, being responsible to the Palestinian people, their national rights and their desire for peace as expressed in the Declaration of Independence issued on November 15, 1988; and in response to the humanitarian quest for international entente, nuclear disarmament and the settlement of regional conflicts by peaceful means, affirms the determination of the Palestine Liberation Organization to arrive at a political settlement of the Arab–Israeli conflict and its core, the Palestinian issue, in the framework of the UN Charter, the principles and rules of international legitimacy, the edicts of international law, the resolutions of the United Nations, the latest of which are Security Council Resolutions 605, 607 and 608, and the resolutions of the Arab summits, in a manner that assures the Palestinian Arab people's right to repatriation, self-determination and the establishment of their independent state on their national soil, and that institutes arrangements for the security and peace of all states in the region.

Towards the achievement of this, the Palestine National Council affirms:

1. The necessity of convening an international conference on the issue of the Middle East and its core, the Palestinian issue, under the auspices of the United Nations and with the participation of the permanent members of the Security Council and all parties to the conflict in the region, including, on an equal footing, the Palestine Liberation Organization, the sole legitimate representative of the Palestinian people; on the understanding that the international conference will be held on the basis of Security Council Resolutions 242 and 338 and the safeguarding of the legitimate national rights of the Palestinian people, foremost among which is the right to self-determination, in accordance with the principles and

provisions of the UN Charter as they pertain to the right of peoples to self-determination, and the inadmissibility of the acquisition of others' territory by force or military conquest, and in accordance with the UN resolutions relating to the Palestinian issue.

2. The withdrawal of Israel from all the Palestinian and Arab territories it occupied in 1967, including Arab Jerusalem.

3. The annulment of all expropriation and annexation measures and the removal of the settlements established by Israel in the Palestinian and Arab territories since 1967.

4. Endeavouring to place the occupied Palestinian territories, including Arab Jerusalem, under the supervision of the United Nations for a limited period, to protect our people, to create an atmosphere conducive to the success of the proceedings of the international conference toward the attainment of a comprehensive political settlement and the achievement of peace and security for all on the basis of mutual consent, and to enable the Palestinian state to exercise its effective authority in these territories.

5. The settlement of the issue of the Palestinian refugees in accordance with the pertinent United Nations resolutions.

6. Guaranteeing the freedom of worship and the right to engage in religious rites for all faiths in the holy place in Palestine.

7. The Security Council shall draw up and guarantee arrangements for the security of all states concerned and for peace between them, including the Palestinian state.

The Palestine National Council confirms its past resolutions that the relationship between the fraternal Jordanian and Palestinian peoples is a privileged one and that the future relationship between the states of Jordan and Palestine will be built on confederal foundations, on the basis of the two fraternal peoples' free and voluntary choice, in consolidation of the historic ties that bind them and the vital interests they hold in common.

The National Council also renews its commitment to the United Nations resolutions that affirm the right of peoples to resist foreign occupation, imperialism and racial discrimination, and their right to fight for their independence; and it once more announces its rejection of terrorism in all its forms, including state terrorism, emphasizing its commitment to the resolutions it adopted in the past on this subject, and to the resolutions of the Arab summit in Algiers in 1988, and to UN Resolutions 42/159 of 1967 and 61/40 of 1985, and to what was stated in this regard in the Cairo Declaration of 7/11/85.

Third: In the Arab and international fields

The Palestine National Council emphasizes the importance of the unity of Lebanon in its territory, its people and its institutions, and stands firmly against the attempts to partition the land and disintegrate the fraternal people of Lebanon. It further emphasizes the importance of the joint Arab effort to participate in a settlement of the Lebanese crisis that helps crystallize and implement solutions that preserve Lebanese unity. The Council also stresses the importance of consecrating the right of the Palestinians in Lebanon to engage in political and informational activity and to enjoy security and protection; and of working against all the forms of conspiracy and aggression that target them and their right to work and live; and of the need to secure the conditions that assure them the ability to defend themselves and provide them with security and protection.

The Palestine National Council affirms its solidarity with the Lebanese nationalist Islamic forces in their struggle against the Israeli occupation and its agents in the Lebanese South; expresses its pride in the allied struggle of the Lebanese and Palestinian peoples against the aggression and toward the termination of the Israeli occupation of parts of the South; and underscores the importance of bolstering this kinship between our people and the fraternal, combative people of Lebanon.

And on this occasion, the Council addresses a reverent salute to the long-suffering people of our camps in Lebanon and its South, who are enduring the aggression, massacres, murder, starvation, air raids, bombardments and sieges perpetrated against the Palestinian camps and Lebanese villages by the Israeli army, air force and navy, aided and abetted by hireling forces in the region; and it rejects the resettlement conspiracy, for the Palestinians' homeland is Palestine.

The Council emphasizes the importance of the Iraq-Iran cease-fire resolution toward the establishment of a permanent peace settlement between the two countries and in the Gulf Region; and calls for an intensification of the efforts being exerted to ensure the success of the negotiations toward the establishment of peace on stable and firm foundations; affirming, on this occasion, the price of the Palestinian Arab people and the Arab nation as a whole in the steadfastness and triumphs of fraternal Iraq as it defended the eastern gate of the Arab nation.

The National Council also expresses its deep pride in the stand taken by the peoples of our Arab nation in support of our Palestinian Arab people and of the Palestine Liberation Organization and of our people's *intifada* in the occupied homeland; and emphasizes the importance of fortifying the bonds of combat among the forces, parties and organizations of the Arab national liberation movement, in defense of the right of the Arab nation and its peoples to liberation, progress, democracy and unity. The Council calls for the adoption of all measures needed to reinforce the unity of struggle among all members of the Arab national liberation movement.

The Palestine National Council, as it hails the Arab states and thanks them for their support of our people's struggle, calls on them to honour the commitments they approved at the summit conference in Algiers in support of the Palestinian people and their blessed *intifada*. The Council, in issuing this appeal, expresses its great confidence that the leaders of the Arab nation will remain as we have known them, a bulwark of support for Palestine and its people.

The Palestine National Council reiterates the desire of the Palestine Liberation Organization for Arab solidarity as the framework within which the Arab nation and its states can organize themselves to confront Israel's aggression and American support of that aggression, and within which Arab prestige can be enhanced and the Arab role strengthened to the point of influencing international policies to the benefit of Arab rights and causes.

The Palestine National Council expresses its deep gratitude to all the states and international forces and organizations that support the national rights of the Palestinians; affirms its desire to strengthen the bonds of friendship and co-operation with the Soviet Union, the People's (Republic of) China, the other socialist countries, the non-aligned states, the Islamic states, the African states, the Latin American states and the other friendly states; and notes with satisfaction the signs of positive evolution in the positions of some West European states and Japan in the direction of support for the rights of the Palestinian people, applauds this development, and urges intensified efforts to increase it.

The National Council affirms the fraternal solidarity of the Palestinian people and the Palestine Liberation Organization with the struggle of the peoples of Asia, Africa and Latin America for their liberation and the reinforcement of their independence; and condemns all American attempts to threaten the independence of the states of Central America and interfere in their affairs.

The Palestine National Council expresses the support of the Palestine Liberation Organization for the national liberation movements in South Africa and Namibia...

The Council notes with considerable concern the growth of the Israeli forces of fascism and extremism and the escalation of their open calls for the implementation of the policy of annihilation and individual and collective expulsion of our people from their homeland, and calls for intensified efforts in all areas to confront this fascist peril. The Council at the same time expresses its appreciation of the role and courage of the Israeli peace forces as they resist and expose the forces of fascism, racism and aggression, support our people's struggle and their valiant *intifada* and back our people's right to self-determination and the establishment of an independent state. The Council confirms its past resolutions regarding the reinforcement and development of relations with these democratic forces.

The Palestine National Council also addresses itself to the American people, calling on them all to strive to put an end to the American policy that denies the Palestinian people's national rights, including their sacred right to self-determination, and urging them to work toward the adoption of policies that conform to the Declaration of Human Rights and the international conventions and resolutions and serve the quest for peace in the Middle East and security for all its peoples, including the Palestinian people.

The Council charges the Executive Committee with the task of completing the formation of the Committee for the Perpetuation of the Memory of the Martyr-Symbol Abu Jihad, which shall initiate its work immediately upon the adjournment of the Council.

The Council sends its greetings to the United Nations Committee on the Exercise of the Inalienable Rights of the Palestinian People, and to the fraternal and friendly international and non-governmental institutions and organizations, and to the journalists and media that have stood and still stand by our people's struggle and *intifada*.

The National Council expresses deep pain at the continued detention of hundreds of combatants from among our people in a number of Arab countries, strongly condemns their continued detention, and calls upon those countries to put an end to these abnormal conditions and release those fighters to play their role in the struggle.

In conclusion, the Palestine National Council affirms its complete confidence that the justice of the Palestinian cause and of the demands for which the Palestinian people are struggling will continue to draw increasing support from honorable and free people around the world; and also affirms its complete confidence in victory on the road to Jerusalem, the capital of our independent Palestinian state.'

DECLARATION OF PRINCIPLES ON PALESTINIAN SELF-RULE

(13 September 1993)

The Government of the State of Israel and the Palestinian team (in the Jordanian-Palestinian delegation to the Middle East Peace Conference) (the 'Palestinian Delegation') representing the Palestinian people, agree that it is time to put an end to decades of confrontation and conflict, recognize their mutual legitimate and political rights, and strive to live in peaceful coexistence and mutual dignity and security and achieve a just, lasting and comprehensive peace settlement and historic reconciliation through the agreed political process.

Accordingly, the two sides agree to the following principles:

Article I

Aim of the negotiations

The aim of the Israeli-Palestinian negotiations within the current Middle East peace process is, among other things, to establish a Palestinian Interim Self-Government Authority, the elected Council, (the 'Council') for the Palestinian people in the West Bank and the Gaza Strip, for a transitional period not exceeding five years, leading to a permanent settlement based on Security Council Resolutions 242 and 338.

It is understood that the interim arrangements are an integral part of the overall peace process and that final status negotiations will lead to the implementation of Security Council Resolutions 242 and 338.

Article II

Framework for the interim period

The agreed framework for the interim period is set forth in the Declaration of Principles.

Article III

Elections

1. In order that the Palestinian people in the West Bank and Gaza Strip may govern themselves according to democratic principles, direct, free and general political elections will be held for the Council under agreed supervision and international observation, while the Palestinian police will ensure public order.

2. An agreement will be concluded on the exact mode and conditions of the elections in accordance with the protocol attached as Annex I, with the goal of holding the elections not later than nine months after the entry into force of this Declaration of Principles.

3. These elections will constitute a significant interim preparatory step toward the realization of the legitimate rights of the Palestinian people and their just requirements.

Article IV

Jurisdiction of the Council will cover West Bank and Gaza Strip territory, except for issues that will be negotiated in the permanent status negotiations. The two sides view the West Bank and the Gaza Strip as a single territorial unit, whose integrity will be preserved during the interim period.

Article V

Transitional period and permanent status negotiations

1. The five-year transitional period will begin upon the withdrawal from the Gaza Strip and Jericho area.

2. Permanent status negotiations will commence as soon as possible, but not later than the beginning of the third year of the interim period, between the Government of Israel and the Palestinian people representatives.

3. It is understood that these negotiations shall cover remaining issues, including Jerusalem, refugees, settlements, security arrangements, borders, relations and co-operation with other neighbours, and other issues of common interest.

4. The two parties agree that the outcome of the permanent status negotiations should not be prejudiced or pre-empted by agreements reached for the interim period.

Article VI

Preparatory transfer of powers and responsibilities

1. Upon the entry into force of this Declaration of Principles and the withdrawal from the Gaza Strip and Jericho area, a transfer of authority from the Israeli military government and its Civil Administration to the authorized Palestinians for this task, as detailed herein, will commence. This transfer of authority will be of preparatory nature until the inauguration of the Council.

2. Immediately after the entry into force of this Declaration of Principles and the withdrawal from the Gaza Strip and Jericho area, with the view to promoting economic development in the West Bank and Gaza Strip, authority will be transferred to the Palestinians in the following spheres: education and culture, health, social welfare, direct taxation, and tourism. The Palestinian side will commence in building the Palestinian police force, as agreed upon. Pending the inauguration of the Council, the two parties may negotiate the transfer of additional powers and responsibilities as agreed upon.

Article VII

Interim agreement

1. The Israeli and Palestinian delegations will negotiate an agreement on the interim period (the 'Interim Agreement').

2. The Interim Agreement shall specify, among other things, the structure of the Council, the number of its members, and the transfer of powers and responsibilities from the Israeli military government and its Civil Administration to the Council. The Interim Agreement shall also specify the Council's executive authority, legislative authority in accordance with Article IX below, and the independent Palestinian judicial organs.

3. The Interim Agreement shall include arrangements, to be implemented upon the inauguration of the Council, for the assumption by the Council of all of the powers and responsibilities transferred previously in accordance with Article VI above.

4. In order to enable the Council to promote economic growth, upon its inauguration, the Council will establish, among other things, a Palestinian Electricity Authority, a Gaza Sea Port Authority, a Palestinian Development Bank, a Palestinian Export Promotion Board, a Palestinian Environmental Authority, a Palestinian Land Authority and a Palestinian Water Administration Authority, and any other authorities agreed upon, in accordance with the Interim Agreement that will specify their powers and responsibilities.

5. After the inauguration of the Council, the Civil Administration will be dissolved, and the Israeli military government will be withdrawn.

Article VIII

Public order and security

In order to guarantee public order and internal security for the Palestinians of the West Bank and the Gaza Strip, the Council will establish a strong police force, while Israel will continue to carry the responsibility for defending against external threats, as well as the responsibility for overall security of the Israelis to protect their internal security and public order.

Article IX

Laws and military orders

1. The Council will be empowered to legislate, in accordance with the Interim Agreement, within all authorities transferred to it.

2. Both parties will review jointly laws and military orders presently in force in remaining spheres.

Article X

Joint Israeli-Palestinian liaison committee

In order to provide for a smooth implementation of this Declaration of Principles and any subsequent agreements pertaining to the interim period, upon the entry into force of this Declaration of Principles, a Joint Israeli-Palestinian Liaison Committee will be established in order to deal with issues requiring co-ordination, other issues of common interest, and disputes.

Article XI

Israeli-Palestinian co-operation in economic fields

Recognizing the mutual benefit of co-operation in promoting the development of the West Bank, the Gaza Strip and Israel, upon the entry into force of this Declaration of Principles, an Israeli-Palestinian Economic Co-operation Committee will be established in order to develop and implement in a co-operative manner the programmes identified in the protocols attached as Annex III and Annex IV.

Article XII

Liaison and co-operation with Jordan and Egypt

The two parties will invite the Governments of Jordan and Egypt to participate in establishing further liaison and co-operation arrangements between the Government of Israel and the Palestinian representatives, on one hand, and the Governments of Jordan and Egypt, on the other hand, to promote co-operation between them. These arrangements will include the constitution of a Continuing Committee that will decide by agreement on the modalities of the admission of persons displaced from the West Bank and Gaza Strip in 1967, together with necessary measures to prevent disruption and disorder. Other matters of common concern will be dealt with by this Committee.

Article XIII

Redeployment of Israeli forces

1. After the entry into force of this Declaration of Principles, and not later than the eve of elections for the Council, a redeployment of Israeli military forces in the West Bank and the Gaza Strip will take place, in addition to withdrawal of Israeli forces carried out in accordance with Article XIV.

2. In redeploying its military forces, Israel will be guided by the principle that its military forces should be redeployed outside the populated areas.

3. Further redeployments to specified locations will be gradually implemented commensurate with the assumption of responsibility for public order and internal security by the Palestinian police force pursuant to Article VIII above.

Article XIV

Israeli withdrawal from the Gaza Strip and Jericho area

Israel will withdraw from the Gaza Strip and Jericho area, as detailed in the protocol attached as Annex II.

Article XV

Resolution of disputes

1. Disputes arising out of the application or interpretation of this Declaration of Principles, or any subsequent agreements pertaining to the interim period, shall be resolved by negotiations through the Joint Liaison Committee to be established pursuant to Article X above.

2. Disputes which cannot be settled by negotiations may be resolved by a mechanism of conciliation to be agreed upon by the parties.

3. The parties may agree to submit to arbitration disputes relating to the interim period, which cannot be settled through conciliation. To this end, upon the agreement of both parties, the parties will establish an Arbitration Committee.

Article XVI

Israel-Palestinian co-operation concerning regional programs

Both parties view the multilateral working groups as an appropriate instrument for promoting a 'Marshall Plan,' the regional programs and other programs, including special programs for the West Bank and Gaza Strip, as indicated in the protocol attached as Annex IV.

Article XVII

Miscellaneous provisions

1. This Declaration of Principles will enter into force one month after its signing.

2. All protocols annexed to this Declaration of Principles and Agreed Minutes pertaining thereto shall be regarded as an integral part hereof.

Annex 1—protocol on the mode and conditions of elections

1. Palestinians of Jerusalem who live there will have the right to participate in the election process, according to an agreement between the two sides.

2. In addition, the election agreement should cover, among other things, the following issues:

a. the system of elections,

b. the mode of the agreed supervision and international observation and their personal composition, and

c. rules and regulations regarding election campaign, including agreed arrangements for the organizing of mass media, and the possibility of licensing a broadcasting and TV station.

3. The future status of displaced Palestinians who were registered on 4th June 1967 will not be prejudiced because they are unable to participate in the election process due to practical reasons.

Annex 2—protocol on withdrawal of Israeli forces from the Gaza Strip and Jericho Area

1. The two sides will conclude and sign within two months from the date of entry into force of this Declaration of Principles, an agreement on the withdrawal of Israeli military forces from the Gaza Strip and Jericho area. This agreement will include comprehensive arrangements to apply in the Gaza Strip and the Jericho area subsequent to the Israeli withdrawal.

2. Israel will implement an accelerated and scheduled withdrawal of Israeli military forces from the Gaza Strip and Jericho area, beginning immediately with the signing of the agreement on the Gaza Strip and Jericho area and to be completed within a period not exceeding four months after the signing of this agreement.

3. The above agreement will include, among other things:

a. Arrangements for a smooth and peaceful transfer of authority from the Israeli military government and its Civil Administration to the Palestinian representatives.

b. Structure, powers and responsibilities of the Palestinian authority in these areas, except, external security, settlements, Israelis, foreign relations, and other subjects mutually agreed upon.

c. Arrangements for assumption of internal security and public order by the Palestinian police force consisting of police officers recruited locally and from abroad (holding Jordanian passports and Palestinian documents issued by Egypt). Those who will participate in the Palestinian police force coming from abroad should be trained as police and police officers.

d. A temporary international or foreign presence, as agreed upon.

e. Establishment of a joint Palestinian-Israeli co-ordination and co-operation committee for mutual security purposes.

f. An economic development and stabilization program, including the establishment of an Emergency Fund, to encourage foreign investment, and financial and economic support. Both sides will co-ordinate and co-operate jointly and unilaterally with regional and international parties to support these aims.

g. Arrangements for a safe passage for persons and transportation between the Gaza Strip and Jericho area.

4. The above agreement will include arrangements for co-ordination between both parties regarding passages:

a. Gaza–Egypt; and

b. Jericho–Jordan.

5. The offices responsible for carrying out the powers and responsibilities of the Palestinian authority under this Annex II and Article VI of the Declaration of Principles will be located in the Gaza Strip and in the Jericho area pending the inauguration of the Council.

6. Other than these agreed arrangements, the status of the Gaza Strip and Jericho area will continue to be an integral part of the West Bank and Gaza Strip, and will not be changed in the interim period.

PROTOCOL ON ISRAELI-PALESTINIAN CO-OPERATION IN ECONOMIC AND DEVELOPMENT PROGRAMS

The two sides agree to establish an Israeli-Palestinian Continuing Committee for Economic Co-operation, focusing, among other things, on the following:

1. Co-operation in the field of water, including a Water Development Program prepared by experts from both sides, which will also specify the mode of co-operation in the management of water resources in the West Bank and Gaza Strip, and will include proposals for studies and plans on water rights of each party, as well as on the equitable utilization of joint water resources for implementation in and beyond the interim period.

2. Co-operation in the field of electricity, including an Electricity Development Program, which will also specify the mode of co-operation for the production, maintenance, purchase and sale of electricity resources.

3. Co-operation in the field of energy, including an Energy Development Program, which will provide for the exploitation of oil and gas for industrial purposes, particularly in the Gaza Strip and in the Negev, and will encourage further joint exploitation of other energy resources. This Program may also provide for the construction of a Petrochemical industrial complex in the Gaza Strip and the construction of oil and gas pipelines.

4. Co-operation in the field of finance, including a Financial Development and Action Program for the encouragement of international investment in the West Bank and the Gaza Strip, and in Israel, as well as the establishment of a Palestinian Development Bank.

5. Co-operation in the fields of transport and communications, including a Program, which will define guidelines for the establishment of a Gaza Sea Port Area, and will provide for the establishing of transport and communications lines to and from the West Bank and the Gaza Strip to Israel and to other countries. In addition, this Program will provide for carrying out the necessary construction of roads, railways, communications lines, etc.

6. Co-operation in the field of trade, including studies, and Trade Promotion Programs, which will encourage local, regional and inter-regional trade, as well as a feasibility study of creating free trade zones in the Gaza Strip and in Israel, mutual access to these zones, and co-operation in other areas related to trade and commerce.

7. Co-operation in the field of industry, including industrial Development Programs, which will provide for the establishment of joint Israeli-Palestinian Research and Development Centers, will promote Palestinian-Israeli joint ventures, and provide guidelines for co-operation in the textile, food, pharmaceutical, electronics, diamonds, computer and science-based industries.

8. A program for co-operation in, and regulation of, labour relations and co-operation in social welfare issues.

9. A Human Resources Development and Co-operation Plan, providing for joint Israeli-Palestinian workshops and seminars, and for the establishment of joint vocational training centres, research institutes and data banks.

10. An Environmental Protection Plan, providing for joint and/or co-ordinated measures in this sphere.

11. A program for developing co-ordination and co-operation in the field of communication and media.

12. Any other programs of mutual interest.

PROTOCOL ON ISRAELI-PALESTINIAN CO-OPERATION CONCERNING REGIONAL DEVELOPMENT PROGRAMS

1. The two sides will co-operate in the context of the multilateral peace efforts in promoting a Development Program for the region, including the West Bank and the Gaza Strip, to be initiated by the G-7. The parties will request the G-7 to seek the participation in this program of other interested states, such as members of the Organization for Economic Co-operation and Development, regional Arab states and institutions, as well as members of the private sector.

2. The Development Program will consist of two elements:

a) an Economic Development Program for the West Bank and the Gaza Strip

b) a Regional Economic Development Program

A. The Economic Development Program for the West Bank and the Gaza Strip will consist of the following elements:

(1) A Social Rehabilitation Program, including a Housing and Construction Program

(2) A Small and Medium Business Development Plan

(3) An Infrastructure Development Program (water, electricity, transportation and communications, etc.)

(4) A Human Resources Plan

(5) Other programs

B. The Regional Economic Development Program may consist of the following elements:

(1) The establishment of a Middle East Development Fund, as a first step, and a Middle East Development Bank, as a second step

(2) The development of a joint Israeli-Palestinian-Jordanian Plan for co-ordinated exploitation of the Dead Sea area

(3) The Mediterranean Sea (Gaza)—Dead Sea Canal

(4) Regional Desalinization and other water development projects

(5) A regional plan for agricultural development, including a co-ordinated regional effort for the prevention of desertification

(6) Interconnection of electricity grids

(7) Regional co-operation for the transfer, distribution and industrial exploitation of gas, oil and other energy resources

(8) A regional Tourism, Transportation and Telecommunications Development Plan

(9) Regional co-operation in other spheres

3. The two sides will encourage the multilateral working groups, and will co-ordinate towards its success. The two parties will encourage international activities, as well as pre-feasibility and feasibility studies, within the various multilateral working groups.

AGREED MINUTES TO THE DECLARATION OF PRINCIPLES ON INTERIM SELF-GOVERNMENT ARRANGEMENTS

A. General Understandings and Agreements

Any powers and responsibilites transferred to the Palestinians pursuant to the Declaration of Principles prior to the inauguration of the Council will be subject to the same principles pertaining to Article IV, as set out in these Agreed Minutes below.

B. Specific Understandings and Agreements

Article IV

It is understood that:

1. Jurisdiction of the Council will cover West Bank and Gaza Strip territory, except for issues that will be negotiated in the permanent status negotiations: Jerusalem, settlements, military locations and Israelis.

2. The Council's jurisdiction will apply with regard to the agreed powers, responsibilities, spheres and authorities transferred to it.

Article VI (2)

It is agreed that the transfer of authority will be as follows:

(1) The Palestinian side will inform the Israeli side of the names of the authorized Palestinians who will assume the powers, authorities and responsibilities that will be transferred to the Palestinians according to the Declaration of Principles in the following fields: education and culture, health, social welfare, direct taxation, tourism, and any other authorities agreed upon.

(2) It is understood that the rights and obligations of these offices will not be affected.

(3) Each of the spheres described above will continue to enjoy existing budgetary allocations in accordance with arrangements to be mutually agreed upon. These arrangements also will provide for the necessary adjustments required in order to take into account the taxes collected by the direct taxation office.

(4) Upon the execution of the Declaration of Principles, the Israeli and Palestinian delegations will immediately commence negotiations on a detailed plan for the transfer of authority on the above offices in accordance with the above understandings.

Article VII (2)

The Interim Agreement will also include arrangements for co-ordination and co-operation.

Article VII (5)

The withdrawal of the military government will not prevent Israel from exercising the powers and responsibilities not transferred to the Council.

Article VIII

It is understood that the Interim Agreement will include arrangements for co-operation and co-ordination between the two parties in this regard. It is also agreed that the transfer of powers and responsibilities to the Palestinian police will be accomplished in a phased manner, as agreed in the Interim Agreement.

Article X

It is agreed that, upon the entry into force of the Declaration of Principles, the Israeli and Palestinian delegations will exchange the names of the individuals designated by them as members of the Joint Israeli-Palestinian Liaison Committee.

It is further agreed that each side will have an equal number of members in the Joint Committee. The Joint Committee will reach decisions by agreement. The Joint Committee may add other technicians and experts, as necessary. The Joint Committee will decide on the frequency and place or places of its meetings.

Annex II

It is understood that, subsequent to the Israeli withdrawal, Israel will continue to be responsible for external security, and for internal security and public order of settlements and Israelis. Israeli military forces and civilians may continue to use roads freely within the Gaza Strip and the Jericho area.

Article XVI

Israeli-Palestinian Co-operation Concerning Regional Programs

Both parties view the multilateral working groups as an appropriate instrument for promoting a 'Marshall Plan,' the regional programs and other programs, including special programs for the West Bank and Gaza Strip, as indicated in the protocol attached as Annex IV.

Article XVII

Miscellaneous Provisions

1. This Declaration of Principles will enter into force one month after its signing.

2. All protocols annexed to this Declaration of Principles and Agreed Minutes pertaining thereto shall be regarded as an integral part hereof.

THE CAIRO AGREEMENT ON THE GAZA STRIP AND JERICHO

(4 May 1994)

The Government of the State of Israel and the Palestine Liberation Organization (hereinafter 'the PLO'), the representative of the Palestinian people;

Preamble

Within the framework of the Middle East peace process initiated at Madrid in October 1991;

Reaffirming their determination to live in peaceful co-existence, mutual dignity and security, while recognizing their mutual legitimate and political rights;

Reaffirming their desire to achieve a just, lasting and comprehensive peace settlement through the agreed political process;

Reaffirming their adherence to the mutual recognition and commitments expressed in the letters dated September 9, 1993, signed by and exchanged between the Prime Minister of Israel and the Chairman of the PLO;

Reaffirming their understanding that the interim self-government arrangements, including the arrangements to apply in the Gaza Strip and the Jericho Area contained in this Agreement, are an integral part of the whole peace process and that the negotiations on the permanent status will lead to the implementation of Security Council Resolutions 242 and 338;

Desirous of putting into effect the Declaration of Principles on Interim Self-Government Arrangements signed at Washington, D.C. on September 13, 1993, and the agreed minutes thereto (hereinafter 'The Declaration of Principles'), and in particular the protocol on withdrawal of Israeli forces from the Gaza Strip and the Jericho Area:

Hereby agree to the following arrangements regarding the Gaza Strip and the Jericho Area:

Article I

DEFINITIONS

For the purpose of this Agreement:

a. The Gaza Strip and the Jericho Area are delineated on Map Nos. 1 and 2 attached to this Agreement (*Maps not reproduced—Ed.*)

b. 'The settlements' means the Gush Katif and Erez settlement areas, as well as the other settlements in the Gaza Strip, as shown on attached Map No. 1

c. 'The military installation area' means the Israeli military installation area along the Egyptian border in the Gaza Strip, as shown on Map No. 1; and

d. The term 'Israelis' shall also include Israeli statutory agencies and corporations registered in Israel

Article II

SCHEDULED WITHDRAWAL OF ISRAELI MILITARY FORCES

1. Israel shall implement an accelerated and scheduled withdrawal of Israeli military forces from the Gaza Strip and from the Jericho Area to begin immediately with the signing of this Agreement. Israel shall complete such withdrawal within three weeks from this date.

2. Subject to the arrangements included in the Protocol concerning withdrawal of Israeli military forces and security arrangements attached as Annex I, the Israeli withdrawal shall include evacuating all military bases and other fixed installations to be handed over to the Palestinian Police, to be established pursuant to Article IX below (hereinafter 'the Palestinian Police').

3. In order to carry out Israel's responsibility for external security and for internal security and public order of settlements and Israelis, Israel shall, concurrently with the withdrawal, redeploy its remaining military forces to the settlements and the military installation area, in accordance with the provisions of this Agreement. Subject to the provisions of this Agreement, this redeployment shall constitute full implementation of Article XIII of the Declaration of Principles with regard to the Gaza Strip and the Jericho Area only.

4. For the purposes of this Agreement, 'Israeli military forces' may include Israeli police and other Israeli security forces.

5. Israelis, including Israeli military forces, may continue to use roads freely within the Gaza Strip and the Jericho Area. Palestinians may use public roads crossing the settlements freely, as provided for in Annex I.

6. The Palestinian Police shall be deployed and shall assume responsibility for public order and internal security of Palestinians in accordance with this Agreement and Annex I.

Article III

TRANSFER OF AUTHORITY

1. Israel shall transfer authority as specified in this Agreement from the Israeli military government and its Civil Administration to the Palestinian Authority, hereby established, in accordance with Article V of this Agreement, except for the authority that Israel shall continue to exercise as specified in this Agreement.

2. As regards the transfer and assumption of authority in civil spheres, powers and responsibilities shall be transferred and assumed as set out in the Protocol concerning civil affairs attached as Annex II.

3. Arrangements for a smooth and peaceful transfer of the agreed powers and responsibilities are set out in Annex II.

4. Upon the completion of the Israeli withdrawal and the transfer of powers and responsibilities as detailed in Paragraphs 1 and 2 above and in Annex II, the Civil Administration in the Gaza Strip and the Jericho Area will be dissolved and the Israeli military government will be withdrawn. The withdrawal of the military government shall not prevent it from continuing to exercise the powers and responsibilities specified in this Agreement.

5. A joint Civil Affairs Co-ordination and Co-operation Committee (hereinafter 'the CAC') and two joint regional civil affairs subcommittees for the Gaza Strip and the Jericho Area respectively shall be established in order to provide for co-ordination and co-operation in civil affairs between the Palestinian Authority and Israel, as detailed in Annex II.

6. The offices of the Palestinian Authority shall be located in the Gaza Strip and the Jericho Area pending the inauguration of the council to be elected pursuant to the Declaration of Principles.

Article IV

STRUCTURE AND COMPOSITION OF THE PALESTINIAN AUTHORITY

1. The Palestinian Authority will consist of one body of 24 members which shall carry out and be responsible for all the legislative and executive powers and responsibilities transferred to it under this Agreement, in accordance with this article, and shall be responsible for the exercise of judicial functions in accordance with Article VI, subparagraph 1.b of this Agreement.

2. The Palestinian Authority shall administer the departments transferred to it and may establish, within its jurisdiction, other departments and subordinate administrative units as necessary for the fulfilment of its responsibilities. It shall determine its own internal procedures.

3. The PLO shall inform the Government of Israel of the names of the members of the Palestinian Authority and any change of members. Changes in the membership of the Palestinian Authority will take effect upon an exchange of letters between the PLO and the Government of Israel.

4. Each member of the Palestinian Authority shall enter into office upon undertaking to act in accordance with this Agreement.

Article V

JURISDICTION

1. The authority of the Palestinian Authority encompasses all matters that fall within its territorial, functional and personal jurisdiction, as follows:

a. The territorial jurisdiction covers the Gaza Strip and the Jericho Area territory, as defined in Article I, except for settlements and the military installation area. Territorial jurisdiction shall include land, subsoil and territorial waters, in accordance with the provisions of this Agreement.

b. The functional jurisdiction encompasses all powers and responsibilities as specified in this Agreement. This jurisdiction does not include foreign relations, internal security and public order of settlements and the military installation area and Israelis, and external security.

c. The personal jurisdiction extends to all persons within the territorial jurisdiction referred to above, except for Israelis, unless otherwise provided in this Agreement.

2. The Palestinian Authority has, within its authority, legislative, executive and judicial powers and responsibilities, as provided for in this Agreement.

3.a. Israel has authority over the settlements, the military installation area, Israelis, external security, internal security and public order of settlements, the military installation area and Israelis, and those agreed powers and responsibilities specified in this Agreement.

b. Israel shall exercise its authority through its military government, which for that end, shall continue to have the necessary legislative, judicial and executive powers and responsibilities, in accordance with international law. This provision shall not derogate from Israel's applicable legislation over Israelis in personam.

4. The exercise of authority with regard to the electromagnetic sphere and airspace shall be in accordance with the provisions of this Agreement.

5. The provisions of this article are subject to the specific legal arrangements detailed in the Protocol concerning legal matters attached as Annex III. Israel and the Palestinian Authority may negotiate further legal arrangements.

6. Israel and the Palestinian Authority shall co-operate on matters of legal assistance in criminal and civil matters through the legal subcommittee of the CAC.

Article VI

POWERS AND RESPONSIBILITIES OF THE PALESTINIAN AUTHORITY

1. Subject to the provisions of this Agreement, the Palestinian Authority, within its jurisdiction:

a. has legislative powers as set out in Article VII of this Agreement, as well as executive powers;

b. will administer justice through an independent judiciary;

c. will have, inter alia, power to formulate policies, supervise their implementation, employ staff, establish departments, authorities and institutions, sue and be sued and conclude contracts; and

d. will have, inter alia, the power to keep and administer registers and records of the population, and issue certificates, licenses and documents.

2.a. In accordance with the Declaration of Principles, the Palestinian Authority will not have powers and responsibilities in the sphere of foreign relations, which sphere includes the establishment abroad of embassies, consulates or other types of foreign missions and posts or permitting their establishment in the Gaza Strip or the Jericho Area, the appointment of or admission of diplomatic and consular staff, and the exercise of diplomatic functions.

b. Notwithstanding the provisions of this paragraph, the PLO may conduct negotiations and sign agreements with states or international organizations for the benefit of the Palestinian Authority in the following cases only:

(1) Economic agreements, as specifically provided in Annex IV of this Agreement;

(2) Agreements with donor countries for the purpose of implementing arrangements for the provision of assistance to the Palestinian Authority;

(3) Agreements for the purpose of implementing the regional development plans detailed in Annex IV of the Declaration of Principles or in agreements entered into in the framework of the multilateral negotiations; and

(4) Cultural, scientific and education agreements.

c. Dealings between the Palestinian Authority and representatives of foreign states and international organizations, as well as the establishment in the Gaza Strip and the Jericho Area of representative offices other than those described in subparagraph 2.a, above, for the purpose of implementing the agreements referred to in subparagraph 2.b above, shall not be considered foreign relations.

Article VII

LEGISLATIVE POWERS OF THE PALESTINIAN AUTHORITY

1. The Palestinian Authority will have the power, within its jurisdiction, to promulgate legislation, including basic laws, laws, regulations and other legislative acts.

2. Legislation promulgated by the Palestinian Authority shall be consistent with the provisions of this Agreement.

3. Legislation promulgated by the Palestinian Authority shall be communicated to a legislation subcommittee to be established by the CAC (hereinafter 'the Legislation Subcommittee'). During a period of 30 days from the communication of the legislation, Israel may request that the Legislation Subcommittee decide whether such legislation exceeds the jurisdiction of the Palestinian Authority or is otherwise inconsistent with the provisions of this Agreement.

4. Upon receipt of the Israeli request, the Legislation Subcommittee shall decide, as an initial matter, on the entry into force of the legislation pending its decision on the merits of the matter.

5. If the Legislation Subcommittee is unable to reach a decision with regard to the entry into force of the legislation within 15 days, this issue will be referred to a Board of Review. This Board of Review shall be comprised of two judges, retired judges or senior jurists (hereinafter 'Judges'), one from each side, to be appointed from a compiled list of three judges proposed by each.

6. Legislation referred to the Board of Review shall enter into force only if the Board of Review decides that it does not deal with a security issue which falls under Israel's responsibility, that it does not seriously threaten other significant Israeli interests protected by this Agreement and that the entry into force of the legislation could not cause irreparable damage or harm.

7. The Legislation Subcommittee shall attempt to reach a decision on the merits of the matter within 30 days from the date of the Israeli request. If this subcommittee is unable to reach such a decision within this period of 30 days, the matter shall be referred to the joint Israeli-Palestinian Liaison Committee referred to in Article XV below (hereinafter 'the Liaison Committee'). This Liaison Committee will deal with the matter immediately and will attempt to settle it within 30 days.

8. Where the legislation has not entered into force pursuant to paragraphs 5 or 7 above, this situation shall be maintained pending the decision of the Liaison Committee on the merits of the matter, unless it has decided otherwise.

9. Laws and military orders in effect in the Gaza Strip or the Jericho Area prior to the signing of this Agreement shall remain in force, unless amended or abrogated in accordance with this Agreement.

Article VIII

ARRANGEMENTS FOR SECURITY AND PUBLIC ORDER

1. In order to guarantee public order and internal security for the Palestinians of the Gaza Strip and the Jericho Area, the Palestinian Authority shall establish a strong police force, as set out in Article IX below. Israel shall continue to carry the responsibility for defence against external threats, including the responsibility for protecting the Egyptian border and the Jordanian line, and for defence against external threats from the sea and from the air, as well as the responsibility for overall security of Israelis and settlements, for the purpose of safeguarding their internal security and public order, and will have all the powers to take the steps necessary to meet this responsibility.

2. Agreed security arrangements and co-ordination mechanisms are specified in Annex I.

3. A Joint Co-ordination and Co-operation committee for mutual security purposes (hereinafter 'the JSC'), as well as three joint district co-ordination and co-operation offices for the Gaza District, the Khan Younis District and the Jericho District respectively (hereinafter 'the DCOS') are hereby established as provided for in Annex I.

4. The security arrangements provided for in this Agreement and in Annex I may be reviewed at the requests of either party and may be amended by mutual agreement of the parties. Specific review arrangements are included in Annex I.

Article IX

THE PALESTINIAN DIRECTORATE OF POLICE FORCE

1. The Palestinian Authority shall establish a strong police force, the Palestinian Directorate of Police Force (hereinafter 'the Palestinian Police'). The duties, functions, structure, deployment and composition of the Palestinian Police, together with provisions regarding its equipment and operation, are set out in Annex I, Article III. Rules of conduct governing the activities of the Palestinian Police are set out in Annex I, Article VIII.

2. Except for the Palestinian Police referred to in this article and the Israeli military forces, no other armed forces shall be established or operate in the Gaza Strip or the Jericho Area.

3. Except for the arms, ammunition and equipment of the Palestinian Police described in Annex I, Article III, and those of the Israeli military forces, no organization or individual in the Gaza Strip and the Jericho Area shall manufacture, sell, acquire, possess, import or otherwise introduce into the Gaza Strip or the Jericho Area any firearms, ammunition, weapons, explosives, gunpowder or any related equipment, unless otherwise provided for in Annex I.

Article X

PASSAGES

Arrangements for co-ordination between Israel and the Palestinian Authority regarding the Gaza-Egypt and Jericho-Jordan passages, as well as any other agreed international crossings, are set out in Annex 1.

Article XI

SAFE PASSAGE BETWEEN THE GAZA STRIP AND THE JERICHO AREA

Arrangements for safe passage of persons and transportation between the Gaza Strip and the Jericho Area are set out in Annex I, Article IX.

Article XII

RELATIONS BETWEEN ISRAEL AND THE PALESTINIAN AUTHORITY

1. Israel and the Palestinian Authority shall seek to foster mutual understanding and tolerance and shall accordingly abstain from incitement, including hostile propaganda, against each other and, without derogating from the principle of freedom of expression, shall take legal measures to prevent such incitement by any organizations, groups or individuals within their jurisdiction.

2. Without derogating from the other provisions of this agreement, Israel and the Palestinian Authority shall co-operate in combating criminal activity which may affect both sides, including offences related to trafficking in illegal drugs and psychotropic substances, smuggling, and offences against property, including offences related to vehicles.

Article XIII

ECONOMIC RELATIONS

The economic relations between the two sides are set out in the Protocol on Economic Relations signed in Paris on April 29, 1994 and the appendixes thereto, certified copies of which are attached as Annex IV, and will be governed by the relevant provisions of this agreement and its annexes.

Article XIV

HUMAN RIGHTS AND THE RULE OF LAW

Israel and the Palestinian Authority shall exercise their powers and responsibilities pursuant to this Agreement with due regard to internationally-accepted norms and principles of human rights and the rule of law.

Article XV

THE JOINT ISRAELI-PALESTINIAN LIAISON COMMITTEE

1. The Liaison Committee established pursuant to Article X of the Declaration of Principles shall ensure the smooth implementation of this Agreement. It shall deal with issues requiring co-ordination, other issues of common interest and disputes.

2. The Liaison Committee shall be composed of an equal number of members from each party. It may add other technicians and experts as necessary.

3. The Liaison Committee shall adopt its rules of procedure, including the frequency and place or places of its meetings.

4. The Liaison Committee shall reach its decision by agreement.

Article XVI

LIAISON AND CO-OPERATION WITH JORDAN AND EGYPT

1. Pursuant to Article XII of the Declaration of Principles, the two parties shall invite the governments of Jordan and Egypt to participate in establishing further Liaison and Co-operation Arrangements between the Government of Israel and the Palestinian Representatives on the one hand, and the governments of Jordan and Egypt on the other hand, to promote co-operation between them. These arrangements shall include the constitution of a Continuing Committee.

2. The Continuing Committee shall decide by agreement on the modalities of admission of persons displaced from the West Bank and the Gaza Strip in 1967, together with necessary measures to prevent disruption and disorder.

3. The Continuing Committee shall deal with other matters of common concern.

Article XVII

SETTLEMENT OF DIFFERENCES AND DISPUTES

Any difference relating to the application of this agreement shall be referred to the appropriate co-ordination and co-operation mechanism established under this agreement. The provisions of Article XV of the Declaration of Principles shall apply to any such difference which is not settled through the appropriate co-ordination and co-operation mechanism, namely:

1. Disputes arising out of the application or interpretation of this agreement or any subsequent agreements pertaining to the interim period shall be settled by negotiations through the Liaison Committee.

2. Disputes which cannot be settled by negotiations may be settled by a mechanism of conciliation to be agreed between the parties.

3. The parties may agree to submit to arbitration disputes relating to the interim period, which cannot be settled through conciliation. To this end, upon the agreement of both parties, the parties will establish an arbitration committee.

Article XVIII

PREVENTION OF HOSTILE ACTS

Both sides shall take all measures necessary in order to prevent acts of terrorism, crime and hostilities directed against each other, against individuals falling under the other's authority and against their property, and shall take legal measures against offenders. In addition, the Palestinian side shall take all measures necessary to prevent such hostile acts directed against the settlements, the infrastructure serving them and the military installation area, and the Israeli side shall take all measures necessary to prevent such hostile acts emanating from the settlements and directed against Palestinians.

Article XIX

MISSING PERSONS

The Palestinian Authority shall co-operate with Israel by providing all necessary assistance in the conduct of searches by Israel within the Gaza Strip and the Jericho Area for missing Israelis, as well as by providing information about missing Israelis. Israel shall co-operate with the Palestinian Authority in searching for, and providing necessary information about, missing Palestinians.

Article XX

CONFIDENCE-BUILDING MEASURES

With a view to creating a positive and supportive public atmosphere to accompany the implementation of this agreement, and to establish a solid basis of mutual trust and good faith, both parties agree to carry out confidence-building measures as detailed herewith:

1. Upon the signing of this agreement, Israel will release, or turn over, to the Palestinian Authority within a period of 5 weeks, about 5,000 Palestinian detainees and prisoners, residents of the West Bank and the Gaza Strip. Those released will be free to return to their homes anywhere in the West Bank or the Gaza Strip. Prisoners turned over to the Palestinian Authority shall be obliged to remain in the Gaza Strip or the Jericho Area for the remainder of their sentence.

2. After the signing of this Agreement, the two parties shall continue to negotiate the release of additional Palestinian prisoners and detainees, building on agreed principles.

3. The implementation of the above measures will be subject to the fulfilment of the procedures determined by Israeli law for the release and transfer of detainees and prisoners.

4. With the assumption of Palestinian Authority, the Palestinian side commits itself to solving the problem of those Palestinians who were in contact with the Israeli authorities. Until an agreed solution is found, the Palestinian side undertakes not to prosecute these Palestinians or to harm them in any way.

5. Palestinians from abroad whose entry into the Gaza Strip and the Jericho Area is approved pursuant to this agreement, and to whom the provisions of this article are applicable, will not be prosecuted for offences committed prior to September 13, 1993.

Article XXI

TEMPORARY INTERNATIONAL PRESENCE

1. The parties agree to a temporary international or foreign presence in the Gaza Strip and the Jericho Area (hereinafter 'the TIP'), in accordance with the provisions of this article.

2. The TIP shall consist of 400 qualified personnel, including observers, instructors and other experts, from 5 or 6 of the donor countries.

3. The two parties shall request the donor countries to establish a special fund to provide finance for the TIP.

4. The TIP will function for a period of 6 months. The TIP may extend this period, or change the scope of its operation, with the agreement of the two parties.

5. The TIP shall be stationed and operative within the following cities and villages: Gaza, Khan Younis, Rafah, Deir al-Balah, Jabalya, Absan, Beit Hanun and Jericho.

6. Israel and the Palestinian Authority shall agree on a special protocol to implement this article, with the goal of concluding negotiations with the donor countries contributing personnel within two months.

Article XXII

RIGHTS, LIABILITIES AND OBLIGATIONS

1.a. The transfer of all powers and responsibilities to the Palestinian Authority, as detailed in Annex II, includes all related rights, liabilities and obligations arising with regard to acts or omissions which occurred prior to the transfer. Israel will cease to bear any financial responsibility regarding such acts or omissions and the Palestinian Authority will bear all financial responsibility for these and for its own functioning.

b. Any financial claim made in this regard against Israel will be referred to the Palestinian Authority.

c. Israel shall provide the Palestinian Authority with the information it has regarding pending and anticipated claims brought before any court or tribunal against Israel in this regard.

d. Where legal proceedings are brought in respect of such a claim, Israel will notify the Palestinian Authority and enable it to participate in defending the claim and raise any arguments on its behalf.

e. In the event that an award is made against Israel by any court or tribunal in respect of such a claim, the Palestinian Authority shall reimburse Israel the full amount of the award.

f. Without prejudice to the above, where a court or tribunal hearing such a claim finds that liability rests solely with an employee or agent who acted beyond the scope of the powers assigned to him or her, unlawfully or with wilful malfeasance, the Palestinian Authority shall not bear financial responsibility.

2. The transfer of authority in itself shall not affect rights, liabilities and obligations of any person or legal entity, in existence at the date of signing of this Agreement.

Article XXIII

FINAL CLAUSES

1. This Agreement shall enter into force on the date of its signing.

2. The arrangements established by this Agreement shall remain in force until and to the extent superseded by the Interim Agreement referred to in the Declaration of Principles or any other Agreement between the parties.

3. The five-year Interim Period referred to in the Declaration of Principles commences on the date of the signing of this Agreement.

4. The parties agree that, as long as this Agreement is in force, the security fence erected by Israel around the Gaza Strip shall remain in place and that the line demarcated by the fence, as shown on attached Map No. 1, shall be authoritative only for the purpose of this Agreement.

5. Nothing in this Agreement shall prejudice or pre-empt the outcome of the negotiations on the Interim Agreement or on the Permanent Status to be conducted pursuant to the Declaration of Principles. Neither party shall be deemed, by virtue of having entered into this Agreement, to have renounced or waived any of its existing rights, claims or positions.

6. The two parties view the West Bank and the Gaza Strip as a single territorial unit, the integrity of which will be preserved during the Interim Period.

7. The Gaza Strip and the Jericho Area shall continue to be an integral part of the West Bank and the Gaza Strip, and their status shall not be changed for the period of this Agreement. Nothing in this Agreement shall be considered to change this status.

8. The preamble to this Agreement, and all Annexes, Appendices and Maps attached hereto, shall constitute an integral part hereof. *[Maps not reproduced here: Ed]*

TREATY OF PEACE BETWEEN THE STATE OF ISRAEL AND THE HASHEMITE KINGDOM OF JORDAN

26 October 1994)

The Treaty was signed by Prime Minister Itzhak Rabin of Israel and the Jordanian premier, Abd al-Salam Majali, in Washington, DC, USA, and was witnessed by President Bill Clinton of the USA. The agreement included 30 Articles, and five Annexes (not reproduced here) dealing with international boundaries, border crossings, and co-operation on the issues of water, crime and drugs-trafficking, and the environment.

The Government of the State of Israel and the Government of the Hashemite Kingdom of Jordan:

Preamble

BEARING in mind the Washington Declaration, signed by them on 25th July 1994, and which they are both committed to honour;

AIMING at the achievement of a just, lasting and comprehensive peace in the Middle East based on Security Council resolutions 242 and 338 in all their aspects;

BEARING in mind the importance of maintaining and strengthening peace based on freedom, equality, justice and respect for fundamental human rights, thereby overcoming psychological barriers and promoting human dignity;

REAFFIRMING their faith in the purposes and principles of the Charter of the United Nations and recognising their right and obligation to live in peace with each other as well as with all states, within secure and recognised boundaries;

DESIRING to develop friendly relations and co-operation between them in accordance with the principles of international law governing international relations in time of peace;

DESIRING as well to ensure lasting security for both their States and in particular to avoid threats and the use of force between them;

BEARING in mind that in their Washington Declaration of 25th July, 1994, they declared the termination of the state of belligerency between them;

DECIDING to establish peace between them in accordance with this Treaty of Peace;

HAVE AGREED as follows:

Article I

ESTABLISHMENT OF PEACE

Peace is hereby established between the State of Israel and the Hashemite Kingdom of Jordan (the 'Parties') effective from the exchange of the instruments of ratification of this Treaty.

Article II

GENERAL PRINCIPLES

The Parties will apply between them the provisions of the Charter of the United Nations and the principles of international law governing relations among states in times of peace. In particular:

1. They recognise and will respect each other's sovereignty, territorial integrity and political independence;

2. They recognise and will respect each other's right to live in peace within secure and recognised boundaries;

3. They will develop good neighbourly relations of co-operation between them to ensure lasting security, will refrain from the threat or use of force against each other and will settle all disputes between them by peaceful means;

4. They respect and recognise the sovereignty, territorial integrity and political independence of every state in the region;

5. They respect and recognise the pivotal role of human development and dignity in regional and bilateral relationships;

6. They further believe that within their control, involuntary movements of persons in such a way as to adversely prejudice the security of either Party should not be permitted.

Article III

INTERNATIONAL BOUNDARY

1. The international boundary between Israel and Jordan is delimited with reference to the boundary definition under the Mandate as is shown in Annex I (a—see below), on the mapping materials attached thereto and co-ordinates specified therein.

2. The boundary, as set out in Annex I (a), is the permanent, secure and recognized international boundary between Israel and Jordan, without prejudice to the status of any territories that came under Israeli military government control in 1967.

3. The Parties recognise the international boundary, as well as each other's territory, territorial waters and airspace, as inviolable, and will respect and comply with them.

4. The demarcation of the boundary will take place as set forth in Appendix (I) to Annex I and will be concluded not later than nine months after the signing of the Treaty.

5. It is agreed that where a boundary follows a river, in the event of natural changes in the course of the flow of the river as described in Annex I (a), the boundary shall follow the new course of the flow. In the event of any other changes the boundary shall not be affected unless otherwise agreed.

6. Immediately upon the exchange of the instruments of ratification of this Treaty, each Party will deploy on its side of the international boundary as defined in Annex I (a).

7. The Parties shall, upon the signature of this Treaty, enter into negotiations to conclude, within 9 months, an agreement on the delimitation of their maritime boundary in the Gulf of Aqaba.

8. Taking into account the special circumstances of the Nayarharim/Baqura area, which is under Jordanian sovereignty, with Israeli private ownership rights, the Parties agreed to apply the provisions set out in Annex I (b).

9. With respect to the Zofar/Al-Ghamr area, the provisions set out in Annex I (c) will apply.

Article IV

SECURITY

1.

a. Both Parties, acknowledging that mutual understanding and co-operation in security-related matters will form a significant part of their relations and will further enhance the security of the region, take upon themselves to base their security relations on mutual trust, advancement of joint interests and co-operation, and to aim towards a regional framework of partnership in peace.

b. Towards that goal the Parties recognise the achievements of the European Community and European Union in the development of the Conference on Security and Co-operation in Europe (CSCE) and commit themselves to the creation, in the Middle East, of a CSCME (Conference on Security and Co-operation in the Middle East). This commitment entails the adoption of regional models of security successfully implemented in the post World War era (along the lines of the Helsinki process) culminating in a regional zone of security and stability.

2. The obligations referred to in this Article are without prejudice to the inherent right of self-defence in accordance with the United Nations Charter.

3. The Parties undertake, in accordance with the provisions of this Article, the following:

a. to refrain from the threat or use of force or weapons, conventional, non-conventional or of any other kind, against each other, or of other actions or activities that adversely affect the security of the other Party;

b. to refrain from organising, instigating, inciting, assisting or participating in acts or threats of belligerency, hostility, subversion or violence against the other Party;

c. to take necessary and effective measures to ensure that acts or threats of belligerency, hostility, subversion or violence against the other Party do not originate from, and are not committed within, through or over their territory (hereinafter the term 'territory' includes the airspace and territorial waters).

4. Consistent with the era of peace and with the efforts to build regional security and to avoid and prevent aggression and violence, the Parties further agree to refrain from the following:

a. joining or in any way assisting, promoting or co-operating with any coalition, organisation or alliance with a military or security character with a third party, the objectives or activities of which include launching aggression or other acts of military hostility against the other Party, in contravention of the provisions of the present Treaty.

b. allowing the entry, stationing and operating on their territory, or through it, of military forces, personnel or materiel of a third party, in circumstances which may adversely prejudice the security of the other Party.

5. Both Parties will take necessary and effective measures, and will co-operate in combating terrorism of all kinds. The Parties undertake:

a. to take necessary and effective measures to prevent acts of terrorism, subversion or violence from being carried out from their territory or through it and to take necessary and effective measures to combat such activities and all their perpetrators.

b. without prejudice to the basic rights of freedom of expression and association, to take necessary and effective measures to prevent the entry, presence and co-operation in their territory of any group or organisation, and their infrastructure, which threatens the security of the other Party by the use of or incitement to the use of, violent means.

c. to co-operate in preventing and combating cross-boundary infiltrations.

6. Any question as to the implementation of this Article will be dealt with through a mechanism of consultations which will include a liaison system, verification, supervision, and where necessary, other mechanisms, and higher level consultation. The details of the mechanism of consultations will be contained in an agreement to be concluded by the Parties within 3 months of the exchange of the instruments of ratification of this Treaty.

7. The Parties undertake to work as a matter of priority, and as soon as possible in the context of the Multilateral Working Group on Arms Control and Regional Security, and jointly, towards the following:

a. the creation in the Middle East of a region free from hostile alliances and coalitions;

b. the creation of a Middle East free from weapons of mass destruction, both conventional and non-conventional, in the context of a comprehensive, lasting and stable peace, characterised by the renunciation of the use of force, reconciliation and goodwill.

Article V

DIPLOMATIC AND OTHER BILATERAL RELATIONS

1. The Parties agree to establish full diplomatic and consular relations and to exchange resident ambassadors within one month of the exchange of the instruments of ratification of this Treaty.

2. The Parties agree that the normal relationship between them will further include economic and cultural relations.

Article VI

WATER

With the view to achieving a comprehensive and lasting settlement of all the water problems between them:

1. The Parties agree mutually to recognise the rightful allocations of both of them in Jordan River and Yarmouk River waters and Araba/Arava ground water in accordance with the agreed acceptable principles, quantities and quality as set out in Annex II, which shall be fully respected and complied with.

2. The Parties, recognising the necessity to find a practical, just and agreed solution to their water problems and with the view that the subject of water can form the basis for the advancement of co-operation between them, jointly undertake to ensure that the management and development of their water resources do not, in any way, harm the water resources of the other Party.

3. The Parties recognise that their water resources are not sufficient to meet their needs. More water should be supplied for their use through various methods, including projects of regional and international co-operation.

4. In light of paragraph 3 of this Article, with the understanding that co-operation in water-related subjects would be to the benefit of both Parties, and will help alleviate their water shortages, and that water issues along their entire boundary must be dealt with in their totality, including the possibility of trans-boundary water transfers, the Parties agree to search for ways to alleviate water shortage and to co-operate in the following fields:

a. development of existing and new water resources, increasing the water availability including co- operation on a regional basis as appropriate, and minimising wastage of water resources through the chain of their uses;

b. prevention of contamination of water resources;

c. mutual assistance in the alleviation of water shortages;

d. transfer of information and joint research and development in water-related subjects, and review of the potentials for enhancement of water resources development and use.

5. The implementation of both Parties' undertakings under this Article is detailed in Annex II.

Article VII

ECONOMIC RELATIONS

1. Viewing economic development and prosperity as pillars of peace, security and harmonious relations between states, peoples and individual human beings, the Parties, taking note of understandings reached between them, affirm their mutual desire to promote economic co-operation between them, as well as within the framework of wider regional economic co-operation.

2. In order to accomplish this goal, the Parties agree to the following:

a. to remove all discriminatory barriers to normal economic relations, to terminate economic boycotts directed at each other, and to co-operate in terminating boycotts against either Party by third parties;

b. recognising that the principle of free and unimpeded flow of goods and services should guide their relations, the Parties will enter into negotiations with a view to concluding agreements on economic co-operation, including trade and the establishment of a free trade area, investment, banking, industrial co-operation and labour, for the purpose of promoting beneficial economic relations, based on principles to be agreed upon, as well as on human development considerations on a regional basis. These negotiations will be concluded no later than 6 months from the exchange of the instruments of ratification of this Treaty.

c. to co-operate bilaterally, as well as in multilateral forums, towards the promotion of their respective economies and of their neighbourly economic relations with other regional parties.

Article VIII

REFUGEES AND DISPLACED PERSONS

1. Recognising the massive human problems caused to both Parties by the conflict in the Middle East, as well as the contribution made by them towards the alleviation of human suffering, the Parties will seek to further alleviate those problems arising on a bilateral level.

2. Recognising that the above human problems caused by the conflict in the Middle East cannot be fully resolved on the bilateral level, the Parties will seek to resolve them in appropriate forums, in accordance with international law, including the following:

a. in the case of displaced persons, in a quadripartite committee together with Egypt and the Palestinians:

b. in the case of refugees, i) in the framework of the Multilateral Working Group on Refugees; and ii) in negotiations, in a framework to be agreed, bilateral or otherwise, in conjunction with and at the same time as the permanent status negotiations pertaining to the territories referred to in Article 3 of this Treaty;

c. through the implementation of agreed United Nations programmes and other agreed international economic programmes concerning refugees and displaced persons, including assistance to their settlement.

Article IX

PLACES OF HISTORICAL AND RELIGIOUS SIGNIFICANCE

1. Each party will provide freedom of access to places of religious and historical significance.

2. In this regard, in accordance with the Washington Declaration, Israel respects the present special role of the Hashemite Kingdom of Jordan in Muslim Holy shrines in Jerusalem. When negotiations on the permanent status will take place, Israel will give high priority to the Jordanian historic role in these shrines.

3. The Parties will act together to promote interfaith relations among the three monotheistic religions, with the aim of working towards religious understanding, moral commitment, freedom of religious worship, and tolerance and peace.

Article X

CULTURAL AND SCIENTIFIC EXCHANGES

The Parties, wishing to remove biases developed through periods of conflict, recognise the desirability of cultural and scientific exchanges in all fields, and agree to establish normal cultural relations between them. Thus, they shall, as soon as possible and not later than 9 months from the exchange of the instruments of ratification of this Treaty, conclude the negotiations on cultural and scientific agreements.

Article XI

MUTUAL UNDERSTANDING AND GOOD NEIGHBOURLY RELATIONS

1. The Parties will seek to foster mutual understanding and tolerance based on shared historic values, and accordingly undertake:

a. to abstain from hostile or discriminatory propaganda against each other, and to take all possible legal and administrative measures to prevent the dissemination of such propaganda by any organisation or individual present in the territory of either Party;

b. as soon as possible, and not later than 3 months from the exchange of the instruments of ratification of this Treaty, to repeal all adverse or discriminatory references and expressions of hostility in their respective legislation;

c. to refrain in all government publications from any such references or expressions;

d. to ensure mutual enjoyment by each other's citizens of due process of law within their respective legal systems and before their courts.

2. Paragraph 1 (a) of this Article is without prejudice to the right to freedom of expression as contained in the International Covenant on Civil and Political Rights.

3. A joint committee shall be formed to examine incidents where one Party claims there has been a violation of this Article.

Articles XII–XXIV

Articles XII–XXIV deal with co-operation between the two countries in the areas of crime and illegal drugs, transportation and roads, access to ports, civil aviation, posts and telecommunications, tourism, the environment, energy, development of the Jordan Rift Valley area, health, agriculture, joint development of the towns of Aqaba (Jordan) and Eilat (Israel), and the settlement of financial claims.

Article XXV

RIGHTS AND OBLIGATIONS

1. This Treaty does not affect and shall not be interpreted as affecting, in any way, the rights and obligations of the Parties under the Charter of the United Nations.

2. The Parties undertake to fulfil in good faith their obligations under this Treaty, without regard to action or inaction of any other party and independently of any instrument inconsistent with this Treaty. For the purposes of this paragraph each Party represents to the other that in its opinion and interpretation there is no inconsistency between their existing treaty obligations and this Treaty.

3. They further undertake to take all the necessary measures for the application in their relations of the provisions of the multilateral conventions to which they are parties, including the submission of appropriate notification to the Secretary General of the United Nations and other depositories of such conventions.

4. Both Parties will also take all the necessary steps to abolish all pejorative references to the other Party, in multilateral conventions to which they are parties, to the extent that such references exist.

5. The Parties undertake not to enter into any obligation in conflict with this Treaty.

6. Subject to Article 103 of the United Nations Charter, in the event of a conflict between the obligations of the Parties under the present Treaty and any of their other obligations, the obligations under this Treaty will be binding and implemented.

Articles XXVI–XXX

Articles XXVI–XXX deal with provisions for the ratification and implementation of the Treaty, interim measures, the settlement of disputes arising out of the application or interpretation of the Treaty, and the registration of the agreement.

ISRAELI-PALESTINIAN INTERIM AGREEMENT ON THE WEST BANK AND THE GAZA STRIP

(28 September 1995)

The Interim Agreement was signed by the Chairman of the PLO, Yasser Arafat, and the Israeli Minister of Foreign Affairs, Shimon Peres, in Washington, DC, USA. The Agreement was witnessed by representatives of the USA, Russia, Egypt, Jordan, Norway and the European Union (EU). Considerable additional detail was contained in seven annexes (not reproduced here) to the Agreement (the most expansive of which—Annex I—concerned redeployment and security arrangements) and a map (also not reproduced here) in which the boundaries of first-phase redeployment areas 'A' and 'B' were defined.

The Government of the State of Israel and the Palestine Liberation Organization (hereinafter the 'PLO'), the representative of the Palestinian people;

Preamble

WITHIN the framework of the Middle East peace process initiated at Madrid in October 1991;

REAFFIRMING their determination to put an end to decades of confrontation and to live in peaceful coexistence, mutual dignity and security, while recognizing their mutual legitimate and political rights;

REAFFIRMING their desire to achieve a just, lasting and comprehensive peace settlement and historic reconciliation through the agreed political process;

RECOGNIZING that the peace process and the new era that it has created, as well as the new relationship established between the two Parties as described above, are irreversible, and the determination of the two Parties to maintain, sustain and continue the peace process;

RECOGNIZING that the aim of the Israeli-Palestinian negotiations within the current Middle East peace process is, among other things, to establish a Palestinian Interim Self-Government Authority, i.e. the elected Council (hereinafter 'the Council' or 'the Palestinian Council'), and the elected Ra'ees of the Executive Authority, for the Palestinian people in the West Bank and the Gaza Strip, for a transitional period not exceeding five years from the date of signing the Agreement on the Gaza Strip and the Jericho Area (hereinafter 'the Gaza-Jericho Agreement') on May 4, 1994, leading to a permanent settlement based on Security Council Resolutions 242 and 338;

REAFFIRMING their understanding that the interim self-government arrangements contained in this Agreement are an integral part of the whole peace process, that the negotiations on the permanent status, that will start as soon as possible but not later than May 4, 1996, will lead to the implementation of Security Council Resolutions 242 and 338, and that the Interim Agreement shall settle all the issues of the interim period and that no such issues will be deferred to the agenda of the permanent status negotiations;

REAFFIRMING their adherence to the mutual recognition and commitments expressed in the letters dated September 9, 1993, signed by and exchanged between the Prime Minister of Israel and the Chairman of the PLO;

DESIROUS of putting into effect the Declaration of Principles on Interim Self-Government Arrangements signed at Washington, DC on September 13, 1993, and the Agreed Minutes thereto (hereinafter 'the DOP') and in particular Article III and Annex I concerning the holding of direct, free and general political elections for the Council and the Ra'ees of the Executive Authority in order that the Palestinian people in the West Bank, Jerusalem and the Gaza Strip may democratically elect accountable representatives;

RECOGNIZING that these elections will constitute a significant interim preparatory step toward the realization of the legitimate rights of the Palestinian people and their just requirements and will provide a democratic basis for the establishment of Palestinian institutions;

REAFFIRMING their mutual commitment to act, in accordance with this Agreement, immediately, efficiently and effectively against acts or threats of terrorism, violence or incitement, whether committed by Palestinians or Israelis;

FOLLOWING the Gaza-Jericho Agreement; the Agreement on Preparatory Transfer of Powers and Responsibilities signed at Erez on August 29, 1994 (hereinafter 'the Preparatory Transfer Agreement'); and the Protocol on Further Transfer of Powers and Responsibilities signed at Cairo on August 27, 1995 (hereinafter 'the Further Transfer Protocol'); which three agreements will be superseded by this Agreement;

HEREBY AGREE as follows:

CHAPTER 1—THE COUNCIL

Article I

TRANSFER OF AUTHORITY

1. Israel shall transfer powers and responsibilities as specified in this Agreement from the Israeli military government and its Civil Administration to the Council in accordance with this Agreement. Israel shall continue to exercise powers and responsibilities not so transferred.

2. Pending the inauguration of the Council, the powers and responsibilities transferred to the Council shall be exercised by the Palestinian Authority established in accordance with the Gaza-Jericho Agreement, which shall also have all the rights, liabilities and obligations to be assumed by the Council in this regard. Accordingly, the term 'Council' throughout this Agreement shall, pending the inauguration of the Council, be construed as meaning the Palestinian Authority.

3. The transfer of powers and responsibilities to the police force established by the Palestinian Council in accordance with Article XIV below (hereinafter 'the Palestinian Police') shall be accomplished in a phased manner, as detailed in this Agreement and in the Protocol concerning Redeployment and Security Arrangements attached as Annex I to this Agreement (hereinafter 'Annex I').

4. As regards the transfer and assumption of authority in civil spheres, powers and responsibilities shall be transferred and assumed as set out in the Protocol Concerning Civil Affairs attached as Annex III to this Agreement (hereinafter 'Annex III').

5. After the inauguration of the Council, the Civil Administration in the West Bank will be dissolved, and the Israeli military government shall be withdrawn. The withdrawal of the military government shall not prevent it from exercising the powers and responsibilities not transferred to the Council.

6. A Joint Civil Affairs Co-ordination and Co-operation Committee (hereinafter 'the CAC'), Joint Regional Civil Affairs Subcommittees, one for the Gaza Strip and the other for the West Bank, and District Civil Liaison Offices in the West Bank shall be established in order to provide for co-ordination and co-operation in civil affairs between the Council and Israel, as detailed in Annex III.

7. The offices of the Council, and the offices of its Ra'ees and its Executive Authority and other committees, shall be located in areas under Palestinian territorial jurisdiction in the West Bank and the Gaza Strip.

Article II

ELECTIONS

1. In order that the Palestinian people of the West Bank and the Gaza Strip may govern themselves according to democratic principles, direct, free and general political elections will be held for the Council and the Ra'ees of the Executive Authority of the Council in accordance with the provisions set out in the Protocol concerning Elections attached as Annex II to this Agreement (hereinafter 'Annex II').

2. These elections will constitute a significant interim preparatory step towards the realization of the legitimate rights of the Palestinian people and their just requirements and will provide a democratic basis for the establishment of Palestinian institutions.

3. Palestinians of Jerusalem who live there may participate in the election process in accordance with the provisions contained in this Article and in Article VI of Annex II (Election Arrangements concerning Jerusalem).

4. The elections shall be called by the Chairman of the Palestinian Authority immediately following the signing of this Agreement to take place at the earliest practicable date following the redeployment of Israeli forces in accordance with Annex I, and consistent with the requirements of the election timetable as provided in Annex II, the Election Law and the Election Regulations, as defined in Article I of Annex II.

Article III

STRUCTURE OF THE PALESTINIAN COUNCIL

1. The Palestinian Council and the Ra'ees of the Executive Authority of the Council constitute the Palestinian Interim Self-Government Authority, which will be elected by the Palestinian people of the West Bank, Jerusalem and the Gaza Strip for the transitional period agreed in Article I of the DOP.

2. The Council shall possess both legislative power and executive power, in accordance with Articles VII and IX of the DOP. The Council shall carry out and be responsible for all the legislative and executive powers and responsibilities transferred to it under this Agreement. The exercise of legislative powers shall be in accordance with Article XVIII of this Agreement (Legislative Powers of the Council).

3. The Council and the Ra'ees of the Executive Authority of the Council shall be directly and simultaneously elected by the Palestinian people of the West Bank, Jerusalem and the Gaza Strip, in accordance with the provisions of this Agreement and the Election Law and Regulations, which shall not be contrary to the provisions of this Agreement.

4. The Council and the Ra'ees of the Executive Authority of the Council shall be elected for a transitional period not exceeding five years from the signing of the Gaza-Jericho Agreement on May 4, 1994.

5. Immediately upon its inauguration, the Council will elect from among its members a Speaker. The Speaker will preside over the meetings of the Council, administer the Council and its committees, decide on the agenda of each meeting, and lay before the Council proposals for voting and declare their results.

6. The jurisdiction of the Council shall be as determined in Article XVII of this Agreement (Jurisdiction).

7. The organization, structure and functioning of the Council shall be in accordance with this Agreement and the Basic Law for the Palestinian Interim Self-Government Authority, which Law shall be adopted by the Council. The Basic Law and any regulations made under it shall not be contrary to the provisions of this Agreement.

8. The Council shall be responsible under its executive powers for the offices, services and departments transferred to it and may establish, within its jurisdiction, ministries and subordinate bodies, as necessary for the fulfillment of its responsibilities.

9. The Speaker will present for the Council's approval proposed internal procedures that will regulate, among other things, the decision-making processes of the Council.

Article IV

SIZE OF THE COUNCIL

The Palestinian Council shall be composed of 82 representatives and the Ra'ees of the Executive Authority, who will be directly and simultaneously elected by the Palestinian people of the West Bank, Jerusalem and the Gaza Strip.

Article V

THE EXECUTIVE AUTHORITY OF THE COUNCIL

1. The Council will have a committee that will exercise the executive authority of the Council, formed in accordance with paragraph 4 below (hereinafter 'the Executive Authority').

2. The Executive Authority shall be bestowed with the executive authority of the Council and will exercise it on behalf of the Council. It shall determine its own internal procedures and decision making processes.

3. The Council will publish the names of the members of the Executive Authority immediately upon their initial appointment and subsequent to any changes.

4.a. The Ra'ees of the Executive Authority shall be an ex officio member of the Executive Authority

b. All of the other members of the Executive Authority, except as provided in subparagraph c. below, shall be members of the Council, chosen and proposed to the Council by the Ra'ees of the Executive Authority and approved by the Council

c. The Ra'ees of the Executive Authority shall have the right to appoint some persons, in number not exceeding twenty percent of the total membership of the Executive Authority, who are not members of the Council, to exercise executive authority and participate in government tasks. Such appointed members may not vote in meetings of the Council

d. Non-elected members of the Executive Authority must have a valid address in an area under the jurisdiction of the Council

Article VI

OTHER COMMITTEES OF THE COUNCIL

1. The Council may form small committees to simplify the proceedings of the Council and to assist in controlling the activity of its Executive Authority.

2. Each committee shall establish its own decision-making processes within the general framework of the organization and structure of the Council.

Article VII

OPEN GOVERNMENT

1. All meetings of the Council and of its committees, other than the Executive Authority, shall be open to the public, except upon a resolution of the Council or the relevant committee on the grounds of security, or commercial or personal confidentiality.

2. Participation in the deliberations of the Council, its committees and the Executive Authority shall be limited to their respective members only. Experts may be invited to such meetings to address specific issues on an ad hoc basis.

Article VIII

JUDICIAL REVIEW

Any person or organization affected by any act or decision of the Ra'ees of the Executive Authority of the Council or of any member of the Executive Authority, who believes that such act or decision exceeds the authority of the Ra'ees or of such member, or is otherwise incorrect in law or procedure, may apply to the relevant Palestinian Court of Justice for a review of such activity or decision.

Article IX

POWERS AND RESPONSIBILITIES OF THE COUNCIL

1. Subject to the provisions of this Agreement, the Council will, within its jurisdiction, have legislative powers as set out in Article XVIII of this Agreement, as well as executive powers.

2. The executive power of the Palestinian Council shall extend to all matters within its jurisdiction under this Agreement or any future agreement that may be reached between the two Parties during the interim period. It shall include the power to formulate and conduct Palestinian policies and to supervise their implementation, to issue any rule or regulation under powers given in approved legislation and administrative decisions necessary for the realization of Palestinian self-government, the power to employ staff, sue and be sued and conclude contracts, and the power to keep and administer registers and records of the population, and issue certificates, licenses and documents.

3. The Palestinian Council's executive decisions and acts shall be consistent with the provisions of this Agreement.

4. The Palestinian Council may adopt all necessary measures in order to enforce the law and any of its decisions, and bring proceedings before the Palestinian courts and tribunals.

5.a. In accordance with the DOP, the Council will not have powers and responsibilities in the sphere of foreign relations, which sphere includes the establishment abroad of embassies, consulates or other types of foreign missions and posts or permitting their establishment in the West Bank or the Gaza Strip, the appointment of or admission of diplomatic and consular staff, and the exercise of diplomatic functions.

b. Notwithstanding the provisions of this paragraph, the PLO may conduct negotiations and sign agreements with states or international organizations for the benefit of the Council in the following cases only:

(1) Economic agreements, as specifically provided in Annex V of this Agreement;

(2) Agreements with donor countries for the purpose of implementing arrangements for the provision of assistance to the Council;

(3) Agreements for the purpose of implementing the regional development plans detailed in Annex IV of the DOP or in agreements entered into in the framework of the multilateral negotiations; and

(4) Cultural, scientific and educational agreements.

c. Dealings between the Council and representatives of foreign states and international organizations, as well as the establishment in the West Bank and the Gaza Strip of representative offices other than those described in subparagraph 5.a above, for the purpose of implementing the agreements referred to in subparagraph 5.b above, shall not be considered foreign relations.

6. Subject to the provisions of this Agreement, the Council shall, within its jurisdiction, have an independent judicial system composed of independent Palestinian courts and tribunals.

CHAPTER 2—REDEPLOYMENT AND SECURITY ARRANGEMENTS

Article X

REDEPLOYMENT OF ISRAELI MILITARY FORCES

1. The first phase of the Israeli military forces redeployment will cover populated areas in the West Bank—cities, towns, villages, refugee camps and hamlets—as set out in Annex I, and will be completed prior to the eve of the Palestinian elections, i.e., 22 days before the day of the elections.

2. Further redeployments of Israeli military forces to specified military locations will commence after the inauguration of the Council and will be gradually implemented commensurate with the assumption of responsibility for public order and internal security by the Palestinian Police, to be completed within 18 months from the date of the inauguration of the Council as detailed in Articles XI (Land) and XIII (Security), below and in Annex I.

3. The Palestinian Police shall be deployed and shall assume responsibility for public order and internal security for Palestinians in a phased manner in accordance with Article XIII (Security) below and Annex I.

4. Israel shall continue to carry the responsibility for external security, as well as the responsibility for overall security of Israelis for the purpose of safeguarding their internal security and public order.

5. For the purpose of this Agreement, 'Israeli military forces' includes Israeli Police and other Israeli security forces.

Article XI

LAND

1. The two sides view the West Bank and the Gaza Strip as a single territorial unit, the integrity and status of which will be preserved during the interim period.

2. The two sides agree that West Bank and Gaza Strip territory, except for issues that will be negotiated in the permanent status negotiations, will come under the jurisdiction of the Palestinian Council in a phased manner, to be completed within 18 months from the date of the inauguration of the Council, as specified below:

a. Land in populated areas (Areas A and B), including government and Al Waqf land, will come under the jurisdiction of the Council during the first phase of redeployment.

b. All civil powers and responsibilities, including planning and zoning, in Areas A and B, set out in Annex III, will be transferred to and assumed by the Council during the first phase of redeployment.

c. In Area C, during the first phase of redeployment Israel will transfer to the Council civil powers and responsibilities not relating to territory, as set out in Annex III.

d. The further redeployments of Israeli military forces to specified military locations will be gradually implemented in accordance with the DOP in three phases, each to take place after an interval of six months, after the inauguration of the Council, to be completed within 18 months from the date of the inauguration of the Council.

e. During the further redeployment phases to be completed within 18 months from the date of the inauguration of the Council, powers and responsibilities relating to territory will be transferred gradually to Palestinian jurisdiction that will cover West Bank and Gaza Strip territory, except for the issues that will be negotiated in the permanent status negotiations.

f. The specified military locations referred to in Article X, paragraph 2 above will be determined in the further redeployment phases, within the specified time-frame ending not later than 18 months from the date of the inauguration of the Council, and will be negotiated in the permanent status negotiations.

3. For the purpose of this Agreement and until the completion of the first phase of the further redeployments:

a. 'Area A' means the populated areas delineated by a red line and shaded in brown on attached map No. 1 (*not reproduced here—Ed.*);

b. 'Area B' means the populated areas delineated by a red line and shaded in yellow on attached map No. 1, and the built-up area of the hamlets listed in Appendix 6 to Annex I; and

c. 'Area C' means areas of the West Bank outside Areas A and B, which, except for the issues that will be negotiated in the permanent status negotiations, will be gradually transferred to Palestinian jurisdiction in accordance with this Agreement.

Article XII

ARRANGEMENTS FOR SECURITY AND PUBLIC ORDER

1. In order to guarantee public order and internal security for the Palestinians of the West Bank and the Gaza Strip, the Council shall establish a strong police force as set out in Article XIV below. Israel shall continue to carry the responsibility for defence against external threats, including the responsibility

for protecting the Egyptian and Jordanian borders, and for defence against external threats from the sea and from the air, as well as the responsibility for overall security of Israelis and Settlements, for the purpose of safeguarding their internal security and public order, and will have all the powers to take the steps necessary to meet this responsibility.

2. Agreed security arrangements and co-ordination mechanisms are specified in Annex I.

3. A Joint Co-ordination and Co-operation Committee for Mutual Security Purposes (hereinafter 'the JSC'), as well as Joint Regional Security Committees (hereinafter 'RSCs') and Joint District Co-ordination Offices (hereinafter 'DCOs'), are hereby established as provided for in Annex I.

4. The security arrangements provided for in this Agreement and in Annex I may be reviewed at the request of either Party and may be amended by mutual agreement of the Parties. Specific review arrangements are included in Annex I.

5. For the purpose of this Agreement, 'the Settlements' means, in the West Bank—the settlements in Area C; and in the Gaza Strip—the Gush Katif and Erez settlement areas, as well as the other settlements in the Gaza Strip, as shown on attached map No. 2 (*not reproduced—Ed.*).

Article XIII

SECURITY

1. The Council will, upon completion of the redeployment of Israeli military forces in each district, as set out in Appendix 1 to Annex I, assume the powers and responsibilities for internal security and public order in Area A in that district.

2.a. There will be a complete redeployment of Israeli military forces from Area B. Israel will transfer to the Council and the Council will assume responsibility for public order for Palestinians. Israel shall have the overriding responsibility for security for the purpose of protecting Israelis and confronting the threat of terrorism.

b. In Area B the Palestinian Police shall assume the responsibility for public order for Palestinians and shall be deployed in order to accommodate the Palestinian needs and requirements in the following manner:

(1) The Palestinian Police shall establish 25 police stations and posts in towns, villages, and other places listed in Appendix 2 to Annex I and as delineated on map No. 3 (*not reproduced—Ed.*). The West Bank RSC may agree on the establishment of additional police stations and posts, if required.

(2) The Palestinian Police shall be responsible for handling public order incidents in which only Palestinians are involved.

(3) The Palestinian Police shall operate freely in populated places where police stations and posts are located, as set out in paragraph b(1) above.

(4) While the movement of uniformed Palestinian policemen in Area B outside places where there is a Palestinian police station or post will be carried out after co-ordination and confirmation through the relevant DCO, three months after the completion of redeployment from Area B, the DCOs may decide that movement of Palestinian policemen from the police stations in Area B to Palestinian towns and villages in Area B on roads that are used only by Palestinian traffic will take place after notifying the DCO.

(5) The co-ordination of such planned movement prior to confirmation through the relevant DCO shall include a scheduled plan, including the number of policemen, as well as the type and number of weapons and vehicles intended to take part. It shall also include details of arrangements for ensuring continued co-ordination through appropriate communication links, the exact schedule of movement to the area of the planned operation, including the destination and routes thereto, its proposed duration and the schedule for returning to the police station or post.

The Israeli side of the DCO will provide the Palestinian side with its response, following a request for movement of policemen in accordance with this paragraph, in normal or routine cases within one day and in emergency cases no later than 2 hours.

(6) The Palestinian Police and the Israeli military forces will conduct joint security activities on the main roads as set out in Annex I.

(7) The Palestinian Police will notify the West Bank RSC of the names of the policemen, number plates of police vehicles and serial numbers of weapons, with respect to each police station and post in Area B.

(8) Further redeployments from Area C and transfer of internal security responsibility to the Palestinian Police in Areas B and C will be carried out in three phases, each to take place after an interval of six months, to be completed 18 months after the inauguration of the Council, except for the issues of permanent status negotiations and of Israel's overall responsibility for Israelis and borders.

(9) The procedures detailed in this paragraph will be reviewed within six months of the completion of the first phase of redeployment.

Article XIV

THE PALESTINIAN POLICE

1. The Council shall establish a strong police force. The duties, functions, structure, deployment and composition of the Palestinian Police, together with provisions regarding its equipment and operation, as well as rules of conduct, are set out in Annex I.

2. The Palestinian police force established under the Gaza-Jericho Agreement will be fully integrated into the Palestinian Police and will be subject to the provisions of this Agreement.

3. Except for the Palestinian Police and the Israeli military forces, no other armed forces shall be established or operate in the West Bank and the Gaza Strip.

4. Except for the arms, ammunition and equipment of the Palestinian Police described in Annex I, and those of the Israeli military forces, no organization, group or individual in the West Bank and the Gaza Strip shall manufacture, sell, acquire, possess, import or otherwise introduce into the West Bank or the Gaza Strip any firearms, ammunition, weapons, explosives, gunpowder or any related equipment, unless otherwise provided for in Annex I.

Article XV

PREVENTION OF HOSTILE ACTS

1. Both sides shall take all measures necessary in order to prevent acts of terrorism, crime and hostilities directed against each other, against individuals falling under the other's authority and against their property, and shall take legal measures against offenders.

2. Specific provisions for the implementation of this Article are set out in Annex I.

Article XVI

CONFIDENCE BUILDING MEASURES

With a view to fostering a positive and supportive public atmosphere to accompany the implementation of this Agreement, to establish a solid basis of mutual trust and good faith, and in order to facilitate the anticipated co-operation and new relations between the two peoples, both Parties agree to carry out confidence building measures as detailed herewith:

1. Israel will release or turn over to the Palestinian side, Palestinian detainees and prisoners, residents of the West Bank and the Gaza Strip. The first stage of release of these prisoners and detainees will take place on the signing of this Agreement and the second stage will take place prior to the date of the elections. There will be a third stage of release of detainees and prisoners. Detainees and prisoners will be released from among categories detailed in Annex VII (Release of Palestinian Prisoners and Detainees). Those released will be free to return to their homes in the West Bank and the Gaza Strip.

2. Palestinians who have maintained contact with the Israeli authorities will not be subjected to acts of harassment, violence, retribution or prosecution. Appropriate ongoing

measures will be taken, in co-ordination with Israel, in order to ensure their protection.

3. Palestinians from abroad whose entry into the West Bank and the Gaza Strip is approved pursuant to this Agreement, and to whom the provisions of this Article are applicable, will not be prosecuted for offences committed prior to September 13, 1993.

CHAPTER 3—LEGAL AFFAIRS

Article XVII

JURISDICTION

1. In accordance with the DOP, the jurisdiction of the Council will cover West Bank and Gaza Strip territory as a single territorial unit, except for:

a. Issues that will be negotiated in the permanent status negotiations: Jerusalem, settlements, specified military locations, Palestinian refugees, borders, foreign relations and Israelis; and

b. Powers and responsibilities not transferred to the Council.

2. Accordingly, the authority of the Council encompasses all matters that fall within its territorial, functional and personal jurisdiction, as follows:

a. The territorial jurisdiction of the Council shall encompass Gaza Strip territory, except for the Settlements and the Military Installation Area shown on map No. 2, and West Bank territory, except for Area C which, except for the issues that will be negotiated in the permanent status negotiations, will be gradually transferred to Palestinian jurisdiction in three phases, each to take place after an interval of six months, to be completed 18 months after the inauguration of the Council. At this time, the jurisdiction of the Council will cover West Bank and Gaza Strip territory, except for the issues that will be negotiated in the permanent status negotiations.

Territorial jurisdiction includes land, subsoil and territorial waters, in accordance with the provisions of this Agreement.

b. The functional jurisdiction of the Council extends to all powers and responsibilities transferred to the Council, as specified in this Agreement or in any future agreements that may be reached between the Parties during the interim period.

c. The territorial and functional jurisdiction of the Council will apply to all persons, except for Israelis, unless otherwise provided in this Agreement.

d. Notwithstanding subparagraph a. above, the Council shall have functional jurisdiction in Area C, as detailed in Article IV of Annex III.

3. The Council has, within its authority, legislative, executive and judicial powers and responsibilities, as provided for in this Agreement.

4.a. Israel, through its military government, has the authority over areas that are not under the territorial jurisdiction of the Council, powers and responsibilities not transferred to the Council and Israelis.

b. To this end, the Israeli military government shall retain the necessary legislative, judicial and executive powers and responsibilities, in accordance with international law. This provision shall not derogate from Israel's applicable legislation over Israelis in personam.

5. The exercise of authority with regard to the electromagnetic sphere and air space shall be in accordance with the provisions of this Agreement.

6. Without derogating from the provisions of this Article, legal arrangements detailed in the Protocol Concerning Legal Matters attached as Annex IV to this Agreement (hereinafter 'Annex IV') shall be observed. Israel and the Council may negotiate further legal arrangements.

7. Israel and the Council shall co-operate on matters of legal assistance in criminal and civil matters through a legal committee (hereinafter 'the Legal Committee'), hereby established.

8. The Council's jurisdiction will extend gradually to cover West Bank and Gaza Strip territory, except for the issues to be negotiated in the permanent status negotiations, through a series of redeployments of the Israeli military forces. The first phase of the redeployment of Israeli military forces will cover populated areas in the West Bank—cities, towns, refugee camps and hamlets, as set out in Annex I—and will be completed prior to the eve of the Palestinian elections, i.e. 22 days before the day of the elections. Further redeployments of Israeli military forces to specified military locations will commence immediately upon the inauguration of the Council and will be effected in three phases, each to take place after an interval of six months, to be concluded no later than eighteen months from the date of the inauguration of the Council.

Article XVIII

LEGISLATIVE POWERS OF THE COUNCIL

1. For the purposes of this Article, legislation shall mean any primary and secondary legislation, including basic laws, laws, regulations and other legislative acts.

2. The Council has the power, within its jurisdiction as defined in Article XVII of this Agreement, to adopt legislation.

3. While the primary legislative power shall lie in the hands of the Council as a whole, the Ra'ees of the Executive Authority of the Council shall have the following legislative powers:

a. The power to initiate legislation or to present proposed legislation to the Council;

b. The power to promulgate legislation adopted by the Council; and

c. The power to issue secondary legislation, including regulations, relating to any matters specified and within the scope laid down in any primary legislation adopted by the Council.

4.a. Legislation, including legislation which amends or abrogates existing laws or military orders, which exceeds the jurisdiction of the Council or which is otherwise inconsistent with the provisions of the DOP, this Agreement, or of any other agreement that may be reached between the two sides during the interim period, shall have no effect and shall be void ab initio.

b. The Ra'ees of the Executive Authority of the Council shall not promulgate legislation adopted by the Council if such legislation falls under the provisions of this paragraph.

5. All legislation shall be communicated to the Israeli side of the Legal Committee.

6. Without derogating from the provisions of paragraph 4 above, the Israeli side of the Legal Committee may refer for the attention of the Committee any legislation regarding which Israel considers the provisions of paragraph 4 apply, in order to discuss issues arising from such legislation. The Legal Committee will consider the legislation referred to it at the earliest opportunity.

Article XIX

HUMAN RIGHTS AND THE RULE OF LAW

Israel and the Council shall exercise their powers and responsibilities pursuant to this Agreement with due regard to internationally-accepted norms and principles of human rights and the rule of law.

Article XX

RIGHTS, LIABILITIES AND OBLIGATIONS

1.a. Transfer of powers and responsibilities from the Israeli military government and its civil administration to the Council, as detailed in Annex III, includes all related rights, liabilities and obligations arising with regard to acts or omissions which occurred prior to such transfer. Israel will cease to bear any financial responsibility regarding such acts or omissions and the Council will bear all financial responsibility for these and for its own functioning.

b. Any financial claim made in this regard against Israel will be referred to the Council.

c. Israel shall provide the Council with the information it has regarding pending and anticipated claims brought before any court or tribunal against Israel in this regard.

d. Where legal proceedings are brought in respect of such a claim, Israel will notify the Council and enable it to participate in defending the claim and raise any arguments on its behalf.
e. In the event that an award is made against Israel by any court or tribunal in respect of such a claim, the Council shall immediately reimburse Israel the full amount of the award.
f. Without prejudice to the above, where a court or tribunal hearing such a claim finds that liability rests solely with an employee or agent who acted beyond the scope of the powers assigned to him or her, unlawfully or with willful malfeasance, the Council shall not bear financial responsibility.
2.a. Notwithstanding the provisions of paragraphs 1.d through 1.f above, each side may take the necessary measures, including promulgation of legislation, in order to ensure that such claims by Palestinians, including pending claims in which the hearing of evidence has not yet begun, are brought only before Palestinian courts or tribunals in the West Bank and the Gaza Strip, and are not brought before or heard by Israeli courts or tribunals.
b. Where a new claim has been brought before a Palestinian court or tribunal subsequent to the dismissal of the claim pursuant to subparagraph a. above, the Council shall defend it and, in accordance with subparagraph 1.a above, in the event that an award is made for the plaintiff, shall pay the amount of the award.
c. The Legal Committee shall agree on arrangements for the transfer of all materials and information needed to enable the Palestinian courts or tribunals to hear such claims as referred to in sub-paragraph b. above, and, when necessary, for the provision of legal assistance by Israel to the Council in defending such claims.

3. The transfer of authority in itself shall not affect rights, liabilities and obligations of any person or legal entity, in existence at the date of signing of this Agreement.

4. The Council, upon its inauguration, will assume all the rights, liabilities and obligations of the Palestinian Authority.

5. For the purpose of this Agreement, 'Israelis' also includes Israeli statutory agencies and corporations registered in Israel.

Article XXI

SETTLEMENT OF DIFFERENCES AND DISPUTES

Any difference relating to the application of this Agreement shall be referred to the appropriate co-ordination and co-operation mechanism established under this Agreement. The provisions of Article XV of the DOP shall apply to any such difference which is not settled through the appropriate co-ordination and co-operation mechanism, namely:

1. Disputes arising out of the application or interpretation of this Agreement or any related agreements pertaining to the interim period shall be settled through the Liaison Committee.
2. Disputes which cannot be settled by negotiations may be settled by a mechanism of conciliation to be agreed between the Parties.
3. The Parties may agree to submit to arbitration disputes relating to the interim period, which cannot be settled through conciliation. To this end, upon the agreement of both Parties, the Parties will establish an Arbitration Committee.

CHAPTER 4—CO-OPERATION

Article XXII

RELATIONS BETWEEN ISRAEL AND THE COUNCIL

1. Israel and the Council shall seek to foster mutual understanding and tolerance and shall accordingly abstain from incitement, including hostile propaganda, against each other and, without derogating from the principle of freedom of expression, shall take legal measures to prevent such incitement by any organizations, groups or individuals within their jurisdiction.

2. Israel and the Council will ensure that their respective educational systems contribute to the peace between the Israeli and Palestinian peoples and to peace in the entire region, and will refrain from the introduction of any motifs that could adversely affect the process of reconciliation.

3. Without derogating from the other provisions of this Agreement, Israel and the Council shall co-operate in combating criminal activity which may affect both sides, including offenses related to trafficking in illegal drugs and psychotropic substances, smuggling, and offenses against property, including offenses related to vehicles.

Article XXIII

CO-OPERATION WITH REGARD TO TRANSFER OF POWERS AND RESPONSIBILITIES

In order to ensure a smooth, peaceful and orderly transfer of powers and responsibilities, the two sides will co-operate with regard to the transfer of security powers and responsibilities in accordance with the provisions of Annex I, and the transfer of civil powers and responsibilities in accordance with the provisions of Annex III.

Article XXIV

ECONOMIC RELATIONS

The economic relations between the two sides are set out in the Protocol on Economic Relations, signed in Paris on April 29, 1994, and the Appendices thereto, and the Supplement to the Protocol on Economic Relations, all attached as Annex V, and will be governed by the relevant provisions of this Agreement and its Annexes.

Article XXV

CO-OPERATION PROGRAMMES

1. The Parties agree to establish a mechanism to develop programmes of co-operation between them. Details of such co-operation are set out in Annex VI.

2. A Standing Co-operation Committee to deal with issues arising in the context of this co-operation is hereby established as provided for in Annex VI.

Article XXVI

THE JOINT ISRAELI-PALESTINIAN LIAISON COMMITTEE

1. The Liaison Committee established pursuant to Article X of the DOP shall ensure the smooth implementation of this Agreement. It shall deal with issues requiring co-ordination, other issues of common interest and disputes.

2. The Liaison Committee shall be composed of an equal number of members from each Party. It may add other technicians and experts as necessary.

3. The Liaison Committee shall adopt its rules of procedures, including the frequency and place or places of its meetings.

4. The Liaison Committee shall reach its decisions by agreement.

5. The Liaison Committee shall establish a subcommittee that will monitor and steer the implementation of this Agreement (hereinafter 'the Monitoring and Steering Committee'). It will function as follows:
a. The Monitoring and Steering Committee will, on an ongoing basis, monitor the implementation of this Agreement, with a view to enhancing the co-operation and fostering the peaceful relations between the two sides.
b. The Monitoring and Steering Committee will steer the activities of the various joint committees established in this Agreement (the JSC, the CAC, the Legal Committee, the Joint Economic Committee and the Standing Co-operation Committee) concerning the ongoing implementation of the Agreement, and will report to the Liaison Committee.
c. The Monitoring and Steering Committee will be composed of the heads of the various committees mentioned above.
d. The two heads of the Monitoring and Steering Committee will establish its rules of procedures, including the frequency and places of its meetings.

Article XXVII

LIAISON AND CO-OPERATION WITH JORDAN AND EGYPT

1. Pursuant to Article XII of the DOP, the two Parties have invited the Governments of Jordan and Egypt to participate in establishing further liaison and co-operation arrangements between the Government of Israel and the Palestinian representatives on the one hand, and the Governments of Jordan and Egypt on the other hand, to promote co-operation between them. As part of these arrangements a Continuing Committee has been constituted and has commenced its deliberations.

2. The Continuing Committee shall decide by agreement on the modalities of admission of persons displaced from the West Bank and the Gaza Strip in 1967, together with necessary measures to prevent disruption and disorder.

3. The Continuing Committee shall also deal with other matters of common concern.

Article XXVIII

MISSING PERSONS

1. Israel and the Council shall co-operate by providing each other with all necessary assistance in the conduct of searches for missing persons and bodies of persons which have not been recovered, as well as by providing information about missing persons.

2. The PLO undertakes to co-operate with Israel and to assist it in its efforts to locate and to return to Israel Israeli soldiers who are missing in action and the bodies of soldiers which have not been recovered.

CHAPTER 5—MISCELLANEOUS PROVISIONS

Article XXIX

SAFE PASSAGE BETWEEN THE WEST BANK AND THE GAZA STRIP

Arrangements for safe passage of persons and transportation between the West Bank and the Gaza Strip are set out in Annex I.

Article XXX

PASSAGES

Arrangements for co-ordination between Israel and the Council regarding passage to and from Egypt and Jordan, as well as any other agreed international crossings, are set out in Annex I.

Article XXXI

FINAL CLAUSES

1. This Agreement shall enter into force on the date of its signing.

2. The Gaza-Jericho Agreement, the Preparatory Transfer Agreement and the Further Transfer Protocol will be superseded by this Agreement.

3. The Council, upon its inauguration, shall replace the Palestinian Authority and shall assume all the undertakings and obligations of the Palestinian Authority under the Gaza-Jericho Agreement, the Preparatory Transfer Agreement, and the Further Transfer Protocol.

4. The two sides shall pass all necessary legislation to implement this Agreement.

5. Permanent status negotiations will commence as soon as possible, but not later than May 4, 1996, between the Parties. It is understood that these negotiations shall cover remaining issues, including: Jerusalem, refugees, settlements, security arrangements, borders, relations and co-operation with other neighbours, and other issues of common interest.

6. Nothing in this Agreement shall prejudice or preempt the outcome of the negotiations on the permanent status to be conducted pursuant to the DOP. Neither Party shall be deemed, by virtue of having entered into this Agreement, to have renounced or waived any of its existing rights, claims or positions.

7. Neither side shall initiate or take any step that will change the status of the West Bank and the Gaza Strip pending the outcome of the permanent status negotiations.

8. The two Parties view the West Bank and the Gaza Strip as a single territorial unit, the integrity and status of which will be preserved during the interim period.

9. The PLO undertakes that, within two months of the date of the inauguration of the Council, the Palestinian National Council will convene and formally approve the necessary changes in regard to the Palestinian Covenant, as undertaken in the letters signed by the Chairman of the PLO and addressed to the Prime Minister of Israel, dated September 9, 1993 and May 4, 1994.

10. Pursuant to Annex I, Article IX of this Agreement, Israel confirms that the permanent check-points on the roads leading to and from the Jericho Area (except those related to the access road leading from Mousa Alami to the Allenby Bridge) will be removed upon the completion of the first phase of redeployment.

11. Prisoners who, pursuant to the Gaza-Jericho Agreement, were turned over to the Palestinian Authority on the condition that they remain in the Jericho Area for the remainder of their sentence, will be free to return to their homes in the West Bank and the Gaza Strip upon the completion of the first phase of redeployment.

12. As regards relations between Israel and the PLO, and without derogating from the commitments contained in the letters signed by and exchanged between the Prime Minister of Israel and the Chairman of the PLO, dated September 9, 1993 and May 4, 1994, the two sides will apply between them the provisions contained in Article XXII, paragraph 1, with the necessary changes.

13.a. The Preamble to this Agreement, and all Annexes, Appendices and maps attached hereto (*not reproduced—Ed.*), shall constitute an integral part hereof.

b. The Parties agree that the maps (*not reproduced—Ed.*) attached to the Gaza-Jericho Agreement as

a. map No. 1 (The Gaza Strip), an exact copy of which is attached to this Agreement as map No. 2 (in this Agreement 'map No. 2');

b. map No. 4 (Deployment of Palestinian Police in the Gaza Strip), an exact copy of which is attached to this Agreement as map No. 5 (in this Agreement 'map No. 5'); and

c. map No. 6 (Maritime Activity Zones), an exact copy of which is attached to this Agreement as map No. 8 (in this Agreement 'map No. 8')

are an integral part hereof and will remain in effect for the duration of this Agreement.

14. While the Jeftlik area will come under the functional and personal jurisdiction of the Council in the first phase of redeployment, the area's transfer to the territorial jurisdiction of the Council will be considered by the Israeli side in the first phase of the further redeployment phases.

THE WYE RIVER MEMORANDUM

(23 October 1998)

The Wye River Memorandum was signed by Israeli Prime Minister Binyamin Netanyahu and Palestinian (National) Authority (PA) President Yasser Arafat, and witnessed by US President Bill Clinton, on 23 October 1998 at the Wye Plantation, Maryland, USA. The Memorandum was to enter into force 10 days after this date. An attachment to the Memorandum detailed a 'time line' for the implementation of the terms of the Interim Agreement and the Memorandum.

The following are steps to facilitate implementation of the Interim Agreement on the West Bank and Gaza Strip of September 28, 1995 (the 'Interim Agreement') and other related agreements including the Note for the Record of January 17, 1997 (hereinafter referred to as 'the prior agreements') so that the Israeli and Palestinian sides can more effectively carry out their reciprocal responsibilities, including those relating to further redeployments and security respectively. These steps are to be carried out in a parallel phased approach in accordance with this Memorandum and the attached time line. They are subject to the relevant terms and conditions of the prior agreements and do not supersede their other agreements.

I. FURTHER REDEPLOYMENTS

A. Phase One and Two Further Redeployments

1. Pursuant to the Interim Agreement and subsequent agreements, the Israeli side's implementation of the first and second F.R.D. will consist of the transfer to the Palestinian side of 13% from Area C as follows:

1% to Area (A)

12% to Area (B)

The Palestinian side has informed that it will allocate an area/areas amounting to 3% from the above Area (B) to be designated as Green Areas and/or Nature Reserves. The Palestinian side has further informed that they will act according to the established scientific standards, and that therefore there will be no changes in the status of these areas, without prejudice to the rights of the existing inhabitants in these areas including Bedouins; while these standards do not allow new construction in these areas, existing roads and buildings may be maintained.

The Israeli side will retain in these Green Areas/Nature Reserves the overriding security responsibility for the purpose of protecting Israelis and confronting the threat of terrorism. Activities and movements of the Palestinian Police forces may be carried out after co-ordination and confirmation; the Israeli side will respond to such requests expeditiously.

2. As part of the foregoing implementation of the first and second F.R.D., 14.2% from Area (B) will become Area (A).

B. Third Phase of Further Redeployments

With regard to the terms of the Interim Agreement and of Secretary Christopher's letters to the two sides of January 17, 1997 relating to the further redeployment process, there will be a committee to address this question. The United States will be briefed regularly.

II. SECURITY

In the provisions on security arrangements of the Interim Agreement, the Palestinian side agreed to take all measures necessary in order to prevent acts of terrorism, crime and hostilities directed against the Israeli side, against individuals falling under the Israeli side's authority and against their property, just as the Israeli side agreed to take all measures necessary in order to prevent acts of terrorism, crime and hostilities directed against the Palestinian side, against individuals falling under the Palestinian side's authority and against their property. The two sides also agreed to take legal measures against offenders within their jurisdiction and to prevent incitement against each other by any organizations, groups or individuals within their jurisdiction.

Both sides recognize that it is in their vital interests to combat terrorism and fight violence in accordance with Annex I of the Interim Agreement and the Note for the Record. They also recognize that the struggle against terror and violence must be comprehensive in that it deals with terrorists, the terror support structure, and the environment conducive to the support of terror. It must be continuous and constant over a long-term, in that there can be no pauses in the work against terrorists and their structure. It must be co-operative in that no effort can be fully effective without Israeli-Palestinian co-operation and the continuous exchange of information, concepts, and actions.

Pursuant to the prior agreements, the Palestinian side's implementation of its responsibilities for security, security co-operation, and other issues will be as detailed below during the time periods specified in the attached time line:

A. Security Actions

1. Outlawing and Combating Terrorist Organizations

a. The Palestinian side will make known its policy of zero tolerance for terror and violence against both sides.

b. A work plan developed by the Palestinian side will be shared with the U.S. and thereafter implementation will begin immediately to ensure the systematic and effective combat of terrorist organizations and their infrastructure.

c. In addition to the bilateral Israeli-Palestinian security co-operation, a U.S.-Palestinian committee will meet biweekly to review the steps being taken to eliminate terrorist cells and the support structure that plans, finances, supplies and abets terror. In these meetings, the Palestinian side will inform the U.S. fully of the actions it has taken to outlaw all organizations (or wings of organizations, as appropriate) of a military, terrorist or violent character and their support structure and to prevent them from operating in areas under its jurisdiction.

d. The Palestinian side will apprehend the specific individuals suspected of perpetrating acts of violence and terror for the purpose of further investigation, and prosecution and punishment of all persons involved in acts of violence and terror.

e. A U.S.-Palestinian committee will meet to review and evaluate information pertinent to the decisions on prosecution, punishment or other legal measures which affect the status of individuals suspected of abetting or perpetrating acts of violence and terror.

2. Prohibiting Illegal Weapons

a. The Palestinian side will ensure an effective legal framework is in place to criminalize, in conformity with the prior agreements, any importation, manufacturing or unlicensed sale, acquisition or possession of firearms, ammunition or weapons in areas under Palestinian jurisdiction.

b. In addition, the Palestinian side will establish and vigorously and continuously implement a systematic programme for the collection and appropriate handling of all such illegal items in accordance with the prior agreements. The U.S. has agreed to assist in carrying out this programme.

c. A U.S.-Palestinian-Israeli committee will be established to assist and enhance co-operation in preventing the smuggling or other unauthorized introduction of weapons or explosive materials into areas under Palestinian jurisdiction.

3. Preventing Incitement

a. Drawing on relevant international practice and pursuant to Article XXII (1) of the Interim Agreement and the Note for the Record, the Palestinian side will issue a decree prohibiting all forms of incitement to violence or terror, and establishing mechanisms for acting systematically against all expressions or threats of violence or terror. This decree will be comparable to the existing Israeli legislation which deals with the same subject.

b. A U.S.-Palestinian-Israeli committee will meet on a regular basis to monitor cases of possible incitement to violence or terror and to make recommendations and reports on how to prevent such incitement. The Israeli, Palestinian and U.S. sides will each appoint a media specialist, a law enforcement representative, an educational specialist and a current or former elected official to the committee.

B. Security Co-operation

The two sides agree that their security co-operation will be based on a spirit of partnership and will include, among other things, the following steps:

1. Bilateral Co-operation

There will be full bilateral security co-operation between the two sides which will be continuous, intensive and comprehensive.

2. Forensic Co-operation

There will be an exchange of forensic expertise, training, and other assistance.

3. Trilateral Committee

In addition to the bilateral Israeli-Palestinian security co-operation, a high-ranking U.S.-Palestinian-Israeli committee will meet as required and not less than biweekly to assess current threats, deal with any impediments to effective security co-operation and co-ordination and address the steps being taken to combat terror and terrorist organizations. The committee will also serve as a forum to address the issue of external support for terror. In these meetings, the Palestinian side will fully inform the members of the committee of the results of its investigations concerning terrorist suspects already in custody and the participants will exchange additional relevant information. The committee will report regularly to the leaders of the two sides on the status of co-operation, the results of the meetings and its recommendations.

C. Other Issues

1. Palestinian Police Force

a. The Palestinian side will provide a list of its policemen to the Israeli side in conformity with the prior agreements.

b. Should the Palestinian side request technical assistance, the U.S. has indicated its willingness to help meet their needs in co-operation with other donors.

c. The Monitoring and Steering Committee will, as part of its functions, monitor the implementation of this provision and brief the U.S.

2. PLO Charter

The Executive Committee of the Palestine Liberation Organization and the Palestinian Central Council will reaffirm the letter of 22 January 1998 from PLO Chairman Yasser Arafat to President Clinton concerning the nullification of the Palestinian National Charter provisions that are inconsistent with the letters exchanged between the PLO and the Government of Israel on 9–10 September 1993. PLO Chairman Arafat, the Speaker of the Palestine National Council, and the Speaker of the Palestinian Council will invite the members of the PNC, as well as the members of the Central Council, the Council, and the Palestinian Heads of Ministries to a meeting to be addressed by President Clinton to reaffirm their support for the peace process and the aforementioned decisions of the Executive Committee and the Central Council.

3. Legal Assistance in Criminal Matters

Among other forms of legal assistance in criminal matters, the requests for arrest and transfer of suspects and defendants pursuant to Article II (7) of Annex IV of the Interim Agreement will be submitted (or resubmitted) through the mechanism of the Joint Israeli-Palestinian Legal Committee and will be responded to in conformity with Article II (7) (f) of Annex IV of the Interim Agreement within the twelve week period. Requests submitted after the eighth week will be responded to in conformity with Article II (7) (f) within four weeks of their submission. The U.S. has been requested by the sides to report on a regular basis on the steps being taken to respond to the above requests.

4. Human Rights and the Rule of Law

Pursuant to Article XI (1) of Annex I of the Interim Agreement, and without derogating from the above, the Palestinian Police will exercise powers and responsibilities to implement this Memorandum with due regard to internationally accepted norms of human rights and the rule of law, and will be guided by the need to protect the public, respect human dignity, and avoid harassment.

III. INTERIM COMMITTEES AND ECONOMIC ISSUES

1. The Israeli and Palestinian sides reaffirm their commitment to enhancing their relationship and agree on the need actively to promote economic development in the West Bank and Gaza. In this regard, the parties agree to continue or to reactivate all standing committees established by the Interim Agreement, including the Monitoring and Steering Committee, the Joint Economic Committee (JEC), the Civil Affairs Committee (CAC), the Legal Committee, and the Standing Co-operation Committee.

2. The Israeli and Palestinian sides have agreed on arrangements which will permit the timely opening of the Gaza Industrial Estate. They also have concluded a 'Protocol Regarding the Establishment and Operation of the International Airport in the Gaza Strip During the Interim Period'.

3. Both sides will renew negotiations on Safe Passage immediately. As regards the southern route, the sides will make best efforts to conclude the agreement within a week of the entry into force of this Memorandum. Operation of the southern route will start as soon as possible thereafter. As regards the northern route, negotiations will continue with the goal of reaching agreement as soon as possible. Implementation will take place expeditiously thereafter.

4. The Israeli and Palestinian sides acknowledge the great importance of the Port of Gaza for the development of the Palestinian economy, and the expansion of Palestinian trade. They commit themselves to proceeding without delay to conclude an agreement to allow the construction and operation of the port in accordance with the prior agreements. The Israeli-Palestinian Committee will reactivate its work immediately with a goal of concluding the protocol within sixty days, which will allow commencement of the construction of the port.

5. The two sides recognize that unresolved legal issues adversely affect the relationship between the two peoples. They therefore will accelerate efforts through the Legal Committee to address outstanding legal issues and to implement solutions to these issues in the shortest possible period. The Palestinian side will provide to the Israeli side copies of all of its laws in effect.

6. The Israeli and Palestinian sides will launch a strategic economic dialogue to enhance their economic relationship. They will establish within the framework of the JEC an Ad Hoc Committee for this purpose. The committee will review the following four issues: (1) Israeli purchase tax; (2) co-operation in combating vehicle theft; (3) dealing with unpaid Palestinian debts; and (4) the impact of Israeli standards as barriers to trade and the expansion of the A1 and A2 lists. The committee will submit an interim report within three weeks of the entry into force of this Memorandum, and within six weeks will submit its conclusions and recommendations to be implemented.

7. The two sides agree on the importance of continued international donor assistance to facilitate implementation by both sides of agreements reached. They also recognize the need for enhanced donor support for economic development in the West Bank and Gaza. They agree jointly to approach the donor community to organize a Ministerial Conference before the end of 1998 to seek pledges for enhanced levels of assistance.

IV. PERMANENT STATUS NEGOTIATIONS

The two sides will immediately resume permanent status negotiations on an accelerated basis and will make a determined effort to achieve the mutual goal of reaching an agreement by May 4, 1999. The negotiations will be continuous and without interruption. The U.S. has expressed its willingness to facilitate these negotiations.

V. UNILATERAL ACTIONS

Recognizing the necessity to create a positive environment for the negotiations, neither side shall initiate or take any step that will change the status of the West Bank and the Gaza Strip in accordance with the Interim Agreement.

SHARM EL-SHEIKH MEMORANDUM ON THE IMPLEMENTATION TIMELINE OF OUTSTANDING COMMITMENTS OF AGREEMENTS SIGNED AND THE RESUMPTION OF PERMANENT STATUS NEGOTIATIONS (WYE TWO)

(4 September 1999)

The implementation of the Wye River Memorandum having stalled under the Netanyahu administration in Israel, in September 1999 the new Israeli Prime Minister, Ehud Barak, and the PA President, Yasser Arafat, met in the Egyptian resort of Sharm el-Sheikh to discuss the possible reactivation of the Memorandum. On 4 September the two leaders signed the Sharm el-Sheikh Memorandum (also known as Wye Two), which detailed a revised timetable for the outstanding provisions of the October 1998 Memorandum. The Memorandum was witnessed by President Hosni Mubarak for Egypt, Secretary of State Madeleine Albright for the USA, and King Abdullah of Jordan.

The Government of the State of Israel and the Palestine Liberation Organization (PLO) commit themselves to full and mutual implementation of the Interim Agreement and all other agreements concluded between them since September 1993 (hereinafter 'the prior agreements'), and all outstanding commitments emanating from the prior agreements. Without derogating from the other requirements of the prior agreements, the two sides have agreed as follows:

1. Permanent Status Negotiations

a. In the context of the implementation of the prior agreements, the two sides will resume the Permanent Status negotiations in an accelerated manner and will make a determined effort to achieve their mutual agenda, i.e. the specific issues reserved for Permanent Status negotiators and other issues of common interest.

b. The two sides reaffirm their understanding that the negotiations on the Permanent Status will lead to the implementation of Security Council Resolutions 242 and 338.

c. The two sides will make a determined effort to conclude a Framework Agreement on all Permanent Status issues in five months from the resumption of the Permanent Status negotiations.

d. The two sides will conclude a comprehensive agreement on all Permanent Status issues within one year from the resumption of the Permanent Status negotiations.

e. Permanent Status negotiations will resume after the implementation of the first stage of release of prisoners and the second stage of the First and Second Further Redeployments and not later than September 13, 1999. In the Wye River Memorandum, the United States has expressed its willingness to facilitate these negotiations.

2. Phase One and Phase Two of the Further Redeployments

The Israeli side undertakes the following with regard to Phase One and Phase Two of the Further Redeployments:

a. On September 5, 1999, to transfer 7% from Area C to Area B.

b. On November 15, 1999, to transfer 2% from Area B to Area A and 3% from Area C to Area B.

c. On January 20, 2000, to transfer 1% from Area C to Area A, and 5.1% from Area B to Area A.

3. Release of Prisoners

a. The two sides shall establish a joint committee that shall follow up on matters related to the release of Palestinian prisoners.

b. The Government of Israel shall release Palestinian and other prisoners who committed their offences prior to September 13, 1993, and were arrested prior to May 4, 1994. The Joint Committee shall agree on the names of those who will be released in the first two stages. Those lists shall be recommended to the relevant Authorities through the Monitoring and Steering Committee.

c. The first stage of release of prisoners shall be carried out on September 5, 1999 and shall consist of 200 prisoners. The second stage of release of prisoners shall be carried out on October 8, 1999 and shall consist of 150 prisoners.

d. The joint committee shall recommend further lists of names to be released to the relevant Authorities through the Monitoring and Steering Committee.

e. The Israeli side will aim to release Palestinian prisoners before next Ramadan.

4. Committees

a. The Third Further Redeployment Committee shall commence its activities not later than September 13, 1999.

b. The Monitoring and Steering Committee, all Interim Committees (i.e. Civil Affairs Committee, Joint Economic Committee, Joint Standing Committee, legal committee, people to people), as well as Wye River Memorandum committees shall resume and/or continue their activity, as the case may be, not later than September 13, 1999. The Monitoring and Steering Committee will have on its agenda, inter alia, the Year 2000, Donor/PA projects in Area C, and the issue of industrial estates.

c. The Continuing Committee on displaced persons shall resume its activity on October 1, 1999 (Article XXVII, Interim Agreement).

d. Not later than October 30, 1999, the two sides will implement the recommendations of the Ad-hoc Economic Committee (article III-6, Wye River Memorandum).

5. Safe Passage

a. The operation of the Southern Route of the Safe Passage for the movement of persons, vehicles, and goods will start on October 1, 1999 (Annex I, Article X, Interim Agreement) in accordance with the details of operation, which will be provided for in the Safe Passage Protocol that will be concluded by the two sides not later than September 30, 1999.

b. The two sides will agree on the specific location of the crossing point of the Northern Route of the Safe Passage as specified in Annex I, Article X, provision c-4, in the Interim Agreement not later than October 5, 1999.

c. The Safe Passage Protocol applied to the Southern Route of the Safe Passage shall apply to the Northern Route of the Safe Passage with relevant agreed modifications.

d. Upon the agreement on the location of the crossing point of the Northern Route of the Safe Passage, construction of the needed facilities and related procedures shall commence and shall be ongoing. At the same time, temporary facilities will be established for the operation of the Northern Route not later than four months from the agreement on the specific location of the crossing-point.

e. In between the operation of the Southern crossing point of the Safe Passage and the Northern crossing point of the Safe Passage, Israel will facilitate arrangements for the movement between the West Bank and the Gaza Strip, using non-Safe Passage routes other than the Southern Route of the Safe Passage.

f. The location of the crossing points shall be without prejudice to the Permanent Status negotiations (Annex I, Article X, provision e, Interim Agreement).

6. Gaza Sea Port

The two sides have agreed on the following principles to facilitate and enable the construction works of the Gaza Sea Port. The principles shall not prejudice or pre-empt the outcome of negotiations on the Permanent Status:

a. The Israeli side agrees that the Palestinian side shall commence construction works in and related to the Gaza Sea Port on October 1, 1999.

b. The two sides agree that the Gaza Sea Port will not be operated in any way before reaching a joint Sea Port protocol on all aspects of operating the Port, including security.

c. The Gaza Sea Port is a special case, like the Gaza Airport, being situated in an area under the responsibility of the Palestinian side and serving as an international passage. Therefore, with the conclusion of a joint Sea Port Protocol, all activities and arrangements relating to the construction of the Port shall be in accordance with the provisions of the Interim Agreement, especially those relating to international passages, as adapted in the Gaza Airport Protocol.

d. The construction shall ensure adequate provision for effective security and customs inspection of people and goods, as well as the establishment of a designated checking area in the Port.

e. In this context, the Israeli side will facilitate on an ongoing basis the works related to the construction of the Gaza Sea Port, including the movement in and out of the Port of vessels, equipment, resources, and material required for the construction of the Port.

f. The two sides will co-ordinate such works, including the designs and movement, through a joint mechanism.

7. Hebron Issues

a. The Shuhada Road in Hebron shall be opened for the movement of Palestinian vehicles in two phases. The first phase has been carried out, and the second shall be carried out not later than October 30, 1999.

b. The wholesale market Hasbahe will be opened not later than November 1, 1999, in accordance with arrangements which will be agreed upon by the two sides.

c. A high-level Joint Liaison Committee will convene not later than September 13, 1999 to review the situation in the Tomb of the Patriarchs/Al Haram Al Ibrahimi (Annex I, Article VII, Interim Agreement and as per the January 15, 1998 US Minute of Discussion).

8. Security

a. The two sides will, in accordance with the prior agreements, act to ensure the immediate, efficient and effective handling of any incident involving a threat or act of terrorism, violence or incitement, whether committed by Palestinians or Israelis. To this end, they will co-operate in the exchange of information and co-ordinate policies and activities. Each side shall immediately and effectively respond to the occurrence of an act of terrorism, violence or incitement and shall take all necessary measures to prevent such an occurrence.

b. Pursuant to the prior agreements, the Palestinian side undertakes to implement its responsibilities for security, security co-operation, ongoing obligations and other issues emanating from the prior agreements, including, in particular, the following obligations emanating from the Wye River Memorandum:

1. continuation of the programme for the collection of the illegal weapons, including reports.

2. apprehension of suspects, including reports.

3. forwarding of the list of Palestinian policemen to the Israeli side not later than September 13, 1999.

4. beginning of the review of the list by the Monitoring and Steering Committee not later than October 15, 1999.

9. The two sides call upon the international donor community to enhance its commitment and financial support to the Palestinian economic development and the Israeli-Palestinian peace process.

10. Recognizing the necessity to create a positive environment for the negotiations, neither side shall initiate or take any step that will change the status of the West Bank and the Gaza Strip in accordance with the Interim Agreement.

11. Obligations pertaining to dates which occur on holidays or Saturdays shall be carried out on the first subsequent working day.

This memorandum will enter into force one week from the date of its signature.

It is understood that, for technical reasons, implementation of Article 2a and the first stage mentioned in Article 3c will be carried out within a week from the signing of this Memorandum.

REPORT OF THE SHARM EL-SHEIKH FACT-FINDING COMMITTEE (THE MITCHELL REPORT)

Violence between Israeli forces and Palestinians broke out in late September 2000, following a visit by the leader of Israel's Likud party, Ariel Sharon, to the site of the Temple Mount/Haram al-Sharif, in East Jerusalem. A period of intense international diplomatic activity ensued, in an attempt to bring about an end to the violent confrontations which had swiftly spread throughout the West Bank and Gaza Strip. On 14 October UN Secretary-General Kofi Annan secured the agreement of the Israeli Prime Minister, Ehud Barak, and the PA President, Yasser Arafat, to lead delegations to a summit meeting in Sharm el-Sheikh, Egypt, with mediation by US President Bill Clinton. The summit duly proceeded on 16 October, concluding the following day with what Clinton termed agreement on 'immediate concrete measures' to end the violence. (Subsequent truce agreements, based on understandings brokered by Clinton at Sharm el-Sheikh, failed to hold, however.) Agreement was reached at the summit on the formation of a US-appointed international fact-finding commission to investigate the clashes. The committee—chaired by former US Senator George Mitchell and comprising also former President Süleyman Demirel of Turkey, Norwegian Minister of Foreign Affairs Thorbjørn Jagland, former US Senator Warren Rudman, and the High Representative for the Common Foreign and Security Policy of the European Union, Javier Solana—was appointed by Clinton in early November. Reproduced is the full text of the committee's report, published on 20 May 2001. [Footnotes to the report—principally references to statements and submissions of the Government of Israel and the PLO, which made submissions to the committee on behalf of the Palestinians—have been omitted].

SUMMARY OF RECOMMENDATIONS

The Government of Israel and the Palestinian Authority (PA) must act swiftly and decisively to halt the violence. Their immediate objectives then should be to rebuild confidence and resume negotiations.

During this mission our aim has been to fulfil the mandate agreed at Sharm el-Sheikh. We value the support given our work by the participants at the summit, and we commend the parties for their co-operation. Our principal recommendation is that they recommit themselves to the Sharm el-Sheikh spirit and that they implement the decisions made there in 1999 and 2000. We believe that the summit participants will support bold action by the parties to achieve these objectives.

The restoration of trust is essential, and the parties should take affirmative steps to this end. Given the high level of hostility and mistrust, the timing and sequence of these steps are obviously crucial. This can be decided only by the parties. We urge them to begin the process of decision immediately.

Accordingly, we recommend that steps be taken to:

End the Violence

The Government of Israel and the PA should reaffirm their commitment to existing agreements and undertakings and should immediately implement an unconditional cessation of violence.

The Government of Israel and PA should immediately resume security co-operation.

Rebuild Confidence

The PA and Government of Israel should work together to establish a meaningful 'cooling-off period' and implement additional confidence-building measures, some of which were detailed in the October 2000 Sharm el-Sheikh Statement and some of which were offered by the US on January 7, 2001 in Cairo [see Recommendations section for further description].

The PA and Government of Israel should resume their efforts to identify, condemn and discourage incitement in all its forms.

The PA should make clear through concrete action to Palestinians and Israelis alike that terrorism is reprehensible and unacceptable, and that the PA will make a 100 percent effort to prevent terrorist operations and to punish perpetrators. This effort should include immediate steps to apprehend and incarcerate terrorists operating within the PA's jurisdiction.

The Government of Israel should freeze all settlement activity, including the 'natural growth' of existing settlements.

The Government of Israel should ensure that the IDF [*Israel Defence Forces*] adopt and enforce policies and procedures encouraging non-lethal responses to unarmed demonstrators, with a view to minimizing casualties and friction between the two communities.

The PA should prevent gunmen from using Palestinian populated areas to fire upon Israeli populated areas and IDF positions. This tactic places civilians on both sides at unnecessary risk.

The Government of Israel should lift closures, transfer to the PA all tax revenues owed, and permit Palestinians who had been employed in Israel to return to their jobs; and should ensure that security forces and settlers refrain from the destruction of homes and roads, as well as trees and other agricultural property in Palestinian areas. We acknowledge the Government of Israel's position that actions of this nature have been taken for security reasons. Nevertheless, the economic effects will persist for years.

The PA should renew co-operation with Israeli security agencies to ensure, to the maximum extent possible, that Palestinian workers employed within Israel are fully vetted and free of connections to organizations and individuals engaged in terrorism.

The PA and Government of Israel should consider a joint undertaking to preserve and protect holy places sacred to the traditions of Jews, Muslims, and Christians.

The Government of Israel and PA should jointly endorse and support the work of Palestinian and Israeli non-governmental organizations involved in cross-community initiatives linking the two peoples.

Resume Negotiations

In the spirit of the Sharm el-Sheikh agreements and understandings of 1999 and 2000, we recommend that the parties meet to reaffirm their commitment to signed agreements and mutual understandings, and take corresponding action. This should be the basis for resuming full and meaningful negotiations.

INTRODUCTION

On October 17, 2000, at the conclusion of the Middle East Peace Summit at Sharm el-Sheikh, Egypt, the President of the United States spoke on behalf of the participants (the Government of Israel, the Palestinian Authority, the Governments of Egypt, Jordan, and the United States, the United Nations, and the European Union). Among other things, the President stated that:

The United States will develop with the Israelis and Palestinians, as well as in consultation with the United Nations Secretary-General, a committee of fact-finding on the events of the past several weeks and how to prevent their recurrence. The committee's report will be shared by the US President with the UN Secretary-General and the parties prior to publication. A final report shall be submitted under the auspices of the US President for publication.

On November 7, 2000, following consultations with the other participants, the President asked us to serve on what has come to be known as the Sharm el-Sheikh Fact-Finding Committee. In a letter to us on December 6, 2000, the President stated that:

The purpose of the Summit, and of the agreement that ensued, was to end the violence, to prevent its recurrence, and to find a path back to the peace process. In its actions and mode of operation, therefore, the Committee should be guided by these overriding goals... [T]he Committee should strive to steer clear of any step that will intensify mutual blame and finger-pointing between the parties. As I noted in my previous letter, 'the Committee should not become a divisive force or a focal point for blame and recrimination but rather should serve to forestall violence and confrontation and provide lessons for the future'. This should not be a tribunal whose purpose is to determine the guilt or innocence of individuals or of the parties; rather, it should be a fact-finding committee whose purpose is to determine what happened and how to avoid it recurring in the future.

After our first meeting, held before we visited the region, we urged an end to all violence. Our meetings and our observations during our subsequent visits to the region have intensified our convictions in this regard. Whatever the source, violence will not solve the problems of the region. It will only make them worse. Death and destruction will not bring peace, but will deepen the hatred and harden the resolve on both sides. There is only one way to peace, justice, and security in the Middle East, and that is through negotiation.

Despite their long history and close proximity, some Israelis and Palestinians seem not to fully appreciate each other's problems and concerns. Some Israelis appear not to comprehend the humiliation and frustration that Palestinians must endure every day as a result of living with the continuing effects of occupation, sustained by the presence of Israeli military forces and settlements in their midst, or the determination of the Palestinians to achieve independence and genuine self-determination. Some Palestinians appear not to comprehend the extent to which terrorism creates fear among the Israeli people and undermines their belief in the possibility of co-existence, or the determination of the Government of Israel to do whatever is necessary to protect its people.

Fear, hate, anger, and frustration have risen on both sides. The greatest danger of all is that the culture of peace, nurtured over the previous decade, is being shattered. In its place there is a growing sense of futility and despair, and a growing resort to violence.

Political leaders on both sides must act and speak decisively to reverse these dangerous trends; they must rekindle the desire and the drive for peace. That will be difficult. But it can be done and it must be done, for the alternative is unacceptable and should be unthinkable.

Two proud peoples share a land and a destiny. Their competing claims and religious differences have led to a grinding, demoralizing, dehumanizing conflict. They can continue in conflict or they can negotiate to find a way to live side-by-side in peace.

There is a record of achievement. In 1991 the first peace conference with Israelis and Palestinians took place in Madrid to achieve peace based on UN Security Council Resolutions 242 and 338. In 1993, the Palestine Liberation Organization (PLO) and Israel met in Oslo for the first face-to-face negotiations; they led to mutual recognition and the Declaration of Principles (signed by the parties in Washington, D.C. on September 13, 1993), which provided a road map to reach the destination agreed in Madrid. Since then, important steps have been taken in Cairo, in Washington, and elsewhere. Last year the parties came very close to a permanent settlement.

So much has been achieved. So much is at risk. If the parties are to succeed in completing their journey to their common destination, agreed commitments must be implemented, international law respected, and human rights protected. We encourage them to return to negotiations, however difficult. It is the only path to peace, justice and security.

DISCUSSION

It is clear from their statements that the participants in the summit of last October hoped and intended that the outbreak of violence, then less than a month old, would soon end. The US President's letters to us, asking that we make recommendations on how to prevent a recurrence of violence, reflect that intention.

Yet the violence has not ended. It has worsened. Thus the overriding concern of those in the region with whom we spoke is to end the violence and to return to the process of shaping a sustainable peace. That is what we were told, and were asked to address, by Israelis and Palestinians alike. It was the message conveyed to us as well by President Mubarak of Egypt, King Abdullah of Jordan, and UN Secretary-General Annan.

Their concern must be ours. If our report is to have effect, it must deal with the situation that exists, which is different from that envisaged by the summit participants. In this report, we will try to answer the questions assigned to us by the Sharm el-Sheikh summit: What happened? Why did it happen?

In light of the current situation, however, we must elaborate on the third part of our mandate: How can the recurrence of violence be prevented? The relevance and impact of our work, in the end, will be measured by the recommendations we make concerning the following:

Ending the Violence.

Rebuilding Confidence.

Resuming Negotiations.

WHAT HAPPENED?

We are not a tribunal. We complied with the request that we do not determine the guilt or innocence of individuals or of the parties. We did not have the power to compel the testimony of witnesses or the production of documents. Most of the information we received came from the parties and, understandably, it largely tended to support their arguments.

In this part of our report, we do not attempt to chronicle all of the events from late September 2000 onward. Rather, we discuss only those that shed light on the underlying causes of violence.

In late September 2000, Israeli, Palestinian, and other officials received reports that Member of the Knesset (now Prime Minister) Ariel Sharon was planning a visit to the Haram al-Sharif/Temple Mount in Jerusalem. Palestinian and US officials urged then Prime Minister Ehud Barak to prohibit the visit. Mr Barak told us that he believed the visit was intended to be an internal political act directed against him by a political opponent, and he declined to prohibit it.

Mr Sharon made the visit on September 28 accompanied by over 1,000 Israeli police officers. Although Israelis viewed the visit in an internal political context, Palestinians saw it as highly provocative to them. On the following day, in the same place, a large number of unarmed Palestinian demonstrators and a large Israeli police contingent confronted each other. According to the US Department of State, 'Palestinians held large demonstrations and threw stones at police in the vicinity of the Western Wall. Police used rubber-coated metal bullets and live ammunition to disperse the demonstrators, killing 4 persons and injuring about 200'. According to the Government of Israel, 14 Israeli policemen were injured.

Similar demonstrations took place over the following several days. Thus began what has become known as the 'Al-Aqsa Intifada' (Al-Aqsa being a mosque at the Haram al-Sharif/ Temple Mount).

The Government of Israel asserts that the immediate catalyst for the violence was the breakdown of the Camp David negotiations on July 25, 2000 and the 'widespread appreciation in the international community of Palestinian responsibility for the impasse'. In this view, Palestinian violence was planned by the PA leadership, and was aimed at 'provoking and incurring Palestinian casualties as a means of regaining the diplomatic initiative.'

The Palestine Liberation Organization (PLO) denies the allegation that the intifada was planned. It claims, however, that 'Camp David represented nothing less than an attempt by Israel to extend the force it exercises on the ground to negotiations', and that 'the failure of the summit, and the attempts to allocate blame on the Palestinian side only added to the tension on the ground...'

From the perspective of the PLO, Israel responded to the disturbances with excessive and illegal use of deadly force against demonstrators; behavior which, in the PLO's view, reflected Israel's contempt for the lives and safety of Palestinians. For Palestinians, the widely seen images of the killing of 12-year-old Muhammad al-Durra in Gaza on September 20, shot as he huddled behind his father, reinforced that perception.

From the perspective of the Government of Israel, the demonstrations were organized and directed by the Palestinian leadership to create sympathy for their cause around the world by provoking Israeli security forces to fire upon demonstrators, especially young people. For Israelis, the lynching of two military reservists, First Sergeant Vadim Novesche and First Corporal Yosef Avrahami, in Ramallah on October 12, reflected a deep-seated Palestinian hatred of Israel and Jews.

What began as a series of confrontations between Palestinian demonstrators and Israeli security forces, which resulted in the Government of Israel's initial restrictions on the movement of people and goods in the West Bank amd Gaza Strip (closures), has since evolved into a wider array of violent actions and responses. There have been exchanges of fire between built-up areas, sniping incidents and clashes between Israeli settlers and Palestinians. There have also been terrorist acts and Israeli reactions thereto (characterized by the Government of Israel as counter-terrorism), including killings, further destruction of property and economic measures. Most recently, there have been mortar attacks on Israeli locations and IDF ground incursions into Palestinian areas.

From the Palestinian perspective, the decision of Israel to characterize the current crisis as 'an armed conflict short of war' is simply a means 'to justify its assassination policy, its collective punishment policy, and its use of lethal force'. From the Israeli perspective, 'The Palestinian leadership have instigated, orchestrated and directed the violence. It has used, and continues to use, terror and attrition as strategic tools'.

In their submissions, the parties traded allegations about the motivation and degree of control exercised by the other. However, we were provided with no persuasive evidence that the Sharon visit was anything other than an internal political act; neither were we provided with persuasive evidence that the PA planned the uprising.

Accordingly, we have no basis on which to conclude that there was a deliberate plan by the PA to initiate a campaign of violence at the first opportunity; or to conclude that there was a deliberate plan by the Government of Israel to respond with lethal force.

However, there is also no evidence on which to conclude that the PA made a consistent effort to contain the demonstrations and control the violence once it began; or that the Government of Israel made a consistent effort to use non-lethal means to control demonstrations of unarmed Palestinians. Amid rising anger, fear, and mistrust, each side assumed the worst about the other and acted accordingly.

The Sharon visit did not cause the 'Al-Aqsa Intifada'. But it was poorly timed and the provocative effect should have been foreseen; indeed it was foreseen by those who urged that the visit be prohibited. More significant were the events that followed: the decision of the Israeli police on September 29 to use lethal means against the Palestinian demonstrators; and the subsequent failure, as noted above, of either party to exercise restraint.

WHY DID IT HAPPEN?

The roots of the current violence extend much deeper than an inconclusive summit conference. Both sides have made clear a profound disillusionment with the behavior of the other in failing to meet the expectations arising from the peace process launched in Madrid in 1991 and then in Oslo in 1993. Each side has accused the other of violating undertakings and undermining the spirit of their commitment to resolving their political differences peacefully.

Divergent Expectations

We are struck by the divergent expectations expressed by the parties relating to the implementation of the Oslo process. Results achieved from this process were unthinkable less than 10 years ago. During the latest round of negotiations, the parties were closer to a permanent settlement than ever before.

None the less, Palestinians and Israelis alike told us that the promise on which the Oslo process is based—that tackling the hard 'permanent status' issues be deferred to the end of the process—has gradually come under serious pressure. The step-by-step process agreed to by the parties was based on the assumption that each step in the negotiating process would lead to enhanced trust and confidence. To achieve this, each party would have to implement agreed-upon commitments and abstain from actions that would be seen by the other as attempts to abuse the process in order to predetermine the shape of the final outcome. If this requirement is not met, the Oslo road map cannot successfully lead to its agreed destination. Today, each side blames the other for having ignored this fundamental aspect, resulting in a crisis in confidence. This problem became even more pressing with the opening of permanent status talks.

The Government of Israel has placed primacy on moving toward a Permanent Status Agreement in a non-violent atmosphere, consistent with commitments contained in the agreements between the parties. 'Even if slower than was initially envisaged, there has, since the start of the peace process in Madrid in 1991, been steady progress towards the goal of a Permanent Status Agreement without the resort to violence on a scale that has characterized recent weeks'. The 'goal' is the Permanent Status Agreement, the terms of which must be negotiated by the parties.

The PLO view is that delays in the process have been the result of an Israeli attempt to prolong and solidify the occupation. Palestinians 'believed that the Oslo process would yield an end to Israeli occupation in five years', the time frame for the transitional period specified in the Declaration of Principles. Instead there have been, in the PLO's view, repeated Israeli delays culminating in the Camp David summit, where, 'Israel proposed to annex about 11.2% of the West Bank (excluding Jerusalem)...' and offered unacceptable proposals concerning Jerusalem, security and refugees. 'In sum, Israel's proposals at Camp David provided for Israel's annexation of the best Palestinian lands, the perpetuation of Israeli control over East Jerusalem, a continued Israeli military presence on Palestinian territory, Israeli control over Palestinian natural resources, airspace and borders, and the return of fewer than 1% of refugees to their homes.'

Both sides see the lack of full compliance with agreements reached since the opening of the peace process as evidence of a lack of good faith. This conclusion led to an erosion of trust even before the permanent status negotiations began.

Divergent Perspectives

During the last seven months, these views have hardened into divergent realities. Each side views the other as having acted in bad faith; as having turned the optimism of Oslo into the suffering and grief of victims and their loved ones. In their statements and actions, each side demonstrates a perspective that fails to recognize any truth in the perspective of the other.

The Palestinian Perspective

For the Palestinian side, 'Madrid' and 'Oslo' heralded the prospect of a State, and guaranteed an end to the occupation and a resolution of outstanding matters within an agreed time frame. Palestinians are genuinely angry at the continued growth of settlements and at their daily experiences of humiliation and disruption as a result of Israel's presence in the Palestinian territories. Palestinians see settlers and settlements in their midst not only as violating the spirit of the Oslo process, but also as an application of force in the form of Israel's overwhelming military superiority, which sustains and protects the settlements.

The Interim Agreement provides that 'the two parties view the West Bank and Gaza as a single territorial unit, the integrity and status of which will be preserved during the interim period'. Coupled with this, the Interim Agreement's prohibition on taking steps which may prejudice permanent status negotiations denies Israel the right to continue its illegal expansionist settlement policy. In addition to the Interim Agreement, customary international law, including the Fourth Geneva Convention, prohibits Israel (as an occupying power) from establishing settlements in occupied territory pending an end to the conflict.

The PLO alleges that Israeli political leaders 'have made no secret of the fact that the Israeli interpretation of Oslo was designed to segregate the Palestinians in non-contiguous enclaves, surrounded by Israeli military-controlled borders, with settlements and settlement roads violating the territories' integrity'. According to the PLO, 'In the seven years since the [Declaration of Principles], the settler population in the West Bank, excluding East Jerusalem and the Gaza Strip, has doubled to 200,000, and the settler population in East Jerusalem has risen to 170,000. Israel has constructed approximately 30 new settlements, and expanded a number of existing ones to house these new settlers.'

The PLO also claims that the Government of Israel has failed to comply with other commitments such as the further withdrawal from the West Bank and the release of Palestinian prisoners. In addition, Palestinians expressed frustration with the impasse over refugees and the deteriorating economic circumstances in the West Bank and Gaza Strip.

The Israeli Perspective

From the Government of Israel perspective, the expansion of settlement activity and the taking of measures to facilitate the convenience and safety of settlers do not prejudice the outcome of permanent status negotiations.

Israel understands that the Palestinian side objects to the settlements in the West Bank and Gaza Strip. Without prejudice to the formal status of the settlements, Israel accepts that the settlements are an outstanding issue on which there will have to be agreement as part of any permanent status resolution between the sides. This point was acknowledged and agreed upon in the Declaration of Principles of 13 September 1993 as well as other agreements between the two sides. There has in fact been a good deal of discussion on the question of settlements between the two sides in the various negotiations toward a permanent status agreement.

Indeed, Israelis point out that at the Camp David summit and during subsequent talks the Government of Israel offered to make significant concessions with respect to settlements in the context of an overall agreement.

Security, however, is the key Government of Israel concern. The Government of Israel maintains that the PLO has breached its solemn commitments by continuing the use of violence in the pursuit of political objectives. 'Israel's principal concern in the peace process has been security. This issue is of overriding importance... [S]ecurity is not something on which Israel will bargain or compromise. The failure of the Palestinian side to comply with both the letter and spirit of the security provisions in the various agreements has long been a source of disturbance in Israel.'

According to the Government of Israel, the Palestinian failure takes several forms: institutionalized anti-Israel, anti-Jewish incitement; the release from detention of terrorists; the failure to control illegal weapons; and the actual conduct of violent operations, ranging from the insertion of riflemen into demonstrations to terrorist attacks on Israeli civilians. The Government of Israel maintains that the PLO has explicitly violated its renunciation of terrorism and other acts of violence, thereby significantly eroding trust between the parties. The Government of Israel perceives 'a thread, implied but nonetheless clear, that runs throughout the Palestinian submissions. It is that Palestinian violence against Israel and Israelis is somehow explicable, understandable, legitimate'.

END THE VIOLENCE

For Israelis and Palestinians alike the experience of the past several months has been intensely *personal*. Through relationships of kinship, friendship, religion, community and profession, virtually everyone in both societies has a link to someone who has been killed or seriously injured in the recent violence. We were touched by their stories. During our last visit to the region, we met with the families of Palestinian and Israeli victims. These individual accounts of grief were heartrending and indescribably sad. Israeli and Palestinian families used virtually the same words to describe their grief.

When the widow of a murdered Israeli physician—a man of peace whose practice included the treatment of Arab patients—tells us that it seems that Palestinians are interested in killing Jews for the sake of killing Jews, Palestinians should take notice. When the parents of a Palestinian child killed while in his bed by an errant .50 calibre bullet draw similar conclusions about the respect accorded by Israelis to Palestinian lives, Israelis need to listen. When we see the shattered bodies of children we know it is time for adults to stop the violence.

With widespread violence, both sides have resorted to portrayals of the other in hostile stereotypes. This cycle cannot be easily broken. Without considerable determination and readiness to compromise, the rebuilding of trust will be impossible.

Cessation of Violence

Since 1991, the parties have consistently committed themselves, in all their agreements, to the path of non-violence. They did so most recently in the two Sharm el-Sheikh summits of September 1999 and October 2000. To stop the violence now, the PA and Government of Israel need not 'reinvent the wheel'. Rather, they should take immediate steps to end the violence, reaffirm their mutual commitments, and resume negotiations.

Resumption of Security Co-operation

Palestinian security officials told us that it would take some time—perhaps several weeks—for the PA to reassert full control over armed elements nominally under its command and to exert decisive influence over other armed elements operating in Palestinian areas. Israeli security officials have not disputed these assertions. What is important is that the PA make an allout effort to enforce a complete cessation of violence and that it be clearly seen by the Government of Israel as doing so. The Government of Israel must likewise exercise a 100 percent effort to ensure that potential friction points, where Palestinians come into contact with armed Israelis, do not become stages for renewed hostilities.

The collapse of security co-operation in early October reflected the belief by each party that the other had committed itself to a violent course of action. If the parties wish to attain the standard of 100 percent effort to prevent violence, the immediate resumption of security co-operation is mandatory.

We acknowledge the reluctance of the PA to be seen as facilitating the work of Israeli security services absent an explicit political context (i.e. meaningful negotiations) and under the threat of Israeli settlement expansion. Indeed, security co-operation cannot be sustained without such negotiations and with ongoing actions seen as prejudicing the outcome of negotiations. However, violence is much more likely to continue without security co-operation. Moreover, without effective security co-operation, the parties will continue to regard all acts of violence as officially sanctioned.

In order to overcome the current deadlock, the parties should consider how best to revitalize security co-operation. We commend current efforts to that end. Effective co-operation depends on recreating and sustaining an atmosphere of confidence and good personal relations.

It is for the parties themselves to undertake the main burden of day-to-day co-operation, but they should remain open to engaging the assistance of others in facilitating that work. Such outside assistance should be by mutual consent, should not threaten good bilateral working arrangements, and should not act as a tribunal or interpose between the parties. There was good security co-operation until last year that benefited from the good offices of the US (acknowledged by both sides as useful), and was also supported indirectly by security projects and assistance from the European Union. The role of outside assistance should be that of creating the appropriate framework, sustaining goodwill on both sides, and removing friction where possible. That framework must be seen to be contributing to the safety and welfare of both communities if there is to be acceptance by those communities of these efforts.

REBUILD CONFIDENCE

The historic handshake between Chairman Arafat and the late Prime Minister Rabin at the White House in September 1993 symbolized the expectation of both parties that the door to the peaceful resolution of differences had been opened. Despite the current violence and mutual loss of trust, both communities have repeatedly expressed a desire for peace. Channelling this desire into substantive progress has proved difficult. The restoration of trust is essential, and the parties should take affirmative steps to this end. Given the high level of hostility and mistrust, the timing and sequence of these steps are obviously crucial. This can be decided only by the parties. We urge them to begin the process of decision immediately.

Terrorism

In the September 1999 Sharm el-Sheikh Memorandum, the parties pledged to take action against 'any threat or act of terrorism, violence or incitement'. Although all three categories of hostilities are reprehensible, it was no accident that 'terrorism' was placed at the top of the list.

Terrorism involves the deliberate killing and injuring of randomly selected non-combatants for political ends. It seeks to promote a political outcome by spreading terror and demoralization throughout a population. It is immoral and ultimately self defeating. We condemn it and we urge that the parties coordinate their security efforts to eliminate it.

In its official submissions and briefings, the Government of Israel has accused the PA of supporting terrorism by releasing incarcerated terrorists, by allowing PA security personnel to abet, and in some cases to conduct, terrorist operations, and by terminating security co-operation with the Government of Israel. The PA vigorously denies the accusations. But Israelis hold the view that the PA's leadership has made no real effort over the past seven months to prevent anti-Israeli terrorism. The belief is, in and of itself, a major obstacle to the rebuilding of confidence.

We believe that the PA has a responsibility to help rebuild confidence by making clear to both communities that terrorism is reprehensible and unacceptable, and by taking all measures to prevent terrorist operations and to punish perpetrators. This effort should include immediate steps to apprehend and incarcerate terrorists operating within the PA's jurisdiction.

Settlements

The Government of Israel also has a responsibility to help rebuild confidence. A cessation of Palestinian–Israeli violence will be particularly hard to sustain unless the Government of Israel freezes all settlement construction activity. The Government of Israel should also give careful consideration to whether settlements that are focal points for substantial friction are valuable bargaining chips for future negotiations or provocations likely to preclude the onset of productive talks.

The issue is, of course, controversial. Many Israelis will regard our recommendation as a statement of the obvious, and will support it. Many will oppose it. But settlement activities must not be allowed to undermine the restoration of calm and the resumption of negotiations.

During the half-century of its existence, Israel has had the strong support of the United States. In international forums, the US has at times cast the only vote on Israel's behalf. Yet, even in such a close relationship there are some differences. Prominent among those differences is the US Government's long-standing opposition to the Government of Israel's policies and practices regarding settlements. As the then Secretary of State, James A. Baker, III, commented on May 22, 1991:

Every time I have gone to Israel in connection with the peace process, on each of my four trips, I have been met with the announcement of new settlement activity. This does violate United States policy. It's the first thing that Arabs—Arab Governments, the first thing that the Palestinians in the territories—whose situation is really quite desperate—the first thing they raise when we talk to them. I don't think there is any bigger obstacle to peace than the settlement activity that continues not only unabated but at an enhanced pace.

The policy described by Secretary Baker, on behalf of the Administration of President George H.W. Bush, has been, in essence, the policy of every American administration over the past quarter century.

Most other countries, including Turkey, Norway, and those of the European Union, have also been critical of Israeli settlement activity, in accordance with their views that such settlements are illegal under international law and not in compliance with previous agreements.

On each of our two visits to the region there were Israeli announcements regarding expansion of settlements, and it was almost always the first issue raised by Palestinians with whom we met. During our last visit, we observed the impact of 6,400 settlers on 140,000 Palestinians in Hebron and 6,500 settlers on over 1,100,000 Palestinians in the Gaza Strip. The Government of Israel describes its policy as prohibiting new settlements but permitting expansion of existing settlements to accommodate 'natural growth'. Palestinians contend that there is no distinction between 'new' and 'expanded' settlements; and that, except for a brief freeze during the tenure of Prime Minister Itzhak Rabin, there has been a continuing, aggressive effort by Israel to increase the number and size of settlements.

The subject has been widely discussed within Israel. The *Ha'aretz* English Language Edition editorial of April 10, 2001 stated:

A government which seeks to argue that its goal is to reach a solution to the conflict with the Palestinians through peaceful means, and is trying at this stage to bring an end to the violence and terrorism, must announce an end to construction in the settlements.

The circumstances in the region are much changed from those which existed nearly 20 years ago. Yet, President Reagan's words remain relevant: 'The immediate adoption of a settlement freeze by Israel, more than any other action, could create the confidence needed [...]'

Beyond the obvious confidence-building qualities of a settlement freeze, we note that many of the confrontations during this conflict have occurred at points where Palestinians, settlers, and security forces protecting the settlers, meet. Keeping both the peace and these friction points will be very difficult.

Reducing Tension

We were told by both Palestinians and Israelis that emotions generated by the many recent deaths and funerals have fuelled additional confrontations, and, in effect, maintained the cycle of violence. We cannot urge one side or the other to refrain from demonstrations. But both sides must make clear that violent demonstrations will not be tolerated. We can and do urge that both sides exhibit a greater respect for human life when demonstrators confront security personnel. In addition, a renewed effort to stop the violence might feature, for a limited time, a 'cooling off' period during which public demonstrations at or near friction points will be discouraged in order to break the cycle of violence. To the extent that demonstrations continue, we urge that demonstrators and security personnel keep their distance from one another to reduce the potential for lethal confrontation.

Actions and Responses

Members of the Committee staff witnessed an incident involving stone throwing in Ramallah from the perspectives, on the ground, of both sides. The people confronting one another were mostly young men. The absence of senior leadership on the IDF side was striking. Likewise, the absence of responsible security and other officials counselling restraint on the Palestinian side was obvious.

Concerning such confrontations, the Government of Israel takes the position that 'Israel is engaged in an armed conflict short of war. This is not a civilian disturbance or a demonstration or a riot. It is characterized by live-fire attacks on a *significant scale* [emphasis added]...[T]he attacks are carried out by a well-armed and organized militia...' Yet, the Government of Israel acknowledges that of some 9,000 'attacks' by Palestinians against Israelis, 'some 2,700 [about 30 percent] involved the use of automatic weapons, rifles, hand guns, grenades, [and] explosives of other kinds'.

Thus, for the first three months of the current uprising, most incidents *did not* involve Palestinian use of firearms and explosives. B'Tselem *[the Israeli Information Centre for Human Rights in the Occupied Territories]* reported that, 'according to IDF figures, 73 percent of the incidents [from September 29 to December 2, 2000] did not include Palestinian gunfire. Despite this, it was in these incidents that most of the Palestinians [were] killed and wounded...' Altogether, nearly 500 people were killed and over 10,000 injured over the past seven months; the overwhelming majority in both categories were Palestinian. Many of these deaths were avoidable, as were many Israeli deaths.

Israel's characterization of the conflict, as noted above, is overly broad, for it does not adequately describe the variety of incidents reported since late September 2000. Moreover, by thus defining the conflict, the IDF has suspended its policy of mandating investigations by the Department of Military Police Investigations whenever a Palestinian in the territories dies at the hands of an IDF soldier in an incident not involving terrorism. In the words of the Government of Israel, 'Where Israel considers that there is reason to investigate particular incidents, it does so, although, given the circumstances of armed conflict, it does not do so routinely'. We believe, however, that by abandoning the blanket 'armed conflict short of war' characterization and by re-instituting mandatory military police investigations, the Government of Israel could help mitigate deadly violence and help rebuild mutual confidence. Notwithstanding the danger posed by stone-throwers, an effort should be made to differentiate between terrorism and protests.

Controversy has arisen between the parties over what Israel calls the 'targeting of individual enemy combatants'. The PLO describes these actions as 'extra-judicial executions', and claims that Israel has engaged in an 'assassination policy' that is 'in clear violation of Article 32 of the Fourth Geneva Convention...' The Government of Israel states that, 'whatever action Israel has taken has been taken firmly within the bounds of the relevant and accepted principles relating to the conduct of hostilities'.

With respect to demonstrations, the Government of Israel has acknowledged 'that individual instances of excessive response may have occurred. To a soldier or a unit coming under Palestinian attack, the equation is not that of the Israeli army versus some stone throwing Palestinian protesters. It is a personal equation'.

We understand this concern, particularly since rocks can maim or even kill. It is no easy matter for a few young soldiers, confronted by large numbers of hostile demonstrators, to make fine legal distinctions on the spot. Still, this 'personal equation' must fit within an organizational ethic; in this case, *The Ethical Code of the Israel Defence Forces*, which states, in part:

The sanctity of human life in the eyes of the IDF servicemen will find expression in all of their actions, in deliberate and meticulous planning, in safe and intelligent training and in proper execution of their mission. In evaluating the risk to self and others, they will use the appropriate standards and will exercise constant care to limit injury to life to the extent required to accomplish the mission.

Those required to respect the IDF ethical code are largely draftees, as the IDF is a conscript force. Active duty enlisted personnel, non-commissioned officers and junior officers—the categories most likely to be present at friction points—are young, often teenagers. Unless more senior career personnel or reservists are stationed at friction points, no IDF personnel present in these sensitive areas have experience to draw upon from previous violent Israeli–Palestinian confrontations. We think it is essential, especially in the context of restoring confidence by minimizing deadly confrontations, that the IDF deploy more senior, experienced soldiers to these sensitive points.

There were incidents where IDF soldiers have used lethal force, including live ammunition and modified metal-cored rubber rounds, against unarmed demonstrators throwing stones. The IDF should adopt crowd-control tactics that minimize the potential for deaths and casualties, withdrawing metal-cored rubber rounds from general use and using instead rubber baton rounds without metal cores.

We are deeply concerned about the public safety implications of exchanges of fire between populated areas, in particular between Israeli settlements and neighbouring Palestinian villages. Palestinian gunmen have directed small arms fire at Israeli settlements and at nearby IDF positions from within or adjacent to civilian dwellings in Palestinian areas, thus endangering innocent Israeli and Palestinian civilians alike. We condemn the positioning of gunmen within or near civilian dwellings. The IDF often responds to such gunfire with heavy calibre weapons, sometimes resulting in deaths and injuries to innocent Palestinians. An IDF officer told us at the Ministry of Defence on March 23, 2001 that, 'When shooting comes from a building we respond, and sometimes there are innocent people in the building'. Obviously, innocent people are injured and killed during exchanges of this nature. We urge that such provocations cease and that the IDF exercise maximum restraint in its responses if they do occur. Inappropriate or excessive uses of force often lead to escalation.

We are aware of IDF sensitivities about these subjects. More than once we were asked: 'What about Palestinian rules of engagement? What about a Palestinian code of ethics for their military personnel?' These are valid questions.

On the Palestinian side there are disturbing ambiguities in the basic areas of responsibility and accountability. The lack of control exercised by the PA over its own security personnel and armed elements affiliated with the PA leadership is very troubling. We urge the PA to take all necessary steps to establish a clear and unchallenged chain of command for armed personnel operating under its authority. We recommend that the PA institute and enforce effective standards of conduct and accountability, both within the uniformed ranks and between the police and the civilian political leadership to which it reports.

Incitement

In their submissions and briefings to the Committee, both sides expressed concerns about hateful language and images emanating from the other, citing numerous examples of hostile sectarian and ethnic rhetoric in the Palestinian and Israeli media, in school curricula and in statements by religious leaders, politicians and others.

We call on the parties to renew their formal commitments to foster mutual understanding and tolerance and to abstain from incitement and hostile propaganda. We condemn hate language and incitement in all its forms. We suggest that the parties be particularly cautious about using words in a manner that suggests collective responsibility.

Economic and Social Impact of Violence

Further restrictions on the movement of people and goods have been imposed by Israel on the West Bank and the Gaza Strip. These closures take three forms: those which restrict movement between the Palestinian areas and Israel; those (including curfews) which restrict movement within the Palestinian areas; and those which restrict movement from the Palestinian areas to foreign countries. These measures have disrupted the lives of hundreds of thousands of Palestinians; they have increased Palestinian unemployment to an estimated 40 percent, in part by preventing some 140,000 Palestinians from working in Israel; and have stripped away about one-third of the Palestinian gross domestic product. Moreover, the transfer of tax and customs duty revenues owed to the PA by Israel has been suspended, leading to a serious fiscal crisis in the PA.

Of particular concern to the PA has been the destruction by Israeli security forces and settlers of tens of thousands of olive and fruit trees and other agricultural property. The closures have had other adverse effects, such as preventing civilians from access to urgent medical treatment and preventing students from attending school.

The Government of Israel maintains that these measures were taken in order to protect Israeli citizens from terrorism. Palestinians characterize these measures as 'collective punishment'. The Government of Israel denies the allegations:

Israel has not taken measures that have had an economic impact simply for the sake of taking such measures or for reasons of harming the Palestinian economy. The measures have been taken for reasons of security. Thus, for example, the closure of the Palestinian territories was taken in order to prevent, or at least minimize the risks of, terrorist attacks...The Palestinian leadership has made no attempt to control this activity and bring it to an end.

Moreover, the Government of Israel points out that violence in the last quarter of 2000 cost the Israeli economy $1.2 billion [US $1,200m.], and that the loss continues at a rate of approximately $150 million per month.

We acknowledge Israel's security concerns. We believe, however, that the Government of Israel should lift closures, transfer to the PA all revenues owed, and permit Palestinians who have been employed in Israel to return to their jobs. Closure policies play into the hands of extremists seeking to expand their constituencies and thereby contribute to escalation. The PA should resume co-operation with Israeli security agencies to ensure that Palestinian workers employed within Israel are fully vetted and free of connections to terrorists and terrorist organizations.

International development assistance has from the start been an integral part of the peace process, with an aim to strengthen the socio-economic foundations for peace. This assistance today is more important than ever. We urge the international community to sustain the development agenda of the peace process.

Holy Places

It is particularly regrettable that places such as the Temple Mount/Haram al-Sharif in Jerusalem, Joseph's Tomb in Nablus, and Rachel's Tomb in Bethlehem have been the scenes of violence, death and injury. These are places of peace, prayer and reflection which must be accessible to all believers.

Places deemed holy by Muslims, Jews, and Christians merit respect, protection and preservation. Agreements previously reached by the parties regarding holy places must be upheld. The Government of Israel and the PA should create a joint initiative to defuse the sectarian aspect of their political dispute by preserving and protecting such places. Efforts to develop inter-faith dialogue should be encouraged.

International Force

One of the most controversial subjects raised during our inquiry was the issue of deploying an international force to the Palestinian areas. The PA is strongly in favour of having such a force to protect Palestinian civilians and their property from the IDF and from settlers. The Government of Israel is just as adamantly opposed to an 'international protection force', believing that it would prove unresponsive to Israeli security concerns and interfere with bilateral negotiations to settle the conflict.

We believe that to be effective such a force would need the support of both parties. We note that international forces deployed in this region have been or are in a position to fulfil their mandates and make a positive contribution only when they were deployed with the consent of all of the parties involved.

During our visit to Hebron we were briefed by personnel of the Temporary International Presence in Hebron (TIPH), a presence to which both parties have agreed. The TIPH is charged with observing an explosive situation and writing reports on their observations. If the parties agree, as a confidence-building measure, to draw upon TIPH personnel to help them manage other friction points, we hope that TIPH contributors could accommodate such a request.

Cross-Community Initiatives

Many described to us the near absolute loss of trust. It was all the more inspiring, therefore, to find groups (such as the Parent's Circle and the Economic Co-operation Foundation) dedicated to cross-community understanding in spite of all that has happened. We commend them and their important work.

Regrettably, most of the work of this nature has stopped during the current conflict. To help rebuild confidence, the Government of Israel and PA should jointly endorse and support the work of Israeli and Palestinian non-governmental organizations (NGOs) already involved in confidence-building through initiatives linking both sides. It is important that the PA and Government of Israel support cross-community organizations and initiatives, including the provision of humanitarian assistance to Palestinian villages by Israeli NGOs. Providing travel permits for participants is essential. Co-operation between the humanitarian organizations and the military/security services of the parties should be encouraged and institutionalized.

Such programmes can help build, albeit slowly, constituencies for peace among Palestinians and Israelis and can provide safety nets during times of turbulence. Organizations involved in this work are vital for translating good intentions into positive actions.

RESUME NEGOTIATIONS

Israeli leaders do not wish to be perceived as 'rewarding violence'. Palestinian leaders do not wish to be perceived as 'rewarding occupation'. We appreciate the political constraints on leaders of both sides. Nevertheless, if the cycle of violence is to be broken and the search for peace resumed, there needs to be a new bilateral relationship incorporating both security co-operation and negotiations.

We cannot prescribe to the parties how best to pursue their political objectives. Yet the construction of a new bilateral relationship solidifying and transcending an agreed cessation of violence requires intelligent risk-taking. It requires, in the first instance, that each party again be willing to regard the other as a *partner*. Partnership, in turn, requires at this juncture something more than was agreed in the Declaration of Principles and in subsequent agreements. Instead of declaring the peace process to be 'dead', the parties should determine how they will conclude their common journey along their agreed 'road map', a journey which began in Madrid and continued—in spite of problems—until very recently.

To define a starting point is for the parties to decide. Both parties have stated that they remain committed to their mutual agreements and undertakings. It is time to explore further implementation. The parties should declare their intention to meet on this basis, in order to resume full and meaningful negotiations, in the spirit of their undertakings at Sharm el-Sheikh in 1999 and 2000.

Neither side will be able to achieve its principal objectives unilaterally or without political risk. We know how hard it is for leaders to act—especially if the action can be characterized by political opponents as a concession—without getting something in return. The PA must—as it has at previous critical junctures—take steps to reassure Israel on security matters. The Government of Israel must—as it has in the past—take steps to reassure the PA on political matters. Israelis and Palestinians should avoid, in their own actions and attitudes, giving extremists, common criminals and revenge seekers the final say in defining their joint future. This will not be easy if deadly incidents occur in spite of effective co-operation. Notwithstanding the daunting difficulties, the very foundation of the trust required to re-establish a functioning partnership consists of each side making such strategic reassurances to the other.

RECOMMENDATIONS

The Government of Israel and the PA must act swiftly and decisively to halt the violence. Their immediate objectives then should be to rebuild confidence and resume negotiations. What we are asking is not easy. Palestinians and Israelis—not just their leaders, but two publics at large—have lost confidence in one another. We are asking political leaders to do, for the sake of their people, the politically difficult: to lead without knowing how many will follow.

During this mission our aim has been to fulfil the mandate agreed at Sharm el-Sheikh. We value the support given our work by the participants at the summit, and we commend the parties for their co-operation. Our principal recommendation is that they recommit themselves to the Sharm el-Sheikh spirit, and that they implement the decisions made there in 1999 and 2000. We believe that the summit participants will support bold action by the parties to achieve these objectives.

End the Violence

The Government of Israel and the PA should reaffirm their commitment to existing agreements and undertakings and should immediately implement an unconditional cessation of violence.

Anything less than a complete effort by both parties to end the violence will render the effort itself ineffective, and will likely be interpreted by the other side as evidence of hostile intent.

The Government of Israel and PA should immediately resume security co-operation.

Effective bilateral co-operation aimed at preventing violence will encourage the resumption of negotiations. We are particularly concerned that, absent effective, transparent security co-operation, terrorism and other acts of violence will continue and may be seen as officially sanctioned whether they are or not. The parties should consider widening the scope of security co-operation to reflect the priorities of both communities and to seek acceptance for these efforts from those communities.

We acknowledge the PA's position that security co-operation presents a political difficulty absent a suitable political context, i.e., the relaxation of stringent Israeli security measures combined with ongoing, fruitful negotiations. We also acknowledge the PA's fear that, with security co-operation in hand, the Government of Israel may not be disposed to deal forthrightly with Palestinian political concerns. We believe that security co-operation cannot long be sustained if meaningful negotiations are unreasonably deferred, if security measures 'on the ground' are seen as hostile, or if steps are taken that are perceived as provocative or as prejudicing the outcome of negotiations.

Rebuild Confidence

The PA and Government of Israel should work together to establish a meaningful 'cooling-off period' and implement additional confidence-building measures, some of which were proposed in the October 2000 Sharm el-Sheikh Statement and some of which were offered by the US on January 7, 2001 in Cairo.

The PA and Government of Israel should resume their efforts to identify, condemn and discourage incitement in all its forms.

The PA should make clear through concrete action to Palestinians and Israelis alike that terrorism is reprehensible and unacceptable, and that the PA will make a 100 percent effort to prevent terrorist operations and to punish perpetrators. This effort should include immediate steps to apprehend and incarcerate terrorists operating within the PA's jurisdiction.

The Government of Israel should freeze all settlement activity, including the 'natural growth' of existing settlements.

The kind of security co-operation desired by the Government of Israel cannot for long co-exist with settlement activity described very recently by the European Union as causing 'great concern' and by the US as 'provocative'.

The Government of Israel should give careful consideration to whether settlements which are focal points for substantial friction are valuable bargaining chips for future negotiations, or provocations likely to preclude the onset of productive talks.

The Government of Israel may wish to make it clear to the PA that a future peace would pose no threat to the territorial contiguity of a Palestinian State to be established in the West Bank and the Gaza Strip.

The IDF should consider withdrawing to positions held before September 28, 2000 which will reduce the number of friction points and the potential for violent confrontations.

The Government of Israel should ensure that the IDF adopt and enforce policies and procedures encouraging non-lethal responses to unarmed demonstrators, with a view to minimizing casualties and friction between the two communities. The IDF should:

Re-institute, as a matter of course, military police investigations into Palestinian deaths resulting from IDF actions in the Palestinian territories in incidents not involving terrorism. The IDF should abandon the blanket characterization of the current uprising as 'an armed conflict short of war', which fails to discriminate between terrorism and protest.

Adopt tactics of crowd-control that minimize the potential for deaths and casualties, including the withdrawal of metal-cored rubber rounds from general use.

Ensure that experienced, seasoned personnel are present for duty at all times at known friction points.

Ensure that the stated values and standard operating procedures of the IDF effectively instil the duty of caring for Palestinians in the West Bank and Gaza Strip as well as Israelis living there, consistent with The Ethical Code of the IDF.

The Government of Israel should lift closures, transfer to the PA all tax revenues owed, and permit Palestinians who had been employed in Israel to return to their jobs; and should ensure that security forces and settlers refrain from the destruction of homes and roads, as well as trees and other agricultural property in Palestinian areas. We acknowledge the Government of Israel's position that actions of this nature have been taken for security reasons. Nevertheless, their economic effects will persist for years.

The PA should renew co-operation with Israeli security agencies to ensure, to the maximum extent possible, that Palestinian workers employed within Israel are fully vetted and free of connections to organizations and individuals engaged in terrorism.

The PA should prevent gunmen from using Palestinian populated areas to fire upon Israeli populated areas and IDF positions. This tactic places civilians on both sides at unnecessary risk.

The Government of Israel and IDF should adopt and enforce policies and procedures designed to ensure that the response to any gunfire emanating from Palestinian populated areas minimizes the danger to the lives and property of Palestinian civilians, bearing in mind that it is probably the objective of gunmen to elicit an excessive IDF response.

The Government of Israel should take all necessary steps to prevent acts of violence by settlers.

The parties should abide by the provisions of the Wye River Agreement prohibiting illegal weapons.

The PA should take all necessary steps to establish a clear and unchallenged chain of command for armed personnel operating under its authority.

The PA should institute and enforce effective standards of conduct and accountability, both within the uniformed ranks and between the police and the civilian political leadership to which it reports.

The PA and Government of Israel should consider a joint undertaking to preserve and protect holy places sacred to the traditions of Muslims, Jews, and Christians. An initiative of this nature might help to reverse a disturbing trend: the increasing use of religious themes to encourage and justify violence.

The Government of Israel and PA should jointly endorse and support the work of Palestinian and Israeli non-governmental organizations (NGOs) involved in cross-community initiatives linking the two peoples. It is important that these activities, including the provision of humanitarian aid to Palestinian villages by Israeli NGOs, receive the full backing of both parties.

Resume Negotiations

We reiterate our belief that a 100 percent effort to stop the violence, an immediate resumption of security co-operation and an exchange of confidence-building measures are all important for the resumption of negotiations. Yet none of these steps will long be sustained absent a return to serious negotiations.

It is not within our mandate to prescribe the venue, the basis or the agenda of negotiations. However, in order to provide an effective political context for practical co-operation between the parties, negotiations must not be unreasonably deferred and they must, in our view, manifest a spirit of compromise, reconciliation and partnership, notwithstanding the events of the past seven months.

In the spirit of the Sharm el-Sheikh agreements and understandings of 1999 and 2000, we recommend that the parties meet to reaffirm their commitment to signed agreements and mutual understandings, and take corresponding action. This should be the basis for resuming full and meaningful negotiations.

The parties are at a crossroads. If they do not return to the negotiating table, they face the prospect of fighting it out for years on end, with many of their citizens leaving for distant shores to live their lives and raise their children. We pray they make the right choice. That means stopping the violence now. Israelis and Palestinians have to live, work, and prosper together. History and geography have destined them to be neighbours. That cannot be changed. Only when their actions are guided by this awareness will they be able to develop the vision and reality of peace and shared prosperity.

UN SECURITY COUNCIL RESOLUTION 1397

(12 March 2002)

Resolution 1397 affirmed for the first time the UN Security Council's 'vision' of both Israeli and Palestinian states. It was the first US-sponsored resolution on the Middle East for some 25 years, and was adopted by 14 votes to none; Syria abstained in the vote.

The Security Council,

Recalling all its previous relevant resolutions, in particular resolutions 242 (1967) and 338 (1973),

Affirming a vision of a region where two States, Israel and Palestine, live side by side within secure and recognized borders,

Expressing its grave concern at the continuation of the tragic and violent events that have taken place since September 2000, especially the recent attacks and the increased number of casualties,

Stressing the need for all concerned to ensure the safety of civilians,

Stressing also the need to respect the universally accepted norms of international humanitarian law.

Welcoming and encouraging the diplomatic efforts of special envoys from the United States of America, the Russian Federation, the European Union and the United Nations Special Co-ordinator and others, to bring about a comprehensive, just and lasting peace in the Middle East,

Welcoming the contribution of Saudi Crown Prince Abdullah,

1. *Demands* immediate cessation of all acts of violence, including all acts of terror, provocation, incitement and destruction;

2. *Calls upon* the Israeli and Palestinian sides and their leaders to co-operate in the implementation of the Tenet work plan and Mitchell Report recommendations with the aim of resuming negotiations on a political settlement;

3. *Expresses* support for the efforts of the Secretary-General and others to assist the parties to halt the violence and to resume the peace process;

4. *Decides* to remain seized of the matter.

UN Document S/Res/1397 (2002).

A PERFORMANCE-BASED ROADMAP TO A PERMANENT TWO-STATE SOLUTION TO THE ISRAELI–PALESTINIAN CONFLICT

(30 April 2003)

The 'roadmap' was presented to both Israeli and Palestinian leaders on 30 April 2003, having been drafted in late 2002 by the Quartet group, comprising the UN, the USA, the EU and Russia. Publication of the roadmap, which was intended to lead to an immediate resumption of Israeli-Palestinian negotiations, followed the naming of a new Palestinian Cabinet by the recently appointed Palestinian Prime Minister, Mahmud Abbas.

The following is a performance-based and goal-driven roadmap, with clear phases, timelines, target dates, and benchmarks aiming at progress through reciprocal steps by the two parties in the political, security, economic, humanitarian, and institution-building fields, under the auspices of the Quartet [the United States, European Union, United Nations, and Russia]. The destination is a final and comprehensive settlement of the Israel–Palestinian conflict by 2005, as presented in President Bush's speech of 24 June, and welcomed by the EU, Russia and the UN in the 16 July and 17 September Quartet Ministerial statements.

A two-state solution to the Israeli–Palestinian conflict will only be achieved through an end to violence and terrorism, when the Palestinian people have a leadership acting decisively against terror and willing and able to build a practising democracy based on tolerance and liberty, and through Israel's readiness to do what is necessary for a democratic Palestinian state to be established, and a clear, unambiguous acceptance by both parties of the goal of a negotiated settlement as described below. The Quartet will assist and facilitate implementation of the plan, starting in Phase I, including direct discussions between the parties as required. The plan establishes a realistic timeline for implementation. However, as a performance-based plan, progress will require and depend upon the good faith efforts of the parties, and their compliance with each of the obligations outlined below. Should the parties perform their obligations rapidly, progress within and through the phases may come sooner than indicated in the plan. Non-compliance with obligations will impede progress.

A settlement, negotiated between the parties, will result in the emergence of an independent, democratic, and viable Palestinian state living side by side in peace and security with Israel and its other neighbors. The settlement will resolve the Israeli–Palestinian conflict, and end the occupation that began in 1967, based on the foundations of the Madrid Conference, the principle of land for peace, UNSCRs 242, 338 and 1397, agreements previously reached by the parties, and the initiative of Saudi Crown Prince Abdullah—endorsed by the Beirut Arab League Summit—calling for acceptance of Israel as a neighbor living in peace and security, in the context of a comprehensive settlement. This initiative is a vital element of international efforts to promote a comprehensive peace on all tracks, including the Syrian-Israeli and Lebanese-Israeli tracks.

The Quartet will meet regularly at senior levels to evaluate the parties' performance on implementation of the plan. In each phase, the parties are expected to perform their obligations in parallel, unless otherwise indicated.

PHASE I: ENDING TERROR AND VIOLENCE, NORMALIZING PALESTINIAN LIFE, AND BUILDING PALESTINIAN INSTITUTIONS—PRESENT TO MAY 2003

In Phase I, the Palestinians immediately undertake an unconditional cessation of violence according to the steps outlined below; such action should be accompanied by supportive measures undertaken by Israel. Palestinians and Israelis resume security co-operation based on the Tenet work plan to end violence, terrorism, and incitement through restructured and effective Palestinian security services. Palestinians undertake comprehensive political reform in preparation for statehood, including drafting a Palestinian constitution, and free, fair and open elections upon the basis of those measures. Israel takes all necessary steps to help normalize Palestinian life. Israel withdraws from Palestinian areas occupied from September 28, 2000 and the two sides restore the status quo that existed at that time, as security performance and co-operation progress. Israel also freezes all settlement activity, consistent with the Mitchell report.

At the outset of Phase I:

Palestinian leadership issues unequivocal statement reiterating Israel's right to exist in peace and security and calling for an immediate and unconditional ceasefire to end armed activity and all acts of violence against Israelis anywhere. All official Palestinian institutions end incitement against Israel.

Israeli leadership issues unequivocal statement affirming its commitment to the two-state vision of an independent, viable, sovereign Palestinian state living in peace and security alongside Israel, as expressed by President Bush, and calling for an immediate end to violence against Palestinians everywhere. All official Israeli institutions end incitement against Palestinians.

SECURITY

Palestinians declare an unequivocal end to violence and terrorism and undertake visible efforts on the ground to arrest, disrupt, and restrain individuals and groups conducting and planning violent attacks on Israelis anywhere.

Rebuilt and refocused Palestinian Authority security apparatus begins sustained, targeted, and effective operations aimed at confronting all those engaged in terror and dismantlement of terrorist capabilities and infrastructure. This includes commencing confiscation of illegal weapons and consolidation of security authority, free of association with terror and corruption.

GOI [*Government of Israel*] takes no actions undermining trust, including deportations, attacks on civilians; confiscation and/or demolition of Palestinian homes and property, as a punitive measure or to facilitate Israeli construction; destruction of Palestinian institutions and infrastructure; and other measures specified in the Tenet work plan.

Relying on existing mechanisms and on-the-ground resources, Quartet representatives begin informal monitoring and consult with the parties on establishment of a formal monitoring mechanism and its implementation.

Implementation, as previously agreed, of US rebuilding, training and resumed security co-operation plan in collaboration with outside oversight board (US–Egypt–Jordan). Quartet support for efforts to achieve a lasting, comprehensive cease-fire.

All Palestinian security organizations are consolidated into three services reporting to an empowered Interior Minister.

Restructured/retrained Palestinian security forces and IDF counterparts progressively resume security co-operation and other undertakings in implementation of the Tenet work plan, including regular senior-level meetings, with the participation of US security officials.

Arab states cut off public and private funding and all other forms of support for groups supporting and engaging in violence and terror.

All donors providing budgetary support for the Palestinians channel these funds through the Palestinian Ministry of Finance's Single Treasury Account.

As comprehensive security performance moves forward, IDF withdraws progressively from areas occupied since September 28, 2000 and the two sides restore the status quo that existed prior to September 28, 2000. Palestinian security forces redeploy to areas vacated by IDF.

PALESTINIAN INSTITUTION-BUILDING

Immediate action on credible process to produce draft constitution for Palestinian statehood. As rapidly as possible, constitutional committee circulates draft Palestinian constitution, based on strong parliamentary democracy and cabinet with empowered prime minister, for public comment/debate. Constitutional committee proposes draft document for submission after elections for approval by appropriate Palestinian institutions.

Appointment of interim prime minister or cabinet with empowered executive authority/decision-making body.

GOI fully facilitates travel of Palestinian officials for PLC and Cabinet sessions, internationally supervised security retraining, electoral and other reform activity, and other supportive measures related to the reform efforts.

Continued appointment of Palestinian ministers empowered to undertake fundamental reform. Completion of further steps to achieve genuine separation of powers, including any necessary Palestinian legal reforms for this purpose.

Establishment of independent Palestinian election commission. PLC reviews and revises election law.

Palestinian performance on judicial, administrative, and economic benchmarks, as established by the International Task Force on Palestinian Reform.

As early as possible, and based upon the above measures and in the context of open debate and transparent candidate selection/electoral campaign based on a free, multi-party process, Palestinians hold free, open, and fair elections.

GOI facilitates Task Force election assistance, registration of voters, movement of candidates and voting officials. Support for NGOs involved in the election process.

GOI reopens Palestinian Chamber of Commerce and other closed Palestinian institutions in East Jerusalem based on a commitment that these institutions operate strictly in accordance with prior agreements between the parties.

HUMANITARIAN RESPONSE

Israel takes measures to improve the humanitarian situation. Israel and Palestinians implement in full all recommendations of the Bertini report to improve humanitarian conditions, lifting curfews and easing restrictions on movement of persons and goods, and allowing full, safe, and unfettered access of international and humanitarian personnel.

AHLC [*Ad-Hoc Liaison Committee*] reviews the humanitarian situation and prospects for economic development in the West Bank and Gaza and launches a major donor assistance effort, including to the reform effort.

GOI and PA continue revenue clearance process and transfer of funds, including arrears, in accordance with agreed, transparent monitoring mechanism.

CIVIL SOCIETY

Continued donor support, including increased funding through PVOs/NGOs [*private voluntary organizations/non-governmental organizations*], for people to people programs, private sector development and civil society initiatives.

SETTLEMENTS

GOI immediately dismantles settlement outposts erected since March 2001.

Consistent with the Mitchell Report, GOI freezes all settlement activity (including natural growth of settlements).

PHASE II: TRANSITION—JUNE 2003–DECEMBER 2003

In the second phase, efforts are focused on the option of creating an independent Palestinian state with provisional borders and attributes of sovereignty, based on the new constitution, as a way station to a permanent status settlement. As has been noted, this goal can be achieved when the Palestinian people have a leadership acting decisively against terror, willing and able to build a practicing democracy based on tolerance and liberty. With such a leadership, reformed civil institutions and security structures, the Palestinians will have the active support of the Quartet and the broader international community in establishing an independent, viable, state.

Progress into Phase II will be based upon the consensus judgment of the Quartet of whether conditions are appropriate to proceed, taking into account performance of both parties. Furthering and sustaining efforts to normalize Palestinian lives and build Palestinian institutions, Phase II starts after Palestinian elections and ends with possible creation of an independent Palestinian state with provisional borders in 2003. Its primary goals are continued comprehensive security performance and effective security co-operation, continued normalization of Palestinian life and institution-building, further building on and sustaining of the goals outlined in Phase I, ratification of a democratic Palestinian constitution, formal establishment of office of prime minister, consolidation of political reform, and the creation of a Palestinian state with provisional borders.

International Conference: Convened by the Quartet, in consultation with the parties, immediately after the successful conclusion of Palestinian elections, to support Palestinian economic recovery and launch a process, leading to establishment of an independent Palestinian state with provisional borders.

Such a meeting would be inclusive, based on the goal of a comprehensive Middle East peace (including between Israel and Syria, and Israel and Lebanon), and based on the principles described in the preamble to this document.

Arab states restore pre-*intifada* links to Israel (trade offices, etc.).

Revival of multilateral engagement on issues including regional water resources, environment, economic development, refugees, and arms control issues.

New constitution for democratic, independent Palestinian state is finalized and approved by appropriate Palestinian institutions. Further elections, if required, should follow approval of the new constitution.

Empowered reform cabinet with office of prime minister formally established, consistent with draft constitution.

Continued comprehensive security performance, including effective security co-operation on the bases laid out in Phase I.

Creation of an independent Palestinian state with provisional borders through a process of Israeli-Palestinian engagement, launched by the international conference. As part of this process, implementation of prior agreements, to enhance maximum territorial contiguity, including further action on settlements in conjunction with establishment of a Palestinian state with provisional borders.

Enhanced international role in monitoring transition, with the active, sustained, and operational support of the Quartet.

Quartet members promote international recognition of Palestinian state, including possible UN membership.

PHASE III: PERMANENT STATUS AGREEMENT AND END OF THE ISRAELI-PALESTINIAN CONFLICT—2004–2005

Progress into Phase III, based on consensus judgment of Quartet, and taking into account actions of both parties and Quartet monitoring. Phase III objectives are consolidation of reform and stabilization of Palestinian institutions, sustained, effective Palestinian security performance, and Israeli-Palestinian negotiations aimed at a permanent status agreement in 2005.

Second International Conference: Convened by Quartet, in consultation with the parties, at beginning of 2004 to endorse agreement reached on an independent Palestinian state with provisional borders and formally to launch a process with the active, sustained, and operational support of the Quartet, leading to a final, permanent status resolution in 2005, including on borders, Jerusalem, refugees, settlements; and, to support progress toward a comprehensive Middle East settlement between Israel and Lebanon and Israel and Syria, to be achieved as soon as possible.

Continued comprehensive, effective progress on the reform agenda laid out by the Task Force in preparation for final status agreement.

Continued sustained and effective security performance, and sustained, effective security co-operation on the bases laid out in Phase I.

International efforts to facilitate reform and stabilize Palestinian institutions and the Palestinian economy, in preparation for final status agreement.

Parties reach final and comprehensive permanent status agreement that ends the Israel–Palestinian conflict in 2005, through a settlement negotiated between the parties based on UNSCR 242, 338, and 1397, that ends the occupation that began in 1967, and includes an agreed, just, fair, and realistic solution to the refugee issue, and a negotiated resolution on the status of Jerusalem that takes into account the political and religious concerns of both sides, and protects the religious interests of Jews, Christians, and Muslims worldwide, and fulfils the vision of two states, Israel and sovereign, independent, democratic and viable Palestine, living side-by-side in peace and security.

Arab state acceptance of full normal relations with Israel and security for all the states of the region in the context of a comprehensive Arab-Israeli peace.

THE GOVERNMENT RESOLUTION REGARDING THE DISENGAGEMENT PLAN

(6 June 2004)

The Israeli Cabinet approved the plan for Israel's disengagement from Palestinians in the Gaza Strip and the northern West Bank on 6 June 2004. The proposals, which were originally outlined by Prime Minister Ariel Sharon at the annual Herzliya Conference in December 2003, required Israel to dismantle most military installations and all 21 Israeli settlements in the Gaza Strip, and to withdraw from four settlements in the West Bank. The Knesset endorsed the plan on 25 October 2004, and the first stage of disengagement entered formal effect from 17 August 2005. The Israel Defence Forces were reported to have completed their withdrawals from the Gaza Strip and the four West Bank settlements, within the framework of the Disengagement Plan, on 12 September and 22 September 2005, respectively. (For further details, see the chapters on Israel and the Palestinian Territories.)

Addendum A—Revised Disengagement Plan—Main Principles

1. BACKGROUND—POLITICAL AND SECURITY IMPLICATIONS

The State of Israel is committed to the peace process and aspires to reach an agreed resolution of the conflict based upon the vision of US President George Bush. The State of Israel believes that it must act to improve the current situation. The State of Israel has come to the conclusion that there is currently no reliable Palestinian partner with which it can make progress in a two-sided peace process. Accordingly, it has developed a plan of revised disengagement (hereinafter—the plan), based on the following considerations:

One. The stalemate dictated by the current situation is harmful. In order to break out of this stalemate, the State of Israel is required to initiate moves not dependent on Palestinian co-operation.

Two. The purpose of the plan is to lead to a better security, political, economic and demographic situation.

Three. In any future permanent status arrangement, there will be no Israeli towns and villages in the Gaza Strip. On the other hand, it is clear that in the West Bank, there are areas which will be part of the State of Israel, including major Israeli population centers, cities, towns and villages, security areas and other places of special interest to Israel.

Four. The State of Israel supports the efforts of the United States, operating alongside the international community, to promote the reform process, the construction of institutions and the improvement of the economy and welfare of the Palestinian residents, in order that a new Palestinian leadership will emerge and prove itself capable of fulfilling its commitments under the Roadmap.

Five. Relocation from the Gaza Strip and from an area in Northern Samaria should reduce friction with the Palestinian population.

Six. The completion of the plan will serve to dispel the claims regarding Israel's responsibility for the Palestinians in the Gaza Strip.

Seven. The process set forth in the plan is without prejudice to the relevant agreements between the State of Israel and the Palestinians. Relevant arrangements shall continue to apply.

Eight. International support for this plan is widespread and important. This support is essential in order to bring the Palestinians to implement in practice their obligations to combat terrorism and effect reforms as required by the Road-map, thus enabling the parties to return to the path of negotiation.

2. MAIN ELEMENTS

A. THE PROCESS:

The required preparatory work for the implementation of the plan will be carried out (including staff work to determine criteria, definitions, evaluations, and preparations for required legislation).

Immediately upon completion of the preparatory work, a discussion will be held by the Government in order to make a decision concerning the relocation of settlements, taking into consideration the circumstances prevailing at that time—whether or not to relocate, and which settlements.

The towns and villages will be classified into four groups, as follows:

1) Group A—Morag, Netzarim, Kfar Darom

2) Group B—the villages of Northern Samaria (Ganim, Kadim, Sa-Nur and Homesh)

3) Group C—the towns and villages of Gush Katif

4) Group D—the villages of the Northern Gaza Strip (Elei Sinai, Dugit and Nissanit)

It is clarified that, following the completion of the aforementioned preparations, the Government will convene periodically in order to decide separately on the question of whether or not to relocate, with respect to each of the aforementioned groups.

3. The continuation of the aforementioned process is subject to the resolutions that the Government will pass, as mentioned above in Article 2, and will be implemented in accordance with the content of those resolutions.

3.1 *The Gaza Strip*

1) The State of Israel will evacuate the Gaza Strip, including all existing Israeli towns and villages, and will redeploy outside the Strip. This will not include military deployment in the area of the border between the Gaza Strip and Egypt ('the Philadelphi Route') as detailed below.

2) Upon completion of this process, there shall no longer be any permanent presence of Israeli security forces in the areas of Gaza Strip territory which have been evacuated.

3.2 *The West Bank*

3) The State of Israel will evacuate an area in Northern Samaria (Ganim, Kadim, Sa-Nur and Homesh), and all military installations in this area, and will redeploy outside the vacated area.

4) Upon completion of this process, there shall no longer be any permanent presence of Israeli security forces in this area.

5) The move will enable territorial contiguity for Palestinians in the Northern Samaria area.

6) The State of Israel will assist, together with the international community, in improving the transportation infrastructure in the West Bank in order to facilitate the contiguity of Palestinian transportation.

7) The process will facilitate normal life and Palestinian economic and commercial activity in the West Bank.

3.3 The intention is to complete the planned relocation process by the end of 2005.

THE SECURITY FENCE:

The State of Israel will continue building the Security Fence, in accordance with the relevant decisions of the Government. The route will take into account humanitarian considerations.

3. SECURITY SITUATION FOLLOWING THE RELOCATION

One. The Gaza Strip:

1) The State of Israel will guard and monitor the external land perimeter of the Gaza Strip, will continue to maintain exclusive authority in Gaza air space, and will continue to exercise security activity in the sea off the coast of the Gaza Strip.

2) The Gaza Strip shall be demilitarized and shall be devoid of weaponry, the presence of which does not accord with the Israeli-Palestinian agreements.

3) The State of Israel reserves its fundamental right of self-defense, both preventive and reactive, including where necessary the use of force, in respect of threats emanating from the Gaza Strip.

Two. The West Bank:

1) Upon completion of the evacuation of the Northern Samaria area, no permanent Israeli military presence will remain in this area.

2) The State of Israel reserves its fundamental right of self-defense, both preventive and reactive, including where necessary the use of force, in respect of threats emanating from the Northern Samaria area.

3) In other areas of the West Bank, current security activity will continue. However, as circumstances require, the State of Israel will consider reducing such activity in Palestinian cities.

4) The State of Israel will work to reduce the number of internal check-points throughout the West Bank.

4. MILITARY INSTALLATIONS AND INFRASTRUCTURE IN THE GAZA STRIP AND NORTHERN SAMARIA

In general, these will be dismantled and evacuated, with the exception of those which the State of Israel decides to transfer to another party.

5. SECURITY ASSISTANCE TO THE PALESTINIANS

The State of Israel agrees that by co-ordination with it, advice, assistance and training will be provided to the Palestinian security forces for the implementation of their obligations to combat terrorism and maintain public order, by American, British, Egyptian, Jordanian or other experts, as agreed therewith. No foreign security presence may enter the Gaza Strip and/or the West Bank without being co-ordinated with and approved by the State of Israel.

6. THE BORDER AREA BETWEEN THE GAZA STRIP AND EGYPT (PHILADELPHI ROUTE)

The State of Israel will continue to maintain a military presence along the border between the Gaza Strip and Egypt (Philadelphi Route). This presence is an essential security requirement. At certain locations, security considerations may require some widening of the area in which the military activity is conducted.

Subsequently, the evacuation of this area will be considered. Evacuation of the area will be dependent, inter alia, on the security situation and the extent of co-operation with Egypt in establishing a reliable alternative arrangement.

If and when conditions permit the evacuation of this area, the State of Israel will be willing to consider the possibility of the establishment of a seaport and airport in the Gaza Strip, in accordance with arrangements to be agreed with Israel.

7. REAL ESTATE ASSETS

In general, residential dwellings and sensitive structures, including synagogues, will not remain. The State of Israel will aspire to transfer other facilities, including industrial, commercial and agricultural ones, to a third, international party which will put them to use for the benefit of the Palestinian population that is not involved in terror.

The area of the Erez industrial zone will be transferred to the responsibility of an agreed upon Palestinian or international party.

The State of Israel will explore, together with Egypt, the possibility of establishing a joint industrial zone on the border of the Gaza Strip, Egypt and Israel.

8. CIVIL INFRASTRUCTURE AND ARRANGEMENTS

Infrastructure relating to water, electricity, sewage and telecommunications will remain in place.

In general, Israel will continue, for full price, to supply electricity, water, gas and petrol to the Palestinians, in accordance with current arrangements.

Other existing arrangements, such as those relating to water and the electro-magnetic sphere shall remain in force.

9. ACTIVITY OF CIVILIAN INTERNATIONAL ORGANIZATIONS

The State of Israel recognizes the great importance of the continued activity of international humanitarian organizations and others engaged in civil development, assisting the Palestinian population.

The State of Israel will co-ordinate with these organizations arrangements to facilitate their activities.

The State of Israel proposes that an international apparatus be established (along the lines of the AHLC), with the agreement of Israel and international elements which will work to develop the Palestinian economy.

10. ECONOMIC ARRANGEMENTS

In general, the economic arrangements currently in operation between the State of Israel and the Palestinians shall remain in force. These arrangements include, inter alia:

One. The entry and exit of goods between the Gaza Strip, the West Bank, the State of Israel and abroad.

Two. The monetary regime.

Three. Tax and customs envelope arrangements.

Four. Postal and telecommunications arrangements.

Five. The entry of workers into Israel, in accordance with the existing criteria.

In the longer term, and in line with Israel's interest in encouraging greater Palestinian economic independence, the State of Israel expects to reduce the number of Palestinian workers entering Israel, to the point that it ceases completely. The State of Israel supports the development of sources of employment in the Gaza Strip and in Palestinian areas of the West Bank, by international elements.

11. INTERNATIONAL PASSAGES

a. The International Passage Between the Gaza Strip and Egypt

1) The existing arrangements shall continue.

2) The State of Israel is interested in moving the passage to the 'three borders' area, south of its current location. This would need to be effected in co-ordination with the Government of Egypt. This move would enable the hours of operation of the passage to be extended.

b. The International Passages Between the West Bank and Jordan:

The existing arrangements shall continue.

12. EREZ CROSSING POINT

The Erez crossing point will be moved to a location within Israel in a time frame to be determined separately by the Government.

13. CONCLUSION

The goal is that implementation of the plan will lead to improving the situation and breaking the current deadlock. If and when there is evidence from the Palestinian side of its willingness, capability and implementation in practice of the fight against terrorism, full cessation of terrorism and violence and the institution of reform as required by the Roadmap, it will be possible to return to the track of negotiation and dialogue.

Addendum C—Format of the Preparatory Work for the Revised Disengagement Plan

1. A process of relocation involves many significant personal repercussions for the relocated residents. In implementing the plan, the Government of Israel is obliged to consider the implications for the relocated residents, assist them, and ease the process for them as much as possible. The difficulties and sensitivities involved in the process must be born in mind by the Government and by those who implement the process.

2. The Government of Israel attributes great importance to conducting a dialogue with the population designated for relocation, regarding various issues relating to the implementation of the plan—including with respect to relocation and compensation—and will act to conduct such a dialogue.

ESTABLISHING AN ORGANIZATIONAL FRAMEWORK

3. An organizational framework will be established with the purpose of addressing and assisting in all matters related to the implementation of the plan.

4. The Ministerial Committee for National Security (The Security Cabinet) will accompany and direct the Revised Disengagement Plan, including acceleration of the construction of the Security Fence, with the exception of the decisions concerning relocation (Article 2.A (2) and (3) in Addendum A).

The Security Cabinet will be responsible for the implementation of this Government Resolution.

5. A Steering Committee is hereby established that will be responsible for co-ordinating the issues pertaining to the Revised Disengagement Plan. The Steering Committee will report to the Security Cabinet on its activities, and bring before it issues which require a decision by the political echelon. The Steering Committee will include the following members:

One. Head of the National Security Council—Chairman

Two. Representatives of the Ministry of Defense, the IDF and the Israel Police

Three. Director-General of the Prime Minister's Office

Four. Director-General of the Ministry of Finance

Five. Director-General of the Ministry of Justice

Six. Director-General of the Ministry of Foreign Affairs

Seven. Director-General of the Ministry of Industry, Trade and Labor

Eight. Director-General of the Ministry of Agriculture and Rural Development

Nine. Director-General of the Ministry of National Infrastructures

Ten. Director-General of the Ministry of the Interior

Eleven. Director-General of the Ministry of Construction and Housing

6. A Committee on Relocation, Compensation, and Alternative Settlement is hereby established which will be charged with the task of preparing legislation regarding relocation and compensation, as well as details of the principles and indexes for compensation, including incentives, advance payments, and compensatory aspects of relocation alternatives in priority areas, in accordance with Government policy. The Committee's recommendations will be presented to the Security Cabinet and serve as a basis for the draft bill on this issue.

This committee will constitute the exclusive authorized body for the co-ordination and conducting of dialogue with the population designated for relocation and compensation, and with all other bodies related to the issue of compensation—until the completion of the legislation. The Committee will be able to establish professional sub-committees, as it deems necessary, for the sake of fulfilling its tasks. The committee will include the following members:

One. Director-General of the Ministry of Justice—Chairman

Two. Representative of the Ministry of Finance

Three. Representative of the Ministry of Industry, Trade and Labor

Four. Representative of the Ministry of Agriculture and Rural Development

Five. Representative of the Prime Minister's Office

7. The Jewish Agency for Israel, as a body involved in settlement, will act in accordance with instructions from the Steering Committee and in co-ordination with the Committee on Relocation, Compensation and Alternative Settlement. The role of the Jewish Agency will be to carry out the activities required for alternative settlement, either agricultural or communal, for those among the relocated civilian population who so desire.

8. a. An Executive Administration is hereby established in the Prime Minister's Office which will be subordinate to the Steering Committee. Its task will be to implement this Government Resolution with regard to the relocation of civilians and compensation.

Two. The Executive Administration will be authorized to grant advance payments to those eligible for compensation—which will be counted against the compensation to be owed to them—according to terms that will be determined by the Committee on Relocation, Compensation, and Alternative Settlement, and in accordance with the instructions and procedures established by the said Committee.

Three. The Head of the Executive Administration will hold the rank of Ministry Director-General.

9. All Government ministries and other governmental bodies will forward, without delay, all information required for the aforementioned organizational frameworks to fulfill their tasks.

LEGISLATION

10. a. The Ministry of Justice will formulate and the Prime Minister will submit, as soon as possible, a draft bill to the Ministerial Committee for Legislation, which will include provisions regarding relocation and compensation for those eligible, as well as the authority necessary for this purpose.

Two. Soon thereafter, the Government will submit the bill to the Knesset.

Three. The IDF Military Commanders in the Areas will issue the Security Legislation necessary for the implementation of the Government's Resolutions.

BUDGET

11. a. Within one month of the adoption of this Resolution, the Director of the Budget Division of the Ministry of Finance, in co-ordination with the Director-General of the Prime Minister's Office and the Director-General of the Ministry of Justice, will allocate the required budget and other resources necessary for the Steering Committee, the Committee on Relocation, Compensation and Alternative Settlement, the Executive Administration and the Jewish Agency to carry out their activities.

Two. The 2005 Budget and subsequent budgets will be adjusted periodically to conform with the process and Government Resolutions on this issue.

Three. For the sake of commencing its activities, the Executive Administration will be allocated, in the first stage, 10 staff positions.

TRANSITION INSTRUCTIONS

12. During the interim period from the date this Resolution is passed, the following instructions will apply to the towns, villages and areas included in the plan (hereafter—the towns and villages), for the purpose of making preparations on the one hand, while maintaining normal and continuous daily life on the other:

One. Municipal and communal activities related to the course of normal life and services to which residents are entitled will continue unaffected, including services provided by the regional council, as well as security, education, welfare, telecommunications, mail, public transportation, electricity, water, gas, petrol, health services, banks and all other services customarily provided to towns and villages prior to this Resolution.

Two. Government plans for construction and development that have yet to commence will not be advanced for implementation.

Three.

Four. Nothing stated in this Resolution is intended to undermine Government Resolution no. 150, dated August 2, 1996, regarding other areas. The aforementioned Government Resolution no. 150 will also apply to towns and villages for the purpose of approval prior to planning and land allocation.

EXCEPTIONAL CASES COMMITTEE

13. An Exceptional Cases Committee will be established which will be authorized to permit the implementation of any plan which was frozen, in accordance with the provisions above, and authorized to decide not to advance plans even if their implementation has already commenced, following an examination of each individual case, and in keeping with criteria that it shall establish.

The Exceptional Cases Committee will be headed by the Director-General of the Prime Minister's Office, and will include the Directors-General of the Ministries of Finance and Justice.

Decisions of the Exceptional Cases Committee may be appealed to the Security Cabinet, in any instance where they are brought before it by a member of the Government.

PRINCIPLES FOR COMPENSATION

14. a. The date which determines the right for compensation is the date of the adoption of this Government Resolution.

b. Those entitled to compensation will receive fair and suitable compensation, as will be set out in the law legislated for this purpose.

JOINT UNDERSTANDING ON NEGOTIATIONS (ANNAPOLIS CONFERENCE)

(27 November 2007)

Following a series of preparatory meetings between US officials and Israeli and Palestinian delegations, an international peace meeting intended officially to relaunch the Middle East peace process was held under US auspices in Annapolis, Maryland, USA, on 27 November 2007. Members of the international Quartet group and the League of Arab States (Arab League) attended the talks, and Syria notably sent a low-level delegation. At the close of the meeting US President George W. Bush read a statement of 'joint understanding' between the Israeli Prime Minister, Ehud Olmert, and the PA Executive President, Mahmud Abbas, who both expressed their commitment to achieving a final settlement of the outstanding issues of contention between Israelis and Palestinians by the end of 2008.

The representatives of the Government of the State of Israel and the Palestine Liberation Organization (PLO), represented respectively by Prime Minister Ehud Olmert and President Mahmoud Abbas, in his capacity as Chairman of the PLO Executive Committee and President of the Palestinian Authority, have convened in Annapolis, Maryland, under the auspices of President George W. Bush of the United States of America, and with the support of the participants of this international conference, having concluded the following Joint Understanding:

We express our determination to bring an end to bloodshed, suffering and decades of conflict between our peoples, to usher in a new era of peace, based on freedom, security, justice, dignity, respect and mutual recognition, to propagate a culture of peace and non-violence, and to confront terrorism and incitement, whether committed by Palestinians or Israelis.

In furtherance of the goal of two states, Israel and Palestine, living side by side in peace and security:

We agree to immediately launch good faith bilateral negotiations in order to conclude a peace treaty resolving all outstanding issues, including all core issues, without exception, as specified in previous agreements.

We agree to engage in vigorous, ongoing and continuous negotiations, and shall make every effort to conclude an agreement before the end of 2008.

For this purpose, a steering committee, led jointly by the head of the delegation of each party, will meet continuously, as agreed.

The steering committee will develop a joint work plan and establish and oversee the work of negotiations teams to address all issues, to be headed by one lead representative from each party.

The first session of the steering committee will be held on 12 December 2007.

President Abbas and Prime Minister Olmert will continue to meet on a bi-weekly basis to follow up the negotiations in order to offer all necessary assistance for their advancement.

The parties also commit to immediately implement their respective obligations under the Performance-Based Road Map to a Permanent Two-State Solution to the Israel-Palestinian Conflict, issued by the Quartet on 30 April 2003 (hereinafter, 'the Roadmap') and agree to form an American, Palestinian and Israeli mechanism, led by the United States, to follow up on the implementation of the Roadmap. The parties further commit to continue the implementation of the ongoing obligations of the Roadmap until they reach a peace treaty. The United States will monitor and judge the fulfillment of the commitments of both sides of the Roadmap.

Unless otherwise agreed by the parties, implementation of the future peace treaty will be subject to the implementation of the Roadmap, as judged by the United States.

In conclusion, we express our profound appreciation to the President of the United States and his Administration, and to the participants of this international conference, for their support for our bilateral peace process.

UN SECURITY COUNCIL RESOLUTION 1860

(8 January 2009)

Resolution 1860 called for a cease-fire in the conflict between Israel and Hamas militants in the Gaza Strip, which had begun in December 2008. The resolution was adopted by 14 votes to none; the USA abstained in the vote.

The Security Council,

Recalling all of its relevant resolutions, including resolutions 242 (1967), 338 (1973), 1397 (2002), 1515 (2003) and 1850 (2008),

Stressing that the Gaza Strip constitutes an integral part of the territory occupied in 1967 and will be a part of the Palestinian state,

Emphasizing the importance of the safety and well-being of all civilians,

Expressing grave concern at the escalation of violence and the deterioration of the situation, in particular the resulting heavy civilian casualties since the refusal to extend the period of calm; and emphasizing that the Palestinian and Israeli civilian populations must be protected,

Expressing grave concern also at the deepening humanitarian crisis in Gaza,

Emphasizing the need to ensure sustained and regular flow of goods and people through the Gaza crossings,

Recognizing the vital role played by UNRWA in providing humanitarian and economic assistance within Gaza,

Recalling that a lasting solution to the Israeli-Palestinian conflict can only be achieved by peaceful means,

Reaffirming the right of all States in the region to live in peace within secure and internationally recognized borders,

1. Stresses the urgency of and calls for an immediate, durable and fully respected ceasefire, leading to the full withdrawal of Israeli forces from Gaza;

2. Calls for the unimpeded provision and distribution throughout Gaza of humanitarian assistance, including of food, fuel and medical treatment;

3. Welcomes the initiatives aimed at creating and opening humanitarian corridors and other mechanisms for the sustained delivery of humanitarian aid;

4. Calls on Member States to support international efforts to alleviate the humanitarian and economic situation in Gaza, including through urgently needed additional contributions to UNRWA and through the Ad Hoc Liaison Committee;

5. Condemns all violence and hostilities directed against civilians and all acts of terrorism;

6. Calls upon Member States to intensify efforts to provide arrangements and guarantees in Gaza in order to sustain a durable ceasefire and calm, including to prevent illicit trafficking in arms and ammunition and to ensure the sustained reopening of the crossing points on the basis of the 2005 Agreement on Movement and Access between the Palestinian Authority and Israel; and in this regard, welcomes the Egyptian initiative, and other regional and international efforts that are under way;

7. Encourages tangible steps towards intra-Palestinian reconciliation including in support of mediation efforts of Egypt and the League of Arab States as expressed in the 26 November 2008 resolution, and consistent with Security Council resolution 1850 (2008) and other relevant resolutions;

8. Calls for renewed and urgent efforts by the parties and the international community to achieve a comprehensive peace based on the vision of a region where two democratic States, Israel and Palestine, live side by side in peace with secure and recognized borders, as envisaged in Security Council resolution 1850 (2008), and recalls also the importance of the Arab Peace Initiative;

9. Welcomes the Quartet's consideration, in consultation with the parties, of an international meeting in Moscow in 2009;

10. Decides to remain seized of the matter.

UN Document S/RES/1860 (2009).

APPLICATION OF PALESTINE FOR ADMISSION TO MEMBERSHIP IN THE UNITED NATIONS

(23 September 2011)

On 23 September 2011, despite opposition from Israel and criticism from Hamas, PA Executive President Abbas presented an application for full membership in the UN on behalf of the State of Palestine. However, on 11 November the Security Council announced that it was unable to recommend the application for consideration by the General Assembly, as only eight of the Council's 15 members were prepared to vote in favour. (An application to membership in the UN must receive the support of at least nine Security Council members, provided that none of the five permanent members indicate their opposition. The USA had previously stated that it would veto the Palestinian application at any formal vote of the Security Council.)

Note by the Secretary-General

In accordance with rule 135 of the rules of procedure of the General Assembly and rule 59 of the provisional rules of procedure of the Security Council, the Secretary-General has the honour to circulate herewith the attached application of Palestine for admission to membership in the United Nations, contained in a letter received on 23 September 2011 from its President (see annex I). He also has the honour to circulate a further letter, dated 23 September 2011, received from him at the same time (see annex II).

Annex I—Letter received on 23 September 2011 from the President of Palestine to the Secretary-General

I have the profound honour, on behalf of the Palestinian people, to submit this application of the State of Palestine for admission to membership in the United Nations.

This application for membership is being submitted based on the Palestinian people's natural, legal and historic rights and based on United Nations General Assembly Resolution 181 (II) of 29 November 1947 as well as the Declaration of Independence of the State of Palestine of 15 November 1988 and the acknowledgement by the General Assembly of this Declaration in Resolution 43/177 of 15 December 1988.

In this connection, the State of Palestine affirms its commitment to the achievement of a just, lasting and comprehensive resolution of the Israeli-Palestinian conflict based on the vision of two States living side by side in peace and security, as endorsed by the United Nations Security Council and General Assembly and the international community as a whole and based on international law and all relevant United Nations resolutions.

For the purpose of this application for admission, a declaration made pursuant to rule 58 of the provisional rules of procedure of the Security Council and rule 134 of the rules of procedure of the General Assembly is appended to this letter (see enclosure).

I should be grateful if you would transmit this letter of application and the declaration to the Presidents of the Security Council and the General Assembly as soon as possible.

(Signed) Mahmoud Abbas

President of the State of Palestine

Chairman of the Executive Committee of the Palestine Liberation Organization

Declaration

In connection with the application of the State of Palestine for admission to membership in the United Nations, I have the honour, in my capacity as the President of the State of Palestine and as the Chairman of the Executive Committee of the Palestine Liberation Organization, the sole legitimate representative of the Palestinian people, to solemnly declare that the State of Palestine is a peace-loving nation and that it accepts the obligations contained in the Charter of the United Nations and solemnly undertakes to fulfill them.

(Signed) Mahmoud Abbas

President of the State of Palestine

Chairman of the Executive Committee of the Palestine Liberation Organization

Annex II—Letter dated 23 September 2011 from the President of Palestine to the Secretary-General

After decades of displacement, dispossession and the foreign military occupation of my people and with the successful culmination of our State-building program, which has been endorsed by the international community, including the Quartet of the Middle East Peace Process, it is with great pride and honour that I have submitted to you an application for the admission of the State of Palestine to full membership in the United Nations.

On 15 November 1988, the Palestine National Council (PNC) declared the Statehood of Palestine in exercise of the Palestinian people's inalienable right to self-determination. The Declaration of Independence of the State of Palestine was acknowledged by the United Nations General Assembly in Resolution 43/177 of 15 December 1988. The right of the Palestinian people to self-determination and independence and the vision of a two-State solution to the Israeli-Palestinian conflict have been firmly established by General Assembly in numerous resolutions, including, *inter alia*, Resolutions 181 (II) (1947), 3236 (XXIX) (1974), 2649 (XXV) (1970), 2672 (XXV) (1970), 65/16 (2010) and 65/202 (2010) as well as by United Nations Security Council Resolutions 242 (1967), 338 (1973) and 1397 (2002) and by the International Court of Justice Advisory Opinion of 9 July 2004 (on the Legal Consequences of the Construction of a Wall in the Occupied Palestinian Territory). Furthermore, the vast majority of the international community has stood in support of our inalienable rights as a people, including to statehood, by according bilateral recognition to the State of Palestine on the basis of the 4 June 1967 borders, with East Jerusalem as its capital, and the number of such recognitions continues to rise with each passing day.

Palestine's application for membership is made consistent with the rights of the Palestine refugees in accordance with international law and the relevant United Nations resolutions, including General Assembly Resolution 194 (III) (1948), and with the status of the Palestine Liberation Organization as the sole legitimate representative of the Palestinian people.

The Palestinian leadership reaffirms the historic commitment of the Palestine Liberation Organization of 9 September 1993. Further, the Palestinian leadership stands committed to resume negotiations on all final status issues—Jerusalem, the Palestine refugees, settlements, borders, security and water—on the basis of the internationally endorsed terms of reference, including the relevant United Nations resolutions, the Madrid principles, including the principle of land for peace, the Arab Peace Initiative and the Quartet Roadmap, which specifically requires a freeze of all Israeli settlement activities.

At this juncture, we appeal to the United Nations to recall the instructions contained in General Assembly Resolution 181 (II) (1947) and that 'sympathetic consideration' be given to application of the State of Palestine for admission to the United Nations.

Accordingly, I have had the honour to present to Your Excellency the application of the State of Palestine to be a full member of the United Nations as well as a declaration made pursuant to rule 58 of the provisional rules of procedure of the Security Council and rule 134 of the rules of procedure of the General Assembly. I respectfully request that this letter be conveyed to the Security Council and the General Assembly without delay.

(Signed) Mahmoud Abbas

President of the State of Palestine

Chairman of the Executive Committee of the Palestine Liberation Organization

UN Document S/2011/592 (2011).

REGIONAL NUCLEARIZATION: SYSTEMIC PRESSURES AND ENDEMIC FEARS

JAMES H. WYLLIE

INTRODUCTION

In June 2013 a new President of Iran was elected. In contemporary Iranian politics, Hassan Rouhani is deemed to be a 'moderate' in social, economic and international issues, in contrast to his controversial predecessor, Mahmoud Ahmadinejad. For over 10 years Iran has been in a state of political conflict with much of the rest of the international community over the opaque character and objectives of its nuclear programme, with profound international anxieties that Iran is intent on procuring nuclear weapons. The election of the new President will have no significant impact on the resolution of this crisis. President Rouhani, a former senior negotiator on the issue, has long been a supporter of Iran's nuclear programme. The key figure in Iran is not the President, but the Supreme Religious Leader, Ayatollah Sayed Ali Khamenei, who exercises close control of all strategic matters. Iran will continue rapidly to develop its nuclear resources, while periodically engaging in desultory international negotiations. Nor has the election of a new Iranian President of reputedly moderate disposition altered the strategic fundamentals of the Middle East. The region continues to be volatile and unpredictable. It is replete with internal rivalries and is deeply penetrated by external great powers with strategic interests of their own. The presence of over 60% of the planet's proven petroleum reserves in the Persian (Arabian) Gulf, and the determination of great powers to sustain access to it, is a dominant strategic characteristic. Equally, the oil-producing states look to protect their vital energy assets and to prolong as much as possible their economic viability. For many oil states, regardless of changes to internal political organization and transitory external allegiances, preserving for as long as possible the valuable energy resources that underpin their fragile societies and brittle power is a constant strategic imperative. According to a recent BP Energy Outlook report, energy use in the Middle East in 1970 was one-half that of other non-Organisation for Economic Co-operation and Development (OECD) countries, but by 2010 it was three times higher. Some 65% of Saudi energy is generated by oil. Unless an alternative power source is utilized, based on current trends Saudi Arabia will become an oil importer before 2040. Irrespective of whatever long-term political transformations occur as a consequence of the 'Arab spring', those states that were clearly intent on a nuclear future prior to the major political upheavals that began in 2011 will continue to pursue one of those rare policies that is popular with both the people and the ruling élites.

The strategic imperatives driving some leading states toward a 'break-out' of nuclear proliferation is hugely challenging. If misunderstood and mismanaged, the issue of nuclear proliferation could wreak damage far in excess of that resulting thus far from all the conflicts of modern times. However, it is the very struggles and vulnerabilities inherent in these issues that oblige governments to protect their vital interests as vigorously as possible. Presently, there are eight definite—and one probable—nuclear weapons states in the world. The probable state is the Democratic People's Republic of Korea (North Korea), and this probable status has contributed to it receiving 'kid-glove' treatment from its protagonists. The stark contrast between recent Western policies towards North Korea and Libya will not have been lost on relatively weak states in the Middle East. The definite nuclear weapons states are the USA, Russia, the People's Republic of China, the United Kingdom, France, India, Pakistan and Israel. The last three are not signatories of the 1968 Non-Proliferation Treaty (NPT), yet have not suffered costly opprobrium for not signing the treaty or subsequently procuring nuclear weapons.

'ROGUE' STATE IMPACT

Since the end of the Cold War, it has been the behaviour of so-called 'rogue' states and, in the light of the attacks of 11 September 2001 in the USA, especially the anxieties over possible strategic links between such states and transnational terrorist groups that have propelled the issue of nuclear proliferation up the Middle East crises agenda. In the eyes of all US administrations, a Middle East government is viewed as dangerous if: it opposes prevalent security arrangements in the region such as US protection for Saudi Arabia; it practises terrorism at home and sponsors terrorism elsewhere; it opposes the Arab-Israeli peace process; it denies Israel's right to exist; and, crucially, it seems intent on procuring nuclear weapons while being a signatory to the NPT. While often using milder rhetoric and different modes of exerting influence, most European governments generally support such a categorization.

The three Middle Eastern states that have alarmed the advanced industrial societies most during the 21st century are Libya, Iraq and Iran. Soon after the US-led military intervention in Iraq in 2003, Libya sensed a new vulnerability. Muammar al-Qaddafi admitted to violations of the NPT and voluntarily relinquished his illegal, clandestine nuclear weapons programme and scaled back his ballistic missile arsenal. From then until the fall of the Qaddafi regime in 2011, the abandonment of European Union (EU) and US economic sanctions and the gradual re-entry of Libya into the economic mainstream were the rewards. This was a rare, peaceful non-proliferation achievement and it yielded valuable intelligence about the covert international nuclear network centred on Prof. Abdul Qadeer Khan from Pakistan.

The military intervention by the 'coalition of the willing' removed Iraq as a nuclear proliferation threat for some time to come. Article 9(E) of the 2005 Iraqi Constitution explicitly prohibits the development, production and use of nuclear weapons. However, there can be no certainty that, driven by the innate insecurities of the region and by future concerns over the protection of its natural resources, an Iraqi government will never again seek nuclear weapons—not least if it comes to be flanked by Saudi and Iranian nuclear forces. The persistence with which Iraq sought nuclear weapons for more than 30 years prior to 2003 suggests a genuine perception of geo-strategic necessity.

Saddam Hussain, while Vice-Chairman of Iraq's Revolutionary Command Council, promoted the nuclear programme, accompanied by chemical and biological programmes, in the early 1970s. Two years into Saddam's presidency, and fearing that Iraqi nuclear fuel enrichment would lead to the production of a nuclear weapon, Israel bombed the Osirak nuclear power station in 1981 before the reactor went critical. Despite this setback, the Saddam Government continued its quest for nuclear weapons. Nuclear equipment and research were provided by France and Russia, with reassurances from Iraq that such help was for nuclear energy only and within the remit of the NPT. Throughout the Iran–Iraq War (1980–88), the Sunni Gulf Arab monarchies, fearful of a Shi'ite Iranian victory, provided Iraq with about US $15,000m. a year for conventional arms. None the less, Saddam Hussain pursued his weapons programmes, with the nuclear programme at the heart of this effort. Soviet missiles were procured and adapted to bring not just Iran but also Israel into range. Taking advantage of the end of the Cold War, and to compensate for the huge political and economic costs of the war with Iran, Saddam's armies invaded and occupied Kuwait in August 1990. One significant outcome of that strategic misadventure was the presence of UN weapons inspectors in Iraq from 1991 until their withdrawal in 1998. As well as extensive chemical and biological warfare programmes, UN inspectors discovered advanced work on nuclear weapons. The programme was immense: several thousand million dollars had been spent, and over 10,000 staff were involved. It had been kept secret from the International Atomic Energy Agency (IAEA), a fact that deeply damaged the agency's inspection credibility. Some estimates indicated that in 1991 Iraq was barely three years away from nuclear weapons status. The UN teams destroyed these facilities as best they could by the mid-1990s, but suspicions remained that elements of the programme remained hidden and awaiting further development when UN teams were absent.

The absence of UN inspection for nearly five years (1998–2003) seriously contributed to the anxieties over weapons of mass destruction that led to the 2003 intervention. Subsequent to the intervention no extant nuclear weapons or major components were discovered, but the official Duelfer Report (the final report issued by the Iraq Survey Group, under the leadership of Charles Duelfer) concluded that other illegal activities regarding long-range missiles, concealed plans and a reservoir of skilled workers made no sense unless the intention was to resume weapons activities quickly after the lifting of sanctions. Mahdi Obeidi, who had directed Iraq's covert uranium enrichment programme and famously hidden plans in his garden, told *The New York Times* that the nuclear programme could have been restarted 'at the snap of Saddam Hussain's fingers'. Duelfer also concluded that fear of Iran was the primary motivation, and that Saddam was reluctant to admit weakness in this area lest Iran exploit this condition. The geo-strategic reality of Arab–Persian rivalry long predates the Saddam regime and will continue far into the future, regardless of which sect of Islam is politically dominant in Iraq.

In 2003 the IAEA discovered that the Islamic Republic of Iran had been engaged in undeclared nuclear activities, contrary to NPT stipulations. Iran was also in possession of illegal documents related to the fabrication of nuclear weapons. These revelations, which came into the open only because of information provided by Iranian dissidents in 2002, reinforced the suspicions of the USA and many others that the Iranian nuclear energy programme was a cover for the development of nuclear weapons.

None the less, since the revival of the nuclear programme the country's leaders have consistently denied the intent to procure nuclear weapons. Despite denials in 2002, it has been confirmed that the Arak nuclear site is a production plant for 'heavy water', used in a type of power plant that produces plutonium—which can be used in the production of nuclear weapons—as a by-product. The Bushehr nuclear energy plant, constructed with essential Russian assistance, is a 'light water' reactor and there is no requirement for 'heavy water'. After numerous delays the new plant began loading fuel in August 2010 and was connected to the national electricity grid in August 2011. It reached full capacity in March 2012, delivering 1,000 MW of electricity to the national grid. Since it is Russian-operated, with Russia supplying the nuclear fuel and removing the waste, there are no anxieties about fuel from Bushehr being diverted for military purposes. However, the Natanz nuclear site, described by an Iranian government spokesman in 2002 as being used for experiments in radioactivity, was confirmed as a major site for the growing centrifuge programme, which allowed Iran to enrich its own uranium as fuel for its projected power stations. However, such enriched uranium could be purchased abroad, as is the arrangement with Russia for the Bushehr plant.

In 2003 Iran agreed to increased IAEA inspection and to suspend the enrichment programme, but with the proviso that it retained the right to resume uranium enrichment. Indeed, this occurred with the inauguration of Mahmoud Ahmadinejad as President in August 2005, even though the 'EU-3' (Germany, France and the United Kingdom) had offered economic and civil nuclear assistance if Iran permanently ceased enrichment. In June 2006, supported by the UN Security Council, more attractive incentives, including the first official bilateral US-Iran talks since 1979, were offered to Tehran but were rejected. Enrichment thus continued. Previously, Russia and China had tilted clearly towards the Iranian case, but from mid-2006 this sympathy began to wane. In 2006 the EU-3 were joined by Russia, China and the USA to form the primary political negotiating unit dealing with the Iranian nuclear issue. This unit is known as 'P5+1' (the five permanent members of the UN Security Council plus Germany). In December 2006 and March 2007 the UN Security Council agreed modest but escalating sanctions against Iran. In July 2007, in an effort to thwart a third, and more severe, set of sanctions, Tehran agreed to allow a delayed IAEA inspection of Arak. The inspectors had been barred from Arak in April, in protest against the second round of sanctions. However, the Iranian Government persisted in its refusal to suspend uranium enrichment. In May 2008 the IAEA produced a report detailing Iran's unrelenting progress and expansion in its uranium enrichment programme. The sombre report included serious concerns about the military dimensions of Iranian nuclear activities. In June the P5+1 offered technological, economic and political incentives to Iran to begin serious negotiations about its nuclear activities. The package included the provision of light-water nuclear reactors and the supply of fuel; assistance with telecommunications infrastructure and modernization of the agricultural sector; trade liberalization; and regional security co-operation. The demand that Iran cease its uranium enrichment programme before such discussions could commence was immediately rejected by the Iranian Government, and it continued to enrich uranium. A fourth round of UN sanctions (Resolution 1929) aimed at forcing Iran to cease uranium enrichment and to allow full IAEA inspection was approved in June 2010. These sanctions included a prohibition on the purchase of certain arms, including ballistic missile material; the imposition of more stringent rules on international financial transactions with Iranian banks and certain individuals; and the implementation of a new regime of cargo inspections to intercept illicit weapons of mass destruction-related material being shipped to Iran. Russia and China only agreed to the new resolution on the understanding that the stricter Western proposals were scaled down. China receives more than 10% of its oil imports from Iran and has over US $120,000m. of investment in the country. Russia is a major supplier of conventional arms and civilian nuclear power technology to Iran, but is also anxious about potential Iranian political meddling in the Caucasus and Central Asia, should Russia fully support Western hardline sanctions. Following the imposition of Resolution 1929, the USA and the EU introduced their own, tougher, economic sanctions against the Iranian regime's nuclear activities, including trade restrictions on various Iranian banking and insurance businesses, and prohibitions on new investments in certain sectors of the Iranian oil and gas industries not covered by Resolution 1929.

The June 2010 UN sanctions and the subsequent US and EU additional sanctions have had little discernible impact on the progress of the nuclear programme. EU-sponsored talks between the P5+1 and Iran in İstanbul, Turkey, in January 2011 proved unsuccessful. The proposal that Iran adopt a confidence-building measure by parting with most of its illicit stockpile of enriched uranium in exchange for the provision of nuclear fuel monitored by the IAEA was rejected by Tehran. In December 2011 EU ministers responsible for foreign affairs applied further pressure by adding 180 individuals and companies to the sanctions list but refrained from imposing an oil embargo at that stage. EU members were buying 450,000 barrels of oil each day from Iran, accounting for 30% of Iran's oil exports. The United Kingdom, France and Germany had favoured the introduction of an immediate embargo, but Italy, Spain and Greece, Iran's largest EU customers, had rejected the proposal.

After a hiatus of more than a year, further negotiations between the P5+1 and Iran took place in İstanbul, followed by Baghdad, Iraq, and then Moscow, Russia, during April–June 2012. The P5+1 aimed to pressure Iran into suspending the enrichment of uranium to 20% purity, sending its current stockpile of 20% enriched uranium abroad, and closing its Fordo enrichment centre. In return, fuel rods for Tehran's nuclear research reactor would be provided and there would be some relaxation of economic sanctions. Iran's 6,000 kg of low-enriched uranium (3.5% purity), which had the potential to provide enough highly enriched uranium to produce five nuclear bombs, would be permitted to remain in the country. However, Iran rejected the offer. Consequently, on 1 July 2012 the EU embargo on Iranian oil came into effect. Given the deals concluded by India and China to buy Iranian oil using their own currencies, and Iran's need to discount its oil prices heavily for other customers, the P5+1 hoped that these tougher sanctions would elicit concessions from Iran in 2013. This was not the case. Although the Iranian economy suffered seriously from the economic sanctions, further tentative negotiations in the early months of 2013 did not deliver any progress. In February the P5+1 offered a slight reduction in sanctions in exchange for restrictions on Iran's uranium enrichment programme, including the suspension of operations at the deeply-buried Fordo facility, and more detailed inspection by the IAEA. This would allow Iran to retain a modest amount of 20% enriched uranium for research purposes. Iran's response was to propose a suspension of all sanctions in return for a temporary halt to 20% enrichment. Given the strategic importance attached to the nuclear programme by the Iranian Government, there appears little prospect that even the most severe of economic sanctions will deliver any resolution acceptable to the Western members of the P5+1.

In April 2006 the successful enrichment of uranium had allowed President Ahmadinejad to assert that Iran had joined the 'nuclear club of nations'. By mid-2007 Iran claimed to have 100 kg of low-enriched uranium at 3.5% purity. This amount could be stockpiled and at a later date enriched to 90% purity, which is weapons-grade level; 50 kg of highly enriched uranium can produce an atomic weapon of the kind which destroyed Hiroshima, Japan, in 1945. According to the IAEA report of May 2010, Iran possessed a stockpile of low-enriched uranium in excess of 2,400 kg. This was enough to allow Iran to refine further a significant quantity of highly enriched uranium necessary to make a bomb. Prior to 2009 the USA's policy had been to demand the cessation of uranium enrichment as a precondition for direct US-Iranian negotiations. The strategy of engagement with adversaries subsequently developed by the Administration of President Barack Obama suggested that the USA would accept Iranian enrichment on condition of Tehran's acceptance of rigorous IAEA inspection, such as real-time, constant, technical surveillance of Iran's enrichment facilities and conduct. In effect, such a new policy could have resulted in Iran being trusted to operate its own enrichment facilities on condition that the process was thoroughly monitored. However, IAEA proposals in mid-2009 for such scrutiny were rejected by Iran. At that time, Russia and China opposed increasing the severity of the regime of modest UN sanctions.

In April 2007 the IAEA confirmed Iranian competence in the complex process of linking 1,300 high-precision centrifuges into eight cascades to produce highly enriched uranium, should it choose to do so. Ahmad Fayazbakhsh, deputy head of the Atomic Energy Organization of Iran, claimed that centrifuge capabilities would soon be expanded to 3,000. The IAEA report of May 2008 confirmed such an increase. A year later, Iran's centrifuges were believed to total more than 5,000. This expanding centrifuge facility is buried 23 m underground, beneath the Dasht-e Kavir desert, 320 km south of Tehran. In September 2009 the existence of another secret nuclear facility was revealed. This uranium-enrichment plant is built into a mountainside at Fordo, outside the holy city of Qom. In February 2010 President Ahmadinejad announced Iran's successful enrichment of uranium to 20% purity, well above the 3.5% level deemed appropriate for nuclear energy purposes. In June 2011 Iran announced its intention to triple its production of 20%-enriched uranium, by commencing output at the Fordo underground site. In November, for the first time, the IAEA explicitly accused Iran of carrying out work to produce atomic weapons. The robust report stated that, while some of Iran's nuclear-related activities had civilian applications, some were 'specific to nuclear weapons', including computer modelling of the core of a warhead, development of a detonator for a nuclear charge and preparatory work for a nuclear test. In February 2012 the IAEA reported a 42% rise in operational centrifuges enriching uranium at the Natanz facility since October 2011, and a 69% increase at Fordo. Once again, Iran had refused to co-operate fully with the IAEA inspection, preventing a visit to a military location in Parchin, where it was suspected that experiments in nuclear weapons detonation had been conducted. Both its February and May 2012 reports stated that 'the Agency is unable to provide credible assurance about the absence of undeclared nuclear material and activities in Iran, and therefore to conclude that all nuclear material in Iran is in peaceful activities'. Many reports indicate a massive increase, by up to 5,000, of Iranian centrifuges in 2013, together with the start of a programme to install IR-2M centrifuges which are three to five times more productive in enriching uranium than Iran's standard IR-1 centrifuges. This development has raised Western anxieties that Iran could soon achieve the critical capability to allow a very rapid development of a nuclear bomb that would preclude sufficient insight by the USA and other concerned states to take appropriate counter-measures quickly.

In 2007 Mohammad el-Baradei, Director-General of the IAEA at that time, suggested that Iran could produce a nuclear weapon within three to eight years. Convictions that Tehran is seeking a nuclear weapon are reinforced by technological links between Iran and North Korea, including a missile programme. As of mid-2012 Iran had the largest surface-to-surface missile arsenal in the Middle East, estimated at 1,000 missiles with ranges of between 150 km and 2,500 km. This arsenal included nuclear-capable *Shahab-3* and *Shahab-4* missiles (based on the North Korean *Rodong* missile), which have the range to strike Israel. In May 2009 President Ahmadinejad announced the successful test-firing of the *Sejil-2* solid-fuelled missile with a range of 2,000 km. It is also reckoned that the *Sejil-2* possesses some capability to evade anti-ballistic missile defences. That this missile is solid-fuelled is of significance. Iran's previous missiles were liquid-fuelled and took hours or even days to prepare for launch. Such missiles are much more vulnerable to pre-emptive strikes than solid-fuelled missiles, which are more mobile and can be launched within minutes. Such an arsenal only makes strategic sense if equipped with nuclear warheads. Political considerations also add weight to the assumption that Iran is intent on nuclear weapons status. Among Iranian nationalists of all political persuasions there are two salient perceptions. One is that Iran embodies the glories of the oldest civilization in the region, and by virtue of its geography and demography as well as its history, it is the rightful leader in the Gulf, with many responsibilities. Not least, one of these responsibilities is to champion the Shi'ite interpretation of Islam and afford protection to all Shi'ite Muslims. The other perception is that, regardless of such rights, Iran is relatively isolated from the mainstream of the Middle East and is unjustly vulnerable to many local and external pressures. If one adopts a 'Tehran strategic perspective' and looks outwards to all points on the compass, then Israeli, Russian, Pakistani, Chinese, Indian and US forces in the Middle East, all equipped with weapons of mass destruction, may be seen to be encircling Iran. The sense of strategic isolation, and the arguments for possession of a nuclear deterrent, were compounded in 2013 by the brutal civil war in Syria, where the Government of President Bashar al-Assad, a rare Middle East ally of Iran, is under severe pressure from rebel groups evidently receiving military and financial support from Saudi Arabia and other Gulf Sunni monarchies.

There is a sense within the country's political élite that it is now appropriate for Iran to be more assertive and robust regarding its national and cultural interests. To this end, Iranian possession of the capital weapons system of the day, under which one-half of the world population enjoys protection, seems only right and proper. That this is a genuine nationalist issue, not a matter of dispute between 'conservative' clerics and secular 'reformists', is underappreciated in the West. The nuclear issue is one on which the nation so far is largely united, while deeply fragmented on a range of social and economic issues. It remains to be seen whether harsh economic sanctions will seriously undermine the national consensus on nuclear policy.

REGIONAL REPERCUSSIONS

The prospect of Iran successfully procuring nuclear weapons has transformed the power perceptions and dynamics of the Middle East. For some time now Iran's nuclear policies have been causing serious disturbance to the hyper-sensitive security antenna of Israel—which, although officially undeclared, remains the only nuclear weapons state in the region. A clear signal of Israeli 'zero tolerance' of regional nuclear threats was the attack against the Iraqi Osirak reactor in 1981. Moreover, there is always the prospect of an Israeli pre-emptive attack on Iran. In May 2010 it was reported by the British *Sunday Times* newspaper that Israel intended to deploy permanently a submarine armed with nuclear cruise missiles close to the Iranian coastline. This action may be viewed as a deterrent to rash Iranian action, or as providing an additional capability should Israel decide to launch long-range air attacks against the Iranian nuclear facilities. For once, Israel has some common cause with the conservative, pro-Western, Gulf Sunni Arab governments, which are deeply anxious about the pace as well as the content of Iran's controversial nuclear programme, coupled with its missile developments. Missile delivery vehicles that are capable of resisting orthodox Arab air defences compound the worries of Iran's Arab neighbours—much more so than 50 years of Israeli possession of nuclear weapons ever did. Arab leaderships may have been resentful, even envious, of Israel's capabilities, but they always reckoned, correctly, that Israel would only use these weapons as a last-resort, defensive measure if the state was ever facing complete defeat and destruction. Hence, an Arab coalition could attack Israel in October 1973 and calculate that there would not be a nuclear response short of Israel's imminent and total defeat. When, in May 2006, Secretary-General of the League of Arab States (Arab League) Amr Moussa called for 'a Middle East free of nuclear weapons', the target of his remarks was not Israel, but Iran. Until the collapse of the presidency of Muhammad Hosni Mubarak in February 2011, Egypt was also anxious about Iranian nuclear developments. Regardless of the modest, immediate post-Mubarak easing of Egyptian-Iranian relations, the regional strategic implications of a possible Iranian nuclear arsenal will oblige any future Egyptian government to pursue countervailing measures.

However, while Iranian capabilities alone may alarm states such as Saudi Arabia, Kuwait and Jordan, when viewed in the context of current and recent Iranian foreign policy the alarm deepens considerably. The foreign policy interests of Iran do not coincide with those of the Sunni Arab leaderships. While a future direct Iranian nuclear attack is deemed improbable, the primary concern is about Iran utilizing its weapons of mass destruction as a shield against US pressure as it supports the ascendancy of the Shi'ite majority in Iraq; provides encouragement and perhaps material backing to large, restive Shi'ite minorities in Kuwait and Saudi Arabia and to the sizeable and disaffected Shi'ite majority in Sunni-ruled Bahrain; strengthens its links with the embattled Shi'ite rulers of largely Sunni Syria; and propels Shi'ite Hezbollah in Lebanon towards even greater, and crucial, overt military assistance for the embattled Syrian Government. This drive by Iran into the heart of the Sunni Middle East led King Abdullah of Jordan in 2006 to warn of the emergence of a radical 'Shi'ite Crescent' stretching from Tehran to Beirut, via Baghdad and Damascus.

Presently, no Arab country has a nuclear power reactor, but over the past seven years there has been a surge of interest in nuclear energy. Saudi Arabia, Egypt and at least four other Arab governments have undertaken serious discussions with the IAEA about how best to progress with nuclear research and development. Those governments that have shown a determination to move beyond past rudimentary nuclear research claim, as Iran often does, that their interest is economic and not military. Preserving oil and gas stocks, and furthering research into nuclear-powered desalination of sea water, are posited as the urgent reasons for revived or new interest in the nuclear industry. It is the case that Saudi Arabia and the United Arab Emirates (UAE) have had a long-standing interest in nuclear-powered desalination, but the political concern in these countries over Iranian behaviour is so acute that to deny that this is not a major motivator, if not the catalyst, of increased interest in nuclear matters requires huge faith in mere coincidence.

In nuclear matters, it makes sense for Saudi Arabia to follow a 'hedging' strategy regarding national security. Assembling trained personnel and creating a nuclear infrastructure facilitates movement towards weapons development at a later date, in the event of Iran proceeding successfully to nuclear weapons status. While it is important to distinguish between the weapons proliferation-prone parts of the nuclear fuel cycle—uranium enrichment and plutonium-reprocessing—and benign, NPT-compliant, civil nuclear energy developments in the current non-nuclear weapons states, the former cannot occur without the latter. If a state such as Saudi Arabia decided no longer to comply with the NPT, civil nuclear energy capabilities would be the essential platform to attain nuclear weapons status. The dual utilities of skills and technical capabilities required for civil and military nuclear advances are virtually impossible to disentangle. Israel, India, Pakistan and North Korea all accessed the nuclear weapons room along the civil nuclear corridor. In April 2010 the creation of the King Abdullah City for Nuclear and Renewable Energy was announced. Evidence of Saudi Arabia's huge commitment to increase its nuclear capabilities was provided by the announcement, in June 2011, of investment of US $100,000m. to construct 16 large reactors by 2030. Agreements for assistance in these developments were signed with France, Argentina, the Republic of Korea (South Korea) and China.

Notwithstanding the huge task of recruiting scientific personnel and creating the technological infrastructure, the national security and foreign policy incentives for Saudi Arabia to undertake serious nuclearization are considerable. Over recent years Saudi Arabia has emerged as the leader of the Arab states, replacing an Egypt still struggling to recover status lost through its peace treaty with Israel and mired in political instability. Spurred by the Iranian foreign policy offensive into the core Middle East, by the uncertainties over Iraq and by Islamist terrorism, King Abdullah of Saudi Arabia has projected his country in a sharp political manner into the heart of Middle Eastern strategic affairs, as demonstrated by its financial and military support for Syrian rebels. With its annual gross domestic product much more than double that of Egypt, Saudi Arabia is increasingly playing a huge role in the region, beyond its traditional religious influence, addressing issues of high relevance to the survival of the unique Saudi state. Being subject to speculation as a nuclear player is important for status, prestige and making a timely signal to Iran. It could also provide the platform for subsequent weapons development, possibly in co-operation with Pakistan, should such a controversial route be taken. A vital element of weapons development is the delivery vehicle component, and in that regard Saudi Arabia is already equipped. In 1986 Saudi Arabia surprised the world by acquiring 50–90 Chinese *CSS-2* missiles and 10–15 mobile launchers. The *CSS-2* missile, which is used by China for its nuclear forces, has a 700-km range and is capable of carrying a 2,500-kg warhead. Given that the missile has a circular error probability accuracy of 1 km–2 km, it only makes strategic sense to have it equipped with a nuclear warhead. Furthermore, the Saudi Government does not allow US or any other inspection.

Even if Iran were a close friend rather than a potential, deadly protagonist, there is a strong strategic argument for a Saudi nuclear force. In terms of conventional security, its relatively small population—given the extent of territory and resources to be protected—makes Saudi Arabia highly vulnerable, regardless of how much is spent on conventional weaponry. A largely Shi'ite Iraq, economically recovered and rearmed, could pose as great a threat as Islamic Iran. Iraq and Iran working together, perhaps even in a tripartite alliance with Shi'ite-governed Syria, to share the Saudi spoils would be a nightmare for Riyadh. In this scenario the USA would either be disenchanted by the Middle East and no longer committed to regional security, or would be deterred by Iranian weapons of mass destruction from offering protection.

Of course, crucial to continuing Saudi confidence in current security arrangements is the sustained commitment of the USA. The Saudi leadership is well aware that it is a realistic measure of national interest that upholds the US security guarantee, rather than any inherent empathy for the regime. Past US 'wobbles' in the region, such as the failure to sustain the Shah, the very close US Senate vote in January 1991 over authorizing the use of force against Saddam Hussain in Kuwait and the political abandonment of President Mubarak of Egypt in 2011, do give pause for strategic thought in Riyadh. If Saudi Arabia were eventually to emulate examples such as Pakistan and Israel, the USA would be mightily displeased, but it and its Western allies could not stop buying Saudi oil. Even if shale gas and 'new oil' technology deeply reduced the USA's dependence on Middle East resources, its allies in Europe and Japan would continue to need Saudi oil for the foreseeable future. Furthermore, by following the examples of Israel and Pakistan, Saudi Arabia would be released from its heavy dependency on the USA for security, which would result in political gains for it throughout the Arab world, not least in countering Islamist criticism of the Saudi royal family inside as well as outside the country.

The next most likely core Middle East state to pursue a 'hedging' nuclear strategy is Egypt. The deeply nationalistic character of the 2011 revolution in Egypt makes it highly unlikely that any new Egyptian government, whether or not based on religious, secular or military platforms, will fail to pursue such a strategy. As with Iran and Saudi Arabia, claims can be made that nuclear interests are being driven by economic considerations. Egypt's limited oil and gas reserves will be depleted in the next 30 years or so. Energy demand is increasing by 7%–8% a year, and population growth continues apace. Egypt's population has doubled since 1977 and is now estimated at around 83m. These trends have been apparent for some time, yet Egypt's rudimentary and troubled nuclear energy research programme was suspended following the disaster at the Chornobyl (Chernobyl) nuclear power plant in Ukraine in 1986. In late 2006 a decision was taken to relaunch the Egyptian nuclear programme. As with Saudi Arabia, Iranian nuclear behaviour must be, at the very least, a salient consideration. Egypt is deeply aware that Shi'ite nuclear capability, providing political as well as military support for Hezbollah and perhaps again for the Islamic Resistance Movement (Hamas), could put an intolerable strain on the Arab-Israeli peace process, and projects Iranian political competition within its sphere of influence. Furthermore, though diminished in Arab politics in recent times, there is a political and intellectual tradition and pride in Egypt that would be offended at being left behind by Saudi Arabia in civilian and, possibly, military nuclear advances. In terms of conventional military power, Egypt remains the strongest presence in the Sunni Arab world. Given Saudi economic dominance, Egypt could not bear to be overtaken also in military terms.

In March 2008 Egypt and Russia signed a nuclear power co-operation treaty and France and China also expressed an interest in providing assistance. There is some urgency to the Egyptian plans, which include the construction of a 1,000-MW reactor at Dabaa on the Mediterranean coast by 2017. This is to be followed by the building of at least three other power plants. In May 2009 the Egyptian Nuclear Power Plants Authority awarded a contract for consultancy work on the Dabaa project to the Australian firm WorleyParsons. The IAEA agreed to provide technical assistance. Under the Mubarak presidency, Cairo made it clear that it had no ambitions to enrich its own fuel, but would import and return reactor fuel under international supervision. There is continuing resentment and regret in high political and scientific circles at Egyptian membership of the NPT, particularly the signing of the 1995 indefinite extension of the Treaty, while Israel remains outside its provisions. Consequently, Egypt has refused to sign the Additional Protocol, allowing more IAEA detailed inspections, until Israel joins the NPT.

Egypt exerted major pressure on the May 2010 NPT Review Conference to aim for a 2012 conference on a nuclear weapons free zone (NWFZ) in the Middle East. Israel was specifically mentioned in the communiqué, while Iran and Syria were not. Iran used its veto to avoid direct censure. Israel, as a non-signatory of the NPT, was not present. Reluctantly, the USA supported the communiqué, but it did manage to restrict the business of any potential 2012 conference to considering the technicalities of a Middle East NWFZ. However, although a process was initiated, the political upheavals and uncertainties in many Arab states have prevented the holding of the conference.

Since 2003 some of the smaller Sunni states in the core Middle East, as well as an increasingly assertive Turkey, have also discovered the attractions of nuclear energy. Jordan, Kuwait, Bahrain, Qatar, UAE, Oman and even impoverished and deeply unstable Yemen have all given notice of nuclear energy ambitions. Given that a large commercial nuclear reactor costs about US $4,000m., such an investment could easily be afforded by a small oil-rich Gulf monarchy, if not easily by Jordan, which frequently announces ambitions for nuclear power plants, or at all by Yemen. In January 2008, during a visit to the UAE by the French President, Nicolas Sarkozy, a bilateral military co-operation accord was signed, which included the establishment of a French military base in Abu Dhabi in 2009 and French assistance in the construction of two nuclear reactors. In May 2009 President Obama signed an agreement to allow US nuclear energy companies to contribute to the UAE's ambitious nuclear energy programme. In December of that year the UAE signed a $40,000m. contract with a consortium led by the Korea Electric Power Corpn, of the Republic of Korea (South Korea), for four nuclear power stations. In the winter of 2012–13 the UAE further enhanced its international nuclear links by agreeing a nuclear assistance contract with Russia. At that time, it appeared likely that the UAE would become the first Arab state to generate nuclear power (2017 was the target date for the plants to commence operations). In 2010 the UAE assured the USA that it would not enrich uranium or reprocess used nuclear fuel, and stated that it would import all fuel for its reactors. The UAE Government describes its nuclear programme as 'peaceful by design' and 'proliferation-proof'. The country is seeking to double its power capacity over the next decade in order to meet the 10% increase in electricity demand from its soaring population, while simultaneously preserving its vital hydrocarbon assets. The UAE is currently one of the world's top five power consumers per head. About 80% of its power is generated from its own natural gas deposits, and the rest from its oil resources. The aim of the UAE is to derive about 25% of its power from its own nuclear plants.

Apart from Saudi Arabia, all the small Gulf states see themselves as potentially 'one bomb targets' in the event of an Iranian-triggered military nuclearization by the larger local states. With the decline in the credibility of the USA and other external security guarantees implicit in such an eventuality, the small Gulf states would have a range of options. Pursuing a 'no foreign bases' and neutral policy similar to that of Austria and Finland in Cold War Europe, and using economic leverage to remain on good terms with all large neighbours, could be an option. Oman could be attracted to that option and feel relatively secure. However, for others such as Kuwait, Bahrain and Qatar, religious, political and geo-strategic considerations could preclude such a choice. In these countries, some relationship with nuclear weapons would be probable. Either a coalition of some smaller member states of the Cooperation Council for the Arab States of the Gulf (Gulf Cooperation Council—GCC) would buy a deterrent 'off the shelf', or it would help to fund an emerging nuclear weapons programme in return for the on-the-spot deterrence presence of nuclear forces operating under a 'dual key' system, whereby any deployment of nuclear missiles would require the approval of all partners. A clear signal of the anxiety over Iran was the tentative agreement between the GCC and the USA to build a regional missile defence system. Details have been under negotiation since mid-2012, and Bahrain's Minister of Foreign Affairs, Sheikh Khalid bin Ahmad Al Khalifa, made it clear that the planned anti-missile system was being developed in response to Iran. Also, separately, Saudi Arabia, Kuwait and the UAE were upgrading their surface-to-air Patriot missile interceptor systems.

Another large state that, again coincidentally with the crisis over Iran, has appeared on the nuclear 'radar screen' is Turkey. Undoubtedly, Turkey has the industrial and scientific capabilities to have a successful nuclear energy programme, and can claim to have legitimate energy needs in an era of high international oil prices. In recent decades Turkey has chosen to focus on its Western links and to keep the states of the old Ottoman Empire at arm's length. Nevertheless, given political disappointments in this Western orientation, and the inability to detach itself strategically from events to the east and south, ranging from the Kurdish question to the 'Arab spring' upheavals, Turkey cannot ignore potential major changes in power relationships in this region. It shares a border, and Kurdish issues, with Iran and has a long-standing, problematic relationship with the regime in Syria, Iran's ally in the core Middle

East, which has deteriorated sharply over the past two years. Construction work on Turkey's proposed first nuclear power plant, at the Black Sea port of Sinop, was scheduled to begin in 2008, but was delayed by local opposition and court rulings. However, this opposition has been quashed, as have concerns about the construction of nuclear plants in earthquake zones arising from the collapse of the Fukushima nuclear reactor following the Japanese earthquake and tsunami in March 2011. The Russian nuclear company Rosatom began construction of Turkey's first nuclear power station, at the Mediterranean port of Mersin, in 2012. In May 2013 the Government signed agreements with a Japanese-French consortium, comprising Mitsubishi Heavy Industries and GDF Suez, under which construction of the second nuclear plant would begin at Sinop in 2017. In the event of Iran achieving nuclear weapons status, the Turkish general staff would begin to ask questions about the value of NATO and US security guarantees in such a new strategic environment. Turkey has an exemplary record in non-proliferation and has signed every appropriate IAEA agreement controlling the spread of nuclear technology. In all likelihood, Turkey will continue to rely on NATO deterrence for its security should Iran acquire nuclear weapons. Given the sharp deterioration in Turkish–Iranian relations since 2012, owing to Iran's vehement support for the Syrian regime of President Bashar al-Assad, NATO should not be seen to waver in its support for Turkey. Any doubt over NATO's commitment could prompt Turkey to consider progressing from civilian nuclear energy technology towards military applications. Many analysts argue that Turkey could have nuclear weapons within a decade, should it choose to do so.

Until a few years ago it was the orthodox view that one major Arab state that, uniquely, would not consider going down the nuclear route, should Iran proliferate, was Syria. Such prestige was assumed to be unimportant to the regime, and the Syrian Government was not engaged in any contest with Egypt and Saudi Arabia for Arab Sunni leadership. The deterrence of Israel was vested in a large, relatively affordable chemical weapons and short-range ballistic missile programme. However, such perceptions were swept away by the unexpected Israeli destruction of a clandestine Syrian nuclear facility at al-Kibar in September 2007. Construction of the isolated and well-concealed nuclear reactor, clearly modelled on the North Korean Yongbyon reactor and being built with apparent North Korean assistance, had been under way since 2001. Given al-Kibar's distance from population centres and the absence of any connections to the Syrian power supply, the facility clearly had military purposes. The IAEA had known nothing of the enterprise, and its inspection of the reactor was stalled until June 2008. By that time the site had been cleared and new non-nuclear construction started.

Concerns over covert Syrian proliferation were exacerbated by an IAEA report published in June 2009, which revealed the discovery of 'anthropogenic' uranium traces not included in Syria's inventory of nuclear material at a UN-monitored research reactor in Damascus. Another IAEA report, published in May 2011, stated that it was very likely that the al-Kibar facility had been a clandestine nuclear reactor under construction and that, when complete, it would have been able to produce nuclear fuel for one or two bombs a year. IAEA frustration with repeated Syrian refusals to co-operate with investigations resulted in the referral of Syria to the UN Security Council in June 2011. A total of 17 IAEA member states voted for the country's referral, while six voted against, including Russia and China. Given that Syria's nuclear misdemeanours took place in the past, and that no nuclear proliferation programme is currently in place, some UN members do not see the Syrian case as constituting an urgent threat, unlike the ongoing and expanding Iranian programme. The popular uprising besetting the Assad regime since 2012, compounded by the divisions in the UN Security Council over an appropriate response, drove the Syrian nuclear issue further down the international agenda.

THE ISRAELI DIMENSION

Following the 1956 Suez War, Israel embarked on a highly secretive nuclear programme, and by 1965 the Dimona nuclear reactor was in operation. In these days before the existence of the NPT it was reported that Israel benefited from some French and South African assistance. According to some estimates, Dimona produces about 20 kg of plutonium a year and Israel has between 75 and 200 nuclear warheads. It has nuclear-capable *Jericho-1* and *Jericho-2* ballistic missiles and advanced combat aircraft. Since 2000 Israel has deployed three German-built *Dolphin*-class submarines, which have nuclear-capable cruise missiles with a range of 1,500 km. Israel's arsenal and strategy is deliberately shrouded in a policy of 'nuclear ambiguity'. Israeli government spokesmen will neither confirm nor deny Israel's nuclear status; their favoured statement is that Israel will not be the first to 'introduce' nuclear weapons to the Middle East. Essentially, this is code for saying that Israel will not, as a matter of strategic and diplomatic routine, brandish its nuclear status in any coercive way to lever advantage; and that such weaponry exists only to deter an overwhelming attack from regional foes.

On occasions, over a period of many years, Arab political rhetoric has been critical of presumed Israeli development of nuclear weapons, but generally the criticism has been muted. There has been a quiet acceptance of the *sotto voce* deterrence posture; awareness in some capitals of the stabilizing contribution of Israeli weapons of mass destruction in limiting some grandiose Arab military ambitions; confidence in Israeli command and control; and certainty that Israel will not proliferate to other states or terrorist groups. Furthermore, persistent criticism of Israel's nuclear success only draws attention to Arab failures. The contrast is very stark, particularly if Iran is successful in procuring nuclear weapons. In this regard it may even be to the future advantage of Arab Sunni governments, whatever their post-'Arab spring' political character and assuming that there is no impulse to procure their own weapons, to have Israel as a 'second centre of nuclear decision-making' *vis-à-vis* Tehran. The USA would be the first centre but, in the event of any crisis with Iran, the Tehran regime must include Israel in its calculations as well as the USA, and it cannot presume that both will pursue similar strategies. Normally, any deterrent effect would be reinforced in such circumstances.

Yet, while 'nuclear ambiguity' seems to have served Israel well until now, the Iranian challenge may require a change to the adoption of a more activist posture. At the very least, it may necessitate the robust and lucid articulation of a deterrent stance, inclusive of secure, second-strike sea-borne deterrents, echoing the Western nuclear deterrent posture towards the Soviet Union during the Cold War. From long before the revelations about Iran's secret nuclear activities in 2002–03, Israel has seen Iran as the existential threat to its national security. The 1979 Islamic Revolution brought an abrupt end to the working relationship between the Shah's Iran and Israel, and witnessed the deliberate 'Islamization' of the Israel issue by Ayatollah Ruhollah Khomenei. Tehran propagated the message that it is the duty of all Muslims to liberate Jerusalem. Fronting the charge legitimized the Tehran regime's religious claim to power and delivered a route into the heart of Middle East politics from which it had normally been excluded by leading Arab Sunni governments. Although the prospect of a direct Iranian nuclear attack is probably low, the Jewish historical experience, the doubts over the viability of mutual deterrence between a small state of 7.6m. people and one of 79m. people, the persistent deep rhetorical hostility of key actors in the Iranian leadership (not only the recent former President) and the prospect, behind its nuclear shield, of even more generous Iranian support for local enemies, cause huge anxieties for Israel.

ADDRESSING PROLIFERATION

The most pressing proliferation challenge remains that of Iran. If, without doubt, it can be established that Iran is not moving towards nuclear weapons procurement, then the prospect of Saudi Arabia, Egypt, Turkey and perhaps others accelerating nuclear energy initiatives and programmes, possibly with a view later to translating them into nuclear weapons developments, is much reduced. However, to date, various multinational efforts towards the engagement of Iran and the restriction of its nuclear activities have proved unproductive. With most assessments reckoning that, as of mid-2013, Iran still remained a year or two away from nuclear-armed status, there may be time for the UN, US and EU sanctions to have an effect. Some previous assessments feared Iranian acquisition of nuclear weapons by about 2011, but the key Iranian uranium enrichment programme at Natanz was reported to have been infiltrated and delayed by the Stuxnet computer virus in 2010. Olli Heinonen, former Deputy Director-General of the IAEA (2005–10), estimated that Stuxnet had disabled 2,000 centrifuges at Natanz. There were strong suspicions that Israel or the USA may have been complicit in this software sabotage. However, the Iranian Government insisted that it had quickly overcome the problems caused by the virus and that its nuclear programme was back on course. It also asserted that the assassination of several Iranian nuclear scientists in 2010–11, and two explosions in November 2011 at, respectively, the Isfahan uranium enrichment facility and a military base close to Tehran (which killed 30 members of the Revolutionary Guard and Gen. Hassan Moghaddam, the head of the Iranian missile defence division), had not hindered the programme. Mossad, Israel's external intelligence agency, was blamed for these attacks (as well as for a number of failed assassinations against Iranian scientists).

Turkey and Brazil (both non-permanent members of the UN Security Council in 2010) did not support UN Resolution 1929 concerning economic sanctions. In May 2010, amid much publicity, these two countries announced an agreement with Iran to receive about one-half of Iran's stockpile of illicit low-enriched uranium, and subsequently return a smaller quantity of more highly enriched uranium for medical research purposes. This arrangement was broadly similar to the P5+1 proposal made to Iran in 2009, which came to nothing following the revelation of the secret Fordo nuclear facility, north of Qom. However, the deal between Iran and Turkey and Brazil was not implemented, and appeared to be an Iranian tactic to deflect and delay the UN Security Council's efforts, as well as an attempt by Turkey and Brazil to project themselves on to the world stage.

To date, the relatively modest UN sanctions, and the much tougher but not universal US and EU sanctions, have not delivered the desired result. Given the circumstances, a military strike—either by Israel or, more likely, by the USA—against Iran's nuclear facilities remains a possibility. Success could not be guaranteed and would be difficult to measure, and the political and strategic ramifications would be manifold. Should Israel be tempted unilaterally to strike Iran, it would find it a much bigger operational challenge than either the Osirak reactor attack in 1981 or the destruction of the al-Kibar facility in 2007. While Israel has long-range F-15 and F-16 bombers, the potential Iranian targets are more than 1,200 km away and the aircraft would require refuelling both en route and on the return journey. Politically, access through Jordanian and Turkish, or even Saudi, airspace could prove problematic, but not impossible. It is unlikely that a Shi'ite-dominated government in Baghdad would wish to grant airspace to Israel, and the authorities in Amman, Ankara and Riyadh, while quietly supportive of such an attack, would prefer not be to seen as complicit. However, given the deep Sunni Arab anxiety over Iran's nuclear development, such sensitivities could well be put aside in some of those capitals. There are multiple sites in Iran, with some, such as the Natanz centrifuge facility, enjoying hard-rock protection deep underground. Iran also defends these sites with an array of anti-aircraft capabilities. Furthermore, many experts are convinced that Iran possessed parallel secret sites that could begin enriching uranium rapidly if the known facilities were destroyed. The IAEA would presumably not be allowed any presence in Iran following an attack, and the Iranian authorities would be incentivized to start producing as many nuclear weapons as possible. Immediate Iranian retaliation, with long-range rockets and, more likely, an escalation of local violence via Hezbollah and perhaps even Hamas, would need to be included in the strategic calculations. In addition, given that nuclear development is a nationalist issue, an Israeli attack could turn many in the Iranian reform movement, previously agnostic about the Israel issue, hostile to Israel and supportive of the Iranian regime. Even assuming a successful attack on the scale that Israel could deliver, Iran could probably revive its nuclear programme relatively quickly. In a few years Israel could be faced with the need to repeat the exercise.

The most likely military strike, to greatest effect, which could be repeated at frequent intervals, would be by the USA. In the past, analysts have looked to deployments of US carrier aircraft in the region as a sign of readiness to attack Iranian nuclear sites. As well as being valuable for coercive diplomacy, such forces would be an important element in any strike. However, local carrier forces are no longer any real measure of US intentions. Immense attacking forces can be delivered 'out of the blue', and are not contingent on the highly visible arrival of extra carrier battle groups. In 2003 the US Strategic Command assumed a global conventional strike role as well as the routine strategic nuclear deterrent role. The objective is to destroy crucial enemy targets with conventional munitions, anywhere on the globe, promptly and with attacks coming from many flanks. Of course, as with any Israeli attack, there is no guarantee that unknown elements of the nuclear programme would be destroyed, and there would be likely costs to be factored into any decision. Undoubtedly, there would be further antagonism against the USA throughout the Muslim world. Iran would attempt to attack tanker traffic in the Gulf and oil infrastructure in the GCC. Iranian oil production would be halted, and no other source could quickly compensate for the loss of Iran's 4.2% of global production. Iranian-sponsored terrorist attacks in the region would escalate, and might even reach into the wider world. In Iraq, the current uneasy domestic peace could be placed in jeopardy by reactivated Shi'ite militias, and there would be the prospect of portable air defence weapons from Iran being deployed by the militant Islamist Taliban organization in Afghanistan. Regardless of the apparent expansion in Iranian nuclear developments over the past four years, for instance the claim of 20% enrichment in February 2010, the reluctance in the USA to use force is genuine and understandable. The Obama Administration's decision to play a 'back-room' role in NATO operations against Libya, and its deep reluctance to have any military involvement in the Syrian civil war, suggest a deep unwillingness to enter into conflict with another Muslim state and compounds US doubts about resorting to force against Iran. Although there is a real appreciation that Iranian nuclear weapons development would cripple the NPT in the Middle East, and probably world-wide, there is also, at the same time, a profound awareness in the US national security establishment of the operational difficulties and probable strategic costs of military interdiction against Iranian nuclear sites.

PROSPECTS

If, despite every indication to the contrary, Iran eventually and clearly accommodates UN requirements to suspend enrichment, or accepts constant IAEA surveillance as the price for continued low-level enrichment, while successfully convincing the P5+1 that it actually has no intention to proceed to nuclear weapons status, then further nuclear developments throughout the region will likely be limited to non-threatening energy and desalination projects. Crucially, barring any new Egyptian Government becoming deeply bellicose, nuclear fuel for most Arab and Turkish civil programmes will be provided from outside the region, and these states will forego the capability to process or enrich plutonium or uranium. As the former Director-General of the IAEA, el-Baradei, warned, when a state can enrich uranium 'it is virtually a nuclear-weapon state'. If, aside from the anomaly of Israel, the states of the turbulent Middle East are to remain confident that it is a zone free of local nuclear weapons actors, not least their bitter rivals, nuclear fuel must either come from external sources, or enrichment must be subject to unfettered inspection.

However, if Tehran proceeds on its current path, as seems most likely regardless of its new President, there are two realistic options, only one of which has any prospect of preventing proliferation. Neither option represents an easy choice. The first is the military strike option discussed above. The second option, accepting the uncomfortable reality that pressures from the UN Security Council, the USA and the EU have failed, is actually a post-proliferation coping strategy. The first option, assuming it is operationally successful, should provide conditions precluding Arab proliferation. However, the political and strategic turbulence arising from such action will always provoke strong argument against utilizing the military instrument.

This being the case, there will be no escaping the second option: the strategic containment of a nuclear Iran. In mid-2007 a US $63,000m. arms package over the following decade for the USA's clients in the Middle East was announced. It was estimated that between 2010 and 2012, Saudi Arabia would spend $50,000m. on advanced weapons; $35,000m. would be spent by the UAE; while Oman and Kuwait would each spend about $10,000m. These expenditure and procurement targets had largely been fulfilled by 2012. In July 2009 Secretary of State Hillary Clinton intimated that the USA would extend a 'defence umbrella' over its allies in the Middle East in the event of Iran continuing its nuclear programme without restraint. As in the Cold War containment of the Soviet Union, the notion is that US nuclear forces will provide a nuclear shield, while local conventional forces will counter any direct or Iranian-sponsored military, insurgent or terrorist adventures. Such security arrangements incorporate a Western expectation that leading Arab states will feel secure enough to forego procuring their own nuclear weapons. Of course, this ignores the precedent set in Cold War Europe, when the United Kingdom and France incurred phases of US displeasure by procuring their own nuclear deterrents. This behaviour demonstrated that in the real world no state can ever be absolutely confident that another will always protect it, whatever the cost.

Such feelings are all the more acute in a nuclear environment, especially in the Middle East. This is clearly how Israel views its security requirements. It is very likely that, should Iran proliferate, regardless of US security guarantees to those fearful of Iran, states such as Saudi Arabia and Egypt will eventually procure their own nuclear weapons. The content of secret US diplomatic cables revealed in 2010 by the WikiLeaks organization quotes King Abdullah of Saudi Arabia warning the US Administration of George W. Bush in 2008 that if Iran acquired nuclear weapons 'everyone in the region would do the same, including Saudi Arabia'. The USA would be deeply displeased with these states but, given that their support for the containment of Iran is essential, US strictures would be muted. So, if the Iranian Government continues down its current nuclear route, as it seems likely to do, and successful military interdiction is not forthcoming, the Middle East will eventually become as nuclearized as Europe, the south Asian sub-continent and north-east Asia. The advanced industrial states will have no alternative but to accept this changed strategic situation. The world will hope that a nuclear 'balance of terror' will emerge, as between East and West in Europe during the Cold War, which will be robust enough to prevent major and deeply disruptive conflict in a tension-ridden region of immense significance to the world economic system.

SELECT BIBLIOGRAPHY

Allison, Graham. *Nuclear Terrorism*. New York, Times Books, 2004.

Bahgat, Gawdat G. 'Iran and the United States: The Emerging Security Paradigm in the Middle East'. *Parameters*. Vol. 37, No. 2, 2007.

BP Statistical Review of World Energy June 2013. London, 2013.

Broad, William J., and Sanger, David E. 'With Eye on Iran, Rivals Also Want Nuclear Power'. *New York Times*, 15 April 2007.

Burke, Jason. 'Riyadh Will Build Nuclear Weapons if Iran Gets Them, Saudi Prince Warns'. *The Guardian*, 29 June 2011.

Chubin, Shahram, and Litwak, Robert S. 'Debating Iran's Nuclear Aspirations'. *Washington Quarterly*. Vol. 26, No. 4, 2003.

Cirincione, Joseph, Wolfsthal, Jon B., and Rajkumar, Miriam. *Deadly Arsenals: Nuclear, Biological, and Chemical Threats*. Washington, DC, Carnegie Endowment for International Peace, revised edn, 2005.

Clawson, Patrick. 'Nuclear Proliferation in the Middle East: Who is Next After Iran?'. April 2003. www.npolicy.org/article_file/Presentation030401_Clawson_Nuclear_Prolif_TB_030211_0552.pdf.

Cordesman, Anthony H., Gold, Bryan, and Coughlin-Schulte, Chloe. *US and Iranian Strategic Competition: Sanctions, Energy, Arms Control and Regime Change*. July 2013. csis.org/files/publication/130722_iransanctions.pdf.

The Economist. 'An Iranian Nuclear Bomb, or the Bombing of Iran?'. *The Economist*, 5 December 2009.

'Keeping it to Themselves'. *The Economist*, 31 March 2012.

'Breakout beckons'. *The Economist*, 22 June 2013.

Follath, Erich. 'The Iranians "Tricked and Misled Us"'. *Der Spiegel*, 6 October 2011.

Guznasky, Yoel. 'Beyond the Nuclear and Terror Threats'. *Strategic Assessment*, INSS, Vol. 13, No. 1. July 2010.

Hibbs, Mark. 'The IAEA and Syria: A New Paradigm for Noncompliance?', *Commentary, Carnegie Endowment for International Peace*, 17 June 2011. www.carnegieendowment.org/publications/index.cfm?fa=-view=44691=zgp=znpp.

International Atomic Energy Agency Board of Governors. *Implementation of the NPT Safeguards Agreement and the Relevant Provisions of Security Council Resolutions in the Islamic Republic of Iran*. Reports of 8 November 2011, 24 February 2012 and 25 May 2012.

International Institute for Strategic Studies. 'Nuclear Energy Expansion in the Middle East: Reactions to Iran?'. *IISS Strategic Comments*. Vol. 12, No. 9, 2006.

Nuclear Programmes in the Middle East. In the Shadow of Iran. London, IISS, 2008.

'Syria's Secret Reactor'. *IISS Strategic Comments*. Vol. 14, No. 5, 2008.

The Military Balance 2013. Abingdon, Routledge, 2013.

Kahl, Colin H. 'Not Time to Attack Iran: Why War Should be the Last Resort'. *Foreign Affairs*, Vol. 92, No. 1, March/April 2012.

Kroenig, Matthew. 'Time to Attack: Why a Strike is the Least Bad Option'. *Foreign Affairs*, Vol. 91, No. 1, January/February 2012.

Land, Thomas. 'Nuclear Reactors invade the Middle East'. *Middle East*, July 2007.

Landler, Mark, and Sanger, David E. 'Clinton Speaks of Shielding Mideast from Iran'. *New York Times*, 22 July 2009.

Lindsay, James M., and Takeyh, Ray. 'After Iran Gets the Bomb'. *Foreign Affairs,* Vol. 89, No. 2, March/April 2010.

Ophir, Noam. 'From Missouri to Natanz: US Global Strike Capability'. *Strategic Assessment*. Vol. 10, No. 1, Jaffee Center for Strategic Studies, 2007.

Russell, Richard L. 'A Saudi Nuclear Option?'. *Survival*. Vol. 43, No. 2, 2001.

Sanger, David E., and Broad, William J. 'Iran Remains Defiant, Nuclear Agency Says'. *New York Times*, 6 September 2010.

Shapir, Yiftah. 'The Saudi Arms Deal', *INSS Insight*, No. 200, 17 August 2010.

Smith, Pamela Ann. 'Nuclear Energy Gains Ground in Arab States'. *The Middle East,* June 2009.

Takeyh, Ray. 'Iran, Israel and the Politics of Terrorism'. *Survival*, Vol. 48, No. 4, 2006–07.

Tripp, Charles. *A History of Iraq*. Cambridge, Cambridge University Press, revised edn, 2002.

Ülgen, Sinan. 'Turkey, Iran and the Bomb'. *Carnegie Endowment for International Peace,* 26 March 2012. carnegieeurope.eu/publications/?fa=47646.

Warrick, Joby. 'UN Inspectors Find Traces of Uranium at Second Site in Syria'. *Washington Post*, 6 June 2009.

POLITICAL ISLAM

GEORGE JOFFÉ

INTRODUCTION

Since the late 1960s political Islam or Islamism—the application of Islamic principle and doctrine to political order—has become an increasingly important phenomenon within the Middle East and North Africa and in the wider Muslim world. More recently, too, it has been perceived by the non-Muslim world as a potential threat to the post-Cold War international order. There was, first, the 1979 Islamic revolution in Iran, closely followed by the anti-Soviet war in Afghanistan and then the events of 11 September 2001 in New York and Washington, DC, USA, together with the subsequent US-led invasion of Afghanistan. The latter events reminded Western states that they were no longer isolated, if indeed they ever were, from the travails of the predominantly Muslim countries, and that political Islam, whether violent or not, could increasingly influence their futures.

Western responses to this evolving global situation have been largely negative. Samuel Huntington, in 1993, seemed to have caught what was to become an increasingly prevalent mood when he argued that wars of the future would be between intrinsically antagonistic civilizations, rather than over ideology or resources. It was an argument that seemed to counter the optimism of the time, captured by Francis Fukuyama in 1989 when he claimed that history had ended in triumph for the Western capitalist system, as expressed politically through democracy and universal humanitarian values. Yet, it was not only Huntington who rejected Fukuyama's millennial optimism, for in the Muslim world too there was growing confidence about alternatives derived from Islam, which would, if need be, confront what that world perceived to be Western arrogance and triumphalism.

However, the unrest in the Arab world during early 2011 called into question the assumptions of both Islamists in the Middle East and North Africa and secularists in the West. Popular demands for radical change, when they came, were not Islamist in nature but were inspired by the much more familiar lineaments of individual political, social and economic rights. They were articulated, moreover, predominantly by the young, as regional demographics would have suggested. As the dust of revolution settled, however, Islamist movements, chastened no doubt by their own miscalculations, still emerged as the most likely inheritors of the new political dispensations that were to appear. They would not, however, be the sole beneficiaries, for they would have to share the new political arenas with non-religious political actors also claiming the right to exercise power. How, then, can we explain both Western and Middle Eastern miscalculations of the potency of political Islam and its persistence in becoming an undeniable element in the new political reality of the region?

REVIVALIST ISLAM

Miscalculation was, perhaps, merely a statement of overconfidence within the region and the power of perceptions of threat in the secular West in the aftermath of the events of 11 September 2001 and the consequent US-led 'war on terror'. Persistence, however, was another matter, for it reflected the complexity of indigenous tradition in which Islam provided cultural consonance. Over the centuries, this had generated alternative views of social and political order, alternatives that were to prove to be complex and manifold, reflecting the richness of intellectual and doctrinal traditions stretching back over almost 1,500 years to the beginnings of Islamic religion. When the Prophet Muhammad moved, with his close companions, from Mecca to Medina, in the *hijra* (the event that formally marks the beginning of the Islamic era), he fashioned the outlines of a political structure in an attempt to bring order to Medinan society and to its relations with its neighbours. Thus, given Islam's dominant public dimension, political issues have always been a major concern. Yet, it is not politics but society that has preoccupied Islamic philosophers and jurists, with the result that concepts of politics in Islam have been relatively elemental, compared with the richness of precepts about law and social order. It has only really been in the modern world that Islamic thinkers have addressed political issues. Political Islam, then, in attempting to address the problems of the contemporary world, is very much a product of late modernity.

The start of the modern era is usually dated in the Middle East to the Napoleonic invasion of Egypt in 1798 and in South Asia to the British victory at the Battle of Plassey in 1757. Prior to that, most political initiatives concerned with Islam in the Muslim world looked back to the supposedly ideal period of the Rashidun ('rightly guided') caliphates, as far as the Sunni world was concerned, in which sovereignty was a divine attribute that the caliph could only articulate if he preserved an Islamic social order and then only with the consent of the community. Of course, over the centuries, the issue of consent to rule and obligations of power were increasingly replaced by main force, but the ideal remained. For Shi'a Muslims, the political ideal was that inherited from the last Rashidun Caliph, Ali, as embodied in the martyrdom of his son, Hussain, and in the persons of his descendants. The 12th *imam*, Muhammad al-Mahdi, disappeared into 'occultation' in 941, to be recalled in future millennial glory, to reward his followers for their submission to authority, whether just or unjust, with a world of justice and prosperity. There, at least, the essential political ideal remained clear.

'Political Islam', in those circumstances, consisted in attempting to revive those ideals, saving Islam, as it were, both from secularism and from the slow corruption of doctrinal purity over time. There were the challenges of the neo-Platonist Mutazilite movement and rationalists such as Ibn Rushd and Ibn Sina, against whom al-Ghazzali raised the baton of faith. Then there were the 'corruptions' of popular religious belief, threatening to prioritize the worship of saints over the unicity of the Muslim ideal. There was also the challenge of Sufism, with its encouragement of mysticism and, alongside it, the group of the Islamic brotherhoods, the *tariqas*, through which such mysticism was expressed.

For the *ulama*, the religious specialists in law, doctrine and philosophy, all these developments that threatened the orthodox corpus were a constant preoccupation. Yet, they were compromised by their subservience to secular power and their willingness to support the state against those who questioned its legitimacy. For some, too, it was not a matter of disputation or debate but of action. Thus, the Assassins in the 12th century engaged in the intensely political activity of eliminating those they deemed to be politically and doctrinally beyond the canon. In the 18th century Wahhabism, a revivalist movement initiated by Muhammad ibn Abd al-Wahhab that was to become the official creed of Saudi Arabia (see the essay on The Religions of the Middle East and North Africa), wasted little time in imposing its vision of Islamic purity based around the principle of unicity and return to an ideal past.

It was this retrospective approach that the clash with European aggressiveness was to change profoundly, as the Islamic world came to grips with the need to formulate a political, rather than a predominantly social, project with which to confront colonialism. It was not just a question of colonial occupation, as it swept away old political orders, but also of the technology that accompanied it. Perhaps the most important example was the printing press, which, as Francis Robinson (see Select Bibliography) has suggested, ultimately destroyed the monopoly of the *ulama* over knowledge and doctrine in a predominantly illiterate society. Now the Koran and the whole corpus of literature associated with Islam would be accessible to all, as levels of literacy increased. The *ulama* lost, too, the monopoly over the interpretation of doctrine in this sudden democratization of religious belief and knowledge, in which anybody could now comment, not just those within the traditionally privileged caste of specialist interpreters.

THE EMERGENCE OF POLITICAL ISLAM

By the 1860s these issues had come to a head and Jamal al-Din al-Afghani initiated the first coherent response to them in what was to become known as the Salafiya movement. It too looked back to the ideal Islamic prototype but did so as a means of constructing a viable response to European technological superiority from within the Muslim cultural tradition. His lead was followed by Muhammad Abduh, formerly Mufti of Egypt, Muhammad Rashid Rida (see Select Bibliography) and Chakib Arslan. Rida, in particular, sought a revival of caliphal governance as the touchstone of political legitimacy, either by a caliph in person or by an enlightened élite capable of legislation consonant with Islamic precept and of popular consultation.

In India similar initiatives had been developed by Sir Sayyid Ahmed Khan, the founder of the Aligarh College, and by the poet and philosopher Muhammad Iqbal. In Turkey even earlier, the Young Ottoman movement had looked back to the *falsafa* tradition of Ibn Sina and Ibn Rushd—the rationalist successor movement to the Mutazilite movement that had been marginalized by al-Ghazzali in the 11th century—to find the inspiration to modernize Islamic culture and doctrine, and to challenge European dominance. Indeed, in the early part of the 20th century, the Salafiya had become the dominant political alternative to European modernity and its challenge to Muslim culture and belief, from south-east Asia to the Atlantic coast.

This was, of course, not the only political current spreading across the Middle East. The Young Ottoman movement was succeeded at the end of the 19th century by the Young Turk movement, which emphasized the nationalist Turkic dimension of the polyglot Ottoman Empire against the pan-Islam of Abdulhamid II who sought legitimacy by reviving the legacy of the Caliphate. However, Mustafa Kemal (Atatürk), as part of his project of constructing a secular, modern Turkey on the remains of empire after the First World War, abolished the Caliphate in 1924, thus ceding a valuable symbol to those who were to see in its revival a political vision of authentic legitimacy derived from Islamic tradition. In the Levant region, even earlier, the European emblem of nationalism was being refashioned into a cultural and linguistic expression of regional identity, Arab nationalism, while in Egypt a territorially based nationalism emerged as a localized challenge to the concept of the *umma*, the Islamic community of believers.

In short, the early form of political Islam, the Salafiya movement, was not unchallenged from within the Muslim world, having to face various secular, nationalist movements, albeit themselves often rooted in Islamic tradition even as they borrowed from European paradigms. There were also the political challenges of Europe itself, as the lineaments of the modern state, with all its political rhetoric and principle, were brought to the region by the colonial powers. It is this background that has given contemporary political Islam much of its sense of reacting to circumstance, of operating within a crowded ideological arena and of its awareness of the dual cultural and political threat that alternative political constructs seem, to it at least, to offer. In addition, threat and response has been a dominant theme of political Islam as it moved into a new world of Muslim nation states, as the 'Imperial moment' came to an end following the Second World War and as India achieved independence from the United Kingdom.

THE MUSLIM BROTHERHOOD

The key stage in the transformation of political Islam into the proliferation of movements currently in evidence was the creation of a political movement, the Muslim Brotherhood (al-Ikhwan al-Muslimun), in Ismailia, Egypt, in 1928. The most important feature of the new movement was not any departure in ideology or doctrine, for it was squarely rooted in the Salafi tradition. Rather, it was the simple fact that the Muslim Brotherhood was a political movement with a clear political objective: to revive Islamic society and values in Egypt against the perceived assault of 'Westernization' and modernity.

In short, the movement was dedicated to what Gilles Kepel (see Select Bibliography) described as 'Islam from below', capturing Egyptian society rather than its polity, although the latter, too, was its ultimate objective. In the fevered atmosphere of the 1930s, the movement also acquired a violent dimension: a secret organization, the Jihaz al-Khazz, dedicated to violent action to capture the political heights—Kepel's 'Islam from above'.

However, after a violent and largely clandestine clash with the authorities during the 1940s that cost the movement's founder, Hasan al-Banna, his life, the violent option was put to one side. Yet, it was not finally and definitively abandoned until the Government of Col Gamal Abd al-Nasir (Nasser) turned against the Muslim Brotherhood in the mid-1950s, accusing the movement of plotting against the state following an assassination attempt against Nasser in 1954. Its point was made with brutal finality in 1966 when one of the movement's most radical ideologues, Sayyid Qutb, was executed for allegedly threatening to overthrow the regime. Consequently, the Muslim Brotherhood, as an organized political movement, was divided between those among its adherents who believed that control of the polity was the primary objective and thus opted for violence, and the majority who declared that recovering society within the constraints imposed by the state was the only viable path.

There was a third consequence, too. Those who accepted the inevitability of a violent confrontation with the state had acquired a martyr. They had also acquired a doctrine of action: Sayyid Qutb left behind an immensely influential book, *Ma'alim fi'l-tariq* (*Milestones*—see Select Bibliography), which laid out an agenda for action and which drew on other, influential modernist thinkers over Islam's political role. He had been particularly influenced by the views of Abu'l 'Ala (Maulana) Maududi, the founder of Pakistan's oldest major political party, Jamaat-e-Islami, whose views had become available in Arabic in the 1950s. Maududi had insisted that the Islamic revival was not just a matter of recapturing the ideal past or defending the Islamic world through *jihad* for the protection of 'Dar al-Islam' ('house of Islam'); unbelief and ignorance (*jahiliyya*) existed in the contemporary world, even in the Muslim world, and countering this, in itself, was the real meaning of *jihad*, whether at the level of government or at the level of society. Qutb argued that such *jihad* should be the duty of organized movements directed towards creating Islamic governance (*hukumiyya*), including through violence, if necessary.

This defined a clear political project, in contradistinction to the social project of the Muslim Brotherhood, now in retreat owing to repression by the Egyptian Government. However, in addition to abandoning the option of violence, the movement had also moved abroad, creating parallel organizations throughout the Muslim world, from Indonesia to Saudi Arabia. In some countries it faced state repression; elsewhere it was tolerated and even welcomed, as in Saudi Arabia. There the welcome given to the Muslim Brotherhood's exiled intellectuals (including Sayyid Qutb's brother, Muhammad, and the future Islamist activist in Pakistan during the war in Afghanistan against the Soviet Union, Abdullah Azzam) brought the Salafi ideals of the Brotherhood into contact with the rigorous unicity of revivalist Wahhabism, the dominant Islamic sect in the Kingdom.

Out of this environment was to arise yet another political vision, encouraged by leading religious thinkers in the Kingdom: that of the Salafist or neo-Salafist movement. This movement, championed by Saudi Arabia's leading Muslim intellectual, Sheikh Abd al-Aziz bin Baz, argued that a truly Islamic society was one dedicated to literally reviving the world and dicta of the Prophet and eschewing political power—a project similar to, but distinct from, Wahhabism itself. Creating such a world could also be considered an intensely political project, despite its claimed indifference to power, so the movement soon proliferated into more activist and political offshoots. In its original form it is an increasingly popular option throughout the present-day Sunni Muslim world. In its more activist versions, combining modernist views of *jihad* with its intense monotheism and doctrinal literalism, it has become the inspiration for violent challenges to established political order. It and the Muslim Brotherhood are paralleled, perhaps, by the Tabligh Jamaat movement, which originated in India in 1926 and seeks a similar pacific re-Islamization of Muslim society world-wide.

THE SHI'A ALTERNATIVE

In the Shi'a world, meanwhile, political Islam had been following a different trajectory, owing partly to doctrinal difference and partly to a different religious history from the Sunni world. Islam had been important within the politics of the state ever since *Ithna'ashara* Shi'ism (see essay on The Religions of the Middle East and North Africa)—the dominant branch of Shi'a theology, which believes that there had been 12 *imams* before the occultation of Muhammad al-Mahdi (see above)—had been adopted by the ruling Safavid dynasty as the official religion of Persia in 1501. This had reversed the traditional pattern of Shi'ism as the religion of the oppressed, who had previously meekly submitted to the autonomous authority of the state while awaiting the return of the 12th *imam*, to revive the fortunes of its adherents. Now the Shi'a religious hierarchy itself was an integral part of the state, although Shi'a divines still maintained a lofty indifference to the actual manipulation of political power. It was only at the beginning of the 20th century that this reality abruptly changed.

The change was forced by the decline in power of the Qajar dynasty, in the face of European and Russian imperial pressure, compounded by the fact that, unlike the preceding Safavid dynasty, it lacked the religious legitimacy of descent from the Prophet. As part of its attempts to reverse the collapse in the financial structure of the state, the Government offered significant concessions to foreign companies to exploit Iran's natural resources, including its reserves of petroleum. Popular reaction to the decision was hostile, and public protests, backed by a significant section of the Shi'a religious hierarchy, culminated in a demand for a constitution designed to limit the Shah's powers. The Shah eventually conceded this demand but was able to withdraw the concession shortly afterwards when another section of the hierarchy opposed it. In other words, the Shi'a hierarchy could now exercise a significant influence over Iran's political life even if, in the end, it decided to return to its traditional indifference. Moreover, it could legitimize popular protest or delegitimize it, as it wished.

It was a lesson that was to come into its own after the US- and British-backed coup against the nationalist Government of Dr Muhammad Musaddeq in 1953. The coup was designed to reverse the effects of the Government's decision, three years previously, to nationalize the Iranian oil industry. It also sought to restore the Shah, Muhammad Reza, to power after he had left the country following disputes with the Government. In the wake of the coup, which reflected the eclipse of British influence in Iran and its replacement by the USA, a segment of the Shi'a hierarchy reacted by protesting against the Shah's pro-US policies and development agenda. This opposition eventually coalesced around a young cleric based in the city of Qom, Ruhollah Khomeini. In November 1964 Ayatollah Khomeini was exiled from Iran, first to Turkey and then to the traditional heartland of Shi'a Islam and burial-place of the Caliph Ali, in Najaf, Iraq.

During his lengthy exile in Najaf and, later, Paris, France, Khomeini was to consider what the processes of governance should be in a state operating in accordance with Islamic principle. His subsequent ideas, collected in a series of lectures entitled '*Hukumat-e Islami*' (Islamic government), culminated in the concept that governance within an Islamic state should be sanctioned, in the absence of the 'occulted' *imam*, by a supreme jurisconsult (*velayat-e faqih*), who would ensure that governance was conducted in accordance with Islamic principles. In effect, Ayatollah Khomeini abandoned the quietist tradition of Shi'a Islam for religious control of governance. It was a principle that echoed Rida's concept of an enlightened élite acting on behalf of the caliph and a development that led the anthropologist and philosopher Ernest Gellner (see Select Bibliography, below) to suggest that Ayatollah Khomeini's vision brought Shi'a and Sunni Islam closer together, at least in terms of political praxis.

Rida, however, had grounded his vision within popular consent and the same concern was to subsequently permeate Ayatollah Khomeini's vision in practice. The response to this came from a sociologist, Ali Shariati, who in the 1960s sought to reconcile Shi'a traditions of submission to authority and discrimination with Marxist concepts of class division and exploitation, as well as Frantz Fanon's and Albert Camus's views of the colonial situation. For Shariati, the eternal Shi'a dialectic between the oppressor and oppressed paralleled the Marxist class struggle between bourgeoisie and proletariat. While Shariati's views mobilized students, Ayatollah Khomeini gained the support of the middle classes and the all-important merchants, or *bazaari*.

The result was that the outcome of the Islamic revolution was to produce a new Constitution for Iran that reflected both of its leading tendencies—clerical conservatism and populist radicalism. The Constitution also reflected the theocratic hierarchy implicit in Ayatollah Khomeini's concept of the *velayat-e faqih* and the idea of popular participation through an electoral process. There were to be presidential elections and elections for the Majlis-e-Shura-e Islami (Islamic Consultative Assembly), although both candidates for the Majlis and the decisions it made were vetted by an appointed council, the Shura-e Nigahban (Council of Guardians). Indeed, this ambivalence in Iran's new constitutional arrangements was to be repeated throughout the structures of the new state, in the courts, the security forces and even in the role of *Shari'a* (Islamic religious law)—in 1988 Khomeini decreed that the interests of the state could override *Shari'a* in instances of conflict between the two, since they could never be in contradiction to the true essence of religious law.

Iran, therefore, only represented a partial Islamic state and one dominated by Shi'a Islam at that, but the Iranian example in 1979 was to have a powerful influence throughout the Sunni world as well, in that it demonstrated the potential of Islam as a political force in challenging government. Just as the result of the Six Day War in 1967 had damaged the concept of Arab nationalism, setting the scene for the growth of political Islam, so the Iranian revolution demonstrated political Islam's potential, whether Sunni or Shi'a in inspiration, and encouraged its adherents throughout the region. It also coincided with two other vitally important events, the Soviet invasion of Afghanistan in 1979 and the assassination in 1981 of President Anwar Sadat in Egypt. Both events gave a major impetus to those groups committed to violent solutions to the problems of governance in the Middle East, encouraging their subsequent proliferation throughout the region.

ISLAMIST VIOLENCE IN EGYPT

This escalation into violent confrontation had begun a few years earlier with the emergence in Egypt of a proliferation of small groups opposed to the state. Some were formalized; many were not, creating a variegated tendency within the population committed to violent action to overthrow the state on grounds legitimized by reference to political Islam, either as described by Sayyid Qutb, or as proposed by other thinkers. One such was Muhammad Farraj, who argued that *jihad* was the sixth obligation of Muslims, an obligation that was, however, largely ignored in the contemporary world, hence the title of his best-known publication, *al-Farida al-Ghaiba* (*The Neglected Duty*—see Select Bibliography), and that he wished to restore. Alongside these appeared more formal movements, including Hizb ut-Tahrir al-Islami (the Islamic Liberation Party), which had been founded in Beirut in 1952 by a Palestinian and which sought to restore the caliphate; Takfir wal-Hijra (Excommunication and Exodus), created in 1977 by Mustapha Shukri; and Tanzim al-Jihad (the Jihad Organization).

The advent of political violence in Egypt, however, can be dated to 1974, when a group linked to the Hizb ut-Tahrir al-Islami attempted to mount a coup in Cairo by attacking the Egyptian Military Academy in Heliopolis. The attempt did not succeed but marked the beginning of a 'third wave' of violent political Islam in Egypt, after the initial bout inspired by the Muslim Brotherhood in the 1940s and the later wave of violence against Nasser after he came to power in 1954. Over the next four years, as President Sadat pursued the aim of peace with Israel, extremist opposition to his initiative mounted and coalesced. Thus, Takfir wal-Hijra, a group that sought both intellectually and morally to distance itself from society and to blend with it by dissembling the appearances, beliefs and objectives of its members, kidnapped and killed a former Minister of Awqaf (religious endowments), Muhammad al-Dhahabi, in 1978, leading to the execution of the group's founder, Mustapha Shukri.

Tanzim al-Jihad was to be involved in the assassination of President Sadat in October 1981 and in a failed parallel uprising in the Upper Egyptian provincial centre of Asyout. Both enterprises had been sanctioned by a radical religious leader, Sheikh Omar Abd al-Rahman. Muhammad Farraj was one of four men executed along with the assassin, Lt Khalid Islambouli, in April the following year. In the wake of the assassination, Tanzim al-Jihad split into two new movements; Islamic Jihad and the Gama'ah al-Islamiyah. The former regarded itself as the vanguard party of an Islamic revolution in Egypt; the latter first directed its attention towards the creation of a mass organization of Islamic protest against government policy, particularly in the universities, before turning to clandestine violence in 1992. Concurrently, the leader of Islamic Jihad, Ayman al-Zawahiri, left Egypt for Afghanistan, where he became integrated into a new movement, al-Qa'ida.

The violent Islamist challenge to the Egyptian Government, organized by the Gama'ah al-Islamiyah and Islamic Jihad, culminated in the November 1997 massacre near Luxor, in which 70 people, including 58 tourists, were killed. The incident destroyed both Egypt's tourist industry and the last remnants of public support for the extremist Islamist campaign. As a result, a final split took place between the imprisoned leadership of Gama'ah al-Islamiyah and Islamic Jihad's exiled leaders in Afghanistan, with the former renouncing violence and even unsuccessfully seeking acceptance as a formal political party. Islamic Jihad, meanwhile, turned its attention to the wider objective of a global struggle until, a decade later, its leading theoretician, Sayyid Imam al-Sharif (al-Fadl), rejected violence in favour of advocacy as well, to the consternation of the movement's leadership, now confined to Afghanistan. Violent political Islam in Egypt, meanwhile, was increasingly marginalized, although attacks have continued, in particular targeting Israelis and other foreign tourists in Sinai.

Popular attention has turned, instead, to the Muslim Brotherhood, which, despite being formally outlawed, successfully contested parliamentary elections, with its candidates standing as independents. At the 2005 parliamentary elections, independent candidates affiliated to the Muslim Brotherhood won 88 seats, making it, in effect, the second largest group in the People's Assembly, after the ruling National Democratic Party. The Government, however, continued to disrupt the Muslim Brotherhood, denying it legal standing and regularly arresting its leadership, while accusing it of involvement in acts of political violence. The Muslim Brotherhood's popularity, however, was bolstered by its ability to respond to social need far faster than the state and to reflect the cultural instincts of Egyptian society at large. Apart from the regime, the only threat to its social hegemony was Salafism, which seemed resolutely non-political in nature and was therefore largely ignored by officialdom.

THE LESSONS OF 2011

Behind this apparent political dominance, though, lay a conundrum that was to be deconstructed at the start of 2011, for it was notable that the Muslim Brotherhood, apparently Egypt's most coherent and powerful opposition movement, took no formal part in the events that led to the overthrow of the Egyptian regime headed by President Hosni Mubarak. Indeed, the demands voiced by the demonstrators, including supporters of the 25 January Movement and its component parts—the Movement for Change, popularly known as Kefaya (Enough), the Al-Ghad (Tomorrow) Party, the 6 April Youth Movement in the Delta and the Khalid Muhammad Said movement in Alexandria—and the vast mass of independent protesters who filled Tahrir Square in Cairo and other Egyptian cities, bore little evidence of an overt commitment to the principles of political Islam beyond a constant demand for social justice and the restoration of a popular sense of dignity and individual rights. Egypt's Islamist movements, led by the Muslim Brotherhood, seemed to have been marginalized during the popular uprising that resulted in the removal of the Mubarak regime from power. However, this alleged marginalization was contested by some observers, who claimed that elements of the Muslim Brotherhood had secretly collaborated in organizing the mass demonstrations after Friday prayers on 28 January, which ultimately gave the protest movement the momentum to overthrow the Mubarak regime.

Similarly, in Tunisia, the country's own Islamist movement, dominated by Hizb al-Nahdah, played virtually no part in the revolution that toppled the regime of Zine al-Abidine Ben Ali in mid-January 2011. Admittedly, it would have been surprising if Islamists had played a major role, since all such movements, particularly al-Nahdah, had been repressed throughout the previous two decades. Yet, it was notable that the demonstrators did not press for the typical demands of the Islamist movements, seeking democratic outcomes instead. In Libya, Islamists, whether moderates or extremists, had been brutally suppressed for decades, so they were unable to take a leading role in the initial insurgency, and, in Syria, the Muslim Brotherhood had been exiled since 1982 and had been unable to spread its message inside the country. In any case, once again, demonstrators sought to replace the regimes under attack with democratic alternatives. In all cases, none the less, organized Islamist movements played little formal part in the initial surge of revolutionary protest.

These events raise important questions about the assumptions of Islamist movements over their relevance in both cultural and religious terms to the political crises that the region confronts. A distinction should, perhaps, be made between political Islam as an intellectual or ideological current and organized political Islam within a social movement. It is true that the latter failed to play a part in the initial insurgencies and that the role of the former was overshadowed by the essentialist and immediate demands of the demonstrators. However, once the first objectives—of overthrowing regimes and demanding basic rights—were achieved, the political discourses that ensued were far more complex and sophisticated, and in these political Islam found its place. Within days, it became evident, both in Tunisia and in Egypt, that the largest and best organized movements to emerge in the wake of regime removal were, in fact, Islamist movements—the Muslim Brotherhood in Egypt and al-Nahdah in Tunisia.

In the subsequent evolution of the political process, Islamism became a major force in the establishment of new regimes. Thus, in Morocco, the approval of a new Constitution in July 2011 enabled the election of a new Government dominated by an Islamist party, while in Tunisia the overthrow of the Ben Ali regime created a power vacuum that was eventually filled by a coalition also headed by an Islamist movement. In Egypt two Islamist parties—the Muslim Brotherhood's Freedom and Justice Party and the Salafist al-Nour Party—secured the largest and second-largest number of seats at legislative elections held in November 2011–January 2012. Although the results of those elections were annulled, Egyptian voters elected Muhammad Mursi of the Muslim Brotherhood as President in June. Only in Libya have elections produced a legislature in which Islamists do not dominate, while in Algeria the electoral process was subverted to marginalize them.

The Egyptian experience, furthermore, should not be viewed simply as an isolated national response to the peace treaty with Israel, for example, or as an outcome of popular frustration with economic disparity and poverty, important though these factors undoubtedly were. The Islamist parties attracted widespread support, partly because they possessed a cultural authenticity and legitimacy that, in contrast to other parties, had not been besmirched by compromises with autocratic regimes or by political or personal corruption. They also often had far more efficient party organizations, frequently honed by their use in providing popular social services, which made them immediately more relevant to populations enjoying democratic choice for the first time.

Although political Islam could be regarded as an attempt to find an alternative, efficient and culturally acceptable political solution to the failure of Arab nationalism and Western politico-economic ideas, it also has to be seen in terms of events in the wider region. One such event was the 1979 Islamic revolution in Iran, as discussed above. The other was the experience, from 1979 until the early 1990s, of the war against the Soviet Union in Afghanistan, which allowed far more extreme interpretations of the Islamist message to flourish.

AFGHANISTAN AND SALAFI-JIHADISM

The conflict in Afghanistan was initiated by the radical measures of social reform espoused by the Afghan Government and popular reaction to it. A short-lived rebellion broke out in 1975 in the Panshir valley but was quickly subordinated. In 1978, however, a much more serious rebellion occurred in Nuristan province, close to the border with Pakistan, and, within one year, 24 of Afghanistan's 28 provinces were in revolt. This was the situation in which the Soviet Union decided to intervene by replacing the Government and confronting the rebellion. The USA, in turn, saw an opportunity to catch its Cold War rival off-balance. It did so by offering finance, arms and training over the next decade to the armed groups opposed to the Soviet presence, led by seven different parties among the massive Afghani diaspora in Pakistan, through Saudi Arabia as intermediary and with Saudi financial help. As part of this initiative, Saudi Arabia also organized the recruitment of up to 40,000 Arab militants across the Middle East and North Africa, using its networks of contacts with mosques and radical Islamists in the region.

The *mujahidin* was in fact made up of a series of constantly warring factions, even as it was successfully confronting Soviet forces. Two major groups emerged, one more radical and the other gradualist but both dedicated to creating an Islamic state in Afghanistan. The radical movement, the Hizb-e Islami of Gulbuddin Hekmatyar, was heavily supported by Pakistan, backed also by Saudi Arabia and the USA. The other, more gradualist group, the Jamiat-i Islami led by Burhanuddin Rabbani, also received some support from those three countries, but relied predominantly on its traditional support among the conservative tribal leaders who had been displaced by the Afghani Government and its Soviet supporters, and wished to restore traditional Islamic governance to the country. A third group, which had started the 1975 rebellion and was now led by Ahmad Shah Masoud, attempted to balance between the two heavyweights, even after the Soviet Union withdrew from the country in 1989 and a civil war between the major Afghani factions broke out, which lasted throughout the first half of the 1990s. The other four factions were essentially secular in nature, except for the Hizb-e Wahdat, which represented the largely Shi'a Hezara and was supported by Iran.

Two aspects of this complex story are relevant to the development of political Islam. The first is the various political agendas of the leading groups in contention and the second is the outcome of foreign intervention in the Afghan conflict, for this was to define the next stage of extremist political Islam and one that essentially defines contemporary Islamist extremism. Olivier Roy (see Select Bibliography) defined the typology of the Islamist groups in Pakistan as traditionalist, fundamentalist or neo-fundamentalist, and—rather confusingly—Islamist. The first of these corresponds to the agenda of tribal leaderships in Afghanistan who were most directly affected by the policies of Afghanistan's radical governments and the Soviet approach to the country. It was perhaps this agenda that best represented the objectives of Ahmad Shah Masoud. The second, still essentially conservative in approach, although in its neo-fundamentalist version as subsequently adopted by the Taliban, powerfully coercive as well, reflects the interests of traditional and conservative Afghan society, as expressed by Rabbani's movement. Gulbuddin Hekmatyar, however, created a radical political machine, as a vanguard party to force through an extreme Islamist agenda and, as such, mirrored Roy's category of 'Islamist' very effectively, with a Salafist, quasi-Wahhabi agenda. It was this agenda that was to be adopted by those Arabs who rallied to the Afghan cause.

Yet, the complexity of Islam in Afghanistan cannot be properly understood if the role of external actors is not included as well. The US position was clear: the USA simply wished to disadvantage the Soviet Union as much as possible and little thought appeared to have been given to the wider implications of the political movements it was fostering. Saudi Arabia had similar objectives, although as an Islamic state itself, it had clear preferences regarding which groups it would encourage. Hekmatyar's group thus also received the bulk of Saudi funding. Pakistan, however, quite apart from the austere ideological agenda of the Government of Gen. Mohammad Zia ul-Haq, also had a geo-strategic agenda. This was to acquire alliances in the region as a defence against the possibility of invasion by India. This, over time, has also become an ideological commitment for certain elements in Pakistan, resulting in tacit support for the Taliban—a Pashtun-patronized, Sunni neo-fundamentalist group inspired by the Deobandi reformist movement—after their victory in Afghanistan in 1996 and following the USA's destruction of the Taliban regime in 2001.

The phenomenon in which these two tendencies came together with baleful effect was that of the *mujahidin* recruited to fight in Afghanistan. Recruitment took place at an unofficial and a semi-official level throughout the Middle East, with mosques as focal points. Popular radical preachers encouraged *jihad* in Afghanistan as a religious duty and popular anger at failures of governance and poverty was easily redirected against the Soviet Union and its invasion of Afghanistan. One such figure was the spiritual leader of Gama'ah al-Islamiyah, Sheikh Omar Abd al-Rahman, who had narrowly avoided punishment for his involvement in the assassination of President Sadat and was later imprisoned in the USA for his role in the 1993 World Trade Center bombing in New York.

The training and indoctrination of the constant stream of recruits was taken in hand in a series of reception centres in Western Pakistan, around Peshawar and in Afghanistan itself. Some of those in charge became major intellectual figures of radical Islamism as well, chief among them a Palestinian who had studied in Egypt, Jordan and Saudi Arabia, Abdullah Azzam. He organized one of the main reception centres for Arab fighters in Peshawar, Afghanistan—the Maktab al-Khidmat—in 1984, with help from a former student of his from Saudi Arabia, Osama bin Laden. In two famous *fatwas*, entitled 'In Defence of Muslim Lands' and 'Follow the Caravan', Azzam modified an orthodox argument about the role of classical *jihad* into an ideology of resistance in the context of Afghanistan. 'Defensive *jihad*', Azzam contended, was a personal obligation of all Muslims in circumstances, such as the Soviet invasion of Afghanistan, which threatened the integrity of the Muslim world. Thus, he prepared the way for 'salafi-jihadism', first as an ideology of resistance and ultimately as a justification for terrorism.

In 1989 Azzam and his two sons were killed in a bomb explosion in Peshawar; their assailants were unknown, although it was reported that Azzam had disagreed with a recent arrival there, Ayman al-Zawahiri. Azzam had wanted to organize a new *jihad* in the Palestinian territories, while al-Zawahiri and his supporters intended to target the Mubarak regime in Egypt. Azzam also disputed the extremist view among the Egyptian's supporters that regarded all Muslims and Muslim governments opposed to their views as apostates. In the aftermath of Abdullah Azzam's death, the Maktab al-Khidmat was taken over formally by Osama bin Laden, who had been involved in a dispute with Azzam the year before over whether Arab *mujahidin* should be integrated with their Afghani counterparts or, as bin Laden believed, formed into a separate fighting force. He had, therefore, created a new organization called al-Qa'ida for this purpose. By now, however, it was clear that the war in Afghanistan was over and, during the next two years, Pakistan—under pressure from the US Administration—began to force the Arab *mujahidin* there to leave. The USA had, by that time, begun to realize the potential danger these Arab militants might eventually represent and many of them were arrested upon returning to their home countries.

Despite these beginnings of an over-arching ideology of universalized defensive *jihad*, the radical Arab Islamist movement created through the war in Afghanistan was by no means a unified entity. Most of the groups concerned still had predominantly national agendas; they wished, as Sayyid Qutb had suggested, to deal with *takfiri* national governments. (For example, the Libyan Islamic Fighting Group embarked upon an unsuccessful campaign against the regime of Muammar al-Qaddafi in the late 1990s.) A much smaller minority was concerned with the new, wider agenda for *jihad*, directed against the West. An even smaller minority, at the end of the 1990s, was to develop the next stage of the radical Islamist agenda, globalized terrorism, as justified by salafi-jihadism.

AL-QA'IDA AND THE GLOBAL BRAND

Although the US security services claim to have identified the first evidence of al-Qa'ida's global ambitions as early as 1990, the organization's activities seem to have been very restrained until the end of the decade. Bin Laden himself returned to Saudi Arabia in 1990 and was strongly opposed to Saudi reliance on Western forces to expel Iraq from Kuwait after the Iraqi invasion there in the August of that year, especially after his offer to recruit Arab *mujahidin* in their place was declined by the Saudi authorities. His increasingly virulent attacks on the Saudi royal family led to his expulsion to Sudan in 1992 and to his loss of Saudi citizenship, as well as his personal fortune, two years later. In 1996, however, bin Laden was forced to leave Sudan, following an assassination attempt against President Mubarak in the Ethiopian capital, Addis Ababa, the previous year in which he was believed to have collaborated with Islamic Jihad. He subsequently returned to Afghanistan, going to Jalalabad, which was by then under the control of the Taliban, led by Mullah Muhammad Omar.

Although bin Laden's personal wealth had been severely curtailed by Saudi government action, his al-Qa'ida organization had been strengthened during the intervening years by its ever-closer links to the Egyptian Islamic Jihad movement and had recovered its financial strength through private donations from the Gulf. The movement had extended Abdullah Azzam's theory of defensive *jihad* as an individual obligation on all Muslims—reminiscent of Muhammad Farraj's contention of the 'neglected obligation'—into a much wider vision. Although, in this new theory, *jihad* was still regarded as a defensive measure, it could also be pre-emptive, a view that was to become a fateful mirror-image of the neo-conservative argument over pre-emptive attack as a legitimate mechanism to ensure national security. Furthermore, the loss of innocent life in such action was no longer seen as a sin but as an unfortunate by-product of a necessary action sanctioned by doctrine. Finally, the 'enemies' of Muslims were clearly identified; in February 1998 bin Laden, in the name of al-Qa'ida, and al-Zawahiri, on behalf of Islamic Jihad, together with four other extremist organizations, issued a *fatwa* identifying 'Crusaders and Jews' as their targets of *jihad*. This followed an earlier decree in 1996, in which bin Laden had threatened the USA alone.

Despite evidence that Osama bin Laden had helped to finance acts of violence up to this time, there had been no unambiguous acts of violence that could be attributed to his organization. However, the February 1998 *fatwa* was followed in August by the bombings of the US embassies in Nairobi, Kenya, and Dar es-Salaam, Tanzania. Then, in January 2000 a suicide bomb attack on a US destroyer, the USS *Cole*, in Aden, Yemen, claimed the lives of 17 US naval personnel. On 11 September 2001 two airliners were seized and flown into the World Trade Center in New York, resulting in the deaths of more than 2,600 people and the destruction of the two towers that comprised the building; another aircraft severely damaged the Pentagon building in Arlington, Virginia, killing 125 people; and a fourth plane, apparently intended for the White House in Washington, DC, crashed in Pennsylvania after the passengers attempted to subdue the group that had hijacked it; a total of 256 people were killed on the four hijacked planes. A month later, the USA, in conjunction with non-Taliban groups in Afghanistan, attacked the Taliban administration there on the grounds that it was allied with al-Qa'ida and had harboured the organization's leadership and hosted its activities.

Although the military victory was rapid, neither the al-Qa'ida leadership nor that of the Taliban was totally dismantled and, although subsequent action severely degraded al-Qa'ida's ability to operate as a cohesive group, particularly after bin Laden was killed by US special forces in the Pakistani garrison town of Abbottabad on 2 May 2011, its ideology has remained intact. Despite its apparent marginalization, the group, now led by Ayman al-Zawahiri, has become what could be termed a global 'brand' for violent movements opposed to the West world-wide, from Indonesia to Europe and the USA itself, as other groups, whether concerned with a national or a global agenda, lay claim to its justification for violence. To a very large extent, the continued vitality of its agenda reflects the growing gulf between Western policy objectives in the Middle East and other Muslim regions and the immense resentment they cause in the Muslim world itself and among minority communities outside it. It also reflects Muslim disgust at the, often pro-Western, activities of autocratic governments within the region. It has been this sentiment that has driven the replication of salafi-jihadi violence during national struggles, as in Iraq or, more recently, in Syria, for instance. The perpetrators of such violence often lay claim to the al-Qa'ida 'brand', or are seen by Western observers to be testament to its continuing vitality, although their activities are confined to the Middle East and North Africa. Indeed, it should always be remembered that violent Islamist extremism is a small and marginalized strand within the overall movement of political Islam, and that those engaged in political violence represent, numerically, an insignificant part of this strand.

DEMOCRATIC EXPERIENCES

One of the consequences of the 'Arab spring' was, initially at least, to push extremist political Islam to the margins of the new Arab political experiences. As mentioned above, even though political Islamic movements had played little part—at least as organized movements—in the actual revolutions themselves, they were certainly to benefit from the early experiments in democratic elections, in Tunisia, Morocco and, particularly, in Egypt. Thus Islamist-dominated Governments came to power at the heads of coalitions in Tunisia and Morocco, while in Egypt, even though legislative elections were partially aborted because the courts decided they were unconstitutional (only the upper chamber of the bicameral legislature was declared properly elected), a presidential election in mid-2012 brought an Islamist candidate to power. North Africa, in short, was to become the laboratory in which Islamists could prove that they understood and accepted the rules of democratic governance—Syria and the Levant region continue to reflect a regional security collapse which is only marginally related to the issue of Islam within the sphere of practical politics.

The outcomes of these experiments have been mixed, to say the least, although it is still not clear whether this is a consequence of ideological clashes or administrative inefficiencies and incompetence. The situation has also been complicated by two other factors: a growth in the activities of extremist organizations, occasioned partly by the continuing lack of security throughout the North African region, particularly in Libya; and a concomitant challenge to moderate political Islam by the entry of Salafist movements into the political arena since the 'Arab spring' began. This has meant that moderate political Islam has not only been challenged in terms of political management by its secularist opponents but it has also had to accommodate an ideological challenge to fundamental doctrinal principle.

The key experience has been Egypt where the Muslim Brotherhood and the political party that it created, the Freedom and Justice Party demonstrated comprehensively that neither organization had really understood the nature of democratic politics. Rather than trying to create a consensus within the disparate Egyptian political scene, the Mursi Government seems to have assumed that its electoral victory, in itself, entitled it to ignore the views of the opposition forces ranged against it, in practising a kind of democratic dictatorship. As a result, it proceeded to impose an Islamist template on Egyptian society irrespective of public attitudes toward such a project. It compounded its errors by gross incompetence, particularly in the economic field, relying on Gulf support, notably from Qatar, to ensure survival.

Within a year it had united the opposition against it and persuaded the army that it could no longer effectively govern the country. As the opposition Tamarrud movement's 22m.-

strong petition, demanding a recall of the President, gathered pace, the army command gave the presidency an ultimatum, that it would intervene if the complaints of the opposition were not addressed. The Mursi presidency, relying on its formal electoral legitimacy, ignored the army's demands, provoking what was, in effect, a coup on 3 July 2013, even if the army's actions themselves were legitimized by popular demand.

The Brotherhood, outraged at the rupture of the power rendered to it by the electoral process, has rejected all compromise that would allow it to play a formal role in the new political system that the army will develop. The Tamarrud opposition, equally outraged by the Brotherhood's inability to compromise, will likely result in the movement being marginalized in the new Egypt that will now emerge. The irony is, of course, that the army that was discredited by its early attempts to manage the Egyptian political scene in 2011 and 2012 is now the essential institution through which the errors of the past may be corrected, thus underlining its saliency to Egypt's political life.

The failure of the Brotherhood's governance in Egypt says more, perhaps, about its habits as an organization than it does about its own political vision. It was its inability to understand that the democratic process requires consensus-building and compromise to succeed, rather than uncompromising majority rule, that determined its downfall. That inability was reinforced by a belief in the need for it to control state institutions, irrespective of popular apprehensions over its intentions. The movement also dramatically under-estimated the anxieties that its electoral success stimulated elsewhere—it was notable that Saudi Arabia, the United Arab Emirates and Kuwait (all hostile to the Brotherhood) were able to fund the new Egyptian Government with grants and loans worth US $12,000m. within days of it being established. Even Qatar, the Brotherhood's mentor in power, now seems to have cooled towards it.

The Brotherhood's failure in Egypt seems to have marked a change in attitudes towards moderate political Islam in power. It was notable, for instance, that a key coalition partner in the majority Islamist Government in Morocco ended its participation in the ruling coalition—apparently with the approval of the King—at the same time. In Tunisia, despite governmental outrage at the military coup in Egypt, there was a general recognition that the Brotherhood had encompassed its own downfall by its political ineptitude. Even in Turkey, the Government of Prime Minister Recep Tayyip Erdoğan encountered severe problems over its intransigent rejection of popular opposition to its attempts to restrain social freedoms. Yet, at the same time this failure also encouraged a widespread view that, to quote a Brotherhood spokesman, 'Democracy is not for Muslims', a sentiment that raised the spectre of extremist violence in future, rather than the slow, patient construction of the 'habits of hearts and minds' that eventually make democratic governance possible.

Indeed, the threat is dual—of violence in the face of perceptions of the absence of democratic options and of radical challenge in terms of the ideological objectives of governance. It is interesting to note that the Muslim Brotherhood in Egypt abandoned the violent option over 40 years ago and, as described above, other Islamist organizations came to similar conclusions during the last 20 years. Despite their frustrations now, it is unlikely that the Brotherhood or its associated organizations will formally abandon their commitment to peaceful protest for, were they to do so, they would invite the Egyptian state to force them underground. However, over the past three years, partly because of a change in the nature of Salafi-jihadism, which now emphasizes its social competence far more that its political ambitions, and partly because of the collapse of security in Libya and throughout the Sahara and the Sahel, other organizations are well-entrenched that could easily take up the baton of violence.

Moderate Islamists now in power are well-aware of the danger and have been forced to accept that they must confront such movements as security threats, rather than to seek to woo them towards moderation as ideological partners—the policy that was initially adopted in Tunisia and Egypt, for example. They still consider that such policies of accommodation are appropriate for Salafists who renounce violence, even if they have now embraced political action, to the disgust of secularists in the Middle East and North Africa. It remains to be seen if, in reality, accommodation and plurality will be possible within the increasingly complex moderate scene, given its recent setbacks, but it does seem certain that a fundamental split has opened between moderates and extremists.

There is one event in the Levant that, however, stands in clear contradistinction to what has been said above about moderate and extremist political Islam. This is the expanding crisis in Syria, which has now reached the status of a civil war and threatens the security of surrounding states, such as Lebanon, Jordan, Iraq and, to a lesser extent, Israel and Turkey. There the dominant role in the struggle against the Assad regime is being increasingly adopted by the al-Nusra Front, a Sunni extremist organization closely linked to al-Qa'ida in Iraq. In Syria, it confronts the moderate Syrian Muslim Brotherhood within the National Coalition for Syrian Revolutionary and Opposition Forces, together with the Free Syrian Army, as well as the pro-Syrian forces of Lebanon's Hezbollah and Iran's Islamic Revolutionary Guards. The latter confrontation also highlights a new and frightening sectarian split within the Levant and the Gulf, between Sunni and Shi'a extremists, which has acquired a new geo-political dimension, pitting the Sunni Arab Gulf states against Iran, Iraq, Syria and Hezbollah in Lebanon.

OUTCOMES

In other words, the events of the past two years have made the mosaic of political Islam in the Middle East and North Africa far more complex than it was at the beginning of the 'Arab spring' in 2011. It has also resulted in the discrediting of Iran as the successful model of Islam-in-power, because of its engagement in Syria and its status as a Shi'a state—a revival of a 14-century-old doctrinal clash. Yet, it is a movement that is still dominated by moderates seeking to find viable solutions to the problems of governance thrown up by the radical and profound changes in the region. Indeed, although extremist groups and actions attract international attention, those reports provide a profoundly misleading image of political Islam, being typical only of a small minority. By far the largest part of this generalized and extremely complex movement is not concerned with seeking to destroy either national governments of which it disapproves in doctrinal or moral terms, or with physically attacking Western states as a response to the policies they have adopted towards the Muslim world. On the contrary, it seeks to engage constructively with the vast social and political complexities of the Muslim world. It may well challenge existing models of governance; it may offer alternative political paradigms; it may seek to reverse what it regards as the moral degeneration of Muslim societies, but it does not seek the violent overthrow of government or the social coercion of the society over which it rules. It does seek to challenge both government and society, but within patterns of political behaviour that should form part of the public sphere and that would be considered legitimate within democratic societies elsewhere, or through social engagement that precludes political action. Indeed, given the evidence of the role it has played in the 'Arab spring' and the support it possesses, the Islamist movement could do nothing else.

Yet, at the same time, political Islam's importance, and a large part of its success, lies in its perceived cultural authenticity; it reflects, in its principles of action, the underlying cultural, moral and religious strata of the world it addresses. Its significance as a political movement, too, is in part a consequence of the Muslim world's variegated history and its brusque encounter, through the colonial experience, with Western alternatives. Since, in many respects, it has been a response to the experiences of that period, it is firmly rooted in late modernity, even if its essential insights appear to come from an idealized past. Indeed, in that respect, it is similar to parallel movements within Christianity and Judaism, both of which have their political dimensions. The difference is, however, that while both the latter seek the refinement of an existing political and moral order, political Islam seeks the revival of an ideal that was once ingrained in a social fabric. It is, perhaps, for this reason that its advocates can appear to be aggressive, even intolerant. Yet, its political objectives are generally and increasingly directed towards political reform and participatory governance.

Quite apart from these political objectives, political Islam has a profound social significance too, especially in the field of civil society. Civil society is usually seen as the intermediary between governance and the private sphere of the family, as it can both supplement the action of government and restrict its excesses. In doing so, it seeks to become the servant of society at large. Institutions stimulated by political Islam—such as Islamic charities, Islamic banks, and social and political associations—play a key role in this respect. They can both supplement and substitute for the deficiencies in state provision, as has occurred in natural disasters throughout the region, including in Egypt during the Cairo earthquake of 1992 and in Algeria following an earthquake in 2003.

The point, however, is that moderate political Islam has widely earned public respect, even if it is deplored by government and élite alike, and as such is now a force to be reckoned with within the Middle East and North Africa. Although it is often still excluded from formal political power—only Saudi Arabia and Iran claim to be Islamic states, although Algeria, Iraq, Jordan, Lebanon and Morocco, and, since 2011, Egypt, Libya and Tunisia, allow explicitly Islamist parties to participate in the electoral process—political Islam is a significant force in the region. Given the electoral success of Islamist parties during 2011 and 2012, it appeared likely that Islamism would remain a major political current throughout the region in the years to come, and the ability of its proponents to engage in participatory governance would be of vital importance. The evidence in this respect had, until 2013, seemed to be encouraging—as perhaps demonstrated in Turkey, where the Adalet ve Kalkınma Partisi (AKP), the ideology of which is derived from political Islam, has been in government since 2002.

This is apparent in both the Sunni and the Shi'a world. The so-called 'Green Movement' that emerged in Iran after the contested presidential election of June 2009 did not seek the violent overthrow of the Iranian Government, but rather attempted to confront it with its own alleged betrayal of the principles on which it claims to be based. Consider, too, how the Islamic Resistance Movement (Hamas), in 2006, participated in elections in the Palestinian territories that were widely considered to be free and fair, and how the Lebanese militant Shi'a organization, Hezbollah, up to 2013 formed part of that country's complex coalition Government. In Iraq, despite the extremist violence there since the US-led invasion in 2003, overtly Islamist parties have taken part in three rounds of legislative elections, and, imperfect though the polls may have been, there is a general consensus in the country that they provide a legitimate basis for governance, even though sectarianism dominates the political process.

Yet, even if the vast majority of Islamist movements seek to operate within a democratic environment—whether or not their host governments are prepared to tolerate their presence—many questions remain as to whether such engagement can endure or whether political Islam is, at root, a potentially totalitarian movement. It is frequently suggested that political Islam is inherently fascist and usually anti-Semitic. It is argued that intrinsic to the Islamist dispensation is a rejection of democracy; after all, democracy requires the sovereignty of the people and political Islam, as the Algerian Islamist Ali Belhadj, the second most prominent leader of the proscribed Front Islamique du Salut, made clear in 1991, can only accept that sovereignty is a divine attribute, so that secular alternatives—and, therewith, democracy—are excluded. Furthermore, the experiences of Islamist movements in power have often seemed to confirm such views, as the collapse of the Mursi Government in Egypt in early July 2013 suggested.

This is, however, only one view among many, which even Belhadj has altered in the intervening years. Rachid Ghannouchi, the leader of Tunisia's previously banned al-Nahdah, has always argued for democratic participation, acknowledging that Islamist movements may lose, as well as win, elections and must abide by democratic outcomes. In Morocco the governing Parti de la Justice et du Développement, together with the banned Al-Adl wal-Ihsan (Justice and Charity) movement, claims that political Islam represents true democratic choice. Abdolkarim Soroush, a leading Iranian political and social philosopher, has posited a very similar view, suggesting that, in reality, few aspects of the public space really engage religious concerns, so there can be no religious bar to democratic political processes. Despite his sometimes controversial views, the Egyptian scholar Yusuf al-Qaradawi has also spoken in support of democracy. Even the gerontocratic leadership of Egypt's Muslim Brotherhood accepts the democratic option, while its younger cohorts have formed the dominant Freedom and Justice Party, which strongly supported President Mursi's regime.

A much more significant reality is that, over the past 50 years, political Islam, particularly in its moderate varieties, has become a complex and dominant element within the Middle East and other Muslim countries, both in terms of politics and in the context of social development. As a movement, it is both intensely political, in that it addresses temporal concerns of the polities in which it is practised, and social through the attempt of its majoritarian trends to address issues of moral social order and adjustment to contemporary modernity. It is also a response in that it has emerged as a putative answer to past political failure, whether in its extremist or its moderate versions. It uses the instruments of civil society to engage with the populations of the countries in which it operates and provides those populations with essential services, in some instances in a far more efficient manner than the state. It is this, as much as its explicitly religious agenda, that engages popular support and has led the movement from the social to the political arena, where it must now compete for attention.

Indeed, alongside the Muslim Brotherhood and the myriad moderate movements derived from it, it is Salafism—that 'non-political' branch of political Islam initiated in Saudi Arabia, with its conscious disdain for political action, which, ironically, is increasingly expressed through new national political parties—that is accruing support today, despite its violent margins. These were in evidence in April and May 2011, when Salafist extremists in Egypt were involved in attacks upon Coptic Christians, thus demonstrating that ideological attitudes claiming to be formally non-political can be intensely political indeed. In addition, ever since the 1970s, regimes in the Middle East and North Africa have implicitly adjusted their policies to accommodate Islamist demands, in a tacit recognition of the demotic power of the message of political Islam. For many observers, political Islam—certainly in its moderate version—is beginning to challenge political discourse throughout the region and is still considered to be a highly influential driver for changes in governance, including democratic choices, despite the sobering experiences of the 'Arab spring'. Indeed, those experiences indicate that the ability to conflate difference into threat has blinded observers in their understanding of a phenomenon that, to a large extent, was simply one political choice among others in the Muslim world. Furthermore, the Islamist movement has had to accept, just like its competitors, that it is predominantly a political movement that has to participate in the pluralistic political arenas now emerging in the Middle East and North Africa. It was, after all, the failure of the Muslim Brotherhood in Egypt to do this that led to its political downfall in mid-2013.

Therein, perhaps, lies the ultimate irony: that a movement born out of a sense of absolute moral outrage at the changes to Muslim society caused by colonialism and late modernity should only be able to achieve its apotheosis in becoming a partner in an indigenous and formally pluralistic political process inside the Middle East and North Africa. It is a transformation that recalls the progress of political movements in Catholic Europe in the second half of the 19th century, which evolved into the Christian democratic political parties of the 20th and 21st centuries. Such changes, furthermore, imply acceptance of the principle that political sovereignty resides with the people, rather than the Divinity. In a similar fashion, the extremist manifestations of Islamism that evolved towards terrorism increasingly recall the waves of political violence and terrorism that have affected Europe since the 1860s, in which similarities in paradigms of political action far outweigh common patterns of doctrinal or ideological justification. By challenging the political process, Islamism has been captivated by it and, in turn, transformed into one political option among many.

SELECT BIBLIOGRAPHY

Algar, Hamid. *Islam and Revolution I: Writings and Declarations of Imam Khomeini*. Berkeley, CA, Mizan Press, 1981.

bin Baz, Abd al-Aziz. Selected writings. www.binbaz.co.uk.

Farraj, Muhammad (trans.). *The Neglected Duty*. Birmingham, Maktabah al-Ansaar Publications, 2000.

Fukuyama, Francis. 'The End of History?' *The National Interest*, Summer 1989.

Gellner, Ernest. *Postmodernism, Reason and Religion*. London, Routledge, 1992.

al-Ghazzali, Abu Hamid Muhammad (trans. Marmura, Michael). *The Incoherence of the Philosophers* (2nd edn). Provo, UT, Brigham Young University Press, 2002.

Huntington, Samuel P. 'The Clash of Civilizations?' *Foreign Affairs*, Summer 1993.

Kepel, Gilles. *The Revenge of God: The Resurgence of Islam, Christianity and Judaism in the Modern World*. Cambridge, Polity Press, 1993.

Maududi, Abu'l 'Ala. *Political Theory of Islam*. Lahore, Islamic Publications, 1976.

Qutb, Sayyid (trans.). *Milestones*. Indianapolis, IN, American Trust Publications, 2005.

Rida, Muhammad Rashid. (Ed.). *al-Manar*. 1898–1935.

Robinson, Francis, 'Crisis of Authority: Crisis of Islam?' *Journal of the Royal Asiatic Society*. Vol. 19, No. 3, July 2009.

Roy, Olivier. *The Failure of Political Islam*. London, I. B. Tauris, 1994.

Shariati, Ali. 'Red Shi'ism (the Religion of Martyrdom) vs. Black Shi'ism (the Religion of Mourning)'. www.iranchamber.com/personalities/ashariati/works/red_-black_shiism.php.

OIL IN THE MIDDLE EAST AND NORTH AFRICA

SIMON CHAPMAN

INTRODUCTION

Most oil industry analysts would agree that the data that indicate the extent of the world's reserves of crude petroleum should be treated with caution. However, no consensus exists on whether they over- or underestimate the abundance of the resource. Given the undeniable flaws in the methods by which the data are compiled, some analysts argue, for instance, that it is in petroleum-producing countries' interest to understate their reserves, in order to keep prices high, while others maintain that it is in the interest of the international oil companies to overstate their reserves, in order to support or boost their share prices. Proven-reserve data are compromised most seriously, it is argued, by a lack of independent corroboration of figures for which the source is often either the producer countries or the international oil companies themselves.

According to the BP *Statistical Review of World Energy 2013*, at 1 January 2013 Middle Eastern countries—including Iran, Iraq, Kuwait, Oman, Qatar, Saudi Arabia, Syria, the United Arab Emirates (UAE) and Yemen—accounted for about 48% of the world's estimated proven reserves of petroleum. With the addition of the reserves of Algeria, Egypt, Libya and Tunisia, that figure rises to approximately 52%. This amounts to about 117,800m. metric tons, or some 872,600m. barrels (1 metric ton = 7.30 barrels, based on world average crude petroleum gravity). Of the 10 countries with the world's largest proven petroleum reserves, six—Saudi Arabia, Iran, Iraq, Kuwait, the UAE and Libya—are located within the region. A history of the discovery of the extent of these resources and of their exploitation in the 20th and early 21st centuries might serve equally well not only as a guide to the region's economic fortunes but also to illuminate key political developments there. Many analysts would contend that oil has been an important factor in many of the region's most significant events: the rise and fall of Arab nationalism; the Iranian Revolution of 1979; Western intervention to liberate Kuwait in 1990–91 and, subsequently, to oust the regime of Saddam Hussain in Iraq; the 2011 civil war in Libya.

In 2012, according to the BP *Statistical Review*, the countries of the Middle East and North Africa, with estimated output of some 1,519m. metric tons (about 11,767m. barrels), accounted for about 37% of world production of crude petroleum totalling an estimated 4,119m. tons. In that year, of the world's leading 10 producer countries, five—Saudi Arabia (first), Iran (sixth), the UAE (seventh), Kuwait (eighth) and Iraq (ninth)—were located in the region. The Middle East and North Africa is the location of eight of the 12 members of the Organization of the Petroleum Exporting Countries (OPEC); founder members Iran, Iraq, Kuwait and Saudi Arabia (Venezuela was the fifth founder member) have since been joined by Algeria, Libya, Qatar and the UAE. OPEC is an intergovernmental body established in 1960 whose stated objective is 'to co-ordinate and unify petroleum policies among Member Countries, in order to secure fair and stable prices for petroleum producers; an efficient, economic and regular supply of petroleum to consuming nations; and a fair return on capital to those investing in the industry'. The history of OPEC closely mirrors the region's foreign relations during the past 50 years, encompassing, for example, decolonization; the struggle of some of the oil-producing countries for sovereignty over their national resources; and key phases of the Arab–Israeli conflict. Such a history, of how OPEC member countries have co-operated, might also elucidate some of the region's most tenacious rivalries, OPEC conferences having frequently provided a stage upon which sub-plots in the struggle between Saudi Arabia and Iran for hegemony in the Muslim world have unfolded, for instance.

In 2013 those eight countries accounted for 115,600m. metric tons—some 68%—of OPEC members' proven reserves of crude petroleum, totalling an estimated 169,900m. tons at 1 January. In 2012 OPEC's Middle Eastern and North African members contributed about 79% of the organization's estimated output of crude petroleum, totalling 1,778.4m. tons. Saudi Arabia's role has been of particular significance within OPEC. The organization has often been described as a type of cartel that aims to increase petroleum prices above the competitive level by restricting its members' production of petroleum via a system of quotas. Similarly to 'textbook' cartels, OPEC has been vulnerable to overproduction and to deception regarding pricing by members whose interests, for a variety of reasons, including extent of reserves and demographic factors, often do not coincide. However, OPEC differs from classic cartels in one important aspect, namely that one of its producers, Saudi Arabia, is geographically much larger than all of the others. This status has meant that Saudi Arabia has assumed the role of OPEC 'swing' producer, i.e. the country modifies its output in order to defend the official world price of oil. This is partly explained by the fact that decreases in the world price of oil impose greater short-term losses on Saudi Arabia than on other member states. Over the longer term, however, Saudi Arabia has pursued a policy that aligns it with OPEC's so-called price 'doves', i.e. those members that favour relatively high production and low prices in order to safeguard markets for oil—Iran and Iraq have traditionally been regarded as OPEC's price 'hawks'. In recent years a debate over so-called 'peak oil' has focused attention on any perceived sign of Saudi Arabia's apparent inability to continue to fulfil this role, as in late 2007, for example, when the price of oil rose to close to US $100 per barrel, far above the level at which OPEC had estimated it could stabilize prices. This caused some analysts to speculate that the country no longer possessed the spare production capacity necessary to maintain stability.

In recent years at least as much attention has been focused on the finite nature of the world's petroleum resources as on their sheer abundance. The concept of 'peak oil' derives from a theory developed by an American geophysicist, Marion King Hubbert, predicting a high point in global output of petroleum, followed by reserve depletion and declining supplies. Among analysts who accept the theory, there is no consensus over whether the 'peak oil' event has already been passed or whether it still lies ahead. Indeed, there are some analysts who argue that, for practical purposes, petroleum is not a finite resource, and the issue is, of course, further complicated by the opacity of proven-reserve data. However, it is noteworthy that the International Energy Agency (IEA) has stated that output of conventional crude petroleum peaked in 2006. While in Western consumer countries the debate over 'peak oil', in tandem with growing environmental concerns, has tended to focus attention on the need to prepare for a post-petroleum age by developing alternative sources of energy on a scale sufficient to maintain the industrial base of their economies and the lifestyles to which their citizens have become accustomed, in the Middle East and North Africa it inevitably highlights the continued overwhelming dependence of most of the region's petroleum-producing countries on their hydrocarbons resources.

This dependence may be quantified in different ways. Macroeconomic data, for instance, indicate that in 2011 petroleum accounted for nearly 90% of Saudi Arabia's export revenues, while in 2010 hydrocarbons production accounted for some 50% of the country's nominal gross domestic product (GDP) at producers' values. Petroleum exports generally account for about 80% of Iran's total export earnings and for about one-half of government revenue. In 2009 the hydrocarbons sector accounted for 55% of Iraq's GDP, and for 68% of government revenue. In 2010 crude petroleum exports also accounted for some 96% of the total value of Iraq's exports, while in 2012 the oil sector was estimated to have accounted for about 70% of Kuwait's total export revenues and about one-half of its GDP. In 2009 the hydrocarbons sector contributed 45.1% of Libya's GDP, while in 2010 exports of hydrocarbons accounted for 90% of the country's total exports. In 2011 Algeria's hydrocarbons industry contributed around 70% of budget revenues and grants, and some 98% of export earnings, according to the IMF. Hydrocarbons, of course, include natural gas. However, it should be noted that much of the natural gas that the region produces is 'associated gas', output of which depends, for the time being at least, on the continued production of petroleum.

The region's oil-producing countries remain highly dependent, too, on petroleum for meeting their own energy requirements that seem certain to increase as 'development' proceeds and economic diversification is pursued. In 2012, of total estimated world consumption of petroleum of 4,130.5m. metric tons, Middle Eastern and North African countries accounted for 427.7m. tons, about 10% of world consumption and equivalent to approximately 49% of total European and Eurasian consumption. Saudi Arabia was the leading regional consumer, accounting for an estimated 129.7m. tons, followed by Iran (89.6m. tons) and Egypt (35.2m. tons). In 2012 the Middle East was estimated to have met about 49% of its primary energy requirements from petroleum. At national level, Iran met some 38% of its estimated total primary energy requirements from petroleum in 2012; Kuwait some 57%; Qatar some 25%; Saudi Arabia some 58%; the UAE some 37%; Algeria some 37%; and Egypt some 40%. However the region's dependence on petroleum is quantified, the reserves-to-production ratios must be taken into account. On the basis of the data cited above, even the reserves of countries such as Iraq and Kuwait, which rank among the most petroleum-rich, are possibly sufficient to allow them to maintain production at the 2012 level for not much longer than another 100 years and 89 years, respectively. Those of the UAE are estimated as being sufficient for another 79 years at the 2012 level; those of Iran for more than 100 years; those of Libya for 87 years; and those of Saudi Arabia for 63 years. On the same basis, Qatar's reserves provide for only another 33 years of production at the 2012 level, and those of Algeria for just 20 years. In those countries in the region where one of the benefits of oil wealth to the general population has been access to modern, high-quality health care, it can be argued that 100 years may not be much longer than the life expectancy of the next generation. General access to high-quality health care, of course, is usually a function of political stability. If, as has often been argued, high-quality health care and other services financed by revenues accruing from oil have been exchanged in some of the countries in the region for a democratically deficient political stability, then it is clear that the region's dependence on the wealth generated by a declining resource poses questions of fundamental significance to their governments.

TRENDS IN PETROLEUM RESERVES AND PRODUCTION

At 1 January 2013 Saudi Arabia's estimated proven reserves of crude petroleum, at 36,500m. metric tons or 265,900m. barrels, were the second largest in the world, after those of Venezuela, accounting for 15.4% of global reserves. Saudi Arabia has additional reserves totalling, according to industry sources, some 2,500m. barrels, in the so-called 'Neutral/Partitioned Zone', which is shared with Kuwait. According to the Energy Information Administration (EIA) of the US Department of Energy, more than one-half of the country's proven reserves are located in only eight out of a total of more than 100 major hydrocarbons fields. These include the world's largest oilfield, the onshore Ghawar field. Other major fields include the offshore Safaniyah, Zuluf and Manifa fields, and the onshore fields of Khurais, Qatif, Shaybah and Abqaiq. Saudi Arabia's hydrocarbons industry is the purview of state-controlled Saudi Aramco, one of the largest oil companies in the world measured by reserves and hydrocarbons output. Supervision of Saudi Aramco is undertaken by the Ministry of Petroleum and Mineral Resources and by a Supreme Council for Petroleum and Mineral Affairs that determines the company's strategy.

Saudi Arabia's output of crude petroleum amounted to an estimated 547.0m. tons in 2012, compared with 526.0m. tons in 2011 and 473.8m. tons in 2010. Production in 2002–12 ranged between 425.2m. tons (2002) and 547.0m. tons (2012). In 2011 the country re-established itself as the leading producer worldwide, replacing Russia (518.5m. tons). Saudi Arabia retained primacy in 2012. In 2012 Saudi Arabia's production capacity was estimated by the EIA to amount to almost 12m. barrels per day (b/d), the largest in the world. About one-half of the country's production is currently generated by the Ghawar field. In the long term Saudi Arabia reportedly aims to increase its output of light crude petroleum grades, which in 2012, according to the EIA, accounted for 65%–70% of total production. Saudi Aramco is also reported to have budgeted US $20,000–$30,000m. up to 2018 to compensate for production declines and maintain/raise capacity. Industry estimates of the annual average rate of decline in Saudi Arabia's oilfields vary. According to the Ministry of Petroleum and Mineral Resources, this is no more than 3%. The Ghawar field is estimated to have produced almost one-half of its proven reserves already.

In 2012, according to the EIA, Saudi Arabia's exports of crude petroleum totalled an estimated 2,738m. barrels. In that year Far Eastern destinations (including the People's Republic of China, India, Japan and the Republic of Korea—South Korea) accounted for an estimated 54% of the country's total exports of crude petroleum. Exports of petroleum liquids to the USA were estimated to have averaged 1.4m. b/d in January–October 2012, compared with 1.2m. b/d for the whole of 2011. Exports depart from the country's three principal terminals at Ras Tanura (the world's largest offshore facility), Ras al-Ju'aymah and Yanbu. The gravity of Saudi Arabian crudes ranges from heavy to super light, and most are rated as 'sour' crudes, i.e. having a relatively high sulphur content. The country's Arab Light crude is one of the 12 constituent crudes of the OPEC reference 'basket' (a weighted average of prices for petroleum blends produced by OPEC member countries). In 2012 the average price of Arab Light was US $110.22 per barrel. The country has two major national pipelines: the East–West Crude Oil Pipeline (Petroline), some 1,200 km in length and with an annual capacity of 1,852m. barrels, which transports mainly Arab Light and other light crudes from refineries at Abqaiq to Yanbu for export to Europe; and the Abqaiq–Yanbu Natural Gas Liquids (NGL) Pipeline, with an annual capacity of some 105m. barrels.

Saudi Arabia is the biggest consumer of oil in the Middle East and North Africa, with consumption totalling an estimated 129.7m. metric tons in 2012, compared with 76.6m. tons in 2002. Fuels for transport and power generation account for the greatest part of consumption, to whose growth high subsidies have contributed substantially in recent years. In 2012 Saudi Arabia met about 58% of its estimated primary energy requirements from petroleum. Plans exist to develop a civil nuclear power programme over the next decade, in order to boost the supplies of petroleum (and natural gas) available for export.

In 2012 Saudi Arabia's refinery capacity was estimated to total 2.1m. b/d—the largest in the Middle East and North Africa—divided among seven facilities. As part of a wider development plan, Saudi Aramco aims to raise its refining capacity from 1.1m. b/d to 3m. b/d, at a cost of US $70,000m. Projects include an export refinery joint venture with Total of France, with projected capacity of 400,000 b/d, scheduled to be operating at capacity by 2014, and a new refinery at Yanbu, with capacity of 400,000 b/d, scheduled to commence operations in 2015. Saudi Arabia's petroleum-processing industry is based around the biggest facility for processing and stabilizing crude in the world, located at Abqaiq, with capacity in excess of 7m. b/d. The Abqaiq complex processes more than 60% of Saudi Arabia's crude petroleum prior to its export or supply to refineries.

Estimated at 21,600m. metric tons, or 157,000m. barrels, at 1 January 2013 the proven petroleum reserves of the Islamic Republic of Iran ranked as the second largest in the region and the fourth largest in world terms. These reserves are divided among a total of 34 producing oilfields—22 onshore and 12 off shore—of which the most important is the Ahvaz field in Khuzestan province, in the south-west of the country. All exploration for and production of petroleum (and natural gas) is undertaken by the state-owned National Iranian Oil Co (NIOC), under the direction of the Ministry of Petroleum. About 80% of production in the provinces of Boyer Ahmad, Bushehr, Fars, Kohkiluyeh and Khuzestan is undertaken by a NIOC subsidiary, the National Iranian South Oil Co (NISOC). International oil companies are allowed to participate in exploration and production development projects on a buyback basis, with an Iranian partner.

Iranian production of crude petroleum totalled an estimated 174.9m. metric tons in 2012, compared with 208.2m. tons in 2011 and 208.8m. tons in 2010. In 2002–12 output ranged between 174.9m. tons (2012) and 214.5m. tons (2008). In 2011 Iran thus ranked as the second largest producer in the region and the sixth largest in the world. Iran also ranked as the second largest producer within OPEC. According to the EIA, Iran's annual production capacity amounted to an estimated 1,424m. b/d in 2009. Prior to the revolution that took place in 1979, Iran's annual output of crude exceeded 1,825m. barrels (production in 2012 was estimated at about 1,343m. barrels). The subsequent decline has been attributed to the combined effects of the war with Iraq (1980–88), insufficient investment due, in part, to economic sanctions imposed on the country, and declining output from mature oilfields. The extension of sanctions in 2012 to include the insurance or re-insurance of Iranian export cargoes of crude petroleum has had a particularly marked effect on production capacity and was one of the main factors behind the decline in estimated output of 16%—to its lowest level since 2002—in that year. In order to counter declines in production, a number of gas reinjection projects have been initiated, notably at the country's Agha Jari oilfield, the largest such project in the world. Iran has set out plans to boost annual production capacity to about 1,862m. barrels by 2015. However, analysts doubt that the country will be able to achieve this goal without the increased participation of foreign oil companies in the development of reserves such as those contained in the Azadegan oilfield, in whose northern section China National Petroleum Corpn (CNPC) has been active since 2009, on a buyback basis. In 2013 almost all activity by Western oil companies was reported to have ceased.

In 2012, according to IEA estimates, Iranian exports of crude petroleum and condensates totalled some 558m. barrels, compared with 916m. barrels in 2011. The IEA estimated that exports to China and India totalled 277m. barrels in 2012, compared with 321m. barrels in 2011. Purchases by Chinese refiners, usually the biggest buyers of Iranian crude, were reported to have declined heavily in January–March 2012, owing to a dispute with NIOC over the terms governing annual purchases. Exports to Greece, Italy, Spain and Turkey were likewise estimated to have fallen steeply in 2012, to an estimated 80m. barrels, compared with some 230m. barrels in 2011. Deliveries to Japan and South Korea, meanwhile, fell to an estimated 116m. barrels in 2012, compared with 200m. barrels in 2011. Iran's main terminals for petroleum exports are Kharg Island, where annual loading capacity amounts to 1,825m. barrels, Lavan Island (73m. barrels), Abadan, Bandar Mahshahr, Kish Island and Neka. Iran Heavy is one of the 12 constituent crudes of the OPEC reference 'basket'. In 2012 the average price of Iran Heavy was US $109.05 per barrel.

Iranian consumption of crude petroleum in 2012, estimated at about 90m. metric tons, was the second largest in the region. In 2002 Iranian consumption amounted to 70m. tons. Most domestic consumption of oil is for the production of gasoline and diesel for fuel. Natural gas is gradually displacing petroleum as the main source of primary energy—in 2012 Iran resorted to petroleum for about 38% of its primary energy needs, while about 60% was met from natural gas.

In 2012 Iran's refinery capacity was estimated to total 1.89m. b/d. According to the EIA, capacity was divided among nine refineries operated by the National Iranian Oil Refining and Distribution Co. Capacity is reportedly insufficient to meet domestic demand. In particular, a shortage of capacity for the manufacture of light fuels has necessitated imports of gasoline on a fairly substantial scale—in 2010 imports of gasoline reportedly totalled some 28m. barrels, thus accounting for about 70% of all petroleum product imports. A rationing system for subsidized gasoline for private and some commercial purposes was in place as of 2010. The Government reportedly aimed to increase refinery capacity to 3m. b/d by 2013, by expanding capacity at existing refineries, constructing new facilities, and via joint ventures elsewhere in Asia, including in China and Singapore. Provided these initiatives were completed as planned, imports of gasoline were expected to cease in 2013.

At an estimated 20,200m. metric tons (or 150,000m. barrels) at 1 January 2013, the oil reserves of Iraq ranked as the third largest in the region and the fifth largest world-wide. Iraq's proven reserves may, in fact, be larger than suggested. Unexplored areas of the country's western and southern deserts are believed to be the location of very substantial additional petroleum resources. Most of Iraq's proven hydrocarbons reserves lie in the north and the south of the country. Out of a total of some 30 oilfields, nine are classified as 'super giant' fields containing more than 5,000m. barrels and 22 are classified as 'giant' fields, containing more than 1,000m. barrels. Super giant fields in the country's south-east are estimated to account for 70%–80% of total proven reserves. Production and development of hydrocarbons is currently the nation-wide remit of Iraq's Ministry of Oil, except in the Kurdish Autonomous Region (KAR) in the north, where the IEA has estimated proven reserves close to the cities of Kirkuk, Khanaqin and Mosul to amount to 4,000m. barrels. (The government of the KAR has claimed the area under its control could contain as much as 45,000m. barrels in unproven reserves.) The Ministry of Oil's operational activities are conducted by the North Oil Co (NOC), the Midland Oil Co (MDOC), the South Oil Co (SOC) and the Missan Oil Co (MOC, operational in the governorate of Maysan and formerly part of the SOC). In the north the Kurdistan administration has enacted its own hydrocarbons legislation, and has concluded exploration, development and production-sharing contracts with international oil companies. In 2012 Iraq was reported to have disqualified the US petroleum corporation Chevron from participation in the oil industry in central and southern Iraq after it acquired two oil-drilling blocks in the KAR from India's Reliance Industries. Another US oil company, ExxonMobil Corpn, had been similarly excluded after concluding a production-sharing agreement with the Kurdish regional government in 2011. In order to maintain complete control of its reserves, Iraq has offered participation in the development of production in the centre and south of the country solely on the basis of less lucrative service contracts. Almost all of the energy needs of Iraq's hydrocarbons sector are reportedly met from petroleum.

In 2012 Iraqi oil production was estimated to have totalled 152.4m. metric tons, compared with 136.7m. tons in 2011 and 121.5m. tons in 2010. Output ranged between 66.0m. tons (2003) and 152.4m. tons in 2002–12. In 2012, according to the EIA, southern oilfields, in particular North and South Rumaila, were the source of about 75% of total output, with the remainder coming from oilfields close to the northern city of Kirkuk, including the Kirkuk field itself. In recent decades, like virtually all other sectors of the economy, Iraq's oil industry has been damaged by the war with Iran (1980–88), the imposition of economic sanctions, and by the wars with multinational forces in 1991 and 2003 and post-war turbulence. A number of obstacles remain to the development of the sector, including the need to modernize the infrastructure and the absence of a clear legal framework for investment in the industry by international oil companies. A more fundamental challenge is the conflicting claims by different ethnic and sectarian groups to exercise control over the country's petroleum resources. The Ministry of Oil is none the less proceeding with a development programme for the sector, and as of mid-2012 international oil companies were reported to have signed contracts to develop 14 of the country's oilfields/blocks. The successful implementation of this programme, for which a deadline of 2017 has been set, would have raised Iraq's annual production capacity to 4,380m. barrels. In 2013, however, the revision of development contracts was reported to have reduced this target to 3,468m. barrels by 2017. Challenges that will have to be overcome if even this lower objective is to be achieved include deficient refinery and export infrastructure, the need for either natural gas- or water-injection programmes in order to maintain oil reservoir pressure and increased electricity generation. In July 2012 Iraq concluded contracts with Pakistan Petroleum, Kuwait Energy and Lukoil (Russia), the leaders of three consortia that had made successful bids in May during the Ministry of Oil's fourth licensing round since 2009. The contracts remained subject to final approval by Iraq's Council of Ministers. Bashneft of Russia, which had also participated in bidding in May as part of a consortium, was subsequently awarded an independent exploration contract by the Ministry of Oil. A fifth licensing round, focused on the development of the Nasiriya oilfield in the governorate of Thi-Qar, together with the construction of a new refinery, was scheduled to be held in 2013.

In 2012, according to the EIA, Iraq's exports of crude petroleum amounted to some 876m. barrels, of which about 767m. barrels departed from the country's Persian (Arabian) Gulf ports and the remainder via the Iraq–Turkey pipeline, which runs from Kirkuk to Ceyhan (see below). In that year 51% of foreign sales of crude were to Asian countries, including China, India and South Korea, 20% to European destinations and 19% to the USA. The most important export terminal is the Basra oil terminal, from where exports totalled about 550m. barrels in 2012, according to the EIA. In order to boost its export capacity, Iraq has begun the Phase One Crude Oil Export Expansion Project to construct three single-point mooring systems, each with annual capacity of some 300m. barrels. The first two of these systems were completed in 2012. Iraq's sole major export pipeline in operation is the Iraq–Turkey pipeline. This conduit comprises two parallel pipelines, with annual combined nameplate capacity of some 600m. barrels. However, the pipeline's operations have been repeatedly disrupted and its infrastructure has reportedly deteriorated to the extent that in 2013 only one of the twin pipelines was fully operational, with maximum annual capacity of about 220m. barrels, according to the IEA. Other pipelines in Iraq include the Iraq–Syria–Lebanon pipeline, which has been closed since 2003, and the Iraq–Saudi Arabia pipeline, which has been closed since 1991. Basra Light is one of the 12 constituent crudes of the OPEC reference 'basket'. In 2012 the average price of Basra Light was US $107.95 per barrel.

In July 2012 Iraq warned Turkey that, by purchasing 'illegal and illegitimate' road-borne deliveries of crude petroleum from the KAR, it was participating in the smuggling of Iraqi oil. The Iraqi Government insisted that oil resources located in the KAR belonged to all Iraqis and that exports of petroleum and the collection of oil revenues should be organized by the central Government.

Iraq's refinery capacity was estimated to total about 1m. b/d in 2012. Much of the country's refining infrastructure is reportedly outdated and in 2009 only about one-half of its refineries were capable of operating at no less than 50% of capacity. Iraq is not currently able to satisfy domestic demand for refined products, in particular for gasoline, 30% of the demand for which is met from imports. Under the strategic plan that covers the period 2008–17 it is aimed to expand refinery capacity to 1.5m. b/d, through the expansion of existing refineries and the construction of four new facilities.

At 1 January 2013 Kuwait's proven reserves of crude petroleum totalled an estimated 14,000m. metric tons, or 101,500m. barrels. Kuwait also shares proven reserves in the 'Neutral/Partitioned Zone', estimated at 5,000m. barrels, on an equal basis with Saudi Arabia. Most of Kuwait's reserves are concentrated in mature fields, including the Greater Burgan field, which is believed to be the second largest oilfield in the world, after Saudi Arabia's Ghawar field. Major fields located in the north of the country include the Raudhatain and Sabriya fields. In recent years reserves have reportedly been boosted by the discovery of light crudes in central areas of the country, although these have yet to be developed. The country's oil policy is determined and the oil industry supervised by the Supreme Petroleum Council (SPC), to which government ministers, including the Prime Minister, and representatives of the private sector are appointed by the Amir of Kuwait. Foreign and domestic investment in the country's oil industry is overseen by the Kuwait Petroleum Corpn (KPC), while KPC subsidiaries are responsible for upstream development (Kuwait Oil Co), the downstream industry (Kuwait National Petroleum Co—KNPC) and the petrochemicals industry (Petrochemicals Industries Co). Foreign trade in petroleum is the remit of KNPC and the Kuwait Oil Tanker Co (KOTC). Meanwhile, the Kuwait Foreign Petroleum Exploration Co manages the KPC's foreign operations, and Kuwait Petroleum International is responsible for international upstream and downstream activities. Separate arrangements govern activities in the 'Neutral/Partitioned Zone', where the Kuwait Gulf Oil Co is active in both onshore and offshore operations.

In 2012 Kuwaiti production of crude petroleum amounted to an estimated 152.5m. metric tons, compared with 139.7m. tons in 2011 and 122.5m. tons in 2010. In 2002–12 Kuwaiti output ranged between 98.9m. tons (2002) and 152.5m. tons. The south-east of the country, in particular the Burgan oilfield, was reportedly the source of more than one-half of Kuwait's output of crude petroleum in 2011. The KPC is pursuing a wide-ranging development programme for the oil sector, which encompasses the expansion of exploration, the construction of new downstream infrastructure and the development of annual crude production capacity so that it totals some 1,460m. barrels by 2020. However, the achievement of this objective will not be possible without the participation of foreign oil companies, which is complicated by a constitutional ban on the ownership of national resources by foreign interests. Attempts to bypass this ban through measures including so-called Enhanced Technical Service Agreements had produced little positive impact on the development of newly-discovered reserves as of mid-2013. A key element of KPC's programme is 'Project Kuwait', for which plans were submitted in 1998 as part of an attempt to make participation in petroleum production more attractive to foreign oil companies. However, the implementation of Project Kuwait has been delayed by legal challenges to the contractual arrangements it proposed. Project Kuwait aims to boost production capacity from the northern fields of Abdali, al-Ratqa, Raudhatain and Sabriya so that total annual capacity reaches some 1,278m. barrels by 2015, as a step towards the 1,460m.-barrel objective. Other measures contained within the project include the development of heavy oil production (most Kuwaiti output is currently of light and medium grades) and the recovery of crude from lakes created by efforts to extinguish fires ignited at Kuwaiti oil wells by the Iraqi army in 1991.

In 2012, according to the EIA, Kuwait's net exports of petroleum liquids totalled about 876m. barrels. In 2011 the main markets for Kuwait's exports of crude petroleum were the Asia-Pacific region (the destination for some 548m. barrels, the USA (some 70m. barrels) and Europe (around 29m. barrels). Kuwait's sole exported crude, Kuwait Export, is a blend of the crudes the country produces, with light Burgan crude the main constituent. Kuwait Export is one of 12 constituent crudes of the OPEC reference 'basket'. In 2012 the average price of Kuwait Export was US $108.93 per barrel. Most Kuwaiti petroleum exports are shipped from the port of Mina al-Ahmadi. There are also terminals at Mina Abdullah, Mina Saud and Shuaiba.

In 2012 Kuwait's consumption of petroleum totalled an estimated 20.9m. metric tons. The vast majority of the country's crude is produced for export. In 2012 Kuwait met about 57% of its primary energy needs from petroleum.

According to an industry source, Kuwait's refinery capacity has remained constant at 936,000 b/d since 2004. Capacity is divided among three refineries—at Abdullah, al-Ahmadi and al-Shuaiba—operated by KNPC. Kuwait's refinery capacity is far in excess of domestic demand and the country is consequently a major exporter of refined petroleum products, in addition to crude. Kuwait has sought to expand its refinery capacity further by means of joint ventures in Asian markets, including in China (with Sinopec), Indonesia and Viet Nam. Completion of a refinery under construction in Guangdong, China, in collaboration with Sinopec, scheduled for 2014, is expected to raise annual export capacity of refined products from 73m. barrels to some 180m. barrels. In mid-2011 the SPC approved two projects—the Clean Fuels Project and a new refinery project at al-Zour—designed to increase Kuwait's ability to meet both growing domestic and foreign demand for high-quality refined products. The new refinery will provide additional annual capacity of some 220m. barrels by 2018.

At 1 January 2013 the proven petroleum reserves of the UAE were estimated to total 13,000m. metric tons or 97,800m. barrels. More than 90% of the UAE's petroleum reserves are located in the emirate of Abu Dhabi, but Dubai, Sharjah and Ras al-Khaimah all possess resources on a smaller scale. The UAE has reportedly been able to maintain its reserves in recent years, thanks, in particular, to the use of enhanced oil recovery technology at mature oilfields. However, exploration projects undertaken in recent years have met with little success. The UAE's oil industry strategy is determined by the Government and implemented by the Supreme Petroleum Council (SPC) via the Abu Dhabi National Oil Co and its subsidiaries. In 2010 the emirate of Sharjah established the Sharjah National Oil Corpn.

The UAE was estimated to have produced 154.1m. metric tons of crude petroleum in 2012, compared with 151.3m. tons in 2011 and 133.3m. tons in 2010. In 2002–12 output ranged between 112.5m. tons (2002) and 154.1m. tons. Foreign participation in petroleum production in the UAE is permitted on the basis of production-sharing agreements. Joint ventures, in which the state takes a majority share, are frequently the vehicle for this participation. In 2012 international oil companies involved in production in the UAE included BP of the United Kingdom, ExxonMobil, Royal Dutch Shell, Total of France and Occidental Petroleum. Petroleum production in the UAE is concentrated on the Zakum oilfields, including the Upper Zakum field, which together were the source of almost 30% of the UAE's total output in 2010. In 2012 production from the Upper Zakum field reportedly amounted to some 200m. barrels. Abu Dhabi's National Petroleum Construction Co and Technip of France are working on a project designed to boost annual output from the Upper Zakum field to around 270m. barrels by 2016. Other major onshore fields include Asab, Bu Hasa, Murban Bab, Sahil and Shah, all of which are operated by the Abu Dhabi Co for Onshore Operations (ADCO). Off shore, the Abu Dhabi Marine Operating Co operates the Lower Zakum and Umm Shaif fields. Annual output from the Lower Zakum field currently amounts to about 110m. barrels, but a project is under way to raise production there to more than 150m. barrels. Production in Dubai is sourced from four fields: Falah; Fateh; South-West Fateh; and Rashid. The Mubarak oilfield is the sole source of output in the emirate of Sharjah. Development projects under way in 2013 included onshore fields at Bab, Bida al-Qemzan and Qusahwira.

In 2010, according to the EIA, the UAE's exports of crude petroleum totalled some 767m. barrels, of which Asian markets, in particular Japan, were the destination for 95%. The UAE has one export terminal at Fujairah, with current storage capacity of 8m. barrels of crude which is planned to be raised to 12m. barrels. In 2012 the Abu Dhabi Crude Oil Pipeline, which links Habshan with Fujairah, commenced operations. The pipeline has substantially boosted the UAE's export capability, having already added almost 550m. barrels of annual capacity. Most importantly, when the pipeline's annual capacity is increased as planned to some 660m. barrels, the UAE will be able to export almost 66% of its daily output of crude, bypassing the strategically vulnerable Strait of Hormuz. The UAE's Murban crude is one of the 12 constituent crudes of the OPEC reference 'basket'. In 2012 the average price of Murban was US $111.75 per barrel.

The UAE consumed an estimated 32.6m. metric tons of petroleum in 2012. Petroleum was used to meet about 37% of the UAE's primary energy needs in that year.

In 2012 the country's refinery capacity was estimated at 710,000 b/d, divided among five facilities. The UAE's two largest refineries, Ruwais (Abu Dhabi) and Jebel Ali (Dubai), have capacities of 400,000 b/d and 120,000 b/d, respectively. The Abu Dhabi Government-owned International Petroleum Investment Co has plans to construct new refining facilities in Fujairah, with annual capacity of some 90m. barrels, at a cost of US $3,000m. In 2012, meanwhile, the Dubai Government-owned Emirates National Oil Co announced the projected expansion of the annual capacity of the Jebel Ali refinery by some 7m. barrels.

At 1 January 2013 Libya's proven reserves of petroleum were estimated to total 6,300m. metric tons, or 48,000m. barrels, the largest in Africa. The Sirte (Surt) basin is the location of the majority of these reserves—about four-fifths—and is also where most of the country's production is concentrated. Prior to the 2011 civil war, which culminated in the fall of the regime led by Muammar al-Qaddafi, the country's oil industry was administered by the National Oil Corpn (NOC). Foreign companies were permitted to participate in the industry, on the basis of exploration and production-sharing agreements. In 2011 international oil companies active in the Libyan oil sector included ConocoPhillips, ExxonMobil, Hess, Marathon, Occidental Petroleum (all USA), BP, OMV (Austria), Repsol (Spain), Eni (Italy), Royal Dutch Shell, StatoilHydro (Norway), Suncor Energy (Canada), Total (France) and Wintershall (Germany). Production, which had been severely disrupted from February as the civil war intensified, began to recover rapidly from September and had reportedly reached about 85% of its pre-conflict level by mid-2012. However, petroleum industry analysts indicated that the future development of the sector would depend on the return to Libya of foreign capital and personnel.

In 2012 Libya's production of crude petroleum was estimated to have amounted to 71.1m. metric tons, compared with only 22.5m. tons in 2011 and 77.7m. tons in 2010. In 2002–10 output ranged between 64.6m. tons (2002) and 85.5m. tons (2008). In the late 1960s, according to the EIA, Libya's output of crude petroleum was as high as 3m. b/d, but has since declined steadily. (In 2010 production totalled about 1.7m. b/d.) Prior to the civil war, the NOC had reportedly aimed to restore output to 2.5m. b/d by 2015. In the wake of the civil conflict, this target was lowered to 2m. b/d by 2017. Any increase in output beyond the pre-civil war level would be dependent on the deployment of enhanced oil recovery technology. Currently, the Sirte (Surt) basin is the source of about two-thirds of total output, complemented by production from the Murzuq basin and, off shore, the Pelagian Shelf basin.

According to the EIA, Libya's net exports (including all liquids) of crude petroleum totalled about 548m. barrels in 2010. IEA data indicated that European markets—in particular France, Italy, Germany and Spain—were the destination of some 85% of these foreign sales. US imports of Libyan crude have also been increasing since the economic sanctions imposed against Libya were lifted in 2004. Libya's foreign sales declined drastically in 2011, but had recovered strongly by mid-2012. Libya produces a total of nine export-grade crudes across a range of densities. European markets are generally the destination for exports of light, sweet crudes, while heavier crudes are frequently marketed in Asia. Libya's Es Sider crude is one of the 12 constituent crudes of the OPEC reference 'basket'. In 2011 the average price of Es Sider was US $111.87 per barrel.

According to the EIA, Libya meets about 72% of its primary energy needs from petroleum. In response to growing demand for electricity, the Government under Qaddafi reportedly planned to increase the share of natural gas at the expense of petroleum.

An industry source reported that Libya's refinery capacity totalled 378,000 b/d in 2011, divided among five facilities. Refinery output was disrupted by the civil war in that year, but by late 2012 all of the country's refineries had resumed operations. Libya reportedly aims to undertake a comprehensive renovation of its refining infrastructure, in order to boost gasoline and other light petroleum-product production capacity. Libya also undertakes refining activities in Europe via its overseas retail unit, Tamoil, producing and distributing refined products in Germany, Italy, the Netherlands, Spain and Switzerland.

At 1 January 2013 Qatar's proven reserves of petroleum were estimated to amount to 2,500m. metric tons, or 23,900m. barrels. Major oilfields in Qatar include the onshore Dukhan field, the country's oldest, and the al-Shaheen field, off shore. Qatar's petroleum industry is administered entirely by state-owned Qatar Petroleum (QP), although some of the country's offshore oilfields are operated by international oil companies on the basis of production-sharing agreements. The Government has reportedly sought to make these agreements more attractive in recent years, in order to boost its oil revenues and offset expenditure on the development of its natural gas industry.

In 2012 Qatar's production of crude petroleum totalled an estimated 83.3m. metric tons, compared with 78.2m. tons in 2011 and 72.1m. tons in 2010. In 2002–12 output ranged between 37.4m. tons (2002) and 83.3m. tons. The offshore al-Shaheen oilfield is the country's most productive, with output amounting to some 110m. barrels in 2011. Output from al-Shaheen in combination with that of Dukhan (about 100m.

barrels in 2011) accounts for about 50% of Qatar's total production of crude petroleum. Although production has risen steadily in recent years, Qatar's major oilfields are maturing. At Dukhan, the largest field in production, output has begun to decline. In order to maintain output Qatar is reportedly deploying enhanced petroleum recovery methods at a number of fields.

According to the EIA, Asian markets, in particular Japan and South Korea, are the principal destinations for Qatar's petroleum exports. Export terminals at Halul Island, Mesaieed and Ras Laffan are the main departure points for these foreign sales. Crude for export is delivered to these terminals via onshore and offshore pipeline networks operated by QP. Qatar's Qatar Marine crude is one of the 12 constituent crudes of the OPEC reference 'basket'. In 2011 the price of Qatar Marine averaged US $109.25 per barrel.

In 2012 Qatar's consumption of crude totalled an estimated 8.0m. metric tons. In that year Qatar met about 25% of its primary energy needs from petroleum. Consumption has increased rapidly since 2000, when it amounted to only 2m. tons, primarily as a consequence of increased demand for petroleum for transportation purposes.

According to the EIA, in 2013 Qatar's refinery capacity totalled 338,700 b/d, divided between two refineries, at Umm Said and Ras Laffan. The condensate facility at Ras Laffan, which has a daily capacity of 138,700 b/d, is operated by Qatargas and is controlled by a consortium of interests including QP (51%); ExxonMobil (10%); Total (10%); and four Japanese companies—Idemitsu Kosan, Cosmo Oil (each 10%), Mitsui Oil Exploration Co and Marubeni (each 4.5%). Plans reportedly exist to double the Ras Laffan refinery's capacity by 2015.

At 1 January 2013 Algeria's proven reserves of petroleum totalled an estimated 1,500m. metric tons, or 12,200m. barrels, located, for the most part, in the country's eastern regions. Sonatrach, a state-owned entity, plays the leading role in the production of crude petroleum—and natural gas—in Algeria, although foreign companies have been allowed to enter the hydrocarbons sector via production-sharing agreements in which Sonatrach is the main stakeholder. Foreign participation in exploration and production was boosted by a number of measures undertaken by the Government from the end of the 1990s, but by the end of the following decade investor enthusiasm had waned owing to unfavourable contractual terms. Amendments to Algeria's Hydrocarbon Act of 2005, enacted in 2006, stipulated, among other things, that Sonatrach's stake in any hydrocarbons venture must amount to at least 51%. In 2013 further amendments to the Act were approved that sought to make the Algerian hydrocarbons sector—in particular offshore exploration—more attractive to foreign investors.

In 2012 Algeria's production of crude petroleum totalled an estimated 73.0m. metric tons, compared with 73.5m. tons in 2011 and 74.1m. tons in 2010. In 2002–12 output ranged between 70.9m. tons (2002) and 86.5m. tons (2007). Major oilfields operated by Sonatrach include Hassi Messaoud, the country's largest, Ait Kheir, Tabankort Ordo, Tin Fouye and Zarzaitine. The Hassi Messaoud field alone accounted for almost 30% of Algeria's output of crude petroleum in 2012, according to the EIA, while the sum of Hassi Messaoud's output and that of the second and third largest fields—Ourhoud and the Hassi Berkine complex—represented about 50% of total output. New areas of the Hassi Messaoud field are reportedly under development in order to boost output there and the development of new fields is also planned, in order to offset declining output at mature fields. Projects scheduled to begin production in 2013 and 2014 include El Merk (Anadarko/Sonatrach), where annual output is eventually expected to reach 36m.–55m. barrels; Bir Seba (PetroVietnam/Sonatrach/PTT Exploration and Production, 13m.–15m. barrels); and Takouazet East and West (Rosneft-Stroytransgaz, 15m.–22m. barrels).

In 2010–12, according to the EIA, Algeria's exports of crude petroleum averaged almost 292m. barrels. Foreign sales to North America, mainly the USA, were estimated to have amounted to some 44m. barrels in that year, compared with more than 160m. barrels in 2007. Algeria's exports to North America accounted for 36% of total foreign sales in 2012, while European destinations received 49% and Asia 12%. Algeria's Saharan Blend crude is one of the 12 constituent crudes of the OPEC reference 'basket'. In 2012 the average price of Saharan Blend was US $111.51 per barrel. Exports depart from seven terminals located at Algiers, Annaba, Arzew, Bejaia, Oran, La Skhirra (Tunisia) and Skikda. The terminals are supplied via a pipeline network totalling more than 3,800 km in length. Since 2008 a US $5,500m. pipeline renovation and extension programme has been under way.

In 2012 domestic consumption of petroleum was estimated to have totalled 16.7m. metric tons. Algeria met about 37% of its primary energy requirements from petroleum in that year.

According to the EIA, in 2013 Algeria's refinery capacity totalled 562,000 b/d, divided among five crude petroleum facilities and one condensate facility. Of these, the refinery at Skikda, with a capacity of 300,000 b/d, was the largest. Plans exist to expand the capacity of the Skikda refinery and of facilities at Algiers and Arzew by a total of 82,000 b/d. Sonatrach has also announced its intention to build four new refineries by 2018, each with a capacity of some 100,000 b/d and located at Biskra, Ghardaia, Hassi Messaoud and Tiaret. In most years Algeria generates an exportable surplus of refined petroleum products. In 2012 the USA was the destination for almost one-half of Algeria's exports of petroleum products, Europe for 24%, Latin America and the Caribbean for 23% and East Asia for 6%.

At 1 January 2013 Oman's proven reserves of crude petroleum were estimated to amount to 700m. metric tons, or 5,500m. barrels. Most of these reserves are located in small onshore oilfields in central and northern regions of the country. Petroleum Development Oman (PDO), in which the state holds a 60% stake, Royal Dutch Shell 34%, Total 4% and Partex (Portugal) 2%, is responsible for applying hydrocarbons policies that are determined by the country's Ministry of Oil and Gas and subject to the approval of Oman's ruler, Sultan Qaboos bin Said al-Said.

In 2012 Oman's production of crude petroleum was estimated to have totalled 45.8m. metric tons, compared with 44.1m. tons in 2011 and 42.9m. tons in 2010. In 2002–12 output ranged between 35.3m. tons (2007) and 45.8m. tons. Owing to the dispersed location of most of the country's petroleum reserves, production costs are high and international oil companies enjoy contractual terms that are among the most generous in the region. Foreign oil firms active in the sultanate include, in addition to those mentioned above, BP, CNPC, Occidental Petroleum and Repsol. Since 2002 PDO has been pursuing a large-scale enhanced oil recovery initiative at mature oilfields, including the use of extraction technologies that have yet to be proven commercially.

According to the EIA, Oman is a significant exporter of crude petroleum, mainly to Asian markets—in particular China, Japan, South Korea and Thailand—via a sole terminal, at Mina al-Fahal. PDO operates a national pipeline network totalling some 1,600 km in length.

Oman's consumption of petroleum products totalled some 36m. barrels in 2011, according to the EIA. In 2012, according to the EIA, Oman's annual refinery capacity amounted to 222,000 b/d. A facility at Sohar is the larger of the country's two refineries, with capacity of about 106,000 b/d. This is complemented by a second refinery at Mina al-Fahal. Both refineries are operated by the Oman Refineries and Petrochemicals Co. Plans exist to expand capacity at Sohar to as much as 170,000 b/d by 2016, and to construct, in a joint venture with international investors, a new refinery with a capacity of 230,000 b/d at al-Duqm, in southern Oman, as well as new petrochemical production facilities and a new export terminal.

At 1 January 2013 Egypt's proven reserves of crude petroleum totalled an estimated 600m. metric tons, or 4,300m. barrels. Most of these reserves are distributed among—for the most part—small, mature oilfields located in the Eastern Desert, the Gulf of Suez, the Mediterranean Sea, the Nile Delta and the Western Desert. Co-ordination of production is undertaken by the state-owned Egyptian General Petroleum Corpn (EGPC), which is also directly responsible for about one-fifth of output. International oil companies play a major role in production, on the basis of production-sharing agreements with the EGPC. Foreign firms active in petroleum production in Egypt in 2012 included Apache Corpn (USA), BG Group, BP, Eni, Hess and Royal Dutch Shell.

In 2012 Egypt's production of crude petroleum was estimated to have totalled 35.4m. metric tons, compared with 35.3m. tons in 2011 and 35.0m. tons in 2010. In 2002–12 output ranged between 33.2m. tons (2005) and 37.2m. tons (2002). Egyptian production has been in decline since the late 1990s, in spite of efforts to introduce enhanced oil recovery techniques at the country's mature oilfields. Political upheaval in Egypt since 2011 has reportedly had little impact on petroleum output owing to the remoteness of the main producing areas from major population centres.

According to the EIA, Egypt exported a total of about 42m. barrels of crude petroleum in 2011. India (which received 22m. barrels) was the principal market in that year, followed by Italy (9m. barrels). US imports of Egyptian crude declined from about 2.6m. barrels in 2010 to around 1.5m. barrels in 2011. The country derives substantial revenues in the form of transit fees for petroleum (and other goods) exported from the Persian (Arabian) Gulf via the Suez Canal and the Suez–Mediterranean pipeline.

In 2012 Egypt's consumption of petroleum was estimated to have totalled 35.2m. metric tons. In that year the country met about 40% of its primary energy requirements from petroleum. Transportation accounts for the greatest part of domestic demand for petroleum. The use of natural gas as a fuel for transportation is being developed through the expansion of compressed natural gas infrastructure.

In 2012, according to the EIA, Egypt's annual refinery capacity was the highest in Africa, amounting to some 265m. barrels distributed among nine refineries, of which the largest was the state-owned El Nasr facility, located at Suez, with an annual capacity of about 53m. barrels. Plans exist to boost capacity—in particular for the production of petrochemicals and high-octane gasoline—by more than 600,000 b/d by 2016. As refining capacity exceeds domestic output of petroleum, some crudes are imported, processed and re-exported.

At 1 January 2013 Syria's proven reserves of petroleum were estimated to total 300m. metric tons, or 2,500m. barrels. The majority of these reserves are located in central and eastern regions of the country, and along the River Euphrates. Syria's two most important oilfields are the Omar and Jbessa fields, complemented by the smaller Gbeibe, Khurbet East, Oudeh, Tishrine and Yousefieh fields. Syria's Ministry of Petroleum and Mineral Resources administers the country's petroleum sector via the Syrian Petroleum Co (SPC). Foreign oil companies are permitted to participate in exploration and production in ventures in which the SPC takes a stake of 50%.

In 2012 Syria's production of crude petroleum was estimated to have amounted to 8.2m. metric tons, compared with 16.3m. tons in 2011 and 19.2m. tons in 2010. In 2002–11 output ranged between 16.3m. tons and 33.7m. tons (2002). The SPC had responded to declines in production since 2000 by seeking to attract foreign investment in exploration and production activities. Most notable among the ventures that resulted from this initiative is the Al Furat Petroleum Co, in which, in addition to the SPC's 50% share, Shell and CNPC both hold stakes. Other foreign companies active in exploration for and production of petroleum in Syria in 2011 included, in addition to CNPC and Royal Dutch Shell, the British firm Gulfsands, India's Oil and Natural Gas Corpn, Tatneft of Russia, and Total. Petro-Canada was also reported to have been awarded an exploration licence in 2011. Civil conflict in Syria since 2011 has severely disrupted the country's petroleum sector, mainly through the impact of sanctions on exploration and development projects, and on foreign trade, both exports, revenues from which have contributed more than one-third of total export earnings in some recent years, and imports. Infrastructure, including pipelines, has also suffered damage.

According to the EIA, in 2010 Syria's (net) exports of petroleum totalled some 40m. barrels. Foreign sales of Syrian petroleum are undertaken exclusively by a state entity, Sytrol, generally via annual contracts. The EIA reported that the principal markets for Syrian crude in 2010 were Germany (which received 32% of the total), Italy (31%), France (11%), the Netherlands (9%), Austria (7%), Spain (5%) and Turkey (5%). In August and September 2011, respectively, the USA and the European Union imposed sanctions on Syria, banning the importation of Syrian crude petroleum and petroleum products. In March 2011–March 2012, according to the same source, almost all of Syria's exports of crude petroleum were to European destinations. In 2012, of only four cargoes exported in total, none was destined for Europe. This loss of European markets owing to sanctions is compounded by the difficulty of finding alternative markets with access to refineries that are capable of processing Syrian Heavy—one of the two crude blends Syria exports. Exports depart via three terminals, at Banias, Latakia and Tartous. The terminals are supplied by a pipeline network that includes the 558-km Tel Adas–Tartous pipeline. Syria's domestic pipeline network is linked with that of Iraq via the Suwe diya–Ain Zalah and Banias–Kirkuk pipelines. However, the Banias–Kirkuk link has not been operational since the US-led invasion of Iraq in 2003.

In 2009, according to the EIA, Syria's consumption of petroleum liquids totalled 252,000 b/d. Domestic demand had risen steadily since the mid-1990s, stimulated by government subsidies. Between 2006 and 2008 a positive trade balance in crude petroleum and petroleum products of some US $1,900m. declined into a deficit of $100m. Syria had planned gradually to withdraw petroleum subsidies, but political upheaval in 2011 and its subsequent degeneration into civil war led to the suspension of this initiative.

Syria's nominal refinery capacity amounted to some 240,000 b/d in 2013, according to the EIA—already insufficient to meet domestic demand for petroleum products and possibly further constrained by damage to supply infrastructure. The country's two refineries are located at Banias and Homs, where capacity is 133,000 b/d and 107,000 b/d, respectively. A project to build a new refinery at Deir al-Zor was at least four years behind schedule by 2010, as was the planned construction of a refinery at Froklos with Venezuelan assistance.

At 1 January 2013 Yemen's proven reserves of petroleum were estimated to total 400m. metric tons, or 3,000m. barrels. The majority of these reserves are believed to lie in the Say'un-Masila basin in the south of the country, while the remainder are located in the Marib-Jawf basin, in the north. Yemen's petroleum sector is administered by several subsidiaries of the General Corpn for Oil, Gas and Mineral Resources, including the General Department of Crude Oil Marketing, the Oil Products Distribution Co, the Petroleum Exploration and Production Authority, Yemen Oil Co and Yemen Refining Co.

In 2012 Yemen's production of petroleum totalled an estimated 8.3m. metric tons, compared with 10.6m. tons in 2011 and 13.5m. tons in 2010. In 2002–12 output ranged between 8.3m. tons and 21.6m. tons (2002). Foreign oil companies are permitted to participate in Yemen's petroleum sector on a production-sharing basis. However, the renewal of contracts is subject to parliamentary approval, which has been withheld in a number of instances. This has prevented resort to the enhanced oil recovery techniques that are needed at Yemen's mature fields, and partly explains the decline in output in recent years. Investment has also been discouraged by security concerns. International oil companies that were active in Yemen's oil industry in 2011 included Norway's DNO International, Total and OMV.

In 2010 the EIA estimated that Yemen's net exports of petroleum totalled about 38m. barrels. Most of these exports were shipped to Asian destinations via three (out of a total of five) export terminals, mainly Ras Isa. The terminals are supplied by a pipeline network totalling some 1,065 km in length. The Ras Isa terminal and the pipeline that supplies it were attacked by suspected anti-Government elements in early 2011, rendering the facility inoperative for several weeks.

According to the EIA, Yemen's consumption of petroleum in 2010 amounted to an estimated 157,000 b/d.

Industry data indicated that Yemen's refinery capacity totalled 140,000 b/d in 2012, divided among two refineries: one, at Aden, operated by Aden Refinery Co; and the other, at Marib, operated by the Yemen Oil Refinery Co. The capacity of the refinery at Aden was reportedly 130,000 b/d, while that of the Marib refinery amounted to 100,000 b/d. The Government of Yemen was said to have initiated talks with its Chinese counterpart in 2011 regarding the renovation of the Aden refinery, where actual capacity was estimated to have declined to only 100,000 b/d. Attacks on its main supply pipeline led to the closure of the Aden refinery in late 2011.

At 1 January 2013 Tunisia's proven reserves of petroleum were estimated to amount to 100m. metric tons, or 400m. barrels. In 2012 Tunisia's production of petroleum was estimated to have totalled 3.1m. tons, compared with 3.2m. tons in 2011 and 3.8m. tons in 2010. In 2002–12 output ranged between 3.1m. tons and 4.6m. tons (2007). In 2009 most of Tunisia's production was from six major fields: Adam; Ashtart; Dalia; El Borma; Hawa; and Oudhna. Exploration for new resources was reported to have declined in 2009 owing to lower world prices for petroleum. A total of 57 Tunisian and international companies, including state-owned Entreprise Tunisienne d'Activités Pétrolières (ETAP) and DualEX Energy International Inc., were reported to be involved in exploration for and production of petroleum in Tunisia in 2009.

OIL STATISTICS

Crude Petroleum Production[1] (million barrels per day)

	2010	2011	2012
Middle East OPEC:			
Iran	4.36	4.36	3.68
Iraq	2.49	2.80	3.12
Kuwait	2.54	2.88	3.13
Qatar	1.68	1.84	1.97
Saudi Arabia	10.08	11.14	11.53
UAE	2.90	3.32	3.38
North Africa OPEC:			
Algeria	1.70	1.68	1.67
Libya	1.66	0.48	1.51
Other OPEC:			
Angola	1.86	1.73	1.78
Ecuador	0.49	0.50	0.51
Nigeria	2.52	2.46	2.42
Venezuela	2.84	2.77	2.73
Other Middle East and North Africa:			
Egypt	0.73	0.73	0.73
Oman	0.87	0.89	0.92
Syria	0.39	0.33	0.16
Tunisia	0.08	0.07	0.07
Yemen	0.29	0.23	0.18
Other producers:			
Argentina	0.72	0.69	0.66
Australia	0.58	0.50	0.46
Brazil	2.14	2.19	2.15
Canada	3.33	3.53	3.74
China, People's Republic	4.08	4.07	4.16
Colombia	0.79	0.92	0.94
Ex-USSR	13.56	13.61	13.66
India	0.87	0.90	0.89
Indonesia	1.00	0.95	0.92
Malaysia	0.70	0.64	0.66
Mexico	2.96	2.94	2.91
Norway	2.14	2.04	1.92
United Kingdom	1.36	1.11	0.97
USA	7.55	7.87	8.91
World total (incl. others)	83.27	84.21	86.15
OPEC total	35.10	35.95	37.41

[1] Includes shale oil, oil sands and natural gas liquids.

Source: BP, *Statistical Review of World Energy 2013*.

Conversion factors based on world average crude petroleum gravity

1 long ton = 7.42 barrels;
1 short ton = 6.63 barrels;
1 metric ton = 7.30 barrels;
1 barrel = 35 imperial gallons;
1 barrel = 42 US gallons;
To convert metric tons per year into b/d, divide by 50.0;
To convert long tons per year into b/d, divide by 49.2.

Proven Published World Reserves as at 1 January 2013
('000 million barrels)

	Reserves	Years of production at 2012 levels*
Middle East and North Africa		
Iran	157.0	>100.0
Iraq	150.0	>100.0
Kuwait	101.5	88.7
Oman	5.5	16.3
Qatar	23.9	33.2
Saudi Arabia	265.9	63.0
Syria	2.5	41.7
UAE	97.8	79.1
Yemen	3.0	46.4
Algeria	12.2	20.0
Egypt	4.3	16.1
Libya	48.0	86.9
Tunisia	0.4	17.9
Middle East and North Africa total	872.0	n.a.

	Reserves	Years of production at 2012 levels*
Other leading producers		
Other OPEC:		
Angola	12.7	19.4
Ecuador	8.2	44.6
Nigeria	37.2	42.1
Venezuela	297.6	>100.0
Total OPEC	1,211.9	88.5
Rest of world:		
Canada	173.9	>100.0
Mexico	11.4	10.7
USA	35.0	10.7
Brazil	15.3	19.5
Ex-USSR	126.0	25.2
Norway	7.5	10.7
United Kingdom	3.1	8.8
China, People's Republic	17.3	11.4
India	5.7	17.5
Indonesia	3.7	11.1
Malaysia	3.7	15.6
World total (incl. others)	1,668.9	52.9

* Including crude oil, shale oil, oil sands and natural gas liquids.

Source: BP, *Statistical Review of World Energy 2013*.

Note: Reserve figures are subject to wide margins of error, and there are considerable differences between sources—including oil companies and governments. Proven reserves do not denote 'total oil in place', but only that proportion of the oil in a field that drilling has shown for certain to be there and to be recoverable with current technology and at present prices. Normally recoverable reserves amount to about one-third of the oil in place. Since the potential of fields is continually being reassessed in the light of production experience and because the production characteristics of a field can (and often do) change as it gets older, proven reserves figures may sometimes be revised upwards or downwards by quite dramatic amounts without any new discoveries being made. Price rises tend inevitably to increase reserves figures by making small fields or more complex recovery techniques economic.

The only exception to the proven commercially recoverable reserves formula used in this table applies to the ex-USSR figures, which, as reported by *Oil and Gas Journal*, refer to 'explored reserves', which include proven, probable and some possible reserves.

Oilfields in the Middle East (reserves of 5,000m. barrels or more)

		Year of discovery	Age of principal reservoirs	Estimated reserves ('000 million barrels)
Ghawar	Saudi Arabia	1948	Jurassic	83
Burgan	Kuwait	1948	Cretaceous	72
Safaniyah-Khafji	Saudi Arabia (Neutral Zone)	1951	Cretaceous	30
Rumaila	Iraq	1953	Cretaceous	20
Ahwaz	Iran	1958	Oligocene, Miocene, Cretaceous	17.5
Kirkuk	Iraq	1927	Oligocene-Eocene, Cretaceous	16
Marun	Iran	1964	Oligocene-Miocene	16
Gach Saran	Iran	1928	Oligocene-Miocene, Cretaceous	15.5
Agha Jari	Iran	1938	Oligocene-Miocene, Cretaceous	14
Abqaiq	Saudi Arabia	1940	Jurassic	12.5
Berri	Saudi Arabia	1964	Jurassic	12
Zakum	Abu Dhabi	1964	Cretaceous	12
Manifah	Saudi Arabia	1957	Cretaceous	11
Fereidoon-Marjan	Iran/Saudi Arabia	1966	Cretaceous	10
Bu Hasa	Abu Dhabi	1962	Cretaceous	9
Qatif	Saudi Arabia	1945	Jurassic	9
Khurais	Saudi Arabia	1957	Jurassic	8.5
Zuluf	Saudi Arabia	1965	Cretaceous	8.5
Raudhatain	Kuwait	1955	Cretaceous	7.7
Shaybah	Saudi Arabia	1968	Cretaceous	7
Abu Saafa	Saudi Arabia/Bahrain	1963	Jurassic	6.6
Asab	Abu Dhabi	1965	Cretaceous	6
Bab	Abu Dhabi	1954	Cretaceous	6
Umm Shaif	Abu Dhabi	1958	Jurassic	5

Source: *Oilfields of the World*, E. N. Tiratsoo (Scientific Press Ltd).

OPEC (Middle East and North Africa) Crude petroleum export revenues, 2001–11 (US $'000m.)

	2001	2002	2003	2004	2005	2006	2007	2008	2009	2010	2011
Algeria	12.1	12.3	17.5	24.3	36.7	45.1	52.0	68.3	42.5	53.2	63.0
Iran	20.5	18.6	23.5	32.4	48.2	55.0	58.4	82.0	55.0	72.8	95.0
Iraq	13.9	13.0	9.0	19.2	23.9	31.5	37.4	60.0	39.1	50.1	71.0
Kuwait	14.4	14.9	19.3	27.4	41.3	50.4	55.3	78.9	47.0	59.7	85.0
Libya	10.9	10.3	12.8	17.9	28.1	35.7	41.2	56.5	33.7	44.1	13.0
Qatar	7.0	6.9	8.4	12.3	19.3	24.3	25.9	37.6	24.2	37.2	57.0
Saudi Arabia	62.4	61.3	81.1	104.9	160.7	187.2	196.9	284.5	156.5	224.7	311.0
UAE	19.0	18.6	23.9	32.2	48.4	59.7	65.7	90.9	53.0	67.2	101.0

Source: US Energy Information Administration.

NATURAL GAS IN THE MIDDLE EAST AND NORTH AFRICA

SIMON CHAPMAN

Based on an original essay by CHRIS CRAGG

The Middle East accounts for 43% of the world's proven reserves of natural gas. With the addition of the reserves of Algeria, Egypt and Libya, that figure rises to about 47%. This amounts to 88,500,000m. cu m, according to the 2013 *BP Statistical Review of World Energy*, but even this figure should be regarded as conservative. The eastern part of the region lies in a trend that many geologists believe contains the bulk of Eurasia's hydrocarbons. This runs from the Yamal peninsula in Russian Siberia to the Caspian Sea, across the 'fertile crescent' into Saudi Arabia, and across the Red Sea towards Sudan. Proven reserves in the region at 1 January 2013 were almost 90% greater than those recorded 20 years earlier, the additional amount alone sufficient for several years of global gross consumption at the 2012 rate. At current levels of production, proven reserves in the Middle East and North Africa could last into the second century of the current millennium, and proven reserves underestimate potential reserves, sometimes by as much as a factor of two.

In spite of these huge reserves, natural gas was, until relatively recently, an under-utilized resource in much of the Middle East and North Africa. In contrast to petroleum, it was difficult to export, requiring either large pipeline systems or very expensive conversion into liquefied natural gas (LNG). Since, in terms of volume, oil has a far greater thermal content than gas, gas produced far less reward than oil for a given capital expenditure. Local markets were generally either dominated by oil burning, or else did not exist. As a result, petroleum companies looking for oil and finding gas shut it in and went elsewhere. Where gas was found with oil—'associated gas'—the oil was used and the gas flared. Some producers did export by liquefying the gas for European, US or Japanese consumption. Yet this was a formidable technical undertaking, requiring liquefaction plants to cool the gas to –165ºC, each costing as much as US $2,000m., and special ships costing more than $100m. each. Constructed in the late 1970s, these plants came into operation at an inopportune moment, since between 1979 and 1982 world gas consumption actually fell. In the USA there was a huge surplus of domestically produced gas, while in Europe large volumes of Soviet gas from Siberia reached the market. Only Japan, with no resources of its own, was obliged to remain in the market.

Many countries, however, began to realize the value of what was being flared. As a substitute for oil, gas could be burnt in power stations, desalination plants and wherever heat was required. Another important consideration in an era of high oil prices was that the increased use of natural gas would free crude petroleum for export. As a result, the flaring of associated gas was gradually reduced, a process which, in some cases, involved the construction of major offshore and onshore gathering grids. Other countries, meanwhile, likewise aware of the waste involved in flaring gas, began to use reinjection techniques in order to facilitate the recovery of oil. In the Middle East and North Africa generally, however, flaring remained high, involving 52,420m. cu m in 1991—an amount almost double Norway's marketed production. A sudden increase in 1991 was largely due to events in Kuwait, where the Iraqi invasion and subsequent war brought about the flaring of 96% of total production in that year. Between 1980 and 1991 gross production in the region had increased by 100%. A greater achievement was to have found a commercial use for the gas. In 1991 the Middle East and North Africa used or exported some 179,760m. cu m of natural gas, more than double the level of consumption seven years earlier. Iran, Abu Dhabi (in the United Arab Emirates—UAE), Saudi Arabia, Bahrain, Oman, Egypt, Libya and Qatar have all more than doubled domestic consumption of natural gas since the mid-1980s, water desalination plants, power stations and even town distribution grids having been constructed near to where the gas used to be flared. Equally, regional petrochemical and metal industries have increasingly utilized gas rather than oil. By 1991 the Middle East and North Africa had more gas-fired power stations than Western Europe and North America combined.

The increase in demand for natural gas has not only occurred in the countries that produce it. In 2012 it was estimated that the countries of the Middle East and North Africa were contracted to export some 222,200m. cu m of natural gas (including LNG), compared with less than 3,000m. cu m annually in the early 1980s. Western Europe has emerged as a major market for North African supplies, especially from Algeria. By 2010 natural gas met some 25.1% of the energy requirements of European Union (EU) member states. Gas is of increasing importance not only to the European economy, however, but also to the global economy. World consumption rose consistently in each year during 2003–08, with utilization world-wide, in terms of oil equivalent, totalling 2,717.7m. metric tons in 2008, compared with 2,647.3m. tons in 2007. In 2009, however, world consumption declined by about 2.3%, compared with the previous year, to 2,655.7m. tons. In 2010 global consumption rebounded by 7.8%, compared with 2009, to reach 2,864.1m. tons. World consumption rose by a further 1.7%, to 2,914.2m. tons, in 2011, and by an additional 2.5%, to 2,987.1m. tons, in 2012. The global market for natural gas, in terms of energy equivalence, is now more than 70% of the size of that for crude petroleum. With regard to the environment, gas has a number of advantages over oil and coal, compared to both of which it produces less carbon dioxide on combustion and generally contains less sulphur. In addition, the use of gas for generating electricity has increased significantly and will continue to do so because the fuel can be used in combined-cycle turbines. Such turbines generate power with a 50% rate of efficiency, compared with the 34% generally achieved by standard, single-cycle oil- or coal-fired power stations. Apart from nuclear energy, gas is the fuel best suited to this process. Natural gas is also a major petrochemical feedstock. With environmental awareness growing, the Middle East and North Africa has quickly realized the value of gas for production of methanol and, from it, methyl-tertiary-butyl ether. With the search now on for cleaner fuels, methanol itself may one day become an important vehicle fuel and it requires a gas feedstock.

The importance of natural gas to the future of the Middle East and North Africa has increased enormously since the early 1970s. A new appreciation of the fuel as clean-burning has created potential demand that has been seen to be a major element in the region's development. In recognition of this, a new spirit of co-operation has developed. Unlike crude petroleum, the production of which is controlled to a large extent by the Organization of the Petroleum Exporting Countries (OPEC) and is thus dominated by the politics of oil pricing and the Organization's internal disputes, gas diplomacy remains largely free of past East–West recriminations, although concerns have been voiced at the increasing dependence of Europe on gas imported from countries perceived to be at risk of political instability and with which amicable diplomatic relations cannot always be guaranteed. The development of reserves, pipelines, liquefaction units and power plants in the region is being aided by Western multinational companies—Royal Dutch Shell Group, Total (formerly TotalFinaElf), Eni SpA (formerly Eni-Agip), BG International and others—while Japanese trading groups such as Mitsui and Mitsubishi have also established themselves in the industry. Gas remains a capital-intensive business, and external assistance is required in both the financial and technical spheres. Gas supply is a central element in the plans of the Cooperation

Council for the Arab States of the Gulf (Gulf Cooperation Council) for economic development, while trade in natural gas with Europe has made a major contribution to the development of Algeria's economy. Despite their apparent vulnerability to civil unrest, the construction of long gas pipelines that extend across the region and beyond, into Europe, seems certain to expand in the foreseeable future.

At 33,600,000m. cu m, Iran's reserves of natural gas at 1 January 2013 were estimated, for the first time in many decades, to have surpassed those of Russia to become the world's largest. (In fact, BP applied a radical downward revision to Russian reserves, to 32,900,000m. cu m, as of 1 January 2013.) Recent discoveries have included those, in 2011, of the Farouz B, Kayyam, Madar and Sardare Jangal fields. Reserves at the Sardare Jangal field, in the Caspian Sea, have been estimated to total as much as 1,400,000m. cu m. However, their exploitation is likely to be complicated by competing claims to their ownership by other Caspian littoral states. In 2004, for the first time, Iran overtook Algeria as the leading regional producer of natural gas, its output amounting to 84,900m. cu m in that year. Iran has subsequently retained regional primacy, with production totalling 151,800m. cu m in 2011 and an estimated 160,500m. cu m in 2012—almost double that of Algeria. (Since 2008 Qatar's output has also risen substantially above that of Algeria.) In 2012, when Iran met 60% of its total primary energy needs from natural gas, domestic consumption totalled an estimated 156,100m. cu m, compared with 153,500m. cu m in 2011.

Iran's potential as a producer and exporter of natural gas is enhanced by the fact that some 80% of its reserves, both offshore and onshore, comprise so-called unassociated gas and have not been developed. The South Pars field (which is part of the same geological formation as Qatar's North Field) contains more than one-quarter of the country's total reserves of gas. It has been estimated that the total cost of the phased development of this offshore field will have reached some US $60,000m. upon its completion, expected by around 2017. In May 2010 Iran announced the award of South Pars development contracts to Chinese, Indian and Malaysian companies, while stating that it planned to exclude Western companies—which it accused of prevarication—from the project in future. Analysts indicated that the reluctance of British, French and Italian companies to make financial commitments to South Pars projects was due to UN and US economic sanctions imposed against Iran as a result of the ongoing dispute over the purpose of its nuclear programme. As well as having been impeded by sanctions and obstructive US legislation that penalizes countries investing in Iran, the development of South Pars has suffered delays owing to technical and financing problems. Production from the first phase commenced in late 2004, several years behind schedule; however, production of gas for domestic consumption from the second and third phases had already commenced in early 2002. At early 2013 10 of the project's scheduled 24 phases had either been completed or were ongoing, with phase 12 scheduled to become operational (before phase 11) in 2014. Most of the natural gas produced from those phases of the South Pars development operational at mid-2013 was either for consumption on the domestic market or for gas reinjection projects. The remainder—which some analysts believe may amount to very little once domestic and reinjection needs have been met—is expected to be traded with South Asian and European destinations and used to produce LNG or for gas-to-liquids schemes.

Domestic Iranian consumption is being boosted by a government investment programme under which the state-controlled price of natural gas to consumers is maintained at a very low level. Despite the doubts expressed by analysts regarding the availability of surplus supplies once growth in domestic demand has been met, the Government remains keen to develop exports of natural gas, and has been committed to a substantial export programme since 2001. Iran's Ministry of Petroleum has forecast that production from South Pars that is destined for export (by pipeline and, once facilities for its production have been developed, as LNG could earn as much as US $11,000m. over a 30-year period. Phases 11–13 of the South Pars project will all reportedly be devoted, in part at least, to the development of LNG production and export, although to realize the potential for those activities will require international partnerships. In 2010, according to the Energy Information Administration (EIA) of the US Department of Energy, the negotiation of such alliances with state and private oil companies that were not affected by sanctions regimes was under way. In June 2009 the China National Petroleum Co (CNPC) signed a $4,700m. contract with the National Iranian Oil Co to develop phase 11 of the South Pars project, from which it is hoped that annual output will, ultimately, rise as high as 18,000m. cu m. In early 2013, however, terms were reported to have been agreed between Iran and CNPC for the termination of this contract. CNPC was reported at that time to have been replaced in the project by Iranian Offshore Engineering and Construction Co.

A natural gas pipeline between Iran and Turkey became operational in 2002, although it remains unclear whether sufficient demand exists in Turkey for imports from Iran on the scale originally planned. In 2012, according to data cited by EIA, Turkish imports of natural gas from Iran totalled some 7,000m. cu m, accounting for about one-fifth of Turkey's total natural gas imports in that year. In 2004 Iran concluded a long-term agreement to supply Armenia with some 37,000m. cu m of natural gas over a 20-year period from 2007, in exchange for electricity generated by using the gas supplied. The first (Armenian) phase of an Iran–Armenia pipeline was inaugurated at Meghri, Armenia, in early 2007. Armenian imports of natural gas from Iran totalled some 454m. cu m in 2012, accounting for about one-quarter of Armenia's total natural gas imports in that year according to data cited by EIA. Under the terms of the bilateral supply agreement, it was originally envisaged that Armenian imports would rise to more than 2,000m. cu m annually by 2019. However, on the basis of volumes traded as of mid-2013, this target appeared unlikely to be met. Azerbaijan was the only other destination for Iranian exports of natural gas in 2012, receiving some 580m. cu m. In late August 2013 Iran signed a Memorandum of Understanding (MOU) with Oman for the export of natural gas over a 25-year period from 2015. According to EIA estimates, Iran generated revenues totalling about US $3,800m. from exports of natural gas in the 12 months to June 2012. In the same period, revenue from Iranian exports of crude oil and condensates was estimated at $84,315m. According to the same source, less than 4% of Iran's total export earnings in 2010 derived from natural gas. In both 2011 and 2012 Iran reportedly accounted for less than 1% of the world's total trade in dry natural gas. In 2002 Iran concluded an agreement with Greece that envisaged the extension into the latter country of the Iran–Turkey pipeline. In 2005 Iran also concluded an agreement on the future supply of gas to Ukraine. The supply of Iranian gas to Switzerland was contracted with Swiss energy trading company Elektrizitäts-Gesellschaft Laufenburg AG to begin in early 2009 via the Iran–Turkey pipeline. Iran seems likely to become a major supplier of natural gas to destinations within the Middle East, and it has been suggested that it may eventually export to the Republic of Korea (South Korea) and the People's Republic of China. In 2004 Iran concluded an agreement with China's Sinopec to supply LNG over a 25-year period. (As of mid-2013, however, Iran still had no liquefaction facilities.)

In 2002 Iran and Pakistan signed a MOU to study the feasibility of constructing a 2,600-km pipeline from southern Iran to south-eastern Pakistan, but the development of the project, the extension to India of which was also envisaged, was impeded by regional geopolitical concerns, not least conflict between Pakistan and India over the disputed region of Kashmir. Improved relations between Iran and Pakistan were reported in 2006 to have prompted both countries, as well as India, to reappraise the pipeline's feasibility. In 2010, despite US attempts to dissuade them from undertaking the project, Iran and Pakistan announced that they had concluded an agreement for its launch. Iran subsequently claimed that it had already completed the construction of a large part of the pipeline located in its territory. In 2011 Pakistan's Minister of Petroleum and Natural Resources was reported to have stated that construction of the Pakistani section of the pipeline would be completed and ready to transport exports of gas from Iran by 2014. In 2012 Pakistan reportedly concluded tendering for commissioning, construction, engineering and procurement for the pipeline, while Iran was reported to have agreed to contribute US $500m. to finance the pipeline's construction in Pakistan. India's role in the project remains uncertain, although in 2010 it did express willingness to pursue further talks with Iran and Pakistan on the pipeline's development. While production and export facilities are under development, Iran continues to import some natural gas for domestic consumption, notably from Turkmenistan and Azerbaijan, which are well situated to supply parts of northern Iran that lie distant from the country's domestic resources. In 2012 these imports totalled some 8,000m. cu m, according to data cited by EIA.

In July 2013 Iran and Iraq were reported to have concluded an agreement under which Iran would supply Iraq with natural gas to be used as a power plant feedstock over a four-year period. This gas, amounting to some 8,700m. cu m annually, was to be supplied by means of a new pipeline between the two countries, construction of which was due for completion in late 2013.

Qatar's proven reserves of natural gas, estimated at 25,100,000m. cu m at 1 January 2013, are the second largest in the region after those of Iran. These reserves include those of Qatar's offshore North Field, the largest resource of non-associated natural gas in the world. Qatari production, which totalled an estimated 157,000m. cu m in 2012 (only 3,500m. cu m less than Iran's estimated output in that year), compared with 145,300m. cu m in 2011, is highly export-orientated. In 2006 Qatar overtook Indonesia as the world's leading exporter of LNG and the country remained the world's leading exporter of LNG (by a huge margin) in 2012, when its foreign sales totalled 105,400m. cu m, compared with sales of 31,800m. cu m by Malaysia, 28,100m. cu m by Australia and 25,000m. cu m by Indonesia. Qatar's trade in LNG is conducted by two companies: Qatar Liquefied Gas Co (Qatargas) and Ras Laffan Liquefied Natural Gas Co (RasGas). As of January 2013 Qatargas and RasGas had a combined total of 14 operational LNG trains, providing annual liquefaction capacity of about 85m. metric tons. In 2012 Japan (21,300m. cu m), India (16,100m. cu m), South Korea (14,200m. cu m), the United Kingdom (13,300m. cu m), the Republic of China (Taiwan—7,900m. cu m), China (6,800m. cu m), Italy (5,800m. cu m) and Belgium (4,500m. cu m) were the principal destinations for supplies of Qatari LNG. Much of the new liquefaction capacity developed by both Qatargas and RasGas was initially focused on supplying US markets. However, low US natural gas prices have led Qatar to pursue contracts to supply other markets, notably China and India. The USA imported just 1,000m. cu m of Qatari LNG in 2012.

The expansion of Qatar's capacity to export natural gas is regarded by the Government as crucial to the country's future economic development. Among the initiatives intended to realize export potential is Qatar's participation in the Dolphin Gas Project, the objective of which is to link the natural gas networks of Oman, the UAE and Qatar to the Gulf region's first natural gas pipeline. A consortium—Dolphin Energy, owned, via the Mubadala Development Co, by the Government of Abu Dhabi (51.0%), Total (24.5%) and Occidental Petroleum (24.5%)—is undertaking the Gas Project, which launched commercial operations in mid-2007. Production by Dolphin Energy was reported to have reached the daily output target for the project of some 53m. cu m in February 2008. The future expansion of Qatar's production of natural gas is expected to derive largely from new projects focused on the country's huge North Field. However, such projects have been subject to a moratorium since 2005, pending the completion of an assessment of the North Field's reservoirs; the moratorium remained in place as of mid-2013. The Qatari Government has also developed gas-to-liquids capacity totalling, as of late 2012, 290,000 barrels per day (b/d) of gas-to-liquids products, condensate and liquefied petroleum gas (LPG). This capacity is divided between the Oryx and Pearl facilities. Qatar Petroleum holds a majority share in the Pearl plant, where Royal Dutch Shell, the plant's other shareholder, commenced operations in early 2011. Full capacity at the facility was reached in late 2012. The Pearl facility is the world's first integrated gas-to-liquids project, joining upstream output of natural gas with conversion facilities on shore. Qatar Petroleum holds a majority stake in the Oryx plant, which has been fully operational since 2009; Sasol-Chevron Gas-to-Liquids is the other shareholder.

From 1991 until 1997, when it was overtaken by Iran, Saudi Arabia was the second largest regional producer of natural gas after Algeria. Saudi Arabia subsequently remained the third largest regional producer until 2009, when, in addition to Iran and Algeria, its output of 78,500m. cu m was also outstripped by that of Qatar. In 2012, as in the two previous years, Saudi Arabia ranked ahead of Algeria as the region's third largest producer, with an estimated output of 102,800m. cu m. At 1 January 2013 Saudi Arabia's proven reserves of natural gas were estimated at 8,200,000m. cu m and thus ranked as the third largest resource in the region and the sixth largest world-wide. According to official sources, moreover, exploration for natural gas has been carried out in less than 20% of Saudi Arabia's territory. More than one-half of the country's reserves are associated with petroleum—nearly 60% of total reserves are associated with petroleum reserves within the onshore Ghawar and the offshore Safaniya and Zuluf oilfields. A key element of the Saudi Government's economic strategy is to substitute gas for oil (for oil production, power generation, desalination, etc.) in order to release greater volumes of oil for export. In late 2006, in order (exclusively) to meet increased domestic demand (consumption of gas amounted to 87,700m. cu m in 2010, 92,300m. cu m in 2011 and an estimated 102,800m. cu m in 2012), the Ministry of Petroleum and Mineral Resources and Saudi Aramco announced plans to boost reserves by some 1,400,000m. cu m of non-associated gas through discoveries by 2016, together, possibly, with an additional 1,400,000m. cu m of associated gas. An exploration initiative was to incorporate the sinking of more than 300 new wells, including about 70 exploratory wells, mainly in non-associated offshore structures.

The most important ventures in the search for non-associated gas are those being pursued by foreign consortiums in Saudi Arabia's Rub al-Khali (the 'Empty Quarter'). For instance, in early 2004 Lukoil of Russia and Sinopec of China were awarded tenders to explore for and produce natural gas in Rub al-Khali. The South Rub al-Khali Company, in which Royal Dutch Shell and Saudi Aramco have equal shares following Total's withdrawal in early 2008, has been exploring concessions adjacent to the Shaybah and Kidan oilfields since mid-2006. In mid-2013 it was reported that only Royal Dutch Shell and Lukoil were reported to have almost completed testing in Rub al-Khali. Industry sources indicated that the development of resources discovered by those companies there would depend on the payment of higher prices for natural gas by the Saudi Arabian Government; however, no significant commercial discoveries had been reported in Rub al-Khali at that time. Outside Rub al-Khali, significant discoveries of non-associated gas have recently been made in the offshore Khuff formation, where the Karan gasfield came on stream in 2011. The offshore Dorra gasfield, located in the Saudi Arabian-Kuwaiti Neutral (Partitioned) Zone, began production in 2008 while remaining under seismic investigation. Saudi Aramco has forecast that annual domestic demand for natural gas will have increased to some 150,000m. cu m by 2030. In 2011 daily domestic gas-processing capacity amounted to some 260m. cu m, including natural gas liquids (NGLs) capacity of 1.1m. b/d. Projects that aimed to raise daily processing capacity to some 350m. cu m were reportedly ongoing in 2013.

At 1 January 2013 the proven reserves of natural gas in the UAE, estimated at 6,100,000m. cu m, were the fourth largest in the Middle East and North Africa, and the seventh largest world-wide. In 2012 the UAE ranked as the sixth largest producer of natural gas in the region, with output of an estimated 51,700m. cu m, compared with 52,300m. cu m in 2011. The emirate of Abu Dhabi is the location of the UAE's largest reserves, including the Khuff reservoirs of non-associated gas, which contain some of the largest deposits in the world. In 2013 the UAE's estimated proven reserves of natural gas were sufficient to last for more than 100 years at the rate of production prevailing in 2012. Domestic consumption rose from 36,400m. cu m in 2002 to an estimated 62,900m. cu m in 2012, boosted, not least, by huge investment in a shift towards the use of natural gas for power generation. Future domestic consumption needs will be met in large part by imports from Qatar, however, as the development of domestic production will focus on NGLs and condensates, and on gas reinjection to facilitate production of crude petroleum from mature oilfields. Moreover, much of the UAE's natural gas is difficult to develop and process economically for domestic consumption, owing to its high sulphur content.

Despite the difficulties of sour gas development, a number of programmes that aim to expand the exploitation of national reserves for domestic consumption have recently been completed or are underway. The most important of these are the onshore gas development, integrated gas development (IGD) and offshore associated gas (OAG) programmes. IGD includes the development of a new facility, Habshan-5, to process associated gas from the UAE's Umm Shaif field and sour gas from the Habshan fields. Costing an estimated US $9,000m., and reportedly 90% complete in mid-2012, Habshan-5 is a key element in the development of national reserves. Construction work on Habshan-5 was due to be completed in late 2013. Meanwhile, OAG, which is being undertaken as part of the IGD programme, involves the construction of two gas processing plants on Das Island to feed additional gas for processing—and, ultimately, domestic consumption—to Habshan. Other ventures include that by Abu Dhabi National Oil Co (ADNOC), in collaboration with Occidental Petroleum, to develop production of sour gas on a large scale at the Shah oilfield. This project is scheduled to become operational in 2014, with projected annual output of some 5,000m. cu m of marketable gas. Exports of Qatari gas to the UAE will be facilitated by the Dolphin Gas Project (see above). The first commercial supply of Qatari gas as part of the project (via pipeline to a receiving facility at Taweelah, Abu Dhabi) commenced in mid-2007; by February 2008 Qatari gas was being transported to the UAE at a daily rate of about 53m. cu m. The UAE is an important exporter of LNG, Abu Dhabi having long been a major supplier to Japan's Tokyo Electric Power Co. In 2012 exports of LNG amounted to 7,600m. cu m, of which 7,500m. cu m were supplied to Japan.

Iraq's proven reserves of natural gas were estimated at 3,600,000m. cu m at 1 January 2013. According to EIA, some 75% of Iraq's reserves of natural gas are associated with petroleum, lying, for the most part, within the oilfields of Kirkuk, Nahr (Bin) Umar, Majnoon, Halfaya, Nasiriya, Rumaila (North and South) and Zubair. Iraqi production has declined enormously from peak levels achieved in the late 1980s. Since the US-led military campaign to oust the regime of Saddam Hussain in March–April 2003, output has fluctuated between an estimated 800m. cu m (2012) and 1,900m. cu m (2008). In 2010, according to EIA, Iraq flared most of the natural gas that it produced, rather than consuming it domestically or exporting it, and ranked fourth in the world in terms of quantity of natural gas flared, as a consequence of inadequate infrastructure. There is also large-scale resort to reinjection in order to aid oil recovery. Iraq aimed to raise annual output of natural gas to some 70,000m. cu m over the term of its strategic plan for 2008–17 and to cease flaring. As part of efforts to achieve these objectives, a bidding process is under way for licences to develop the unassociated al-Mansuriyah, Akkas and Siba gasfields. Successful bidders in the four rounds that took place up to May 2012 were KazMunayGas (Akkas), Korea Gas Corpn (Akkas and al-Mansuriyah), Kuwait Energy (al-Mansuriyah and Siba) and Turkish Petroleum Corpn (al-Mansuriyah and Siba). The Iraqi Ministry of Oil has also signalled that a fifth round of bidding was to be held for exploration licences by the end of 2013. In 2011 the Iraqi Ministry of Oil, Royal Dutch Shell and Mitsubishi Corpn signed an agreement to establish the Basra Gas Co joint venture to capture flared gas at the southern Rumaila, Zubair and West Qurna Phase One oilfields over a 25-year period. The state-owned South Gas Co holds a 51% stake in the joint venture, Royal Dutch Shell 44% and Mitsubishi Corpn the remaining 5%. Over the lifetime of the project Basra Gas Co is to invest a total of US $17,200m. in infrastructure ($12,800m.) and in the construction of an LNG facility ($4,400m.) with a daily exporting capacity of some 17m. cu m. Under the terms of the agreement, Basra Gas Co must sell processed gas to South Gas Co to meet local demand. However, it will be allowed to export any gas that is surplus to the needs of Iraqi power plants. The project's stakeholders announced the commencement of operations in May 2013. Official sources have stated that by 2017 the project will be able to process all of the gas that was being lost daily to flaring at the southern oilfields as of mid-2013.

The attack by Islamist militants on Algeria's Tigantourine gas-processing plant near In Amenas (see below) in January 2013 highlighted the country's key role as a supplier—the fourth largest—of natural gas to Europe. At 1 January 2013 Algeria's proven reserves of natural gas, standing at an estimated 4,500,000m. cu m, were the second largest in Africa, after those of Nigeria. More than one-half of Algeria's reserves, which consist largely of associated gas, lie in the huge Hassi R'Mel field. Algeria also possesses vast, undeveloped reserves of shale gas that, according to a survey published in 2011, totalled an estimated 6,500,000m. cu m. In 2012 Algeria's production of natural gas was estimated at 81,500m. cu m—about one-third more than that of Egypt, the country's closest African rival in terms of output; however, this represented a decline from 82,700m. cu m in 2011 and 88,200m. cu m in 2005. Owing to the depletion of its mature fields and, as a consequence of delays, the failure of new projects to compensate for this, Algeria's output of dry natural gas has declined fairly steadily since 2005. Several projects are now scheduled to become operational in 2014–16, most notably the Southwest Gas Project, which includes ventures in which GDF Suez (Touat), Repsol (Reggane Nord) and Total (Timimoun) are involved in partnership with the state-owned Société Nationale pour la Recherche, la Production, le Transport, la Transformation et la Commercialisation des Hydrocarbures (Sonatrach). (Legislation enacted in 2005 stipulates that Sonatrach—the Algerian agency responsible for, *inter alia*, the production and wholesale distribution of natural gas—must hold a stake of at least 51% in any natural gas venture.) The Southwest Gas Project also encompasses the construction of new infrastructure, including a pipeline—GR5—linking new gas collection and treatment plants to the Hassi R'Mel gasfield. An additional major initiative in the south-west is the Menzel Ledjmet East project, which became operational in early 2013 under the leadership of Italy's Eni. It has been estimated that, provided the necessary funding is forthcoming and infrastructural shortcomings are repaired, these and other new projects in preparation could boost Algeria's production of natural gas by almost 30,000m. cu m annually before 2020. In 2012 Algerian consumption of natural gas amounted to an estimated 30,900m. cu m. Domestic consumption is focused largely on electricity generation and petrochemical feedstock uses. Foreign investment in the country's gas sector has been allowed to increase gradually, and foreign interests are partners with Sonatrach in many production and wholesale distribution initiatives. Investors' reluctance to tender for new projects on the prevailing terms was reported in mid-2013 to have prompted the Algerian Government to introduce fiscal incentives intended to encourage foreign participation in hydrocarbons exploration ventures off shore, and in the development of onshore shale resources. Plans also exist to allow foreign participation in gas retailing projects. Algeria exports gas to Europe via the Enrico Mattei (formerly Transmediterranean or Transmed) pipeline to Italy (via Tunisia) and via the Pedro Duran Farell (formerly Maghreb–Europe Gas) pipeline to Spain (via Morocco). Western Europe is the most important destination for exports of Algerian natural gas, and it was hoped that these could be increased through the development—via an innovative joint venture between Statoil of Norway, Sonatrach and BP—of seven proven gasfields that were already in production in the In Salah region.

Output resulting from this joint venture finally began in 2004, having been delayed by several factors, including slower growth in demand in potential European markets, such as Spain, and new EU legislation governing re-exports of natural gas. As the liberalization of EU gas markets has occurred, so-called 'destination clauses' in gas delivery contracts that prevented the resale of the gas delivered have been subject to legal challenges. In 2007 an agreement was reached between Algeria and the European Commission for the removal of 'destination clauses' from contracts pertaining to both pipeline and LNG supplies. Output from the joint venture In Salah gasfields, whose annual capacity amounts to some 9,000m. cu m, is being marketed in Europe, Turkey and North Africa. Since 2002 Sonatrach and BP have collaborated on an initiative—the largest wet gas project in Algeria—to increase production in In Amenas, in the Illizi basin of south-eastern Algeria, where four wet gasfields have been developed. Output from In Amenas commenced in 2007 and was expected to rise to an annual level of 9,000m. cu m of gas and 50,000 barrels of gas liquids. In 2004 Repsol YPF and Gas Natural (now Gas Natural Fenosa) won a tender to develop a project at Gassi Touil, from which supplies to Spain and other European markets were scheduled to commence in 2009. However, the contract was terminated in November 2009, following a contractual dispute between the two Spanish companies and Sonatrach that had precipitated the suspension of the project in 2007. The project, now being undertaken solely by Sonatrach, is scheduled to become operational in 2014.

Work on a new pipeline—Medgaz—linking Algeria directly to Spain and, thereafter, France, commenced in 2007, proceeding to the construction of the deepwater pipeline beneath the Mediterranean Sea in March 2008. Medgaz came on stream in May 2011, with an annual capacity amounting to 8,000m. cu m. As of mid- 2013 Sonatrach held the largest stake in the project (42%). Pipelines to extend Medgaz from Spain to France were reported to be at the planning stage in early 2012 and were expected to become operational in 2013–15. In 2002 Sonatrach concluded an agreement with ENEL of Italy and Wintershall of Germany to form a consortium to construct another pipeline—GALSI—from Algeria to Italy. Construction was initially scheduled to begin in 2012, but was delayed owing to seismic problems discovered in 2008, which forced the routes first proposed for GALSI to be changed. (It was originally envisaged that GALSI would run to Cagliari in Sardinia, and from there onwards, both onshore and offshore, to Olbia, Sardinia, and Castiglion della Pescaia, in mainland Italy. At mid-2013 GALSI's route remained undetermined, pending the completion of ongoing feasibility studies.) Wintershall withdrew from the GALSI project in 2008, leaving as stakeholders Sonatrach (41.6%), Edison SpA (20.8%), ENEL (15.6%), Sardinia Autonomous Region (via Sfirs, 11.6%) and Hera Trading (10.4%).

Since 2002 the Trans-Saharan Natural Gas Consortium, comprising Sonatrach and the Nigerian Natural Gas Petroleum Corpn (NNGPC), which together hold a 90% stake, and the Republic of Niger (10%), has been conducting a study into the feasibility of constructing a trans-Saharan natural gas pipeline from Warri, Nigeria, through Niger, to Hassi R'Mel. The so-called NIGAL project, a formidable undertaking of some 4,000 km in length, would carry Nigerian natural gas to European markets after linking with Medgaz and the Enrico Mattei pipeline. The Algerian Government has reportedly set 2015 as the target date for the completion of the project, which is expected to cost US $20,000m. In early 2009, following a meeting between officials from Sonatrach and NNGPC, plans for NIGAL were reported to be close to completion. The Presidents of Algeria and Nigeria met in June 2011 to discuss a detailed timetable for the construction of the pipeline. OAO Gazprom, Total and Eni were among the companies that were said to have expressed an interest in the NIGAL project at that time. Algeria pioneered the production of LNG and in 2012 was the seventh largest exporter in the world after Qatar, Malaysia, Australia, Nigeria, Indonesia and Trinidad and Tobago, meeting about 5% of world demand. France was the most important destination for Algerian LNG in 2012, followed by Turkey and Spain. Algerian contracted exports of natural gas by pipeline totalled 34,800m. cu m in 2012. Italy was the destination for about 60% of Algerian natural gas exports by pipeline in that year, while Spain accounted for 29% of the total.

In 2012 Egypt, after Algeria, was the second largest African producer of natural gas, with output, estimated at 60,900m. cu m, slightly lower than confirmed production of 61,400m. cu m in 2011. Output has increased rapidly in recent years—in 2002 it amounted to only 27,300m. cu m. Production soared by 29% in both 2005 and 2006. At 1 January 2013 Egypt's proven reserves of natural gas were estimated to total 2,000,000m. cu m. These reserves have been boosted very substantially in recent years by the discovery of rich deposits in the Mediterranean, the Nile Delta—together the location of more than 80% of total reserves and 70% of production, according to EIA—and the Western Desert. Further exploration and development activity, especially in the Nile Delta, is being undertaken by the International Egyptian Oil Co (which belongs to Italy's Eni), in partnership with foreign interests. In 2012 Egyptian consumption of natural gas totalled an estimated 52,600m. cu m, compared with 49,600m. cu m in 2011, and representing a significant increase from 2002, in which year consumption had amounted to only 26,500m. cu m. Growth in consumption has occurred largely as a result of the conversion of Egypt's thermal power plants to the use of gas for generating purposes, but the Ministry of Petroleum is also pursuing a strategy of expanding natural gas usage for industrial, commercial and domestic purposes in all of the country's governorates. In 2007 the Egyptian Natural Gas Holding Co concluded an agreement with a consortium of banks, led by the Arab International Bank, to provide finance totalling £E512m. for the construction of gas supply infrastructure linking Taba to Sharm el-Sheikh and Shokhair to Hurghada. The aim of the project was to provide natural gas to 6m. housing units by 2013. In 2008 the World Bank approved loans for the Natural Gas Connections Project, which aims to convert consumption of LPG to natural gas by investing in new connections, and to boost the use of natural gas in densely populated residential areas.

With reserves and production both regarded as ample to meet growing domestic demand in the near term, the priority of the Egyptian Government in recent years has been to realize the export potential of the natural gas sector in order to compensate for declining revenues from oil exports. However, the development of exports has been constrained by the pursuit of a policy whereby reserves of natural gas are divided equally between domestic consumption, future generations and exports. In 2008, in response to rising domestic demand and low international prices for natural gas, the Government applied a two-year moratorium on new export contracts. In 2010, according to EIA, Egypt's exports of natural gas by pipeline and as LNG combined fell by 20%, to some 15,000m. cu m. Development of the resource's export potential has taken place mainly within the framework of the Arab Gas Pipeline (AGP) project, under which Egypt undertook, in 2001, to supply Jordan, Lebanon and Syria with natural gas over a 30-year period. The total cost of the 1,200-km AGP has been estimated at more than US $1,200m. In 2008 Egypt was reported to be supplying Jordan with 2,800m. cu m of natural gas annually, under a 15-year contract, from the project's first two phases. Meanwhile, the third phase of the AGP, running from Rihad, Jordan, to Syria's Deir Ali power station, south of Damascus, became operational. Under this third phase Egypt was initially to supply Syria with natural gas at a daily rate of 2.5m. cu m, and was then to increase the amount gradually, to total 6m. cu m by 2016. A fourth phase of the AGP runs from Syria to Lebanon. A branch of the AGP that runs from Arish, in the Sinai Peninsula, to Ashkelon, Israel, was reported in 2010 to have resumed operations, having been closed as a result of domestic opposition to the contractual terms for, and the pricing of gas exports to, Israel, in addition to technical problems. In 2006 Egypt, Syria, Jordan, Turkey, Lebanon and Romania agreed that the AGP should be extended to Turkey, in preparation for its eventual connection to the planned Nabucco pipeline, which would allow natural gas to be transported via Turkey to Austria and other European destinations. However, owing to increasing political instability in the region (not least the conflict in Syria), this project has not progressed since 2011. Moreover, politically motivated sabotage in Egypt has interrupted the operation of the AGP on numerous occasions since 2011.

In addition to the pipeline project, foreign partners, including Gas Natural Fenosa of Spain, Royal Dutch Shell and Eni, are involved in LNG export projects. A liquefaction facility constructed at Damietta by Unión Fenosa became operational in early 2005. Output from a two-train LNG export project, constructed at Idku by BG, in partnership with Petronas, also commenced at that time. Gaz de France is the main purchaser from Idku's first train. BG LNG Services agreed to supply LNG from Idku's second train to the USA from mid-2006, but the destination for these supplies was subsequently to be switched to a terminal at Brindisi, Italy. In 2012 Egypt's contracted exports of LNG totalled 6,700m. cu m (compared with 8,600m. cu m in 2011), the country thus ranking as the world's 13th largest exporter. Japan was the principal destination for these exports, accounting for 1,400m. cu m (about 21% of the total), followed by France, which received 900m. cu m (13%).

Libya's proven reserves of natural gas were estimated at 1,500,000m. cu m at 1 January 2013. There was little annual variation in output during the 1990s and early 2000s, up to 2003, when production ranged, approximately, between 5,000m. cu m and 6,000m. cu m. Subsequently, output increased steadily, rising to 8,100m. cu m in 2004 and totalling 15,900m. cu m in both 2008 and 2009. Production increased again, to 16,800m. cu m, in 2010, but fell sharply, to only 7,900m. cu m, in 2011 as a consequence of civil war. Output of natural gas was halted entirely for long periods during that year, but was reported in mid-2012 to have recovered swiftly since the collapse of the regime of Muammar al-Qaddafi. Production for 2012 as a whole was estimated at 12,200m. cu m. Official Libyan sources regard current estimates of proven reserves as an inadequate indication of the country's wealth in natural gas, since relatively little exploration for it has been undertaken. Where it has been pursued, considerable success has been achieved. Exploration has intensified greatly in recent years as the Government has sought to implement policies of substituting, where possible, gas for petroleum for the purposes of domestic consumption, in order to release greater quantities of petroleum for export, and of increasing its exports of natural gas to European markets. The flaring of associated gas, which reportedly totalled some 3,400m. cu m in 2010, is also being reduced. Until 2005 Spain was the only European market to be supplied by Libya. Since that time, however, Italy and other European destinations have been supplied with Libyan natural gas through the Western Libyan Gas Project (WLGP), an equal joint venture between Eni and Libya's National Oil Corpn (NOC), and through 'Greenstream', an underwater pipeline running from the Libyan coast to Sicily. Under the WLGP, Libya aims, for a period of some 25 years, to export about 8,000m. cu m per year from facilities on its Mediterranean coast to Italy and France. Since 2007 this amount of gas has indeed been exported annually from Melitah via the Greenstream link to south-eastern Sicily. The volume of gas exported via Greenstream declined sharply in 2011, to only 2,300m. cu m, for the reason noted above, but by April 2012 Italian import data indicated that it had recovered to 75% of the pre-civil war level.

Libya is also a potential participant in a project to transport, by means of a new pipeline, gas from Egypt, Libya, Tunisia and Algeria to southern Europe, via Morocco. A long-standing agreement exists between Libya and Tunisia for the formation of a joint venture to construct a natural gas pipeline running from Mellitah to Gabès, Tunisia. The two countries' respective Governments were reported at mid-2013 to be considering plans to construct the Mellitah–Gabès link. Libya was the second country, after Algeria, to commence exporting LNG, but this trade has never realized its full potential. One reason for this has been a lack of access to the technological solutions to make good the deficiencies of Libya's sole LNG facility at Marsa el-Brega, owing to the sanctions regimes that have been applied to Libya in recent years. In 2011 the facility suffered a further setback when it was damaged in the civil war. Prior to the conflict Enagás of Spain had been the sole recipient of Libyan LNG—it took delivery of 100m. cu m in 2011. In 2005 Royal Dutch Shell concluded an agreement with Libya's state-owned NOC in which it undertook, among other things, to develop Libya's LNG export capacity. Royal Dutch Shell reportedly intended to develop Marsa el-Brega and, possibly, also to create new LNG export facilities. Shell's decision in 2011 to withdraw from natural gas exploration owing to disappointing results, in combination with other issues potentially affecting feedstock availability, meant that the status of this initiative remained uncertain at mid-2013. In 2012 Libya's exports of natural gas were estimated to have totalled 6,500m. cu m, all of which was supplied via pipeline. Italy was consequently the sole recipient of Libyan gas exports in 2012.

Elsewhere in the Middle East and North Africa, at 1 January 2013 the proven reserves of natural gas of Kuwait were estimated at 1,800,000m. cu m, and those of Oman at 900,000m. cu m. In 2012 Kuwait's production of natural gas totalled an estimated 14,500m. cu m, while that of Oman amounted to some 29,000m. cu m. Most of Kuwait's proven reserves are of associated gas and output therefore fluctuates in line with changes to the country's OPEC oil production quota. The country is pursuing a strategy to raise the proportion of electric power that it derives from natural gas, and to increase the use of natural gas in water desalination and petrochemical production, in order to release more petroleum for export; and to boost domestic production by utilizing associated gas that has hitherto largely been flared. The Kuwait Oil Co aims to raise annual production of natural gas to some 40,000m. cu m by 2030. Development of natural gas output is focused on recent discoveries of non-associated reserves in the north of the country, in particular the Jurassic field, the exploitation of whose estimated 990,000m. cu m in proven reserves has been ranked as among the most technically challenging in the world. In 2013 the first phase of the Jurassic project was producing natural gas at an annual rate of some 1,400m. cu m—less than had been envisaged initially. A second phase of the project was projected to raise annual output by some 5,000m. cu m in 2013. Kuwait has sought to initiate the development of the offshore Dorra gasfield, but this is complicated by conflicting claims to it by—as well as Kuwait itself—Saudi Arabia and Iran. Kuwait and Saudi Arabia have signalled their intention to generate annual output ranging between some 5,000m. cu m and 8,000m. cu m from Dorra by 2017, while Iran has said that it will independently pursue the development of reserves therein. Kuwait's consumption of natural gas now outstrips domestic production and demand for (natural gas-derived) electricity reportedly regularly exceeds output in the summer months. In 2009 Qatar agreed to supply Kuwait with approximately 2,000m. cu m of LNG in the summer months for a five-year period beginning in mid-2009. In the same year Kuwait reportedly concluded an agreement with Royal Dutch Shell to import LNG to the Mina al-Ahmadi regasification terminal—the first such facility of its kind in the Persian (Arabian) Gulf. Supplementary summer supplies are also acquired on the LNG 'spot' market.

Exploration, which remains ongoing, has substantially boosted Oman's proven reserves of natural gas in recent years and the resource is now regarded as a key element of the country's economic diversification strategy. Foreign interests have been allowed to participate in the exploration for, and production of, Oman's natural gas, and are also involved in the expansion of the country's pipeline network. In 2007 BP was reported to have signed a production-sharing contract focused on the Khazzan and Makarem so-called tight natural gas reservoirs, which had remained undeveloped since their discovery in 1993, owing to the technical difficulties involved in their exploitation. Resources contained by these reservoirs have been estimated to total as much as 2,800,000m. cu m, and their output is expected to amount to some 10,000m. cu m annually by 2017. Oman is a participant in the Dolphin Gas Project, from which conduit it receives about 2,000m. cu m annually of Qatari gas for generating electricity. Although domestic consumption of natural gas has risen rapidly since 2000, Oman continues to export more than one-half of its output (exclusively as LNG) owing to long-term contractual commitments. In 2000, for instance, Oman commenced exporting natural gas to South Korea, whose national Gas Corpn has agreed to purchase Omani LNG for 25 years. Exports of LNG amounted to 11,200m. cu m in 2012, of which South Korea received 5,700m. cu m and Japan 5,400m. cu m. A third gas liquefaction train commenced operations in early 2006, and the construction of a fourth, in which India may participate financially, has been proposed.

At 1 January 2013 Yemen's proven reserves of natural gas totalled an estimated 500,000m. cu m. In 2009 Yemeni production of natural gas for export commenced, totalling 800m. cu m. Output rose to 6,200m. cu m in 2010, and increased further, to 9,400m. cu m, in 2011. However, production was estimated to have declined, to 7,600m. cu m, in 2012. Output had previously been restricted to associated gas that was utilized for oilfield reinjection. The development of this resource has been spurred by a 20-year LNG sales contract concluded with Korea Gas Corpn in 2005. Similar long-term contracts were subsequently signed with GDF Suez Co, and with Total, which has led the Yemen LNG project, the country's largest industrial initiative, in which Yemen Gas Co has a 23% stake. Yemen's first liquefaction train, at Balhaf, which receives supplies via pipeline from a gasfield in the country's Marib-Jawf basin, became operational in late 2009, and a second train was brought into production there in 2010. Yemen's contracted LNG exports totalled 7,100m. cu m in 2012, compared with 8,900m. cu m in 2011, Yemen thus ranking as the world's 12th largest exporter. South Korea was the principal destination for Yemeni LNG in 2012, receiving 3,600m. cu m. Other markets included China (800m. cu m), the USA (600m. cu m), India (600m. cu m) and Thailand (500m. cu m). The USA was expected eventually to be the destination of about two-thirds of the Balhaf facility's output, with the remainder being exported to Asia. Domestic consumption of natural gas is expected to rise substantially if projects to expand Yemen's natural gas infrastructure—notably, the construction of an industrial centre at Hodeida, announced in late 2009—proceed.

Syria's proven reserves of natural gas were estimated at 300,000m. cu m at 1 January 2013, and production totalled an estimated 7,600m. cu m in 2012, compared with 8,700m. cu m in 2011. In 2010 output had risen by some 43% compared with the previous year, to 8,000m. cu m. Syrian output has been boosted by the recent completion of new projects, such as the South Central Area gas facility, constructed by Stroytransgaz of Russia, and the Ebla gas plant, operated by Suncor Energy. Total and Petro-Canada were granted licences to explore for onshore resources after participating in a bidding round in early 2010. In 2011 Syria also invited bids for the development of three offshore blocks. However, since 2011, like many other activities in the Syrian energy sector, exploration was reported virtually to have ceased owing to a combination of the continued civil conflict and the resultant imposition of sanctions against the Syrian regime. In August 2011 the USA imposed sanctions prohibiting the importation of Syrian gas products, and in January 2012 the EU banned the importation of key equipment related to the exploration, production and liquefaction of natural gas. As in countries with much larger resources, local supplies have rapidly been put to use for the production of electricity in Syria. The country had announced its intention to switch from imported refined petroleum products to natural gas for all domestic power generation and industrial purposes by 2014, but this target is now unlikely to be met. Domestic consumption rose by one-third between 2000 and 2011, according to EIA.

GAS STATISTICS

Gas: Reserves and Production (t.c.m. = trillion cu metres)

Country	Reserves 1 Jan. 2013 (t.c.m.)	Production 2012 (m. tons oil equivalent)
Iran	33.6	144.5
Iraq	3.6	0.7
Kuwait	1.8	13.1
Qatar	25.1	141.3
Saudi Arabia	8.2	92.5
UAE	6.1	46.5
Algeria	4.5	73.4
Egypt	2.0	54.8
Libya	1.5	11.0
Indonesia	2.9	64.0
Nigeria	5.2	38.9
Venezuela	5.6	29.5
Canada	2.0	140.9
Mexico	0.4	52.6
USA	8.5	619.2
Netherlands	1.0	57.5
Norway	2.1	103.4
Russian Federation	32.9	533.0
Turkmenistan	17.5	57.9
United Kingdom	0.2	36.9
Asia Pacific (excl. Indonesia)	12.6	377.2
World total (incl. others)	187.3	3,033.5
OPEC total	95.2	591.4
OPEC % world total	50.8	19.5

Source: BP, *Statistical Review of World Energy 2013*.

Notes: Figures in the Reserves column are for gas recoverable with present technology and at present prices. Figures for reserves of gas—like reserves of oil—may be subject to wide margins of error.

Definitions: Natural gas may be found on its own ('unassociated gas') or with oil ('associated gas'). 'Associated gas' exists partly as a gas cap above the oil and partly dissolved in oil—it is the presence of gas under pressure in new oilfields which drives the oil to the surface. 'Associated gas' is unavoidably produced with oil and may be flared, reinjected or used as fuel.

Natural gas is a mixture of numerous hydrocarbons and varying amounts of inert gases, including nitrogen, carbon dioxide and sulphur compounds. (Gas containing large quantities of sulphur is known as sour gas; gas without sulphur is sweet gas.) By far the biggest component of all natural gas by volume (at least 75%) is methane, CH_4. Other components are ethane—C_2H_6, propane—C_3H_8, and butane—C_4H_{10}. All of these hydrocarbons are gases at normal temperatures and pressures. Suspended in the gas are various heavier hydrocarbons, pentane (C_5H_{12}), octane, etc., which are liquids at normal temperatures and pressures. Gas with a relatively high proportion of propane, butane and the heavier hydrocarbons is known as wet gas. 'Associated natural gas' tends to be wetter than 'unassociated gas'.

Methane is the normal pipeline natural gas used for domestic and industrial purposes. It liquefies at very low temperatures (−160°C) and very high pressures, and in this condition is known as *liquefied natural gas* (LNG).

Ethane is either kept with methane and used as a fuel, or is separated and used as a feedstock for petrochemicals production. Ethane is not traded on its own internationally.

Propane and butane are used as cylinder gases for a large number of industrial and domestic purposes—camping gas and cigarette lighter gas is either propane or butane. The two gases liquefy at higher temperatures and lower pressures than methane. In their liquid state they are known as *liquefied petroleum gases* (LPGs).

Pentane and other heavier liquids are used for a variety of purposes, including the spiking of heavy crude oils and as petrochemical feedstocks. These hydrocarbons, liquid at normal temperatures and pressures, are known as *natural gasolines* or *condensate*.

Together, liquefied petroleum gases and natural gasolines are referred to as *natural gas liquids* (NGLs).

Natural Gas Consumption (millions of metric tons of oil equivalent*)

	2010	2011	2012
Canada	85.5	90.8	90.6
Mexico	65.2	69.0	75.3
USA	619.3	626.5	654.0
North America total	770.1	786.2	820.0
Belgium-Luxembourg	17.0	14.9	15.2
France	42.7	36.8	38.2
Germany	75.0	67.1	67.7
Italy	68.5	64.2	61.8
Netherlands	39.2	34.3	32.8
Romania	12.2	12.5	12.1
Spain	31.2	29.0	28.2
Turkey	35.1	41.2	41.7
United Kingdom	89.3	74.5	70.5
Europe total (incl. others)	503.8	466.0	459.0
Africa	97.0	102.6	110.5
Australia	23.1	23.0	22.9
China, People's Republic	96.2	117.5	129.5
Former USSR	521.7	539.2	526.4
Japan	85.1	95.0	105.1
Middle East	339.1	355.3	370.6
South and Central America	137.0	140.8	148.6
World total	2,864.1	2,914.2	2,987.1

* One metric ton of oil equivalent = 1,120 cu m of gas.

Source: BP, *Statistical Review of World Energy 2013*.

THE RELIGIONS OF THE MIDDLE EAST AND NORTH AFRICA

ISLAM

R. B. SERJEANT

Islam is a major world religion and the faith predominating throughout the Middle East (with the exception of Israel) and North Africa. There are substantial Christian minorities in some countries (e.g. Lebanon and Egypt) and communities of oriental Jews and other faiths, for centuries integrated with the Muslim majority. Islam is not only a highly developed religious system, but also an established and distinctive culture embracing every aspect of human activity from theology, philosophy and literature to the visual arts and even the individual's routine daily conduct. Its characteristic intellectual manifestation, therefore, is in the field of Islamic law, the *Shari'a*. Though in origin a Semitic Arabian faith, Islam was also the inheritor of the legacy of classical Greek and Roman civilization and, in its major phase of intellectual, social and cultural development after its emergence from its Arabian womb, it was affected by Christian, Jewish and Persian civilization. In turn, Greek scientific and philosophical writings—in the form of direct translations into Arabic or as a principal element in the books of Arab scholars—began to enter medieval Europe in Latin renderings about the early 12th century from the brilliant intellectual circles of Islamic Spain, and formed a potent factor in the little Renaissance of Western Europe.

Islamic civilization had, by about the 18th century, clearly lost its initiative to the ascendant West and has not since regained it. Today, however, certain oil-rich Arab states of the Persian (Arabian) Gulf, notably Saudi Arabia and Kuwait, have made significant progress in the world of international finance and mercantilism, engaging in activities such as the provision of Islamic banking services—for which there has been a significant increase in demand since the latter part of the 20th century. The tiny kingdom of Bahrain has also become a leading centre of Islamic banking and finance in recent years, while other countries in the region are promoting considerable growth in this area.

History

The founder of the religion of Islam was the Prophet Muhammad b. 'Abdullah, born about AD 570, a member of the noble house of Hashim, belonging to the 'Abd Manaf clan, itself a part of the Quraish tribal confederation of Mecca. 'Abd Manaf may be described as semi-priestly, since they had the privilege of certain functions during the annual pilgrimage to the Meccan Ka'ba—a cube-shaped temple set in the sacred enclave (*haram*). Quraish controlled this enclave, which was maintained inviolate from war or killing, and they had established a pre-eminence and even loose hegemony over many Arabian tribes which they had induced to enter a trading alliance extending over the main Arabian land routes, north and south, east and west. Muhammad clashed with the powerful Quraish leaders in Mecca (temple guardians, chiefs and merchant adventurers), when, aged about 40, he began to proclaim the worship of one God, Allah, as against their multiplicity of gods. The Quraish leaders were contemptuous of his mission.

While his uncle Abu Talib, head of the house of Hashim, lived, he protected Muhammad from physical harm, but after Abu Talib's death Muhammad sought protection from tribes outside Mecca. However, even after he had asked to remain quietly without preaching, they would not accept him and Thaqif of Taif (al-Ta'if, south of Mecca) drove him away. Ultimately, pilgrims of the Aws and Khazraj tribes of Yathrib (Medina), some 200 miles north of Mecca, agreed to protect him there, undertaking to associate no other god with Allah and accepting certain moral stipulations. Muhammad left Mecca with his Companion, Abu Bakr, in 622—this is the year of the *Hijra* or Hegira ('flight' or migration).

Arriving in Yathrib, Muhammad formed a federation or community (*umma*) of Aws and Khazraj known as the 'Supporters' (*Ansar*), followed by their Jewish client tribes, and the 'Emigrants' (*Muhajirun*—his refugee Quraish adherents), with himself as the ultimate arbiter of the *umma* as a whole. However, there remained a local opposition covertly antagonistic to him, the *Munafiqun*, rendered as 'Hypocrites'. Two internal issues had now to be fought by Muhammad—the enforcement of his position as theocratic head of the federation, and the acquisition of revenue to maintain his position; externally, he adopted an aggressive attitude towards the Meccan Quraish.

In Yathrib Muhammad's disposal of the Jewish tribes who made common cause with the 'Hypocrites' improved his financial position. Muhammad overcame the Meccan Quraish more as a result of skilful political manoeuvring than of occasional armed clashes, and in year 8 he entered Mecca peacefully. He had previously declared Yathrib a *haram*, renaming it *Madinat al-Nabi* (Medina, the City of the Prophet)—the two cities, known as al-Haraman, have become the holy land of Islam. Muhammad was conciliatory towards his defeated Quraish kinsmen, and, after his success in al-Ta'if, deputations came from the Arabian tribes to make terms with the Prophet—the heritor of the influence of the Meccan Quraish.

EARLY ISLAM

The two main tenets of Islam are embodied in the formula of the creed, 'There is no god but Allah and Muhammad is the Apostle of God'. Unitarianism (*tawhid*), as opposed to polytheism (*shirk*) or making partners with God, is Islam's basic principle, coupled with the authority conferred on Muhammad by God. Muhammad made little change to the ancient Arabian religion—he abolished idolatry but confirmed the pilgrimage to the Ka'ba; the Koran, the sacred Book in Arabic revealed to Muhammad for his people, lays down certain social and moral rules. Among these are the condemnation of usury or interest (*riba*) on loans and the prohibition of wine (*khamr*)—both ordinances have always been difficult to enforce. In many respects, the similarities between the old and new faiths enabled Arabia to embrace Islam with relative ease. While there is incontrovertible evidence of Muhammad's contact with Judaism, and even with Christianity, and the Koran contains versions of narrative known to the sacred books of these faiths, these are used to point to purely Arabian morals. The limited social law laid down by the Koran is supplemented by a body of law and precept derived from the *Hadith* or Tradition of Muhammad's practice (*Sunna*) at Medina, and welded into the Islamic system, mainly in its second and third centuries.

SUBSEQUENT HISTORY

Immediately after Muhammad's death in 632, Abu Bakr, delegated by the Prophet to lead the prayer during his last indisposition, became his successor or Caliph. Some Medinan 'Supporters' had attempted a breakaway from Quraish overlordship, but Abu Bakr adroitly persuaded them to accept his succession. Office in Arabia, generally speaking, is hereditary within a family group, though elective within that group, and Abu Bakr's action had taken no account of the claims of 'Ali, the Prophet's cousin and son-in-law. The house of Hashim, to which Muhammad and 'Ali belonged, was plainly aggrieved that a member of a minor Quraish clan, not of the 'house' (*bayt*) of their ancestor, Quṣaiy, the holder of religious offices in Mecca which he bequeathed to his descendants, should have snatched supreme power. Muhammad's Arabian coalition also weakened, the tribes particularly objecting to paying taxes to Medina, but Abu Bakr's uncompromising leadership re-asserted cohesion. Expansionist campaigns beyond Arabia undertaken during his Caliphate were continued under his successors 'Umar and 'Uthman, diverting tribal energies to profitable warfare in Mesopotamia, Palestine-Syria, Egypt and Persia. Muslim armies were eventually to conquer North Africa, much of Spain, parts of France, and even to besiege

Rome, while in the east they later penetrated as far as Central Asia and India.

During 'Uthman's tenure the pace of conquest temporarily slackened and the turbulent tribes, now settled in southern Iraq and Egypt, began to dispute the Caliph's disposal of plunder and revenue, maintaining that he favoured members of his own house unduly. A delegation of tribal malcontents from Egypt murdered 'Uthman in the holy city of Medina, and in the resultant confusion 'Ali, Muhammad's cousin, was elected Caliph with the support of the tribesmen responsible for the murder. This raised grave constitutional problems for the young Muslim state, and is regarded as the origin of the first and greatest schism in Islam.

If legitimist arguments were the sole consideration, 'Ali's claims to succession would appear to be superior, but his claim had already been superseded by 'Uthman—whose father belonged to the Umaiya clan which had opposed Muhammad, but whose mother was of Hashim ancestry. 'Uthman naturally appointed Umaiya men loyal to him to commands in the Empire, notably Mu'awiya—the son of Abu Sufyan who had led Quraish opposition to Muhammad at Mecca, but was later reconciled with him—as governor of Syria. Mu'awiya demanded that 'Uthman's murderers be brought to justice in accordance with the law, but 'Ali, unable to deliver the murderers from among his supporters, was driven by events to take up arms against Mu'awiya. When they clashed at Siffin, Syria, 'Ali was forced, against his better judgement, to submit to the arbitration of the Koran and *Sunna*, thus automatically losing the position of supreme arbiter, inherited by the Caliphs from Muhammad. Although history is silent as to what the arbiters actually judged upon, it was most likely as to whether 'Ali had broken the law established by Muhammad, and that he was held to have sheltered unprovoked murderers. The arbiters deposed him from the Caliphial office, though historians allege that trickery entered into their action.

'Ali was murdered shortly afterwards by one of a group of his former supporters which had come out against the arbitration it had first urged upon him. This group, the Khawarij, is commonly held to be the forerunner of the Ibadis of Oman and elsewhere. Mu'awiya became Caliph and founder of the Umaiyad dynasty, with its capital in Damascus. The ambitions of the Hashim house were not allayed, however, and when Umaiyad troops slew 'Ali's son, Husain, at Karbala in southern Iraq, they created the greatest Shi'a martyr (see Religious Groupings).

The house of Hashim also included the descendants of 'Abbas, the Prophet's uncle, but 'Abbas had opposed Muhammad until late in his life. The 'Abbasids made common cause with the 'Ali-id Shi'a against the Umaiyads, but were evidently more able in the political field. In the Umaiyad empire the Arabian tribes formed a kind of military élite, but were constantly at factious war with one another. The Hashemites rode to power on the back of a rebellion against the Umaiyads which broke out in Khorasan in eastern Persia; however, it was the 'Abbasid branch of Hashim which assumed the Caliphate and ruled from the capital they founded at Baghdad.

The 'Abbasid Caliphate endured up to the destruction of Baghdad in 1258 by the devastating Mongol invaders of the eastern empire, but the Caliphs had long been mere instruments in the hands of Turkish and other mercenaries, and the unwieldy empire had fragmented into independent states which rose and fell, though they mostly conceded nominal allegiance to the 'Abbasid Caliphs.

The Mongol Ilkhanid sovereigns, now converted to Islam, were in turn displaced by the conquests of Tamerlane at the end of the 14th century. In fact the Islamic empire had largely been taken over by Turkic soldiery. The Mameluke or Slave rulers of medieval Egypt, who followed the Aiyubid (Kurdish) dynasty of Salah ul-Din (Saladin), were mainly Turks or Circassians. It was they who checked the Mongol advance at 'Ain Jalut in Palestine (1260). The Ottoman Turks captured Constantinople in 1453, and seized Egypt from the Mamelukes in 1516, subsequently occupying the Hedjaz where the Ashraf, descendants of the Prophet, ruled in Mecca and Medina, under first Mameluke then Turkish suzerainty. In 1533 the Turks took Baghdad, and Iraq became part of the Ottoman Empire. The Ottoman Sultans assumed the title of Caliph—though in Islamic constitutional theory it is not easy to justify this. The Ottoman Caliphs endured until the Caliphate was abolished by Mustafa Kemal (later called Atatürk, or 'Father of the Turks') in 1924. The Turks have always been characterized by their adherence to Sunni orthodoxy.

Throughout history the 'Ali-ids have constantly asserted their right to be the Imams or leaders of the Muslim community—this in the religious and political senses, since Islam is fundamentally theocratic. The Shi'a, or followers of 'Ali and his descendants, were in constant rebellion against the 'Abbasids and came to form a distinct schismatic group of legitimist sects—at one time the Fatimid Shi'a rulers of Egypt were close to conquering the main part of the Islamic world. The principal Shi'a sects today are the Ithna'asharis, the Isma'ilis and the near-orthodox Zaidis of Yemen. The Safavids who conquered Persia at the beginning of the 16th century brought it finally into the Shi'a fold. Sunni Hashemite dynasties flourish today in Jordan and Morocco, as they did until fairly recently in Iraq and Libya, and the Shi'a Zaidi ruler of Yemen was only displaced in 1962. The main difference between Sunnis and Shi'a concerns the Imamate, i.e. the temporal and spiritual leadership of Islam: for Sunnis, while they respect the Prophet's house, do not consider that the Imam must be a member of it; the Shi'a, on the other hand, insist on an Imam of the descendants of 'Ali and his wife Fatima, daughter of the Prophet.

It has been too readily assumed that, during the later Middle Ages and long Turkish domination, the Islamic Middle East was completely stagnant. The shift in economic patterns after the discovery of the New World and the Cape route to India, coupled with widening Western intellectual horizons and the development of science and technology, did push European culture far ahead of the Muslim Middle East. It was confronted by a vigorous and hostile Christianity intent on proselytizing in its very homelands. Muslim thinkers like Muhammad Abduh (1849–1905) of Egypt and his school asserted that Islam had become heavily overlaid with false notions—hence its decline; like earlier reformers, they were convinced that the present difficulties could be resolved by reversion to an (idealized) pure, primitive Islam. Sometimes, in effect, this meant reinterpreting religious literature to suit attitudes and ideas of modern times—as for instance when the virtual prohibition of polygamy was identified in the restrictions which define the practice. Since the earlier modern days political leaders such as Atatürk have often taken drastic measures, secularizing the state itself even in the sensitive field of education, and accusing the more conservative forms of Islam of blocking progress. In recent years the Islamic Middle East has witnessed regimes ranging from the firm supporters of traditional Islam—for example Saudi Arabia and Libya—to the anti-religious Marxist group which controlled Aden (the People's Democratic Republic of Yemen) until 1990. In Libya, nevertheless, Muammar al-Qaddafi in the 1970s published *The Green Book*, embodying his personal, socialist solution of problems of democracy and economics. Theocratic Shi'a Iran has a distinctive character of its own.

Islamic Law

Orthodox Sunni Islam finds its main expression in *Shari'a* law, which it regards with great veneration. The Sunnis have crystallized into four schools or rites (*madhhab*), all of which are recognized as valid. Although in practice the adherents of one school can sometimes have profound disagreement with another, in modern times it is claimed that the law of any one of these rites can be applied to a case. The schools, named after their founders, are the Hanbali, regarded as the strictest, with adherents mainly in Saudi Arabia; the Shafi'is, the widest in extent, with adherents in Egypt, Palestine-Syria, South Arabia and the Far East; the moderate Hanafi school, which was the official rite of the Ottoman Turkish empire and to which most Muslims in the Indian sub-continent belong; and the Malikis of the North African states, as well as Nigeria and Sudan. The Shi'ite sects have developed their own law and give prominence to *ijtihad*, the forming of independent judgement, whereas the Sunnis are more bound by *taqlid* or following ancient models. However, since the law of Sunnis, the moderate Shi'a and the Ibadis is basically derived from the same sources, the differences are generally more of emphasis than of principle.

The completely Islamic state as the theorists envisage it, organized in total conformity with the rules of the *Shari'a*, has probably never been achieved, and people's practice is often at variance with some or other requirements of *Shari'a*. Nevertheless, the imprint of Islam is unmistakably evident, in one way or another, on virtually every country in the region.

CIVIL COURTS

In modern states of the Islamic world there exists, side by side with the *Shari'a* court (judging cases on personal status, marriage, divorce, etc.), the secular court which has a wide jurisdiction (based on Western codes of law) in civil and criminal matters. This court is competent to give judgment irrespective of the creed or race of the defendant.

ISLAMIC LAW AS APPLYING TO MINORITIES

In cases of minorities (Christian or Jewish) residing as a community in Muslim countries, spiritual councils are established where judgment is passed according to the law of the community, in matters concerning personal status, under the jurisdiction of the recognized head of that community.

TRIBAL COURTS

In steppe and mountain areas of some countries a proportion of the population maintain tribal courts which administer law and justice in accordance with ancient custom and tribal procedure. Among tribes these courts are often more popular than *Shari'a* courts, because justice is swifter. Conciliation (*sulh*) is generally their objective. There is, none the less, constant pressure to eliminate customary practices where these are unequivocally seen to be contrary to Islamic principles.

AWQAF

In Muslim countries the law governing *awqaf* (singular, *waqf*), called in North Africa *habous* (*hubus*), is the law applied to religious and charitable endowments, trust and settlements. This important Islamic institution is administered in most Muslim countries by a special ministry of *awqaf*. *Awqaf*, or endowments, are pious bequests made by Muslims for the upkeep of religious institutions, public benefits, etc. Family *awqaf* provide an income partly for religious purposes and partly for the original donor's family.

Sufis

In common with other religions where simple observance of a code of law and morals proves spiritually unsatisfying, some Muslims have turned to mysticism. From early times Islamic mystics existed, known as Sufis, allegedly owing to their wearing a woollen garment. They seek complete identification with the Supreme Being, and annihilation of the self—the existence of which they term polytheism (*shirk*). The learned doctors of Islam often think ill of the Sufis, and indeed rogues and wandering mendicants found Sufism a convenient means of livelihood. Certain Sufi groups allowed themselves dispensations and, as stimulants, even used hashish and opium, which are not sanctioned by the Islamic moral code. The Sufis became organized in what are loosely called brotherhoods (*turuq*; singular, *tariqa*), and have to a large extent been incorporated into the structure of orthodox Islamic society. Some *turuq* induce ecstatic states by their performance of the *dhikr*, meaning, literally, the mentioning (of Allah). Today there is much disapproval of the more extravagant manifestations of the Sufis, and in some places these have been banned entirely.

Belief and Practice

'Islam' means the act of submitting or resigning oneself to God, and a Muslim is one who resigns or submits himself to God. Muslims disapprove of the term 'Muhammadan' for the faith of Islam, since they worship Allah, and Muhammad is only the Apostle of Allah whose duty it was to convey revelation, though he is regarded as the 'Best of Mankind'. He is the Seal (*Khatam*) of the prophets, i.e. the ultimate Prophet in a long series in which both Moses and Jesus figure. They are revered, but, like Muhammad the Prophet, they are not worshipped.

Nearly all Muslims agree on acceptance of six articles of the faith of Islam: Belief (i) in God; (ii) in His angels; (iii) in His revealed books; (iv) in His Apostles; (v) in the Resurrection and Day of Judgement; and (vi) in His predestination of good and evil.

Faith includes works, and certain practices are obligatory for the Muslim believer. These are five in number.

1. The recital of the creed (*Shahada*)—'There is no god but God (Allah) and Muhammad is the Apostle of God.' This formula is embodied in the call to prayer made by the *muezzin* (announcer) from the minaret of the mosque before each of the five daily prayers.
2. The performance of the Prayer (*Salat*) at the five appointed canonical times—in the early dawn before the sun has risen above the horizon, in the early afternoon when the sun has begun to decline, later when the sun is about midway in its course towards setting, immediately after sunset, and in the evening between the disappearance of the red glow in the west and bedtime. In prayer Muslims face towards the Ka'ba in Mecca. They unroll prayer mats and pray in a mosque (place of prostration), at home or wherever they may be, bowing and prostrating themselves before God and reciting set verses in Arabic from the Koran. On Fridays it is obligatory for men to attend congregational Prayer in the central mosque of the quarter in which they live; women do not normally attend. On this occasion formal prayers are preceded by a sermon.
3. The payment of the legal alms (*Zakat*). In early times this contribution was collected by officials of the Islamic state, and devoted to the relief of the poor, debtors, travellers and to other charitable and state purposes, and it often became, in effect, a purely secular tax on crops. Nowadays the fulfilment of this religious obligation is left to the conscience of the individual believer. The *zakat* given at the breaking of the fast at the end of Ramadan, for example, is a voluntary gift of provisions.
4. The 30 days of the fast in the month of Ramadan, the ninth month in the lunar year. As the lunar calendar is shorter by 11 days than the solar calendar, Ramadan moves from the hottest to the coldest seasons of the solar year. It is observed as a fast from dawn to sunset each day by all adults in normal health, during which time no food or drink may be taken. The sick, pregnant women, travellers and children are exempt; some states exempt students, soldiers and factory workers. The fast ends with one of the two major Muslim festivals, 'Id al-Fitr.
5. The pilgrimage (*Hajj*) to Mecca. Every Muslim is obliged, circumstances permitting, to perform this at least once in his lifetime, and when accomplished he may assume the title, *Hajji*. More than 2m. pilgrims go each year to Mecca (including some 1.5m. non-Saudi Muslims), but the holy cities of Mecca and Medina are prohibited to non-Muslims.

Before entering the sacred area around Mecca by the seventh day of Dhu'l-Hijja, the 12th month of the Muslim year, pilgrims must don the *ihram*, consisting of two unseamed lengths of white cloth, indicating that they are entering a state of consecration and casting off what is ritually impure. The pilgrims circumambulate the Ka'ba seven times, endeavouring to kiss the sacred Black Stone. Later they run seven times between the nearby twin hills of Safa and Marwah (now covered in by an immense hall), thus recalling Hagar's desperate search for water for her child Ishmael (from whom the Arabs claim descent). On the eighth day of the month the pilgrims leave the city for Mina, a small town six miles to the east. Then, before sunrise of the next day, all make for the plain below Mount 'Arafat, some 12 miles east of Mecca, where they pass the day in prayers and recitation until sunset. This point is the climax of the pilgrimage when the whole gathering returns, first to Muzdalifah where it spends the night, then to Mina where pilgrims stone the devil represented by three heaps of stones (*jamra*). The devil is said to have appeared to Abraham here and to have been driven away by Abraham throwing stones at him. This day, the 10th of Dhu'l-Hijja, is 'Id al-Adha, the Feast of the Sacrifice, and the pilgrims sacrifice an animal, usually a sheep, and have their heads shaved by one of the barbers at Mina. They return to Mecca that evening. In recent years the increasing number of pilgrims arriving (especially by air) has presented the Saudi authorities, guardians of the Holy Places, with major problems of organization, supply, health and public order. In 1988, following the tragic events of July 1987, when 402 people (including 275 Iranian pilgrims) lost their lives in clashes between the Iranians and Saudi security forces, and in order to reduce overcrowding, the Saudi Government imposed national quotas for the numbers of pilgrims performing the *Hajj*. However, overcrowding has continued to present serious problems, and tragic incidents similar to that of 1987 have not been infrequent in recent years. In January 2006 at least 345 pilgrims died in a stampede near the Jamarat Bridge in Mina. As a result of such accidents, restructuring of the bridge area was undertaken; the final stage of this work was completed in November 2009.

The Holy War (*Jihad*) against the infidel was the means whereby Arab Muslim rule made its immense expansion in the first centuries of Islam, but despite pressures to do so, it has never been elevated to form a sixth Pillar of Islam. Today some theologians interpret *jihad* in a less literal sense as the combating of evil, but it is significant that the Afghan guerrillas who resisted the Soviet presence in their country called themselves *mujahidin*, i.e. those who wage the *jihad* against the enemies of Islam.

The Koran (*Quran*—'recital' or 'reading') is for Muslims the very Word of God. The Koran consists of 114 chapters (*surah*) of uneven length, the longest coming first after the brief opening chapter called *al-Fatiha*. (The Koran is about as long as the Christian New Testament.) *Al-Fatiha* (The Opener) commences (as does every chapter) with the words, *'Bismillahi 'l-Rahmani 'l-Rahim'*, 'In the name of God, the Compassionate, the Merciful', and forms part of the ritual five prayers (*Salat*). Other special verses and chapters are also used on a variety of occasions, and Muslim children are taught to recite by heart a portion of the Koran or, preferably, the whole of it. The Koran has been the subject of vast written commentaries, but translation into other languages is not much approved by Muslims, although interlinear translations (a line of Koran underneath which is a line of translation) are used, and a number of modern translations into English and most other languages exist. The earlier (Meccan) chapters of the Koran speak of the unity of God and his wonders, of the Day of Judgement and Paradise, while the Medinan chapters tend to be occupied more with social legislation for marriage, divorce, personal and communal behaviour. The definitive redaction of the Koran was ordered by the Caliph 'Uthman (644–56).

Holy Places

Mecca (Makkah): Hedjaz province of Saudi Arabia. Mecca is centred around the Ka'ba, the most venerated building in Islam, traditionally held to have been founded by Abraham, recognized by Islam also as a prophet. It stands in the centre of the vast courtyard of the Great Mosque and has the form of a cube; its construction is of local grey stone and its walls are draped with a black curtain embroidered with a strip of writing containing verses from the Koran. In the eastern corner is set the famous Black Stone. The enlarging of the Great Mosque commenced under the second Caliph 'Umar. Both the Ka'ba and Great Mosque have undergone many renovations, notably since 1952. Mecca is the centre of the annual pilgrimage (*Hajj*) from all Muslim countries.

Medina (*Al-Madinah—The City*, i.e. of the Prophet): Hedjaz province of Saudi Arabia. Medina, formerly called Yathrib, was created as a sacred enclave (*haram*) by Muhammad, who died there in the year 11 of the *Hijra* ('flight' or migration) and was buried in the Mosque of the Prophet. Close to his tomb are those of his companions and successors, Abu Bakr and 'Umar, and a little further away, that of his daughter Fatima. Frequently damaged, restored and enlarged, the mosque building was extensively renovated by the Saudi Government in 1955.

Jerusalem (Arabic *al-Quds* or *Beit al-Maqdis*, The Hallowed/Consecrated): West Bank (annexed by Israel). Jerusalem is Islam's next most holy city after al-Haraman (Mecca and Medina), not only because it is associated with so many pre-Islamic prophets, but because Muhammad himself is popularly held to have made the 'Night Journey' there. Jerusalem contains the magnificent Islamic shrine, the Dome of the Rock (688–91), built by the Caliph 'Abd al-Malik, and the famous al-Masjid al-Aqsa (al-Aqsa Mosque).

Hebron (Al-Khalil): West Bank. The Mosque of Abraham, called al-Khalil, the 'Friend of God', is built over the tomb of Abraham, the Cave of Machpelah; it also contains the tombs of Sarah, Isaac, Rebecca, Jacob and Leah. The shrine is revered by Muslims and Jews, and is also important to Christians.

Qairawan (Kairouan): Tunisia. The city is regarded as a holy place for Muslims, seven pilgrimages to the Great Mosque of Sidi 'Uqbah b. Nafi' (an early Muslim general who founded Qairawan as a base for the Muslim invaders of North Africa) being considered the equivalent of one pilgrimage to Mecca.

Muley Idris: Morocco. The shrine at the burial place of the founder of the Idrisid dynasty in the year 687, at Walili, near Fez.

Every Middle Eastern country has a multitude of shrines and saints' tombs held in veneration, except Wahhabi states which consider saint cults to be polytheism (*shirk*). In Turkey, however, the policy of secularization led to Aya Sofya Mosque (St Sophia) being turned into a museum.

The following shrines are associated with the Shi'a or Legitimist sects of Islam.

Meshed (Mashad): Iran. The city is famous for the shrine of Imam 'Ali al-Rida/Riza, the eighth Imam of the Ithna'ashari group, which attracts many thousands of pilgrims each year. The shrine is surrounded by buildings with religious or historical associations.

Qom: Iran. A Shi'a centre, it is venerated as having the tomb of Fatima, the sister of Imam al-Rida/Riza, and those of hundreds of saints and kings including Imams 'Ali b. Ja'far and Ibrahim, Shah Safi and Shah 'Abbas II. Following the Iranian Revolution of 1979 it became the centre favoured by Ayatollah Khomeini.

Najaf (Al-Najaf): Iraq. Mashhad 'Ali, reputed to be constructed over the place where 'Ali b. Abi Talib, fourth Caliph, the cousin and son-in-law of Muhammad, is buried, is a most venerated Shi'a shrine, drawing many pilgrims.

Kerbala (Karbala): Iraq. The shrine of Husain b. 'Ali where, at Mashhad Husain, he was slain with most of his family, is today more venerated by the Shi'a than the Mashhad 'Ali. 'Ashoura Day (10th Muharram), when Husain was killed, is commemorated by passion plays (*ta'ziya*) and religious processions during which the drama of his death is re-enacted with extravagant expressions of emotion.

Baghdad: Iraq. The Kazimain/Kadhimain Mosque is a celebrated Shi'a shrine containing the tomb of Musa al-Kazim/Kadhim, the seventh Imam of the Ithna'asharis.

Religious Groupings

SUNNIS

The great majority, probably over 80% of Muslims, are Sunni, followers of the *Sunna*, i.e. the way, course, rule or manner of conduct of the Prophet Muhammad; they are generally called 'orthodox'. The Sunnis recognize the first four Caliphs (Abu Bakr, 'Umar, 'Uthman and 'Ali) as Rashidun, i.e. following the right course. They base their *Sunna* upon the Koran and 'Six Books' of Traditions, and are organized in four orthodox schools or rites (*madhhab*), all of equal standing within the orthodox fold. Many Muslims today prefer to avoid identification with any single school and simply call themselves Muslim or Sunni.

WAHHABIS

The adherents of 'Wahhabism' strongly disapprove of this title by which they are known outside their own group, for they call themselves Muwahhidun or Unitarians. In fact they belong to the strict Hanbali school, following its noted exponent, the 13th/14th century Syrian reformer Ibn Taimiyah. The founder of 'Wahhabism', Muhammad ibn Abd al-Wahhab of Arabian Najd (1703–87), sought to return to the pristine purity of early Islam, freed from all accretions and from what he regarded as innovations contrary to its true spirit, such as saint worship, lax sexual practices and superstition. His doctrine was accepted by the chief Muhammad ibn Sa'ud of Dar'iya (near Riyadh). Ibn Sa'ud and his son Abd al-Aziz—who proved a capable general—conquered much of Arabia. Medina fell in

1804 and Mecca in 1806 to Sa'ud, son of Abd al-Aziz, but after his death in 1814 the Wahhabis were gradually broken by the armies of the Pasha of Egypt, Muhammad 'Ali, acting nominally on behalf of the Ottoman Sultan of Turkey. After varying fortunes in the 19th century, the Wahhabis emerged as an Arabian power in the opening years of the 20th century. By the close of 1925 they held the Holy Cities and Jeddah, and are today the strongest power in the Arabian Peninsula. Though Wahhabism remains the strictest of the orthodox groups, Saudi Arabia has made some accommodation to modern times.

THE TURUQ OR RELIGIOUS ORDERS

In many Middle Eastern countries the religious orders (*turuq*) have important political-cum-religious roles in society. There are the widely spread Qadiriya who, with Tijaniya, are found in North Africa, the Khatmiya in Sudan, and the Rifa'iya in Egypt and Syria, to name a few. The West has no organizations exactly equivalent to these Sufi orders into which an individual has to be initiated, and in which, by dint of ascetic exercises and study, he may attain degrees of mystical enlightenment—this can also bring moral influence over his fellow men. The Orders may be Sunni or Shi'a; some few Orders are even so unconventional as to be hardly Islamic at all. Although Sufism is essentially uninterested in worldly politics, the *turuq* have, at times, been drawn into the political arena. It was the orthodox reformist Sanusi Order that played the most significant role in our time. The Grand Sanusi, Muhammad ibn Ali, born at Mustaghanem in Algeria of a Sharif family, founded the first *zawiya* or lodge of the Sanusis in 1837. The Sanusi *tariqa* is distinguished for its exacting standards of personal morality. The Sanusis established a network of lodges in Cyrenaica (Libya) and put up strong resistance to Italian colonization. The Grand Sanusi was recognized as King Idris of Libya in 1951, but lost his throne in the military revolt led by Qaddafi in 1969.

SHI'A

The Legitimist Shi'a pay allegiance to 'Ali, as mentioned above. 'Ali's posterity, which must number at least hundreds of thousands scattered all over the Muslim world, are customarily called Sharifs if they trace descent to his son al-Hasan, and Sayyids if descended from his second son al-Husain, but while the Sharifs and Sayyids, the religious aristocracy of Islam, are traditionally accorded certain privileges in Islamic society, not all are Shi'a, many being Sunnis. By the ninth century many strange sects, and even pagan beliefs, had become associated with the original Shi'a or Party of 'Ali; however, these extremist sects, called *ghulat*, have vanished except for a few, often practising a sort of quietism or dissimulation (*taqiyya*) for fear of persecution. All Shi'a accord 'Ali an exalted position, the extreme (and heretical) Shi'a at one time even according him a sort of divinity. Shi'ite Islam does not in the main differ on fundamental issues from the Sunni orthodox since they draw from the same ultimate sources, but Shi'a *mujtahids* have, certainly in theory, greater freedom to alter the application of law since they are regarded as spokesmen of the Hidden Imam.

THE ITHNA'ASHARIS (TWELVERS)

The largest Shi'a school or rite is the Ithna'ashariya or Twelvers, acknowledging a succession of 12 Imams. From 1502 Shi'ism became the established school in Iran under the Safavid ruler Sultan Shah Isma'il, who claimed descent from Musa al-Kazim. There are also Ithna'ashariya in southern Iraq, al-Hasa (Saudi Arabia), Bahrain and the Indian subcontinent.

The last Shi'a Imam, Muhammad al-Mahdi, disappeared in 878, but the Ithna'asharis believe that he is still alive and will reappear in the last days before the Day of Judgement as the Mahdi (Guided One)—a sort of Messiah—who will rule personally by divine right.

The 12 Imams recognized by the Twelver, Ithna'ashari Shi'a are:

(1) 'Ali b. Abi Talib, cousin and son-in-law of the Prophet Muhammad.
(2) Al-Hasan, son of 'Ali.
(3) Al-Husain, second son of 'Ali.
(4) 'Ali Zain al-'Abidin, son of Husain.
(5) Muhammad al-Baqir, son of 'Ali Zain al-'Abidin.
(6) Ja'far al-Sadiq, son of Muhammad al-Baqir.
(7) Musa al-Kazim, son of Ja'far al-Sadiq.
(8) 'Ali al-Rida, son of Musa al-Kazim.
(9) Muhammad al-Taqi, son of 'Ali al-Rida.
(10) 'Ali al-Naqi, son of Muhammad al-Taqi.
(11) Al-Hasan al-Zaki, son of 'Ali al-Naqi, al-'Askari.
(12) Muhammad al-Mahdi, son of al-Hasan b. 'Ali, al-'Askari, known as al-Hujja, the Proof.

ISMA'ILIS

This group of Shi'a does not recognize Musa al-Kazim as the seventh Imam, but holds that the last Imam visible on earth was Isma'il, the other son of Ja'far al-Sadiq. For this reason they are also called the Sab'iya or Seveners. There is, however, much disagreement among the Seveners as to whether they recognized Isma'il himself as the seventh Imam, or one of his several sons, and the Fatimids of Egypt (10th–12th centuries) in fact recognized a son of Isma'il's son Muhammad. Schismatic offshoots from the Fatimid-Isma'ili group are the Druzes, the Musta'lians, first settled in Yemen but now with their main centre in Mumbai, India—where the Daudi section, under the chief 'missionary' (Da'i al-Du'a), is known as Bohoras, but who are properly called the Fatimi Taiyibi Da'wa—and the Nizari Isma'ilis, of whom the Agha Khan is the spiritual head. These sects have a secret literature embodying their esoteric philosophies. Both groups are very active and a large Isma'ili Institute, sponsored by the Agha Khan, was opened in London, United Kingdom, in 1985. Small groups of Isma'ilis are to be found in north-west Syria, Iran, Afghanistan, East Africa and Zanzibar, and larger numbers in India and Pakistan.

'ALAWIS (NUSAIRIS)

The 'Alawis believe that Muhammad was a mere forerunner of 'Ali and that the latter was an incarnation of Allah. This extremist Shi'a sect, established in the ninth century, has also adopted practices of both Christian and pagan origin. Most of its members today live in north-west Syria.

DRUZE

The Druze are heretics, an offshoot of the Fatimid-Isma'ilis, established in Lebanon and Syria. Their name (Duruz) derives from al-Darazi, a missionary of Persian origin who brought about the conversion of these Syrian mountaineers to the belief of the divine origin of the Fatimid Caliph al-Hakim. The origins of this sect and its subsequent expansion are still obscure. Hamza b. 'Ali, a Persian contemporary of al-Darazi, is the author of several of the religious treatises of the Druze. This community acknowledges one God and believes that he has on many occasions become incarnate in man. His last appearance was in the person of the Fatimid Caliph al-Hakim (disappeared 1020). The Druze have played a distinctive role in the political and social life of their country and are renowned for their independence of character. They engaged ardently in *jihad* against the Israeli invaders of Lebanon and their Christian allies. Druze morale is reinforced by the inspiration of the Islamic Revolution in Shi'ite Iran.

ZAIDIS

The Zaidis are a liberal and moderate sect of the Shi'a, close enough to the Sunnis to call themselves the 'Fifth School' (*al-madhhab al-khamis*). Their name is derived from a grandson of al-Husain b. 'Ali called Zaid b. 'Ali, whom they recognize as the fifth Imam. They reject religious dissimulation (*taqiyya*) and are extremely warlike. Zaidism is the dominant school of Islam in Yemen, its main centres being San'a and Dhamar, but Shafi'is form roughly one-half of the population.

IBADIS

The Ibadis are commonly held to have their origins in the Khawarij, who disassociated themselves from 'Ali b. Abi Talib when he accepted arbitration in his quarrel with Mu'awiya; however, this is open to question. They broke off early from the mainstream of Islam and are usually regarded as heretics, though with little justification. Groups of the sect, which has often suffered persecution, are found in Oman (where Ibadism is the majority religion), Zanzibar, Libya and Algeria, mainly in the Mzab.

CHRISTIANITY

Development in the Middle East

Christianity was adopted as the official religion of the Roman empire in AD 313, and the Christian Church came to be based on the four leading cities, Rome, Constantinople (capital from AD 330), Alexandria and Antioch. From the divergent development of the four ecclesiastical provinces there soon emerged four separate churches: the Roman Catholic or Latin Church (from Rome), the Greek Orthodox Church (from Constantinople), the Syrian or Jacobite Church (from Antioch) and the Coptic Church (from Alexandria).

Later divisions resulted in the emergence of the Armenian (Gregorian) Church, which was founded in the fourth century, and the Nestorian Church, which grew up in the fifth century in Syria, Mesopotamia and Iran, following the teaching of Nestorius of Cilicia (d. 431). From the seventh century onwards followers of St Maron began to establish themselves in northern Lebanon, laying the foundations of the Maronite Church.

Subsequently, the Uniate Churches were brought into existence by the renunciation by formerly independent churches of doctrines regarded as heretical by the Roman Church and by the acknowledgement of Papal supremacy. These churches—the Armenian Catholic, Chaldean (Nestorian) Catholic, Greek Catholic, Coptic Catholic, Syrian Catholic and Maronite Church—did, however, retain their Oriental customs and rites. The independent churches continued to exist alongside the Uniate Churches, with the exception of the Maronites who reverted to Rome.

Holy Places

Bethlehem (Beit Lahm): West Bank. The traditional birthplace of Jesus is enclosed in the Basilica of the Nativity, revered also by Muslims. Christmas is celebrated here by the Roman and Eastern Rite Churches on 25 December, by the Greek Orthodox, Coptic and Syrian Orthodox Churches on 6 and 7 January, by the Ethiopian Church on 8 January, and by the Armenian Church on 19 January. The tomb of Rachel, important to the three faiths, is just outside the town.

Jerusalem: West Bank (annexed by Israel). The most holy city of Christianity has been a centre for pilgrims since the Middle Ages. It is the seat of the patriarchates of the Roman, Greek Orthodox and Armenian Churches, who share the custodianship of the Church of the Holy Sepulchre and who each own land and buildings in the neighbouring area.

The Church of the Holy Sepulchre stands on the hill of Golgotha in the higher, north-western part of the Old City. In the central chamber of the church is the Byzantine Rotunda built by 12th century crusaders, which shelters the small shrine of the traditional site of the tomb. Here the different patriarchates exercise their rights in turn. Close by is the Rock of Calvary, revered as the site of Jesus's Crucifixion.

Most pilgrims devoutly follow the Way of the Cross, leading from the Roman Praetorium through several streets of the Old City to the Holy Sepulchre. Franciscan monks, commemorating the journey to the Crucifixion, follow the course of this traditional route each Friday; on Good Friday this procession marks a climax of the Easter celebrations of the Roman Church.

Outside the Old City stands the Mount of Olives, the scene of Jesus's Ascension. At the foot of its hill is the Garden of Gethsemane, which is associated with the vigil on the eve of the Crucifixion. The Cenaculum, or traditional room of the Last Supper, is situated on Mount Zion in Israel.

Nazareth: Israel. This town, closely associated with the childhood of Jesus, has been a Christian centre since the fourth century AD. The huge, domed Church of the Annunciation has recently been built on the site of numerous earlier churches to protect the underground Grotto of the Annunciation. Nearby the Church of St Joseph marks the traditional site of Joseph's workshop.

Galilee: Israel. Many of the places by this lake (the Sea of Galilee, or Lake Tiberias) are associated with the life of Jesus: Cana, scene of the miracle of water and wine, which is celebrated by an annual pilgrimage on the second Sunday after Epiphany; the Mount of Beatitudes; Tabgha, scene of the multiplication of the loaves and fish; and Capernaum, scene of the healing of the Centurion's servant.

Mount Tabor: Israel. The traditional site of the Transfiguration, which has drawn pilgrims since the fourth century, is commemorated by a Franciscan Monastery and a Greek Basilica, where the annual Festival of the Transfiguration is held.

Jericho (Ariha): West Bank. The scene of the baptism of Jesus; nearby is the Greek Monastery of St John the Baptist.

Nablus (Nabulus): West Bank. This old town contains Jacob's Well, associated with Jesus, and the Tomb of Joseph.

Qubaibah (Emmaus): Jordan. It was near this town that two of the Disciples encountered Jesus after the Resurrection.

'Azariyyah (Bethany): Jordan. A town frequented by Jesus, the home of Mary and Martha, and the scene of the Raising of Lazarus.

Mount Carmel: Haifa, Israel. The Cave of Elijah draws many pilgrims, including Muslims and Druzes, who celebrate the Feast of Mar Elias on 20 July.

Ein Kerem: Israel. Traditional birthplace of John the Baptist, to whom a Franciscan church is dedicated; nearby is the church of the Visitation.

Ephesus: Turkey. The city was formerly a great centre of pagan worship, where Paul founded the first of the seven Asian Churches. The Basilica, built by Justinian, is dedicated to John the Evangelist, who, according to legend, died here; a fourth-century church on Aladag Mountain commemorating Mary's last years spent here now draws an annual pilgrimage in August.

JUDAISM

There are two main Jewish communities, the Ashkenazim and the Sephardim. The former originate from central, northern and eastern Europe (Ashkenaz being the old Hebrew word for Germany), while the latter come from the historic Spanish community and their descendants (Sepharad being the old Hebrew word for Spain). In popular use, however, the term Sephardim is often expanded to include all Jews of non-European origin and thus those communities from the Balkans, the Middle East and North Africa. The term Mizrahim (meaning 'easterners') has also emerged in Israel to describe Jews descended from communities in Asia and Africa. The majority of immigrants into Israel were from the Ashkenazim, and their influence predominates there, although the Hebrew language follows Sephardim usage. There is no doctrinal difference between the two communities, but they observe distinct rituals.

Holy Places

Wailing Wall: Jerusalem. This last remnant of the western part of the wall surrounding the courtyard of Herod's Temple, finally destroyed by the Romans in 70 AD, is visited by devout Jews, particularly on the Fast Day of the ninth of Av, to grieve at the destruction of the First and Second Temples which had once stood on the same site.

Mount Zion: Israel. A hill to the south-west of the Old City of Jerusalem, venerated particularly for the tomb of David, acknowledged by Muslims as Abi Dawud (the Jebuzite hill on which David founded his Holy City is now known as Mount Ophel, and is in Jordan just to the east of the modern Mount Zion). Not far from the foot of the hill are the rock-cut tombs of the family of King Herod.

Cave of Machpelah: West Bank. The grotto, over which was built a mosque, contains the tombs of Abraham and Sarah, Isaac and Rebecca, Jacob and Leah.

Bethlehem: West Bank. The traditional tomb of Rachel is in a small shrine outside the town, venerated also by Muslims and Christians.

Mount Carmel: Israel. The mountain is associated with Elijah, whose Cave in Haifa draws many pilgrims. (See Christianity.)

Safad: Israel. Centre of the medieval Cabbalist movement, this city contains several synagogues from the 16th century associated with these scholars, and many important tombs, notably that of Rabbi Isaac Louria.

Meiron: Israel. The town contains the tombs of Shimon bar Yohai, reputed founder in the second century of the medieval Cabbalist movement, and his son Eleazer. A yearly Hassidic pilgrimage is held to the tomb to celebrate Lag Ba'Omer with a night of traditional singing and dancing in which Muslims also participate.

Tiberias: Israel. An ancient city containing the tombs of Moses Maimonides and Rabbi Meir Baal Harness. Famous as a historical centre of Cabbalist scholarship, it is—with Jerusalem, Safad and Hebron—one of the four sacred cities of Judaism, and once accommodated a university and the Sanhedrin.

OTHER COMMUNITIES

Zoroastrians

Zoroastrianism developed from the teaching of Zoroaster, or Zarathustra, who lived in Iran some time between 700 and 550 BC. Later adopted as the official religion of the Persian empire, Zoroastrianism remained predominant in Iran until the rise of Islam. Many adherents were forced by persecution to emigrate, and the main centre of the faith is now Mumbai, where followers are known as Parsees. Technically a monotheistic faith, Zoroastrianism retained some elements of polytheism. It later became associated with fire-worship.

Yazd: Iran. This city was the ancient centre of the Zoroastrian religion, and was later used as a retreat during the Arab conquest. It contains five fire temples and still remains a centre for this faith, of which an estimated 30,000–60,000 adherents live in Iran.

Bahá'ís

Bahá'ísm developed in the mid-19th century from Babism. The Bab, or Gateway (to Truth), Saiyid Ali Muhammad of Shiraz (1821–50), was opposed to the corrupt Shi'a clergy in the Iran of his day and was executed in 1850. His remains were later taken to Haifa and buried in a mausoleum on the slopes of Mount Carmel. Mirza Husain Ali Bahá'ullah ('Splendour of Allah', 1817–92), a follower of Babism, experienced a spiritual revelation while in prison and in 1863 declared himself to be 'he whom Allah shall manifest' as predicted by the Bab. A member of the Persian nobility, he devoted his life to preaching against the corruption endemic in Persian society and as a result spent many years in exile. He died at Acre in Palestine in 1892 and is buried in a shrine adjacent to the mansion in which the Bab died, at Bahji, some miles north of Acre on the road to Beirut.

It was in the will and testament of Abdul Bahá, the eldest son and successor of Bahá'ullah, that after his death (in 1921) the head of the Bahá'í faith would be Shoghi Effendi, known as the Guardian of the Bahá'í faith ('Guardian of Allah's Command'), and that he would be the 'President' of the Universal House of Justice which would be elected in due course. In fact Shoghi Effendi died in London in 1957 after 36 years as Guardian, but the Universal House of Justice was not elected from the Bahá'í world until 1963. The presidency was never assumed and there is no possibility of a second Guardian being appointed.

In 1846 the Babis declared their secession from Islam, and the Bahá'ís claim independence from all other faiths. They believe that the basic principles of the great religions of the world are in complete harmony and that their aims and functions are complementary. Other tenets include belief in the brotherhood of man, opposition to racial and colour discrimination, equality of the sexes, progress towards world peace, monogamy, chastity and the encouragement of family life. Bahá'ísm has no priesthood and discourages asceticism, monasticism and mystic pantheism. The number of Bahá'ís world-wide is reported to be more than 5m., some 2.2m. of whom live in India. Most of Bahá'ísm's Middle Eastern adherents live in Iran and, on a temporary basis, Israel, but since the 1979 Islamic Revolution those in Iran have suffered from severe official persecution.

Haifa: Israel. Shrine and gardens of the Bab on Mount Carmel, the world centre of the Bahá'í faith. Pilgrims visit the Bahá'í holy places in Haifa and in and around Acre. The Pilgrimage lasts for nine days and the pilgrimage period extends over the whole year, with the exception of August and September.

PART TWO

Country Surveys

ALGERIA

Physical and Social Geography

Algeria is the largest of the three countries in north-western Africa that comprise the Maghreb, as the region of mountains, valleys and plateaux lying between the sea and the Sahara desert is known. It is situated between Morocco and Tunisia, with a Mediterranean coastline of nearly 1,000 km and a total area of some 2,381,741 sq km (919,595 sq miles), over four-fifths of which lies south of the Maghreb proper and within the western Sahara. Its extent, both from north to south and west to east, exceeds 2,000 km. The Arabic name for the country, el-Djezaïr (the Islands), is said to derive from the rocky islands along the coastline.

The total population of Algeria increased from 23,038,942 in April 1987 to 29,100,867 (excluding 171,476 Sahrawi refugees in camps) at the census of June 1998. At a new census conducted in April 2008, the total population was recorded at 34,080,030. As at January 2013, the population was estimated to be 37,900,000. The great majority of the inhabitants reside in the northern part of the country, particularly along the Mediterranean coast where both the capital, Algiers or el-Djezaïr (including suburbs, estimated at 2,915,700 in mid-2011), and the second largest town, Oran or Ouahran are located. Many settlements reverted to their Arabic names in 1981. The population is almost wholly Muslim. A majority speak Arabic and the remainder Tamazight, the principal language of the Berber minority who were the original inhabitants of the Maghreb. Many Algerians also speak French.

PHYSICAL FEATURES

The major contrast in the physical geography of Algeria is between the mountainous, relatively humid terrain of the north, which forms part of the Atlas mountain system, and the vast expanse of desert to the south, which is part of the Saharan tableland. The Atlas Mountains extend from south-west to north-east across the whole of the Maghreb. Structurally, they resemble the 'Alpine' mountain chains of Europe and, like them, they came into existence during the Tertiary era. They remain unstable and liable to severe earthquakes, such as those which devastated el-Asnam in 1954 and 1980. The mountains consist of rocks, now uplifted, folded and fractured, that once accumulated beneath an ancestral Mediterranean sea. Limestone and sandstone are particularly extensive and they often present a barren appearance in areas where the topsoil and vegetation is thin or absent altogether.

In Algeria the Atlas mountain system comprises three broad zones running parallel to the coast: the Tell Atlas, the High Plateaux and the Saharan Atlas. In the north, and separated from the Mediterranean only by a narrow and discontinuous coastal plain, is the complex series of mountains and valleys that encompass the Tell Atlas. Here individual ranges, plateaux and massifs vary in height from about 500 m to 2,500 m above sea level and are frequently separated from one another by deep valleys and gorges which divide the country into self-contained topographic and economic units. Most distinctive of these are the massifs of the Great and Little Kabylia between Algiers and the Tunisian frontier, which have acted as mountain retreats where Berber ways of village life persist.

South of the Tell Atlas lies a zone of featureless plains known as the High Plateaux of the Shotts. To the west, near the Moroccan frontier, they form a broad, monotonous expanse of level terrain about 160 km across and more than 1,000 m above sea level. They gradually narrow and descend eastwards to end in the Hodna basin, a huge enclosed depression, the bottom of which is only 420 m above sea level. The surface of the plateaux consists of alluvial debris from erosion of the mountains to the north and south. The plateaux owe their name to the presence of several vast basins of internal drainage, known as shotts, the largest of which is the Hodna basin. During rainy periods water accumulates in the shotts to form extensive shallow lakes which give way, as the water is absorbed and evaporated, to saline mudflats and swamps.

The southern margin of the High Plateaux is marked by a series of mountain chains and massifs that form the Saharan Atlas. They are more interrupted than the Tell Atlas and present no serious barrier to communication between the High Plateaux and the Sahara. From west to east the chief mountain chains are the Ksour, Amour, Ouled Naïl, Ziban and Aurès. The latter, the most impressive massif in the whole Algerian Atlas system, includes the highest peak: Djebel Chelia, 2,328 m (7,638 ft). The relief of the Aurès is extremely bold, with narrow gorges cut between sheer cliffs surmounted by steep bare slopes, and to the east and north of the Hodna basin its ridges merge with the southernmost folds of the Tell Atlas. North-eastern Algeria thus forms a compact block of high relief in which the two Atlas mountain systems cease to be clearly separated. Here there are a number of high plains studded with salt flats but their size is insignificant compared with the enormous shotts to the west.

CLIMATE AND VEGETATION

The climate of northernmost Algeria, including the narrow coastal plain and the Tell Atlas southwards to the margin of the High Plateaux, is of 'Mediterranean' type with warm, wet winters and hot, dry summers. Rainfall varies from over 1,000 mm annually on some coastal mountains to less than 130 mm in sheltered situations, and occurs mostly during the winter. Complete drought lasts for three to four months during the summer, when the notorious sirocco (Chehili) also occurs. This is a scorching, dry and dusty southerly wind blowing from the Sahara, prevailing for some 40 days a year over the High Plateaux, although nearer the coast its duration is closer to 20 days. With the arrival of the sirocco, shade temperatures often rise rapidly to more than 40°C (104°F), while vegetation and crops, unable to withstand the intensity of evaporation, may die within a few hours. As a result of low and uneven rainfall combined with high rates of evaporation, the rivers of the Tell tend to be short and to suffer large seasonal variations in flow. Many run completely dry during the summer and are full only for brief periods following heavy winter rains. The longest perennially flowing river is the Oued Chélif, which rises in the High Plateaux and crosses the Tell to reach the Mediterranean Sea east of Oran.

Along the northern margin of the High Plateaux 'Mediterranean' conditions give way to a semi-arid or steppe climate, in which summer drought lasts from five to six months and winters are colder and drier. Rainfall is limited to 200 mm–400 mm annually and tends to occur in spring and autumn rather than in winter. It is, moreover, variable from year to year, and under these conditions the cultivation of cereal crops without irrigation becomes unreliable. South of the Saharan Atlas annual rainfall decreases to below 200 mm and any regular cultivation without irrigation becomes impossible. There are no permanent rivers south of the Tell Atlas and any surface run-off following rain is carried by temporary watercourses towards local depressions, such as the shotts.

The soils and vegetation of northern Algeria reflect the climatic contrast between the humid Tell and the semi-arid lands farther south, but they have also suffered widely from the destructive effects of over-cultivation, over-grazing and deforestation. In the higher, wetter and more isolated parts of the Tell Atlas relatively thick soils support forests of Aleppo pine, cork oak and evergreen oak, while the lower, drier and more accessible slopes tend to be bare or covered only with thin soils and a scrub growth of thuya, juniper and various drought-resistant shrubs. Only a few remnants survive of the once extensive forests of Atlas cedar, which have been exploited for timber and fuel since classical times. They are found chiefly above 1,500 m in the eastern Tell Atlas. South of the Tell there is very little woodland except in the higher and wetter parts of the Saharan Atlas. The surface of the High Plateaux is bare or covered only with scattered bushes and clumps of esparto and other coarse grasses.

SAHARAN ALGERIA

South of the Saharan Atlas, Algeria extends for over 1,500 km into the heart of the desert. Structurally, this huge area consists of a resistant platform of geologically ancient rocks against which the Atlas Mountains were folded. Over most of the area relief is slight, with occasional plateaux, such as those of Eglab, Tademaït and Tassili-n-Ajjer, rising above vast spreads of gravel, such as the Tanezrouft plain, and huge sand accumulations, such as the Great Western and Eastern Ergs. In the south-east, however, the great massif of Ahaggar rises to a height of 2,918 m (9,573 ft). Here, erosion of volcanic and crystalline rocks has produced a lunar landscape of extreme ruggedness. Southwards from the Ahaggar the massifs of Adrar des Iforas and Aîr extend into neighbouring Mali and Niger.

The climate of Saharan Algeria is characterized by extremes of temperature, wind and aridity. Daily temperature ranges reach 32°C, and maximum shade temperatures of over 55°C have been recorded. Sometimes very high temperatures are associated with violent dust storms. Mean average rainfall, although extremely irregular, is everywhere less than 130 mm, and in some central parts of the desert it falls to less than 10 mm. These rigorous conditions are reflected in the extreme sparseness of the vegetation and in a division of the population into settled cultivators, who occupy oases dependent on permanent supplies of underground water, and nomadic pastoralists who make use of temporary pastures which appear after rain.

History

Revised for this edition by AHMED AGHROUT and YAHIA ZOUBIR

EARLY HISTORY

The Berber people have comprised the majority of the population of this part of Africa since the earliest times. From 208 to 148 BC Numidia occupied most of present-day Algeria north of the Sahara. After the destruction of Carthage in 146 BC Numidia, greatly reduced in extent, was transformed into a Roman vassal-state, while the rest of the area formed a loose confederacy of tribes, which maintained their independence by frequent revolt. After a brief period of Vandal dominance, Roman rule was restored in the provinces of Africa (modern Tunisia) and Numidia, and parts of the coast. Elsewhere, the Berber confederacies, centred in the Aurès and Kabylia, maintained their independence.

The rise of Islam in Arabia was soon followed by its penetration of North Africa, the first Arab raids taking place in about the middle of the seventh century. Kairouan (in present-day Tunisia) was founded by the Arabs in 670 as a base; the other towns remained under Byzantine control, and the Berber tribes founded a state centred on the eastern Maghreb. Increasing Arab immigration towards the end of the seventh century finally overcame Berber and Byzantine resistance; the Berbers gradually converted to Islam, and the whole of the area was incorporated into the Ummayad Empire. In 756 the Berbers freed themselves from the control of the recently established Abbasid Caliphate, and for the next three centuries power was disputed between various Arab dynasties and Berber tribes. After the invasion in c. 1050 of the Banu Hilal, a confederation of nomadic Arab tribes dislodged from Egypt, a period of anarchy ensued, but the Berber dynasty of the Almoravids, from Morocco, temporarily restored order in the area of modern Algiers (el-Djezaïr) and Oran (Ouahran). In c. 1147 the Almoravids were succeeded by the Almohads, who unified the whole of the Maghreb and Muslim Spain, bringing cultural and economic prosperity to North Africa. From the middle of the 13th century, however, the region entered a period of decline, both economic and in terms of its political influence, which persisted for more than two centuries.

In the closing years of the 15th century the Spanish monarchy carried its crusade against Muslim power to North Africa, the fragmented political state of that area offering little resistance. On the death of Ferdinand of Castile in 1516, the Algerines sought the assistance of the Turkish corsair Aruj, who took possession of Algiers and proclaimed himself Sultan. In 1518 he was succeeded by his brother, Khayr al-Din (Barbarossa), who placed all his territories under the nominal protection of the Ottoman Sultan. This decisive act may be said to mark the emergence of Algiers as a political entity. After numerous efforts to re-establish their position, the Spanish finally withdrew in 1541 and Algeria was left for three centuries to the Muslims. Power in Algiers lay in the hands of the *dey* and there was a rapid succession of *deys*, often as the result of an assassination. Each *dey* established his relationship with the Sultan by sending him tribute. Real power in Algiers was held by two bodies—the janissary corps and the guild of corsair captains. The Regency of Algiers reached its peak in the 17th century, the profitable trade of piracy bringing great wealth. Despite Turkish attempts to control the interior, several of the Berber tribes most distant from Algiers retained their independence. During the 18th century the growth of European sea power in the Mediterranean brought a period of decline to the littoral, while in the interior a period of relative economic prosperity ensued.

THE FRENCH CONQUEST

On 5 July 1830 Algiers fell to a French expedition, and the *dey* and most of the Turkish officials were sent into exile. The pretext for the intervention was an insult perceived to have been offered by the *dey* to the French consul in 1827; the real cause was the pressing need of Polignac, the chief minister under Charles X, to secure some credit for his administration from the French public and to provide employment for the Napoleonic veterans. However, the Bourbon dynasty and its Government were subsequently overthrown by revolution, and Polignac's plan to hand over the rest of the country, and decisions on its future, to a European congress was abandoned. In Algeria the absence of any central authority increased the prestige of the tribal chiefs. In 1834, however, the French decided upon the further conquest and annexation of Algeria, and a governor-general was appointed.

Over the next quarter of a century, France pursued its conquest of Algeria, despite bitter opposition. Constantine (Qacentina), the last Turkish stronghold, was captured in 1837, and by 1841 French rule had been consolidated in most of the ports and their immediate environs. By 1844 much of the eastern part of Algeria was under French control, but in the west the conquerors encountered the formidable Abd al-Kadir, a skilful diplomat and military commander, who at first concluded treaties with the French, consolidating his position as leader of the Berber confederacies in the west. In 1839, however, he declared war on France and united Berbers and Arabs against the invaders. Resistance was maintained until 1847, when Abd al-Kadir was defeated by Gen. Bugeaud, the real architect of French rule in Algeria. During the late 1840s and 1850s the tribes on the edge of the Sahara were pacified, while the conquest was effectively completed by the submission of the hitherto independent Berber confederacies of Kabylia in 1857. Nevertheless, further rebellions were to occur throughout the 19th century.

Meanwhile, a policy of colonization, with widespread confiscation of land and the transference thereof to settler groups, had been adopted. Bugeaud at first encouraged colonization in the coastal plains, and after 1848 the influx of colonists accelerated. Further stimulus to colonization was provided by the widespread confiscation of lands after an unsuccessful Muslim rebellion in 1871. French settlers had, by that time, become the dominant power in Algeria, owning much of the best land and initiating extensive agricultural development.

After the revolt of 1871 the situation was regularized by a new French administration under Adolphe Thiers. A civil administration with the status of a French *département* was established for much of Algeria, while the amount of territory under military rule steadily declined. From 1871 to 1900 there was considerable economic development in Algeria and increasing European immigration, notably from Italy. A feature of this period was the growth of large-scale agricultural and industrial enterprises, which further concentrated power in the leaders of the settler groups. In 1900 Algeria secured administrative and financial autonomy, to be exercised through the so-called 'Financial Delegations', composed of two-thirds European and one-third Muslim members, which were empowered to set the annual budget and to raise loans for economic development.

Within 70 years the Muslim people of Algeria had been reduced from relative prosperity to economic, social and cultural subordination. Some 3m. inhabitants had died, tribes had been disbanded and the traditional economy altered during the prolonged 'civilizing' campaigns. In particular, the production of wine for export had replaced the growing of cereals for domestic consumption. By contrast, the settlers enjoyed a high level of prosperity in the years before the First World War.

BIRTH OF NATIONALISM

The spirit of nationalism, which was spreading throughout the Middle East, emerged among Algerian Muslims after the First World War. Nationalist aspirations were voiced not only by Algerian veterans of the war in Europe but also by Algerians who had gone to France to study or work. In 1924 one of these students, Messali Hadj, in collaboration with the Parti Communiste Français (French Communist Party), founded in Paris, France, the first Algerian nationalist newspaper; however, the link with the Communists was severed in 1927. Hadj and his movement were forced into hiding by the French Government, but re-emerged in 1933 to sponsor a congress on the future of Algeria—demanding full independence, the recall of French troops, the establishment of a revolutionary government, large-scale reforms in land ownership and the nationalization of industrial enterprises.

More moderate doctrines were advanced by an influential body of French-educated Muslims, formalized in 1930 as the Federation of Muslim Councillors. Under the leadership of Ferhat Abbas, it sought integration with France on a basis of complete equality. The victory of the Front Populaire (Popular Front) in the French elections of 1936 gave rise to the hope that some of these aspirations might be achieved peaceably. However, the Blum-Viollet Plan, which would have granted full rights of citizenship to an increasing number of Algerian Muslims, was abandoned by the French Government as it was fiercely opposed by French settlers and the Algerian civil service.

The years immediately prior to the Second World War were characterized by growing nationalist discontent, in which Hadj played a significant part with the formation of the Parti du Peuple Algérien (PPA—Algerian People's Party). The outbreak of war in 1939 suspended the nationalists' activities, but the war greatly strengthened their position. Although the Vichy administration in Algeria, strongly supported by the French settlers, was hostile to nationalist sentiment, the Allied landings in North Africa in 1942 provided an opportunity for the Algerian nationalists to present constitutional demands. A group led by Abbas submitted to the French authorities and the Allied military command a memorandum demanding the post-war establishment of an Algerian constituent assembly, to be elected by universal suffrage. However, no demand was made for Algerian independence outside the French framework.

These proposals, to which the French authorities remained unresponsive, were followed early in 1943 by the 'Manifesto of the Algerian People', which demanded immediate reforms, including the introduction of Arabic as an official language and the end of colonial rule. Further proposals, submitted in May, envisaged the post-war creation of an Algerian state, with a constitution to be determined by a constituent assembly, and anticipated an eventual North African Union, comprising Tunisia, Algeria and Morocco. The newly established Free French administration in Algiers categorically rejected the Manifesto and the subsequent proposals.

Confronted by growing Muslim discontent, and following a visit to Algiers by Gen Charles de Gaulle, a new statute for Algeria came into effect in March 1944. Membership of the French electoral college was opened to 60,000 Muslims, but there were still 450,000 European voters, and only 32,000 Muslims registered to vote. The Muslim share of the seats in the *communes mixtes* was restricted to 40%. All further discussion of Algeria's future relationship with France was rejected.

Shortly afterwards, Abbas founded the Amis du Manifeste de la Liberté (AML—Friends of the Freedom Manifesto), which aimed to establish an autonomous Algerian republic linked federally with France. The movement was based mainly on the support of middle-class Muslims, and also gained a certain following among the masses, who comprised the main support of the PPA in 1944–45.

FRENCH INTRANSIGENCE

All possibility of a gradually negotiated settlement was destroyed by blunders in post-war French policy and the opposition of the French settlers to any concessions to Muslim aspirations. Riots at Sétif (Stif) in May 1945 were ruthlessly suppressed. This action, the subsequent arrest of Abbas and the dissolution of the AML served to convince many nationalist leaders that force was the only means by which they could gain their objective.

Nevertheless, attempts to reach a compromise continued. In March 1946 Abbas, released under an amnesty, launched the Union Démocratique du Manifeste Algérien (UDMA—Democratic Union of the Algerian Manifesto), with a programme providing for the creation of an autonomous, secular Algerian state within the French Union. Despite successes in elections to the French Assembly, the UDMA failed to achieve its objectives. It withdrew from the Assembly in September and refused to participate in the next elections. The breach was filled by the more radical Mouvement Pour le Triomphe des Libertés Démocratiques (MTLD—Movement for the Triumph of Democratic Freedoms), formed by Hadj at the end of the war, which demanded the creation of a sovereign constituent assembly and the withdrawal of French troops.

In another attempt at compromise, the French Government introduced a new Constitution, adopted on 20 September 1947, granting French citizenship, and therefore the right to vote, to all Algerian citizens, both men and women, and recognizing Arabic as an official language. However, the proposed new Algerian Assembly was to be divided into two colleges, each comprising 60 members, one to represent the 1.5m. resident Europeans, the other the 9m. Algerian Muslims. Other provisions excluded any legislation contrary to the interest of the colonists.

The new Constitution was never brought fully into operation. Following MTLD successes in the municipal elections of October 1947, there was open interference with the elections to the Algerian Assembly: many candidates were arrested and polling stations were operated improperly. As a result only one-quarter of the members returned to the second college in April 1948 belonged to the MTLD or the UDMA; the remainder, known as the 'Béni-Oui-Oui', were nominally independent, but easy to manipulate. Such methods continued to be employed in local and national elections during the next six years, as well as in the Algerian elections to the French National Assembly in June 1951, and some of the improvements envisaged under the 1947 Constitution were never put into effect. The aim was to destroy, or at least render harmless, opposition to French rule;

the result was that the main forces of nationalism were forced to operate clandestinely.

As early as 1947 several of the younger members of the MTLD had formed the Organisation Spéciale (OS—Special Organization), which collected arms and money and organized a network of cells throughout Algeria in preparation for armed insurrection and the establishment of a revolutionary government. Two years later the OS felt itself strong enough to launch an attack in Oran. The movement was subsequently discovered and most of its leaders were arrested, but a nucleus survived in the Kabylia region and the organizer of the attack, Ahmed Ben Bella, escaped to Cairo, Egypt, in 1952.

A decisive split was opening in the ranks of the MTLD, and the veteran Hadj, who now embraced nebulous doctrines of Pan-Arabism, was gradually losing control of the party organization to more activist, pro-independence members. In March 1954 nine former members of the OS formed the Comité Révolutionnaire d'Unité et d'Action (CRUA—Revolutionary Committee of Unity and Action) to prepare for an immediate revolt against French rule.

WAR OF INDEPENDENCE

Plans for the insurrection were formulated at a series of CRUA meetings in Switzerland during March–October 1954. Algeria was divided into six *wilayat* (administrative districts) and a military commander was appointed for each. When the revolt was launched on 1 November the CRUA changed its name to the Front de Libération Nationale (FLN—National Liberation Front), its armed forces being known as the Armée de Libération Nationale (ALN—National Liberation Army). Beginning in the Aurès, by early 1955 the revolt had spread to the Constantine area, Kabylia and the Moroccan frontier, west of Oran. By the end of 1956 the ALN was active throughout the settled areas of Algeria.

Abbas and Ahmad Francis of the more moderate UDMA and the *ulema* (Muslim scholars/lawyers) joined the FLN in April 1956, thereby integrating all sectors of Algerian nationalist feeling with the exception of Hadj's Mouvement National Algérien (MNA—Algerian National Movement). In August a secret congress of the FLN established a central committee and formed the National Council of the Algerian Revolution. A socialist programme for the future Algerian republic and plans for a violent offensive in Algiers were also approved.

Between September 1956 and June 1957 bomb explosions engineered by the FLN caused great loss of life. This violence was halted only by severe French repression of the Muslim population, including the use of torture and internment. Guerrilla activities continued, but electrified barriers were erected along the Tunisian and Moroccan borders and bands of ALN fighters attempting to cross into Algeria suffered heavy losses.

In June 1957 the French Government introduced legislation to link Algeria indissolubly with France, but the measure was not approved. Following the FLN conference of August 1956, a joint Moroccan-Tunisian plan had been announced for the establishment of a North African federation linked with France. FLN leaders began negotiations in Morocco in October 1957. However, Ben Bella and his companions were kidnapped en route from Morocco to Tunisia, when the French pilot of their aircraft landed at Algiers. The French authorities could hardly ignore this, and the captured leaders were arrested and interned in France. However, neither the internment of FLN leaders nor the bombing by French aircraft, in February 1958, of a Tunisian border village, in which 79 villagers were killed, weakened the resolve or the capacity of the FLN to continue fighting, and the failure of these desperate measures only made the possibility of French negotiations with the FLN more likely. This, in turn, provoked a violent reaction from the Europeans in Algeria (only about one-half of whom were of French origin).

In May 1958 the colonists instigated the overthrow of the discredited Fourth French Republic and celebrated de Gaulle's return to power, in the belief that he would further their aim of complete integration of Algeria with France. Although de Gaulle intensified military action against the FLN, this was achieved only at the cost of increased terrorism in Algiers and growing tension on the Tunisian and Moroccan borders. The FLN responded in August by establishing in the Tunisian capital, Tunis, the Provisional Government of the Algerian Republic (GPRA), headed by Abbas and including Ben Bella and the other leaders who had been interned in France. De Gaulle was now beginning to recognize the strength of Algerian nationalism and was moving cautiously towards accepting FLN demands.

NEGOTIATIONS AND THE COLONISTS' OPPOSITION

Initially de Gaulle's public statements on Algeria were vague. When he did make an unequivocal pronouncement in September 1959, upholding the right of Algerians to determine their own future, the colonists reacted swiftly. In January 1960 they rebelled again, this time against de Gaulle, and erected barricades in Algiers. However, without the support of the army the insurrection collapsed within nine days. Provisional talks between French and FLN delegates, held in secret near Paris in mid-1960, were inconclusive.

In November 1960 de Gaulle announced that a referendum was to be held on the organization of government in Algeria, pending self-determination, and the following month he visited Algeria to prepare the way. In the referendum the electorate was asked to approve a draft law providing for self-determination and immediate reforms to give Algerians the opportunity to participate in government. However, there were mass abstentions from voting in Algeria and in February 1961 new French approaches to the FLN were made through the President of Tunisia. Direct negotiations between French and FLN representatives began in May at Evian, on the Franco–Swiss border, but foundered in August over the issue of control over petroleum reserves in the Sahara and because of a French attack on the blockaded French naval base at Bizerta, Tunisia, which resulted in the deaths of 800–1,300 Tunisians.

Europeans in Algeria and sections of the French army had, meanwhile, formed the Organisation de l'Armée Secrète (OAS—Secret Army Organization) to resist a negotiated settlement and the transfer of power from European hands. In April 1961 four generals organized the seizure of Algiers, but this attempt at an army coup proved abortive as most regular officers remained loyal to de Gaulle. Offensive operations against the Algerian rebels, suspended upon the commencement of the Evian talks, were resumed by the French Government and fighting continued, although on a reduced scale. At the same time the OAS initiated a campaign of indiscriminate terrorist violence against native Algerians. The Mayor of Evian had already been killed by an OAS bomb, and attacks were now also mounted in Paris.

Secret contacts between the French Government and the FLN were re-established in October 1961. Negotiations resumed in December and in January 1962 in Geneva, Switzerland, and Rome, Italy, with the five members of the GPRA interned in France taking part through a representative of the King of Morocco. Ministerial-level meetings were held in strict secrecy in Paris in February and the negotiations were concluded at Evian in March with the signing of a cease-fire agreement and a declaration of future policy that provided for the establishment of an independent Algerian state after a transitional period, and for the safeguarding of individual rights and liberties. Other declarations issued subsequently dealt with the rights of French citizens in Algeria and with future Franco-Algerian co-operation. In the military sphere, France was to retain the naval base at Mers el-Kebir for 15 years and the nuclear testing site in the Sahara, together with various landing rights, for five years.

In accordance with the Evian accords, a provisional Government was formed on 28 March 1962, with Abderrahman Farès as President and an executive composed of FLN members, other Muslims and Europeans. The USSR and many East European, African and Asian countries quickly gave *de jure* recognition to the GPRA.

The signing of the Evian accords provoked renewed opposition by the OAS. A National Council of French Resistance in Algeria was formed, with Gen. Raoul Salan (one of the leaders of the attempted coup in 1961) as Commander-in-Chief. OAS commando units launched attacks on the Muslim population and on public buildings in an attempt to provoke a general breach of the cease-fire. After the failure of the OAS to establish an 'insurrectional zone' in the Orléansville (El-Asnam) area and Salan's capture in April 1962, and with a renewal of FLN terrorist activity and reprisals, increasing numbers of Europeans began to leave Algeria for France. Secret negotiations between OAS leaders and the FLN, aimed at securing guarantees for the European population, revealed a division in the OAS, heralding the virtual end of European terrorist activity. By late June more than one-half of the European population of Algeria had left the country.

The final steps towards Algerian independence were taken at a referendum on 1 July 1962, at which 91% of participants voted for independence. Algerian independence was proclaimed by Gen. de Gaulle on 3 July.

THE INDEPENDENT STATE

The achievement of power by the FLN revealed serious tensions within the Government, while the problems facing the new state after eight years of civil war were formidable.

The dominant position in the GPRA of the 'centralist' group, headed by Ben Khedda and comprising former members of the MTLD, was threatened by the release in March 1962 of the five GPRA members who had been detained in France—Ben Bella, Muhammad Khider, Muhammad Boudiaf, Hocine Aït Ahmed and Rabah Bitat. Boudiaf and Aït Ahmed rallied temporarily to the support of Ben Khedda, while the others formed yet another opposition faction besides that of Abbas, who had been removed from the GPRA leadership in 1961.

The ALN leadership was also split, with the commanders of the main armed forces in Tunisia and Morocco opposing the politicians of the GPRA, and the commanders of the internal guerrilla groups hostile to all external and military factions.

Serious differences emerged when the National Council of the Algerian Revolution met in Tripoli, Libya, in May 1962 to consider policies for the new state. A commission headed by Ben Bella produced a programme envisaging large-scale agrarian reform, a state monopoly of external trade and a foreign policy aimed towards Maghreb unity, neutrality and anti-colonialism. Despite the opposition of Ben Khedda's group, the Tripoli programme became the official FLN policy.

After independence the GPRA Cabinet, with the exception of Ben Bella, flew to Algiers, where they installed themselves alongside the official Provisional Executive. Ben Khedda attempted to reassert control over the ALN by dismissing the Commander-in-Chief, Col Houari Boumedienne, but Ben Bella flew to Morocco to join Boumedienne, and in July 1962 they crossed into Algeria and established their headquarters in Tlemcen, where Ben Bella instituted the Political Bureau as the chief executive organ of the FLN and a rival to the GPRA. After negotiations, he was joined by some of the GPRA leaders, leaving Ben Khedda isolated in Algiers, with Boudiaf and Aït Ahmed in opposition.

However, several *wilaya* leaders felt that, having provided the internal resistance, it was they who represented the true current of the revolution, and they opposed the Political Bureau and Boumedienne. While ALN forces loyal to the Bureau occupied Constantine and Bône (renamed Annaba) in the east in July 1962, Algiers remained in the hands of the leadership of *wilaya* IV, who refused the Bureau entry. When Boumedienne's forces marched on Algiers from Oran in September there were serious clashes with *wilaya* IV troops. Total civil war was averted, partly because of mass demonstrations against the fighting, which were organized by the Union Générale des Travailleurs Algériens (UGTA—General Union of Algerian Workers).

The struggle for power proved costly for Ben Khedda. Before the elections were held on 20 September 1962, one-third of the 180 candidates on the single list drafted in August had been purged (including Ben Khedda himself) and replaced with lesser-known figures. Some 99% of the electorate were declared to have voted in favour of the proposed powers of the Constituent Assembly. The functions of the GPRA were transferred to the Assembly when it convened on 25 September, and Abbas was elected its President. The Algerian Republic was proclaimed, and on the following day Ben Bella was elected Prime Minister. He subsequently appointed a cabinet comprising his personal associates and former ALN officers.

BEN BELLA IN POWER

The new Government acted immediately to consolidate its position. Hadj's PPA (formerly the MNA), the Parti Communiste Algérien (Algerian Communist Party) and Boudiaf's Parti de la Révolution Socialiste (Socialist Revolution Party) were all banned in November 1962; the *wilaya* system was abolished the following month, and, apart from the UGTA, all organizations affiliated to the FLN were brought firmly under control.

The country's economic plight was severe. Some 90% (1m.) of the Europeans, representing virtually all the entrepreneurs, technicians, administrators, teachers, doctors and skilled workers, had left the country. Factories, farms and shops had closed, leaving 70% of the population unemployed. Public buildings and records had been destroyed by the OAS. At the end of the war, in which more than 1m. people had died, 2m. people were interned and 500,000 were refugees in Tunisia and Morocco. An austerity plan was formulated in December 1962, and extensive loans and technical assistance from France, plus other emergency foreign aid, enabled the Government to remain in power.

By filling the first UGTA congress with FLN militants and unemployed, the FLN managed in January 1963 to gain control of the UGTA executive, which had been opposed to the dictatorial nature of the new Government. In March the workers' committees, which, aided by the UGTA, had taken over the operation of many of the abandoned European estates, were legalized; the remaining estates were nationalized in 1963. The system of workers' management, known as *autogestion*, under which the workers elected their own management board to work alongside a state-appointed director, became the basis of 'Algerian socialism'.

In April 1963 Ben Bella assumed the post of Secretary-General of the FLN. In August he secured the adoption by the Assembly of a draft constitution providing for a presidential regime, with the FLN as the sole political party. The new Constitution was approved by referendum, and on 13 September Ben Bella was elected President for a five-year period, taking the title of Commander-in-Chief of the Armed Forces as well as becoming Head of State and head of government. These moves towards dictatorial government aroused opposition. Abbas, the leading proponent of a more liberal policy, resigned from the presidency of the Assembly and was subsequently expelled from the FLN.

THE BOUMEDIENNE ERA

On 19 June 1965 Ben Bella was deposed and arrested in a swift and bloodless military *coup d'état*, led by the Minister of Defence, Boumedienne. Supreme political authority in Algeria passed to the Council of the Revolution, which consisted mostly of military figures and was presided over by Boumedienne. The Boumedienne regime enjoyed a remarkable degree of stability after the debilitating rivalries and uncertainties of the early years of independence. The majority of the Algerian population greeted the new regime with indifference, and most active opposition was crushed after an abortive coup in 1967. There was no real attempt to democratize the structure of political control, and Algeria continued to be governed by a few men and a few institutions—with the army and the administration having central executive importance. The FLN, once a successful mass political movement, ceased to play an effective role. Although elected local and provincial assemblies were created in the late 1960s, their role was essentially advisory and they operated within a framework determined by the central Government.

The personal authority of Boumedienne increased in the 1970s, and in 1975 he announced that elections for a National Assembly and a President were to be held, and that a national charter would be drafted to provide the state with a new constitution. Public discussion of the national charter was vigorous and often critical of local and central government, but it received the approval of 98.5% of the population at a referendum held in June 1976. The essence of the charter was the irreversible commitment of Algeria to socialism, albeit a socialism specifically adapted to Third World conditions. The dominant role of the FLN was reasserted, but, as a concession to conservative elements, Islam was recognized as the state religion. In November a new Constitution, embodying the principles of the charter, was also approved by referendum, and in December Boumedienne was elected unopposed as President, taking 99% of the votes cast. To complete the new formal structure of power, a 261-member National People's Assembly was elected in February 1977 from 783 candidates selected by a committee of the FLN.

During the Boumedienne era Algeria's participation in international affairs was as ambitious as its development strategy. Boumedienne's ministers often expressed a grand concept of Algeria's role in the world, and the Minister of Foreign Affairs, Abdelaziz Bouteflika, described Algeria as the 'central country' in the Maghreb, on the borders of the Mediterranean, with an attachment to both Africa and the Arab world, and thus ideally placed at the crossroads of Europe, Asia and Africa. The country's major successes in world affairs during the 1970s were in oil politics and within the Non-aligned Movement. Algeria joined the Organization of the Petroleum Exporting Countries (OPEC) in 1969 and, as a minor producer, quickly became one of the organization's leading 'hawks', consistently campaigning for the maintenance of high prices for the commodity. Among the Non-aligned states, Algeria argued persuasively in favour of nationalization and producer cartels and used the example of its own experience to demonstrate that the struggle for development should be seen as an extension of the struggle for liberation. These policies were promoted energetically at the fourth conference of the Non-aligned Movement held in Algiers in September 1973, and again in April 1974 when Boumedienne addressed a special session of the UN General Assembly. His call for a 'new international economic order' to redress the economic disparities between the Western industrialized countries and the developing world heralded Algeria's efforts to establish an international forum to tackle these problems through dialogue rather than confrontation. Algeria's mobilization of the Non-aligned world, the 'seventy-seven' developing countries, the UN and OPEC in support of these initiatives, even though the practical outcome was negligible, won it new prestige and almost universal recognition as a diplomatic leader of the Third World.

In spite of the militancy of Algerian rhetoric in international affairs and its vociferous support for liberation movements, in practice Algeria's foreign relations were tempered by a good deal of pragmatism. Anxieties in the West that Algeria might fall within the Soviet sphere of influence proved unfounded, and co-operation with the USSR was limited essentially to the supply of military equipment for Algeria's armed forces, while technology for its economic development programme was purchased mainly from the USA and Western Europe. Although Algeria was critical of US actions in Latin America, the Middle East and Viet Nam, by 1976 the USA had replaced France as Algeria's principal trading partner. Increasing contact with the English-speaking world inevitably produced new strains in Algeria's intense but uneasy relations with its former colonial power. Bilateral relations had already been aggravated by the nationalization, in 1971, of French oil interests—responsible for some two-thirds of Algeria's total production—and France's decision to impose a boycott of Algerian petroleum, and by the inability, or unwillingness, of the French police to protect Algerian workers living in France. In 1973, following a series of racially motivated incidents in the south of France directed against Algerians, the Algerian Government suspended all new emigration to France.

The dispute over French oil interests was resolved in late 1974, and in April 1975 Valéry Giscard d'Estaing became the first French President to visit Algeria since independence. However, a new source of friction arose later in 1975 when Spanish Sahara was annexed by Morocco and Mauritania following their Tripartite Agreement with Spain. Algeria denounced the annexation and gave active support to the Saharan liberation movement, the Frente Popular para la Liberación de Saguia el-Hamra y Río de Oro (the Polisario Front), which proclaimed the Sahrawi Arab Democratic Republic (SADR) in 1976. France, on the other hand, supported Morocco, and in May 1978 French military aircraft intervened by carrying out bombing raids against Polisario guerrillas. The prospect of full-scale war between Morocco and Algeria over Western Sahara quickly receded, although Algeria continued to provide military and diplomatic assistance to Polisario and refuge for displaced persons and Polisario fighters near Tindouf.

CHADLI IN POWER

Boumedienne died suddenly on 27 December 1978 without naming a successor. The choice of Col Ben Djedid Chadli, the commander of the Oran military district, as the new President—rather than Minister of Foreign Affairs Bouteflika or the administrative head of the FLN, Muhammad Salah Yahiaoui, both of whom had been regarded as more obvious potential candidates—came as a surprise both inside and outside the country, but unquestionably reaffirmed the political primacy of the armed forces. Chadli was inaugurated as President on 9 February 1979, after his candidature had been approved by 94% of the electorate.

Initially the Chadli Government appeared weak as the President's own supporters were in a minority. However, the existence of a number of factions within the regime gave Chadli some room for manoeuvre and enabled him gradually to exert his control over the state apparatus. Bouteflika, Yahiaoui and other influential personalities from the Boumedienne era were dismissed first from the Political Bureau and then from the Central Committee of the FLN. For the first time since independence a Prime Minister was named: Col Muhammad Ben Ahmed Abd al-Ghani. This nomination preceded constitutional changes, adopted by the National People's Assembly in June 1979, which made the appointment of a Prime Minister obligatory and also reduced the President's term of office from six to five years.

Following his re-election as party Secretary-General at the FLN's fifth party congress in December 1983, Chadli automatically became the party's candidate in the presidential election held in January 1984, at which he was re-elected for a second five-year term with 95% of the vote.

On coming to power, Chadli had declared that he would uphold the policies of his predecessor, but it soon became clear that, despite the official rhetoric about 'continuity', Boumedienne's policies were to be revised, reversed or abandoned. In foreign affairs Boumedienne's aim of presenting Algeria as one of the leaders of the developing world was abandoned. Chadli forged close links with conservative states while attempting not to alienate radicals. Algeria earned high regard as a mediator, notably in negotiations that secured the release of US hostages detained in Iran after the 1979 Islamic Revolution. Much attention was paid to improving relations with Algeria's Maghreb neighbours, especially Morocco, and in February 1989 Algeria signed the treaty creating the Union du Maghreb Arabe (UMA—Union of the Arab Maghreb) with Libya, Mauritania, Morocco and Tunisia.

In domestic politics the Chadli regime devoted most of its attention to the economy, introducing a range of reforms. However, the impact of the liberalization programme was uneven and had unintended consequences. Restructuring state-owned industrial enterprises did not improve productivity. Far from transforming the pattern of trade, the country became almost completely dependent on petroleum and gas for its export revenues. The liberalization of the deeply troubled agricultural sector failed to stimulate food production, although it paved the way for the enrichment of certain private farmers specializing in speculative products. By the early 1990s Algeria had the most precarious food security situation in the region, with as much as 80% of its food supply being imported. The private sector, both formal and informal, legal and illegal, expanded dramatically. The entrepreneurs who benefited most from economic liberalization were those close to the state who could avoid the stifling bureaucracy because of their association with government officials. This produced serious corruption at the highest levels, led by what Algerians referred to as the 'mafia', within the informal economy.

The dramatic collapse in oil prices in 1986, together with the depreciation of the US dollar, had a devastating effect on the Algerian economy. Receipts from sales of crude oil dropped by 80% in real terms and, as prices for Algeria's exports of natural gas were linked to that of crude petroleum, overall hydrocarbon export receipts declined from US $12,970m. in 1985 to $7,633m. in 1986 and remained depressed for the rest of the decade. Algeria was particularly vulnerable because it had incurred heavy foreign debt during the 1970s in order to finance its ambitious development programme and, following the decrease in petroleum prices, debt-servicing costs accounted for a growing proportion of the country's export revenues. The Government responded to the crisis by taking measures to reduce both imports and public spending. A second phase of reforms was introduced to accelerate economic liberalization. Subsidies on basic consumer goods were reduced and price controls were lifted from state industrial and agricultural sectors in order to allow market forces to regulate resource distribution. The social costs of these reforms were high, particularly for the vulnerable strata of society. Inequalities in income widened and, while a privileged minority was enriched, unemployment rose and the purchasing power of the majority of families declined drastically.

THE 1988 RIOTS AND THE RE-EMERGENCE OF THE ISLAMIST MOVEMENT

The tensions that had been mounting in Algerian society erupted in widespread rioting in October 1988. The disturbances, affecting Algiers and other cities, proved difficult to control, and the eventual deployment of the army gave rise to intense popular anger at the brutal manner in which the rioters were subdued. Hundreds were killed and thousands injured, and there were reports that some detainees had been tortured. It was rumoured at the time that the clandestine communist party, the Parti d'Avant-garde Socialiste (PAGS—renamed Ettahaddi in 1993), which was influential in the main trade union, the UGTA, had been responsible for provoking these disturbances in an attempt to force the Government to decelerate its economic liberalization programme. The riots rapidly became an opportunity for the release of feelings of intense frustration and alienation among the Algerian youth against a regime that was perceived to have marginalized and abandoned them.

The riots also saw the re-emergence of the Islamist movement in mainstream Algerian political life. Islamist militants had not instigated the riots but they represented the only organized movement to voice the frustration of those involved, and Islamists became prominent targets for the security forces in the subsequent repression. Unlike their opposition rivals, the Islamists did not hesitate to employ violence to promote their cause. The first armed resistance was launched by a former FLN war veteran, Mustafa Bouiali, who during 1981–87 embarked on an armed struggle against 'the impious state' in the name of *jihad*. Bouiali was killed by the security forces in 1987.

INTRODUCTION OF A MULTI-PARTY SYSTEM

Chadli responded to the October 1988 riots by accelerating economic reforms and introducing wide-ranging political changes. In late October he proposed that the identification of the state with the FLN be ended by allowing non-party candidates to contest elections. Furthermore, the Prime Minister and the Government would no longer be responsible to the President, who would stand above party politics, but to the National People's Assembly. To demonstrate that these measures would not be merely superficial, five days later Chadli dismissed his uncompromising FLN deputy, Muhammad Cherif Messaâdia, replacing him with the more liberal Abd al-Hamid Mehiri, who had been the Algerian ambassador to France and Morocco. On 3 November the proposed reforms were approved at a referendum by 92.3% of the votes cast.

After Chadli's re-election as President in December 1988 (when he received 81% of the votes cast) further constitutional changes were approved by 73.4% of the votes cast at a referendum in February 1989, signalling a clear ideological break with the past. The 'irreversible commitment to socialism' was abandoned, and freedoms of expression, association and organization were guaranteed, as were the rights to unionize and strike. Executive, legislative and judicial functions were separated and no longer controlled by the FLN; instead they were to be supervised by a Constitutional Council. Mouloud Hamrouche, hitherto a senior figure in the presidential office, was appointed Prime Minister in September 1989.

However, the most notable of the changes in progress was that 'associations of a political nature' were allowed to compete with the FLN provided their platforms were neither religious nor regionalist. A law on political associations was passed in July 1989, and a new electoral law adopted later that month paved the way to a controlled multi-party system. Within a short time some 30 political parties, representing a wide range of ideological tendencies, had been officially registered. Apart from the previously outlawed Front des Forces Socialistes (FFS—Socialist Forces' Front), led by Hocine Aït Ahmed (one of the *chefs historiques* of the Algerian revolution), and Saïd Saâdi's newly created Rassemblement Pour la Culture et la Démocratie (RCD—Union for Culture and Democracy), both of which drew their support predominantly from the Berber-speaking Kabylia region, together with Ben Bella's Mouvement Pour la Démocratie en Algérie (MDA—Movement for Democracy in Algeria), most parties were relatively small and insignificant—with the exception of the fundamentalist Front Islamique du Salut (FIS—Islamic Salvation Front), which quickly emerged as the only serious nation-wide competitor to the FLN. Although other Islamist parties emerged, the FIS gathered together the major, yet diverse, elements of the Islamist movement into a political coalition which had a well-organized and well-financed party network, strongly rooted at the local level in the many neighbourhood mosques. The party attracted support from the so-called 'pious bourgeoisie', some members of the technical and intellectual élite, and from the deprived and frustrated urban youth from the city slums, the main victims of the regime's economic reforms.

LOCAL AND NATIONAL ELECTIONS

The new multi-party system was put to the test in June 1990 when municipal and provincial elections were held—the first free elections in Algeria since independence. Disregarding a high rate of voter abstention (estimated at 35%–40%), the FIS won a sweeping victory—obtaining some 55% of the votes cast and securing control of 853 municipalities, including the three major cities, Algiers, Oran and Constantine, and 32 *wilayat*. Only in Kabylia and in the south did the FIS fail to win convincingly. In contrast, its chief rival, the FLN, which had entered the elections deeply divided, was comprehensively defeated, obtaining only 32% of the vote and taking control of only 487 municipalities and 14 *wilayat*. Prior to the elections the former Prime Minister, Abd al-Hamid Brahimi, had alleged that FLN and government officials had received US $26,000m. ($2,000m. more than the entire national debt) in bribes during the previous decade. The FIS's victory was widely interpreted as a crushing rejection of rule by the FLN establishment, rather than an endorsement of the project and world view of radical Islamism.

In December 1990 the National People's Assembly approved a vote of confidence in Prime Minister Hamrouche, the first such vote for 20 years. At the end of the month the Assembly approved a law stipulating that, after 1997, Arabic would become Algeria's official language and that the use of the French and Berber languages by private companies and political parties would thereafter incur heavy fines. The new law was regarded as an attack on Algeria's Western-educated élite and the Berber people, and some 500,000 people demonstrated in Algiers against religious and political intolerance. The FIS regarded the adoption of the 'Arabization' law as a political triumph, but it no longer held a monopoly on Islamist activism. There were now two new political parties which aimed to recruit people dissatisfied with the intolerance of the FIS and those who saw no incompatibility between Islam and liberal economics—the Islamic Renaissance Movement (Al-Nahda) and Hamas. The FIS, which was also losing support to the MDA, claimed that these new parties had been sponsored by the Government. The FIS itself appeared to be undermined by divisions between the organization's leader, Abbassi Madani, and another senior figure, Ali Belhadj, notably on the issue of the crisis arising from Iraq's invasion of Kuwait: while the latter urged his supporters to prepare to give military support to Iraq in the face of the US-led military build-up in the Gulf region, Madani argued that military training should be restricted to the army and that the FIS should gain power through electoral means.

The Government announced in April 1991 that the long-awaited parliamentary elections would be held in two rounds in June and July, and introduced major revisions to the country's electoral law. In constituencies where no candidate obtained an absolute majority in the first round of voting, second ballots were to be conducted; campaigning in mosques and proxy voting were to be restricted; and the number of constituencies was increased from 290 to 542. The FIS regarded these changes as a deliberate ploy to reduce its chances of victory in the forthcoming elections, and demanded that a presidential election be held concurrently with the legislative elections. In protest at the new electoral law, in May the FIS urged an indefinite general strike and numerous FIS supporters took to the streets of Algiers as part of a campaign of peaceful protest. However, when riot police were ordered to clear the streets, fierce fighting erupted as armed FIS supporters set up barricades in two of the city's main squares.

At the beginning of June 1991 Chadli declared a 'state of siege' and suspended the elections indefinitely. Tanks were deployed in Algiers and a curfew was imposed. Armed with extensive powers, the military subsequently restored relative calm on the streets of the capital. Shortly afterwards the FIS leadership abandoned the general strike, declaring that the President had agreed to hold both legislative and presidential elections before the end of the year and to change the disputed electoral laws to ensure that elections would be 'clean and fair'. What appeared to be a victory for the FIS antagonized elements within the army bitterly hostile to the Islamists. Army leaders demanded a crackdown on the radical fringe of the Islamist movement, and later in June, when troops removed Islamic slogans from FIS-controlled municipal buildings, further violent clashes erupted as FIS militants confronted the security forces. At the end of June Madani, Belhadj and some 2,500 of their supporters (8,000 according to opponents of the Government) were arrested. The two FIS leaders were accused of leading an armed conspiracy against the state in an attempt to take power. Despite rumours that an army-backed regime was to be installed, the army did not take power at this time but waited a further six months before intervening decisively. Some analysts have argued that leading members of the military hierarchy were persuaded that the FIS would not be able to repeat its success in the forthcoming legislative elections; others maintained that the army leadership was poised to take over but that, aware of international opinion, the military was waiting until it could claim that the incompetent Chadli regime had allowed the political situation to escalate out of control and that it had been forced to intervene to protect the integrity of the state against the threat of an Islamist take-over.

In October 1991 the National People's Assembly approved amendments to the electoral law, establishing the number of single-member parliamentary constituencies at 430. Independent candidates would in future need to obtain only 300 (rather than 500) signatures in support of their candidacy, and the minimum age for parliamentary candidates was lowered from 35 to 28 years. President Chadli announced that the first round of voting in the general election would take place on 26 December, with a second round of voting on 16 January 1992 in constituencies where there had been no outright winner at the first round. The FIS threatened to boycott the elections unless its leaders were released, but agreed to participate at the last minute.

The 430 seats in the National People's Assembly were contested by 5,712 candidates representing 49 political parties and by more than 1,000 independents. In the first round of voting, in which some 59% of the electorate participated, the FIS took an apparently unassailable lead, winning 188 seats outright, although it received just 3.2m. votes (1.5m. fewer than in the municipal elections) from an electorate of 13.3m. The FFS took 25 seats, while the former ruling party, the FLN, was relegated to a humiliating third place with only 15 seats (although it won about one-half as many votes as the FIS). The FLN complained of intimidation and malpractice in 340 constituencies in which officials of FIS-controlled municipalities had distributed voting papers. A second round of voting was required for 199 seats, with the FIS needing to win only 20 to secure an absolute majority in the Assembly. The other three Islamist parties, Al-Nahda, Hamas and El-Oumma, instructed their supporters to vote for the FIS against the FLN in the second round, but the secular parties failed to declare their support for the FLN. President Chadli, who had resigned from the FLN the previous year, reaffirmed that he would respect the election results and indicated his willingness to 'cohabit' with an FIS government. The FIS, however, confident of winning at least two-thirds of the seats in the new Assembly, rejected the possibility of power-sharing and demanded the appointment of Abbassi Madani as Prime Minister and an immediate presidential election. Meanwhile, there were widespread demonstrations in defence of democracy and against the potential establishment of an 'Iranian-style' fundamentalist regime.

THE MILITARY TAKE-OVER

On 4 January 1992 the National People's Assembly was dissolved by presidential decree. One week later, and five days before the scheduled second round of the election, President Chadli, apparently under intense pressure from the army chiefs, resigned 'to safeguard the interests of the country'. Tanks and heavily armed troops were deployed around key buildings in the capital, and the High Security Council, dominated by three senior generals—the Minister of Defence, Maj.-Gen. Khaled Nezzar, the Minister of the Interior, Larbi Belkheir, and the Chief of Staff of the Army, Abdelmalek Guenaïzia—and also including the Prime Minister, and the Ministers of Justice and Foreign Affairs—took power with the declared aim of maintaining public order and national security. They appointed Abd al-Malek Benhabiles, the Chairman of the Constitutional Council, as acting Head of State. The second round of the election was cancelled and a 'state of exception' was declared.

On 14 January 1992 a five-member High Council of State (HCS) was appointed to operate as a collegiate presidency until the expiry of Chadli's term of office in December 1993. The leading figure in the Council was clearly Nezzar, but its Chairman was Muhammad Boudiaf, one of the historic leaders of the War of Independence who now returned from self-imposed exile in Morocco, where he had lived since 1964.

On taking power, the military junta moved swiftly against municipalities, newspapers and mosques controlled by the FIS. Security forces seized control of the FIS offices and arrested leading FIS officials, who were accused of inciting soldiers to desert. Violent clashes broke out between the army and demonstrators across the country, and on 9 February 1992 the HCS declared a 12-month state of emergency giving the security services sweeping powers of arrest and detention. Thousands of FIS supporters were arrested, and by the end of March some 9,000 were being held in special detention camps set up in remote parts of the Sahara. Already, more than 100 people had been killed in clashes between Islamist militants and the security forces. Some within the FIS leadership insisted that the party would fight the military take-over through democratic means, but this moderate line was unacceptable to militants and to those who had always had doubts about the party's electoral strategy.

In early March 1992, following a court ruling, the FIS was outlawed 'for pursuing by subversive means goals that endanger public order'. Madani and Belhadj were brought before a military court in June, accused of aggression and conspiracy against the state, and sentenced to 12 years in prison. The security situation continued to deteriorate, and in August a series of bombings, including an attack on Algiers international airport that killed nine people, marked a dangerous escalation in the cycle of violence. New security laws were introduced as the authorities declared 'total war' against supporters of the proscribed FIS. A curfew was imposed in Algiers and surrounding areas, and was later extended to 10 other provinces. Three state security courts were established with the authority to impose harsh sentences including the death penalty. In January 1993 the first two Islamist militants, both of them former soldiers, were put to death, and more executions followed—including that of Hocine Abderramane, a close associate of Madani. In February the state of emergency was renewed indefinitely. The London-based human rights organization Amnesty International reported a dramatic increase in the use of torture by the security forces. These tough policies found support among some elements within Algerian society, but for the vast majority of the population, especially the urban poor, the crude techniques of mass repression provoked popular resentment and merely increased their support for the Islamists.

EMERGENCE OF ARMED ISLAMIST GROUPS

Following the proscription of the FIS and the dismantling of its political organization in early 1992, the Islamist initiative passed to a number of armed clandestine opposition groups, some of which derived from the earlier phase of armed Islamist resistance led by Mustafa Bouiali in the 1980s. The precise relationship of these groups with the FIS political leadership was unclear. The Mouvement de l'Etat Islamique (MEI—Movement of the Islamic State), under the leadership of Abdelkader Chebouti, a former associate of Bouiali, and Said Mekhloufi, a founder member of the FIS, attracted a certain number of militants from the dissolved FIS. Well-organized and with a clear command structure, the MEI directed its struggle primarily against the state and its representatives. Its more radical rival, the Groupe Islamique Armé (GIA—Armed Islamic Group), linked together several largely autonomous cells, including many Algerian Islamists who had fought with the *mujahidin* (holy warriors) against the Soviet occupation in Afghanistan, and groups that had opposed the electoral strategy of the political wing of the FIS. The GIA condemned as impious those pacifist FIS members who refused to take up arms, calling for a *jihad*, following the Afghan model, to establish a 'caliphate' in Algeria. The GIA targeted not only the security services but also sought to remove prominent public figures, intellectuals, journalists and teachers, not all of whom were linked to the regime, as well as 'impious' foreign nationals. Its statements accelerated the exodus of foreign nationals. Armed Islamist groups attracted mainly young men from the poor urban quarters. At first they received voluntary contributions from members of the 'pious bourgeoisie', hostile to a regime that had robbed them of electoral victory. However, they quickly resorted to extortion and intimidation, alienating their middle-class supporters and thus dividing and eventually weakening the Islamist movement.

THE ASSASSINATION OF BOUDIAF

Boudiaf, who had been installed as Chairman of the HCS to give a measure of legitimacy to the new regime, was assassinated in Annaba on 29 June 1992. Widely respected as a man of integrity, he had begun to give indications of a personal political agenda. In particular, his efforts to eradicate corruption had threatened many at the highest levels of the ruling establishment, and he had ensured that at least one senior army officer, Maj.-Gen. Mustafa Beloucif, was charged before a military tribunal for the embezzlement of millions of dinars. Although there was television footage of Boudiaf's killing, and the assassin was seized on the spot, it was by no means certain whether the assassination was the action of a lone killer or part of a conspiracy; nor was the motive for the killing clear. The HCS declared seven days of mourning and ordered a commission of inquiry into the assassination. Islamist extremists applauded the killing but did not claim credit for it. The inquiry's report was made available to the media in December, but with 76 of its 111 pages missing. Its conclusion was that the assassin had not acted alone but on behalf of an unspecified organization that was increasingly identified with the FLN. It was not until June 1995 that Lt Lembarek Boumaârafi, a member of the special anti-terrorist unit responsible for the President's security on the day of his assassination, was sentenced to death for Boudiaf's murder. Little new information was revealed at the trial, and the authorities maintained that Boumaârafi had acted alone. However, popular suspicion fell on the 'mafia' and its allies in the administration and army, often referred to as the *hizb fransa*—the 'party of France'.

There was speculation that Maj.-Gen. Nezzar would succeed Boudiaf as Chairman of the HCS, but he was in poor health and apparently unwilling to make too obvious the military's control of the state. After consulting with party leaders, another member of the HCS, Ali Kafi, the head of the Algerian War Veterans' Organization, was nominated for the chairmanship of the HCS. Kafi pledged adherence to Boudiaf's programme but showed no signs of implementing it. Sid-Ahmed Ghozali resigned as Prime Minister and was replaced by Belaid Abd el-Salam, who had been in charge of Algeria's hydrocarbons and industrial policy under Boumedienne. On the anniversary of the military take-over Kafi promised that a new constitution would be drafted, after consultation with groups not committed to violence, and that the resultant document would be pluralist and allow genuinely democratic elections. There would be a referendum on the balance of power between the President and the Government. Regarded as a further pretext for postponing elections, this proposal was greeted with scepticism by the main political parties.

In July 1993 Maj.-Gen. Nezzar was replaced as Minister of Defence by Gen. Liamine Zéroual, although he remained a member of the HCS. Gen. Muhammad Lamari, who had been responsible for organizing anti-terrorist units, was appointed Chief of Staff. In August, after only a year in office, Abd el-Salam was replaced as Prime Minister by the Minister of Foreign Affairs, Redha Malek, a former career diplomat. The appointment of Mourad Benachenhou, a former Algerian representative at the World Bank, as Minister of the Economy, apparently signalled a return to the reform programme. A senior army officer, Col Sélim Saâdi, was appointed Minister of the Interior, and this was followed by the reorganization of the security forces and the creation of a unified command of the military and police forces in an attempt to combat Islamist violence.

LIAMINE ZÉROUAL BECOMES HEAD OF STATE

The mandate of the HCS was scheduled to expire on 31 December 1993, and in October the formation of an eight-member National Dialogue Commission (NDC) was announced, to oversee the transition to an elected government. The appointment of three generals to the commission openly brought the military into the political process for the first time. However, little progress was made by the NDC in its negotiations with opposition parties regarding the creation of a transitional regime. The only significant legal parties, the FLN and the FFS, had strongly opposed the 1992 coup and the interruption of the electoral process and had refused to co-operate with the military-backed governments installed since then. After 1992 the power structure had become deeply divided, with two tendencies confronting one another: the so-called *éradicateurs*—who rejected any compromise with the FIS and the Islamist militants and insisted on the brutal suppression of the Islamist movement—and the *conciliateurs*, who believed that the political crisis could only be solved by compromise and dialogue with the Islamist opposition. The main *éradicateurs* were those senior army officers who had served in the French army before independence and who had occupied key positions in the army high command since 1988. Support outside the army for this hardline tendency was limited to the leadership of the trade union movement, the Berber RCD, the former communist party (Ettahaddi), women's groups and most of the francophone press. The *conciliateurs* could count on less formal support among the senior officer class, but included all the main political parties, human rights activists, and intellectuals and journalists grouped around the journal *Naqd* and the weekly *La Nation*.

In December 1993 the HCS stated that it would not disband until a new presidential body had been inaugurated. It proposed the convening of a national dialogue conference in January 1994 to choose a new collective leadership. The conference proved to be an abject failure as it was boycotted by almost all the main political parties. The HCS then appeared to have abandoned the idea of a presidential triumvirate to rule during the transitional period from 1994–96 in favour of a single, strong hand intended to restore confidence and coherence to government policy. Hardliners in the regime, such as Gens Nezzar, Belkheir, Benabbes Gheziel and Muhammad 'Tewfik' Medienne, favoured Abdelaziz Bouteflika, Boumedienne's Minister of Foreign Affairs, but he declined the invitation to take control. Eventually the HCS named the Minister of Defence, Liamine Zéroual, as Head of State. Zéroual, who was sworn in on 31 January 1994, was one of the most respected members of the senior officer corps and was believed to share the views of the *conciliateurs*. Zéroual derived a measure of personal legitimacy from the fact that he had joined the ALN at the age of 16 and had fought in the guerrilla struggle for independence inside Algeria. In his first public statement the new President appealed for 'serious dialogue' to find a way out of the country's crisis and made cautious overtures to those members of the banned FIS who renounced violence. In April he removed the *éradicateurs* Malek and Saâdi from the Government, appointing a new administration comprised mainly of technocrats and senior civil servants, and headed by Mokdad Sifi, hitherto Minister of Equipment. During the following month Zéroual made changes to senior posts in the military, but security operations remained under the control of hardliners such as Gens Lamari, Medienne and Muhammad Touati.

DIALOGUE FAILS

Efforts to promote dialogue proved cautious. In May 1994 Zéroual inaugurated the National Transition Council (NTC), an interim legislature of 200 appointed members intended to provide a forum for debate until new parliamentary elections were held. Of the main political parties, only the 'moderate' Islamist Hamas agreed to participate in the new body, which became the target of ridicule in the media. It was not until August that the President managed to persuade five leading legalized parties to join talks aimed at drawing up an acceptable peace formula, and even then there was disagreement among the parties over whether or not to include the banned FIS. Earlier in the year two high-ranking FIS members, Ali Djeddi and Abdelkader Boukhamkham, had been released from prison in order for the possibilities for dialogue with the Islamist opposition to be explored, but little progress was made. Finally, in late August a breakthrough appeared to have been made. In a letter to Zéroual, imprisoned FIS leader Abbassi Madani agreed to respect the 1989 Constitution and the principle of the alternation of power, and, while not explicitly renouncing violence, referred to the possibility of a truce. In September 1994 Zéroual ordered the release of both Madani and Belhadj from prison and their transfer to house arrest.

Several factors are thought to have prompted the change in the FIS's intransigent stance towards the military-backed regime, but most important may have been its fear of marginalization by the extremist GIA. In May 1994 the MEI and a number of other armed groups linked to the FIS had agreed to merge with the GIA and accept the leadership of the GIA's 'national emir', Cherif Gousmi. However, unwilling to let the extremists gain the upper hand, the head of the FIS Executive Committee Abroad, Rabah Kebir, rejected the agreement and in July announced the creation of the Armée Islamique du Salut (AIS—Islamic Army of Salvation) under the leadership of Madani Mezrag. The AIS brought together, under the authority of the FIS and its imprisoned leadership, armed Islamist groups active in the west and east of Algeria. Thus the FIS political leadership sought to create its own armed wing, distinct from the radical GIA, in order to negotiate with the military-backed regime from a position of strength. The GIA, which had its stronghold in the centre of the country, especially in and around Algiers, immediately denounced the FIS leadership's decision to negotiate with Zéroual's Government, and opposed the establishment of democracy by means of a moderate Islamist regime. There was to be no truce and no dialogue. Instead, the country had to be purified of the 'impious' and an Islamic state established by *jihad*.

The transfer of the two FIS leaders to house arrest failed to break the impasse between the regime and the FIS. In October 1994 Zéroual announced that neither Madani nor Belhadj was willing to renounce violence or participate in negotiations. In a speech later that month Zéroual spoke of the failure of dialogue with the FIS, and announced his decision to hold a presidential election in 1995 before the end of his mandate. He also used the occasion to announce the promotion of Gen. Muhammad Lamari, a leading *éradicateur*, to the highest rank in the Algerian military.

THE SANT' EGIDIO PACT

Zéroual's plan to hold a presidential election towards the end of 1995 was rejected by many leading legalized opposition parties and condemned by the exiled FIS leadership. Unexpectedly, the opposition parties seized the initiative and—after talks in Rome under the aegis of the Sant' Egidio Roman Catholic community in November 1994 and again in January 1995—the main Algerian opposition parties agreed a 'platform for a national contract', presenting the basis for a negotiated end to the conflict and a return to democracy. The document was signed by representatives of the FIS, the FLN and the FFS, together with the MDA, Al-Nahda, the Parti des Travailleurs (PT—Workers' Party) and the Algerian League for the Defence of Human Rights (ALDHR).

The Sant' Egidio pact made an urgent appeal to all parties in the conflict to end hostilities and allow the restoration of civil peace. It recommended the establishment of a transitional government, in which both the regime and the political parties would be represented, to prepare the way for free, multi-party elections. All parties were asked to guarantee to respect the results of the elections. Before any negotiations, the participants appealed for the release of the FIS leadership and of all political detainees, the restoration of the legal status of the FIS, and an immediate end to the use of torture and attacks on civilians, foreigners and public property. The parties to the pact also agreed certain general principles including the renunciation of violence as a means to achieve or retain power, together with respect for human rights, multi-party democracy and the alternation of power, and the guarantee of fundamental liberties. They recognized the importance of Islamic, Arab and Berber culture in Algeria, and demanded that both the Arab and Berber languages be recognized as national languages. Finally, they appealed for the withdrawal of the army from politics. Belhadj and Madani endorsed the Sant' Egidio pact, whereas the GIA condemned it and reaffirmed its commitment to the establishment of a 'caliphate' by armed struggle.

Zéroual's regime condemned the Sant' Egidio meeting even before it had begun, claiming foreign interference in Algeria's national affairs, and after the pact was announced a government spokesman categorically rejected its proposals. The French, Italian, Spanish and US Governments expressed support for the Rome talks, while avoiding putting any pressure on the Algerian regime even to consider some aspects of the pact. Whereas some analysts argued that the Sant' Egidio pact confirmed that the FIS was distancing itself from the Islamist radicals, anti-Islamist organizations in Algeria saw the pact as no more than a ploy by the Islamists to take power; with the army neutralized they would abandon all pretence at democracy and impose fundamentalist rule. This would become the leitmotif some sectors of Algerian society utilized to justify the continued repression of the FIS.

Meanwhile, President Zéroual continued to prepare for a presidential election. In April 1995 he attempted to regain the initiative by resuming talks with the legalized opposition parties. However, talks with the FLN and the FFS quickly collapsed when Zéroual again refused to include the FIS in any dialogue. The FLN and the FFS agreed to take part in the presidential election only if the FIS was allowed to participate. The Government reiterated its demand that the FIS renounce violence and accept the Constitution before it could participate in the election. There was speculation that unofficial talks were continuing between the Government and the FIS leadership, but in July Zéroual issued a statement announcing the collapse of dialogue with the FIS. In June Abbassi Madani and Ali Belhadj were once again returned to prison.

THE 'DIRTY WAR'

For all the talk of dialogue during 1994, the descent into civil war continued, and some of the barbarous acts reported recalled the worst days of the struggle for independence. Indiscriminate terror tactics by both Islamist guerrillas and the security forces turned the conflict into a 'dirty war'. The regime admitted in September 1994 that 10,000 people had died in the conflict since early 1992. Amnesty International estimated the death toll at 20,000, one-half of them ordinary civilians. These figures almost certainly underestimate the death toll, as daily killings went unreported in the heavily censored media. As many as 30,000 lives had probably been lost since February 1992, with around 1,000 killed every week by the end of 1994.

An Amnesty International report released in October 1994 painted the grim picture of a country where civilians were living in a state of fear, threatened and killed by Islamists for not obeying their orders, and by the security forces in retaliation for Islamist raids. Damage to the country's infrastructure as a result of the conflict was estimated at US $3,000m., although the oil and gas industry and infrastructure did not suffer any significant damage as the security forces made their protection a priority. In fact, in mid-April 1995 security measures were reinforced in the four 'exclusion zones' at Ouargla, Laghouat, el-Oued and Illizi—established to protect the Saharan oil- and gasfields, which provided 95% of Algeria's export revenues. Certain towns, and entire neighbourhoods in some cities, were virtually controlled by armed Islamist groups, and Islamist attacks on government officials, politicians, judges, intellectuals, journalists and teachers continued. In addition to their campaign of assassinations, Islamist guerrillas burnt down schools and colleges and instituted a reign of terror in areas under their control; anyone violating Islamist diktats risked mutilation or murder. Foreign nationals continued to be targeted, forcing many of them to flee, and some countries closed their embassies and consulates.

The security forces intensified their campaign against armed Islamist groups, undertaking air attacks using napalm, and conducting punitive raids, torture and psychological warfare in their efforts to eradicate the militants. Army repression was particularly harsh in the more densely populated quarters of Algiers and other large cities, where many young men suspected of Islamist sympathies were apprehended in raids by the security forces, tortured and summarily executed. 'Death squads' emerged, carrying out 'revenge' killings against victims selected at random. In Kabylia, a region traditionally alienated from the regime but strongly opposed to the Islamists, Berber villages began organizing their own armed militias. After the failure of dialogue with the Islamist opposition, the army embarked on the most extensive military operations of the conflict, seemingly having abandoned all restraint in its efforts to uncover Islamist sympathizers and guerrilla units. In October 1994 Djamel Zitouni became the GIA's new 'national emir', following the murder of Gousmi the previous month.

On 24 December 1994 four GIA guerrillas hijacked an Air France aircraft at Algiers airport and murdered three passengers. The aircraft was stormed by French counter-terrorist police after it landed at Marseille and the hijackers were killed. It was claimed that the guerrillas had intended to blow up the aircraft over Paris. The GIA called for war on France, and in 1995 carried out a series of attacks in that country, including the bombing of the Paris metro. By launching a campaign of violence in France, the GIA sought to demonstrate that the FIS had no control over the armed struggle and was therefore incapable of negotiating an agreement with the military junta that would end the violence.

THE PRESIDENTIAL ELECTION OF NOVEMBER 1995

Algeria's first multi-party presidential election since independence was held on 16 November 1995 and resulted in a clear victory for the incumbent President Zéroual, who won 61.0% of the votes cast. Sheikh Mahfoud Nahnah, the leader of Hamas, took 25.6% of the vote, followed by Saïd Saâdi, Secretary-General of the RCD (9.6%) and Nourreddine Boukrouh, leader of the Parti du Renouveau Algérien (PRA—3.8%). The FIS, the FLN and the FFS had all urged a boycott of the election. Notwithstanding their demand, and threats by Islamist militants to 'turn the ballot boxes into coffins', official figures stated that 75.7% of the electorate participated in the election. Considering the circumstances, turn-out was very high and demonstrated that ordinary Algerians favoured the ideas of dialogue and national reconciliation that Zéroual appeared to represent. The main legal opposition parties, together with the proscribed FIS, were forced to acknowledge the political implications of the election, and there were appeals for a renewal of dialogue. At his inauguration on 27 November Zéroual reiterated his commitment to national dialogue and pledged to hold pluralist legislative and municipal elections, although he offered no precise timetable. The FFS announced that it would end its boycott of the electoral process and participate in legislative elections. The FLN, under a new leader, Boualem Benhamouda, was publicly reconciled with Zéroual and also indicated that it was prepared to contest future elections. Immediately after the presidential election, Rabah Kebir, the senior FIS spokesman in exile, acknowledged Zéroual's victory and appealed for new negotiations with the regime. In April and July 1996 Zéroual held talks with leaders of the main opposition parties, the UGTA and other associations, culminating in a national conference in September to ratify his political reform programme.

A referendum followed on 28 November 1996 to amend the 1989 Constitution in preparation for general and local elections in 1997. The proposed changes included the creation of a bicameral parliament with the new upper house, the Council of the Nation, appointed either directly or indirectly by the President, a ban on political parties based on religion or language, and the introduction of proportional representation. According to official figures, some 79.8% of the electorate participated in the referendum, with 85.9% voting in favour of the constitutional changes. A number of opposition parties claimed that the results had been manipulated by the Government. Opposition to the proposed reforms was particularly strong in Kabylia, where residents staged protests against the designation of Arabic as the sole 'national language'.

THE GENERAL AND LOCAL ELECTIONS OF 1997

Some 39 political parties qualified to take part in legislative elections held on 5 June 1997, when more than 7,000 candidates contested the 380 seats in the National People's Assembly. They included a new political party, the Rassemblement National Démocratique (RND—National Democratic Union), created only a few months before and led by Abdelkader Bensalah, former President of the NTC. The RND brought together a range of anti-Islamist organizations, self-defence groups, trade unions and women's associations, and its electoral lists included Ahmed Ouyahia, who had replaced Mokdad Sifi as Prime Minister in December 1995, and numerous other government ministers. The party was permitted to use official buildings for its electoral campaign and benefited from other public facilities, drawing accusations of favouritism from opposition parties. According to official results, the RND won 156 of the 380 seats contested; the Mouvement de la Société Pour la Paix (MSP—Society's Movement for Peace, as Hamas had been renamed in May, in compliance with new legislation) 69, the FLN 62, Al-Nahda 34, the FFS 20, the RCD 19 and the PT four, with the remainder being taken by independent candidates and other small political groupings. The RND did not achieve an overall majority in the new lower house, but it was generally assumed that it could rely on the support of the FLN. The two Islamist parties, the MSP and Al-Nahda, won more than 100 seats and, according to official figures, received over 20% of all the votes cast. The level of voter participation was officially put at 65.5%, although less than one-half of eligible voters in Algiers took part in the election. Opposition parties insisted that the turn-out had been lower than the official figures indicated, and complained of numerous and deliberate abuses. In mid-June President Zéroual asked Ouyahia to form a government; the FLN and the MSP received seven portfolios in the new Council of Ministers, while the RND took the remainder.

Elections to restore regional and municipal councils, which had not existed since 1992, followed in October 1997. The RND won more than one-half of the seats contested, with seven other parties winning seats on the regional councils and 33 securing representation on municipal councils. According to official results, some 62.7% of the electorate participated in regional elections and 67.7% in municipal elections. The Government expressed satisfaction at the result, and sought to portray the polls as the final stage in the restoration of the democratic process in Algeria. However, all major political parties complained of widespread electoral fraud and, in the weeks following the elections, opposition parties organized mass demonstrations on a scale not seen for many years. President Zéroual refused to annul the results, and street protests continued. In December an electoral college selected two-thirds of the seats in the new 144-member Council of the Nation from members of the regional and municipal councils; of the 96 seats, the RND took 80, the FLN 10, the FFS four and the MSP two. The remaining 48 members were nominated by Zéroual. Henceforth, legislation drafted by the lower house would not be promulgated unless approved by two-thirds of members in the Council of the Nation. In April 1998 a new Constitutional Council was installed.

POLITICAL VIOLENCE INTENSIFIES

The presidential election of November 1995 did not bring an end to political violence, which continued to claim an estimated 100 victims every week. Nevertheless, military analysts argued that the new strategies introduced by the security forces were more effective than in the past, that anti-terrorist intelligence was better co-ordinated, and that the self-defence groups—numbering some 18,000 men—had become increasingly integrated with the regime's security apparatus. They claimed that the security forces had made it more difficult for Islamist guerrilla bands to regroup and obtain weapons, and that they had fragmented into small groups unable to mount operations against major military targets. As a result, Islamist militants increasingly favoured the use of car bombs: it was estimated that in the six weeks after the start of Ramadan in January 1996 some 80 car bombs had exploded. After the presidential election the internment camp in the Sahara for alleged Islamist militants was closed and its inmates were released. However, some 17,000 Algerians remained imprisoned—the majority without trial—for alleged terrorist activities. Human rights organizations continued to condemn both the Islamist militants and the security forces for human rights abuses. Journalists still suffered violence and intimidation from Islamist extremists and harassment by the authorities, and several were killed in a wave of car bomb attacks in early 1996.

Meanwhile, the armed Islamist movement remained deeply divided, and, under the leadership of Djamel Zitouni, the GIA was characterized by growing internal dissent. During 1995 several senior figures in the group—notably Ezzedine Baa, Abderrazaq Redjem and Muhammad Saïd—were eliminated after they defected to the AIS. Zitouni had earlier accused them of attempting a coup against him. Further defections followed after the GIA murdered and mutilated seven French Trappist monks who had been kidnapped from their monastery near Médéa in May. A number of local GIA commanders abandoned their support for Zitouni, and in June 1996 the GIA's principal ideologues, the Palestinian Abu Qatada and the Syrian Abu Mous'ab, both based in London, United Kingdom, announced that they were withdrawing support from Zitouni, who was killed the following month following clashes between rival factions. The FIS leadership and several independent commentators asserted that, under Zitouni's leadership, the GIA had been infiltrated by the Algerian secret services and manipulated by them in order to discredit and divide the Islamist movement.

As the violence intensified, support for the Islamists' armed struggle diminished and the population became increasingly weary of a conflict that appeared to be leading nowhere. Zitouni was succeeded as the GIA's 'national emir' by Antar Zouabri, a close ally. Zouabri carried out further purges within the GIA, eliminating those who challenged his authority. Early in 1997 Zouabri acquired a new ideologue in the form of the London-based Egyptian militant Abu Hamza, who published a pamphlet entitled *Le sabre tranchant*, in which he admitted that *jihad* had become unpopular and that only a tiny minority of Algerians affirmed their religion by participating in the armed struggle. Under Zouabri's leadership many of the violent acts perpetrated by the GIA factions were aimed at punishing the civilian population for betraying the cause. In 1997 acts of brutality against civilians occurred on a scale hitherto unprecedented in the civil war. Beginning in January and February and intensifying in August and September, a series of massacres took place in villages to the south and west of Algiers. In some villages several hundred people—men, women and children, even babies—were slaughtered. Some victims had their throats cut or were burned alive, and many were horribly mutilated. The security forces appeared unable or unwilling to prevent the bloodshed; on several occasions the military failed to assist the local population during attacks that took place in the vicinity of army barracks.

In September 1997, in a communiqué published by Abu Hamza in the periodical *Al-Ansar*, Zouabri claimed responsibility for the massacres in the name of the GIA and justified them by declaring all Algerians who did not join the GIA to be *kuffar* (unbelievers) and thus legitimate targets of attack. Shortly afterwards Abu Hamza ended his support for Zouabri and the GIA because of this pronouncement of *takfir* against virtually the whole of Algerian society. In the opinion of some commentators, from the end of 1997 the GIA ceased to have a coherent command structure at the national level and fragmented into a number of 'autonomous' factions, some reduced to simple banditry. Nevertheless, the violence continued unabated. Further massacres were perpetrated in December in the days preceding the start of Ramadan, and during the holy month more than 1,300 civilians were killed—including 400 civilians slaughtered in one night in villages near Relizane. In September, meanwhile, the AIS leader, Madani Mezrag, called for all militants under his command to observe a unilateral cease-fire effective from 1 October. Although details of the agreement struck between the military high command and the AIS that led to the cease-fire were not revealed, there was speculation that it included the incorporation of some AIS fighters into regular units of the armed forces. Always much weaker militarily than its rival the GIA, the AIS considered a cease-fire preferable to defeat or surrender. In spite of official claims that the conflict was nearly over and that GIA groups had incurred significant losses as a result of operations by the security forces, massacres, ambushes and bomb attacks continued during late 1998 and into 1999.

In April 1998 more than 100 people, including police officers, leaders of self-defence groups and local government officials, were arrested for alleged involvement in the massacres of civilians. Those arrested were alleged to have been involved not only in eliminating suspected Islamists but also in killings linked to criminal activities and tribal rivalries. In early 2003 it emerged that one of the accused, Muhammad Fergane, the mayor of Relizane at the time, although expelled from the RND, had never been brought to justice. While officials admitted that some abuses were committed by the security forces and their allies, they insisted that such incidents were rare. The horrific massacres of civilians in 1997 had led to appeals from several European states for international intervention to resolve the conflict. Two European Union (EU) delegations visited Algiers in early 1998, but Algerian officials continued to reject all offers of foreign mediation or assistance for the victims of violence and opposed any form of independent inquiry into the massacres. A senior-level UN 'fact-finding' mission, led by former Portuguese President Mário Soares, visited Algiers in July and, in addition to consultations with government officials and representatives of political parties and civil society, it was allowed access to sites of recent massacres. The mission's report was strongly criticized by Amnesty International for failing to address the human rights crisis.

ZÉROUAL RESIGNS: THE PRESIDENTIAL ELECTION OF APRIL 1999

In a dramatic television address in September 1998, President Zéroual announced that he would stand down after a presidential election to be held in February 1999, almost two years before the end of his five-year term of office. The date of the election was subsequently postponed until April, officially to give political parties time to participate fully in the electoral process. Although Zéroual was suffering from poor health, it was widely acknowledged that he was being forced out as a result of renewed infighting in the army high command. His announcement followed a series of vitriolic articles in sections of the press against Gen. Muhammad Betchine, Zéroual's presidential adviser and closest political ally, which were clearly aimed at the President himself. Betchine resigned in October 1998, as did the Minister of Justice, Muhammad Adami, another of Zéroual's allies. Both strongly denied press allegations of corruption. The episode was regarded as a victory for the 'clan' led by Lt-Gen. Muhammad Lamari and the powerful head of military security, Gen. Muhammad Medienne. In December Prime Minister Ouyahia resigned and was replaced by Smaïl Hamdani. A new, largely unaltered Council of Ministers was appointed.

Of 47 potential candidates for the presidential election, only seven reached the final list: Abdelaziz Bouteflika; Ahmed Taleb Ibrahimi, a leading member of the establishment's Arab/Islamic wing; Sheikh Abdallah Djaballah, who had formed the Mouvement de la Réforme Nationale (MRN—National Reform Movement) after being ousted as leader of Al-Nahda by members who supported Bouteflika's candidacy; Hocine Aït Ahmed; Mouloud Hamrouche, the leader of the FLN's liberal reformist wing; former premier Mokdad Sifi; and Youcef Khateb, a hero of the war of independence reported to have close links with some of the 'patriotic' militias. This time the senior generals did not present one of their own number for the post, as they had Zéroual, deciding that the new President should be a civilian. During the electoral campaign Bouteflika swiftly emerged as the leading candidate and was widely seen as the '*candidat privilégié*'. On 13 April 1999, two days before the first round of the presidential election, a crisis developed when four of the candidates—Aït Ahmed, Hamrouche, Ibrahimi and Djaballah—issued a communiqué accusing the authorities of initiating a 'massive fraud' in favour of Bouteflika. They claimed that a large number of additional ballot papers with the name of Bouteflika selected had been deposited in the *wilayat*, and that the security forces had been instructed to prevent representatives of the other candidates from being present at polling stations on the day of the first round of voting. The next day they were joined in their allegations by Khateb and Sifi. The Minister of the Interior rejected the allegations of fraud, accusing the candidates of seeking to discredit the administration and mislead the public. The protesting candidates responded by withdrawing from the election. Bouteflika decided to continue as the sole candidate, but on the day of the election he announced that he would not assume the presidency unless he received substantial support from the electorate.

According to official results, Bouteflika won 73.8% of the votes cast at the presidential election of 15 April 1999, followed by Ibrahimi (12.5%), Djaballah (4.0%), Aït Ahmed (3.2%), Hamrouche (3.1%), Sifi (2.2%) and Khateb (1.2%). Although Bouteflika's opponents had withdrawn, they did not formally call for a boycott and ballot papers including all seven contestants were provided at the polling stations. According to official figures, the rate of participation was recorded at 60.9% of the electorate, but there were sharp regional disparities. On 16 April Bouteflika accepted the presidency; he took office on 27 April. The opposition, which had already refused to accept the legitimacy of the results, immediately challenged the official rate of participation, with the FFS claiming that a mere 23.3% of the electorate had voted. The French daily *Le Monde*, quoting a military source, estimated turn-out at 23%, with Bouteflika obtaining only 28% of the votes cast (little more than 1m.), Ibrahimi 20%, Aït Ahmed 13.3%, Djaballah 12.8% and Hamrouche 12.2%. The opposition called for a peaceful protest march in Algiers against military dictatorship, but the rally was banned by the authorities. Clashes took place between demonstrators and security forces in central Algiers and several arrests were made.

BOUTEFLIKA'S PRESIDENCY

Bouteflika's first priority on assuming the presidency was the restoration of peace in the country. He established contacts with senior members of the outlawed FIS, and in June 1999 the movement's military wing, the AIS, agreed to make its ceasefire (in place since October 1997) permanent. Furthermore, it offered to co-operate with the security forces against other armed Islamist groups notably its rival, the GIA, which had refused to join the truce. Abbassi Madani, the FIS leader, who remained under house arrest, and the FIS Constitutional Council endorsed the agreement, but some FIS supporters complained that it did not provide a political solution to the conflict. Others demanded that *jihad* should continue until an Islamic state was finally achieved. On 5 July (Independence Day) the President pardoned 5,000 imprisoned Islamist sympathizers and drew up a Law on Civil Concord, which was unanimously adopted by the National People's Assembly on 13 July. The new legislation offered an amnesty for Islamist militants not implicated in mass killings, rapes or bomb attacks on public places, and reduced the sentences of those who had taken part in such crimes provided they surrendered to the authorities within a period of six months (i.e. by 13 January 2000). At a referendum held on 16 September, official figures indicated that 98.6% of those who voted endorsed the President's peace initiative. Turn-out was reported at 85% of registered voters, although the opposition FFS insisted that it had been only 45%. Families of victims of Islamist attacks denounced the new Law on Civil Concord, which was condemned by the French-language press as 'a shameful capitulation to Islamist violence'. An editorial in the independent daily *Le Matin* accused Bouteflika of handing the 'terrorists' a political victory 'on a silver platter' just when they had been defeated militarily. Given the controversial circumstances of his election, some politicians accused Bouteflika of using the referendum to bolster his own legitimacy.

In early January 2000, following urgent high-level negotiations between the Government and the AIS leadership, which had reportedly threatened to withdraw from the President's peace initiative, a new agreement was reached providing for a full amnesty for the group's estimated 3,000 fighters, financial compensation for their families, housing for those whose homes had been destroyed by the security forces, and assistance in securing employment. On 19 January the Minister of the Interior announced that 80% of the members of armed groups had surrendered to the authorities. At the same time a pro-Government newspaper, *El Khabar*, reported that in addition to the AIS fighters, some 4,200 militants may have given themselves up. Other sources put the total figure at 6,000.

Meanwhile, in November 1999 Abdelkader Hachani, the third most senior figure in the FIS hierarchy and the most senior member of the leadership still at liberty and politically active, was assassinated in Algiers by a lone gunman. Hachani had favoured dialogue with all political movements and was rumoured to have been involved in secret political contacts between the Government and the FIS. In the following month Fouad Boulemia, a member of the main GIA faction headed by Antar Zouabri, was reported to have confessed to the murder, after having been found in possession of the alleged murder weapon and identity documents belonging to Hachani.

In the months following his inauguration Bouteflika gave numerous speeches across the country and participated in several radio and television interviews in which he pronounced on a wide range of issues, some of them highly controversial, and made promises, some of which appeared contradictory. The new President denounced weaknesses in the country's educational system, spoke out on the sensitive language issue, promised to reform the justice system, urged that national reconciliation should include Algeria's Jewish community, the 'pieds-noirs' (the pre-independence population of French origin) and the 'harkis' (those Algerians who had served in the French army prior to independence), and in particular condemned corruption, which he stated paralysed the administration and undermined the economy. In August 1999 Bouteflika dismissed 22 of the country's 48 *walis* (prefects or provincial governors) on the grounds of alleged corruption or other abuses of power. Although Bouteflika gave his first speech to the nation in May 1999 in classical Arabic, he later gave many of his speeches—both within Algeria and abroad—in French, angering those seeking to promote 'Arabization'.

While frequently praising the army for its loyalty and for preserving 'territorial integrity', Bouteflika repeatedly emphasized that he did not intend to be manipulated by the generals, and that he was determined to exercise power as Head of State following the model of his mentor, the late President Boumedienne. However, six months after he assumed office there were few signs that Bouteflika exercised real power. In December 1999 he finally announced the formation of a new Government headed by Ahmed Benbitour, a former Minister of Finance. Although the President succeeded in placing members of his own entourage in a number of key positions, most of the ministers were drawn from the political parties and were considered to be 'clients' of the various army factions.

In February 2000 President Bouteflika announced the most wide-ranging changes to the military high command since 1988. These included the replacement of the commanders of four of the country's six military regions. However, the most senior positions remained unchanged. Lt-Gen. Muhammad Lamari (who remained Chief of Staff), Maj.-Gen. Muhammad Medienne (head of military intelligence and security) and Maj.-Gen. Smaïn Lamari (head of counter-espionage and internal security) were regarded as the principal architects of the repressive policies against the Islamist movement after 1992. In August 2000 Benbitour resigned the premiership amid rumours that he considered himself to have been excluded by Bouteflika from the decision-making process. There had been fundamental differences between the two men on economic policy, and the President had publicly criticized the Government's '*immobilisme*'. Bouteflika appointed one of his closest associates, Ali Benflis, as Prime Minister. The composition of the new Government was little changed and most senior ministers retained their posts.

In December 2000 a new wave of massacres, attributed to the GIA, provoked the strongest public criticism of President Bouteflika since he took office, articulated not only in the private press but also by several political parties, including two members of the governing coalition, the RCD and the ANR. Sections of the press declared that the massacres demonstrated that the President's peace initiative had failed, and some claimed that the amnesty had actually encouraged terrorism. At the same time some analysts attributed the resurgence in violence to the latest power struggle between Bouteflika and the senior generals. The country's military *décideurs*, it was claimed, had lost confidence in Bouteflika, accusing him of seeking to make peace with the Islamists at the military's expense. Rumours circulated that the senior generals were planning to replace Bouteflika, naming former premier Ghozali as his most likely successor. It was suggested that matters had reached a climax when in November a delegation from Amnesty International, which had been granted permission by Bouteflika to visit Algiers, requested to hear from Gens Muhammad Lamari, Muhammad Medienne and Smaïn Lamari about human rights abuses in Algeria and the question of the 'disappeared'—a request reported to have caused indignation and panic among senior military figures. The generals, it was claimed, considered that Bouteflika was using Amnesty International against them and had decided that he had to be replaced. In September Bouteflika had decided to publish the full version of a confidential memorandum by Amnesty International, which referred openly to abuses of power, disappearances and unlawful killings. There were also reports of tensions over the President's determination to reform state institutions and establish control over the economy, moves which challenged the vested interests carefully built up by the military over many years.

Bouteflika appeared to be more isolated than ever at the beginning of 2001, and was subject to continued criticism of his autocratic style both in the press and from within the coalition Government. There were also reports of growing frustration and disillusionment with Bouteflika among ordinary Algerians as a result of the continuing violence and his failure to implement effective economic and social reforms. As relations between the President and the Government became increasingly strained, Bouteflika accused several ministers of being more interested in their portfolios and privileges than in the welfare of the country, while the coalition parties, for their part, criticized the President for excluding them from the decision-making process and marginalizing the National People's Assembly. Amendments to the penal code in May introduced harsh penalties for articles or caricatures judged to be defamatory, with prison sentences and heavy fines for offending the Head of State. There were protests in Algiers and other cities against the new amendments.

VIOLENCE ERUPTS IN KABYLIA

In April 2001 violent clashes broke out between young protesters and security forces in several villages in Kabylia following the killing of a secondary school student while in police custody at Beni Douala near the regional capital, Tizi Ouzou. The local head of the gendarmerie referred to a 'regrettable shooting incident', claiming that the victim had been among a group of youths apprehended for committing an assault during a robbery. This version of events angered both local inhabitants and the family of the victim, and thousands of people signed a petition demanding a full inquiry into the incident. Three days after the student was killed the situation was further inflamed when three other young Kabyles were brutally assaulted by gendarmes near Béjaïa. These incidents coincided with demonstrations traditionally held to mark the anniversary of the 'Berber spring' protests in 1980. Appeals by the two main political parties in the region, the FFS and the RCD, failed to calm an increasingly tense situation, and the violence quickly escalated. By the end of April 2001 over 60 people were reported to have been killed, and more than 600 wounded, in rioting, which spread from the Béjaïa area to the *wilayat* of Bouira, Tizi Ouzou, Borj Bou Arreridj and parts of Sétif. Tensions also increased in the capital—especially on university campuses, where meetings were organized to condemn the killings in Kabylia, and the extreme brutality employed, particularly by the gendarmerie, to restore order was widely denounced. In the past resentment in Kabylia had focused on the Government's refusal to recognize the Berber Tamazight as a national language, but some observers argued that despair born out of lack of economic opportunities and mounting hostility to the central Government were the underlying causes of the rioting. For many Kabyles the gendarmerie in particular was seen as the representative of the central Government and an occupying force which regularly committed abuses against the local population.

On 30 April 2001 President Bouteflika made an address to the nation on the crisis in Kabylia and announced the establishment of a national commission of inquiry, which would include representatives of civil society, to investigate recent events. He indicated that the question of the Tamazight language would be considered as part of his future plans to revise the Constitution, and that he intended to adopt a proposal making instruction in the Berber language compulsory in Berber-speaking areas. Bouteflika subsequently appointed Mohand Issad, a lawyer originally from Kabylia, to head the commission of inquiry. However, the President's address was strongly criticized by the main political groupings in the region and in early May the leader of the RCD, Saïd Saâdi, announced his party's withdrawal from the coalition Government.

In early May 2001 the FFS organized a demonstration in Algiers, which was attended by some 10,000–30,000 people, to condemn the authorities and denounce the repression in Kabylia. Later in the month rioting in Kabylia again intensified and spread. The protests appeared to have been organized by local committees without links to the traditional political parties represented in the region. In the face of a mounting cycle of rioting and repression the authorities remained silent until late May, when President Bouteflika made a second speech in which he called for vigorous sanctions against those who had instigated the tragic events and against all those responsible for excesses, irrespective of their origins.

Furthermore, Bouteflika emphasized that Islam united all Algerians and referred to a 'plot hatched from inside and outside the country to destabilize the entire nation'. However, the speech did little to reduce tensions in Kabylia and sections of the press strongly criticized the authorities for their handling of the situation. Earlier the heads of the gendarmerie and civil police, as well as the Ministry of the Interior and Local Authorities, had admitted the existence of abuse in Kabylia but denied that it was systematic and widespread. At the end of May some 300,000 people (600,000 according to the organizers) took part in a 'march of democratic hope' in Algiers organized by the FFS. The scale of the demonstration surprised many commentators; over the last decade only the Islamists of the FIS had succeeded in mobilizing such large numbers.

In June 2001 the Coordination des Aârchs, Daïras et Communes (CADC) organized a large demonstration in Algiers to protest against repression and injustice. Village committees (*aarush*), which have traditionally played a key role in the social fabric of Kabylia, began to assume a political role in an effort to assert their authority over the currents of protest in the region. While the two main political parties active in Kabylia, the FFS and the RCD, appeared remote from the daily concerns of marginalized youths in the region, the CADC explicitly identified itself with their main demand, namely the withdrawal of all gendarmerie brigades from the region, and the demonstration—the largest since independence—attracted some 500,000 people. Although intended as a peaceful protest, the demonstration degenerated into violence after the route was blocked by the security forces, and rioting and looting of shops took place in the capital's main commercial street. Appeals for calm from the main political parties in the region and from local popular committees went unheeded. By the end of June the unrest had spread beyond Kabylia to the Berber-speaking Aurès region, as well as to Annaba and to Biskra (Beskra) in the south of the country. Reports suggested that at least 100 people had been killed, and several hundred more wounded, since the violence first erupted.

The provisional report of the Issad commission into the violence in Kabylia was made public in July 2001. It strongly criticized the gendarmerie for the violent methods used against unarmed civilians and stated that it had by its actions deliberately provoked and prolonged the violence. The report concluded that either the senior gendarmerie commanders in Kabylia had lost control of the situation, or they were being exploited by 'external forces'. As the commission dismissed any foreign involvement in the crisis, the reference to external forces appeared to point to one of the clans within the military hierarchy. The report was criticized by the FFS and local leaders, who insisted that the commission should have named those individuals responsible for the repression. Nevertheless, this was the first time that an official report had condemned part of the armed forces for excesses against the civilian population. The commission resumed its work in August, but, lacking the authority to insist that politicians and military officers give evidence before it, it was unable to make further progress, and in December it declared that its task was at an end.

After months of political paralysis, in October 2001 Bouteflika announced that Tamazight would be designated a national language alongside Arabic in a forthcoming constitutional amendment, and gave Prime Minister Benflis, a Berber from the Aurès region, responsibility for dealing with the crisis in Kabylia. Benflis sought dialogue with the CADC, but by this time the citizens' movement was deeply divided and it was sometimes unclear who was authorized to speak on behalf of the protesters. In December Benflis held talks with one of the movement's factions but the so-called 'radicals', who appeared to be in the majority, rejected all negotiations with the Government.

In January 2002 Benflis reported that a series of resolutions had been adopted during discussions with the *dialoguistes* of the CADC, including one for the establishment of a special ministerial council to implement the Kabyles' main demands as set out in their 15-point 'El-Kseur platform': notably the creation of decentralized government councils at *wilaya* level in Kabylia and the granting of 'martyr' status to victims of the crisis. However, no reference was made to the Kabyles' demand that the gendarmerie be withdrawn from the region. The radicals continued to insist that their demands were not negotiable, and maintained pressure on the authorities by means of strikes and demonstrations. They also threatened to boycott legislative elections scheduled for May. Meanwhile, Kabylia was slowly descending into anarchy as the authority of the central Government in the region weakened.

The final report of the Issad commission was leaked to the press in January 2002. It expressed deep pessimism regarding the immediate future of Kabylia and emphasized the difficulty of carrying out an in-depth study of recent events in the region because many witnesses were afraid to come forward. At a broader level the report highlighted the weakening of the powers of the civil authorities in Algeria in favour of the military since 1992, and claimed that during the last decade there had been a subtle slide from a state of emergency to a state of siege. On questions of public order the responsibilities of civil and military authorities had become blurred, and respect for the law had not yet become part of the culture of the country's officials. Finally, the report suggested that the spontaneous and rapid appearance of a citizens' movement in Kabylia emphasized the urgent need for Algerians to have real and effective political representation. In early February 2002 Benflis declared that the authorities had no intention of sending military units to restore order in Kabylia, and insisted that the Government was committed to resolving the crisis through dialogue. The Prime Minister held another meeting with the *dialoguistes* from the CADC, but this faction appeared to have little influence over actual events in the region. On 12 February the region was paralysed by a general strike called by the CADC in protest at the reappearance of units of the gendarmerie, which had begun to man road-blocks in some parts of the region.

In early March 2002 President Bouteflika announced the formal recognition of Tamazight as a national language without putting the issue to a referendum; local sources suggested that he feared that Algerians might not support the proposal. However, Bouteflika rejected demands for the withdrawal of the gendarmerie from Kabylia, although he indicated that he might consider re-examining the deployment of the force at some future date. Furthermore, he reported that 24 gendarmes, including five officers, had been jailed for murder and the misuse of firearms during the riots in the spring of 2001. Victims of the rioting would be compensated but they would not be granted the status of 'martyrs'. The radical faction of the CADC rejected the conciliatory gestures made by the President, and announced that they would prevent legislative elections being held in the region.

Tensions mounted after further clashes between young protesters and the gendarmerie in late March 2002, in which a number of youths were killed. At this time some 15 gendarmerie units were withdrawn from Kabylia and replaced by police. Official sources insisted that other units would be withdrawn and that this was part of a 'redeployment'. On 8 April the National People's Assembly voted almost unanimously in favour of amending the Constitution to grant Tamazight the status of a national language. In late April, on the anniversary of the 1980 'Berber spring', numerous demonstrations were held across Kabylia, the largest in Tizi Ouzou, which was attended by some 100,000 people.

However, unrest was not limited to Kabylia. The deepening socio-economic crisis led to rioting in several small towns in different parts of the country in late 2001 and early 2002, as youths took to the streets to protest about the lack of employment opportunities, housing shortages, inadequate infrastructure and corruption among local officials. Particularly disturbing for the authorities was the fact that the unrest had spread to the south of the country, which had previously been relatively peaceful.

THE LEGISLATIVE ELECTIONS OF MAY 2002

In February 2002 President Bouteflika announced that parliamentary elections would be held on 30 May, and expressed his determination to respect the results of the poll and to guarantee that voters had freedom of choice. In April he announced the establishment of a national commission to supervise the elections, whose members were drawn entirely from representatives of opposition parties and independent personalities.

Official campaigning for the legislative elections began on 9 May 2002, with 23 political parties taking part together with 129 independent lists. The number of seats in the National People's Assembly was increased from 380 to 389 to take account of population growth. Amid general indifference on the part of the majority of Algerians, the main issue debated in political circles was the scale of participation in the forthcoming poll. President Bouteflika embarked on a nation-wide campaign in an effort to counter appeals from the FFS, the RCD and the CADC for Algerians to boycott the elections. Campaigning was a lacklustre affair, with only the FLN and the MSP reported to have made any significant impact. The most notable feature of the election was the low rate of voter participation: only 46.2% of the 18m. eligible voters reportedly took part—compared with 65.5% in 1997 and 59% in 1991—the lowest rate since independence.

The lowest levels of voter participation were recorded in Kabylia, where the boycott organized by the CADC, the FFS and the RCD proved highly effective. The participation rates in Tizi Ouzou and Béjaïa were 1.8% and 2.6%, respectively. Most polling stations in Kabylia remained closed, and some came under attack by rioters who burnt ballot boxes. There were disturbances throughout the region as riot police clashed with demonstrators, reportedly resulting in the death of at least one person. According to the Ministry of the Interior and Local Authorities, 707 out of 880 polling stations in the Tizi Ouzou *wilaya* and 455 out of 488 in Béjaïa remained closed. Elsewhere, voting proceeded peacefully, with participation rates highest in the south and lowest in the major cities. In Algiers, where polling stations were heavily guarded because of fears of attacks by armed Islamist groups, turn-out was recorded at only 30%. Both the FFS and the RCD challenged the official figures on voter turn-out, claiming that it had reached no more than 15%–20%, and declaring that, for the first time since independence, a section of the Algerian people (those in Kabylia) would be excluded from parliamentary representation.

The election results proved surprising as the FLN secured 199 of a total of 389 seats, giving the former single party an absolute majority in the new National People's Assembly. The FLN had finished third in the 1997 elections, after the RND and the MSP, and held only 62 seats in the outgoing legislature. The RND was relegated to second place, retaining only 48 seats (compared with 155 in 1997). Of the two Islamist parties, the MSP (which had won 69 seats in 1997) secured only 38 seats, while Sheikh Abdallah Djaballah's MRN took 43 seats. (Djaballah's former party, Al-Nahda, had won 34 seats in 1997.) Independent candidates won 30 seats (compared with only 11 in 1997), while the PT increased its representation from four to 21. Political commentators attributed the FLN's success to the energetic leadership of Benflis and to the changes introduced since he became the party's Secretary-General in September 2001, notably his efforts to open the party to young people and women. They also believed that the record level of abstentions had worked in favour of the FLN, which also benefited from the collapse of the RND—seen as the voice of the military *décideurs* and held responsible for the bad management of the many municipalities it controlled. Leaders of opposition parties stated that voting had been sullied by fraud, and that the results had no significance because they would not help to resolve the political, economic and social difficulties confronting the country. The FFS, the RCD and the CADC called for the elections to be annulled.

In June 2002 Benflis formed a new coalition Government of 38 ministers, comprising mainly FLN deputies but with the RND and the MSP retaining some portfolios. However, the Prime Minister failed to persuade other political parties, notably the PT and the MRN, to join the new administration. The ministerial posts that remained unchanged included Noureddine Yazid Zerhouni, a close ally of Bouteflika, who retained the interior portfolio despite widespread criticism of his handling of the crisis in Kabylia, and Abdelaziz Belkhadem, a strong supporter of dialogue with the Islamists, as Minister of State for Foreign Affairs. There was general agreement that the new appointments (almost one-half of the Government) suggested that Benflis had been given somewhat greater room to manoeuvre in forming his new administration.

THE LOCAL ELECTIONS OF OCTOBER 2002

In August 2002 President Bouteflika announced a special amnesty for some 60 Kabyle demonstrators—including several members of the CADC leadership—detained during recent rioting. The release of the detainees had been one of the conditions outlined by the FFS for the party's participation in local elections, scheduled for 10 October. The FFS announced subsequently that it would take part in the elections, stating that a boycott would undermine the unity and stability of the country. However, the CADC called for a boycott of the poll and later declared their determination to prevent voting from taking place. Among the parties not taking part were the RCD, the ANR and the MDS, while the PT announced that it would only participate in elections for provincial councils. A national commission to supervise the municipal elections was established, comprising representatives from all participating parties. President Bouteflika declared that the establishment of the commission reflected the state's determination to ensure transparent and free elections. Campaigning began on 15 September and the Government announced that members of the army, police, gendarmerie and customs officers would no longer be required to vote at special polling stations at their place of work but at the main polling stations along with ordinary voters. This measure, commentators suggested, would allow almost 1m. people to vote without any kind of pressure.

When the preliminary results of the elections were announced on 11 October 2002 the FLN had repeated its success achieved in the parliamentary elections in May, winning control of 668 of the 1,541 municipal assemblies and of 43 of the 48 provincial assemblies. The party's success was again attributed to the energetic leadership of Ali Benflis. The RND, which had controlled one-half of the country's municipalities following the 1997 local elections, suffered another crushing defeat, gaining control of only 171 municipal councils and failing to secure control of any provincial councils. Independent lists won control of 77 municipal councils and the FFS secured power in 65 municipal councils, with a majority of seats on two provincial councils—Tizi Ouzou and Béjaïa. The main Islamist parties, including the MSP, together won control of 58 municipal councils. In terms of the number of votes cast, the MRN came third in municipal elections and second in provincial elections, while a relatively new party, the Algerian National Front (FNA), achieved control of 26 municipalities.

According to official figures, national turn-out at the elections was 50.1%, excluding the provinces of Tizi Ouzou and Béjaïa in Kabylia, where the rate was officially recorded at 7.6% and 15.6%, respectively. Bouteflika blamed 'irresponsible extremists' for obstructing voting and inciting riots in Kabylia. In the run-up to the elections there had been numerous clashes between protesters and the police and a number of FFS offices in the region were ransacked; threats were issued against the party's candidates and attempts made to disrupt party meetings. Although some 20,000 members of the security forces were deployed in the region to protect the ballot boxes, reporters claimed that they had only intervened to defend polling stations in and around the main towns and that elsewhere some polling stations without a police presence had fallen to the rioters; at least two had been burnt down. The CADC leadership announced that it did not recognize the results of the elections. Efforts by associates of Benflis to engage in a dialogue with the CADC met with no response.

In April 2003 Kabylia was paralysed by a general strike, and tens of thousands of people hostile to the central Government demonstrated in Tizi Ouzou on the 23rd anniversary of the 1980 'Berber spring' and the 'Black spring' of April 2001. Demonstrations across the region were organized by the CADC and clashes broke out between protesters and the security forces in Tizi Ouzou and Béjaïa.

BOUTEFLIKA DISMISSES BENFLIS AND APPOINTS OUYAHIA PREMIER

The FLN's eighth party congress, held in March 2003, revealed evidence of a serious rift between Benflis and President Bouteflika. Delegates elected a new Central Committee and Political Bureau and re-elected Benflis as the party's Secretary-General for another five years (with considerably increased powers). Observers noted that in his address to delegates Benflis made no reference to Bouteflika and that the President failed to send a message of goodwill to the congress. Benflis also spoke out against the unpopular privatization policy and the draft hydrocarbons law, publicly distancing himself from the Head of State and the Ministers of Energy and Mining and of Participation and Investment Promotion. Indeed, there were reports that before the congress Benflis had indicated that he wanted to dismiss the two ministers, known as the President's ministers, but that Bouteflika had refused and insisted that, if he did so, the entire Government would have to be relieved of its duties and a new administration formed. In response, Benflis had stated that as leader of the largest parliamentary party he had the right to remain as head of government. On 5 May 2003 Bouteflika dismissed Benflis and appointed as Prime Minister the leader of the RND, former premier Ahmed Ouyahia, one of the most unpopular politicians in Algeria. Ouyahia had close links to the military *décideurs* and it was suggested that his main task as Prime Minister would be to reassure the army chiefs and manage the country's affairs until the presidential election in April 2004. In June 2003 the FLN announced that Benflis would stand as a candidate in the forthcoming presidential election.

In late May 2003 Ouyahia, himself a Kabyle, called on local leaders in Kabylia to negotiate with the authorities to bring an end to the violence in the region. In early June those members of the CADC who had been imprisoned in October 2002 were released. These moves appeared to indicate that Bouteflika was keen to resolve the long-running crisis in Kabylia before the presidential election in 2004, and that the President had accepted the CADC as a key interlocutor. However, the CADC showed little enthusiasm for renewed negotiations with the Algerian Government, and many activists demanded that those responsible for the murder of civilians be brought to justice. Later in June 2003 Ouyahia repeated his offer of dialogue, although again no positive response was received.

The two leaders of the proscribed FIS, Abbassi Madani and Ali Belhadj, were released in early July 2003 after completing their 12-year sentences for aggression and conspiracy against the state. Madani had been under house arrest at Belcourt in Algiers and Belhadj had been held in a military prison in Blida. Both were issued with a court order banning them from engaging in any political activity, including contact with the media.

The Government announced at the end of July 2003 that it had agreed to reintroduce the use of the Berber language, Tamazight, into Algeria's educational system, thereby fulfilling one of the demands of the Berber minority who had staged a series of violent protests against the authorities in Kabylia during 2001.

SPLIT IN THE FLN

The FLN congress in March 2003 had brought about a serious rift in the party and the creation of a 'Corrective Movement', which challenged the legitimacy of the resolutions passed at the congress. A meeting held in Algiers in August by the Corrective Movement resulted in violent clashes as the pro-Benflis faction attempted to prevent the meeting from taking place and the security forces had to intervene to restore order. The Corrective Movement held a further meeting in September and appointed a provisional executive with Abdelaziz Belkhadem, the Minister of State for Foreign Affairs, as its Co-ordinator-General. Benflis described the dissidents as an 'artificial creation' destined to disappear and, without mentioning him by name, strongly criticized Bouteflika for his autocratic rule. He declared that under his leadership the FLN stood for democracy, liberty and progress. The so-called *bouteflikistes*, for their part, accused Benflis of being a puppet manipulated by the military hierarchy. Meanwhile, Bouteflika announced a reorganization of the Council of Ministers, in which he dismissed a number of ministers, several of whom were supporters of Benflis.

The day before the FLN's extraordinary congress in October 2003, Benflis withdrew the remaining FLN ministers loyal to him from the Council of Ministers. Bouteflika replaced the majority of them with members of the anti-Benflis group within the FLN. The congress was held despite a court ruling, made at the request of the Corrective Movement, which attempted to prevent the meeting from taking place. Reports indicated that the circumstances under which the court order had been obtained had been highly irregular. The congress voted overwhelmingly to support Benflis as the party's candidate in the 2004 presidential election. Benflis stated that the party must close ranks and remain an 'autonomous party serving democracy and pluralism', while a party spokesman announced that the anti-Benflis group were no longer members of the organization. In November Belkhadem claimed that 75 of the FLN's 203 deputies had joined the Corrective Movement, together with 3,000 members of local assemblies.

In December 2003 a court froze the activities and funds of the FLN and ruled the results of the eighth party congress in March null and void. The ruling, later upheld by the State Council, was condemned by politicians from across the political spectrum, who accused the Government of using the judiciary for political purposes. Benflis publicly accused Bouteflika of being behind the decision and insisted that he would continue with his electoral campaign. Belkhadem repeated his call for a new FLN congress to unify the party, but this was rejected by Benflis, who stated that Belkhadem did not have the authority to speak for the FLN and accused him of seeking to take over the post of Secretary-General. A number of pro-Benflis FLN deputies subsequently demanded the President's resignation, declaring that he represented a threat to the country's stability, a danger to public order and an insult to the dignity of the Algerian people.

In January 2004 the Corrective Movement held a congress in Algiers, which was attended by some 2,000 delegates. Belkhadem insisted that the principal aim of the congress was to return the party to its correct path, and the reunification of the FLN, but the meeting ended with a declaration of support for Bouteflika even though he had still not officially announced that he would seek a second mandate. Supporters of Benflis, who had attempted to disrupt the meeting, were forcibly expelled.

Meanwhile, in October 2003 Bouteflika had announced the establishment of a 35-member commission under the chairmanship of Muhammad Zaghloul Bouterene, the President of the Supreme Court, to formulate amendments to the controversial family code of 1984. Several observers argued that the establishment of the new commission was a cynical move by Bouteflika to gain support in the run-up to the presidential election and questioned whether proper and effective revisions to the code could be made in such a short period of time. At the same time Bouteflika replaced some 21 judges and announced that the Minister of Justice and Attorney-General, Tayeb Belaïz, had established a working group on prison reform. A commission under Mohand Issad had been established in 1999 to advise on reform of the justice system but no action had been taken following the completion of its report. Bouteflika's critics stated that the appointment of new judges was a political act and accused him of removing those judges favourable to Benflis and replacing them with his own supporters. Elections to the Council of the Nation in December 2003, incomplete largely because of the unrest in Kabylia, confirmed the dominant position of the RND in the upper house, where it had a total of 52 senators.

THE PRESIDENTIAL ELECTION OF APRIL 2004

Bouteflika won a landslide victory in the presidential election held in April 2004, securing 85.0% of the votes cast, according to official results. His re-election bid had been supported by the Corrective Movement of the FLN, the RND and the MSP, together with the powerful UGTA and the National Mujahidin Organization (former fighters in Algeria's war of independence). Benflis, meanwhile, won only 6.4% of the vote; and Sheikh Abdallah Djaballah, Secretary-General of the Islamist MRN, came third, with 5.0%. Saïd Saâdi, leader of the RCD, received 1.9% of the vote, Louisa Hanoune, leader of the small PT and the first woman to contest a presidential election in Algeria (or indeed elsewhere in the Arab world) 1.0%, and Ali Fawzi Rebaïne, the President of Ahd 54, 0.6%. In March the Constitutional Court had disqualified on a technicality three candidates: Ahmed Taleb Ibrahimi of Wafa; Sid-Ahmed Ghozali, a former Prime Minister and leader of the Front démocratique; and Moussa Touati of the FNA.

Voter participation was officially recorded at 58.1%, with the lowest participation rate in Kabylia where only 17.8% voted, according to official figures. Although talks between the faction of the CADC in favour of dialogue with the Government and Prime Minister Ouyahia had taken place in early January 2004 and progress had been made concerning some of the demands set out in the El-Kseur platform, negotiations had quickly broken down when Ouyahia insisted that the issue of making Tamazight an official language had to be put to a referendum. The *dialoguistes* within the CADC called for a boycott of the presidential election. Earlier, the FFS had stated that it would not take part in the election.

Despite suspicions regarding Bouteflika's large majority, most international observers stated that there had been no obvious vote-rigging and that the election result represented the clear will of the majority. French President Jacques Chirac was one of the first foreign leaders to congratulate Bouteflika on his re-election, complimenting Algeria for holding free and fair elections. Chirac declared in an interview with *Le Monde* that he could not see how 'in all good faith' he could fault the electoral process. In January 2004 the National People's Assembly had adopted a number of amendments to the electoral law, the most significant being a ban on the use of special polling stations for the military, gendarmerie and police. Opposition groups had claimed that the special polling stations in military barracks were impossible to monitor and made it easier for the Government to perpetrate electoral fraud. Benflis, Djaballah and Saâdi immediately challenged the election result and claimed widespread fraud. These accusations, which were echoed by the anti-Bouteflika private press, were dismissed by the President's representatives, who accused his rivals of seeking to 'disobey the popular will'. Some independent Algerian observers insisted that the result was suspect but that this would be difficult to prove. Ali Yahia Abdennour, President of the ALDHR, later stated that the key to the electoral fraud was the fact that the administration had controlled the election 'from top to bottom' under the benevolent eye of military security. Candidates opposed to Bouteflika had welcomed a statement in January by the Chief of Staff, Lt-Gen. Muhammad Lamari, that the army was not involved in the election, had no candidate of its own and did not oppose any candidate. However, opposition candidates accused Bouteflika and his clan of using public funds to support his re-election campaign, of suppressing the press, and monopolizing state television and employing it as an instrument of propaganda.

BOUTEFLIKA'S SECOND TERM

On 19 April 2004 Bouteflika was sworn in for his second five-year term of office at the Palais des Nations. In his address he pledged to continue to promote 'true national reconciliation', modernization and sustained economic development. He extolled the Civil Concord but stressed that terrorism had become international and that the struggle against it must go on undiminished. On the crisis in Kabylia, Bouteflika called for dialogue and urged the CADC to return to the negotiating table. He urged Kabyles not to listen to extremists who advocated violence and destruction, insisting that an acceptable solution would be found. He also promised emancipation to women subjected to a repressive Islamic family code. To mark his inauguration, Bouteflika pardoned some 5,670 prisoners, although those released did not include detainees convicted of terrorism, violent crimes, fraud or drugs-trafficking.

Following Bouteflika's inauguration, as required under the Constitution, Ouyahia and his Council of Ministers resigned. Bouteflika immediately reappointed Ouyahia to the premiership and the new Government, announced in late April 2004, contained few changes. The unpopular and much criticized Noureddine Yazid Zerhouni remained Minister of State for the Interior and Local Authorities, while Abdelaziz Belkhadem was reappointed Minister of State for Foreign Affairs. The Ministry of Communications and Culture was divided into two separate ministries, with Khalida Toumi-Messaoudi retaining the culture portfolio. Of the 39 ministerial posts, 15 were taken by Bouteflika loyalists within the FLN, six by members of the RND and four by members of the MSP; the remaining 14 had no party affiliation.

The opposition dubbed it an administration of the status quo, whose role was to maintain the balance between the clients of the regime. At its first meeting Bouteflika told the Council of Ministers that achieving national reconciliation was an absolute priority for the country's stability. Presenting the new Government's programme to the National People's Assembly, Ouyahia devoted most of his address to the theme of reconciliation, emphasizing that this required continued efforts in the war against terrorism. The actual programme differed little from that of his previous administration and he declared that 85% of Algerians had voted for continuity on 8 April 2004. There were pledges to continue the reform programme, notably of the justice and educational systems, to create 2m. new jobs and to build 1m. new homes. Ouyahia also stated that his Government was determined to resolve the long-running crisis in Kabylia and called on the CADC to resume dialogue. In May the RND, the MSP and the Corrective Movement of the FLN agreed to establish structures to facilitate and co-ordinate co-operation between the three parties within both legislative chambers.

Bouteflika moved to consolidate his position in mid-2004 by making a number of changes among senior ranks of the armed forces, promoting a number of his own protégés to key posts. Also in August Gen. Larbi Belkeir, Director of the President's Office since 2000, was named as the new ambassador to Morocco. This was seen as an 'honourable exit' for a man regarded as the key interlocutor between the President and the military *décideurs*. By this time only three of the senior military officers who had taken power in January 1992 remained in post: Abdelmalek Guenaïzia, appointed to the new post of Minister-delegate to the Minister of National Defence in May 2004, and most notably Muhammad Medienne and Smaïn Lamari, in charge of the Département de Renseignement et de Securité (DRS), the powerful structure controlling Algerian society.

In mid-August 2004 the Council of Ministers approved amendments to the family code of 1984, as proposed in the final report of the commission established by the President in October 2003. It recommended that the legal age of marriage for both men and women should be 19 years; a woman should no longer require the permission of a male guardian in order to marry; polygamous marriages must be authorized by a judge; a woman should be able to initiate divorce proceedings; and following a divorce the husband should be obliged to ensure that his wife and children were supported financially. The PT, the RCD and feminist associations argued that the proposed amendments did not go far enough and that the 'infamous' family code should be abolished. On the other hand, the main Islamist parties—the MSP and the MRN—denounced the proposals as a violation of the precepts of Islam, and threatened to vote against them in the National People's Assembly. In October 2004 Bouteflika expressed his determination to pursue the ratification of the amendments; however, at a cabinet meeting in February 2005, which he chaired, the proposed amendments were reviewed and in the final text submitted to the Assembly the requirement for a woman to marry in the presence of a male guardian was reinserted. Women's associations condemned the change and stated that it was a concession to the Islamists. The amendments, in the form of a presidential decree, were approved, without debate, by the Assembly in March.

The resignation of Ali Benflis as Secretary-General of the FLN in April 2004, followed by that of Karim Younès as President of the National People's Assembly in June and of Abbas Mekhalif as leader of the party's parliamentary group (both of whom were Benflis supporters), was seen as an important victory for the party's Corrective Movement, and defections from the pro-Benflis camp increased after Bouteflika's victory. The leaders of the Corrective Movement assumed control over the preparations for a new, 'reunifying' eighth congress, but the party remained deeply divided. Opening the congress, Abdelaziz Belkhadem, who had been elected as the new Secretary-General of the FLN, called for unity and insisted that the party's priority was to support President Bouteflika's programme of national reconciliation and the general amnesty.

After proposing no new initiatives for almost a year to resolve the crisis in Kabylia, in January 2005 Prime Minister Ouyahia made a new and successful appeal to the CADC to resume dialogue with the Government on the basis of the agreement reached in January 2004. After two days of negotiations it was announced that agreement had been reached to establish joint working groups to implement the El-Kseur platform 'within the framework of the Constitution and the laws of the country'. In April 2005 Ouyahia visited Kabylia on the fourth anniversary of the 'Black spring'. In July local and regional assemblies in Kabylia were dissolved by presidential decree and new local elections were scheduled for November. This had been one of the principal demands of the CADC because of the very low turn-out in the 2002 local elections. Both the RCD and the FFS denounced the decision as arbitrary and illegal but later announced that they would take part in new elections.

ARMED ISLAMIST GROUPS WEAKENED BUT STILL ACTIVE

Despite President Bouteflika's peace initiative, launched in July 1999, the killing of civilians, soldiers and policemen by the GIA and its splinter groups continued during the second half of 1999, albeit at a much lower level than in previous years. An estimated 150 people were reported to have been killed during the month of Ramadan—only a fraction of the killings recorded during the same period in the years since the conflict began. The security forces continued to mount increasingly successful offensives against GIA strongholds, and greatly reduced the threat posed by radical Islamist forces. However, the GIA itself, while apparently weakened and more divided than ever, remained extremely dangerous. In response to the AIS announcement in June that it was to make its cease-fire (in place since October 1997) permanent, the main GIA faction, headed by Antar Zouabri, threatened to intensify its campaign of violence inside Algeria and abroad. Nevertheless, official sources claimed that by the mid-January 2000 deadline large numbers of GIA militants had surrendered to the authorities under the President's amnesty programme. Despite numerous security force offensives against rebel Islamist groups' strongholds throughout 2000, in July of that year, 12 months after the launch of Bouteflika's initiative for national reconciliation, thousands of Islamist guerrillas remained at large. Bouteflika had acknowledged in August 1999 that at least 100,000 people had died in the previous seven years as a result of the civil conflict (rather than the 30,000 previously claimed by the Government), and the number of victims continued to rise during 2000.

Although relative calm prevailed in the capital and in most major cities, large areas of the countryside remained insecure, with around 200 civilians killed every month. However, at the end of 2000 there was a marked upsurge in the level of violence, with some 300 civilians killed during the first two weeks of December; the renewed violence was attributed to the GIA, especially to the faction led by Zouabri. The authorities released no information about the latest atrocities, but they were widely reported in the independent press—which voiced strong criticisms of the President and claimed that certain Islamist militants had taken advantage of the amnesty to re-establish their networks. Questions were raised about the high degree of mobility of the armed groups and their apparent access to sophisticated weapons. Some analysts argued that the resurgence of violence reflected the latest power struggle between Bouteflika and the high-ranking military *éradicateurs*, suggesting that the GIA was the creation of military security and was acting on orders to discredit Bouteflika's policy of reconciliation.

In his book published in November 2000, Nesroulah Yous, a survivor of the massacre of almost 400 people in a suburb of Algiers in 1997 (which had been attributed to the GIA), implied that a special death squad attached to the security forces was in fact behind the killings. In early 2001 a former officer in the Algerian army published a book in which he presented first-hand accounts of alleged massacres of civilians by soldiers disguised as 'terrorists', summary executions and the burning of bodies, and the routine torture of suspected Islamists at one of the army's interrogation centres, although, in an interview with the French daily *Le Figaro* in April, former Minister of Defence Maj.-Gen. Khaled Nezzar categorically rejected the allegations. Meanwhile, in January 2001 the authorities discovered the bodies of four Russian engineers employed by a state company near the eastern city of Annaba. The murders—the first killings of foreign nationals since 1996—were attributed to Islamist rebels. There was a renewed resurgence of violence in late August and September 2001, when some 80 people were killed during a two-week period. Massacres again took place in areas that were understood to have been 'pacified' and new bomb attacks were carried out in Algiers, following a two-year period of relative calm in the capital.

Ongoing criticism in the francophone press of the President's Civil Concord intensified after the terrorist attacks on New York and Washington, DC, USA, on 11 September 2001, as the *éradicateurs* condemned Bouteflika for maintaining a dialogue with the country's radical Islamists. In the aftermath of the attacks against the USA, both the GIA and the Groupe Salafiste pour la Prédication et le Combat (GSPC—Salafist Group for Preaching and Combat)—which had broken away from the GIA in October 1998—appeared on the USA's list of alleged international terrorist organizations whose assets were to be frozen. The GSPC leader, Hassan Hattab, warned shortly after the attacks that if the Americans attacked Muslims they could expect reprisals that would be much worse than those inflicted on New York and Washington. Meanwhile, security forces in a number of European countries—notably Spain, France and Italy—made a number of arrests of suspected members of GSPC cells. Investigators alleged that the GSPC network in Europe, which included not only Algerians but also Tunisians and Moroccans, was providing logistical support for the militant Islamist al-Qa'ida network—believed by the USA to be principally responsible for the September 2001 attacks—and for the Algerian *maquis* (guerillas), and was plotting terrorist attacks in Europe under directions from the al-Qa'ida leadership. After the events of 11 September a number of Algerian sources suggested that close links had existed between the al-Qa'ida leader, Osama bin Laden, and the Algerian Islamist movement from the early 1990s, and that several Algerians working directly for al-Qa'ida ran a series of 'charitable' organizations and Islamic centres in Europe which acted as fronts for the organization's activities. A number of sources, including *El Khabar*, claimed that bin Laden had engineered the schism in the GIA in 1998 that had led to the creation of the GSPC.

After a period of relative calm during Ramadan in late 2001, violence erupted again in early 2002. Unofficial reports indicated that some 150 people were killed by armed Islamist groups during January alone, predominantly in the so-called 'triangle of death' between Blida, Aïn Delfa and Médéa. There were reports that some *repentis* (members of armed Islamist groups who had surrendered to the authorities under the Civil Concord) had taken up arms again and returned to the *maquis*. In February security forces killed Antar Zouabri, the GIA's 'national emir' since 1996, along with two other senior members of the organization. Rachid Abou Tourab, named as the new national emir in March 2002, vowed to continue the violent methods of his predecessor until an Islamic state had been established in Algeria, later reiterating that there would be no respite in the killings and massacres. In April 21 soldiers engaged in a military operation against the GIA were killed in an ambush near Saïda. On 5 July, the 40th anniversary of Algerian independence, armed Islamist groups carried out a series of bomb attacks across the country. The most serious was at Larba, south-east of Algiers, where a bomb exploded in a busy market, killing up to 50 people.

In October 2002 the Minister of State for the Interior and Local Authorities, Noureddine Yazid Zerhouni, declared that the armed Islamist groups were 'melting away' and that the number of terrorist attacks had declined dramatically. He estimated that in total the armed groups numbered 400–500 fighters, compared with 25,000 in the mid-1990s, and that they no longer attracted new recruits. However, he acknowledged that, although the groups were smaller and much weaker, their attacks, especially those against civilians, had become more violent to ensure maximum coverage in the media.

In January 2003 more than 40 soldiers were killed when their convoy was attacked in the Aurès Mountains. It was the most devastating attack inflicted on the security forces since the civil war began. The Algerian press accused al-Qa'ida of involvement in the planning of the assault. Algerian officials had claimed that a number of senior members of al-Qa'ida were present in the country to make contact with armed Islamist groups and that one of them, a Yemeni citizen named Emad Abdelwahid Ahmed Alwan, had been killed in the Batna region in September 2002. In response to the ambush of the military convoy in the Aurès, the security forces carried out a major operation in the area and announced that they had killed 40 Islamist militants and captured several others, including a number of foreign nationals from Pakistan, Afghanistan and Yemen. It was reported that the militants had succeeded in smuggling weapons into the country through neighbouring Mali.

A high-level Algerian army source admitted in April 2003 that 32 European tourists, who had disappeared in the Algerian Sahara between February and March, had been kidnapped by a faction of the GSPC, although the Algerian authorities refused to confirm this. Some reports suggested that the tourists had been taken as hostages to be exchanged for Islamist militants imprisoned in Europe. In May the Algerian army rescued 17 of the hostages, and the remainder (with the exception of one tourist, who had died while being held hostage) were released from captivity in August amid rumours that a large ransom had been paid to secure their release. The leader of the GSPC faction responsible for the kidnappings, Amari Saifi (also known as Abderrezak le Para), was handed over to the Algerian authorities by Libya in October 2004 and sentenced to life imprisonment in June 2005.

In October 2003 the press reported that Hassan Hattab had been deposed as the GSPC's 'national emir' and replaced by Nabil Sahraoui (also known as Abu Ibrahim Mustafa). A communiqué signed by the new emir pledged allegiance to all Muslim combatants in the Palestinian territories and Afghanistan and to al-Qa'ida. Sahraoui was killed in June 2004, along with at least three of his senior aides, in a large-scale operation by the security forces in the Béjaïa region after an ambush during which 12 soldiers were killed. Shortly before the GSPC had issued a communiqué in which it declared war on 'everything that is foreign and atheistic within Algeria's borders, whether against individuals, interests or installations'. The day after Sahraoui's death was announced, a large explosion occurred at the Hamma power station near Algiers. The Government insisted that it was a 'technical incident', but the GSPC later claimed to have carried out a bomb attack against the plant and promised that other actions would follow. Abdelmalek Droukdal (also known as Abu Musab Abd al-Wadud) was named as the group's new leader in September.

GIA NEUTRALIZED

In January 2005 the Ministry of the Interior and Local Authorities announced that during an operation beginning in November 2004 the security services had arrested the national leadership of the GIA, including the current 'national emir', and had recovered an important cache of arms and money. On the basis of information obtained from those arrested, the security forces had succeeded in almost totally neutralizing the terrorist group: only 30 militants remained in two strongholds. Nevertheless, in April 2005 two members of the GIA were apprehended after killing 14 civilians in the Blida region.

Immediately prior to the summit meeting of the League of Arab States (Arab League) held in Algiers in March 2005, a statement signed by GSPC leader Droukdal warned Arab leaders that their policies clearly indicated that they were standing with the USA against the interests of their own peoples and nations. It urged Arab peoples to disavow these 'apostate regimes' and take up *jihad*, while reiterating the group's loyalty to bin Laden. The GSPC, considered to be the main armed Islamist group still active in the country, praised the kidnapping and execution of two Algerian diplomats in Iraq in July by the Base of Holy War in Mesopotamia militant group (also known as al-Qa'ida in Iraq), then led by Abu Musab al-Zarqawi. Indeed, the Algerian authorities claimed that the GSPC had established links with al-Zarqawi's group and was affiliated to the al-Qa'ida network, a view supported by French intelligence services but rejected by several specialists on armed Islamist groups. Strongly embedded in the north-east of the country and using funds stolen from banks and post offices to finance its operations, the group also remained active on Algeria's southern borders and in Europe, where it declared France to be the 'enemy number one of Islam'.

In the run-up to the referendum on the President's Charter for Peace and National Reconciliation on 29 September 2005, the GSPC stepped up its attacks and issued a communiqué rejecting the President's peace offer, reiterating its commitment to follow *jihad* until the establishment of an Islamic state in Algeria. During the first half of October it was estimated that over 55 people had been killed in violence attributed to armed Islamist groups. Prime Minister Ouyahia stated that 10,000 terrorists had surrendered to the authorities under the amnesties of 1997 and 1999, and predicted that, although the GSPC had rejected the President's latest peace offer, some 200–300 armed Islamists would surrender under the terms of the new charter. In March 2006 Ouyahia stated that 17,000 'terrorists' had been killed by the security forces since 1992 and that another 180,000 people had died in the violence. He also admitted that the authorities had deliberately given a much lower figure for the number of people killed in a massacre near Relizane in January 1998 to avoid provoking disquiet abroad, where accusations had been made that Algeria could not protect its own citizens. Some 1,000 civilians had been killed in a single night, but the official figure issued for those who died was 100–150. Meanwhile, a senior member of the GSPC who had been Abderrezak le Para's second-in-command before surrendering to the authorities in 2000 was murdered in el-Oued, in what appeared to be a targeted assassination by the GSPC. He was reported to have assisted the security services in persuading members of GSPC factions to surrender their arms and negotiate with the authorities. In April 2006 reports indicated that more than 65 people had died, including 13 customs officers killed near Ghardaïa in the south and nine *gardes communaux* killed in an ambush near Skikda. Both attacks were attributed to the GSPC. At the end of April Ouyahia announced that 200 'terrorists' had surrendered since the presidential decree in February, more than double the figure cited earlier by Zerhouni.

HUMAN RIGHTS AND THE QUESTION OF THE 'DISAPPEARED'

In late 1999 President Bouteflika agreed to allow Amnesty International to send a delegation to Algeria. The organization had been banned from visiting the country for some four years. The delegation visited Algeria in May 2000, and another mission followed in November. Amnesty International criticized the President's peace initiative, arguing that in practice neither side in the conflict would be punished for acts of brutality, and urged the authorities to investigate all past and present atrocities, publish the results of the investigations and bring those responsible to justice.

By the beginning of 2003 little progress had been made in resolving the issue of the several thousand Algerians who 'disappeared' during the 1990s, many after being arrested by the security forces on suspicion of being Islamists or of being sympathetic to the Islamist cause. In January 2002 Bouteflika, concerned that the issue was tarnishing Algeria's image abroad, had appointed the respected lawyer Farouk Ksentini as head of the Commission Nationale Consultative de Promotion et de Protection des Droits de l'Homme, with instructions to give priority to this dossier and report back by the end of the year. Associations bringing together the families of the 'disappeared' accused Ksentini of seeking to bury a troublesome dossier rather than cast new light on the issue, but nevertheless, public discussion about the issue was no longer taboo—previously the families of the 'disappeared' had often been portrayed by the press as being in league with the 'terrorists'—and a number of new facts had emerged. The gendarmerie (responsible for co-ordinating the dossier since 1995) officially admitted that some 7,046 complaints had been lodged relating to people who had 'disappeared' during the 1990s. They insisted that all complaints had been investigated and that in 4,740 cases their inquiries had proved 'fruitless'. For the rest they maintained that the responsibility of the security forces had never been proved. An authorized military source claimed that no one was being held in secret anywhere in the country, suggesting that there were no survivors among the 'disappeared', but this was still to be confirmed officially. The same army source stated that at the height of the civil war victims on both sides had been buried in communal graves and that 3,030 bodies had been buried at one site. The authorities were prepared to pay compensation to the families in order to 'turn the page', but were not prepared to accept guilt or concede to demands for truth and justice. One human rights activist insisted that the problem of the 'disappeared' could not be resolved by Ksentini or indeed the President himself because those responsible for the majority of the disappearances, the military high command and especially those in charge of military security, were still in power. At the same time Muhammad Smain, the ALDHR representative in Relizane, stated that military security personnel remained above the law, a state within a state. He insisted there was evidence that members of the security forces continued to arrest people who then disappeared. When family members made enquiries they were often told that their relative had 'escaped'.

In September 2003 Amnesty International published a new report concerning Algeria following a visit to the country in February. The report stated that there had been some improvement in the country's human rights record since the mid-1990s but that violence continued, with killings, torture and abductions being carried out by both armed Islamist groups and the security services; civilians were the main victims. Recent reforms and initiatives had often not been implemented and the authorities were criticized for the lack of progress towards truth and justice. Amnesty International called on the authorities to order full and independent investigations into disappearances and executions. It also referred to thousands of abductions and rapes of girls and women by armed groups since 1992 and thousands of cases of torture of men, women and children who had been detained by the state authorities. In late September 2003 President Bouteflika announced the establishment of a commission to liaise with the families of the 'disappeared'. The seven-member commission, chaired by Farouk Ksentini, would not launch an inquiry, as requested by human rights groups, but would open a dialogue with the families by examining cases brought before it and helping them to obtain aid and compensation. The commission's work was to be completed in 18 months. Ksentini told the press that there were 10,000 cases of forced disappearances attributed to 'terrorist' groups and 7,200 to state organizations, according to allegations by the families involved. This was the first time that the Algerian state had acknowledged that it had responsibilities regarding the question of the 'disappeared'. Nevertheless, the ALDHR described the commission as a 'cover-up' to protect those who had ordered these crimes against humanity, while several commentators accused the President of using this initiative for electoral gain in order to rally the Islamist vote and weaken the military hierarchy.

An inquiry was initiated in December 2003 after Smain discovered a mass grave in the Relizane region and identified the remains of a man known to have been kidnapped in September 1996 by local militias. However, before any of the bodies were exhumed, Smain accused gendarmes, aided by local militias, of removing all traces of the contents of the grave. In February 2004 Amnesty International called on the Algerian authorities to implement urgent measures to protect the sites of mass graves which, they insisted, contained vital evidence for inquiries into crimes against humanity during the 1990s.

In January 2005 Amnesty International presented a report to the UN concerning violence against women in Algeria and the lack of political will on the part of the authorities to protect them. Highlighting the case of some 40 women attacked in Hassi Messaoud in July 2001 by a gang of more than 400 individuals, the report condemned the absence of any thorough inquiry into rape allegations or legal proceedings against those responsible. The report stated that training was needed for police, judges and others responsible for dealing with such cases and that refuges should be opened for women who had been subjected to violence. It also criticized the fact that no member of the security services or armed militias had been prosecuted in connection with the thousands of 'disappearances' during the 1990s, and stated that the suffering of the mothers and wives of the 'disappeared' merited the description 'acts of torture'. The MSP criticized Amnesty International's report on the grounds that it showed a lack of understanding of relations between men and women in a Muslim society.

In April 2005 the Ksentini Commission set up to examine the issue of civilian disappearances during the 1990s presented its report to President Bouteflika. It stated that members of the security services were responsible for 6,146 disappearances, but emphasized that these were individual acts perpetrated during a period of violent upheaval and a breakdown in the chain of command. It recommended that the families of victims should receive compensation and that state agents responsible for disappearances should not be excluded from the proposed general amnesty. The report 'invited' the authorities to tell the truth about the fate of the 'disappeared'. This was the first official admission of the role of state agents in the disappearances; however, organizations campaigning on behalf of the families insisted that the disappearances were part of a centrally controlled policy and not isolated acts by individuals. Their estimates for the number of 'disappeared' were 10,000 taken by armed Islamist groups and 8,000 by the security forces and militias. In an interview, Ksentini stated that those civilians abducted by terrorists had been executed and buried in mass graves, as these groups took no prisoners; consequently, they had not disappeared in a legal sense. It was essential to distinguish between these two categories of the 'disappeared'.

REFERENDUM ON THE CHARTER FOR PEACE AND NATIONAL RECONCILIATION

In August 2005 Bouteflika finally announced details of his Charter for Peace and National Reconciliation. After a vigorous campaign throughout the country by the President and his ministers to promote the project, it was put to a referendum on 29 September. According to official sources, the Charter was approved by 97.4% of voters with a turn-out of 79.6%, although this figure was challenged by the opposition as being 'inconceivable'. Under the terms of the Charter, members of armed Islamist groups who surrendered voluntarily to the authorities would be pardoned together with those already condemned, imprisoned or sought for acts of terrorism, with the exception of those implicated in collective massacres, rapes or bomb attacks on public places. The security forces were exonerated from serious human rights abuses, notably on the issue of the thousands who had 'disappeared' during the 1990s, and all allegations of a deliberate state policy of disappearances were rejected. Indeed, the President gave fulsome praise for the sacrifices made by the security forces and all 'patriots', who had 'saved Algeria from the hydra of terrorism and preserved Republican institutions'. The Charter referred to the 'disappeared' as 'victims of the national tragedy' and stated that their families would receive compensation; they had to accept the heavy but inevitable price for the peace and security for all Algerians. Without direct reference to the FIS, the party was held responsible for the tragic events of the 1990s and was forbidden from ever resuming its political activities.

The referendum was strongly opposed by some political parties, notably the FFS and the RCD, human rights organizations and support groups for the families of the 'disappeared'. They called for a massive and active boycott, and accused the authorities of denying them access to the state media and harassment and intimidation of their activists during campaigning against the referendum. Opponents insisted that there should be no pardon without truth and justice and that no one should benefit from impunity. The Charter, like the 1999 Law of Civil Concord, would not bring about an end to the violence because that required a political solution; only democracy would save Algeria. The President was accused of using the referendum as a plebiscite to reinforce his power and as a prelude to constitutional amendments that would allow him to stand for a third mandate in 2009.

In troubled Kabylia, voters boycotted the referendum in large numbers and turn-out was the lowest in the country, at only 11% in the two main cities, Tizi Ouzou and Béjaïa. In January 2005 talks between the pro-dialogue wing of the CADC and Ouyahia had resumed and agreement reached to implement the El-Kseur platform, including making Tamazight an official language, 'within the framework of the Constitution and the laws of the country'. Yet only limited progress was made, apart from a presidential decree in July dissolving municipal and provincial councils in Kabylia and scheduling new local elections. A widespread boycott of the 2002 local elections meant that some councils had been elected on a turn-out of less than 1%. Four days after the referendum, during a speech in Constantine, President Bouteflika insisted that Arabic would remain the country's only official language, contradicting the agreement made by his Prime Minister. The anti-dialogue wing of the CADC insisted that the negotiations with Ouyahia had been a deception and that from the outset the central authorities had no intention of conceding to the demands set out in the El-Kseur platform.

In local elections in Kabylia on 24 November 2005 the FFS and its fraternal rival, the RCD, won over one-half of all seats on municipal and provincial councils. Nevertheless, the FLN and the RND improved on their performance and seemed likely to benefit from the deep divisions between their opponents (the FFS, the RCD and the CADC). According to official figures, turn-out in the municipal elections was 33%, while this was slightly lower in the provincial elections, at 31%. No single party secured a majority of seats on most councils, requiring tactical alliances to ensure that they could function properly. It was later reported that the majority of alliances had been between the FFS and the FLN on the one hand, and the RCD and the RND on the other. The FFS boycotted by-elections to the Council of the Nation held in Kabylia in late February 2006.

After the local elections there was speculation about the future of the CADC following the success of the region's traditional political parties. However, a spokesman for the pro-dialogue wing of the CADC denied that the movement was running out of steam and stated that it had moved from a phase of confrontation to one of partnership with the authorities. It was ready to resume negotiations with the Prime Minister to capitalize on the achievements made under the January 2005 agreement, while acknowledging that a number of outstanding problems remained—notably the question of making Tamazight an official language. Celebrations in April 2006 to mark the fifth anniversary of the 'Black spring' passed peacefully and reports indicated that a measure of stability had returned to the troubled region. Belkhadem, who replaced Ouyahia as Prime Minister in May, had stated after the local elections in November 2005 that dialogue with the CADC was of no value now that Kabylia had new elected representatives.

In February 2006 a presidential decree outlining measures to implement the provisions of the Charter on Peace and National Reconciliation was approved by the Council of Ministers, thereby bypassing a parliamentary debate. Members of armed Islamist groups who gave themselves up within six months would receive a presidential pardon and be reintegrated into Algerian society or receive compensation if they were unable to go back to their former jobs. Those members of armed groups who had surrendered between 13 January 2000 (the deadline set by the 1999 Law on Civil Concord) and the date when the new law was promulgated would also receive a presidential pardon. Those sentenced and imprisoned on terrorism charges would be pardoned and released, and those still sought or sentenced *in absentia* would also be pardoned. Those involved in massacres, rapes and bomb attacks on public places were excluded from the amnesty. All members of the security forces and militias armed by the state were given immunity from prosecution for actions carried out 'while protecting and safeguarding the nation and preserving its institutions'. Families of the 'disappeared' and those of terrorists killed by the security forces would be eligible for compensation. The decree explicitly banned any person responsible for the manipulation of religion that led to the national tragedy, i.e. members of the former FIS, from taking part in any form of political activity. Anyone 'who exploited the wounds of the national tragedy to harm state institutions, weaken the state, undermine the good reputation of its agents or tarnish the image of Algeria abroad' would be punished by three to five years' imprisonment and a fine of AD 300,000–AD 500,000. The President was granted sweeping powers to take any other measures required in order to implement the Charter.

In response, Amnesty International, Human Rights Watch, the International Centre for Transitional Justice and the International Federation for Human Rights issued a joint statement in which they described the decree as a major setback for human rights in Algeria. The new measures, it stated, amounted to a denial of truth and justice to the victims of abuses and to their families, and contravened Algeria's obligations under international law. Particular concern was expressed about the blanket amnesty extended to the security forces and state-armed militias, and the fact that no details were given about mechanisms to determine whether members of armed Islamist groups who surrendered were 'eligible' for amnesty. Fears were expressed that members of armed groups who were not involved in collective killings but who had committed serious crimes such as torture and kidnapping would go free. It noted that the 1999 Law on Civil Concord had created a screening mechanism that operated arbitrarily and with a lack of transparency, resulting in de facto wide-ranging impunity for abuses committed by armed groups. The communiqué also criticized the fact that families would only receive compensation if they obtained death certificates for their 'disappeared' relatives, something that many were opposed to so long as the state was unable or unwilling to provide them with the truth about the fate of their loved ones. Moreover, it noted that the decree threatened to penalize families of the 'disappeared' who continued to campaign for disclosure of the truth about the fate of their relatives and to muzzle open debate by criminalizing all public discussion about the tragic events of the 1990s.

The decree enraged families of the 'disappeared' and human rights activists, who described the new measures as a scandal. Many families of victims stated that they would risk imprisonment rather than abandon their campaign for truth and justice and demanded that the Charter be annulled. In March 2006 the authorities began releasing Islamist prisoners: Ali Belhadj, the second-in-command of the former FIS, and Abdelhak Layada, one of the founders of the GIA and its second 'national emir', were the first among some 2,200 Islamist prisoners released under the terms of the Charter. Shortly after his release, Belhadj gave an interview to *Le Monde* denouncing the authorities as 'illegitimate', declaring that national reconciliation had been imposed by those responsible for the 1992 coup and insisting that no one could deny Islamist activists their right to take part in political life.

BELKHADEM APPOINTED PREMIER

At the end of May 2006 Ouyahia resigned the premiership and Bouteflika appointed Abdelaziz Belkhadem, the Secretary-General of the FLN and hitherto Minister of State and Special Representative of the President, to succeed him. The Council of Ministers remained virtually unchanged, suggesting that Bouteflika was keen to keep the presidential alliance (of the FLN, the RND and the MSP) intact. During the preceding months there had been a struggle within the alliance between Belkhadem (allied to the MSP) and Ouyahia, who was strongly criticized for not pushing forward with reforms to combat poverty and unemployment at a time when Algeria was in receipt of huge revenues from hydrocarbon exports due to high petroleum prices. Belkhadem had also called publicly for a change in the Constitution to give Algeria a presidential regime and allow the Head of State to serve for three mandates, whereas Ouyahia favoured more discrete amendments. Some sections of the Algerian press indicated surprise at Bouteflika's choice of Belkhadem as Prime Minister ahead of one of the technocrats in the Council of Ministers. Belkhadem, a leading member of the FLN's Islamo-conservative wing, had long demonstrated his complete loyalty to Bouteflika, and this appeared to have been his main qualification for attaining the premiership.

GSPC RESTYLED 'AL-QA'IDA ORGANIZATION IN THE LAND OF THE ISLAMIC MAGHREB'

Despite the Algerian authorities' implementation of provisions outlined in the Charter on Peace and National Reconciliation, the threat of Islamist violence continued during 2006, and attacks attributed to militants of the GSPC resulted in the deaths of a number of Algerian security officials during April of that year. The six-month amnesty for militant Islamists who had surrendered to the authorities expired in late August, by which time the Minister of State for the Interior and Local Authorities, Noureddine Yazid Zerhouni, stated that only some 250–300 militants had given up their weapons; it was estimated that up to 800 Islamist fighters remained at large, most of these being members of the GSPC. In October three people were killed in co-ordinated bomb explosions outside police stations in Réghaïa and Dergana. In December the GSPC claimed responsibility for a roadside bomb attack near Algiers on two vehicles carrying employees of a US- and Algerian-owned engineering company, in which one man was killed and nine others, including six foreigners, were injured.

It was reported in January 2007 that the GSPC had restyled itself as the al-Qa'ida Organization in the Land of the Islamic Maghreb (AQIM). The announcement followed reports in September 2006 that the GSPC had 'joined' the international al-Qa'ida network led by Osama bin Laden. One of al-Qa'ida's most senior leaders, Ayman al-Zawahiri, described the development as a 'blessed union' during a video broadcast on the internet on the occasion of the fifth anniversary of the September 2001 attacks in the USA. Days after the GSPC had announced its name change, 15 people were killed following clashes between Algerian security forces and Islamist militants in Batna. During February 2007 at least six people died when a series of explosions targeting police stations were launched in eastern Algeria. In March seven police officers and four pipeline construction workers (from Russia and Ukraine), together with three Algerians, died in two separate militant attacks, in Tizi Ouzou and Aïn Defla, south-west of Algiers, respectively, for which AQIM claimed responsibility. The same group declared that it had carried out co-ordinated car bomb attacks targeted at sites in the capital in early April, in which 33 people were killed and more than 200 wounded; one of the bombs exploded close to the Prime Minister's office. Later that month Algerian military officials announced that the AQIM second-in-command, Samir Saioud (also known as Samir Moussaâb), had been killed during fighting to the east of Algiers. In June the Italian authorities announced that at least 10 suspected militant Islamists thought to have been involved in the planning of the Algiers car bombings had been detained in Milan, Italy.

It appeared in the early part of 2007 that an intensification of Islamist violence was simultaneously taking place in neighbouring Morocco and Tunisia, and there were widespread fears that attacks across the region were being co-ordinated by militant groups with an al-Qa'ida connection. Indeed, many observers noted that the renaming of the GSPC effectively to join the al-Qa'ida 'franchise' was clearly aimed at attracting a wider pool of support across the whole of North Africa and at recruiting new members to the cause. The apparent radicalization of the GSPC appeared to be in direct contrast to the willingness of many of Algeria's militant groups to lay down their weapons and renounce violence under President Bouteflika's Charter on Peace and National Reconciliation.

A suicide bombing apparently intended to coincide with the opening of the All-Africa Games in early July 2007—one of the continent's most important sporting events, which was being held in Algeria for the second time—resulted in the deaths of at least eight people. The driver of a truck detonated his explosives at a military barracks near the town of Bouira, south-east of Algiers, in the Kabylia region. AQIM claimed responsibility for the attack, prompting Minister of State Zerhouni to declare defiantly that such violence would not prevent the Government from continuing its 'relentless fight against terrorism'. Two further suicide bombings apparently carried out by the al-Qa'ida offshoot in Batna and Algiers in early September claimed some 57 lives. The latest bomb attacks, one of which appeared to have targeted President Bouteflika, resulted in an anti-violence demonstration in the capital by thousands of Algerians.

The security forces appeared to have had some success against militant Islamism in early October 2007, when it was reported that they had killed the deputy leader of AQIM, Hareg Zoheir (or Sofiane Abu Fasila), in Tizi Ouzou; Zoheir was thought to have been responsible for many of Algeria's recent bombings. Nevertheless, the violence continued at an alarming rate: on 11 December two suicide car bombings in separate districts of Algiers resulted in a large number of fatalities. (Estimates for the number of those killed ranged between an official figure of 26 and reports from other sources, such as medical personnel, who claimed that around 70 people had lost their lives.) The first bomb exploded outside the Constitutional Court, while the second targeted UN offices, killing 17 people. This reportedly brought to 15 the number of terrorist attacks perpetrated in the country since the start of 2007; an estimated 491 people were believed to have died as a result of political violence by the end of that year. Many commentators noted that the leadership of AQIM, which was said to be experiencing considerable levels of dissent within its various factions, had chosen to adopt suicide bombing as its principal method of operation, in contrast with the tactics traditionally used by militant Islamist groups in Algeria, and that civilians were increasingly being targeted as well as the armed forces, police and other state officials. In early January 2008 a car bomb attack against a police station and an ambush on a military convoy, both in the Algiers region, resulted in the deaths of four police officers and five soldiers, respectively. The authorities responded to this renewed violence, for which AQIM again claimed responsibility, by arresting many suspected militants and implementing a further tightening of security measures.

THE LEGISLATIVE ELECTIONS OF 2007

The Government announced in February 2007 that elections to the National People's Assembly would be held on 17 May and that, in preparation for the polls, the country's electoral lists were to be revised. The FFS responded by announcing in March that it intended to boycott the elections, as had been the case in 2002, citing its lack of confidence in the Algerian parliamentary system as a means of bringing about real political change.

As at the legislative elections of 2002, the FLN retained its dominance of the legislature following the 17 May 2007 polls, winning 136 of the 389 seats and thus an overall majority. However, this was a poorer result for the party than had been the case in the previous election, when the FLN had 199 representatives in the National People's Assembly. The RND again held the second highest number of seats, with 62 (compared with 48 in 2002), while the MSP increased its representation, taking 51 seats (against 38 in 2002). The PT fared well at the polls, with a gain of five seats, from 21 to 26. A notable result was the relative success of the RCD, which had boycotted the previous election: the party achieved a total of 19 seats in the legislature. In contrast, the MRN, which had been the principal opposition movement in the outgoing Assembly, won only three seats. Independent candidates secured 33 seats (against 29 in 2002). Although the rate of voter participation was reported to have been the lowest since Algeria's independence, at only 36% (compared with the official figure of 46.2% recorded in 2002), Zerhouni asserted that similar rates were not unusual in some Western democracies and denied that the new legislature would lack credibility.

In early June 2007 President Bouteflika appointed a new, 38-member Council of Ministers, with Abdelaziz Belkhadem being renamed as Prime Minister. Notable changes in the composition of the Government were the replacement of Muhammad Bedjaoui as Minister of Foreign Affairs by the Minister of Finance, Mourad Medelci, while Karim Djoudi was chosen to replace Medelci in his former post.

At local elections held in late November 2007 (postponed from October owing to the month of Ramadan) the FLN obtained some 30.0% of the seats, against 24.5% for the RND and 11.3% for the Front National Algérien. Recent changes to electoral legislation had restricted the number of parties eligible to participate in the polls and, as in the general election held in May, the FIS was not permitted to field candidates. However, most of Algeria's political organizations considered the local elections to have been conducted fairly. In early 2008 opposition politicians, academics and journalists launched a petition against plans by supporters of President Bouteflika to amend the Constitution (which stipulated that a President may only renew his term of office once) in order to allow Bouteflika to seek a third presidential term.

OUYAHIA APPOINTED PRIME MINISTER AMID RISING ISLAMIST VIOLENCE

The threat of violence by Islamist militants continued to escalate in early 2008: eight Algerian gendarmes were killed in a suspected ambush by Islamist extremists in el-Oued on 8 February. AQIM subsequently claimed responsibility for the attack, which was the deadliest since the double car bombings of 11 December 2007. Following a period of relative calm, there was a further outbreak of violence in June 2008: 19 people were reportedly killed (including several members of the security forces) and many more were injured in a series of bomb attacks to the east of Algiers during 4–8 June. While no claim of responsibility was made in the immediate aftermath of the attacks, suspicion fell on AQIM—particularly as those targeted in the bombings were again members of the armed forces and other state officials. Two further bomb attacks, on 23 July and 3 August (targeting a military convoy in Lakhdaria, and a police station and military barracks in Tizi Ouzou, respectively), were subsequently claimed by AQIM. A series of arrests of AQIM militants in early 2008 did not diminish the organization's ability to launch attacks. In August the organization carried out 10 attacks in four separate provinces, mostly against military and security personnel, killing at least 90 people and injuring a further 150. These included a suicide bombing outside a military training college in Issers on 19 August, in which 48 people were killed and a further 38 were injured. Despite the efforts of the security forces to disrupt AQIM, the organization appeared to retain the capacity to recruit. Analysts attributed this principally to the rising rate of youth unemployment in Algeria. In mid-2009 AQIM claimed responsibility for a number of attacks, including the ambush in June of a convoy of security personnel escorting a group of Chinese construction workers near Bordj Bou Arreridj, in which 18 Algerian gendarmes and one Chinese national were killed.

In a presidential decree issued on 23 June 2008 President Bouteflika effected a surprise cabinet reorganization, which included the appointment of Ahmed Ouyahia to succeed Abdelaziz Belkhadem as Prime Minister. Ouyahia—who had previously served in the post from 1995–98, and again from 2003–06—was known for his firm stance against Islamist militants, and his appointment was understood, in part, as a reaction to the recent increase in Islamist violence.

BOUTEFLIKA'S THIRD TERM—THE PRESIDENTIAL ELECTION OF 2009

In a move that opposition parties widely condemned, the National People's Assembly approved a constitutional amendment in November 2008 abolishing the two-term limit for the post of President. Bouteflika had sought the removal of the two-term limit and had specifically chosen Ouyahia as Prime Minister in order to steer the amendment through parliament. Two months before the election, which was scheduled for 9 April 2009, Bouteflika finally announced that he would indeed be seeking a third term and that he would contest the election as an independent. Bouteflika's electoral campaign focused largely on the issue of national security and reconciliation, with the President stating that an amnesty for AQIM fighters could be envisaged if they renounced violence. The state of the economy was the other important issue in the campaign. Bouteflika announced that he would undertake a number of measures to boost employment and improve the country's infrastructure. The opposition parties, including the RCD and the FFS, accused the President of a return to authoritarianism and eventually decided to boycott the election. The final results were unsurprising as Bouteflika, amid accusations of government interference and intimidation of voters, was re-elected with 90.2% of the votes. Meanwhile, Louisa Hanoune was second, receiving a meagre 4.5% of the votes, while the remaining four candidates each received between 2.0% and 0.9% of the votes. Before the election, Bouteflika had stated that only a high turn-out would give legitimacy to his third term and, according to the official figures, turn-out was indeed high at 74.6%. This figure was disputed by opposition parties and by some of the other presidential candidates. Despite the controversies generated by the constitutional change allowing him to contest a third term and the accusations of fraud, Bouteflika was congratulated by the international community, including French President Nicolas Sarkozy.

Shortly after the election, Bouteflika announced that the Council of Ministers was to remain virtually unchanged, with Ouyahia continuing as Prime Minister. In May 2009 Ouyahia presented the Government's programme, which emphasized increasing efforts towards national reconciliation, political pluralism and the development of links between elected officials and civil society.

DRIFT TOWARDS ECONOMIC NATIONALISM

The first noteworthy step taken by the new Government was the adoption of an amended budget in July 2009. This was regarded by some observers as a reversal of previous commitments to a liberal economic policy and signalling a step towards economic nationalism. In line with earlier pronouncements by Bouteflika and members of the Government, the revised budget contained measures requiring at least 51% of any new joint venture and 30% in any foreign imports company to be held by Algerian interests. The new regulations also limited the payment of all imports by letters of credit and banned credit to consumers, both of which measures were intended to control the flow of imports.

The new regulations, however, prompted dissatisfaction within local and foreign business groups. In August 2009 Algeria's largest employers' organization, the Forum des Chefs d'Entreprises, depicted the measures as engendering a 'grave situation' and considered that 'the absence of consultation and the authoritarianism which dictates economic decisions reduce the credibility of these measures and may lead to paralysis of the country'. At the international level, the country's two largest trading partners, the USA and the EU, expressed their unease over the restrictive measures. Despite those concerns, a delegation of representatives of 24 American companies operating in various industry sectors and led by the US Assistant Secretary of Commerce for Manufacturing and Services visited Algeria in February 2010 for discussions regarding potential investment in the country. Earlier that month a 12-person EU delegation had arrived in Algiers for discussions on trade, as well as to review the 2005 Association Agreement. However, in its April 2010 quarterly bulletin the Agence Nationale de Développement de l'Investissement asserted that only four new projects were recorded in 2009, compared with 102 in 2008.

INCREASING SOCIAL DISCONTENT

During 2009–10 there were several protests and strikes in the country, reflecting popular grievances over the quality of housing, the level of unemployment, low wages and deteriorating purchasing power. On 19 October 2009 violent protests, fuelled by inadequate housing and high unemployment, broke out in the Diar Echems district of Algiers and lasted for several days. By March 2010 more than 500 of the 1,500 families living in the district were reported to have been rehoused. In an attempt to tackle the housing problem and persistently high levels of youth unemployment, the Government pledged to build 1m. new housing units and to create 3m. jobs in 2010–14.

For several months, demonstrations and strikes also disrupted vital sectors such as education, health care and industry. In an article published in January 2010, the daily *L'Expression* estimated the total number of workers on strike in the country at 600,000 in various sectors. In November 2009 teachers, mobilized by independent teaching unions, began a series of strikes over pay and working conditions. While the Government agreed to a pay rise, the teachers insisted on this being backdated. The strike was ended in March, however, after the Minister of Education threatened to suspend the participants. Public health practitioners also went on strike for almost four months, demanding a review of their status and improved wages. Similarly to the teachers' strike, the trade unions representing those participating in the industrial action decided to end the strike at the end of March, following pressure from the Government. In early January workers at the state-owned Entreprise Nationale des Véhicules Industriels plant in Rouiba began a strike to demand an increase in salaries, as well as a reversal of changes in the retirement system. Following a commitment made by the UGTA to satisfy their demands, the strike was ended later that month. Also in January workers at a steel plant owned by the Luxembourg-based ArcelorMittal in El-Hadjar commenced industrial action against the proposed closure of a coking plant at the site and related loss of 320 jobs; ArcelorMittal subsequently agreed on a project to renovate the plant.

CAMPAIGN AGAINST CORRUPTION

In a speech in mid-April 2009 to mark the inauguration of his third term of office, President Bouteflika promised a sweeping anti-corruption campaign. Thus, the first year of his term was marked by a number of major corruption scandals involving state officials. In its 2009 *Corruption Perception Index*, the German-based non-governmental organization (NGO) Transparency International ranked Algeria 111th of 180 countries surveyed. The two largest cases were concerned with the so-called 'east-west' highway project and the state-owned oil and gas company Sonatrach. While the campaign was officially proclaimed as a 'clean-out' operation, commentators suggested that it could be connected to a power struggle within the country's élite. The involvement of the country's powerful security services, the DRS, was regarded by some observers as a political manoeuvre intended to discredit the President and his closest allies in the Government, and those high-profile cases seemed to have, in some measure, served this purpose.

The 'east-west' highway project, designed to link the Algeria-Tunisia border to the east and the Algeria-Morocco border to the west, was officially launched in March 2007. In October 2009, however, at least four people, including the Secretary-General of the Ministry of Public Works, were arrested following an investigation by the DRS into allegations of financial and managerial irregularities. The DRS, in conjunction with the police authorities in Algiers, later extended their investigations to the railways sector, and claimed to have uncovered other cases of irregularities in the awarding of contracts. As a result, contracts valued at some US $2,500m. which had been awarded to the Railway Construction Company in July 2009 were cancelled in May 2010 by the Agence Nationale d'Etudes et de Suivi de la Réalisation des Investissements Ferroviaires—the government agency in charge of awarding contracts aimed at modernizing and extending Algeria's railway network.

Following an initial inquiry conducted by the DRS, a number of management officials at Sonatrach were either placed under judicial investigation or arrested on charges of 'violation of public procurement regulations, association with criminals and corruption'. The most senior executive to be implicated was Muhammad Meziane, who had held the role of President and Director-General at the company since 2003. The accusations reportedly concerned the misappropriation of funds in the awarding of contracts. In May 2011 Meziane was sentenced to two years' imprisonment for his role in the scandal; four other executives each received prison sentences of up to a year.

The most significant ramification of the scandal that engulfed Sonatrach had been the replacement of the Minister of Energy and Mining, Chakib Khelil, by Youcef Yousfi—himself a former head of Sonatrach—in a cabinet reorganization announced by President Bouteflika in May 2010. Khelil had hitherto been regarded as one of Bouteflika's close allies, having held the role since 1999.

The assassination on 25 February of the head of the Direction Générale de la Sûreté Nationale, Col Ali Tounsi, was widely rumoured to be related to issues of corruption. Tounsi was reportedly shot dead after a verbal confrontation with a high-ranking police officer. Immediately after the incident, the Minister of the Interior and Local Authorities, Noureddine Yazid Zerhouni, announced that a judicial inquiry had been opened into the circumstances surrounding Tounsi's death. Although the inquiry concluded in July, no significant details of its conclusions were reported.

In December 2009 President Bouteflika issued a directive in which he instructed the Government to implement a number of urgent and preventive anti-corruption measures. Among these was the creation of a national anti-corruption observatory, which was announced in February 2010. Moreover, in August the Government announced the formation of an anti-corruption agency, the Office Central de Répression de la Corruption. The adoption in July of new regulations regarding the award of public sector contracts was also intended as part of an overall national strategy to curb corrupt practices.

POPULAR PROTESTS CONTINUE

Between July 2010 and July 2011 Algeria witnessed more than 9,000 riots and disturbances, according to Maj.-Gen. Abdelghani Hamel, who had replaced Tounsi as head of the Direction Générale de la Sûreté Nationale in July 2010. Sporadic and localized protests occurred in response to various social and economic problems. For example, in late December in the Algiers district of Les Palmiers, riots erupted over the issue of inadequate housing and subsequently spread to other suburbs. In an attempt to quell the unrest, the authorities promised to deliver more housing in 2011.

These protests were soon followed by another series of more violent disturbances sparked off this time by the spiralling prices of basic foodstuffs, particularly cooking oil and sugar. The protests, which started in a western suburb of Algiers on 5 January 2011, spread to other parts of the capital and then to several other cities within a few days. It was reported that about one-half of the country's 48 *wilayat* were affected by rioting and looting of businesses and public buildings. According to the Government, during several days of violence five people were killed, 800 (including 763 police officers) were wounded and 1,100 people were arrested, most of whom were minors.

In fact, the eruption of these riots was, to a considerable degree, related to the population's immediate problems such as the high cost of living, poor housing conditions and absent or limited employment opportunities. They were also exacerbated by the rioters' sense of *hogra*—a local word used to describe what was seen as the authorities' contempt for the concerns of ordinary people. In response to the unrest, the Government decided to reduce duties on oil and sugar by 41%.

In addition to the riots, several cases of self-immolation—seemingly inspired by a similar act in Tunisia in December 2010 (see the chapter on Tunisia)—were reported across the country, the most prominent of which was that of Mohsen Bouterfif, who died four days after setting himself on fire because the authorities refused to deal with his grievances relating to housing and employment. The protest movement took a new turn with the establishment on 21 January 2011 of the Coordination Nationale pour le Changement et la Démocratie (CNCD), a loose umbrella organization incorporating various opposition groups such as the RCD and the Ligue Algérienne pour la Défense des Droits de l'Homme (LADDH), as well as unofficial trade unions. Seeking a systemic change in the country, the CNCD called for a mass protest march on 12 February in the capital, which was met with a massive police deployment of some 30,000 officers. This did not deter the CNCD, as one of its main founders, the human rights activist Ali Yahia Abdelnour, vowed to hold further protest marches every Saturday in Algiers. However, owing to a split within the organization, and the effects of the government crackdown, its ability to mobilize demonstrators was subsequently impeded.

Strikes, demonstrations and sit-ins continued to affect a wide range of sectors, however, and included action by medical personnel, teachers and lecturers, students, former soldiers, local government workers, post office staff and the unemployed. For the most part, the demands were for higher wages and better working conditions. In an effort to avert further large-scale upheaval in the country, the Government deployed its reserves from the proceeds of petroleum exports to satisfy these demands, as well as to subsidize basic foodstuffs, increase investment and create jobs. The cost was reflected in the government amendment of the 2011 budget, which was expected to increase public spending by 25%, resulting in a budget deficit of almost 34% of GDP.

LIFTING OF THE STATE OF EMERGENCY

The state of emergency—which had been imposed immediately following the annulment of the country's first multi-party legislative elections in February 1992—was widely denounced by opposition groups and human rights organizations. With violence having abated in the country in recent years, keeping emergency rules was considered by these groups as a mechanism to justify the restriction and suppression of civil liberties. Thus, it was unsurprising that the ending of the 19-year state of emergency became one of the main rallying points for protesters who staged demonstrations in the country from early January 2011. These demonstrations prompted the authorities to revoke the legislation, something which the Minister of the Interior and Local Authorities, Dahou Ould Kablia, seemed uneasy about when he stated that 'the idea of removing the state of emergency was rather old and not taken because of events the country witnessed early January'.

President Bouteflika announced at a meeting of the Council of Ministers held on 3 February 2011 that the state of emergency was to be lifted shortly. The announcement came two days after a group of 21 members of the National People's Assembly (from the FLN, the MSP, the MRN, the FNA and dissidents from the RCD) submitted a draft bill to parliament to repeal the emergency law. The next cabinet meeting, which took place later that month, adopted a number of legislative texts, including the ordinance aimed at ending the state of emergency.

The official announcement to end the state of emergency was met with mixed reactions by the various political forces. Parties of the governing alliance—the FLN, the RND and the MSP, along with the PT—welcomed the decision. On the contrary, the other parties of the opposition were sceptical; the RCD saw it as 'a manoeuvre' meant 'to create diversion' while the LADDH described it as 'a manoeuvre to deceive international public opinion'. The FFS viewed the move as a positive signal, but considered that new anti-terrorist legislation would 'generate anxiety and suspicion'. Indeed, the legislation, adopted to remove the state of emergency was accompanied by new legislation permitting the armed forces to continue their role, as they did under emergency rules, to fight terrorism and subversion. In addition, a June 2001 order (part of the emergency rules) remained in force, prohibiting demonstrations in Algiers.

CONSULTATION ON POLITICAL REFORM

On 15 April 2011 President Bouteflika announced, in a televised speech, that the country was to carry out a number of major reforms. In order to 'strengthen democracy', his promised reform 'roadmap' would include constitutional amendments and the revision of the legislative framework relating to electoral law, the law governing political parties and the media. He also announced the establishment of a commission—the Commission Nationale de Consultation sur les Réformes Politiques (CNCRP)—whose mission would be 'to strive to provide an opportunity for all parties consulted to express their opinions'. The CNCRP would then make proposals to the President to be submitted for approval either by means of a referendum or a parliamentary vote.

Abdelkader Bensalah, the President of the Council of the Nation, was appointed as chairman of the CNCRP along with two co-chairmen, Gen. Muhammad Touati and Muhammad Ali Boughazi, both Bouteflika's personal advisers. Once Bouteflika had clarified the agenda for political and constitutional reform and the consultation process, which banned those the authorities call the 'proponents of violence' from participation, the commission was launched on 21 May 2011. During the first month, the CNCRP held discussions with more than 200 political parties, national figures, trade unionists and civil society organizations. Political parties within the presidential alliance all expressed their support for the initiative, and almost all of those who took part in the consultations were unanimous in advocating the revision of the Constitution, a process regarded as a 'prelude to further democracy and freedom'. Restricting the presidential mandate to two terms and promoting alternation in power were also issues which many of the participants believed would enable better governance in the country. Moreover, some recommended the establishment of a provisional government and a constituent assembly to carry out the reform package.

However, the debate about the reforms was marred by disagreements. Several of the key national personalities, political parties and civil society groups turned down the CNCRP's invitation to take part in the debate. Veteran political personalities, such as former presidents (Ben Djedid Chadli, Ali Kafi and Liamine Zéroual) and former prime ministers (Mokdad Sifi, Mouloud Hamrouche, Ahmed Benbitour and Ali Benflis) all declined to participate, with some criticizing the whole process or arguing for a wider national dialogue. For instance, Hocine Aït Ahmed, the historic leader of the FFS, saw the consultation process as a political move by the regime to buy time during a period marked by heightened social tensions; his party branded the process a 'political circus'. Like the FFS, other opposition parties, such as the RCD, Ahd 54 and the Parti Socialiste des Travailleurs (PST—Socialist Workers' Party), also boycotted the talks. The RCD called the regime's initiative a 'monologue against change' and 'an insult to the suffering and anger of Algerians who aspire to dignity, freedom and prosperity'.

On 21 June 2011 the CNCRP concluded its consultation work. At a meeting of the Council of Ministers on 10 July the Government was instructed to continue elaborating the draft laws on political reforms, expected to be submitted to parliament at its next session. In early September Bouteflika announced further reforms that would permit the creation of private radio and television broadcasters.

ADOPTION OF THE REFORM AGENDA

In successive meetings, held on 28 August and on 11–12 September 2011, the Council of Ministers endorsed a number of proposed pieces of legislation, concerning, *inter alia*, the electoral system, women's representation in elected bodies, cases of incompatibility with the parliamentary mandate, political parties, associations and information. These legislative texts were debated and approved by both chambers of parliament, and were officially promulgated in mid-January 2012. The reforms, as embodied in the proposed legislative package, were intended to 'deepen the democratic process in the country', according to the assertions of President Bouteflika. However, it was noted by some observers that, with the exception of female representation in elected institutions and cases of incompatibility with parliamentary mandate, the substance of the other texts (electoral code, political parties, associations and information) was already included in existing legislation.

There was little public debate with regard to these reforms. Nevertheless, the 'heated' parliamentary debate over the political reform package brought to notice differing partisan predilections among the major political forces—this was particularly the case when the first series of legislative acts was debated. The proposed draft electoral bill was decried by the FLN, especially in its stipulations relating to 'prohibition of political nomadism' and 'conditions for cabinet ministers running for election' (although the same text and others, including the one on women's political representation, had previously been approved, on 28 August 2011, by an FLN-dominated Government). The FLN, supported by its ally in the ruling presidential coalition, the RND, succeeded in securing the removal of both provisions before the bill was adopted in parliament. The stipulation prohibiting 'crossing the floor' (changing party affiliation) had been championed by several opposition parties, such as the PT and the FNA, which suffered the majority of the defections during the legislature of 2007–12, mostly to the governing FLN and RND. These governing parties also opposed the proviso requiring ministers wishing to stand for election to resign from their positions three months beforehand. This was perceived by the opposition as favouring the ruling parties, whose ministers could make use of government machinery during electioneering. Even after the adoption of the electoral law, the PT's leader, Hanoune, continued to demand that ministers standing for election resign from the Government prior to the campaign for the legislative polls.

The draft law on increasing women's political representation proposed, in its original version, electoral list quotas for women of 33%—their under-representation was reflected in the fact that women comprised only 7.7% of the 389-member National People's Assembly and less than 5% of the 144-member Council of the Nation. Yet again, the ruling FLN and RND were able to introduce amendments setting variable quotas of 20%–40% in the final text of the bill, the percentage being directly proportional to the number of seats in each electoral constituency. The ALDHR, in a critical report concerning the political reform legislation package, issued in April 2012, contended that the law was designed neither to ensure equal representation between women and men in elected assemblies nor to promote women's full participation in the country's political and public life.

The adoption of the reform legislation, with its revision of the law on political parties, appeared to have prompted the legalization of a multitude of new organizations. By March 2012 the number of new parties formally recognized by the Ministry of the Interior and Local Authorities had risen to 21 prior to the legislative elections. Several of these political formations were set up by dissidents from established political parties such as the FLN, the RND, the FNA, the RCD and the MSP. This proliferation of new political parties continued as the country prepared for local elections, scheduled to take place on 29 November. In August a further three new parties were legally recognized and 14 others authorized to hold their constituent congresses prior to their accreditation. Some observers were predicting that this rapid increase in newly established parties would result in the fragmentation of the country's political landscape, with the likely effect of reducing the willingness of an already disaffected electorate to participate in polls.

2012 LEGISLATIVE ELECTIONS: MAINTAINING THE STATUS QUO

The three-week parliamentary electoral campaign was officially launched on 15 April 2012 and involved some 44 political parties and 185 lists of independent candidates. In general, the campaign went off without any major incident. There were reports that meetings and rallies were cancelled, owing to widespread disinterest among voters, and also allegations of parties and candidates bribing people to attend. Overall, the campaign seemed to have had no significant effect on the apathetic mood of the electorate. Unemployment, declining purchasing power, shortage of affordable housing, insecurity and need for change were recurrent issues raised during the campaign. The invitation by the authorities of about 500 foreign observers—from the UN, the EU, the African Union (AU), the Arab League and the Organisation of Islamic Cooperation (OIC)—to monitor the voting was intended to provide a guarantee that the elections would be conducted according to democratic standards.

With almost 25,000 candidates contesting seats in the enlarged 462-member National People's Assembly, the elections took place on 10 May 2012, as scheduled. Of more than 21.6m. registered voters, only about 9.3m, participated, giving an official voter turn-out rate of 43.1%—including the vote of the diaspora whose electorate numbered almost 1m. This was without doubt a satisfactory figure for the authorities, compared with the rate of 35.7% obtained in the previous legislative elections of 2007. However, this turn-out includes invalid votes, the largest proportion of which was likely to be a result of intentional spoiling, which represented over 18% of the total votes cast (more than 1.7m.). When this is taken into account as a form of protest vote—which was clearly the case—voter turn-out would amount to only about 35.3%.

Contrary to expectations, these elections allowed the FLN—the party in power since independence in 1962—to register the greatest gains, by securing 221 of the 462 seats in the lower parliamentary chamber. Even though this represented 49% of the total seats, however, the FLN only received 17.3% of the total valid votes (more than 7.6m.). The RND, of Prime Minister Ouyahia, was placed second with 70 seats. The other party that performed relatively well was the FFS, the country's longest-standing opposition party, which, after boycotting national elections for more than a decade, had decided to contest the polls and succeeded in securing 21 seats. Obtaining 17 seats, Hanoune's PT registered a slight decline in support compared with the 2007 legislative elections. However, the worst performing group in the elections was the Alliance de l'Algérie Verte (Green Alliance of Algeria, AAV)—comprising three Islamist parties, the MSP, Mouvement de la Renaissance Islamique (Al-Nahda) and Mouvement de la Réforme Nationale (El-Islah) that had been formed in March 2012 to contest the elections—which received 47 seats. Much to its chagrin, the Alliance was unable to replicate the electoral success attained by Islamist parties across the region (in Egypt, Morocco and Tunisia), as the results confounded their early expectations. In response, the AAV accused the Government of manipulating the elections with the intention to benefit the ruling FLN and RND. Its leader, Bouguerra Soltani, contended that the results were 'illogical, unreasonable and unacceptable' and signalled 'a return to single-party rule'. Moreover, the newly elected deputies from the AAV and other smaller Islamist parties withdrew from the inaugural session of the newly elected legislature on 26 May to denounce what they claimed were fraudulent elections.

It is evident that a number of combined considerations made it possible for the FLN to achieve such electoral success in terms of parliamentary representation. Many people of the old generation interpreted President Bouteflika's appeals for a high voter turn-out on two symbolic dates (24 February and 8 May 2012) as an urge to vote for the FLN. Also several parties, notably the newly established ones, were unable to obtain the 5% of the votes cast to be eligible for a proportional distribution of seats, a factor that clearly benefited long-established parties, principally the FLN. Those who voted for the FLN opted for continuity rather than change, which, in their view, would be tantamount to a risky undertaking in times of uncertainty in the Arab region.

Even though the election results consolidated the power of the existing regime, the international reaction to them was, on the whole, positive: the international election monitors all maintained that the polls were 'free and transparent', while the USA, France and other Western countries praised the conduct of the elections as a step towards democratic reform. In early September 2012, after nearly four months of delay, Bouteflika announced the appointment of a new Government, under the premiership of a long-standing ally, Abdelmalek Sellal (hitherto Minister of Water Resources). Overall, however, it appeared that the elections and their results had only served to maintain the status quo and ensure the regime's survival, while giving the impression that things were changing. Furthermore, on 27 April 2013 Bouteflika suffered a stroke, and was transferred for treatment to the Val de Grace military hospital in France. With his health still causing concern after his return to Algiers, some opposition parties and politicians called for Article 88 of the Constitution to be invoked; the article states that when the President is incapacitated, power is temporarily transferred to the President of the Council of the Nation. The issue of succession continued to be the subject of much speculation, following a reorganization of the Council of Ministers in mid-September. Notably, the chief of staff of the armed forces, Lt-Gen. Ahmed Gaid Salah, was appointed to the Government as Vice-Minister of National Defence, effectively taking charge of that ministry, which was nominally headed by Bouteflika. Many of the most senior portfolios were reallocated: Tayeb Belaïz replaced Kablia as Minister of State and Minister of the Interior and Local Authorities, Ramtane Lamamra took Medelci's place as Minister of Foreign Affairs and Tayeb Louh became Minister of Justice and Attorney-General.

MORE CORRUPTION SCANDALS

Recent years have been marked by a succession of corruption scandals. The most recent again involved the state hydrocarbons company and was therefore referred to as 'Sonatrach 2'. The case came to light in January 2013 when Italian prosecutors announced an investigation into the Italian oil and gas company Eni and its subsidiary Saipem. It was reported that, in order to win lucrative contracts in Algeria, Saipem may have paid large bribes to Sonatrach executives and intermediaries. Indeed, Saipem had secured seven contracts in Algeria, with a total value of €8,000m., during 2007–10. In return, the prosecutors alleged, Saipem had paid a total of US $197m. to Pearl Partners Ltd, a company based in Hong Kong, and owned by Farid Bedjaoui, the nephew of Muhammad Bedjaoui (Algeria's Minister of Foreign Affairs in 2005–07), and Chakib Khelil (Algeria's Minister of Energy and Mining in 1999–2010).

The state news agency Algérie Presse Service reported on 3 July 2013 that, while attending a recent parliamentary session, the Minister of Justice and Attorney-General, Muhammad Charfi, declared that the investigation had revealed the existence of a 'truly international corruption network whose ramifications extend to all continents'. It is worth pointing out that the Italian justice authorities were first to issue an international arrest warrant against Farid Bedjaoui in July. The Italian authorities are attempting to recover US $123m., believed to be held in accounts in Singapore and Hong Kong, and belonging to Bedjaoui. On 12 August the Algerian authorities followed suit in issuing international arrest warrants against nine people, including Khelil, his wife and their two sons, Khelil's nephew, Muhammad Réda Hemche, and Bedjaoui.

In mid-2013 the Algerian authorities were also reported to be investigating another case, this time involving Canada's SNC-Lavalin Group. Its offices in Algiers were raided by the police in May 2013 in connection with 'allegations of bribery and kickbacks involving public officials and agents hired by SNC-Lavalin to procure a number of large infrastructure projects'. The Canadian company is believed to have won an estimated US $6,000m. worth of contracts in Algeria, the most recent of which was a $1,200m. deal in 2009 to design and build a natural gas processing plant in the Sahara. However, Algerian media have reported that the police investigation was related to a contract the Canadian company won in 2005 to build the Hadjret Ennous power plant near Algiers.

Further allegations concerned two other power plants built for Sonelgaz—the state-owned electricity and gas firm—by Alstom/Orascom and General Electric/Iberdrola groups. Indeed, in mid-June, some local newspapers reported that the CEO of Sonelgaz, Noureddine Bouterfa, his predecessor, Abdelkrim Boughanem, and several other senior executives were under formal investigation. The conditions under which the contracts were awarded were the subject of the allegations. The construction of the Terga (Ain Témouchent) and Koudiet Edraouech (El Tarf) power plants was estimated to have cost a total of some US $5,500m.; a cost which was not only excessive when compared to $3,400m. which Sonelgaz had set as the maximum amount, but three times higher than the cost of Hadjret Ennous power plant built by SNC-Lavalin. In reaction to the media reports, Sonelgaz defended the decisions, but stressed that the final decision came from the Ministry of Energy and Mining.

THE HOSTAGE CRISIS OF IN AMENAS

The armed attack on In Amenas gas plant—located about 1,300 km south-east of Algiers—in January 2013 was the most serious security challenge to have faced the Algerian authorities in recent years. On 16 January a militant Islamist group, believed to be affiliated to AQIM, perpetrated an attack on the Tiguentourine gas plant—owned and operated by Sonatrach, BP and Norway's Statoil. The militant group, calling itself the 'Signed in Blood Battalion', was led by Mokhtar Belmokhtar, who was believed to be a founder member of AQIM.

Hundreds of workers, including both Algerians and foreign nationals, were taken hostage. Reports gave no single explanation for the attack, which occurred days after the French military intervention in neighbouring Mali. In this respect, some reports quoted Belmokhtar as claiming to have 'carried out the assault on In Amenas to punish the West for intervening in Mali'. The British Secretary of State for Foreign and Commonwealth Affairs, William Hague, however, expressed doubts about such a claim, citing the complexity of the attack and high degree of planning involved. Other reports indicated that the assailants' demands were concerned with the release of fellow militants held in gaols in both Algeria and the USA.

Speaking on state television, the Minister of the Interior and Local Authorities, Dahou Ould Kablia, insisted that the Algerian authorities would not negotiate or respond to the militants' demands. Even though many of the Algerian workers were released in small groups, the militants continued to hold a significant number of hostages. Several countries—particularly France, Japan, Norway, the United Kingdom and USA—whose nationals were detained offered to provide technical and military assistance, while urging the Algerian Government to resolve the crisis peacefully. However, the Algerian Government continued to refuse any assistance, a stance that stemmed from Algeria's fierce protection of its national sovereignty and wariness over outside interference in its domestic affairs.

The following day the Algerian authorities launched an assault on the site, claiming that the hostage-takers were not only planning to leave the country with their hostages, but also intended to destroy the gas facility. During the security forces' rescue operation, 38 foreign hostages and one Algerian were killed. Official reports also stated that 29 militants had been killed and three captured alive.

Prime Minister Sellal hailed the rescue operation as a success. Yet, some countries, including Japan and the United Kingdom, expressed frustration with the approach adopted by the Algerian Government and its perceived lack of co-operation with those countries whose citizens were represented among the hostages.

EXTERNAL RELATIONS AFTER THE 1992 COUP

Following the army's cancellation of the second round of parliamentary elections in January 1992, Western governments were reluctant to be seen to offer political support to the new military-backed regime. Nevertheless, in view of the potential consequences of an Islamist victory in Algeria—EU member states in particular were afraid of a massive influx of Algerian immigrants—discreet contacts were maintained and the junta was provided with urgently needed financial assistance by Western governments and by international agencies such as the IMF. However, relations were frequently strained, and Algerian officials repeatedly criticized Western governments for granting Algerian Islamists political asylum and allowing Islamist groups in their countries to raise funds to support terrorist activities in Algeria. The GIA in particular developed extensive support networks in several European countries to raise money and purchase weapons. France, the former colonial power, quickly became Algeria's leading supporter in the West, lending political and economic support to the military regime, although persistent reports of French military assistance were strongly denied by French officials. After the hijacking of a French airliner by GIA militants in December 1994, the GIA issued a statement declaring war on France because of its 'support to the oppressive regime, in addition to its military presence in Algeria'. During July–October 1995 the GIA launched a series of bomb attacks in France, in which seven people were killed and 160 wounded, with the aim of persuading the French Government to withdraw its support for the junta and thus hasten its collapse, but the plan had the opposite effect. The French authorities increased their support for the military-backed regime and quickly moved to dismantle FIS and GIA cells and support networks across France and elsewhere in Europe.

France remained Algeria's chief interlocutor with the EU. In December 1996 the EU had agreed to begin talks on the admission of Algeria to the Euro-Mediterranean free trade zone, although Algerian and EU officials admitted that they expected the negotiations to be difficult. In January 1998 the EU presidency expressed grave concern at the dramatic increase in violence in Algeria and later that month sent a delegation of ministers from the United Kingdom, Luxembourg and Austria to Algiers. Yet despite growing unease in Europe at the escalating violence, and concerns that the Algerian authorities might have been involved in the bloodshed, the EU appeared reluctant to antagonize the Algerian regime and risk jeopardizing member states' substantial economic interests there.

There was speculation in 1994 that the USA was adjusting its policy towards Algeria and that, in order to avoid the mistakes made in the case of Iran, it was preparing for a possible Islamist regime to assume power there in the future. In June US President Bill Clinton confirmed that there had been low-level contacts between US officials and the FIS in the USA and Germany, and stated that his Administration was not opposed to some form of power-sharing between the Zéroual regime and 'dissident groups who are not involved in terrorism'. In March 1996 US Assistant Secretary of State Robert Pelletreau visited Algiers and reaffirmed his country's support for Zéroual's policy of dialogue. It was also reported that the US Department of State had ended contacts with FIS spokesman Anwar Haddam, and in December 1996 Haddam was taken into custody by US immigration officials pending his deportation.

Algeria's North African neighbours, particularly Tunisia, did not disguise their relief that a possible Islamist take-over had been averted by the military's intervention in 1992. Nevertheless, relations with Morocco remained strained owing to Algeria's continued support for the Polisario Front, while each country accused the other of sponsoring terrorism to destabilize its neighbour. Elsewhere in the Middle East, those Arab states that had their own problems, or perceived problems, with militant Islamists generally welcomed the new regime in Algiers. Iran, however, which had previously warned that force should not be used against the FIS, declared the postponement of the second round of voting to be illegal. Algeria accused Iran of interfering in its internal affairs and severed relations completely in March 1993.

FOREIGN RELATIONS DURING BOUTEFLIKA'S FIRST TERM

In July 1999, less than three months after Bouteflika assumed the presidency, Algeria hosted a summit meeting of the Organization of African Unity (OAU, now African Union—AU) in Algiers, which was attended by representatives of 43 of the 53 member states and was widely regarded as a success. Algeria assumed the presidency of the organization for the next year, and in the following months Algerian envoys were dispatched on peace initiatives to various parts of Africa where conflicts remained unresolved. In May 2000 President Bouteflika, in his capacity as Chairman of the OAU Assembly of Heads of State, visited the Horn of Africa to mediate in the war between Ethiopia and Eritrea. Representatives of both countries subsequently attended peace talks in Algiers, and a peace agreement was eventually signed there in December.

During the 1999 election campaign Bouteflika pledged to restore Algeria to its role as a leading regional power. However, on assuming the presidency he adopted a more conciliatory stance towards Algeria's Maghreb neighbours, especially Morocco. Bouteflika responded positively to King Hassan's message of congratulation on his election victory, and following the King's death in July the Algerian President held talks with his successor, Muhammad VI, in the Moroccan capital, Rabat, after attending Hassan's funeral. However, despite an undertaking to work towards a further improvement in bilateral relations, this co-operation proved short-lived. In August, following the GIA's massacre of 29 civilians in the Béchar region near the Moroccan border, Bouteflika accused Morocco of providing sanctuary for those responsible for the attack and also extended accusations to drugs-trafficking and arms-dealing on the joint border. Renewed tensions prevented the long-awaited reopening of the land border between the two countries, scheduled for late August.

However, it was the Western Sahara issue that remained the main obstacle to improved relations. While Algeria continued to support a solution to the conflict by means of the proposed UN referendum on self-determination, many Moroccans remained convinced that Polisario was only a force to be reckoned with because of Algerian backing. Indeed, in an interview, King Muhammad later asserted that the Western Sahara dispute was of Algeria's creation. Algeria and Polisario rejected autonomy proposals for Western Sahara put forward by the UN Security Council in June 2001.

In February 2002, following a report to the Security Council by the UN Secretary-General, Kofi Annan, in which he stated that partition was one option in the Western Sahara issue, relations between Algeria and Morocco deteriorated further. Morocco categorically rejected the proposal, claiming that it was an Algerian plan designed to create a Sahrawi 'mini-state' under Algerian protection, thus providing Algeria with an outlet to the Atlantic Ocean. Algeria's representative at the UN denied that he had formulated the proposal, but there was speculation that it had been a personal initiative of President Bouteflika. On 27 February Bouteflika became the first Algerian President to visit the Sahrawi refugee camps around Tindouf in south-western Algeria. The visit, on the 26th anniversary of the establishment of the SADR, was described by Morocco as 'provocative'. Algeria subsequently supported the revised peace plan put forward by the UN Secretary-General's Personal Envoy for Western Sahara, James Baker (and consequently referred to as the Baker Plan), and persuaded Polisario to accept it. However, Morocco rejected the new proposals. Although the revised plan, providing for immediate self-government for the territory for a period of four to five years followed by a referendum on self-determination, was adopted by the UN Security Council in July 2003, the resolution refrained from imposing the plan on the parties concerned and merely called on them to work constructively towards acceptance and implementation of Baker's proposals. In December the US Secretary of State, Colin Powell, on a visit to Algiers, stated that the USA was encouraging negotiations between Morocco and Algeria, although Bouteflika stated that while Algeria was willing to contribute to solving the issue through its continued contacts with Morocco and Polisario, the problem should be settled within the framework of a referendum on self-determination for the Sahrawi people as set out in UN resolutions.

Despite much rhetoric about reviving the virtually moribund UMA, little progress was made—largely because of continuing tensions between Algeria and Morocco. Bouteflika regarded a revived UMA as essential because it would enable the Maghreb states to bargain collectively with the EU, thus strengthening their hand. However, a UMA summit meeting scheduled for the end of 1999 was cancelled. The Moroccan Minister of Foreign Affairs, Muhammad Benaïssa, did attend a meeting of UMA ministers responsible for foreign affairs in Algiers in January 2002, although on the sensitive issue of Western Sahara Benaïssa made it clear that there was no question of Morocco sacrificing its 'national cause for the sake of building a Greater Maghreb'. A summit meeting of UMA heads of state, scheduled to take place in Algiers in June, was postponed indefinitely after King Muhammad of Morocco announced his refusal to attend, and another attempt to hold a UMA heads of state summit meeting in Algiers in December 2003 was cancelled when King Muhammad again indicated that he would not attend.

President Zine al-Abidine Ben Ali of Tunisia made an official visit to Algiers in February 2002 to discuss bilateral relations and measures to revive the UMA. In April and November 2001 Lt-Gen. Muhammad Lamari, Algeria's Chief of Staff, had held talks in Tunis with Ben Ali and his military and security officials on issues regarding the campaign against Islamist militants, improving border surveillance—notably to prevent Algerian and Tunisian members of al-Qa'ida from returning to their country of origin—and dismantling North African Islamist cells in Europe. It was reported that numerous alleged Islamist activists from Tunisia, who had taken refuge in Algeria and joined local GIA groups, had been arrested by the Algerian authorities and handed over to the Tunisian security forces.

Algeria's negotiations with the EU over admission to the Euro-Mediterranean free trade zone resumed after the 1999 presidential election. Further discussions made substantial progress and in December 2001 President Bouteflika signed an association agreement between Algeria and the EU in Brussels, Belgium; a formal signing took place in April 2002. Bouteflika became the first Algerian Head of State to visit the North Atlantic Treaty Organization (NATO) headquarters in December 2001, where he promised to maintain closer relations with NATO 'for the sake of regional stability'. Algeria was to negotiate an accord with NATO for the secure exchange of military information. Among a senior-level EU delegation that visited Algiers in June 2002 was the Spanish Minister of Foreign Affairs, who stated that discussions had been very useful and that Algeria had recorded a clear improvement in the sphere of human rights. However, in an open letter to the EU, Amnesty International stated that there was no sign of improvement in Algeria's human rights situation and criticized the EU for failing to impose changes on the Algerian authorities.

Tensions that had developed between Algeria and France following the 1999 presidential election soon eased. (In response to allegations of massive fraud, the French authorities had expressed concern and regretted that the electoral process was not as transparent and pluralist as promised. For his part, President-elect Bouteflika had accused France of regarding his country as a 'protectorate', asserting that it should abandon its 'fixation' with Algeria.) French Minister of the Interior Jean-Pierre Chevènement and Minister of Foreign Affairs Hubert Védrine visited Algiers in June and July 1999, respectively. In September Bouteflika met President Chirac at the UN in New York (the first meeting between the leaders of the two countries since 1992). To mark the improvement in bilateral relations, France agreed substantially to increase the number of visas issued to Algerians wishing to visit France. A delegation from the French Senate visited Algeria in December, and in January 2000 Algeria's new Minister of Foreign Affairs, Youcef Yousfi, became the first member of an Algerian government to make an official visit to France for six years when, acting as Bouteflika's special envoy, he held talks with Prime Minister Lionel Jospin in Paris. France subsequently initiated discussions on bilateral military co-operation. Bouteflika made a full state visit to Paris in June—the first of its kind by an Algerian President—during which he was received with full ceremony, including a personal welcome by Chirac at the airport and an invitation to address the French National Assembly. None the less, sections of the French press published unflattering assessments of Bouteflika's presidency and highlighted criticism of his country's human rights record. The visit produced few tangible results, but was interpreted in Algiers as an important step towards ending the diplomatic isolation imposed on Algeria after the 1992 military take-over.

In May 2001, in response to the rioting in Kabylia, Védrine told the French National Assembly that France could not remain silent about the violent repression by the Algerian authorities of demonstrations at which many young people had been killed, and called for 'political dialogue'. His Algerian counterpart, Abdelaziz Belkhadem, described the remarks as 'unacceptable'. In mid-June the Algerian embassy in Paris urged the French media to respect 'truth and objectivity' in the reporting on events in Kabylia and in Algeria in general, emphasizing that as millions of Algerians listened to broadcasts from France, this gave the French media a 'considerable responsibility'. Two days later thousands of people demonstrated in Paris to express their anger at the conduct of the Algerian regime, and there were calls for an end to the military junta and the departure of President Bouteflika. Shortly afterwards, during a speech at Illizi in southern Algeria, Bouteflika—without explicitly naming France—blamed the former colonial power for the violence in Kabylia. Since the outbreak of rioting in that region in April Bouteflika had repeatedly claimed the existence of a plot or conspiracy in part directed from abroad to exploit Kabyle separatism. However, Bouteflika stated subsequently that the accusations of French involvement in the rioting were not directed at the French people or the French Government but at 'secret business circles' and their networks in Algeria.

There was a marked improvement in relations between France and Algeria following the suicide attacks on the USA in September 2001. Védrine visited Algiers in October, as part of a tour of the Maghreb to discuss co-operation in the fight against terrorism. Both Algeria and France agreed that, in response to the attacks on New York and Washington, DC, the USA and its allies were justified in taking reprisals. Védrine's Algerian counterpart supported a strengthening of co-operation with France against terrorism in all areas, notably the dismantling of transnational networks, the freezing of their sources of finance and the exchange of information on the prevention of terrorist crimes. In December 2001 Jacques Chirac (the first French President to visit Algeria since 1989) made a rapid tour of Maghreb capitals to discuss the US-led military campaign against al-Qa'ida and the Taliban regime in Afghanistan, and the international repercussions of the so-called 'war on terror'. President Chirac stated that the French and Algerian authorities were in full agreement on the need to eradicate international terrorism, including al-Qa'ida, and both rejected the notion of a 'clash of civilizations', which the French President described as 'absurd, dangerous and unfounded', as well as any attempt to equate Islam with terrorism. In February 2002 AirLib inaugurated a twice-daily service from Paris to Algiers, the first time that a French airline had made scheduled flights to Algeria since the hijacking of an Air France Airbus by the GIA in December 1994. Meanwhile, during 2001 a number of Algerians and French nationals of Algerian origin were arrested during a crackdown on Islamist networks operating in France and suspected of having links with al-Qa'ida.

Algerians reacted with horror and disbelief when the extreme right-wing National Front leader, Jean-Marie Le Pen, came second to the incumbent Jacques Chirac at the first round of the French presidential election in April 2002 (thus proceeding to the second round). For four decades Le Pen's name had been associated with bitter memories of the Algerian war of independence, and his views on immigration aroused particular fears for the future of Algerians and their families living in France. Chirac's victory in the second round of the presidential election and the success of the centre-right in legislative elections in June were welcomed in most political and media circles in Algeria.

In March 2003 Chirac made a full state visit to Algeria, the first at this level by a French President since Algerian independence in 1963. Between 500,000 and 1m. Algerians turned out to welcome him, many demanding visas to visit France. In his address to the Algerian National People's Assembly Chirac invited the French and the Algerians to respect all the victims of the Algerian war, the fighters for independence and those who chose exile, in particular referring to the 'pieds-noirs' and the 'harkis'. During the visit the two Presidents signed the Declaration of Algiers, which was to initiate an 'exceptional partnership' between the two countries and strengthen co-operation in all areas. The partnership would lead to a treaty of friendship similar to that which existed between France and Germany. Sections of the Algerian press claimed that Bouteflika was using Chirac's visit to strengthen his own position in order to secure a second presidential mandate by demonstrating to the military *décideurs* that he had the support of France. In June 2003 Air France resumed flights to Algeria, which had been suspended since December 1994.

Meanwhile, Germany reopened its visa and consular divisions in Algeria, and Denmark announced that from February 2000 its new embassy in Algiers would become the regional base for diplomatic services covering Morocco, Libya, Tunisia and Mauritania. A British Minister of the Foreign and Commonwealth Office visited Algiers in October 2001 to discuss security and co-operation in the fight against terrorism, and in February 2002 Ahmed Ouyahia, Algeria's Minister of Justice, made an official visit to London. For some years Algeria had criticized the British Government for granting refuge to its Islamist opponents. At least 20 Algerians condemned to death for acts of terrorism were living in the United Kingdom.

In August 2002 the Berlin, Germany, correspondent of the Qatar-based satellite broadcaster Al Jazeera claimed that the FIS had recently held a secret congress in Belgium at which delegates from across the world had participated either directly or via the internet in discussions to elect a new executive and determine the party's future strategy. While the Belgian Minister of Foreign Affairs expressed his disquiet at the revelations, the Minister of the Interior stated that he was not particularly concerned. The Director of the Minister's Office told a local newspaper that Belgium adopted a pragmatic attitude to the FIS, which according to him had renounced violence. These views were strongly opposed by some political parties, and one senator called for an inquiry into the country's intelligence services. In October Mourad Dhina, who had been living in exile in Geneva since 1995, announced that he had been elected as interim head of the FIS executive in place of Abbassi Madani and Ali Belhadj. Algeria's ambassador to the UN delivered a protest to his Swiss counterpart stating that Dhina had been tried *in absentia* in Algeria in 1997 on criminal charges and sentenced to 20 years in prison, and that Algeria had requested his extradition from Switzerland in December 2001. Dhina, considered to be a hardliner, claimed that the FIS only supported armed groups that did not attack civilians. His request for political asylum had been rejected by the Swiss authorities in 1996, but officially his presence had been tolerated.

In October 2002 President Bouteflika made an official visit to Spain, where he signed an agreement on increased co-operation in the struggle against terrorism. The Spanish authorities stated that, in contrast to other countries in the region, co-operation with Algeria on the sensitive issue of immigration was very satisfactory. As Spanish–Moroccan relations deteriorated sharply during the year, relations between Algeria and Spain became more cordial and in January 2003 a Spanish delegation, including members of parliament and organizations supporting the Sahrawi people, visited Algiers for talks at the National People's Assembly on the Western Sahara conflict. In November the Spanish Prime Minister, José María Aznar, visited Algiers and agreed to convert US $50m.–$100m. of Algerian debt into shares in local small industries and the fishing industry.

In January 2000 two Algerians, suspected of having links with the GIA and with Osama bin Laden, were arrested in the USA and charged with conspiring to carry out a bomb attack. In December 1999 another Algerian national had been arrested while attempting to cross the US–Canadian border carrying bomb-making equipment. The US authorities believed that the two incidents were linked to a bomb plot involving bin Laden and other Islamist extremists. In February 2000 US Secretary of Defense William Cohen announced that the USA intended to expand military co-operation with Algeria. President Bouteflika made an official visit to the USA in July 2001 (the first by an Algerian Head of State for more than a decade), accompanied by several government ministers. Talks between Bouteflika and the new US President, George W. Bush, were described as 'very positive'. There were also reports of increased intelligence co-operation between Algeria and the USA, with Algerian military intelligence providing information to US officials regarding Algerian citizens who were suspected of belonging to al-Qa'ida.

President Bouteflika condemned in the strongest terms the suicide attacks on New York and Washington, DC, of 11 September 2001, and sent a message of condolence to President Bush. Shortly after the attacks the two radical Algerian Islamist groups, the GIA and the GSPC, both of which were alleged to have close links with al-Qa'ida, appeared on an official US list of terrorist organizations whose assets were to be frozen. Algeria voiced support for the US-led international 'coalition against terror', without participating in military operations. However, the US-led bombing of Afghanistan was condemned by several political parties in Algeria, notably the FLN, while a senior member of the proscribed FIS declared that all Arab and Muslim allies of the USA were traitors to their religion, people and nation. Algeria's Muslim leaders recalled that it was forbidden for a Muslim state to support or assist in an attack against another Muslim state, but, in contrast to the 1991 Gulf War, there were no street protests against the US-led military action in Afghanistan or in support of bin Laden and his allies.

President Bouteflika made a second official visit to Washington, DC, in November 2001, where he reiterated his support for the US-led military campaign in Afghanistan. The Algerian authorities declared that they felt less isolated after the 11 September attacks, and considered that there was now greater understanding in the West of their own 'struggle' against terrorism. This growing rapprochement with the West, notably the USA, apparently exemplified Algeria's successful emergence from a decade of diplomatic isolation after the military take-over in 1992. Co-operation between the Algerian security services and the US Federal Bureau of Investigation (FBI) in tracking down terrorists of Algerian origin based in Europe continued. The USA declared that the Algerian parliamentary elections held in May 2002 were evidence of the 'development of democracy'.

In December 2002 the USA announced that it would lift its ban on arms sales to Algeria and that it had agreed to supply military equipment for use in the anti-terrorism campaign. The US Under-Secretary of State for Commerce, who visited Algiers in October, had indicated the USA's interest in Algeria's hydrocarbon sector and hinted that its opening up to foreign capital could lead to further co-operation in military technology and defence. His strong support for controversial new legislation on hydrocarbons currently under discussion in Algeria angered Bouteflika's critics, who stated that they were determined to prevent the President from handing over control of the country's petroleum and gas to his 'American friends'. In January 2003 the leadership of the two Islamist parties, the MRN and the MSP, condemned US threats to attack Iraq and organized protest meetings and demonstrations denouncing the preparations for war 'against the Iraqi people'. There were violent incidents during an MSP march in Algiers in February, and in March security forces prevented demonstrators from marching to the National People's Assembly. Pro-Iraqi demonstrations continued during the US-led military action in Iraq, although the authorities continued to prohibit marches in the capital and remained largely silent on the issue of Iraq.

In December 2003 US Secretary of State Colin Powell made his first visit to Algiers as part of a brief tour of the Maghreb states. During his visit Powell stated that the USA's relationship with Algeria had never been stronger, as a result of exceptional co-operation in the 'war on terror' and the expanding economic links between the two countries. However, on a visit to the Algerian capital in January 2004 the US Assistant Secretary of State for Democracy, Human Rights and Labour expressed concern at government actions against certain independent newspapers.

President Bouteflika visited Moscow, Russia, in April 2001, and in June, after his return from a visit to Algiers, the Russian vice-premier, Ilya Klebanov, announced the beginning of a 10-year programme of military and technical co-operation. In December Algeria took delivery of a number of new Russian military aircraft, under the first part of a major military contract with Russia to modernize and upgrade the country's ageing air force. Visiting Moscow in April 2002, Algeria's Chief of Staff, Lt-Gen. Muhammad Lamari, signed a new agreement on arms purchases.

Diplomatic relations with Iran were restored in January 2001 after a meeting between Bouteflika and President Muhammad Khatami at the UN Millennium Summit in New York, USA, in September 2000. In October 2002, during a visit to the Iranian capital, Tehran, Lamari met the Iranian Minister of Defence and Logistics and signed a declaration of military co-operation under which the two countries would exchange military knowledge and expertise. In October 2003 Bouteflika visited Iran—the first visit by an Algerian head of state for 20 years. He held talks with Khatami and the Supreme Religious Leader, Ayatollah Sayed Ali Khamenei, and several co-operation agreements were signed. Sections of the independent press in Algeria strongly criticized the visit. They claimed that during the 1990s the Iranian embassy in Algiers had become a 'marketing bureau' for political Islamism and pointed to alleged links between the Iranian authorities and radical Algerian Islamism.

At the invitation of the Lebanese President, Bouteflika attended the ninth Francophone summit in Beirut in October 2002, the first time that an Algerian Head of State had participated. Since independence Algeria had deliberately avoided any participation in 'La Francophonie'. Bouteflika did not announce that Algeria would join the Organisation internationale de la francophonie, but he emphasized that French, which had been the language of colonialism, must now become the language of emancipation and progress in Africa. As language remains a sensitive issue in Algeria, some sections of the local press strongly criticized Bouteflika for breaking with tradition and attending the summit.

FOREIGN POLICY DURING BOUTEFLIKA'S SECOND TERM

At his inauguration ceremony in April 2004 Bouteflika stated that the struggle against Islamist extremists in Algeria would continue within the framework of the international 'war on terror'. He also emphasized the importance of promoting the UMA and stated that his Government would also seek to strengthen co-operation with members of the AU to seek to eliminate poverty and end the ongoing civil wars in Africa. There were also references to offering support to the Palestinians.

Relations with France continued to strengthen in 2004. President Chirac made a brief visit to Algiers in April to congratulate Bouteflika on his 'brilliant re-election', and was followed by a procession of senior ministers, including in July Michèle Alliot-Marie, the French Minister of Defence, who spoke of establishing an extensive partnership in the area of military co-operation. In October 2004 sources close to Chirac stated that the President gave high priority to Franco-Algerian rapprochement and hoped that a strong Franco-Algerian axis could serve as the driving force in relations with the Maghreb and Arab-Muslim world. However, some observers interpreted France's renewed interest in Algeria as a sign of growing competition between France and the USA for influence in the Maghreb. Relations with France deteriorated sharply after the French National Assembly passed a law in February 2005 that included an article emphasizing the positive role of the French presence in Algeria. Bouteflika subsequently denounced the law as an act of 'mental blindness' and even compared the actions of the French colonial authorities with those of the Nazis. As a result of the dispute, the treaty of friendship between the two countries, which was scheduled to have been signed by the end of the year, remained blocked. In early May 2006 Lt.-Gen. Ahmed Gaid Salah became the first Algerian Chief of Staff to make an official visit to France. He discussed bilateral military co-operation with his French counterpart and met with Alliot-Marie. Later in May Bouteflika stated publicly that France must offer an official apology to the Algerian people for the years of French colonialism before negotiations over the treaty of friendship could proceed. In mid-November the French Minister of the Interior and Land Management, Nicolas Sarkozy, met Bouteflika for talks in Algiers but refused to apologize to the Algerian people on behalf of France, commenting to Prime Minister Abdelaziz Belkhadem that 'you can't ask sons to say sorry for their fathers' mistakes'. By late 2006 discussions regarding the treaty of friendship appeared to have reached an impasse. Following his election to the French presidency in May 2007, Sarkozy visited Algeria and Tunisia in July, apparently to demonstrate the intention of his administration to forge even closer ties with the countries of the Maghreb (see below). President Sarkozy undertook a further visit to Algiers in December, during which his failure to offer an explicit apology on behalf of the French nation for the era of colonial rule again angered some Algerian officials. Nevertheless, Sarkozy did acknowledge that France's colonization of Algeria had been 'profoundly unfair', and the two countries signed several important bilateral agreements in the fields of petroleum, gas and nuclear energy. At the end of a two-day visit by the French Prime Minister, François Fillon, to Algiers in June 2008, a further agreement was signed between the two countries concerning civil nuclear co-operation, as well as a military co-operation accord and memorandum of understanding (MOU) on bilateral financial matters. However, the economic agreements signed with France did not modify Algeria's position regarding the supposedly beneficial impact of French colonialism and on 8 May 2009, during the commemoration ceremony for the victims of the 1945 Sétif massacre, Bouteflika once again stated that glorifying colonialism did not render justice for the suffering of Algeria, although he recognized that the entire people of France should not bear the responsibility and guilt of the colonial enterprise. These more conciliatory remarks were widely regarded as a prelude to an official state visit to France scheduled for late 2009. Speaking after a meeting with the President of the Foreign Affairs Committee of the French National Assembly, Axel Poniatowski, the Algerian Minister of Foreign Affairs, Medelci, indicated that the discussions between Sarkozy and Bouteflika would mainly focus on the Algerian community in France, the movement of people between the two countries and French investment in Algeria.

In May 2005 the newly appointed Spanish Minister of Foreign Affairs and Co-operation, Miguel Angel Moratinos, visited the Algerian capital for talks on bilateral relations. However, a visit to Algiers by the new Spanish premier, José Luis Rodríguez Zapatero, in July revealed differences over the question of Western Sahara; the Algerian press accused Spain's new Socialist Government of a shift in policy so that it was now aligned with France in supporting Morocco's stance on the disputed territory. However, these political differences did not negatively influence economic co-operation, as the two ministers jointly announced that construction work on the MEDGAZ pipeline between Algeria and Spain, which was to transport Algerian gas to southern Europe, had been completed. The pipeline became operational in March 2011.

In October 2004 the German Federal Chancellor, Gerhard Schröder, visited Algiers and stated that Germany wanted to support Algeria on the path towards democracy and a market economy. During a visit to Algeria by the Portuguese Prime Minister, Pedro Santana Lopes, in January 2005, a treaty of friendship and co-operation was signed between the two countries, providing for an annual summit between their leaders and regular consultations between their ministers of foreign affairs. Co-operation was to cover economic, political, military, cultural and scientific matters. Meanwhile, Algeria's association agreement with the EU, having been ratified by the National People's Assembly in March and the requisite EU member states by April, came into effect in September.

In February 2006 the British Secretary of State for Foreign and Commonwealth Affairs, Jack Straw, visited Algiers for talks with President Bouteflika and senior ministers. Straw stated that much progress had been made in negotiations for an MOU to allow the British Home Office to deport Algerian nationals held on suspicion of involvement in terrorist activities, and that he hoped it would be concluded as quickly as possible. However, in March Zerhouni criticized the United Kingdom for refusing to hand over the head of the Khalifa Group, Abdelmoumen Rafik Khalifa, who was subject to an international arrest warrant, while it sought to deport Algerian nationals and insisted on checking whether they were being tortured by the Algerian authorities. (The trial of more than 100 officials of the Khalifa Group ended in March 2007, with Khalifa himself being sentenced *in absentia* to life imprisonment, having been convicted of fraud, corruption, theft and forgery, and at least 50 other defendants receiving prison terms of between 18 months and 15 years.) The memorandum on extradition was signed in early June during a visit to Algiers by the British Minister of State for the Middle East, Dr Kim Howells. Later that month two Algerian terror suspects were deported to Algeria, and a further five reportedly agreed to be extradited in January 2007. Bouteflika made an official visit to the United Kingdom in July 2006, during which a formal agreement was concluded to form a joint commission to diversify and strengthen bilateral relations. Meeting in Oran in November 2004, ministers responsible for foreign affairs of the so-called '5+5' states (the five UMA countries and Portugal, Spain, Italy, France and Malta) expressed their desire to relaunch the Euro-Mediterranean partnership programme.

In May 2006 Maj.-Gen. Gaid visited NATO headquarters in Brussels to participate in a meeting of the Chiefs of Staff of NATO countries and their counterparts in the Mediterranean dialogue. The following year the issue of Euro-Mediterranean co-operation once more became the focus of discussion when Nicolas Sarkozy proposed the idea of a Mediterranean Union as part of his election campaign for the French presidency. Envisaged as an international body capable of fostering economic, political and cultural links between Mediterranean states, the initiative was described by Sarkozy as building upon the Barcelona Process launched by Euro-Mediterranean foreign ministers in November 1995. By the beginning of 2008 the project had been modified to encompass not just those nations bordering the Mediterranean Sea, but all EU member states, and had been renamed the Union for the Mediterranean. Several Arab states, including Algeria, expressed reservations about the project—namely that it would undermine the work of the Arab League and represent something of a return to colonial rule. In an effort to allay such concerns, the French Minister of Foreign and European Affairs, Bernard Kouchner, visited Algeria for discussions with President Bouteflika in mid-May 2008. However, Algeria reportedly remained sceptical about the economic sapience of the union and the danger of it becoming enmeshed in the Israeli–Palestinian conflict. None the less, when the Union for the Mediterranean was officially inaugurated at a summit meeting in Paris on 13 July 2008, Bouteflika was among the many heads of state of the 43 EU and Mediterranean member nations to be in attendance (with the notable exception of the Libyan leader, Muammar al-Qaddafi, who remained staunchly opposed to the project). The initial difficulties of the Union for the Mediterranean were compounded by the reactions of some of its member countries to the conflict in the Gaza Strip between December 2008 and January 2009. In April 2009 the Minister of Foreign Affairs, Medelci, stated that, while Algeria remained interested in developing co-operation within the Union, Israeli military actions in Gaza remained a significant obstacle to progress.

President Bush congratulated Bouteflika on his re-election in April 2004 and described the presidential election as another step on the road towards democracy. On a visit to Algiers in May, the US Assistant Secretary of State for Near Eastern Affairs, William Burns, praised the presidential election as a 'landmark democratic step' and pledged support for economic reforms through US technical assistance and membership of the World Trade Organization (WTO). Bouteflika was one of a number of Arab and African leaders invited by President Bush to take part in the Group of Eight (G8—comprising the G7 group of Western industrialized nations and Russia) meeting held in Georgia, USA, in June. It was reported in August that, following a visit to the USA by the Director-General of National Security, Ali Tounsi, an agreement had been signed for Algerian police officers to receive specialized training in the USA to help them tackle organized crime and terrorism. In October an Algerian-US Parliamentary Friendship Group was established. Bouteflika warmly welcomed President Bush's re-election in November, in sharp contrast to the reaction of the Algerian public to the US election result.

In August 2005 Senator Richard Lugar, Chairman of the US Senate Foreign Relations Committee, visited Algiers accompanied by a high-level delegation, including senior US military officers. He was in the region as President Bush's personal envoy to oversee the release of the final group of Moroccan prisoners of war held by Polisario. Lugar stated that the USA supported a rapprochement between Algeria and Morocco and a peaceful solution to the Western Sahara dispute within a UN framework that honoured the principle of self-determination. He reiterated that the USA strongly supported Algeria's application to join the WTO. In October the USA reopened its consular services for issuing temporary visas for the USA, a move described by the US ambassador as a new step in bilateral relations. Later that month a US delegation visited Algeria to discuss the case of 30 Algerians held in detention in Guantánamo Bay, Cuba, and it was reported that negotiations were planned to discuss the return of the prisoners to Algeria. In February 2006 the Director of the FBI, Robert Mueller, visited Algeria to discuss security co-operation. Shortly afterwards Donald Rumsfeld, at the head of a high-level military delegation, made his first visit to Algeria since becoming US Secretary of Defense, as part of a tour of Maghreb states. Claims in the French press that the USA had established a base near Tamanrasset in southern Algeria to combat terrorism were denied by both the USA and Algeria. In March David Welch, the Assistant Secretary of State for Near Eastern Affairs, visited Algiers for talks with Bouteflika and senior ministers, shortly after Algeria had signed a major arms deal with Russia (see below). On the question of the sale of US weapons to Algeria, Welch stated that any requests would be considered on a case-by-case basis. In April Bedjaoui made an official visit to Washington for talks with the US Secretary of State, Condoleezza Rice, and other senior officials. Shortly afterwards Maj.-Gen. Gaid became the first Algerian Chief of Staff to visit the USA, where he held talks with senior US generals on military co-operation. In September 2008 Rice made her first visit to Algeria, during which she held discussions regarding the Algerian citizens detained at the US detention camp at Guantánamo Bay, anti-terrorism co-operation and democratization, after which she emphasized the good relations between the two countries. In April 2009 the US Special Envoy to the Middle East, George Mitchell, arrived in Algiers for meetings with Medelci and President Bouteflika to discuss the Middle East peace process. The inclusion of North Africa as part of his tour of consultations with Arab leaders was warmly welcomed by Bouteflika, as Algeria sought to rebuild its reputation as a mediator in Middle East disputes.

During an official visit to Algiers by the Russian President, Vladimir Putin, in March 2006 the two countries signed a major arms agreement bringing the value of total contracts for delivery of Russian military equipment to Algeria to US $7,500m. At the same time Russia agreed to cancel debts incurred by Algeria to the former USSR during the 1960s and 1970s, which were estimated at $4,700m., or one-quarter of Algeria's total external debt. Reports indicated that Russia was to sell up to 100 of the most modern combat aircraft to Algeria, including *MiG-29* fighter planes, together with sophisticated anti-missile air defences. The new agreement was reported to have caused disquiet among Algeria's neighbours, especially Morocco and Libya, and concern in both the USA and France. Algeria also attempted to strengthen its commercial links with traditionally friendly countries, including Cuba. The President of the Cuban Council of State, Gen. Raúl Castro, visited Algeria in February 2009 and signed a number of trade agreements, including the creation of a joint facility to produce vaccines. Raúl Castro returned to Algeria for a second visit in July. Similar agreements were also signed with Brazil and the Republic of Korea (South Korea).

King Muhammad of Morocco was one of the first leaders to congratulate Bouteflika on his election victory, stating that he hoped to work with him to create a better understanding and solidarity between their two countries. In May 2004, while attending a session of the Arab Parliamentary Union in Rabat, Abdelkader Bensalah, the President of the Council of the Nation, held talks with the Moroccan Prime Minister, Driss Jettou, on promoting bilateral relations. In October 2004 relations deteriorated sharply as a new war of words erupted over Western Sahara. Algeria strongly supported the new UN Security Council Resolution (No. 1570) on Western Sahara at the end of October because it emphasized the validity of the Baker Plan as the most suitable political solution and reaffirmed the right of the Sahrawi people to self-determination Morocco responded by accusing Algeria of blocking a solution by its 'unfounded demand for the acceptance and implementation of the Baker Plan'. King Muhammad attended the Arab League summit in Algiers in March 2005—his first visit to Algeria since becoming King and the first visit by a Moroccan monarch since 1991. The Algerian Minister of State for Foreign Affairs, Abdelaziz Belkhadem, confirmed that the King and Bouteflika had held a private meeting that had helped to 'thaw' relations between the two countries, although no details were given. In April 2005 Algeria announced that it was abolishing visa requirements for Moroccans visiting the country as a gesture of 'goodwill'.

However, in May 2005 relations deteriorated again after King Muhammad announced that he would not be attending the UMA heads of state summit meeting in Tripoli, following recent comments by President Bouteflika reiterating Algeria's support for Polisario. In June a visit by Prime Minister Ouyahia to Rabat was cancelled at Morocco's request and a new war of words erupted between the two countries. By October, when the UN Secretary-General's new Personal Envoy for Western Sahara, Peter van Walsum, made his first visit to the region, he concluded that the position of the key players was 'quasi-irreconcilable'. The issue of Western Sahara continued to hinder relations between Morocco and Algeria. However, in an interview with the Algerian daily *El Khabar* in February 2009, the Moroccan Minister of Communication indicated his country's willingness to normalize relations with Algeria. For his part, Bouteflika reiterated Algeria's support for Polisario. In March 2005 Algeria hosted the Arab League summit meeting amid tight security. Bouteflika promised an 'exceptional summit'; however, only 13 heads of state of the 22 member nations attended and an impression of unity was only maintained by avoiding some of the most controversial issues. At the end of the Arab summit the ministers responsible for foreign affairs of the UMA held a meeting, but the long-awaited heads of state summit scheduled to be held in Tripoli at the end of May was cancelled after King Muhammad announced at the last minute that he would not be attending. In November, during the World Summit on the Information Society in Tunis, Bouteflika met President Ben Ali of Tunisia and Muammar al-Qaddafi, the Libyan leader, to examine ways of strengthening co-operation and solidarity between the Maghreb countries.

In July 2005 two Algerian diplomats, including the chargé d'affaires, the country's most senior envoy to Iraq, were kidnapped in Baghdad and executed by al-Qa'ida in Iraq. In its communiqué the group stated that the envoys represented a state that did not apply Islamic law (*Shari'a*) and was allied to Jews and Christians. Bouteflika condemned the executions as a 'monstrous and barbarous act'. The Algerian authorities had always expressed doubts about US policy in Iraq while co-operating closely with the US Administration in the 'war on terror'.

In May 2004 the Iranian Minister of Foreign Affairs, Kamal Kharrazi, visited Algiers at the head of a high-ranking delegation, and in October Iranian President Khatami made an official visit to Algeria at the invitation of Bouteflika, during which he addressed the National People's Assembly on the importance of 'dialogue among civilizations' and the promotion of democracy. In August 2008 Bouteflika visted Tehran at the invitation of Iran's President, Mahmoud Ahmadinejad. Leading a high-ranking economic and political delegation, Bouteflika held a series of talks with his Iranian counterpart and other senior officials on issues of regional and international co-operation. The two leaders also expressed their support for the solidarity of the Palestinian nation and denounced terrorism in all its forms.

FOREIGN POLICY DURING BOUTEFLIKA'S THIRD TERM

In his inauguration speech on 19 April 2009 President Bouteflika stated that Algeria would persist in its appeal for more balanced economic relations that favoured genuine economic, social and technological progress in the developing countries. He also reaffirmed Algeria's position in the Arab world and Africa, and reiterated its support for 'just' causes, citing in particular Western Sahara and the Palestinians.

On 25 April 2009 Minister of Foreign Affairs Medelci announced that Bouteflika had accepted an invitation by French President Sarkozy for a state visit to France. However, both countries agreed to postpone the visit, ostensibly owing to difficulties in preparing the agenda. In May Bouteflika had hinted that the question of France's repentance could be put aside, which suggested that relations might be allowed to restart on a good footing. However, other ongoing issues complicated the already tense relations between the two countries. The arrest in France in 2008 of the Algerian diplomat Muhammad Ziane Hasseni, who was accused of involvement in the assassination in 1987 of the Paris-based Algerian dissident Ali Mecili, was yet another controversial issue in Franco-Algerian relations. The diplomat, who had held the role of Head of Protocol in the Algerian Ministry of Foreign Affairs, was imprisoned for his alleged role in the killing and later put under judicial control. In February 2010, following an announcement by the French authorities that there was no evidence to charge Hasseni with the assassination, the Algerian Government expected that all charges would be dismissed. However, the magistrate hearing the case decided to designate Hasseni as an assisted witness in the investigation. In April France's Ambassador to Algeria, Xavier Driencourt, was summoned to the Ministry of Foreign Affairs to receive a formal complaint from the Algerian Government expressing Algeria's 'great surprise' and 'deep concern' about the case.

A further contentious issue related to nuclear weapons testing conducted by France in the Sahara during the 1960s. In May 2009 Medelci declared that France should not just pay compensation to those Algerians whose health was alleged to have been affected by the tests, but that it should also take measures to decontaminate the area where the tests were undertaken.

In January 2010 France announced its decision to add Algeria to a list of countries whose citizens were deemed to represent a threat to French national security; visitors arriving in France coming from Algeria were henceforth to be subject to increased security measures upon their arrival at French air and seaports. The decision prompted strong protests within Algeria. In an attempt to alleviate the crisis, in February Sarkozy dispatched the Secretary-General of the Presidency, Claude Guéant, for talks with Prime Minister Ouyahia, Medelci and other high-level officials. In June Guéant again travelled to Algeria to meet President Bouteflika, Ouyahia, and the Minister-delegate to the Minister of Foreign Affairs, in charge of Maghreb and African Affairs, Abdelkader Messahel, to review relations between the two countries.

In January 2010 President Bouteflika paid a state visit to Spain, where he co-chaired with Spanish premier Zapatero the fourth high-level Algerian-Spanish summit meeting. The ministers who accompanied Bouteflika, including Zerhouni, Medelci, Minister of Energy and Mining Chakib Khelil and Minister of Public Works Amar Ghoul, also held working sessions with their Spanish counterparts.

In October 2009 Bouteflika met the British Secretary of State for Defence, Bob Ainsworth, who was on a two-day visit to Algiers. The two delegations exchanged views on recent developments regarding the Western Sahara in advance of the second round of informal meetings held in Armonk, New York, USA, in February 2010, between representatives of Polisario and Morocco, as well as the forthcoming visit to the Maghreb region. The two countries also discussed the security situation in the Sahel region. There was convergence of views on both the analysis of the situation and the assessment of threats and dangers to regional security. The two sides underlined their confidence in the aptitude of the countries of the region to overcome the problem of terrorism and organized crime. The two delegations insisted on the adherence by all countries to UN resolutions and conventions relating to combating terrorism, particularly Resolution 1904, which condemned and criminalized the payment of ransom fees to terrorist groups.

During the fifth meeting of the EU-Algeria Association Council, held in Luxembourg in mid-June 2010, Medelci urged the EU to modify the schedule for tariff elimination under the terms of the Association Agreement. He reiterated Algeria's desire to develop ties covering political, economic, commercial, cultural, social and human development co-operation, claiming that, thus far, only the commercial aspect of the Agreement had received particular attention. He insisted that the level of direct investment by EU countries had been well below that expected by the Algerian Government, claiming that Algeria had incurred significant losses of revenue since the dismantling of trade tariffs. In 2005–09 lost customs revenue reportedly amounted to nearly US $2,500m., while the losses in 2010–17 were forecast to reach almost $8,500m.

In April 2009 Bouteflika met with US President Barack Obama's Special Envoy to the Middle East, George Mitchell, and in December Medelci visited Washington, DC, for talks with US Secretary of State Hillary Clinton. In January 2010 the US Department of Justice announced that two Algerian detainees, Hasan Zemiri and Adil Hadi al-Jazairi bin Hamlili, had been transferred from the US detention facility at Guantánamo Bay to the custody and control of the Algerian authorities.

In June 2009 Bouteflika attended tripartite consultations with Egyptian President Hosni Mubarak and Qaddafi in Cairo, Egypt. On 2 November Medelci and his Egyptian counterpart, Ahmad Aboul Gheit, called on the media of both countries to address the upcoming qualification match for the football World Cup between Egypt and Algeria in the context of sportsmanship and fraternal spirit. (Previous matches between the two countries had been marked by fierce rivalry and violent clashes between supporters.) Two days before the match, a vehicle transporting the Algerian players to a hotel in the Egyptian capital was attacked by Egyptian supporters; three members of the Algerian squad were injured in the attack. Following Egypt's victory in the match, violence erupted in Algiers, with Egyptian business interests reportedly being attacked by Algerian supporters. The result of that match necessitated a play-off game between the two countries in Khartoum, Sudan, later that month, prompting fears of an escalation in violence. The conclusion of the match, which was won by Algeria, did not end the tension. The following month Medelci rejected calls for mediation, while also rejecting an Egyptian demand for an apology for Algeria's role in the diplomatic dispute. On 4 July, however, President Mubarak attended the funeral of Bouteflika's brother, Mustapha, in Algiers, while Aboul Gheit and Medelci held talks the same day, amid signs of a tentative rapprochement.

On 31 August–1 September 2009 Bouteflika effected a state visit to Libya, where he also attended festivities held to mark the 40th anniversary of Qaddafi's seizure of power. On 2 December Medelci visited Tunis to review bilateral relations with Tunisia. Following the meeting, the two countries announced an agreement on the delimitation of their respective maritime boundaries. In February 2010 Messahel heralded the 13th session of the Algerian-Libyan joint commission, co-presided by Prime Minister Ouyahia and the Libyan Secretary of the General People's Committee, Dr al-Baghdadi Ali al-Mahmoudi, as a new beginning for co-operation between the two countries, stressing in particular the importance of a project to establish a common customs checkpoint at the land border crossings of Ghadamès and Dabdab. By the end of the 13th session of the joint commission, the two delegations had signed 12 agreements and MOUs, in addition to a programme covering various areas of socio-economic and cultural policy.

Algeria took a leading role in combating terrorism in the Sahel-Sahara region. In March 2010 the Algerian Government hosted a ministerial conference of Sahel-Saharan African countries in Algiers, which was attended by the ministers responsible for foreign affairs of Burkina Faso, Libya, Mali, Mauritania, Niger and Chad. The conference was principally devoted to an assessment of the security situation in the region, particularly focusing on the resurgence of militant groups, including AQIM, and transnational criminal organizations. The conference was followed a month later by a meeting of the military Chiefs of Staff of the Sahel-Sahara countries, the objective of which was to formulate a co-ordinated anti-terrorist strategy for the region. Algeria's foreign policy at the mid-point of Bouteflika's third term in office seemed to focus primarily on relations with the major powers and with Africa. With respect to the major powers, the most high-profile activities concerned relations with France and the USA. Critics suggested that the country had neglected its traditionally strong relations with the African continent and that the main beneficiary had been Morocco, Algeria's contender in the continent. This partly explained the intense diplomatic activities in Africa at the bilateral level, as well as within multilateral organizations, such as the AU and the G8. The Sahel-Sahara region remains of great concern for Algeria's security; therefore, not only has Algeria worked closely with the Sahel-Sahara states, but has also sought support within the AU for Algeria's position concerning the region. With regard to its immediate neighbours, Algeria has faced serious challenges since January 2011, owing to the spectacular changes prior and subsequent to the fall of Tunisia's President Ben Ali, and the civil war in Libya whose repercussions represented a security threat for Algeria.

Relations with the EU and its members, particularly the United Kingdom, Germany, Italy, Spain and Portugal, have also been quite strained. The most notable development in Algeria's foreign relations has been its apparent willingness to improve relations, as is the case with France, or to consolidate ties, as has become evident with the USA and the United Kingdom. Relations with France have improved noticeably. Both sides have sought to overcome the major hurdles that poisoned relations since February 2005, when the French National Assembly passed a law in which an article emphasized the positive role of French colonialism in Algeria. A series of visits from senior officials to Algiers from late 2010 created a new dynamic in those relations. The first sign of this was Bouteflika's decision to attend the 25th Africa-France Summit held in Nice, France, in May–June 2010. One of the main objectives of the summit was to explore ways to enhance Africa's role in the new architecture of global governance. In addition, the summit aimed to understand how the collective security system put in place by the AU with EU support could achieve greater peace, security, and stability in Africa. Following the conclusion of the Hasseni affair, which was resolved in the courts with the acquittal of the Algerian diplomat in August 2010, a series of official visits took place between senior representatives of the French and Algerian Governments. Both sides emphasized the constructive nature of these visits. Some commentators believed that France was especially anxious to increase co-operation in the Sahel-Sahara region, where it has considerable interests, and where some of its citizens had been a target for kidnappings by AQIM. Former Prime Minister Jean-Pierre Raffarin's trip to Algiers, as Sarkozy's special envoy, was the strongest signal of improved relations between the two states. Sarkozy's assigned mission (as of September 2010) for Raffarin, known as 'Monsieur Algérie', was to coordinate the development of economic co-operation between France and Algeria, as well as to encourage bilateral investment. His main task was to restart a number of important projects between the two countries that had become stalled. These projects covered areas as diverse as transportation, infrastructure, energy, industry, insurance and banking. Raffarin returned for a second visit in February 2011 and was received by both Bouteflika and Ouyahia. His working sessions with the Minister of Industry, Small and Medium-sized Enterprises and Investment Promotion, Muhammad Benmeradi, were hailed as successful by both parties. Economic relations between France and Algeria, its principal economic partner in Africa, were seen to have received a considerable boost, thus highlighting the willingness of both sides to begin relations afresh. At the political level, the main area of disagreement was France's intervention in Libya. Algeria's sacrosanct opposition to foreign interventions in sovereign states' domestic affairs was at loggerheads with France's rather imposing intervention in Libya in March 2011. Algeria called for a resolution of the conflict through a ceasefire and negotiations between the warring parties. Algeria's position coincided with that of the AU and of other powers, including the People's Republic of China. The French Minister of State, Minister of Foreign and European Affairs, Alain Juppé, and Medelci discussed the issue in a telephone conversation on 18 April 2011. The conversation focused on relations between the two countries, but also concerned accusations that the Algerian authorities had provided assistance to the Qaddafi regime. Algiers rejected the accusations vehemently. Juppé made an official visit to Algiers in June for talks with Bouteflika and Ouyahia. Both sides agreed that the Libyan crisis should be resolved politically, although it was clear that differences remained on a number of long-standing issues, particularly the restriction of visas to Algerians wishing to travel to France. In late August the Algerian Government was the subject of international criticism after it confirmed that members of Qaddafi's immediate family, including two of his sons, Muhammad and Hannibal, had crossed the border into Algeria after the capture of Tripoli by forces loyal to the Libyan opposition National Transitional Council (NTC). However, in an interview with a French radio station in early September Medelci indicated

Algeria's willingness to recognize a future NTC government in Libya.

Algeria's relations with the USA have also intensified. Although these relations cover a range of issues, by far the most dominant among these is security. In recent economic affairs, the most notable event was the visit in December 2010 of Jose W. Fernandez, US Assistant Secretary of State for Economic, Energy and Business Affairs. Discussions centred on the possibility of US involvement in Algeria's five-year economic plan for 2010–14, particularly as the USA had expressed a desire to have greater business presence in Algeria. Fernandez also discussed with Medelci co-operation in the Maghreb region and how US experience could assist in the development of an integrated economic zone in the region. Fernandez insisted on President Obama's commitment to enhance relations with the Maghreb countries, particularly with Algeria. A month after Fernandez's visit, John O. Brennan, Obama's chief counterterrorism adviser, made an official visit to Algiers, where he met Messahel, Medelci, Bouteflika and Kamel Rezzag-Bara, Presidential Adviser and Co-ordinator of Inter-Ministerial External Counterterrorism and Security Co-operation, along with other senior officials, to discuss the security situation in the Sahel-Sahara and Somalia, as well as illicit trafficking of all kinds in the region.

Under-Secretary of State for Political Affairs William J. Burns toured the Maghreb countries in early 2011, visiting Algiers in late February. During his stay in Algiers, Burns held talks with Messahel, Medelci, and Bouteflika. The discussions focused on bilateral issues regarding political, economic and security issues. Given the developments that were taking place in Tunisia and Egypt, which Burns had just visited, Algerians and Americans shared their respective assessments of the current circumstances in the region. A security co-operation agreement signed by the two countries in April 2010, as well as further official visits, paved the way for perhaps the most important security gathering between officials of the countries. During an official visit in March 2011, Daniel Benjamin, Co-ordinator for Counterterrorism at the US Department of State, co-chaired, with Rezzag-Bara, the first meeting of the Bilateral Contact Group on Algerian-American Counterterrorism and Security Co-operation. The objective of the meeting was to exchange information and analyses on the development of the terrorist threat in Algeria, the USA and worldwide. They also examined the growing relationship between terrorism and various types of organized crime. Algeria and the USA also agreed to explore their counterterrorism co-operation within multilateral organizations. In May Medelci visited Washington, DC, where he held further discussions with Benjamin, Brennan and Burns on security and counterterrorism co-operation, political and economic reforms in Algeria (announced by Bouteflika on 15 April), the deterioration of the situation in Libya and its security consequences, the situation in the Sahel-Sahara and developments in Tunisia. Medelci also briefed Brennan on the meeting, held in Bamako the week before, of the Operational Joint Chiefs of Staff Committee (CEMOC), which brings together the Sahel-Sahara neighbours, Algeria, Mali, Niger and Mauritania. Medelci later met Secretary of State Clinton and both sides reiterated the closeness of the two states' relations, especially in the fight against terrorism. It was agreed that Clinton would visit Algeria later in 2011. Upon his return to Algiers, Medelci declared that numerous US companies were planning to come to Algeria to explore the Algerian market.

In relations with the EU, the main issue remained the implementation of the 2005 Association Agreement, which Algerians felt was unfairly weighted in favour of the EU. Medelci, who attended the sixth session of the Association Council, held in Luxembourg (19–20 June 2011), declared that Algeria sought to arrive rapidly at an agreement with the EU. Algeria requested assistance from the EU, its main trading partner, to support the reforms and the diversification of the country's economy. Algerians also complained that the direct investments that were anticipated from the Association had not materialized. The EU promised that it would study the factors that had impeded foreign direct investments in Algeria. The EU had sought co-operation with Algeria to address the security situation in the Sahel-Sahara, a region of great concern to the EU. At a meeting in June 2011 Messahel and EU Counterterrorism Co-ordinator Gilles de Kerchove agreed that the situation needed to be addressed not just through security measures, but also through development in order to divert disaffected young people in the region from engaging in terrorism or in organized crime.

Co-operation in counter-terrorism has also been strengthened at the bilateral level between Algeria and EU countries. This is particularly the case with the United Kingdom, whose trade relations with Algeria have grown significantly; total trade between the two countries amounted to US $2,000m. in 2010. Parliamentary Under-Secretary of State at the Foreign and Commonwealth Office Alistair Burt made an official visit to Algiers in November 2010. The two countries shared similar views on the situation in the Sahel. Burt returned to Algiers in April 2011 to attend the fifth session of the Algerian-British Bilateral Commission. The two sides described relations as being excellent and expressed the desire to expand them to all sectors. Algeria was appreciative of the British Government's efforts in the UN Security Council to include the supervision of human rights in the mandate of the UN peace-keeping mission in Western Sahara. Algeria's relations with Germany have also made progress. In December 2010 Bouteflika, Medelci and other senior officals visited Berlin. During a meeting with the German Federal Chancellor, Angela Merkel, Bouteflika and Medelci appealed to Germany to invest in Algeria, to share its expertise and to train Algerians. Bouteflika announced the immediate creation of a joint bilateral commission to enable German companies to establish operations in Algeria. The commission held its first session in Algiers in March 2011. At the political level, relations between the two countries have been exemplary. Algeria has also maintained excellent relations with Italy, Spain and Portugal. Italy's Minister of Foreign Affairs Franco Frattini visited Algeria twice in 2010 and 2011, when the country agreed to convert a portion of Algeria's debt into 34 projects. In May 2011 Algeria and Spain established a bilateral contact group for co-operation in the fight against terrorism and other related crimes. Meanwhile, relations between Algeria and Portugal were strengthened in November 2010, following the third High-Level Algerian-Portuguese Commission, held in the Portuguese capital, Lisbon, and presided jointly by Ouyahia and the Portuguese Prime Minister, José Sócrates; nine major accords of co-operation and partnership were signed. On 1 March 2011 Bouteflika received Portugal's Minister of Foreign Affairs, Luís Filipe Marques Amado.

Although Bouteflika has reduced his official foreign visits in recent years, he has always attempted to attend the AU's major gatherings. In July 2010 he attended the AU Summit held in Kampala, Uganda. His speech during the summit was focused on peace and security in the continent. In November of that year he attended the third Africa-Europe Summit held in Tripoli. Like his African peers, he encouraged the consolidation of the economic partnership between the two continents as a way to enhance the overall partnership with the EU. In his address, Bouteflika dealt with the question of migration. He argued that human exchanges should constitute a bridge between the two continents and insisted on the respect of the rights of migrant workers. In late June 2011 Bouteflika attended the 17th AU Summit held in Malabo, Equatorial Guinea. Bouteflika also participated in the 35th session of the Forum of the Heads of State and Government of the African Peer Review Mechanism, which was held concurrently with the AU Summit.

Algerian relations with Russia have been consolidated in recent years. At the end of President Dmitrii Medvedev's visit to Algiers in October 2010, a 17-point Algerian-Russian communiqué was issued. The communiqué highlighted the foundations and principles that underlie their bilateral relations. Minister of Foreign Affairs Sergei V. Lavrov visited Algiers in March 2011; both sides insisted on a timetable for the execution of various projects in a range of sectors, notably, energy, nuclear energy and infrastructure. The two sides also reiterated their long-standing co-operation in defence affairs and in the fight against terrorism.

Algeria's ties with China have also been strengthened. In July 2010 State Councillor Dai Bingguo came to Algiers for a three-day official visit during which he met Bouteflika and various senior officials. In February 2011 the two countries signed a co-operation agreement covering technical assistance and the transfer of technology and expertise. In the following month the Deputy Minister of Foreign Affairs, Zhai Jun, held official talks, reiterating the strategic relations between the two countries.

At the Conference of the Non-aligned Movement held in Bali, Indonesia, in May 2011, Medelci insisted on the intensification of multilateralism, contending that it is the best mechanism for the defence of the interests of developing countries. He also appealed for a global and profound reform of the UN, in essence a revitalization of the UN General Assembly and a reform of the Security Council.

In the Maghreb region, relations with Morocco, notwithstanding some positive rhetoric, remained frosty. In September 2010 Moroccan authorities implicated Algeria in the arrest in Western Sahara of Ould Sidi Mouloud, a pro-Moroccan Sahrawi, by the Polisario Front. Algeria responded to Moroccan accusations by stating that Morocco had used the incident to divert attention from its occupation of Western Sahara and to escape its obligation under UN resolutions. On 21 October Medelci stated unequivocally that Morocco was responsible for the absence of a peaceful resolution of the Western Sahara conflict. He accused Morocco of obstructing the negotiation process led by UN Special Envoy Christopher Ross between Moroccans and Sahrawis. Medelci also deplored the fact that, despite Polisario's call on the UN to undertake supervision of human rights in the camps and in the occupied territory, the organization had not given a clear response. The uprisings in Tunisia and Egypt in January and February 2011, respectively, prompted Algerian and Moroccan authorities to moderate their hostile rhetoric. Moreover, in February 2011 Medelci spoke of the rejuvenation of relations between the two countries. Three Algerian ministers visited Morocco in April to propel the new dynamic, at least at the economic level. Moroccan ministers also visited Algeria during that period. Bouteflika declared on 17 April, while in Tlemcen, a city very close to the border with Morocco, that no problem existed between Algeria and Morocco and that the conflict of Western Sahara was a question for the UN. The new dynamic resulted in the announcement in newspapers in both countries that the Algerian-Morocco border, closed since August 1994, would be reopened on 2 June. On 29 May Ouyahia declared that the reopening of the border was not on the agenda but that it would be reopened at some point in the future. He insisted that resolution of the conflict in Western Sahara was not a precondition for the reopening of the border; this was a way of putting the ball in Morocco's court since the latter has insisted that normalization of bilateral relations presupposes resolution of the disputed territory. In addition, Ouyahia accused the Moroccan Government of attempting through its state media to implicate Algeria in the Libyan crisis by alleging that Algeria was sending mercenaries and supplying weapons to Qaddafi's forces.

While Algeria was rather silent about events in Tunisia, relations with the new Tunisian Government were cordial. The new interim Prime Minister, Beji Caïd Essebsi, chose Algeria as the destination for his first foreign visit. He arrived in Algiers on 15 March 2011 to meet Bouteflika, Ouyahia, Medelci, Messahel and numerous other officials. In July Tunisia's Minister of Foreign Affairs, Muhammad Mouldi Kéfi, paid a working visit to Algiers. The objective was to co-chair, with Medelci, the sixth session of the Algerian-Tunisian Commission for Political Consultation. He also briefed Algerian authorities on the transformations in Tunisia. The two sides held a common position on the crisis in Libya, insisting on a political, peaceful solution along the 'roadmap' elaborated by the AU. On 11 July the two countries signed an agreement on the demarcation of their maritime borders; the agreement was the result of a long and arduous process that had begun years before. The parties declared that the finalization of the demarcation of their borders would strengthen their bilateral relations and give them a strategic dimension. Undoubtedly, the Libyan crisis has brought Algeria and Tunisia (which both share borders with the country) even closer. From the inception of the uprising in Libya, Algerian officials called on the Libyan authorities to listen to the protest movement. The Government in Algiers was greatly concerned about the consequences of the Libyan crisis and shared those fears with European governments, the USA, Russia and China. Not only was the Government concerned about massive migration into Algeria and Tunisia, but also about the likelihood of AQIM having access to arms depots, weapons from which could be used in the Sahel-Sahara and against targets in Algeria. Messahel argued that with the desertion of the barracks, Libya had become 'an open skies [arms] depot'.

The Sahel-Sahara region has remained a constant preoccupation for Algiers. Algeria has worked on both the bilateral and multilateral levels to secure regional and international co-operation on the matter and has sought to convince the international community about the dangerous situation prevailing there. In September 2010 Messahel declared that African states must play their part in protecting their populations against the threat of terrorism in the Sahel. He also called on the international community to provide expertise, strengthening of logistical support capacities, and exchange of intelligence and training for Africans. Moreover, he asked that the decisions made by the UN with respect to terrorism, particularly the payment of ransoms, be more effective. He believed that Europeans could not simply state that they were against the payment of ransoms, but that European institutions should also take measures to criminalize their payment. In October Ouyahia stated that the Sahel states need development and that the northern part of the region needed to strengthen its administrative capacities, which would require foreign assistance. However, he also argued that foreign presence would be the worst scenario, as it would turn the terrorists into *mujahidin*. Mali's relations with Algeria had been strained owing to Mali's perceived ambivalence toward the counterterrorism effort; in February 2010 Mali released four terrorists (two of whom were Algerian members of AQIM) in exchange for the liberation of AQIM-held French hostage Pierre Camatte. Gradually, ties between the two countries improved, particularly following the appointment on 7 April 2011 of Soumeylou Boubèye Maïga, an expert in counterterrorism, as Mali's new Minister of Foreign Affairs and International Co-operation. Under his leadership Mali engaged more decisively in counterterrorism. In addition to its participation in CEMOC and other regional security arrangements, Mali benefited from Algerian financial largesse: in May 2011 Algeria pledged US $10m. to stimulate socio-economic development in the impoverished northern part of Mali.

The turbulent developments in the Maghreb and in the Sahel regions since early 2011 induced Algerian policy-makers to respond to the events as best as they could through bilateral, regional, and international actions. Unsurprisingly, Algeria's foreign policy demonstrated new activism in Maghreb affairs; in the face of adversity, not only Algeria but all its Maghreb neighbours sought greater co-operation. The intensification of the civil war in Libya preoccupied Algeria, as the acquisition of weapons by AQIM was facilitated and the number of refugees fleeing the country reached high levels. During an international conference on terrorism, held in Algiers on 7–8 September, Algerian policy-makers and their Sahel partners highlighted the risks arising from the Libyan civil war. They also insisted on the geopolitical implications of the situation in Libya and their impact on terrorism in the Sahel. The participation of jihadist militias was particularly worrisome to Algeria, which feared that the NTC in Libya would not have the same determination in fighting terrorist groups as Qaddafi. Algerian diplomats urged greater regional and international co-operation in fighting terrorism in the area, but also in addressing the socio-economic needs of the populations of the Sahel countries in order to counteract AQIM's propaganda. Algeria repeated continually that AQIM exploits the poverty of those populations and the lack of public services to gain the sympathy of those populations and recruit among the youths. Algeria, like many other countries, including the USA, concluded that the 'war on terrorism' must be conducted globally. Thus, in September 2001 Algeria had been among the 30 founding members of the US-inspired Global Counterterrorism Forum (GCTF), which was launched in New York on the margins of the UN General Assembly meetings. Algeria pledged to make a contribution to and share its anti-terrorist experience with the GCTF; it also committed to mobilize the regional actors against terrorism within the framework of the AU and the UN. Algeria has since co-chaired (2011–13), together with Canada, one of the GCTF's five committees, which focuses on the means to strengthen the economic and security capacities in the Sahel. In early November 2011 high-ranking security officials and diplomats from the 'core countries' of the Sahel region, Algeria, Mali, Mauritania and Niger, met US Defense and State Department counterparts in Washington, DC. The meeting was a follow-up to the Algiers conference two months earlier. The objective was to execute concrete military and economic actions to re-establish security in the Sahara-Sahel region and defining the terms of international co-operation. On 16 November the GCTF held a closed-door conference in Algiers that brought together 150 international experts on terrorism from 30 countries, UN agencies, and NGOs. The Algerian authorities highlighted the need to eliminate the funding of terrorism, which has drawn assets from the payment of ransoms for the freeing of Western hostages, as well as its connections with organized crime networks. The situation in the Sahel alarmed Algerian authorities, as the security in their vast southern and eastern borders became vulnerable due not only to the collapse of the Libyan regime in October, but also to the return of armed Tuaregs to the Azawad region in northern Mali. Algeria attempted to mediate in February 2012 between the Tuaregs of the National Movement for the Liberation of the Azawad (MNLA) and the Malian Government. The defeat of the Malian troops by the Tuareg forces and the subsequent military coup on 22 March, coupled with the proclamation of independence of the Azawad by the MNLA and the presence of other competing jihadist groups, created a complicated situation for Algeria. The kidnapping of seven Algerian diplomats, including the Consul, in Gao, northern Mali, presented Algeria with serious challenges.

The Arab uprisings resulted in intense diplomatic activity in the Maghreb; in an unexpected move, Algeria declared on 22 September 2011 that it recognized the Libyan interim administration as the legitimate representatives of the Libyan people and that it was ready to work closely with the NTC, with which relations had hitherto been rather tense. Algeria's decision to grant asylum on humanitarian grounds to members of the Qaddafi family (who were not indicted by the International Criminal Court) had worsened relations between the NTC and the Algerian Government, which refused to extradite them to Libya. In November 2011 Bouteflika met the Chairman of the NTC, Mustafa Muhammad Abd al-Jalil, twice on the margin of the first summit of heads of state and government of the Forum of Gas Exporting Countries held in Doha, Qatar; although nothing material transpired, it is expected that Bouteflika used the opportunity to explain Algeria's policy towards Libya during the uprising and to discuss the necessity of securing the borders to avoid the dispersion of weapons into Algeria, Tunisia and the Sahel. Although Algerian diplomats rejected reports that Qatar had played a mediation role, it seems that the Amir of Qatar, Sheikh Hamad bin Khalifa Al Thani, did in fact have such involvement. In any case, by March 2012 relations between the two countries had gradually improved. Medelci visited Tripoli to review the contentious issues with high-level officials, including Abd al-Jalil. The two parties made a solid commitment to end past differences and to give a new dynamic to relations between the two countries. Soon after the visit, an agreement was signed between the two Ministers of the Interior in Algiers on joint border control patrols. In mid-April, Abd al-Jalil made an official visit to Algiers at the invitation of Bouteflika. At the end of the visit on 16 April, the two sides issued a joint communiqué, which provided broad perspectives on bilateral relations (security and military co-operation, joint economic projects, infrastructural developments and trade).

An improvement in Algeria's relations with Morocco became apparent in November 2011, when Medelci and Messahel met the Moroccan Minister of Foreign Affairs and Co-operation, Taieb Fassi Fihri, in Rabat; the two sides declared that they were considering ways to increase bilateral co-operation. Algerian and Moroccan ministers in different sectors had held productive meetings in Algiers and in Rabat and reported the concrete steps that had been taken. The determination of the two sides to strengthen their bilateral relations and to revive the UMA was none the less hampered by the continued issues of the closed common border and the conflict in Western Sahara. However, in the interests of progress, these contentious issues were not discussed during a visit by the new Moroccan Minister of Foreign Affairs and Co-operation, Saâd-eddine el-Othmani, to Algiers on 23 January 2012. While the two sides insisted that their bilateral relations were strategic, Algeria argued that the border issue must be treated within a 'global perspective'. In other words, the opening of the border would not be a precondition but would only be resolved through a comprehensive resolution of the other contentious issues. With regard to the question of Western Sahara, both Algeria and Morocco agreed that it was to be addressed by the UN and should not hinder the development of good relations between the two countries. Algeria began to suggest a programme to invigorate bilateral relations in all sectors with Morocco. During his visit to Rabat in mid-February to attend the 30th session of the UMA's council of foreign affairs ministers, Medelci signed an MOU with el-Othmani for the institution of a commission for political consultations.

Relations with Tunisia have also witnessed a new dynamic. On 21 November 2011 Bouteflika received a visit by Rachid Ghannouchi, the leader of the ruling Parti de la renaissance/Hizb al-Nahdah movement, who favoured even better relations with Algeria. In January 2012 Bouteflika attended the first anniversary celebrations of the abdication of President Ben Ali. During the visit, he met Tunisia's interim President, Moncef Marzouki. He also conducted discussions with Amir of Qatar Sheikh Hamad, Mauritanian President Mohamed Ould Abdel Aziz, and Chairman of the NTC Abd al-Jalil. The following month Marzouki made an official visit to Algiers, where he met Bouteflika and the most senior members of the Government. The two sides emphasized the good relations between the two countries, Marzouki appealing to Algeria to assist in reviving the Tunisian economy.

Algeria's relations with the USA maintained their steady trajectory, particularly in the area of military and security. President Bouteflika met the commander of the US African Command (AFRICOM), Gen. Carter F. Ham, who attended the Algiers conference on terrorism (entitled Partnership, Security and Development) in September 2011. On 24 September Messahel attended the launching of the Global Counterterrorism Forum in New York, in the presence of Secretary of State Hillary Clinton and the ministers responsible for foreign affairs of the member states of the GCTF. In January 2012 Medelci made an official visit to the USA, meeting Clinton, and reportedly briefing her on the state of Algeria's relations with Morocco and on the question of Western Sahara. Medelci expressed his satisfaction regarding US-Algerian relations in the economic sphere (the USA being a main partner of Algeria) and in military co-operation. On 25 February Hillary Clinton made a brief visit to Algiers, where she met Medelci and Bouteflika. The following month the US Acting Under Secretary of State for Public Diplomacy and Public Affairs, Kathleen Stephens, also visited Algiers. In early April Gen. Ham, accompanied by Assistant Secretary of State for African Affairs Johnnie Carson, made a further visit to Algiers, during which he met Bouteflika in the presence of senior government officials.

Algeria's relations with France failed to improve greatly during 2011; the Libyan crisis had exacerbated the tensions that already existed between the two countries, with France criticizing Algeria's 'ambiguous position'. By the end of that year, however, the bilateral strains appeared to have eased. On 4 December France's Minister of the Interior, Claude Guéant, visited Algiers in order to discuss the issue of the French hostages detained by AQIM in the Sahel, as well as the control of immigration to France, which the Government sought to reduce by 10%, and the attribution of visas to Algerians. On 7 December Medelci addressed the Foreign Relations Commission of the French National Assembly, when he provided a lengthy exposé on the reforms undertaken in Algeria. Both sides encouraged the development of stronger bilateral relations in the economic, cultural and scientific fields. They also agreed that the 50th anniversary of Algerian independence should mark the start of even better relations between the two nations. In February 2012 France's Minister in charge of Co-operation, Henri de Raincourt, insisted during a visit to Algiers that there was convergence of views between the two Governments on the situation in the Sahel and that France supported Algeria's role in seeking a resolution to the problems prevailing in that region, especially in northern Mali. Following the election of François Hollande as French President in May, Algeria indicated its hope that bilateral relations would improve. During a visit by French Minister of Foreign Affairs Laurent Fabius to Algiers in July, both sides agreed to expedite the implementation of accords regarding the industrial sectors, such as pharmaceuticals, construction and automobiles.

The issue of regional security has been high on the agenda of the member countries of the AMU. Given the continued instability and the increasing threats posed by the proliferation of arms and drugs, terrorism and organized crime, the prime ministers of Algeria, Libya and Tunisia met on 12 January in Ghadames, Libya, to discuss the enhancement of security along their shared borders, agreeing to co-ordinate border patrols and to improve the exchange of information. In the same vein, the ministers responsible for internal affairs of the AMU member states gathered on 21 April in Rabat to converse about the need for joint consultation and co-ordination to address these security issues; and a draft security strategy was adopted in this respect. However, some observers cautioned that because of the member states' political differences, the measures agreed to may prove difficult to put into practice.

Bilateral relations between Algeria and Morocco, after signs of optimism, were strained again in late 2012. Representatives of both countries had previously spoken of their commitment to reaffirming the ties linking them. However, a speech given by King Muhammad VI in November on the occasion of the celebration of the 37th anniversary of Morocco's annexation of Western Sahara, in which he appeared to accuse Algeria of complicity in human rights violations in Tindouf damaged hopes of any meaningful improvement in relations in the near future.

However, relations between Algeria and Tunisia have, by and large, developed amicably since the Tunisian 'revolution'. Attending an official celebration marking the second anniversary of the Tunisian uprising on 14 January 2013, the President of the Council of the Nation, Abdelkader Bensalah, stressed Algeria's support for Tunisia's transition. The strengthening and co-ordination of security co-operation dominated the diplomatic activity between both countries. During a visit to Algeria on 29 April the Tunisian Prime Minister, Ali Laârayedh, affirmed the two countries' common interests, not least over security. Accompanying Laârayedh, the Chief of Staff of the Tunisian armed forces, Gen. Rachid Ammar, held talks with his Algerian counterpart, Lt-Gen. Salah. Both sides also welcomed the finalization of a preferential trade agreement, pledged to develop their shared border regions, and called for greater progress in areas such as energy, industry, small and medium enterprises and investment promotion.

After a period of discord, diplomatic visits appeared to have improved bilateral relations between Algeria and Libya; the most important of these was the visit of Libyan Prime Minister Ali Zidan to Algiers in December 2012. Algeria pledged to provide support to the Libyan Government in the area of security. More recently, the focus has been on ways to improve border security co-operation in order to confront the movement of arms and militants.

The situation in the Sahel in general, and in Mali in particular, remained a major priority in Algeria's diplomatic activity, not least because of the potential negative consequences on regional stability and security. Algeria continued its attempts to reach a negotiated political solution to the conflict in Mali. Its disapproval of any military intervention to settle this conflict was consistent with its principle of non-interference in the internal affairs of other states, a hallmark of Algerian foreign policy. More importantly, Algeria was very much concerned about the potential destabilizing effect of such an intervention. Algeria sought to promote dialogue, especially between the Islamist militant group Ansar Dine and the Malian Government. However, in early January 2013 Ansar Dine withdrew its offer of ceasefire and proclaimed the north of Mali an autonomous region. This put an end to the diplomatic solution that Algeria had been seeking to achieve and, in a way, provided the justification for the military intervention. Opening its airspace to French military aircraft and closing its borders with Mali in early January 2013 signalled Algeria's change of approach to the conflict.

Relations with the EU witnessed further developments. In response to Algeria's intention to join the European Neighbourhood Policy—by concluding an EU–Algeria Action Plan—the first round of negotiations with the EU took place on 17–18 October 2012. Negotiations were successfully brought to a close with the signing of an MOU on a strategic energy partnership in July 2013. This agreement was of paramount importance to Algeria, as a reassuring signal to companies operating in the oil and gas sector, especially following the hostage crisis at In Amenas), and also as a confirmation of Algeria's position as a favoured supplier to the European energy market, particularly at a time of increasing international competition.

Algeria continued to pursue positive relations with France. Two prominent members of the new French Government—Minister of Foreign Affairs Laurent Fabius, and Minister of the Interior Manuel Valls—visited Algiers in July and October 2012, respectively. Issues of common interest, including economic projects with French companies and the movement of people between the two countries, were discussed. Moreover, their visits were intended to prepare for President François Hollande's visit in December. A visit which, as stated by Valls, was expected to inaugurate a new stage in the relationship between the two countries. During his trip, the French President denounced the suffering endured by Algerians throughout the colonial period, but stopped short of a full and official apology. Many saw the trip as an attempt by France to give renewed impetus to the bilateral economic relations. Probably the most important and widely publicized deal concluded was the building of a Renault factory in Algeria, to manufacture 75,000 cars a year.

Co-operation on security and counter-terrorism continued to dominate bilateral relations between Algeria and the USA. In late September 2012 Carter F. Ham made a two-day visit to Algeria to meet Bouteflika and senior diplomatic and military officials. The discussions focused mainly on the deteriorating security situation in the Sahel region in general and Mali in particular. Part of their regular consultations, this visit reflected not only the key role of Algeria in the region but the apparent convergence in their respective positions *vis-à-vis* the Malian issue.

A significant indication of the rapprochement between the countries was the launching of a first-ever 'bilateral strategic dialogue' in October 2012 in Washington, DC. Approximately 90% of bilateral trade, which totalled US $13,600m. in 2012, consisted of energy exports to the US market. Hence the official visit to the USA of the Algerian Minister of Commerce, Mustapha Benbada, was intended—in addition to garnering support for Algerian accession to the WTO—to reactivate the countries' joint council on trade and investment.

Relations with Russia were marked by the working visit made by Medelci on 24 June 2012. The main focus of discussions was on taking stock of the progress in their bilateral co-operation. Thus the implementation of the Declaration on Strategic Partnership—signed by Algeria and Russia on 4 April 2001 in Moscow—was reviewed to further boost the 'privileged relations' between them. The Russian Minister of Foreign Affairs, Sergei V. Lavrov, stated that 'Algeria is a key traditional partner in North Africa, and with which we intend to strengthen our co-operation, especially in the economic, trading and energy areas'. International issues, such as the human rights situation in Western Sahara, the crisis in the Sahel, and the peace process in the Middle East were also discussed. It emerged that both countries were in agreement on several key international issues, especially in relation to the supremacy of law and the central role of the UN and its organs in settling conflicts.

Algeria's relations with China remained, for the most part, focused on economic ties. In terms of commercial exchanges,

Algeria's trade deficit with China reached nearly US $3,200m. in 2012, the largest among its trading partners—China was the second largest supplier of imports after France. As part of the regular political consultations between the two countries, the Minister-delegate to the Minister of Foreign Affairs, in charge of Maghreb and African Affairs, Abdelkader Messahel, visited Beijing on in December 2012 for talks on international and regional issues, notably the situation in Mali.

Economy

RICHARD GERMAN and ELIZABETH TAYLOR

Algeria covers an area of 2,381,741 sq km (919,595 sq miles), of which a large part is desert. The country is divided into 48 *wilayat* (departments) for administrative purposes. At the 1977 census the population (excluding Algerians abroad) was 16,948,000. By 1987 it had reached 23,038,942, in addition to about 1m. Algerians living abroad (mainly in France). The 1998 census gave a population of 29,100,867 (excluding 171,476 Sahrawi refugees in camps) and the 2008 count indicated that the figure had increased to 34,080,030. According to official estimates, the population stood at 37.9m. by January 2013.

Algeria has varied natural resources. In the coastal region are fertile plains and valleys, where profitable returns are made from cereals, wine, olives and fruit. The remainder of the country supports little agriculture, though in the mountains grazing and forestry produce a small income, and dates are cultivated in the oases of the Sahara. Mineral resources, in particular petroleum and natural gas, are abundant, and dominate Algeria's export trade—the hydrocarbons sector accounting for some 36.7% of Algeria's gross domestic product (GDP) in 2011.

GOVERNMENT STRATEGY

From independence in 1962 Algerian governments sought to promote economic growth as a foundation for a socialist society, and acquired either a complete or a controlling interest in most foreign-owned companies. Having initiated a series of development plans from 1970, the Government in 1971 assumed control of the hydrocarbons sector export revenues, which generated an average annual GDP growth rate of 6%–6.5% during the 1970s. The 1980–84 Development Plan aimed for a more diversified economy, easing state control and encouraging private investment and enterprise. The 1985–89 Plan placed greater emphasis on investment in agriculture and social infrastructure, reflecting the need to satisfy the requirements of a rapidly expanding population. It also sought to promote non-hydrocarbon exports following falls in prices and quotas sponsored by the Organization of the Petroleum Exporting Countries (OPEC). However, the erosion of government income resulting from the collapse in petroleum prices in 1986 prevented the achievement of the Plan's investment targets. Algeria's economic position was further undermined by the level of foreign debt (the highest in the Arab world in 1985), many development projects having been financed through borrowings on the international capital markets since the 1970s.

Legislation enacted in 1987 eased restrictions on commercial bank lending to private companies, and opened the way for public sector enterprises to adopt their own annual plans, to determine the prices of their products, and to invest their profits freely. By mid-1989 three-quarters of Algeria's state-controlled enterprises, including banks, insurance companies and industrial, commercial and service organizations, had become autonomous *entreprises publiques économiques* (EPEs). Formal ownership of state shareholdings in EPEs was vested in eight state holding companies (*fonds de participation*), established in 1988 to take responsibility for different sectors of the economy. Regulations restricting access to convertible currency were modified in 1988 to attract investment in productive sectors and improve the export marketing capabilities of EPEs. In 1990 the importing of goods for resale on the Algerian domestic market ceased to be a state monopoly. Foreign manufacturers and traders who established import businesses in Algeria were offered tax incentives to reinvest their profits in the country's production facilities.

In June 1989 Algeria made its first ever use of IMF resources, securing a 12-month stand-by credit worth US $187m. (to support the Government's economic programme) and a compensatory financing allocation of $378m. (to assist with trade financing). In June 1991 the IMF agreed to make $404m. of stand-by credit available in the period to March 1992, while the World Bank approved a $350m. structural adjustment loan. In March 1992 a group of international banks agreed to refinance $1,457m. of Algeria's short-term commercial debt.

A government recovery programme, announced in February 1992, gave priority to key sectors of the economy, such as agriculture, public works and construction, which were targeted in a structured import programme. In August 1993 a new Government introduced an investment code, intended to stimulate foreign and domestic private investment in areas outside the mining and hydrocarbon sectors (which were covered by separate legislation introduced in late 1991), providing protection for investors who were to be offered a range of tax and duty reductions for certain categories of investment.

In December 1993 negotiations recommenced with the IMF for a loan linked to a stabilization programme. In January 1994 the IMF approved a 12-month package, providing a US $500m. stand-by loan and a $300m. compensatory and contingency financing facility (CCFF). The agreement committed Algeria to a number of reforms, including a 40% devaluation and a sharp increase in interest rates. In June 1994 the 'Paris Club' of official creditors agreed to refinance a total of about US $5,400m. of sovereign debt incurred by Algeria prior to September 1993, with repayments to be rescheduled over a period of 15 years following a four-year grace period. In July 1996 the Banque d'Algérie (the central bank) finalized an agreement with the 'London Club' of creditor banks to reschedule $3,200m. of long-term commercial debt contracted by Algerian state-owned banks and the state energy company, the Société Nationale pour la Recherche, la Production, le Transport, la Transformation et la Commercialisation des Hydrocarbures (Sonatrach).

Meanwhile, in April 1994 the IMF indicated its approval of government initiatives, and acknowledged that economic performance had to be assessed in the context of violence and political uncertainty, which continued to discourage investment. Algeria's GDP declined by 1.8% in real terms in 1994 (the ninth consecutive year of negative growth), compared with a planning target of 3% positive growth. In May 1995 the IMF approved a US $1,800m. three-year extended credit facility for Algeria. The Government agreed to continue a wide-ranging programme of structural reforms and to eliminate subsidies on food and other commodities. A comprehensive privatization law was enacted in August 1995.

In May 1995 the European Union (EU) agreed to lend Algeria US $268m. on conditions similar to those of the IMF, and in July the 'Paris Club' agreed to a refinancing of debts worth over $7,000m. Payments due between June 1995 and May 1997 were rescheduled over 15 years from 1999. Unlike the June 1994 'Paris Club' agreement, which dealt only with repayments of debt principal, the July 1995 agreement included some rescheduling of interest payments. In April 1996 the World Bank approved a loan of $300m. to support the Government's structural adjustment programme. Higher agricultural output and stronger international petroleum prices contributed to a 3.8% increase in real GDP in 1995 (the first year of real growth since 1985).

To expedite the restructuring of public sector enterprises, the system of ownership through *fonds de participation* was replaced in October 1996 by a new structure of 11 holding companies. These were authorized not only to hold shares in state enterprises, but also to offer shares for sale and to take action to close unprofitable enterprises. In December the Government published amendments to the 1995 privatization law, designed to stimulate private sector interest in the purchase of fully operational companies. Amongst the changes, eligibility for privatization (hitherto limited to EPEs) was to be extended to enterprises controlled by Algerian local government bodies.

There was a fall in the end-year inflation rate to 15% in 1996, compared with 22% in 1995 and 39% in 1994, reflecting the economy's adjustment to more stable conditions after the 1994 currency devaluation and the subsequent withdrawal of price subsidies. The freeing of prices had by early 1997 produced what the World Bank described as 'one of the most liberal trade regimes in the region'. Increases in both the volume and unit value of hydrocarbon exports, coupled with a record cereals harvest, gave Algeria a significant trade surplus and a positive current account balance in 1996, underpinning the achievement of 4% real GDP growth in that year. Following the rescheduling agreements with foreign creditors, debt-servicing as a proportion of export earnings decreased to 27.9% in 1996 (down from 77.7% in 1993). Despite the positive macroeconomic achievements, the output of non-hydrocarbon industries shrank by 8% in 1996 and GDP grew by just 1.3% in 1997, well below the official target of 5%, as a result of a decline in both agricultural and industrial production.

In May 1998 the Government listed 89 companies to be privatized from June, affecting enterprises in the tourism, construction, services, agri-business and transport sectors. The partial privatization, in early 1999, of the state-owned pharmaceuticals company, SAIDAL, and the cereals distributor, Eriad-Sétif, raised more than AD 4,000m.

In March 1999 the Arab Monetary Fund agreed to provide a loan of US $131m. to help Algeria to finance economic reforms in 1999–2000 and to provide balance of payments support. In May the IMF approved a further credit of $300m. under the CCFF to enable Algeria to offset the sharp decline in its hard currency earnings that had resulted from low oil prices in 1998.

Abdelaziz Bouteflika assumed the presidency in April 1999. Although seen as a strong supporter of state institutions, he promised an acceleration in the privatization programme, while insisting that only non-competitive firms in the public sector would be sold off. Despite the rhetoric from successive governments on the urgency of economic reforms, however, agreement on their implementation remained elusive, while advocates of reform continued to encounter strong resistance from the state bureaucracy, the labour movement and powerful commercial cartels linked to senior figures in the military.

The Banque d'Algérie reported real GDP growth of 3.8% in 2000 (substantially below the official projection of 5.6%). It also cautioned that growth of 6%–7% would be required in order significantly to reduce unemployment. Official statistics indicated that some 2.4m. Algerians were unemployed at mid-2000, two-thirds of whom were under the age of 30.

In April 2001 the Government announced an economic revival plan, committing US $700m. in expenditure to stimulate growth for the period 2001–04. The IMF commended the Government for its fiscal discipline, careful monetary policy and management of the exchange rate float. However, it emphasized the need for further privatization and banking reform to sustain growth, while lowering tariffs aimed at protecting domestic industry and reducing dependence on hydrocarbons. Algeria's overall GDP growth in 2001 decreased to 2.1%, which reflected higher spending and a decline in hydrocarbon revenues owing to reduced OPEC quotas. Economic activity improved in 2002: GDP growth reached 4.2%, and a fall in food prices resulted in a decrease in the average inflation rate.

In 2003 GDP growth reached 6.8%, reflecting increased hydrocarbons production and good agricultural output, and the average rate of inflation was 3.5%. Significant hydrocarbon exports led to a positive balance of payments position and a steady rise in foreign exchange reserves. The IMF welcomed the improved economic performance, but stated that structural and institutional reforms remained a prerequisite for higher and sustainable growth. Although a third GSM licence (see Telecommunications) was sold to a private investor in 2003, there were difficulties in completing other major privatization projects.

The IMF gave a generally favourable assessment of the economy for 2004. Real GDP growth was estimated at 5.5%, and inflation at 4%. However, unemployment remained high, particularly among the younger population, and was unevenly distributed across the country, with almost 60% of unemployed people residing in urban areas. As the economy continued to benefit from high hydrocarbon revenues, in 2005 the Government decided to raise the funding of the Budget and Growth Consolidation Plan (targeting social infrastructure, housing, education and employment needs—see Budget) to US $60,000m.—the UN's 2005 Human Development Index having ranked Algeria an undistinguished 103rd out of 177 countries.

Real GDP growth for 2005 was just over 5% and, while welcoming the performance, the IMF again underlined the importance of accelerating the promotion of private sector investment and job creation. Meanwhile, the Government announced plans to develop the non-hydrocarbon economy and to attract additional foreign investment through the modernization of the banking system and further privatization. In 2006 a new privatization programme was launched to attract investment in more than 1,000 companies (although those in strategic sectors, such as Air Algérie and Sonatrach, remained exempt from sale).

According to the IMF, GDP growth decreased to 2.0% in 2006 (owing to a decline in hydrocarbon output for technical reasons), but increased to 3.0% in 2007, reflecting stronger growth in the construction and service sectors. Inflation increased in the first half of 2007, due mainly to rising food prices and greater liquidity in the banking system. As unemployment reached an estimated 13.8% during that year (up from 12.3% in 2006), the IMF continued to urge the Government to bolster growth in non-hydrocarbon industries. Meanwhile, the Government began to implement the recommendations of a review (conducted with the World Bank in 2005–06) of the financial management and quality of public investments under the Budget and Growth Consolidation Plan, and established a supervisory National Agency for Investment Development.

In July 2008 President Bouteflika, claiming that foreign investors were not acting in Algeria's best interests, stated that they would henceforth be limited to minority stakes in projects with local companies, and that they would be subject to new land ownership restrictions. This apparent reversal of the economic liberalization policy also included the introduction of new tax regulations on the repatriation of capital by foreign-owned companies. However, the Government backtracked on a requirement that local subsidiaries of foreign companies importing goods into Algeria for resale cede 30% of their capital to a local company. It was announced in early 2009 that this measure would not be applied retroactively, and would be applied only to new ventures. Bouteflika, meanwhile, rejected the creation of a sovereign wealth fund, preferring instead to invest state resources in domestic infrastructure projects under a new five-year plan for 2009–13 (see also Budget).

Despite IMF warnings to the contrary, the non-hydrocarbons sector continued to expand, reflecting a good cereal harvest and robust government investment, and, according to the IMF, increased by about 9% in 2009. Inflation averaged an estimated 5.8% in that year, largely owing to elevated food prices. The overall rate of unemployment declined to 10.2%, although youth unemployment remained high, at about 24%. During 2009 the Government implemented further measures to restrict foreign involvement in the economy and to reduce the level of imports, in an attempt to promote the role of domestic companies.

Overall GDP growth in 2010 was projected by the IMF at 3.3% (increases of 2.4% having been recorded in both 2008 and 2009), with growth of some 5% in the non-hydrocarbons sector. Average inflation for the year was meanwhile estimated to have declined to 3.9% (although food prices again started to surge at the end of 2010). The IMF acknowledged Algeria's good overall economic performance in 2010, but emphasized the need for the Government to continue structural reforms in order to encourage private investment and economic diversification, and to strengthen the financial sector so as to create job opportunities, particularly for the young. The Fund also continued to criticize the stringent foreign investment regulations (which were extended to the banking sector in 2010 in a supplementary budget—see Budget). The number of foreign investment projects had fallen sharply, from 102 in 2008 to just four in 2009.

Having revoked the long-standing state of emergency in February 2011, in May of that year the Government announced an increase in budget expenditure in support of measures to counter rising prices and to promote employment, in an attempt to assuage public discontent and pre-empt the kind of political challenges being mounted against other regimes across the Arab world.

Algeria maintained a solid economic performance in 2011, as higher oil prices strengthened the current account and improved fiscal revenues. The IMF estimated overall growth for the year at 2.4%, with non-oil expansion at 5.3%. The Government's main challenge remained to ensure sustainable, diversified and private investment-led growth in order to reduce unemployment. Average inflation rose to 4.5%, partly because of the rise in food prices, and the IMF warned that the increased budget expenditure could, if not moderated, result in excessive inflationary pressures ¬in 2012.

Meanwhile, in mid-2011 the Government announced that it would no longer continue with its targeted privatization programme, because of the lack of progress to date and limited interest from foreign investors. New stakes in state-owned companies would in future be offered on an ad hoc basis. The World Bank continued to rank Algeria poorly (148th of 183 countries) in its *Doing Business 2012* report.

The IMF projected growth of 2.5% in 2012, rising to 3.4% in 2013. The Fund commended Algeria's continued economic resilience in the face of the difficult external environment, but reiterated that surging inflation (which averaged 8.4% in 2012, fuelled by price increases in food and manufactured goods and by excess liquidity), hydrocarbon reliance, high public spending and unemployment remained significant challenges to be addressed. The IMF also urged the Government to make use of financial markets to finance its deficits, rather than relying heavily on its oil stabilization fund, and to address the high level of food, employment and housing subsidies (which accounted for 13.6% of GDP in 2012).

In October 2012 the new Prime Minister, Abdelmalek Sellal, presented his Government's programme, which focused on the promotion of sustainable economic growth, attracting private investment, rehabilitating the public sector and investing in infrastructure in order to meet growing social demands. The IMF had, meanwhile, encouraged the authorities to review and reform Algeria's restrictive foreign direct investment regime, and in January 2013 a new hydrocarbons law, including amendments to the tax system, changes in ownership rules and exploration incentives, was adopted by the National People's Assembly in an effort to attract investors. There was, however, likely to be a negative impact on the investment outlook for the oil and gas sector, owing to security concerns generated by a militant Islamist attack on a gas plant near the south-eastern town of In Amenas in January 2013, in which Algerian and foreign workers were killed.

AGRICULTURE

The agricultural sector employed roughly 11% of Algeria's labour force and accounted for some 8.2% of GDP in 2011. More than 90% of the land consists of arid plateaux, mountains or desert, supporting herds of sheep, goats or camels. Only the northern coastal strip, 100 km–200 km wide, is suitable for arable farming. Most of the Sahara is devoted to semi-desert pasturage. Cultivated land produces cereals, principally wheat and barley; other crops include citrus fruits, vegetables, grapes, olives and dates.

Under President Houari Boumedienne, agricultural production was organized increasingly on a co-operative basis from 1971. However, poor productivity and the high cost of food imports prompted the Chadli administration to relax this policy during the 1980s, assigning land to private farmers, easing price controls and allocating increased public funds for agricultural infrastructure. Despite liberalization of the agricultural sector, Algeria's dependence on food imports continued, reaching as much as 80% of the country's requirements by the early 1990s. In 1994 the Government announced the creation of a lending agency, Crédit Mutuel Agricole, to provide private sector farmers with financial assistance and measures to reschedule their outstanding debts. At the World Bank's insistence, land reform legislation was presented to the National People's Assembly in 1998 to allow the privatization of state-owned farms. However, little progress was made, largely reflecting the influence of powerful political factions opposed to privatization.

Production of cereals has fluctuated considerably, mainly because of frequent droughts. In 2000 the Government introduced the National Agricultural and Rural Development Plan to promote food security, identify resources with potential growth, and protect the environment. Improved cereal harvests were recorded in 2004, 2006 (both 4.0m. metric tons) and 2007 (3.6m. tons). A severe lack of rainfall meant that the 2008 harvest was expected to total only about 2m. tons, necessitating substantial imports to meet domestic needs at a time of high cereal prices on the international market; in the event, however, total cereal output was better than initially anticipated, at 3.6m. tons. Cereal production in 2009 was projected at a record 6m. tons (owing to favourable weather and government incentives to stimulate domestic production), and the Government announced that Algeria had become a net exporter of barley for the first time in 40 years. The cereal crop then decreased to about 4.5m. tons in 2010 and 4m. tons in 2011, and the country continued to rely on wheat imports from the international market to cover its consumption needs. According to FAO, the 2012 cereal harvest, at 5.2m. tons, was the second highest on record, following that of 2009. In November 2012 the Government announced plans to increase grain storage capacity by 1m. tons, as irrigation incentives to farmers were expected to contribute to further larger harvests.

Olives are grown mainly in the western coastal belt and in the north-eastern region of Kabylia. Output fluctuates because of the two-year flowering cycle of the olive. According to FAO estimates, production of olives totalled 420,000 metric tons in 2011. Dates form one of the country's most important non-hydrocarbon exports, despite much of the yield being consumed locally.

Sheep, goats and cattle are raised, but improvements are needed in stock-rearing methods, disease control and water supply if increasing consumer demand for meat is to be fulfilled. FAO data for 2011 estimated that there were 24.0m. sheep, 4.5m. goats and 1.8m. cattle.

The area covered by forests declined rapidly during 1970–90, and areas of forest covering the mountainous regions along the Mediterranean coast have since been destroyed, some as a result of operations carried out by the security forces against Islamist militants.

During the 1990s the Government sought to exploit the country's fishing potential. The total catch rose annually from 92,600 metric tons in 1998 to 141,900 tons in 2003, but decreased to 114,000 tons in 2004. By 2008 it had recovered to 141,615 tons, before falling again to 95,366 tons in 2010 but then rising to 104,000 tons in 2011, according to FAO estimates. Most local fishing activity is carried out in small, family-owned boats, and commercial fishing remains marginal.

PETROLEUM AND NATURAL GAS

Algeria is a major producer and exporter of hydrocarbons. According to the 2013 BP *Statistical Review of World Energy*, its proven and recoverable petroleum reserves at the end of 2012 totalled 12,200m. barrels, while proven reserves of natural gas—mostly unassociated with oilfields—totalled 4,500,000m. cu m. Sonatrach, which is owned by the Algerian Government, has dominated the oil and gas industry since independence, but there is still extensive foreign participation in hydrocarbons development.

Petroleum

Production of crude petroleum in the Algerian Sahara began on a commercial scale, in 1958. The principal producing areas were at Hassi Messaoud, in central Algeria, and around Edjeleh-Zarzaitine in the Polignac Basin, near the Libyan frontier. In the 1960s, with extra pipeline capacity, output of crude petroleum was increased by substantial quantities from oilfields at Gassi Touil, Rhourde el-Baguel and Rhourde Nouss. Subsequent discoveries of petroleum were made at Nezla, Hoaud Berkaoui, Ouargla, Mesdar, el-Borma, Hassi Keskessa, Guellala, Tin Fouyé and el-Maharis.

By 1979 output had reached around 1.2m. barrels per day (b/d). Thereafter, production was restricted in order to prolong the life of the oilfields and, after 1983, to conform to the production quotas set by OPEC. Production of other hydrocarbons, particularly gas, liquefied natural gas (LNG), natural gas liquids (a category including condensates) and refined products, assumed greater importance as a source of government revenues. By 1986 production of crude petroleum had fallen to an average of 670,000 b/d, mainly from the Hassi Messaoud oilfield. However, by the mid-1990s, as new oilfields came into production, output began to rise. In 1999, according to industry figures, production averaged 1.51m. b/d, and output continued to rise annually to reach 1.99m. b/d in 2005, remaining around that level in the following two years. From late 2008, as the international financial crisis precipitated a global economic downturn, petroleum prices declined dramatically from their record mid-year levels. OPEC sought to end the price decline through cuts in output from late 2008, with consequent reductions in Algeria's production quota. Average output was 1.97m. b/d in 2008, 1.77m. b/d in 2009, 1.70m. b/d in 2010, 1.68m. b/d in 2011 and 1.67m. b/d in 2012.

The country's major pipeline carries oil from Hassi Messaoud to coastal export terminals at Arzew, Skikda, Algiers, Annaba, Oran and Béjaia. Another pipeline connects the In Amenas field, in southern Algeria, to an export terminal at La Skhirra, Tunisia. Sonatrach has expanded the existing Hassi Messaoud–Arzew pipeline capacity with the construction of a second, parallel line.

There are petroleum refineries at Algiers, Hassi Messaoud, Skikda, Arzew and Adrar, operated by Naftec (a subsidiary of Sonatrach). The Skikda refinery provides the bulk of Algeria's refined products. The Hassi Messaoud facility supplies products to southern Algeria, while the Algiers refinery processes crude petroleum from Hassi Messaoud for consumption in the capital. The Arzew refinery produces for both domestic consumption and export. In 2003 Sonatrach contracted the National Oil and Gas Exploration and Development Corpn of the People's Republic of China to build a new facility at Adrar, and also announced plans to build a condensate facility at Skikda and to modernize existing refineries. In 2006 the Adrar refinery was brought on stream. In November 2008 a US $400m. contract to upgrade the Arzew refinery was awarded to a consortium from the Republic of Korea (South Korea), which included Hyundai Engineering and Construction, and in May 2009 South Korea's Samsung Engineering won the $2,600m. contract to modernize the Skikda refinery. However, further progress of refinery projects was delayed from early 2010, following investigations into alleged corruption involving Sonatrach's senior management, until September that year, when the company awarded a $908m. contract to France's Technip to refurbish the Algiers refinery. In early 2012 Sonatrach announced plans to expand the country's refining capacity by 360,000 b/d, in order to meet rising domestic demand, by constructing up to four new refineries and also by rehabilitating existing facilities. In March 2013 it was disclosed that the first two new plants, costing $14,000m., would be located at Tiaret and at Biskra, with a proposed capacity of about 100,000 b/d each.

Natural Gas

Most of Algeria's gas comes from the Hassi R'Mel region, 400 km south of Algiers. The field was discovered in 1956, and is still considered to be one of the largest in the world. Unassociated gas is also found near In Amenas, Alrar, Gassi Touil, Rhourde Nouss, Tin Fouyé and In Salah. The Government invested heavily in the development of these gasfields. Pipelines were laid to the coast, to supply local gas distribution systems, and LNG exports began in 1965. The export of dry natural gas to Italy began in 1983, following the inauguration of the Transmediterranean (Transmed—subsequently renamed Enrico Mattei) pipeline running from Algeria to Sicily via Tunisia and the Mediterranean.

Before 1962 Algeria exported relatively small amounts of LNG from the Camel liquefaction plant at Arzew. The next phase of gas development began in the 1970s, with the negotiation of major new export contracts with companies including the USA's Distrigas, Trunkline and El Paso, Belgium's Distrigaz, Enagas of Spain and Italy's Società Nazionale Metanodotti (Snam). However, Algeria lost several customers in the early 1980s as a result of an aggressive pricing policy (linking natural gas prices to those of crude petroleum) before adopting a more flexible approach to win new orders. In the early 1990s Sonatrach signed long-term contracts with Ente Nazionale per l'Energia Elettrica (ENEL) of Italy to deliver gas (as well as LNG supplies) through the Enrico Mattei pipeline, and with Enagas and the Portuguese consortium Transgas for gas via the new Maghreb-Europe pipeline (also known as the Pedro Duran Farell pipeline). In 2000 Sonatrach extended two LNG contracts with Gaz de France to 2013, and in 2003 it signed an agreement with Italy's Mogest to supply natural gas until 2019. Also in 2003 Sonatrach, in partnership with BP, finalized a long-term capacity contract with National Grid to export LNG to the United Kingdom. In 2005 Sonatrach signed a 20-year agreement with National Grid to double its delivery of LNG, and also signed supply agreements with Sempra Energy of the USA and with Occidental Energy Ventures for exports to Mexico. In 2007 Sonatrach and Petrobras of Brazil signed an LNG delivery accord and a co-operation agreement covering oil exploration. Sonatrach also agreed to form a strategic partnership with Energias de Portugal (EDP) for the provision and distribution of natural gas and electricity in the Iberian peninsula. In November of that year Sonatrach signed a long-term agreement to supply EDP with up to 1,600m. cu m of gas annually, and in December it reached an agreement to extend Gaz de France's LNG supply contracts to 2019. In January 2013 long-term LNG contract with Turkey was extended for another 10 years from 2014.

There are gas liquefaction facilities at Skikda and Arzew. In January 2004 three of the Skikda plant's six liquefaction units (trains) were destroyed when a boiler exploded. In September Sonatrach launched a reconstruction project, including the building of a single 4m.-metric-tons per year LNG train. The US $600m.–$700m. project would be financed mainly by a $500m. insurance pay-out, with the remaining costs to be funded by Sonatrach. In 2007 Sonatrach and a Japanese consortium of Ishikawajima-Harima Heavy Industries and Itochu Corpn signed a $1,100m. contract to build three new petroleum gas trains in Arzew, as well as a new refining plant and storage facilities. Also in 2007 Italy's Saipem was awarded the $500m. contract to build a 505-km LPG pipeline between the Hassi R'Mel gasfield and the petrochemical complex at Arzew; United Arab Emirates (UAE)-based Petrofac International was awarded the $600m. contract to build gas compression facilities at the In Salah field; and Sonatrach awarded the $2,900m. engineering, procurement and construction (EPC) contract for the new LNG train at Skikda to US-based Kellogg Brown and Root. During 2008 Saipem won a $1,700m. contract to build an LPG processing facility at Hassi Messaoud; and an Italian-Japanese consortium of Snamprogetti and Chiyoda won a $4,500m. contract to build a new LNG plant at Arzew. In October of that year a cracked pipeline forced Sonatrach to cut LNG production from its Arzew plant, disrupting shipments to Europe. The oldest train at Arzew was closed down in early 2011, having been deemed too dangerous for further operation. The reconstructed LNG train at Skikda (see above) was commissioned in late 2012 and came on stream in April 2013.

There are three gas export pipelines between Algeria and Europe. The Enrico Mattei pipeline runs between Algeria and Italy, the Pedro Duran Farell line runs from Algeria to Spain via Morocco and the Mediterranean, and the Medgaz pipeline links Algeria to Spain. In 2002 Sonatrach signed an agreement with ENEL and Germany's Wintershall to form Galsi, a consortium to build another natural gas pipeline from Hassi R'Mel in Algeria to the Italian mainland via Sardinia. In March 2005 the Government signed 12 letters of intent for the sale of gas through the Galsi pipeline, and in 2007 Rete Gas, a subsidiary of Italy's ENI, signed a memorandum of understanding (MOU) to build the Italian section of the pipeline. However, the Galsi consortium announced in 2009 that the start-up of the pipeline had been delayed to 2014, because of amendments to the planned route and delays in the authorization process. Meanwhile, plans for the Medgaz line had been initiated in 2000, and the project was officially launched in November 2006. The process of laying the 450-km pipeline between Beni Saf in Algeria and Almería in Spain was completed in December 2008, and the pipeline, with an annual capacity of 20,000m. cu m, became commercially operational in April 2011. Sonatrach meanwhile formalized 20-year agreements for the supply of natural gas through the Medgaz line with the Spanish companies Cepsa, Endesa and Iberdrola, and with GDF Suez of France. During 2009 Sonatrach signed contracts worth more than US $1,400m. with Saipem of Italy and Petroleum Projects and Technical Consultations Co (PETROJET) of Egypt for the construction of gas pipelines to increase delivery capacity from the Hassi R'Mel field and feed power stations and export terminals. Contracts were also awarded to SNC Lavalin of Canada (worth $1,100m.) for gas-processing infrastructure in southern Algeria, and to JGC Corpn of Japan (worth $1,500m.) for the construction of gas-gathering facilities at Gassi Touil.

By 2005, with production of natural gas having increased to 88,200m. cu m, exports (mainly to Western Europe, particularly France and Spain) had reached 71,300m. cu m (including 29,500m. cu m of LNG). Production decreased to 84,500m. cu m in 2006, before increasing to 84,800m. cu m in 2007 and further, to 85,800m. cu m, in 2008. However, in 2009 production declined to 79,600m. cu m, largely reflecting decreased international demand as a result of the global economic downturn. In 2010 a slight increase in output, to 80,400m. cu m, was recorded, but production again fell to 78,000m. cu m in 2011. An increase, to 81,500m. cu m, was recorded in 2012. Doubts have arisen regarding Algeria's ability to increase gas exports, owing to rapidly rising domestic demand, infrastructure problems (particularly affecting LNG capacity), and a low level of interest in licensing rounds (see Foreign Participation) that reflected stringent contract terms.

In March 2011 the Government announced that Algeria was interested in developing its extensive shale gas reserves, in view of the increase in domestic demand for gas and the consequent pressure on export capacity. Later that year Sonatrach signed a co-operation agreement with Italy's ENI for the exploration and exploitation of the country's shale gasfields, and in 2012 Talisman Energy and Shell also signed exploration accords.

Sonatrach

Following its establishment in 1963, Sonatrach expanded to become Algeria's largest, most complex and economically most important state company once the petroleum and gas sector had been nationalized in 1971. In 1998 Sonatrach was converted into a joint-stock company with capital entirely subscribed by the state (to prevent foreign investors from acquiring stakes). It has since sought to become a global energy company by forging links with multinational and state oil companies in petrochemicals, refining and power generation. During 2000 a new international holding section was established for Sonatrach's overseas subsidiaries and expansion.

In 2001 the Government proposed legislation ending Sonatrach's monopoly in the domestic petroleum market. Initially shelved owing to widespread opposition from the labour organizations and from within Sonatrach's management, the legislation was reintroduced in 2004 and finally approved in March 2005 with some amendments—including a provision that domestic energy prices would not be liberalized for five to 10 years. Under the law, Sonatrach's function as the country's hydrocarbons regulator and its responsibility for the tendering process for oil and gas exploration blocks were to be assumed by two new autonomous regulatory agencies: the Agence Nationale pour la Valorisation des Ressources en Hydrocarbures (Alnaft), responsible for managing the tendering process, awarding future exploration and production contracts, and the payment of taxes and royalties; and the Agence Nationale de Contrôle et de Régulation des Activités dans le Domaine des Hydrocarbures, responsible for administrative and regulatory activities in the sector. Sonatrach would henceforth compete for licences with international oil companies, which were no longer required to form a partnership with the company when operating exploration contracts. Instead of taking a 50% interest in projects, Sonatrach would have an exploitation option in all future commercial discoveries and pipelines, enabling it to take an equity stake of 25%. In July 2006, however, the Council of Ministers approved an amendment to the hydrocarbons law, which would allow Sonatrach to hold a 51% stake in all commercial discoveries and development projects, thereby restoring Sonatrach's monopoly over energy projects. In December 2011 the Minister of Energy and Mining announced that the Government was to review the hydrocarbons law (see Foreign Participation).

In line with its policy of expanding international co-operation, in 2005 Sonatrach announced that it would pursue hydrocarbon exploration contracts in Libya, Niger, Peru and Tunisia, and confirmed its commitment to a partnership with Nigeria for the development of a gas pipeline linking the two countries. The Governments of Algeria, Niger and Nigeria formally approved the latter US $10,000m. project in July 2009. During 2006 Algeria and Egypt agreed to establish a joint venture to prospect for oil and gas, and Sonatrach secured a 20% interest in an Egyptian offshore concession in the Nile Delta in partnership with Norway's Statoil. In the same year Sonatrach signed accords with the Russian companies Gazprom and Lukoil to co-operate in hydrocarbon exploration and development. This Algerian-Russian partnership prompted concerns within the EU about the potential creation of a gas supply cartel and a consequent rise in prices.

In a scandal that was damaging for Sonatrach and the Algerian Government alike, a number of senior figures in the company's leadership, including President and Director-General Muhammad Meziane, were suspended from their posts in January 2010. The suspensions were announced amid ongoing investigations into alleged corruption in the awarding of contracts, and several other senior staff were subsequently arrested (see History). The Government subsequently introduced regulations restricting the awarding of directly negotiated contracts by Sonatrach and other public organizations, in order to prevent special treatment being given to companies close to the authorities. Restrictions were also placed on the granting of service contracts in the energy sector. Upon the appointment of a new management team, Sonatrach issued a new code of conduct for staff, which set out ethical standards in an effort to draw a line under the scandal. In May 2011 Meziane and other senior executives received various terms of imprisonment, having been convicted of the embezzlement of public funds. At the end of 2011 President Bouteflika inaugurated a new body, the Office Central de Répression de la Corruption, to investigate cases of alleged corruption by public officials.

In mid-2010 Sonatrach won an international arbitration case, dating back to 2007, against Spain's Gas Natural, upholding its right to increase the price of gas supplied to the Spanish company through the Pedro Duran Farell pipeline. In June 2011 Sonatrach agreed to take a 3.85% stake in Gas Natural, and the Spanish utility also paid US $1,300m. to Sonatrach, in compensatory payments to resolve the dispute. Sonatrach in turn agreed to cede 10% of its stake in the Medgaz pipeline to Gas Natural.

Foreign Participation

Following the fall in international petroleum prices in the mid-1980s, the Government was forced to seek much needed foreign investment to improve recovery rates and increase production. New hydrocarbon laws were introduced in 1986 and 1991 to attract foreign investors engaged in oil exploration by offering better terms for concession agreements, service contracts or production-sharing. In December 1987 Italy's Agip became the first foreign company to sign an exploration and production agreement with Sonatrach under the 1986 law. Despite the deteriorating security situation, other foreign companies steadily increased their participation in Algeria's hydrocarbons sector from the early 1990s. These included Mobil of the USA, Repsol of Spain, the United Kingdom's BP and Petro-Canada. In March 1996 the US company Atlantic Richfield Co (Arco) signed a contract with Sonatrach to rehabilitate the Rhourde el-Baguel oilfield, Algeria's second largest field. This was the country's first enhanced oil recovery scheme, and involved the drilling of additional wells and the use of gas injection techniques to increase production.

In 1995 Sonatrach signed a gas exploration and production agreement with BP, the country's first gas production-sharing agreement with a private company. The project (estimated to cost US $2,700m.) identified unexploited fields in the In Salah region to bring a further 9,000m. cu m of gas on stream by 2004. Sonatrach agreed that the gas would be marketed with BP in a 50:50 joint-venture company. Progress in the project was slow initially, owing to the depressed price of gas (which remained linked to that of oil) and the need to sign more gas purchase agreements. Despite the signing of agreements with Italy's Edison and ENEL, negotiations with other European countries were hampered by EU legislation of 1998 that prevented the original importer from reselling the gas to another EU country. Nevertheless, in 2001 contracts were awarded to enable the project to go ahead—Japan's JGC Corpn and US-based Kellogg Brown and Root were selected for the main EPC project; Bechtel of the USA for in-field pipelines and a pipeline link to Hassi R'Mel; and the Sonatrach subsidiary Enefor for the drilling development programme. In July 2004 BP announced that the In Salah project had come on stream. (In 2003 Statoil had acquired 50% of BP's interest in the In Salah project, together with 50% of BP's holding in another development at In Amenas.)

In 1996 Total of France and Repsol signed a production agreement with Sonatrach to develop the Tin Fouye Tabankort gasfield, the second agreement of its kind between the state energy company and private investors. After a total investment of US $700m., the field came on stream in 1999. In 1998 Cepsa announced investment of more than $1,000m. to develop the new Ourhoud field, in co-operation with Sonatrach. Production from the field began in 2002. Also in 1998 the US-headquartered company Anadarko announced a major investment programme to develop three oilfields, and began producing oil at Hassi Berkine South.

In 1999 Mobil announced that, as a result of depressed world petroleum markets, it had stopped all exploration and production in Algeria. However, following a sharp rise in oil prices later that year, a number of other international oil companies confirmed that they were proceeding with major development projects in the country. By then, Arco and Sonatrach had invested more than US $1,000m. in the redevelopment of the Rhourde el-Baguel oilfield. In 2000 Anadarko signed agreements with contractors for the development of facilities (completed in 2002) for the Hassi Berkine South field and for Hassi Berkine North to increase total output capacity. Also in 2000 Burlington Resources of the USA announced a major new oil and gas discovery in the Berkine Basin, and, after more than two years of negotiations, Amerada Hess (now Hess Corpn) of the USA signed an agreement with Sonatrach to invest $500m. over 25 years in enhanced recovery from the Zotti, El-Gassi and El-Agreb fields, south-east of Hassi Messaoud (with Sonatrach retaining a 51% stake in the production-sharing contract).

In 2000 Australia's BHP acquired a 60% stake in the Ohanet gas condensate project being developed with Japan Ohanet Oil and Gas and Petrofac Resources. With reserves estimated at 96,300m. cu m, the project was expected to produce 30,400 b/d of condensate, 27,700 b/d of LPG and 665m. cu m of natural gas, commencing in 2003. The contract to design and build a gas processing plant and a 236-km pipeline for the project was awarded to ABB and Petrofac International of the United Kingdom. BHP also announced that it was proceeding with the Rhourde Ouled Djemma integrated development project near Ohanet, at a cost of US $500m., in partnership with Agip Algeria Exploration and Sonatrach.

In October 2000 Sonatrach opened its first public licensing round for six exploration blocks—four in the Berkine Basin and one each at In Salah and Constantine. In March 2001 the Ministry of Energy and Mining awarded contracts for three of the blocks—to the Russian companies Rosneft and Stroytransgaz in the Illizi Basin; to Gulf Keystone Petroleum of the UAE in the Constantine region; and to Anadarko in the Berkine Basin—but no bids were received for the remaining three blocks. A second international bidding round for 15 oil and gas blocks was launched in May of that year. Participation was lower than expected, and there were no offers for blocks in frontier areas outside Berkine. Companies receiving blocks included Anadarko, Burlington Resources, First Calgary Petroleums of Canada, TotalFinaElf and Repsol-YPF.

In 2002, following a third international bidding round, Sonatrach signed oil and gas exploration contracts valued at US $105m. Companies granted blocks included Anadarko in the Berkine Basin; Petrovietnam in Oued Mya; a consortium of Germany's RWE-DEA, Cepsa, Repsol and Edison in Reggane; Gaz de France in the Sbaâ Basin; TotalFinaElf (renamed Total in 2003) and Cepsa in Timimoum; and Cyprus-based Medex Petroleum in Illizi. In 2003 Anadarko formed a partnership with the Kuwait Foreign Petroleum Exploration Co and announced a new oil discovery at Sif Fatima South West well, near the Berkine Basin. In November 2002 Sonatrach and BP signed an agreement for a second major gas and condensate project at In Amenas in the Illizi Basin. The project, which also included the construction of three pipelines to carry the gas to the Ohanet distribution system, came on stream in June 2006.

In 2003 Sonatrach and First Calgary Petroleums reached an agreement to develop the Menzel Ledjmet East gas and condensate field in the Berkine Basin. Sonatrach also reported a new oil discovery in the Hassi Dzabat region, in the north-east of Rhourde el-Baguel, and Anadarko and its partners reported a discovery in the Berkine Basin North East field area. Gas discoveries included a major field, with reserves estimated at 20,000m. cu m per year, in the Reggane Basin in south-west Algeria, and a major condensate gas deposit north of the Gassi Touil field. In May 2004 Sonatrach also announced the discovery of a new gas deposit in the Timimoun Basin in the south-west.

In December 2003, meanwhile, Sonatrach awarded five new oil and gas exploration contracts as part of the fourth licensing round: two blocks in Chelif and Oued Mya Basins were awarded to the China National Petroleum Co; Amguid in Hassi Messaoud was awarded to Petro-Canada; the Ahnet Basin in Ohanet went to the Repsol-Edison international consortium; and the Béchar block in the Sahara desert was awarded to Total Algérie and Cepsa. However, seven blocks remained without bids, including two offshore Mediterranean blocks and blocks in the Berkine Basin and Sahara desert. At the end of 2004 a US $2,100m. contract for the integrated Gassi Touil LNG project in the southern Berkine Basin was awarded to a Spanish consortium of Repsol and Gas Natural, but this was later terminated in 2007.

In July 2004, following the opening of the fifth international licensing round in April, Sonatrach awarded eight (of 10) licences: the largest permit, Hassi Mouina in the Gourara Basin, was awarded to Statoil; Agreb in the Amguid Messaoud Basin went to Amerada Hess; of three blocks in the Oued Mya Basin, El-M'zaid was awarded to CNPC, and Guerara and El Hadjira to Sinopec of China; Ireland's Petroceltic International was awarded the Isarene permit in the Illizi Basin; Repsol and Gas Natural were awarded Gassi Chergui West in the Berkine Basin; and a joint venture of Australia's BHP Billiton and Woodside won the Ksar Hirane block in the Benoud Basin. In late 2004 new gas discoveries were reported by First Calgary Petroleums in the Berkine Basin, south-east of Hassi Messaoud, and by a consortium led by Total in the Timimoun Basin, south of Hassi R'Mel.

In April 2005 nine (of 10) exploration contracts were awarded in the sixth international licensing round: BP was awarded two blocks—Bourarhat South and South East Illizi—in the Illizi Basin, and a third block at Hassi Matmat in the Oued Mya Basin; Shell, returning to Algeria after an absence of almost two decades, was awarded Reggane Hirane in the Reggane Basin and Zerafa in the Timimoun Basin; BHP Billiton was awarded Hassi Bir Rekais in the Berkine Basin and Oudoume in the Illizi Basin; and Gulf Keystone Petroleum was awarded the Bottena block in the South East Constantine Basin and Hassi Ba Hamou in the Béchar Oued Namous Basin.

Sonatrach and ENI reported new hydrocarbon reserves in the Berkine Basin and the northern Saharan region in late 2005, and a discovery in Amguid Messaoud in early 2006. In the same period, further oil discoveries were confirmed by Petrovietnam in Touggourt, and by First Calgary Petroleums in the Tagi zone. The Edison consortium reported a gas discovery in the Reggane Nord concession, and signed an agreement to establish a new company, Sociedad de Licuefacción, to build and operate a gas liquefaction terminal. Total also reported a discovery in the Timimoun gas perimeter in south-western Algeria.

There were 17 oil and gas discoveries made by Sonatrach and its partners in 2006. In 2007 a further 18 discoveries were made, including in the Berkine, Illizi, Oued Mya and Gourara Basins, by First Calgary Petroleums, Medex Petroleum (North Africa), Petroceltic International, China National Petroleum Co, Anadarko and Statoil. The Russian energy companies Rosneft and Stroytransgaz also announced plans to invest US $1,300m. in hydrocarbon exploration and development. In October it was confirmed that Sonatrach would develop the Gassi Touil project alone, following the cancellation of the contract with Repsol and Gas Natural because of delays, higher cost projections and technical complications.

In January 2008 the Ministry of Energy and Mining's Agence Nationale pour la Valorisation des Ressources en Hydrocarbures (Alnaft) invited companies to prequalify for the country's long-awaited seventh international licensing round, which had been delayed several times to allow for the implementation of the hydrocarbons law. However, when bids were finally opened in December, just nine were tendered for a total of four blocks (won by ENI and BG in the Gourara Basin, and by Russia's Gazprom and Germany's E.ON Ruhrgas in the Berkine Basin). Although international companies criticized the contract conditions and the complexity of the prequalification and bidding criteria, the Government stated that the lack of bids was attributable to the prevailing economic downturn rather than to its terms. Also in 2008 Sonatrach announced new gas discoveries in partnerships with Statoil, BP, BG and Gulf Keystone, while Repsol made discoveries in the Reggane, Ahnet and Berkine Basins. A major joint venture between Sonatrach and Anadarko to develop a US $3,800m. central hydrocarbons processing facility in the el-Merk Basin in the Sahara progressed in early 2009 with the award of construction contracts to Petrofac International, ABB and Egypt's Orascom Construction Industries (OCI).

The eighth international licensing round was launched, mainly for gas exploration, by Alnaft in June 2009. However, the results, announced in December, were similarly disappointing, with only three of the 10 licences on offer being awarded: the Ahnet field to Total; the Hassi Bir Rekaiz permit in the Berkine Basin to the China National Offshore Oil Corpn; and the South East Illizi licence to Repsol. Although the Government attributed the outcome to the depressed state of the world gas market, international companies still regarded the contractual terms as harsh.

In 2009 Alnaft approved gas exploration and development plans with the Russian companies Rosneft and Stroytransgaz in the Illizi Basin, with GDF Suez of France in the Touat field and with Total and Cepsa in the Timimoun field. It also gave approval to operators for three other oil developments: to Petrovietnam Investment and Development Co for the Bir Sbaa field near Hassi Messaoud; to Rosneft and Stroytransgaz for the Takouezet East and Takouezet West fields; and to ConocoPhillips for the Menzel Ledjmet South East oilfield. In August of that year BP announced plans to invest US $2,000m. by 2014 in order to maintain production at the In Salah and In Amenas fields and to carry out further exploration work in its Bouraret field. In November 2009 Sonatrach and Hess Corpn launched a further phase, valued at $400m., of their programme to enhance recovery at the El-Agreb, El-Gassi and Zotti fields. Sonatrach announced in December 2009 that it had made five new hydrocarbon discoveries in the Berkine, Illizi and Amguid Messaoud basins. In total, 16 new hydrocarbons discoveries were made in 2009—nine by Sonatrach itself and the remainder in co-operation with foreign companies. Sonatrach, Gazprom and E.ON Ruhrgas announced further discoveries in the Berkine Basin during 2010.

In September 2010 Alnaft opened another international licensing round for 10 blocks. However, the results were again disappointing as only two licences were awarded in early 2011: one to Sonatrach for the Rhourde Fares concession in the Berkine Basin; and the other to Cepsa for the Rhourde Rouni concession in the Sbâa Basin. As in previous rounds, many of the areas on offer went unclaimed, in part because of resistance among international energy firms to Algeria's tough contract terms, and perhaps also reflecting the uncertainty of the political situation across the Arab world from early 2011.

After a long delay, in early 2011 the Government approved Repsol's development plans (submitted in 2009) for the Reggane North gasfield in partnership with Sonatrach, RWE and Edison. The contract, worth US $3,000m., was finally signed in February 2012. The Government also endorsed plans for Gulf Keystone Petroleum and BG to develop the Hassi Bahamou field, and for ENI to develop Rhourde Messaoud Nord. In January 2011 Petrofac International was awarded a $1,200m. contract to develop southern fields (Garet el Befinat, Hassi Moumene, In Salah and Gour Mohmoud) in the In Salah development, with the aim of increasing production at the gasfields to 9,000m. cu m annually by 2013. Also in 2011 Sonatrach and E.ON Ruhrgas announced an oil and gas discovery at Rhourde Yacoub in the Berkine Basin; Alnaft awarded Sonatrach an exploration licence for the offshore Béjaïa-Annaba perimeter; and JGC Corpn of Japan was awarded a $400m. EPC services contract for the Bir Sbaa field development project.

In December 2011 the Minister of Energy and Mining announced that the hydrocarbons law would be revised in 2012. The revision, adopted by the National People's Assembly in January 2013, was intended to make the terms and conditions for exploration projects more attractive to foreign investors in advance of the next licensing round. The Government planned to tax international oil companies on their profits rather than turnover. The law was also designed to promote investment in offshore reserves and unconventional resources such as shale gas (see Natural Gas, above). Future contracts would additionally take account of the degree of difficulty and risk in hydrocarbon exploration.

In December 2012 Sonatrach agreed a contract with French firm CGG Veritas to start offshore exploration. Also that month Alnaft approved Petroceltic International's development plan for the Ain Tsila gas condensate field in the Illizi basin. Hydrocarbon discoveries in 2012 and early 2013 included a gas find in the South East Illizi block by Repsol, the location of a new oil and gas reservoir in the El Assel field in the Berkine Basin by a Gazprom consortium, and a further oil find in the Berkine Basin at the Hassi Bir Rekaiz field by a group led by Thailand's PTTEP. Meanwhile, the Menzel Ledjmet South East field in the Berkine Basin began gas production in December 2012, and ConocoPhillips announced plans to sell its Algerian interests to Pertamin of Indonesia. In January 2013 ENI began production at the Menzel Ledjmet East field (formerly operated by First Calgary Petroleum).

An unprecedented militant attack on the In Amenas gas facility in January 2013 (see History) prompted uncertainty over future investment in the hydrocarbons sector as foreign energy firms sought security guarantees from the Government, and in May BP was reported to be reviewing its major gas projects in the country.

OTHER MINERALS

Algeria has rich deposits of iron ore, phosphates, lead, zinc and antimony. Legislation adopted in 1991 (and amended in 1999) encouraged local private sector and foreign investment in the mining sector, which had been nationalized in 1966. The aim was to increase exploration and reverse declining production. In 2000 the Minister of Energy and Mining announced that 48 small mines (producing gold, semi-precious stones and marble) would be put out to tender for local investors. At the end of the first phase of the programme 24 licences, mainly for marble, sand and gold projects, had been awarded. In 2001 a new mining law provided for the creation of two organizations—the Agence Nationale du Patrimoine Minier (ANPM) and the Agence Nationale du Contrôle des Mines—to manage the mining sector, leaving the state to act as a regulator rather than an operator. The legislation put all investors—local and foreign, public and private—on an equal footing, no longer insisting on the state taking a 51% stake in all discoveries. In early 2011 the Government approved the establishment of a new public mining group, Manadjim El Djazair (Manal), comprising five state companies—Ferphos, Eng, Enof, Enasel and Enamarbre; Manal was to oversee increased exploration and exploitation of Algeria's mineral resources.

In January 2007 the Government issued tenders for 18 mineral prospecting permits, covering gold, copper, lead and zinc deposits. Exploration permits were subsequently issued to three Chinese companies (Shaolin, CGC Overseas Construction Co and China Geo-Engineering Corpn) and Canada's Cancor Mines. At the first international mining conference in Algiers in December 2007 (attended by representatives from more than 20 countries and 50 foreign companies) the Government launched a second exploration licensing round, covering a range of minerals including gold, diamond, copper, lead and zinc. This was aimed at developing the south-eastern area of the country and diversifying the economy away from hydrocarbons. Some 29 licences were awarded in 2009, and in early 2010 the Government invited expressions of interest for up to 54 new mineral exploration and mine operating permits. In December 2011 Sonatrach announced that it was seeking a new investor for the development of the Tirek-Amesmessa gold mine following the withdrawal of its former partner, GMA Resources of Australia. In the previous month Qatar Mining signed an MOU with Manal to co-operate in the mining sector. In early 2012 the ANPM opened an international bidding round for 18 mining sites, and in October the Government announced plans to open lead-zinc mines at Sétif, Batna and Béjaïa, a barite mine at Béchar and a gold mine at Tamanrasset. In December the ANPM issued a tender for a further 20 sites with clay, limestone and sandstone resources, and in April 2013 it awarded four local companies exploration permits in the provinces of Ghardaïa, Naâma, Souk Ahras and Laghouat.

Iron ore is mined at Beni-Saf, Zaccar, Timezrit and near the eastern frontier at Ouenza and Bou Khadra. The average grade of ore is 50%–60%. Production has fluctuated greatly since independence, reaching 2.1m. metric tons (metal content) in 1974, falling to 897,000 tons in 1981 and then rising again to 2.1m. tons in 2008. In late 2007 the Government announced proposals to develop an iron ore mine as part of a major steel-processing project. The project would involve the exploitation of iron ore deposits in Gara Djebilet (near the border with Mauritania), construction of a railway line to transport the ore, and a steel plant to process the iron. In late 2009 it was reported that Sonatrach was in the process of seeking partners to develop the project.

Production of lead and zinc ores at el-Abed, on the Algerian–Moroccan frontier, and at the Kherzet Youcef mine, in the Sétif region, ended in 2004. In 2006 a consortium led by Terramin Australia announced plans to develop zinc resources at Oued Amizour, on the north coast, after securing an exploration permit for an area of 125 sq km. Terramin held 65% in the Western Mediterranean Zinc Spa (WMZ) consortium, with the remaining 35% held by two Algerian government-owned companies. Preliminary studies in 2007 indicated potential production of 2m. metric tons a year, representing one of the largest prospective zinc deposits in the Mediterranean region. A favourable feasibility study for the most significant Tala Hamza deposit, estimated at 68m. tons, was completed in September 2010.

Exploitation of large phosphate deposits at Djebel-Onk began in 1960. Total phosphate rock output was 1.8m. metric tons in 2008, but the depressed world market meant that production declined to just over 1m. tons in 2009. Algeria's other mineral resources include tungsten, manganese, mercury, copper and salt.

ELECTRICITY AND WATER

Conventional thermal sources, predominantly natural gas, provide almost all of Algeria's electricity supply, supplemented by a small amount of hydroelectricity. With an installed generating capacity of 11,390 MW in 2010, Algeria faces accelerating domestic demand for electricity, which, according to the state power company, the Société Algérienne de l'Electricité et du Gaz (SONELGAZ), is expected to increase at a rate of about 10% per year up to 2020. In response, and following civil disturbances over major power outages in mid-2012, the Government announced plans in August that year to invest up to US $30,000m. to almost double the generating capacity to 19,000 MW, partly through renewable energy resources.

By the early 1990s most of Algeria's installed electricity capacity was supplied by gas-fired power plants in Algiers, Annaba and Oran, although there were also a number of small hydroelectric stations in Kabylia. Gas turbine plants came on stream at Hassi Messaoud in 1999, and at Hamma and Aïn M'Lila in 2002. The first stage of a 300-MW gas turbine plant in Hassi Berkine, the country's first privately financed project, was completed in 2001 and the other two units became operational in 2002.

In 2002 new legislation to deregulate the power sector and open it up to private investment was ratified by the National People's Assembly. Under its provisions SONELGAZ lost its monopoly status, becoming a joint-stock company in which the state retained a majority shareholding, with 30% open to private investment. In 2004 three new SONELGAZ subsidiaries were created: Gestionnaire du Réseau de Transport Gaz, Gestionnaire du Réseau de Transport d'Electricité and Gestionnaire du Réseau de Production d'Electricité. An independent regulatory authority, the Commission de Régulation de l'Electricité et du Gaz, assumed responsibility for regulating the power sector in 2005, and was charged with administering legislation intended to open up 30% of the retail market to private competition.

The Algerian Energy Company (AEC), established as a joint venture in 2001 between SONELGAZ and Sonatrach, is responsible for a range of generation projects and for pursuing partnerships with foreign investors. Reflecting Algeria's policy to attract private investment for power projects, the construction of a 1,200-MW independent water and power plant at Arzew in a joint venture between AEC and Black & Veatch of the USA was completed in 2005, an 800-MW independent power plant at Skikda undertaken by Canada's SNC Lavalin came into operation in 2006, a 490-MW gas-fired plant at Berroughia was completed in 2007 in partnership with Germany's Siemens and Italy's Saipem, and a 1,200-MW combined-cycle power plant at Hadjret Ennous in Tipaza has been built by SNC Lavalin in a joint venture with Abu Dhabi (UAE)-based Mubadala Development Co. Meanwhile, the renewable energy agency New Energy Algeria (NEAL) has developed the country's first solar/gas hybrid power plant (with a 25-MW solar component) at Hassi R'Mel, inaugurated in 2011. In 2007 SONELGAZ had awarded contracts for projects at Terga and Koudiet Draouch—two combined cycle plants with a total capacity of 2,400 MW—to a consortium of Alstom of France and OCI of Egypt. The Terga plant was completed in 2012, while the Koudiet Draouch facility was expected to be operational in 2013. In 2012 SONELGAZ awarded Daewoo of South Korea a contract for a 1,200-MW combined-cycle power plant in Boumerdès.

In response to an initiative by the mainly German consortium Desertec to develop solar energy in North Africa for the supply of electricity to Europe, in October 2009 the Algerian Government announced that it would only work with the consortium if the latter agreed to partnerships with Algerian firms. However, at a meeting in December 2010, President Bouteflika and Germany's Federal Chancellor, Angela Merkel, agreed to create a joint economic commission aimed at developing renewable energy sources as part of the Desertec project. In that month the Algerian Government announced that it aimed to generate as much electricity from renewable energy sources as from gas by 2030, and that it would draw up a national plan for renewables development. In July 2011 the Government released details of the plan, with the target of installing up to 22,000 MW of generating capacity from renewable sources by 2030. The investment programme envisaged 67 projects, including solar plants, photovoltaic facilities, hybrid power stations and wind farms. In April 2012 a German consortium was awarded the contract to build a photovoltaic manufacturing facility at Rouiba.

From the mid-1980s Algeria's development, with Chinese assistance, of a 15-MW nuclear reactor at Birine prompted speculation that the facility was for military use. In response, the Government submitted to inspection by the International Atomic Energy Agency from 1992. Following the inauguration of the reactor in December 1993, Algeria acceded to the Treaty on the Non-Proliferation of Nuclear Weapons in 1995. In December 2007 the Government announced plans for a uranium exploration programme to increase reserves and boost the use of nuclear energy, and for a regulatory agency. In May 2010 the Government signed a civil nuclear energy co-operation agreement with its South African counterpart.

In 2001 the Government announced plans to invest US $3,500m. in the water sector to ease severe shortages, of which $1,200m. would provide an emergency fund for projects in the north of the country. In 2002 AEC began several projects for integrated seawater desalination units coupled with power stations, including the water and power plant at Arzew (developed jointly by Black & Veatch and AEC, see above) and a plant at Hamma, which came into service in 2007.

In 2005 the Government announced plans to award contracts to private companies to manage the provision of water services in the major cities. Suez Environnement of France won the five-year management contract for the capital's water services in December of that year. The contract was renewed for a further five years and extended to the province of Tipaza in 2011.

Investment plans were announced by the Government in 2006 to relieve drinking water shortages. The projects included a US $1,000m. water transfer pipeline to link the southern city of Tamanrasset to In Salah (which was completed in April 2011) and a dam to provide drinking water and irrigation. The Government planned to have 15 desalination plants in operation by 2015, supplying up to 1m. cu m of water per day, and also to oversee the construction of 20 new dams, beginning in 2010, to meet water requirements to 2040. Singapore-based Hyflux was awarded contracts in 2006 and 2008 to build desalination plants at Tlemcen (which was inaugurated in 2011) and Magtaa (expected to be operational in 2013), respectively, while in 2007 the Spanish consortium Geida won a contract to build a plant in Honaine (which was under trial in 2012). A further facility, at Fouka, was inaugurated in July 2011.

TRANSPORT

Rail routes within Algeria are managed by the state railway company, the Société Nationale des Transports Ferroviaires (SNTF), and include Algiers–Oran, Béchar–Mohammedia, Mohammedia–Mostaganem, Algiers–Annaba, Constantine–Touggourt, Constantine–Skikda, Algiers–Tizi Ouzou, Annaba–Tébessa and Djelfa–Blida. There are international rail links to Morocco and Tunisia.

In 2003 SNTF awarded a US $74m. contract to a consortium of local and Turkish companies to construct a rail link between Tizi Ouzou and Oued Aissi. Spain's Obrascon Huarte Lain was subsequently awarded a €248m. contract to upgrade the rail link between Annaba and Ramdane Djamel in the north-east. In 2007 Thales of France won a €268m. contract to supply signalling and telecommunications equipment for three sections of the North Railway Bypass project serving the main cities of Oran, Algiers and Constantine along the northern coastal region. Development plans for an east–west railway line along the High Plateau region, south of the Atlas Mountains, were announced during 2008, and the SNTF invited bids for the $1,500m. project during 2009. Also in 2009 two suburban rail lines were inaugurated in Algiers, as were a 256-km line between Algiers and Béjaia, and a 300-km line linking the capital with Sétif. In May 2010 Spain's Fomento de Construcciones y Contratas (FCC) won a $1,330m. contract to build a 185-km railway line running west of Algiers and connecting the towns of Relizane, Tiaret and Tissemsilt. The Government's 2010–14 development plan (see Budget) allocated some $30,000m. to the railways, with the aim of increasing the coverage of the national network from 3,500 km to 10,500 km. In early 2011 contracts were awarded to a joint venture of FCC with the local company ETRHB Haddad to build a new 66-km line between Tlemcen and Akkid Abbas; to two local consortia for a 150-km line between Boughezoul and M'Sila, and a 139-km line to connect Boughezoul and Tissemsilt; and to an Italian joint venture led by Astaldi for the Saïda–Tiaret section of the High Plateau line. In November 2012 the Government announced plans for further new rail projects, worth an estimated $4.500m., to construct over 600 km of new track and to modernize existing lines. New routes would include Djelfa–Boughezoul (140 km), Touggourt–Hassi Messaoud (154 km) and Mecheria–El Bayadh (130 km), with new suburban lines in Arzew and Beni-Saf and a connection from Algiers airport to Bab Ezzouar.

Long-standing plans for the construction of a metro system for Algiers were revived in 2000, when Entreprise du Métro d'Alger (EMA) invited international construction companies to bid for two projects: a 9-km underground network with 10 stations; and a 4.3-km network with four stations. A consortium led by Siemens won the €400m. underground contract in 2005. The first line of the Algiers metro commenced operations in November 2011. The Government had meanwhile appointed Semaly-Ingerop of France to conduct a feasibility study for a tramway system in Algiers to carry up to 200,000 passengers: on an eastbound link to Aïn Taya and Borj el Kiffan; and westbound to Bab el-Oued and Aïn Benian. In March 2006 a consortium led by France's Systra won the contract to manage construction of the eastbound link. In 2008 EMA awarded contracts worth €662m. to two European consortia led by Alstom to build tram systems in Oran (an 18-km line serving 32 stations, which was inaugurated in May 2013) and Constantine (an 8-km line serving 11 stations), and in 2010 it invited bids for the construction of a new 12-km tram line at Mostaganem.

The main international airport—Houari Boumedienne—is at Algiers, with some international services also using Annaba, Constantine and Oran airports. A new international terminal at Houari Boumedienne, operated by Aéroports de Paris and with an annual capacity in excess of 6m. passengers, opened in 2006. In 2007 the Ministry of Transport confirmed that the domestic aviation sector would remain closed to private companies (thereby confirming the monopoly of the national airline, Air Algérie).

The principal seaports are Algiers, Oran, Annaba, Mostaganem, Arzew, Béjaia, Skikda and Jijel. In 1996 a multipurpose container terminal opened at Annaba, and in 1998 a new port at Djen-Djen, near Jijel, opened to serve Algeria's first free zone (see Manufacturing). By the end of 2000 a new 17.5 ha container terminal had opened at Algiers, which was subsequently expanded to handle some 450,000 containers per year. In 2004 Entreprise Portuaire d'Alger announced plans to double the capital's port capacity to 20m. tons per year by 2010 by building a new container terminal and upgrading the main quay superstructure. The Compagnie Nationale Algérienne de Navigation (CNAN) is the state shipping line, offering freight, chartering and transit services. In March 2009 Dubai (UAE)-based maritime terminal operator DP World won the contract to run the Port of Algiers (renamed DP World Djazair) for a period of 30 years. The operator also assumed responsibility for the port at Djen-Djen. In 2009 the Ministry of Transport awarded a construction contract for the expansion of Djen-Djen port to South Korea's Daewoo Engineering and Construction Co Ltd. In October 2011 the Government announced plans for the construction of a new deepwater seaport, expected to be located between Algiers and Tenes, to relieve the congestion at the country's other major ports.

In 2000 the Government announced plans to privatize all road transport, and indicated that it was seeking private investment in the national road system. New financing from the European Investment Bank (EIB) was approved in 2000 and 2002 to support the further development of the motorway network, including an 80-km motorway in the Algiers region, and improvements to the Greater Algiers road system. During the 1990s the Government had revived plans for an east–west motorway system, linking Annaba and Tlemcen and forming part of a trans-Maghreb motorway, with funding from the EIB and the African Development Bank. An Asian consortium was awarded the estimated US $7,000m. contract for the project in 2006. The Consortium Japonais pour l'Autoroute Algérienne (COJAAL) was to construct the 399-km eastern section, and a Chinese consortium comprising the CITIC Group and the China Railway Construction Corpn was to build the 359-km western section. In 2008 the state roads agency issued tenders for a contract to undertake technical studies for a 1,000-km road across the north of the country (in addition to the east–west motorway system). The project was to be divided into three parts: an eastern section between Batna and Tébessa, near the border with Tunisia; a western section linking Tiaret and El-Aricha, near the Moroccan border; and a 495-km central section connecting the two. In 2010 the contracts awarded to CITIC/CRCC were cancelled, following an investigation into alleged corruption (see History). In early 2011 the Government announced plans for 15 new road construction projects in Algiers, at a cost of about $400m., in an effort to reduce traffic congestion in the capital. Eleven new road projects scheduled to be launched in 2013 were to include links between Algeria's seaports and the east–west motorway system.

TELECOMMUNICATIONS

In 2000 a posts and telecommunications bill was ratified by the National People's Assembly, removing the state's monopoly over this sector and redefining its role to that of a supervisory authority. The new legislation provided for the appointment of an independent regulator, and opened up both the fixed-line and mobile sectors to foreign competition. In 2001 the Government announced the creation of a new joint-stock company, Algérie Télécom, to be responsible for the country's fixed-line services and existing GSM licence—functions previously undertaken by the Ministry of Posts and Telecommunications.

In July 2001 a second GSM licence, valued at US $737m., was awarded to the Egyptian company Orascom Telecom, to provide services in Algiers and in 11 other cities in the north-east. The service, which was to operate under the brand name Djezzy, was officially launched in 2002. The country's third GSM licence, worth $421m., was awarded to Kuwait National Mobile Telecommunications (Wataniya Telecom) in 2003. The GSM network, known as Nedjma, was inaugurated in the following year, covering the provinces of Algiers, Boumerdès, Tipaza, Oran and Constantine.

In March 2005 a 15-year fixed-line licence was awarded to an Egyptian consortium of Orascom Telecom and Telecom Egypt for its US $65m. bid. The licence included a two-year exclusivity period to operate both national and international network services, ending Algérie Télécom's monopoly. The two companies held equal stakes in the project company. Algérie Télécom announced plans in November 2009 to spend $6,000m. in order to upgrade its mobile and fixed-line operations by 2014. Meanwhile, in early 2009 the Government had announced that it would no longer consider privatizing Algérie Télécom, and that the company's capital would not be opened to private investors. In early 2010 an appeal lodged by Orascom Telecom against rulings that Djezzy owed outstanding taxes and penalties was rejected by the Algerian tax authorities. In mid-2010 the Government refused Orascom's proposed sale of Djezzy to MTN of South Africa, claiming that the state had a pre-emptive right to purchase the company according to foreign ownership rules. Orascom then agreed to enter into negotiations with the Government regarding Djezzy's nationalization and to resolve the dispute centring on Orascom's settling of its liabilities in Algeria. In January 2011 the Government appointed international law firm Shearman & Sterling to provide a valuation and advice concerning the selection of a partner for its acquisition of Djezzy. In August 2011 the Government announced that it would begin the licensing process for third generation (3G) mobile phone networks. The tender was to be open to Algeria's three existing mobile operators, but the award of the licences was then postponed until the future of Djezzy was resolved. Negotiations over Djezzy—now also involving the Russian operator Vimpelcom, which had acquired a stake in 2011—were further complicated in early 2012, after the Government rejected Shearman & Sterling's valuation and an Algerian court imposed a $1,300m. fine on Djezzy for breaches of currency regulations. Djezzy's status remained unresolved as of mid-2013 and the 3G licensing process had yet to be launched.

MANUFACTURING

At independence the Algerian manufacturing sector was very small, being confined mainly to food processing, building materials, textiles and minerals. The departure of the French entailed loss of demand, capital and skill, thereby decelerating the industrialization process. Foreign firms became increasingly reluctant in the 1960s to invest in Algeria because of the risk of nationalization. At the start of the 1970s the Government implemented a highly centralized industrialization programme, funded largely by hydrocarbon export revenues. However, the decline in world oil prices in the 1980s adversely affected investment in what had become an inefficient structure, where many of the new industrial plants were running substantially below capacity. The Government therefore sought to stimulate foreign investment, and to allow the private sector a greater role in establishing manufacturing industries.

Algeria's first free zone for industrial development opened in 1998 on a site at Bellara, near Jijel international airport and 40 km from a new harbour.

In 1992 the Government announced measures to open state sector industries to local (private) and foreign participation, recognizing that income from hydrocarbons was insufficient to finance the recovery of Algeria's industrial base and that privatization was essential to provide investment and new technology. The only exceptions would be industries classified as strategic, such as the Entreprise Nationale de Sidérurgie (SIDER), SONELGAZ and agro-industrial companies. A new Ministry of Industrial Restructuring and Participation was created in 1994 to oversee the restructuring of state companies, as required by the agreements signed with the IMF in 1994 and 1995 (see Government Strategy). In 1999 the Ministry presented a report outlining major policy objectives for the manufacturing sector during the period to 2015. The report emphasized the need to achieve sustained industrial growth, improve the competitiveness of industrial enterprises, diversify products and promote a competitive export sector. Industrial production had meanwhile increased by 10.5% in 1998, representing the first recorded annual growth since 1991.

Despite ambitious plans to expand the country's petrochemical industries, technical and financial problems have in the past hindered progress. The largest petrochemical plants are: a high-density polyethylene plant (with an ethylene cracker and aromatics complex) at Skikda, which came into operation in 1999 after long delays in its construction; a fertilizer plant at Arzew, producing ammonia, urea and ammonium nitrate; and an ammonium nitrate facility and nitric acid complex at Annaba. Following its decision in 1998 to open the downstream oil and gas sector to foreign investment, the Government had started negotiations with several international companies wishing to invest in petrochemicals. In that year a US $500m. joint venture was agreed between Fertiberia of Spain and Sonatrach, together with the state-owned fertilizer and phosphate companies Enterprise Publique Economique Asmidal, SpA and the Entreprise Nationale du Fer et du Phosphate (Ferphos), to produce fertilizers and ammonia products for the Algerian market and for export. Both Asmidal and Ferphos were to be opened to foreign investors under the privatization programme. During 2006 Sonatrach issued invitations for international companies to take a majority stake in Enterprise Nationale de la Pétrochimie and take over the renovation of facilities at Skikda and Arzew, and in 2007 it awarded Oman's Suhail Bahwan Group a contract for the construction of an ammonia and urea complex at Arzew. In July of that year France's Total was awarded the contract to build a $3,000m. ethane cracker, and the local Almet consortium was selected to construct a $700m. methanol plant, both located at Arzew (although the ethane cracker project has reportedly since been delayed until 2014). In early 2008 the Government announced plans for a $1,500m. fertilizer production facility at Guelma, in the first of a series of projects designed to increase exports substantially by 2020. Société des Mines des Phosphates, SpA (Somiphos—a subsidiary of Ferphos) was to develop the plant in a joint venture with Pakistan's Engro Corpn. In March 2013 Algeria signed accords with Norway and Qatar to build fertilizer factories. Yara International of Norway agreed to invest in a $2,000m. facility in partnership with a Sonatrach subsidiary. Norway also planned to join Qatar in the construction of a $3,000m. ammonium plant in Hadjar Essed and a phosphoric acid factory in Oued Koubrite.

The Mubadala Development Co of Abu Dhabi and the Dubai Aluminium Co signed a US $5,000m. contract in March 2007 to develop Algeria's first aluminium smelter. Located at Beni Saf, the plant was expected to produce around 700,000 metric tons of high-grade primary aluminium per year, largely for export. In early 2012 Qatar Steel and Qatar Mining formed a joint venture to build an integrated steel, mining and power project at Bellara. In another venture the Algerian Government in May 2013 reached an agreement with ArcelorMittal for a $1,000m. expansion of capacity at the El Hadjar steel plant in Annaba to 2.2m tons per year

Since the late 1980s the Government has encouraged the local manufacture of vehicle components by Algerian companies and joint ventures with other countries. The importing of vehicles to meet domestic demand was opened to the private sector in 1990–91, allowing foreign manufacturers (including Peugeot, Renault, Fiat, Daewoo, Honda and Nissan) to establish local distribution agencies. Following the introduction of supplementary budget measures in mid-2009 in an attempt to reduce the cost of imports (see Budget), the Government and Abu Dhabi-based investment firm Aabar concluded a memorandum of understanding with five German companies to establish vehicle manufacturing plants in Tiaret, Aïn Smara and Oued Hamimine to produce up to 10,000 cars and trucks per year in joint ventures with local companies. In late 2010 Renault announced that it intended to expand its operations in Algeria, and in December 2012 concluded an agreement to establish a car assembly plant, with an initial capacity of 25,000 vehicles per year, near Oran. Another French company, Peugeot, set up a light-duty vehicles transformation unit in Algiers in the same month.

Construction work was begun by OCI in 2002 on a cement plant, with an annual capacity of 3.6m. metric tons, in the M'Sila region south-east of Algiers. The new plant was inaugurated in 2003, and in 2004 OCI announced that its wholly owned subsidiary, the Algerian Cement Company, had signed a contract for the construction of a second production line at M'Sila to increase the total plant capacity to 4.4m. tons per year. In 2008 it was announced that the French cement group Lafarge would build a 2.5m.-tons per year plant at Oum el-Bouaghi, in the north-east, as part of a programme to double Algeria's cement production. In November 2011, following lengthy negotiations with the authorities, Lafarge agreed to continue the project as a minority partner with a 49% interest, in accordance with foreign ownership regulations.

In early 2012 the Government announced that it would invest US $250m. in the pharmaceutical sector, in support of its strategic aim to provide 70% of domestic demand for medicines through local production by 2014.

TRADE

Exports of petroleum and natural gas have transformed the pattern of Algerian exports since the 1970s, and by the mid-1990s restrictions on external trade had been eliminated, allowing public and private importers to finance their transactions from their own foreign exchange holdings or through official cash and credit lines. In 1997 the Government established an export promotion agency (PROMEX), and introduced a range of financial incentives to stimulate the growth of non-hydrocarbon exports.

By 2000 the overall value of exports had reached US $22,030m. ($18,800m. of which was from hydrocarbons), while imports totalled $9,170m.—giving a significant trade surplus of $12,860m. The value of exports shrank to $20,040m. in 2001, as a result of the decrease in world prices for petroleum over the year, while imports increased to $9,760m., narrowing the surplus to $10,280m. In 2002 exports decreased to $18,420m. ($17,690m. from hydrocarbons) and imports rose to $11,750m., giving a reduced surplus of $6,670m. The trade balance in 2003 recorded a surplus of $10,830m., with exports increasing by 26.6%, to $23,840m., and imports to some $13,000m. In 2004 the surge in petroleum prices on international markets further strengthened Algeria's external position. Exports were estimated at $33,300m. and imports at $17,600m. The value of exports in 2005 reached $42,600m. ($41,740m. from hydrocarbons) and that of imports rose to $20,000m., generating a surplus of $22,600m. In 2006, further buoyed by the high price of hydrocarbons, exports reached an estimated $54,600m. The value of imports rose to $21,450m., resulting in a trade surplus of $33,150m. Figures for 2007 indicated that exports continued to increase in value, to $59,518m., with imports at $27,439m.

In 2008 exports rose to US $79,298m., with imports at $39,479m., generating a current account surplus estimated at 25% of GDP. According to the IMF, the value of exports was projected to fall by some 40%, to $44,900m., in 2009, reflecting in the main falling hydrocarbon revenues, with imports declining to $37,500m. For 2010, the Fund forecast that exports would rise substantially again, to reach $57,600m. (as hydrocarbon revenues rebounded following a recovery in world oil prices), and that imports would increase marginally, to $38,000m. The IMF projected a further rise in exports in 2011, to $71,900m., and an increase in the value of imports to $45,100m. Again reflecting higher oil prices, the current account surplus continued to improve, increasing to 9.5% of GDP (from 7.5% in 2010), despite strong import growth. High oil prices also contributed to an increase in the trade surplus, to $26,800m. The trade surplus increased by 3.6% in 2012. Exports rose to $73,980m. (with hydrocarbons representing 97% of the total), while imports fell to $46,800m. The current account remained in surplus at about 8% of GDP.

In 1989 the Union of the Arab Maghreb (UMA) was formed by Algeria, Libya, Mauritania, Morocco and Tunisia, with a focus on industrial co-operation and economic integration. The UMA sought to establish a customs union and a single monetary exchange currency, with the ultimate aim of allowing all UMA members to establish industries in each of the five countries. Despite a great deal of rhetoric, however, little progress was recorded in the late 1990s and the early years of the 21st century (see History). None the less, in November 2008 Algeria finalized a preferential trade agreement with Tunisia.

The EU has become Algeria's main trading partner (accounting for more than one-half of the country's trade by 2012). In April 2002 the EU-Algeria Euro-Mediterranean Association Agreement was formally signed in Valencia, Spain. With Algerian manufactures already having duty-free access to the EU, the main focus of the free trade component of the agreement was the phasing out of Algerian import duties on EU manufactures over 12 years. Algeria was also to introduce tariff reductions on EU agricultural products. The Association Agreement came into effect in September 2005. The Government subsequently sought a postponement of the timetable for dismantling tariffs on products imported from the EU to 2020, and an agreement on revising the schedule was reached in October 2012.

Algeria has continued to pursue its application for membership of the World Trade Organization, and accession negotiations were ongoing at mid-2013.

Following the Chinese Premier's visit to Algeria in 2002, Algeria and China signed an economic co-operation agreement; China has since significantly increased its industrial and construction involvement in Algeria. In October 2011 the Government awarded a US $1,400m. building contract to China State Construction Engineering Corpn for the Algiers Grand Mosque project.

BANKING AND FINANCE

The Banque d'Algérie (the central bank) started its operations (as the Banque Centrale d'Algérie) on 1 January 1963, issuing currency, regulating and licensing banks, and supervising all foreign transactions. A state monopoly on all foreign financial transactions was imposed in November 1967. State-run banks included the Banque Nationale d'Algérie, founded in 1966, traditionally services sector based; Crédit Populaire d'Algérie (CPA), founded in 1966, strong in the construction sector; the Banque Extérieure d'Algérie (BEA), founded in 1967, dealing with foreign trade; the Caisse Nationale d'Epargne et de Prévoyance, specializing in savings and housing loans; the Banque de l'Agriculture et du Développement Rural, founded in 1982, providing finance for the agricultural sector; and the Banque de Développement Local, founded in 1985, which has traditionally provided loans for companies run by local government.

Under legislation introduced in the mid-1980s, lending policy and banking control was strictly controlled by the Government, and state banks were constrained to give priority to state-run companies in order to finance investments that were part of a central plan. In 1988 banks were included in the group of more than 70 state-controlled companies that gained autonomy and became EPEs. The BEA was the first state bank to become fully autonomous under the scheme. A new banking law in 1990 granted the central bank the authority to formulate and implement monetary and foreign exchange policies, removed controls on foreign investment in most sectors, allowed full foreign ownership of new investment projects, and encouraged unrestricted joint ventures between foreign companies and Algerian private concerns.

By 1993 legislation permitting the establishment of local private banks was in place. The country's first local private bank, the Union Bank, was established in 1995. Two further local private banks were authorized in 1998: the El-Khalifa Bank and the El-Mouna Bank, established in Oran. Meanwhile, Citibank of the USA upgraded its representative office in the capital to a full branch; the Arab Banking Corpn of Bahrain became the first major international Arab bank to open an office in Algiers; and France's Natexis Groupe, Société Générale and BNP received clearance to set up operations in Algeria. In 2001 the Banque d'Algérie gave approval for the establishment of BNP Paribas El Djazaïr (a wholly owned subsidiary of BNP Paribas), and EFG Hermes of Egypt applied for a licence to open a commercial bank in the country. In 2003, however, the Banque d'Algérie appointed an administrator to manage the El-Khalifa Bank, and withdrew its accreditation from the privately owned Commercial and Industrial Bank of Algeria, because of alleged violations of the currency and banking laws. Their operating licences were subsequently withdrawn.

In 2001 a ministerial commission was appointed to review the banking sector. The state-owned banking system was regarded as one of the major obstacles to economic reform, and its privatization was unlikely to be achieved without far-reaching reforms. During 2002 a financial restructuring of state-owned banks was completed, reform of the payments system was initiated, and new private banks were licensed. Further proposed reforms envisaged greater partnership between state-owned and private banks, and the IMF recommended that the Government should rescind the decree prohibiting public entities from dealing with private banks.

In 2010 restrictions on foreign direct investment, which had been introduced from 2009, were extended to the banking sector in a supplementary budget; this prompted criticism from the IMF, which considered that the action could prevent the entry of new banks with majority foreign ownership, or the takeover of public banks, and thereby hamper growth.

During 2011 and 2012 the central bank sought to contain the growing liquidity in the banking system generated by higher hydrocarbon revenues and increased government expenditures, and to limit their impact on inflation. In order to ensure stability, it also announced in June 2012 that it would start to monitor the banking sector from 2013 by assessing banks' solvency ratios, yields on capital and investments, and their liquidity and risk management. The reserves requirement rate, which had been raised from 9% to 11% in 2012, was again increased, to 12%, in May 2013 in order to absorb excess liquidity in the banking system.

The Algiers Stock Exchange began trading in 1999, amendments to the banking law having given foreign investors free access to the exchange and the right to expatriate profits from stock trading. In late 2010 the local Alliance Assurances became the first private company to be listed on the exchange, following the implementation of legislation that exempted companies from paying tax on capital gains made on stock market transactions for five years. In early 2012 the Government embarked on plans to modernize the financial markets, including legislation to relax requirements for market entry and the establishment of a Commission of the Supervision of the Stock Exchange Operations. The exchange is to be opened up to foreign investors, as a means of adding liquidity and to encourage more local companies to participate. However, foreign involvement is to be limited to partnerships with local businesses.

The level of foreign exchange reserves fluctuated considerably through the 1990s, but the surge in revenues from hydrocarbons since that time has resulted in reserves rising dramatically, to reach US $190,660m. at the end of 2012. In October it was announced that the Government would contribute $5,000m. to the IMF through the purchase of special drawing rights.

BUDGET

The 2001 budget projected spending at AD 1,251,000m. and revenue at AD 1,234,000m., based on an average oil price of US $19 per barrel, resulting in an expected deficit of AD 17,000m. However, oil prices were expected to be well in excess of $19 per barrel, and any revenues above the projected level were to be transferred to a stabilization fund established within the treasury in 2000 to support the budget should oil prices fall in the future. It was reported in September that the Banque d'Algérie had transferred some $3,000m. to the fund. The budget included a 33% increase to the monthly minimum wage effective from 1 January 2001 and a 15% increase in the monthly salaries of public sector workers. Furthermore, value-added tax was to be simplified, and shopkeepers and small vendors were now to be exempt from the tax.

The budget for 2002 projected spending at AD 1,559,850m. and revenue at AD 1,475,750m. (63% of which was to be derived from hydrocarbon revenues, based on an average oil price of US $22 per barrel). The 2003 budget projected revenue at AD 1,451,450m. and spending at AD 1,711,110m., based on an average oil price of $19 per barrel. It authorized a 12% increase in capital expenditure, and also included measures to update the tax system and reorganize the tax and customs administration. Having narrowed in 2001 and 2002, high hydrocarbon revenues meant that the overall budget surplus strengthened again in 2003, exceeding 3% of GDP. A supplementary budget law was introduced to provide additional funding for appropriations related to the earthquake in May of that year. In the 2004 budget expenditure was projected at AD 1,920,000m. and revenue at AD 1,528,000m., based on an oil price of $19 per barrel.

In late 2004 the Government launched the Budget and Growth Consolidation Plan, a capital expenditure programme worth AD 3,800,000m. (61% of that year's GDP) for the period 2005–09. The plan aimed to channel increased spending into improving public services—16% for human resources projects, 23% for infrastructure, 15% to support economic activity (mainly agriculture) and 25% for housing. At the same time current spending was to be curbed by reducing the public wage bill, by active public debt management and by the reduction of subsidies. Funding committed to the Plan was increased to US $60,000m. in 2005.

According to the IMF, the 2005 budget recorded revenue and grants at AD 3,082,700m. and expenditure at AD 2,052,000m. The 2006 budget forecast revenue and grants at AD 3,512,000m. and expenditure at AD 2,514,000m., while the 2007 budget projected revenue at AD 3,813,000m. and expenditure at AD 2,920,000m. Strong hydrocarbon revenues were expected to finance substantial capital spending allocations for infrastructure projects, including road networks and social housing. A windfall tax on international oil company profits was also expected to raise an additional US $1,500m. Profits accrued by oil companies when prices exceed $30 a barrel became taxable at between 5% and 50%, depending on total output. The windfall tax was backdated to August 2006, applying to existing production agreements between the state and private operators as well as those signed in the future. A supplementary budget law was introduced in July 2007 to take account of higher hydrocarbon revenues and increased expenditure on capital investment programmes.

The 2008 budget forecast revenue and grants at AD 4,871,000m. and total expenditure at AD 3,357,000m., according to the IMF. Revenue from hydrocarbons was forecast at AD 3,786,000m. The budget assumed GDP growth of 5.8% and inflation of 3.0%, and included an increase in the threshold for general income tax and other measures to simplify Algeria's tax system. A supplementary budget was introduced in July 2008, lowering the GDP growth forecast to 3.5% and amending the reference price for oil from US $19 to $37 per barrel. Additional expenditure was allocated for food subsidies to offset the impact of rising world prices, and there were also increases in tax thresholds and some reductions in corporation tax.

The 2009 budget forecast a GDP growth rate of 4.1% (6.6% in the non-hydrocarbon sector). Inflation was forecast at 3.5%. Expenditure was projected at AD 4,417,000m. and revenue at AD 3,332,000m., based on an oil price of US $37 per barrel. The budget also included allocations for food subsidies, tax incentives for local business, a new tax on the repatriation of capital by foreign companies, a dividend tax on capital transferred abroad by the local branches of foreign companies, and regulations removing the right of foreign companies to own the land on which they develop projects. A supplementary budget introduced in July was widely criticized. The measures included a ban on consumer lending (except for mortgages) to limit household indebtedness, stringent measures to reduce imports in order to correct the deteriorating trade balance, and restrictions on foreign investment. For all new investments, the majority stake (51%) was required to be held by a domestic partner, and the Government and public enterprises had a preemptive purchase right for all sales by or to foreign investors. The supplementary budget also incorporated measures to assist social development projects, including tax incentives and support for low-income families. According to the IMF, Algeria was expected to post its first budget deficit in a decade in 2009, reaching as much as 8% of GDP, as the fiscal position was impacted by the decline in hydrocarbon revenues while expenditures remained at a high level.

The IMF forecast that expenditure under the 2010 budget would increase to AD 5,022,000m., and revenue to AD 4,255,000m., based on a still-conservative oil price of US $37 per barrel. Despite the decline in revenues from hydrocarbon exports, there were increased spending allocations for health, education and employment, and additional funding to cover a controversial increase in the minimum wage. In August 2010 the Government agreed a supplementary budget, which included new regulations further restricting the operation of foreign companies in Algeria, in line with its policy of promoting the development of domestic companies. The regulations extended the 49% restriction on foreign holdings in joint ventures with local partners to the banking sector. There was also a requirement for foreign bidders for state contracts to form a joint venture with a local partner. Despite Algeria's increased hydrocarbon revenues in 2010, the IMF forecast a second consecutive budget deficit, but at a significantly lower level (an estimated 4% of GDP) than in 2009.

Earlier in 2010 the Government had approved a US $286,000m. development plan (additional to annual budgeted expenditure) for 2010–14, which aimed to diversify the economy away from its dependency on hydrocarbons, improve infrastructure, and promote social and human resource development. Under the plan, $156,000m. would be invested in new projects, while $130,000m. would be spent on existing programmes. It would be financed internally and thus without recourse to international borrowing.

According to the IMF, the 2011 budget projected an increase in total expenditure to AD 5,514,000m., and in revenue and grants to AD 5,075,000m., still based on the reference oil price of US $37 per barrel. The budget assumed GDP growth of 4% (6% in non-hydrocarbon development) and inflation of 3.5%. In May 2011 the Government announced a draft supplementary budget to increase public expenditure by 25%, in support of emergency measures first announced in February to offset rising prices, promote employment and assist small businesses.

The budget for 2012, which was approved in November 2011 and again based on an assumed oil price of US $37 per barrel, forecast expenditure of AD 6,214,000m. and revenue and grants of AD 5,347,000m. The Government anticipated GDP growth of 4.7% in 2012, with an inflation rate of 4%, and the budget projected a 10.2% reduction in expenditure compared with the supplementary budget of 2011. However, an additional spending allocation of AD 317,000m. to cover a 20% increase in the minimum wage for civil servants and some revision of pension benefits was subsequently introduced in a further supplementary measure in 2012.

The budget for 2013 projected total expenditure at AD 6,743,000m. (current spending accounting for 64% and capital spending for 24%), and revenue and grants at AD 6,623,000m., with a growth rate of 5% in 2013, according to the Government, and inflation of 4%. Measures in the budget aimed to promote private investment and provided for the introduction of new tax exemptions, while seeking to curb tax evasion. The IMF welcomed the fiscal consolidation in the budget, but urged the Government to resist any further wage bill increases which would generate further inflationary pressures.

FOREIGN DEBT

From 1983 Algeria borrowed heavily on the international markets, and by 1993 the cost of servicing the country's external debt was equivalent to 78% of total export earnings. Major rescheduling of sovereign debt (through the 'Paris Club') and of commercial debt (through the 'London Club') had been completed by 1996 (see Government Strategy). The first repayment of Algeria's 'London Club' debt was made in March 1998. Total external debt declined in that year, to US $30,676m., and again in 1999, to $28,005m. There was a further decline in 2000, to $25,002m. (according to World Bank data). At the end of that year the Governor of the Banque d'Algérie forecast that most of the foreign debt would be erased by 2011, provided no new borrowing was undertaken. External debt continued to decrease—to $22,600m. at the end of 2001—and the debt-to-GDP ratio was projected to decline from 35% in 2003 to 25% in 2004. Following early debt repayments in 2005, the ratio was expected to fall to 16.5% in that year. External debt stood at $17,800m. in September 2005, down from $21,400m. in December 2004. In May 2006 the Government announced that it was to pay back all of the $8,000m. debt owing to 'Paris Club' creditors, and in November this was finalized. The external debt-to-GDP ratio has declined from 4.9% in 2006 to less than 2.0% in 2012.

Statistical Survey

Source (unless otherwise stated): Office National des Statistiques, 8 rue des Moussebilines, BP 202, Ferhat Boussad, Algiers; tel. (21) 63-99-74; fax (21) 63-79-55; e-mail ons@ons.dz; internet www.ons.dz.

Area and Population

AREA, POPULATION AND DENSITY

Area (sq km)	2,381,741*
Population (census results)	
25 June 1998	29,100,867
16 April 2008	
Males	17,232,747
Females	16,847,283
Total	34,080,030
Population (official estimates at mid-year)	
2010	35,978,000
2011	36,717,000
2012	37,495,000
Density (per sq km) at mid-2012	15.7

* 919,595 sq miles.

POPULATION BY AGE AND SEX

(UN estimates at mid-2013)

	Males	Females	Total
0–14	5,549,248	5,314,779	10,864,027
15–64	13,412,550	13,119,282	26,531,832
65 and over	860,257	952,078	1,812,335
Total	19,822,055	19,386,139	39,208,194

Source: UN, *World Population Prospects: The 2012 Revision.*

POPULATION BY WILAYA (ADMINISTRATIVE DISTRICT)

(2008 census)

	Area (sq km)	Population	Density (per sq km)
Adrar	439,700	399,714	0.9
Aïn Defla	4,897	766,013	156.4
Aïn Témouchent	2,379	371,239	156.0
Algiers (el-Djezaïr)	273	2,988,145	10,945.6
Annaba	1,439	609,499	423.6
Batna	12,192	1,119,791	91.8
el-Bayadh	78,870	228,624	2.9
Béchar	162,200	270,061	1.7
Béjaïa	3,268	912,577	279.2
Biskra (Beskra)	20,986	721,356	34.4
Blida (el-Boulaïda)	1,696	1,002,937	591.4
Borj Bou Arreridj	4,115	628,475	152.7
Bouira	4,439	695,583	156.7
Boumerdès	1,591	802,083	504.1
Chlef (el-Cheliff)	4,795	1,002,088	209.0
Constantine (Qacentina)	2,187	938,475	429.1
Djelfa	66,415	1,092,184	16.4
Ghardaïa	86,105	363,598	4.2
Guelma	4,101	482,430	117.6
Illizi	285,000	52,333	0.2
Jijel	2,577	636,948	247.2
Khenchela	9,811	386,683	39.4
Laghouat	25,057	455,602	18.2
Mascara (Mouaskar)	5,941	784,073	132.0
Médéa (Lemdiyya)	8,866	819,932	92.5
Mila	9,375	766,886	81.8
Mostaganem	2,175	737,118	338.9
M'Sila	18,718	990,591	52.9
Naâma	29,950	192,891	6.4
Oran (Ouahran)	2,121	1,454,078	685.6
Ouargla	211,980	558,558	2.6
el-Oued	54,573	647,548	11.9
Oum el-Bouaghi	6,768	621,612	91.8
Relizane (Ghilizane)	4,870	726,180	149.1
Saïda	6,764	330,641	48.9
Sétif (Stif)	6,504	1,489,979	229.1
Sidi-bel-Abbès	9,096	604,744	66.5
Skikda	4,026	898,680	223.2
Souk Ahras	4,541	438,127	96.5

—*continued*	Area (sq km)	Population	Density (per sq km)
Tamanrasset (Tamanghest)	556,200	176,637	0.3
el-Tarf	3,339	408,414	122.3
Tébessa (Tbessa)	14,227	648,703	45.6
Tiaret (Tihert)	20,673	846,823	41.0
Tindouf	159,000	49,149	0.3
Tipaza	2,166	591,010	272.9
Tissemsilt	3,152	294,476	93.4
Tizi Ouzou	3,568	1,127,607	316.0
Tlemcen	9,061	949,135	104.7
Total	2,381,741	34,080,030	14.3

PRINCIPAL TOWNS

(population at 1998 census)

Algiers (el-Djezaïr, capital)	1,519,570	Tébessa (Tbessa)	153,246
Oran (Ouahran)	655,852	Blida (el-Boulaïda)	153,083
Constantine (Qacentina)	462,187	Skikda	152,335
Batna	242,514	Béjaïa	147,076
Annaba	215,083	Tiaret (Tihert)	145,332
Sétif (Stif)	211,859	Chlef (el-Cheliff)	133,874
Sidi-bel-Abbès	180,260	el-Buni	133,471
Biskra (Beskra)	170,956	Béchar	131,010
Djelfa	154,265		

Mid-2011 ('000, incl. suburbs, UN estimate): Algiers 2,915.7 (Source: UN, *World Urbanization Prospects: The 2011 Revision*).

BIRTHS, MARRIAGES AND DEATHS*

	Registered live births†		Registered marriages		Registered deaths†	
	Number	Rate (per 1,000)	Number	Rate (per 1,000)	Number	Rate (per 1,000)
2005	703,000	21.4	279,548	8.5	147,000	4.5
2006	739,000	22.1	295,295	8.8	144,000	4.3
2007	783,000	23.0	325,485	9.6	149,000	4.4
2008	817,000	23.6	331,190	9.6	153,000	4.4
2009	849,000	24.1	341,321	9.7	159,000	4.5
2010	888,000	24.7	344,819	9.6	157,000	4.4
2011	910,000	24.8	369,031	10.1	162,000	4.4
2012	978,000	26.1	371,280	9.9	170,000	4.5

* Figures refer to the Algerian population only, and include adjustment for underenumeration.

† Excluding live-born infants dying before registration of birth.

Life expectancy (years at birth): 73.1 (males 71.6; females 74.6) in 2011 (Source: World Bank, World Development Indicators database).

ECONOMICALLY ACTIVE POPULATION

('000 persons aged 15 years and over at September)

	2003	2004
Agriculture, hunting, forestry and fishing	1,411.8	1,616.2
Mining and quarrying	82.9	135.1
Manufacturing	616.7	846.7
Electricity, gas and water	104.6	79.1
Construction	799.9	967.6
Trade; repair of motor vehicles, motorcycles and personal household goods	880.9	1,174.4
Hotels and restaurants	102.5	164.8
Transport, storage and communications	405.4	435.9
Financial intermediation	67.6	68.8
Real estate, renting and business activities	68.0	72.4
Public administration and defence; compulsory social security	1,071.2	1,104.1

—continued	2003	2004
Education	627.7	634.0
Health and social work	245.0	235.5
Other community, social and personal service activities	183.4	208.9
Households with employed persons	12.2	34.9
Extra-territorial organizations and bodies	2.9	3.9
Sub-total	6,682.7	7,782.2
Activities not adequately defined	1.4	16.2
Total employed	6,684.1	7,798.4
Unemployed	2,078.0	1,671.5
Total labour force	8,762.1	9,469.9

Source: ILO.

2011 (sample survey at July, '000 persons aged 15 years and over): Agriculture 1,034; Industry 2,962 (Mining and quarrying 192, Manufacturing 1,175; Construction 1,595); Services 5,603; *Total employed* 9,599; Unemployed 1,063; *Total labour force* 10,662.

Health and Welfare

KEY INDICATORS

Total fertility rate (children per woman, 2011)	2.2
Under-5 mortality rate (per 1,000 live births, 2011)	30
HIV/AIDS (% of persons aged 15–49, 2011)	0.1
Physicians (per 1,000 head, 2002)	1.1
Hospital beds (per 1,000 head, 2004)	1.7
Health expenditure (2010): US $ per head (PPP)	364
Health expenditure (2010): % of GDP	4.3
Health expenditure (2010): public (% of total)	79.9
Access to water (% of persons, 2011)	84
Access to sanitation (% of persons, 2011)	95
Total carbon dioxide emissions ('000 metric tons, 2009)	121,311.7
Carbon dioxide emissions per head (metric tons, 2009)	3.5
Human Development Index (2012): ranking	93
Human Development Index (2012): value	0.713

For sources and definitions, see explanatory note on p. vi.

Agriculture

PRINCIPAL CROPS

('000 metric tons)

	2009	2010	2011
Wheat	2,953	3,100*	2,800*
Barley	2,203	1,500*	1,350*
Oats	96	140*	126†
Potatoes	2,636	3,310	3,993†
Broad beans, dry	36	36	37†
Chick peas	18	23	29†
Almonds	47	39†	50†
Olives	475	410†	420†
Rapeseed†	37	39	45
Cabbages	47	51	55†
Artichokes	40	39†	39†
Tomatoes	641	718	790†
Cauliflowers and broccoli	82	88	93†
Pumpkins, squash and gourds	190	228*	240†
Cucumbers and gherkins	190	116	100†
Aubergines (Eggplants)	76	91	105†
Chillies and peppers, green	319	383*	400†
Onions, dry	980	1,001	1,000†
Garlic	60	64	66†
Beans, green	45	53	61†
Peas, green	103	125	145†
Carrots and turnips	271	324	375†
Oranges	626	583	600†
Tangerines, mandarins, clementines and satsumas	157	152	150†
Lemons and limes	60	52	55†

—continued	2009	2010	2011
Apples	267	379	450†
Pears	160	168	180†
Apricots	203	201*	205†
Peaches and nectarines	147	163*	175†
Plums and sloes	74	85*	85†
Grapes	493	561	650†
Watermelons	1,035	1,224	1,350†
Figs	84	124	150†
Dates	601	645	690*
Tobacco, unmanufactured	8	8†	7†

* Unofficial figure.
† FAO estimate(s).

Aggregate production ('000 metric tons, may include official, semi-official or estimated data): Total cereals 5,253 in 2009, 4,742 in 2010, 4,278 in 2011; Total roots and tubers 2,636 in 2009, 3,310 in 2010, 3,993 in 2011; Total vegetables (incl. melons) 4,748 in 2009, 5,175 in 2010, 5,514 in 2011; Total fruits (excl. melons) 2,992 in 2009, 3,239 in 2010, 3,528 in 2011.

Source: FAO.

LIVESTOCK

('000 head, year ending September, unless otherwise indicated)

	2009	2010	2011*
Sheep	21,405	22,669	24,000
Goats	3,962	4,287	4,544
Cattle	1,717†	1,778†	1,800
Horses	45	44	43
Asses*	150	150	150
Mules*	40	40	40
Camels	301†	314†	315
Chickens (million)*	125	126	127

* FAO estimates.
† Unofficial figure.

Source: FAO.

LIVESTOCK PRODUCTS

('000 metric tons)

	2009	2010	2011
Cattle meat*	131	137	127
Goat meat*	15	16	15
Chicken meat*	254	255	256
Rabbit meat*	7	8	8
Sheep meat*	197	213	182
Cows' milk*	1,750	1,811	1,811
Sheep's milk*	260	265	265
Goats' milk*	221	248	248
Hen eggs	194	194	195*
Honey*	3	3	3
Wool, greasy*	26	26	26

* FAO estimate(s).

Source: FAO.

Forestry

ROUNDWOOD REMOVALS

('000 cubic metres, excl. bark, FAO estimates)

	2009	2010	2011
Sawlogs, veneer logs and logs for sleepers	0	29	28
Pulpwood	51	64	59
Other industrial wood	52	52	52
Fuel wood	8,072	8,176	8,246
Total	8,175	8,321	8,385

Sawnwood production ('000 cubic metres, incl. railway sleepers, FAO estimates): 13 per year in 1975–2011.

Source: FAO.

Fishing

('000 metric tons, live weight)

	2009	2010	2011
Capture	127.5	93.6	101.8
Bogue	6.6	6.5	7.3
Jack and horse mackerels	18.5	11.1	11.3
Sardinellas	16.2	11.1	13.4
European pilchard (sardine)	55.3	31.2	40.0
European anchovy	3.2	2.0	2.7
Aquaculture*	2.2	1.8	2.2
Total catch*	130.0	95.4	104.0

* FAO estimates.

Source: FAO.

Mining

('000 metric tons unless otherwise indicated)

	2009	2010	2011
Crude petroleum*	77,200	74,122	73,538
Natural gas (dry basis, million cu m)*	79,550	80,412	82,700
Iron ore (gross weight)	1,307	1,469	1,400
Phosphate rock†	1,017	1,525	1,287
Barite (Barytes)	3368	40	30
Salt (unrefined)	109	107	170
Gypsum (crude)	1,757	1,610	1,610

* Source: BP, *Statistical Review of World Energy*.

† Figures refer to gross weight. The estimated phosphoric acid content (in '000 metric tons, estimated) was 305 in 2009; 458 in 2010; 386 in 2011.

Mercury (kilograms): 73,451 in 2005.

2012: Crude petroleum 73,046,000 metric tons; Natural gas 81,500m. cu m (Source: BP, *Statistical Review of World Energy*).

Source (unless otherwise indicated): US Geological Survey.

Industry

SELECTED PRODUCTS

('000 metric tons unless otherwise indicated)

	2007	2008	2009
Olive oil (crude)	22	36	n.a.
Naphthas	3,698	3,641	4,913
Motor spirit (petrol)	2,100	2,780	2,517
Jet fuel	1,034	988	977
Gas-diesel (distillate fuel) oils	6,388	7,403	7,533
Residual fuel oils	5,518	6,009	5,581
Lubricating oils	143	89	140
Petroleum bitumen (asphalt)	331	315	310
Liquefied petroleum gas	9,183	9,240	8,896
Pig iron for steel-making	1,193	690	680
Crude steel (ingots)	1,278	646	543
Electric energy (million kWh)	37,196	40,236	42,769

Source: UN Industrial Commodities Statistics Database.

Finance

CURRENCY AND EXCHANGE RATES

Monetary Units

100 centimes = 1 Algerian dinar (AD).

Sterling, Dollar and Euro Equivalents (31 May 2013)

£1 sterling = 120.150 dinars;
US $1 = 78.973 dinars;
€1 = 102.713 dinars;
1,000 Algerian dinars = £8.32 = $12.66 = €9.74.

Average Exchange Rate (dinars per US $)

2010 74.386
2011 72.938
2012 77.536

GOVERNMENT FINANCE

(central government operations, '000 million AD)

Summary of Balances

	2009	2010	2011
Revenue and grants	3,676	4,393	5,790
Less Expenditure	4,221	4,440	5,853
Budget balance	–545	–47	–63
Special accounts balance	508	11	26
Less Net lending by Treasury	642	184	153
Overall balance	–679	–220	–190

Revenue and Grants

	2009	2010	2011†
Hydrocarbon revenue	2,413	2,905	3,980
Sonatrach dividends	85	85	150
Other revenue	1,263	1,488	1,810
Tax revenue	1,147	1,298	1,527
Taxes on income and profits	462	562	685
Taxes on goods and services	478	515	573
Customs duties	170	182	222
Registration and stamps	36	40	47
Non-tax revenue	117	190	283
Total	3,676	4,393	5,790

Expenditure

Expenditure by economic type	2009	2010	2011†
Current expenditure	2,275	2,632	3,879
Personnel expenditure	880	1,193	1,740
War veterans' pensions	131	151	163
Material and supplies	113	122	130
Current transfers	1,114	1,130	1,808
Interest payments	37	36	38
Capital expenditure	1,946	1,808	1,974
Total	4,221	4,440	5,853

Sectoral allocation of capital expenditure*	2009	2010	2011†
Agriculture and fishery	25.8	22.4	17.6
Irrigation and waterworks	256.6	272.1	284.2
Industry and energy	0.1	0.2	0.2
Economic infrastructure	398.5	381.7	400.0
Housing	230.8	293.5	137.8
Education and professional training	144.9	153.5	127.6
Social infrastructure	68.5	71.2	77.7
Administrative infrastructure	85.7	113.7	116.3
Urban development	77.6	65.3	47.4
Unallocated	136.7	134.4	126.2
Total	1,425.5	1,508.6	1,335.1

* Commitment basis.

† Preliminary figures.

Source: IMF, *Algeria: Statistical Appendix* (February 2013).

CENTRAL BANK RESERVES
(US $ million at 31 December)

	2010	2011	2012
Gold*	301	300	300
IMF special drawing rights	1,653	1,649	1,651
Reserve position in IMF	394	599	636
Foreign exchange	160,568	180,574	189,010
Total	162,916	183,122	191,597

* National valuation.

Source: IMF, *International Financial Statistics*.

MONEY SUPPLY
('000 million AD at 31 December)

	2010	2011	2012
Currency outside depository corporations	2,098.63	2,571.48	2,952.20
Transferable deposits	2,804.41	3,591.19	3,520.11
Other deposits	2,524.28	2,732.49	3,191.40
Broad money	7,427.32	8,895.16	9,663.72

Source: IMF, *International Financial Statistics*.

COST OF LIVING
(Consumer Price Index; base: 2000 = 100)

	2010	2011	2012
Food	157.1	166.5	188.0
All items (incl. others)	145.9	154.3	169.3

Source: ILO.

NATIONAL ACCOUNTS
('000 million AD at current prices)

Expenditure on the Gross Domestic Product

	2009	2010	2011
Government final consumption expenditure	514.2	655.6	1,006.1
Private final consumption expenditure	3,677.6	4,043.1	4,475.5
Gross fixed capital formation	3,811.4	4,350.9	4,617.7
Changes in inventories	864.4	555.6	494.2
Total domestic expenditure	8,867.5	9,605.2	10,593.6
Exports of goods and services	3,525.9	4,610.1	5,630.6
Less Imports of goods and services	3,583.8	3,768.0	4,114.7
GDP at purchasers' values	8,809.6	10,447.3	12,109.5

Gross Domestic Product by Economic Activity

	2009	2010	2011
Agriculture	931.3	1,015.3	1,173.7
Mining (including associated industries)	3,203.9	4,243.7	5,312.8
Construction	1,000.1	1,194.1	1,262.6
Other industry	577.0	616.7	663.3
Transport and communications	911.3	991.4	1,049.8
Trade	1,151.6	1,279.5	1,444.6
Other services	318.6	359.0	396.1
Sub-total	8,093.8	9,699.6	11,302.9
Taxes on products (net)	715.8	747.7	806.6
GDP at purchasers' values	8,809.6	10,447.3	12,109.5

BALANCE OF PAYMENTS
(US $ '000 million)

	2009	2010	2011
Exports of goods f.o.b.	45.2	57.1	72.9
Imports of goods f.o.b.	–37.4	–38.9	–44.9
Trade balance	7.8	18.2	27.9
Exports of services	3.0	3.6	3.8
Imports of services	–11.7	–11.9	–12.6
Balance on goods and services	–0.9	9.9	19.2
Other income received	4.7	4.6	4.5
Other income paid	–6.1	–5.0	–6.5
Balance on goods, services and income	–2.3	9.5	17.2
Transfers (net)	2.7	2.7	2.6
Current balance	0.4	12.2	19.7
Direct investment (net)	2.5	3.5	2.0
Official capital (net)	1.5	0.1	–0.6
Short-term capital and net errors and omissions	–0.6	–0.4	–1.2
Overall balance	3.9	15.9	20.1

Source: IMF, *Algeria: Statistical Appendix* (February 2013).

External Trade

Note: Data exclude military goods. Exports include stores and bunkers for foreign ships and aircraft.

PRINCIPAL COMMODITIES
(distribution by HS, US $ million)

Imports c.i.f.	2010	2011	2012
Dairy products, eggs, honey, edible animal products, etc.	994.0	1,543.3	1,268.7
Milk and cream (concentrated or sweetened)	903.1	1,363.2	1,093.4
Cereals	1,950.6	4,019.9	3,259.4
Wheat and meslin	1,251.6	2,846.9	2,129.0
Pharmaceutical products	1,673.1	1,961.4	2,240.7
Medicament mixtures	1,459.4	1,618.2	1,754.8
Plastics and plastic products	1,319.0	1,676.7	1,696.0
Iron and steel	1,967.3	2,996.4	3,440.8
Bars of iron, etc.	1,094.0	1,816.2	2,098.4
Iron or steel products	4,797.7	2,901.4	1,722.8
Tubes, pipes and related products	2,015.7	701.5	308.5
Machinery, boilers, etc.	8,845.3	8,217.0	6,404.9
Electrical and electronic equipment	3,010.2	3,479.9	3,310.1
Vehicles (other than railway and tramway)	4,083.8	5,034.4	7,739.2
Cars and station wagons	1,455.7	2,108.5	3,908.7
Trucks, motor vehicles for the transport of goods	1,303.6	1,568.1	2,205.5
Total (incl. others)	41,000.0	47,219.7	47,484.1

Exports f.o.b.	2010	2011	2012
Mineral fuels, lubricants, etc.	56,087.3	72,212.5	70,716.2
Crude petroleum oils, etc.	24,779.4	35,027.5	32,879.4
Petroleum gases	22,462.0	25,278.8	27,001.3
Petroleum oils, other than crude oil	8,282.0	11,070.6	9,921.6
Total (incl. others)	57,051.0	73,436.3	71,865.7

Source: Trade Map-Trade Competitiveness Map, International Trade Centre, www.intracen.org/marketanalysis.

PRINCIPAL TRADING PARTNERS
(US $ million)

Imports c.i.f.	2010	2011	2012
Argentina	1,230.7	1,782.4	1,802.7
Austria	313.8	347.0	352.6
Belgium	776.7	830.1	633.8
Brazil	902.4	1,758.8	1,343.8
Canada	329.7	258.2	523.6
China, People's Republic	4,605.1	4,737.3	5,964.8
Egypt	346.9	452.0	384.4
France (incl. Monaco)	6,119.7	7,115.4	6,092.0
Germany	2,382.0	2,558.0	2,591.2
India	777.5	1,092.6	1,107.6
Italy	4,114.1	4,675.3	4,566.1
Japan	1,570.2	1,072.9	929.7
Korea, Republic	1,987.8	1,615.1	1,260.1
Mexico	231.7	289.0	202.8
Netherlands	481.0	701.6	785.8
Spain	2,643.6	3,427.2	4,194.0
Sweden	393.0	462.4	533.0
Switzerland	588.2	600.8	403.2
Turkey	1,522.3	1,398.4	1,798.3
United Kingdom	767.6	1,011.6	853.4
Ukraine	150.5	251.3	331.9
USA	2,125.5	2,176.8	1,684.1
Total (incl. others)	41,000.0	47,219.7	47,484.1

Exports f.o.b.	2010	2011	2012
Belgium	1,920.0	2,119.2	1,922.6
Brazil	2,415.4	3,233.9	3,395.5
Canada	2,970.8	4,458.6	5,082.1
China, People's Republic	1,173.4	2,173.8	2,596.7
Egypt	427.0	650.9	764.9
France (incl. Monaco)	3,776.1	6,533.6	6,124.2
India	1,565.1	2,236.8	1,067.1
Italy	8,779.3	10,440.8	11,512.6
Japan	126.0	235.7	854.5
Korea, Republic	1,157.5	257.0	357.9
Morocco	713.2	922.1	993.3
Netherlands	4,163.5	4,916.2	5,256.7
Portugal	1,014.6	1,848.5	1,711.0
Spain	5,908.6	7,186.1	7,809.4
Tunisia	536.3	650.3	1,018.7
Turkey	2,703.6	2,524.9	2,624.6
United Kingdom	1,290.0	2,855.0	3,668.1
USA	13,827.3	15,127.3	10,778.2
Total (incl. others)	57,051.0	73,436.3	71,865.7

Source: Trade Map-Trade Competitiveness Map, International Trade Centre, www.intracen.org/marketanalysis.

Transport

RAILWAYS
(traffic)

	2007	2008	2009
Passengers carried ('000)	19,052	24,744	27,843
Freight carried ('000 metric tons)	6,185	6,901	5,252
Passenger-km (million)	758	937	1,141
Freight ton-km (million)	1,425	1,562	1,184

Source: Société Nationale des Transports Ferroviaires.

ROAD TRAFFIC
(motor vehicles in use at 31 December)

	2009	2010
Passenger cars	2,593,310	2,691,075
Lorries and vans	1,247,300	1,282,970
Buses and coaches	70,070	72,538
Motorcycles and mopeds	10,978	12,109

Source: IRF, *World Road Statistics*.

SHIPPING

Flag Registered Fleet
(at 31 December)

	2010	2011	2012
Number of vessels	159	168	174
Total displacement ('000 grt)	809.5	815.1	787.4

Source: Lloyd's List Intelligence (www.lloydslistintelligence.com).

CIVIL AVIATION
(traffic on scheduled services)

	2007	2008	2009
Kilometres flown (million)	46	53	53
Passengers carried ('000)	2,813	4,428	4,371
Passenger-km (million)	2,941	3,962	3,814
Total ton-km (million)	281	394	382

Source: UN, *Statistical Yearbook*.

Passengers carried ('000) 3,372 in 2010; 3,544 in 2011 (Source: World Bank, World Development Indicators database).

Tourism

FOREIGN TOURIST ARRIVALS BY COUNTRY OF ORIGIN*

	2008	2009	2010
France	170,538	171,314	140,129
Germany	10,961	12,148	9,244
Italy	15,477	18,824	16,886
Libya	13,940	16,359	19,313
Mali	18,100	23,907	30,648
Morocco	14,852	17,300	17,115
Spain	20,000	23,746	25,633
Tunisia	148,157	197,911	245,222
United Kingdom	8,703	9,375	8,024
Total (incl. others)	556,697	655,810	654,987

* Excluding arrivals of Algerian nationals resident abroad: 1,215,052 in 2008; 1,255,696 in 2009; 1,415,509 in 2010.

Total visitor arrivals ('000, incl Algerian nationals resident abroad): 2,395 in 2011 (provisional).

Tourism receipts (US $ million, excl. passenger transport): 267 in 2009; 219 in 2010.

Source: World Tourism Organization.

Communications Media

	2010	2011	2012
Telephones ('000 main lines in use)	2,922.7	3,059.3	3,202.0
Mobile cellular telephones ('000 subscribers)	32,780.2	35,615.9	37,692.0
Broadband subscribers ('000)	900	1,000	1,111

2009: Internet users ('000) 4,700.

Source: International Telecommunication Union.

Education

(2010/11 unless otherwise indicated)

	Institutions*	Teachers	Pupils
Pre-primary	n.a.	19,323	490,035
Primary	17,680	144,537	3,363,236
Secondary	6,529	176,375	4,572,513
Tertiary	n.a.	42,265	1,188,562

* 2009/10.

Sources: UNESCO, Institute for Statistics, and Ministère de l'Education nationale.

1998/99 (Pre-primary and primary): 15,729 institutions; 170,562 teachers; 4,843,313 pupils.

Pupil-teacher ratio (primary education, UNESCO estimate): 23.3 in 2010/11 (Source: UNESCO Institute for Statistics).

Adult literacy rate (UNESCO estimates): 75.4% (males 84.3%; females 66.4%) in 2007 (Source: UNESCO Institute for Statistics).

Directory

The Constitution

A new Constitution for the People's Democratic Republic of Algeria, approved by popular referendum, was promulgated on 22 November 1976. The Constitution was amended by the National People's Assembly on 30 June 1979. Further amendments were approved by referendum on 3 November 1988, on 23 February 1989 and on 28 November 1996. On 8 April 2002 the Assembly approved an amendment that granted Tamazight, the principal language spoken by the Berber population of the country, the status of a national language. On 12 November 2008 the Assembly approved an amendment to abolish the limit on the number of terms a President may serve. The main provisions of the Constitution, as amended, are summarized below:

The preamble recalls that Algeria owes its independence to a war of liberation which led to the creation of a modern sovereign state, guaranteeing social justice, equality and liberty for all. It emphasizes Algeria's Islamic, Arab and Amazigh (Berber) heritage, and stresses that, as an Arab Mediterranean and African country, it forms an integral part of the Great Arab Maghreb.

FUNDAMENTAL PRINCIPLES OF THE ORGANIZATION OF ALGERIAN SOCIETY

The Republic

Algeria is a popular, democratic state. Islam is the state religion, and Arabic and Tamazight are the official national languages.

The People

National sovereignty resides in the people and is exercised through its elected representatives. The institutions of the state consolidate national unity and protect the fundamental rights of its citizens. The exploitation of one individual by another is forbidden.

The State

The state is exclusively at the service of the people. Those holding positions of responsibility must live solely on their salaries and may not, directly or by the agency of others, engage in any remunerative activity.

Fundamental Freedoms and the Rights of Man and the Citizen

Fundamental rights and freedoms are guaranteed. All discrimination on grounds of sex, race or belief is forbidden. Law cannot operate retrospectively, and a person is presumed innocent until proved guilty. Victims of judicial error shall receive compensation from the state.

The state guarantees the inviolability of the home, of private life and of the person. The state also guarantees the secrecy of correspondence, the freedom of conscience and opinion, freedom of intellectual, artistic and scientific creation, and freedom of expression and assembly.

The state guarantees the right to form political associations (on condition that they are not based on differences in religion, language, race, gender or region), the right to join a trade union, the right to strike, the right to work, to protection, to security, to health, to leisure, to education, etc. It also guarantees the right to leave the national territory, within the limits set by law.

Duties of Citizens

Every citizen must respect the Constitution, and must protect public property and safeguard national independence. The law sanctions the duty of parents to educate and protect their children, as well as the duty of children to help and support their parents. Every citizen must contribute towards public expenditure through the payment of taxes.

The National Popular Army

The army safeguards national independence and sovereignty.

Principles of Foreign Policy

Algeria subscribes to the principles and objectives of the UN. It advocates international co-operation, the development of friendly relations between states, on the basis of equality and mutual interest, and non-interference in the internal affairs of states.

POWER AND ITS ORGANIZATION

The Executive

The President of the Republic is Head of State, Head of the Armed Forces and responsible for national defence. He must be of Algerian origin, a Muslim and more than 40 years old. He is elected by universal, secret, direct suffrage. His mandate is for five years, and there is no limit on the number of terms he may serve. The President embodies the unity of the nation. The President presides over meetings of the Council of Ministers. He decides and conducts foreign policy and appoints the Prime Minister, who is responsible to the National People's Assembly. The Prime Minister must appoint a Council of Ministers. He drafts, co-ordinates and implements his government's programme, which he must present to the Assembly for ratification. Should the Assembly reject the programme, the Prime Minister and the Council of Ministers resign, and the President appoints a new Prime Minister. Should the newly appointed Prime Minister's programme be rejected by the Assembly, the President dissolves the Assembly, and a general election is held. Should the President be unable to perform his functions, owing to a long and serious illness, the President of the Council of the Nation assumes the office for a maximum period of 45 days (subject to the approval of a two-thirds' majority in the National People's Assembly and the Council of the Nation). If the President is still unable to perform his functions after 45 days, the Presidency is declared vacant by the Constitutional Council. Should the Presidency fall vacant, the President of the Council of the Nation temporarily assumes the office and organizes presidential elections within 60 days. He may not himself be a candidate in the election. The President presides over a High Security Council, which advises on all matters affecting national security.

The Legislature

The legislature consists of the Assemblée Populaire Nationale (National People's Assembly) and the Conseil de la Nation (Council of the Nation, which was established by constitutional amendments approved by national referendum in November 1996). The members of the lower chamber, the National People's Assembly, are elected by universal, direct, secret suffrage for a five-year term. Two-thirds of the members of the upper chamber, the Council of the Nation, are elected by indirect, secret suffrage from regional and municipal authorities; the remainder are appointed by the President of the Republic. The Council's term of office is six years; one-half of its members are replaced every three years. The deputies enjoy parliamentary immunity. The legislature sits for two ordinary sessions per year, each of not less than four months' duration. The commissions of the legislature are in permanent session. The two parliamentary chambers may be summoned to meet for an extraordinary session on the request of the President of the Republic, or of the Prime Minister, or of two-thirds of the members of the National People's Assembly. Both the Prime Minister and the parliamentary chambers may initiate legislation, which must be deliberated upon respectively by the National People's Assembly and the Council of the Nation before promulgation. Any text passed by the Assembly must be approved by three-quarters of the members of the Council in order to become legislation.

The Judiciary

Judges obey only the law. They defend society and fundamental freedoms. The right of the accused to a defence is guaranteed. The Supreme Court regulates the activities of courts and tribunals, and the State Council regulates the administrative judiciary. The Higher Court of the Magistrature is presided over by the President of the Republic; the Minister of Justice is Vice-President of the Court. All magistrates are answerable to the Higher Court for the manner in which they fulfil their functions. The High State Court is empowered to judge the President of the Republic in cases of high treason, and the Prime Minister for crimes and offences.

The Constitutional Council

The Constitutional Council is responsible for ensuring that the Constitution is respected, and that referendums, the election of the President of the Republic and legislative elections are conducted in accordance with the law. The Constitutional Council comprises nine members, of whom three are appointed by the President of the Republic, two elected by the National People's Assembly, two elected by the Council of the Nation, one elected by the Supreme Court and one elected by the State Council. The Council's term of office is six years; the President of the Council is appointed for a six-year term and one-half of the remaining members are replaced every three years.

The High Islamic Council

The High Islamic Council is an advisory body on matters relating to Islam. The Council comprises 15 members and its President is appointed by the President of the Republic.

Constitutional Revision

The Constitution can be revised on the initiative of the President of the Republic (subject to approval by the National People's Assembly and by three-quarters of the members of the Council of the Nation), and must be approved by national referendum. Should the Constitutional Council decide that a draft constitutional amendment does not in any way affect the general principles governing Algerian society, it may permit the President of the Republic to promulgate the amendment directly (without submitting it to referendum) if it has been approved by three-quarters of the members of both parliamentary chambers. Three-quarters of the members of both parliamentary chambers, in a joint sitting, may propose a constitutional amendment to the President of the Republic, who may submit it to referendum. The basic principles of the Constitution may not be revised.

The Government

HEAD OF STATE

President and Minister of National Defence: ABDELAZIZ BOUTEFLIKA (inaugurated 27 April 1999; re-elected 8 April 2004 and 9 April 2009).

COUNCIL OF MINISTERS

(September 2013)

Prime Minister: ABDELMALEK SELLAL.

Minister of State and Minister of the Interior and Local Authorities: TAYEB BELAÏZ.

Vice-Minister of National Defence and Chief of Staff of the People's National Army: Lt-Gen. AHMED GAID SALAH.

Minister of Foreign Affairs: RAMTANE LAMAMRA.

Minister of Justice and Attorney-General: TAYEB LOUH.

Minister of Finance: KARIM DJOUDI.

Minister of Energy and Mining: YOUCEF YOUSFI.

Minister of Water Resources: HOCINE NECIB.

Minister of Religious Affairs and Awqaf (Religious Endowments): BOUABDALLAH GHLAMALLAH.

Minister of War Veterans: MUHAMMAD CHÉRIF ABBES.

Minister of Territorial Planning and the Environment: DALILA BOUDJEMAÂ.

Minister of Transport: AMAR GHOUL.

Minister of National Education: ABDELATIF BABA AHMED.

Minister of Agriculture and Rural Development: ABDELWAHAB NOURI.

Minister of Public Works: FAROUK CHIALI.

Minister of National Solidarity, the Family and Women: SOUAD BENDJABALLAH.

Minister of Culture: KHALIDA TOUMI.

Minister of Commerce: MUSTAPHA BENBADA.

Minister of Higher Education and Scientific Research: MUHAMMAD MEBARKI.

Minister of Relations with Parliament: MAHMOUD KHEDRI.

Minister of Vocational Training and Education: NOUREDINE BEDOUI.

Minister of Housing, Urban Planning and Towns: ABDELMADJID TEBBOUNE.

Minister of Labour, Employment and Social Security: MUHAMMAD BENMERADI.

Minister of Health, Population and Hospital Reform: ABDELMALEK BOUDIAF.

Minister of Tourism and Handicrafts: MUHAMMAD AMINE HADJ SAID.

Minister of Youth and Sports: MUHAMMAD TAHMI.

Minister of Industrial Development and Investment Promotion: AMARA BENYOUNES.

Minister of Postal Services and Information and Communications Technologies: ZOHRA DERDOURI.

Minister of Fisheries and Marine Resources: SID AHMED FERROUKHI.

Minister of Communication: ABDELKADER MESSAHEL.

Minister-Delegate to the Minister of Foreign Affairs, in charge of Maghreb and African Affairs: ABDELMADJID BOUGHERRA.

Minister-delegate to the Minister of Finance, in charge of the Budget: MUHAMMAD DJELLAB.

Secretary-General to the Government: AHMED NOUI.

MINISTRIES

Office of the President: Présidence de la République, el-Mouradia, Algiers; tel. (21) 69-15-15; fax (21) 69-15-95; e-mail president@el-mouradia.dz; internet www.el-mouradia.dz.

Office of the Prime Minister: rue Docteur Saâdane, Algiers; tel. (21) 73-23-40; fax (21) 71-79-29; internet www.cg.gov.dz.

Ministry of Agriculture and Rural Development: 12 blvd Col Amirouche, Algiers; tel. (21) 71-17-12; fax (21) 74-51-29; internet www.minagri.dz.

Ministry of Commerce: Cité Zerhouni Mokhtar les El Mohamadia, Algiers; tel. (21) 89-00-74; fax (21) 89-00-34; e-mail info@mincommerce.gov.dz; internet www.mincommerce.gov.dz.

Ministry of Culture: BP 100, Palais de la Culture 'Moufdi Zakaria', Plateau des Annassers, Kouba, Algiers; tel. (21) 29-10-10; fax (21) 29-20-89; e-mail contact@m-culture.gov.dz; internet www.m-culture.gov.dz.

Ministry of Energy and Mining: BP 677, Tower A, Val d'Hydra, Alger-Gare, Algiers; tel. (21) 48-85-26; fax (21) 48-85-57; e-mail info@memalgeria.org; internet www.mem-algeria.org.

Ministry of Finance: Immeuble Ahmed Francis, Ben Aknoun, Algiers; tel. (21) 59-51-51; e-mail mfmail@mf.gov.dz; internet www.mf.gov.dz.

Ministry of Fisheries and Marine Resources: route des Quatre Canons, Algiers; tel. (21) 43-31-74; fax (21) 43-31-68; e-mail info@mpeche.gov.dz; internet www.mpeche.gov.dz.

Ministry of Foreign Affairs: place Mohamed Seddik Benyahia, el-Mouradia, Algiers; tel. (21) 29-12-12; fax (21) 50-43-63; internet www.mae.dz.

Ministry of Future Planning and Statistics: Algiers.

Ministry of Health, Population and Hospital Reform: 125 rue Abderrahmane Laâla, el-Madania, Algiers; tel. (21) 67-53-15; fax (21) 65-36-46; internet www.sante.gov.dz.

Ministry of Higher Education and Scientific Research: 11 chemin Doudou Mokhtar, Ben Aknoun, Algiers; tel. (21) 91-23-23; e-mail webmaster@mesrs.dz; internet www.mesrs.dz.

Ministry of Housing and Urban Planning: 135 rue Mourad Didouche, Algiers; tel. (21) 74-07-22; e-mail mhabitat@wissal.dz; internet www.mhu.gov.dz.

Ministry of Industry, Small and Medium-sized Enterprises and Investment Promotion: Immeuble de la Colisée, 2 rue Ahmed Bey, el-Biar, Algiers; tel. (21) 23-91-43; fax (21) 23-94-88; internet www.mipi.dz.

Ministry of Information: Algiers.

Ministry of the Interior and Local Authorities: 18 rue Docteur Saâdane, Algiers; tel. (21) 73-76-81; fax (21) 73-61-54.

Ministry of Justice: 8 place Bir Hakem, el-Biar, Algiers; tel. (21) 92-41-83; fax (21) 92-17-01; e-mail contact@mjustice.dz; internet www.mjustice.dz.

Ministry of Labour, Employment and Social Security: 44 rue Muhammad Belouizdad, 16600 Algiers; tel. and fax (21) 65-99-99; e-mail informa@mtess.gov.dz; internet www.mtess.gov.dz.

Ministry of National Defence: Les Tagarins, el-Biar, Algiers; tel. (21) 71-15-15; fax (21) 64-67-26.

Ministry of National Education: 8 rue de Pékin, el-Mouradia, Algiers; tel. (21) 60-55-60; fax (21) 60-67-02; e-mail education@men.dz.

Ministry of National Solidarity and Family: BP 31, route nationale no 1, Les Vergers, Bir Khadem, Algiers; tel. (21) 44-99-46; fax (21) 44-97-26; e-mail cellulemassn@massn.gov.dz; internet www.massn.gov.dz.

Ministry of Postal Services and Information and Communications Technologies: 4 blvd Krim Belkacem, Algiers 16027; tel. (21) 71-12-20; fax (21) 73-00-47; e-mail contact@mptic.dz; internet www.mptic.dz.

Ministry of Public Works: 6 rue Moustafa Khalef, Ben Aknoun, Algiers; tel. (21) 91-49-47; fax (21) 91-35-85; e-mail info@mtp-dz.com; internet www.mtp.gov.dz.

Ministry of Religious Affairs and Awqaf (Religious Endowments): 4 rue de Timgad, Hydra, Algiers; tel. (21) 76-18-60; fax (21) 69-15-69; e-mail redaction@marwakf-dz.org; internet www.marwakf-dz.org.

Ministry of Territorial Planning, the Environment and Towns: rue des Quatre Canons, Bab-el-Oued, Algiers; tel. (21) 43-28-01; fax (21) 43-28-55; e-mail deeai@ifrance.com.

Ministry of Tourism and Handicrafts: Algiers.

Ministry of Transport: 1 chemin ibn Badis el-Mouiz (ex Poirson), el-Biar, 16300 Algiers; tel. (21) 92-98-85; fax (21) 92-98-94; internet www.ministere-transports.gov.dz.

Ministry of Vocational Training and Education: rue des frères Aîssou, Ben Aknoun, Algiers; tel. (21) 91-15-03; fax (21) 91-22-66; e-mail contacts@mfep.gov.dz; internet www.mfep.gov.dz.

Ministry of War Veterans: 2 ave du Lt Muhammad Benarfa, el-Biar, Algiers; tel. (21) 92-23-55; fax (21) 92-35-16; e-mail sinformatique@m-moudjahidine.dz; internet www.m-moudjahidine.dz.

Ministry of Water Resources: 3 rue du Caire, Kouba, Algiers; tel. (21) 28-39-01; e-mail deah@mre.gov.dz; internet www.mre.gov.dz.

Ministry of Youth and Sports: 3 rue Muhammad Belouizdad, Algiers; tel. (21) 68-33-50; fax (21) 65-77-78; e-mail contact@mjs.dz; internet www.mjs.dz.

President and Legislature

PRESIDENT

Presidential Election, 9 April 2009

Candidate	Votes	% of votes
Abdelaziz Bouteflika	13,019,787	90.23
Louisa Hanoune	649,632	4.50
Moussa Touati	294,411	2.04
Muhammad Djahid Younsi	208,549	1.45
Mohand Oussaïd Belaïd	133,315	0.92
Ali Fawzi Rebaïne	124,559	0.86
Total	14,430,253*	100.00

* Excluding 925,711 invalid votes.

LEGISLATURE

National People's Assembly

18 blvd Zighout Youcef, 16000 Algiers; tel. (21) 73-86-00; internet www.apn-dz.org.

President: Dr MUHAMMAD LARBI OULD KHELIFA.

General Election, 10 May 2012

	Seats
Front de libération nationale (FLN)	221
Rassemblement national démocratique (RND)	70
Alliance de l'Algérie verte (AAV)	47
Front des forces socialistes (FFS)	21
Parti des travailleurs (PT)	17
Front national algérien (FNA)	9
Front pour la justice et le développement (FJD-El-Addala)	7
Mouvement populaire algérien (MPA)	6
Parti el-Fedjr el-Jadid (PFJ)	5
Parti national pour la solidarité et le développement (PNSD)	4
Front du changement (FC)	4
Ahd 54	3
Alliance nationale républicaine (ANR)	3
Front national pour la justice sociale (FNJS)	3
Union des forces démocratiques et sociales (UFDS-El-Ittihad)	3
Rassemblement algérien (RA)	2
Rassemblement patriotique républicain (RPR)	2
Mouvement national de l'espérance (MNE)	2
Front El-Moustakbel (FM)	2
Parti El-Karama (PK)	2
Mouvement des citoyens libres (MCL)	2
Parti des jeunes (PJ)	2
Parti Ennour el-Djazairi (PED)	2
Others	4
Independents	19
Total	462

Council of the Nation

7 blvd Zighout Youcef, 16000 Algiers; tel. (21) 74-60-85; fax (21) 74-60-79; e-mail hamrani@majliselouma.dz; internet www.majliselouma.dz.

President: ABDELKADER BENSALAH.

Elections, 29 December 2009 and 29 December 2012*

	Seats
Rassemblement national démocratique (RND)	44
Front de libération nationale (FLN)	40
Front des forces socialistes (FFS)	2
Mouvement de la société pour la paix (MSP)	2
Ahd 54	1
Front El-Moustakbel (FM)	1
Front national algérien (FNA)	1
Mouvement populaire algérien (MPA)	1
Rassemblement pour la culture et la démocratie (RCD)	1
Independents	3
Appointed by the President†	48
Total	144

* Deputies of the 144-member Council of the Nation serve a six-year term; one-half of its members are replaced every three years. Elected representatives are selected by indirect, secret suffrage from regional and municipal authorities.

† 30 new members were appointed by the President on 6 January 2013.

Political Organizations

Until 1989 the FLN was the only legal party in Algeria. Amendments to the Constitution in February of that year permitted the formation of other political associations, with some restrictions. The right to establish political parties was guaranteed by constitutional amendments in November 1996; however, political associations based on differences in religion, language, race, gender or region were proscribed. Some 27 political parties contested the legislative elections of May 2012. The most prominent political organizations are listed below.

Ahd 54 (Oath 54): 53 rue Larbi Ben M'Hedi, Algiers; tel. (21) 73-00-83; fax (21) 73-00-82; e-mail info@ahd54.com; internet www.ahd54.com; f. 1991; small nationalist party; Pres. ALI FAWZI REBAÏNE.

Alliance de l'Algérie verte (AAV): Algiers; f. 2012; electoral alliance including three Islamist parties: Mouvement de la société pour la paix (MSP), Mouvement de la renaissance islamique (Al-Nahda) and Mouvement pour la réforme nationale; Leader BOUGUERRA SOLTANI.

Alliance nationale républicaine (ANR): 202 blvd Bougara, el-Biar, Algiers; tel. (21) 91-69-30; fax (21) 91-48-34; e-mail contact@anr.dz; f. 1995; anti-Islamist; Leader REDHA MALEK; Sec.-Gen. BELKACEM SAHLI.

Front de libération nationale (FLN): 7 rue du Stade, 16405 Hydra, Algiers; tel. (21) 69-42-81; fax (21) 69-47-07; e-mail contact@pfln.dz; internet www.pfln.dz; f. 1954; sole legal party until 1989; socialist in outlook, the party is organized into a Secretariat, a National Council, an Executive Committee, Federations, Kasmas and cells; under the aegis of the FLN are various mass political orgs, incl. the Union Nationale de la Jeunesse Algérienne and the Union Nationale des Femmes Algériennes; Pres. ABDELAZIZ BOUTEFLIKA; Sec.-Gen. AMMAR SAÏDANI.

Front démocratique libre (FDL) (Free Democratic Front): Algiers; f. 2012; Pres. BRAHMI RABAH.

Front des forces socialistes (FFS): 56 ave Souidani Boudjemaâ, el-Mouradia, 16000 Algiers; tel. (21) 69-41-41; fax (21) 69-41-42; e-mail ffscomdz@gmail.com; internet www.ffs-dz.com; f. 1963; revived 1989; seeks greater autonomy for Berber-dominated regions and official recognition of the Berber language; Leader HOCINE AÏT AHMED; Sec.-Gen. ALI LASKRI.

Front du changement (FC): Algiers; Chair. ABDELMADJID MENASRA.

Front El-Moustakbel (FM): Algiers; internet www.frontelmoustakbal.dz; f. 2012; Pres. ABDELAZIZ BELAÏD.

Front national algérien (FNA): 18 rue Chaib Ahmed, 16100 Algiers; tel. (21) 73-07-88; fax (21) 73-30-96; e-mail touatimoussa@yahoo.fr; internet www.fna.dz; f. 1999; advocates eradication of poverty and supports the Govt's peace initiative; Pres. MOUSSA TOUATI.

Front national démocratique (FND): Algiers; Pres. MABROUK SASSI.

Front national des indépendants pour la concorde (FNIC): Algiers; Pres. Dr LEKAL YACINE.

Front national pour la justice sociale (FNJS): Algiers; f. 2012; Pres. KHALED BOUNEDJMA.

Front pour la justice et le développement (FJD—El-Addala): Algiers; f. 2012; Leader ABDELLAH DJABALLAH.

Mouvement des citoyens libres (MCL): Algiers; f. 2012; Pres. MUSTAPHA BOUDINA.

Mouvement El-Infitah (ME): Algiers; Pres. OMAR BOUACHA.

Mouvement pour l'autonomie de la Kabylie (MAK): Tizi Ouzou; e-mail info@makabylie.info; internet mak.makabylie.info; f. 2001; advocates autonomy for the north-eastern region of Kabylia within a federal Algerian state; Pres. BOUAZIZ AIT-CHEBIB.

Mouvement démocratique et social (MDS): 67 blvd Krim Belkacem, 16200 Algiers; tel. (21) 63-86-05; fax (21) 63-89-12; e-mail mds-algerie@orange.fr; f. 1998 by fmr mems of Ettahaddi; left-wing party; 4,000 mems; Sec.-Gen. AHMED MELIANI.

Mouvement El Islah (MRN) (Mouvement de la réforme nationale): Algiers; internet www.elislah.net; f. 1998; radical Islamist party; contested May 2012 legislative elections as part of Alliance de l'Algérie verte; Sec.-Gen. HAMLAOUI AKOUCHI.

Mouvement populaire algérien (MPA): 53 Coopérative des médecins, Ben Aknoun, Algiers; tel. (21) 94-67-07; fax (21) 94-67-27; internet mouvementpopulairealgerien.org; Sec.-Gen. AMARA BENYOUNES.

Mouvement de la renaissance islamique (Al-Nahda) (Harakat al-Nahda al-Islamiyya): blvd des Martyrs, 16100 Algiers; tel. (21) 74-85-14; fundamentalist Islamist group; contested May 2012 legislative elections as part of Alliance de l'Algérie verte; Leader FATEH REBAI.

Mouvement de la société pour la paix (MSP) (Harakat Mujtamaa al-Silm): 63 rue Ali Haddad, Algiers; e-mail info@hmsalgeria.net; internet hmsalgeria.net; fmrly known as Hamas; adopted current name in 1997; moderate Islamist party, favouring the gradual introduction of an Islamic state; contested May 2012 legislative elections as part of Alliance de l'Algérie verte; Pres. ABDERREZAK MOKRI.

Parti algérien vert pour le développement (PAVD) (Algerian Green Party for Development): Algiers; f. 2012; Sec.-Gen. AMARA ALI.

Parti des fidèles à la patrie (PFP) (Party of Patriots): Algiers; f. 2012; Pres. MUSTAPHA KAMEL.

Parti des jeunes (PJ): Algiers; f. 2012; Gen. Coordinator HAMANA BOUCHERMA.

Parti des travailleurs (PT): 2 rue Belkheir Hassan Badi, el-Harrach, 16000 Algiers; tel. (21) 52-62-45; fax (21) 52-89-90; e-mail contact@pt-dz.com; internet www.pt-dz.com; workers' party; Leader LOUISA HANOUNE.

Parti du renouveau algérien (PRA): 8 ave de Pékin, 16209 el-Mouradia, Algiers; tel. (21) 59-43-00; Sec.-Gen. KAMEL BENSALEM; Leader NOUREDDINE BOUKROUH.

Parti El-Karama (PK): Algiers; f. 2012; Pres. MUHAMMAD BENHAMOU.

Parti Ennour el-Djazairi (PED): Algiers; Sec.-Gen. BADREDDINE BELBA.

Parti national pour la solidarité et le développement (PNSD): BP 110, Staouéli, Algiers; tel. and fax (21) 39-40-42; e-mail cherif_taleb@yahoo.fr; f. 1989 as Parti social démocrate; Leader MUHAMMAD CHÉRIF TALEB.

Rassemblement algérien (RA): cité Ahcène Mahiouz, BP 158, Ben Aknoun, 16000 Algiers; e-mail info@rassemblement-algerien.com; internet www.rassemblement-algerien.com; f. 2008; Pres. Dr ALI ZEGHDOUD.

Rassemblement national démocratique (RND): BP 10, Cité des Asphodèles, Ben Aknoun, Algiers; tel. (21) 91-64-10; fax (21) 91-47-40; e-mail contact@rnd-dz.com; internet www.rnd-dz.com; f. 1997; centrist party; Sec.-Gen. ABDELKADER BENSALAH (acting).

Rassemblement patriotique républicain (RPR): Algiers; Pres. ABDELKADER MERBAH.

Union des forces démocratiques et sociales (UFDS-El-Ittihad): Algiers; internet www.ufds-algerie.com; Sec.-Gen. NOUREDDINE BAHBOUH.

The following groups are in armed conflict with the Government:

Al-Qa'ida Organization in the Land of the Islamic Maghreb (AQIM): f. 1998 as the Groupe salafiste pour la prédication et le combat (GSPC), a breakaway faction from the Groupe islamique armé; adopted current name in Jan. 2007, when it aligned itself with the militant Islamist al-Qa'ida network; particularly active to the east of Algiers and in Kabylia; as the GSPC, traditionally responded to preaching by Ali Belhadj, the second most prominent member of the proscribed Front islamique du salut; Leader ABDELMALEK DROUKDAL (also known as Abu Musab Abd al-Wadud).

Groupe islamique armé (GIA): f. 1992; was the most prominent and radical Islamist militant group in the mid-1990s, but has reportedly split into several factions that do not all adhere to one leader.

Diplomatic Representation

EMBASSIES IN ALGERIA

Angola: 12 rue Mohamed Khoudi, el-Biar, Algiers; tel. (21) 92-21-43; fax (21) 92-04-18; e-mail ngolamd@wissal.dz; Ambassador JOSÉ ANTONIO CONDESA DE CARVALHO.

Argentina: Lotissement el-Feth, Villa 68, el-Biar, 16030 Algiers; tel. (21) 92-31-18; fax (21) 92-31-08; e-mail earge@mrecic.gov.ar; Ambassador MIGUEL ANGEL HILDMANN.

Austria: 17 chemin Abd al-Kader Gadouche, 16035 Hydra, Algiers; tel. (21) 69-10-86; fax (21) 69-12-32; e-mail algier-ob@bmeia.gv.at; internet www.aussenministerium.at/algier; Ambassador ALOISIA WÖRGETTER.

Belgium: BP 341, 16030 el-Biar, Algiers; tel. (21) 92-26-20; fax (21) 92-50-36; e-mail algiers@diplobel.fed.be; internet www.diplomatie.be/algiersfr; Ambassador FRÉDÉRIC MEURICE.

Benin: BP 103, 16 Lot du Stade Birkhadem, Algiers; tel. (21) 56-52-71; Ambassador LEONARD ADJIN.

Brazil: 55 Bis, chemin Cheikh Bachir el-Ibrahimi, el-Biar, 16030 Algiers; tel. (21) 92-44-37; fax (21) 92-41-25; e-mail brasemb.argel@itamaraty.gov.br; internet argel.itamaraty.gov.br; Ambassador HENRIQUE SARDINHA PINTO.

Bulgaria: 13 blvd Col Bougara, el-Biar, Algiers; tel. (21) 23-00-14; fax (21) 23-05-33; e-mail Embassy.Algiers@mfa.bg; internet www.mfa.bg/embassies/algeria; Chargé d'affaires a.i. MAXIM BLAGOEV.

Burkina Faso: BP 212, 23 Lot el-Feth, chemin ibn Badis el-Mouiz (ex Poirson), el-Biar, Didouche Mourad, Algiers; tel. (21) 92-33-39; fax (21) 92-73-90; e-mail abfalger@yahoo.fr; Ambassador DOMINIQUE DJINDJÉRÉ (designate).

Cameroon: 15 lotissement el-Feth, 16134 el-Biar, Algiers; tel. (21) 92-11-24; fax (21) 92-11-25; e-mail ambacamalger@yahoo.fr; Ambassador CLAUDE JOSEPH MBAFOU.

Canada: BP 464, 18 rue Mustapha Khalef, Ben Aknoun, 16306 Algiers; tel. (770) 08-30-00; fax (770) 08-30-40; e-mail alger@international.gc.ca; internet www.international.gc.ca/world/embassies/algeria; Ambassador GENEVIÈVE DES RIVIÈRES.

Chad: Villa 18, Cité DNC, chemin Ahmed Kara, Hydra, Algiers; tel. (21) 69-26-62; fax (21) 69-26-63; Ambassador OUSMANE MATAR BREME.

Chile: 8 rue F. les Crêtes, Hydra, Algiers; tel. (21) 48-31-63; fax (21) 60-71-85; e-mail embachileargelia@gmail.com; Ambassador PABLO MUÑOZ ROMERO.

China, People's Republic: 34 blvd des Martyrs, Algiers; tel. (21) 69-27-24; fax (21) 69-30-56; e-mail chinaemb_dz@mfa.gov.cn; internet dz.chineseembassy.org; Ambassador LIU YUHE.

Congo, Republic: 13 rue Rabah Noel, Algiers; tel. (21) 58-06-13; Ambassador JEAN-PIERRE LOUYEBO.

Côte d'Ivoire: BP 260, Immeuble 'Le Bosquet', Parc Paradou, Hydra, Algiers; tel. (21) 69-23-78; fax (21) 69-28-28; Ambassador SIA BI SEI.

Croatia: 26 bis, rue Hadj Ahmed Mohamed, Hydra, 16405 Algiers; tel. (21) 48-49-07; fax (21) 48-48-98; e-mail croemb.algeria@mvep.hr; Ambassador MARIN ANDRIJAŠEVIĆ.

Cuba: 22 rue Larbi Allik, Hydra, Algiers; tel. (21) 69-21-48; fax (21) 69-32-81; e-mail embacubargelia@assila.net; Ambassador EUMELIO CABALLERO RODRÍGUEZ.

Czech Republic: BP 358, Villa Koudia, 3 chemin Ziryab, Alger-Telemly, Algiers; tel. (21) 23-00-56; fax (21) 23-01-33; e-mail algiers@embassy.mzv.cz; internet www.mzv.cz/algiers; Ambassador PAVEL KLUCKÝ.

Egypt: BP 297, 8 chemin Abd al-Kader Gadouche, 16300 Hydra, Algiers; tel. (21) 69-16-73; fax (21) 69-29-52; Ambassador EZZ EL-DIN FAHMI MAHMOUD.

Finland: 10 rue des Cèdres, el-Mouradia, Algiers; tel. (21) 69-29-25; fax (21) 69-16-37; e-mail sanomat.alg@formin.fi; internet www.finlandalgeria.org; Ambassador HANNELE VOIONMAA.

France: 25 chemin Abd al-Kader Gadouche, 16035 Hydra, Algiers; tel. (21) 98-17-17; fax (21) 98-17-09; e-mail contact@ambafrance-dz.org; internet www.ambafrance-dz.org; Ambassador ANDRÉ PARANT.

Gabon: BP 125, Rostomia, 21 rue Hadj Ahmed Mohamed, Hydra, Algiers; tel. (21) 69-24-00; fax (21) 60-25-46; Ambassador YVES ONGOLLO.

Germany: BP 664, 165 chemin Sfindja, Alger-Gare, 16000 Algiers; tel. (21) 74-19-56; fax (21) 74-05-21; e-mail zreg@algi.diplo.de; internet www.algier.diplo.de; Ambassador GÖTZ LINGENTHAL.

Ghana: 62 rue des Frères Benali Abdellah, Hydra, Algiers; tel. (21) 60-64-44; fax (21) 69-28-56; Ambassador ADOLPHUS KINGSLEY ARTHUR.

Greece: 60 blvd Col Bougara, 16030 el-Biar, Algiers; tel. (21) 92-34-91; fax (21) 92-34-90; e-mail gremb.alg@mfa.gr; internet www.mfa.gr/algiers; Ambassador VASILIOS MOUTSOGLOU.

Guinea: 43 blvd Central Saïd Hamdine, Hydra, Algiers; tel. (21) 69-36-11; fax (21) 69-34-68; e-mail ambaga49@yahoo.fr; Ambassador OUSMANE DIAO BALDÉ.

Guinea-Bissau: BP 32, 17 rue Ahmad Kara, Colonne Volrol, Hydra, Algiers; tel. (21) 60-01-51; fax (21) 60-97-25; Ambassador IBRAIMA SANO.

Holy See: 1 rue Noureddine Mekiri, 16021 Bologhine, Algiers (Apostolic Nunciature); tel. (21) 95-45-20; fax (21) 95-40-95; e-mail nuntiusalger2@yahoo.fr; Apostolic Nuncio Most Rev. THOMAS YEH SHENG-NAN (Titular Archbishop of Leptis Magna).

Hungary: BP 68, 18 ave des Fréres Oughlis, el-Mouradia, Algiers; tel. (21) 69-79-75; fax (21) 69-81-86; e-mail alg.missions@kum.hu; Ambassador JÓZSEF HAJGATÓ.

India: BP 108, 14 rue des Abassides, 16030 el-Biar, Algiers; tel. (21) 92-32-88; fax (21) 92-40-11; e-mail amb.algiers@mea.gov.in; internet www.indianalg.org; Ambassador Dr KULDEEP SINGH BHARDWAJ.

Indonesia: BP 62, 17 chemin Abd al-Kader Gadouche, 16070 el-Mouradia, Algiers; tel. (21) 69-49-15; fax (21) 69-49-10; e-mail kbrialger@indonesia-dz.org; internet algiers.kemlu.go.id; Ambassador AHMAD NI'AM SALIM.

Iraq: BP 249, 4 rue Abri Arezki, Hydra, Algiers; tel. (21) 69-31-25; fax (21) 69-10-97; e-mail algemb@iraqmofamail.com; Ambassador ABDULLAH AL-KHAIRALLAH.

Italy: 18 rue Muhammad Ouidir Amellal, 16030 el-Biar, Algiers; tel. (21) 92-23-30; fax (21) 92-59-86; e-mail segretaria.algeri@esteri.it; internet www.ambalgeri.esteri.it; Ambassador MICHELE GIACOMELLI.

Japan: BP 80, 1 chemin el-Bakri (ex Macklay), Ben Aknoun, el-Biar, Algiers; tel. (21) 91-20-04; fax (21) 91-20-46; internet www.dz.emb-japan.go.jp; Ambassador TSUKASA KAWADA.

Jordan: 47 rue Ammani Belkalem, Hydra, Algiers; tel. (21) 69-20-31; fax (21) 69-15-54; e-mail jordan@wissal.dz; Ambassador MUHAMMAD SALAMAH NUEIMAT.

Korea, Democratic People's Republic: Algiers; tel. (21) 62-39-27; Ambassador PAK HO IL.

Korea, Republic: BP 92, 39 ave Mohamed Khoudi, el-Biar, Algiers; tel. (21) 79-34-00; fax (21) 79-34-04; e-mail koemal@mofat.go.kr; internet dza.mofat.go.kr/kor/af/dza/main/index.jsp; Ambassador KIM JONG-HOON.

Kuwait: chemin Abd al-Kader Gadouche, Hydra, Algiers; tel. (21) 59-31-57; Ambassador SAUD FAISAL SAUD AL-DAWEESH.

Lebanon: 9 rue Kaïd Ahmad, el-Biar, Algiers; tel. (21) 78-20-94; Ambassador BASSAM ALI TARABAH.

Libya: 15 chemin Cheikh Bachir el-Ibrahimi, Algiers; tel. (21) 92-15-02; fax (21) 92-46-87; Ambassador ABD AL-MOULA EL-GHADHBANE.

Madagascar: BP 65, 22 rue Abd al-Kader Aouis, 16090 Bologhine, Algiers; tel. (21) 95-03-74; fax (21) 95-17-76; e-mail ambamadalg@yahoo.fr; Ambassador VOLA DIEUDONNÉ RAZAFINDRALAMBO.

Mali: Villa 15, Cité DNC/ANP, chemin Ahmed Kara, Hydra, Algiers; tel. (21) 69-13-51; fax (21) 69-20-82; Ambassador BOUBACAR KARAMOKO COULIBALY.

Mauritania: 107 Lot Baranès, Aire de France, Bouzaréah, Algiers; tel. (21) 79-21-39; fax (21) 78-42-74; Ambassador BOULAH OULD MOGUEYE.

Mexico: BP 329, 25 chemin El-Bakri, Ben Aknoun, 16306 Algiers; tel. (21) 91-46-00; fax (21) 91-46-01; e-mail embamexargelia@gmail.com; internet embamex.sre.gob.mx/argelia; Chargé d'affaires a.i. GERARDO ALFREDO FERIA AMAYA.

Morocco: 8 rue Abd al-Kader Azil, el-Mouradia, Algiers; tel. (21) 60-57-07; fax (21) 60-50-47; e-mail ambmaroc-alg@maec.gov.ma; Ambassador ABDELLAH BELKEZIZ.

Netherlands: BP 72, 23/27 chemin Cheikh Bachir el-Ibrahimi, el-Biar, Algiers; tel. (21) 92-28-28; fax (21) 92-29-47; e-mail alg@minbuza.nl; internet alger.nlambassade.org; Ambassador FRANCISCUS GIJSBERTUS (FRANS) BIJVOET.

Niger: 54 rue Vercors Rostamia, Bouzaréah, Algiers; tel. (21) 78-89-21; fax (21) 78-97-13; Ambassador MAHAMIDOU ELHADJI YAHAYA.

Nigeria: BP 629, 27 bis rue Blaise Pascal, Algiers; tel. (21) 69-18-49; fax (21) 69-11-75; Ambassador HARUNA GINSAU.

Norway: 7 chemin Doudou Mokhtar, Ben Aknoun, 16035 Algiers; tel. (21) 94-65-65; fax (21) 94-64-65; e-mail emb.alger@mfa.no; internet www.norvege-algerie.org; Ambassador ARILD RETVEDT ØYEN.

Oman: BP 201, 52 rue Djamel Eddine, el-Afghani, Bouzaréah, Algiers; tel. (21) 91-28-35; fax (21) 91-47-37; e-mail algeria@mofa.gov.om; Ambassador ALI ABDULLAH AL-ALAWI.

Pakistan: BP 395, Villa no 18, rue des Idrissides, el-Biar, Algiers; tel. (21) 79-37-56; fax (21) 79-37-58; e-mail pakembagiers@yahoo.com; internet www.mofa.gov.pk/algeria; Ambassador KHALID DURRANI.

Peru: 2 et 4 Capitaine Salah Moghni, El Biar, 16406 Algiers; tel. (21) 92-38-54; fax (21) 92-38-56; e-mail ambaperou@yahoo.fr; Ambassador LUIS FELIPE GÁLVEZ VILLARROEL.

Poland: rue Olof Palme, Nouveau-Paradou, Hydra-Algiers; tel. (21) 60-99-50; fax (21) 60-99-59; e-mail algier.amb.sekretariat@msz.gov.pl; internet algier.msz.gov.pl; Ambassador MICHAŁ RADLICKI.

Portugal: 4 rue Mohamed Khoudi, el-Biar, Algiers; tel. (21) 92-53-14; fax (21) 92-53-13; e-mail embportdz@yahoo.fr; internet www.embaixadaportugalargel.com; Ambassador ANTÓNIO GAMITO.

Qatar: BP 35, Quartier Diplomatique, Dely Ibrahim, Algiers; tel. (21) 91-08-84; fax (21) 91-09-44; e-mail algeria@mofa.gov.qa; Ambassador ABDULLAH NASSER ABDULLAH AL-HUMAIDI.

Romania: 24 rue Abri Arezki, Hydra, 16035, Algiers; tel. (21) 60-08-71; fax (21) 69-36-42; e-mail alger@mae.ro; Ambassador MARCEL ALEXANDRU.

Russia: 7 chemin du Prince d'Annam, el-Biar, Algiers; tel. (21) 92-31-39; fax (21) 92-28-82; e-mail ambrussie@yandex.ru; internet www.algerie.mid.ru; Ambassador ALEKSANDR Y. ZOLOTOV.

Saudi Arabia: BP 256, 5 chemin Doudou Mokhtar, Ben Aknoun, el-Biar, Algiers; tel. (21) 60-35-18; e-mail dzemb@mofa.gov.sa; Ambassador Dr SAMI IBN ABDULLAH IBN OTHMAN AL-SALEH.

Senegal: 1 chemin Mohamed Drarni, Hydra, Algiers; tel. (21) 54-90-90; fax (21) 54-90-94; e-mail senegal@wissal.dz; Ambassador PAPA OUSMANE SEYE.

Serbia: BP 366, 7 rue des Frères Ben-hafid, 16035 Hydra, Algiers; tel. (21) 69-12-18; fax (21) 69-34-72; e-mail ambasada@ambserbie-alger.com; internet www.ambserbie-alger.com; Ambassador MIROSLAV ŠESTOVIĆ.

South Africa: 21 rue du Stade, Hydra, Algiers; tel. (21) 48-44-18; fax (21) 48-44-19; e-mail teffahim@foreign.gov.za; internet www.saealgiers.com; Ambassador JOSEPH KOTANE.

Spain: BP 142, 46 bis, rue Muhammad Chabane, el-Biar, Algiers; tel. (21) 92-27-13; fax (21) 92-27-19; e-mail emb.argel@mae.es; Ambassador GABRIEL BUSQUETS APARICIO.

Sudan: Algiers; tel. (21) 56-66-23; fax (21) 69-30-19; Ambassador MADJI MUHAMMAD TAHA EL-HASSAN.

Sweden: BP 263, rue Olof Palme, Nouveau Paradou, Hydra, Algiers; tel. (21) 54-83-33; fax (21) 54-83-34; e-mail ambassaden.alger@gov.se; internet www.swedenabroad.se/algersv; Ambassador EVA EMNÉUS.

Switzerland: Villa 5, rue no 4, Parc du Paradou, 16035 Hydra, Algiers; tel. (21) 60-76-80; fax (21) 60-98-54; e-mail alg.vertretung@eda.admin.ch; internet www.eda.admin.ch/alger; Ambassador JEAN-CLAUDE RICHARD.

Syria: Domaine Tamzali, 11 chemin Abd al-Kader Gadouche, Hydra, Algiers; tel. (21) 91-20-26; fax (21) 91-20-30; Ambassador NAMIR WAHIB GHANEM.

Tunisia: 5 rue du Bois, Hydra, 16405 Algiers; tel. (21) 60-13-88; fax (21) 69-23-16; e-mail ambassade@ambtunisie-dz.com; Ambassador MUHAMMAD EL-FADHAL KHALIL.

Turkey: 21 Villa Dar el-Oued, chemin de la Rochelle, blvd Col Bougara, 16000 Algiers; tel. (21) 23-00-04; fax (21) 23-01-12; e-mail ambassade.alger@mfa.gov.tr; internet www.algiers.emb.mfa.gov.tr; Ambassador ADNAN KEÇECI.

Ukraine: 19 rue des Frères Benhafid, Hydra, Algiers; tel. (21) 69-13-87; fax (21) 69-48-87; e-mail emb_dz@mfa.gov.ua; internet algeria.mfa.gov.ua; Ambassador VALERIY KIRDODA.

United Arab Emirates: BP 165, Alger-Gare, 14 rue Muhammad Drarini, Hydra, Algiers; tel. (21) 54-96-99; fax (21) 54-96-66; e-mail algeria@mofa.gov.ae; internet uae-embassy.ae/Embassies/dz; Ambassador MUHAMMAD ALI NASSER AL-WALI AL-MAZROUEI.

United Kingdom: 3 chemin Capitaine Hocine Slimane, Hydra, Algiers; tel. (770) 08-50-00; fax (770) 08-50-99; e-mail britishembassy.algiers@fco.gov.uk; internet ukinalgeria.fco.gov.uk; Ambassador MARTYN ROPER.

USA: BP 549, 5 chemin Cheikh Bachir el-Ibrahimi, el-Biar, 16030 Algiers; tel. (770) 08-20-00; fax (770) 08-20-64; e-mail algiers_webmaster@state.gov; internet algiers.usembassy.gov; Ambassador HENRY S. ENSHER.

Venezuela: BP 297, 3 impasse Ahmed Kara, Hydra, Algiers; tel. (21) 54-74-14; fax (21) 54-73-96; e-mail hector.mujica@mre.gob.ve; Ambassador HECTOR MICHEL MUJICA.

Viet Nam: 30 rue de Chenoua, Hydra, Algiers; tel. (21) 60-88-43; fax (21) 69-37-78; e-mail sqvnalgerie@yahoo.com.vn; internet www.vietnamembassy-algerie.org; Ambassador TRONG CUONG DO.

Yemen: 18 chemin Mahmoud Drarnine, Hydra, Algiers; tel. (21) 54-89-50; fax (21) 54-87-40; Ambassador JAMAL AWADH NASSER.

Judicial System

Justice is exercised through 183 courts (Tribunaux) and 31 appeal courts (Cours d'appel), grouped on a regional basis. The highest court of justice is the Supreme Court (Cour suprême). New legislation, promulgated in March 1997, provided for the eventual establishment of 214 courts and 48 appeal courts. The Court of Accounts (Cour des comptes) was established in 1979. Algeria adopted a penal code in 1966, retaining the death penalty. In February 1993 three special courts were established to try suspects accused of terrorist offences; however, the courts were abolished in February 1995. Constitutional amendments introduced in November 1996 provided for the establishment of a High State Court (empowered to judge the President of the Republic in cases of high treason, and the Head of Government for crimes and offences), and a State Council to regulate the administrative judiciary. In addition, a Conflicts Tribunal has been established to adjudicate in disputes between the Supreme Court and the State Council.

Supreme Court: rue du 11 décembre 1960, Ben Aknoun, Algiers; tel. (21) 92-58-52; fax (21) 92-96-44; e-mail sg_coursupreme@mjustice.dz; internet www.coursupreme.dz; f. 1963; comprises 150 judges; Pres. KADDOUR BERRADJA.

Attorney-General: MUHAMMAD CHARFI.

Religion

ISLAM

Islam is the official religion, and the vast majority of Algerians are Muslims.

High Islamic Council

16 rue du 11 décembre 1960, Ben Aknoun, 16030 Algiers; tel. (21) 91-54-10; fax (21) 91-54-09; e-mail hci@hci.dz; internet www.hci.dz.

President of the High Islamic Council: Dr CHEIKH BOUAMRANE.

CHRISTIANITY

The majority of the European inhabitants, and a few Arabs, are Christians.

The Roman Catholic Church

Algeria comprises one archdiocese and three dioceses (including one directly responsible to the Holy See). The Bishops' Conference of North Africa (Conférence des Evêques de la Région Nord de l'Afrique—CERNA) moved from Algiers to Tunis, Tunisia, in 2004.

Archbishop of Algiers: Most Rev. GHALEB ABDULLAH MOUSSA, 22 chemin d'Hydra, 16030 el-Biar, Algiers; tel. (21) 92-56-67; fax (21) 92-55-76; e-mail evechealger@yahoo.fr.

Protestant Church

Eglise Réformée d'Alger: 31 rue Reda Houhou, 16110 Alger-HBB, Algiers; tel. and fax (21) 71-62-38; e-mail protestants_alger@yahoo.com; 38 parishes; 7,000 mems; Pres. MOUSTAFA KRIM.

The Press

In 2008 there were an estimated 290 newspapers in circulation, including more than 60 dailies.

DAILIES

El Acil: 1 rue Kamel Ben Djelit, Constantine; tel. and fax (31) 92-46-13; e-mail elacilquotidien@yahoo.fr; f. 1993; French; Dir GHALIB DJABBOUR.

Akher Sâa: Intersection Bougandoura Miloud et Sakhri Abdelhamid, Annaba; tel. (38) 86-02-41; fax (38) 86-47-19; e-mail saidbel@hotmail.com; internet www.akhersaa-dz.com; Arabic; Dir SAÏD BELHADJOUDJA.

L'Authentique: 4 rue Abane Ramdane, Algiers; tel. (17) 06-13-80; fax (21) 74-27-15; e-mail lauthentiqueredaction@yahoo.fr; French; Editorial Dir TAHAR AKEZOUH.

Ech-Cha'ab (The People): 1 ave Pasteur, 16000 Algiers; tel. (21) 60-70-40; fax (21) 60-67-93; e-mail webmaster@ech-chaab.com; internet www.ech-chaab.com; f. 1962; Arabic; journal of the Front de libération nationale; Dir AZZEDINE BOUKERDOUSSE; circ. 24,000.

Echorouk El-Youmi: Maison de la presse Abdelkader Safir, Kouba, Algiers; tel. and fax (21) 29-89-41; e-mail contact@echoroukonline.com; internet www.echoroukonline.com; f. 2000; Arabic; Dir ALI FOUDIL.

Le Courier d'Algérie: Maison de la presse Abdelkader Kouba, Algiers; tel. (21) 46-25-12; fax (21) 46-25-13; e-mail redactioncourrier@yahoo.fr; internet www.lecourrier-dalgerie.com; f. 2003; French; Dir AHMED TOUMIAT.

La Dépêche de Kabylie: Maison de la presse Tahar Djaout, place du 1er mai, 16016 Algiers; tel. (21) 66-38-05; fax (21) 66-37-87; e-mail info@depechedekabylie.com; internet www.depechedekabylie.com; f. 2001; Dir IDIR BENYOUNÈS.

Djazair News: Maison de la presse Tahar Djaout, place du 1er mai, 16016 Algiers; tel. (21) 66-36-93; fax (21) 66-36-93; e-mail djazairnews@gmail.com; internet www.djazairnews.info; f. 2003; Arabic; Man. Dir HMIDA AYACHI.

L'Expression: Maison de la presse Abdelkader Safir, Kouba, Algiers; tel. (21) 68-94-55; fax (21) 28-02-29; e-mail laredaction@lexpressiondz.com; internet www.lexpressiondz.com; f. 2000; French; Editor AHMED FATTANI; circ. 70,000.

Al-Fedjr: Maison de la presse Tahar Djaout, place du 1er mai, 16016 Algiers; tel. and fax (21) 65-76-60; e-mail fadjr@al-fadjr.com; internet www.al-fadjr.com; f. 2000; Arabic; Dir ABDA HADDA HAZEM.

Horizons: 20 rue de la Liberté, Algiers; tel. (21) 73-67-24; fax (21) 73-61-34; e-mail administration@horizons-dz.com; internet www.horizons-dz.com; f. 1985; evening; French; Dir NAÂMA ABBAS; circ. 35,000.

Le Jeune Indépendant: Maison de la presse Tahar Djaout, 1 rue Bachir Attar, place du 1er mai, 16016 Algiers; tel. (21) 67-07-48; fax (21) 67-07-46; e-mail redaction@jeune-independant.net; internet www.jeune-independant.net; f. 1990; French; Man. Dir ALI MECHERI; Editor NAÏMA NEFLA; circ. 60,000.

El-Joumhouria (The Republic): 6 rue Bensenouci Hamida, Oran; tel. (41) 39-04-97; fax (41) 39-10-39; e-mail djoumhouria@yahoo.fr; internet www.eldjoumhouria.dz; f. 1963; Arabic; Editor BENAMEUR BOUKHALFA; circ. 20,000.

El Khabar: 32 rue El Feth Ibn Khlakane, Hydra, Algiers; tel. (21) 48-44-37; fax (21) 48-44-31; e-mail cherif_dz@hotmail.com; internet www.elkhabar.com; f. 1990; Arabic; Dir-Gen. CHERIF REZKI; circ. 470,000.

Liberté: BP 178, 37 rue Larbi Ben M'Hidi, Alger-Gare, Algiers; tel. (21) 64-34-25; fax (21) 64-34-29; e-mail infos@liberte-algerie.com;

internet www.liberte-algerie.com; f. 1992; French; independent; Dir ALI OUAFEK; Editors SALIM TAMANI, AMAR OUALI; circ. 20,000.

El-Massa: Maison de la presse Abdelkader Safir, Kouba, 16000 Algiers; tel. (21) 74-57-99; fax (21) 74-57-90; e-mail info@el-massa.com; internet www.el-massa.com; f. 1977; evening; Arabic; Dir ABDERRAHMANE TIGANE; circ. 45,000.

Le Matin: Maison de la Presse Tahar Djaout, 1 rue Bachir Attar, place du 1er mai, 16016 Algiers; tel. (21) 66-07-08; fax (21) 66-20-97; e-mail redactionlematin@gmail.com; internet www.lematindz.net; French; Dir MUHAMMAD BENCHICOU.

El-Moudjahid (The Fighter): 20 rue de la Liberté, Algiers; tel. (21) 73-70-81; fax (21) 73-56-70; e-mail elmoudja@elmoudjahid.com; internet www.elmoudjahid.com; f. 1965; govt journal in French and Arabic; Dir ABDELMADJID CHERBAL; circ. 392,000.

An-Nasr (The Victory): BP 388, Zone Industrielle, La Palma, Constantine; tel. (31) 66-82-61; fax (31) 66-81-45; e-mail contact@annasronline.com; internet www.annasronline.com; f. 1963; Arabic; Dir LARBI OUANOUGHI; circ. 340,000.

La Nouvelle République: Maison de la presse Tahar Djaout, 1 rue Bachir Attar, place du 1er mai, 16016 Algiers; tel. (21) 67-10-44; fax (21) 67-10-75; e-mail inr98@yahoo.fr; internet www.lanouvellerepublique.com; French; Dir ABDELWAHAB DJAKOUNE; Editor MEHENNA HAMADOUCHE.

Ouest Tribune: 13 Cité Djamel, 31007 Oran; tel. (41) 45-31-30; fax (41) 45-34-62; e-mail redaction@ouestribune-dz.com; internet www.ouestribune-dz.com; French; Dir ABDELMADJID BLIDI.

Le Quotidien d'Oran: BP 110, 63 ave de l'ANP, 1 rue Laid Ould Tayeb, Oran; tel. (41) 32-63-09; fax (41) 32-51-36; e-mail infos@lequotidien-oran.com; internet www.lequotidien-oran.com; French; Dir-Gen. MUHAMMAD ABDOU BENABBOU.

Sawt al-Ahrar: 6 ave Pasteur, Algiers; tel. (21) 73-47-76; fax (21) 73-47-65; e-mail sawtalahrar@hotmail.com; internet www.sawt-alahrar.net; Arabic; Dir MUHAMMAD NADIR BOULAGROUNE.

Le Soir d'Algérie: Maison de la presse Tahar Djaout, 1 rue Bachir Attar, place du 1er mai, 16016 Algiers; tel. (21) 67-06-58; fax (21) 67-06-76; e-mail info@lesoirdalgerie.com; internet www.lesoirdalgerie.com; f. 1990; evening; independent information journal in French; Dir FOUAD BOUGHANEM; Editor NACER BELHADJOUDJA; circ. 80,000.

La Tribune: Maison de la presse Tahar Djaout, 1 rue Bachir Attar, place du 1er mai, 16016 Algiers; tel. (21) 68-54-21; fax (21) 68-54-22; e-mail latribun@latribune-online.com; internet www.latribune-online.com; f. 1994; current affairs journal in French; Dir HASSAN BACHIR-CHERIF; Editorial Dir ABDELKRIM GHEZALI.

La Voix de l'Oranie: 3 rue Rouis Rayah, Haï Oussama, 31000 Oran; tel. (41) 32-22-18; fax (41) 35-18-01; e-mail contact@voix-oranie.com; internet www.voix-oranie.com; French; Dir RAFIK CHARRAK.

El Watan: Maison de la presse, 1 rue Bachir Attar, place du 1er mai, 16016 Algiers; tel. (21) 68-21-83; fax (21) 68-21-87; e-mail admin@elwatan.com; internet www.elwatan.com; f. 1990; French; Dir OMAR BELHOUCHET; circ. 140,000.

El-Youm: Maison de la presse Tahar Djaout, 1 rue Bachir Attar, place du 1er mai, 16016 Algiers; tel. (21) 66-70-82; fax (21) 67-57-05; e-mail pubelyoum@yahoo.fr; internet www.elyawm.com; Arabic; Dirs MAHFOUD HADJI, AMINA HADJI; Editor KHALED LAKHDARI; circ. 54,000.

WEEKLIES

Les Débats: 2 blvd Muhammad V, Algiers; tel. (21) 63-73-05; fax (21) 63-70-05; e-mail lesdebats@hotmail.com; internet www.lesdebats.com; French; Dir AÏSSA KHELLADI.

Al-Mohakik Assiri (The Secret Enquirer): 2 ave Nafaâ Hafaf, Algiers; tel. (21) 71-05-58; e-mail almohakik@yahoo.fr; internet www.almohakik.com; f. 2006; Arabic; Dir HABET HANNACHI.

La Nation: 33 rue Larbi Ben M'hidi, Algiers; tel. (21) 43-21-76; f. 1992; French; Dir ATTIA OMAR; Editor SALIMA GHEZALI; circ. 35,000.

Révolution Africaine: Algiers; tel. (21) 59-77-91; fax (21) 59-77-92; current affairs journal in French; socialist; Dir FERRAH ABDELLALI; circ. 50,000.

OTHER PERIODICALS

Al-Acala: 4 rue Timgad, Hydra, Algiers; tel. (21) 60-85-55; fax (21) 60-09-36; f. 1970; publ. by the Ministry of Religious Affairs and Awqaf (Religious Endowments); fortnightly; Arabic; Editor MUHAMMAD AL-MAHDI.

Algérie Médicale: Algiers; f. 1964; publ. of the Union médicale algérienne; 2 a year; French; circ. 3,000.

Alouan (Colours): 119 rue Didouche Mourad, Algiers; f. 1973; cultural review; monthly; Arabic.

L'Auto Marché: 139 blvd Krim Belkacem; tel. (21) 74-44-59; fax (21) 74-14-63; e-mail contact@lautomarche.com; internet www.lautomarche.com; f. 1998; fortnightly; French; motoring; Dir MOURAD CHEBOUB.

Bibliographie de l'Algérie: Bibliothèque Nationale d'Algérie, BP 127, Hamma el-Annasser, 16000 Algiers; tel. (21) 67-57-81; fax (21) 67-23-00; e-mail contact@biblionat.dz; internet www.biblionat.dz; f. 1963; lists books, theses, pamphlets and periodicals publ. in Algeria; bi-annual; Arabic and French; Dir-Gen. MUHAMMAD AÏSSA OUMOUSSA.

Le Buteur: Maison de la presse Tahar Djaout, 1 rue Bachir Attar, place du 1er mai, 16016 Algiers; tel. (21) 73-25-76; fax (21) 73-99-71; e-mail contact@lebuteur.com; internet www.lebuteur.com; Mon., Thur. and Sat.; French; sports; Dir BOUSAÂD KAHEL.

Al-Cha'ab al-Thakafi (Cultural People): Algiers; f. 1972; cultural monthly; Arabic.

Al-Chabab (Youth): Algiers; journal of the Union Nationale de la Jeunesse Algérienne; bi-monthly; Arabic and French.

Al-Djeich (The Army): Office de l'Armée Nationale Populaire, Algiers; f. 1963; monthly; Arabic and French; Algerian army review; circ. 10,000.

IT Mag: 5è groupe, Bat J, 1er Mai, Algiers; tel. (21) 66-29-92; fax (21) 65-03-28; e-mail info@itmag-dz.com; internet www.itmag.dz; f. 2002; French; telecommunications and IT in North Africa; Dir ABDERRAFIQ KHENIFSA.

Journal Officiel de la République Algérienne Démocratique et Populaire: pl. Seddik Ben Yahia, el-Mouradia, Algiers; tel. (21) 68-65-50; internet www.joradp.dz; f. 1962; Arabic and French.

Révolution et Travail: Maison du Peuple, 1 rue Abdelkader Benbarek, place du 1er mai, Algiers; tel. (21) 66-73-53; journal of the Union Générale des Travailleurs Algériens (central trade union) with Arabic and French edns; monthly; Editor-in-Chief RACHIB AÏT ALI.

Revue Algérienne du Travail: 28 rue Hassiba Bouali, Algiers; f. 1964; labour publ; quarterly; French; Dir A. DJAMAL.

Al-Thakafa (Culture): 2 place Cheikh Ben Badis, Algiers; tel. (21) 62-20-73; f. 1971; every 2 months; cultural review; Editor-in-Chief CHEBOUB OTHMANE; circ. 10,000.

NEWS AGENCIES

Agence Algérienne d'Information (AAI): Maison de la presse Tahar Djaout, 1 rue Bachir Attar, place du 1er mai, 16016 Algiers; tel. (21) 67-07-44; fax (21) 67-07-32; e-mail aai@aai-online.com; f. 1999; Dir HOURIA AÏT KACI.

Algérie Presse Service (APS): BP 444, 58 ave des Frères Bouadou, Bir Mourad Raïs, 16300 Algiers; tel. (21) 56-44-44; fax (21) 44-03-12; e-mail aps@aps.dz; internet www.aps.dz; f. 1961; provides news reports in Arabic, English and French.

Publishers

BERTI Editions: Lot el-Nadjah no 24, 16320 Dely Ibrahim, Algiers; tel. (21) 33-50-75; fax (21) 33-53-65; e-mail berti@berti-editions.com; internet www.berti-editions.com; f. 1995; publishes books on medicine, law, finance and IT; Dir MUHAMMAD GACI.

Casbah Editions: Lot Saïd Hamdine, Hydra, 16012 Algiers; tel. (21) 54-79-10; fax (21) 54-72-77; f. 1995; literature, essays, memoirs, textbooks and children's literature; Dir-Gen. SMAÏN AMZIANE.

CHIHAB Diffusion (CHIDIF): BP 74/4, Zone industriel de Reghaia, 16000 Algiers; tel. (21) 84-87-02; fax (21) 85-83-25; e-mail chidif@chihab.com; internet www.chihab.com; f. 1989; publishes educational textbooks.

Editions Bouchène: 4 rue de l'oasis, Algiers; tel. (21) 59-69-23; e-mail edbouchene@wanadoo.fr; internet www.bouchene.com; f. 1998; publishes books on the Maghreb region.

Editions Dahlab: 18 rue d'Auzia, Hydra, Algiers; tel. and fax (21) 69-40-06; e-mail editiondahlab@yahoo.fr; internet editions-dahlab.com; history, social sciences, economics; Dir ABDELLAH CHEGHNANE.

Editions du Tell: 3 rue des Frères Yacoub Torki, 09000 Blida; tel. (25) 31-10-35; fax (25) 31-10-36; e-mail contact@editions-du-tell.com; internet www.editions-du-tell.com; f. 2002; publishes books on literature, history, economics and social sciences.

Entreprise Nationale des Arts Graphiques (ENAG): BP 75, Zone industriel de Réghaia, Algiers; tel. (21) 84-86-11; fax (21) 84-80-08; e-mail edition@enag.dz; internet www.enag.dz; f. 1983; art, literature, social sciences, economics, science, religion, lifestyle and textbooks; Dir-Gen. HAMIDOU MESSAOUDI.

Maison d'Édition El Amel: Cité 600, Logement EPLF 53, 15000 Tizi Ouzou; tel. (26) 21-96-55; fax (26) 21-07-21; law and political science publishers.

Office des Publications Universitaires (OPU): 1 place Centrale de Ben Aknoun, 16306 Algiers; tel. (21) 91-23-14; fax (21) 91-21-81;

e-mail info@opu-dz.com; internet www.opu-dz.com; publishes university textbooks; Dir-Gen. NOUREDDINE LACHEB.

Sedia: Cité les Mandariniers, Lot 293, al-Mohammadia, 16211 Algiers; tel. 770973861 (mobile); fax (21) 21-90-16; e-mail sedia@sedia-dz.com; internet www.sedia-dz.com; f. 2000; literature and educational textbooks; Pres. and Dir-Gen. BRAHIM DJELMAMI-HANI.

Broadcasting and Communications

TELECOMMUNICATIONS

New legislation approved by the National People's Assembly in August 2000 removed the state's monopoly over the telecommunications sector and redefined its role to that of a supervisory authority. Under the legislation, an independent regulator for the sector was created, and both the fixed-line and mobile sectors were opened to foreign competition.

Algérie Télécom: route Nationale 5, Cinq Maisons, Mohammadia, 16130 Algiers; tel. (21) 82-38-38; fax (21) 82-38-39; e-mail contact@algerietelecom.dz; internet www.algerietelecom.dz; f. 2001 to manage and develop telecommunications infrastructure; Pres. and Dir-Gen. AZOUAOU MEHMEL.

Mobilis: Site Sider, 7 rue Belkacem Amani, Paradou, Hydra, Algiers; tel. (21) 54-71-63; fax (21) 54-72-72; e-mail commercial@mobilis.dz; internet www.mobilis.dz; f. 2003; subsidiary of Algérie Télécom; Pres. and Dir-Gen. BERTRAND DE TALHOUËT.

Djezzy GSM: Orascom Telecom Algérie, rue Mouloud Feraoun, Lot no. 8A, el-Beida, Algiers; tel. (70) 85-00-00; fax (70) 85-70-85; e-mail djezzy.entreprises@otalgerie.com; internet www.djezzy.com; f. 2002; operates mobile cellular telephone network; some 17m. subscribers (2013); Exec. Pres. VINCENZO NESCI.

Wataniya Telecom Algérie (Nedjma): BP 74, Algiers; e-mail mtouati@wta.dz; internet www.nedjma.dz; f. 2004; owned by Nat. Mobile Telecommunications Co KSC (Kuwait); offers mobile cellular telecommunications services under brand name Nedjma; Dir-Gen. JOSEPH GED.

Regulatory Authority

Autorité de Régulation de la Poste et des Télécommunications (ARPT): 1 rue Kaddour Rahim, Hussein Dey, 16008 Algiers; tel. (21) 47-02-05; fax (21) 47-01-97; e-mail info@arpt.dz; internet www.arpt.dz; f. 2001; Pres. DERDOURI ZOHRA; Dir-Gen. MUHAMMAD AMGHAR.

BROADCASTING

Radio

Radiodiffusion Algérienne (ENRS): 21 blvd des Martyrs, Algiers; tel. (21) 48-37-90; fax (21) 23-08-23; e-mail info@algerian-radio.dz; internet www.radioalgerie.dz; govt-controlled; operates 30 local radio stations; Dir-Gen. AZZEDINE MIHOUBI.

Arabic Network: transmitters at Adrar, Aïn Beïda, Algiers, Béchar, Béni Abbès, Djanet, El Goléa, Ghardaïa, Hassi Messaoud, In Aménas, In Salah, Laghouat, Les Trembles, Ouargla, Reggane, Tamanrasset, Timimoun, Tindouf.

French Network: transmitters at Algiers, Constantine, Oran and Tipaza.

Kabyle Network: transmitter at Algiers.

Television

The principal transmitters are at Algiers, Batna, Sidi-Bel-Abbès, Constantine, Souk-Ahras and Tlemcen. Television plays a major role in the national education programme.

Télévision Algérienne (ENTV): BP 16070, 21 blvd des Martyrs, Algiers; tel. (21) 60-23-00; fax (21) 60-19-22; e-mail alger-contact@entv.dz; internet www.entv.dz; f. 1986; govt-controlled; Dir-Gen. ABDELKADER LALMI.

Finance

(cap. = capital; res = reserves; dep. = deposits; brs = branches; m. = million; amounts in Algerian dinars)

BANKING

Central Bank

Banque d'Algérie: Immeuble Joly, 38 ave Franklin Roosevelt, 16000 Algiers; tel. (21) 23-00-23; fax (21) 23-03-71; e-mail ba@bank-of-algeria.dz; internet www.bank-of-algeria.dz; f. 1962 as Banque Centrale d'Algérie; present name adopted 1990; bank of issue; cap. 40m., res 74,367.5m. (March 2006); Gov. MUHAMMAD LAKSACI; 48 brs.

Nationalized Banks

Banque Al-Baraka d'Algérie: Haï Bouteldja Houidef, Villa 1, Ben Aknoun, Algiers; tel. (21) 91-64-50; fax (21) 91-64-57; e-mail info@albaraka-bank.com; internet www.albaraka-bank.com; f. 1991; Algeria's first Islamic financial institution; owned by the Saudi Arabia-based Al-Baraka Investment and Devt Co (56%) and the local Banque de l'Agriculture et du Développement Rural (44%); cap. 10,000m., res 1,011m., dep. 76,554m. (Dec. 2009); Chair. ADNANE AHMAD YOUCEF; Gen. Man. HAFID MUHAMMAD SEDDIK; 8 brs.

Banque Extérieure d'Algérie (BEA): 48 rue des Trois Frères Bouadou, Bir Mourad Raïs Algiers; tel. (21) 44-90-25; fax (21) 56-17-40; e-mail dircom@bea.dz; internet www.bea.dz; f. 1967; chiefly concerned with energy and maritime transport sectors; cap. 24,500m., res 94,297m., dep. 2,059,089m. (Dec. 2010); Pres. and Dir-Gen. MUHAMMAD LOUKAL; 80 domestic brs, 1 abroad.

Banque du Maghreb Arabe pour l'Investissement et le Commerce (BAMIC): 7 rue Dubois, Hydra, Algiers; tel. (21) 69-45-43; fax (21) 60-19-54; e-mail bamic@bamic-dz.com; internet www.bamic-dz.com; f. 1988; owned by Libyan Arab Foreign Bank (50%) and by Banque Extérieure d'Algérie, Banque Nationale d'Algérie, Banque de l'Agriculture et du Développement Rural and Crédit Populaire d'Algérie (12.5% each); cap. 50m., res 16.2m. (Dec. 2005); Pres. MUHAMMAD DJELLAB; Dir-Gen. TAHER NEFFATI.

Crédit Populaire d'Algérie (CPA): BP 411, 2 blvd Col Amirouche, 16000 Algiers; tel. (21) 63-57-05; fax (21) 63-57-13; e-mail info@cpa-bank.com; internet www.cpa-bank.dz; f. 1966; specializes in light industry, construction and tourism; cap. and res 28,002m., total assets 367,847m. (Dec. 2002); Pres. and Dir-Gen. MUHAMMAD DJELLAB; 128 brs.

Development Banks

Banque de l'Agriculture et du Développement Rural (BADR): BP 484, 17 blvd Col Amirouche, 16000 Algiers; tel. (21) 63-49-22; fax (21) 63-51-46; e-mail dcm@badr-bank.net; internet www.badr-bank.net; f. 1982; wholly state-owned; finance for the agricultural sector; cap. 33,000m., res 9,610m., dep. 720,945m. (Dec. 2009); Pres. and Dir-Gen. BOUALEM DJEBBAR; 270 brs.

Banque Algérienne de Développement (BAD): 21 blvd Zighout Youcef, Algiers; tel. (21) 73-99-04; e-mail bad@ist.cerist.dz; f. 1963; a public establishment with fiscal sovereignty; aims to contribute to Algerian economic devt through long-term investment programmes; cap. and res 7,125.4m., total assets 132,842.3m. (Dec. 2003); Dir-Gen. SADEK ALILAT; 4 brs.

Banque de Développement Local (BDL): 5 rue Gaci Amar, Staouéli, 16000 Algiers; tel. (21) 39-28-58; fax (21) 39-37-57; e-mail clientele@bdl.dz; internet www.bdl.dz; f. 1985; regional devt bank; cap. 15,800m., res 11,026m., dep. 231,417m. (Dec. 2009); CEO MUHAMMAD ARSLANE BACHTARZI; 15 brs.

Caisse Nationale d'Epargne et de Prévoyance (CNEP-Banque): 42 rue Khélifa Boukhalfa, Algiers; tel. (21) 71-33-53; fax (21) 71-70-22; e-mail infos@cnepbanque.dz; internet www.cnepbanque.dz; f. 1964; savings and housing bank; cap. and res 22.6m., total assets 443,239.6m. (Dec. 2001); Pres. and Dir-Gen. DJAMEL BESSA.

Private Banks

Arab Banking Corporation-Algeria (ABC Bank): BP 367, 54 ave des Trois Frères Bouadou, Algiers; tel. (21) 54-15-37; fax (21) 54-16-04; e-mail abc.general_management@arabbanking.com.dz; internet www.arabbanking.dz; f. 1998; cap. 10,000m., res 1,432m., dep. 25,580m. (Dec. 2010); Chair. Dr MUHAMMAD ABD EL-SALAM SHOKRI.

Arab Leasing Corpn: 3, rue Ahmed Ouaked, Dély Ibrahim, Algiers; tel. (21) 33-63-93; fax (21) 33-63-90; e-mail Contact@arableasing-dz.com; internet www.arableasing-dz.com; f. 2001; owned by Arab Banking Corpn (41%), The Arab Investment Co (25%), CNEP (27%) and other small shareholders; cap. and res 758m., total assets 801.6m. (Dec. 2002); Dir-Gen. ABDENOUR HOUAOUI.

BNP Paribas El-Djazair: 8 rue de Cirta, 16405 Hydra, Algiers; tel. (21) 60-39-42; fax (21) 60-39-29; e-mail mounir.belaidene@bnpparibas.com; internet www.bnpparibas.dz; f. 2001; cap. 10,000m., res 2,888m., dep. 122,771m. (Dec. 2010); Dir-Gen. LAURENT DUPUCH.

Gulf Bank Algeria: BP 26, route de Chérage, Dély Ibrahim, Algiers; tel. (21) 91-00-31; fax (21) 91-02-37; e-mail agbank_dz@hotmail.com; internet www.ag-bank.com; f. 2004; owned by United Gulf Bank, Bahrain (60%), Tunis Int. Bank (30%) and Jordan Kuwait Bank (10%); cap. 10,000m., res 268m., dep. 43,726m. (Dec. 2011); Pres. ABDELKRIM AL-KABARITY; Man. Dir MUHAMMAD LOUAB.

Trust Bank Algeria: 70 chemin Larbi Allik, Hydra, Algiers; tel. (21) 54-97-55; fax (21) 54-97-50; e-mail direction@trust-bank-algeria.com; internet www.trust-bank-algeria.com; f. 2002; Dir-Gen. REIDH SLIMANE TALEB; 3 brs.

Banking Association

Association des banques et des établissements financiers (ABEF): 03 chemin Romain, Val d'Hydra, el-Biar, Algiers; tel. (21) 91-55-77; fax (21) 91-56-08; e-mail abenkhalfa@gmail.com; f. 1995; serves and promotes the interests of banks and financial institutions in Algeria; Del.-Gen. ABDERRAHMANE BENKHALFA.

STOCK EXCHANGE

Bourse d'Alger (Algiers Stock Exchange): 27 blvd Col Amirouche, 16000 Algiers; tel. and fax (21) 63-47-99; e-mail sgbv-email@sgbv.dz; internet www.sgbv.dz; f. 1999; Pres. MILOUD GHOLLAM; Dir-Gen. MUSTAPHA FERFERA.

Commission d'Organisation et de Surveillance des Opérations de Bourse (COSOB): 17 Campagne Chkiken, 16045 Hydra, Algiers; tel. and fax (21) 59-10-13; e-mail contact@cosob.org; internet www.cosob.org; f. 1993; Pres. ABD EL-HAKIM BERRAH.

INSURANCE

The insurance sector is dominated by the state; however, in 1997 regulations were drafted to permit private companies to enter the Algerian insurance market.

L'Algérienne des Assurances (2a): 1 rue de Tripoli, Hussein-Dey, Algiers; tel. (21) 47-68-72; fax (21) 47-65-78; e-mail info@assurances-2a.com; internet www.assurances-2a.com; f. 1999; general; Pres. ABDELWAHAB RAHIM; Dir-Gen. TAHAR BALA.

Caisse Nationale de Mutualité Agricole (CNMA): 24 blvd Victor Hugo, Algiers; tel. (21) 74-33-28; fax (21) 73-34-79; e-mail cnma@cnma.dz; internet www.cnma.dz; f. 1972; Dir-Gen. KAMEL ARBA; 62 brs.

Cie Algérienne d'Assurances (CAAT): 52 rue des Frères Bouaddou, Bir Mourad Raïs, Algiers; tel. (21) 44-90-75; fax (21) 44-92-03; e-mail info@caat.dz; internet www.caat.dz; f. 1985; general; majority state ownership; Pres. and Dir-Gen. ABDELKRIM DJAFRI.

Cie Algérienne d'Assurance et de Réassurance (CAAR): 48 rue Didouche Mourad, 16000 Algiers; tel. (21) 63-20-72; fax (21) 63-13-77; e-mail caaralg@caar.com.dz; internet www.caar.com.dz; f. 1963 as a public corpn; partial privatization pending; Pres. and Dir-Gen. BRAHIM DJAMEL KASSALI.

Cie Centrale de Réassurance (CCR): Lot Saïd Hamdine, Bir Mourad Raïs, 16012 Algiers; tel. (21) 54-70-33; fax (21) 54-75-06; e-mail contact@ccr.dz; internet www.ccr.dz; f. 1973; general; Pres. and Dir-Gen. HADJ MUHAMMAD SEBA.

Société Nationale d'Assurances (SAA): 5 blvd Ernesto Ché Guévara, Algiers; tel. (21) 71-47-60; fax (21) 71-22-16; internet www.saa.dz; f. 1963; state-sponsored co; Pres. and Dir-Gen. AMARA LATROUS.

Trust Algeria Assurances-Réassurance: 70 chemin Larbi Allik, 16405 Hydra, Algiers; tel. (21) 54-88-00; fax (21) 54-71-36; e-mail secretariat@trustalgerians.com; f. 1987; 60% owned by Trust Insurance Co (Bahrain), 17.5% owned by CAAR; Pres. and Dir-Gen. ABD AL-SALAM ABU NAHL.

Trade and Industry

GOVERNMENT AGENCIES AND DEVELOPMENT ORGANIZATIONS

Agence Algérienne de Promotion du Commerce Extérieur (ALGEX): 5 rue Nationale, Algiers; tel. (21) 52-12-10; fax (21) 52-11-26; e-mail info@algex.dz; internet www.algex.dz; f. 2004; Dir-Gen. MUHAMMAD BENNINI.

Agence Nationale de l'Aménagement du Territoire (ANAT): 30 ave Muhammad Fellah, Kouba, Algiers; tel. (21) 68-78-16; fax (21) 68-85-03; e-mail anat@anat.dz; f. 1980; Dir-Gen. MUHAMMAD MEKKAOUI.

Agence Nationale de Développement de l'Investissement (ANDI): 27 rue Muhammad Merbouche, Hussein-Dey, Algiers; tel. (21) 77-32-62; fax (21) 77-32-57; e-mail dg@andi.dz; internet www.andi.dz; Dir-Gen. ABDELKARIM MANSOURI.

Institut National de la Productivité et du Développement Industriel (INPED): 35000 Boumerdès; tel. (24) 81-77-50; fax (24) 81-59-14; e-mail dg@inped.edu.dz; internet www.inped.edu.dz; f. 1967; Dir-Gen. ABDERRAHMANE MOUFEK.

Office National de Recherche Géologique et Minière (ORGM): BP 102, Cité Ibn Khaldoun, 35000 Boumerdès; tel. (24) 81-75-99; fax (24) 81-83-79; e-mail orgm-dg@orgm.com.dz; f. 1992; mining, cartography, geophysical exploration; Dir-Gen. ESSAID AOULI.

CHAMBERS OF COMMERCE

Chambre Algérienne de Commerce et d'Industrie (CACI): BP 100, Palais Consulaire, 6 blvd Amilcar Cabral, place des Martyres, 16003 Algiers; tel. (21) 96-77-77; fax (21) 96-70-70; e-mail infos@caci.dz; internet www.caci.dz; f. 1980; Pres. TAHER KELLIL; Dir-Gen. YAHIA SAHRAOUI.

Chambre Française de Commerce et d'Industrie en Algérie (CFCIA): Villa Clarac, 3 rue des Cèdres, 16070 el-Mouradia, Algiers; tel. (21) 48-08-00; fax (21) 60-95-09; e-mail jf.heugas@cfcia.org; internet www.cfcia.org; f. 1975; c. 24,500 mems; Pres. JEAN MARIE PINEL.

INDUSTRIAL ASSOCIATIONS

Centre d'Etudes et de Services Technologiques de l'Industrie des Matériaux de Construction (CETIM): BP 93, Cité Ibn Khaldoun, 35000 Boumerdès; tel. (24) 81-99-72; fax (24) 81-72-97; e-mail contact@cetim-dz.com; f. 1982; CEO ABDENNOUR ADJTOUTAH.

Institut National Algérien de la Propriété Industrielle (INAPI): 42 rue Larbi Ben M'hidi, 16000 Algiers; tel. (21) 73-01-42; fax (21) 73-55-81; e-mail info@inapi.org; internet www.inapi.org; f. 1973; Dir-Gen. ABD EL-HAFID BELMEHDI.

Institut National des Industries Manufacturières (INIM): 35000 Boumerdès; tel. (21) 81-62-71; fax (21) 82-56-62; f. 1973; Dir-Gen. YOUSUF OUSLIMANI.

STATE TRADING ORGANIZATIONS

Since 1970 all international trading has been carried out by state organizations, of which the following are the most important:

Entreprise Nationale d'Approvisionnement en Outillage et Produits de Quincaillerie Générale (ENAOQ): 5 rue Amar Semaous, Hussein-Dey, Algiers; tel. (21) 23-31-83; fax (21) 47-83-33; tools and general hardware; Dir-Gen. SMATI BAHIDJ FARID.

Entreprise Nationale de Produits Alimentaires (ENAPAL): 29 rue Larbi Ben M'hidi, Algiers; tel. (21) 76-10-11; f. 1983; monopoly of import, export and bulk trade in basic foodstuffs; brs in more than 40 towns; Chair. LAÏD SABRI; Man. Dir BRAHIM DOUAOURI.

Office Algérien Interprofessionnel des Céréales (OAIC): 5 rue Ferhat-Boussaad, Algiers; tel. (21) 23-73-04; fax (21) 23-70-83; e-mail oaic@ist.cerist.dz; f. 1962; responsible for the regulation, distribution and control of the national market and the importation of cereals and vegetables; Dir-Gen. MUHAMMAD KACEM.

Office National de Commercialisation des Produits Viti-Vinicoles (ONCV): 112 Quai Sud, Algiers; tel. (21) 73-82-59; fax (21) 73-72-97; e-mail info@oncv-dz.com; internet www.oncv-groupe.com; f. 1968; monopoly of importing and exporting products of the wine industry; Man. Dir MAJID AMZIANI.

Société des Emballages Fer Blanc et Fûts (EMB-FBF): BP 245, Kouba, route de Baraki, Gué de Constantine, Algiers; tel. (21) 83-94-23; fax (21) 83-05-29; e-mail info@emb-fbf.com; internet www.emb-fbf.com; Dir-Gen. HAMID ZITOUN.

UTILITIES

Regulatory Authority

Commission de Régulation de l'Electricité et du Gaz (CREG): Immeuble du Ministère de l'Energie et des Mines, Tour B, Val d'Hydra, Algiers; tel. (21) 48-81-48; fax (21) 48-84-00; e-mail contact@creg.mem.gov.dz; internet www.creg.gov.dz; f. 2005; Pres. NADJIB OTMANE.

Electricity and Gas

Linde Gas Algérie SpA (GI): BP 247, 23 ave de l'ALN, Hussein-Dey, Kouba, Algiers; tel. (21) 49-85-99; fax (21) 49-71-94; internet www.gaz-industriels.com.dz; f. 1972 as Entreprise Nationale des Gaz Industriels; production, distribution and commercialization of industrial and medical gas; Pres. and Dir-Gen. LAHOCINE BOUCHERIT.

Société Algérienne de l'Electricité et du Gaz (Sonelgaz SpA): 2 blvd Col Krim Belkacem, Algiers; tel. (21) 72-31-00; fax (21) 71-26-90; e-mail n.boutarfa@sonelgaz.dz; internet www.sonelgaz.dz; f. 1969; production, distribution and transportation of electricity, and transportation and distribution of natural gas; Chair. and CEO NOUREDDINE BOUTARFA.

Société de Travaux d'Electrification (KAHRIF): Villa Nour, Aïn d'Heb, Médéa; tel. (25) 58-51-67; fax (25) 61-31-14; e-mail hadjeb.mohamed@kahrif.com; internet www.kahrif.com; f. 1982; planning and maintenance of electrical infrastructure; Pres. and Dir-Gen. MUHAMMAD HADJEB.

Water

L'Algérienne des Eaux (ADE): BP 548, 3 rue du Caire, Kouba, 16016 Algiers; tel. (21) 28-28-07; fax (21) 28-10-06; internet www.ade

.dz; f. 1985 as Agence Nationale de l'Eau Potable et Industrielle et de l'Assainissement; state-owned co; Dir-Gen. Abdelkrim Mechia.

STATE HYDROCARBONS AGENCIES AND COMPANIES

Agence Nationale pour la Valorisation des Ressources en Hydrocarbures (Alnaft): Ministère de l'Energie et des Mines, Tour B, Val d'Hydra, Algiers; tel. (21) 48-82-67; fax (21) 48-82-76; e-mail firstender-alnaft@alnaft.mem.gov.dz; f. 2005; Dir Sid Ali Betata.

Autorité de Régulation des Hydrocarbures (ARH): Ministère de l'Energie et des Mines, Tour B, Val d'Hydra, Algiers; tel. (21) 48-81-67; fax (21) 48-83-15; e-mail arh@arh.mem.gov.dz; internet www.arh.gov.dz; f. 2005; Dir Noureddine Cherouati.

Société Nationale pour la Recherche, la Production, le Transport, la Transformation et la Commercialisation des Hydrocarbures (Sonatrach): Djenane el-Malik, Hydra, Algiers; tel. (21) 54-70-00; fax (21) 54-77-00; e-mail sonatrach@sonatrach.dz; internet www.sonatrach-dz.com; f. 1963; exploration, exploitation, transport and marketing of petroleum, natural gas and their products; Pres. and Dir-Gen. Abdelhamid Zerguine; Gen. Sec. Abdelmalek Zitouni.

The following companies are wholly owned subsidiaries of Sonatrach:

Entreprise Nationale de Canalisation (ENAC): 132 rue Tripoli, Algiers; tel. (21) 77-04-63; fax (21) 53-85-53; internet www.enac-dz.com; piping; Vice-Pres. Hocine Chekired.

Entreprise Nationale de Forage (ENAFOR): BP 211, Hassi Messaoud, W. Ouargla; tel. (29) 73-81-85; fax (29) 73-21-70; e-mail zoubir@enafor.dz; internet www.enafor.dz; f. 1981; drilling; CEO Abdelkader Zoubiri.

Entreprise Nationale de Géophysique (ENAGEO): BP 140, 30500 Hassi Messaoud, Ouargla; tel. (29) 73-77-00; fax (29) 73-72-12; e-mail engeoh1@wissal.dz; internet www.enageo.com; f. 1981; seismic acquisition, geophysics; Dir-Gen. Réda Rahal.

Entreprise Nationale des Grands Travaux Pétroliers (ENGTP): BP 09, Zone Industrielle, Reghaïa, Boumerdès; tel. (21) 84-86-26; fax (21) 84-80-34; e-mail engtpcommunication@engtp.com; internet www.engtp.com; f. 1980; major industrial projects; Dir-Gen. Muhammad Seghir Laouissi.

Société Nationale de la Pétrochimie (ENIP): BP 215, Zone industrielle, 21000 Skikda; tel. (38) 74-52-94; fax (38) 74-52-80; e-mail inr@enip-dz.com; internet www.enip-dz.com; f. 1984; design and construction for petroleum-processing industry; Dir-Gen. N. Kourdache.

Entreprise Nationale des Services aux Puits (ENSP): BP 83, 30500 Hassi Messaoud, Ouargla; tel. (29) 73-73-33; e-mail info@enspgroup.com; internet www.enspgroup.com; f. 1981; oil-well services; Pres. and Dir-Gen. Abdelwahab Oubira.

Entreprise Nationale des Travaux aux Puits (ENTP): BP 206–207, Base du 20 août 1955, 30500 Hassi Messaoud, Ouargla; tel. (29) 73-88-50; fax (29) 73-84-06; e-mail contact@entp-dz.com; internet www.entp-dz.com; f. 1981; oil-well construction; Pres. and Dir-Gen. Bachir Ben Amor.

Société Nationale de Commercialisation et de Distribution des Produits Pétroliers (NAFTAL, SpA): BP 73, route des Dûnes, Chéraga, Algiers; tel. (21) 38-13-13; fax (21) 38-19-19; e-mail webmaster@naftal.dz; internet www.naftal.dz; f. 1987; international marketing and distribution of petroleum products; Pres. and Dir-Gen. Saïd Akretche.

Société Nationale de Génie Civil et Bâtiment (GCB, SpA): BP 110, blvd de l'ALN, Boumerdès-Ville; tel. (24) 41-41-50; fax (24) 81-38-80; e-mail contact@gcb.dz; internet www.gcb.dz; civil engineering.

NATIONALIZED INDUSTRIES

A large part of Algerian industry is nationalized. Following the implementation of an economic reform programme in the 1980s, however, privatizations were undertaken during the 1990s, and it was further planned to transfer more than 180 companies to private control by 2004. The sale of 50 small and medium-sized enterprises was reported during that year. In 2006 a new privatization programme was launched to attract investment in over 1,000 companies (although some were unprofitable and in need of restructuring and those in strategic sectors remained exempt from sale). The Ministry of Industry and Investment Promotion is responsible for the Government's privatization programme.

Direction Générale des Forêts: chemin Doudou Mokhtar, Ben Aknoun, Algiers; tel. (21) 91-52-90; fax (21) 91-53-14; e-mail dgf@wissal.dz; internet www.dgf.gov.dz; f. 1971; production of timber, management of forests; Dir-Gen. Muhammad Seghir Noual.

Entreprise Nationale d'Approvisionnement en Bois et Dérivés (ENAB): 2 blvd Muhammad V, 16026 Algiers; tel. (21) 63-77-35; fax (21) 63-77-37; e-mail info@enab-dz.com; internet www.enab-dz.com; f. 1970; import and distribution of wood and wood products; Pres. El Hadj Rekhroukh.

Entreprise Nationale d'Ascenseurs (ENASC): 86 rue Hassiba Ben Bouali, 16014 Algiers; tel. (21) 66-75-23; fax (21) 66-82-50; internet www.enasc-dz.com; f. 1983; manufacture of elevators and escalators; Pres. Saïd Brahimi.

Entreprise Nationale de Bâtiments Industrialisés (BATIMETAL): BP 88, Zone Industrielle de Oued-Smar, 16270 Algiers; tel. (21) 48-26-02; fax (21) 48-46-38; e-mail batimetal@wissal.dz; internet www.batimetal.com.dz; f. 1983; study and commercialization of buildings; Dir-Gen. Boudjema Talai.

Entreprise Nationale de Charpentes et de Chaudronnerie (ENCC): BP 435, 8 rue Capitaine Azzoug, Hussein-Dey, Algiers; tel. (21) 49-72-69; fax (21) 49-78-95; e-mail dg@encc-group.dz; internet www.encc-group.dz; f. 1983; 6 subsidiary cos, mnaufacturing, supplying and maintaining industrial equipment; Pres. and Dir-Gen. Belkacem Saâda.

Entreprise Nationale de Construction de Matériaux et d'Equipements Ferroviaires (Ferrovial): BP 63, route d'El Hadjar, Annaba; tel. (38) 52-19-65; fax (38) 52-16-73; e-mail ferrovial@ferrovial.dz; internet www.ferrovial.dz; f. 1983; production, import and export of railway equipment; Dir-Gen. Salah Melek.

Entreprise Nationale de Distribution du Matériel Electrique (Edimel): 4–6 blvd Muhammad V, Algiers; tel. (21) 63-78-59; fax (21) 63-78-32; f. 1983; distribution of electrical equipment; Pres. and Dir-Gen. Bourai Achour.

Entreprise Nationale de Produits Miniers Non-Ferreux et des Substances Utiles (ENOF): 31 rue Muhammad Hattab, Belfort, Algiers; tel. (21) 52-52-36; fax (21) 52-15-27; e-mail info@enof-mines.com; f. 1983; production and distribution of minerals; Pres. and Dir-Gen. Abderrahmane Tahrat.

Entreprise Nationale de Sidérurgie (SIDER): BP 342, 23000 Annaba; tel. (38) 87-28-83; fax (38) 87-29-12; e-mail pdg@sider.dz; internet www.sider.dz; f. 1964 as Société Nationale de Sidérurgie; restructured 1983; steel, cast iron, zinc and products; Pres. and Dir-Gen. Amar Belkacemi.

Entreprise Nationale des Appareils de Mesure et de Contrôle (AMC): BP 248, route de Djemila, el-Eulma, Sétif; tel. (36) 87-34-24; fax (36) 87-49-72; e-mail amcdg@amc-dz.com; internet www.amc-dz.com; f. 1984; production of measuring, checking and regulation equipment; partial privatization pending; Dir-Gen. Noureddine Hammouda.

Entreprise Nationale des Industries de l'Electroménager (ENIEM): BP 71a, blvd Stiti Ali, Chikhi, Tizi Ouzou; tel. (26) 21-87-46; fax (26) 20-04-24; e-mail commercial@eniem.com.dz; internet www.eniem.com.dz; consortium of mfrs of household equipment; Pres. and Dir-Gen. Dahmane Yadaden.

Entreprise Nationale des Matériels de Travaux Publics (ENMTP): BP 67, Aïn Smara, Constantine; tel. and fax (31) 97-47-10; fax (31) 97-34-29; e-mail info@enmtp.com; internet www.enmtp.com; f. 1983; Dir Slimane Boulebd.

Entreprise Nationale des Véhicules Industriels (SNVI): BP 153, RN 5, Rouiba, Algiers; tel. (21) 81-24-36; fax (21) 81-13-92; f. 1981; manufacture of industrial vehicles; Pres. and Dir-Gen. Mokhtar Chahboub.

Entreprise Nationale du Fer et du Phosphate (FERPHOS): 8 rue Souahi Madani, 23000 Annaba; tel. (38) 84-63-60; fax (21) 38-65-08; e-mail ferphos@ferphos.com; internet www.ferphos.com; f. 1983; production, import and export of iron and phosphate products; Pres. and Dir-Gen. Farid Ben Hadji.

Entreprise Publique Economique Asmidal, SpA: BP 326, route des Salines, 23000 Annaba; tel. (38) 52-29-90; fax (38) 52-24-00; e-mail asmidal@asmidal-dz.com; internet www.asmidal-dz.com; f. 1985; production of ammonia, fertilizers, pesticides and sodium tripolyphosphate.

Entreprise de Transformation des Produits Longs (TPL): BP 1005, 19 rue Mekki Khelifa, el-Manouar, Oran; tel. (41) 34-37-05; fax (41) 34-19-50; e-mail tplsiege@tpl-algeria.com; internet www.tpl-algeria.com; f. 1983; production and distribution of girders; Dir-Gen. Abd al-Hamid Benahmed.

Groupe Boissons d'Algérie (GBA): BP 417, 21 rue Belhouchat Mouloud, 16040 Hussein-Dey, Algiers; tel. (21) 23-18-17; fax (21) 23-18-15; e-mail gba@cojub.com; internet www.cojub.com/gba/gba.htm; f. 1983; mineral water, carbonated beverages and beer.

Groupe Industriel du Papier et de la Cellulose (GIPEC): route de la Gare, Baba Ali, Algiers; tel. (21) 30-98-84; fax (21) 30-91-94; internet www.gipec.dz; pulp and paper; Pres. and Dir-Gen. Mustapha Merzouk.

SAIDAL Production Pharmaceutique: BP 141, 11 route de Wilaya, A16100 Dar el-Beida, Algiers; tel. (21) 50-60-42; fax (21) 50-52-68; e-mail r.zaouani@saidalgroup.com; internet www

.saidalgroup.dz; f. 1982 as Entreprise Nationale de Production Pharmaceutique; name changed as above in 1985; production of pharmaceuticals; partially privatized; Pres. and Dir-Gen. BOUMEDIENE DERKAOUI.

Société des Emballages et Arts Graphiques (EMBAG): BP 490, route d'Alger, 34000 Bordj Arréridj; tel. (35) 68-59-46; fax (35) 68-53-47; e-mail embag@embag.dz; f. 1985; packaging; subsidiary of GIPEC; Pres. and Dir-Gen. ZITOUN HAMID.

TRADE UNIONS

Syndicat National des Journalistes (Algerian Journalists' Union): Maison de la presse Tahar Djaout, 1 rue Bachir Attar, place du 1er mai, 16016 Algiers; tel. and fax (21) 67-36-61; e-mail snjalgerie2006@yahoo.fr; f. 2001; Sec.-Gen. KAMEL AMARNI.

Union Générale des Entrepreneurs Algériens (UGEA): Villa 28, Quartier Aïn Soltane, les Oliviers, Birkhadem, Algiers; tel. and fax (21) 54-10-82; e-mail contact@ugea-dz.com; internet www.ugea-dz.com; f. 1989; Pres. Dr ABDELMADJID DENNOUNI.

Union Générale des Travailleurs Algériens (UGTA): Maison du Peuple, place du 1er mai, Algiers; tel. (21) 65-07-36; e-mail sgeneral@ugta.dz; internet www.ugta.dz; f. 1956; there are 10 national 'professional sectors' affiliated to the UGTA; Sec.-Gen. ABDELMADJID SIDI SAÏD.

Union Nationale des Paysans Algériens (UNPA): f. 1973; 700,000 mems; Sec.-Gen. MUHAMMAD ALIOUI.

Transport

RAILWAYS

In 2010 the total length of Algerian railways was 3,512 km.

Entreprise du Métro d'Alger (EMA): 170 rue Hassiba Ben Bouali, Algiers; tel. (21) 66-17-47; fax (21) 66-17-57; e-mail contact@metroalger-dz.com; internet metroalger-dz.com; initial 9-km section (10 stations) commenced operations Nov. 2011; construction of a second line currently underway, as well as extensions to line 1; Pres. and Dir-Gen. OMAR HADBI.

Infrafer (Entreprise Publique Economique de Réalisation des Infrastructures Ferroviaires): BP 208, 15 rue Col Amirouche, 35300 Rouiba; tel. (21) 85-67-02; fax (21) 85-49-62; e-mail info@infrafer.com; internet www.infrafer.com; f. 1986; responsible for construction and maintenance of track; Dir-Gen. ABDERAHMANE AKTOUF.

Société Nationale des Transports Ferroviaires (SNTF): 21–23 blvd Muhammad V, Algiers; tel. (21) 71-15-10; fax (21) 63-32-98; e-mail dg-sntf@sntf.dz; internet www.sntf.dz; f. 1976 to replace Société Nationale des Chemins de Fer Algériens; daily passenger services from Algiers to the principal provincial cities and services to Tunisia and Morocco; Dir-Gen. OMAR BENAMEUR.

ROADS

In 2010 there were an estimated 113,655 km of roads, including 29,468 km of highways, main or national roads, 24,108 km of secondary, regional roads and 60,079 km of other roads. The French administration built a good road system (partly for military purposes), which, since independence, has been allowed to deteriorate in places. New roads have been built linking the Sahara oilfields with the coast, and the Trans-Sahara highway is a major project. Construction of the 1,216-km East–West motorway, linking el-Tarf with Tlemcen, at an estimated cost of more than US $11,000m., was scheduled for completion by the end of 2010. However, by early 2012 only around 1,000 km of the route was open to traffic. It was subsequently reported that the remaining sections would not open until late 2013.

Agence Nationale des Autoroutes (ANA): BP 72M Mohammadia, El Harrach, Algiers; tel. (21) 53-09-63; fax (21) 53-09-62; e-mail dgana@ana.org.dz; internet www.ana.org.dz; f. 2005 to manage the construction and maintenance of the motorway network; Dir-Gen. MUHAMMAD ZIANI.

Société Nationale des Transports Routiers (SNTR): 27 rue des Trois Frères Bouadou, Bir Mourad Raïs, Algiers; tel. (21) 54-06-00; fax (21) 54-05-35; e-mail dg-sntr@sntr-groupe.com; internet www.sntr-groupe.com; f. 1967; goods transport by road; maintainance of industrial vehicles; Pres. and Dir-Gen. ABDELLAH BENMAÂROUF.

Société Nationale des Transports des Voyageurs (SNTV): Algiers; tel. (21) 66-00-52; f. 1967; long-distance passenger transport by road; Man. Dir MUHAMMAD DIB.

SHIPPING

Algiers is the main port, with anchorage of between 23 m and 29 m in the Bay of Algiers, and anchorage for the largest vessels in Agha Bay. The port has a total quay length of 8,610 m. In November 2008 United Arab Emirates-based DP World signed a 30-year contract with the Algerian Government to manage and redevelop the ports at Algiers and Djen-Djen. The proposed redevelopment at Algiers port included an expansion of capacity from 500,000 20-ft equivalent units (TEUs) to 800,000 TEUs. DP World officially commenced operations at Algiers in March 2009 and at Djen-Djen in June. There are also important ports at Annaba, Arzew, Béjaïa, Djidjelli, Ghazaouet, Mostaganem, Oran, Skikda and Ténès. Petroleum and liquefied gas are exported through Arzew, Béjaïa and Skikda. Algerian crude petroleum is also exported through the Tunisian port of La Skhirra. At 31 December 2012 Algeria's flag-registered fleet totalled 174 vessels, with an aggregate displacement of 787,387 grt. Of those vessels, four were bulk carriers, seven were fish carriers, 11 were gas tankers and 10 were general cargo ships.

Port Authorities

Entreprise Portuaire d'Alger (EPAL): BP 259, 2 rue d'Angkor, Alger-Gare, Algiers; tel. (21) 42-36-14; fax (21) 42-36-03; e-mail epal@portalger.com.dz; internet www.portalger.com.dz; f. 1982; responsible for management and growth of port facilities and sea pilotage; Dir-Gen. ABDELAZIZ GUERRAH.

Entreprise Portuaire d'Annaba (EPAN): BP 1232, Môle Cigogne, quai Nord, 23000 Annaba; tel. (38) 86-31-31; fax (38) 86-54-15; e-mail epan@annaba-port.com; internet www.annaba-port.com; Pres. and Dir-Gen. DJILANI SALHI.

Entreprise Portuaire d'Arzew (EPA): BP 46, 7 rue Larbi Tebessi, 31200 Arzew; tel. and fax (41) 47-21-27; e-mail contact@arzew-ports.com; internet www.arzewports.com; Pres. and Dir-Gen. NOUREDDINE HADJIOUI.

Entreprise Portuaire de Béjaïa (EPB): BP 94, 13 ave des frères Amrani, 06000 Béjaïa; tel. (34) 21-18-07; fax (34) 20-14-88; e-mail portbj@portdebejaia.dz; internet www.portdebejaia.dz; Dir-Gen. DJELLOUL ACHOUR.

Entreprise Portuaire de Djen-Djen (EPJ): BP 87, El Achouat Taher-Wilaya de JIJEL, 18000 Jijel; tel. (34) 44-21-64; fax (34) 44-21-60; e-mail contact@djendjen-port.com; internet www.djendjen-port.com; f. 1984; Dir-Gen. ABDERREZAK SELLAMI.

Entreprise Portuaire de Ghazaouet (EPG): BP 217, Wilaya de Tlemcen, 13400 Ghazaouet; tel. (43) 32-32-37; fax (43) 32-32-55; e-mail contact@portdeghazaouet.com; internet www.portdeghazaouet.com; f. 1982; Pres. and Dir-Gen. BRAHIM ABDELMALEK.

Entreprise Portuaire de Mostaganem (EPM): BP 131, quai du Maghreb, 27000 Mostaganem; tel. (45) 21-14-11; fax (45) 21-78-05; e-mail epm@port-mostaganem.dz; internet www.port-mostaganem.dz; Pres. and Dir-Gen. MOKHTAR CHERIF.

Entreprise Portuaire d'Oran (EPO): 1 rue du 20 août, 31000 Oran; tel. (41) 33-24-49; fax (41) 33-24-98; e-mail pdg@port-oran.dz; internet www.port-oran.dz; Dir-Gen. MUHAMMAD BOUTOUIL (acting).

Entreprise Portuaire de Skikda (EPS): BP 65, 46 ave Rezki Rahal, 21000 Skikda; tel. (38) 75-68-50; fax (38) 75-20-15; e-mail epskikda@skikda-port.com; internet www.skikda-port.com; Man. Dir LAÏDI LEMRABET.

Entreprise Portuaire de Ténès (EPT): BP 18, Wilaya de Chlef, 02200 Ténès; tel. (27) 76-61-96; fax (27) 76-61-77; e-mail porttenes@yahoo.fr; internet www.portdetenes.dz; f. 1985; Man. Dir ALI ASSENOUNI.

Principal Shipping Companies

Cie Algéro-Libyenne de Transport Maritime (CALTRAM): 19 rue des Trois Frères Bouadou, Bir Mourad Raïs, Algiers; tel. (21) 54-17-00; fax (21) 54-21-04; e-mail caltram@wissal.dz; f. 1974; Man. Dir A. KERAMANE.

Cie Nationale de Navigation (CNAN Group): BP 280, 2 quai no 9, Nouvelle Gare Maritime, Algiers; tel. (21) 42-33-89; fax (21) 42-31-28; f. 2003 as part of restructuring of the Société Nationale de Transports Maritimes/Compagnie Nationale Algérienne de Navigation (SNTM/CNAN); state-owned; fleet of 12 freight ships; includes CNAN Maghreb Lines; rep. offices in Marseille (France) and La Spezia (Italy), and rep. agencies in Antwerp (Belgium), Barcelona (Spain), Hamburg (Germany) and the principal ports in many other countries; Dir-Gen. ALI BOUMBAR.

Entreprise Nationale de Réparation Navale (ERENAV): quai no 12, Algiers; tel. (21) 42-37-83; fax (21) 42-30-39; e-mail azzedine.bourouga@erenav.com; f. 1987; ship repairs; Pres. and Dir-Gen. A. BOUROUGA.

Entreprise Nationale de Transport Maritime de Voyageurs—Algérie Ferries (ENTMV): BP 467, 5–6 rue Jawharlal Nehru, 16001 Algiers; tel. (21) 42-46-50; fax (21) 42-98-74; e-mail entmv@algerieferries.com; internet www.algerieferries.com; f. 1987 as part of restructuring of SNTM-CNAN; responsible for passenger transport; operates car ferry services between Algiers, Annaba, Skikda,

Alicante (Spain), Marseille (France) and Oran; Dir-Gen. AHCÈNE GRAÏRIA.

HYPROC Shipping Co (HYPROC SC): BP 7200, Zone des Sièges 'ZHUN-USTO', el-Seddikia, 31025 Oran; tel. (41) 42-62-62; fax (41) 42-32-75; e-mail hyproc@hyproc.com; internet www.hyproc.com; f. 1982 as Société Nationale de Transports Maritimes des Hydrocarbures et des Produits Chimiques; name changed as above in 2003; wholly owned subsidiary of Sonatrach; Pres. and Dir-Gen. MOSTEFA MUHAMMADI.

Société Générale Maritime (GEMA): BP 368, 2 rue Jawharlal Nehru, 16100 Algiers; tel. (21) 74-73-00; fax (21) 74-76-73; e-mail gemadg@gema-groupe.com; internet www.gema-groupe.com; f. 1987 as part of restructuring of SNTM/CNAN; shipping, ship-handling and forwarding; Pres. and Dir-Gen. ALI LARBI CHÉRIF.

CIVIL AVIATION

Algeria's principal international airport, Houari Boumedienne, is situated 20 km from Algiers. Other international airports are situated at Constantine, Annaba, Tlemcen and Oran. There are, in addition, 65 aerodromes, of which 20 are public, and a further 135 airstrips connected with the petroleum industry.

Air Algérie (Entreprise Nationale d'Exploitation des Services Aériens): BP 858, 1 place Maurice Audin, Immeuble el-Djazair, Algiers; tel. (21) 74-24-28; fax (21) 61-05-53; e-mail contacts@airalgerie.dz; internet www.airalgerie.dz; f. 1953 by merger; state-owned from 1972; internal services and extensive services to Europe, North and West Africa, and the Middle East; flies to more than 70 destinations; Dir-Gen. and CEO MUHAMMAD SALAH BOULTIF.

Tassili Airlines: BP 301, blvd Mustapha Ben Boulaïd, 30500 Hassi Messaoud; tel. (29) 73-80-25; fax (29) 73-84-24; internet www.tassiliairlines.dz; f. 1997; wholly owned by Sonatrach; domestic passenger services; Chair. and Man. Dir FAIÇAL KHELIL.

Tourism

Algeria's tourist attractions include the Mediterranean coast, the Atlas mountains and the Sahara desert. According to provisional data, in 2011 there were 2.4m. visitors to Algeria. Receipts from tourism totalled US $219m. in 2010. It was announced in early 2007 that the Government was investing some $1,000m. in the tourism sector; the construction of 42 new resorts was scheduled to be completed by 2015.

Agence Nationale de Développement Touristique (ANDT): BP 78, Sidi Fredj Staoueli, Algiers; tourism promotion; Dir-Gen. NOUREDDINE NEDRI.

Office National du Tourisme (ONT): 2 rue Ismail Kerrar, 16000 Algiers; tel. (21) 43-80-60; fax (21) 43-80-59; e-mail ont@ont-dz.org; internet www.ont-dz.org; f. 1988; state institution; oversees tourism promotion policy; Dir-Gen. HADJ SAÏD MUHAMMAD AMINE.

ONAT (Entreprise Nationale Algérienne de Tourisme): 126 bis A, rue Didouche Mourad, 16000 Algiers; tel. (21) 74-44-48; fax (21) 74-32-14; e-mail direction-marketing@onatalgerie.com; internet www.onatalgerie.com; f. 1983; Dir-Gen. SELATNIA MUHAMMAD CHÉRIF.

Touring Club d'Algérie (TCA): 30 rue Hassène Benaâmane, Les Vergers, Bir Mourad Raïs, Algiers; tel. (21) 54-13-13; fax (21) 54-15-11; e-mail sg_touring@algeriatouring.dz; internet www.algeriatouring.dz; f. 1963; Pres. ABDERRAHMANE ABDEDAÏM.

Touring Voyages Algérie: Centre commercial 'el-Hammadia', Bouzaréah, Algiers; tel. (21) 54-13-13; fax (21) 94-26-87; e-mail contact@touring-algerie.com; internet www.touringvoyagesalgerie.dz; f. 1995 to manage the commercial activities of Touring Club d'Algérie; 89% owned by Touring Club d'Algérie; Pres. and Dir-Gen. TAHAR SAHRI.

Defence

Chief of Staff of the People's National Army: Lt-Gen. AHMED GAID SALAH.

Commander of the Land Force: Maj.-Gen. AHCÈNE TAFER.

Commander of the Air Force: Maj.-Gen. ABDELKADER LOUNES.

Commander of the Naval Forces: Maj.-Gen. MALEK NECIB.

Commander of the Territory Air Defence Forces: Maj.-Gen. AMAR AMRANI.

Commander of the National Gendarmerie: Maj.-Gen. AHMED BOUSTEILA.

Commander of the Republican Guard: Maj.-Gen. AHMED MOULAY MILIANI.

Defence Budget (2012): AD 723,000m.

Military Service: 18 months (army only).

Total Armed Forces (as assessed at November 2012): 130,000: army 110,000 (75,000 conscripts); navy est. 6,000; air force 14,000. Reserves 150,000.

Paramilitary Forces (as assessed at November 2012): est. 187,200 (National Security Forces 16,000; Republican Guards 1,200; an est. 150,000 self-defence militia and communal guards, and a gendarmerie of 20,000).

Education

Education, in the national language (Arabic), is officially compulsory for a period of nine years, for children between six and 15 years of age. Primary education begins at the age of six and lasts for five years. Secondary education begins at 11 years of age and lasts for up to seven years, comprising first cycle of four years and a second of three years. In 2009/10 the total enrolment at primary schools included 96% of children in the relevant age-group. The comparable ratio for secondary enrolment in 2008/09 was equivalent to 95% of students in the relevant age-group. In 2012 the Algerian Government allocated AD 821,000m. to education (equivalent to 20% of the national budget).

There were some 500,165 pupils at pre-primary schools in 2009/10, while in 2009/10 some 3,312,440 pupils attended primary schools (compared with about 800,000 in 1962). In 2008/09 some 4,585,189 pupils attended secondary schools. Most education at primary level is in Arabic, but at higher levels French is still widely used. In mid-2003 the Government agreed to permit the use of the Berber language, Tamazight, as a language of instruction in Algerian schools. The majority of foreign teachers in Algeria come from Egypt, Syria, Tunisia and other Arab countries.

In 2009/10 the number of students receiving higher education (including post-graduate) was 1,144,271. In addition to the 27 main universities, there are 16 other *centres universitaires* and a number of technical colleges. Several thousand students go abroad to study. Efforts have been made to combat adult illiteracy by means of a large-scale campaign in which instruction is sometimes given by young people who have only recently left school, and in which the broadcasting services are widely used.

Bibliography

Ageron, Charles-Robert. *Modern Algeria: A History from 1830 to the Present*. London, Hurst, 1992.

Aghrout, Ahmed, with Bougherira, Redha (Eds). *Algeria in Transition: Reforms and Development Prospects*. London, Routledge, 2004.

Aissaoui, Ali. *Algeria: The Political Economy of Oil and Gas*. New York and Oxford, Oxford University Press, 2001.

Aït-Chaalal, Amine. *Algérie–Etats-Unis; des relations denses et complexes*. Louvain-la-Neuve, CERMAC, 1998.

Al-Ahnaf, M., Botiveau, B., and Frégosi, F. *L'Algérie par ses islamistes*. Paris, Editions Karthala, 1992.

Allais, M. *Les Accords d'Evian, le référendum et la résistance algérienne*. Paris, 1962.

Amrane-Minne, Danièle Djamila. *Des femmes dans la guerre d'Algérie*. Paris, Editions Karthala, 1996.

Aron, Raymond. *La tragédie algérienne*. Paris, 1957.

Aussaresses, Gen. Paul. *Services spéciaux Algérie 1955–1957: Mon témoignage sur la torture*. Paris, Perrin, 2001.

The Battle of the Casbah: Terrorism and Counter-Terrorism in Algeria 1955–1957. Silver Spring, MD, Enigma Books, 2004.

Baduel, Pierre R. *L'Algérie incertaine*. Aix-en-Provence, Edisud, 1993.

Balta, Paul, and Rulleau, Claudine. *L'Algérie des algériens*. Paris, Editions Ouvrières, 1982.

Bedjaoui, Youcef, *et al.* (Eds). *An Inquiry into the Algerian Massacres*. Geneva, Hoggar, 1999.

Belarbi, Ahcene. *Demain, la mémoire: Chroniques de l'Algérie massacrée.* Paris, Editions des Ecrivains, 2000.

Benamou, Georges-Marc. *Un mensonge français: Enquête sur la guerre d'Algérie.* Paris, Laffont, 2003.

Bencherif, Osman. *The Image of Algeria in Anglo-American Writings 1785–1962.* Lanham, MD, University Press of Algeria, 1997.

Bennoune, M. *The Making of Contemporary Algeria (1830–1987).* Cambridge, Cambridge University Press, 1988.

Bonner, Michael, Reif, Megan, and Tessler, Mark (Eds). *Islam, Democracy and the State in Algeria: Lessons for the Western Mediterranean and Beyond.* Abingdon, Routledge, 2005.

Bonora, C. *France and the Algerian Conflict.* Aldershot, Ashgate Publishing Ltd, 2000.

Boudiaf, Muhammad. *Où va l'Algérie?* Algeria, Rahma, 1992.

Bougherira, Redha M., and Agrout, Ahmed (Eds). *Algeria in Transition: Reforms and Development Prospects.* London, Routledge, 2004.

Boukhobza, M'Hammed. *Ruptures et transformations sociales en Algérie.* Algiers, OPU, 1989.

Boukra, Liess. *Algérie: La terreur sacrée.* Paris, Favre, 2002.

Bourdieu, Pierre. *The Algerians.* Boston, 1962.

Sociologie de l'Algérie. Paris, Que Sais-je, 1958.

Brace, R., and Brace, J. *Ordeal in Algeria.* New York, 1960.

Cavatorta, Francesco. *The International Dimension of the Failed Algerian Transition: Democracy Betrayed?* Manchester, Manchester University Press, 2009.

De Gaulle, Charles. *Mémoires d'espoir: Le Renouveau 1958–1962.* Paris, Plon, 1970.

Derradji, A. *The Algerian Guerrilla Campaign: Strategy and Tactics.* Edwin Mellen Press, 1997.

Duquesne, Jacques. *Pour comprendre la guerre d'Algérie.* Paris, Perrin, 2002.

Encyclopaedia of Islam. *Algeria.* New edn, Vol. I. London and Leiden, 1960.

Evans, Martin. *Algeria: France's Undeclared War.* Oxford, Oxford University Press, 2011.

Evans, Martin, and Phillips, John. *Algeria: Anger of the Dispossessed.* New Haven, CT, Yale University Press, 2007.

Eveno, P., and Planchais, J. *La guerre d'Algérie.* Paris, La Découverte, 1989.

Faivre, Maurice. *Les archives inédites de la politique algérienne 1958–1962.* Paris, L'Harmattan, 2000.

Favrod, Ch.-H. *Le FLN et l'Algérie.* Paris, 1962.

Forestier, Patrick, with Salam, Ahmed. *Confession d'un émir du GIA.* Grasset et Fasquelle, Paris, 1999.

Francos, Avia, and Séréri, J.-P. *Un Algérien nommé Boumedienne.* Paris, 1976.

Fuller, Graham E. *Algeria: The Next Fundamentalist State.* Rand Corporation, 1996.

Gacemi, Baya. *Moi, Nadia, femme d'un émir du GIA.* Seuil, Paris, 1999.

Garon, Lise. *L'obsession unitaire et la Nation trompée: La fin de l'Algérie socialiste.* Montreal, University of Laval Press, 1993.

Gillespie, Joan. *Algeria.* London, Benn, 1960.

Gordon, David. *The Passing of French Algeria.* Oxford, 1966.

Goytisolo, Juan. *Argelia en el vendaval.* Madrid, El País-Aguilar, 1994.

Harbi, Muhammad. *L'Algérie et son destin.* Paris, Arcantère, 1992.

Hassan. *Algérie, histoire d'un naufrage.* Paris, Seuil, 1995.

Henissart, Paul. *Wolves in the City: The Death of French Algeria.* London, Hart-Davis, 1971.

Hill, J. N. C. *Identity in Algerian Politics: The Legacy of Colonial Rule.* Boulder, CO, Lynne Rienner Publishers, 2009.

Horne, Alistair. *A Savage War of Peace: Algeria 1954–1962.* London, Macmillan, 1977.

House, Jim, and McMaster, Neil. *Paris 1961: Algerians, State Terror, and Memory.* New York, NY, Oxford University Press, 2009.

Humbaraci, Arslan. *Algeria: A Revolution that Failed.* London, Pall Mall, 1966.

Ibrahimi, A. Taleb. *De la décolonisation à la révolution culturelle (1962–72).* Algiers, SNED, 1973.

Jeanson, F. *La révolution algérienne: Problèmes et perspectives.* Milan, 1962.

Joesten, Joachim. *The New Algeria.* New York, 1964.

Joffé, George. *Algeria: The Failed Revolution.* Abingdon, Routledge, 2009.

Julien, Charles-André. *Histoire de l'Algérie contemporaine, conquête et colonisation, 1827–1871.* Paris, Presses Universitaires de France, 1964.

Keenan, Jeremy. *The Lesser Gods of the Sahara.* London, Frank Cass, 2004.

Kettle, Michael. *De Gaulle and Algeria.* London, Quartet, 1993.

Khelladi, A. *Les islamistes algériens face au pouvoir.* Algiers, Alfa, 1992.

Lacheraf, Mostepha. *L'Algérie, nation et société.* Paris, Maspéro, 1965.

Laffont, Pierre. *L'Expiation: De l'Algérie de papa à l'Algérie de Ben Bella.* Paris, Plon, 1968.

Lakehal, M. *Algérie: De l'indépendance à l'Etat d'urgence.* Paris, L'Harmattan, 1992.

Lambotte, R. *Algérie, naissance d'une société nouvelle.* Paris, Editions Sociales, 1976.

Laremont, Ricardo René. *Islam and the Politics of Resistance in Algeria 1783–1992.* Trenton, NJ, Africa World Press, 2000.

Lassassi, Assassi. *Non-alignment and Algerian Foreign Policy.* Aldershot, Dartmouth, 1988.

Lawless, Richard I. *Algeria.* World Bibliographical Series Vol. 19. Denver, CO, Clio Press, 1995.

Lazreg, Marnia. *The Eloquence of Silence: Algerian Women in Question.* London, Routledge, 1994.

Le Sueur, James D. *Uncivil War: Intellectuals and Identity Politics during the Decolonization of Algeria.* Philadelphia, PA, University of Pennsylvania Press, 2001.

Between Terror and Democracy: Algeria since 1989. London, Zed Books, 2010.

Lebjaoui, Mohamed. *Vérités sur la Révolution Algérienne.* Paris, Gallimard, 1970.

Leca, Jean, and Vatin, Jean-Claude. *L'Algérie politique, institutions et régime.* Paris, Fondation nationale des sciences politiques, 1974.

Liverani, Andrea. *Civil Society in Algeria: The Political Functions of Associational Life.* Abingdon, Routledge, 2008.

Lorcin, Patricia M. E. *Imperial Identities: Stereotyping, Prejudice and Race in Colonial Algeria.* London and New York, I. B. Tauris, 1999.

(Ed.). *Algeria and France, 1800–2000: Identity, Memory, Nostalgia.* New York, Syracuse University Press, 2006.

Lowi, Miriam R. *Oil Wealth and the Poverty of Politics: Algeria Compared.* Cambridge, Cambridge University Press, 2009.

Lyotard, Jean-François. *La guerre des Algériens: Ecrits 1956–1963.* Paris, Galilée, 1989.

McDougall, James. *History and the Culture of Nationalism in Algeria.* Cambridge, Cambridge University Press, 2008.

Majumdar, Margaret A., and Saad, Mohammed. *Transition and Development in Algeria: Economic, Social and Cultural Challenges.* Bristol, Intellect Books, 3rd edn, 2005.

Mallarde, Etienne. *L'Algérie depuis 1962.* Paris, La Table Ronde, 1977.

Malley, Robert. *The Call from Algeria: Third Worldism, Revolution and the Turn to Islam.* Berkeley, CA, University of California Press, 1996.

Mandouze, André. *La révolution algérienne par les textes.* Paris, 1961.

Martens, Jean-Claude. *Le modèle algérien de développement (1962–1972).* Algiers, SNED, 1973.

Martin, Claude. *Histoire de l'Algérie française 1830–1962.* Paris, 1962.

Martinez, Luis. *The Algerian Civil War, 1990–1998.* London, C. Hurst and Co., 2000.

Mouilleseaux, Louiz. *Histoire de l'Algérie.* Paris, 1962.

Nabi, Muhammad. *L'Algérie aujhourd'hui ou l'absence d'alternatives à l'Islam politique.* Paris, L'Harmattan, 2000.

Ottaway, David and Marina. *Algeria. The Politics of a Socialist Revolution.* Berkeley, CA, University of California Press, 1970.

Ouzegane, Amar. *Le Meilleur Combat.* Paris, Julliard, 1962.

Pierre, Andrew J., and Quandt, William B. *The Algerian Crisis, Policy Options for the West.* Washington, DC, The Brookings Institution, 1997.

Porch, Douglas. *The Conquest of the Sahara.* New York, Farrar, Straus and Giroux, 2005.

Quandt, William B. *Revolution and Political Leadership: Algeria, 1954–1968.* MIT Press, 1970.

Between Ballots and Bullets: Algeria's Transition from Authoritarianism. Brookings Institution Press, 1998.

Algeria, 1830-2000: A Short History. New York, Cornell University Press, 2004.

Redjala, R. *L'opposition en Algérie depuis 1962*. Paris, L'Harmattan, 1988.

Rey-Goldzeiguer, Annie. *Aux origines de la guerre d'Algérie 1940–1945. De Mers el-Kébir aux massacres du Nord-Constantinois*. Paris, La Découverte, 2002

Rivet, Daniel. *Le Maghreb à l'épreuve de la colonisation*. Paris, Hachette Littératures, 2002.

Roberts, Hugh. *The Battlefield: Algeria, 1988–2002. Studies in a Broken Polity*. London, Verso, 2003.

Robson, P., and Lury, D. *The Economics of Africa*. London, Allen and Unwin, 1969.

Ruedy, John D. *Land Policy in Colonial Algeria: The Origins of the Rural Public Domain*. Berkeley, CA, University of California Press, 1967.

Modern Algeria: The Origins and Development of a Nation. Bloomington, IN, Indiana University Press, 2nd edn, 2005.

Sa'dallah, A. Q. *Studies on Modern Algerian Literature*. Beirut, Al Adab, 1966.

Samraoui, Muhammad. *Chronique des années de sang*. Paris, Denoël, 2003.

Schiemla, E. *Unbowed: An Algerian Woman Confronts Islamic Fundamentalism. Interviews with Khalida Messaoudi*. Philadelphia, PA, University of Pennsylvania Press, 1998.

Sivan, Emmanuel. *Communisme et Nationalisme en Algérie (1920–1962)*. Paris, 1976.

Smith, Tony. *The French Stake in Algeria 1945–1962*. New York, Cornell University Press, 1978.

Souaïda, Habib. *La sale guerre*. Paris, La Découverte, 2001.

Stone, Martin. *The Agony of Algeria*. London, C. Hurst & Co Ltd, 1998.

Stora, Benhamin. *Histoire de l'Algérie coloniale*. Cheltenham, Gallimard-Jenmesse, 1998.

Sulzberger, C. L. *The Test, de Gaulle and Algeria*. London and New York, 1962.

Talbott, John. *France in Algeria, 1954–1962*. New York, Knopf, 1980.

Vatin, Jean-Claude. *L'Algérie politique, histoire et société*. Paris, Fondation nationale des sciences politiques, 1974.

Vidal-Naquet, Pierre. *L'Affaire Audin*. Paris, Les éditions de Minuit, 1989.

Face à la raison d'Etat: Un historien dans la guerre d'Algérie. Paris, La Découverte, 1989.

Volpi, Frédéric. *Islam and Democracy: The Failure of Dialogue in Algeria*. London, Pluto Press, 2002.

Wall, Irwin M. *France, the United States and the Algerian War*. Berkeley, CA, University of California Press, 2001.

Werenfels, Isabelle. *Managing Instability in Algeria: Elites and Political Change since 1995*. Abingdon, Routledge, 2009.

Willis, Michael. *The Islamist Challenge in Algeria*. Reading, Ithaca Press, 1996.

Yous, Nesroulah. *Qui a tué à Bentalha?* Paris, La Découverte, 2000.

Zahraoui, Saïd. *Entre l'horreur et l'espoir 1990–1999: Chronique de la nouvelle guerre d'Algérie*. Paris, Laffont, 2000.

BAHRAIN

Geography

The Kingdom of Bahrain consists of a group of some 36 islands, situated midway along the Persian (Arabian) Gulf, about 24 km from the east coast of Saudi Arabia and 28 km from the west coast of Qatar.

The total area of the Bahrain archipelago is 757.5 sq km (292.5 sq miles). Bahrain itself, the principal island, is about 50 km long and between 13 km and 25 km wide. To the north-east of Bahrain, and linked to it by causeway and road, lies Muharraq island, which is approximately 6 km long. A causeway also links Bahrain island to Sitra island. Other islands in the state include Nabih Salih, Jeddah, Hawar, Umm Nassan and Umm Suban. A causeway linking Bahrain and Saudi Arabia was opened in November 1986. The construction of a causeway linking eastern Bahrain to Qatar was scheduled to commence by the end of 2009; however, following delays as a result of financial difficulties, construction had yet to commence at mid-2013. It had initially been envisaged that the project would be completed by 2014.

Between April 1971 and the census of 7 April 2001 the total population of Bahrain increased from 216,078 to 650,604, of whom 405,667 were Bahraini citizens. According to results of the latest census of April 2010, the population had increased further, to 1,234,571 (males 768,414, females 466,157). Of the total, 568,399 were Bahrainis (males 287,246, females 281,178) and 666,172 non-Bahraini nationals (males 481,175, females 184,997). About 80% of the population are thought to be of Arab ethnic origin, and 20% Iranian. In 2001 the port of Manama (on Bahrain island)—the capital and seat of government—had a population of 153,395; the UN estimated that this had increased to 261,782 by mid-2011. Bahrain's Muslim population (70.2% of the total in 2010) is estimated to consist of almost 60% Shi'ites and just over 40% Sunnis. The ruling family are Sunnis. The Bahraini labour force was forecast to have doubled between 1989 and the end of the 20th century: some 75.8% of the employed population were estimated to be of non-Bahraini origin in 2008.

History

Revised for this edition by AURORA SOTTIMANO

EARLY HISTORY

After several centuries of independence, Bahrain passed first under the rule of the Portuguese (1521–1602) and then under periodic Persian rule (1602–1782). The Persians were expelled in 1783 by the Utub tribe from Arabia, whose leading family, the Al Khalifas, became the independent sheikhs of Bahrain and have ruled Bahrain ever since, except for a brief period before 1810. Nevertheless, claims based on the Persian occupation of the islands were renewed intermittently.

In the 19th century European powers began to take an interest in the area of the Persian (Arabian) Gulf. Britain was principally concerned with protecting the route to India, and suppressing the trade in slaves and weapons. In 1861 the Sheikh of Bahrain undertook to abstain from the prosecution of war, piracy and slavery by sea, in return for British support in case of aggression. In 1880 and 1892 the Sheikh also pledged not to cede, mortgage or otherwise dispose of parts of his territories to anyone except the British Government, or to enter into relations with any other government without British consent. A convention acknowledging Bahrain's independence was signed by the British and Ottoman Governments in 1913, although the islands remained under British control.

Under Sheikh Sulman bin Hamad Al Khalifa (who became ruler of Bahrain in 1942) social services and public works were extended considerably. Sheikh Sulman was succeeded on his death in November 1961 by his eldest son, Sheikh Isa bin Sulman Al Khalifa. In February 1956 elections were held for members of an Education and Health Council (the first election in Bahrain had been held in 1919 for the Municipal Council). In 1967 the United Kingdom transferred its principal Arabian military base from Aden to Bahrain, but by 1968 the British Government had decided to withdraw all forces 'East of Suez' before the end of 1971.

Extensive administrative and political reforms came into effect in January 1970, when a 12-member Council of State was established. The formation of this new body, which became the state's supreme executive authority, represented the first formal derogation of the ruler's powers. Sheikh Khalifa bin Salman Al Khalifa, the ruler's eldest brother, became President of the Council. Only four of the initial 12 'Directors' were members of the royal family, but all were Bahrainis, and the British advisers were reduced to the status of civil servants. Equal numbers of Sunni and Shi'ite Muslims were included (the royal family apart) to reflect Bahrain's religious balance. When Bahrain became fully independent, in August 1971, the Council of State became the Cabinet of the State of Bahrain (with Sheikh Khalifa as Prime Minister), with authority to direct the country's internal and external affairs.

After 1968 Bahrain officially agreed to membership of the embryonic Federation of Arab Emirates. The Bahraini Government, however, failed to agree on the terms of the federal constitution with the richer, but less developed, sheikhdoms in the region. Bahrain's position was strengthened in May 1970, when Iran accepted the findings of a UN report that the Bahraini people overwhelmingly favoured complete independence rather than union with Iran.

DOMESTIC POLITICS AND INTERNAL UNREST

On 15 August 1971 Bahrain achieved full independence; a new treaty of friendship was signed with the United Kingdom, and Sheikh Isa assumed the title of Amir. Bahrain became a member of both the League of Arab States (the Arab League) and the UN. In December 1972 elections were held for a Constituent Assembly. This body drafted a new Constitution, which came into force on 6 December 1973. Elections to a 44-member National Assembly took place the following day. Of its members, 30 were chosen by the all-male electorate, the remainder being members of the Government. A delay in the establishment of trade unions, for which the Constitution made provision, and a sharp rise in the cost of living provoked industrial unrest in 1974. In August 1975 the Prime Minister submitted his resignation, complaining that the National Assembly was preventing the Government from exercising its functions. The Amir invited him to form a new government, and, two days later, dissolved the National Assembly and suspended the Constitution. Although the traditional institution of *majlis* (council), where citizens and non-citizens present petitions to the Amir, remained, it was not until November 1992 that the Amir announced the formation of a new, 30-member Consultative Council. The Council, whose establishment met with scant popular enthusiasm, had little scope to question or alter government policy, and power remained with the Amir and the ruling Al Khalifa family.

In September 1979 Iranian Shi'ite elements exhorted Bahraini Shi'ites, who are in the majority with many of Iranian descent, to demonstrate against the Sunni Amir. Calm was restored, but it was apparent that the new regime in Iran was interested in reviving the Iranian claim to Bahrain. In December 1981 at least 50 people, mainly Bahrainis, were arrested on charges of conspiring to overthrow the Government. Despite subsequent improvements in relations, Bahrain continued to monitor carefully its own domestic stability and the political situation in Iran. Strict censorship was imposed, and political parties were banned. The Government has been severely criticized by human rights organizations for its alleged use of torture and detention without trial.

Fears of unrest among Bahrain's Shi'ite majority have continued to preoccupy the ruling regime and to elicit an uncompromising response to popular disaffection. In December 1993 the human rights organization Amnesty International published a highly critical report claiming that Bahraini Shi'ites had been deprived of their nationality and forcibly exiled by their own Government. In response to such criticism, the Amir issued a decree in March 1994 pardoning 64 Bahrainis exiled since the 1980s and permitting them to return to Bahrain. In November 1994, however, 12 Shi'ite villagers were reported to have been arrested in Jidd Hafs, to the west of Manama, following the violent disruption of a charity running event in which a group of expatriate men and women were participating. In early December police arrested a young Shi'ite cleric, Sheikh Ali Salman, imam of the main Shi'ite mosque in Manama, who had demanded the release of those arrested at Jidd Hafs and had also condemned the participation of women in the race. Moreover, he had called for the restitution of the National Assembly and criticized the ruling family, the large number of foreign workers employed on the island and the decline of moral standards. Despite an attempt by the Amir to defuse the crisis, widespread rioting ensued, especially in Shi'ite areas, where demonstrators appealed for the release of Sheikh Salman; several people died in clashes with armed police. The crisis was particularly embarrassing for the Government since it occurred as Bahrain was preparing to host a summit meeting of the Cooperation Council for the Arab States of the Gulf (Gulf Cooperation Council—GCC). The authorities acknowledged the existence of political unrest and blamed Sheikh Salman and certain 'foreign interests'—a coded reference to Iran. The police proceeded to make a large number of arrests: according to opposition sources, some 2,500 Bahrainis, mainly Shi'ites, had been arrested by mid-January 1995.

In mid-January 1995 Sheikh Salman, together with two associates, was deported from Bahrain; he subsequently sought, and was granted, political asylum in the United Kingdom. In August the Amir issued a decree pardoning 150 people detained since the disturbances. In the same month the Government initiated talks with Shi'ite opposition leaders in an apparent attempt at reconciliation, although by mid-September the talks had collapsed. Nevertheless, more than 40 Shi'ite detainees were released shortly afterwards.

In June 1995 the Prime Minister, Sheikh Khalifa bin Sulman Al Khalifa, announced the first major cabinet reorganization in nearly 20 years. Cabinet changes had been expected since the outbreak of political unrest, although the regime insisted that the reallocation of portfolios had been planned for some time. There were no changes, however, to the key defence, foreign affairs, interior, and finance and national economy portfolios. It was also announced that the Bahrain Defence Force (BDF) would be expanded.

Meanwhile, the opposition maintained that the authorities had agreed, in the course of the reconciliation talks initiated in mid-1995, to release all detainees and to allow the return of political exiles. In return, the opposition pledged to end the violence. By early October some 400 political prisoners had been released. However, accusing the Government of having failed to fulfil its promise to release all detainees, in October seven opposition leaders led by influential Shi'ite cleric Sheikh Abd al-Amir al-Jamri began a hunger strike. Their demands included an agreement by the authorities to resume open talks with the opposition regarding the restoration of the 1973 Constitution. The Government itself had denied that earlier meetings with the opposition had actually taken place. Sheikh al-Jamri and the other protesters ended their hunger strike at the beginning of November 1995 without achieving their objectives.

Disturbances erupted again in November 1995 (especially among students) and, according to opposition sources, the police made hundreds of arrests. The authorities sought assistance from Saudi Arabia, and it was reported that Saudi security officers were dispatched to reinforce the Bahraini police. In January and February 1996 the conflict escalated when a number of bombs exploded in Manama's business district. The security forces had closed mosques where prominent leaders had continued to urge the authorities to restore democracy, and in late January eight opposition leaders, including Sheikh al-Jamri, were rearrested on charges of inciting unrest. For the first time in the recent disturbances the authorities also detained a prominent Sunni member of the Committee for Popular Petition; Ahmad al-Shamlan, a lawyer, was arrested after distributing a statement criticizing the Government's authoritarian action. Al-Shamlan was released in May, following strong representation by international organizations. The closure of mosques provoked renewed clashes between protesters and police. Mass arrests were reported, and at the beginning of February the Ministry of the Interior admitted that some 600 people had been detained, while the opposition estimated the number of arrests at 2,000. Reports suggested that most of those detained (including women and children) were held without charge or trial.

In March 1996 the Amir issued a decree transferring jurisdiction for a range of offences from ordinary courts to the Higher Court of Appeal, sitting as the State Security Court. This effectively introduced a 'fast-track' system, denying the accused any right of appeal and greatly limiting the role of the defence. In late March Isa Ahmad Hassan Qambar was executed by firing squad for killing a police officer during clashes with security forces in March 1995. The first execution in Bahrain for almost 20 years, this provoked mass protests, with police using tear gas to disperse young Shi'ite protesters. In April 1996 the Government announced the creation of a Higher Council of Islamic Affairs, appointed by the Prime Minister and headed by the Minister of Justice and Islamic Affairs, to supervise religious activities in the country, including those of the Shi'ite population. Leading Shi'ites immediately condemned the move as an attempt to interfere in their affairs. At the end of April the Government announced that the State Security Court had imprisoned 11 people on charges connected with the disturbances, including arson, sabotage and membership of illegal organizations. It was reported that large numbers of defendants had been tried in groups and sentenced to long terms of imprisonment by the Court. In May, following the death of a demonstrator after security forces opened fire on a crowd of protesters, a number of bombs exploded throughout the country, killing several people (including two policemen).

In June 1996 the Government announced that some 10 prisoners had confessed to belonging to the military branch of Hezbollah Bahrain, a previously unknown organization. The prisoners were reported to have admitted that this group had been created on the instruction of, and had received financial support from, Iran's Revolutionary Guards. Despite the insistence of the authorities that the dissidents had foreign backers, most observers considered that the pro-democracy movement was locally rooted, unifying various sections of Bahraini society with no outside support. Independent sources questioned the validity of the confessions, while also pointing out that recent acts of sabotage were not professionally executed and therefore not consistent with the presence of a movement such as Hezbollah. This was the first time that the Bahraini Government had directly accused Iran of supporting the unrest, allegations that Iran persistently denied. Bahrain recalled its ambassador from the Iranian capital, Tehran, and downgraded its diplomatic representation there.

In September 1996, in what was interpreted as a move to counter opposition demands, the Amir expanded the membership of the Government-appointed Consultative Council from 30 to 40 and allowed up to one-half of the members to be elected indirectly through professional and cultural organizations. The new Council comprised 22 members of the previous body and 18 new members nominated by the Amir. Appointed for a four-year term, the Council was to comment on most areas of government policy (the previous Council had been restricted to consideration of Cabinet-proposed legislation), but would still enjoy very limited powers since its recommendations would continue to be non-binding on the Government. A new decree, issued by the Amir in June, divided Bahrain into four new administrative regions, or *mohafadat*, with the aim of improving services and making officials more accountable. However, opponents argued that the new system would enable the Ministry of the Interior to intensify security measures, particularly following reports that the ministry was to be reorganized and the intelligence service expanded. In January 1997 the Amir issued a decree establishing a National Guard to provide support for the BDF and the security forces of the interior ministry. Crown Prince Hamad, already Commander-in-Chief of the Defence Force, was also appointed to command the new force, and there was speculation that its primary duty would be to protect the ruling family.

Growing concern for human rights in Bahrain resulted in unprecedented scrutiny of its internal affairs by the international community (the European Parliament in particular urged the Bahraini Government to release political prisoners and to grant access to human rights organizations), and sentences imposed on political opponents became noticeably more lenient. In April 1997 the trial of 81 Bahrainis accused of membership of Hezbollah Bahrain ended unexpectedly with relatively light sentences: the maximum terms of imprisonment imposed (on the alleged leaders) were 15 years. A lawsuit filed by the Government in October against eight Shi'ite members of the opposition resident abroad followed a similar course, despite the severity of the charges, which included inciting violence, establishing Hezbollah Bahrain and attempting to overthrow the regime. During 1997 the authorities released a substantial number of political detainees (some 3,000, according to unofficial sources).

In February 1998 Ian Henderson, the long-serving British-born head of the State Security Investigation Directorate, was replaced by Khalid bin Muhammad Al Khalifa, a close associate of the Crown Prince. The dismissal of Henderson, considered to be central to the apparatus of state repression, was welcomed by opponents of the Government, who stated that a precondition for dialogue with the Government was the 'Bahrainization' of the security forces: in 1997 opposition sources had estimated that as many as 50,000 non-Bahrainis were employed in the country's security services.

In July 1998 the death in Lebanon, under mysterious circumstances, of a Bahraini national, Tawfiq Abd al-Nabi Ibrahim al-Baharinah, prompted speculation about efforts on the part of the Bahraini Government to trace links between the internal opposition and Hezbollah. Initial reports, endorsed by the Lebanese Minister of Foreign Affairs, suggested that al-Baharinah had been a Bahraini intelligence agent, although Bahrain subsequently denied this. Independent observers suggested that al-Baharinah might have been a member of an opposition group, the Islamic Front for the Liberation of Bahrain, believed to have a strong support base in Lebanon. Renewed concerns over the possible involvement of Lebanese Hezbollah in Bahrain's internal affairs coincided with the explosion of a car bomb in central Manama in November. A few days earlier a Lebanese Shi'ite had been arrested, together with five Bahraini citizens, on terrorist charges, for allegedly having smuggled explosives into Bahrain via Syria and Saudi Arabia following intensive training at a Hezbollah camp in southern Lebanon.

Following widespread international media attention focusing on criticism of alleged legal abuses in Bahrain, in February 1999 the State Security Court finally began legal proceedings against Sheikh al-Jamri. (Under the terms of the security legislation, which provided for the imprisonment of suspects without trial for a period of up to three years, al-Jamri was due to be released in early 1999.) In July the Court sentenced al-Jamri to 10 years' imprisonment and imposed a substantial fine on him, although he was granted an official pardon the following day.

ACCESSION OF SHEIKH HAMAD AND POLITICAL REFORM

On 6 March 1999 Crown Prince Sheikh Hamad bin Isa Al Khalifa was appointed Amir upon the death of his father. His accession encouraged expectations of political change among the opposition, who welcomed the change of leadership as an opportunity to renew negotiations with the Government and urged a temporary cessation of popular protest as a gesture of respect for the late Amir. Sheikh Hamad's first official address to the nation, in mid-March, was emphatic in its high regard for the armed forces as the guardians of both internal security and regional stability. In May Sheikh Hamad effected a cabinet reorganization. Sheikh Khalifa bin Sulman Al Khalifa remained Prime Minister, despite his long-standing power struggle with the new Amir. Abdullah Hassan Saif, formerly Governor of the Bahrain Monetary Agency (BMA), entered the Cabinet as Minister of Finance. Sheikh Salman bin Hamad Al Khalifa, eldest son of the Amir, became Crown Prince.

In a National Day address in December 1999, Sheikh Hamad stated his intention to hold elections for municipal councils, on the basis of universal suffrage. However, no timetable was announced for these elections, and the extent of the Amir's desire to introduce some form of democracy remained unclear.

In May 2000 Prime Minister Sheikh Khalifa announced that women, as well as a number of non-Muslims, would for the first time be appointed to the Consultative Council, which was to be elected by popular vote from 2004. This unexpected announcement intensified the struggle between the Prime Minister and the Amir over issues of domestic policy and placed the extension of political participation at the top of the Government's agenda. In September 2000 the appointment by Sheikh Hamad of a Jewish businessman, together with a Bahraini of Indian origin and four women (one of whom was a Christian), to the Consultative Council was welcomed by foreign governments, especially the US Administration.

Progress towards political reform gathered momentum in November 2000, when the Amir appointed a 46-member Supreme National Committee (SNC), charged with drafting a document outlining the further evolution of Bahrain's political system. The proposed National Action Charter (NAC), published in December, included recommendations by the SNC that there should be a transition from an emirate to a constitutional monarchy, with a directly elected bicameral parliament (with women allowed both to vote and to seek election), a consultative chamber appointed by the Government from all sections of society, and an independent judiciary. The Amir, who approved the proposals, announced that the reforms outlined in the NAC would be submitted to a national referendum. However, the British-based opposition questioned the legal basis for the Charter, and urged the reinstatement of the 1973 Constitution as the legitimate framework for democratic development.

The referendum (in which Bahraini women voted for the first time) was conducted on 14–15 February 2001. Having secured a resounding popular endorsement of the NAC, with some 98.4% of those who participated approving its terms, the Government announced that the first parliamentary elections would be held by 2004. This was widely understood to be a significant victory for Sheikh Hamad, as it trumped the proposed elections to the Consultative Council that the Prime Minister had announced in May 2000. In late February 2001 Sheikh Hamad formed two committees. The first, the Committee for the Activation of the National Charter, chaired by Crown Prince Sheikh Salman, was charged with implementing the NAC and with defining the respective responsibilities of the parliament and the monarchy. The second committee, chaired by the Minister of Justice and Islamic Affairs, Sheikh Abdullah bin Khalifa Khalid Al Khalifa, was required to oversee amendments to the Constitution and, in the view of many commentators, was to act as a crucial arbiter on the role of the Consultative Council, whose likely position with regard to the future legislature had generated fierce debate within Bahrain.

The national referendum won the praise of the international community and of human rights organizations, and received an unprecedented degree of support from Bahraini opposition groups. Moreover, in February 2001 the 1974 Decree Law on State Security Measures, together with the State Security Court, was abolished. Shortly before the referendum the Amir ordered the release of all political prisoners, including the Shi'ite cleric Sheikh al-Jamri, who had been under house arrest since July 1999. After the Cabinet removed travel restrictions for members of the opposition, by mid-March 2001 dozens of political exiles had returned to Bahrain, among them Sheikh Ali Salman, the Shi'ite cleric deported in 1995, and Abd al-Rahman al-Naimi, the former leader of the Bahrain Popular Liberation Front. In early March 2001, prior to a visit by representatives of Amnesty International, the Government licensed the independent Bahrain Society for Human Rights and announced that henceforth it would look favourably on the establishment of NGOs. Full Bahraini citizenship was also to be granted to Shi'ite Muslims of Iranian descent whose ancestors had lived in Bahrain for several generations.

Meanwhile, in June 2001 Mansour al-Jamri, leader of the London-based Bahrain Freedom Movement (BFM), endorsed the NAC during his first visit to Bahrain in 15 years. Al-Jamri's support for the Charter boosted domestic and international confidence in the Government's commitment to reform, despite several restrictions imposed by the authorities on public gatherings. In May Sheikh Hamad separated the Public Prosecution Office from the Ministry of the Interior, in a further step to dismantle the state security system after the abolition of the relevant legislation in February.

Despite Sheikh Hamad's announcement that political activities would be restricted to broadly based, non-sectarian political groups, the Government began to grant licences to local non-governmental organizations (NGOs) irrespective of their religious orientation in October 2001. From early 2002 the Al-Wefaq National Islamic Society (or the Islamic National Accord Association), headed by Sheikh Ali Salman, emerged as a leading opposition group. It was widely considered that the establishment of political groups under the aegis of local NGOs represented a significant step towards the formation of a multi-party system.

During 2001 the Government continued to remain silent over the constitutional aims of the NAC, particularly with regard to the responsibilities of the elected parliament (Council of Representatives or Majlis al-Nuab) and of the Consultative Council (Majlis al-Shura). In an announcement on state-owned television on 14 February 2002—the first anniversary of the referendum in which the NAC proposals were approved—Sheikh Hamad declared Bahrain to be a constitutional monarchy and proclaimed himself King. The new King signed the constitutional amendments into law and set the dates of the municipal and legislative elections for 9 May and 24 October 2002, respectively.

The prospect of imminent parliamentary elections (which had not been expected until 2004) received universal praise from the international media, but encountered substantial criticism in Bahraini opposition circles. King Hamad's decision to enact an amended Constitution and to grant the new Consultative Council legislative powers equal to those of the elected Council of Representatives was rebuffed by members of the opposition as a 'constitutional putsch' in betrayal of the spirit of the 1973 Constitution (under which the National Assembly was unicameral and included exclusively elected members). Furthermore, Article 73 of the new Constitution gave the King the right to make amendments without the approval of the two chambers.

Municipal elections were duly held in May 2002. A decree issued in December 2001 added new responsibilities to Bahrain's municipal councils, while for electoral purposes the country was divided into five districts, with each district to provide 10 elected representatives. Despite concerns over the 'sectarian approach' employed by the Government in the distribution of seats, in March 2002 five of the major NGO-based political organizations, including Al-Wefaq, affirmed their intention to take part in the ballot. Groups of Islamist orientation performed well, while nationalist and leftist elements failed to win consistent support.

In preparation for the forthcoming legislative elections, in June 2002 a draft electoral law was approved by the Bahraini Government. However, the new legislation was criticized by opposition groups since it barred all overtly political organizations from participating in the ballot. In July King Hamad ordered the establishment of an independent financial auditing court with far-reaching powers to monitor state spending. Later in that month the creation of a Constitutional Court was also approved by the Government.

At the parliamentary elections held on 24 October 2002—the first for almost 30 years—21 of the 40 seats in the Council of Representatives were won by independents and 'moderate' Sunni candidates, with the remaining 19 taken by more radical Islamists. According to official figures, electoral turn-out was 53.2% despite calls for a boycott by four political associations led by the main Shi'ite association, Al-Wefaq. The eight female candidates failed to win any seats and no international human rights organization was allowed to monitor the electoral process. Opposition groups criticized the new legislature as being unrepresentative of Bahraini society, and continued to condemn the policy of political naturalization adopted by the Government. In particular, they accused the King of having granted voting rights to Sunnis from the neighbouring Eastern Province of Saudi Arabia.

On 17 November 2002 the new Consultative Council, headed by Dr Faisal Radhi al-Mousawi, hitherto Minister of Health, was sworn in by the King: the body comprised 40 appointed members, including four women. Earlier in the month King Hamad named an expanded Cabinet, which included two Shi'ites, the former opposition figure Dr Majid bin Hassan al-Alawi and Sheikh Jawad bin Salem al-Oraid, as Minister of Labour and Social Affairs and Minister of Justice, respectively. Sheikh Khalifa bin Sulman Al Khalifa remained Prime Minister, while for the first time two Deputy Prime Ministers were appointed: Sheikh Abdullah bin Khalid Al Khalifa, who also held the position of Minister of Islamic Affairs, and Sheikh Muhammad bin Mubarak Al Khalifa, who retained the foreign affairs portfolio.

After the disputed election, the opposition continued to instigate public debate on issues of constitutional reform, naturalization and corruption. In April 2003 news of the impending collapse of two pension funds managed by the Government led to a parliamentary inquiry. In March 2004 the Cabinet granted land and monetary compensation to the two funds, and in April the Minister of Finance and National Economy, Abdullah bin Hassan Saif, faced questions in the Council of Representatives regarding allegations of corruption. While the Bahrain Centre for Human Rights (BCHR) continued to accuse the Government of discrimination against the Shi'ite majority, in February 2004 opposition groups organized a controversial conference on constitutional rights and continued to press for the repeal of constitutional changes made in 2002. In April 2004 several arrests were made in connection with a petition calling for constitutional reform. To restore the confidence of both tourists and investors, the authorities declared 'zero tolerance' on violence and threatened to dissolve political associations. In May protests against US-led operations in Iraq and Israel's military offensive in the Gaza Strip left several people injured, including Jawad Fairooz, a prominent member of Al-Wefaq. The King launched a swift investigation and dismissed the Minister of the Interior, Sheikh Muhammad bin Khalifa Al Khalifa, who had held the post since 1974; Maj.-Gen. (later Lt-Gen.) Sheikh Rashid bin Abdullah bin Ahmad Al Khalifa was appointed in his stead.

Meanwhile, new legislation on the establishment of trade unions was ratified in November 2002. The General Federation of Bahrain Trade Unions (GFBTU), led by opposition groups, held its inaugural conference in January 2004 with an agenda dominated by the issue of 'Bahrainization' of the work-force. In April Dr Nada Haffadh replaced Dr Khalil bin Ibrahim Hassan as the Minister of Health, thereby becoming Bahrain's first female cabinet minister.

A dialogue between the Government and the extra-parliamentary opposition that had been launched in July 2004 was postponed indefinitely in October following alleged contacts between the four political societies and the British ambassador to Bahrain, which had brought accusations of their involvement with a foreign country. Confrontation with the Government had resumed in September upon the arrest of Abd al-Hadi al-Khawaja, the co-founder and director of the BCHR, after he had publicly called for the resignation of the Prime Minister on the grounds of his poor record on human rights and economic management. The sentencing of al-Khawaja to one year in prison and the disbanding of the BCHR caused further unrest and attracted widespread international scrutiny. Mounting tension was eased by the intervention of the King, who pardoned the activist and asked Crown Prince Salman to hold a 'national dialogue' with all elements of society. Meanwhile, the Government proposed new legislation to restrict the activities of extra-parliamentary political groups.

In January 2005 the King reorganized the Cabinet. Responsibility for the Ministry of Finance and National Economy was divided between the new Minister of Finance and National Economy, Sheikh Ahmad bin Muhammad Al Khalifa, formerly the Governor of the BMA, and the Crown Prince in his capacity as head of the Economic Development Board. This move weakened the influence over economic policy of the Prime Minister, the leading conservative figure who has strong ties with the business community, while increasing the influence of the Crown Prince. In January 2005 the King rejected a petition signed by 75,000 Bahrainis, who were demanding that the constitutional law comply with principles established in 1973, on the grounds that the Council of Representatives should address the issue.

Following concerns expressed in early 2005 by international humanitarian organizations, the Government intensified its efforts to implement reforms. However, on 17 May members of the Council of Representatives voted against allowing the Constitutional Court (which had opened in April) to examine the legality of the controversial Decree 56 of 2002, which granted immunity to officials responsible for abuses perpetrated before the 2001 general amnesty—a move that, in the view of deputies, would be destructive to national unity. Unemployment remained the major social problem in Bahrain: despite the Government's repeated denials, the issue went beyond purely economic concerns, since most unemployed workers were from the Shi'ite community. During mid-2005 riot police forcibly stopped several rallies by protesters demanding recognition of rights for the jobless as well as employment opportunities for Bahrainis in the Ministries of the Interior and of Defence, which mostly recruit Sunni expatriates.

After heated parliamentary debates, a new political societies law was finally approved by the Council of Representatives in July 2005. In October the principal opposition groups chose to register their societies under the new law; the radical Al-Wefaq divided and some members formed a new forum, Al-Haq ('Right'), which appeared to attract cross-sectarian support from dissatisfied members of various opposition groups. The split within the opposition camp was deepened by divergent views on participation in municipal and legislative elections, scheduled for between September and December 2006. Al-Wefaq voted in favour of contesting the elections, after having boycotted parliament in 2002, while Al-Haq refused on the grounds that voting would lend credibility to an illegitimate Government. In mid-2005 the National Audit Court published a report revealing irregularities in the accounts of ministries and public bodies during 2003–04. The allegations gave the King justification for a limited cabinet reorganization: September saw the closure of the Ministry of Oil and its replacement by the National Oil and Gas Authority—a move that was allegedly intended to weaken the authority of the Prime Minister. Following the audit report, parliamentary deputies put forward a bill to tackle corruption in the higher echelons of government. However, the bill was postponed in November, and, reversing an earlier decision, the legislature voted in May 2006 to cross-examine ministers behind closed doors.

International developments in 2006 placed renewed pressure on the Government. The bombing in February of the al-Askari Mosque (or Golden Mosque) in Samarra, one of the holiest Shi'ite shrines in Iraq, prompted the largest demonstration in Bahrain for many years. Tension persisted as new restrictions on public meetings and the controversial counter-terrorism law, introduced in July, imposed serious limitations on the exercise of human rights. In September a row erupted over alleged Government efforts to alter the Sunni-Shi'ite balance, which included the mass naturalization of pro-Government Asians. A report by Salah al-Bandar, a British national and consultant to the Government of Bahrain, documented secret operations by senior government officials to manipulate the vote and undermine Shi'ite opposition activities. These allegations prompted the opposition to call for an independent investigation of al-Bandar's allegations and raised sectarian tensions a few weeks before the elections. The opposition intensified its campaign for electoral reform, for the easing of restrictions on free expression and for better access to jobs and housing. In response to continued demonstrations, the Government proposed legislation in October implementing state financial support for unemployed Bahraini citizens, based on plans first announced in 2005.

Elections for the Council of Representatives and for municipal councils were held in two rounds in November and December 2006. The main opposition group, the Shi'a-based Al-Wefaq, participated for the first time after ending a four-year boycott of parliamentary proceedings and won 17 out of 40 seats, thereby becoming the largest group in the Council of Representatives. The two leading Sunni Islamist groups, al-Asala (a *Salafi* group) and al-Menbar (an offshoot of the Muslim Brotherhood), also won all the seats they contested (five and seven, respectively), while secular and nationalist groups failed to secure a single seat. Whereas the previous Council was roughly divided between secularists and Islamists, Sunni and Shi'ite Islamists collectively now held a clear majority. However, religious and political differences continued to limit their ability to co-operate, with Sunni representatives being generally more sympathetic to the royal family. No member of Al-Wefaq was appointed to the new Cabinet announced in mid-December, prompting the group to boycott the inaugural session of the legislature. In its absence, Sunni Islamists were appointed as speaker and first and second deputy speakers of the Council of Representatives. None the less, the Government did appoint Bahrain's first Shi'ite Deputy Prime Minister, Jawad bin Salem al-Arrayed, a Government supporter and former minister. A second Shi'ite, Nizar al-Baharna, was given a junior portfolio as Minister of State for Foreign Affairs. As expected, the ruling family continued to hold most key cabinet posts, with Sheikh Khalifa bin Salman Al Khalifa remaining as Prime Minister, while Sheikh Khalid bin Ali Al Khalifa assumed the position of Minister of Justice and Islamic Affairs after the merging of the two portfolios. The opposition gained representation on parliamentary committees elected in January 2007, with Al-Wefaq deputies heading two of the five committees. Following the elections, the Consultative Council was reappointed by the King and included Houda Nonoo, a human rights activist and the first Jewish woman to sit in Bahrain's parliament.

In the new legislature the opposition continued to prioritize electoral and constitutional reform, an inquiry into allegations of vote-rigging and the provision of jobs and housing. The new Council of Representatives adopted a less co-operative attitude towards government policy, with mixed results. Numerous attempts were made by Al-Wefaq deputies to question the Minister of State for Cabinet Affairs, Sheikh Ahmad bin Atiyatallah Al Khalifa, over his alleged involvement in electoral manipulation and activities to undermine Shi'ite opposition activities. Meanwhile, in April 2007 the Council launched investigations into claims of mismanagement and errors at the Ministry of Health. In an effort to defuse the growing unrest among deputies, the Government removed the Minister of Health, Nada Haffadh, one of only two women in the Cabinet, and the Minister of Information, Muhammad Abd al-Gaffar, from their posts in September. They were succeeded by Faisal al-Hamer, and Jihad Bu Kamal, respectively.

Meanwhile, in February 2007 the arrest of prominent activists associated with Al-Haq and the outlawed BCHR provoked angry demonstrations. Following increased violence in May, King Hamad ordered that the case be dropped. During that summer the issue of access to public land and water, along with the proportion of private land held by the ruling family, became a focal point for months of protests. Bahrain witnessed another series of riots in December 2007, after the Government refused permission for a rally to commemorate the victims of human rights abuses perpetrated during the 1990s. In July 2008 the sentencing of 11 men convicted of having taken part in the

December riots ignited further protests. In an attempt to calm the unrest, the King included six of the 11 in a broad royal pardon for 225 prisoners, granted on the occasion of Ramadan.

The King took steps to strengthen the position of his son and boost the reform process in early 2008. In January he announced the disbandment of the Ministry of Defence and the appointment of Crown Prince Salman to the newly created position of Deputy Supreme Commander of the BDF. The outgoing Minister of Defence, Sheikh Khalifa bin Ahmad Al Khalifa, was appointed to the post of Commander-in-Chief of the Army, and the administration of matters pertaining to the military was placed under the control of the Minister of State for Defence Affairs. In the same month King Hamad made a public statement reaffirming the overriding authority of the EDB, chaired by the Crown Prince, on matters of economic policy. Prince Salman subsequently expanded the board of directors of the EDB to include most Cabinet ministers, thereby creating something of a parallel cabinet. These moves were welcomed by most opposition leaders, despite the potential erosion of the Council of Representatives' authority (the EDB—unlike ministers—was not directly accountable to parliament). While strengthening the position of the Crown Prince, the King also appeared to be extending his influence over security, nominally the Prime Minister's remit. Following the death of a policeman in a firebomb attack on a police car in the village of Karzakan in April, Sheikh Khalifa bin Ahmed Al Khalifa, who was considered to be a close ally of the King, was appointed as the new head of the country's national security body.

Although the Council of Representatives continued to be a showcase for sectarian divisions, which impaired its ability to compel the executive to solve grievances about human and civil rights, its members continued to question ministers, and investigative committees were formed to examine public policies. In early 2008 attempts to question the Shi'ite Minister of Municipalities and Agriculture Affairs, Mansoor bin Rajab, and the Sunni Minister of State for Cabinet Affairs, Sheikh Ahmad bin Atiyatallah Al Khalifa, over claims of financial and administrative irregularities created divisions between the respective parliamentary groups and brought parliament to a virtual stalemate. Sheikh Atiyatallah was eventually questioned in his capacity as head of the national statistics agency, the Central Informatics Organization, about recently published population figures that estimated the number of Bahrainis in 2007 at 529,446 and the overall population at over 1m. These data showed an unexpected 41% increase in Bahrain's population and a 15% increase in the number of nationals, fuelling suspicions among the Bahrain Shi'ite community that the Government had been accelerating the naturalization process for Sunni Muslims from abroad in an effort to alter the sectarian balance. In May Sheikh Atiyatallah was cleared by an investigative committee of any wrongdoing, prompting Al-Wefaq deputies to walk out of parliament. Although cleared of any wrongdoing by a parliamentary committee in May, bin Rajab was replaced as Minister of Municipalities and Agriculture Affairs by Juma al-Ka'abi in October. A financial transparency bill was presented to parliament in November, following the arrests of several officials at state-owned companies who were suspected of financial irregularities. In April 2008 both Sunni and Shi'ite deputies voted to amend the bill to ensure that the Prime Minister would not be excluded from its requirements.

In November 2008 both the chief executive of the Bahrain Radio and Television Corpn, and the Minister of Culture and Information, Jihad Bu Kamal, were removed from office, following the broadcast of a television programme in which opposition politicians accused the ruling élite of concealing information concerning oil revenues and expenditure on security.

Despite the appointment of women to some senior positions, including that of Bahrain's first female diplomat, Sheikha Haya Rashid Al Khalifa, as President of the UN General Assembly in September 2006, the issue of women's rights continued to be a source of concern. Islamic political societies and conservatives had long blocked plans to promulgate a codified family status law that would limit the discretion of clerics in family courts and strengthen women's rights. In May 2009 the Council of Representatives finally endorsed a law that covers only Sunni family matters, as the Shi'ite members maintained that only religious leaders were qualified to decide on matters rooted in religious jurisprudence. Women's rights activists and various NGOs argued that the legislation would slow efforts to issue a unified family law and deepen sectarian divisions in Bahraini society.

In late 2007 the Government presented draft legislation allowing licensed societies for the first time to be involved in political affairs, to receive finances from abroad and to establish unions. Several amendments have since been proposed to remove the remaining restrictions, including the Ministry of Social Development's control over minutes of meetings and all forms of financial aid. Meanwhile, in May 2008 the Consultative Council approved an amendment to the press and publications law that would abrogate all prison sentences for journalists convicted of press offences. The move was heralded by Sheikh Atiyatallah as a positive step towards ensuring freedom of expression in Bahrain. However, at mid-2013 the amendment still awaited approval by the Council of Representatives.

Anti-Government demonstrations occurred in numerous Shi'ite villages around the country on an almost weekly basis during 2008–09, protesting at the slow pace of reform allowed by the ruling family. In December 2008 the authorities announced the arrest of 15 men, all from Shi'ite villages, accused of plotting bomb attacks in central Manama to disrupt the celebration of Bahrain's National Day on 16 December. A crackdown on opposition activists followed, including the arrest in January 2009 of senior opposition figures, including the leader of Al-Haq, Hassan Mesheima, on suspicion of links with groups attempting to overthrow the Government. The arrest and subsequent trial of the activists—even though it was adjourned—and the televised alleged confession of some of the suspects in advance of the trial led to renewed protests and social unrest in Shi'ite areas during the following months. In an attempt to end the stalemate between the Government and the opposition, and to defuse rising social unrest, in April the King granted pardons to 178 detainees held on security grounds, including the leaders of Al-Haq, who were 'pardoned' before a verdict was reached in their trials.

In 2009 Bahrain instituted a series of ambitious measures to reorganize the labour market as part of the Vision 2030 long-term development plan prepared by the EDB, Bahrain's main economic policy-making agency. With effect from 1 August 2009 the Government amended the sponsorship system for immigrant workers; under the new system, the Labour Market Regulatory Authority rather than private employers would sponsor foreign workers, who would be granted the legal right to change jobs without seeking permission from their existing employer. The move was intended not only to reduce the risk of exploitation and abuse of immigrant workers, but also to increase employment opportunities for Bahraini nationals.

In November 2009 the Bahrain Chamber of Commerce and Industry signed a memorandum of understanding (MOU) with the GFBTU that was aimed at curbing strikes. Among other improvements on the agenda were an increase in the annual number of private sector vacation days, from 24 to 30 days, and an increase in statutory maternity leave, from 45 to 60 days. In March 2010 the legislature approved a proposal to introduce a voluntary pension scheme. In the same month the authorities tightened restrictions on visas for expatriates in order to reduce the number of people entering Bahrain on a short-term visa and outstaying the stipulated period. The GFBTU estimated in February 2010 that there were around 46,000 illegal visitors in the country.

In September 2009 the Minister of the Interior announced a review of the country's naturalization law. Expatriates accounted for nearly one-half of the population, and the vast majority of recently naturalized Bahrainis were Sunnis, rendering the issue of naturalization ever more sensitive for sectarian as well as economic reasons.

Demonstrations and protests had intensified in late 2009, following the Government's refusal to authorize celebration of a 'Martyrs' Day', which opposition groups had planned to stage on 16 December, the country's National Day, in commemoration of opposition activists who had died or disappeared during the 1990s. Furthermore, in August the authorities had reportedly dispersed people attending an 'alternative' celebration commemorating the 38th anniversary of independence. On both occasions, clashes between police officers and would-be protesters from the Shi'ite villages around Manama lasted for days.

A report published in February 2010 by Human Rights Watch offered the most detailed account to date of allegations that Bahraini officials had, since 2007, repeatedly resorted to torture in order to secure confessions in a number of high-profile cases. Although government spokespeople were adamant that the claims were unfounded, the report contended that the allegations were credible. Moreover, a few weeks prior to the publication of the report, Freedom House, the US-based human rights organization, downgraded Bahrain's rating in terms of civil liberties and political rights from 'partially free' to 'not free' in its annual *Freedom in the World* report.

During April 2010 further civil unrest flared up in the vicinity of Karzakan village, over the controversial trial of 19 men accused of murdering a police officer in 2008. In October 2009 the men had been acquitted by the High Criminal Court, owing to a lack of evidence. However, in March 2010 the Supreme Criminal Appeals Court overturned the High Criminal Court's ruling, and the men were all given three-year prison sentences.

Tensions between the Government and Al-Wefaq, the mainly Shi'ite opposition bloc, were exacerbated by remarks made by Sheikh Ali Salman during Al-Wefaq's annual conference in February 2010. The Al-Wefaq leader had declared that Bahrain needed a real constitutional monarchy, as pledged in the National Charter; that the Government was not elected by the people; and that the Al Khalifa family monopolized government ministries and large corporations. Sheikh Ali Salman's comments provoked a strong reaction from Sunni legislators and other prominent figures within Sunni communities, who condemned what they considered to be an insult to the King and the rest of the royal family. The Minister of Justice and Islamic Affairs, Sheikh Khalid bin Ali Al Khalifa, threatened to pursue Al-Wefaq under the societies law, and the Minister of Culture and Information, Sheikha Mai bint Muhammad Al Khalifa, was reported to have asked newspaper editors not to publish any response from Al-Wefaq to the criticism that it received.

In March 2010 the Ministry of Culture and Information intercepted a live broadcast by Bahrain's official radio station of a parliamentary session during which legislators were discussing land property. A report submitted by a committee headed by Al-Wefaq members pointed to the involvement of government officials and members of the Al Khalifa family in an extensive corruption scandal involving public land, valued at some BD 14,000m. (US $37,100m.), which had allegedly been transferred to private ownership by dubious means.

In June 2010 the Government removed the Information department from the Ministry of Culture and Information, and created a new Bahrain Media Authority (BMA) with responsibility for all media-related affairs, including broadcast media and the Bahrain News Agency. Sheika Mai retained her post at the renamed Ministry of Culture. Fawwaz bin Mohammad Al Khalifa, a former Minister of Youth and Sports, was appointed in charge of the BMA.

Meanwhile, ahead of the elections scheduled to be held in late 2010, a number of amendments to the legislature were introduced to increase the accountability of the Consultative Council while strengthening the relatively limited powers of the directly elected Council of Representatives. In April the Consultative Council voted to force ministers to attend parliamentary committees in which matters under their ministry's competence were due to be debated. In addition, legislators were granted the right to discuss any matter of general interest, as well as the power to order the Financial Audit Bureau to investigate any organization suspected of misconduct; previously, the Bureau did not have the power to monitor public organizations.

Further legislation was introduced that required senior public figures, including members of the both legislative councils, government ministers, and high-ranking public servants, to declare their assets and those of their families. The legislation was designed to increase transparency and limit the opportunities for corruption in state affairs, and was in part a response to charges of money-laundering brought against Minister of State without portfolio Mansoor bin Rajab, who was removed from office in March 2010, despite repudiating the charges against him. (Bin Rajab had been questioned by parliament in 2008 over possible illegal financial activities, but he was subsequently cleared of any wrongdoing.) As he is a member of the Shi'ite community, the scandal involving bin Rajab stoked some sectarian tensions, with certain elements within the media accusing him of handling financial transactions for Iran's Islamic Revolutionary Guards Corps.

In June 2010 the two main Sunni societies, al-Asala and al-Menbar, announced that they were co-ordinating their election campaigns to ensure maximum representation. In August King Hamad issued a decree, scheduling the election for 23 October. At the same time, the Government took an increasingly hard-line approach towards dissidents, and launched a political crackdown on mostly Shi'ite opposition activists. By the end of August the authorities had arrested 23 prominent dissidents, charging them with attempting to overthrow the Government and planning terrorist acts. Among those arrested were the Shi'ite opposition leader Abd al-Jalil al-Singace and leading figures in Al-Haq and the Al-Wafa Islamic Party, two unregistered opposition groups that had publicly campaigned for the restoration of the 1973 Constitution and its provisions for a fully elected parliament. Meanwhile, the website and newsletter of Al-Wefaq, the largest Shi'ite society in the Council of Representatives, were banned intermittently.

Moreover, in early September 2010 the Government announced its decision to reassert state control over mosques, and revoked the Bahraini citizenship of Ayatollah Muhammad Najati, the representative in Bahrain of Iraq's Grand Ayatollah Ali al-Sistani, who in the past had openly criticized the Bahraini Government. Although the citizenship of Ayatollah Najati was subsequently reinstated, the original act sent a signal to Shi'ite clerics who urged their followers to vote as a religious duty. The leading Shi'ite cleric in Bahrain—Sheikh Issa Qassim, who was considered to be the religious leader of Al-Wefaq—took a passive stance and appealed for dialogue.

This crackdown on dissidents was not limited to Bahrain's Shi'ite community. A range of opposition movements was targeted, including the secular, leftist political society Al-Waad, which had its campaigns disrupted, while independent NGOs and human rights activists also suffered increasing repression.

The opposition accused the Government of intimidation before the elections. Sheikh Ali Salman, the head of Al-Wefaq, declared that the crackdown had 'in one week destroyed 10 years of progress'. Amnesty International appealed for an investigation into allegations of ill treatment and torture made by several detainees. The Government maintained that the detainees had been arrested for security and terrorism violations, not for expressing dissident political views. Yet, the authorities allegedly banned the media from reporting on detentions, and took an increasingly critical stance towards the work of NGOs dealing with human rights, including Human Rights Watch, which was accused of 'interfering' in Bahrain's elections by Minister of Development and Social Affairs Fatima Muhammad al-Blushi. The minister also announced in September 2010 the dismissal of the entire board of the Bahrain Human Rights Society and its replacement by a government-appointed administration board.

Ahead of the October 2010 elections, the Islamic Action Society, a registered political society, announced that it was to boycott the poll. The three main movements targeted in the September crackdown—Al-Wafa, Al-Haq and the BFM, all of which the authorities considered unauthorized—issued a joint statement appealing for a boycott of the elections 'as a form of civil disobedience and peaceful resistance'.

THE OCTOBER 2010 PARLIAMENTARY ELECTIONS

A general election for the 40-member Council of Representatives was held over two rounds on 23 and 30 October 2010. A relatively high overall turn-out of 67% was recorded. The weeks of unrest and arrests of largely Shi'ite opposition activists that preceded the election probably contributed to the strong turn-out among Bahraini Shi'ites, to the benefit of Al-Wefaq, which emerged as the largest group in the legislature after winning all of the 18 seats that it contested in the first round, with 53% of the votes cast. Nevertheless, the opposition failed to gain a majority of seats in the elected chamber because the electoral districts were divided in such a way as to dilute the Shi'ite vote. Thus, Al-Wefaq's ability to manoeuvre within parliament depended on its relations with a number of newly elected (Sunni) independents.

The second largest group in parliament, with 17 seats, was mainly composed of pro-Government independents. Al-Waad failed to win any seats. Its three candidates were undermined when the Government shut down the organization's publications and removed its posters from public display during the campaign.

Various other irregularities were reported during the elections, and no international observers were permitted to monitor the conduct of the polls. Opposition groups raised concerns about the use of 'general' voting stations, where people could vote outside their own constituencies; about reports of people from Saudi Arabia using a polling station on the Bahraini–Saudi causeway; about the bribery of voters; and about the unequal division of constituency boundaries. Sheikh Ali Salman, leader of Al-Wefaq, alleged that at least 2,000 voters were prevented from casting ballots, but did not challenge the result of the election.

Following the elections, King Hamad reappointed most of the Cabinet to their posts, including Sheikh Khalifa, who remained Prime Minister. Sheikh Khalid bin Abdullah Al Khalifa, a former Minister of Housing, was appointed as a Deputy Prime Minister. Fahmi Ali al-Jouder moved from the Ministry of Works to the reinstated Ministry of Electricity and Water, and was replaced by Isam bin Abdullah Khalaf.

THE PEARL ROUNDABOUT REVOLT

Tension had been simmering for years in Bahrain, due in part to the stalled political reform process, and the kingdom experienced more protests than any other GCC state. The escalation of protest and violence that commenced in late 2010 came to a head during February 2011 in unprecedented anti-Government protests inspired by the downfall of the Tunisian and Egyptian regimes and the civil unrest that followed across the Arab world. Using social networking websites, Bahraini activists appealed for a large demonstration in Manama on 14 February, marking both the 10th anniversary of the nationwide referendum on the King's NAC, which had promised sweeping political reforms, and the anniversary of his promulgation of constitutional amendments in 2002. Echoing other Arab anti-Government protests, the opposition appealed for a 'day of rage' on 14 February 2011, and demanded political reforms to empower the parliament; respect for human rights; an improvement in living standards; and action against corruption and nepotism. It was the first sign of post-Egypt unrest in the wealthy Gulf states, but was clearly rooted in local factors, particularly the anger at discrimination against the Shi'ite majority by the Sunni Al Khalifa dynasty.

On 14 February 2011 riot police used tear gas to disperse groups of 200–300 protesters who were seeking to converge on Manama for a larger rally, and one man was shot dead in the village of Daih. On the 15 February riot police used tear gas against the participants in a huge funeral procession for Mushaima, and reportedly shot dead a second man. In spite of a short televised speech broadcast later that day, in which King Hamad offered condolences to the families of the two men killed and promised an independent inquiry, protesters vehemently shouted anti-Government slogans, demanding a democratically elected government and an end to anti-Shi'ite discrimination. The political protests centred on the Pearl (Lu'lu') Roundabout near Manama, and a makeshift camp was established, emulating the one erected in Tahrir Square in Cairo, Egypt.

Political tensions rose dramatically throughout the following days, with thousands of people reportedly taking to the streets, but there was also a dramatic escalation of violence against protesters, which destroyed hopes for peaceful political change. A heavy-handed response by the authorities began on 17 February 2011, when police stormed the Pearl Roundabout protest camps, killing at least two people and injuring many others. On the following day, according to international press reports, armed military forces were deployed on the streets of the capital, with tanks, armoured vehicles and helicopters firing on demonstrators and prayer groups. At least seven people were killed during 14–17 February, and hundreds were injured. Despite a ban on further gatherings, protesters regained control of Pearl Roundabout, where they camped for weeks.

On 18 February 2011 Crown Prince Salman appeared on state television appealing for calm and dialogue. On the following day, amid international condemnation of the violent crackdown, King Hamad appointed the Crown Prince to lead a national dialogue with the opposition, and ordered the withdrawal of the security forces. As a result of pressure from sponsors and teams involved in the Formula One motor-racing Grand Prix, which was to be held in Bahrain in March, Sheikh Salman also announced in mid-February that the season-opening race would be cancelled.

Bahrain's opposition groups have been divided over whether they should engage in discussions with the regime and over the terms of such a dialogue. The violence appeared to have radicalized parts of the opposition, with increasingly vocal demands for the overthrow of the Al Khalifa monarchy itself. On 16 February 2011 seven opposition groups announced an alliance in support of the so-called '14 February movement'. In the following days, the leaders demanded, as preconditions for any dialogue, the release of prisoners; the resignation of the Government; an independent investigation into the deaths of the seven protesters; and a commitment to reform, including the establishment of a constitutional monarchy and an elected government. Unlicensed groups, with their considerable street credibility, rejected any kind of dialogue with the regime. A central issue for the opposition was the dismissal of the Prime Minister, who was widely seen as representative of the conservative old guard who had run the country before King Hamad began to initiate reforms in 2001.

On 18 February 2011 all 18 Al-Wefaq deputies resigned from the elected Council of Representatives in protest over the violence used against demonstrators. None the less, they averred that they remained ready to engage in discussions about political reform. The Government announced that by-elections to replace them would be held on 24 September.

The regime portrayed the uprising as a Shi'ite revolt inspired by Iran, and asked for the support of the other Gulf states, especially Saudi Arabia. Like other governments throughout the Arab world, the authorities in Bahrain responded to the popular uprising with a mix of increased repression, token concessions and increases in public spending. As a conciliatory gesture, the Government released a number of political prisoners, including al-Singace (although he was detained again when tensions escalated in mid-March 2011) and 22 other prominent opposition activists who had been imprisoned on terrorism charges in August and September 2010. In addition, exiled Shi'ite opposition leader Hasan Mesheima was allowed to return to Bahrain.

In an effort to defuse tensions and bolster the legitimacy of his regime, the King announced a number of economic measures, including a grant of BD 1,000 (US $2,660) for each Bahraini family to coincide with 14 February, the anniversary of the approval of the 2002 Constitution; an increase in food subsidies; an exemption from university fees for 1,000 students; and a two-year extension of the monthly 'anti-inflation' grant of BD 50 ($133), which he had introduced in 2008 as a temporary measure to compensate for the rise in international food prices.

On 26 February 2011 King Hamad carried out a limited cabinet reorganization that changed the heads of key economic ministries—including housing, labour and energy—but did not replace any of those ministers responsible for internal security. Notably, in a Cabinet in which important portfolios were traditionally held by members of the Al Khalifa family, Minister of Labour Majid al-Alawi, a Shi'ite former opposition activist in the BFM, was moved to the Ministry of Housing. A new Ministry of Energy was created by the merger of the

Ministry for Oil and Gas Affairs with the Ministry of Electricity and Water. Abd al-Hussain bin Ali Mirza, the former Minister for Oil and Gas Affairs, assumed responsibility for the merged portfolio. Al-Alawi announced in March that up to 50,000 new homes would be built over the next five years, in an attempt to reduce the number of people waiting for government housing. The housing shortage was a key economic grievance, which had worsened in recent years owing to rapid population growth. The reorganization suggested that the Government hoped to address the unrest by improving public services.

Another notable change was the replacement of the Minister of Health, Dr Faisal al-Hamer, by Nizar al-Baharna. Opposition activists had demanded al-Hamer's dismissal after many doctors reported that they had been prevented from taking ambulances to the wounded at Pearl Roundabout, the focal point of the anti-Government protests, on 17 and 18 February 2011. Meanwhile, the dismissal of Minister of State Ahmad bin Atiyatallah Al Khalifa, who had been named in the so-called 'Bandargate' scandal of 2006, and who was accused of promoting anti-Shi'ite sentiment, was also a significant development.

INTERVENTION OF THE GCC PENINSULA SHIELD FORCE

For a period of three weeks in late February and early March 2011, talks between the Government and opposition representatives stalled because the various opposition groups remained divided over whether to seek the overthrow of the monarchy, favoured by Al-Haq and Al-Wafa, or a constitutional monarchy, favoured by Al-Wefaq. On 4 March Al-Wefaq and six other societies demanded the resignation of the entire Government before they would engage in any dialogue.

On 13 March 2011, while Crown Prince Salman bin Hamad Al Khalifa appealed for a wide-ranging debate about such issues as corruption, fair electoral representation and naturalization policy, protesters blocked access to the Bahrain Financial Harbour, where many major financial institutions maintain offices, and the Qatar-based television channel Al Jazeera broadcast footage of a police officer firing indiscriminately into a crowd of protesters. On the same day King Hamad requested the deployment of troops from other GCC member states under the terms of the GCC joint defence agreement signed in 2000.

On 14 March 2011 an estimated 1,000 Saudi troops crossed the causeway from Saudi Arabia, with some 500 United Arab Emirates (UAE) police officers and additional troops from Qatar, precipitating a new security crackdown on the continuing anti-Government protests. On 15 March King Hamad announced a three-month 'state of national safety', during which protests were banned; a curfew was imposed; inter- and intra-island movement was restricted; and reporting on actions taken by the security forces was forbidden. Al-Wefaq, the main Shi'ite opposition party, denounced the moves as 'an overt occupation of the Kingdom of Bahrain', while government supporters claimed that the country was on the brink of anarchy and civil war.

In the following two days the streets of Manama again erupted in violence. At least two policemen and five protesters were killed, and hundreds injured, as Bahraini security forces launched a second crackdown to clear protesters from the Pearl Roundabout area. On 18 March 2011 the hub of rebellion and its symbol—the monument of the pearl in the middle of Pearl Roundabout—were destroyed and the roundabout was renamed. A new wave of arrests of activists and suspected activists followed, including the leaders of two opposition groups that had appealed for the overthrow of the monarchy, Mesheima and Abd al-Wahhab. The arrest of Ibrahim Sharif, the leader of Al-Waad, and of Al-Singace, demonstrated clearly that the regime intended to use this opportunity to suppress the widest possible range of critics.

The official mission of the Saudi-led Peninsula Shield Force was to guard strategic sites. None the less, Bahraini protesters claimed that the Saudi army staffed checkpoints and participated in the continuing violent repression of unarmed civilians, particularly Shi'ites. An independent international NGO, Physicians for Human Rights, denounced systematic and co-ordinated attacks by the security forces against medical professionals who treated injured protesters during the months of unrest. In late February and early March 2011 the main medical centre at Salmaniya became an unofficial centre for protests after security forces tried to prevent doctors from tending to the wounded.

On March 2011 King Hamad was forced to make further changes to the Government, following the resignations of al-Baharna and al-Alawi, reportedly in protest against the treatment of the demonstrators. Bassem bin Yacoub al-Hamer was appointed as Minister of Housing, while the Minister of Social Development, Dr Fatima Muhammad al-Blushi, assumed additional responsibility for the health portfolio. (In June the King announced the creation of a new Ministry of Human Rights and Social Development; al-Blushi retained responsibility for the revised portfolio, as well as that of health.)

A wide-ranging crackdown continued during April and May 2011, with hundreds of demonstrators, opposition leaders, human rights activists and health professionals being detained. Hundreds more working in public sector companies and institutions were dismissed or suspended for taking part in protests and strikes. In early April the deaths of four activists in custody lent substance to rumours of torture in Bahrain's prisons, reported by human rights groups but always denied by the Bahraini authorities. On 28 April a Bahraini military court, meeting *in camera*, sentenced four dissidents to death and three to life imprisonment for killing two policemen during the March demonstrations. Human rights activists claimed that the men did not receive a fair trial and had been tortured into making false confessions. On 3 May the Ministry of Justice and Islamic Affairs charged 47 medical workers with acting against the state, causing the deaths of two protesters, and denying care to Sunni Bahrainis and expatriate workers. Throughout the month the military court sentenced activists to prison terms ranging from five to 20 years.

Due to the extensive deployment of army and security forces, and repeated appeals for calm by Sheikh Issa Qassim and Sheikh Ali Salman, protests had virtually ceased by mid-2011. Meanwhile, the Government organized a day of public celebration in recognition of the part played by Saudi Arabia in 'restoring calm' to Bahrain. Citing the improved security situation, King Hamad lifted the three-month 'state of national safety' on 1 June, two weeks ahead of schedule. The Minister of Foreign Affairs, Sheikh Khalid bin Ahmad Al Khalifa, declared in April that the Peninsula Shield Force would remain in Bahrain until every external threat had dissipated. The trials of dozens of opposition figures, human rights activists and Shi'ite professionals continued even after the emergency laws had been lifted. International media access to Bahrain remained restricted, and media repression continued, with the arrest of several journalists from the formerly independent newspaper *al-Wasat*. Moreover, the Bahraini authorities demolished a number of Shi'ite mosques and *matams* (mourning houses), important social spaces in the Shi'ite community, claiming that they had been built illegally, even though residents asserted that some of the buildings were over 300 years old, thus predating the building permit system and the rule of the Al Khalifas. Since Bahrain had generally been a country where freedom of religion was respected, this was a marked departure from previous policies.

Opposition groups gave a cool reception to the King's appeal for a dialogue which was scheduled to begin in July 2011. In an apparent effort to draw opposition groups into government-sponsored reconciliation talks, the Bahraini authorities reportedly moved the trials of anti-Government protesters to civilian courts, and King Hamad announced the creation of an independent commission of inquiry to investigate allegations that dissidents' rights were violated during what he described as the 'unfortunate events' of February and March. The main Shi'ite opposition group, Al-Wefaq, announced its withdrawal from the national dialogue with the ruling monarchy, amidst widespread criticism of both the commission and the talks as mere expedients, which sought to quell criticism from abroad whilst promoting peace at home. Moreover, the Government continued to repress demonstrations, and sentenced 13 prominent opposition figures to imprisonment, thus further undermining the credibility of its initiative. Meanwhile, renewed protests erupted in and around Manama. On 22 July one person was reported to have been killed and several injured when security forces used tear gas to disperse demonstrators. On 31 August a youth was reportedly killed by police during the suppression of an anti-Government protest in Sitra.

While demonstrations and violent clashes continued, the Shi'ite opposition groups Al-Wefaq and Al-Waad announced that they would not participate in the parliamentary by-election that was scheduled for 24 September 2011 to replace the 18 Al-Wefaq deputies who had resigned their seats in March. As a result of the boycott, voter turn-out was only 17.4%, reflecting widespread scepticism regarding the ability of the legislature to influence decisions. The resulting Council of Representatives largely comprised pro-Government figures, with only eight Shi'ites among the 40 elected deputies, and the total number of women rising to four.

Acknowledging that controversial political issues could be raised in neither the national dialogue process nor in the legislature, five major opposition societies (Al-Wefaq, Al-Waad, the Nationalist Democratic Assembly, the National Democratic Assemblage and the Ekha National Society) published a joint 'Manama Document' on 12 October 2011. In this declaration, they demanded a comprehensive reform of the political system, to include an elected government, a fair electoral system, and a parliament with full legislative powers. The document has become the opposition manifesto for a Bahraini constitutional monarchy.

Anti-Government protests continued in the second half of 2011 on an almost daily basis, and were violently suppressed by security forces. On 6 October a 16-year-old demonstrator died, following clashes between pro-reform activists and police in the Shi'ite village of Abu Saiba, west of Manama. On 23 November a demonstrator was killed in Manama when police dispersed protesters. Meanwhile, trials of protesters and activists in military courts continued. In early October 33 activists were sentenced for up to 15 years in prison on charges that included attempted murder during the anti-Government protests. In the face of international criticism, a civilian retrial was announced for the high-profile case of 20 Shi'ite medical personnel from the Salmaniya Medical Complex, who, having assisted those attacked in the riots, were charged with crimes ranging from killing protesters to seeking to overthrow the Government. None the less, other civilians continued to be tried in military courts, including the head and deputy head of the Bahrain Teachers Association, Magdi Abu Dee and Jalila Saman, who were sentenced to 10 and five years, respectively, for having organized a strike earlier in the year. Moreover, the General Federation of Bahrain Trade Unions (GFBTU) announced that nearly 3,000 workers had been summarily dismissed for participating in a strike in March, in contravention of Bahrain's labour laws. Among them were 55 trade union leaders and six members of the GFBTU executive.

On 23 November 2011 the royally-appointed Bahrain Independent Commission of Inquiry (BICI), which had been charged with investigating human rights violations committed during the unrest in early 2011, released a report giving detailed evidence of the systematic use of excessive force, including torture, by security forces. The BICI report concluded that the authorities condoned arbitrary arrests and prosecutions, as well as the illegal dismissal of workers, but failed to implicate any one senior official, thereby falling short of the opposition's demand for full accountability. The report also stated that there was no evidence of Iranian involvement in fomenting unrest in the country, contrary to allegations by the state-controlled media and pro-Government groups. The recommendations offered a major opportunity for reform and national reconciliation, and opposition groups have continued to cite them as a benchmark for dialogue. In response, the King pledged to initiate reforms and established a new National Committee to oversee their implementation. Other measures taken since November have included revoking the arrest powers of the National Security Agency, and the introduction of legislative amendments to expand the definition of torture; pledges were also issued to rebuild Shi'ite mosques destroyed by the regime during the crackdown, and to reinstate workers dismissed on the grounds of their political beliefs.

By the beginning of 2012 political talks had come to a halt. Waves of repression, followed by attempts at dialogue and limited reforms, failed to placate the opposition, and ongoing clashes between protesters and security forces continued unabated, with more than 10 protesters having been killed since November. The Ministry of the Interior stated that 41 policemen had been injured over the weekend of 20–21 January. Riot police had apparently increased their use of tear gas in Shi'ite villages, allegedly causing deaths and miscarriages. The BCHR demanded investigations into four deaths on 25 January, which were allegedly due to suffocation from tear gas after police brutality. In late January Amnesty International urged the Bahraini Government to investigate a number of deaths following the misuse of tear gas by security forces.

In March 2012 the Bahraini authorities claimed that 90% of the reform measures recommended by the BICI report had been implemented. In late April the authorities announced the retrial of 13 opposition leaders who had been imprisoned for their roles in the 2011 uprising. On 14 June the Court of Appeals acquitted nine of the 20 health professionals from the Salmaniya Medical Complex whom the authorities had placed on trial for sedition, and sentenced the others to prison terms of between one month and five years.

Nevertheless, rallies continued during April and May 2012 to protest against the proposed Saudi Arabia-Bahrain union (see Regional Relations in 2011–13), and in support of detained activists, particularly a group of 14 prominent militants arrested in April 2011. These included Al-Waad leader Sharif, and human rights activist Abd al-Hadi al-Khawaja, whose 110-day-long hunger strike to protest at his conviction for 'plotting against the state' made him a symbol of resistance for many Bahrainis. In June 2012 security forces arrested Nabil Rajab, President of the BCHR, after his organization published a report that documented human rights violations since the release of the November BICI report, including 11 extrajudicial killings. Rajab had previously been arrested and released several times between March and May on charges of organizing illegal demonstrations. On 16 August Rajab was convicted by a court in Manama for 'involvement in illegal practices and inciting gatherings and calling for unauthorized marches through social networking sites', 'participation in an illegal assembly', and 'participation in an illegal gathering and calling for a march without prior notification', and was sentenced to three years' imprisonment. An appeal against an earlier prison sentence for libel was ongoing.

In contrast to the continuing political impasse, the Bahraini uprising itself appeared to have crossed a significant threshold. After months of largely peaceful demonstrations calling for constitutional reform, protesters were increasingly using homemade explosives to attack police. Sectarian tensions mounted, after the explosion of a bomb in the Shi'ite village of Akar on 9 April 2012 injured several policemen, and pro-Government Sunni groups retaliated by vandalizing the properties of a Shi'a-owned company accused of supporting the protests. In early June Bahrain's Ministry of Justice and Islamic Affairs dissolved the Islamic Action Society (known as Amal) for following 'hostile clerical authority' in calling for violence. Bahrain's Office of Political Associations Affairs warned all other political associations to comply with the requirements set for political groups. Later in the month security forces opened fire with rubber bullets, in addition to the use of tear gas, against protesters, wounding Al-Wefaq leader Sheikh Ali Salman and other opposition figures. Also in July, Nabeel Rajab, the President of the Bahrain Centre for Human Rights (BCHR), was arrested; in mid-August he was sentenced to three years' imprisonment for instigating and participating in unauthorized protests.

Protests intensified in Bahrain during mid-2012, with demands for an end to the reign of the ruling monarchy becoming widespread, amid allegations of police abuses. The BCHR compared the heightened police presence, with checkpoints and house raids, to an imposition of martial law. Opposition groups claimed that at least 25 demonstrations had occurred daily in the kingdom since the holy month of Ramadan began in late July. Amid an escalation of protests against a ban on opposition rallies that was announced by the Ministry of the Interior in mid July, Crown Prince Salman ordered the police to exercise restraint in dealing with protesters. Nevertheless, a teenage protester was killed on 18 August during clashes with riot police. More demonstrations followed his funeral, leading to the arrest of eight activists.

Protests and repression continued in an escalation of violence during a series of demonstrations in many towns across Bahrain during August and September 2012. In August the leading activist Zainab al-Khawaja was arrested, together with some 40 others, following protests near Manama demanding reforms. On 31 August several thousand participated in the first authorized opposition protest, again near Manama, to demand reforms.

In an effort to appease its critics both inside and outside the country, the Ministry of the Interior announced on 29 July 2012 the opening of investigations into possible rights violations committed by security forces during their repression of protesters; Bahrain's public prosecutor, Nawaf Hamza, announced in early August that 15 policemen would be charged with mistreating a group of detained Shi'ite medics. Also in July, the Bahraini Information Affairs Authority released information regarding what it called 'strenuous efforts' to implement the recommendations of the BICI, which had been created by the Government to investigate alleged abuses since protests started in 2011. Moreover, in September 2012 the Government officially pledged to fulfil the 158 recommendations included in the UN Universal Periodic Review regarding human rights abuses and prisoner conditions. In September seven policemen were charged with the torture of detainees.

Nevertheless, the Bahrain authorities continued to react to dissent with violent measures against protesters. In September 2012 an appeals court upheld lengthy prison sentences for 20 opposition and human rights activists on charges ranging from espionage to conspiring to overthrow the Government. Among the confirmed sentences were seven terms of life imprisonment for prominent activists, including Abd al-Jalil Singace, Abd al-Jalil Ridha and Abd al-Hhadi al-Khawaja, whose 110-day hunger strike had drawn international attention earlier in 2012. Human rights groups joined Al-Wefaq and lawyers of the defendants in criticizing the court's decision, which followed months of contested hearings and allegations of forced confessions. These verdicts precipitated further protests. On 28 September, when thousands of anti-Government protesters demonstrated in Shi'ite villages near the capital, a teenage activist was killed by riot police allegedly acting in self-defence. Thousands of mourners chanted anti-Government slogans at the subsequent funeral march, whilst riot police fired tear gas and stun grenades at protesters throwing stones. Other clashes erupted at the funeral of another activist, who had died in custody on 2 October, allegedly after having been denied medical treatment.

King Hamad's call for dialogue in his address at the National Assembly on 14 October 2012, a few days after security forces used tear gas to disperse protesters in Manama, did little to quell mounting tensions in the country. A policeman was killed on 19 October in an explosion in Eker, south of Manama; clashes broke out in the following days, after security forces arrested seven people and prevented activists and medics from entering the village. The BCHR reported violent raids and arbitrary arrests of activists, including Zainab al-Khawaja, after security forces blocked access to the village. Refuting the claims of abuse, the Bahraini Information Affairs Authority condemned the attack as a 'domestic terror act'. On 30 October the Minister of the Interior, Sheikh Rashid bin Abdullah bin Ahmad Al Khalifa, announced a ban on all public protests and gatherings, as a response to alleged repeated abuse of the freedom of speech and expression in the country. This move represented the most sweeping attempt to suppress anti-Government protest since martial law was enacted during the early months of the uprising in 2011, and attracted the criticism of several international human rights organizations, as well as Bahrain's Western allies.

By the first anniversary of the release of the groundbreaking BICI report (see above) in November 2012, the Government announced that most of the 26 listed recommendations for reform in the kingdom had already been implemented, thus suggesting that it saw little room for improvement in these areas. Nevertheless, many independent observers, including Amnesty International, the International Federation of Human Rights, Human Rights Watch and the BCHR, considered the Government's efforts insufficient and disappointing while a majority of Bahrainis were still denied fundamental rights on a daily basis. The political situation in Bahrain continued to deteriorate, with frequent eruptions of violence, including a series of explosions in central Manama in early November, in which two expatriate workers were killed. Although no group claimed responsibility for the bombings, the Bahrain authorities blamed the mainstream opposition, whilst the Minister of State for Information Affairs, Sameera Rajab, suggested the involvement of Hezbollah. A number of repressive measures followed, including a halt to political dialogue and the withdrawal of the Bahraini citizenship of 31 Shi'ite activists, clerics and human rights lawyers, including dissidents Saeed al-Shehabi and Ali Mushaima, on the ground of repeated abuse of the rights to freedom of speech and expression. Also in November, a Bahraini court sentenced 23 medical workers to three months' imprisonment for participation in unauthorized demonstrations during 2011.

Opposition groups called again for mass protests ahead of Bahrain's National Day celebrations on 16 December 2012, shortly after the ban on demonstrations was lifted. A weekend of unrest followed the King's speech, with protesters urging reforms and the liberation of political prisoners, including Yousef al-Muhafedha, the acting head of the BCHR, who had been arrested a few days before. The opposition group Al-Wefaq joined four other political societies in a statement that called the political and humanitarian situation in Bahrain 'the worst ever', despite a number of conciliatory moves on part of the authorities, including a seven-year prison sentence for eight policemen charged with killing Shi'ite activists in custody, and the reduction from three to two years of the prison term imposed on Nabeel Rajab.

In January 2013 King Hamad announced a new plan to revive the moribund 'national consensus dialogue' between various groups, excluding the banned movements that had called for a republican government. Bahrain's six main opposition parties, as well as loyalist parties, such as the National Unity Gathering and the Islamist group al-Asala, participated in the first round of the dialogue on 10 February. Despite calls from opposition groups for government representatives to take part in the talks, the Government itself only served as a facilitator, rather than an interlocutor, in the dialogue. In an interview with the British Broadcasting Corporation, Sheikh Ali Salman, the leader of Al-Wefaq, declared that he would welcome the participation of Crown Prince Salman Al Khalifa, who was widely viewed as a moderate, as a representative of the ruling family. Crown Prince Salman had been dominated by hardliners in previous months; his appointment, on 11 March, to the new post of First Deputy Prime Minister was regarded by opposition groups as an effort to expedite the reform programme. Two Sunni factions, al-Saff al-Islami and al-Minbar al-Islami, boycotted the second session of the dialogue to protest at the refusal of the opposition to condemn street violence, on the grounds that violence from all parties needed to be denounced. The scope of the talks remained limited to resolving political differences and building trust between all participating groups. One month into the dialogue process and after 10 rounds of talks, the parties had yet to set the agenda and the atmosphere deteriorated, as participants accused each other of being unco-operative, leaking updates and receiving instructions from abroad.

Meanwhile, protests and heavy repression continued. In January 2013 the Court of Cassation upheld the prison sentences imposed on 13 leaders of the 2011 uprising, including Abd al-Hadi al-Khawaja. Later in the month a bomb blast injured three policemen at a roundabout west of Manama. As with previous attacks, no group claimed responsibility for the bombing. Protests intensified on the second anniversary of the beginning of the protest movement calling for democratic change. On 14 February a teenage protester and a policeman were reported killed in Daih, west of Manama, and another protester later died from injuries. A number of protesters and two policemen were injured in protests marking the second anniversary of the intervention of Saudi and other GCC forces to suppress the Bahraini uprising. Clashes between opposition forces and police continued during March, leaving several injured on both sides. Violence against the police increased in response to the abuse of power by security forces, which used tear gas and stun grenades to disperse gatherings. Following four small explosions in Manama on 14 April, for the first time the Coalition of February 14 Youth, one of the more confrontational opposition groups formed in 2011, claimed responsibility for the attack.

In February 2013 a BCHR report entitled 'Two Years of Death and Detentions' stated that the human rights situation in the country had become 'more serious'. Meanwhile, Human Rights Watch released its *World Report 2013*, in which it denounced Bahrain's escalating campaign to silence human rights defenders, and denounced the Government's claims that it was carrying out promised reforms as fraudulent—conclusions that Bahrain's Ministry of the Interior rejected as 'wrong and contradictory'. Amid continuing negative publicity, the Government increased the penalty for insulting the King to five years' imprisonment and postponed indefinitely a visit by the UN Special Rapporteur on Torture. The decision followed the release of the latest US State Department human rights report on 19 April, which contained allegations of torture and repressive behaviour by Bahraini security forces (see Other International Relations in 2011–13).

The prosecution of a member of Bahrain's royal family, Princess Noura bint Ibrahim Al Khalifa, who was brought to trial in February 2013 on charges of torturing anti-Government protesters whilst she was working as a police officer during the 2011 protests, as well as the acquittal of 21 medics of charges linked to anti-Government protests in 2011, were widely viewed as encouraging signs of the Government's commitment to justice. Nevertheless, earlier trials of low-ranking policemen had resulted in few convictions, whilst activists had received long sentences, including life imprisonment. The harshest sentence against security forces for abuses committed during unrest, which by mid-2013 had claimed more than 88 lives, according to the BCHR, was given to two police officers, who were sentenced in mid March to 10 years in prison for torturing an anti-Government protester to death.

The political climate further deteriorated during May 2013. Opposition societies suspended their participation in the national dialogue for two weeks and protests were staged against a security forces' raid on the residence of a senior Shi'a cleric, Isa Qasim. Later in the month seven policemen were wounded in a bomb attack in Bani Jamri. As violence intensified, the legislature proposed a draft law on rallies which would require organizers to deposit US $53,000 to gain authorization to demonstrate and the authorities banned political groups from contact with Hezbollah, which they viewed as a terrorist organization instigating Shi'ite anti-Government rebellion. On 28 May 22 people were arrested for their role in anti-Government protests. Also in May, six users of social-networking site Twitter were sentenced to imprisonment of one year for remarks made against the King.

The Ministry of the Interior announced in June 2013 that it had identified members of the February 14 Youth Coalition who were allegedly responsible of 'a string of crimes' committed over the last few months, and named 11 arrested suspects, as well as 13 individuals 'who were leading the coalition from abroad', with links to armed groups in Iraq and Lebanon, and receiving 'direct financial support and field instructions' from leaders in Iran. These included Bahraini national Saeed Abd al-Nabi al-Shahabi, who was subsequently tried *in absentia* and sentenced to life imprisonment. The authorities maintained that 'extremist religious and political leaders from outside and inside Bahrain' had an active role in inciting acts of terrorism. In late September 2013 five opposition groups, including al-Wefaq, withdrew from the national dialogue process. This followed the arrest of Khalil al-Marzuq, a former member of the Council of Representatives and a senior figure in al-Wefaq, on suspicion of 'inciting and promoting terrorist acts'.

TERRITORIAL DISPUTE WITH QATAR

In April 1986 a long-standing territorial dispute between Bahrain and Qatar erupted into military confrontation. Qatari military forces raided the island of Fasht al-Dibal, a coral reef situated midway between Bahrain and Qatar, over which both claimed sovereignty. During the raid Qatar seized 29 foreign workers (all of whom were subsequently released), who were constructing a coastguard station for Bahrain on the island. Officials of the GCC attempted to reconcile the two states and avoid a split within the organization. Fasht al-Dibal was one of three areas of contention, the others being Zubarah, on mainland Qatar, and the Hawar islands. In July 1991 Qatar unilaterally instituted proceedings at the International Court of Justice (ICJ) in The Hague, Netherlands, in an attempt to resolve the dispute over the potentially oil-rich Hawar islands, the shoals of Dibal and Qit'at Jaradah and the delineation of the maritime boundary. In mid-1992 Qatar rejected Bahrain's attempt to broaden the issue to include its claim to part of the Qatari mainland, around Zubarah, which had been Bahraini territory until the early 20th century. Despite the ICJ's declaration that it did have authority to adjudicate in the dispute, Bahrain continued to insist that a bilateral solution be sought, rejected the jurisdiction of the ICJ in the matter and welcomed a Saudi offer to act as mediator.

At the end of 1995 Qatar criticized Bahrain's decision to build a tourist resort on the Hawar islands, and urged co-operation with the ICJ on the resolution of the dispute. Bahrain, however, maintained that the islands were 'sovereign territory', and again refused to accept the ICJ's jurisdiction on this issue. Bahrain boycotted the GCC annual summit convened in the Qatari capital, Doha, in December 1996, at which it was decided to establish a quadripartite committee (comprising those GCC countries not involved in the dispute) to facilitate a solution. Attempts by the committee to foster improved relations between Bahrain and Qatar achieved a degree of success, and meetings between prominent government ministers from both countries in the United Kingdom and in Manama in February and March 1997 resulted in the announcement that they were to establish diplomatic relations at ambassadorial level by mid-1997. However, there were renewed bilateral tensions in mid-1997, after the Bahrain authorities failed to appoint a diplomatic representative to Doha and opened a new hotel on the Hawar islands while announcing plans to build a housing complex there. In February 1998 the Amir made a widely publicized visit to the islands. There were repeated regional attempts to find a solution to the dispute. However, the opposition of Saudi Arabia and the UAE to Qatar's stance encouraged Bahrain to extend its occupation of the islands. Bahrain repeatedly stated that it would disregard any final decision made by the ICJ, and dismissed as forgeries a series of documents submitted to the Court by the Qatari Government in support of its own claim (Qatar subsequently agreed to withdraw them from evidence). In mid-1998 Bahrain's plans to build a causeway linking the islands to the mainland fuelled speculation about a future military escalation between the two countries.

Relations with Qatar remained tense following the accession of Sheikh Hamad in March 1999. In June Bahrain notably attempted to pressure other GCC members into censuring Al Jazeera, which had broadcast interviews with members of the Bahraini opposition. In late 1999, however, there was a marked rapprochement, and the Amir of Qatar made his first official visit to Manama. In the course of the visit it was agreed that a joint committee, headed by the Crown Princes of Bahrain and Qatar, would be established to encourage co-operation and to seek a bilateral solution to the territorial disputes. A second senior-level meeting was held in January 2000, when Sheikh Hamad made his first visit to Qatar. The two countries agreed to expedite the opening of embassies in Manama and Doha. In February, following the first meeting of the Bahrain-Qatar Supreme Joint Committee, Qatar officially named its ambassador to Bahrain. In May, however, Bahrain unilaterally suspended the Committee, pending the ruling of the ICJ.

Hearings by the ICJ began in late May 2000 and were completed by the end of June. The Court's final verdict was delayed until March 2001, when it confirmed Bahrain's sovereignty over the Hawar islands and Qit'at Jaradah, while the town of Zubarah, Janan island and Fasht al-Dibal were to remain under Qatari control. This arbitration, which ended the 60-year dispute, was accepted by both sides and hailed by Bahrain's Amir as a 'historic victory'. In late March the two countries agreed to resume the activities of the Supreme Joint Committee, after a high-profile visit by Sheikh Hamad to Doha. After the ICJ ruling, Sheikh Hamad renewed pledges to transform the Hawar islands into a major tourist resort, and from early 2002 international oil companies were invited to submit bids to drill for oil and gas off the islands. Bahrain's relations with Qatar remained steady throughout 2003, despite several arrests of Bahraini fishermen who had entered Qatari waters. The visits of King Hamad to Doha in December and again in April 2004 revived bilateral co-operation.

Following the signing of an MOU in February 2005, the two Governments established a public commission to oversee the construction of a 40-km causeway linking Bahrain and Qatar (or the Friendship Bridge, as it was officially named). The project was formally approved by the Crown Princes of Qatar and Bahrain in July 2008. The causeway was expected to have a dramatic effect on the Bahraini economy, particularly in promoting tourism, reducing commuting times from five hours to just 30 minutes, and providing an alternative route for imports by land, thereby lessening Bahrain's dependence on the King Fahd Causeway that links it with Saudi Arabia. Construction work on the Friendship Bridge—which, upon completion, would be the world's longest fixed link—was initially expected to begin in early 2009, but this was subsequently delayed owing to financial difficulties, and construction had yet to commence as of mid-2013.

Meanwhile, in May 2005 the Qatari authorities confirmed their decision to supply Bahrain with natural gas, a development hailed as a cornerstone for the building of strong bilateral ties. Talks were held in late 2007 with a view to constructing a pipeline in order to import the gas; however, thus far there has been little indication of progress, and Qatar has placed a moratorium on new gas export deals until 2014.

OTHER INTERNATIONAL RELATIONS

Concern over regional security was one of the reasons why Bahrain joined five other Gulf states in forming the GCC in 1981. Bahrain's reliance on collective defence has also been emphasized by the country's participation in joint naval manoeuvres with Qatar and other Gulf states, and in the GCC's 'Peninsula Shield' military exercises.

In August 1990 Bahrain assumed new strategic importance as a result of Iraq's occupation and annexation of Kuwait. Following the annexation, Bahrain firmly supported the implementation of UN economic sanctions against Iraq, and permitted the stationing of US combat aircraft in Bahrain. British armed forces participating in the multinational force for the liberation of Kuwait were also stationed in Bahrain during 1990–91. In June 1991 it was announced that Bahrain would remain a regional support base for the USA, but would not become the headquarters of a Gulf-based US military command and control centre. In October Bahrain and the USA signed a defence co-operation agreement allowing for joint military exercises, the storage of equipment and the use of Bahraini port facilities by US forces. In January 1994 MOUs on military co-operation were signed with the USA and the United Kingdom.

In July 1992 Bahrain's Prime Minister expressed the hope that the country's relations with Iraq would improve and that, eventually, both Iraq and Iran would be incorporated into the GCC. This was the first time that the government of a GCC state had openly promoted the restoration of contacts with Iraq. However, in the final communiqué of the GCC summit held in Riyadh, Saudi Arabia, in December 1993, the six heads of state demanded that international pressure on Iraq to observe all UN resolutions pertaining to it should be maintained, and that the sovereignty of Kuwait should be respected. It was also decided to double the size of the Saudi-based 'Peninsula Shield' joint defence force. In October 1994, when Iraqi troops were again positioned in the Iraq–Kuwait border area, Bahrain deployed combat aircraft and naval units to join GCC and US forces in the defence of Kuwait.

Since the 1990s Saudi Arabia has remained Bahrain's most steadfast ally, in both political and economic respects. Increasingly, Saudi Arabia has linked Bahrain's stability to its own internal security, owing to the large Shi'ite population in its oil-rich Eastern Province. A number of other GCC countries have also offered their support for maintaining the status quo in Bahrain, apparently accepting Bahrain's argument that, if the dissidents succeed there, unrest would spread across the region.

Bahrain attended the Arab League summit meeting held in Cairo in June 1996, where the final communiqué criticized Iran for its 'interference in the internal affairs of Bahrain'. Relations with Iran improved steadily, however, following the election of Sayed Muhammad Khatami as President of Iran in May 1997. The new Iranian Minister of Foreign Affairs, Kamal Kharrazi, visited Bahrain in November and discussed the expansion of diplomatic, cultural and economic relations between the two countries with his Bahraini counterpart. Increased diplomatic contacts between Bahrain and Iran, encouraged by Saudi Arabia, culminated in the nomination of an Iranian ambassador to Bahrain in December 1998. The Iranian Government came under increasing pressure from Saudi Arabia to control the activities of uncompromising Shi'ite clerics in Bahrain, particularly following the tentative rapprochement between Saudi Arabia and Iran, which gathered momentum during 1998. Following talks in December 1999, relations at ambassadorial level were re-established between Bahrain and Iran, and in March 2000 the Ministers of Foreign Affairs of the two countries met in Manama to discuss regional security as well as political and economic co-operation. A joint economic commission held its inaugural meeting in that month.

The first official Israeli delegation to visit Bahrain arrived in September 1994, and in the following month the Israeli Minister of the Environment, Yossi Sarid, attended multilateral regional talks on environmental issues held in Manama. During his visit Sarid met Bahrain's Minister of Foreign Affairs, marking the first contact at ministerial level between Bahrain and Israel. Despite further ministerial-level contacts, however, Bahrain has appeared to follow the example of Saudi Arabia in refusing a move towards diplomatic relations until a comprehensive Middle East peace settlement, including a solution to the problem of the status of Jerusalem, is achieved. Bahrain, unlike Qatar and Oman, declined to send a representative to the funeral of Israeli Prime Minister Itzhak Rabin, assassinated in November 1995. Allegations in late 1999 of secret diplomatic and commercial contacts between the Bahraini Government and Israel were promptly denied by Manama. In early 2000 Crown Prince Salman held semi-official talks with former Israeli Prime Minister Shimon Peres during the World Economic Forum summit in Davos, Switzerland. After widespread criticism in the Arab press, on this occasion the Bahraini Government made it clear that the meeting was contingent on progress in the Middle East peace process.

In December 1995, with some reluctance, Bahrain agreed to a request from the USA to allow the temporary stationing of US military aircraft in Bahrain. In March 1996 an agreement was reached with the USA to supply Bahrain with an advanced frigate and air defence system. The USA condemned Iran for interfering in Bahrain's internal affairs, and in June, after the Bahraini authorities denounced an alleged Iranian-backed plot to destabilize the archipelago, Bahrain made public US President Bill Clinton's assurances to the Amir that the USA pledged its 'total support to his Government, his sovereignty and the security of Bahraini territories'. However, in early 1998 a US Department of State review of human rights was extremely critical of Bahrain's record. Relations deteriorated further in February when Bahrain opposed any military intervention in Iraq and advocated a diplomatic solution to the impasse between weapons inspectors of the UN Special Commission (UNSCOM) and the Iraqi authorities. In March the Bahraini Government agreed to accept a continued US military presence, and in April US forces replaced combat and air support units in Bahrain, in order to strengthen US offensive capabilities; Bahraini forces also participated in naval exercises with both US and British units. Following a meeting of Bahraini and US officials in Washington, DC, in October, the US Secretary of Defense, William Cohen, visited Bahrain in an attempt to promote the purchase of a US anti-ballistic missile system. Although the Bahraini Government supported the US-led military campaign against Iraq in December (the operation was centred in Manama, where the Fifth Fleet has its headquarters), it maintained a low profile and refrained from any public endorsement of the air-strikes.

Following his accession in March 1999, Sheikh Hamad strengthened military co-operation with the USA in an attempt to consolidate his international credentials. In mid-1999, however, it was reported that Bahrain desired both a reduction of the US military presence in Bahrain, particularly the Fifth Fleet, and the closure of the UNSCOM office in Manama. Despite local discontent, a prolonged visit by Cohen in April 2000 confirmed the importance of Bahrain to US regional policy. The renewed Palestinian *intifada* (uprising) against Israel in late 2000 channelled popular opinion in Bahrain against the USA, and riot police intervened to disperse demonstrations outside the US embassy in Manama. In June 2001 US forces in Bahrain were again alerted following the indictment of 13 Saudi Shi'ites by the US Department of Justice for a 1996 bombing launched against US military personnel in the Saudi town of al-Khobar, which is linked to Bahrain by the King Fahd Causeway.

In common with the other GCC states, Bahrain condemned the devastating terrorist attacks on New York and Washington on 11 September 2001, and pledged to co-operate with the USA's attempts to forge an international 'coalition against terror', notably by freezing the financial assets of individuals or organizations allegedly linked to the militant Islamist al-Qa'ida organization of Osama bin Laden, held by the USA to be principally responsible for the attacks. As elsewhere in the region, there was concern that US-led military action should not be directed against any Muslim target in the Middle East. Bahrain joined the US-led military offensive against al-Qa'ida and the fundamentalist Taliban regime in Afghanistan (which began in early October), contributing a frigate for rescue and humanitarian operations. The extent of Bahrain's support for Washington's 'war on terror' won the praise of the US Administration of George W. Bush, which, in November, described Bahrain as a 'major non-NATO ally'; nevertheless, there was subsequent evidence of renewed antipathy towards the USA in some quarters.

In late 2002 and early 2003, as the momentum grew towards a US-led military campaign to oust the regime of Saddam Hussain in Iraq, the second phase of the USA's 'war on terror', anti-war riots broke out with increasing frequency in Bahrain. However, Bahrain announced that it would contribute a frigate and an unspecified number of troops to the defence of Kuwait from possible Iraqi retaliation should the military campaign proceed. In March the Bahraini Government lent its support to an appeal by the UAE for Saddam Hussain to go into exile in order to save his country from the consequences of the US pursuit of 'regime change', and offered him asylum in Bahrain. Following the commencement of US-led military action in Iraq, in April the Government ordered the expulsion from Manama of an Iraqi diplomat who was alleged to be linked to an explosion outside the Fifth Fleet base. In the aftermath of the conflict Bahrain moved rapidly to build strong ties with the US-installed Iraqi Governing Council, while pressing for the restoration of Iraq's sovereignty and a more consistent role for the UN. King Hamad's participation at a summit meeting of the Group of Eight (G8) leading industrialized nations in June on Sea Island, Georgia, USA, at the invitation of President Bush, was intended to become a showcase for the Government's reform efforts and a platform to promote Bahrain as a model for democratization in the Arab world. In the same month six Bahrainis suspected of having links to al-Qa'ida were arrested in Manama.

Although the occupation of Iraq remained highly unpopular with Bahrainis, relations with the USA were strengthened in the economic sphere from 2004. Negotiations launched in January of that year regarding a free trade agreement (FTA) were completed in May, and the deal, which was signed in September, was endorsed by the Bahrain parliament in July 2005. After ratification by the US Congress in December, in January 2006 President Bush signed the legislation into law. To comply with conditions that the USA attached to the agreement, Bahrain ended its economic embargo of Israel in October 2005 (while strongly denying that this represented the first step towards the establishment of diplomatic relations with Israel) and enacted legislation in 2006 to extend protection of intellectual property rights. In November 2005 three of the six Bahraini detainees in the US detention camp at Guantánamo Bay, Cuba, were released. A fourth was freed in October 2006, and the two remaining detainees were released in July and August 2007.

Relations with the United Kingdom were somewhat strained by the election in that country, in May 1997, of a new Government, which announced its intention to place greater importance on human rights considerations in its foreign policy dealings, while the activities of the London-based opposition continued to frustrate the Bahraini authorities. In September a British government delegation on a visit to Manama encountered considerable opposition to a decision by the British authorities to grant refugee status to three prominent Bahraini opposition figures. Earlier in September Ali Salman Ahmed, Hamza Ali al-Dayri and Haidar Hasan al-Sitri, each of whom had been sentenced *in absentia* to five years' imprisonment by a Bahraini court in November 1997, were allowed to extend their period of residence in the United Kingdom. Visiting London in April 1999, Bahrain's Minister of Foreign Affairs, Sheikh Muhammad bin Mubarak Al Khalifa, demanded the immediate expulsion of his Government's political opponents from the United Kingdom.

The announcement in July 1999 of a new military co-operation accord between Bahrain and France was widely interpreted as an indication of Bahrain's growing dissatisfaction with the United Kingdom's attitude towards members of the exiled Bahrain opposition. None the less, official sources described the first visit as Amir of Sheikh Hamad to the United Kingdom in November as 'constructive', despite renewed protests from human rights groups. During 2000 bilateral relations improved considerably, particularly after dissidents were allowed to return to Bahrain. A new bilateral agreement on military co-operation was expected to facilitate an increase in joint exercises, as well as the sale to Bahrain of defence systems and equipment produced in the United Kingdom. In July 2001 Bahrain signed a number of bilateral agreements with the United Kingdom. Meanwhile, military agreements with the USA and the United Kingdom apparently mirrored efforts to increase military capability and co-operation in the region, an issue that was discussed during the 21st GCC summit meeting, held in Manama in December 2000. Co-operation with the United Kingdom continued despite the Bahraini Government's criticism of the British ambassador in connection with his alleged contacts with opposition societies in 2004. Amid the tense domestic political climate of March 2005, the British Government officially endorsed the Constitution of 2002 and praised King Hamad for his reformist agenda. In August 2005, however, Bahraini authorities reacted angrily to an opposition seminar held in London, only weeks after King Hamad had met British Prime Minister Tony Blair during a visit to the United Kingdom. In 2006 and 2007 relations remained close, despite British rejection of repeated demands by Bahrain to restrict the activity of Bahraini opposition groups in London. In February 2010 the United Kingdom came under further criticism for its contacts with Bahraini political societies, following a meeting between the British ambassador to Bahrain, Jamie Bowden, and Al-Wefaq. The meeting was condemned as foreign interference in the political life of Bahrain, and all ambassadors were warned by the Minister of Foreign Affairs to adhere to international conventions. Nevertheless, the United Kingdom remained an influential political ally and business partner. In March Bahrain and the United Kingdom signed their first double-taxation agreement, which included a zero rate of withholding tax on royalties, dividends and interest for non-residents. The new agreement was expected to encourage United Kingdom-based companies to set up subsidiaries in Bahrain.

In May 2004 the member states of the GCC signed a counter-terrorism pact intended to improve regional security co-operation. The accord was hailed as the most important agreement since the foundation of the GCC in 1981. Saudi Arabia did not participate in the 25th GCC summit meeting held in Manama in December 2004 after Bahrain signed an FTA with the USA. The pact allegedly violated GCC tariff policies and Saudi Arabia perceived it as a means of giving the USA trade advantages over GCC member states. Nevertheless, in May 2005 Gulf ministers responsible for finance reportedly decided to allow bilateral commercial accords between individual GCC countries and the USA.

Ministers from the GCC and the European Union (EU) met in Manama in April 2005 to discuss terrorism and regional security, while relaunching negotiations for a bilateral FTA. Further negotiations concerning the FTA were held in Riyadh, Saudi Arabia, in May 2007, following which it was envisaged that the agreement would soon be concluded. Yet at the end of 2008 talks were suspended owing to disagreements over democracy and human rights, and only resumed in April 2009.

Relations with Iran steadily improved from the end of the 1990s and were consolidated by King Hamad's visit to Tehran in 2002, which was reciprocated by President Khatami in June 2003. Relations suffered in 2005, however, following the publication in the Bahraini daily newspaper *Al-Ayam* of a caricature that was considered to be insulting to Ayatollah Sayed Ali Khamenei. Moreover, many in Bahrain were offended by the display, by some Bahraini citizens, of posters of Iranian religious leaders during Bahrain's own celebrations to mark the festival of Ashoura in February. By mid-2006 Bahrain and Iran had taken steps to repair ties, with reciprocal visits of the two countries' respective ministers responsible for foreign affairs. In May Bahrain's Minister of Foreign Affairs, Sheikh Khalid bin Ahmad Al Khalifa, allegedly rejected the use of any military action against Iran over its nuclear programme, while urging Iran to abide by international treaties.

Tensions between Iran and Bahrain increased in 2007, when long-standing suspicions about the perceived Iranian influence over Bahraini Shi'ites and concerns about Iran's nuclear programme emerged in the press. In July an editorial in an Iranian state-owned newspaper described Bahrain as 'a province of Iran', while in early November two British newspapers reported that Crown Prince Salman had stated in interviews that Iran was developing a nuclear bomb—a claim denied by Iran. Bahrain's Minister of Foreign Affairs, Sheikh Khalid bin Ahmad Al Khalifa, was subsequently reported to have described the Crown Prince's comments as 'distorted'. Despite these incidents, parliament and public opinion proved persuasive in ensuring that the Bahraini Government and Iran maintain cordial relations. During the official visit of President Mahmoud Ahmadinejad to Bahrain in November—only the second by an Iranian President since the Islamic Revolution of 1979—the two Governments expressed support for Iran's right to peaceful nuclear technology. Bahrain became an official member of the International Atomic Energy Agency in September 2007, and the Government subsequently drafted a law to allow the use of nuclear energy for peaceful purposes. Iranian and Bahraini officials also signed a co-operation agreement for the gas sector, which included an option for Bahrain to import Iranian gas. The ongoing talks on a gas deal were briefly suspended in February 2009 owing to another disagreement following remarks by a senior Iranian official who referred to Bahrain as the 14th province of Iran. Moreover, an Iranian parliamentarian suggested that, in the event of a referendum, most Bahrainis would choose to be part of Iran. In October 2009 the Bahraini Minister of Oil and Gas, Abd al-Husayn Mirza, indicated Bahrain's intention to resume negotiations. However, by mid-2013 the talks had yet to recommence.

In December 2009 Bahrain hosted a major annual security conference organized by the International Institute for Strategic Studies (IISS) and attended by representatives of Gulf Arab countries, Iran and the permanent members of the UN Security Council. During the conference, Minister of Foreign Affairs Sheikh Khalid bin Ahmad Al Khalifa urged greater involvement of the GCC countries in the negotiations with Iran over its nuclear programme, arguing that their absence was hindering progress.

During 2008 the long-standing alliance between Bahrain and the USA was reinforced by the visits of President Bush in January and of Secretary of State Condoleezza Rice in April, when she met with the foreign ministers of the GCC, Jordan, Egypt and Iraq. King Hamad paid an official visit to the USA in March, during which he signed an agreement on civil nuclear energy co-operation with the US Administration. Responding to US pressure, but wary of domestic opposition, the Bahraini authorities also agreed to open an embassy in Baghdad. In August Salah al-Maliki, a former diplomat to the UN, was appointed as Bahrain's first ambassador to Iraq since the injury of Hassan Ansari during an attempted kidnap in 2005.

At the December 2009 GCC summit, held in Kuwait, Bahrain, Kuwait, Qatar and Saudi Arabia announced an agreement to enter into a monetary union. Bahrain's legislature had ratified the accord in November. The Gulf Monetary Authority, which was due to be established by the end of 2010, was to be the precursor to a joint central bank. The introduction of a single currency was not expected to occur before 2013.

At a time when tension was mounting between the USA and Iran, Bahrain, together with Kuwait, Qatar and the UAE, was reported in February 2010 to have received land-based *Patriot* defence missiles from the USA within the framework of a US military build-up in the region. In late May construction work commenced on a project to expand the US naval base in Bahrain at Juffair, Manama. The base hosts the US Naval Forces Central Command/US Fifth Fleet and is the primary naval base supporting US regional maritime operations in the Arabian Gulf. The US $580m. expansion project, the stated aim of which was to protect US forces and allies in the region, was scheduled to be completed within five years, and included new ports, administrative buildings, barracks, ship-support facilities and a flyover bridge to connect the base to the new port facilities.

Although Bahrain's leaders publicly maintained that they harboured no ill will towards Iran, the online publication of secret US diplomatic cables in late 2010 by the WikiLeaks organization undermined the credibility of those statements. The cables quoted King Hamad as demanding that the USA take 'action' to prevent Iran from developing nuclear weapons. Bahrain's Minister of Foreign Affairs, Sheikh Khalid bin Ahmad Al Khalifa, stated in November that the leaks reflected US officials' 'interpretations', while the Iranian President, Mahmoud Ahmadinejad, declared that the leaks were 'mischief' and did not reflect the real state of bilateral relations. The Iranian Minister of Foreign Affairs, Manouchehr Mottaki, visited Bahrain in early December to attend the Manama Dialogue, an annual Middle East security forum organized by the IISS.

REGIONAL RELATIONS IN 2011–13

The Tunisian and Egyptian uprisings in early 2011 raised questions about the stability of the region's authoritarian regimes. Following the overthrow of the Tunisian President, Zine al-Abidine Ben Ali, the Ministry of Foreign Affairs expressed Bahrain's support for both a return to calm and stability in Tunisia, and the aspirations of the Tunisian people for reform. The removal of the Egyptian President, Muhammad Hosni Mubarak, who supported the Gulf states in their policies of co-operation with Western powers and the containment of Iran, was much more concerning for Bahrain. On 12 February, one day after Mubarak's departure, the Bahraini Ministry of Foreign Affairs issued a statement that offered assurances of support and respect for the hopes and aspirations of the Egyptian people while expressing the confidence of the Government in the ability of the Egyptian army to ensure stability and security.

Bahrain's 'day of rage' on 14 February 2011 was the first sign of post-Egypt unrest in the wealthy Gulf states, and regional dynamics clearly intensified Bahrain's own domestic tensions. The GCC clearly stated its collective interest in guaranteeing the status quo in Bahrain as something essential to Gulf stability. At an emergency meeting held in Manama on 17 February, the GCC ministers responsible for foreign affairs issued a statement supporting the Bahraini Government and warning against 'foreign meddling'. Nevertheless, there was little evidence that outsiders had shaped the political objectives of the Bahraini Shi'ite community. There appeared to be no direct Iranian involvement beyond a rhetorical escalation in Iranian media coverage denouncing moves by Bahrain's Sunni Government against mainly Shi'ite protesters. Moreover, although the Minister of Foreign Affairs stated that there was evidence that Bahraini activists had been trained by Hezbollah, the armed Lebanese Shi'ite political group, he failed to share this evidence with the country's Western allies. None the less, diplomatic tensions between Bahrain and Iran did intensify after the dispatch of the Saudi-led PSF to Bahrain, ostensibly to 'guard key economic installations' and strategic sites against foreign sabotage.

The intervention of Saudi-led troops in Bahrain on 14 March 2011 marked the first time that GCC forces had been used to help quell an internal uprising in a member state. The Bahraini Government formally requested armed intervention under the terms of the GCC joint defence agreement signed in December 2000. The agreement stipulated that external aggression against any one of its members—Saudi Arabia, Kuwait, Bahrain, Qatar, Oman and the UAE—would be considered as aggression against the GCC as a whole and would lead to collective military assistance. The PSF was created in 1986, but was disbanded as an integrated military force after proving its ineffectiveness during the 1990 Iraqi invasion of Kuwait. In 2006 Saudi Arabia had proposed that each GCC state designate certain army and police units located in its own territory as part of the PSF under unified command.

The political significance of the PSF deployment was greater than simply helping the BDF, some 12,000 strong and well equipped, to quell a domestic uprising. Invocation of the common defence pact provided a useful means to highlight King Hamad's claim—in remarks widely understood to be referring to Iran—that over the past 20–30 years a 'foreign' government had fomented a plot to destabilize Bahrain, but had now failed. Moreover, the despatch of GCC troops sent a strong political message to actual and potential protesters across the Arab Gulf area that the Al Khalifas were part of a close-knit group of Sunni tribal monarchs, who were prepared to use any means necessary—despite US and EU disapproval—to guarantee the survival of the regional status quo. In a May 2011 interview with the Kuwaiti newspaper *al-Rai*, the head of the BDF, Field Marshal Sheikh Khalid bin Ahmad Al Khalifa, suggested that a permanent PSF base could be established in Bahrain if the GCC member states agreed.

Bahrain's need for military support from Saudi Arabia to suppress the uprising sent ominous signals throughout the region. Saudi Arabia was certainly concerned about the possibility that the Bahraini protests could influence its own Shi'ite citizens in Eastern Province. Moreover, the move marked a new stage in Saudi Arabia's emergence as the key regional policeman. The two main regional powers—Saudi Arabia and Iran—accused each other of using the Arab world's smallest state as an arena for their broader agendas. Saudi Arabia is a key ally, since most of Bahrain's crude petroleum comes from a shared, but Saudi-operated, offshore field, and the causeway to Saudi Arabia is Bahrain's only land link. Saudi Arabia has became even more integral to Bahrain's security following the PSF intervention, since Saudi troops formed the largest component of the Force. On 18 April 2011 the Bahraini Prime Minister, Sheikh Khalifa bin Sulman Al Khalifa, received a high-level reception during a visit to Riyadh. The ties between the ruling families of the two countries were reaffirmed by the marriage of a son of King Hamad to a daughter of King Abdullah ibn Abd al-Aziz Al Sa'ud of Saudi Arabia on 16 June.

Relations with Iran soured during the Bahrain uprising, particularly after the GCC intervention. Bahrain's leaders blamed the Iranian Government for encouraging the uprising of Bahraini Shi'ites, although no clear evidence emerged to support the charges, which were also rejected by the BICI report. Iranian-owned media channels stridently denounced the repressive measures against protesters, and Iran's Supreme Religious Leader, Ayatollah Sayed Ali Khamenei, strongly condemned the deployment of troops; yet at the same time, the Iranian Government denied allegations of interference. Following a statement by the Iranian Minister of Foreign Affairs that Bahrain's rulers and the Gulf states needed to act with 'wisdom and caution', both Bahrain and Iran engaged in the reciprocal expulsions of each other's diplomats.

The entry of GCC troops into Bahrain inflamed sectarian tensions in the Middle East. Sheikh Hasan Nasrallah, the Secretary-General of Hezbollah, strongly condemned the deployment of troops and expressed his support for the Bahraini opposition. Radical Iraqi cleric Muqtada al-Sadr, in turn, urged his followers in Iraq to demonstrate in support of their fellow Shi'ites in Bahrain, and Iraq's Prime Minister Nuri al-Maliki warned that foreign intervention in Bahrain might draw the entire region into a sectarian war.

Against this background of regional turmoil and fears over the growing influence of Iran, the 32nd GCC summit was held in Riyadh in December 2011. During the meeting, King Abdullah urged the formation of a Gulf union with a common foreign and defence policy. The proposal was greeted with scepticism by most GCC member states, which regarded such a move as encouraging greater Saudi influence both in the region and over their own domestic affairs. The Saudi King and some members of the Bahraini Government were among the strongest proponents of such a union. Prior to the Gulf Arab leaders meeting held in Riyadh on 14 May 2012, Sheikh Khalifa argued that the matter of a GCC union had become urgent to ensure security in the region. Nevertheless, Arab Gulf leaders delayed any final decision. It emerged that any political integration was likely to involve Saudi Arabia and Bahrain only, before any merger with other GCC states. Following the summit, the Bahraini media reported increasing speculation that the creation of a Saudi Arabia-Bahrain union might be announced by the end of the year. At the end of the 33rd GCC heads of state summit in Manama in November, the Council approved the common internal security pact agreed by GCC ministers a month earlier, which established a single GCC military command. Although this was presented as a move in line with the Gulf union aspiration, the Saudi proposal to create a deeper political union failed to progress.

None the less, maintaining good relations with the other GCC countries remained a priority for Bahrain, as it relies on its regional partners for both security and economic stability. In the short term, Bahrain's economic policy focuses on restoring its reputation as a safe, stable financial hub, a reputation that was severely damaged by the recent political unrest. The currency union between Bahrain, Kuwait, Qatar and Saudi Arabia, which was first proposed in 2010, has been delayed as the member states pursued policy convergence and observed the outcome of the eurozone crisis. Meanwhile, the central bank maintained the Bahraini dinar's peg to the dollar. In March 2011 the GCC announced that it had established a US $20m. bail-out fund to boost development in Bahrain and Oman, the member states with the lowest levels of oil production and the most instability. Both countries would receive $10m. to spend on housing and infrastructure. Saudi Arabia and the UAE have traditionally been the main sources of financial assistance to Bahrain. In February 2013 Bahrain signed a memorandum of understanding with the Abu Dhabi Development Fund, which was to grant Bahrain $2,500m. over the following 10 years to help fund development projects in the kingdom.

Within Bahrain, the proposed unification with Saudi Arabia has further increased tensions. On 18 May 2012 several thousand protesters chanting 'Bahrain is not for sale' stretched for more than five km along a major highway outside Manama in order to denounce the proposal. Shi'ite leaders denounced the plan as a betrayal of the country's independence and an expedient to give Saudi security forces greater powers in repressing anti-Government protests. Al-Wefaq leader Sheikh Ali Salman demanded that the proposal be referred to a referendum.

The Saudi proposal also aggravated tensions with Iran. The Iranian Government responded by increasing its rhetorical support for the Bahrain uprising and resurrected its own claim to Bahrain. In May 2012 *Kayhan*, an Iranian newspaper believed to be close to Ayatollah Ali Khamenei, claimed that most Bahrainis would prefer to be ruled by Iran—a statement promptly refuted by the main Shi'ite group, Al-Wefaq. In Tehran, a government-supported protest decried the proposed union as a conspiracy aimed at the annexation of Bahrain by Iran's main regional rival, Saudi Arabia. The 33rd GCC heads of state summit, held in Manama in November, was intended primarily to condemn Iran's alleged interference in domestic affairs that 'violate the sovereignty and independence of GCC member states', according to the Secretary-General of the GCC, Al-Zayani, in an interview published in *Al-Ayam*. GCC ministers at the Joint Defence Council in Manama explicitly condemned violence by the Bahraini opposition. As part of a GCC effort to re-engage with Iran diplomatically, Bahrain reinstated its ambassador to Tehran in August 2012, 17 months after it had withdrawn the envoy in protest at Iran's strong condemnation of the Gulf-supported suppression of pro-democracy protests. However, bilateral relations remained strained, as Bahrain and the GCC countries perceived the domestic unrest as a result of Iranian interference. In October the Bahraini authorities strongly rejected an Iranian offer to mediate in the kingdom's internal crisis and accused Iran of inciting Bahraini sects against one another, after Iranian officials met Sheikh Isa Qassim, a leading Bahrain Shi'a cleric. The Iranian Government continued to deny taking any role in Bahrain's crisis.

In May 2013 the Iranian authorities stated that they regretted Bahrain's decision to ban the Sunni-ruled kingdom's opposition groups from having contact with Hezbollah, Lebanon's Shi'ite militant movement and close ally of Tehran. Earlier in the month Bahrain's Minister of Foreign Affairs, Sheikh Khalid bin Ahmad Al Khalifa, called the head of Hezbollah a 'terrorist', after its leader Nasrallah declared that his fighters would help bring victory to the Syrian President, Bashar al-Assad, against radical Sunni Islamists. The comment showed the widening sectarian divisions in the region over the war in Syria. Bahrain's rulers blamed the regional Shi'a power, Iran, Hezbollah's main backer, of fomenting the domestic crisis, and projected it as a clash between Shi'a and Sunni—a view largely propagated by Saudi Arabia and the Gulf Emirates.

Relations with Iraq remained tense during 2012, as Muqtada al-Sadr condemned Bahrain for staging the motor-racing Formula 1 Grand Prix while 'blood was being shed', and his followers demonstrated in Basra in support of the Bahraini opposition. In early February the Bahraini Government announced that it would not attend the Arab League summit scheduled to take place in Baghdad in March, in protest at the sympathetic position taken by Iraq towards the protesters, which the Bahraini authorities considered to be an interference in their internal affairs.

Bahrain's relations with Qatar have been uneven during the past few years, owing to disputes over maritime boundaries, as well as to an assertive Qatari foreign policy. In early August 2011 the Bahraini authorities protested to Qatar, after the Qatari government-funded satellite television broadcaster Al Jazeera released a documentary on the Bahrain uprising which highlighted human rights abuses by the regime. Nevertheless, bilateral relations continue to develop as progress on the long-delayed project to build a transport link between Bahrain and Qatar has resumed, owing to an US $350m. loan offered by Qatar to cover Bahrain's share in the project's equity. The contracts to build the 40-km Friendship Bridge were signed in 2008, but the start of work has been delayed, because of presumed Bahraini financial difficulties. It is expected that the causeway will be completed ahead of the football World Cup tournament, which is to be hosted by Qatar in 2022.

OTHER INTERNATIONAL RELATIONS IN 2011–13

Whilst both the USA and the EU expressed concern about the tactics used by the Bahraini Government to suppress internal dissent, the US position has been ambivalent owing to the kingdom's strategic importance. The USA repeatedly emphasized its alliance with Bahrain, and made it clear that the presence of its naval base, which is doubling the area of its onshore facilities near Manama, was a deterrent against an assertive Iranian foreign policy. In mid-April 2011 the US Secretary of Defense, Robert Gates, maintained that the USA did not believe that Iran was behind the protests in any Arab country, but expressed concern that Iran was seeking to exploit the unrest, 'particularly in Bahrain'. Yet, at the same time, the USA criticized the violent response of the Bahraini Government to the protests and encouraged the monarchy to meet some of the demands voiced by the opposition. US President Barack Obama criticized Bahrain's human rights record in a key speech on 19 May, in which he outlined US foreign policy priorities in the Middle East. Obama expressed concern about the detention of opposition leaders and reports of the destruction of Shi'ite mosques. Subsequently, in mid-June the USA included Bahrain on its list of countries to be scrutinized by the UN Human Rights Council (UNHRC); strikingly, Bahrain was the only US ally on that list. Nonetheless, the USA has not downgraded any aspects of its military, economic or diplomatic relationship with Bahrain since the crackdown. On 29 June the USA welcomed King Hamad's announcement of the establishment of an independent international commission of human rights experts to investigate the uprising, and urged all participants in the 'national dialogue' to 'engage constructively in an effort to produce reforms that will respond to the legitimate aspirations of the Bahraini people'. Relations remained cordial despite the arrest and deportation in February 2012 of several members of a US group known as Witness Bahrain, who had entered the country to monitor protests, and the subsequent tightening of visa restrictions on the part of the Bahraini authorities. Only when the hunger strike of al-Khawaja elicited denunciations from the international community did the US Administration issue a statement expressing 'continued concern' for the health of the human rights activist, and urging 'all parties to reject violence'.

In September 2011 the US Department of Defense notified Congress of a proposed sale of US $53m. in armoured vehicles and other equipment to the BDF, as well as the provision of $15m. in military financing for Bahrain. The proposed arms sale deal was suspended, due to concerns from the US Congress over the ongoing domestic repression and the stalled reform process. Nevertheless, the USA failed to link conditions to aid, and on 11 May 2012 the US Administration announced the partial resumption of arms shipments during a visit by Crown Prince Sheikh Salman bin Hamad Al Khalifa, to Washington, DC, where he met US Secretary of State Hillary Clinton. The US Department of State declared that the equipment and services had been released to help Bahrain to maintain its external defence capabilities, and stressed that the deal would not include any items that could be used for internal repression. The Obama Administration's quiet criticism of Bahrain's human rights abuses has been deemed insufficient by human rights activists, who have remarked that Bahrain has been able to maintain strong ties with Western governments without embarking on political reforms or negotiation with the opposition. The USA continued to alternate between declaring support for the democratization process and backing a Government that hosts the US Navy's Fifth Fleet. However, Bahrain's ban on all protests, announced on 30 October, was condemned by the US State Department in unusually strong terms: its spokesman, Mark Toner, urged the Government of Bahrain to uphold its international commitments and ensure that its citizens are able to exercise their rights without fear of arrest or detention. On 19 April the US State Department released its latest human rights report, which detailed harsh repression in Bahrain during 2012, including arbitrary arrests and detention, torture, lack of due judicial process, and a systematic violation of freedom of speech, assembly and association.

Previously harmonious relations with such European partners as France and the United Kingdom were also strained by the Bahraini authorities' violent suppression of the protests. In an effort to repair the damage to Bahrain's international reputation, and to garner international support for the 'national dialogue' process, Crown Prince Salman and other high-level Bahraini delegations visited the USA, the United Kingdom, France and Belgium during the second half of 2011. After the initial condemnation of the shooting of protesters, the two European permanent members of the UN Security Council supported the Crown Prince-led dialogue initiative, reflecting an optimistic hope that dialogue would eventually take place. On 12 December King Hamad met British Prime Minister David Cameron in London, the first such visit since the protests began. The French Government discreetly received the King and continued its co-operation policy with him. In May 2012 the King, together with other world leaders, attended the Diamond

Jubilee celebrations of the British monarch, Queen Elizabeth II, at official invitation which was strongly criticized by human rights campaigners and Bahraini opposition groups. Traditionally, such groups have been fairly sympathetic to the United Kingdom, partly because Bahraini dissidents have taken refuge in London over the years. Nevertheless, they were angered by what they perceived as a limited British response to the repression. Security ties between the two countries were strengthened in October, when the United Kingdom signed a new defence co-operation agreement with Bahrain, and in April 2013 British Defence Attaché Christopher Murray met the Bahraini Minister of State for Defence Affairs, Sheikh Muhammad bin Abdullah Al Khalifa, in Manama to discuss bilateral military co-operation. According to the organization Campaign Against Arms Trade, during 2008–12 the United Kingdom licensed the sale to Bahrain of weapons valued at almost £13m., including more than £4m. of small arms. However, King Hamad's further visits to London, in August 2012 and May 2013, had a much lower profile than previously.

A number of European states have been more outspoken in their criticism of Bahrain's dire human rights record and brutal suppression of protest. Denmark suggested that Europe should consider sanctions against regime members over the detention of al-Khawaja, who holds dual Bahraini and Danish nationality. Moreover, Bahrain rulers have faced strong criticism from several international human rights organizations, including Human Rights Watch and Amnesty International, over their ongoing attacks on Bahraini citizens' human and civil rights.

During 2011 UN representatives expressed cautious criticism of Bahrain's violent actions. When high-profile cases attracted international attention, UN Secretary-General Ban Ki-Moon has condemned the excessive force used by the police, while evincing concern about the violent behaviour of protesters. In a new development, at the UN's Universal Periodic Review (UPR) of human rights, held in Geneva, Switzerland, in May 2012, many European states, including France and Germany, issued vigorous criticism of the Bahraini Government for its abuse of human rights. At the 21st session of the UN Human Rights Council, Michael Posner, US Assistant Secretary of State for Democracy, Human Rights and Labour, welcomed the UPR of Bahrain. However, neither the United Kingdom nor the USA signed the UN Human Rights Council document, which condemned the ongoing abuses of human and civil rights in Bahrain and demanded that the Bahraini authorities make greater efforts to protect civil liberties. In September the UN High Commissioner for Human Rights, Navi Pillay, included Bahrain among the governments accused of undertaking 'reprisals and intimidation' against activists critical of regimes, as well as restricting the activities of NGOs. Perhaps in retaliation for such criticism, in April 2013 the Bahraini authorities postponed indefinitely a visit by the UN Special Rapporteur on Torture, which had been discussed since September 2011. Although such a unilateral decision was unlikely to harm Bahrain's international relations, it raised deep concerns about the prospects of political reconciliation in the country.

Economy

Revised for this edition by RICHARD GERMAN and ELIZABETH TAYLOR

INTRODUCTION

During the 1970s and 1980s the exploitation of Bahrain's hydrocarbon resources was the basis for considerable economic diversification, particularly in the construction, industrial and banking sectors, as a result of which Bahrain became the leading banking and financial centre in the Persian (Arabian) Gulf region. Having encountered some difficulties in the wake of the 1990–91 Gulf crisis, Bahrain regained economic momentum from the late 1990s. Nevertheless, a rapid rate of population growth—particularly in the number of non-Bahraini nationals—has resulted in a persistent problem of unemployment. According to the 2010 census, the total population of Bahrain stood at 1,234,571, representing an almost 90% increase compared with 2001. Bahrainis comprised only 46% of the population. In 2011 the Central Informatics Organization estimated the population at 1,195,000.

Throughout the early 1990s the Government implemented a range of measures designed to attract new investors, including tax concessions, rebates on rent and power charges to small and medium-sized businesses, and a subsidy for every Bahraini national employed. Official procedures were simplified, and full foreign ownership of companies was allowed, provided they were engaged in industrial activities or were establishing a base for the sale of manufactured goods and services in the Gulf region. There was also duty-free access to the wider market of the Cooperation Council for the Arab States of the Gulf (Gulf Cooperation Council, GCC)—of which Bahrain is a member—for Bahrain-based industries whose products met GCC eligibility criteria.

Having encouraged new private industrial investment, Bahrain was forced to consider the expansion of infrastructure to meet rising demand. The Government was reluctant to embark on a major capital spending programme as long as it continued to experience problems in containing the budget deficit. In 1996, however, the Government's financial situation (already benefiting from higher petroleum export prices) was greatly strengthened by Saudi Arabia's decision to allocate its share of that year's output of petroleum from the jointly owned Abu Saafa oilfield to Bahrain (see Petroleum and Gas). By early 1997 the Government had approved a medium-term investment programme totalling more than US $3,000m., including a new port and industrial area, giving rise to expectations of a period of strong growth after several years of relative stagnation. Subsequently, the decline in world petroleum prices resulted in a budget deficit of 3% of gross domestic product (GDP) in 1998, the largest for many years, and some development plans were cancelled or scaled down.

On his accession to power in 1999, the new Amir, Sheikh Hamad bin Isa Al Khalifa (who subsequently became King, in 2002, upon declaring Bahrain a kingdom—see History), declared his intention to continue to promote established lines of economic policy, including the privatization of state assets, while adopting a more interventionist approach to economic decision-making. Bahrain benefited from the sharp upturn in world oil prices in late 1999, which had the effect of reducing the budget deficit and stimulating a resumption of economic growth. In 2000 a Supreme Council for Economic Development was established, under the chairmanship of the Prime Minister; this became the Economic Development Board (EDB) in 2001. Its stated priorities included the privatization of some state-owned industries, and economic diversification. Restructured in 2003, the EDB was given responsibility for attracting inward investment into Bahrain, focusing on six key economic sectors—financial services, downstream hydrocarbon industries, tourism, business services, logistics, and education and training.

A report commissioned by the EDB in 2004 highlighted the unemployment level among a workforce dominated by cheap expatriate labour. In response, in April 2005 the Government approved the creation of a Labour Market Regulatory Authority and a Labour Fund Authority to begin a series of reforms; these included new labour permit levies on expatriate workers, with the objective of moving more Bahraini nationals into private sector employment (although the levies were suspended in 2011). In October 2008 King Hamad launched a new plan for economic diversification, entitled Economic Vision 2030. The document, which was formulated by the

EDB, outlined a series of initiatives aimed at reducing dependency on oil revenues and doubling the level of disposable income held by Bahrainis by 2030. This was to be achieved principally by encouraging further private investment, as well as by reducing subsidies on basic commodities.

Having increased at an average annual rate of 5.8% during 1998–2005, GDP growth reached 6.5% in 2006, according to the IMF. Official figures indicated that the rate of GDP growth increased further, to some 8.4%, in 2007. Despite this buoyant economic performance and rising per caput income, continuing concerns among the local population over unemployment and rising inflation were manifested in civil unrest during December 2007. By March 2008 inflation exceeded 5% (more than double the 2006 average of 2.1%), reflecting excess liquidity in the economy and several reductions in interest rates as Bahrain maintained its currency peg to the weak US dollar. Meanwhile, Bahrain's banking sector was adversely affected by the sharp reduction in availability of credit owing to the global financial crisis that took hold from the second half of 2008, and this began to affect the wider economy. The Central Bank of Bahrain estimated that GDP growth declined to 6.3% in 2008; and there was a further sharp decrease, to just over 3%, in 2009, as a result of global financial conditions and a significant decline in international petroleum prices.

There was an upturn in Bahrain's economic fortunes in 2010, with real GDP growing by 4.1%. In a report published in December, the IMF considered that the near-term outlook was favourable following the increase in petroleum prices and the continuing recovery in the global economy. However, in February 2011, inspired by the popular uprisings that led to the removal of the authoritarian regimes in Tunisia and Egypt, anti-Government demonstrators took to the streets in Manama. The authorities forcibly suppressed the uprising with the backing of security forces from neighbouring GCC countries (see History). Major factors behind the discontent among the majority Shi'ite community included high unemployment, a shortage of housing, and inadequate social benefits for the poor. The Government announced a series of reforms, in an attempt to curb this dissatisfaction, including a one-time grant of BD 1,000 (US $2,660) for families and an increase in some food subsidies (thus adding to the existing subsidy burden), and also revealed plans to build up to 50,000 new homes. In May 2011 parliament approved an expansionary, populist budget for the 2011 and 2012 fiscal years, which was endorsed by King Hamad in June. Nevertheless, the international credit rating agency Moody's Investors Service stated that the unrest and the use of force by the Bahraini authorities (which, despite the ending in June of the state of national safety imposed in March, continued intermittently throughout the rest of the year and into 2012) were likely to damage growth prospects significantly, potentially derailing efforts to diversify the economy.

Bahrain's reputation as a business and investment hub was undermined by the political turmoil, and the IMF sharply reduced its GDP growth estimate for 2011 from 5% to 2.1%. The financial and tourism sectors suffered the most, with banks reporting a deterioration in asset quality, growth and profitability, and tourism data indicating that airport arrivals and hotel occupancy rates had declined. Nevertheless, the oil sector, contributing over 85% of fiscal and external receipts, was largely unaffected, and this cushioned the macroeconomic impact of the unrest.

According to the EDB, GDP growth was expected to reach 3.9% in 2012 (although the IMF projected a higher figure of 4.8%). There was a rise in production across the non-oil economy, and there were indications that bank lending was increasing. The IMF noted that the economic situation had improved in 2012, but that the outlook depended on the restoration of stability on the domestic political front in order to promote investor confidence, and that it was vulnerable to oil price fluctuations. Despite the better-than-expected budget deficit of 2.6% of GDP in 2012 (resulting from higher oil prices, capital spending consolidation and the reduction of gas subsidies for industrial users) and the expected grants from the GCC, the Government needed to cut spending, which had been increased to quell political unrest, or risk an unsustainable level of public debt as the fiscal deficit widened. The IMF proposed a gradual retargeting of subsidies, the containment of public sector wage increases and the further diversification of the economy away from oil. Inflation, meanwhile, averaged 2.8% in 2012, as higher prices for foodstuffs were largely offset by continued depressed rents.

AGRICULTURE

Agriculture has declined rapidly since the 1960s, and by 2011 the sector contributed only 0.3% of GDP. The Bahrain islands are largely barren and have never been able to support farming on more than a limited scale. About three-quarters of the agricultural land in traditional farming areas in the north had been abandoned by the end of the 1970s. By 2011 just 0.6% of the labour force was engaged in agriculture, according to FAO. This reduction in agricultural activity was caused both by the increasing salinity of traditional supplies of water and by the attractions of other sectors of the economy. The value of agricultural output reached BD 20.8m. in 2009. In 2011 there were an estimated 10,000 cattle, 40,000 sheep and 19,000 goats in the country.

PETROLEUM AND GAS

Bahrain's petroleum and gas industries are controlled by the state-owned Bahrain Petroleum Co (BAPCO), created by royal decree in December 1999. The National Oil and Gas Authority (NOGA, which replaced the Supreme Oil Council in 2005) is the regulatory and policy-making body for the sector. A NOGA holding company administers the Government's shares in various energy companies, including BAPCO, the Bahrain National Gas Co (BANAGAS), the Bahrain Aviation Fuelling Co, the Gulf Petrochemical Industries Corpn (GPIC) and Tatweer Petroleum.

At 1 January 2012 Bahrain's proven onshore reserves of petroleum were estimated to be about 120m. barrels, all located in the Awali field. Bahrain also shares production from the Abu Saafa offshore field with Saudi Arabia (with a long-standing entitlement to a 50% share in revenues). Average production of petroleum from the Awali field peaked at 76,639 barrels per day (b/d) in 1970, but has since decreased steadily as reserves have been depleted. To offset this decline and to boost production, BAPCO has undertaken a major expansion programme, with the aim of increasing total output to 100,000 b/d by 2020. In November 2007 it received eight bids from international oil companies for the expansion of the Awali field, and in April 2009 Occidental Petroleum of the USA and the Abu Dhabi-based Mubadala Development Co signed an agreement with the Bahraini Government to create a joint venture company, Tatweer Petroleum, to undertake infrastructure upgrading projects. In March 2007 NOGA had opened a new licensing round for four offshore exploration and production concessions (although one was later withdrawn): in early 2008 Thailand's PTT Exploration and Production was awarded one offshore licence, and Occidental was awarded two. According to the US Energy Information Administration, Bahrain's total oil production was 48,000 b/d in 2012, despite the negative impact of protracted disruption in the Abu Saafa oilfield during that year.

A refinery at Sitra, established in 1936 and therefore the oldest operational refinery in the Gulf, processes all Bahrain's onshore output and supplies the country's domestic requirements. However, most of its crude supply is imported via an underwater pipeline from Saudi Arabia, and the bulk of its output is exported via tanker—chiefly to Asian markets. It was originally operated by BAPCO, owned from 1981 by the Bahraini Government (60%) and Caltex (40%) until 1997, when the Government became the sole owner. The Government thus assumed complete control of Bahrain's oil exports, and became the sole decision-maker on the question of implementing a major refinery modernization programme, which was repeatedly deferred during the 1990s. Eventually, in 1998 the Supreme Oil Council approved a refurbishment and expansion programme for the Sitra refinery, including a 40,000 b/d low sulphur diesel production (LSDP) hydrocracker, intended to reduce the sulphur content in diesel produced by the refinery, and a new, US $120m.–$150m. refinery gas desulphurization unit with a capacity of 45,000 b/d. The LSDP facility was commissioned in 2007, and the gas desulphurization project was completed in 2008. In May 2012 the Minister of

Energy announced that the Government intended to invest up to $8,000m. to further boost refining capacity. Meanwhile, in August 2008 Bahrain Base Oil Co, a joint venture between BAPCO, NOGA and the Finnish company Neste Oil, awarded a contract to Samsung Engineering of the Republic of Korea (South Korea) for the construction of a $430m. lubricant base oil manufacturing plant at Sitra. In March 2013 BAPCO completed studies for a new pipeline from Saudi Arabia, which would be the key element of the wider programme to increase capacity at the Sitra refinery. The total cost of the project was at some $6,000m. Japan's JGC Corpn was awarded the engineering, procurement and construction management contract.

According to BP's *Statistical Review of World Energy 2013*, Bahrain's proven reserves of natural gas were estimated at 200,000m. cu m at the end of 2012, while production totalled 14,200m. cu m in that year. Natural gas comes mainly from the Khuff zone, commercial development of which began in 1969. Bahrain's gas output is consumed locally by power stations, by the Aluminium Bahrain (ALBA) aluminium smelter (see Industry and Manufacturing), by the Sitra oil refinery, and (as feedstock) by the local petrochemicals industry. The 75% state-owned BANAGAS processes gas to produce liquefied products (propane, butane and naphtha) for export, and dry gases (mainly methane and ethane) for local use as industrial fuels. The Governments of Bahrain and Qatar announced the signing of an agreement in May 2005 for the purchase of natural gas by Bahrain. A memorandum of understanding (MoU) regarding the purchase of natural gas was also signed with Iran in November 2007; however, the Bahraini Government suspended the negotiations in February 2009. In October 2010 NOGA signed a gas co-operation agreement with Gazprom of Russia, which could lead to Gazprom exporting natural gas to Bahrain as well as engaging in petroleum and gas exploration in the country. Also in 2010 the Bahraini Government announced plans to construct a US $1,000m. liquefied natural gas (LNG) import terminal; in early 2011 BAPCO shortlisted nine companies to become the strategic partner for the project, and the award of the tender was expected in 2013. In December 2010 the USA's Occidental Petroleum was awarded a contract for deep gas exploration at Awali, and a further exploration agreement was announced in March 2012.

INDUSTRY AND MANUFACTURING

In the mid-1990s government efforts were concentrated on encouraging private foreign investment in the industrial sector to achieve greater diversification and to promote more export-orientated industries. Investment was sought in downstream industries related to aluminium and pharmaceuticals, as well as in new activities. The Government's Incentive Programme, introduced in 1993, offered a wide range of concessions and incentives to attract foreign investment, and official procedures were greatly simplified.

The aluminium industry remains central to the Government's strategy to expand the country's export-orientated industries. The development of the industry began in 1968 with the incorporation of ALBA, a government-led consortium (currently including the Bahrain Mumtalakat Holding Company, together with Saudi Arabia's SABIC Industrial Investments and Breton Investments of Germany). Production at the ALBA smelter, initially at 120,000 metric tons per year using imported alumina from Australia, began in 1971. Following a significant expansion of capacity between 1992 and 1997, the plant could produce more than 500,000 tons a year. A fifth potline was commissioned in 2005, raising annual production capacity to 860,000 tons. ALBA's plans for further expansion have been hindered by concerns regarding the company's ability to secure new gas supplies from overseas, but the 2010 gas agreement with Gazprom (see Petroleum and Gas, above) is expected to provide the necessary feedstock through a new LNG terminal scheduled to open by 2015. In June 2012 ALBA appointed the BNP Paribas banking group to assess the financing requirements for a sixth potline.

Several major secondary enterprises related to aluminium exist in Bahrain. The first downstream venture was Bahrain Atomizer International, established in 1973 with 51% government ownership in association with a German company, which produces atomized aluminium powder. The Bahrain Aluminium Extrusion Co was established under state ownership in 1977 and transferred to the private sector in 1995. It produces aluminium profiles and sections for domestic and foreign markets. Midal Cables was established under private ownership in 1978 to produce aluminium rods and coils. Its subsidiary, Metal Form, was set up in 1994 to produce products from Midal's own aluminium rods. Another subsidiary, Alu-wheel, was established in 1992 to produce semi-finished aluminium wheel hubs for European and US car manufacturers. Gulf Aluminium Rolling Mill Co (GARMCO, established in 1981 under the auspices of the Gulf Organization for Industrial Consulting) had an annual production capacity of 165,000 metric tons in 2005. The company subsequently announced that it would stop using ALBA as its sole supplier of aluminium after 2012 and would source its material from other smelters in the GCC region. In March 2012 GARMCO revealed plans to triple its production capacity to 600,000 tons per year by 2022 and to build the region's largest recycling plant. Bahrain Alloys Manufacturing Co was established by overseas investors in 1994 to produce alloys for the automotive and aerospace industries.

It was announced in 2000 that a consortium of Egon Eertz of Germany and private GCC investors had secured a preliminary licence for a US $47m. joint venture steel mill in the Hidd industrial zone, with an annual capacity of 300,000 metric tons of iron beams and rods for the construction industry. In 2005 the United Stainless Co was established to oversee the construction of a new steel mill at Hidd. The project was to have a production capacity of 90,000 tons per year of cold-rolled stainless steel. In 2005 Germany's RUF-Automobile agreed to form a joint venture with local businessmen to establish a $50m. car manufacturing facility near Bahrain's Formula 1 motor-racing track at Sakhir. In March 2010 Bahrain's Gulf United Steel Holding Co and Japan's Yamato Kogyo announced plans to invest $1,200m. in a joint venture to develop a large integrated steel mill in Bahrain. The contract to execute the project was awarded to Nass Contracting of Bahrain in mid-2011, and operations by the United Steel Company (SULB) were expected to commence by the second half of 2012.

GPIC built a petrochemicals plant at Sitra in 1985 with a capacity of 1,200 metric tons per day each of ammonia and methanol. The complex was a joint venture between the Bahrain National Oil Co, the Saudi Basic Industries Corpn and Kuwait's Petrochemical Industries Corpn. A new plant was commissioned in 1998 to produce urea using ammonia feedstock from the existing GPIC facility.

In 1993 the National Chemical Industries Corpn–majority owned by Bahrain's United Gulf Industries Corpn–signed a contract with United Engineers International of the USA to build a sulphur derivatives plant near the refinery at Sitra. The plant was to produce 18,000 metric tons of sodium sulphite and sodium metabisulphite each year. In 2004 the Bahraini Government reached a preliminary understanding with Kuwait Finance House (KFH) to establish Bahrain's first integrated petrochemicals, power and water complex, at an estimated cost of US $1,500m. Following the successful completion of feasibility studies, KFH received approval to locate the site at Sitra. The plant was to have an annual production capacity of 315,000 tons of ethylene dichloride (EDC), 500,000 tons of caustic soda and 167,000 tons of liquefied petroleum gas (LPG). Offtake agreements were signed with Mitsubishi Corpn of Japan for the plant's EDC output and with BANAGAS for the LPG. The facility was also to produce 30m. gallons of water per day and 1,000 MW of power. KFH was to take a 10% stake in the project.

The Arab Shipbuilding and Repair Yard (ASRY) Co's dry dock, financed by the members of the Organization of Arab Petroleum Exporting Countries, was opened in 1977. In 1992 ASRY invested US $61m. in two floating docks, giving the yard (which originally had a single, 500,000-metric-ton graving dock) increased flexibility, and in 2000 it announced its intention to diversify into higher-value 'niche' markets for specialized services, including the conversion and fitting out of vessels for the offshore oil and gas industry. In 2006 work on the construction of two slipways, each with a length of 255 m and a capacity of up to 15,000 tons, commenced; the slipways became operational in 2008. In that year ASRY repaired 133 vessels, and the company recorded sales of about $207m. In November 2011 an Italian shipbuilder, Rodriquez Cantieri Navalli, signed an MoU with the EDB to construct a new shipyard in the kingdom.

Light industry, including the production of supplementary gas supplies, asphalt, prefabricated buildings, plastics, soft drinks, air-conditioning equipment and paper products, developed during the 1980s. In 1987 Wires International became the first Bahraini company to export an industrial product (aluminium fly mesh) to the Far East. Following the introduction of the Government's Incentive Programme in 1993, two joint ventures were agreed, including a tissue paper mill—a joint venture between Olayan of Saudi Arabia and Kimberly-Clark of the USA—which began production in 1995.

In 1994 Bahrain became the first Gulf state to secure access to European Union (EU) equity investment funds for small and medium-sized industrial joint ventures. Up to 20% of the equity for joint ventures between local and European partners could be provided by the EU, as well as concessionary funding for feasibility studies and human resource development. In 1995 the Government launched a programme to encourage investment in medium-scale industrial projects in order to strengthen economic diversification.

Government infrastructure schemes and private sector investment projects have generated increased activity in the construction sector. The number of construction permits issued increased from 3,844 in 2001 to 11,391 in 2005, before declining to 10,313 in 2009, 10,260 in 2010 and 7,770 in 2011. Permits relating to reclamation work rose from two in 2001 to 53 in 2003, but decreased to nine in 2009 and 12 in 2010. As a result of the political instability in Bahrain in early 2011, some construction work in the private sector was postponed or cancelled. According to the *Middle East Economic Digest*, the total value of projects planned or under way declined from US $80,600m. in March to $66,700m. in April that year.

In 2004 it was announced that the Bahrain World Trade Center, a 50-storey, twin-tower development costing US $150m., would be located in Manama; the building was officially inaugurated in 2008. In 2005 a tender was issued for the contract to build a 47-storey tower called the Blue Pearl in central Manama, and for the $250m. contract to build the three-storey Bahrain City Centre mall in al-Seef district. Meanwhile, in 2002 a French consortium was awarded a contract to manage the North Bahrain New Town project, providing homes for 120,000 residents. Land reclamation work for the project commenced in 2005, following the award of a contract to a consortium comprising two Dutch firms, Royal Boskalis Westminster and Van Oord. Tackling the shortage of housing has remained a key priority for the Government, and the country's first public-private partnership social housing project was tendered in April 2010 to develop 5,000 residential units in al-Buhari (east of Rifa'a), North Bahrain New Town and al-Luzil. The Government awarded the contract to the local Naseej consortium in early 2012. Also in 2012 a $1,000m. technology city was under construction at the Bahrain International Investment Park at Hidd, in a joint venture between the EDB and KFH.

POWER AND WATER

All of Bahrain's electricity generating capacity is derived from conventional thermal sources (mostly natural gas). In 2007 a new Electricity and Water Authority (EWA) was created to take over responsibility for power and water provision in the kingdom (replacing the Ministry of Electricity and Water and its directorates) and to prepare a new strategic plan for the period to 2020 to meet growing consumer demand.

In response to increasing pressure from industry and the impact of rapid population growth on electricity and water supplies, expansion of the sector had commenced in 1991. The steam-fired 120-MW station at Sitra was refurbished, and in 1994 the ALBA aluminium complex's 1,500-MW power plant (raised in 2005 to a 2,200-MW capacity) was linked to the national grid, giving the Ministry of Electricity and Water access to an additional 250 MW of generating capacity for a period of 10 years (until 2003, when the agreement expired). In 1997 the Government signed a US $530m. contract to construct a 280-MW power station and associated desalination plant, with a capacity of 30m. gallons (136,380 cu m) per day, at Hidd. The first of two 140-MW gas turbines was commissioned at Hidd in 1999, and the second in 2000, while four 7.5m.-gallons-per-day desalination units were also installed. In 2001 Alstom Power of France signed a $300m. EPC contract for a major second-phase expansion of the complex, to add between 630 MW and 750 MW of new generating capacity; the expansion was completed in 2004. In 2005 the Government approved the privatization of the Hidd power and desalination complex, as part of a plan to accelerate the sale of the state's existing power generation assets. A privatization agreement for the complex was signed by the Ministry of Finance and a consortium of International Power (United Kingdom), Sumitomo Corpn (Japan) and Suez Energy International (France) in 2006, with the total project being valued at $1,250m. The consortium thus assumed responsibility for a third phase of expansion at the complex, which was completed in March 2009, increasing total desalination capacity at the plant to 90m. gallons per day.

In 2002 the Government announced plans to build the first privately operated power plant—the Al-Ezzal plant—on a site adjacent to Hidd. The contract for the plant was awarded to a joint venture of Belgium's Tractebel and Kuwait's Gulf Investment Corpn in 2004. The plant began commercial operation in 2006, with an initial capacity of 470 MW, and a further 480 MW was added during 2007. In November of that year the Government announced plans for a major new independent power and water desalination plant at Addur, costing US $2,000m. The contract for the project was awarded to a consortium of Gulf Investment Corpn and France's GDF Suez in 2008, and financing for the project was successfully completed in 2009. Although construction was reportedly hampered by the unrest in early 2011, the project was completed later that year. The plant, which began commercial operations in February 2012 and was officially inaugurated in May, had the potential to produce 1,200 MW of electricity and 48m. gallons of fresh water per day, equivalent to about 33% of the kingdom's installed power capacity and 33% of its water needs. In 2012 EWA was evaluating bids for a contract to develop a 15-year master plan for the power and water sectors, including adding 1,500 MW to power capacity by 2015.

In addition to increasing electricity generation, the Government has sought to improve the power transmission and distribution infrastructure. In 2007 the Electricity and Water Authority announced a programme of improvements to the transmission network, including the installation of 51 sub-stations. In June 2009 four contracts valued at US $305m. were awarded for the supply and installation of cables and transformers for the new substations, two to Areva of France for the manufacture and installation of transformers, and one each to South Korea's LS Cable and the Saudi Cable Co.

In 1999 the Gulf Council Interconnection Authority (GCIA) was formed by the GCC to oversee the connection of the national grids of its six member states, the aim being to reduce the cost of power generation. Work on the project began in 2005 and was expected to be completed in three phases. The first stage, connecting the electricity grid of Bahrain with those of Kuwait, Qatar and Saudi Arabia, was completed in July 2009.

Plans for a US $500m. waste-to-energy plant, to be constructed and operated by Constructions Industrielles de la Méditerranée of France, reached commercial close in mid-2010. Contracts were also awarded to South Korea's GS Engineering & Construction in October 2010 for a waste-water project at the Sitra refinery, and to a consortium of South Korea's Samsung Engineering, Invest AD of Abu Dhabi (United Arab Emirates—UAE) and the United Kingdom's United Utilities in early 2011 for a sewage treatment plant and waste-water system in Muharraq.

TRANSPORT AND COMMUNICATIONS

Bahrain International Airport (BIA) was opened in 1971 on Muharraq island, and it has also become the headquarters of the Bahraini carrier Gulf Air. The airline had been co-owned with the Governments of Qatar, Abu Dhabi and Oman until they withdrew their stakes in 2002, 2005 and 2007, respectively; shares were later transferred to Mumtalakat. In January 2008 the airline shelved its plans to float on the stock market to raise funds, having reduced its losses through a company restructuring programme and having secured fresh credit facilities to upgrade its fleet (with an order for new Dreamliner aircraft from the US company Boeing). In 2009, however, the company posted a substantial loss for the year, despite having received extensive government subsidies, prompting demands for an investigation into its finances. In February 2010 Mumtalakat announced that it would transfer its investment in Gulf Air back to the Government, in view of the airline's need for significant financing and because of its strategic importance to the country. Gulf Air subsequently embarked on a new strategic plan, with a capital injection from the Government in October of US $1,000m. The carrier reduced its workforce, took delivery of new Airbus A320s to phase out older models, and added new destinations to its network. In March 2012 it was reported that the Government had again agreed to provide the airline with financial support (of almost $1,800m.) following a decline in visitor numbers to Bahrain in 2011 and the temporary suspension of air services to Iran and Iraq—both important Gulf Air markets—for political and security reasons. The closure of some loss-making routes was announced in January 2013, and the airline was expected to reduce its fleet.

Plans for a US $80m. expansion of facilities at BIA were pursued in 1999–2000, including the construction of a new airport hotel and an aircraft repair and maintenance facility. In 2001 the Department of Civil Aviation Affairs received consultants' proposals for the construction of an additional terminal at BIA. In 2004 work was completed on a new duty-free hall, a multi-storey car park and a shopping mall, while a project for a satellite building, an air traffic control tower and runway upgrades was initiated. The airport handled 105,931 flights, 8.5m. passengers and 256,826 metric tons of cargo in 2012. Construction work on the expansion was scheduled to begin in 2013. Upon completion of the 30-year expansion project, the annual passenger capacity at BIA was expected to reach 13.5m.

The Bahrain Telecommunications Co (BATELCO), in which the Bahraini Government held a 36.6% stake, was formed in 1981 with capital of BD 60m. In 1986 it introduced a cellular telephone system, and the digitization of Bahrain's 120,000-line domestic network was completed in 1992. In 1999 BATELCO embarked on a US $118m. investment programme to increase its mobile telephone capacity to 230,000 lines by the end of 2001 and to upgrade its internet access service. In 2001 a contract was awarded to expand BATELCO's mobile subscriber capacity further to 340,000. At the same time, the Bahraini Government announced that plans were being drawn up to end BATELCO's monopoly in Bahrain's telecommunications sector, which was to be opened up to other (including foreign) companies. A law was enacted in 2002 to liberalize the sector, which became fully competitive in July 2004 when licences for fixed-line and full international services were opened for applications.

From the beginning of 2002 BATELCO reduced its mobile telephone tariffs and registration fees, with the result that by April it had 330,000 mobile subscribers—equivalent to a 50% share of the available market. In 2003 the new independent regulator, the Telecommunications Regulatory Authority (TRA), awarded a licence to operate a second GSM network to MTC Vodafone Bahrain (restyled as Zain Bahrain in 2007), a 60:40 joint venture between Kuwait's Mobile Telecommunications Co (MTC) and the Bahraini Government. BATELCO lost its monopoly for the provision of services to the local market at the end of 2003, and in May 2004 the Bahraini Government appointed HSBC as the financial adviser for the sale of its stake in the company. In March 2004, meanwhile, the TRA awarded an internet service provider licence to Bahrain Internet Exchange and also issued an interconnection order to the two GSM operators. In January 2009 the TRA awarded a third GSM licence to the Saudi Telecommunications Co—Saudi Telecom, which launched its operating company, Viva, in March 2010. In February that year Tata Communications of India signed an agreement with several Middle Eastern telecommunications operators, including Bahrain Internet Exchange, to build a new international submarine cable, providing a direct connection between the Gulf and India.

In August 2010 the TRA instructed the mobile telephone networks to register all prepaid subscribers in Bahrain. Unregistered mobile lines were to be disconnected.

Khalifa Bin Salman Port (KBSP), constructed on 110 ha of reclaimed land in Hidd's industrial area at a cost of some BD 136.3m., was officially inaugurated in late 2009 (operations having begun there in April that year). With a handling capacity of 1.1m. 20-ft equivalent units (TEU), four times greater than that of Mina Salman—to which it is linked by a 5-km causeway—and incorporating container, passenger, general cargo and roll-on, roll-off facilities, it has replaced the latter as Bahrain's principal sea port. Both KBSP and Mina Salman are operated by the multinational APM Terminals (part of A. P. Møller—Mærsk of Denmark), under the supervision of the Ports and Maritime Affairs division of Bahrain's Ministry of Transportation, in accordance with a 25-year concession agreement signed in 2006 with the Government of Bahrain. Bahrain intends that KBSP will become the principal transshipment hub for the northern Gulf region.

The inauguration in 1987 of a causeway between Bahrain and Saudi Arabia led to increased motor traffic in Bahrain, in the light of which the road network was upgraded and traffic management studies were undertaken. Following the completion of a 2.5-km causeway from Manama to Muharraq in 1997, a second causeway, linking Hidd (on Muharraq island) and Manama, opened in 2003. The settlement, in March 2001, of Bahrain's long-standing territorial dispute with Qatar (see History) led the two Governments to accelerate plans to build a 40-km causeway between their countries, at an estimated cost of US $3,000m. The design-and-build contract for the causeway was awarded in 2008 to a consortium of France's Vinci Construction Grands Projets, Germany's Hochtief, Greece-based Consolidated Contractors Co, and Middle East Dredging Co of Qatar. However, the project has been delayed owing to design alterations and financial disputes.

In 2003 the Government appointed a new management team at the Ministry of Public Works to expedite road improvement projects. These included the widening of the Sitra causeway, expansion of arterial roads and flyovers at al-Seef and Wali al-Ahed, a highway link from Manama to Durrat al-Bahrain and an access road to the Amwaj Islands. The consultancy contract for the Sitra causeway and the BD 17.6m. construction contract for the Durrat al-Bahrain highway link were awarded in 2004. In 2005 bids were invited for the construction of bridges linking the various portions of the Durrat al-Bahrain resort and for the consultancy contract on the first phase of the Government's plans for the improvement of roads, particularly of interchanges, in Manama. In 2010 Belgium's Six Construct and the local Haji Hassan won the BD 100m. contract to build the North Manama Causeway and Bridge project, linking Manama, the Bahrain Financial Harbour complex and Muharraq.

The GCC countries have approved plans for an integrated regional railway network by 2017, and work on a new rail link between Bahrain and Saudi Arabia, to complement the existing motorway connection, is scheduled to begin following a feasibility study.

BUDGET, INVESTMENT AND FINANCE

The Bahrain Monetary Agency (BMA) exercised all the powers of a central bank from 1975 until the establishment of the Central Bank of Bahrain in 2006. The BMA oversaw the issuing of currency, regulated exchange control and credit policy, licensed and controlled the banking and financial system, and, from 2002, was responsible for the management and regulation of the insurance sector and capital markets. In 2007 the Central Bank outlined a new regulatory strategy aimed at strengthening the country's financial framework. The new regulations were designed to nurture conditions for high-risk investments by hedge funds and leveraged buyout companies—firms that purchase others either exclusively or predominantly with borrowed funds, with the debt being secured against the assets of that being acquired. In early 2008 it was reported that the Central Bank, in view of the repercussions of the US mortgage crisis, planned to tailor lending rules for local finance houses to reflect their risk exposure, assigning banks individual capital adequacy ratios based on their business model, strength of risk management procedures and investment strategies. In 2009 the Central Bank formalized its liquidity management guidelines for banks, discouraging them from increasing their exposure to property and construction projects, setting a loan-to-deposit ratio requirement, and reducing its reserve requirement ratio. A new corporate governance code, which was intended to improve board management and increase transparency, entered into effect on 1 January 2011. By April 2013 there were 410 licensed financial institutions in the kingdom, including 26 Islamic banks.

As part of its efforts to promote Bahrain as a centre for Islamic banking, the BMA announced in 2000 that capital adequacy requirements would be introduced for Islamic banks, similar to the ratios applicable to conventional banks. The Islamic Credit Company was licensed by the BMA in May 2001 to issue the world's first Islamic finance-compliant credit card. In September of that year the BMA made an inaugural issue of five-year Islamic leasing instruments worth a total of US $100m., with the aim of developing the ability of the Islamic financial community to handle medium- to long-term exposures. In January 2002 the BMA introduced more comprehensive regulations for its Islamic banks, covering capital adequacy ratios, risk management, asset quality, liquidity management and auditing. The world's first International Islamic Financial Market, with a liquidity management centre and Islamic ratings agency, was officially established in Bahrain in August, as a joint venture by the Islamic Development Bank and the monetary authorities of Bahrain, Brunei, Indonesia, Malaysia and Sudan. In 2003 the Liquidity Management Centre launched a $250m. five-year Islamic leasing bond, bringing the total value of such bonds issued to $730m. Also in 2003 the BMA signed an MoU with the London Metal Exchange (LME) to facilitate trading on the LME by Islamic financial institutions, and appointed Citi Islamic Investment Bank (Bahrain) and Citigroup Global Markets to manage its first international $250m. *sukuk* (Islamic leasing) issue. According to the Central Bank, total assets of Islamic banks increased from $1,900m. in 2000 to $26,300m. at the end of the decade. The market share of Islamic banks also increased, from 1.8% of total banking assets in 2000 to 11.1% in June 2009. The Accounting and Auditing Organization for Islamic Financial Institutions is sited in Bahrain, and prepares accounting, governance and Islamic law (*Shari'a*) compliance standards for Islamic financial institutions.

Important investment banks in Bahrain—owned by shareholders in the Gulf, but having most of their earning assets outside the region—include Arab Banking Corpn, Gulf International Bank and Ahli United Bank. In 2002 there was a sharp decline in the assets of banks operating in Bahrain, to US $73,996m. (from $102,700m. in 2001). According to the BMA, this was caused by a $30,000m. decline in the consolidated balance sheet of offshore banking units (OBUs) following the withdrawal of Citibank's assets from Bahrain as a precautionary measure against political uncertainties in the Middle East region, and in particular in Iraq. The consolidated balance sheet of the banks recovered to $118,913m. in 2004, and in 2005 to some $140,400m. The BMA granted 30 new banking licences in 2003 (compared with 24 in 2002 and 15 in 2001), and a licence to the Bank of China to establish a representative office in Bahrain—the first such venture in the Middle East by a Chinese bank—in 2004. In 2002, meanwhile, the Government launched the Bahrain Financial Harbour project, intended to revitalize the redundant Manama port area and provide a centre for the 'offshore' financial sector. Gulf Finance House, together with the GCC and local investors, was to own and finance the project, the first phase of which was formally inaugurated in May 2007.

At the end of 2010 banking sector assets stood at US $222,178m. Although Bahrain had avoided some of the worst effects of the global financial crisis and the Central Bank had tightened bank regulations, the investment banks were more seriously affected by uncertainty surrounding debt problems in Dubai, UAE, and a general downturn in property development in the GCC countries. The Central Bank was forced to take control of The International Banking Corpn and Awal Bank (owned by two Saudi conglomerates) after they defaulted on financial obligations. Additionally, significant losses were announced in 2009 by two of the largest Bahrain investment banks—Gulf Finance House and Arcapita Bank—causing concerns about the resilience of the sector generally. Gulf Finance House, which narrowly escaped defaulting, restructured its debt, and sold its 50% stake in Bahrain Financial Harbour in May 2010. However, Arcapita filed for bankruptcy protection in the USA in March 2012, after the failure of rescheduling negotiations with its creditors. In late 2009 Moody's Investors Service downgraded its credit ratings for the National Bank of Bahrain and BBK (formerly the Bank of Bahrain and Kuwait), having reassessed the Bahraini Government's ability to provide support to the domestic banking sector; and in August 2010 Moody's downgraded Bahrain's sovereign credit rating, amid concerns about the financial sector. In early 2011 Moody's and two other international ratings agencies—Standard & Poor's and Fitch—further downgraded Bahrain's sovereign ratings, in response to the political turmoil in the country and the wider region. None the less, a $1,500m. Eurobond issue by the Government in June 2012 was four times oversubscribed, and was described by the Central Bank as confirmation of continuing global investor confidence in Bahrain. In January 2013 Standard & Poor's upgraded Bahrain's outlook from negative to stable, although its rating remained constrained by continuing domestic political tensions in Bahrain and the fiscal dependency on sustained high oil prices and international donor support.

In June 2012 the Government announced a new two-year development plan for housing, education, health care and infrastructure projects, to be financed with GCC assistance. Over the following months the Kuwait Fund for Arab Economic Development and the Abu Dhabi Fund for Development both offered US $2,500m. in grants on an annual $250m. basis, while the Saudi Fund for Development pledged $448m.

The two-year budget for 2001–02 provided for a deficit of BD 154m. in 2001 and a deficit of BD 160m. in 2002. The two-year budget for 2003–04 was approved by the new legislature in May 2003, and provided for a deficit of BD 262m. in 2003 and a deficit of BD 383m. 2004, based on an average oil price of US $18 per barrel. To finance a number of infrastructure projects, the Government raised a $600m. sovereign loan in 2002, and issued an inaugural $500m. five-year Eurobond (equivalent to 6% of GDP) in 2003. The 2005–06 budget provided for deficits of BD 303m. and BD 208.6m. in 2005 and 2006, respectively. However, owing to significant oil revenues resulting from continued high prices on the international market, an actual budget surplus was recorded for both years. For 2007–08 the Government projected a deficit of BD 194.0m. in 2007 and BD 184.0m. in 2008. The 2009–10 budget provided for large deficits of BD 684.0m. in 2009 and BD 728.8m. in 2010. The increases were attributed principally to the decline in international oil prices and the slowdown in foreign trade as a result of the global financial crisis. In October 2009 parliament ratified a government request for a supplementary budget to increase expenditure by about 8%, in order to cover financing for a range of public projects. Earlier, in June, the Government had successfully issued a $750m. sovereign *sukuk*, and in March 2010 it issued a $1,250m. 10-year bond, which was six times oversubscribed, indicating that the economy had retained the confidence of international financial markets.

The two-year draft budget for the 2011 and 2012 fiscal years projected revenue of BD 4,636m. (BD 2,288m. for 2011 and BD 2,348m. for 2012) and expenditure of BD 6,199m. (BD 3,124m. for 2011 and BD 3,075m. for 2012), with fiscal deficits envisaged in both years. The assumed average oil price of US $80 per barrel was higher than that applied in budget formulations by most of Bahrain's more conservative neighbours, and was considerably greater than the cautious price levels applied in previous budget projections. According to the Ministry of Finance, the Government was implementing a policy of strategic funding in the new budget, which linked financial allocations to key national development priorities.

The budget plan for 2013–14, as approved by parliament in June 2013, provided for revenue of BD 2,788m. in 2013 and BD 2,790m. in 2014, based on an oil price of US $90 per barrel. Expenditure for both years, approved at BD 3,620m. for 2013 (compared with actual spending of BD 3,260m. in 2012) and BD 3,710m. in 2014, was higher than the levels originally proposed by the Ministry of Finance, and notably included provision for increased pension payments and higher subsidies for food and other goods; however, proposals for a 15% increase in public sector salaries, which had been opposed by the Cabinet and which had blocked passage of the budget, were excluded from the approved spending. The budget deficit was estimated at BD 833.2m. for 2013, compared with an out-turn of BD some 227m. in 2012, and BD 914.4m. for 2014. Considerable additional project spending was to take place outside the budget, through GCC assistance (see above).

The Bahrain Stock Exchange (BSE) opened in June 1989, with an initial market capitalization of BD 1,121m. Since the end of 1994 the stock exchanges of Bahrain and Oman have listed each other's shares under a reciprocal agreement. Bahrain and Jordan made similar reciprocal listing arrangements in 1996. Under liberalized rules introduced in 1997, and further amended by decree in 1999, non-GCC investors may hold up to 49% of shares in any listed company provided that they have resided in Bahrain for at least one year or are resident outside Bahrain; GCC nationals may hold up to 100% shares in a company listed on the BSE. The volume of shares traded on the BSE had reached 336.5m. (from 45 listed companies, with a combined value of BD 174.6m.) by 2004, increasing progressively to 458.3m. (47 companies; BD 268.1m. in value) in 2005, 727.6m. (50 companies; BD 522.9m.) in 2006, and 851.1m. (51 companies; BD 403.1m.) in 2007. Despite the global financial crisis, the volume of shares traded increased significantly in 2008, to BD 1,675.8m. (51 companies; BD 787.4m.). However, the volume traded in 2009 decreased sharply, by almost 50%, to BD 852.2m. (49 companies; BD 178.4m.), and declined by a further 28% in 2010. Following a restructuring and a change in its legal status in December of that year, the BSE was renamed the Bahrain Bourse and converted into a closed shareholding company fully owned by the Government and supervised by the Central Bank. Meanwhile, in May 2010 Citigroup, through its Global Transaction Services business, signed a depository agreement with the BSE, enabling the bank to provide custody of BSE-listed securities to institutional investors from September of that year, and thereby helping to broaden the exchange's investor base. The Bahrain Financial Exchange, the first multi-asset class exchange in the Middle East region, was launched in February 2011. The Bourse underperformed compared with all other countries in the GCC in 2012.

Bahrain's first private placement of shares was announced in 2001, following the introduction of a property law permitting non-GCC nationals to acquire limited ownership rights in designated sites in Bahrain. In the same year the National Bank of Bahrain and the TAIB Bank combined to provide direct-access online share-trading services for investors. A decree allowing non-Bahrainis to own property in selected locations was issued in August 2003.

FOREIGN TRADE AND BALANCE OF PAYMENTS

By 2005 foreign trade figures showed a positive trade balance of BD 319.2m., from exports of BD 3,851.0m. and imports of BD 3,531.8m. The oil trade surplus increased to BD 1,359m. and the non-oil deficit to BD 1,143.5m. The current account recorded a surplus of BD 554.3m. Provisional figures for 2006 indicated a trade surplus of BD 663.5m.; exports increased to BD 4,587.2m. and imports to BD 3,953.7m. The oil trade surplus and the non-oil deficit were BD 1,622.8m. and BD 1,109.1m., respectively, and the current account surplus reached BD 822.5m. Oil exports increased to BD 3,465.8m. as a result of the continuing increase in international petroleum prices. Further provisional figures for 2007 recorded a trade surplus of BD 806.8m., from exports of BD 5,126.2m. and imports of BD 4,319.3m., and the current account increased to BD 1,092.9m. According to provisional figures, in 2008 the value of exports increased to BD 7,975.9m., while that of imports increased to BD 6,119.9m. The current account surplus declined to BD 848m. in that year. As a result of the global financial and economic downturn, the surplus decreased further, to BD 210.6m., in 2009, according to provisional data. Exports decreased in value to BD 4,464.5m. (with oil exports at BD 3,351.5m.), while imports declined to BD 3,614.5m. Provisional figures for 2010 put the current account surplus at BD 289.5m. in 2010. Exports in that year were valued at BD 5,131.3m. (including oil exports of BD 3,828.0m.), and imports at BD 4,207.6m. In 2011, according to provisional data, the current account surplus widened to BD 1,220.9m., reflecting higher petroleum earnings, which, at BD 5,824.5m., offset the poorer performance of the services sector. Overall, export earnings stood at BD 7,388.5m., and imports at BD 4,551.8m. In 2012 the current account narrowed to BD 835.4m., according to provisional data. The value of exports reached BD 7,432.8m., including oil exports of BD 5,712.8m., and that of imports BD 4,978.0m.

Bahrain was a signatory of a GCC agreement in 1999 that provided for the creation of a full customs union by 2005, with a common external tariff of 5.5% on basic goods and of 7.5% on luxury items. The Government abolished import duties on foodstuffs and applied a 25% reduction in tariffs on 53 essential commodities with effect from January 2000, and from January 2003 restrictions were removed on all goods and services traded within the GCC. The six GCC member states later announced plans for the creation of a single market and currency by January 2010. The UAE withdrew from the initiative in May 2009 (Oman had backed out in 2006). None the less, an accord on Gulf Monetary Union was signed in June of that year by Bahrain, Kuwait, Qatar and Saudi Arabia, and was formally approved by GCC Supreme Council in December.

In September 2004 Bahrain and the USA signed a free trade agreement abolishing all customs duties (with a few exceptions) on consumer and industrial products. On agricultural products, 98% of trade was to be duty-free, with the remainder of Bahraini tariffs phased out over 10 years. Market access was also to be liberalized in the service sectors, particularly in financial services, telecommunications, health care and construction.

TOURISM

Tourism has been systematically promoted by the Government since 1985, and increasingly from the mid-1990s, as various major projects have been initiated that seek to capitalize on Bahrain's island location in warm waters. Annual visitor numbers reached 8.6m. by 2008, although there was a 19% decline, to 7m., in the following year.

Inaugurated in 1991, the purpose-built Bahrain International Exhibition Centre underwent a major expansion programme in 1998–99. A new International Convention Centre was opened at Bahrain's Gulf Hotel in 1997. In 1999 the local EBH Holdings and India's Oberoi Group announced plans for the development of a luxury hotel and resort, at a cost of US $70m., on the man-made Lulu Island.

In January 2001 the Government announced that it was setting up a holding company, with paid-up capital of BD 100m. (20% to be invested by the Government and the remainder raised through share offers to local and foreign investors), as a vehicle for joint-venture projects to develop tourism facilities on three sites on Bahrain island. As part of its strategy of making Bahrain a centre for international sporting events, the Government also invited bids for the contract to build a US $80m. multi-purpose racetrack complex near Manama, featuring a motor racing circuit, a drag-racing track and permanent seating for up to 62,000 spectators. In 2002 the Government signed a six-year agreement with the Formula 1 authorities for inclusion in the international Grand Prix circuit, starting in 2004. Cybarco was awarded the $100m. contract to build the racetrack (the first in the Middle East), which was completed on schedule for the inaugural Bahrain Formula 1 motor racing Grand Prix in April. In 2005 the Government approved the establishment of a BD 250m. company to acquire the state's stakes in tourism projects, as part of a wider policy to place the private sector at the forefront of economic development.

The confirmation of Bahrain's sovereignty over the Hawar islands in March 2001 accelerated the elaboration of plans by the South Area Development Company for the development of these and adjacent islands for tourism, at a projected total cost of some US $100m. In March 2002 seven international companies submitted bids for the first-phase dredging and reclamation work on the islands, involving the reclamation from the sea of 300,000 sq m of land; it was aimed to create 32 islets and one large new island, on which building plots would be created for sale to private investors—including non-Bahraini nationals.

New tourism projects launched in 2005 included the Asdaf Islands development, consisting of a number of interlinked islands with a commercial district, luxury hotels, residential properties, leisure facilities and marinas. In 2008 KFH announced that it was to develop the Diyar al-Muharraq resort, off the coast of Muharraq, extending over 12m. sq m and including hotels, residential properties, schools, hospitals and marinas. A scheme was also under way to develop the artificially created Amwaj islands (north-east of Muharraq island) as an integrated, self-contained resort complex covering 2.7m. sq m, including hotels, leisure facilities and residential units. The project, to be developed in three phases at a total cost of US $1,000m., was under the control and direction of Bahrain's OSSIS Property Developers. In addition, the Bahraini Government and Gulf Finance House formed a joint venture to establish the Al-Areen Desert Spa and Resort near Sakhir, a project costing $600m. and including themed hotels, a residential village and an aqua park. The first phase of the development ended in 2007.

The civil unrest in early 2011 had a detrimental effect on the tourism sector, and prompted the cancellation, for security reasons, of that year's motor racing Grand Prix. Despite a resurgence in pro-democracy agitation, the 2012 season's Grand Prix was held in April, amid tightened security, and the 2013 event similarly went ahead despite extensive protests (see History).

Statistical Survey

Sources (unless otherwise stated): Central Informatics Organization (formerly Central Statistics Organization), POB 33305, Manama; tel. 17727722; e-mail ciohelpdesk@cio.gov.bh; internet www.cio.gov.bh; Central Bank of Bahrain, POB 27, Bldg 96, Block 317, Rd 1702, Manama; tel. 17547777; fax 17530399; e-mail info@cbb.gov.bh; internet www.cbb.gov.bh; Ministry of Finance, POB 333, Diplomatic Area, Manama; tel. 17575000; fax 17532713; e-mail mofne@batelco.com.bh; internet www.mofne.gov.bh.

Area and Population

AREA, POPULATION AND DENSITY

Area (sq km)	757.5*
Population (census results)	
7 April 2001	650,604
27 April 2010	
Males	768,414
Females	466,157
Total	1,234,571
Bahrainis	568,399
Non-Bahrainis	666,172
Population (official estimate at mid-year)	
2011	1,195,020
Density (per sq km) at mid-2011	1,577.6

* 292.5 sq miles.

POPULATION BY AGE AND SEX
(official estimates at mid-2011)

	Males	Females	Total
0–14	127,890	122,147	250,037
15–64	600,312	317,904	918,216
65 and over	13,281	13,486	26,767
Total	741,483	453,537	1,195,020

REGIONS
(population at 2001 census)

	Area (sq km)	Population	Density (per sq km)
Hidd	17.1	11,637	731.9
Muharraq	39.0	91,939	3,024.3
Manama	31.2	153,395	5,096.2
Jidd Hafs	25.0	52,450	2,098.8
Northern	45.6	43,691	995.2
Sitra	31.0	43,910	1,435.0
Central	35.5	49,969	1,407.6
Isa Town	12.4	36,833	2,963.2
Rifa'a	297.9	79,985	271.1
Western	157.6	26,149	166.1
Hawar	52.1	3,875	74.4
Hamad Town	13.1	52,718	4,018.1
Total*	757.5	650,604	877.5

* Area as at 2008; total population includes 4,053 nationals residing abroad.

PRINCIPAL TOWNS
(at 2001 census)

Manama (capital)	153,395	Hamad Town	52,718
Muharraq	91,939	Jidd Hafs	52,450
Rifa'a	79,985		

Mid-2011 (incl. suburbs, UN estimate): Manama 261,782 (Source: UN, *World Urbanization Prospects: The 2011 Revision*).

BIRTHS, MARRIAGES AND DEATHS

	Registered live births		Registered marriages		Registered deaths	
	Number	Rate (per 1,000)	Number	Rate (per 1,000)	Number	Rate (per 1,000)
2002	13,576	19.1	4,909	7.3	2,035	2.9
2003	14,560	19.0	5,373	7.8	2,114	2.8
2004	14,968	18.2	4,929	7.0	2,215	2.7
2005	15,198	17.1	4,669	6.4	2,222	2.5
2006	15,053	15.7	4,724	6.4	2,317	2.4
2007	16,062	15.4	4,914	4.8	2,270	2.2
2008	17,022	15.4	4,896	4.4	2,390	2.2
2009	n.a.	n.a.	5,067	4.3	2,314	2.0

Registered marriages: 4,960 in 2010.

Life expectancy (years at birth): 75.2 (males 74.5; females 75.8) in 2011 (Source: World Bank, World Development Indicators database).

ECONOMICALLY ACTIVE POPULATION
(persons aged 15 years and over, at 2010 census)

	Males	Females	Total
Agriculture, fishing and animal husbandry	7,479	72	7,551
Mining and quarrying	1,678	58	1,736
Manufacturing	77,137	7,237	84,374
Electricity, gas and water	1,109	60	1,169
Construction	155,042	5,666	160,708
Trade and repairs	95,771	13,723	109,494
Restaurants and hotels	29,318	6,194	35,512
Transport, storage and communications	19,961	4,080	24,041
Banks, insurance and finance	12,330	5,023	17,353
Real estate and business	34,624	6,733	41,357

—continued	Males	Females	Total
Government, defence, social affairs and security	67,824	15,233	83,057
Education	10,710	13,563	24,273
Health	1,427	1,989	3,416
Community, social and personal services	11,723	4,098	15,821
Households with employed persons	24,666	59,737	84,403
Sub-total	550,799	143,466	694,265
Activities not adequately defined	7,145	1,797	8,942
Total employed	557,944	145,263	703,207
Unemployed	2,466	5,557	8,023
Total labour force	560,410	150,820	711,230

Mid-2013 (estimates in '000): Agriculture and animal husbandry 4; Total labour force 682 (Source: FAO).

Health and Welfare

KEY INDICATORS

Total fertility rate (children per woman, 2011)	2.5
Under-5 mortality rate (per 1,000 live births, 2011)	10
HIV/AIDS (% of persons aged 15–49, 2003)	0.2
Physicians (per 1,000 head, 2010)	2.6
Hospital beds (per 1,000 head, 2010)	2.1
Health expenditure (2010): US $ per head (PPP)	937
Health expenditure (2010): % of GDP	4.3
Health expenditure (2010): public (% of total)	71.1
Total carbon dioxide emissions ('000 metric tons, 2009)	24,220.5
Carbon dioxide emissions per head (metric tons, 2009)	20.7
Human Development Index (2012): ranking	48
Human Development Index (2012): value	0.796

For sources and definitions, see explanatory note on p. vi.

Agriculture

PRINCIPAL CROPS
('000 metric tons)

	2009	2010*	2011*
Lettuce	0.7	0.7	0.7
Tomatoes	4.2	3.9	3.8
Onions, dry	0.7	0.7	0.8
Bananas	0.9*	0.9	0.9
Lemons and limes	0.9*	1.1	1.1
Dates	12.9	14.2	14.6

* FAO estimate(s).

Aggregate production ('000 metric tons, may include official, semi-official or estimated data): Total vegetables (incl. melons) 16.3 in 2009, 16.5 in 2010, 18.4 in 2011; Total fruits (excl. melons) 19.1 in 2009, 20.7 in 2010, 21.8 in 2011.

Source: FAO.

LIVESTOCK
('000 head, year ending September)

	2009	2010	2011*
Cattle	7	10*	10
Sheep	41	40†	40
Goats	20	19†	19
Chickens*	525	530	540

* FAO estimate(s).
† Unofficial figure.

Source: FAO.

LIVESTOCK PRODUCTS
('000 metric tons)

	2009	2010*	2011*
Cattle meat	1.0*	1.0	1.0
Sheep meat	14.4*	16.6	16.8
Goat meat	0.2*	0.2	0.2
Chicken meat	6.2	6.3	6.3
Cows' milk	9.0	9.3	9.3

* FAO estimate(s)

Source: FAO.

Fishing

('000 metric tons, live weight)

	2009	2010	2011
Capture	16.4	13.5	9.9
Spangled emperor	0.5	0.3	0.2
Spinefeet (Rabbitfishes)	1.4	1.7	1.1
Blue swimming crab	4.1	3.9	3.0
Green tiger prawn	3.4	4.6	2.5
Aquaculture	0.0	0.0	0.0
Total catch	16.4	13.5	9.9

Source: FAO.

Mining

	2009	2010	2011
Crude petroleum ('000 barrels)*	66,510.0	66,376.0	69,452.0
Natural gas ('000 million cu ft)	543.4	556.6	552.1

* Including a share of production from the Abu Saafa offshore oilfield, shared with Saudi Arabia (54,760,000 barrels in 2009, 54,741,000 barrels in 2010 and 53,936,000 in 2011).

Industry

SELECTED PRODUCTS
('000 barrels unless otherwise indicated)

	2008	2009	2010
Liquefied petroleum gas	1,095	1,132	1,132
Butane	920	907	908
Propane	949	953	990
Naptha	1,699	1,730	1,760
Motor spirit (petrol)	7,300	7,600	7,600
Kerosene and jet fuel	21,557	21,827	21,827
Distillate fuel oil	32,850	32,886	32,886
Residual fuel oil*	15,002	14,856	14,856
Aluminium (unwrought, metric tons)	871,658	847,738	850,700
Electric energy (million kWh)	11,657	12,120	13,757

* Estimates.

2011: Electric energy (million kWh) 13,826.

2012: Electric energy (million kWh) 14,104.

Source: mainly US Geological Survey.

Finance

CURRENCY AND EXCHANGE RATES

Monetary Units

1,000 fils = 1 Bahraini dinar (BD).

Sterling, Dollar and Euro Equivalents (31 May 2013)

£1 sterling = 572 fils;
US $1 = 376 fils;
€1 = 489 fils;
10 Bahraini dinars = £17.48 = $26.60= €20.45.

Average Exchange Rate

Note: This has been fixed at US $1 = 376 fils (BD 1 = $2.6596) since November 1980.

BUDGET

(BD million)

Revenue	2010	2011	2012
Petroleum and gas	1,852.1	1,930.7	2,133.1
Taxation and fees	179.0	238.0	269.2
Government goods and services	52.0	33.6	35.6
Investments and government properties	19.4	12.9	12.2
Grants	28.6	37.6	37.6
Sale of capital assets	0.4	0.4	0.4
Fines, penalties and miscellaneous	44.1	42.1	34.9
Total	2,175.6	2,295.4	2,523.0

Expenditure	2010	2011	2012
Recurrent expenditure	1,868.0	2,585.5	2,666.6
Manpower	868.1	984.6	1,105.1
Services	130.5	138.4	139.8
Consumption	79.7	87.2	89.8
Assets	20.8	20.7	21.5
Maintenance	44.4	51.2	54.0
Transfers	529.4	1,000.2	832.1
Grants and subsidies	195.1	303.2	424.4
Projects	767.4	635.0	885.0
Total	2,635.4	3,220.5	3,551.6

INTERNATIONAL RESERVES

(US $ million at 31 December)

	2009	2010	2011
Gold (national valuation)	6.6	6.6	6.6
IMF special drawing rights	200.0	196.8	196.7
Reserve position in IMF	111.6	109.7	109.3
Foreign exchange (central bank)*	3,533.5	4,782.2	4,238.6
Total*	3,851.8	5,095.2	4,551.1

* Excluding foreign exchange reserves held by government.

2012: IMF special drawing rights 197.6; Reserve position in IMF 109.4.

Source: IMF, *International Financial Statistics*.

MONEY SUPPLY

(BD million at 31 December)

	2009	2010	2011
Currency outside banks	323.0	349.6	402.2
Demand deposits at commercial banks	1,835.3	1,954.3	2,234.7
Total money	2,158.3	2,303.9	2,636.9

2012: Demand deposits at commercial banks 2,189.7.

Source: IMF, *International Financial Statistics*.

COST OF LIVING

(Consumer Price Index; base: 2006 = 100)

	2010	2011	2012
Food and non-alcoholic beverages	132.5	135.5	140.7
Alcoholic beverages and tobacco	117.5	124.5	139.7
Clothing	106.4	108.7	111.0
House-related expenses, water, electricity, gas and other fuels	108.2	94.8	91.7
Goods for home service	113.2	115.4	121.1
Transport	105.7	107.3	111.9
Education	112.7	114.8	116.9
Health	105.9	109.2	110.3
Culture, entertainment and recreation	105.4	112.8	135.9
Communication	94.3	92.3	88.5
Other goods and services	117.5	131.2	135.9
All items	112.1	111.6	114.7

NATIONAL ACCOUNTS

(BD million at current prices)

National Income and Product

	2009	2010	2011*
Compensation of employees	2,547.2	2,785.8	2,958.3
Operating surplus	5,312.5	6,022.5	7,023.3
Domestic factor incomes	7,859.7	8,808.3	9,981.6
Consumption of fixed capital	487.7	540.9	613.4
Gross domestic product (GDP) at factor cost	8,347.4	9,349.2	10,595.0
Indirect taxes, less subsidies	277.4	319.0	305.7
GDP in purchasers' values	8,624.8	9,668.2	10,900.7
Primary income (net)	–902.3	–892.3	–1,415.5
Gross national income	7,722.5	8,775.9	9,485.2
Less Consumption of fixed capital	487.7	540.9	613.4
Net national income	7,234.8	8,235.0	8,871.8
Current transfers (net)	–523.0	–617.3	–770.8
Net national disposable income	6,711.8	7,617.7	8,101.0

* Provisional figures.

Expenditure on the Gross Domestic Product

	2009	2010	2011*
Government final consumption expenditure	1,205.6	1,249.9	1,374.5
Private final consumption expenditure	3,528.4	3,981.7	4,131.7
Gross fixed capital formation	2,178.6	2,518.1	1,938.1
Change in stocks	76.2	120.0	49.4
Total domestic expenditure	6,988.8	7,869.7	7,493.7
Exports of goods and services	5,905.0	6,723.0	8,627.5
Less Imports of goods and services	4,269.1	4,924.5	5,220.5
GDP in purchasers' values	8,624.8	9,668.2	10,900.7
GDP at constant 2010 prices	9,266.3	9,668.2	9,847.8

* Provisional figures.

Gross Domestic Product by Economic Activity

	2009	2010	2011*
Agriculture and fishing	29.1	28.8	31.5
Mining	1,712.7	2,099.8	2,947.9
Petroleum and gas	1,661.4	2,041.5	2,890.5
Manufacturing	1,205.9	1,400.2	1,695.5
Electricity and water	117.2	128.7	137.5
Construction	681.6	719.8	654.0
Transport and communications	551.7	647.1	656.3
Trade	411.3	451.9	447.6
Hotels and restaurants	226.4	260.6	201.7
Real estate and business activities	551.5	598.4	559.7

—continued	2009	2010	2011*
Finance and insurance	1,609.6	1,696.3	1,715.0
Government services	977.6	1,014.3	1,180.2
Education	218.5	232.7	258.3
Health	123.9	127.8	138.5
Other social and personal services	389.7	442.3	499.3
Private non-profit institutions serving households	3.2	3.4	3.9
Households with employed persons	74.0	75.7	78.6
Sub-total	8,541.5	9,567.2	10,808.6
Import duties	83.3	101.0	92.1
GDP in purchasers' values	8,624.8	9,668.2	10,900.7

* Provisional figures.

Note: Totals may not be equal to the sum of components, owing to rounding.

2012 (BD million at current prices, provisional figures): Agriculture and fishing 36.7; Mining and quarrying 2,874.8; Manufacturing 1,735.7; Electricity and water 143.9; Construction 688.9; Trade and repairs 465.8; Hotels and restaurants 277.1; Transport and communications 726.9; Real estate and business activities 580.6; Finance and insurance 1,797.9; Government services 1,299.7; Other social and personal services 583.3; Private non-profit institutions serving households 4.6; Households with employed persons 89.2; *Sub-total* 11,305.1; Import duties 109.1; *GDP in purchasers' values* 11,414.2.

BALANCE OF PAYMENTS
(US $ million)

	2009	2010	2011
Exports of goods	11,873.7	13,647.1	19,650.3
Imports of goods	−9,613.0	−11,190.4	−12,105.9
Balance on goods	2,260.6	2,456.6	7,544.4
Exports of services	3,831.1	4,233.2	3,295.7
Imports of services	−1,741.0	−1,905.1	−1,778.5
Balance on goods and services	4,350.8	4,784.8	9,061.7
Primary income received	1,680.1	1,467.6	6,821.8
Primary income paid	−4,080.0	−3,840.6	−10,586.2
Balance on goods, services and primary income	1,950.9	2,411.8	5,297.3
Secondary income (net)	−1,391.0	−1,641.8	−2,050.0
Current balance	560.0	770.1	3,247.3
Capital account (net)	50.0	50.0	76.1
Direct investment assets	1,791.5	−334.0	−893.6
Direct investment liabilities	257.1	155.8	780.9
Portfolio investment assets	6,710.1	2,051.6	5,164.1
Portfolio investment liabilities	1,565.5	2,704.2	419.1
Other investment assets	18,123.8	2,739.7	17,327.4
Other investment liabilities	−28,926.4	−6,964.8	−26,780.1
Net errors and omissions	−250.0	107.1	71.5
Overall balance	−118.5	1,279.5	−587.3

Source: IMF, *International Financial Statistics*.

External Trade

PRINCIPAL COMMODITIES
(distribution by SITC, US $ million)

Imports f.o.b	2008	2009	2010*
Food and live animals	965.3	879.9	1,010.4
Crude materials, except fuels	1,226.6	818.8	2,375.9
Metalliferous ore and metal scrap	1,076.4	668.6	2,243.6
Mineral fuels, lubricants and related materials	8,166.4	5,384.6	223.7
Petroleum and related materials	8,151.6	5,378.2	215.2
Crude petroleum	7,850.7	5,147.4	0.1
Chemicals and related products	700.2	640.6	682.8
Basic manufactures	2,190.6	1,375.0	1,337.2
Iron and steel	965.7	306.2	373.1
Machinery and transport equipment	4,028.2	3,251.9	3,593.5
Road vehicles	1,461.1	1,099.9	1,158.8
Miscellaneous manufactured articles	881.7	733.3	715.8
Total (incl. others)	18,414.6	13,260.0	10,142.9

Exports (incl. re-exports) f.o.b.	2008	2009	2010*
Food and live animals	263.4	266.0	283.2
Crude materials, except fuels	657.5	280.7	1,239.1
Metalliferous ore and metal scrap	652.4	275.1	1,231.2
Mineral fuels, lubricants and related materials	8,685.8	5,425.8	n.a.
Petroleum and related materials	8,676.9	5,425.4	n.a.
Non-crude petroleum	8,636.2	5,372.4	n.a.
Chemicals and related products	593.1	312.5	111.0
Basic manufactures	2,136.0	1,390.4	2,115.1
Non-ferrous metals	1,494.9	934.8	1,574.4
Machinery and transport equipment	535.9	517.4	539.4
Road vehicles	226.9	194.0	226.9
Miscellaneous manufactured articles	188.8	151.8	215.6
Total (incl. others)	13,083.0	8,365.2	4,554.4

* Full data for petroleum imports and exports were not available.

Source: UN, *International Trade Statistics Yearbook*.

2011 (excluding petroleum, BD million, provisional): Total imports 3,825.5; Total exports 2,295.5; Total re-exports 342.3.

PRINCIPAL TRADING PARTNERS
(excluding petroleum, BD million)

Imports	2009	2010*	2011*
Australia	228.6	234.9	158.7
Brazil	106.9	687.5	473.0
Canada	24.6	18.0	40.3
China, People's Republic	307.6	442.9	514.0
France	74.4	101.7	90.9
Germany	134.1	202.6	188.0
India	96.5	130.1	149.1
Italy	70.5	90.5	117.7
Japan	218.2	283.5	221.5
Korea, Republic	78.2	136.8	10.6
Kuwait	51.2	33.6	34.2
Malaysia	35.9	42.8	39.2
Netherlands	38.1	53.6	49.8
Pakistan	28.1	32.1	33.3
Russian Federation	2.2	0.7	49.8
Saudi Arabia	227.4	181.8	233.7
Spain	26.5	35.1	65.7
Switzerland	58.2	63.0	61.1
Thailand	44.9	47.3	70.1
Turkey	34.3	79.3	55.4
United Arab Emirates	137.9	140.9	217.0
United Kingdom	98.5	142.8	116.1
USA	176.6	269.7	314.1
Total (incl. others)	2,574.1	3,813.9	3,825.8

Exports	2009	2010*	2011*
Algeria	9.6	20.7	22.5
Australia	20.2	30.8	40.8
China, People's Republic	21.5	65.6	98.3
Egypt	23.4	47.2	29.4
France	10.7	19.6	13.9
Germany	6.5	21.3	16.6
India	81.9	210.1	182.4
Indonesia	2.1	18.3	35.1
Italy	16.2	45.0	59.2
Jordan	21.6	16.7	16.9
Kuwait	30.5	38.2	41.3
Malaysia	1.5	16.8	24.7
Morocco	12.1	28.6	36.7
Netherlands	16.0	31.1	50.9
Oman	30.6	71.9	283.9
Peru	3.3	1.6	38.5
Qatar	78.1	235.9	279.5
Saudi Arabia	280.2	361.8	476.7
Syria	15.2	18.6	23.0
Taiwan	1.8	11.8	34.2
United Arab Emirates	101.4	124.9	192.0
USA	75.8	103.9	101.1
Total (incl. others)	1,112.1	1,956.5	2,637.8

* Provisional figures.

Transport

ROAD TRAFFIC
(motor vehicles in use at 31 December, estimates)

	2009	2010	2011
Passenger cars	315,265	328,536	342,218
Buses and coaches	9,460	10,134	10,621
Lorries and vans	55,850	58,622	61,571
Motorcycles and mopeds	6,086	7,136	8,120

SHIPPING

Flag Registered Fleet
(at 31 December)

	2010	2011	2012
Number of vessels	312	321	343
Total displacement ('000 grt)	775.8	781.8	757.7

Source: Lloyd's List Intelligence (www.lloydslistintelligence.com).

International Sea-borne Freight Traffic ('000 metric tons, 1990): *Goods loaded:* Dry cargo 1,145; Petroleum products 12,140. *Goods unloaded:* Dry cargo 3,380; Petroleum products 132 (Source: UN, *Monthly Bulletin of Statistics*).

CIVIL AVIATION
(traffic on scheduled services)

	2007	2008	2009
Kilometres flown (million)	79	100	105
Passengers carried ('000)	4,451	5,643	5,668
Passenger-km (million)	10,505	13,656	13,949
Total ton-km (million)	1,504	1,837	1,849

Source: UN, *Statistical Yearbook*.

2011: Passengers carried ('000) 5,591 (Source: World Bank, World Development Indicators database).

Tourism

FOREIGN VISITOR ARRIVALS BY NATIONALITY
('000)

	2005	2006	2007
India	466.8	590.2	718.4
Kuwait	239.5	298.6	309.3
Philippines	143.6	198.3	225.6
Saudi Arabia	3,864.6	4,225.6	4,366.6
United Kingdom	210.1	245.1	263.7
USA	137.3	168.4	187.2
Total (incl. others)	6,313.2	7,288.7	7,833.6

Receipts from tourism (US $ million, incl. passenger transport, unless otherwise indicated): 1,927 in 2008; 1,873 in 2009; 1,362 in 2010 (excl. passenger transport).

Source: World Tourism Organization.

Communications Media

	2010	2011	2012
Telephones ('000 main lines in use)	228.0	276.5	290.0
Mobile cellular telephones ('000 subscribers)	1,567.0	1,693.6	2,123.9
Internet subscribers ('000)	67.6	183.0	n.a.
Broadband subscribers ('000)	67.6	183.0	173.2

Source: International Telecommunication Union.

Education

(state schools only, 2009/10 unless otherwise indicated)

	Institutions	Teachers	Students
Primary	109	4,788	54,433
Primary/Intermediate	21	1,165	13,429
Intermediate	36	2,141	24,496
Intermediate/Secondary	2	218	2,306
Secondary	30	3,385	29,059
Religious institutes	3	167	1,880
University level*	16	1,240	29,678

* 2005/06 figures.

2012/13 (state schools): *Students:* 63,648 in primary education; 31,921 in intermediate education; 31,167 in secondary education; 2,005 in religious institutes.

Private education (2009/10): *Pre-primary:* 143 schools; 1,084 teachers; 16,593 infants. *Other:* 65 schools; 3,768 teachers; 56,078 students.

Pupil-teacher ratio (primary education, UNESCO estimate): 16.4 in 2001/02 (Source: UNESCO Institute for Statistics).

Adult literacy rate (UNESCO estimates): 91.9% (males 92.8%; females 90.2%) in 2010 (Source: UNESCO Institute for Statistics).

Directory

The Constitution

The 108-article Constitution that came into force on 6 December 1973 stated that 'all citizens shall be equal before the law' and guaranteed freedom of speech, of the press, of conscience and of religious beliefs. Other provisions included compulsory free primary education and free medical care. The Constitution also provided for a National Assembly, composed of 14 members of the Cabinet and 30 members elected by popular vote, although this was dissolved in August 1975. A National Action Charter was approved in a nation-wide referendum held on 14–15 February 2001. (The Charter had been prepared by a Supreme National Committee, created by Amiri decree in late 2000 with the task of outlining the future evolution of Bahrain's political system.) Principal among the Committee's recommendations were that there should be a transition from an emirate to a constitutional monarchy (the Amir proclaimed himself King on 14 February 2002), with a bicameral parliament (comprising a directly elected legislature and an appointed consultative chamber) and an independent judiciary. Bahraini women were to be permitted for the first time to hold public office and to vote in elections. The amended Constitution, promulgated on 14 February 2002, guaranteed the provisions of the National Action Charter. The kingdom's first direct elections to the 40-member Majlis al-Nuab (Council of Representatives) took place on 24 October 2002, and the new Majlis al-Shura (Consultative Council), also comprising 40 members, was appointed by the King on 17 November. Members of both chambers are appointed for terms of four years. Members of the lower house are required to be Bahraini nationals of at least 30 years of age, while those of the appointed chamber—who must also be Bahraini citizens—are to be aged at least 35.

The Government

HEAD OF STATE

King and Supreme Commander of the Bahrain Defence Force: HM Sheikh HAMAD BIN ISA AL KHALIFA (acceded as Amir 6 March 1999; proclaimed King 14 February 2002).

CABINET
(September 2013)

Prime Minister: Sheikh KHALIFA BIN SULMAN AL KHALIFA.

First Deputy Prime Minister: Crown Prince Sheikh SALMAN BIN HAMAD AL KHALIFA.

Deputy Prime Ministers: Sheikh MUHAMMAD BIN MUBARAK AL KHALIFA, Sheikh ALI BIN KHALIFA AL KHALIFA, Sheikh KHALID BIN ABDULLAH AL KHALIFA, JAWAD BIN SALEM AL-ARRAYED.

Minister of Foreign Affairs: Sheikh KHALID BIN AHMAD AL KHALIFA.

Minister of the Interior: Lt-Gen. Sheikh RASHID BIN ABDULLAH BIN AHMAD AL KHALIFA.

Minister of Justice and Islamic Affairs: Sheikh KHALID BIN ALI AL KHALIFA.

Minister of the Royal Court: Sheikh KHALID BIN AHMAD BIN SALMAN AL KHALIFA.

Minister of the Royal Court for Follow-up Affairs: Sheikh AHMAD BIN ATIYATALLAH AL KHALIFA.

Minister of Royal Court Affairs: Sheikh ALI BIN ISA AL KHALIFA.

Minister of Municipal Affairs and Urban Planning: Dr JUMA AL-KA'ABI.

Minister of Energy and Minister of State for Electricity and Water Affairs: Dr ABD AL-HUSSAIN BIN ALI MIRZA.

Minister of Works: ISAM BIN ABDULLAH KHALAF.

Minister of Housing: BASSEM BIN YACOUB AL-HAMER.

Minister of Finance and Minister of Oil and Gas Affairs: Sheikh AHMAD BIN MUHAMMAD AL KHALIFA.

Minister of Culture: SHEIKA MAI BINT MUHAMMAD AL KHALIFA.

Minister of Industry and Commerce: Dr HASSAN BIN ABDULLAH FAKHRO.

Minister of Education: Dr MAJID BIN ALI AL-NO'AIMI.

Minister of Labour: JAMIL HUMAIDAN.

Minister of Social Development: Dr FATIMA MUHAMMAD AL-BLUSHI.

Minister of Health: SADIQ BIN ABD AL-KARIM AL-SHEHABI.

Minister of Transportation: KAMAL BIN AHMAD MUHAMMAD.

Minister of Shura Council and Parliament Affairs: ABD AL-AZIZ BIN MUHAMMAD AL-FADHIL.

Minister of State for Interior Affairs: Maj.-Gen. ADEL BIN KHALIFA AL-FADHUL.

Minister of State for Foreign Affairs: GHANEM FADHUL AL-BUAINAIN.

Minister of State for Human Rights Affairs: SALAH ALI.

Minister of State for Information Affairs: SAMEERA RAJAB.

Minister of State for Defence Affairs: Dr SHEIKH MUHAMMAD BIN ABDULLAH AL KHALIFA.

Minister of State for Follow-up Affairs: MUHAMMAD BIN IBRAHIM AL-MUTAWA.

Minister of State for Telecommunications Affairs: Sheikh FAWAZ BIN MUHAMMAD AL KHALIFA.

MINISTRIES

Royal Court: POB 555, Riffa Palace, Manama; tel. 17666666; fax 17663070.

Prime Minister's Court: POB 1000, Government House, Government Rd, Manama; tel. 17253361; fax 17533033.

Ministry of Culture: POB 253, Manama; tel. 17871111; fax 17682777; e-mail webmaster@info.gov.bh; internet www.moci.gov.bh.

Ministry of Education: POB 43, Manama; tel. 17278727; fax 17273656; e-mail moe@moe.gov.bh; internet www.education.gov.bh.

Ministry of Energy: Manama.

Ministry of Finance: POB 333, Diplomatic Area, Manama; tel. 17575000; fax 17532713; e-mail mofne@batelco.com.bh; internet www.mofne.gov.bh.

Ministry of Foreign Affairs: POB 547, Government House, Government Rd, Manama; tel. 17227555; fax 17212603; e-mail info@mofa.gov.bh; internet www.mofa.gov.bh.

Ministry of Health: POB 12, Bldg 1228, Rd 4025, Juffair 340, Manama; tel. 17288888; fax 17286691; e-mail webmaster@health.gov.bh; internet www.moh.gov.bh.

Ministry of Housing: Manama; tel. 17533000; fax 17534115; internet www.housing.gov.bh.

Ministry of Industry and Commerce: POB 5479, Diplomatic Area, Manama; tel. 17574777; fax 17530151; e-mail info@moic.gov.bh; internet www.moic.gov.bh.

Ministry of the Interior: POB 13, Police Fort Compound, Manama; tel. 17254699; fax 17233482; internet www.interior.gov.bh.

Ministry of Justice and Islamic Affairs: POB 450, Diplomatic Area, Manama; tel. 175313000; fax 17536343; internet www.moj.gov.bh.

Ministry of Labour: POB 32333, Isa Town; tel. 17873777; fax 17686954; e-mail web.contain@mol.gov.bh.

Ministry of Municipal Affairs and Urban Planning: POB 53, Manama; tel. 17501565; fax 17293694; e-mail helpdesk@mun.gov.bh; internet www.mun.gov.bh.

Ministry of Oil and Gas Affairs: Manama.

Ministry of Social Development: POB 32868, Isa Town; tel. 17873999; fax 17682248; e-mail info@social.gov.bh; internet www.social.gov.bh.

Ministry of Transportation: POB 10325, Diplomatic Area, Manama; tel. 17534534; fax 17534041; internet www.transportation.gov.bh.

Ministry of Works: POB 5, Manama; tel. 17545555; fax 17545608; e-mail info@works.gov.bh; internet www.works.gov.bh.

Legislature

Majlis al-Shura
(Consultative Council)

POB 2991, Manama; tel. 17748888; fax 17714583; e-mail info@shura.bh; internet www.shura.bh.

The new 40-seat Consultative Council was appointed by King Hamad on 25 November 2010.

Chairman: ALI BIN SALEH AL-SALEH.

Majlis al-Nuab
(Council of Representatives)

POB 54040, Manama; tel. 17748444; fax 17748445; e-mail fshehabi@almajlis.gov.bh; internet www.nuwab.gov.bh.

Speaker: KHALIFA BIN AHMAD AL-DHAHRANI.

Election, 23 and 30 October 2010

Groups	Seats
Al-Wefaq National Islamic Society	18
Al-Asala Islamic Society	3
Al-Menbar Islamic Society	2
Independents	17
Total	40

Political Organizations

Political parties are still prohibited in Bahrain. However, several political and civic societies (many of which were previously in exile) are now active in the country, and a number of new groups have been established since 2001. Restrictions on campaigning by political groups were revoked prior to the first elections to the new Majlis al-Nuab (Council of Representatives), held in October 2002. By mid-2009 it was reported that there were 18 political alliances or blocs functioning in Bahrain. Organizations currently represented in the Majlis include:

Al-Asala Islamic Society: Manama; Sunni Islamist; promotes the implementation of strict Salafi principles in society and law; Pres. GHANEM FADHUL AL-BUAINAIN.

Al-Menbar Islamic Society (Islamic National Tribune Society): Bldg 30, Sheikh Salman St, Muharraq; tel. 17324996; fax 17324997; internet www.almenber.bh; Sunni Islamist; political wing of the al-Islah Soc., affiliated with the Muslim Brotherhood; Sec.-Gen. Dr ALI AHMED ABDULLAH.

Al-Wefaq National Islamic Society (Islamic National Accord Association): POB 1553, Manama; tel. 17406020; fax 17406024; e-mail info@alwefaq.org; internet www.alwefaq.org; f. 2001; Shi'a Islamist; mems of the soc. won 18 out of 40 seats in the 2010 elections; Sec.-Gen. SHEIKH ALI SALMAN AHMAD SALMAN.

Other prominent groups include Al-Adala (National Justice Movement—a secular, liberal society established in 2006), Al-Haq (Movement for Liberty and Democracy—a radical breakaway faction of Al-Wefaq, opposed to participation in parliamentary politics), the Islamic Action Society (Shi'a Islamist), Al-Meethaq (liberal, pro-democracy) and Al-Waad (National Democratic Action—secular, left-wing).

Diplomatic Representation

EMBASSIES IN BAHRAIN

Algeria: Villa 1220, Rd 3324, Blk 333, Umm al-Hassam, Manama; tel. 17740659; fax 17740652; e-mail algerian.embassy@gmail.com; Ambassador NADJIB SENOUSSI.

Bangladesh: POB 26718, Bldg 71, Rd 56, Blk 356, al-Qufool, Manama; tel. 17233925; fax 17233683; e-mail bangla@batelco.com.bh; internet www.bdembassy.org.bh; Ambassador MUHAMMAD ALI AKBAR.

Brunei: POB 15700, Bldg 892, Rd 3218, Blk 332, al-Mahooz, Manama; tel. 17720222; fax 17741757; e-mail kbbhhom@batelco.com.bh; Ambassador Haji AHMAD Haji JUMAAT.

China, People's Republic: POB 3150, Bldg 158, Rd 4156, Blk 341, Juffair Ave, Manama; tel. 17723800; fax 17727304; e-mail chinaemb_bh@mfa.gov.cn; internet bh.china-embassy.org; Ambassador LEE CHEN.

Egypt: POB 818, Villa 18, Rd 33, Blk 332, al-Mahooz, Manama; tel. 17720005; fax 17721518; e-mail egyembbh@batelco.com.bh; Ambassador ESSAM SALEH AWAD MUSTAPHA.

France: POB 11134, Bldg 51A, Rd 1901, Blk 319, Diplomatic Area, Manama; tel. 17298660; fax 17298607; e-mail chancellerie.manama-amba@diplomatie.gouv.fr; internet www.ambafrance-bh.org; Ambassador CHRISTIAN TESTOT.

Germany: POB 10306, Bldg 39, Rd 322, Blk 327, Salmaniya Ave, Manama; tel. 17745277; fax 17714314; e-mail info@manama.diplo.de; internet www.manama.diplo.de; Ambassador SABINE TAUFMANN.

India: POB 26106, Bldg 182, Rd 2608, Blk 326, Adliya, Manama; tel. 17712785; fax 17715527; e-mail indemb@batelco.com.bh; internet indianembassybahrain.com; Ambassador Dr MOHAN KUMAR.

Indonesia: Villa 2113, Rd 2432, Blk 324, Juffair, Manama; tel. 17400164; fax 17400267; e-mail indonesia.manama@batelco.com.bh; internet www.kemlu.go.id/manama; Ambassador CHILMAN ARISMAN.

Iran: POB 26365, Bldg 1034, Rd 3221, Blk 332, al-Mahooz, Manama; tel. 17722880; fax 17722101; internet bahrain.mfa.ir; Ambassador (vacant).

Iraq: POB 26477, Bldg 396, Rd 3207, Blk 332, al-Mahooz, Manama; tel. 17741472; fax 17720756; e-mail bhremb@iraqmofamail.com; Ambassador AHMAD NAIF RASHID AL-DULAIMI.

Italy: POB 347, Villa 1554, Rd 5647, Blk 356, Manama; tel. 17252424; fax 17277060; e-mail ambasciata.manama@esteri.it; internet www.ambmanama.esteri.it; Ambassador ALBERTO VECCHI.

Japan: POB 23720, Bldg 55, Blk 327, Salmaniya Ave, Manama; tel. 17716565; fax 17715059; e-mail japan@bh.mofa.go.jp; internet www.bh.emb-japan.go.jp; Ambassador SHIGEKI SUMI.

Jordan: POB 5242, Bldg 43, Rd 1901, Blk 319, Manama; tel. 17291109; fax 17291980; e-mail jordemb@batelco.com.bh; Ambassador MUHAMMED ALI ABD AL-HAMID SIRAJ.

Korea, Republic: POB 20554, Rd 915, Villa 401, Blk 309, Salmaniya, Manama; tel. 17531120; fax 17531140; e-mail koreanembassy.bahrain@gmail.com; internet nma.mofat.go.kr/english; Chargé d'affaires YU JOON-HA.

Kuwait: POB 786, Rd 1703, Blk 317, Manama; tel. 17534040; fax 17536475; e-mail almanama@mofa.gov.kw; Ambassador Sheikh AZZAM MUBARAK AL-SABAH.

Lebanon: POB 32474, Villa 1556, Rd 5647, Blk 356, al-Barhama, al-Salihia, Manama; tel. 17579001; fax 17232535; e-mail lebembassy@gmail.com; Chargé d'affaires a.i. IBRAHIM ELIAS AASAF.

Libya: POB 26015, Villa 787, Rd 3315, Blk 333, Umm al-Hassam, Manama; tel. 17722252; fax 17722911; e-mail libyan_bbb@hotmail.com; Ambassador FAWZI EL-TAHIR AHMAD ABD AL-A'ALI.

Malaysia: POB 18292, Bldg 2305, Rd 2835, Blk 428, al-Seef District, Manama; tel. 17564551; fax 17564552; e-mail malmnama@kln.gov.my; internet www.kln.gov.my/perwakilan/manama; Ambassador Dato' AHMAD SHAHIZAN.

Morocco: POB 26229, Villa 2743, Rd 2771, Blk 327, Manama; tel. 17740566; fax 17740178; e-mail sifamana@batelco.com; Ambassador AHMAD RASHID KHATTABI.

Oman: POB 26414, Bldg 37, Rd 1901, Blk 319, Diplomatic Area, Manama; tel. 17293663; fax 17293540; e-mail oman@batelco.com.bh; Ambassador Dr SULAIMAN BIN SAUD AL-JABRI.

Pakistan: POB 563, Bldg 35, Rd 1901, Blk 319, Manama; tel. 17244113; fax 17255960; e-mail parepbah@batelco.com.bh; Ambassador JUAHER SALEEM.

Philippines: POB 26681, Villa 939, Rd 3220, Blk 332, al-Mahooz, Manama; tel. 17721234; fax 17720827; e-mail manamape@batelco.com.bh; internet philembassy-bahrain.com; Ambassador CORAZON YAP-BAHJIN.

Qatar: POB 15105, Villa 814, Rd 3315, Blk 333, al-Mahooz, Manama; tel. 17722922; fax 17740662; Ambassador Sheikh ABDULLAH BIN THAMIR AL THANI.

Russia: POB 26612, Villa 877, Rd 3119, Blk 331, Zinj, Manama; tel. 17725222; fax 17725222; fax 17725921; e-mail bahrain@mid.ru; internet www.bahrain.mid.ru; Ambassador VICTOR YU. SMIRNOV.

Saudi Arabia: POB 1085, Bldg 82, Rd 1702, Blk 317, Diplomatic Area, Manama; tel. 17537722; fax 17533261; e-mail bhemb@mofa.gov.sa; internet embassies.mofa.gov.sa/sites/bahrain; Chargé d'affaires a.i. MUHAMMAD IBN ABD AL-RAHMAN AL-BDIWI.

Senegal: Villa 25, Rd 33, Blk 333, Umm-Shoom Ave, al-Mahooz, Manama; tel. 17821060; fax 17721650; e-mail sengemb@batelco.com.bh; Ambassador ABDOU LAHAT SOURANG.

Sudan: POB 5438, Villa 423, Rd 3614, Blk 336, al-Adliya, Manama; tel. 17717959; fax 17710113; e-mail norabousen@hotmail.com; Ambassador ABDULLA AHMED OSMAN.

Syria: POB 11585, Villa 867, Rd 3315, Blk 333, al-Mahooz, Manama; tel. 17722484; fax 17740380; e-mail syremb@batelco.com.bh; Chargé d'affaires a.i. FAYZEH ISKANDAR AHMAD.

Thailand: POB 26475, Villa 132, Rd 66, Blk 360, Zinj, Manama; tel. 17246242; fax 17272714; e-mail thaimnm@mfa.go.th; internet www.thaiembassy.org/manama; Ambassador VICHAI VARASIRIKUL.

Tunisia: POB 26911, Villa 54, Rd 3601, Blk 336, Adliya, Manama; tel. 17714149; fax 17715702; e-mail atmanama@batelco.bh; Ambassador ZINE EL-ABIDINE EL-TERRAS.

Turkey: POB 10821, Suhail Centre, 5th Floor, Bldg 81, Rd 1702, Blk 317, Manama; tel. 17533448; fax 17536557; e-mail turkemb.manama@mfa.gov.tr; internet www.manama.emb.mfa.gov.tr; Ambassador AHMET ÜLKER.

United Arab Emirates: POB 26505, Villa 270, Rd 2510, Blk 325, Manama; tel. 17748333; fax 17717724; e-mail uaeembassybahrain@hotmail.com; Ambassador MUHAMMAD SULTAN SAIF AL-SUWEIDI.

United Kingdom: POB 114, Blk 306, 21 Govt Ave, Manama; tel. 17574100; fax 17574101; e-mail british.embassy@batelco.com.bh; internet ukinbahrain.fco.gov.uk; Ambassador IAIN LINDSAY.

USA: POB 26431, Bldg 979, Rd 3119, Blk 331, Zinj, Manama; tel. 17242700; fax 17270547; e-mail manamaconsular@state.gov; internet bahrain.usembassy.gov; Ambassador THOMAS C. KRAJESKI.

Yemen: POB 26193, Villa 442, Rd 3512, Blk 335, Umm al-Hassam, Manama; tel. 17822110; fax 17822078; e-mail yemenmb@batelco.com.bh; Ambassador (vacant).

Judicial System

Since the termination of British legal jurisdiction in 1971, intensive work has been undertaken on the legislative requirements of Bahrain. All nationalities are subject to the jurisdiction of the Bahraini courts, which guarantee equality before the law irrespective of nationality or creed. The 1974 Decree Law on State Security Measures and the State Security Court were both abolished in February 2001. The adoption of the amended Constitution in 2002 provided for the establishment of an independent judiciary; however, all judges are appointed by royal decree. The Criminal Law is at present contained in various Codes, Ordinances and Regulations; a new Code of Criminal Procedure was introduced in 2002.

Constitutional Court: POB 18380, Manama; tel. 17578181; fax 17224475; e-mail info@constitutional-court.bh; internet www.constitutional-court.org.bh; f. 2002 to undertake review of, and to settle disputes concerning the constitutionality of laws and regulations; consists of seven members appointed by the King; Chair. SALEM MUHAMMAD SALEM AL-KUWARI.

Court of Cassation: f. 1990; serves as the final court of appeal for all civil and criminal cases; Pres. Sheikh KHALIFA BIN RASHID AL KHALIFA.

Civil Law Courts: All civil and commercial cases, including disputes relating to the personal affairs of non-Muslims, are settled in the Civil Law Courts, which comprise the Higher Civil Appeals Court, Higher Civil Court and Lesser Civil Courts.

Criminal Law Courts: Higher Criminal Court, presided over by three judges, rules on felonies; Lower Criminal Courts, presided over by one judge, rule on misdemeanours.

Religious Courts: *Shari'a* Judiciary Courts operate according to Islamic principles of jurisprudence and have jurisdiction in all disputes relating to the personal affairs of Muslims, including marriage contracts and inheritances. They are structured according to the following hierarchy: Higher *Shari'a* Appeals Court, Greater *Shari'a* Court, Lesser *Shari'a* Court; each court has separate Sunni and Shi'a departments.

Supreme Judicial Council: Founded in 2000, and further regulated by law decree in 2002, the Supreme Judicial Council, headed by the King, is made up of the most senior figures from each branch of the judiciary. The Council supervises the performance of the courts and recommends candidates for judicial appointments and promotions.

Attorney-General: Dr ALI BIN FADHUL AL-BUAINAIN.

Religion

At the 2010 census the total population was recorded at 1,234,571, of whom 866,888 were Muslims. According to the census data, Bahraini citizens totalled some 568,399, of whom some 99.8% were Muslims. Of the 666,172 non-Bahrainis resident in the country, 55.0% were classified as adhering to religions other than Islam.

ISLAM

Muslims are divided between the Sunni and Shi'ite sects. The ruling family is Sunni, although the majority of the Bahraini Muslim population are Shi'ite.

CHRISTIANITY

The Anglican Communion

Within the Episcopal Church in Jerusalem and the Middle East, Bahrain forms part of the diocese of Cyprus and the Gulf. There are two Anglican churches in Bahrain: St Christopher's Cathedral in Manama and the Community Church in Awali. The congregations are entirely expatriate. The Dean of St Christopher's Cathedral is the Archdeacon in the Gulf, while the Bishop in Cyprus and the Gulf is resident in Cyprus.

Archdeacon in the Gulf: Very Rev. ALAN HAYDAY, St Christopher's Cathedral, POB 36, al-Mutanabi Ave, Manama; tel. 17253866; fax 17246436; e-mail cathedra@batelco.com.bh; internet www.stchcathedral.org.bh.

Roman Catholic Church

A small number of adherents, mainly expatriates, form part of the Apostolic Vicariate of Northern Arabia.

The Press

DAILIES

Akhbar al-Khaleej (Gulf News): POB 5300, Manama; tel. 17620111; fax 17621566; e-mail editor@aaknews.com; internet www.aaknews.com; f. 1976; Arabic; Chair. and Editor-in-Chief ANWAR ABD AL-RAHMAN; circ. 32,000.

Al-Ayam (The Days): POB 3232, Manama; tel. 17617777; fax 17617111; e-mail alayam@batelco.com.bh; internet www.alayam.com; f. 1989; Arabic; publ. by Al-Ayam Establishment for Press and Publications; Editor-in-Chief ISA AL-SHAIJI; circ. 36,000.

Bahrain Tribune: POB 3232, Manama; tel. 17827111; fax 17827222; e-mail tribune@batelco.com.bh; internet www.bahraintribune.com; f. 1997; English; Editor-in-Chief JALIL OMAR; circ. 13,000.

Gulf Daily News: POB 5300, Manama; tel. 17620222; fax 17622141; e-mail gdn1@batelco.com.bh; internet www.gulf-daily-news.com; f. 1978; English; publ. by Al-Hilal Publishing and Marketing Group; Chair. ANWAR ABD AL-RAHMAN; Editor-in-Chief GEORGE WILLIAMS; circ. 11,000.

Khaleej Times: POB 26707, City Centre Bldg, Suite 403, 4th Floor, Government Ave, Manama; tel. 17213911; fax 17211819; e-mail ktimesbn@batelco.com.bh; internet www.khaleejtimes.com; f. 1978; English; based in Dubai (United Arab Emirates); circ. 72,565.

Al-Meethaq: Manama; tel. 17877777; fax 17784118; f. 2004; Arabic; supports the Govt's reform programme; publ. by Al-Meethaq Media and Publishing House; Editor-in-Chief MUHAMMAD HASSAN AL-SATRI; circ. 35,000.

Al-Wasat: Dar al-Wasat for Publishing and Distribution, POB 31110, Manama; tel. 17596999; fax 17596900; e-mail news@alwasatnews.com; internet www.alwasatnews.com; Editor-in-Chief MANSOOR AL-JAMRI.

Al-Watan: Rifa'a; tel. 17496666; fax 17496667; e-mail malaradi@alwatannews.net; internet www.alwatannews.net; f. 2005; Arabic; Editor-in-Chief YUSSEF AL-BINKHALIL.

WEEKLIES

Al-Adhwaa' (Lights): POB 250, Old Exhibition Rd, Manama; tel. 17290942; fax 17293166; f. 1965; Arabic; publ. by Arab Printing and Publishing House; Chair. RAID MAHMOUD AL-MARDI; Editor-in-Chief MUHAMMAD QASSIM SHIRAWI; circ. 7,000.

The Gulf: POB 224, Manama; tel. 17293131; fax 17293400; e-mail editorial@thegulfonline.com; internet www.thegulfonline.com; f. 2008; English; business and current affairs; publ. by Al-Hilal Publishing and Marketing Group; Editor DIGBY LIDSTONE; circ. 7,500.

Gulf Weekly: POB 5300, Manama; tel. 17293131; fax 17293400; e-mail editor@gulfweekly.com; internet www.gulfweekly.com; f. 2002; English; publ. by Al-Hilal Publishing and Marketing Group; Editor STAN SZECOWKA; circ. 13,000.

Huna al-Bahrain (Here is Bahrain): POB 26005, Isa Town; tel. 17870166; fax 17686600; e-mail bahrainmag@info.gov.bh; internet www.moci.gov.bh/en/PressandPublications/; f. 1957; Arabic; publ. by the Ministry of Culture; Editor ABD AL-QADER AQIL; circ. 3,000.

Al-Mawakif (Attitudes): POB 1083, Manama; tel. 17231231; fax 17271720; e-mail mwmradhi@batelco.com.bh; f. 1973; Arabic; general interest; Editor-in-Chief MANSOOR M. RADHI; circ. 6,000.

Oil and Gas News: POB 224, Bldg 149, Exhibition Ave, Manama; tel. 17293131; fax 17293400; e-mail editor@oilandgasnewsworldwide.com; internet www.oilandgasnewsworldwide.com; f. 1983; English; publ. by Al-Hilal Publishing and Marketing Group; Editor-in-Chief CLIVE JACQUES; circ. 5,000.

Sada al-Usbou (Weekly Echo): POB 549, Manama; tel. 17291234; fax 17290507; f. 1969; Arabic; Owner and Editor-in-Chief ALI ABDULLAH SAYYAR; circ. 40,000 (in various Gulf states).

OTHER PERIODICALS

Arab Agriculture: POB 10131, Bahrain Tower, 8th Floor, Manama; tel. 17213900; fax 17211765; e-mail fanar@batelco.com.bh; f. 1984; annually; English and Arabic; publ. by Fanar Publishing WLL; Editor-in-Chief ABD AL-WAHED ALWANI; circ. 13,000.

Arab World Agribusiness: POB 10131, Bahrain Tower, 8th Floor, Manama; tel. 17213900; fax 17211765; e-mail fanar@batelco.com.bh; internet www.fanarpublishing.com; f. 1985; 9 per year; English and Arabic; publ. by Fanar Publishing WLL; Editor-in-Chief ABD AL-WAHED ALWANI; circ. 18,000.

Bahrain Telegraph: POB 55055, Manama; tel. 17530535; fax 17530353; e-mail info@bahraintelegraph.com; internet www.bahraintelegraph.com; f. 2009; monthly; English; news, business and politics; Editor-in-Chief SOMAN BABY.

Al-Bahrain ath-Thaqafia: POB 2199, Manama; tel. 17290210; fax 17292678; e-mail zahraam@info.gov.bh; internet www.moc.gov.bh; quarterly; Arabic; publ. by the Ministry of Culture; Editor ABD AL-QADER AQIL.

Bahrain This Month: POB 20461, Manama; tel. 17813777; fax 17813700; e-mail redhouse@batelco.com.bh; internet www.bahrainthismonth.com; f. 1997; monthly; English; publ. by Red House Marketing; Publr and Man. Dir GEORGE F. MIDDLETON; circ. 10,000.

Gulf Construction: POB 224, Exhibition Ave, Manama; tel. 17293131; fax 17293400; e-mail editor@gulfconstructionworldwide.com; internet www.gulfconstructionworldwide.com; f. 1980; monthly; English; publ. by Al-Hilal Publishing and Marketing Group; Editor BINA PRABHU GOVEAS; circ. 26,539.

Gulf Industry: POB 224, Manama; tel. 17293131; fax 17293400; e-mail editor@gulfindustryworldwide.com; internet www.gulfindustryworldwide.com; English; industry and transport; publ. by Al-Hilal Publishing and Marketing Group; Editor SALVADOR ALMEIDA; circ. 10,924.

Al-Hayat at-Tijariya (Commerce Review): POB 248, Manama; tel. 17229555; fax 17224985; e-mail bcci@bcci.bh; monthly; English and Arabic; publ. by Bahrain Chamber of Commerce and Industry; Editor KHALIL YOUSUF; circ. 7,500.

Al-Hidayah (Guidance): POB 450, Manama; tel. 17727100; fax 17729819; f. 1978; monthly; Arabic; publ. by Ministry of Justice and Islamic Affairs; Editor-in-Chief ABD AL-RAHMAN BIN MUHAMMAD RASHID AL KHALIFA; circ. 5,000.

Al-Mohandis (The Engineer): POB 835, Manama; tel. 17727100; fax 17729819; e-mail mohandis@batelco.com.bh; internet www.mohandis.org; f. 1972; quarterly; Arabic and English; publ. by Bahrain Society of Engineers; Editor SHAHRABAN SHARIF.

Al-Musafir al-Arabi (Arab Traveller): POB 10131, Bahrain Tower, 8th Floor, Manama; tel. 17213900; fax 17211765; e-mail fanar@batelco.com.bh; internet www.fanarpublishing.com; f. 1985; 6 per year; Arabic; publ. by Fanar Publishing WLL; Editor-in-Chief ABD AL-WAHED ALWANI; circ. 36,000.

Al-Quwwa (The Force): POB 245, Manama; tel. 17291331; fax 17659596; e-mail dgcdf@gmail.com; internet www.bdf.gov.bh; f. 1977; monthly; Arabic; publ. by Bahrain Defence Force; Editor-in-Chief Maj. AHMAD MAHMOUD AL-SUWAIDI.

Travel and Tourism News Middle East: POB 224, Exhibition Ave, Manama; tel. 17293131; fax 17293400; e-mail editor@ttnworldwide.com; internet www.ttnworldwide.com; f. 1983; monthly; English; travel trade; publ. by Al-Hilal Publishing and Marketing Group; Publishing Dir KIM THOMPSON; circ. 12,370.

Woman This Month: POB 20461, Manama; tel. 17813777; fax 17813700; e-mail editor@womanthismonth.com; internet www.womanthismonth.com; f. 2003; English; monthly; publ. by Red House Marketing; Editor KIRSTY EDWARDS-HARRIS; Publr and Man. Dir GEORGE F. MIDDLETON.

NEWS AGENCY

Bahrain News Agency (BNA): Information Affairs Authority, POB 5421, Manama; tel. 17871602; fax 17681874; e-mail info@bna.bh; internet www.bna.bh; f. 2001 to cover local and foreign news; replaced Gulf News Agency as national news agency; Dir MUHANNAD SULEIMAN.

PRESS ASSOCIATION

Bahrain Journalists' Association (BJA): 2057, Rd 4156, Block 0341, Juffair, Manama 332; tel. 17811770; e-mail bja@batelco.com.bh; internet www.bja-bh.org; f. 2000; Chair. ISA AL-SHAIJI; Sec.-Gen. JAWAD ABD AL-WAHAB; 250 mems.

Publishers

Arabian Magazines Group: POB 26810, Villa 910, Rd 3316, Opp. Qatar Embassy, Blk 333, Mahooz, Manama; tel. 17822388; fax 17721722; e-mail info@arabianmagazines.com; internet www.arabianmagazines.com; f. 2001; publs include *Bahrain Confidential*, *Areej*, *Gulf Insider*, *Shout Confidential*; CEO NICHOLAS COOKSEY.

Fanar Publishing WLL: POB 10131, Manama; tel. 17213900; fax 17211765; e-mail fanar@batelco.com.bh; internet www.fanarpublishing.com; f. 1985; Editor-in-Chief ABD AL-WAHED ALWANI.

Al-Hilal Publishing and Marketing Group: POB 1100, Manama; tel. 17293131; fax 17293400; e-mail hilalad@tradearabia.net; internet www.alhilalgroup.com; f. 1978; specialist magazines, newspapers and websites of commercial interest, incl. *Gulf Daily News*, *Gulf Weekly*, *Gulf Construction*, *Gulf Industry*, *Travel & Tourism News*, etc.; Man. Dir RONNIE MIDDLETON.

Al-Maseerah Printing & Publishing House Co WLL: POB 5981, Manama; tel. 17258882; fax 17276178; e-mail info@almaseerahprintings.com; internet www.almaseerahprintings.com; f. 1981.

Primedia International BSC: POB 2738, Manama; tel. 17490000; fax 17490001; e-mail info@primediaintl.com; internet www.primedia.com.bh; f. 1977; fmrly Tele-Gulf Directory Publications WLL; publrs of, *inter alia*, annual *Gulf Directory* and *Arab Banking and Finance*, as well as *Bahrain Telephone Directory with Yellow Pages*, *Qatar Telephone Directory with Yellow Pages* and *Banks in Bahrain*; CEO MIKE ORLOV.

Red House Marketing: POB 20461, Manama; tel. 17813777; fax 17813700; e-mail redhouse@batelco.com.bh; internet www.redhousemarketing.com; British-owned; publs include *Bahrain This Month*, *Woman This Month*, *Bahrain Hotel & Restaurant Guide*, maps, tourist guides and various specialist trade publs; Man. Dir and Publr GEORGE F. MIDDLETON.

GOVERNMENT PUBLISHING HOUSE

Directorate of Press and Publications: POB 253, Manama; tel. 17717525; e-mail jamaldawood@hotmail.com; internet www.info.gov.bh/en/PressandPublications; publs include *Official Gazette* and *Huna Al-Bahrayn Magazine*; Dir JAMAL DAWOOD AL-JLAHMA.

Broadcasting and Communications

TELECOMMUNICATIONS

The telecommunications sector in Bahrain was fully opened to private sector competition in 2002. Since liberalization of the sector Bahrain has been at the forefront of the development of new infrastructure and technologies in the region. Several companies provide fixed-line services. Three providers have been awarded mobile telecommunications licences; the third mobile licence was awarded to Saudi Telecom (STC) in January 2009.

Bahrain Telecommunications Co BSC (BATELCO): POB 14, Manama; tel. 17881881; fax 17311120; e-mail batelco@btc.com.bh; internet www.batelco.com.bh; f. 1981; cap. BD 120m.; 100% owned by Govt of Bahrain, financial institutions and public of Bahrain; launched mobile cellular telecommunications service, Sim Sim, in 1999; provides fixed-line and mobile telephone services, broadband internet and data services; Chair. Sheikh HAMAD BIN ABDULLAH BIN MUHAMMAD AL KHALIFA; CEO PETER KALIAROPOULOS.

Nuetel Communications: POB 50960, Amwaj Islands; tel. 16033000; fax 16033001; e-mail info@nue-tel.com; internet www.nue-tel.com; f. 2006; provides fixed-line telephone, broadband internet, internet telephony and data services; CEO MARK NIXON.

2Connect Bahrain WLL: POB 18057, 12th Floor, NBB Tower, Government Ave, Manama; tel. 16500110; fax 16500109; e-mail info@2connectbahrain.com; internet www.2connectbahrain.com; f. 2004; provides fixed-line telephone, broadband internet and data-hosting services; Man. Dir FAHAD SHIRAWI.

VIVA Bahrain: Bldg 15, Blk 428, Seef, Manama; internet www.viva.com.bh; f. 2010; subsidiary of Saudi Telecommunications Co—Saudi Telecom; mobile telephone and broadband internet services; CEO ULAIYAN AL-WETAID.

Zain Bahrain: POB 266, Manama; tel. 36107107; e-mail customercare@bh.zain.com; internet www.bh.zain.com; f. 2003 under the name MTC Vodafone Bahrain; present name adopted 2007; acquired Celtel International (Netherlands) in 2005; 60% owned by Mobile Telecommunications Co (Kuwait), 40% by Bahraini Govt; provides mobile telephone services; Group CEO Dr SAAD AL-BARRAK; CEO (Middle East) MAHMOUD HASHISH; Gen. Man. MUHAMMAD ZAIN AL-ABDEEN.

Regulatory Authority

Telecommunications Regulatory Authority (TRA): POB 10353, Taib Tower, 7th Floor, Diplomatic Area, Manama; tel. 17520000; fax 17532125; e-mail contact@tra.org.bh; internet www.tra.org.bh; f. 2002; Chair. Dr MUHAMMAD AHMAD AL-AMER; Gen. Dir MUHAMMAD HAMAD BUBSHAIT.

BROADCASTING

Radio

Bahrain Radio and Television Corpn: POB 702, Manama; tel. 17871405; fax 17681622; e-mail ceobrtc@batelco.com.bh; internet www.bahraintv.com; f. 1955; state-owned; two 10-kW transmitters;

programmes are in Arabic and English, and include news, drama and discussions; CEO Sheikh RASHID BIN ABD AL-RAHMAN AL KHALIFA.

Radio Bahrain: POB 702, Manama; tel. 17871585; fax 17780911; e-mail info@radiobahrain.fm; internet www.radiobahrain.fm; f. 1977; English-language commercial radio station; Head of Station SALAH KHALID.

Television

Bahrain Radio and Television Corpn: POB 1075, Manama; tel. 17686000; fax 17681544; e-mail ceobrtc@batelco.bh; internet www.bahraintv.com; commenced colour broadcasting in 1973; broadcasts on 5 channels, of which the main Arabic and the main English channel accept advertising; offers a 24-hour Arabic news and documentary channel; covers Bahrain, eastern Saudi Arabia, Qatar and the United Arab Emirates; an Amiri decree in early 1993 established the independence of the Corpn, which was to be controlled by a committee; CEO Sheikh RASHID BIN ABD AL-RAHMAN AL KHALIFA.

Finance

(cap. = capital; res = reserves; dep. = deposits; m. = million; br.(s) = branch(es); amounts in Bahraini dinars unless otherwise stated)

BANKING

Central Bank

Central Bank of Bahrain (CBB): POB 27, Bldg 96, Block 317, Rd 1702, Diplomatic Area, Manama; tel. 17547777; fax 17530399; e-mail info@cbb.gov.bh; internet www.cbb.gov.bh; f. 1973 as Bahrain Monetary Agency; in operation from Jan. 1975; name changed as above Sept. 2006; controls issue of currency, regulates exchange control and credit policy, organization and control of banking and insurance systems, bank credit and stock exchange; cap. 200m., res 276m., dep. 1,156m. (Dec. 2009); Chair. QASSIM MUHAMMAD FAKHRO; Gov. RASHID MUHAMMAD AL-MARAJ.

Locally Incorporated Commercial Banks

Ahli United Bank BSC (AUB): POB 2424, Bldg 2495, Rd 2832, al-Seef District 428, Manama; tel. 17585858; fax 17580549; e-mail info@ahliunited.com; internet www.ahliunited.com; f. 2001 by merger of Al-Ahli Commercial Bank and Commercial Bank of Bahrain; cap. US $1,367m., res $671m., dep. $22,547m. (Dec. 2011); Chair. FAHAD AL-RAJAAN; Group CEO and Man. Dir ADEL EL-LABBAN; 130 brs.

Awal Bank BSC: POB 1735, Manama; tel. 17203333; fax 17203355; e-mail info@awal-bank.com; internet www.awal-bank.com; f. 2004; owned by Saad Group (Saudi Arabia); placed into administration July 2009; cap. US $2,000m., res $72.2m., dep. $4,861.2m. (Dec. 2008); Chair. MAAN A. AL-SANEA; CEO and Dir ALISTAIR MACLEOD (acting).

Bahrain Islamic Bank BSC: POB 5240, Al-Salam Tower, Diplomatic Area, Manama; tel. 17546111; fax 17535808; e-mail info@bisbonline.com; internet www.bisb.com; f. 1979; cap. 93m., res 51m., dep. 723m. (Dec. 2011); Chair. KHALID ABDULLAH AL-BASSAM; CEO MUHAMMAD EBRAHIM MUHAMMAD; 13 brs.

BBK BSC: POB 579, 43 Government Ave, Area 305, Manama; tel. 17223388; fax 17229822; e-mail swar@bbkonline.com; internet www.bbkonline.com; f. 1971 as Bank of Bahrain and Kuwait BSC; name changed as above 2005; cap. 85m., res 123m., dep. 2,218m. (Dec. 2011); Chair. MURAD ALI MURAD; Chief Exec. ABD AL-KARIM AHMAD BUCHEERY; 20 brs.

Future Bank BSC: POB 785, Government Rd, Manama; tel. 17505000; fax 17224402; e-mail info@futurebank.com.bh; internet www.futurebank.com.bh; f. 2004; owned by Ahli United Bank BSC, Bank Melli Iran and Bank Saderat Iran; cap. 83m., res 5m., dep. 372m. (Dec. 2011); Chair. MAHMOUD REZA KHAVARI; CEO and Man. Dir GHOLAM SOURI; 3 brs.

Ithmaar Bank BSC: POB 2820, 10th Floor, Addax Tower, Manama; e-mail info@ithmaarbank.com; internet www.ithmaarbank.com; f. 1984 as Faisal Investment Bank of Bahrain EC, a wholly owned subsidiary of Shamil Bank of Bahrain BSC; acquired by Dar al-Maal al-Islami and assumed name as above in 2003; merged with Shamil Bank of Bahrain in April 2010; cap. US $670m., res. $236m., dep. $2,722m. (Dec 2011); Chair. Prince AMR MUHAMMAD AL-FAISAL; CEO MUHAMMAD ABD AL-RAHMAN BUCHEEREI; 11 brs.

National Bank of Bahrain BSC (NBB): POB 106, Government Ave, Manama; tel. 17228800; fax 17228998; e-mail nbb@nbbonline.com; internet www.nbbonline.com; f. 1957; 49% govt-owned; cap. 85m., res 101m., dep. 2,032m. (Dec. 2011); Chair. FAROUK YOUSUF AL-MOAYYED; CEO and Dir ABD AL-RAZAK A. HASSAN AL-QASSIM; 25 brs.

Al-Salam Bank Bahrain BSC: POB 18282, Bldg 22, Ave 58, al-Seef District, Manama; tel. 17560000; fax 17560003; internet www.alsalambahrain.com; f. 2006; acquired Bahraini Saudi Bank in July 2009; Islamic bank; cap. 149m., res 8m., dep. 597m. (Dec 2011); Chair. MUHAMMAD ALI AL-ABBAR; CEO and Dir YOUSUF ABDULLAH TAQI; 2 brs.

Specialized Financial Institutions

Bahrain Development Bank (BDB): POB 20501, Manama; tel. 17511111; fax 17534005; e-mail info@bdb-bh.com; internet www.bdb-bh.com; f. 1992; invests in manufacturing, agribusiness and services; cap. 50m., res 1m., dep. 50m. (Dec. 2009); Chair. Sheikh MUHAMMAD BIN ISSA BIN MUHAMMAD AL KHALIFA; CEO NEDHAL S. AL-AUJAN.

First Energy Bank BSC: POB 209, Manama; tel. 17100001; fax 17100002; internet www.1stenergybank.com; f. 2008; owned by Gulf Finance House BSC and other Gulf shareholders; Islamic wholesale bank providing investment and advice for energy projects; cap. US $1,000m., res. $4m., dep. $171m. (Dec. 2009); CEO MUHAMMAD SHUKRI GHANEM (acting); Chair. KHADEM ABDULLAH AL-QUBAISI.

'Offshore' Banking Units

Bahrain has been encouraging the establishment of 'offshore' banking units (OBUs) since 1975. An OBU is not permitted to provide local banking services, but is allowed to accept deposits from governments and large financial organizations in the area and make medium-term loans for local and regional capital projects. In late 2006 there were 49 OBUs in operation in Bahrain.

ABC Islamic Bank EC: POB 2808, ABC Tower, Diplomatic Area, Manama; tel. 17543000; fax 17536379; e-mail webmaster@arabbanking.com; internet www.arabbanking.com; f. 1987 as ABC Investment and Services Co (EC); name changed as above in 1998 when converted into Islamic bank; 100% owned by Arab Banking Corpn BSC; cap. US $132m., res $14m. (Dec. 2011), dep. $1,133m. (Dec. 2009); Pres. and Chief Exec. HASSAN ALI JUMA; Chair. SADDEK EL-KABER.

Allied Banking Corpn (Allied Bank); Philippines: POB 20493, Bahrain Tower, 11th Floor, Government Ave, Manama; tel. 17224707; fax 17210506; e-mail ally3540@batelco.com.bh; internet www.alliedbank.com.ph; f. 1980; Chair. DOMINGO T. CHUA; Gen. Man. RAMON R. LANDINGIN.

Alubaf Arab International Bank BSC: POB 11529, Sheraton Tower 13F, Manama; tel. 17517722; fax 17540094; e-mail info@alubafbank.com; internet www.alubafbank.com; f. 1982; 99.5% owned by Libyan Foreign Bank; cap. US $200m., res $26m., dep. $755m. (Dec. 2011); Chair. Dr MUHAMMAD ABDULLAH BAIT ELMAL; CEO HASAN ABULHASAN.

Arab Bank PLC (Jordan): POB 813, Manama; tel. 17549000; fax 17541116; e-mail arabbank@batelco.com.bh; internet www.arabbank.bh; f. 1930; Chair. SABIH AL-MASRI.

Arab Banking Corpn BSC: POB 5698, ABC Tower, Diplomatic Area, Manama; tel. 17543000; fax 17533062; e-mail webmaster@arabbanking.com; internet www.arabbanking.com; f. 1980; cap. US $3,110m., res $332m., dep. $16,615m. (Dec. 2011); Chair. MUHAMMAD HUSAIN LAYAS; Pres. and Chief Exec. HASSAN ALI JUMA.

Arab Investment Co SAA (Saudi Arabia): POB 5559, Bldg 2309, Rd 2830, al-Seef District 428, Manama; tel. 17588888; fax 17588885; e-mail taic@taicobu.com; internet www.taic.com; f. 1974; cap. US $700m., res $141m., dep. $1,184m. (Dec. 2011); Chair. YOUSEF BIN IBRAHIM AL-BASSAM; Gen. Man. NABIL A. AL-SAHAF.

BNP Paribas (France): POB 5253, Bahrain Financial Harbour, West Tower, Manama; tel. 17866223; fax 17866601; e-mail jean-christophe.durand@mideastbnpparibas.com; internet www.bahrain.bnpparibas.com; f. 1975; Regional Man. JEAN-CHRISTOPHE DURAND.

Gulf International Bank BSC (GIB): POB 1017, Al-Duwali Bldg, 3 Palace Ave, Area 317, Manama; tel. 17534000; fax 17522633; e-mail info@gibbah.com; internet www.gibonline.com; f. 1975; cap. US $2,500m., res $246m., dep. $10,069m. (Dec. 2011); Chair. Sheikh JAMMAZ BIN ABDULLAH AL-SUHAIMI; CEO YAHYA AL-YAHYA.

Korea Exchange Bank (Repub. of Korea): POB 5767, Yateem Centre Bldg, 5th Floor, Manama; tel. 17229333; fax 17225327; e-mail bahrain@keb.co.kr; internet www.keb.co.kr; f. 1977; Pres. and CEO YUN YONG-RO.

MCB Bank Ltd (MCB) (Pakistan): POB 10164, Diplomatic Area, Manama; tel. 17533306; fax 17533308; e-mail mcbobubh@batelco.com.bh; internet www.mcb.com.pk; f. 1947 as Muslim Commercial Bank Ltd, name changed as above in 2005; Chair. MUHAMMAD MANSHA.

National Bank of Abu Dhabi (UAE): POB 5886, Manama 304; tel. 17214450; fax 17210086; e-mail Hassan.Bahzad@nbad.com; internet www.nbad.com; f. 1977; Regional Man. HASSAN BEHZAD.

National Bank of Kuwait SAK: POB 5290, Bahrain BMB Centre, Diplomatic Area, Manama; tel. 17532225; fax 17530658; e-mail nbkbah@batelco.com.bh; f. 1977; Gen. Man. ALI Y. FARDAN.

Standard Chartered Bank (United Kingdom): POB 29, Manama; tel. 17223636; fax 17225001; internet www.standardchartered.com/bh; f. 1976; cap. US $1,192m., res $16,355m., dep. $439,780m. (Dec. 2011); CEO HASSAN JARRAR.

State Bank of India: POB 5466, GBCorp Tower, Bahrain Financial Harbour, Manama; tel. 17505177; fax 17224692; e-mail opns.wbbbah@statebank.com; internet www.sbibahrain.com; f. 1977; CEO ASHWINI KUMAR SHUKLA.

Yapi ve Kredi Bankasi AS (Turkey): POB 10615, c/o Bahrain Development Bank, Diplomatic Area, Manama; tel. 17530313; fax 17530311; internet www.yapikredi.com; f. 1982; Chair. TAYFUN BAYAZIT.

Investment Banks

Arcapita Bank BSC: POB 1406, Manama; tel. 17218333; fax 17217555; internet www.arcapita.com; f. 1997; cap. US $311m., res $879m., dep. $1,440m. (June. 2011); Chair. MUHAMMAD ABD AL-AZIZ AL-JOMAIH; CEO ATIF A. ABD AL-MALIK; 1 domestic br., 3 abroad.

Bahrain Middle East Bank BSC (BMB Investment Bank): POB 797, BMB Centre, Diplomatic Area, Manama; tel. 17532345; fax 17530526; e-mail requests@bmb.com.bh; internet www.bmb.com.bh; f. 1982; fmrly Bahrain Middle East Bank EC; cap. US $60m., res $19m., dep. $14m. (Dec. 2011); Chair. WILSON S. BENJAMIN; CEO AKBAR A. HABIB; 1 br.

Al-Baraka Islamic Bank BSC (EC): POB 1882, Diplomatic Area, Manama; tel. 17535300; fax 17533993; e-mail baraka@batelco.com.bh; internet www.barakaonline.com; f. 1984 as Al-Baraka Islamic Investment Bank BSC (EC); current name adopted 1998; owned by Al-Baraka Banking Group BSC; cap. 122m., res 19m., dep. 1,284m. (Dec. 2011); Chair. KHALID RASHID AL-ZAYANI; CEO MUHAMMAD AL-MUTAWEH; 240 brs.

Capital Management House (CMH): POB 1001, Manama; tel. 17540454; fax 17540464; e-mail info@capitalmh.com; internet www.capitalmh.com; f. 2006; cap. US $47.7m.; Islamic investment co licensed with the powers of an investment bank; Chair. KHALID ABDULLAH AL-BASSAM; Man. Dir and CEO KHALID MUHAMMAD NAJIBI.

First Investment Bank: 7th Floor, Euro Tower, al-Seef District, POB 10016, Manama; tel. 17389089; fax 17556621; e-mail info@first-ibank.com; internet www.first-ibank.com; f. 2007; Islamic investment bank; jt venture between 8 Gulf investors; cap. US $200m.; Chair. MUHAMMAD A. AL-ALLOUSH; Dep. CEO YOUSIF AL-THAWADI.

Global Banking Corpn (GBCORP): POB 1486, GBCORP Tower, Bahrain Financial Harbour, Manama; tel. 17200200; fax 17200300; e-mail info@gbcorponline.com; internet www.gbcorponline.com; f. 2007; Islamic investment bank; cap. p.u. US $250m; Chair. SALEH AL-ALI AL-RASHED; Vice-Chair. and Man. Dir ABD AL-RAHMAN MUHAMMAD AL-JASMI.

Gulf Finance House BSC: POB 10006, Bahrain Financial Harbour, Manama; tel. 17538538; fax 17540006; e-mail info@gfh.com; internet www.gfhouse.com; f. 1999 as Gulf Finance House EC, name changed as above in 2004; cap. US $145m., res $272m., dep. $128m. (Dec. 2010); Chair. ESAM Y. JANAHI; CEO TED PRETTY.

INVESTCORP Bank BSC: POB 5340, Investcorp House, Diplomatic Area, Manama; tel. 17532000; fax 17530816; e-mail info@investcorp.com; internet www.investcorp.com; f. 1982 as Arabian Investment Banking Corpn (Investcorp) EC, current name adopted in 1990; cap. US $711m., res $209m., dep. $436m. (June 2011); Exec. Chair. and CEO NEMIR A. KIRDAR.

Nomura Investment Banking (Middle East) EC: POB 26893, BMB Centre, 7th Floor, Diplomatic Area, Manama; tel. 17530531; fax 17530365; f. 1982; cap. US $25.0m., res $46.3m., dep. $0.3m. (Dec. 2007); Chair. TAKUYA FURUYA.

TAIB Bank BSC: POB 20485, TAIB Tower, 79 Rd 1702, Diplomatic Area, Manama 317; tel. 17549494; fax 17533174; e-mail taibprivatebank@taib.com; internet www.taibdirect.com; f. 1979 as Trans-Arabian Investment Bank EC, renamed TAIB Bank EC in 1994, current name adopted in 2004; cap. US $112m., res $11m., dep. $133m. (Dec. 2011); Chair. ABD AL-RAHMAN HAREB RASHED AL-HAREB; Dir ABD AL-RAHMAN ABDULLAH MUHAMMAD.

United Gulf Bank BSC: POB 5964, UGB Tower, Diplomatic Area, Manama; tel. 17533233; fax 17533137; e-mail info@ugbbah.com; internet www.ugbbah.com; f. 1980; cap. US $208m., res $211m., dep. $292m. (Dec. 2011); Chair. MASAUD M. J. HAYAT; CEO RABIH SOUKARIEH (acting).

Venture Capital Bank BSC: POB 11755, Manama; tel. 17518888; fax 17518880; e-mail info@vc-bank.com; internet www.vc-bank.com; f. 2005; Islamic investment bank; cap. US $250m., res $22m. (Dec. 2011); Chair. Dr GHASSAN AHMED AL-SULAIMAN; CEO ABD AL-LATIF MUHAMMAD JANAHI.

Other investment banks operating in Bahrain include Al-Amin Bank, Amex (Middle East) EC, Capital Union EC, Daiwa Securities SMBC Europe Ltd (Middle East), Global Banking Corpn BSC, Investors Bank EC, Al-Khaleej Islamic Investment Bank (BSC) EC and Merrill Lynch Int. Bank Ltd.

STOCK EXCHANGES

Bahrain Bourse: POB 3203, Manama; tel. 17261260; fax 17256362; e-mail info@bahrainbourse.com.bh; internet www.bahrainbourse.com.bh; f. 1989; 51 listed cos at Dec. 2008; scheduled for privatization; Chair. YOUSUF ABDULLA HUMOOD; Dir FOUAD A. RAHMAN RASHID.

Bahrain Financial Exchange (BFX): POB 1936, 12th Floor, East Tower, Bahrain Financial Harbour, Manama; tel. 16511511; fax 16511599; e-mail info@bfx.bh; internet www.bfx.bh; f. 2009; trading in securities, derivatives, commodities, foreign exchange and *Shari'a*-compliant financial products; owned by Financial Technologies Group (India); Chair. JIGNESH SHAH; Man. Dir and CEO ARSHAD KHAN.

INSURANCE

In 2009 there were 25 locally incorporated insurance firms operating in Bahrain, including:

Al-Ahlia Insurance Co BSC: POB 5282, Chamber of Commerce Bldg, 4th Floor, King Faisal Rd, Manama; tel. 17225860; fax 17224870; e-mail alahlia@alahlia.com; internet www.alahlia.com; f. 1976; Chair. HUSSAIN ALI SAJWANI; Gen. Man. TAWFIQ SHEHAB.

Arab Insurance Group BSC (ARIG): POB 26992, Arig House, Diplomatic Area, Manama; tel. 17544444; fax 17531155; e-mail info@arig.com.bh; internet www.arig.net; f. 1980; owned by Govts of Kuwait, Libya and the United Arab Emirates (49.5%), and other shareholders; reinsurance and insurance; Chair. KHALID ALI AL-BUSTANI; CEO YASSIR ALBAHARNA.

Bahrain Kuwait Insurance Co BSC: POB 10166, Diplomatic Area, Manama; tel. 17542222; fax 17530799; e-mail info@bkic.com; internet www.bkic.com; f. 1975; CEO IBRAHIM SHARIF AL-RAYES; Chair. ABDULLAH HASSAN BUHINDI.

Bahrain National Holding Co BSC (BNH): POB 843, BNH Tower, al-Seef District; tel. 17587300; fax 17583099; e-mail bnh@bnhgroup.com; internet www.bnhgroup.com; f. 1999 by merger of Bahrain Insurance Co and Nat. Insurance Co; all classes incl. life insurance; Chair. FAROUK Y. AL-MOAYYED; Chief Exec. MAHMOUD AL-SOUFI.

Gulf Union Insurance and Reinsurance Co: POB 10949, Manama Centre, Ground Floor, Manama; tel. 17215622; fax 17215421; e-mail guirco@batelco.com.bh; internet www.thyra.com/Sites/gulfunion; Chair. Sheikh IBRAHIM BIN HAMAD AL KHALIFA.

Solidarity Insurance Co: POB 18668, Seef Tower, 11th Floor, al-Seef District, Manama; tel. 17585222; fax 17585200; e-mail mail@solidarity.cc; internet www.solidarity.cc; f. 2004 by Qatar Islamic Bank; Chair. KHALID ABDULLAH JANAHI; CEO ASHRAF BSEISU.

Takaful International Co: POB 3230, B680 R2811, al-Seef District 428, Manama; tel. 17565656; fax 17582688; internet www.takafulweb.com; f. 1989 as Bahrain Islamic Insurance Co; restructured and renamed as above in 1998; Chair. BARA'A ABD AL-AZIZ AL-QENAEI; CEO YOUNIS J. AL-SAYED.

Insurance Association

Bahrain Insurance Association (BIA): POB 2851, Manama; tel. 17532555; fax 17536006; e-mail biabah@batelco.com.bh; internet www.bia-bh.com; f. 1993; 43 mems; Chair. YOUNIS JAMAL AL-SAYED.

Trade and Industry

GOVERNMENT AGENCIES

Economic Development Board (EDB): POB 11299, Manama; tel. 17589999; fax 17589900; e-mail info@bahrainedb.com; internet www.bahrainedb.com; f. 2000; assumed duties of Bahrain Promotions and Marketing Board (f. 1993) and Supreme Council for Economic Devt (f. 2000) in 2001; provides national focus for Bahraini marketing initiatives; attracts inward investment; encourages devt and expansion of Bahraini exports; Chair. Sheikh SALMAN BIN HAMAD AL KHALIFA; CEO Sheikh MUHAMMAD BIN ISSA AL KHALIFA.

National Oil and Gas Authority (NOGA): POB 1435, Manama; tel. 17312644; fax 17293007; e-mail info@noga.gov.bh; internet www.noga.gov.bh; f. 2005 for the regulation and devt of oil- and gas-related industries in the kingdom; Chair. Dr ABD AL-HUSSAIN BIN ALI MIRZA.

CHAMBER OF COMMERCE

Bahrain Chamber of Commerce and Industry: POB 248, Bldg 122, Rd 1605, Block 216, Manama; tel. 17576666; fax 17576600; e-mail bcci@bcci.bh; internet www.bcci.bh; f. 1939; 12,023 mems

(Jan. 2007); Chair. Dr ESSAM ABDULLAH YOUSUF FAKHRO; CEO NABIL ABD AL-RAHMAN AL-MAHMOOD (acting).

STATE HYDROCARBONS COMPANIES

Bahrain National Gas Co BSC (BANAGAS): POB 29099, Rifa'a; tel. 17756222; fax 17756991; e-mail bng@banagas.com.bh; internet www.banagas.com.bh; f. 1979; responsible for extraction, processing and sale of hydrocarbon liquids from associated gas derived from onshore Bahraini fields; 75% owned by Govt of Bahrain, 12.5% by Caltex and 12.5% by Boubyan Petrochemical Co; produces approx. 2,900 barrels per day (b/d) of propane, 2,700 b/d of butane and 5,200 b/d of naphtha; Chair. ALI BIN MUHAMMAD AL-JALAHMA; Chief Exec. Dr Sheikh MUHAMMAD BIN KHALIFA AL KHALIFA.

Bahrain Petroleum Co BSC (BAPCO): POB 25555, Awali; tel. 17704040; fax 17704070; e-mail info@bapco.net; internet www.bapco.com.bh; f. 1999 by merger of Bahrain Nat. Oil Co (f. 1976) and Bahrain Petroleum Co (f. 1980); 100% govt-owned; fully integrated co responsible for exploration, drilling and production of oil and gas; supply of gas to power-generating plants and industries, refining crude petroleum, international marketing of crude petroleum and refined petroleum products, supply and sale of aviation fuel at Bahrain International Airport, and local distribution and marketing of petroleum products; Chair. Dr ABD AL-HUSSAIN BIN ALI MIRZA (Minister of Energy); CEO FAISAL MUHAMMAD AL-MAHROOS.

Gulf Petrochemical Industries Co BSC (GPIC): POB 26730, Manama; tel. 17731777; fax 17731047; e-mail gpic@gpic.com; internet www.gpic.com; f. 1979 as jt venture between the Govts of Bahrain, Kuwait and Saudi Arabia, each with one-third equity participation; a petrochemical complex at Sitra, inaugurated in 1981; produces 1,200 metric tons of both methanol and ammonia per day; Chair. Sheikh ISA BIN ALI AL KHALIFA; Gen. Man. A. RAHMAN A. HUSSEIN JAWAHERI.

UTILITIES

Electricity and Water Authority: POB 2, King Faisal Rd, Manama; tel. 17546767; fax 17541182; e-mail publicrelations@ewa.bh; internet www.mew.gov.bh; f. 2007; privatization of electricity production was approved in December 2003; CEO Sheikh NAWAF BIN IBRAHIM AL KHALIFA.

MAJOR COMPANIES

Aluminium Bahrain BSC (Alba): POB 570, 150 Hawar Ave, Asker 951, Manama; tel. 17830000; fax 17830083; e-mail alba@alba.com.bh; internet www.aluminiumbahrain.com; f. 1971; operates a smelter owned by the Govt of Bahrain (77%), Saudi Public Investment Fund (20%) and Breton Investments Ltd (3%); capacity 840,000 metric tons per year; Chair. MAHMOOD HASHIM AL-KOOHEJI; CEO TIM MURRAY; 3,000 employees.

Awal Dairy Co WLL: POB 601, Manama; tel. 17598598; fax 17591150; e-mail info@awaldairy.com; internet www.awaldairy2.com; f. 1963 as Bahrain Danish Dairy Co WLL; current name adopted 2006; 51% owned by Gen. Trading and Food Processing Co BSC; sales BD 8.25m. (2005); processing, packaging and distribution of milk, ice cream and fruit juice; Chair. IBRAHIM MUHAMMAD ALI ZAINAL; Gen. Man. GEORGE THOMAS; 289 employees.

Bahrain Aluminium Extrusion Co BSC (BALEXCO): POB 1053, Manama; tel. 17730073; fax 17736929; e-mail balexco@batelco.com.bh; internet www.balexco.com.bh; f. 1977; supplies aluminium profiles in mill finish, powder coated and anodized; capacity 25,000 metric tons per year; cap. BD 10m.; Chair. HISHAM ALRAYE; CEO JASSIM MUHAMMAD SAYADI; 302 employees.

Bahrain Atomizers International BSC (BAI): POB 5328, Manama; tel. 17830880; fax 17830025; e-mail bai1@batelco.com.bh; f. 1973; produces 7,000 metric tons of atomized aluminium powder per year; owned by the Govt of Bahrain (51%) and Eckart Austria GmbH (49%); Chair. MUHAMMAD AL-KOOHEJI; Gen. Man. TIM McLAUGHLIN; 55 employees.

General Trading and Food Processing Co BSC (TRAFCO): POB 20202, Manama; tel. 17729000; fax 17727380; e-mail info@trafco.com; internet www.trafco.com; f. 1978; importation and distribution of food products; subsidiaries include Awal Dairy Co WLL, Food Supply Co WLL, Bahrain Water Bottling and Beverage Co BSC; Chair. IBRAHIM MUHAMMAD ALI ZAINAL; Gen. Man. S. SRIDHAR.

Gulf Aluminium Rolling Mill Co BSC (GARMCO): POB 20725, Manama; tel. 17734600; fax 17730542; e-mail wajdi@garmco.com; internet www.garmco.com; f. 1981 as a jt venture between the Govts of Bahrain, Saudi Arabia, Kuwait, Iraq, Oman and Qatar; annual production 165,000 metric tons; Chair. AREF SALEH KHAMIS; CEO ADEL HAMAD A. RAHMAN HAMAD; 800 employees.

Al-Khajah Establishment and Factories: POB 5042, Manama; tel. 17730811; fax 17731340; e-mail alkhajah@alkhajahfactory.com; internet www.alkhajahfactory.com; f. 1972; contracting, trading and manufacture of switchgear and light fittings; numerous subsidiaries within the Gulf; Gen. Man. ESAM AL-KHAJAH; over 800 employees.

Maskati Bros and Co BSC: POB 24, 321 Delmon House, Rd 1506, Bahrain International Investment Park, Manama; tel. 17464646; fax 17464600; e-mail info@maskatibros.com; internet www.maskatibros.com; f. 1956; paper converters, polyethylene manufacture, injection moulders; Chair. HUSSAIN M. MASKATI; Deputy Chair. and Man. Dir KHALID H. MASKATI; over 600 employees.

Midal Cables Ltd: POB 5939, Manama; tel. and fax 17832832; e-mail midalcbl@midalcable.com; internet www.midalcable.com; f. 1977; manufacture of aluminium and aluminium alloy electrical and mechanical rods and conductors for overhead transmission and distribution lines; Man. Dir HAMID R. AL-ZAYANI; CEO MUHAMMAD MUSTAFA; 350 employees.

Nass Group: POB 669, Bldg 453, Rd 4308, Blk 343, Mina Salman Industrial Area, Manama; tel. 17725522; fax 17728184; e-mail nassbah@batelco.com.bh; internet www.nassgroup.com; f. 1963; construction and associated industries, incl. manufacturing, marine transport, offshore engineering and ship repair; 34 subsidiary cos, incl. Nass Corpn BSC, Nass Int. Trading and Gulf Devt Corpn; 6 associated cos; affiliated offices in Kuwait, Qatar, Saudi Arabia and the United Arab Emirates; Chair. ABDULLA AHMED NASS.

Shaheen Group: POB 405, Manama; tel. 17814615; e-mail arehman@shaheengroup.com; internet www.shaheengroup.com; f. 1958 as AWALCO Group; 3 subsidiary cos: Awal Products (heating and ventilation), Gulf Services (security and safety), Gypsum Products (manufacture and installation of gypsum products); Chair. SHAHEEN SAGER SHAHEEN; CEO and Man. Dir SAGER SHAHEEN.

TRADE UNIONS

In November 2002 legislation was ratified to permit the establishment of independent trade unions. There were reported to be more than 50 trade unions operating within Bahrain by early 2007. In July 2012 the Bahrain Labour Union Free Federation (now Bahrain Free Labour Unions Federation) was launched, following disagreement within the General Federation of Bahrain Trade Unions over its alleged political activities.

Bahrain Free Labour Unions Federation: POB 32806, Villa 3776, Rd 915, Blk 809, Isa, Manama; tel. 17226522; fax 17226422; e-mail bflufbh@bflufbh.com; internet www.bflufbh.com; f. 2012; Chair. YAQOOB MUHAMMAD YOUSIF.

General Federation of Bahrain Trade Unions (GFBTU): Manama; tel. 17727333; fax 17729599; internet www.gfbtu.org; f. 2002; Sec.-Gen. SALMAN JAFFAR AL-MAHFOUD.

Transport

RAILWAYS

There are no railways in Bahrain. In early 2011 a detailed feasibility study began into plans for a 184-km domestic rail network, to be constructed in three phases by 2030. The Bahraini project was expected to form part of a planned regional rail network, connecting Bahrain with member countries of the Cooperation Council for the Arab States of the Gulf (or Gulf Cooperation Council—GCC). In early 2013 a feasibility study into plans for a railway connecting Bahrain and Saudi Arabia was also under way, and was due to be completed by 2014.

ROADS

In 2011 Bahrain had 4,147 km of roads, including 576 km of highways, main or national roads, 585 km of secondary or regional roads and 2,256 km of other roads; 82.4% of roads were paved. The King Fahd Causeway, a 25-km causeway link with Saudi Arabia, was opened in 1986. A three-lane dual carriageway links the causeway to Manama. Other causeways link Bahrain with Muharraq island and with Sitra island. The Strategic Roads Masterplan 2021, launched by the Ministry of Works in 2005, outlined plans for the modernization of Bahrain's road network in anticipation of significant increases in road traffic volume. Approval for the construction of a causeway linking Askar in eastern Bahrain with Ras Ishairij in Qatar (the Friendship Bridge) was given in 2004. The project was to be supervised by a committee established in February 2005 by the Governments of both countries. After protracted discussions and numerous delays, in May 2008 the contract to design and build the causeway, at a cost of some US $3,000m., was awarded to a France-based consortium. The decision, in late 2008, to incorporate a dual railway line into the project necessitated substantial design revisions that were expected to add up to $1,000m. to the cost of the causeway. Construction work had been expected to begin in early 2009, with a projected completion date of 2013; however, following further delays as a result of financial difficulties, by mid-2013 construction work had yet to commence.

Responsibility for the management and development of Bahrain's roads is divided between the Ministry of Works (Roads Projects and Maintenance Directorate, and Roads, Planning and Design Directorate) and the Ministry of the Interior (Directorate of Traffic).

SHIPPING

Numerous shipping services link Bahrain and the Gulf with Europe, the USA, Pakistan, India, the Far East and Australia.

The deep-water harbour of Mina Salman was opened in 1962. However, following the opening of Khalifa bin Salman port in 2009 (see below), commercial operations at Mina Salman were phased out and plans for an expanded US Navy base at the port were under discussion.

In 1999 work began on the construction of a new port and industrial zone at Hidd, on Muharraq island. Incorporating the Bahrain Gateway Terminal, the new port, Khalifa bin Salman, which became operational in April 2009 (at an estimated cost of over US $350m.), has an annual handling capacity of 1.1m. 20-foot equivalent units (TEUs). The port, which has 1,800 m of quayside walls and a quayside depth of 12.8 m (due to be increased to 15 m), includes a general cargo berth and two container berths with roll-on roll-off facilities. Khalifa bin Salman is managed and operated by APM Terminals Bahrain, under the terms of a 25-year contract awarded in 2007. At 31 December 2012 Bahrain's flag registered fleet totalled 343 vessels, with an aggregate displacement of 757,656 grt. Of those vessels, three were bulk carriers, one was a fish carrier and two were general cargo ships.

Port and Regulatory Authorities

APM Terminals Bahrain BSC: PO Box 50490, Khalifa bin Salman Port, Hidd; tel. 17365500; fax 17365505; e-mail bahapmtcom@apmterminals.com; internet www.apmterminals.com/africa-mideast/bahrain; f. 2006; 80% owned by APM Terminals Management BV, 20% by Yusuf bin Ahmad Kanoo Holdings; management and operation of Bahrain's commercial port; Man. Dir STEEN DAVIDSEN.

General Organization of Sea Ports: POB 75315, Manama; tel. 17359595; fax 17359359; e-mail info@gop.gov.bh; internet www.gop.bh; responsible for regulation, devt and promotion of maritime and logistics zones; Chair. Sheikh DAIJ BIN SALMAN BIN DAIJ AL KHALIFA; Dir-Gen. HASSAN ALI AL-MAJID.

Principal Shipping Companies

Alsharif Group WLL: POB 1322, Manama; tel. 17515055; fax 17537637; e-mail alsharif@batelco.com.bh; internet www.alsharifbahrain.com; f. 1957; shipping agency; Man. Dir ALI ABD AL-RASOOL AL-SHARIF; Gen. Man. BALAJI ARDHANARI.

Arab Shipbuilding and Repair Yard Co (ASRY): POB 50110, Hidd; tel. 17671111; fax 17670236; e-mail asryco@batelco.com.bh; internet www.asry.net; f. 1974 by OAPEC mems; 500,000-ton dry dock opened 1977; 2 floating docks in operation since 1992; new twin slipway completed 2008; repaired 139 ships in 2006; Chair. Sheikh DAIJ BIN SALMAN BIN DAIJ AL KHALIFA; Chief Exec. CHRIS POTTER.

The Gulf Agency Co (Bahrain) WLL: POB 412, Rd 20, 224 Muharraq Area, GLS Premises, Manama; tel. 17339777; fax 17320498; e-mail bahrain@gac.com; internet www.gacworld.com/bahrain; f. 1957; shipping agency; operates at Sitra, Mina Salman and Hidd ports; Man. Dir MIKAEL LEIJONBERG.

Al-Jazeera Shipping Co WLL: POB 302, Mina Salman Industrial Area, Manama; tel. 17728837; fax 17728217; e-mail almelaha@batelco.com.bh; internet www.ajsco.com; operates a fleet of tugboats and barges; Man. Dir ALI HASSAN MAHMOUD.

Kanoo Shipping: POB 45, Al Khalifa Ave, Manama; tel. 17220220; fax 17229122; e-mail kanoomgt@batelco.com.bh; internet www.ybakanoo.com; f. 1890; owned by Yusuf bin Ahmad Kanoo Group; air and shipping cargo services, commercial and holiday services; Chair. MUBARAK JASIM KANOO; Shipping Man. DON BANNERMAN.

Nass Marine Services: POB 669, Manama; tel. 17467722; fax 17467773; e-mail nassmarine@batelco.com.bh; internet www.nassgroup.com; f. 2006; part of Nass Group; shipbuilding and ship-repair; Chair. ABDULLAH AHMAD NASS.

UCO Marine Contracting WLL: POB 1074, Manama; tel. 17730816; fax 17732131; e-mail ucomarin@batelco.com.bh; owns and operates a fleet of bulk carriers, tugboats, barges and dredgers; Man. Dirs BADER AHMAD KAIKSOW, HASSAN SABAH AL-BINALI, ALI AL-MUSALAM.

CIVIL AVIATION

Bahrain International Airport (BIA) has a first-class runway, capable of taking the largest aircraft in use. In 2012 BIA handled some 8.5m. passengers. Plans for a two-phase project to expand the airport's capacity through the construction of two new passenger terminals, at an estimated total cost of US $4,700m., were finalized in late 2009. However, in 2011 it was announced that plans for a second terminal had been abandoned. The project to expand the existing terminal to accommodate up to 13.5m. passengers per year was to continue and was due to be completed by 2015.

Department of Civil Aviation Affairs: POB 586, Manama; tel. 17321110; fax 17339066; e-mail prelation@caa.gov.bh; internet www.caa.gov.bh; Under-Sec. Capt. ABD AL-RAHMAN MUHAMMAD AL-GAOUD.

Gulf Air: POB 138, Manama; tel. 17339339; fax 17224494; e-mail gfpr@batelco.com.bh; internet www.gulfair.com; f. 1950 as Gulf Aviation Co; name changed 1974; wholly owned by the Govt of Bahrain; services to the Middle East, South-East Asia, the Far East, Australia, Africa and Europe; Chair. Sheikh KHALID BIN ABDULLAH AL KHALIFA (Deputy Prime Minister); CEO MAHER SALMAN JABER AL-MUSALLAM (acting).

Tourism

There are several archaeological sites of importance in Bahrain, which is the site of the ancient trading civilization of Dilmun. Qal'at al-Bahrain, the ancient capital of Dilmun, was designated a UNESCO World Heritage Site in 2005. In early 2012 major hotel and resort developments were ongoing at Bahrain Bay, City Centre Mall, Al-Areen, the Amwaj Islands and Durrat al-Bahrain. The Government is currently promoting Bahrain as a destination for sports and leisure activities. The Bahrain Grand Prix, held annually since 2004, was the first Formula One event to be held in the Middle East. In 2011 the event was cancelled owing to unrest in the country, but in 2012 and 2013 the Grand Prix took place as scheduled, despite continued protests within Bahrain and international criticism. In 2007 Bahrain received 7.8m. foreign visitors. Income from tourism (excluding passenger transport) totalled US $1,362m. in 2010.

Bahrain Exhibition and Convention Authority: POB 11644, Manama; tel. 17558800; fax 17555513; e-mail info@bahrainexhibitions.com; internet www.bahrainexhibitions.com; Chair. Dr HASSAN BIN ABDULLAH FAKHRO (Minister of Industry and Commerce); CEO HASSAN JAFFAR MUHAMMAD.

Bahrain Tourism Co (BTC): POB 5831, Manama; tel. 17530530; fax 17530867; e-mail btc@alseyaha.com; internet www.alseyaha.com; f. 1974; Chair. QASSIM MUHAMMAD FAKHROO; CEO ABD AL-NABI DAYLAMI.

Tourism Affairs: Ministry of Culture, POB 26613, Manama; tel. 17201244; fax 17211717; e-mail azizisherida@info.gov.bh; internet www.moc.gov.bh/en/TourismAffairs; Asst Under-Sec. for Tourism SHAFIQA SHAHIN.

Defence

Supreme Commander of the Bahrain Defence Force: HM Sheikh HAMAD BIN ISA AL KHALIFA.

Commander-in-Chief of the Bahrain Defence Force: Field Marshal Sheikh KHALIFA BIN AHMAD AL KHALIFA.

Chief of Staff of the Bahrain Defence Force: Maj.-Gen. Sheikh DUAIJ BIN SALMAN BIN AHMAD AL KHALIFA.

Defence Budget (2012): BD 383m.

Military Service: voluntary.

Total Armed Forces (as assessed at November 2012): 8,200 (army 6,000; navy 700; air force 1,500).

Paramilitary Forces (as assessed at November 2012): est. 11,260 (police 9,000; national guard est. 2,000; coastguard some 260).

Education

Although education is not compulsory, it is provided free of charge up to secondary level. Basic education, from the ages of six to 14, is divided into two levels: children attend primary school from six to 11 years of age and intermediate school from 12 to 14. Secondary education, beginning at the age of 15, lasts for three years; students choose to follow a general (science or literary), commercial, technical or vocational curriculum. In 1996 enrolment at primary, intermediate and secondary levels was 97.8%, 96.0% and 95.0% of the relevant age-groups, respectively. According to UNESCO, in 2008/09 the total enrolment at primary schools included 97% of children in the relevant age-group, while the comparable ratio for secondary enrolment in 2008/09 was 89%. Private and religious education are also available. In 2011 recurrent expenditure by the Ministry of Education totalled BD 245.8m. (equivalent to 10.2% of total recurrent government expenditure).

The University of Bahrain, established by Amiri decree in 1986, comprises nine Colleges: of Engineering, Arts, Science, Information Technology, Law, Applied Studies, Business Administration,

Bahrain Teachers College and the Academy of Physical Education and Physiotherapy. Some 12,709 students were enrolled at the University in 2010/11. Higher education is also provided by the College of Health Sciences. The Arabian Gulf University (AGU), funded by seven Arab Governments, also provides higher education. The AGU comprises the College of Medicine and Medical Sciences, and the College of Graduate Studies. The Royal College of Surgeons in Ireland Medical University of Bahrain was founded in 2004, and construction of a new campus at Muharraq was completed in 2008, at an estimated cost of US $78.9m. In addition, ambitious plans to establish a Higher Education City, at a projected cost of $1,000m., were finalized in December 2006; the development was to include a full branch of a leading US university, an international research centre and a specialist academy.

Bibliography

Adamiyat, Fereydoun. *Bahrain Islands: A Legal and Diplomatic Study of the British-Iranian Controversy*. New York, Praeger, 1955.

Al-Arayed, Jawad Salim. *A Line in the Sea: The Qatar Versus Bahrain Border Dispute in the World Court*. Berkeley, CA, North Atlantic Books, 2003.

Belgrave, Charles. *Personal Column*. Beirut, Librarie du Liban, 2nd edn, 1972.

Belgrave, James H. D. *Welcome to Bahrain*. Stourbridge, Mark and Moody, 4th edn, 1960.

Burton, Paul, and Hassan, Omar. *Bahrain and its Development Philosophy*. London, Gulf Centre for Strategic Studies, 1998.

Clarke, Angela. *Bahrain: Oil and Development, 1929–1989*. London, Immel, 1998.

Cordesman, Anthony H. *Bahrain, Oman, Qatar and the UAE: Challenges of Security*. Boulder, CO, Westview Press, 1997.

Crawford, Harriet (Ed.). *The Dilmun Temple at Saar: Bahrain and its Archeological Inheritance*. London, Kegan Paul International, 1997.

Dilmun and its Gulf Neighbours. Cambridge University Press, 1998.

Dabrowska, Karen. *Bahrain Briefing: The Struggle for Democracy*. London, Colourmast, 1997.

Farah, Talal T. *Protection and Politics in Bahrain, 1869–1915*. American University of Beirut, 1985.

Fuccaro, Nelida. *Histories of City and State in the Persian Gulf: Manama since 1800*. Cambridge, Cambridge University Press, 2009.

Al-Ghatam, Dr Mohammed, and Galal, Dr Mohammed Nomal. *A Strategic Outlook on Bahrain and the Arab Region in an International Context (No. 3)*. Manama, Bahrain Centre for Studies and Research, 2006.

Hakima, A. M. *Eastern Arabia: Bahrain*. International Book Centre, 1984.

The Rise and Development of Bahrain and Kuwait. Beirut, 1965.

Hamad bin Isa Al Khalifa, Sheikh. *First Light: Modern Bahrain and its Heritage*. London, Kegan Paul International, 1995.

Hassan, Omar. *Border Dispute Between Bahrain and Qatar and the Challenges of Gulf Co-operation*. London, Gulf Centre for Strategic Studies, 1997.

Insoll, Timothy R. *The Land of Enki in the Islamic Era: Pearls, Palms, and Religious Identity in Bahrain*. Columbia University Press, 2004.

Khuri, F. I. *Tribe and State in Bahrain*. Chicago University Press, 1981.

Lahn, Glada. *Democratic Transition in Bahrain: A Model for the Arab World*. London, Gulf Centre for Strategic Studies, 2004.

Lawson, Fred H. *The Modernization of Autocracy*. Boulder, CO, Westview Press, 1989.

Marlowe, John. *The Persian Gulf in the 20th Century*. London, Cresset Press, 1962.

Miles, S. B. *The Countries and Tribes of the Persian Gulf*. London, Frank Cass, 3rd edn, 1970.

Mohammed, Nadeya Sayed Ali. *Population and Development of the Arab Gulf States: The Case of Bahrain, Oman and Kuwait*. Aldershot, Ashgate Publishing, 2003.

Mojtahedzadeh, Pirouz. *Security and Territoriality in the Persian Gulf: A Maritime Political Geography*. Richmond, Curzon Press, 1999.

Moore, Philip. *Bahrain: A New Era*. London, Euromoney Books, 2001.

Nakhleh, Emile A. *Bahrain: Political Development in a Modernizing Society*. Lexington, MA, Lexington Books, 1976.

Routine Abuse, Routine Denial: Civil Rights and the Political Crisis in Bahrain. New York, Human Rights Watch, 1997.

Payne, Anna, and Steele, Katie (Eds). *Foreign Policy in Bahrain*. London, Gulf Centre for Strategic Studies, 2004.

Radhi, Hassan Ali (Ed.). *Judiciary and Arbitration in Bahrain: A Historical and Analytical Study*. New York, Kluwer Law International, 2003.

al-Rumaihi, Mohammed. *Bahrain: Social and Political Change since the First World War*. Durham Univ., Bowker, in association with the Centre for Middle Eastern and Islamic Studies, 1977.

Terterov, Marat, and Shoult, Anthony (Eds). *Doing Business with Bahrain*. London, GMB Publishing, revised edn, 2005.

Wheatcroft, Andrew. *The Life and Times of Sheikh Salman bin Hamad Al Khalifa: Ruler of Bahrain 1942–61*. London, Kegan Paul International, 1995.

Winkler, David F. *Amirs, Admirals and Desert Sailors: Bahrain, the U.S. Navy and the Arabian Gulf*. Annapolis, MD, Naval Institute Press, 2007.

CYPRUS

Physical and Social Geography

W. B. FISHER

The island of Cyprus, with an area of 9,251 sq km (3,572 sq miles), is situated in the north-eastern corner of the Mediterranean Sea, closest to Turkey (which is easily visible from its northern coast), but also less than 160 km (100 miles) from the Syrian coast. Its greatest length (including the long, narrow peninsula of Cape Andreas) is 225 km. The census of 1 October 1982, which was held only in Greek Cypriot areas, but included an estimate for the Turkish-occupied region, recorded a total population of 642,731. The census of 1 October 2001 (excluding the Turkish-occupied region) recorded a total population of 703,529. At the census of October 2011, the population was recorded at 840,407 (excluding the Turkish-occupied region), giving a population density for Greek Cyprus of 90.8 per sq km.

A census conducted in the 'Turkish Republic of Northern Cyprus' ('TRNC') on 15 December 1996 recorded a total population of 200,587. By the time of the census held on 30 April 2006, the population in the 'TRNC' had increased to 256,644. According to official estimates, the population was 286,973 at mid-2010, giving a density for the 'TRNC' of 87.5 per sq km.

PHYSICAL FEATURES

Cyprus owes its peculiar shape to the occurrence of two ridges that were once part of two much greater arcs running from the mainland of Asia westwards towards Crete. The greater part of these arcs has disappeared, but remnants are found in Cyprus and on the eastern mainland, where they form the Amanus range of Turkey. In Cyprus the arcs are visible as two mountain systems—the Kyrenia range of the north, and the much larger and imposing Troödos massif in the centre. Between the two mountain systems lies a flat lowland, open to the sea in the east and west and spoken of as the Mesaoria. Here also lies the chief town, Nicosia (Lefkoşa in Turkish).

The mountain ranges are actually very different in structure and appearance. The Kyrenia range is a single narrow fold of limestone, with occasional deposits of marble, and its maximum height is 900 m. As it is mainly porous rock, rainfall soon seeps below ground, and so its appearance is rather arid, but very picturesque, with white crags and isolated pinnacles. The soil cover is thin. The Troödos, on the other hand, has been affected by folding in two separate directions, so that the whole area has been fragmented, and large quantities of molten igneous rock have forced their way to the surface from the interior of the earth, giving rise to a great dome that reaches 1,800 m above sea level. As it is impervious to water, there are some surface streams, rounder outlines, a thicker soil, especially on the lower slopes, and a covering of pine forest.

CLIMATE

The climate in Cyprus is strongly Mediterranean in character, with the usual hot dry summers and warm, wet winters. As an island with high mountains, Cyprus receives a fair amount of moisture, and up to 1,000 mm of rain falls in the mountains, with the minimum of 300 mm–380 mm in the Mesaoria. Frost does not occur on the coast, but may be sharp in the higher districts, and snow can fall fairly heavily in regions over 900 m in altitude. In summer, despite the proximity of the sea, temperatures are surprisingly high, and the Mesaoria, in particular, can experience over 38°C (100°F). There is a tendency for small depressions to form over the island in winter, giving a slightly greater degree of changeability in weather than is experienced elsewhere in the Middle East.

Cyprus is noteworthy in that between 50% and 60% of the total area is under cultivation—a figure higher than that for most Middle Eastern countries. This is partly to be explained by the relatively abundant rainfall, the expanses of impervious rock that retain water near the surface, and the presence of rich soils derived from volcanic rocks which occur around the Troödos massif. The potential of the tourist trade and the export markets in wine and early vegetables add to the incentives to development. In the southern (Greek) part of the island economic recovery after partition has been considerable; however, economic development has been far slower in the north.

History

Revised for this edition by RICHARD GERMAN and ELIZABETH TAYLOR

EARLY HISTORY

Cyprus first became important in recorded history when the island fell under Egyptian control in the second millennium BC. After a long period during which the Phoenicians and the Mycenaeans founded colonies there, Cyprus, in the eighth century BC, became an Assyrian protectorate at a time when the Greeks of the mainland were extending their settlements on the island. From the sixth century BC it was a province of the Persian empire and took part in the unsuccessful Ionian revolt against Persian rule in 502 BC. Despite the Greek victory over the Persian emperor Xerxes in 480 BC, subsequent efforts by the Greek city states of the mainland to free Cyprus from Persian control met with little success, largely because of dissension among the Greek cities of Cyprus itself. For more than two centuries after 295 BC the Ptolemies of Egypt ruled in Cyprus until it became part of the Roman Empire.

Cyprus prospered under the rule of the Roman emperor Augustus, for trade flourished while the Romans kept the seas free of piracy. When Jerusalem fell to the Emperor Titus in AD 70, many Jews found refuge in Cyprus, where they became numerous enough to undertake a serious revolt in 115. Christianity, apparently introduced into the island during the reign of the Emperor Claudius (41–54), grew steadily in the next three centuries, during which Cyprus, isolated from a continent frequently ravaged by barbarian inroads, continued to enjoy a relative degree of prosperity. From the time of Constantine the Great, Cyprus was a province governed by officials appointed from Antioch and formed part of the diocese of the East. In the reign of Theodosius I (379–95) the Greek Orthodox Church was firmly established there and in the fifth century proved strong enough to resist the attempts of the Patriarchs of Antioch to control the religious life of the island.

The Arab attack of 649 began a new period in the history of Cyprus, which now became, for more than 300 years, the object of dispute between the Byzantines (Eastern Romans) and the Muslims. Whenever the Byzantine fleet was weak, the Empire's continuing possession of Cyprus was placed in jeopardy. After the decisive Byzantine re-conquest of 964–65, Cyprus enjoyed, for more than two centuries, a period of relative calm.

WESTERN RULE

In 1192 King Richard I of England, having taken the island from the usurping Byzantine governor, Isaac Comnenus, sold it to the Knights Templar, who, in turn, sold it to Guy de Lusignan, formerly King of Jerusalem. Thus began almost 400 years of Western rule, which saw the introduction of Western feudalism and of the Latin Church into a land that hitherto had been Greek in its institutions and Orthodox in its religious beliefs.

In the period from 1192 to 1267 (when the direct line of the Lusignan house became extinct) the new regime was gradually elaborated. The Lusignan monarchy was limited in character, for royal power was effective only in the military sphere. All other important business of state was decided in a high court, which consisted of the nobles, the fief-holders and the great officers of state. This court applied a highly developed code of feudal law derived from the Assizes of Jerusalem, although Cypriots were allowed to retain their own laws and customs in so far as these did not conflict with the feudal law. The period was also marked by the determined efforts of the Latin clergy, supported by the Papacy, to establish complete control over the Orthodox Church—a policy carried out with much harshness, which the Crown and the feudal nobility often sought to mitigate in order to keep the loyalty of the subject population. The dominance of the Latin Church was finally assured by the *Bulla Cypria* of Pope Alexander IV (1260).

During the second half of the 13th century the kingdom of Cyprus (now ruled by the house of Antioch-Lusignan) played an important role in the final struggle to maintain the Latin states in Syria against the Mamluk offensive. The influence of the monarchy was further strengthened in this period, and when, in 1324, Hugh IV became King, the great age of feudal Cyprus had begun. Cyprus was now of great importance in the commerce that the Italian republics maintained with the East, and Famagusta became a flourishing port. The Papacy, however, always anxious to weaken the power of Mamluk Egypt, placed severe limitations on the trade of the Italian republics with that state and charged Cyprus and Rhodes with their enforcement. Thus began a conflict between the kings of Cyprus and the great republics of Venice and Genoa. This did not endanger Cyprus provided that the Papacy could mobilize sentiment in the West to support the crusading state of the Lusignans. However, as the 14th century advanced, the Papacy lost its power to command such support in the West and Cyprus was left to face its enemies unaided, and was powerless to withstand the ambitions of Genoa and Venice.

Before this decline began, Cyprus enjoyed a brief period of military success under the crusading King Peter I (1359–69). In 1361 he occupied the port of Adalia on the south coast of Asia Minor, then held by the Turkish emirate of Tekke, and in 1362–65 he toured Europe in an effort to win adequate support for a new crusade. His most memorable exploit came in 1365, when he captured Alexandria in Egypt, sacking it so completely that even as late as the 16th century it had not recovered its former splendour. With his assassination in 1369 the fortune of the Lusignan house began to decline.

The reign of King Janus I (1398–1432) witnessed a long struggle to drive out the Genoese, who had seized Famagusta during the war with Cyprus in 1372–74, and to repel the attacks of Mamluk Egypt, which had become weary of the repeated sea-raids undertaken from the ports of Cyprus. After plundering Larnaca and Limassol in 1425, the Mamluks crushed the army of Cyprus in a battle at Khoirakoitia in 1426. King Janus was captured, and his capital, Nicosia, sacked. The King was released in 1427, after promising the payment of a large ransom and of an annual tribute. The last years of Lusignan power were marked by dissension in the ruling house and by the increasing domination of Venice, which, with the consent of Caterina Cornaro, the Venetian widow of the last Lusignan king, annexed Cyprus in 1489.

TURKISH RULE

Venice held Cyprus until 1570, when the Ottoman Turks began a campaign of conquest, which led to the fall of Nicosia in September 1570 and of Famagusta in August 1571. The Turks restored to the Greek Orthodox Church its independence and ended the former feudal status of the peasantry. The Cypriots paid a tax for the freedom to follow their own religion, and were allowed to cultivate their land as their own and to hand it down to their descendants on payment of a portion of the produce. About 30,000 Turkish soldiers were also given land on the island, thus establishing a Turkish element in the population, which was later reinforced by immigration from Asia Minor.

The 17th and 18th centuries were a rather melancholy period in the history of Cyprus. Repeated droughts and ravages of locusts preceded a famine in 1640 and an outbreak of plague in 1641. In 1660 the Ottoman Government, in order to limit the extortions of its officials and of the tax-farmers, recognized the Orthodox Archbishop and his three suffragans as guardians of the Christian peasantry, but this did not prevent revolts in 1665 and 1690. A great famine in 1757–58 and a severe plague in 1760 reduced the numbers of the peasantry very considerably, causing widespread distress, which culminated in the revolt of 1764–66. From 1702 Cyprus had been a fief of the Grand Vizier, who normally sold the governorship to the highest bidder—usually for a period of one year. This practice created great opportunities for financial oppression. Perhaps the most striking development of the period was the growing power of the Orthodox bishops, whose influence was so great in the late 18th century that the Turkish administration depended on their support for the collection of revenues. The Turkish elements in Cyprus, resenting the dominance of the Orthodox bishops, accused them in 1821 of having a secret understanding with the Greeks of the Morea (the inhabitants of the Peloponnese peninsula who had revolted against Turkish rule) and carried out a massacre of the Christians at Nicosia and elsewhere, which brought the supremacy of the bishops to an end.

In 1833 the Sultan granted Cyprus to Muhammad Ali, Pasha of Egypt, who was forced to renounce possession of it in 1840 at the demand of the Great Powers. During the period of reforms initiated by Sultan Mahmud II (1808–39) and continued by his immediate successors, efforts were made to improve the administration of the island. The practice of farming out taxes was abolished (although later partially reintroduced) and the Governor became a salaried official, ruling through a *divan* that was half-Turkish and half-Christian in composition.

BRITISH RULE

At the Congress of Berlin of 1878 the Great Powers endorsed an agreement between the United Kingdom and the Sultan of Turkey whereby Cyprus was placed under British control, to be used as a base from which to protect the Ottoman Empire against the ambitions of Russia. Control of Cyprus was now regarded as vital, since the opening of the Suez Canal (1869) had made the eastern Mediterranean an area of great strategic importance. Under the 1878 agreement, Cyprus remained legally a part of the Ottoman Empire, to which a tribute was paid, consisting of the surplus revenues of the island, calculated at less than £93,000 per annum.

From 1882 until 1931 the island had a legislative council which was partly nominated and partly elected. Various reforms were carried out in this first period of British rule: the introduction of an efficient judicial system and of an effective police force, and considerable improvements in agriculture, roads, education and other public services.

When Turkey joined the Central Powers in the First World War, the United Kingdom immediately annexed Cyprus (1914) and then offered it to Greece (1915), provided that the latter joined the Allies: this offer was refused, however, and was not repeated when Greece eventually joined the hostilities, on the side of the Allies, in 1917. Under the terms of the Treaty of Lausanne of 1923, both Greece and Turkey recognized British sovereignty over Cyprus, which became a Crown Colony in 1925. Thereafter, discontent among the Greek Cypriots began to assume serious proportions, culminating in anti-British riots in 1931 and the suspension of constitutional rule.

In the period after 1931 the desire to achieve self-government within the British Commonwealth grew stronger, but the movement for *Enosis* (union with Greece) became the dominant influence in the political life of the island. Following the Second World War, during which Cypriot troops served,

Cyprus was used as a place of detention for illegal Jewish immigrants into Palestine, the last of such detention camps being closed in 1949. Following his election as head of the Orthodox Church of Cyprus in 1950, Archbishop Makarios III assumed the leadership of the *Enosis* movement. An unofficial plebiscite, conducted by the Church in that year, demonstrated overwhelming support for *Enosis* among Greek Cypriots.

CONSTITUTIONAL PROPOSALS

In July 1954 the United Kingdom made known its intention of preparing a restricted form of constitution for Cyprus, with a legislature containing official, nominated and elected members. The Greek Cypriots, insisting that their ultimate goal was *Enosis*, viewed the proposed constitution with disfavour, whereas the Turkish Cypriots declared their readiness to accept it. The Greek Government now brought the problem of Cyprus before the UN. It was the view of the United Kingdom, however, that the question was one with which it alone was competent to deal. In December the UN resolved to take no immediate action in the matter.

The more extreme advocates of *Enosis*, grouped together in EOKA (National Organization of Cypriot Combatants) under the leadership of Gen. George Grivas (Dhigenis), now began a campaign of guerrilla activities against the British administration. A conference including British, Greek and Turkish representatives met in London, United Kingdom, in August 1955. The British offer of substantial autonomy for Cyprus failed to win the approval of Greece, since it held out no clear prospect of self-determination for the island, and the conference ended in frustration.

The campaign of violence intensified in November 1955, and a state of emergency was declared. All public assemblies of a political nature were forbidden; the British troops in Cyprus (about 10,000 in all) assumed the status of active service in wartime. The Governor now ruled the island through an executive council consisting of four officials from the administration, two Greek Cypriots and one Turkish Cypriot.

At the beginning of 1956 the Governor, Sir John Harding, discussed the situation with Archbishop Makarios. Since the United Kingdom was now willing to accept the principle of ultimate independence for Cyprus, agreement seemed to be within reach. In March, however, the discussions were suspended, and Archbishop Makarios, implicated in the activities of EOKA, was deported to Seychelles.

RELEASE OF MAKARIOS

In March 1957 Archbishop Makarios was released from detention in Seychelles and, since he was not allowed to return to Cyprus, went to Athens, Greece. The British authorities also relaxed some of the emergency laws, such as the censorship of the press and the mandatory death penalty for the bearing of arms. These measures facilitated the holding of further discussions, but little progress was made.

High levels of violence persisted during the first half of 1958. EOKA carried out an intensive campaign of sabotage, especially in Nicosia and Famagusta. Meanwhile, strife between the Greek Cypriots and the Turkish Cypriots was becoming more frequent and severe, with particularly serious outbreaks in June. There was increased tension, too, between the Greek and Turkish Governments.

In June 1958 the United Kingdom made public a new scheme for Cyprus, which came into force in October. The island was to remain under British control for seven years; full autonomy in communal affairs would be granted, under separate arrangements, to the Greek Cypriots and the Turkish Cypriots; internal administration was to be reserved for the Governor's Council, which would include representatives of the Greek Cypriot and Turkish Cypriot communities and also of the Greek and Turkish Governments.

INDEPENDENCE

Following the holding of a conference in Zürich, Switzerland, it was announced in February 1959 that Greece and Turkey had devised a compromise settlement concerning Cyprus. A further conference in London decided that Cyprus was to become an independent republic with a Greek Cypriot President and a Turkish Cypriot Vice-President. There would be a Council of Ministers (comprising seven Greeks and three Turks) and a House of Representatives (70% Greek, 30% Turkish) elected by universal suffrage for a term of five years. Communal Chambers (one Greek and one Turkish) were to exercise control in matters of religion, culture and education. The Turkish inhabitants in five of the main towns would be allowed to establish separate municipalities for a period of four years. Cyprus was not to be united with another state, nor was it to be subject to partition. The United Kingdom, Greece and Turkey guaranteed the independence, the territorial integrity and the Constitution of Cyprus. Greece received the right to station a force of 950 men on the island, and Turkey a force of 650 men. The United Kingdom retained under its direct sovereignty two base areas in Cyprus (at Akrotiri and at Dhekelia).

In November 1959 agreement was reached regarding the delimitation of the executive powers to be vested in the President and Vice-President of Cyprus. A further agreement defined the composition of the Supreme Constitutional Court. In December the state of emergency came to an end, and Archbishop Makarios was elected the first President of Cyprus. The post of Vice-President was awarded, unopposed, to the Turkish Cypriot leader, Dr Fazil Küçük. After lengthy negotiations, concluded in July 1960, the United Kingdom and Cyprus reached agreement over the precise size and character of the two military bases under British sovereignty.

Cyprus formally became an independent republic on 16 August 1960, and was admitted to the UN in the following month and to the Commonwealth in March 1961.

CONSTITUTIONAL PROBLEMS

As Cyprus achieved independence, serious problems began to arise over the interpretation and working of the Constitution. There was a divergence of opinion between Greek and Turkish Cypriots over the formation of a national army, particularly regarding the degree of integration to be established between the two ethnicities. In October 1961 Vice-President Küçük used his power of veto to ban full integration, which President Makarios favoured at all levels of the armed forces.

The year 1962 saw the development of a serious crisis over the system of separate Greek and Turkish municipalities in the five main towns of Cyprus (Nicosia, Famagusta, Limassol, Larnaca and Paphos). In December the Turkish Communal Chamber adopted a law maintaining the Turkish municipalities in the five towns from 1 January 1963 (when their original four-year mandate expired), and also establishing a similar municipality in the predominantly Turkish town of Lefka. President Makarios issued a decree stating that, from that date, government-appointed bodies would control municipal organizations throughout the island—a decree denounced by the Turkish Cypriots as an infringement of the Constitution.

The Constitutional Court of Cyprus, sitting in judgment on the consequent financial disputes, ruled in February 1963 that taxes could be imposed on the people of the island, but that no legal mechanism existed for the collection of such taxes. In April 1963 the court declared that the Government had no power to control the municipalities through bodies of its own choosing, and that the decision of the Turkish Communal Chamber to maintain separate Turkish municipalities in defiance of the Cyprus Government was also invalid.

Negotiations between President Makarios and Vice-President Küçük to resolve the deadlock ended in failure in May 1963. Accordingly, in November, Makarios put forward proposals for a number of reforms. However, these proved to be unacceptable to the Turkish Cypriots.

CIVIL WAR

Meanwhile, underground organizations, prepared for violence, had been formed among both the Greek and the Turkish communities. In December 1963 serious conflict broke out. The United Kingdom suggested that a joint force composed of British, Greek and Turkish troops should be established to restore order. The Cypriot, Greek and Turkish Governments gave their assent to this scheme. As a result of the December crisis, co-operation between Greek Cypriot and Turkish

Cypriot officials virtually came to an end, most notably in the form of a Turkish Cypriot boycott of the House of Representatives.

There was renewed violence in February 1964, especially in Limassol. Considerable quantities of arms were being smuggled into the island for both sides, and the number of armed 'irregulars' was increasing rapidly. These developments also gave rise to further friction between the Greek and Turkish Governments.

ESTABLISHMENT OF UN PEACE-KEEPING FORCE

In March 1964 the UN Security Council adopted a resolution establishing the UN Peace-keeping Force in Cyprus (UNFICYP), and by May the UN headquarters at Nicosia controlled 6,931 military personnel.

There was more fighting between Greek and Turkish Cypriots in March and April 1964. In June the Cyprus House of Representatives approved legislation establishing a National Guard and rendering all male Cypriots between the ages of 18 and 59 liable to six months' service. Only members of the National Guard, of the regular police and of the armed forces would now have the right to bear arms. One purpose of the legislation was to suppress the 'irregular bands' that were becoming increasingly difficult to control.

Under the agreements concluded for the independence of Cyprus in 1959–60, Turkey maintained a contingent of troops on the island, the personnel of this force being renewed on a system of regular rotation. A new crisis arose in August–September 1964 when the Cyprus Government refused to allow such a rotation of personnel. After much negotiation through the UN officials on the island, the Government agreed to raise its ongoing blockade of the Turkish Cypriots entrenched in the Kokkina district and to allow the normal rotation of troops for the Turkish force stationed on Cyprus. The Turkish Government now consented that this force should come under UN command on the island.

GENERAL GRIVAS

There was further tension in Cyprus during March 1966 over the position of Gen. Grivas, the former head of EOKA. Grivas had returned to the island in June 1964 at a time when it was felt that he might be able, with his high personal prestige, to bring to order the small 'private armies' and 'irregular bands' that had emerged among the Greek Cypriots and were violently defying the Cyprus Government.

In March 1966 President Makarios attempted to limit the functions of Gen. Grivas in Cyprus and to end a situation whereby political control was vested in himself, while command of the armed forces (both the Greek Cypriot National Guard and also the 'volunteer' Greek troops stationed in Cyprus) rested with the General, who took his orders from Greece. The President's proposal that the National Guard should be transferred to the control of the Cyprus Minister of Defence found favour neither with Gen. Grivas nor the Government in Athens, where it provoked a serious political crisis.

The military coup in Greece in April 1967 was followed by a brief improvement in Greco-Turkish relations. The Prime Ministers and ministers responsible for foreign affairs of Greece and Turkey met in Thrace in September, but failed to reach an agreement on Cyprus. Greece rejected any form of partition, which was implicit in the Turkish proposal to accept *Enosis* in return for military bases and 10% of the island's territory.

TURKISH CYPRIOT ADMINISTRATION

On 29 December 1967 Turkish Cypriot political leaders announced the establishment of a 'Transitional Administration' to administer their community's affairs until the provisions of the 1960 Constitution were implemented. Measures were approved to establish separate executive, legislative and judicial authorities, and Küçük, who remained the official Vice-President of Cyprus, was appointed President of the Transitional Administration, with Rauf Denktaş as Vice-President. A legislative body was established, consisting of the Turkish Cypriot members of the House of Representatives elected in 1960 and the members of the Turkish Communal Chamber, and a nine-member executive council was formed. President Makarios described the Transitional Administration as 'totally illegal', but it proceeded to function as the de facto Government of the Turkish community in Cyprus.

INTERCOMMUNAL TALKS

In early 1968 the Cypriot Government gradually relaxed the measures it had adopted against the Turkish community. With the exception of the Turkish area in Nicosia, freedom of movement for Turkish Cypriots was restored, checkpoints were removed and unrestricted supplies to Turkish areas were permitted. In April Denktaş was allowed to return from exile in Turkey, and in May he began talks with Glavkos Klerides, the President of the House of Representatives. These negotiations were intended to form the basis of a settlement of the constitutional differences between the Greek and Turkish communities, but very little progress was made. There was still an impasse—the Turks demanding local autonomy and the Greeks rejecting any proposals tending towards a federal solution, fearing that this might lead to partition.

TERRORISM AND ELECTIONS, 1969–70

There was a marked reduction in intercommunal violence while the talks between the Greek and Turkish communities continued. However, the Greek population of the island was divided between supporters of Makarios and his aim of an independent unitary state, and those who demanded union with Greece. In 1969 the National Front, an organization advocating immediate *Enosis*, embarked on a campaign of violence, raiding police stations to steal arms, bombing British military buildings and vehicles, shooting and wounding the chief of police, and launching several (unsuccessful) bomb attacks against government ministers. An attempt in March 1970 to assassinate President Makarios was attributed to the National Front, and a week later Polykarpos Georghadjis, a former Minister of the Interior, was found shot dead. At the trial of the President's would-be assassins, Georghadjis was named as a party to the conspiracy.

Despite the activities of the National Front, the Government decided to hold a general election on 5 July 1970. The dissolved House of Representatives had been in existence since 1960, and the elections, which should have been held in 1965, according to the Constitution, had been postponed from year to year. The continued absence of the 15 Turkish members, who met as part of the Turkish Legislative Assembly, meant that the House of Representatives contained only the 35 Greek Cypriot members. Fifteen of the Greek Cypriot seats were won by the Unified Party, led by Klerides, with a policy of support for President Makarios and a united, independent Cyprus. The communist Progressive Party of the Working People (AKEL) won nine seats, to become the second largest in the House. The elections held at the same time by the Turkish Cypriots to their own legislature resulted in a victory for the National Solidarity Party, led by Denktaş.

RETURN OF GRIVAS AND EOKA-B, 1971–72

The ideal of *Enosis* remained attractive to many Greek Cypriots, despite the lack of success for pro-union candidates in the election. Gen. Grivas denounced the President in an article in an Athens newspaper, demanding his resignation on the grounds that, by abandoning *Enosis*, the President had betrayed EOKA's struggle for freedom.

In September 1971 Grivas returned secretly to Cyprus and began to hold meetings with the leaders of the National Front and with his erstwhile followers from the EOKA movement of the 1950s. President Makarios threatened to arrest the General for setting up armed bands, and declared his opposition to the achievement of *Enosis* by violent means. For their part, pro-*Enosis* Greek Cypriots condemned the intercommunal talks and rejected the idea of a negotiated compromise with the Turkish community.

Makarios had been under pressure for some time from the Greek Government to dismiss ministers it considered hostile. In February 1972 it was suggested in Athens that a Cypriot government of national unity should be formed, including the more moderate representatives of Gen. Grivas's movement. For some months the President resisted this pressure, and it seemed that the Greek Government, in alliance with dissident bishops and Grivas, was intent on forcing his resignation. In May the Minister of Foreign Affairs, Spyros Kyprianou, who had been the main target of Greek hostility and one of the President's closest associates, resigned, and in June the President capitulated and carried out an extensive reorganization of his Council of Ministers. Grivas organized a new guerrilla force, EOKA-B, and launched a series of attacks on the Makarios Government similar to those against British rule in the 1950s.

1973 PRESIDENTIAL ELECTION

The demand for a plebiscite from supporters of Gen. Grivas was put forward as an alternative to the election for the presidency, called by President Makarios as a test of strength. The President set out his position in February 1973: while believing in *Enosis*, he considered that talks with the Turkish community on the basis of an independent Cyprus were the only practical possibility. He condemned terrorism and violence as counter-productive, likely to lead to Turkish intervention. The Greek Government also repudiated terrorism and expressed its support for a constitutional solution.

On 8 February 1973 Makarios was returned unopposed for a third five-year term as President, and in the Turkish quarter of Nicosia Denktaş was declared elected Vice-President, following the withdrawal of Ahmet Berberoğlu from the poll.

EOKA-B continued its campaign throughout 1973, concentrating on bombings and raids on police stations. In July the Minister of Justice, Christos Vakis, was kidnapped, prompting an escalation in violence. The President rejected the terms put forward by Grivas for the release of Vakis. Numerous police and National Guard officers, suspected of being Grivas sympathizers, were dismissed, and Vakis was released in August. Action by security forces against secret EOKA-B bases resulted in many arrests, the seizure of quantities of munitions and the discovery of plans to assassinate the President. President Georgios Papadopoulos of Greece publicly condemned the activities of 'the illegal organization of Gen. Grivas', which undermined the Greek policy of 'support for the finding of a solution to the Cyprus problem through the enlarged local talks aimed at ensuring an independent, sovereign and unitary state'.

ABORTIVE MILITARY COUP OF 1974

The deposition of three bishops of the Orthodox Church of Cyprus for attempting to remove Archbishop Makarios from the Church, and the resultant demonstrations of popular support for the President, enabled the Cyprus Government to take strong measures against other supporters of Gen. Grivas. Forces loyal to the President conducted a military campaign against EOKA-B, and carried out a purge of the armed forces and police—some of whose members had collaborated with the guerrillas and helped in their raids. The Grivas campaign of terrorism seemed to have been checked by the beginning of 1974, and when Grivas died as a result of a heart attack in January the President granted an amnesty to 100 of his imprisoned supporters, hoping to restore normality in Cyprus.

In June 1974 President Makarios ordered a purge of EOKA supporters in the police, civil service, schools and National Guard, and on 2 July he accused the Greek military regime of giving arms and subsidies to EOKA and of using the Greek army officers attached to the Cyprus National Guard for subversion. The President demanded that the Greek officers who had collaborated with EOKA should be withdrawn, and began to take steps to ensure that the Guard was loyal to Cyprus, rather than to Greece and *Enosis*. The National Guard, apparently with Greek support, then staged a coup, and on 15 July a former EOKA militant, Nikos Sampson, was appointed President. Makarios fled to the United Kingdom, the resistance of his supporters was crushed, and Greece sent more officers to reinforce the National Guard.

Denktaş, the Turkish Cypriot leader, appealed for military action by the United Kingdom and Turkey, as guarantors of Cypriot independence, to prevent Greece imposing *Enosis*. Having failed to induce the United Kingdom to intervene, Turkey acted unilaterally. Turkish troops landed in Cyprus on 20 July 1974 and seized the port of Kyrenia and a corridor connecting it to the Turkish sector in Nicosia. A cease-fire on 22 July did not prevent further Turkish advances, and the UN peace-keeping force had little success in its efforts to interpose itself between the two Cypriot communities. Massacres and other atrocities were reported from many bi-communal villages, reinforcing the hostility between the Greeks and Turks.

TURKEY OCCUPIES NORTHERN CYPRUS

The successful Turkish invasion had foiled Greek plans to take over Cyprus using the National Guard, and when the military Government in Greece resigned on 23 July 1974, Sampson did likewise. Klerides, the moderate Speaker of the House of Representatives, was appointed President, and promptly began negotiations with Denktaş. The United Kingdom, Greece and Turkey also held talks (in Geneva, Switzerland), but these were unsuccessful, owing to Turkish demands for the establishment of a cantonal federation giving almost one-third of the area of Cyprus to the Turkish Cypriots.

On 14 August 1974, the day after the Geneva talks ended, the war was renewed. Turkish forces seized the whole of Cyprus north of what became the 'Attila Line', or 'Green Line', running from Morphou through Nicosia to Famagusta, and the new civilian Government in Greece announced its inability to intervene. Turkey proclaimed that, by this fait accompli, the boundaries of an autonomous Turkish Cypriot administration had been established. For his part, Denktaş spoke of establishing a completely independent Turkish Cypriot state north of the Green Line and of encouraging the immigration of Turkish Cypriots from areas still under Greek Cypriot control, to produce a permanent ethnic and political partition of the island. An important round of peace talks on the Cyprus problem began in Vienna, Austria, between Klerides and Denktaş in January 1975, under the aegis of UN Secretary-General Dr Kurt Waldheim. However, there remained considerable distance between the two sides regarding the political future of the island: the Turkish Cypriots sought a bi-regional federation with strong regional governments, whereas the Greeks favoured a multi-regional or cantonal federation with a strong central government.

On 13 February 1975 a 'Turkish Federated State of Cyprus' ('TFSC') was proclaimed in the part of the island under Turkish occupation. The new 'state' was not declared an independent republic, but rather a restructuring of the Autonomous Turkish Cypriot Administration, a body established after the invasion, 'on the basis of a secular and federated state until such time as the 1960 Constitution of the Republic . . . is amended in a similar manner to become the Constitution of the Federal Republic of Cyprus'. Denktaş was appointed President of the new 'state'. Greece denounced this move as a threat to peace and declared that the issue would be taken to the UN Security Council, which, in March, adopted a resolution (No. 367) regretting the unilateral decision to establish a Turkish Federated State.

The flight of Turkish Cypriots to British bases after the National Guard coup, and the withdrawal of Greek Cypriot civilians before the advancing Turkish army, had created a major problem in Cyprus. In August 1974 the UN estimated that there were some 225,600 refugees in Cyprus, of whom 183,800 were Greek Cypriots. In the southern part of Cyprus, under Greek Cypriot control, there were 198,800 refugees, of whom 35,000 were Turkish Cypriots, including prisoners of war. This problem persisted in 1976, when an estimated 200,000 refugees remained on the island. However, in August 1975 9,000 Turkish Cypriots were given the opportunity to move to the northern sector. In return, the Turkish Cypriot authorities allowed 800 relatives of Greeks who remained in the north to join them in the Turkish sector. The concern over the treatment of Greeks in the Turkish-occupied area gave rise in that month to an investigation by the European Commission of Human Rights, which in a report published in January 1977 found Turkey guilty of committing atrocities in Cyprus.

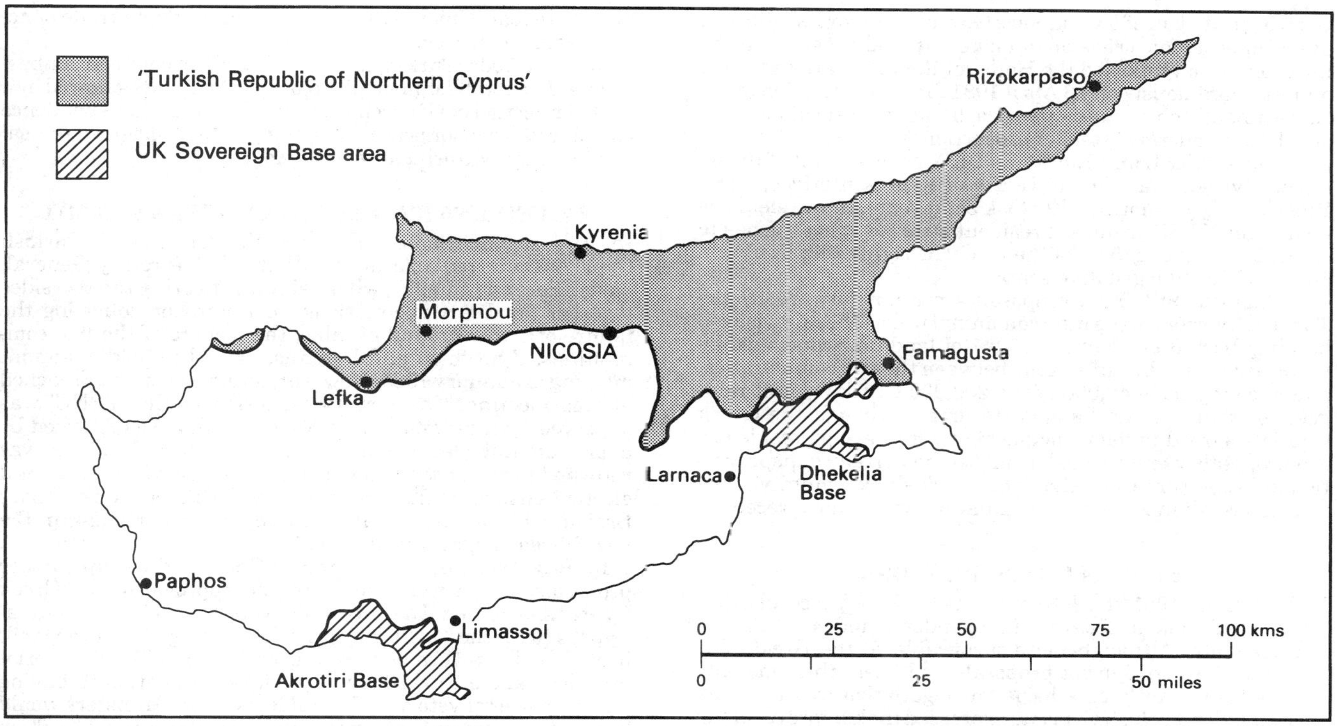

Cyprus, showing the 'Turkish Republic of Northern Cyprus'

In December 1974 Archbishop Makarios returned to Cyprus and resumed the presidency. In January 1975 the United Kingdom decided to permit the resettlement of more than 9,000 Turkish Cypriot refugees from the British Sovereign Base at Akrotiri. In retaliation for the alleged ill-treatment of Turkish Cypriots still living in Greek areas, and in order to force a decision on the release of the refugees and their resettlement, the Turks threatened to expel all remaining Greek Cypriots in northern Cyprus and initiated a scheme to colonize the area, bringing thousands of farmers and peasants from mainland Turkey and settling them in Greek-owned property.

ELECTIONS AND INTERCOMMUNAL TALKS, 1975–76

In September 1975 talks between the two sides resumed in New York, USA. However, these and further discussions in February 1976 were completely unproductive.

During 1976 general elections were held on both sides of the Green Line. In June Denktaş was elected President of the 'TFSC'. His election placed him constitutionally above party politics, but in fact his position depended upon the support of the National Unity Party (UBP). Under the terms of the Constitution promulgated by the Turkish Cypriot authorities, 40 deputies were elected to a legislative assembly, with the UBP gaining a majority. Nejat Konuk, the Secretary-General of the UBP, was appointed Prime Minister.

In September a general election was conducted in the government-controlled area. A new party under Spyros Kyprianou, the Democratic Front (supporting the policies of Archbishop Makarios), won a decisive victory, taking 21 of the 35 seats. The party of Klerides, the Democratic Rally (DISY), failed to secure representation.

In January 1977 Denktaş initiated a meeting with Makarios to establish preliminaries for resuming intercommunal talks (suspended since February 1976); Makarios made it clear that he was prepared to accept a bi-zonal federation provided that the Turkish authorities made territorial concessions, and only if there was provision for a central government with adequate powers. A sixth round of talks, which opened in Vienna in March, broke down, was resumed in Nicosia in May, but was then suspended until after the general election due in Turkey in June.

DEATH OF MAKARIOS, ACCESSION OF KYPRIANOU

The death of Archbishop Makarios on 3 August 1977 put an end to hopes for an immediate continuation of negotiations, and gave rise to fears about the stability of the Greek Cypriot regime in his absence. Kyprianou, the President of the House of Representatives, was elected on 31 August to serve the remainder of Makarios's presidential term. In the presidential election of January 1978 he was returned to office unopposed. Shortly afterwards EOKA-B announced its dissolution, but in April, after the discovery of a destabilization plot, 22 of its members were arrested.

In April 1978, following criticism in the Turkish Cypriot press about rising prices, Nejat Konuk resigned as Prime Minister of the 'TFSC' and was replaced by Osman Orek, the former President of the National Assembly. In December factional disputes within the UBP prompted the resignation of Prime Minister Orek and his Government. A new Council of Ministers was formed under Mustafa Çağatay, previously the Minister of Labour, Social Affairs and Health. In April 1979 a new party, the Democratic Party, was formed by Konuk, as the UBP lost support in the legislature.

On 19 May 1979 Kyprianou and Denktaş drew up a 10-point agenda, based on the Makarios-Denktaş agreement of February 1977. However, intercommunal talks in June were adjourned after a week, due to differences in the interpretation of the agreement, which Turkish Cypriots saw as providing for bi-zonality on the island. Meanwhile, the UNFICYP mandate continued to be extended at six-monthly intervals.

On 9 September 1980 a reorganization of the Greek Cypriot Government led to the appointment of seven new ministers. As a result, President Kyprianou came under criticism from the communist AKEL and from the right-wing opposition under Klerides, thus losing his overall majority in the House of Representatives. During the next three months three new 'centrist' political parties were established: the Pan-Cypriot Renewal Front (PAME), the Democratic Party (DIKO) and the Centre Union.

ELECTIONS AND FURTHER TALKS, 1980–81

On 16 September 1980, in the shadow of the military coup in Turkey, the intercommunal peace talks were resumed after an interval of 15 months, and continued intermittently thereafter.

Growing criticism of Kyprianou's Government for its failure to avert an economic crisis or to make any real progress in the intercommunal talks led the House of Representatives to vote almost unanimously on 16 April 1981 for the dissolution of the Government. In the subsequent parliamentary elections, held on 24 May under a system of proportional representation, the communist AKEL and Klerides's DISY each won 12 of the 35 Greek Cypriot seats in the House of Representatives, while President Kyprianou's DIKO took eight seats. In the elections held in the 'TFSC' in June, President Denktaş was returned to office, but with only 52% of the vote. His right-wing UBP won 18 out of the 40 legislative seats.

In August 1981 fresh proposals were put forward by the Turkish Cypriots in the intercommunal talks. These envisaged handing back 3%–4% of the 35.8% of land now controlled by them, as well as the buffer zone between the two communities, and allowing some 40,000 of the 200,000 Greek Cypriot refugees to return to the Famagusta area. Although the Greek Cypriots agreed to the principle of an alternating presidency, the proposals were rejected owing to the perceived disproportionate representation that the Turkish community, who formed less than 20% of the population, would have received.

NEW UN PEACE PROPOSAL

In November 1981 the UN presented a new peace plan, or 'evaluation', for a federal, independent and non-aligned Cypriot state. Although more favourable to the Greek side than the Turkish Cypriot proposals had been, this was only accepted reluctantly as a basis for negotiation by the Greek Cypriots. The Turkish Cypriots expressed their approval of the UN's plan.

With a presidential election in view, President Kyprianou and his DIKO party formed an electoral alliance with AKEL in April 1982, based on a 'minimum programme' of continuance of the non-aligned status quo, defence of the mixed economy and support for the intercommunal talks. This put a strain on relations with the Greek Government, since it was contrary to the policy recently laid down by both Governments.

In the 'TFSC' the Çağatay Government resigned in December 1981. A period of political crisis ensued, and it was not until March 1982 that a coalition Government was formed under the leadership of Çağatay comprising his own UBP, the Democratic People's Party and the Turkish Unity Party.

In February 1983 President Kyprianou was re-elected, with 56.5% of the vote, for a five-year term. The DISY candidate, Klerides, polled 34.0%.

In May 1983 the UN General Assembly voted overwhelmingly in favour of the withdrawal of Turkish troops from Cyprus, although the USA and the United Kingdom abstained in protest against the perceived partisan wording of the resolution. In retaliation, Denktaş threatened to boycott any further intercommunal talks and to call a referendum in the 'TFSC' to decide whether to make a unilateral declaration of independence and seek international recognition. The Cyprus pound was replaced by the Turkish lira as legal tender in the 'TFSC'.

DECLARATION OF 'TURKISH REPUBLIC OF NORTHERN CYPRUS'

On 15 November 1983 the 'TFSC' made a unilateral declaration of independence as the 'Turkish Republic of Northern Cyprus' ('TRNC'), with Denktaş as President. Later that month Çağatay resigned as Turkish Cypriot Prime Minister and as leader of the UBP. On 2 December the Legislative Assembly of the 'TRNC' adopted legislation for the establishment of a 70-member constituent assembly (comprising the 40 elected members of the Legislative Assembly and 30 others appointed from representative groups within the community), which met for the first time on 6 December. The following day Denktaş appointed the President of the 'TRNC' Legislative Assembly, Konuk, as Prime Minister of an interim Council of Ministers, pending elections in 1984. Like the 'TFSC', the 'TRNC' was recognized only by Turkey, and the declaration of independence was condemned (in Resolution 541) by the UN Security Council. However, the European Community (EC, now European Union—EU) resolved not to apply trade sanctions against the 'TRNC'.

In April 1984 Turkey and the 'TRNC' exchanged ambassadors. The establishment of diplomatic links was followed by a formal rejection of UN proposals for a freezing of independence as a precondition for peace talks, along with a continued refusal to return the Varosha area of Famagusta.

FAILED 1985 KYPRIANOU-DENKTAŞ SUMMIT

In August and September 1984 the Greek and Turkish Cypriots conferred separately with the UN Secretary-General, Javier Pérez de Cuéllar, whose aim was to bring the two sides together for direct negotiations. In December, following the failure of a third round of talks, the leaders of the two communities, Kyprianou and Denktaş, agreed to hold a summit meeting in January 1985. However, no agreement was reached at this meeting. The new Constitution of the 'TRNC' was approved by a referendum in May, and this was followed by a presidential election on 9 June, at which Denktaş was returned to power with more than 70% of the votes. A general election ensued on 23 June, with the UBP, led by Dr Derviş Eroğlu, winning more seats than any other party (24) in the new 50-seat Legislative Assembly.

In July 1985 the UN Secretary-General drew up further proposals, which were met with the approval of the Greek Cypriots. The new UN proposals were for a bi-zonal federal Cyprus (with the Turkish Cypriots occupying 29% of the land) in which the government would be led by a Greek Cypriot president and a Turkish Cypriot vice-president, both having limited power of veto over federal legislation. Ministers would be appointed in a ratio of seven Greek Cypriots to three Turkish Cypriots. One 'major' ministry would always be held by a Turkish Cypriot, and a special working party would consider demands that the minister of foreign affairs should always be a Turkish Cypriot. There would be two assemblies: an upper house, with a 50:50 community representation, and a lower house, with 70:30 representation in favour of the Greek Cypriots. Legislation on important issues would require 'separate majorities in both chambers'. A tripartite body, including one non-Cypriot voting member, would have the final say in constitutional disagreements concerning the extent of federal power. However, the Turkish Cypriots rejected the proposals, as they wanted Turkish troops to remain on the island indefinitely to protect their interests, and believed that any peace settlement should include Turkey as a guarantor. They had also revised their opinion on allowing Greek Cypriot refugees to return to the 'TRNC'.

1985 GREEK CYPRIOT ELECTIONS

President Kyprianou had come under severe criticism within the House of Representatives over the failure of the summit in January 1985. He reorganized the Council of Ministers and terminated his alliance with AKEL, which had become increasingly strained, mainly because of Kyprianou's unyielding attitude to the intercommunal talks. In November, following an acrimonious debate over Kyprianou's leadership, the House of Representatives was dissolved.

An early general election was held on 8 December 1985 for an enlarged House of 56 Greek Cypriot seats (compared with 35 previously), while the nominal allocation of seats to the Turkish Cypriot community was increased from 15 to 24. DISY replaced AKEL as the largest party in the House by winning 19 seats, with 33.6% of the vote. Significant gains were also made by DIKO, which won 16 seats and increased its share of the vote to 27.6%. AKEL, meanwhile, took only 15 seats, and its share of the vote declined to 27.4%. The EDEK Socialist Party of Cyprus (EDEK), which supported Kyprianou's stance on peace negotiations, won six seats with 11.1% of the vote.

Further meetings to discuss the UN peace plan were conducted in March 1986. On this occasion, the Turkish Cypriots accepted the draft peace plan, while the Greek Cypriots declared their opposition to the proposals.

In July 1986 Turgut Özal, the Prime Minister of Turkey, made his first visit to the 'TRNC' and urged the adoption of an economic model similar to that in Turkey. The Communal Liberation Party (TKP) disagreed with this policy, and in

August it withdrew from the 'TRNC' coalition Government. In September the Prime Minister, Eroğlu, formed a new administration in coalition with the New Dawn Party.

In an address to the UN General Assembly in October 1987, Kyprianou proposed an international peace-keeping force to replace the armed forces of both the Greek and Turkish Cypriots. Denktaş, however, maintained that negotiations on the establishment of a federal bi-zonal republic should precede any demilitarization.

ELECTION OF VASSILIOU AS PRESIDENT

The first round of voting in a presidential election took place in the Greek Cypriot zone on 14 February 1988. However, since no candidate received more than 50% of the total vote, a second round was held a week later to decide between the two leading candidates at the first round—the leader of DISY, Glavkos Klerides, with 33.3% of the total vote, and Georghios Vassiliou, an independent who had the unofficial support of AKEL, with 30.1%. Kyprianou, seeking a third consecutive term, was third, with 27.3%. This unexpected defeat was widely interpreted as a result of the failure of Kyprianou's uncompromising stance on reunification. In the second round of voting, Vassiliou, with the backing of EDEK and a significant number of Kyprianou supporters (the outgoing President had declared that he would not support either candidate), was elected as the new President by a narrow margin, taking 51.6% of the total votes cast.

President Vassiliou, unlike Kyprianou, quickly expressed his willingness to enter into direct informal dialogue with the Turkish Cypriot leader. Vassiliou also promised to re-establish the National Council (originally convened by President Makarios), which was to include representatives from all the main Greek Cypriot parties, to negotiate plans for the settlement of the Cyprus problem. On 28 February 1988 Vassiliou was officially sworn in as the new President and named a new Council of Ministers.

RESUMPTION OF INTERCOMMUNAL TALKS

After a meeting with the newly revived National Council in June 1988, President Vassiliou agreed to a proposal by the UN Secretary-General to resume intercommunal talks, without pre-conditions, with President Denktaş. Following a meeting with the Turkish Government in July, Denktaş also approved the proposal. Consequently, the impasse between the two sides was ended and a UN-sponsored summit meeting proceeded in Geneva on 24 August. At this summit, Vassiliou and Denktaş resumed direct talks on a settlement of all aspects of the Cyprus problem. As a result of the meeting, the two leaders began the first formal round of substantive direct negotiations, under UN auspices, in Nicosia on 15 September 1988. However, despite several rounds of intensive talks, held in Nicosia and New York, it became apparent by June 1989 that no progress had been achieved.

In May 1989, under the supervision of UNFICYP, a non-confrontation agreement (reached in March) was implemented, which involved the withdrawal of Greek Cypriot and Turkish Cypriot troops from 24 military posts along the central Nicosia sector of the Green Line. In July, however, tensions increased when more than 100 protesters were arrested by the Turkish Cypriot forces during demonstrations against the continuing partition of the island.

ABORTIVE 1990 VASSILIOU-DENKTAŞ SUMMIT

A new round of UN-sponsored talks, which began in February 1990 in New York, came to a premature end in March, following disagreement arising from demands by President Denktaş that the right to self-determination of the Turkish Cypriots be recognized by the Greek Cypriot community. President Vassiliou accused Denktaş of deliberately frustrating hopes of a settlement by introducing new conditions to the negotiations and implicitly advocating some form of partition or secession. Denktaş, in turn, accused Vassiliou of refusing to consider any form of compromise. A resolution approved by the UN Security Council later in March rejected Denktaş's stance and reaffirmed the UN's commitment to a resolution based on a bi-communal federal republic.

Later in March 1990 Denktaş resigned the presidency of the 'TRNC' and called an early presidential election for 22 April. Denktaş, standing as an independent, received 66.7% of the votes cast, while Ismail Bozkurt, who also stood as an independent, received about 32%. Denktaş's victory was widely interpreted as a sign of Turkish Cypriot approval of the President's stance throughout the recent negotiations with President Vassiliou, although opposition parties advocating a more conciliatory approach commanded significant support.

The UBP retained its majority in the 'TRNC' Legislative Assembly at a general election on 6 May 1990, securing 34 of the 50 seats. In June Denktaş approved the appointment of several newcomers to the Council of Ministers, which Eroğlu continued to head as Prime Minister.

In July 1990 Cyprus formally applied for full membership of the EC. International observers regarded the political division within the island as a major obstacle to Cyprus's achieving member status, while President Denktaş declared that the 'unilateral' application by the Greek Cypriots on behalf of the whole island would further complicate the search for a political settlement for Cyprus. In July and October, in retaliation for the EC application, the 'TRNC' Government and Turkey signed an agreement envisaging the creation of a customs union, the abolition of passport controls and the introduction of a 'TRNC' currency backed by the Turkish central bank. These 'unilateral' steps were condemned by the Greek Cypriot Government.

1991 GREEK CYPRIOT ELECTIONS

In a general election for the 56 Greek Cypriot seats in the House of Representatives held on 19 May 1991, the conservative DISY, in alliance with the Liberal Party, received 35.8% of the votes cast and secured 20 seats. The AKEL communists unexpectedly achieved the biggest advance, with 30.6% of the vote and 18 seats. The EDEK socialists also gained ground by securing seven seats in the House, while support for the 'centrist' DIKO decreased to 19.5% of the vote and just 11 seats.

RESUMPTION OF UN-SPONSORED TALKS, 1991–92

US diplomatic efforts resulted in an announcement by President George Bush in August 1991 that the Greek and Turkish Prime Ministers had confirmed their willingness to attend a UN-sponsored conference in New York with the aim of finding a solution to the Cyprus question. However, although Presidents Vassiliou and Denktaş declared their support for this initiative, hopes of a breakthrough receded when the UN Secretary-General, Javier Pérez de Cuéllar, made it clear that the conference would not be convened unless progress had been made on resolving outstanding differences.

On taking office on 1 January 1992, the new UN Secretary-General, Dr Boutros Boutros-Ghali, initiated another attempt to establish the basis for a high-level conference on Cyprus. To this end, UN envoys visited Cyprus, Turkey and Greece in February, and Boutros-Ghali held meetings in New York with Vassiliou and Denktaş in January and March. However, in a report to the Security Council in April, the UN Secretary-General advised that no progress had been made towards resolving basic disagreements and that 'there has even been regression'.

In accordance with Security Council instructions, Boutros-Ghali held further separate talks with Vassiliou and Denktaş in New York in June 1992, when deliberations centred on UN proposals for the demarcation of Greek Cypriot and Turkish Cypriot areas of administration under a federal structure. In view of the reluctance of the parties to discuss lines on a map, the cartographic ideas put forward by Boutros-Ghali were described as a 'non-map'. The 'non-map' showed that the proposed area of Turkish administration would be about 25% smaller than the 'TRNC', from the existing territory of which the Greek Cypriots would recover Morphou and Varosha (although not old Famagusta) and a total of 34 villages. According to the published details, the new division would, *inter alia*, create a Turkish enclave to the east of Nicosia and a Greek enclave in the north-eastern tip of the island. Some 60,000 displaced Greek Cypriots were expected to be able to return to their pre-1974 homes and remain under Greek Cypriot administration.

Following further unsuccessful UN-sponsored talks, conducted in New York during October and November 1992, the Secretary-General took the unusual step of publishing a tabulation of the respective responses to his settlement ideas. This revealed that, whereas the Greek Cypriot side accepted the proposals and the UN map as the basis for a negotiated settlement, the Turkish Cypriot side had reservations with regard to nine of the 100 articles, all of which dealt with crucial matters. The tabulation demonstrated that, apart from the basic issues of sovereignty and territorial division, the Turkish Cypriots were continuing to insist that the posts of federal president and vice-president should rotate between the two communities and that the federal government should comprise an equal number of Greek Cypriot and Turkish Cypriot ministers. The Greek Cypriots proposed that the two most senior positions should be decided by 'federation-wide and weighted universal suffrage', and also endorsed the UN proposal that there should be a 7:3 ratio of Greek Cypriot and Turkish Cypriot ministers, although they accepted that a Turkish Cypriot should normally hold one of the three main portfolios of foreign affairs, finance and defence. Moreover, while both sides accepted the 'security and guarantees' section of the UN proposals (including provisions for the withdrawal of all non-Cypriot forces), considerable disagreement persisted as to whether or not the 1959 treaty of guarantee afforded Turkey a unilateral right of intervention in Cyprus.

GREEK CYPRIOT AND TURKISH CYPRIOT ELECTIONS, 1993

The veteran DISY leader, Klerides, was the unexpected victor in the Greek Cypriot presidential election conducted in two rounds on 7 and 14 February 1993, narrowly defeating Vassiliou. Again standing as an independent with AKEL support, Vassiliou led the first-round voting with 44.2%, compared with 36.7% for Klerides. During the campaign Klerides had distanced himself from the Government's stance regarding the settlement negotiations, enabling DIKO and EDEK, both strongly opposed to the UN plan, to transfer their support to Klerides, who won 50.3% of the second-round vote. The new Government, appointed by the President-elect on 25 February, contained six DISY ministers and five from DIKO.

Although the new Turkish President, Süleyman Demirel, recommended that Denktaş should adopt a more conciliatory approach to the intercommunal negotiations, Denktaş failed to meet the UN Secretary-General's deadline of June 1993 for acceptance of the proposed confidence-building measures. A mission to Athens, Cyprus and Ankara, Turkey, undertaken by the UN Secretary-General's new Special Representative in Cyprus, Joe Clark, failed to foster any significant new initiative for peace.

An early general election in the 'TRNC' on 12 December 1993 partially resolved a long power struggle between Denktaş and Prime Minister Eroğlu, in the former's favour. The UBP, once led by Denktaş but now advocating Eroğlu's openly pro-partition stance, remained the largest party in the Legislative Assembly, but failed to win an overall majority. The pro-Denktaş Democrat Party (DP) and the left-wing Republican Turkish Party (CTP) thereupon agreed to form a coalition, under the premiership of Hakki Atun, the DP leader. The new coalition supported the Denktaş stance that talks should continue, while at the same time confirming policy positions likely to ensure continued stalemate.

DEADLOCK ON CONFIDENCE-BUILDING MEASURES

Negotiations in the first half of 1994 on the UN-sponsored confidence-building measures centred on the proposed transfer to UN administration of the Turkish-held Varosha suburb of Famagusta (so that its former Greek Cypriot inhabitants might then return) and the reopening of Nicosia airport for use by both sides. Despite a further visit by Clark in May, no agreement could be reached. In a report subsequently submitted to the Security Council, the UN Secretary-General again censured the Turkish Cypriots for failing to show the political will needed to produce a settlement. In the following month, however, he amended this verdict by stating that there was 'a very substantial measure of agreement' and that the only obstacle to implementation of the confidence-building measures was disputed methodology. The Greek Cypriots countered that this assessment did not give 'the true picture' of the persisting differences between the two sides.

In a concurrent deterioration, at the end of May 1994 Denktaş warned that if Greek Cyprus was admitted to the EU without reference to the Turkish Cypriots, the 'TRNC' would opt for integration with Turkey. However, this warning did not deter the Greek Cypriots from openly welcoming an EU decision, in June, to include Cyprus in the next phase of enlargement. The Greek Cypriot Government was also gratified in July by a ruling of the European Court of Justice banning EU members from importing goods from the 'TRNC'. This ruling was condemned by the 'TRNC' authorities. In August the 'TRNC' Legislative Assembly sought co-ordination with Turkey on defence and foreign policy, and rejected a federal solution, urging instead 'political equality and sovereignty' for the Turkish Cypriots.

In Resolution 939, adopted on 29 July 1994, the UN Security Council effectively conceded that confidence-building measures were not a realistic possibility in the absence of agreement on fundamental issues. Following a November 1993 agreement placing Cyprus within 'the Greek defence area', joint Greek-Greek Cypriot military exercises were held for the first time in October 1994, matching similar military co-operation between the 'TRNC' and Turkey.

TURKISH CYPRIOT PRESIDENTIAL ELECTION, 1995

Atun resigned as 'TRNC' Prime Minister on 24 February 1995, after the CTP had opposed Denktaş's offer, made in advance of the scheduled presidential election, to distribute to 'TRNC' citizens the title deeds to property in the north owned by Greek Cypriots; however, following the rejection by the UBP leader, Eroğlu, of an invitation to form a government, the DP leader was reappointed in the following month. At the presidential election, conducted on 15 and 22 April, Denktaş for the first time failed to win an outright majority in the first round (receiving only 40.4% of the vote), although he achieved a comfortable 62.5% victory over Eroğlu in the second round. Protracted inter-party negotiations were then required prior to the formation of a new Government, which was a further DP-CTP coalition under Atun's premiership.

In a statement issued on 2 May 1995, Denktaş suggested that war might result from unilateral Greek Cypriot accession to the EU, because this would constitute a form of *Enosis* with Greece (already an EU member) and would be in breach of international treaty stipulations that Cyprus was barred from joining any supranational grouping that did not include both Greece and Turkey. Two days later President Klerides led a visit to Athens by the Greek Cypriot National Council (consisting of the main party leaders) for a 'unity' meeting with Greek government leaders, at which he expressed gratitude for Greek support for his administration's EU application.

1996 GREEK CYPRIOT ELECTIONS—NEW 'TRNC' GOVERNMENT

Greek Cypriot elections to the House of Representatives were held on 26 May 1996. DISY remained the largest single party, with 20 seats (34.5% of the vote), slightly ahead of the opposition AKEL, which took 19 seats (33.0%). DIKO lost one of its 11 seats (16.4%), while EDEK retained only five seats (8.1%) and the new Movement of Free Democrats (KED), led by former President Vassiliou, won the remaining two seats (3.7%). DISY remained the dominant party in the new coalition Government that was subsequently formed with DIKO.

UN and EU endeavours to bring the sides together continued parallel to an ongoing US initiative, while in May 1996 the British Government appointed Sir David Hannay, the United Kingdom's former ambassador to the UN, to be its own special representative for Cyprus.

Following policy disagreements, the DP-CTP coalition Government in the 'TRNC' resigned in July 1996; the UBP authorized Eroğlu to begin talks with the DP, now headed by Serdar Denktaş (the President's son, who had been elected to the party leadership in May), on forming a new government. After a successful conclusion to the negotiations, the protocol of the new DP-UBP coalition Government was signed in mid-August; ministers assumed their duties shortly thereafter, with Eroğlu replacing Atun as Prime Minister and Serdar Denktaş becoming Deputy Prime Minister.

1996 VIOLENCE IN THE UN BUFFER ZONE—CRISIS OVER RUSSIAN MISSILES

From mid-1996 intercommunal relations descended to some of their most hostile levels since 1974, as the result of a series of violent incidents in the UN buffer zone. In June 1996 Turkish Cypriot forces shot and killed an unarmed Greek Cypriot soldier in the Nicosia sector, and in August a Greek Cypriot anti-partition demonstrator was beaten to death by Turkish nationalist extremists during a protest rally, at which an estimated 50 people were injured. The victim's funeral was followed by further violence, in which a Greek Cypriot was shot dead by Turkish Cypriot guards and a further 11 people, including two UN officials, were injured. Tensions were further exacerbated in September when a Turkish Cypriot soldier was shot and killed, and another wounded, across the buffer zone, in the south-eastern sector, and in October another Greek Cypriot was shot dead by Turkish Cypriot forces near the British military base at Dhekelia.

In a landmark judgment delivered on 18 December 1996, the European Court of Human Rights (ECHR) ruled that Turkey, as the effective power in the 'TRNC', had breached the European Convention on Human Rights by denying a Greek Cypriot woman, Titina Loizidou, access to her property in Kyrenia since the 1974 invasion. The ruling opened the way for compensation claims against Turkey by other displaced persons, although Turkey rejected the ruling and also refused to comply with the ECHR's decision in 1998 to award some US $900,000 to Loizidou in damages and costs.

A further severe crisis developed in January 1997, when it was confirmed that the Greek Cypriot Government had signed an agreement to purchase Russian *S-300* surface-to-air missiles. Amid international criticism of the purchase, particularly by the USA, the 'TRNC' authorities described the agreement as an 'act of aggression', while the Turkish Government warned that it would be prepared to use military force to prevent deployment of the system. Mediation by the USA and other foreign governments succeeded in defusing the immediate crisis on the basis of an assurance by the Greek Cypriot Government that the missiles would not be deployed for at least 13 months. However, indications of continuing tension included a 'TRNC'-Turkish commitment to a joint defence strategy, whereby an attack on the 'TRNC' would be regarded as an attack on Turkey itself.

1997 KLERIDES–DENKTAŞ TALKS—EU ACCESSION NEGOTIATIONS SCHEDULED

Renewed international attempts at mediation prompted by the intercommunal crisis of mid-1996 in Cyprus resulted in meetings between Sir David Hannay and the two Cypriot leaders in October, as a result of which the British special representative announced that adequate progress had been made to enable direct negotiations to resume, under UN auspices, in 1997. At the same time senior military commanders from both sides began UN-sponsored talks with the aim of defusing tension along the demarcation line.

Following proximity talks, which had begun in March 1997, Klerides and Denktaş attended their first direct discussions for three years on 9–12 July at Troutbeck, New York. The meetings were chaired by UN Special Representative Diego Córdovez and were attended by the UN Secretary-General, Kofi Annan, and other Security Council representatives. Sufficient progress was made for further direct talks to be held by the two leaders in late July, in Nicosia, where agreement was reached regarding the implementation of measures to establish the fate of persons missing since the hostilities both prior to and during the 1974 invasion.

Meanwhile, the Greek Cypriot Government's objective of EU membership became a critical source of dissension in July 1997, when an EU summit in the Netherlands formally agreed that Cyprus would be included in the next phase of EU enlargement, on which negotiations were to begin in 1998. The decision was to apply to Cyprus as a whole, and was regarded by the EU as a possible device for bringing about a settlement that would preserve Cyprus as a single sovereign entity. However, the Turkish Cypriot authorities categorically rejected any EU negotiations not based on Turkish Cypriot sovereignty, while the Turkish Government also opposed any accession by Cyprus to the EU that did not accommodate Turkish Cypriot demands or preceded the admittance of Turkey itself. On 20 July President Denktaş and the Turkish Deputy Prime Minister, Bülent Ecevit, signed a joint declaration threatening to integrate the 'TRNC' into Turkey if EU negotiations with the Greek Cypriot administration commenced as planned.

Another round of formal intercommunal talks, which took place in Switzerland in August 1997, broke down after a matter of days, with Denktaş claiming that the Cypriot application for EU membership was illegal since it had not been made on behalf of the population of the whole island. Relations worsened in December when an EU summit in Luxembourg issued a formal invitation to Cyprus to begin accession negotiations in 1998; the 'TRNC' responded by suspending its participation in intercommunal talks.

RE-ELECTION OF KLERIDES, 1998—MILITARY TENSIONS

The five DIKO ministers resigned from the coalition Greek Cypriot Government in November 1997 (and were replaced by non-partisan technocrats), following an announcement by Klerides that he intended to seek a second presidential term with the endorsement of DISY. In the first round of the presidential election, conducted on 8 February 1998, Georghios Iacovou (with the support of AKEL and DIKO) achieved a narrow lead over Klerides. However, in the second round of voting, conducted on 15 February, Klerides defeated Iacovou with 50.8% of the vote, owing principally to EDEK's decision to offer its support. A new Government of national unity was sworn in on 28 February, including ministers from DISY, EDEK and the United Democrats (EDI) as well as several DIKO dissidents, although DIKO officially joined AKEL in opposition. Vassiliou was appointed chief negotiator for Cyprus at the EU accession talks, which were formally inaugurated on 31 March.

Meanwhile, there had been renewed tensions in January 1998, following the completion of a new Greek Cypriot military airfield at Paphos. In the absence of a Cypriot air force, the airfield was intended to be an emergency base for Greek war planes, and was to be protected by the controversial missiles being purchased from Russia. Vociferous opposition from President Denktaş prompted the Greek Government to emphasize that the new site had the status of a Greek military base, and thus any assault on the site would be regarded as an attack on a mainland military installation. There was further tension in mid-June when six Turkish war planes landed at a 'TRNC' airfield, in response to the landing of Greek military aircraft at Paphos the previous week. While Greek Cypriot and Greek spokesmen described the Turkish action as 'completely illegal', the US Department of State condemned both deployments as unhelpful to the peace process and urged an end to such actions.

At the end of June 1998 President Konstantinos Stefanopoulos of Greece paid an official visit to Cyprus (the first such visit by a Greek head of state since independence in 1960), during which he publicly envisaged 'a free and truly independent Cyprus', with equality for all its citizens. Stefanopoulos also appealed to the Turkish Cypriots to seize the opportunity offered by the prospective accession to the EU. Denktaş responded in August by elaborating his proposal for a confederation based on two sovereignties, and by again rejecting the resumption of intercommunal talks unless the Greek Cypriot Government suspended accession negotiations with the EU.

Parliamentary elections in the 'TRNC', conducted on 6 December 1998, resulted in gains for the UBP, which won 24 of the 50 seats, followed by the DP with 13, the TKP with seven and the CTP with six. At the end of the month UBP leader Eroğlu was reappointed Prime Minister, at the head of a new Government formed in coalition with the TKP.

NON-DEPLOYMENT OF RUSSIAN MISSILES

Following intense pressure from the UN, the USA and the countries of the EU, on 29 December 1998 President Klerides announced that Russian-supplied *S-300* missiles would not after all be deployed in Cyprus. A crucial factor in this decision had been the adoption by the UN Security Council (on 22 December) of two new resolutions pertaining to Cyprus: Resolution 1217 renewed the UNFICYP mandate and urged reunification as a single sovereign state, while Resolution 1218 expressed 'grave concern at the lack of progress towards an overall political settlement' based on UN resolutions, and advocated a phased demilitarization of the island. For the first time the resolutions incorporated a requirement for compliance by the parties involved, although they contained no timetable for a settlement. After consultations with the Greek and Russian authorities, in January 1999 the Greek Cypriot Government confirmed that the missiles would instead be deployed on the Greek island of Crete. Klerides's decision aroused strong domestic criticism and prompted the withdrawal from the ruling coalition of EDEK, which had favoured adherence to the original plan. A reorganization of the Government was announced in March, following the resignation of the Minister of the Interior, Dinos Michaelides, as a result of allegations of corruption (which he strenuously denied).

UN-SPONSORED PROXIMITY TALKS—RE-ELECTION OF DENKTAŞ

Denktaş and Klerides attended UN-sponsored proximity talks in New York in December 1999, which focused on the key issues of the distribution of powers, property rights, territorial issues and security arrangements. However, not least because of the continuing insistence of the Turkish Cypriots on recognition of 'TRNC' sovereignty, no substantive progress was made. The negotiations were also undermined by the EU summit in Helsinki, Finland, in December, which agreed that Turkey (now accorded official candidate status for membership of the Union) could not block the accession of Cyprus to the EU if the island were to remain divided. A second round of talks followed in Geneva in January–February 2000, but failed to break the deadlock.

A presidential election held in the 'TRNC' in April 2000 went to a second round of voting, after Rauf Denktaş won 43.7% of the vote in the first round, thus failing to secure the 50% necessary for an outright victory. However, Denktaş was subsequently declared to have won the election by default after his second-round challenger, Eroğlu, withdrew three days before the vote, in protest against what he alleged was 'interference' in the electoral process. In July thousands of Turkish Cypriots joined a demonstration in Nicosia to demand that Denktaş resign. The demonstration followed the arrest, some 10 days previously, of six people (including four journalists employed by a daily newspaper) on charges of spying for the Greek Cypriots; shortly before the arrests, the newspaper had criticized the role of the Turkish military in the running of the 'TRNC'. The six detainees were released shortly before the demonstration began.

The UNFICYP mandate had continued to be renewed at six-monthly intervals, and in June 2000 the UN Security Council approved a further six-month renewal, urging all states to respect the sovereignty, independence and territorial integrity of Cyprus. However, the approval of Resolution 1303 caused some controversy after the UN altered its wording to accommodate Greek Cypriot concerns that it implicitly recognized the legitimacy of the 'TRNC'. In protest against the amendments (the resolution now excluded any reference to the authority of the 'TRNC'), in July Turkish troops advanced into the UN buffer zone near the Greek Cypriot village of Strovilia and established a checkpoint on the main road, refusing to withdraw despite UN and other appeals.

A third round of proximity talks opened in Geneva in July 2000. The talks were chaired by Alvaro de Soto, the Special Adviser on Cyprus to the UN Secretary-General, who indicated afterwards that the discussions had moved from procedural issues to a more substantive phase; however, two further rounds held in September and November ended without progress.

TURKISH CYPRIOT WITHDRAWAL FROM TALKS—GREEK CYPRIOT ELECTIONS, 2001

The UN-sponsored peace process came to a halt in November 2000, when the Turkish Cypriots announced that they would not participate in the sixth round of proximity talks scheduled to begin in January 2001. Denktaş cited the continuing refusal of the international community to accord recognition to the 'TRNC' as the reason for his withdrawal. A further crucial factor was the Turkish Government's expressed annoyance at the inclusion in newly published draft EU requirements for Turkish accession to the Union of a stipulation that Turkey should expedite a settlement of the Cyprus problem. In December 2000 Turkey secured adjustments to the EU text specifying that the Cyprus impasse would be covered by EU-Turkish 'dialogue' rather than in accession negotiations, although the Turkish Cypriots subsequently remained unyielding to international pressure concerning their refusal to rejoin the UN talks.

The gulf between the Cypriot sides was further emphasized by an ECHR judgment in May 2001 that found Turkey guilty of extensive violations of human rights in the Turkish-occupied area—in which it was deemed to have 'effective overall control'. Whereas the Greek Cypriot Government described the ruling as 'historic', and as its most significant legal victory over Turkey since the 1974 invasion, Turkey dismissed it as 'wrong', while Denktaş claimed that it justified his refusal to participate in further talks.

The Greek Cypriot general election, held on 27 May 2001, produced small but significant changes in the composition of the House of Representatives. AKEL became the largest single party, with 20 of the 56 seats (and 34.7% of the votes cast), overtaking DISY, which retained 19 seats (with 34.0% of the vote). DIKO's representation was reduced to nine seats (14.8%), the Movement of Social Democrats (KISOS—the successor party to EDEK) held only four seats (6.5%) and EDI one (2.6%). Three other parties secured one seat each. When the new House convened in June, the AKEL leader, Demetris Christofias, was elected as its President, receiving crucial support from the DIKO members to defeat the DISY leader, Nikos Anastasiades.

In the 'TRNC' the ruling coalition between the UBP and the TKP was terminated by the former in May 2001. It was replaced in the following month by a coalition of the UBP and the DP, with Eroğlu continuing as Prime Minister and Salih Coşar of the DP becoming Minister of State and Deputy Prime Minister.

RESUMPTION OF UN-SPONSORED TALKS—PUBLICATION OF UN PLAN

International diplomatic pressure on Turkey resulted in an agreement on the part of the Turkish Cypriot side to return to UN-sponsored negotiations, on the basis of the 'Nicosia Agreement' concluded between Klerides and Denktaş on 4 December 2001. This specified that there would be no pre-conditions to renewed talks; that all issues would be open for discussion; that the negotiations would continue 'in good faith' until a comprehensive settlement had been reached; and that 'nothing will be agreed until everything is agreed'. Formal, direct talks between the two leaders began in mid-January 2002 in the UN buffer zone in Nicosia, with Alvaro de Soto in attendance. In February the UN Security Council expressed the hope that a settlement would be reached by June, and this target date for a resolution of 'core' issues (defined as governance, security, territory and property) was reiterated by Secretary-General

Kofi Annan during an official visit to Cyprus in May, despite growing pessimism regarding the progress of the talks. Although Klerides and Denktaş had held 51 separate negotiating sessions by the end of August, they failed to make any breakthrough, with the key obstacle continuing to be the Turkish Cypriot side's insistence on separate sovereignty for the 'TRNC'.

The UN Secretary-General made a further attempt to break the deadlock in New York in October 2002, and persuaded Klerides and Denktaş to agree to the creation of two bilateral committees that would make recommendations on the settlement plan and provide the legislative ingredients of an agreement without prejudicing the positions of the two leaders on the core issues. However, the hospitalization of Denktaş in New York for major heart surgery and his lengthy convalescence prevented the committees from beginning substantive work. Also complicating the situation was the general election in Turkey in early November and the victory of the moderate Islamist Justice and Development Party (AKP). Although the new Turkish Government declared its support for continued negotiations on Cyprus, the Greek Cypriot Government regarded the change of administration in Ankara as making a settlement less likely, especially since the powerful Turkish military establishment continued to back Denktaş in his demand for separate sovereignty. Undeterred, on 11 November Annan presented the full text of his plan for a Cyprus settlement and requested that the two sides sign up to its key provisions in advance of the EU summit to be held in Copenhagen, Denmark, in mid-December, at which Cyprus's candidacy for EU membership was due to be formally approved.

The 137-page 'Annan Plan' proposed the creation of a 'common state' of Cyprus, consisting of equal Greek Cypriot and Turkish Cypriot 'component states', each with its own administration and legislature responsible for all spheres not reserved to the federal government. The 'common state' would have a single international legal personality and sovereignty, with a single citizenship, and would join the EU as such. It would have a parliament consisting of a senate and a chamber of deputies, each with 48 members popularly elected for five-year terms. The senate would have 24 members from each 'component state', while the chamber would be composed in proportion to population, subject to neither 'component state' having fewer than 12 seats. Decisions of the parliament would require the approval of both houses by simple majority, subject in the senate to the majority including at least one-quarter of those voting from each 'component state' (and at least two-fifths in certain special cases). Executive power in the 'common state' would be vested in a six-member presidential council elected by the senate. Each 'component state' would provide at least two members and contentious decisions would require the support of at least one member from each 'component state'. After a three-year transitional period, a president and vice-president of the 'common state', who could not be from the same 'component state', would be drawn from the presidential council, rotating every 10 months, subject to neither 'component state' providing more than two consecutive presidents. During the transitional period the leaders of the two communities would exercise executive power as co-presidents, assisted by a council of ministers. Cyprus would be demilitarized, but Greece and Turkey, as guarantor powers (together with the United Kingdom), would each be entitled to deploy up to 9,999 troops on the island. The UNFICYP would remain. On the crucial question of territorial adjustment, the plan proposed that the area under Turkish Cypriot control should be reduced from about 37% to around 28.5% and the Greek Cypriot area increased to some 71.5%. An estimated 85,000 Greek Cypriot refugees, out of some 200,000 displaced in 1974, would be able to return to their former homes.

Annan's goal of securing agreement on the core elements of his plan before the EU summit in Copenhagen in December 2002 was not achieved. Whereas the Greek Cypriot side was prepared to accept the plan with some modifications, Denktaş described its territorial provisions as 'utter nonsense' and continued to insist that the separate sovereignty of the Turkish Cypriot area must be recognized. Accordingly, the EU summit, in approving Cyprus's membership application and reiterating its preference for the accession of a reunited island on 1 May 2004, confirmed that in the absence of a settlement the EU's *acquis communautaire* would not apply in the Turkish Cypriot area when Cyprus became a member. Disappointment at the failure to reach a settlement was particularly acute among ordinary Turkish Cypriots, who in late 2002 and early 2003 staged massive demonstrations in support of the entry of a reunified Cyprus into the EU and urging Denktaş to accept the Annan Plan or resign.

2003 GREEK CYPRIOT PRESIDENTIAL ELECTION—COLLAPSE OF UN PROCESS

The Annan Plan and the Government's conduct of negotiations on the proposals inevitably dominated the Greek Cypriot presidential election in February 2003. At the last minute Klerides decided to run for a limited third term as an independent, stating that he wished to remain in office for a further 16 months so that he could effect a settlement and ensure that Cyprus became a member of the EU on 1 May 2004. His main opponent was Tassos Papadopoulos, the DIKO leader, who was backed by AKEL and KISOS, on a platform that was highly critical of the settlement terms proposed and of the Government's handling of the negotiations. In the event, Papadopoulos won the election outright in the first round of voting on 16 February 2003, taking 51.5% of the vote against 38.8% for Klerides. A new Government appointed by Papadopoulos included four ministers from AKEL (which entered government for the first time), three from DIKO and two from KISOS. The new Minister of Foreign Affairs was the non-partisan Georghios Iacovou, who had previously held the portfolio in 1983–93.

President-elect Papadopoulos was immediately confronted with the need to make a decision on the Annan Plan, as the UN Secretary-General visited Cyprus at the end of February 2003 and requested the two Cypriot leaders to meet him at The Hague, Netherlands, in the following month to tell him whether they would submit the latest version of his settlement proposals to popular referendums in the two communities. Annan's aim was that endorsement should be given to the plan before the scheduled signing of Cyprus's EU Accession Treaty in Athens in April. As a result of comments and objections submitted by the two sides since the tabling of the plan, the latest, amended text specified that the proposed 'common state' would be called the United Cyprus Republic and would consist of Greek Cypriot and Turkish Cypriot 'constituent states'. An important new feature was that, as a result of an unexpected British offer, about one-half of the territory of the British sovereign base areas (SBAs) in Cyprus would be transferred to Cypriot sovereignty on condition that a definitive settlement was concluded. Under the British offer, 46% of the 99 sq miles of the Dhekelia and Akrotiri SBAs would be ceded, about 90% to the Greek Cypriot 'constituent state' and 10% to the Turkish Cypriot 'constituent state'. However, the meeting held on 10–11 March ended in failure. Papadopoulos agreed to call a referendum on the UN plan, provided that the legislative framework for the proposed 'common state' was in place beforehand and on condition that the Turkish Cypriots also agreed. In contrast, Denktaş refused to commit himself to a referendum because he had what Annan called 'fundamental objections to the plan on basic points'. In his final statement, the UN Secretary-General stated that 'we have reached the end of the road' and made it clear that the UN settlement effort would not be revived unless the current deadlock was resolved.

SIGNATURE OF EU ACCESSION TREATY—OPENING OF INTERNAL BORDER

Greek Cypriot disappointment at the failure of the UN process was offset to some extent by the signing of Cyprus's Treaty of Accession with the EU in Athens on 16 April 2003, which Iacovou described as the most significant date in the island's history since independence. Cyprus's accession to the EU was unanimously approved by the Greek Cypriot House of Representatives on 14 July 2003, and the ratification instrument was signed by President Papadopoulos on 28 July. In the absence of a settlement with the Turkish Cypriots, a special protocol was annexed to the treaty specifying that on accession the *acquis communautaire* would not apply in the area not under the effective control of the Government of the Republic of Cyprus. It also specified that the suspension would be lifted in the event of a settlement being reached and that the EU Council of Ministers would then decide how to adapt Cyprus's accession terms to the Turkish Cypriots.

In what was widely viewed as an attempt to deflect domestic and international criticism of his intransigent stance in the negotiations, in April 2003 Denktaş unexpectedly relaxed restrictions on the movement of people across the Green Line of control in Cyprus, describing the decision as 'an experiment' to improve intercommunal relations. Cypriots subsequently undertook crossings in large numbers (some 400,000 by the end of May), many of them Greek Cypriots anxious to see their ancestral homes in the Turkish-occupied north for the first time since 1974. The Greek Cypriot Government initially described the opening of the Green Line as an illegal move, but, when its citizens reacted with enthusiasm, quickly changed its stance to one of guarded approval. At the end of April 2003 the Government sought to recapture the initiative by announcing extensive economic, social and legal measures of its own, intended 'to give Turkish Cypriots, who live mainly in the occupied areas, the opportunity to enjoy to the extent possible the rights and benefits that the Republic of Cyprus offers its citizens'.

2003 TURKISH CYPRIOT ELECTIONS

Parliamentary elections in the 'TRNC' on 14 December 2003 attracted much international attention since a three-party opposition coalition, headed by the CTP, mounted a strong challenge, campaigning with a policy of advocating reunification on the basis of the Annan Plan, to enable a reunified island to join the EU, and the replacement of Denktaş as the Turkish Cypriots' chief negotiator on the Cyprus problem. In the event, the opposition coalition secured 50.3% of the vote, but only 25 of the 50 seats, with the CTP becoming the largest single party with 19 seats. The ruling coalition of the UBP and the DP also won 25 seats, so that the CTP leader, Mehmet Ali Talat, was obliged to form a coalition Government with the DP (holding seven seats), in which Serdar Denktaş (the DP leader and son of the President) became Deputy Prime Minister and Minister of Foreign Affairs. Under the coalition agreement, Rauf Denktaş remained the Turkish Cypriots' chief negotiator, although the new Government was also committed to seeking a rapid settlement and EU membership.

In an effort to avert possible expulsion from the Council of Europe, the Turkish Government announced in December 2003 that it would comply with the 1996 ECHR ruling in the Loizidou case by paying the Greek Cypriot plaintiff US $1.3m. in compensation (including additional costs and accrued interest) for her expropriated property in Turkish-occupied Kyrenia.

RESUMPTION OF SETTLEMENT TALKS—REFERENDUMS ON REUNIFICATION

A new initiative by the UN Secretary-General resulted in an agreement between Papadopoulos and Denktaş, reached in New York in February 2004, to resume bilateral negotiations on the basis of the Annan Plan. This time, however, Annan not only imposed a timetable designed to produce a settlement before EU accession on 1 May, but also secured agreement that a final version of his plan would be submitted to simultaneous Greek Cypriot and Turkish Cypriot referendums, whether or not the political leaders resolved their differences. Accordingly, when talks between Papadopoulos and Denktaş again reached an impasse, on 24 March Annan convened a final negotiating effort in Bürgenstock, Switzerland, involving the Greek and Turkish Prime Ministers in addition to the two Cypriot sides. Significantly, the Turkish Cypriot delegation was headed by Talat, after Denktaş himself refused to participate on the grounds that there was no prospect of an acceptable agreement being reached. In contrast, the Turkish Government now appeared to support a settlement and to believe that one was possible.

When the Bürgenstock talks also ended without agreement, on 31 March 2004 Annan presented a fifth and supposedly final version of his plan, providing for the creation of a federal United Cyprus Republic, comprising Greek Cypriot and Turkish Cypriot 'constituent states', which would join the EU on 1 May, subject to popular approval by the two communities. To the dismay of EU governments and the USA, in April President Papadopoulos issued a declaration strongly urging Greek Cypriots to vote against the plan, on the grounds that it enshrined much of the illegal status quo resulting from three decades of Turkish military occupation of northern Cyprus. The powerful AKEL party, DIKO and KISOS also favoured a 'no' vote, with only a majority faction of the opposition DISY and some small parties appealing for the plan to be approved. The outcome of the referendums held on 24 April was a rejection of the plan by an overwhelming 75.8% of Greek Cypriot voters, whereas 64.9% of Turkish Cypriots voted in favour, as recommended by the TKP and other parties, as well as by business leaders and trade unions. Despite having himself urged a vote against the plan, Denktaş subsequently dismissed demands for his resignation as 'TRNC' President.

DIVIDED ISLAND JOINS THE EU—EU DECISIONS AFFECTING CYPRUS

As a result of the Greek Cypriots' rejection of the Annan Plan, the still divided island acceded to the EU on 1 May 2004, the *acquis communautaire* being suspended in the Turkish Cypriot area pending a future political settlement. A special EU regulation stipulated that the Green Line of effective control in Cyprus was not an external border of the EU and recognized the primary role of the Cyprus Government in authorizing the movement of goods, services and people across the Line. In May a reorganization of the Greek Cypriot Government was effected, after the Minister of Finance, Markos Kyprianou, became the island's first EU Commissioner. At elections for Cyprus's six seats in the European Parliament on 13 June, the DISY won two, AKEL two, DIKO one and the For Europe coalition (established by former DISY members and later reconstituted as a parliamentary caucus, European Democracy) one seat. Although all Turkish Cypriots were theoretically entitled to participate in the elections, only 503 registered to vote and the sole Turkish Cypriot candidate was not elected.

In July 2004 the Greek Cypriot Government announced a series of measures aimed at improving security on the island, including a partial withdrawal of troops from the Green Line, the clearing of minefields and the opening of more crossing-points. Also announced were proposals to stimulate intra-island trade for the benefit of the Turkish Cypriots, which led to the implementation in August of a new EU Green Line regulation intended to allow certificated Turkish Cypriot goods to enter the Greek Cypriot area. However, amid bureaucratic confusion and accusations by each side that the other did not really want more commercial exchanges, the subsequent increase in intra-island trade was minimal. Moreover, a proposal by the European Commission for 'direct trade' between EU countries and the Turkish Cypriots was strongly resisted by the Greek Cypriot side, which viewed it as a means of bypassing the authority of the Cyprus Government and upgrading the status of the 'TRNC'. As a result of this impasse, a related Commission plan to grant special EU financial aid of €259m. to the Turkish Cypriots was also blocked. Nevertheless, the UN Security Council decided in October that the security situation had improved sufficiently for the size of UNFICYP to be reduced from 1,224 to 860 troops. (In June 2005 the mandate of UNFICYP, which had actually been scaled down to 875 troops, was extended for a further six months; the contingent was to remain at that size until the civilian police component could be fully expanded.)

Turkey's quest to join the EU, and its relationship to the Cyprus problem, came to the fore in December 2004, when an EU summit in Brussels, Belgium, agreed that formal accession negotiations would open with Turkey in October 2005, subject to certain requirements being met. These included Turkey's signature of a protocol extending its customs union with the EU to the 10 new member states, including Cyprus, although it was left unclear whether signature would constitute recognition by Turkey of the (Greek Cypriot) Republic of Cyprus. In post-summit statements, the Turkish Government maintained that signature of the protocol would not amount to abandonment of the claim of the 'TRNC' to sovereignty and would not oblige Turkey to open its ports and airports to Cypriot ships and aircraft. Papadopoulos responded that, while his Government continued to favour the eventual admission of Turkey to the EU, signature and full implementation of the protocol was a minimum requirement for accession negotiations to start with Turkey, failing which he reserved the right to use Cyprus's veto.

2005 TURKISH CYPRIOT ELECTIONS—EFFORTS TO REVIVE TALKS

Months of political instability in the 'TRNC' resulted in the holding of early legislative elections on 20 February 2005. Again campaigning on a pro-unification, pro-EU platform, Talat's CTP advanced to 24 of the 50 seats with 44.5% of the vote, while the UBP won 19, the DP six and the Peace and Democracy Movement (BDH) one. (Following a by-election held on 25 June 2006 to fill two vacant seats in the Turkish Cypriot legislature, its composition was as follows: the CTP held 25 seats, the UBP 17, the DP seven and the BDH one. One representative of the UBP subsequently became an independent deputy.) The outcome of the legislative elections was the formation in March 2005 of a further coalition between the CTP and the DP, with Talat again retaining the premiership. However, at a presidential election held in the following month, Talat was elected President of the 'TRNC', winning outright with 55.8% in the first round of voting on 17 April, whereupon a new CTP-DP coalition was formed, with Ferdi Sabit Soyer of the CTP as Prime Minister. Talat's victory brought to an end the long dominance of Rauf Denktaş as Turkish Cypriot leader, although Denktaş, who had not sought re-election, declared that he would continue to oppose the Annan Plan.

A further landmark ruling by the ECHR in April 2005 on a Greek Cypriot property claim again went against Turkey, whose contention that the 'TRNC' authorities had provided adequate domestic remedy for such claims by establishing a 'property commission' was unanimously rejected. The case highlighted the Greek Cypriot side's increasing concern about a property boom in the 'TRNC' involving the sale of houses and land legally owned by Greek Cypriots, which was seen as greatly complicating prospects of a political settlement. Nevertheless, the accession of Talat to power in the 'TRNC' gave rise to some hopes of a resumption of settlement talks, which were boosted by an impromptu discussion between Papadopoulos and the Turkish Prime Minister in Moscow, Russia, in May, following which Papadopoulos sent an envoy to New York to explain the Greek Cypriot position to UN officials. The result was a visit to Cyprus, Athens and Ankara in late May and early June by the UN Under-Secretary-General for Political Affairs, Sir Kieran Prendergast, to assess whether conditions were conducive to Annan reviving his mission. On the basis of his findings, Annan reported to the Security Council in June that conditions were not right for a resumption of UN-sponsored talks, although he emphasized that the situation would be kept under review.

Developments over the next few months centred on the planned accession negotiations between Turkey and the EU. In July 2005 Turkey signed, as required, the protocol extending its customs union to the new EU member states. However, it also issued a declaration that this did not imply recognition of the Greek Cypriot Government and that a comprehensive settlement for the whole island would have to be reached first. Turkey, meanwhile, continued to ban Greek Cypriot aircraft and ships from entering its airspace and ports. Reflecting the considerable hostility among some EU states towards Turkish membership, the French Prime Minister, Dominique de Villepin, declared in August that it was inconceivable that membership talks could begin with a country that failed to recognize all 25 member states. Nevertheless, accession negotiations commenced, on schedule, in October in Luxembourg. However, Turkish recognition of Cyprus at some future date would remain a prerequisite for eventual EU membership, and Turkey would also need to fulfil all the complex legal conditions of entry to the satisfaction of all 25 member states, including Cyprus, over the long negotiating period, or else risk a veto.

2006 GREEK CYPRIOT LEGISLATIVE ELECTIONS

On 21 May 2006 legislative elections were held for the 56 Greek Cypriot seats in the House of Representatives, resulting in no major changes in its composition. Voters again demonstrated support for parties opposed to the idea of reviving the UN reunification plan that had been rejected in 2004, which implied little prospect of further diplomatic progress. According to official results released by the Ministry of the Interior, AKEL won 18 seats, with 31.1% of the votes cast; DISY also won 18 seats, with 30.3% of the vote, and President Papadopoulos's DIKO increased its representation to 11 seats, with a 17.9% share of the vote. The three other parties securing seats were KISOS, with five seats, the European Party (Evro.Ko—for the first time contesting an election), with three, and the Cyprus Green Party (KOP), with one seat.

In June 2006 President Papadopoulos announced changes to the Greek Cypriot Council of Ministers. These included Georghios Iacovou's replacement as Minister of Foreign Affairs by Giorgos Lillikas and the appointment of Phivos Klokkaris as Minister of Defence.

INTERNATIONAL AND DOMESTIC DEVELOPMENTS

Hopes of some progress towards Cypriot reunification were rekindled on 8 July 2006, when Presidents Papadopoulos and Talat reached agreement at a UN-sponsored meeting on a set of principles to revitalize the peace process. In addition to committing to a settlement based on a bi-zonal, bi-communal federation and political equality, the two leaders agreed to a negotiating framework that envisaged the establishment of technical committees to tackle issues affecting the day-to-day lives of the people and, concurrently, of expert working groups to discuss substantive matters. They also expressed their commitment to ending mutual recriminations. At the end of July Greek and Turkish Cypriot negotiators exchanged lists of issues that would form a basis for future discussions.

However, Turkey continued to block Greek Cypriot shipping and air traffic from its territory while the trade embargo on northern Cyprus remained in force, prompting criticisms from the European Parliament in September 2006 and from the European Commission in November, and rejected an EU deadline to open its ports by 6 December. Consequently, ahead of a European Council summit in mid-December, the EU ministers responsible for foreign affairs agreed to a partial suspension of Turkey's accession negotiations for failing to fulfil its obligations.

In a more positive, if largely symbolic, development, both communities in early 2007 demolished parts of the barrier that had divided Nicosia for over 30 years, preparing the way for a buffer zone pedestrian crossing in the capital.

Within the Greek Cypriot Council of Ministers, Klokkaris's tenure as Minister of Defence was short-lived, as he resigned in September 2006. Nikos Symeonidas assumed the portfolio in the following month, but died in May 2007 and was replaced by Christodoulos Pasiardis. Also in September 2006 Andreas Christou resigned as Minister of the Interior, to be replaced by Neoklis Silikiotis. A further reorganization of the Government was effected in July 2007, following the withdrawal of AKEL from the coalition in order for its Secretary-General, Demetris Christofias, to contest the Greek Cypriot presidential election scheduled for early 2008.

Meanwhile, in the 'TRNC', the CTP-DP Government collapsed in September 2006 and a new coalition was formed, between the CTP and the Freedom and Reform Party (ORP). The ORP had been established earlier in the year by parliamentary deputies from the UBP and the DP, and was headed by Turgay Avcı, who became Deputy Prime Minister and Minister of Foreign Affairs.

On 15 June 2007 and again in mid-December the UNFICYP mandate was extended for further six-month periods. On both occasions the Security Council noted with concern the lack of progress in the initiative begun in July of the previous year and urged all parties to engage constructively with the UN's efforts at brokering a settlement. Having received approval from EU ministers responsible for finance in July 2007, Cyprus formally adopted the single currency, the euro, from 1 January 2008.

2008 GREEK CYPRIOT PRESIDENTIAL ELECTIONS—NEW OPTIMISM

The first quarter of 2008 was dominated by the elections for the Greek Cypriot presidency. The incumbent, Papadopoulos, AKEL leader Christofias, and the DISY-backed independent candidate, Ioannis Kasoulides, were the leading contenders in the first round of voting on 17 February. In a close result, Kasoulides won 33.5% of the votes cast, and Christofias, who had pledged as a priority to renew talks with Turkish Cypriots to find a solution to the island's division, secured 33.3%, thus eliminating Papadopoulos, who took 31.8%—a result attributed by many to increasing levels of popular frustration at his perceived intractability with regard to the Cyprus problem. In the second round of voting on 24 February Christofias, with support from DIKO, secured 53.4% of the ballot to defeat Kasoulides and become the country's first (nominally) communist President. He was sworn in on 28 February and subsequently announced a new Council of Ministers—a coalition comprising AKEL, DIKO and KISOS, together with AKEL-backed independents—which included Markos Kyprianou (DIKO) as Minister of Foreign Affairs and Charilaos Stavrakis (independent), hitherto Chief Executive of the Bank of Cyprus, as Minister of Finance.

It was announced soon after the Greek Cypriot presidential election that Christofias and Turkish Cypriot President Talat had agreed to meet under UN auspices in the buffer zone on 21 March 2008. The meeting generated considerable optimism as the two leaders declared their intention to relaunch formal reunification talks. A plan was drawn up for the establishment of six bi-communal working groups and seven technical committees, whose task would be to consider a range of issues in preparation for fully fledged negotiations. It was announced on 26 March that the new working groups would study governance and power-sharing; EU matters; security and guarantees; territory; property; and economic matters. The technical committees would oversee crime/criminal matters; economic and commercial matters; cultural heritage; crisis management; humanitarian matters; health; and the environment. Christofias and Talat also agreed to remove the Ledra Street barricade in the centre of Nicosia, one of the most enduring symbols of partition, in order to create a new crossing point across the Green Line; this occurred on 3 April in the presence of officials from both communities. In the same month Tayé-Brook Zerihoun of Ethiopia was appointed as the UN Secretary-General's new Special Representative in Cyprus.

Christofias and Talat conducted a second meeting, hosted by the UN, in Nicosia on 23 May 2008. While acknowledging their different views on the commencement of peace negotiations, the statement issued at the conclusion of the meeting noted that the Greek and Turkish Cypriot leaders 'reaffirmed their commitment to a bi-zonal, bi-communal federation with political equality, as defined by relevant Security Council resolutions' and asserted that this partnership would 'comprise a Federal Government with a single international personality, along with a Turkish Cypriot Constituent State and Greek Cypriot Constituent State, which will be of equal status'. The two Presidents also agreed to reconvene in June (subsequently moved back to July) to assess the progress of the working groups and technical committees. Commenting on the meeting, Zerihoun noted that 'there is broad agreement that there is a new environment, conducive to the re-engagement, and a commitment to see the process through'. Meanwhile, in his report to the Security Council on the work of UNFICYP in June, UN Secretary-General Ban Ki-Moon declared that 'a window of opportunity for Cypriots to finally resolve the Cyprus problem is clearly open'. UNFICYP's mandate was extended for a further six-month period on 13 June.

Christofias and Talat met for a third time in the presence of Zerihoun in Nicosia on 1 July 2008. The two leaders discussed the progress of the working groups and technical committees, and reiterated their commitment—in principle at least—to issues of single sovereignty and citizenship. On the same day it was reported that Alexander Downer, hitherto the Australian Minister for Foreign Affairs, had been appointed as the UN Secretary-General's Special Adviser on Cyprus. Christofias and Talat reconvened in Nicosia for a final review in mid-July and announced that in September they would commence direct negotiations concerning a mutually acceptable reunification settlement that would be put to separate and simultaneous referendums on both sides of the island. The two leaders met, as agreed, in Nicosia in September, where the foundations were laid for more substantive negotiations under UN auspices later that month.

PROGRESS OF NEGOTIATIONS

The negotiations concentrated initially on governance and power-sharing, since the resolution of other complex issues—particularly territorial adjustment and security guarantees (also involving Turkey, which had thousands of troops stationed in northern Cyprus) and disputed property ownership rights—was likely to prove more difficult. While both sides were reportedly in agreement on a rotating presidency and vice-presidency (with one from each community), Christofias' preference was for them to be elected directly by popular vote, while Talat favoured election by parliament.

Following a meeting on 11 September 2008, there was a four-week break in the talks. During that time, the fragility of the peace process became evident as both leaders adopted a more critical and provocative stance in their public statements and through the media, possibly in recognition of the scepticism about the negotiations that existed among sections of their communities. More positively, in mid-October Christofias and Talat announced the cancellation of annual military exercises on either side of the Green Line, which had proved a source of tension in previous years. They also agreed to a UN recommendation that they delegate some of the more detailed negotiations to their respective advisers in an effort to accelerate the process.

Progress was slow during the last two months of 2008, but the momentum of negotiations appeared to have increased with the announcement on 5 January 2009 by UN Special Representative Zerihoun that the negotiating parties had reached an agreement on the issue of co-operation between the various constituent parts of a future federal state, although some outstanding aspects remained under discussion. Earlier, in December 2008, the UN Security Council had extended UNFICYP's mandate for a further six months, to 15 June 2009, and urged an intensification in the pace of the talks.

From February 2009 attention turned to the highly contentious and litigious issue of the ownership of land in northern Cyprus. A high-profile test case for restitution centred on Meletis Apostolides, a displaced Greek Cypriot whose land in northern Cyprus had been bought by a British couple. A decision in 2008 by a Greek Cypriot court that the land should be returned to Apostolides was subsequently upheld in a landmark ruling by the European Court of Justice on 28 April 2009, with implications for similar pending cases and a potentially negative impact on Turkish Cypriot attitudes to the peace process.

2009 TURKISH CYPRIOT LEGISLATIVE ELECTIONS

Doubts about the prospects for a reunification settlement increased when the UBP, led by former Prime Minister Derviş Eroğlu, won legislative elections held in the 'TRNC' on 19 April 2009. In the elections, held a year early reportedly because Talat's ruling CTP feared losing ground to nationalist parties, the hard-line opposition UBP won 44.0% of the vote and 26 of the 50 seats to secure an overall parliamentary majority. The CTP's vote share declined to 29.3%, with only 15 seats. The DP won five seats, and two smaller centre-left parties—the Communal Democracy Party (TDP), established in 2007, and the ORP—each took two seats. In May Eroğlu formed a new Government that included among its most notable appointees Hüseyin Özgürgün as Minister of Foreign Affairs and İlkay Kamil as Minister of Interior Affairs and Local Administrations.

Reflecting the Turkish Government's concerns about Eroğlu's attitude to the peace process (and the fact that facilitating a settlement would enhance its prospects of EU accession), two days after the election the Turkish Prime Minister, Recep Tayyip Erdoğan, warned the new Turkish Cypriot administration not to end or reorientate the negotiations. The Turkish President, Abdullah Gül, similarly endorsed Talat's representation of the Turkish Cypriot community at the talks. In response, Eroğlu confirmed that his party would support Talat as chief negotiator, but insisted that he would also appoint a representative to attend the negotiations.

SETTLEMENT PROSPECTS FALTER

Intercommunal negotiations resumed in September 2009 and intensified through October, but little significant progress had been achieved by the end of the year. With few exceptions, most of the major issues of contention remained unresolved, reinforcing a general mood of pessimism about the prospects of reaching a settlement.

After further talks in January 2010, progress appeared to have been made on the issue of governance and power-sharing. Media reports claimed that agreement had been reached on a rotation regime for the presidency and on the intercommunal composition of the council of ministers and the ratio of parliamentary representation. However, these arrangements proved unacceptable to KISOS, one of the two partner parties in Christofias' AKEL-led Greek Cypriot coalition, which withdrew from the Government, prompting further doubts about the attainment of a durable solution. None the less, in February Erdoğan cited for the first time the bi-zonal, bi-communal basis for a Cypriot settlement and referred to the possibility of a Turkish military withdrawal.

Disputes and litigation over property ownership in the 'TRNC'—and two court rulings in particular—continued to cast a shadow over the settlement negotiations. In January 2010 the United Kingdom's Court of Appeal backed an earlier Greek Cypriot court ruling in the case of displaced Greek Cypriot Apostolides, requiring a British couple to demolish the house that they had built in northern Cyprus because it was built on land belonging to Apostolides. The ruling implied that many foreigners could face prosecution if they had purchased properties in the north that had been abandoned by Greek Cypriots in 1974. The Turkish Cypriot Government responded by stating that it would not enforce the ruling. In March 2010 the ECHR decreed that the Turkish Cypriot Immovable Property Commission (IPC—established in 2005) constituted an accessible framework of redress for some 1,400 Greek Cypriot property claims filed at the court (effectively ordering all Greek Cypriots with cases filed at the ECHR to pursue their claims through the IPC or await a political solution to the division of the island).

Meanwhile, in November 2009 the British Government offered to cede about one-half of the British SBAs on the island to a united Cyprus in the event of a solution being achieved. The concession would make it easier for the Greek Cypriots to acquire the percentage of land that they sought.

2010 TURKISH CYPRIOT PRESIDENTIAL ELECTION

Further settlement negotiations were suspended in March 2010 until after the Turkish Cypriot presidential election. At the poll held on 18 April, Prime Minister Eroğlu took 50.4% of the vote in the first ballot, rendering a run-off poll unnecessary; Talat, secured 42.8% of the vote, ahead of five other candidates. Eroğlu took office as the new President on 23 April, and on 10 May he appointed İrsen Küçük as Prime Minister. Küçük's Council of Ministers, which retained the key ministers of the outgoing administration, was approved by the President on 17 May.

Given his opposition to Cypriot reunification, Eroğlu's election victory heightened concerns that the change of leadership might not only undermine what had been achieved during the previous two years of negotiations but also further complicate Turkey's EU membership aspirations. However, Eroğlu pledged to maintain the dialogue with Christofias, and UN Special Adviser Downer and Turkish Prime Minister Erdoğan stressed that they expected the settlement process to continue within the same parameters. Negotiations duly resumed in Nicosia in late May 2010.

In June 2010 UN Secretary-General Ban Ki-Moon announced the appointment of Lisa Buttenheim of the USA as his new Special Representative in Cyprus and head of UNFICYP. UNFICYP's mandate was subsequently extended by the UN Security Council for a further six months to December.

UN CONCERNS OVER NEGOTIATIONS

Talks from May 2010 onwards concentrated on the complex issue of property ownership. However, there was scant evidence of any substantial progress being made in this regard, although there was some advance in confidence-building when a seventh crossing point, at Limnitis/Yeşilırmak, on the buffer zone was opened in October and annual (provocative) military exercises were cancelled by both sides.

On 18 November 2010 Ban Ki-Moon held a tripartite meeting with the two Cypriot leaders in New York in an effort to instil new momentum into the negotiations. Both leaders said that they recognized the need to move more decisively and agreed to intensify their contacts over the following weeks ahead of a further meeting with the Secretary-General scheduled for January 2011 in Geneva. However, Ban Ki-Moon's frustration at the slow pace of progress was apparent in his report on the UN mission in Cyprus and the settlement process published in November 2010. In this document the Secretary-General stated: 'It is my concern that the political environment in the second quarter of 2011 will likely not be conducive to constructive negotiations', in reference to forthcoming parliamentary elections in Greek Cyprus in May and in Turkey in June.

Taking note of Ban Ki-Moon's report, the UN Security Council on 14 December 2010 extended UNFICYP's mandate for another six months, to June 2011, while simultaneously urging the Cypriot leaders to accelerate the negotiations and develop a means for overcoming remaining obstacles. However, the meeting in Geneva in January 2011 again made little progress in respect of core differences over property, territory, security and guarantees, and the prospect of any further significant advance being made ahead of the Greek Cypriot and Turkish elections became increasingly unlikely. In March another status report by Ban Ki-Moon warned that negotiations 'cannot be an open-ended process, nor can we afford interminable talks for the sake of talks'. He, nevertheless, subsequently recommended that UNFICYP's mandate be extended for a further six-month period from June. (The mandate was duly extended until 15 December.)

GENERAL STRIKES IN THE 'TRNC'—2011 GREEK CYPRIOT LEGISLATIVE ELECTIONS

On 28 January 2011 tens of thousands of Turkish Cypriot public sector workers undertook a general strike and held a mass protest in Nicosia against economic austerity measures introduced earlier that month, which included significant reductions in the salaries of civil servants and the privatization of several public sector institutions. The protesters claimed that the austerity measures were in fact being imposed at the behest of Turkey, which was seeking to reduce its own expenditure on financing the budget deficit of the 'TRNC'. Further general strikes and rallies took place on 2 March and 7 April. On 6 April, meanwhile, Prime Minister Küçük announced a reorganization of the Government. Most notably, Nazım Çavuşoğlu was appointed as Minister of Interior Affairs and Local Administrations.

On 22 May 2011 parliamentary elections were held for the 56 Greek Cypriot seats in the House of Representatives, from which DISY and AKEL again emerged as the two largest parties with, respectively, 20 and 19 seats (and 34.3% and 32.7% of the votes cast). Both parties increased their share of the vote, compared with the corresponding percentage achieved in the 2006 poll. DIKO, AKEL's coalition partner in government, took nine seats (with a 15.8% vote share), while KISOS won five (with 8.9%), Evro.Ko two (3.9%) and the KOP one (2.2%). The turn-out was 78.7%, indicating a higher than average abstention rate.

EVANGELOS FLORAKIS EXPLOSIONS—GREEK CYPRIOT GOVERNMENT REORGANIZATION

President Christofias and the Government came under severe pressure in mid-July 2011, following a series of explosions at the Evangelos Florakis naval base on 11 July 2011, in which 13 people were killed and extensive damage was caused to the country's main power station at Vassiliko. Both the commander of Cyprus's naval force and the base commander were among those killed in the incident. It subsequently emerged that the explosions had been caused by some 98 containers of munitions that had been stored in the open air at the base since being seized in 2009 from a ship thought to be travelling from Iran to Syria. Following the incident, the Minister of Defence, Costas Papacostas of AKEL, and the Commander of the National Guard resigned from office. Criticism of the Government's apparent failure to dispose of the containers after seizure increased and protests were held in Nicosia throughout the following week. On 19 July the Minister of Foreign Affairs, Kyprianou, also announced his resignation from the Government. As protests against Christofias and the Government continued to increase in scale, on 28 July Christofias requested the resignation of the entire Council of Ministers to facilitate a reorganization. Following an announcement two days earlier that DIKO was to withdraw from the governing coalition, a new Council of Ministers comprising members of AKEL and independents was sworn in on 5 August. Eratou Kozakou-Marcoullis became Minister of Foreign Affairs, while Demetris Eliades was appointed as Minister of Defence. Kikis Kazamias joined the Government as Minister of Finance. Other notable appointees included Efthymios Flourentzos, who replaced Kozakou-Marcoullis as Minister of Communications and Works, and EDI President Praxoulla Antoniadou Kyriakou, who took the post of Minister of Commerce, Industry and Tourism. In further changes announced in March 2012, prompted by the resignation of Kazamias on health grounds, Vasos Shiarlis, a banker, was appointed as Minister of Finance, while Eleni Mavrou, a former Mayor of Nicosia, became Minister of the Interior in place of Neoklis Sylikiotis. Kyriakou was replaced as Minister of Commerce, Industry and Tourism by Sylikiotis.

STALLED NEGOTIATIONS AND POLITICAL UNCERTAINTY

The negative repercussions of the Evangelos Florakis disaster, a worsening banking crisis in the wake of Cypriot exposure to Greece's financial instability and inconclusive intercommunal negotiations left Christofias politically weakened and increasingly isolated during the remainder of 2011 and the first half of 2012. Additional uncertainty was generated by electoral upheaval in Greece in May–June, Cyprus' assumption of the rotating six-month presidency of the EU from 1 July and the pending Greek Cypriot presidential election, scheduled for February 2013.

Meanwhile, in June 2011 the UN Security Council extended the UNFICYP mandate for another six months. The Council urged the leaders of both Cypriot communities to 'foster positive public rhetoric', encouraging them to explain the benefits of a settlement as well as the need for increased flexibility and compromise.

In July 2011 the UN Secretary-General announced that, while reunification talks should continue to be 'Cypriot-owned and Cypriot-led', both leaders had accepted his offer of an enhanced UN mediation role in intensified negotiations. Ban Ki-Moon acknowledged that both sides had strived to take the process forward since he had last met with them in January but that progress had been far too slow. He added that he hoped Christofias and Eroğlu would reach convergence on the core issues by October, which could pave the way towards convening an international conference, bringing together Greece, Turkey and the United Kingdom, to finalize a durable settlement. Media reports speculated that if this goal was not reached the UN might declare the mediation effort at an end.

Meanwhile, the political atmosphere was complicated by increasing tensions over the Greek Cypriot Government's plans to exploit the potentially vast natural gas reserves in its exclusive economic zone and to launch a second exploration licensing round (which took place in February 2012). Turkish Cypriots and the Turkish Government objected to the drilling plans on the grounds that the island's natural resources should be shared by both communities and that a comprehensive political settlement should first be achieved. In defiance, the 'TRNC' signed an agreement with Turkey in September 2011 to delimit the continental shelf and then issued its own exploration licences to the Turkish Petroleum Corpn.

In October 2011 Ban Ki-Moon hosted two days of talks with Christofias and Eroğlu in New York. Despite some agreement on economic and policing matters, there was little advance on the more divisive political and property issues. At the same time, the Secretary-General noted that, with Cyprus due to assume the obligations of the EU presidency from July 2012, opportunities for further progress in the negotiations would be limited. The newly re-elected Turkish Prime Minister had declared in July 2011 that he would suspend negotiations with the EU if the Greek Cypriots assumed the presidency without having first resolved the Cyprus dispute. In December 2011 the UN Security Council extended the UNFICYP mandate until 19 July 2012; the mandate was subsequently extended further, incrementally, until 31 January 2014.

After another round of tripartite talks in New York in January 2012, focusing on governance, power-sharing, property rights and citizenship, Ban Ki-Moon again acknowledged the lack of substantive progress. Reporting to the UN Security Council in March, he noted that the negotiations were 'close to deadlock' on the core issues, and, following a review meeting with Special Adviser Downer, he confirmed in April that the common ground that had been achieved between the two sides to date was not sufficient to warrant holding an international conference. Later that month Downer informed the two Cypriot leaders of the UN's decision to downgrade its involvement in negotiations from high-level mediation to technical-level discussions and confidence-building measures in view of the fact that the core issue talks had stalled. Nevertheless, he affirmed that it remained the Secretary-General's ambition to call a multilateral conference to conclude negotiations if the Cypriot leaders were to reach a working convergence. Media opinion, however, considered that substantive developments were unlikely until after the Cypriot EU presidency and the Greek Cypriot presidential election had concluded.

THE 2013 GREEK CYPRIOT PRESIDENTIAL ELECTION—EARLY LEGISLATIVE ELECTIONS IN THE 'TRNC'

In late June 2012 the Cypriot Government confirmed that it needed to apply to the European Financial Stability Facility (EFSF) for financial assistance to recapitalize the struggling banking sector, which was highly exposed to Greek sovereign debt and to the broader Greek economy, and to offset a growing budget deficit (see Economy). It was also reported that Cyprus had requested a US $5,000m. loan from Russia, although this was not to be forthcoming. The country's economic and financial concerns were to dominate much of the following year, which also heralded the election of a more hardline Greek Cypriot President, further tensions with Turkey over oil and gas exploration and stagnation on core intercommunal issues.

Strict conditions were to be attached to any international financial support, including fiscal consolidation and structural reforms to the Cypriot economy, and the Government's negotiations in this respect with a 'troika' comprising the European Commission, the IMF and the European Central Bank largely overshadowed its presidency of the EU in the second half of 2012. At the same time, Turkey suspended contacts with the EU presidency (although not with other EU institutions) during the Cypriot tenure. However, in November the Government announced that it had reached a deal in principle with the troika on a financial bail-out package, although final agreement would be determined by the outcome of an independent investigation into Cypriot bank capital requirements and would depend on ratification by some other EU member states' parliaments.

Meanwhile, President Christofias confirmed that he would not seek a second term in the February 2013 election. Nikos Anastasiades was widely expected to win the poll as the leader and presidential nominee of DISY, the main opposition, having also secured support from DIKO, the third-largest party. In the first round of voting on 17 February, Anastasiades secured 45.5% of the votes cast, while the AKEL-backed candidate, Stavros Malas, took 26.9%, necessitating a second round, which was held on 24 February. Anastasiades won 57.5% of votes cast in that poll, and was sworn in as President on 28 February. His new appointments to the Council of Ministers included Michalis Sarris as Minister of Finance, Ioannis Kasoulides as Minister of Foreign Affairs, Fotis Fotiou as Minister of Defence and Socrates Hasikos as Minister of the Interior.

The new Government's attention promptly focused on the international financial bail-out plan for Cyprus. After further fraught negotiations and considerable parliamentary hostility, a revised, but still controversial, agreement was reached in late March with the EU and the IMF on a €10,000m. rescue package to avert a financial collapse and keep Cyprus within the European single currency zone. The deal entailed the closure and restructuring, respectively, of Laiki Bank and Bank of Cyprus (the country's two largest banks), with heavy losses for uninsured depositors, particularly Russian account holders. Then, at the beginning of April, Minister of Finance Sarris resigned, only weeks after his appointment, having attracted criticism over his former supervision of the collapsed Laiki Bank and his perceived mishandling of the international bail-out negotiations, which were to be investigated by a committee of judges. He was replaced by Haris Georgiades. The Government received the first instalment of its bail-out funding in May.

With Greek Cypriot attention concentrated on the negative economic situation, Minister of Foreign Affairs Kasoulides announced, prior to his first official meeting in early May with the UN Secretary-General, that the Government hoped to be able to resume negotiations on the financial crisis in the autumn. Following that meeting, Kasoulides stressed that, while negotiations would not have to start from the beginning, there were some issues that President Anastasiades would not be bound by, implying a more hardline future approach. Kasoulides also noted that it was necessary to make some 'major moves' to restore the lack of confidence between the two communities, proposing that Turkish-occupied Famagusta be restored to its former Greek Cypriot residents, in return for which the Greek Cypriot Government would allow the Turkish Cypriots to carry out direct trade through the city's port under EU supervision.

On 14 June 2013 Sibel Siber, of the CTP, was sworn into office as interim 'TRNC' Prime Minister and early legislative elections were scheduled for late July. Her appointment followed the Küçük Government's defeat at a vote of no confidence in the Legislative Assembly. The vote had been prompted by the decision of eight UBP deputies to join the opposition DP. Siber's Council of Ministers was approved by the legislature on 23 June. Elections to the Assembly were duly held on 28 July. The CTP secured the largest representation, winning 21 seats. The UBP secured 14 seats and the DP 12. The three remaining seats were allocated to the TDP. On 15 August President Eroğlu asked CTP Leader Özkan Yorgancıoğlu to form a new government. A coalition agreement between the CTP and DP was subsequently approved by members of both parties, and a new Government took office on 2 September. Yorgancıoğlu was appointed as Prime Minister, and Serdar Denktaş Deputy Prime Minister and Minister of the Economy, Tourism and Sports.

Economy

Revised for this edition by CHARLES CHARALAMBOUS

Note: The Cyprus pound (C£) was formerly in use. The government-controlled area of Cyprus adopted the euro (€) on 1 January 2008, and this became the sole legal tender in this area from the end of the same month. Some historical data in this essay continues to be presented in terms of Cyprus pounds, with the euro equivalent at the prevailing conversion rate indicated in brackets.

Since July 1974 Cyprus has been divided into two areas, one to the north and one to the south of the UN-monitored buffer zone, also known as the 'Attila Line', or 'Green Line'. The northern two-fifths of the country, under Turkish Cypriot control, is closely linked to the economy of Turkey, and has had little economic contact with the south of the island since partition, despite recent attempts to stimulate intra-island trade. The unilateral declaration of independence by the 'Turkish Republic of Northern Cyprus' ('TRNC') in November 1983 and subsequent international court judgments reinforced the economic separation, which has caused serious problems for the northern sector. Both areas suffered severe disruption as a result of the events of 1974. The collapse of essential services in many places reduced economic activity to a low level. Crops were not harvested, tourism ceased, and industrial buildings and plants were destroyed or lost their work-force.

THE SOUTHERN ECONOMY

Since 1974 the economies to the north and the south of the Green Line have diverged sharply. For many years, the economy in the south has largely been driven by tourism, but also by business services to international companies that historically have taken advantage of the low corporate tax rate. Construction and overall consumer demand have also played important roles. The economy of the south made a remarkable recovery following partition, despite having lost 38% of the island's territory, 70% of its productive resources, 30% of its factories, 60% of the tourist installations, the main port (Famagusta), 66% of the grain-producing land and 80% of the citrus fruit groves, all of which were on the northern side of the line. By 1979 gross domestic product (GDP) in the southern part of the island was almost double that for the whole of Cyprus in 1973. Unemployment was reduced from almost 30% of the labour force in late 1974 to just 1.7% in 1979, partly by the emigration of workers but largely through the promotion of labour-intensive industry and massive expansion of the construction sector, both for private housing and for development projects.

By 1980, however, it became clear that the post-1976 boom had concealed a deeper instability in the economy. Recovery was based on labour-intensive production by a low-wage work-force, but, with full employment from 1977, wage rises escalated. Rising wages and the growing cost of imported petroleum, among other factors, contributed to an increase in inflation, from an annual average of 3.8% in 1976 to 13.5% in 1980. The (Greek Cypriot) Republic of Cyprus Government was also faced confronted with widening balance of payments and budgetary deficits, as revenue failed to keep pace with expenditure. Despite loans from international agencies and foreign governments, and extensive borrowing abroad, Cyprus's reserves in 1980 were perilously low. The Government adopted a stabilization programme designed to reduce imports, to cut the budget deficit and to limit inflation. As a result, inflation declined to 5% by 1985.

By 1980, however, it became clear that the post-1976 boom had concealed a deeper instability in the economy. Recovery was based on labour-intensive production by a low-wage work-force, but, with full employment from 1977, wage rises escalated. Rising wages and the growing cost of imported petroleum, among other factors, contributed to an increase in inflation. The Greek Cypriot Government was also confronted with widening balance of payments and budgetary deficits, as revenue failed to keep pace with expenditure. Despite loans from international agencies and foreign governments, and extensive borrowing abroad, Cyprus's reserves in 1980 were perilously low. The Government adopted a stabilization programme and begun efforts to diversify the economy, with less reliance being placed on the agricultural sector and increased emphasis on the development of more broadly based services and industrial sectors, particularly tourism, shipping and financial services.

The Government's Five-Year Economic Plan for 1989–93, adopted in June 1989, envisaged average annual growth of 5%. The actual growth rate was slightly higher, at 5.2%. However, during that period annual growth rates were extremely volatile. For example, in 1993 the growth rate was only 0.7%, owing to the effects on the economy of the European recession, whereas in 1994 and 1995 it was 5.9% and 6.5%, respectively. The average annual growth rate in 1991–95 was 4.6%. This decreased to 3.8% in 1996–2000, largely as a result of controversy in 1996–97 over a Russian missile system, when the Government's plan to deploy missiles on the island provoked threats from Turkey (see History), which damaged the tourism sector. The average annual growth rate decreased again during 2001–05, largely owing to the September 2001 suicide attacks in the USA, the consequences in 2002 of the crash that followed a poorly regulated stock market boom and the US-led military campaign in Iraq in 2003. A revival in the tourism industry, as well as an upsurge in construction fuelled by rising credit, contributed to a recovery over the next few years, with GDP growth averaging 4.3% per year in 2004–08 and peaking at 5.1% in 2007.

However, by the end of 2008 the economy had started to decelerate as a result of the global economic downturn, with the bursting of the real estate 'bubble' and declining consumer demand contributing to a slowdown, to 3.6%, of GDP growth for the year as a whole. The economy went into recession during 2009; a GDP contraction of 1.9% in that year was in part attributable to very poor performances by the tourism and construction sectors. GDP grew by 1.3% in 2010 and, according to provisional figures, by 0.5% in 2011, buoyed up by increased activity in real estate services and the hotels and restaurants sector. However, the manufacturing and construction sectors contracted for a third consecutive year, by 3.0% and 10.3%, respectively, in 2011. Although the banking sector continued to show relatively healthy profits into 2010, by the end of 2011 a substantial write-down of high exposure to Greek sovereign and commercial debt by the island's two largest banks had resulted in serious capitalization issues (see Industry, Manufacturing and Services). This, coupled with the economic cost of the disaster at the Mari naval base and continuing international concerns over the Government's fiscal policy, which had resulted in a rapid downgrading of Cyprus's credit rating to a level which shut it out of the international financial markets in June 2011, obliged the Government to apply on 25 June 2012 for aid from the European Financial Stability Facility (EFSF—see Budget, Investment and Finance). According to provisional data, there was a 2.4% GDP contraction in 2012, with notably large contractions in the construction (19.6%) and mining and quarrying sectors (27.8%); manufacturing also continued to decline (by 6.8%).

In August 1991, in view of measures taken by the Greek Cypriot Government to encourage economic performance, the World Bank removed Cyprus from its official list of developing countries, thereby ending Cyprus's qualification for development loans at preferential rates. According to figures revised in 2013, GDP in the Greek Cypriot sector, at current market prices, increased from €7,088m. in 1995 to €9,756m. in 2000 and to €13,402m. in 2005. GDP grew further in 2008 to reach €17,157m., but declined to €16,854m. in 2009, before growing again, to €17,406m., in 2010. GDP rose to a provisionally estimated €17,979m. in 2011 and €17,887m. in 2012. At purchasing-power parity (PPP), gross national income (GNI) per caput, at current prices, in the Greek Cypriot area was estimated by the World Bank at US $29,790 in 2008, rising to $30,940 in 2009; it then fluctuated between $30,010 in 2010, $31,020 in 2011 and $29,400 in 2012. According to the most up-to-date national sources, GNI per caput, at current prices, in the Greek Cypriot area rose from €13,129 in 2000 to €17,394 in 2005 and to €21,544 in 2008, before declining to €19,974 in 2009. This figure increased to €20,308 in 2010 and, according to provisional data, to €21,218 in 2011, before declining to €19,676 in 2012. According to official data, GNI per caput, at current prices, in the Turkish Cypriot sector had risen to $16,158 by 2008 (based on revised population figures), as a result of strong economic growth. This level of income was equivalent to around 60% of that in the Greek Cypriot sector, up from about 30% in 1995. However, GNI per caput in northern Cyprus declined to $13,930 in 2009, before recovering to $14,703 in 2010, equivalent to 56% of that in the south. No figures for PPP are produced for the north, but it has been suggested that, given the area's lower cost of living, its GNI per caput at PPP would be closer to that in the south.

The average level of unemployment in the Greek Cypriot sector fluctuated during the early 1990s and stood at 2.6% in 1995, before rising to reach an average rate of 3.4% (10,934 persons) in 2000. By 2005 it was only slightly higher, at 3.6%, but thereafter the Statistical Service ceased to produce a registered unemployment rate, preferring instead the broader definition based on the labour force surveys. According to this definition, the unemployment rate decreased from 4.7% in 2004 (16,685 persons) to 3.7% (14,523 persons) in 2008. By the end of 2009 unemployment had risen to 6.0% (24,273 persons), mainly driven by the downturn in the construction and hospitality sectors; for the first time, the unemployment rate among males (6.1%) was higher than the comparable rate among females (5.7%). Unemployment reached an historic high of 7.2% (29,618 persons) in the first quarter of 2010, decreasing steadily to 5.4% (21,899 persons) by the end of the year. However, by the end of 2011 unemployment had spiked at 7.9% (31,432 persons), with large year-on-year increases in the construction, manufacturing, and wholesale and retail trade sectors. This sharp upward trend continued in 2012, ending at a seasonally adjusted 11.9% (40,184 persons), with further significant job losses in the hotels and restaurants sector, construction and manufacturing. The seasonally-adjusted number of registered unemployed reached a new high of 51,291 persons in August 2013; significant sectoral increases occurred in trade, education, financial and insurance activities, construction and manufacturing, as well as newcomers to the labour market. The annual rate for 2013 was expected to near 14%.

An increase in economic activity caused the rate of inflation to rise in the early 1990s, reaching an average of 4.7% a year during 1991–95. In 1996–2000 the inflation rate was fairly subdued, averaging 2.9% per year, but in 2000 inflation accelerated sharply, to 4.1%. Minimal price increases for local products and many imports resulted in the overall inflation rate being reduced to its underlying core rate of 2.0% in 2001, but two successive increases in value-added tax (VAT) rates raised it to 2.8% in 2002 and 4.1% in 2003. A fairly strong euro-linked Cyprus pound helped to contain inflation thereafter, so that in the period 2001–05 the average annual inflation rate was only 2.8%. The inflation rate was 2.5% in 2006 and 2.4% in 2007. High global petroleum and food prices, combined with the mild upward effect on prices of the introduction of the euro, pushed the rate up to 4.7% in 2008. However, dual declines in consumer confidence and demand caused inflation to decrease to just 0.3% in 2009, before rising again, to 2.4% in 2010 and 3.3% in 2011. According to national data, inflation was 2.4% in 2012. Measured by the EU Harmonized Index of Consumer Prices (HICP), Cyprus achieved an inflation rate of 2.2% in both 2006 and 2007. Based on the HICP, the European Commission stated in May 2007 that Cyprus had met the inflation criterion, as well as all of the other Maastricht convergence criteria, allowing Cyprus to adopt the euro on 1 January 2008. As measured by the HICP, the rate of inflation increased to 4.4% in 2008, declining to 0.2% (mainly owing to a decrease in petroleum and electricity prices) in 2009; it then rose sharply, to 2.6% in 2010 and 3.5% in 2011, before falling to 3.1% in 2012.

An important feature of economic policy since 1992 has been the gradual adaptation of economic practices and procedures to prepare for full membership of the European Community (EC, now EU), followed by the adoption of the euro in January 2008. The Cyprus Government had applied for membership in July 1990 (having achieved customs union with the EC from 1 January 1988) and joined the EU on 1 May 2004. In addition to the introduction of VAT, in June 1992 the Government linked the Cyprus pound initially to the European Currency Unit (ECU) and then to the euro at a rate of C£1 = €1.708601. This proved to be a remarkably successful policy for currency stability as the pound traded very closely to this rate for well over a decade and joined the Exchange Rate Mechanism (ERM) at the same rate (inverted, therefore, at C£0.585274 per euro) in May 2005. It was also the rate at which the Cyprus pound was converted to the euro.

Cyprus's formal accession to the EU on 1 May 2004 was overshadowed by the failure to reach a political settlement, with the result that only the (de facto) Greek Cypriot area came under the EU's *acquis communautaire* (this remained suspended in the northern part of the island in late 2013), and that the potential economic benefits of a reunified island being in the EU—in particular, building commercial relations with the island's largest neighbouring market—were deferred. On the other hand, the Cyprus Government was not obliged to meet the cost of reunification, estimates of which varied wildly (for political reasons), from a low of about C£4,000m. (€6,834m.) to a high of some C£16,000m. (€27,337m.), at a time when its finances were in substantial deficit. In an early warning to Cyprus, the European Commission announced in May 2004 that the Government's fiscal consolidation plans had significantly diverged from targets, resulting in levels of budget deficit and public debt well above the Maastricht convergence criteria. The high budget deficit prompted the European Commission to launch a formal 'excessive deficit procedure', which effectively delayed Cyprus's entry into the ERM, and thus adoption of the euro, by a year. The Government responded to the Commission in June by announcing new measures for the progressive reduction of the deficit, which had the effect of reducing it from 6.3% of GDP in 2003 to 2.3% in 2005. On 2 May 2005 the Cyprus pound was admitted to the ERM, beginning the obligatory minimum two-year transitional stage towards adoption of the euro (see Budget, Investment and Finance). On 16 May 2007 the Commission recommended that Cyprus should adopt the euro on 1 January 2008, which it duly did, at a rate of €1 = C£0.585274.

Declining share prices in early 2000 culminated in a major correction to the Cyprus Stock Exchange (CSE) index in March. Market capitalization of quoted companies decreased to less than C£8,000m. (€13,669m.), while the CSE index declined by more than one-half. Further significant decreases in the following months effectively wiped out the substantial gains registered in the previous year and inflicted heavy losses on new investors, some of whom staged angry demonstrations in protest against what they alleged were fraudulent activities by brokers with the connivance of the CSE authorities. The Government responded in August 2000 by announcing various measures to restore investor confidence, including a strengthening of the CSE's legal framework and the introduction of greater transparency in its operations. Nevertheless, the CSE all-share index continued on a downward trend and reached a low of about 70 in October 2004.

Investor confidence was further damaged in that month by the report of an official inquiry into the 2000 CSE collapse, which detailed evidence of fraud and the failure of CSE regulatory procedures, although no one was ever made to bear responsibility for the widespread malpractices. In March 2005 the CSE and the Athens Stock Exchange agreed to create a common trading platform, which became operational in October 2006 and resulted in the switch from trading in Cyprus pounds to trading in euros. By the end of 2005 the new main index had risen by 70%, to 1,728, and it rose by a further 150% in 2006, to 3,983; the rally continued into 2007, to total 4,821 by the end of that year, owing to rising bank profits and mergers in the banking sector. However, the global downturn led to a 77% decline in the index in 2008, to just 1,101. By the end of 2009 the index had recovered modestly, to 1,597, but ended 2010 at only 1,055, with continuing concern over the wider impact on the economy of the commercial banks' substantial exposure to Greek sovereign debt. In 2011 a lack of confidence in the market generally and growing concerns over the banking sector in particular resulted in the CSE closing the year at a mere 296. Following the country's application in June 2012 for aid from the EFSF and a worsening of commercial prospects, the CSE had fell to just 115 at the end of that year.

Given the resolution of Cyprus Popular Bank and the radical restructuring of shares in the Bank of Cyprus (BoC) in 2013 (see Industry, Manufacturing and Services), the future of the CSE is in doubt, since trading in the shares of those two institutions accounted for the bulk of daily transactions. A potential basis for revival may lie in the privatization of semi-governmental organizations, as called for under the Memorandum of Understanding (MOU) signed by the Government and the 'troika' of international organizations (the European Commission, the IMF and the European Central Bank) in April 2013 (see Budget, Investment and Finance).

THE NORTHERN ECONOMY

Since 1974 the economy of the area north of the Green Line has not made nearly as much progress as the Greek Cypriot area, primarily owing to restrictions on external trade in goods and services that have transpired as a by-product of its non-recognized status. This has led to heavy dependence on Turkey for transfers, which in turn has bred a dependency culture, as well as corruption (including money-laundering) and poor economic governance. These problems have been aggravated by the legal uncertainty relating to property titles, which also limited property development, at least until 2004. In recent years Turkey's extensive programme of development in northern Cyprus is estimated to amount to some 20% of projected Turkish Cypriot budget expenditure.

Owing to Turkey's economic difficulties, its annual subsidy to the 'TRNC' was reportedly reduced in 2002–03, although the budget figures published by the 'TRNC' authorities do not bear this out. Under a protocol signed in April 2003 (and revised in June 2005), Turkey pledged direct financial support of US $550m. to the 'TRNC' for the period 2004–06. In addition, in May 2006 Turkey promised a further $135m. Between 2000 and 2005 budgetary aid from Turkey amounted to an annual of 7.5% of the north's gross national product (GNP) per year, while credits (often not repaid) amounted to an average of 11.7% of GNP per year. In 2008 aid from Turkey totalled 294m. new Turkish lira (YTL—now Turkish lira), representing 5.7% of GNP, which stood at YTL 5,128.3m. ($3,995.6m.). In the same year, credits—which were technically earmarked for infrastructure expenditure—amounted to YTL 433m. (8.4% of GNP). The most recent consolidated official data show YTL 273m. (5.0% of GNP) and YTL 303m. (5.4%) in aid from Turkey for 2009 and 2010, respectively, while credits from Turkey amounted to YTL 659m. (12.2% of GNP) in 2009 and YTL 48m. (9.7%) in 2010. In 2010 and 2011 the 'TRNC' administration implemented an extensive austerity and privatization package designed by the Turkish Government, following the latter's concern over the high fiscal burden of the public sector. The measures, which included the eventual closure of the publicly run airline Kıbrıs Türk Hava Yollari (Cyprus Turkish Airlines), led to significant industrial conflict in the north during 2012.

An economic protocol signed by the 'TRNC' and Turkey in December covers the period 2013-15. This aims to direct most of the aid that will come from Turkey during this period (a projected US $1,200m. in 2014-15) away from the public sector (currently the largest employer) and towards boosting growth in the private sector through investment (which is widely expected to come predominantly from Turkey). The protocol places emphasis on the privatization of state-owned enterprises; it is likely that the power generation, telecommunications, seaport and education sectors will be targeted. Assessment of the real performance of the 'TRNC' economy has been notoriously difficult, owing to a relative lack of data and statistics and to the fact that what is published is not compiled according to EU norms. For example, GNP figures expressed in constant prices refer to 1977 as the base year. However, the available statistics generally conform to physical and anecdotal evidence. According to official 'TRNC' figures, between 1978 and 2009 the north suffered seven years of contraction in GNP. By contrast, prior to 2009, the last time that the economy had contracted in the south was in 1974–75. The Five-Year Plan for the years 1988–92 (the third such plan to be launched since 1978) targeted an average growth rate of 7% per year. However, the actual rate was only 4.6%, largely owing to a contraction of 5.3% in 1991. Real GNP growth averaged 1.3% per year in 1991–95 and 3.9% in 1996–2000. However, macroeconomic instability in Turkey, followed by a devaluation of the Turkish lira, led to a decline in annual GNP of 0.7% in 2000 and a much more severe decrease of 5.4% in 2001.

Growth accelerated from 2002, first as a result of the devaluation of the Turkish lira in 2001 and then of the opening of the Green Line checkpoints in April 2003, which brought tourists from the south, as well as incomes from the many Turkish Cypriots who began to cross daily to work. By 2009 an estimated 3,000–5,000 Turkish Cypriots were crossing the Green Line daily to work in the south. The Greek Cypriot rejection of the reunification plan in April 2004 in contrast with its acceptance by Turkish Cypriots—also led to an acceleration of building on Greek Cypriot-titled land until a court case brought by a Greek Cypriot against a British couple who had built on land he claimed to own (see History), as well as a number of scandals and liquidity problems, resulted in a slowdown in the construction sector. Real GNP therefore rose at an average annual rate of 12.1% in 2002–06, peaking at 15.4% in 2004, before a sharp decline in construction activity (from sectoral growth of 68.1% in 2006 to just 4.2% in 2007) led to overall real growth of just 1.5% in 2007. Many economic sectors contracted dramatically in 2008, particularly agriculture (18.2%), manufacturing (13.4%), industry (10.3%) and construction (8.0%), resulting in an overall reduction in GNP of 3.4%. Despite a marked improvement in the agricultural sector, official figures for 2009 indicated an overall contraction of 5.7% in GNP, driven notably by severe decreases in output in the sectors of construction (18.5%), wholesale and retail trade (11.4%), industry (9.1%) and tourism (8.7%). In 2010 there was 3.6% growth in GNP, with relatively healthy growth in wholesale and retail trade (21.5%), tourism (18.3%), agriculture (10.0%) and construction (3.8%). Industry and manufacturing contracted further, but by lesser amounts (0.2% and 1.6%, respectively).

Frequent recessions kept per caput incomes lower than in the Greek Cypriot south. Nevertheless, the unprecedented period of growth in 2003–06 brought annual GNP per head in the north from US $4,401, or 30.6% of the Greek Cypriot average, in 2002 to $16,158, or some 60% of the Greek Cypriot average, in 2008. A census carried out on 30 April 2006 revealed that population growth had been much higher than expected, with the total population reaching more than 260,000 by that date. Since 2006 the official population figure has been drawn from mid-year de jure population projections based on the General Population and Housing Unit Census. According to this measure, the population reached 274,436 in 2008, representing an annual increase of 2.4%. The official population figure for 2010 was 286,973. A census performed in December 2011 resulted in an official population figure of 294,906, but this has been disputed by local political parties, labour unions and media outlets, amid accusations that the Government had deliberately under-counted the population.

Based on official figures at current market prices, the contribution to GDP of the agriculture sector rose from 7.9% in 2001 to 9.4% in 2003, then declined steadily, to just 6.5% in 2010. Manufacturing declined steadily from 5.4% of GDP in 2001 to 2.6% in 2010. The contribution of the construction sector to GDP increased from 3.6% in 2001 to 7.9% in both 2006 and 2007, before decreasing to 6.4% in 2010. The contribution of other sectors remained fairly stable during the same period, culminating in the following contributions in 2010: public services (23.2%), business and personal services (12.8%), wholesale and retail trade (11.8%), other industry (8.3%) and financial services (8.0%). Education, for which no separate figures are available, was also an important generator of revenue; from 2005 some three-quarters of the total number of students enrolled in tertiary institutions (41,230 for the academic year 2010/11) hailed from abroad (mainly Turkey).

Until recently, the 'TRNC' experienced a persistently high level of inflation, much of it 'imported' from Turkey, in that the Turkish lira is the currency in use and the local authorities have no control over the money supply. The average annual inflation rate was 83.7% in 1991–95, 68.3% in 1996–2000 and 23.2% in 2001–05. The inflation rate in 2005 was only 2.7%, at that time the lowest on record, owing to a stronger Turkish lira. However, further weaknesses in the Turkish lira led to an inflation rate of 19.2% in 2006. A marked improvement in foreign exchange rates in 2007 was partially offset by an increase in VAT, higher prices of diesel fuel, meat and services, and higher costs in vegetable and fruit production, resulting in an inflation rate of 9.4%. Inflation rose to 14.5% in 2008 (peaking at 17.8% in mid-year), but declined steadily in 2009, reaching 5.7% in December, and fluctuated between 3.2% and 5.4% during 2010, ending the year at 3.3%. The inflation rate rose significantly throughout 2011, ending at a peak of 14.7% against a background of spiralling consumer debt and the impact of the austerity measures. However, January 2012 marked the beginning of a gradual fall, ending the year at 3.6%.

Owing, in part, to the large public sector, the official unemployment rate has remained very low in the 'TRNC'. According to official figures, the unemployment rate was just 1.2% in 1990, 1.3% in 2000 and 1.0% in 2005. However, it was widely accepted that the real unemployment rate was in fact much higher, and in 2008 the authorities appeared to acknowledge this by reporting a revised rate of 8.2% in 2005. This rose to 9.4% in 2006, remaining largely unchanged in 2007–08; at the end of 2008 the rate stood at 9.8%. Unemployment increased to 12.4% in 2009, decreasing to 11.9% in 2010. The administration's plans to privatize various public sector enterprises were expected to produce a sharp rise in the unemployment rate. Household labour force surveys, which were introduced in 2004, showed an increase in the number of employed persons from 86,914 in 2004 to 93,498 in 2010.

The liberal trade policies adopted by the 'TRNC' since the late 1980s have resulted in the establishment of trading relations with over 60 countries, mostly via Turkey, owing to the non-recognition of the 'TRNC' as a political entity. The volume of trade (exports plus imports) was recorded at $447.0m. in 1990, $475.3m. in 2000 and $1,764.4m. in 2008, decreasing to an estimated $1,700.6m. in 2010. The trade deficit grew from $316.0m. in 1990, $374.5m. in 2000 and $1,597.0m. in 2008, but then contracted to an estimated $1,507.8m. in 2010. Net tourism revenues rose from $198.3m. in 2000 to $328.8m. in 2005, before decreasing sharply to $303.2m. in 2006. Revenues grew again to $381.0m. in 2007, increasing slightly, to $383.7m., in 2008. Net tourism revenues for 2010 were estimated at $405.8m., a 3.9% increase on the previous year's estimate of $390.7m. Other net invisible earnings increased by 19.2% to $582.3m. in 2005 and by 37.6% to $801.3m. in 2006; however, growth in net invisible earnings contracted to just 2.8% ($824.1m.) in 2007, and in the following year a contraction of 0.1% ($823.0m.) was recorded. Estimated figures for 2009 and 2010 are $799.0m. and $826.2m., respectively. Services and invisibles inflows have not normally been high enough to cover the trade deficit, so that since 1990 the current account has only been in surplus twice (in 2002 and 2003).

With the exception of 1998 and 1999, the annual current account deficit has tended to be modest; however, it spiked from $14.1m. in 2004 to $276.3m. in 2005, peaking at $390.3m. in 2008. According to estimated figures, the current account deficit decreased to $65.4m. in 2009, then rose to $275.8m. in 2010. In the absence of foreign direct investment (FDI) or inflows that a sovereign country would attract, such as stock market purchases, most of this deficit is covered by foreign aid and other credits from Turkey, which has kept the overall balance of payments in surplus and totalled an estimated $363.9m. in 2010. Foreign exchange reserves rose steadily from $183.7m. in 1990 to $631.9m. in 2000, $1,597.6m. in 2005 and $2,072.1m. in 2007. Reserves declined to $1,802.6m. in 2008, then rose to $2,069.1m. in 2010.

From August 1990 the northern economy encountered major difficulties as a result of the collapse, with debts of some £1,300m., of Polly Peck International, a fruit-packaging, tourism and publishing conglomerate based in the United Kingdom but with substantial interests in the 'TRNC'. In December 1990 66 charges covering false accounting and the theft of £360m. were brought against the Turkish Cypriot Chairman of the conglomerate, Asil Nadir, whose various companies were estimated to have provided more than one-third of annual GDP in the 'TRNC', accounting for 60% of total exports. In May 1993 Nadir fled to the 'TRNC', claiming that he could not expect a fair trial from the British authorities. It was reported that he intended to revive the remnants of the Polly Peck empire in northern Cyprus. Whether or not he had the official support of the 'TRNC' authorities in this endeavour remained unclear. Nadir was also the owner of Kıbrıs (Cyprus), the newspaper with the largest circulation in the north. In August 2010 Nadir announced that he was prepared to return to the United Kingdom, and in early September he appeared at the Central Criminal Court in London for a bail hearing. His trial on 13 specimen counts of theft relating to the transfer of £34m. out of Polly Peck between 1987 and 1990 commenced in January 2012. In August Nadir was found guilty of 10 of the 13 charges, and was sentenced to 10 years' imprisonment for unlawfully taking a total of £28.6m. from the company's accounts.

Further damage was incurred following a European Court of Justice ruling in July 1994, which had the effect of drastically reducing the competitiveness of Turkish Cypriot exports. The Court of Justice ruled that EU member states could not accept movement and phytosanitary certificates that were issued by authorities other than the competent authorities of the Republic of Cyprus. This meant that henceforth Turkish Cypriot goods would be subject to high tariffs. The cost of exports was also raised by the fact that exports could not come directly from northern Cyprus but had to be stamped in Turkey. The immediate consequence of the ruling was that hundreds of 'TRNC' textile workers were made redundant, while in the longer term it increased the dependence of the 'TRNC' on Turkey.

In January 2000 the Turkish Ministry of Finance issued a decree setting an official exchange rate between the Turkish lira and the Cyprus pound (TL 952,000 = C£1) for the first time since 1974. The main factor in this decision was the need to discourage Turkish Cypriots from changing Cyprus pounds (in which they are often paid) illegally. In practice, however, the Cyprus pound (and now the euro) was exchanged at market rates.

The major financial crisis in Turkey in February 2001 and the 30% devaluation of the Turkish lira directly affected the 'TRNC', where resultant price increases and non-payment of state salaries and pensions provoked demonstrations and opposition calls for the Government to move away from economic dependence on Turkey. The crisis therefore strengthened Turkish Cypriot elements that favoured participation in Cyprus's accession negotiations with the EU and the restoration of economic unity in the island. The new administration that took office in June 2001 undertook to pursue free market policies and to accelerate privatization, while 'keeping in mind the country's social structure', and also to pursue the creation of a joint economic zone with Turkey.

The relaxation of restrictions on movement in Cyprus from April 2003 brought significant economic benefits to the Turkish Cypriot area, allowing large numbers of Turkish Cypriots to work in the south, Greek Cypriot visitors to spend money in the 'TRNC' (particularly in the casinos, which were banned in the south), and foreign visitors on holiday in the south to cross to the north.

In April 2004 the European Commission adopted the so-called 'Green Line regulation'. This was a new authorization system that would allow selected Turkish Cypriot goods to be sold in the south, and (in theory) to be exported through ports controlled by the Greek Cypriot Government. Goods began to be traded in August 2004 and the Turkish Cypriot administration reciprocated with similar rules. Initially trade volumes were low, but they accelerated in 2008, with north–south trade reaching €6.8m. in that year, before declining by 11.5%, to €6.0m., in 2009, and then by 6.5%, to €5.2m., in 2010. In 2011 trade across the Green Line, with the exception of the sale of electricity, declined further, to €4.8m., which could be ascribed to the slowdown in the construction sector and the subsequent reduction in demand for quarried rock, bricks and other building materials. However, electricity to the value of €24,085,775 (82% of the total trade for that year), was sold by the north following the explosion at the Mari naval base in July 2011, which destroyed large parts of the nearby Vassiliko power station. The sale of electricity to the south ended in March 2012, amounting to €4.8m. (53% of the north-south trade for the whole year). With the exception of electricity, the value of goods traded across the Green Line in 2012 declined to €4.0m. Until 2010 potatoes were the largest single component of Green Line trade, accounting for up to 30% of overall trade. In 2011, however, the potato trade represented less than 1% of total trade. In 2012, after electricity, plastic products were the most traded item, followed by building materials/articles of stone and fresh fish.

Owing to the suspension in the Turkish Cypriot area of the EU's *acquis communcutaire*, the European Commission, encouraged by a European Council request made shortly before Cyprus joined the EU, proposed two regulations to mitigate that area's resulting financial disadvantage. The 'financial aid' regulation envisaged aid of €259m. (the same amount as had been designated for the Turkish Cypriots for the 2004–06 period, in the event of a solution). The 'direct trade' regulation envisaged preferential trade in what would amount to the lifting of restrictions on exports from the port of Famagusta, which the Greek Cypriots had declared closed. Owing to Greek Cypriot objections and the Turkish Cypriots' desire not to decouple the two regulations, the two proposed regulations remained blocked for almost two years. The financial aid regulation was finally approved in early 2006, and €311m. was programmed in aid between 2006 and the end of 2012. In total, €204m. (66% of the overall amount contracted since the start of the programme) was disbursed during that period, with 402 contracts remaining open. However, it remained unclear at mid-2013 whether the direct trade regulation would ever enter into effect. Meanwhile, on 1 January 2005 the Turkish Government established a new monetary unit, known as the new Turkish lira, which was equivalent to 1,000,000 of the former units. (The name of the currency reverted to Turkish lira on 1 January 2009.)

Economic prospects in the north remain uncertain, as the political ramifications of reduced funding from Turkey for infrastructure projects and the administration's privatization policy are played out. Demonstrations involving tens of thousands of people (a significant proportion of the population) were held in north Nicosia on 28 January and 2 March 2011 to protest against the austerity measures imposed by Turkey, coupled with 24-hour general strikes on both days. In June 2010 Cyprus Turkish Airlines (the 'state-operated' carrier) was closed down after efforts to sell it to the private sector Turkish carrier Atlasjet Havacilik AŞ collapsed. Plans to privatize other 'state' enterprises, such as the electricity and telecommunications utilities and Ercan airport, were prepared during 2011, and a draft law was submitted to the legislature. When the authorities introduced plans to privatize the Cyprus Turkey Electricity Corpn (KIB-TEK) in January 2012, the main trade union started an indefinite strike, stopping production and thus causing power cuts. Within a week the union was invited to negotiate, and the privatization plan was dropped shortly afterwards in favour of a restructuring. Following its defeat at a parliamentary vote of no confidence in June 2013, the National Unity Party (UBP) Government scheduled early legislative elections for the following month. The UBP's subsequent defeat in those elections was widely interpreted as a vote against its cuts in public sector spending and the privatization of publicly-owned companies envisaged by the 'TRNC'-Turkey protocol. However, given the Turkish Cypriot area's financial dependence on Turkey, it is unlikely that the new coalition Government will have many options. (For further details on the 'TRNC' elections, see History.)

AGRICULTURE

Until only a few decades ago agriculture was the single most important economic activity in Cyprus, but—following the economic dislocation caused by the 1974 invasion—it has since been superseded on both sides of the island by tourism and manufacturing and in the south also by financial services. In 1974 some 36% of the island's labour force was gainfully employed in agriculture, which accounted for 16.7% of GDP. According to the household labour force survey, by 2008 only 3.5% of the Turkish Cypriot employed labour force was engaged in agriculture, down from 8.4% in 2004; however, this increased to 5.7% (5,300 persons) in 2010. In the Greek Cypriot area, 6.8% of the employed population was engaged in agriculture (including hunting, forestry and fishing) in 2008; since 2009, this figure has remained constant at just over 7.0%. The main crops in both parts of the island are citrus fruits, potatoes, olives, carobs, wheat and barley.

After the division of the island in 1974, the Government of the Republic of Cyprus initiated a series of emergency development plans in which agriculture and irrigation featured prominently. Loans were given to farmers, and agricultural production responded rapidly. Most of the island's citrus trees were in the north, so they were replaced as the main agricultural product in the south by potatoes and other vegetables.

Periodic drought conditions have made agricultural production volatile, and have led environmentalists to question the logic of producing crops that need large amounts of water, such as citrus fruits. The average annual increase in agricultural production was 3.2% in 1991–95, but production contracted by 1.1% per year on average in 1996–2000, by 0.1% in 2001–05 and by 3.0% in 2006. There were droughts in 1994, 1997 and 2000, and also a four-year drought in 2004–08. Gross value added as a share of GDP at current prices showed a gradual decline, from 7.2% in 1990 to 5.3% in 1995, 3.4% in 2000, 2.5% in 2005 and 1.9% in 2009, according to provisional data. Overall agricultural production was relatively stable during 2000–07. Production of cereals declined from 127,100 metric tons in 1999 to 47,600 tons in the drought year of 2000. Having recovered to 164,280 tons in 2003, production declined to 65,732 tons by 2010. The potato crop peaked at 234,000 tons in 1995. Since then production has fluctuated year by year, but has been on a general declining trend, reaching just 82,000 in 2010, before increasing, to 109,600 tons, in 2011. The production of grapes, bananas and olives has declined markedly since 2003, in part owing to the trend for sizeable tracts of agricultural land in certain areas to be sold for property development, and stood at 24,700 tons, 5,900 tons and 15,300 tons, respectively, in 2011. The production of oranges, the main citrus fruit, declined from 63,000 tons in 1990 to 37,700 tons in 2011. The main livestock products are pork and poultry, with production of 57,600 tons and 27,400 tons, respectively, in 2011. Exports of products of agricultural origin, such as halloumi cheese, are becoming more important to the agricultural sector. Domestic exports of industrial products of agricultural origin increased steadily from €14.9m. in 2008 to €17.2m. in 2012.

By mid-2013 five desalination plants were in operation in the Greek Cypriot-controlled area. The first plant, at Dhekelia on the southern coast, became operational in 1997, providing 20,000 cu m of water per day. A second permanent desalination plant, located near Larnaca airport and having a capacity of 52,000 cu m per day, was inaugurated in April 2001. On assuming office in 2003, President Tassos Papadopoulos decided to cancel the desalination plant programme that had been planned by his predecessor, Glavkos Klerides. However, there followed several years of drought, leading to empty dams by 2008 and emergency measures being implemented, including water cuts, importing water by ship from Greece (at a cost of over €50m.), using mobile temporary desalination units and finally starting the process to award new desalination contracts. Construction of two more desalination plants (at Vassiliko, near Larnaca, and at Kouklia in Paphos district) commenced in 2009, while another, to be built in Limassol, was in the process of being contracted. The desalination unit at Kouklia was inaugurated in May 2011, and the Vassiliko unit commenced operations before the end of the year. The fifth desalination plant was inaugurated in Limassol in August 2013. Although the total output capacity of the five plants (approximately 220,000 cubic metres of water per day) would be sufficient to meet the projected demands of the Cypriot consumer for good quality potable water (independent of rainfall considerations) until 2018, exceptionally heavy rainfall in the winters of 2009 and 2011 raised water levels in reservoirs to 91% of capacity in June 2012, compared with 60% a year previously. By January 2012 all desalination units had reduced or halted production, as they would only have to cover roughly one-third of drinking water needs. Citing the development of new, less energy-consuming methods of desalination, the Government indicated in August 2013 that it would proceed with the construction of further plants in order to cover growing consumer needs. This announcement may be viewed in political terms, as the possibility of water being supplied from the north has been proposed as an element of future negotiations over reunification.

The Turkish Cypriot north inherited about 80% of the island's citrus groves, all the tobacco fields, 40% of the carobs, 80% of carrots and 10%–15% of potatoes. Nevertheless, agriculture in the north has lagged behind that of the south. In the chaos that followed the fighting, many citrus trees were neglected and died, or contracted diseases. Production resumed gradually in the 1980s, but the collapse of Polly Peck International (see The Northern Economy) seriously disrupted the northern citrus fruit industry, resulting in the closure of some processing plants and severely reducing export volumes.

The European Court of Justice ruling in July 1994, effectively barring the direct import of 'TRNC' goods and produce by EU countries unless certificated by the recognized Cypriot authorities, also had damaging consequences. From 1997 there was a steep decline in the value of agricultural exports and by 2001 the total value of exports of agricultural production from the 'TRNC', at current prices, had decreased to just $12.3m. (35.5% of the total). A shift of concentration to Middle East markets, as well as a strengthening Turkish lira after 2001, helped raise the value of agricultural exports gradually in dollar terms to a high of $30.7m. in 2007; this contracted back to $28.4m. in 2008 and $20.9m. in 2009, before recovering to $36.8m. in 2010. The agricultural sector's share of GDP was 10.2% in 1995; it decreased from 7.0% in 2005 to 6.5% in 2010, with crop production accounting for 3.0%, livestock production 2.4% and fishing 0.4%. Raw agricultural exports represented 38.2% of total exports by value in 2010, while processed agricultural goods represented 40.8%.

Water shortage has also been a persistent problem in the 'TRNC', necessitating the importation of water from Turkey. In January 2000 a Turkish-led international consortium announced that construction of a water pipeline between Turkey and the 'TRNC' would begin later that year. However, the first-phase construction of the Alaköprü Dam near the Turkish coastal town of Anamur only commenced in March 2011, with completion projected by March 2014. The remainder of the project was due to be constructed in three phases, including a second dam, on the island, at the town of Geçitköy (Panagra in Greek), and the 107-km pipeline was scheduled to be operational by November 2014, delivering 75m. cu m of water annually.

INDUSTRY, MANUFACTURING AND SERVICES

Industry was likewise severely affected by the war of 1974, which resulted in the Greek Cypriots losing an estimated 70% of gross domestic manufacturing output. However, Government incentives for investment, combined with a decline in real wages, stimulated a rapid expansion of manufacturing industry thereafter, especially in small-scale labour-intensive plants producing goods for export.

During 1989–92 the output of the manufacturing sector increased at an average rate of 3% per year, compared with the planning target of 5% annually. Failure to attain the desired growth rate was attributed to adverse conditions in major markets, such as the United Kingdom and the Arab states. However, the real problem was the diminishing price competitiveness of the sector, which was exacerbated by inflation-linked wages. This meant that the sector was ill-prepared for the competition that followed the gradual abolition of import tariffs under the Additional Protocol of the Cyprus–EU Association Agreement, which came into force in January 1988. The continued weak performance of the broad industrial sector (manufacturing, mining, and electricity, gas and water) was reflected during 1995–2000, when the output index rose from 100 in 1995 to only 100.1 in 2000, having reached a nadir of 94.3 in 1997. Rising prices meant that the aggregate value of manufacturing output at current market prices rose from

C£1,296m. (€2,214m.) in 1995 to C£1,581m. (€2,701m.) in 2000. Within the sector, food products, beverages and tobacco formed substantially the largest component in 2000, with gross output valued at C£578m. (€988m.), followed by chemicals, petroleum, and rubber and plastics products (C£291m. or €497m.), other non-metallic mineral products (C£145m. or €248m.), and basic metals and fabricated metal products (C£124m. or €212m.). During 1995–2000 clothing and textiles lost their status as the largest manufacturing category, the value of output at current market prices declining from C£150m. (€256m) in 1995 to C£98m. (€167m.) in 2000, while footwear and leather, in decline since the late 1980s owing to Asian competition based on cheaper labour, shrank from an output value of C£31m. (€53m.) to C£16m. (€27m.). The value of domestic manufactured exports rose from C£164m. (€280m.) in 1995 (including C£44m. or €75m. from clothing and textiles as the largest category) to C£187m. (€320m.) in 2000 (when the most important category was pharmaceuticals, at C£31m. or €53m.).

The following five years saw a strong recovery for the overall industrial sector, mainly as a result of growth in mining and quarrying and electricity, gas and water, but only a modest recovery for the sub-sector of manufacturing. The 2000–05 period was characterized by a sharp decline in output from the traditional manufacturing sectors, such as clothing, textiles and leather products, as these sectors failed to compete with lower-cost manufacturers abroad, and a strong increase in certain higher value-added sectors such as pharmaceuticals and machinery and equipment. The manufacturing index rose from 100 in 2000 to 104.8 in 2005. However, output of petroleum refining declined by 35.3% in 2001–05, owing to the closure of the oil refinery in April 2004. The fortunes of various sub-sectors are reflected in figures for domestic exports of manufactured goods. Exports of chemicals products, including pharmaceuticals, rose from C£41.2m. (€70.4m.) in 2000 to C£59.4m. (€101.5m.) in 2005. By contrast, exports of textiles contracted from C£24m. (€41.0m.) in 2000 to C£4.8m. (€8.2m.) in 2005 and exports of leather products decreased from C£6.3m. (€10.8m.) to C£1.2m. (€2.1m.). Exports of domestically produced food, beverages and tobacco increased slightly, from C£50.3m. (€85.9m.) in 2000 to C£53.1m. (€90.7m.) in 2005. Within this sub-category, there was a sharp decline in exports of cigarettes, from C£16.2m. (€27.7m.) in 2000 to C£7.9m. (€13.5m.) in 2005, and a large increase in sales of halloumi cheese, from C£7.6m. (€13.0m.) to C£15.3m. (€26.1m.).

In 2006–08 the overall trend continued. A decline in output of textiles and pulp and paper products offset the healthy increase in output of chemicals (including pharmaceuticals), electrical and optical equipment, and transport equipment. The manufacturing index therefore rose to 108.7 by 2008, but then began to decline steadily, to 96.2 in 2009 and 76.4 in 2012. The contribution of manufacturing to GDP at current market prices declined steadily from 14.4% in 1995 to 10.4% in 2000, 7.6% in 2005, and 5.9% in 2012.

In contrast to the relative decline in the contribution of the manufacturing sector, the services sector has broadly maintained its share of GDP over recent years, based on constant annual growth in total gross value added. It rose from 64.7% of GDP in 1995 to 69.6% in 2000, then declined gradually to 66.4% of GDP in 2008 as construction boomed. When this sector declined sharply in 2009, the contribution of the services sector rose accordingly to 69.9%. Services contributed 71.6% of GDP in 2010 and, according to provisional data, 82.3% in 2012.

From the late 1980s, service industries such as banking, insurance and consultancy grew at a remarkable rate and emerged as an important part of the Greek Cypriot economy. By the end of 1994 more than 17,000 foreign companies were registered in the Greek Cypriot sector, although only about 10% of those maintained offices on the island. In 1996–2000 the financial intermediation (mainly banking) sector expanded rapidly, at an average annual rate of 12.6%, compared with 4.9% for the tourism-related restaurants and hotels sector, and 3.0% for wholesale and retail trade.

The next five years saw a reversal of fortunes for both the financial and tourism services, owing to the stock market downturn and weak tourism market. In 2001–05 value added in hotels and restaurants contracted by 2.4%; by contrast, value added in retail and wholesale trade, helped by buoyant consumer demand, rose by 5.0% over the same period. Value added in financial intermediation grew marginally from 5.1% in 2000 to 5.8% in 2006, declining to 5.3% in 2007, 4.9% in 2008, 5.0% in 2009 and an estimated 4.9% in 2010. However, a combination of sustained low interest rates for the euro and large inward flows of Russian capital with light European regulation in the period 2005–08 encouraged a bullish view in banking circles based on attractive short-term returns on investments. This surge in lending, bolstered by increased deposits attracted by relatively high deposit interest rates, took the form of personal loans, credit cards and commercial loans, but also mortgages and commercial real estate (re-)financing on a scale that fed a real estate 'bubble'.

The virtual standstill of both the construction and real estate sectors from 2009 raised concerns over the commercial banks' exposure to property developers, evidenced by a significant rise in the rescheduling of loans and provision for non-performing loans. Given the crucial role of the banking sector in the economy (with total assets of around eight times GDP in 2011), a far greater worry emerged in 2010 and deepened in 2011 regarding the Cypriot commercial banks' substantial exposure to the crisis-ridden economy of Greece. In April 2011 Standard & Poor's estimated this exposure at some €6,400m. in Greek sovereign and bank debt, in addition to significant amounts lent to Greek companies and households through the Cypriot banks' substantial networks in Greece. Most Greek-related exposure was held by the three largest Cypriot banks: BoC, Marfin Popular Bank (MPB) and the Hellenic Bank. Up to 40% of their combined total lending was to Greece, compared with approximately one-third of the whole banking system's assets, including those of Greek subsidiaries based in Cyprus. Despite the banks' apparent compliance with the Central Bank of Cyprus's instruction to improve capital adequacy ratios to levels that would accommodate 50% write-offs as the loans fell due and were rolled over, the Bank of Cyprus and MPB proved unable to cope with the impact of the 76.4% 'haircut' on their sovereign Greek assets as part of bailout plan agreed by Greece with the so-called troika (the European Commission, IMF and European Central Bank) in October 2011. In particular, they failed to raise their capital by 30 June 2012 to comply with a minimum Core Tier 1 requirement of 9.0% set by the European Banking Authority (EBA).

The banks' continuing exposure to Greece and the likelihood of a Greek exit from the eurozone, the resulting increase in the likely amount of support that the Government might have to extend to Cypriot banks, the existing strain on the country's finances and the later denial to Cyprus of access to the international markets were cited by the main credit ratings agencies as major reasons for a series of downgrades of Cyprus's sovereign rating in 2010, 2011 and 2012; the Government's apparent reluctance to finalize the terms of a bailout deal in 2012 was also cited. Further deterioration in the health of both the banking sector and the Government's economic prospects resulted in further downgrades in 2013. As of August 2013, Cyprus's long-term sovereign debt was rated Caa3 by Moody's Investors Service, B- by Fitch Ratings and CCC+ by Standard & Poor's.

MPB had bought heavily into Greek sovereign debt between 2007 and 2009, adding to a large commercial and consumer debt portfolio—amounting to the biggest Greek exposure of all the Cypriot banks. Non-Executive Chairman Andreas Vgenopoulos was forced to resign in November 2011, just before MPB posted a record net loss for that year of €2,830m., which included a 65% write-down (€1,969m.) of its €3,052m. Greek sovereign debt holding. In April 2012 the now-renamed Cyprus Popular Bank (CPB) revised its final 2011 losses upwards to €3,650.4m., incorporating a write-down of the full 76.4% (€2,331m.) of the nominal value of its Greek government bond holdings. By May 2012 it was evident that CPB would not be able to raise from a strategic investor the €1,800m. it needed for recapitalization—the EBA had set the replenishment at €1,970m.—and appealed to the Government for assistance, which agreed to underwrite the €1,800m. capital issue. The state bought €1,797m. of the share issue in June, gaining an interest in the bank of 84%, and named new board members in July. According to bank officials, its total lending to the

Greek private sector stood at €11,500m. in the first quarter of 2012, and the non-performing loan (NPL) ratio in Greece rose to 22.8%, up by 3.3% compared with the fourth quarter of 2011. Loans in Cyprus rose to €10,600m. in the first quarter of 2012, but NPLs also rose by €141m., to 9.4%, up by 1.3% on the fourth quarter of 2011. In the second quarter of 2012 the NPL ratio rose to 32.6% in Greece and to 13.6% in Cyprus (up by €486m.). In November 2012 CPB announced a nine-monthly gross operating profit of €638m. (24% lower on a yearly basis), but a net loss of €1,091m., after a €1,285m. provision for NPLs (503% higher on a yearly basis, of which €967m. on Greek loans) and a €166m. impairment of debt and equity holdings. Taking into account impairment of goodwill and other intangible assets (mainly in Greece), the total attributable loss amounted to €1,671m. In the third quarter of 2012 the NPL ratio rose to 40.1% in Greece and to 17.2% in Cyprus (up by €387m.). In August 2012 CPB employed 2,500 staff in Cyprus; it planned to reduce its payroll by 12% by the end of the year and was also reported to be preparing to close 65 branches in Cyprus and Greece as part of a restructuring of its consumer business. By the end of 2012 CPB had cut its branch network in Greece by 42 to 132 branches.

However, CPB's difficulties increased, as concerned depositors began to withdraw their funds, leaving it increasingly dependent on the emergency liquidity assistance (ELA) provided by the central bank. In early 2013 CPB began selling assets—including loans in Serbia and Ukraine, and part of a €2,000m. shipping loan portfolio in Greece—at a 15% discount. Following the February 2013 presidential election, the new Government announced that the publication of CPB's financial results for 2012 would be postponed until the total recapitalization requirements of the banking sector were finalised by external consultants. The terms of the bailout agreed by the Government with the troika in late March 2013 (see Budget, Investment and Finance) specified the winding down of CPB. This involved the full contribution of equity shareholders, bond holders and uninsured depositors (i.e. with deposits of more than €100,000); the sale of CPB's business in Cyprus (excluding its subsidiaries and branches abroad) to BoC; and the division of CPB into a 'good' bank with performing loans (to be absorbed by BoC) and a 'bad' bank with non-performing loans (to be run down over time). CPB would only enter into liquidation after selling its subsidiaries in Romania, Russia, Malta and Serbia, and winding down its operations in Ukraine for the benefit of its creditors. Although BoC received around €4,000m. from CPB in insured deposits (i.e. less than €100,000), it was also required to assume some of CPB's obligations, including the €9,200m. that the latter had accumulated in ELA debt, adding to BoC's own ELA liability of around €2,000m. At the Government's insistence, 2,390 CPB employees in Cyprus were also transferred to BoC's payroll, prior to an eventual reduction of the total work-force and branch network. In mid-2012 it emerged publicly that BoC had bought over €2,000m. in high-yield Greek government bonds from German banks at 68% of face value during 2010, just a few months after complying with a Central Bank instruction to reduce its Greek exposure. Following the Greek bailout agreement in October 2011 with its attached 'haircut', BoC posted post-tax losses of €1,380m. in its 2011 full-year results, incorporating a €1,682m. write-down (74.0% impairment plus hedging costs) of the €2,083m. nominal value of its Greek sovereign debt holdings, leaving a carrying value of €616m. The bank's 2011 annual report showed €10,014m. of other on-balace sheet Greek exposure, plus €2,209m. in off-balance sheet Greek exposure. In April 2012 BoC revised its losses for 2011 upwards, by €360m. Group CEO Andreas Eliades resigned in July 2012, after the BoC board had assured shareholders at its annual general meeting in June that the bank was confident it could raise from private funds the relatively modest shortfall of €200m. in its €1,560m. core Tier 1 recapitalization target, mooting the sale of two subsidiary insurance businesses. In fact, the bank announced on 27 June that it needed €500m., which it could only secure through temporary state assistance.

Under the initial terms of the March 2013 bailout agreement, uninsured depositors with BoC were subjected to a 'bail-in', involving the automatic conversion of 37.5% of net funds into Class A shares in BoC, with voting rights and dividends. A further 22.5% of uninsured depositors' net funds were temporarily frozen against eventual conversion into Class A shares when the final bail-in figure was agreed; this was set at 47.5% in July. The existing ordinary shares were converted into new shares of Class D, existing securities which were convertible into shares were converted into new shares of Class C, and existing bonds were converted into new shares of Class B. Under the new structure, former CPB depositors now own some 18% of BoC—but they can only sell those shares when the 'bad' part of CPB is finally wound down. The bank employees' union became BoC's second-largest shareholder after the bail-in of its provident fund deposits. As part of the CPB resolution process, in March both banks' boards were dismissed by the central bank in its capacity as the resolution authority to facilitate the restructuring of the banking sector; the central bank appointed an interim board of directors at BoC in April, and a new CEO the following month. In June BoC had a total (combined) work-force of 5,640 and 202 branches (having taken over 85 CPB branches); in August it announced that 1,370 employees had applied for voluntary retirement under a scheme launched two months previously. On 30 July BoC formally exited administration by the resolution authority and it regained access to cheaper liquidity via the Eurosystem the following day. In mid-September a new 16-member Board of Directors was elected at the bank's AGM, including six Russians. In 2011 Hellenic Bank posted a gross operating profit of €56m., and a loss before tax of €87m. after including provisions for NPLs and a €77m. write-down (70% of nominal value) of its Greek sovereign debt holding. Hellenic was reported to have €900m. in loans to Greek businesses and households going into 2012. In 2012, gross operating profit was €149m., but €162 provisions for increasing NPLs in Cyprus (up 45%) resulted in a loss before tax of €13m. Accumulated provisions for NPLs amounted to €812m. as at 31 December 2012 (up from €645m. in 2011) and represented 14.6% of total gross loans and advances (up from 11.5% in 2011).

The operations abroad of the three largest Cypriot banks began to be curtailed in the second quarter of 2013, with BoC taking steps to sell its units in Romania, Russia and Ukraine. In March 2013 representatives from BoC, CPB and Hellenic were informed by the central bank that, under the terms set by the Eurogroup for the bailout agreement, they were expected to sign a document detailing the sale of their Greek operations to an as-yet-unknown Greek bank on unspecified terms, in order to remove the risk of further losses on Greek loans. Together the three banks held 8% of Greek banking deposits, 10% of loans and operated 312 branches in that country. One week later Piraeus Bank was chosen by the Greek Government to assume the Greek units of the Cypriot banks, with the total price set at €524m. The deal was approved, despite opposition from the boards of both BoC and CPB. The BoC board reportedly refused to sign off on the sale; as the state owned 84% of CPB, the Governor of the central bank signed the deal on its behalf. In May Hellenic announced that it booked a €10.2m. loss in the first quarter of 2013 from the sale of its Greek unit in a deal valued at €29m. Piraeus reported a net profit of €3,620m. compared with €46m. in the same period a year earlier. The figure included €3,410m. goodwill write-back from the Cypriot takeover and a deferred tax asset of €540m. Excluding the one-off gain, Piraeus said it lost €336m. before tax. Piraeus also said its ratio of NPLs would rise to 26% from 21% after the branch takeover. It emerged in June that due to an oversight by the Cypriot authorities, BoC had been left with the obligation to honour €700m. in letters of credit or guarantee, while the assets used as collateral for them were transferred to Piraeus Bank; Piraeus subsequently agreed to assume €300m. in obligations. Meanwhile, a substantial part of CPB's ELA liability had originally been required to cover deposit outflows from CPB's Greek branches; however, the enforced sale of the Cypriot banks' Greek units resulted in CPB selling to Piraeus Bank assets that were pledged against its ELA liability, without Piraeus assuming the corresponding ELA liability. CPB was therefore left with an 'unsecured' ELA liability amounting to some €3,800m., which was then imposed on BoC as a result of the Eurogroup decision. As part of the rescue programme agreed by the troika with the Government, which provides €1,500m. for co-operative banks to correct a capital shortfall, the number of co-op banks must be reduced from 96 to 18, mainly through mergers. Some 150 branches must also be closed, leaving 250. Supervision of co-operative banks was moved to the Central Co-operative Bank from the Ministry of Commerce and Industry; the central bank will also have a role. Under an approved arrangement designed to recapitalize and restructure the co-operative credit sector before the end of 2013 without a depositor 'bail-in', the state will use the bailout funds to buy 99% of shares, effectively becoming the exclusive owner of the sector, and thus liable for any losses, but also eligible for dividends. The Government has agreed to receive 10% annual interest on the capital, allowing the co-ops to use any surplus to buy back shares.

In April 2012 the Governor of the central bank, Athanasios Orphanides, came to the end of his five-year term, during which he had frequently disagreed publicly with the Government's reluctance to correct what he argued were structural imbalances in the public finances. The Government's very late announcement that Orphanides would not be given a second term was in keeping with its subsequent accusations that the former Governor had been negligent in his oversight of the banking sector's exposure to Greece and had not kept President Christofias informed of any negative developments. In a further twist, in July CPB's newly appointed Chairman, Michalis Sarris—who, as a former Minister of Finance, had been openly critical of the Government's fiscal policy—was forced to resign by the new central bank Governor, Panicos Demetriades, for unnamed reasons. Following Christofias's defeat in the February 2013 presidential election, Sarris was once again appointed Minister of Finance. However, upon concluding the bailout deal with international lenders in early April, Sarris resigned, citing the potential for his previous role as chairman of CPB to come under scrutiny.

The construction sector grew rapidly after the 1974 Turkish invasion, partly owing to the need to house refugees from the north. The manufacturing and construction sectors were hampered, in the early 1980s, by the adverse effects of the Government's deflationary measures and by the accumulated results of wage inflation over several years. However, the construction sector enjoyed a period of rapid growth in the second half of the decade.

That rapid expansion led to over-supply, however, and during 1990–94 growth in the construction sector decelerated overall and actually declined in value-added terms in 1993–94. The number of authorized building permits decreased each year from 8,159 in 1990 to 6,924 in 1993, before rising slightly, to 6,988, in 1994. The next five-year-period was little better. During 1995–99 value added in construction rose only in 1995, and the number of building permits authorized decreased from 7,259 in 1995 to 6,429 in 1999 and 6,096 in 2000. Gross output in construction was valued at C£714.6m. (€1,221.0m.) in 2000. One of the reasons for the poor performance of construction in 1999–2000 was the stock market 'bubble', which diverted money temporarily into investment in (over-valued) stocks. The spectacular crash of the stock market, combined with restrictions on taking money out of Cyprus that were only fully lifted in 2004, led Cypriots to return to the more traditional investment in land. Thus, a long recovery in the construction sector began from 2001, assisted initially by a decrease in interest rates and later by increased foreign demand for holiday homes. The number of authorized building permits rose from 6,096 in 2000 to 9,794 in 2006.

The first signs of another slowdown became evident in 2007, when authorized building permits declined to 9,521. Permits decreased further, to 8,896, in 2008, increased slightly, to 8,950, in 2009, and then decreased again in 2010, to 8,777. The downward trend continued into 2011, with 7,506 permits issued, and 2012, during which 7,172 permits were issued. Value added in the construction sector expanded in real terms at an average annual rate of 5.2% in 2001–05 and 7.4% in 2006–07; growth decelerated to 1.9% in 2008. A large contraction of 18.7% was recorded in value added in the construction sector in 2009; this was followed by a contraction of 8.3% in 2010 and, according to provisional data, further contractions of 10.3% in 2011 and 19.6% in 2012, due to over-supply built up during the boom period and tighter credit conditions thereafter. Total gross output in construction and land development at current market prices was €4,277.5m. in 2008, declining (for the first time since 1995) to €3,376.3m. in 2009. This decline in output continued in 2010 (down to €3,186.6m.) and 2011 (down to €2,834.3m., close to 2005 levels). Unemployment in the construction sector has increased significantly, with the monthly average of unemployed workers rising from 902 in 2008 to 6,177 in 2012. A major concern of both the industry and banking sector in 2010 was the extent to which construction completed in 2009 had remained unsold. The significant devaluation of pound sterling against the euro, combined with heightened concern over delays in the issuing of title deeds for properties already purchased, greatly reduced demand from British buyers for new holiday homes in 2009. Despite the sharp economic downturn, offer prices for real estate during that year remained high in a stagnant market, resulting in a 44% decrease in sales, according to Land Registry data, with purchase prices only beginning to decline in 2010. The decrease in residential property prices continued and intensified during 2011, declining by 5.6% year-on-year in the last quarter. This trend continued into 2012: according to the RICS Cyprus property price index, purchase prices declined in the last quarter, on a yearly basis, by 7.9% for apartments, 5.7% for houses, 15.5% for retail premises, 10.0% for offices and 9.3% for warehouses. As the economy continued to contract and unemployment grew against a backdrop of radical restructuring to the banking sector, the decline of purchase prices accelerated in the second quarter of 2013, resulting in a decrease of 12.6% for apartments, 11.2% for houses, 23.3% for retail, 13.0% for offices, and 14.8% for warehouses. The number of property sales contracts recorded by the Department of Lands and Surveys increased steadily between 2000 and 2007, from 12,664 to a high of 21,245. A sharp decline (to 14,667) began in 2008, as spiralling land prices forced many local buyers out of the market. Only 8,170 sales were recorded in 2009; in 2012 the number of sales fell to 6,269.

In the years after 1974, the Government encouraged the temporary emigration of workers as a solution to unemployment. Subsequently the emphasis was more on encouraging workers, especially those skilled in research and development, to return. By 1992 renewed labour shortages had induced the Greek Cypriot Government to authorize the recruitment of 8,000 foreign workers (some 2%–3% of the labour force), although the maximum contract period was restricted to two years because of fears that permanent immigration might engender social problems. In 1999 the Government imposed a moratorium on the issuing of work permits to foreigners, announcing in July 2000 that the freeze would be maintained for the foreseeable future, although with some exceptions for the tourism industry and certain other sectors. In addition, under the Government's labour market plan for 2003–07, reducing the number of foreign workers was identified as a major priority. However, demand for foreign labour continued to rise, reaching 34,500 in 2001—more than 30% higher than in 2000 and equivalent to some 10% of the total labour force. Accession to the EU provided another boost, because as a new member state Cyprus did not impose restrictions on labour from other EU member states. In 2008, registered foreign workers numbered 96,324 (25.5% of the gainfully employed population of 378,100). Their number grew by 10.2% in 2009 to 106,110, equivalent to 28.3% of the gainfully employed population (375,400). The upward trend slowed down in 2010 (up 7.2%), with 113,720 registered foreign workers out of 376,100 gainfully employed (30.2%), and slowed further in 2011 (up 5.4%), with 119,867 registered foreign workers out of 378,300 gainfully employed (31.7%). Although the ratio of EU citizens to third-country nationals has tended to remain constant at approximately two-thirds of registered foreign workers, more recently there has been a slight proportionate increase in the number of third-country nationals. This latter trend and the overall figures appear to confirm that in practice, jobs for foreign labour have been restricted to low-paid, lower-skilled work: in 2011 21.8% of foreign workers were domestic servants, 16.6% worked in hotels and restaurants, 14.4% in trade, 11,0% in construction and 8.4% in manufacturing. Most third-country nationals tend to be from Asia (mainly the Philippines and Sri Lanka) and the former USSR (mainly Georgia and, to a lesser extent, Belarus and Ukraine). Despite the Government easing conditions for hiring skilled, non-EU labour in early 2007, international companies still complained that it was difficult to hire skilled foreign labour. One of the Government's responses to an unprecedented rise in unemployment in 2009 was to increase the number of labour inspections of workplaces, with the aim of combating the illegal employment of foreign workers; this initiative was extended during 2010 and 2011. In October 2012 the Minister of Labour and Social Insurance proposed a moratorium on work permits for third-country nationals employed in certain sectors in an attempt to reduce unemployment among Cypriots and other EU citizens, but this was opposed by employers' organizations.

The 'TRNC' has few industrial resources, its industrial sector (excluding construction) accounting for 12.4% in 1990, 10.5% in 2000, 9.2% in 2005 and 10.9% in 2010. Manufacturing has been affected both by cheaper Asian competitors and by the 1994 European Court of Justice ruling. However, with raw agricultural output declining, the share of industrial products in total 'TRNC' exports tended to rise, from 53.7% in 1990 to 67.9% in 2000. Nevertheless, the average annual share was 60.5% during the period 2001–05 and 57.0% during 2006–10. The value of such exports has displayed the same basic trend in the past 20 years: at US $35.2m. in 1990, $34.2m. in 2000, $41.1m. in 2005 and $52.1m. in 2010. The textile and clothing industry grew rapidly in the 1980s (although most of the raw material had to be imported), roughly matching citrus fruit as the largest single source of export revenue during the 1990s. However, as a result of the effective exclusion of the EU market, combined with global competition, the sector subsequently declined to an annual share of some 10% during the period 2000–05, with a further steady decline to just 4.2% ($4.0m.) of total exports in 2010, compared with 28.2% ($27.2m.) for citrus fruits.

The 'TRNC', which lacked electricity-generating capacity, was supplied with electricity from the south from 1974 until its first power plant opened in Kyrenia in 1996. The cost of the electricity supplied over this period totalled US $162m., which the Electricity Authority of Cyprus (EAC) claimed was never paid. The EAC supplied electricity again in 2006, following an explosion at the Kyrenia plant. Gross electricity production in the Greek Cypriot area rose from 3,370 GWh in 2000 to 5,205 GWh in 2010.

In January 2001 the Greek Cypriot Government approved plans for the concentration of all refining and energy production facilities at Vassiliko on the southern coast. The Vassiliko Energy Centre was ultimately to host all existing and new electricity generation and oil-refining installations. The Government subsequently confirmed that, owing to cost and environmental grounds, and to meet the requirements of EU membership, Cyprus would eventually switch to the use of natural gas rather than petroleum for generating electricity. To that end, it entered into talks with Syria and Egypt on the supply of Egyptian natural gas to Cyprus via Syria and an underwater pipeline, stating that this was its preferred solution. However, in the light of cost and supply uncertainties, the Government announced in December 2002 that it had chosen the option of importing liquefied natural gas (LNG) by tanker. International tenders would be invited for contracts to bring LNG to Cyprus and also for the construction of a terminal at Vassiliko on a build-operate-transfer basis. Estimated as likely to cost up to US $250m., the Vassiliko terminal would be equipped with a plant to convert the LNG back into gas, initially for use in generating electricity and eventually to supply industry and households. New plans to create an offshore as well as an onshore unit for converting LNG prompted EAC workers to go on strike in June 2007.

The possibility that Cyprus might be able to exploit recently discovered gas reserves in its exclusive economic zone was one of the reasons for an extended pause in the LNG terminal project. The Natural Gas Public Company (DEFA), which was established in 2007, invited expressions of interest for a supplier in November 2009, and in January 2011 the Government announced that Royal Dutch Shell had made the best competitive offer (worth €4,500m.) for a 20-year supply line of LNG starting from 2014; however, the Government added that a political decision had not yet been taken. In June 2011 the EAC announced that it had begun talks with Israeli oil and gas exploration company Delek Energy regarding the supply of natural gas to Cyprus from offshore reserves in the Eastern Mediterranean possibly as early as 2014, for use in electricity production but also to be liquefied for export. In June 2012 ministerial-level talks between Cyprus and Israel continued to focus on an 'interim solution' for natural gas—the possibility of importing natural gas from Israel until such time as Cyprus could exploit its own gas reserves. This followed the announcement by the Minister of Commerce, Industry and Tourism, Neoklis Sylikiotis, that a political decision had been taken to build an onshore facility for liquefying and storing natural gas, projected to be completed by 2019 at an estimated cost of €6,000–€7,000m. (revised five months later to €7,000m.–€8,000m.). In late September 2012 DEFA invited expressions of interest for the supply of natural gas covering a five-year period to 2018; in addition to supplying the fuel, interested parties would make all infrastructure arrangements based on liquefied natural gas (LNG), compressed natural gas (CNG), or any other technology. Having received 17 expressions of interest, in January 2013 DEFA invited tenders from the 14 companies that met its minimum criteria, with a view to beginning negotiations in February. In April DEFA's Chairman was removed, reportedly in connection with lobbying activities in 2009; this delayed the opening of negotiations with the preferred bidder, the Russian company Itera, amid accusations relayed by the media that the fuel-importing companies were using their political leverage to postpone a switch by the EAC from heavy fuel oil to natural gas for as long as possible. Itera's bid was rejected in September, on the grounds that it would not allow the EAC to meet the Government's target of reducing the cost of electricity to the end-consumer by at least 10% via the switch to gas; this failure was partly due to the fact that the EAC anticipated a sharp drop in electricity demand in 2013, and hence needed to purchase less fuel oil. In September DEFA's options were to allow Itera to submit an adjusted bid; to open negotiations with the Dutch-owned multinational Vitol, whose original bid was placed second; to pursue a proposal by Noble Energy to set up a spar platform; to support a further a proposal by the Israeli Electricity Co to provide cheaper electricity to Cyprus through a small dedicated underwater cable from Israel; or agree to a ship 'taxi service' for compressed natural gas purchased from Israel, whose Tamar gasfield was expected to come onstream in the second half of 2013 (see the chapter on Israel).

Against a background of austerity measures and severe economic recession that is expected to persist at least into 2015, hopes for future economic growth were vested in the confirmed existence of major gas deposits to the south of Cyprus, within its 200-mile exclusive economic zone (EEZ). Having had its EEZ mapped out in detail and signed EEZ delimitation agreements with Egypt, Israel and Lebanon (although the latter has not yet been ratified, owing to Lebanon's disputation of the Cyprus-Israel agreement), the Greek Cypriot Government is now intent on exploiting at least an estimated gross mean 7,000,000m. cu ft (198,240,000m. cu m) of natural gas.

The presence of these first reserves was confirmed in December 2011 by US company Noble Energy, which holds the concession to a 2,000-sq-km area known as Block 12 following the first licensing round in 2007. This block is located some 60 km from Israel's Leviathan gasfield, which contains some 19,000,000m. cu ft of natural gas. The proximity of Israeli gasfields and the collaboration between Noble Energy and Israeli company Delek Energy in the Israeli gas finds led naturally to high-level contact between Cyprus and Israel over the possibility of co-operating on the exploitation of their respective gas resources. In February 2013 the Government signed an agreement transferring 30% of Noble Energy's gas exploitation rights on offshore Block 12 to Avner Oil & Gas and Delek Drilling, the US firm's Israeli partners. In March Noble confirmed that it would explore a second prospect within Block 12, believed to hold up to 5,000,000m. cu ft of natural gas, and began an appraisal well in June. In September Noble began the first production tests of natural gas in Block 12: a month-long drill stem test to verify the pressure and quality of the identified deposits, and a flare test. The preliminary results were expected in October, while the assessment of the quantities present would only be known in early 2014.

Despite threats from Turkey, which disputes Cyprus's right to exploit the its EEZ for hydrocarbons, in May 2012 the Greek Cypriot Government closed a second licensing round for the remaining 12 blocks in its EEZ, receiving 15 bids from five companies and 10 consortiums, including Malaysia's Petronas, Russia's Gasprom, Total of France, the Korea Gas Corpn (KOGAS) of the Republic of Korea—South Korea—among others. In October 2012 the Government announced the award of four licences for contiguous blocks to the north and north-east of Block 12: for Blocks 2 and 3, licences were awarded to a consortium of Italy's ENI and KOGAS; the licence for Block 9 went to a consortium comprising Total E&P Activities Petrolières, NOVATEC Overseas Exploration & Production GMbH and GPB Global Resources BV from Russia; and the licence for Block 11 went to Total E&P Activities Petrolières. In February 2013 the Government signed an exploration agreement with Total to for oil and gas in Blocks 10 and 11. At that point, around ten exploratory drillings were scheduled to take place within the island's EEZ over the next three years.

According to the US Geological Survey, the Levant Basin—an area which includes the coastal areas near Cyprus, Israel, Lebanon and Syria—held an estimated 120,000,000m. cu ft of undiscovered, recoverable natural gas, as well as an estimated 1,700m. barrels of undiscovered, recoverable oil. Cyprus has already begun to sign co-operation agreements with its neighbours in various related areas, including a memorandum of co-operation (MOC) between CERA and Greece's Regulatory Authority for Energy in May 2012; an MOC between the EAC and Greece's DEH Quantum Energy relating to the EuroAsia Interconnector project; and several agreements with the Israeli Government in the areas of energy, water, trade and tourism. The immediate focus of discussions from a Cypriot point of view is when the gas can begin to be brought onshore and processed for domestic energy production and for export, and what interim solutions could be employed until a permanent solution is in place. The question of how to cover the significant development costs will be key in the choice of course to follow; potentially, bigger finds elsewhere in the world and falling market prices could render the Cypriot finds unviable commercially. Alternatively, if Israel decides to pursue other options in the region for political or other reasons, Cyprus's lack of a strategic partner may tip the balance against it. Meanwhile, in late 2012 the Christofias Government began creating the legal entities that will manage and regulate what will become a new industrial sector, setting up a State Hydrocarbons Company (KRETYK) as a public entity governed by private law. However, the Anastasiades Government announced in August 2013 that KRETYK and DEFA would be merged into a single entity that will act as the commercial arm of the Government on hydrocarbon issues.

Delek Energy's proposal to create an LNG facility on Cyprus to process the natural gas deposits that Israel has already discovered off shore and those which Cyprus hopes to exploit was discussed further by the Government and Israel in December 2012, and then confirmed by President Anastasiades during an official trip to Israel in May 2013. The Greek Cypriot Government signed a statement of intent with Delek Group and Noble Energy, as well as Avner Oil Exploration Ltd Partnership, for the construction of an LNG facility in June 2013. Meanwhile, Total indicated in June that it would be interested in investing in an LNG facility in Cyprus if by mid-2014 it had decided to drill for gas as well as oil in its two blocks.

In a separate development, the Turkish Petroleum Corpn (Türkiye Petrolleri Anonim Ortaklığı—TPAO) was reported in early 2011 to be planning to begin exploring for offshore reserves of oil and natural gas in the area between Antalya Bay and the north coast of Cyprus. It was reported that TPAO would conduct seismic surveys in an area of 2,100 sq km, within the framework of the Taurus-Mediterranean District Hydrocarbon Potential Evaluation Project. In April 2012 the Turkish Government authorized TPAO to conduct offshore exploration in waters to the north, west and east of the island, and launched an onshore drill near Singrasi village in Famagusta. Having reached a depth of 4km without results, the onshore drill was closed down in November 2012 after the local water supply became contaminated. Establishing legal ownership of any discoveries in the north could become another vital component in the search for a settlement of the Cyprus problem.

In July 2012 the EAC signed a MOC with the Israel Electric Corpn regarding the use of their countries' respective hydrocarbons discoveries in the eastern Mediterranean. The MOC include provisions for connecting the two organizations' electricity grids via submarine cable and jointly developing electricity production stations using natural gas, for export to third countries. The MOC was motivated partly by progress in feasibility studies for the EuroAsia Interconnector project, which aimed to construct a submarine cable to carry 2,000 MW between Israel, Cyprus and Greece in both directions. The initial feasibility studies were completed in late 2012 and a revised proposal was presented to the three governments in May 2013, with a view to completing the project in 2016. It was estimated to take three years to build at a cost of €1,500m., with the Israel-Cyprus section accounting for €500m. The project would be funded and developed by DEH Quantum Energy, a joint venture established in 2011 and consisting of Greece's state-run public power corporation DEH, Cyprus's Quantum Energy and the BoC as a minority shareholder. In July 2013 the project was recognised by the EU as a cross-border project of common interest, which qualifies it for EU funding.

Electricity production capacity rose gradually after the first phase of the Vassiliko power station was commissioned in 2000. At the beginning of July 2011 the EAC owned and operated three power stations with a total nominal capacity of 1,558 MW: Vassiliko (878 MW, of which 220 MW was not yet online), Dhekelia (360 MW) and Moni (330 MW). The EAC also distributed electricity generated by three operational privately owned wind farms: Orites (82 MW), Ayia Anna (20 MW) and Alexigros (31.5 MW).

On 11 July 2011 98 containers holding munitions at the Evangelos Florakis naval base in Mari exploded, killing 13 firefighters and sailors, and injuring 60 others. The blast from the explosion severely damaged the Vassiliko power station, which was just 300 m away. The explosion coincided with the hottest months of the year, when demand can reach up to 1,200 MW; rolling power cuts thus ensued until mid-August. An agreement was reached for the supply, from mid-July, of up to 120 MW from the main power company in northern Cyprus to the end of February 2012, as covered by the Green Line trade regulation. In August 2011 the EAC installed temporary generating units with a total capacity of 72 MW at Vassiliko, and temporary generating units with an additional 95 MW capacity at the Dhekelia and Moni power stations.

The EAC took further steps to boost capacity in 2012 in order avert potential power cuts during periods of high demand, including the installation of 95 temporary power generators (120 MW) at Moni, which were to operate for three months from 15 June. Meanwhile, it continued with the restoration of Vassiliko: its black start gas turbine (38 MW) resumed operation in August 2011; Unit 5 (220 MW), which was not online in July 2011, became fully operational again in August 2012; Unit 4 (220 MW) resumed operation in stages, starting in August 2012; restoration of Unit 3 (130 MW) was completed in early 2013, and Units 1 and 2 (260 MW) in July and August 2013, respectively. An added benefit of the repair was that all the units were made more efficient and were fully prepared to work with natural gas. Although experts from the EU solidarity fund who had visited the station in 2011 had predicted that the repair costs would be between €330m. and €700m., the final cost of the full repair was only €165m. The EAC received an agreed €132.5m. from its insurers, who in turn reached an out-of-court settlement with the Government for the reimbursement of some €99m.

Although more than 95% of the Greek Cypriot sector's energy still comes directly from oil, the Government is promoting renewable energy sources (RES) subsidy schemes, involving primarily the exploitation of solar and wind energy, as part of its European obligation to increase energy production through RES to 13% by 2020. According to official figures, the contribution of RES in energy consumption reached 8.6% in 2012, exceeding the national target of 4.9%. Since 2008 licences for seven wind farms have been issued to private owners/operators, the last of these in June 2011. By September 2013 six wind farms were operational, producing a total of 147 MW. In June 2011 the Government announced a plan to increase the installed capacity of solar-sourced energy from 7 MW to 10 MW by the end of the year, rising to 25 MW by 2014 and 192 MW by 2020. In May 2012 the Government announced new subsidy schemes for RES, focusing on photovoltaic (PV) units for household and commercial purposes. That same month private Greek energy company Easypower announced plans for the construction of a 25.5-MW PV park complex in Potamia-Ayios Sozomenos (Nicosia district) and a 21-MW solar thermal station (named the Nicosia Sterling Engine Park) in the Ayios Sozomenos area. The solar thermal station, in which the EAC is a partner, is expected to take two years to reach full capacity. In January 2013 the University of Cyprus (UCY) announced it had received permission to build a 10 MW PV park within the UN-controlled buffer zone in Aglandjia; construction was scheduled to be completed in the second half of 2013, at a cost of €14m. In May UCY announced it had signed a MOC with the Bishopric of Tamasos and Orini of the Church of Cyprus, to develop a second 10MW PV park in the Agrokipia area of the capital Nicosia. In August 2012 CERA announced plans for a pilot net-metering scheme for households using PV systems, with a view to rolling out installation of PV systems in all Cypriot homes on a self-financing basis from 2014. In July 2013 the Government launched the first programme, offering 50% subsidies of the installation costs of 3-kW units from a €5m. special fund to eligible households selected from a list of financially vulnerable groups, up to a maximum of €2,700 per household. The Cyprus Energy Regulatory Authority (CERA) stated that it expected between 2,000 and 2,500 homes to take up the offer, with a combined output of 6 MW. However, by September only 887 households had lodged applications, apparently put off by the 50% investment tied to the offer; a second round of applications was therefore invited. A second programme with a combined output of 9 MW—corresponding to roughly 3,000 households at a maximum of 3 kW each—was made available for applicants without subsidy and therefore not subject to income criteria; this had attracted 614 applications by September, with the deadline set for mid-November. CERA's initial target was 60,000 net metering systems within three years.

TRANSPORT AND COMMUNICATIONS

As part of a programme of economic diversification, the Greek Cypriot sector has become a major maritime trading centre. From 1989 to mid-1992 the number of shipping companies registered in Cyprus doubled to more than 700, while the number of ships registered was 2,733, making the Cyprus registry the fastest growing in the world. By the end of 1996 Cyprus had climbed to fifth position in terms of displacement, which totalled more than 26m. grt. However, the ship registry has since been in decline. Under a new policy introduced in January 2000 to improve the safety record of Cyprus-registered ships, the age limit for registration was reduced from 17 to 15 years. These and other quality improvements, as well as a ban imposed by Turkey on Cyprus-flagged ships docking in Turkish ports, resulted in the Cyprus registry slipping by December 2004 to ninth position in the world (third in the EU), with a register of 1,913 ships and 23.1m. grt. The registered fleet shrank further, to 1,802 ships, in 2005 and 1,790 by 2007. The number of ships recovered slightly, to 1,869, in 2008, and remained relatively stable in 2010, at 1,862, before falling to 1,840 in 2011. In 2007 value added of water transport amounted to €73.0m, marginally greater than in the two previous years. In 2008 the figure rose to €106.3m., and in 2009 to €133.2m. (a 25.2% increase), equivalent to 0.8% of GDP at current market prices. It remained stable at €131.9m. in 2010 (0.8% of GDP at current market prices).

Famagusta formerly handled 83% of Cyprus's freight traffic, but since becoming Turkish-controlled it was declared closed by the Cypriot Government and has been superseded by Larnaca and Limassol for shipments from the Republic of Cyprus-controlled area. In 1996 a total of 5,088 vessels visited Greek Cypriot ports, of which 3,668 visited Limassol. The number of vessels calling at Greek Cypriot ports rose from 4,743 in 1990 to 5,289 in 2000, but has since declined, totalling only 3,607 by 2010 and 3,319 in 2011. Gross tonnage of goods loaded increased from 1,631.1m. metric tons in 2000 to 1,901.9m. tons in 2005, but decreased sharply from a 2006 high of 2,060.9m. tons to 1,374.7m. tons in 2010, before rising to 1,693.3m. tons in 2011. Gross tonnage of goods unloaded rose from 5,270.0m. tons in 2000 to 6,135.0m. tons in 2005, peaking at 8,110.7m. tons in 2008, before decreasing to 6,418.0m. tons in 2010 and 5,842.3.m. tons in 2011. Port development schemes have been instituted at Larnaca and Limassol, and new marina projects are under way in Paphos, Larnaca, Limassol and Ayia Napa.

Meanwhile, plans were announced in July 2010 for the construction, at an estimated cost of €100m., of an oil products import and distribution terminal in the industrial area of Vassiliko. Work commenced in April 2012, with completion projected by mid-2014. The initial plan of owner/operator Vitol Tank Terminals International (VTTI) was to focus on storing and consolidating oil products for re-export to the region—which would involve obtaining a bonded licence from the Government—with a view also to supplying the local market in Cyprus. Phase One of the project will create 19 tanks and capacity of 357,000 cu mof storage for petrol, diesel, jet fuel and fuel oil. In April 2013, with 12 tanks completed in Phase One, VTTI reaffirmed its commitment to the project, with the possibility of a further €100m. investment in Phase Two, which would create 34 tanks and a capacity of 643,000 cu m at the new facility in the medium term. In December 2012 the Government announced it had awarded the tender for a second fuel terminal and storage facility in Vassilikos to Dutch company VOPAK Oil EMEA.

In 2001 the Government secured parliamentary approval for plans to privatize the operation and development of the two international airports, at Larnaca and Paphos, and in 2003 a contract was awarded to the Alterra Consortium (including Manchester Airport, Bechtel International and the Royal Bank of Scotland). However, owing to contractual disputes, work was delayed and the contract was eventually awarded in 2005 to the second preferred bidder, an international consortium, Hermes Airports Ltd, which secured a 25-year concession from the Cypriot Government for the development and management of the two airports. Work to construct new passenger terminals and associated infrastructure at both airports finally began in 2006. The new terminal building at Paphos airport opened in November 2008, while the new Larnaca airport was inaugurated in November 2009. Apart from a dip in 2009 due to a reduction in tourist arrivals, the numbers of air passenger arrivals and departures have grown steadily over recent years, with both numbers recorded at 3.8m. in 2011.

Rising incomes and a poor public transport service led to a rapid increase in the number of licensed motor vehicles, from 316,437 in 1990 to 444,183 in 2000 and to 648,143 in 2010. Of those, 462,652 were passenger cars. New registrations have been influenced in recent years by changes in taxation. As a result of changes in excise duties, total vehicle registrations increased by 34% in 2004, compared with the previous year, to 54,037. Further tax cuts in November 2006 led to a 33.1% rise in 2007, to 64,405. A more modest increase of 5.2% was recorded in 2008, with total registrations reaching 67,722. In 2009 total registrations decreased by 25.7%, to 50,291, reflecting the slump in consumer demand owing to the economic downturn. In 2010 a further 12.5% decrease, to 44,025, was recorded, followed by a 17.6% decrease in 2011, to 36,264. Continuing credit restrictions contributed to a further 28.8% decrease in 2012, to 25,829.

The Greek Cypriot Government has given priority to establishing Cyprus as a centre for regional telecommunications and as a staging post for satellite communications between Europe, the Middle East and Asia. In a major step towards achieving this objective, in May 2003 Cyprus and Greece jointly launched the Hellas Sat satellite from Cape Canaveral, Florida, USA, using a US rocket to provide voice, digital television, internet and broadband services to as many as 25 countries. The telecommunications sector was traditionally dominated by the state-owned Cyprus Telecommunications Authority (CYTA), but in March 2003 CYTA's monopoly effectively ended, with the granting of licences to four Cyprus-registered information technology (IT) companies for the provision of various land-line services. In August the Telecommunications and Post Office Commission awarded a 20-year special licence to the EAC for the provision of land-line telephone services and in October the Lebanese-funded Scancom (Cyprus) group won an auction for a 20-year mobile telephone licence, operating first under the name Areeba and then as MTN, for which it paid the Government C£12.75m. (€21.8m.) In April 2004 another licence for the provision of telephone services was awarded to the private enterprise Callsat. Complying with EU requirements, in June 2013 the Government announced a tender for a third mobile network operator licence, despite protests from CYTA and MTN that the island's market was too small to accommodate it. In 2002 there were 598 fixed analogue telephone lines and 584 mobile telephone subscriptions per 1,000 people. By 2011 the number of fixed analogue telephone lines per 1,000 people had declined to 466 and mobile telephone subscriptions had risen to 1,266 subscribers per 1,000 people. According to official figures, an increasing number of households (61.8% in 2012) had internet access, most of which (97%) via broadband.

TOURISM

Tourism was one of the areas of the Greek Cypriot economy that was most adversely affected by the 1974 war, as 90% of the island's hotels came under Turkish Cypriot control. However, the sector expanded rapidly in the 1980s, becoming the Republic of Cyprus's largest source of income.

By 1990 the annual total of tourist arrivals had increased to 1,561,479. Receipts from tourism in that year totalled C£573m. (€979.0m.). In promoting the industry, the Greek Cypriot authorities tried somewhat unsuccessfully to lay emphasis on the desirability of developing 'high-value' tourism (as opposed to the 'package' holiday trade) and on sustainable tourism development. Tourist arrivals in 1996 declined slightly, to 1,950,000, compared with 2,100,000 in 1995, partly owing to tensions with Turkey over the Government's plans to bring Russian missiles to the island. Tourism revived in 1997, as arrivals increased to 2,088,000. The sector accounted for some 20% of GDP and 12% of employment in that year. Tourist arrivals and revenue continued to rise in 1998–2001, reaching a peak of 2,696,732 arrivals and C£1,272m. (€2,173.3m.) in revenue in 2001.

Tourism then entered a difficult period, with either declining arrivals or dwindling revenue in many of the years after 2001. Occasional indirect factors included the outbreak of severe acute respiratory syndrome (SARS) in Asia in 2002 and the onset of the Iraq crisis in 2003, but industry experts more often cite an ageing product and a comparative lack of infrastructure. Despite a short-lived recovery in 2004–05, tourist arrivals in 2005, at 2,470,063, were still less than their 2001 peak and revenue was also lower, at C£1,005.7m. (€1,718.3m.) Moreover, annual arrivals declined on average in 2006–08, reaching 2,403,750 in 2008, with revenues of C£1,049m. (€1,793m.). Revenue from tourism had thus decreased to only 10.6% of GDP in 2008, from a peak of 20.6% of GDP in 2000.

The global economic crisis, the full effects of which did not manifest in Cyprus until 2009, hit the tourism sector especially hard; total arrivals declined to 2,141,193 (down 10.9% from 2008), and receipts from tourism decreased by 16.7% to €1,493.2m. The volcanic dust cloud emanating from Iceland, which severely disrupted air traffic across Europe in April 2010, resulted in an estimated €7m.–€10m. loss in revenues at the traditional start of the high season. Despite this setback, total arrivals for the year rose to 2,172,998, a 1.5% increase on a particularly poor 2009. Significant decline in the number of arrivals from the United Kingdom was offset by a revival in the number of arrivals from Germany, France and Switzerland, with arrivals from Russia increasing by more than 50%. Receipts from tourism in 2010 rose to €1,549.8m. (an increase of 3.8% on 2009), and average per caput spending climbed to €713. Total arrivals in 2011 rose by 10.1% to 2,392,228, marking a return to 2008 levels. The largest increase was in the number of Russian arrivals, up by 49% to 334,083, followed by British arrivals, which rose by 2.5% to 1,020,709. Arrivals from Romania, Germany, Greece and the Netherlands also rose significantly. Receipts from tourism in 2011 rose by 12.9% to €1,749.3m. (9.8% of GDP), and average per caput spending increased by 2.5% to €731. Total arrivals in 2012 rose by 3.0% to 2,464,908, the highest level since 2001. The largest increase (and the most significant change by far) was in the number of Russian arrivals, up by 42.0% to 474,426. British arrivals fell by 6.0% to 959,463, as did arrivals from Germany (down 8.6% to 144,407) and Greece (down 4.1% to 132,990). Receipts from tourism in 2012 rose by 10.2% to € 1,927.7m. (10.8% of GDP), and average per caput spending increased by 7.7%, to €787.

The Government's attempts to upgrade the quality of tourism on offer have been slow to get off the ground. For example, in May 2000 approval was given for the construction of six new marinas by the end of 2002, as part of the Government's strategy of promoting 'high-value' tourism. However, it was not until September 2010 that the foundation stone for the first marina was laid in Limassol; work on this €350m. project was expected to be mostly completed by the end of 2013, with the marina facilities and linked commercial area becoming fully operational in the first half of 2014. Securing finance for the other marina projects, notably the €700m. project in Larnaca, became increasingly difficult in 2013. The Christofias Government consistently opposed the licensing of casinos in the south of the island. However, the new Government indicated at the beginning of its term that it would include casinos in its strategy to encourage foreign investment. The Cyprus Tourism Organisation commissioned a study by private consultants into the potential impact of casinos on tourism, and in July 2013 it announced a plan to grant a licence for an integrated casino resort that would have a large bed capacity and offer a number of auxiliary services, including theme parks, restaurants and retail space.

Tourism in the north has also expanded since the division of the island, but it is restricted by the fact that the airport does not enjoy international recognition and therefore flights must first land in Turkey. Many of the best hotels remained unused and derelict after the 1974 invasion. Some have, however, been taken over, much against the will of the Greek Cypriot owners. Since 2004, when the Greek Cypriots rejected the UN-sponsored reunification plan, companies have been less reticent about building on Greek Cypriot-titled land and bed capacity has increased. The late 1980s were characterized by a rapid growth in arrivals from both Turkey and elsewhere, reaching 300,810 and 57,541, respectively, in 1990, resulting in revenues of $224.8m. While Turkish arrivals remained flat during the period 1991–95, the number of other visitors grew steadily (298,026 and 87,733, respectively, in 1995), but revenues fluctuated, reaching $218.9m. in 1995. The trend in arrivals was reversed during the next five-year period, with 347,712 Turkish arrivals and 85,241 others in 2000; this was reflected in revenues, which dipped sharply in 1996 and then rose gradually, to $198.3m. in 2000. The four years following an exceptionally bad 2001—when total arrivals decreased to 365,097 and revenues more than halved year-on-year to $93.7m.—showed strong growth driven by foreign investment, with 488,023 Turkish arrivals and 164,756 others (almost double the 2000 figure) in 2005; revenues also grew strongly, to $328.8m. The five years to 2010 saw a marked steady increase in Turkish arrivals (741,925 in 2010), while other arrivals dipped to 143,116 in 2006 before gradually rising to 160,465 in 2010. The record number of total arrivals of 902,390 in 2010 also resulted in record revenues of $405.8m.

The opening of the internal Cyprus border from late April 2003 gave an unexpected boost to the tourism sector in the north, as large numbers of Greek Cypriots and many foreign tourists undertook crossings to the Turkish Cypriot area. Most Greek Cypriot visits are day trips, with surveys showing that those who spend large amounts of money spend them in the (largely Turkish-owned) casinos. Foreign tourists took advantage of an initial permission to stay for up to three nights, which was later fully liberalized for EU citizens. The opening of the Ledra Street crossing in central Nicosia in 2008 provided a particular boost, reflected in a subsequent increase in the use of credit cards on both sides of the Green Line. Prospects for further infrastructure development in the north were compromised in 2009 both by the economic crisis and by court rulings in cases brought by Greek Cypriots disputing the use of their land. Despite this, work on the Karpaz Gate Marina, located near the village of Yialousa in the Karpas (Karpaz) peninsula, was completed on schedule in June 2011 and received its first yachts that year. The marina offers 300 berths with space for maintenance and storage, next to a restaurant and a beach club. In February 2013 a €300m. project was launched to add a four- and a five-star hotel, two spas, a conference centre, a casino and a number of bars and restaurants.

BUDGET, INVESTMENT AND FINANCE

Budget policy in the last 10–15 years has been defined by EU membership requirements. (Cyprus having joined the EU on 1 May 2004 and the eurozone on 1 January 2008.)

The 2000 budget unified the three traditional budget accounts (ordinary, development and resettlement) into a single measure, providing for expenditure of C£2,007.4m. (€3,429.8m.), net revenue of C£1,348.1m. (€2,303.4m.) and a projected budget deficit equivalent to 4.3% of GDP (although in the event the deficit was contained at 2.7% of GDP as a result of subsequent austerity measures). In May the Government secured approval for a programme of tax cuts and other measures designed to compensate the lower paid for an increase in VAT from 8% to 10%, which came into effect on 1 July 2000, as the first step towards the minimum 15% rate required by EU accession. The VAT rate rose from 10% to 13% on 1 July 2002, and to 15% on 1 January 2003. In the same context, legislation adopted in December 1999 provided for the existing 9% statutory ceiling on interest rates to be removed with effect from 1 January 2001.

The budget for 2001 provided for expenditure of C£2,426m. (€4,145.1m.) and net revenue of C£1,553m. (€2,653.5m.), envisaging a fiscal deficit of 2.5%–3.0% of GDP. In March 2001 the Government set itself the objective of reducing the fiscal deficit to 2% in 2002 and achieving a balanced budget in 2004. At that stage public debt as a proportion of GDP had been brought down to 59.8%, from more than 62% in mid-2000. In November 2001 the Government announced major reforms in taxation policy, including cuts in personal income tax, an increase in VAT from 10% to 13% in the course of 2002 and a reduction of corporation tax to a standard rate of 10%. 'Offshore' companies were to lose their preferential 4.5% corporation tax rate and be required to pay the 10% rate by the end of 2005; as of August 2012, this was still the applicable rate for all companies. In the 2002 budget total expenditure was set at C£2,700m. (€4,613.2m.), while revenue was projected at C£2,400m. (€4,100.6m.). However, a deterioration in economic conditions in 2002 resulted in a budget deficit out-turn of 3.6% of GDP, owing in particular to lower than anticipated revenue from the tourism sector. Under constitutional amendments enacted in June 2002, the Central Bank of Cyprus became fully independent from the Government on 1 July, in accordance with the norm in EU member states. The Government's 2003 budget forecast a return to significant economic growth of over 4% and a reduction in the budget deficit to 2.1% of GDP, on the basis of expenditure of C£3,081m. (€5,264.2m.) and revenue of C£2,401m. (€4,102.4m.) However, it quickly became apparent, after the change of government in February 2003 and the start of the conflict in Iraq, that budgeted commitments could not be met, with the result that the House of Representatives in July adopted a supplementary budget providing for additional expenditure of C£312m. (€533.1m.) Nevertheless, the budget deficit rose sharply to 6.3% of GDP in 2003 and the level of public debt to 72.6%.

The Government's 2004 budget provided for expenditure of C£3,400m. (€5,809.2m.) and revenue of C£2,800m. (€4,784.1m.), with the resultant deficit of C£600m. (€1,025.2m.) being projected at 3.7% of GDP. Overall expenditure was forecast to increase by only 2% in 2004, mainly as a result of lower outlays for defence, whereas development expenditure was to rise by 24%, to C£346m. (€591.2m.). It became evident in the first half of 2004, however, that the budget deficit was running at double the 3.7% target, with the result that in June the Government, under pressure from the European Commission, announced new austerity measures intended to contain the deficit to 5.2% of GDP in 2004 and then to reduce it to less than 3% in 2005 and to under 2% by 2007, to allow Cyprus to qualify for entry into the euro.

In June 2005 the Government approved legislation to increase the retirement age of civil servants from 60 to 63, on a voluntary basis; plans to make this mandatory by July 2008 were not implemented. These measures helped to restrain the 2004 deficit to 4.2% of GDP, creating a platform for the target of a further reduction to 2.9% in 2005, under a budget providing for expenditure of C£3,551m. (€6,067.2m.) and revenue of C£2,719m. (€4,645.7m.). Owing to receipts of C£70m. (€119.6m.) from an income tax amnesty that expired on 31 March, the out-turn for 2005 was a budget deficit of 2.4% of GDP. The 2006 budget provided for an overall deficit of 1.9% of GDP. The fiscal performance in 2006 would be one of the main criteria used for assessing whether Cyprus had fulfilled all the preconditions for adopting the euro on 1 January 2008 as planned. In the event, the budget deficit out-turn was only 1.5% of GDP, well below the 3% ceiling. The 2007 budget aimed for a budget deficit of 1.6% of GDP, but in the event a large surplus of €537.4m., or 3.4% of GDP, was recorded. On 16 May 2007 the European Commission declared that Cyprus had met all of the (Maastricht) criteria for adoption of the euro, and Cyprus duly adopted the euro on 1 January 2008.

In 2008 GDP grew by 3.6%, while there was a fiscal surplus of €160.6m., equivalent to 0.9% of GDP, and public debt was reduced to 48.9% of GDP, from 59.4% in 2007. The surplus was soon applied to raising state pensions closer in line with EU norms and to increasing other welfare allowances to mitigate the initial effects of the economic downturn. The Government expressed public optimism that the economy could ride out the economic crisis in 2009 without serious difficulties, forecasting growth of 2.0% and a budget deficit of less than 1.0% of GDP. However, by mid-2009 the Ministry of Finance had downwardly revised both forecasts, to 1.0% and 2.0%–2.5% of GDP, respectively. In the event, Cyprus's economy contracted by 1.9% in 2009, while public debt increased to 58.5% of GDP and the budget deficit amounted to €1,030.7m., equivalent to 6.1% of GDP. In March 2010 the Ministry of Finance announced that the Government expected the fiscal deficit to increase to around 7% in that year. In June the European Commission recommended opening an Excessive Deficit Procedure (EDP) for Cyprus, owing to the sizeable 2009 budget deficit and a forecast increase in public debt to 62.3% of GDP in 2010. The out-turn for 2010 was a budget deficit decrease to 5.3% of GDP (lower than the anticipated 6.0%–7.0%, owing to the unforeseen profit made on an interest-swap agreement and the transfer of higher than usual central bank profits), and public debt equivalent to 61.5% of GDP (marginally less than projected). The economy grew by 1.1% in 2010, with the Government forecasting 1.5% growth for 2011. The Government also predicted that the budget deficit would decrease to 4.0% of GDP in 2011 and that there would be a slight rise in public debt as a ratio of GDP to 63.3%. This latter forecast reflected the Government's plan to increase the maximum amount that it could borrow under its current medium-term euro-denominated note (EMTN) programme, from €6,000m. to €9,000m. in 2011, with a view to tapping the international markets in November.

As of 30 June 2012, Cyprus only had €3,829m. in EMTN debt, reflecting the unavailability of the international capital markets since June 2011 due to its poor credit rating. Other foreign debt included a €2,500m. loan extended by Russia at a below-market interest rate of 4.5% in late 2011, disbursed in three tranches from December 2011 to April 2012; this loan was designed to cover state financing requirements for 2012. Based on provisional data, the out-turn for 2011 was 0.5% growth; it was estimated that the severe damage to the Vassiliko power station caused by the Mari naval base explosion had cost the economy 1.0% of GDP. However, the budget deficit amounted to €1,132.4m., equivalent to 6.3% of GDP, and public debt rose sharply to €12,778.4m., equivalent to 71.1% of GDP. This was despite two austerity packages adopted in September and December 2011, which saw a 10% cut in salary for senior government officials, a two-year freeze in basic civil service salaries, a freeze on new recruitment in the civil service and a staggered increase in income tax rates. As annual budget revenue fluctuated from €7,388.6m. in 2008 to €6,763.6m. in 2009, then up to €7,139.3m. in 2011, compensation for state employees remained constant at over 34% of annual expenditure, or 15%–16% of GDP.

The targets for 2012 declared by the Government under its EDP in April 2012 were a budget deficit of €473m. (2.6% of projected GDP of €18,212m.) and public debt of €13,656m., equivalent to 75% of GDP. The Government also projected a 0.5% contraction in GDP, followed by 0.5% growth in 2013. In its May 2012 review of Cyprus's stability programme, the European Commission forecast a 3.4% budget deficit by the end of 2012, only expecting the economy to hit the target of a 2.5% deficit in 2013. Public debt was forecast to increase to 76.5% in 2012 and 78.1% in 2013. The European Commission also expected GDP to contract by 0.8% by the end of 2012, followed by 0.3% growth in 2013. In its report, the Commission said that Cyprus had experienced an internal imbalance due to its banking sector—heavily exposed to Greece—and the indebtedness of the corporate sector and an external and internal imbalance in its fiscal dynamics and competitiveness. It referred to a number of areas that required action to ensure the long-term sustainability of public finances, notably in the area of pensions. Government figures showed a 1.6% contraction, year-on-year, in the first quarter of 2012, largely due to negative growth in the sectors of construction, manufacturing and electricity; negative growth in the same sectors also contributed to a 2.3% contraction in the second quarter of 2012.

During the first half of 2012 increased government efforts to secure a large bilateral loan (of up to €5,000m.) focused on China and Russia, but without success. The decision by Fitch Ratings on 25 June to cut Cyprus's sovereign rating to 'junk' status meant that the country lost its investment grade status with all three of the largest rating agencies, obliging the European Central Bank to stop accepting Cypriot government bonds as collateral for commercial bank borrowing. Having already had to rely heavily on short-term borrowing for its own refinancing needs by turning to the domestic bank markets and semi-governmental organizations like CyTA and the EAC (short-term borrowing represented just 19% of the state's overall loans in 2010, but increased to 46% in 2011), and with yields on its 10-year benchmark bond of around 16%, the Government had little option but to apply on 27 June for aid from the EFSF for both the state and the banks.

The projected size of the European bail-out grew very rapidly from the minimum €2,300m. needed for the recapitalization of CPB and the BoC to include some €4,500m. for state (re-)financing needs into 2013; the European authorities were reported to be urging a 'once and for all' loan of the order of €10,000m. When Standard & Poor's announced in August 2012 its further downgrading of Cyprus to BB, the agency referred to a base case scenario involving a €11,000m. financial support package—the state absorbing €6,590m. to cover maturing debt and underlying deficits during 2012–14, €2,300m. going towards recapitalization of the Bank of Cyprus and CPB to comply with EBA standards, and an additional €2,180m. for the banks as a buffer for further potential credit losses during 2012 and 2013—but it said that given the uncertainty in Greece and the likely need for further buffers, it did not rule out a total package in excess of €15,000m. As a result, it estimated that Cyprus's net general government debt burden would increase by nearly 12% of GDP on average in 2012 and 2013, peaking at over 105% of GDP in 2013.

A troika delegation visited Cyprus on two fact-finding missions in July 2012, conducting discussions with all concerned parties that focused on three main areas: public finances; structural economic issues; and the banking sector. In August a 10-member committee was appointed to select an international firm to carry out diagnostic checks on the loan portfolios of the BoC, CPB and Hellenic Bank, as well as the Cypriot subsidiaries of the Greek-based Alpha Bank and Eurobank. A representative sample of co-operative banks were also to be audited. The audit was scheduled for completion by October, with an exact figure for the capital needs of the Cyprus banking system being fixed in early November (in the event, investment company PIMCO delivered a preliminary report in December and a final report in February 2013). In late August 2012 the economy was officially estimated to have contracted by 1.5% in the first half of the year, compared with the previously projected 0.5% contraction. The Government also revised its budget deficit forecast upwards from 3.5% to 4.5% without additional corrective measures. This was due to a lower than expected increase in revenues (1.3%)—ascribed to a combination of lower production and a decline in consumption—and a lower than expected reduction in government spending (1.4% instead of the projected 3%), which in turn was ascribed in part to the rising cost of borrowing.

By the time the Government and the troika resumed negotiations in November 2012 on the specifics of the MOU relating to the financial support package, the European Commission had revised downward its forecast on Cyprus's economy. It now expected a contraction by 2.3% in 2012 and by another 1.7% in 2013, citing record unemployment (especially in the construction sector) and a high degree of economic uncertainty which had reduced private consumption—a trend that it expected to continue into 2014. The state budget for 2013 submitted to the House of Representatives by the Ministry of Finance later that month—which reflected the terms agreed with the troika at that point by cutting expenditure by 5.8% on an annualized basis and raising indirect taxation—projected that the economy would contract by 3.5% in 2013, with the Government aiming for a 4.4% budget deficit. Based on provisional data, the out-turn for 2012 was a budget deficit of €1,127.3m., equivalent to 6.3% of GDP (as in 2011); the economy contracted by 2.4% and public debt reached 85.8% of GDP. In its economic forecast published in February 2013, the European Commission doubled its recession forecast for Cyprus to a 3.5% contraction, with a further 1.3% contraction in 2014, due to further declines in domestic demand and investment activity.

By January 2013, six months after Cyprus made its formal request for a bailout and still without a final agreement (despite the fact that the House of Representatives had approved a series of bills to implement the terms of the November interim agreement), it had become clear that the rescue programme would need to be delayed by at least two more months, amid mounting disagreement over how to reduce the cost to a manageable level for the debt-laden Government. (The bailout amount was unofficially estimated at around €7,500m.–€10,000m. to recapitalize the banks, €6,000m. for maturing state debt and €1,500m. for public finances.) Within the troika, the IMF was insisting on significant amounts of debt relief before it agreed to participate, and the option of a 'bail-in' of creditors began to be promoted strongly by some actors.

At the beginning of March, EU ministers responsible for financial affairs pledged to agree a bailout for Cyprus by the end of the month; meanwhile, a controversial money-laundering audit (advocated mainly by Germany) of Cypriot banks would be carried out jointly by the private accountancy firm Deloitte and the Council of Europe's MONEYVAL, under the supervision of the central bank (the report was finally delivered in April). At the newly-elected President Anastasiades's first European Council meeting in mid-March, he was presented with the ultimatum of an unprecedented levy on all deposits (6.7% on deposits under €100,000 and 9.9% on those over €100,000) held by all Cypriot banks as a precondition for a rescue programme. This proposal was rejected by the House of Representatives. Ten days later, the Eurogroup withdrew the proposal and decided to close Cyprus Popular Bank and seize a large proportion of uninsured deposits held by the Bank of Cyprus. Banks remained closed between the first and second Eurogroup meetings to prevent a bank run; the closure compounded the uncertainty, as businesses could not use their cashflow.

PIMCO's assessment of the capital shortfall of the Cypriot financial institutions which were included in its review had amounted to €5,980m. in a baseline scenario and €8,860m. in an adverse scenario. However, the amount that Cyprus was called upon to contribute on its own account to the financial support package had increased from the initial estimate of €7,500m. to €13,000m. (out of a total gross financing needs of an estimated €23,000m. from the second quarter of 2013 to the first quarter of 2016). Of the €10,000m. from international lenders: €2,500m. was for recapitalising what is left of the Cypriot banking sector after the closure of CPB and the restructuring of BoC; €4,100m. was for redeeming maturing government debt; and €3,400m. would cover the Government's fiscal needs during the three-year period. The breakdown of

Cyprus's €13,000m. contribution was up to €10,600m. from the resolution of CPB and the 'bail-in' of BoC's uninsured depositors; up to €600m. through raising the rate of corporate tax by 2.5% to 12.5% and doubling the rate of capital gains tax to 30%; around €400m. from the sale of gold reserves; up to €1,000m. through an enforced 'rollover' of short-term debt held by domestic investors; an estimated €1,400m. from the privatization of semi-governmental organizations such as CYTA and EAC; and up to €100m. released through the rescheduling of the €2,500m. loan from Russia (the rescheduling agreement signed in September 2013 provided for repayment of the loan in eight biannual instalments between 2018 and 2021, in place of a one-off payment in 2016, at 2.5% interest instead of 4.5%).

In its April 2013 assessment of Cyprus's debt sustainability, the European Commission forecast that real GDP would contract by 8.7% in 2013 and by 3.9% in 2014, and that there would be 1.1% growth in 2015, rising to 1.9% in 2016. It forecast budget deficits equivalent to 6.0% of GDP in 2013, 7.9% in 2014, 5.7% in 2015 and 2.5% in 2016. Gross government debt was forecast at 109.0% of GDP in 2013, rising to 123.0% in 2014, 126.3% in 2015, before declining slightly to 121.9% in 2016.

The 'TRNC' budget is characterized by large subsidies from Turkey in the form of aid and credits. Together these typically account for more than 10% of GNP in any given year and thus reduce what would otherwise be a very large budget deficit to an average of only around 3% of GNP since 1977. By 2005 local revenue had reached 33.2% of GNP (YTL 1,042m.) and total expenditure had reached 47.7% of GNP (YTL 1,745m.), implying a budget deficit without aid and credits of 15.2% of GNP, although the official budget reported a surplus of 1.4%. By 2010 local revenue had reached 31.7% of GNP (YTL 1,791.3m.) and total expenditure had reached 47.1% of GNP (YTL 2,661.0m.), implying a budget deficit without aid and credits of 10.0% of GNP. On 1 July 1992, in partial parallel to Greek Cypriot policy, the 'TRNC' Government introduced VAT on consumer goods at a rate of 10% (compared with the introductory rate of 5% in the south). There are now six VAT rates in operation in the 'TRNC', with the standard rate being 16% (compared with 18% in the south). The corporate tax rate is 10%.

FOREIGN TRADE AND BALANCE OF PAYMENTS

Cyprus has experienced a persistent trade deficit for many years (with imports regularly being three or four times as great as exports in terms of value), only partly offset by an 'invisibles' balance, arising mainly from earnings from tourism and, more recently, income from accounting and legal services. The effect in recent years has been a growing current account deficit, which is primarily funded by inflows of bank deposits from non-residents (the traditional offshore sector) and partly by FDI. In 1990 the trade deficit was C£842.9m. (€1,440.2m.), or 32.5% of GDP. The trade deficit rose in nominal terms to C£1,810.1m. (€3,092.7m.) or 31.3% of GDP in 2000, and the current account deficit reached C£303.8m. (€519.1m.) or 5.3% of GDP. In 2007, owing to high oil prices, the trade deficit increased to C£2,756.9m. (€4,710.4m.) or 29.7% of GDP, pushing the current account deficit to C£1,091.5m. (€1,865.0m.) or 11.7% of GDP. The trade deficit grew to a record €6,176.3m. (36.0% of GDP) in 2008, producing a current account deficit of €2,679.0m. (15.6% of GDP). Weak demand for imports in 2009 meant that the trade deficit decreased to €4,721.3m. (28.0% of GDP) and the current account deficit to €1,808.0m. (10.7% of GDP). In 2010 the trade deficit increased to €5,380.6m. (30.9% of GDP) but the current account deficit decreased to €1,711.9m. (9.8% of GDP). Stronger exports in 2011 resulted in a trade deficit of €4,906.6m (27.3% of GDP) and a current account deficit of €848.9m. (4.7% of GDP), while in 2012 a drop in imports against firm exports reduced the trade deficit to €4,320.0m. (24.2% of GDP), with a current account deficit of €2,092.3 (11.7% of GDP).

Cyprus acts as a trans-shipment centre, meaning that total exports and total imports exceed goods produced or consumed domestically. Total exports amounted to C£435.6m. (€744.3m.) in 1990, of which domestically produced exports were C£255.8m. (€437.1m.), and total imports reached C£1,278.5m. (€2,184.4m.), of which imports for home consumption were C£1,084.5m. (€1,853.0m.). In 2000 total exports were C£591.9m. (€1,011.3m.), of which domestic exports were C£224.0m. (€382.7m.), while total imports were C£2,402.0m. (€4,104.1m.), and imports for home consumption C£1,968.7m. (€3,363.7m.). In 2009 total exports amounted to €970.5m., compared with €1,190.4m. the previous year, carrying on a downward trend from a peak of €1,228.7m. in 2005. Total exports recorded an increase of 17.1% in 2010, to €1,136.8m., and a further increase of 23.7% in 2011, to €1,406.0m. A more modest increase of 1.2%, to €1,420.5m., was recorded in 2012. Domestic exports, however, followed a different course, rising annually from €406.2m. in 2005 to €546.5m. in 2008; after dipping to €479.5m. in 2009, they rose 18.2% to €566.7m. in 2010, €627.3m. (up 10.7%) in 2011 and 649.0m. (up 3.5%) in 2012. This trend also applied to imports, which increased annually from €5,069.1m. in 2005 (of which €4,427.0m. was for home consumption) to €7,366.7m. in 2008 (€6,925.1m. for home consumption); after decreasing to €5,691.8m. (€5,430.4m. for home consumption) in 2009, in line with the contraction in domestic demand, they increased to €6,517.4m. (€6,218.8m. for home consumption) in 2010 before decreasing again to €6,310.5m. (€5,951.2m. for home consumption) in 2011, and to €5,740.5m. (€5,448.5m. for home consumption) in 2012.

Having stood at C£518.2m. (€885.4m.) in 1995, foreign exchange reserves rose to C£1,153.3m. (€1,970.5m.) in 2000 and to C£2,426m. (€4,146m.) in 2007. However, total reserves declined to €721m. (including €421m. in foreign exchange) at the end of 2008, owing to the fact that, since Cyprus had joined the eurozone at the start of the year, all euro-denominated reserves and all reserves in foreign currency but held within other eurozone countries were excluded. Total reserves rose to €895m. (€391m. foreign exchange) in December 2009, decreased to €858m. (€207m. foreign exchange) in December 2010, rose to €932m. (€126m. in foreign exchange) in 2011 and then decreased to €903.7m. (€108m. in foreign exchange) in 2012.

There was a significant alteration in the Greek Cypriot trading pattern in the late 1980s, with EC countries taking over the dominant role from Arab countries (chiefly Lebanon, Egypt, the states of the Arabian peninsula, and Libya). Greek Cypriot exports to EC countries increased from 32.4% of total domestic export revenue in 1985 to 53.2% in 1990, although they declined in the succeeding years, to 41.7% in 1993. EC countries were also the main suppliers of goods to the Greek Cypriot sector, their share of the region's total imports, by value, rising to 60.8% in 1986, before decreasing slightly, to 57.0% in 1987 and 54.0% in 1990, only to increase again, to 58.0%, in 1992. Imports from Arab countries, in turn, declined after 1985 (when they accounted for 10.1% of total import costs), to 6.1% in 1987 and to 5.0% in 1993. In 1995 the United Kingdom was Cyprus's largest individual trading partner, supplying 11.7% of its imports and taking 13.3% of total Cypriot exports. However, by 2007 it had fallen as a supplier to third place behind Greece and Italy. In 2009 EU countries received 60.4% of Greek Cypriot exports and supplied 71.8% of imports. In 2010 EU countries received 51.3% of exports and supplied 69.1% of imports; in 2011 the figures showed a decrease to 50.6% and 67.6%, respectively.

In November 1985 the EC Council of Ministers approved the admission of Cyprus to a customs union with the EC. Accordingly, a protocol with the EC was signed in October 1987 and entered into effect on 1 January 1988. The protocol defined an initial 10-year phase (1988–98) during which tariffs on imports to Cyprus were to be reduced by 10% annually, leading to their complete removal by 1998. For some products of importance to the island's economy (e.g. clothing and footwear), tariffs were to decrease by only 4% annually in the first phase. The EC agreed to waive quantitative restrictions on exports of Cypriot garments to the EC and to make concessions to Cypriot agricultural exports, particularly potatoes, grapes, wine and citrus fruit. Cyprus, in turn, agreed to dismantle its quantitative restrictions on imports of industrial products from EC countries, yet was to be allowed to retain a 20% tariff on up to 15% of imports that competed with local products. A second phase, of four to five years' duration, which was to be introduced after a review of the first phase, was to remove all remaining restrictions and trade barriers on products covered by the agreement.

Cyprus was then expected to adopt the EC's common customs tariff, in accordance with its Third Country provisions, freeing it of restrictions within the EC. The President of the 'TRNC', Rauf Denktaş, denounced the customs union, claiming that the EC was not entitled to negotiate the agreement without consulting representatives of the Turkish sector of the island. The EC, however, made it clear that the union would apply to the whole island, reiterating this assertion in a report published by the Commission in June 1993, which confirmed Cyprus's eligibility for EC membership.

Under the fourth EU-Cyprus financial protocol, signed in June 1995 in the framework of the existing association agreement, the island was to receive €74m. in loans and grants over five years, in support of efforts to promote economic integration and to prepare for EU membership. In December 2000 agreements were signed whereby Cyprus would receive €57m. in pre-accession assistance from the EU. Following accession to the EU on 1 May 2004, Cyprus discovered that, under European Commission proposals, it would be the only one of the 10 new member states expected to be a net contributor to the EU budget at the start of the 2007–13 budget cycle.

ECONOMIC PROSPECTS

Although the economy in the southern part of Cyprus appears at face value to have been unaffected in the long term by the division of the island, it does carry the opportunity cost of not trading with the large emerging market of Turkey. A report published by the Cyprus Centre at the International Peace Research Institute, in Oslo, Norway, in 2008 estimated that a reunited economy stood to gain an average of €1,800m. per year in the first seven years after a settlement, largely through additional trade in goods and services with its large neighbour. The potential for development in the north, meanwhile, remains severely constrained by the political situation, exacerbated by the close fiscal and political control exercised by the Turkish Government. In view of the Turkish Cypriots' vote in favour of the Annan Plan at the 2004 referendum, the EU declared its aim of developing economic relations with the Turkish Cypriot area to reduce the wide economic disparities between the two parts of Cyprus. Although this aim is in principle supported by the Greek Cypriot Government, in practice the Government has resisted any attempt to lift restrictions on exports from, or flights to, northern Cyprus.

Israel's efforts to market its gas reserves fully in the region, combined with Turkey's energy needs as its economy continues to grow strongly, could potentially act as a catalyst for some degree of rapprochement between the Greek Cypriot Government and Turkey. Conversely, Turkey's vehement opposition to an exclusively Greek Cypriot exploitation of Cyprus's gas reserves could serve to reinforce entrenched views.

In the absence of a political solution to the island's division, its two economies are expected to diverge even further, with the Turkish Cypriot economy increasing its dependence on Turkey, with few incentives for structural reform, and the Greek Cypriot economy becoming more closely integrated with the EU. In the longer term, and in order to respond to the challenges of being in the eurozone, the Republic of Cyprus Government has sought to promote higher value-added tourism, and investment in research and development, especially in the areas of environment and water, while continuing to promote Cyprus as a regional financial centre—in 2011 Cyprus had double-taxation treaties with 44 countries, 10 of which had been signed in the last three years. However, in practice there has often been a significant gap between rhetoric and action, and the tendency has been for viable projects—for example, luxury marinas—to remain suspended for several years before ground is broken. In recent years, efforts to attract FDI in infrastructure and other projects have resulted in some very public failures, such as the proposed Qatari investment in a luxury hotel and commercial complex in Nicosia, or the proposed Chinese involvement in redeveloping the old Larnaca airport site. Today, such considerations appear increasingly to be hypothetical, as the Cypriot economy focuses on digesting the measures that must be implemented as part of the bailout programme agreed with the troika in March 2013. However one may view the European institutions' handling of the Cypriot bailout, and leaving aside questions such as the long-term future of the euro, the fact remains that the Cypriot economy has suffered catastrophic damage at the hands of the troika. The banking sector, which dominated economic activity and contributed massively to years of growth, has been savaged and dislocated. The capital controls imposed by the EU institutions failed to prevent capital flight: according to the IMF, net outflows reached around €8,000m. between March and August 2013, counting for 12.6% of deposits, or nearly one-half of the country's GDP. Meanwhile, the newly-restructured BoC is illiquid and may well confront more severe challenges in the short term as it struggles to restore its health. More fundamentally, Cypriots have every reason not to trust the banks, those who run and supervise them, and those who make the political decisions determining their future.

It is difficult to see where economic growth might come from in the short- and medium-term. The construction sector has gone from stagnation to near-collapse, the tourism sector continues predominantly to offer a tired and uncompetitive product, and the real estate sector—far from offering prospects of recovery—threatens to trigger a new banking crisis as the scale of property-related NPLs emerges more clearly.

As the European Commission itself put it in a report published in early 2013, real GDP is expected to decline sharply by 8.7%, affected in particular by the immediate restructuring of the banking sector, which affects net credit growth, fiscal consolidation, and the high degree of economic uncertainty which weighs on domestic demand and investment. In addition, the temporary imposition of capital controls and withdrawal restrictions are expected to hamper international capital flows and to reduce business volumes in both domestic and internationally-oriented companies. The bail-in of uninsured depositors implies a loss of wealth, which will also affect private consumption and investment'.

The current record levels of unemployment can only worsen over the coming years as the public sector is reduced in size, placing greater emphasis on private consumption and investor sentiment. Moreover, as things stand, the economy has no flexibility to deal with domestic or external shocks; this increases the probability of the need for further remedial action in the case of failure to implement the terms of the financial support package.

It could be contended that the bailout agreement is imposing the kind of fiscal and commercial policy that could never have been introduced by an overwhelmingly populist and opportunistic political class. The same argument applies to reform of the public sector, which for decades has been overstaffed, inefficient and subject to cronyism and clientelism. Meanwhile, the requirement to privatize at least some of Cyprus's semi-governmental organizations could help to encourage a general change in attitude among the population, as well as contribute to more immediate improvements in the public finances.

However, the danger remains that the conservatism of significant parts of Cypriot society, which it could be suggested helped to create today's painful situation, is deeply ingrained, and will continue to be an obstacle to building a healthier economy.

Statistical Survey

Source (unless otherwise indicated): Statistical Service of Cyprus (CYSTAT), Ministry of Finance, Michalakis Karaolis St, 1444 Nicosia; tel. 22602102; fax 22661313; e-mail enquiries@cystat.mof.gov.cy; internet www.cystat.gov.cy.

Note: Since July 1974 the northern part of Cyprus has been under Turkish occupation. As a result, some of the statistics relating to subsequent periods do not cover the whole island. Some separate figures for the 'TRNC' are also given.

AREA AND POPULATION

Area: 9,251 sq km (3,572 sq miles), incl. Turkish-occupied region; 5,896 sq km (2,276 sq miles), government-controlled area only.

Population: 703,529, excl. Turkish-occupied region, at census of 1 October 2001 (adjusted figures); 867,600, incl. 88,900 in Turkish-occupied region, at 31 December 2006 (official estimate); 840,407 (males 408,780, females 431,627), excl. Turkish-occupied region, at census of 1 October 2011. Note: Figures for the Turkish-occupied region exclude settlers from Turkey, estimated at 115,000 in 2001.

Density (at 2011 census): 90.8 per sq km.

Population by Age and Sex (excl. Turkish-occupied region, population at 2011 census): *0–14:* 134,948 (males 69,161, females 65,787); *15–64:* 593,593 (males 287,904, females 305,689); *65 and over:* 111,866 (males 51,715, females 60,151); *Total* 840,407 (males 408,780, females 431,627).

Ethnic Groups (31 December 2001, estimates): Greeks 639,400 (80.6%), Turks 87,600 (11.1%), Others 66,100 (8.3%); Total 793,100.

Districts (excl. Turkish-controlled region, population at 2011 census): Ammochostos 46,629; Larnaka (Larnaca) 143,192; Lefkosia 326,980; Lemesos (Limassol) 235,330; Pafos (Paphos) 88,276; *Total* 840,407.

Principal Towns (population at 31 December 2011): Nicosia (capital) 244,500 (excl. Turkish-occupied portion); Limassol 183,555; Larnaca 85,874; Paphos 63,541.

Births, Marriages and Deaths (government-controlled area, 2011): Registered live births 9,622 (birth rate 11.3 per 1,000); Registered marriages 13,248 (incl. 6,210 residents of Cyprus); Registered deaths 5,504 (death rate 6.5 per 1,000).

Life Expectancy (years at birth): 79.6 (males 77.4; females 81.8) in 2011. Source: World Bank, World Development Indicators database.

Economically Active Population (government-controlled area, '000 persons aged 15 years and over, excl. armed forces, labour force survey 2012): Agriculture, forestry and fishing 11.3; Mining and quarrying 0.9; Manufacturing 29.1; Electricity, gas and water 7.6; Construction 40.7; Wholesale and retail trade; repair of motor vehicles, motor cycles and personal and household goods 72.7; Restaurants and hotels 30.0; Transport, storage and communications 25.4; Financial intermediation 23.3; Real estate, renting and business activities 35.3; Public administration and defence 25.0; Education 28.8; Health and social work 16.2; Other community, social and personal service activities 17.1; Private households 23.7; Extra-territorial organizations 1.4; *Total* 388.6; Unemployed 52.0; *Total labour force* 440.6.

HEALTH AND WELFARE

Key Indicators

Total Fertility Rate (children per woman, 2011): 1.5.

Under-5 Mortality Rate (per 1,000 live births, 2011): 3.

HIV/AIDS (% of persons aged 15–49, 2007): 0.25.

Physicians (per 1,000 head, 2008): 2.6.

Hospital Beds (per 1,000 head, 2008): 3.8.

Health Expenditure (2010): US $ per head (PPP): 2,218.

Health Expenditure (2010): % of GDP: 7.4.

Health Expenditure (2010): public (% of total): 43.3.

Total Carbon Dioxide Emissions ('000 metric tons, 2009): 8,199.4.

Carbon Dioxide Emissions Per Head (metric tons, 2009): 7.5.

Human Development Index (2012): ranking: 31.

Human Development Index (2012): index: 0.848.

For sources and definitions, see explanatory note on p. vi.

AGRICULTURE

Principal Crops (government-controlled area, '000 metric tons, 2011): Wheat 19.7; Barley 45.7; Potatoes 109.6; Olives 15.3; Cabbages and other brassicas 3.8; Tomatoes 14.8; Cucumbers and gherkins 11.7; Onions, dry 6.7; Bananas 5.9; Oranges 37.7; Tangerines, mandarins, etc. 42.0; Lemons and limes 14.0; Grapefruit and pomelos 24.2; Apples 7.0; Grapes 24.7; Cantaloupes and other melons 8.7.

Livestock (government-controlled area, '000 head, 2011): Cattle 56.9; Sheep 355.9; Goats 290.3; Pigs 438.9; Chickens 3,058.0.

Livestock Products (government-controlled area, '000 metric tons, 2011): Sheep meat 2.6; Goat meat 2.4; Pig meat 57.6; Chicken meat 27.4; Cows' milk 152.6; Hen eggs 9.7.

Forestry (government-controlled area, '000 cubic metres, 2011): Roundwood removals (excl. bark) 8.5; Sawnwood production (incl. railway sleepers) 2.9.

Fishing (government-controlled area, metric tons, live weight, 2011): Capture 1,184 (FAO estimate—Bogue 109; Picarels 82); Aquaculture 4,745 (European seabass 1,517; Gilthead seabream 3,113); *Total catch* 5,929 (FAO estimate).

Source: FAO.

MINING

Selected Products (government-controlled area, '000 metric tons, 2010): Sand and gravel 13,413.0; Gypsum 240.3; Bentonite 128.0; Umber 7.7.

INDUSTRY

Selected Products (government-controlled area, 2012 unless otherwise indicated): Wine 10.7m. litres (2010); Beer 33.5m. litres; Soft drinks 32.1m. litres; Cigarettes 3,803m. (2001); Footwear 125,674 pairs (2010); Bricks 103.3m (2008); Floor and wall tiles 320,000 sq m (2004); Cement 1,080,019 metric tons; Electric energy 4,929.1m. kWh (2011).

FINANCE

Currency and Exchange Rates: 100 cent = 1 euro (€). *Sterling and Dollar Equivalents* (31 May 2013): £1 sterling = €1.170; US $1 = €0.769; €10 = £8.55 = US $13.01. *Average Exchange Rate* (euros per US dollar): 0.7550 in 2010; 0.7194 in 2011; 0.7779 in 2012. Note: The Cyprus pound (C£) was formerly in use. On 1 January 2008 the government-controlled area of Cyprus adopted the euro, which became the sole legal tender in that area from the end of the same month.

Budget (government-controlled area, € million, 2012): *Revenue:* Taxation 5,585.4 (Direct taxes 2,072.7, Indirect taxes 2,499.9, Social security contributions 1,012.7); Other current revenue 911.0; Total 6,496.4, excl. grants from abroad (105.7). *Expenditure:* Current expenditure 7,100.0 (Wages and salaries 1,907.2, Other goods and services 513.7, Social security payments 1,497.1, Subsidies 95.5, Interest payments 652.6, Pensions and gratuities 635.8, Social pension 64.4, Other current transfers 1,664.0, Unallocated 69.8); Capital expenditure (investments) 376.7; Total 7,476.7. Source: Budgets and Fiscal Control Directorate, Ministry of Finance, Nicosia.

International Reserves (government-controlled area, US $ million at 31 December 2012): Gold (national valuation) 742.1; IMF special drawing rights 177.2; Reserve position in IMF 127.9; Foreign exchange 142.5; Other reserve assets 1.3; Total 1,191.0. Source: IMF, *International Financial Statistics*.

Money Supply (incl. shares, government-controlled area, € million at 31 December 2012): Currency issued 1,739 (Currency issued by the Central Bank of Cyprus 1,739); Demand deposits 10,081; Other deposits 33,145; Securities other than shares 1,758; Shares and other equity 16,078; Other items (net) –862; *Total* 61,939. Source: IMF, *International Financial Statistics*.

Cost of Living (government-controlled area, Retail Price Index; base: 2005 = 100): 112.9 in 2010; 116.6 in 2011; 119.4 in 2012.

Gross Domestic Product (government-controlled area, € million at current prices): 17,406.0 in 2010; 17,979.3 in 2011 (provisional figure); 17,886.8 in 2012 (provisional figure).

Expenditure on the Gross Domestic Product (government-controlled area, € million at current prices, 2012, provisional figures): Government final consumption expenditure 3,587.9; Private final consumption expenditure 11,948.1; Increase in stocks 46.1; Gross fixed capital formation 2,294.8; *Total domestic expenditure*

17,876.9; Exports of goods and services 8,136.7; *Less* Imports of goods and services 8,126.8; *GDP in market prices* 17,886.8.

Gross Domestic Product by Economic Activity (government-controlled area, € million at current prices, 2012, provisional figures): Agriculture, forestry and fishing 366.6; Mining and quarrying 29.2; Manufacturing 953.0; Electricity, gas and water supply 513.3; Construction 1,017.3; Wholesale and retail trade 1,915.5; Restaurants and hotels 1,114.4; Transport, storage and communications 1,460.1; Financial intermediation 1,499.6; Real estate, renting and business activities 3,092.7; Public administration and defence 1,824.4; Education 1,105.1; Health and social work 687.3; Other community, social and personal services 510.4; Private households with employed persons 194.4; *Sub-total* 16,283.5; Import duties 57.4; Value-added tax 1,545.9; *GDP in market prices* 17,886.8.

Balance of Payments (government-controlled area, US $ million, 2011): Exports of goods 2,748; Imports of goods –7,950; *Balance on goods* –5,202; Exports of services 7,933; Imports of services –3,790; *Balance on goods and services* –1,059; Primary income received 2,822; Primary income paid –2,662; *Balance on goods, services and primary income* –900; Secondary income received 834; Secondary income paid –1,1,03; *Current balance* –1,169; Capital account (net) 65; Direct investment assets –633; Direct investment liabilities 1,080; Portfolio investment assets 7,933; Portfolio investment liabilities 123; Financial derivatives and employee stock options assets 508; Financial derivatives and employee stock options liabilities –881; Other investment assets –4,153; Other investment liabilities –2,618; Net errors and omissions –311; *Reserves and related items* –56. Source: IMF, *International Financial Statistics*.

EXTERNAL TRADE

Principal Commodities (government-controlled area, US $ million, distribution by SITC, 2010): *Imports c.i.f.:* Food and live animals 935.5; Mineral fuels and lubricants 1,742.8 (Petroleum and products 1,694.8); Chemicals and related products 837.9; Basic manufactures 1,102.3 (Iron and steel 239.6); Machinery and transport equipment 2,167.3 (Passenger cars 481.1); Miscellaneous manufactured articles 1,211.7 (Clothing and accessories 361.1); Total (incl. others) 8,569.8. *Exports f.o.b.:* Food and live animals 244.0 (Vegetables and fruit 120.6); Beverages and tobacco 97.0; Mineral fuels and lubricants 215.1; Chemicals and related products 355.5 (Medicinal and pharmaceutical products 237.4); Machinery and transport equipment 259.3 (Road vehicles 23.9); Miscellaneous manufactured articles 166.1; Total (incl. others) 1,516.4. Source: UN, *International Trade Statistics Yearbook 2011* (€ million): Total imports 6,310.5; Total exports 1,404.0.

Principal Trading Partners (government-controlled area, US $ million, 2010): *Imports c.i.f.:* Belgium 177.8; Brazil 19.8; China, People's Repub. 455.0; France (incl. Monaco) 437.2; Germany 763.6; Greece 1,615.1; Ireland 154.7; Israel 677.0; Italy 802.5; Japan 91.3; Malta 133.9; Netherlands 387.0; Spain 239.0; Switzerland-Liechtenstein 103.9; United Kingdom 710.1; USA 124.1; Total (incl. others) 8,569.8. *Exports f.o.b.* (incl. re-exports): China, People's Republic 20.8; Egypt 26.5; France (incl. Monaco) 17.2; Germany 139.6; Greece 323.4; Israel 27.9; Italy 34.3; Lebanon 49.8; Netherlands 24.7; Romania 17.4; Russia 26.2; Saudi Arabia 19.1; Sweden 16.2; Syria 32.2; United Arab Emirates 27.5; United Kingdom 113.5; USA 21.0; Total (incl. others) 1,516.4. Source: UN, *International Trade Statistics Yearbook. 2011* (€ million): Imports c.i.f.: China, People's Republic 300.3; Egypt 71.9; France 348.9; Germany 506.8; Greece 1,338.3; Israel 637.9; Italy 505.8; Netherlands 282.0; Spain 197.7; United Kingdom 550.2; USA 155.9; Total (incl. others) 6,310.5; Exports f.o.b. (incl. re-exports): China, People's Republic 19.0; Egypt 24.2; Germany 67.2; Greece 331.5; Israel 29.1; Italy 40.2; Lebanon 47.7; Netherlands 17.6; Russia 19.1; United Kingdom 125.2; USA 18.2; Total (incl. others) 1,404.0.

TRANSPORT

Road Traffic (government-controlled area, licensed motor vehicles, 31 December 2011): Private passenger cars 460,085; Taxis and self-drive cars 9,458; Buses and coaches 3,461; Lorries and vans 118,003; Motorcycles 39,803; Total (incl. others) 651,671.

Shipping (government-controlled area, freight traffic, '000 metric tons, 2011): Goods loaded 1,693, Goods unloaded 5,842. *Flag Registered Fleet:* At 31 December 2012 a total of 1,146 merchant vessels (combined displacement 20,616,268 grt) were registered in Cyprus (Source: Lloyd's List Intelligence, www.lloydslistintelligence.com).

Civil Aviation (government-controlled area, 2011): Overall passenger traffic 7,233,428; Total freight transported 38,503 metric tons.

TOURISM

Foreign Tourist Arrivals (government-controlled area, '000): 2,173.0 in 2010; 2,392.2 in 2011; 2,464.9 in 2012 (estimate).

Arrivals by Country of Residence (government-controlled area, '000, 2012, estimates): Germany 144.4; Greece 133.0; Norway 69.4; Russia 474.4; Sweden 117.3; United Kingdom 959.5; Total (incl. others) 2,464.9.

Tourism Receipts (government-controlled area, € million): 1,549.8 in 2010; 1,749.3 in 2011; 1,927.7 in 2012.

COMMUNICATIONS MEDIA

Telephones (main lines in use, 2012): 373,200.

Mobile Cellular Telephones (subscribers, 2012): 1,110,900.

Personal Computers: 324,000 (383.4 per 1,000 persons) in 2006.

Internet Subscribers (2011): 212,100.

Broadband Subscribers (2012): 217,100.

Source: International Telecommunication Union.

EDUCATION

2010/11 (government-controlled area): Pre-primary: 680 institutions, 2,203 teachers, 28,582 pupils; Primary: 368 institutions, 4,821 teachers, 54,083 pupils; Secondary (Gymnasiums and Lyceums): 166 institutions, 7,603 teachers, 63,764 pupils; Tertiary (incl. University of Cyprus): 43 institutions, 1,803 teachers, 32,118 students (of whom 10,026 were foreign students). Note: 19,199 Cypriot students were studying abroad.

Pupil-teacher Ratio (primary education): 11.2 in 2010/11.

Adult Literacy Rate (2011 census): 98.7% (males 99.3%; females 98.1%).

'Turkish Republic of Northern Cyprus'

Source: Statistics and Research Dept, State Planning Organization, Prime Ministry, Lefkoşa (Nicosia), Mersin 10, Turkey; tel. (22) 83141; fax (22) 85988; e-mail trnc-spo@management.emu.edu.tr; internet www.devplan.org.

AREA AND POPULATION

Area: 3,242 sq km (1,251 sq miles).

Population: 256,644 (males 138,568, females 118,076) at census of 30 April 2006. *Mid-2010:* 286,973.

Density (at mid-2010): 87.5 per sq km.

Population by Age and Sex (at census of 30 April 2006): *0–14:* 47,595 (males 24,489, females 23,106); *15–64:* 189,686 (males 105,421, females 84,265); *65 and over:* 19,363 (males 8,658, females 10,705); *Total* 256,644 (males 138,568, females 118,076).

Population by Country of Nationality (self-declaration at census of 30 April 2006): 'TRNC' 135,106; Joint 'TRNC' and other 42,925 (with Turkey 34,370, with United Kingdom 3,854, with Other 4,701); Turkey 70,525; United Kingdom 2,729; Bulgaria 797; Iran 759; Pakistan 475; Moldova 354; Germany 181; Other 2,793; *Total* 256,644.

Districts (population at census of 30 April 2006): Lefkoşa 84,776; Mağusa 63,603; Girne 57,902; Güzelyurt 29,264; İskele 21,099.

Principal Towns (population within the municipal boundary at census of 30 April 2006): Lefkoşa (Nicosia) 49,868 (Turkish-occupied area only); Gazi Mağusa (Famagusta) 35,381; Girne (Kyrenia) 23,839; Güzelyurt 12,391.

Births, Marriages and Deaths (registered, 2001): Live births 2,550 (birth rate 15.0 per 1,000); Marriages 1,090 (marriage rate 5.2 per 1,000); Deaths 781 (death rate 8.0 per 1,000). *2010:* Birth rate 15.2 per 1,000; Death rate 6.9 per 1,000.

Life Expectancy (years at birth, 2010): Males 72.0; Females 76.7.

Employment (labour force survey, October 2010): Agriculture, forestry and fishing 5,300; Mining and quarrying 73; Manufacturing 8,393; Construction 7,746; Electricity, gas and water 1,051; Wholesale and retail trade 16,547; Hotels and restaurants 7,470; Transport, storage and communications 5,026; Financial institutions

3,498; Real estate and renting 4,686; Public administration 15,669; Education 9,149; Health 2,481; Other community services 6,408; *Total employed* 93,498. *2010:* Total unemployed 12,619.

HEALTH AND WELFARE

Key Indicators

Total Fertility Rate (children per woman, 2010): 1.9.

Under-5 Mortality Rate (per 1,000 live births, 2006): 13.9.

Physicians (per 1,000 head, 2010): 2.7.

Hospital Beds (per 1,000 head, 2010): 5.6.

AGRICULTURE

Principal Crops ('000 metric tons, 2001): Wheat 7.6; Barley 102.1; Potatoes 14.0; Legumes 2.5; Tomatoes 8.3; Onions 1.7; Artichokes 1.2; Watermelons 9.7; Melons 3.0; Cucumbers 2.1; Carobs 2.8; Olives 3.1; Lemons 10.7; Grapefruit 15.8; Oranges 61.6; Tangerines 2.0.

Livestock ('000 head, 2001): Cattle 34.2; Sheep 202.7; Goats 54.8; Chickens 4,238.

Livestock Products ('000 metric tons, unless otherwise indicated, 2001): Sheep's and goats' milk 11.4; Cows' milk 66.5; Sheep meat 3.3; Goat meat 0.8; Cattle meat 2.1; Chicken meat 6.8; Wool 0.2; Eggs (million) 13.4.

Fishing (metric tons, 2001): Total catch 400.

FINANCE

Currency and Exchange Rates: Turkish currency: 100 kuruş = 1 Turkish lira. *Sterling, Dollar and Euro Equivalents* (31 December 2012): £1 sterling = 2.812 liras; US $1 = 1.782 liras; €1 = 2.351 liras; 100 Turkish liras = £35.56 = $56.12 = €42.53. Note: A new currency, the new Turkish lira, equivalent to 1,000,000 of the former units, was introduced on 1 January 2005. Figures in this survey have been converted retrospectively to reflect this development. (The name of the currency reverted to Turkish lira on 1 January 2009, although new Turkish lira banknotes and coins were to remain in circulation for a further year.) *Average Exchange Rate* (liras per US dollar): 1.503 in 2010; 1.675 in 2011; 1.796 in 2012.

Budget ('000 Turkish liras, 2010): *Revenue:* Local revenue 1,791,246.8 (Direct taxes 584,146.9, Indirect taxes 687,951.4, Other income 170,387.4, Fund revenues 348,761.0); Foreign aid 303,637.3; Total 2,094,884.1. *Expenditure:* Personnel 947,401.5; Other goods and services 192,648.5; Transfers 1,169,441.2; Investments 188,138.6; Defence 163,327.2; Total 2,660,957.0.

Cost of Living (Consumer Price Index, annual averages; base: 2008 = 100): 110.3 in 2010; 120.9 in 2011; 130.6 in 2012.

Expenditure on the Gross Domestic Product ('000 Turkish liras at current prices, 2003, provisional figures): Government final consumption expenditure 482,674; Private final consumption expenditure 1,071,916; Increase in stocks 30,900; Gross fixed capital formation 300,218; *Total domestic expenditure* 1,885,707; Net exports of goods and services –56,763; *GDP in purchasers' values* 1,828,944; *GDP at constant 1977 prices* (million liras) 9,523.6.

Gross Domestic Product by Economic Activity ('000 Turkish liras, 2010): Agriculture, forestry and fishing 330,292.7; Mining and quarrying 35,628.4; Manufacturing 130,888.7; Electricity and water 386,319.1; Construction 312,118.7; Wholesale and retail trade 598,030.0; Restaurants and hotels 302,003.6; Transport and communications 525,213.2; Finance 404,371.0; Ownership of dwellings 220,581.2; Business and personal services 652,317.3; Government services 1,180,064.6; *Sub-total* 5,077,828.4; Import duties 536,308.5; *GDP in purchasers' values* 5,614,136.9.

Balance of Payments (US $ million, 2008): Merchandise exports f.o.b. 83.7; Merchandise imports c.i.f. –1,680.7; *Trade balance* –1,597.0; Services and unrequited transfers (net) 1,206.7; *Current balance* –390.3; Foreign aid and loans from Turkey 337.1; Other short-term capital movements 73.4; Net errors and omissions –289.7; *Overall balance* –269.5.

EXTERNAL TRADE

Principal Commodities (US $ million, 2010): *Imports c.i.f.:* Food and live animals 176.9; Beverages and tobacco 86.7; Mineral fuels, lubricants, etc. 328.1; Basic manufactures 331.1; Machinery and transport equipment 362.2; Miscellaneous manufactured articles 149.8; Total (incl. others) 1,604.2. *Exports f.o.b.:* Food and live animals 36.8; Industrial products 52.1; Minerals 7.5; Total 96.4.

Principal Trading Partners (US $ million, 2010): *Imports c.i.f.:* Turkey 1,137.4; United Kingdom 74.7; USA 11.7; Total (incl. others) 1,604.2. *Exports f.o.b.:* Turkey 44.7; United Kingdom 4.8; Total (incl. others) 96.4.

TRANSPORT

Road Traffic (registered motor vehicles, 2001): Saloon cars 76,850; Estate cars 9,168; Pick-ups 3,825; Vans 9,131; Buses 2,077; Trucks 1,593; Lorries 6,335; Motorcycles 16,424; Agricultural tractors 6,594; Total (incl. others) 134,454.

Shipping (2001): Freight traffic ('000 metric tons): Goods loaded 247.2, Goods unloaded 898.1; Vessels entered 3,220.

Civil Aviation (2001): Passenger arrivals and departures 691,431; Freight landed and cleared (metric tons) 4,297.

TOURISM

Visitors (2010): 902,390 (including 741,925 Turkish visitors).

Tourism Receipts (US $ million, 2010): 405.8.

COMMUNICATIONS MEDIA

Radio Receivers (2001, provisional): 82,364 in use.

Television Receivers (2001, provisional): 70,960 in use.

Telephones (2010): 359,000 subscribers.

Mobile Cellular Telephones (2010): 1,832,000 subscribers.

EDUCATION

2010/11: *Pre-primary schools:* 145 institutions, 487 teachers, 6,229 pupils; *Primary schools:* 94 institutions, 1,567 teachers, 18,053 pupils; *Secondary Schools:* 36 institutions, 1,108 teachers, 10,487 students; *General High Schools:* 27 institutions, 973 teachers, 7,786 students; *Vocational Schools:* 11 institutions, 524 teachers, 3,080 students; *Universities:* 8 institutions, 41,230 students (of which 12,666 Turkish Cypriots, 24,319 from Turkey, 4,245 from other countries). Note: 2,620 'TRNC' students were studying abroad.

Pupil-teacher Ratio (primary education): 12.6 in 2010/11.

Adult Literacy Rate (at census of 15 December 1996): 93.5%.

Directory

The Constitution

The Constitution, summarized below, entered into force on 16 August 1960, when Cyprus became an independent republic.

THE STATE OF CYPRUS

The State of Cyprus is an independent and sovereign Republic with a presidential regime.

The Greek Community comprises all citizens of the Republic who are of Greek origin and whose mother tongue is Greek or who share the Greek cultural traditions or who are members of the Greek Orthodox Church.

The Turkish Community comprises all citizens of the Republic who are of Turkish origin and whose mother tongue is Turkish or who share the Turkish cultural traditions or who are Muslims.

The official languages of the Republic are Greek and Turkish.

The Republic shall have its own flag of neutral design and colour, chosen jointly by the President and the Vice-President of the Republic.

The Greek and the Turkish Communities shall have the right to celebrate respectively the Greek and the Turkish national holidays.

THE PRESIDENT AND VICE-PRESIDENT

Executive power is vested in the President and the Vice-President, who are members of the Greek and Turkish Communities respectively, and are elected by their respective communities to hold office for five years.

The President of the Republic as Head of the State represents the Republic in all its official functions; signs the credentials of diplomatic envoys and receives the credentials of foreign diplomatic envoys; signs the credentials of delegates for the negotiation of international treaties, conventions or other agreements; signs the letter relating to the transmission of the instruments of ratification of any international treaties, conventions or agreements; confers the honours of the Republic.

The Vice-President of the Republic, as Vice-Head of the State, has the right to be present at all official functions; at the presentation of the credentials of foreign diplomatic envoys; to recommend to the President the conferment of honours on members of the Turkish Community, which recommendation the President shall accept unless there are grave reasons to the contrary.

The election of the President and the Vice-President of the Republic shall be direct, by universal suffrage and secret ballot, and shall, except in the case of a by-election, take place on the same day but separately.

The office of the President and of the Vice-President shall be incompatible with that of a Minister or of a Representative or of a member of a Communal Chamber or of a member of any municipal council including a Mayor or of a member of the armed or security forces of the Republic or with a public or municipal office.

The President and Vice-President of the Republic are invested by the House of Representatives.

The President and the Vice-President of the Republic in order to ensure the executive power shall have a Council of Ministers composed of seven Greek Ministers and three Turkish Ministers. The Ministers shall be designated respectively by the President and the Vice-President of the Republic who shall appoint them by an instrument signed by them both. The President convenes and presides over the meetings of the Council of Ministers, while the Vice-President may ask the President to convene the Council and may take part in the discussions.

The decisions of the Council of Ministers shall be taken by an absolute majority and shall, unless the right of final veto or return is exercised by the President or the Vice-President of the Republic or both, be promulgated immediately by them.

The executive power exercised by the President and the Vice-President of the Republic conjointly consists of:

Determining the design and colour of the flag.

Creation or establishment of honours.

Appointment of the members of the Council of Ministers.

Promulgation by publication of the decisions of the Council of Ministers.

Promulgation by publication of any law or decision passed by the House of Representatives.

Appointments and termination of appointments as in Articles provided.

Institution of compulsory military service.

Reduction or increase of the security forces.

Exercise of the prerogative of mercy in capital cases.

Remission, suspension and commutation of sentences.

Right of references to the Supreme Constitutional Court and publication of Court decisions.

Address of messages to the House of Representatives.

The executive powers which may be exercised separately by the President and Vice-President include: designation and termination of appointment of Greek and Turkish Ministers respectively; the right of final veto on Council decisions and on laws concerning foreign affairs, defence or security; the publication of the communal laws and decisions of the Greek and Turkish Communal Chambers respectively; the right of recourse to the Supreme Constitutional Court; the prerogative of mercy in capital cases; and addressing messages to the House of Representatives.

THE COUNCIL OF MINISTERS

The Council of Ministers shall exercise executive power in all matters, other than those which are within the competence of a Communal Chamber, including the following:

General direction and control of the government of the Republic and the direction of general policy.

Foreign affairs, defence and security.

Co-ordination and supervision of all public services.

Supervision and disposition of property belonging to the Republic.

Consideration of Bills to be introduced to the House of Representatives by a Minister.

Making of any order or regulation for the carrying into effect of any law as provided by such law.

Consideration of the Budget of the Republic to be introduced to the House of Representatives.

THE HOUSE OF REPRESENTATIVES*

The legislative power of the Republic shall be exercised by the House of Representatives in all matters except those expressly reserved to the Communal Chambers.

The number of Representatives shall be 50, subject to alteration by a resolution of the House of Representatives carried by a majority comprising two-thirds of the Representatives elected by the Greek Community and two-thirds of the Representatives elected by the Turkish Community.

Out of the number of Representatives 70% shall be elected by the Greek Community and 30% by the Turkish Community separately from among their members respectively, and, in the case of a contested election, by universal suffrage and by direct and secret ballot held on the same day.

The term of office of the House of Representatives shall be for a period of five years.

The President of the House of Representatives shall be a Greek, and shall be elected by the Representatives elected by the Greek Community, and the Vice-President shall be a Turk and shall be elected by the Representatives elected by the Turkish Community.

* Following a constitutional amendment in 1985, the number of seats in the House of Representatives was increased to 80 (of which 56 were allocated to Greek Cypriot deputies and 24 reserved for Turkish Cypriots).

THE COMMUNAL CHAMBERS

The Greek and the Turkish Communities respectively shall elect from among their own members a Communal Chamber.

The Communal Chambers shall, in relation to their respective Community, have competence to exercise legislative power solely with regard to the following:

All religious, educational, cultural and teaching matters.

Personal status; composition and instances of courts dealing with civil disputes relating to personal status and to religious matters.

Imposition of personal taxes and fees on members of their respective Community in order to provide for their respective needs.

THE PUBLIC SERVICE AND THE ARMED FORCES

The public service shall be composed as to 70% of Greeks and as to 30% of Turks.

The Republic shall have an army of 2,000 men, of whom 60% shall be Greeks and 40% shall be Turks.

The security forces of the Republic shall consist of the police and gendarmerie and shall have a contingent of 2,000 men. The forces shall be composed as to 70% of Greeks and as to 30% of Turks.

OTHER PROVISIONS

The following measures have been passed by the House of Representatives since January 1964, when the Turkish members withdrew:

The amalgamation of the High Court and the Supreme Constitutional Court (see Judicial System section).

The abolition of the Greek Communal Chamber and the creation of a Ministry of Education.

The unification of the municipalities.

The unification of the police and the gendarmerie.

The creation of a military force by providing that persons between the ages of 18 and 50 years can be called upon to serve in the National Guard.

The extension of the term of office of the President and the House of Representatives by one year intervals from July 1965 until elections in February 1968 and July 1970 respectively.

New electoral provisions; abolition of separate Greek and Turkish rolls; abolition of post of Vice-President, which was re-established in 1973.

The Government

HEAD OF STATE

President: NIKOS ANASTASIADES (took office 28 February 2013).

COUNCIL OF MINISTERS
(September 2013)

A coalition Government formed by the Democratic Rally (DISY), the Democratic Party (DIKO), the European Party (Evro.Ko) and independents (Ind.).

Minister of Foreign Affairs: IOANNIS KASOULIDES (DISY).

Minister of Finance: HARIS GEORGIADES (DISY).

Minister of the Interior: SOCRATES HASIKOS (DISY).

Minister of Defence: FOTIS FOTIOU (DIKO).

Minister of Education and Culture: KYRIAKOS KENEVEZOS (DIKO).

Minister of Communications and Works: TASOS MITSOPOULOS (DISY).

Minister of Commerce, Industry and Tourism: GEORGIOS LAKKOTRYPIS (DIKO).

Minister of Agriculture, Natural Resources and the Environment: NIKOS KOUYALIS (Evro.Ko).

Minister of Labour and Social Insurance: GEORGIA (ZETA) EMILIANIDOU (Ind.).

Minister of Justice and Public Order: IONAS NICOLAOU (DISY).

Minister of Health: PETROS PETRIDES (DIKO).

Government Spokesman: CHRISTOS STYLIANIDES (DISY).

Note: Under the Constitution of 1960, the position of Vice-President and three posts in the Council of Ministers are reserved for Turkish Cypriots. However, there has been no Turkish Cypriot participation in the Government since December 1963.

MINISTRIES

Office of the President: Presidential Palace, Demosthenis Severis Ave, 1400 Nicosia; tel. 22867400; fax 22663799; e-mail info@presidency.gov.cy; internet www.presidency.gov.cy.

Ministry of Agriculture, Natural Resources and the Environment: Loukis Akritas Ave, 1411 Nicosia; tel. 22408307; fax 22781156; e-mail registry@moa.gov.cy; internet www.moa.gov.cy.

Ministry of Commerce, Industry and Tourism: 6 Andreas Araouzos St, 1421 Nicosia; tel. 22867100; fax 22375120; e-mail perm.sec@mcit.gov.cy; internet www.mcit.gov.cy.

Ministry of Communications and Works: 28 Achaeon St, Agios Andreas, 1424 Nicosia; tel. 22800288; fax 22776266; e-mail ipiresia.politi@mcw.gov.cy; internet www.mcw.gov.cy.

Ministry of Defence: 4 Emmanuel Roides Ave, 1432 Nicosia; tel. 22807724; fax 22429392; e-mail othellos4@cytanet.com.cy; internet www.mod.gov.cy.

Ministry of Education and Culture: Kimonos and Thoukididis, 1434 Nicosia; tel. 22800600; fax 22426349; e-mail minister@moec.gov.cy; internet www.moec.gov.cy.

Ministry of Finance: Cnr Michalakis Karaolis St and Gregoriou Afxentiou St, 1439 Nicosia; tel. 22601104; fax 22602741; e-mail registry@mof.gov.cy; internet www.mof.gov.cy.

Ministry of Foreign Affairs: Presidential Palace Ave, 1447 Nicosia; tel. 22401000; fax 22661881; e-mail minforeign1@mfa.gov.cy; internet www.mfa.gov.cy.

Ministry of Health: 1 Prodomou and 17 Chilonos, 1448 Nicosia; tel. 22605300; fax 22605487; e-mail perm.sec@moh.gov.cy; internet www.moh.gov.cy.

Ministry of the Interior: Demosthenis Severis Ave, Ex Secretariat Compound, 1453 Nicosia; tel. 22867800; fax 22671465; e-mail info@moi.gov.cy; internet www.moi.gov.cy.

Ministry of Justice and Public Order: 125 Athalassa Ave, 1461 Nicosia; tel. 22805955; fax 22518356; e-mail registry@mjpo.gov.cy; internet www.mjpo.gov.cy.

Ministry of Labour and Social Insurance: 7 Byron Ave, 1463 Nicosia; tel. 22401600; fax 22670993; e-mail administration@mlsi.gov.cy; internet www.mlsi.gov.cy.

President and Legislature

PRESIDENT

Presidential Election, First Ballot, 17 February 2013

Candidate	Valid votes	%
Nikos Anastasiades (DISY)	200,591	45.46
Stavros Malas (Ind., with AKEL support)	118,755	26.91
Giorgos Lillikas (Ind., with KISOS support)	109,996	24.93
Georgios Charalambous (ELAM)	3,899	0.88
Praxoula Antoniadou Kyriakou (EDI)	2,678	0.61
Makaria-Andri Stylianou (Ind.)	1,898	0.43
Lakis Ioannou (LASOK)	1,278	0.29
Solon Gregoriou (Ind.)	792	0.18
Kostas Kyriacou (Ind.)	722	0.16
Andreas Efstratiou (Ind.)	434	0.10
Loukas Stavrou (Ind.)	213	0.05
Total	441,256*	100.00

* Excluding 12,278 blank or invalid votes (2.7% of the total votes cast).

Presidential Election, Second Ballot, 24 February 2013

Candidate	Votes	%
Nikos Anastasiades (DISY)	236,965	57.48
Stavros Malas (Ind., with AKEL support)	175,267	42.52
Total*	412,232	100.00

* Excluding 32,777 blank or invalid votes (7.36% of total votes cast).

House of Representatives

1402 Nicosia; tel. 22407300; fax 22668611; e-mail vouli@parliament.cy; internet www.parliament.cy.

The House of Representatives originally consisted of 50 members, 35 from the Greek community and 15 from the Turkish community, elected for a term of five years. In January 1964 the Turkish members withdrew and set up the 'Turkish Legislative Assembly of the Turkish Cypriot Administration'. At the 1985 elections the membership of the House was expanded to 80 members, of whom 56 were to be from the Greek community and 24 from the Turkish community (according to the ratio of representation specified in the Constitution).

President: YIANNAKIS OMIROU.

Elections for the Greek Representatives, 22 May 2011

Party	Votes	% of Votes	Seats
Democratic Rally (DISY)	138,682	34.28	20
Progressive Party of the Working People (AKEL)	132,171	32.67	19
Democratic Party (DIKO)	63,763	15.76	9
Movement of Social Democrats EDEK (KISOS)	36,113	8.93	5
European Party (Evro.Ko)	15,711	3.88	2
Cyprus Green Party (KOP)	8,960	2.21	1
Others	9,177	2.27	—
Total*	404,577	100.00	56

* Excluding 8,701 invalid votes and 4,969 blank votes.

Political Organizations

Agonistiko Dimokratiko Kinima (ADIK) (Fighting Democratic Movement): POB 216095, 80 Archbishop Makarios III Ave, 2085 Nicosia; tel. 22765353; fax 22375737; e-mail info@adik.org.cy; internet www.adik.org.cy; f. 1999; centre-right; supports independent and united Cyprus and a settlement based on UN resolutions; Pres. DINOS MICHAELIDES; Gen. Sec. SPYROS STEFOU.

Anorthotiko Komma Ergazomenou Laou (AKEL) (Progressive Party of the Working People): POB 21827, 4 E. Papaioannou St, 1075 Nicosia; tel. 22761121; fax 22761574; e-mail k.e.akel@cytanet.com.cy; internet www.akel.org.cy; f. 1941; successor to the Communist Party of Cyprus (f. 1926); Marxist-Leninist; supports united, sovereign, independent, federal and demilitarized Cyprus; over 14,000 mems; Sec.-Gen. ANDROS KYPRIANOU.

Dimokratiko Komma (DIKO) (Democratic Party): POB 23979, 50 Grivas Dhigenis Ave, 1080 Nicosia; tel. 22873800; fax 22873801; e-mail diko@diko.org.cy; internet www.diko.org.cy; f. 1976; absorbed Enosi Kentrou (Centre Union, f. 1981) in 1989; supports settlement of the Cyprus problem based on UN resolutions; Pres. MARIOS KAROYIAN; Gen. Sec. KYRIAKOS KENEVEZOS.

Dimokratikos Synagermos (DISY) (Democratic Rally): POB 25305, 25 Pindarou St, 1308 Nicosia; tel. 22883000; fax 22753821; e-mail disy@disy.org.cy; internet www.disy.org.cy; f. 1976; absorbed Democratic National Party (DEK) in 1977, New Democratic Front (NEDIPA) in 1988 and Liberal Party in 1998; advocates the reunification of Cyprus on the basis of a bizonal federation; also advocates market economy with restricted state intervention and increased state social role; 40,000 mems; Pres. AVEROF NEOPHYTOU; Dir-Gen. DEMETRIS STYLIANOU.

Enomeni Dimokrates (EDI) (United Democrats): POB 23494, 1683 Nicosia; tel. 22663030; fax 22664747; e-mail edicy@spidernet.com.cy; internet www.edi.org.cy; f. by merger of Ananeotiko Dimokratiko Socialistiko Kinima (ADISOK—Democratic Socialist Reform Movement) and Kinima ton Eleftheron Dimokraton (KED—Movement of Free Democrats); Pres. PRAXOULA ANTONIADOU KYRIAKOU; Gen. Sec. DR GEORGE D. CHRISTODOULIDES.

Epalxi Anasygrotisis Kentrou (EPALXI) (Political Forum for the Restructuring of the Centre): 1 Lambousa St, 1095 Nicosia; POB 22119, 1517 Nicosia; tel. 22777000; fax 22779939; e-mail info@epalxi.com; internet www.epalxi.com; f. 1998; aims to achieve a wider grouping of all centrist social-democratic movements; supports a settlement to the Cyprus problem based on the principles of the Rule of Law, international law and respect for human rights for all citizens, and the establishment of a democratic federal system of govt; Pres. KYPROS CHRYSOSTOMIDES.

Ethniko Laiko Metopo (ELAM) (National People's Front): Nicosia; e-mail ethnikolaikometwpo@gmail.com; internet www.elamcy.com; right-wing, nationalist; Leader CHRISTOS CHRISTOU.

Evropaiko Komma (Evro.Ko) (European Party): Stasandrou 27, 1060 Nicosia; tel. 22460033; fax 22761144; e-mail evropaiko.komma@cytanet.com.cy; internet www.evropaikokomma.org; f. 2005 by fmr mems of Neoi Orizontes (NEO) and other political orgs; Pres. DEMETRIS SYLLOURIS.

Kinima Oikologon Perivallontiston (KOP) (Cyprus Green Party): POB 29682, 1722 Nicosia; tel. 22518787; fax 22512710; e-mail greenparty@cytanet.com.cy; internet www.greenpartycy.com; f. 1996; advocates the reunification of Cyprus; promotes the principles of sustainable devt; Sec.-Gen. GEORGE PERDIKIS.

Kinima Sosialdimokraton EDEK (KISOS) (Movement of Social Democrats): POB 21064, 40 Byron Ave, 1096 Nicosia; tel. 22476000; fax 22678894; e-mail tipos@edek.org.cy; internet www.edek.org.cy; f. 2000 as successor to Socialistico Komma Kyprou (EDEK—Socialist Party of Cyprus, f. 1969); supports independent, non-aligned, unitary, demilitarized Cyprus; Pres. YIANNAKIS OMIROU; Hon. Pres. Dr VASSOS LYSSARIDES.

Diplomatic Representation

EMBASSIES AND HIGH COMMISSIONS IN CYPRUS

Australia: 27 Pindarou St, Blk 4, Alpha Business Centre, 7th Floor, 1060 Nicosia; tel. 22753001; fax 22766486; e-mail nicosia.ahc@dfat.gov.au; internet www.cyprus.embassy.gov.au; High Commr TREVOR PEACOCK.

Austria: POB 23961, 34 Demosthenis Severis Ave, 1080 Nicosia; tel. 22410151; fax 22680099; e-mail nicosia-ob@bmeia.gv.at; internet www.bmeia.gv.at/botschaft/nikosia; Ambassador Dr KARL MÜLLER.

Belgium: 2A Chilonos St, Office 102, 1101 Nicosia; tel. 22449020; fax 22774717; e-mail nicosia@diplobel.fed.be; internet www.diplomatie.be/nicosia; Ambassador GUY SEVRIN.

Brazil: 14 Acheon St, Ayios Andreas, 1101 Nicosia; tel. 22592300; fax 22354538; e-mail brasemb.nicosia@itamaraty.gov.br; Ambassador DANTE COELHO DE LIMA.

Bulgaria: POB 24029, 13 Konst. Paleologos St, 2406 Engomi, Nicosia; tel. 22672486; fax 22676598; e-mail bulgaria@cytanet.com.cy; internet www.mfa.bg/embassies/cyprus; Ambassador VESSELIN VALCHEV.

China, People's Republic: POB 24531, 30 Archimedes St, 2411 Engomi, Nicosia; tel. 22352182; fax 22353530; e-mail chinaemb_cy@mfa.gov.cn; internet cy.china-embassy.org; Ambassador LIU XINSHENG.

Cuba: POB 28173, 51-A Kratinou St, 2040 Strovolos, 1st Floor, Nicosia; tel. 22769743; fax 22753820; e-mail embacuba@spidernet.com.cy; Ambassador ARAMIS FUENTE HERNÁNDEZ.

Czech Republic: POB 25202, 48 Arsinois St, 1307 Nicosia; tel. 22421118; fax 22421059; e-mail nicosia@embassy.mzv.cz; internet www.mzv.cz/nicosia; Chargé d'affaires a.i. PETR KAVÁN.

Denmark: POB 20995, 7 Dositheou St, Parabldg Blk C, 4th Floor, 1071 Nicosia; tel. 22377417; fax 22377472; e-mail nicamb@um.dk; internet cypern.um.dk; Ambassador CASPER KLYNGE.

Egypt: POB 21752, 14 Ayios Prokopios St, Engomi, 1512 Nicosia; tel. 22449050; fax 22449081; e-mail info@egyptianembassy.org.cy; Ambassador MENHA MAHROUZ BAKHOUM.

Finland: POB 21438, 9 Arch. Makarios III Ave, 1508 Nicosia; tel. 22458020; fax 22477880; e-mail sanomat.nic@formin.fi; internet www.finland.org.cy; Ambassador ANU SAARELA.

France: 14–16 Saktouri St, 2nd Floor, Agioi Omologitai, 1080 Nicosia; tel. 22585353; fax 22585350; e-mail ambafrance@cytanet.com.cy; internet www.ambafrance-cy.org; Ambassador JEAN-LUC FLORENT.

Georgia: 46 Themistocles Dervis St, Medcon Tower, 5th Floor, 1066 Nicosia; tel. 22357327; fax 22357307; e-mail geoembassy@cytanet.com.cy; internet cyprus.mfa.gov.ge; Chargé d'affaires a.i. GAIOZ JAPARIDZE.

Germany: 10 Nikitaras St, Ay. Omoloyitae, 1080 Nicosia; POB 25705, 1311 Nicosia; tel. 22451145; fax 22665694; e-mail info@nikosia.diplo.de; internet www.nikosia.diplo.de; Ambassador Dr GABRIELA GUELLIL.

Greece: POB 21799, 8–10 Byron Ave, 1096 Nicosia; tel. 22445111; fax 22680649; e-mail grembnicosia@cytanet.com.cy; internet www.mfa.gr/cyprus; Ambassador VASSILIS PAPAIOANNOU.

Holy See: POB 21964, Holy Cross Catholic Church, Paphos Gate, 1010 Nicosia (Apostolic Nunciature); tel. 22662132; fax 22660767; e-mail holcross@logos.cy.net; Apostolic Nuncio Most Rev. GIUSEPPE LAZZAROTTO (Titular Archbishop of Numana—also Apostolic Delegate to Jerusalem and Palestine and Apostolic Nuncio to Israel, resident in Jerusalem).

Hungary: 2 Prodromou and Demetrakopoulou, Zenios Tower, 3rd Floor, 1090 Nicosia; tel. 22459132; fax 22459134; e-mail huembnic@cytanet.com.cy; Ambassador BALÁZS BOTOS.

India: POB 25544, 3 Indira Gandhi St, Engomi, 2413 Nicosia; tel. 22351741; fax 22352062; e-mail hicomind@spidernet.com.cy; internet www.hcinicosia.gov.in; High Commr ASHOK KUMAR.

Iran: POB 28908, 42 Armenias St, 2003 Acropolis, Nicosia; tel. 22314459; fax 22315446; e-mail iranemb@cytanet.com.cy; Ambassador Dr ALI AKBAR REZAEI.

Ireland: 7 Aiantas St, Ayios Omoloyites, 1082 Nicosia; POB 23848, 1686 Nicosia; tel. 22818183; fax 22660050; e-mail nicosiaembassy@dfa.ie; internet www.embassyofireland.com.cy; Ambassador PATRICK SCULLION.

Israel: POB 25159, 4 Ioanni Grypari St, 1090 Nicosia; tel. 22369500; fax 22369555; e-mail ambass-sec@nicosia.mfa.gov.il; internet nicosia.mfa.gov.il; Ambassador MICHAEL HARARI.

Italy: POB 27695, 11 25th March St, Engomi, 2408 Nicosia; tel. 22357635; fax 22357616; e-mail ambnico.mail@esteri.it; internet www.ambnicosia.esteri.it; Ambassador GUIDO CERBONI.

Kuwait: 38 Armenias St, Strovolos, 2003 Nicosia; tel. 22466656; fax 22454424; e-mail nicosia@mofa.gov.kw; Ambassador AHMAD SALEM AL-WEHAIB.

Lebanon: POB 21924, 6 Chiou St, Ayios Dhometios, 1515 Nicosia; tel. 22878282; fax 22878293; e-mail lebanon.emb@cytanet.com.cy; Ambassador YOUSSEF SADAKA.

Libya: POB 22487, 7 Stassinos Ave, 1060 Nicosia; tel. 22460055; fax 22452710; e-mail info@libyanembassy.com.cy; Chargé d'affaires a.i. NUR AL-DIN M. S. EJLEDI.

Netherlands: POB 23835, 34 Demosthenis Severis Ave, 1080 Nicosia; tel. 22873666; fax 22872399; e-mail nic@minbuza.nl; internet www.cyprus.nlembassy.org; Ambassador BRECHJE SCHWACHÖFER.

Oman: Hilton Cyprus Hotel, Nicosia; tel. 22376064; fax 22374436; e-mail embassyofoman@cytanet.com.cy; Ambassador Sheikh KHALIFA BIN ALI BIN ISA AL-HARTHI.

Poland: POB 22743, 12–14 Kennedy Ave, 1087 Nicosia; tel. 22751980; fax 22751981; e-mail nikozja.amb.sekretariat@msz.gov.pl; internet www.nikozja.polemb.net; Ambassador PAWEŁ DOBROWOLSKI.

Portugal: 9 Arch. Makarios III Ave, Severis Bldg, 5th Floor, POB 27407, 1645 Nicosia; tel. 22375131; fax 22756456; e-mail embportugal@nicosia.dgaccp.pt; Chargé d'affaires JOÃO BERNARDO WEINSTEIN.

Qatar: 10 Agathonos St, Lykavittos, 1070 Nicosia; tel. 22466864; fax 22466893; e-mail qatarembassy@cytanet.com.cy; Ambassador HUSSEIN BIN AHMAD MUHAMMAD IBRAHIM AL-HMEID.

Romania: POB 22210, 27 Pireos St, Strovolos, 2023 Nicosia; tel. 22495333; fax 22517383; e-mail embrom@cytanet.com.cy; internet www.nicosia.mae.ro; Ambassador ION PASCU.

Russia: POB 21845, Ayios Prokopias St and Archbishop Makarios III Ave, Engomi, 2406 Nicosia; tel. 22774622; fax 22774854; e-mail russia1@cytanet.com.cy; internet www.cyprus.mid.ru; Ambassador STANISLAV V. OSADCHII.

Serbia: 2 Vasilissis Olgas St, Engomi, 1101 Nicosia; tel. 22777511; fax 22775910; e-mail nicosia@serbia.org.cy; Ambassador SAVO DJURICA.

Slovakia: POB 21165, 4 Kalamatas St, 2002 Strovolos, Nicosia; tel. 22879681; fax 22311715; e-mail skembassy@cytanet.com.cy; Ambassador Dr OKSANA TOMOVA

Spain: POB 28349, 32 Strovolos Ave, 2018 Strovolos, Nicosia; tel. 22450410; fax 22491291; e-mail emb.nicosia@maec.es; internet www.exteriores.gob.es/embajadas/nicosia; Ambassador ANA MARÍA SÁLOMON PÉREZ.

Sweden: POB 21621, 9 Archbishop Makarios Ave, Severis Bldg, 2nd Floor, 1065 Nicosia; tel. 22458088; fax 22374522; e-mail ambassaden.nicosia@gov.se; internet www.swedenabroad.se/nicosia; Ambassador KLAS GIEROW.

Switzerland: 46 Themistocles Dervis St, Medcon Tower, 1066 Nicosia; POB 20729, 1663 Nicosia; tel. 22466800; fax 22766008; e-mail nic.vertretung@eda.admin.ch; internet www.eda.admin.ch/nicosia; Ambassador GABRIELA NUTZI SULPIZO.

Syria: POB 21892, 24 Nikodimos Mylona St, Ayios Antonios, 1071 Nicosia; tel. 22817333; fax 22756963; e-mail syrianembassy@cytanet.com.cy; Chargé d'affaires a.i. ZOUHEIR JABBOUR.

Ukraine: 10 Andrea Miaouli St, Makedonitissa, Engomi, 2415 Nicosia; tel. 22464380; fax 22464381; e-mail emb_cy@mfa.gov.ua; internet www.mfa.gov.ua/cyprus; Ambassador BORYS HUMENIUK.

United Kingdom: POB 21978, Alexander Pallis St, 1587 Nicosia; tel. 22861100; fax 22861125; e-mail brithc.2@cytanet.com.cy; internet ukincyprus.fco.gov.uk; High Commr MATTHEW KIDD.

USA: Metochiou and Ploutarchou St, Engomi, 2407 Nicosia; POB 24536, 1385 Nicosia; tel. 22393939; fax 22780944; e-mail info@americanembassy.org.cy; internet cyprus.usembassy.gov; Ambassador JOHN M. KOENIG.

Venezuela: POB 23367, 12 Andrea Zakou St, Engomi, 2402 Nicosia; tel. 22445332; fax 22662975; e-mail embaven_chipre@hotmail.com; Chargé d'affaires a.i. JEANPIER ANAYA SALAS.

Judicial System

As required by the Constitution, a law was adopted in 1960 providing for the establishment, jurisdiction and powers of courts of civil and criminal jurisdiction, i.e. of six District Courts and six Assize Courts. In accordance with the provisions of new legislation, approved in 1991, a permanent Assize Court, with powers of jurisdiction in all districts, was established.

In addition to a single Military Court, there are specialized courts concerned with cases relating to industrial disputes, rent control and family law.

Supreme Council of Judicature: Nicosia; tel. 22865716; fax 22304500; The Supreme Council of Judicature is composed of the President and Judges of the Supreme Court. It is responsible for the appointment, promotion, transfer, etc., of the judges exercising civil and criminal jurisdiction in the District Courts, the Assize Courts, the Family Courts, the Military Court, the Rent Control Courts and the Industrial Dispute Court.

Supreme Court: Charalambos Mouskos St, 1404 Nicosia; tel. 22865741; fax 22304500; e-mail chief.reg@sc.judicial.gov.cy; internet www.supremecourt.gov.cy; f. 1964; final appellate court and adjudicator in matters of constitutional and administrative law, including recourses on conflict of competence between state organs on questions of the constitutionality of laws, etc. It deals with appeals from Assize Courts, District Courts and other inferior courts as well as from the decisions of its own judges when exercising original jurisdiction in certain matters such as prerogative orders of *habeas corpus, mandamus, certiorari*, etc., and in admiralty cases; Pres. PETROS ARTEMIS.

Attorney-General: PETROS CLERIDES.

'Turkish Republic of Northern Cyprus'

The Turkish intervention in Cyprus in July 1974 resulted in the establishment of a separate area in northern Cyprus under the control of the Autonomous Turkish Cypriot Administration, with a Council of Ministers and separate judicial, financial, police, military and educational machinery serving the Turkish community.

On 13 February 1975 the Turkish-occupied zone of Cyprus was declared the 'Turkish Federated State of Cyprus', and Rauf Denktaş declared President. At the second joint meeting held by the Executive Council and Legislative Assembly of the Autonomous Turkish Cypriot Administration, it was decided to set up a Constituent Assembly, which would prepare a constitution for the 'Turkish Federated State of Cyprus' within 45 days. This Constitution, which was approved by the Turkish Cypriot population in a referendum held on 8 June 1975, was regarded by the Turkish Cypriots as a first step towards a federal republic of Cyprus. The main provisions of the Constitution are summarized below:

The 'Turkish Federated State of Cyprus' is a democratic, secular republic based on the principles of social justice and the rule of law. It shall exercise only those functions that fall outside the powers and functions expressly given to the (proposed) Federal Republic of Cyprus. Necessary amendments shall be made to the Constitution of the 'Turkish Federated State of Cyprus' when the Constitution of the Federal Republic comes into force. The official language is Turkish.

Legislative power is vested in a Legislative Assembly, composed of 40 deputies, elected by universal suffrage for a period of five years. The President is Head of State and is elected by universal suffrage for a period of five years. No person may be elected President for more than two consecutive terms. The Council of Ministers shall be composed of a Prime Minister and 10 Ministers. Judicial power is exercised through independent courts.

Other provisions cover such matters as the rehabilitation of refugees, property rights outside the 'Turkish Federated State', protection of coasts, social insurance, the rights and duties of citizens, etc.

On 15 November 1983 a unilateral declaration of independence brought into being the 'Turkish Republic of Northern Cyprus', which, like the 'Turkish Federated State of Cyprus', was not granted international recognition.

The Constituent Assembly, established after the declaration of independence, prepared a new Constitution, which was approved by the Turkish Cypriot electorate on 5 May 1985. The new Constitution is very similar to the old one, but the number of deputies in the Legislative Assembly was increased to 50.

HEAD OF STATE

President of the 'Turkish Republic of Northern Cyprus': Dr DERVIŞ EROĞLU (inaugurated 23 April 2010).

COUNCIL OF MINISTERS

(September 2013)

A coalition Government formed by the Republican Turkish Party (CTP) and the Democrat Party (DP).

Prime Minister: ÖZKAN YORGANCIOĞLU (CTP).

Deputy Prime Minister and Minister of Economy and Tourism: SERDAR DENKTAŞ (DP).

Minister of Foreign Affairs: ÖZDIL NAMI (CTP).

Minister of Interior Affairs and Local Administrations: TEBERRÜKEN ULUÇAY (CTP).

Minister of Finance: ZEREN MUNGAN (CTP).

Minister of Education, Youth and Sport: Dr MUSTAFA ARABACIOĞLU (DP).

Minister of Health: Dr AHMET GÜLLE (CTP).

Minister of Food, Agriculture and Energy: ÖNDER SENNAROĞLU (CTP).

Minister of Public Works and Transport: Dr AHMET KAŞIF (DP).

Minister of Labour and Social Security: AZIZ GÜRPINAR (CTP).

Minister of Environment and Natural Resources: HAMIT BAKIRCI (DP).

MINISTRIES

Office of the President: Şht Selahattin Sonat Sok., Lefkoşa (Nicosia), Mersin 10, Turkey; tel. 2283444; fax 2272252; internet www.kktcb.eu.

Prime Minister's Office: Selçuklu Rd, Lefkoşa (Nicosia), Mersin 10, Turkey; tel. 2283141; fax 2287280; e-mail info@kktcbasbakanlik.org; internet www.kktcbasbakanlik.org.

Ministry of Agriculture and Natural Resources: Salih Mecit Sok. 16, Lefkoşa (Nicosia), Mersin 10, Turkey; tel. 2283735; fax 2286945; e-mail info@kktob.org; internet www.kktob.org.

Ministry of Economy and Energy: Lefkoşa (Nicosia), Mersin 10, Turkey; tel. 2289629; fax 2273976.

Ministry of Education, Youth and Sport: Lefkoşa (Nicosia), Mersin 10, Turkey; tel. 2284505; fax 2282334; e-mail info@mebnet.net; internet www.mebnet.net.

Ministry of Finance: Lefkoşa (Nicosia), Mersin 10, Turkey; tel. 2283116; fax 2278230; e-mail bim@kktcmaliye.com; internet www.kktcmaliye.com.

Ministry of Foreign Affairs: Selçuklu Rd, Lefkoşa (Nicosia), Mersin 10, Turkey; tel. 2283241; fax 2284290; e-mail bakanlik@trncinfo.org; internet www.trncinfo.org.

Ministry of Health: Lefkoşa (Nicosia), Mersin 10, Turkey; tel. 2283173; fax 2283893; e-mail saglik@kktc.net; internet www.saglikbakanligi.com.

Ministry of Interior Affairs and Local Administrations: Lefkoşa (Nicosia), Mersin 10, Turkey; tel. 2283344; fax 2283043.

Ministry of Labour and Social Security: 7 İplik Pazarı Sok., Lefkoşa (Nicosia), Mersin 10, Turkey; tel. 2273643; fax 2283776; e-mail calismadairesi@gmail.com; internet www.csgb.eu.

Ministry of Public Works and Transport: Lefkoşa (Nicosia), Mersin 10, Turkey; tel. 2283666; fax 2281981; e-mail info@kktculastirma.com; internet www.kktculastirma.com.

Ministry of Tourism, Environment and Culture: Selçuklu Rd, Lefkoşa (Nicosia), Mersin 10, Turkey; tel. 2289629; fax 2285625; internet www.turizmcevrekultur.org.

PRESIDENT

Election, 18 April 2010

Candidates	Votes	%
Dr Derviş Eroğlu (National Unity Party)	61,422	50.35
Mehmet Ali Talat (Ind.)	52,294	42.87
Tahsin Ertuğruloğlu (Ind.)	4,647	3.81
Zeki Besiktepeli (Ind.)	1,967	1.61
Mustafa Kemal Tümkan (Ind.)	964	0.79
Arif Salih Kirdag (Ind.)	520	0.43
Ayhan Kaymak (Ind.)	168	0.14
Total*	121,982	100.00

* Excluding 3,312 invalid votes.

LEGISLATIVE ASSEMBLY

Speaker: HASAN BOZER (UBP).

General Election, 28 July 2013

Party	Votes	% of votes	Seats
Republican Turkish Party (CTP)	477,209	38.38	21
National Unity Party (UBP)	339,864	27.33	14
Democrat Party (DP)	288,021	23.16	12
Communal Democracy Party (TDP)	92,110	7.41	3
United Cyprus Party (BKP)	39,127	3.15	—
Total (incl. others)	1,243,441	100.00	50

ELECTORAL COMMISSION

Yüksek Seçim Kurulu (YSK) (Higher Council of Elections): Lefkoşa (Nicosia), Mersin 10, Turkey; internet ysk.makhemeler.net; Pres. METIN A. HAKKI.

POLITICAL ORGANIZATIONS

Birleşik Kıbrıs Partisi (BKP) (United Cyprus Party): Ali Paşa Sok. 4, Çağlayan, Lefkoşa (Nicosia), Mersin 10, Turkey; tel. 2281845; fax 2281617; e-mail bkp@birlesikkibris.com; internet birlesikkibrispartisi.net; f. 2002; Marxist-Leninist; Sec.-Gen. İZZET İZCAN.

Cumhuriyetçi Türk Partisi (CTP) (Republican Turkish Party): 99 Şehit Salahi, Şevket Sok., Lefkoşa (Nicosia), Mersin 10, Turkey; tel. 2273300; fax 2274476; e-mail ctp@ctp-bg.org; internet www.ctp-bg.org; f. 1970 by mems of the Turkish community in Cyprus; district orgs at Gazi Mağusa (Famagusta), Girne (Kyrenia), Güzelyurt (Morphou) and Lefkoşa (Nicosia); Leader ÖZKAN YORGANCIOĞLU; Gen. Sec. ASIM AKANSOY.

Demokrat Parti (DP) (Democrat Party): Hasane Ilgaz Sok. 13A, Lefkoşa (Nicosia), Mersin 10, Turkey; tel. 2283795; fax 2287130; e-mail basin@demokratparti.net; internet www.demokratparti.net; f. 1992 by disaffected representatives of the Ulusal Bırlık Partisi; merged with the Yeni Doğuş Partisi (New Dawn Party; f. 1984) and Sosyal Demokrat Partisi (Social Democrat Party) in May 1993; Leader SERDAR DENKTAŞ; Gen. Sec. ERTUĞRUL HASIPOĞLU.

Kıbrıs Adalet Partisi (KAP) (Cyprus Justice Party): 1 Osman Paşa Ave, Köşklüçiftlik, Lefkoşa (Nicosia), Mersin 10, Turkey; tel. 2270274; fax 2289938; Leader OĞUZ KALEIOĞLU.

Kıbrıs Sosyalist Partisi (KSP) (Cyprus Socialist Party): Lefkoşa (Nicosia), Mersin 10, Turkey; e-mail ksp@kibrissosyalistpartisi.org; internet www.kibrissosyalistpartisi.org; Gen. Sec. MEHMET BIRINCI.

Milliyetçi Bariş Partisi (MBP) (National Peace Party): Lefkoşa (Nicosia), Mersin 10, Turkey; f. 2003; Leader ERTUĞRUL HASIPOĞLU.

Özgürlük ve Reform Partisi (ORP) (Özgür Parti—Freedom and Reform Party): Lala Mustafa Paşa Sok. 18, Köşklüçiftlik, Lefkoşa (Nicosia), Mersin 10, Turkey; tel. 2290593; fax 2270537; f. 2006 by breakaway parliamentary deputies; Leader Dr TURGAY AVCI.

Toplumcu Demokrasi Partisi (TDP) (Communal Democracy Party): 11 Selim Cad., 44 Köşklüçiftlik, Lefkoşa (Nicosia), Mersin 10, Turkey; tel. 2272555; fax 2287539; e-mail tdp@kktc.net; internet www.toplumcudemokrasipartisi.com; f. 2007, by merger between the Bariş ve Demokrasi Hareketi (Peace and Democracy Movement) and the Toplumcu Kurtuluş Partisi (Communal Liberation Party); Pres. MEHMET ÇAKICI.

Ulusal Bırlık Partisi (UBP) (National Unity Party): 9 Atatürk Meydanı, Lefkoşa (Nicosia), Mersin 10, Turkey; tel. 2273972; fax 2288732; e-mail ubp@kibris.net; internet www.ubp-kktc.org; f. 1975; right of centre; opposes reunification of Cyprus; Pres. İRSEN KÜÇÜK; Sec.-Gen. FUAT NAMSOY.

Yeni Kıbrıs Partisi (YKP) (New Cyprus Party): Tahir Hussain Bldg, Lefkoşa (Nicosia), Mersin 10, Turkey; tel. 2274917; fax 2288931; e-mail ykp@ykp.org.cy; internet www.ykp.org.cy; f. 1989; operated as Yurtsever Bırlık Hareketi (YBH) between 1998–2004; publishes weekly newsletter *Yeniçag*; Gen. Sec. MURAT KANATLI.

Yeni Partisi (New Party): Lefkoşa (Nicosia), Mersin 10, Turkey; f. 2004; Leader NURI ÇEVIKEL.

DIPLOMATIC REPRESENTATION

Embassy in the 'TRNC'

Turkey: Bedrettin Demirel Cad., T. C. Lefkoşa Büyükelçisi, Lefkoşa (Nicosia), Mersin 10, Turkey; tel. 2272314; fax 2282209; e-mail buyukelcilik.lefkosa@mfa.gov.tr; internet www.tclefkosabe.org; Ambassador HALIL İBRAHIM AKÇA.

Turkey is the only country officially to have recognized the 'Turkish Republic of Northern Cyprus'.

JUDICIAL SYSTEM

Supreme Court: Lefkoşa (Nicosia), Mersin 10, Turkey; tel. 2287535; fax 2285265; e-mail erkancoskun@kamunet.net; internet www.mahkemeler.net; The Supreme Court is the highest court in the 'TRNC', and functions as the Constitutional Court, the Court of Appeal and the High Administrative Court. The Supreme Court, sitting as the Constitutional Court, has exclusive jurisdiction to adjudicate finally on all matters prescribed by the Constitution. The Supreme Court, sitting as the Court of Appeal, is the highest appellate court in the 'TRNC' in both civil and criminal cases. It also has original jurisdiction in certain matters of judicial review. The Supreme Court, sitting as the High Administrative Court, has exclusive jurisdiction on matters relating to administrative law; The Supreme Court is composed of a President and seven judges; Pres. NEVVAR NOLAN.

Subordinate Courts: Judicial power other than that exercised by the Supreme Court is exercised by the Assize Courts, District Courts and Family Courts.

Supreme Council of Judicature: The Supreme Council of Judicature, composed of the president and judges of the Supreme Court, a member appointed by the President of the 'TRNC', a member appointed by the Legislative Assembly, the Attorney-General and a member elected by the Bar Association, is responsible for the appointment, promotion, transfer and matters relating to the discipline of all judges. The appointments of the president and judges of the Supreme Court are subject to the approval of the President of the 'TRNC'.

The Attorney-General's Office: The office of the Attorney-General is not attached to any Ministry. The Deputy Attorney-General acts for the Attorney-General in case of his absence; Attorney-General ASKAN ILGEN.

Religion

Greeks form 77% of the population, and most of them belong to the Orthodox Church, although there are also adherents of the Armenian Apostolic Church, the Anglican Communion and the Roman Catholic Church (including Maronites). Most Turks (about 18% of the population) are Muslims.

CHRISTIANITY

The Orthodox Church of Cyprus

The Autocephalous Orthodox Church of Cyprus, founded in AD 45, is part of the Eastern Orthodox Church; the Church is independent, and the Archbishop, who is also the Ethnarch (national leader of the Greek community), is elected by representatives of the towns and villages of Cyprus. The Church comprises 16 dioceses, and in 1995 had an estimated 600,000 members.

Archbishop of Nova Justiniana and all Cyprus: Archbishop CHRYSOSTOMOS II, POB 1130, Archbishop Kyprianos St, Nicosia; tel. 22554600; fax 22431796; e-mail office@churchofcyprus.org.cy; internet www.churchofcyprus.org.cy.

Metropolitan of Kitium: Bishop CHRYSOSTOMOS.

Metropolitan of Kyrenia: Bishop KYKKOTIS.

Metropolitan of Limassol: Bishop ATHANASIOS.

Metropolitan of Morphou: Bishop NEOPHYTOS.

Metropolitan of Paphos: Bishop GEORGIOS.

The Roman Catholic Church

Latin Rite

The Patriarchate of Jerusalem covers Israel, Jordan and Cyprus. The Patriarch is resident in Jerusalem (see the chapter on Israel).

Vicar Patriarchal for Cyprus: Fr UMBERTO BARATO, Holy Cross Catholic Church, Paphos Gate, POB 21964, 1010 Nicosia; tel. 22662132; fax 22660767; e-mail holcross@logos.cy.net.

Maronite Rite

Most of the Roman Catholics in Cyprus are adherents of the Maronite rite. Prior to June 1988 the Archdiocese of Cyprus included part of Lebanon. At 31 December 2006 the archdiocese contained an estimated 10,000 Maronite Catholics.

Archbishop of Cyprus: Most Rev. JOSEPH SOUEIF, POB 22249, Maronite Archbishop's House, 8 Ayios Maronas St, Nicosia; tel. 22678877; fax 22668260; e-mail archmar@cytanet.com.cy.

The Anglican Communion

Anglicans in Cyprus are adherents of the Episcopal Church in Jerusalem and the Middle East, officially inaugurated in January 1976. The Church has four dioceses. The diocese of Cyprus and the Gulf includes Cyprus, Iraq and the countries of the Arabian peninsula.

Bishop in Cyprus and the Gulf, President Bishop of the Episcopal Church in Jerusalem and the Middle East: Right Rev. MICHAEL LEWIS, c/o POB 22075, Diocesan Office, 2 Grigoris Afxentiou St, 1516 Nicosia; tel. 22671220; fax 22674553; e-mail cygulf@spidernet.com.cy; internet www.cypgulf.org; Archdeacon in Cyprus Very Rev. STEPHEN COLLIS.

Other Christian Churches

Among other denominations active in Cyprus are the Armenian Apostolic Church and the Greek Evangelical Church.

ISLAM

Most adherents of Islam in Cyprus, of whom the majority reside in the 'TRNC', are Sunni Muslims of the Hanafi sect. In 2011 an estimated 98% of Turkish Cypriots were Muslims. The religious head of the Muslim community in the 'TRNC' is the Grand Mufti.

Grand Mufti of the 'TRNC': Sheikh AL-SAYYID MUHAMMAD NAZIM ADIL AL-QUBRUSI AL-HAQQANI, PK 142, Lefkoşa (Nicosia), Mersin 10, Turkey.

The Press

GREEK CYPRIOT DAILIES

Alithia (Truth): 26A Pindaros and Androklis St, 1060 Nicosia; POB 21695, 1512 Nicosia; tel. 22763040; fax 22763945; e-mail news@alithia-news.com; internet www.alithia.com.cy; f. 1952 as a weekly, 1982 as a daily; morning; Greek; right-wing; Man. Dir FRIXOS N. KOULERMOS; Editor-in-Chief PAMBOS CHARALAMBOUS; circ. 11,000.

Cyprus Mail: 24 Vassilios Voulgaroktonos St, 1010 Nicosia; POB 21144, 1502 Nicosia; tel. 22818585; fax 22676385; e-mail mail@cyprus-mail.com; internet www.cyprus-mail.com; f. 1945; morning; English; independent; Man. Dir KYRIACOS IAKOVIDES; Editor JEAN CHRISTOU; circ. 6,000.

Haravgi (Dawn): ETAK Bldg, 6 Ezekia Papaioannou St, 1075 Nicosia; POB 21556, 1510 Nicosia; tel. 22766666; fax 22765154; e-mail haravgi@spidernet.com.cy; internet www.haravgi.com.cy; f. 1956; morning; Greek; organ of AKEL; Dir and Chief Editor ANDROULLA GIOUROV; Publr KYPROS KOURTELLARIS; circ. 10,000.

MAXH (Combat): POB 27628, 1st Floor, Block D, 109 office, 2113 Engomi, Nicosia; tel. 22356676; fax 22356701; e-mail newsmaxi@spidernet.com.cy; internet www.maxhnews.com; f. 1960; weekly; Greek; right-wing; Gen. Man. MINA SAMPSON; Chief Editor FROSSO GEORGIOU; circ. 5,000.

O Phileleftheros (Liberal): POB 21094, 1501 Nicosia; tel. 22744000; fax 22590122; e-mail mailbox@phileleftheros.com; internet www.phileleftheros.com.cy; f. 1955; morning; Greek; independent; moderate; Exec. Dir MYRTO MARKIDOU-SELIPA; Sr Editor ARISTOS MICHAELIDES; circ. 28,000.

Politis (Citizen): 8 Vassilios Voulgaroktonos St, 1010 Nicosia; POB 22894, 1524 Nicosia; tel. 22861861; fax 22861871; e-mail info@politis-news.com; internet www.politis.com.cy; f. 1999; morning; Greek; independent; Publr YIANNIS PAPADOPOULOS; Chief Editors GEORGE KASKANIS, SOTIRIS PAROUTIS.

Simerini (Today): POB 21836, 31 Archangelos Ave, Strovolos, 2054 Nicosia; tel. 22580580; fax 22580570; e-mail mail@simerini.com; internet www.simerini.com; f. 1976; morning; Greek; right-wing; supports DISY; Pres. KOSTAS HADJIKOSTIS; Publr PETROS ZACHARIADES; circ. 17,000.

TURKISH CYPRIOT DAILIES

Afrika: Lefkoşa (Nicosia), Mersin 10, Turkey; tel. 2271338; fax 2274585; e-mail avrupa@kktc.net; internet www.afrikagazetesi.net; fmrly *Avrupa*; Turkish; independent; Editor ŞENER LEVENT; circ. 3,000.

Halkın Sesi (Voice of the People): 172 Girne Cad., Lefkoşa (Nicosia), Mersin 10, Turkey; tel. 22856453141; fax 2272612; e-mail halkinsesi@superonline.com; internet www.halkinsesi.org; f. 1942; morning; Turkish; independent Turkish nationalist; Editor SEFA KARAHASAN.

Kıbrıs (Cyprus): Dr Fazil Küçük Bul., Yeni Sanayi Bölgesi, Lefkoşa (Nicosia), Mersin 10, Turkey; tel. 2252555; fax 2255176; e-mail kibris@kibrisgazetesi.com; internet www.kibrisgazetesi.com; Turkish; Editor BAŞARAN DÜZGÜN; circ. 13,000.

Ortam (Political Conditions): 7 Cengiz Han Sok, Köskluciflik, Lefkoşa (Nicosia), Mersin 10, Turkey; tel. 2280852; fax 2283784; e-mail ortam@north-cyprus.net; internet www.ortamgazetesi.com; f. 1981; Turkish; organ of the TDP; Editor-in-Chief MEHMET DAVULCU; circ. 1,250.

Vatan (Homeland): 46 Müftü Ziyai Sok., PK 842, Lefkoşa (Nicosia), Mersin 10, Turkey; tel. 2277557; fax 2277558; e-mail atekman@vatangazetesi.net; internet www.vatangazetesi.com; f. 1991; Turkish; Editor ALI TEKMAN.

Yeni Düzen (New System): Organize Sanayi Bölgesi, Lefkoşa (Nicosia), Mersin 10, Turkey; tel. 2256658; fax 2253240; e-mail yeniduzen@defne.net; internet www.yeniduzengazetesi.com; f. 1975; Turkish; organ of the CTP; Chief Editor CENK MUTLUYAKALI; circ. 1,250.

GREEK CYPRIOT WEEKLIES

Athlitiki tis Kyriakis (Sunday Sports News): 53 Demosthenis Severis Ave, 9th Floor, 1080 Nicosia; tel. 22664344; fax 22664543; e-mail fellouka@cytanet.com.cy; f. 1996; Greek; athletics; Dir PANAYIOTIS FELLOUKAS; Chief Editor NICOS NICOLAOU; circ. 4,000.

Cyprus Weekly: POB 24977, 1 Diogenous St, Engomi, 2404 Nicosia; tel. 22744400; fax 22744440; e-mail info@cyprusweekly.com.cy; internet www.cyprusweekly.com.cy; f. 1979; English; independent; Publishing Dirs ALEX EFTHYVOULOS, ANDREAS HADJIPAPAS; Chief Editor MARTYN HENRY; circ. 17,000.

Dimosios Ypallilos (Civil Servant): 3 Demosthenis Severis Ave, 1066 Nicosia; tel. 22844445; fax 22668639; e-mail pasydy@spidernet.com.cy; internet www.pasydy.org; f. 1927; Greek; publ. by the Cyprus Civil Servants' Trade Union (PASYDY); circ. 15,000.

Ergatiki Phoni (Workers' Voice): POB 25018, SEK Bldg, 23 Alkeou St, Engomi, 2018 Nicosia; tel. 22849849; fax 228498508; e-mail sekxenis@cytanet.com.cy; f. 1947; Greek; organ of SEK trade union; Dir NICOS MOYSEOS; Chief Editor XENIS XENOFONTOS; circ. 10,000.

Ergatiko Vima (Workers' Tribune): POB 21185, 1514 Nicosia; tel. 22866400; fax 22349381; e-mail ergatiko-vima@peo.org.cy; f. 1956; Greek; organ of PEO trade union; Chief Editor LEFTERIS GEORGIADIS; circ. 14,000.

Financial Mirror: POB 16077, 2085 Nicosia; tel. 22678666; fax 22678664; e-mail info@financialmirror.com; internet www.financialmirror.com; f. 1993; English (with Greek-language supplement); independent; Publr and Dir MASIS DER PARTHOGH; circ. 4,000.

Official Gazette: Printing Office of the Republic of Cyprus, 1445 Nicosia; tel. 22405811; fax 22303175; e-mail entorzi@gpo.mof.gov.cy; internet www.mof.gov.cy/gpo; f. 1960; Greek; publ. by the Govt of the Republic of Cyprus; circ. 5,000.

Selides (Pages): POB 21094, 1 Diogenous St, Engomi, 2404 Nicosia; POB 21094, 1501 Nicosia; tel. 22744000; fax 22590516; e-mail mailbox@phileleftheros.com; internet www.phileleftheros.com; f. 1991; Greek; Exec. Dir MYRTO MARKIDOU-SELIPA; Chief Editor MARIA MENIKOU; circ. 16,500.

Tharros (Courage): POB 27628, 14A Danaes St, Engomi, Nicosia; tel. 22356676; fax 22356701; e-mail newsmaxi@spidernet.com.cy; internet www.maxinewspaper.com; f. 1961; Greek; right-wing; Gen. Man. MINA SAMSON; circ. 5,500.

To Periodiko: POB 21836, 23 Alkeou St, 4th Floor, 2404 Nicosia; tel. 22580670; fax 22662247; e-mail psillidesc@toperiodiko.com; f. 1986; Greek; general interest; Dir ANTIS HADJIKOSTIS; Chief Editor POPI VAKI; circ. 16,000.

TURKISH CYPRIOT WEEKLIES

Cyprus Observer: 18 Aytekin Zekai Sok., Kyrenia (Girne), Mersin 10, Turkey; POB 29085, Nicosia; tel. 8155387; fax 8155585; e-mail news@observercyprus.com; internet www.observercyprus.com; f. 2005; English; Exec. Editor HASAN ERCAKICA; Editor UMUT URAS.

Cyprus Today: Dr Fazil Küçük Bul., PK 831, Lefkoşa (Nicosia), Mersin 10, Turkey; tel. 2252555; fax 2253708; e-mail cyprustoday@yahoo.com; f. 1991; English; political, social, cultural and economic; Editor GILL FRASER; circ. 6,000.

Ekonomi (The Economy): 90 Bedrettin Demirel Cad., Lefkoşa (Nicosia), Mersin 10, Turkey; tel. 2283760; fax 2283089; f. 1958;

Turkish; publ. by the Turkish Cypriot Chamber of Commerce; Editor-in-Chief SAMI TAŞARKAN; circ. 3,000.

Safak: PK 228, Lefkoşa (Nicosia), Mersin 10, Turkey; tel. 2271472; fax 2287910; f. 1992; Turkish; circ. 1,000.

Yeniçağ: 28 Ramadan Cad., Lefkoşa (Nicosia), Mersin 10, Turkey; tel. 2274917; fax 2271476; e-mail irtibat@yenicaggazetesi.com.tr; internet www.yenicaggazetesi.com.tr; f. 1990; Turkish; organ of the YKP; Editor MURAT KANATLI; circ. 600.

OTHER WEEKLIES

The Blue Beret: POB 21642, HQ UNFICYP, 1590 Nicosia; tel. 22614550; fax 22614461; e-mail unficyp-blue-beret@un.org; internet www.unficyp.org; bi-monthly journal of the UN Peace-keeping Force in Cyprus (UNFICYP); English; f. 1965; circ. 1,500; Editor JOSÉ DIAZ.

The Cyprus Lion: 55 AEC Episkopi, BFPO 53; tel. 25962052; fax 25963181; e-mail lioncy@cytanet.com.cy; distributed to British Sovereign Base Areas, UN Forces and principal Cypriot towns; includes British Forces Broadcasting Services programme guide; Editor LOUISE CARRIGAN; circ. 5,000.

Middle East Economic Survey: Middle East Petroleum and Economic Publications (Cyprus), POB 24940, 23 Alkeos St, Politica Business Centre, 1355 Nicosia; tel. 22665431; fax 22671988; e-mail info@mees.com; internet www.mees.com; f. 1957 (in Beirut, Lebanon); review and analysis of petroleum, finance and banking, and political devts; Publr Dr SALEH S. JALLAD; Editor-in-Chief DAVID KNOTT.

GREEK CYPRIOT PERIODICALS

Cool: POB 8205, 86 Iphigenias St, 2091 Nicosia; tel. 22378900; fax 22378916; f. 1994; Greek; youth magazine; Chief Editor PROMETHEAS CHRISTOPHIDES; circ. 4,000.

Cypria (Cypriot Woman): POB 28506, 56 Kennedy Ave, 11th Floor, Strovolos, 2080 Nicosia; tel. 22494907; fax 22427051; e-mail pogo@spidernet.com.cy; f. 1983; every 2 months; Greek; Owner MARO KARAYIANNI; circ. 7,000.

Cyprus P.C.: POB 24989, 6th Floor, 1 Kyriakou Matsi St, 1306 Nicosia; tel. 22765999; fax 22765909; e-mail pc@infomedia.cy.net; f. 1990; monthly; Greek; computing magazine; Dir LAKIS VARNAVA; circ. 5,000.

Cyprus Time Out: POB 3697, 4 Pygmalionos St, 1010 Nicosia; tel. 22472949; fax 22360668; f. 1978; monthly; English; Dir ELLADA SOPHOCLEOUS; Chief Editor LYN HAVILAND; circ. 8,000.

Cyprus Today: c/o Ministry of Education and Culture, Cultural Services, Ifighenias 27, 2007 Strovolos, Nicosia; tel. 22809845; fax 22809876; e-mail plyssioti@pio.moi.gov.cy; f. 1963; quarterly; English; cultural and information review; publ. and distributed by Press and Information Office; Chair. PAVLOS PARASKEVAS; circ. 15,000.

Cyprus Tourism: POB 51697, Limassol; tel. 25337377; fax 25337374; f. 1989; bi-monthly; Greek and English; tourism and travel; Man. Dir G. EROTOKRITOU; circ. 250,000.

Enosis (Union): 71 Piraeus & Tombazis, Nicosia; tel. 22756862; fax 22757268; f. 1996; monthly; Greek; satirical; Chief Editor VASOS FTOCHOPOLILOS; circ. 2,000.

Eva: 6 Psichikou St, Strovolos, Nicosia; tel. 22322959; fax 22322940; f. 1996; Greek; Dir DINOS MICHAEL; Chief Editors CHARIS PONTIKIS, KATIA SAVVIDOU; circ. 4,000.

Hermes International: POB 24512, Nicosia; tel. 22570570; fax 22581617; f. 1992; quarterly; English; lifestyle, business, finance, management; Chief Editor JOHN VICKERS; circ. 8,500.

I Kypros Simera (Present Day Cyprus): 1 Apellis St, 1456 Nicosia; tel. 22801186; fax 22666123; e-mail kvrahimis@pio.moi.gov.cy; f. 1983; fortnightly; Greek; publ. by the Press and Information Office of the Ministry of the Interior; Principal Officers MILTOS MILTIADOU, MICHALAKIS CHRISTODOULIDES; circ. 3,500.

Nicosia This Month: POB 20365, 2 Agathokleous St, Strovolos, Nicosia; tel. 22441922; fax 22519743; e-mail info@gnora.com; internet www.gnora.com; f. 1984; monthly; English; Publr MARINOS MOUSHIOTTAS; Man. Dir ANDREAS HADJKYRIACOS; circ. 4,000.

Omicron: POB 21094,1 Diogenous St, Engomi, 1501 Nicosia; tel. 22744000; fax 22590516; f. 1996; Greek; Dir NIKOS CHR. PATTICHIS; Chief Editor MARIANNA KARAVALI; circ. 10,000.

Paediki Chara (Children's Joy): POB 136, 18 Archbishop Makarios III Ave, 1065 Nicosia; tel. 22817585; fax 22817599; e-mail poed@cytanet.com.cy; f. 1962; monthly; for pupils; publ. by the Pancyprian Union of Greek Teachers; Dir FILIOS FILAKTOU; circ. 15,000.

Synergatiko Vima (The Co-operative Tribune): Kosti Palama 5, 1096 Nicosia; tel. 22680757; fax 22660833; e-mail coop.confeder@cytanet.com.cy; internet confederation.coop.com.cy; f. 1983; monthly; Greek; official organ of Pancyprian Co-operative Confed. Ltd; circ. 5,000; Pres. ANDREAS MOUSKALLIS.

Synthesis (Composition): 6 Psichikou St, Strovolos, Nicosia; tel. 22322959; fax 22322940; f. 1988; every 2 months; Greek; interior decorating; Dir DINOS MICHAEL; circ. 6,000.

Tele Ores: POB 28205, 4 Acropoleos St, 1st Floor, 2091 Nicosia; tel. 22513300; fax 22513363; f 1993; fortnightly; Greek; television guide; Chief Editor PROMETHEAS CHRISTOPHIDES; circ. 17,000.

TV Kanali (TV Channel): POB 25603, 5 Aegaleo St, Strovolos, Nicosia; tel. 22353603; fax 22353223; f. 1993; Greek; Dirs A. STAVRIDES, E. HADJIEFTHYMIOU; Chief Editor CHARIS TOMAZOS; circ. 13,000.

TURKISH CYPRIOT PERIODICALS

Güvenlik Kuvvetleri Magazine: Lefkoşa (Nicosia), Mersin 10, Turkey; tel. 2275880; publ. by the Security Forces of the 'TRNC'.

Halkbilimi (Folklore): Hasder, PK 199, Lefkoşa, Mersin 10, Turkey; tel. 8534983; fax 2287798; e-mail hasder@hasder.org; internet www.hasder.org; f. 1986; annual; publ. of Hasder Folk Arts Foundation; academic, folkloric; Turkish, with a short summary in English; Chief Editor ALI NEBIH; circ. 750.

Kıbrıs—Northern Cyprus Monthly: Ministry of Foreign Affairs, Lefkoşa (Nicosia), Mersin 10, Turkey; tel. 2283365; fax 2287641; e-mail pio@trncpio.org; internet www.trncpio.org; f. 1963; Editor GÖNÜL ATANER.

Kıbrıslı Türkün Sesi: 44 Mecidiye St, Lefkoşa (Nicosia), Mersin 10, Turkey; tel. 2278520; fax 2287966; monthly; political; Exec. Dir DOGAN HARMAN; Gen. Co-ordinator CEVDET ALPARSLAN.

Kuzey Kıbrıs Kültür Dergisi (North Cyprus Cultural Journal): PK 157, Lefkoşa (Nicosia) Mersin 10, Turkey; tel. 2231298; f. 1987; monthly; Turkish; Chief Editor GÜNSEL DOĞASAL.

NEWS AGENCIES

Cyprus News Agency: 21 Akademias Ave, 2107 Aglantzia, Nicosia; tel. 22556009; fax 22556103; e-mail director@cna.org.cy; internet www.cna.org.cy; f. 1976; Greek, Turkish and English; Dir and Editor-in-Chief GEORGE PENINTAEX (acting); Chair. of Bd LARKOS LARKOU.

Kuzey Kıbrıs Haber Ajansı (Northern Cyprus News Agency): Alirizin Efendi Cad., Vakıflar Işhani, Kat 2, No. 3, Ortaköy, Lefkoşa (Nicosia), Mersin 10, Turkey; tel. 2281922; fax 2281934; f. 1977; Dir-Gen. M. ALI AKPINAR.

TürkAjansı-Kıbrıs (TAK) (Turkish News Agency of Cyprus): PK 355, 30 Mehmet Akif Cad., Lefkoşa (Nicosia), Mersin 10, Turkey; tel. 2282773; fax 2271213; e-mail tak@emu.edu.tr; internet kktc.gov.nc.tr/tak; f. 1973; Dir EMIR HÜSEYN ERSOY.

Publishers

GREEK CYPRIOT PUBLISHERS

Andreou Chr. Publishers: POB 22298, 67A Regenis St, 1520 Nicosia; tel. 22666877; fax 22666878; e-mail andreou2@cytanet.com.cy; f. 1979; biography, literature, history, regional interest.

KY KE M (Cyprus Research Centre): POB 22687, 1523 Nicosia; tel. 22668848; fax 22667816; e-mail kykem@cytanet.com.cy; Pres. TONIS TOUMAZIS.

Anastasios G. Leventis Foundation: 40 Gladstonos St, POB 22543, 1095 Nicosia; tel. 22667706; fax 22675002; e-mail leventcy@zenon.logos.cy.net; internet www.leventisfoundation.org; f. 1980; Dir CHARALAMBOS BAKIRTZIS.

MAM Ltd (The House of Cyprus and Cyprological Publications): POB 21722, 1512 Nicosia; tel. 22753536; fax 22375802; e-mail mam@mam.com.cy; internet www.mam.com.cy; f. 1965.

Nikoklis Publishing House: POB 20300, 2150 Nicosia; tel. 22334918; fax 22330218; history, geography, culture, travel; Man. Dr ANDREAS SOPHOCLEOUS.

Pierides Foundation: POB 40025, 6300 Larnaca; tel. 24814555; fax 24817868; e-mail centrart@spidernet.com.cy; internet www.pieridesfoundation.com.cy; f. 1974.

TURKISH CYPRIOT PUBLISHERS

Action Global Communications: 6 Kondilaki St, 1090 Lefkoşa (Nicosia), Mersin 10, Turkey; tel. 22818884; fax 22873633; e-mail action@actionprgroup.com; internet www.actionprgroup.com; f. 1971; affiliate of Weber Shandwick; has 44 offices in the emerging markets; travel, aviation and hospitality; Man. Dir TONY CHRISTODOULOU.

Bolan Matbaası: 35 Pençizade Sok., Lefkoşa (Nicosia), Mersin 10, Turkey; tel. 2274802.

Devlet Basımevi (Turkish Cypriot Government Printing House): Şerif Arzik Sok., Lefkoşa (Nicosia), Mersin 10, Turkey; tel. 2272010; Dir SONGUC KÜRŞAD.

Güneş Gazetesi: Yediler Sok., Lefkoşa (Nicosia), Mersin 10, Turkey; tel. and fax 2272959; e-mail gunesgazetesi@kibris.net; f. 1980; Dir EROL ÖNEY.

Halkın Sesi Ltd: 172 Girne Cad., Lefkoşa (Nicosia), Mersin 10, Turkey; tel. 2285645; fax 2272612; e-mail halkinsesi@superonline.com; internet www.halkinsesi.org.

Kıbrıs Araştırma ve Yayın Merkezi (North Cyprus Research and Publishing Centre—CYREP): PK 327, Lefkoşa (Nicosia), Mersin 10, Turkey; tel. 8555179; fax 2272592; e-mail gazioglu@kktc.net; Dir AHMET C. GAZIOĞLU.

K. Rüstem & Bro.: 22–24 Girne Cad., Lefkoşa (Nicosia), Mersin 10, Turkey; tel. 2271418; fax 2283641.

Tezel Matbaası: 35 Şinasi Sok., Lefkoşa (Nicosia), Mersin 10, Turkey; tel. 2271022.

Broadcasting and Communications

TELECOMMUNICATIONS

Greek Cypriot Operators

Cyprus Telecommunications Authority (CYTA): POB 24929, Telecommunications St, Strovolos, 1396 Nicosia; tel. 22701000; fax 22494940; e-mail enquiries@cyta.com.cy; internet www.cyta.com.cy; provides fixed-line telecommunications services and broadband internet access; signed partnership agreement with Vodafone PLC (United Kingdom) in 2004 to offer mobile cellular telecommunications services under brand name Cytamobile-Vodafone; Chair. STATHIS KITTIS; CEO PHOTIOS SAVVIDES.

MTN Cyprus: Nicosia; e-mail contactus@mtn.com.cy; internet www.mtn.com.cy; f. 2004 as Areeba; 51% owned by MTN Group, 49% by Amaracos Holding; provides mobile cellular telecommunications services; Group Pres. and CEO PHUTHUMA NHLEKO.

PrimeTel PLC: POB 51490, The Maritime Center, 141 Omonia Ave, 3506 Limassol; tel. 22027300; fax 22102211; e-mail info@prime-tel.com; internet www.prime-tel.com; f. 2003; provides fixed-line telecommunications services, broadband internet access and cable television to domestic customers under brand name PrimeHome; Man. Dir HERMES N. STEPHANOU.

Turkish Cypriot Operators

KKTC Telsim: Girne Cad. 81, Lefkoşa (Nicosia), Mersin 10, Turkey; tel. 4440542; fax 2280181; e-mail info@kktctelsim.com; internet www.kktctelsim.com; f. 1995; provides mobile cellular telecommunications services; subsidiary of Vodafone Turkey.

Kuzey Kıbrıs TURKCELL (KKTCell): Bedrettin Demirel Cad., Salih Mecit Sok. 1, Kızılay, Lefkoşa (Nicosia), Mersin 10, Turkey; tel. 6001030; internet www.kktcell.com; f. 1999; subsidiary of Turkcell; provides mobile cellular telecommunications services; 318,000 subscribers (March 2009).

Telekomünikasyon Dairesi Müdürlüğü (Directorate of Telecommunications): Lefkoşa (Nicosia), Mersin 10, Turkey; tel. 2281888; fax 2288666; f. 1963; state-owned; admin. and operation of telecommunications services; Gen. Man. MUSTAFA BERKTUĞ.

BROADCASTING

Radio

British Forces Broadcasting Service, Cyprus: Akrotiri, BFPO 57; tel. 25278518; fax 25278580; e-mail cyprus@bfbs.com; internet www.ssvc.com/bfbs/radio/cyprus; f. 1948; broadcasts daily radio and television services in English; Station Man. CHRIS PEARSON; Engineering Man. GEORGE MATSANGOS.

Cyprus Broadcasting Corporation (CyBC): POB 24824, CyBC St, 2120 Nicosia; tel. 22862000; fax 22314050; e-mail rik@cybc.com.cy; internet www.cybc.com.cy; f. 1952; four 24-hour radio channels, two of which are mainly Greek; channel 2 broadcasts programmes in Turkish, English and Armenian; Pres. MAKIS SYMEOU; Dir-Gen. THEMIS THEMISTOCLEOUS.

Kanali Exi: POB 54845, 69 Irinis St, 3041 Limassol; tel. 25820500; fax 25820550; e-mail info@kanali6.com; internet www.kanali6.com.cy; Dir MICHALIS PAPAEVAGOROU.

Logos: Church of Cyprus, POB 27400, 1644 Nicosia; tel. 22477965; fax 22352349; e-mail a.lambrou@logosradio.com.cy; internet www.logosradio.com.cy; Pres. KOSTAS KATSAROS; Dir-Gen. MIXALIS SPYROU.

Radio Astra: Arch. Makarios III Ave 33, 2220 Latsia, Nicosia; tel. 22368888; fax 22319262; e-mail astra@cytanet.com.cy; internet www.astra.com.cy; Chair. YIANNAKIS KOLOKASIDES; Dir GEORGE PAVLIDES.

Radio Proto: POB 21836, 31 Archangelos St, Parissinos, 2057 Nicosia; tel. 22580400; fax 22580425; e-mail web@radioproto.com; internet www.radioproto.com; Chair. KOSTAS HADJIKOSTIS; Gen. Man. MANOS MOYSEOS.

Super FM: POB 22795, 4 Annis Komninis St, Solea Court, 6th Floor, 1060 Nicosia; tel. 22460150; fax 22769516; e-mail studio@superfmradio.com; internet www.superfmradio.com; Gen. Man. MANOS MOYSEOS.

Bayrak Radio and TV Corpn (BRTK): BRTK Sitesi, Dr Fazıl Kucuk Bul., Lefkoşa (Nicosia), Mersin 10, Turkey; tel. 2255555; fax 2254581; e-mail info@brtk.net; internet www.brtk.net; f. 1963 as Bayrak Radio; became independent Turkish Cypriot corpn, partly financed by the 'TRNC' Govt, in July 1983; now has five radio stations on air: Radio Bayrak, Bayrak International (international music, 24-hour, and news in English, Greek, Russian, Arabic and German), Bayrak FM (popular music, 24-hour), Bayrak Classic (classical music, 24-hour) and Bayrak Turkish Music (Turkish classical and folk music, 18-hour); Chair. YILMAZ BAŞKAYA; Gen. Man. ÖZER KANLI.

First FM and Interfirst FM: Lefkoşa (Nicosia), Mersin 10, Turkey; tel. 2289308; fax 2276363; f. 1996.

Kıbrıs FM / Kıbrıs TV: Dr Fazil Küçük Blvd, Yeni Sanayi Bolgesi, Lefkoşa (Nicosia), Mersin 10, Turkey; tel. 2252555; fax 2253707; e-mail kibris@kibrisgazetesi.com; Dir ERDINCH GUNDUZ.

Radio Emu: Eastern Mediterranean University, Gazi Mağusa (Famagusta), Mersin 10, Turkey; e-mail radio@emu.edu.tr; internet www.emu.edu.tr.

Television

Greek Cypriot viewers have access to Greek television channels via satellite. Several Turkish channels are transmitted to the 'TRNC'. Digital Video Broadcasting replaced analogue transmission networks in Cyprus in July 2011.

Antenna TV Cyprus (ANT1 Cyprus): POB 20923, 1665 Nicosia; tel. 22200200; fax 22200210; e-mail infowebsite@antenna.com.cy; internet www.antenna.com.cy; f. 1983; Chair. LOUKIS PAPAPHILIPPOU; Gen. Man. STELIOS MALEKOS.

British Forces Broadcasting Service, Cyprus: BFPO 57, Akrotiri; tel. 25952009; fax 25278580; e-mail dusty.miller@bfbs.com; internet www.bfbs.com/tv; f. 1948; broadcasts a daily TV service; Station Man. IAN NOAKES; Engineering Man. ADRIAN ALMOND.

Cyprus Broadcasting Corporation (CyBC): POB 24824, CyBC St, 1397 Nicosia; tel. 22862000; fax 22314050; e-mail rik@cybc.com.cy; internet www.cybc.com.cy; f. 1957; Pik 1 (CyBC 1) one Band III 100/10-kW transmitter on Mount Olympus; Pik 2 (CyBC 2) one Band IV 100/10-kW ERP transmitter on Mount Olympus; ET1 one Band IV 100/10-kW ERP transmitter on Mount Olympus for transmission of the ETI Programme received, via satellite, from Greece; the above three TV channels are also transmitted from 80 transposer stations; Pres. MAKIS SYMEOU; Dir-Gen. THEMIS THEMISTOCLEOUS; Dir of Television GREGORIS MALIOTIS.

Lumiere TV Public Co Ltd: POB 25614, 1311 Nicosia; tel. 22357272; fax 22354638; e-mail administration@ltv.com.cy; internet www.ltv.tv; f. 1992; encoded signal; Exec. Chair. AKIS AVRAAMIDES; Man. Dir GEORGE XINARIS.

MEGA TV: POB 27400, 1644 Nicosia; tel. 22477777; fax 22477737; e-mail newsdpt@megatv.com.cy; internet www.megatv.com; Gen. Man. GEORGE CHOULIARAS.

Sigma Radio TV Ltd: POB 21836, 2054 Nicosia; tel. 22580100; fax 22358645; e-mail programme@sigmatv.com; internet www.sigmatv.com; f. 1995; island-wide coverage; Chair. and Dir KOSTAS HADJICOSTIS.

Bayrak Radio and TV Corpn (BRTK): BRTK Sitesi, Dr Fazıl Kucuk Bul., Lefkoşa (Nicosia), Mersin 10, Turkey; tel. 2255555; fax 2254581; e-mail info@brtk.net; internet www.brtk.cc; f. 1976; in July 1983 it became an independent Turkish Cypriot corpn, partly financed by the 'TRNC' Govt; Bayrak TV; transmits programmes in Turkish, Greek and English; Chair. of Bd YILMAZ BAŞKAYA; Dir-Gen. ÖZER KANLI.

Kanal T: Üsteğmen Mustafa Orhan Sok., Lefkoşa (Nicosia), Mersin 10, Turkey; tel. 2271666; fax 2234979; e-mail kanalt@kibris.net; internet www.kanaltkibris.net; Owner ERSIN TATAR.

Kıbrıs Genç TV: Şehit Ecvet Yusuf Cad. 8, Yenişehir, Lefkoşa (Nicosia), Mersin 10, Turkey; tel. 2280790; fax 2276363; e-mail iletisim@kibrisgenctv.com; internet www.kibrisgenctv.com; Dir ERTAN BIRINCI.

Finance

(br.(s) = branches; cap. = capital; res = reserves; dep. = deposits; m. = million; amounts in euros unless otherwise indicated, except for Turkish Cypriot banks)

BANKING

Central Banks

Central Bank of Cyprus: POB 25529, 80 Kennedy Ave, 1076 Nicosia; tel. 22714100; fax 22714959; e-mail cbcinfo@centralbank.gov.cy; internet www.centralbank.gov.cy; f. 1963; became fully independent from govt control in July 2002; cap. 30m., res 33m., dep. 3,713m. (Dec. 2009); Gov. PANICOS DEMETRIADES.

Central Bank of the 'Turkish Republic of Northern Cyprus': POB 857, Bedreddin Demirel Ave, Lefkoşa (Nicosia), Mersin 10, Turkey; tel. 2283216; fax 2285240; e-mail ileti@kktcmb.trnc.net; internet www.kktcmb.trnc.net; f. 1984; Pres. AHMET TUGAY.

Greek Cypriot Banks

Alpha Bank Cyprus Ltd: POB 21661, 3 Lemesos Ave, 1596 Nicosia; tel. 22888888; fax 22334868; e-mail secretariat@alphabank.com.cy; internet www.alphabank.com.cy; f. 1960 as Lombard Banking (Cyprus) Ltd; name changed to Lombard NatWest Banking Ltd in 1989 and as above in 1998; locally incorporated although foreign-controlled; 100% owned by Alpha Bank (Greece); cap. 118m., res 15m., dep. 7,475m. (Dec. 2010); Chair. SPYROS N. FILARETOS; Man. Dir GEORGE GEORGIOU; 35 brs and three international units.

Bank of Cyprus Public Company Ltd: POB 21472, 51 Stassinos St, Ayia Paraskevi, 2002 Strovolos 140, 1599 Nicosia; tel. 22842100; fax 22378111; e-mail info@cy.bankofcyprus.com; internet www.bankofcyprus.com; f. 1899; reconstituted 1943 by the amalgamation of Bank of Cyprus, Larnaca Bank Ltd and Famagusta Bank Ltd; cap. 899m., res 2,030m., dep. 30,654m. (Dec. 2011); Chair. ANDREAS ARTEMIS; 143 brs in Cyprus, 452 brs abroad.

Co-operative Central Bank Ltd: POB 24537, 8 Gregoris Afxentiou St, 1389 Nicosia; tel. 22743000; fax 22670261; e-mail coopbank.gm@ccb.com.cy; internet www.ccb.coop.com.cy; f. 1937 under the Co-operative Societies Law; banking and credit facilities to mem. societies, importer and distributor of agricultural requisites, insurance agent; cap. 86m., res 27m., dep. 3,939m. (Dec. 2010); Chair. GEORGE JOSEF; CEO and Gen. Man. EROTOKRITOS CHLORAKIOTIS; 4 brs.

Cyprus Popular Bank Public Co Ltd (Laiki Bank): POB 22032, Laiki Bank Bldg, 154 Limassol Ave, 1598 Nicosia; tel. 22552000; fax 22811496; e-mail laiki.telebank@laiki.com; internet www.laiki.com; f. 1901 as People's Savings Bank of Limassol; fmrly Marfin Popular Bank; name changed as above in Apr. 2012; full commercial banking; cap. 1,369m., res 2,132m., dep. 29,786m. (Dec. 2011); Chair. ANDREAS PHILLIPOU; Group CEO CHRISTOS STYLIANIDIS; 114 brs in Cyprus, 5 brs abroad.

Hellenic Bank Public Company Ltd: 200 cnr Limassol and Athalassa Ave, 2025 Nicosia; tel. 22500000; fax 22500050; e-mail hellenic@hellenicbank.com; internet www.hellenicbank.com; f. 1974; financial services group; cap. 132m., res 263m., dep. 7,180m. (Dec. 2011); Chair. Dr ANDREAS P. PANAYIOTOU; CEO MAKIS KERAVNOS; 70 brs in Cyprus, 27 abroad.

National Bank of Greece (Cyprus) Ltd: 15 Arch. Makarios III Ave, 1597 Nicosia; tel. 22840000; fax 22840010; e-mail cloizou@nbg.com.cy; internet www.nbg.com.cy; f. 1994 by incorporating all local business of the National Bank of Greece SA; full commercial banking; Chair. ALEXANDROS TOURKOLIAS; Man. Dir NICHOLAOS BEIS; 24 brs.

USB Bank PLC: 83 Dhigenis Akritas Ave, 1070 Nicosia; tel. 22883333; fax 22875899; e-mail usbmail@usb.com.cy; internet www.usbbank.com.cy; f. 1925 as Yialousa Savings Ltd (closed 1974, reopened 1990), renamed Universal Savings Bank Ltd 2001, became Universal Bank Public Ltd 2004, restyled as above 2009; cap. 34m., res 27m., dep. 658m. (Dec. 2011); Chair. MAURICE SEHNAOUI; 16 brs.

Turkish Cypriot Banks

(amounts in Turkish liras)

Asbank Ltd: 8 Mecidiye Sok., PK 448, Lefkoşa (Nicosia), Mersin 10, Turkey; tel. 2283023; fax 2287790; e-mail info@asbank.com.tr; internet www.asbank.com.tr; f. 1986; cap. 17m., res 3m., dep. 334m. (Dec. 2010); Chair. ALTAY ADADEMIR; Gen. Man. TASTAN M. ALTUNER; 8 brs.

CreditWest Bank Ltd: Şehit Mustafa A. Ruso Cad. No. 27, Lefkoşa (Nicosia), Mersin 10, Turkey; tel. 6780000; fax 6780026; e-mail pazarlama@creditwestbank.com; internet www.creditwestbank.com; f. 1993 as Kıbrıs Altinbaş Bank Ltd; name changed as above Oct. 2006; cap. 10m., res 21m., dep. 457m. (Dec. 2010); Pres. SOFU ALTINBAŞ; Gen. Man. SÜLEYMAN EROL; 13 brs.

Kıbrıs Continental Bank Ltd: 35–37 Girne Cad., Lefkoşa (Nicosia), Mersin 10, Turkey; tel. 2273220; fax 2286334; e-mail info@kibriscontinentalbank.net; internet www.kibriscontinentalbank.net; f. 1998; cap. 10m., res –5m., dep. 47m. (Dec. 2009); Chair. OSMAN KARAISMAILOĞLU; Gen. Man. SERACETTIN BAKTAY.

Kıbrıs Iktisat Bankasi Ltd (Cyprus Economy Bank Ltd): 151 Bedreddin Demiral Cad., Lefkoşa (Nicosia), Mersin 10, Turkey; tel. 6004000; fax 2281311; e-mail info@iktisatbank.com; internet www.iktisatbank.com; f. 1990; cap. 21m., res 11m., dep. 606m. (Dec. 2010); Chair. METE OZMERTER; 17 brs.

Kıbrıs Türk Kooperatif Merkez Bankası Ltd (Cyprus Turkish Co-operative Central Bank): PK 823, 49–55 Mahmut Paşa Sok., Lefkoşa (Nicosia), Mersin 10, Turkey; tel. 2273398; fax 2276787; e-mail info@koopbank.com; internet www.koopbank.com; f. 1959; cap. 18m., res 121m., dep. 1,870m. (Dec. 2009); banking and credit facilities to mem. societies and individuals; Chair. ÜSTÜN TURAN; Gen. Man. GÜLHAN ALP; 20 brs.

Kıbrıs Vakiflar Bankası Ltd (Cyprus Vakiflar Bank Ltd): PK 212, 66 Atatürk Cad., Yenisehir, Lefkoşa (Nicosia), Mersin 10, Turkey; tel. 2275169; fax 2285872; e-mail kvb@kktc.net; internet www.vakiflarbankasi.com; f. 1982; cap. 40m., res 15m., dep. 667m. (Dec. 2011); Chair. MEHMET SALIH YILDIRIR; 13 brs.

Limassol Turkish Co-operative Bank Ltd: 10 Orhaneli Sok., Kyrenia, PK 247, Mersin 10, Turkey; tel. 2280333; fax 2281350; e-mail info@limasolbank.com.tr; internet www.limasolbank.com; f. 1939; cap. 11m., res -2m., dep. 196m. (Dec. 2009); Chair. HÜSEYIN KEMALER; Gen. Man. AHMET GÜNDÜZ.

Türk Bankası Ltd (Turkish Bank Ltd): 92 Girne Cad., PK 242, Lefkoşa (Nicosia), Mersin 10, Turkey; tel. 2283313; fax 2282432; e-mail info@turkishbank.net; internet www.turkishbank.com; f. 1901; cap. 61m., res 24m., dep. 654m. (Dec. 2010); Chair. HAKAN BORTECENE; CEO ERHAN ÖZÇELIK; 21 brs.

Viyabank Ltd: Atatürk Cad., 16 Muhtar Yusuf Galleria, Lefkoşa (Nicosia), Mersin 10, Turkey; tel. 2285286; fax 2285878; e-mail gm@viyabank.com; internet www.viyabank.com; f. 1998; cap. 40m., res 11m., dep. 19m. (Dec. 2010); Pres. and Chair. SALVO TARAGANO; 1 br.

Yakin Dogu Bank Ltd (Near East Bank Ltd): POB 47, 1 Girne Cad., Lefkoşa (Nicosia), Mersin 10, Turkey; tel. 2283834; fax 2284180; e-mail ydbank@kktc.net; internet www.yakindogubank.com; cap. 24m., res 2m., dep. 246m. (Dec. 2011); Chair. Dr SUAT I. GÜNSEL; Gen. Man. SELCUK BURAT; 7 brs.

Yeşilada Bank Ltd: POB 626, 11 Atatürk Ave, Lefkoşa (Nicosia), Mersin 10, Turkey; tel. 2281789; fax 2277106; e-mail info@yesilada-bank.com; internet www.yesilada-bank.com; cap. 8m., res –8m., dep. 28m. (Dec. 2009); Chair. and Pres. ISMET KOTAK; Gen. Man. MUSTAFA UZUN.

Investment Organization

The Cyprus Investment and Securities Corpn Ltd: POB 20597, 1660 Nicosia; tel. 22881700; fax 22338488; e-mail info@cisco.bankofcyprus.com; internet www.cisco-online.com.cy; f. 1982 to promote the devt of capital market; brokerage services, fund management, investment banking; mem. of Bank of Cyprus Group; issued cap. 22m. (2004); Chair. DEMETRIS IOANNOU; Gen. Man. ANNA SOFRONIOU.

Development Bank

The Cyprus Development Bank Public Company Ltd: POB 21415, Alpha House, 50 Archbishop Makarios III Ave, 1065 Nicosia; tel. 22846500; fax 22846600; internet www.cyprusdevelopmentbank.com; f. 1963; cap. 21m., res 19m., dep. 304m. (Dec. 2009); aims to accelerate the economic devt of Cyprus by providing medium- and long-term loans for productive projects, developing the capital market, encouraging jt ventures, and providing technical and managerial advice to productive private enterprises; Chair. RENA ROUVITHA PANOU; CEO KYRIACOS IACOVIDES; 1 br.

STOCK EXCHANGE

Cyprus Stock Exchange: POB 25427, 71–73 Lordou Vyronos Ave, 1309 Nicosia; tel. 22712300; fax 22570308; e-mail info@cse.com.cy; internet www.cse.com.cy; f. 1996; official trading commenced in March 1996; 135 cos listed in Feb. 2009; Chair. GIORGOS KOUFARIS; Dir-Gen. NONDAS METAXAS.

INSURANCE

Insurance Companies Control Service: Ministry of Finance, POB 23364, 1682 Nicosia; tel 22602952; fax 22660135; e-mail insurance@mof.gov.cy; internet www.mof.gov.cy; f. 1969 to control insurance cos, insurance agents, brokers and agents for brokers in Cyprus; Superintendent VICTORIA NATAR.

Greek Cypriot Insurance Companies

Atlantic Insurance Co Public Ltd: POB 24579, 15 Espiridon St, 1301 Nicosia; tel. 22886000; fax 22886111; e-mail atlantic@atlantic

.com.cy; internet www.atlantic.com.cy; f. 1983; general, non-life; Chair. and Man. Dir EMILIOS PYRISHIS.

Cosmos Insurance Co Public Ltd: Cosmos Tower, 46 Griva Digeni St, 1080 Nicosia; POB 21770, 1513 Nicosia; tel. 22796000; fax 22022000; e-mail info@cosmosinsurance.com.cy; internet www.cosmosinsurance.com.cy; f. 1981; present name adopted 2004; general; Pres. ANDREAS P. EROTOKRITOU; Man. Dir ANDREAS K. TYLLIS.

Eurolife Ltd: POB 21655, Eurolife House, 4 Evrou, 1511 Nicosia; tel. 22474000; fax 22341090; e-mail info@eurolife.bankofcyprus.com; internet www.eurolife.com.cy; wholly owned subsidiary of Bank of Cyprus; life, accident and health; CEO ARTEMIS PANTELIDOU.

General Insurance of Cyprus Ltd: POB 21668, 2–4 Themistoklis Dervis St, 1511 Nicosia; tel. 22128705; fax 22676682; e-mail general@gic.bankofcyprus.com; internet www.gic.com.cy; f. 1951; wholly owned subsidiary of Bank of Cyprus; general, non-life; CEO STELIOS CHRISTODOULOU.

Hellenic Alico Life Insurance Ltd: POB 20672, 38 Kennedy Ave, 1662 Nicosia; tel. 22450650; fax 22450750; e-mail life@hellenicalico.com; internet www.hellenicbank.com; f. by merger of Hellenic Bank PCL and Alico AIG Life; 72.5% stake owned by Hellenic Bank PCL; Chair. and Man. Dir CHRISTOS A. ANTONIOU.

Laiki Cyprialife Ltd: POB 20819, 64 Archbishop Makarios III Ave and 1 Karpenisiou St, 1077 Nicosia; tel. 22887300; fax 22374460; e-mail pmichaelides@laiki.com; internet www.laiki.com; f. 1995; wholly owned subsidiary of Marfin Popular Bank; life, accident and health; CEO POLIS MICHAELIDES.

Laiki Insurance Co Ltd: POB 25218, 45 Vyzantiou St, Strovolos, 1307 Nicosia; tel. 22887600; fax 22887501; e-mail anstylianou@cnpmarfin.com; internet www.laiki.com; f. 1981; subsidiary of Marfin Popular Bank and CNP Assurances; general; Gen. Man. ANDREAS STYLIANOU.

Minerva Insurance Co Public Ltd: POB 23544, 1684 Nicosia; tel. 22551616; fax 22551717; e-mail minerva@minerva.com.cy; f. 1970; general and life; CEO COSTAKIS KOUTSOKOUMNIS.

Pancyprian Insurance Ltd: POB 21352, Pancyprian Tower, 66 Grivas Dhigenis Ave, 1095 Nicosia; tel. 22743743; fax 22677656; e-mail pancyprian@hellenicbank.com; internet www.pancyprianinsurance.com; f. 1992; wholly owned subsidiary of Hellenic Bank PCL; general, non-life; CEO SOCRATES DEMETRIOU.

Prime Insurance Co Ltd: POB 22475, 1522 Nicosia; tel. 22896000; fax 22767768; e-mail info@primeinsurance.eu; internet www.primeinsurance.eu; acquired by Demco Insurance Ltd (Greece) May 2011; fmrly Interlife Insurance Co; present name adopted Sept. 2011; life and general; Man. Dir MICHALIS MICHAELIDES.

Universal Life Insurance Public Company Ltd: POB 21270, Universal Tower, 85 Dhigenis Akritas Ave, 1505 Nicosia; tel. 22882222; fax 22882200; e-mail info@unilife.com.cy; internet www.universallife.com.cy; f. 1970; life, accident, health and general; Chair. PHOTOS PHOTIADES; CEO and Man. Dir ANDREAS GEORGHIOU.

Greek Cypriot Insurance Association

Insurance Association of Cyprus: POB 22030, Insurance Centre, 23 Zenon Sozos St, 1st Floor, 1516 Nicosia; tel. 22452990; fax 22374288; e-mail info@iac.org.cy; internet www.iac.org.cy; 29 mem. cos; Chair. PHILIOS ZACHARIADES; Dir-Gen. STEPHIE DRACOS.

Turkish Cypriot Insurance Companies

Akfinans Sigorta Insurance Ltd: 16 Osman Paşa Cad., Lefkoşa (Nicosia), POB 451, Mersin 10, Turkey; tel. 2284506; fax 2285713; e-mail akfinans@akfinans.com; internet www.akfinans.com; f. 1996; Gen. Man. MEHMET KADER.

Anadolu Anonim: Memduh Asaf Sokak 8, Lefkoşa (Nicosia), Mersin 10, Turkey; tel. 2279595; fax 2279596; e-mail bolge50@anadolusigorta.com.tr; internet www.anadolusigorta.com.tr.

Ankara Sigorta: PK 551, Bedrettin Demirel Cad., Lefkoşa (Nicosia), Mersin 10, Turkey; tel. 2285815; fax 2283099; internet www.ankarasigorta.com.tr.

ERGOİSVİÇRE Sigorta AŞ: Şehit Mustafa Ahmet Ruso Cad. Küçükkaymaklı, Lefkoşa (Nicosia), Mersin 10, Turkey; tel. 2282125; fax 2288236; internet www.ergoisvicre.com.tr; acquired by ERGO Versicherungsgruppe AG (Germany) in 2008.

Gold Insurance Ltd: Salih Mecit Sok. 9, Lefkoşa (Nicosia), Mersin 10, Turkey; tel. and fax 2286500; fax 2286300; e-mail info@gold-insurance.com; internet www.gold-insurance.com; f. 1996; Man. Dir ULKER FAHRI.

Groupama Sigorta: Mehmet Akif Cad. 95, Lefkoşa (Nicosia), Mersin 10, Turkey; tel. 2280208; fax 2286160; e-mail n.kural@groupama.com.tr; internet www.groupama.com.tr; Man. NAMIK KEMAL KURAL.

Güneş Sigorta AŞ: Şehit Mustafa Ahmet Ruso Cad., Küçükkaymaklı, Galeria Muhtar İş Merkezi 218, Lefkoşa (Nicosia), Mersin 10, Turkey; tel. 2286690; fax 2292657; internet www.gunessigorta.com.tr.

Kıbrıs Sigorta STI Ltd (Cyprus Insurance Co Ltd): Abdi İpekçi Cad., Eti Binaları, Lefkoşa (Nicosia), Mersin 10, Turkey; tel. 2283022; fax 2279277; e-mail info@kibris-sigorta.com; internet www.kibris-sigorta.com; Man. Dir MEHMET UĞUR KIRAZ.

Ray Sigorta AŞ: Bedrettin Demirel Cad., Arabacıoğlu Apt 7, Lefkoşa (Nicosia), Mersin 10, Turkey; tel. 2270380; fax 2270383; internet www.raysigorta.com.tr.

Şeker Sigorta (Kıbrıs) Ltd: Mahmut Paşa Sok. 14/A, PK 664, Lefkoşa (Nicosia), Mersin 10, Turkey; tel. 2285883; fax 2274074; e-mail bilgi@sekersigorta-kibris.com; internet www.sekersigorta-kibris.com; Man. Dir AHMET ERASLAN.

Turkish Cypriot Insurance Association

Kuzey Kıbrıs Sigorta ve Reasürans Şirketleri Birliği (Insurance and Reinsurance Association of Northern Cyprus): Selim Cad. 49, Arca Apartment No. 3, Lefkoşa (Nicosia), Mersin 10, Turkey; tel. 2280937; fax 2286483; e-mail info@kksrsb.org; internet www.kksrsb.org; 32 mem. cos; Pres. ÜLKER FAHRI.

Trade and Industry

GREEK CYPRIOT CHAMBERS OF COMMERCE AND INDUSTRY

Cyprus Chamber of Commerce and Industry: POB 21455, 38 Grivas Dhigenis Ave, 1509 Nicosia; tel. 22889800; fax 22669048; e-mail chamber@ccci.org.cy; internet www.ccci.org.cy; f. 1927; Pres. MANTHOS MAVROMMATIS; Sec.-Gen. PANAYIOTIS LOIZIDES; 8,000 mems, 120 affiliated trade asscns.

Famagusta Chamber of Commerce and Industry: POB 53124, 339 Ayiou Andreou St, Andrea Chambers Bldg, 2nd Floor, Office No. 201, 3300 Limassol; tel. 25370165; fax 25370291; e-mail chamberf@cytanet.com.cy; internet www.famagustachamber.org.cy; f. 1952; Pres. GEORGE MICHAELIDES; Sec. and Dir IACOVOS HADJIVARNAVAS; 400 mems and 200 assoc. mems.

Larnaca Chamber of Commerce and Industry: POB 40287, 12 Gregoriou Afxentiou St, Skouros Bldg, Apt 43, 4th Floor, 6302 Larnaca; tel. 24655051; fax 24628281; e-mail lcci@spidernet.com.cy; f. 1954; Pres. ANDREAS LOUROUTZIATIS; Sec. GEORGE PSARAS; 600 mems and 25 assoc. mems.

Limassol Chamber of Commerce and Industry: 170 Franklin Roosevelt Ave, 3045 Limassol; POB 55699, 3781 Limassol; tel. 25877350; fax 25661655; e-mail info@limassolchamber.eu; internet www.limassolchamber.eu; f. 1962; Pres. PHILOKYPROS ANDREOU; Sec. and Dir CHRISTOS ANASTASSIADES; 800 mems.

Nicosia Chamber of Commerce and Industry: POB 21455, 38 Grivas Dhigenis Ave, Chamber Bldg, 1509 Nicosia; tel. 22889600; fax 22667433; e-mail reception@ncci.org.cy; internet www.ncci.org.cy; f. 1952; Pres. COSTAS GEORGALLIS; Dir SOCRATES HERACLEOUS; 1,520 mems.

Paphos Chamber of Commerce and Industry: POB 82, Tolmi Court, 1st Floor, cnr Athinon Ave and Alexandrou Papayou Ave, 8100 Paphos; tel. 26818173; fax 26944602; e-mail evepafos@cytanet.com.cy; internet www.pcci.org.cy; Pres. THEODOROS ARISTODEMOU; Sec. KENDEAS ZAMPIRINIS; 530 mems and 6 assoc. mems.

TURKISH CYPRIOT CHAMBERS OF COMMERCE AND INDUSTRY

Turkish Cypriot Chamber of Commerce: 90 Bedrettin Demirel Cad., PK 718, Lefkoşa (Nicosia), Mersin 10, Turkey; tel. 2283645; fax 2283089; e-mail ktto@ktto.net; internet www.ktto.net; f. 1958; Pres. GÜNAY ÇERKEZ; Sec.-Gen. JANEL BURCAN; more than 9,000 mems.

Turkish Cypriot Chamber of Industry: 126 Mehmet Akif Cad., Lefkoşa (Nicosia), Mersin 10, Turkey; tel. 2258131; fax 2258130; e-mail info@kibso.org; internet www.kibso.org; f. 1977; Pres. ALI ÇIRALI; Sec.-Gen. DOĞA DÖNMEZER; 600 mems.

GREEK CYPRIOT EMPLOYERS' ORGANIZATION

Cyprus Employers' & Industrialists' Federation: POB 21657, 2 Acropoleos Ave, 1511 Nicosia; tel. 22665102; fax 22669459; e-mail info@oeb.org.cy; internet www.oeb.org.cy; f. 1960; 64 mem. trade asscns, 500 direct and 4,500 indirect mems; Chair. PHILIOS ZACHARIADES; Dir-Gen. MICHAEL PILIKOS; the largest of the trade asscn mems are: Cyprus Building Contractors' Asscn; Land and Building Developers' Asscn; Asscn of Cyprus Tourist Enterprises; Cyprus Shipping Asscn; Cyprus Footwear Mfrs' Asscn; Cyprus Metal Industries Asscn; Cyprus Bankers Employers' Asscn; Cyprus Asscn of Business Consultants; Mechanical Contractors Asscn of Cyprus; Union of Solar Energy Industries of Cyprus.

TURKISH CYPRIOT EMPLOYERS' ORGANIZATION

Kıbrıs Türk İşverenler Sendikası (Turkish Cypriot Employers' Association): PK 674, Lefkoşa (Nicosia), Mersin 10, Turkey; tel. 2273673; fax 2277479; Chair. HASAN SUNGUR.

GREEK CYPRIOT UTILITIES

Electricity

Electricity Authority of Cyprus (EAC): POB 24506, 1399 Nicosia; tel. 22201000; fax 22201020; e-mail eac@eac.com.cy; internet www.eac.com.cy; generation, transmission and distribution of electric energy in govt-controlled area; also licensed to install and commercially exploit wired telecommunication network; total installed capacity 1,118 MW in 2008; Chair. CHARALAMBOS TSOURIS; Gen. Man. STELIOS STYLIANOU.

Water

Water Development Department: 100–110 Kennenty Ave, 1047 Pallouriotissa, Nicosia; tel. 22609000; fax 22675019; e-mail eioannou@wdd.moa.gov.cy; internet www.moa.gov.cy/wdd; f. 1939; owned by Ministry of Agriculture, Natural Resources and the Environment; dam storage capacity 327.5m. cu m; Dir Dr KYRIACOS KYROU.

TURKISH CYPRIOT UTILITIES

Electricity

Cyprus Turkish Electricity Corpn: Lefkoşa (Nicosia), Mersin 10, Turkey; tel. 2283730; fax 2291318; e-mail info@kibtek.com; internet www.kibtek.com; Chair. MUSTAFA HARUTOĞLU.

MAJOR COMPANIES

Greek Cypriot Companies

Covotsos Textiles Ltd: POB 51090, Kato Polemidia Industrial Area, Acharnon St, 4180 Limassol; tel. 25391344; fax 25390754.

Cyprus Canning Co Ltd: POB 50209, 1 Franklin Roosevelt Ave, 3602 Limassol; tel. 25853100; fax 25573429; f. 1954.

Cyprus Forest Industries Public Ltd: POB 24043, 1700 Nicosia; tel. 22872700; fax 22833564; e-mail cfi@cfi.com.cy; internet www.cfi.com.cy; Pres. STELIOS PAPADOPOULOS; CEO PETROS VRAHIMIS.

Cyprus Phassouri Plantations Co Ltd: POB 50180, 3601 Limassol; tel. 25876000; fax 25952225; e-mail info@redseal-quality.com; internet www.redseal-quality.com.

Cyprus Trading Corporation Public Ltd: POB 21744, Shacolas House, 1589 Nicosia; tel. 22740300; fax 22485385; e-mail ctc@ctcgroup.com; internet www.ctcgroup.com; Exec. Chair. NICOLAS K. SHACOLAS; Man. Dir MARIOS LOUCAIDES.

Keo PLC: POB 50209, 1 Franklin Roosevelt Ave, 3602 Limassol; tel. 25853100; fax 25573429; e-mail keo@keogroup.com; internet www.keogroup.com; f. 1927 as Keo Ltd; renamed as above in 2006; cap. C£7.1m.; mfrs of wine, beer and spirits, fruit juices, canned vegetables and mineral water; Chair. COSTAS KOUTSOS; Man. Dir CHARALAMBOS PANAGIOTOU; 440 employees.

Vassiliko Cement Works Ltd: POB 22281, 1519 Nicosia; tel. 24845555; fax 24332651; e-mail info@vassiliko.com; internet www.vassiliko.com; f. 1963; cap. C£63.8m.; cement mfrs; Exec. Chair. ANTONIS ANTONIOU; Gen. Man. GEORGE A. SIDERIS; 200 employees.

Turkish Cypriot Companies

Cypfruvex Ltd: Güzelyurt, PK 433, Lefkoşa (Nicosia), Mersin 10, Turkey; tel. 2243495; e-mail info@cypfruvex.com; internet www.cypfruvex.com; f. 1974; state-owned; fruit exporters; Gen. Man. HÜSEYIN KOZAL (acting).

Eti Ltd: Abdi İpekci Cad., PK 452, Lefkoşa (Nicosia), Mersin 10, Turkey; tel. 2273610; fax 2272873; e-mail etisatinalma@yahoo.com; state-owned; import and distribution of foodstuffs.

Hilmi Toros Industry Ltd: Mehmet Akif Ave, PK 526, Lefkoşa (Nicosia), Mersin 10, Turkey; tel. 2272412; fax 2287574; textile and clothing mfrs.

Kıbrıs Türk Petrolleri Ltd, Şti (Turkish Cypriot Petroleum Co Ltd): Gazi Mağusa (Famagusta), PK 117, Mersin 10, Turkey; tel. 3832645; fax 2365230; import, storage and distribution of petroleum and petroleum derivatives.

Kıbrıs Türk Tütün Endüstri Ltd (Turkish Cypriot Tobacco Industry Ltd): 27 Atatürk Cad., Lefkoşa (Nicosia), Mersin 10, Turkey; tel. 2273403; fax 2273394; state-owned; cigarette mfrs.

Learned Ltd: Lefkoşa (Nicosia), Mersin 10, Turkey; hotels, packaging, fruit processing; Dir SIDIKA ATALAY.

TAŞEL (Turkish Spirits and Wine Enterprises Ltd): Gazi Mağusa (Famagusta), PK 48, Mersin 10, Turkey; tel. 2365440; fax 2366330; f. 1961; state-owned; mfrs of alcoholic beverages; Gen. Man. HASAN YUMUK.

Toprak Ürünleri Kurumu (Agricultural Products Board): PK 773, Lefkoşa (Nicosia), Mersin 10, Turkey; tel. 2283211; e-mail info@toprakkurumu.org; internet www.toprakkurumu.org; state-owned; potato exporters; Chair. AHMET İZZI TÜRKEL; Man. Dir RAĞIB RATIP.

TRADE UNIONS

Greek Cypriot Trade Unions

Cyprus Civil Servants' Trade Union (PASYDY): 3 Demosthenis Severis Ave, 1066 Nicosia; tel. 22844445; fax 22668639; e-mail pasydy@spidernet.com.cy; internet www.pasydy.org; f. 1927; regd 1966; restricted to persons in the civil employment of the Govt and public authorities; 6 brs with a total membership of 15,383; Pres. ANTONIS KOUTSOULIS; Gen. Sec. GLAFKOS HADJIPETROU.

Dimokratiki Ergatiki Omospondia Kyprou (DEOK) (Democratic Labour Federation of Cyprus): POB 21625, 40 Byron Ave, 1511 Nicosia; tel. 22872177; fax 22670494; e-mail deok@cytanet.com.cy; internet www.deok.org.cy; f. 1962; 5 workers' unions with a total membership of 9,220; Gen. Sec. DIOMEDES DIOMEDOUS.

Pankypria Ergatiki Omospondia (PEO) (Pancyprian Federation of Labour): POB 21885, 31–35 Archermos St, Nicosia 1045; tel. 22886400; fax 22349382; e-mail info@peo.org.cy; internet www.peo.org.cy; f. 1946; regd 1947; previously the Pancyprian Trade Union Cttee (f. 1941, dissolved 1946); 8 unions and 176 brs with a total membership of 75,000; affiliated to WFTU; Gen. Sec. PAMBIS KYRITSIS.

Pankypria Omospondia Anexartition Syntechnion (Pancyprian Federation of Independent Trade Unions): 168 Athalassa Ave, Office 401, Minos Court; 2025 Nicosia; tel. and fax 22516600; fax 22516717; e-mail info@poas.org.cy; internet www.poas.org.cy; f. 1957; regd 1957; has no political orientation; 10 unions with a total membership of 1,842; Gen. Sec. GREGORY KATSELLIS.

Synomospondia Ergazomenon Kyprou (SEK) (Cyprus Workers' Confederation): POB 25018, 11 Strovolos Ave, 2018 Strovolos, 1306 Nicosia; tel. 22849849; fax 22849850; e-mail sek@sek.org.cy; internet www.sek.org.cy; f. 1944; regd 1950; 7 federations, 5 labour centres, 47 unions, 12 brs with a total membership of 65,000; affiliated to ITUC and the European Trade Union Confed; Gen. Sec. NIKOS MOYSEOS.

Union of Cyprus Journalists: POB 23495, Rik Ave 12, 1683 Nicosia; tel. 22446090; fax 22446095; e-mail cyjourun@logosnet.cy.net; internet www.esk.org.cy; f. 1960; Pres. ANDREAS KANNAOUROS; Gen. Sec. ANDROULA GEORGIADOU.

Turkish Cypriot Trade Unions

Devrimci İşçi Sendikaları Federasyonu (Dev-İş) (Revolutionary Trade Unions' Federation): 6 Serabioğlu Sok., 748 Lefkoşa (Nicosia), Mersin 10, Turkey; tel. 2272640; fax 2286463; e-mail dev-is@defne.net; internet www.dev-is.org; f. 1976; 4 unions with a total membership of 1,850 (2002); affiliated to WFTU; Pres. MEHMET SEYIS; Gen. Sec. HASAN FELEK.

Kıbrıs Türk İşçi Sendikaları Federasyonu (TÜRK-SEN) (Turkish Cypriot Trade Union Federation): POB 829, 7–7A Şehit Mehmet R. Hüseyin Sok., Lefkoşa (Nicosia), Mersin 10, Turkey; tel. 2272444; fax 2287831; e-mail erkan.birer@turk-sen.org; internet www.turk-sen.org; f. 1954; regd 1955; affiliated to ITUC, the European Trade Union Confed., the Commonwealth Trade Union Council and the Confed. of Trade Unions of Turkey (Türk-İş); Pres. ARSLAN BIÇAKLI; Gen. Sec. ERKAN BIRER.

Transport

RAILWAYS

There are no railways in Cyprus.

ROADS

According to the International Road Federation, in 2010 there were 12,483 km of roads in the government-controlled areas, of which 2,186 km were motorways, 257 km were highways and main or national roads, and 3,226 km were secondary or regional roads. The Nicosia–Limassol four-lane dual carriageway, which was completed in 1985, was subsequently extended with the completion of the Limassol and Larnaca bypasses. Highways also connect Nicosia and Larnaca, Nicosia and Anthoupolis-Kokkinotrimithia, Larnaca and Kophinou, Aradippo and Dhekelia, Limassol and Paphos, and Dhekelia and Ammochostos (Famagusta). The north and south are now served by separate transport systems, and there are no services linking the two sectors.

SHIPPING

Until 1974 Famagusta, a natural port, was the island's most important harbour, handling about 83% of the country's cargo. Since its capture by the Turkish army in August of that year the port has been officially declared closed to international traffic. However, it continues to serve the Turkish-occupied region.

The main ports that serve the island's maritime trade at present are Larnaca and Limassol. There is also an industrial port at Vassiliko, and there are three specialized petroleum terminals, at Larnaca, Dhekelia and Moni. In August 2012 the Government awarded a contract for a three-phase redevelopment (on a build-operate-transfer basis) of Larnaca port and its subsequent management to the international Zenon Consortium. Construction was expected to commence in 2013, and to cost an estimated €700m.

In addition to serving local traffic, Limassol and Larnaca ports act as transshipment load centres and as regional warehouse and assembly bases. Both Kyrenia and Karavostassi are under Turkish occupation and have been declared closed to international traffic. A hydrofoil service operates between Kyrenia and Mersin on the Turkish mainland.

At 31 December 2012 the Greek Cypriot shipping registry comprised 1,146 flag registered vessels, with an aggregate displacement of 20.6m. grt, of which 287 were bulk carriers, six were fish carriers, 10 were gas tankers and 185 were general cargo ships.

Port and Regulatory Authorities

Department of Merchant Shipping: POB 56193, Kylinis St, Mesa Geitonia, 4007 Limassol; tel. 25848100; fax 25848200; e-mail maritimeadmin@dms.mcw.gov.cy; internet www.shipping.gov.cy; f. 1977; Dir SERGHIOS S. SERGHIOU.

Cyprus Ports Authority: POB 22007, 23 Crete St, 1516 Nicosia; tel. 22817200; fax 22765420; e-mail cpa@cpa.gov.cy; internet www.cpa.gov.cy; f. 1973; Chair. CHRYSIS PRENTZAS.

Greek Cypriot Shipping Companies

Ahrenkiel Shipmanagement (Cyprus) Ltd: POB 53594, 4th Floor, O & A Tower, 25 Olympion St, 3033 Limassol; tel. 25854000; fax 25854001; e-mail infocy@ahrenkiel.net; internet www.ahrenkiel.net; f. 1977; Man. Dir VASSOS STAVROU.

Amer Shipping Ltd: POB 27363, 701 Ghinis Bldg, 58–60 Dhigenis Akritas Ave, 1644 Nicosia; tel. 22875188; fax 22756556; e-mail ateam@amershipping.com; internet www.amershipping.com; f. 1989; Man. Dir ANIL DESHPANDE.

Bernhard Schulte Shipmanagement (Cyprus) Ltd: Hanseatic House, 111 Spyrou Araouzou St, POB 50127, 3036 Limassol; tel. 25846400; fax 25745245; e-mail cy-sdc-man@bs-shipmanagement.com; internet www.bs-shipmanagement.com; f. 1972; CEO ANDREAS J. DROUSSIOTIS.

Columbia Shipmanagement Ltd: Dodekanissou St, 4043 Limassol; tel. 25843100; fax 25320325; e-mail marketing@csmcy.com; internet www.columbia.com.cy; f. 1978; Man. Dir DIRK FRY.

Cyprus Shipping Chamber: POB 56607, City Chambers, 1st Floor, 6 Regas Fereos St, 3309 Limassol; tel. 25360717; fax 25358642; e-mail csc@csc-cy.org; internet www.csc-cy.org; f. 1989; Dir-Gen. THOMAS A. KAZAKOS.

Interorient Navigation Co Ltd: POB 51309, 142 Franklin Roosevelt Ave, 3504 Limassol; tel. 25840300; fax 25575895; e-mail management@interorient.com.cy; internet www.interorient.com; Man. Dir JAN LISSOW.

Louis Cruise Lines: 11 Lemessos Ave, 2112 Nicosia; tel. 22588168; fax 22442957; e-mail investors@louisgroup.com; internet www.louisgroup.com; f. 1935; Exec. Chair. COSTAKIS LOIZOU.

Marlow Navigation Co Ltd: POB 54077, 13 Alexandrias St, 3720 Limassol; tel. 25882588; fax 25882599; e-mail marlow@marlow.com.cy; internet www.marlownavigation.com.cy; f. 1982; Chair. HERMANN EDEN; Man. Dirs ANDREAS NEOPHYTOU, JAN MEYERING.

Oldendorff Ltd, Reederei 'Nord' Klaus E: POB 56345, Libra Tower, 23 Olympion St, 3306 Limassol; tel. 25841400; fax 25345077; e-mail mail@rnkeo.com.cy; internet www.rnkeo.com; f. 1964; Chair. and Man. Dir CHRISTIANE E. OLDENDORFF; Gen. Man. Capt. KEITH V. OBEYESEKERA.

Turkish Cypriot Shipping Companies

Ak-Günler Co Ltd: Girne (Kyrenia), Mersin 10, Turkey; tel. 8156002; fax 8153268; e-mail denizcilik@akgunler.com.tr; internet www.akgunler.com.tr; f. 1978; operates a fleet of 8 passenger and cargo vessels; Man. Dir İÇIM KAVUKLU; Gen. Man. HAMIT GÖRGÜN.

Armen Shipping Ltd: Altun Tabya, St 10/1, Gazi Mağusa (Famagusta), Mersin 10, Turkey; tel. 3664086; fax 3665860; e-mail armen@armenshipping.com; internet www.armenshipping.com; provides transportation services, shipping agency services and customer clearance facilities; Dir VARGIN VARER.

Fergün Shipping Co: Girne Yeni Liman Yolu, Fergün Apt 1, Girne (Kyrenia), Mersin 10, Turkey; tel. 8151770; fax 8151989; e-mail info@fergun.ne; internet www.fergun.net; ferries to Turkish ports; Owner FEHIM KÜÇÜK.

Kıbrıs Türk Denizcilik Ltd, Şti (Turkish Cypriot Maritime Co Ltd): 3 Bülent Ecevit Bul., Gazi Mağusa (Famagusta), Mersin 10, Turkey; tel. 3665995; fax 3667840; e-mail cypship@superonline.com.

Tahsin Transtürk ve Oğlu Ltd: 11 Kizilkule Yolu, Gazi Mağusa (Famagusta), Mersin 10, Turkey; tel. 3665409; fax 3660330.

CIVIL AVIATION

There is an international airport at Nicosia, which has been closed since 1974, following the Turkish invasion. A new international airport was constructed at Larnaca, from which flights operate to Europe, the USA, the Middle East and Asia. Another international airport at Paphos began operations in 1983. A project to expand and modernize Larnaca and Paphos airports commenced in June 2006; by November 2008 the new terminal at Paphos airport was fully operational, and the new Larnaca airport, with an annual capacity of 7.5m. passengers, was inaugurated in November 2009.

In 1975 the Turkish authorities opened Ercan (fmrly Tymbou) airport, and a second airport was opened at Geçitkale (Lefkoniko) in 1986. However, only Turkey and Azerbaijan recognize the airports as legitimate points of entry; flights from all other countries involve a preliminary stopover at one of Turkey's airports.

Cyprus Airways: POB 21903, 21 Alkeou St, Engomi, 2404 Nicosia; tel. 22661800; fax 22663167; e-mail webcenter@cyprusairways.com; internet cyprusair.com; f. 1947; jointly owned by Cyprus Govt (93.67%) and local interests; services throughout Europe and the Middle East; Chair. STAVROS STAVROU; CEO GEORGE MAVROCOSTAS.

Tourism

In 2012 an estimated 2.5m. foreign tourists visited the Greek Cypriot area, while receipts from tourism amounted to some €1,927.7m.

In 2010 some 902,390 tourists, 741,925 of whom were from Turkey, visited the Turkish Cypriot area, while revenue from tourism amounted to US $405.8m.

Cyprus Tourism Organisation (CTO): POB 24535, 19 Leoforos Lemesou, Aglantzia, 1390 Nicosia; tel. 22691100; fax 22334696; e-mail cytour@visitcyprus.com; internet www.visitcyprus.com; Chair. ALECOS OROUNTIOTIS.

North Cyprus Tourism Centre: Ministry of Tourism, Environment and Culture, Selçuklu Rd, Lefkoşa (Nicosia), Mersin 10, Turkey; tel. 2289629; fax 2285625; e-mail info@northcyprus.cc; internet www.northcyprus.cc; headquarters based in London, United Kingdom.

Defence

The House of Representatives authorized the formation of the National Guard in 1964, after the withdrawal of the Turkish members. Men aged between 18 and 50 years are liable to 24 months' conscription. As assessed at November 2012, the National Guard comprised an army of 12,000 regulars, mainly composed of Cypriot conscripts (some 9,100) but with an estimated 200 seconded Greek Army officers and NCOs, and 50,000 reserves. A further 950 Greek army personnel were stationed in Cyprus at that time. There is also a Greek Cypriot paramilitary police force of some 750. In 2012 the defence budget for the Greek Cypriot area was some €204m. As assessed at November 2012, the 'TRNC' had an army of an estimated 3,500 regulars and 26,000 reserves. There was also a paramilitary armed police force of about 150. Men between 18 and 50 years of age are liable to 24 months' conscription. The 'TRNC' forces were being supported by an estimated 36,000 Turkish troops. In 2010 the defence budget for the 'TRNC' was TL 163.3m. A UN peace-keeping force is also based in Cyprus, and there are British military bases at Akrotiri, Episkopi, Ayios Nikolaos and Dhekelia.

Commander of the Greek Cypriot National Guard: Lt-Gen. STYLIANOS NASIS.

Commander of 'TRNC' Security Forces: Brig.-Gen. BAKI KAVUN.

UNITED NATIONS PEACE-KEEPING FORCE IN CYPRUS (UNFICYP)

POB 21642, 1590 Nicosia; tel. 22464000; e-mail unficyp-public-information-office@un.org; internet www.unficyp.org.

UNFICYP was established for a three-month period in March 1964 by a UN Security Council resolution (subsequently extended at intervals of three or six months by successive resolutions) to keep the peace between the Greek and Turkish communities and help to solve outstanding issues between them. In mid-1993, following an announcement by troop-providing countries that they were to withdraw a substantial number of troops, the Security Council introduced a system of financing UNFICYP by voluntary and assessed contributions. Following a significant reduction in the size of UNFICYP, as prescribed by a UN Security Council resolution adopted in October 2004, the contingent numbered 922 uniformed personnel (854 troops, 68 police), supported by 145 local and international civilian staff, at the end of July 2013.

Commander: Maj.-Gen. CHAO LIU (People's Republic of China).

Special Representative of the UN Secretary-General and Head of Mission: LISA M. BUTTENHEIM (USA).

See also the section on UN Peace-keeping Operations in the Regional Organizations section of Part Three.

BRITISH SOVEREIGN BASE AREAS

Akrotiri and Dhekelia

Headquarters British Forces Cyprus, Episkopi 3370, BFPO 53; tel. 25967295; fax 25963521; e-mail cosba@cytanet.com.cy; internet www.sba.mod.uk.

Under the Cyprus Act 1960, the United Kingdom retained sovereignty in two base areas and this was recognized in the Treaty of Establishment signed between the United Kingdom, Greece, Turkey and the Republic of Cyprus in August 1960. The base areas cover 99 sq miles. The Treaty also conferred on Britain certain rights within the Republic, including rights of movement and the use of specified training areas. As assessed at November 2012, military personnel in the sovereign base areas numbered 2,620.

Administrator: Air Vice-Marshal GRAHAM STACEY.

Education

Until 1965 each community in Cyprus managed its own schooling through a Communal Chamber. In March, however, the Greek Communal Chamber was dissolved and a Ministry of Education was established to take its place. Intercommunal education has been placed under this Ministry. Public expenditure on education by the central Government in the Greek Cypriot area was €1.390,9m. (equivalent to 8.0% of GDP) in 2010, according to official figures.

GREEK CYPRIOT EDUCATION

Primary education is compulsory and is provided free in six grades to children between five-and-a-half and 12 years of age. In some towns and large villages there are separate junior schools consisting of the first three grades. Apart from schools for the deaf and blind, there are also seven schools for handicapped children. In 2010/11 there were 680 kindergartens, with 2,203 teachers and 28,582 pupils. There were 368 primary schools, with 4,821 teachers and 54,083 pupils in that year. According to UNESCO estimates, enrolment in primary education in 2009/10 included 99% of children in the relevant age-group.

Secondary education is also free for all years of study and lasts for six years, with three compulsory years at a general secondary school (gymnasium) being followed by three non-compulsory years at a technical school or lyceum. Pupils at the lyceums may choose one of five main fields of specialization: humanities, science, economics, commercial/secretarial and foreign languages. At technical schools students may undertake one of several specializations offered within two categories of courses—technician and craft; the school-leaving certificate awarded at the end of the course is equivalent to that of the lyceums. In 2010/11 there were 166 secondary schools (gymnasiums and lyceums), with 7,603 teachers and 63,764 pupils. In addition, there were numerous privately operated secondary schools, where instruction is in English. According to UNESCO estimates, in 2009/10 enrolment in secondary education included 96% of children in the relevant age-group.

Post-secondary education is provided at a total of 42 tertiary institutions in 2009/10, including schools in the humanities and social sciences, pure and applied sciences, and economics and management. The University of Cyprus was established in 1992. The Higher Technical Institute offers sub-degree courses, leading to a diploma, in civil, electrical, mechanical and marine engineering and in computer studies. Other specialized training is provided at the Cyprus Forestry College, the Higher Hotel Institute, the Mediterranean Institute of Management and the School of Nursing. In 2010/11 32,118 students (including 10,026 foreign pupils) were enrolled in tertiary education, while a total of 19,199 students from the Greek Cypriot area were studying at universities abroad, mainly in Greece, the USA and the United Kingdom.

TURKISH CYPRIOT EDUCATION

With the exception of private kindergartens, a vocational school of agriculture attached to the Ministry of Agriculture and Natural Resources, a training school for nursing and midwifery attached to the Ministry of Health, and a school for hotel catering attached to the Ministry of Tourism, Environment and Culture, all schools and educational institutes are administered by the Ministry of National Education, Youth and Sport.

Education in the Turkish Cypriot zone is divided into two sections, formal and adult (informal) education. Formal education covers nursery, primary, secondary and higher education. Adult education caters for special training outside the school system.

Formal education is organized into four categories: pre-primary, primary, secondary and higher education. Pre-primary education is provided by kindergartens for children between the ages of 5 and 6. Primary education lasts for five years and caters for children aged 7–11. In 2010/11 there were 239 pre-primary and primary schools, with 2,054 teachers and 24,282 pupils. Secondary education is provided in two stages. The first stage (junior), lasting three years, is intended for pupils aged 12–14. In 2010/11 there were 36 secondary schools, with 1,108 teachers and 10,487 pupils. The second stage consists of a three-year programme of instruction for pupils aged 15–17. Pupils elect either to prepare for higher education, to prepare for higher education with vocational training, or to prepare for vocational training only. This stage of education is free, but not compulsory. In 2010/11 there were 27 general high schools, with 973 teachers and 7,736 pupils. There were also 11 vocational schools, with 524 teachers and 3,080 pupils.

Cyprus's first university, The Eastern Mediterranean University, which is located near Gazi Mağusa (Famagusta), was opened in 1986. A total of 13,255 students attended the university in 2008/09. Other institutions providing higher education in the Turkish Cypriot zone are: the Near East University in Lefkoşa (Nicosia); the Girne (Kyrenia) American University; the Anadolu University; the European University of Lefke (Levka); the International American University; the Cyprus International University; and the Teachers' Training College in Lefkoşa (Nicosia), which trains teachers for the elementary school stage. In 1982 an International Institute of Islamic Banking and Economics was opened to provide postgraduate training. In 2010/11 some 41,230 students were studying at universities in the 'TRNC', while 2,620 students were pursuing higher education studies abroad, mainly in Turkey, the USA and the United Kingdom.

Bibliography

Akçali, Emel. *Chypre: un enjeu géopolitique actuel*. Paris, L'Harmattan, 2009.

Aktar, Ayhan, Kızılyürek, Niyazi, and Özkırımlı, Umut (Eds). *Nationalism in the Troubled Triangle: Cyprus, Greece and Turkey*. Basingstoke, Palgrave Macmillan, 2010.

Alastos, D. *Cyprus in History*. London, 1955.

Anastasiou, Harry. *The Broken Olive Branch: Nationalism, Ethnic Conflict and the Quest for Peace in Cyprus*. Two vols, Syracuse, NY, Syracuse University Press, 2006.

Arnold, Percy. *Cyprus Challenge*. London, Hogarth Press, 1956.

Asmussen, Jan. *Cyprus at War: Diplomacy and Conflict during the 1974 Crisis*. London, I. B. Tauris, 2008.

Barker, Dudley. *Grivas*. London, Cresset Press, 1960.

Borowiec, Andrew. *Cyprus: A Troubled Island*. Westport, CT, Praeger Publishers, 2000.

Bryant, Rebecca. *Imagining the Modern: The Cultures of Nationalism in Cyprus*. New York, I. B. Tauris, 2004.

Byford-Jones, W. *Grivas and the Story of EOKA*. London, Robert Hale, 1960.

Calotychos, Vangelis (Ed.). *Cyprus and its People: Nation, Identity and Experience in an Unimaginable Community, 1955–97*. Boulder, CO, Westview Press, 1998.

Casson, S. *Ancient Cyprus*. London, 1937.

Christou, George. *The European Union and Enlargement: The Case of Cyprus*. New York, Palgrave, 2004.

Crawshaw, Nancy. *The Cyprus Revolt: An Account of the Struggle for Union with Greece*. London, Allen & Unwin, 1978.

Cyprus: Documents Relating to Independence of Cyprus and the Establishment of British Sovereign Base Areas. London, Cmnd 1093, HMSO, July 1960.

Cyprus: Treaty of Guarantee. Nicosia, 16 August 1960.

Denktaş, Rauf R. *The Cyprus Triangle*. London, K. Rüstem and Bros, 1988.

Diez, Thomas, and Tocci, Nathalie. (Eds). *Cyprus: A Conflict at the Crossroads*. Manchester, Manchester University Press, 2009.

Dodd, Clement H. *The Cyprus Imbroglio*. Huntingdon, Eothen Press, 1998.

Storm Clouds over Cyprus (A Briefing). Huntingdon, Eothen Press, 2001.

(Ed.). *The Political, Social and Economic Development of Northern Cyprus*. Huntingdon, Eothen Press, 1993.

(Ed.). *Cyprus: The Need for New Perspectives*. Huntingdon, Eothen Press, 1999.

The History and Politics of the Cyprus Conflict. Basingstoke, Palgrave Macmillan, 2010.

Esin, Emel. *Aspects of Turkish Civilization in Cyprus*. Ankara, Ankara University Press, 1965.

Faustmann, Hubert, and Varnava, Andrekos (Eds). *Reunifying Cyprus: The Annan Plan and Beyond*. London, I. B. Tauris, 2009.

Foley, Charles. *Island in Revolt*. London, Longmans Green, 1962.

Legacy of Strife. London, Penguin, 1964.

Foot, Sir Hugh. *A Start in Freedom*. London, 1964.

Foot, Sylvia. *Emergency Exit*. London, Chatto and Windus, 1960.

Green, Pauline (with Collins, Ray). *Embracing Cyprus: The Path to Unity in the New Europe*. London, I. B. Tauris, 2002.

Grivas (Dhigenis), George. *Guerrilla Warfare and EOKA's Struggle*. London, Longman, 1964.

Memoirs of General Grivas. London, Longman, 1964.

Hakkı, Murat Metin. *The Cyprus Issue: A Documentary History, 1878–2006*. London, I. B. Tauris, 2007.

Hannay, David. *Cyprus: The Search for a Solution*. London, I. B. Tauris, 2005.

Harbottle, Michael. *The Impartial Soldier*. Oxford, Oxford University Press, 1970.

Henn, Francis. *A Business of Some Heat: The United Nations Force in Cyprus before and during the 1974 Turkish Invasion*. Barnsley, Pen and Sword Books, 2004.

Hill, Sir George. *A History of Cyprus*. 4 vols, London, 1940–1952.

Hitchens, Christopher. *Hostage to History: Cyprus from the Ottomans to Kissinger*. London, Verso Books, 1997.

Holland, Robert. *Britain and the Revolt in Cyprus, 1954–59*. Oxford, Clarendon Press, 1998.

Joseph, Joseph S. *Cyprus: Ethnic Conflict and International Politics: From Independence to the Threshold of the European Union*. New York, St Martin's Press, 1999.

Ker-Lindsay, James. *EU Accession and UN Peacekeeping in Cyprus*. Basingstoke, Macmillan, 2005.

The Cyprus Problem: What Everyone Needs to Know. Oxford, Oxford University Press, 2011.

Ker-Lindsay, James, Faustmann, Hubert, and Mullen, Fiona. (Eds). *An Island in Europe: The EU and the Transformation of Cyprus*. London, I. B. Tauris, 2011.

Koumoulides, John A. *Cyprus: The Legacy*. Bethesda, MA, University Press of Maryland, 1999.

Kyriakides, S. *Cyprus—Constitutionalism and Crisis Government*. Philadelphia, PA, University of Pennsylvania Press, 1968.

Leventis, Yiorghos. *The Struggle for Self-Determination in the 1940s: Prelude to Deeper Crisis*. New York, Peter Lang Publishing, 2002.

Luke, Sir Harry C. *Cyprus under the Turks 1571–1878*. Oxford, 1921.

Cyprus: A Portrait and an Appreciation. London, Harrap, 1965.

Mallinson, William. *Cyprus: A Modern History*. Revised edn, London, I. B. Tauris, 2008.

Partition through Foreign Aggression: The Case of Turkey in Cyprus (Minnesota Mediterranean and East European Monographs). Minneapolis, MN, Modern Greek Studies, University of Minnesota, 2010.

Markides, Diana Weston. *Cyprus 1957-1963: From Colonial Conflict to Constitutional Crisis: The Key Role of the Municipal Issue* (Minnesota Mediterranean and East European monographs). Minneapolis, MN, Modern Greek Studies, University of Minnesota, 2001.

Mehmet, Ozay. *Sustainability of Micro-States: The Case of North Cyprus*. Salt Lake City, UT, University of Utah Press, 2009.

Mirbagheri, Farid. *Cyprus and International Peacemaking, 1964–86*. London, Routledge, 1998.

Moran, Michael (Ed.). *Rauf Denktash at the United Nations: Speeches on Cyprus*. Huntingdon, Eothen Press, 1997.

Morgan, Tabitha. *Sweet and Bitter Island: A History of the British in Cyprus*. London, I. B. Tauris, 2010.

Newman, Philip. *A Short History of Cyprus*. 1940.

O'Malley, Brendan, and Craig, Ian. *The Cyprus Conspiracy: America, Espionage and the Turkish Invasion*. New York, St Martin's Press, 2000.

Panteli, Dr Stavros. *The Making of Modern Cyprus*. Interworld, 1990.

Historical Dictionary of Cyprus. Lanham, MD, Scarecrow Press, 1995.

Place of Refuge: A History of the Jews in Cyprus. Sarasota, FL, Elliot & Thompson, 2004.

The History of Modern Cyprus. London, Interworld Publications, 2005.

Papadakis, Yiannis. *Echoes from the Dead Zone: Across the Cyprus Divide*. London, I. B. Tauris, 2005.

Papadakis, Yiannis, Peristianis, N., and Welz, Gisela. (Eds). *Divided Cyprus: Modernity, History and an Island in Conflict*. Bloomington, IN, Indiana University Press, 2006.

Papadopoullos, T. *The Population of Cyprus (1570–1881)*. Nicosia, 1965.

Pericleous, Chrysostomos. *The Cyprus Referendum: A Divided Island and the Challenge of the Annan Plan*. London, I. B. Tauris, 2009.

Purcell, H. D. *Cyprus*. London, Benn, 1969.

Richmond, Oliver P. *Mediating in Cyprus: The Cypriot Communities and the United Nations*. London, Frank Cass, 1998.

Richmond, Oliver P., and Ker-Lindsay, James. *The Work of the UN in Cyprus: Promoting Peace and Development*. New York, Palgrave Macmillan, 2001.

Rossides, Eugene T. (Ed.). *The United States, Cyprus and the Rule of Law: Twenty Years of Turkish Aggression and Occupation*. New York, Melissa Media, 1999.

Salih, H. Ibrahim. *Cyprus: Ethnic Political Counterpoints*. Lanham, MD, University Press of America, 2005.

Sevcenko, Nancy P., and Moss, Christopher F. *Medieval Cyprus*. Princeton, NJ, Princeton University Press, 1999.

Sonyel, Salahi R. *Cyprus: The Destruction of a Republic. British Documents 1960–65*. Huntingdon, Eothen Press, 1997.

Spyridakis, Dr C. *A Brief History of Cyprus*. Nicosia, 1964.

Stefanidis, Ioannis D. *Isle of Discord: Nationalism, Imperialism and the Making of the Cyprus Problem*. New York, New York University Press, 1999.

Stefanou, Constantin. *Cyprus and the EU: The Road to Accession*. London, Ashgate Publishing, 2005.

Storrs, Sir Ronald. *A Chronology of Cyprus*. Nicosia, 1930.

Stylianou, A., and Stylianou, J. *Byzantine Cyprus*. Nicosia, 1948.

Theophylactou, Demetrios A. *Security, Identity and Nation Building: Cyprus and the European Union in Comparative Perspective*. Aldershot, Avebury, 1995.

Tocci, Nathalie. *EU Accession Dynamics and Conflict Resolution: Catalysing Peace or Consolidating Partition in Cyprus?* London, Ashgate Publishing, 2004.

Uslu, Nasuh. *Cyprus Question as an Issue of Turkish Foreign Policy and Turkish-American Relations, 1959–2003*. New York, Nova Science Publishers, 2003.

Yennaris, Costas. *From the East: Conflict and Partition in Cyprus*. Sarasota, FL, Elliot & Thompson, 2004.

EGYPT

Physical and Social Geography

W. B. FISHER

SITUATION

The Arab Republic of Egypt occupies the north-eastern corner of the African continent, with an extension across the Gulf of Suez into the Sinai region, which is usually regarded as lying in Asia. The area of Egypt is 1,009,450 sq km (389,751 sq miles) but only 5.5% can be said to be permanently settled or cultivated, the remainder being desert or marsh. Egypt lies between latitudes 22°N and 32°N; the greatest distance from north to south is about 1,024 km (674 miles), and that from east to west is 1,240 km (770 miles), giving the country a roughly square shape, with the Mediterranean and Red Seas forming, respectively, the northern and eastern boundaries. Egypt has political frontiers on the east with Israel, on the south with the Republic of Sudan and on the west with Libya. The actual frontiers run, in general, as straight lines drawn directly between defined points, and do not normally conform to geographical features. Between June 1967 and October 1973 the de facto frontier with Israel was the Suez Canal. As a result of the 1979 Peace Treaty, the frontier reverted to a line much further to the east (Documents on Palestine, see p. 71).

PHYSICAL FEATURES

The remarkable persistence of cultural cohesion among the Egyptian people may largely be explained by the geography of the country. Egypt consists essentially of a narrow, trough-like valley, some 3 km–15 km wide, cut by the Nile river in the plateau of north-east Africa. At an earlier geological period a gulf of the Mediterranean Sea probably extended as far south as Cairo, but deposition of silt by the Nile has entirely filled this gulf, producing the fan-shaped Delta region (22,000 sq km in area), through which flow two main distributary branches of the Nile—the eastern, or Damietta, branch (240 km long) and the western, or Rosetta, branch (235 km), together with many other minor channels. As deposition of silt takes place, large stretches of water are gradually impounded to form shallow lakes, which later become firm ground. At present there are four such stretches of water in the north of the Delta: from east to west, and in order of size, lakes Menzaleh, Brullos, Idku and Mariut.

Upstream from Cairo the Nile Valley is at first 10 km–15 km in width, and, as the river tends to lie close to the eastern side, much of the cultivated land, and also most of the major towns and cities, lie on the western bank. Towards the south the river valley gradually narrows until, at about 400 km from the border with Sudan, it is no more than 3 km wide. Near Aswan there is an outcrop of resistant rock, chiefly granite, which the river has not been able to erode as quickly as the rest of the valley. This gives rise to a region of cascades and rapids that is known as the First Cataract. Four other similar regions occur on the Nile, but only the First Cataract lies within Egypt. The cataracts form a barrier to human movement upstream and serve to isolate the Egyptian Nile from territories further south. In Ancient Egypt, when river communications were of paramount importance, there was a traditional division of the Nile Valley into Lower Egypt (the Delta), Middle Egypt (the broader valley above the Delta) and Upper Egypt (the narrower valley as far as the cataracts). Nowadays, however, it is usual to speak merely of Upper and Lower Egypt, with the division occurring at Cairo.

The fertile strip of the Nile Valley is separated to the south by the cataracts and by the deserts and swamps of Sudan; to the north by the Mediterranean Sea; and to the east and west by desert plateaux. The land immediately to the east of the Nile Valley, known as the Eastern Highlands, is a complex region with peaks that rise 1,800 m to 2,100 m, but also deep valleys, which make travel difficult. Owing to aridity the whole region is sparsely populated, with a few partly nomadic shepherds, one or two monasteries and a number of small towns associated chiefly with the exploitation of minerals—petroleum, iron, manganese and granite—that occur in this region. Difficult landward communications mean that contact is mostly by sea, except in the case of the iron-fields. The Sinai, separated from the Eastern Highlands by the Gulf of Suez, is structurally very similar, but the general plateau level is tilted, giving the highest land (again nearly 2,100 m in elevation) in the extreme south, where it rises in bold scarps from sea level. Towards the north the land gradually slopes down, ultimately forming the low-lying sandy plain of the Sinai desert, which fringes the Mediterranean Sea. Owing to its low altitude and accessibility, the Sinai, in spite of its desert nature, has been for many centuries an important corridor linking Egypt with Asia.

West of the Nile occur the vast expanses known as the Western Desert. Though by no means uniform in height, the land surface is much lower than that to the east of the Nile, and within Egypt rarely exceeds 300 m above sea level. Parts are covered by extensive masses of light, shifting sand, which often form dunes, but in addition there are a number of large depressions, some of which actually reach to below sea level. These depressions seem to have been hollowed out by wind action, breaking up rock strata that were weakened by the presence of underground water, and most hollows still contain supplies of artesian water. In some instances (as, for example, the Qattara depression and the Wadi Natrun, respectively south-west and south-east of Alexandria) the subterranean water is highly saline and consequently useless for agriculture; however, in others—notably the oases of the Fayum, Siwa, Dakhlia, Behariya and Farafra—the water is suitable for irrigation purposes, and settlements have grown up within the desert.

CLIMATE

The main feature of the Egyptian climate is the almost uniform aridity. Alexandria, the wettest part, receives only 200 mm of rain annually, and most of the south has 80 mm or less. In many districts rain may fall in quantity only once every two or three years; consequently, throughout most of Egypt, including Cairo itself, the majority of the people live in houses made of unbaked, sun-dried brick. During the summer temperatures are extremely high, sometimes reaching 38°C–43°C and even 49°C in the southern and western deserts. The Mediterranean coast has cooler conditions, with a maximum of 32°C; as a result, the wealthier classes tend to move to Alexandria for the three months of summer. Winters are generally warm, with very occasional rain, but cold spells occur from time to time and light snow is not unknown. Owing to the large expanse of desert, hot dry sand-winds (called *khamsin*) are fairly frequent, particularly in spring, and much damage can be caused to crops; it has been known for the temperature to rise by 20°C in two hours, and the wind to reach 150 km per hour. Another unusual condition is the occurrence of early morning fog in Lower Egypt during spring and early summer. This has a beneficial effect on plant growth since it supplies moisture and is a partial substitute for rainfall.

IRRIGATION

With insufficient rainfall over the entire country, human existence in Egypt is heavily dependent on irrigation from the Nile. It may be stated, in summary, that the river rises in the highlands of East Africa, with its main stream issuing from Lakes Victoria and Albert. In southern Sudan it flows sluggishly across a flat, open plain, where the fall in level is only 1:100,000. Here the shallow waters become a vast swamp, full of dense masses of papyrus vegetation, and this section of the Nile is called the Sudd ('blockage'). Finally, in the north of Sudan, the Nile flows in a well-defined channel and enters Egypt. In Upper Egypt the river is in the process of cutting its bed deeper into the rock floor, but in the lower part of its course silt is deposited, and the level of the land is rising—in some places by as much as 10 cm per century.

The salient feature of the Nile is its annual flood, which is caused by the onset of summer rains in East Africa and Ethiopia. The flood waters travel northward, reaching Egypt during August, and within Egypt the normal rise in river level was at first 6.4 m, declining to 4.6 m as irrigation works developed. This cycle of flooding had been maintained for many thousands of years until, in 1969, construction of the Aswan High Dam made it a feature of the past so far as Egypt is concerned.

Originally, the flood waters were simply retained in specially prepared basins with earthen banks, and the water could then be used for three to four months after the flood. Within the last century, the building of large barrages, holding water all the year round, has allowed cultivation in any season. The old (basin) system allowed one or two crops per holding per year; the newer (perennial) system allows three or even four. In the past, barley and wheat were the main crops; under perennial irrigation maize and cotton, which can tolerate the great summer heat, provided they are watered, have assumed equal importance.

The transfer from basin to perennial irrigation allowed a considerable population increase in Egypt, from about 2.5m. in 1800 to 83.7m. at the beginning of 2013, giving rural densities of over 2,500 per sq km in some areas; and, as 99% of all Egyptians live within the Nile Valley (only 4% of the country's area), there is considerable pressure on the land.

With most Egyptians entirely dependent upon Nile water, almost all the water entering Egypt is fully utilized. However, there are enormous losses by evaporation, which at present amount to some 70% of the total flow. Difficulties and opportunities over the use of Nile water were exemplified by the High Dam scheme at Aswan, which created a lake 500 km in length and 10 km wide that extends southwards across the Sudanese border. The High Dam is 3,600 m across, with a girth of 980 m at the river bed and 40 m at the top. It holds back one of the largest artificial lakes in the world (Lake Nasser), and enables large-scale storage of water from year to year, and the regular planned use of all Nile water independently of the precise amount of annual flood. The irrigation potential of the High Dam is 2m. feddans for Lower Egypt alone, and the provision for the Nile valley (including Upper Egypt) was expected to add 30% to the total cultivable area of Egypt. Furthermore, 12 generator units incorporated into the dam give considerable quantities of low-cost electric power. This power has been a most important aid to industrialization, especially for the new metal industries. The dam was completed in July 1970 and officially inaugurated in January 1971.

However, adverse effects were soon noticed: scouring of the Nile bed below the dam; increased salinity in the lower stretches; reduced sedimentation below the dam and heavy deposition within the basin, resulting in the need for greater use of artificial fertilizers, which must be imported; and, perhaps more seriously, the disappearance of fish (particularly sardines) off the Mediterranean coast of Egypt. Possibly the most disturbing effect of all was a notable rise in the water table in some areas, owing to hydrostatic pressures, and the year-round presence of water. Besides disturbing irrigation systems (which are adapted to pre-existing conditions), salinity and gleying of a more permanent nature began to appear; reports of bilharzia and other parasitic diseases increased; and the appearance of the plant water hyacinth threatened to choke irrigation systems.

LANGUAGE

Arabic is the language of almost all Egyptians, although there are very small numbers of Berber language-speaking villages in the western oases. The traditional French interest in Egypt is reciprocated: government decrees are sometimes published in French, as well as Arabic, and newspapers in French have an important circulation in Cairo and Alexandria. Small colonies of Greeks and Armenians are also a feature of the larger Egyptian towns. The Arabic name for Egypt, Misr, is always used within the country itself.

History

Revised by DENIS J. SULLIVAN and KIMBERLY JONES

EGYPT—SHAPED BY CONQUEST

Egypt is well known for its ancient history replete with the rule of its ancient pharaohs, such as Hatshepsut, Tutankhamun (Tut Ankh Amon) and Ramses II, as well as the construction of its pyramids. The Nile Valley, which abuts the country's aqueous lifeline, the Nile River, has been inhabited for more than 7,000 years. However, Egypt's more recent history has been shaped by conquest and external rulers.

Prior to the arrival of the Arabs in the mid-seventh century AD, the Assyrians and Persians (sixth century BC) left their mark in Egypt. These empires were followed by the ascendancy of individual rulers such as Alexander the Great, after whom the Mediterranean port city of Alexandria is named, and Cleopatra. Thereafter was the rise and rule of the Roman and Byzantine empires, the latter ruling from Constantinople (modern-day İstanbul). Mark, 'the Evangelist,' founded Christianity in Egypt in the middle of the first century AD, and Alexandria became one of Christianity's greatest centres of learning.

With the birth and advance of Islam, the Arab-Muslims arrived in Egypt in 640 AD. Over time, Egypt became an Arabic-speaking country with a Muslim majority, and a Coptic Christian minority. The early centuries of Arab and Islamic rule were characterized by the rise (and fall) of various empirical powers and dynasties—from the Abbasids (Sunni Muslim) to the Fatimids (Shi'a Muslim).

Under the early Fatimids, the city of Cairo was developed and the mosque of Al-Azhar was established in 970–972 AD. The Kurdish leader Salah al-Din ibn Ayyub, known as Saladin, rose to prominence, returning Egypt to a Sunni orientation and successfully battling against the Crusaders. When Saladin died in 1193, his empire was divided among his heirs, one branch of which, the Egyptian Ayyubids, reigned in Cairo.

Louis IX of France led an attack on Egypt in 1249, but was halted at the battle of al-Mansura in 1250. Thereafter, Egypt was ruled by Mamluk (non-Egyptian) sultans until the Ottoman advance at the beginning of the 16th century. Egypt then became a province of the Ottoman Empire, until Napoleon's invasion in 1798.

At the end of the 18th century Egypt became a pawn in the war between France and Britain. Napoleon wished to disrupt British commerce and eventually overthrow British rule in India. He landed at Alexandria in 1798, but in 1801 the French were forced to capitulate by British and Ottoman forces. The expulsion of the French was followed by a struggle for power, with the victor an officer in the Ottoman forces, Muhammad Ali Pasha, who is regarded by many as a great modernizer (or to some 'Westernizer') of Egyptian state and society.

In 1854 Muhammad Ali's fourth son, Said Pasha, (as the new ruler of Egypt) granted a concession to a French engineer and diplomat, Ferdinand de Lesseps, to build the Suez Canal; work began in 1859 and the Canal was opened in 1869. In addition to the canal, railroads and telegraph lines were also constructed.

During this period of growth, Egyptian indebtedness rose dramatically. In 1875 Egypt averted financial bankruptcy by selling shares in the Suez Canal to the British Government.

By the late 1800s Egyptian nationalist sentiment against external influences was taking root and demands for independence were lodged. The most significant movement (and failed attempt) to secure Egypt's independence came in 1882, when Col Ahmed 'Urabi led a revolt, with support from leading Islamists as well as liberal nationalists. British forces quashed the 'Urabi Revolt' and placed forces along the Suez Canal Zone in August 1882. Nationalism ebbed and flowed in succeeding decades, as did British power and control. The next important effort to gain independence from Britain came after the First World War, when Saad Zaghlul (who had participated in the 1882 Revolt) led a delegation (or Wafd) to the Paris Peace Conference in 1919. Eventually, Egypt moved from a British protectorate to gain conditional independence in 1922, and adopt a constitution in 1923.

INDEPENDENCE FOLLOWED BY REVOLUTION

Between conditional independence and the Second World War, years of struggle ensued between the British, Egyptian King Fouad, installed with British assistance, and those who wanted revolution or at least significant change. Among those fighting for change were the Wafd (now a nationalist movement) and the Muslim Brotherhood (Al-Ikhwan al-Muslimun), an organization that had been formed in 1928 with the aim of establishing an Islamic society.

In 1936 King Fouad was succeeded by his son, Farouk. That same year a 20-year Anglo-Egyptian treaty was signed, which terminated Britain's occupation but empowered it to station forces in the Suez Canal Zone until the Egyptian army was in a position to ensure the waterway's security.

During the Second World War Egypt played a vital strategic role as the British base in the Middle East. However, Egyptian support for the Allied cause was by no means total. The Wafd favoured co-operation with the British, and Britain forced Farouk's acquiescence in the formation of a Wafdist Government under Nahas Pasha in 1942, which lasted two years. Nahas became increasingly enthusiastic about Arab unity and was instrumental in establishing the League of Arab States (the Arab League) in the final months of the Second World War.

In the aftermath, Britain receded as an empire from the Middle East. Included therein was its withdrawal from the conflict-ridden Palestinian Mandate (previously granted under the League of Nations) in May 1948. That same month Egypt joined Iraq, Syria and Jordan in a less than successful military action against Israel following its declaration of statehood. Subsequent years were tumultuous: The King's early popularity declined; the Muslim Brotherhood gained strength as a movement, and communism had gained new adherents. Nahas, again in power, then abrogated the 1936 treaty with Britain. A range of tactics—from the violent to the economic—followed, in an attempt to compel the British forces to withdraw from the Suez Canal Zone.

On 23 July 1952 a group of young army officers, termed the 'Free Officers', who had long planned a coup, seized power in Cairo. They invited the veteran politician Ali Maher to form a government under their control, and secured the abdication of King Farouk in favour of his infant son, Ahmad Fuad II, on 26 July.

Gen. Muhammad Neguib, who had incurred the enmity of King Farouk and who had gained popularity by condemning the British, was made commander-in-chief of the armed forces and head of the military junta. A Council of Regency was formed in August 1952. On 7 September, after an attempt by the Wafd and other parties to resume the political battle on their own terms, a new Cabinet, with Gen. Neguib as Prime Minister, replaced that of Ali Maher. Real power, however, lay with the nine officers who formed the Revolutionary Command Council (RCC).

The revolution soon gained momentum. On 10 December 1952 the Constitution was abolished, and on 16 January 1953 all political parties were dissolved. It was announced that there would be a three-year transitional period before representative government was restored. On 18 June the monarchy was abolished and Egypt was declared a republic, with Neguib as President and Prime Minister, as well as Chairman of the RCC. Col Gamal Abd al-Nasir (Nasser), who, although leader of the Free Officers, had hitherto remained in the background, became Deputy Prime Minister and Minister of the Interior.

Internal powers struggles followed, including those between Gen. Neguib and Col Nasser. On 25 February 1954 Neguib was relieved of his posts as President, Prime Minister and Chairman of the RCC, accused of having attempted to concentrate power in his own hands. Nasser briefly became Prime Minister and Chairman of the RCC, but Neguib was restored to the three posts, only to be ousted again as Prime Minister by Nasser in April. In October a member of the Muslim Brotherhood attempted to assassinate Nasser. Its leaders and several thousand alleged supporters were arrested, and in subsequent trials a number of death sentences were imposed. On 14 November Neguib was again relieved of the presidency, this time accused of being involved in a Muslim Brotherhood conspiracy against the regime. He was placed under house arrest and Nasser became acting Head of State. In January 1956 a new Constitution providing for a strong presidency was proclaimed. In June it was approved in a public referendum, and Nasser was elected President.

External relations also changed. An Anglo-Egyptian agreement, signed in February 1953, ended the Condominium (according to which the British and Egyptians had exercised joint authority over Sudan since 1899) and offered the Sudanese the choice of independence or union with Egypt. Egyptian expectation that they would choose the latter was disappointed. Additionally, an agreement on Suez was signed on 19 October 1954; this provided for the withdrawal of British troops from the Canal Zone within 20 months. The agreement recognized the international importance of the Suez Canal (which was described as 'an integral part of Egypt') and expressed the determination of both parties to uphold the 1888 Constantinople Convention, which provided that the Suez Canal should be open to vessels of all nationalities, in war and peace.

Under Nasser, Egypt began to assert its importance in world affairs. He sought influence in four circles: the Islamic, the African, the Arab, and the non-aligned. Egypt led certain Arab states in opposing the Baghdad Pact (later to become the Central Treaty Organization—CTO), which was a US-led alliance against the expansionism of the USSR and in favour of mutual defence. In October 1955 Egypt concluded its own defence agreements with Syria and with Saudi Arabia, and in April 1956 a military pact was signed between Egypt, Saudi Arabia and Yemen. Tension with its neighbour Israel, however, remained high. As the USA denied Nasser arms owing to his refusal to join the Baghdad Pact, he announced an arms deal with Czechoslovakia in September 1955, for the supply of large quantities of military equipment in return for cotton and rice.

THE SUEZ CRISIS AND ITS CONSEQUENCES

President Nasser's adoption of a policy of non-alignment, which implied a willingness to deal with competing power blocs, was followed by his attempt to obtain funds for the ambitious High Dam project at Aswan. With this endeavour, the Egyptian Government aimed to augment the area of cultivable land and generate electricity for industrialization, which was seen as a main solution to Egypt's increasing population problem. Following offers of assistance from the USA and the United Kingdom, the World Bank offered Egypt a loan of US $200m. However, as further punishment for Nasser's failure to join their Baghdad Pact and 'fight Communism', the USA and United Kingdom withdrew their offers of finance for the High Dam on 20 July 1956. Their rationale centred around first, the lack of an agreement between the riparian states on the Dam, and second, that Egypt's ability to devote adequate resources to the project was doubtful. On 26 July President Nasser announced that the Suez Canal Company had been nationalized and that revenue from the canal would be used to finance the High Dam, which the USSR had offered to construct.

The United Kingdom, France and the USA protested strongly at Nasser's nationalization of the Suez Canal Company. After an international conference met in London, United Kingdom, in August 1956, a committee, under Australian chairmanship, went to Cairo to submit proposals for the operation of the Canal under an international system. The Egyptian Government rejected these proposals. At a second London conference, held in September, a Suez Canal Users' Association was formed; it was later joined by 16 states. On 13 October the UN Security Council voted on an Anglo-French resolution embodying basic principles for a settlement agreed earlier between the British, French and Egyptian ministers of foreign affairs. The first part of this, outlining the agreed principles, was adopted unanimously; the second, endorsing the proposals of the first London conference and inviting Egypt to make prompt proposals providing no less effective guarantees to users, was vetoed by the USSR.

The United Kingdom and France, frustrated in their attempts to retain some measure of control over the Suez Canal, reached a then-secret understanding with Israel involving military action. Israeli forces crossed into Sinai on 29 October 1956, ostensibly to attack Palestinian *fedayeen* (militants), and advanced towards the Suez Canal. On 30 October France and the United Kingdom called on Israel and Egypt to cease warlike action and withdraw their forces from either side of the Canal. Egypt was asked to agree to an Anglo-French force moving temporarily into key positions at Port Said, Ismailia and Suez; Israel agreed but Egypt refused. At a meeting of the UN Security Council on the same day, the United Kingdom and France vetoed US and Soviet resolutions that requested an immediate Israeli withdrawal and called on all UN members to refrain from the use of force or the threat of force.

Anglo-French air operations against Egypt began on 31 October 1956, but paratroops and sea-borne forces landed in the Port Said area only on 5 November. On 2 November the UN General Assembly called for a cease-fire and two days later adopted a Canadian proposal to create a UN Emergency Force to supervise the ending of hostilities. On 6 November, following considerable US pressure, British Prime Minister Anthony Eden announced that, subject to confirmation that Egypt and Israel had accepted an unconditional cease-fire, the armed conflict would end at midnight.

The organization of the UN force was rapidly undertaken, and the first units reached Egypt on 15 November 1956. The withdrawal of the Anglo-French forces was completed in December. Israeli forces, which had occupied the entire Sinai Peninsula, withdrew from all areas except the Gaza Strip, owing to stated security concerns regarding militants, and Sharm el-Sheikh, at the entrance to the Gulf of Aqaba, which commanded the seaway to the port of Eilat. After considerable US pressure on Israel, these areas were returned to Egyptian control in March 1957.

The Suez Canal, which had been blocked by the Egyptians, was cleared by a UN salvage fleet and reopened in late March 1957. The terms under which the Canal reopened were full control by the Egyptian Canal Authority and respect for the Constantinople Convention of 1888. Disputes would be settled in accordance with the UN Charter, or referred to the International Court of Justice.

REGIONAL STRIFE

In the wake of the Suez crisis, elections to the Egyptian National Assembly, provided for in the 1956 Constitution, were held in July 1957. Only candidates approved by President Nasser and his colleagues were permitted to stand, and it was clear that the 350 elected members were not expected to exert much influence on the Government.

Early the following year, in February 1958, Egypt and Syria formed a union, under the title of the United Arab Republic (UAR). The union was the product of talks that began in conjunction with mutual defence agreements of 1956. Both countries were aligned against the West and looked to the USSR and the communist bloc for support, and in Syria pro-Egyptian elements were ascendant. In July 1960 the first National Assembly of the UAR, consisting of deputies from both Egypt and Syria, was opened in Cairo by President Nasser.

An invitation was extended to other Arab states to join the new union, and in March 1958 the UAR and Yemen entered into a loose association called the United Arab States. However, this association did not flourish, and it was terminated by the UAR in December 1961.

President Nasser's antipathy towards the West found favour with the USSR, which established closer ties with the UAR during these years. Soviet military and industrial aid was granted, and in December 1958 an agreement was concluded that ensured Soviet assistance for the building of the Aswan High Dam. Work on the first stage of the High Dam began in January 1960.

Relations with the West also improved during 1959–60. Through the mediation of the World Bank, an agreement with the United Kingdom was signed on 1 March 1959 providing for the payment by the UAR of £27.5m. as compensation for British private property taken over at the time of the Suez crisis in 1956. Diplomatic relations with the United Kingdom were resumed at chargé d'affaires level in December 1959 and raised to ambassadorial level in early 1961. A loan of US $56.5m. to improve the Suez Canal was obtained from the World Bank in 1959, and other aid came from the USA in 1960.

Syria had by now become dissatisfied with the union and on 28 September 1961 the Syrian army seized control in Damascus, resulting in Syria's withdrawal from the UAR. Nasser at first called for resistance to the coup in Syria, but, when the insurgents were seen to be in firm control, Nasser stated that he would not oppose recognition of Syria's independence. The loss of Syria was a bitter blow to President Nasser and his Egyptian colleagues, who now set about a re-examination of their policies, which resulted in a renewal of revolutionary fervour.

The UAR Government (Egypt retained the full title) was reformed on 18 October 1961 and a National Congress of Popular Forces, consisting of 1,750 delegates, representing economic and professional interests and other social groups, rather than geographical areas, met in Cairo on 21 May 1962. President Nasser presented the National Congress with a draft National Charter outlining his programme for developing the UAR according to Arab socialist principles. A new 'democratic' system of government was introduced, based on a new political organization, the Arab Socialist Union (ASU—replacing the National Union, which had been established in 1956), and including popular councils of which at least one-half of the members would be workers or *fellahin* (peasants).

The Syrian coup had been preceded by the overthrow in February 1963 of the regime of Gen. Abd al-Karim Kassem in Iraq. These changes in power brought Syria and Iraq into closer alignment with Egypt, and it was announced on 17 April that agreement had been reached on the formation of a federation of the three countries under the name of the United Arab Republic. Rivalries, however, arose in both Baghdad and Damascus between supporters of the Baath Party and 'Nasserists', and by August President Nasser withdrew from the agreement, claiming that the Baathists had established one-party dictatorships in Syria and Iraq and ignored his insistence on wider nationalist representation. A month later President Abd al-Salam Muhammad Aref of Iraq called for a Baathist union of the three countries but, after the expulsion of Baath leaders from Iraq in November and the consolidation of power in Aref's hands, the unity movement between Iraq and Syria collapsed and Iraq and Egypt again moved closer together. A Unified Political Command between Iraq and Egypt began work in early 1965, but progress towards unity was slow.

The Arab reconciliation and presentation of a united front lasted until early 1965. Iraq, Kuwait, Yemen (Arab Republic), Algeria and Lebanon continued to follow President Nasser's lead, with only Syrian critics complaining that UAR policy was not sufficiently anti-Israeli. Relations between the UAR and Jordan improved markedly and, after a conference of heads of Arab governments was held in Cairo in January to discuss co-ordination of Arab policies, Jordan's King Hussein, previously denounced by the UAR, visited Cairo.

In Yemen, despite Egyptian support, the republican regime seemed no closer to victory in its war against the royalists, who held the mountainous regions of the north-east and were assisted by Saudi Arabian finance and supplies of arms. In February 1966 the British Government announced that British forces would leave Aden and South Arabia when that territory became independent in 1968. The same day, President Nasser stated that Egyptian troops would not be withdrawn until the revolution in Yemen could 'defend itself against the conspiracies of imperialism and reactionaries.'

The years 1964 and 1965 were marked by a deterioration of UAR relations with the West, in particular the USA and the United Kingdom, and increasing dependence on the USSR. Relations with the USSR had been strengthened in May 1964 when the Soviet leader, Nikita Khrushchev, made a 16-day visit to Egypt to attend the ceremony marking the completion of the first stage of the Aswan High Dam, being built with Soviet aid. President Nasser paid his third visit to the USSR in August 1965 and the new Soviet premier, Aleksei Kosygin, visited the UAR in May 1966, expressing support for UAR policies and again demonstrating Soviet interest in the Middle East.

Although Nasser obtained over 99% of the votes cast in the presidential referendum in March 1965, there were subsequently more signs of discontent in the UAR than at any time since he had come to power. In a speech to Arab students during his visit to Moscow in August, he disclosed that a plot against his life had been discovered, in which the proscribed Muslim Brotherhood was thought to have been involved.

The years 1965 and 1966 were ones of internal changes and challenges. Taxation was increased and measures of retrenchment were introduced owing to growing economic difficulties. Nevertheless, the level of imports, particularly food to sustain the growing population, and the debt-service burden represented a continuing drain on foreign exchange reserves, and the UAR faced a balance of payments crisis. When the UAR defaulted on repayments due to the IMF in December 1966 the country was on the verge of bankruptcy.

Regional shifts were also underway. A rift between the UAR and Saudi Arabia widened. In February 1966 Nasser expressed opposition to an Islamic grouping that King Faisal ibn Abd al-Aziz Al Sa'ud was promoting, and in subsequent months propaganda warfare between the two countries was intensified. In October Tunisia severed relations with the UAR in response to continued differences over Arab League policies. In Yemen, Egyptian forces withdrew from northern and eastern areas and concentrated in the triangle between San'a, Hodeida and Taiz. Egyptian control over the republican armed forces and administration was increased.

EGYPT AND ISRAEL: WAR AND OCCUPATION

The events of May-June 1967 transformed the Middle East. There had been an increase in Syrian guerrilla activities against Israel during the previous six months, and in April the tension led to fighting in the Lake Tiberias (Sea of Galilee) area; six Syrian aircraft were shot down. Israeli warnings to the Syrian Government, culminated with Israeli Prime Minister Levi Eshkol's threat of severe reprisals if terrorist activities were not controlled. This prompted Syrian allegations that Israel was about to mount a large-scale attack.

President Nasser, who was reproached for not aiding Syria in prior fighting in accordance with the mutual defence agreement, responded immediately, moving large numbers of troops to the Israeli border. The UN Emergency Force, which depended on Egyptian permission for its presence on the Egyptian side of the frontier, was removed by UN Secretary General U Thant. Nasser later justified these steps by claiming that he had received Syrian and Soviet warnings that Israeli troops were concentrated on the Syrian border and that an invasion of Syria was imminent.

When President Nasser closed the Straits of Tiran to Israeli shipping, thereby effectively blockading the port of Eilat, his prestige in the Arab world increased considerably. The United Kingdom and the USA protested that the Gulf of Aqaba was an international waterway; Israel regarded the blockade of the Straits as an unambiguous act of war. As tension increased, King Hussein of Jordan concluded a mutual defence pact with the UAR and was immediately joined by Iraq. On 5 June Israel launched large-scale air attacks on Egyptian, Jordanian, Syrian and Iraqi airfields, and Israeli ground forces made rapid advances into the Gaza Strip, Sinai and western Jordan; there was also fighting on the Israeli–Syrian border. The outcome was decided within hours by the air strikes, which destroyed most of the Arab air forces, and by the Israeli ground forces' success. By 10 June, when all participants had accepted the UN Security Council's demand for a cease-fire, Israeli troops were in control of the entire Sinai peninsula (including Sharm el-Sheikh) as far as the Suez Canal, the West Bank of Jordan (including the Old City of Jerusalem), the Gaza Strip and Syrian territory extending 12 miles from the Israeli border (the Golan Heights).

In the wake of his defeat, President Nasser offered to resign, but popular support led him to withdraw his resignation. He dismissed a number of senior army officers and assumed the duties of Prime Minister and Secretary-General of the ASU. The implications of Egypt's 1967 catastrophe were only gradually realized. It was estimated that the loss of revenue from the Suez Canal, from oil produced in Sinai, and from tourism, amounted to some £E12.5m. per month, or almost one-half of Egypt's foreign currency earnings. In addition, the withdrawal of a large part of the Egyptian force in Yemen reduced Nasser's ability to influence affairs both in that country and in Aden and South Arabia (which became independent as the Republic of Southern Yemen on 30 November 1967, after the withdrawal of British troops). The USSR, which had given the Arab cause strong verbal support throughout the crisis, continued its staunch pro-Arab stand at the UN; it also replaced about one-half of the lost Egyptian aircraft and provided other military supplies and instructors.

After repeated violations of the cease-fire by both sides, on 22 November 1967 the UN Security Council adopted a resolution (242) that laid down the principles for a just and lasting peace in the Middle East and authorized the appointment of a UN special representative to assist in the achievement of a settlement. Resolution 242 has subsequently formed the basis of most peacemaking attempts in the Middle East.

Meanwhile, President Nasser faced daunting economic difficulties and an unstable political situation in Egypt. An austerity budget had been framed in July 1967. The cost of re-equipping the armed forces required reductions in investment, despite Soviet aid and assistance from other Arab governments. Socialist policies were still pursued, as demonstrated by the decision, announced in October, to nationalize wholesale trade. The continuing shortage of foreign exchange made it prudent to improve the UAR's relations with the West, and in December diplomatic relations with the United Kingdom were resumed. A bridging loan from British, West German and Italian banks, obtained in February 1968, enabled the UAR to make the repayments to the IMF that had been outstanding since the end of 1966, and in March the Fund approved further drawings.

Demonstrations by students and workers took place in Cairo and Helwan towards the end of February 1968. The protests were initially organized against the leniency of court sentences passed against senior air force officers for their failure to prevent the destruction of the UAR air force on 5 June 1967, however, they revealed widespread discontent. Several people were killed in clashes with police, and the universities were closed. President Nasser realized the need for immediate conciliatory action. Retrials were ordered and comprehensive changes to the Cabinet were announced, including the introduction of a number of civilian experts.

Military expenditures remained high in 1968 and 1969; Soviet arms deliveries continued, as did the presence in Egypt of some 3,000 Soviet military advisers and instructors. A pattern of sporadic action, involving artillery duels across the Suez Canal, commando raids and air combat developed throughout 1969 and into 1970, with growing Soviet involvement in Egypt's defence. In mid-1970 US Secretary of State William Rogers presented a set of proposals for solving the continuing Middle East crisis, which resulted in an uneasy cease-fire but did not achieve a permanent solution.

FROM NASSER TO SADAT

Although President Nasser had clear differences with the Palestinian guerrillas over their rejection of US peace proposals and the hijacking of Western airliners at the beginning of September 1970, one of his final acts was to secure agreement in Cairo between King Hussein of Jordan and the Palestinian leader, Yasser Arafat, for an end to the fighting between the Jordanian army and Palestinian guerrillas.

Nasser's sudden death on 28 September 1970 came as a profound shock, which precipitated fears that prospects for conflict resolution in the Middle East would be jeopardized. Col Anwar Sadat, a close associate of Nasser, and the incumbent Vice-President, was immediately appointed provisional President by the Cabinet and the ASU, later being elected President in a national referendum. By mid-1971 he was firmly in control of the Government.

Sadat lacked strong commitment to any particular ideology. He was a pragmatist rather than an ideologue, so he could engage in war in order to make peace with Israel more likely. He did, however, attempt to create an image of himself as 'the Believer President,' perhaps not out of true religious duty as much as to develop his own constituency, rather than one dedicated to Nasser. Through his policy of *infitah* (economic opening), he promoted an image of himself as pro-capitalist—but not because he was committed to those policies. Indeed, Sadat maintained the Nasserist policies of state control over the economy. Sadat envisioned Arab capital (especially from Saudi Arabia) combined with Western technology as the way to promote fiscal development in an economy that had long been stagnant, owing to Nasser's policies and Sadat's own inability to change them fundamentally as well as the seemingly impossible task of tackling the demographic challenge of Egypt's high birth rate.

In November 1970 President Sadat agreed to the creation of a federation with Sudan and Libya. Sudan, however, later postponed its membership in the union. In April 1971 Syria agreed to become the third member of the federation. The federation proposals, together with Sadat's plan for the reopening of the Canal, precipitated a crisis in the Egyptian leadership, which led to a comprehensive purge by Sadat of opponents (including many Nasserists) at all government levels; this purge and new policy approach became known as the 'Corrective Revolution'. A new Constitution was approved in September 1971. It contained important clauses governing personal freedoms and replaced the name of the United Arab Republic with that of the Arab Republic of Egypt.

Legislative changes followed as did unrest: a law enacted in August 1972 provided for severe penalties, such as life imprisonment, for offences including the endangerment of national unity, forcible opposition to the Government and incitement of violence between Muslims and the Coptic Christian minority. Clashes between these two communities were becoming more frequent and, along with growing student unrest, were seen as an expression of dissatisfaction with the state of no-peace-no-war. In January 1973 there were violent clashes between police and students. In February a number of left-wing elements were expelled from the ASU; student unrest continued and in March President Sadat took over as Prime Minister (while retaining the presidency).

In terms of its international relations, Egypt had become increasingly dependent on the USSR, both militarily and economically, and intensified efforts to diversify sources of development aid and armaments. The Suez–Alexandria (Sumed) oil pipeline received promises of Western backing, and in May 1972 a five-year preferential trade agreement was concluded with the European Community (EC, now European Union—EU). However, the most striking event of 1972 was the dismissal of more than 10,000 Soviet military advisers from Egypt in July. Notably, this neither led to a major rupture in Egyptian-Soviet relations nor resulted in any significant rapprochement with the West. A new round of diplomacy to state Egypt's case, particularly in the West and the Far East, ensued, and arms supplies were requested from France and Britain. Contacts with the USSR continued and economic relations appeared unaffected by the events of July, although it was evident that the USSR was looking elsewhere to maintain its presence in the Mediterranean.

THE OCTOBER WAR AND ITS AFTERMATH

Between the June 1967 war and October 1973 Egyptian leaders frequently stated that the war against Israel would be resumed, but when Egyptian forces crossed the Suez Canal on 6 October 1973 to recover the territory lost to Israel, it came as a surprise both to Israel and the rest of the world. For President Sadat the war, which ended in a cease-fire after 18 days of fighting, represented a considerable triumph; it appeared to end the years of stalemate with Israel, and his personal reputation was greatly enhanced. As a result of the Disengagement Agreement signed by Israel and Egypt, Egyptian forces regained a strip of territory to the east of the Suez Canal.

Another result of the October War was Egypt's improved relations with the USA. Diplomatic relations between the two countries were restored in November 1973 and the US Secretary of State, Henry Kissinger, maintained a cordial relationship with President Sadat during the disengagement talks between Egypt and Israel. US peace-making initiatives were generally welcomed by Egypt, while the USA became more conscious of the extent of its dependence on Arab oil.

Significant internal political changes also took place. In early 1974 an amnesty was initially granted to a number of important political prisoners. This was further extended to more than 2,000 persons who had been imprisoned for political or criminal offences. Press censorship ended in February, and in May, at a national referendum, more than 8m. voters endorsed a programme of economic and social reform which focused on reconstruction, attracting foreign investment, the introduction of a private enterprise sector in the economy and limiting police interference in everyday life. However, increases in the cost of living and the slow pace of economic reform provoked riots in Cairo on 1 January 1975, and further disturbances in March. As a result of the unrest, Dr Abd al-Aziz Higazi, who had assumed the role of Prime Minister in September 1974, resigned the premiership and was replaced in April 1975 by Gen. Mamdouh Muhammad Salem, hitherto Deputy Prime Minister and Minister of the Interior.

During the first eight months of 1975 Kissinger engaged in considerable 'shuttle diplomacy', and in September Egypt and Israel signed the Second Interim Peace Agreement. In brief, Israel withdrew from the Giddi and Mitla passes and Egypt recovered the Abu Rudeis oilfield in Sinai, while Article I of the Agreement stated that the two countries agreed that 'the conflict between them and in the Middle East shall not be resolved by military force but by peaceful means'. This agreement brought upon President Sadat the strong disapproval of other Arab interests, particularly Syria, Jordan, Iraq and the Palestinian Liberation Organization (PLO), as it appeared to them that Egypt was seeking to commit the whole Arab world to a policy of peace with Israel. The position was complicated by the PLO's formal recognition as 'the sole, legitimate representative of the Palestinian people' at the Arab League summit in Rabat, Morocco, in October 1974. In May 1976 Egypt attempted to improve relations with the PLO by asking the Arab League to admit the PLO as a full member.

Despite the regional turmoil during 1976 and most of 1977, President Sadat was forced to concentrate increasingly on domestic issues. In March 1976 three political 'platforms' were allowed to form within the ruling ASU, and in the November 1976 elections to the People's Assembly these 'platforms' entered the contest as full-scale political parties. The Arab Socialist Party (a party of the centre, supporting Sadat) won 280 seats, while the Liberal Socialist Party (LSP, supporting political and economic liberalization) won 12 seats. The left-wing National Progressive Unionist Party (NPUP, or Tagammu) won two seats. After the elections, President Sadat announced that the ASU would take a less active political role in the future, acting more as a supervisory body for the three parties' activities.

Disturbed by the revival of the Wafd Party (as the New Wafd Party) and the criticisms of the NPUP, Sadat won approval in a referendum for new regulations on political parties that resulted in the disbanding of the New Wafd Party and the suspension of the NPUP. In July Sadat announced the creation of a new political party, the National Democratic Party (NDP), with himself as leader, which in practice replaced the Arab

Socialist Party. In September 1978 an official opposition party, the Socialist Labour Party (SLP), was formed.

THE ROAD TO A 'COLD' PEACE

In November 1977 President Sadat attracted international controversy with his announcement that he would 'go to Jerusalem' if it meant advancing peace talks with Israel. He further disturbed regional relations when he visited Israel and addressed its parliament, the Knesset. Notably, much of the Arab world was opposed to Egypt's unilateral engagement with Israel, regarding it as detrimental to Arab unity. Egypt had pre-empted action being considered by Syria, Libya, Algeria, Iraq and the People's Democratic Republic of Yemen, by severing diplomatic relations with these countries in December 1977.

In September 1978 an unexpected breakthrough was achieved at talks at the US presidential retreat at Camp David, Maryland, in the USA. Under the auspices of US President Jimmy Carter, Sadat and the Israeli Prime Minister, Menachem Begin, signed two agreements. The first was a 'framework for peace in the Middle East' (Documents on Palestine, see p. 69) and the second was a 'framework for the conclusion of a peace treaty between Egypt and Israel'. The first agreement provided for a five-year transitional period during which the inhabitants of the Israeli-occupied West Bank and the Gaza Strip would obtain full autonomy and self-government, and the second provided for the signing of a peace treaty within three months. The signing of the peace treaty was delayed because there was a question about whether there should be any linkage between the conclusion of the peace treaty and progress towards autonomy in the Israeli-occupied areas. However, on 26 March 1979, after another intervention by President Carter, the signing took place. The treaty (Documents on Palestine, see p. 71) provided for a phased Israeli withdrawal from Sinai over a period of 3 years. This withdrawal went according to plan (but for a lengthy negotiation over Taba), and, for the first time, diplomatic relations between Egypt and Israel were established on 26 February 1980 and the countries exchanged ambassadors.

The Camp David agreements and the subsequent peace treaty resulted in Egypt's isolation in the Arab world. Syria, Algeria, Libya and the PLO had met in Damascus in September 1978 and strongly condemned the Camp David agreements, and in March 1979, after the signing of the peace treaty, the Arab League Council met in Baghdad, Iraq, and passed a series of resolutions that addressed the withdrawal of Arab ambassadors to Egypt, the severing of economic and political links with Egypt, the withdrawal of Arab aid and the removal of the headquarters of the Arab League from Cairo to Tunis, Tunisia. Some Arab states were reluctant to implement these decisions, but when Saudi Arabia also broke off diplomatic relations with Egypt in late April, Egypt's isolation became potentially serious, although private Arab investment continued. (Of the Arab League countries, only Oman, Sudan and Somalia then maintained diplomatic relations with Egypt.) As a result, Egypt became increasingly dependent on US financial and military aid.

MUBARAK SUCCEEDS SADAT

After the signing of the Camp David agreements in September 1978, Sadat appointed a new Government, designed to further the peace process, with Mustafa Khalil as Prime Minister, who later became Minister of Foreign Affairs. Elections, held in June 1979, resulted in a win for Sadat's NDP, which obtained 302 seats in the expanded 392-seat People's Assembly (lower house of parliament).

Constitutional amendments were then proposed and approved in 1980, the most important of which provided for six-year renewable presidential terms, recognized Islamic jurisprudence as the basis of Egyptian law, and provided for the election of a 210-member Majlis al-Shura (Advisory Council) to replace the former Central Committee of the ASU. Elections for the new body took place in September, during which the NDP won all 140 elective seats. The remaining 70 members were appointed by the President.

Despite the legalization of political parties, power remained with Sadat's NDP; opposition, however, was never far beneath the surface. In mid-1981 there were clashes between Copts and Islamists, resulting in numerous arrests and the closure of various newspapers. Sadat attempted to stifle the opposition with little regard for religious or political persuasion.

On 6 October 1981, while attending a military parade celebrating the 1973 'victory' over Israel, Sadat was assassinated by a group of militants led by Khaled Islambouli. Islambouli was captured and later convicted and executed with four associates on 15 April 1982. Much of the world assumed Sadat was killed owing to his pursuit of peace with Israel. In reality, the assassination was more about his increasingly autocratic policies at home—including his censorship of the press and mass arrest of opponents, including Islambouli's younger brother, Muhammad.

Vice-President Muhammad Hosni Mubarak was confirmed as President in a referendum on 13 October 1981 and a state of emergency was declared and repeatedly extended in the years that followed. Although Mubarak released some who had been detained by Sadat, he continued to arrest Islamists, several hundred of whom were tried on charges of belonging to the extreme Islamist organization Gama'ah al-Islamiyah, which had plotted to overthrow the Government in 1981. In September 1984, 174 of the 302 people arrested in connection with Sadat's murder were acquitted of conspiring to overthrow the Government; 16 were sentenced to hard labour for life and the remainder received prison sentences ranging from two to 15 years.

In early 1984 Mubarak promised 'free, honest and sincere' elections in the hope that he could consolidate his authority and also establish himself as a popular leader who was tolerant, within limits, of opposition. NDP dominance was effectively assured as the absolute majority system (for individual candidates) was replaced with an electoral law establishing a system of proportional representation, which required parties to gain a minimum of 8% of the total vote in order to be represented in the People's Assembly. The size of the new Assembly was increased from 392 seats to 448, elected from 48 constituencies. (The President appointed 10 additional members.)

Elections to the People's Assembly took place on 27 May 1984, and the NDP accordingly took 72.9% of the total vote (the official turn-out was only 43% of eligible voters), entitling it to 389 seats. Of the four participating opposition parties, only the New Wafd (which had only been granted legal status in January), in strategic alliance with the outlawed Muslim Brotherhood, crossed the 8% threshold, winning a combined 15.1% of the vote, entitling them to 58 seats in the legislature (New Wafd had 50 seats and the Muslim Brotherhood eight).

The 1984 elections left Mubarak firmly in power, with a viable, yet politically brittle, opposition in the New Wafd, and the subversive Muslim Brotherhood in a relatively open political role, in which their activities could more easily be monitored. The opposition claimed that the elections were undemocratic, and accused the Government of widespread fraud and intimidation of voters. Moreover, the campaign by Egypt's Islamists for the legal system fully to adopt the principles of Islamic law (*Shari'a*) intensified and became part of a wider resurgence of Islamic consciousness in Egypt. Mubarak was wary of alienating the country's Coptic Christians (many of whom occupied important positions in commerce, industry and the professions). The President responded by imposing tighter censorship on books and films. However, at the same time he continued to adopt measures to prevent Islamist agitation from destabilizing the country by banning rallies, arresting militant, Islamist leaders and, in July 1985, placing all mosques under the control of the Ministry of Awqaf (Islamic Endowments). Islamists, however, were not Mubarak's only concern.

In foreign affairs, the early months of Mubarak's presidency were preoccupied with the question of the return of Sinai by Israel under the Camp David process. After many last-minute problems, the last section was returned to Egypt on 25 April 1982, although a dispute persisted until 1989 (resolved through international arbitration) concerning the 1 sq km of the Taba enclave on the Egypt–Israel border, north of the Gulf of Aqaba and adjacent to the Israeli city of Eilat.

Relations between the two countries were subsequently soured, most significantly by Israel's invasion of Lebanon in June 1982 and by Israel's suppression of the Palestinian uprising in the Occupied Territories. For its part, Egypt withdrew its ambassador from Tel-Aviv. There were signs during 1983—such as the readiness of Iraq and the PLO to restore normal diplomatic links, the resumption of trade with Jordan and with Iraq, and the increased flow of Arab money into Egyptian banks—that the period of the country's ostracism by other Arab states (with the exception of those with the most uncompromising regimes, such as Algeria, Libya and Syria) was drawing to a close. President Mubarak had openly supported Yasser Arafat when a Syrian-inspired revolt against his leadership of the PLO erupted in 1983 in the Beqa'a Valley, in Lebanon. In recognition of Egypt's support, Arafat visited Mubarak for talks in Cairo in December 1983, his first visit to Egypt for six years, marking the end of the rift between Egypt and the PLO. Substantial proof of Egypt's rehabilitation was provided by its readmission to the Organization of the Islamic Conference (OIC, now the Organization of Islamic Cooperation) in March 1984, although several countries, notably Libya and Syria, opposed the move.

Elsewhere in the region, an Egypt-Sudan Nile Valley Parliament, a Higher Integration Council and a Joint Fund, based on the two countries' common interests in the Nile River, were established by charter in October 1982. The parliament, comprising 60 Egyptian and 60 Sudanese members, was inaugurated in May 1983. Relatively powerless in itself, it was designed as the first step towards economic integration and an ultimate federation of the two states. The Higher Integration Council was to meet regularly to organize and review joint economic projects and to plan all aspects of the transition to the hoped-for federation. It was also to be used as a forum to coordinate policy on Pan-Arab questions. In October 1984 Egypt unilaterally withdrew from the confederation agreement for a 'Union of Arab Republics', which it had entered into with Syria and Libya in 1971.

In April 1985 the Sudanese President was deposed in a relatively bloodless coup, which was endorsed by the Libyan leader Muammar al-Qaddafi, who urged Arabs to overthrow other 'reactionary' regimes, implicitly including Egypt. Bilateral links between Sudan and Egypt were eventually placed on a more secure footing in February 1987, when a 'Brotherhood Charter' was signed in Cairo. This was understood to supersede an integration charter of October 1982 and to form the basis for future relations between the two countries.

The full resumption of diplomatic relations with the USSR was achieved during 1984, following the visit to Cairo in May of Vladimir Polyakov, the last Soviet ambassador to Egypt, who had been expelled with 1,000 or more experts by President Sadat in 1981. Mubarak had previously allowed the experts to return, and had signed trade and cultural agreements with the USSR. While it sought improved relations with the USSR, Egypt now stood second only to Israel in the amount of economic and military aid that it received from the USA.

OLD 'FRIENDS' AND NEW ELECTIONS

Egypt's engagement with the Israelis and Palestinians was ongoing. Arafat responded to pressure from King Hussein of Jordan and President Mubarak who called for the PLO to renounce violence (after a series of violent attacks implicating Arafat). The Palestinian leader reiterated a PLO decision of 1974 to confine military operations to Israel and the Occupied Territories; however, this was hardly the unequivocal statement that the Egyptian and Jordanian leaders had sought. In September 1986 President Mubarak met with Israel's Prime Minister, Shimon Peres, in Alexandria to discuss reviving the Middle East peace process. That same month, the two countries signed the Taba arbitration agreement).

It was largely as a result of its links with Israel that a new rift occurred between Egypt and the PLO in 1987. The crisis in relations was precipitated by the reunification of the Palestinian movement that took place at a session of the Palestine National Council (PNC) in Algiers in April. One of the conditions that dissident PLO factions exacted as the price for their return to the mainstream of the movement, under Arafat's leadership, was the weakening of Arafat's links with Egypt, making future contacts dependent on Egypt's abrogation of the Camp David accord and the 1979 peace treaty with Israel. President Mubarak responded by closing all the PLO's offices in Egypt at the end of April 1987. However, just a few months later, President Mubarak and Yasser Arafat held discussions in Addis Ababa, Ethiopia; the PLO's offices in Egypt were formally reopened at the end of November 1987. At the talks both leaders endorsed proposals (already supported by Egypt and Jordan) for convening an international peace conference on the Middle East, under UN auspices, involving the five permanent members of the UN Security Council and all parties to the conflict, including the PLO. President Mubarak and the Israeli Minister of Foreign Affairs, Shimon Peres, had agreed in principle on the need for an international conference when the latter visited Egypt in February, although the issue of PLO representation remained an obstacle to further progress. The Israeli Prime Minister, Itzhak Shamir, was opposed to a peace conference in any form, and suggested direct talks between Israel, Egypt, a Jordanian-Palestinian delegation and the USA. Mubarak urged the PLO to devise a formula for its inclusion in an international peace conference, and, during a visit to Israel in July, the Egyptian Minister of Foreign Affairs appealed to the Israeli Government to participate.

In November 1987, at a summit conference in Amman, Jordan, the Syrian President, Hafiz al-Assad, obstructed proposals to readmit Egypt to membership of the Arab League. However, recognizing Egypt's support for Iraq in its war against Iran and acknowledging the influence that Egypt (as the most populous and, militarily, the most powerful Arab nation) could bring to bear on the problems of the region, the conference approved a resolution putting the establishment of diplomatic links with Egypt at the discretion of member governments. One week after the conference ended, nine Arab states (the United Arab Emirates, Iraq, Kuwait, Morocco, the Yemen Arab Republic, Bahrain, Saudi Arabia, Mauritania and Qatar) had re-established full diplomatic relations with Egypt. Of the remaining 12 members of the League, three (Sudan, Somalia and Oman) had maintained diplomatic links with Egypt throughout the period of the boycott, Jordan and Djibouti had re-established them in 1985 and 1986, respectively, and the PLO (to which the League accorded nation status) had recently begun to settle its differences with Egypt. In February 1988 the People's Democratic Republic of Yemen restored full diplomatic relations with Egypt, leaving Algeria, Lebanon, Libya and Syria as the only Arab League members not to have done so. Libya was the most outspoken critic of the change in the League's policy towards Egypt, on the grounds that the 1979 peace treaty with Israel, the original reason for Egypt's ostracism, remained in force. In November 1988 Algeria announced that it would re-establish diplomatic relations with Egypt, and in June 1989 full diplomatic relations with Lebanon were restored.

In May President Mubarak represented Egypt at an emergency summit meeting of the Arab League in Casablanca, Morocco. The meeting, convened to rally support for the diplomatic initiatives of Yasser Arafat following the Palestinian declaration of independence (which Egypt recognized), was preceded by a meeting of ministers responsible for foreign affairs of the majority of the League's members, which endorsed Egypt's formal readmission to the Arab League after an absence of 10 years. Despite Libya's opposition to Egypt's readmission to the League, Qaddafi attended the meeting, and held separate talks with Mubarak. In June it was announced that Egypt was preparing to reopen its border with Libya, and in October Qaddafi visited Egypt, the first such visit for 16 years, for further discussions with Mubarak.

As Egypt moved towards elections, the requirement for political parties to obtain 8% of the total vote in order to enter the People's Assembly effectively prevented individual opposition parties from gaining significant representation in the legislature, and necessitated the formation of electoral alliances. After a failed attempt to unify all opposition parties under the banner of the New Wafd in January 1987, the SLP, the LSP and the Muslim Brotherhood agreed to form an alliance, which came to be known as the 'Islamic Alliance.' The New Wafd and the NPUP entered the 1987 election campaign unaligned.

Polling resulted in a large, though reduced, majority for the NDP in the People's Assembly. The ruling party won 346 seats (compared with 389 at the previous election in 1984), while the opposition parties won a total of 95 seats and independents seven. The 'Islamic Alliance' won a combined total of 60 seats, of which the Muslim Brotherhood took 37, making it the largest single opposition group in the new Assembly, while the New Wafd Party won 35 seats. The NPUP again failed to obtain representation in the legislature, winning only 2.2% of the vote. Overall, the election campaign was marred by sectarian clashes between Muslims and Christians in several towns in February and March 1987, and the opposition parties accused the Government of electoral fraud, the intimidation of opposition candidates and other forms of corruption.

In July 1987 Mubarak was nominated by the necessary two-thirds' majority of People's Assembly members to seek a second six-year term as President. Mubarak, the sole candidate, was duly confirmed in office by national referendum on 5 October, polling 97.1% of the votes cast.

DOMESTIC DISCONTENT

In December 1988 more than 500 Islamist students in Cairo and Asyout were arrested on suspicion of involvement in 'anti-state activities'. A few months later, facing mounting popular discontent over price increases and food shortages, the Government acted to pre-empt disturbances during the month of Ramadan by detaining more than 2,000 Islamists it viewed as extremists.

In July and August 1989, in a further attempt to suppress political opposition, members of the proscribed Egyptian Communist Workers' Party, Shi'ite Muslims, and prominent members of the Muslim Brotherhood were arrested on charges of subversion. By early September, following international protests, it was reported that most of the detainees had been released. In December there was speculation that Islamists had been responsible for the attempted assassination of the Minister of the Interior, Maj.-Gen. Zaki Badr, who had conducted the Government's ruthless campaign against political dissent. In January 1990 Badr was dismissed from his post and replaced by Muhammad Abd al-Halim Moussa.

The assassination of Dr Rifa'at el-Mahgoub, the Speaker of the People's Assembly, on 12 October 1990 increased tensions and led to the most comprehensive security operation since President Sadat's murder in 1981: hundreds of suspected Islamists were arrested and detained. The Ministry of the Interior claimed that the militant group, Islamic Jihad, was responsible for the assassination.

In May 1990 a constitutional crisis arose after Egypt's Supreme Constitutional Court ruled that elections to the People's Assembly in 1987 had been unconstitutional because the electoral law promulgated in 1986 unfairly discriminated against independent candidates. Legislation subsequently passed by the Assembly was deemed to be valid, but the Court declared that any new laws approved after 2 June 1990 could not be endorsed. A referendum was held in October, at which 94.3% of participating voters approved the dissolution of the People's Assembly.

At the legislative elections, held in November–December 1990, the former requirement for political parties to win a minimum of 8% of the total vote in order to gain representation in the Assembly was abolished, and restrictions on independent candidates were removed. Reverting to the 1979 electoral law, the new Assembly was elected on the basis of an absolute majority system for individual candidates. In addition, the size of the Assembly was decreased slightly, from 448 to 444 elective seats in 222 constituencies. However, opposition groups, including the New Wafd, the SLP, the LSP and the Muslim Brotherhood, boycotted the elections. The NPUP was the only major opposition party that took part in the polling, criticizing the boycott as being counter-productive. The elections resulted in a clear victory for the ruling NDP: of the 444 elective seats in the new Assembly, the NDP won 348 (compared with 346 at the 1987 general election), the NPUP six, and independent candidates won 83 (of whom 60 were affiliated to the NDP, 14 to the New Wafd Party, eight to the SLP and one to the LSP). Voting in the remaining seven seats was suspended. Voter turn-out was estimated at only 20%–30%.

REGIONAL REALIGNMENTS

In December 1989 Egypt and Syria restored full diplomatic relations, after a rift of 12 years. The rapprochement was widely regarded as signaling a shift away from the balance of power that had prevailed in the Arab world throughout the 1980s.

Prior to the crisis in the Persian (Arabian) Gulf region precipitated by Iraq's invasion and annexation of Kuwait in August 1990, Egypt attempted to mediate between Iraq and Kuwait. Following the invasion of Kuwait, Egypt sought initially to maintain its role as a mediator, immediately proposing a summit meeting of Arab leaders. At the meeting, Egypt firmly demanded the withdrawal of Iraqi forces from Kuwait, and 12 of the 20 Arab League member states participating in the meeting voted to send an Arab deterrent force to the Gulf in support of US efforts to deter an Iraqi invasion of Saudi Arabia. By late August about 5,000 Egyptian troops were reported to be in Saudi Arabia.

Egypt's quick success in mobilizing the support of moderate Arab states for the economic sanctions imposed on Iraq by the UN, and for the defence of Saudi Arabia, emphasized the extent of the improvement in relations with Syria. While it condemned Iraq's invasion of Kuwait, however, the Muslim Brotherhood demanded the immediate withdrawal of US forces from the Gulf and opposed the dispatch of Egyptian troops to Saudi Arabia as part of an Arab deterrent force. It was feared, too, that Egyptian expatriate workers (totalling some 800,000 in Iraq and 100,000 in Kuwait before the Iraqi invasion) returning in large numbers to almost certain unemployment in Egypt might have a destabilizing effect. Some 600,000 were reported to have returned to Egypt by January 1991.

Following the outbreak of hostilities between Iraq and a UN multinational force in January 1991, the Egyptian Government continued to support the anti-Iraq coalition. Egypt's contingent within the multinational force, eventually 35,000-strong, sustained only light casualties in the fighting. Egypt emerged from the conflict in the Gulf with its international reputation enhanced, largely as a result of President Mubarak's leadership of moderate Arab opinion. Moreover, the economy benefited from the waiving of almost US $14,000m. of Egypt's debts to the USA and other Western and Gulf states at an early stage in the crisis, and by the signing of an agreement with the IMF in May 1991, which, later in the same month, led to the rescheduling of $10,000m. of Egypt's debt to the 'Paris Club' of Western creditor governments, and the cancellation of the remaining $10,000m. over a three-year period.

Following the Gulf crisis, the Government's foreign policy continued to focus on the twin themes of Arab reconciliation and a settlement of the Arab–Israeli dispute, with particular emphasis being given to the Palestinian dimension. Egypt participated in the inaugural meeting of the Middle East peace conference in Madrid, Spain, in October 1991. In later stages it attended bilateral sessions as an observer and multilateral sessions as a participant. The appointment of Egypt's former Deputy Prime Minister, Dr Boutros Boutros-Ghali, as the new Secretary-General of the UN was regarded by Egypt as recognition of its moderating regional influence. President Mubarak welcomed the change of government in Israel in June 1992, and in July Israeli Prime Minister Itzhak Rabin visited Cairo for talks with President Mubarak, who reportedly emphasized that progress in the peace process was dependent on halting Jewish settlement construction in the Occupied Territories.

Egyptian mediators played an active role during the secret negotiations that led to the signing of the Declaration of Principles on Palestinian Self-rule between Israel and the PLO on 13 September 1993 (Documents on Palestine, see p. 76). The agreement made provision for limited Palestinian self-rule in the Gaza Strip and the town of Jericho on the West Bank. Once the agreement was announced, Egypt was the first Arab state that the PLO looked to for support. In October the

PLO and Israeli negotiating teams began meeting regularly in Egypt to discuss the detailed implementation of the agreement. In December, when talks became deadlocked, President Mubarak convened an emergency summit meeting in Cairo between the Israeli Prime Minister and the PLO leader, Yasser Arafat. However, the meeting failed to achieve an agreement on the withdrawal of Israeli armed forces from Gaza and Jericho, which had been scheduled to begin on 13 December.

The massacre of more than 40 Palestinians in Hebron on the West Bank by an Israeli settler on 25 February 1994 provoked several days of angry demonstrations in Cairo. Egypt withdrew its ambassador from Israel for consultations, but Egyptian diplomats tried to persuade both the PLO and Israel to resume their negotiations. Talks between Israel and the PLO recommenced in Cairo at the end of March. In early April President Assad of Syria visited Cairo for talks with President Mubarak, reportedly concerning Syria's dissatisfaction with Egypt's support for the Israeli-PLO agreement. On 4 May, after months of negotiations, the Israeli Prime Minister and the PLO Chairman signed an agreement on Palestinian self-rule in Gaza and Jericho at a ceremony presided over by President Mubarak.

UPSURGE IN VIOLENCE

From early 1992, militant Islamist groups intensified their campaign and the Government responded. Militant strongholds included the Asyout governorate in Upper Egypt and the poorer districts of Cairo, such as Imbaba. In June approximately 5,000 members of the security forces were deployed in Asyout, one of the most extensive military operations against militants in years. In July the People's Assembly adopted new anti-terrorism legislation that imposed the death sentence for some crimes.

The leader of Gama'ah al-Islamiyah publicly denounced the very concept of foreign tourism in Egypt and threatened to destroy the country's major tourist attractions, the Pharaonic sites. Attacks on foreign tourists occurred regularly during 1993, seriously damaging the country's vital tourism industry. As a result of the campaign of violence, many international tour operators withdrew from Egypt, and revenues from tourism fell dramatically.

The problem of militant violence became more acute in 1993, and attempts to control it came to dominate the domestic political agenda. In April the Minister of Information narrowly escaped death when his car was ambushed. Ironically, the minister had been criticized by liberals for filling the television schedules with religious programmes, which was regarded as a crude and unconvincing attempt to appease Islamist opinion. The Minister of the Interior, Hassan Muhammad al-Alfi, was seriously wounded in an assassination attempt in August. In November Prime Minister Atif Sidqi escaped unharmed when a car bomb exploded near his residence. Harsh measures were employed by the security forces to counter the escalation of violence, and those arrested were increasingly tried by military courts, which were seen as more effective than civil courts in securing quick convictions. During 1993 military courts sentenced 38 alleged militant Islamists to death and 29 were hanged, the largest number of political executions in Egypt's recent history.

Policing methods and the use of military courts in the campaign against Islamist violence provoked widespread international criticism. In May 1993 the United Kingdom-based human rights organization Amnesty International published a report which stated that, in response to the increased killings of police officers and others, the security forces appeared to have been given 'a licence to kill with impunity'. It criticized the military courts as 'a travesty of justice'. In November the UN Committee against Torture accused the Egyptian security forces of carrying out systematic torture against suspects in security cases and in ordinary criminal cases.

Militant groups intensified their attacks on tourists and also targeted foreign investors. Gama'ah al-Islamiyah sent a series of warnings to international news agencies to the effect that tourists and foreign investors should leave Egypt, and that anyone helping a regime that opposed Islam would receive 'the same punishment as the oppressors'. In February and March 1994 there were several attacks on tourist trains in Upper Egypt, and in early March a German tourist was killed when shots were fired at Nile cruise ships. Gama'ah al-Islamiyah also carried out a series of bomb attacks on banks in Cairo and towns in Upper Egypt.

The crackdown by the security forces was unrelenting. Figures released by the Ministry of the Interior showed that 29,000 suspected militants had been incarcerated following mass arrests. In April 1994 a new law was enacted abolishing local elections and granting the Ministry of the Interior powers to appoint village mayors (*omdas*). In response to criticism from opposition deputies, the Government claimed that many mayors had refused to co-operate in security matters and were corrupt. The following day the emergency laws, which gave the security forces wide powers to arrest and detain suspects, were renewed for a further three years. The authorities also redoubled their efforts to curb the activities of leaders of extremist groups living abroad. In early April an extradition treaty was signed with Pakistan, and there were reports that the authorities in Yemen and Saudi Arabia were co-operating with Egypt in security matters. Local and Western journalists were warned to ensure that their articles conformed with official guidelines or they would face arrest or expulsion. A propaganda offensive against the Islamists launched in the state-controlled media included televised 'confessions' by alleged former militants.

Stringent security measures remained in force, and the continued use of special military courts to try suspected Islamists was criticized by human rights groups. Since 1992 scores of Islamists had been sentenced to death by military courts. Mass arrests continued: among those detained in December 1994 was the Secretary-General of the pro-Islamist SLP, Adel Hussein, a former Marxist turned Islamist, who was accused of having links with militant extremist groups and of supporting Gama'ah al-Islamiyah in its efforts to overthrow the Government. A prominent journalist, Hussein had written several articles vehemently denouncing official corruption. He was detained for one month and only released after strong protests from journalists, intellectuals and opposition leaders.

During 1995–97 militants wreaked havoc on Egypt in a series of attacks, which left dozens dead and even more wounded. One of their more brazen attacks was the June 1995 attempted assassination of President Mubarak in Addis Ababa, Ethiopia. Gama'ah al-Islamiyah claimed responsibility, but Islamic Jihad was implicated. Following the attempt on President Mubarak's life in Addis Ababa, militants continued their struggle abroad, which included an attack on the Egyptian embassy in Islamabad, Pakistan.

In February 1997 the People's Assembly approved a presidential decree whereby emergency law provisions were extended for a further three years. Human rights groups insisted that the emergency measures were being used not only to counter militancy but also to undermine support for political groups opposed to the regime. In the early months of 1997 there were a number of reports of attacks by Islamist groups against Coptic Christians in Upper Egypt.

The most infamous militant attack in Egypt occurred in November 1997, when 70 people, including 58 foreign tourists, were killed by members of Gama'ah al-Islamiyah in Luxor. The damage to the Egyptian tourism industry was apparent in the immediate aftermath of the attack as foreign tour operators cancelled bookings and foreign governments advised their citizens to leave the country. Militants, Islamists and others were aggrieved with the Arab–Israeli peace process and frustrated at the lack of legitimate means to express political opposition, economic hardship caused by the country's programme of fiscal reform, and at the corruption resulting from that programme. A spokesman of the Muslim Brotherhood condemned the attack at Luxor, but emphasized the need for the Government to engage in dialogue with those among its political opponents who rejected violence, as part of a wider process of political, economic and social reform. Following the attack at Luxor, President Mubarak ordered a heightened security presence at all tourist sites, and placed the Prime Minister at the head of a special committee that was to devise a plan to safeguard the tourism industry.

POLITICAL DEVELOPMENTS

Against this backdrop of state insecurity and violence, President Mubarak was formally nominated for a third six-year term of office in July 1993. None of the opposition parties, nor the proscribed but tolerated Muslim Brotherhood, endorsed his candidature. Mubarak's nomination was 'approved' by nation-wide referendum on 4 October. Mubarak immediately promoted the Minister of Defence, Gen. Muhammad Hussain Tantawi, to the rank of Field Marshal, an honour accorded to only four other generals since the revolution. Senior air force and air defence officers were also promoted. Some observers saw this as a move to placate the army—the ultimate power behind the regime—after Mubarak's refusal to appoint a Vice-President, a post that the military had traditionally regarded as its own. In a newspaper interview in October, Tantawi stated that he would deploy the army against militants if they threatened the security of the nation. This was the first time that the army had publicly declared its readiness to involve itself in the campaign against militant Islamist groups which had been largely the purview of the Ministry of the Interior.

As elections to the People's Assembly in November 1995 approached, the political opposition remained weak and divided. After many months of negotiations the different parties were unable to agree on terms for a united front against the ruling NDP. Despite the opposition's outspoken lack of confidence in the electoral process, in August 1995 the New Wafd Party formally announced that it would participate in the elections and the other parties quickly followed suit. The main disagreement, however, appeared to be between the secular and pro-Islamist opposition parties. Meanwhile, the Government moved to isolate the Muslim Brotherhood and to weaken its political influence in the approach to the parliamentary elections. Several leading members of the Brotherhood were arrested earlier in the year, and the Government claimed that there was evidence of links between it and more extreme groups. After the attempted assassination of President Mubarak in June, pre-election security operations against the Muslim Brotherhood intensified. At the end of August Mubarak's decision to refer 49 leading members of the Brotherhood for trial by military courts attracted widespread criticism, even from the movement's political opponents. The NPUP, the (Arab Democratic) Nasserist Party and the New Wafd Party, among others, endorsed a statement of protest against the military trials, observing that the Muslim Brotherhood was committed to dialogue. Just days before the elections, dozens of the Brothers, including many parliamentary candidates, received prison sentences of three to five years for 'unconstitutional activities' from a military court that also closed down the movement's headquarters in Cairo. In November the Minister of the Interior repeated his claim to have evidence of close links between the Brotherhood and the Islamist militants, and accused the Brotherhood, Gama'ah al-Islamiyah and Islamic Jihad of, ultimately, being part of one single organization.

The combined results of the first and second rounds of voting, held on 29 November and 6 December 1995, were as follows: the NDP won 316 of the total 444 seats, independent candidates 115 and the opposition parties combined just 13—the New Wafd Party six, the NPUP five, and the LSP and the Nasserist Party one each. For the first time the NDP pitted powerful government ministers against prominent Islamist candidates, most of whom were defeated in the first round. After the vote 99 independent deputies were reported to have joined the NDP, giving the ruling party an overwhelming victory with 93% of all parliamentary seats. Five women won seats, all of them candidates of the NDP. The newly formed Independent Commission for Electoral Review (ICER) noted that 56 Coptic candidates contested the elections, but that no Copts were included on NDP nomination lists. No Copts were elected, but of the 10 deputies appointed by the President, six were Copts. Voter participation was officially registered at around 50% in both rounds of voting, but the ICER claimed that fear of violence and lack of faith in the fairness of the elections had resulted in a considerable increase in voter abstention in the second round. Despite government assurances that the elections would be fair, they were widely denounced as the most fraudulent in Egypt's recent history. Furthermore, the ICER and other sources claimed that they had been characterized by unprecedented violence and bloodshed.

In January 1996 President Mubarak appointed the Deputy Prime Minister and Minister of Planning, Dr Kamal al-Ganzouri, to head a new Government, in place of the long-serving Atif Sidqi. After the parliamentary elections Mubarak came under pressure to improve the Government's image by creating a more efficient administration with less ministerial conflict. Although regarded as an economic conservative, international institutions expressed the hope that, with strong support from the President, the new Prime Minister would prove more decisive than Sidqi in implementing reforms. Al-Ganzouri, who retained the planning portfolio, stated that he would give priority to job creation, accelerating economic development and encouraging foreign investment.

The Government's intimidation of the Muslim Brotherhood continued after the parliamentary elections. Following allegations of financial mismanagement, the Lawyers' Syndicate, which had been dominated by members of the Muslim Brotherhood, was placed under the control of court-appointed custodians, leaving the Medical Syndicate as the only major professional union controlled by Islamists. In May 1996 the Supreme Constitutional Court upheld a decree, issued by the Minister of Education in July 1994, prohibiting girls from wearing the *niqab* (veil) in schools. In December the People's Assembly made it an offence to preach in a mosque that had not been licensed by the Ministry of Awqaf. The Government thereby intended to extend its control over the country's many private mosques, which it claimed were used by 'fundamentalist' Islamist groups, such as the Brotherhood, for their political activities.

In March 1997 the Brotherhood announced that it was not contesting the forthcoming local elections because it did not expect them to be free or fair. The other main opposition party, the New Wafd, also indicated that it would boycott the elections. As expected, at the local elections held on 7 April 1997 the ruling NDP won the vast majority of seats. Although the NDP faced little to no opposition, there were widespread claims of electoral fraud. Two days before the elections the State Security Prosecutor ordered the arrest of 27 members of the Muslim Brotherhood, which claimed that hundreds of its followers had been detained to prevent them from participating.

Attempts by the Government to suppress the activities of Islamist groups intensified during 1998, with further arrests and security trials. However, the Government also moved closer to moderating its approach towards some militants—accused and actual. In the meantime, internal dissent within Gama'ah al-Islamiyah remained evident. In early 1999 one of the group's founders denied reports that the organization was planning to establish a political party. Nevertheless, speculation continued during that year, and it was predicted that the political programme of the new party (reportedly to be called Al-Islah or Reform) would shortly be presented to the Political Parties Committee (PPC). Meanwhile, in March Gama'ah al-Islamiyah declared a unilateral cease-fire and announced a new strategy of exerting maximum political pressure on the Government without the use of violence. The cease-fire had reportedly been endorsed by Sheikh Abd al-Rahman, its Advisory Council and the leaders in exile. However, it remained unclear as to whether its military commanders would end their campaign of violence.

Despite the apparent development of a fragile truce between the Government and some militants, state security trials, prison sentences of between one year and life, all with hard labour, and death sentences were handed down. Relatively few defendants were acquitted. Among those sentenced to death, having been tried *in absentia* (as were most of the defendants), was a senior leader of Islamic Jihad, Ayman al-Zawahiri. In response to the verdicts, Islamic Jihad pledged to continue its actions against the state, despite Gama'ah al-Islamiyah's cease-fire declaration in March 1999. The Egyptian Organization for Human Rights (EOHR) claimed that there had been insufficient evidence for the defendants to be sentenced. In September the Government stated that it had released more than 5,000 Islamist detainees since the beginning of the year. Human rights groups noted that this still left approximately

15,000 in detention, two-thirds of whom had no 'extremist', Islamist connections. Moreover, most of these detainees were being held without charge or trial.

Meanwhile, labour unrest in Egypt had reached its highest level since the 1952 revolution. Despite legal restrictions on strike action, public sector workers staged an estimated 80 protests in 1998, and 10 strikes were organized in February 1999. This increase in industrial action, which particularly affected the road and air transport and textiles sectors, was believed to reflect public concerns about a proposed labour law that would facilitate the termination of employment contracts. In addition, legislation concerning the activities of non-governmental organizations (NGOs), approved by the People's Assembly in May, attracted strong criticism from both the committee charged with preparing recommendations on the proposed law and from human rights groups which claimed that the legislation would compromise the independence of the organizations. The new Law on Associations and Civil Institutions imposed stringent state regulation on such bodies, including the right of state intervention to dismiss board members and appoint government representatives in their place, and prevented NGOs from receiving funding from abroad.

EGYPT STRIVES TO REASSERT ITS REGIONAL STATUS

The Middle East peace process continued to dominate Egypt's foreign policy. In July 1994 President Mubarak travelled to Damascus in an effort to break the deadlock in the negotiations between Syria and Israel, and before returning to Cairo he met with the Israeli Prime Minister. The first official visit by an Israeli President, Ezer Weizman, happened in December, although relations were becoming more tenuous as Egypt grew concerned about Israel's intransigence.

The situation deteriorated as Mubarak reiterated that Egypt would not sign the Treaty on the Non-Proliferation of Nuclear Weapons (the Non-Proliferation Treaty—NPT), which was due for renewal in April, unless Israel also agreed to sign it; Mubarak urged other Arab states to follow Egypt's example. Israel, meanwhile, accused Egypt of attempting to use the non-proliferation issue to disrupt its efforts to normalize relations with other Arab states. In March 1995 Israel offered to sign the NPT once it had concluded peace treaties with all the Arab states and Iran, and to allow Egypt to inspect its research nuclear reactor at Nahal Shorek but not the nuclear facility at Dimona. Egypt rejected both offers, but adopted a more conciliatory stance on the issue.

Egypt's position regarding the NPT antagonized the USA, which insisted that the continuation of US aid depended on Egypt's signing of the Treaty. When President Mubarak visited Washington, DC, USA, in April 1995, Egypt's relations with the USA had reached their lowest level for many years. The dispute with Israel over the NPT dominated discussions during the visit, at the end of which President Mubarak pledged that Egypt would not withdraw from the Treaty nor persuade other states to suspend their membership. However, the possibility of a reduction in US aid to Egypt continued to be discussed openly.

As the dispute over the NPT came to a head at the UN in New York in May 1995, Egypt led the Arab states in demanding a resolution requiring Israel to sign the Treaty. However, under US pressure, the Arab states agreed to a resolution that did not mention Israel by name but instead urged all states in the Middle East without exception to sign the NPT and accept inspection of their nuclear facilities by the International Atomic Energy Agency (IAEA).

Back on the Israeli-Palestinian front, Egypt continued its intermediary role in the complex negotiations that eventually led to the signing of the Israeli-Palestinian Interim Agreement on the West Bank and the Gaza Strip in Washington, DC, in September 1995. On 6 November Mubarak made his first visit to Israel as President of Egypt, in order to attend the funeral of Prime Minister Itzhak Rabin, who had been assassinated two days earlier by Yigal Amir, an Israeli law student opposed to peace with Palestinians (see the chapter on Israel). Egypt also participated in meetings leading to the start of more substantive talks between Israel and Syria at the end of 1995.

Disputes over Israel's nuclear capability and the execution of Egyptian prisoners of war continued, however. In April 1996, following reports of a possible leak of nuclear waste from Israel's Dimona reactor, Egypt's Minister of Foreign Affairs, Amr Moussa, urged that the reactor should be dismantled and rejected any co-operation on security with Israel while it retained a nuclear capability. In that month the African Nuclear-Weapon-Free Zone Treaty (or Pelindaba Treaty) was signed in Cairo. At the signing ceremony President Mubarak urged all Middle Eastern countries to make the region a nuclear-free zone by signing the NPT.

By April of 1996, Egypt's relations with Israel deteriorated further when Israeli forces launched air and artillery attacks on Hezbollah bases in Lebanon, inflicting heavy casualties on Lebanese civilians. The Lebanese Prime Minister, Rafiq Hariri, visited Cairo to seek assistance against Israeli aggression; however, diplomatic efforts by the Egyptian Minister of Foreign Affairs to achieve a cease-fire were unsuccessful, and in exasperation he complained that Israel's actions threatened the credibility of the entire peace process. Relations did not improve when it was announced, in April, that Israel and Turkey had concluded a military agreement in February allowing Israeli aircraft to fly from Turkish airbases and Israeli warships to use Turkish ports during joint naval manoeuvres. The Egyptian Minister of Foreign Affairs denounced the agreement, arguing that it did not serve the interests of peace or stability in the region. Military strategists in Egypt regarded it as the creation of 'a second front against the Arabs' while other observers maintained that a new strategic partnership was emerging in the region between Israel, the USA, Jordan and Turkey that could only serve to increase Egypt's marginalization.

In June 1996, after Israeli Prime Minister Benjamin Netanyahu rejected the principle of 'land for peace', President Mubarak convened an emergency summit meeting of the Arab League in Cairo—the first full-scale summit meeting in six years. (Iraq was not invited owing to what President Mubarak referred to as 'continuing sensitivities'.) The summit reaffirmed Egypt's central role in the Arab world, where Egyptian efforts at reconciliation created some semblance of unity.

Although Netanyahu was invited for talks with President Mubarak in Cairo in July 1996, relations with Israel became increasingly strained. In September there were popular demonstrations in Egypt after the Israeli Government opened the ancient Hasmonean tunnel in East Jerusalem, close to Muslim religious sites. Violent clashes erupted between Israeli troops and Palestinians and public anger prevented Egypt from acting as mediator in the crisis. Although Prime Minister Netanyahu, King Hussein of Jordan and the President of the Palestinian (National) Authority (PA), Yasser Arafat, attended a summit meeting in Washington, DC, to try to defuse the crisis, President Mubarak resisted US pressure to participate, stating that an immediate resolution was unlikely to be achieved. Despite a goodwill visit to Cairo by President Weizman in October, his reassurances about Israel's peace commitments failed to ease tensions between the two countries.

The year 1997 was another one of vicissitudes. When, in March 1997, the ministers of foreign affairs of the Arab League member states met in Cairo, it was decided to reintroduce the economic boycott of Israel and to halt the normalization of relations. Egypt was exempt from the boycott, however, owing to its peace treaty with Israel. In early April President Mubarak insisted that relations with Israel would remain secure. Indeed, Egypt wished to maintain its intermediary role and its economic links with the country. Nevertheless, there were many signs of popular dissatisfaction with the normalization of relations with Israel. Although President Mubarak tried to restart the peace process through consultation with a range of parties, Israel's continued building of settlements in East Jerusalem appeared to prolong the deadlock, and for the remainder of the year the Egyptian Government, in its role as principal mediator, attempted unsuccessfully to revive the peace process. By September Egypt's relations with Israel were further impaired when an

Egyptian State Security Court sentenced an Israeli Arab, Azam Azam, to 15 years' imprisonment with hard labour, having convicted him of spying for the Israeli intelligence services (which the Israeli Government denied). In October Egypt announced a prohibition of imports of Israeli goods produced in the Occupied Territories, and in the following month joined several other Arab countries and boycotted the fourth Middle East and North Africa economic conference in Doha, Qatar, to protest Israel's failure to honour its commitments to the Palestinians under the terms of the Oslo accords.

President Mubarak and Prime Minister Netanyahu of Israel held talks in Cairo in April 1998. The focus of their discussions was reportedly a US initiative to restart the peace process, which proposed that Israel should withdraw from a further 13.1% of West Bank territory. Prior to his meeting with Mubarak, Netanyahu had rejected the US proposal. In Mubarak's view, Israel's acceptance of the proposal would facilitate the resumption of final status negotiations between Israel and the Palestinians, as well as Israel's negotiations with Syria and Lebanon. In June, after talks were held with Arafat to discuss an Israeli proposal for a new Madrid peace conference, President Mubarak accused Netanyahu of 'destroying the peace process' by seeking to annul the first Madrid agreement. By July bilateral relations were reported to have deteriorated to their worst level since 1979. President Mubarak cautiously welcomed the Wye River Memorandum signed by Arafat and Netanyahu in the USA, in October 1998 (Documents on Palestine, see p. 92). However, in January 1999 the Egyptian Government froze all contacts with Israel's Likud Government over its decision to suspend the implementation of the agreement.

President Mubarak attended the funeral of King Hussein of Jordan in February 1999. In March, following a trilateral meeting with Palestinian representatives, Egypt and Jordan made a joint declaration in support of the Palestinians' right to declare an independent state after the expiry of the Oslo accords on 4 May. However, in the light of an increasingly volatile security situation in the Occupied Territories, and of the Israeli general election scheduled for 17 May, Egypt and Jordan subsequently joined the EU, the USA and other countries in urging Arafat to postpone the planned declaration of Palestinian statehood.

In July 1999 the new Israeli Prime Minister, Ehud Barak, held talks with Egyptian, Jordanian, Palestinian and US leaders to seek to advance the peace process. It was considered to be a clear sign of Egypt's crucial role in the negotiations—especially after the death of King Hussein—that President Mubarak should be chosen as the first Arab leader to meet the new Israeli premier.

Meanwhile, relations with the USA remained strained. Egypt was convinced that the Clinton Administration had forfeited its role as impartial mediator in the Middle East peace process owing to its close alliance with Israel. Visiting Cairo in April 1996, the US Secretary of Defense, William Perry, denied rumours that the USA had signed a secret defence agreement with Israel. During his visit Perry announced that his country would supply advanced military equipment to Egypt, including 21 F-16 fighter aircraft, in acknowledgement of its key role in the peace process. However, in December the US veto of a second term of office as UN Secretary-General for Boutros Boutros-Ghali provoked widespread outrage in the Egyptian media. Egypt was also highly critical of US military air strikes against alleged terrorist strongholds in Afghanistan, and a pharmaceuticals factory in Khartoum, Sudan. The US Government claimed the factory was being used by associates of Osama bin Laden to manufacture chemical weapons components. Moreover, air strikes against Iraq undertaken by US and British forces in December 1998 exacerbated existing tensions between Egypt and the USA, since Mubarak had consistently urged a diplomatic solution to the crisis.

Egypt frequently sought to mediate in disputes between Iraq and the UN after 1991. In September 1997, in a joint declaration with Russia, Egypt urged the restoration of Iraq's status as a full member of the international community, while insisting that it should comply with pertinent UN resolutions. In February 1998, following consultations with other Arab leaders, President Mubarak presented the US Secretary of State, Madeleine Albright, with an 'integrated' Arab plan to resolve Iraq's latest conflict with the UN over weapons inspections. In January 1999 Arab League ministers responsible for foreign affairs, meeting in Cairo, made a formal request for Iraq to comply with all pertinent UN Security Council resolutions and apologize to Kuwait for the 1990 invasion.

Egypt's relations with Libya slowly improved after 1996. Egypt played an important role as mediator in Libya's discussions with the USA and the United Kingdom over the Lockerbie affair (see the chapter on Libya), the repercussions of which had dominated Egyptian-Libyan relations. In April 1999 the two Libyans suspected of organizing the Lockerbie bomb were extradited to the Netherlands to stand trial. In the same month, as a result of this development, UN sanctions imposed against Libya in 1992 were suspended indefinitely.

DOMESTIC POLITICS AS USUAL?

In June 1999 President Mubarak was formally nominated for a fourth six-year term of office; once again, he did not face an opponent. In the national referendum, held on 26 September, President Mubarak's re-election was approved by some 93.8% of the valid votes cast. In August opposition parties and human rights groups had urged the President to carry out significant constitutional and political reforms, notably the abolition of emergency laws and restrictions on the formation of political parties and trade unions, increased press freedom and the guarantee of free and fair elections. There was, however, little substantive change to reinforce hopes of political liberalization in the coming year.

On 5 October 1999 Mubarak appointed Dr Atif Muhammad Obeid, previously the Minister of the Public Enterprise Sector and responsible for the Government's programme of privatization, as the new Prime Minister. The appointment of Obeid was widely interpreted as an indication that economic reforms would be accelerated, since the new premier was viewed as being far more pro-liberalization and pro-privatization than his predecessor. When, on 10 October, Obeid announced his new Council of Ministers, which included 13 new ministers, Mubarak's trusted 'old guard' retained control over the strategic defence, interior and foreign affairs portfolios.

In political terms, the first year of Mubarak's fourth term was characterized by far more continuity than change. The Government undertook a series of arrests and harassment of potential candidates during October 1999. In that month 20 members of the Muslim Brotherhood were arrested on charges of plotting to overthrow the Government and of infiltrating professional syndicates (including the Medical and Engineers' Syndicates), in order to undermine national security. The subsequent trial—the biggest against the Muslim Brotherhood since 1995—opened in December 1999, but was postponed for procedural reasons and resumed in January 2000, at a military base outside Cairo.

In December 1999 the authorities released 1,200 Gama'ah al-Islamiyah prisoners (and hundreds more, including Islamic Jihad prisoners, were released the following March). During that month there were reports of a renewed power struggle within the organization's leadership. In January 2000 there were also rumours that a 'coup' had occurred within Islamic Jihad whereby one of the leaders of the organization, Dr Ayman al-Zawahiri, had been removed (allegedly owing to his links with Osama bin Laden). In February it was reported that the Islamic Jihad leadership had called on its members both in Egypt and abroad to cease their military activities. This was the first time that Islamic Jihad leaders had called for a cease-fire, and it was reportedly backed by the group's imprisoned leaders. This appeared to be confirmed when, in July, 11 leaders of Jihad's military wing, who were imprisoned in Egypt, officially declared an end to their armed operations against the Government. Meanwhile, in June the cease-fire that had been declared by Gama'ah al-Islamiyah was called into question when Sheikh Abd al-Rahman announced from detention in the USA that he was withdrawing his support for it, claiming that the cease-fire had achieved nothing. Although some of the group's founders stressed subsequently that Gama'ah al-Islamiyah remained committed to pursuing solely peaceful means, some observers feared a return to violence.

In February 2000 observers learned that EOHR's Secretary-General, Hafiz Abu Sa'ada, would be tried before the Higher State Security Court for accepting US $25,000 from the British embassy in Cairo without obtaining official permission from the Ministry of Social Affairs. Some observers saw a connection between this development and the EOHR's investigations into the worst incidence of sectarian violence in Egypt for decades. In January 2000 three days of violent clashes had taken place between Muslims and Coptic Christians in the predominantly Christian village of el-Kosheh in Upper Egypt. An estimated 21 people, 20 Copts and one Muslim, died as a result of the violence, and more than 30 others were injured. The EOHR's report, released in February, identified the primary cause of the violence as 'economic inequalities' between the relatively prosperous Coptic majority and the poorer Muslim minority. The EOHR claimed that during 1991–98 about 99 Copts were killed by militant Islamist organizations. The report criticized the security forces and drew attention to allegations that they had used oppressive measures against the Coptic community during investigations in mid-1998 into the murder of two Copts in el-Kosheh, which the EOHR felt had contributed to communal tensions. In June 2000 the trial began of 96 men in connection with January's violence. In February 2001 the Coptic Church announced that it would appeal against the criminal court verdict: four Muslim men were sentenced to between one and 10 years' imprisonment, while the remaining 92 defendants were acquitted.

In early February 2000 President Mubarak appointed his son, Gamal, to the general secretariat of the ruling NDP, as part of a wider reorganization of the party. Gamal Mubarak, however, later denied rumours that he was preparing to stand for the People's Assembly in the forthcoming general election. On 26 February a presidential decree was issued extending until 2003 the state of emergency in place since President Sadat's assassination in 1981.

In late May 2000 the PPC suspended the Islamist-orientated SLP and its newspaper Al-Shaab, on the grounds that the party had exceeded its political mandate. This followed a campaign by Al-Shaab against *Banquet for Seaweed*, a novel (first published in 1983) by the Syrian author Haidar Haidar, which the newspaper claimed was blasphemous. The SLP was held responsible for clashes in early May 2000 outside the Al-Azhar University between police and hundreds of students protesting at the decision, taken in November 1999 by the Ministry of Culture, to approve the reprinting of the book. As a result of the riots, the Government banned all sales of the book. In mid-July 2,000 charges were initiated against leaders of the SLP, including the editor of Al-Shaab, Magdi Ahmad Hussein; these included having links with the Muslim Brotherhood and disturbing public order. However, in late July a court ruling stated that the action of banning the party and closing down its newspaper were unconstitutional. The SLP's activities remained officially frozen, but in September a Judicial Administrative Court ruled against the suspension of Al-Shaab and referred the issue of the disbandment of the SLP to the High Administrative Court.

There were minor successes for human rights groups and other NGOs in 2000. In May the Arab Organization for Human Rights, a regional group unofficially based in Cairo since 1989, was legalized. Moreover, in early June 2000 the Supreme Constitutional Court annulled the controversial Law on Associations and Civil Institutions, enacted in May 1999, declaring it to be unconstitutional. Nevertheless, at the end of June 2000 the Government ordered the closure of the Ibn Khaldoun Center for Social and Development Studies in Cairo and arrested five of its members, including the academic and democracy activist, Prof. Saad Eddin Ibrahim. It was alleged that Ibrahim had accepted more than US $220,000 from the European Commission to produce a documentary on the electoral process in Egypt ahead of the parliamentary elections scheduled for late 2000. Western governments condemned the action, and expressed renewed concerns over the Egyptian authorities' apparent crackdown on human rights activists in the approach to the elections. In August Ibrahim was also charged by the Egyptian Government with involvement in espionage activities on behalf of the USA. Ibrahim and his colleagues were released on bail in the same month. However, in May 2001 Ibrahim was sentenced to seven years' imprisonment, with hard labour, having been convicted on charges of defaming Egypt, embezzlement, forgery and receiving unauthorized funds. Following widespread international protest, Ibrahim faced two retrials and was finally acquitted of all charges in March 2003.

In July 2000 the Supreme Constitutional Court ruled that the incumbent People's Assembly, elected in 1995, was invalid since the constitutional requirement that the judiciary have sole responsibility for the supervision of elections had been ignored. In response, President Mubarak held an extraordinary session of the Assembly on 16 July 2000, at which deputies unanimously approved several amendments to the existing Political Rights Law, granting the judiciary the authority to supervise the elections at both main and auxiliary polling stations and the right to select its own members for the task. In an earlier amendment of the same law, approved in April 2000, the Government had merely extended judicial supervision to the counting stations and assigned one judge to monitor several auxiliary stations. The amendments were welcomed by opposition leaders.

The amendments to the electoral law providing for sole judicial supervision raised hopes that the elections, to be held in three rounds on 18 October, 29 October and 8 November 2000, would be the most transparent and credible for more than a decade. However, the announcement in September that the Minister of the Interior had been given the authority to name the judges who would chair local election committees, and that the Prosecutor-General—a government official—would chair the National Election Committee, prompted protests from the judiciary, which claimed that these decisions violated the Supreme Constitutional Court ruling. The Government furthermore announced that the presence of judges would be restricted to the counting stations. Ongoing arrests of Muslim Brotherhood activists also demonstrated the limits that remained upon free electoral campaigning.

Almost one-half of the ruling NDP candidates contested seats in the legislature for the first time, while 100 of its candidates for the 444 elective seats in the People's Assembly were reported to be under 40 years of age. Nevertheless, despite these efforts to create the impression of renewal within the NDP, the old guard remained solidly in control of the party. It was noted that there were only two Copts among the NDP candidates, and that (contrary to wide expectation) Gamal Mubarak did not seek election. Many nominally independent candidates were believed to be NDP sympathizers, while the Muslim Brotherhood fielded almost 100 candidates as independents, apparently in an effort to avert official harassment. Those parties established in 1999 by Islamists who had renounced violence were unable to present candidates because their applications for legal recognition were denied.

While the new system of judicial supervision was considered to have had a positive impact in terms of improving the fairness of the elections, it did not prevent numerous incidents of harassment, aimed particularly at candidates believed to be sympathetic to the Muslim Brotherhood. At least 14 people reportedly died in election-related violence, and hundreds were injured. The NDP once again secured a resounding victory, with (according to official results) candidates of the ruling party taking 353 of the 444 elective seats. Nominally independent candidates secured 72 seats, but it was reported that 35 of these had either joined or rejoined the NDP shortly after the elections; 17 other 'independents' were reported to be Muslim Brotherhood supporters. The New Wafd party won seven seats, the NPUP six, the Nasserist Party three and the LSP one seat. (Voting for the two seats in one constituency in Alexandria was postponed following the arrest of some 20 Muslim Brotherhood activists.) The rate of participation by voters at the three stages was officially stated to be between 15% and 40%.

In November 2000 the trial of 20 members of the Muslim Brotherhood ended with 15 of the defendants being sentenced to between three and five years' imprisonment; the remainder were acquitted. The Brothers were arrested in October 1999 on charges of plotting to overthrow the Government and of infiltrating professional syndicates, in order to undermine national security. This constituted a clear signal from the Government that it would not acquiesce in the apparent growth of Islamist political support and representation. In January 2001, however, writer Salah el-Din Mohsin was sentenced by the State Security Court to three years' imprisonment for 'offending religion'; he had, in a book published privately in early 2000, described the Koran as promoting 'ignorance'. His original trial had resulted in July in a six-month suspended sentence, but the authorities had ordered a retrial on the grounds that the sentence was too lenient.

Much attention in the immediate aftermath of the 2000 general election focused on the likely strategy and tactics of the Muslim Brotherhood as it succeeded once again in achieving significant representation in the People's Assembly. Many commentators judged that, in concentrating excessively on cultural and religious issues at the expense of wider political and economic concerns, it had failed to make the most of previous periods of parliamentary influence.

Partial elections were held to the Shura (Advisory) Council, the upper house of the legislature, on 16 and 22 May 2001. In the weeks prior to the poll, there were a number of arrests involving alleged members of the Muslim Brotherhood. In the elections the NDP won 74 of the 88 contested seats, while independent candidates won the remaining 14 seats. The opposition parties failed to win any seats.

MIDDLE EAST PEACE

The Middle East peace process continued to be a central preoccupation of Egypt's foreign policy during President Mubarak's fourth term. Mubarak placed strong emphasis on ensuring that any final settlement would be truly comprehensive. He was particularly concerned that the Israeli-Syrian track not become separated from the Israeli-Palestinian track. The poor state of Palestinian–Syrian relations meant that this could never be fully ruled out as a possibility. Egypt reiterated its stance that until a comprehensive peace settlement had been achieved in the region, the full normalization of relations with Israel was impossible. As the Israeli-Palestinian track reached crisis point in late 2000, Egypt sought to balance its solidarity with the Palestinian cause with desperate efforts to revive the peace process.

Egypt hosted the signing of the revised Wye River Memorandum by Ehud Barak and Yasser Arafat, which took place at Sharm el-Sheikh in early September 1999. The Sharm el-Sheikh agreement, or Wye II, effectively removed the obstacles to an Israeli transfer of a further 5% of the West Bank to the PA. Egyptian mediation had been influential in the discussions between Israeli and Palestinian negotiators that led to an agreement, and Mubarak called for immediate moves towards negotiations on a final peace settlement.

Nevertheless, relations between the Egyptian and Israeli Governments remained strained in late 1999, as Egypt became increasingly concerned about the growing number of Jewish settlements in the Occupied Territories. Although 'final status' negotiations between Israel and the Palestinians opened at Ramallah on the West Bank on 8 November, they were broken off once again in early December.

In January 2000 Mubarak made an unscheduled visit to Damascus, amid increased optimism that substantive negotiations on both tracks in the Middle East peace process were about to resume once again. However, the momentum did not last. The resumption of peace negotiations between the Israeli Prime Minister and the Syrian Minister of Foreign Affairs, Farouk al-Shara', had taken place at Shepherdstown, West Virginia, USA, on 15 December 1999 and continued during early January 2000. Nevertheless, further negotiations were postponed indefinitely, owing to a lack of agreement regarding a possible Israeli withdrawal from the Golan Heights. The death of President Assad of Syria on 10 June further stalled the Israeli-Syrian track of the peace process. Mubarak attended Assad's funeral on 13 June, where he pledged his support to the late President's son and designated successor, Bashar.

After Israel launched a series of air raids on infrastructural targets in Lebanon in early February 2000, destroying three major power stations, President Mubarak, who denounced the Israeli attacks as 'criminal acts' which required an 'urgent global response', made his first ever visit to Beirut on 19 February, where he held talks with Lebanese President Emile Lahoud. The purpose of the visit was ostensibly to demonstrate Egypt's solidarity with Lebanon. Over the next two months, Egypt's involvement in the peace process increased. In March 2000 President Mubarak hosted a tripartite summit meeting at Sharm el-Sheikh between PA President Yasser Arafat and Israeli Prime Minister Ehud Barak, at which both sides gave a commitment to meet in the USA in April and announced a timetable for achieving a framework peace agreement by the end of May—this was a step towards the final settlement due to be agreed by September. However, as adherence to the timetable quickly slipped again, Mubarak emphasized that Egypt would recognize Arafat's threated unilateral declaration of Palestinian statehood (scheduled for September) if they failed to reach a final settlement.

On 10 July 2000 Barak held talks with Mubarak in Cairo prior to entering into a summit meeting to work towards a final agreement with Yasser Arafat at Camp David, hosted by Bill Clinton. Egyptian Minister of Foreign Affairs Amr Moussa urged Israel to make concessions for peace. Following the failure of the Camp David talks, which took place during 11–25 July, Mubarak continued to consult other Arab and Western leaders in the hope that the momentum of peace talks could be maintained. However, the Egyptian President emphasized that he would not pressure Arafat into making concessions over the status of Jerusalem, which had proved to be the principal stumbling block in the talks. He appealed for a united Arab stance in support of the Palestinians until they regained all their legitimate rights in accordance with the pertinent UN resolutions. As the 13 September deadline for a final settlement passed without a declaration of independent statehood, Mubarak proposed a resolution of the dispute over Jerusalem that would make it an 'open city', with Israeli sovereignty over the West and Palestinian sovereignty over the East of the city.

From late September 2000 President Mubarak played a leading role in the intense international diplomacy aimed at preventing what was the most serious violence for many years between Israeli forces and Palestinians in the West Bank and Gaza Strip from escalating into a major regional conflict. A US-brokered summit meeting between Barak and Arafat was convened at Sharm el-Sheikh on 16 October. A statement was issued at the end of the summit in which both sides were said to have agreed measures to end the violence. However, this fragile agreement was rapidly overtaken by further escalations in violence in what had become known as the al-Aqsa intifada. On 21–22 October an emergency meeting of Heads of State of Arab League countries was convened in Cairo. Mubarak's main objective was to promote a unified Arab position in support of the Palestinians. However, he was keen to avoid any decision to sever diplomatic relations with Israel. Measures adopted at the summit—including a call for an international tribunal to investigate Israeli 'war crimes'—were regarded by the Palestinians as 'tokenism', although the establishment of an Arab solidarity fund to support the families of Palestinian victims of the conflict was welcomed. The summit's final communiqué held Israel solely to blame for the violence, and 'for any steps taken in regard to relations with Israel by Arab countries, including their cancellation'.

As the violence escalated, President Mubarak found it increasingly difficult to justify to the Egyptian public his unwillingness to implement diplomatic sanctions against Israel. Finally, on 21 November 2000, following Israeli air attacks on offices of the PA in the Gaza Strip, Egypt withdrew its ambassador to Israel. Egypt also gave its support to Palestinian efforts to secure a UN resolution that would send a UN protection force to the region. At an Arab League summit on the Palestinian situation, held in Jordan on 26-28 March 2001, President Mubarak was again successful in dampening demands from more radical Arab states that Egypt and Jordan should break off diplomatic relations with Israel entirely. The summit appointed Amr Moussa as the new Secretary-General of the Arab League.

In April 2001 Egypt and Jordan tabled a joint peace plan that called for an immediate halt to Israeli construction of settlements and a withdrawal of Israeli forces to pre-intifada positions, as a basis for both sides taking steps to end the violence and with a view to the resumption of 'final status' talks. This initiative was an attempted revival of the 'understandings' first reached by Israel and the Palestinians at the Sharm el-Sheikh meeting in October 2000. Israel argued that it would be willing only to restrict settlement building to 'natural growth', and claimed that the plan did not place enough weight upon the responsibility of the Palestinian security forces to end what it called 'terrorist attacks' on Israel. However, the plan was supported by the new US Administration of President George W. Bush, the EU and the Arab world. President Mubarak urged the Bush Administration to adopt a more active engagement in the Middle East peace process. Egypt had criticized the USA's use of its veto in the UN Security Council in late March to defeat the long-awaited resolution to send an international protection force to the region.

Escalating violence rather than diplomatic progress characterized the following months. Egypt condemned the use by Israel of F-16 fighter aircraft to bomb Palestinian targets in mid-May 2001, and President Mubarak warned that the violence was close to reaching a 'point of no return'. Arab ministers responsible for foreign affairs met in Egypt on 19 May and agreed to suspend all political contacts with Israel until Israel's attacks on Palestinians halted. Once again, with Egyptian influence evident, they stopped short of breaking diplomatic ties entirely.

With the installation of the new US Administration it appeared inevitable that US-Egyptian relations would have to be renegotiated. Egypt expressed frustration at the new Administration's apparent reluctance to become fully engaged in diplomatic efforts to revive the Middle East peace process. During a visit to the USA in April 2001, President Mubarak met with Bush for the first time and urged the USA to support the Egyptian-Jordanian peace plan. Meanwhile, Bush, who had indicated that Iraq would be his Administration's priority in terms of Middle East policy, expressed his unease at Egypt's lack of support for continuing international sanctions against Saddam Hussain; he also urged Egypt to return its ambassador to Israel. A further inhibitor of relations was the conviction in May 2001 of civil rights activist Saad Eddin Ibrahim, who held US citizenship.

TERRORISM, SECURITY AND DEMOCRATIC MOVES

Relations with the USA were further complicated by the attacks against the USA on 11 September 2001, which President Mubarak was swift to condemn. However, the Egyptian Government was unwilling to participate directly in the US-led military campaign against Osama bin Laden and the Taliban regime in Afghanistan, which commenced in October. Egypt, however, pronounced itself satisfied that the US evidence establishing responsibility for the attacks was compelling. Nonetheless, President Mubarak expressed concern that the phrase 'war on terror' was being used too indiscriminately by the USA to shape its foreign policy. He particularly opposed its use as a template for the Israeli–Palestinian conflict or for resolving tensions with Iraq.

Relations between Egypt and Iraq had improved markedly during Mubarak's fourth term, and Egypt became a principal advocate of an end to the international sanctions in force from 1990 to 2003 and a critic of US-British air-strikes against Iraqi targets. In January 2001 the Iraqi Vice-President visited Cairo; he was the highest ranking Iraqi official to visit Egypt since 1990. During the visit the two countries signed a trade agreement, which came into effect in August 2001. By early 2002 Iraq had become an increasingly important market for Egyptian exporters. During a meeting with the US Vice-President, Dick Cheney, in Cairo in March 2002, President Mubarak urged the US Administration not to embark on a military campaign to overthrow Iraqi President Saddam Hussain, asserting that the priority must be to ensure the return to Iraq of UN weapons inspectors. Egypt exerted pressure on the Iraqi Government to readmit weapons inspectors and co-operate fully with them. However, as diplomatic efforts to resolve the crisis collapsed in March 2003, Egypt joined with other Arab states in declaring that it would not participate in any US-led campaign against Iraq. Egypt was concerned to avoid appearing hostile to either the USA or the Iraqi Government.

As the USA's rhetorical commitment to promoting democratization in the Arab world intensified after the US-led overthrow of Saddam Hussain in Iraq in April 2003, Egypt's response was ambivalent. It refused an invitation to attend a US-sponsored conference on political reform in the Middle East in June 2004, and sought to play a constructive role in the Middle East peace process in part to deflect US pressure to implement domestic political reform. It combined an official position of support for the interim Iraqi Government with calls for the earliest possible withdrawal of the US-led occupying military forces. While unwilling to deploy its military forces there, in July 2004, following a visit to Cairo of the US Secretary of State, Colin Powell, Egypt offered to assist in training the new Iraqi police force. In June 2005 a new Egyptian diplomatic envoy, Ihab al-Sherif, was dispatched to Iraq and designated ambassador, representing the upgrading of diplomatic ties between the two countries. In the following month, however, al-Sherif was kidnapped and murdered in Baghdad by a militant group claiming to represent al-Qa'ida in Iraq. It was subsequently announced that Egypt would reduce its diplomatic presence in Iraq.

As bilateral and international relations were becoming more tumultuous, the domestic political scene failed to offer Egyptians any respite. In November 2001 some 22 members of the Muslim Brotherhood were arrested on charges of incitement to violence and belonging to an illegal organization. In the same month the trial, by military court, commenced of 94 Islamists accused of conspiring to assassinate President Mubarak and seize power. Guilty verdicts were imposed on 51 of the defendants in September 2002: their sentences ranged from two years' to 15 years' imprisonment.

In July 2002 a process of internal elections at the neighbourhood, district and governorate levels began within the ruling NDP. This represented an attempt to revive what had become an ossified institution, despite its ostensible mass membership, ahead of the NDP's eighth party congress in September. Gamal Mubarak was appointed Secretary-General for Policy, effectively making him the third most senior figure in the party. The following month Gamal publicly proposed the abolition of the controversial State Security Courts, as well as of the punishment of hard labour in the penal code, and the establishment of a National Council for Human Rights. Speculation continued that Gamal Mubarak would stand for the presidency after his father's scheduled retirement in 2005. Prior to the US-led campaign to oust the regime of Saddam Hussain in Iraq, the Egyptian authorities actively obstructed efforts to hold large-scale public demonstrations. They were forced to relent once the campaign began in March 2003, but demonstrations were heavily policed and hundreds of anti-war activists were detained (most being swiftly released). The Government resisted calls to close the Suez Canal to ships of the US-led coalition, but felt unable to resist pressure to endorse the right of Muslims to volunteer to fight on the side of Iraq.

Notably, a month prior the People's Assembly had voted to extend the state of emergency for another three years, despite almost universal opposition among other political parties and civil society groups. The Egyptian authorities cited the fact that Western democracies were tightening security following the attacks on the USA in September 2001. At the NDP's first annual party conference, held in September 2003, President Mubarak announced that all military orders issued under the emergency laws, which had been in place since the assassination of President Sadat in 1981, would be abolished, except those that were deemed 'necessary to maintain public order and security.' However, a committee established by the Prime Minister to review the existing emergency powers recommended that only six of the 13 military orders could be withdrawn. Nevertheless, restrictions and limitations pertaining to the formation of new political parties and the activities of existing political organizations were also to be reviewed, and Gamal Mubarak pledged to take steps to ensure that all Egyptians would receive the fundamental rights of participatory democracy and equality.

At partial elections to the Advisory Council held in May and June 2004, the NDP won 70 out of the 88 'contested' seats, while 17 seats were secured by NDP members standing as independents and one was taken by the NPUP. A further 44 seats were filled by presidential appointees.

In early July 2004 Prime Minister Obeid announced the resignation of his entire administration. Dr Ahmad Nazif, the former Minister of Communications and Information Technology, was appointed Prime Minister. Several appointees in the new Council of Ministers were regarded as having close links with Gamal Mubarak, among them Ahmad Aboul Gheit, hitherto Egypt's Permanent Representative to the UN, who assumed the post of Minister of Foreign Affairs. Notable changes intended to assist the process of economic reform included the creation of a Ministry of Investment and the merger of the Ministries of Foreign Trade and of Industry and Technological Development.

In October 2004, with strong US encouragement in the context of its push for political reform across the Middle East, it approved the registration of a new political party, the liberal al-Ghad (Tomorrow), led by Ayman al-Nour, an independent member of the People's Assembly. The Government also displayed a greater tolerance of small-scale street demonstrations and proposed a 'national dialogue' on reform issues between the NDP and opposition parties. Al-Ghad stated that its political programme would focus on constitutional reform and the repeal of the state of emergency.

With a presidential election on the horizon in late 2005, Al-Ghad called for the Egyptian people to be given a genuine choice by allowing opposition candidates to stand. In these calls it was joined by the Muslim Brotherhood and by a new coalition called the Egyptian Movement for Change—popularly known as Kefaya (Enough).

As with previous political thaws, the Government's apparent easing of the restrictions on opposition parties was largely conditional upon the degree to which the power and interests of the NDP remained unchallenged. Ayman al-Nour was arrested in January 2005, two days after having met with former US Secretary of State Madeleine Albright. Alleged by the authorities to have forged many of the signatures required to register his party, he was placed under preventive detention for 45 days and stripped of his parliamentary immunity. Al-Ghad's newspaper was also closed down. However, within weeks of al-Nour's arrest, there was an apparent reversal by President Mubarak. Following the cancellation of a visit to Cairo by the new US Secretary of State, Condoleezza Rice, on 26 February, President Mubarak announced that he now supported the idea of a multi-candidate presidential election later in the year and stated that the Constitution would be amended to provide for this. On 12 March al-Nour was released on bail and declared that he would stand in the presidential election provided that all candidates had an equal chance of success; however, on 23 March he was formally charged with forgery. At his trial, which commenced in June, al-Nour pleaded not guilty to the charges, and two days later, one of his co-defendants withdrew his testimony, stating that his confession had been obtained under duress. In July it was announced that the trial would be postponed until after the election in September.

The spring of 2005 was one of significant changes. In March, the Muslim Brotherhood held the largest pro-reform demonstration ever seen in Cairo. In April the Judges' Club stated that its members would only oversee future elections provided that they could do so without political interference. On 10 May 2005 the People's Assembly approved amendments to Article 76 of the Constitution to allow for multi-candidate presidential elections. Independent candidates seeking to run for the presidency were henceforth required to obtain 250 signatures in support of their nomination, including 65 from parliamentarians, 25 from members of the Advisory Council and 10 from local councillors in each of Egypt's 14 provinces. Parties wishing to nominate candidates were required to hold at least 5% of the seats in both the People's Assembly and the Advisory Council. The amended Article also mandated that parties seeking to contest any future presidential elections would need to have been in existence for at least five years at the time of the poll and would have to nominate candidates who had held a senior leadership position within the party for at least one year. Given that none of the existing opposition parties at that time held 5% of the seats in both chambers of parliament, a clause was added to the constitutional amendment, which allowed all legalized political parties to nominate candidates for the 2005 elections.

This constitutional provision did not go unnoticed. The three main opposition parties in the People's Assembly—the New Wafd, the NPUP and the Nasserist Party—declared two days later that they would boycott the forthcoming referendum on the constitutional amendments. In a joint statement, the parties criticized the severe restrictions imposed on candidates, arguing that these made it impossible for individual opposition figures and parties to contest any future presidential elections. On the same day the Muslim Brotherhood declared its own boycott of the referendum, citing similar reasons. On 13 May 2005 the General Assembly of the Egyptian Judges' Club issued a statement threatening to boycott the forthcoming elections should the Government fail to grant the judiciary full supervisory authority over the elections.

Despite the opposition's call for a boycott, on 25 May 2005 the amendments to Article 76 of the Constitution were endorsed in a national referendum. According to official figures, 53.6% of all registered voters went to the polls, of whom 83% voted in favour of the amendments. The results were met in the opposition press by claims that the referendum process had been marred by fraud and that the voter turn-out was much lower than the official figure. On 1 July the Egyptian Judges' Club published a report denouncing the lack of adequate judicial supervision of the referendum process.

Between June and July 2005 a series of political reform measures were adopted by the legislature, including revisions to the laws regulating political parties, political rights, the People's Assembly and the Advisory Council. A new Presidential Election Law was promulgated, which laid down the campaigning regulations for presidential elections and established an independent 10-member Presidential Election Commission (PEC), to be headed by the Chairman of the Supreme Constitutional Court. In early July changes to the Political Rights Law led to the establishment of another election commission for parliamentary elections. In contrast to the PEC, which contained no representative of the executive branch, the 11-member Higher Election Commission (HEC) was to include the Minister of Justice and a representative of the Ministry of the Interior. In early July changes to the Political Rights Law led to the establishment of another election commission for parliamentary elections. While the NDP hailed the package of reforms as a further step towards democracy, more critical voices noted that in substance these reforms did not significantly reduce the regime's control of the political system.

During June and July 2005 several new reform coalitions and groupings emerged on the domestic political scene, joining a growing number of protest movements that had appeared since the foundation of Kefaya in 2004. On 30 June 2005 former Prime Minister Aziz Sidqi, together with several former government ministers and academics, founded the National Coalition for Democratic Transformation (NCDT). In July the Muslim Brotherhood combined forces with various leftist groups to form the National Coalition for Reform. Both coalitions campaigned for an end to corruption, the abrogation of the emergency law and the instigation of far-reaching constitutional and political reforms.

The summer of political upheaval was marred by violence in the Sinai. On 23 July 2005 at least 60 people, including several foreigners, were killed and some 200 injured in three bomb attacks in the resort of Sharm el-Sheikh. Three different Islamist groups initially claimed responsibility for the blasts; however, the Egyptian authorities believed the attacks to be linked to bombings, which had occurred in Taba in October 2004.

MUBARAK WINS A FIFTH TERM

In late July 2005 President Mubarak declared his intention to seek a fifth term of office in the forthcoming election, which was subsequently scheduled for early September. In the same declaration, and throughout his election campaign, Mubarak also committed himself to further political reforms, promising, most notably, the replacement of the state of emergency by a new, anti-terrorism law. Mubarak appeared at this time to retain the political initiative, although the Egyptian landscape was more fluid and unpredictable than it had been for decades. In August the New Wafd broke ranks with the NPUP and the Nasserist Party, and announced that its Chairman, No'man Gomaa, would contest the presidential election. Until that time the three opposition parties had remained united in their decision not to contest the election, on the grounds that the poll would be neither free nor fair. Moreover, in a last-minute decision, the PEC reversed course and announced that local monitors would be granted unrestricted access to all polling stations.

At the election held on 7 September 2005 Mubarak secured a fifth consecutive term of office, having won an overwhelming 88.6% of the votes cast. Ayman al-Nour came second, with 7.6% of the vote, and No'man Gomaa of the New Wafd party came third, with 2.9%. Seven other candidates stood in the election, all receiving less than 0.5% of the vote. The election was marred by a low turn-out (only 23% of registered voters participated), attributed in part to the scepticism of the voting public that their vote would do anything to influence a result that had seemed inevitable since the start of the election campaign. Moreover, there were allegations of widespread electoral abuses at polling stations, although calls by al-Nour for a re-run of the ballot were rejected by the country's electoral commission.

Shortly after the presidential election a leadership crisis erupted within Al-Ghad that split the party into rival factions. The dispute, which had been ignited by four founding members of the party, sparked a series of manoeuvres to depose al-Nour from the party chairmanship. The four dissenters claimed that al-Nour had mismanaged the party and carried personal responsibility for the dismal performance of al-Ghad at the presidential poll. After being dismissed from al-Ghad for violating party statutes, the dissenters submitted a memorandum to the PPC, demanding al-Nour's dismissal. With no response forthcoming, the dissenting Ghadists organized a general assembly of their rival faction, during which al-Nour was voted out of office and replaced by Moussa Moustafa Moussa (the party's former Deputy Chairman). Meanwhile, in order to diffuse the crisis, al-Nour called his own party conference, at which he was reconfirmed as the legitimate Chairman of al-Ghad. In the midst of the al-Ghad crisis, on 25 September the court trying al-Nour and three co-defendants for forgery adjourned the proceedings until 8 October.

After the dismal performance of the opposition in the presidential election, and in the realization that none of the opposition parties could take on the NDP individually, concerted efforts were undertaken by the political opposition to create a broad-based electoral alliance for the upcoming elections to the People's Assembly. In October 2005 these efforts culminated in the formation of the United National Front for Change (UNFC), a loose coalition of 11 parties and groupings, which agreed to field a single list of candidates against the NDP. Led by No'man Gomaa, the coalition included the NPUP, the Nasserist Party, the LSP, two non-licensed political parties (Al-Wasat and Karama), Kefaya, the Popular Campaign for Change, the National Alliance for Reform and Change and the NCDT. The UNFC's election manifesto called for wide-ranging political, social and constitutional reforms, including the abrogation of the emergency law, full judicial independence, an end to corruption, the establishment of equality between the sexes and the elimination of poverty.

While the Muslim Brotherhood subscribed to the UNFC's platform of domestic reform, the group declined to participate in the coalition's list of candidates to contest the legislative elections. Stating that it had completed its nomination process before the creation of the alliance, the Muslim Brotherhood decided to nominate its own candidates. The ruling NDP fielded 432 candidates in 222 constituencies and the UNFC 213 candidates in 180 constituencies (New Wafd 114, NPUP 47, Nasserist Party 22, LSP 13, Karama eight, others nine). The Muslim Brotherhood nominated 150 candidates, Ayman al-Nour's al-Ghad 60, and several fringe parties also contested the elections.

Polling took place in three stages between 9 November and 1 December 2005 (with run-off elections held after each stage). As anticipated, the NDP retained a significant majority in the People's Assembly, winning 311 of the 444 elective seats (this number includes candidates who contested the election as independents and rejoined the NDP after their victory). The UNFC won 11 seats (New Wafd six, NPUP two, Karama two, others one), independents 21 and the Muslim Brotherhood 88. Although al-Nour lost the seat that he had held since 1995, al-Ghad managed to retain its presence in the Assembly, winning one seat. Neither the Nasserist Party nor any of the other minor parties achieved representation in the new Assembly. Owing to alleged voting irregularities and violence at polling stations, 12 seats remained vacant, with fresh elections to be scheduled at a future date. According to the HEC, only 26% of all registered voters participated in the elections.

Despite judicial supervision and local monitoring, the 2005 legislative elections were marred by widespread electoral fraud, an upsurge in violence and the arrest of scores of opposition members and supporters. According to the EOHR, during the elections 12 people were killed and 500 wounded in violent clashes involving supporters of different candidates, voters and the security forces. The EOHR also reported widespread election irregularities, including vote-buying, the closure of voting stations to opposition supporters and assaults on supervising judges and media representatives. According to the Muslim Brotherhood, about 1,250 of its supporters were arrested by the security forces during the polls.

Apart from the fact that a significant number of veteran NDP candidates lost their seats, the elections produced two surprising results. The first was the dismal performance of the secular opposition, which, despite the formation of a unified list and a relatively open political climate, failed to increase its representation in the People's Assembly. In fact, between 2000 and 2005 the combined share of the secular opposition parties declined from 17 seats to 10. An even greater surprise was the performance of the Muslim Brotherhood, which achieved a five-fold increase in its share of parliamentary seats, from 17 to 88. Observers have pointed to various contributing factors to this unprecedented electoral success, noting in particular: the group's grassroots support and organizational strength; the weakness of the secular opposition; the waning legitimacy of the NDP; and international pressure, which made it increasingly difficult for the regime to manipulate the electoral process.

RETREAT FROM 'REFORM'

In an unexpected development, on 5 December 2005, an Egyptian criminal court ordered the detention of Ayman al-Nour and his co-defendants in a Cairo prison. In mid-December al-Nour began a hunger strike in protest against his detention and ill treatment in prison. On 24 December he was sentenced to five years' imprisonment, having been found guilty of the forgery charges. The verdict provoked widespread condemnation, not least from local human rights organizations, the USA and the EU, which questioned the integrity of the trial and demanded al-Nour's immediate release. On 18 May, however, the Court of Cassation ruled against an appeal by al-Nour's defence team. Furthermore, in February 2007 a team of government-appointed medical experts concluded that al-Nour (who had undergone heart surgery in December 2006) was fit to serve his full term in prison.

In a development that was widely seen as a further attempt to bolster the chances of dynastic succession to the presidency, on 1 February 2006 Mubarak announced a major reorganization of the NDP leadership. His son, Gamal Mubarak, was promoted to one of the three posts of Deputy Secretary-General, further cementing his influential position within the party (he also retained the chairmanship of the policy secretariat, which he had held since 2000). In an attempt to strengthen the reformist movement within the party, the President also replaced the majority of Chairmen of the NDP's secretariats with known supporters of Gamal Mubarak.

In January 2006 a group of 'reformist' Wafdists, led by Mounir Abd al-Nour and Mahmoud Abaza, removed No'man Gomaa from the party chairmanship, promising to hold new leadership elections within 60 days. Condemning Gomaa's leadership style as dictatorial, the group argued that he carried full responsibility for the New Wafd's dismal performance in the 2005 presidential and parliamentary elections, and that a younger, reform-minded Chairman was needed to reinvigorate the party. Gomaa's subsequent refusal to accept his removal spurred a three month-long factional struggle within the New Wafd, which almost led to the collapse of the party. In late January Gomaa filed a lawsuit against Abaza with the Administrative Court, contesting his 'unconstitutional and illegal' removal from the chairmanship; however, on 10 February Moustafa al-Tawil was elected by the High Committee of the New Wafd as interim Chairman of the party. The dispute turned to violent confrontation on 1 April when Gomaa and several of his supporters attempted to seize the party headquarters in the Dokki district of Cairo. In the ensuing clashes between supporters of the two rival factions, 21 people were injured and the party premises were severely damaged. Gomaa and five of his supporters were subsequently arrested and held in custody for four days on suspicion of crimes including attempted murder and the possession of firearms. On 2 June elections were held at the party headquarters to select a new High Committee and Chairman; Mahmoud Abaza stood unopposed and was duly elected.

A marked change in the Government's attitude towards the process of political reform was evident from early 2006. With the 2005 elections having taken place and the US Administration preoccupied by events in Iraq, the Egyptian Government showed little inclination to meet its pre-election pledges of further constitutional and political change. In a period reminiscent of the mid-1990s, the first half of 2006 was instead characterized by a strict clampdown on opponents of the regime and pro-democracy activists, and a serious dispute regarding the independence of the judiciary.

One of the first signs that the Government was stepping back from further political reform was the postponement of the municipal council elections, which had been scheduled to take place in April 2006. Amid severe domestic and international criticism, on 14 February the People's Assembly passed an amendment to the 1979 Local Council Law, which extended the mandate of the sitting councils for another two years, to 2008. Officially, the two-year postponement was justified by the need to revamp the existing Local Council Law, which had become inadequate after the amendment of Article 76 of the Constitution. Among the opposition, however, the delay was interpreted as a deliberate move by the administration to prevent the Muslim Brotherhood from replicating its success in the 2005 parliamentary elections at the local level.

In an unprecedented move, on 17 February 2006 the Government stripped four liberal judges of their immunity from prosecution and referred them to the State Security Prosecutor for interrogation. The four judges, Hisham el-Bastawisi, Ahmad Mekki, Mahmoud Mekki and Muhammad el-Khodeiri, were accused of slandering the reputation of fellow judges by implicating them in vote-rigging during the 2005 parliamentary elections. The judges, two of whom were deputy heads of the Court of Cassation, belonged to a group of liberal-minded judges who, in previous months, had strongly criticized the Government's handling of the 2005 elections and demanded greater judicial independence. On 17 March 2006 the Egyptian Judges' Club issued a statement, declaring its view that the judges should not have to appear before the State Security Prosecutor for interrogation. On the same day the Syndicate of Journalists issued a statement, expressing solidarity with the demands of the judges. On 18 April the Government referred Mahmoud Mekki and el-Bastawisi to the disciplinary board of the Supreme Judicial Council for possible expulsion from the judiciary. A month later the Supreme Judicial Council ruled against el-Bastawisi, warning him that he would be dismissed if he committed any further offence; however, Mahmoud Mekki was cleared of all the charges.

The decision by the Government to prosecute the two judges sparked a series of mass protests in Cairo in April–May 2006, drawing together representatives of the country's legal profession, syndicates, civil society organizations, advocacy groups and political parties. On 24 April 50 judges protesting at the headquarters of the Judges' Club were forcibly removed by the police. Many of those who attended the protest claimed to have been beaten by the security forces and 15 people were reportedly arrested. At the disciplinary hearing of Mekki and el-Bastawisi on 18 May a crowd of protesters gathered outside the High Court in support of the judges was dispersed by the police and hundreds of people were arrested, including around 400 members of the Muslim Brotherhood, according to the group's own estimates.

In late June 2006 both houses of the legislature approved a new Judicial Authorities Law, which, according to government officials, was intended further to strengthen the independence of the Egyptian judiciary. The passage of the law was secured by the NDP's overwhelming majority in the People's Assembly, despite severe criticism by members of the opposition and an opposition boycott of the actual vote. Critics decried the new law as being part of the Government's assault on the judiciary, arguing that it further eroded, rather than strengthened, judicial independence from the executive. The judicial profession was particularly outraged by the failure of the legislation to: provide clear guidelines regarding the appointment of justices and the assignment of cases to judges; recognize the right of judges to form or join associations representing their interests; and incorporate fair trial guarantees in the case of disciplinary procedures against judges. It was feared that these omissions would provide the Government with additional tools by which to meddle in judicial affairs, and thus undermine the constitutional separation of powers.

Dr Osama al-Ghazali Harb, a former member of the NDP's policy secretariat and close ally of Gamal Mubarak, announced his resignation from the party on 7 March 2006. Al-Ghazali Harb strongly criticized the Government for its failure to implement meaningful political reforms and the NDP for its inability to transform itself into a modern democratic party. On 16 July al-Ghazali Harb announced that he had joined with 75 fellow opposition figures to form a new secular party, the Democratic Front, to promote the 'build up of a true and democratic system' and a liberal economic policy. The new party received its operating licence from the PPC on 24 May 2007, thereby bringing to 24 the number of legalized political parties in Egypt.

On 23 April 2006 the People's Assembly approved a request by the Government to renew the state of emergency for a further two years. Prime Minister Nazif, who in March had indicated that the law would soon be replaced by new anti-terrorism legislation, justified the volte-face by citing the need for the state to retain extraordinary powers in light of tensions and violence.

A new round of sectarian violence erupted in Alexandria in April 2006. In the worst outbreak of inter-communal strife since October 2005, 12 people were wounded and 67 detained by the security forces as enraged groups of Coptic Christian and Muslim protesters clashed in heavy street fighting. The clashes were triggered by a series of attacks on Coptic churches, in which two worshippers were killed and another eight injured. According to human rights activists, the recurrence of sectarian violence in Egypt has its root cause in a number of factors, including the Government's discriminatory policies towards the Coptic minority, the failure to promote a liberal religious education in schools and the absence of liberal-minded Muslim and Christian preachers.

On 24 April 2006 three bombs exploded in co-ordinated attacks in the Red Sea tourist resort of Dahab, leaving 23 people dead and some 150 injured (among them several foreigners). A day later two attacks were carried out in the northern Sinai Peninsula, one near the town of El-Arish and the other near al-Gorash airport, which is used by the Multinational Force and Observers (MFO—an organization created to supervise the implementation of security provisions of the 1979 Camp David agreement between Egypt and Israel). With no group claiming responsibility, it was initially unclear whether the blasts had been carried out by local militants or an international terrorist organization such as al-Qa'ida. After the prompt arrest of 10 suspects in connection with the Dahab blasts and the killing in May of the suspected mastermind behind the bombings, the Egyptian authorities confirmed that the Dahab attack had been carried out by a local militant group called Tawhid wa al-Jihad (Unification and Holy War), which was also responsible for the Taba and Sharm el-Sheikh bombings. Throughout May–June further members of the group were arrested or killed by the security forces in operations targeting Islamist militants on the Sinai Peninsula.

In late May 2006 the Criminal Court charged three journalists from *Sawt Al-Umma* and *Afaq Arabia* for having published the names of judges allegedly involved in vote-rigging during the 2005 elections and for slandering the head of a local election commission. The prosecution of the journalists for slander, which came only months after the Government had promised to decriminalize libel in a revision of the Press Law, was widely interpreted as yet another attempt by the Egyptian authorities to silence critics of the regime. The editor-in-chief and a reporter of *Al-Dustour* were each sentenced to a year's imprisonment and fined on 26 June 2006 for 'insulting and harming the President'. In April 2005 the newspaper had reported a lawsuit that accused President Mubarak of misusing public funds during the privatization of state-owned companies. The journalists' co-defendant who had filed the lawsuit was also fined and received a one-year prison sentence.

A government-sponsored bill proposing revisions to the existing Press Law received parliamentary approval in July 2006. As had been promised, the revised law abolished custodial sentences for some publishing offences, including libel. To the outrage of journalists, the Syndicate of Journalists and pro-reform activists, however, the law also increased the fines payable by journalists convicted of libel, and retained provisions that prison sentences could be handed down to those deemed to have insulted the Egyptian President or foreign heads of state. In addition, the revised Press Law introduced custodial sentences for journalists who published information on the property or funds of public employees and government officials. This latter provision was widely seen as an attempt by the regime to protect corrupt officials from prosecution. A day before its ratification in the legislature, on 8 July, more than 20 independent and opposition newspapers took part in a nation-wide strike to protest against the proposed amendments. Within the profession the revisions to the Press Law were widely interpreted as a significant step backwards, further eroding freedom of the press in Egypt.

CONSTITUTIONAL OVERHAUL

Following through on his 2005 election pledge, in late 2006 Mubarak initiated an overhaul of the 1971 Constitution. Based on his own recommendations, in early December 2006 the President instructed the NDP's Policy Secretariat to draw up a detailed proposal of constitutional amendments, which was then to be debated both in the legislature and in public. According to the Government, the amendment process was to involve a broad range of civil society organizations and to end in the holding of a national referendum. The constitutional changes themselves were presented to the public as part of an ongoing process of political reform.

In late December 2006 the draft constitutional amendments were submitted for debate and fine-tuned in the committees and plenary sessions of the People's Assembly and the Advisory Council. Although the Government had kept its promise to consult opposition representatives and other civil society organizations on the amendments, a widespread sentiment persisted among these groups that their input in the drafting process had been more cosmetic than substantial. This sentiment was later confirmed by the passage of a final draft set of constitutional amendments that in substance deviated little from the initial proposals put forward by the President and the NDP leadership. Following two months of parliamentary debate, on 14 March 2007 the proposed constitutional changes were approved by the Advisory Council, and on 20 March they were ratified by the People's Assembly. Despite strong opposition to the amendments, their passage was never seriously endangered, given the numerical predominance of the NDP in both upper and lower chambers. Nevertheless, more than 110 deputies had voted against the proposals, including all members of the parliamentary opposition, several independent deputies and one NDP representative.

The final draft of the proposed amendments, as presented to the public in late March 2007, contained a total of 34 changes to the 1971 Constitution. Of these, the most far-reaching, and indeed most controversial, amendments were focused on the nature of the Egyptian economy; the organization of elections and party political activities; as well as the incorporation of stringent new anti-terrorism provisions. With regard to the economy, the proposed amendments withdrew all reference to the 'socialist character of the state' stipulated in the 1971 Constitution. In line with economic realities, the revised Constitution now stated that Egypt's economy rested on 'market principles'. On the political front, in turn, important changes were made to four articles of the Constitution. Article Five, which defines Egypt as a multi-party system, was amended explicitly to prohibit the formation of political parties and the pursuit of political activities on the basis of religion. Also changed was Article 76, which lays down the candidacy requirements for presidential elections. According to the new provisions, political parties seeking to participate would need to hold at least 3% of all seats in either the People's Assembly or the Advisory Council, as opposed to a previous requirement of 5% in both upper and lower chambers. No changes were made, however, to any of the stringent requirements for independent candidates. Changes to Article 88 involved the establishment of an 11-member government-appointed HEC, which was to replace full judicial supervision of elections. Government officials justified the move by pointing to the undue strains that this supervision of elections had placed on the judiciary and the delays it had caused to the normal workings of the courts. To prepare for new anti-terrorism legislation, which was to replace the existing emergency law, the regime amended Article 179 of the Constitution. Introducing new anti-terrorism measures, the revised article confirmed the President's right to refer civilians to military courts and significantly broadened the police's powers of surveillance, interrogation and arrest. Some human rights advocates termed this part of an entrenchment of the emergency regime. Other notable amendments to the Constitution concerned the President's right unilaterally to dissolve parliament without calling for a national referendum; the rebalancing of executive legislative powers; and the introduction of quotas for female representation in local councils.

While the Government presented the amendments as a step towards political reform, many opposition groups and pro-reform activists took the view that they were intended to achieve precisely the opposite effect: namely further to erode political and civil liberties and to enhance the powers of the executive. Most opposition activists agreed, for instance, that key stipulations of the revised Constitution directly targeted the Muslim Brotherhood, making it literally impossible for the group to pursue any political activities and put forward candidates for future elections. Moreover, there was a widespread sentiment that the regime had intentionally abolished full judicial supervision so as to secure future NDP victories by means of widespread electoral fraud and malpractice. Some commentators even went as far as to claim that the amendments were engineered primarily to facilitate a smooth succession to the presidency of Gamal Mubarak. In their view, by reducing judicial oversight over the electoral process and barring the most credible opponent—the Muslim Brotherhood—from contesting future presidential elections, the NDP would be able to retain control over both the nomination and election of future presidents.

Shortly after being ratified by the People's Assembly on 19 March 2007, the Government announced that the package of 34 constitutional amendments would be put to a national referendum on 26 March (a week earlier than anticipated). According to opposition representatives, the timing of the referendum illustrated the fact that the Government was seeking to hasten the amendment process, without facilitating any proper awareness campaign and public debate on the constitutional reforms and their implications. In the weeks leading up to the poll, and on the day itself, Kefaya and other opposition forces organized a series of nation-wide demonstrations to protest against the amendments and the Government's handling of the ratification process.

The referendum itself was organized and supervised by the HEC and observed by a number of Egyptian human rights groups. The referendum was boycotted by a broad coalition of opposition parties, civil society organizations and prominent individuals. According to the official results, 27.1% of all registered voters had taken part in the referendum, of whom 75.9% voted in favour of the constitutional amendments.

Casting doubt on the integrity of the poll, however, independent observers and opposition representatives were quick to question the official results. Some argued that the sight of empty polling stations across the country, and the fact that turn-out in Egypt had never surpassed 20% of all registered voters, rendered the official figure implausible. Instead, they suggested that actual turn-out had been around 5%–7%. As in past elections, there were numerous reports that the referendum process had been marred by widespread voter intimidation and vote tampering at the polling stations.

In an effort to bring ordinary legislation into line with the country's new constitutional realities, in May 2007 parliament adopted revisions to the Political Rights Law, which included new procedures for future elections. According to the revised legislation, elections to the People's Assembly and the Advisory Council were henceforth to be held on a single day instead of taking place over several days, as had been the case since 2000. Furthermore, the revised legislation specified the composition and functions of the HEC, which was to be headed by the President of the Cairo Court of Appeal and to be renewed every three years. In accordance with Article Five of the revised Constitution, the new Political Rights Law also stipulated that the use of religious slogans in elections was to be prohibited. As with the constitutional amendments themselves, the parliamentary opposition strongly criticized their lack of involvement in the drafting process of the new law and rejected its content.

GOVERNMENT SUPPRESSION OF CRITICS

Throughout the ratification process of the constitutional changes and beyond, the Government continued its clampdown on critics of the regime and their activities. As in the past, the prime target of official repression was the Muslim Brotherhood, which since the 2005 elections had become the most vocal critic of the Egyptian authorities within and outside of parliament. According to estimates by the Brotherhood, between June 2006 and March 2007 more than 300 of its members were arrested, including leadership cadres and prominent financiers of the group. Most of the detainees were charged with being members of an outlawed organization and/or with possessing illegal literature. In an attempt to disconnect the group from its constituency, the regime also targeted the Muslim Brotherhood website, repeatedly preventing access to it for extended periods of time.

Probably the most severe crackdown on the group since 2005 occurred in the aftermath of the student demonstrations at Al-Azhar University in December 2006. During these demonstrations students affiliated to the Muslim Brotherhood had protested against the Government's interference in the student union elections, particularly against the removal of politically active students from the list of candidates. Most of the demonstrators had appeared in military-style outfits, thereby outraging a regime increasingly concerned about a recurrence of Islamist militancy on Egyptian soil. Although vehemently refuted by the Muslim Brotherhood leadership, the Government treated the incident as a clear indication that the group was harbouring the establishment of its own military wing, a belief which triggered the series of mass arrests that shook the Brotherhood in subsequent months. By mid-April 2007 the state security police had arrested another 80 members of the organization, including two parliamentary deputies. Legal experts contended that the arrest of sitting lawmakers constituted a violation of the immunity provisions for holders of public office enshrined in the Egyptian Constitution.

Seemingly undeterred by the Government's measures against its members and assets, and possibly in a show of defiance, the Muslim Brotherhood announced on 27 December 2006 that it intended to seek status as a legalized political party. High-ranking Brotherhood officials asserted that this move would sharpen the profile of the group, which was in the process of developing a comprehensive manifesto for the new party. Acknowledging the virtual impossibility of obtaining a licence from the PPC, the Muslim Brotherhood asserted that it would not submit a formal licensing application, but would simply inform the PPC of its transformation into a fully fledged political party.

In late April 2007 40 senior members of the Muslim Brotherhood were tried on charges of leading an illegal group that participated in terrorist activities. A renewed and widespread crackdown on the activities of the group was reported by officials of the Brotherhood in August, amid fresh reports about the organization's preparations to establish a political party. In the following month the editors of four independent newspapers were given one-year prison sentences and also fined, after they had been found guilty by a court in Cairo of defamation against President Mubarak and his son Gamal. In early 2008 Muslim Brotherhood leaders protested that further mass arrests of their members represented a concerted campaign by the authorities to prevent them from contesting the local elections scheduled for April (having been postponed from 2006). The organization claimed in late February 2008 that up to 500 activists were in detention, and on 7 April announced that they would boycott the polls. In the event, the local elections, held the following day, saw NDP candidates return unchallenged to some 70% of the 52,000 council seats.

Between late 2006 and mid-2007 the Government also intensified its crackdown on internet sites and blogs where discussions of a politically sensitive, religious or government-critical matter were taking place. As part of these measures, the authorities resorted to a variety of repressive tools, including the closure of websites, the confiscation of hardware and the intimidation and even arrest of political bloggers. The first arrest took place on 6 November 2006, involving a former student of Al-Azhar University who was accused of defaming the President and Islam on his blog. At the end of his trial, which lasted until February 2007, the blogger was found guilty and handed down a four-year prison term by a court in Alexandria. Incensed by the harsh sentence against the blogger, numerous domestic and international human rights groups organized a series of protests in support of the defendant and against the Government's suppression of activity on the internet, which was decried as yet another attempt to stifle freedom of speech.

Late 2006 and early 2007 also saw a renewal of labour unrest, this time at a textile factory in the Delta town of Mahalla al-Kobra. The strike, which was organized outside the formal labour union framework, drew around 27,000 workers, who were demanding the payment of their annual bonus by the factory management. Although eventually a compromise was reached concerning the payment, the Government sought to punish those whom it held responsible for inciting the strike. In early April the Ministry of Social Affairs ordered the closure of three branches of the Centre for Trade Union and Workers Services, a advocacy group that the Government accused of having organized the strike.

In spite of the threat of disciplinary action, in early April 2008 a series of further strikes were organized by workers seeking to make public sector salaries more commensurate with soaring food and commodity prices. Rioting broke out in Mahalla al-Kobra after police prevented industrial action by textile workers; two people died in the clashes and more than 100 were injured. Meanwhile, in a move indicative of the wider sense of economic unrest felt by many Egyptians, students and professionals across the country staged demonstrations in solidarity with the protesters. By the end of April President Mubarak, keen to avert the possibility of a nation-wide strike, capitulated to public pressure and proposed a 30% increase in the salaries of public sector employees. However, given the steep rate of inflation in Egypt, scepticism remained about whether the measure was sufficient to address the growing problem of economic and social polarization in the country. Moreover, concerns were also raised about the likely changes to wider economic policy necessary to accommodate the diversion of extra funds into public sector salaries.

Meanwhile, opposition politics in Egypt also underwent a number of noteworthy developments in the early part of 2007. Continuing its restrictive practice, in early January the PPC rejected the applications of 13 new political parties, including those of Al-Wasat and Karama, both of which had been part of the UNFC alliance in the 2005 elections to the People's Assembly. Following their rejection, 12 of the parties filed an appeal against the decision with the Supreme Administrative Court in

Cairo. On 6 January the Court rejected the appeals, upholding the initial PPC ruling.

In a significant step towards gender equality in Egypt, in December 2006 the Supreme Judicial Council approved a request by the Ministry of Justice to permit the appointment of female judges. Previously, women, with few exceptions (and then by presidential decree) had only been allowed to serve as consultants on judicial councils. Amid strong opposition from conservative judges and activists, who asserted that female judges violated key tenets of Islamic law, on 15 March 2007 the Supreme Judicial Council announced the appointment of 31 women to judicial posts in Egypt's courts. In early April their appointment was confirmed by presidential decree. Some observers contended that the Government's renewed interest in gender equality was meant to showcase the regime's willingness to continue on the path of political reform.

In other judicial matters, on 9 May 2007 an administrative court in Cairo ruled that the transfer of civilians to military tribunals was unconstitutional, resulting in the acquittal of 33 Muslim Brotherhood detainees who were, at that time, to stand trial in a military court. Pro-reform activists celebrated the bold ruling as a major setback for the Government, which in the past had made ample use of such transfers to try critics of the regime. Following an appeal by the Government, however, on 14 May the Supreme Administrative Court in Cairo reversed the initial ruling, confirming the President's right to refer civilians to military courts for trial. The Government's immediate appeal also meant that the Muslim Brotherhood detainees previously acquitted by a lower court were to remain in custody.

On the electoral front, in May 2007 the Egyptian Government announced that elections to 88 of the elective seats in the Advisory Council would be held in two rounds on 11 June and 18 June. Days after the announcement, on 18 May, the NDP published its list of candidates for the Council, putting forward a total of 97 candidates for the elective seats. Within the ranks of Egypt's legalized opposition, the announcement of the elections was greeted with little enthusiasm. Of all the opposition parties, only the NPUP and a handful of minor political forces decided to participate in the poll. Both the New Wafd and Nasserist parties announced their formal withdrawal from the elections, with the Wafd leadership citing the need to focus all its energies on restructuring the party as the principal reason for non-participation. Condemning the prospect of widespread electoral fraud and malpractice, the SLP meanwhile proclaimed a boycott of the elections.

Seemingly undeterred by the ongoing security crackdown on its members, and in contrast to most legalized parties, the Muslim Brotherhood announced in mid-April 2007 that it would participate in the forthcoming Advisory Council elections. The announcement was widely interpreted as a first show of defiance by the group following the passage of constitutional amendments that severely curtailed its rights to political participation. The 19 candidates of the Muslim Brotherhood, while formally running as independents, were to campaign under the slogan of 'Islam is the Solution'. The election campaign itself was marked by widespread popular apathy and an intensification of repressive measures taken by the authorities against the Muslim Brotherhood and its candidates. Scores of its members were arrested for belonging to an outlawed organization and for campaigning on religious slogans. According to Brotherhood sources, in the two weeks leading up to the poll more than 600 members of the group were detained by Egypt's security services.

As expected, the NDP overwhelmingly won the June 2007 elections. In the two rounds of voting the ruling party won 84 of the 88 elective seats. Of the remaining four seats, three went to so-called NDP independents and one to the NPUP. The Muslim Brotherhood failed to win a seat. According to the HEC, voter turn-out stood at over 30% in the first and at 23% in the second round of voting. In early November Mubarak was re-elected unchallenged as leader of the NDP at the party's ninth congress; it was the first time since the President assumed the NDP leadership in 1981 that members had voted by secret ballot. There was renewed speculation concerning the likelihood of Gamal Mubarak succeeding his father as President after it was revealed that the party's Politburo and Secretariat-General had been merged to form a new Supreme Council. Some commentators noted that the change meant that Gamal consequently met the constitutional requirement that presidential candidates must either stand as independents or be members of the governing body of a legal political party. However, party officials were swift to deny that this had been the reason for the reform. Shortly after the local elections of 8 April 2008 Mubarak announced an administrative reorganization. He appointed 12 new governors and created two new governorates (Helwan and Sixth of October), bringing the total number of governorates in Egypt to 29.

Meanwhile, in mid-January 2008 the Egyptian Government summoned EU ambassadors to protest against a draft resolution that had been adopted by the European Parliament. The resolution criticized Egypt's emergency legislation (subsequently renewed later that year until 2010), police practices, especially the use of torture against detainees, and official treatment of religious minorities. The EU also demanded the immediate release of the al-Ghad leader, Ayman al-Nour, who was finally set free in February 2009. The authorities asserted that he was released owing to ill health: however, it was widely believed that ongoing pressure from the international community—particularly the EU and the USA—and from human rights organizations was the principal reason behind the dissident's early release from gaol. In May, a day after announcing his intention to stand as a candidate in the presidential election scheduled to take place in 2011, al-Nour was injured in a firebomb attack on his car in Cairo; he was reported to have suffered first-degree burns.

EGYPT AS INTERNATIONAL MEDIATOR

Egypt's efforts to mediate in the Middle East peace process continued to dominate the foreign policy agenda during Mubarak's fifth term in office. On 28 August 2005, shortly before the planned Israeli withdrawal from Gaza, Egypt and Israel successfully concluded negotiations over the security arrangements at the Palestinian–Egyptian border and the Rafah crossing. According to the agreement reached between the two parties, 750 Egyptian troops were to take over from the MFO and secure the Gaza border against smuggling and the infiltration of militants into Palestinian territory. The MFO had patrolled the border between Israel and Egypt since 1981, charged with the implementation and supervision of the 1979 Camp David agreement. Minister of Foreign Affairs Ahmad Aboul Gheit welcomed the Israeli disengagement as a positive step towards the resumption of peace negotiations between the two sides and a full withdrawal of Israel from the territories occupied during the 1967 war.

In a turn of events that complicated Egypt's efforts to revive the peace process, on 25 January 2006 Hamas (an organizational off-shoot of the Muslim Brotherhood) claimed victory in the Palestinian legislative elections, defeating the Fatah administration that had ruled the PA since 1996. In contrast with Fatah, which had negotiated all previous agreements with Israel and formally accepted a two-state solution, Hamas had repeatedly refused to accept Israel's right of existence. On 31 January 2006, in its first official response to the election results, Egypt signalled its readiness to work with a future Hamas administration. While they rejected Western calls to boycott a Hamas-led administration, the Egyptian authorities made it clear that any co-operation would be contingent upon Hamas's willingness to renounce violence and to work within the framework of the Oslo accords and the roadmap for peace.

In the months following Hamas's victory, Egypt pursued a two-pronged diplomatic strategy, pressuring Hamas officials to alter their stance towards Israel, while urging Israeli and Western governments not to boycott the possible formation of a Hamas-led authority. In a statement issued on 14 February 2006, President Mubarak expressed confidence that Hamas would eventually recognize Israel's right to exist and promised that Egypt and its Middle Eastern partners would exert every pressure on the organization to do so. In the same month Mubarak warned that a freeze of Palestinian assets by the Israeli Government would only lead to a further deterioration in living conditions in the Palestinian territories and spark further violence and unrest in the territories. After talks with

Hamas representatives, on 7 March Dr Osama al-Baz, Mubarak's senior adviser, issued a statement condemning Western plans to withhold financial aid to a Hamas-led administration, calling instead on Israel and the West to 'give the new Palestinian administration a chance'.

Throughout the spring of 2006 Egyptian officials met with representatives from various Arab and European governments, in an effort to ensure continued international financial support for the PA and to revive the Middle East peace process. Mubarak urged the EU to continue its financial assistance to the PA, while insisting that Hamas adhere to the Saudi peace initiative, which had been formally adopted by the member states of the Arab League in 2002. On 26 March 2006 Mubarak met with Palestinian President Mahmud Abbas in Sharm el-Sheikh to discuss the peace process and the formation of a Hamas administration. Egyptian diplomatic efforts to reinvigorate the moribund peace process were further intensified after the election of a new Israeli Government led by Prime Minister Ehud Olmert on 28 March. Mubarak and Olmert convened a bilateral summit on 4 June in Sharm el-Sheikh, at which Mubarak reiterated Egypt's objection to any unilateral disengagement from Palestinian territories, emphasizing the need to find a negotiated solution to the Israeli–Palestinian conflict. On 17 June Abbas travelled to Egypt for further talks regarding the peace process. During the meeting Abbas and Mubarak discussed the ongoing negotiations between the new Hamas administration and Fatah to formulate a common position towards Israel and Abbas's call for a national referendum should Hamas fail to recognize Israel's right to exist. After the meeting Mubarak announced that preparations were under way to hold a three-way meeting between the leaders of Egypt, Israel and the PA.

From mid-June 2006 Egyptian efforts to resume peace negotiations between Abbas and Olmert were seriously derailed by the outbreak of factional fighting between Hamas and Fatah militias in the Palestinian territories only months after the swearing-in of a Hamas-led administration, a hostage crisis in Gaza, and the war between Israel and Hezbollah in Lebanon. Between October 2006 and February 2007 the Mubarak Government was heavily involved in attempts to bring about an end to the factional fighting between Hamas and Fatah militias. Egyptian diplomats and security experts repeatedly travelled to the Gaza Strip to help negotiate a lasting cease-fire between the two sides. Egyptian diplomats, alongside their Saudi counterparts, were also involved in efforts to broker a national unity administration between Hamas and Fatah, which was seen as the only feasible way to bring to an end both the violence and international economic embargo that had crippled the Palestinian territories since Hamas's election victory.

In late June 2006 prospects for a broader regional peace were further dented after an Israeli soldier was kidnapped in the Gaza Strip and a further two were kidnapped (and several others killed) in northern Israel. According to various sources, the kidnapping in Gaza had been masterminded by the Syrian leader of Hamas, Khalid Meshaal, and was carried out by a number of armed Palestinian groups, including the military wing of Hamas. In an attempt to free the soldier and in retaliation for his capture, the Olmert Government launched the largest incursion of Israeli forces into Gaza since the withdrawal of Israeli settlers from the territory in 2005. Throughout the hostage crisis, Egyptian security officials were deeply involved in negotiations with the hostage-takers in Gaza and with Meshaal in Syria in an effort to secure the soldier's release. Their efforts centred on a possible prisoner exchange, which would see the Israeli soldier freed in return for a release of Palestinian women and children from Israeli prisons. In October 2011 the soldier kidnapped in Gaza, Gilad Shalit, was released by Hamas in exchange for 1,027 Palestinian prisoners held in Israel.

Even more dramatic in their impact than the hostage crisis in Gaza were the kidnappings in June 2006 of the two Israeli soldiers by Hezbollah militias in northern Israel. As in Gaza, Israel retaliated with attacks on Hezbollah positions in Lebanon, sparking a month-long war between the Israeli armed forces and Hezbollah militias on Lebanese territory. Despite its limited diplomatic sway over the warring parties, throughout the war Egypt urged both sides to end the fighting and agree to a cease-fire. With the war raging into August, Mubarak condemned what he perceived as undue Israeli aggression against Lebanon, warning that the Middle East peace process was being seriously endangered. According to Mubarak, the root cause of the war, which ended with a UN-brokered cease-fire agreement on 14 August, lay with the unresolved Palestinian–Israeli conflict.

In early February 2007, at a summit meeting held in Mecca under Saudi auspices, an agreement was reached between Fatah and Hamas to form a power-sharing administration. The agreement and subsequent establishment of a national unity Cabinet in March were welcomed across the region, although Arab leaders differed in their demands towards the new administration. While Jordan reiterated the view that it must adhere to the principles of the Quartet (comprising the UN, the EU, the USA and Russia), Egypt—in a volte-face to its previous position—asserted that no conditions should be imposed on the new power-sharing administration. Despite widespread regional support, the unity administration collapsed only three months later, amid renewed fighting between Hamas and Fatah militias that had left Hamas in full control of the Gaza Strip. In response to the Hamas takeover of Gaza, President Abbas dismissed the Cabinet, instead forming an emergency administration that was immediately recognized by the Egyptian and other Arab governments.

In March 2007, at a summit meeting of the Arab League in Riyadh, Saudi Arabia, regional leaders agreed to revive the 2001 'land-for-peace' plan, which promised Israel full Arab recognition in return for its withdrawal from all territories occupied in 1967 and the establishment of a Palestinian state, with East Jerusalem as its capital. At the summit it was decided that the two countries with full diplomatic relations with Israel—Egypt and Jordan—would lead discussions with the Olmert administration on the Arab peace initiative. In contrast to the Sharon Government, which at the time had dismissed the Saudi initiative, this time around it received a cautious welcome from the Israeli Prime Minister. However, during a visit to Cairo in May 2007, the Israeli Minister of Foreign Affairs expressed several reservations about the initiative, most notably on the issues of refugees and borders. Meanwhile, in the Palestinian territories Hamas also voiced its objection to the 'land-for-peace' plan, arguing that the promise of full Arab recognition of Israel ran counter to its ideological tenets. On 24 June Egypt hosted a summit meeting of regional leaders in Sharm el-Sheikh, in an effort to resume peace negotiations between the new Abbas administration and the Israeli Government. At the summit, which was attended by King Abdullah of Jordan, President Abbas and Prime Minister Olmert, Mubarak also called on Hamas and Fatah to begin talks on how to end their stand-off.

In early 2007 a series of incidents placed further strains on the already tense bilateral relations between Cairo and Jerusalem. In February the Egyptian authorities charged three Israeli intelligence officers *in absentia* with spying for Israel, a charge that the Olmert Government was quick to refute as groundless. In March an Israeli television station aired a documentary on the 1967 war, which alleged that during the fighting Israeli troops had massacred about 250 Egyptian prisoners-of-war on the Sinai Peninsula. The allegations caused widespread outrage among both the Egyptian public and the Government, which demanded an official Israeli inquiry into the incident. Denying all accusations, the Israeli Government, meanwhile, maintained that those killed by Israeli forces in 1967 had not been Egyptian prisoners-of-war but Palestinian militia.

Initial hopes were high for an improvement in the regional situation following the international peace conference held in Annapolis, Maryland, USA, in late November 2007. At the same time, Mubarak was highly critical of Israel's continued expansion of Jewish settlements in the West Bank, which he said would seriously hinder the achievement of a comprehensive peace deal by the US Administration's deadline of the end of 2008.

Further hampering peace prospects, the Israeli Deputy Prime Minister and Minister of Defence, Ehud Barak, ordered virtually a complete blockade on the Gaza Strip in mid-

January 2008, in an attempt to counter the growing number of rockets being launched against Israeli border towns from the Strip by militants of the Hamas group. In late January Palestinian fighters succeeded in breaching the Rafah crossing that divides Gaza from Egypt and hundreds of thousands of Palestinians entered Egypt in search of food, fuel and medical supplies. The crossing had been virtually closed since Hamas's takeover of the Strip in June 2007 because the Egyptian Government, like Israel, refused to recognize Hamas as the legitimate administration in Gaza. Egyptian officials responded by offering their backing to a plan proposed by President Abbas that would allow for the PA, rather than Hamas, to assume control of the Egypt–Gaza border. The breaches in the border were repaired in early February 2008; however, there were subsequent reports of exchanges of gunfire between Egyptian security forces and Palestinian gunmen as tensions continued.

Relations between Egypt and Hamas deteriorated in August, when Hamas officials declared that they were suspending negotiations concerning the release of the Israeli soldier kidnapped in Gaza in June 2006 until Israel completely lifted its blockade of the territories. The Israeli military offensive in the Gaza Strip in December 2008–January 2009 further exacerbated tensions between Egypt and Hamas, with the latter—along with many in the Arab world—accusing Egypt of being complicit in the conflict as well as the conditions faced by Palestinians living in the enclave. Under significant pressure from the USA and Israel to tackle the problem, pressure intensified by the US Congress's decision in December 2007 to withhold US $100m. of aid to Egypt, Egypt took measures to placate the US authorities refusing to open its Rafah crossing-point on the Egypt–Gaza border to anything other than non-humanitarian goods. This implicit support for the Israeli-imposed blockade against the Palestinian enclave incensed many in Egypt and the wider region, prompting accusations against the Egyptian Government of pandering to 'enemies' of the Arab world.

In Israel, the appointment in February 2009 to the position of Prime Minister of the Likud leader, Binyamin Netanyahu (the Prime Minister in 1996–99), threatened further to impede already strained relations between Israel and Egypt. Prior to June 2009 Netanyahu, unlike his predecessor, Olmert, had notably refused to lend his support to the two-state solution and was instead a proponent of an approach based on economic co-operation, contending that political accord must be preceded by 'economic peace' in the Palestinian territories. However, in June, shortly after an address to the international Muslim community by US President Barack Obama, Netanyahu appeared to effect a volte-face; in a speech broadcast live in both Israel and many Arab countries, the Israeli Prime Minister endorsed the notion of a Palestinian state for the first time. However, many commentators dismissed the about-turn as little more than an attempt to appease the US Administration. Netanyahu continued to reject a right of return for Palestinian refugees, arguing that this would compromise 'Israel's continued existence as the state of the Jewish people', and declared that Jewish settlements in the West Bank would remain and expand in line with population growth. Given these qualifications of Netanyahu's endorsement of a Palestinian state, it seemed likely that Egypt's position as mediator in the Middle East peace process would remain a difficult one.

EGYPT AND THE USA—A COMPLICATED 'FRIENDSHIP'

Relations between the USA and Egypt remained uneasy during the early months of Mubarak's fifth term. The key issue of contention on the part of the USA was Egypt's retreat from democratic reform and its stance towards the crises in Iran and Iraq, which contravened that of the Bush Administration. Egypt neither supported the use of sanctions in the nuclear dispute with Iran nor the possible deployment of Egyptian troops in Iraq. Meanwhile, Egyptian policy-makers showed increasing frustration over US interference in domestic affairs and its failure to reignite the Middle East peace process.

Following the Egyptian presidential and parliamentary polls, in December 2005 the US House of Representatives passed a strongly worded resolution condemning the two elections as fraud-ridden and demanding more far-reaching political reforms. During the visit of a congressional delegation to Cairo in January 2006, the USA (Egypt's largest trading partner) delayed the completion of a bilateral free trade agreement with Egypt, apparently owing to a lack of progress towards political reform.

Apart from the occasional criticism of Egypt's human rights record, the tone of bilateral relations between the USA and Egypt improved markedly from July 2006. In mid-2006 both countries agreed to resume the strategic dialogue discussions on regional, economic and domestic developments that had been introduced under the Clinton Administration in 1999. Two months later, in an interview given to the *Wall Street Journal*, President Bush openly praised the Mubarak regime, expressing admiration for the 'young reformers' in the Nazif Government. In Egypt these comments were widely interpreted as signalling unconditional US support for the ruling party and its young cadre around Gamal Mubarak. This sentiment was further reinforced by the lack of any mention of Egypt's human rights record during a series of visits by Condoleezza Rice to Cairo between October 2006 and March 2007. All three visits during this period focused exclusively on regional matters, including the situation in the Palestinian territories, the Palestinian-Israeli peace process and the security situation in Iraq. Observers contended that the toning down of the Bush Administration's agenda to promote democracy in the Arab world was driven in large measure by the need to bolster 'moderate' regimes friendly with the USA against radical Islamist forces in the region.

Nevertheless, the importance of US-Egyptian relations to both countries appeared to have waned by mid-January 2008, when President Bush visited Egypt only briefly at the end of an eight-day tour of the Middle East intended principally to accelerate the relaunch of the peace process and to secure Arab support in the US Administration's ongoing efforts to persuade Iran to abandon its nuclear programme. The US leadership had been strongly critical of Egypt for its failure to secure its border with the Gaza Strip following the takeover of the territory by Hamas militants in June 2007 and to prevent Palestinian militants from smuggling weapons into Gaza for use in attacks against Israeli targets. As noted above, in December 2007 the US Congress voted to withhold US $100m. in aid to Egypt until the USA had received assurances that the authorities in Cairo had imposed sufficient measures to bring to an end the cross-border arms-smuggling and had also taken steps to improve the country's human rights record.

The election of Barack Obama to the US presidency in November 2008 was accompanied by a discernible change in US-Egyptian relations. In contrast to the Bush Administration, perceived as having sidelined Egypt in its efforts to relaunch the Middle East peace process, the Obama Administration made it clear that it would seek engagement with Egypt on regional issues. The US Special Envoy for Middle East Peace, George Mitchell, visited Egypt to meet with President Mubarak during a regional tour in July 2009 aimed at reviving the stalled peace talks. In August Obama hosted a visit from Mubarak in Washington, DC—the first time that the Egyptian President had attended a White House summit since 2004. The two heads of states expressed optimism over the possibility of moving forward with the peace process. Other issues discussed included Iranian nuclear developments, the situation in Iraq, and co-operative efforts on economy, education and health. President Mubarak also offered assurances that the Egyptian Government was committed to furthering the process of democratic reform and improving the country's human rights record.

Egypt continued to position itself as a regional peace-maker, a role that required a delicate balancing act between Israeli and Palestinian leaders and between the different Palestinian groups. It aimed to promote reconciliation between the two main Palestinian factions—Hamas, which was in de facto control of the Gaza Strip, and Fatah, which dominated the internationally recognized PA Government in the West Bank. This proved problematic, however, as Egypt was widely seen as being much closer to Fatah, and any 'reconciliation' it promoted was perceived as being designed to reinforce Fatah's dominance of Palestinian politics.

Following the international reaction to the incident on 31 May 2010, during which Israeli security forces boarded a Turkish-registered ship that formed part of a flotilla of vessels attempting to break the Israeli blockade of the Gaza Strip and deliver humanitarian supplies (see the chapter on Israel), Egypt reopened the Rafah crossing on its border with Gaza, allowing tens of thousands of Palestinians to enter Egypt's Sinai Peninsula for a few hours to purchase food and other supplies. Egypt also allowed medical and humanitarian aid through the crossing, and the Egyptian Ministry of Foreign Affairs issued a statement condemning an Israeli plan to close all of Israel's land crossings with Gaza, which would leave the Egyptian border as the only access point for the movement of people, food and supplies.

Meanwhile, concern was raised in both the USA and Egypt, and the wider Arab world, by comments made by US Secretary of Defense Robert Gates in May 2009, following a meeting with President Mubarak. In response to the question of whether US military aid to Egypt would be linked to progress on democracy and human rights, as was the case during the Bush Administration, Gates' reply included the comment that, while the USA was always supportive of human rights, 'the debate over funding conditions is essentially over'. This response prompted concerns that, for all the promising rhetoric, the Obama Administration might not veer as comprehensively as many had hoped from the previous Administration's implicit strategy of ignoring human rights abuses by Arab leaders in exchange for co-operation on defence and security matters.

DIPLOMATIC DEVELOPMENTS IN THE REGION

On 16 March 2006, shortly before the annual Arab League summit meeting in Khartoum, Egypt announced that the member states had agreed to re-elect Amr Moussa as Secretary-General of the organization for a second five-year term. At the summit on 28 March regional leaders focused their discussions on the crisis in Iraq, the Darfur region of Sudan and the Palestinian territories. The meeting also addressed a Saudi-Egyptian initiative to convene two summits per year and for Sharm el-Sheikh to be designated as the permanent seat for Arab League summit meetings. According to Saudi and Egyptian officials, the permanent move of Arab League meetings to Egypt (which was formally agreed on 5 April) would reduce the costs of organizing such events and enhance the security provisions for visiting heads of state.

Continuing its role as regional mediator in Sudan, Egypt sustained its efforts to facilitate a peaceful resolution to the deepening crisis in Darfur throughout Mubarak's fifth presidential term. With historically close ties to Sudan, Mubarak's diplomatic involvement was primarily geared towards finding a regional solution to the conflict and a solution that was acceptable to the Government in Khartoum. Following the establishment of a joint African Union-UN peace-keeping force, Egypt deployed 1,200 troops to Darfur in January 2008. In April the Egyptian Government announced the provision of US $1m. in aid to the Darfur region and granted $1m. of food aid to Sudan in July. In addition, Egypt continued to meet with high-level Sudanese officials and Darfur rebel group leaders to discuss the advancement of conflict resolution negotiations.

In early 2006 Egypt continued its diplomatic efforts to facilitate reconciliation between the different Iraqi groups and to encourage the formation of a national unity government. On 28 March, however, Egypt rejected a US proposal gradually to replace coalition troops with Arab or Muslim forces, arguing that Arab governments were neither ready nor keen to become involved in Iraq. Egyptian efforts to resolve the deepening crisis in Iraq were seriously undermined by comments made by President Mubarak in an interview on 8 April. Mubarak stated that Iraq was in the grip of civil war and that Shi'ite Muslims around the world showed a greater allegiance to Iran than to their respective home countries. Infuriated by the comments, leaders across the region strongly denied the claims. Iranian officials asserted that the country's influence over Iraq was 'spiritual' rather than political; while the Iraqi Government rejected the claim that Iraq was gripped by civil war and that its Shi'ite population was disloyal to the country. In response to Mubarak's comments, the Iraqi Government declined to attend a meeting of Arab ministers responsible for foreign affairs, scheduled for 12 April. The meeting's agenda included the security situation in Iraq, provision of Arab aid and the progress being made in the formation of a unity government.

Bilateral relations between Egypt and Iraq were further tested in the months that followed the Mubarak interview. To the outrage of the Baghdad administration, in mid-October 2006 the Egyptian Minister of Foreign Affairs reiterated the President's earlier warning that Iraq stood on the brink of all-out civil war. Three months later, in yet another thinly veiled criticism of the new Iraqi Government, President Mubarak called the execution of Saddam Hussain 'ill-timed, barbaric and illegal'. The execution of the former Iraqi leader took place amid the festivities of Id al-Adha (Feast of the Sacrifice), a fact that caused a public outcry in many Sunni Arab regimes. In March 2007 Egypt played host to a regional summit on Iraq in Sharm el-Sheikh. The summit, which was attended by some 49 countries—including Iraq's neighbours and all five permanent members of the UN Security Council—discussed ways to improve domestic security and reduce sectarian violence in Iraq. In October 2008 Ahmad Aboul Gheit became the first Egyptian Minister of Foreign Affairs to visit Iraq since 1989, reflecting a gradual amelioration of bilateral relations, culminating in the announcement that Egypt was to send an ambassador to Baghdad for the first time since the assassination in 2005 of Ihab al-Sherif. Meanwhile, several memorandums of understanding intended to bolster bilateral co-operation on, *inter alia*, military, security and investment matters were signed by Egyptian and Iraqi representatives in July–August 2008. Also in August it was announced that Iraqi Prime Minister Nouri al-Maliki was to visit Egypt in late September, in a further sign of improving relations between the two countries.

Despite its limited diplomatic influence over Iran (diplomatic relations between the two countries had been severed in 1979) Egypt adopted a strong stance regarding the dispute between Iran and the USA, which had worsened following the election of Mahmoud Ahmadinejad as President of Iran in June 2005 and which threatened further to destabilize the region. The dispute was exacerbated in late 2005 when it transpired that Iran was apparently working on a secret nuclear weapons programme, in breach of the NPT, to which it had been a signatory since 1970 (for further details, see the chapter on Iran). In February 2006 Egypt voted alongside the USA and a majority of the member states of the UN General Assembly to refer Iran to the Security Council, while at the same time calling for a peaceful solution to the dispute. On 1 March President Mubarak urged the USA to refrain from using military force against Iran, fearing a further destabilization of the Middle East. While acknowledging Iran's right to peaceful nuclear technology, Mubarak also reiterated Egypt's long-standing demand that the Middle East, including Israel, become free of nuclear weapons.

In a rare diplomatic move, on 21 April 2006 the Iranian Minister of Foreign Affairs, Manouchehr Mottaki, made a telephone call to his Egyptian counterpart to discuss Iran's position on the nuclear issue. Mottaki reportedly expressed Iran's willingness to find a peaceful solution to the crisis, while retaining the right to develop peaceful nuclear technology. Further direct talks between the two countries took place during a visit of the Iranian Secretary of the Supreme Council for National Security and chief nuclear negotiator, Ali Ardeshir Larijani, to Cairo on 10 June, although Larijani refused to reveal whether the visit indicated a step towards the normalization of relations between the two countries.

In late 2006 and early 2007 the Mubarak administration continued its mediation efforts in the nuclear stand-off between the UN and Iran, reiterating its position that both Iran and Israel must halt their nuclear programmes in order to prevent a nuclear arms race in the region. Although there were strong indications in the first half of 2007 that Iran was considering the resumption of full diplomatic relations with Egypt, Egyptian diplomats remained cautious, pointing to the erratic behaviour of the Iranian President with regard to foreign policy. Despite the holding of 'constructive' discussions between senior Egyptian and Iranian officials from mid-2007, it appeared that the Egyptian leadership was reluctant to proceed with the normalization of relations until Iran first ended what Egypt deemed to be Iranian interference in the internal affairs of several Arab countries, notably Iraq, Lebanon and the Palestinian territories.

The improvement in Egyptian-Iranian relations was largely nullified during the course of 2008 and into 2009. Egyptian officials were incensed by the airing in July 2008 by Iran's state television network of a documentary on the assassination of Sadat that pilloried the former Egyptian President as a 'treacherous Pharoah' while depicting his killer, Khaled Islambouli, in a favourable light. In January 2009 Egypt acted to prevent an Iranian ship, which was allegedly transporting arms to the Gaza Strip, from passing through the Suez Canal. None the less, in June Egypt announced that it would not stop ships carrying aid to Gaza from the Iranian Red Crescent Society. Israel had earlier asked Egypt to prevent the passage of certain vessels through the Canal, but Egypt had rejected the request stating that, owing to international agreements, it could not stop any ship from passing through the canal, unless it were a ship from a state at war with Egypt. In April 2009 49 people were arrested in connection with an alleged Hezbollah plot to carry out terrorist attacks in Egypt; the Egyptian authorities accused Iran of being behind the operation, a claim that was vehemently denied by the Iranian Government.

Despite months of discussions in 2009–10, Egypt and Sudan remained at odds with the other countries that belong to the Nile Basin Initiative (NBI), a World Bank-funded programme aimed at finding consensus among the states that draw on the waters of the Nile. (Egypt relies on the Nile for 95%–97% of all its water requirements.) A total of nine NBI states were involved in negotiations over the fair use of the Nile waters: Egypt, Sudan, Ethiopia, Kenya, Uganda, Tanzania, Burundi, the Democratic Republic of Congo (DRC) and Rwanda. Egypt and Sudan consistently sought to prevent changes to their historical rights to use 85% of the Nile waters, which were based on two colonial agreements signed with Britain in 1929 and 1959, while the upstream countries advocated new arrangements to allow them greater use of Nile water for development projects.

In May 2010, following a meeting in Entebbe, Uganda, five of the NBI countries—Kenya, Ethiopia, Rwanda, Uganda and Tanzania—signed a new Nile water-sharing accord, which reversed the colonial agreements; Egypt and Sudan refused to sign the document. The agreement required a sixth signature—from either the DRC or Burundi—to move closer to implementation; Egypt, which was adamant about protecting what it saw as its right to use most of the water of the Nile, determinedly lobbied both countries in an attempt to prevent them from joining the other five African states in signing the accord.

The division of Sudan following a referendum on 9 January 2011 presented a further complication of the issue of Egypt's national security. While Egypt had experienced decades of conflict with a unified Sudan—involving utilization of the Nile waters, border disputes (such as that over the Halaib triangle), and refugees—the two countries had, none the less, always remained closely aligned in opposition to the upstream Nile countries. A divided Sudan meant that Egypt would have to contend with one more state in negotiations over access to Nile waters.

A THREATENING POLITICAL STORM

On 22 February 2009 an explosive device was detonated in the Khan el-Khalili market in central Cairo, killing one French teenager and injuring more than 20 people, including many European tourists. A second bomb, discovered nearby by the authorities, was safely defused. On the following day seven alleged members of the Islamic Army of Palestine (IAP—a militant, Islamist organization with alleged links to al-Qa'ida) were reportedly arrested by the Egyptian authorities in connection with the attack. The incidents were seen by some as militants' response to the Egyptian Government's perceived support of the Israeli blockade of the Gaza Strip. However, with no group actually claiming responsibility for the attack in Cairo, some attributed blame to the Government itself, citing the imminence of a parliamentary debate, scheduled for the following month, on whether the national state of emergency should be renewed beyond 2010. Proponents of such 'conspiracy theories' argued that Mubarak and the Government were becoming increasingly nervous about their waning popularity and hold on power. However, others dismissed this idea, pointing to the primitive nature of the explosive device used in the attack, arguing that such a contraption suggested the involvement of disaffected individuals or an ad hoc group with little experience or organizational support.

Militancy was not the only domestic threat on Egypt's agenda. Despite the absence of cases of the swine influenza variant pandemic (H1N1) 2009 (commonly referred to as swine flu) in Egypt, in April 2009 concerns about the virus prompted the Government to order the cull of the entire pig population in the country, estimated to number some 300,000. Angry at the decision, pig farmers held several street demonstrations, many of which were forcibly dispersed by the authorities, with dozens of protesters reportedly arrested. The cull particularly angered the members of the Coptic Christian population, who owned the vast majority of the pigs and who contended that the Government had used the threat of swine flu as an excuse to attack the Coptic minority.

The Government was also accused of attempting to cull political opponents. Controversial legislation expanding the number of seats in the National Assembly from 454 to 518, with all 64 new seats to be reserved for female candidates, was passed in June 2009, to take effect at the legislative elections scheduled for 2010. The Minister of State for Legal and Parliamentary Councils, Dr Mufid Mahmoud Shehab, argued that the law would 'ensure parity for women and promote their role in society'. The new legislation was intended to remain in place for the duration of the next two five-year parliamentary sessions, after which the Government hoped that such affirmative action would no longer be required. However, opponents of the new legislation, who included the Muslim Brotherhood, argued that it ran counter to the laws of equality enshrined within the country's Constitution, and contended that the actual reason behind the new law was the fact that it would bolster the ruling party's parliamentary majority since the only women likely to secure election would be NDP candidates. The legislation was also interpreted by some as an overture to the West, where women's rights are an ongoing important issue.

In October 2009 opposition groups began a campaign against the possible candidacy of Gamal Mubarak to succeed his father at the end of the presidential term in 2011. A new opposition movement, Mayihkomsh ('he will not rule'), was formed under the leadership of Ayman al-Nour. Its first conference was held in Cairo on 14 October 2009 and was attended by, among others, representatives of the Muslim Brotherhood, the Democratic Front Party and Kefaya.

Muhammed el-Baradei, the former Director-General of the IAEA, returned to Egypt in February 2010 and helped mobilize this effort. His campaign for reform of the political, electoral and constitutional system included calls for changes to the Constitution to allow for wider participation in presidential elections; the restoration of judicial oversight of the electoral process; and the abolition of the state of emergency. In an attempt to galvanize widespread anger and frustration with the Egyptian Government, el-Baradei founded the National Association for Change (NAC—also referred to as the National Front for Change), to serve as a co-ordinating body and to develop strategy among a range of individuals and organizations—including liberals, conservatives, Islamists, secular parties and Coptic Christians—who shared his goals. For months following his return, el-Baradei held meetings with various opposition leaders and others from across the political spectrum. However, during those few months, divisions emerged among the disparate elements of the NAC. Concerted attacks were made on him by state-owned media outlets, which attempted to portray him as an outsider with little knowledge of contemporary Egyptian society. El-Baradei was eventually ousted from the organization's leadership.

In early May 2010 President Mubarak (with the support of parliament) extended the state of emergency for another two years. Although new limits to the legislation were introduced (for the first time since its implementation), the extension of the emergency law again elicited widespread condemnation from human rights activists and political opposition leaders. Protests were held outside the People's Assembly. In the same month members of trade unions, public workers and opposition groups demonstrated outside various government ministers' offices, demanding an increase in the minimum wage, which had not officially been raised since 1984. The protests were part of a series of riots and peaceful demonstrations that occurred in Egypt throughout the year.

In June 2010 protests erupted following allegations that members of the police force had tortured and beaten to death a young man from Alexandria, Khalid Muhammad Said, who was reportedly about to make public a video containing footage of corrupt practices by police officers. Images purporting to show Said's body displaying severe injuries were distributed on the internet. An official Egyptian government 'investigation' concluded that he died while attempting to swallow a plastic bag containing illegal drugs. Many viewed this account as a fabrication. The incident provoked large anti-Government protests in Alexandria, inside the city's largest mosque, and outside the internal security headquarters in Cairo, as well as other areas of the capital. In June two police officers were arrested in connection with Said's death. The trial of the two men on charges of illegal arrest and excessive use of force commenced at a court in Alexandria in late July; following several adjournments, the two defendants were found guilty and each sentenced to seven years' imprisonment in October 2011.

Earlier in the year, the Muslim Brotherhood elected a new and more conservative leadership, following a meeting of its own internal Shura (Advisory) Council. Muhammad Badie was elected as Supreme Guide, replacing Muhammad Mahdi Akif (who had led the Brotherhood since 2004). Analysts suggested that the change in leadership would prompt the organization to focus on ideological education of youth, religious duties and social work in place of political engagement and activism. However, the election caused a rift within the movement since the previous leadership, under Akif, had brought a semblance of unity across generations as well as between moderates and conservatives, and urban and rural activists. Young activists had also been energized by the Brotherhood's success in the 2005 parliamentary elections, in which it secured its largest ever representation in the People's Assembly.

In February 2010 Badie stated that the Brotherhood would participate (as independents) in the November People's Assembly elections. However, on 1 June the Brotherhood's new leaders experienced their first setback when the group failed to gain a single seat in elections to the Advisory Council, the upper house of Parliament. The leadership of the Brotherhood denounced the conduct of the poll, claiming that the elections were neither free nor fair.

In October 2010 President Mubarak announced that elections to the People's Assembly were to be held on 28 November, with run-off elections to take place on 5 December. In September el-Baradei had appealed for an electoral boycott, claiming that the elections would doubtlessly be rigged by the Government and that taking part in the process would accordingly constitute an insult to democratic principles. However, the proscribed Muslim Brotherhood subsequently announced its intention to field candidates as independents. On 25 November the NDP stated that it had filed complaints against 52 nominally independent candidates whom it believed to be linked to the Muslim Brotherhood; dozens of Brotherhood-affiliated candidates had already been disqualified and more than 1,000 of the group's supporters were reported to have been arrested in the weeks preceding the poll. On 26 November administrative courts ordered the cancellation of polling in 24 districts after the HEC had ignored previous court orders demanding the reinstatement of disqualified opposition and independent candidates; however, the cancellation orders appeared to go similarly unheeded.

In the first round of voting, held as scheduled on 28 November 2010, the NDP was reported to have won the vast majority of seats, with independent candidates affiliated to the Muslim Brotherhood failing to secure a single seat. The second round of voting was boycotted by the New Wafd Party and associates of the Muslim Brotherhood, who alleged widespread voting irregularities during the first round. According to final results released by the HEC, the NDP secured 420 seats of the 508 contested seats in the People's Assembly, the New Wafd Party obtained six, the NPUP won five, and the Democratic Generation Party, al-Ghad, al-Salam and the Social Justice Party each won one seat; independent candidates took 69 seats, of which only one was won by an affiliate of the Muslim Brotherhood (compared with 88 in the 2005 elections). The results appeared to preclude the possibility of any of the opposition parties putting forward a candidate at the 2011 presidential election: according to the Constitution, in order to field a candidate, a political party had to have obtained 3% of the total number of seats in the People's Assembly and 5% of seats in the Advisory Council; the chances of an independent candidate being able to stand also appeared highly unlikely, with such candidates being required to obtain the endorsement of 250 elected members from Egypt's representative bodies. The New Wafd Party ordered its six elected deputies to tender their resignation from parliament, while the Muslim Brotherhood withdrew its support for Magdi Ashour, the sole affiliate of the group to win a seat. In the meantime, the Government continued to deny any accusations of vote-rigging, acknowledging only 'minor irregularities' that it asserted had no bearing on any results. Election monitors, however, reported widespread polling violations, and two people were killed as violent clashes between the supporters of rival candidates erupted in some polling districts.

Protests against the allegedly fraudulent nature of the elections persisted throughout December 2010 and into 2011. In mid-December 2010 a group of approximately 20 opposition party members who had failed to secure election, including members of the Muslim Brotherhood and the New Wafd Party, announced the establishment of a shadow parliament, pledging allegiance to the Constitution and 'the will of the people'. There were also widespread popular protests. While the Muslim Brotherhood remained ambivalent to the demonstrations, in a video recording posted on the internet in mid-December, el-Baradei implicitly approved of the demonstrators' actions and warned of possible violence if their demands were not met. One month later el-Baradei announced that he did not intend to contest the presidential poll due later in the year, asserting that it would be 'meaningless under current circumstances'; he appealed for a boycott of the elections in an attempt to 'erode the regime's legitimacy'.

THE FALL OF MUBARAK AND THE RISE OF THE SCAF

As 2010 came to an end, there was little indication that the Middle East was on the verge of serious popular protest, let alone what many have termed 'revolution'. Since President Mubarak's election to a fifth term in 2005, speculation had centred on the issue of the presidential succession. Although the military did come to power in 2011, it was not in the manner anticipated.

The Egyptian protests that led to the resignation of President Mubarak were mainly motivated by domestic discontent, although some were undoubtedly moved to action by witnessing insurgents in neighbouring Tunisia remove President Zine al-Abidine Ben Ali on 14 January 2011 (see the chapter on Tunisia). The initial 'day of rage', which took place on 25 January (coinciding with National Police Day), was marked by thousands of Egyptians taking to the streets. Prior to that date, youth groups had begun a virtual mobilization via social media pages. These forms of 'new media' (including mobile cellular telephones and social networking websites) were the primary vehicles in mobilizing thousands (and, ultimately, millions) to demonstrate on the streets of Cairo and other major cities. The Government briefly cut off all mobile telephone lines, as well as internet services, across the country on 26 January. The services were restored a few days later, but their suspension seemed to encourage more people to join the protests.

During the weeks that followed, Egyptians from all sections of society came together, primarily in Tahrir (Liberation) Square in Cairo, to demand the 'ending of the regime' and Mubarak's immediate resignation. Such mass protests spawned similar demonstrations across Egypt—in Alexandria, Ismailia and in numerous cities and villages in the Nile Delta and Nile Valley. While the protests themselves were mostly peaceful, the interaction between supporters of the Mubarak regime and those seeking the removal of the President were not. The resultant violence was instigated by the pro-Mubarak forces (especially by the undercover police and other elements affiliated with the regime, known as *baltagiyya*, or thugs). During the principal days of protests (on 25 January–11 February 2011), hundreds were killed and even more injured in Tahrir Square, and elsewhere throughout Egypt.

In the course of the uprising, the Egyptian Government offered a series of concessionary measures—including a pledge by President Mubarak not to seek re-election, the replacement of Prime Minister Nazif's Government by a new administration under Gen. Ahmad Muhammad Shafiq, the appointment of a Vice-President (the chief of the General Intelligence Service, Omar Suleiman), the release of political prisoners and increases in salaries and pensions. The protesters, however, were not appeased by the offer, which was widely considered to be only a half-measure. Many believed that the real problem was systemic and required fundamental change. The Egyptian armed forces found themselves in a precarious position during the protests. Popular ire was not directed at the military, at this point. In fact, the army was perceived as protecting the protesters.

The US Administration of Barack Obama was also in an awkward position. As noted above, although there had been issues of contention, the USA has enjoyed long-term positive diplomatic relations with Egypt. Moreover, US and Egyptian militaries had co-operated regularly in a range of joint exercises.

The Obama Administration was not obliged to consider this dilemma for too long, however: Mubarak resigned the presidency on 11 February 2011, just 18 days after the uprising began. He transferred his powers to the Supreme Council of the Armed Forces (SCAF), under the leadership of the Commander-in-Chief of the Armed Forces, Deputy Prime Minister and Minister of Defence, Field Marshal Muhammad Hussein Tantawi.

In a communiqué issued on 13 February 2011, the SCAF announced the dissolution of parliament, the suspension of the Constitution, and declared that it would 'run the affairs of the country on a temporary basis for six months or until the end of parliamentary and presidential elections'. A judicial committee was instructed to formulate amendments to the Constitution in preparation for a national referendum in March. The communiqué also confirmed that Tantawi, as Chairman of the SCAF, was to act as de facto Head of State. Despite the installation of the SCAF, the Government of Prime Minister Shafiq was requested to remain in office, pending the conclusion of elections. The judicial committee on constitutional reform published its draft amendments on 28 February, including revisions to those articles regarding political parties and the criteria of eligibility for presidential candidates; on 4 March the Council decreed that a referendum was to take place on 19 March. Meanwhile, on 3 March Shafiq's resignation was announced; former Minister of Transport Dr Essam Sharaf was subsequently appointed to replace him. Sharaf named his new Council of Ministers on 7 March. These arrangements, however, were unacceptable to many of the 'revolutionaries', and protests continued in Cairo.

The draft amendments to the Constitution included provisions for the judicial supervision of elections, the limiting of a four-year presidency to two terms, and the mandated appointment of a Vice-President. Other amended articles stipulated the removal of a controversial counter-terrorism provision and the narrowing of the criteria under which a President can institute a state of emergency. Questions were, however, raised about whether the constitutional amendments should be approved before the elections (or vice versa), and whether the Constitution could or should be amended at all or a new document drawn up in its entirety. There were concerns about who benefited from the process of reform, which was perceived by some as being rather hasty and secretive. Allegations were made that the NDP and the Muslim Brotherhood, both of which supported the constitutional amendments, were best poised to capitalize on the electoral changes since they were the country's best organized political groups.

On 19 March 2011, despite opposition from prominent figures in the anti-Mubarak protest movement, including el-Baradei, and from various youth movements, the constitutional amendments were approved by some 77.3% of voters; voter turn-out was recorded at 41.2% (a remarkable showing given Egypt's historically low voter participation). Accordingly, on 23 March the SCAF issued a Constitutional Declaration—including the amendments approved at the referendum—which was temporarily to replace the former Constitution until a new document could be formulated. Legislative elections were scheduled for later in the year.

At the end of March 2011 former President Mubarak and his family were placed under house arrest at their residence in Sharm el-Sheikh, and early the following month the Prosecutor-General requested that the former President and his sons, Gamal and Alaa, be questioned with regard to allegations of corruption and the deaths of protesters during the February uprising. On 17 April the High Administrative Court approved the dissolution of the NDP and the return of its assets to the state, while two days later the Prosecutor-General announced that former Prime Minister Nazif and former Minister of Finance Yousuf Boutros-Ghali had been charged with corruption and misuse of public funds. In late April a government committee established to investigate the deaths of protesters published a report, in which it confirmed that a total of 846 people had been killed during the unrest of early 2011. The report also accused the security forces of using 'excessive' force in their efforts to curb the protests.

After the revolution the masses stopped gathering on a daily basis in Tahrir Square, although significant protests continued. Increasingly, the new military rulers were criticized for not delivering change in an expeditious manner—on the one hand promising reform, while on the other undertaking repressive measures against their opponents, many of whom were sentenced to death.

Notably, the SCAF's use of military tribunals (already widely employed during Mubarak's regime) reached new heights during its first eight months, when it was widely reported that more than 12,000 were subjected to military trials on charges ranging from curfew violations to insulting the military.

The SCAF was also particularly criticized by domestic and international organizations for the violent treatment of protesters. Substantiated allegations involved the military beating unarmed protesters, firing live ammunition at protesters, assaulting medics attempting to render aid to the injured, and physically attacking journalists covering its actions. The arrest and detention of demonstrators and others questioning the legitimacy of the SCAFs rule are considered commonplace.

The events of 9 March 2011 proved a turning point in Egyptian citizens' attitudes towards the SCAF and the military. On that day Egyptian soldiers, supported by *baltagiyya*, destroyed a tent camp established by demonstrators in Tahrir Square and beat the protesters, many of whom were subsequently detained in the Egyptian Museum and tortured. One of the most widely denounced episodes of the military abuse on 9 March was the use of 'virginity tests' on many women; this was a way of intimidating and abusing female protesters, with male 'doctors' examining the women in front of soldiers. After 9 March attitudes towards the SCAF shifted dramatically, albeit over a period of several months, and it was generally viewed in a negative light thereafter.

In October 2011 state-society relations were further destabilized by sectarian violence, as soldiers killed about 25 Coptic Christian protesters in Cairo, injuring hundreds more (following similar incidents earlier that year). After the ouster of Mubarak, many Copts were uncertain about their social, political and legal future in the new Egypt, and staged protests against the perceived discrimination of their religious community.

Late November and December 2011 were marked by further conflict, as the police violently suppressed continuing protests against the SCAF. The police, with the support of the army, used tear gas, batons, and live ammunition to disperse the protesters; it was reported that several hundred demonstrators had been killed and thousands injured since the beginning of the unrest.

Domestic and international NGOs also came under attack from the SCAF. By late 2011 17 groups had been raided at the order of the Prosecutor's Office, and numerous foreign staff were prohibited from leaving the country and/or faced criminal proceedings. The SCAF was reportedly concerned that the NGOs were fomenting unrest, and 43 employees were charged with operating without a licence and with the illegal receipt of foreign funds. The US-based Freedom House, the International Republican Institute (IRI) and the National Democratic Institute (NDI) were among the organizations affected. A small number of US workers sought refuge in the US embassy in Egypt. The USA consequently threatened to withhold its substantial annual foreign aid package (including US $1,300m. in military assistance), and in February 2012 sent former US presidential candidate and senior Senator John McCain (who was also the Chairman of the IRI) to attempt to settle the diplomatic dispute. By early March the situation was were somewhat resolved, as Egypt agreed to allow the US citizens to leave the country after bail was posted. Trials *in absentia* were scheduled for those foreign nationals who had returned home.

In May 2012 the SCAF announced the end of the state of emergency, which had been imposed following President Sadat's assassination. However, weeks later it declared that military officers were empowered to detain civilians engaged in criminal activities and refer them to military tribunals. The decree was, however, successfully challenged in court by a number of groups.

THE NEW POLITICAL LANDSCAPE

Egypt has developed a new political landscape, although it is still too early to determine which figures and parties will prove lasting. Predictions are difficult because the system in which they will interact in the long run is still an unknown. As described below, a new parliament and President have been elected, but both electoral cycles were fraught with difficulty. The SCAFs willingness to relinquish power remains a huge question which dominates the politics of Egypt. And, last but not least, Egypt is constitutionally lacking.

The Muslim Brotherhood continues to be a source of concern among Egyptians as well as on the part of external observers, especially after its candidate won the 2012 presidential election. Questions continue to be asked about the nature of the group's Islamist agenda, its long-term political ambitions, its tolerance for non-Muslims (especially Coptic Christians), its relations with its organizational offspring Hamas, and its willingness to abide by international agreements, especially with Israel.

Until early 2011 the Muslim Brotherhood largely faced these questions as a socio-religious organization, despite the fact that it had won seats in the Egyptian parliament (with its deputies officially being elected as independents). However, in April 2011 the Brotherhood entered a new era by forming a political party, the Freedom and Justice Party (FJP), an organizationally distinct entity but with strong links to the Brotherhood. The FJP subsequently formed a coalition with a range of secular and other religious political parties, including the liberal New Wafd Party, the leftist NPUP and a newly formed Salafist group, the Al-Nour (Light) Party. The durability of this coalition, constituting an unlikely assortment of allies, as well as its electoral agenda, remained uncertain.

At the same time, the Muslim Brotherhood faced internal dissension. As part of its strategy to reassure the sceptics, the organization stated that the FJP was not seeking a parliamentary majority in the forthcoming elections (it would present candidates for only 50% or less of the seats in the legislature), and that it would not put forward a candidate in the forthcoming presidential election. However, it appeared that not all of the Brotherhood's members were in agreement with this stance.

Prior to the revolution, questions had surfaced about divisions within the Brotherhood. In early 2010 the election of Muhammad Badie as the group's new Supreme Leader had proved controversial—observers had warned of a possible organizational bifurcation between the new and old guard, reformists and conservatives. One year on, during the 2011 uprising, questions had been raised about the Brotherhood's position on the momentous events. Some wondered whether the group was strategically staying on the sidelines—in order that the revolution be perceived as of the people rather than of the Islamists. Others thought that the Brotherhood was being too pragmatic—waiting to see what ultimately evolved from the political upheaval before declaring its unconditional support for the revolution. A few even questioned whether the Muslim Brotherhood was secretly orchestrating events from behind the scenes.

After the formation of the FJP and the revolution, dissenters openly emerged within the Muslim Brotherhood. Senior Muslim Brotherhood member Abd el-Monim Abou el-Fotouh declared his intention to contest the presidency as an independent; he was consequently expelled from the organization. Key members of the Brotherhood's youth movement formed a new party, apparently outside the influence of the FJP, and named it the Al-Tayar al-Masry—the Egyptian Current (or Stream) Party.

Also of significance was the emergence of two other Islamist parties—the Al-Nour Party and the Al-Wasat (New Centre) Party. Al-Wasat was granted official recognition as a party immediately after Mubarak's fall from power; it had sought official approval since its formation in 1996 by breakaway members of the Muslim Brotherhood who were seeking to present a more moderate Islamist front. These developments confirmed that the Brotherhood does not hold a monopoly on Islamist social or political expression in Egypt.

Voting for the new People's Assembly began in late November 2011 and was concluded in early January 2012. The election results were announced on 21 January: the Muslim Brotherhood's FJP won 235 of the 498 elective seats, the Al-Nour Party 123 seats, and the New Wafd Party 38 seats. Some 12 other parties also secured representation. The remaining 132 seats were reserved for independent candidates, while 10 additional members were appointed by the SCAF. Reports indicated that there were irregularities—ranging from closed polling stations to procedural violations.

In January and February 2012 elections for the Advisory Council were held; the FJP won 105 of the 180 contested seats, the Al-Nour Party 45 seats, and the New Wafd Party 14 seats, although voter turn-out was reportedly very low. Meanwhile, tensions over the forthcoming presidential election increased. In mid-January el-Baradei stated that he was withdrawing his candidacy for the presidency, having declared that 'the old regime had not fallen yet'. On 23 January the new People's Assembly held its inaugural session. The FJP's nomination of its Secretary-General, Muhammad Saad el-Katatni, as the chamber's Speaker, was approved with overwhelming support.

Only five months later, however, on 14 June 2012, the Supreme Constitutional Court declared the legislation under which the People's Assembly had been elected to be unconstitutional, and also ruled that former members of Mubarak's regime were permitted to run for office. The decision was widely considered to be a direct reverse for the Muslim Brotherhood specifically, and Islamists generally, as they dominated the People's Assembly and were well positioned to succeed in the presidential contest. On 15 June the SCAF dissolved the Assembly and assumed legislative powers on an interim basis.

The period preceding the presidential poll proved highly eventful. In March 2012 the Muslim Brotherhood nominated Khairat al-Shater as its presidential candidate, despite previous Brotherhood statements that it would not seek the presidency. Less than one month later, the election commission had disqualified some 10 candidates, including al-Shater (due to a previous criminal conviction), as well as Omar Suleiman, Mubarak's former head of intelligence (owing to a signature requirement), and conservative Salafist Hazem Abu Ismail (on the grounds that his mother had held US citizenship, contravening a legal requirement that a candidate be solely of Egyptian parentage).

Voting for Egypt's first presidential election after the overthrow of Mubarak was conducted on 23–24 May 2012, with 13 candidates participating. Voter turn-out was reported as just under 50%. Since no single candidate secured a majority of the votes cast, a second round was scheduled between the two leading candidates, FJP leader Muhammad Mursi (who had received 24.8% of the vote) and former Prime Minister Shafiq (23.7%).

The second round of the presidential election took place on 16–17 June 2012; announcement of the results was delayed for several days owing to allegations of electoral irregularities. The delay was a major concern in Egypt, as citizens and observers wondered whether the SCAF would manipulate the results and to what end. On 24 June the election results were officially released: FJP candidate Mursi was declared the victor, after he narrowly defeated Shafiq with 51.7% of the votes cast. While the second round was taking place, the SCAF restricted presidential powers through amendments to the Constitutional Declaration (issued in March 2011), thereby asserting its authority over legislation, the army budget and declarations of war, as well as the forthcoming constitutional process.

Mursi was sworn in at the Supreme Constitutional Court on 30 June 2012. In a speech delivered shortly afterwards at Cairo University, President Mursi declared that: 'The army is now returning to its original role, protecting the nation and its borders'. However, only 10 days before the election, a leading member of the SCAF had stated: 'The good of the country requires a presence for the armed forces in the street to protect the country since the police are still unable to fully perform'.

In the midst of the turmoil surrounding the presidential election, former President Mubarak was sentenced to life imprisonment in early June 2012. Judge Ahmed Rifaat described Mubarak's era as '30 years of darkness'. In late June reports emerged that Mubarak had died, after suffering a stroke; these subsequently proved to be false, although he was believed to be in ill health.

CHANGES IN FOREIGN POLICY

Following the ouster of Mubarak, Egypt appeared to be charting a somewhat new course in regional foreign policy. This was demonstrated by adjustments in its relations with Iran, a change of position regarding the border with Gaza, and seemingly more enthusiastic efforts at nurturing positive relations between Hamas and Fatah.

In February 2011, just days after of the fall of Mubarak, Egypt permitted two Iranian naval vessels to pass through the Suez Canal in relatively close proximity to Israel. This transit was the first time that Egypt had allowed Iran access to the Canal since the deterioration of relations between the two countries following the Iranian revolution of 1979. Although Iran denied any hostile or provocative intentions in the vessels to pass through the Canal, Israel expressed great consternation. At that time the Israeli authorities were already perturbed by the upheaval in the region, the unpredictability of future developments and particularly by the fact that Israel's neighbour Egypt, with which it had a long-standing peace agreement, was undergoing radical changes. The USA attempted to strike a diplomatic balance—expressing concern about potential Iranian military motives while extolling the virtues of open navigation.

Since the imposition of the blockade of the Gaza Strip in 2006, Egypt had largely complied with Israel's policy, earning it the displeasure of Palestinians along with the guarded appreciation of the Israeli Government. Following the appointment of the Sharaf Government in March 2011, however, Egypt appeared to adopt a more independent approach towards this issue. At the end of May, much to the disapproval of Israel, the Government declared the Rafah border crossing open for people, although not for goods. However, the opening of the crossing encountered various problems. Quotas and permits for Palestinians, as well as checkpoint staffing and opening hours, have all proved to be issues requiring attention.

Meanwhile, in early May, under the auspices of Egypt, Hamas and Fatah signed an accord offering possibilities for longer-term reconciliation between the rival factions. The provisions of the agreement included proposals for the establishment of an interim Palestinian government pending elections in 2012. Egypt's role as mediator was not a new development, although the positive result in this case was a departure from previous attempts at reconciliation. For many years President Mubarak had sought to be a Palestinian kingmaker, hosting numerous rounds of talks. However, these efforts had achieved only limited results, partly owing to the view of some observers and participants that Mubarak had attempted to empower Fatah at the expense of Hamas. The provisional Egyptian Government offered the Palestinians a fresh start, or at least a new context in which the parties could negotiate. Nevertheless, by mid-2013 the formation of a non-partisan government for Gaza and the West Bank had yet to be finalized.

Following his election in June 2012, President Mursi stated that he would abide by all international agreements, including the peace treaty with Israel, while asserting that he regarded Israel as failing fully to comply with such agreements. Some observers also consider that Mursi challenged Egypt's relations with the USA by stating that he sought the release of the Egyptian cleric Sheikh Omar Abd al-Rahman, who was convicted by a US court in the aftermath of the first World Trade Center bombing in 1993.

THE MURSI GOVERNMENT

In July 2012, less than two weeks after taking office, President Mursi contravened the June ruling of the Supreme Constitutional Court and subsequent SCAF decree by ordering the reconstitution of the People's Assembly. However, the Supreme Constitutional Court countered that: 'all the rulings and decisions of the Supreme Constitutional Court are final and not subject to appeal ... and are binding for all state institutions'. The crisis seemed likely to escalate with the intervention of the elected deputies of the People's Assembly, who met in defiance of the Supreme Constitutional Court and the SCAF. Although the meeting was brief and symbolic, it attracted significant attention and caused further consternation. Ultimately, Mursi conceded the dissolution of the People's Assembly until new elections could be held.

In the following months Mursi continued to provoke controversy, and by the end of 2012 many Egyptians began to believe that the country had exchanged one authoritarian leader for another. A new Government, in which the Muslim Brotherhood held four portfolios, was formed by Mursi in early August; Hisham Muhammad Qandil, the Minister of Water Resources and Irrigation in the outgoing, interim cabinet, was confirmed as Prime Minister. However, political chaos increased on 12 August, when Mursi dismissed senior members of the SCAF, including Tantawi, and, revoking amendments to the Constitutional Declaration issued by the SCAF in June, adopted the legislative powers that the body had assumed following the dissolution of the People's Assembly. A few months later, on 22 November, the President issued an interim Constitutional Declaration adopting new powers to protect the revolution 'by any means necessary'. The decree eliminated judicial oversight over presidential decision-making, and removed the authority of the Supreme Constitutional Court to dissolve the Advisory Council and the Constituent Assembly, which had been elected by the Council to prepare a new constitution. The 100-member Constituent Assembly, which had been formed in March and then re-formed in July, had been strongly criticized for failing to reflect the opinions of a range of Egyptians, in particular those of women and Coptic Christians, and had been hampered by boycotts and protests. Although in early December Mursi rescinded the declaration in the interim, the Constituent Assembly had quickly drafted a constitution, which was hurriedly presented for approval at a national referendum.

At the national referendum, which was held in two rounds on 15 and 22 December 2012, the draft Constitution was adopted with 63.8% of the votes cast. Voter turn-out was low—at just under 32.9% (of the registered electorate of approximately 52m.). President Mursi signed the Constitution into law on

26 December. Significant changes included a reduction in the presidential term of office from six years to four; a restriction on the President to two terms in office; the abolition of the post of Vice-President; and a requirement for a parliamentary vote of confidence in candidates for the office of Prime Minister. The Constitution also contained what amounted to a temporary provision regarding the existent state of government, prescribing that the Advisory Council, as elected, would assume the legislative functions for the country until a new People's Assembly could be formed. At that time legislative authority would temporarily be transferred to the lower house until the election of a new Advisory Council.

Islam remained the official religion of the state, although new provisions were added about interpretative tools and the prominence of Sunni erudition. The Al-Azhar University, the foremost institution of Sunni jurisprudence, was also empowered through the Constitution as self-governing, with a formal role in Islamic legal matters. Followers of Christianity and Judaism were newly guaranteed freedom of worship in the Constitution. The Constitution formally prohibited parties that discriminated on the basis of religion, as well as gender and origin.

After Mubarak's tenure as President had been enforced by a long-standing state of emergency, a constitutional article provided for a new separation of authorities: the President was empowered to declare a state of emergency after consultation with the cabinet, but within seven days the declaration was to be be submitted for approval by the People's Assembly (or the Advisory Council if the house was not constituted at that time). Any state of emergency extending beyond six months required approval in a public referendum.

On 2 June 2013, nearly a year after the President first clashed with the SCAF and the Supreme Constitutional Court, the latter issued another ruling—that the Advisory Council election was unconstitutional owing to issues stemming from the governing electoral law at the time. However, the Court also determined that the Advisory Council could remain in place until a election to a new People's Assembly could be held and representatives returned to the lower house. In the same ruling, the Supreme Constitutional Court also declared the Constituent Assembly that had drafted the Constitution to be invalid.

UNREST IN THE SINAI PENINSULA AND REGIONAL TENSIONS

As noted above, the Sinai Peninsula is a source of ongoing and intermittent concerns, not only for Egypt, but also for its neighbouring states. Since the uprising against President Mubarak, the security situation in that region has further deteriorated. Notably, in July 2012 militants blew up a gas pipeline in the Sinai that connected to both Israel and Jordan. Jordan, which was highly dependent on natural gas from Egypt for its energy needs, was seriously affected by the explosion and subsequent suspension in supplies.

Concerns about the region were again dramatically, if briefly, heightened in May 2013, when a militant group kidnapped seven security personnel in the Sinai, and issued demands for the release of family members and militants held by the state. Egypt increased its military engagement in the Peninsula, and within a week the hostages had been released. President Mursi thanked not only the security services, but also the people and tribes of the Sinai, who apparently had played a role in securing their release. In addition, since Mursi came to power there have been numerous attacks on a checkpoint near the Rafah border crossing into the Gaza Strip, and also against security personnel, resulting in deaths and injuries.

Meanwhile, the evolving relationship between the Muslim Brotherhood and Hamas, which continues to dominate in the Gaza Strip, prompted much speculation. The network of illegal tunnels connecting Egypt to Gaza has recently caused particular contention. Israel has long sought to destroy the tunnels, which are used to smuggle people, livestock and consumer goods and supplies. Hamas has viewed the tunnels as a valuable transport link, a way to raise funds, and a mechanism for garnering support, by helping to provide Palestinians with staple goods during the Israeli blockade. In February 2013 the Government unexpectedly flooded a number of the smuggling tunnels, citing security concerns regarding the flow of militants and weapons. Notably, the action also sent a message to the USA and Israel about its willingness to deal with cross-border issues with Gaza, albeit in a fractional way. This was, in fact, the beginning of a prolonged effort to thwart the tunnel trafficking industry, and the campaign increased prior to the opposition protests on 30 June. The result has been a significant reduction in operational tunnels and sharp price increases for some critical goods in Gaza. Overall, the response of Hamas, which has its own internal concerns about the flow of people and weapons to those not affiliated with the organization, has been relatively muted. In general, Egyptians have also been wary of the close organizational relationship between Hamas and the Muslim Brotherhood because Hamas is perceived to support Mursi—even to the point of allegedly sending in Palestinians through the tunnels to rally in support of the President during the 30 June opposition protests.

Egypt has also been actively engaged in broader regional relations. From some perspectives, Mursi has served as an 'honest broker', helping to negotiate a cease-fire in a conflict between Israel and Hamas in November 2012. Egypt condemned Israeli air raids in Syria in May 2013, while the following month Mursi suspended relations with Syria and criticized Hezbollah for its engagement in that conflict.

There have also been regional tensions with Ethiopia over the latter's construction of a dam, diverting part of the Nile River, which is strongly opposed by Egypt. The Grand Ethiopian Renaissance Dam, if completed as planned, will be the continent's largest hydroelectric power plant. Mursi has tried to use the issue to rally popular opinion and national unity, by claiming it to be a threat to national security.

THE USA AND EGYPT—AN UNEASY ALLIANCE

US-Egyptian relations proceeded following the election of Mursi, but have been less than cordial. The USA demonstrated concerns about regional relations, including how a Muslim Brotherhood-dominated Government would maintain a balance with Israel, as well as about the pace of democratization (or at least the upholding of the associated human rights associated). US foreign assistance to Egypt continued, but members of Congress expressed concerns and sought to place new limits on funding.

A key domestic concern has been the targeting of international and domestic NGO workers. On 4 June 2013 sentences were imposed on the 43 NGO employees charged in late 2011 (of whom 19 were Americans, 16 Egyptians, and the remainder from Germany, Serbia, Norway, the Palestinian territories and Jordan). Some 27 were sentenced *in absentia* to five years in prison, 11 received one-year suspended sentences; and five received two-year terms. Additionally, several US NGOs, including the NDI and the IRI, were closed and their assets seized. Although the initial raid that led to the trials took place before Mursi's election, the new Government failed to intervene in the proceedings. The convictions followed a controversial new NGO law under debate by the Advisory Council. The draft law, which had been proposed by the President and strongly condemned by domestic and international human rights organizations, would allow for state control over NGO funding and activities—much as had been the case under Mubarak.

THE 'NEW REBELS'

The Tamarrud ('Rebel') initiative was launched in late April 2013 to campaign for an early presidential election in an effort to remove Mursi. According to Tamarrud leaders, the President had failed the Egyptian people in terms of the provision of justice, the deterioration of the economy and a lack of security. Tamarrud was formed by members of the Kefaya movement and was supported by the National Salvation Front, the secular opposition alliance established by Muhammad el-Baradei. By late June the Tamarrud group claimed that it had collected 15m. signatures from across Egypt in support of a new presidential election. Protests were planned across Egypt for 30 June, the anniversary of Mursi's assumption of presidential duties.

In the period preceding the demonstrations, the country anticipated an impending clash between members and supporters of the Muslim Brotherhood and the President, and those rebelling against Mursi and his failing policies. Mursi actually gave his opponents more political ammunition, and a boost to their campaign to oust him, when on 17 June 2013 he appointed Adel al-Kahyat, a member of a political party associated with Gama'ah al-Islamiyah, as Governor of Luxor. Members of Gama'ah al-Islamiyah had been responsible for the killing of tourists in Luxor in 1997, a terrorist attack that had turned popular opinion against the group, and Egyptians—including many Islamist allies of Mursi—were shocked by the appointment. Although al-Khayat's subsequent resignation stemmed the criticism in the immediate term, the episode further damaged Mursi's reputation among his opponents.

MURSI'S REMOVAL FROM POWER

As planned by the Tamarrud campaign, on 30 June 2013 mass popular demonstrations were staged to protest against Mursi's rule and demand an early presidential election. As the demonstrations continued, the Egyptian military gave the President a 48-hour ultimatum, threatening intervention unless the demands of the people were met. On 3 July Mursi was accordingly removed from office, in what was widely termed a coup, and the military again assumed control of the country, albeit with civilians serving as the official 'face' of the Government. The Commander-in-Chief of the Armed Forces, and Minister of Defence and Defence Production, Gen. Abd al-Fatah al-Sisi, appointed the President of the Supreme Constitutional Court, Adli Mahmoud Mansour, as interim President, amid calls for another constitution-drafting process and for new parliamentary and presidential elections. On 9 July Hazem al-Biblawi, the Deputy Prime Minister for Economic Affairs and Minister of Finance in the transitional Government of Essam Sharaf in 2011, was designated as Prime Minister, and on 16 July a new administration was installed. El-Baradei was named as Vice-President in the new Government, but resigned in early August, amid a violent campaign to suppress supporters of Mursi. In early September, after a 50-member constitutional revision committee was announced, few Islamists were included among its members, although the Salafist al-Nour Party agreed to participate. Amr Moussa, the former Secretary-General of the Arab League and Minister of Foreign Affairs in 1991–2001, was elected to preside over the committee.

Meanwhile, outside government chaos continued in the streets, as supporters and opponents of Mursi (and the Muslim Brotherhood) engaged in rhetorical and physical conflict in Cairo and elsewhere. From the time the coup was announced to mid-August 2013, well over 1,000 Egyptians had been killed, mainly by state forces, and thousands more were injured. Many were killed when state security forces took action to disperse pro-Mursi protest camps that were largely peaceful in nature, although there were credible reports of some violence emanating from within the pro-Mursi camps. Amnesty International and other organizations reported that human rights abuses were committed by both sides, from pro-Mursi demonstrators to state security forces, and thugs who viewed themselves as aligned with the state.

In the wake of Mursi's ouster, many Brotherhood members and supporters were arrested and detained, with estimates ranging from 1,000 to more than 10,000. Among those detained were Mursi, Supreme Leader Badie and deputy Leader Khairat al-Shater. Notably, at the end of August Badie was reported to have suffered a heart attack while in detention. While members of the Brotherhood were reported to be in disarray, fugitive and divided about its future direction, the organization was widely expected to continue to survive. However, the new Egyptian leadership took immediate measures to repress the Brotherhood. Charges, including incitement to murder, were announced against key Brotherhood leaders, among them former President Mursi. A judicial panel also recommended that the organization be disbanded. Meanwhile, former President Mubarak, was released to house arrest while he awaited new judicial proceedings.

International reactions to the removal of Mursi and subsequent violence have been varied. Some Gulf states initially congratulated Mansour on his new post, while the EU urged Egypt to return to the 'democratic process', and Turkey was more outspoken in condemning the effective coup. As the situation unfolded, the USA refrained from terming the military's overthrow of the Mursi Government as a coup but was critical of the subsequent violence and the perceived marginalization of democratization efforts. In a gesture of dissatisfaction, the USA cancelled its bi-annual joint military operations. However, some US politicians believed that stronger action should have been taken. Others were critical of the US Administration's apparent lack of attention towards violence originating from supporters of the Brotherhood and the precarious situation of Egypt's Copts. The relatively limited response of the USA was partly attributed to concerns about pushing Egypt into alliances with states perceived to be more dangerous. Additionally, some policy-makers feared that Egypt would respond to any penalties by threatening regional stability with regard to its peace agreement with Israel.

As of early September 2013 the state continued its campaign of repression, with the use of military trials and imprisonment. Additionally, the Government made it more difficult for citizens to access critical and opposing reports by preventing access to several news sources. Thus, many ordinary Egyptians felt caught between the military that seeks to control the country's political space and the Islamists, who have fallen dramatically from power and are desperate to return, in some cases by any means possible. At this time it is unclear whether Egypt will remain on this reverse political course, rapidly moving away from democratization and back towards its authoritarian past. What is clear is that the 2011 uprising welcomed by many remains incomplete—it is a revolution interrupted.

Economy

RICHARD GERMAN and ELIZABETH TAYLOR

INTRODUCTION

From the mid-20th century Egypt's economy has been fundamentally influenced by political circumstances. In particular, external relations with Israel have had major repercussions on the nature of public expenditure and foreign aid, while the orientation of domestic policy has shifted from state socialism towards a market economy. There have also been significant constraints on development arising from rapid population growth, the dearth of land available for agriculture and lack of water for irrigation.

The total area of Egypt is 1,009,450 sq km (389,751 sq miles), but more than 90% of the country is desert. There is no forestry and hardly any permanent meadows or pastures, and arable land is scarce. At the 1976 census the population was 38.2m., but by 2006 the figure had risen to almost 72.8m. The lack of employment opportunities has driven people from the country into already overcrowded cities (particularly Cairo) since the 1970s, and hastened the emigration of qualified personnel whom the country could ill afford to lose. The rising population has tended to offset increases in economic growth and depress average standards of living. According to official estimates, the total population reached 83.7m. at 1 January 2013.

During the 1960s Egypt, under the presidency of Col Gamal Abd al-Nasir (Nasser), followed an economic policy based on socialist planning. However, Nasser's death and conflict with Israel heralded a period of change in Egypt's economic relations with both its Arab neighbours and the wider international community. The 1970s saw a significant increase in foreign aid from the petroleum-rich Arab states until Egypt's peace treaty with Israel in 1979. The League of Arab States (Arab League) agreed on a policy of economic and political isolation of Egypt, and the Arab Fund for Economic and Social Development suspended aid and credit assistance. The impact of the Arab trade boycott was nevertheless alleviated by increased aid from Western Europe, Japan and, particularly, the USA (as Egypt became the second largest recipient of US aid, after Israel). By the late 1980s Egypt was reconciled with the Arab world, being readmitted to the Arab League and the Organization of Arab Petroleum Exporting Countries (OAPEC). Later, in 1998, it was admitted to the Common Market for Eastern and Southern Africa, and in 2001 Egypt signed an association agreement with the European Union (EU) (see Foreign Trade and Payments).

The average annual growth of Egypt's gross domestic product (GDP) was 7.3% in 1965–80, slowing to 5.4% in 1980–90 and to 4.4% in 1990–2000. GDP growth then fell to an estimated 2.0% by 2003, before achieving a recovery in the financial year (July to June) 2004/05, to 5.1%. In 2005/06 GDP grew by 6.8%, underpinned by high oil and gas prices and by the effects of structural reforms introduced by the Government in 2004 (see Policy and Planning). However, unemployment (at 9.0% of the labour force according to official figures for the end of 2006, but much higher by independent estimates) and rising inflation remained a concern. According to the IMF, economic growth accelerated to 7.1% in 2006/07, but inflation continued to rise, particularly as a result of rising prices for wheat and other basic commodities, which prompted civil unrest in early 2008 and a substantial increase in the Government's subsidy allocation. The GDP growth rate for 2007/08 was again robust, at 7.2%. Despite the international financial crisis that erupted in the latter half of 2008, the country's economic performance in 2008/09 was better than initially anticipated—with GDP expanding by 4.7%, according to official figures. Reforms since 2004 had reduced Egypt's monetary and external vulnerabilities, and improved the investment climate, while targeted fiscal stimulus packages and cuts in interest rates helped to deflect the effects of the international financial turbulence. A strengthening economic recovery led to growth of 5.1% in 2009/10, according to the Central Bank of Egypt; and the Government expected a return to pre-crisis levels in 2010/11, as average growth rates of 5.6% were recorded in the first two quarters. However, unprecedented civil unrest in January 2011, inspired by protests in Tunisia but fuelled by longer-term grievances about poor living conditions, corruption and lack of economic opportunity, heralded the demise of President Hosni Mubarak's rule (see History) and resulted in a contraction in GDP of 4.2% in the January–March quarter in the wake of the turmoil. Continuing sporadic violence, particularly in Cairo, and the volatility surrounding the political transition led to capital flight and sharp reductions in foreign direct investment (FDI) and tourism revenues—two key sources of international reserves. Real GDP growth slowed to 1.8% in 2010/11, while annual headline inflation rose to 11.8% in June 2011, up from 10.1% in June 2010. The rate of unemployment increased to 11.8% at the end of 2010/11, from 9.0% in the previous year (partly reflecting the displacement of up to 1.5m. Egyptians formerly working in Libya, which had also experienced a popular uprising during 2011). The Government estimated the economic cost of the civil upheaval at £E40,000m. (about 2.9% of GDP) for 2010/11 and £E65,000m. (4.9% of GDP) for 2011/12. Slightly increased growth of 2.2% was recorded for 2011/12, according to the Central Bank, although unemployment rose further, to 12.3%, while FDI, tourist inflows and foreign reserves all declined. In the first half of the 2012/13 financial year the growth rate reached 2.4%. Nevertheless, unfavourable global and domestic circumstances have continued to disrupt the macroeconomic picture, keeping growth below potential.

POLICY AND PLANNING

Following Nasser's death in 1970, President Anwar Sadat embarked on a gradual distancing from old-style socialist economic policies and sought to encourage private enterprise and foreign investment to aid development. Under President Mubarak (who took office following Sadat's assassination in 1981), a long-term national socio-economic development programme (broken down into a series of five-year plans) was devised. The 1982–87 plan aimed to reduce the proportion of private consumption and of imports in total expenditure, so as to mobilize domestic resources for investment and reduce the growing trade deficit. However, these objectives were undermined by the adverse effects of the collapse in the price of petroleum (Egypt's principal export commodity) on the country's balance of payments in the mid-1980s.

The 1987–92 plan sought to encourage public sector production and raise the level of exports. It also devoted more resources to the development of the private sector, and aimed to improve agricultural output and so reduce food imports (which met 60% of Egypt's requirements). However, in addition to the lack of funds available to finance development projects, the 1990–91 Gulf crisis undermined the plan's targets as thousands of expatriate Egyptian workers returned home, causing a loss of remittance revenue and a rise in domestic unemployment. By contrast, the Iraqi invasion of Kuwait also resulted in a sharp increase in aid to Egypt, in addition to the waiver or rescheduling of certain Egyptian debts to other countries.

Further plans were drawn up for 1992–97 and 1997–2002. The latter envisaged total investment of around £E400,000m. over five years and an average annual rate of growth of 6.8%. At the same time the Government outlined targets for the 20 years up to 2017. These envisaged a doubling of GDP between 1997 and 2007 and the same rate of increase for 2007–17. The budget deficit was to be eliminated and, if possible, replaced by a surplus before the end of 2017, while the target rate for the creation of new jobs would be 550,000 per year throughout the period. In the event, the growth target for 1997–2002 was not reached, largely owing to the economic crisis in Asia, the decline in world prices for petroleum and reduced revenues from tourism following a terrorist attack at Luxor in 1997.

The 2002–07 plan envisaged total investment of £E445,000m., including £E73,000m. from the private sector. In 2002, however, as the threat of renewed conflict in Iraq eroded global economic confidence, FDI and tourism revenues both declined significantly. The Government's decision to adopt a floating exchange rate regime in 2003 (see Banking, Finance and Exchange Rates) was seen as an important step in the long-term recovery of the economy. However, as the Egyptian pound fell against the US dollar, the continued shortage of hard currency prompted the Government to intervene in the foreign exchange markets and to introduce anti-inflationary measures. In 2004 the Government took steps to reduce tax liability across almost all economic activities, as well as cutting the tax burden of those on low incomes; restructure the customs and tariff regime to encourage international trade; and accelerate the privatization programme (see Privatization). FDI increased from US $407m. in 2004 to $3,900m. in 2005, as a result of the revitalized privatization programme and also a promotional campaign to attract overseas capital.

The 2007–12 plan envisaged average annual economic growth of 8%, an annual increase in average real income per head of 6%, the creation of 750,000 jobs per year, and a reduction in the unemployment rate to 5.5%. The Government expected the private sector to provide up to about 60% of its targeted £E1,295,000m. investment programme, and aimed to provide new opportunities through long-term concessions, leasing schemes and public-private partnerships (PPPs). Tourism was expected to achieve a 10% growth rate and to generate US $12,000m. in revenue. The Government proposed investment of £E122,000m. in regional development projects, with

Greater Cairo to receive 25% of the investment, Upper Egypt 22%, Alexandria 21%, Suez 19% and the Nile Delta 13%.

However, the international financial crisis meant that there was a marked slowdown in economic activity during the latter half of 2008. As global credit markets froze, the value of FDI fell sharply, to US $4,000m. in July–December 2008 from $7,700m. in the corresponding period in 2007. Receipts from the Suez Canal dropped, as did Egyptian workers' remittances from overseas. The tourism sector also began to suffer, and there was a significant reduction in exports. In response to the difficult economic environment, the Government announced a $2,700m. stimulus package in November 2008, consisting of $1,900m. in investment expenditure, combined with export subsidies and tax exemptions for capital and intermediary goods. A second stimulus package of the same value was announced in March 2009, including $1,400m. for infrastructure investment and $710m. for export subsidies. Although providing a timely boost to the economy, both packages were to be funded through loans, and the Government consequently forecast that the already large budget deficit would widen further in 2009/10. Also in March 2009 the Government announced that it would not make planned subsidy cuts in that year, or impose additional taxes. A third stimulus package, of $1,800m., was approved by the Government in November. Despite the global downturn, analysts considered that the Egyptian economy was well placed to recover relatively quickly, given its diversified foundations, strong financial sector and large consumer base.

Precipitated by the Tunisian revolution but underpinned by economic grievances, Egyptians began an uprising, concentrated largely in Cairo, in January 2011. President Mubarak dismissed the Government of Ahmad Nazif, seeking to distance himself from its economic policies, and called on a new administration to step up subsidies, control inflation and provide more jobs. However, despite attempts to placate the protesters, Mubarak was forced to relinquish office in February.

The uprising disrupted economic life, undermining tourism, consumption and business activity. Given the consequent decline in revenues, the interim Government needed funding of US $10,000m.–$12,000m. in order to finance the budget deficit, and requested assistance from the IMF, the World Bank, the African Development Bank (AfDB) and several bilateral development partners. In June 2011 the IMF agreed a 12-month $3,000m. loan package. Later in the month, however, the Government approved a significantly revised draft of the 2011/12 budget, which lowered the budget deficit target and sought to rely on domestic, rather than external, borrowing (see National Budget), and declined the IMF aid on the grounds that an interim administration did not have a popular mandate to accept the loan. Subsequent budgetary pressures and gloomy economic prospects prompted the Government to resume loan negotiations with the IMF from January 2012, in order to boost confidence in the country's creditworthiness. The Fund declared its readiness to support a reform programme that would maintain macroeconomic stability and promote growth, and that commanded broad-based political support following Egypt's parliamentary elections. Other pledges of international financial support in 2011/12 were made by the World Bank, the AfDB, the Arab Monetary Fund, the Islamic Development Bank, Qatar, Saudi Arabia and the United Arab Emirates (UAE). Financial assistance from the EU was reportedly subject to the successful conclusion of an agreement with the IMF.

A second preliminary agreement was reached between the Government and the IMF in November 2012, providing for a US $4,800m. credit facility, subject to structural economic reforms—including increased taxes on a range of goods and transactions, and reductions in costly energy subsidies and in public sector employment. In anticipation of the advance, the Government announced an economic development plan, and was to prepare a revised budget for 2012/13 with the intention of reducing the fiscal deficit. However, confirmation of the IMF loan was delayed, as planned tax increases and austerity measures were put on hold owing to the political unrest that followed President Mursi's decision to accelerate the implementation of a new constitution. Talks with the IMF resumed in January 2013, as the Government announced a revised economic programme—although this appeared to dilute the previously agreed tax reforms and subsidy cuts. In March the Fund suggested that Egypt could qualify for emergency short-term financing that was not conditional on prior approval of a medium-term economic strategy. However, the Mursi Government ruled out such assistance, having received pledges of support from Qatar and Libya, and no further agreement with the IMF had been finalized by September 2013. In May two experienced ministers who had been involved in the negotiations with the Fund had left the Government.

NATIONAL BUDGET

The 2002/03 budget provided for expenditure of £E141,600m. and revenue of £E111,400m. The net budget deficit was expected to be £E17,200m., compared with £E9,600m. in 2001/02. The 2003/04 budget forecast a 12% rise in total spending, to £E159,600m., including an increase in subsidy payments from £E6,700m. to £E8,000m. and significantly higher foreign debt-servicing, while total consolidated revenue was projected to rise to £E130,900m. The net budget deficit was set to rise to about 7.0% of GDP, compared with 5.4% in 2002/03. The 2004/05 budget provided for total expenditure of £E177,400m. and total revenue of £E140,000m., leaving a deficit of £E37,400m., equivalent to some 7.0% of GDP.

The 2005/06 budget provided for expenditure of £E187,000m. and revenue of £E130,100m., leaving the budget deficit equivalent to 9.2% of GDP. In anticipation of a reduction in revenue resulting from tax and customs reforms, the Government started to reduce the burden of subsidies, increasing diesel retail prices by 50% and cutting subsidies on fuel and electricity. Under the 2006/07 budget, operating expenditure was projected to rise to £E217,300m. and revenue to £E163,900m., leaving a forecast budget deficit equivalent to 8.1% of GDP. Notwithstanding the budget, the Government also submitted to parliament a five-year fiscal consolidation plan to bring down the deficit by 1% per year until 2010/11. This included reform of the domestic fuel subsidy system, and in July 2006 the Government increased the price of petrol for the first time in more than 20 years.

The draft budget for 2007/08 projected that operating expenditure would rise to £E241,500m., including £E59,500m. for wages and salaries, and revenue to £E184,700m. Subsidies would increase to £E64,540m. The 2008/09 draft budget provided for total expenditure of £E331,000m., including increased spending on education (to £E35,000m.) and food subsidies (£E20,000m.), and a 15% wage increase for public sector workers (affecting 5.7m. people); total revenue was forecast at £E259,000m. However, in response to a slowdown in the economy arising from the international financial crisis, the Government introduced an additional stimulus package worth US $2,700m. in November 2008. The final budget for 2009/10, projecting twin decreases in revenue and expenditure, to an estimated £E224,990m. and £E323,920m., respectively, was approved in June 2009. Further stimulus packages were also approved that year, the first in March and the second in November. Under the 2010/11 draft budget, approved in March 2010, revenue and expenditure were both projected to increase, to £E280,700m. and £E399,000m. respectively, resulting in a deficit equivalent to 7.9% of GDP. The budget also allowed for an 11% increase in wages and a 22% rise (to £E116,000m.) in subsidies (mainly for energy and food). In June 2011 the Ministry of Finance set out a draft budget for the 2011/12 fiscal year, under which public expenditure was forecast to increase to £E515,500m., while revenue was projected at £E350,300m. However, the interim Government approved the budget only after sharp reductions in spending were made. The Government also took the decision not to accept foreign loans, including a proposed US $3,000m. credit facility from the IMF (see Policy and Planning). The revised budget included a lower overall deficit target of 8.6% of GDP (as opposed to almost 11% in the original draft), and expenditure was reduced to £E490,600m. The energy subsidies bill was projected to decrease from £E99,000m. to £E95,500m., while the threshold for income tax was to be raised and a new top rate of tax introduced, although the Government later postponed levying a new property tax until January 2013 and subsequently until July of that year.

The draft budget for 2012/13 initially provided for expenditure of £E537,700m. and revenue of £E393,400m., with the deficit set to contract to 7.9% of GDP. A growth rate of 4%–4.5% was targeted. In the absence of a parliament, the Supreme Council of the Armed Forces approved the budget in July 2012. As part of the proposed loan agreement in November 2012 with the IMF (see Policy and Planning), the new Mursi Government then sought to prepare a revised budget with a new deficit target of 10.4% of GDP, entailing cuts in fuel subsidies and some tax increases. However, these measures were subsequently suspended following further public unrest.

Assuming a real GDP growth rate of 3.8% for the coming year, the Government presented its draft budget for 2013/14 in April 2013 with revenue projected at £E497,100m. and expenditure at £E692,400m., leaving a shortfall of £E195,300m. Proposed expenditure included an increased allocation of £E172,000m. for public sector remuneration and £E205,500m. in subsidies and social benefits, elements that would be difficult to reconcile with the loan conditions previously set by the IMF.

AGRICULTURE

Egypt's agriculture is dominated by the Nile river and the need for irrigation. The main summer crops are cotton, rice, maize and sorghum, and in winter the chief crops are wheat, beans, berseem (Egyptian clover, used for animal feed) and vegetables. During the 1970s agriculture's contribution to GDP remained fairly constant at just under 30%, but it has fallen steadily since then, to 14.8% by 2011/12. The number of Egyptians employed in the sector has also declined. While there is self-sufficiency in fruit and vegetables (some of which are exported to the EU), shortages are encountered in basic grains. Egypt has one of the highest per head wheat consumption levels in the world, and relies heavily on imports. Cereal production in 2010 was estimated at 21.9m. metric tons, close to the annual average of about 22.5m. tons recorded in the previous few years. However, a sharp rise in international wheat prices, exacerbated by Russia's temporary suspension of exports, added substantially to the cost of Egypt's wheat imports in 2010, and to state expenditure on bread subsidies. In March 2011 the Government raised procurement prices for key agricultural products, in an effort to encourage farmers to increase production. Cereals output in 2011 reached 22.3m. tons (with wheat production at about 8.4m. tons) and 23.1m. tons in 2012 (wheat output increasing to 8.8m. tons). While the Government forecast a record wheat crop in 2013, concerns nevertheless remained regarding Egypt's declining foreign currency reserves and the possible impact its ability to meet import requirements for wheat, fuel and fertilizer.

Long-staple cotton is the most important field crop, but the area under cultivation has declined since the late 1960s. Egypt produces about one-third of the world crop of long-staple cotton (1.125 ins and longer), and is a major exporter. Cotton provides considerable agricultural employment and helps to support a substantial textile industry. The Government liberalized Egypt's internal trade in cotton in 1993–94, and ended the public sector monopoly of cotton exports in 1996. Forming part of a deregulation programme agreed with the World Bank, the cotton industry reforms were designed to improve the crop's financial appeal to farmers and to encourage wider use of high-yield cultivation techniques. In 2008–09 cotton farmers were severely affected by the impact of the economic downturn, with prices for higher grade cotton falling by about one-third.

Rice is another important crop and foreign currency earner. Annual output has averaged over 6m. metric tons in recent years, although production reached 7.3m. tons in 2008. In 2006 FAO co-ordinated a hybrid rice breeding project, intended to help Egypt to increase output using less water and land. In 2008 the Government suspended rice exports for six months, in order to meet increasing domestic demand. In March 2009 the Minister of Trade and Industry announced an extension of the moratorium to October, and it was later further extended to October 2011. Rice production dropped by 18% in 2009/10, as the Government sought to reduce the land area planted for rice in order to restrict water use (in the wake of the dispute with other African countries concerning Nile water rights—see History). The export ban was again renewed in October 2011 to ensure domestic supply. The Government finally withdrew the ban on exports with effect from October 2012, at which time domestic output was sufficient to meet domestic demand. In May 2013, however, it was reported that exports had again been suspended until the new harvest in September, in an effort to control domestic price increases and to address low stocks.

Many kinds of fruit, vegetables and horticultural products are grown and are important as exports. Efforts have been made to promote the production of these items, especially citrus fruit, and special areas are allocated along the Mediterranean coast for their cultivation.

Attention has been given to animal husbandry, in an attempt to raise dairy and meat production, but Egypt remains a net importer of meat to supplement its own output. Avian influenza (bird flu) first appeared in Egyptian poultry in early 2006, and by mid-2007 the effects of the virus had cost the industry some £E1,000m. In April 2009 the Government announced that all pigs in the country would be culled, in an attempt to prevent the spread of the swine influenza variant pandemic (H1N1) 2009 (commonly referred to as swine flu). A major outbreak of foot-and-mouth disease affected the livestock sector in 2011. According to FAO data, 6.3m. buffalo and 7.5m. sheep and goats were at risk as the Government and FAO sought to institute a national strategy to control the disease.

The increasing pressure of population on the land has meant that the extension of the cultivable area through reclamation and irrigation has remained at the forefront of government policy. Important schemes have included the 'Suez Siphon' (to convey Nile water under the Suez Canal into the Sinai desert), the New Valley project, the Oweinat project in the Western Desert and the al-Salaam Canal development project in North Sinai. More recently, in 2006 the Government launched the US $500m. West Delta Water Conservation and Irrigation Rehabilitation Project to carry water from the Nile to farmers in the Western Delta.

The Aswan High Dam project was started in 1960 and officially inaugurated in 1971. The dam's primary purpose is to store the annual Nile flood (which reaches its peak in August) in Lake Nasser, a large artificially created lake, allowing yearly control of the downstream flow for perennial irrigation and further land reclamation. Historically, 70% of the flow at Aswan originates from the Blue Nile in Ethiopia. In June 2013 it was reported that Egypt's Minister of Water Resources and Irrigation had warned that a controversial dam-building project in Ethiopia posed a threat to Egypt's Nile water rights, and would have an adverse impact on the Aswan High Dam's capacity to produce hydroelectricity.

In January 1997 the Government inaugurated the New Valley project to build a 30-m-wide canal from Lake Nasser to the oasis regions in the central Western Desert. A new pumping station, costing £E1,200m., was completed in 2003 to extract water from Lake Nasser, just north of the outfall of the Toshka reservoir, in order to fill the canal to facilitate the irrigation of up to 500,000 feddans (210,000 ha) of land and to open up adjacent areas for development. Overall, it was hoped that the New Valley project would resettle 3m. Egyptians around the oases over a 20-year period, at a cost of up to £E300,000m.

Regarding the system of land tenure, the first agrarian reform law was issued in 1952, and was aimed at breaking the feudal power of the deposed regime. This law and subsequent measures limited individual and family landholding and widened the land ownership base, although legislation introduced in 1997 met with widespread disapproval owing to its abolition of fixed rents and security of inherited tenure.

MANUFACTURING AND INDUSTRY

In 2005 the Government inaugurated a new 20-year development strategy to upgrade Egypt's industrial base and capability. Initially targeting industrial expansion and the creation of employment through the promotion of exports and foreign investment, the strategy's longer-term objective was to encourage innovation and achieve a gradual shift towards medium- and high-technology production and exports. As part of this strategy, the Government was to develop 10 new industrial zones. In late 2008 the Government announced a US $1,300m. support package to help exporters to maintain the level of sales to traditional markets and encourage exports to new markets. There was also funding for small businesses and industrial modernization schemes.

Textiles have traditionally been a significant part of the manufacturing sector. In 2003/04 the textile sector accounted for 13% of total Egyptian exports. Following the abolition of textile quotas by the World Trade Organization in January 2005, the sector began to lose the quasi-guaranteed market access into the EU and was forced to compete with international companies. The value of textile exports decreased to US $650m. in 2004/05, although government figures reported a growth in exports of ready-made clothes. In 2006 the EU approved a £E195m. grant to help to restructure the spinning industry. By 2011/12 the sector accounted for about 7.2% of total exports.

The food-processing industry has been one of Egypt's fastest-growing manufacturing sectors. According to the Industrial Development Authority (IDA), output grew by 37% between 2001 and 2007. In May 2013 the Government announced investment plans for a new US $370m. sugar production facility, to be located in Sharkia governorate, with a proposed refining capacity of more than 500,000 metric tons annually.

The heavy industry sector has been gradually developed since the early 1970s, when the Egyptian Iron and Steel Co complex at Helwan began operations. More recently, Ezz Steel Rebars, a large independent steel producer, achieved a market share of over 60%. Suez Steel, producing about 1m. metric tons of flat steel sheeting annually, was privatized in 2006 (with local steel company Attaka acquiring the state's 82% stake). In 2008 the IDA issued steel production licences to Luxembourg's Arcelor Mittal and Kuwait's Al-Kharafi Group. In 1998 the Government announced plans to establish a company to develop iron ore deposits south of Aswan: the Aswan Iron and Steel Co subsequently constructed a £E2,600m. processing plant. The Aluminium Co of Egypt, whose complex at Naga Hammadi opened in 1975, is the country's primary aluminium producer. It was partially privatized in 1997. In 2010 the IDA launched a tender for new steel production licences, reflecting the Government's plans to boost production to meet growing demand from the construction industry and to stabilize prices. In July 2011 four companies—IIC for Steel Plants Management, El-Marakby Steel, Port Said National Co for Steel and Al-Watania—were granted licences to produce a combined total of 2m. tons of foundation steel and 1m. tons of steel billets. In September 2011 a court controversially revoked licences awarded in 2008 for five steel-manufacturing projects, affecting Ezz Steel and three other local companies—Beshay Steel, Suez Steel and Taibeh Steel. At the same time the former heads of Ezz Steel and the IDA, and a former Minister of Trade and Industry in the Mubarak regime were convicted and sentenced on related corruption charges. The court ruled that the award of the licences without payment of fees had been illegal and unfair to the unsuccessful bidders.

Egypt's cement industry underwent rapid development in the 1980s. New cement works were built, and steps were taken to expand output at existing plants. By the early 1990s local supply had been brought more closely into balance with demand. In 2005 Lafarge of France controlled the Alexandria Portland Cement Co (and 25% of the market), and Ciments Français took a controlling interest in the Suez Cement Co. Also in 2005 Vicat of France acquired a controlling stake in Sinai Cement, the Italcementi Group purchased a majority share in ASEC Cement, and the Government opened the bidding to sell the last state-owned producer, the National Cement Co. The Government banned cement exports for six months from March 2008, in response to shortages in the local market, and also awarded licences for six new plants. The ban was reimposed for four months from April 2009, and was later extended to 1 October 2010, owing to increased domestic demand for cement products. A 5% sales tax was imposed on local producers from July 2010. In the following month the Government approved the issue of 12 new licences for cement plants, with the aim of boosting output by 40% by 2015.

During 2004 the Anglo-Swedish company AstraZeneca applied for a licence to build a pharmaceuticals factory in 6 October City; Orascom Construction Industries (OCI) was awarded the contract to build the plant. In 2005 Dubai-based Emaar Properties and the local El-Nasr Housing and Development Co announced plans to develop the Cairo Heights project at an estimated cost of US $4,000m. In 2006 the Government announced a PPP project to build 50 new schools, and also sold the state retail chain Omar Effendi (following three earlier attempts since 1999) to the Saudi company Anwal for £E589m. With a work-force of 6,000 and a high-profile history as Egypt's flagship store, the sale generated more controversy than any other privatization to date. However, a court annulled the transaction in 2011, with critics having long argued that the chain had been undersold.

In early 2010 a joint venture comprising Hill International of the USA and the local EHAF Consulting Engineers was appointed to manage the construction of the US $550m. Grand Egyptian Museum, which upon completion would be the largest museum in the country.

Within the motor industry, the El Nasr Automotive Manufacturing Co had a virtual monopoly on production until it was opened up to the private sector in the 1980s. General Motors Egypt was established in 1985, and other companies began developing local assembly plants for makes of passenger and commercial vehicles such as Hyundai, Suzuki, Peugeot, Citroën, Mercedes-Benz, Škoda, Daewoo, Nissan and BMW. Hyundai and Daewoo became the leading passenger vehicle assemblers in Egypt, and General Motors the leading assembler of light commercial vehicles. In 2002 the Egyptian-German Auto Company agreed to export cars to the People's Republic of China, and the Russian company AvtoVAZ announced plans to open an assembly plant. Arab American Vehicles began assembly of the Japanese company Toyota's sports utility vehicles in early 2012.

ELECTRICITY

From the early 1980s increasing demand for electric power underlined the need for more power generation than that supplied by the Aswan High Dam. The Government has since sought steadily to expand installed capacity, mainly through thermal power generation. It has also pursued a policy of converting power stations to use natural gas (minimizing domestic use of petroleum that could be used to generate valuable export revenue). At the start of the 1982–87 five-year plan, Egypt had about 3,700 MW of installed capacity. By 2004 this had risen to about 17,000 MW, with plans to add some 13,000 MW by 2012 and a further 46,500 MW between 2013 and 2027.

Egypt's power sector is comprised of nine state-owned power production and distribution companies. These were held by the Egyptian Energy Authority, which in 2002 was converted into a holding company, the Egyptian Electricity Holding Co (EEHC), still under state ownership. EEHC-owned projects have included a 1,500-MW plant at Nubariya, near Alexandria, and a 750-MW addition to the Cairo North combined-cycle power complex. The Ministry of Electricity and Energy revised its generation expansion programme in 2004, launching three new power projects: a 650-MW plant at el-Tebine (estimated to cost US $250m.), a second 750-MW unit at Kureimat ($350m.) and a 650-MW plant at Cairo West.

In 2008 the Ministry of Electricity and Energy revived its plans for private sector involvement in power generation, with new legislation that would allow investors to develop plants, independent of the Government, on a build-own-operate-transfer (BOOT) basis and, for the first time, encourage private sector companies to develop renewable energy schemes as independent power projects. Government involvement would be limited to the collection of a tariff for the transmission of electricity through the national grid and the provision of back-up power. In early 2010 the EEHC announced plans to develop several independent power projects with a combined capacity of 3,500 MW. A new 1,500-MW scheme was launched at Dairut, and a 750-MW combined-cycle power plant was proposed in

Banha (north of Cairo). The Kuwait Fund for Arab Economic Development also agreed to contribute towards the financing of a 1,300-MW plant at Ain Sokhna.

Rising demand for electricity has nevertheless continued to outstrip capacity, and extreme summer temperatures have contributed to widespread and frequent power shortages, as well as disruption to other utility services. In response to public anger, the Government announced in September 2010 that it would invite bids to build eight more power generators, with a combined capacity of 1,000 MW, as part of an initiative to increase emergency capacity by mid-2011. It also planned to upgrade the Aswan hydroelectric turbines to supply an additional 175 MW, and to accelerate the launch of the Nubariya plant. The longer-term strategy included the development of nuclear power and renewable energy sources. In 2010 the Government also began investigating a project, expected to cost about US $1,600m., to link the power grids of Egypt and Saudi Arabia, with a carrying capacity of 3,000 MW; an agreement to proceed was signed in June 2013. In September 2011 the EEHC signed agreements with US-based multinational conglomerate General Electric and China's Sepco for two new combined-cycle power projects, at Giza North and Banha, which would add 2,250 MW of generating capacity. Also in 2011 the AfDB signed a $550m. loan agreement to finance a new 650-MW plant in Suez. In February 2012 the World Bank approved $240m. of additional financing for the Giza project.

In mid-2012 the Government warned that the country might be subject to electricity rationing owing to the continuing shortfall in generating capacity and ever-rising demand. Despite the Government's reluctance to underwrite the financing of independent power projects, the Central Bank nevertheless agreed in December 2012 to provide guarantees amounting to US $3,500m. for a 2,250 MW combined-cycle plant at Dairut and a wind farm in the Gulf of Suez with a capacity of 250 MW. Both projects had attracted interest from prospective investors before the 2011 revolution, but had stalled owing to concerns about their financial viability in the absence of any sovereign guarantees.

In 2006 President Mubarak had stated that Egypt needed to investigate new sources of energy, including nuclear power—pursuit of which had been abandoned following the accident at the Chornobyl (Chernobyl) nuclear power plant in Ukraine in 1986. The Supreme Council for Energy was subsequently convened for the first time in nearly 20 years, and plans were put forward for a nuclear power station at Dabaa, on Egypt's Mediterranean coast. The Mubarak administration announced in 2010 that construction of the plant would proceed; and this was reaffirmed by the interim Government in January 2012, despite local protests.

Reflecting the Government's intention to produce 20% of electricity from renewable sources by 2020, a 60-MW wind-powered electricity farm was built at Zaafarana; and construction of an integrated solar-thermal power plant at Kureimat was completed in December 2010, with financing from the World Bank. In 2009 the New and Renewable Energy Authority awarded to Italy's Italcementi a contract for the construction of a 250-MW wind farm on the Gulf of Suez. In 2011 the Government invited bids for the construction of a 1,000-MW wind energy park in the Gabal el-Zeit area of the Gulf of Suez, supported by funding from the European Investment Bank (EIB).

PETROLEUM AND GAS

The development of Egypt's hydrocarbons sector has had a major impact on the economy. Although petroleum production is declining and remains relatively low by Middle Eastern standards, offshore gas is increasingly being found and developed: Egypt has become Africa's second largest natural gas producer. At the end of 2012, according to the BP *Statistical Review of World Energy 2013*, the country's proven petroleum reserves totalled 4,300m. barrels. The sector is managed by the Ministry of Petroleum, under which four companies—the Egyptian General Petroleum Corpn (EGPC), the Egyptian Natural Gas Holding Co (EGAS), the Egyptian Petrochemicals Holding Co (ECHEM) and Ganope (the South Valley Development Co, established in 2003)—function as government agencies in oil, gas, petrochemical and Upper Egypt development activities. Oil production increased markedly in the early 1980s, mainly reflecting the return by Israel of the Alma oilfield (renamed the Shaab Ali field) in the Gulf of Suez in 1979 and the Sinai oilfields (notably the Abu Rudeis area) in 1982, and the increase in concessions and finds particularly in the Gulf of Suez and the Eastern and Western Deserts. From the mid-1990s production declined gradually, with output down to 672,000 barrels per day (b/d) in 2005. By 2009 production had again risen to 730,000 b/d, although there was a marginal decline thereafter. Output in 2012 averaged 728,000 b/d.

Egypt has made numerous oil concession and exploration agreements with foreign companies (exploration having been stimulated by the oil price rises of the early 1970s).

Egypt was readmitted to OAPEC in 1989, and it subsequently sought to increase co-operation with Libya, Syria, Jordan, Yemen and the Gulf states. Companies from Kuwait and the UAE invested in exploration concessions in Egypt. In the early 1990s improvements in bidding terms included increased block sizes, improved cost recovery formulas and flexible withdrawal options. Production-sharing terms (which were negotiable on a case-by-case basis) reportedly envisaged a reduction in EGPC's share of output to 70%–80%, compared with its entitlements of 80%–89% under existing agreements.

New discoveries were made in 2001 in the north-eastern Abu Gharadiq concession, in the Western Desert by Shell Egypt and the USA's Apache Corpn, in the Gulf of Suez by Ocean Energy of the USA (in the East Zeit block), and by Canada's Cabre Exploration in the West Esh el-Mallaha block. In 2003 BP announced the largest oil discovery in the Gulf of Suez in 14 years at its Saqqara well. Discoveries were, meanwhile, reported in Ras Gharib-Amr on the western shore of the Gulf of Suez, at the el-Tamad field in the Nile Delta (the first oil discovery in the Delta) and at the el-Diyur concession in the Western Desert. BP reported a discovery in the South Mansoura concession and the Balayeem Co discovered a new field in South Sinai.

In 2006 further discoveries were reported in Beni-Suef and Matruh governorates and in the Gulf of Suez to the north-west of the South Sinai city of el-Tour. Later in 2006 EGPC launched a new licensing round for six blocks in the Gulf of Suez and the Western Desert, with concessions awarded to Naftogaz of Ukraine, PICO International Petroleum and Kuwait Foreign Petroleum Exploration Co. In 2007 Ganope awarded concessions in the Eastern and Western Deserts to Aminex Petroleum Egypt Ltd, Pan Pacific Petroleum of Australia, Al Thani Corpn of the UAE, the United Kingdom's Melrose Resources, Syria's United Oil Co and Gujarat State Petroleum Corpn Ltd, and to Petrocorp in the Gulf of Suez. Discoveries in that year included the first in Upper Egypt, made by Dana Gas of the UAE. In March 2008 Ganope launched a licensing round for 12 blocks in the Gulf of Sinai, the Red Sea, and the Eastern and Western Deserts. In 2009 discoveries were reported by Apache Corpn in the Western Desert, and by Circle Oil of Ireland in the Gamsa area of the Gulf of Suez. Also that year Italy's Eni agreed to invest US $1,500m. in exploration and production in Egypt over five years. In July EGPC offered eight exploration blocks in the Gulf of Suez, while Ganope offered three blocks (one in the Gulf of Suez, and two in the Eastern Desert). In August six oil and gas concessions worth $2,000m. were awarded to BP, the International Egyptian Oil Co (IEOC—Eni's Egyptian affiliate) and the local Tharwa Petroleum Co, covering the Eastern Desert, the Gulf of Suez, the Nile Delta and North Sinai. In early 2010 Dana Gas made an oil discovery at its Komombo concession in the south of Egypt. Other companies reported discoveries at around the same time, including Kuwait Energy in East Ras Qattara, Canada's Transglobe Energy Corpn in East Ghazalat, in the Western Desert, and Apache Corpn in the Faghur Basin, also in the Western Desert. Circle Oil and partners, meanwhile, started production from the North-West Gemsa concession in the Gulf of Suez.

In September 2011 EGPC launched another licensing round for 15 exploration blocks, including three off shore, in the Gulf of Suez, the Eastern and Western Deserts, and the Sinai sedimentary basins. Most had been offered in previous rounds, generating little interest, but it was announced in April 2012 that 25 bids had been received from 12 international companies. Apache Corpn stated that, despite the political unrest in the country, it had invested US $1,000m. in Egypt in 2011 and would invest a further $1,000m. in 2012. In February 2012 Shell also announced plans to invest $600m. in exploration and the development of existing wells. In early 2012 Kuwait Energy reported further discoveries in the Gulf of Suez and the Abu Sennan concession in the Western Desert, and in May Eni announced a 'significant' find at the Emry Deep prospect in the Western Desert.

The 320-km Suez–Mediterranean (Sumed) crude oil pipeline, operated by the Arab Petroleum Pipelines Co (50% owned by Egypt and 50% by Saudi Arabia, Kuwait, Qatar and Abu Dhabi, mostly through state oil companies), opened in 1977. In 2004 Lukoil Overseas opened a new 24,000-b/d pipeline to convey crude oil from its concession near Hurghada to export terminals on the Red Sea.

Egypt's largest refinery is the En-Nasr refinery at Suez. The Midor refinery at Sidi Krier, near Alexandria, was originally constructed as an export-orientated Egyptian-Israeli joint venture project. However, when it started trial production in 2001, Arab countries refused to supply oil until the Israeli company Merhav sold its 20% stake in Midor to the National Bank of Egypt (NBE). In 2009 Sokhna Refining & Petrochemicals was seeking the necessary finance for a proposed integrated refining and petrochemicals plant at Ain Sokhna, while in May 2010 EGPC also agreed to develop a US $2,000m. refinery in partnership with two Chinese companies. The Egyptian Refining Co—a joint venture between EGPC, Qatar Petroleum and Citadel Capital—announced a project to build a $3,700m. refinery in the Greater Cairo area, which was expected to produce over 4m. metric tons of refined products per year and could be operational in 2015, although the collapse of the Mubarak regime in February 2011 delayed financial closure with the investors in the deal until mid-2012.

Egypt's proven reserves of natural gas at the end of 2012 totalled 2,000,000m. cu m. In tandem with substantial discoveries, the production sector has expanded rapidly since the first natural gasfield came on stream in 1974 at Abu Madi, with annual output having reached 62,690m. cu m by 2009. Until the late 1980s gas pipelines were developed primarily to serve heavy industrial plants; thereafter power stations became the largest consumers, most of the steep rise in gas consumption in the early 1990s being attributable to a national strategy to substitute gas for oil wherever possible. At the same time foreign oil companies began more active exploration for natural gas, finding a series of significant natural gas deposits in the Nile Delta, offshore from the Nile Delta, and in the Western Desert.

By the early 1990s most of Egypt's gas output came from the Abu Madi and El Qara fields in the Nile Delta, and the Badr el-Din field in the Western Desert. The most important new gas discovery in that period was made by Shell Egypt in 1992 in the coastal region of the Western Desert, involving the Obaiyed field. Having significantly improved its financial terms for gas development and production in 1988, the Government further enhanced the return to producing companies in 1993, when it raised its main reference price by 12.5%—bringing it roughly in line with European gas prices. In 1994 EGPC, Amoco and IEOC signed an agreement to establish an Egypt Trans-Gas Co to take charge of a project to build a 500-km gas pipeline from Port Said to Gaza and Israel, to handle proposed exports of gas to these markets, and to assess the potential for the eventual development of further markets in Lebanon and Turkey. In 2001 a project was announced to construct a US gas pipeline between Egypt and Jordan, Syria and Lebanon. The link between Egypt and Jordan was inaugurated in July 2003.

Further discoveries of natural gas deposits off the Nile Delta were made in 2000–01. BP reported a new find in the offshore North Alexandria concession. Also in 2001 BG Group (formerly British Gas) brought the Rosetta oil- and gasfield on stream, and was developing new fields in the West Delta Deep Marine Concession. New discoveries were reported by Apache Corpn in the Khalda concession in the Western Desert and by Centurion Energy International of Canada in the El Manzala concession, in the Nile Delta. Apache Corpn's discovery was subsequently described as its most significant to date, and was appraised as the biggest in the Western Desert. The gas discoveries, and the launch of the Jordanian pipeline, led to a search for further export options, since the Government believed that one-third of reserves would be sufficient to meet domestic needs. To manage the sector, the Government established EGAS in 2002. The company took responsibility for the assets previously held by EGPC, and for a programme to export 8.6m. metric tons per year of gas to Europe by 2005 with the start-up of a number of liquefied natural gas (LNG) export terminals along the Mediterranean coast. A new company, Tharwa, was established in 2004 to provide exploration and engineering services for companies involved in upstream gas development in Egypt. The principal shareholders in the company are EGPC, the NIB and EGAS.

In 2002–03 discoveries of gas deposits were made by Apache Corpn in its West Mediterranean and Ras el-Hekma concessions, by a consortium of Italian companies at a deep-water natural gasfield off Damietta, and by Melrose Resources in the Mansoura concession in the onshore Nile Delta. In 2004 discoveries were reported by BP Egypt in the Ras el-Barr concession in the Nile Delta region, by Shell in the Nemed deep-water concession and by Edison International in the Rosetta concession (the Rashid North). New gas discoveries in 2005 were reported by Apache Corpn on the Mediterranean coast and in the Western Desert (in the latter, the discovery at Syrah being described as one of the region's largest). BP also announced a new find in the West Nile Delta region. In June 2005 the Governments of Egypt and Israel signed a Memorandum of Understanding (MOU) under which Eastern Mediterranean Gas (EMG—an Egyptian-Israeli consortium) would export gas from Egypt to Israel via an undersea pipeline to be built between el-Arish and the southern Israeli city of Ashkelon, which was expected to transport 7,000m. cu m of gas annually for 20 years. In December the second phase of the gas pipeline linking Egypt and Jordan was completed. During 2006 the Government signed a gas supply agreement with Turkey; the two countries agreed jointly to establish a pipeline company, Tergas, to transport and market Egyptian gas to Turkey and on to Europe. In late 2009 the Government signed a 15-year agreement to supply gas by pipeline to Lebanon via Syria.

In early 2008 BP announced significant gas discoveries in Taurus and a concession shared with Eni in the Nile Delta. Further discoveries were reported in 2008/09 by RWE Dea of Germany in the West Nile Delta, Dana Gas in the El Manzala and West Qantara concessions, and by Abuqir Petroleum (a joint venture between EGPC and Edison) in the Abu Qir concession offshore from Alexandria. A new offshore exploration licensing round in the Mediterranean was launched in August 2008 with improved gas pricing terms. In May 2009 EGAS awarded four of seven exploration blocks on offer to BG in the North Gamasa field, to BP in the North Tineh field, to BP in partnership with Shell and Malaysia's Petronas in the North Damietta field, and to Total of France and Enel of Italy in the El Burullus field. EGAS did not award three other blocks (covering the El Mamura, El Dabaa and Sidi Barrani fields), owing to insufficient bids.

In 2009/10 Dana Gas reported gas discoveries in the Nile Delta and West Qantara concession and started production from its Sondos field in El Manzala; Melrose Resources reported a discovery in South East Mansoura concession; IEOC started production from its North Bardawil field in the Mediterranean; and BG and the local Burullus Gas Co produced the first gas from the offshore Sequoia project, north-east of Alexandria.

There are two LNG plants. The first, controlled by Unión Fenosa (now Gas Natural Fenosa) of Spain and Eni, shipped its first cargo from Egypt's first LNG export terminal at Damietta in 2005. The second LNG export project—Egyptian LNG at Idku—is led by BG in partnership with EGPC, EGAS, Gaz de France and Petronas. The latter project is tied in to natural gas reserves from BG's Simian Sienna offshore fields. The first train began production in March 2005 and the entire output was sold to Gaz de France under a 20-year agreement. In July BG reached an agreement on a financing package for a second LNG train at Idku. In June 2006 Unión Fenosa and Eni signed the agreement to build a second train at Damietta (although these plans were delayed by EGAS in 2009 pending the discovery of new gas reserves).

In 2010 BG announced that it would invest US $2,000m. in an offshore pipeline and new wells in the West Delta concession to meet the rising domestic gas demand, and in drilling three exploratory wells in offshore concessions in the el-Manzala and el-Burg blocks over two years. In July that year BP and RWE Dea signed a $9,000m. investment agreement with the Government to develop gas resources in the offshore North Alexandria and West Mediterranean Deepwater concessions. The structure of the contract, giving BP and RWE Dea control over production from the field and making investment more attractive to the two companies, represented a significant departure from previous production-sharing formats. Earlier, in May, RWE Dea announced an offshore gas find in the North el-Amriya concession, and in November BP declared that it had made a significant discovery in the West Mediterranean Deepwater concession. In May 2011 Dana Gas discovered additional reserves in the Nile Delta.

In April 2011 the interim Government announced that it would review gas export agreements with other countries, including Israel and Jordan, amid accusations that the deposed Mubarak regime had improperly negotiated the sale of gas at preferential prices. Later that month supplies to Israel were disrupted for several weeks by an armed attack on a gas pipeline in North Sinai. Further attacks on gas installations in Sinai continued to impede exports. In April 2012 Egypt's state-owned energy companies controversially cancelled the supply contract with Israel. EGAS complained that it had not been paid by EMG, although Israel denied the claim and warned Egypt that it was violating an economic provision of the 1979 peace treaty. The Egyptian Government had, meanwhile, revised its gas agreement with Jordan in 2011, increasing the price of exports.

In June 2012 EGAS launched a licensing round for 15 exploration blocks in the Mediterranean and Nile Delta basins. In total, 13 bids were received from international companies, and eight blocks were provisionally awarded. Among the successful bidders were Petroceltic, Edison, BP, Dana Gas, Sea Dragon and IEOC. In October the Government reached a general agreement to import gas from Algeria, and in November it invited companies to tender for a project to import LNG, establish a regasification facility and market the gas to local customers. The Government would therefore be in the unusual position of both importing and exporting LNG. By early 2013 EGAS had received five bids from investors. In April Qatar agreed to supply natural gas to Egypt during the summer months to help meet the seasonal surge in demand for electricity. Meanwhile, concerns about the lack of new gas output and the rapid rise in demand led to a curtailment of the operations of the Damietta and Idku LNG facilities, as the Government sought to channel gas supplies to the domestic market rather than sending it to the plants for liquefaction and export. Also in April BG Group announced plans to proceed with a US $1,500m. project to drill new production wells in the West Delta Deep Marine concession with its Malaysian partner, Petronas, with the aim of bringing new gas supplies on stream during 2014 to be sold to EGAS for home consumption.

In 2002 the Government established ECHEM to assume the functions previously held by EGPC as the first step in a plan to rationalize the fragmented petrochemical sector. ECHEM assumed responsibility for an investment programme costing some US $10,000m. Covering the period 2004–21, it aimed to increase total petrochemical production to 15m. metric tons per year and identified five core projects valued at $2,500m. for the first phase period up to 2009. In 2003 the company signed shareholder agreements for a polypropylene plant at Suez (originated by Oriental Petrochemicals Co) and a linear alkyl benzene plant in Alexandria. ECHEM was also to conduct a revised feasibility study for two other core projects: a 1.7m.-ton-per-year methanol plant and a styrene/polystyrene plant. The main fertilizer plants using Egypt's hydrocarbon feedstocks are Talkha I in Lower Egypt, producing nitrogenous fertilizers; Talkha II producing ammonia, which is then used for making urea (both plants use gas from the Abu Madi field); the Suez plant, producing nitrogenous fertilizer, using gas from Abu Gharadeq; the plant at Dakahlia, using Abu Qir gas and producing urea and ammonium nitrate; and the Abu Qir fertilizer works, in Alexandria, producing ammonia and urea.

In 2005 it was announced that the second phase of the Government's petrochemicals investment programme, running from 2009–15 at an estimated cost of US $3,300m., would include the addition of styrene, polyester, aromatics, terephthalic acid and ethoxylates units, as well as further olefins and methanol plants. Meanwhile, the Government sold 20% stakes in two profitable joint ventures in the energy sector, SIDPEC and AMOC. SIDPEC is Egypt's largest producer of ethylene and polyethylene, while AMOC operates plants for the production of mineral oils and paraffin wax.

In early 2009 India's TCI Sanmar Chemicals secured US $565m. in financing for a new $868m. chloride petrochemicals plant at Port Said, while in March 2010 ECHEM announced plans to build a $2,000m. petrochemicals complex at Alexandria. In October 2011 ECHEM awarded Japan's Toyo Engineering a $600m. contract to build an ethylene cracker in Alexandria. A $3,700m. project by Egypt's Carbon Holdings to establish a petrochemicals complex at Ain Sokhna is planned for completion in 2017. The engineering, procurement and construction contract had been awarded in 2011 to the US Shaw Group and South Korea's SK Engineering, and finance was agreed in principle in 2012 with the US and South Korean export credit agencies.

OTHER MINERALS

Egypt's principal mineral reserves are phosphate, iron ore and gold. There are also coal deposits in Sinai. Iron ore was traditionally mined from the Aswan area, but new and better-quality reserves were discovered in the Bahariya Oasis region. Phosphate is mined at Isna, Hamrawein, Safaga, Abu Tartur in the Western Desert, in the Nile Valley between Edfu and Qena, and on the Red Sea coast.

In 1997 a new gold discovery was announced in the far south-west of Egypt at Jabal Kamel, where Egyptian geologists had been prospecting for iron ore. In 2001 substantial gold reserves were discovered by Centamin Egypt in its Sukari concession in the Eastern Desert. Commercial production began in 2009; however, the concession was annulled by an administrative court ruling in October 2012, as the judicial authorities challenged some commercial agreements made under President Mubarak.

From 2008 a new regulatory framework and code was being prepared by the Egyptian Mineral Resource Authority (formerly the Egyptian Geological Survey and Mining Authority), in consultation with the World Bank, to encourage greater investment by international companies in developing the country's largely untapped resources, particularly gold. The code was to replace existing joint venture partnerships and production-sharing agreements with a system based on royalty payments, more closely reflecting mining laws in other countries.

BANKING, FINANCE AND EXCHANGE RATES

Foreign banks have been welcome in Egypt since it began liberalizing its economy in the mid-1970s, making their biggest impact on the banking system through joint ventures established with local banks. Other significant banking developments around that time included the opening in Cairo in 1979 of the Faisal Islamic Bank of Egypt—the first Egyptian bank to do business according to *Shari'a* (Islamic law)—and of Egypt's first international bank, the Egyptian International Bank, in 1980. Also in 1980 a National Investment Bank was established to monitor public investment.

During the 1980s the Government became concerned about the growth of Islamic investment companies; these attracted a significant proportion of private savings, including remittances from Egyptians working abroad, and channelled domestic funds and foreign exchange away from the official banking system—effectively constituting a large, unregulated financial sector in competition with the official banking institutions. In 1988 legislation was enacted requiring Islamic investment companies to become regular shareholding companies, and placing a limit of £E50m. on their authorized capital. The measures provoked strong resistance and, with the collapse that year of a number of Islamic finance houses, thousands of small investors lost their savings.

Several new banking laws were introduced from the start of the 1990s. Legislation in 1991 tightened the financial regulations relating to banks and strengthened the supervisory powers of the Central Bank. Under the measure, Egyptian banks were required to have paid-up capital of at least £E50m. (as against £E500,000 previously), while foreign banks had to have at least US $10m. Further legislation in 1998 allowed the Egyptian or international private sector to invest in Egypt's four state-owned banks (although private sector shares were restricted to 10%). In 2000 legislation was approved allowing banks to extend loans for the purchase of houses under a mortgage system, and in 2003 another law was adopted to unify banking sector regulations and reinforce the Central Bank's role in monitoring and supervising credit practices (in response to a series of high-profile bad loan cases). A Monetary Policy Committee was also established. The legislation additionally included a provision for foreign companies to own more than 50% of local banks, and a stipulation that banks would not be permitted to merge without prior approval from the Central Bank. A single regulatory body for the financial services industry, the Egyptian Financial Supervisory Authority, was established in 2009, replacing the Capital Markets Authority, the Egyptian Insurance Supervisory Authority and the Mortgage Finance Authority. However, responsibility for the banking sector remained with the Central Bank.

Following a major devaluation of the Egyptian pound against the US dollar in 1979, a 'black market' in currency developed, as Egypt maintained a complex system of multiple exchange rates. By 1987 the Government was under considerable pressure—particularly from the IMF—to unify these rates, and in May of that year it announced the partial flotation of the currency. Under reforms agreed with the IMF, which became operative in 1991, a new exchange system was introduced. This provided for the determination by the commercial banks of a free market rate of exchange, although an 'official' Central Bank rate continued to be set.

The drive towards liberalization during the late 1990s came at a cost. After a sharp rise in January 2000, the stock market stagnated, reflecting Egypt's ongoing liquidity problems—the major causes of which were the government arrears to the private sector, increased expenditure by the previous Government of Kamal al-Ganzouri on major infrastructure projects, and a depletion in the main sources of hard currency (principally petroleum sales, tourism and Suez Canal revenues). Eventually, intervention by the Government and the Central Bank in mid-2000 resulted in the informal abandonment of the Egyptian pound's fixed exchange rate against the US dollar. The value of the national currency subsequently declined substantially, from US $1 = £E3.40 in May 2000 to $1 = £E4.09 at the beginning of January 2001.

In January 2001 Prime Minister Atif Obeid announced the transfer of control of the rate of exchange to the Central Bank. A new, 'managed peg' system was introduced, whereby the currency would be allowed to fluctuate within a narrow band (initially of 1%) either side of the official rate set by the Central Bank: this rate was initially established at US $1 = £E3.85. While the adoption of what was considered a more appropriate official rate of exchange was broadly welcomed, the trading band was considered by some analysts as being too restrictive to eradicate the black market for the currency. In August the Bank adjusted the official rate to $1 = £E4.15, and widened the trading band to 3% either side of the new rate. In December, in response to the difficulties caused by the collapse in tourism after the 11 September attacks on the mainland USA, the Central Bank announced a further 7.5% devaluation in the currency, to a central rate of $1 = £E4.50, with the trading band maintained and proposals to inject $500m. into the market immediately and a further $1,500m. over the following six months. Also in 2001 Egypt issued its first sovereign Eurobond; heavily oversubscribed, it raised a total of $1,500m.

Regional instability surrounding political developments in Iraq and the discrepancy between the official and parallel markets prompted the Government to adopt a new floating foreign exchange system in January 2003, in an attempt to revive export and tourism revenues. However, shortages of foreign currency prompted the Central Bank to intervene in the foreign exchange markets, including the provision of US $1,200m. in reserves to commercial banks. The additional imposition of stringent capital controls in March prompted criticism from local banks.

In 2004 the Government announced proposals for further reform of the banking sector by reintegrating small banks into their parent companies, reorganizing public banks, broadening the capital base of mixed-ownership banks, merging some banks and reinforcing regulations. The Central Bank subsequently approved the merger of Misr Exterior Bank with its state-owned parent Banque Misr, and the mergers of both the local branch of American Express with Egyptian American Bank (EAB) and the local Crédit Lyonnais branch with Crédit Agricole Indosuez. During 2005 the divestiture of government shares in mixed-ownership banks progressed, with the National Société Générale Bank (NSGB) acquiring a majority stake in Misr International Bank (the enlarged entity becoming the country's biggest private sector bank in terms of assets). The Government also announced the merger of both the state-owned Bank of Commerce and Development and Mohandes Bank with the NBE. In addition, several local banks attracted increasing foreign interest, the largest deal being the purchase by France's Société Générale of a £E714m. stake in NSGB. Banking consolidation continued during 2006, with Calyon Corporate and Investment Bank of France purchasing some 75% of the EAB, and the NBE concluding the sale of Commercial International Bank to a US consortium led by Ripplewood Holdings. The Islamic International Bank for Investment and Development, the Nile Bank and the United Bank of Egypt were merged into the United Bank; and, in the first privatization of an Egyptian state-owned bank, 80% of the Bank of Alexandria was sold to Gruppo Sanpaolo IMI of Italy for US $1,600m. The Central Bank and a number of private and public institutions meanwhile established the Egyptian Company for Mortgage Refinancing to promote home ownership, and Egypt's first credit bureau, Estealam, was formed.

Although not immune from the global downturn, Egypt's banks were generally able to withstand the onset of the international financial crisis in the latter half of 2008, and the steep decline in the stock market in October of that year. The Central Bank increased interest rates six times during 2008 owing to rising inflation, which reached a peak of almost 24% in August, before cutting rates four times in early 2009. By June inflation had receded to 9.9%. The Central Bank continued to cut interest rates through to September in support of economic recovery, and in October it launched its own measure of inflation, the core inflation index, which excluded prices for the most volatile food items and regulated goods. In December the annual core inflation rate stood at 6.85%.

Following a period of structural reform and relative stability, the banking sector was adversely affected by the political unrest in early 2011. Banks were closed, and only reopened a week after President Mubarak's departure from office to prevent panic-induced capital flight. The Government limited daily cash withdrawals by individuals, and the Central Bank introduced measures to maintain bank liquidity. The benchmark interest rate remained unchanged, as the need for economic stability outweighed concerns about inflation. The Government raised US $2,200m. from the sale of treasury bills—although Egyptian banks purchased virtually all of the debt, as international investors proved reluctant to enter the market. Foreign exchange reserves meanwhile declined from $36,000m. in December 2010 to $28,000m. in April 2011. In the latter month the international credit rating agency Moody's downgraded its outlook for the Egyptian banking sector, citing the sovereign debt exposure and the effect of political uncertainty on the economy. Having apparently stabilized by late 2011, the Egyptian pound then declined sharply against the US dollar in November following further serious unrest, prompting the Central Bank to raise interest rates for the first time since 2008 to support the currency, encourage local currency deposits and contain inflationary pressures. Also in November 2011 the Central Bank issued dollar-denominated, one-year treasury bills to the value of $1,530m., and in December it raised $1,000m. from the sale of five-year bonds. The Government announced plans in August 2012 to increase the average maturity of securities by issuing more treasury bonds, and issued its first floating-rate bond, raising £E1,000m., in September. A greater dependence was evident on the issue of treasury bills and bonds to finance the deficit, with Egyptian banks increasingly investing in such instruments. According to the Central Bank, holdings of government securities by commercial banks rose by 39% between 2010 and 2012. In February 2013 legislation was approved enabling the Government and companies to issue Islamic bonds.

Meanwhile, foreign reserves had declined further by July 2012, to US $14,400m., as the Government made scheduled debt repayments, but they recovered in August following a $1,000m. deposit with the Central Bank from Saudi Arabia and a pledge from Qatar of a further $2,000m. However, the Central Bank struggled to contain the depreciation of the Egyptian pound, and it introduced currency auctions and other foreign currency controls in December. Despite a deposit by Qatar that month, reserves fell again, and the pound's exchange rate tumbled against the US dollar. From a new low of $13,400m. at the end of March 2013, reserves then rose in April to reach $14,400m. During that month Qatar pledged a further $3,000m. to buy government bonds, while Libya made a $2,000m. deposit with the Central Bank to support the Egyptian economy. In May reserves reached $16,000m.—a level described by the Central Bank as the critical minimum, and sufficient to cover three months of imports. However, the Egyptian pound continued to slide against the dollar, despite Central Bank intervention to try to slow the rate of depreciation. Faced with a weakening currency and rising inflation, the Central Bank raised interest rates in March 2013 for the first time since 2011, and also introduced measures to absorb excess liquidity. According to the Ministry of Finance, gross domestic public debt reached £E1,341.2m. at the end of March 2013 (equivalent to some 77% of GDP), while external debt of $38,800m. was recorded in December 2012. In March 2013 Moody's downgraded Egypt's sovereign foreign currency credit rating, citing continuing unsettled political conditions.

FOREIGN TRADE AND PAYMENTS

Egypt's merchandise trade deficit has traditionally been offset by surpluses in the services account, including tourism and Suez Canal revenues. By the end of the 1990s a marked improvement in the balance of payments was evident, with the overall current account in deficit by only US $8.5m. in 2001/02.

In 2002/03 there was a visible trade deficit of US $6,615m., from exports of $8,205m. and imports of $14,821m. Sustained high petroleum prices led to a 33% increase in petroleum export revenues to $3,161m. The current account recorded a surplus of $1,883m. Receipts from the Suez Canal reached $2,300m., and earnings from tourism $3,423m. In 2003/04 the visible trade deficit reached $7,833m. Exports increased by 27%, to reach $10,453m., and imports increased by 21%, to $18,286m. Petroleum exports increased by 23.7%, to reach $3,910m. The overall current account recorded an increased surplus of $3,418m., which was mainly attributed to the better performance in service industries. Suez Canal revenues contributed $2,848m. and tourism revenues $5,475m. The visible trade deficit reached $10,400m. in 2004/05, as exports increased to $13,800m. and imports to $24,200m. The current account continued to show a surplus, reaching $2,900m. Invisible earnings contributed most to this as revenues from tourism increased by 17.4%, to $6,400m., Suez Canal receipts increased to $3,300m., and remittances from overseas workers reached $4,330m. In 2005/06 the visible trade deficit widened to almost $12,000m., with exports at $18,500m. and imports at $30,400m., but the current account balance maintained a surplus of $1,800m. There were strong performances in the services account, as tourism revenues increased to $7,200m., Suez Canal earnings reached $3,600m. and remittances from workers abroad increased to over $5,000m. FDI and inward portfolio flows also rose sharply, and, according to the results of a UN survey of global FDI flows, Egypt was among the top recipients of foreign investment in Africa. In 2006/07 the trade deficit increased to $15,800m., from exports of $22,000m. and imports of $37,800m., while the current account surplus reached $2,700m. The services account recorded a surplus of $11,400m., and FDI inflows totalled $11,000m. In 2007/08 exports increased to $29,400m., and imports to $52,800m. Non-oil goods accounted for most of the rise in exports, while the higher value of imports reflected spiralling prices of some foods and petroleum. The current account surplus narrowed considerably, to $900m., but FDI inflows increased to $13,200m. According to the Central Bank, there was a trade deficit of $3,400m. in 2008/09. Exports declined to $25,200m., reflecting a 24% decline in oil exports, while imports declined to $50,300m. The services balance fell by 16.5%, to $12,500m.—attributable to the 8.4% decline in revenue from the Suez Canal, to $4,700m., and a 3.1% contraction in tourism revenues, to $10,500m. The surplus from remittances also declined by 11.7%, to $4,200m. FDI inflows stood at $8,100m., a figure hailed by the Government as an achievement, in view of the global economic slowdown.

According to the Central Bank, Egypt's external position improved in 2009/10. The balance of payments recorded a US $3,360m. surplus, compared with an overall deficit of $3,380m. the previous financial year. The current account deficit declined by 2.4%, to $4,300m., while the capital and financial account realized a net inflow of $8,300m. The trade deficit remained relatively stable, at $25,100m., with export proceeds declining to $23,900m. and imports to $49,000m. The balance of payments then recorded a deficit of $9,800m. in 2010/11, reflecting the repercussions of the political turmoil and the ousting of the Mubarak regime in early 2011 in terms of lost tourist revenue and foreign investment. None the less, the current account deficit narrowed to $2,800m., reflecting a reduction in the trade deficit (with exports valued at $26,992.5m. and imports at $50,776.5m.). The capital and financial account registered a deficit of $4,800m., following a significant reversal of portfolio investment, which decreased to $2,600m. from $7,900m. in the previous year. There was an 8.6% contraction in tourism receipts, to $10,600m., in 2010/11, as revenues declined for the first time in a decade. Remittances from Egyptians abroad rose to $14,300m., although external debt had increased to $34,900m. by the end of June 2011.

According to the Central Bank, the balance of payments deficit for the 2011/12 fiscal year widened to US $11,300m., while the trade deficit increased sharply, as imports rose to $58,673.8m. against exports valued at $26,975.9m. The current account deficit widened to $7,900m., and would have been greater but for a 43.5% increase in private transfers from the Egyptian diaspora, to $17,800m. The capital and financial account recorded a net outflow of $1,400m., and tourism revenues fell to $9,400m. In March 2013 President Mursi authorized changes to customs levies, including increased tariffs on non-essential imports, in an effort to generate further revenues to support the economy.

In 2001 Egypt signed a trade partnership agreement with the EU. During the initial 12–16-year transitional period, the EU would lift quotas on imports of Egyptian textiles and agricultural goods. The agreement would also phase out tariffs on EU exports; tariffs on exports of raw materials and capital goods would be eliminated over the first three years, those on intermediate goods would be phased out between years four and nine, and duties on finished goods would be removed between years six and 13. Egypt, Jordan, Tunisia and Morocco also signed an agreement to establish a free trade zone from 2006. In 2004 the Governments of Egypt, Israel and the USA signed a qualifying industrial zone (QIZ) trade agreement (the QIZ programme having been established by the USA in 1996 to encourage economic ties). Under its terms, goods manufactured at three designated QIZs in Egypt—covering Greater Cairo, Alexandria and the Suez Canal—are permitted to enter the USA without customs tariffs, provided 35% of the end product comes from co-operation between Egyptian and Israeli companies. In 2005 Egypt and Turkey signed a free trade agreement, the value of bilateral trade between the two countries having reached US $726m. in 2004. Although Egypt's main trading partners in 2006/07 were the EU (accounting for some 34% of total trade) and the USA (25%), trade with China was increasing rapidly. In 2009 the Government asked the USA for an extension of its QIZ programme into Upper Egypt and parts of the south. In August 2010 Egypt signed a free trade agreement with the South American trading bloc Mercado Común del Sur (Mercosur), envisaging the gradual removal of duties over a 10-year period.

TRANSPORT AND COMMUNICATIONS

The Suez Canal is an important international waterway, and a major source of foreign exchange for Egypt. After the October 1973 war, the most pressing need was to restore and reopen the Canal. Expansion was made all the more urgent by the vast increase in oil tanker sizes after June 1967, which the closure of the Canal helped to precipitate. At President Sadat's initiative, it was reopened in June 1975. Transit dues for ships using the waterway in the first year of operation was US $230m. By the late 1980s total annual revenue was almost $1,500m. Despite the introduction of selective discounts, the number of vessels using the Canal fell gradually during the 1990s (from 17,318 in 1993 to 13, 490 by 1999), largely owing to increased competition from pipelines as a means of transporting oil. In 1998 the Government placed the Suez Canal Authority (SCA) under the auspices of the Prime Minister as part of an initiative to improve efficiency. In 2003 the Canal was used by 14,610 vessels, and in 2004 the number of ships rose to 16,174. Increased trade flows from Asia, especially India and China, were partially responsible for the rise in revenues to $3,458m. in 2005, as were higher global oil prices, which made shorter transport routes more desirable. In that year the Suez Canal was used by 18,176 vessels. In 2006, although the SCA increased transit fees and reduced discounts for empty oil tankers from 40% to 20%, 18,664 ships passed through the Canal, raising $3,600m. in revenue. Revenues in 2007 increased to $4,600m., as 20,384 ships passed through the Canal. A series of major dredging operations have deepened the Canal to accommodate larger vessels. Since 1980 its maximum depth has increased from 38 ft to 62 ft, and work to increase this further, to 66 ft, was completed in 2010. A total of 21,415 ships passed through the Canal in 2008, in which year revenue increased to $5,380m. However, a reduction in traffic in the last quarter of the year, owing to the global economic downturn, as well as Somali piracy in the Gulf of Aden (which has led many shippers, particularly oil tankers, to reroute around South Africa's Cape of Good Hope), prompted the SCA to freeze its tariffs for 2009 at 2008 levels. The number of ships passing through the Canal in 2008/09 fell to 17,228, resulting in a decline in revenues to $4,700m. There was a further fall in earnings in 2009/10, to $4,500m., although shipping traffic increased to 17,993. Canal trade was largely unaffected by the political disruption in 2011 and 2012; the volume of traffic was maintained at 17,799 in 2011, and revenue increased to $5,100m.; and, while the number of vessels using the Canal dropped to 17,298 in 2012, revenues rose to $5,208m.

Egypt's principal ports are at Alexandria, Port Said and Suez. From 1998 the Government started a modernization policy, initially forming the Egyptian Company for Port Said Area Ports to develop a hub port on the east bank of the Suez Canal. By 2007 the first phase of renovation of Alexandria port, aided by a World Bank loan, had been completed, and Safaga on the Red Sea had also been developed. In 2004 the International Finance Corpn approved funding to the Sokhna Port Development Co to expand the facilities at Ain Sokhna port (where the company has a 25-year concession agreement awarded by the Government in 1999). In 2005 the Alexandria Port Authority awarded Hong Kong-based Hutchison Port Holdings contracts to develop and manage the Dakahlia and Alexandria container terminals, and the Damietta Port Authority signed an MOU with Kuwait and Gulf Link Transport Co for a new US $1,000m. container terminal at the port.

River transport on the Nile and its related waterways is being expanded to relieve the load on roads and railways for internal distribution. In 2005 the River Transport Authority (RTA) was developing a strategy to increase the share of cargo transported by river by up to 70% by 2020. In addition to modernizing existing waterways, the RTA planned to increase the river traffic to Cairo from industrial areas near Port Said, Port Suez and Damietta. It also intended to attract private investment, offering new port management and construction projects on a PPP basis.

Egypt has more than 5,000 km of railway track. Following a series of rail crashes since the turn of the century, the Ministry of Transport in 2007 was awarded £E8,500m. to upgrade the national rail system and make it economically sustainable in association with the private sector. Further upgrading measures were announced after another major accident in January 2013. In early 2012 the World Bank approved a US $330m. loan to upgrade the 250-km railway line between Beni-Suef and Asyout. The French-designed Cairo metro system currently consists of two lines. The first, a 44-km line running from el-Marg el-Gedida in the north to Helwan in the south, opened in 1987, and was the first underground transport system in the Middle East and North Africa. The second, running from the suburb of Shoubra el-Kheima to Cairo University (Giza), was completed in 2000. Two further lines are under construction, with finance from the Agence Française de Développement, the EIB and the Japan Bank for International Cooperation. The third line, to run from Cairo international Airport to Imbaba and Giza, is due to open in 2019; and the fourth, connecting Greater Cairo from east to west, in 2020.

Good roads connect Cairo with Alexandria, the canal towns and Upper Egypt. In 2000 two 2.6-km road tunnels beneath Old Cairo were completed, and in 2001 a 2.9-km suspension bridge over the Suez Canal opened. In 2006 the Government proposed a US $3,000m. project to build a causeway across the Strait of Tiran from Sharm el-Sheikh to Saudi Arabia, and in 2010 the Government proposed the construction of a tunnel under the Suez Canal at Port Said, with the projected cost of $1,000m. to be funded by private investors. In January 2011 the Government invited pre-qualified groups to submit bids for the construction, on a PPP contract basis, of the 35-km Rod el-Farag highway in Greater Cairo.The project was subsequently suspended until after the legislative and presidential elections, but in mid-2012 it was reported that the Government had approved the resumption of the tender process.

In 2001 plans for the construction of a new airport to the west of Cairo were abandoned in favour of a long-delayed project to build a third passenger terminal and a new runway to increase the existing airport's annual handling capacity. The US $347m. construction contract for the third terminal was awarded to a Turkish contractor in 2004, and commercial operations began at the new terminal in 2009. In 2003 the Ministry of Civil Aviation ended the separate status of the Cairo Airport Authority, placing it under the management of the Egyptian Holding Co for Airports and Air Navigation. With the exception of Cairo's third terminal, the largest expansion projects are the construction of new international airport facilities at Borg el-Arab, and the upgrade of three airports at Luxor, Sharm el-Sheikh and Hurghada. Airport management contracts were awarded to Aéroports de Paris for the airports at Sharm el-Sheikh, Hurghada, Luxor, Aswan and Abu Simbel from 2005, and to Frankfurt Airport Services Worldwide (Fraport) for Cairo International Airport, also from 2005. In that year the Saudi Binladin Group was awarded the $65m. Sharm el-Sheikh expansion contract, and in 2007 a contract for the Borg el-Arab modernization project was awarded to OCI. In early 2010 the Egyptian Holding Co for Airports and Air Navigation invited consultants to prepare a master plan for Cairo Airport City, for which the World Bank had pledged funding.

EgyptAir is the state airline, operating a network of domestic and international routes. In 2005 the Ministry of Civil Aviation announced plans to sell a 20% share of the airline through an initial public offering. Meanwhile, the company signed a US $850m. contract with Boeing for 12 new 737-800 passenger aircraft, and Air Cairo (40% owned by EgyptAir) ordered four new A320 Airbus aircraft. In 2006 the Civil Aviation Authority approved the creation of five new civil airlines to boost charter business, and EgyptAir launched a low-cost airline called EgyptAir Express to serve its domestic routes. In addition, in 2007 the Ministry of Civil Aviation established a new company, Smart Aviation Co, to serve the business community.

In the telecommunications sector, under 1998 legislation Telecom Egypt became a service operator and joint-stock company owned by the Government, while the National Telecommunications Regulatory Authority (NTRA) was established to undertake regulatory functions. The Government established the Ministry of Communications and Information Technology in 1999 to formulate policy. The first private GSM licence was awarded in 1998 to Vodafone Egypt and the second to the Egyptian Co for Mobile Services (commonly known by its brand name MobiNil). In 2000 the new Ministry announced a US $1,000m. plan to modernize Egypt's telecommunications infrastructure over a three-year period. Telecom Egypt was prepared for privatization; however, the transaction was suspended owing to market conditions. In 2001 the NTRA granted the company a $470m. licence to launch its own global system for mobile communications (GSM) service when the four-year exclusivity agreement with the existing operators expired the following year. After a period of speculation, during which time the NTRA indicated that establishing a third mobile phone company was not feasible in light of the weak Egyptian pound, Telecom Egypt announced in December 2003 that it was to become a partner in an existing mobile service and acquired a 25.5% stake in Vodafone Egypt (so recouping the licence fee and relinquishing its rights to the country's third GSM licence). At the same time Vodafone Egypt was listed on the stock exchange. Telecom Egypt and Vodafone formed a new joint venture called Wataniya Consortium. To attract foreign investment and expand the fixed-line system, Telecom Egypt selected the US-Kuwaiti Raneen consortium to set up a wireless local loop system at a cost of $700m.–$900m., on a revenue-sharing basis. In 2005 the Government approved an international auction for the licence to establish a third-generation (3G) mobile telephone network. Also in 2005 the Government signed co-operation agreements with the US chip-maker Intel to establish a regional centre in Egypt for developing Intel products, and with the USA's Microsoft to set up joint ventures to train young people in new technology.

In November 2005 the Government successfully launched an initial public offering of 20% of its shares in Telecom Egypt, also terminating the company's monopoly over international calls. In the auction launched in 2006 for the third GSM licence, where international applicants were expected to bid in partnership with an Egyptian company, a consortium headed by the UAE's Emirates Telecommunications Corpn (Etisalat) made the successful bid of £E16,700m. for the contract. The licence included both second-generation (2G) and 3G services. To maintain its commitment to the mobile market, Telecom Egypt acquired a further 23.5% stake in Vodafone Egypt from minority shareholders during 2006. In 2007 the NTRA allowed Vodafone Egypt to upgrade its mobile phone licence to 3G services for a total of US $581m., and granted MobiNil a 3G mobile licence for $585m. It also offered licences to mobile operators to provide international call services to their subscribers. The Government had intended to issue a second fixed-line licence, ending Telecom Egypt's monopoly, but postponed the publication of tender documents in January 2008 as it was still debating whether to open the market to greater competition by giving foreign operators access to Telecom Egypt's existing network. The NTRA then postponed tendering for the second licence indefinitely in September 2008 owing to the turbulent financial climate. In 2009 Orascom Telecom had become involved in a tax dispute with its Algerian subsidiary, Djezzy GSM, and in early 2010 an appeal lodged by the latter against the ruling that Djezzy owed outstanding taxes and penalties was rejected by the Algerian tax authorities. In mid-2010 the Algerian Government rejected Orascom's proposed sale of Djezzy to MTN of South Africa; Orascom then agreed to enter into negotiations for Djezzy's nationalization and to resolve the dispute centring on Orascom's settlement of its liabilities in Algeria. In April Orascom reached an agreement with France Télécom to end a protracted dispute relating to the sale of shares in MobiNil. In early 2011 Russia's VimpelCom acquired a 51% stake in Orascom Telecom, following its merger with Orascom's parent company, Wind Telecom. In early 2012 VimpelCom had agreed to sell a 51% stake in Djezzy to the Algerian Government, subject to a valuation and on the understanding that it would remain as operator; negotiations were ongoing in early 2013, although in May of that year there were conflicting reports concerning their future.

TOURISM

Although one of the most dynamic sectors of the Egyptian economy, tourism has equally been one of the most immediately vulnerable to political uncertainty. Following the Gulf crisis in 1990–91, the industry experienced further downturns in 1992/93, when a violent domestic campaign by Islamist militants included foreign tourists as targets; and in 1997, following the massacre of 58 tourists and four Egyptians in Luxor (see History). Nevertheless, the development of new tourism resorts continued, particularly on the Red Sea and South Sinai coasts.

Despite the reverberations of the September 2001 suicide attacks on the USA and the outbreak of hostilities in Iraq two years later, overall visitor arrivals totalled 6.0m. in 2003, while 2004 was reported to be a record year for tourism in Egypt—with tourist arrivals reaching 8.1m. However, fears for the short-term prospects of the industry were again expressed in July 2005, following three further, co-ordinated bomb attacks at the popular resort of Sharm el-Sheikh, and in April 2006 at the resort town of Dahab in Sinai. Nevertheless, visitor numbers continued to grow, reaching 8.6m. in 2005 and 9.1m. in 2006, and the Government announced plans to increase this figure to 14m. by 2011. In 2006 the Egyptian Tourist Authority launched a global marketing campaign to promote Egypt as a year-round destination, as well as a national campaign to educate Egyptians about the importance of tourism to the economy. Property investment restrictions were relaxed, permitting foreign investors unlimited ownership rights in most of Egypt (or 99-year lease agreements in Sinai). Tourist arrivals increased to 12.8m. in 2007/08. Visitor numbers fell in each of the last four months of 2008, and the trend continued into 2009 in the wake of the global economic slowdown and further security problems in September 2008 and February 2009. However, during 2009 as a whole there was only a modest drop in overall tourist arrivals, to 12.5m. Total arrivals rose to 13.8m. in the fiscal year 2009/10. The Government had anticipated up to 16m. arrivals in 2011, but the political unrest that erupted during that year prompted many visitors to leave the country or cancel reservations. Arrivals fell to 9.8m. in 2011, before increasing, to 11.5m., in 2012. The consequent loss of revenue had a severe impact on the current account deficit in those years.

Statistical Survey

Sources (unless otherwise stated): Central Agency for Public Mobilization and Statistics, POB 2086, Cairo (Nasr City); tel. (2) 4020574; fax (2) 4024099; e-mail misr@capmas.gov.eg; internet www.capmas.gov.eg; Central Bank of Egypt, 31 Sharia Qasr el-Nil, Cairo; tel. (2) 27702770; fax (2) 23925045; e-mail info@cbe.org.eg; internet www.cbe.org.eg.

Area and Population

AREA, POPULATION AND DENSITY

Area (sq km)	1,009,450*
Population (census results)†	
31 December 1996	59,312,914
21 November 2006	
Males	37,219,056
Females	35,578,975
Total	72,798,031
Population (official estimates at 1 January, preliminary)	
2011	79,617,517
2012	81,395,541
2013	83,661,000
Density (per sq km) at 1 January 2013	82.9

* 389,751 sq miles.

† Excluding Egyptian nationals abroad, totalling an estimated 2,180,000 in 1996 and an estimated 3,901,396 in 2006.

POPULATION BY AGE AND SEX

('000, official estimates at 1 January 2013, preliminary)

	Males	Females	Total
0–14	13,509	12,505	26,014
15–64	27,443	26,516	53,959
65 and over	1,821	1,867	3,688
Total	42,773	40,888	83,661

GOVERNORATES

(official estimates at 1 January 2013, preliminary)

	Area (sq km)	Population ('000)	Density (per sq km)	Capital
Cairo*	214.20	8,943	41,750.7	Cairo
Alexandria	2,679.36	4,609	1,720.2	Alexandria
Port Said	72.07	640	8,880.3	Port Said
Ismailia	1,441.59	1,136	788.0	Ismailia
Suez	17,840.42	592	33.2	Suez
Damietta	589.17	1,271	2,157.3	Damietta
Dakahlia	3,470.90	5,668	1,633.0	El-Mansoura
Sharkia	4,179.55	6,163	1,474.6	Zagazig
Kalyoubia	1,001.09	4,881	4,875.7	Banha
Kafr el-Sheikh	3,437.12	3,029	881.3	Kafr el-Sheikh
Gharbia	1,942.21	4,538	2,336.5	Tanta
Menoufia	1,532.13	3,759	2,453.4	Shebien el-Kom
Behera	10,129.48	5,481	541.1	Damanhour
Giza†	85,153.56	7,175	84.3	Giza
Beni-Suef	1,321.50	2,687	2,033.3	Beni-Suef
Fayoum	1,827.10	2,994	1,638.7	El-Fayoum
Menia	2,261.70	4,864	2,150.6	El-Menia
Asyout	1,553.00	4,008	2,580.8	Asyout
Suhag	1,547.20	4,345	2,808.3	Suhag
Qena	1,795.60	2,882	1,605.0	Qena
Luxor	55.00	1,092	19,854.5	Luxor
Aswan	678.45	1,383	2,038.5	Aswan
Red Sea	203,685.00	328	1.6	Hurghada
El-Wadi el-Gidid	376,505.00	215	0.6	El-Kharga
Matruh	212,112.00	404	1.9	Matruh
North Sinai	27,574.00	406	14.7	El-Areesh
South Sinai	33,140.00	168	5.1	El-Tour
Total	997,738.40‡	83,661	83.9‡	—

* Including territory designated as the governorate of Helwan in April 2008 and consisting of 1,713,278 persons at 2006 census.

† Including territory designated as the governorate of Sixth of October in April 2008 and consisting of 2,581,059 persons at 2006 census.

‡ The official, rounded national total is 1,009,450 sq km, producing an overall density figure of 82.9 per sq km.

Note: Totals may not be equal to the sum of components, owing to rounding.

PRINCIPAL TOWNS

(population at 1996 census)*

Cairo (Al-Qahirah, the capital)	6,789,479	Zagazig (Al-Zaqaziq)	267,351
Alexandria (Al-Iskandariyah)	3,328,196	El-Fayoum (Al-Fayyum)	260,964
Giza (Al-Jizah)	2,221,868	Ismailia (Al-Ismailiyah)	254,477
Shoubra el-Kheima (Shubra al-Khaymah)	870,716	Kafr el-Dawar (Kafr al-Dawwar)	231,978
Port Said (Bur Sa'id)	469,533	Aswan	219,017
Suez (Al-Suways)	417,610	Damanhour (Damanhur)	212,203
El-Mahalla el-Koubra (Al-Mahallah al-Kubra)	395,402	El-Menia (Al-Minya)	201,360
Tanta	371,010	Beni-Suef (Bani-Suwayf)	172,032
El-Mansoura (Al-Mansurah)	369,621	Qena (Qina)	171,275
Luxor (Al-Uqsor)	360,503	Suhag (Sawhaj)	170,125
Asyout (Asyut)	343,498	Shebien el-Kom (Shibin al-Kawn)	159,909

* Figures refer to provisional population. Revised figures include: Cairo 6,800,992; Alexandria 3,339,076; Port Said 472,335; Suez 417,527.

Mid-2011 ('000, incl. suburbs, UN estimate): Cairo 11,169 (Source: UN, *World Urbanization Prospects: The 2011 Revision*).

BIRTHS, MARRIAGES AND DEATHS

	Registered live births		Registered marriages		Registered deaths	
	Number ('000)	Rate (per 1,000)	Number	Rate (per 1,000)	Number ('000)	Rate (per 1,000)
2003	1,777	26.2	537,092	7.9	440	6.5
2004	1,780	25.7	550,709	7.9	442	6.4
2005	1,801	25.5	522,751	7.4	451	6.4
2006	1,854	25.7	522,887	7.3	452	6.3
2007	1,950	26.5	614,848	8.5	451	6.1
2008	2,051	27.3	660,000	8.8	462	6.1
2009	2,217	28.8	759,004	9.9	477	6.2
2010	2,261	28.7	864,857	11.0	483	6.1
2011	2,442	30.4	894,040	11.1	493	6.1

Life expectancy (official estimates, years at birth, 2012): Males 69.0; Females 71.8.

ECONOMICALLY ACTIVE POPULATION

('000 persons aged 15–64 years, labour force sample survey, 2011)

	Male	Female	Total
Agriculture, hunting, forestry and fishing	4,806.0	2,004.3	6,810.3
Mining and quarrying	49.0	0.5	49.5
Manufacturing	2,104.3	188.1	2,292.4
Electricity, gas and water supply (incl. water support, drainage and recycling)	403.7	28.9	432.6
Construction	2,697.8	18.2	2,716.0
Wholesale and retail trade; repair of motor vehicles, motorcycles, and personal and household goods	2,296.7	275.0	2,571.7
Hotels and restaurants	447.5	17.1	464.6
Transport, storage and communications	1,724.9	75.1	1,800.0
Financial intermediation	152.2	48.9	201.1
Real estate, renting and business activities	506.7	84.6	591.3
Public administration and defence; compulsory social security	1,432.8	429.3	1,862.1

—continued	Male	Female	Total
Education	1,099.5	1,023.7	2,123.2
Health and social work	262.4	362.7	625.1
Other community, social and personal service activities	594.7	36.1	630.8
Private households with employed persons	90.4	28.4	118.8
Extra-territorial organizations and bodies	1.4	0.9	2.3
Sub-total	18,670.0	4,621.8	23,291.8
Activities not adequately defined	48.6	5.6	54.2
Total employed	18,718.6	4,627.4	23,345.9
Unemployed	1,822.0	1,361.2	3,183.4
Total labour force	20,540.6	5,988.4	26,529.0

Note: Totals may not be equal to the sum of components, owing to rounding.

2012 ('000 persons aged 15–64 years, October–December, preliminary): Total employed 23,506 (males 18,882, females 4,624); Unemployed 3,519 (males 2,003, females 1,516); Total labour force 27,025 (males 20,885, females 6,140).

Health and Welfare

KEY INDICATORS

Total fertility rate (children per woman, 2011)	2.7
Under-5 mortality rate (per 1,000 live births, 2011)	21
HIV/AIDS (% of persons aged 15–49, 2011)	<0.1
Physicians (per 1,000 head, 2009)	2.8
Hospital beds (per 1,000 head, 2010)	1.7
Health expenditure (2010): US $ per head (PPP)	293
Health expenditure (2010): % of GDP	4.7
Health expenditure (2010): public (% of total)	39.2
Access to water (% of persons, 2011)	99
Access to sanitation (% of persons, 2011)	95
Total carbon dioxide emissions ('000 metric tons, 2009)	216,136.6
Carbon dioxide emissions per head (metric tons, 2009)	2.7
Human Development Index (2012): ranking	112
Human Development Index (2012): value	0.662

For sources and definitions, see explanatory note on p. vi.

Agriculture

PRINCIPAL CROPS
('000 metric tons)

	2009	2010	2011
Wheat	8,523.0	7,177.4	8,407.1
Rice, paddy	5,520.5	4,329.5	5,675.0
Barley	148.4	117.1	122.3
Maize, green	7,686.1	7,041.1	6,876.5
Sorghum	780.9	701.6	839.2
Potatoes	3,659.3	3,643.2	4,338.4
Sweet potatoes	357.3	370.9	274.9
Taro (Coco yam)	114.3	119.4	103.1
Sugar cane	15,482.2	15,708.9	15,765.2
Sugar beet	5,333.5	7,840.3	7,486.1
Broad beans, horse beans, dry	297.6	233.5	174.6
Groundnuts, with shell	198.0	202.9	206.6
Olives	449.0	390.9	459.7
Cabbages and other brassicas	740.4	690.6	626.0
Artichokes	209.6	215.5	202.5
Lettuce and chicory	80.1	97.7	94.3
Tomatoes	10,278.5*	8,545.0	8,105.3
Cauliflowers and broccoli	99.5	117.9	201.2
Pumpkins, squash and gourds	624.9	658.2	633.6
Cucumbers and gherkins	600.0	631.4	665.1
Aubergines (Eggplants)	1,290.2	1,229.8	1,166.4
Chillies and peppers, green	792.8	655.8	670.4
Onions, dry	2,128.6	2,208.1	2,304.2
Garlic	195.7	244.6	295.8
Beans, green	282.3	270.7	305.6
Peas, green	282.9	270.7	225.7
Carrots and turnips	175.9	139.0	150.3
Okra	134.7	86.2	84.0
Bananas	1,120.5	1,029.0	1,054.2
Oranges	2,372.3	2,401.0	2,577.7
Tangerines, mandarins, clementines and satsumas	809.8	796.9	848.0
Lemons and limes	809.8	318.1	296.8
Apples	508.8	493.1	455.8
Peaches and nectarines	363.2	273.3	332.5
Strawberries	242.8	238.4	240.3
Grapes	1,370.2	1,360.3	1,320.8
Watermelons	1,653.2	1,637.1	1,508.9
Cantaloupes and other melons	918.4	1,076.8	1,038.4
Figs	286.7	185.0	165.5
Guavas, mangoes and mangosteens	534.4	505.7	598.1
Dates	1,270.5	1,353.0	1,373.6

* FAO estimate.

Aggregate production ('000 metric tons, may include official, semi-official or estimated data): Total cereals 22,756.9 in 2009, 19,450.5 in 2010, 22,014.9 in 2011; Total roots and tubers 4,135.1 in 2009, 4,137.7 in 2010, 4,721.2 in 2011; Total vegetables (incl. melons) 21,350.5 in 2009, 19,487,1 in 2010, 18,945.5 in 2011; Total fruits (excl. melons) 10,299.0 in 2009, 9,581.2 in 2010, 9,922.3 in 2011.

Source: FAO.

LIVESTOCK
('000 head, year ending September)

	2009	2010	2011
Cattle	4,525	4,729	4,803*
Buffaloes	3,839	3,818	3,800†
Sheep	5,592	5,530	5,488*
Goats	4,139	4,175	4,207†
Pigs†	11	12	11
Horses	66	65	64†
Asses†	3,350	3,350	3,350
Camels	137	111	107†
Chickens†	105,500	106,000	108,000
Ducks†	14,800	15,200	15,500
Geese and guinea fowls†	6,975	7,450	7,450
Turkeys†	1,360	1,360	1,400

* Unofficial figure.
† FAO estimate(s).

Source: FAO.

LIVESTOCK PRODUCTS
('000 metric tons)

	2009	2010	2011
Cattle meat	447.0	457.3	454.5
Buffalo meat	411.9	398.4	395.8
Sheep meat	85.2	75.1	73.6
Goat meat	59.3	52.7	53.5
Pig meat	1.0	1.0	0.5*
Camel meat	36.8	48.0†	47.3*
Rabbit meat	51.0	52.3	53.3
Chicken meat	671.1	744.0	796.0
Cows' milk	2,803.3	2,995.3	2,995.3*
Buffaloes' milk	2,696.7	2,653.2	2,653.2
Sheep's milk*	108.0	113.0	113.0
Goats' milk*	16.0	18.0	18.0
Hen eggs	249.3	291.2	305.5
Honey	7.0	6.0	6.0*
Wool, greasy	11.2	12.0*	12.0*

* FAO estimate(s).
† Unofficial figure.

Source: FAO.

Forestry

ROUNDWOOD REMOVALS
('000 cubic metres, excluding bark, FAO estimates)

	2008	2009	2010
Sawlogs, veneer logs and logs for sleepers	134	134	134
Other industrial roundwood	134	134	134
Fuel wood	17,283	17,397	17,511
Total	17,551	17,665	17,779

2011: Production assumed to be unchanged from 2010 (FAO estimates).

Source: FAO.

SAWNWOOD PRODUCTION
('000 cubic metres, incl. railway sleepers)

	2003	2004	2005
Total (all broadleaved)	3	35	12

2006–11: Output assumed to be unchanged from 2005 (FAO estimates).

Source: FAO.

Fishing

('000 metric tons, live weight)

	2009	2010	2011
Capture	387.4	385.2	375.4
Grass carp	26.1	21.4	32.2
Nile tilapia	105.0	130.3	120.2
Mudfish	37.8	29.2	30.1
Mullets	21.9	31.6	23.5
Aquaculture	705.5	919.6*	986.8*
Cyprinids	62.3	100.0*	100.0*
Nile tilapia	390.3	557.0	610.6
Flathead grey mullet	210.0	116.0	114.0
Total catch	1,092.9	1,304.8*	1,362.2*

* FAO estimate.

Note: Figures exclude capture data for sponges, estimated by FAO at 1 metric ton per year.

Source: FAO.

Mining

('000 metric tons unless otherwise indicated, year ending 30 June)

	2009	2010	2011
Crude petroleum	35,260	35,030	35,250
Natural gas (million cu m)	62,690	61,320	61,448
Aluminium	265*	359	360*
Iron ore†	195	256	250
Salt (unrefined)	2,666	2,460	2,800
Phosphate rock	6,227	3,435	4,700
Gypsum (crude)	735	942	1,000
Kaolin	523	304	304
Granite (cu m)	59,000	480,000	480,000
Marble (cu m)	284,000	1,400,000	1,400,000

* Estimated production.

† Figures refer to gross weight. The estimated iron content is 50%.

2012: Crude petroleum ('000 metric tons) 35,393; Natural gas (million cu m) 60,881.

Sources: US Geological Survey; BP, *Statistical Review of World Energy*.

Industry

SELECTED PRODUCTS
('000 metric tons unless otherwise indicated)

	2007	2008	2009
Jet fuels	2,422	2,319	2,016
Kerosene	143	133	151
Distillate fuel oils	8,803	8,666	8,267
Motor spirit (gasoline)	4,195	4,240	4,384
Residual fuel oil (mazout)	10,989	9,529	9,166
Petroleum bitumen (asphalt)	831	783	738
Electric energy (million kWh)	128,129	134,565	142,690

2006: Cigarettes (million) 55,123; Mineral water ('000 hl) 6,164; Caustic soda 95.

Source: UN Industrial Commodity Statistics Database.

Cement ('000 metric tons): 46,900 in 2009; 44,592 in 2010; 43,884 in 2011 (Source: US Geological Survey).

Finance

CURRENCY AND EXCHANGE RATES

Monetary Units
1,000 millièmes = 100 piastres = 5 tallaris = 1 Egyptian pound (£E).

Sterling, Dollar and Euro Equivalents (30 April 2013)
£1 sterling = £E10.765;
US $1 = £E6.936;
€1 = £E9.066;
£E100 = £9.29 sterling = $14.42 = €11.03.

Note: From February 1991 foreign exchange transactions were conducted through only two markets, the primary market and the free market. With effect from 8 October 1991, the primary market was eliminated, and all foreign exchange transactions are effected through the free market. In January 2001 a new exchange rate mechanism was introduced, whereby the value of the Egyptian pound would be allowed to fluctuate within narrow limits: initially, as much as 1% above or below a rate that was set by the Central Bank of Egypt, but would be adjusted periodically in response to market conditions. The trading band was widened to 3% in August, and in January 2003 the Government adopted a floating exchange rate.

Average Exchange Rate (Egyptian pound per US $)
2009 5.545
2010 5.622
2011 5.933

GOVERNMENT FINANCE
(budgetary central government operations, £E million, year ending 30 June)

Revenue

	2010/11	2011/12	2012/13*
Tax revenue	192,072	207,410	266,905
Income tax	89,593	91,245	121,654
Property tax	9,452	13,089	19,403
Taxes on goods and services	76,068	84,594	100,702
Taxes on international trade and transactions	13,858	14,788	20,759
Other taxes	3,102	3,694	4,388
Non tax revenue	73,214	96,212	129,941
Grants	2,287	10,103	10,057
Other revenue	70,927	86,109	119,884
Total	265,286	303,622	396,847

Expense

Expense by economic type	2010/11	2011/12	2012/13*
Compensation of employees	96,271	122,818	136,627
Use of goods and services	26,148	26,826	28,765
Interest payments	85,077	104,441	133,612
Subsidies, grants and social benefits	123,125	150,193	145,838
Other payments	31,364	30,796	33,325
Purchases of non-financial assets	39,881	35,918	55,618
Total	401,866	470,992	533,785

* Budget figures.

Source: Ministry of Finance, Cairo.

INTERNATIONAL RESERVES
(US $ million at 31 December)

	2010	2011	2012
Gold (national valuation)	2,180	2,743	3,303
IMF special drawing rights	1,261	1,258	1,260
Foreign exchange	32,351	13,658	10,368
Total	35,792	17,659	14,931

Source: IMF, *International Financial Statistics*.

MONEY SUPPLY
(£E million at 31 December)

	2010	2011	2012
Currency outside depository corporations	143,632	176,578	205,020
Transferable deposits	113,895	119,852	133,903
Other deposits	716,434	742,440	828,237
Broad money	973,962	1,038,871	1,167,160

Source: IMF, *International Financial Statistics*.

COST OF LIVING
(Consumer Price Index; base: January 2010 = 100)

	2009	2010	2011
Food and non-alcoholic beverages	109.9	126.5	138.1
Alcoholic beverages and tobacco	121.9	171.2	201.5
Clothing and footwear	101.1	103.6	108.4
Housing and utilities	99.1	102.9	110.1
Health	100.3	102.0	103.7
Education	106.2	127.7	140.8
Transport	100.5	101.6	103.3
Communication	99.9	98.7	95.9
Recreation and culture	102.0	109.8	118.8
All items (incl. others)	105.4	116.4	125.0

NATIONAL ACCOUNTS
(£E million at current prices, year ending 30 June)

Expenditure on the Gross Domestic Product

	2010/11	2011/12
Government final consumption expenditure	157,000	179,000
Private final consumption expenditure	1,036,000	1,223,200
Changes in inventories	5,400	22,000
Gross fixed capital formation	229,100	236,100
Total domestic expenditure	1,427,500	1,660,300
Exports of goods and services	282,000	286,100
Less Imports of goods and services	338,500	404,100
GDP in purchasers' values	1,371,000	1,542,300

Note: Figures are rounded to the nearest £E hundred million.

Gross Domestic Product by Economic Activity

	2010/11	2011/12
Agriculture, hunting, forestry and fishing	190,159	218,216
Mining and quarrying	195,136	228,384
Manufacturing	216,184	238,369
Electricity, gas and water	21,544	24,373
Construction	60,070	67,382
Wholesale and retail trade, restaurants and hotels	192,413	212,113
Transport, storage and communications	122,681	133,438
Suez Canal	29,311	31,203
Finance, insurance, real estate and business services	126,527	141,439
Public administration and defence	133,688	153,984
Other services	51,503	57,628
GDP at factor cost	1,309,906	1,475,326
Indirect taxes, *less* subsidies*	61,094	66,974
GDP in purchasers' values	1,371,000	1,542,300

* Figures obtained as residuals.

BALANCE OF PAYMENTS
(US $ million)

	2009	2010	2011
Exports of goods	23,089	25,024	27,913
Imports of goods	-39,907	-45,145	-47,312
Balance on goods	-16,818	-20,120	-19,398
Exports of services	21,520	23,807	19,140
Imports of services	-13,935	-14,718	-14,070
Balance on goods and services	-9,233	-11,031	-14,328
Primary income received	992	534	318
Primary income paid	-3,068	-6,446	-6,695
Balance on goods, services and primary income	-11,309	-16,943	-20,705
Secondary income received	8,305	12,836	15,566
Secondary income paid	-345	-397	-345
Current balance	-3,349	-4,504	-5,484
Capital account (net)	-19	-39	-45
Direct investment assets	-571	-1,176	-626
Direct investment from liabilities	6,712	6,386	-483
Portfolio investment assets	-267	-445	-220
Portfolio investment liabilities	-260	10,887	-10,431
Other investment assets	-5,879	-11,185	2,876
Other investment liabilities	1,601	2,003	-2,467
Net errors and omissions	398	-2,145	-2,855
Reserves and related items	-1,635	-218	-19,736

Source: IMF, *International Financial Statistics*.

External Trade

Note: Figures exclude trade in military goods.

PRINCIPAL COMMODITIES
(distribution by HS, US $ million)

Imports c.i.f.	2010	2011	2012
Cereals	3,483.9	5,452.7	5,349.1
Wheat and meslin	2,181.9	3,199.2	3,196.9
Mineral fuels, oils, distillation products, etc.	7,130.7	9,280.3	13,061.1
Crude petroleum oils	1,321.2	1,700.2	2,933.3
Non-crude petroleum oils	3,656.7	5,119.3	7,718.7
Petroleum gases	1,806.2	2,055.6	2,230.9
Plastics and articles thereof	2,296.1	2,915.0	3,112.1
Iron and steel	3,125.8	3,600.3	4,307.4
Iron ingots, wastes and scraps	669.4	1,032.9	934.4
Articles of iron or steel	2,787.1	2,598.4	2,583.0
Machinery, boilers, etc.	5,613.3	5,452.7	5,570.9
Electrical, electronic equipment	3,376.1	3,655.3	3,713.4
Vehicles other than railway, tramway	3,768.2	3,093.8	3,555.1
Total (incl. others)	53,003.4	62,282.0	69,865.6

Exports f.o.b.	2010	2011	2012
Vegetables, roots and tubers	834.3	986.0	804.3
Fruit, nuts, peel of citrus fruit and melons	955.1	1,020.6	990.3
Mineral fuels, oils, distillation products, etc.	7,593.9	9,242.0	8,872.0
Crude petroleum oils	1,777.5	3,014.0	3,022.6
Non-crude petroleum oils	2,962.0	3,507.3	3,150.4
Petroleum gases	2,266.6	2,030.2	2,179.9
Fertilizers	1,152.3	1,443.2	1,284.0
Nitrogenous fertilizers	1,080.8	1,354.5	1,184.9
Plastics and articles thereof	886.5	1,098.1	1,266.8
Non-knitted articles of apparel and accessories	821.0	994.3	770.5
Pearls, precious stones, metals, coins, etc.	1,037.4	1,725.8	1,330.7
Gold, unwrought or semi-manufactured	1,033.8	1,715.2	1,318.7
Iron and steel	872.9	1,157.6	775.0
Electrical and electronic equipment	816.4	1,166.6	1,153.7
Total (incl. others)	26,331.8	31,582.4	29,417.0

Source: Trade Map-Trade Competitiveness Map, International Trade Centre, www.intracen.org/marketanalysis.

PRINCIPAL TRADING PARTNERS
(US $ million)*

Imports c.i.f.	2010	2011	2012
Algeria	412.8	684.0	968.4
Argentina	888.2	1,859.3	1,103.1
Australia	538.5	521.7	457.0
Belgium	861.6	1,336.5	1,692.8
Brazil	1,736.2	2,404.5	2,783.6
China, People's Republic	4,901.8	5,708.3	6,590.7
France (incl. Monaco)	1,886.1	2,053.2	2,278.0
Germany	4,023.9	3,930.0	4,670.0
India	1,557.8	1,642.4	2,251.6
Indonesia	532.6	903.7	774.6
Italy	2,962.6	3,123.8	3,464.6
Japan	1,440.2	1,375.7	1,591.8
Korea, Republic	1,906.0	1,735.3	1,763.2
Kuwait	1,524.1	2,786.8	2,690.9
Malaysia	784.6	768.7	557.7
Malta	1,053.8	208.3	226.2
Netherlands	831.5	1,656.3	1,452.5
Russia	1,835.1	2,634.1	3,988.8
Saudi Arabia	2,120.1	2,546.4	2,722.4
Spain	847.9	1,106.1	1,352.6
Sweden	623.3	707.2	913.3
Switzerland	542.4	657.0	731.3
Thailand	749.1	701.7	911.3
Turkey	1,880.0	2,638.7	3,490.1
Ukraine	1,624.8	1,946.0	3,861.4
United Arab Emirates	730.2	804.7	810.1
United Kingdom	1,269.0	1,270.6	1,265.1
USA	4,961.9	6,470.1	5,276.5
Total (incl. others)	53,003.4	62,282.0	69,865.6

Exports f.o.b.	2010	2011	2012
Algeria	262.4	386.9	391.9
Belgium	351.2	550.9	398.0
China, People's Republic	431.6	623.3	747.1
France (incl. Monaco)	924.1	1,288.6	1,152.5
Germany	573.4	792.5	644.5
Greece	271.9	400.6	225.8
India	1,227.9	2,265.4	2,039.5
Iraq	382.9	450.5	569.9
Italy	2,199.2	2,719.7	2,324.5
Japan	188.9	362.2	1,007.4
Jordan	711.8	864.4	695.0
Korea, Republic	531.3	433.6	278.7
Lebanon	523.9	964.7	843.1
Libya	1,220.4	556.7	1,439.3
Morocco	402.1	492.6	397.3
Netherlands	558.8	701.2	405.6
Russia	213.3	353.2	225.1

Exports f.o.b.—*continued*	2010	2011	2012
Saudi Arabia	1,549.0	1,977.7	1,832.8
South Africa	395.6	1,008.5	526.3
Spain	1,621.4	1,312.9	1,008.2
Sudan	559.2	537.0	452.2
Switzerland	398.1	272.5	344.5
Syria	800.5	762.0	391.7
Taiwan	337.8	377.1	94.8
Turkey	985.3	1,528.8	1,570.2
United Arab Emirates	613.4	867.0	721.7
United Kingdom	813.4	965.9	840.5
USA	1,547.1	1,819.4	2,015.5
Total (incl. others)†	26,331.8	31,582.4	29,417.0

* Imports by country of consignment, exports by country of destination. Totals include trade in free zones, not classifiable by country.

† Including bunkers and ships' stores (US $ million): 948.2 in 2010; 1,114.0 in 2011; 1,236.5 in 2012.

Source: Trade Map-Trade Competitiveness Map, International Trade Centre, www.intracen.org/marketanalysis.

Transport

RAILWAYS
(traffic, year ending 30 June)

	2001/02	2002/03	2003/04
Passenger-km (million)	39,083	46,185	52,682
Net ton-km (million)	4,188	4,104	4,663

Source: UN, *Statistical Yearbook*.

2005 (million): Passengers carried 451.1; Freight carried (metric tons) 10.1; Passenger-km 40,837; Freight ton-km 3,917 (Source: World Bank, World Development Indicators database).

2009/10 (million): Passengers carried 805; Freight ton-km 1,889.

ROAD TRAFFIC
(licensed motor vehicles in use at 31 December)

	2010	2011	2012
Passenger cars	3,169,329	3,434,114	3,538,679
Buses and coaches	104,131	109,466	106,617
Lorries and vans	937,234	978,731	1,026,476
Motorcycles and mopeds	1,374,775	1,509,373	1,674,812
Total (incl. others)	5,814,385	6,278,728	6,607,432

SHIPPING

Flag Registered Fleet
(at 31 December)

	2010	2011	2012
Number of vessels	450	449	449
Displacement ('000 grt)	1,283.3	1,345.9	1,281.4

Source: Lloyd's List Intelligence (www.lloydslistintelligence.com).

International sea-borne freight traffic ('000 metric tons, incl. ships' stores, 2005, figures are rounded): Goods loaded 21,230; Goods unloaded 42,410 (Source: UN, *Monthly Bulletin of Statistics*).

SUEZ CANAL TRAFFIC

	2010	2011	2012
Transits (number)	17,993	17,798	17,298
Displacement ('000 net tons)	846,400	928,900	928,500
Total cargo volume ('000 metric tons)	646,100	691,800	739,911

Source: Suez Canal Port Authority.

CIVIL AVIATION
(traffic on scheduled services)

	2007	2008	2009
Kilometres flown (million)	90	110	113
Passengers carried ('000)	5,829	6,689	6,216
Passenger-km (million)	12,001	14,266	14,801
Total ton-km (million)	1,429	1,631	1,670

Source: UN, *Statistical Yearbook*.

Passengers carried ('000): 9,179 in 2010; 7,141 in 2011 (Source: World Bank, World Development Indicators database).

Tourism

ARRIVALS BY NATIONALITY
('000)

	2008	2009	2010
France	586.9	551.7	599.4
Germany	1,202.5	1,202.3	1,329.0
Israel	213.1	203.3	226.5
Italy	1,073.2	1,048.0	1,144.4
Libya	481.5	410.2	451.1
Netherlands	279.8	249.0	291.2
Palestinian Territories	68.4	104.7	177.3
Russia	1,825.3	2,035.3	2,855.7
Saudi Arabia	402.3	348.0	374.9
United Kingdom	1,201.9	1,346.7	1,455.9
USA	319.1	321.3	361.5
Total (incl. others)	12,835.4	12,535.9	14,730.8

Tourism receipts (US $ million, incl. passenger transport unless otherwise indicated): 12,104 in 2009; 12,528 (excl. passenger transport) in 2010; 8,707 (excl. passenger transport, provisional) in 2011.

Source: World Tourism Organization.

Total tourist arrivals ('000): 9,845 in 2011; 11,532 in 2012.

Communications Media

	2010	2011	2012
Telephones ('000 main lines in use)	9,618.1	8,714.3	8,557.5
Mobile cellular telephones ('000 subscribers)	70,661.0	83,425.1	96,798.8
Internet subscribers ('000)	2,118.2	2,165.8	n.a.
Broadband subscribers ('000)	1,426.1	1,843.6	2,287.2

Personal computers: 3,197,036 (39.2 per 1,000 persons) in 2008.

Source: International Telecommunication Union.

Education

(2011/12 unless otherwise indicated, estimates)

	Schools	Teachers	Students
Pre-primary	8,928	31,768	874,730
Primary	17,249	376,745	9,644,456
Preparatory	10,372	225,861	4,158,845
Secondary:			
general	2,780	96,514	1,324,440
technical	1,892	139,195	1,628,168
University*	42	78,596	1,722,968

* 2010/11 figures.

Sources: Ministry of Education.

Al-Azhar (2011/12): *Primary:* 3,465 schools; 1,175,183 students. *Preparatory:* 3,131 schools; 489,703 students. *Secondary:* 2,068 schools; 316,306 students.

Pupil-teacher ratio (primary education, UNESCO estimate): 27.7 in 2009/10 (Source: UNESCO Institute for Statistics).

Adult literacy rate (UNESCO estimates): 72.0% (males 80.3%; females 63.5%) in 2010 (Source: UNESCO Institute for Statistics).

Directory

The Constitution

A new Constitution for the Arab Republic of Egypt was approved by referendum on 11 September 1971. Amendments to the Constitution were endorsed by the People's Assembly on 30 April 1980, 10 May 2005 and 19 March 2007, and subsequently approved at national referendums.

Following the ouster of former President Muhammad Hosni Mubarak and his Government in early February 2011, the 1971 Constitution was suspended pending the approval of amendments at a national referendum held on 19 March 2011. At the referendum, the proposed amendments were approved by 77.3% of participating voters and a temporary Constitutional Declaration was subsequently published by the Supreme Council of the Armed Forces (SCAF). A draft for a new, permanent constitution was presented to President Muhammad Mursi by the outgoing Constituent Assembly on 1 December 2012. At a referendum, held in two rounds on 15 and 22 December, the document was approved by 63.8% of participating voters, according to official results. The total rate of participation was recorded at 32.9%. The new Constitution entered into effect on 26 December.

However, the Constitution was suspended on 3 July 2013, following Mursi's removal from office, and on 8 July a 33-article Constitutional Declaration was announced by Interim President Adli Mahmoud Mansour. Under the provisions of the Declaration, Mansour was to appoint a committee of judges to study amendments to the 2012 Constitution within 25 days of his assumption of office; the recommendations of this committee were then to be submitted to a second committee, comprising representatives of the armed forces and of religious institutions, for approval in September. The second committee was to agree on a draft within 30 days. A national referendum to approve the final draft was scheduled to take place by the end of November 2013.

The Government

HEAD OF STATE

President: ADLI MAHMOUD MANSOUR (ad interim; took office 4 July 2013).

COUNCIL OF MINISTERS
(September 2013)

On 3 July 2013 President Muhammad Mursi was removed from office by the armed forces, following popular protests in the capital, Cairo, and other cities demanding his resignation. The protests had commenced on 30 June to mark the one-year anniversary of Mursi's assumption of office, and had been prompted by concerns over Mursi's increasing authoritarianism and his failure to address social and economic problems. The Commander-in-Chief of the Armed Forces, Minister of Defence and Defence Production Gen. Abd al-Fatah al-Sisi, announced the suspension of the Constitution and the appointment of the President of the Supreme Constitutional Court, Adli Mahmoud Mansour, as interim President. On 9 July Hazem al-Biblawi, who had served as Deputy Prime Minister for Economic Affairs and Minister of Finance in the transitional Government of Essam Sharaf in 2011, was designated as Prime Minister, and on 16 July a new administration was sworn into office.

Prime Minister: Dr HAZEM AL-BIBLAWI.

First Deputy Prime Minister and Minister of Defence: Gen. ABD AL-FATAH AL-SISI.

Deputy Prime Minister and Minister of Higher Education: Dr HOSSAM EISSA.

Deputy Prime Minister and Minister for International Co-operation: ZIAD BAHAA AL-DIN.

Minister of Finance: AHMAD GALAL.

Minister of Electricity and Energy: Dr AHMAD EMAM.

Minister of Planning: ASHRAF AL-ARABI.
Minister of Housing and Urban Development: IBRAHIM MEHLEB.
Minister of Education: MAHMOUD ABUL NASR.
Minister of State for Antiquities: MUHAMMAD IBRAHIM.
Minister of Investment: OSAMA SALEH.
Minister of Tourism: MUHAMMAD HISHAM ABBAS ZAAZOU.
Minister of Supply: MUHAMMAD ABU SHADI.
Minister of the Interior: Maj.-Gen. MUHAMMAD IBRAHIM.
Minister of Manpower and Immigration: KAMAL ABU EITAH.
Minister of Culture: MUHAMMAD SABER ARAB.
Minister of Petroleum and Metallurgical Wealth: SHERIF ISMAIL.
Minister of Information: DORRAYA SHARAF AL-DIN.
Minister of State for Scientific Research: Dr RAMZI GEORGE STINO.
Minister of Military Production: Air Marshal REDA MAHMOUD HAFIZ.
Minister of Awqaf (Islamic Endowments): MUHAMMAD MOKHTAR GOMAA.
Minister of Foreign Affairs: NABIL FAHMI.
Minister of Civil Aviation: ABD AL-AZIZ FADIL.
Minister of Agriculture and Land Cultivation: AYMAN FARID ABU HADID.
Minister of Water Resources and Irrigation: MUHAMMAD ABD AL-MUTTALIB.
Minister of Health and Population: Dr MAHA AL-RABAT.
Minister of Transport: IBRAHIM AL-DOMEIRI.
Minister of Industry and Foreign Trade: MOUNIR FAKHRI ABD AL-NOUR.
Minister of Communications and Information Technology: ATIF HELMI.
Minister of State for Youth Affairs: KHALID ABD AL-AZIZ.
Minister of Local Development: ADIL LABIB.
Minister of State for Environmental Affairs: Dr LAILA RASHID ISKANDAR.
Minister of State for Sports: TAHIR ABU ZEID.
Minister of Transitional Justice and National Reconciliation: MUHAMMAD AMIN AL-MAHDI.
Minister of Social Solidarity: AHMAD AL-BORAI.

MINISTRIES

Office of the Prime Minister: 2 Sharia Majlis al-Sha'ab, Cairo; tel. (2) 27935000; fax (2) 27958048; e-mail questions@cabinet.gov.eg.

Ministry of Agriculture and Land Cultivation: 1 Sharia Nadi el-Seid, Cairo (Dokki); tel. (2) 33372970; fax (2) 33372435; e-mail info@agr-egypt.gov.eg; internet www.agr-egypt.gov.eg.

Ministry of Awqaf (Islamic Endowments): Sharia Sabri Abu Alam, Bab el-Louk, Cairo; tel. (2) 23929403; fax (2) 23929828; e-mail awkafministry@yahoo.com; internet www.awkaf.org.

Ministry of Civil Aviation: Sharia Cairo Airport, Cairo; tel. (2) 22688342; fax (2) 22688341; e-mail info@civilaviation.gov.eg; internet www.civilaviation.gov.eg.

Ministry of Communications and Information Technology: Smart Village, km 28, Sharia Cairo–Alexandria, Cairo; tel. (2) 35341300; fax (2) 35341111; e-mail info@mcit.gov.eg; internet www.mcit.gov.eg.

Ministry of Culture: 2 Sharia Shagaret el-Dor, Cairo (Zamalek); tel. (2) 27380761; fax (2) 27353947; e-mail ecm@idsc.net.eg; internet www.ecm.gov.eg.

Ministry of Defence and Military Production: Sharia 23 July, Kobri el-Kobba, Cairo; tel. (2) 4032159; fax (2) 2906004; e-mail mod@afmic.gov.eg.

Ministry of Drinking Water and Sanitation Facilities: Cairo.

Ministry of Education: 12 Sharia el-Falaky, Cairo; tel. (2) 27947363; fax (2) 27947502; e-mail info@mail.emoe.org; internet www.emoe.org.

Ministry of Electricity and Energy: POB 222, 8 Sharia Ramses, Abbassia Sq., Cairo (Nasr City); tel. (2) 22616317; fax (2) 22616302; e-mail info@moee.gov.eg; internet www.moee.gov.eg.

Ministry of Finance: Ministry of Finance Towers, Cairo (Nasr City); tel. (2) 23428886; fax (2) 26861561; e-mail finance@mof.gov.eg; internet www.mof.gov.eg.

Ministry of Foreign Affairs: Corniche el-Nil, Cairo (Maspiro); tel. (2) 25749820; fax (2) 25748822; e-mail info@mfa.gov.eg; internet www.mfa.gov.eg.

Ministry of Health and Population: 3 Sharia Majlis al-Sha'ab, Lazoughli Sq., Cairo; tel. (2) 27942865; fax (2) 27953966; e-mail webmaster@mohp.gov.eg; internet www.mohp.gov.eg.

Ministry of Higher Education: 101 Sharia Qasr el-Eini, Cairo; tel. (2) 27920323; fax (2) 27941005; e-mail mohe.info@gmail.com; internet www.egy-mhe.gov.eg.

Ministry of Housing and Urban Planning: 1 Sharia Ismail Abaza, 3rd Floor, Qasr el-Eini, Cairo; tel. (2) 27921440; fax (2) 27957836; internet www.moh.gov.eg.

Ministry of Industry and Foreign Trade: 2 Sharia Latin America, Cairo (Garden City); tel. (2) 27921167; fax (2) 27955025; e-mail inquiry@mti.gov.eg; internet www.mti.gov.eg.

Ministry of Information: Radio and TV Bldg, Corniche el-Nil, Cairo (Maspiro); tel. (2) 25757164; fax (2) 25746928; e-mail info@moinfo.gov.eg; internet www.moinfo.gov.eg.

Ministry of the Interior: 25 Sharia Sheikh Rihan, Bab el-Louk, Cairo; tel. (2) 27955005; fax (2) 27960682; e-mail center@iscmi.gov.eg; internet www.moiegypt.gov.eg.

Ministry of Investment: 3 Salah Salem St, Cairo; tel. (2) 24055628; fax (2) 24055635; internet www.investment.gov.eg.

Ministry of Manpower and Immigration: 3 Sharia Yousuf Abbas, Cairo (Nasr City); tel. (2) 22609359; fax (2) 23035332; e-mail manpower@mome.gov.eg; internet www.manpower.gov.eg.

Ministry of Petroleum and Metallurgical Wealth: 1 Sharia Ahmad el-Zomor, Cairo (Nasr City); tel. (2) 26706401; fax (2) 26706419; e-mail contactus@petroleum.gov.eg; internet www.petroleum.gov.eg.

Ministry of Planning: POB 11765, Sharia Salah Salem, Cairo (Nasr City); tel. (2) 24014526; fax (2) 24014732; e-mail moed.egypt@gmail.com; internet www.mop.gov.eg.

Ministry of State for Scientific Research: Cairo.

Ministry of State for Antiquities: Cairo; tel. (2) 27358761; fax (2) 27357239.

Ministry of State for Environmental Affairs: 30 Sharia Misr Helwan el-Zirai, Maadi, Cairo; tel. (2) 25256452; fax (2) 25256490; e-mail eeaa@eeaa.gov.eg; internet www.eeaa.gov.eg.

Ministry of Local Development: Sharia Nadi el-Seid, Cairo (Dokki); tel. (2) 37497470; fax (2) 37497788; internet www.mld.gov.eg.

Ministry of Military Production: 5 Sharia Ismail Abaza, Qasr el-Eini, Cairo; tel. (2) 27948739; fax (2) 27953063; e-mail mmpisscc@idsc.gov.eg.

Ministry of Social Solidarity: Cairo.

Ministry of State for Sports: Sharia 26 July, Sphinx Sq., Mohandessin, Cairo (Giza).

Ministry of State for Youth Affairs: Sharia 26 July, Sphinx Sq., Mohandessin, Cairo (Giza).

Ministry of Supply: 99 Sharia Qasr el-Eini, Cairo; tel. (2) 7958481; fax (2) 7956442; e-mail Info@mss.gov.eg; internet www.mss.gov.eg.

Ministry of Tourism: Cairo International Conferences Center, Cairo (Nasr City); tel. (2) 22611732; fax (2) 26859551; e-mail mot@idsc.gov.eg; internet www.visitegypt.gov.eg.

Ministry of Transitional Justice and National Reconciliation: Sharia Majlis al-Sha'ab, Cairo.

Ministry of Transport: Nasr Road, Nasr City, Cairo; tel. (2) 2604884; fax (2) 2610510; internet www.mot.gov.eg.

Ministry of Water Resources and Irrigation: Sharia Gamal Abd al-Nasser, Corniche el-Nil, Imbaba, Cairo; tel. (2) 35449420; fax (2) 35449470; e-mail minister@mwri.gov.eg; internet www.mwri.gov.eg.

President and Legislature

Following the resignation from office of former President Muhammad Hosni Mubarak on 11 February 2011, the Supreme Council of the Armed Forces (SCAF), under the chairmanship of Field Marshal Muhammad Hussein Tantawi, assumed the president's powers on an interim basis. The Constitution was suspended and both the People's Assembly (Majlis al-Sha'ab) and the Advisory Council (Majlis al-Shura) dissolved. Elections to the People's Assembly were held in three stages, from 28 November–11 January 2012, while elections to a new Advisory Council took place on 29 January–22 February. A presidential election was held on 23–24 May, at which Muhammad Mursi of the Freedom and Justice Party (with 24.8% of the total valid votes) and former Prime Minister Ahmad Shafiq (23.7%) secured the largest support. At a second round of voting on 16–17 June, Mursi was elected President, securing 51.7% of the valid votes cast, and was sworn into office on 30 June. Meanwhile, following a ruling by the Supreme Constitutional Court that declared the legislation under which the People's Assembly had been elected to be unconstitutional, on 15 June the SCAF dissolved the Assembly and assumed legislative powers on an interim basis. On 8 July President Mursi issued a decree reinstating the People's Assembly; however, the Supreme Constitutional Court insisted that its decision could not be revoked. On 12 August Mursi issued a further decree revoking amendments to the Constitutional Declaration, under which the SCAF had assumed legislative powers. A new Constitution was promulgated in late December 2012, following its approval at a national referendum.

On 3 July 2013 President Mursi was removed from office by the armed forces and the 2012 Constitution was suspended. The Advisory Council was dissolved on 6 July and two days later a Constitutional Declaration was announced by the Interim President, Adli Mahmoud Mansour. According to the Declaration, elections to the People's Assembly were expected to take place in January–February 2014 and presidential elections in February–March.

PRESIDENT

Presidential Election, First Ballot, 23–24 May 2012

Candidates	Votes	%
Muhammad Mursi	5,764,952	24.77
Ahmad Shafiq	5,505,327	23.66
Hamdeen Sabbahi	4,820,273	20.71
Abd el-Monem Aboul Foutouh	4,065,239	17.47
Amr Moussa	2,588,850	11.12
Muhammad Salim el-Awwa	235,374	1.01
Khalid Ali	134,056	0.57
Aboul Ezz al-Hariri	40,090	0.17
Hisham al-Bastawisi	29,189	0.12
Mahmoud Hossam	23,992	0.10
Muhammad Fawzi Essa	23,889	0.10
Hossam Khairallah	22,036	0.09
Abdullah al-Ashaal	12,249	0.05
Total*	23,265,516	100.00

* Excluding 406,720 invalid votes (1.74% of total votes cast).

Presidential Election, Second Ballot, 16–17 June 2012

Candidate	Votes	% of votes
Muhammad Mursi	13,230,131	51.73
Ahmad Shafiq	12,347,380	48.27
Total	25,577,511	100.00

LEGISLATURE

People's Assembly
(Majlis al-Sha'ab)

Cairo; tel. (2) 27945000; fax (2) 27943130; e-mail contact-us@parliament.gov.eg; internet www.parliament.gov.eg.

Speaker: (vacant).

Elections, 28–29 November and 5–6 December 2011, 14–15 December and 21–22 December 2011, 3–4 January and 10–11 January 2012

	Seats
The Freedom and Justice Party (FJP)	235
Al-Nour Party	123
New Wafd Party	38
Egyptian Bloc	34
Al-Wasat Party	10
The Reform and Development Party	9
The Revolution Continues Alliance	7
National Party of Egypt	5
Freedom Party	4
Egyptian Citizen Party	4
Union Party	2
Others	4
Independents	23
Total*	508†

* There are, in addition, 10 representatives appointed by the Supreme Council of the Armed Forces.

† Of the 498 elective seats, 332 seats are allocated to party lists under a system of proportional representation, while the remaining 166 seats are allocated to individual candidates who may or may not be affiliated to political organizations. (List candidates are elected from 46 constituencies and individual candidates from 83 constituencies.)

Advisory Council
(Majlis al-Shura)

Cairo; tel. (2) 27955492; fax (2) 27941980; e-mail gsecretariat@parliament.gov; internet www.shoura.gov.eg.

In September 1980 elections were held for an advisory body, the **Advisory (Shura) Council**, which replaced the former Central Committee of the Arab Socialist Union. Two-thirds of the 270 members of the Advisory Council are elected by direct suffrage; the remainder are appointed by the Head of State (in 2012, by the Supreme Council of the Armed Forces). The Council's term in office is six years, with one-half of its members being replaced every three years. At a two-stage election held from 29 January to 22 February 2012 the Muslim Brotherhood's Freedom and Justice Party secured 105 of the 180 contested seats, while the Al-Nour Party took 45 seats. The New Wafd Party secured 14 seats and the Egyptian Bloc eight seats. The Freedom Party and the Democratic Peace Party, both offshoots of the defunct National Democratic Party, won three seats and one seat, respectively, while the remaining four seats went to independent candidates.

Speaker: (vacant).

Election Commissions

Higher Election Commission (HEC): Cairo; tel. (2) 4142613; fax (2) 4142615; e-mail info@elections.gov.eg; regulates legislative elections; comprises 11 mems; Chair. SAMIR ABU AL-MAATI; Sec.-Gen. ABD AL-MALIK AL-QOMMOS.

Supreme Presidential Election Commission (PEC): 3rd Floor, 117 Sharia Abd al-Aziz Fahmy, Cairo (Heliopolis); f. 2005; independent; comprises 10 mems, presided over by the Chief Justice of the Supreme Constitutional Court and 4 other ex officio mems of the judiciary; of the remaining 5 mems (who are independent, public figures), 3 are appointed by the People's Assembly and 2 by the Advisory Council; Chair. Hon. FAROUK AHMED SULTAN.

Political Organizations

Following the removal from office of President Muhammad Hosni Mubarak in February 2011, new legislation governing the licensing of political organizations was promulgated in late March. A number of new parties were granted official recognition—including the Freedom and Justice Party (see below), which was founded in April by the Muslim Brotherhood—and participated in legislative elections held from November. Meanwhile, in mid-April the National Democratic Party of former President Mubarak was dissolved, following a ruling by the High Administrative Court.

Arab Democratic Nasserist Party: 8 Sharia Talaat Harb, Cairo; f. 1992; advocates maintaining the principles of the 1952 Revolution, achieving a strong national economy and protecting human rights; Chair. DIAA EL-DIN DAOUD; Sec.-Gen. AHMED HASSAN.

Democratic Front Party (Hizb al-Gabha al-Dimuqrati): 14 el-Muhammad Shafiq, Nile Valley, Cairo; tel. (3) 3050552; fax (3) 33050547; e-mail info@democraticfront.org; internet www.democraticfront.org; f. 2007 by fmr mems of the National Democratic Party; seeks to promote liberal democracy, the rule of law and a civil society; Founder and Pres. Dr OSAMA AL-GHAZALI HARB; Sec.-Gen. SAMI IBRAHIM.

Democratic Generation Party (Hizb al-Geel al-Dimuqrati): Bldg 26, Ismail Abaza St, Saad Zaghloul Metro Station, Cairo; internet www.hzpelgeel.com; tel. and fax (2) 27960814; f. 2002; advocates improvements in education and youth-based policies; Chair. NAGUI EL-SHEHABY.

Democratic Peace Party: Cairo; f. 2005; Chair. AHMAD MUHAMMAD BAYOUMI AL-FADALI.

The Egyptian Arab Association Party: Cairo.

Egyptian Arab Socialist Party (Hizb Misr al-Arabi al-Ishtiraki): f. 1976; seeks to maintain principles of the 1952 Revolution and to preserve Egypt's Islamic identity; f. 1985; Leader WAHID FAKHRY AL-UQSURI.

The Egyptian Bloc: e-mail kotla-masreya@info.com; internet www.elkotlaelmasreya.com; f. 2011; originally formed as a coalition of 15 political parties; secular, liberal; currently comprises the Free Egyptians Party, the Egyptian Social Democratic Party and the National Progressive Unionist Party—Tagammu.

Egyptian Citizen Party (Hizb al-Mowaten al-Masri): f. 2011; offshoot of the former National Democratic Party; Leader MUHAMMAD RAGAB.

Egyptian Green Party (Hizb al-Khudr al-Misri): 9 Sharia al-Tahrir, Cairo (Dokki); tel. and fax (2) 33364748; fax (2) 33364748;

e-mail awad@egyptiangreens.com; internet www.egyptiangreens.com; f. 1990; Pres. MUHAMMAD AWAD.

Egyptian Islamic Labour Party: 12 Sharia Awali el-Ahd, Cairo; e-mail magdyahmedhussein@gmail.com; internet www.el3amal.net; f. 1978; official opposition party; pro-Islamist; seeks establishment of economic system based on *Shari'a* (Islamic) law, unity between Egypt, Sudan and Libya, and the liberation of occupied Palestinian territory; Sec.-Gen. MUHAMMAD MAGDI AHMAD HUSSEIN.

Freedom Party (Hizb al-Horreya): Center Amwalimomat St, Housing Sheraton, Cairo; tel. (2) 2660325; fax (2) 2660390; internet www.alhoriaparty.com; f. 2011; offshoot of the former National Democratic Party; Chair. MAMDOUH HASSAN; Sec.-Gen MOATAZ HASSAN.

Free Social Constitutional Party: f. 2004; seeks introduction of further political, social and economic reforms; Chair. MAMDOUH QENAWI.

Al-Ghad (Tomorrow) Party: Cairo; e-mail info@elghad.org; f. 2004; aims to combat poverty and to improve the living conditions of Egypt's citizens; Chair. MOUSSA MOUSTAFA MOUSSA.

Misr el-Fatah (Young Egypt Party): f. 1990; pursues a socialist, nationalist and reformist agenda; Chair. ABD AL-HAKIM ABD AL-MAJID KHALIL.

Muslim Brotherhood (Al-Ikhwan al-Muslimun): internet www.ikhwanonline.com; f. 1928, with the aim of establishing an Islamic society; banned in 1954; transnational org.; moderate; advocates the adoption of *Shari'a* (Islamic) law as the sole basis of the Egyptian legal system; founded Freedom and Justice Party to contest at least one-half of the seats at 2011–12 legislative elections; Supreme Guide MAHMOUD IZZAT (acting).

Freedom and Justice Party (FJP): Cairo; internet www.fjponline.com; f. 2011; Islamist party committed to democracy and social equality; member of the Democratic Alliance for Egypt; Chair MUHAMMAD SAAD EL-KATATNI; Sec.-Gen. HUSSEIN IBRAHIM.

National Party of Egypt (Hizb Masr al-Qawmi): f. 2011; offshoot of the former National Democratic Party.

National Progressive Unionist Party (NPUP) (Hizb al-Tagammu' al-Watani al-Taqadomi al-Wahdawi—Tagammu): 1 Sharia Karim el-Dawlah, Cairo; tel. (2) 5791629; fax (2) 5784867; e-mail khaled@al-ahaly.com; internet www.al-ahaly.com; f. 1976; left-wing; seeks to defend the principles of the 1952 Revolution; Founder KHALED MOHI EL-DIN; Chair. SAYID ABD AL-AAL; 160,000 mems.

New Wafd Party (New Delegation Party): POB 357, 1 Boulos Hanna St, Cairo (Dokki); tel. (2) 3383111; fax (2) 3359135; e-mail info@alwafdparty.com; internet www.alwafd.org; f. 1919 as Wafd Party; banned 1952; re-formed as New Wafd Party Feb. 1978; disbanded June 1978; re-formed 1983; seeks further political, economic and social reforms, greater democracy, the abolition of emergency legislation, and improvements to the health and education sectors; Chair. SAYED EL-BADAWI.

Al-Nour Party: Zezenia, Alexandria; tel. (3) 5741310; fax (3) 5741317; e-mail info@alnourparty.org; internet www.alnourparty.org; f. 2011; Salafist; Chair YOUNIS MAKHYOUN.

The Reform and Development Party (al-Islah wa al-Tanmiya): 28 Samir Mokhtar St, Ard El Golf, Cairo; tel. (2) 4185545; fax (2) 4184920; e-mail info@rdpegypt.org; internet www.rdpegypt.org; f. 2009; was denied licence in 2010; formed by merger of the Reformation and Development Party with the Masrena Party; Chair. MUHAMMAD ANWAR ESMAT EL-SADAT.

The Revolution Continues Alliance (RCA): Cairo; f. 2011; comprises the Socialist Popular Alliance Party, the Egyptian Current Party, the Revolution Youth Coalition, the Egyptian Socialist Party, the Egyptian Alliance Party, the Freedom Egypt Party and the Equality and Development Party.

Solidarity Party (Hizb al-Takaful): f. 1995; advocates imposition of 'solidarity' tax on the rich in order to provide for the needs of the poor; Chair. Dr OSAMA ABD AL-SHAFI SHALTOUT.

Ummah (People's) Party (Hizb al-Umma): f. 1983; social democratic party; Leader AHMAD AL-SABAHI KHALIL.

Union Party (Hizb al-Ittihad): f. 2011; offshoot of the former National Democratic Party; Leader HOSSAM BADRAWI.

Al-Wasat Party: 8 Pearl St, Mokattam, Cairo; tel. (2) 5044151; internet www.alwasatparty.com; f. 2011; originally formed in 1996 but denied licence under rule of former President Hosni Mubarak; Pres. ABUL ELA MADI; Sec.-Gen. MUHAMMAD ABD AL-LATIF.

Diplomatic Representation

EMBASSIES IN EGYPT

Afghanistan: 59 Sharia el-Orouba, Cairo (Heliopolis); tel. (2) 4177236; fax (2) 4177238; e-mail info@afghanembassy-egypt.com; internet www.afghanembassy-egypt.com; Ambassador FAZLURRAHMAN FAZIL.

Albania: Ground Floor, 27 Sharia Gezira al-Wissta, Cairo (Zamalek); tel. (2) 27361815; fax (2) 27356966; e-mail embassy.cairo@mfa.gov.al; Ambassador NURI DOMI.

Algeria: 14 Sharia Bresil, Cairo (Zamalek); tel. (2) 7368527; fax (2) 7364158; e-mail nov54@link.net; Ambassador NAZEER AL-ARBAWI.

Angola: 12 Midan Fouad Mohi ed-Din, Mohandessin, Cairo; tel. (2) 3377602; fax (2) 708683; e-mail angola@access.com.eg; Ambassador ANTÓNIO DA COSTA FERNANDES.

Argentina: 1st Floor, 8 Sharia el-Saleh Ayoub, Cairo (Zamalek); tel. (2) 27351501; fax (2) 27364355; e-mail eegip@mrecic.gov.ar; Chargé d'affaires a.i. DIEGO SADOFSCHI.

Armenia: 20 Sharia Muhammad Mazhar, Cairo (Zamalek); tel. (2) 27374157; fax (2) 27374158; e-mail armegyptembassy@mfa.am; internet egypt.mfa.am; Ambassador Dr ARMEN MELKONIAN.

Australia: 11th Floor, World Trade Centre, Corniche el-Nil, Cairo 11111 (Boulac); tel. (2) 27706600; fax (2) 27706650; e-mail cairo.austremb@dfat.gov.au; internet www.egypt.embassy.gov.au; Ambassador Dr RALPH KING.

Austria: 5th Floor, Riyadh Tower, 5 Sharia Wissa Wassef, cnr of Sharia el-Nil, Cairo 11111 (Giza); tel. (2) 35702975; fax (2) 35702979; e-mail kairo-ob@bmeia.gv.at; internet www.bmeia.gv.at/kairo; Ambassador Dr FERDINAND MAULTASCHL.

Azerbaijan: Villa 16/24, Sharia 10, Maadi Sarayat, Cairo; tel. (2) 23583761; fax (2) 23583725; e-mail azsefqahira@link.net; internet www.azembassy.org.eg; Ambassador SHAHIN ABDULLAYEV.

Bahrain: 15 Sharia Bresil, Cairo (Zamalek); tel. (2) 27350642; fax (2) 27366609; e-mail cairo.mission@mofa.gov.bh; Ambassador Sheikh RASHID BIN ABD AL-RAHMAN AL KHALIFA.

Bangladesh: POB 136, 20 Sharia Geziret el-Arab, Mohandessin, Cairo; tel. (2) 33462003; fax (2) 33462008; e-mail bdoot@link.net; Ambassador MIZANUR RAHMAN.

Belarus: 26 Sharia Gaber Ibn Hayan, Cairo (Dokki); tel. (2) 37499171; fax (2) 33389545; e-mail egypt@mfa.gov.by; internet egypt.mfa.gov.by; Ambassador IGOR FISSENKO.

Belgium: POB 37, 20 Sharia Kamal el-Shennawi, Cairo 11511 (Garden City); tel. (2) 27947494; fax (2) 27943147; e-mail cairo@diplobel.fed.be; internet www.diplomatie.be/cairo; Ambassador GILLES HEYVAERT.

Bolivia: 21 New Ramses Centre, Sharia B. Oman, Cairo 11794 (Dokki); tel. (2) 37624362; fax (2) 37624360; e-mail embolivia_egipto@yahoo.com; Chargé d'affaires a.i. RAÚL PALZA ZEBALLOS.

Bosnia and Herzegovina: 42 Sharia al-Sawra, Cairo (Dokki); tel. (2) 37499191; fax (2) 37499190; e-mail ambbih@link.net; Ambassador BORIVOJ MAROJEVIĆ.

Brazil: Nile City Towers, North Tower, 2005 C, Corniche el-Nil, Cairo; tel. (2) 24619837; fax (2) 24619838; e-mail administ.cairo@itamaraty.gov.br; internet cairo.itamaraty.gov.br; Ambassador MARCO ANTONIO DINIZ BRANDÃO.

Brunei: 14 Sharia Sri Lanka, Cairo (Zamalek); tel. (2) 27366651; fax (2) 27360240; e-mail cairo.egypt@mfa.gov.bn; Ambassador Haji MAHDI PEHIN Dato' Haji ABDULLAH RAHMAN.

Bulgaria: 6 Sharia el-Malek el-Afdal, Cairo (Zamalek); tel. (2) 27363025; fax (2) 27363826; e-mail embassy.cairo@mfa.bg; internet www.mfa.bg/embassies/egypt; Ambassador RUMEN PETROV.

Burkina Faso: POB 306, Ramses Centre, 22 Sharia Wadi el-Nil, Mohandessin, Cairo 11794; tel. (2) 23898056; fax (2) 23806974; Ambassador MOUSSA B. NEBIE.

Burundi: 27 Sharia el-Ryad, Mohandessin, Cairo; tel. (2) 33024301; fax (2) 33441997; Ambassador MUSA SOLEIMANI.

Cambodia: 2 Sharia Tahawia, Cairo (Giza); tel. (2) 3489966; Ambassador IN SOPHEAP.

Cameroon: POB 2061, 15 Sharia Muhammad Sedki Soliman, Mohandessin, Cairo; tel. (2) 3441101; fax (2) 3459208; e-mail ambcam@link.net; Ambassador Dr MOHAMADOU LABARANG.

Canada: POB 57, 26 Kamel el-Shenawy, Cairo (Garden City); tel. (2) 27918700; fax (2) 27918860; e-mail cairo@dfait-maeci.gc.ca; internet www.canadainternational.gc.ca/egypt-egypte; Ambassador DAVID DRAKE.

Central African Republic: 41 Sharia Mahmoud Azmy, Mohandessin, Cairo (Dokki); tel. and fax (2) 33445942; Ambassador HENRY KOBA.

Chad: POB 1869, 12 Midan al-Refaï, Cairo 11511 (Dokki); tel. (2) 3373379; fax (2) 3373232; Ambassador EL HADJ MAHMOUD ADJI.

Chile: 19 Sharia Gabalaya, Apt 92, Cairo (Zamalek); tel. (2) 27358711; fax (2) 27353716; e-mail embchile.eg@gmail.com; Ambassador ALEX GEIGER SOFFIA.

China, People's Republic: 14 Sharia Bahgat Ali, Cairo (Zamalek); tel. (2) 27380466; fax (2) 27359459; e-mail webmaster_eg@mfa.gov.cn; internet eg.china-embassy.org/eng; Ambassador Song Aiguo.

Colombia: 6 Sharia Guezira, Cairo (Zamalek); tel. (2) 27364203; fax (2) 27357429; e-mail ccairo@cancilleria.gov.co; internet mre.cancilleria.gov.co/wps/portal/embajada_egipto; Ambassador Mario Germán Iguarán Arana.

Congo, Democratic Republic: 5 Sharia Mansour Muhammad, Cairo (Zamalek); tel. (2) 3403662; fax (2) 3404342; Ambassador Rafael Malonga.

Côte d'Ivoire: 9 Sharia Shehab, Mohandessin, Cairo; tel. (2) 33034373; fax (2) 33050148; e-mail acieg@ambaci-egypte.org; internet www.ambaci-egypte.org; Ambassador Bernard Tanoh Boutchoue.

Croatia: 3 Sharia Abou el-Feda, Cairo (Zamalek); tel. (2) 27383155; fax (2) 27355812; e-mail croemb.cairo@mvpei.hr; internet eg.mfa.hr; Ambassador Darko Javorski.

Cuba: Apartment 1, 13th Floor, 10 Sharia Kamel Muhammad, Cairo (Zamalek); tel. (2) 7360651; fax (2) 7360656; e-mail cubaemb@link.net; Ambassador Otto Vaillant Frías.

Cyprus: 17 Sharia Omar Tosson, Ahmed Orabi, Mohandessin, Cairo; tel. (2) 33455967; fax (2) 33455969; e-mail cairoembassy@mfa.gov.cy; Ambassador Sotos A. Liasides.

Czech Republic: 1st Floor, 4 Sharia Dokki, Cairo 12511 (Giza); tel. (2) 33339700; fax (2) 37485892; e-mail cairo@embassy.mzv.cz; internet www.mfa.cz/cairo; Ambassador Pavel Kafka.

Denmark: 12 Sharia Hassan Sabri, Cairo 11211 (Zamalek); tel. (2) 27396500; fax (2) 27396588; e-mail caiamb@um.dk; internet www.egypten.um.dk; Ambassador Pernille Dahler Kardel.

Djibouti: 11 Sharia el-Gazaer, Aswan Sq., Cairo (Agouza); tel. (2) 3456546; fax (2) 3456549; Ambassador Sheikh Moussa Mohamed Ahmed.

Ecuador: 33 Sharia Ismail Muhammad, Cairo (Zamalek); tel. (2) 27372776; fax (2) 27361841; e-mail ecuademb@link.net; Ambassador Edwin Johnson.

Eritrea: 6 Sharia el-Fallah, Mohandessin, Cairo; tel. (2) 3033503; fax (2) 3030516; e-mail eritembe@yahoo.com; Ambassador Osman Muhammad Omar.

Estonia: 8th Floor, Abou el-Feda Bldg, 3 Sharia Abou el-Feda, Cairo 11211 (Zamalek); tel. (2) 27384190; fax (2) 27384189; e-mail embassy.cairo@mfa.ee; internet www.kairo.vm.ee; Ambassador Paul Teesalu.

Ethiopia: Mesaha Sq., Villa 11, Cairo (Dokki); tel. (2) 3353693; fax (2) 3353699; e-mail ethio@ethioembassy.org.eg; Ambassador Mahmoud Drir.

Finland: 13th Floor, 3 Sharia Abou el-Feda, Cairo 11211 (Zamalek); tel. (2) 27363722; fax (2) 27371376; e-mail sanomat.kai@formin.fi; internet www.finland.org.eg; Ambassador Roberto Tanzi-Albi.

France: POB 1777, 29 Sharia Charles de Gaulle, Cairo (Giza); tel. (2) 35673200; fax (2) 35718498; e-mail questions@ambafrance-eg.org; internet www.ambafrance-eg.org; Ambassador Nicolas Galey.

Gabon: 17 Sharia Mecca el-Moukarama, Cairo (Dokki); tel. (2) 3379699; Ambassador Joseph Mamboungou.

Georgia: 11 Sharia Tanta, Aswan Sq., Mohandessin, Cairo; tel. (2) 33044798; fax (2) 33044778; e-mail cairo.emb@mfa.gov.ge; internet www.egypt.mfa.gov.ge; Ambassador Archil Dzuliashvili.

Germany: 2 Sharia Berlin (off Sharia Hassan Sabri), Cairo (Zamalek); tel. (2) 27282000; fax (2) 27282159; internet www.kairo.diplo.de; Ambassador Michael Bock.

Ghana: 1 Sharia 26 July, Cairo (Zamalek); tel. (2) 3444455; fax (2) 3032292; Ambassador Alhaji Said Sinare.

Greece: 18 Sharia Aicha al-Taimouria, Cairo 11451 (Garden City); tel. (2) 27950443; fax (2) 27963903; e-mail gremb.cai@mfa.gr; internet www.mfa.gr/egypt; Ambassador Christodoulos Lazaris.

Guatemala: 5th Floor, 17 Sharia Port Said, Maadi, Cairo; tel. (2) 23802914; fax (2) 23802915; e-mail embegipto@minex.gob.gt; internet www.embaguategypt.com; Ambassador Lars Pira.

Guinea: 46 Sharia Muhammad Mazhar, Cairo (Zamalek); tel. (2) 7358109; fax (2) 7361446; Ambassador El Hadj Ibrahima Sori Traoré.

Holy See: Apostolic Nunciature, Safarat al-Vatican, 5 Sharia Muhammad Mazhar, Cairo (Zamalek); tel. (2) 27352250; fax (2) 27356152; e-mail nunteg@yahoo.com; Apostolic Nuncio Most Rev. Jean-Paul Aimé Gobel (Titular Archbishop of Calatia).

Honduras: 8th Floor, 5 Sharia el-Israa, Mohandessin, Cairo; tel. (2) 3441337; fax (2) 3441338; e-mail hondemb@idsc.net.eg; Ambassador Nelson Valencia.

Hungary: 29 Sharia Muhammad Mazhar, Cairo 11211 (Zamalek); tel. (2) 27358659; fax (2) 27358648; e-mail mission.cai@kum.hu; internet mfa.gov.hu/emb/cairo; Ambassador Dr Péter Kveck.

India: 5 Sharia Aziz Abaza, Cairo (Zamalek); tel. (2) 27363051; fax (2) 27364038; e-mail embassy@indembcairo.com; internet www.indembcairo.com; Ambassador Navdeep Suri.

Indonesia: POB 1661, 13 Sharia Aicha al-Taimouria, Cairo (Garden City); tel. (2) 27947200; fax (2) 27962495; e-mail pwkcairo@access.com.eg; internet cairo.kemlu.go.id; Ambassador Dr Nurfaizi Suwandi.

Iraq: 1 Sharia Abd al-Moneim Riad, Thawra Sq., Cairo; tel. (2) 7358087; fax (2) 7622517; e-mail caiemb@iraqmofamail.com; Ambassador Zia Hadi Mahmoud Dabbas.

Ireland: 22 Sharia Hassan Assem, Cairo (Zamalek); tel. (2) 27358264; fax (2) 27362863; e-mail cairoembassy@dfa.ie; internet www.embassyofireland.org.eg; Ambassador Isolde Moylan.

Israel: 6 Sharia Ibn el-Malek, Cairo (Giza); tel. (2) 33321500; fax (2) 33321555; e-mail info@cairo.mfa.gov.il; Ambassador Yaakov Amitai.

Italy: 15 Sharia Abd al-Rahman Fahmi, Cairo (Garden City); tel. (2) 27943194; fax (2) 27940657; e-mail ambasciata.cairo@esteri.it; internet www.ambilcairo.esteri.it; Ambassador Maurizio Massari.

Japan: POB 500, 2nd Floor, 81 Sharia Corniche el-Nil, Maadi, Cairo; tel. (2) 25285903; fax (2) 25285906; e-mail culture@ca.mofa.go.jp; internet www.eg.emb-japan.go.jp; Ambassador Toshiro Suzuki.

Jordan: 6 Sharia Juhaini, Cairo; tel. (2) 37485566; fax (2) 37601027; e-mail jocairo2@ie-eg.com; internet www.jordanembassycairo.gov.jo; Ambassador Dr Bishr Khasawneh.

Kazakhstan: 9 Wahib Doss St, Maadi, Cairo; tel. (2) 23809804; fax (2) 23586546; e-mail cairo@mfa.kz; Ambassador Berik Aryn.

Kenya: POB 362, 29 Sharia al-Quds al-Sharif, Mohandessin, Cairo (Giza); tel. (2) 33453907; fax (2) 33026979; e-mail info@kenemb-cairo.com; internet kenemb-cairo.com; Ambassador Dave Arunga.

Korea, Democratic People's Republic: 6 Sharia al-Saleh Ayoub, Cairo (Zamalek); tel. (2) 3408219; fax (2) 3414615; Ambassador Ri Hyok-Chol.

Korea, Republic: 3 Sharia Boulos Hanna, Cairo (Dokki); tel. (2) 3611234; fax (2) 3611238; e-mail egypt@mofat.go.kr; internet egy.mofat.go.kr; Ambassador Kim Young-So.

Kuwait: 21 Sharia Muhammad Mazhar, Cairo (Zamalek); tel. (2) 7372120; fax (2) 7371199; Ambassador Salem Ghassab al-Zamanan.

Latvia: 8th Floor, Abou el-Feda Bldg, 3 Sharia Abou el-Feda, Cairo (Zamalek); tel. (2) 27384188; fax (2) 27384189; e-mail embassy.egypt@mfa.gov.lv; Ambassador Iveta Šulca.

Lebanon: 22 Sharia Mansour Muhammad, Cairo (Zamalek); tel. (2) 7382823; fax (2) 7382818; Ambassador Khaled Ziadeh.

Lesotho: 5 Sharia Ahmed el-Meleby, Cairo (Dokki); tel. (2) 33369161; fax (2) 25211437; e-mail lesotho-cairo@foreign.gov.ls; Ambassador Thabo Khasipe.

Liberia: 4th Floor, 9 Ahmad Samy el-Sayeh Sq., Mohandessin, Cairo; tel. (2) 37626794; fax (2) 37627194; e-mail liberiaembassy1@yahoo.com; Ambassador Alexander Wallace.

Libya: 4 Sharia Patrice Lumumba, Cairo; tel. (2) 4940286; fax 3934643; Ambassador Muhammad Fayez Abd al-Aziz Jibril.

Lithuania: 23 Muhammad Mazhar, Cairo (Zamalek); tel. (2) 27366461; fax (2) 27365130; e-mail amb.eg@mfa.lt; internet eg.mfa.lt; Ambassador Dainius Junevičius.

Malaysia: 21 Sharia el-Aanab, Mohandessin, Cairo (Giza); tel. (2) 37610013; fax (2) 37610216; e-mail malcairo@kln.gov.my; internet www.kln.gov.my/web/egy_cairo; Ambassador Datuk Ku Jaafar Ku Shaari.

Mali: POB 844, 3 Sharia al-Kansar, Cairo (Dokki); tel. and fax (2) 3371841; e-mail mali.eg@ie.eg.com; Ambassador Mamadou Kaba.

Malta: 1 Sharia el-Saleh Ayoub, Cairo (Zamalek); tel. (2) 27362368; fax (2) 27362371; e-mail maltaembassy.cairo@gov.mt; internet www.foreign.gov.mt/egypt; Ambassador George Cassar.

Mauritania: 114 Mohi el-Din, Abou-el Ezz, Mohandessin, Cairo; tel. (2) 37490671; fax (2) 37491048; Ambassador Mohamed Weld Abdulaziz.

Mauritius: 1st Floor, 33 Sharia Ismail Muhammad, Cairo (Zamalek); tel. (2) 7365208; fax (2) 7365206; e-mail cairoemb@mail.gov.mu; internet cairo.mauritius.gov.mu; Ambassador D. I. Fakim.

Mexico: 5th Floor, Apt 502–503, 17 Sharia Port Said, Maadi, 11431 Cairo; tel. (2) 23580256; fax (2) 3780059; e-mail oficial@embamexcairo.com; internet www.sre.gob.mx/egipto; Ambassador María Carmen Oñate Muñoz.

Mongolia: 14 Sharia 152, Maadi, Cairo; tel. and fax (2) 3586012; Ambassador Banzragch Odonjil.

Morocco: 10 Sharia Salah el-Din, Cairo (Zamalek); tel. (2) 27359849; fax (2) 27361937; e-mail morocemb@link.net; Ambassador Muhammad Saad al-Alami.

Mozambique: 2 Sharia Tahran, Cairo (Dokki); tel. (2) 7605505; fax (2) 7486378; e-mail tombolane2000@yahoo.com; Ambassador Artur Josefa Jamo.

Myanmar: 24 Sharia Muhammad Mazhar, Cairo (Zamalek); tel. (2) 27362644; fax (2) 7357712; Ambassador THET OO MAUNG.

Nepal: 23 Sharia al-Hassan, Mohandessin, Cairo (Dokki); tel. (2) 37612311; fax (2) 33374447; e-mail ne@nepalembassyegypt.com; Ambassador PRAHLAD KUMAR PRASAI.

Netherlands: 18 Sharia Hassan Sabri, Cairo (Zamalek); tel. (2) 27395500; fax (2) 27365249; e-mail kai@minbuza.nl; internet egypt.nlembassy.org; Ambassador GERARD STEEGHS.

New Zealand: North Tower, 8th Floor, Nile City Bldg, Sharia Corniche el-Nil, Cairo (Boulac); tel. (2) 24616000; fax (2) 24616099; e-mail enquiries@nzembassy.org.eg; internet www.nzembassy.com/egypt; Ambassador DAVID STRACHAN.

Niger: 101 Sharia Pyramids, Cairo (Giza); tel. (2) 3865607; Ambassador MOULOUD AL-HOUSSEINI.

Nigeria: 13 Sharia Gabalaya, Cairo (Zamalek); tel. (2) 3406042; fax (2) 3403907; Ambassador LAWAN GANA GUBA.

Norway: 8 Sharia el-Gezirah, Cairo (Zamalek); tel. (2) 27358046; fax (2) 27370709; e-mail emb.cairo@mfa.no; internet www.norway-egypt.org; Ambassador TOR WENNESLAND.

Oman: 52 Sharia el-Higaz, Mohandessin, Cairo; tel. (2) 27350792; fax (2) 27373188; e-mail cairo@mofa.gov.om; Ambassador Sheikh KHALIFA BIN ALI BIN ISSA AL-HARTHY.

Pakistan: 8 Sharia l-Salouli, Cairo (Dokki); tel. (2) 37487806; fax (2) 37480310; e-mail parepcairo@hotmail.com; Ambassador (vacant).

Panama: POB 62, 4A Sharia Ibn Zanki, Cairo 11211 (Zamalek); tel. (2) 3400784; fax (2) 3411092; Chargé d'affaires a.i. ROY FRANCISCO LUNA GONZÁLEZ.

Peru: 8 Sharia Kamel el-Shenawi, Cairo (Garden City); tel. (2) 3562973; fax (2) 3557985; Ambassador MANUEL VERAMENDI I. SERRA.

Philippines: Villa 28, Sharia 200, Cairo (Degla Maadi); tel. (2) 25213062; fax (2) 25213048; e-mail pe.cairo@dfa.gov.ph; Ambassador CLARO S. CRISTOBAL.

Poland: 5 Sharia el-Aziz Osman, Cairo (Zamalek); tel. (2) 27367456; fax (2) 27355427; e-mail cairo.secretariat@msz.gov.pl; internet www.kair.polemb.net; Ambassador PIOTR PUCHTA.

Portugal: 1 Sharia el-Saleh Ayoub, Cairo (Zamalek); tel. (2) 27350779; fax (2) 27350790; e-mail embpcai@link.net; Ambassador FERNANDO MACHADO.

Qatar: 10 Sharia al-Thamar, Midan al-Nasr, Madinet al-Mohandessin, Cairo; tel. (2) 7604693; fax (2) 7603618; e-mail qa.emb.cai@gmail.com; internet www.qatarembassyegypt.com; Ambassador SAIF BIN MUQADAM AL-BUAINAIN.

Romania: 6 Sharia el-Kamel Muhammad, Cairo (Zamalek); tel. (2) 27360107; fax (2) 27360851; e-mail roembegy@link.net; internet cairo.mae.ro; Ambassador CORNEL ALECSE.

Russia: 95 Sharia Giza, Cairo (Dokki); tel. (2) 37489353; fax (2) 37609074; e-mail ruemeg@tedata.net.eg; internet www.egypt.mid.ru; Ambassador SERGEI KIRPICHENKO.

Rwanda: 23 Sharia Babel, Mohandessin, Cairo (Dokki); tel. (2) 3350532; fax (2) 3351479; Ambassador (vacant).

Senegal: 46 Sharia Abd al-Moneim Riad, Mohandessin, Cairo (Dokki); tel. (2) 3460946; fax (2) 3461039; e-mail mamadousow@hotmail.com; Ambassador MAMADOU SOW.

Serbia: 33 Sharia Mansour Muhammad, Cairo (Zamalek); tel. (2) 27354061; fax (2) 27353913; e-mail serbia@serbiaeg.com; Ambassador DRAGAN BISENIĆ.

Singapore: 40 Sharia Adnan Omar Sedki, Cairo 11511 (Dokki); tel. (2) 37490468; fax (2) 37480562; e-mail singemb@link.net; internet www.mfa.gov.sg/cairo; Ambassador PREMJITH SADASIVAN.

Slovakia: 3 Sharia Adel Hussein Rostom, Dokki, Cairo (Giza); tel. (2) 33358240; fax (2) 33355810; e-mail zukahira@tedata.net.eg; Ambassador PETER ZSOLDOS.

Slovenia: 6th Floor, 21 Sharia Soliman Abaza, Mohandessin, Cairo; tel. (2) 37498171; fax (2) 37497141; e-mail vka@gov.si; internet cairo.embassy.si; Ambassador Dr ROBERT KOKALJ.

Somalia: 27 Sharia el-Somal, Cairo (Dokki), Giza; tel. (2) 3374577; Ambassador ABDULLAHI ALI HASSAN.

South Africa: Bldg 11, Intersection Rd 200 and 203, Maadi, Cairo; tel. (2) 25353000; fax (2) 25213278; e-mail saembcai@tedata.net.eg; internet saembassyinegypt.com; Ambassador NOLUTHANDO MAYENDE-SIBIYA.

Spain: 41 Sharia Ismail Muhammad, Cairo (Zamalek); tel. (2) 27356462; fax (2) 27352132; e-mail emb.elcairo@maec.es; internet www.exteriores.gob.es/embajadas/elcairo; Ambassador FIDEL SENDAGORTA GÓMEZ DEL CAMPILLO.

Sri Lanka: POB 1157, 8 Sharia Sri Lanka, Cairo (Zamalek); tel. (2) 27350047; fax (2) 27367138; e-mail slembare@menanet.net; Ambassador (vacant).

Sudan: 4 Sharia el-Ibrahimi, Cairo (Garden City); tel. (2) 3545043; fax (2) 3542693; Ambassador KAMAL HASSAN ALI.

Sweden: POB 131, 13 Sharia Muhammad Mazhar, Cairo (Zamalek); tel. (2) 27289200; fax (2) 27354357; e-mail ambassaden.kairo@gov.se; internet www.swedenabroad.com/cairo; Ambassador MALIN KÄRRE.

Switzerland: POB 633, 10 Sharia Abd al-Khalek Sarwat, 11511 Cairo; tel. (2) 25758284; fax (2) 25745236; e-mail cai.vertretung@eda.admin.ch; internet www.eda.admin.ch/cairo; Ambassador MARKUS LEITNER.

Syria: 18 Sharia Abd al-Rehim Sabry, POB 435, Cairo (Dokki); tel. (2) 3358806; fax (2) 3358232; Ambassador YOUSUF AL-AHMAD.

Tanzania: 10 Anas Ibn Malek St, Mohandessin, Cairo; tel. (2) 3374155; fax (2) 3374446; Ambassador ALI SHAURI HAJI.

Thailand: 9 Tiba St, Cairo (Dokki); tel. (2) 37603553; fax (2) 37605076; e-mail royalthai@link.net; Ambassador CHALIT MANITYAKUL.

Tunisia: 26 Sharia el-Jazirah, Cairo (Zamalek); tel. (2) 27352032; fax 27362479; e-mail tunisiacairo@link.net; Ambassador ABDELKADER AL-HAJJAR.

Turkey: 25 Sharia Felaki, Cairo (Bab el-Louk); tel. (2) 27978400; fax (2) 27978477; e-mail embassy.cairo@mfa.gov.tr; internet cairo.emb.mfa.gov.tr; Ambassador HÜSEYIN AVNI BOTSALI.

Uganda: 66 Rd 10, Maadi, Cairo; tel. (2) 3802514; fax (2) 3802504; e-mail ugembco@link.net; internet www.uganda-embassy.com; Ambassador RICHARD LAUS ANGUALIA.

Ukraine: 50 Sharia 83, Maadi, Cairo; tel. (2) 23786871; fax (2) 23786873; e-mail emb_eg@mfa.gov.ua; internet mfa.gov.ua/egypt/en; Ambassador YEVHEN KYRYLENKO.

United Arab Emirates: 4 Sharia Ibn Sina, Cairo (Giza); tel. (2) 7766102; fax 5700844; e-mail info.cairo@mofa.gov.ae; Ambassador MUHAMMAD BIN NAKHIRA AL-DAHERI.

United Kingdom: 7 Sharia Ahmad Ragheb, Cairo (Garden City); tel. (2) 27916000; fax (2) 27916135; e-mail information.cairo@fco.gov.uk; internet ukinegypt.fco.gov.uk; Ambassador JAMES WATT.

USA: 5 Sharia Tawfik Diab, Cairo (Garden City); tel. (2) 27973300; fax (2) 27973200; e-mail pressinfoegypt@state.gov; internet cairo.usembassy.gov; Ambassador ANNE W. PATTERSON.

Uruguay: 6 Sharia Lotfallah, Cairo (Zamalek); tel. (2) 7353589; fax (2) 7368123; e-mail urugemb@idsc.gov.eg; Ambassador CÉSAR WALTER FERRER BURLE.

Uzbekistan: 18 Sharia Sad el-Aali, Cairo (Dokki); tel. (2) 3361723; fax (2) 3361722; Ambassador MINOVAROV SHAAZIM SHAISLAMOVICH.

Venezuela: 43, Rd 18, el-Nahda Sq., Maadi, Cairo; tel. (2) 9812141; fax (2) 3809291; e-mail embvenez@tedata.net.eg; internet www.embavenezegypt.com; Ambassador VÍCTOR R. CARAZO.

Viet Nam: Villa 47, Sharia Ahmed Heshmat, Cairo (Zamalek); tel. (2) 7364326; fax (2) 7366091; e-mail vnembcairoeg@yahoo.com.vn; internet www.vietnamembassy-egypt.org; Ambassador DAO THANH CHUNG.

Yemen: 28 Sharia Amean al-Rafai, Cairo (Dokki); tel. (2) 3614224; fax (2) 3604815; e-mail info@yemenembassy-cairo.com; internet www.yemenembassy-cairo.com; Ambassador ABD AL-WALI ABD AL-WALITH AL-SHAMIRI.

Zimbabwe: 40 Sharia Ghaza, Mohandessin, Cairo; tel. (2) 3030404; fax (2) 3059741; e-mail zimcairo@thewayout.net; Ambassador MARGARET MUSKWE (designate).

Judicial System

The Courts of Law in Egypt are principally divided into two juridical court systems: Courts of General Jurisdiction and Administrative Courts. Since 1969 the Supreme Constitutional Court has been at the top of the Egyptian judicial structure.

Supreme Constitutional Court: Corniche el-Nil, Maadi, Cairo; tel. (2) 5246323; fax (2) 7958048; e-mail info@sccourt.gov.eg; has specific jurisdiction over: (i) judicial review of the constitutionality of laws and regulations; (ii) resolution of positive and negative jurisdictional conflicts and determination of the competent court between the different juridical court systems, e.g. Courts of General Jurisdiction and Administrative Courts, as well as other bodies exercising judicial competence; (iii) determination of disputes over the enforcement of two final but contradictory judgments rendered by two courts each belonging to a different juridical court system; (iv) rendering binding interpretation of laws or decree laws in the event of a dispute in the application of said laws or decree laws, always provided that such a dispute is of a gravity requiring conformity of interpretation under the Constitution; Pres. ADLI MAHMOUD MANSOUR.

Court of Cassation: f. 1931; highest court of general jurisdiction. Its sessions are held in Cairo. Final judgments rendered by Courts of Appeal in criminal and civil litigation may be petitioned to the Court of Cassation by the Defendant or the Public Prosecutor in criminal litigation and by any of the parties in interest in civil litigation on grounds of defective application or interpretation of the law as stated in the challenged judgment, on grounds of irregularity of form or procedure, or violation of due process, and on grounds of defective reasoning of judgment rendered. The Court of Cassation is composed of the President, 41 Vice-Presidents and 92 Justices.

Courts of Appeal: Cairo; Each Court of Appeal has geographical jurisdiction over one or more of the governorates of Egypt, and is divided into Criminal and Civil Chambers. The Criminal Chambers try felonies, and the Civil Chambers hear appeals filed against such judgment rendered by the Tribunals of First Instance where the law so stipulates. Each Chamber is composed of three Superior Judges. Each Court of Appeal is composed of the President, and sufficient numbers of Vice-Presidents and Superior Judges.

Tribunals of First Instance: In each governorate there are one or more Tribunals of First Instance, each of which is divided into several Chambers for criminal and civil litigations. Each Chamber is composed of: (a) a presiding judge, and (b) two sitting judges. A Tribunal of First Instance hears, as an Appellate Court, certain litigations as provided under the law.

District Tribunals: Each is a one-judge ancillary Chamber of a Tribunal of First Instance, having jurisdiction over minor civil and criminal litigations in smaller districts within the jurisdiction of such a Tribunal of First Instance.

Public Prosecution: Cairo; represented at all levels of the Courts of General Jurisdiction in all criminal litigations and also in certain civil litigations as required by the law. It also controls and supervises enforcement of criminal law judgments; Prosecutor-General HISHAM BARAKAT.

Administrative Courts System (Conseil d'Etat): has jurisdiction over litigations involving the State or any of its governmental agencies. It is divided into two courts: the Administrative Courts and the Judicial Administrative Courts, at the top of which is the High Administrative Court; Pres. Hon. SAMIR ABD AL-HALIM AHMAD AL-BADAWI.

The State Council: an independent judicial body, which has the authority to make decisions in administrative disputes and disciplinary cases within the judicial system; Chair. MUHAMMAD AHMAD EL-HUSSEINI.

The Supreme Judicial Council: reinstituted in 1984, having been abolished in 1969. It exists to guarantee the independence of the judicial system from outside interference and is consulted with regard to draft laws organizing the affairs of the judicial bodies; Pres. and Chair. HAMAD ABDULLAH.

Religion

According to the 1986 census, some 94% of Egyptians are Muslims (and almost all of these follow Sunni tenets). According to government figures published in the same year, there are about 2m. Copts (a figure contested by Coptic sources, whose estimates range between 6m. and 7m.), forming the largest religious minority, and about 1m. members of other Christian groups. There is also a small Jewish minority.

ISLAM

There is a Higher Council for the Islamic Call, on which sit: the Grand Sheikh of al-Azhar (Chair.); the Minister of Awqaf (Islamic Endowments); the President and Vice-President of Al-Azhar University; the Grand Mufti of Egypt; and the Secretary-General of the Higher Council for Islamic Affairs.

Grand Sheikh of Al-Azhar: Sheikh AHMED MUHAMMAD EL-TAYEB.

Grand Mufti of Egypt: Sheikh ALI GOMAA.

CHRISTIANITY

Orthodox Churches

Armenian Apostolic Orthodox Church: POB 48, 179 Sharia Ramses, Faggalah, Cairo; tel. (2) 25901385; fax (2) 25906671; e-mail armpatrcai@yahoo.com; Prelate Bishop ASHOT MNATSAKANIAN; 7,000 mems.

Coptic Orthodox Church: St Mark Cathedral, POB 9035, Anba Ruess, 222 Sharia Ramses, Abbassia, Cairo; tel. (2) 2857889; fax (2) 2825683; e-mail coptpope@copticpope.org; internet www.copticpope.org; f. AD 61; Patriarch Pope TAWADROS II; c. 13m. followers in Egypt, Sudan, other African countries, the USA, Canada, Australia, Europe and the Middle East.

Greek Orthodox Patriarchate: POB 2006, Alexandria; tel. (3) 4868595; fax (3) 4875684; e-mail patriarchate@greekorthodox-alexandria.org; internet www.greekorthodox-alexandria.org; f. AD 43; Pope and Patriarch of Alexandria and All Africa THEODOROS II; 3m. mems.

The Roman Catholic Church

Armenian Rite

The Armenian Catholic diocese of Alexandria is suffragan to the Patriarchate of Cilicia. The Patriarch is resident in Beirut, Lebanon.

Bishop of Alexandria: Rt Rev. KRIKOR-OKOSDINOS COUSSA, Patriarcat Arménien Catholique, 36 Sharia Muhammad Sabri Abou Alam, 11121 Cairo; tel. (2) 23938429; fax (2) 23932025; e-mail pacal@tedata.net.eg.

Chaldean Rite

Bishop of Cairo: Rt Rev. YOUSUF IBRAHIM SARRAF, Evêché Chaldéen, Basilique-Sanctuaire Notre Dame de Fatima, 141 Sharia Nouzha, 11316 Cairo (Heliopolis); tel. and fax (2) 26355718; e-mail fatimasarraf@yahoo.com.

Coptic Rite

Egypt comprises the Coptic Catholic Patriarchate of Alexandria and five dioceses.

Patriarch of Alexandria: Cardinal ANTONIOS NAGUIB, Patriarcat Copte Catholique, POB 69, 34 Sharia Ibn Sandar, Koubbeh Bridge, 11712 Cairo; tel. (2) 22571740; fax (2) 24545766; e-mail p_coptocattolico@yahoo.it.

Latin Rite

Egypt comprises the Apostolic Vicariate of Alexandria (incorporating Heliopolis and Port Said).

Vicar Apostolic: Rt Rev. ADEL ZAKY, 10 Sharia Sidi el-Metwalli, Alexandria; tel. (3) 4876065; fax (3) 4878169; e-mail latinvic@link.net.

Maronite Rite

Bishop of Cairo: Rt Rev. FRANÇOIS EID, Evêché Maronite, 15 Sharia Hamdi, Daher, 11271 Cairo; tel. (2) 26137373; fax (2) 25939610; e-mail feid43@yahoo.com.

Melkite Rite

His Beatitude Grégoire III Laham (resident in Damascus, Syria) is the Greek-Melkite Patriarch of Antioch and all the East, of Alexandria, and of Jerusalem.

Patriarchal Exarchate of Egypt and Sudan: Greek Melkite Catholic Patriarchate, 16 Sharia Daher, 11271 Cairo; tel. (2) 25905790; fax (2) 25935398; e-mail grecmelkitecath_egy@hotmail.com; 6,200 adherents (31 December 2007); General Patriarchal Vicar for Egypt and Sudan Most Rev. Archbishop GEORGES BAKAR (Titular Archbishop of Pelusium).

Syrian Rite

Bishop of Cairo: Rt Rev. CLÉMENT-JOSEPH HANNOUCHE, Evêché Syrien Catholique, 46 Sharia Daher, 11271 Cairo; tel. (2) 25901234; fax (2) 25923932.

The Anglican Communion

The Anglican diocese of Egypt, suspended in 1958, was revived in 1974 and became part of the Episcopal Church in Jerusalem and the Middle East, formally inaugurated in January 1976. The Province has four dioceses: Jerusalem, Egypt, Cyprus and the Gulf, and Iran, and its President is the Bishop in Egypt. The Bishop in Egypt has jurisdiction also over the Anglican chaplaincies in Algeria, Djibouti, Eritrea, Ethiopia, Libya, Somalia and Tunisia.

Bishop in Egypt: Rt Rev. Dr MOUNEER HANNA ANIS, Diocesan Office, POB 87, 5 Sharia Michel Lutfalla, 11211 Cairo (Zamalek); tel. (2) 7380829; fax (2) 7358941; e-mail diocese@link.net; internet www.dioceseofegypt.org.

Other Christian Churches

Coptic Evangelical Organization for Social Services: POB 162, 11811 El Panorama, Cairo; tel. (2) 26221425; fax (2) 26221434; e-mail gm@ceoss.org.eg; internet www.ceoss.org.eg; Chair. Dr MERVAT AKHNOUKH ABSAKHROUN; Dir-Gen. Dr NABIL SAMUEL ABADIR.

Other denominations active in Egypt include the Coptic Evangelical Church (Synod of the Nile) and the Union of the Armenian Evangelical Churches in the Near East.

JUDAISM

The 1986 census recorded 794 Jews in Egypt, and there were reported to be around 40 remaining by the 2013.

Jewish Community: Main Synagogue, Shaar Hashamayim 17, Adly St, Cairo; tel. (2) 4824613; fax (2) 7369639; e-mail bassatine@yahoo.com; f. 19th century; Pres. MAGDA HAROUN.

The Press

Despite a fairly high illiteracy rate in Egypt, the country's press is well developed. Cairo is one of the region's largest publishing centres.

All newspapers and magazines are supervised, according to law, by the Supreme Press Council. The four major state-owned publishing houses of Al-Ahram Establishment, Dar al-Hilal, Dar Akhbar el-Yom and El-Tahrir Printing and Publishing House operate as separate entities and compete with each other commercially.

DAILIES

Al-Ahram (The Pyramids): Sharia al-Galaa, Cairo 11511; tel. (2) 5801600; fax (2) 5786023; e-mail ahramdaily@ahram.org.eg; internet www.ahram.org.eg; f. 1875; morning, incl. Sun.; Arabic; international edn publ. in London, United Kingdom; North American edn publ. in New York, USA; Chair. ABD EL-MONEIM SAÏD; Chief Editor ABD EL-NASSER SALAMA; circ. 900,000 (weekdays), 1.1m. (Fri.).

Al-Ahram al-Massa'i (The Evening Al-Ahram): Sharia al-Galaa, Cairo 11511; e-mail massai@ahram.org.eg; internet massai.ahram.org.eg; f. 1990; evening; Arabic; Editor-in-Chief MURSI ATALLAH.

Al-Ahrar: 58 Manshyet al-Sadr, Kobry al-Kobba, Cairo; tel. (2) 4823046; fax (2) 4823027; e-mail sawtalahrar@hotmail.com; internet www.sawt-alahrar.net; f. 1977; organ of Liberal Party; Editor-in-Chief SALAH QABADAYA.

Al-Akhbar (The News): Dar Akhbar el-Yom, 6 Sharia al-Sahafa, Cairo; tel. (2) 25782600; fax (2) 25782530; e-mail akhbarelyom@akhbarelyom.org; internet www.elakhbar.org.eg; f. 1952; Arabic; Chair. MUHAMMAD MAHDI FADLI; Editor-in-Chief MUHAMMAD HASSAN EL-BANNA; circ. 850,000.

Arev: 10 Sharia Menouf, Cairo; tel. (2) 24170204; e-mail arev@intouch.com; f. 1915; evening; Armenian; official organ of the Armenian Liberal Democratic Party; Editor ASSBED ARTINIAN.

Al-Dustour (The Constitution): nr Kobri al-Gamaa, Cairo (Giza); tel. (2) 33379008; fax (2) 33379766; internet www.dostor.org; f. 1995; banned by the authorities in 1998; relaunched in 2005; daily and weekly edns; independent; Editor-in-Chief IBRAHIM ISSA.

The Egyptian Gazette: 111–115 Sharia Ramses, Cairo; tel. (2) 5783333; fax (2) 5784646; e-mail ask@egyptiangazette.net.eg; internet www.egyptiangazette.net.eg; f. 1880; morning; English; Chair. MUHAMMAD ABD AL-HADEED; Editor-in-Chief RAMADAN A. KADER; circ. 90,000.

Al-Gomhouriya (The Republic): 24 Sharia Zakaria Ahmad, Cairo; tel. (2) 25781515; fax (2) 25781717; e-mail eltahrir@eltahrir.net; internet www.algomhuria.net.eg; f. 1953; morning; Arabic; mainly economic affairs; Chair. MUHAMMAD ABU HADID; Editor-in-Chief ABD EL-AZIM EL-BABLI; circ. 800,000.

Al-Masry al-Youm: Cairo; tel. (2) 27980100; fax (2) 27926331; e-mail admin@almasry-alyoum.com; internet www.almasry-alyoum.com; f. 2003; Arabic; independent, privately owned; Editor-in-Chief MAGDY AL-GALAD; circ. 100,000.

Al-Misaa' (The Evening): 24 Sharia Zakaria Ahmad, Cairo; tel. (2) 5781010; fax (2) 5784747; e-mail eltahrir@eltahrir.net; internet www.almessa.net.eg; f. 1956; evening; Arabic; political, social and sport; Editor-in-Chief MUHAMMAD FOUDAH; Man. Dir ABD AL-HAMROSE; circ. 450,000.

Le Progrès Egyptien: 24 Sharia Zakaria Ahmad, Cairo; tel. (2) 5783333; fax (2) 5781110; e-mail ask@progres.net.eg; internet www.progres.net.eg; f. 1893; morning incl. Sun.; French; Chair. ALI HACHEM; Editor-in-Chief AHMED AL-BARDISSI; circ. 60,000.

La Réforme: 8 Passage Sherif, Alexandria; French.

Al-Wafd: 1 Sharia Boulos Hanna, Cairo (Dokki); tel. (2) 33383111; fax (2) 33359135; e-mail contact@alwafd.org; internet www.alwafd.org; f. 1984; organ of the New Wafd Party; Editor-in-Chief ABBAS AL-TARABILI; circ. 220,000.

PERIODICALS

Al-Ahaly (The People): Sharia Kareem al-Dawli, Tala'at Harb Sq., Cairo; tel. (2) 7786583; fax (2) 3900412; internet www.al-ahaly.com; f. 1978; weekly; publ. by Nat. Progressive Unionist Party; Chair. LOTFI WAKID; Editor-in-Chief ABD AL-BAKOURY.

Al-Ahram al-Arabi: Sharia al-Galaa, Cairo 11511; tel. (2) 5786100; e-mail arabi@ahram.org.eg; internet arabi.ahram.org.eg; f. 1997; weekly (Sat.); Arabic; political, social and economic affairs; Editor-in-Chief ABD EL-ATTI MUHAMMAD.

Al-Ahram al-Dimouqratiyah (Democracy Review): Sharia al-Galaa, Cairo 11511; tel. (2) 25786960; fax (2) 27705238; e-mail democracy@ahram.org.eg; internet democracy.ahram.org.eg; f. 2001; quarterly; politics; Arabic and English; publ. by Al-Ahram Establishment; Editor-in-Chief HALA MUSTAFA.

Al-Ahram Hebdo: POB 1057, Sharia al-Galaa, Cairo 11511; tel. (2) 27703100; fax (2) 27703314; e-mail hebdo@ahram.org.eg; internet hebdo.ahram.org.eg; f. 1993; weekly (Wed.); French; publ. by Al-Ahram Establishment; Editor-in-Chief MUHAMMAD SALMAWI.

Al-Ahram al-Iqtisadi (The Economic Al-Ahram): Sharia al-Galaa, Cairo 11511; tel. (2) 25786100; fax (2) 25786833; e-mail ik@ahram.org.eg; internet ik.ahram.org.eg; Arabic; weekly (Mon.); economic and political affairs; publ. by Al-Ahram Establishment; Chief Editor ISSAM RIFA'AT; circ. 10,000.

Al-Ahram Weekly (The Pyramids): Al-Ahram Bldg, Sharia al-Galaa, Cairo 11511; tel. (2) 5786100; fax (2) 5786833; e-mail weeklyweb@ahram.org.eg; internet weekly.ahram.org.eg; f. 1989; English; weekly; publ. by Al-Ahram Establishment; Man. Editor GALAL NASSER; Editor-in-Chief ASSEM EL-KERSH; circ. 150,000.

Akhbar al-Adab: 6 Sharia al-Sahafa, Cairo; tel. (2) 5795620; fax (2) 5782510; e-mail akhbarelyom@akhbarelyom.org; internet www.akhbarelyom.org.eg/adab; f. 1993; literature and arts for young people; Editor-in-Chief ABLA AL-RUWAYNI.

Akhbar al-Hawadith: 6 Sharia al-Sahafa, Cairo; tel. (2) 5782600; fax (2) 5782510; e-mail akhbarelyom@akhbarelyom.org; internet www.akhbarelyom.org.eg/hawadeth; f. 1993; weekly; crime reports; Editor-in-Chief MUHAMMAD BARAKAT.

Akhbar al-Nogoom: 6 Sharia al-Sahafa, Cairo; tel. (2) 5782600; fax (2) 5782510; e-mail akhbarelyom@akhbarelyom.org; internet www.akhbarelyom.org.eg/nogoom; f. 1991; weekly; theatre and film news; Editor-in-Chief AMAL OSMAN.

Akhbar al-Riadah: 6 Sharia al-Sahafa, Cairo; tel. (2) 5782600; fax (2) 5782510; e-mail akhbarelyom@akhbarelyom.org; internet www.akhbarelyom.org.eg/riada; f. 1990; weekly; sport; Editor-in-Chief IBRAHIM HEGAZY.

Akhbar al-Sayarat: 6 Sharia al-Sahafa, Cairo; e-mail akhbarelyom@akhbarelyom.org; internet www.akhbarelyom.org.eg/sayarat; f. 1998; car magazine; Editor-in-Chief SOLIMAN QENAWI.

Akhbar el-Yom (Daily News): 6 Sharia al-Sahafa, Cairo; tel. (2) 25782600; fax (2) 25782520; e-mail akhbarelyom@akhbarelyom.org; internet www.akhbarelyom.org.eg; f. 1944; weekly (Sat.); Arabic; Chair. MUHAMMAD MAHDI FADLI; Editor-in-Chief SOLIMAN EL-QENAWI; circ. 1,184,611.

Akher Sa'a (Last Hour): Dar Akhbar el-Yom, Sharia al-Sahafa, Cairo; tel. (2) 5782600; fax (2) 5782530; e-mail akhbarelyom@akhbarelyom.org; internet www.akhbarelyom.org.eg/akhersaa; f. 1934; weekly (Sun.); Arabic; independent; consumer and news magazine; Editor-in-Chief MAHMOUD SALAH; circ. 150,000.

Aqidaty (My Faith): 24–26 Sharia Zakaria Ahmad, Cairo; tel. (2) 5783333; fax (2) 5781110; e-mail eltahrir@eltahrir.net; internet www.aqidati.net.eg; weekly; Arabic; Islamic newspaper; Editor-in-Chief ABD AL-RAOUF EL-SAYED; circ. 300,000.

Business Monthly: 33 Soliman Abaza St, Cairo (Giza); tel. (2) 33381050; fax (2) 33381060; e-mail publications@amcham.org.eg; internet www.amcham.org.eg/resources_publications/publications/business_monthly; f. 1985; English; monthly; business; publ. by the American Chamber of Commerce in Egypt; Editor-in-Chief BERTIL G. PETERSON; circ. 9,000.

Business Today Egypt: 3A Sharia 199, IBA Media Bldg, Degla, Maadi, Cairo; tel. (2) 27555000; fax (2) 27555050; e-mail editor@businesstodayegypt.com; internet www.businesstodayegypt.com; f. 1994; English; monthly; business, economics and politics; publ. by IBA Media Group; Editor PATRICK FITZPATRICK.

Al-Da'wa (The Call): Cairo; monthly; Arabic; organ of the Muslim Brotherhood.

Egypt Today: 3A Sharia 199, IBA Media Bldg, Degla, Maadi, Cairo; tel. (2) 27555000; fax (2) 27555050; e-mail editor@egypttoday.com; internet www.egypttoday.com; f. 1979; monthly; English; current affairs; publ. by IBA Media Group; Editor-in-Chief Dr MURSI SAAD EL-DIN; circ. 11,500–14,500.

Egyptian Cotton Gazette: POB 1772, 12 Muhammad Talaat Nooman St, Ramel Station, Alexandria; tel. (3) 4806971; fax (3) 4873002; e-mail alcotexa@tedata.net.eg; internet www.alcotexa.org; f. 1947; 2 a year; English; organ of the Alexandria Cotton Exporters' Asscn; Chief Editor GALAL AL-REFAI.

El-Elm Magazine (Sciences): 24 Sharia Zakaria Ahmad, Cairo; tel. (2) 5781010; fax (2) 5784747; e-mail ask@elm.net.eg; internet www.elm.net.eg; f. 1976; monthly; Arabic; publ. with the Academy of Scientific Research in Egypt; circ. 70,000.

The Employer: 4 el-Marwa Bldgs, blk 2, Ahmad Taysir St, Heliopolis, Cairo; tel. and fax (2) 24189939; e-mail info@the-employer.com; internet www.the-employer.net; English; bi-monthly; employment; Man. Dir DINA MAKKAWI.

El-Fagr (The Dawn): Cairo; tel. (2) 33442306; fax (2) 33032344; e-mail info@elfagr.net; internet www.elfagr.org; f. 2005; Arabic; weekly; independent; Editor-in-Chief ADEL HAMMOUDA.

El Gouna Magazine: 66 Abu el-Mahasen el-Shazli St, 4th Floor, Agouza, Cairo; tel. (2) 33034654; e-mail editor@elgounamag.com;

internet www.elgounamag.com; f. 2000; English; quarterly; lifestyle; Gen. Man. MARYSE RAAD.

Hawa'a (Eve): Dar al-Hilal, 16 Sharia Muhammad Ezz el-Arab, Cairo 11511; tel. (2) 3625450; fax (2) 3625469; f. 1892; weekly (Sat.); Arabic; women's magazine; Chief Editor EKBAL BARAKA; circ. 210,502.

Al-Hilal: Dar al-Hilal, 16 Sharia Muhammad Ezz el-Arab, Cairo 11511; tel. (2) 3625450; fax (2) 3625469; f. 1895; monthly; Arabic; literary; Editor MAIDI AL-SAYID AL-DAQAQ.

Horreyati: 24 Sharia Zakaria Ahmad, Cairo; tel. (2) 5781010; fax (2) 5784747; e-mail eltahrir@eltahrir.net; internet www.horreyati.net.eg; f. 1990; weekly; social, cultural and sport; Editor-in-Chief MUHAMMAD NOUR EL-DIN; circ. 250,000.

Al-Kawakeb (The Stars): Dar al-Hilal, 16 Sharia Muhammad Ezz el-Arab, Cairo 11511; tel. (2) 3625450; fax (2) 3625469; f. 1952; weekly; Arabic; film magazine; Editor-in-Chief FAWZI MUHAMMAD IBRAHIM; circ. 86,381.

El-Keraza (The Sermon): St Mark Cathedral, POB 9035, Anba Ruess, 222 Sharia Ramses, Abbassia, Cairo; e-mail coptpope@tecmina.com; internet www.copticpope.org; fortnightly newspaper of the Coptic Orthodox Church; Arabic and English; Editor-in-Chief (vacant).

Al-Kora wal-Malaeb (Football and Playgrounds): 24 Sharia Zakaria Ahmad, Cairo; tel. (2) 5783333; fax (2) 5784747; internet www.koura.net.eg; f. 1976; weekly; Arabic; sport; circ. 150,000.

Al-Liwa' al-Islami (Islamic Standard): 11 Sharia Sherif Pasha, Cairo; f. 1982; weekly; Arabic; govt paper to promote official view of Islamic revivalism; Propr AHMAD HAMZA; Editor MUHAMMAD ALI SHETA; circ. 30,000.

Magallat al-Mohandessin (The Engineer's Magazine): 30 Sharia Ramses, Cairo; e-mail info@eea.org.eg; internet www.eea.org.eg; f. 1945; publ. by The Engineers' Syndicate; 10 a year; Arabic and English; Editor and Sec. MAHMOUD SAMI ABD AL-KAWI.

Medical Journal of Cairo University: Qasr el-Eini Hospital, Sharia Qasr el-Eini, Cairo; tel. and fax (2) 3655768; internet www.medicaljournalofcairouniversity.com; f. 1933; Qasr el-Eini Clinical Society; quarterly; English; Editor-in-Chief AHMAD SAMEH FARID.

The Middle East Observer: 41 Sharia Sherif, Cairo; tel. and fax (2) 3939732; e-mail info@meobserver.com; internet middleeastobserver.com; f. 1954; weekly; English; specializes in economics of Middle East and African markets; also publishes supplements on law, foreign trade and tenders; agent for IMF, UN and IDRC publs, distributor of World Bank publs; Publr AHMAD FODA; Chief Editor HESHAM A. RAOUF; circ. 20,000.

Al-Mussawar: Dar al-Hilal, 16 Sharia Muhammad Ezz el-Arab, Cairo 11511; tel. (2) 3625450; fax (2) 3625469; f. 1924; weekly; Arabic; news; Chair. and Editor-in-Chief ABD AL-KADER SHUHAYIB; circ. 130,423.

Nesf al-Donia: Sharia al-Galaa, Cairo 11511; tel. (2) 5786100; internet www.ahram.org.eg; f. 1990; weekly; Arabic; women's magazine; publ. by Al-Ahram Establishment; Editor-in-Chief AFKAR EL-KHARADLI.

October: Dar al-Maaref, 1119 Sharia Corniche el-Nil, Cairo; tel. (2) 25777077; fax (2) 25744999; internet www.octobermag.com; f. 1976; weekly; Arabic; Chair. and Editor-in-Chief ISMAIL MUNTASSIR; circ. 140,500.

Al-Omal (The Workers): 90 Sharia al-Galaa, Cairo; internet www.etufegypt.com; weekly; Arabic; publ. by the Egyptian Trade Union Federation; Chief Editor AHMAD HARAK.

Le Progrès Dimanche: 24 Sharia al-Galaa, Cairo; tel. (2) 5781010; fax (2) 5784747; e-mail ask@progres.net.eg; internet leprogresdimanche.newspaperdirect.com; weekly; French; Sun. edition of *Le Progrès Egyptien*; Editor-in-Chief KHALED ANWAR BAKIR; circ. 35,000.

La Revue d'Egypte: 3A Sharia 199, IBA Media Bldg, Degla, Maadi, Cairo; tel. (2) 27555000; fax (2) 27555050; e-mail courrier@iba-media.com; internet www.larevuedegypte.com; f. 2002; monthly; French; current affairs, culture, lifestyle; publ. by IBA Media Group; Editor-in-Chief FRÉDÉRIC MIGEON.

Rose al-Yousuf: 89A Sharia Qasr el-Eini, Cairo; tel. (2) 7923514; fax (2) 7925540; e-mail info@rosaonline.net; internet www.rosaonline.net; f. 1925; weekly; Arabic; political; circulates throughout all Arab countries; Editor-in-Chief ABDULLAH KAMAL EL-SAYED; circ. 35,000.

Sabah al-Kheir (Good Morning): 89A Sharia Qasr el-Eini, Cairo; tel. (2) 27950367; fax (2) 27923509; e-mail noor@rosaonline.net; internet www.rosaonline.net/Sabah; f. 1956; weekly (Tue.); Arabic; light entertainment; Chief Editor MUHAMMAD ABD AL-NOUR; circ. 70,000.

Al-Shaab (The People): 313 Sharia Port Said, Sayeda Zeinab, Cairo; tel. (2) 3909716; fax (2) 3900283; e-mail elshaab@idsc.gov.eg; internet www.alshaab.com; f. 1979; bi-weekly (Tue. and Fri.); organ of Socialist Labour Party; pro-Islamist; Editor-in-Chief MAGDI AHMAD HUSSEIN; circ. 130,000.

Shashati (My Screen): 24 Sharia Zakaria Ahmad, Cairo; tel. (2) 5781010; fax (2) 5784747; e-mail eltahrir@eltahrir.net; internet www.shashati.net.eg; weekly; art, culture, fashion and television news.

Al-Siyassa al-Dawliya: Al-Ahram Bldg, 12th Floor, Sharia al-Galaa, Cairo 11511; tel. (2) 25786071; fax (2) 25792899; e-mail siyassa@ahram.org.eg; internet www.siyassa.org.eg; f. 1965; quarterly; politics and foreign affairs; publ. by Al-Ahram Establishment; Man. Editor KAREN ABOUL KHEIR; Editor-in-Chief MUHAMMAD ABD EL-SALAM.

Tabibak al-Khass (Family Doctor): Dar al-Hilal, 16 Sharia Muhammad Ezz el-Arab, Cairo; tel. (2) 3625473; fax (2) 3625442; monthly; Arabic.

Watani (My Country): 27 Sharia Abd al-Khalek Sarwat, Cairo; tel. (2) 23927201; fax (2) 23935946; e-mail watani@watani.com.eg; internet www.wataninet.com; f. 1958; weekly (Sun.); Arabic and English, with French supplement; independent newspaper addressing Egyptians in general and the Christian Copts in particular; Editor-in-Chief YOUSSEF SIDHOM; circ. 60,000–100,000.

NEWS AGENCY

Middle East News Agency (MENA): POB 1165, 17 Sharia Hoda Sharawi, Cairo; tel. (2) 3933000; fax (2) 3935055; e-mail newsroom@mena.org.eg; internet www.mena.org.eg; f. 1955; regular service in Arabic, English and French; Chair. and Editor-in-Chief ABDULLAH HASSAN ABD AL-FATTAH.

PRESS ASSOCIATIONS

Egyptian Press Syndicate: Cairo; Chair. MAKRAM MUHAMMAD AHMED.

Foreign Press Association: 2 Sharia Ahmad Ragheb, Cairo (Garden City); tel. (2) 27943727; fax (2) 27943747; e-mail info@fpaegypt.net; internet www.fpaegypt.net; f. 1972; Chair. VOLKHARD WINDFUHR.

Publishers

The General Egyptian Book Organization: POB 235, Sharia Corniche el-Nil, Cairo (Boulac) 11221; tel. (2) 25779283; fax (2) 25789316; e-mail info@egyptianbook.org.eg; internet www.egyptianbook.org.eg; f. 1961; affiliated to the Ministry of Culture; editing, publishing and distribution; organizer of Cairo International Book Fair; Chair. AHMED MEGAHED; Gen. Dir AHMAD SALAH ZAKI.

Al-Ahram Establishment: Al-Ahram Bldg, 6 Sharia al-Galaa, Cairo 11511; tel. (2) 5786100; fax (2) 5786023; e-mail ahram@ahram.org.eg; internet www.ahram.org.eg; f. 1875; state-owned; publishes newspapers, magazines and books, incl. *Al-Ahram*; Chair. ABD EL-MONEIM SAÏD; Dep. Chair. and Gen. Man. ALI GHONEIM.

Dar Akhbar el-Yom: 6 Sharia al-Sahafa, Cairo; tel. (2) 5748100; fax (2) 5748895; e-mail akhbarelyom@akhbarelyom.org; internet www.akhbarelyom.org.eg; f. 1944; state-owned; publs include *Al-Akhbar* (daily), *Akhbar el-Yom* (weekly) and *Akher Sa'a* (weekly); Chair. MUHAMMAD MAHDI FADLI.

American University in Cairo Press: 113 Sharia Qasr el-Eini, POB 2511, Cairo 11511; tel. (2) 27976926; fax (2) 27941440; e-mail aucpress@aucegypt.edu; internet aucpress.com; f. 1960; political history, economics, Egyptology and Arabic literature in English translation; Dir Dr NIGEL FLETCHER-JONES.

Boustany's Publishing House: 4 Sharia Aly Tawfik Shousha, Cairo (Nasr City) 11371; tel. and fax (2) 2623085; e-mail boustany@link.net; internet www.boustanys.com; f. 1900; fiction, poetry, history, biography, philosophy, language, literature, politics, religion, archaeology and Egyptology; Chief Exec. FADWA BOUSTANY.

Elias Modern Publishing House: 1 Sharia Kenisset al-Rum El-Kathulik, Daher, Cairo 11271; tel. (2) 25903756; fax (2) 25880091; e-mail info@eliaspublishing.com; internet www.eliaspublishing.com; f. 1913; publishing, printing and distribution; publ. dictionaries, children's books, and books on linguistics, poetry and arts; Chair. NADIM ELIAS; Man. Dir LAURA KFOURY.

Dar al-Farouk: 12 Sharia Dokki, 6th Floor, Cairo (Giza); tel. (2) 37622830; fax (2) 33380474; e-mail support@darelfarouk.com.eg; internet www.darelfarouk.com.eg; wide range of books incl. educational, history, science and business; Chair. FAROUK M. AL-AMARY; Gen. Man. Dr KHALED F. AL-AMARY.

Dar al-Gomhouriya: 24 Sharia Zakaria Ahmad, Cairo; tel. (2) 5781010; fax (2) 5784747; e-mail eltahrir@eltahrir.net; internet www.algomhuria.net.eg; state-owned; affiliate of El-Tahrir Printing and Publishing House; publs include the dailies *Al-Gomhouriya*, *Al-Misaa'*, *The Egyptian Gazette* and *Le Progrès Egyptien*; Pres. MUHAMMAD ABOUL HADID.

Dar al-Hilal: 16 Sharia Muhammad Ezz el-Arab, Cairo 11511; tel. (2) 3625450; fax (2) 3625469; f. 1892; state-owned; publs include *Al-*

Hilal, Kitab al-Hilal, Tabibak al-Khass (monthlies); *Al-Mussawar, Al-Kawakeb, Hawa'a* (weeklies); Chair. ABD AL-KADER SHUHAYIB.

Dar al-Kitab al-Masri: POB 156, 33 Sharia Qasr el-Nil, Cairo 11511; tel. (2) 3922168; fax (2) 3924657; e-mail info@daralkitabalmasri.com; internet www.daralkitabalmasri.com; f. 1929; publishing, printing and distribution; publrs of books on Islam and history, as well as dictionaries, encyclopaedias, textbooks, children's and general interest books; Pres. and Dir-Gen. Dr HASSAN EL-ZEIN.

Dar al-Maaref: 1119 Sharia Corniche el-Nil, Cairo; tel. (2) 25777077; fax (2) 25744999; e-mail maaref@idselgov.eg; internet www.octobermag.com; f. 1890; publishing, printing and distribution of wide variety of books in Arabic and other languages; publrs of *October* magazine; Chair. ISMAIL MUNTASSIR.

Maktabet Misr: POB 16, 3 Sharia Kamal Sidki, Cairo; tel. (2) 5898553; fax (2) 7870051; e-mail info@misrbookshop.com; f. 1932; fiction, biographies and textbooks for schools and universities; Man. AMIR SAID GOUDA EL-SAHHAR.

Dar al-Masri al-Lubnani: 16 Sharia Abd al-Khalek Sarwat, Cairo; tel. (2) 3910250; fax (2) 3909618; e-mail info@almasriah.com; internet www.almasriah.com; Arabic literature, history, sciences, textbooks and children's books; Chair. MUHAMMAD RASHED.

Nahdet Misr Group: al-Nahda Tower, 21 Sharia Ahmad Orabi, Sphinx Sq., Mohandessin, Cairo (Giza); tel. (2) 33464903; fax (2) 33462576; e-mail publishing@nahdetmisr.com; internet www.nahdetmisr.com; f. 1938; fiction, children's literature and educational books; also publishes magazines, incl. *Mickey* (weekly); Chair. MUHAMMAD AHMAD IBRAHIM.

Dar al-Nashr (fmrly Les Editions Universitaires d'Egypte): POB 1347, 41 Sharia Sherif, Cairo 11511; tel. (2) 3934606; fax (2) 3921997; f. 1947; university textbooks, academic works and encyclopaedias.

National Centre for Educational Research and Development: 12 Sharia Waked, el-Borg el-Faddy, POB 836, Cairo; tel. (2) 3930981; f. 1956; fmrly Documentation and Research Centre for Education (Ministry of Education); bibliographies, directories, information and education bulletins; Dir Prof. ABD EL-FATTAH GALAL.

National Library Press (Dar al-Kutub): POB 11638, 8 Sharia al-Sabtteya, Cairo; tel. (2) 5750886; fax (2) 5765634; e-mail info@darelkotob.org; internet www.darelkotob.org; bibliographic works; Chair. Dr MUHAMMAD SABER ARAB.

Safeer Publishing: POB 425, Cairo (Dokki); tel. (2) 37608703; fax (2) 37608650; internet www.safeer.com.eg; f. 1982; children's books; Pres. MUHAMMAD ABD EL-LATIF.

Dar al-Shorouk: 8 Sibaweh al-Masri, Cairo (Nasr City) 11371; tel. (2) 24023399; fax (2) 24037567; e-mail dar@shorouk.com; internet www.shorouk.com; f. 1968; publishing, printing and distribution; publrs of books on current affairs, history, Islamic studies, literature, art and children's books; Chair. IBRAHIM EL-MOALLEM.

El-Tahrir Printing and Publishing House: 24 Sharia Zakaria Ahmad, Cairo; tel. (2) 5781222; fax (2) 2784747; e-mail eltahrir@eltahrir.net; internet www.eltahrir.net; f. 1953; state-owned; Pres. and Chair. of Bd ALI HASHIM.

Dar el-Thaqafa: Coptic Evangelical Organization for Social Services, Sharia Dr Ahmed Zaki, Cairo; tel. (2) 6221425; internet www.darelthaqafa.com; publishing dept of the Coptic Evangelical Org. for Social Services; publishes books on social issues as well as on spiritual and theological topics; Dir Rev. Dr ANDREA ZAKI STEPHANOUS.

Broadcasting and Communications

TELECOMMUNICATIONS

Egyptian Company for Mobile Services (MobiNil): The World Trade Center, 2005C, Corniche el-Nil, Boulaq, Cairo; tel. (2) 25747000; fax (2) 25747111; e-mail customercare@mobinil.com; internet www.mobinil.com; began operation of the existing state-controlled mobile telecommunications network in 1998; owned by France Télécom (93.9%) and Orascom Telecom (5%); 32.9m. subscribers (2011); Chair. ISKANDER N. (ALEX) SHALABY; CEO YVES GAUTHIER.

Etisalat Misr: POB 11, S4 Down Town, Sharia 90, 5th Compound, New Cairo; tel. (2) 35346333; internet www.etisalat.com.eg; f. 2007 as Egypt's third mobile telephone service provider; subsidiary of Etisalat (United Arab Emirates); Chair. GAMAL EL-SADAT; CEO SALEH EL-ABDOULI.

Orascom Telecom: 2005A Nile City Towers, South Tower, Corniche el-Nil, Ramlet Beaulac, 11221 Cairo; tel. (2) 24615050; fax (2) 24615054; e-mail info@orascom.com; internet www.orascomtelecom.com; Chair. JO LUNDER; Group CEO AHMED ABU DOMA.

Telecom Egypt: POB 2271, Sharia Ramses, Cairo 11511; tel. (2) 25793444; fax (2) 25744244; e-mail telecomegypt@telecomegypt.com.eg; internet www.telecomegypt.com.eg; f. 1957; provider of fixed-line telephone services; CEO and Man. Dir TAREK ABOU ALAM; Chair. AKIL HAMED BESHIR.

Vodafone Egypt: 7A Corniche el-Nil, Maadi, 11431 Cairo; tel. (2) 25292000; e-mail public.relations@vodafone.com; internet www.vodafone.com.eg; f. 1998 by the MisrFone consortium; mobile telephone service provider; majority-owned by Vodafone Int. (United Kingdom); 36.3m. subscribers (Dec. 2011); Chair. IAN GRAY; CEO HATEM DOWIDAR.

Regulatory Authority

National Telecommunications Regulatory Authority (NTRA): Smart Village, Bldg No. 4, km 28, Sharia Cairo–Alexandria, Cairo; tel. (2) 35344000; fax (2) 35344155; e-mail info@tra.gov.eg; internet www.ntra.gov.eg; f. 2000; Chair. ATIF HELMI (Minister of Communications and Information Technology); Exec. Pres. Dr AMR BADAWI.

BROADCASTING

Radio and Television

Egyptian Radio and Television Union (ERTU): POB 11511, Cairo 1186; tel. (2) 5787120; fax (2) 746989; e-mail info@ertu.org; internet www.ertu.org; f. 1928; home service radio programmes in Arabic, English and French; foreign services in Arabic, English, French, German, Spanish, Portuguese, Italian, Swahili, Hausa, Urdu, Indonesian, Pashtu, Farsi, Turkish, Somali, Uzbek, Albanian, Afar, Amharic; operates 2 national and 6 regional television channels; also owns the satellite television network Nile TV, which offers 12 specialized channels; Pres. AHMAD ANIS.

Dreams TV: 23 Polis Hana St, Cairo (Giza); tel. (2) 7492817; fax (2) 7410949; e-mail urquestions@dreams.tv; internet www.dreams.tv; f. 2001; privately owned satellite television station; broadcasts on Dream 1 and Dream 2 networks, providing sports, music and entertainment programmes; Chair. Dr AHMAD BAHGAT.

El-Mehwar TV: Cairo; e-mail ElMehwar@ElMehwar.tv; internet www.elmehwar.tv; f. 2001; privately owned; entertainment and current affairs programmes; Founder Dr HASSAN RATEB.

Middle East Radio: Société Egyptienne de Publicité, 24–26 Sharia Zakaria Ahmad, Cairo; tel. (2) 5781010; fax (2) 5784747; e-mail radioinfo@ertu.org; internet ertu.org/radio/mideast.html.

Finance

(cap. = capital; res = reserves; dep. = deposits; m. = million; brs = branches; amounts in Egyptian pounds, unless otherwise stated)

BANKING

Central Bank

Central Bank of Egypt (CBE): 31 Sharia Qasr el-Nil, Cairo; tel. (2) 27702770; fax (2) 23925045; e-mail info@cbe.org.eg; internet www.cbe.org.eg; f. 1961; controls Egypt's monetary policy and supervises the banking sector; cap. 1,000m., res 1,543.7m., dep. 211,861.5m. (June 2007); Gov. and Chair. Dr FAROUK ABD EL-BAKY EL-OKDAH; 4 brs.

Commercial and Specialized Banks

Bank of Alexandria: 49 Sharia Qasr el-Nil, Cairo; tel. (2) 23913822; fax (2) 23919805; e-mail info@alexbank.com; internet www.alexbank.com; f. 1957; 80% stake acquired by Gruppo Sanpaolo IMI (Italy) in Oct. 2006; cap. 800m., res 977m., dep. 31,640m. (Dec. 2011); Chair. and Man. Dir BRUNO GAMBA; 196 brs.

Banque du Caire, SAE: POB 9022, Banque du Caire Tower, 6 Sharia Dr Moustafa Abu Zahra, Nasr City, Cairo 11371; tel. (2) 2647400; fax (2) 403725; e-mail intl.division@bdc.com.eg; internet www.bdc.com.eg; f. 1952; state-owned; privatization pending; cap. 1,600m., res 991m., dep. 39,224m. (June 2010); Chair. and CEO MOUNIR ABD EL-WAHAB EL-ZAHID; 216 brs.

Banque Misr, SAE: 151 Sharia Muhammad Farid, Cairo; tel. (2) 3912711; fax (2) 3919779; e-mail staff@banquemisr.com.eg; internet www.banquemisr.com.eg; f. 1920; merger with Misr Exterior Bank in 2004; privatization pending; cap. 5,000m., res 1,609m., dep. 157,611m. (June 2011); Chair. MUHAMMAD KAMAL AL-DIN BARAKAT; 438 brs.

Commercial International Bank (Egypt), SAE: POB 2430, Nile Tower Bldg, 21–23 Sharia Charles de Gaulle, Cairo (Giza); tel. (2) 37472000; fax (2) 25701945; e-mail info@cibeg.com; internet www.cibeg.com; f. 1975 as Chase Nat. Bank (Egypt), SAE; adopted present name 1987; Nat. Bank of Egypt has 19.91% interest, Bankers Trust

Co (USA) 18.76%, Int. Finance Corpn 5%; cap. 5,934m., res 1,525m., dep. 74,808m. (Dec. 2011); Chair. and Man. Dir HISHAM EZZ AL-ARAB; 112 brs.

Egyptian Arab Land Bank: 78 Sharia Gameat al-Dowal al-Arabia, Mohandessin, Cairo 12311; tel. (2) 33368075; fax 33389218; e-mail foreign@eal-bank.com; internet www.eal-bank.com; f. 1880; state-owned; Chair. ABD EL-MEGUID MOHIE EL-DIN; 26 brs in Egypt, 15 abroad.

Export Development Bank of Egypt (EDBE): 108 Mohi el-Din Abou al-Ezz, Cairo 12311 (Dokki); tel. (2) 7619006; fax (2) 3385938; e-mail info@edbebank.com; internet www.edbebank.com; f. 1983 to replace Nat. Import-Export Bank; cap. 1,440m., res 31m., dep. 10,228m. (June 2011); Chair. MAJID FAHMI ATTIA; 15 brs.

HSBC Bank Egypt, SAE: POB 126, Abou el-Feda Bldg, 3 Sharia Abou el-Feda, Cairo (Zamalek); tel. (2) 27396001; fax (2) 27364010; e-mail hsbcegypt@hsbc.com; internet www.egypt.hsbc.com; f. 1982 as Hong Kong Egyptian Bank; name changed to Egyptian British Bank in 1994, and as above in 2001; 94.5% owned by Hongkong and Shanghai Banking Corpn; cap. 1,508m., res 1,144m., dep. 40,662m. (Dec. 2010); Chair. ABD AL-SALAM EL-ANWAR; CEO ANDREW LONG; 78 brs.

National Bank for Development (NBD): POB 647, 5 Sharia el-Borsa el-Gedida, Cairo 11511; tel. (2) 23959291; fax (2) 23936039; e-mail nbd@internetegypt.com; internet www.nbdegypt.com; f. 1980; 16 affiliated Nat. Banks for Devt merged with NBD in 1992; 51% share bought by Abu Dhabi Islamic Bank in 2007; cap. 2,000m., res 1,322m., dep. 12,822m. (Dec. 2011); Man. Dir and CEO NEVINE LOUTFY; 70 brs.

National Bank of Egypt (NBE): POB 11611, National Bank of Egypt Tower, 1187 Corniche el-Nil, Cairo; tel. (2) 25749101; fax (2) 25762672; e-mail nbe@nbe.com.eg; internet www.nbe.com.eg; f. 1898; merged with Mohandes Bank and Bank of Commerce and Devt in 2005; privatization pending; handles all commercial banking operations; cap. 7,000m., res 4,741m., dep. 270,691m. (June 2011); Chair. HUSSEIN ABDEL AZIZ HUSSEIN; 401 brs.

Principal Bank for Development and Agricultural Credit (PBDAC): 110 Sharia Qasr el-Eini, 11623 Cairo; tel. (2) 27951229; fax (2) 27948337; e-mail pbdac@pbdac.com.eg; internet www.pbdac.com.eg; f. 1976 to succeed former credit orgs; state-owned; cap. 1,500m., res 314m., dep. 28,464m. (June 2010); Chair. ALI ISMAEL SHAKER; 172 brs.

Société Arabe Internationale de Banque (SAIB): 56 Sharia Gamet el-Dowal al-Arabia, Mohandessin, Cairo (Giza); tel. (2) 37499464; fax (2) 37603497; f. 1976; 46% owned by Arab Int. Bank; cap. US $150m., res $45m., dep. $1,644m. (Dec. 2011); Chair. MUHAMMAD NAGUIB IBRAHIM; Man. Dir HASSAN ABD AL-MEGUID; 20 brs.

Union National Bank-Egypt SAE: el-Gamaa Bldg, 57 Sharia el-Giza, Alexandria 21519; tel. (2) 33385073; fax (2) 33384983; e-mail foreign@acmb.com.eg; internet www.acmb.com.eg; f. 1981 as Alexandria Commercial and Maritime Bank, SAE; adopted present name Dec. 2007; 94.8% owned by Union Nat. (United Arab Emirates); cap. 637m., res 123m., dep. 3,628m. (Dec. 2011); Chair. Sheikh NAHAYAN MUBARAK AL NAHAYAN; Man. Dir RAMADAN ANWAR; 25 brs.

The United Bank (UBE): Cairo Center, 106 Sharia Qasr el-Eini, Cairo; tel. (2) 33326010; fax (2) 27920153; e-mail info@ube.net; internet www.theubeg.com; f. 1981 as Dakahlia Nat. Bank for Devt; renamed United Bank of Egypt 1997; current name adopted 2006, when merged with Nile Bank and Islamic Int. Bank for Investment and Devt; privatization mooted in 2008; cap. 1,000.0m., res –11.0m., dep. 10,390.8m. (Dec. 2008); Chair. and Man. Dir MUHAMMAD ASHMAWY; 41 brs.

Social Bank

Nasser Social Bank: POB 2552, 35 Sharia Qasr el-Nil, Cairo; tel. (2) 3924484; fax (2) 3921930; f. 1971; state-owned; interest-free savings and investment bank for social and economic activities, participating in social insurance, specializing in financing co-operatives, craftsmen and social institutions; cap. 20m.; Chair. NASSIF TAHOON.

Multinational Banks

Arab African International Bank: 5 Midan al-Saray al-Koubra, POB 60, Majlis el-Sha'ab, Cairo 11516 (Garden City); tel. (2) 27924770; fax (2) 27925599; internet www.aaib.com; f. 1964 as Arab African Bank; renamed 1978; acquired Misr-America Int. Bank in 2005; cap. US $100m., res $99m., dep. $7,221m. (Dec. 2010); commercial investments and retail banking; shareholders are Central Bank of Egypt, Kuwait Investment Authority (49.37% each), and individuals and Arab institutions; Chair. MAHMOUD A. AL-NOURI; Vice-Chair. and Man. Dir HASSAN E. ABDALLA; 27 brs in Egypt, 3 abroad.

Arab International Bank: POB 1563, 35 Sharia Abd al-Khalek Sarwat, Cairo; tel. (2) 23918794; fax (2) 23916233; internet www.aib.com.eg; f. 1971 as Egyptian Int. Bank for Foreign Trade and Investment; renamed 1974; owned by Egypt, Libya, Oman, Qatar, the United Arab Emirates and private Arab shareholders; cap. US $450m., res $200m., dep. $3,032m. (Dec. 2011); 'offshore' bank; aims to promote trade and investment in shareholders' countries and other Arab countries; Chair. GAMAL NEGM; Dep. Chair. and Man. Dir MUHAMMAD IBRAHIM ABD AL-JAWAD; 7 brs.

Commercial Foreign Venture Banks

Ahli United Bank (Egypt): POB 1159, 9th Floor, World Trade Center, 1191 Corniche el-Nil; tel. (2) 25801200; fax (2) 25757052; e-mail info@deltabank-egypt.com; internet www.ahliunited.com; f. 1978 as Delta Int. Bank; name changed as above in 2007; 89.3% stake owned by Ahli United Bank BSC (Bahrain) and other Gulf-based financial institutions; cap. 750m., res 89m., dep. 11,531m. (Dec. 2011); Chair. FAHAD AL-RAJAAN; CEO and Man. Dir NEVINE EL-MESSEERI; 28 brs.

alBaraka Bank Egypt, SAE: POB 455, 60 Sharia Mohi el-Din Abu al-Ezz, Cairo (Dokki); tel. (2) 37481777; fax (2) 37611436; e-mail centeral@esf-bank.com; internet www.albaraka-bank.com.eg; f. 1980 as Pyramids Bank; renamed Egyptian-Saudi Finance Bank 1988; current name adopted April 2010; 73.7% owned by Al-Baraka Banking Group (Bahrain); cap. 534m., res 165m., dep. 12,269m. (Dec. 2010); Chair. ADNAN AHMAD YOUSUF ABD AL-MALEK; Vice Chair. and CEO ASHRAF AHMAD MOUSTAFA EL-GHAMRAWY; 23 brs.

Bank Audi SAE: Pyramid Heights Office Park, km 22, Cairo–Alexandria Desert Rd, Cairo; tel. (2) 35343300; fax (2) 35362120; e-mail contactus.egypt@banqueaudi.com; f. 1978 as Cairo Far East Bank SAE; name changed as above in 2006, when acquired by Bank Audi SAL (Lebanon); cap 1,123m., res 117m., dep. 13,788m. (Dec. 2010); Chair. and Man. Dir HATEM A. SADEK; 34 brs.

Barclays Bank Egypt, SAE: POB 110, 12 Midan el-Sheikh Yousuf, Cairo (Garden City); tel. (2) 23662600; fax (2) 23662810; internet www.barclays.com.eg; f. 1975 as Cairo Barclays Int. Bank; renamed Banque du Caire Barclays Int. in 1983 and Cairo Barclays Bank in 1999; name changed as above in 2004; wholly owned by Barclays Bank; acquired 40% stake held by Banque du Caire in 2004; cap. 995m., res 193m., dep. 15,054m. (Dec. 2010); Chair. OMAR EL-SAYEH; Man. Dir KHALID EL-GIBALY; 65 brs.

Blom Bank Egypt: 64 Sharia Mohi el-Din Abou al-Ezz, Cairo (Dokki); tel. (2) 33039825; fax (2) 33039804; e-mail mail@blombankegypt.com; internet www.blombankegypt.com; f. 1977 as Misr Romanian Bank, name changed as above in 2006; 99.7% owned by Blom Bank SAL (Lebanon); cap. 750m., res 102m., dep. 6,226m. (Dec. 2010); Chair. SAAD AZHARI; CEO and Man. Dir MUHAMMAD OZALP; 25 brs.

BNP Paribas SAE: POB 2441, 3 Latin America St, Cairo (Garden City); tel. (2) 27948323; fax (2) 27942218; e-mail bnppegypt@bnpparibas.com; internet www.egypt.bnpparibas.com; f. 1977 as Banque du Caire et de Paris SAE, name changed to BNP Paribas Le Caire in 2001 and as above in 2006; BNP Paribas (France) has 95.2% interest and Banque du Caire 4.8%; cap. 1,700m., res 24m., dep. 14,934m. (Dec. 2010); Chair. JEAN THOMAZEAU; Man. Dir JANY GEROMETTA; 8 brs.

Crédit Agricole Egypt, SAE: POB 1825, 4 Hassan Sabri St, Cairo 11511 (Zamalek); tel. (2) 27382661; fax (2) 27380450; internet www.ca-egypt.com; f. 2006 by merger of Calyon Bank Egypt (Egyptian affiliate of Crédit Agricole Group—France) and Egyptian American Bank; owned by Crédit Agricole Groupe, Mansour and Maghrabi Investment and Devt, and Egyptian investors; cap. 1,148m., res 133m., dep. 22,600m. (Dec. 2011); Chair. and Man. Dir FRANÇOIS EDOUARD DRION; 44 brs.

Egyptian Gulf Bank: POB 56, El-Orman Plaza Bldg, 8–10 Sharia Ahmad Nessim, Cairo (Giza); tel. (2) 33368357; fax (2) 37490002; e-mail h.r.egb@mst1.mist.com.eg; internet www.egbbank.com.eg; f. 1981; Misr Insurance Co has 19.3% interest; cap. 906m., res 79m., dep. 5,473m. (Dec. 2011); Chair. MUHAMMAD GAMAL EL-DIN MAHMOUD; CEO and Man. Dir ALI ISMAIL SHAKER; 16 brs.

Faisal Islamic Bank of Egypt, SAE: POB 2446, 149 Sharia el-Tahrir, Galaa Sq., Cairo (Dokki); tel. (2) 37621285; fax (2) 37621281; e-mail foreigndept@faisalbank.com.eg; internet www.faisalbank.com.eg; f. 1979; all banking operations conducted according to Islamic principles; cap. 1,059m., res 631m., dep. 32,239m. (Dec. 2011); Chair. Prince MUHAMMAD AL-FAISAL AL-SAOUD; Gov. ABD AL-HAMID ABU MOUSSA; 29 brs.

Piraeus Bank Egypt SAE: POB 92, 4th Floor, Evergreen Bldg, 10 Sharia Talaat Harb, Majlis al-Sha'ab, Cairo; tel. (2) 25764644; fax (2) 25799862; internet www.ecb.com.eg; f. Jan. 2006, following acquisition of Egyptian Commercial Bank by Piraeus Bank Group (Greece) in June 2005; cap. 978m., res 390m., dep. 10,322m. (Dec. 2010); Chair. ILIAS MILIS; CEO and Man. Dir NAYERA AMIN; 49 brs.

Suez Canal Bank, SAE: POB 2620, 7 Abd el-Kader Hamza St, Cairo (Garden City); tel. (2) 27943483; fax (2) 27926476; e-mail info@

scbank.com.eg; f. 1978; cap. 2,000m., res 145m., dep. 13,719m. (Dec. 2010); Chair. and Man. Dir TAREQ KANDIL; 29 brs.

Al-Watany Bank of Egypt: POB 63, 13 Sharia Semar, Dr Fouad Mohi el-Din Sq., Gameat el-Dewal al-Arabia, Mohandessin, Cairo 12655; tel. (2) 33388816; fax (2) 33362763; internet www.alwatany.net; f. 1980; 51% owned by Nat. Bank of Kuwait; cap. 1,000m., res 177m., dep. 13,573m. (Dec. 2011); Chair. ISAM AL-SAGER; Man. Dir Dr YASSER ISMAIL HASSAN; 39 brs.

Non-Commercial Banks

Arab Banking Corporation—Egypt: 1 Sharia el-Saleh Ayoub, Cairo (Zamalek); tel. (2) 27362684; fax (2) 27363643; e-mail abcegypt@arabbanking.com.eg; internet www.arabbanking.com.eg; f. 1982 as Egypt Arab African Bank; acquired by Arab Banking Corpn (Bahrain) in 1999; Arab Banking Corpn has 93% interest, other interests 7%; cap. 600m., res 212m., dep. 3,702m. (Dec. 2010); commercial and investment bank; Chair. HASSAN ALI JUMA; Man. Dir and CEO AKRAM TINAWI; 28 brs.

Arab Investment Bank (Federal Arab Bank for Development and Investment): POB 826, Cairo Sky Center Bldg, 8 Sharia Abd al-Khalek Sarwat, Cairo; tel. (2) 5768097; fax (2) 5770329; e-mail arinbank@mst1.mist.com.eg; internet www.aibegypt.com; f. 1978 as Union Arab Bank for Devt and Investment; Egyptian/Syrian/Libyan jt venture; cap. 500m., res 5m., dep. 3,240m. (Dec. 2010); Chair. and Exec. Man. Dir MUHAMMAD HANI SEIF EL-NASR; 13 brs.

EFG-Hermes: 58 Sharia el-Tahrir, Cairo 12311 (Dokki); tel. (2) 33383626; fax (2) 33383616; e-mail corporate@efg-hermes.com; internet www.efg-hermes.com; f. 1984; offices in Cairo, Alexandria and Mansoura; cap. 405.4m., res 109.0m., dep. 1,166.6m. (Dec. 2005); Chair. MONA ZULFICAR; CEO YASSER EL-MALLAWANY; 11 brs.

Housing and Development Bank, SAE: POB 234, 12 Sharia Syria, Mohandessin, Cairo (Giza); tel. (2) 37492013; fax (2) 37600712; e-mail hdbank@hdb-egy.com; internet www.hdb-egy.com; f. 1979; cap. 670m., res 164m., dep. 6,568m. (Dec. 2009); Chair. and Man. Dir FATHY EL-SEBAIE MANSOUR; 40 brs.

Industrial Development and Workers Bank of Egypt (IDWBE): 110 Sharia al-Galaa, Cairo 11511; tel. (2) 25772468; fax (2) 25751227; e-mail cs@idbe-egypt.com; internet www.idbe-egypt.com; f. 1947 as Industrial Bank; re-established as above in 1976; cap. 500m., res 608m., dep. 2,055m. (Dec. 2009); Chair. and Man. Dir EL-SAYED MUHAMMAD EL-KOSAYER; 19 brs.

Misr Iran Development Bank: POB 219, Nile Tower Bldg, 21 Charles de Gaulle Ave, Cairo 12612 (Giza); tel. (2) 35727311; fax (2) 35701185; e-mail midb@mst1.mist.com.eg; internet www.midb.com.eg; f. 1975; Iran Foreign Investment Co has 40.14% interest, Bank of Alexandria and Misr Insurance Co each have 29.93% interest; cap. 714m., res 477m., dep. 7,907m. (Dec. 2010); Chair. and Man. Dir ISMAIL HASSAN MUHAMMAD; 12 brs.

National Société Générale Bank, SAE (NSGB): POB 2664, 5 Sharia Champollion, 11111 Cairo; tel. (2) 27707000; fax (2) 27707799; e-mail info@nsgb.com.eg; internet www.nsgb.com.eg; f. 1978; Société Générale (France) has 78.38% interest, other interests 21.62%; merged with Misr Int. Bank SAE in 2006; cap. 4,032m., res 1,985m., dep. 51,819m. (Dec. 2011); Chair. and Man. Dir MUHAMMAD OSMAN EL-DIB; Vice-Chair. and Man. Dir JEAN-PHILIPPE COULIER; 138 brs.

REGULATORY AUTHORITY

Egyptian Financial Supervisory Authority (EFSA): Unit 84B, Bldg 5A, Alexandria Desert Rd, km 28, Cairo 12577; tel. (2) 35370040; fax (2) 35370041; e-mail info@efsa.gov.eg; internet www.efsa.gov.eg; f. 2009, following the merger of the Capital Market Authority, the Egyptian Insurance Supervisory Authority and the Mortgage Finance Authority; also assumed the regulatory functions of the General Authority for Investment and Free Zones, and the Egyptian Exchange; supervision of all non-banking financial markets and institutions, incl. the stock exchange, the capital market, and the insurance and mortgage sectors; Chair. Dr ASHRAF EL-SHARKAWY.

STOCK EXCHANGE

The Egyptian Exchange (EGX): 4A Sharia el-Sherifein, Cairo 11513; tel. (2) 23928698; fax (2) 23924214; e-mail webmaster@egx.com.eg; internet www.egx.com.eg; f. 1883 as the Cairo and Alexandria Stock Exchanges; present name adopted 2008; Chair. Dr MUHAMMAD OMRAN.

INSURANCE

Allianz Egypt: POB 266, Saridar Bldg, 92 Sharia el-Tahrir, Cairo (Dokki); tel. (2) 37605445; fax (2) 37605446; e-mail info@allianz.com.eg; internet www.allianz.com.eg; f. 1976 as Arab Int. Insurance Co; Allianz AG (Germany) purchased 80% stake in 2000; name changed as above in 2004; general and life insurance; Chair. RAYMOND SEMAAN EL-CHAM.

MetLife Alico: 28th Floor, Nile City Bldg, North Tower, Ramlet Beualac, Cairo; tel. (2) 4619020; fax (2) 4619015; e-mail service-egypt@metlifealico.com; internet www.eg.alico.com; f. 1997; first multinational insurance company to be granted licence to offer life insurance service in Egypt; CEO MICHEL KHALAF.

Misr Insurance Co: POB 950, 7 Sharia Abd al-Latif Boltia, Cairo; tel. (2) 7918300; fax (2) 797041; e-mail quality@misrins.com.eg; internet www.misrins.com.eg; f. 1934; merged with Al-Chark Insurance Co and Egyptian Reinsurance Co in Dec. 2007; scheduled for privatization; all classes of insurance and reinsurance; Chair. Prof. ADEL HAMMAD.

Mohandes Insurance Co: POB 62, 3 el-Mesaha Sq., Cairo (Dokki); tel. (2) 3352547; fax (2) 3361365; e-mail chairman@mohandes-ins.com; internet www.mohandes-ins.com; f. 1980; privately owned; insurance and reinsurance; Chair. and Man. Dir MUHAMMAD AHMED BARAKA.

Al-Mottahida: POB 804, 9 Sharia Sulayman Pasha, Cairo; f. 1957.

National Insurance Co of Egypt, SAE: POB 592, 41 Sharia Qasr el-Nil, Cairo; tel. (2) 3910731; fax (2) 3933051; internet www.ahlya.com; f. 1900; cap. 100m.; scheduled for privatization; Chair. SADEK HASSAN SADEK.

Provident Association of Egypt, SAE: POB 390, 9 Sharia Sherif Pasha, Alexandria; f. 1936; Man. Dir G. C. VORLOOU.

Trade and Industry

GOVERNMENT AGENCIES

Egyptian Mineral Resource Authority (EMRA): 3 Sharia Salah Salem, Abbassia, 11517 Cairo; tel. (2) 6828013; fax (2) 4820128; e-mail info@egsma.gov.eg; f. 1896 as the Egyptian Geological Survey and Mining Authority; state supervisory authority concerned with geological mapping, mineral exploration and other mining activities; Chair. HUSSEIN HAMOUDA.

General Authority for Investment (GAFI): Sharia Salah Salem, 11562 Cairo (Nasr City); tel. (2) 24055452; fax (2) 24055425; e-mail investorcare@gafinet.org; internet www.gafinet.org; Chair. OSAMA SALEH.

CHAMBERS OF COMMERCE

Federation of Egyptian Chambers of Commerce (FEDCOC): 4 el-Falaki Sq., Cairo; tel. (2) 7951136; fax (2) 7951164; e-mail fedcoc@menanet.net; internet www.fedcoc.org.eg; f. 1955; Chair. MUHAMMAD EL-MASRY.

Alexandria

Alexandria Chamber of Commerce: 31 Sharia el-Ghorfa Altogariya, Alexandria; tel. (3) 4837808; fax (3) 4837806; e-mail acc@alexcham.org; internet www.alexcham.org; f. 1922; Chair. AHMAD EL-WAKIL.

Cairo

American Chamber of Commerce in Egypt: 33 Sharia Sulayman Abaza, Cairo (Dokki) 12311; tel. (2) 33381050; fax (2) 33381060; e-mail info@amcham.org.eg; internet www.amcham.org.eg; f. 1981; Pres. OMAR MOHANNA; Exec. Dir HISHAM A. FAHMY.

Cairo Chamber of Commerce: 4 el-Falaki Sq., Cairo; tel. and fax (2) 27962091; f. 1913; Pres. MAHMOUD EL-ARABY; Sec.-Gen. MOSTAFA ZAKI TAHA.

In addition, there are 24 local chambers of commerce.

EMPLOYERS' ORGANIZATION

Federation of Egyptian Industries: 1195 Corniche el-Nil, Ramlet Boulal, Cairo; and 65 Gamal Abd al-Nasir Ave, Alexandria; tel. (2) 25796950; fax (2) 25796953 (Cairo); tel. and fax (3) 34916121 (Alexandria); e-mail info@fei.org.eg; internet www.fei.org.eg; f. 1922; Chair. GALAL ABD AL-MAKSOOD EL-ZORBA.

STATE HYDROCARBONS COMPANIES

Egyptian General Petroleum Corpn (EGPC): POB 2130, 4th Sector, Sharia Palestine, New Maadi, Cairo; tel. (2) 7065358; fax (2) 7028813; e-mail info@egpc.com.eg; state supervisory authority generally concerned with the planning of policies relating to petroleum activities in Egypt with the object of securing the devt of the petroleum industry and ensuring its effective administration; Chair. TARIQ AL-MOLLA.

Arab Petroleum Pipelines Co (SUMED): POB 158, el-Saray, 431 el-Geish Ave, Louran, Alexandria; tel. (3) 5835152; fax (3) 5831295; internet www.sumed.org; f. 1974; EGPC has 50% interest, Saudi Arabian Oil Co 15%, Int. Petroleum Investment Co (United Arab Emirates) 15%, Kuwait Real Estate Investment

Consortium 14.22%, Qatar Petroleum 5%, other Kuwaiti cos 0.78%; Suez–Mediterranean crude oil transportation pipeline (capacity: 117m. metric tons per year) and petroleum terminal operators; Chair. and Man. Dir Eng. SHAMEL HAMDI.

Belayim Petroleum Co (PETROBEL): POB 7074, Sharia el-Mokhayam, Cairo (Nasr City); tel. (2) 2621738; fax (2) 2609792; f. 1977; capital equally shared between EGPC and Int. Egyptian Oil Co, which is a subsidiary of Eni of Italy; petroleum and gas exploration, drilling and production; Chair. and Man. Dir MEDHAT EL-SAYED.

Egyptian Natural Gas Co (GASCO): Ring Rd, Exit 12, Sharia el-Tesien, 5th Settlement, Cairo; tel. (2) 6171911; fax (2) 6172824; e-mail gassupplyaffairs@gasco.com.eg; internet www.gasco.com.eg; f. 1997; 70% owned by EGPC, 15% by Petroleum Projects and Technical Consultations Co (PETROJET), 15% by Egypt Gas; transmission and processing of natural gas; operation of the national gas distribution network; Chair. and Man. Dir Eng. YAHIA AL-RIDI.

General Petroleum Co (GPC): POB 743, 8 Sharia Dr Moustafa Abou Zahra, Cairo (Nasr City); tel. (2) 4030975; fax (2) 4037602; f. 1957; wholly owned subsidiary of EGPC; operates mainly in Eastern Desert; Chair. HUSSEIN KAMAL.

Gulf of Suez Petroleum Co (GUPCO): POB 2400, 4th Sector, Sharia Palestine, New Maadi, Cairo 11511; tel. (2) 3520985; fax (2) 3531286; f. 1965; jt venture between EGPC and BP Egypt (United Kingdom/USA); developed the el-Morgan oilfield in the Gulf of Suez, also holds other exploration concessions in the Gulf of Suez and the Western Desert; Chair. Eng. MUHAMMAD ABOUL WAFA; Man. Dir L. D. MCVAY.

Middle East Oil Refinery (MIDOR): POB 2233, 22 Sharia el-Badeya, Cairo (Heliopolis) 11361; tel. (2) 24195501; fax (2) 24145936; e-mail info@midor.com.eg; internet www.midor.com.eg; f. 1994; 78% owned by EGPC, 10% by Engineering for the Petroleum and Process Industries (Enppi), 10% by Petroleum Projects and Technical Consultations Co (PETROJET), 2% by Suez Canal Bank; operation of oil-refining facilities at Ameriya, Alexandria; capacity 100,000 b/d; Chair. and CEO MEDHAT YOUSUF MAHMOUD.

Western Desert Petroleum Co (WEPCO): POB 412, Borg el-Thagr Bldg, Sharia Safia Zagloul, Alexandria; tel. (3) 4928710; fax (3) 4934016; f. 1967 as partnership between EGPC (50% interest) and Phillips Petroleum (35%) and later Hispanoil (15%); developed Alamein, Yidma and Umbarka fields in the Western Desert and later Abu Qir offshore gasfield in 1978, followed by NAF gasfield in 1987; Chair. MUHAMMAD MOHI EL-DIN BAHGAT.

Egyptian Natural Gas Holding Co (EGAS): POB 8064, 85C Sharia Nasr, 11371 Cairo (Nasr City); tel. (2) 24055845; fax (2) 24055876; e-mail egas@egas.com.eg; internet www.egas.com.eg; f. 2001 as part of a restructuring of the natural gas sector; strategic planning and promotion of investment in the natural gas industry; Chair. Dr SHERIF SOUSA.

UTILITIES

Electricity

In 1998 seven new electricity generation and distribution companies were created, under the direct ownership of the Egyptian Electricity Authority (EEA). In 2000 the EEA was restructured into a holding company (the Egyptian Electricity Holding Co—see below) controlling five generation and seven distribution companies. A specialized grid company was to manage electricity transmission. The Government commenced partial privatizations of the generation and distribution companies in 2001–02, while retaining control of the hydroelectric generation and grid management companies. In 2006 the Ministry of Electricity and Energy announced a five-year plan to add 7,800 MW of capacity to the national grid by 2012. Nine electricity distribution companies, six generation companies and a transmission company were administered by the Egyptian Electricity Holding Co in 2008.

Egyptian Electricity Holding Co: Sharia Ramses, Cairo (Nasr City); tel. (2) 24030681; fax (2) 24031871; e-mail info@egelec.com; internet www.egelec.com; fmrly Egyptian Electricity Authority; renamed as above 2000; Chair. MUHAMMAD MUHAMMAD AWAD.

Gas

Egypt Gas: Corniche el-Nil, Warak-Imbaba, Cairo; tel. and fax (2) 5408882; e-mail info@egyptgas.com.eg; internet www.egyptgas.com.eg; f. 1983; Chair. and Man. Dir NABIL HASHEM.

Water

Holding Co for Water and Wastewater: Corniche el-Nil, Cairo; tel. (2) 24583590; fax (2) 24583884; e-mail hcww@hcww.com.eg; internet www.hcww.com.eg; f. 2004; operation, maintenance and devt of water and wastewater facilities; oversees the operations of 20 affiliated regional water cos; Chair. Dr ABD EL-KAWI KHALIFA.

National Organization for Potable Water and Sanitary Drainage (NOPWASD): 6th Floor, Mogamma Bldg, el-Tahrir Sq., Cairo; tel. (2) 3557664; fax (2) 3562869; f. 1981; water and sewerage authority; Chair. MUHAMMAD KHALED MOUSTAFA.

STATE HOLDING COMPANIES

The following holding companies, under the supervision of the Ministry of Investment, are responsible for the management of the public sector companies and state investments in the relevant sectors. In addition, the holding companies promote and implement the Government's privatization programme.

Holding Co for Chemical Industries: POB 38, 11516 Cairo (Garden City); tel. (2) 27954006; fax (2) 27964597; e-mail chairman@cihc-eg.com; internet www.cihc-eg.com; 22 affiliated cos incl. Egyptian Chemical Industries Co (KIMA), Misr Chemical Industries Co, National Cement Co, Rakata Paper Co, Eastern Tobacco Co; mfrs of industrial chemicals; fertilizers; tyres, rubber and leather; cement; paper and packaging; cigarettes; vehicle components; cap. p.u. £E1,641m., revenue £E653.4m. (2007/08); Chair. MUHAMMAD ADEL EL-MOUZI.

Holding Co for Food Industries: Cairo; tel. (2) 22845573; fax (2) 22842620; internet www.food-industries.com.eg; 23 affiliated cos; 12 jt ventures; manufacture, processing and distribution of foodstuffs and agricultural commodities; Chair. AHMED AL-RAKAIBI.

Holding Co for Metallurgical Industries: 5 Sharia Ittihad el-Mohameen el-Arab, Cairo (Garden City); tel. (2) 27954844; fax (2) 27956976; e-mail micor1@micor.com.eg; internet www.micor.com.eg; affiliated cos incl. Egypt Aluminium Co, Egyptian Iron and Steel Co, El-Nasr Mining Co, Egyptian Ferro Alloys Co; Chair. Eng. ZAKI A. BASSYONI.

Holding Co for Pharmaceuticals, Chemicals and Medical Appliances (HoldiPharma): 12 Sharia Waked, 2078 Cairo; tel. (2) 25912825; fax (2) 25916866; e-mail holdi@holdipharma.com.eg; internet www.holdipharma.com.eg; 12 affiliated cos incl. Nile Co for Pharmaceuticals, Kahira Co for Pharmaceuticals and Chemical Industries, Alexandria Co for Pharmaceuticals and Chemical Industries; Chair. Dr MAGDI HASSAN.

Holding Co for Tourism, Hotels and Cinema: 4 Sharia Latin America, Cairo (Garden City); tel. (2) 27940036; fax (2) 27952056; e-mail info@hotac.com.eg; internet www.hotac.com.eg; nine affiliated cos incl. Egyptian General Co for Tourism and Hotels (EGOTH), Misr Travel Co, Misr Hotels Co; Chair. and CEO ALI ABD EL-AZIZ.

National Co for Construction and Development: Cairo (Heliopolis); tel. (2) 2660952; fax (2) 2663160; e-mail tacts@link.com.eg; internet www.nccd-construction.com; 21 affiliated cos; revenue £E7,197m. (2007/08); Chair. AHMED MUHAMMAD EL-SAYED.

MAJOR COMPANIES

(Figures for revenue and sales, etc., are in Egyptian pounds, unless otherwise stated.)

Abu Qir Fertilizer Co: Alexandria 21911; tel. (3) 5603053; fax (3) 5603032; e-mail afc@abuqir.com; internet www.abuqir.com; f. 1976; production of nitrogen-based fertilizers; capacity urea 5.9m. metric tons per year (t/y), urea ammonium nitrate 300,000 t/y, bulk-blended fertilizers 200,000 t/y; revenue 2,200m. (2008); Man. Dir SAAD IBRAHIM ABU AL-MAATI; 3,312 employees.

AJWA Group Egypt: 5C Sharia Merghany, Cairo (Heliopolis); tel. (2) 24178182; fax (2) 24146721; e-mail orouba@orouba.ajwa.com; internet www.ajwagroup.com; f. 1985; processing, distribution and marketing of edible oils and food products; Pres. Sheikh MUHAMMAD BIN ISSA AL-JABER.

Alexandria Mineral Oils Co (AMOC): POB 5, Sharia el-Sad el-Ali, Wadi el-Qamar, el-Max, Alexandria; tel. (3) 2205646; fax (43) 2205637; e-mail amoc@amocalex.com; internet www.amocalex.com; major shareholders include Alexandria Petroleum Co 20%, Al-Ahly Capital Holding Co 18.8%, Banque Misr 14.3%, Misr Insurance Co 9.79%; manufacture and distribution of refined petroleum products incl. paraffin wax, transmission fluid, lubricants and base oils; Chair. FATHI MUHAMMAD HUSSEIN EID (acting).

Alexandria Spinning and Weaving Co: al-Bar al-Kebli, al-Mahmoudaya, el-Nozha, Alexandria; tel. (3) 3818046; fax (3) 3818045; e-mail spinalexco@yahoo.com; internet www.spinalex.com; f. 1959; production of cotton yarns; operates four mills; Chair. and Man. Dir RIFAAT HELAL; 2,400 employees.

Amiral Group: 29 Sharia Farid, Cairo (Heliopolis) 11341; tel. (2) 4149944; fax (2) 4148877; e-mail info@amiral.com; internet www.amiral.com; active in maritime, livestock, engineering and technology, and bio-fuels industries; most of group's operations based at Sokhna Port; subsidiaries incl. Royal Logistics, Omnia Investments Group, Amiral Management Corpn, Amiral BioEnergy; Pres. and CEO OSAMA AL-SHARIF.

Cairo Poultry Co: POB 42, Cairo (Giza); tel. (2) 5714124; fax (2) 5726485; internet www.cpg.com.eg; f. 1977; breeding and distribution of poultry and poultry products; controls 18 subsidiary cos (2007); sales 1,627.4m. (2007); Chair. MAMDOUH SHARAF EL-DIN; Vice-Chair. and Man. Dir AHMED EL-KHAYAT.

Eastern Tobacco Co: POB 1543, 450 Sharia al-Ahram, Cairo (Giza); tel. (2) 35724711; fax (2) 35687434; e-mail egypt@easternegypt.com; internet www.easternegypt.com; f. 1920; partial privatization began in 1995; currently 55% state-owned; manufacture and distribution of tobacco and associated products; Chair. NABIL ABD EL-AZIZ; 12,054 employees.

Egypt Aluminium Co (Egyptalum): 48–50 Sharia Abd el-Khalek Sarwat, Cairo; tel. (2) 23904710; fax (2) 23919623; e-mail info@egyptalum.com.eg; internet www.egyptalum.com.eg; f. 1972; operates a smelting plant at Nag Hammady; Chair. and CEO SAYED A. EL-WAHAB; 9,000 employees.

Egyptian Cement Co (Lafarge Egypt Cement): Nile City Towers, Corniche el-Nil, Cairo; tel. (2) 24612400; fax (2) 24611995; f. 1996; annual capacity 10m. metric tons; majority shareholder Lafarge SA (France), following acquisition of Orascom Construction Industries cement division by Lafarge in 2007; Chair. BRUNO LAFONT; 1,200 employees.

Egyptian Financial and Industrial Co: 23–25 Sherif St, Cairo; tel. (2) 23928651; fax (2) 23938578; e-mail efic.ir@Sfie.com.eg; internet www.sfie.com.eg; f. 1929; fmrly 100% state-owned; initial public offering of 65% of shares issued in 1996; production of phosphate fertilizers and sulphuric acid; cap. 520m. (2007), revenue 931m. (2008); Chair. YAHIYA KOTB.

Egyptian International Pharmaceutical Industries Co (EIPICO): POB 149, Zone B1, 10 Ramadan City, Cairo (Giza); tel. (15) 361663; fax (15) 364377; e-mail eipico@eipico.com.eg; internet www.eipico.com.eg; f. 1985; production and marketing of pharmaceutical products; Chair. and Gen. Man. Dr A. BORHAN EL-DIN ISMAIL.

Egyptian Iron and Steel Co (HADISOLB): 54 Sharia Abd el-Khalek Sarwat, Cairo; tel. (2) 5011599; e-mail micor2@micor.com.eg; internet www.micor.com.eg; f. 1954; state-owned; affiliate of the Holding Co for Metallurgical Industries; Chair. Eng. ZAKI A. BASIONI.

Elsewedy Electric: POB 311, Plot 27, District 1, Settlement 5, New Cairo 11835; tel. (2) 27599700; fax (2) 25799739; e-mail info@elsewedy.com; internet www.elsewedyelectric.com; f. 1984; privately owned; mfrs of cables and electrical products for the telecommunications and energy industries; revenue 12,902m. (2009); CEO SADEK AHMED EL-SEWEDY.

Al-Ezz Steel Rebars (ezzsteel): 10 Sharia Shehab, Mohandessin, Cairo; tel. (2) 33046060; fax (2) 33470059; e-mail ir@ezzsteel.com; internet www.ezzindustries.com; f. 1994; mfrs of long and flat steel products; subsidiaries include Al-Ezz Dekheila Steel Co; annual capacity 5.3m. metric tons; revenue 21,800m. (2008); Chair. and Man. Dir PAUL CHEKAIBAN; 6,300 employees.

Ghabbour Auto Group (GB Auto): POB 120 Giza, Abu Rawash Industrial Zone, km 28, Cairo–Alexandria Desert Rd, Cairo; tel. (2) 35391201; fax (2) 35391198; e-mail ir@ghabbour.com; internet www.ghabbourauto.com; f. 1956 as Ghabbour Brothers; automotive assembly and distribution; Chair. and CEO RAOUF GHABBOUR; 6,000 employees.

Olympic Group for Financial Investment: IDEAL, Ramses St Extension, Cairo (Nasr City); tel. (2) 24880880; fax (2) 24880888; internet www.olympicgroup.com; f. 1995; manufacture and marketing of household appliances; subsidiaries include Delta Industrial Co (IDEAL); working cap. 677m., sales 2,707m. (2008); Chair. and CEO AHMED EL-BAKRY.

Orascom Construction Industries: Nile City Towers, Corniche el-Nil, 11221 Cairo; tel. (2) 24611111; fax (2) 24619409; e-mail hassan.badrawi@orascomci.com; internet www.orascomci.com; f. 1976; international construction contractor with operations in the Middle East, Africa, Europe and Cen. Asia; three construction divisions: Orascom Construction, BESIX Group, Contrack Int; also active in the manufacture of fertilizer products through subsidiaries incl. Egyptian Fertilizers Co; revenue 20,252.6m., total assets 43,025.5m. (2008); Chair. and CEO NASSEF SAWIRIS.

Oriental Weavers Carpet Co: 8 Sharia Zakaria Khalil, Cairo (Heliopolis); tel. (2) 22672121; fax (2) 22672242; e-mail owc@orientalweavers.com; internet www.orientalweavers.com; f. 1980; mfrs of rugs, carpets and associated products; sales 3,442m. (2008); Chair. and CEO MUHAMMAD FARID KHAMIS.

Pharco Corpn: POB 12, Sidi Gaber, Alexandria; tel. (3) 5823745; fax (3) 5830958; e-mail contact@pharco.org; internet www.pharcocorporation.com; f. 1987; devt, manufacturing, marketing, distribution and exporting of pharmaceutical products; subsidiaries include Pharco Pharmaceuticals, Amriya Pharmaceutical Industries, European Egyptian Pharmaceutical Industries, Safe Pharma, Technopharma Egypt; Chair. Dr HASSAN ABBAS HELMY; 5,700 employees (2011).

Sidi Krier Petrochemicals (Sidpec): km 36, Cairo–Alexandria Desert Rd, el-Ameriya, Alexandria; tel. (3) 4770141; fax (3) 4770129; e-mail info@sidpec.com; internet www.sidpec.com; f. 1997; 20% owned by Egyptian Petrochemicals Holding Co, 21% by Misr Bank; mfrs of polyethylene products; Chair. and CEO AHMAD AL-BORDINI.

Suez Cement: POB 2691, Ein Sokhna Rd, Cairo (Helwan); tel. (2) 25222000; fax (2) 25222067; e-mail info@suezcem.com; internet www.suezcement.com.eg; f. 1977; 55% owned by Italcementi Group (Italy); five production facilities; annual capacity 4m. metric tons; Man. Dir BRUNO CARRÉ; Chair. OMAR MOHANNA; more than 5,000 employees.

Talaat Moustafa Group Holding (TMG): 34–36 Sharia Mussadak, Cairo; tel. (2) 33016701; fax (2) 33362198; e-mail talaatmostafa@tmg.com.eg; internet www.talaatmoustafa.com; f. 1975; community real estate devt, and devt of hotels and resorts; 21 subsidiary cos, in the real estate, construction and agriculture sectors; Chair. and Man. Dir TAREK TALAAT MOSTAFA; more than 100,000 employees.

TRADE UNIONS

Until early 2011 the Egyptian Trade Union Federation was the sole trade union federation in Egypt. However, following the removal from power of former President Hosni Mubarak in February 2011, two new organizations, the Egyptian Federation of Independent Trade Unions and Egyptian Democratic Labour Congress, were formed.

Egyptian Trade Union Federation (ETUF): 90 Sharia al-Galaa, Cairo; tel. (2) 5740362; fax (2) 5753427; internet www.etufegypt.com; f. 1957; govt-controlled; affiliated to Int. Confed. of Arab Trade Unions and to the Org. of African Trade Union Unity; 23 affiliated unions; 5m. mems; Pres. AHMED ABD AL-ZAHIR; Gen. Sec. MUHAMMAD IBRAHIM AZHARI.

Egyptian Federation of Independent Trade Unions (EFITU): Cairo; f. 2011; Pres. KAMAL ABU EITA; 261 affiliated unions and 2.4m. mems.

Egyptian Democratic Labour Congress (EDLC): 88 Sharia Qasr al-Eini, 1st Floor, Apt no. 7, Downtown, Cairo; tel. (2) 7962564; e-mail edlc.labourcongress@gmail.com; f. 2011; Leader KAMAL ABBAS; 271 affiliated unions and more than 1m. mems.

Transport

RAILWAYS

The area of the Nile Delta is well served by railways. Lines also run from Cairo southward along the Nile to Aswan, and westward along the coast to Salloum. As part of an integrated transport strategy being developed by the Government, up to US $1,500m. was allocated for the upgrading of Egypt's ageing railway infrastructure from 2007. A feasibility study into construction of a high-speed rail connection between Cairo and Alexandria was initiated in mid-2009. In 2010 the total length of Egyptian railways was 5,195 route-km.

Egyptian National Railways: Station Bldg, Midan Ramses, Cairo 11794; tel. (2) 5751000; fax (2) 5740000; e-mail support@enr.gov.eg; internet enr.gov.eg; f. 1852; length over 5,000 km; 42 km electrified; a 346-km line to carry phosphate and iron ore from the Bahariya mines, in the Western Desert, to the Helwan iron and steel works in south Cairo, was opened in 1973, and the Qena–Safaga line (length 223 km) came into operation in 1989; restructured in 2012.

Alexandria Passenger Transport Authority: POB 466, Aflaton, el-Shatby, Alexandria 21111; tel. (3) 5975223; fax (3) 5971187; e-mail apta@link.net; internet www.alexapta.org; f. 1860; controls City Tramways (28 km), Ramleh Electric Railway (16 km), suburban buses and minibuses (1,688 km); 119 tram cars, 519 suburban buses and minibuses; 362 suburban buses and minibuses from private sector; Chair. and Tech. Dir Eng. SHERINE KASSEM.

Cairo Metro: National Authority for Tunnels, POB 466, Ramses Bldg, Midan Ramses, Cairo 11794; tel. (2) 5742968; fax (2) 5742950; e-mail chairman@nat.org.eg; internet www.nat.org.eg; construction of the first electrified, 1,435-mm gauge underground transport system in Africa and the Middle East began in Cairo in 1982; Line 1, which opened to the public in 1987, has a total of 35 stations (5 underground), connects el-Marg el-Gedida with Helwan and is 44 km long with a 4.7-km tunnel beneath central Cairo; Line 2 links Shoubra el-Kheima with Giza, at el-Monib station, totalling 21.6 km (13 km in tunnel), and with 20 stations (12 underground), two of which interconnect with Line 1; the first section of Line 3, which will connect Imbaba and Mohandessin with Cairo International Airport and will total 34.2 km (30.3 km in tunnel) with 29 stations (27 underground), opened in early 2012, with completion of the line scheduled for late 2013; Chair. Eng. ATTA A. R. EL-SHERBINY.

Cairo Transport Authority: Sharia Ramses, el-Gabal el-Ahmar, Cairo (Nasr City); tel. (2) 6845712; fax (2) 8654858; owned by the Governorate of Cairo; provider of public transport services in Greater

Cairo, incl. tram, surface metro, bus and ferry services; rail system length 78 km (electrified); gauge 1,000 mm; operates 16 tram routes and 24 km of light railway; 720 cars; Chair. SALAH FARAG.

ROADS

The estimated total length of the road network in 2010 was 137,430 km, of which 836 km were motorways, 23,143 km were highways, main or national roads, and 113,451 km were secondary or regional roads. There are good metalled main roads as follows: Cairo–Alexandria (desert road); Cairo–Banha–Tanta–Damanhour–Alexandria; Cairo–Suez (desert road); Cairo–Ismailia–Port Said or Suez; and Cairo–Fayoum (desert road). The Ahmad Hamdi road tunnel (1.64 km) beneath the Suez Canal was opened in 1980. A second bridge over the Suez Canal was completed in 2001. A project to develop the Cairo–Alexandria highway into a 231-km motorway was under way in 2013. Other road projects at the planning or construction stage in 2013 included the Mediterranean coastal highway, linking Port Said with Mersa Matruh, and the Shoubra el-Kheima–Banha and Kafr el-Zayat–Alexandria highways.

General Authority for Roads, Bridges and Land Transport—Ministry of Transport (GARBLT): 105 Sharia Qasr el-Eini, Cairo; tel. (2) 7957429; fax (2) 7950591; e-mail garblt@idsc.gov.eg; Chair. Eng. TAREK EL-ATTAR.

SHIPPING

Egypt's principal ports are Alexandria, Port Said and Suez. A port constructed at a cost of £E315m., and designed to handle up to 16m. metric tons of cargo per year in its first stage of development, was opened at Damietta in 1986. By mid-2008 handling capacity at Damietta had increased to 19.7m. tons. Egypt's first privately operated port was opened in 2002 at Ain Sokhna on the Red Sea coast, near the southern entrance of the Suez Canal. Sokhna's capacity was projected to increase from 6m. tons in 2005 to 90m. tons by 2020. The modernization of the quays at Alexandria port and the construction of two new container terminals at the adjacent Dakahlia port were completed during the first half of 2007. The first phase of a major expansion of the Suez Canal Container Terminal at Port Said, which envisaged a new container terminal with a total capacity of 5.4m. 20-foot equivalent units per year, was inaugurated in August 2010; the second phase was ongoing in mid-2013.

At 31 December 2012 Egypt's flag registered fleet totalled 449 vessels, with an aggregate displacement of 1.3m. grt, of which 15 were bulk carriers, three were fish carriers and 16 were general cargo ships.

Port and Regulatory Authorities

Maritime Transport Sector: Ministry of Transport, 4 Sharia Ptolemy, Bab Sharqi, 21514 Alexandria; tel. (3) 4869836; fax (3) 4874674; e-mail mmt@idsc.net.eg; internet www.mts.gov.eg; supervision of the maritime sector; Dir-Gen. Rear-Adm. MUHAMMAD ABD AL-MENEM.

Alexandria Port Authority: 106 Sharia el-Hourriya, Alexandria 26514; tel. (3) 4800359; fax (3) 4807098; e-mail info@apa.gov.eg; internet www.apa.gov.eg; f. 1966; management of Alexandria and Dakahlia ports; Chair. Rear-Adm. AL-SAYED HAMAD SHAKER HEDAYA; Vice-Chair. Rear-Adm. ADEL YASSIN HAMAD.

Damietta Port Authority: POB 13, Damietta; tel. (57) 2290006; fax (57) 2290930; e-mail chairman@damietta-port.gov.eg; internet www.damietta-port.gov.eg; Chair. Adm. IBRAHIM FLAIFEL.

Port Said Port Authority: Intersection Sharia Moustafa Kamel and Sharia Azmy, Port Said; tel. (66) 3348270; fax (66) 3348262; e-mail info@psdports.org; internet www.psdports.org; Chair. Adm. IBRAHIM MUHAMMAD SADEK.

Red Sea Ports Authority: POB 1, Port Tawfik, Suez; tel. (62) 3190731; fax (62) 3191117; e-mail rspsite@emdb.gov.eg; responsible for ports incl. Suez, Sokhna and Hurghada; Chair. Gen. MUHAMMAD ABD EL-KADER.

Principal Shipping Companies

Arab Maritime Petroleum Transport Co (AMPTC): POB 143, 9th Floor, Nile Tower Bldg, 21 Sharia Giza, 12211 Giza; tel. (2) 35701311; fax (2) 33378080; e-mail amptc.cairo@amptc.net; internet www.amptc.net; f. 1973; affiliated to the Org. of Arab Petroleum Exporting Countries; 11 vessels; Gen. Man. SULAYMAN AL-BASSAM.

Canal Shipping Agencies Co: 26 Sharia Palestine, Port Said; tel. (66) 3227500; fax (66) 3239896; e-mail csaagencies@canalshipping.net; internet www.canalshipping.net; f. 1965; shipping agency, cargo and forwarding services; affiliated cos: Assuit Shipping Agency, Aswan Shipping Agency, Damanhour Shipping Agency, El-Menia Shipping Agency; Chair. FOUAD EL-SAYED EL-MULLA.

Egyptian Navigation Co (ENC): 2 el-Nasr St, el-Gomrok, Alexandria; tel. (3) 4800050; fax (3) 4871345; e-mail enc@dataxprs.com.eg; internet www.enc.com.eg; f. 1961; owners and operators of Egypt's mercantile marine; international trade transportation; 12 vessels; Chair. and Man. Dir AMR GAMAL EL-DIN ROUSHDY.

Holding Co for Maritime and Land Transport: POB 3005, Alexandria; tel. (3) 4865547; fax (3) 4872647; e-mail holding@hcmlt.com; internet www.hcmlt.gov.eg; govt-owned; 17 affiliated cos, incl. General Co for River Nile Transportation, Port Said Container and Cargo Handling Co, General Egyptian Warehouses Co; Chair. Adm. MUHAMMAD YOUSUF.

International Maritime Services Co: 20 Sharia Salah Salem, Alexandria; tel. (3) 4840817; fax (3) 4869177; e-mail agency@imsalex.com; internet www.imsalex.com; f. 1986; shipping agency, freight-forwarding, transshipment contractor, marine surveyor; subsidiary: Egyptian Register of Shipping Co; Chair. Capt. MONTASSER EL-SOKKARY.

National Navigation Co: 4 Sharia El-Hegaz, Cairo (Heliopolis); tel. (2) 24525575 fax (2) 24526171; e-mail nnc@nnc.com.eg; internet www.nnc.com.eg; f. 1981; specializes in bulk cargoes; operates passenger services between Egypt and Saudi Arabia; 18 vessels; Chair. and Man. Dir TAMER ABD EL-ALIM.

Pan-Arab Shipping Co: POB 39, 404 ave el-Hourriya, Rushdi, Alexandria; tel. (3) 5468835; fax (3) 5469533; internet www.pan-arab.org; f. 1974; Arab League Co; bulk handling, forwarding and warehousing services; 5 vessels; Chair. Adm. MUHAMMAD SHERIF EL-SADEK; Gen. Man. Capt. MAMDOUH EL-GUINDY.

Red Sea Navigation Co: 10 Gowhar el-Khaled St, Port Tawfik, Suez; tel. (62) 3196971; fax (62) 9136915; e-mail suez@rdnav.com; internet www.rdnav.com; f. 1986; operates a fleet of eight cargo vessels; shipping agency, Suez Canal transit and stevedoring; Chair. ABD EL-MAJID MATAR.

THE SUEZ CANAL

In 2012 a total of 17,225 vessels, with a net displacement of 739.9m. tons, used the Suez Canal linking the Mediterranean and Red Seas.

Length of canal: 190 km; maximum permissible draught: 20.73 m (68 ft); breadth of canal at water level and breadth between buoys defining the navigable channel at −11 m: 365 m and 225 m, respectively, in the northern section, and 305 m and 205 m in the southern section.

Suez Canal Authority (Hay'at Canal al-Suways): Irshad Bldg, Ismailia; Cairo Office: 6 Sharia Lazoughli, Cairo (Garden City); tel. (64) 3392010; fax (64) 3392834; e-mail info@suezcanal.gov.eg; internet www.suezcanal.gov.eg; f. 1956; govt-owned; Chair. and CEO Vice-Adm. MOHAB MUHAMMAD HUSSEIN MAMISH.

Suez Canal Container Terminal: POB 247, Port Said; tel. (66) 3254960; fax (66) 3254970; e-mail scct@scctportsaid.com; internet www.scctportsaid.com; f. 2000, with 30-year concession to operate the East Port Said container terminal; Man. Dir KLAUS HOLM LAURSEN.

CIVIL AVIATION

The main international airports are at Cairo (located at Heliopolis, 23 km from the centre of the city), Sharm el-Sheikh and Hurghada. A major programme of expansion at Cairo International Airport commenced in 2004: a third terminal was formally inaugurated in December 2008 and became fully operational in June 2009, while a fourth runway was completed in October 2010. Meanwhile, Cairo's Terminal Two was closed in April 2010 in preparation for the commencement of a US $400m. expansion project to increase the terminal's annual capacity to 7.5m. passengers; construction was expected to be completed by 2013. Construction work on a new international airport at Borg el-Arab (40 km south-west of Alexandria) was inaugurated in November 2010. The completion of a second terminal at Sharm el-Sheikh airport in 2007 increased capacity from 3m. to 7.5m. passengers per year; plans for a third terminal, which would increase annual passenger-handling capacity to 15m., were under way in mid–2013.

EgyptAir: Administration Complex, Cairo International Airport, Cairo (Heliopolis); tel. (2) 22674700; fax (2) 22663773; e-mail callcenter@egyptair.com; internet www.egyptair.com.eg; f. 1932 as Misr Airwork; known as United Arab Airlines 1960–71; restructured as a holding co with nine subsidiaries 2002; operates internal services in Egypt and external services throughout the Middle East, Far East, Africa, Europe and the USA; Chair. and CEO HUSSEIN MASSOUD (EgyptAir Holding Co); Chair. and CEO Capt. ALAA ASHOUR (EgyptAir Airlines).

Egyptian Civil Aviation Authority: ECAA Complex, Sharia Airport, Cairo 11776; tel. (2) 2677610; fax (2) 2470351; e-mail info@civilaviation.gov.eg; internet www.civilaviation.gov.eg; f. 2000; Pres. Capt. SAMEH EL-HEFNI.

Egyptian Holding Co for Airports and Air Navigation (EHCAAN): EHCAAN Bldg, Airport Rd, Cairo; tel. (2) 6352442; fax (2) 2663440; e-mail info@ehcaan.com; internet www.ehcaan.com;

f. 2001; responsible for management and devt of all Egyptian airports; Chair. MUHAMMAD FATHALLAH REFAAT.

Cairo Airport Company: Cairo International Airport, 11776 Cairo (Heliopolis); tel. (2) 2474245; fax (2) 2432522; e-mail cac@cairo-airport.com; internet www.cairo-airport.com; under management of Egyptian Holding Co since 2003; Chair. Dr AHMAD HAFIZ; Exec. Dir PETER DIENSTBACH.

Egyptian Airports Co: Cairo; tel. (2) 22739417; fax (2) 22739416; e-mail info@eac-airports.com; internet www.eac-airports.com; f. 2001; management and devt of 19 regional airports; Chair. and Man. Dir YUSRI GAMAL EL-DIN.

Tourism

Tourism is currently Egypt's second largest source of revenue, generating an estimated US $8,707m. (excluding passenger transport) in 2011. Despite further terrorist attacks in the Sinai region during 2004–06, the number of tourists visiting the country increased significantly in the following years, reaching some 14.7m. by 2010. The industry was severely affected by the political unrest of 2011; according to official estimates, just 9.8m. tourists visited Egypt in that year. The sector recovered somewhat in 2012, with the number of arrivals increasing to 11.5m. However, the outbreak of violence in mid-2013 was expected to prompt a further decline.

Egyptian Tourist Authority: Misr Travel Tower, 32 Sharia Emtidad Ramses, Abbassia Sq., Cairo; tel. (2) 2854509; fax (2) 2854363; e-mail user@egypt.travel; internet www.egypt.travel; f. 1965; brs at Alexandria, Port Said, Suez, Luxor and Aswan; Chair. AMR EL-EZABI.

Egyptian General Co for Tourism and Hotels (EGOTH): 4 Sharia Latin America, 11519 Cairo (Garden City); tel. (2) 27942914; fax (2) 27943531; e-mail info@egoth.com.eg; internet www.egoth.com.eg; f. 1961; affiliated to the Holding Co for Tourism, Hotels and Cinema; Chair. and Man. Dir NABIL SELIM.

Defence

Commander-in-Chief of the Armed Forces: Gen. ABD AL-FATAH AL-SISI.

Chief of Staff of the Armed Forces: Lt-Gen. SIDKI SAYED AHMED.

Commander of the Air Force: Lt-Gen. YOUNES HAMED.

Commander of Air Defence Forces: Lt-Gen. ABD EL-MONEIM IBRAHIM.

Commander-in-Chief of the Navy: Lt-Gen. OSAMA AHMED EL-GENDI.

Budgeted Defence Expenditure (2013): £E26,300m.

Military service: one–three years, selective.

Total armed forces (as assessed at November 2012): 438,500: army 310,000; air defence command 80,000; navy 18,500 (10,000 conscripts); air force 30,000 (10,000 conscripts). Reserves 479,000.

Paramilitary Forces (as assessed at November 2012): est. 397,000 (Central Security Forces 325,000; National Guard 60,000 and Border Guard 12,000).

Education

Education is compulsory for eight years between six and 14 years of age. Primary education, beginning at six years of age, lasts for five years. Secondary education, beginning at 11 years of age, lasts for a further six years, comprising two cycles (the first being preparatory) of three years each. In 2009/10, according to UNESCO estimates, primary enrolment included an estimated 94% of children in the relevant age-group, while the comparable ratio for secondary enrolment was estimated at 70%. In 2009/10 there were an estimated 2,004,870 students enrolled at universities. The Al-Azhar University and its various preparatory and associated institutes provide instruction and training in several disciplines, with emphasis on adherence to Islamic principles and teachings. Education is free at all levels. In 2008/09 a total of £E39,880m. (some 11.2% of total expenditure) was allocated to education by the central Government.

Bibliography

General and Historical Context

Abdel-Malek, Anwar. *Egypte, société militaire.* Paris, 1962.

Idéologie et renaissance nationale / L'Egypte moderne. Paris, 1969.

Adly, Amr. *State Reform and Development in the Middle East: Turkey and Egypt in the Post-Liberalization Era.* Abingdon, Routledge, 2013.

Ahmed, J. M. *The Intellectual Origins of Egyptian Nationalism.* London, Royal Institute of International Affairs, 1960.

Aldridge, James. *Cairo: Biography of a City.* London, Macmillan, 1970.

Amin, Galal. *Whatever Happened to the Egyptian Revolution?* (trans. by Jonathan Wright). Cairo, American University of Cairo Press, 2013.

Avram, Benno. *The Evolution of the Suez Canal State 1869–1956. A Historico-Juridical Study.* Geneva, Librairie E. Droz, and Paris, Libraire Minard, 1958.

Baddour, Abd. *Sudanese-Egyptian Relations. A Chronological and Analytical Study.* The Hague, Nijhoff, 1960.

Badeau, J. S. *The Emergence of Modern Egypt.* New York, 1953.

Baer, Gabriel. *A History of Landownership in Modern Egypt 1800–1950.* London, Oxford University Press, 1962.

The Evolution of Landownership in Egypt and the Fertile Crescent. The Economic History of the Middle East 1800–1914. Chicago, IL, and London, University of Chicago Press, 1966.

Studies in the Social History of Modern Egypt. Chicago, IL, and London, University of Chicago Press, 1969.

Bagnall, Roger S., and Rathbone, Dominic W. (Eds). *Egypt from Alexander to the Early Christians: An Archaeological and Historical Guide.* Los Angeles, CA, J. Paul Getty Museum, 2005.

Berger, Morroe. *Islam in Egypt Today: Social and Political Aspects of Popular Religion.* Cambridge, Cambridge University Press, 1970.

Berque, Jacques. *Egypt: Imperialism and Revolution.* London, Faber, 1972.

Blunt, Wilfred Scawen. *Secret History of the English Occupation of Egypt.* London, Martin Secker, 1907.

Cannuyer, Christian. *Les Coptes.* Turnhout, Editions Brepols, 1991.

Chevillat, Alain and Evelyne. *Moines du désert d'Egypte.* Lyons, Editions Terres du Ciel, 1991.

Chih, Rachida. *Le Soufisme au quotidien: confréries d'Egypte au XXe siècle.* Arles, Sinbad: Actes Sud, 2000.

Collins, Robert O. *The Nile.* New Haven, CT, Yale University Press, 2003.

Cromer, Earl of. *Modern Egypt.* 2 vols, London, 1908.

Dawisha, A. I. *Egypt in the Arab World.* London, Macmillan, 1976.

Dodwell, H. *The Founder of Modern Egypt.* Cambridge, 1931, reprinted 1967.

Driault, E. *L'Egypte et l'Europe.* 5 vols, Cairo, 1935.

Efendi, Husein. *Ottoman Egypt in the Age of the French Revolution* (trans. and with introduction by Stanford J. Shaw). Cambridge, MA, Harvard University Press, 1964.

Empereur, Jean-Yves. *Alexandria. Past, Present and Future.* London, Thames and Hudson, 2002.

Garzouzi, Eva. *Old Ills and New Remedies in Egypt.* Cairo, Dar al-Maaref, 1958.

Haeri, Niloofar. *Sacred Language, Ordinary People. Dilemmas of Culture and Politics in Egypt.* Basingstoke, Palgrave Macmillan, 2004.

Harris, C. P. *Nationalism and Revolution in Egypt: The Role of the Muslim Brotherhood.* The Hague, Mouton and Co, 1964.

Harris, J. R. (Ed.). *The Legacy of Egypt.* Oxford, Oxford University Press, 2nd edn, 1972.

Holt, P. M. *Egypt and the Fertile Crescent.* London, Longman, 1966.

Hopkins, Harry. *Egypt, The Crucible.* London, Secker and Warburg, 1969.

Hurst, H. E. *The Nile.* London, 1952.

The Major Nile Projects. Cairo, 1966.

Iskandar, Adel. *Egypt in Flux: Essays on an Unfinished Revolution.* Cairo, American University of Cairo Press, 2013.

Kepel, Gilles. *The Prophet and the Pharaoh: Muslim Extremism in Egypt.* London, Al Saqi Books, 1985.

King, Joan Wucher (Ed.). *An Historical Dictionary of Egypt.* Metuchen, NJ, Scarecrow Press, 1984.

Kinross, Lord. *Between Two Seas: The Creation of the Suez Canal.* London, John Murray, 1968.

Lacouture, Jean and Simonne. *Egypt in Transition.* London, Methuen, 1958.

Lauterpacht, E. (Ed.). *The Suez Canal Settlement.* London, Stevens and Sons, under the auspices of the British Institute of International and Comparative Law, 1960.

Lengye, Emil. *Egypt's Role in World Affairs.* Washington, DC, Public Affairs Press, 1957.

Lia, Brynjar. *The Society of the Muslim Brothers in Egypt: The Rise of an Islamic Mass Movement 1928–1942.* Reading, Ithaca Press, 2006.

Little, Tom. *Modern Egypt.* London, Ernest Benn, and New York, Praeger, 1967.

Lloyd, Lord. *Egypt since Cromer.* 2 vols, London, 1933–34.

Makari, Peter E. *Conflict and Cooperation: Christian-Muslim Relations in Contemporary Egypt.* Syracuse, NY, Syracuse University Press, 2007.

Marlowe, J. *Anglo-Egyptian Relations.* London, 1954.

Mehrez, Samia. *Egypt's Culture Wars: Politics and Practice.* Abingdon, Routledge, 2008.

Morkot, Robert. *Egyptians: An Introduction.* Abingdon, Routledge, 2005.

Osman, Ahmed. *Christianity: An Ancient Egyptian Religion.* Rochester, VT, Inner Traditions International Ltd, 2005.

Owen, Robert, and Blunsum, Terence. *Egypt, United Arab Republic. The Country and its People.* London, Queen Anne Press, 1966.

Pollard, Lisa. *Nurturing the Nation: The Family Politics of Modernizing, Colonizing, and Liberating Egypt, 1805–1923.* Berkeley, CA, University of California Press, 2005.

Richmond, J. C. B. *Egypt, 1798–1952: Her Advance towards a Modern Identity.* London, Methuen, 1977.

Safran, Nadav. *Egypt in Search of Political Community: An Analysis of the Intellectual and Political Evolution of Egypt, 1804–1952.* Cambridge, MA, Harvard University Press, and London, Oxford University Press, 1961.

Stewart, Desmond. *Cairo.* London, Phoenix House, 1965.

Viollet, Roger, and Doresse, Jean. *Egypt.* New York, Cromwell, 1955.

Waterfield, Gordon. *Egypt.* London, Thames and Hudson, 1966.

Watt, D. C. *Britain and the Suez Canal.* London, Royal Institute of International Affairs, 1956.

Wavell, W. H. *A Short Account of the Copts.* London, 1945.

Weaver, Mary Ann. *A Portrait of Egypt: A Journey Through the World of Militant Islam.* New York, Farrar, Straus and Giroux, 1998.

Wilson, John A. *The Burden of Egypt.* Chicago, IL, 1951.

Zaki, Abdel Rahman. *Histoire Militaire de l'Epoque de Mohammed Ali El-Kebir.* Cairo, 1950.

Contemporary Political History

Alexander, Anne. *Nasser.* London, Haus Publishing, 2005.

Arafat, Alaa al-Din. *Hosni Mubarak and The Future of Democracy in Egypt.* New York, NY, Palgrave Macmillan, revised edn, 2011.

Baker, Raymond William. *Egypt's Uncertain Revolution under Nasser and Sadat.* Cambridge, MA, Harvard University Press, 1979.

Baker, Raymond William. *Sadat and After: Struggles for Egypt's Political Soul.* London, I. B. Tauris, 1990.

El-Baraway, Rashed. *The Military Coup in Egypt.* Cairo, Renaissance Bookshop, 1952.

Barraclough, Geoffrey (Ed.). *Suez in History.* London, 1962.

Berger, Morroe. *Bureaucracy and Society in Modern Egypt: A Study of the Higher Civil Service.* Princeton, NJ, Princeton University Press, 1957.

Bradley, John R. *Inside Egypt: The Land of The Pharaohs on the Brink of a Revolution.* New York, NY, Palgrave Macmillan, 2009.

Brehony, Noel, and el-Desouky, Ayman Ahmed (Eds). *British-Egyptian Relations from Suez to the Present Day.* London, Saqi Books, 2007.

Brown, Nathan J. *Peasant Politics in Modern Egypt: The Struggle against the State.* New Haven, CT, and London, Yale University Press, 1990.

Carter, B. L. *The Copts in Egyptian Politics.* London, Croom Helm, 1986.

Cohen, Raymond. *Culture and Conflict in Egyptian-Israeli Relations: A Dialogue of the Deaf.* Bloomington, IN, Indiana University Press, 1994.

Connell, John. *The Most Important Country. The Story of the Suez Crisis and the Events leading up to it.* London, Cassell, 1957.

Cook, Steven A. *The Struggle for Egypt: From Nasser to Tahrir Square.* New York, Oxford University Press, 2012.

Cooper, Mark N. *The Transformation of Egypt.* London, Croom Helm, 1982.

Fahmy, Ninette S. *The Politics of Egypt: State-Society Relationship.* London, RoutledgeCurzon, 2002.

Farnie, D. A. *East and West of Suez. The Suez Canal in History, 1854–1956.* Oxford, Clarendon Press, 1969.

Fawzi, Mahmoud. *Suez 1956.* London, Shorouk International, 1986.

Finklestone, Joseph. *Anwar Sadat: Visionary Who Dared.* London, Frank Cass, 1998.

Heikal, Muhammad. *The Road to Ramadan.* London, Collins, 1975.

Sphinx and Commissar. The Rise and Fall of Soviet Influence in the Arab World. London, Collins, 1978.

Autumn of Fury: The Assassination of Sadat. London, André Deutsch, 1983.

Cutting the Lion's Tail: Suez through Egyptian Eyes. London, André Deutsch, 1986.

Hirst, David, and Beeson Irene. *Sadat.* London, Faber, 1981.

Holt, P. M. *Political and Social Change in Modern Egypt.* Oxford, Oxford University Press, 1967.

Iskander, Elizabeth. *Sectarian Conflict in Egypt: Coptic Media, Identity and Representation.* Abingdon, Routledge, 2012.

Ismael, Tareq Y., and El-Said, Rifa'at. *The Communist Movement in Egypt 1920–1988.* Syracuse, NY, Syracuse University Press, 1990.

Issawi, Charles. *Egypt in Revolution.* Oxford, 1963.

Joesten, Joachim. *Nasser: The Rise to Power.* London, Odhams, 1960.

Kamel, Muhammad Ibrahim. *The Camp David Accords: A Testimony by Sadat's Foreign Minister.* London, Routledge and Kegan Paul, 1986.

Kassem, Maye. *In the Guise of Democracy: Governance in Contemporary Egypt.* Reading, Ithaca Press, 1999.

Egyptian Politics: The Dynamics of Authoritarian Rule. Boulder, CO, Lynne Rienner, 2004.

Kassem, Maye, and Kraetzschmar, Hendrik J. *Egypt.* Abingdon, Routledge, 2006.

Kienle, Eberhard. *A Grand Delusion: Democracy and Economic Reform in Egypt.* London, I. B. Tauris, 2001.

Krause, Wanda. *Civil Society and Women Activists in the Middle East: Islamic and Secular Organizations in Egypt.* London, I. B. Tauris, 2012.

Kyle, Keith. *Suez: Britain's End of Empire in the Middle East.* London, I. B. Tauris, 2002.

Lacouture, Jean. *Nasser: A Biography.* London, Secker and Warburg, 1973.

Love, K. *Suez: The Twice-fought War.* Longman, 1970.

Mansfield, Peter. *Nasser's Egypt.* London, Penguin, 1965.

Nasser. London, Methuen, 1969.

The British in Egypt. London, Weidenfeld and Nicolson, 1971.

Marsot, Afaf Lutfi al-Sayyid. *Egypt and Cromer: A Study in Anglo-Egyptian Relations.* London, John Murray, and New York, Praeger, 1968.

A History of Egypt: From the Arab Conquest to the Present. Cambridge, Cambridge University Press, 2nd edn, 2007.

Moustafa, Tim. *The Struggle for Constitutional Power: Law, Politics and Economic Development in Egypt.* Cambridge, Cambridge University Press, 2007.

Nasser, Gamal Abdel. *Egypt's Liberation: The Philosophy of the Revolution.* Washington, DC, 1955.

Neguib, Mohammed. *Egypt's Destiny: A Personal Statement.* New York, 1955.

Nutting, Anthony. *No End of a Lesson; The Story of Suez.* London, Constable, 1967.

Nasser. London, Constable, 1972.

O'Ballance, E. *The Sinai Campaign 1956.* London, Faber, 1959.

Osman, Tarek. *Egypt on the Brink: From Nasser to Mubarak.* New Haven, CT, Yale University Press, 2010.

Quandt, William B. *Camp David: Peacemaking and Politics.* Washington, DC, Brookings Institution, 1986.

Riad, Hassan. *L'Egypte Nassérienne.* Paris, Editions de Minuit, 1964.

Rubin, Barry. *Islamic Fundamentalism in Egyptian Politics.* London, Macmillan, 1990.

Rutherford, Bruce K. *Egypt after Mubarak: Liberalism, Islam, and Democracy in the Arab World.* Princeton, NJ, Princeton University Press, 2008.

Al-Sadat, Anwar. *Revolt on the Nile.* London, Allen Wingate, 1957.

Schonfield, Hugh A. *The Suez Canal in Peace and War, 1869–1969*. London, Vallentine Mitchell, 2nd edn, 1969.

Scott, Rachel M. *The Challenge of Political Islam: Non-Muslims and the Egyptian State*. Stanford, CA, Stanford University Press, 2010.

El-Shazly, Gen. Saad. *The Crossing of Suez: The October War (1973)*. London, Third World Centre for Research and Publishing, 1980.

Shehata, Dina. *Islamists and Secularists in Egypt: Opposition, Conflict and Co-operation*. Abingdon, Routledge, 2009.

Sirrs, Owen L. *A History of the Egyptian Intelligence Service: A History of the Mukhabarat, 1910–2009*. Abingdon, Routledge, 2010.

Soueif, Ahdaf. *Cairo: My City, Our Revolution*. London, Bloomsbury, 2012.

Stephens, R. *Nasser*. London, Allen Lane and Penguin, 1971.

Tadros, Mariz. *The Muslim Brotherhood in Contemporary Egypt: Democracy Redefined or Confined?* Abingdon, Routledge, 2012.

Takeyh, Ray. *The Origins of the Eisenhower Doctrine: The US, Britain and Nasser's Egypt, 1953–57*. London, Macmillan, 2000.

Tal, Nachman. *Radical Islam in Egypt and Jordan*. Eastbourne, Sussex Academic Press, 2005.

Vatikiotis, P. J. *A Modern History of Egypt*. New York, Praeger, 1966; London, Weidenfeld and Nicolson, 1969, revised edn, 1980.

The Egyptian Army in Politics. Bloomington, IN, Indiana University Press, 1961.

Vaucher, G. *Gamal Abdel Nasser et son Equipe*. 2 vols, Leiden, Brill, 1950.

Waterbury, John. *The Egypt of Nasser and Sadat: The Political Economy of Two Regimes*. Princeton, NJ, Princeton University Press, 1983.

Wilbur, D. N. *The United Arab Republic*. New York, 1969.

Wynn, Wilton. *Nasser of Egypt: The Search for Dignity*. Cambridge, MA, 1959.

Zahid, Mohammed. *The Muslim Brotherhood and Egypt's Succession Crisis: The Politics of Liberalisation and Reform in the Middle East*. London, I. B. Tauris, 2010.

Economy

Farah, Nadia Ramsis. *Egypt's Political Economy: Power Relations in Development*. Cairo, American University of Cairo Press, 2009.

El Ghonemy, M. Riad. *Economic and Industrial Organization of Egyptian Agriculture since 1952, Egypt since the Revolution*. London, Allen and Unwin, 1968.

Egypt in the Twenty-First Century: Challenges for Development. London, Routledge, 2003.

Hopkins, Nicholas, and Westergaard, Kirsten (Eds). *Directions of Change in Rural Egypt*. New York, Columbia University Press, 1999.

Hvidt, Martin. *Water, Technology and Development: Upgrading Egypt's Irrigation System*. London, Tauris Academic Studies, 1997.

Ikram, Khalid. *The Egyptian Economy 1952–2000: Performance, Policies and Issues*. Abingdon, Routledge, 2005.

El Kammash, M. M. *Economic Development and Planning in Egypt*. London, 1967.

Kardouche, G. S. *The UAR in Development*. New York, Praeger, 1967.

Mabro, Robert. *The Egyptian Economy 1952–1972*. London, Oxford University Press, 1974.

Mead, Donald C. *Growth and Structural Change in the Egyptian Economy*. Homwood, IL, Irwin, 1967.

O'Brien, Patrick. *The Revolution in Egypt's Economic System 1952–65*. Oxford, 1966.

Posusney, Marsha Pripstein. *Labour and the State in Egypt: Workers, Unions and Economic Restructuring*. New York, Columbia University Press, 1998.

Saab, Gabriel S. *The Egyptian Agrarian Reform 1952–1962*. London and New York, Oxford University Press, 1967.

Utvik, Bjørn Olav. *Islamist Economics in Egypt: The Pious Road to Development*. Boulder, CO, Lynne Rienner Publishers, 2006.

Warriner, Doreen. *Land Reform and Economic Development*. Cairo, 1955.

Land Reform and Development in the Middle East—A Study of Egypt, Syria and Iraq. London, Oxford University Press, 2nd edn, 1962.

IRAN

Physical and Social Geography

W. B. FISHER

SITUATION

The Islamic Republic of Iran is bounded on the north by the Caspian Sea, Armenia, Azerbaijan and Turkmenistan, on the east by Afghanistan and Pakistan, on the south by the Persian (Arabian) Gulf and the Gulf of Oman, and on the west by Iraq and Turkey.

PHYSICAL FEATURES

Structurally, Iran is an extremely complex area and, owing partly to political difficulties and partly to the difficult nature of the terrain itself, complete exploration and investigation have not so far been achieved. In general, Iran consists of an interior plateau, 1,000 m to 1,500 m above sea level, ringed on almost all sides by mountain zones of varying height and extent. The largest mountain massif is that of the Zagros, which runs from the north-west, first south-westwards to the eastern shores of the Persian Gulf, and then eastwards, fronting the Arabian Sea, and continuing into Baluchistan (Pakistan). Joining the Zagros in the north-west, and running along the southern edge of the Caspian Sea, is the narrower but equally high Alborz range; along the eastern frontier of Iran are several scattered mountain chains, less continuous and imposing than either the Zagros or the Alborz, but sufficiently high to act as a barrier.

The Zagros range begins in north-western Iran as an alternation of high tablelands and lowland basins, the latter containing lakes, the largest of which is Lake Urmia. This lake, having no outlet, is saline. Further to the south-east the Zagros becomes much more imposing, consisting of a series of parallel hog's-back ridges, some of which reach over 4,000 m in height. In its southern and eastern portions the Zagros becomes distinctly narrower, and its peaks much lower, though a few exceed 3,000 m. The Alborz range is very much narrower than the Zagros, but equally, if not more, abrupt, and one of its peaks, the volcanic cone of Mt Damavand, at 5,604 m, is the highest in the country. There is a sudden drop on the northern side to the flat plain occupied by the Caspian Sea, which lies about 27 m below sea level. The eastern highlands of Iran consist of isolated massifs separated by lowland zones, some of which contain lakes from which there is no outlet, the largest being the Hirmand Basin, on the border with Afghanistan.

The interior plateau of Iran is partly covered by a salt swamp (termed *kavir*) and partly by loose sand or stones (*dasht*), with stretches of better land mostly round the perimeter, near the foothills of the surrounding mountains. In these latter areas much of the cultivation of the country is practised, but the lower-lying desert and swamp areas, towards the centre of the plateau, are largely uninhabited. The Kavir is an extremely forbidding region, consisting of a surface formed by thick plates of crystallized salt, which have sharp, upstanding edges. Below the salt lie patches of mud, with, here and there, deep drainage channels—all of which are very dangerous to travellers and are hence unexplored. Owing to the presence of an unusually intractable 'dead heart', it has proved difficult to find a good central site for the capital of Iran—many towns, all peripheral to a greater or lesser degree, have in turn fulfilled this function, but none has proved completely satisfactory. The choice of the present capital, Tehran, dates only from the end of the 18th century.

Iran suffers from occasional earthquakes, which can cause severe loss of life, damage to property and disruption of communications. A particularly bad earthquake occurred around Tabas in the north-eastern Khurasan province in September 1978, when an estimated 20,000 lives were lost; severe damage was inflicted, extending over 2,000 sq km. Even more devastating was the major earthquake that struck north-western Iran (principally the provinces of Gilan and Zanjan) in June 1990. Estimates put the total number of those killed during the quake and a series of severe tremors and aftershocks at some 40,000. In December 2003 more than 26,000 people were killed by an earthquake in the region of the ancient city of Bam, in south-eastern Iran.

The climate of Iran is one of great extremes. Owing to its southerly position, adjacent to Arabia and near the Thar Desert, the summer is extremely hot, with temperatures in the interior rising possibly higher than anywhere else in the world—certainly a temperature exceeding 55°C has been recorded. In winter, however, the great altitude of much of the country and its continental situation result in far lower temperatures than one would expect to find in such low latitudes. Temperatures of −30°C have been recorded in the north-western Zagros, and −20°C is common in many places.

Another unfortunate feature is the prevalence of strong winds, which intensify the temperature contrasts. Eastern Iran is subject to the so-called 'Wind of 120 Days', which blows regularly throughout the summer, occasionally reaching a velocity of more than 160 km per hour and raising sand to such an extent that the stone walls of buildings are sometimes scoured away and turn to ruins.

Most of Iran is arid; but in contrast, parts of the north-west and north receive considerable rainfall—up to 2,000 mm along parts of the Caspian coast, producing very special climatic conditions in this small region, recalling conditions in the lower Himalayas. The Caspian coast has a hot, humid climate and this region is by far the most densely populated of the whole country. Next in order of population density comes the north-western Zagros area—the province of Azerbaijan, with its capital, Tabriz, the fourth city of Iran. Then, reflecting the diminished rainfall, next in order come the central Zagros area, and adjacent parts of the interior plateau, around Esfahan, Hamadan, Shiraz and Bakhtaran (Kermanshah), with an extension as far as Tehran. The extreme east and south, where rainfall is very scarce, were historically extremely lightly populated, except, in the few parts where water is available, by nomadic groups.

ECONOMIC LIFE

Owing to the difficulties of climate and topography, there are few districts, apart from the Caspian plain, that are continuously cultivated over a wide area. Settlement tends to occur in small clusters, close to water supplies, or where there are especially favourable conditions—a good soil, shelter from winds or easy communications. Away from these cultivated areas, which stand out like oases among the barren expanses of desert or mountain, most of the population live as nomads, by the herding of animals. The nomadic tribesmen have had great influence on the life of Iran. Their principal territory is the central Zagros, where the tribal system is strongly developed; but nomads are found in all the mountain zones, though their numbers are very few in the south and east. Reza Shah (see History) made considerable efforts to break the power of the nomadic tribes and to force them to settle as agriculturalists. Now, with the development of the economy, many nomads have moved into towns.

Economic activity has suffered from the handicaps of topography and climate, prolonged political and social insecurity (with constant pressure by foreign powers), and widespread devastation in the later Middle Ages by Mongol invaders. Agricultural methods in particular are primitive, so that yields are low; but the drawbacks to efficient production—archaic systems of land tenure, absentee landlords, lack of education, and shortage of capital—are gradually being overcome. In the north and west, which are by far the most productive regions, a wide variety of cereals (including wheat, barley and rice) and much fruit are grown, but in the south and east dates are the principal source of food.

Iran has a number of mineral resources, some of which are exploited on a commercial scale. Copper deposits at Sar Cheshmeh are among the largest in the world. Iran also has very significant oil and natural gas resources; and there are large deposits of good-quality coal and iron ore near Kerman. Iranians have always had a good reputation as craftsmen—particularly in metalwork and carpet making. Although Reza Shah attempted to develop modern mechanized industry by siting state-owned factories in most large towns—some of which proved successful, others not—bazaar manufactures have retained their importance. Tehran is now a major manufacturing centre, with a considerable spread of activities from the processing of foodstuffs to the manufacture of consumer and construction goods as well as an increasing range of more complex items: electronic and motor manufactures and high-grade chemicals.

The adverse nature of geographical conditions has greatly restricted the growth of communications in Iran. The country is very large in relation to the size of its population—it is 2,250 km from north-west to south-west—and, because of the interior deserts, many routes must follow a circuitous path instead of attempting a direct crossing. Moreover, the interior is isolated by ranges that are in parts as high as the Alps of Europe, but far less broken up by river valleys. Road construction is generally difficult, but since the mid-1960s increasing effort has been devoted to providing all-weather trunk routes between major cities for which special allocations have been made in the five-year plans. An important link is the railway constructed with great effort before the Second World War between the Caspian coast, Tehran and the Gulf. Other rail links with bordering countries already exist or are under construction. Although there are mountain streams, many flowing in deep, inaccessible gorges, only one, the Karun river, is navigable. The Caspian ports are subject to silting, while most of the harbours in the south are either poorly sheltered or difficult of access from the interior. However, there has been a deliberate focusing of development on the Gulf, in response to the enhanced economic and political status of the region, now one of the wealthiest in the world. Development was undertaken in the region of the Shatt al-Arab during the last years of the Shah's regime. However, the war between Iran and Iraq, beginning in September 1980, greatly impeded economic prospects, both there and in the Persian Gulf. Overall, the effect of the Revolution of 1979 was to reduce, though not entirely to terminate, the sophisticated industrial developments that were initiated under the Shah, and to shift external trading more towards imports of basic raw materials and food, balanced (often by direct exchange approaching barter) by exports of petroleum.

LANGUAGE

Several languages are current in Iran. Persian (Farsi), an Indo-Aryan language related to the languages of Western Europe, is spoken in the north and centre of the country, and is the only official language of the state. As the north is by far the most densely populated region of Iran, the Persian language has an importance somewhat greater than its territorial extent would suggest. Various dialects of Kurdish are current in the north and central Zagros mountains, and alongside these are found several Turki-speaking tribes. Baluchi is spoken in the extreme south-east.

History

Revised by JALIL ROSHANDEL

EARLY HISTORY

The Achaemenid empire, the first Persian empire, was founded by Cyrus, who revolted against the Median empire in 533 BC. After the defeat of the Median empire, Babylon was taken in 529 BC. Then in 525 BC the successor of Cyrus, Cambyses, conquered Egypt. This period of conquest was completed by Darius, who reduced the tribes of the Pontic and Armenian mountains while extending the Persian dominion to the Caucasus. The main work of Darius, however, lay not in the conquest but in the organization that he gave to the empire. During his reign, wars with Greece broke out and in 490 BC the Persian army suffered a major defeat at Marathon; an expedition under Xerxes, the successor of Darius, which set out to avenge this defeat was eventually defeated at Salamis in 480 BC. The empire was finally overthrown by Alexander of Macedon, who defeated the Persian army at Arbela in 331 BC and then burnt Persepolis, the Achaemenid capital; the last Darius then fled and was killed in 330 BC. Alexander thereafter regarded himself as the head of the Persian empire. His death in 323 BC was followed by a struggle between his generals, one of whom, Seleucus, took the whole of Persia, apart from northern Media, and founded the Seleucid empire. About 250 BC a reaction against Hellenism began with the rise of the Parthian empire of the Arsacids. Although by origin nomads from the Turanian steppe, the Arsacids became the wardens of the north-east marches and were preoccupied in defending themselves in the east against the Scythians who, with the Tocharians and Sacae, attacked the Parthian empire; they were engaged in fending off attacks by the Romans in the west.

The Arsacids were succeeded by the Sasanians, who, like the Achaemenids, came from Fars and were Zoroastrians. Ardashir Babakan subdued the neighbouring states (c. AD 212) and made war on Arsacid Artabanus V, eventually defeating him. The empire that he founded largely continued the traditions of the Achaemenids, although it never equalled the Achaemenid empire in extent. The monarchy of the Sasanian period was a religious and civil institution. The monarch, who ruled by divine right, was absolute but his autocracy was limited by the powers of the Zoroastrian hierarchy and the feudal aristocracy. During the reign of Qubad (488–531), a movement of social and religious revolt, led by Mazdak, gained ground. Under Qubad's successor, Anushiravan (531–79), orthodoxy was restored, but at the cost of the imposition of a military despotism. Like the Arsacids, the Sasanians were occupied in the west with wars against Rome and in the east with repelling the advances of nomads from Central Asia.

MUSLIM PERSIA

By the beginning of the seventh century AD Persia had been weakened by these conflicts, so when the Muslim Arabs attacked at Qadisiyya (637) and Nihavand (c. 641), little effective resistance was offered. Persia did not re-emerge as a political entity until the 16th century, although with the decline of the Abbasid empire semi-independent and independent dynasties arose in different parts of Persia. At times they even incorporated under their rule an area extending beyond the confines of present-day Iran. As a result of the Arab conquest Persia became part of the Muslim world. However, local administration remained in the hands of the indigenous population, allowing many local customs to continue to be observed. In due course a new civilization developed in Persia, the unifying force of which was Islam.

With the transfer of the capital of the Islamic empire from Damascus to Baghdad (c. 750), Persian influence began to be felt in the life of the empire. Islam had already replaced Zoroastrianism and by the 10th century modern Persian, written in the Arabic script and including a large number of

Arabic words in its vocabulary, became established. Its emergence was of immense importance; the literary tradition for which it became the vehicle kept alive a national consciousness among the Iranians and preserved the memory of the great Persian empires of the past.

By the early ninth century the Abbasid caliphate began to disintegrate. In the 11th century control of the north-eastern frontiers broke down and the Ghuzz Turks invaded Persia. This movement was ethnologically important since it altered the balance of population. The Turkish element became second to the Persian in numbers and influence, and it was in the Seljuq empire that the main lines of the politico-economic structure were developed. The basis of this structure was the land assignment, the holder of which was often a petty, territorial ruler who was required to provide the ruler with a military contingent.

The Seljuq empire disintegrated in the 12th century into a number of successor states; the 13th century saw the Mongol invasion and in 1258 Hulagu, the grandson of Chinghiz (Jenghiz) Khan, sacked Baghdad and destroyed the caliphate. For some years the Ilkhan dynasty, founded by Hulagu, ruled Persia as vassals of the Great Khan in Qaraqorum, but from the reign of Abaqa (1265–81) onwards they became a Persian dynasty, having also converted to Islam. Their empire, like that of the Seljuqs before them—and for the same reason—broke up at the beginning of the 14th century into a number of lesser states. Towards the end of the century Persia again fell under the dominion of a military conqueror, when Timur, who had started his career as the warden of the marches in the Oxus-Jaxartes basin against the nomads of Central Asia, undertook a series of military campaigns against Persia between 1381 and 1387. Timur's kingdom was short-lived and rapidly disintegrated upon the death of his son Shahrukh, with the western part falling first to the Turkomans of the Black Sheep and then to the Turkomans of the White Sheep, while Transoxania passed into the hands of the Uzbegs.

THE PERSIAN MONARCHY

The 16th century saw the foundation of the Safavid empire, which was accompanied by an eastward movement of the Turkomans from Asia Minor back into Persia. For the first time since the Muslim conquest Persia reappeared as a political unit. The foundations of the Safavid empire were laid by Isma'il Safavi (1502–24). He fostered a sense of separateness and of national unity vis-à-vis the Ottoman Turks, with whom the Safavids were engaged in a struggle for supremacy in the west, using Shi'ism as his main weapon to accomplish this purpose. Not only the Turks but also the majority of his own subjects were Sunni Muslims at the time—nevertheless, Safavi imposed Shi'ism upon them by force and created a sense of national unity as Persians among the population of his dominions, many of whom, especially among his immediate followers, were Turks. Apart from a brief interlude under Nadir Shah, Shi'ism has remained the majority rite in Persia and is still the official rite of the country today. Under Shah Abbas (1587–1629) the Safavid empire reached its zenith, allowing Persia to enjoy a power and prosperity that it has not regained since.

GREAT POWER RIVALRY

During the Safavid period contact with Europe increased. Various foreign embassies interested in the silk trade reached the Safavid court via Russia and the Persian (Arabian) Gulf. In the early years of the 16th century a struggle for supremacy developed between the British and the Dutch in the Gulf, where 'factories' began to be established by the East India Company.

Under the later Safavids internal decline set in and during 1722–30 Persia was subject to Afghan invasion and occupation, while in the west and north it was threatened by Turkey and Russia. After the death of Peter the Great there was a temporary slackening of Russian pressure, but the Turks continued to advance and took Tabriz in 1725, peace eventually being made at Hamadan in 1727. The Afghans were finally evicted in 1736 by Nadir Shah Afshar, who was known for his military exploits and reigned during 1736–47. The Afsharids were succeeded by Karim Khan Zand (1750–79), whose peaceful reign was followed by the rise of the Qajars, who continued to rule until 1925. Under them the capital was transferred from Esfahan to Tehran. During the Qajar period events in Persia became increasingly affected by Great Power rivalry, which came to dominate Persia's foreign policy and internal politics.

With the growth of British influence in India in the late 18th and early 19th centuries the main emphasis in Anglo-Persian relations began to shift from commerce to strategy. The region of Persia and the Persian Gulf became regarded as one of the main bastions protecting British India, and the existence of an independent Persia as a major British interest. In the early 19th century fear of a French invasion of India through Persia exercised the minds of the British in India and Whitehall. French envoys were active in Persia and Mesopotamia from 1796 to 1809, and to counter possible French activities Captain (later Sir) John Malcolm was sent to Persia in 1800 by the Governor-General of India. He concluded a political and commercial treaty with Fath Ali Shah, with the purpose of ensuring that the Shah should not receive French agents and would do his utmost to prevent French forces from entering Persia. With the defeat of Napoleon in Egypt the matter was no longer regarded as urgent, and the agreement was not ratified. Subsequently, the French made proposals to Persia for an alliance against Russia, and in 1807 Persia concluded the Treaty of Finkenstein with France, after which a military mission under Gen. Gardanne came to Persia. In 1808 another British mission was sent under Malcolm. Its object was primarily to detach the Court of Persia from the French alliance and to prevail on that Court to refuse the passage of French troops through the territories subject to Persia, or the admission of French troops into the country. Malcolm's task was complicated by the almost simultaneous arrival of a similar mission from Whitehall. In 1809 after the Treaty of Tilsit, which debarred the French from aiding the Shah against Russia, Gardanne was dismissed.

WARS WITH RUSSIA, TURKEY AND THE UNITED KINGDOM

Meanwhile, the formal annexation of Georgia by Russia in 1801 was followed by a campaign against Russia. This proved disastrous to Persia and was temporarily brought to an end by the Treaty of Gulistan (1813), by which Persia ceded Georgia, Qara Bagh and seven other provinces. British policy remained concerned with the possibility of an invasion of India via Persia, and in 1814 the Treaty of Tehran was concluded with Persia—by which the United Kingdom undertook to provide troops or a subsidy in the event of unprovoked aggression against Persia. Although the treaty provided for defence against any European power, it was intended to counteract the designs of Russia. In fact it proved ineffective: when the Perso–Russian war recommenced in 1825 the United Kingdom did not interfere except as a peacemaker and discontinued the subsidy to Persia, which was the aggressor. The war was concluded in 1828 by the Treaty of Turkomanchai, under the terms of which Persia ceded Erivan and Nakhjivan and agreed to pay an indemnity; in addition, it was prohibited from having armed vessels on the Caspian Sea.

During this period Persia was also engaged in hostilities with Turkey. Frontier disputes in 1821 culminated in the outbreak of war, which was concluded by the Treaty of Erzurum (1823).

By the 19th century the Persian Government had ceased to exercise effective control over the greater part of Khurasan. Russian policy encouraged the Shah to reimpose Persian rule on the eastern provinces. British policy, on the other hand, came to regard Afghanistan as an important link in the defence of India and urged moderation upon the Persian Government. After the accession of Muhammad Shah in 1834, an expedition was sent against Herat. The siege of Herat began in 1837, but was lifted when the Shah was threatened with British intervention. Subsequently, local intrigues enabled the Persians to enter Herat. The seizure of the city by Persia led to the outbreak of the Anglo–Persian war in 1856.

In the second half of the century Russia's subjection of the Turkoman tribes, its capture of Marv in 1854 and the occupation of the Panjeh meant that Russian influence became dominant in Khurasan in the same way as the advance of Russia to the Araxes after the Persian wars in the early part of the 19th century made Russian influence dominant in Azerbaijan.

INCREASED FOREIGN INTERVENTION

Internally, the second half of the 19th century was remarkable chiefly for the beginnings of the modernist movement, which was stimulated on the one hand by internal misgovernment and on the other by increased intervention in the internal affairs of the country by Russia and the United Kingdom. Towards the end of the century numerous concessions were granted to foreigners, largely in order to pay for the extravagances of the court. The most fantastic of these was the Reuter concession. In 1872 a naturalized British subject, Baron de Reuter, was given by the Shah a monopoly for 70 years of railways and tramways in Persia, all the minerals except gold, silver and precious stones, irrigation, road, factory and telegraph enterprises, and the farm of customs dues for 25 years. Eventually he received only a Persian state bank with British capital, which was to have the exclusive right to issue banknotes: thus in September 1889 the Imperial Bank of Persia began trading. In the same year Prince Dolgoruki obtained for Russia the first option of a railway concession for five years. In November 1890 the railway agreement with Russia was changed into one interdicting all railways in Persia. By the turn of the century there had been a pronounced sharpening of Anglo–Russian hostility. In 1900 a Russian loan was given to Persia. Subsequently, various short-term advances and subsidies from the Russian treasury, including advances to the heir apparent, Muhammad Ali, were made so that by 1906 some £7.5m. was owed to the Russians. Under the 1891 Russo-Persian tariff treaty bilateral trade had increased, and when, under the 1901 Russo-Persian commercial treaty, a new customs tariff was announced in 1903, Russian exports to Persia were considerably aided, and, up to 1914, Russian commerce with Persia continued to grow.

These concessions to foreigners and the raising of foreign loans led to growing anxiety on the part of the Persian public. Furthermore, large numbers of Persians fled the country and were living in exile. When a tobacco monopoly was granted to a British subject in 1890, various elements of the population, including the intellectuals and religious classes, combined to oppose it. Strikes and riots threatened and the monopoly was rescinded. No effective steps, however, were taken to allay popular discontent. In 1901 protests were made against the loans and mortgages from Russia which were being contracted to pay for Muzaffar ul-Din Shah's journeys to Europe. Demand for reform increased, and finally, on 5 August 1906, after 12,000 people had taken sanctuary in the British legation, a constitution was granted. A long struggle then began between the constitutionalists and the Shah. The Cossack Brigade, formed during the reign of Nasir ul-Din Shah, which was under Russian officers and was the most effective military force in the country, played a major part in this struggle and was used by Muhammad Ali Shah to suppress the National Assembly in 1908. Civil war ensued, and Muhammad Ali Shah's abdication was forced in 1909.

Meanwhile, in 1907 the Anglo-Russian convention was signed. The convention, which included a mutual undertaking to respect the integrity and independence of Persia, divided the country into three areas: that lying to the north of a line passing from Qasr-e-Shirin to Kakh, where the Russian, Persian and Afghan frontiers met in the east; that lying to the south of a line running from Qazik, on the Perso–Afghan frontier, through Birjand and Kerman to Bandar Abbas on the Persian Gulf; and that lying outside these two areas. Great Britain gave an undertaking not to seek or support others looking for political or economic concessions in the northern area, while Russia gave a similar undertaking with reference to the southern area. In the central area the freedom of action of the two parties was not limited, and their existing concessions were maintained. The conclusion of this convention—which had taken place partly because of a change in the relative strength of the Great Powers and partly because the British Government hoped thereby to terminate Anglo–Russian rivalry in Persia and to prevent further Russian encroachments—came as a shock to Persian opinion, which had hoped for much from the support the British Government had given to the constitutional movement. It was believed that Persian interests had been bartered away by Britain for a promise of Russian support in the event of a European war. In fact, the convention failed in its objective. Russian pressure continued to be exercised on Persia directly and indirectly, leading, in 1911, to the suspension of the National Assembly and the forced resignation of the Administrator-General of the Finances, W. Morgan Shuster, who had been appointed in the hope of bringing order to Persia's finances.

THE FIRST WORLD WAR

During the First World War (1914–18) Persia was officially neutral but, in fact, pro-Turkish. By the end of the war the internal condition of Persia was chaotic. To the British Government the restoration of order was desirable; with this end in view the Agreement of 1919 was drawn up whereby personnel were to be lent to reorganize the Persian army and to reform the Ministry of Finance, and a loan of £2m. was to be given. However, there was opposition to this agreement in the USA,France and in Persia itself, and the treaty was not ratified. A *coup d'état* took place in 1921, with Reza Khan (later Reza Shah) becoming Minister of War. In February of that year the Soviet-Persian Treaty was signed whereby the Soviet authorities declared all treaties and conventions concluded with Persia by the Tsarist Government null and void.

REZA SHAH, 1925–41, AND AFTER

In 1923 Reza Khan became Prime Minister. His first task was to restore the authority of the central Government throughout the country, and place Persia's relations with foreign countries on a basis of equality. All extra-territorial agreements were terminated from 1928. Lighterage and quarantine duties on the Persian littoral of the Gulf, hitherto performed by Britain, were transferred to the Persian Government in 1930. The Indo-European Telegraphy Company, which had been in operation since 1872, had been almost entirely withdrawn by 1931, and the British coaling stations were transferred from Basidu and Henjam to Bahrain in 1935.

In 1932 the cancellation of the Anglo-Persian Oil Co's concession was announced by Persia. The original concession obtained by William Knox D'Arcy in 1901 had been taken over by the Anglo-Persian Oil Co in 1909 and the British Government acquired a controlling interest in the company in 1914. The Persian Government's action in cancelling the concession was referred to the League of Nations. Eventually an agreement was reached in 1933 for a new concession whereby the concession area was reduced and the royalty paid to the Persian Government increased. The concession was to run until 1993.

Internally, Reza Shah's policy was aimed at modernization, though it later edged towards totalitarianism. The introduction of compulsory military service led to the expansion of the army, while communications were greatly improved and the construction of a trans-Persian railway was begun. In 1935 Reza Shah, facing internal dissent, officially changed the name of the country to Iran. Education was remodelled on Western lines and women were no longer obliged to wear the full-face veil (*niqab*) after 1936. Foreign trade was made a state monopoly, and currency and clearing restrictions were established. These arrangements were compatible with the economy of Germany, and, by the outbreak of the Second World War in 1939 Germany had acquired considerable commercial and political influence in Iran.

Although Iran declared its neutrality at the outbreak of war, by 1941 the Allies had become exasperated by the extent of German influence in Iran and demanded the expulsion of German nationals. This demand was not met, and on 26 August the Allies invaded Iran; hostilities lasted for some two days, leading to Reza Shah's abdication in favour of his son Muhammad Reza on 16 September. In January 1942 a Tripartite Treaty of Alliance was concluded with Britain and the USSR whereby those countries undertook jointly and severally 'to respect the territorial integrity, sovereignty and political independence of Iran' and 'to defend Iran by all means in their command from aggression'. According to the terms of the agreement, the Iranian Government undertook to give the Allies, for military purposes, access to and control of all means of communications in Iran. Allied forces were to be withdrawn not later than six months after the conclusion of hostilities between the Allied Powers and Germany and its associates. However, it soon became clear that the division of administrative powers among the occupying Allied forces was significantly reducing both freedom of movement and the effectiveness of government.

In September 1944, in reaction to proposals made by foreign oil companies, the Iranian Cabinet issued a decree deferring the granting of oil concessions until after the war. Meanwhile, the USSR prevented Iranian security forces from entering Azerbaijan or the Caspian provinces, and an autonomous government was established in Azerbaijan in December 1945. In January 1946 the Iranian Government had recourse to the UN Security Council, and though British and US forces evacuated Iran after the expiration of the Tripartite Treaty in March, Soviet forces remained. The Iranian Government again appealed to the Security Council, and in April an understanding was reached whereby a joint Soviet-Iranian company to exploit the oil in the northern provinces was to be formed. Although Soviet forces evacuated the country in May, Soviet pressure continued to be exerted through the communist Tudeh Party, the Democrat movement in Azerbaijan and the Kurdish autonomy movement, and the Iranian Government was unable to re-enter Azerbaijan until December. In October 1947 an agreement was signed with the USA, providing for a US military mission in Iran to co-operate with the Iranian Ministry of War in 'enhancing the efficiency of the Iranian army'.

NATIONALIZING THE OIL INDUSTRY

A nationalist movement came to the fore in 1950 in reaction to civil unrest and discontent prompted by internal misgovernment. Initially, opposition was brought about by the Supplemental Oil Agreement signed with the Anglo-Iranian Oil Co (as the Anglo-Persian Oil Co had been renamed in 1935) in July 1949, and in November 1950 the oil commission of the National Assembly recommended its rejection. Meanwhile, Iran received a loan of US $25m. from the Export-Import Bank of Washington and a grant of $500,000 under the Point IV allocation. Subsequently, in 1952 the Point IV aid programme was expanded. In April 1951 the National Assembly enacted legislation for the nationalization of the oil industry, and in May Dr Muhammad Musaddeq, who had led the campaign for nationalization of oil, became Prime Minister. In spite of efforts to involve the International Court of Justice (ICJ), the status quo could not be maintained in Iran and the Anglo-Iranian Oil Co, unable to continue operations, evacuated the country later that year.

The dispute between Anglo-Iranian and the Iranian Government soon became enmeshed in US policy. A joint offer by British Prime Minister Sir Winston Churchill and US President Harry S Truman, concerning proposals to assess the compensation to be paid to the Anglo-Iranian Oil Co, and the resumption of the flow of oil to world markets, was rejected by the Iranian Government. In October 1952 the Iranian Government broke off diplomatic relations with Britain and further Anglo-American proposals for an oil settlement were rejected by the Iranian Government in February 1953. Meanwhile, dissension between Musaddeq and some of his supporters broke out, and a rift also developed between the Prime Minister and the Shah. Iran's economic situation began to deteriorate, culminating in the overthrow of Musaddeq by Gen. Zahedi in August. Musaddeq was tried and sentenced to three years in prison for allegedly trying to overthrow the regime and illegally dissolving the Majlis e-Shura (Consultative Assembly).

GROWING POWER OF THE SHAH AND HIS REFORMS

Although internal order was initially restored, the failure of the Government to push forward with reform led to a further outbreak of civil unrest. In April 1955 Zahedi resigned and was succeeded by Hussein Ala; in November an attempt was made to assassinate the Prime Minister. The country had not recovered from the financial difficulties brought on by the Musaddeq regime in spite of considerable financial aid (more than US $800m.) granted by the USA. In March 1959 a bilateral defence agreement was signed in Ankara, Turkey, between the USA and Iran. Under the agreement, the US Government would 'in case of aggression, take such appropriate action, including the use of armed force, as may be mutually agreed, and as envisaged in the Joint Resolution to promote peace and security in the Middle East'. (The Joint Resolution refers to the 'Eisenhower Doctrine'.)

Relations with the USSR in the years following the fall of Musaddeq were not cordial, but in December 1954 an agreement was reached concerning the repayment of Soviet debts to Iran for goods supplied and services rendered.

In April 1957 Hussein Ala resigned and was succeeded as Prime Minister by Dr Manoutchehr Egbal, who immediately declared an end to martial law and announced his intention to form a democratic two-party system in accordance with the wishes of the Shah. In February 1958 a pro-Government Nation Party was formed. An opposition Mardom (People's) Party had been established in 1957. Elections contested by both these political parties disclosed electoral irregularities, and in August 1960 Dr Jaafar Sharif-Emami replaced Egbal as Prime Minister. In May 1961, however, Sharif-Emami resigned as a result of criticism of his handling of a teachers' strike, and the Shah called upon Dr Ali Amini, the leader of the opposition, to form a new government. Amini took uncompromising measures to halt the political and economic chaos in Iran, instigating a drive against corruption in the government and civil service. Both houses of parliament were dissolved pending the enactment of a new electoral law that would make free and fair elections possible. Postponement of elections in July 1962 gave rise to disorder in Tehran, and the added difficulty of producing a reasonably balanced budget led Dr Amini to resign.

A new Government was formed by Assadollah Alam, the leader of the Mardom Party. Alam, one of Iran's largest landowners and administrator of the Pahlavi Foundation, was renowned for redistributing much of his own land among the peasants, and pledged to continue the land reform programme and the struggle against internal political corruption. Elections in September 1963 resulted in an overwhelming victory for Alam's coalition group, the National Union. The elections were the first in which women were allowed to vote, but were held in the face of strong opposition from the left-wing parties of Iran, which campaigned unsuccessfully for a boycott. The Shah called on the new parliament to inaugurate a 20-year programme of economic and social reform and political development, and also announced a second phase of the land reform programme, whereby it was hoped that another 20,000 villages would be added to the 10,000 already ceded to the tenants. The Government continued to be in power until March 1964, when Alam resigned. The new leader, Hassan Ali Mansur, a former minister and founder of the Progressive Centre, had played a prominent part in Alam's coalition in the previous year. In December 1963 Mansur formed the New Iran Party, which by then had the support of some 150 members of the Majlis. The second stage of the land reform plan was placed before the Majlis in May 1964, aiming to break down the great estates more thoroughly: the maximum permissible size was to range from 120 ha in arid regions to 30 ha in more fertile areas.

On 21 January 1965 Mansur was assassinated by members of the right-wing religious sect Fedayin Islam. The assassins were reportedly followers of the Ayatollah Ruhollah Khomeini, a Shi'a Muslim religious leader who had been exiled to Iraq in 1964 for his opposition to the Shah's reforms. Amir Abbas Hoveyda, the Minister of Finance, was immediately appointed Prime Minister, while retaining his ministerial post. He pledged the continuation of his predecessor's policies, and was given the support of the Majlis.

The Shah had begun distributing his estate among the peasants in 1950. By the end of 1963 he had disposed of all his Crown Properties. In January 1963 a referendum gave overwhelming approval to the Shah's six-point plan, which included the distribution of lands among the peasants, the promotion of literacy and the emancipation of women. The dismantling of great estates began almost immediately, and the programme was finally completed in September 1971.

FOREIGN RELATIONS UNDER THE SHAH

Mansur was keen for Iran to maintain links with the USSR. During 1964–65 various bilateral trade and technical agreements were signed, resulting in the establishment of a regular commercial air service between Tehran and Moscow. In June 1965 the Shah visited Moscow, and in October an agreement was signed for the construction of a steel mill by Soviet engineers. November 1967 saw the formal ending of US economic aid under the Point IV programme. Iran, which had been the first country to accept this aid in 1951, was now the second—after Taiwan (Republic of China)—able to dispense with it; US military aid, however, continued. At the same time economic co-operation with the USSR was developed, and an agreement was made for the purchase of £40m. of munitions, the first occasion on which the USSR had concluded an arms transaction with an ally of the Western powers.

In January 1968 the British Government announced its decision to withdraw all of its forces from the Gulf by the end of 1971, raising fears of a revival of the ancient rivalry between the Arabs and Persians over supremacy in the Gulf. The Iranian Government continued to reiterate its claim to Bahrain, but it did welcome the proposed Federation of Arab Emirates (which it was thought would incorporate Bahrain). In June 1970 a dispute with other Gulf states arose over Iran's claim to the islands of Abu Musa and the Tunbs—belonging to Sharjah and Ras al-Khaimah, respectively. The dispute was settled in December 1971. The Sheikh of Sharjah agreed to share sovereignty of Abu Musa with Iran. The Sheikh of Ras al-Khaimah was less accommodating, so Iran invaded his possessions of the Greater and Lesser Tunbs and took them by force. After occupying Abu Musa and the Tunbs, Iran developed them into military bases, which commanded the Strait of Hormuz at the neck of the Gulf. Iran regarded the maintenance of freedom of passage through the Strait of Hormuz as vital to its strategic and economic interests.

Iran's relations with the more radical Arab states were less friendly under the Shah. These states had long been suspicious of Iran's close ties with the West, and especially of the generous US military aid to the powerful Iranian armed forces. Moreover, the Arab states distrusted Iran's attitude towards Israel. Although no formal diplomatic links existed, petroleum trading was conducted with Israel. The frontier with Iraq along the Shatt al-Arab waterway—the estuary of the Tigris and Euphrates that flows into the Gulf—had been delineated by a 1937 treaty. Under its terms the frontier followed the eastern—i.e. Iranian—bank: thus, Iraq legally had sovereignty over the whole waterway. In April 1969 Iran decided to abrogate the treaty, sending Iranian vessels through the waterway while naval forces stood ready to intervene; there were further border clashes in September. In January 1970 Iraq accused the Iranian Government of supporting an abortive coup in Iraq, and diplomatic relations between the two countries were severed. Once again in 1975, Iran and Iraq almost started a war on the Shatt al-Arab waterway, but finally the Shah of Iran managed signing the 1975 Algiers Agreement (dividing the Shatt al-Arab waterway) between Iran and Iraq.

INTERNAL UNREST AND THE FALL OF THE SHAH

Signs of domestic opposition to the Shah's regime became increasingly evident as the celebrations for the 2,500th anniversary of the Persian monarchy were being prepared for October 1971. The lavishness of the festivities and the extent of the accompanying security precautions compounded ill feelings that arose from the unequal distribution of oil revenue and the suppression of dissent. From then until the final fall of the Shah in early 1979 there were numerous accounts of the stifling of opposition by the ruthless activities of SAVAK, the government security agency. In March 1975 the Shah, dissatisfied with the current structure of party politics in Iran, sought to bring together those who supported the principles of his 'White Revolution' policy (later known as the 'Revolution of the Shah and People'), and announced the formation of a single-party system, the Iran National Resurgence Party (Rastakhiz), with the Prime Minister, Hoveyda, as Secretary-General. By 1978 it became clear that the single-party Rastakhiz system was not solving the problem of internal opposition in Iran.

Throughout 1977 and 1978 the universities became the focus of demonstrations, and acts of political violence increased. Attempts by the Shah to control the situation, first by greater liberalization and then through firmer suppression, proved ineffective. In August 1977 Amouzegar, who had earlier been appointed Secretary-General of Rastakhiz, replaced the long-serving Hoveyda as Prime Minister, but he resigned a year later. In August 1978 Jaafar Sharif-Emami was appointed Prime Minister (an office he had previously held in 1960–61) and promised that his Government would observe Islamic tenets. However, unrest continued; martial law was introduced in September, and in November the Shah established a military Government headed by the army Chief of Staff, Gen. Gholamreza Azhari. Censorship was imposed, but industrial action undertaken by workers in the oil industry and public services left the Shah in a desperate situation, and in early January 1979 he charged Dr Shapour Bakhtiar, a former deputy leader of the National Front, with forming a 'last-chance' government. Dr Bakhtiar attempted to dissolve SAVAK, halt the export of oil to South Africa and Israel, and support the Palestinians. However, opposition to the Shah continued to such an extent that he left the country on 15 January, never to return.

The opposition within Iran had stemmed from two main sources. By the time of the Shah's departure, opposition from the left and the more 'liberal' National Front had been overshadowed by the success of the opposition movement surrounding the exiled fundamentalist leader Ayatollah Khomeini. He conducted his campaign from France, where he arrived in October 1978 after 14 years of exile in Iraq for opposing the Shah's 'White Revolution'. In January 1979 Khomeini formed an Islamic Revolutionary Council from his base near the French capital, Paris; in Iran pressure grew for his return. The Bakhtiar Government tried to delay this for as long as possible, but on 1 February Khomeini arrived in Tehran from Paris to a tumultuous welcome from the Iranian people. Bakhtiar refused to recognize Khomeini, but, after several demonstrations and outbreaks of violence, the army withdrew its support from Bakhtiar and he resigned on 11 February. Dr Mehdi Bazargan, named 'Provisional Prime Minister' by Khomeini on 6 February, formed a provisional government later in the month; however, it was evident that real power rested with Khomeini's 15-member Islamic Revolutionary Council.

IRAN UNDER AYATOLLAH KHOMEINI

Although Khomeini became the de facto leader of Iran, the difficulties of putting into practice the ideals of the Islamic Revolution tested the Revolutionary Government. There was conflict between members of the Islamic Revolutionary Council and also between the new rulers in Tehran and the country's ethnic minorities. Most serious was the demand for autonomy from the Kurds in the north-west, which often led to open warfare in that area. Conflict with the Arabs in the south-west also interacted with hostile relations with Iraq, which subsequently culminated in the Iran–Iraq War in September 1980. The position was complicated by the fact that these minorities were Sunni Muslims, while the Khomeini regime and the majority of Iranians were Shi'a.

Khomeini's regime from the outset condemned previous US interference in Iranian affairs, and when, on 4 November 1979, Iranian students seized 53 hostages in the US embassy in Tehran, Khomeini was quite ready to offer his support to the students who demanded the return of the Shah (then in the USA) to Iran to face trial. This problem dominated relations with the USA for the next 14 months, and was not resolved by the death of the Shah in Egypt on 27 July 1980. In April 1980 the USA launched an airborne military operation to free the hostages (code-named Operation Eagle Claw), landing a commando force in eastern Iran. The operation was aborted at an early stage, however, due to equipment failure. Eight men died when a helicopter collided with a transport aircraft as the force prepared to abandon the mission. Internal disagreements meant that the first Islamic Majlis was slow to address the problem of the hostages; they were not released until 20 January 1981. Meanwhile, one of the first actions of the Khomeini regime in early 1979 was to end all ties with Israel and to align Iran firmly with the Arab cause, by allowing, for example the Palestine Liberation Organization (PLO) to open an office in Tehran.

At the end of March 1979 Ayatollah Khomeini held a referendum to ascertain the level of popular support for the creation of an Islamic republic. The result was almost unanimously in favour, and on 1 April the Islamic Republic of Iran was declared. A draft constitution proposed that Iran be governed by a president, prime minister and a single-chamber Majlis-e-Shura-e Islami (Islamic Consultative Assembly) of 270 deputies. Although there was pressure in Iran to submit the draft constitution to a newly elected Constituent Assembly, Khomeini presented it for revision to a Majlis-e Khobregan (Assembly of Experts), comprising 75 members who were elected on 3 August. The most important feature of the draft constitution was provision for a *Wali Faqih* (supreme religious leader—initially Khomeini), whose extensive powers accorded him the most important executive influence in Iran. The new Constitution was approved with minimal opposition.

Presidential elections followed on 27 January 1980, and resulted in a convincing victory for Abolhasan Bani-Sadr, with about 75% of the votes cast. Until then the Islamic Revolutionary Council had effectively been administering the country, although there was a Government headed by Dr Mehdi Bazargan until his resignation in mid-November 1979 over Khomeini's support for the retention of the US hostages. Thereafter the Islamic Revolutionary Council ruled more openly, appointing ministers to run the country until elections to the Majlis. It was clear that the Islamic Republican Party (IRP), aligned with the policies of Ayatollah Khomeini, was in a majority, claiming 130 seats in the Islamic Revolutionary Council. The IRP leader, Ayatollah Beheshti, was perceived as a threat to the leadership of President Bani-Sadr. On 7 May Khomeini gave Bani-Sadr authority to appoint a Prime Minister until the Majlis convened, but Beheshti successfully prevented this, insisting that the appointment of a premier should be the responsibility of the Majlis.

The Islamic Revolutionary Council was dissolved on 18 July 1980, but there followed a delay in forming a government. Many of the candidates for ministerial office who were proposed by the Majlis and supported by the IRP were unacceptable to President Bani-Sadr. The President reluctantly agreed to the appointment of Muhammad Ali Rajai as Prime Minister, although a feud subsequently developed between President Bani-Sadr, and Rajai and the IRP. In June 1981 Khomeini dismissed Bani-Sadr as Commander-in-Chief of the Armed Forces; soon afterwards Bani-Sadr was deprived of the presidency, and later fled to France, where he formed a 'National Council of Resistance' in alliance with Massoud Rajavi, the former leader in Iran of the opposition guerrilla group, the Mujahidin-e-Khalq. A three-man Presidential Council replaced Bani-Sadr until new presidential elections could be held. However, on 28 June a bomb exploded at the headquarters of the IRP, killing Ayatollah Beheshti (the Chief Justice and head of the IRP), four cabinet ministers, six deputy ministers and 20 parliamentary deputies.

The presidential election on 24 July 1981 resulted in a victory for Muhammad Ali Rajai. Muhammad Javad Bahonar then succeeded Rajai as Prime Minister. A further bomb exploded on 29 August, killing both the President and the Prime Minister. Ayatollah Muhammad Reza Mahdavi Kani became Prime Minister in September, and another round of presidential elections was held on 2 October. Ali Khamenei, a leading figure of the IRP, was elected President, winning more than 16m. of the 16.8m. votes cast. At the end of October, after the resignation of Ayatollah Muhammad Reza Mahdavi Kani, Mir Hossein Mousavi was appointed Prime Minister.

THE IRAN–IRAQ WAR, 1980–86

After the Iranian Revolution came to an end and tensions within the region began to diminish, Iraq's President, Saddam Hussain, began to seek ways of expanding Iraq's influence in the Middle East with the aim of making it a strong regional power. Hussain and his supporters believed that one way to do this was through the invasion of Iran. They calculated that an attack would increase Iraq's potential oil reserves and prove that it was a force to be reckoned with following a period of great instability within Iran.

Months of rhetorical manoeuvring were met with real threats—in late April and early May 1980 Iran's embassy in London, United Kingdom, was attacked by a militant group campaigning for autonomy for the largely Arab region of Khuzestan. However, Iraq's desire for territorial gain and isolated incidents of violence all came to a head in March 1980 following the attempted assassination of Iraqi Deputy Prime Minister and Minister of Foreign Affairs Tareq Aziz. Hussain blamed 'Iranian agents', in reference to the Iranian-supported, largely Shi'a Al-Dawah organization. This event served as the pretext for the larger conflict to come.

In late September 1980 Saddam Hussain unilaterally abrogated the treaty between Iran and Iraq and attacked the capital, Tehran, and other major cities in Iran. Soon both sides launched a campaign of bombing raids, which were followed by sustained combat on the ground. To Hussain's great surprise, Iran's Arab minority remained loyal to Tehran despite his belief that the Iraqi invasion of Khuzestan would result in an outpouring of discontent and rejection of Khomeini's fundamentalist regime.

By the time of Mousavi's appointment as Prime Minister, expectations grew outside Iran that the Islamic Revolution was about to disintegrate. Yet, by mid-1983, following early periods of stalemate, Iran was seemingly making the greater territorial gains. Separate offensives in early 1982 had resulted in advances in the region of Shush-Dezful and the recapture of the port of Khorramshahr. A further Iranian offensive in July saw its forces entrenched 15 km within northern Iraq. Iraq escalated its response in the second half of 1983, increasing missile and aircraft raids against Iranian towns and petroleum installations. Iran countered by declaring its intention to make the Gulf impassable to all shipping should Iraqi military action render it unable to export oil from the Gulf via the Strait of Hormuz.

In March 1984 a further Iranian offensive succeeded in taking part of the marshlands around the southern Iraqi island of Majnoun, the site of rich oilfields, though only at great human cost. Iraq subsequently retook some of the territory it had lost, but seemed more intent on consolidating its defences than making further ground. As the year progressed, with the war on the ground once more at stalemate, Iraq resumed its assaults on Iranian cities.

In April 1985 the UN Secretary-General, Javier Pérez de Cuéllar, visited both Tehran and Baghdad in an attempt to establish a basis for peace negotiations, but Iran's terms remained the same. The Iranian claim for Iraqi war reparations was US $350,000m., and although there was less official insistence on the removal of Hussain and his Baathist regime from power as a condition of peace, it was expected by the Iranian Government that, if all the other conditions (the payment of reparations, an Iraqi admission of responsibility for starting the war, and the withdrawal of Iraqi troops from all Iranian territory) were met, he would fall anyway. In August Iraq made the first of a concentrated series of raids upon the main Iranian oil export terminal on Kharg Island. By the end of 1985 it was reported that exports from Kharg had ceased.

On 9 February 1986 Iran launched the Wal-Fajr (Dawn) 8 offensive—so called to commemorate the month of Ayatollah Khomeini's return to Iran in 1979 from exile in France. Iranian forces crossed the Shatt al-Arab waterway and on 11 February occupied the disused Iraqi port of Faw, and, according to Iran, about 800 sq km of the Faw peninsula. When Iraq launched a counter-offensive on Faw in mid-February, Iran opened up a second front in Iraqi Kurdistan, hundreds of miles to the north, with the Wal-Fajr 9 offensive. In Resolution 582, adopted at the end of February, the UN Security Council, while urging a cease-fire, cited Iraq for the first time as being responsible for starting the war.

It emerged in November 1986 that the USA, despite its official discouragement of arms sales to Iran by other countries, had been conducting secret negotiations with the Islamic Republic since July 1985, and had made three shipments of weapons and spare parts to Iran. The shipments were allegedly in exchange for Iranian assistance in securing the release of US hostages who had been kidnapped by Shi'a extremists in Lebanon. The talks were reportedly conducted on the Iranian side by the Speaker of the Majlis, Ali Akbar Hashemi Rafsanjani, with Ayatollah Khomeini's consent but without the knowledge of other senior government figures, including the Prime Minister and the President. It was estimated that businesses or governments in 44 countries, including both the USA and the USSR, sold armaments to Iran over the course of the war. The People's Republic of China became the leading supplier of military equipment to Iran.

INTERNAL DEVELOPMENTS

Contrary to perceived global opinion, the Iranian regime was able to withstand both the bomb outrages of 1981 and the opening stages of the war. Internal opposition was dealt with harshly: an extended, and often ferocious, campaign against the main anti-Government guerrilla group, the Mujahidin-e-Khalq, eventually achieved some success, and in February 1982 the Mujahidin leader in Iran, Musa Khiabani, was killed. In 1983 the Government turned its attention to the communist Tudeh Party, which was banned under the Shah but had re-emerged after the 1979 Revolution. In February the party's Secretary-General, Nour el-Din Kianuri, was arrested on charges of spying for the USSR; he became the first of a number of party members to confess to this and other crimes against the state on television. Thus the Tudeh Party was officially banned again in April.

An intense rivalry within the Government became increasingly apparent after the Revolution. The two rival groups were the right-wing Hojjatieh, identified with the traditionalist clerical and merchant ('*bazaari*') communities, and the radical technocrats. The Hojjatieh were opposed to radical economic reforms such as the nationalization programme and the reform of laws governing land ownership, and had extensive representation in the first Majlis. In April 1982 an anti-Government plot was uncovered in which Ayatollah Shariatmadari, one of Iran's leading mullahs, was accused of involvement. He denied this, but admitted knowledge of the plot, in which the former Minister of Foreign Affairs, Sadeq Ghotbzadeh, was deeply implicated. Ghotbzadeh was tried and executed in September. Ayatollah Shariatmadari died in April 1986, after two years of house arrest in Qom.

Elections to the second Majlis took place on 15 April and 17 May 1984, significantly altering the distribution of influence in the assembly. Slightly more than one-half of the outgoing Majlis were clerics, and that majority had given them the power to determine policy according to largely religious considerations. A high proportion of the 1,230 or more candidates who contested the elections were markedly secular: they included doctors, scientists and engineers. However, despite the success of these candidates—who were believed to have secured more than one-half of the seats in the new assembly—the Shura-e-Nigahban (Council of Guardians, which was founded in 1980 to supervise elections and to examine legislation adopted by the Majlis) was of a 'conservative', clerical nature and proved to be a major obstacle to economic reform. The 'conservatives' also asserted their authority in the field of justice, and from 1985 they began rigidly to enforce Islamic codes of correction including the dismembering of a hand for theft; flogging for more than 50 offences, including forgery, consumption of alcohol, fornication and violations of the strict code of dress for women; and stoning to death for adultery. Suppression of opposition to the Government continued. In 1985, according to the human rights organization Amnesty International, 399 people were executed in Iran in the period to the end of October, bringing the total to 6,426 deaths by execution since the Revolution. A report by the UN Commission on Human Rights, published in February 1987, estimated the number of executions at a minimum of 7,000 between 1979 and 1985.

President Ali Khamenei was due to complete his four-year term of office in September 1985 and a presidential election was held on 16 August, which comprised only three candidates, including the incumbent. The Council of Guardians rejected almost 50 candidatures, including that of Dr Mehdi Bazargan. Ali Khamenei was re-elected President, with 85.7% of the votes cast. Mousavi was confirmed as Prime Minister by the Majlis on 13 October.

THE IRAN–IRAQ WAR, 1987

The war entered a potentially explosive new phase in 1987. In January Iran rejected Saddam Hussain's offer of a cease-fire and peace talks, and in the following months mounted a series of offences that demonstrated its ability to launch attacks from one end to the other of its 1,200-km frontier with Iraq. In reprisal for Kuwait's support for Iraq, Iranian attacks were concentrated on Kuwaiti shipping and on neutral vessels and tankers carrying oil or other cargoes to and from Iraq via Kuwait. Kuwait subsequently sought the protection of the leading powers for its shipping in the Gulf. In May the USA agreed to re-register 11 Kuwaiti tankers under its flag and to increase its naval presence in the Gulf in order to protect them. This decision followed the apparently accidental attack in the Gulf by an Iraqi *Mirage* F-1 fighter plane on the USS *Stark* on 17 May. Iran made it clear that it considered the US naval presence in the Gulf to be provocative, and fears of a military confrontation grew.

The escalation of tension in the Gulf resulted in a rare display of unanimity in the UN Security Council, which adopted a 10-point resolution (No. 598) on 20 July 1987, urging an immediate cease-fire in the Iran–Iraq War; the withdrawal of all forces to internationally recognized boundaries; and the co-operation of Iran and Iraq in mediation efforts to achieve a peace settlement.

POLITICAL AND DIPLOMATIC DEVELOPMENTS, 1987–88

During 1987 the conviction grew among the international community that Iran was attempting to spread the Islamic Revolution through a network of agents operating in diplomatic missions abroad which were controlled by the Iranian Ministry of Intelligence and Internal Security. In March Tunisia broke off diplomatic relations with Iran, accusing it of fomenting Islamist fundamentalist opposition to the Tunisian Government, and of recruiting Tunisians for terrorist operations abroad through its embassy in Tunis. On 17 July France severed its diplomatic relations with Iran in the midst of a protracted crisis over a translator at the Iranian embassy in Paris wanted in connection with a bombing campaign in the city in 1986. France and Iran resumed diplomatic relations and exchanged ambassadors in June 1988.

In June 1987 Ayatollah Khomeini approved a proposal by Rafsanjani, the Speaker of the Majlis, which was reluctantly supported by President Khamenei, to disband the IRP. In a letter to Khomeini the two leaders stated that, the institutions of the Islamic Republic having been established, 'party polarization under the present conditions may provide an excuse for discord and factionalism'.

Just two months later in August 1987 Hojatoleslam Mehdi Hashemi, a close associate of Grand Ayatollah Ali Hossain Montazeri, one of the leaders of the 1979 Revolution, was tried by a specially appointed Islamic court and convicted on charges of murder,the kidnapping of a Syrian diplomat in Tehran, forming a private army, and planning explosions in Mecca during the *Hajj* in July 1987. Hashemi was executed on 28 September.

In April 1988, following further Iranian attacks on Saudi and other neutral shipping in the Gulf, Saudi Arabia severed its diplomatic relations with Iran. Iran hadinsisted that it was intending to send as many as 150,000 pilgrims on the *Hajj* to Mecca, Saudi Arabia, in 1988, despite the events of July 1987 and the subsequent deterioration in bilateral relations. A meeting of the Organization of the Islamic Conference (OIC, now Organization of Islamic Cooperation) in Amman, Jordan, agreed to a formula for 1988, whereby each Muslim nation would be permitted to send 1,000 pilgrims per 1m. citizens, giving Iran a quota of 45,000. Ultimately, Iran decided that it would send no pilgrims on the *Hajj* at all.

CEASE-FIRE AND POLITICAL UNCERTAINTY, 1988–89

Divisions within the Government over the conduct of the war with Iraq became more apparent, as Ayatollah Khomeini grew increasingly frail and the political struggle for the succession intensified. The elections to the third Majlis in April and May 1988 provided a further boost for the 'reformers'. The elections were the first not to be contested by the IRP, which had been dissolved in June 1987. Instead, all 1,600 candidates for the 270 seats in the Majlis were examined for eligibility by local committees and sought election as individuals. In June, Rafsanjani was re-elected as Speaker of the Majlis and Mousavi was overwhelmingly endorsed as Prime Minister. He presented a new Council of Ministers to the Majlis in July.

During 1987–88, due to poor mobilization, disorganization and a shortage of volunteers, Iran was unable to launch a major winter offensive and began to lose ground to Iraqi advances along the length of the war front (offsetting the gains that it had made during the previous few years). On 3 July 1988 the USS *Vincennes*, the US Navy's most sophisticated guided-missile destroyer, which had recently been deployed in the Gulf to counter the threat to shipping of Iran's *Silkworm* missiles, mistakenly shot down an IranAir Airbus A300B over the Strait of Hormuz, having, according to official statements, assumed it to be an attacking F-14 fighter-bomber; all 290 passengers and crew were killed. On 20 July the world was taken by surprise when, after 12 months of prevarication, Iran agreed, unconditionally, to accept Resolution 598 in all its parts.

UN-sponsored negotiations between Iran and Iraq for a comprehensive peace settlement began at foreign ministerial level in Geneva, Switzerland, on 25 August 1988. One of the most contentious issues to be decided at these talks was the status of the 1975 Algiers Agreement (dividing the Shatt al-Arab waterway) between Iran and Iraq, which Iran insisted should be the basis for negotiations butwhich Iraq rejected. The matter of determining responsibility for starting the war was another potential obstacle to the negotiation of a lasting peace. It was generally accepted that Iraq initiated the conflict by invading Iran on 22 September 1980. Iraq, however, maintained that the war had begun on 4 September with Iranian shelling of Iraqi border posts. Resolution 598 provided for the establishment of an impartial body to apportion responsibility for the war. Iraq rejected Iranian demands for the payment of reparations, for which Resolution 598 made no provisions. The peace negotiations soon became deadlocked in disputes concerning sovereignty over the Shatt al-Arab and the right of navigation in the waterway and the Gulf, the exchange of prisoners of war, and the withdrawal of troops to within international borders.

THE SALMAN RUSHDIE AFFAIR

On 14 February 1989 Ayatollah Khomeini issued a *fatwa* (religious edict), pronouncing a death sentence on a British writer, Salman Rushdie, and his publishers, and exhorting all Muslims to carry out the sentence. Khomeini's edict followed demonstrations in India and Pakistan in protest at the imminent publication in the USA of Rushdie's novel *The Satanic Verses*, the content of which was considered to be blasphemous by some Muslims owing toits irreverent depiction of the Prophet Muhammad. (Rushdie, born a Muslim himself, was therefore guilty of apostasy, an offence punishable by death under *Shari'a* law.) The *fatwa*, which has never been rescinded, led to a sharp deterioration in relations between Iran and the United Kingdom and other Western countries.

While the significance of the Rushdie affair was initially defined in terms of its effect on Iran's foreign relations, it soon became apparent that the issue was being used tactically by competing factions within the Iranian leadership. In a speech on 22 February 1989 Khomeini referred explicitly to a division in the Iranian leadership (between 'liberals', who sought Western participation in Iran's post-war reconstruction, and 'conservatives', who opposed Western involvement) in terms that implied that *The Satanic Verses* was the culmination of a Western conspiracy against Islam, and declared that he would never allow the 'liberal' faction to prevail.

By late March 1989 it was clear that Khomeini's intervention had decisively strengthened the hand of the 'conservatives'. In early April Khomeini's designated successor, Grand Ayatollah Montazeri, perceived as a 'liberal', resigned. On 24 April a 20-member council was appointed by Ayatollah Khomeini to draft amendments to the Iranian Constitution.

IRAN AFTER KHOMEINI

Ayatollah Khomeini died on 3 June 1989. In an emergency session on 4 June the Assembly of Experts elected President Khamenei to succeed him as Iran's Supreme Religious Leader, and on 5 June Prime Minister Mousavi declared his support, and that of all government institutions, for Khamenei. On 8 June Rafsanjani reiterated his intention to stand as a candidate at the forthcoming presidential election, and on 12 June he was re-elected for a further one-year term as Speaker of the Majlis.

Despite the apparent intensification in the struggle for power within the Iranian leadership in the months preceding Ayatollah Khomeini's long-anticipated death, both 'conservatives' and 'liberals' gave their support to the candidacy of Rafsanjani for the presidency. The presidential election, held on 28 July 1989, was contested by only Rafsanjani and Abbas Sheibani, a former minister who was widely regarded as a 'token' candidate. According to official figures, Rafsanjani received some 15.5m. (95.9%) of a total 16.2m. votes cast. At the same time 95% of voters approved 45 proposed amendments to the Constitution, the most important of which were the elevation of the President to the Government's Chief Executive and the abolition of the post of Prime Minister. Mousavi was given a ceremonial position as Vice-President and member of the Supreme Council of Cultural Revolution. Rafsanjani was sworn in as President on 17 August. The new Council of Ministers was regarded as a balanced coalition of 'conservatives', 'liberals' and technocrats, and its endorsement by the Majlis was viewed as a mandate for Rafsanjani to conduct a more conciliatory foreign policy towards the West and to introduce economic reforms. Western support was regarded as vital to Iran's economic reconstruction by Rafsanjani and his supporters within the Iranian leadership, but was regarded as anathema by his opponents, who feared that it would lead to the erosion of Islamic values and the betrayal of the Revolution. The amendments to the Constitution that gave Rafsanjani radically different powers to those held by previous Presidents were later seen as a precedent for further changes that were made shortly after the re-election of Mahmoud Ahmadinejad in 2009.

FOREIGN RELATIONS

Although the death sentence on Salman Rushdie remained in force, the tension created by its initial pronouncement in February 1989 lessened somewhat in the ensuing months. In March European Community (EC, now European Union—EU) ministers of foreign affairs agreed that member states should be allowed to reinstall their ambassadors in Tehran. There was evidence, too, of an improvement in relations between Iran and the communist bloc. In June, Rafsanjani visited the USSR, where he and the Soviet leader, Mikhail Gorbachev, signed a 'declaration on the principles of relations' between Iran and the USSR. These relations were strained in January 1990, however, when Iranian politicians voiced support for the Muslim Azerbaijani revolt against the Soviet central Government in the Nakhichevan enclave, on the Iranian border.

In July 1989 the USA unexpectedly offered to pay compensation directly to the families of the 290 passengers and crew of the IranAir Airbus mistakenly shot down by the USS *Vincennes* a year earlier. However, the Iranian Government insisted that the compensation should be distributed through its agencies, rather than privately, and took the matter to the

ICJ. The fragility of Iran's relations with the USA was underlined in August when, in response to the abduction by Israeli forces of the Lebanese Shi'a Muslim leader Sheikh Abd al-Karim Obeid, a US hostage in Lebanon, Lt-Col William Higgins, was executed by his captors, who threatened the execution of more hostages if Sheikh Obeid was not released. The USA immediately engaged in urgent negotiations with Iranian leaders in order to prevent further killings. In November the USA agreed to release US $567m. of the total of $810m. of Iranian assets that had been seized 10 years previously, at the time of the siege of the US embassy in Tehran, in order to secure US bank claims on Iran. In April 1990, following the release of two US citizens who had been held hostage by pro-Iranian groups in Lebanon, the USA thanked both the Syrian and the Iranian Governments for their role in securing the hostages' release. In May the USA and Iran concluded a 'small claims agreement', whereby US claimants were to be repaid for losses incurred during the Iranian Revolution in 1979. Moreover, in June 1990 Iran agreed to pay the US company Amoco $600m. in compensation for US oil operations expropriated during the Revolution.

In February 1990 the United Kingdom expelled nine Iranian diplomats for security reasons, and, in a retaliatory gesture, Iran closed the office of the British Broadcasting Corporation (BBC) in Tehran. In the same month, however, President Rafsanjani described the *fatwa* against Rushdie as an exclusively Islamic issue, while trade between the two countries was reported to be increasing. In May the United Kingdom was said to have been involved in indirect contacts with Iran concerning four British nationals held hostage by pro-Iranian groups in Lebanon, and the United Kingdom announced that it was prepared to resume direct talks with the Iranian Government. In June, however, Ayatollah Khamenei declared that the *fatwa* against Rushdie could never be repealed.

IRAQ CONCEDES IRAN'S PEACE TERMS

In early 1990 Iran and Iraq agreed to resume negotiations in the USSR, at the invitation of the Soviet Ministry of Foreign Affairs. In July the Iraqi and Iranian Ministers of Foreign Affairs conferred at the UN in Geneva. However, this breakthrough in the peace process was quickly overtaken by the consequences of Iraq's invasion and annexation of Kuwait in August.

On 16 August 1990 Saddam Hussain abruptly sought an immediate, formal peace with Iran by accepting all the claims that Iran had pursued since the declaration of a cease-fire, including the reinstatement of the 1975 Algiers Agreement. While these concessions were transparently dictated by expediency and thus left the conflicts underlying the Iran–Iraq War unresolved, they were welcomed by Iran—which none the less insisted that the issue of peace with Iraq was separate from that of Iraq's occupation of Kuwait. On 11 September 1990 Iran and Iraq re-established diplomatic relations.

The publication in August 1991 of the report of a UN delegation sent to Iran—in accordance with the terms of Resolution 598—to assess the level of human and material damage caused by the war with Iraq seemed to indicate that the UN was once again considering the need for a comprehensive peace settlement. The Iranian Government released its own assessment of the damage caused by the war: it estimated that Iran had experienced direct damage amounting to IR 30,811,000m.; that 50 towns and 4,000 villages were destroyed or badly damaged; and that 14,000 civilians were killed and 1.25m. people displaced.

IRAN AND THE CONFLICT OVER KUWAIT

Iran condemned Iraq's invasion of Kuwait in August 1990 and offered to defend other Gulf states from Iraqi aggression, but it welcomed Iraq's offer of a formal settlement of the Iran–Iraq War on Iran's terms. While Iran stated that it would observe the economic sanctions imposed on Iraq by the UN, Iraq was believed to have tried to persuade Iran to trade oil for food. However, the Iranian Government adhered to its pledge to implement economic sanctions for the duration of the conflict over Kuwait, sending only supplies of food and medicine to Iraq on a humanitarian basis.

As the deployment of a multinational force (assembled in accordance with Article 51 of the UN Charter) for the defence of Saudi Arabia gathered pace, Iran urged the simultaneous and unconditional withdrawal of Western—above all of US—armed forces from the Gulf region, and of Iraqi armed forces from Kuwait. In September 1990 Ayatollah Khamenei came close to endorsing the demands of 'conservatives', such as Hojatoleslam Ali Akbar Mohtashemi, for Iran to ally itself with Iraq in a *jihad* (holy war) against Western forces in the Gulf. President Rafsanjani's position was that the presence of these forces was tolerable on condition that they withdrew as soon as the conflict in Kuwait had been resolved.

Following the outbreak of military hostilities between Iraq and the multinational force in January 1991, Iran attempted, unsuccessfully, to intercede, urging an 'Islamic solution' to the conflict. In February President Rafsanjani announced that the terms of an Iranian peace proposal had been conveyed to Saddam Hussain during the visit to Tehran by Iraq's Deputy Prime Minister, Sa'adoun Hammadi, three days earlier. President Rafsanjani claimed that the terms of Iran's proposal were consistent with resolutions adopted by the UN Security Council. An immediate cease-fire was to be followed by the simultaneous and complete withdrawal of Iraqi armed forces from Kuwait, and of all foreign forces from the Gulf region. In deference to Iraq's insistence on the 'linkage' of the conflict in Kuwait with other conflicts in the Middle East (in particular the continuing Israeli occupation of the West Bank and Gaza Strip), Iran also urged the immediate cessation of new Israeli settlements in the Occupied Territories.

On 8 February 1991, in a letter to President Rafsanjani, Saddam Hussain dismissed the proposal, stating that Iraq had no intention of withdrawing from Kuwait. Iran claimed some of the credit for the concessions offered in an Iraqi peace proposal on 15 February, and urged the multinational force not to initiate hostilities on the ground until the limits of Iraq's flexibility had been determined. However, the countries contributing to the multinational force were unwilling, by this stage, to allow Iraq the opportunity to procrastinate.

Relations between Iran and Iraq deteriorated after the conclusion of hostilities between Iraq and the multinational force at the end of February 1991. In response to the suppression, by Iraqi armed forces loyal to President Saddam Hussain, of the Shi'a-led rebellion in southern and central Iraq, Iran declared its commitment to the territorial integrity of Iraq but demanded the resignation of Saddam Hussain and protested at the damage inflicted by Iraqi armed forces on Shi'a shrines at Najaf, Karbala and Samarra. Iraq accused Iran of providing material and human support for the southern and central rebellions, citing the involvement of the Tehran-based Supreme Council for the Islamic Revolution in Iraq (SCIRI—renamed the Islamic Supreme Council of Iraq in 2007). The Iraqi regime later resumed support for the military activities of the largest Iranian dissident groups, the Mujahidin-e-Khalq and the Kurdish Democratic Party (KDP). Iraq's suppression of the internal rebellions led to a mass flight of Iraqi Kurds and Shi'a Muslims across the Iranian border. By May 1991 more than 1m. Iraqi Kurds had fled to Iran, while the number of Shi'a refugees still in Iran was estimated at 65,000. Iran backed Western initiatives to establish 'safe havens' for Iraqi Kurds in the north of Iraq and unsuccessfully sought support for Iraqi refugees in Iran.

DOMESTIC REFORM UNDER RAFSANJANI

The onset of the Gulf crisis in August 1990 led to further friction between the rival factions in the Iranian leadership, but President Rafsanjani gradually asserted his authority and began the long process of seeking to reduce the power of the 'conservatives'. Elections to the fourth Majlis in April and May 1992 seemed to provide Rafsanjani with the opportunity to shift further the balance of power against the 'conservatives'. An estimated 70% of the deputies elected to the new Majlis were supporters of the President. The incoming deputies appeared to be highly educated, younger and more technocratic in orientation than their predecessors. Rafsanjani installed a new Speaker of the Majlis, Ali Akbar Nateq Nouri, who replaced the 'conservative' Mahdi Karrubi. However, it subsequently became clear that assessments predicting the support of the majority of the new deputies for Rafsanjani's policies were incorrect.

The atmosphere of political malaise was further deepened in June 1994 by the bombing of the Imam Reza shrine in Mashad, which left at least 24 dead. A crisis threatened in the following month when, in the space of a few days, two Iranian Christian leaders were assassinated in Tehran and bombs wreaked havoc against Jewish targets in London, United Kingdom, and Buenos Aires, Argentina; it was widely suspected that the two bomb attacks had been carried out by pro-Iranian militants.

FOREIGN RELATIONS UNDER RAFSANJANI

Efforts at domestic reform under Rafsanjani were accompanied by periodic diplomatic initiatives by Iran, aimed at securing its reintegration into the international community. The greatest single obstacle to improved relations with Western countries was initially Iran's perceived complicity in the holding of Western hostages in Lebanon by groups linked to the pro-Iranian Hezbollah. Between August and December 1991, with Iran, Syria, Israel and the UN diplomatically active, all remaining British and US hostages were released. While the aim of the captors was to trade the release of such hostages for the release of Shi‘a hostages held by Israel, it was decided ultimately to release them unconditionally. The last remaining Western hostages were freed in June 1992.

The release of US hostages, accompanied by some progress at the US-Iran Claims Tribunal in The Hague, Netherlands, temporarily removed some of the tension between the USA and Iran. Bilateral relations deteriorated, however, after President Bill Clinton took office in the USA in January 1993. Throughout the year the Clinton Administration pressed initially reluctant Western allies to reduce levels of economic assistance to Iran and sought to block Iranian efforts to reschedule the country's international debts.

In early 1995 the USA, the United Kingdom and Israel expressed alarm at the possibility that Iran might be able to manufacture nuclear weapons within a few years. The International Atomic Energy Agency (IAEA) stated that it had found no evidence to suggest that Iran was seeking to develop nuclear weapons; however, under an agreement concluded in January, Russia was reportedly determined to sell at least one 1,000-MW nuclear reactor to Iran, despite the objections of the USA. This agreement concerned Russia's eventual completion of the unfinished nuclear power plant at Bushehr, in south-western Iran.

On 30 April 1995 US efforts to isolate Iran internationally culminated in the announcement of a complete ban on trade with Iran within 30 days: all US companies and their foreign subsidiaries would also be prevented from investing in Iran. There was little international support for such an embargo, and without the support of Iran's European trading partners and of Japan it was far from clear how the embargo would damage Iran's long-term economic interests. Furthermore, the USA subsequently conceded that US oil companies active in the Caucasus and in Central Asia would be allowed to participate in exchange deals with Iran in order to facilitate the marketing of petroleum from former Soviet states. In the immediate aftermath of the announcement of the embargo, however, the value of the Iranian rial declined by about one-third. In 1995 the US Congress pressured other countries to support the trade ban, and in March 1996 Iran was accused of actively supporting the Palestinian Islamist group Hamas; Iran denied involvement.

In June 1996 the US House of Representatives approved legislation seeking to penalize companies operating in US markets that were investing US $40m. or more in Iran's oil and gas industry. The sanctions received presidential assent despite sustained protests from Japan and the EU.

During the conflict over Kuwait in 1990–91 and its aftermath, Iran sought to normalize its relations with Egypt, Tunisia, Jordan and the Gulf states, while reasserting itself as a regional power. In March 1991 it re-established diplomatic relations with Saudi Arabia, allowing about 115,000 Iranian pilgrims to participate in that year's *Hajj*. Thereafter, however, relations between Iran and Saudi Arabia were characterized by mistrust. In August, meanwhile, Iran and Iraq met directly for talks on a comprehensive settlement to the 1980–88 war, but little was achieved.

Iran reacted negatively to efforts based on the Damascus Declaration of March 1991 to create a regional security structure in the Gulf from which it was itself excluded. Opposing the defence agreements that the Gulf states subsequently negotiated with the USA, Iran focused its diplomatic efforts on improving its relations with them, though significant progress was thwarted in a dispute between Iran and the United Arab Emirates (UAE) over control of the Abu Musa islands in 1992.

The dramatic developments in the USSR after August 1991 opened up a new arena for Iranian diplomacy in Central Asia, as Iran, Saudi Arabia and Turkey vied for influence in the newly independent states of the region. Iran sought to strengthen its position in Central Asia through bilateral agreements and institutions such as the Tehran-based Economic Co-operation Organization (ECO). In September 1994 the Tajikistani Government and its opponents in the civil war that had erupted in the country in 1992 signed a cease-fire agreement in Tehran. In July 1995 Iran sponsored further talks between the two sides, which resulted in an extension of the cease-fire.

During 1996 Iran became increasingly interested in events in Afghanistan, owing to the military advancement of Sunni fundamentalist Taliban guerrilla fighters. Following the Taliban capture of the Afghan capital, Kabul, in September, Iran accused the group of being a proxy for US, Saudi and Pakistani interests in the country. The Iranian Government refused to recognize the Taliban-sponsored authorities in Kabul, and continued to express support for ousted President Rabbani.

In July 1995 Iran was reported to have organized a month-long extension of a cease-fire between rival Kurdish groups in northern Iraq, prompting Iraq to denounce Iranian interference in its internal affairs. In September 1996 Iran appealed for international assistance to provide emergency aid to as many as 500,000 Kurdish refugees who had fled towards the Iranian border in response to inter-Kurdish hostilities around the towns of Irbil (Arbil) and Al-Sulaimaniyah (Sulaimaniya) in the Kurdish 'safe haven' in northern Iraq. Supporting the Patriotic Union of Kurdistan (PUK) in these hostilities, Iran apparently aimed to defeat US allies in Iraqi Kurdistan and to assert its own influence.

ELECTION OF KHATAMI

The months following the 1996 Majlis elections were something of an interregnum, as 'liberals' and 'conservatives' manoeuvred in anticipation of the presidential elections scheduled for May 1997 and it became clear that the Constitution would not be amended to allow Rafsanjani to seek re-election for a third term. In March Rafsanjani was appointed Chairman of the Shura-ye Tashkhis-e Maslahat-e Nezam (Council to Determine the Expediency of the Islamic Order—which was established in 1988 to arbitrate in disputes between the Majlis and the Council of Guardians) for a further five-year term, indicating that he would continue to play an influential role in political life upon the expiry of his presidential mandate. The Council of Guardians approved four candidates for the presidential election, which took place on 23 May 1997. The selected candidates were Ali Akbar Nateq Nouri (Speaker of the Majlis); Sayed Muhammad Khatami (a presidential adviser and former Minister of Culture and Islamic Guidance); Muhammad Muhammadi Reyshahri (previously Minister of Intelligence and Internal Security, Prosecutor-General and, of late, Khamenei's representative in *Hajj* and pilgrimage affairs); and Sayed Reza Zavarei (hitherto vice-president of the judiciary and a member of the Council of Guardians). Despite early expectations that Nateq Nouri would secure an easy victory, Khatami took some 69.1% of the total votes cast, ahead of Nouri, with 24.9%. Khatami was sworn in on 3 August and took the presidential oath of office before the Majlis on the following day. The new President stated that it would be the responsibility of his administration to create a safe forum for free speech, within the framework of regulations defined by Islam and the Constitution, and to promote 'easy and transparent' relations between the people and the organs of state.

INTERNAL POLITICAL RIVALRIES

Although Khatami pledged his allegiance to Khamenei as Iran's spiritual leader, the new President's assumption of office revived long-standing rivalries among the senior clergy. The focus of the opposition to Khamenei was Ayatollah Montazeri (Khomeini's designated successor prior to March 1989), who began openly to question Khamenei's authority and to demand that Khatami be allowed to govern without interference. In April 1998 the Mayor of Tehran, Gholamhossein Karbaschi, became the focus of political rivalry when he was arrested on charges of fraud and mismanagement. Karbaschi was a popular national figure and a prominent supporter of President Khatami, and on the day of his arrest the Council of Ministers issued a public statement criticizing the decision to detain him. Later in the month students demonstrating in support of Karbaschi were involved in violent clashes with the police. Karbaschi's trial, broadcast in full on Iranian television, commenced in June and achieved unprecedented publicity. The following month Karbaschi was sentenced to five years' imprisonment and 60 lashes. He was also fined and banned from holding public office for 20 years. Following an appeal, in December the duration of the custodial sentence was reduced to two years and the punishment of 60 lashes commuted to a fine. Karbaschi was released in January 2000, shortly before the legislative elections, having been pardoned by President Khatami.

Several months of factional tensions preceded the next major test of strength between 'conservatives' and 'liberals', the elections to the Assembly of Experts (the body responsible for the appointment of the country's spiritual leader), held on 23 October 1998. The 'conservatives' retained control of the Council, but, to many observers, the low turn-out at the polls significantly undermined the legitimacy of their victory. Although the 'conservatives' had done their best to mobilize voters, it appeared that public disillusion with the electoral process had led to a poor level of participation. The number of voters was estimated at between 15m. and 18m.—about 40% of all eligible voters. (In the 1997 presidential elections 29m. had voted.) None the less, the figures apparently confirmed that the 'conservatives' retained a real social base, estimated at around 30% of the population. The day after the results were announced the Ministry of the Interior, which remained in the hands of the 'reformists', declared that the first local council elections were to be held in early 1999, thus immediately precipitating another round of factional struggles.

In the final weeks of 1998 the murders of a number of political dissidents engendered an atmosphere of terror among Iran's intelligentsia. The first, and most prominent, victim was Dariush Foruhar, who was killed with his wife at their home in Tehran. Foruhar had founded the Iranian People's Party, and had for some time also edited a newsletter that was critical of the regime. In subsequent weeks three more dissidents were kidnapped and murdered: all three were writers and campaigners against censorship, who were attempting to revive the secular Writers' Association. The murders prompted outcry both within Iran and abroad, and it was immediately rumoured—and widely believed—that a radical right-wing group, possibly with links to elements within the State, was responsible. President Khatami and members of his Government denounced the crimes, and Ayatollah Khamenei also condemned the killings and urged the intelligence service to arrest and punish the culprits.

President Khatami and his supporters made another significant advance after their victory in the local council elections on 26 February 1999; the elections themselves were generally accepted to have been among the most transparent in the country's history. Three propensities competed for votes, the 'left-wing' pro-Khatami Islamic Iran Participation Front (Jebbeh-ye Mosharekat-e Iran-e Islami), the 'centrist' pro-Rafsanjani Servants of Construction Party and the 'conservative' Green Coalition. The Participation Front and the Servants of Construction, which both campaigned on a 'reformist' platform, secured a decisive victory in Tehran and the larger cities. In the capital they won all 15 seats, thus ensuring that the next mayor of Tehran would also be a 'reformist'.

In early July 1999 a serious challenge to the regime erupted on the streets of Tehran. The crisis began when the 'conservative'-dominated Majlis approved legislation aimed at curbing press freedom. The new press law was an integral part of efforts by 'conservatives' to ensure their success in the forthcoming Majlis elections. The judiciary immediately seized the opportunity to ban the publication of *Salam*, Iran's oldest pro-reform newspaper, on 7 July. The same night hundreds of Tehran university students held a demonstration in support of the suppressed daily. The response to this relatively minor disturbance followed early the next morning, with the right-wing vigilantes of the Ansar-e Hezbollah, assisted by police, forcibly entering halls of residence. Their assaults on the students left at least one person dead and several hundred injured; about 200 arrests were made. In subsequent days thousands of students gathered in Tehran, and unrest spread to other cities. Student leaders clashed repeatedly with riot police, demanded radical change and openly criticized Ayatollah Khamenei. Supporters of President Khatami came to the defence of the students, and Tehran university chancellors resigned in protest at the police violence. Khamenei also distanced himself from the attacks on the students, and the Shura-ye Ali-ye Amniyyat-e Melli (Supreme National Security Council—SNSC) ordered the dismissal of two senior police officers.

The student movement was regarded as an important element of the pro-Khatami coalition, with several effective networks mostly controlled by 'moderate' Islamists. In the course of the demonstrations, however, leftist and secular elements emerged more clearly, and the split between the 'moderate' and 'radical' wings of the student movement became more apparent. Khatami appealed for restraint, and the unrest subsided when the students dispersed for the summer vacation. However, it was announced in September 1999 that four students had been sentenced to death for their part in the July riots, although the death sentences were commuted to 15 years' imprisonment in April 2000.

In September 1999 the 'conservatives' intensified their campaign against pro-reform elements to coincide with the official announcement of the next legislative elections by the Ministry of the Interior. As the electoral campaign got under way, the judiciary became the focus of this rivalry: the strategy of the 'conservatives' was, broadly, to use the courts to restrain the press and to weaken public enthusiasm for reform, in preparation for low-profile elections in which they hoped to minimize their losses. In October the 'conservatives' reinforced their effort to prevent a landslide victory for 'reformers' in the forthcoming elections by attempting, via the judiciary, to bring about the downfall of former Minister of the Interior Abdollah Nuri, a leading 'reformist' figure associated with the Servants of Construction. Nuri was indicted by the Special Clerical Court on charges that he had insulted religious sanctities, attempted to establish relations with the USA, encouraged the recognition of Israel, campaigned for the proscribed 'liberal' group Nehzat-e Azadi-ye Iran (Liberation Movement of Iran) and supported Grand Ayatollah Montazeri, Iran's most senior dissident cleric. The 'conservatives' further accused Nuri of using his position as managing editor of the popular pro-reform newspaper *Khordad* to undermine Islamic and revolutionary values, and demanded that he change the newspaper's editorial board in order to avoid standing trial. In November the Special Clerical Court sentenced Nuri to a term of five years' imprisonment, having found him guilty of a number of charges—among them insulting religious beliefs, deviating from the teachings of Ayatollah Khomeini, undermining public confidence and working against the Islamic Republic.

The registration of candidates for the forthcoming legislative elections (scheduled to be held in February 2000) commenced in December 1999. The decision of former President Ali Akbar Hashemi Rafsanjani to participate aroused alarm in 'reformist' circles and prompted an alliance of 12 'conservative' factions to place him at the head of their list of 160 candidates. Rafsanjani based his decision to stand for election on the hope that he would be able to consolidate 'centrist' tendencies and contain the rivalry between 'reformers' and 'conservatives'. In Tehran, where voting is regarded as the most accurate indicator of national trends, nine joint candidates of the two major pro-reform parties—the 'left-wing' Participation Front and the more 'centrist' Servants of Construction—secured the 25% of votes necessary to secure election. The Participation Front was the clear overall winner, its exclusive candidates faring much better than those of the Servants of Construction. Rafsanjani, the leading candidate of both the Servants of Construction and the 'conservatives', fared badly. Muhammad Reza Khatami, brother of President Khatami and Secretary-General of the Participation Front, polled first among the Tehran candidates, and his success was regarded as a renewal of the popular mandate for the President's 'reformist' programme. The 'conservatives', meanwhile, suffered a devastating defeat in the capital: not one of their candidates was elected. In Mashad, Iran's second largest city, 'reformist' candidates gained all five seats, as they did in Esfahan; they also achieved decisive victories in Shiraz and Tabriz. There was a marked increase in the proportion of Majlis seats won by women; by contrast, the number of clerics in the new assembly declined. For seats where the result was inconclusive in the first round of voting, supplementary elections were held in May 2000.

In the aftermath of the elections to the Majlis fears were expressed that right-wing elements might resort to violence, and rumours circulated of a possible *coup d'état* by units of the Revolutionary Guards. In an apparent effort to demonstrate that the state would not tolerate acts of provocation, 20 police officers (including the former Tehran chief of police, Brig.-Gen. Farhad Nazari) were arraigned on charges of involvement in the assaults on students that had triggered the unrest of July 1999. (Nazari and 17 co-defendants were acquitted in July 2000, while two police officers received custodial sentences.) In May 2000 five men (including alleged religious activists and members of the Revolutionary Guards) were found guilty of having carried out the attempted assassination of the prominent 'reformist' Saeed Hajjarian in March and were sentenced to prison terms ranging from three to 15 years; three other defendants were acquitted.

Following the legislative elections tensions had arisen regarding the future of Rafsanjani, who, with fewer votes than any of the other candidates elected outright in Tehran, had barely achieved election to the Majlis. After complaints about electoral malpractice, the Council of Guardians ordered that almost one-third of the votes cast in Tehran should be re-counted. In May 2000 the Council invalidated 726,000 votes cast in the capital and rearranged the order of the successful candidates. Rafsanjani, who was believed to have been in 30th place after the preliminary results were announced, was now ranked 20th in Tehran, while three 'reformers' were deprived of their seats. The veracity of the revised count was challenged both by the public and by 'reformist' politicians, who argued that Rafsanjani's unpopularity among young voters and other key sections of the electorate meant that he was unlikely to have achieved such a position. Rafsanjani himself, publicly humiliated by the apparent machinations of the Council of Guardians, resigned his seat, thus relinquishing his ambition to become the new Speaker of the Majlis, a powerful position which the 'conservatives' were expected to use to obstruct reform. Nevertheless, Rafsanjani retained a power base as Chairman of the Council to Determine the Expediency of the Islamic Order.

On 23 December 2000 the trial of those accused of the murders of the four dissident writers and intellectuals in 1998 began before a military tribunal. A group of 18 defendants, some of them senior intelligence officers, were charged with ordering or participating in the murders. Public interest in the case was profound. Only a few weeks previously the journalist Akbar Ganji had at his own trial repeated in open court accusations that the former information minister, Ali Falahian, hadordered the murders with the approval of senior 'hardline' clerics. The verdict was announced on 27 January 2001. Three of the accused—intelligence agents who admitted to having physically carried out the killings—were condemned to death; five others were sentenced to life imprisonment, some of them several times over; seven accomplices received prison terms of up to 10 years; and three of the defendants were acquitted. Although the sentences were correct in terms of Iranian law, Iran's largest 'reformist' faction, the Participation Front, denounced the outcome of the trial, claiming that it left too many questions unanswered. The victims' families also rejected the court's decision, asserting that the proceedings had been designed to conceal the extent of the murders and the true burden of responsibility. In August the Supreme Court ordered a retrial of the 15 agents. In January 2003 it was reported that two of the agents had hadtheir death sentences commuted to terms of life imprisonment; of those given life sentences, two now received prison terms of 10 years, while seven of the agents were given gaol terms of between two and 10 years. The remaining agents were to have their cases reviewed.

Meanwhile, 17 'reformists' were prosecuted for attending a conference in Berlin, Germany,during April 2000 to discuss Iran's political future. The trial culminated with severe sentences being handed down by the Tehran Revolutionary Court on 13 January 2001. Seven of the defendants, including Akbar Ganji and two feminist activists, Shahla Lahiji and Mehrangiz Kar, received prison sentences; the politician Jamileh Kadivar, however, was among the six to be acquitted. Appeals were immediately lodged by all those convicted, resulting in a reduction in some of the prisoners' sentences by a Tehran court in December. In mid-2005 Ganji spent more than two months on hunger strike in an attempt to force the authorities to order his unconditional release. The pro-reform movement was united in viewing the sentences against the Berlin conference participants as another politically motivated blow at an awkward time when President Khatami remained undecided as to whether, and, if so, on what terms to seek re-election in June 2001. Meanwhile, the judiciary continued its campaign against the 'reformers': more than two dozen prominent journalists, politicians and even Majlis deputies were brought to trial during a two-week period in February 2001. There was then a new wave of arrests in April, including the detention of 42 prominent 'liberals', mostly members of the Liberation Movement of Iran, on charges of conspiracy to overthrow the Islamic regime.

On 4 May 2001, just two days before the deadline for the registration of presidential candidates, President Khatami finally declared himself as a candidate for the Islamic Republic's eighth presidential election. Pressure from the President's supporters had apparently persuaded him to stand, although in late 2000 he had admitted publicly that the presidency lacked the requisite powers to safeguard the Constitution. Although Khatami may have been hoping to wring a deal out of the 'conservatives' in return for continuing to confer legitimacy on the system, Ayatollah Khamenei remained aloof from endorsing Khatami's candidacy. A total of 814 people put themselves forward as presidential candidates, including 45 women. However, in mid-May the Council of Guardians reduced the number of candidates to a shortlist of 10, resulting in the 'conservatives' failing to agree on a single candidate, although several independent 'conservatives' were running for election.

KHATAMI RE-ELECTED

Khatami was returned to office on 8 June 2001 with 21.7m. votes, exceeding the record 20m. votes he had received in 1997 and thus becoming the first Iranian President to win more votes for his second term than his first. This was significant because the 'conservatives', were thus unable to argue that the 'reform' movement had lost its legitimacy. The incumbent President had faced nine opponents, all of whom were 'conservatives' but none of whom had received the official endorsement of the 'conservative' hierarchy, which did not wish to be identified with a humiliating defeat. The election, therefore, had rather the character of a referendum on the reform programme.

Khatami's election in 1997 had, to some extent, been seen as the result of a protest vote against the system. This time, however, the voting was interpreted as a positive expression of support for the President personally, and for his reform programme. This endorsement gave Khatami the strength to return to the struggle with the 'conservatives', but also put him under greater pressure from his own constituency to achieve certain concrete goals.

FOREIGN RELATIONS UNDER KHATAMI

The success of President Khatami's 'reformist' project depended on ending Iran's isolation—both political and economic—by seeking an improvement in relations with the West. Any such improvement would be determined by the course of Iran's relations with the USA. This key area of foreign policy was also, however, the one most likely to provoke conflict between opposing factions within the Iranian leadership. In August 1997 President Khatami identified Iran's need for 'an active and fresh presence' in the sphere of foreign relations. The US Department of State greeted the announcement of a new Iranian Council of Ministers in that month with a statement of its willingness to engage in dialogue, provided that Iran would discuss the issues of nuclear weapons, 'terrorism' and the Middle East peace process. This was tantamount to setting impossible conditions for dialogue: Iran's definition of 'terrorism', for instance, was substantially different to that of the USA, and Iran had long regarded the Middle East peace process as dead.

In mid-1997 official US attitudes towards Iran continued to be dominated by concern about the country's weapons programmes. In July the announcement that Russia was to assist Iran with completion of the nuclear power plant at Bushehr prompted the USA to reiterate its concern that Iran might attempt to exploit civilian nuclear technology for the development of nuclear weapons. Yet despite unrelenting pressure from the USA and Israel to withdraw from the project in 1998, Russia was determined to continue with its programme of nuclear co-operation with Iran. In Tehran the Russian minister responsible for nuclear power, Yevgenii Adamov, signed an agreement with Muhammad Aghazadeh, head of the Atomic Energy Organization of Iran, committing Russia to complete the installation of the first reactor at Bushehr and to conduct a feasibility study for the construction of three additional units at the site. Although Iran had signed and ratified the Treaty on the Non-Proliferation of Nuclear Weapons (the Non-Proliferation Treaty—NPT) and given the IAEA full access to Bushehr, the USA and Israel repeatedly alleged that the reactor could give Iran the technology it needed to develop nuclear weapons. Adamov, however, reiterated assurances that Bushehr could not be used for military purposes. In December 2000 Russia agreed to resume military co-operation with Iran, although during an official visit to Russia by President Khatami in March 2001, his Russian counterpart, Vladimir Putin, emphasized that Russia would only export weapons to Iran to be used for defensive purposes. As part of a bilateral security and co-operation agreement, it was also confirmed that Russia would assist Iran with the completion of the Bushehr power plant. In May Russia agreed to the sale of advanced ship-borne cruise missiles to Iran. A military co-operation accord—reportedly amounting to annual sales to Iran of Russian weaponry worth some US $300m.—was signed by the two sides in October.

The election of President Khatami and the appointment, in August 1997, of a new Minister of Foreign Affairs apparently led to a relaxation of tensions in EU–Iranian relations. In November a compromise arrangement was finally reached allowing the return of all ambassadors from EU countries to Iran. However, the EU's policy of 'critical dialogue' remained in suspension. In September 1998, following intensive negotiations between the British Secretary of State for Foreign and Commonwealth Affairs, Robin Cook, and the Iranian Minister of Foreign Affairs, Kamal Kharrazi, it was announced that the British Government had secured verbal assurances from the Iranian Government that it would not support the bounty on Rushdie's head, although the 1989 *fatwa* could not be formally revoked. In February 1998 the EU revoked its ban on high-level ministerial contacts between member states and Iran, stating that it wished to encourage moderate political forces in the Islamic Republic. Moreover, the Rushdie affair and the US-imposed 1996 Iran and Libya Sanctions Act (ILSA) notwithstanding, European companies were actively pursuing opportunities in the energy industries of the Caspian Basin and in Iran.

The 'active and fresh presence' in the sphere of foreign relations to which President Khatami referred in August 1997 had, by mid-1998, yielded results in the field of Iranian–Arab relations. The OIC Conference held in Tehran in December 1997 illustrated how far the Arab position had shifted towards Iran. Saudi Arabia has long been the target of Iranian criticism for the style of its guardianship of the holy cities of Mecca and Medina, along with its dependence on the USA for its security. The kingdom was represented at the OIC summit meeting by Crown Prince Abdullah ibn Abd al-Aziz Al Sa'ud and by its Minister of Foreign Affairs. Their attendance represented a significant further stage in the process of reconciliation, which had begun with the visit of a Saudi Arabian ministerial delegation to Iran in July, and culminated, in February 1998, in an official visit by former Iranian President Rafsanjani to Saudi Arabia.

In May 1999 President Khatami embarked on a tour of Arab capitals, beginning with Syria, where he reaffirmed the alliance with President Hafiz al-Assad. The Iranian President then proceeded to Saudi Arabia, a visit that marked the culmination of the steady improvement in relations between these two countries. There were, however, fewer signs of improvement in Iran's relations with the UAE, which had deteriorated further in 1996 after Iran opened an airport on Abu Musa in March and a power station on Greater Tunb in April. Both countries continued to assert their sovereignty over the three disputed islands. The apparent rapprochement between Iran and Saudi Arabia during 1999 caused a bitter crisis within the Cooperation Council for the Arab States of the Gulf (or Gulf Cooperation Council—GCC). A June meeting of GCC ministers responsible for foreign affairs was unable to agree a common stand on the UAE's dispute with Iran over the three Gulf islands. This resulted in Tehran interpreting the meeting as evidence of Saudi Arabia's desire to pursue closer relations with Iran.

Following the election of President Khatami in 1997 there were also signs of an improvement in relations with Iraq. In September of that year Iraq opened its border with Iran in order to allow Iranian pilgrims access to its Shi'a shrines for the first time in 17 years. At the end of the month, however, Iranian aircraft violated the air exclusion zone over southern Iraq in order to bomb two bases of the Mujahidin-e-Khalq in that country. Despite a protest lodged with the UN by Iraq in June 2002, stating that Iran was continuing to violate agreements reached at the end of the Iran–Iraq War, a general thaw in bilateral relations was evident.

In September 1997 the Taliban leadership in Afghanistan accused Iran of providing military assistance to its opponents and threatened retaliatory action. In late 1997 it was reported that, since the election of President Khatami, Iran had begun to participate in meetings at the UN with (among others) US officials in an attempt to identify ways of ending the Afghan civil war. Iran's principal concerns with regard to Afghanistan had been the containment of any instability resulting from the conflict there, and to remove the strain placed on its domestic resources by the presence in Iranian territory of large numbers of Afghan refugees. Following the alleged kidnapping by Taliban forces in August of more than 40 Iranian nationals, Iran organized large-scale military exercises near the border with Afghanistan and by September had posted some 250,000 troops to the border region. Overt military conflict with Afghanistan was ultimately averted, although Iran maintained a significant military presence on the border.

In the second half of 1999 there were new indications of a possible resumption of relations between Iran and the USA. In August the Iranian Deputy Minister of Foreign Affairs, Mohsen Aminzadeh, stated that Iranian policy towards the USA had changed. He was reported to favour Iran's approaching the USA from a position of strength in order to gain as many concessions as possible, particularly with regard to Azerbaijani oil contracts and the lifting of economic sanctions. Although Aminzadeh later complained that his remarks had been quoted out of context, and that he had also criticized US policy, his views were none the less regarded as an accurate reflection of the official policy. On 19 March 2000 US Secretary of State

Madeleine Albright delivered a well-publicized address in which she announced an end to import restrictions on Iranian carpets and foodstuffs; she also acknowledged Iran's importance, the failure of US policy towards the country and the prospects for improved future relations. Besides praising Iranian 'reformers', Albright came close to apologizing for the role the USA had played in the overthrow of Muhammad Musaddeq in 1953 and for its support for Iraq in the Iran–Iraq War.

However, any improvements in US-Iranian relations again faltered when, in June 2001, 14 men were indicted *in absentia* by the US Government, having been charged with involvement in the bombing at al-Khobar, Saudi Arabia, in June 1996. The accused men—13 Saudis and one Lebanese—included the leader of Saudi Hezbollah and prominent members of Hezbollah's military wing. Announcing the list, US Attorney-General John Ashcroft alleged that members of the Iranian Government 'inspired, supported and supervised' Saudi Hezbollah, and that the terrorists 'reported surveillance activities to Iranian officials'. However, the list was noteworthy for its omission of any Iranian names. This was a considerable climbdown for the US Federal Bureau of Investigation (FBI), whose outgoing Director, Louis Freeh, had for years insisted that the organization possessed enough information to indict senior members of Iran's intelligence services and its spiritual leader, Ayatollah Khamenei.

Although Iranian officials welcomed early indications that the new Administration of President George W. Bush, inaugurated in January 2001, was reviewing US policy on sanctions, the USA confirmed in August that ILSA was to be extended for a further five years. (The legislation incorporated an option for President Bush to review the sanctions in 2003.) In July 2001 the USA had, for the second time since May, blocked Iran's bid to enter negotiations regarding membership of the World Trade Organization (WTO). By December 2004 the USA had vetoed 20 such Iranian applications, although in March 2005 President Bush announced a series of economic incentives, including the removal of the ban on Iran's membership of the WTO, in an attempt to persuade Iran to suspend permanently its nuclear energy programme.

In the immediate aftermath of the devastating suicide attacks on 11 September 2001, in New York and Washington, DC, there was considerable speculation among Western observers as to Iran's likely response to the US prosecution of a campaign against the al-Qa'ida organization and its leader, the Saudi-born fundamentalist dissident Osama bin Laden, who was then based in Afghanistan.

President Khatami was swift to offer his 'deep sympathy . . . to the American nation', asserting that terrorism was 'condemned' while urging the international community to take 'effective measures against it'. In a letter to the UN Secretary-General, Khatami stated that he regarded the UN as the most appropriate mechanism to achieve the eradication of terrorism. Ayatollah Khamenei, for his part, remained initially silent on the issue. When he did comment, almost a week after the attacks, he condemned the atrocities in the strongest terms but cautioned against a military offensive against Afghanistan that might result in the deaths of innocent civilians and create a new refugee exodus. Khamenei stressed that Iran would similarly condemn any 'catastrophe' brought about in Afghanistan by US-led conflict, also warning that the USA's problems would multiply if the country sought to establish a presence in Pakistan and send troops into Afghanistan. Khamenei's views were echoed in Iran's 'conservative' press. While it was considered by many that some form of co-operation against bin Laden, and potentially his Taliban hosts, could be advantageous to both Iran and the USA, influential forces within both the Iranian and US administrations remained implacably opposed to such a pragmatic approach. By late September indications that the USA was seeking to establish a channel of communication with authorities in Tehran. This was confirmed when it was announced that the British Secretary of State for Foreign and Commonwealth Affairs, Jack Straw, was to bring forward an official visit to Iran that had been planned for November. However, Iran emphasized that it would not lend military assistance to the US-led campaign against Afghanistan, and both 'liberals' and 'conservatives' in the Iranian regime strongly condemned the commencement of hostilities in early October.

KHATAMI'S SECOND TERM: TENSIONS WITHIN THE ISLAMIC REGIME—REPERCUSSIONS OF THE 'WAR ON TERROR'

Amid the general preoccupation with events in Afghanistan, the struggle between Iran's 'reformists' and 'conservatives' continued. In October 2001 President Khatami issued a formal constitutional warning to the Head of the Judiciary, Ayatollah Hashemi Shahrudi, regarding the prosecution of pro-reform Majlis deputies despite their parliamentary immunity under the terms of the Constitution. At least two deputies had received prison sentences for remarks made during a session of the Majlis, although they had not yet actually been imprisoned. By the end of 2001 the number of deputies facing charges for their speeches in the Majlis had reached 60. All had been summoned to court, and in December Hossein Loqmanian, a 'reformist' deputy, was the first actually to be gaoled. In January 2002, however, Majlis Speaker Karrubi made a dramatic intervention when he forced the release of Hossein Loqmanian by walking out of parliament and essentially going on strike until Khamenei was obliged to intervene and pardon the imprisoned deputy; Loqmanian was duly released.

The internal power struggle was undoubtedly affected by the international crisis over Afghanistan, with some 'reformists' hoping that the conflict there might help to open the way for a dialogue with the US Administration. Iran's long border with Afghanistan and its influence over the Western-backed opposition forces, known collectively as the United National Islamic Front for the Salvation of Afghanistan (or the Northern Alliance), especially the Shi'a Hizb-i Wahdat, gave it a key role in the Afghan situation.

Iran had a number of concerns relating to the outcome of the Afghan campaign. Already host to an estimated 2.3m. Afghans, it feared an influx of thousands of new refugees. In late September 2001, as the USA began preparations for military action against al-Qa'ida and its Taliban hosts, Iran moved to stem the refugee tide by closing its eastern border with Afghanistan and sending a large contingent of troops there. The Iranian leadership was also suspicious of the potential installation of another hostile, US-engineered regime in Kabul (as a replacement for the Taliban), and was anxious about the instability that might result from a long and inconclusive conflict. Some 'reformers' insisted that talking to all parties in the conflict, including the USA, was essential to securing Iran's national interests and a favourable formula for Afghanistan's future. Iran was already involved in the long-standing 'Six plus Two' group, which brought together, under UN auspices, Afghanistan's neighbours with Russia and the USA. Iran continued to assert that the UN should play a pivotal role in the construction of a post-war government in Afghanistan, pressing this view on the UN Secretary-General's Special Envoy to Afghanistan, Lakhdar Brahimi, during his talks in Tehran.

Any hopes entertained by 'reformists' in Tehran and 'doves' in Washington that the Afghan crisis might lead to a rapprochement between the two countries were discouraged by US President Bush's annual State of the Union address on 29 January 2002, where he linked Iran, Iraq and the Democratic People's Republic of Korea (North Korea) in what he termed an 'axis of evil'. Iran was particularly aggrieved since even the Bush Administration conceded that the country had played a constructive role during the November–December 2001 conference in Bonn, Germany, which led to the formation of a new interim Afghan administration under Hamid Karzai (Iran had pledged more than US $500m. to Kabul), and during the fund-raising conference in Tokyo, Japan.

As 2002 progressed, the perception among Iranians across the political spectrum was one of threat posed from abroad. US armed forces and their allies had established a considerable presence and authority in Afghanistan; a similar campaign in Iraq to remove Saddam Hussain from power was apparently only being delayed by the tense situation in Israel and the Palestinian territories; while the pro-Israeli lobby in the USA was constantly campaigning against Iran. The appropriate response to the US position remained a highly controversial issue within Iran, and in April the Deputy Foreign Minister for Education and Research, Sadegh Kharrazi, was forced to resign amid rumours of contacts with US officials. (Although a handful of 'reformists' within Iran still favoured talks with the USA, it became clear that the broad Iranian establishment did not. In May the judiciary in Tehran issued a warning to newspapers that the publication of any material favouring the idea of negotiations with US officials would be deemed a criminal offence.) Meanwhile, a further source of external pressure was added in April 2002, when a summit of the five littoral states failed to resolve the legal status of the Caspian Sea.

During mid-2002 US President Bush again sought to persuade his Russian counterpart, Vladimir Putin, to cease the transfer of Russian nuclear knowledge and technology to Iran by ending its involvement with the power plant at Bushehr. In late July Russian officials angered the US Administration by signing a draft development and co-operation accord with Iran, which was reported to include the proposed construction of three more nuclear reactors at the Bushehr plant. Iran did, nevertheless, accept an offer of humanitarian aid from the USA following a major earthquake in the north-west of the country in late June 2002. However, the deterioration in Iranian–US relations was evident when, towards the end of July, Khatami openly condemned US plans to use military force to bring about 'regime change' in Iraq, warning that such action posed a serious risk to regional stability.

Towards the end of 2002 the belief was growing in Tehran that, despite the outcome in Iraq, there would be an intensification of US pressure on Iran in a post-Saddam Hussain era. Accordingly, there was an increased emphasis on military preparedness and also on healing internal divisions in order to withstand this pressure. On a visit to Madrid, Spain, in October, Khatami accused the USA of having rebuffed all Iran's gestures of 'goodwill' and of pursuing policies that undermined moderate Islam and actually recruited for al-Qa'ida, declaring that, alongside the people, the Islamic Republic's armed forces would defend the country's rights and freedoms. Iranian officials also saw the need for a strengthening of regional ties, and early in 2003 they were involved in a flurry of regional contacts over the Iraq crisis. Additionally, there were signs that most of those involved in the internal struggles were preparing to lay aside their disputesin the national interest.

In January 2003 Grand Ayatollah Montazeri was released from house arrest in Qom, where he had remained since 1997. Once the designated successor to Ayatollah Khomeini, Montazeri had displeased Khamenei by publicly questioning both the latter's religious qualifications and the manner in which he was interpreting and conducting his role.

Municipal elections were held throughout Iran in February 2003. At the polls the 'reformists' suffered a crushing blow at the hands of the 'conservatives'. The turn-out was generally low—at only 39% of the 41m. eligible voters—but was particularly disappointing in Tehran, where only about 10% of the electorate voted. It was apparently this low turn-out that enabled a group of unknown 'conservatives' to sweep the capital's 15-member council, and for opponents of the 'reformists' to make substantial gains in other cities. This surprising result represented a severe setback for President Khatami, whose allies blamed the loss of public support on the slow pace of change. 'Conservative' newspapers, however, were quick to point out that the defeat of the 'reformers' at the ballot-box meant that they could no longer claim a popular mandate.

INCREASED DOMESTIC AND INTERNATIONAL TENSION FOLLOWING THE COLLAPSE OF THE REGIME IN IRAQ

The increasingly clear determination of the USA to attack Iraq represented a major dilemma for Tehran. The official line, propagated by figures from both the 'conservative' and the 'reformist' camps, was that a unilateralist US attack against the Iraqi regime would be both morally wrong and regionally destabilizing, and that the UN should be the only framework for dealing with Baghdad. In late 2002 a high-ranking delegation from the Iraqi Kurdish party, the KDP, had visited Tehran for talks with political, military and security officials from across the Iranian spectrum. The negotiators left Iran with the strong impression that, notwithstanding public rhetoric, Iranian leaders of all political leanings would be delighted by the removal of Saddam Hussain and would support the Iraqi opposition to that end. This impression was reinforced by the fact that Tehran had placed no obstacles in the way of Ayatollah Muhammad Baqir al-Hakim's Iran-based Supreme Council for Islamic Revolution in Iraq (SCIRI) when it joined five other Iraqi opposition groups in talks with the US Administration in Washington, DC, in August.

By May 2003, following the start of the campaign to oust Saddam Hussain, it seemed that the 'hawks' in the Bush Administration were also setting their sights on 'regime change' in Tehran. The USA accused Iran of sheltering al-Qa'ida leaders who had masterminded a series of suicide bombings against expatriate compounds in Riyadh, Saudi Arabia, on 12 May. Iranian officials vehemently denied the charge, although they admitted that a small number of al-Qa'ida suspects, detained prior to the Riyadh bomb attacks, were in Iranian custody. Relations between the USA and Iran had also deteriorated because of Iraq. During the conflict, stern US warnings were issued to Iran not to get involved, but the large numbers of exiles returning to Iraq from Iran—not only clergy but also leaders of SCIRI (which in May 2007 changed its name to the Islamic Supreme Council of Iraq) and its armed militia, the Badr Brigade (subsequently renamed Badr Organization)—carried Iranian influence deep into southern Iraq and beyond. These warnings presaged the US Administration's increased focus on Iran following the collapse of the regime in Baghdad. Discreet direct contacts between the USA and Iran had reportedly been taking place in Geneva to discuss the problems arising on the ground in Iraq, including the continuing presence there of the Mujahidin-e-Khalq and its military wing, the National Liberation Army (NLA), and the repatriation of Iraqi exiles in Iran. However, these contacts were abruptly broken off following the allegations that Iran was sheltering al-Qa'ida militants, and US officials began accusing Iran of 'interfering' in Iraqi affairs. US Secretary of Defense Donald Rumsfeld, in particular, warned that any Iranian attempt to create a new Iraq in the image of the Islamic Republic would be 'aggressively put down'. In June nearly 160 members of the Mujahidin were arrested by the authorities in Paris, amid claims that they were plotting attacks. The detainees included Maryam Rajavi, co-leader of the organization and the wife of Massoud Rajavi, and resulted in protests in Tehran and by Iranian *émigrés* in several European cities. Maryam Rajavi was later released without charge.

An ongoing source of contention was the USA's accusation that Iran was secretly trying to develop nuclear weapons, a charge that has been routinely denied by Tehran. On 9 February 2003 President Khatami announced the discovery and extraction of uranium deposits in central Iran, and the establishment of processing facilities in Esfahan and Kashan—sites that were due for inspection by the IAEA later that month. The USA attempted to pressure both the IAEA to declare that Iran was in violation of the NPT and Russia to abandon its involvement in Iran's nuclear power plant at Bushehr. The Russians refused, instead urging Iran to submit to greater international scrutiny by agreeing to sign the Additional Protocol to the NPT. There was also confusion at the beginning of June regarding the status of Russian exports of nuclear fuel to Iran: President Vladimir Putin's assertion that Russia would indeed cease such exports was later contradicted by Alexandr Rumyantsev, the Russian Minister of Atomic Energy, who announced ongoing contractual negotiations for Russia to commence the re-processing of Iranian nuclear waste in early 2004. Questions were raised about Iran's nuclear policy, yet Iran insisted that it would only accept the rigorous inspection conditions in exchange for a lifting of the ban of access to nuclear technology. Meanwhile, in Washington it appeared that US 'hawks' were being prevented from pressing for an escalation of the antagonistic situation between the USA and Iran amid doubts about the military feasibility of any attack against the Islamic regime and the lack of any credible pro-US Iranian opposition.

Inside Iran, the conflict between 'conservatives' and 'reformers', and dissent within the pro-reform camp, continued. In May 2003, following the refusal of the Council of Guardians to ratify the two key bills presented to the Majlis by President Khatami the previous September and subsequently passed by that body, 127 'reformist' deputies wrote to Khamenei urging him to intervene to unblock the stalled reform process and also calling for a referendum on proposed reforms. The internal tensions led to a wave of large student demonstrations in June. The demonstrations were provoked by plans to privatize Iran's universities, but quickly took on a more political and anti-regime complexion, with regular clashes between students, riot police and pro-Government vigilante groups. Iranian officials reacted with outrage to President Bush's public backing for the demonstrations. Up to 4,000 arrests were made during the disturbances, prompting four members of the Majlis to stage a sit-in in protest at the treatment of some of the student leaders. The crisis continued into early July, with student leaders planning mass rallies for 9 July, the anniversary of the huge protests of 1999. However, amid a deteriorating domestic situation and severe external threat, and following a request from five reformist deputies, the official protests were cancelled (although spontaneous and sporadic demonstrations still took place).

IAEA DEADLINE AND SUBSEQUENT NEGOTIATIONS

The 31 October 2003 deadline set by the IAEA for Iran's signature of the Additional Protocol posed a dilemma for the Iranian regime. If it complied with the deadline, it would appear to be capitulating to US pressure at a time when Muslim opinion was incensed by events in the Palestinian territories and Iraq. However, if it resisted, the regime risked finding itself in a position of North Korean-style isolation, with severely negative implications for its relations with Europe and its regional status. Some 'hardline' newspaper editorials, Friday sermons, and declarations from 'conservative' figures advocated withdrawal from the NPT as the only way of securing national independence. However, most 'conservatives' seemed in favour of compliance, although attempts to put forward a more pragmatic approach were undermined by the overt nature of US pressure on the IAEA and by the failure of Washington to live up to its own NPT commitments. None the less, the 'reformist' Participation Front issued a statement arguing strongly in favour of compliance. The Front argued that signing the Additional Protocol, which would allow intrusive, unannounced IAEA inspections, would enhance international confidence in Iran.

Iran's strategic decision to co-operate with the IAEA was confirmed by a statement that emerged from the visit by the ministers responsible for foreign affairs of France, Germany and the United Kingdom on 21 October 2003. Iran stated for the first time without equivocation that it had decided to sign the Additional Protocol and pledged to 'address and resolve with full transparency' all the IAEA's remaining questions and to 'clarify and correct any possible failures and deficiencies' with the agency. While emphasizing its right to develop peaceful nuclear energy under safeguards, Iran also announced that it had decided 'voluntarily to suspend all uranium enrichment and reprocessing activities, as defined by the IAEA'. In return, Iran received an indication that, if it abided by its commitments, the current crisis could be resolved within the IAEA context, and the rather vaguely worded assurance that 'once international concerns are fully resolved Iran could expect easier access to modern technology in a range of areas'. This assurance was the closest the three European ministers came to promising Iran access to the technology and enriched fuel it needed to sustain a civil nuclear power programme, and Jack Straw, the British Secretary of State for Foreign and Commonwealth Affairs, later stated that no promises of specific nuclear technology had been given at this stage.

Under pressure from the IAEA and the international community, and after days of deliberations and negotiations, Iran eventually handed over full documentation concerning all the issues under investigation by the IAEA, including information relating to Iran's attempts to enrich uranium. In an address to senior officials on 2 November 2003, Khamenei declared his backing for the decision, and appeared to defuse 'conservative' opposition. On 20 November the IAEA Board of Governors met in Vienna, Austria, adopting a resolution five days later which criticized Iran for past 'failures to report' but did not declare Iran to be in non-compliance of its NPT obligations, and therefore did not refer it to the UN Security Council for further action.

During the early part of 2004 negotiations continued between Iran and the IAEA, despite an IAEA resolution that criticized Iran's failure to co-operate with inspectors. Iran reacted furiously and directed the thrust of its criticism at the trio of European states that had drafted the resolution. It accused the United Kingdom, France and Germany of reneging on their side of the October 2003 agreement, and offailing to provide the technology and trade in return for which Iran had pledged to freeze its uranium enrichment. By the end of June 2004 Iran announced that it would resume elements of its uranium enrichment programme.

DEVELOPMENTS IN IRAQ

The capture of Saddam Hussain in December 2003 was warmly welcomed by Iran, which made official demands that the former Iraqi President face an international trial at which Iran and other countries with grievances against the Baathist regime could lodge their complaints, and where 'those parties who equipped the Iraqi dictator' could also be identified. As with other international and regional events, Saddam Hussain's capture became an indicator of domestic tensions within the Islamic regime. The 'hardline' press emphasized the USA's support for the Iraqi leader during the 1980s, when he was at the height of his excesses, while the 'reformists' focused on the significance of his fate for those who lose popular support.

By early 2004 the tone of official Iranian pronouncements on US policy and actions in Iraq was becoming increasingly vituperative. In an address on 14 April, Ayatollah Khamenei was scathing about US accusations that the Iranian regime was inciting the unrest in Iraq. Although Iran continued to regard a US withdrawal from Iraq as both desirable and inevitable, its policy was directed towards achieving calm and stability in that country in order to expedite a US evacuation. Officials steadfastly denied that any Iranian element, including the Revolutionary Guards, was assisting the radical Shi'a movement led by Muqtada al-Sadr. None the less, the 'conservative' press was fiercely critical of US attacks against al-Sadr's forces and opposed any attempt by Iran to mediate between the USA and Iraqi Shi'a. On 15 April Khalil Naimi, first secretary at the Iranian embassy in Baghdad, was shot and killed by three unknown assailants. The assassination occurred a day after the arrival in Baghdad of an Iranian diplomatic mission which was intended to attempt to defuse the stand-off around Najaf between US troops and al-Sadr's forces (see the chapter on Iraq). The Iranian mission, headed by the Director for Gulf Affairs at the Ministry of Foreign Affairs, Hussein Sadeghi, was recalled early.

ELECTIONS TO THE SEVENTH MAJLIS

On 11 January 2004 a crisis erupted in Tehran over the legislative elections scheduled for 20 February, when the Council of Guardians barred almost one-half of the 8,000 candidates wishing to stand. The ban was principally directed at the 'reformists', including 80 incumbent Majlis deputies, most notably the President's brother, Muhammad Reza Khatami, leader of the Participation Front. The Council of Guardians, which had blocked 'reformist' candidates in the past (although never on such a scale), deemed that those barred from standing were insufficiently respectful either towards the Islamic Republic's Constitution or to Ayatollah Khamenei. One hundred 'reformist' deputies began a sit-in at the Majlis to protest against what they saw as a pre-emptive strike by their 'conservative' opponents, while President Khatami, pro-reform ministers and all 27 provincial Governors threatened to resign. As the crisis intensified, the Government asked the Council of Guardians to postpone the elections as the Ministry of the Interior had argued that free and fair elections were currently impossible, but the Council refused. This left the 'reformist' camp with a dilemma as to whether to participate in the elections or not. Finally, eight of the 22 groups that originally constituted the Second of Khordad movement decided to contest the elections, including the 'reformist' Majma'-e Ruhaniyun-i Mobarez (Militant Clergy Association), to which both Khatami and Karrubi belonged. These eight groups formed a loose alliance called the Coalition for Iran, but candidates continued to withdraw in protest at the conduct of the elections. Even with the addition of some moderate 'conservatives' and independents, the Coalition for Iran was unable to field a sufficient number of candidates to contest all 290 seats.

Campaigning for the elections was a low-key affair with widespread public indifference. In the first round of voting on 20 February 2004, national turn-out was officially estimated at some 51% (with polling in Tehran recorded at only 28%); 229 candidates were elected directly to the Majlis, with the remainder of the 290 seats to be filled at a second round of voting, held on 7 May. Those 'reformists' who had decided to stand fared particularly badly, at least in the important Tehran constituency: Mahdi Karrubi, Jamileh Kadivar and other well-known 'reformist' figures all finished outside the top 30; Karrubi subsequently withdrew rather than be humiliated further by losing a run-off for one of the undecided bottom-ranking seats. Furthermore, electoral turn-out was not so low as to be regarded as a great success for those who had advocated a boycott. (The Council of Guardians maintained that turn-out was in fact around 60%.) Following the two rounds of voting, the 'conservatives' emerged with a clear majority in the seventh Majlis; they reportedly secured more than 190 seats, while 'reformists' took fewer than 50 seats, and the remainder went to 'independents'. The new legislature was inaugurated on 27 May and the 'conservatives', including Gholam-Ali Haddad-Adel, who had achieved the best result in the Tehran ballot and had later become the new Speaker, took steps to reassure domestic opinion that there would be no crackdown in the social and political arena, and the international community that there would be no sudden reversal of the *détente* pursued by the 'reformists'.

DEVELOPMENTS IN THE NUCLEAR ISSUE, 2004–05

Throughout 2004 the wrangling over Iran's nuclear programme continued. On 18 September an IAEA resolution gave Iran until 25 November, the organization's next board meeting, to suspend its enrichment programme and prove its peaceful intent or face the possibility of being referred to the UN Security Council. Inside Iran the mood remained defiant, with senior officials repeating that the country would never surrender its right to fuel self-sufficiency. Even 'reformists' were adamant that Iran should not back down, while the Majlis Energy Commission called for Iran's civil nuclear programme to be stepped up. On the day before the meeting of the IAEA board, a deal was struck between Iran and the three European countries most involved in negotiations, the United Kingdom, France and Germany. After weeks of talks, Iran agreed once again to suspend enrichment voluntarily while it discussed fresh proposals to end the deadlock. On 29 November the IAEA passed a resolution recognizing that Iran had suspended all enrichment activities as a voluntary gesture of 'goodwill'. The USA stated that it might take Iran to the Security Council independently of the IAEA, but seemed aware that it would find it difficult to push through a sanctions resolution. Iranian-European talks resumed, and continued into 2005. Following an eight-month suspension, due to the resumption of uranium conversion at Esfahan, the IAEA passed a resolution on 11 August, urging Iran to halt all uranium enrichment and nuclear-reprocessing activities.

Meanwhile, in February 2005 it was revealed that the USA had been flying unmanned spy planes over Iran since early 2004, to test Iranian radar and air defence systems and to seek out nuclear facilities as potential targets for air strikes. However, it was widely presumed that the USA's continuing military and political difficulties in Iraq precluded any imminent attack on Iran.

THE 2005 PRESIDENTIAL ELECTION

On 22 May 2005 the Council of Guardians barred 1,008 candidates for the presidential election, including the most prominent 'reformist', Moustafa Moin, prompting his supporters in the largest pro-reform factions to call for a boycott. Former President Ali Akbar Hashemi Rafsanjani had announced his intention to contest the presidency in mid-May and was regarded as the most likely victor, followed by Muhammad Baqir Qalibaf, the former police chief, and former head of state broadcasting Ali Ardeshir Larijani. The other candidates included Mahdi Karrubi, the former Speaker of the Majlis, who was on the right wing of the 'reformist' camp, and Mahmoud Ahmadinejad, the populist mayor of Tehran. Following criticism from the Ministry of the Interior and the Supreme Leader, Ayatollah Khamenei, the Council of Guardians reversed its ban on the candidacies of Moin and another 'reformist', Mohsen Mehr-Alizadeh. Observers believed this was meant to complicate the outcome of the election by further dividing votes.

Opinion polls gave Rafsanjani the lead, with more than 20% of the vote, none of his rivals having more than 15%. However, since no single candidate was expected to win the 50% of votes cast necessary for outright victory, a second round of voting appeared inevitable; thus the race for second place became crucial. Several candidates were vying for the 'reformist' votes, including Rafsanjani himself. Mahdi Karrubi, who, apart from Rafsanjani, was the only cleric in the contest, modelled his image on his close colleague, President Khatami, but suffered from the popular perception of the latter's timidity and failure. It was Moin, however, who was the main 'reformist' hope, basing his campaign on human rights and democratization.

The first round of polling took place on 17 June 2005. The result was quite contrary to the expectations of both Iranian and foreign analysts. The only correct prediction was Rafsanjani's place at the top of the poll: from 29.3m. votes cast, Rafsanjani took 6.2m. (21.0%). Of the other 'conservative' candidates, Ahmadinejad polled 5.7m. votes (19.5%), Qalibaf 4.1m. and Larijani 1.7m. Of the 'reformist' candidates, Karrubi finished in third place, with 5.1m. votes, Moin fifth, with 4.1m., and Mehr-Alizadeh last, with 1.3m. The turn-out, at 62%, also exceeded expectations. The closeness and unpredictability of the poll brought people out to participate, with Rafsanjani, the 'conservatives' and the 'reformists' offering three clearly defined and differing positions.

The second round of polling took place on 24 June 2005, giving a clear victory to Ahmadinejad, who won with over 17m. votes (61.7% of total votes cast) against Rafsanjani's 10m. It appeared that the former Tehran mayor's large majority was based on a combination of populist economics and the electoral appeal of a perceived political outsider. The poor were attracted by Ahmadinejad's promises of greater distribution of wealth, improved social justice, strong continued subsidies, more public sector employment and cheaper food, while many who voted in the first round for 'reformist' candidates were unwilling to switch to Rafsanjani, whom they mistrusted and associated with corruption. Ahmadinejad formally assumed the office of President on 6 August, having been sworn in before the Majlis; he nominated his first Council of Ministers, subject to legislative approval, on 14 August. On 24 August the Majlis voted to approve 17 of Ahmadinejad's 21 nominees, all of whom were reported to be 'hardliners'. However, although Ahmadinejad's victory was widely interpreted as a victory of the 'conservatives' over 'moderates' and 'reformists', it also seemed to mark the emergence of a new division within 'conservative' ranks between the *bazaari* and the clergy on the one hand, and the new Islamic populists on the other.

DEVELOPMENTS IN THE NUCLEAR ISSUE, 2005–06

From late 2005 and into 2006 the tensions surrounding Iran's nuclear issue escalated. In November 2005 the EU accused Iran of having documents that served no other purpose than that of producing nuclear arms, and warned Iranian officials of possible future referral to the UN Security Council at a meeting of the IAEA. The main issue was Iran's continuing refusal to give up its right to uranium enrichment. In its statement, the EU offered new negotiations aimed at defusing tensions over this issue. A recent plan had foreseen moving any Iranian enrichment project to Russia. There, in theory, Russia would supervise the process to ensure that enrichment was limited to the level necessary to produce fuel. Iran, however, rejected the proposals, and Minister of Foreign Affairs Manouchehr Mottaki told reporters in Tehran that, while his country was willing to resume formal talks with key European powers concerning its nuclear programme, 'naturally we aim to have enrichment on Iran's territory'.

The three EU countries most involved in negotiations (the United Kingdom, France and Germany) hoped to restart talks which had been broken off in August 2005, when the Iranians had resumed nuclear-related activities at the Esfahan plant. These hopes were dissolved in December, when Iran announced plans to construct two more nuclear power plants. Ali Larijani, Iran's senior nuclear negotiator, stated that he did not expect the plans to affect the resumption of the nuclear talks with the three EU nations.

The dispute reached fresh heights when, on 10 January 2006, Iran removed the IAEA seals from its uranium enrichment equipment at the Natanz plant, south of Tehran, announcing that it would restart the programme. In response, the USA, Russia, China, the United Kingdom and France agreed to move the Iranian dispute to the UN Security Council. However, the significance of this decision was limited as the agreement, deferring to Russian demands, only 'reported' rather than 'referred' Iran to the Security Council. The agreement also stipulated that the Security Council would undertake no action for at least a month, until after the next IAEA board meeting, scheduled for 6 March. The EU at this point declared talks with Iran to be at a 'dead end', especially with Iran threatening to abandon the NPT.

An announcement made by Iran on 14 February 2006 stated that the country had resumed small-scale uranium enrichment. This represented the first resumption of small-scale enrichment since two-and-a-half years previously, when enrichment at the Natanz plant had been abandoned under an agreement with the three main EU negotiating powers. On the following day the Bush Administration responded by making an emergency request to the US Congress for a sevenfold increase in funding to mount the biggest ever propaganda campaign against the Tehran Government. Condoleezza Rice, the US Secretary of State, declared that the US $75m. in extra funds, in addition to the $10m. already allocated, would be used to broadcast US radio and television programmes into Iran, help fund Iranians to study in the USA and support pro-democracy groups inside Iran.

On 19 March 2006 the UN Security Council issued a formal demand for Iran to abandon its uranium enrichment efforts. The statement, passed unanimously, called on the IAEA to report back in 30 days on Tehran's compliance, but did not make clear what the Security Council would do if Iran refused to co-operate. The stakes were raised in the nuclear stand-off when, on 2 April, Iran fired what it described as the world's fastest underwater missile, during a week of Iranian military exercises in the Gulf.

Meanwhile, some progress was made towards direct talks between Iran and the USA with regard to Iraq. On 21 March 2006 Ayatollah Khamenei gave his backing to such talks, saying that if his officials could make the USA 'understand some issues about Iraq', then there would be 'no problem with the negotiations'. This statement marked the first time that Khamenei, holder of the final say on all state matters in the country, had come out publicly in favour of direct discussions.

President Ahmadinejad announced on 11 April 2006 that his country had succeeded in enriching uranium, though insisting that Tehran had no plans to produce nuclear weapons. He declared that Iran intended to reach industrial levels of nuclear production and demanded that Western countries respect his country's right to nuclear technology. His announcement came shortly after the Vice-President and Head of the Iranian Atomic Energy Organization, Gholamreza Aghazadeh, declared that Iran had stockpiled 110 metric tons of uranium gas and had begun operations at a pilot enrichment plant at Natanz. The next day bells rang out in schools across Tehran in response to an order from the Islamic regime for a day of rejoicing.

In response to Ahmadinejad's announcement, Javier Solana, Secretary-General of the Council of the EU and High Representative for the Common Foreign and Security Policy, recommended limited sanctions against Iran, including visa bans imposed on leading figures, if Tehran continued to defy the UN over its disputed nuclear programme. Other proposed sanctions included a block on the transfer of civilian nuclear technology, an arms embargo and the suspension of negotiations with Iran on a free trade pact. The EU would also fund propaganda broadcasts against Tehran. In Luxembourg, the sanctions were discussed at a closed meeting of foreign ministers from the EU's 25 member states, but a decision was postponed until the expiry of a 30-day deadline set by the UN Security Council on 29 March 2006 for Iranian compliance.

This deadline, however, was ignored, and on 28 April 2006 the Director-General of the IAEA, Muhammed el-Baradei, released a report concluding that the deadline had not been complied with. The next stage was for the UN Security Council to discuss possible punitive measures, including sanctions. On 4 May the Security Council met to discuss a draft resolution on Iran's alleged nuclear weapons programme. This came soon after an announcement by Vice-President Aghazadeh that Iran had in fact enriched uranium to 4.8%, in contrast with the 3.6% earlier announced by President Ahmadinejad. Even this, however, fell well short of the levels needed to achieve nuclear weapons capability.

On 8 May 2006 President Ahmadinejad surprised the international community by sending a letter to President Bush, offering an analysis of global issues and 'new ways of getting out of the current delicate situation in the world'. The USA immediately rejected the letter as having no relevance, prompting an immediate rebuke from Russian President Vladimir Putin. Russia doubted that Iran was actively attempting to produce a nuclear bomb. Meanwhile, President Ahmadinejad remarked that the countries criticizing Iran's nuclear project were themselves involved in nuclear activities that were 'expanding day by day'.

By mid-May 2006 the EU was prepared to offer a 'bold package' of incentives to Iran, including possible security guarantees, provided that Tehran could ensure that its nuclear programme was not being used to produce weapons. This offer was ridiculed by Iran, which compared European incentives to suspend uranium enrichment to 'trading gold for chocolate'. President Ahmadinejad then countered with an offer of better trade deals for Europe if it dropped opposition to the programme. Meanwhile, on 23 May the Bush Administration ruled out previously authorized direct talks between Tehran and the US ambassador in Baghdad, which were supposed to have focused on the situation in Iraq. A US official said that although the US envoy had originally been granted a mandate for talks with Iran, 'we have decided not to pursue it'.

None the less, on 31 May 2006 the USA offered to join multilateral talks on Iran's nuclear programme, on the condition that Iran suspended uranium enrichment and co-operated with UN inspectors. This approach, which President Bush labelled 'robust diplomacy', was contingent on Russia and China agreeing to sanctions if the offer was rejected by Iran. On 6 June the EU again offered Iran an ambitious package of rewards, including the right to retain some uranium enrichment activities, if it reached agreement with the USA, Russia, the EU and China on its nuclear programme. Under the proposal Iran would have to freeze uranium enrichment activities before and during the talks. Javier Solana travelled to Tehran to present the initiative. After two hours of talks with the EU High Representative, Larijani affirmed that the package contained positive elements and could form the basis for renewed negotiations.

However, the possibility of an end to the dispute receded on 27 June 2006 when Ayatollah Khamenei reiterated that his country had an unalienable right to develop nuclear technology, stating that Iran would have 'nothing to gain' from talks with Washington on the issue. President Ahmadinejad indicated that a more considered reply by Iran would be forthcoming on 22 August. Yet President Bush expected a response within a matter of weeks. By the end of July the five permanent members of the UN Security Council were already showing signs of impatience, with US ambassador to the UN John

Bolton indicating that failure to take action would lead to sanctions on Iran. On 22 August Iran offered its response, stating that it was willing to hold 'serious talks' on the issue, while continuing to insist that suspending uranium enrichment was not on the agenda. While China and Russia agreed that the issue should be resolved through diplomatic means, the USA stated that the offer fell short of the conditions set by the Security Council.

INTERNATIONAL DIPLOMACY AND EXTERNAL TENSIONS

In response to US efforts to isolate Iran, President Ahmadinejad engaged in an energetic diplomatic counter-offensive during 2005. Iranian officials pursued increased political and economic co-operation with their counterparts from various countries, including Venezuela, and held high-level meetings with Russia, China and numerous Arab and Muslim states. Iran also attended the summit of the Shanghai Co-operation Organization which brought together the leaders of 10 nations. The support given by Iran to the newly elected Hamas in the Palestinian territories boosted Ahmadinejad's regional standing. This backing also served to exacerbate hostility between Iran and Israel, which during 2005–06 became more overt. In December 2005 President Ahmadinejad made remarks questioning whether the Holocaust had taken place and stating that Israel should be moved to Europe. He later reiterated his belief that the Holocaust was 'a myth', a statement that prompted a storm of international criticism. In February 2006 protests broke out in Iran over anti-Islamic cartoons published in the Danish press. Demonstrators attacked the Danish embassy in Tehran, and the Iranian Government imposed a formal trade ban on Danish imports. Iran's best-selling newspaper, *Hamshahri*, announced that it would retaliate for the cartoons by running images satirizing the Holocaust. The In May a Canadian newspaper was forced to apologize for publishing an erroneous story suggesting that Iran had passed a law requiring Jews and Christians to wear badges identifying them as religious minorities. The story, quoting Iranian expatriates and published in *The National Post*, a conservative national daily, stirred up an international row, resulting in the Iranian Government summoning Canada's ambassador to the Ministry of Foreign Affairs in Tehran.

Tensions between Iran and Israel were further fuelled when conflict erupted between the Lebanon-based militant organization Hezbollah and Israel in July. The Israeli campaign of launching massive air strikes on Lebanese towns in response to the abduction and killing by Hezbollah of some of its soldiers (for further details, see the chapter on Lebanon) prompted Maj.-Gen. Yahya Rahim-Safavi, head of the Revolutionary Guards, to call on God to 'arouse the dignity of Muslims and destroy America, Israel and their associates'. Although many Western governments and media reports accused Iran of financing and supplying arms to Hezbollah, Iran's Ministry of Foreign Affairs vigorously denied the claims.

INTERNAL DEVELOPMENTS, 2005–06

During 2005–06 President Ahmadinejad appeared to be growing in domestic popularity, due partly to the perceptions that he had stood up to the USA over Iran's right to nuclear power, supported the Palestinians, and also because of his own populist style and fortnightly tours of the country. By June 2006 Ahmadinejad had become the clear favourite to win a second term in 2009. In April 2006, in a move especially appealing to Iranian youth, Ahmadinejad announced that women would be allowed to attend football matches in large stadiums (where national and other important matches were held) for the first time since the 1979 Islamic Revolution. Under a decree reported on state television, the President ordered the head of the country's Physical Education Organization to provide separate areas for women. None the less, Western media reports in the same month suggested that Iran's Islamic authorities were preparing a crackdown on women who flouted the strict Islamic dress code, and that Tehran police would be ordered to arrest women who failed to comply.

Meanwhile, internal discontent and dissent continued to simmer. In November 2005 a power struggle broke out between the President and the Majlis after deputies refused to accept the President's choice for the post of Minister of Petroleum. In March 2006, trouble erupted at Tehran's universities when the authorities began a programme of burying the bodies of unknown soldiers on university campus grounds around the capital. Student leaders described this as a thinly disguised attempt to bring religious extremists into the universities on the pretext of holding 'martyrs' ceremonies'. Students feared that such a presence would be used violently to suppress their activities. In one incident, students at Tehran's Sharif University were attacked by plain-clothed *Basij* (paramilitary volunteers) during an unsuccessful attempt to prevent the burial of three soldiers from the 1980–88 Iran–Iraq War inside the campus mosque. The incident was overseen by Mehrdad Bazrpash, a close aide to President Ahmadinejad and a former *Basij* leader.

In March 2006 Akbar Ganji was freed after six years in prison. However, in May a prominent Iranian-Canadian philosopher and writer, Ramin Jahanbegloo, was arrested on unspecified charges. He was held in a Tehran prison for four months before being released on bail in August. Provincial and ethnic unrest also took place around this time. In March Iran accused the United Kingdom of attempting to stir unrest after armed rebels ambushed a party of government officials. Also, in May a caricature in a popular newspaper provoked large-scale disturbances, particularly among the Azeri minority, resulting in the newspaper's closure.

UN IMPOSES SANCTIONS

On 23 December 2006 the UN Security Council imposed limited sanctions on Iran and gave the country 60 days to end its uranium enrichment or face further punitive measures. Just before the new deadline of 21 February 2007, Iran rejected the Security Council's demand. President Ahmadinejad said at a rally that Iran was willing to enter fresh talks on its nuclear activities, but that it would suspend its uranium enrichment only if Iran's negotiating partners in the West took the same step. By mid-March the five permanent members of the UN Security Council and Germany (widely referred to as the P5+1) had agreed a deal to expand sanctions against Iran after the Iranian regime ignored the deadline established by the earlier resolution. President Ahmadinejad responded by declaring that sanctions would only stiffen his country's resolve. Although the new UN resolution (No. 1747, approved on 24 March) was a compromise between those countries in the P5+1 group, the additional sanctions were still significant. They introduced a complete embargo on arms exports by Iran, discouraged the sale of large weapons items to Iran, including tanks, aircraft and helicopters, and broadened the scope of travel and financial restrictions on a wider number of Iranian businesses and individuals. In a further effort to isolate the regime, the text of the resolution called on all states and international financial institutions to withhold further economic assistance to the Iranian Government, including any new loans, unless they were clearly directed at humanitarian needs. Iran immediately responded by announcing a partial suspension of co-operation with the IAEA. President Ahmadinejad described the sanctions as illegal and stated that Iran would not end what he called its 'peaceful and legal' nuclear programme but would 'adjust' its ties with those behind the resolution.

The Iranian President announced in April 2007 that the Natanz facility had begun 'industrial-scale' production of nuclear fuel—thus a major advance in Iran's uranium enrichment programme—and declared that Iran had joined the 'nuclear club of nations'. Workers were believed to have begun injecting uranium gas into a new array of 3,000 centrifuges, a notable development from the 328 centrifuges known to be in operation at Natanz. Meanwhile, IAEA inspectors visited the Natanz plant. Following the inspection, Olli Heinonen, the IAEA's Deputy Director-General, confirmed in a letter on 18 April that Iran had crossed a new threshold by producing fuel in its underground plant. The letter said that Iran was running more than 1,300 centrifuges and had begun feeding small amounts of uranium gas into them. The IAEA also reported that Iran had managed to link the centrifuges into eight cascades, suggesting that scientists had mastered a further stage in the process. Additionally, the IAEA complained about Iran's refusal to allow UN inspectors to visit the country's heavy water reactor. However, the IAEA did not confirm that all 1,300 centrifuges were operational. Experts claimed that the Iranians were experiencing difficulties in sustaining the project. Iran, for its part, continued to insist that it intended to enrich uranium only to lower levels suitable for civilian power, and that it was not seeking weapons-grade uranium.

On 23 May 2007, the day before another UN Security Council deadline, the IAEA reported that Iran was still in defiance of the UN and admitted that its knowledge of Iran's nuclear programme was deteriorating. This report by the agency followed complaints from US, British, French and German officials that the Director-General of the IAEA, Muhammad el-Baradei, was insufficiently critical of Iran. A few days later el-Baradei stated that Iran was between three and eight years away from producing a nuclear weapon, should it choose to do so. He affirmed that the IAEA had seen no evidence that Iran was seeking to use nuclear material to produce weapons or that there existed undeclared nuclear facilities in the country.

DOMESTIC ISSUES, 2007–08

By mid-2007 the Iranian population was already feeling the strain from the UN sanctions. Prices were being driven up, inflation had risen to an estimated 20%–30%, and on 23 May the Government announced that it would introduce petrol rationing to ease the burden of providing subsidized petrol. A lack of refining capacity in the country means that Iran imports most of its petrol from the UAE and fuel subsidies result in a large state budget deficit.

Meanwhile, US firms were already banned from doing business with Iran, and the US Administration exerted pressure on non-US businesses to sever ties as well. International banks were cutting back their operations in Iran under threat that their US business might be affected. In February 2007 Germany's Commerzbank halted dollar transactions with Iran in response to reported US pressure. On 24 May Iran's financial system suffered a major jolt when President Ahmadinejad abruptly ordered banks to cut interest rates sharply, despite surging inflation. The order, which went against expert advice, triggered warnings of a financial crisis amid fears of a capital flight from the country's lending institutions. The decision caused panic selling on the Tehran Stock Exchange. The interest rate reduction was designed to help poorer social groups, who had put Ahmadinejad into office, by giving them access to cheaper loans.

In May 2007 the Government also increased petrol prices, and in June suddenly introduced fuel rationing. Motorists were restricted to a monthly limit of 100 litres of petrol. The short notice was apparently aimed at preventing hoarding. In response, angry consumers launched arson attacks on at least a dozen petrol stations in Tehran. Banks, supermarkets and fire engines were also attacked, and further disturbances were reported in other big cities, including Esfahan and Shiraz. Although the Majlis had already approved the plan, parliamentary deputies urged the Government to delay the scheme amid fears over its social and economic impact. In July President Hugo Chávez of Venezuela announced that his country would sell petrol to Iran to alleviate its fuel shortage and to bolster their common front against the USA.

RELATIONS BETWEEN IRAN AND THE USA

Tensions between Iran and the USA were heightened following events in Iraq. In January 2007 US forces detained five Iranians at the Iranian consulate in Arbil. The USA claimed that the men were Revolutionary Guards who were in Iraq to assist and finance insurgents; however, Iran insisted that they were diplomats. This incident was quickly followed by renewed US claims that Iran was supplying weapons and training to Iraqi militias that had attacked US troops, although no detailed evidence was provided. President Ahmadinejad repeatedly denied the US accusations. In February an Iranian diplomat in Baghdad, Jalal Sharafi, was kidnapped by gunmen dressed in Iraqi security force uniforms. Iran announced that it was holding the US Administration directly responsible for his arrest and safe return.

On 4 May 2007 a conference was held at Sharm el-Sheikh, Egypt, at which the US Secretary of State, Condoleezza Rice, discussed with ministers responsible for foreign affairs from the states neighbouring Iraq how they might help in restoring that country's security. The Iranian Minister of Foreign Affairs, Manouchehr Mottaki, attended the conference and said that the USA had to take responsibility for the ongoing terrorism in Iraq due to its occupation of the country. Mottaki also demanded the immediate release of the five Iranians arrested at Arbil, describing their abduction as a 'brazen contravention of international conventions'. The Iraqi Government had been urging Rice to meet Mottaki for bilateral talks; however, the widely anticipated meeting failed to take place amid public acrimony over the arrested Iranians and the nuclear issue. In July the USA publicly accused Iran of intervening in the Iraq conflict, claiming that its Revolutionary Guards had played a role in an attack that killed five Americans and were using Lebanese militants to train Iraqi insurgents. The public accusation marked a significant escalation in tensions between the two sides since previous claims had mostly been made 'off the record'.

None the less, on 28 May 2007 talks took place between the Iranian and US ambassadors in Baghdad—the first formal discussions between the two countries since the USA severed diplomatic ties in 1980. The agenda was strictly confined to Iraq, with no mention of the nuclear issue, the abducted Iranians or the recent Iranian arrests of US-Iranian academics. The talks took place amid rising tension as the USA assembled nine warships off the Iranian coast to perform military exercises in what was the largest daytime assembly of ships in the Gulf since the US-led invasion of Iraq in 2003. In response, the Iranian Minister of Defence and Armed Forces Logistics, Moustafa Muhammad-Najar, who was not notified in advance of the exercises, stated that his country would resist any threat from its enemies. In mid-August 2007 unnamed sources announced that the USA was preparing to designate all or part of Iran's Revolutionary Guards as a foreign terrorist organization, owing to the group's alleged support for Shi'a militias in Iraq. Brig.-Gen. Muhammad Ali Jafari was appointed as the new Chief of Staff of the Islamic Revolutionary Guards early in the following month, replacing Maj.-Gen. Yahya Rahim-Safavi in the post.

In late October 2007 Iran's Deputy Foreign Minister for European and American Affairs, Saeed Jalili, was chosen to replace Larijani as Secretary of the SNSC and principal negotiator on the nuclear issue, after Larijani had tendered his resignation. It was widely reported that the appointment of Jalili, who was closely affiliated with President Ahmadinejad, would result in Iran taking a firmer stance in the ongoing negotiations with the IAEA and international community regarding its nuclear capabilities. Towards the end of October the USA imposed further unilateral sanctions against Iran, which principally targeted state-owned banks, organizations and agencies deemed to be involved in a clandestine nuclear programme or to sponsor terrorism abroad, and in particular named affiliates of the Revolutionary Guards and its élite Quds Force.

The IAEA reported in November 2007 that Iran had installed 3,000 centrifuges capable of enriching uranium, although the report also stated that Tehran had been co-operating with agency inspectors. In the following month the US Secretary of Defense, Robert Gates, speaking in Bahrain, claimed that Iran might secretly have resumed efforts to develop a nuclear weapon; Gates demanded intensified economic, financial and diplomatic international pressure against the Islamic regime, and urged Saudi Arabia and other Gulf states to develop a joint air and missile shield to ward off future Iranian threats. His stance drew sharp public criticism from several Gulf leaders, who favoured negotiations with the Iranian Government.

In December 2007 Russia delivered the first 80-metric ton shipment of fuel to the Bushehr power station, construction of which was completed in March 2009, a few months later than originally planned. It was reported that production was to commence by October, but the head of the Atomic Energy Organization, Ali Akbar Salehi, declined to confirm this speculation. The delivery of Russian fuel in late 2007 appeared to signal a weakening of the US-led coalition's opposition to Iran's nuclear plans. Momentum for a new UN Security Council resolution that would produce another embargo had certainly slowed after a recent report published by 16 US intelligence agencies.

LEGISLATIVE ELECTIONS OF 2008

On 30 January 2008 the Head of the Judiciary, Ayatollah Hashemi Shahrudi, moved to curb the increasingly common spectacle of public executions by banning the practice, except in cases personally approved by himself. The order followed a dramatic rise in public hangings, and a general increase in the use of the death penalty. Around 300 executions were reportedly carried out in Iran during 2007. In late April 2008 Hossein Samsami replaced Davoud Danesh-Ja'afari as the Minister of Economic Affairs and Finance, in an acting capacity. In mid-May President Ahmadinejad dismissed the Minister of the Interior, Moustafa Pour-Muhammadi; Mehdi Hashemi was subsequently named as the caretaker minister. Finally, in early August the Majlis endorsed the nomination of Shamseddin Hosseini as Minister of Economic Affairs and Finance, Ali Kordan as Minister of the Interior and Hamid Behbahani as Minister of Roads and Transport.

Elections to the eighth Majlis were held on 14 March 2008. In advance of the polls, hundreds of 'reformist' candidates had been disqualified from standing by the Council of Guardians for 'lacking Islamic authenticity', leaving the 'reformist' bloc able to contest only one-half of the 290 seats in the legislature. President Ahmadinejad did not run his own list, but in early March it was reported that 'conservatives' had split into two separate lists to contest the polls: the United Principlist Front was formed by traditionalists who supported President Ahmadinejad's policies, while the Broad Principlist Coalition consisted of those who were more critical of the President's foreign and economic policies. The latter group included: Ali Larijani, the previous Secretary of the SNSC and senior nuclear negotiator; Muhammad Baqir Qalibaf, the mayor of Tehran; and Mohsen Rezai, an ex-Revolutionary Guards commander. This group was dissatisfied with Ahmadinejad's style of government, his economic policies and provocative performance on the world stage. However, the Supreme Leader, Ali Khamenei, delivered a clear endorsement of the President.

Turn-out in the elections appeared low, especially in Tehran, although the Ministry of the Interior reported that almost 60% of eligible voters had participated in the first ballot. Following a second round of voting on 25 April 2008 for some 82 undecided Majlis seats, the 'conservatives' ended with a clear majority, with 70% of the seats; 'reformists' secured some 15% of the seats, with the remainder being held by independents. Opposition politicians, as well as US and EU officials, were strongly critical of the conduct of the elections. On 1 June Larijani was elected to the influential position of Speaker of the Majlis, in succession to Gholam-Ali Haddad-Adel.

The announcement in October 2008 of an end to the execution of juveniles in Iran was enthusiastically welcomed by international human rights organizations. However, in the following month any restoration of the Iranian Government's public image was undermined by the impeachment for deception of Minister of the Interior Ali Kordan, who reportedly had confessed to holding a forged law degree from the United Kingdom's University of Oxford. Despite claiming to be a fierce opponent of government corruption, President Ahmadinejad spoke out in defence of Kordan, insisting that his 30 years of public service should not be compromised by a 'piece of torn paper'. Of the 247 legislators who attended the parliamentary session, 188 voted in favour of impeaching Kordan, 45 voted against the motion and 18 abstained. Following his impeachment, Kordan was replaced as Minister of the Interior by Sadeq Mahsouli.

UN TIGHTENS SANCTIONS

On 3 March 2008 the UN Security Council adopted Resolution 1803, approving a third round of sanctions against Iran with near unanimous support (14-0, with one abstention from Indonesia). Just before the vote Iran's UN ambassador told the Council that the Government would not comply with the 'unlawful action' against its nuclear programme, stating that Iran could not and would not accept a requirement that was legally defective and politically coercive. For the first time, the resolution prohibited trade with Iran in goods that had both civilian and military uses. It also authorized inspections of shipments to and from Iran by sea and air that were suspected of carrying banned items. Resolution 1803 introduced financial monitoring of two banks with suspected links to nuclear proliferation activities, Bank Melli and Bank Saderat. It called on all countries 'to exercise vigilance' in entering into new trade commitments with Iran, including granting export credits, guarantees or insurance. The resolution also ordered countries to freeze the assets of 12 additional companies and 13 individuals with links to Iran's nuclear or ballistic missile programmes—requiring countries to report the travel or transit of those Iranians. It imposed a travel ban on five individuals linked to Iran's nuclear effort.

Meanwhile, in early March 2008 President Ahmadinejad became the first Iranian President to visit Iraq since the Iranian Revolution of 1979. During a high-profile state visit, Ahmadinejad declared the start of a new era in bilateral relations, and he held hands with his Iraqi counterpart, Jalal Talabani, as their two nations' national anthems were played. Many commentators noted that the visit underlined Iran's growing influence in the region and, in particular, its influence with Iraq's Shi'a-led Government. It was also deemed significant that the Iranian President's motorcade travelled along the road from Baghdad airport to the presidential palace, rather than the Iranian delegation taking the safer trip via helicopter that was usually used by foreign dignitaries. In addition to signalling its political influence, the Iranian regime was believed to be emphasizing its growing economic and commercial links with Iraq, with Iran involved in providing loans for a number of Iraqi infrastructural projects, including the construction of an airport close to the Shi'a shrines of Najaf and Karbala.

In late April and early May 2008 the US Administration intensified its allegations that the Iranian regime was arming insurgents in Iraq, and increased its naval presence in the region with a second aircraft carrier; Iran consistently rejected the US claims. According to reports in the US media, the Bush Administration had significantly expanded the number of covert military operations being carried out inside Iran with the aim of destabilizing the Government.

On 6 June 2008 Shaul Mofaz, Israel's Deputy Prime Minister and Minister of Transport and Road Safety, as well as a former Chief of Staff of the Armed Forces, issued the threat that Israel would attack Iran if the latter succeeded in developing nuclear weapons. Also in the first week of June, according to US officials, Israel mounted a major long-range military air exercise—involving more than 100 *F-15* and *F-16* fighter aircraft—as a rehearsal for a potential strike on Iran's nuclear facilities. The aircraft, together with refuelling tankers and helicopters able to rescue pilots who had been shot down, were mobilized over the eastern Mediterranean Sea and Greece in an exercise monitored by foreign intelligence agencies. Again according to US officials, the tankers and helicopters were reported to have flown around 1,500 km from their bases in Israel—roughly the same distance as that between Israel and Iran's uranium enrichment plant at Natanz. On 30 June an Iranian revolutionary court sentenced a businessman, Ali Ashtari, to death after he was convicted of spying on Iran's military and nuclear programmes on behalf of the Israeli authorities.

Meanwhile, in early June 2008 the EU's High Representative for the Common Foreign and Security Policy, Javier Solana, travelled to Tehran, offering a package of energy and trade incentives to the Iranian Government in exchange for an agreement to suspend uranium enrichment and processing activities. However, the official Iranian response to the offer was ambiguous. Later that month the EU approved the imposition of fresh sanctions against Iranian financial institutions. In early July the US Chairman of the Joint Chiefs of Staff, Adm. Michael Mullen, visited Israel for talks with

Israeli military commanders, and warned publicly on his return to Washington, DC, that an Israeli attack on Iran's nuclear facilities would destabilize the region. It was reported that US exports to Iran had risen dramatically during President Bush's term in office, in spite of the US Administration's tough rhetoric and imposition of tighter economic sanctions against the Iranian regime. An analysis of US government trade figures published in the US media revealed that US sales to Iran had increased more than 10-fold over the past seven years.

In early July 2008 Iran conducted tests involving nine missiles, including a new *Shahab-3* long-range missile that could easily reach Israel and a number of US bases situated in the Gulf region. The *Shahab-3* has an estimated range of at least 1,200 km. Hossein Salami, the air force commander of the Revolutionary Guards stated that the missile test was not routine, but was a demonstration of resolve amid growing international pressure over Iran's nuclear programme. Many regional analysts interpreted the Iranian missile tests as a direct response to the Israeli military exercises held over the Mediterranean in the previous month. On 10 July Iran carried out a second ballistic missile test, leading Israel to respond by displaying a new spy and early-warning plane that was capable of reaching Iran.

DEVELOPMENTS IN THE NUCLEAR ISSUE, 2008–09

Despite comments in October 2008 made by the Iranian Chief Representative to the IAEA that, if guaranteed nuclear fuel for use in its power stations, Iran would consider suspending its uranium enrichment programme, the Iranian Government continued to stress that it would neither halt its programme under any conditions, including economic incentives, nor discuss its nuclear programme outside the framework of the IAEA's regulations. In mid-April 2009 Ahmadinejad announced an increase in the number of centrifuges at its uranium enrichment facility and officially opened Iran's first nuclear fuel production plant, in Esfahan. US Secretary of State Hillary Clinton had declared just one day previously, that the US Government would henceforth fully participate in nuclear talks held under the remit of the UN. Opponents of Iran's nuclear programme contended that the plant at Esfahan could reprocess fuel into plutonium for a nuclear warhead. Further consternation was provoked in the following month by the successful launch of a surface-to-surface missile with a range of about 2,000 km, which would, therefore, be able to reach both Israel and US military bases in the Gulf region. While the USA gave little public response, the Israeli Prime Minister, Binyamin Netanyahu, who repeatedly insisted that Iran rather than the Israeli–Palestinian issue was the single largest threat to Middle East peace, cited the missile launch as further evidence that Iran's eventual goal was to initiate a nuclear attack against Israel. The USA sent Central Intelligence Agency (CIA) Director Leon Panetta to Israel to meet with Netanyahu and Ehud Barak, seeking assurances that the Iranian missile launch would not result in a pre-emptive Israeli strike.

In June 2009 French President Nicolas Sarkozy met with Iranian Minister of Foreign Affairs Mottaki in Tehran to discuss Iran's nuclear programme. Sarkozy warned that Iran risked increasing isolation from the international community should it fail to agree to negotiations regarding its programme. It had been reported in October 2008 that the USA and European countries were discussing the possible formation of a 'coalition of the willing', which would impose more stringent sanctions against Iran if it refused to enter into dialogue about the nuclear issue. Ignoring the warnings levelled against the Iranian Government, in September 2009 Ahmadinejad repeated his insistence that 'from our point of view, Iran's nuclear issue is over'. Speaking at a press conference, he stated that Iran was prepared to discuss nuclear developments only in so far as it was relevant to the prevention of nuclear proliferation and 'creating peaceful nuclear energy for all countries'.

IRANIAN–US RELATIONS FOLLOWING THE ELECTION OF OBAMA

In March 2009 Barack Obama, who had been inaugurated as US President in January, issued a recorded video message addressing the Iranian people in an attempt to communicate his Administration's departure from the policy of isolating Iran. Referring to the country as 'the Islamic Republic of Iran', Obama offered the prospect of an end to years of diplomatic impasse between the two nations, stating that he was keen to engage Iran in bilateral discussions, provided that the Iranian Government moderated its belligerent tone. Following this, Ahmadinejad did appear to soften his customary anti-Western rhetoric, stating that, if re-elected in the forthcoming presidential elections, he would be prepared to enter into dialogue with the USA, provided that the talks were based on 'justice and respect'. However, hopes of thawing bilateral relations were reduced after the publication in April of a report by the US Department of State which asserted that Iran remained the 'most active state sponsor of terrorism', and singled out the Quds special unit of the Iranian Revolutionary Guards as the primary channel through which such support was provided. Obama was reported to have said that the Iranian Government had until the end of September to decide whether or not it wished to engage with his administration, but threatened that a refusal to acquiesce to the request might lead to a tightening of sanctions against Iran and an intensification of that country's isolation from the international community.

PRE-ELECTION VIOLENCE

In the fortnight before the presidential elections in Iran, which took place on 12 June 2009, a series of violent attacks occurred in Zahedan, Sistan and Baluchestan province. On 28 May a suicide bomber targeted the Amir al-Momenin mosque, a large Shi'a mosque that was crowded with people commemorating the anniversary of the death of the Prophet Muhammad's daughter, Fatima Zahra. More than 20 people were killed and another 125 injured in the explosion, for which a local Sunni insurgency group—Jundallah (Soldiers of God), which was strongly opposed to the predominantly Shi'a Iranian Government and was thought to have links to al-Qa'ida—was reported to have claimed responsibility. Some Iranian officials claimed that Jundallah had been supported by the US Government, which they alleged had hired mercenaries to carry out the attack—claims adamantly denied by the Obama Administration. On the following day gunmen burst into Ahmadinejad's presidential election campaign office in Zahedan, opening fire and injuring three people, including one child. Police officers were reported to have arrested the men as they attempted to flee the scene. On 30 April, just two days after the mosque bombing, three members of Jundallah were executed, having been arrested and convicted of involvement in the attack. The authorities insisted that the men had received a fair trial and had confessed to having supplied the suicide bomber with the explosives used in the attack. A further 14 members of Jundallah were reported to have been executed on 14 July, including the second-in-command Abdolhamid Rigi, brother of the group's leader Abdolmalek Rigi, for involvement in the killings of dozens of police officers and civilians in various attacks over the preceding few years and for involvement in the mosque bombing the previous month. Amnesty International had pleaded for a stay of execution for the defendants, claiming that they had not received a fair trial. Meanwhile, on 30 May a bomb was reported to have been discovered on a domestic flight bound for Tehran from Ahraz, in Khuzestan province, and on 1 June five people were killed in an arson attack on the Mehr Financial and Credit Institute in Zahedan. On the latter day Ayatollah Khamenei warned of an 'enemies' conspiracy' that was attempting to 'harm national unity. It was claimed by some that the Iranian Government was manipulating the handling and reporting of the violence, in the knowledge that any unrest in the run-up to the presidential elections was likely to scare borderline voters into supporting the hardline President over the more moderate Mir Hossein Mousavi, Prime Minister in 1981–89 and Ahmadinejad's principal challenger.

THE PRESIDENTIAL ELECTION OF 2009

On 12 June 2009 the presidential election was held as scheduled and contested between Ahmadinejad and his main rival Mousavi, as well as Mohsen Rezai and Mahdi Karrubi. According to official results published by the Iranian Ministry of the Interior on 13 June, Ahmadinejad won a landslide victory, receiving 24,527,516 votes, equivalent to 62.63% of the total and almost double the number of votes reported to have been cast for his nearest rival, Mousavi (who garnered 13,216,411 votes—33.75% of the total). Rezai and Karrubi attracted just 1.73% and 0.85% of the total number of votes, respectively. Turn-out was reported to have been high, at 85% of the electorate. The USA, the United Kingdom and the EU all expressed serious concern over irregularities in the election, implying that the results might not be authentic. Mobile telephone services and a number of internet sites were blocked, while reports indicated that some polling locations had recorded a turn-out of more than 100%. The official results were rejected by all three opposition candidates, who claimed that electoral misconduct had occurred. Ayatollah Khamenei's subsequent approval of the results and declaration of support for Ahmadinejad appeared to have intensified the situation.

The large margin of victory for Ahmadinejad in what had been almost universally predicted to be a close-run contest prompted many people—both within Iran and abroad—to suspect that the results had been manipulated in favour of the incumbent. Mousavi, whose election campaign had made it clear that he wished to improve relations with the West (including, notably, the USA) in the hope of ending Iran's isolation, had been expected to garner a significantly higher percentage of the vote. Together with Rezai, Mousavi filed an official complaint with the Council of Guardians on 14 June 2009, alleging that there had been severe irregularities in the vote-counting process and calling for the results to be nullified. On 15 June Ayatollah Khamenei announced that there was to be an investigation into the alleged irregularities, and on the following day the Council of Guardians announced that a partial recount, of 10% of the ballots, was to be organized. The announcement, however, did little to placate supporters of Mousavi, who insisted that such a recount—especially in light of the large margin of victory and given that up to 14m. ballots were reported to be missing—would accomplish nothing, and continued to call for fresh, and fair, elections.

Widespread protests gathered pace in the following few days. Mousavi stressed that he did not wish his supporters to engage in any violence in protest at the results, even cancelling a planned rally having received information that the authorities intended forcibly to disperse the crowds. None the less, hundreds of demonstrators were arrested as thousands took to the streets, clashing with security forces in exchanges that were reported to have left more than 30 people dead—although some protesters claimed that the figure was actually closer to 100. Several foreign journalists were arrested and expelled from the country; reports of the violence were notably lacking from the vast majority of Iranian news sources; and local and international fixed-line and mobile telephone services were disrupted. The way in which the authorities were seen to be dealing with the unrest provoked international censure, with the EU and UN Secretary-General Ban Ki-Moon expressing their dismay at the unfolding situation. However, US President Obama and British Prime Minister Gordon Brown—both sensitive to accusations of interference in Iranian internal affairs—were, at least initially, notably reserved in their comments about the election and the resultant turmoil, although perceived Iranian provocations were soon to result in an escalation in their disapproval.

On 29 June 2009 the Council of Guardians announced that the partial recount of ballots had been completed and revealed no irregularities in the vote, having ruled earlier that the detection of any improprieties would not affect the outcome of the vote in any case. For many Iranians and observers around the world, this decision confirmed the fraudulent nature of Ahmadinejad's victory, and protests continued to occur. The emergence of public criticism of the Supreme Leader, who had repeatedly insisted that he would not succumb to public pressure for him to reconsider the results of the vote, suggested that divisions within Iranian society reached into the upper echelons of the Iranian establishment.

No independent investigation of the election was permitted, only that of the Council of Guardians, which confirmed the official result. The contested election sparked widespread protests and clashes. The Qatar-based television broadcaster Al Jazeera reported that the outbursts were the largest since the 1979 Revolution. The size of the demonstrations increased and, on 15 June 2009, more than 100,000 protesters held a vigil in Tehran after Mousavi called for a day of mourning for those killed and injured during the protests. Unconfirmed reports claimed that up to 70 people had been killed and several hundred injured in the post-election unrest. An unknown number of detainees were held in various locations, including the Evin prison in Tehran. Several people were reported to have been killed and tortured in the Kahrizak detention centre in Tehran; after their release, some of the detainees claimed that they had been sexually assaulted. More than 100 individuals filed complaints following their detention at the Kahrizak facility, prompting an order by Ayatollah Khamenei to close the centre; nevertheless, claims by detainees of mistreatment persisted.

Anti-regime demonstrations ensued at Iranian embassies around the world, notably in Turkey, the UAE and several European capitals. Nationally and internationally, anti-Government demonstrations continued into 2010. The protests in Iran frequently resulted in public events being cancelled or postponed. In what was regarded by some observers as an attempt to avoid further public action, the Majlis approved the principles of a bill to postpone (by two years) city and town council elections due to take place in 2010.

GOVERNMENT CHANGES

On 16 July 2009 the Vice-President and Head of the Iranian Atomic Energy Organization, Gholam Reza Aghazadeh, formally resigned from both positions, having reportedly tendered his resignation three weeks previously. While Aghazadeh, a long-time supporter of Mousavi, did not publicly cite a reason for his decision to stand down, it was widely assumed that it was in protest at Ahmadinejad's re-election. On the following day Ali Akbar Salehi was appointed as Aghazadeh's replacement, an appointment that was greeted with cautious optimism by the West owing to Salehi's reputation as a moderate figure who had signed a protocol in December 2003 allowing the IAEA a freer hand in inspecting Iran's nuclear sites. Meanwhile, on 16 July Ahmadinejad announced the appointment of close confidant Esfandiar Rahim-Mashaei to the position of First Vice-President, provoking strong disapproval even from allies of the President. Rahim-Mashai, previously Head of the Cultural Heritage, Handicrafts and Tourism Organization, had attracted severe criticism in 2008 when he referred to Iran as being 'a friend of the Israeli people'. Disapproval of Rahim-Mashai's appointment extended to the upper echelons of the Islamic Republic, with Ayatollah Khamenei writing a stern letter to the President demanding he be removed. On 24 July 2009, almost certainly at the behest of Ahmadinejad in an attempt to rescue the situation, Rashim-Mashai tendered his resignation from his new post, although Ahmadinejad further angered his critics by retaining Rashim-Mashai as an adviser and Head of the Presidential Office.

Ahmadinejad appeared to have prompted a constitutional crisis on 26 July 2009 when it was announced that he had dismissed four government ministers—the Ministers of Intelligence and Security, Culture and Islamic Guidance, Labour and Social Affairs, and Health and Medical Education—following disagreements with the four over the appointment of Rahim-Mashai. According to the terms of the Iranian Constitution, should more than 50% of the Council of Ministers be replaced during the tenure of a Government, the administration would be required to seek a parliamentary vote of confidence; prior to the most recent dismissals Ahmadinejad had replaced nine of his original 22-member Council of Ministers appointed at the start of his presidential term in 2005. Ahmadinejad swiftly revoked the dismissals of all but the Minister of Intelligence and Security. However, Minister of Culture and Islamic Guidance Muhammad Hossein Saffar-

Harandi tendered his resignation on 27 July in a letter that accused Ahmadinejad of reinstating the three ministers merely to avoid a vote of confidence. Ahmadinejad refused to accept Saffar-Harandi's resignation, and was thus able to avoid a potentially embarrassing defeat in a vote of confidence just days before his inauguration on 5 August.

On 20 August 2009 Ahmadinejad announced the composition of his new Council of Ministers, which, for the first time in the Islamic Republic's 30-year history, included female ministers. Mostafa Muhammad-Najjar, formerly Minister of Defence and Armed Forces Logistics, was appointed Minister of the Interior. Heydar Moslehi was nominated as Minister of Intelligence and Security, while Manouchehr Mottaki was to retain the foreign affairs portfolio. The list included three females: Marzieh Vahid Dastjerdi was awarded the health and medical education portfolio; Fatemeh Ajorlou was to head the welfare and social security ministry; and Sousan Keshavarz was to assume responsibility for education. All three female nominees had ties with the Revolutionary Guards. To the surprise of some observers, 18 of Ahmadinejad's 21 nominees were approved by parliament on 3 September, including Dastjerdi. The newly appointed Council of Ministers held its first meeting on 7 September; Ahmadinejad subsequently announced three new nominees for the posts left vacant, including one woman. The nominations received parliamentary approval in November.

On 13 December 2010 President Ahmadinejad suddenly announced his decision to dismiss Minister of Foreign Affairs Manouchehr Mottaki while the latter was on a diplomatic mission to Senegal. Mottaki, who was widely believed to have been Ahmadinejad's chief political opponent within the Government, claimed that his dismissal was 'undiplomatic, un-Islamic, and offensive'. He also stated that he had spoken to the President immediately prior to his departure for Senegal and had not been informed of his imminent ousting, despite government claims that this had been planned for some time. Mottaki was temporarily replaced by the head of the Atomic Energy Organization, Ali Akbar Salehi, who assumed the post on a permanent basis in January 2011. On 13 February President Ahmadinejad appointed Fereydoon Abbasi as Head of the Atomic Energy Organization to succeed Salehi.

Amid revolutionary protests in a number of Arab states (see Other External Relations), on 9 February 2011 Iranian opposition groups requested permission from the Ministry of the Interior to organize pro-democratic and anti-Government protests in Tehran under the supervision of the state police; the protests were scheduled to commence on 14 February. However, the Ministry forbade the holding of such demonstrations and began to crack down on members of the opposition parties. The authorities shut down or blocked opposition websites and placed opposition party leaders under house arrest. The Government also warned that protesters would be forcibly stopped by the Revolutionary Guards. Despite the threats, the protests proceeded as planned. It was reported that the Revolutionary Guards deployed around 10,000 security personnel to prevent protesters from gathering in Azadi Square in the capital. Three demonstrators were injured in clashes with the police and dozens were arrested.

In April 2011 Ahmadinejad forced Heydar Moslehi, the Minister of Intelligence and Security, to resign. There was speculation that Moslehi had been pressurized into standing down following a dispute with Esfandiar Rahim-Mashaei over attempts by Moslehi to dismiss an intelligence official. However, Ayatollah Khamenei reinstated Moslehi to his position. Ahmadinejad responded by refusing to attend cabinet meetings since he declined to be in the same room as Moslehi. However, the President returned to work at the beginning of May, publicly declaring his support for Khamenei and denying the existence of any tension between the two of them. None the less, many government officials were angry that it had taken Ahmadinejad so long to confirm his support for Khamenei's decision.

In May 2011 escalating confrontation between the President and Supreme Leader led to the simultaneous dismissal of three cabinet ministers—those of petroleum, of welfare and social security, and of industries and mines. Ahmadinejad announced his plan to reshape the Government in stages by merging eight of the ministries into four. This proposal was strongly opposed by the influential 'conservative' faction in parliament which held that the imposition of such a measure would not be in Iran's national interest. Ahmadinejad initially appointed temporary acting officials in a number of ministries subject to the merger proposals, but in June the creation of four new ministries—Co-operatives, Labour and Social Welfare; Industries, Mines and Trade; Roads and Urban Development; and Sport and Youth Affairs—was approved by the Majlis. In August Rostam Ghasemi, a former commander in the Revolutionary Guards, was named as the new Minister of Petroleum. Many observers suggested that this appointment was another example of the way in which the Revolutionary Guards were extending their influence within Iran's key economic institutions.

THE FINANCIAL CRISIS OF 2012–13 AND THE END OF AHMADINEJAD'S PRESIDENCY

Despite the Iranian Government's insistance that sanctions against Iran were ineffective and that they were not harming the economy, during the second half of 2012, somewhat unexpectedly, Iran's national currency (the rial) lost a significant proportion of its value against other foreign currencies. This was particularly evident in its ability to buy hard currencies like the US dollar, the euro or the United Kingdom's pound sterling. The rial's devaluation immediately provoked considerable anger on the part of the Iranian people towards President Ahmadinejad. It also caused much resentment against the Iranian leadership and against the incapability of the regime to confront a financial crisis such as a currency devaluation. As a result, and within a short period of time, the value of the US dollar on the Iranian market rose from IR 1,000 per dollar to IR 3,700. Indeed, the Iranian rial lost more than 15% of its exchange value in a single day during early October 2012, by which time it had lost 80% of its value since the same period of 2011.

Many people rushed to compare the current situation with the time of the Shah, when a US dollar was worth no more than IR 68. Many others viewed their loss as the direct result of US and UN sanctions, but a third group saw the collapse of the Iranian currency as a by-product of the corruption and mismanagement of Iran's domestic economic policy by Ahmadinejad's inner circle.

The collapse of the rial affected the entire Iranian market, with the value of properties and gold experiencing a dramatic rise; in the property market, some rents increased fourfold. Many Iranians thus chose not to rent, or to rent their houses using payments in US dollars or an equivalent currency. The value of the US dollar on the Iranian market was slightly higher than IR 10,000 in early 2012 and in mid-2013 it stood at IR 33,000.

FOREIGN RELATIONS AND THE 'BALUCH FACTOR'

In late February 2009 Morocco recalled its ambassador to Iran, having been angered by 'inappropriate language' used against Morocco in a communiqué reported by the state-controlled Islamic Republic News Agency. In early March Morocco announced that it had severed diplomatic relations with Iran following comments made by an adviser to Ayatollah Khamenei that Bahrain was a province of Iran, a claim denounced as 'absurd' by Morocco's King Muhammad VI.

During an address at a UN conference on racism in April 2009, President Ahmadinejad continued his anti-Israeli rhetoric, accusing the USA and Europe of having created Israel in the aftermath of the Second World War and branding Israel the 'most cruel and repressive racist regime' in history, prompting dozens of European diplomats to walk out of the conference in protest. Several Western countries, including the USA and Canada, had refused to attend the conference in protest at Ahmadinejad's invitation. Ahmadinejad was reported to have repeated the claim and labelled the Holocaust 'an historical deception' in June; during a meeting on the following day between French President Nicolas Sarkozy and Iranian Minister of Foreign Affairs Mottaki primarily to discuss Iran's nuclear ambitions, Sarkozy—who had refused to meet with

Ahmadinejad owing to his overtly anti-Israeli rhetoric—branded the statements as 'unacceptable and deeply shocking'.

In mid-March 2009 Iran's ambassador to the EU, Ali-Asghar Khaji, held informal discussions with NATO's Assistant Secretary-General for Political Affairs and Security Policy, Martin Erdmann, with the primary subject of the talks reported to have been the situation in Afghanistan. The meeting, the first between an Iranian diplomat and a NATO official in three decades, together with the attendance of an Iranian representative at a US-backed international conference on Afghanistan held in The Hague a few days later, were heralded as encouraging steps towards re-integrating Iran within the international community. Later that month, Ayatollah Khamenei spoke out against the USA, saying that President Obama was following the 'same misguided track' as his immediate predecessor with regard to US policies in the Middle East.

Meanwhile, in May 2009 Italian Minister of Foreign Affairs Franco Frattini cancelled a planned visit to Tehran to meet with Ahmadinejad just moments before boarding his plane, upon being informed of Iran's successful launch of a surface-to-surface missile (see Developments in the Nuclear Issue: 2008–09). It was subsequently reported that Frattini had wanted to avoid the possibility of Ahmadinejad using the visit as a propaganda tool for his presidential election campaign. News of the planned meeting had initially prompted surprise from other EU members, including France and the United Kingdom, the governments of which had applied pressure on Frattini not to meet with the Iranian President lest it aid Ahmadinejad's re-election ambitions and suggest a disunited approach to Iran among EU member states. In July the Iranian Chief of Staff of the Armed Forces, Maj.-Gen. Hassan Firouzabadi, declared that the EU had 'lost its qualification to hold nuclear talks with Iran due to its members' interference in Iran's internal affairs in the post-election riots', after the governments of various EU member states had issued public statements of dismay at Iran's handling of the unrest precipitated by Ahmadinejad's re-election.

Unrest has been a constant factor in the south-eastern province of Baluchestan. Between 2008 and 2010 the Iranian authorities had considerable success in their attempts to subdue the armed Sunni separatist group Jundullah and leading figures within the organization, including Abdolmalek and Abdolhamid Rigi. In 2008 Abdolhamid was arrested and handed over to Iran by the Pakistani security authorities, and was later charged with kidnapping, murder, armed robbery, propaganda, links with foreign intelligence services and counter-revolutionary activities. The following year he made several televised confessions that also implicated Abdolmalek in the organization's activities. In February 2010 Abdolmalek, the founder and leader of the group, was arrested onboard an airline travelling from Dubai to Kyrgyzstan after it was intercepted by the Iranian air force and forced to land at Iran's Bandar Abbas airport.

On 29 May 2010, following two postponements, Abdolhamid Rigi was executed in Zahedan, and less than one month later Abdolmalek was also executed, at Tehran's Evin prison. On 15 July, in an apparent response to the death of its leader, Jundullah claimed responsibility for two suicide bombings that targeted the Shi'a mosque of Jamia in Zahedan. The bombings were reported to have killed 27 people and injured 100 people, including members of the Revolutionary Guards.

TENSIONS WITH THE OBAMA ADMINISTRATION, 2009–12

In a television interview broadcast in late July 2009 US Secretary of State Hillary Clinton commented that if Iran's goal was to acquire nuclear weapons, the pursuit would be 'futile'. The stated goal of the comments was 'to send a message to whoever is making these decisions that if you're pursuing nuclear weapons for the purpose of intimidating, of projecting your power, we're not going to let that happen'. Previously, Secretary of State Clinton had spoken of the possibility of placing a 'defence umbrella' over the Middle East to protect the region from an expansionist Iran. She further stated that Iran had a right to pursue nuclear power for civil use, but maintained that Iran did not have the right to retain control over the entire enrichment cycle.

This language was exceptionally direct and forceful in diplomatic terms and it indicated without ambiguity that the Obama Administration was going to take a harder approach towards Iran's nuclear programme. The hedging made clear that the Administration was not implacable when it came to civil nuclear power, but the comment on the enrichment cycle control was indicative of the USA's continued distrust of the Iranian Government.

In July 2009 three US citizens were detained by Iranian border guards during a hiking trip to Iraq's Kurdish Autonomous Region. The Iranian authorities claimed that the group had crossed the border, while the hikers insisted that they had been in Iraqi territory when they were arrested. The three were subsequently held at Tehran's Evin Prison and were unable to communicate with their families until May 2010. On 9 November 2009 the three hikers were charged with espionage. President Ahmadinejad stated that, while he hoped the US detainees would be found to be innocent of the charge, they must be punished for entering Iran without permission.

This case was not, however, the sole recent example of Iran detaining US citizens. In January 2009 US journalist Roxana Saberi was arrested and sentenced to four months' imprisonment on charges of espionage. Following Saberi's release in May, the USA released the five Iranian diplomats it had arrested in Arbil, Iraq, in 2007 (see Relations between Iran and the USA), prompting speculation that Iran might seek to facilitate an exchange for the hikers. In mid-September 2010 one of the hikers, Sarah Shourd, returned to the USA, following her release on bail for humanitarian reasons (citing health concerns). Although she was ordered to return to Iran for the judicial proceeding, she refused to do so. In her absence, the Iranian court delayed the trial three times. The Iranian lawyer of the US detainees, Masoud Shafiee, lodged a formal protest claiming that the court should not delay the trial of all three of the hikers just because one was absent. The US Department of State issued a statement following the third postponement urging a swift resolution to the case. In addition, Amnesty International called for the release of the two remaining US prisoners, asserting that the judicial proceedings of the case had not met the international standards for a fair trial. Some observers alleged that the delayed judicial process amounted to a political detainment that could be considered a 'hostage taking'.

In February 2011 the two remaining defendants, Shane Bauer and Joshua Fattal, appeared for trial in the Iranian court; the Government banned outside observers from the proceedings. Both of the young Americans pleaded not guilty to the charge of espionage and maintained that they were merely on a hiking holiday. With Shourd's continued refusal to return to Iran to face trial, the proceedings were again adjourned. The trial was recommenced in May 2011, but no verdict was reached until 20 August when it was finally announced that all three of the defendants had been sentenced to eight years in prison on charges of spying and illegal entry into Iranian territory. However, in late September Bauer and Fattal were released from Iranian custody and allowed to return to the USA, following mediation by Oman.

DEVELOPMENTS IN IRAN'S NUCLEAR PROGRAMME, 2009–12

On 5 June 2009 the IAEA released a report indicating that the number of centrifuges used to enrich uranium at the Natanz fuel enrichment plant had increased by some 2,132 since its last report in March. In addition, the report highlighted Iran's 'continued refusal' to allow the IAEA access to the nuclear reactor sites under construction and said that Iran had made no progress on other issues.

As international speculation and concern over Iran's ambitions for nuclear weapons mounted, Iran admitted, in September 2009, that it was building a hitherto undisclosed uranium enrichment plant near Qom. However, Ahmadinejad insisted that the plant was to be used for peaceful purposes. Later that month, to the concern of the USA, Iran successfully test-fired a series of medium- and long-range missiles, indicating that Iran was capable of targeting Israel, as well as US military bases in the Gulf.

On 21 October 2009 the IAEA, along with delegates from the USA, France, Iran and Russia, agreed a draft fuel swap deal intended to provide the energy needed for the Tehran Research Reactor, which produces medical radioisotopes for diagnostic and therapeutic procedures. The deal would allow Iran to send its low-enriched uranium outside of the country for further enrichment under international supervision, which would then be returned to Iran for use in the medical reactor. This was widely considered a confidence-building gesture allowing some degree of hope that Iran would commence bringing its programme back into the international fold. However, Iran's only response was to issue a counter-offer after the allotted deadline and it appeared to have attempted to stall the talks.

The following month the IAEA passed a resolution that condemned Iran for developing the Qom uranium enrichment site without disclosing the details of the operation. Iran, in turn, suggested that the reprimands were 'political' in nature and, to show its disregard for the international restrictions, announced plans to create a further 10 uranium enrichment facilities. However, some observers suggested that the plans to build 10 more facilities did not accurately reflect Iran's true capabilities. Economic and technical obstacles, including the fact that Iran had just 8,000 centrifuges (only one-half of which were capable of producing reactor uranium), would make such plans difficult, if not impossible.

In February 2010 Iran indicated that it was prepared to send its uranium abroad for further enrichment in exchange for nuclear fuel. On 17 May Brazil, Turkey and Iran announced an agreement along the lines of the October 2009 IAEA recommendation that Iran send its low-enriched uranium abroad. Under the terms of the deal, Iran claimed to have agreed to transfer 1,200 kg of its low-enriched uranium to Turkey within a month and would receive 120 kg of 20%-enriched uranium for use in its medical research reactor within a year. This agreement was widely criticized as being insufficient, since 1,200 kg was only about one-half of the total amount of Iran's uranium that was available for enrichment. Questions also remained as to whether or not Iran would continue the enrichment process in the hope of acquiring the highly enriched uranium necessary to construct a nuclear weapon.

Although initially optimistic about the possibilities of such exchanges, the USA reacted with ambivalence, suggesting that, despite the fact that this represented a positive step, there remained much scepticism regarding Iran's intentions. In mid-June 2010 the UN Security Council voted in favour of a resolution that would impose tighter and more rigid sanctions against Iran. The resolution was passed with 12 votes in favour; Turkey and Brazil voted against it and Lebanon abstained from voting. The measures adopted in Resolution 1929 were intended to freeze the funds and assets of the Revolutionary Guards and the Islamic Republic of Iran Shipping Lines, preventing the import of weapons or the financing of anything that could be related to weapons. The severity of these sanctions was unexpected, especially given the political manoeuvring that was required to prevent a Chinese or Russian veto. Iran immediately responded by characterizing the sanctions as 'illegal', while Ahmadinejad himself stated that 'we do not recognize sanctions'.

Following the Security Council decision, on 22 June 2010 the US Congress urged the Obama Administration to endorse legislation that would significantly reinforce US sanctions on Iran. The measures contained in the Comprehensive Iran Sanctions, Accountability, and Divestment Act of 2010 were described as the 'toughest ever'. They extended the sanctions the USA had already imposed on Iran, targeting in particular Iran's petroleum imports. Although Iran is one of the world's largest producers of crude oil, the sector requires significant investment in infrastructure in order to meet domestic demand. Goods and services for the modernization of the oil and natural gas sectors were also targeted by the sanctions. The EU followed suit in July, placing further restrictions on Iran's foreign trade, financial services, and the oil and gas sector.

In addition to the economic sanctions, the USA imposed further sanctions on eight Iranian officials, including several leading cabinet members and the commander of the Revolutionary Guards, in September 2010. These sanctions specified that the assets of the eight individuals were subject to seizure by the USA and banned any transaction between them and US citizens. They also invoked the human rights clause incorporated in one of the sanctions passed earlier that year. President Obama claimed that the sanctioned officials had been involved in human rights abuses during and after the disputed 2009 election. Officials in Tehran subsequently requested international support against the sanctions, claiming that the USA did not have the right to be involved in Iranian domestic affairs and that the sanctions represented a clear misuse of the phrase 'human rights abuses'.

In December 2010, in Geneva, Iran met with officials from the P5+1 countries for further talks on the nuclear issue. The negotiations were intended once again to encourage Iran to comply with international obligations. However, the only agreement reached was that another round of talks would be held in İstanbul, Turkey, in January 2011. At these talks the P5+1 proposed two different types of solution. One type offered suggestions on how Iran could improve its transparency so that IAEA officials were able better to answer any lingering questions about the country's nuclear programme. The other type of solution was to continue reactor fuel swaps, such as the one carried out at the Bushehr plant between Russia and Iran. The P5+1 claimed that these proposals met Iran's demands that the international community respect its right to conduct a peaceful nuclear energy programme. However, no practical progress was made during the talks, which ended with no plans being made for future discussions. In May Iran offered to resume talks in Turkey with the P5+1, but as of mid-September no decision had been made regarding if or when Iran's offer would be accepted.

In May 2011 the IAEA released a report claiming that Iran had made progress in its nuclear programme and that its total output of low-enriched uranium now stood at 4.1 metric tons—enough to produce two nuclear weapons if further refined. The report also asserted that the IAEA had evidence that Iran had been working on a sophisticated nuclear triggering device. The IAEA cited this alleged finding as proof that Iran was working on the development of nuclear weapons, since this sort of technology is only applicable in the triggering of such weapons.

In November 2011 the IAEA issued a report stating that Iran had recently carried out research that could only be used to develop a nuclear bomb trigger, and indicating for the first time that it was likely that such research was ongoing. The Iranian Government rejected the findings as politically motivated; however, the report prompted the extension of EU and US sanctions. International attention was increasingly focused on the Parchin military site, south of Tehran, as the location of possible major nuclear activities by the Iranian authorities. The Iranian Government, while denying the allegations, refused to allow the IAEA to visit the site. In February 2012 a group of IAEA inspectors were permitted to travel to Tehran, but left Iran after being denied access to the Parchin site. The IAEA reported that Iran had begun uranium enrichment at its underground Fordo plant near Qom.

Meanwhile, between 2010 and 2012 a number of leading Iranian scientists working in the field of the Government's nuclear programme were killed in gun or bomb attacks. In all cases, Iran accused the USA and Israel's external intelligence service, Mossad, of responsibility for the killings. Notably, in January 2012 a university professor and prominent scientist, Mostafa Ahmadi Roshan, who worked at the Natanz fuel enrichment plant, was killed in a car bomb explosion in Tehran. In July the Iranian Minister of Intelligence, Heydar Moslehi, accused Mossad, the CIA, and the British secret services of ordering the killing of Iranian scientists, and claimed that his forces had arrested 30 terrorists who were trained by Mossad.

INCREASE IN US AND EU SANCTIONS

Amid an intensification of the dispute concerning Iran's nuclear programme during 2011, in May the EU added a further 100 Iranian firms and individuals to its list of those subject to sanctions (again extending the list in October and

December). At the end of November Iranian demonstrators attacked and partly occupied the British embassy and a residential compound in Tehran, in protest against the imposition by the British Government earlier that month of further economic sanctions—which included a virtual ban on British banks doing business with Iranian banks and on firms involved in Iran's energy sector. Following this incident, the British Government closed its embassy, withdrew diplomatic staff from Iran and expelled Iranian diplomats from the United Kingdom, and bilateral relations have since remained suspended. On 23 January 2012 the EU approved an embargo on imports of petroleum from Iran, which entered into effect on 1 July, and also froze assets belonging to the Central Bank.

In late November 2011, following the significant report issued by the IAEA, the USA extended its bilateral sanctions in force against firms engaged in business deals with the Iranian oil and petrochemical sectors. At the end of December the USA imposed sanctions restricting foreign companies that engaged in business with Iran's Central Bank, thereby making international currency transfers and transactions on Iranian oil even more difficult.

Further sanctions were imposed by the USA against Iran in early 2012, and not only against its nuclear programme. The USA's sanctions against Iran's Central Bank were further expanded in early February, when all Iranian government assets in the USA were frozen. In the same month the USA announced the imposition of sanctions on Iran's Ministry of Intelligence, which it accused of supporting terrorism, abusing the human rights of Iranian citizens and supporting the Syrian Government's violent repression of protests (see Other External Relations). According to the US Treasury's Under Secretary for Terrorism and Financial Intelligence, David Cohen, the Ministry of Intelligence also provided support to al-Qa'ida, Hezbollah and Hamas, 'exposing the extent of Iran's sponsorship of terrorism as a matter of Iranian state policy'.

In July 2012 Mitt Romney, the Republican candidate in the US presidential election scheduled for November, visited Israel, where he openly stated that if he were to become President the USA would support Israeli unilateral military action against Iran's nuclear sites. By contrast, Obama had urged caution regarding a military attack. Shortly afterwards US Secretary of Defense Leon Panetta visited Jerusalem and confirmed that the US Administration was prepared to consider all options against Iran's nuclear programme, although analysts also suggested that his message to the Israeli leaders reiterated the President's exhortation to wait until all other means of pressure were exhausted. Meanwhile, at the end of July the USA announced a new series of sanctions which were designed to enforce the economic embargo on Iran's petrochemical industry and oil exports by penalizing firms or individuals that helped Iran to circumvent the existing prohibitions. According to the US Treasury Department, penalties were imposed on two financial institutions, Bank of Kunlun in China and Elaf Islamic Bank in Iraq, both of which were accused of assisting Iran's petroleum sales. The Chinese Government rapidly rejected the allegations and urged the USA to revoke the imposition of sanctions against the Bank of Kunlun.

During President Obama's second term of office from January 2013 (Obama having defeated Romney in the US presidential vote of November 2012), US support for more aggressive sanctions against the Iranian regime continued, despite a policy of verbal support for the Iranian people. In the course of a week during May–June 2013 the Obama Administration escalated its sanctions against Iran in order to exert additional pressure on the regime.

This last action further weakened the country's already devalued currency, seriously disrupted its automotive industry, and created a significant disturbance in domestic employment and revenue generation for the Iranian Government. A US presidential executive order effective from 1 July 2013 was a response to what the US Administration called Iran's 'continued failure to meet its international obligations', i.e. the country's international obligations regarding its controversial nuclear programme.

2012 PARLIAMENTARY ELECTIONS

By 2012 the anti-Government protests, known as the 'Green Movement', had lost strength and virtually ended. Since the elections, Mousavi, together with his wife, and Karrubi had been detained, at times in their own homes and most recently in unknown locations, while any one remotely connected with Mousavi had been arrested or had fled the country. These included high-profile former government members such as former Minister of Culture and Islamic Guidance Mohajerani, who had joined the dissidents living outside Iran, and former Minister of Science, Research and Technology and presidential candidate Moin, who in June 2012 was sentenced to one year's imprisonment for anti-regime propaganda. (His sentence was subsequently reduced to an IR 2m. fine.)

Elections to the ninth Majlis took place on 2 March 2012, with a second round on 4 May. Over 5,000 candidates had registered, of whom more than one-third were banned from contesting the polls by the Council of Guardians. Many of those candidates were parliamentary members, but were not recognized as being qualified for seats in the next Majlis. Nonetheless, about 3,400 candidates contested the 290 parliamentary seats. Some observers described the process as a contest between the President and the Supreme Leader. Since pro-Ahmadinejad candidates had been subject to the official restrictions, in the absence of many of the moderate 'reformists' the new Majlis overwhelmingly comprised followers of the Supreme Leader.

Meanwhile, President Ahmadinejad's confrontation with the Ayatollah Khamenei and the Majlis continued; in some cases, he was obliged to cede to pressure from the Supreme Leader. In July 2012 the Majlis announced that a faction within the chamber aimed to bring about closer parliamentary scrutiny of the Government by adopting a 'parliamentary system' in place of a 'presidential system', which would involve the abolition of the presidential office and the possible restoration of the post of Prime Minister.

OTHER EXTERNAL RELATIONS

Initially, the Iranian Government expressed mixed feelings about the revolutions in Egypt and Tunisia that took place in early 2011, fearing that the unrest would spread to their own territory. Supreme Leader Ayatollah Khamenei none the less publicly referred to the revolutions as an 'Islamic awakening'. The Iranian Government welcomed the election of Muhammad Mursi of the Muslim Brotherhood as President of Egypt in June 2012.

Iran was also indirectly involved in the revolutionary protests in Bahrain which commenced in February 2011. One of the aims of the demonstrations in Sunni-controlled Bahrain was to achieve political equality between the country's Shi'a and Sunnis. The Bahraini Government approved the deployment of the armed forces, supplemented by troops and police officers from Saudi Arabia, Qatar and the UAE, to suppress the protests through the use of force and arrests. Iran strongly denounced the actions of the Bahraini authorities, which, in turn, warned Iran against interfering in the internal affairs of Bahrain. In March hundreds of Iranian protesters stoned the Saudi consulate in the north-eastern city of Mashhad and the Iranian authorities expelled a Bahraini diplomat from the country (following the earlier expulsion of the Iranian chargé d'affaires from Manama). In addition, Iran dispatched a 'solidarity flotilla' of vessels to Bahrain in May in a show of support for the mainly Shi'a protesters. However, these ships, which were carrying humanitarian aid, turned back before reaching Bahrain.

Iran has had longstanding close relations with Syria since the presidency of Hafiz al-Assad (the father of incumbent President Bashar al-Assad). In addition to supporting Iran against Iraq under Saddam Hussain, Syria facilitated Iran's access to Hezbollah in South Lebanon. Since the confrontation in Syria between Assad's regime and the opposition, Iran has always declared its support for the Syrian Government and its view that the opposition was a creation of the West. Reports have emerged that the Revolutionary Guards have assisted President Assad in suppressing the insurgent protests. At least in the initial stage of the Syrian demonstrations, there was some similarity in the action taken by the regime to the events in Iran during the unrest following the presidential election of 2009.

In April 2012 President Ahmadinejad unexpectedly visited Abu Musa, when he reiterated Iran's claim of sovereignty over the island and insisted that 'the Persian Gulf is Persian'. In response, the UAE recalled its ambassador from Tehran, condemning Ahmadinejad's visit as a violation of its sovereign territorial rights. Following the controversy precipitated by the visit, UAE Crown Prince and the Deputy Supreme Commander of the Armed Forces, Sheikh Muhammad bin Zayed Al Nahyan, met US President Obama in June to discuss regional issues. Obama declared his support for a resolution through direct bilateral negotiations between the UAE and Iran, or at the ICJ or another appropriate international forum.

In response to the new oil embargo announced by the EU, Iran renewed threats to prevent the transport of oil through the Straits of Hormuz. In fact, since Rafsanjani's presidency Iran had on occasion warned that it would close the Straits of Hormuz if its interests were threatened, but the Government's rhetoric increased from late December 2011. The USA responded to Iranian naval exercises in the region by sending an aircraft carrier to the Straits of Hormuz in early 2012. By July the US navy had deployed four additional Avenger-class mine counter-measure ships (increasing the number to eight), as well as a large number of submarine vessels, to the Persian Gulf and Arabian Sea, in anticipation of a confrontation with Iran. Although the Iranian Government has modified its bellicose tone and language, the Revolutionary Guards have repeatedly claimed that they have a plan to mine the Straits of Hormuz.

URANIUM ENRICHMENT

In mid-November 2012 a leaked IAEA report stated that Iran was ready to double the amount of enriched uranium at the Fordo underground nuclear facility. The facility is intended to hold approximately 3,000 centrifuges, with 2,710 centrifuges installed in 2013, according to IAEA records. The number of centrifuges actually in operation is believed to be above 1,400. Fordo has been a source of escalation in Iran's chaotic relationship with the West since its existence was identified in September 2009.

After several leaked IAEA reports claiming that Iran was ready to double the output of uranium at the Fordo facility, Iran finally informed the IAEA in January 2013 that it planned to upgrade its uranium enrichment centrifuges at its Natanz plant. This would allow the regime to refine uranium at a faster rate, thus bringing forward the timeline of its nuclear programme.

Almost immediately after this Iranian announcement, in January 2013 Iran arrested 11 journalists whom it accused of co-operating with a foreign Persian-language media organization. These arrests were part of a clampdown against the BBC and Voice of America, which Tehran considers to be 'hostile' organizations. Both media outlets were accused of inciting unrest after the disputed re-election of President Mahmoud Ahmadinejad in 2009, by broadcasting online videos and interviews with anti-Government protesters, who described deaths, injuries and arbitrary arrests being carried out by security forces. These arrests continue to show the tightening of restrictions by the Iranian leadership on the media ahead of June's presidential election.

In February 2013 the US Administration offered to hold direct talks with the Iranian Government concerning Tehran's nuclear programme; however, the prospect of such discussions was dismissed by Ayatollah Khamenei because of the continuing US sanctions in place against Iran. Despite several announcements being made by President Ahmadinejad that he was ready for direct talks with the USA, Khamenei has the final say on all key issues in the Islamic Republic, including Iran's sensitive nuclear activities and foreign policy, and was thus able to override Ahmadinejad's wishes.

In April 2013 Iran announced defiantly that it had begun operations at two uranium mines and a uranium ore-processing plant, thereby furthering its capacity to produce nuclear material. These twin sites reflect the regime's goal of greater self-sufficiency through the entire nuclear fuel cycle from uranium mines to enrichment laboratories. This announcement, which was made just days after the latest round of negotiations with the P5+1 group of countries again ended in stalemate, reinforces a broader suggestion that Iran plans to push ahead with its nuclear project even at the potential risk of threatening its dialogue with US and other envoys. Iran's gambit appears to be built around its drive for formal acknowledgement from Washington and other capitals of its 'right' to enrich uranium, while in tandem wanting the West to pull back on sanctions in exchange for some nuclear compromises.

THE 2013 PRESIDENTIAL ELECTION

While the leaders of the opposition Green Movement had remained in gaol for over 1,000 days, in March 2013 Hassan Rouhani, a moderate politician and former Secretary of the SNSC, launched his presidential campaign. On 15 June Rouhani was elected as Iran's President with 50.7% of the total number of votes. Nearly 37m. Iranian voted in the presidential poll (some 72% of eligible voters). Muhammad Baqir Qalibaf, the mayor of Tehran, finished second with 16.6% of the votes. Several other 'conservative' candidates also contested the election: most notably, Saaed Jalili, the incumbent Secretary of the SNSC, won 11.4% of the vote, and Mohsen Rezai 10.6%.

Rouhani was regarded as more of a centrist than a liberal, and his policies differed substantially from those of President Ahmadinejad, in that Rouhani appeared to be more willing to do whatever is necessary to ensure Iran's economic growth, even it if means conceding to the requests of the West. Iran's new President considers the country's existing problems in the field of the economy and other sectors to be due to incorrect management by the incumbent administration. He has stated that with proper planning, production units can be activated and jobs can be created, but that this requires stability.

As far as Iran's nuclear programme is concerned, Rouhani defended his track record as Iran's chief nuclear negotiator from October 2003 to August 2005. He claimed that he prevented Iran from facing additional international sanctions, further UN Security Council resolutions and even the prospect of war. However, Rouhani's current view on the nuclear programme and its relationship with Iran's economic problems due to sanctions revolves around the idea that a nuclear programme for the production of weapons is a waste of time, while its achievement of producing nuclear power for electricity is not. Rouhani has pledged greater transparency about what he says is Iran's peaceful nuclear enrichment programme, aimed at producing fuel for nuclear reactors to generate electricity.

Additionally, Rouhani has promised more effective diplomacy with the West, stating that 'The Iran–US relationship is a complex and difficult issue. A bitter history, filled with mistrust and animosity, marks this relationship. It has become a chronic wound whose healing is difficult but possible, provided that good faith and mutual respect prevail… As a moderate, I have phased a plan to de-escalate hostility to a manageable state of tension and then engage in promotion in interactions and dialogue between the two peoples to achieve *détente*, and finally reach to the point of mutual respect that both peoples deserve.'

After the confirmation by the Supreme Leader of the results of the election on 3 August 2013, Rouhani took office, before a formal confirmation ceremony in parliament the following day. President Rouhani used his speech to the Majlis to announce his nominees for the Council of Ministers. After four days of debate and discussions, on 15 August the Iranian parliament entered into a vote of confidence session and approved all but three of the President's 18 nominees. Muhammad Ali Najafi, Jafar Mili-Monfared and Massoud Soltani-Far—the respective candidates for Minister of Education, Minister of Science, Research and Technology and Minister of Sport and Youth Affairs—all failed to win the endorsement of the Majlis. Their support for the Green Movement was cited as the main point of divergence with 'conservative' deputies. Among the 18 candidates presented were six former ministers, the most notable being Bijan Namdar Zanganeh, who was approved as the new

Minister of Petroleum. He had already served as both the Minister of Petroleum and of Energy for a combined total of 17 years under Presidents Khatami and Rafsanjani. Another approved nominee who faced significant opposition during the parliamentary debates was Muhammad Javad Zarif, who finally received 232 votes in favour of his appointment to the Ministry of Foreign Affairs, with only 36 'hardline' deputies voting against his candidacy. Zarif is internationally well-known and respected, and served as Iran's permanent head of delegation at the UN under President Khatami. Rouhani was swift to appoint former President Ahmadinejad's Minister of Foreign Affairs, Ali Akbar Salehi, as a vice-president, in charge of the country's disputed nuclear programme. It appeared, however, that Rouhani intended to make the Ministry of Foreign Affairs the sole authority in negotiations on the nuclear issue and thereby avoid the interference that used to come from a variety of authorities.

One month into his presidency, it appeared that Rouhani was focused on plans to tackle urgent economic priorities, such as controlling inflation, increasing purchasing power and reducing the high level of unemployment. However, there was concern among the international community that the new President would continue the Iranian regime's support for Syrian President Assad. Nevertheless, during President Rouhani's first press conference after winning the election, he asserted that 'the ultimate responsibility to resolve the Syrian civil war should be in the hands of the Syrian people'.

Economy

SARA BAZOOBANDI

INTRODUCTION

Iran is among the largest economies of the Middle East and North Africa region. With a gross domestic product (GDP) of some US $482,000m. in 2012, Iran is ranked the second in the region after Saudi Arabia. The main driver of Iran's economy is its large hydrocarbon sector. Iran is known to possess the world's largest reserves of natural gas and the fourth largest reserves of petroleum. Until 2011 Iran was the fourth largest producer of crude petroleum globally. However, this trend has changed as a result of international economic sanctions, and in 2012 Iran was the sixth largest producer. Hydrocarbons are the main source of foreign exchange, and, according to central bank data, earnings from oil and gas exports accounted for almost 50% of general budget receipts in the year to March 2012, down from some 53% in 2010/11. The country has small private and agriculture sectors, with a strong government presence in both manufacturing industry and the financial sector. Despite high international oil prices, the economy has been struggling with various macroeconomic issues, including high inflation and relatively low rates of growth. Moreover, while most of the oil producing countries in the Middle East have accumulated a considerable volume of assets in commodity-based foreign reserves, Iran has historically had a very poor record in this respect—although a new National Development Fund was established in 2011 in an effort to address this.

The medium-term outlook for Iran's economic growth is negative as a result of the recent strengthening of international economic sanctions, with government revenues from oil exports having dropped significantly. In addition to the international economic sanctions, Iran's heavy reliance on revenue from oil exports means that fluctuations in world oil prices have also affected the Iranian economy. According to World Bank data, Iran's annual GDP growth declined from 7.8% in 2007 to 2.3% in 2008, and further, to 1.8%, in 2009, reflecting the impact on the Iranian economy of the oil price decline as a result of the global financial crisis. The IMF, in its April 2013 World Economic Outlook, assessed that Iran's economy contracted by 1.9% in 2012, and projected a further contraction, of 1.3%, in 2013. It forecast growth of 1.1% for 2014, however. This suggests the Iranian economy was expected to be able to find domestic sources of demand to compensate for the negative impact of the sanctions particularly on its export industry.

The Iranian Government has increased its efforts to attract foreign direct investment (FDI), which has been hard hit by economic sanctions imposed over the country's disputed nuclear programme. According to the UN Conference on Trade and Development (UNCTAD), Iran attracted US $4,870m. in FDI in 2012, an increase of 17.3% compared with the previous year. In July 2013 the Vice-Minister of Economic Affairs and Finance, Behrouz Alishiri, stated that the country was to offer tax exemptions in order to attract foreign investors. The largest of these were to be in the agriculture sector, with a 100% tax exemption for an unlimited period. Up to 80% tax exemption would be offered in mining and industry, potentially increasing to 100% for a 10-year period in underdeveloped areas of the country. Moreover, Alishiri indicated that tax exemptions in free trade zones would be extended for 20 years.

Iran has experienced significantly high inflation since 2011, particularly reflected in the price of imported items, arising from the devaluation of the rial. Controlling inflation in Iran will require tightly co-ordinated monetary and fiscal policies. While the Government has claimed to put a strong emphasis on prudent policies in recent years, the devaluation of Iran's currency since the announcement of tighter international sanctions has triggered upward and rapidly increasing inflation. The official inflation rate in urban areas was recorded at 21.5% in the year to March 2012, although government data are widely thought to understate actual inflation. Furthermore, various official sources have published different inflation rates for the same period. For example, the Central Bank of Iran announced that inflation in the year to June 2013 was 35.9%, while the Statistical Centre of Iran (SCI) put the inflation rate at 32.6% for the same period.

The value of rial against the US dollar declined significantly from December 2011, imposing inflationary effects on the economy to which the property market has immediately responded. A key factor contributing to the devaluation of the currency is the application of tougher sanctions by the West, which affected foreign currency transactions for the country's trade; particularly the oil exports income. Since sanctions were tightened in late 2011 Iran has found it difficult to receive funds from Asian buyers—including the People's Republic of China and India, whose purchases account for some 65% of Iran's oil exports. In order to address the issue of devaluation of the national currency, the Iranian Government has applied a multi-rate foreign exchange system, previously used during the Iran–Iraq war. During that period Iran was suffering low income from oil exports as a result of damage to oil production sites and the high cost of conflict. Iran abandoned the multi-rate system few years after the end of the war, but reintroduced it from 2011. In July 2013 the Government's Money and Finance Working Group announced its decision to revert to a single foreign exchange rate system.

The Iranian economy has been characterized by high unemployment. As with inflation, official data on unemployment are widely considered to be understated. In mid-2011 a new definition of employment was introduced: this designates as employed an individual aged 10 years and above who is working at least one hour per week'. Even based on this definition, the unemployment rate for the age group of 15–29 years was still high, at 24.2%, in the period between December 2012 and March 2013, according to the Statistical Centre of Iran (SCI). Unemployment of persons aged 10 years and above was put at 12.4% in 2012/13.

PETROLEUM AND NATURAL GAS

Oil production has declined significantly since 2009: according to the *BP Statistical Review of World Energy 2013*, Iran produced 214.5m. metric tons of oil in 2008; output had slowed to 208.2 tons by 2011, and dropped to just 174.9m. tons in 2012. The economic sanctions imposed by the USA and the European Union (EU) during the presidency of Mahmoud Ahmadinejad (2005–13) have restricted international companies' interactions with Iran and reduced the number of markets for exports of Iranian crude oil.

As a result of the sanctions, Iran's break-even prices have become the highest in the region. The IMF projected a break-even price for Iranian oil output of US $150 per barrel in 2013, up from $134 per barrel in 2012. This compares with a projected break-even price for Saudi Arabia of $85.2 per barrel in 2013, from $74.4 per barrel in 2012.

Although four rounds of UN sanctions have been imposed on Iran, the tougher measures introduced by the USA and the EU have severely hampered Iran's ability to export its oil. Moreover, the US and EU measures banned foreign investment in the country's oil and gas sector, and cut off Iran's access to EU and US financial networks. Further sanctions have banned EU protection and indemnity clubs from providing Iranian crude tankers with insurance and reinsurance. The implementation of insurance-related sanctions was particularly effective in stemming Iranian exports, which specifically forced Iran's Asian customers to reduce their imports from Iran. The US House of Representatives was reportedly working on a new sanctions bill in mid-2013 requesting that the US President arrive at a strategy within two months to cut Iran's remaining export sales. The proposed new US sanctions would no longer allow exemptions to be granted to countries such as China, Japan, Turkey and the Republic of Korea (South Korea), which have continued to import oil supplies from Iran. Companies in those countries had previously been given a 'waiver' against being cut off from the US economy should they do business with Iran. Exemptions granted to companies from Japan and 10 EU countries were extended by six months in September 2013, in return for a pledge to reduce imports from Iran during that period. Exemptions granted to China, India, South Korea and Turkey, as well as five other countries, were due to expire in December. However, by September no announcement had been made regarding any US decision on their renewal.

At April 2013 China, Japan, India, South Korea and Turkey were together importing about 750,000 b/d of Iranian oil, down from 1.1m. b/d the previous month. The biggest drop came from Japan, which bought virtually no Iranian crude after April 2013 as it reduced the number of tankers with sovereign insurance from 13 to eight. The fall in imports from these countries continued in May, forcing Iran to store oil in tankers off shore and then, after reaching full capacity, to reduce output. Iranian oil production was expected to decline to 2.5m. b/d–2.6m. b/d in early 2013. Such a low level was last seen in 1989, during the Iran–Iraq war.

The Iranian Government has been putting a significant effort into easing the effect of sanctions. However, macroeconomic challenges such as the devaluation of the national currency, low growth and high inflation prove that the Government's effort has not been particularly fruitful. Iran's newly elected President, Hassan Rouhani, has appointed Bijan Namdar Zanganeh as Minister of Petroleum. Following his nomination, Zanganeh, who previously held that portfolio during the presidency of Muhammad Khatami (1997–2005), pledged to restore the country's oil production capacity to 2005 levels.

AGRICULTURE AND FOOD

Iran is confronted by a serious water problem. According to FAO, annual rainfall averages 228 mm. Approximately 90% of the country is arid or semi-arid, with annual rainfall ranging from less than 50 mm in desert areas to 2,275 mm at Rasht on the Caspian Sea, and about two-thirds of rainfall evaporates before reaching Iran's rivers. According to the Iran Water Resources Management Company, average rainfall declined by some 16% in the 2010/11 farming year (October/September) compared with the previous year, and the long-term trend has been negative Water shortage means that the agricultural sector in Iran has been severely affected. However, the Government has apparently been reluctant to confirm the challenge facing agriculture sector, perhaps to avoid any social unrest.

Official production statistics for the sector are considered by some analysts to be overstated. For example, government data show that the country produced 14.3m. metric tons of wheat in 2012 and imported about 6.7m. tons in the same year. This would mean that Iran had 21m. tons of wheat in 2012. The Government puts total domestic consumption of wheat at roughly 8m. tons. Assuming about 1m. tons was used as seed and 1m. tons as food stock in poultry production, and 1m. tons was smuggled to neighbouring countries, Iran would thus have had around 10m. tons of surplus wheat for the year. However, the Government has never mentioned having created a strategic reserve stock that might account for the 10m. tons missing in the official data for 2012, which suggests that the domestic production data may well be overestimated.

Preliminary data from the Ministry of Agricultural Jihad put Iran's gross agricultural output at just under 76m. metric tons in 2012, representing a 2.7% decline from the previous year. According to central bank data, trade in agricultural products on the Iran Mercantile Exchange in 2011/12 was about 549,000 tons, a fall of some 66.4% compared with the previous year, although in value terms (IR 3,800,000m.), there was a 1.7% increase. Wheat accounted for about 45.6% percent of total domestic agricultural trading by volume. Total credit extended to the agriculture sector, both public and private, increased by some 17% in the 2011/12 fiscal year, to IR 338,279,000m.: this represented about 9.8% of total credit extended to all the sectors. The state agricultural insurance fund paid IR 10,200,000m. in compensation to local agricultural producers in the 2010/11 farming year, an increase of some 77.6% over the previous year.

The total deficit in the balance of trade in agricultural products reached US $4,878m. in 2011/12, an increase of 9% compared with the previous year. Iran imported 13.6m. metric tons of agricultural products (about $10,400m. in US dollar terms) in 2011/12, representing a decrease of 15.4 % by volume and an increase of 6.1% by value. The average cost of each ton of agricultural products imported in 2011/12 was about $767, an increase of 25.3% compared with the previous fiscal year. This is mainly due to the decline of the rial. Total grain imports (wheat, barley, rice and corn) were about 6.3m. metric tons in 2011/12, largely unchanged from the previous year, while the cost increased about 32%. These imports supplied nearly 20% of Iran's aggregate demand for grains. Iran also imported about 193,000 tons of meat in 2011/12, accounting for around 16% of total domestic consumption.

The Government has supported the agriculture sector extensively. In the years following the 1979 Islamic Revolution self-sufficiency in every sector, and in particular in agriculture, was a main focus of government policy. Between 1990 and 2010 the Iranian authorities encouraged the creation of 1,850 new farming co-operatives. The Government also introduced a crop insurance scheme through which it purchases agricultural products at guaranteed prices. The state is obliged to insure at least 50% of a year's crop if requested to do so by a farmer. In addition, the Government has been offering to purchase forage crops, fertilizers, seeds, fuel and machinery at reduced prices.

Another key challenge facing Iranian agriculture and food sector is the contamination of food items. The principal source of food contamination in Iran has been through two factors: the importing of contaminated food (mainly rice) and the unregulated use of pesticides by domestic farmers. The flow of sewage water into rice farms and the use of expired pesticides are known to be the main reasons for domestic farm pollution. Most of the expired pesticides are reportedly imported from China in exchange for oil. As a result of the international sanctions, Iran has been forced to exchange oil for goods because the conventional transaction channels have been blocked. Local farmers have not receive any training in the use of dangerous chemical products, and the authorities have not provided adequate instructions. Imported contaminated food items are also reported often to have been traded for oil, and Iran's health and safety authorities have failed to examine such items in order to identify the issue and reject consignments if necessary. There have been similar reports on the high level of chemical contamination of imported wheat in Iran. Iranian analysts have blamed the chemical contamination of imported grain as a main cause of various diseases, including different types of cancer. It is worth mentioning that some types of contamination are reportedly caused by delays at customs arising from the devaluation of the rial, which has put pressure on Iranian traders as a result of the sanctions. Some food shipments to Iran are held at sea for long periods before clearing customs, and it has been suggested that cargos that are delayed in this way are more likely to have (or develop) contamination. The Government has denied the problem, but the opposition and some former government officials who did not support the Ahmadinejad administration have frequently discussed the topic in various online and print media and have criticized government efforts in dealing with the issue of food safety.

POWER AND WATER

Iran, located in an arid/semi-arid zone, is expected to suffer severe water shortage as a result of a combination of mismanagement of water resources and ongoing environmental changes. Desertification is already taking place and poses a major threat to country, which has no notable watersheds and is heavily reliant on non-renewable fossil water and imported water. Around half of Iran's water comes from underground sources, but in some parts of the country underground supplies are drying up. Iran depends greatly on 'virtual' water imports by importing water-intensive agricultural goods such as meat, fruit and vegetables.

The water crisis, which is expected to worsen in the coming decades, and the issue of water has already started to provoke small-scale social unrest in some parts of the country. After a drought period in early 2013 there were clashes between police and hundreds of farmers in a town in Esfahan province following an attack on a water pipeline that was diverting water from the Zayandeh river to the city of Yazd in the neighbouring province of the same name.

Before the 1979 Revolution, 14 large dams were constructed in Iran with the assistance of foreign banks and companies. The dam construction industry then gained momentum after 1988, with the commencement of post-war reconstruction and development. According to the International Commission on Large Dams (ICOLD) non-governmental organization, Iran had some 541 dams by 2013, both large and small. Existing water storage capacity in Iran's dams is 52,000m. cu m, and the scheduled inauguration of 15 new dams by March 2014 would contribute a further 6,000m. cu m to overall capacity.

The Lake Urmia Basin, located in a mountainous area in north-west Iran, is one of the best known cases of environmental change. Urmia is the largest lake in the Middle East, and world's third largest salt lake. However, to date, it has lost some 60% of its volume, and it is under serious threat of drying up completely. The death of the lake has catastrophic implications for the wildlife of the region, and will permanently change the climate of that part of the country, potentially eventually leading to the displacement of some 14m. inhabitants. There has been a national debate over the issue, with campaigners accusing the Government of being directly responsible for the lake's desiccation and demanding urgent action. Several government projects, including a highway bridge completed in 2008, have become a barrier to the circulation of water, contributing to the fast disappearance of the lake. Moreover, a number of dam-building projects, financed and run by the Government, on rivers that supply the lake, as well as misguided irrigation policies that have allowed farmers to extract underground water that also supplies the lake, are known to be key causes of the problem.

Iran's power sector is state-controlled, and the government-owned Iran Power Generation, Transmission and Distribution Company (Tavanir) is the sole distributor of electricity. As a part of the Government's economic reform programme, pricing models for power and water have been reviewed in order to reduce government expenditures in these sectors. In 2009 the Iran Water Resources Management Company conducted a review of the pricing model for electricity production by the country's hydroelectric and thermal power plants. Traditionally, Tavanir bought electricity from the power plants and distributed it to consumers at a highly subsidized rate. The study recommended that the actual price of distributed electricity must be significantly higher, as the environmental and production costs were underestimated in the model that then applied. As a result, the price of electricity has been significantly increased during the first stage of a programme to phase out subsidies. (For further details of subsidies reform, see Monetary and Fiscal Policy, and Macroeconomic Reform.)

AUTOMOTIVE INDUSTRY

The car manufacturing industry was established in 1962, and has developed to become Iran's second largest industry, after oil and gas, and thus the largest non-oil sector of the Iranian economy. Iran's automotive industry is among the 10 largest in Asia, and is the leading such industry in the Middle East region. Until 2012, when the international sanctions targeted its car manufacturing industry, the country was producing almost 1m. cars annually, In 2013 Iran was reported by official media to have 39 automobile manufacturing companies and 1,200 auto part makers, providing about 1.2m. jobs. With the tightening of international sanctions, output by Iranian car producers was reported by the *Financial Times* to have fallen to 677,000 vehicles in the first nine months of the 2012/13 Iranian year, compared with 1.2m. during the same period in 2011/12. The rate of decline in the sector was thus greater than that experienced during the Iran–Iraq war in 1980–88. More than 110 auto part makers were reported to have closed in 2012, and thousands of workers in the sector lost their jobs. The sanctions have reportedly led to a rise of some 40% in production costs for Iranian car manufacturers, which were not fully offset by sharp increases in car prices (the price increases in themselves creating a further problem for the economy). The Government owns the two major production companies, Iran Khodro and Saipa, and the combined losses of these firms reached some US $407m. in 2012 as a result of a fivefold increase in prices for raw materials.

The sanctions have forced most foreign partners previously operating the Iranian car manufacturing sector to withdraw from Iran. South Korean and French suppliers were previously the main exporters of car parts to the country. In February 2012 France's PSA Peugeot Citroën ceased the trade of car parts with Iran and halted its exports of vehicles to the country. Iranian car producers announced the closure of six production lines for foreign models, including Nissan (Japan)'s Maxima and Qashqai, Hyundai (South Korea)'s Avante and Verna, and Kia (South Korea)'s Rio and Lifan 520.

The car manufacturing sector has incurred significant losses as a result of a combination of government macroeconomic policies and the international sanctions. While the Government undertook to pay some US $814m. to Iran Khodro and Saipa to help them meet their obligations to suppliers, the pressure created by the sanctions meant that the state might be restricted in its efforts to assist the sector—not least because domestic banks, the potential supporters of any bailout, were struggling under the impact of international sanctions.

MONETARY AND FISCAL POLICY, AND MACROECONOMIC REFORM

The government relies heavily on income from petroleum in order to finance its budget, and taxes have not traditionally been a large source of government revenue. The ratio of taxes to government expenditure was low in 2002–05, averaging about 20%. Budgetary policy and economic activity has, therefore, been unduly vulnerable to shocks in international oil markets, and the lack of an efficient tax system undermined income redistribution policies intended to lower income inequality, which had been a government priority since the 1979 revolution. The Government has for several decades proposed the reform of the tax system, including the introduction of a value-added tax, but progress in implementation has been slow.

The Economic Transformation Bill, enacted in January 2010, provided for the phased withdrawal of subsidies for energy products and other basic goods by 2015. In addition to cuts in fuel subsidies, prices for water, electricity, gas and essential foods were all to rise incrementally to global levels over the five-year period. The reform was intended to help address the fiscal shortfall: subsidies were estimated to absorb US $30,000m.–$100,000m. annually. The implementation of the subsidy reductions was reflected in the rate of inflation, with consumer prices in urban areas, according to official data, increasing by an average of 12.4% in 2010/11 and 21.5% in 2011/12.

The new legislation required the Government to redistribute some US $30,000m. in cash from the price increases to lower income households during the first year of implementation. About 70m. people were estimated to be in receipt of such payments in early 2011. In addition, some $15,000m.–$18,000m. was to be disbursed to businesses in order to finance their restructuring to reduce energy intensity, and about $10,000m.–$12,000m. was to be paid to the Government to assist the public sector in meeting higher fuel bills and improving energy efficiency.

The reduction in fuel subsidies also contributed to Iran's efforts to reduce reliance on imported oil products. Although Iran is a net exporter of oil, it lacks sufficient domestic refining capacity and capabilities to meet domestic requirements. The *New York Times* reported in 2010 that the Government had ordered domestic petrochemical plants to shift to production of petrol (gasoline). The motor fuel produced has higher levels of particulates than are allowed by law, and this has apparently exacerbated a chronic smog issue and attendant health issues.

In parallel with the subsidies cut, the Iranian Government has implemented another significant policy in its effort to reduce imports, in the form of a series of fuel rationing exercises that have at times led to shortages and distortions in the domestic fuel market. In 2006 about 40% of Iran's refined fuel was imported, leaving the country vulnerable to sanctions as global banks refused to issue letters of credit for Iranian importers.

Comprehensive market-based reforms have been adopted in order to fulfil the Government's 20-year Vision 2025 project and the Fifth Five-Year Development Plan (2011–15). None the less, the state still plays a key role in the economy. The Government owns a number of large public and quasi-public enterprises, which to some extent dominate the manufacturing and commercial sectors. A central policy has been privatization, facilitated under the Ahmadinejad presidency after Iran's Supreme Religious Leader, Ayatollah Sayed Ali Khamenei, decreed a new reinterpretation of Article 44 of the Constitution in 2005 to permit the transfer of state enterprises to private ownership.

Under the privatization programme, it was aimed to divest some 20% of state-owned enterprises annually. According to the Iranian Privatization Organization, 177 state-owned enterprises were wholly or partially sold in 2005/06–2010/11, to the value of US $82,770m. Some of these sales were conducted through the Tehran Stock Exchange (TSE), but the procedures for many of the larger, strategic privatizations—including the sale of a controlling stake in the Telecommunications Company of Iran in 2011—were more opaque. Notably, the Islamic Revolutionary Guards Corps and semi-governmental enterprises were reported to have acquired majority holdings in several key state enterprises that were presented to private investors on the TSE via intermediary co-operatives.

SOVEREIGN WEALTH AND FINANCE

Iran has historically spent most of its oil revenues on subsidies and on large infrastructure projects. The country's earnings from oil sales have offset its difficulty in accessing capital, with loans being made from oil income to finance private sector development. Moreover, the Government frequently accessed the assets its Oil Stabilization Fund—established in 2000 to collect above-projected oil revenues—to support the budget and cover foreign exchange liabilities. While the Government has been reluctant to provide detailed information on the operation of the fund, Iran has apparently lagged far behind other regional oil producers in saving its surplus hydrocarbon revenues. Under the terms of the Fifth Five-Year Development Plan, the assets of the Oil Stabilization Fund were transferred to a new National Development Fund that was established in 2011. The mandate of the new fund was explicitly to transform a proportion of revenues from oil and gas into sustainable wealth and productive investments, as well as to save for future generations. At least one-fifth of the new fund's reserves were to be invested abroad. From an initial investment of 20% in 2011/12, 26% of oil and gas revenues were to be transferred to the National Development Fund in 2013/14, rising to 32% by 2015/16. The fund reported its value at some US $54,000m. in July 2013.

The international economic pressure on Iran has influenced the country's strategy for oil revenue management. In 2010 Mahmoud Bahmani, the head of the central Bank Markazi, stated that the bank had withdrawn Iranian banks' assets from Europe. Moreover, Iran was estimated to have bought more than US $6,000m. of gold from Turkey in 2012, almost 10 times more than was purchased in 2011. This followed the expulsion of Iranian banks from the international SWIFT banking transactions mechanism in March of that year, making it virtually impossible for money to flow into or from Iran via standard banking channels. It has also been reported that a significant amount of gold has been shipped from countries in Africa and South America, and from Switzerland to Iran via transit points such as İstanbul, Turkey, and Dubai, United Arab Emirates.

BANKING

Iran's is the largest Islamic financial system in the world. With the licensing of private banks and the sale of several large public commercial banks in 2008–09, private bank assets have become the largest in Iran's banking system, according to an IMF study published in 2011. The study noted the role of the financial system in supporting growth in the context of the country's relative isolation under sanctions. However, the banking system remains in need of significant structural reform. The banks' aggregate capital buffers are inadequate given the inherent volatility of the Iranian economy and a relatively high rate of non-performing loans. A critical reform must be a regulatory requirement for banks to have a higher minimum capital adequacy and a higher provision for non-performing loans. The IMF study recommended the implementation of policies aimed at limiting dividend distribution on the part of undercapitalized banks and strengthening profitability, allowing banks greater flexibility in setting rates of return on assets and liabilities, and reducing operating costs. The IMF noted that the Fifth Five-Year Development Plan provided for the extension of Bank Markazi's regulatory reach and supervisory authority, especially in the domain of public banks. Progress was also noted in improving banking practices and standards of information disclosure and governance. The Plan also made provision for public banks to retain after-tax profits as capital, rather than accruing them to the budget. However, the IMF advised that it remained critical that the central bank be given full autonomy in exercising prompt enforcement powers, which were restricted by mandatory recourse to a separate banking disciplinary committee.

Statistical Survey

The Iranian year runs from approximately 21 March to 20 March

Sources (except where otherwise stated): Statistical Centre of Iran, POB 14155-6133, Dr Fatemi Ave, Tehran 14144; tel. (21) 88965061; fax (21) 88963451; e-mail sci@sci.org.ir; internet www.amar.org.ir; Bank Markazi Jomhouri Islami Iran (Central Bank), POB 15875-7177, 144 Mirdamad Blvd, Tehran; tel. (21) 29954855; fax (21) 29954780; e-mail g.secdept@cbi.ir; internet www.cbi.ir.

Area and Population

AREA, POPULATION AND DENSITY

Area (sq km)	1,648,195*
Population (census results)	
28 October 2006	70,495,782
24 October 2011	
Males	37,905,669
Females	37,244,000
Total	75,149,669
Density (per sq km) at 2011 census	45.6

* 636,372 sq miles.

POPULATION BY AGE AND SEX

(population at 2011 census)

	Males	Females	Total
0–14	8,979,259	8,582,519	17,561,778
15–64	26,756,132	26,488,668	53,244,800
65 and over	2,141,760	2,155,009	4,296,769
Unknown	28,518	17,804	46,322
Total	37,905,669	37,244,000	75,149,669

PROVINCES

(population at 2011 census)

Province (Ostan)	Area (sq km)*	Population	Density (per sq km)	Provincial capital
Tehran (Teheran)†	13,692	12,183,391	889.8	Tehran (Teheran)
Markazi (Central)	29,127	1,413,959	48.5	Arak
Gilan	14,042	2,480,874	176.7	Rasht
Mazandaran	23,842	3,073,943	128.9	Sari
Azarbayejan-e-Sharqi (East Azerbaijan)	45,651	3,724,620	81.6	Tabriz
Azarbayejan-e-Gharbi (West Azerbaijan)	37,411	3,080,576	82.3	Orumiyeh
Bakhtaran (Kermanshah)	25,009	1,945,227	77.8	Bakhtaran
Khuzestan	64,055	4,531,720	70.7	Ahvaz
Fars	122,608	4,596,658	37.5	Shiraz
Kerman	180,726	2,938,988	16.3	Kerman
North Khorasan	28,434	867,727	30.5	Bojnurd
South Khorasan	95,385	662,534	6.9	Birjand
Razavi Khorasan	118,851	5,994,402	50.4	Mashhad
Esfahan	107,018	4,879,312	45.6	Esfahan
Sistan and Baluchestan	181,785	2,534,327	13.9	Zahedan
Kordestan (Kurdistan)	29,137	1,493,645	51.3	Sanandaj
Hamadan	19,368	1,758,268	90.8	Hamadan
Chaharmahal and Bakhtiyari	16,328	895,263	54.8	Shahr-e-Kord
Lorestan	28,294	1,754,243	62.0	Khorramabad
Ilam	20,133	557,599	27.7	Ilam
Kohgiluyeh and Boyerahmad	15,504	658,629	42.5	Yasuj
Bushehr	22,743	1,032,949	45.4	Bushehr
Zanjan	21,773	1,015,734	46.7	Zanjan
Semnan	97,491	631,218	6.5	Semnan
Yazd	129,285	1,074,428	8.3	Yazd
Hormozgan	70,697	1,578,183	22.3	Bandar Abbas
Ardebil	17,800	1,248,488	70.1	Ardebil
Qom	11,526	1,151,672	99.9	Qom
Qazvin	15,567	1,201,565	77.2	Qazvin
Golestan	20,367	1,777,014	87.2	Gorgan
Alborz†	5,122	2,412,513	471.0	Karaj
Total	1,628,771	75,149,669	46.1	—

* Excluding inland water; densities are calculated on basis of land area only.
† In June 2010 the legislature enacted a law dividing the existing province of Tehran to create a new province, Alborz, with the city of Karaj as its capital.

PRINCIPAL TOWNS

(population at 2011 census)

Tehran (Teheran, the capital)	8,154,051	Kerman	534,441
Mashad (Meshed)	2,766,258	Hamadan	525,794
Esfahan (Isfahan)	1,756,126	Yazd	486,152
Karaj	1,614,626	Arak	484,212
Tabriz	1,494,998	Ardabil (Ardebil)	482,632
Shiraz	1,460,665	Bandar Abbas	435,751
Ahvaz	1,112,021	Eslamshahr (Islam Shahr)	389,102
Qom	1,074,036	Zanjan	386,851
Bakhtaran (Kermanshah)	851,405	Qazvin	381,598
Orumiyeh	667,499	Sanandaj	373,987
Rasht	639,951	Khorramabad	348,216
Zahedan	560,725		

BIRTHS, MARRIAGES AND DEATHS

(annual averages, UN estimates)

	1995–2000	2000–05	2005–10
Birth rate (per 1,000)	20.7	18.9	18.8
Death rate (per 1,000)	5.4	5.2	5.3

Source: UN, *World Population Prospects: The 2012 Revision*.

Births ('000): 1,154 in 2004/05; 1,239 in 2005/06; 1,254 in 2006/07; 1,287 in 2007/08; 1,300 in 2008/09; 1,349 in 2009/10; 1,364 in 2010/11; 1,382 in 2011/12.

Marriages ('000): 724 in 2004/05; 788 in 2005/06; 778 in 2006/07; 841 in 2007/08; 882 in 2008/09; 890 in 2009/10; 892 in 2010/11; 875 in 2011/12.

Deaths ('000): 369 in 2003/04; 355 in 2004/05; 364 in 2005/06; 409 in 2006/07; 413 in 2007/08; 418 in 2008/09; 394 in 2009/10; 441 in 2010/11; 341 in 2011/12.

Life expectancy (years at birth): 73.0 (males 71.2; females 74.9) in 2011 (Source: World Bank, World Development Indicators database).

ECONOMICALLY ACTIVE POPULATION
('000 persons aged 10 years and over, excl. armed forces, 2008)

	Males	Females	Total
Agriculture, hunting and forestry	3,232	1,034	4,266
Fishing	76	2	78
Mining and quarrying	123	5	128
Manufacturing	2,630	882	3,512
Electricity, gas and water supply	171	9	180
Construction	2,762	27	2,791
Wholesale and retail trade; repair of motor vehicles, motorcycles and personal and household goods	2,821	160	2,981
Hotels and restaurants	194	17	211
Transport, storage and communications	2,021	46	2,067
Financial intermediation	243	41	284
Real estate, renting and business activities	444	77	521
Public administration and defence; compulsory social security	1,216	116	1,332
Education	618	601	1,219
Health and social work	244	204	448
Other community, social and personal service activities	303	140	443
Private households with employed persons	5	14	19
Extra-territorial organizations and bodies	1	1	2
Sub-total	17,105	3,376	20,481
Activities not adequately defined	14	5	19
Total employed	17,119	3,381	20,500
Unemployed	1,715	677	2,392
Total labour force	18,834	4,058	22,892

Source: ILO.

2012/13 (labour force survey, December 2012–March 2013, '000 persons aged 10 years and over, incl. armed forces and unpaid family workers): Agriculture 3,496.1; Industry 7,118.9; Services 10,094.8; Total employed 20,709.8 (males 17,369.6, females 3,340.3); Unemployed 2,918.5 (males 2,104.8, females 813.7); Total labour force 23,628.3 (males 19,474.4, females 4,154.0).

Health and Welfare

KEY INDICATORS

Total fertility rate (children per woman, 2011)	1.6
Under-5 mortality rate (per 1,000 live births, 2011)	25
HIV/AIDS (% of persons aged 15–49, 2011)	0.2
Physicians (per 1,000 head, 2005)	0.9
Hospital beds (per 1,000 head, 2009)	1.7
Health expenditure (2010): US $ per head (PPP)	797
Health expenditure (2010): % of GDP	5.3
Health expenditure (2010): public (% of total)	41.6
Access to water (% of persons, 2011)	95
Total carbon dioxide emissions ('000 metric tons, 2009)	602,055.4
Carbon dioxide emissions per head (metric tons, 2009)	8.2
Human Development Index (2012): ranking	76
Human Development Index (2012): value	0.742

For sources and definitions, see explanatory note on p. vi.

Agriculture

PRINCIPAL CROPS
('000 metric tons)

	2009	2010	2011*
Wheat	13,484.5	13,500.0	14,361.4
Rice, paddy	2,253.4	3,012.7	3,217.3
Barley	3,446.2	3,579.6	3,919.0
Maize	1,642.7	2,144.9	2,200.0
Potatoes	4,107.6	4,274.5	4,822.1
Sugar cane	2,823.1	5,685.1	5,685.1
Sugar beet	2,015.9	4,095.6	4,095.7
Beans, dry	181.4	267.8	246.1
Chick-peas	208.9	267.8	290.2
Lentils	84.0	100.2	98.5
Almonds, with shell	140.0*	158.1	167.6
Walnuts, with shell*	463.0	475.0	485.0
Pistachios	446.6	446.6	472.1
Soybeans (Soya beans)	207.5	162.7	170.0
Cabbages and other brassicas*	360.6	391.7	508.6
Lettuce and chicory	390.8	424.2*	550.8
Tomatoes	5,887.7	5,256.1	6,824.3
Pumpkins, squash and gourds*	675.0	732.7	951.3
Cucumbers and gherkins	1,603.7	1,811.6	2,352.1
Aubergines (Eggplants)	862.2	935.8	1,215.0
Chillies and peppers, green	35.5	38.6*	50.1
Onions, dry	1,522.2	1,923.0	2,496.7
Garlic	64.0	69.5*	90.2
Watermelons	3,074.6	3,466.9	4,501.3
Cantaloupes and other melons	1,278.5	1,387.8*	1,801.8
Oranges	2,000.0*	1,502.8	1,200.9
Tangerines, mandarins, clementines and satsumas	276.1	276.1	261.5
Lemons and limes*	673.4	689.8	560.1
Apples	2,000.0*	1,662.4	1,651.8
Pears	153.4	153.4	145.1
Apricots	371.8	371.8	453.0
Sweet cherries	225.0	242.7*	241.1
Peaches and nectarines	496.1	496.1	498.3
Plums and sloes	269.1	269.1	288.2
Grapes	2,255.7	2,255.7	2,241.3
Figs	76.4	76.4	75.9
Dates	1,023.1	1,023.1	1,016.6
Tea	165.7	165.7	162.5

* FAO estimate(s)

Aggregate production ('000 metric tons, may include official, semi-official or estimated data): Total cereals 20,835.8 in 2009, 22,247.0 in 2010, 23,707.4 in 2011; Total roots and tubers 4,107.6 in 2009, 4,274.5 in 2010, 4,822.1 in 2011; Total vegetables (incl. melons) 18,421.5 in 2009, 19,995.3 in 2010, 25,961.1 in 2011; Total fruits (excl. melons) 12,325.6 in 2009, 11,561.9 in 2010, 11,233.5 in 2011.

Source: FAO.

LIVESTOCK
('000 head, FAO estimates)

	2009	2010	2011
Horses	140	140	140
Asses	1,600	1,600	1,600
Mules	175	175	175
Cattle	8,400	8,500	8,600
Buffaloes	390	375	375
Camels	154	153	152
Sheep	50,000	49,500	49,000
Goats	22,500	23,000	23,500
Chickens	873,704	880,000	900,000
Ducks	1,600	1,600	1,600
Geese and guinea fowl	1,000	1,000	1,000
Turkeys	2,000	2,000	2,000

Source: FAO.

LIVESTOCK PRODUCTS
('000 metric tons)

	2009	2010	2011*
Cattle meat	247	222	235
Buffalo meat	5	3	3
Sheep meat	114	90	93
Goat meat	137†	140*	142
Chicken meat	1,995	1,650	1,686
Turkey meat*	6	6	6
Cows' milk*	6,620	6,391	6,391
Buffaloes' milk*	150	140	140
Goats' milk*	293	306	306
Hen eggs	725	741*	741
Honey	46	47*	47
Wool: greasy*	75	60	60

* FAO estimate(s).
† Unofficial figure.

Source: FAO.

Forestry

ROUNDWOOD REMOVALS
('000 cubic metres, excl. bark)

	2009	2010	2011
Sawlogs, veneer logs and logs for sleepers	275	263	254
Pulpwood	222	199	176
Other industrial wood	296	235	230
Fuel wood	60	53	45
Total	853	750	705

Source: FAO.

SAWNWOOD PRODUCTION
('000 cubic metres, incl. railway sleepers)

	2009	2010	2011
Total (all broadleaved)	40	32	31

Source: FAO.

Fishing

('000 metric tons, live weight)

	2009	2010	2011
Capture	419.9	443.7	487.8
Caspian sprat	25.5	27.1	20.7
Indian oil sardine	21.2	20.8	35.4
Kawakawa	17.8	16.3	22.2
Skipjack tuna	44.8	22.3	17.4
Longtail tuna	49.5	64.5	80.9
Yellowfin tuna	22.6	31.5	28.8
Aquaculture	179.6	220.0	247.3
Silver carp	55.2	66.9	72.7
Rainbow trout	73.6	91.5	106.4
Total catch	599.5	663.7	735.1

Source: FAO.

Production of caviar (metric tons, year ending 20 March): 9 in 2009/10; 7 in 2010/11; 6 in 2011/12.

Mining

CRUDE PETROLEUM
('000 barrels per day, year ending 20 March)

	2009/10	2010/11	2011/12
Total production	3,557	3,536	3,619

Total production ('000 barrels per day, estimate): 3,680 in 2012 (Source: BP, *Statistical Review of World Energy*).

NATURAL GAS
(excluding reinjection gas; million cu metres, year ending 20 March)

	2005/06	2006/07	2007/08
Consumption (domestic)*	102,200	109,800	122,500
Flared	15,800	15,100	15,000
Regional uses and wastes	7,400	5,000	7,300
Gas for export	4,800	5,700	5,600
Less Net imports	5,200	6,300	6,200
Total production	125,000	129,300	144,200

* Includes gas for household, industrial, generator and refinery consumption.

Natural gas consumption (domestic): 141,200 in 2009/10; 150,800 in 2010/11; 152,700 in 2011/12.

Gas injection (year ending 20 March, million cu metres): 26,663 in 2006/07; 25,971 in 2007/08; 28,448 in 2008/09; 28,840 in 2009/10.

OTHER MINERALS
('000 metric tons, unless otherwise indicated, year ending 20 March)

	2008/09	2009/10	2010/11*
Iron ore: gross weight	34,034	35,000*	35,000
Iron ore: metal content*	16,000	16,500	16,500
Copper concentrates*†	260	265	255
Bauxite	522	681	600
Lead concentrates*†	20	35	35
Zinc concentrates†	72	80*	80
Manganese ore‡	126	132	130
Chromium concentrates§	225	45	100
Molybdenum concentrates (metric tons)*†	2,500	3,900	3,900
Silver (metric tons)*†	15	15	15
Gold (kilograms)†	2,000	2,000	2,000
Bentonite	387	350	350
Kaolin	907	1,480	1,400
Other clays*	530	550	550
Magnesite	131	130*	130
Fluorspar (Fluorite)	71	72*	70
Feldspar	635	652	650
Barite (Barytes)	361	326	330
Salt (unrefined)	2,816	3,291	3,000
Gypsum (crude)	13,000	11,914	12,000
Pumice and related materials*	1,500	1,500	1,500
Mica (metric tons)	6,797	2,860	2,900
Talc	66	96*	90
Turquoise (kilograms)*	19,000	20,000	20,000
Coal	2,181	2,300*	2,300

* Estimate(s).
† Figures refer to the metal content of ores and concentrates.
‡ Figures refer to gross weight. The estimated metal content ('000 metric tons) was: 45 in 2008/09, 46 in 2009/10, 46 in 2010/11.
§ Figures refer to gross weight. The estimated chromic oxide content ('000 metric tons) was: 110 in 2008/09, 22 in 2009/10, 50 in 2010/11.

Source: US Geological Survey.

Industry

PETROLEUM PRODUCTS
(average cu m per day, year ending 20 March)

	2007/08	2008/09	2009/10
Liquefied petroleum gas	7,723	8,071	8,362
Motor spirit (petrol)	45,080	51,496	59,515
Burning oil (for electricity)	21,680	21,347	18,519
Jet fuel	3,426	3,519	4,188
Gas-diesel (distillate fuel) oil	81,549	84,957	88,702
Residual fuel oils	73,020	77,132	76,101
Petroleum bitumen (asphalt)	976	616	698

OTHER PRODUCTS
(year ending 20 March)

	2007/08	2008/09	2009/10
Refined sugar ('000 metric tons)	1,841	1,656	1,409
Soft drinks (million bottles)	4,252	4,471	3,849
Malt liquor (million bottles)	356	597	870
Cigarettes (million)	17,387	22,436	26,898
Threads ('000 metric tons)	417	348	324
Finished fabrics (million metres)	325	338	293
Machine-made carpets ('000 sq m)	30,583	57,935	75,642
Hand-woven carpets (moquette—'000 sq m)	68,510	62,699	71,995
Paper ('000 metric tons)	455	502	466
Detergent powder ('000 metric tons)	584	505	594
Soap (metric tons)	72,616	72,791	57,750
Cement ('000 metric tons)	40,189	44,253	49,471
Washing machines ('000)	774	807	667
Radio receivers ('000)	702	637	656
Television receivers ('000)	355	298	389
Water meters ('000)	823	877	1,611
Electricity meters ('000)	689	1,294	1,757
Passenger cars and jeeps ('000)	946	1,258	1,442
Electric energy (million kWh)	203,983	214,530	221,314

Electric energy (million kWh): 232,994 in 2010/11; 240,064 in 2011/12.

Finance

CURRENCY AND EXCHANGE RATES

Monetary Units
100 dinars = 1 Iranian rial (IR).

Sterling, Dollar and Euro Equivalents (31 May 2013)
£1 sterling = 18,652.4 rials;
US $1 = 12,260.0 rials;
€1 = 15,945.4 rials;
100,000 Iranian rials = £5.36 = $8.16 = €6.27.

Average Exchange Rate (rials per US $)
2010 10,254.18
2011 10,616.31
2012 12,175.55

Note: In March 1993 the former multiple exchange rate system was unified, and since then the exchange rate of the rial has been market-determined. The foregoing information on average exchange rates refers to the base rate, applicable to receipts from exports of petroleum and gas, payments for imports of essential goods and services, debt-servicing costs and imports related to large national projects. There was also an export rate, set at a mid-point of US $1 = 3,007.5 rials in May 1995, which applied to receipts from non-petroleum exports and to all other official current account transactions not effected at the base rate. In addition, a market rate was determined by transactions on the Tehran Stock Exchange: at 31 January 2002 it was US $1 = 7,924 rials. The weighted average of all exchange rates (rials per US $, year ending 20 December) was: 3,206 in 1997/98; 4,172 in 1998/99; 5,731 in 1999/2000. A new unified exchange rate, based on the market rate, took effect from 21 March 2002.

BUDGET
(consolidated accounts of central government and Oil Stabilization Fund—OSF, '000 million rials, year ending 20 March)

Revenue	2007/08	2008/09*	2009/10†
Oil and gas revenue	578,708	569,951	436,159
Budget revenue	444,278	559,589	498,071
Transfers from OSF	209,098	184,235	223,099
Revenues transferred to OSF	134,430	10,362	–61,912
Non-oil budgetary revenue	237,893	283,918	354,315
Tax revenue	162,579	203,042	240,454
Taxes on income, profits and capital gains	97,097	130,453	153,994
Domestic taxes on goods and services	16,663	15,900	29,771
Taxes on international trade and transactions	48,819	56,689	56,689
Non-tax revenue	75,314	80,876	113,861
Non-oil OSF revenues	4,551	6,038	6,223
Total	821,152	859,906	796,697

Expenditure	2007/08	2008/09*	2009/10†
Central government expenditures	710,022	841,093	884,798
Current expenditure	562,306	595,254	676,682
Wages and salaries	151,583	211,000	229,000
Interest payments	7,371	5,982	5,982
Subsidies	62,862	61,000	68,000
Goods and services	39,119	55,000	71,600
Grants	13,823	50,800	28,700
Social benefits	64,492	139,605	181,000
Gasoline imports	33,820	60,867	34,300
Other expenses	189,236	11,000	58,100
Capital expenditure	147,716	245,839	208,116
OSF expenditures	40,289	19,148	—
Total	750,311	860,240	884,798

* Estimates.
† Projections.

Source: IMF, *Islamic Republic of Iran: 2009 Article IV Consultation—Staff Report; Staff Supplement; Public Information Notice on the Executive Board Discussion; and Statement by the Executive Director for Iran* (March 2010).

2010/11 ('000 million rials, estimates): *Revenue:* Tax revenue 272,382 (Taxes on income, profits and capital gains 145,470; Domestic taxes on goods and services 37,894; Taxes on international trade and transactions 77,886); Other revenue 714,731; Total 987,113. *Expenditure:* Current expenditure 710,957 (Compensation of employees 204,463; Goods and services 79,147; Subsidies 118,720; Social benefits 191,272); Net acquisition of non-financial assets 205,107; Total 916,064 (Source: IMF—see below).

2011/12 ('000 million rials, projections): *Revenue:* Tax revenue 344,867 (Taxes on income, profits and capital gains 180,355; Domestic taxes on goods and services 59,072; Taxes on international trade and transactions 91,639); Other revenue 1,115,309; Total 1,460,176. *Expenditure:* Current expenditure 1,032,775 (Compensation of employees 278,355; Goods and services 107,750; Subsidies 166,600; Social benefits 260,397); Net acquisition of non-financial assets 278,600; Total 1,311,375 (Source: *Islamic Republic of Iran: 2011 Article IV Consultation—Staff Report; Public Information Notice on the Executive Board Discussion; and Statement by the Executive Director for Iran*,—August 2011).

INTERNATIONAL RESERVES
(US $ million at 31 December)*

	1993	1994	1995
Gold (national valuation)	229.1	242.2	251.9
IMF special drawing rights	144.0	142.9	133.6
Total	373.1	385.1	385.5

* Excluding reserves of foreign exchange, for which no figures have been available since 1982 (when the value of reserves was US $5,287m.).

IMF special drawing rights (US $ million at 31 December): 2,365 in 2010; 2,359 in 2011; 2,368 in 2012.

Source: IMF, *International Financial Statistics*.

MONEY SUPPLY

('000 million rials at 20 December)

	2008	2009	2010
Currency outside banks	122,603	147,878	210,289
Non-financial public enterprises' deposits at Central Bank	16,978	15,496	18,353
Demand deposits at commercial banks	300,451	317,415	150,432
Total money	440,031	480,790	379,073

Source: IMF, *International Financial Statistics*.

COST OF LIVING

(Consumer Price Index in urban areas, year ending 20 March; base: 2004/05 = 100)

	2009/10	2010/11	2011/12
Food and beverages	218.6	254.1	320.0
Clothing	179.7	200.9	245.4
Housing, water, electricity, gas, and other fuels	220.2	236.2	279.3
All items (incl. others)	203.0	228.2	277.2

NATIONAL ACCOUNTS

('000 million rials at current prices, year ending 20 March, preliminary)

Expenditure on the Gross Domestic Product

	2008/09	2009/10	2010/11
Final consumption expenditure	1,812,176	1,985,948	2,248,482
Private	1,420,657	1,540,628	1,767,132
Public	391,519	445,320	481,350
Changes in inventories	313,386	475,472	639,312
Gross fixed capital formation	957,271	949,354	1,146,917
Total domestic expenditure	3,082,833	3,410,774	4,034,711
Exports of goods and services	1,015,562	923,411	1,194,391
Less Imports of goods and services	741,949	756,788	896,016
GDP at market prices	3,356,447	3,577,397	4,333,087
GDP at constant 1997/98 prices	492,520	511,975	542,174

Gross Domestic Product by Economic Activity

	2008/09	2009/10	2010/11
Hydrocarbon GDP	850,642	729,282	977,799
Non-hydrocarbon GDP	2,528,082	2,833,007	3,326,466
Agriculture	302,210	365,976	436,975
Industry	632,263	653,751	837,475
Mining	27,919	26,696	31,903
Manufacturing	345,806	374,950	509,150
Construction	215,877	210,176	244,337
Electricity, gas and water	42,660	41,930	52,085
Services	1,691,955	1,919,083	2,200,733
Transport and communication	317,512	350,949	389,426
Banking and insurance	102,718	120,059	167,403
Trade, restaurants and hotels	364,661	411,353	503,048
Ownership and dwellings	506,828	558,834	607,934
Public services	312,611	380,926	411,745
Private services	87,624	96,962	121,177
Less Imputed bank service charge	98,344	105,803	148,717
GDP at factor prices	3,378,724	3,562,289	4,304,264
Net indirect taxes	−22,277	15,108	28,823
GDP at market prices	3,356,447	3,577,397	4,333,087

BALANCE OF PAYMENTS

(US $ million, year ending 20 March)

	2009/10	2010/11	2011/12
Exports of goods f.o.b.	88,326	112,788	144,874
Petroleum and gas	69,957	90,191	118,232
Non-petroleum and gas exports	18,369	22,596	26,642
Imports of goods f.o.b.	−69,247	−75,458	−77,805
Trade balance	19,079	37,330	67,069
Exports of services	8,074	8,853	8,621
Imports of services	−17,656	−18,893	−17,053
Balance on goods and services	9,497	27,263	58,637
Income received	1,791	1,952	2,171
Income paid	−1,912	−1,873	−1,849
Balance on goods, services and income	9,375	27,369	58,960
Transfers (net)	101	185	423
Current balance	9,477	27,554	59,383
Capital account (net)	−744	−986	−684
Financial account (net)	−5,716	−23,310	−37,291
Overall balance	3,016	3,259	21,409

External Trade

PRINCIPAL COMMODITIES

(US $ million, year ending 20 March)

Imports c.i.f. (distribution by SITC)	2009/10	2010/11	2011/12
Food and live animals	6,409	6,790	7,388
Cereals and cereal preparations	3,517	2,278	2,998
Crude materials (inedible) except fuels	2,055	2,156	2,300
Animal and vegetable oils and fats	989	1,444	1,625
Vegetable oils and fats	983	1,440	1,620
Chemicals and related products	6,029	7,011	7,441
Chemical elements and compounds	1,248	1,434	1,440
Plastic, cellulose and artificial resins	1,835	2,190	2,536
Basic manufactures	12,590	14,231	13,442
Iron and steel	8,166	9,235	8,357
Machinery and transport equipment	18,060	20,713	22,136
Non-electric machinery	9,552	10,692	10,291
Electrical machinery, apparatus, etc.	3,973	4,400	5,456
Transport equipment	4,535	5,620	6,388
Miscellaneous manufactured articles	1,867	1,788	1,809
Total (incl. others)	55,287	64,450	61,808

Exports f.o.b.*	2009/10	2010/11	2011/12
Agricultural and traditional goods	4,133	5,056	5,181
Carpets	495	557	559
Fruits (fresh and dried)	1,779	2,194	2,204
Industrial manufactures	17,017	20,194	27,590
Oil and gas products	3,925	4,892	8,485
Iron and steel	1,041	1,015	1,522
Total (incl. others)	21,891	26,551	33,819

* Excluding exports of crude petroleum and associated gas (US $ million): 69,957 in 2009/10; 90,191 in 2010/11; 118,232 in 2011/12 (preliminary).

Note: Imports include registration fee, but exclude defence-related imports and imports of refined petroleum products.

PRINCIPAL TRADING PARTNERS
(US $ million, year ending 20 March)

Imports c.i.f.	2007/08	2008/09	2009/10
Austria	1,071	1,131	736
Belgium	536	994	569
Brazil	563	570	614
Canada	149	672	312
China, People's Republic	4,292	4,945	4,846
France	1,894	1,992	1,688
Germany	5,328	5,369	4,688
India	1,457	1,819	1,793
Italy	1,902	1,979	1,898
Japan	1,325	1,344	1,423
Korea, Republic	2,456	3,105	3,468
Netherlands	537	535	1,092
Russia	863	1,405	1,016
Saudi Arabia	500	n.a.	n.a.
Singapore	575	882	1,015
Sweden	451	716	600
Switzerland	2,779	3,542	2,137
Taiwan	519	464	467
Turkey	1,246	1,508	2,025
United Arab Emirates	11,509	13,491	16,187
United Kingdom	2,002	2,039	1,654
Total (incl. others)	48,439	56,042	55,287

Exports f.o.b.	2007/08	2008/09	2009/10
Afghanistan	543	633	1,047
Azerbaijan	350	369	374
Belgium	223	406	509
China, People's Republic	1,244	2,051	3,126
Ecuador	20	224	n.a.
Germany	374	319	349
Hong Kong	292	150	200
India	837	1,159	1,264
Indonesia	206	321	368
Iraq	1,842	2,762	4,560
Italy	522	325	436
Japan	927	589	360
Korea, Republic	552	821	543
Kuwait	319	133	138
Malaysia	31	186	97
Netherlands	234	346	298
Pakistan	274	296	435
Philippines	47	108	222
Russia	367	358	333
Saudi Arabia	310	388	177
Spain	234	175	169
Syria	330	316	379
Taiwan	205	376	184
Tajikistan	171	187	163
Turkey	566	530	593
Turkmenistan	189	249	358
United Arab Emirates	2,166	2,322	2,934
Total (incl. others)	15,312	18,334	21,891

Note: Exports exclude crude petroleum and associated gas.

Transport

RAILWAYS
(traffic, year ending 20 March)

	2009/10	2010/11	2011/12
Passengers carried ('000)	27,710	28,814	28,560
Passenger-km (million)	16,814	17,611	17,877
Freight carried ('000 metric tons)	32,817	33,458	33,104
Freight ton-km (million)	20,247	21,779	21,008

ROAD TRAFFIC
(registered motor vehicles, year ending 20 March)

	2009/10	2010/11	2011/12
Passenger cars*	1,170,581	1,104,304	1,378,860
Pick-ups and light trucks	202,200	189,302	200,035
Motorcycles	591,318	835,711	813,386
Total (incl. others)	2,005,475	2,179,517	2,482,718

* Including ambulances.

SHIPPING

Flag Registered Fleet
(at 31 December)

	2010	2011	2012
Number of vessels	520	533	619
Total displacement ('000 grt)	1,053.8	787.6	2,394.7

Source: Lloyd's List Intelligence (www.lloydslistintelligence.com).

International Sea-borne Freight Traffic
(year ending 20 March, '000 metric tons)*

	2009/10	2010/11	2011/12
Goods loaded	42,230	54,910	57,188
Crude petroleum and petroleum products	14,376	18,014	21,029
Goods unloaded	77,744	72,102	65,471
Petroleum products	29,997	24,045	20,605

* Cargo loaded onto and from vessels with a capacity of 1,000 metric tons or greater only.

CIVIL AVIATION
(year ending 20 March)

	2009/10	2010/11	2011/12
Passengers ('000):			
domestic flights	14,440	16,104	16,481
international arrivals	3,714	3,847	4,379
international departures	3,704	4,053	4,404
Freight (excl. mail, metric tons):			
domestic flights	37,688	47,158	56,413
international arrivals	53,506	65,274	61,221
international departures	29,034	30,762	24,806
Mail (metric tons):			
domestic flights	5,211	5,785	3,843
international arrivals	8,247	8,708	7,842
international departures	2,724	3,038	4,180

Tourism

FOREIGN TOURIST ARRIVALS
(year ending 20 March)

Country of nationality	1997/98	1998/99	1999/2000
Afghanistan	69,793	125,189	146,322
Azerbaijan	302,574	383,123	447,797
Kuwait	19,642	26,472	30,941
Pakistan	100,427	115,431	134,916
Russia	16,466*	10,191*	11,911
Saudi Arabia	17,406	21,093	24,654
Turkey	93,105	160,959	188,130
Total (incl. others)	764,092	1,007,597	1,320,905

* Including Belarus.

Total arrivals (year ending 20 March): 2,272,575 in 2009/10; 3,121,283 in 2010/11; 3,294,126 in 2011/12.

Tourism receipts (US $ million, excl. passenger transport): 2,012 in 2009; 2,707 in 2010 (Source: World Tourism Organization).

Communications Media

	2010	2011	2012
Telephones ('000 main lines in use)	25,815.2	27,766.9	28,758.5
Mobile cellular telephones ('000 subscribers)	54,051.8	56,043.0	58,157.5
Internet subscribers ('000)	n.a.	5,240.2	n.a.
Broadband subscribers ('000)	962.2	1,772.9	3,076.2
Book production*:			
titles	64,606	61,724	n.a.
copies ('000)	198,593	173,592	n.a.

* Twelve months beginning 21 March of year stated.

Newspapers and periodicals (number of titles, year ending 20 March 2006): Daily 183; Other 4,528.

Personal computers: 7,420,791 (105.9 per 1,000 persons) in 2006.

Source: partly International Telecommunication Union.

Education

(2011/12)

	Institutions	Teachers	Students ('000) Males	Females	Total
Special	1,750	11,421	50.5	31.9	82.3
Pre-primary	16,113	1,898	232.6	242.8	475.4
Primary	57,619	235,193	2,932.3	2,769.2	5,701.5
Lower secondary:					
mainstream	25,451	165,764	1,693.3	1535.1	3,228.4
adult	787		12.1	13.9	26.0
Upper secondary:					
mainstream	14,697	189,803	1,567.7	1,389.6	2,957.3
adult	4,034		242.6	153.6	396.2
Pre-university:					
mainstream	8,593	n.a.	177.3	263.3	440.6
adult	1,068		24.1	19.3	43.4
Teacher training	98	n.a.	16.6	18.9	35.5
Islamic Azad University	n.a.	82,113	1,004.6	626.4	1,631.0
Other higher	n.a.	171,271	1,252.0	1,576.3	2,828.3

Pupil-teacher ratio (primary education, UNESCO estimate): 20.5 in 2008/09 (Source: UNESCO Institute for Statistics).

Adult literacy rate (UNESCO estimates): 85.0% (males 89.3%; females 80.7%) in 2008 (Source: UNESCO Institute for Statistics).

Directory

The Constitution

A draft constitution for the Islamic Republic of Iran was published on 18 June 1979. It was submitted to an Assembly of Experts, elected by popular vote on 3 August, to debate the various clauses and to propose amendments. The amended Constitution was approved by a referendum on 2–3 December 1979. A further 45 amendments to the Constitution were approved by a referendum on 28 July 1989.

The Constitution states that the form of government of Iran is that of an Islamic Republic, and that the spirituality and ethics of Islam are to be the basis for political, social and economic relations. Persians, Turks, Kurds, Arabs, Balochis, Turkomans and others will enjoy completely equal rights.

The Constitution provides for a President to act as Chief Executive. The President is elected by universal adult suffrage for a term of four years. Legislative power is held by the Majlis (Islamic Consultative Assembly), with 290 members (effective from the 2000 election) who are similarly elected for a four-year term. Provision is made for the representation of Zoroastrians, Jews and Christians.

All legislation passed by the Islamic Consultative Assembly must be sent to the Council for the Protection of the Constitution (Article 94), which will ensure that it is in accordance with the Constitution and Islamic legislation. The Council for the Protection of the Constitution consists of six religious lawyers appointed by the Wali Faqih and six lawyers appointed by the High Council of the Judiciary and approved by the Islamic Consultative Assembly. Articles 19–42 deal with the basic rights of individuals, and provide for equality of men and women before the law and for equal human, political, economic, social and cultural rights for both sexes.

The press is free, except in matters that are contrary to public morality or insult religious belief. The formation of religious, political and professional parties, associations and societies is free, provided they do not negate the principles of independence, freedom, sovereignty and national unity, or the basis of Islam.

The Constitution provides for a Wali Faqih (religious leader) who, in the absence of the Imam Mehdi (the hidden Twelfth Imam), carries the burden of leadership. The amendments to the Constitution that were approved in July 1989 increased the powers of the Presidency by abolishing the post of Prime Minister, formerly the Chief Executive of the Government.

The Government

SUPREME RELIGIOUS LEADER

Wali Faqih: Ayatollah SAYED ALI KHAMENEI.

HEAD OF STATE

President: HASSAN ROUHANI (assumed office 3 August 2013).

First Vice-President: ESHAQ JAHANGIRI.

Executive Vice-President: MORTEZA BANK.

Vice-President in charge of Legal Affairs: ELHAM AMINZADEH.

Vice-President in charge of Parliamentary Affairs: TEIMOUR ALI ASGARI.

Vice-President for Supervision and Strategic Affairs: MUHAMMAD BAGHER NOBAKHT.

Vice-President and Head of the Cultural Heritage, Handicrafts and Tourism Organization: MUHAMMAD-ALI NAJAFI.

Vice-President and Head of the Atomic Energy Organization: ALI AKBAR SALEHI.

Vice-President for Political and Security Affairs: ALI YOUNESI.

Vice-President and Head of the Organization for the Protection of the Environment: MASSOUMEH EBTEKAR.

The Head of Presidential Office and the Cabinet Secretary also have full ministerial status.

COUNCIL OF MINISTERS
(September 2013)

Minister of Education: ALI ASGHAR FANI (acting).

Minister of Communications and Information Technology: MAHMOUD VAEZI.

Minister of Intelligence: MAHMOUD ALAVI.

Minister of Economic Affairs and Finance: ALI TAYEBNIA.

Minister of Foreign Affairs: MUHAMMAD JAVAD ZARIF.

Minister of Health and Medical Education: HASSAN QAZIZADEH HASHEMI.

Minister of Agricultural Jihad: MAHMOUD HOJJATI.

Minister of Justice: MOSTAFA POUR-MUHAMMADI.

Minister of Defence and Armed Forces Logistics: HOSSEIN DEHQAN.

Minister of Roads and Urban Development: ABBAS AHMAD AKHOUNDI.

Minister of Science, Research and Technology: JAFAR TOFIGHI DARIAN (acting).

Minister of Culture and Islamic Guidance: ALI JANNATI.

Minister of Labour and Social Affairs: ALI RABEI.

Minister of the Interior: ABDOLREZA RAHMANI FAZLI.

Minister of Petroleum: BIJAN NAMDAR ZANGANEH.

Minister of Energy: HAMID CHITCHIAN.

Minister of Sport and Youth Affairs: REZA SALEHI AMIRI (acting).

Minister of Industries, Mines and Trade: MUHAMMAD REZA NEMATZADEH.

MINISTRIES

Office of the President: POB 1423-13185, Pasteur Ave, Tehran 13168-43311; tel. (21) 64451; e-mail webmaster@president.ir; internet www.president.ir.

Ministry of Agricultural Jihad: 20 Malaei Ave, Vali-e-Asr Sq., Tehran; tel. (21) 81363301; fax (21) 81363345; e-mail pr@maj.ir; internet www.maj.ir.

Ministry of Communications and Information Technology: POB 15875-4415, Shariati St, Tehran 16314; tel. (21) 88114315; fax (21) 88467210; e-mail khajeh@ict.gov.ir; internet www.ict.gov.ir.

Ministry of Culture and Islamic Guidance: POB 5158, Baharestan Sq., Tehran 11365; tel. (21) 38512583; fax (21) 33117535; e-mail info@ershad.gov.ir; internet www.ershad.gov.ir.

Ministry of Defence and Armed Forces Logistics: Shahid Yousuf Kaboli St, Sayed Khandan Area, Tehran; tel. (21) 26126988; e-mail info@mod.ir; internet www.mod.ir.

Ministry of Economic Affairs and Finance: Sour Esrafil Ave, Nasser Khosrou St, Tehran 11149-43661; tel. (21) 22553401; fax (21) 22581933; e-mail info@mefa.gov.ir; internet mefa.gov.ir.

Ministry of Education: Si-e-Tir St, Imam Khomeini Sq., Tehran; tel. (21) 32421; fax (21) 675503; e-mail negah@medu.ir; internet www.medu.ir.

Ministry of Energy: POB 19968-32611, Niayesh Highway, Vali-e-Asr Ave, Tehran; tel. (21) 81606757; fax (21) 81606552; e-mail info@moe.org.ir; internet www.moe.org.ir.

Ministry of Foreign Affairs: Imam Khomeini Sq., Tehran; tel. (21) 61151; fax (21) 66743149; e-mail matbuat@mfa.gov.ir; internet www.mfa.gov.ir.

Ministry of Health and Medical Education: POB 310, Jomhouri Islami Ave, Hafez Crossing, Tehran 11344; tel. (21) 88363560; fax (21) 88364111; e-mail webmaster@mohme.gov.ir; internet www.mohme.gov.ir.

Ministry of Industries, Mines and Trade: Shahid Kalantari, Ostad Negatollahi St, Ferdosi Sq., Tehran; tel. (21) 88906563; fax (21) 88903650; e-mail intl@mim.gov.ir; internet www.mim.gov.ir.

Ministry of Intelligence: POB 16765-1947, Second Negarestan St, Pasdaran Ave, Tehran; tel. (21) 233031; fax (21) 23305.

Ministry of the Interior: Jahad Sq., Fatemi St, Tehran; tel. (21) 84866031; fax (21) 88964678; e-mail ravabetomomi@moi.gov.ir; internet www.moi.ir.

Ministry of Justice: Panzdah-e-Khordad Sq., Tehran 14158-55139; tel. (21) 88383201; fax (21) 3904986; e-mail info@justice.ir; internet www.justice.ir.

Ministry of Labour and Social Affairs: Azadi St, Tehran; tel. (21) 88977415; fax (21) 88951536; e-mail support@irimlsa.ir; internet www.irimlsa.ir.

Ministry of Petroleum: Hafez Crossing, Taleghani Ave, Tehran 15936-57919; tel. (21) 66152606; fax (21) 66154977; e-mail public-relations@nioc.ir; internet www.mop.ir.

Ministry of Roads and Urban Development: Dadman Tower, Africa Blvd, Tehran; tel. (21) 88646130; internet www.mrud.ir.

Ministry of Science, Research and Technology: POB 15875-4375, Central Bldg, Ostad Nejatollahi Ave, Tehran; tel. (21) 82231000; fax (21) 88827234; e-mail zahedi@msrt.ir; internet www.msrt.ir.

Ministry of Sport and Youth Affairs: Tehran.

President and Legislature

PRESIDENT

Presidential Election, 14 June 2013

Candidates	Votes	%
Hassan Rouhani	18,613,329	50.71
Muhammad Baqir Qalibaf	6,077,292	16.56
Saeed Jalili	4,168,946	11.36
Mohsen Rezai	3,884,412	10.58
Ali Akbar Velayati	2,268,753	6.18
Muhammad Gharazi	446,015	1.22
Total	36,704,156*	100.00

* Including 1,245,409 invalid votes (3.39% of total votes cast).

Majlis-e-Shura-e Islami—Islamic Consultative Assembly
Baharestan Sq., Tehran; tel. (21) 33440236; fax (21) 33440309; internet www.parliran.ir.

Elections to the eighth Majlis took place in early 2008. Prior to the elections the Council of Guardians and the Ministry of the Interior barred at least 1,700 of the 7,168 registered candidates from standing, including a number of current Majlis deputies. The majority of the barred candidates were recognized as being 'reformists'. At the first round of voting, held on 14 March, 208 deputies received a sufficient number of votes to be elected directly to the Majlis; at the second round, on 25 April, a further 79 deputies were elected. Three seats remained vacant following both rounds, after election officials had annulled the results for unspecified reasons; by-elections for these seats were to be held at a later date. According to official reports, 'conservatives' controlled the eighth Majlis, with an estimated 198–200 seats; 'reformists' secured around 46–50 seats, and some 40–43 seats were held by 'independents'. A reported 29 of the 30 seats in Tehran were filled by 'conservatives', with only one seat going to a 'reformist' candidate. However, despite the 'conservatives' having consolidated their control of the Majlis, some of the new deputies were reported to be critical of President Mahmoud Ahmadinejad's policies. On 2 March 2012 the first round of elections to the ninth Majlis took place. Of the 290 seats, 'conservatives' secured 143 seats, while 'reformists' took 59 seats. Candidates representing religious minorities held 14 seats and nine seats went to 'independents'. A second round of voting for the 65 remaining seats was held on 4 May, at which 'conservatives' secured 41 seats, 'reformists' secured 13 seats and 11 seats went to 'independents'.

Speaker: ALI ARDESHIR LARIJANI.

First Deputy Speaker: MUHAMMAD REZA BAHONAR.

Second Deputy Speaker: MASOUD MIR KAZEMI.

Shura-ye Ali-ye Amniyyat-e Melli—Supreme National Security Council

Formed in July 1989 (in place of the Supreme Defence Council) to co-ordinate defence and national security policies, the political programme and intelligence reports, and social, cultural and economic activities related to defence and security. The Council is chaired by the President and includes a representative of the Wali Faqih, the Minister of the Interior, the Speaker of the Majlis, the Head of the Judiciary, the Chief of the Supreme Command Council of the Armed Forces, the Minister of Foreign Affairs, the Head of the Management and Planning Organization, and the Minister of Intelligence and Security.

Secretary: SAEED JALILI.

Majlis-e Khobregan—Assembly of Experts
Tehran; e-mail info@majleskhobregan.com; internet www.majlesekhobregan.ir.

Elections were held on 10 December 1982 to appoint an Assembly of Experts which was to choose an eventual successor to the Wali Faqih (then Ayatollah Khomeini) after his death. The Constitution provides for a three- or five-man body to assume the leadership of the country if there is no recognized successor on the death of the Wali Faqih. The Council comprises 86 clerics, who are elected to serve an eight-year term. Elections to a fourth term of the Council were held on 15 December 2006.

Speaker: Ayatollah MUHAMMAD REZA MAHDAVI KANI.

First Deputy Speaker: Ayatollah SAYED MAHMOUD HASHEMI SHAHROUDI.

Second Deputy Speaker: Ayatollah MUHAMMAD YAZDI.

Secretaries: Ayatollah AHMAD KHATAMI, Ayatollah QORBANALI DORRI NAJAFABADI.

Shura-e-Nigahban—Council of Guardians

The Council of Guardians, composed of six qualified Muslim jurists appointed by Ayatollah Khomeini and six lay Muslim lawyers, appointed by the Majlis from among candidates nominated by the Head of the Judiciary, was established in 1980 to supervise elections and to examine legislation adopted by the Majlis, ensuring that it accords with the Constitution and with Islamic precepts.

Chairman: Ayatollah AHMAD JANNATI.

Shura-ye Tashkhis-e Maslahat-e Nezam—Council to Determine the Expediency of the Islamic Order

Formed in February 1988, by order of Ayatollah Khomeini, to arbitrate on legal and theological questions in legislation approved by the Majlis, in the event of a dispute between the latter and the supervisory Council of Guardians. Its permanent members, defined in March 1997, are Heads of the Legislative, Judiciary and Executive Powers, the jurist members of the Council of Guardians, and the Minister or head of organization concerned with the pertinent arbitration. In October 2005 the powers of the Expediency Council were extended, allowing it to supervise all branches of government. Four new members were appointed to the Expediency Council in February 2007, when Rafsanjani was reappointed as Chairman; the term of the Council is five years.

Chairman: Hojatoleslam ALI AKBAR HASHEMI RAFSANJANI.

Secretary: Maj.-Gen. MOHSEN REZAI.

Hey'at-e Peygiri-ye Qanun Asasi Va Nezarat Bar An—Committee for Ensuring and Supervising the Implementation of the Constitution

Formed by former President Khatami in November 1997; members are appointed for a four-year term. Two new members were appointed to the Committee in April 2002.

Members: Dr GUDARZ EFTEKHAR-JAHROMI, MUHAMMAD ISMAÏL SHOUSHTARI, HASHEM HASHEMZADEH HERISI, Dr HOSSEIN MEHRPUR, Dr MUHAMMAD HOSSEIN HASHEMI.

Political Organizations

Numerous political organizations were registered in the late 1990s, following the election of former President Khatami, and have tended to be regarded as either 'conservative' or 'reformist', the principal factions in the legislature. There are also a small number of centrist political parties. Under the Iranian electoral system, parties do not field candidates *per se* at elections, but instead back lists of candidates, who are allowed to be members of more than one party. In the mid-2000s there were estimated to be more than 100 registered political organizations, some of which are listed below:

Democratic Coalition of Reformists: Tehran; f. 2010; Sec.-Gen. MASOUMEH EBTEKAR.

Eslahteleban-e Motedel (Moderate Reformists): Tehran; Leader ALI MOTAHARI.

Jebhe-ye Besiret ve Bidari-ye Eslami (Insight and Islamic Awakening Front): Tehran; Leader SHAHABEDDIN SADRI.

Jebhe-ye Istadegi (Resistance Front): Tehran.

Jebhe-ye Mottehed-e Osulgeraian (United Front of Principalists): Tehran; officially formed in 2008; reformed in 2012; Leader MUHAMMAD REZA MAHDAVI KANI.

Jebhe-ye Paydari-ye Enghelab-e Eslami (Front of Islamic Revolution Stability): Tehran; internet www.jebhepaydari.ir; f. 2011; Leader GHOLAM-HUSSEIN ELHAM; Sec.-Gen. MORTEZA AGHA-TEHRANI.

Jebhe-ye Seda-ye Mellet (People's Voice Front): Tehran; f. 2011; Leader MOHSEN REZAI; Sec.-Gen. ALI MOTAHARI.

Jebhe-ye Touhid ve Edalet (Monotheism and Justice Front): Tehran; f. 2012; Leader MANOUCHEHR MOTTAKI; Sec.-Gen. ESFANDIAR RAHIM MASHAI.

Labour Coalition (LC): Tehran; f. 2000; Leader HOSSEIN KAMALI; Sec.-Gen. SOHEILA JOLODARZADEH.

Most of the following are either registered political parties that have boycotted elections to the Majlis-e-Shura-e Islami (Islamic Consultative Assembly) in the 2000s, or are unregistered organizations or guerrilla groups:

Ansar-e Hezbollah (Helpers of the Party of God): f. 1995; militant, ultra-conservative youth movement; pledges allegiance to the Wali Faqih (supreme religious leader).

Daftar-e Tahkim-e Vahdat (Office for Strengthening Unity): Tehran; f. 1979; org. of Islamist university students who supported Khatami in the presidential election of 1997 and reformist candidates in the Majlis elections of 2000; Spokesman ALI NIKUNESBATI.

Democratic Party of Iranian Kurdistan: 17 ave d'Italie, Paris 75013, France; tel. 1-45-85-64-31; fax 1-45-85-20-93; e-mail pdkiran@club-internet.fr; internet www.pdki.org; f. 1945; seeks a federal system of govt in Iran, in order to secure the national rights of the Kurdish people; consultative mem. of the Socialist International; 95,000 mems; Sec.-Gen. MUSTAFA HIJRI.

Fedayin-e-Khalq (Organization of the Iranian People's Fedayeen—Majority): Postfach 260268, 50515 Köln, Germany; e-mail info@fadai.org; internet www.fadai.org; f. 1971; Marxist; Leader BEHROUZ KHALIQ.

Fraksion-e Hezbollah: f. 1996 by deputies in the Majlis who had contested the 1996 legislative elections as a loose coalition known as the Society of Combatant Clergy; Leader ALI AKBAR HOSSAINI.

Free Life Party of Kurdistan (Parti Jiyani Azadi Kurdistan—PJAK): f. 2004; militant org. that operates in mountainous areas of Iran and northern Iraq; apparently has close links with the Kurdistan Workers' Party (PKK—Partiya Karkeren Kurdistan) of Turkey; seeks a federal, secular system of govt in Iran, in order to secure the national rights of the Kurdish people; Sec.-Gen. RAHMAN HAJI AHMADI.

Hezb-e Etemad-e Melli (National Confidence Party—NCP): Tehran; tel. (21) 88373305; fax (21) 88373306; e-mail info@etemademelli.ir; f. 2005 by Mahdi Karrubi, fmrly of the Militant Clergy Association, shortly after his defeat in the presidential election of June; reformist, centrist; Sec.-Gen. MAHDI KARRUBI.

Hezb-e Hambastegi-ye Iran-e Islami (Islamic Iran Solidarity Party): f. 1998; reformist; Sec.-Gen. EBRAHIM ASGHARZADEH.

Hezb-e-Komunist Iran (Communist Party of Iran): POB 70445, 107 25 Stockholm, Sweden; e-mail cpi@cpiran.org; internet www.cpiran.org; f. 1979 by dissident mems of Tudeh Party; Sec.-Gen. 'AZARYUN'.

Iran National Front (Jebhe Melli Iran): US Section, POB 136, Audubon Station, New York, NY 10032, USA; e-mail contact@jebhemelli.net; internet www.jebhemelli.net; f. late 1940s by the late Dr Muhammad Mussadeq; secular, pro-democracy opposition group, which also seeks to further religious freedom within Iran; Leader ADIB BOROUMAND.

Jame'e-ye Eslaami-e Mohandesin (Islamic Society of Engineers): f. 1988; conservative; mems incl. fmr President Mahmoud Ahmadinejad; Sec.-Gen. MUHAMMAD REZA BAHONAR.

Jebbeh-ye Mosharekat-e Iran-e Islami (Islamic Iran Participation Front): e-mail mail.emrooz@gmail.com; f. 1998; reformist, leftist; reportedly proscribed by the Iranian authorities in March 2010; Sec.-Gen. MOHSEN MIRDAMADI.

Komala Party of Iranian Kurdistan: e-mail secretariat@komala.org; internet www.komala.org; f. 1969; Kurdish wing of the Communist Party of Iran; Marxist-Leninist; Sec.-Gen. ABDULLAH MOHTADI.

Marze Por Gohar (Glorious Frontiers Party): 1351 Westwood Blvd, Suite 111, Los Angeles, CA 90024, USA; tel. (310) 473-4763; fax (310) 477-8484; e-mail info@marzeporgohar.org; internet www.marzeporgohar.org; f. 1998 in Tehran; nationalist party advocating a secular republic in Iran; Chair. ROOZBEH FARAHANIPOUR.

Mujahidin-e-Khalq (Holy Warriors of the People): e-mail mojahed@mojahedin.org; internet www.mojahedin.org; Marxist-Islamist guerrilla group opposed to clerical regime; since June 1987 comprising the National Liberation Army; mem. of the National Council of Resistance of Iran; based in Paris, France 1981–86 and in Baghdad, Iraq, 1986–2003; Leaders MARYAM RAJAVI, MASSOUD RAJAVI.

National Democratic Front: f. March 1979; Leader HEDAYATOLLAH MATINE-DAFTARI (based in Paris, France, Jan. 1982–).

Nehzat-e Azadi-ye Iran (Liberation Movement of Iran): e-mail nehzateazadi1340@gmail.com; f. 1961; emphasis on basic human rights as defined by Islam; Sec.-Gen. Dr IBRAHIM YAZDI.

Pan-Iranist Party: POB 31535-1679, Karaj; internet www.paniranist.org; calls for a Greater Persia; Leader REZA KERMANI.

Sazeman-e Mujahidin-e Enqelab-e Islami (Organization of the Mujahidin of the Islamic Revolution): reformist; Sec.-Gen. MUHAMMAD SALAMATI.

Sazmane Peykar dar Rahe Azadieh Tabaqe Kargar (Organization Struggling for the Freedom of the Working Class): Marxist-Leninist.

Tudeh Party of Iran (Party of the Masses): POB 100644, 10566 Berlin, Germany; tel. (30) 3241627; e-mail mardom@tudehpartyiran.org; internet www.tudehpartyiran.org; f. 1941; declared illegal 1949; came into open 1979; banned again April 1983; First Sec., Cen. Cttee ALI KHAVARI.

The National Council of Resistance (NCR) was formed in Paris, France, in October 1981 by former President Abolhasan Bani-Sadr and Massoud Rajavi, the leader of the Mujahidin-e-Khalq in Iran. In 1984 the Council comprised 15 opposition groups, operating either clandestinely in Iran or from exile abroad. Bani-Sadr left the Council in that year because of his objection to Rajavi's growing links with the Iraqi Government. The French Government asked Rajavi to leave Paris in June 1986 and he moved his base of operations to Baghdad, Iraq. In June 1987 Rajavi, Secretary of the NCR, announced the formation of a 10,000–15,000-strong National Liberation Army as the military wing of the Mujahidin-e-Khalq. However, the status of the Mujahidin was initially uncertain following the invasion of Iraq by the US-led coalition in March 2003 (see the chapter on Iraq) and firmer measures being taken against the activities of the organization by the authorities in Paris in mid-2003. In July 2004 the USA declared a group of 3,800 members of the Mujahidin-e-Khalq interned in Iraq to have 'protected status' under the Geneva Convention. There is also a National Movement of Iranian Resistance, based in Paris.

Diplomatic Representation

EMBASSIES IN IRAN

Afghanistan: Dr Beheshti Ave, cnr of 4th St, Pakistan St, Tehran; tel. (21) 88737050; fax (21) 88735600; e-mail info@afghanembassy.ir; internet www.afghanembassy.ir; Ambassador Dr NASIR AHMADNOUR.

Algeria: No. 6, 16th Alley, Velenjak Ave, Velenjak, Tehran; tel. (21) 22420015; fax (21) 22420017; e-mail ambalg_teheran@yahoo.fr; Ambassador SOFIANE MIMOUNI.

Argentina: POB 15875-4335, 11 Ghoo Alley, Yar Mohammadi Ave, Darrous, Tehran; tel. (21) 22577433; fax (21) 22577432; e-mail eiran@mrecic.gov.ar; internet www.eiran.mrecic.gob.ar; Chargé d'affaires GUILLERMO NICOLÁS.

Armenia: 32 Ostad Shahriar St, Razi St, Jomhouri Islami Ave, Tehran 11337; tel. (21) 66740199; fax (21) 66700657; e-mail armiranembassy@mfa.am; Ambassador GRIGOR ARAKELYAN.

Australia: POB 15875-4334, No. 2, 23rd St, Khalid Islambuli Ave, Tehran 15138; tel. (21) 83863666; fax (21) 88720484; e-mail dfat-tehran@dfat.gov.au; internet www.iran.embassy.gov.au; Ambassador PAUL FOLEY.

Austria: 6–8 Bahonar St, Moghaddasi St, Ahmadi Zamani St, Tehran; tel. (21) 22750040; fax (21) 22705262; e-mail teheran-ob@bmeia.gv.at; internet www.bmeia.gv.at/botschaft/teheran; Ambassador Dr THOMAS M. BUCHSBAUM.

Azerbaijan: 16 Ratovan St, Sherzad Ave, Ehteshamie, Tehran; tel. (21) 22563146; fax (21) 22558183; e-mail az.embassy.ir@gmail.com; Ambassador JAVANSHIR AKHUNDOV.

Bahrain: POB 33111-15186, Tehran; tel. (21) 88773383; fax (21) 88880276; e-mail tehran.mission@mofa.gov.bh; internet www.mofa.gov.bh/tehran; Ambassador RASHID BIN SAAD AL-DOSARI.

Bangladesh: POB 11365-3711, Bldg 58, cnr Maryam Alley, Vanak St, Tehran; tel. (21) 88063073; fax (21) 88039965; e-mail info@bangladoot.ir; Ambassador KHANDAKAR ABDUS SATTAR.

Belarus: House 1, Azar Alley, Shahid Taheri St, Fallahi St, Zafaranieyeh Ave, Tehran 19887; tel. (21) 22752229; fax (21) 22751382; e-mail iran@mfa.gov.by; internet iran.mfa.gov.by; Ambassador VIKTOR RYBAK.

Belgium: POB 11365-115, 82–157 Shahid Fayyaz Bakhsh Ave, Elahieh, Tehran 16778; tel. (21) 22041617; fax (21) 22044608; e-mail teheran@diplobel.fed.be; internet www.diplomatie.be/tehran; Ambassador FRANÇOIS DEL MARMOL.

Bosnia and Herzegovina: No. 485, Aban Alley, 4th St, Iran Zamin Ave, Shahrak-e-Ghods, Tehran; tel. (21) 88086929; fax (21) 88092120; e-mail bhembasy@parsonline.net; Ambassador EMIR HADŽIKADUNIĆ.

Brazil: POB 19886-33854, 2 Yekta St, Vali-e Asr Ave, Zafaranieh, Tehran; tel. (21) 22753010; fax (21) 22752009; e-mail brasemb.teera@itamaraty.gov.br; internet teera.itamaraty.gov.br; Ambassador SANTIAGO IRAZABAL MOURÃO.

Brunei: No. 7 Mina Blvd, Africa Ave, Tehran; tel. (21) 88797946; fax (21) 88770162; e-mail tehran.iran@mfa.gov.bn; Ambassador Pengiran Haji SAHARI Pengiran Haji SALEH.

Bulgaria: POB 11365-7451, Vali-e-Asr Ave, Tavanir Ave, 40 Nezami-e-Ganjavi St, Tehran; tel. (21) 88775662; fax (21) 88779680; e-mail embassy.tehran@mfa.bg; internet www.mfa.bg/embassies/iran; Chargé d'affaires STILIYAN VARBANOV.

China, People's Republic: POB 11365-3937, 13 Narenjestan 7th, Pasdaran Ave, Tehran; tel. (21) 22291240; fax (21) 22290690; e-mail chinaemb_ir@mfa.gov.cn; internet ir.china-embassy.org; Ambassador YU HONGYANG.

Comoros: No. 10 Malek St, Shariati Ave, Tehran; tel. (21) 77624400; fax (21) 77624411; e-mail ambacomoresthn@yahoo.fr; Ambassador AHMAD NADJID AL-MARZOUQI.

Croatia: No. 25, 1st Behestan, Pasdaran St, Tehran; tel. (21) 22589923; fax (21) 22549199; e-mail vrhteh@mvpei.hr; Chargé d'affaires IVAN PERKOVIĆ.

Cuba: Bldg 54, 17th West, Khodaverdi St, Niavaran Sq., Tehran; tel. and fax (21) 22282749; e-mail embajada@embacuba.ir; internet www.cubadiplomatica.cu/iran; Ambassador WILLIAM CARBÓ RICARDO.

Cyprus: POB 18348-44681, 328 Shahid Karimi, Dezashib, Tajrish, Tehran; tel. (21) 22219842; fax (21) 22219843; e-mail cyprus@parsonline.net; internet www.mfa.gov.cy/embassytehran; Ambassador ANDREAS IGNATIOU.

Czech Republic: POB 11365-4457, No. 36, Nastaran Alley, Bostan St, North Pasdaran Ave, Upper Farmaniyeh Crossroads, Tehran; tel. (21) 26118851; fax (21) 22802079; e-mail teheran@embassy.mzv.cz; internet www.mfa.cz/tehran; Chargé d'affaires JOSEF HAVLAS.

Denmark: POB 19395-5358, 10 Dashti St, Dr Shariati Ave, Hedayat St, Tehran 1914861144; tel. (21) 28155000; fax (21) 22640007; e-mail thramb@um.dk; internet iran.um.dk; Ambassador ANDERS CHRISTIAN HOUGÅRD.

Finland: POB 19395-1733, No. 2, Haddadian Alley, Mirzapour St, Dr Shariati Ave, Tehran 19336; tel. (21) 23512000; fax (21) 22215822; e-mail sanomat.teh@formin.fi; internet www.finland.org.ir; Ambassador HARRI KÄMÄRÄINEN.

France: 64–66, rue Neauphle-le-Château, Tehran; tel. (21) 64094000; fax (21) 64094092; e-mail contact@ambafrance-ir.org; internet www.ambafrance-ir.org; Ambassador BRUNO FOUCHER.

The Gambia: No. 10, Malek St, Shariati Ave, Tehran; tel. (21) 77500074; fax (21) 77529515; e-mail gambiaembassy_tehran@yahoo.co.uk; Ambassador SAEED ZARE.

Georgia: 92, 2nd Golestan St, Pasdaran Ave, Tehran; tel. and fax (21) 22782386; fax (21) 22542692; e-mail tehran.emb@mfa.gov.ge; internet www.iran.mfa.gov.ge; Ambassador GIORGI JANJGAVA.

Germany: POB 11365-179, 320–324 Ferdowsi Ave, Tehran; tel. (21) 39990000; fax (21) 39991890; e-mail info@tehe.diplo.de; internet www.teheran.diplo.de; Ambassador MICHAEL FREIHERR VON UNGERN-STERNBERG.

Greece: POB 11155-1151, 43 Esfandiar Ave, Africa Expressway, Tehran 19679; tel. (21) 22050533; fax (21) 22057431; e-mail gremb.teh@mfa.gr; internet www.mfa.gr/tehran; Ambassador NIKOLAOS GARILIDIS.

Guinea: POB 11365-4716, Dr Shariati Ave, Malek St, No. 10, Tehran; tel. (21) 77535744; fax (21) 77535743; e-mail ambaguinee_thr@hotmail.com; Ambassador (vacant).

Holy See: Apostolic Nunciature, POB 11155-178, 84 Razi Ave, Crossroad Neauphle-le-Château Ave, Tehran; tel. (21) 66403574; fax (21) 66419442; e-mail nuntius_fars@fastmail.fm; Apostolic Nuncio (vacant).

Hungary: POB 6363-19395, No. 16, Shadloo St, Hedayat Sq., Darrous, Tehran; tel. (21) 22550460; fax (21) 22550503; e-mail mission.thr@kum.hu; internet www.mfa.gov.hu/kulkepviselet/ir; Ambassador GYULA PETHŐ.

India: POB 15875-4118, 22 Mir-Emad St, cnr of 9th St, Dr Beheshti Ave, Tehran; tel. (21) 88755103; fax (21) 88755973; e-mail hoc.tehran@mea.gov.in; internet www.indianembassy-tehran.ir; Ambassador DINKAR PRAKASH SRIVASTAVA.

Indonesia: POB 11365-4564, Ghaem Magham Farahani Ave, No. 210, Tehran; tel. (21) 88716865; fax (21) 88718822; e-mail kbritehran@safineh.net; internet www.indonesian-embassy.ir; Ambassador DIAN WIRENGJURIT.

Iraq: Vali-e-Asr Ave, Vali-e-Asr Sq., Tehran; tel. (21) 88938865; fax (21) 88938877; e-mail info@iraqembassy.ir; internet www.iraqembassy.ir; Ambassador MUHAMMAD MAJID ABBAS AL-SHEIKH.

Italy: POB 4813-4863, 81 Neauphle-le-Château Ave, Tehran 1134834814; tel. (21) 66726955; fax (21) 66726961; e-mail segreteria.teheran@esteri.it; internet www.ambteheran.esteri.it; Ambassador LUCA GIANSANTI.

Japan: POB 11365-814, Bucharest Ave, cnr of 5th St, Tehran; tel. (21) 88717922; fax (21) 88713515; e-mail infoeoj@th.mofa.go.jp; internet www.ir.emb-japan.go.jp; Ambassador KOJI HANEDA.

Jordan: No. 1553, 2nd Alley, North Zarafshan, Phase 4, Shahrak-e-Ghods, Tehran; tel. (21) 88088356; fax (21) 88080496; e-mail tehran@fm.gov.jo; Chargé d'affaires JANTI GLAZOGA.

Kazakhstan: 82 North Hedayet St, cnr of Masjed Alley, Darrous, Tehran; tel. (21) 22565933; fax (21) 22546400; e-mail iran@mfa.kz; Ambassador BAGDAD K. AMREYEV.

Kenya: POB 19395-4566, 46 Golshar St, Africa Ave, Tehran; tel. (21) 22049355; fax (21) 22058372; e-mail kenemteh@irtp.com; Ambassador Dr RASHID ALI.

Korea, Democratic People's Republic: 349 Shahid Dastjerdi Ave, Africa Ave, Tehran; tel. (21) 22357300; fax (21) 22089718; Ambassador JO IN-CHOL.

Korea, Republic: POB 11155-3581, No. 2, West Daneshvar St, Shaikhbahai Ave, Vanak Sq., Tehran; tel. (21) 88054900; fax (21) 88064899; e-mail emb-ir@mofat.go.kr; internet irn.mofat.go.kr; Ambassador SONG WOONG-YEOB.

Kuwait: Africa Ave, Mahiyar St, No. 15, Tehran; tel. (21) 88785997; fax (21) 88788257; Ambassador MAJDI AL-DHUFAIRI.

Kyrgyzstan: POB 19579-35611, Bldg 12, 5th Naranjestan Alley, Pasdaran St, Tehran; tel. (21) 22830354; fax (21) 22281720; e-mail krembiri.mydatak@gmail.com; Ambassador HAN CHERYIKOLOV.

Lebanon: POB 11365-3753, No. 31, Shahid Kalantari St, Gharani Ave, Tehran; tel. (21) 88908451; fax (21) 88907345; Ambassador FADI HAJALI.

Libya: 2 Maryam Alley, South Kamranieh St, Tehran; tel. (21) 22201677; fax (21) 22236649; Ambassador SAAD MOJBAR.

Macedonia, former Yugoslav republic: No. 7, 4th Alley, Intifada Ave, Tehran; tel. and fax (21) 88720810; Ambassador CVETKO SOFKOVSKI.

Malaysia: No. 6, Changizi Alley, Alef St, Mahmoodieh, Tehran; tel. (21) 22046873; fax (21) 22046972; e-mail malthran@kln.gov.my; internet www.kln.gov.my/web/irn_tehran; Ambassador MUHAMMAD SADIK KETHERGANY.

Mali: No. 16, Aroos Alley, Istanbul St, Shariati Ave, Tehran; tel. (21) 22207278; fax (21) 22234631; e-mail malimissiontehran@yahoo.com; Ambassador (vacant).

Mexico: POB 19156, No. 12, Golfam St, Africa Ave, Tehran; tel. (21) 22012921; fax (21) 22057589; e-mail embiran@sre.gob.mx; internet embamex.sre.gob.mx/iran; Chargé d'affaires a.i. MARTÍN TORRES GUTIÉRREZ-RUBIO.

Netherlands: POB 11155-138, No. 7 Sonbol, Tehran; tel. (21) 23660000; fax (21) 23660190; e-mail teh@minbuza.nl; internet iran.nlambassade.org; Ambassador JOS DOUMA.

New Zealand: No. 1, 2nd Park Alley, 34 Sousan St, North Golestan Complex, Aghdassiyeh Ave, Niavaran, Tehran; tel. (21) 26122175; fax (21) 26121973; e-mail nzembassytehran@hotmail.co.nz; internet www.nzembassy.com/iran; Ambassador BRIAN SANDERS.

Nicaragua: Tehran; tel. (21) 88685070; fax (21) 88685073; e-mail mbarquero@cancilleria.gob.ni; Ambassador MARIO BARQUERO.

Nigeria: 11 Sarvestan St, Elahieh, Tehran; tel. (21) 22009119; fax (21) 88799783; e-mail ngrembtehran@yahoo.com; Ambassador TUKUR MANI.

Norway: No. 54, Dr Lavasani St, cnr of Salmanpoor Zahir St, Tehran 1953694483; tel. (21) 22291333; fax (21) 22292776; e-mail emb.tehran@mfa.no; internet www.norway-iran.org; Ambassador JENS-PETTER KJEMPRUD.

Oman: No. 12, Tandis Alley, Africa Ave, Tehran; tel. (21) 22056831; fax (21) 22044672; e-mail tehran@mofa.gov.om; Ambassador Sheikh YAHYA BIN ABDULLAH AL-FANA AL-ARAIMI.

Pakistan: No. 1, Ahmed Eitmadzadeh St, West Dr Fatemi Ave, Tehran 14118; tel. (21) 66941388; fax (21) 66944898; e-mail eoptehran@gmail.com; Ambassador KHALID AZIZ BABAR.

Philippines: POB 19395-4797, 5 Khayyam St, Vali-e-Asr Ave, Tehran; tel. (21) 22668774; fax (21) 22668990; e-mail tehranpe@yahoo.com; Chargé d'affaires a.i. ROSARIO P. LEMQUE.

Poland: POB 11155-3489, No. 2, Pirouz St, Africa Expressway, Tehran; tel. (21) 88787262; fax (21) 88788774; e-mail teheran.amb.sekretariat@msz.gov.pl; internet teheran.msz.gov.pl; Ambassador JULIUSZ JACEK GOJŁO.

Portugal: No. 13, Rouzbeh St, Hedayat Ave, Darrous, Tehran; tel. (21) 22582760; fax (21) 22552668; e-mail teerao@mne.pt; internet www.portugueseembassy.ir; Ambassador Dr MARIO FERNANDO DAMAS NUNES.

Qatar: POB 11155-1631, No. 4, Golazin St, Africa Ave, Tehran; tel. (21) 22029336; fax (21) 22058478; e-mail tehran@mofa.gov.qa; Ambassador Dr IBRAHIM BIN ABD AL-RAHMAN AL-MEGHAISEEB.

Romania: 89 Shahid Meshki, Baharestan Ave, Tehran; tel. (21) 77647570; fax (21) 77535291; e-mail teheran@mae.ro; Ambassador CRISTIAN TEODORESCU.

Russia: 32 Neauphle-le-Château Ave, Tehran; tel. (21) 66728873; fax (21) 66701676; e-mail teheran@dks.ru; internet www.rusembiran.ru; Ambassador LEVAN S. DZHAGARYAN.

Saudi Arabia: No. 1, Niloufar St, Boustan St, Pasdaran Ave, Tehran; tel. (21) 22288543; fax (21) 22294691; e-mail iremb@mofa.gov.sa; Ambassador MUHAMMAD BIN ABBAS AL-KILABI.

Serbia: POB 11365-118, Velenjak Ave, No. 9, 9th St, Tehran 19858; tel. (21) 22412571; fax (21) 22402869; e-mail serbembteh@parsonline.net; Ambassador ALEXANDER TASIĆ.

Sierra Leone: POB 11365-1689, No. 4, Bukan St, Sadeghi Ghomi St, Bahonar Ave, Niavaran, Tehran; tel. (21) 22721474; fax (21) 22721485; e-mail slembsy_tehran@yahoo.com; Ambassador MUHAMMAD FUFANA.

Slovakia: POB 19395-6341, 34 Sarlashgar Fallahi St, Tehran 19887; tel. (21) 22411164; fax (21) 22409719; e-mail emb.tehran@mzv.sk; internet www.tehran.mfa.sk; Ambassador JÁN BÓRY.

Slovenia: POB 19575-459, 30 Narenjestan 8th Alley, Pasdaran Ave, Tehran 19576; tel. (21) 22836042; fax (21) 22290853; e-mail vte@gov.si; internet tehran.embassy.si; Chargé d'affaires KRISTINA RADEJ.

Somalia: 1 Hadaiyan St, Mirzapour St, Dr Shariati Ave, Tehran; tel. and fax (21) 22245146; e-mail safarian@hotmail.com; Ambassador KHALIFA MOUSSA.

South Africa: POB 11365-7476, 5 Yekta St, Bagh-e-Ferdows, Vali-e-Asr Ave, Tehran; tel. (21) 22702866; fax (21) 22719516; e-mail tehran.admin@foreign.gov.za; Ambassador WILLIAM MAX WHITEHEAD.

Spain: No. 10 Shadi St Abbas Asadi St, Sharzad Blvd, Darrous, Tehran; tel. (21) 22568681; fax (21) 22568018; e-mail emb.teheran@maec.es; internet www.exteriores.gob.es/embajadas/teheran/es/paginas/inicio.aspx; Ambassador PEDRO ANTONIO VILLENA PÉREZ.

Sri Lanka: No. 66, Kafiabadi Alley, Shahid Fallahi St, Zafaranieh, Tehran; tel. (21) 22569179; fax (21) 22175471; e-mail slemb@aframail.com; Ambassador MUHAMMAD FEISAL RAZIN.

Sudan: No. 39, Babak Bahrami St, Africa Ave, Tehran; tel. (21) 88781183; fax (21) 88792331; e-mail sudanembassytehran@sap-it.net; internet www.sudanembassyir.com; Ambassador (vacant).

Sweden: POB 19575-458, 27 Nastaran St, Boostan Ave, Tehran; tel. (21) 23712200; fax (21) 22296451; e-mail ambassaden.teheran-visum@ gov.se; internet www.swedenabroad.com/tehran; Ambassador PETER TEJLER.

Switzerland: POB 19395-4683, 2 Yasaman St, Sharifimanesh Ave, Elahieh, Tehran 19649; tel. (21) 22008333; fax (21) 22006002; e-mail teh.vertretung@eda.admin.ch; internet www.eda.admin.ch/tehran; Chargé d'affaires a.i. GEORGE STEINER.

Syria: 19 Iraj St, Africa Ave, Tehran; tel. (21) 22052780; fax (21) 22059409; e-mail tehran@mofa.gov.sy; Ambassador Dr ADNAN MAHMOUD.

Tajikistan: No. 10, 3rd Alley, Shahid Zeynali St, Niavaran, Tehran; tel. (21) 22299584; fax (21) 22809299; e-mail tajemb-iran@tajikistanir.com; Ambassador DAVLATALI HOTAMOV.

Thailand: POB 11495-111, No. 4 Esteghlal Alley, Baharestan St, Tehran; tel. (21) 77531433; fax (21) 77532022; e-mail info@thaiembassy-tehran.org; Ambassador UDOMSAK SRITANGOS.

Tunisia: No. 12, Shahid Lavasani Ave, Farmanieh, Tehran; tel. (21) 2706699; fax (21) 22631994; e-mail at-teheran@neda.net; Ambassador KHALED ZITOUNI.

Turkey: POB 11365-8758, No. 337 Ferdowsi Ave, Africa Ave, Tehran; tel. (21) 35951100; fax (21) 33117928; e-mail embassy.tehran@mfa.gov.tr; internet tehran.emb.mfa.gov.tr; Ambassador ÜMIT YARDIM.

Turkmenistan: 5 Barati St, Vatanpour St, Tehran; tel. (21) 22206731; fax (21) 22206732; e-mail tmnteh@afranet.com; Ambassador AKHMED GURBANOV.

Uganda: 3rd Floor, 10 Malek St, Shariati Ave, Tehran; tel. (21) 77643335; fax (21) 77643337; e-mail uganda_teh@yahoo.com; Ambassador Dr MUHAMMAD AHMAD KISULE.

Ukraine: 101 Vanak St, Vanak Sq., Tehran; tel. (21) 22404081; fax (21) 22417921; e-mail emb_ir@mfa.gov.ua; internet mfa.gov.ua/iran; Ambassador OLEKSANDR SAMARSKY.

United Arab Emirates: POB 19395-4616, No. 355, Vahid Dastjerdi Ave, Vali-e-Asr Ave, Tehran; tel. (21) 88781333; fax (21) 88789084; e-mail uae_emb_thr@universalmail.com; Ambassador SAIF MUHAMMAD OBAID AL-ZAABI.

Uruguay: POB 19395-4718, No. 6, Mina Blvd, Africa Ave, Tehran; tel. (21) 88679690; fax (21) 88782321; e-mail uruter@uruter.com; Ambassador CARLOS OJEDA.

Uzbekistan: No. 6, Nastaran Alley, Boustan St, Pasdaran Ave, Tehran; tel. (21) 22299780; fax (21) 22299158; internet www.uzbekembassy.ir; Ambassador ELHAM AKRAMOV.

Venezuela: No. 17 Tajiki St, Kamranieh St North, Tehran; tel. (21) 22284450; fax (21) 26124886; e-mail embve.irthr@mre.gob.ve; internet emveniran.net; Ambassador AMENHOTEP ZAMBRANO CONTRERAS.

Viet Nam: No. 6, East Ordibehesht, Zaferanieh, Peysian St, M. Ardabili Vali-e-Asr Ave, Tehran; tel. (21) 22411670; fax (21) 22416045; e-mail vnemb.ir@mofa.gov.vn; internet www.vietnamembassy-iran.org; Ambassador TRAN TRONG KHANH.

Yemen: No. 15, Golestan St, Africa Ave, Tehran; tel. (21) 22042701; e-mail yem.emb.ir@neda.net; Ambassador JAMAL ABDULLAH AL-SOLAL.

Zimbabwe: 6 Shad Avar St, Mogghadas Ardabili, Tehran; tel. (21) 22027555; fax (21) 22049084; e-mail zimtehran@yahoo.com; Ambassador NICHOLAS KITIKITI.

Judicial System

In August 1982 the Supreme Court revoked all laws dating from the previous regime that did not conform with Islam; in October all courts set up prior to the Islamic Revolution of 1979 were abolished.

In June 1987 Ayatollah Khomeini ordered the creation of clerical courts to try members of the clergy opposed to government policy. A new system of *qisas* (retribution) was established, placing the emphasis on swift justice. Islamic codes of correction were introduced in 1983, including the dismembering of a hand for theft, flogging for fornication and violations of the strict code of dress for women, and stoning for adultery. The Islamic revolutionary courts try those accused of crimes endangering national security, corruption, drugs-trafficking, and moral and religious offences. The Supreme Court has 33 branches, each of which is presided over by two judges.

Supreme Court: Chief Justice Ayatollah MOHSENI GORKANI.

Head of the Judiciary: Hojatoleslam SADEQ ARDESHIR LARIJANI.

Prosecutor-General: GHOLAM-HOSSEIN MOHSENI EJEIE.

Religion

According to the 1979 Constitution, the official religion is Islam of the Ja'fari sect (Shi'a), but other Islamic sects, including Zeydi, Hanafi, Maleki, Shafe'i and Hanbali, are valid and will be respected. Zoroastrians, Jews and Christians will be recognized as official religious minorities. According to the 2006 census, there were 70,097,741 Muslims, 109,415 Christians (mainly Armenian), 19,823 Zoroastrians and 9,252 Jews in Iran.

ISLAM

The great majority of the Iranian people are Shi'a Muslims, but there is a minority of Sunni Muslims. Persians and Azerbaijanis are mainly Shi'a, while the other ethnic groups are mainly Sunni.

CHRISTIANITY

The Roman Catholic Church

Armenian Rite

Bishop of Esfahan: (vacant), Armenian Catholic Bishopric, POB 11318, Khiaban Ghazzali 65, Tehran; tel. (21) 66707204; fax (21) 66727533; e-mail arcaveso@yahoo.com.

Chaldean Rite

Archbishop of Ahvaz: HANNA ZORA, Archbishop's House, 334 Suleiman Farsi St, Ahvaz; tel. (61) 2224980.

Archbishop of Tehran: RAMZI GARMOU, Archevêché, Enghelab St, Sayed Abbas Moussavi Ave 91, Tehran 15819; tel. (21) 88823549; fax (21) 88308714.

Archbishop of Urmia (Rezayeh) and Bishop of Salmas (Shahpour): THOMAS MERAM, Khalifagari Kaldani Katholiq, POB 338, 7 Mirzaian St, Orumiyeh 57135; tel. (441) 2222739; fax (441) 2236031; e-mail thmeram@yahoo.com.

Latin Rite

Archbishop of Esfahan: IGNAZIO BEDINI, Consolata Church, POB 11155-445, 73 Neauphle-le-Château Ave, Tehran; tel. (21) 66703210; fax (21) 66724749; e-mail latin.diocese@gmail.com.

The Anglican Communion

Anglicans in Iran are adherents of the Episcopal Church in Jerusalem and the Middle East, formally inaugurated in January 1976. The Bishop in Cyprus and the Gulf is resident in Cyprus.

Bishop in Iran: Rt Rev. AZAD MARSHALL, POB 135, 81465 Esfahan; tel. (21) 88801383; fax (21) 88906908; internet dioceseofiran.org; diocese founded 1912.

Presbyterian Church

Synod of the Evangelical (Presbyterian) Church in Iran: POB 14395-569, Assyrian Evangelical Church, Khiaban-i Hanifnejad, Khiaban-i Aramanch, Tehran; tel. (21) 88006135; Moderator Rev. ADEL NAKHOSTEEN.

ZOROASTRIANS

There are an estimated 30,000–60,000 Zoroastrians, a remnant of a once widespread religion.

OTHER COMMUNITIES

Communities of Armenians, and somewhat smaller numbers of Jews, Assyrians, Greek Orthodox Christians, Uniates and Latin Christians are also found as officially recognized faiths. The Bahá'í faith, which originated in Iran, has about 300,000 Iranian adherents, although at least 10,000 are believed to have fled since 1979 in order to escape persecution. The Government banned all Bahá'í institutions in August 1983.

The Press

Tehran dominates the media, as many of the daily papers are published there, and the bi-weekly, weekly and less frequent publications in the provinces generally depend on the major metropolitan dailies as a source of news. A press law announced in August 1979 required all newspapers and magazines to be licensed, and imposed penalties of imprisonment for insulting senior religious figures. Offences against the Act will be tried in the criminal courts. Under the Constitution, the press is free, except in matters that are contrary to public morality, insult religious belief, or slander the honour and reputation of individuals. An intense judicial campaign since the late 1990s has sought to curb freedom of the press; some sources estimate that more than 100 publications were closed down during Muhammad Khatami's presidency (1997–2005).

PRINCIPAL DAILIES

Aftab-e-Yazd (Sun of Yazd): POB 13145-1134, Tehran; tel. (21) 66495833; fax (21) 66495835; internet www.aftab-yazd.com; f. 2000; Farsi; pro-reform; Chief Editor SAYED MOJTABA VAHEDI; circ. 100,000.

Alik: POB 11365-953, 26 Shahid Mohebi Ave, North Sohrevardi Ave, Tehran 155588; tel. (21) 88768567; fax (21) 88760994; e-mail alikmail@hyenet.ir; internet www.alikonline.com; f. 1931; afternoon; Armenian; political, literary, cultural, social, sport; Editor DERENIK MELIKIAN; circ. over 4,500.

Donya-e-Eqtesad (Economic World): POB 14157-44344, Tehran; tel. (21) 87762511; fax (21) 87762516; e-mail info@donya-e-eqtesad.com; internet www.donya-e-eqtesad.com; Farsi; Editor Dr MOUSA GHANINEJAD.

Entekhab (Choice): 12 Noorbakhsh Ave, Vali-e-Asr Ave, Tehran; tel. (21) 88893954; fax (21) 88893951; e-mail info@tiknews.net; online only; Farsi; centrist; Man. Dir Dr TAHA HASHEMI.

Etemad (Confidence): e-mail info@etemaad.com; internet www.etemaad.ir; Farsi; pro-reform; Man. Dir ELIAS HAZRATI; Editor BEHROUZ BEHZADI.

Ettela'at (Information): Ettela'at Bldg, Mirdamad Ave, South Naft St, Tehran 15499; tel. (21) 29999; fax (21) 22258022; e-mail ettelaat@ettelaat.com; internet www.ettelaat.com; f. 1925; evening; Farsi; political and literary; operates under the direct supervision of *wilayat-e-faqih* (religious jurisprudence); Editor SAYED MAHMOUD DO'AYI; circ. 500,000.

Hambastegi (Solidarity): Tehran; e-mail info@hambastegi-news.com; internet www.hambastegidaily.com; Farsi; pro-reform; Editor SALEH ABADI.

Ham-Mihan (Compatriot): Tehran; e-mail info@hammihan.com; internet www.hammihan.com; f. 2000; Farsi; independent, pro-reform; Founder and Man. Dir GHOLAMHOSSEIN KARBASCHI; Chair. of Bd MUHAMMAD ATRIANFAR; Editor MUHAMMAD GHOUCHANI.

Hamshahri (Citizen): POB 19395-5446, Tehran; tel. (21) 23023453; fax (21) 23023455; e-mail adjigol@hamshahri.org; internet www.hamshahrilinks.org; f. 1993; Farsi; conservative; economics, society and culture; owned by the Municipality of Tehran; Editor-in-Chief HOSSEIN GORBANZADEH; circ. 400,000.

Iran: POB 15875-5388, Tehran; tel. (21) 88761720; fax (21) 88761254; e-mail iran-newspaper@iran-newspaper.com; internet www.iran-newspaper.com; Farsi; conservative; connected to the Islamic Republic News Agency; Man. Dir HOSSEIN ZIYAEI; Editor-in-Chief BIJAN MOGHADDAM.

Iran Daily: Iran Cultural and Press Institute, 208 Khorramshahr Ave, Tehran; tel. (21) 88755761; fax (21) 88761869; e-mail iran-daily@iran-daily.com; internet www.iran-daily.com; English.

Iran News: POB 15875-8551, No. 13, Pajouhesh Lane, Golestan St, Marzdaran Blvd, Tehran; tel. (21) 44253450; fax (21) 44253478; e-mail info@irannewsdaily.com; internet www.irannewsdaily.com; f. 1994; English; Man. Dir MAJID AQAZADEH; circ. 35,000.

Jam-e Jam: Tehran; tel. (21) 22222511; fax (21) 22226252; e-mail info@jamejamonline.ir; internet www.jamejamonline.ir; online only; Farsi, English and French; conservative; linked to Islamic Republic of Iran Broadcasting; Man. Editor B. MOGHADDAM.

Jomhouri-e-Eslami (Islamic Republic): tel. (21) 33916111; fax (21) 33117552; e-mail info@jomhourieslami.com; internet www.jomhourieslami.com; f. 1980; Farsi; conservative; Man. Dir MASIH MOHAJERI.

Kalameh-ye Sabz (Green Word): f. 2009; Man. Dir MIR HOSSEIN MOUSAVI; Editor-in-Chief SAYED ALI REZA BEHESHTI.

Kayhan (Universe): Institute Kayhan, POB 11365-3631, Shahid Shahcheraghi Alley, Ferdowsi Ave, Tehran 11444; tel. (21) 33110251; fax (21) 33111120; e-mail kayhan@kayhannews.ir; internet www.kayhannews.ir; f. 1941; evening; Farsi; political; also publishes *Kayhan International* (f. 1959; daily; English; Editor HAMID NAJAFI), *Kayhan Arabic* (f. 1980; daily; Arabic), *Kayhan Persian* (f. 1942; daily; Farsi), *Zan-e Rooz* (Today's Woman; f. 1964;

weekly; Farsi), *Kayhan Varzeshi* (World of Sport; f. 1955; daily and weekly; Farsi), *Kayhan Bacheha* (Children's World; f. 1956; weekly; Farsi), *Kayhan Farhangi* (World of Culture; f. 1984; monthly; Farsi); owned and managed by Mostazafin Foundation from October 1979 until January 1987, when it was placed under the direct supervision of *wilayat-e-faqih* (religious jurisprudence); Editor-in-Chief HOSSEIN SHARIATMADARI; circ. 350,000.

Khorasan: Mashad; Head Office: Khorasan Daily Newspapers, 14 Zohre St, Mobarezan Ave, Tehran; tel. (511) 7634000; fax (511) 7624395; e-mail info@khorasannews.com; internet www.khorasannews.com; f. 1948; Farsi; Propr MUHAMMAD SADEGH TEHERANIAN; Editor MUHAMMAD SAEED AHADI; circ. 40,000.

Quds Daily: POB 91735-577, Khayyam Sq., Sajjad Blvd, Mashad; tel. (51) 7685011; fax (511) 7684004; e-mail info@qudsdaily.com; internet www.qudsdaily.com; f. 1987; Farsi; owned by Astan Quds Razavi, the org. that oversees the shrine of Imam Reza at Mashad; also publ. in Tehran; Man. Dir GHOLAMREZA GHALANDARIAN; Editor-in-Chief MUHAMMAD HADI ZAHEDI.

Resalat (The Message): POB 11365-777, 53 Ostad Nejatollahi Ave, Tehran; tel. (21) 88902642; fax (21) 88900587; e-mail info@resalat-news.com; internet www.resalat-news.com; f. 1985; organ of right-wing group of the same name; Farsi; conservative; political, economic and social; Propr Resalat Foundation; Man. Dir SAYED MORTEZA NABAVI; circ. 100,000.

Shargh (East): Tehran; f. 2003; Farsi; reformist; publ. suspended in in August 2009, allowed to resume in March 2010; Man. Dir MEHDI RAHMANIAN; Editor AHMAD GHOLAMI.

Tehran Times: POB 14155-4843, 32 Bimeh Alley, Ostad Nejatollahi Ave, Tehran; tel. (21) 88800789; fax (21) 88800788; e-mail info@tehrantimes.com; internet www.tehrantimes.com; f. 1979; English; independent; Man. Dir REZA MOGHADASI; Editor-in-Chief ABOLFAZI AMOUEI.

PRINCIPAL PERIODICALS

Acta Medica Iranica: Bldg No. 8, Faculty of Medicine, Tehran University of Medical Sciences, Poursina St, Tehran 14174; tel. (21) 88973667; fax (21) 88962510; e-mail acta@sina.tums.ac.ir; internet acta.tums.ac.ir; f. 1956; monthly; English; Editors-in-Chief AHMAD REZA DEHPOUR, M. SAMINI; circ. 2,000.

Ashur (Assyria): Ostad Motahari Ave, 11–21 Kuhe Nour Ave, Tehran; tel. (21) 622117; f. 1969; Assyrian; monthly; Founder and Editor Dr WILSON BET-MANSOUR; circ. 8,000.

Bukhara: POB 15655-166, Tehran; tel. 9121300147 (mobile); fax (21) 88958697; e-mail dehbashi.ali@gmail.com; internet www.bukharamag.com; bi-monthly; Farsi; arts, culture and humanities; Editor ALI DEHBASHI.

Bulletin of the National Film Archive of Iran: POB 11155, Baharestan Sq., Tehran 11499-43381; tel. (21) 38512583; fax (21) 38512710; e-mail khoshnevis_nfai@yahoo.com; f. 1989; English; Editor M. H. KHOSHNEVIS.

Daneshmand (Scientist): POB 15875-3649, Tehran; tel. (21) 88497883; fax (21) 88497880; e-mail info@daneshmandonline.ir; f. 1963; monthly; Farsi; owned by Mostazafari Foundation; science and technology in Iran and abroad; CEO YAGHOUB MOSHFEGH; Editor-in-Chief MINOO MEHRALI.

Donyaye Varzesh (World of Sports): Tehran; tel. (21) 3281; fax (21) 33115530; weekly; sport; Editor G. H. SHABANI; circ. 200,000.

The Echo of Iran: POB 14155-1168, 4 Hourtab Alley, Hafez Ave, Tehran; tel. (21) 22930477; e-mail info@iranalmanac.com; internet www.iranalmanac.com; f. 1952; monthly; English; news, politics and economics; Man. FARJAM BEHNAM; Editor JAHANGIR BEHROUZ.

Echo of Islam: POB 14155-3899, Tehran; tel. (21) 88897663; fax (21) 88902725; e-mail info@echoofsalam.com; internet www.echoofsalam.com; quarterly; English; publ. by the Islamic Thought Foundation; Man. Dir Dr MAHDI GOLJAN; Editor-in-Chief S. MOUSAVI.

Economic Echo: POB 14155-1168, 4 Hourtab Alley, Hafez Ave, Tehran; tel. (21) 22930477; e-mail info@iranalmanac.com; internet www.iranalmanac.com; f. 1998; English; Man. FARJAM BEHNAM.

Ettela'at Haftegi: 11 Khayyam Ave, Tehran; tel. (21) 311238; fax (21) 33115530; f. 1941; general weekly; Farsi; Editor F. JAVADI; circ. 150,000.

Ettela'at Javanan: POB 15499-51199, Ettela'at Bldg, Mirdamad Ave, South Naft St, Tehran; tel. (21) 29999; fax (21) 22258022; f. 1966; weekly; Farsi; youth; Editor M. J. RAFIZADEH; circ. 120,000.

Farhang-e-Iran Zamin: POB 19575-583, Niyavaran, Tehran; tel. (21) 283254; annual; Farsi; Iranian studies.

Film International, Iranian Film Quarterly: POB 11365-875, Tehran; tel. (21) 66709374; fax (21) 66719971; e-mail info@film-international.com; internet www.film-international.com; f. 1993; quarterly; English; Editor-in-Chief MASSOUD MEHRABI; circ. 15,000.

Iran Almanac: POB 14155-1168, 4 Hourtab Alley, Hafez Ave, Tehran; tel. and fax (932) 9139201; e-mail behnam.f@iranalmanac.com; internet www.iranalmanac.com; f. 2000; English; reference; history, politics, trade and industry, tourism, art, culture and society; Researcher and Editor FARJAM BEHNAM.

Iran Tribune: POB 111244, Tehran; e-mail matlab@iran-tribune.com; internet www.iran-tribune.com; monthly; English and Farsi; socio-political and cultural.

Iran Who's Who: POB 14155-1168, 4 Hourtab Alley, Hafez Ave, Tehran; e-mail info@iranalmanac.com; internet www.iranalmanac.com; annual; English; Editor FARJAM BEHNAM.

Iranian Cinema: POB 11155, Baharestan Sq., Tehran 11499-43381; tel. (21) 35812583; fax (21) 35812710; e-mail khoshnevis-nfai@yahoo.com; f. 1985; annual; English.

Kayhan Bacheha (Children's World): Institute Kayhan, POB 11365-3631, Shahid Shahcheraghi Alley, Ferdowsi Ave, Tehran 11444; tel. (21) 33110251; fax (21) 33111120; f. 1956; weekly; illustrated magazine for children; Editor AMIR HOSSEIN FARDI; circ. 150,000.

Kayhan Varzeshi (World of Sport): Institute Kayhan, POB 11365-3631, Shahid Shahcheraghi Alley, Ferdowsi Ave, Tehran 11444; tel. (21) 33110246; fax (21) 33114228; e-mail info@kayhanvarzeshi.com; internet www.kayhanvarzeshi.com; f. 1955; weekly; Farsi; Dir MAHMAD MONSETI; circ. 125,000.

Mahjubah: POB 14155-3899, Tehran; tel. (21) 88897662; fax (21) 88902725; e-mail mahjubah@iran-itf.com; internet www.itf.org.ir; Islamic family magazine; publ. by the Islamic Thought Foundation; Editor-in-Chief TURAN JAMSHIDIAN.

Soroush: POB 15875-1163, Soroush Bldg, Motahari Ave, Mofatteh Crossroads, Tehran; tel. and fax (21) 88847602; e-mail cultural@soroushpress.com; internet www.soroushpress.com; f. 1972; one weekly magazine; four monthly magazines, one for women, two for adolescents and one for children; one quarterly review of philosophy; all in Farsi; Editor-in-Chief ALI AKBAR ASHARI.

Tavoos: POB 19395-6434, 6 Asgarian St, East Farmanieh Ave, Tehran 19546-44755; tel. (21) 22817700; fax (21) 22825447; e-mail info@tavoosmag.com; internet www.tavoosmag.com; quarterly; Farsi and English; arts; Man. Dir MANIJEH MIREMADI; circ. 5,000.

Tchissta: POB 13145-593, Tehran; tel. (21) 678581; e-mail daneshvamardom@tchissta.com; internet tchissta.com; Farsi; politics, society, science and literature; Editor-in-Chief PARVIZ SHAHRIARI.

ZamZam: POB 14155-3899, Tehran; tel. (21) 88897663; fax (21) 88902725; internet www.itf.org.ir; children's magazine; English; publ. by the Islamic Thought Foundation; Man. Dir. Dr MAHDI GOLJAN; Editor-in-Chief SHAGHAYEGH GHANDEHARI.

Zan-e Rooz (Today's Woman): Institute Kayhan, POB 11365-3631, Shahid Shahcheraghi Alley, Ferdowsi Ave, Tehran 11444; tel. (21) 33911575; fax (21) 33911569; e-mail kayhan@istn.irost.com; f. 1964; weekly; women's; circ. over 60,000.

NEWS AGENCIES

Fars News Agency: Tehran; e-mail info@farsnews.com; internet www.farsnews.com; f. 2003; independent; news in Farsi and English; Man. Dir HAMID REZA MOQADDAMFAR.

Iranian Quran News Agency (IQNA): 97 Bozorgmehr St, Qods Ave, Tehran; tel. (21) 66470212; fax (21) 66970769; e-mail info@iqna.ir; internet www.iqna.ir; f. 2003; general news and news on Koranic activities.

Islamic Republic News Agency (IRNA): POB 764, 873 Vali-e-Asr Ave, Tehran; tel. (21) 88902050; fax (21) 88905068; e-mail irna@irna.com; internet www.irna.com; f. 1934; state-controlled; Man. Dir MAJID OMIDI SHARAKI.

Mehr News Agency: 32, Bimeh Alley, Nejatollahi St, Tehran; tel. (21) 88809500; fax (21) 88805801; e-mail info@mehrnews.com; internet www.mehrnews.com; f. 2003; news in Farsi, English and Arabic; Man. Dir PARVIZ ESMAEILI.

PRESS ASSOCIATION

Association of Iranian Journalists: No. 87, 7th Alley, Shahid Kabkanian St, Keshavarz Blvd, Tehran; tel. (21) 88956365; fax (21) 88963539; e-mail generalsecretary@aoij.org; Pres. RAJABALI MAZROOEI; Sec. BADRALSADAT MOFIDI.

Publishers

Amir Kabir Book Publishing and Distribution Co: POB 11365-4191, Jomhouri Islami Ave, Esteghlal Sq., Tehran; tel. (21) 33900751; fax (21) 33903747; e-mail info@amirkabir.net; internet www.amirkabir.net; f. 1948; historical, philosophical, social, literary and children's books; Dir AHMAD NESARI.

Avayenoor Publications: 31 Roshan Alley, Vali-e-Asr Ave, Tehran; tel. (21) 55136353; fax (21) 88907452; e-mail info@avayenoor.com; internet www.avayenoor.com; f. 1988; sociology, politics and economics; Editor-in-Chief SAYED MUHAMMAD MIRHOSSEINI.

Caravan Books Publishing House: POB 186-14145, 18 Salehi St, Sartip Fakouri Ave, Northern Karegar Ave, Tehran 14136; tel. (21) 88007421; fax (21) 88029486; e-mail info@caravan.ir; internet caravan.ir; f. 1997; fiction and non-fiction; Chief Editor ARASH HEJAZI.

Echo Publishers & Printers: POB 14155-1168, 4 Hourtab Alley, Hafez Ave, Tehran; tel. and fax (21) 22930477; e-mail info@iranalmanac.com; internet www.iranalmanac.com; f. 2000; politics, economics and current affairs; Man. FARJAM BEHNAM.

Eghbal Publishing Organization: 273 Dr Ali Shariati Ave, Tehran 16139; tel. (21) 77500973; fax (21) 7768113; f. 1903; Man. Dir SAEED EGHBAL.

Farhang Moaser: 43 Khiaban Daneshgah, Tehran 13147; tel. (21) 66465520; fax (21) 66417018; e-mail info@farhangmoaser.com; internet www.farhangmoaser.com; dictionaries.

Gooya Publications: 139 Karimkhan-e Zand Ave, Tehran 15856; tel. (21) 8838453; fax (21) 8842987; e-mail info@goyabooks.com; internet www.gooyabooks.com; f. 1981; art; Dir NASER MIR BAGHERI.

Iran Chap Co: Ettela'at Bldg, Mirdamad Ave, South Naft St, Tehran; tel. (21) 29999; fax (21) 22258022; e-mail ettelaat@ettelaat.com; internet www.ettelaat.com; f. 1966; newspapers, books, magazines, book-binding and colour printing; Man. Dir MAHMOUD DOAEI.

Iran Exports Publication Co Ltd: POB 16315-1773, 41 First Mehr Alley, Mirzapour St, Shariati Ave, Tehran; tel. (21) 22200646; fax (21) 22888505; e-mail info@iranexportsmagazine.com; internet www.iranexportsmagazine.com; f. 1987; business and trade publs in English; Editor-in-Chief and Dir of Int. Affairs AHMAD NIKFARJAM.

Ketab Sara Co: POB 15117-3695, Tehran; tel. (21) 88711321; fax (21) 88717819; e-mail ketabsara@ketabsara.org; internet www.ketabsara.org; f. 1980; Dir SADEGH SAMII.

Kowkab Publishers: POB 19575-511, Tehran; tel. (21) 22949834; fax (21) 22949834; e-mail info@kkme.com; internet www.kkme.com; engineering, science, medicine, humanities, reference; Man. Dir Dr AHMAD GHANDI.

The Library, Museum and Documentation Center of the Islamic Consultative Assembly (Ketab-Khane, Muze va Markaz-e Asnad-e Majlis-e-Shura-e Islami): POB 11365-866, Ketab-Khane Majlis-e-Shura-e Islami No. 2, Baharestan Sq., Tehran; tel. (21) 33130911; fax (21) 33130920; e-mail info@majlislib.com; internet www.majlislib.com; f. 1912 as Majlis Library; renamed as above in 1996; arts, humanities, social sciences, politics, Iranian and Islamic studies; Dir SAYED MOHAMMAD ALI AHMADI ABHARI.

Ofoq Publishers: 181 Nazari St, 12th Farvardin St, Tehran 13145-1135; tel. (21) 66413367; fax (21) 66414285; e-mail info@ofoqco.com; internet www.ofoqco.com; f. 1990; illustrated books for children and teenagers, adult fiction and non-fiction; Dir REZA HASHEMINEJAD.

Qoqnoos Publishing House: 111 Shohadaye Jandarmeri St, Enghelab Ave, Tehran; tel. (21) 66408640; fax (21) 66413933; e-mail qoqnoos@morva.net; internet www.qoqnoos.ir; f. 1977; fiction, history, philosophy, law, sociology and psychology; privately owned; Owner and Gen. Man. AMIR HOSSEINZADEGAN; Editor-in-Chief ARSALAN FASIHI.

Sahab Geographic and Drafting Institute: POB 11365-617, 30 Somayeh St, Hoquqi Crossroads, Dr Ali Shariati Ave, Tehran 16517; tel. (21) 77535651; fax (21) 77535876; internet www.sahabmap.com; f. 1936; maps, atlases, and books on geography, science, history and Islamic art; Man. Dir MUHAMMAD REZA SAHAB.

Soroush Press: POB 15875-1163, Soroush Bldg, Motahari Ave, Mofatteh Crossroads, Tehran; tel. and fax (21) 88847602; fax (21) 88300760; e-mail cultural@soroushpress.com; internet www.soroushpress.ir; part of Soroush Publication Group, the publs dept of Islamic Republic of Iran Broadcasting; publishes books, magazines and multimedia products on a wide range of subjects; Man. Dir ALI AKBAR ASHARI.

Tehran University Press: 16th St, North Karegar St, Tehran; tel. (21) 88012080; fax (21) 88012077; e-mail press@ut.ac.ir; internet press.ut.ac.ir; f. 1944; univ. textbooks; Man. Dir Dr MUHAMMAD SHEKARCIZADEH.

Broadcasting and Communications

TELECOMMUNICATIONS

The Mobile Communications Company of Iran, a subsidiary of the Telecommunications Company of Iran, previously had a monopoly over the provision of mobile cellular telecommunications services in the country. However, in February 2004 Iran's second GSM licence was awarded to Irancell, a consortium led by Turkcell (Turkey). The contract was subsequently revised by the Majlis and the Council of Guardians to require that domestic firms hold a majority stake in the consortium, and Turkcell was replaced as the foreign partner by the second-placed bidder, the South African company MTN. The licence award was eventually signed in November 2005, and initial services commenced in October 2006. A consortium led by the Emirates Telecommunications Corpn (Etisalat—United Arab Emirates) was named as the successful bidder for Iran's third GSM licence in January 2009. However, in May the award was revoked by the regulatory authority. In April 2010 the third GSM licence was reallocated to Tamin Telecom, an Iranian company that had formed part of the previous Etisalat-led consortium. Tamin began offering third-generation mobile telecommunications services, under the brand name RighTel, in 2013.

Telecommunications Company of Iran (TCI): POB 3316-17, Dr Ali Shariati Ave, Tehran; tel. (21) 88113938; fax (21) 88405055; e-mail info@irantelecom.ir; internet www.irantelecom.ir; fmrly 100% state-owned; 51% stake acquired by Etemad-e-Mobin consortium Sept. 2009; 24.3m. fixed-line subscribers (Sept. 2008); Chair. VAFA GHAFFARIAN; Man. Dir SABER FEIZI.

Mobile Communications Company of Iran (MCCI): Tehran; e-mail info@mci.ir; internet www.mci.ir; f. 2004; wholly owned subsidiary of TCI; 27.8m. subscribers (Sept. 2008); CEO VAHID SADOUGHI.

MTN Irancell: 12 Anahita Alley, Africa St, Tehran; internet www.irancell.ir; f. 2004 as Irancell, name changed as above 2005; mobile telecommunications; consortium of Iran Electronic Devt Co (51%) and MTN (South Africa—49%); 18.2m. subscribers (March 2009); Chair. Dr IBRAHIM MAHMOUDZADEH; Man. Dir ALIREZA GHALAMBOR DEZFOULI.

Regulatory Authority

Radio Communications and Regulations Organization: f. 2005; affiliated to the Ministry of Communications and Information Technology (see Ministries).

BROADCASTING

Article 175 of Iran's Constitution prohibits the establishment of private television channels and radio stations that are deemed to be 'un-Islamic'. However, in addition to the channels operated by the state-controlled Islamic Republic of Iran Broadcasting, many Iranians have access to foreign television programmes transmitted via satellite dishes (although ownership of these is officially banned).

Islamic Republic of Iran Broadcasting (IRIB): POB 19395-3333, Jam-e Jam St, Vali-e-Asr Ave, Tehran; tel. (21) 22041093; fax (21) 22014802; e-mail infopr@irib.ir; internet www.irib.com; semi-autonomous authority, affiliated with the Ministry of Culture and Islamic Guidance; non-commercial; operates seven national and 30 provincial television stations, and nine national radio networks; broadcasts world-wide in 27 languages; launched Al-Alam (international Arabic-language news channel) in 2002 and Press TV (English-language satellite channel) in 2007; Pres. SAYED EZZATOLLAH ZARGHAMI.

Radio

Radio Network 1 (Voice of the Islamic Republic of Iran): Covers the whole of Iran and also reaches Europe, Asia, Africa and part of the USA via short-wave and the internet; medium-wave regional broadcasts in local languages: Arabic, Armenian, Assyrian, Azerbaijani, Balochi, Bandari, Dari, Farsi, Kurdish, Mazandarani, Pashtu, Turkish, Turkoman and Urdu; external broadcasts in English, French, German, Spanish, Italian, Turkish, Bosnian, Albanian, Russian, Georgian, Armenian, Azeri, Tajik, Kazakh, Arabic, Kurdish, Urdu, Pashtu, Dari, Hausa, Bengali, Hindi, Japanese, Mandarin, Kiswahili, Indonesian and Hebrew.

Television

Television Network 1 (Vision of the Islamic Republic of Iran): 625-line, System B; Secam colour; two production centres in Tehran producing for national networks and 30 local television stations.

Finance

(cap. = capital; res = reserves; dep. = deposits; brs = branches; m. = million; amounts in rials, unless otherwise stated)

BANKING

Banks were nationalized in June 1979 and a revised commercial banking system was introduced consisting of nine banks (subsequently expanded to 11). Three banks were reorganized, two (Bank Tejarat and Bank Mellat) resulted from mergers of 22 existing small banks, three specialize in industry and agriculture, and one, the

Islamic Bank of Iran (now Islamic Economy Organization), set up in May 1979, was exempt from nationalization. The 10th bank, the Export Development Bank, specializes in the promotion of exports. Post Bank of Iran became the 11th state-owned bank upon its establishment in 2006. A change-over to an Islamic banking system, with interest (forbidden under Islamic law) being replaced by a 4% commission on loans, began on 21 March 1984. All short- and medium-term private deposits and all bank loans and advances are subject to Islamic rules.

A partial liberalization of the banking sector was implemented by the administration of former President Khatami during 1997–2005, beginning with the establishment of four private banks after 2001. Two further private banks were granted licences to commence operations in 2005. Notable banks included in the Government's privatization programme are Mellat, Refah, Saderat, Tejarat and Post Bank of Iran.

Although the number of foreign banks operating in Iran has decreased dramatically since the Revolution, some 21 are still represented, in the form of representative offices. However, it was announced in 2007 that legislation to enable foreign banks to establish actual branches in Iran was to be presented to the Majlis. During 2007–08 the UN, USA and the European Union imposed various sanctions against Banks Mellat, Melli, Saderat and Sepah, owing to their suspected involvement in nuclear proliferation and/or terrorism-related activities.

Central Bank

Bank Markazi Jomhouri Islami Iran (Central Bank): POB 15875-7177, 144 Mirdamad Blvd, Tehran; tel. (21) 29954855; fax (21) 29954780; e-mail g.secdept@cbi.ir; internet www.cbi.ir; f. 1960; Bank Markazi Iran until Dec. 1983; issuing bank, govt banking; cap. 15,000,000m., res 102,794,098m., dep. 782,499,933m. (March 2009); Gov. Dr VALIOLLAH SEIF.

State-owned Commercial Banks

Bank Keshavarzi (Agricultural Bank): POB 14155-6395, 129 Patrice Lumumba Ave, Jalal al-Ahmad Expressway, Tehran 14454; tel. (21) 88250135; fax (21) 88262313; e-mail info@agri-bank.com; internet www.agri-bank.com; f. 1980 by merger of Agricultural Co-operative Bank of Iran and Agricultural Devt Bank of Iran; cap. 8,021,118m., res 7,712,383m., dep. 212,812,146m. (March 2011); Chair. and Man. Dir Dr MUHAMMAD TALEBI; 1,870 brs.

Bank Mellat (Nation's Bank): Head Office Bldg, 327 Taleghani Ave, Tehran 15817; tel. (21) 82962043; fax (21) 88834417; e-mail info@bankmellat.ir; internet www.bankmellat.ir; f. 1980 by merger of 10 fmr private banks; cap. 13,100,000m., res 4,136,267m., dep. 447,222,510m. (March 2010); Chair. and Man. Dir Dr ALI DIVANDARI; 1,905 brs in Iran, 5 abroad.

Bank Melli Iran (National Bank of Iran): POB 11365-171, Ferdowsi Ave, Tehran; tel. (21) 6414; fax (21) 33912813; e-mail intlrel@bankmelli-iran.com; internet www.bankmelli-iran.com; f. 1928; present name since 1943; cap. 22,400,000m., res 7,460,824m., dep. 508,409,899m. (March 2009); Chair. and Man. Dir FARSHAD HEIDARI; 3,300 brs in Iran, 16 abroad.

Bank Refah Kargaran: 186 Northern Shiraz Ave, Molla Sadra Ave, Vanak Sq., Tehran 19917; tel. and fax (21) 88042875; e-mail info@bankrefah.ir; internet www.refah-bank.ir; f. 1960; cap. 895,000m., res 302,259m., dep. 56,545,320m. (March 2008); Chair. and Man. Dir SAYYED ZIA IMANI; 1,117 brs.

Bank Saderat Iran: POB 15745-631, Bank Saderat Tower, 43 Somayeh Ave, Tehran; tel. (21) 88302699; fax (21) 88839539; e-mail info@bsi.ir; internet www.bsi.ir; f. 1952; cap. 20,164,000m., res 8,445,000m., dep. 465,818,000m. (March 2011); Chair. MUHAMMAD REZA PISHRO; 3,300 brs in Iran, 21 abroad.

Bank Sepah: 7 Africa Ave, Argentina Sq., Tehran 15149-47111; tel. (21) 88646980; fax (21) 88646979; e-mail info@banksepah.ir; internet www.banksepah.ir; f. 1925; nationalized in June 1979; cap. 7,821,522m., res 1,516,259m., dep. 219,092,869m. (March 2011); Chair. and Man. Dir RAMIN PASHAEE FAM; 1,891 brs in Iran, 3 abroad.

Bank Tejarat (Commercial Bank): POB 11365-5416, 130 Taleghani Ave, Nejatoullahie, Tehran 15994; tel. (21) 88826690; fax (21) 88893641; internet www.tejaratbank.ir; f. 1979 by merger of 12 banks; cap. 10,437,384m., res 5,121,248m., dep. 291,238,243m. (March 2010); Chair. and Man. Dir Dr MAJID REZA DAVARI; 1,971 brs in Iran, 2 abroad.

Islamic Economy Organization: Ferdowsi Ave, Tehran; f. 1980 as the Islamic Bank of Iran; cap. 2,000m.; provides interest-free loans and investment in small industry; 1,200 funds under its supervision.

Post Bank of Iran (PBI): 237 Motahari Ave, Tehran 15876-18118; tel. (21) 88502024; fax (21) 88502027; e-mail info@postbank.ir; internet www.postbank.ir; f. 2006; cap. 561,143m., res 11,559m., dep. 8,236,617m. (March 2009); Chair. and Man. Dir Dr M. H. MOHEBIAN; 404 brs.

Private Commercial Banks

Bank Pasargad: POB 19697-74511, 430 Mirdamad Ave, Tehran; tel. (21) 88649502; fax 88649501; e-mail info@bankpasargad.com; internet fa.bpi.ir; f. 2005; cap. 23,100,000m., res 2,874,177m., dep. 139,727,884m. (March 2011); Chair. SAYED KAZEM MIRVALAD; CEO Dr MAJID GHASEMI; 233 brs.

Bank Sarmaye: POB 19395-6415, 24 Arak St, Gharani Ave, Tehran; tel. (21) 88803632; fax (21) 88890839; e-mail info@sbank.ir; internet www.sbank.ir; f. 2005; cap. 3,535,000m., res 373,434m., dep. 23,174,471m. (March 2010); Chair. PARVIZ KAZEMI; CEO ALI BAKHSHAYESH; 61 brs.

Eghtesad Novin Bank (EN Bank): 28 Esfandiar Blvd, Vali-e-Asr Ave, Tehran 196865-5944; tel. (21) 82330000; fax (21) 88880166; e-mail info@enbank.ir; internet www.en-bank.com; granted operating licence in 2001; cap. 5,500,000m., res 1,585,908m., dep. 120,235,940m. (March 2011); Chair. MUHAMMAD SADR HASHEMI NEJAD; CEO Dr MUHAMMAD HASHEM BOTSHEKAN; 244 brs.

Karafarin Bank: POB 1966916461, No. 97, West Nahid St, Valiasr Ave, Tehran; tel. (21) 26215000; fax (21) 26214999; e-mail info@karafarinbank.com; internet www.karafarinbank.com; f. 1999 as Karafarin Credit Institute; converted into private bank in 2001; cap. 3,000,000m., res 1,026,021m., dep. 33,776,307m. (March 2011); Chair. ALI A. AFKHAMI; Man. Dir VALIOLLAH SEIF; 81 brs.

Parsian Bank: 65 Keshavarz Blvd, Tehran; tel. (21) 88979333; fax (21) 88979344; e-mail info@parsian-bank.net; internet www.parsian-bank.com; f. 2002; cap. US $1,061m., res $347m., dep. $22,469m. (March 2011); Chair. JAVAD NAJM-E-DIN; Man. Dir ALI SOLEIMANI SHAYESTEH; 155 brs.

Saman Bank Corpn: Bldg No. 1, 879 Kaledge Junction, Engheleb St, Tehran; tel. (21) 66959050; fax (21) 26210911; e-mail info@sb24.com; internet www.sb24.com; f. 2001; cap. 2,990,997m., res 617,024m., dep. 69,667,613m. (March 2011); Chair. ALLAHVERDI RAJAEE SALMASI; 54 brs.

Development Banks

Bank of Industry and Mine (BIM): POB 15875-4456, Firouzeh Tower, 2917 Vali-e-Asr Ave (above Park Way Junction), Tehran; tel. (21) 22029838; fax (21) 22029894; e-mail info@bim.ir; internet w3.bim.ir; f. 1979 by merger of Industrial Credit Bank, Industrial and Mining Devt Bank of Iran, Devt and Investment Bank of Iran, and Iranian Bankers Investment Co; state-owned; cap. 20,722,472m., res 3,203,074m., dep. 46,425,865m. (March 2011); Chair. and Man. Dir MUHAMMAD REZA PISHROW; 31 brs.

Export Development Bank of Iran (EDBI): POB 151674-7913, Tose'e Tower, 15th St, Ahmad Ghasir Ave, Argentina Sq., Tehran; tel. (21) 88702130; fax (21) 88798259; e-mail info@edbi.ir; internet www.edbi.ir; f. 1991; state-owned; cap. 16,418,554m., res 3,550,743m., dep. 23,421,570m. (March 2010); Chair. and Man. Dir BAHMAN VAKILI; 34 brs.

Housing Bank

Bank Maskan (Housing Bank): POB 19947-63811, 14 Attar St, Vanak Sq., Tehran; tel. (21) 88797822; fax (21) 82932735; e-mail intl_div@bank-maskan.ir; internet bank-maskan.ir; f. 1979; state-owned; cap. 14,074,157m., res 3,271,780m., dep. 351,558,983m. (March 2011); provides mortgage and housing finance; Chair. and Man. Dir GHODRATOLLAH SHARIFI; 1,214 brs.

STOCK EXCHANGE

Tehran Stock Exchange: 192 Hafez Ave, Tehran 11355; tel. (21) 66719535; fax (21) 66710111; e-mail int@tse.ir; internet www.tse.ir; f. 1967; cap. 1,726,000m.; 322 listed cos (2012); Chair. HAMID REZA RAFIEI KESHTELI; CEO and Pres. Dr HASSAN GHALIBAF ASL.

INSURANCE

The nationalization of insurance companies was announced in June 1979. However, as part of the reforms to the financial sector undertaken by the former Khatami administration, four new private insurance companies were licensed to commence operations in May 2003. By the end of 2008 there were 16 privately owned insurance and reinsurance companies operating in Iran. There were also four state-owned insurance companies in operation.

Bimeh Alborz (Alborz Insurance Co): POB 4489-15875, Alborz Bldg, 234 Sepahbood Garani Ave, Tehran; tel. (21) 88803821; fax (21) 88908088; e-mail info@alborzins.com; internet www.alborzinsurance.ir; f. 1959; state-owned; all types of insurance; Chair. and Man. Dir MUHAMMAD EBRAHIM AMIN; 39 brs.

Bimeh Asia (Asia Insurance Co): POB 15815-1885, Asia Insurance Bldg, 299 Taleghani Ave, Tehran; tel. (21) 88800950; fax (21) 88898113; e-mail info@bimehasia.ir; internet www.bimehasia.com; f. 1959; state-owned; all types of insurance; Man. Dir M. ALIPOUR; 83 brs.

Bimeh Dana (Dana Insurance Co): 25 15th St, Ghandi Ave, Tehran 151789-5511; tel. (21) 88770971; fax (21) 88792997; e-mail info@dana-insurance.com; internet www.dana-insurance.com; f. 1988; 56% govt-owned; life, personal accident and health insurance; Chair. and Man. Dir H. O. HOSSEIN.

Bimeh Day (Day Insurance Co): 241 Mirdamad Blvd, Tehran; tel. (21) 22900551; fax (21) 22900516; e-mail info@dayins.com; internet www.dayins.com; f. 2004; privately owned; all types of insurance.

Bimeh Iran (Iran Insurance Co): POB 14155-6363, 107 Dr Fatemi Ave, Tehran; tel. (21) 88954712; e-mail info@iraninsurance.ir; internet www.iraninsurance.ir; f. 1935; state-owned; all types of insurance; Chair. and Man. Dir JAVAD SAHAMIAN MOGHADDAM; 246 brs in Iran, 14 brs abroad.

Bimeh Karafarin (Karafarin Insurance Co): POB 15875-8475, No. 9, 17th St, Ahmad Ghasir Ave, Argentina Sq., Tehran; tel. (21) 88723830; fax (21) 88723840; e-mail karafarin@karafarin-insurance.com; internet www.karafarin-insurance.com; f. 2003; privately owned; all types of insurance; 14 brs; Chair. Dr PARVIZ AGHILI-KERMANI; Man. Dir ABDOLMAHMOUD ZARRABI.

Bimeh Novin (Novin Insurance Co): POB 19119-33183, 11 Behrouz St, Madar (Mohseni) Sq., Mirdamad Blvd, Tehran; tel. (21) 22258046; fax (21) 22923844; e-mail info@novininsurance.com; internet www.novininsurance.com; f. 2006; privately owned; all types of insurance; Chair. Dr GHOLAMALI GHOLAMI.

Bimeh Saman (Saman Insurance Co): 113 Khaled Eslamboli Ave, Tehran 15138-13119; tel. (21) 88700205; fax (21) 88700204; e-mail info@samaninsurance.com; internet www.samaninsurance.com; f. 2005; privately owned; Chair. MUHAMMAD ZRABYH.

Bimeh Sina (Sina Insurance Co): 343 Beheshti Ave, Tehran; tel. (21) 88706701; fax (21) 88709654; e-mail info@sinainsurance.com; internet www.sinainsurance.com; f. 2003; privately owned.

Mellat Insurance Co: 48 Shahid Haghani Expressway, Vanak Sq., Tehran; tel. and fax (21) 88878814; e-mail info@mellatinsurance.com; internet www.mellatinsurance.com; privately owned; property, life, engineering, aviation and marine insurance; Chair. ABDOLHOSSEIN SABET; Man. Dir MASOUD HAJJARIAN KASHANI.

Regulatory Authority

Bimeh Markazi Iran (Central Insurance of Iran): POB 19395-5588, 72 Africa Ave, Tehran 19157; tel. (21) 22050001; fax (21) 22054099; e-mail pr@centinsur.ir; internet www.centinsur.ir; f. 1971; regulates and supervises the insurance market and tariffs for new types of insurance cover; the sole state reinsurer for domestic insurance cos, which are obliged to reinsure 50% of their direct business in life insurance and 25% of business in non-life insurance with Bimeh Markazi Iran; Pres. Dr JAVAD FARSHBAF MAHERIYAN.

Trade and Industry

CHAMBERS OF COMMERCE

Iran Chamber of Commerce, Industries and Mines: 254 Taleghani Ave, Tehran 15875-4671; tel. (21) 88846031; fax (21) 88825111; e-mail dsg@iccim.ir; internet www.iccim.ir; supervises the affiliated 32 local chambers; Pres. Dr MUHAMMAD NAHAVANDIAN.

Esfahan Chamber of Commerce, Industries and Mines: POB 81656-336, Feyz Sq., Tehran; tel. (311) 6611467; fax (311) 6615099; e-mail m.eslamian@eccim.com; internet www.eccim.com; Pres. KHORSO KARAEIYAN.

Shiraz Chamber of Commerce, Industries and Mines: Zand St, Shiraz; tel. (711) 6294901; fax (711) 6294910; e-mail info@sccim.org; internet www.sccim.ir; Chair. FERIDOUN FORGHANI.

Tabriz Chamber of Commerce, Industries and Mines: 65 North Artesh Ave, Tabriz; tel. (411) 5264111; fax (411) 5264115; e-mail info@tzccim.ir; internet www.tzccim.ir; f. 1906; privately owned; Chair. RAHIM SADEGHIAN.

Tehran Chamber of Commerce, Industries and Mines: 285 Motahari Ave, Tehran; tel. (21) 88701912; fax (21) 88715661; e-mail into@tccim.ir; internet www.tccim.ir; Chair. Dr YAHYA ALE-ESHAGH.

INDUSTRIAL AND TRADE ASSOCIATIONS

National Iranian Industries Organization (NIIO): POB 15875-1331, No. 11, 13th Alley, Miremad St, Tehran; tel. (21) 88744198; fax (21) 88757126; f. 1979; owns 400 factories in Iran; Man. Dir ALI TOOSI.

National Iranian Industries Organization Export Co (NECO): No. 8, 2nd Alley, Bucharest Ave, Tehran; tel. (21) 44162384; fax (21) 212429.

STATE HYDROCARBONS COMPANIES

The following are subsidiary companies of the Ministry of Petroleum:

National Iranian Gas Co (NIGC): POB 6394-4533, 7th Floor, No. 401, Saghitaman, Taleghani Ave, Tehran; tel. (21) 88133347; fax (21) 88133456; e-mail webmaster@nigc.org; internet www.nigc.ir; f. 1965; Chair. BIJAN NAMDER ZANGANEH (Minister of Petroleum); Man. Dir JAVAD OJI.

National Iranian Oil Co (NIOC): POB 1863, Taleghani Ave, Tehran 15875-1863; tel. (21) 66154975; fax (21) 66154977; e-mail public-relations@nioc.com; internet www.nioc.com; f. 1948; controls all upstream activities in the petroleum and natural gas industries; incorporated April 1951 on nationalization of petroleum industry to engage in all phases of petroleum operations; in Feb. 1979 it was announced that in future Iran would sell petroleum directly to the petroleum companies, and in Sept. 1979 the Ministry of Petroleum assumed control of the NIOC; Chair. BIJAN NAMDAR ZANGANEH (Minister of Petroleum); Man. Dir SEIFOLLAH JASHNSAZ; subsidiary cos include the following:

Iranian Offshore Oil Co (IOOC): POB 5591, 38 Tooraj St, Vali-e-Asr Ave, Tehran 19395; tel. (21) 22664402; fax (21) 22664216; e-mail M.Khandan@iooc.co.ir; internet www.iooc.co.ir; f. 1980; devt, exploitation and production of crude petroleum, natural gas and other hydrocarbons in all offshore areas of Iran in the Persian (Arabian) Gulf and the Caspian Sea; Chair. Dr MUHAMMAD JAVAD ASEMI POOR; Man. Dir MAHMOUD ZIRAKCHIAN ZADEH.

Pars Oil and Gas Co (POGC): POB 14141-73111, 1 Parvin Etesami Alley, Dr Fatemi Ave, Tehran; tel. (21) 88966031; fax (21) 88989273; e-mail info@pogc.ir; internet www.pogc.ir; f. 1999; Man. Dir ALI VAKILI.

National Iranian Oil Refining and Distribution Co (NIORDC): POB 15815-3499, NIORDC Bldg, 140 Ostad Nejatollahi Ave, Tehran 15989; tel. (21) 88801001; fax (21) 66152138; e-mail info@niordc.ir; internet www.niordc.ir; f. 1992 to assume responsibility for refining, pipeline distribution, engineering, construction and research in the petroleum industry from NIOC; Chair. BIJAN NAMDAR ZANGANEH (Minister of Petroleum); Man. Dir NOUREDDIN SHAHNAZIZADEH.

National Iranian Petrochemical Co (NIPC): POB 19395-6896, North Sheikh Bahaei St, Tehran; tel. (21) 88620000; fax (21) 88059702; e-mail webmaster@nipc.net; internet www.nipc.net; f. 1964; oversees the devt and operation of Iran's petrochemical sector; directs activities of over 50 subsidiaries; Chair. BIJAN NAMDAR ZANGANEH (Minister of Petroleum); Man. Dir ABDOLHOSSEIN BAYAT.

CO-OPERATIVES

Central Union of Rural and Agricultural Co-operatives of Iran: POB 14155-6413, 78 North Palestine St, Opposite Ministry of Energy, Tehran; tel. (21) 88978150; fax (21) 88964166; internet www.trocairan.com; f. 1963; educational, technical, commercial and credit assistance to rural co-operative societies and unions; Chair. and Man. Dir SAYED MUHAMMAD MIRMUHAMMADI.

UTILITIES

Electricity

Iran Power Generation, Transmission and Distribution Co (Tavanir): POB 19988-36111, Tavanir Blvd, Rashid Yasami St, Vali-e-Asr Ave, Tehran; tel. (21) 88774088; fax (21) 88778437; e-mail ceo@tavanir.org.ir; internet www.tavanir.org.ir; f. 1979; state-owned; operates a network of 16 regional electricity cos, 27 generating cos and 42 distribution cos; also responsible for electricity transmission; Man. Dir MUHAMMAD ALI VAHDATI.

Water

Iran Water Resources Management Co: 517 Felestin Ave, Tehran; tel. (21) 88901081; fax (21) 88916600; e-mail waterpr@wrm.ir; internet www.wrm.ir; f. 2003; govt agency reporting to the Ministry of Energy; in charge of Iran's Regional Water Authorities; Chair. HAMID CHITCHIAN (Minister of Energy).

MAJOR COMPANIES

Aabsal Public Co: No. 54, 40th St, Narmak Ave, Tehran; tel. (21) 77451002; fax (21) 77451009; e-mail info@aabsal.com; f. 1956; mfrs of domestic appliances.

Alborz Darou Pharmaceutical Co: Qazvin Industrial City, Tehran; tel. (21) 2221001; fax (21) 2223700; internet www.alborzdarouco.com; f. 1976; as International Products Co; renamed as above in 1989; engaged in formulation, development, manufacturing and marketing of pharmaceutical products.

Alborz Tire Manufacturing Co: 545 Azadi Ave, Tehran; tel. (21) 66008030; fax (21) 66008038; e-mail info@alborz-tire.com; f. 1958; mfrs of vehicle tyres.

Ama Industrial Co: POB 37515-355, Km 17, Jaddeh Makhsoos Karaj, Tehran; tel. (21) 44983935; fax (21) 44987769; e-mail contact@

ama-co.com; internet www.ama-co.com; f. 1959; mfrs of arc welding consumables; Commercial Man. AKBAR ALIZADEH RAD.

Arak Petrochemical Corpn: POB 19689-13751, 3 Taban St, Vali-e-Asr Ave, Tehran; tel. (21) 82120; fax (21) 82121; e-mail infoarpc@arpc-ir.net; internet www.arpc.ir; mfrs of plastics, rubber and chemicals; Man. Dir MOHSEN MUHAMMAD MEHRZAD.

Bahman Group (Sherkat-e Iran Vanet): 37 Africa Ave, Saba Blvd, Tehran; tel. (21) 22018570; fax (21) 22023607; e-mail info@bahmangroup.com; internet www.bahmangroup.com; f. 1952 as Iran Khalidj Co, renamed Iran Vanet Co in 1984; in 1998 became a holding co under the name Bahman Group; mfrs of pick-up trucks and other motor vehicles, automotive spare parts; 18 subsidiaries; sales 1,383,000m. rials (2004); Man. Dir MUHAMMAD REZA SOROUSH; 950 employees.

Behnoush Iran Co: POB 13185-571, Mahmoud Poori St, Km 7, Karaj Special Rd, Tehran; tel. (21) 44504781; fax (21) 44504776; e-mail info@behnoushiran.com; internet www.behnoushiran.com; f. 1966; mfrs of non-alcoholic beverages.

Behpak Industrial Co: Shahid Hashemi-nejad Blvd, Behshahr; tel. (152) 5226302; fax (152) 5226310; e-mail info@behpak.com; internet www.behpak.com; mfrs of soya protein and vegetable oils; Chair. A. MIRMORTAZAVI; Man. Dir Dr ALI SHARIFI.

Behran Oil Co: POB 15815-1633, 27 Dastgerdi St, Shariati Ave, Tehran 191184-6611; tel. (21) 22264124; fax (21) 22264131; e-mail info@behranoil.com; internet www.behranoil.com; f. 1963; mfrs of engine and industrial lubricants, anti-freeze and paraffin wax; Man. Dir HOJJATOLLAH AMANI DOWLATSARA; 580 employees.

Borujerd Textile Co: 65 West Farzan St, Africa Blvd, Tehran; tel. (21) 88794431; fax (21) 88783564; e-mail info@borujerdtextile.com; internet www.borujerdtextile.com; f. 1983; textile mfrs; Pres. J. SOLEIMANI; 1,200 employees.

Chemi Darou Industrial Co: POB 16765-1189, Abali Rd, Km 3, Tehran; tel. (21) 77330300; fax (21) 77336458; e-mail info@chemidaro.com; internet www.chemidarou.com; f. 1965; publicly owned; mfrs of pharmaceuticals and chemicals; Man. Dir Dr ASEF YAGHOUBI; 361 employees.

Damafin Thermal Technology Co: Zamyad St, Iran Khodro Blvd, Km 14, Karaj Special Rd, Tehran; tel. (21) 44922498; fax (21) 44922494; e-mail sales@damafin.com; internet www.damafin.com; f. 1992; mfrs of air coolers and finned tubes; Man. Dir M. A. SIAHPOUSH.

Darou Pakhsh Pharmaceutical Chemical Co: POB 13185-877, Talaghani Ave, Darou Pakhsh Ave, Km 18, Karaj Freeway, Tehran; tel. (21) 44981191; fax (21) 44985053; e-mail dppc@dppcco.com; internet www.dppcco.com; f. 1956; mfrs of human and veterinary pharmaceuticals; Chair. and Man. Dir MAHMOUD N. ARAB; 2,000 employees.

Defence Industries Organization (DIO): POB 19585-777, Pasdaran St, Permanent Expo of Defence Industries Organization, Tehran; tel. (21) 22562883; fax (21) 22551961; e-mail marketing@dio1.org; internet www.diomil.ir; f. 1981; subsidiary of the Ministry of Defence and Armed Forces Logistics; supplies the Iranian armed forces; exports weapons, engineering and technical services.

Esfahan Petrochemical Co: POB 81395-313, Petrochemical Blvd, Tehran Rd, Esfahan; tel. (311) 33804250; fax (311) 33804244; e-mail info@epciran.com; internet www.epciran.com; f. 1992; mfrs of aromatics; Man. Dir MANOUCHEHR AGHANEJAD.

Exir Pharmaceutical Co: POB 14335-379, No. 22, Rahmati Alley, Vlieasr St, Tehran; tel. (21) 88918461; fax (21) 88899358; e-mail info@exir.co.ir; internet exir.co.ir; f. 1984; mfrs over 180 pharmaceutical products.

Fars & Khuzestan Cement Co: POB 15875-3343, No. 4, 4th Alley, Pakistan St, Dr Beheshti Ave, Tehran 15317; tel. (21) 88737115; fax (21) 88736323; e-mail info@fkcco.com; internet www.fkcco.com; f. 1950; cap. 2,600,000m. rials (2005); mfrs of cement.

Fars Chemical Industries Co (FCIC): Marvdasht Rd, Zarghan Area, Shiraz; tel. (712) 4224658; fax (712) 4222144; e-mail info@farschemical.com; internet www.farschemical.com; f. 1974; mfrs of melamine, formalin and glue; Chair. AKBAR HENDIZADEH; Man. Dir DAVOUD RAKHSHANPOURI.

Firouza Engineering Co: Km 9, Karaj Makhsous Rd, 1399617911 Tehran; tel. (21) 44522415; fax (21) 44504875; e-mail info@firouzacranes.com; internet www.firouzacranes.com; f. 1967; cranes and load-handling machines; Chair. MAHMOUD SADEGHI ZAMANI; Man. Dir GHASEM EBRAHIMI MAJD.

Ghazvin Glass Co: 34 Shahid Sarafraz St, Ostad Motahari, Tehran; tel. (21) 88730832; fax (21) 88735762; e-mail info@ghazvinglass.net; f. 1965; mfrs of sheet glass; Man. Dir H. ESFAHBODI.

Glass Wool Co of Iran: 221 Motahari Ave, Tehran 15876; tel. (21) 26213520; fax (21) 26216272; e-mail export@iranglasswool.com; internet www.iranglasswool.com; f. 1964; mfrs of glass fibre insulation; Man. Dir ARDESHIR AMINI.

Golgohar Mining & Industrial Co: No. 231, Opp. Laleh Hotel, Dr Fatemi Ave, Tehran; tel. (21) 88977260; e-mail info@golgohar.com; internet www.golgohar.com; f. 1969; mfrs of different types and forms of iron ore; Chair. KOUROSH PARVIZIAN; Man. Dir MUHAMMAD JALALMAAB.

Hakim Pharmaceutical Co: POB 11365-5465, 1452 Dr Shariati Ave, Gholhak, Tehran; tel. (21) 22263051; fax (21) 22267978; e-mail info@hakinpharm.com; internet www.hakimpharm.com; f. 1962; mfrs of pharmaceutical products.

Hamadan Glass Co: 2 Ghazali St, Hafez St, Tehran; tel. (21) 66704528; fax (21) 66713016; e-mail info@hamadanglass.com; internet www.hamadanglass.com; f. 1975; mfrs of glass bottles and jars; Man. Dir. KHOSROW FAKHIM HASHEMI; 1,000 employees.

Iran Cable Manufacturing Co: 16th Km, Karaj Old Rd, Tehran; tel. (21) 66282706; fax (21) 66282574; e-mail info@irancable.com; f. 1965; cap. 25,200m. rials; mfrs of power cables and earthing wires; 500 employees.

Iran Diesel Engine Manufacturing Co (IDEM): POB 51335-4688, Tehran; tel. (21) 88770116; fax (21) 88777412; e-mail info@idem.ir; internet www.idem.ir; f. 1969; 47.5% owned by Iran Khodro Diesel Co, 30% owned by Daimler Chrysler and 22.5% owned by Iran Khodro Co; mfrs of diesel engines and spare parts; Man. Dir HASHEM YEKE ZAARE.

Iran Electronics Industries (IEI): POB 19575-365, Tehran; tel. (21) 22988006; fax (21) 22549664; e-mail marketing@ieicorp.com; internet www.ieimil.ir; f. 1973; mfrs of electronic products, incl. audio-visual, communications, IT, optics, security systems, training aids and electro-medical; six subsidiaries: Shiraz Electronics Industies, Iran Communications Industries, Information Systems of Iran, Electronic Components Industries, Isfahan Optics Industries and Iran Electronics Research Center; Man. Dir EBRAHIM MAHMOUDZADEH; 5,000 employees.

Iran Insulator Co: 4 Niloofar Alley, South Bahar St, Enghelab Ave, Tehran; tel. (21) 77528642; fax (21) 77523311; e-mail iic@iraninsulator.com; internet www.iraninsulator.com; mfrs and exporters of ceramic insulators; Man. Dir HASSAN KHORSAND MOADAB.

Iran International Engineering Co (IRITEC): POB 19395-3344, 3 North Gandi St, Tehran; tel. (21) 88778116; fax (21) 88678750; e-mail info@iritec.com; internet www.iritec.com; f. 1975; 56% privately owned; engineering consultancy and contracting; Man. Dir MEHDI KOHIE.

Iran Khodro Industrial Group: Gate 1, Km 14, Karaj Rd, Tehran; tel. (21) 48901; fax (21) 44907202; e-mail info@ikco.com; internet www.ikco.com; f. 1962; publicly owned; mfrs of cars, pick-ups, ambulance minibuses and buses; Dir JAVAD NAJMEDDIN; 17,000 employees.

Iran Office Machines Industries (IOMInd): POB19395/1415, NO 3, Aftab St, Khoddami St, Tehran; tel. (21) 88623700; fax (21) 88623730; e-mail sanaye@maadiran.com; internet www.maadiran.com; f. 1963; 100% privately owned; mfrs of office machines; mem. of Maadiran Group; Chair. MASOUD AMIRI.

Iran Power Plants Project Management Co (MAPNA): POB 19395-6448, 231 Mirdamad Blvd, Tehran; tel. (21) 81981001; fax (21) 22908597; e-mail info@mapna.com; internet www.mapnagroup.com; f. 1999; devt and implementation of power plant projects; other fields of activity include construction, engineering, manufacturing, oil and gas, petrochemicals, rail transportation; 33 subsidiary cos; Chair. Dr ABBAS ALIABADI.

Iran Tire Manufacturing Co: Opposite Ghods Air Industries, Km 5, Karaj Makhsoos Rd, Tehran; tel. (21) 44503460; fax (21) 44503490; e-mail info@irantire.com; internet www.irantireco.com; f. 1964; mfrs of vehicle tyres.

Iran Tractor Manufacturing Co (Sherkat-e Teraktor Sazi-e Iran): POB 51335-4687, No. 14, 17th St, Mirzay-e Shirazi Ave, Tehran; tel. (21) 4245891; fax (21) 4246048; e-mail export@itm.co.ir; internet www.itm.co.ir; f. 1967; publicly owned; mfrs of tractors; CEO ABOLFATH EBRAHIMI; 2,321 employees.

Iran Zinc Mines Development Co: No. 10, 8th St, Ghaemmagham-e-Farahani Ave, Tehran; tel. (21) 88730772; fax (21) 88540093; e-mail info@izmdc.com; internet www.izmdc.com; f. 1997; zinc mining; 10 subsidiary cos; CEO JACOB KARGRZADH.

Iranian Aluminum Co: Km 31.5, Qom Rd, Arak; tel. (861) 44130430; fax (861) 44130238; e-mail info@iralco.net; internet www.iralco.net; mfrs of aluminium ingots and alloys.

Iranian Offshore Engineering and Construction Co (IOEC): 18 Shahid Dehghani St, Gharani Ave, Tehran; tel. (21) 88832990; fax (21) 88812180; e-mail info@ioec.com; internet www.ioec.com; f. 1993; owned by Nat. Iranian Oil Co and Industrial Devt and Renovation Org. of Iran; designs, procures, builds, installs and services offshore infrastructure for the offshore petroleum and gas industry; Pres. NOSRATOLLAH ESPIARI; Vice-Pres. and Man. Dir ALI TAHERI MOTLAGH; over 400 employees.

Khorasan Steel Complex Co: Neyshabur; tel. (21) 2453234; fax (21) 2453270; internet www.khorasansteel.com; operates steel making and rolling mill plants; also maintains several auxiliary plants; Chair. SHEYKHNIA HASAN; Man. Dir AHMADI SEYED HOSEIN.

Loabiran Co: POB 15855-316, Shahid Sanei St, North Gandi Ave, Vanak Sq., Tehran 19699-45311; tel. (21) 88795141; fax (21) 88882883; e-mail info@loabiran.com; internet www.loabiran.com; f. 1987; mfrs of glazes and coatings for the ceramics and tile industries; Man. Dir ABDOLREZA RAJAEE.

Margarine MFG Co: POB 18735-348, Km 8, Fath Freeway, Tehran; tel. (21) 3400431; fax (21) 3400430; e-mail info@margarine-co.com; f. 1953; mfrs of margarine, edible vegetable oils and fats; Man. Dir MUHAMMAD ABASALIPOOR.

Melli Agrochemical Co (MAC): Adi Sq., Mokhberi St, Asharafi Isfahani, Tehran; tel. (21) 44471636; fax (21) 44471361; e-mail info@melliagrochemical.ir; internet www.melliagrochemical.ir; f. 1984; mfrs of agrochemicals; Man. Dir M. S. NOSRATLU.

Minoo Industrial Group: POB 15875-3189, Km 10, Tehran–Karaj Rd, Tehran 139973-6311; tel. (21) 44543011; fax (21) 44543004; e-mail info@minoogroup.com; internet www.minoogroup.com; f. 1959; foodstuffs, pharmaceuticals, cosmetics and hygiene products; consists of 12 separate cos.

Mobarakeh Steel Co: tel. (311) 33325325; fax (311) 33324324; e-mail info@msc.ir; internet www.mobarakeh-steel.ir; f. 1993; iron and steel milling; Chair. MUHAMMAD MASOUD SAMIEINEJAD.

Motogen MFG Co: POB 1767-15875, Tehran; tel. (21) 88730844; fax (21) 88730840; e-mail info@motogen.com; internet www.motogen.com; f. 1973; mfrs of industrial and household electrical motors; Chair. NASSER BAGHINEJAD; 1,251 employees.

National Iranian Copper Industries Co (NICICO): POB 15115-416, No. 1091, Vali-e-Asr Ave, Tehran 15115; tel. (21) 82138000; fax (21) 88717965; e-mail info@nicicocongress.ir; internet www.nicico.com; f. 1972 as Sarcheshmeh Copper Mine Co of Kerman; copper extraction and mfrs of copper products; Man. Dir NEAMATOLLAH POOSTINDOOZ.

Navard Aluminum Manufacturing Group: 2 Anahita St, Africa Ave, Tehran; tel. (21) 88653780; fax (21) 88653790; e-mail info@navardaluminum.com; internet www.navardaluminum.com; f. 1972; mfrs and exporters of rolled aluminium.

Niroumokarekeh Machine Tools Co (NMT): 103 Passage Vanak, Vanak Ave, Vanak Sq., Tehran 19919; tel. (21) 88796991; fax (21) 88775402; e-mail nfo@nmt-co.com; internet www.nmt-co.com; f. 1990; mfrs of machine tools; Chair. ABD AL-RAHMAN HADDAD.

Osvah Pharmaceutical Co: 17 Shahrivar St, Shad Abad, Karaj Old Rd, Tehran; tel. (21) 66801075; fax (21) 66808454; e-mail info@osvahpharma.com; internet www.osvahpharma.com; f. 1966 as Iran Merck; adopted present name 1981.

Pak Dairy Co: POB 13865-364, Shir Sq., Old Karaj Rd, Tehran; tel. (21) 66808051; fax (21) 66809535; e-mail info@pakdairy.com; internet www.pakdairy.com; f. 1959; producers of dairy products and ice cream; 1,375 employees.

Pars Appliance MFG Co (Lavazem Khanegi Pars): 181 Taleghani Ave, Tehran; tel. (21) 88302096; fax (21) 88304077; e-mail info@parsappliance.com; internet www.parsappliance.com; f. 1975; domestic appliances; Man. Dir S. A. M. FAYYAZI; 802 employees.

Pars Darou Co: POB 11365-4688, Tehran; tel. (21) 77704061; fax (21) 77877700; e-mail parsdarou@parsdarou.ir; internet www.parsdarou.ir; f. 1960; mfrs of pharmaceuticals; 250 employees.

Pars Shahab Lamp Co (PSLC): 49 Sepahbod Gharani Ave, Tehran; tel. (21) 88838143; fax (21) 88837996; e-mail parslamp@parsshahab.com; f. 1969; jt venture with Toshiba (Japan); mfrs and exporters of light bulbs.

Pars Vegetable Oil Co: 375 Nofel Loshatoo Cross Rd, Hafez Ave, Tehran 1497-11365; tel. (21) 66701012; fax (21) 66708584; e-mail info@parsvegoil.com; internet www.parsvegoil.com; f. 1954; mfrs of vegetable oil.

Paxan PLC: POB 13774, 8th Km, Fath Highway, Tehran; tel. (21) 64562325; fax (21) 66258382; e-mail info@paxanco.com; internet www.paxanco.com; f. 1963; household and personal hygiene products; CEO H. BALAZADH NAYERI; 1,316 employees.

Petrochemical Industries Investment Co: Hoveyze St, North Sohrevardi Ave, Tehran; tel. (21) 88524497; fax (21) 88524502; e-mail info@piicgroup.com; internet www.piicgroup.com; f. 1991; finance/investment; subsidiary of state-owned Nat. Petrochemical Co; Chair. of Bd AMIR HASAN FALAH ALIVERDI; Man. Dir MOHSEN HABIB.

Pumpiran Co: Vali-e-Asr Ave, Mirdamad Junction, Eskan Tower 2, Tehran 1969613313; tel. (21) 88654811; fax (21) 88798942; e-mail info@pumpiran.com; internet www.pumpiran.com; f. 1973; mfrs of household pumps, industrial pumps and industrial electric motors; Man. Dir AHMAD CHERAGH; 550 employees.

Radiator Iran Co: POB 13445-159, Km 15, Old Karaj Rd, Tehran; tel. (21) 44922719; fax (21) 44922725; e-mail info@irradiator.com; internet www.irradiator.com; mfrs of radiators and heat exchangers; CEO A. KMYZY; 700 employees.

Razak Laboratories Co: POB 13185-1671, Km 10 Karaj Rd, Tehran; tel. (21) 44525413; fax (21) 44525410; e-mail razak@razak-labs.com; internet www.razak-labs.com; f. 1964; mfrs of human and veterinary drugs; Man. Dir AHAMAD KARBASI.

Rehabilitation and Maintenance of Petrochemical Co (RAMPCO): 1st Floor, 16 Tandis St, Africa Blvd, Tehran; tel. (21) 22044244; fax (21) 22048227; e-mail info@rampco-ir.com; internet www.rampco-ir.com; f. 1992; repair, rehabilitation and installation of machinery and equipment in petrochemical plants and other industries; over 5,000 employees.

Sadra (Iran Marine Industrial Co): POB 14665-495, Shafagh Ave, Pounak Khavari Blvd, Shahrak Ghods, Tehran 14669; tel. (21) 83362000; fax (21) 88073118; e-mail info@sadra.ir; internet www.sadra.ir; f. 1968; shipbuilding and repairs; Man. Dir MEHDI ETESAM.

Saipa Diesel Co: POB 13895-141, Km 14, Karaj Makhsous Rd, Tehran 138618-1198; tel. (21) 44196513; fax (21) 44196518; e-mail info@saipadiesel.com; internet www.saipadiesel.com; f. 1963; mfrs of motor vehicles; Chair. RIAHEE CHALESHTARY; Man. Dir ALI MALEK; 1,727 employees.

Sepahan Cement Co: 235 East Vahid Dastgerget St, Tehran; tel. (21) 22277465; fax (21) 22250336; e-mail info@sepahancement.com; internet www.sepahancement.com; f. 1970; mfrs and exporters of cement; Man. Dir ARAEI HOSSEIN.

Sepahan Industrial Group Co: POB 15857-6617, 1 Ahmad Ghassir Ave, Tehran 1514613146; tel. (21) 88739010; fax (21) 88738061; e-mail info@sepahan.com; internet www.sepahan.com; f. 1973; mfrs of industrial pipes and scaffolding tubes; over 880 employees.

Shahdiran Inc: POB 91775-1174, 72 Milad St, Sajad Blvd, Mashhad; tel. (511) 6514300; fax (511) 6514494; e-mail info@shahdiran.ir; internet www.shahdiran.ir; f. 1982; fruit juice mfrs; Man. Dir SADEGH MORTAZAVI ALAVI.

Shahid Bahonar Copper Industries Co (CSP): No. 19, Gandhi St, 7th Alley (Palizvani), Tehran; tel. (21) 82166705; fax (21) 82166979; e-mail export@csp.ir; internet www.csp.ir; f. 1983; Commercial Dir MAHMOUD SHAHRASEBI.

Shargh Cement Co: 2/1 Asrar St, Mashhad; tel. (511) 8449956; fax (511) 8430848; e-mail info@sharghcement.ir; internet www.sharghcement.ir; f. 1953; mfrs of Portland cement; Man. Dir ALI TAVAKOLI.

Sina Chemical Industrial Co: POB 15875-8537, No. 12, 6th St, Bucharest Ave, Tehran 15146-45711; tel. (21) 88501038; fax (21) 88732998; e-mail sci@sinachem.com; internet www.sinachem.com; f. 1989; mfrs of formalin, hexamine and paraformaldehyde; Man. Dir EHSAN BAYAT; 198 employees.

Sina Darou Laboratories Co: POB 11155-3851, Km 15, Makhsoos Karaj Rd, Iran Ave, Tehran 13561; tel. (21) 44194521; fax (21) 44196603; e-mail info@sinadarou.com; internet www.sina-darou.com; f. 1962; mfrs of pharmaceuticals.

Soufian Cement Co: POB 51335-4713, Km 33, Marand Rd, Tabriz 51335-4713; tel. (472) 3227100; fax (472) 3227140; e-mail gd@soufiancement.com; internet www.soufiancement.com; f. 1966; mfrs of Portland cement; Man. Dir V. AKHLAGHI FARD.

Varziran Co: 12-1 Amdi St, Africa Expressway, Tehran 15189; tel. (21) 88773124; fax (21) 88730963; e-mail info@varziran.co.ir; internet www.varziran.co.ir; f. 1982; mfrs of pipe coating, waterproofing membranes and bitumen for use in pipelines, building and road construction; Man. Dir HOSSEIN AZIZI.

Wagon Pars Co: POB 14155-5814, 76 Taleghani Ave, Tehran 14168; tel. (21) 88524997; fax (21) 66400263; e-mail info@wagonpars.com; internet www.wagonpars.com; f. 1974; mfrs and exporters of railway wagons; Man. Dir REZA MOKHTARI.

Zahravi Pharmaceutical Co: POB 15175-335, No. 8, Hoveyzeh Gharbi St, Shahid Abdolhamid Saboonchi Ave, Shahid Dr Beheshti Ave, Tehran 15336; tel. (21) 88756014; fax (21) 88758735; e-mail info@zahravipharma.com; internet www.zahravipharma.com; f. 1986.

Zamyad Company: POB 13185-943, Km 15, Old Karaj Rd, Tehran; tel. (21) 66028111; fax (21) 66028795; e-mail info@zamyad.co.ir; f. 1963; part of the Saipa Group; mfrs of vans, trucks and minibuses; Man. Dir HOSSEIN ABED.

Transport

RAILWAYS

In 2010 the total length of Iranian railways was 6,073 route-km. In 2007 it was reported that the Government planned to expand the rail network to 28,000 km by 2020. However, the expansion programme has been severely impeded by a shortage of foreign investment and the impact of US-led sanctions. None the less, construction of a 506-

km rail link between Esfahan and Shiraz was completed in June 2009. In the same month a 250-km Zahedan–Kerman line was inaugurated, linking the rail networks of Iran and Pakistan and facilitating the launch of a direct Islamabad (Pakistan)–Tehran–Istanbul (Turkey) freight service in August. Construction of a 1,350-km railway along Iran's eastern border, linking Mashad, in the north-east, with Chabahar on the Persian (Arabian) Gulf, commenced in May 2010. A 51-km railway linking Khorramshahr with Basra in southern Iraq was also under construction. In February 2011 a US $12,860m. contract to build eight new lines—totalling some 5,300 km—was awarded to the People's Republic of China.

Islamic Republic of Iran Railways: Railways Central Bldg, Argentina Sq., Africa Blvd, Tehran; tel. (21) 88646568; fax (21) 88646570; e-mail iranrai@rai.ir; internet www.rai.ir; f. 1934; affiliated to Ministry of Roads and Urban Development; Pres. ABDOL-ALI SAHEB MUHAMMADI.

Raja Passenger Trains Co: POB 15875-1363, 1 Sanaie St, Karimkhan Zand Ave, Tehran; tel. (21) 88310880; fax (21) 88834340; e-mail info@raja.ir; internet www.raja.ir; f. 1996; state-owned; affiliated to Iranian Islamic Republic Railways; Chair. and Man. Dir NASER BAKHTIARI.

Underground Railway

Construction of the Tehran underground railway system commenced in 1977. By 2013 the system consisted of five lines: Line 1, a 32-km line linking north and south Tehran; Line 2, a 25-km line running east–west across the city; Line 4, an 8.5-km line serving five stations in the city centre; and Line 5, a 41.5-km suburban line, linking Tehran with the satellite city of Karaj. A further three lines—3, 6 and 7—were under construction. In March 2010 the Tehran Urban and Suburban Railway Company announced plans for an additional six underground lines—8 and 9, and four suburban lines linking central Tehran to satellite cities. It was envisaged that construction work on these additional lines would commence in 2018, following the completion of existing projects.

Tehran Urban and Suburban Railway Co (Tehranmetro) (TUSRC): 37 Mir Emad St, Tehran 15878-13113; tel. (21) 88740110; fax (21) 88740114; e-mail info@tehranmetro.com; internet www.tehranmetro.com; f. 1976; CEO HABIL DARVISH.

ROADS

In 2010 there were an estimated 198,866 km of roads, including 1,957 km of motorways, 31,945 km of highways, main or national roads, 43,264 km of secondary or regional roads and 121,700 km of other roads. There is a paved highway (A1, 2,089 km) from Bazargan on the Turkish border to the Afghanistan border. The A2 highway runs 2,473 km from the Iraq border to Mir Javeh on the Pakistan border. A new highway linking the eastern city of Dogharun to Herat in Afghanistan was opened in January 2005.

INLAND WATERWAYS

Lake Urmia (formerly Lake Rezaiyeh): 80 km west of Tabriz in north-western Iran; from Sharafkhaneh to Golmankhaneh there is a regular service of tugs and barges for the transport of passengers and goods.

Karun River: Flowing south through the oilfields into the Shatt al-Arab waterway, and thence to the head of the Persian (Arabian) Gulf near Abadan; there is a regular cargo service, as well as a daily motor-boat services for passengers and goods.

SHIPPING

At 31 December 2012 Iran's flag registered fleet comprised 619 vessels, with an aggregate displacement of 2.3m. grt, of which 21 were bulk carriers, 26 were fish carriers and 160 were general cargo ships.

The main oil terminal on the Persian (Arabian) Gulf is at Kharg Island. The principal commercial non-oil ports are Bandar Shahid Rajai (which was officially inaugurated in 1983 and handles a significant proportion of the cargo passing annually through Iran's Gulf ports), Bandar Imam Khomeini, Bushehr, Bandar Abbas and Chabahar. The Bandar Abbas port complex, which predates the 1979 Islamic Revolution, comprises two separate ports, Shahid Rajai and Shahid Bahonar. A major expansion of Chabahar port, which was expected to increase annual handling capacity from 100,000 to 500,000 20-ft equivalent units, was under way in 2013. Iran's principal ports on the Caspian Sea include Bandar Anzali (formerly Bandar Pahlavi) and Bandar Nowshahr.

Port Authority

Ports and Maritime Organization (PMO): POB 158754574-158753754, South Didar St, Shahid Haghani Highway, Vanak Sq., Tehran; tel. (21) 88809280; fax (21) 88651191; e-mail info@pmo.ir; internet www.pmo.ir; f. 1960 as Ports and Shipping Org.; affiliated to Ministry of Roads and Urban Development; Man. Dir ATAOLLAH SADR.

Principal Shipping Companies

Bonyad Shipping Agencies Co (BOSCO): POB 15875-3794, 24 Gandhi Ave, 15177 Tehran; tel. (21) 88795211; fax (21) 88776951; e-mail bosaco@bosaco.ir; internet www.bosacoir.com; f. 1991; Man. Dir ALI SAFARALI.

Iran Marine Services: 151 Mirdamad Blvd, Tehran 19116; tel. (21) 22222249; fax (21) 22223380; e-mail center@ims-ir.com; internet www.ims-ir.com; f. 1981; Chair. and Man. Dir MUHAMMAD HASSAN ASHRAFIAN LAK.

Irano–Hind Shipping Co (IHSC): POB 15875-4647, 18 Sedaghat St, Vali-e-Asr Ave, Tehran; tel. (21) 22058095; fax (21) 22057739; e-mail admin@iranohind.com; internet www.iranohind.com; f. 1974; jt venture between Islamic Republic of Iran and Shipping Corpn of India; Man. Dir Capt. C. P. ATHAIDE.

Islamic Republic of Iran Shipping Lines (IRISL): POB 19395-1311, 37 Asseman Tower, Sayyad Shirazee Sq., Pasdaran Ave, Tehran; tel. (21) 20100369; fax (21) 20100367; e-mail e-pr@irisl.net; internet www.irisl.net; f. 1967; Man. Dir MUHAMMAD HOSSEIN DAJMAR.

National Iranian Tanker Co (NITC): POB 19395-4833, 67–68 Atefis St, Africa Ave, Tehran; tel. (21) 23803325; fax (21) 22058761; e-mail souri@nitc.co.ir; internet www.nitc.co.ir; Chair. and Man. Dir MUHAMMAD SOURI.

CIVIL AVIATION

The principal international airport is the Imam Khomeini International Airport (IKIA), to the south of Tehran. IKIA opened fully in May 2005, and, by mid-2006, had taken over all international flights from Mehrabad airport (west of Tehran). There are several other international airports, including those at Esfahan, Mashad, Shiraz and Tabriz.

Civil Aviation Organization (CAO): POB 13445-1798, Taleghani Ave, Tehran; tel. (21) 66025131; fax (21) 44665496; e-mail info@cao.ir; internet www.cao.ir; affiliated to Ministry of Roads and Urban Development; Pres. HAMID REZA PAHLEVANI.

Caspian Airlines: 5 Sabonchi St, Shahid Beheshti Ave, Tehran; tel. (21) 88751671; fax (21) 887516676; internet www.caspian.aero; f. 1992; operates more than 50 flights per week from Tehran to other cities in Iran, as well as scheduled flights to the United Arab Emirates, Lebanon, Syria, Turkey and several European destinations; rep. offices abroad; Gen. Dir Capt. ASGAR RAZZAGHI.

IranAir (Airline of the Islamic Republic of Iran): POB 13185-755, IranAir HQ, Mehrabad Airport, Tehran; tel. (21) 46624256; fax (21) 46628222; e-mail pr@iranair.com; internet www.iranair.com; f. 1962; serves the Middle East and Persian (Arabian) Gulf area, Europe, Asia and the Far East; Chair. and Man. Dir FARHAD PARVARESH.

Iran Airtours: POB 1587997811, 183 Motahari St, Dr Mofatteh Cross Rd, Tehran; tel. (21) 88755535; fax (21) 88755884; e-mail info@iranairtours.com; internet iranairtours.ir; f. 1992; low-cost subsidiary of IranAir, offering flights from Tehran and Mashad; serves domestic routes and the wider Middle East; Chair. ABBAS POUR-MUHAMMADI; Man. Dir SAYED MAHDI SADEGHI.

Iran Aseman Airlines: POB 141748, Mehrabad Airport, Tehran 13145-1476; tel. (21) 66035310; fax (21) 66002810; e-mail public@iaa.ir; internet www.iaa.ir; f. 1980 as result of merger of Air Taxi Co (f. 1958), Pars Air (f. 1969), Air Service Co (f. 1962) and Hoor Asseman; domestic routes and charter services to destinations in Central Asia and the Middle East; Chair. and Man. Dir ALI ABEDZADEH.

Kish Air: POB 19395-4639, 215 Africa Ave, Tehran 19697; tel. (21) 44665639; fax (21) 44665221; e-mail info@kishairline.com; internet www.kishairline.com; f. 1989, under the auspices of the Kish Devt Org.; domestic routes and flights to the United Arab Emirates and Turkey; Chair. and CEO Capt. REZA NAKHJAVANI.

Mahan Air: POB 14515-411, Mahan Air Tower, 21 Azadegan St, Karaj Highway, Tehran 14816-55761; tel. (21) 48041111; fax (21) 48041112; e-mail international@mahanairlines.com; internet www.mahan.aero; f. 1992; domestic routes and charter services to other Middle Eastern, Asian and European destinations; Man. Dir HAMID ARABNEJAD.

Qeshm Air: 17 Ghandi Ave, Tehran; tel. (21) 88776012; fax (21) 88786252; e-mail qeshmair@farazqeshm.com; operates regular flights from Qeshm Island to the Iranian mainland and the United Arab Emirates.

Saha Airlines: POB 13865-164, Karadj Old Rd, Tehran 13873; tel. (21) 66696200; fax (21) 66698016; e-mail saha2@iran-net.com; f. 1990; owned by the Iranian Air Force; operates passenger and cargo charter domestic flights and services to Europe, Asia and Africa; Man. Dir Capt. MANSOUR NIKUKAR.

Tourism

Iran's principal attraction for tourists is its wealth of historical sites, notably Esfahan, Shiraz, Persepolis, Tabriz and Shush (Susa). The country also possesses a wide variety of natural landscapes, and skiing or hiking are popular activities in the Alborz Mountains close to Tehran. In 2006 it was announced that Iran was seeking to attract tourists from neighbouring Muslim countries by developing the tourism industry on Kish island, declared a free trade zone in 1992. The Government plans to attract 20m. foreign tourists each year to Iran by 2018. Tourist arrivals totalled 3,294,126 in 2011/12 (year ending 20 March). Receipts from tourism in 2010 were recorded at US $2,707m. (excluding passenger transport).

Iran Tourism and Touring Organization (ITTO): 154 Keshavarz Blvd, Tehran; tel. (21) 88737065; fax (21) 88736800; e-mail info@itto.org; internet www.itto.org; f. 1985; administered by Ministry of Culture and Islamic Guidance.

Defence

Secretary of the Supreme National Security Council: Rear Adm. Ali Shamkani.

Chief of Staff of the Armed Forces: Maj.-Gen. Hassan Firouzabadi.

Commander of the Army: Brig.-Gen. Ataollah Salehi.

Commander of the Air Force: Brig.-Gen. Hassan Shahsafi.

Commander of the Navy: Rear-Adm. Habibollah Sayyari.

Chief of Staff of the Islamic Revolutionary Guards Corps (Pasdaran Inqilab): Brig.-Gen. Muhammad Ali Jafari.

Commander of the Islamic Revolutionary Guards Corps Ground Forces: Brig.-Gen. Muhammad Pakpour.

Commander of the Islamic Revolutionary Guards Corps Air Force: Brig.-Gen. Amir Ali Hejizadeh.

Commander of the Islamic Revolutionary Guards Corps Navy: Rear-Adm. Ali Fadavi.

Commander of Basij (Mobilization) War Volunteers Corps: Brig.-Gen. Muhammad Reza Naghdi.

Budgeted defence expenditure (2012): (year ending 20 March) est. IR 310,000,000m.

Total armed forces: As assessed at November 2012, Iran's regular armed forces totalled an estimated 523,000 (excluding 350,000 reserves): army 350,000 men; navy 18,000; air force 30,000; Islamic Revolutionary Guards Corps (*Pasdaran Inqilab*, which has its own land, navy and marine units) some 125,000; membership of Basij War Volunteers Corps estimated to include up to 1m. combatants; there were also some 40,000 paramilitary forces under the command of the Ministry of the Interior.

Education

PRIMARY AND SECONDARY EDUCATION

Primary education, beginning at the age of six and lasting for five years, is compulsory for all children and provided free of charge. Secondary education, from the age of 11, lasts for up to seven years, comprising a first cycle of three years and a second of four years. According to the Government, 24,000 schools were built between the 1979 Revolution and 1984. According to official figures, 5,701,500 pupils were enrolled in primary education in 2011/12, while 6,185,700 were engaged in secondary education. In 2006/07, according to UNESCO estimates, primary enrolment included 99% of children in the relevant age-group, while in 2009/10 enrolment at secondary schools included 86% of the appropriate age-group.

HIGHER EDUCATION

Iran has 39 universities, including 16 in Tehran. Universities were closed by the Government in 1980 but have been reopened gradually since 1983. According to official sources, some 2,828,300 students were enrolled at Iran's public colleges and universities in the 2011/12 academic year, in addition to the 1,631,000 students enrolled at the Islamic Azad University. Apart from Tehran, there are universities in Bakhtaran, Esfahan, Hamadan, Tabriz, Ahwaz, Babolsar, Meshed, Kermanshah, Rasht, Shiraz, Zahedan, Kerman, Shahrekord, Urmia and Yazd. There are c. 50 colleges of higher education, c. 40 technological institutes, c. 80 teacher-training colleges, several colleges of advanced technology, and colleges of agriculture in Hamadan, Zanjan, Sari and Abadan. Vocational training schools also exist in Tehran, Ahwaz, Meshed, Shiraz and other cities. Budgetary expenditure on education by the central Government in the financial year 2004/05 was IR 31,518,000m. (8.2% of total spending).

Bibliography

General and Historical Context

Abisaab, Rula Jurdi. *Converting Persia: Religion and Power in the Safavid Empire*. London, I. B. Tauris, 2004.

Afkham, Mahnaz, and Friedl, Erika (Eds). *In the Eye of the Storm: Women in Post-Revolutionary Iran*. London, I. B. Tauris, 1998.

Afshar, Haleh. *Islam and Feminism: An Iranian Case Study*. London, Macmillan, 1998.

Akram, A. I. *The Muslim Conquest of Persia*. Karachi, Oxford University Press Pakistan, 2004.

Alavi, Nasrin. *We are Iran*. London, Portobello Books, 2006.

Amanat, Abbas. *Apocalyptic Islam and Iranian Shi'ism*. London and New York, I. B. Tauris, 2009.

Amirahmadi, Hooshang, and Entessar, Nader. *Iran and the Arab World*. Basingstoke, Macmillan, 1993.

Amirsadeghi, Hossein. *Twentieth Century Iran*. London, Heinemann, 1977.

Arberry, A. J. (Ed.). *The Legacy of Persia*. London and New York, 1953.

Shiraz: The Persian City of Saints and Poets. Norman, OK, University of Oklahoma Press, 1960.

(Ed.). *The Cambridge History of Iran*. Cambridge University Press, 1969.

Axworthy, Michael. *Iran, Empire of the Mind: A History from Zoroaster to the Present Day*. London, Penguin Books, 2008.

Banani, Amin. *The Modernization of Iran, 1921–1924*. Stanford, CA, 1961.

Brosius, Maria. *The Persians*. Abingdon, Routledge, 2006.

Bunya, Ali Akbar. *A Political and Diplomatic History of Persia*. Tehran, 1955.

Cambridge History of Iran (8 vols). Cambridge University Press, reissued edn, 1993.

Colledge, M. A. R. *The Parthians*. London, Thames and Hudson, 1968.

Culican, William. *The Medes and the Persians*. 1965.

Daniel, Elton L. *The History of Iran*. Westport, CT, Greenwood Press, 2000.

De Bellaigue, Christopher. *In the Rose Garden of the Martyrs: A Memoir of Iran*. London, HarperCollins, 2005.

De Groot, Joanna. *Religion, Culture and Politics in Iran: From the Qajars to Khomeini*. London, I. B. Tauris, 2007.

Ebadi, Shirin. *Iran Awakening: A Memoir of Revolution and Hope*. London, Rider, 2006.

Refugee Rights in Iran. London, Saqi Books, 2008.

Ehteshami, Anoushiravan, and Hinnebusch, Raymond. *Syria and Iran: Middle Powers in a Penetrated Regional System*. London and New York, Routledge, 1997.

Elwell-Sutton, L. P. *Modern Iran*. London, 1941.

A Guide to Iranian Area Study. Ann Arbor, 1952.

Persian Oil: A Study in Power Politics. London, 1955.

Eskelund, Karl. *Behind the Peacock Throne*. New York, Alvin Redman, 1965.

Forbes Manz, Beatrice. *Power, Politics and Religion in Timurid Iran*. Cambridge University Press, 2007.

Frye, Richard N. *Persia*. London, Allen and Unwin, 3rd edn, 1969.

Ghirshman, R. *L'Iran: des Origines à Islam*. Paris, 1951 (trans. as *Iran from the Earliest Times to the Islamic Conquest*. London, 1954).

Iran. New York, 1964.

Goodarzi, Jubin M. *Syria and Iran: Diplomatic Alliance and Power Politics in the Middle East*. London, I. B. Tauris, 2009.

Herzfeld, E. *Iran in the Ancient East*. Oxford, 1941.

Hiro, Dilip. *Iran Today*. London, Politico's Publishing Ltd, 2006.

Hovannisian, Richard, and Sabagh, Georges. *The Persian Presence in the Islamic World*. Cambridge, Cambridge University Press, 1999.

Humphreys, Eileen. *The Royal Road: A Popular History of Iran*. London, Scorpion, 1991.

Huot, Jean Louis. *Persia* Vol. I. London, Muller, 1966.

Keddie, Nikki R. *Iran. Religion, Politics and Society*. London, Frank Cass, 1980.

(Ed. with Gasiorowski, Mark). *Neither East nor West: Iran, the Soviet Union and the United States*. New Haven, CT, Yale University Press, 1990.

Khazeni, Arash. *Tribes and Empire on the Margins of Nineteenth-century Iran*. Seattle, WA, University of Washington Press, 2010.

Khomeini, Ayatollah Ruhollah. *A Clarification of Questions*. Boulder, CT, Westview Press, 1985.

Lambton, A. K. S. *Landlord and Peasant in Persia*. New York, 1953.

Islamic Society in Persia. London, 1954.

The Persian Land Reform 1962–66. Oxford, Clarendon Press, 1969.

Lockhart, L. *Famous Cities of Iran*. London, 1939.

The Fall of the Safavi Dynasty and the Afghan Occupation of Persia. Cambridge, Cambridge University Press, 1958.

Marlowe, John. *Iran, A Short Political Guide*. London and New York, Pall Mall Press, 1963.

Martin, Vanessa (Ed.). *Anglo-Iranian Relations since 1800*. Abingdon, Routledge, 2009.

Melville, Charles (Ed.). *Safavid Persia*. 1996.

Millspaugh, A. C. *Americans in Persia*. Washington, DC, 1946.

Minoui, Delphine (Ed.). *Jeunesse d'Iran: Les voix du changement*. Paris, Autrement, 2001.

Mohammadi, Ali, and Ehteshami, Anoushiravan (Eds). *Iran and Eurasia*. London, Ithaca Press, 2000.

Olmstead, A. T. *History of the Persian Empire, Achaemenid Period*. Chicago, IL, 1948.

Ramazani, Rouhollah K. *The Foreign Policy of Iran 1500–1941*. Charlottesville, VA, University Press of Virginia, 1966.

The Persian Gulf: Iran's Role. Charlottesville, VA, University Press of Virginia, 1972.

Rice, Cyprian. *The Persian Sufis*. London, Allen and Unwin, 1964.

Sabahi, Hushang. *British Policy in Persia 1918–1925*. London, Frank Cass, 1990.

Sanghvi, Ramesh. *Aryamehr: The Shah of Iran*. London, Macmillan, 1968.

Sansarian, Eliz. *Religious Minorities in Iran*. Cambridge, Cambridge University Press, 2000.

Savory, Roger. *Iran under the Safavids*. Cambridge, Cambridge University Press, 1980.

Sciolino, Elaine. *Persian Mirrors: The Elusive Face of Iran*. New York, Free Press, 2000.

Shah of Iran. *Mission for My Country*. London, Hutchinson, 1961.

Shearman, I. *Land and People of Iran*. London, 1962.

Sirdar, Ikbal Ali Shah. *Persia of the Persians*. London, 1929.

Stark, Freya. *The Valleys of the Assassins*. London, 1934.

East is West. London, 1945.

al-Suwaidi, Jamal S. (Ed.). *Iran and the Gulf: A Search for Stability*. Abu Dhabi, Emirates Centre for Strategic Studies and Research, 1996. (Distrib. I. B. Tauris, London).

Sykes, Sir Percy. *Persia*. Oxford, 1922.

A History of Persia (2 vols; 3rd edn, with supplementary essays). London, 1930.

Tapper, Richard, and Thompson, Jon. *The Nomadic Peoples of Iran*. London, Azimuth Editions, 2002.

Thomas, L. V., and Frye, R. N. *The United States and Turkey and Iran*. Cambridge, MA, 1951.

Wiesehofer, Josef. *Ancient Persia*. London, I. B. Tauris, 2001.

Wilber, Donald N. *Iran: Past and Present: From Monarchy to Islamic Republic*. Princeton University Press, 1955, 9th edn 1982.

Wright, Robin B. *The Last Great Revolution: Turmoil and Transformation in Iran*. New York, Alfred A. Knopf, 2000.

Yildiz, Kerim, and Taysi, Tanyel B. *The Kurds in Iran: The Past, Present and Future*. London, Pluto Press, 2007.

Zabih, Sepehr. *The Communist Movement in Iran*. Berkeley, CA, University of California Press, 1967.

Contemporary Political History

Abrahamian, Ervand. *Radical Islam: The Iranian Mojahedin*. London, I. B. Tauris, 1989.

Khomeinism: Essays on the Islamic Republic. Berkeley, CA, University of California Press, 1993.

A History of Modern Iran. Cambridge, Cambridge University Press, 2008.

Adib-Moghaddam, Arshin. *Iran in World Politics: The Question of the Islamic Republic*. New York, Columbia University Press, 2008.

Akhavi, Shahrough. *Religion and Politics in Contemporary Iran*. State University of New York Press, 1980.

Alikhani, Hossein. *Sanctioning Iran: Anatomy of a Failed Policy*. London, I. B. Tauris, 2000.

Amirahmadi, Hooshang, and Entessar, Nader. *Reconstruction and Regional Diplomacy in the Persian Gulf*. London, Routledge, 1992.

Ansari, Ali M. *Iran, Islam and Democracy: The Politics of Managing Change*. London, Royal Institute for International Affairs, 2nd edn, 2006.

Confronting Iran: The Failure of American Foreign Policy and the Roots of Mistrust. London, C. Hurst & Co, 2006.

Modern Iran since 1921: The Pahlavis and After. Harlow, Longman, 2nd edn, 2007.

Iran under Ahmadinejad: The Politics of Confrontation. Abingdon, Routledge, 2007.

Arjomand, Saïd Amir. *The Turban for the Crown: The Islamic Revolution in Iran*. New York, Oxford University Press, 1989.

After Khomeini: Iran Under His Successors. New York, Oxford University Press, 2009.

Assadollah, Alam. *The Shah and I: The Confidential Diaries of Iran's Royal Court, 1969–77*. London, I. B. Tauris, 1991.

Azimi, Fakhreddin. *Iran: The Crisis of Democracy 1941–1953*. London, I. B. Tauris, 1990.

Bakhash, Shaul. *The Reign of the Ayatollahs*. London, I. B. Tauris, 1984.

Bani-Sadr, Abol-Hassan. *My Turn to Speak: Iran, the Revolution and Secret Deals with the US*. New York, Brassey's, 1991.

Behrouz, Maziar. *Rebels with a Cause: the Failure of the Left in Iran*. London and New York, I. B. Tauris, 2000.

Benard, Cheryl, and Khalilzad, Zalmay. *The Government of God: Iran's Islamic Republic*. New York, Columbia University Press, 1984.

Bill, James A. *The Lion and the Eagle: the Tragedy of American-Iranian Relations*. New Haven, CT, Yale University Press, 1988.

Brumberg, Daniel. *Reinventing Khomeini: The Struggle for Reform in Iran*. University of Chicago Press, 2001.

Byman, Daniel L., Chubin, Shamran, Ehteshami, Anoushiravan, and Green, Jerrold. *Iran's Security Policy in the Post-Revolutionary Era*. Santa Monica, CA, RAND, 2001.

Byrne, Malcolm, and Gasiorowski, Mark J. (Eds). *Mohammad Mossadeq and the 1953 Coup in Iran*. Syracuse, NY, Syracuse University Press, 2004.

Chaqueri, Cosroe. *Origins of Social Democracy in Modern Iran*. Seattle, WA, University of Washington Press, 2001.

Chubin, Shahram. *Iran's Nuclear Ambitions*. Carnegie Endowment for International Peace, 2006.

Chubin, Shahram, and Tripp, Charles. *Iran and Iraq at War*. London, I. B. Tauris, 1988.

Chubin, Shahram, and Zabih, Sepehr. *The Foreign Relations of Iran: A Developing State in the Zone of a Great-Power Conflict*. Berkeley, CA, University of California Press, 1975.

Cohen, Ronen A. *The Rise and Fall of the Mojahedin Khalq, 1987–1997: Their Survival After the Islamic Revolution and Resistance to the Islamic Republic of Iran*. Brighton, Sussex Academic Press, 2008.

Cordesman, Anthony H. *The Iran–Iraq War and Western Security 1984–87*. London, Jane's Publishing Company, 1987.

Iran's Developing Military Capabilities (Significant Issues Series). Washington, DC, Center for Strategic and International Studies, 2005.

Cottam, Richard W. *Nationalism in Iran*. Pittsburgh University Press, 1964.

Iran and the United States: a cold war case study. Pittsburgh, PA, University of Pittsburgh Press, 1988.

Cronin, Stephanie. *The Army and the Creation of the Pahlavi State in Iran 1910–1926*. London and New York, I. B. Tauris, 1997.

The Making of Modern Iran: State and Society under Riza Shah, 1921–1941. London, Routledge, 2003.

(Ed.). *Reformers and Revolutionaries in Modern Iran: New Perspectives on the Iranian Left*. London, RoutledgeCurzon, 2004.

Tribal Politics in Iran: Rural Conflict and the New State, 1921–1941. Abingdon, Routledge, 2006.

De Bellaigue, Christopher. *The Struggle for Iran*. New York, New York Review of Books, 2007.

Delannoy, Christian. *Savak*. Paris, Editions Stock, 1991.

Delpech, Thérèse. *Iran and the Bomb: The Abdication of International Responsibility*. London, C. Hurst & Co, 2006.

Ehteshami, Anoushiravan. *After Khomeini: The Iranian Second Republic*. London and New York, Routledge, 1995.

Ehteshami, Anoushiravan, and Molavi, Reza. (Eds). *Iran and the International System*. Abingdon, Routledge, 2011.

Ehteshami, Anoushiravan, and Zweiri, Mahjoob. *Iran and the Rise of its Neoconservatives: The Politics of Tehran's Silent Revolution*. London, I. B. Tauris, 2007.

Ehteshami, Anoushivaran, and Zweiri, Mahjoob. (Eds). *Iran's Foreign Policy: From Khatami to Ahmadinejad*. Reading, Ithaca Press, 2012.

Elling, Rasmus Christian. *Minorities in Iran: Nationalism and Ethnicity after Khomeini*. New York, Palgrave Macmillan, 2013.

Esposito, John L., and Ramazani, R. K. *Iran at the Crossroads*. Basingstoke, Palgrave, 2001.

Fayazmanesh, Sasan. *The United States and Iran: Sanctions, Wars and the Policy of Dual Containment*. Abingdon, Routledge, 2008.

Fischer, M. J. *Iran: From Religious Dispute to Revolution*. Cambridge, MA, Harvard University Press, 1980.

Fitzpatrick, Mark. *The Iranian Nuclear Crisis: Avoiding Worst-case Outcomes*. Abingdon, Routledge, 2008.

Furtig, Henner, and Ehteshami, Anoushiravan. *Iran's Rivalry with Saudi Arabia between the Gulf Wars*. Reading, Ithaca Press, 2001.

Gheissari, Ali. (Ed.). *Contemporary Iran: Economy, Society, Politics*. Oxford, Oxford University Press, 2009.

Gheissari, Ali, and Nasr, Vali. *Democracy in Iran: History and the Quest for Liberty*. New York, Oxford University Press, 2006.

Goode, James F. *The United States and Iran, 1946–51: The Diplomacy of Neglect*. New York, St Martin's Press, 1989.

Halliday, Fred. *Iran: Dictatorship and Development*. London, 1978.

Harney, Desmond. *The Priest and the King: An Eyewitness Account of the Iranian Revolution*. London, I. B. Tauris, 1999.

Heikal, Muhammad. *The Return of the Ayatollah*. London, André Deutsch, 1981.

Herzig, Edmund. *Iran and the Former Soviet South*. London, Chatham House, 1996.

Heydemann, Steven, and Leenders, Reinoud (Eds). *Middle East Authoritarianisms: Governance, Contestation, and Regime Resilience in Syria and Iran*. Redwood City, CA, Stanford University Press, 2013.

Hiro, Dilip. *Iran under the Ayatollahs*. London, Routledge and Kegan Paul, 1984.

The Longest War: The Iran–Iraq Military Conflict. London, Grafton, 1989.

Neighbours, Not Friends: Iraq and Iran after the Gulf Wars. London, Routledge, 2001.

The Iranian Labyrinth: Journeys through Theocratic Iran and its Furies. New York, Nation Books, 2005.

Hooglund, Eric, and Stenberg, Leif. (Eds). *Navigating Contemporary Iran: Challenging Economic, Social and Political Perceptions*. Abingdon, Routledge, 2012.

Hoveyda, Ferydoun. *The Fall of the Shah*. London, Weidenfeld and Nicolson, 1979.

Ismael, Tareq Y. *Iran and Iraq: Roots of Conflict*. Syracuse, NY, Syracuse University Press, 1983.

Jafarzadeh, Alireza. *The Iran Threat: President Ahmadinejad and the Coming Nuclear Crisis*. London, Palgrave Macmillan, 2008.

Kapuściński, Ryszard. *Shah of Shahs*. San Diego, CA, Harcourt Brace Jovanovich, 1985.

Karsh, Efraim. *The Iran–Iraq War: 1980–1988 (Essential Histories)*. Oxford, Osprey, 2002.

Katouzian, Homa. *State and Society in Iran: the Eclipse of the Qajars and the Emergence of the Pahlavis*. London and New York, I. B. Tauris, 2000.

Musaddiq and the Struggle for Power in Iran. London, I. B. Tauris, 2000.

Katouzian, Homa, and Shahidi, Hossein. *Iran in the 21st Century: Politics, Economics and Conflict*. Abingdon, Routledge, 2007.

Katzman, Kenneth. *The Warriors of Islam: Iran's Revolutionary Guard*. Boulder, CO, and Oxford, Westview Press, 1994.

Keddie, Nikki R. *Modern Iran: Roots and Results of Revolution*. New Haven, CT, Yale University Press, revised edn, 2006.

Khan, Saira. *Iran and Nuclear Weapons: Protracted Conflict and Proliferation*. Abingdon, Routledge, 2009.

Khomeini, Ayatollah Ruhollah. *Islam and Revolution: Writings and Declarations of Imam Khomeini* (trans. and ed. by Hamid Algar). Berkeley, CA, Mizan Press, 1982.

Kinzer, Stephen. *All the Shah's Men: An American Coup and the Roots of Middle Eastern Terror*. John Wiley & Sons, Inc, 2004.

Krause, Joachim (Ed.). *Iran's Nuclear Programme: Strategic Implications*. Abingdon, Routledge, 2011.

Kurzman, Charles. *The Unthinkable Revolution in Iran*. Cambridge, MA, Harvard University Press, 2004.

Laing, Margaret. *The Shah*. London, Sidgwick and Jackson, 1977.

Lenczowski, George. *Russia and the West in Iran*. New York, Cornell University Press, 1949.

(Ed.). *Iran under the Pahlavis*. Stanford, CA, Hoover Institution Press, 1978.

Malek-Ahmadi, Farshad. *Trapped by History: 100 Years of Struggle for Constitutionalism and Democracy in Iran*. Abingdon, Routledge, 2006.

Martin, Vanessa. *Creating an Islamic State: Khomeini and the Making of a New Iran*. London and New York, I. B. Tauris, 2000.

Menashri, David. *Post-Revolutionary Politics in Iran: Religion, Society, Power*. London, Frank Cass, 2001.

Milani, Abbas. *The Persian Sphinx: Amir Abbas Hoveyda and the Riddle of the Iranian Revolution*. London, I. B. Tauris, 2000.

Mir-Hosseini, Ziba, and Tapper, Richard. *Islam and Democracy in Iran: Eshkevari and the Quest for Reform*. London, I. B. Tauris, 2006.

Mirsepassi, Ali. *Democracy in Modern Iran: Islam, Culture and Political Change*. New York, New York University, 2010.

Mohammadi, Ali (Ed.). *Iran Encountering Globalization: Problems and Prospects*. Abingdon, Routledge, 2006.

Moin, Baqer. *Khomeini: Life of the Ayatollah*. London and New York, I. B. Tauris, 1999.

Mojtahedzadeh, Pirouz. *Security and Territoriality in the Persian Gulf: A Maritime Political Geography*. Richmond, Curzon, 1999.

Moslem, Mehdi. *Factional Politics in Post-Khomeini Iran*. Syracuse, NY, Syracuse University Press, 2002.

Mottahedeh, Roy. *The Mantle of the Prophet: Religion and Politics in Iran*. London, Chatto and Windus, 1985.

Mousavian, Seyyed Hossein. *Iran-Europe Relations: Challenges and Opportunities*. Abingdon, Routledge, 2010.

Murray, Donette. *US Foreign Policy and Iran: American-Iranian Relations since the Islamic Revolution*. Abingdon, Routledge, 2007.

Naji, Kasra. *Ahmadinejad: The Secret History of Iran's Radical Leader*. Berkeley, CA, University of California Press, 2008.

Nasr, Vali and Gheissari, Ali. *Democracy in Iran: History and the Quest for Liberty*. Oxford University Press, 2006.

Omid, Homa. *Islam and the Post-Revolutionary State in Iran*. London, Macmillan, 1993.

Paidar, Parvin. *Women and the Political Process in Twentieth-Century Iran*. Cambridge University Press, 1995.

Parsa, Misagh. *Social Origins of the Iranian Revolution*. New Brunswick, NJ, and London, Rutgers University Press, 1989.

Parsons, Sir Anthony. *The Pride and the Fall: Iran 1974–79*. London, Jonathan Cape, 1984.

Patrikarakos, David. *Nuclear Iran: The Birth of an Atomic State*. London, I. B. Tauris, 2012.

Pedram, Ali M. *Parliament and the Process of Democratization in the Islamic Republic of Iran*. Reading, Ithaca Press, 2009.

Pelletiere, Stephen. *The Iran–Iraq War: Chaos in a Vacuum*. London and New York, Praeger Publishers, Inc, 1992.

Perkes, Volker. *Iran—Eine politische Herausforderung: die Prekäre Balance von Vertrauen und Sicherheit*. Berlin, Suhrkamp Verlag, 2008.

Pipes, Daniel. *The Rushdie Affair: The Novel, the Ayatollah, and the West*. New York, Birch Lane Press, 1990.

Potter, Lawrence G., and Sick, Gary G. (Eds). *Iran, Iraq and the Legacies of War* London, Palgrave Macmillan, 2006.

Rahnema, Saeed, and Bedad, Sohrab (Eds). *Iran After the Revolution: Crisis of an Islamic State*. London, I. B. Tauris, 1995.

Rajaee, Farhang (Ed.). *The Iran–Iraq War: The Politics of Aggression*. Gainsville, FL, University Press of Florida, 1994.

Islamism and Modernism: The Changing Discourse in Iran. Austin, TX, University of Texas Press, 2007.

Rakel, Eva Patricia. *Power, Islam, and Political Elite in Iran: A Study on the Iranian Political Elite from Khomeini to Ahmadinejad*. Boston, MA, Brill, 2009.

Rezun, Miron (Ed.). *Iran at the Crossroads: Global Relations in a Turbulent Decade*. Oxford, Westview Press, 1990.

Roosevelt, Kermit. *Countercoup: the Struggle for the Control of Iran.* McGraw-Hill, 1980.

Sadeghinia, Mahboubeh. *Security Arrangements in the Persian Gulf: With Special Reference to Iran's Foreign Policy*. Reading, Ithaca Press, 2011.

Samore, Gary (Ed.). *Iran's Strategic Weapons Programmes: A Net Assessment.* Abingdon, Routledge, 2005.

Schirazi, Asghar. *The Constitution of Iran: Politics and the State in the Islamic Republic*. London, I. B. Tauris, 1998.

Sick, Gary. *All Fall Down: America's Tragic Encounter with Iran.* New York, Random House, 1985.

October Surprise. New York, Random House, 1991.

Stempel, John D. *Inside the Iranian Revolution.* Bloomington, IN, Indiana University Press, 1982.

Taheri, Amir. *The Spirit of Allah: Khomeini and the Iranian Revolution.* London, Hutchinson, 1985.

Takeyh, Ray. *Guardians of the Revolution: Iran and the World in the Age of the Ayatollahs*. New York, Oxford University Press, 2009.

Upton, Joseph M. *The History of Modern Iran: An Interpretation.* Cambridge, MA, Harvard University Press, 1960.

Villiers, Gerard de. *The Imperial Shah: An Informal Biography.* London, Weidenfeld and Nicolson, 1977.

Zonis, Marrin. *Majestic Failure: The Fall of the Shah.* Chicago, IL, University of Chicago Press, 1991.

Economy

Alizadeh, Parvin (Ed.). *The Economy of Iran: The Dilemmas of an Islamic State*. London, I. B. Tauris, 2001.

Amid, Mohammad Javad. *Poverty, Agriculture and Reform in Iran.* London, Routledge, 1990.

Amuzegar, Jahangir. *An Economic Profile.* Middle East Institute, 1977.

The Dynamics of the Iranian Revolution. SUNY Press, 1991.

Iran's Economy under the Islamic Republic. London, I. B. Tauris, 1993.

Baldwin, George B. *Planning and Development in Iran.* Baltimore, MA, Johns Hopkins Press, 1967.

Bharier, Julian. *Economic Development in Iran 1900–1970.* London, Oxford University Press, 1971.

Elm, Mostafa. *Oil, Power and Principle: Iran's Oil Nationalization and its Aftermath.* Syracuse, NY, Syracuse University Press, 1992.

Ghosh, Sunil Kanti. *The Anglo–Iranian Oil Dispute.* Calcutta, 1960.

Gupta, Raj Narain. *Iran: An Economic Study.* New Delhi, 1947.

Heiss, Mary Ann. *Empire and Nationhood: The United States, Great Britain and Iranian Oil, 1950–1954.* New York, Columbia University Press, 1998.

Issawi, Charles. *The Economic History of Iran, 1800–1919.* University of Chicago Press, 1972.

Mason, F. C. *Iran: Economic and Commercial Conditions in Iran.* London, HMSO, 1957.

Mofid, Kamran. *The Economic Consequences of the Gulf War.* London, Routledge, 1990.

Nahai, L., and Kibell, C. L. *The Petroleum Industry of Iran.* Washington, DC, US Department of the Interior, Bureau of Mines, 1963.

Shakoori, Ali. *The State and Rural Development in Post-Revolutionary Iran*. New York, St Martin's Press, 2001.

IRAQ

Physical and Social Geography

W. B. FISHER

Iraq is bounded on the north by Turkey, on the east by Iran, on the south by Kuwait and the Persian (Arabian) Gulf, on the south-west by Saudi Arabia and Jordan, and on the north-west by Syria. The actual frontier lines present one or two unusual features. First, there exists between Iraq, Kuwait and Saudi Arabia a 'Neutral Zone', rhomboidal in shape, which was devised to facilitate the migrations of pastoral nomads, who cover great distances each year in search of pasture for their animals and who move regularly between several countries. Hence the stabilization or closing of a frontier could be for them a matter of life and death. Second, the frontier with Iran in its extreme southern portion, below al-Basrah (Basra), follows the course of the Shatt al-Arab waterway (the confluence of the Tigris and Euphrates), which flows into the Gulf, but from 1936 until March 1975 the frontier was at the left (east) bank, placing the whole of the river within Iraq. This situation had become increasingly unacceptable to Iran, and under the Algiers Agreement of March 1975 the border was restored to the Thalweg Line in the middle of the deepest shipping channel in the Shatt al-Arab estuary. The dispute over the precise position of this border was one of the causes of the war with Iran that began in 1980. Third, the inclusion of the northern province of al-Mawsil (Mosul) within Iraq was agreed only in 1926. Owing to its petroleum deposits, this territory was in dispute between Turkey, Syria and Iraq. Again, the presence of large numbers of migratory nomads, journeying each season between Iran, Turkey, Syria and Iraq, was a further complicating factor. In March 1984 a treaty was signed by Jordan and Iraq that finally demarcated the border between the two countries and under which Iraq ceded some 50 sq km to Jordan.

PHYSICAL FEATURES

The old name of Iraq (Mesopotamia = land between the rivers) indicates the main physical aspect of the country—the presence of the two river valleys of the Tigris and Euphrates, which merge in their lower courses. On the eastern side of this double valley the Zagros Mountains appear as an abrupt wall, overhanging the riverine lowlands, particularly in the south, below Baghdad. North of the latitude of Baghdad the rise to the mountains is more gradual, with several intervening hill ranges, such as the Jebel Hamrin. These ranges are fairly low and narrow at first, with separating lowlands, but towards the main Zagros topography becomes more imposing, and summits over 3,000 m in height occur. This region, lying north and east of Baghdad, is the ancient land of Assyria; nowadays the higher hill ranges lying in the extreme east are known as Iraqi Kurdistan, since many Kurdish tribes inhabit them.

On the western side of the river valley the land rises gradually to form the plateau that continues into Syria, Jordan and Saudi Arabia, and its maximum height in Iraq is about 1,000 m. In places it is possible to trace a cliff formation, where a more resistant bed of rock stands out prominently, and from this the name of the country is said to be derived (Iraq = cliff). There is no sharp geographical break between Iraq and its western neighbours comparable with that between Iraq and Iran; the frontier lines are artificial.

THE RIVERS

The Tigris, 1,850 km (1,150 miles) in length, rises in Turkey, and is joined by numerous and often large tributaries both in Turkey and Iraq. The Euphrates, 2,350 km in length, also rises in Turkey and flows first through Syria and then Iraq, joining the Tigris in its lower course at Qurnah, to form the stream known as the Shatt al-Arab (or Arvand river, as it is called by the Iranians), which is 185 km in length. Unlike the Tigris, the Euphrates receives no tributaries during its passage of Iraq. Above the region of Baghdad both rivers flow in well-defined channels, with retaining valley walls. Below Baghdad, however, the vestiges of a retaining valley disappear, and the rivers meander over a vast open plain with only a slight drop in level—in places merely 1.5 m or 2.0 m in 100 km. Here the rivers are raised on great levees, or banks of silt and mud (which they themselves have laid down), and now lie several feet above the level of the surrounding plain. One remarkable feature is the change in the relative level of the two river beds—water can be led from one to the other according to the actual district, and this possibility, utilized by irrigation engineers for many centuries, still remains the basic principle of present-day development. Old river channels, fully or partially abandoned by the river, are also a feature of the Mesopotamian lowland, associated with wide areas of swamp, lakes and sandbars. The Tigris, though narrower than the Euphrates, is swifter, and carries far more water.

As the sources of both rivers lie in the mountains of Turkey, the current is very fast, and upstream navigation is difficult in the middle and upper reaches. In spring, following the melting of snows in Asia Minor, both rivers begin to rise, reaching a maximum in April (Tigris) and May (Euphrates). During the season floods of 3.6 m to 6.0 m occur, and 10 m is known—this in a region where the land may fall only 4 m or less in level over 100 km. Immense areas are regularly inundated, levees often collapse, and villages and roads, where these exist, must be built on high embankments. The Tigris is particularly liable to sudden flooding, and can rise at the rate of one foot per hour. In lower Iraq wide expanses are inundated every year. Construction of the Wadi Tharthar control scheme, however, greatly reduced the incidence of severe flooding, particularly along the Tigris.

Roads were formerly difficult to maintain because of floods, and the rail system was of different gauges. New standard-gauge rail links have now been constructed: north–south from Mosul to Basra via Baghdad; various cross-country lines; and an extension along the Euphrates valley towards north-eastern Syria.

As a result of the former difficulties in communication, many communities of differing cultures and ways of life have persisted. Minority groups have thus been a feature in Iraq.

CLIMATE AND ECONOMIC ACTIVITY

The summers are overwhelmingly hot, with shade temperatures of over 43°C. Winters may be surprisingly cold: frost, though very rare in the south, can be severe in the north. Sudden hot spells during winter are another feature in the centre and south of Iraq. Rainfall is scanty over all of the country, except for the north-east (Assyria), where annual falls of 400 mm–600 mm occur—enough to grow crops without irrigation. Elsewhere farming is entirely dependent upon irrigation from river water. The great extent of standing water in many parts of Iraq leads to an unduly high air humidity, which explains the notorious reputation of the Mesopotamian summer.

The unusual physical conditions outlined present a number of obstacles to human activity. The flood waters are rather less 'manageable' than in Egypt, for example, and there is less of the regular deposition of thick, rich silt that is such a feature of the Nile. The effects of this are strikingly visible in the relatively small extent of land actually cultivated—at most, only one-sixth of the potentially cultivable territory and 3% of the total area of the country. Owing to the easy availability of agricultural land, wasteful, 'extensive' farming methods are often followed, giving a low yield. On the whole, Iraq is underpopulated, and could support larger numbers of inhabitants.

The unusual physical conditions have greatly restricted movement and the development of communications of all kinds. In the upper reaches of the rivers, boat journeys can only be made downstream, while nearer the sea the rivers are wider and slower but often very shallow. Roads and railways are difficult to maintain because of the floods.

PEOPLE AND LANGUAGE

In the marshes of the extreme south there are several boat- and raft-based Arab communities. Other important minorities live in, or close to, the hill country of the north: the Kurds, who number an estimated 4m. and migrate extensively into Syria, Turkey and Iran (see History); the Yazidis of the Jebel Sinjar; the Assyrian Christians (the name refers to their geographical location, and has no historical connection); and various communities of Uniate and Orthodox Christians. In addition, there were important groups of Jews—more than in most other Muslim countries—though, since the establishment of the State of Israel, much emigration has taken place. Nowadays only a tiny, and rapidly dwindling, Jewish community remains in Baghdad. It should be noted that, while the majority of the Muslims follow Shi'a rites, the wealthier Muslims have tended to be of Sunni adherence.

According to the new Constitution, which was ratified in 2005, both Arabic and Kurdish are the official languages of Iraq. Arabic is the most widely used language and the first language in the Arab provinces, while Kurdish is the primary language in the Kurdish autonomous regions. Dialects of Turkish are also current in the north, while variants of Persian are spoken by tribes in the east. An estimate, probably overly generous to the Arabic speakers, puts the relative proportions at Arabic 79%, Kurdish 16%, Persian 3% and Turkish 2% of the total population, which was estimated by the UN to total 33,765,232 at mid-2013.

History

LIAM ANDERSON

EARLY HISTORY

By the advent of Islam in the seventh century AD Iraq had already experienced more than 3,500 years of civilization. The Sumerians were, in turn, succeeded by the Elamites, the Amorites, the Mittani, the Hittites and the Assyrians, until in 612 BC the subject peoples rose and sacked Nineveh. Iraq then became the centre of a neo-Babylonian state, which, under Nebuchadnezzar (604–538 BC), included much of the Fertile Crescent (from the Euphrates to the Nile Valley), but soon fell to the Persians, who seized Babylon in 539–538 BC.

Iraq thus became a province of the Achaemenid Empire, until the military successes of Alexander the Great in 334–327 BC. After about 100 years of Seleucid rule, Iraq became a frontier province of the Parthian Empire against the might of Rome. Between AD 113 and 117 the Emperor Trajan conquered much of Iraq, but his successor, Hadrian, withdrew, although a Roman reoccupation later took place. Parthian rule eventually gave way before the emergence of the Persian Sasanid regime in the second century AD. Frontier wars with Rome broke out from time to time, but by the seventh century both Persia and the Eastern Persian Empire (Byzantium) were exhausted, and the way was open to conquest from the south.

THE RISE OF ISLAM

The spectacular birth and growth of Islam in the first quarter of the seventh century set the Arabs on the path of conquest outside Arabia. In 637, at the battle of Jalula, the Arabs virtually ended Sasanid power in Iraq. There immediately followed a period of struggle between Ali, the son-in-law of the Prophet, and Mu'awiya, who had been governor of Syria. Ali fell in battle in 661, making way for the Umayyad dynasty, based in Damascus, Syria, until 750. A movement arose known as the Shi'atu Ali (i.e. the party of Ali) and most new converts gave their allegiance to the Shi'a, partly as an expression of their social and political grievance against the established order. In 750 Umayyad rule was replaced by that of the Abbasid dynasty, with Iraq becoming the dominant and most prosperous part of the empire. The second Abbasid, al-Mansour (754–775), quickly abandoned the Shi'ite extremists who had brought the Abbasids to power. However, by the early eighth century, the Abbasid caliphs had become subordinate to the Turkish Mamluks (slave soldiers), and thereafter the Caliphate, while retaining its spiritual hegemony, was dependent for its survival upon a series of client rulers and dynasties, notably the Shi'ite Buyids and the Seljuq Turks.

MONGOL INVASIONS

In 1253 Hulagu, a grandson of Chinghiz (Jenghiz) Khan, moved westwards in force, captured Baghdad in 1258 and brought to an end the Abbasid Caliphate in Baghdad. Now part of the Ilkhanate, ruled by the Mongol Ilkhans of Persia, Iraq became a mere frontier province. After the death of the Ilkhan Abu Sa'id in 1335, Iraq passed to the Jala'irids who ruled until the early years of the 15th century. Iraq then passed successively under the power of two rival Turkoman confederations (the Black Sheep and the White Sheep) until, in 1499–1508, the White Sheep regime was destroyed by the Safavid Ismail, who made himself Shah of Persia. The Sunni Ottoman Turks considered the Shi'ite Ismail to be a threat, and the Sultan Suleyman I (Suleyman the Magnificent), in the course of his campaign against Persia, conquered Baghdad in 1534–35.

OTTOMAN IRAQ

Although Persian control was restored for a brief period between 1623 and 1638, Iraq was to remain, at least nominally, under Ottoman control until the First World War. A series of Mamluk pashas in the 18th century engaged in wars with Persia, and towards the end of the century had to contend with Kurdish insurrection in the north and raids by Wahhabi tribesmen from the south. In the early 19th century the Ottoman Sultan decided to regain direct possession of Iraq and end the Mamluk system. Sultan Mahmoud II sent Ali Ridha Pasha to perform this task in 1831. A severe outbreak of plague hampered the Mamluks, Da'ud Pasha was deposed, and the Mamluk regiments were exterminated.

WESTERN INFLUENCE

Although some of the European nations had long been in contact with Iraq through their commercial interests in the Persian (Arabian) Gulf, Western influences were slow to penetrate the province. By 1800 there was a British Resident at Basra and two years later a British Consulate in Baghdad. France also maintained agents in these cities, and French and Italian religious orders had settlements in the land. During the *tanzimat* reform period of the mid-19th century, the Ottoman Government did much to impose direct control over Kurdistan and the mountainous areas close to the Persian border, but serious reform did not begin until 1869, when Midhat Pasha arrived in Baghdad. After his departure in 1872, reform and European influence continued to advance, although slowly.

In November 1914 the United Kingdom and the Ottoman Empire were at war. British troops occupied the Shatt al-Arab region and, through the necessity of war, transformed Basra into an efficient and well-equipped port. A premature advance on Baghdad in 1915 ended in the retreat of the British forces to Kut, their prolonged defence of that town and, when all attempts to relieve it had failed, capitulation to the Ottomans in April 1916. A new offensive launched from Basra in late 1916 brought about the capture of Baghdad in March 1917. Kirkuk was taken in 1918, but, before the Allies could seize Mosul, the Ottoman Government sought and obtained an armistice in October. For two years, until the winter of 1920, the Commander-in-Chief of the British forces, acting through a civil commissioner, continued to be responsible for the administration of Iraq from Basra to Mosul, all the apparatus of a modern system of rule being created in Baghdad.

The last phase of Ottoman domination in Iraq, especially during the years after the Young Turk Revolution in 1908, had witnessed a marked growth of Arab nationalist sentiment. The prospect of independence, which the Allies held out to the Arabs in the course of the war, strengthened and extended the nationalist movement. In April 1920 the United Kingdom received a mandate for Iraq from the conference at San Remo, Italy. This news was soon followed by a serious insurrection among the tribesmen of the south. The revolt, caused partly by instinctive dislike of foreign rule but also by vigorous nationalist propaganda, was not wholly suppressed until early in the next year. Nevertheless, in October 1920 military rule in Iraq was formally terminated. An Arab Council of State, advised by British officials and responsible for the administration, now came into being and in March 1921 the Amir Faisal ibn Hussain agreed to rule as King in Baghdad. His ceremonial accession took place on 23 August 1921.

The Najdi (Saudi Arabian) frontier with Iraq was defined in the Treaty of Mohammara in May 1922. Saudi concern over loss of traditional grazing rights resulted in further talks between Ibn Sa'ud and the British Civil Commissioner in Iraq, and a Neutral Zone of 7,000 sq km was established adjacent to the western tip of the Kuwait frontier. A further agreement concerning the administration of this zone was signed between Iraq and Saudi Arabia in May 1938.

MODERN IRAQ

Despite the opposition of the more extreme nationalists, an Anglo-Iraqi Treaty was signed on 10 October 1922. It embodied the provisions of the mandate, safeguarded the judicial rights of foreigners and guaranteed the special interests of the United Kingdom in Iraq. An electoral law facilitated the choice of a constituent assembly, which met in March 1924 and, despite strong opposition by the nationalists, ratified the treaty with the United Kingdom. It accepted, too, an organic law declaring Iraq to be a sovereign state with a constitutional hereditary monarchy and a representative system of government. In 1925 the League of Nations recommended that the *wilaya* (administrative district) of Mosul, to which the Turks had laid claim, be incorporated into the new kingdom, a decision finally implemented in the treaty of July 1926 between the interested parties: the United Kingdom, Turkey and Iraq. By 1926 a fully constituted parliament was in session in Baghdad and all the ministries, as well as most of the larger departments of the administration, were in effective control. In 1930 a new treaty was signed with the United Kingdom, which established a close alliance between the two countries for a period of 25 years and granted the United Kingdom the use of airbases at Shuaiba and Habbaniya. On 3 October 1932 Iraq entered the League of Nations as an independent power, the mandate now being terminated.

Numerous difficulties confronted the kingdom in the period after 1932: for example, the animosities between the Sunni Muslims and the powerful Shi'ite tribes on the Euphrates, which tended to divide and embitter political life; the problem of relations with the Kurds, some of whom wanted a separate Kurdish state, and with other minorities such as the Assyrians; and the complicated task of reform in land tenure and of improvement in agriculture, irrigation, flood control, public services and communications. During these years the Government was little more than a façade of democratic forms concealing faction and intrigue. It is not surprising, therefore, that the first years of full independence made rather halting progress towards efficient rule. The dangerous nature of domestic tensions was demonstrated by the Assyrian massacre of 1933, perpetrated by troops of the Iraqi army. Political intrigue from Baghdad was partly responsible for the outbreak of tribal revolt along the Euphrates in 1935–36. The army crushed the insurrection without much difficulty and then, under the leadership of General Bakr Sidqi, and in alliance with disappointed politicians and reformist elements, brought about a *coup d'état* in October 1936. The new regime failed to fulfil its assurances of reform; its policies alienated the tribal chieftains and gave rise to serious tensions even within the armed forces, tensions which led to the assassination of Bakr Sidqi in August 1937.

In 1937 Iraq joined Turkey, Iran (as Persia had been renamed in 1935) and Afghanistan in the Sa'dabad Pact, which arranged for consultation in all disputes that might affect the common interests of the four states. A treaty signed with Iran in July 1937 and ratified in the following year provided for the specific acceptance of the boundary between the two countries as it had been defined in 1914. Relations with the United Kingdom deteriorated in the period after 1937, mainly because of the growth of anti-Zionist feeling and of resentment at British policy in Palestine. German influence in Iraq increased very much at this time, especially among those political and military circles associated with the army group later to be known as the Golden Square. Iraq severed its diplomatic connections with Germany at the beginning of the Second World War, but in 1941 the army commanders carried out a new *coup d'état*, establishing, under the nominal leadership of Rashid Ali al-Gaylani, a regime that announced its non-belligerent intentions. A disagreement over the passage of British troops through Iraq left no doubt of the pro-German sympathies of the Gaylani Government and led to hostilities that ended with the Allied occupation of Basra and Baghdad in May 1941. Thereafter, Iraq co-operated with the Allies and declared war on the Axis powers in 1943.

Iraq, during the years after the Second World War, was to experience much internal tension and unrest. In January 1948 a new Anglo-Iraqi agreement was signed. The agreement was designed to replace that of 1930 and incorporated substantial concessions, among them the British evacuation of the airbases at Shuaiba and Habbaniya and the creation of a joint board for the co-ordination of all matters relating to mutual defence. The animosities arising from the situation in Palestine provoked riots in Baghdad, directed against the new agreement with the United Kingdom, which were sufficiently disturbing to oblige the Iraqi Government to repudiate the settlement.

FOREIGN RELATIONS, 1955–58: THE BAGHDAD PACT AND THE SUEZ CRISIS

Iraq during these years found itself caught between the growing presence of the USSR in Middle Eastern (specifically Arab) affairs and the efforts of the Western Powers to counter that presence. In February 1955 Iraq made an alliance with Turkey for mutual co-operation and defence, a pact to which the United Kingdom acceded in the following April, agreeing also to end the Anglo–Iraqi agreement of 1930 and to surrender its airbases at Shuaiba and Habbaniya. When Pakistan and Iran followed suit in late 1955, the so-called Baghdad Pact was completed—a defensive cordon now existed along the southern fringe of the USSR.

The outbreak of hostilities between Israel and Egypt on 29 October 1956, and the armed intervention of British and French forces against Egypt (31 October–6 November) emboldened opposition in Iraq to all connections with the Western Powers. Indeed, Iraq broke off diplomatic relations with France and announced that it could give no assurance of taking part in further sessions of the Council of the Baghdad Pact, if delegates from the United Kingdom were present. However, the equivocal attitude of the Baghdad Government during the Suez crisis provoked unrest in Iraq, with fatal disturbances at Najaf and Mosul. Martial law was imposed on 31 October and was not raised until 27 May 1957.

In February 1958 King Faisal of Iraq and King Hussein of Jordan joined together in an abortive Arab Federation (see the chapter on Jordan).

OVERTHROW OF THE MONARCHY AND INTERNAL UPHEAVAL, 1958–68

King Faisal II, the Crown Prince of Iraq and Gen. Nouri al-Said were all killed during a *coup d'état*, initiated on 14 July 1958 by units of the Iraqi army. Iraq became a republic and power was placed in the hands of a Council of Sovereignty exercising presidential authority, and of a Cabinet led by Brig. Abd al-Karim Kassem, with the rank of Prime Minister. However, a power struggle soon developed between the two main architects of the coup—Brig. (later Gen.) Kassem, the Prime Minister, and Col (later Field-Marshal) Abd al-Salam Muhammad Aref, the Deputy Prime Minister and Minister of the Interior. Col Aref was associated with the influential Baath Party and had shown himself to be a supporter of union between Iraq and the United Arab Republic (UAR—the union of Egypt and Syria). In September he was dismissed from his offices and, in November, was tried on a charge of plotting against the interests of Iraq. Upon its reconstitution in February 1959 the new regime proved to be hostile to the UAR and inclined to favour a form of independent nationalism with left-wing tendencies. One of the new regime's earliest acts, in March, was to withdraw from the Baghdad Pact. Shortly afterwards, the British Royal Air Force contingent at Habbaniya was recalled.

In early 1959 the Iraqi communists, operating mainly under the aegis of the so-called People's Resistance Force, were refused representation in the Government, but had otherwise already infiltrated into the armed forces and the civil service. Gen. Kassem now began to introduce measures to limit communist influence inside the Government and the administration of the country. In July fighting occurred at Kirkuk between the Kurds (supported by the People's Resistance Force) and the Turkomans, with the result that Kassem disbanded the People's Resistance Force. More important for the Government was the fact that, in March 1961, a considerable section of the Kurdish population in northern Iraq rose in rebellion under Mustafa Barzani, the President of the Kurdistan Democratic Party (KDP—a party established in 1958 after the return of Barzani from an exile occasioned by an earlier unsuccessful revolt in 1946), owing to the Government's refusal to accede to repeated demands for Kurdish autonomy; Barzani proclaimed an independent Kurdish state. By September the rebels controlled the mountainous territory for some 400 km along the Iraq–Turkey and Iraq–Iran frontiers, from Zakho in the west to Sulaimaniya in the east. The Kurds were able to consolidate their hold over much of northern Iraq during the course of 1962, using guerrilla tactics to isolate and deprive the government garrisons in the north of supplies, and by December 1963 Kurdish forces had advanced south towards the Khanaqin area and the main road linking Iraq with Iran. Negotiations for peace began near Sulaimaniya in January 1964 and led to a cease-fire on 10 February. The national claims of the Kurds were to be recognized in a new provisional constitution for Iraq, but the Kurdish tribes refused to lay down their arms until their political demands had been granted. Despite the negotiation of this settlement, no definitive solution to the Kurdish problem had emerged.

Gen. Kassem was killed on 8 February 1963 in a military coup against his regime that had been planned by nationalist army officers and the Baath Party. Col Aref was now promoted to the office of President and a new Cabinet was created under Brig. (later Gen.) Ahmad Hassan al-Bakr. The Baath Party, founded in 1941 (in Syria) and dedicated to the ideas of Arab unity, socialism and freedom, drew its main support from military elements, intellectuals and the middle classes, but in Iraq it was divided into a pro-Egyptian wing advocating union with the UAR and a more independent wing disinclined to accept authoritarian control from Egypt. The coup triggered the arrest of pro-Kassem and communist elements, mass trials, a number of executions, confiscations of property and a purge of the officer corps and civil service.

The schism between the extremist and the more moderate Baath elements soon widened. At the end of September 1963 the extremists dominated the Baath Regional Council in Iraq, and their position was strengthened by an international Baath conference held at Damascus in October, which supported a federal union between Syria and Iraq and put forward more radical social and economic policies. Nevertheless, a further Baathist conference at Baghdad in November enabled the moderates to elect a new Baath Regional Council in Iraq with their own adherents in control. At this juncture the extremists attempted a *coup d'état*, in the course of which air force elements attacked the presidential palace and the Ministry of Defence. On 18 November President Aref assumed full powers in Iraq, with the support of the armed forces, and a new Revolutionary Command was established in Baghdad.

In July 1965 a number of pro-Egyptian ministers resigned, and at the beginning of September a new administration was installed, with Brig. Aref Abd al-Razzaq as Prime Minister. Abd al-Razzaq, reputed to be pro-Egyptian, tried to seize full power in Iraq, but his attempted *coup d'état* failed, and on 16 September he, together with some of his supporters, found refuge in Cairo, Egypt. On 13 April 1966 President Abd al-Salam Aref was killed in a helicopter crash. His brother, Maj.-Gen. Abd al-Rahman Aref, succeeded him as President with the approval of the Cabinet and of the National Defence Council. In late June Abd al-Razzaq led a second abortive coup. Meanwhile, the war against the Kurds continued during 1964–66, and fighting in December 1965 close to the Iraq–Iran border led to a number of frontier violations, which exacerbated tensions between the two states.

THE 1968 COUP AND ITS AFTERMATH

Popular perceptions of the regime were that it was corrupt and inefficient, and consequently the sudden bloodless *coup d'état* of 17 July 1968 did not surprise many observers. Former Prime Minister al-Bakr became President; the deposed President Aref went into exile and his Prime Minister, Taher Yahya, was imprisoned on corruption charges. A new Government was soon dismissed by the President, who accused it of 'reactionary tendencies'. He then appointed himself Prime Minister and Commander-in-Chief of the Armed Forces. However, by November there were frequent reports of a purge directed against opponents of the new regime, and freedom of political comment seemed to have disappeared. A former Minister of Foreign Affairs, Dr Nasser al-Hani, was found murdered, and former Prime Minister Dr Abd al-Rahman al-Bazzaz was arrested as a 'counter-revolutionary leader'. Open hostilities with the Kurds erupted in October 1968 for the first time since the June 1966 cease-fire, and continued on an extensive scale throughout the winter. The Baghdad Government had little success in gaining military control of the situation, claiming that the rebels were receiving aid from Iran and Israel. Fighting continued unabated through 1969, the Kurds demanding autonomy within the state and asking for UN mediation.

In June 1972 Iraq nationalized the interests of the Iraq Petroleum Co (IPC), and agreement on outstanding points of dispute was finally reached on 28 February 1973. The company agreed to settle Iraqi claims for retrospective royalties by paying £141m., and to waive its objections to Law No. 80 under which the North Rumaila fields were seized in 1961.

In July 1973 an abortive coup took place, led by the security chief, Nazim Kazzar, in which the Minister of Defence, Gen. Hammad Shehab, was killed. There was some speculation that the coup had been attempted by a civilian faction within the Baath Party in an attempt to eliminate President Bakr and the military faction. Consequences of the attempted coup included an amendment to the Constitution giving more power to the President, and the formation of a National Front between the Baath Party and the Iraqi Communist Party (ICP).

SETTLEMENT WITH THE KURDS

In March 1970 a 15-article peace plan was announced by the Revolutionary Command Council (RCC) and the Kurdish leaders. The plan conceded: that the Kurds should participate fully in government; that Kurdish officials should be appointed in areas inhabited by a Kurdish majority; that Kurdish should be the official language, along with Arabic, in Kurdish areas; that development of Kurdish areas should be implemented; and that the Provisional Constitution should be amended to incorporate the rights of the Kurds. The agreement was widely accepted by the Kurdish community and fighting ceased, thus ending a war that had proved costly to Iraq and had seriously delayed the national development programme.

According to the agreement, the deadline for implementation of the accord was 11 March 1974. On expiry of the deadline, Saddam Hussain al-Tikriti, the Vice-President of the RCC, announced the granting of autonomy to the Kurds. The KDP felt that the Iraqi offer did not fulfil its demands for full government representation, which included membership of the RCC, but a minority of Kurds welcomed the proposals. Barzani and his *peshmerga* ('those who confront death') militia commenced an armed insurgency in northern Iraq. By August 1974 the Kurdish war had reached a new level of intensity; the Government in Baghdad was directing large military resources against the *peshmerga*, deploying tanks, field guns and bombers. About 130,000 Kurds, largely civilians, took refuge in Iran, which was also supplying arms to the *peshmerga*. However, the Kurdish rebellion collapsed after Iraq and Iran signed an accord at the meeting of the Organization of the Petroleum Exporting Countries (OPEC) in Algiers, Algeria, on 6 March 1975, ending their border dispute and agreeing to end 'infiltrations of a subversive character'; Barzani decided that he could not continue his struggle without Iran's aid, and fled to the Iranian capital, Tehran. (He died in the USA in 1979 and was succeeded as leader of the KDP by his son, Masoud.)

On 16 July 1979 Saddam Hussain replaced Ahmad Hassan al-Bakr as President of Iraq and Chairman of the RCC. A few days later an attempted coup was reported, and several members of the RCC were sentenced to death for their alleged part in the plot.

WAR WITH IRAN

Iraq was dissatisfied with the 1975 peace agreement with Iran (though from a domestic aspect it had virtually ended the Kurdish rebellion), and wanted to re-establish the Shatt al-Arab boundary whereby it controlled the whole waterway. The Iranian Revolution of 1979 increased tensions as the new regime in Tehran accused Iraq of fomenting demands for Arab autonomy in the Iranian province of Khuzestan (also known as 'Arabistan'). Additionally, Iraq's Sunni leadership feared that the Islamic Revolution in Iran might inspire Iraq's Shi'ite majority. Fighting on the border between Iran and Iraq occurred frequently as 1980 progressed, and open warfare began on 22 September when Iraqi forces advanced into Iran along a 480-km front. Iran had ignored Iraqi diplomatic demands for the withdrawal of Iranian forces from Zain ul-Qos on the border, Iraq maintaining that this territory should have been returned by Iran under the 1975 agreement. Iraq therefore abrogated the Shatt al-Arab agreement on 16 September.

Most commentators agree that Saddam Hussain's real intention when he invaded Iran was to topple the Islamic revolutionary regime. However, resistance was fiercer than he expected and a stalemate was soon reached along the invasion front, while various international peace missions sought in vain for a solution. In early 1982 Iranian forces launched successful counter-offensives, one in the region of Dezful in March, and another in April that resulted in the recapture of Khorramshahr by the Iranians in May. By late June Saddam Hussain had to acknowledge that the invasion of Iran had been a failure, and he arranged for the complete withdrawal of Iraqi troops from Iranian territory. In July the Iranian army crossed into Iraq, giving rise to the heaviest fighting of the war thus far.

From October 1983 Iran launched a series of attacks across its northern border with Iraq. About 700 sq km of Iraqi territory were gained, threatening the last outlet for Iraqi exports of petroleum through the Kirkuk pipeline. Iraq intensified its missile attacks and bombing raids against Iranian towns and petroleum installations.

In February 1984 Iran launched an offensive in the marshlands around Majnoon Island, the site of rich oilfields in southern Iraq, near the confluence of the Tigris and Euphrates rivers. Iraq failed to regain control of this territory, and was condemned for using mustard gas in the fighting. Iraq subsequently established extensive and formidable defences, including a system of dams and embankments, along the southern front, near Basra, in anticipation of a possibly decisive offensive by Iran, which massed some 500,000 men there.

The anticipated offensive occurred in March 1985, when Iran committed an estimated 50,000 troops to an attack on the southern front in the region of the Hawizah marshes, east of the Tigris. Iranian forces succeeded in crossing the Tigris and for a time closed the main road connecting Baghdad and Basra before being repulsed. Iraq was again accused of using chemical weapons during this engagement.

Until mid-1985 Iraq had failed to launch attacks against the main Iranian oil export terminal on Kharg Island of sufficient frequency or intensity seriously to threaten the continuation of oil exports. In August, however, Iraq made the first of a concentrated series of raids on Kharg, causing a reduction in Iranian oil exports from 1.2m. barrels per day (b/d)–1.5m. b/d, in the months leading up to the raids, to less than 1m. b/d in September. By the end of 1985 exports from Kharg had reportedly been reduced to a trickle compared with its 6.5m.-b/d capacity.

From mid-1986 Iran launched a series of offensives along the length of the Iraqi border and, in the south, the Karbala-5 offensive brought Iranian troops to within 10 km of Iraq's second most populous city, Basra. Iraq, meanwhile, continued to attack tankers shuttling Iranian oil from Kharg Island to the floating terminals at Sirri and Larak islands during the first half of the year. However, an apparently accidental attack in the Gulf by an Iraqi *Mirage* F-1 fighter plane on the frigate USS *Stark*, part of the US naval force, which had been deployed in the Gulf to protect shipping, created a crisis in Iraqi–US relations. The fighter fired two *Exocet* missiles at the *Stark*, only one of which exploded, killing 37 US sailors. Iraq apologized for the 'error' and desisted from attacks on tankers for the next five weeks.

Tension in the Gulf escalated in May 1987 after the USA's decision to accede to a request from Kuwait for 11 Kuwaiti tankers to be re-registered under the US flag, entitling them to US naval protection. Apart from the financial aid it gave Iraq, Kuwait was a transit point for goods (including military equipment) destined for Iraq, and for exports of oil sold on Iraq's behalf. Iran warned Kuwait on several occasions of dire consequences if it continued to support Iraq, and between October 1986 and April 1987 15 ships bound to or from Kuwait were attacked in the Gulf by Iran, and several Kuwaiti cargoes were seized. After the USA made its navy available to escort re-registered Kuwaiti tankers through the Gulf, Iran announced that it would not hesitate to sink US warships if provoked.

Contrary to advice from Western governments, Iraq resumed attacks on Iranian oil installations and industrial targets, and on tankers in the Gulf transporting Iranian oil, on 29 August 1987.

CEASE-FIRE IN THE IRAN–IRAQ WAR

During 1987–88, for the first time in six years, owing to poor mobilization, disorganization and a shortage of volunteers, Iran was unable to launch a major winter offensive and began to lose ground to Iraqi advances along the length of the war front. However, this was not before Kurdish guerrillas, in February 1988, had advanced into government-controlled territory in Iraqi Kurdistan, where Iranian forces, with Kurdish assistance, had established bridgeheads, particularly in the Mawat region, along the Iranian border. The Kurdish part in these operations represented the largest Kurdish offensive since 1974–75, uniting forces from the KDP and the Patriotic Union of Kurdistan (PUK), which, in November 1986, had agreed to co-ordinate their military and political activities and were in the process of forming a coalition of Kurdish nationalist groups. In March 1988, in a retaliatory attack against the captured town of Halabja, Iraq used chemical weapons to kill 4,000 Kurdish civilians. In mid-April 1988 Iraqi forces regained control of the Faw peninsula, where the Iranians, who had been unable to make further territorial gains since capturing the area in 1986, had scaled down their presence. Then, in May 1988, Iraq recaptured the Shalamcheh area, south-east of Basra, driving the Iranians back across the Shatt al-Arab.

Following a series of military defeats in 1988, Iran accepted the terms of a cease-fire which came into force on 20 August, monitored by a specially created UN observer force of 350 officers, the UN Iran–Iraq Military Observer Group. On 16 August 1990 Saddam Hussain abruptly sought an immediate, formal peace with Iran (for full details, see the chapter on Iran) by accepting almost all of the claims that Iran had pursued since the declaration of a cease-fire. On 10 September 1990 Iran and Iraq formally agreed to resume diplomatic relations.

IRAQI SUPPRESSION OF THE KURDS

The introduction of a cease-fire in the Iran–Iraq War in August 1988 allowed Iraq to divert more troops and equipment to Kurdistan, apparently in an attempt to effect a final military solution to the problem of the Kurdish separatist movement. At the end of August an estimated 60,000–70,000 Iraqi troops launched a new offensive to conquer guerrilla bases near the borders with Iran and Turkey, bombarding villages, allegedly using chemical weapons, and forcing thousands of Kurdish civilians and *peshmerga* to escape into Iran and Turkey. By mid-September more than 100,000 Kurdish refugees were believed to have fled across the border into Turkey, while Iraqi Kurds seeking refuge in Iran joined an estimated 100,000 others from their country, some 40,000 of whom had escaped from Halabja after the chemical attack on the city in March. The death toll from the new offensive was estimated at 15,000 in early September.

In September 1988 the Government began to evacuate inhabitants of the Kurdish Autonomous Region to the interior of Iraq as the first step towards the creation of a 30 km-wide uninhabited 'security zone' along the whole of Iraq's border with Iran and Turkey.

IRAQ'S INVASION OF KUWAIT

Prior to a meeting of the OPEC ministerial council in Geneva on 25 July 1990, Iraq had implied that it might take military action against countries that continued to flout their oil production quotas. It had also accused Kuwait of violating the Iraqi border in order to steal Iraqi oil resources worth US $2,400m., and suggested that Iraq's debt to Kuwait, accumulated largely during the Iran–Iraq War, should be waived.

Direct negotiations between Iraq and Kuwait commenced in Saudi Arabia at the end of July 1990, with the aim of resolving disputes over territory, oil pricing and Iraq's debt to Kuwait. Kuwait was expected to accede to Iraqi demands for early negotiations to draft a border demarcation treaty, and Iraq was expected to emphasize a claim to the strategic islands of Bubiyan and Warbah, situated at the mouth of the Shatt al-Arab. On 1 August, however, the talks collapsed, and on 2 August Iraq invaded Kuwait, taking control of the country and establishing a (short-lived) Provisional Free Government.

The immediate response, on 2 August 1990, of the UN Security Council to the invasion of Kuwait was to convene and to adopt unanimously a resolution (No. 660) which: condemned the Iraqi invasion of Kuwait; demanded the immediate and unconditional withdrawal of Iraqi forces from Kuwait; and appealed for a negotiated settlement of the conflict. On 6 August the UN Security Council convened again and adopted a further resolution (No. 661), which imposed mandatory economic sanctions on Iraq and on occupied Kuwait, affecting all commodities with the exception of medical supplies and foodstuffs 'in humanitarian circumstances'.

On 7 August 1990, at the request of King Fahd of Saudi Arabia, the USA dispatched combat troops and aircraft to Saudi Arabia to secure the country's border with Kuwait against a possible attack by Iraq. US troops began to occupy positions in Saudi Arabia on 9 August, one day after Iraq announced its formal annexation of Kuwait. On the same day the UN Security Council convened and adopted a unanimous resolution (No. 662), which declared the annexation of Kuwait to be null and void, and urged all states and institutions not to recognize it.

The dispatch of US troops signified the beginning of 'Operation Desert Shield' for the defence of Saudi Arabia, in accordance with Article 51 of the UN Charter. By the end of January 1991 some 30 countries had contributed ground troops, aircraft and warships to the multinational force in Saudi Arabia and the Gulf region. By far the biggest contributor was the USA, which, it was estimated, had deployed some 500,000 military personnel. Arab countries participating in the multinational force were Egypt, Syria, Morocco and the members of the Cooperation Council for the Arab States of the Gulf (Gulf Cooperation Council—GCC)—Bahrain, Kuwait, Oman, Qatar, Saudi Arabia and the United Arab Emirates (UAE). It was estimated that Iraq had deployed some 555,000 troops in Kuwait and southern Iraq by the end of January 1991.

On 29 November 1990 the UN Security Council convened and adopted a resolution (No. 678), drafted by the USA, which, with reference to its previous resolutions regarding Iraq's occupation of Kuwait, authorized all necessary means to enforce the removal of Iraqi forces from Kuwait. The declared aim of the multinational force in Saudi Arabia, in the initial phase of Operation Desert Storm, was to gain air superiority, and then air supremacy, over Iraqi forces, in order to facilitate air attacks on Iraqi military and industrial installations. Hostilities commenced on 16–17 January 1991 with air raids on Baghdad. On 30 January the multinational force claimed air supremacy over Iraq and Kuwait, and air attacks were refocused on the fortified positions of Iraqi ground troops in Kuwait, in preparation for a ground offensive.

During the night of 23–24 February 1991 the multinational force launched a ground offensive for the liberation of Kuwait. Iraqi troops defending Kuwait's border with Saudi Arabia were quickly defeated, offering little resistance to the multinational force. A flanking movement, far to the west, by French and US forces succeeded in severing the main road west from Basra, while the road leading north from Basra was breached by repeated bombing. Divisions of Iraq's élite Republican Guards in the Kuwait area were thus isolated to the south of the Tigris and Euphrates rivers and prevented from retreating towards Baghdad. On 28 February US President George Bush announced that the war to liberate Kuwait had been won, and he declared a cease-fire. Iraq had agreed to renounce its claim to Kuwait and to release all prisoners of war. It also indicated that it would comply with the remaining relevant UN Security Council resolutions. On 3 March Iraq accepted the cease-fire terms that had been dictated, at a meeting with Iraqi military commanders, by the commander of the multinational force, Gen. Norman Schwarzkopf of the US army.

On 3 April 1991 the UN Security Council adopted a resolution (No. 687) that stipulated the terms for a full cease-fire in the Gulf. Among these was the requirement that Iraq dismantle its weapons of mass destruction stockpiles and production facilities. A UN Special Commission (UNSCOM) was created by the UN to monitor Iraq's compliance. These terms were accepted on 5 April by Iraq's RCC, and on the following day by the National Assembly.

INTERNAL REVOLT

Following the rout of the Iraqi army by the UN-sponsored multinational force in February 1991, armed rebellion broke out among the largely Shi'ite population of southern Iraq and the Iraqi Kurds in the Kurdish northern provinces. In the south, Basra was the centre of the rebellion. On 4 March it was reported that supporters of the Tehran-based Supreme Council for the Islamic Revolution in Iraq (SCIRI) had gained control of the towns of Basra, Amarah, Samawah and al-Nasiriyah (Nasiriya). Already, on 5 March, the assessment of US intelligence sources that the southern rebellion lacked sufficient organization to succeed appeared to be corroborated: armed forces loyal to the Government were reported to be regaining control of the cities that had fallen to the rebels. Crucially, there was no military intervention by the multinational force in support of the rebellion. By mid-March armed forces loyal to the Government had effectively crushed the rebellion in the south, but their deployment there had allowed a simultaneous revolt by Kurdish guerrilla groups in the Kurdish northern provinces of Iraq to gather momentum. In late March it was reported that Kurdish rebels had gained control of Kirkuk and of important oil installations to the west of the city, and in early April Kurdish leaders claimed that as many as 100,000 guerrillas were involved in hostilities against government forces.

However, lacking military support from the multinational force, the Kurdish guerrillas were unable to resist the onslaught of the Iraqi armed forces, which were redeployed northwards as soon as they had crushed the uprising in southern Iraq. By early April 1991 government forces had recaptured Kirkuk, Irbil (Arbil), Dohuk and Zakho. Some 50,000 Kurds were reported to have been killed in the hostilities, and, fearing genocide, an estimated 1m.–2m. Kurds fled before the Iraqi army across the northern mountains into Turkey and Iran.

As the 'Kurdish crisis' had developed, France, the United Kingdom and the USA had all committed troops to maintain a 'safe haven' for the Kurds in northern Iraq. On 8 April 1991 a proposal by the British Prime Minister, John Major, that a UN-supervised enclave be created in northern Iraq for the protection of the Kurdish population was approved by the leaders of the member states of the European Community (now European Union—EU). The US Government withheld its formal approval of the proposal, but on 10 April it warned Iraq that any interference in relief operations north of latitude 36°N would prompt military retaliation. The UN response to the proposal to create Kurdish 'safe havens' under its auspices also remained cautious. On 17 April the UN Secretary-General, Javier Pérez de Cuéllar, warned that the Iraqi Government's permission would have to be obtained before foreign troops were deployed in northern Iraq, and that the UN Security Council would need to approve the policing of the Kurdish enclave by a UN-backed force. Nevertheless, in late April UN relief agencies reported that Kurdish refugees were returning to Iraq in large numbers.

As international diplomacy sought to create secure conditions for Iraqi Kurds within Iraq, negotiations between the leaders of Kurdish groups and the Iraqi Government soon collapsed and, in the absence of a negotiated autonomy agreement with the Iraqi Government, the Kurds organized elections to a 105-member Iraqi Kurdistan National Assembly, and for a paramount Kurdish leader.

CONCLUSION OF AGREEMENT ON PETROLEUM SALES

After rejecting the UN's initial plan to allow Iraq to export oil in return for supplies of essential civilian goods, in January 1996 Iraq finally indicated its willingness to 'enter into a dialogue' on an oil-for-food agreement with the UN, provided that no conditions were attached to it. Under the conditions of Resolution 986, Iraq had to accept UN monitoring of the distribution of humanitarian supplies and to agree to the supply of specified amounts of food and medicine to the Kurdish-controlled enclave in the north—and on 20 May Iraq accepted the UN terms. The memorandum of agreement, which had to be renewed every six months, detailed stringent conditions for the sale of up to US $4,000m. of Iraqi oil a year in order to fund the purchase of food and medicine and to finance UN operations in Iraq. Petroleum began to flow through the pipeline to Turkey on 10 December. Part of Iraq's oil revenue was to be allocated to the UN Compensation Commission, which had been unable to settle the majority of Gulf War compensation claims because of inadequate funds. The first shipments of food and humanitarian supplies purchased under the new agreement reached Iraq in March 1997.

On 21 June 1998 the UN Security Council unanimously adopted Resolution 1115, condemning the Iraqi authorities for repeatedly refusing to allow inspection teams access to sites and indicating that failure to co-operate could prompt the imposition of further sanctions. Relations between UNSCOM and the Iraqi Government deteriorated rapidly, provoked mainly by an ongoing dispute over the inspection of presidential palaces. More broadly, Iraq continued to insist that it had destroyed all its weapons of mass destruction but was unable to verify this to the satisfaction of UNSCOM.

ECONOMIC CRISIS, MILITARY INSTABILITY AND CONFLICTS WITHIN THE REGIME

By October 1994 the living standards of large sections of the Iraqi population had reportedly been reduced to subsistence level. The Iraqi Government appeared increasingly desperate to maintain order in the face of this economic crisis. Dissatisfaction within the armed forces was a particular source of concern for the regime. An unsuccessful coup attempt in January 1995 prompted a comprehensive reorganization of military ranks. In March another coup attempt, organized by the former head of Iraqi military intelligence during the 1990–91 hostilities in the Gulf, and supported by Kurdish insurgents in the north and Shi'ite rebels in the south, was also thwarted.

A new Minister of Defence and a new Chief of the General Staff were appointed in July 1995 in an attempt to consolidate support for the President. However, in August further significant divisions within Saddam Hussain's power base became apparent following the defection to Jordan of two of the President's sons-in-law, Lt-Gen. Hussain Kamel al-Majid and his brother Col Saddam Kamel, together with their wives. Hussain Kamel had been Minister of Industry and Military Production, responsible for Iraq's weapons development programme, and Saddam Kamel the head of the Presidential Guard, responsible for presidential security. It was rumoured that they had become alarmed at the increasing concentration of power in the hands of Saddam Hussain's two sons, Uday and Qusay, and that they feared for their lives. The two men were immediately granted political asylum by King Hussein of Jordan. From Amman, Hussain Kamel urged the Iraqi army to overthrow Saddam Hussain's regime, and Iraqi opposition groups to unite and form a government-in-exile. There was speculation that he himself was regarded as a possible successor to Saddam Hussain. Hussain Kamel also met Rolf Ekeus, the head of UNSCOM, and was believed to have provided further information on Iraq's biological weapons development programmes. Iraq condemned both men as traitors and a wave of arrests and executions followed their defection as Saddam Hussain ordered a purge of senior army officers and government officials who had been close to the two brothers.

In February 1996 the two defectors, Hussain and Saddam Kamel, returned to Baghdad, having been granted a pardon by Saddam Hussain. Immediately after their return to Iraq the two men (who were promptly divorced from their wives) were assassinated, allegedly by men under the command of Saddam Hussain's son, Uday. In June reports emerged of a new coup plot involving senior officers of the Republican Guard and close associates of Saddam Hussain from Tikrit. More than 100 officers, including two army commanders, were arrested and subsequently executed. Mounting opposition to the President from within the armed forces was widely considered to have prompted his decision to transfer responsibility for the national military intelligence department from the Ministry of Defence, and to create new paramilitary units entrusted with the protection of his own family.

Tensions in the south of Iraq were greatly exacerbated in February 1999 when Ayatollah al-Sadr was assassinated in the holy city of Najaf, becoming the third senior Shi'a cleric to be murdered in less than a year. In his last sermon, a week before his death, al-Sadr had called on the authorities to release immediately an estimated 100 Shi'a clerics who had been arbitrarily arrested. The Iraqi Government again denied any involvement in the murder, and swiftly suppressed widespread riots among Shi'ites throughout the southern provinces, as well as in at least one major suburb of Baghdad, which erupted following al-Sadr's murder.

OPERATION DESERT FOX

In December 1998 the head of UNSCOM, Richard Butler, submitted a new report to the UN Security Council that was critical of Iraq's attitude towards UNSCOM. On 16 December, as the Security Council considered Butler's report, the USA and the United Kingdom launched an intensive bombing campaign against Iraq over four consecutive nights, involving cruise missiles, fighter aircraft and heavy bombers. The stated aim of the campaign—termed Operation Desert Fox—was to diminish and degrade Saddam Hussain's ability to use and deploy weapons of mass destruction.

Operation Desert Fox signalled the end of any effort by Iraq to co-operate with UNSCOM. It was also the last significant attempt by the Administration of US President Bill Clinton to precipitate the downfall of Hussain's regime through military force. Instead, the emphasis shifted to containment, specifically through the vigorous enforcement of the two 'no-fly' zones. US and British forces continued to attack military targets in both zones, extending the range from surface-to-air missile batteries to their command and control infrastructure, and began attacking some oil-related installations. (Iraq insisted that these attacks had resulted in civilian casualties.)

IRAQ IN THE AFTERMATH OF 11 SEPTEMBER 2001

Following the swift victory of US-led forces against the Taliban regime in Afghanistan in late 2001, demands within the US political establishment for a similar campaign in Iraq increased. By the end of the year statements made by senior US officials appeared to suggest that, if Iraq did not agree to the prompt return of UN weapons inspectors, the Administration of US President George W. Bush was prepared to resort to military action.

On 8 November 2002, following months of tension between the USA and Iraq regarding the re-admittance of weapons inspectors, the UN Security Council unanimously adopted Resolution 1441. The resolution demanded that Iraq must, first, declare all details of its weapons programmes; and, second, provide immediate and unconditional access to weapons inspectors. It concluded that Iraq would face serious consequences if it continued to 'violate its obligations'. The resolution did not authorize the automatic use of force against Iraq. Hans Blix, in charge of weapons inspections, presented his first report to the UN Security Council on 27 January 2003, amid a tense political atmosphere. The report, which highlighted Iraqi co-operation, but also indicated areas in need of improvement, only served to heighten the already fraught divisions within the Security Council. Blix's second report, on 14 February, offered similarly ambiguous conclusions. The report stated that, while no Iraqi weapons of mass destruction had been found, inspectors doubted Saddam Hussain's intentions to disarm. With the British Prime Minister, Tony Blair, particularly insistent upon at least attempting to secure a UN resolution authorizing the use of military force against Iraq, the USA, the United Kingdom and Spain submitted a draft resolution on 24 February emphasizing the serious consequences faced by Iraq as a result of its 'continued violation of its obligations'. After the French threatened to veto any resolution authorizing the use of force, it became clear that any attack on Iraq would proceed without UN backing.

OPERATION IRAQI FREEDOM

The military undertaking to remove Saddam Hussain started from a weakened position, owing to the refusal of the Turkish Grand National Assembly to permit the use of Turkish territory as a base for an attack on the Iraqi regime. This left Kuwait as the US-led coalition's only base of operations for land forces. With plans already in need of modernization, the coalition command seized the opportunity to eliminate Saddam Hussain at the start of the hostilities and Operation Iraqi Freedom commenced on 20 March 2003 with a swift air-strike at the centre of Baghdad in an attempt to assassinate the Iraqi President. The attack failed but was followed by a precise but overwhelming onslaught of aerial firepower in a strategy that came to be labelled as 'shock and awe'. The land assault began almost simultaneously. The coalition forces remained convinced that Saddam Hussain enjoyed little popular support from the Iraqi people and expected little opposition on the ground. British forces tentatively occupied Basra on 6 April, though failed for several days adequately to secure the city. The US conquest of Baghdad commenced on 3 April, with US forces consolidating their hold on the capital by 9 April. Coalition forces were left exposed to guerrilla attacks, with daily losses being announced. The removal of Saddam Hussain from power was symbolized by the toppling of his statue in the centre of Baghdad. However, it soon became apparent that the lightning speed with which the coalition forces had entered and occupied Iraq had bypassed significant pockets of pro-Saddam Hussain groups.

POST-WAR TURBULENCE

The ousting of Saddam Hussain's Government was followed by a period of civil unrest. In particular, in the security vacuum that emerged after the disintegration of Saddam Hussain's regime, the looting of Iraq's infrastructure reached epidemic proportions. The USA moved quickly to place an administrator for Iraq in Baghdad in order to bring order to the city and country. A retired general, Jay Garner, and the Office of Reconstruction and Humanitarian Assistance (ORHA) were given the task of restoring basic services and law and order to Iraq. Arriving in the country on 21 April 2003, Garner proved to be unable to resolve the immediate problems facing Iraqi society and was subsequently replaced by the State Department's appointee, Paul Bremer, on 12 May. Bremer was to head the Coalition Provisional Authority (CPA), the replacement for the OHRA. Bremer made clear his intent to remove the last vestiges of Saddam Hussain's authority by outlawing the Baath Party and demobilizing the Iraqi army and institutions of state deemed to be corrupted by the Baathists, including the Ministries of Defence and of Information, and the security apparatus. Nevertheless, attacks attributed by the US-led coalition to remnants of Saddam Hussain's regime, including the *Fedayeen Saddam*, grew in number and intensity: 31 US troops were killed in guerrilla attacks between 1 May (when President Bush announced the end of major combat operations in Iraq) and 21 July. Towards the end of April the Sunni-dominated town of Fallujah, 35 miles west of Baghdad, became the focal point for anti-US attacks. The subsequent response by US forces, which resulted in 13 Iraqis being killed on 28 April alone, only served to heighten the tension. The security situation in Fallujah deteriorated further, with US forces regularly coming under fire. The British army faced a less intense, but no less damaging, response in Basra.

Rejecting Garner's plan to select an interim Leadership Council, Bremer instead empowered the leaders of the seven most prominent political parties in Iraq. Subsequently, on 13 July 2003 a 25-member Governing Council was established in Baghdad; unelected, and with no executive power, its remit was three-fold: to draw up a new constitution; to appoint ministers and diplomatic representatives; and to set a date for free elections. It was a situation that satisfied none of the political parties, but one they had little choice but to accept. However, it put the occupying powers in the unenviable position of committing themselves to an extended period of administrative involvement in an Iraqi state galvanized more by an anti-occupation sentiment than by acceptance of US hegemony.

In the first of three major attacks against non-coalition targets in August 2003, 19 people were killed when the Jordanian embassy was severely damaged by a car bomb on 7 August. More worrying, from an international viewpoint, was the destruction of the UN building in Baghdad on 19 August. The UN Special Representative for Iraq, Sergio Vieira de Mello, and more than 20 others were killed when a truck laden with explosives was driven into the UN compound and detonated. On 29 August a car bomb exploded in the city of Najaf, killing the Shi'a cleric and leader of SCIRI Muhammed Bakir al-Hakim and up to 125 of his followers. Abd al-Aziz al-Hakim, a member of the Governing Council and brother of the murdered cleric, assumed the leadership of SCIRI. By early September 139 US troops had reportedly been killed in Iraq since President Bush had formally announced the cessation of major combat operations on 1 May—this exceeded the number of soldiers who had died during the conflict itself. In late September Aquila al-Hashimi, one of only three female members of the Governing Council, was assassinated by unidentified gunmen in Baghdad.

THE RETURN OF SOVEREIGNTY TO IRAQ

The upsurge in attacks committed by Iraqi insurgent forces against the CPA, the Governing Council and US-led coalition military targets continued unabated throughout mid-2003. In a security environment increasingly characterized by sporadic bombings and shootings, structures of local governance rapidly broke down, and political life within Iraq became inherently localized and communalized. In the south of the country, clerics loyal to Muqtada al-Sadr gained prominence in the town councils of Basra and Kut al-Amara. In the Sunni-dominated areas of Tikrit, Mosul and Baquba, religious groups associated with Sheikh Kubaisi continued to consolidate their support base, and Baghdad itself became increasingly divided according to sectarian identity. The predominantly Shi'ite slums in north-eastern Baghdad, formerly known as Saddam City, were renamed Sadr City, clearly reflecting the allegiances of its inhabitants. In the north of Iraq, the Kurds continued to exist autonomously from the rest of the country, but were increasingly concerned about how to maintain this autonomy in the future. The Governing Council failed to gain support from the majority of Iraqis, who viewed it as a US creation, staffed solely by returning exiles. Even when it did make decisions, these still had to be accepted by the CPA before they were made law.

Apparently unable to improve the security situation within Iraq, and still facing criticism from the international community at large regarding the occupation of the country, the USA moved toward the handover of sovereignty to Iraqis at the earliest opportunity. In this atmosphere of heightened violence (US casualties alone reached 500 by January 2004), the CPA revealed that the creation of a TNA would not take place as planned. Instead, the CPA extended the remit of the Governing Council and gave it the task of drafting a Transitional Administrative Law (TAL) to serve as an interim constitution. In the finished document the Kurds succeeded in including reference to the autonomous region governed by the Kurdistan Regional Government (KRG) while the Shi'a compromised by having Islam cited as 'a' source of legislation rather than 'the' source. The TAL also contained a provision by which a two-thirds' majority vote in any three governorates (provinces) could block the adoption of a new constitution, referred to by Arab Iraqis as 'the Kurdish veto'. The TAL, which was to serve as Iraq's constitution until a permanent replacement could be approved by the Iraqi people, was signed on 8 March 2004.

A new phase of anti-coalition attacks commenced at the end of March 2004, and this time included Shi'a groups in addition to the Sunni groups already identified. On the Shi'a side, Muqtada al-Sadr remained a dangerous focal point for many Shi'a Iraqis opposed to coalition forces, and he had steadily consolidated his hold on Sadr City and Kufa, as well as becoming increasingly influential in Basra, Najaf and Karbala. Following the closure of his newspaper, *al-Hawza*, and the arrest of his close aide Mustafa Yacoubi, widespread demonstrations were held in Baghdad, Najaf, Nasiriya and Karbala, resulting in the deaths of nine coalition troops and some 50 Iraqis. What became known as the 'Sadr Insurgency' gained momentum and Sadr's 'Mahdi Army' fought openly with coalition forces across Iraq.

The Sunni-associated insurgency also gained increased notoriety on 31 March 2004 as four civilian contractors from the CPA were captured and killed in Fallujah, and their corpses put on public display. The killings caused outrage in the USA, forcing the CPA to take an increasingly aggressive line towards the Sunni insurgents. The Shi'a and Sunni insurgents were not unified save in the common cause of opposing the occupying coalition forces. Insurgents quickly gained control of many areas outside Baghdad, and in Fallujah widespread fighting left approximately 450 Iraqis (including many civilians) and 40 US soldiers dead. Several foreign workers were kidnapped, beginning a dynamic that would continue to haunt foreigners working in Iraq. The scale of the Shi'a insurgency and the failure of the US Marine Corps to pacify Fallujah forced the USA to back down on several of its threats. Instead of capturing al-Sadr, as threatened, the USA proved unwilling to venture into the Shi'a strongholds of Najaf and Kufa for fear of consolidating Shi'a support behind al-Sadr. Instead, US forces struck a deal with the cleric in June, bringing his insurgency to an end but leaving his forces intact. In Fallujah, the US Marine Corps were replaced with Iraqis under the command of one of Saddam Hussain's former generals. In addition, the CPA announced in April that it would be reinstating members of the former Baathist security forces.

In May 2004 security concerns were further compounded by the disclosure of alleged human rights abuses against Iraqi prisoners in coalition prisons, including the notorious Abu Ghraib. Graphic photographs of abuse were shown on television across the USA and the Middle East. Meanwhile, the timetable for handing over sovereignty to Iraqis progressed relentlessly. Dr Ayad Allawi, leader of the opposition Iraqi National Accord (INA), was appointed Prime Minister of the new Interim Government (IG) on 28 May. The position of President was awarded to the Sunni tribal figure Sheikh Ghazi Mashal Ajil al-Yawar on 1 June. The positions of Vice-President went to Ibrahim al-Ja'fari, spokesman of the Shi'a Islamic Dawa Party, and to the KDP member Dr Rozh Nuri Shawais.

As the handover date of 30 June 2004 approached, there was a significant increase in the number of attacks launched by insurgency forces and in the kidnapping and killing of foreigners in Iraq. In an attempt to forestall what many believed would be a large-scale assault by the insurgency forces, the handover of sovereignty to the IG was brought forward in secret to 28 June.

THE INSURGENCY CONTINUES

Security remained the most pressing concern of the new Government. Most of the indigenous security forces that had been trained in the year preceding the IG's selection had demonstrated their unwillingness to fight against fellow Iraqis during the siege of Fallujah in April 2004. Most units had either deserted or defected to join the insurgents. The only Iraqi troops that actually fought during the siege were reported to be elements of the Kurdish *peshmerga*. In the absence of capable Iraqi security forces, US troops were forced to confront a stubbornly persistent threat from al-Sadr's Mahdi Army, and an increasingly violent 'Sunni Triangle'. The Mahdi Army continued its sporadic attacks on coalition forces throughout mid-2004. Notably, Baghdad's Sadr City became virtually inaccessible and there was a major Mahdi Army uprising in August in the holy cities of Karbala and Najaf. Al-Sadr's supporters succeeded in occupying the Imam Ali mosque (Shi'ism's most sacred shrine) and fought running battles with US troops for control of Najaf. Ultimately, it required the direct intervention of Grand Ayatollah Sistani to broker a truce between the two sides, and once again al-Sadr escaped punishment with his Mahdi Army depleted, but intact. Two months later the city of Fallujah was once more the scene of an intense battle between US troops and insurgents. Unlike the earlier siege (in which only about 2,000 US marines had participated), during the November siege the US military amassed close to 15,000 troops to attack the city. After a fierce battle that resulted in the deaths of over 50 US troops and perhaps 1,000 insurgents, Fallujah was eventually 'pacified'.

THE JANUARY 2005 ELECTIONS

With attacks on coalition forces running at upwards of 70 per day by January 2005, there seemed little likelihood that the elections to the TNA scheduled for 30 January could safely be conducted in all parts of Iraq, still less that they would constitute a crucial turning point in Iraq's democratic development. Prominent Sunni groups—most notably, the Association of Muslim Scholars—denounced the entire electoral process as illegitimate and urged Sunnis to boycott the elections. At the opposite end of the spectrum, Grand Ayatollah Sistani issued a *fatwa* declaring it to be the religious obligation of every Shi'a to vote, while Kurds in the relative security of the north prepared to participate in massive numbers. Meanwhile, Abu Musab al-Zarqawi, a Jordanian national, with suspected links to al-Qa'ida, thought to be the leader of an insurgent network responsible for numerous kidnappings, executions and bomb attacks, reportedly 'declared a fierce war on this evil principle of democracy' and threatened to 'wash the streets with blood' on election day.

Within the Shi'a community, the dominant political force was the United Iraqi Alliance (UIA), an uneasy coalition of primarily religious groupings that included SCIRI and its armed faction, the Badr Organization (previously named the Badr Brigades), the Islamic Dawa Party and a variety of individuals with ties to Muqtada al-Sadr. Also included was Ahmad Chalabi and the remnants of the INC, and a scattering of representatives of other ethnicities and sects.

The main secular Shi'a alternative was Ayad Allawi's Iraqi List, a coalition that included Sunnis and former Baathists. The two main Kurdish parties—the PUK and the KDP—pooled resources to form the Democratic Patriotic Alliance of Kurdistan (DPAK). From the Sunni Arab community, only interim President Ghazi al-Yawar's Iraqis Party opted to participate seriously in the election.

The results represented a clear triumph for the religious Shi'a bloc, which succeeded in obtaining an overall majority of seats (140 out of a total 275) in the TNA on the basis of just under 48% of the valid votes cast. Overall, overtly religious parties and coalitions of various parties obtained almost 54% of the Assembly's seats. The Kurdish list also performed disproportionately well relative to the numerical presence of Kurds in the population as a whole, winning 75 of the Assembly's seats on just under 26% of the valid votes cast. Conversely, Allawi's Iraqi List, and a host of other moderate, secular parties performed poorly. The Iraqi List, which had been widely considered to be the UIA's major challenger prior to the election, obtained only 40 seats in the Assembly on the basis of less than 14% of the valid votes cast. The only Sunni Arab party represented in the Assembly was al-Yawar's Iraqis, which gained five seats on a share of valid votes of less than 2%.

On the same day as the elections for the National Assembly, Iraqis also voted to elect 18 provincial councils, and in the Kurdish region to choose a Kurdistan National Assembly (KNA). The outcome followed much the same pattern as the results at the national level, with the Kurds and religious Shi'a parties emerging as dominant. Kurdish parties won majorities in all five of the northernmost provinces, including Kirkuk and Nineveh, while all provinces south of Baghdad fell to religious parties. The remaining four provinces produced highly fragmented councils, with the exception of Anbar province, where voter turn-out was so low (less than 0.5% of the electorate) that the results were meaningless. Unsurprisingly, voting for the KNA was completely dominated by a joint PUK-KDP list.

Much of the upsurge in violence emerge in the aftermath of the elections can be attributed to a vacuum in legitimacy that arose because of a three-month delay in the formation of the new government. This delay was largely due to the rules on forming the new administration that were written into the TAL requiring (effectively) a two-thirds' majority of votes in the National Assembly to endorse a new government. This meant that the UIA controlled too few votes to form a government on its own, despite controlling a majority in the Assembly, and was forced to rely on a tactical alliance with the Kurdish list. As kingmakers in this process, the Kurds managed to secure the presidency in the person of PUK leader Jalal Talabani, who assumed office on 7 April 2005. Including Sunnis in a government of national unity was deemed essential to the country's future stability, but there were only 17 potential candidates to choose from, and it was not clear that any spoke credibly for the broader Sunni population. The eventual compromise deal saw the UIA's Ibrahim al-Ja'fari emerge as the Prime Minister, with Talabani as President, Dr Adil Abd al-Mahdi (Shi'a Arab) as one Vice-President and Ghazi al-Yawar (Sunni Arab) as the other. Sunnis were awarded seven of the 37 ministerial portfolios, including the Ministry of Defence, while the remaining portfolios were allocated (broadly) on the basis of seat percentage in the Assembly.

In addition to combating the insurgency and trying to rebuild Iraq's still dilapidated infrastructure, the major task of the elected Transitional Government was to organize the drafting of Iraq's permanent constitution. The timeline for this envisaged in the TAL was for the drafting process to be completed by mid-August 2005. Subsequently, a referendum on the new constitution was scheduled for 15 October, with elections to follow by 15 December. The initial three-month delay in forming the new Government, combined with disagreements concerning the composition of the 55-member constitutional council, made it unlikely that this timetable would be met. The initial decision of al-Ja'fari's Government to allocate places on the constitutional council in proportion to each party's share of seats in the Assembly meant that 28 seats on the council went to the UIA, 15 to the Kurds, eight to Allawi's faction and one seat each to a communist, a Turkman, a Christian and a Sunni Arab. The almost total absence of Sunni Arabs from the body charged with drafting Iraq's permanent constitution was an obvious source of concern in that it ran the risk of further marginalizing the Sunni community. To alleviate this problem, the Government asked groups believed to represent at least some proportion of the broader Sunni community, such as the IIP and the National Dialogue Council, to propose a slate of 15 Sunnis to sit on a panel that would operate alongside the main council. Reportedly, consensus was to be sought between the Sunni panel and the main council on all issues.

It soon became clear that on several core issues, the interests of Sunni Arab members were opposed to those of the Kurds and Shi'a and that a consensus among all groups would be difficult, if not impossible, to obtain. Nevertheless, following a series of extensions beyond the original deadline of 15 August 2005, the parliamentary committee charged with drafting the constitution presented a finalized text to the TNA for consideration on 28 August.

Much of the text of the draft constitution was imported unchanged from the TAL, and the institutional structure of government remained much as before. The constitution outlined a parliamentary system in which primary executive authority was vested in the Prime Minister and the Council of Ministers. With respect to federalism, Chapter Four of the constitution detailed certain 'exclusive' powers to be exercised solely by the federal Government, together with a number of 'duties' to be shared by the federal and regional authorities. The powers listed as being exclusive to the federal Government included foreign policy, national defence, finance and trade policy. According to Article 115, 'all that is not written in the exclusive powers of the federal authorities is in the authority of the regions'. The powers reserved for the regions included, according to Article 121, the regulation of internal security forces for the region. Ambiguities remained regarding the division of powers between the federal and regional governments. The constitution was not clear regarding which level of government had the power to tax, for example, or whether the revenues generated by newly exploited or discovered oil and gas fields would belong to the host regions or to the federal Government. However, arguably the most controversial feature of the federal structure concerned the way in which provinces joined together to form larger regions. Article 119 of the constitution stated that 'one or more governorates shall have the right to establish a region', a provision from which only Baghdad was excluded. This seemingly minor change in wording meant that there was now no longer an upper limit on the number of provinces that could amalgamate into regions, thereby opening up the possibility of a Shi'a 'super-region' composed of all the provinces south of Baghdad. Another controversial item, Article 140, envisaged a three-stage process for the resolution of the status of Kirkuk and the other disputed territories in northern Iraq. The third stage, a referendum to determine the will of the people, was to be held no later than 31 December 2007. Finally, as a last-minute concession to Sunnis, the Constitution contained a provision for a four-month period for proposing constitutional amendments following the investiture of the central Government elected in December 2005. For this limited period, amendments could be ratified by a majority of the population in a referendum rather than by the more onerous regular procedure. It was hoped that as part of a broader reconciliation package, Kurdish and Shi'a leaders would make concessions on those elements of the Constitution deemed most objectionable to the Sunni Arab community; but while the final draft of the constitution satisfied most of the aspirations of Shi'a and Kurdish leaders, it offered almost nothing to Sunni Arabs.

Hence, the referendum on the draft Constitution yielded predictable results. The Constitution was endorsed in Shi'a- and Kurdish-dominated provinces by large margins. In the multi-communal provinces, the vote in favour of the Constitution prevailed by narrower margins, and in two Sunni-dominated provinces (Anbar and Salah al-Din) the vote went overwhelmingly against it. Voters in Nineveh province (ethnically mixed, but with a Sunni Arab majority) rejected the

Constitution, but the vote failed to reach the necessary two-thirds' threshold. Overall, the Constitution was approved with the endorsement of 79% of voters.

The legislative elections of 15 December 2005 did not differ greatly from those held the previous January. Ongoing violence again precluded any meaningful campaigning on the part of candidates, party platforms were largely non-existent, parties coalesced around ethno-sectarian identities and the UIA once more dominated proceedings. However, the crucial difference was the participation of the Sunni Arab community in the December elections. Having boycotted the January elections and paid a heavy price in terms of loss of influence over the drafting of the Constitution, Sunni Arab leaders were determined not to repeat their mistake. As was the case in January, parties standing for election were dominated by ethno-sectarian identity. The UIA, the major Shi'a religious grouping, suffered the defection of Ahmed Chalabi's INC faction, which opted to run as an independent party, but was joined by the Sadrists. The major secular Shi'a alternative, Ayad Allawi's Iraqi National List (INL), was strengthened by the inclusion of two factions that had run independently in January—Ghazi al-Yawar's Iraqis and the communist People's Union. With the exception of the Kurdistan Islamic Union (KIU), most of the major Kurdish parties ran on the same ticket as before, namely the DPAK. Two significant coalitions represented the interests of the Sunni Arab community. The Iraqi Accord Front (IAF) comprised an amalgam of Sunni religious groupings including, most notably, Adnan al-Dulaimi's General Council for the People of Iraq and Tariq al-Hashimi's IIP. The Iraqi Front for National Dialogue (IFND), meanwhile, purported to offer a 'non-sectarian' alternative, but was generally thought to represent the interests of secular Sunnis and former Baathists.

When the Independent Electoral Commission of Iraq finally certified the results of the elections, nearly two months after the polls, the composition of the new parliament was remarkably similar to that of the old. With just over 41% of the votes, the UIA emerged as the largest single party, claiming 128 of the 275 available seats, while the Kurdish alliance secured 53 seats on a vote of 22%. The participation of the two Sunni Arab parties meant that both the UIA and the Kurdish alliance experienced declines in their share of the popular vote, and, as a consequence, their share of seats. The IAF performed well, polling over 15% of the vote and obtaining 44 seats, while the IFND's 4% of the vote yielded 11 seats. Of the other parties organized around ethnic or sectarian identity, the Turkmen Front, the National Rafidain List (Assyrians) and the Al-Ezediah Movement for Progress and Reform (a Yazidi grouping) obtained one seat each. The performance of Allawi's INL (25 seats from a vote of 8%) was a major disappointment for those who had hoped to see a consolidation or strengthening of the moderate, secular vote. Likewise, Chalabi's INC polled close to 0% of the vote and achieved no representation in parliament. Overall, this pattern of results accurately reflected the prevailing reality of Iraq's political climate. By December 2005 the politics of communal identity had, if anything, become even more deeply entrenched than it had been in January.

As inter-communal violence intensified in early 2006, political leaders in Baghdad struggled to forge a government of national unity that might help avert all-out civil war. In principle, all political leaders favoured a unity government, but in practice this proved difficult to achieve. The deadlock persisted for over six weeks until, finally, Ayatollah Sistani was able to broker a deal between various factions within the UIA to coalesce behind the nomination of a compromise candidate, Nuri Kamal (Jawad) al-Maliki. Like former Prime Minister al-Ja'fari, al-Maliki came to prominence as a leading member of the Islamic Dawa Party and, ideologically, the two were virtually indistinguishable. Al-Maliki's ties to Iran ran less deep than al-Ja'fari's, but ultimately, his major selling point was that he was not unacceptable to anyone.

The Government of national unity officially came into being on 20 May 2006, when the National Assembly finally approved al-Maliki's 37-member cabinet. The major factions participating in the Government were the UIA, the Kurdish alliance, the IAF and the INL. Together with three smaller parties, the Government controlled 240 of the 275 seats in the Council of Representatives.

FROM INSURGENCY TO CIVIL WAR

As politicians in Baghdad struggled to form a consensus on the contours of a new government, the violence in Iraq began to shift in an ominous direction. The problem of sectarian violence was not unknown before 2005. Al-Zarqawi had made attacks on Iraq's Shi'a population central to his campaign to destabilize the country. The ultimate goal, many observers concluded, was to provoke all-out civil war between Sunni and Shi'a communities. Under strict instructions from Ayatollah Sistani and other Shi'a clerics, the Shi'a community mostly refrained from exacting revenge. However, following the formation of the UIA-dominated Government in March 2005, this restraint began to erode rapidly. Prime Minister al-Ja'fari's appointment of prominent SCIRI hardliner Bayan Jabr as Minister of the Interior led to a dramatic reorganization of the Ministry's security forces. Significant elements of the Badr Organization were incorporated into counter-insurgency commando units that swiftly acquired a reputation for brutality and violent excesses. Adopting names such as the Volcano, Scorpion or Wolf Brigades, these units conducted a vicious, but effective, counter-insurgency campaign against Iraq's Sunni population. Viewed by the Sunni community as little more than state-sponsored death squads, these commando units were heavily criticized by human rights organizations for indiscriminate violence and the use of torture. The low-level civil war gathered momentum throughout the latter months of 2005, then escalated in February 2006 when insurgents, believed to be associated with al-Zarqawi's group, destroyed the golden dome of the Al-Askari Mosque in Samarra. Over the next few days mobs of Shi'a militia forces, led by al-Sadr's Mahdi Army, exacted revenge on the Sunni community, torching dozens of Sunni mosques and assassinating Sunni clerics. During the first five days after the attacks the official death toll was 1,300, but unofficially the figure was believed to be much higher. Once the first wave of intense violence had petered out, it initially seemed that the attacks might actually serve to bring Iraq's communities together in a common cause. However, rather than dissipating, the violence instead moved underground, ushering in a period of shadowy, but intense, sectarian warfare. By the end of June a UN report estimated that over 150,000 Iraqis had been displaced by the violence since February.

THE SURGE

The results of the November 2006 congressional elections in the USA dealt a crushing blow to the Bush Administration, delivering control over both the House of Representatives and the Senate to the Democrats. In the wake of these results, the subsequent resignation of the war's main architect, Secretary of Defense Donald Rumsfeld, the repeated failure of various military operations to impose security on Iraq, and the apparent inability (or unwillingness) of Iraq's political leaders to compromise on key issues, most observers expected President Bush to announce a major change in US strategy early in the new year. However, to the surprise of many, the President used an address to the nation on 10 January 2007 to announce an increase in US troop levels of between 20,000 and 30,000. The majority of these troops were to be deployed to Baghdad, with a smaller number (approximately 4,000) of marines assigned to Anbar province. The essentials of the new 'surge' strategy marked a major departure from the Rumsfeld approach of US forces leaving a 'light footprint' while 'standing up' Iraqi forces to bear the brunt of counter-insurgency operations.

By October 2007 clear evidence from multiple sources indicated that violence of all types was on the decline. During this month 38 US troop deaths were recorded, compared with more than 100 during every month from April to June. Iraqi civilian deaths, meanwhile, declined from nearly 2,000 during January (the start of the surge) to fewer than 900 for the month of October. By mid-2008 almost every available indicator showed that violence in Iraq had declined to its lowest level since the declared end of combat operations in May 2003. In May 2008, for example, the US military experienced fewer combat deaths

(19) than at any time during the post-war period. Over the February–May 2008 period insurgent attacks in Baghdad were more than 50% lower than the levels experienced during May–July 2007, and in the once volatile Anbar governorate attacks had ceased almost entirely. Civilian deaths and sectarian killings had also declined significantly. Judged on the basis of declining violence, therefore, the surge was an unambiguous success. However, among many experts questions remained about what factors had led to the diminution in violence, and whether the broader surge strategy would carry long-term costs that outweighed the short-term benefits.

An important reason for the significant decline in sectarian killings in Baghdad was that by the end of 2007, the city was almost completely segregated into sectarian neighbourhoods. Many of the remaining Sunni Arab neighbourhoods had been sealed off from surrounding Shi'a districts through the construction of vast walls that enabled security forces to control points of entry and exit. Thus, one plausible reason for the decline in sectarian killings was that there were few remaining neighbourhoods in which Sunnis and Shi'a co-existed. Another plausible reason for the decline in violence was the USA's strategy of empowering Sunni Arab militias through the so-called 'Awakening' (*sahwa*) movement, which clearly had a dramatic impact on violence levels in Sunni Arab areas. From its beginnings in 2005 in Anbar governorate, the movement spread throughout north-central Iraq and into Baghdad, and by mid-2008 had nearly 100,000 members. Many of these were former insurgents, paid by the USA to join an alliance of convenience against Islamist insurgent groups. The short-term benefit of the *sahwa* movement was the virtual elimination of attacks on coalition forces and the defeat of radical Islamist insurgent groups in places like Anbar.

LEGISLATIVE AND CONSTITUTIONAL IMPASSE

Despite the reduction in violence associated with the surge, politics in Baghdad remained gridlocked. The fundamental problem confronting Iraq's political leaders was a deepening divide between those (mainly the Kurds and the ISCI) who perceived Iraq's permanent Constitution to be a largely finished document, and those who sought major amendments to its provisions. This division reflected the broader 'federalist versus nationalist' confrontation, and was viewed by many Western observers as a positive development for the Iraqi political system because it suggested that Iraqis were moving beyond the politics of ethnicity and sect and towards a more ideologically driven brand of politics. None the less, the depths of this division made it almost impossible for Iraq's political leaders to compromise on constitutional amendments. The Constitutional Review Committee (CRC), which had laboured since November 2006 to arrive at a set of mutually acceptable amendments, appeared to have thrown in the towel when it issued its 'final report' in July 2008. No agreement could be reached over several issues, including the powers of the President, which Sunni members of the CRC had sought to strengthen by granting the President power over Iraq's armed forces. The CRC was also divided over those articles of the Constitution that dealt with the management of the hydrocarbons sector, and the powers of regions and governorates relative to the federal government. Finally, the CRC was utterly divided about how to proceed with Article 140. The inability of the CRC to reach consensus on these core issues had at least three important implications for Iraqi politics. First, a CRC at impasse demonstrated that Iraq's major political factions were still bitterly divided over the very structure of governance in the country, including the nature of executive power, the federal system, and the future status of territories disputed by the Iraqi Kurdistan Region and the federal Government. Second, in the absence of a finished founding document that enjoyed popular legitimacy, it had been almost impossible to make progress in areas such as oil and gas legislation. Third, the absence of consensus on the CRC left Iraq without an upper house of parliament (the Federation Council) and, critically, without a constitutional court (the Federal Supreme Court), which both remained hostage to the stalled constitutional revision process. The lack of a constitutional court was particularly troubling because it meant there was no obvious way to determine whether pieces of legislation, or the actions of political leaders, were in accord with the letter and spirit of the Constitution. With no constitutional court, Iraq's political system lacked a vital check on the power of its political leaders, particularly the Prime Minister, and the integrity of the Constitution itself was progressively eroding.

THE ASCENT OF NURI AL-MALIKI

One of the more remarkable political developments of the 2008–09 period was the emergence of Prime Minister Nuri al-Maliki as the single most powerful political leader in Iraq. Once regarded as a weak and ineffectual politician, al-Maliki had originally been a compromise candidate for Prime Minister and was generally assumed to be a pliable puppet of the Shi'a religious establishment. However, from early 2008 al-Maliki began to use the powers of his office to assert his authority. In February 2008, for example, the Prime Minister announced his intention to mount a major military operation in Basra 'to take on criminals and gang leaders' in the city. The operation, dubbed 'Charge of the Knights', involved over 40,000 Iraqi troops who were intended to operate without the assistance of coalition forces. The assault on Basra was accompanied by serious clashes between the Mahdi Army and Iraqi troops in several major cities in the south, including Amarah, Kut and Nasiriya. Subsequently, US forces sealed off the Sadrist stronghold of Sadr City in Baghdad and joint US-Iraqi attacks commenced in April 2008. The attack on Sadr City continued for seven weeks and resulted in an estimated 1,000 deaths of (mainly) civilians. In mid-May al-Sadr announced a cease-fire and agreed to allow Iraqi government troops, but not US forces, to enter Sadr City. The attacks on al-Sadr's militia forces in various locations were indecisive from a military perspective, but they demonstrated al-Maliki's willingness to confront militias within the Shi'a community, and thereby enhanced his claims to be a champion of the Iraqi nationalist cause.

In the wake of his military campaigns against rival militias in the south, al-Maliki established a network of so-called 'tribal support councils' (*isnad*) throughout the region. Modelled on the Awakening movement in the predominantly Sunni parts of the country, these *isnad* operated outside any legal or constitutional framework and received their funding directly from the office of the Prime Minister. As they proliferated throughout the south, al-Maliki acquired what he and his Islamic Dawa Party had previously lacked—a support base, and an organizational means through which to challenge the power of the Islamic Supreme Council of Iraq (ISCI—as SCIRI had been renamed) in the south. In July 2008 al-Maliki turned his attention northwards, launching a large-scale military offensive in the troubled province of Diyala on 29 July. Termed Operation Promise of Good, the offensive involved up to 30,000 Iraqi troops and police supported by US forces, and initially focused on the provincial capital, Baquba. The stated target of the operation was al-Qa'ida in Iraq, but the operation soon developed into a confrontation between Iraqi government forces and local Sunni insurgent (Sons of Iraq—SOI) groups, and more dangerously, with the forces of the Kurdish *peshmerga* stationed in the disputed northern districts of the province. What started as a counter-insurgency operation, therefore, soon took on the appearance of an attempt by the Prime Minister to eliminate rivals and impose his will on the province, including the arrests of five key SOI leaders and hundreds of fighters, along with members of the Sunni IAF. Matters came to a head in mid-August when Iraqi forces reached the northern district of Khanaqin, a mostly Kurdish district, and threatened a confrontation with the 4,000-strong *peshmerga* brigade stationed there. The stand-off was only resolved when the President of the Kurdish Autonomous Region, Masoud Barzani, visited Baghdad to negotiate a deal directly with al-Maliki. The result was an agreement whereby security in the city of Khanaqin would be provided by local police, *peshmerga* forces would withdraw to positions some 25 km north and south of the city, and control over Arab sub-districts in the south of the city would be transferred to Iraqi forces. Though military confrontation was thereby avoided, the situation in northern Diyala remained tense.

The effectiveness of this strategy was evident in the January 2009 provincial elections when al-Maliki's State of Law alliance won sweeping victories from Baghdad southwards, and the ISCI was reduced to a minor political force in much of the south. Of the 14 provinces in which elections were held, al-Maliki's State of Law alliance won in nine, including Basra and Baghdad, either by capturing more seats than any other coalition, or by winning an outright majority. Consequently, the State of Law alliance secured control (either alone or in a coalition) of eight of the 14 provinces. By contrast, the ISCI fared badly in almost every southern province and emerged from the election in control of only one council—Muthanna. These results represented a personal triumph for al-Maliki and his brand of Iraqi nationalism and suggested that al-Maliki was emerging as exactly the sort of powerful, centralizing leader that most Arab Iraqis (but few Kurds) appeared to favour.

In Baghdad, meanwhile, al-Maliki consolidated his hold on power by establishing a network of security institutions, such as the Baghdad Brigade and the National Counterterrorism Force, which were directly funded by, and answerable to, the office of the Prime Minister. Moreover, the constitutional and legal constraints that required, for example, the approval of the Iraqi parliament for the appointment of senior army officers, had been routinely ignored; in practice this meant that the upper ranks of the armed forces were beholden to the Prime Minister personally for their career progression (or regression). In a classic example of his emerging strategy, al-Maliki ordered a new military offensive, Operation Promise of Good II, in Diyala in May 2009. Much like the operation in July 2008, the sequel was portrayed as an attempt to root out remaining al-Qa'ida forces in the province, but morphed swiftly into an attack on Diyala's Sunni political leaders, who had excluded al-Maliki's State of Law alliance from participating in the provincial Government. On 18 May 2009 the regional head of the IAF in Diyala, Abd al-Jabbar al-Khazraji and SOI leader Sheikh Riyad al-Mujami, were arrested following accusations of attacks on civilians.

THE DEMISE OF ARTICLE 140

The major political victims of the emerging nationalist bloc were the Kurds. Already facing harsh criticism from all sides in Baghdad for circumventing the federal Government in the signing of oil contracts, the Kurdish negotiators only barely managed to hold on to the Kurds' 17% share of revenues during budget negotiations and singularly failed to receive financial compensation to help cover the costs of *peshmerga* deployments in support of Iraqi government troops. However, the major casualty of the upsurge in anti-Kurdish sentiment was the Kurds' effort to secure a favourable resolution to the issue of Kirkuk and other 'disputed territories'. Article 140 of the Constitution had envisaged a three-stage process leading to a resolution of Kirkuk's final status. Stage one—normalization—involved the return of those Kurds deliberately displaced by Saddam Hussain as part of his campaign to change the demography of Kirkuk, and the return to their governorates of origin of Arabs brought into the region as part of the same campaign. Upon the completion of normalization, stage two involved a census, and stage three a referendum on the future status of the territories, to be conducted by 31 December 2007.

Of the various territories generally considered to be 'disputed', Kirkuk was by far the most controversial, both because of its large oil resources and because the city (and governorate) contained sizeable populations of Kurds, Arabs and Turkmen. The Kurdish effort to incorporate Kirkuk into the territory of the Kurdish region was bitterly opposed by almost every non-Kurdish group in Iraq, as well as by most states in the region (especially Turkey), and the Kurds faced determined opposition at all levels of government to their drive to complete the necessary stages in time for a December 2007 vote. Although the political decision to reverse the effects of Arabization was approved by Prime Minister al-Maliki in March, it was not until September that the necessary finances were made available to compensate those Kurds and Arabs affected. Consequently, the normalization stage of Article 140 had barely begun by the time that the referendum deadline came around. In addition, only about 5% of the tens of thousands of Kirkuk property disputes had been resolved, and no agreement had been reached on the restoration of Kirkuk governorate to its pre-Baathist boundaries. Saddam Hussain had repeatedly manipulated the boundaries of Kirkuk to make it demographically less Kurdish and more Arab, and it was not clear that the Kurds had the numbers to win a vote on Kirkuk's future status without these heavily Kurdish-populated districts being reattached to the governorate.

When the deadline expired without the completion of even stage one of the process, the future of Article 140 was thrown into political limbo. Many in the federal Government deemed the Article to be 'null and void'. In previous cases where constitutional deadlines had been missed, as had occurred with the work of the Constitutional Review Committee (CRC), for example, the deadline had been extended by a vote in parliament. This was not an option for Article 140 because the Kurds were opposed in parliament by the overwhelming majority of lawmakers In the absence of a favourable resolution to the Kirkuk issue, the Kurds refused to sign off on the package of constitutional amendments recommended by the CRC. As a consequence of this, the single most important dimension of the political reconciliation process, namely, amending the Constitution to assuage Sunni Arab concerns, cannot be completed without a resolution to the Kirkuk issue.

The status of the disputed territories remained one of the most divisive and contentious issues facing Iraq's political leaders and the most likely trigger for an Arab–Kurdish confrontation. In this context, the passage through the Kurdish regional parliament of a draft Constitution for the Kurdish Autonomous Region in June did little to alleviate tensions. The draft, which has yet to be approved in a popular referendum, included Kirkuk and other disputed territories within the boundaries of the Kurdish Autonomous Region, and asserted the right of the *peshmerga* to maintain security.

US WITHDRAWAL

With the UN mandate authorizing the presence of coalition forces in Iraq set to expire on 31 December 2008, the latter half of that year saw an intensifying effort on the part of the outgoing Bush Administration and the Iraqi Government to craft a mutually acceptable status of forces agreement (SOFA) to provide a legal basis for a continued US military presence beyond that date. Naturally, the process was fraught with complexity and controversy. The agreement that eventually emerged appeared to offer a number of important concessions to Iraq. The most significant articles were Article 27, which prohibited Iraqi 'land, sea, and air' from being used as a 'launching or transit point for attacks against other countries' (i.e. Iran), and Article 24, which appeared to establish an unambiguous timetable for the withdrawal of US forces: Section 3 required all US 'combat' forces to withdraw from Iraqi cities no later than 30 June 2009, and the withdrawal of all 'United States Forces' from Iraqi territory by 31 December 2011. In August 2010 US President Barack Obama officially declared an end to combat operations in Iraq. In the process, the military-led Operation Iraqi Freedom was transformed into the civilian-led Operation New Dawn. The new mission of the 50,000 remaining US troops in Iraq was to train, equip and advise Iraqi military forces and to protect the remaining US civilian presence in the country. Meanwhile, the US Administration worked diligently behind the scenes to convince Iraqi politicians of the need to retain some form of US military presence beyond the deadline. The politics of this was complicated, however. Ending the war in Iraq was a key pledge of Obama's presidential electoral campaign, while Prime Minister al-Maliki used the signing of the SOFA, complete with its requirement for a withdrawal of all US troops, to strengthen his credentials as an Iraqi nationalist; neither found it easy to justify reneging on this commitment. Hence, both sides sought an agreement that would allow for the longer-term presence of US forces while retaining the support of the public.

This idea of a long-term deployment appeared to gain momentum in October 2011, when a meeting of Iraq's key leaders in Baghdad authorized the Government to allow an unspecified number of US trainers to remain in Iraq beyond

December. However, the legal status of these trainers was disputed. While the USA insisted on immunity from Iraqi law for any remaining trainers, there appeared to be a consensus among Iraqi leaders that this should not be granted. Despite lengthy talks between the USA and Iraq during the following months, a proposal to maintain a US military presence in the country under the auspices of the North Atlantic Treaty Organization (NATO) was rejected in December for the same reason. Hence, all remaining US military units departed Iraq ahead of schedule on 19 December.

ELECTIONS IN THE KURDISH AUTONOMOUS REGION

In July 2009 Kurds went to the polls in northern Iraq to elect the Kurdish Autonomous Region's President and legislature. As in previous polls, the PUK and KDP formed an electoral alliance (the Kurdistan List); however, many of the lesser parties that had previously participated in the DPAK ran in direct opposition to the PUK-KDP alliance.

Leading the assault on the status quo was the Movement for Change (Gorran), founded by former Deputy Secretary-General of the PUK Nawshirwan Mustafa, following his defection from that party in protest against its failure to address internal corruption. Formally registered as a political party in February 2009, Gorran campaigned on an anti-establishment platform that was overtly critical of the PUK and KDP for their alleged corruption and failure to establish a clear distinction between their own institutions and those of government. In its emphasis on the failings of the dominant parties, Gorran tapped into popular discontent that had been festering in the Kurdish Autonomous Region since the 2005 elections. Also prominent among the opposition was the Service and Reform List (SRL), an alliance of Islamist and left-wing parties, spearheaded by the increasingly influential KIU, and also including the Islamic Group of Kurdistan (IGK), the Kurdistan Socialist Democratic Party and the Future Party.

A further 23 parties, alliances and individuals contested the 111 parliamentary seats on offer at the polls on 25 July 2009. Turn-out was relatively high, at nearly 80% of the registered electorate. As expected, the Kurdistan List garnered the most votes (57% of the total), to secure 59 seats; however, this was over 20% fewer votes, and 45 fewer seats, than the DPAK had obtained in 2005. Gorran, meanwhile, polled nearly 24% of the total ballot, securing 25 seats, including the PUK's own home base of Sulaimaniya. The SRL also performed creditably, securing nearly 13% of the vote to win 13 seats. The Islamic Movement in Iraqi Kurdistan took two seats, and the Freedom and Social Justice List one seat, while the remaining 11 seats were reserved for representatives of various minority groups. In the concurrent presidential election, the KDP's Masoud Barzani was re-elected by a comfortable margin, securing 69.6% of the vote.

To the extent that the ascendancy of Gorran injected competition into Kurdish politics and served as a check on the excesses of the two major parties, the net effect on the Kurdish Autonomous Region was positive. Less clear was the long-term impact that Gorran's rise would have on the balance of power between the two major parties. The PUK and KDP had run on joint slates in almost every election since 2003, and had divided up the spoils of office (whether parliamentary seats or executive posts) with studious egalitarianism. This spirit of strict equality of power-sharing was embodied in the 2006 unification agreement, which detailed which posts in the KRG 'belonged' to each of the two main parties. However, the success of Gorran, which came largely at the expense of the PUK, raised important questions regarding the continued viability of this sort of arrangement.

THE MARCH 2010 LEGISLATIVE ELECTIONS

Unlike the 2005 national election, in which most of the Shi'a parties had joined forces to form the UIA, the 2010 elections saw an important split in Shi'a ranks. In August 2009 the remnants of the UIA, most notably the ISCI and the Sadrists, combined under the Iraqi National Alliance banner, along with an assortment of both religious and secular Shi'a independents, including former premier Ibrahim al-Ja'fari's small National Reform Movement, Ahmad Chalabi's Iraqi National Congress (INC), a breakaway faction of the Islamic Dawa Party, Fadillah, and even a Sunni Arab leader of the Anbar awakening, Hamed al-Hayes. The ISCI-Sadrist alliance was undeniably a marriage of convenience. The two movements represented starkly different constituencies within the Shi'a community, with the ISCI drawing support mainly from the middle class, and the Sadrists from the poor and dispossessed. Moreover, the respective positions of the two parties on a variety of key ideological issues—federalism, for example—bordered on the mutually incompatible. However, they were united in a shared hostility toward al-Maliki and a mutual determination to prevent him from securing another term as Prime Minister. In contrast to the obviously sectarian flavour of the Iraqi National Alliance, al-Maliki reassembled his State of Law alliance with the stated intent of transcending ethno-sectarian boundaries. However, after failing to attract much interest from within either the Sunni or Kurdish communities, the finalized State of Law alliance was arguably no less sectarian than the Iraqi National Alliance: its core was al-Maliki's own Islamic Dawa Party, to which was added two other Dawa factions, an independent bloc led by Minister of Oil Dr Hussain al-Shahristani, and various other individuals with localized appeal.

Pitted against the two Shi'a-dominated lists were two secular, nationalist alliances, Iraqiya and the Iraqi Unity Coalition (IUC). Forged by Minister of the Interior Jawad al-Bulani in October 2009, the IUC had genuine trans-sectarian appeal; as well as al-Bulani (a secular Shi'a), it included several prominent Sunni tribal leaders, including Ahmad Abu Risha, who had helped to initiate the Anbar awakening. Meanwhile, Allawi's Iraqiya, formed in January 2010, attempted to secure a broader appeal than the now-defunct INL, particularly in the Sunni-dominated provinces in northern Iraq, by the addition of a number of prominent Sunni Arab movements and individuals, including Saleh al-Mutlaq and his IFND, Vice-President al-Hashimi and the influential al-Hadbaa list from Nineveh. Collectively, the fusion of these groups and individuals into a single bloc created a powerful political force to challenge the established Shi'a parties.

The most prominent Kurdish contender—the Kurdistan Alliance—was contesting the 2010 elections as a two-party alliance of the KDP and PUK. Also competing for Kurdish votes were Gorran and the two Islamic parties (the KIU and IGK), all three of which ran on separate slates.

According to the final results (including compensatory seats) announced by the IHEC in late March 2010, Allawi's Iraqiya had secured 91 seats with 24.7% of the vote, narrowly defeating the State of Law alliance, which won 89 seats, having garnered 24.2% of the vote. The Iraqi National Alliance won 70 seats (18.0% of the vote), while the Kurdistan Alliance obtained 43 seats (14.6%). The Kurdistan Alliance's loss of 10 seats from the 2005 elections was mainly due to the performance of the three other Kurdish parties—Gorran (which won eight seats), the KIU (four seats) and the IGK (two seats). Other than the eight seats reserved for minorities, only two other parties achieved representation in parliament—the IAF (which earned six seats) and the Iraqi Unity Coalition (four). The pattern of results across Iraq as a whole served to reinforce the impression that Iraqi voters had yet to transcend the politics of ethno-sectarianism. The Shi'a Arab-dominated parties (the State of Law alliance and the Iraqi National Alliance) won all but 17 of the 119 seats on offer in the nine predominantly Shi'a provinces south of Baghdad, but only one seat in the provinces north of Baghdad. Meanwhile, the Sunni Arab-dominated parties (Iraqiya and the IAF) won convincing victories in all the Sunni Arab majority provinces in the north, and, predictably, the Kurdish parties swept the board in the Kurdish Autonomous Region.

In the absence of a clear legislative majority, the Constitution required the President to assign the responsibility for government formation to 'the biggest bloc in parliament in numerical terms', which appeared to be Allawi's Iraqiya. However, the Constitution failed to define the term 'bloc' and, crucially, whether or not one could be formed after an election. In an attempt to capitalize on this constitutional loophole, the State of Law alliance and the Iraqi National Alliance announced that they had agreed to form a unified parliamentary bloc—the National Alliance (NA)—in early May 2010. With a combined total of 159 seats, the NA would have the right to form a new government as the largest parliamentary bloc.

Though nominally a unified force, the NA's major problem concerned the nomination of the new premier: the ISCI and the Sadrists were prepared to accept any candidate from the State of Law alliance other than al-Maliki, while al-Maliki insisted that the State of Law would only participate in government if he continued as Prime Minister. In August 2010 Kurdish leaders had issued a list of 19 demands that would have to be satisfied in order to earn Kurdish support. One of the key Kurdish demands was that any government formed must include all key groups. This meant that both Iraqiya and the State of Law would have to be included in government for the Kurds to lend their support. At the end of October 2010 a series of meetings between the leaders of the major blocs as part of the so-called Barzani initiative resulted in the establishment of the Arbil Agreement. Although the details of this agreement were not published, and there was some doubt, indeed, as to whether an actual document existed, the broad principles of the accord were believed to involve the retention of al-Maliki as Prime Minister, the establishment of a new National Council for Strategic Policy, to be headed by Allawi, and the maintenance of 'balance' in terms of government appointments among Iraq's various communities. The Arbil Agreement succeeded in preparing for a broad consensus on government formation. Accordingly, on 11 November the Council of Representatives was reconvened to re-elect Jalal Talabani as President; Talabani then invited al-Maliki to form a new governing coalition. In accordance with the Agreement, Iraqiya's Osama al-Nujaifi was elected Speaker. With the principal posts filled, attention turned to the onerous task of allocating ministries to the various parties.

Three days prior to the expiration of a 25 December deadline for government formation, Prime Minister al-Maliki presented an incomplete list of ministers to the Council of Representatives for approval. Controversially, al-Maliki did not name anyone to head the three crucial security ministries—those of defence, national security affairs and the interior—opting instead to nominate himself as temporary head of all three. The major winners in the division of government positions were the State of Law, with 11 ministries, and the Sadrists, with six. In stark contrast, the once all-powerful ISCI emerged from the process in control of just one ministry (transportation). On 22 December al-Maliki's new (partial) Government was approved by the necessary majority.

The failure of Iraq's political leaders to agree on the appointment of candidates to head ministries as critical as defence and the interior reflected a fundamental disagreement about who had the right to control which of the three security ministries. Allawi claimed that the defence portfolio was promised to Iraqiya, while al-Maliki maintained that the agreement was to have a Sunni (regardless of party affiliation) in the defence ministry and two Shi'a in the interior and national security affairs portfolios. For their part, Kurdish leaders demanded the appointment of a Kurd as Minister of National Security Affairs in order to maintain an ethno-sectarian balance in the security ministries. In the mean time, there was no progress at all on the establishment of a National Council for Strategic Policy, which was a key part of the deal that brought Iraqiya into the Government.

The common theme linking these disputes was the desire on the part of al-Maliki's rivals to prevent the Prime Minister from concentrating too much power in his own hands. Al-Maliki's autocratic tendencies were clearly displayed during the 2008–10 period, as was his preference for ignoring constitutional limitations on his power. Fears that this behaviour would be repeated were heightened in January 2011, as a result of a Federal Supreme Court decision to place certain critical institutions, including the Iraqi High Election Commission and the Central Bank, under the control of the executive branch. This measure, constituting a massive extension of the powers of the Prime Minister, appeared to contravene directly the Constitution, which stated that these bodies were 'considered independent commissions subject to monitoring by the Council of Representatives'. This was just the latest of a series of court decisions that had favoured al-Maliki. In conjunction with al-Maliki's tendency to create new security and intelligence offices that were solely responsible to the Office of the Prime Minister, and his demonstrated willingness to utilize these against political opponents, there was an understandable concern among opponents of al-Maliki that his intentions were not benign.

A second dynamic that shaped the post-election political landscape was the sharp deterioration in the relationship between al-Maliki and Allawi. Since the conclusion of the coalition agreement that allowed the establishment of the unity Government, al-Maliki had done nothing to indicate that he was serious about sharing power with Allawi. He rejected all of Allawi's nominations for Minister of Defence and stated clearly that creating a National Strategic Policy Council with meaningful powers (i.e. the capacity to check the Prime Minister) would violate the Constitution. By mid-2011 communications between the two had ended. Simultaneously, the US departure from Iraq in 2011 left Prime Minister al-Maliki virtually unchecked in his exercise of power. Within hours of the exit of the last US troops and just days after al-Maliki's visit to Washington, DC, to meet with President Obama, Iraq's Higher Judicial Council issued an arrest warrant for Vice-President Tariq al-Hashimi on terrorism. In response to the charges, al-Hashimi fled to the Kurdish Autonomous Region, where he enjoyed the protection of Kurdish leaders until he departed for Qatar in April 2012, and thereafter travelled to Turkey. Al-Hashimi's trial on 150 separate terrorism-related charges began, in absentia, in May. On 9 September al-Hashimi was found guilty of planning and facilitating the murder of two men and sentenced to death by hanging. Al-Hashemi rejected the verdict as 'unjust', while Iraqiya issued a statement in which it claimed that the court's decision had been politically motivated.

POLITICAL OPPOSITION TO AL-MALIKI

Prime Minister al-Maliki's capacity to confront and outmanoeuvre his opponents continued to be a defining feature of politics in Baghdad. The most serious threat to al-Maliki gathered pace in April 2012 when the leaders of the major opposition blocs—the Kurds, Iraqiya and the Sadrists—met in Arbil to plan a strategy for confrontation. The result was a nine-point letter, delivered in the form of an ultimatum, which demanded that the premiership be limited to two terms and that al-Maliki adhere to the Arbil Agreement. The Prime Minister was given a deadline of 15 days to deliver a satisfactory response, in the absence of which a vote of no confidence would be organized in the Council of Representatives. Following the expiry of the deadline, a concerted effort began to mobilize enough votes to remove al-Maliki from office. In June it was revealed that a petition had been submitted to President Jalal Talabani requesting that he authorize a vote of no confidence in the Prime Minister, but the number of signatories to the petition, 160, fell three short of the absolute majority of 163 votes required to remove the Prime Minster and his Government.

Besides al-Maliki's strategic use of patronage, his control of the coercive instruments of state and his network of allies throughout the south, the key to his survival was the weakness and incoherence of the opposition. For example, the move to oust al-Maliki divided the Kurdish parties, with some PUK members and the entire Gorran delegation refusing to participate in what had originally been an initiative of Kurdish Autonomous Region President Barzani. Iraqiya was equally divided over the move and continued its process of gradual fragmentation. The occasions on which the opposition has been sufficiently unified to present a genuine check on the power of the Prime Minister have been rare. They include the Council of Representatives' successful blocking of al-Maliki's ongoing efforts to curb Iraq's Election Commission. After first attempting and failing to remove perceived adversaries from the Commission through accusations of corruption in 2012, the Prime Minister then tried to 'pack' the Commission by expanding its membership from nine to 15 in September. The move was thwarted when the Council of Representatives rejected the proposal and elected nine new members, under the chairmanship of the KDP's Sarbas Mustafa Rashid.

Iraq's other nominally independent commissions have proved less resilient in the wake of the Supreme Court's January 2011 decision. In 2011 the Chairman of the Trade Bank of Iraq, Hussein al-Azri, was forced to flee to Lebanon, after al-Maliki launched a corruption investigation against him and the bank. Al-Azri was later sentenced to 15 years' imprisonment and replaced by al-Maliki's nominee, Hamdiyah al-Jaff. Iraq's Integrity Commission, the body charged with investigating government corruption, was targeted next. After facing the familiar corruption charges levelled by the Prime Minister, Judge Rahim al-Ogaili resigned, to be replaced by an al-Maliki ally, Izzat Tawfiq. Finally, accusations of money-laundering and the irregular conduct of foreign exchange auctions against the Governor of Iraq's Central Bank, Sinan al-Shabibi, led to his formal removal in October 2012, together with the resignation of many of his staff. Within two years, therefore, al-Maliki had succeeded in replacing the heads of virtually all of Iraq's nominally independent institutions with his own allies.

This sustained drive to expand executive power was seemingly halted in February 2013, when the Accountability and Justice Commission (AJC), the successor body to the de-Baathification Commission, announced that the Chief Justice and head of Iraq's Higher Judicial Council, Medhat al-Mahmoud, had been removed from office on account of his extensive record of judicial service under both al-Bakr and Saddam Hussein. Since al-Mahmoud's rulings had been instrumental in facilitating al-Maliki's expansion of executive power, this move was widely viewed as an attempt by the Commission to take action against the Prime Minister. Al-Maliki's response was to dismiss the head of the AJC and appoint a more amenable replacement. Subsequently, an appeals court overturned the decision to remove al-Mahmoud.

POPULAR OPPOSITION TO AL-MALIKI

While the political opposition in Baghdad struggled to rise against the increasingly authoritarian tendencies of the Prime Minister, a more serious threat to al-Maliki's authority began to emerge in mid-2010 in the form of widespread popular demonstrations against the Government. Initially, popular discontent was directed at government officials for their failure to provide basic services and exacerbated by the widespread, and largely accurate, perception that corruption was endemic in the entire governing edifice. In June 2010, for example, major demonstrations erupted in several Iraqi cities in protest against the Government's failure to deliver adequate supplies of electricity. While sporadic anti-Government protests continued throughout late 2010, it was not until February 2011 that large-scale, organized demonstrations began to take place. In keeping with the wave of popular uprisings throughout the Middle East, protest organizers in Iraq designated 25 February as a 'day of rage' and urged 1m. Iraqis to participate. Prime Minister al-Maliki's response to the impending protests was to claim they were being manipulated by Baathists and al-Qa'ida, and to ban all traffic in Baghdad on the day of the protests on security grounds. In the end, protests took place in 18 cities across Iraq, although attendance fell far short of 1m. Several of the protests became violent, with the result that up to 50 people were killed by security forces across Iraq. Al-Maliki's main approach to addressing the protest movement was repression. By March it had become almost impossible to obtain permission to demonstrate; political parties supporting the protests, such as the ICP, were being forced to suspend operations, while journalists reporting on the demonstrations were routinely being beaten and arrested by security forces.

From December 2012 onwards, the protests assumed a more dangerous form. In that month arrest warrants were issued for several bodyguards of the Minister of Finance, Fallujah-born Rafie al-Issawi. This action prompted large-scale protests in Fallujah and Ramadi the same month, which later spread to cities throughout the Sunni-populated areas of the country. The initial demands of the protesters were predictable—a reversal of de-Baathification, the release of prisoners and the resignation of al-Maliki. In January 2013, however, events escalated when the Iraqi army opened fire on protesters in Fallujah, killing nine and wounding more than 50. Then, in April an attack on a police checkpoint outside Hawija (in Kirkuk governorate) prompted Iraqi security forces to attack a protest site in Hawija. In the resulting confrontation, approximately 40 protesters were killed and over 150 injured. Over the following days violence escalated throughout central Iraq as insurgent groups, such as al-Qa'ida and the Baathist Naqshibandi group, capitalized on the Hawija incident to launch a wave of attacks against government forces and Shi'a civilians. As a result, April and May were the most violent months in Iraq, in terms of the number of deaths, since 2008. The main threat presented by the 2013 protest movement was that, unlike in 2010–11, when demonstrations were staged throughout Iraq, the 2013 protests were exclusively conducted in the Sunni part of the country and were overtly sectarian in nature. Hence, the sectarian attacks that followed raised fears of a return to the large-scale violence of the civil war years (2005–08). What prevented the protests from coalescing into something more threatening to al-Maliki's Government were the internal divisions among the protesters, both in terms of their ultimate aims and the means that they were prepared to use to achieve them.

RELATIONS WITH THE KURDISH AUTONOMOUS REGION

Along with the future status of the disputed territories, the other key concern that has dominated relations between the central Government and the Kurdish authorities is the management of Iraq's oil and gas sector, particularly whether the KRG has the constitutional right to sign contracts with international oil companies (IOCs) without the approval of the Ministry of Oil in Baghdad. Efforts to adopt a comprehensive package of legislation relating to the hydrocarbons sector in Iraq began during mid-2006, with the completion of the first draft of the proposed law. Almost immediately there was controversy over issues such as the terms of private sector involvement in Iraq's petroleum industry, whether oil revenues should be controlled by the central or regional governments, and the mechanism by which revenues would ultimately be distributed across the country as a whole. The failure of Iraq's political leaders to pass a national oil and gas law prompted the KRG to pass its own regional oil and gas law in 2007. This offered more favourable terms to IOCs than those being offered by Baghdad. Subsequently, the KRG signed contracts with more than 40 IOCs to develop the hydrocarbons sector in the Kurdistan region. In response, the Ministry of Oil declared the contracts to be illegal and threatened to blacklist any company that signed an agreement with the KRG.

Initially, most of the IOCs that signed contracts were small-scale operations, such as the USA's Hunt Oil and Norway's DNO, but in November 2011 several petroleum exploration agreements were signed by US oil giant ExxonMobil and the KRG to develop a number of fields in the Kurdish region. At least three of these fields were wholly or partially situated in disputed areas of Nineveh and Kirkuk outside the recognized Kurdish Autonomous Region. Predictably, the central Government condemned the agreements as 'illegal' and in violation of the Constitution, and threatened ExxonMobil with a variety of negative consequences, including the termination of its existing participation in the exploitation of the large-scale West Qurna field in Basra. Moreover, the company was banned from a hydrocarbons bidding round in May 2012. In June al-Maliki reportedly urged President Obama to intervene directly to halt ExxonMobil's dealings with the KRG, claiming that they were having a negative impact on Iraq's stability. The involvement of ExxonMobil had the potential to change the dynamics of the relationship between the Kurdish Autonomous Region and the authorities in Baghdad in a fundamental way. ExxonMobil may be powerful enough, especially if backed by the USA, to resist this government pressure and change the business environment in the hydrocarbons sector. The company's apparent success in concluding agreements with the Kurds while retaining its West Qurna contract could inspire other major oil and gas firms to pursue the significantly better deals offered by the KRG. Indeed, in June 2012 French oil company Total announced that it was beginning oil exploration in the region and the same month, US oil giant Chevron signed a deal with the KRG to develop two exploration blocs north of Arbil. Two months later, the oil arm of Russia's Gazprom, the world's largest gas producer, also acquired two exploration blocs in the Kurdish region. The major problem facing the KRG and IOCs operating in the Kurdish region was how to transport oil to market without relying on Iraq's existing infrastructure. A potential solution to this problem emerged in May 2012, when it was announced that the KRG and Turkey had agreed to export Kurdish crude petroleum via a new pipeline to the Turkish border from 2013–14. This new outlet would allow the KRG to bypass the Ministry of Oil's monopoly on the country's oil infrastructure and attain an unprecedented level of independence for the region's petroleum industry.

Despite these promising developments for the Kurds, the Iraqi authorities retain de facto control over the oil industry in the Kurdish region, not just via its control of the pipeline network, but also because the Government decides the distribution of all oil and gas revenues. The KRG relies on Baghdad for over 90% of its income, including the revenue necessary to compensate IOCs for the costs of hydrocarbons development in the region. In an attempt to loosen this hold, in July 2012 the KRG negotiated an agreement with the Turkish Government to export oil to Turkey by truck in exchange for supplies of fuel. In response, Prime Minister al-Maliki threatened to deduct the value of these exports from the Kurdish administration's guaranteed 17% share of the national budget. The dispute was apparently resolved in September, when the KRG and Iraqi authorities reached an agreement for the Kurds to produce 200,000 barrels of oil per day for export via the pipeline system, and in return for which the Iraqi Government would pay nearly US $1,000m. to IOCs working in the region. Like the two oil deals that preceded it, however, this agreement soon broke down, due to the failure of the Kurdish administration to meet its export quota and the consequent refusal of the Iraqi Government to release the full amount of funds needed to compensate IOCs. The oil and gas issue also adversely affected negotiations over Iraq's 2013 budget. When the final budget was passed by the Council of Representatives in March 2013, it included less than $700m. to compensate IOCs working in the Kurdish region, significantly less than the $3,500m. demanded by the KRG. After boycotting the original vote in protest, the Kurdish parties then announced a formal boycott of the legislature and the Council of Ministers on 18 March. The boycott was eventually brought to an end with the signing of a new seven-point agreement between the Iraqi and Kurdish authorities, which included the creation of several committees to manage mutual relations in the disputed territories and a renewed commitment on all sides to the adoption of a national oil and gas law. The likelihood that anything concrete will result from this agreement is remote, however.

THE 2013 PROVINCIAL ELECTIONS

The April 2013 provincial elections took place against a background of increasing violence in Sunni-dominated regions. As a result of the violence, the elections in Anbar and Nineveh provinces were postponed until July by the Government, which used the grave security situation as the justification. With the three Kurdish-dominated provinces still avoiding elections, and the status of Kirkuk too controversial for the authorities to risk organizing a vote, balloting actually took place in only 12 of Iraq's 19 provinces on 20 April. The elections did very little to disturb the existing balance of power. Al-Maliki's State of Law, which was joined by the Badr Organization, the Islamic Virtue Party and a number of Shi'a members of Iraqiya, was placed first in seven provinces, including Baghdad and Basra, and took joint first place with the ISCI in Wasit. In Najaf and Salah al-Din, local independent lists (the Alliance of Iraqi People and Loyalty to Najaf, respectively) prevailed, while the Sadrists were successful in Maysan. In Diyala, a pan-Shi'a list that included the ISCI, the Sadrists and the State of Law was placed first. Although it secured the highest number of provincial council seats across Iraq as a whole, however, the State of Law actually lost representation compared with its performance in 2009, and in no province was the party's margin of victory sufficient to govern without coalition partners. The main group to suffer a loss of support in the elections was the remnants of Allawi's Iraqiya. Despite being the only list to present candidates in all 12 provinces, Iraqiya's best result was fourth place in Diyala and Salah al-Din. The main beneficiary appeared to be a coalition assembled by Parliamentary Speaker Osama al-Nujaifi, known as the Uniters, which was placed second in Baghdad, Salah al-Din and Diyala (in alliance with Saleh al-Mutlaq's Iraqi Front for National Dialogue).

FOREIGN RELATIONS IN THE POST-SADDAM HUSSAIN ERA

The removal of Saddam Hussain's regime in April 2003 heralded a new era in Iraq's relations with its neighbours. Iraq was no longer considered to be an immediate military threat to the Gulf states, and UN sanctions were lifted following the former President's deposition. Superficially, Iraq's relations with its neighbours appeared to have benefited from the change of regime, since virtually all of the neighbouring states had reason to oppose or fear Saddam Hussain's Iraq. However, with Saddam removed, Iraq's relations with its neighbours were governed by new parameters.

During the period leading up to the removal of Saddam Hussain, the Iranian Government had been divided over whether US plans for Iraq should be welcomed or opposed. In general, 'hardline' religious clerics feared the potential success of a US mission to bring democracy to Iraq. Iranian 'reformists' viewed the arrival of the USA as a welcome force, encouraging Iran's own democratic process. Within Iraq, the Iranian Government had a great deal of influence, which the USA initially underestimated. As Iran shared the same Shi'a beliefs as the majority of the population of southern Iraq, there existed a complex web of linkages between Iraqi and Iranian society and government. However, the relationship was far from being dominated by Tehran. Within Shi'ism, the principal holy cities are Najaf and Karbala, both in Iraq. With the removal of the constraints imposed upon the Iraqi Shi'a religious establishment by Saddam Hussain's regime, the traditional Iraqi centres of Shi'ism were again able to resume their position as the focal points of the religion, much to the consternation of the Iranian Shi'a establishment in Qom and Mashad.

However, the Iranian Government had in place many groups that it had supported since the 1980s, including the SCIRI and its Badr Brigades (now Organization) militia. In addition to political groups and their militias, there was also an extensive network of charities and religious offices within Iraq that were funded by Iran. This complex tapestry of interlinked systems meant that Iran was perhaps the most influential foreign element in Iraq after the removal of Saddam Hussain, perhaps even more influential than the USA itself. Observers reported from the early part of 2004 that Iran had established a network of agents from Zakho in Iraqi Kurdistan through to Umm al-Khasib in the south. US administration sources indicated that Iran had perhaps as many as 14,000 operatives in Iraq, making the Iranian presence substantially larger than that of, say, the British.

The extent of direct Iranian influence in Iraq following the overthrow of Saddam Hussain's regime was almost impossible to establish, but throughout the period of US occupation repeated allegations were made by both Iraqi government officials and British and US military sources that Iran was actively aiding the insurgency. Relations between Iraq and Iran improved dramatically following the Iraqi elections in January 2005. The sweeping victory of the UIA, a coalition dominated by Shi'a religious parties such as SCIRI, brought to power a Government dominated by groups and individuals with long-standing ties to Tehran. Iraq's new Prime Minister, Ibrahim al-Ja'fari, had, like many Iraqi Shi'a, spent the years of the Iran–Iraq War in Tehran. Representatives of SCIRI took control of the two key Ministries of the Interior and of Oil, and the Iranian-financed, -equipped and -trained Badr Organization became the unofficial militia of the Ministry of the Interior.

From the USA's perspective, Iran's growing influence over political life in Iraq was regarded as both a stabilizing factor, in that Iran had a clear strategic interest in promoting a stable, Shi'a-dominated government, and a worrying development, in that it undermined US efforts to isolate Iran in the region. Tensions between the USA and Iran escalated rapidly after Mahmoud Ahmadinejad's election as Iranian President in June 2005. A hardliner, known for his fiery rhetoric and hostile stance towards the USA and Israel, Ahmadinejad had vigorously defended Iran's right to pursue a nuclear programme. Iran claimed that its nuclear intentions were entirely peaceful, a claim given little credence by the USA. Meanwhile, Iran's involvement in Iraq, particularly its suspected support for various Shi'a militia groups and insurgent factions, continued to be a source of concern for the USA and the United Kingdom. In August both countries formally protested to Iran over its alleged involvement in training insurgents and smuggling sophisticated explosives across the border, which, they claimed, were being used against coalition forces. Bayan Jabr, Iraq's Minister of the Interior, dismissed the accusations as 'an exaggeration'. The Iraqi legislative elections of December 2005 did not produce the ideal outcome from the Iranian Government's point of view. Though the UIA, many factions of which had close ties to Iran, won a plurality of seats, the internal squabble over the premiership resulted in a significant diplomatic defeat for Iran. The Iranians backed al-Ja'fari for the leadership and SCIRI's Bayan Jabr for the interior portfolio, neither of whom was appointed. While al-Maliki was not known to be actively hostile towards Tehran, unlike al-Ja'fari and the leadership of SCIRI, he had spent most of his exiled years in Syria rather than Iran.

Iran's primary concern in the run-up to the 2010 Iraqi national elections was to ensure the election of a government that would be amenable to Iranian interests. Consequently, high-level Iranian officials played an active role in the formation of the ISCI- and Sadrist-dominated INA.

As Iraq's election campaign gained momentum in January and February 2010, Iran's involvement became more controversial. In January news emerged that Iran's ambassador-designate to Iraq, Hassan Danafar, was actually a member of the Quds Force. Subsequently, US Generals David Petraeus and Ray Odierno both accused the Quds Force of manipulating Iraq's de-Baathification process in order to eliminate rivals to the INA, and of providing the ISCI and the Sadrists with millions of dollars a month to support their campaigns. In the event, the victory in the March polls of former interim premier Allawi's Iraqiya was the worst possible outcome from an Iranian perspective. Subsequently, the main Iranian objective was to sideline Allawi by brokering a reconstruction of the ruling Shi'a-Kurdish coalition. In the end, Iran played a critical role in the formation of the post-election Government by helping to convince al-Sadr to support a second prime ministerial term for al-Maliki. Experts suggested that a fatwa issued by al-Sadr's long-term mentor, Iranian-based Ayatollah Khadem al-Haeri, supporting al-Maliki's bid for a second term in office was critical in changing al-Sadr's stance. While the new Government was not precisely the one wanted by Iran, its least preferred regime in Iraq was thereby avoided. For the Government of Turkey, the removal of Saddam Hussain brought with it the spectre of a Kurdish national revival. Since 1991 the Iraqi Kurds had governed their own affairs independently from the rest of Iraq. They had become key components of the Iraqi opposition movement and had succeeded in gaining support for the creation of a federal Iraqi state with a Kurdish component. For some sections of the Turkish Government and military, a federal Iraq would be the first stage in the collapse of the Iraqi state and the emergence of an independent Kurdistan. Fearing the example such a development would set for its own Kurdish population, the Turkish Government's relations towards Iraq following Saddam Hussain's removal focused on maintaining the territorial integrity of the state at all costs.

Initial attempts by Turkey to station forces in Iraq to assist the US military were blocked by Kurds within the Governing Council. Relations between the Iraqi Kurds and the Turkish Government remained particularly tense throughout 2003, and were heightened by the question of the status of Kirkuk, which the Kurds continued to claim as their capital. However, following a change of senior staff within the military, it appeared that the Turkish Government had become increasingly resigned to the inevitability of an autonomous Kurdish entity in northern Iraq. Having once strongly resisted the idea of a form of federalism in Iraq that would recognize a distinct Kurdish region, from 2004 the Turkish Government adopted a more realistic approach to the issue. There were even indications from within the Government that outright Kurdish independence from Iraq would be a tolerable outcome for Turkey, though not if this included the annexation of Kirkuk. The prospect of a major Turkish military intervention in northern Iraq diminished considerably as a consequence of Turkey's ongoing efforts to secure membership of the EU; in December 2004 Turkey was finally permitted to begin official accession talks with the EU, which began in October 2005. However, the presence of an estimated 3,000–5,000 PKK guerrillas in the mountains of northern Iraq, and their resumption of (low-level) attacks on Turkish security forces in April–May 2005, was likely to perpetuate tensions in the region, especially as the USA seemed unwilling (or unable) to act decisively to eliminate the PKK threat from Iraq. The results of the January 2005 elections in Iraq represented a blow to Turkey's interests in the country. The results strengthened both Kurdish nationalists and Shi'a fundamentalist parties, thus leaving Turkey deprived of natural allies in the Iraqi Government. For the time being, therefore, Turkey had little option but to co-operate with the two major Kurdish parties, and little capacity to alter the trajectory of events in Iraq in its own favour.

While clearly uncomfortable with the degree of autonomy afforded to the Kurds by the new Iraqi Constitution, Turkey appeared ready to accept the inevitable and 'normalize' relations with the Kurdish entity in northern Iraq. In November 2005 an Iraqi Airways flight landed in İstanbul's Atatürk airport to complete the first Iraq–Turkey flight in 14 years. Two months later the Turkish Government authorized chartered flights by a private company to two Kurdish cities for the first time, a move that symbolized to many a change in Turkey's approach to its failed Iraq policy. This failure was graphically illustrated by the poor performance of the Turkish-backed umbrella party, the Iraqi Turkmen Front (ITF), in the December elections. The virtual collapse of Turkey's efforts to influence Iraq's politics directly by mobilizing the Turkmen population through the ITF left the Turks with next to no leverage over political events in Iraq. Accordingly, government statements, even on the explosive issue of Kirkuk, were toned down considerably.

Two issues—the future status of Kirkuk and the activities of the PKK—continued to dominate Turkey's agenda with respect to Iraq throughout the post-war period. Regarding the situation in Kirkuk, events unfolded broadly in accordance with Article 140 of the Iraqi Constitution, leaving Turkey with few concrete options, other than hostile rhetoric. Regarding the PKK, the rhetoric was, if anything, even more bellicose. As the PKK stepped up attacks against both civilian targets and security forces, pressure mounted on the Turkish Government to authorize an incursion into northern Iraq to destroy the PKK's bases. On 17 October the Turkish Grand National Assembly voted overwhelmingly to approve a military incursion into Iraq to track down PKK militants, and in December the Turkish air force launched a sustained bombing campaign against PKK bases inside Iraqi territory. In February 2008 the Turkish military invaded Iraqi territory with a force of more than 10,000 troops. The incursion lasted for a week and led to the deaths of 240 PKK rebels and 27 Turkish troops, according to the Turkish Government. The Iraqi Government claimed to have been informed about the incursion 'at the last minute', and had not approved it. While tensions between Iraq and Turkey over the latter's persistent violations of Iraqi sovereignty continued, a more harmonious relationship appeared to be on the horizon after the visit of Turkish Prime Minister Erdoğan to Iraq in July. The two countries signed a series of deals on energy and border security, and announced the establishment of a 'high-level strategic co-operation council' between their Governments that would help to forge a 'long-term strategic partnership'. Accordingly, in November 2008 Iraq, Turkey and the USA formed a permanent trilateral commission (with Iraqi Kurdish involvement) in order to 'enact forceful measures to stop all activities undertaken by this organization inside Iraqi territory or in any region adjacent to the Turkish–Iraqi border'. Although Turkey continued to mount sporadic strikes on PKK bases in northern Iraq during the latter part of 2008 and early 2009, the establishment of this commission, and better relations between the Turkish Government and the Iraqi Kurds, suggested that a consensus on the PKK issue was emerging. In March 2009, during a visit by Turkish President Gül to Baghdad, Iraqi President Talabani issued an ultimatum to the PKK to either 'lay down its guns or leave Iraq'. According to media reports, the trilateral commission had, by this time, made significant progress on a deal under the terms of which Turkey would offer an amnesty to PKK fighters willing to lay down their arms.

Progress was also made on another traditional source of tension between Turkey and Iraq during 2009. In June Turkey finally agreed to increase the water flow of the Euphrates River into Iraq by up to 50%. The flow of water into Iraq had decreased dramatically over recent years as a result of Turkey's ambitious Southeast Anatolia Project, which involved building a network of 22 dams on the Tigris and Euphrates rivers to irrigate thousands of acres of land and generate some 1,200 MW of electricity. The project was scheduled for completion in 2013, making water a possible cause of bilateral tension in the coming years.

Relations between Iraq and Turkey began to deteriorate during late 2011 as a result of al-Maliki's targeting of prominent Sunni political leaders Saleh al-Mutlaq and Tariq al-Hashimi. Erdoğan warned that these actions could precipitate a sectarian civil war, while al-Maliki condemned the Turkish Prime Minister for interfering in Iraq's internal affairs. In April 2012 Erdoğan accused al-Maliki of 'fanning' sectarian tensions through his 'self-centred' approach to governance. In response, al-Maliki accused Turkey of 'flagrant interference' and declared the country a 'hostile state'. Relations soured further when Turkey extended sanctuary to al-Hashimi in April and began accepting unauthorized exports of crude petroleum from the Kurdish Autonomous Region in May.

Iraq's relations with its Arab neighbours entered a distinctly uneasy phase following the US-led removal of Saddam Hussain from power. For Jordan, the problem was quite simply how to maintain good relations with the USA, while satisfying the inherently anti-US position of Jordanian and Palestinian society. The Jordanian Government recognized its dependency upon the Iraqi economy for Jordan's own economic prosperity, and therefore could not adopt an anti-US position. However, with approximately one-half of the Jordanian population being Palestinian and, on the whole, supporters of an anti-US position, King Abdullah ibn al-Hussein had to find a careful balance. A generally pro-US stance was tied to the King's appeal for a resolution of the Palestinian issue, emphasizing the balance the Jordanian Government sought to achieve. This move by the Jordanian Government was heavily influenced by the fact that many of the foreign insurgents travelling to Iraq to fight against coalition forces passed through Jordan, while US forces in Iraq believed that a Jordanian national and suspected al-Qa'ida operative, Abu Musab al-Zarqawi, was co-ordinating many of the attacks against them. The involvement of Jordanians in the insurgency, and Jordan's apparent inability to prevent their crossing into Iraq, was a continual source of tension in relations between the two countries. In March 2005, following a major terrorist attack, allegedly perpetrated by Jordanian national Raed Mansour al-Banna, which killed 125 Shi'a Arabs in the Iraqi city of Hilla, Shi'a demonstrators protested against the killings by storming the Jordanian embassy in Baghdad and raising the Iraqi flag over the building. A spokesman for the UIA accused the Jordanian Government of complicity in the attack by failing to seal its border, and both Iraq and Jordan withdrew their diplomatic representatives from each others' capital city.

Syria did not possess the initial good relationship with the USA that Jordan enjoyed. Indeed, the strained bilateral relations meant that Syria was immediately accused of assisting in the disappearance of Saddam Hussain's family at the commencement of military operations. The USA further accused Syria of assisting insurgents logistically and by facilitating their travel from Syria into Iraq, charges that the Syrian Government strenuously denied. The heightened tension between Syria and the USA resulted in the US Administration applying economic sanctions against Syria in May 2004, after Syria refused to expel Palestinian militants operating from the country. Overall, relations between Syria and the various Iraqi governments following the fall of Saddam Hussain's regime were characterized by the same uncertainty and inconsistency that plagued Iraq's relations with all its neighbours. In May 2005, for example, interim Prime Minister Ayad Allawi issued a statement praising Syria for its efforts to control its border with Iraq. Barely a month later Iraq's Minister of Foreign Affairs, Hoshyar al-Zibari, condemned the Syrians for failing to stem the flow of insurgents across its border. In June 2006 the Syrian Minister of Foreign Affairs, Walid Mouallem, announced plans to visit Baghdad with a view to restoring full diplomatic relations with Iraq for the first time since 1980. Full diplomatic relations were restored in November 2006, and in the following month concurrent ceremonies were held in Damascus and Baghdad to announce the reopening of the two countries' respective embassies. A more difficult issue for Syria was the rapidly growing refugee crisis caused by escalating sectarian tensions in Iraq. By mid-2007 there were an estimated 1.4m. Iraqi refugees in Syria, with 40,000 more arriving every month, putting an immense strain on the country's social and economic infrastructure.

The outbreak of hostilities in Syria in March 2011 and the country's subsequent descent into civil war placed the Iraqi Government in a difficult position. On the one hand, many of Iraq's Shi'a political parties feared the consequences of a regime change in Syria that would almost certainly result in yet another Sunni-dominated government on its borders; on the other, Iraq risked diplomatic isolation if it publicly supported the regime of Syrian President Bashar al-Assad. Initially, there were strong declarations of support for the Assad regime from a variety of sources within Iraq, most notably Muqtada al-Sadr. There were also reports that members of al-Sadr's Mahdi Army were actively fighting in Syria on the side of President Assad. Iraq abstained from an Arab League vote to suspend Syria's membership in November 2011, and adopted an official policy of 'neutrality' in the conflict thereafter.

Saudi Arabia's relations with Iraq after Saddam Hussain's removal from power appeared to be driven by petroleum considerations, Iraq's future political structure and Saudi Arabia's own relations with the USA. The stability of the House of Sa'ud had increasingly been called into question, and many observers speculated as to whether it could survive the emergence of a democratic Iraq. Another cause for concern in bilateral relations focused on the emergence of a strong Shi'a political identity in Iraq. For the first time in Iraq's recent history the holy cities of Najaf and Karbala were effectively reopened to the world-wide Shi'a community, and this remained a cause of concern for Saudi Arabia with its considerable Shi'a minority, living mainly in the oil-producing regions. The Shi'a of Saudi Arabia followed Ayatollah Sistani of Iraq as their spiritual leader, and had tribal links with southern Iraq. For Saudi Arabia, the emergence of a Shi'a-dominated Iraq was viewed with trepidation, as was the potential fragmentation of the state. For this reason, the Saudi Government spoke openly throughout 2004 of the need to maintain the territorial integrity of Iraq. During a speech to the Council on Foreign Relations in Washington, DC, in November, the Saudi Minister of Foreign Affairs, Prince Nayef ibn Abd al-Aziz Al Sa'ud, warned against the dangers of marginalizing Iraq's Sunni population during constitutional negotiations. He also spoke out against growing Iranian influence in Iraq, stating that 'we fought a war to keep Iran out of Iraq ... now we are handing the whole country over to Iran without reason'. In a furious response, Iraq's Minister of the Interior branded the Saudis as 'tyrants who think they are king and God' and castigated the Saudi Government for discriminatory policies against its own Shi'a population. Saudi Arabia subsequently toned down its rhetoric and focused attention on diplomacy.

Efforts to tempt Arab ambassadors to Iraq, which would imply full diplomatic recognition of the legitimacy of the new Government, were dealt a serious blow in July 2005 when Egypt's envoy to Iraq Ihab al-Sharif, was kidnapped and later killed. Responsibility for the killing was claimed by al-Qa'ida in Iraq, the organization reportedly led by al-Zarqawi. Al-Sharif was to have been the first full Arab ambassador stationed in Iraq since the war in 2003. By mid-2008, however, with Iraq's security continuing to improve, a number of Arab states made moves to restore full diplomatic relations. In June the UAE's Minister of Foreign Affairs, Sheikh Abdullah bin Zayed Al Nahyan, became the first minister from the Gulf state to visit Baghdad since 2003. During the visit it was announced that the UAE had appointed an ambassador to Iraq and that its embassy would open in the near future. In the same week both Bahrain and Kuwait made similar statements, and Saudi Arabia dispatched a delegation to Baghdad to assess the security environment with a view to opening an embassy.

In August 2008 King Abdullah of Jordan flew to Baghdad to hold talks with Prime Minister al-Maliki. Issues discussed at the meeting included the plight of the hundreds of thousands of Iraqi refugees who remained stranded in Jordan, the renewal of an agreement to supply Jordan with cheap oil, and security co-operation. However, the real importance of the visit was its symbolism: this was the first time that an Arab head of state had visited the Iraqi capital since the fall of the previous regime. For this reason, the visit was hailed as a 'breakthrough' by the Iraqi Minister of Foreign Affairs, Hoshyar al-Zibari. For his part, the King urged Arab governments to 'extend their hand to Iraq'. The appeal was apparently answered barely two weeks later when the Lebanese Prime Minister, Fouad Siniora, arrived in Baghdad to hold talks with al-Maliki. That the first two Arab leaders to visit post-war Baghdad were two of the USA's closest allies in the region did not escape attention, and it was commonly assumed that the visits were at least partly due to the exertion of considerable pressure by the US Administration on the region's Arab leaders to forge closer ties with Iraq as a means of countering the growing influence of Iran. During the latter months of 2008, however, the number of Arab states willing to appoint ambassadors to Baghdad increased significantly. By the end of the year, Bahrain, Jordan, Kuwait, the UAE and Syria had all dispatched ambassadors to Baghdad. In October the Egyptian Minister of Foreign Affairs, Ahmad Aboul Gheit, arrived in Baghdad for a one-day visit, and in June 2009 President Mubarak appointed Sherif Kamal Shahin as Egypt's first ambassador to Iraq since the killing of Ihab al-Sharif in July 2005.

The most significant dissenting voice remained Saudi Arabia. Suspicions that the Saudi Government continued to be a major source of funding and training to armed groups operating in Iraq and elsewhere were further fuelled in July 2010, when it was reported that a military base had been established on the Saudi–Jordanian border for the purpose of training militants to conduct attacks in Iraq. This followed previous allegations within the media that a leaked Saudi government document appeared to confirm that the Kingdom was financing al-Qa'ida in Iraq. The Saudi Government refused to comment on the allegations, but instead ordered the arrest of 37 intelligence officers supposedly responsible for the leak. In late 2010 classified US diplomatic communications released by the WikiLeaks organization provided a significant insight into the nature of relations between Saudi Arabia and Iraq, revealing, for example, that Saudi King Abdullah believed Prime Minister al-Maliki to be an agent of Iran and that the Saudi Arabian Government had contributed substantial funds to the organization of the 2010 Iraqi elections, in an effort to avoid a victory by Shi'a-dominated parties. There were more favourable developments with respect to Kuwait. In January 2011 Kuwait's Prime Minister, Sheikh Nasser al-Muhammad al-Ahmad al-Sabah, became the highest-ranking Kuwaiti to visit Baghdad since the 1990 war. The difficult nature of relations between Iraq and its Sunni neighbours in the region was demonstrated in March and April 2011, when many prominent Iraqi politicians declared support for the mainly Shi'a anti-Government protesters in Bahrain. In response to the Bahraini Government's violent suppression of demonstrations, the Iraqi Council of Representatives suspended sessions temporarily to register its disapproval, Muqtada al-Sadr mobilized mass rallies in Baghdad, and Ahmad Chalabi organized a 'Popular Committee in Iraq to Support the People of Bahrain' in order to co-ordinate the Iraqi response.

In spite of tensions between Iraq's Shi'a-dominated Government and many of its Sunni Arab neighbours, some evidence of an improvement in relations emerged during 2012. First, Saudi Arabia announced the posting of its new ambassador to Iraq in February, thereby establishing high-level Saudi representation in Baghdad for the first time in over two decades. Second, Iraq hosted the Arab League summit in March. The low-level representatives that were sent by many Arab countries and the lack of any concrete decisions on, for example, the crisis in Syria should not obscure the symbolic importance of the summit for Iraq. Iraq's status in the region may have declined, but the country was no longer the Arab region's diplomatic pariah.

Economy

Revised for this edition by the editorial staff; based on an earlier essay by MOIN SIDDIQI

INTRODUCTION

Abundant natural and human resources coupled with a thriving agricultural sector (Iraq was a net food exporter) enabled Iraq to attain the status of a middle-income economy in the 1970s and 1980s. It is an oil-rich country and developed a good basic infrastructure and efficient health care and educational systems, which were widely regarded as the best in the Middle East. Gross domestic product (GDP) per head rose to over US $3,700 in 1980, according to the World Bank. However, since that time the once prosperous economy has been gripped by a series of structural and man-made problems, including severe misrule; rampant institutionalized corruption; internal repression; pervasive state intervention; gross under-investment in physical infrastructure, industries (including the all-important petroleum industry) and social services; two costly wars—the 1980–88 Iran–Iraq conflict, and the Iraqi invasion of Kuwait in August 1990 and the subsequent multinational coalition campaign to liberate Kuwait in early 1991—and prolonged international trade sanctions; as well as more than nine years of political strife and conflict (which has claimed thousands of civilian lives) following the removal from power of the Baathist regime by the US-led coalition in April 2003.

Consequently, Iraq's human development indicators, which two decades ago exceeded regional averages, are now among the lowest in the Arab region, and income per head has continued to decline, a fact clearly incompatible with the country's status as the world's third largest holder of proven petroleum reserves, after Saudi Arabia and Iran. Iraq's per caput GDP of US $2,531 in 2010 was the second lowest in the Middle East. The country's decrepit infrastructure is a reflection of the lack of real capital investments since the early 1980s. A survey of living conditions in the period prior to the US invasion, commissioned by the UN Development Programme (UNDP) and compiled by the Iraqi Central Organization for Statistics and Information Technology (COSIT), highlighted acute problems of social deprivation. About one-half of the population said that they had unsatisfactory water supplies and more than 40% were deprived of good sanitation facilities. Furthermore, the survey reported that one-third of households were living on the equivalent of less than US $70 per week, and 5% of Iraqis lived in absolute poverty. Three-fifths of the population were relying totally on food aid for subsistence.

According to the 2007 Household Survey commissioned by the World Bank, only 12.5% of persons—those whose dwellings were connected to the public network—had a reliable water supply, while 22.4% relied on the national grid for electricity to their housing unit. Iraq's National Strategy for Poverty Reduction estimated the incidence of poverty at 23%; however, the 'poverty gap'—i.e. the gap between average incomes and the poverty threshold—was only 4.5%. Hence, a small increase in people's incomes would lift many of those classed as poor above the poverty threshold; conversely, a relatively minor deterioration of economic conditions would increase the rate of poverty. About 15% of all household income derives from government transfers, including pensions, in-kind transfers through the state Public Distribution System and cash transfers.

Iraq's once reputable education and health systems now compare unfavourably with those of neighbouring countries, reflecting the impact of sanctions and chronic under-funding. The mortality rate of children aged under five was reported at 38 (per 1,000 live births) in 2011. In 2011 life expectancy was assessed by the World Bank at 69 years—an improvement on the 2007 figure of 59 years, but still below the regional average of 72 years. Health expenditure rose from 3.2% of GDP in 2008 to 8.5% of GDP in 2010 (equivalent to US $ 346 per head), while the number of hospital beds (per 1,000 head) stood at 1.3. In 2011 access to sanitation facilities (as a percentage of the total population) was reported at 84%. The literacy rate among those aged over 15 years was 78.2% in 2010, according to UNESCO. The World Bank has estimated that 4,500 new schools are needed and 10,000 of the existing ones require renovation. The Government has pledged to spend US $5,200m. and $9,300m., respectively, over the next five years in improving the country's health care and educational sectors.

Mass under-employment, especially among young males, and widespread social deprivation have led to lawlessness and violent insurgency across Iraq. An estimated 140,000 people, including college graduates, enter the labour market every year. The unemployment rate in 2011 was officially estimated at 16%, but anecdotal evidence suggested that it was even higher. Increased job creation holds the key to much-needed socio-political stability. According to World Bank figures, the total labour force stood at 7.8m. in 2011. According to the IMF, the public sector employs about one-half of the country's labour force.

The US-led invasion generated an unparalleled movement of the Iraqi population, the largest in the Middle East since 1948. The United Nations High Commissioner for Refugees (UNHCR) estimated in January 2010 that over 3.8m. Iraqis had left their homes; of these, 1.6m. Iraqis were displaced internally, while the remainder had sought refuge in Jordan and Syria. However, displacement has subsided as the security situation in some locations (including the Baghdad area) has slowly improved. According to a report published by the International Office for Migration in April 2009, approximately 18% of total internally displaced persons (IDPs) had returned to their place of origin. None the less, the precarious living conditions and generally lower wages in Iraq have resulted in the emigration of professionals and skilled labour, hindering economic development and reconstruction efforts. Poor governance and reported cases of corruption are also problems that affect the economy: the German-based Transparency International rated Iraq 169th out of 176 countries in its 2012 Corruption Perception Index. According to local media reports, Iraq lost an estimated US $1,000m. through corruption in 2010.

Power generation, water and sewage treatment are operating below 2003 levels. Iraq's installed generating capacity is estimated at about 9,000 MW, of which 6,200 MW is fired by gas, stream or hydropower. Nonetheless, total present capacity falls far short of the nation-wide demand, estimated at 13,500 MW (excluding Iraqi Kurdistan) in 2012. Consequently, Iraqis face continual power outages (especially in the area around Baghdad) and rationing, affecting both the industrial and the residential sectors, and causing considerable popular discontent. A survey of 30,000 households commissioned by the Ministry of Planning's Iraq Knowledge Network found that 82% received an electricity supply for 10 hours or fewer a day.

Iraq currently imports some 16,000m. MWh of electricity per day from Iran and Turkey. Problems are caused by a combination of factors, notably widespread sabotage, looting, obsolete technology, disruptions in fuel supplies for power stations and the fragility of the grid. It is estimated that chronic power shortages cost the economy as much as US $40,000m. per year. The Baghdad area consumes 27% of the total electricity supply. Basra, in the south, and Mosul, in the north, account for 9% and 8%, respectively, of the total supply. The remaining 56% is distributed among Iraq's 18 governorates. About one-third of total energy is derived from heavy fuel oil, 27.8% from crude oil, and 13.3% from gas oil. Natural gas fires around 26% of Iraq's power generation capacity.

The Government's 20-year strategy—approved by the World Bank and UNDP—to overhaul the power sector requires about US $27,300m. of fixed investment, of which $4,500m. will be spent on installing new generation plants and rehabilitating existing ones. Between 2012 and 2017 Iraq's energy master plan aims to install 24,400 MW of new capacity; however, such an ambitious target will require annual investments of $4,500m. over the next five years. Overall, $35,000m. is the sum projected as necessary for rebuilding the dilapidated power sector.

The Government has pledged over the longer term to install up to 30,000 MW of generating capacity and favours private sector capital based on build-own-operate-transfer, build-operate-transfer and independent power projects—as in the countries of the Persian (Arabian) Gulf. In December 2008 GE Energy of the USA and Siemens of Germany received contracts worth $4,900m. for the delivery of 56 heavy-duty gas turbines to 10 sites across Iraq, with a combined generating capacity of 10,150 MW. Further to this, the Ministry of Electricity has signed a $3,200m. agreement with a company from the Republic of Korea (South Korea) to build 25 power stations with a total capacity of 2,500 MW in different parts of Iraq, as well as a $762m. contract with Jordanian-based Elite to construct several power plants with a total capacity of 600 MW. Baghdad is also offering four 25-year build-own-operate concessions to develop gas-fired plants at Amara, Diwaniya, Samawa and Shatt al-Basra—each with an installed capacity of 500 MW, except for the larger 1,250 MW independent power project at Basra.

According to a master plan for the country's power sector devised by US-based Parsons Brinckerhoff, Iraq needs to install US $29,000m. worth of new generating capacity between 2015 and 2030, calculated at constant 2009 prices. Once investments into transmission and distribution projects are included, the total amount required for upgrading the power infrastructure rises to $55,000m. The plan envisages that the private sector, including foreign investors, will provide the bulk of new financing, while power demand (under best-case scenarios) could reach 20,000 MW, 24,000 MW and 32,000 MW by 2019, 2024 and 2029, respectively.

For drinking water, Iraq relies heavily on extraction and treatment of water from the Euphrates and Tigris rivers, which is then piped to urban areas and rural communities. However, according to the World Bank, many water treatment plants are operating well below 50% capacity, reflecting a shortage of spare parts and electricity. Since 2004 the US Government has spent about US $2,460m. on water and sanitation projects, which have added more than 2.5m. cu m per day (m/d) of water treatment capacity, plus 1.2m. cu m/d of sewage treatment capacity. Much of the work was carried out by the US Army Corps of Engineers. A joint UN-World Bank report estimated the cost of rehabilitating Iraq's water and sanitation infrastructure at $6,800m.

Iraq's economy has experienced sharp fluctuations in output in the past three decades. According to the IMF, GDP per head declined steeply from over US $3,600 in the early 1980s to a mere $200 in the early 1990s. Although per caput GDP recovered to an estimated $800 in 2001, it slumped again, to about $500 in 2003, having been affected by post-invasion turmoil. Moreover, taking into account projected export earnings capacity and the much-depleted monetary value (expressed in US dollar terms) of the economy—measured by GDP—Iraq was also ranked among the most heavily externally indebted countries in the world (see Finance and Banking).

The Centre for Strategic and International Studies, a research institute based in Washington, DC, USA, estimated Iraq's pre-2003 total external obligations (including compensation claims) at $383,000m., equivalent to $15,506 per head—the largest in the Middle East—hence the need for enhanced debt relief.

Iraq faces a formidable task of rebuilding its infrastructure. Total long-term reconstruction costs could exceed US $100,000m., with a joint UN-World Bank Iraq assessment report in October 2003 estimating that the country needed $56,100m. for its infrastructure rebuilding programme up to 2007. The World Bank projected that restoring the national electricity system and providing a clean water supply and sanitation would require $12,000m. and $6,000m., respectively, in fixed investment, while the telecommunications and transport sectors would require $3,400m. The education system needs at least $8,000m. for building new schools and colleges, training teachers and creating a productive workforce. The World Bank's Iraq Economic Transition Report assessed the direct monetary cost of the war, including the 'spill-over' effects, to be as much as $1,300,000m.

According to estimated national accounts statistics compiled by the UN Economic and Social Commission for Western Asia in 2001, Iraq's nominal GDP was about ID 4,874,160m. in 2000, rising to ID 5,361,576m. in 2001 and ID 5,924,542m. in 2002. Real GDP growth was estimated at 9.0% for 2001 and 7.0% for 2002. The military action undertaken by the US-led coalition in March 2003, and subsequent widespread looting and sabotage, brought about a virtual halt to economic activity for the rest of the year. As a consequence, Iraq dipped into a cycle of 'stagflation'—i.e., a combination of rising inflation and rapid contractions in GDP.

Estimates from the Central Bank of Iraq (CBI) suggest that economic output fell from US $23,100m. in 2002 to $17,400m. in 2003, while the IMF and the World Bank estimated that nominal GDP decreased by about one-third in 2003, to $12,603m., reflecting a decline in petroleum output to 1.34m. barrels per day (b/d)—from an average of 2.4m. b/d during 1998–2002, and a severe contraction in the non-petroleum sectors of the economy. Electricity production declined by 30%. However, inflation, as recorded by an increase in the consumer price index (CPI), was contained at 34% by the end of 2003, aided by subsidized prices for energy, water and basic foodstuffs.

The Coalition Provisional Authority (CPA) attempted to implement structural adjustment reforms similar to the 'shock therapy' programmes of the mid-1990s in some former eastern European economies. The main goals of market-friendly reforms backed by appropriate legal and regulatory frameworks were to facilitate reconstruction and kick-start economic activity, as well as encouraging private investment. Reforms were orientated toward creating an attractive climate for foreign investors and a new economy. Iraq's state-owned enterprises, except those in the hydrocarbons sector, were to be privatized. In 2004 real GDP escalated by 46.5%, underpinned by a strong recovery in non-petroleum output, which exceeded its pre-war level, while petroleum output, which comprised two-thirds of the economy, increased by 52%, to 2.01m. b/d, according to sources within the Organization of the Petroleum Exporting Countries (OPEC). Nominal GDP in 2004 rebounded to US $25,800m.

The US Agency for International Development (USAID) estimated that the Iraqi economy grew by about 18% in 2005, with GDP expanding to US $33,000m. Income per head rose to $1,500, but still represented less than one-third of Iraq's 1980 national annual income. The inflation rate in the year to December 2005 was estimated at 20%. Real GDP growth for 2006, which was initially projected at 10.5%, ended the year at 6.2%, reflecting lower investments in basic infrastructure and oil capacity expansion projects. The investment execution rate in the petroleum sector was estimated at about 40%. The CBI reported that the average inflation rate surged from 37% at the end of 2005 to 53% a year later, exacerbated by a significant reduction in fuel subsidies and increasing transport and security costs, as well as shortages of key commodities, especially fuel products.

In late 2006 the Government took steps to combat inflationary pressures. The CBI raised its policy interest rate sharply from 12% in November 2006 to 20% in early January 2007 and permitted a gradual appreciation of the dinar. These measures were intended to 'de-dollarize' the economy, thus enhancing the CBI's control over monetary conditions, and also to reduce imported inflation Strong policy actions proved effective in restoring some confidence in the local currency and reducing inflation. The annual CPI rate fell from an average of 53.2% in 2006 to 30.8% during 2007. Additionally, the Government facilitated private fuel imports of petroleum products, with a view to easing supply bottlenecks and reducing 'black market' prices. Despite the perilous security situation, significant progress has been achieved in areas of fiscal sustainability and prudent economic policies, with support from the IMF and the World Bank. Real GDP growth rose steeply from 1.5% in 2007 to 9.5% in 2008. Non-oil activity also regained some momentum in 2008, registering a 5.4% expansion, after a 2% contraction over the previous year. Per caput income was estimated at US $2,845 in 2008, up from $1,720 in 2006. Since 2004 Iraq has successfully completed three economic reform programmes supported by the IMF: one under the Emergency Post Conflict Assistance facility and two (precautionary) Stand By Arrangements (SBAs). The main objectives of these programmes were to preserve hard-won macroeconomic stability, facilitate higher investment and output in the oil sector, and expedite structural reforms and institution building. Priority reforms include strengthening public sector budgetary management and the accounting framework of the CBI, the restructuring of the financial sector and improving governance in the oil industry. During this period Iraq has made tangible progress under harsh conditions, by reducing inflation to single digits, showing fiscal probity, rebuilding economic institutions and tackling deficiencies in the public sector. These achievements have helped to obtain generous debt relief from the 'Paris Club' of western official creditors and others.

The decline in oil prices from their July 2008 peak seriously impacted Iraq's economy, with nominal GDP contracting by almost 25% in 2009 to US $65,200m. Real GDP growth was estimated to have more than halved, to 4.2%, despite an improvement in oil production towards the end of the year as a result of efforts to address bottlenecks. However, the gradually improving security situation has revived commercial activity in the non-oil sector. COSIT estimated that real non-oil GDP grew by about 5.5% over 2008/09. The CBI proved successful in controlling inflation, by managing the exchange rate and keeping the policy interest rate positive in real terms. When inflationary pressures emerged during 2008, the CBI allowed appreciation of the dinar vis-à-vis the US dollar (rising by 0.5% per month until late 2008), which also helped counter-dollarization. Headline inflation remained well below the target of 6% in 2009, with prices actually decreasing by 4.4%, mainly owing to cheaper fuel and food prices.

To preserve macroeconomic stability and foster growth and employment, Iraq adopted an economic adjustment programme for 2010–11, for which it received support from the IMF under a new two-year SBA, as well as financial assistance from other multilateral institutions and donor countries. Real GDP growth was estimated at 8.4% in 2012 (down slightly from 8.6% in 2011), largely underpinned by expanding hydrocarbons production and buoyant fixed investment activity, especially in the housing and energy sectors. Meanwhile, consumer prices grew by 6.0% in 2012, up from 2.4% in 2010. Iraq's national output grew more than two-fold over the period 2007–12, representing a compound annual growth rate (CAGR) of 30.5%—making Iraq the eighth largest economy in the Middle East and North Africa region.

The Iraqi authorities are set to encounter significant challenges in the years ahead. The main priority is to accelerate reconstruction and to combat civil strife and sabotage activities. It will also be imperative to develop efficient state institutions to support a diversified market economy and deliver public services (notably electricity, water and sanitation, education and health care), and strengthen administrative capacity and the rule of law, rebuilding social cohesion, as well as completing the political transition. The country's population—

growing rapidly at 3% a year—is projected to reach 50m. by 2030, compared with official estimates of 33m. in 2011.

Diversifying the economy is the cornerstone of Iraq's new National Development Plan (NDP), which was unveiled in December 2010. The plan seeks to invest US $186,000m. between 2010 and 2014 in expanding public services, housing, utilities and general infrastructure, with the aims of raising annual GDP growth by 9.4%, creating 4.5m. new jobs and reducing poverty by 30% from 2007 levels. A total of $86,000m. (almost one-half of the planned investment) was expected to come from Iraq's private sector and foreign investment, with the remainder from state and federal sources. The Government allocated 17%, 15%, 10%, 9%, and 5%, respectively, of the NDP's capital spending for the housing, hydrocarbons, electricity, transport and communications and agriculture sectors. Estimates put the national housing deficit at 3.5m and two-thirds of Iraq's population live in urban areas. Large-scale reconstruction activities, however, depend on the restoration of lasting security. The country will need to improve the business climate to nurture a vibrant private sector in order to sustain higher output growth and provide much-needed new jobs, as well as to reintegrate Iraq into the global economy. The World Bank report *Doing Business 2013* rated Iraq 165th out of 185 economies in terms of the ease of doing business. To facilitate private investments, efforts will be required to reduce red tape and start-up costs for new businesses, and to improve physical infrastructure.

There is no easy solution to Iraq's many structural deficiencies, and nation-building could take a decade, even under the best-case scenario: higher inflows of official development assistance, debt cancellation, foreign investment into sectors besides petroleum, and sustained political stability. Post-conflict Iraq will probably remain underdeveloped for some years to come and relative poverty still affects almost a quarter of Iraq's population. In addition, many structural reforms have yet to be finished in the areas of public financial management, bank restructuring, planning processes and strategy design (at central and provincial levels), as well as deregulation of energy and services. However, despite the unfavourable political situation, there have been some encouraging signs in the past two years. The IMF estimated per caput GDP at US $6,300 for 2012 (compared with $4,278 in 2009), largely due to increased revenues from petroleum. Moreover, compared with other troubled states, Iraq's future creditworthiness appeared more solid. This reflects vast (untapped) hydrocarbons resources, fertile agricultural land, a plentiful water supply, a skilled and educated work-force and, by regional standards, technical sophistication.

SANCTIONS AND THE 'OIL-FOR-FOOD' PROGRAMME

The mandatory economic sanctions imposed on Iraq (and Iraqi-controlled Kuwait) by the UN Security Council on 6 August 1990 (and subsequently revised and expanded) included: bans on the purchase or trans-shipment of Iraqi petroleum and other commodities, and bans on the sale or supply of all goods and products to Iraq (with possible humanitarian exceptions for medical supplies and foodstuffs); the proscription of new investment in Iraq and Kuwait; the freezing of Iraqi and Kuwaiti assets abroad; and the interdiction of air traffic and the obligatory detention of Iraqi-registered ships violating the trade embargo. The effect of the sanctions was to place the Iraqi economy in almost total isolation, except that the land route from Jordan remained open for certain supplies. Particularly damaging for Iraq was the abrupt cessation of its oil and gas exports, its prime source of revenue. The Government responded by introducing the rationing of basic food items and adopted various emergency measures to promote economic self-sufficiency. Moreover, under Law 57 of 1990, announced on 18 September but backdated to 8 August, the Government declared Iraq's non-recognition of all seizures of Iraqi assets and decreed the seizure of the assets of all countries and organizations that 'issued arbitrary decisions' against Iraq. As part of this strategy, Iraq suspended debt repayments to the USA and other members of the multinational coalition.

The maintenance of most UN sanctions after the cease-fire agreement of 3 March 1991 (except those on food and medical supplies) meant that the Iraqi Government was obliged to begin its reconstruction efforts within those constraints, involving the continued non-availability of crucial oil revenues. (In the event, Iraqi resistance to full observance of the UN cease-fire resolution terms meant that the UN embargo was still in force up until the commencement of hostilities by the US-led coalition in March 2003.)

In February 1996 Iraq opened negotiations with the UN to establish terms for the possible export of oil to finance a UN-supervised humanitarian programme for the import and distribution of medical and food supplies. On 20 May, after four months of talks, the Iraqi Government signed a memorandum of understanding accepting the terms of UN Security Council Resolution 986 of April 1995. An implementation plan was eventually approved by the sanctions committee in early August 1996, and it was expected that all the required procedures and personnel would be established by mid-September. However, a new crisis in US–Iraqi relations at the start of September 1996 caused a temporary suspension of UN preparatory work within Iraq, and it was not until late November that arrangements to monitor oil sales under the terms of Resolution 986 were completed.

Production of petroleum for export under the UN-supervised 'oil-for-food' programme began on 10 December 1996. The export of oil to the value of some US $2,000m. was to be permitted over a period of 180 days, and all proceeds were to be paid into a special UN escrow account in New York, USA. Of the $2,000m., $20m. was allocated for the operation of the escrow account, $44.32m. for UN operational and administrative costs, $15m. for the UN Special Commission (tasked with verifying compliance with cease-fire conditions) and $600m. for the UN Compensation Commission's fund for war reparations. This left $1,320.68m. available for spending on humanitarian supplies, of which $260m. was assigned for the UN co-ordinated relief programme in Kurdish-controlled areas of Iraq and $1,060.68m. for supplies to the remainder of Iraq. Some 61% of total humanitarian spending was allocated for imports of foodstuffs, 16% for medicines and 8% for soaps and detergents. Priority imports for the electricity, agricultural and educational sectors accounted for 11% of authorized humanitarian spending, compared with 3% for water and sanitation services and 1% for health infrastructure -and nutrition.

Upon assuming office in January 2001, the US Administration of George W. Bush swiftly made clear its intention to influence a reform of the sanctions regime and the oil-for-food programme—the terms of which were being bypassed with considerable success by Iraq and an increasing number of international partners. It was estimated that the Iraqi Government was able to procure some US $1,000m. annually beyond the control of the UN, but it was clear that the Iraqi people were not benefiting from these additional revenues in terms of improved health and nutritional provision. A 'smart' sanctions initiative was therefore promoted by the USA and the United Kingdom as a means of removing restrictions on the flow of food and other consumer goods, while strengthening controls on the sale of military goods and on oil-smuggling. A British-drafted resolution for the introduction of 'smart' sanctions had failed to secure support from the UN Security Council by the time of the expiry of the ninth phase of the oil-for-food programme in early June, and was eventually withdrawn. Agreement was then reached by the permanent members of the Security Council (except Russia) on a compromise list of products that Iraq was forbidden to import under an eventual new sanctions regime; in order to secure acceptance of the list by the People's Republic of China, the USA had agreed to withdraw its block on some $90m. in Chinese contracts, including a major telecommunications project, which it had been delaying at the UN Security Council's sanctions committee. On 10 July Iraq resumed oil exports from both of its UN-authorized outlets, and on 29 November the oil-for-food programme was renewed for a further six months, to 30 May 2002 (the 11th phase). In mid-May, after intensive negotiations between the USA and Russia, the UN Security Council unanimously approved Resolution 1409 establishing the 12th phase of the programme (which expired on 25 November 2002) and revised the UN sanctions regime to allow Iraq to import all humanitarian goods not included on the new goods review list with only minimal checks. Goods featured on the list were only to be sold to Iraq after contracts had been screened and approved by the UN Monitoring, Verification and Inspection Commission and the International Atomic Energy Agency. The list was to be reviewed regularly by the Security Council. The embargo on all arms sales to Iraq remained in place.

In October 2001 the UN Office of the Iraq Programme alleged that Iraq had exported additional crude petroleum valued at some US $10m. by topping up officially approved shipments after UN inspectors had completed their checks. Iraq rejected these allegations, but the UN proposed a tightening of loading procedures at the officially designated export terminals. Furthermore, industry sources estimated that some 410,000 b/d of Iraq's total oil production of 2.31m. b/d in January 2002 was being exported illegally (180,000 b/d to Syria, 110,000 b/d to Jordan, 80,000 b/d to Turkey and 40,000 b/d to the Gulf region), making illicit exports effectively equivalent to more than one-quarter of the total amount of petroleum exported under the oil-for-food programme. UN censure was stymied by wider political considerations in the region. The UN Office of the Iraq Programme also expressed concern about the continuing number of contracts (particularly those for humanitarian purposes) under the oil-for-food programme stalled by the UN Security Council's sanctions committee because of administrative difficulties or suspicions that the goods requested might be used for military purposes; in contrast, virtually all contracts relating to the Kurdish Autonomous Region had been approved and processed. In an assessment of the situation published on 28 September 2001 by the UN Secretary-General, it was conceded that lower than projected oil revenues, the erratic way contracts were submitted by Iraq and delays in approving and processing some contracts by the sanctions committee had resulted in some sectors being fully funded according to the agreed distribution plan, while other sectors—particularly agriculture, education, electricity, health and water—had experienced shortages and delays.

Exports under the oil-for-food programme increased from 120m. barrels in phase one (December 1996–June 1997) to almost 390m. barrels during phase six (June–December 1999), falling to 293m. barrels under the ninth phase (December 2000–July 2001, before rising again, to slightly more than 300m. barrels, under the 10th phase (July–November 2001), only to decline once more, to some 226m. barrels, under the 11th phase (December 2001–May 2002). Revenues increased from US $2,150m. under the first phase to $9,564m. during the eighth phase (June–December 2000) following a significant rise in world petroleum prices from the second half of 1999, but dwindled thereafter (to $5,638m. under the ninth phase, $5,350m. under the 10th phase and $4,589m. under the 11th phase) as a result of a slump in world oil prices and Iraq's suspension of petroleum exports for five weeks beginning in June 2001. Iraq ceased all oil exports again in early 2002 in protest at Israel's uncompromising military intervention in Palestinian-controlled areas of the West Bank, but resumed in May. Finally, exports were put on hold during the US-led military campaign in Iraq from March 2003, approximately halfway through the 13th phase of the oil-for-food programme. As the ousting of Saddam Hussain from power also removed the *raison d'être* for the programme, on 22 May the UN Security Council adopted Resolution 1483, bringing an end to sanctions and setting a closure date for the programme of 21 November, as well as designating a UN special representative to assist in the reconstruction of Iraq. Up to 20 March 2003 5,633.5m. barrels of petroleum, with a value of $64,231m., were exported under the oil-for-food programme. (In April 2004 the UN Security Council approved an investigation into allegations that the former regime had used proceeds from the oil-for-food programme to bribe foreign government officials and corporations. The report published by the investigating committee in September 2005 found 'serious instances of illicit, unethical and corrupt behaviour within the United Nations' and blamed the Secretary-General, Kofi Annan, for mismanagement of the programme, although Annan was subsequently cleared of corruption charges.)

AGRICULTURE AND FOOD

Despite the increasing dominance of oil and gas production, the Government continued through the 1980s to allocate substantial resources to the development of agriculture, with the aim of achieving food self-sufficiency and even surpluses for export. At the same time state control of the agricultural sector was steadily relaxed in favour of allowing a greater role for private initiatives and for private sector investment from both Iraqi and other Arab sources. However, like the rest of the economy, agriculture suffered major disruption during the Gulf crisis and hostilities of 1990–91, one consequence of which was a return to state control and direction. Statistics reflect the impact of that conflict and of the sanctions imposed in the 1990s: by 2002 the percentage of the labour force engaged in agriculture had decreased to 9.2%, compared with 50% in 1965 and 53% in 1960; and at the time of the removal from power of Saddam Hussain in 2003, FAO estimated that there were some 600,000 farmers in Iraq, but that only 38% of irrigated land was under cultivation.

According to a report by the UN Secretary-General, published in November 2001, all parts of the agricultural sector were hampered by the large number of contracts for agricultural inputs submitted by the Iraqi Government under the oil-for-food programme (introduced in 1995) but placed 'on hold' by the sanctions committee of the UN Security Council. Ultimately, food prices began to decrease and ration sizes increased following the arrival in March 1997 of Iraq's first food imports under the long-delayed oil-for-food scheme. Grain production totalled an estimated 2.5m. metric tons in 1998, but declined to only 795,000 tons in 2000.

The removal of the regime of Saddam Hussain in early 2003 was expected (depending on political developments) to precipitate a complete reversal of the former government policy of state subsidies for agriculture. An early act of the US-led CPA was to divide the Ministry of Agriculture and Irrigation into two ministries (as they had been until their merger in 1987) and the 15 companies controlled by the new Ministry of Agriculture were expected to be privatized under a future programme of reform. In the first full-year budget for 2004 agricultural subsidies were estimated to be in the region of US $100m., down from $230m. under Saddam Hussain. War damage to irrigation systems and interruptions in the power supply affected farmers' production capabilities. An important element in Iraq's agricultural revival is trade with its neighbours. Iran, Syria and Turkey all provide Iraq with agricultural imports, while Kuwait, which is estimated to import 98% of its food requirements, should become an important market for exports of Iraqi agricultural products.

A wide variety of crops are grown, but the most important are barley and wheat. Production estimates vary considerably. A good crop is dependent on favourable rains, and in 2011, according to FAO estimates, 2.8m. metric tons of wheat were produced, while barley production was estimated at 820,000 tons. Overall, output of cereals was estimated to have reached 4.3m. in 2011.

Other crops grown include rice, vegetables, maize and millet, sugar cane and beet, oil seeds, pulses, dates and other fruits (principally melons), fodder, tobacco and cotton. In 2011 Iraq produced an estimated 235,000 metric tons of paddy rice and 336,000 tons of maize. In that year production of vegetables was estimated at 3.9m. tons. Iraq produced an estimated 1.1m. tons of tomatoes in 2011, while production of potatoes was 557,000 tons.

The livestock sector was developed in the 1980s with the assistance of Dutch, British, West German and Hungarian companies. A significant decline in livestock products was witnessed in the mid-1990s, owing to reduced production of animal feed. According to FAO estimates, Iraq produced 197,200 metric tons of meat in 2011 (of which 87,200 tons was chicken meat), 287,300 tons of milk and 50,900 tons of eggs. The sector has suffered from decades of under-investment coupled with distorted input and output prices. In April 2010 the Ministry of Agriculture announced a development programme comprising 48 projects, including the construction of dairy factories, storage facilities, abattoirs, fish farms and facilities for date production, at a projected total cost of some US $18,000m. The NDP for 2010–14 allocated US $9,300m. for improving food security.

PETROLEUM AND NATURAL GAS

A largely underexploited hydrocarbons sector is regarded as the basis of future prosperity, permitting vastly improved security in the oil-belt regions and massive foreign direct investment (FDI) by major energy conglomerates. Iraq holds the world's fifth largest petroleum reserves, estimated at 150,000m. barrels at the end of 2012 (9.0% of the world's total), according to the BP *Statistical Review of World Energy 2013*, an increase of 24% on the 2002 estimate of 115,000m. barrels.

The country's oil sector has highly attractive potential, with only 27 oilfields out of 78 discovered now on stream and a further 25 close to production, while 26 fields are not yet developed. Exploration and production (E&P) costs in Iraq—estimated at below US $2 per barrel—are among the lowest in the world. Deep oil-bearing formations in the vast Western Desert (along the border with Saudi Arabia and Jordan) and north-western regions are as yet untapped. Geologists reckon that the western and southern deserts may hold an estimated additional 45,000m. to 100,000m. barrels of recoverable petroleum. Thus far, 120 of the 530 oil-bearing structures have been drilled, representing less than one-quarter of total oil prospects identified to date. Compared with major Middle Eastern Gulf producers, Iraq has fewer oil wells (about 2,300), but they are among the world's most productive, yielding on average 3,500 b/d.

Moreover, only 10% of Iraq has been explored and statistics for its resource base are mainly derived from 2-D seismic data from 30 years ago. Therefore, with aggressive E&P of known hydrocarbons provinces, increased FDI and the application of enhanced oil recovery technologies, 'probable reserves' should ultimately yield 300,000m. barrels. Iraq, in fact, boasts the world's highest reserves-to-production ratio—estimated at over 100 years of E&P. The British-based energy consultancy firm Bayphase Ltd has predicted that Iraq's hydrocarbons resources in the coming decades may reach 330,000m. barrels of crude petroleum and 324,000,000m. cu ft of natural gas.

Crude petroleum was first discovered at the Kirkuk field, in the northern Kurdish region, in October 1927 by the Turkish Petroleum Co (TPC). In 1929 TPC was renamed the Iraqi Petroleum Co (IPC). Most of the oil lies in the Shi'a-dominated south and the Kurdish north of the country. By 1938 Iraq was exporting oil at an average rate of 80,000 b/d. Rumaila field (near the border with Kuwait) was discovered in 1953. In 1972 the Government nationalized all the remaining holdings of IPC and transferred them to the Iraq National Oil Co (INOC), which was responsible for E&P, transportation and marketing of crude petroleum. In 1987 INOC was dissolved and merged with the Ministry of Oil. Under the new structure, oil exploration and production, transport and refineries were managed by 14 operating companies reporting to the ministry, while marketing activities fell under the State Oil Marketing Organization. Iraq was one of the founding members of OPEC, but its output has remained outside OPEC quotas since August 1990.

Iraq owns seven 'supergiant' fields (over 5,000m. barrels) and 22 'giant' fields (over 1,000m. barrels). The 'supergiant' onshore fields are Majnoon (with estimated reserves of 12,000m.–30,000m. barrels); South and North Rumaila (a combined total of 17,000m. barrels); West Qurna-1 (12,900m. barrels); East Baghdad (11,000m. barrels); Kirkuk (10,000m. barrels); West Qurna-2 (8,700m. barrels); and Nahr-Umr (6,000m. barrels). The 'giant' oilfields include Halfaya (4,600m. barrels); Zubair (4,000m. barrels); Rattawi (3,100m. barrels); Al-Nasiriyah (Nasiriya—2,600m. barrels); Bai Hassan (2,300m. barrels); Suba-Luhais (2,200m. barrels); Tuba (1,500m. barrels); Gharaf (1,100m. barrels); and Khurmala (1,000m. barrels). About 70%–80% of Iraq's recoverable crude reserves are deposited within Basra region.

According to BP figures, Iraq's crude oil production fell in 2012, to 3.68m. b/d, compared with 4.36m. b/d in 2011. Restoring and maintaining production levels from matured fields presents a challenge, but Iraq has the potential to expand output rapidly from undeveloped fields. About two-thirds of production comes from the southern fields, with the remainder from the north-central fields near Kirkuk. There are 16 oil sector companies in Iraq: Northern Oil Company, Maysan Oil Company, Southern Oil Company, Oil Exploration Company, Iraq Oil Tanker Company, Iraq Excavation Company, Oil Products Distribution Company, Oil Pipelines Company, Gas Bottling Company, Al Wasit Refineries Company, Northern Refineries Company, Southern Refineries Company, Southern Gas Company, Northern Gas Company, Oil Projects Company and Oil Marketing Company. Presently, the Ministry of Oil has a monopoly over hydrocarbons production and development in all but the Kurdish territory.

In early 2010 the Ministry of Oil announced that it planned to boost oil production from 2.5m. b/d to 12.0m. b/d by 2017, after awarding 11 development contracts for 'giant' oilfields to a number of international oil companies (IOCs)—including the 'supermajors' (BP, ExxonMobil, Royal Dutch Shell, Eni and Total). Industry experts believe Iraq needs to drill some 1,000 wells a year and build transport, storage and export facilities in order to achieve such an ambitious target, which would rival Saudi Arabia, currently the world's largest oil producer. However, a report by IHS Energy Cambridge Energy Research Associates noted that for Iraq to attain even one-half of its longer-term targets would still represent a 'significant expansion'. The current outlook is that production will reach 4.5m. b/d in 2015, rising to 6.5m. b/d by 2020, just over half of what the Iraqi Government had originally targeted. Boosting oil capacity is critical in order to provide much-needed resources for reconstruction and to support economic growth over the medium term.

Before the first Gulf War petroleum output had reached 3.5m. b/d, of which 3m. b/d were exported. However, Iraq's petroleum exports were then brought to a virtual halt by the UN embargo, imposed as a consequence of its invasion of Kuwait, and in the Gulf hostilities of early 1991 the massive damage sustained by Iraqi oil installations brought production to a standstill. Between 1992 and 1996 oil output averaged just 520,000 b/d. With Iraq's acceptance in 1996 of UN Resolution 986, which permitted limited exports in exchange for food and other supplies, the country's oil output began rising more rapidly, averaging 2.19m. b/d during 1997–2002. Production ceased for the duration of the US-led invasion to remove Saddam Hussain from power in March–April 2003. Output in 2003 averaged 1.34m. b/d, a decline of 36.5% from the previous year.

The smuggling of crude petroleum and refined products to neighbouring countries cost Iraq an estimated US $4,200m. during 2005. A report published in December 2006 by the bipartisan Iraq Study Group found that as much as 500,000 b/d of petroleum had been stolen. The US Government Accountability Office (GAO) estimated that smuggling and theft were costing Iraq $15m. in potential oil revenues each day: 'about 10 percent to 30 percent of refined fuels is diverted to the black market or is smuggled out of Iraq and sold for profit', according to the US Department of State's findings cited by GAO. In fact, the country lost an estimated $24,700m. in oil exports after the US-led 2003 invasion, mainly owing to corruption and violence. A report by accountants Ernst & Young found that in 2007 13.9m. barrels of oil, or 38,000 b/d, could not be accounted for.

Iraq has begun work to upgrade and expand the country's oil infrastructure. In the near term, the increase in exports, however, will remain constrained by existing bottlenecks, including ageing pipelines and export terminals, and limited storage capacity. Major pipelines are the Kirkuk–Ceyhan (Dortyol) Pipeline (with an installed capacity of 1.6m. b/d); the Iraqi–Saudi Arabian Pipeline (1.65m. b/d); the Iraq Strategic Pipeline (under 1.4m. b/d); and the Banias–Tripoli Pipeline (300,000 b/d). However, the latter is currently closed and the Iraq–Saudi Arabia Pipeline (closed since 1990) is now being used for domestic natural gas shipments. The Ministry of Oil is reportedly preparing to embark upon a massive US $50,000m. project (in three phases) to rehabilitate its oil/gas export pipelines. Phase-1 will entail the construction of a 1.7m. b/d pipeline from the Persian (Arabian) Gulf port of Basra to Haditha, in the western governorate of Anbar. Phase-2 will involve the building of a 1.5m. b/d heavy crude pipeline from Basra to North Baghdad and then connecting to the Syrian port of Tartus on the Mediterranean coast. The final phase of expansion involves the construction of oil product pipelines from Iraq's current refineries and from four planned refineries to depots across the country. Iraq has also expressed an interest in building a 500,000 b/d crude pipeline from Haditha to the port of Aqaba, Jordan.

Iraq has three oil ports: Basra (formerly Mina al-Bakr), Khor al-Amaya and Khor al-Zubair (which handles minimal oil volumes, natural gas liquids and liquefied petroleum gas). Iraq exported about 2.2m. b/d in February 2011, of which1.7m. b/d came from Basra, with the rest exported via the Iraq–Turkey pipeline in the north. Refineries in Asia, including China and India, import the bulk of Iraq's oil. Iraq is also investing in storage facilities and in new desalination plants to produce water for injection into the oilfields. In mid-2008 the State Company for Oil Projects announced plans to expand crude petroleum storage capacity in the country by 86%, from 14.7m. barrels to 27.3m. barrels, and to expand products storage capacity from 10.8m. barrels to 15.5m. barrels.

Over the last 30 years the petroleum industry has been starved of new capital spending and vital technological transfers. The Iraqi Energy Council puts the cost of rebuilding Iraq's dilapidated oil sector at US $38,000m. Bayphase Ltd has estimated that Iraq's hydrocarbons industry—encompassing the upstream (oil and gasfields), midstream (pipelines and terminals) and downstream (refineries and petrochemicals) sectors—would require between $100,000m. and $150,000m. in long-term investments. However, much-needed foreign capital to revive Iraq's hydrocarbons industry remains on hold until the persistent violence and political wrangling end, since the IOCs will only invest within a stable environment. Most industry experts believe that Iraq's optimal longer-term capacity may not be reached because of operational and infrastructure challenges and insecurity.

The Iraqi parliament has yet to approve a draft hydrocarbons law (first proposed in February 2007), which allocates oil revenues between the 18 governorates according to population levels and specifies methods for external participation in the oil industry. Disputes between political parties over provisions have so far blocked its implementation. When it is eventually approved, the long-delayed law will give the regions the right to award contracts to foreign companies (notably Western oil majors), while restructuring INOC as an independent holding entity, as well as establishing a Federal Council as a forum for national oil policy. Furthermore, as part of the Government's efforts to strengthen governance in the hydrocarbons sector, Iraq became a candidate member to the Extractive Industries Transparency Initiative in February 2010.

The draft hydrocarbons law was intended to attract foreign investment. IOCs are keen to acquire E&P rights for prized oilfields (notably Majnoon, West Qurna, Ratawi, Bin Umar and Nasiriya, among others). Despite the lack of a national Iraqi law governing hydrocarbons investment, the Kurdistan Regional Government has signed oil production sharing, E&P contracts with foreign firms—namely DNO (Norway), Genel Enerji (Turkey) and Canadian-based Heritage Oil, Western Oil Sands and Addax Petroleum. Kurdistan is seeking to achieve a production capacity of 1m. b/d by 2012. The US Geological Survey estimates that the Kurdish region may contain 40,000m. barrels of reserves.

The natural gas sector remains severely under-exploited, although Iraq held the world's 12th largest proven reserves of 126,700,000m. cu ft (3,600,000m. cu m) at the end of 2012, according to BP figures, in addition to an estimated 150,000,000m. cu ft in probable reserves—70% of which are thought to lie in the Basra region. Its recoverable gas reserves are equivalent to 4.5% of the Middle East and North Africa's total, and 1.9% of the world's. About two-thirds of natural gas resources are associated with crude petroleum and so future petroleum E&P projects will also directly affect the upstream gas sector. Non-associated and salt 'dome' gas, meanwhile, comprise 20% and 10%, respectively, of aggregate reserves.

The main non-associated gasfields are Al-Anfal, Chemchamal, Jaria Pika, Khashm Al-Ahmar and Mansuriya, located in northern Iraq. For decades as much as 70% of associated gas from Kirkuk, as well as the southern Nahr-Umr, Majnoon, Halfaya, Nasiriya, Rumaila, Qurna and Zubair oilfields (among others), has been simply flared off, reflecting the lack of infrastructure to utilize it for power generation and other industrial usages. The flaring of the natural gas has also meant the loss of an estimated 300,000 metric tons of output per day of liquefied petroleum gas and 20m. tons of carbon dioxide per year. Flaring, estimated at 700m. cu ft per day in the south of the country, costs the Government more than US $1,000m. in lost revenues each year.

Under the Government's 10-year Strategic Plan (2008–17) for the hydrocarbons industry, production of natural gas was expected to reach some 2,500,000m. cu ft by 2017, while the practice of flaring natural gas was to be discontinued. As part of this plan, in April 2010 Iraq formally launched a third bidding round, in an effort to develop three untapped gasfields—Akkas in western Anbar governorate (the largest of the three fields), al-Mansuriyah located in eastern Diyala governorate and the Siba field in the Basra region—the combined reserves of which were reported at 22,000,000 cu ft. A consortium comprising the Korea Gas Corpn (KOGAS) and Kazakhstan's KazMunaiGas was awarded a contract to develop the Akkas gasfield in October 2010. However, following the decision of KazMunaiGas to withdraw its participation, in June 2011 the Government requested KOGAS to continue the project. According to BP figures, Iraq's gas production had declined to just 800m. cu m in 2012, compared with 1,300m. cu m in 2010. Nevertheless, plentiful untapped gas reserves offer the potential for downstream activities, such as iron, steel and aluminium smelting and the rapid expansion of the petrochemicals industry, as well as reinjection for enhanced oil recovery programmes.

Iraq has 10 ageing refineries, of which the three largest are Baiji North (built in 1982), Basra (1972) and Daura (1955). Pre-1990 nameplate capacity was 785,000 b/d, but all the refineries suffered heavy damage during the 1991 Gulf War. In recent years refineries have operated well below optimal capacity, requiring the country to import 200,000 b/d of refined products from Kuwait, Jordan, Syria, Turkey and Iran, costing about US $3,000m.–$5,000m. a year. More than one-quarter of fuel requirements are met by imports. According to BP, total installed nameplate capacity in 2012 was 1.0m. b/d (up from 996,000 b/d in 2011). Rising pollution levels (reflecting a lack of water treatment facilities), a lack of light-end products (gasoline, diesel, lubricants), frequent power outages and post-invasion looting and sabotage, as well as poor maintenance and equipment, have continued to undermine Iraq's refining sector. Operating rates from smaller older refineries across the country are reportedly as low as 60%.

The Strategic Plan for 2008–17 outlined the Government's intention to expand refining capacity to 1.5m. b/d. At mid-2010 plans were under way to construct five new refineries, adding a total capacity of some 840,000 b/d, and also to upgrade existing facilities at Basra, Baiji and Daura—costing more than US $23,000m. The largest of the five refineries, with a capacity of 300,000 b/d, was to be built at Nasiriya in southern Iraq (at an estimated cost of $8,000m.). The front-end engineering and design (FEED) contract was awarded to US-based Foster Wheeler. The second and third refineries, each with 150,000 b/d capacity, were to be built in Kirkuk and Missan. Shaw & Webster of the USA won the FEED contracts for both these plants (each costing over $5,000m. Meanwhile, two new refineries were under construction—a 200,000 b/d facility in Karbala governorate and a 100,000 b/d facility in eastern Baghdad.

INDUSTRY

Until the 1970s Iraq had few large industries apart from petroleum. In greater Baghdad the larger enterprises were concerned with electricity and water supply and the building materials industry. In addition, there were a large number of smaller-unit industries concerned with food- and drinks-processing (date-packing, breweries, etc.), cigarette-making, textiles, chemicals, furniture, shoe-making, jewellery and various metal manufactures. However, greater priority was subsequently given to industrial developments, as the Government sought to reduce Iraq's dependence on the petroleum industry. Inevitably, the Gulf War of 1990–91 and the UN sanctions regime of the 1990s caused the degradation of the industrial sector, with further damage caused by hostilities and looting during the US-led campaign to oust Saddam Hussain in early 2003. In June of that year it was reported that the 48 state companies controlled by the Ministry of Industry and Minerals were to be part-privatized within the next year.

Iraq's mineral resources, apart from hydrocarbons, include sulphur and phosphate rock. Mining for sulphur at Mishraq, near Mosul, began in 1972. The mining complex, including a sulphuric acid plant, had a design capacity of 1.25m. metric tons per year. In 1988 proven reserves of sulphur stood at 515m. tons, the largest in the world, according to the Iraqi Government. According to the US Geological Survey, in 2011 total sulphur production was only an estimated 20,000 tons, decidedly below production capacity.

Phosphate rock reserves, mostly in the Akashat area, and in the Marbat region, north-west of Baghdad, were estimated at 10,000m. metric tons in 1988. The phosphate fertilizer plant at al-Qaim was built by Sybetra of Belgium, which also installed the phosphate mine in Akashat. In 2004 estimated phosphate rock production was 30,000 tons (compared with 100,000 tons in 2002). Daily production of 1,000 tons of ammonia and 1,700 tons of urea also commenced at a fourth nitrogenous fertilizer factory at Baiji. Production of urea at the Khor al-Zubair fertilizer plant, with a production capacity of 1m. tons per year of ammonia and urea, resumed in April 2004.

Other major state-owned industrial enterprises included: a textile factory at Mosul, producing calico from local cotton; three sugar refineries, at Karbala, Sulaimaniya and Mosul, with another four planned; a tractor assembly plant; a paperboard factory at Basra; a synthetic fibres complex at Hindiya; and a number of flour mills. Shoe and cigarette factories served the domestic market. Other developments in the manufacturing sector included factories to produce pharmaceuticals, electrical goods, telephone cables and plastics, together with additional food-processing plants. Production of cement reached 13m. metric tons in 1989, when 5.4m. tons were exported, mainly to other Arab countries; by 2000–01, however, output had fallen considerably, to 2m. tons. In November 2003 the CPA announced plans for the upgrade of the cement plant of Tasluja, north of Sulaimaniya. The plant had been producing 100,000 tons of cement a year since 1998. The Ministry of Industry and Minerals issued 19 licences in 2005 for the construction of cement plants across the country. Existing plants currently produce below 3m. tons a year, compared with their capacity of 20m. tons.

Of the proposals made by the Interim Government in September 2003 for the reform of Iraq's economic and industrial sectors, perhaps the most radical was to allow foreign companies to have 100% ownership of Iraqi companies, effectively opening up the Iraqi industrial sector to foreign investment. In October the Ministry of Industry and Minerals released tenders for the privatization of 18 state-owned companies. The list included companies producing wool, cotton, tobacco, paper, chemicals, electrical goods and pharmaceuticals. Given new investments and a stable security environment, Iraqi industry led by petrochemicals and agro-business has the potential to contribute one-fifth of GDP in future years. According to the IMF, manufacturing value added in 2006 was ID 1,288,000m. The neglected manufacturing sector comprised a mere 2.3% of GDP in 2010. Industrial production recorded a steep fall of 6% per year between 1998 and 2008.

TRANSPORT AND COMMUNICATIONS

Iraq currently has six international airports, at Baghdad, Basra, Arbil, Mosul, Najaf and Sulaimaniya, with a combined annual capacity of 16.4m. passengers. In 2003 Saddam International Airport was renamed Baghdad International Airport by the occupying US forces. The contract to run the airports at Baghdad, Basra and Mosul was awarded to the US company SkyLink. Arbil International Airport opened in December of that year to facilitate flights between the Kurdish Autonomous Region and neighbouring countries; passenger flights to destinations in Europe commenced in 2005. An expansion of the airport, including a new terminal building and runway, was completed in mid-2010, while construction work on a new airport in Karbala began in March of that year. Meanwhile, Iraqi Airways resumed flights in late 2004, and by mid-2013 was operating services to 36 destinations, including airports in Egypt, India, Iran, Jordan, Lebanon, Malaysia, Pakistan, Sweden, Syria, Turkey, the United Arab Emirates (UAE) and the United Kingdom. At mid-2013 several international carriers were also operating flights to Iraq, including Germany's Lufthansa, Emirates Airline and Etihad Airways of the United Arab Emirates, Qatar Airways and Turkish Airlines.

To cope with future increases in air traffic, the Iraqi National Aviation Plan was unveiled in May 2011, with projected costs of more than US $60,000m. It entails the rehabilitation and upgrade of existing airports, and the construction of logistics centres, cargo and warehousing facilities, as well as new regional airports. This large-scale project has the potential to create 1m. new jobs over the next 10 years. Total annual passenger traffic in Iraq is forecast to reach 22.5m. and in excess of 25m. by 2016 and 2022, respectively. Moreover, annual cargo volume at Iraqi airports is predicted to reach 700,000 metric tons in 2016, before rising to 900,000 tons by 2022. The Government is expected to contribute $17,000m. (or around one-quarter of the total) towards funding the project, with the rest coming from the private sector.

Iraq is virtually landlocked, and its main port at Basra (on the Shatt al-Arab waterway) was effectively disabled during the Iran–Iraq War. Before the outbreak of hostilities with Iran two new ports were developed, at Umm Qasr and Khor al-Zubair (the latter linked to Umm Qasr and the Gulf via a 40-km ship canal). Umm Qasr (Iraq's only deep-sea facility) was an early and important target for US-led coalition forces in March 2003, and was secured by British troops after heavy fighting. The contract to run the port at Umm Qasr was awarded in late March to the US firm Stevedore Services of America. The port reopened on 16 June and was handed back to Iraqi control when sovereignty was transferred from the CPA to the Interim Government at the end of June 2004.

The Iraqi Ports Authority estimated that Iraq's ports would require investment of US $1,000m., and major projects were expected to include expansions in the number of berths at Umm Qasr (at an estimated cost of $250m.), Khor al-Zubair ($450m.) and Mina Maqal ($50m.). In April 2009 Iraq signed a contract with an Italian consortium for building a $3,700m. port complex near Basra. In 2012 there were 43 commercial port docks with a capacity of 15.9m. tons a year in operation.

In 2010 the total length of Iraq's roads, excluding municipalities, was just under 42,000 km, of which highways comprised 1,006 km

Iraq's railway network of 2,025 km (in 2010) depends on three major lines, Baghdad–Basra–Umm Qasr, Baghdad–Mosul–Tel Kotchek and Baghdad–Kirkuk–Arbil. After a decade of sanctions the railway infrastructure was in considerable disrepair by the early 2000s, with services infrequent and unreliable. Although passenger rail services between the northern city of Mosul and Aleppo in Syria resumed in August 2000—after an interval of 20 years—they were discontinued again in 2004 after persistent insurgent attacks. In July 2001 it was announced that a weekly rail link with south-eastern Turkey, via Syria, had also been restored. As in 1991, the railway infrastructure was targeted by US-led coalition forces in March 2003, and a programme of repair and upgrading was subsequently planned.

Before 1991 considerable emphasis had been put on road construction; good progress was made on a number of international expressways designed to link Iraq to the Mediterranean and the Gulf states, and several urban motorways were built in Baghdad. During the Iran–Iraq War many roads in the eastern part of the country (towards the Iranian border) were upgraded for military purposes. However, numerous roads and bridges were destroyed during 'Operation Desert Storm' in 1991, and in the immediate aftermath of the war the only viable surface transport link to the outside world was the route through Amman, Jordan, to the Jordanian port of Aqaba. Repair work to the country's 39,000-km paved road network and bridges was given priority in the post-war period, and considerable progress was made, but road transport, essential for the distribution of humanitarian supplies, continued to be affected by the shortage of trucks and spare parts for motor vehicles. Similar effects were felt during the US-led campaign to oust Saddam Hussein in March 2003. The US company Bechtel Group was charged with overseeing the rebuilding of Iraq's roads and bridges.

A US $3,000m. project to construct a 22-km metro line in Baghdad reportedly stalled in mid-2011, owing to a lack of available funds. However, by mid-2012 preliminary engineering work had started, undertaken by France's Alstom.

Prior to the 1990–91 Gulf conflict, Iraq had been modernizing its telecommunications systems, introducing crossbar telephone switching, a telex system, a microwave link between major cities and an earth satellite connection for international communications. Colossal damage was inflicted on the internal and external telephone networks during Operation Desert Storm; almost 50% of the country's telephone lines were destroyed during the hostilities. In addition, the imposition of sanctions produced a severe shortage of spare parts for repair and maintenance, so that only a small fraction of the telephone system was operational. Following the conflict in early 2003, the Bechtel Group began the task of reconnecting Baghdad's main fixed-line connection with other cities, setting up international call access and establishing switch stations. Licences for global system for mobile communications (GSM) mobile services were awarded to three consortia: Asiacell, led by the Iraqi Kurdish company Asiacell Telecom, was to operate services in the northern region; Orascom Telecom Iraq Corpn, led by Orascom Telecom of Egypt, would do likewise for the central region; and Atheer Telecom Iraq, led by Mobile Telecommunications Company (MTC) of Kuwait, would provide services for the southern region. The telecoms industry is regulated by an independent body, the Commission of Media and Communications, which was formed in 2004.

In 2010 fixed mainlines and mobile phone subscribers per 100 people were estimated at 5.1 and 75.8, respectively, according to the International Telecommunication Union, while the number of internet users per 100 people was merely 2.5. Iraq's mobile operators now serve almost 27m. customers. The Government allocated US $16,700m. for new investments in the transport and communications sector between 2010 and 2014.

FINANCE AND BANKING

Iraq's external debt continued to swell during the 1990s, reflecting the accumulation of payments arrears (principal and interest) and hefty penalties. In the early 1990s total debt stock (including war reparations claims) was estimated at between US $200,000m. and $250,000m. The IMF estimated total obligations (excluding war reparations) at the end of 2003 at $125,000m. (about 700% of GDP), of which $42,000m. were owed to the 'Paris Club', $67,400m. to non-'Paris Club' bilateral creditors (notably Arab and eastern European countries), $15,000m. to private creditors (including Western banks) and $500m. to multilateral organizations. Major sovereign creditors were Saudi Arabia ($25,000m.), Kuwait ($12,500m.), Russia ($8,000m.), Japan ($7,100m.), the UAE and Qatar ($7,000m.) and Germany ($4,300m.).

The post-Saddam Hussein Government argued that loans from Gulf states were 'gifts' to fund the war against Iran, though Saudi Arabia insisted that these were 'soft' loans, not grants. Scheduled debt service obligations were between US $7,000m. and $8,000m. per year, which were clearly unsustainable in relation to Iraq's external and fiscal accounts. The IMF, in its assessment of Iraq's external liabilities, calculated that a write-off in the range of 65%–95% of total outstanding debt was warranted. Following the demise of the Baathist regime, oil export revenues—under the UN Security Council Resolution 1483—were immune from legal proceedings, such as debt collections, until the end of 2007.

Iraq's debt-restructuring over recent years has proved highly successful. In November 2004 the 19-strong 'Paris Club' agreed to cancel, in three stages, up to 80% of Iraq's US $42,600m. worth of debts. Under the accord, 30% ($12,780m.) was cancelled immediately, with a further 30% cancelled in December 2005, following an IMF SBA. The final tranche of 20% was effective in December 2008, after successful completion of the three-year structural adjustment programme. The agreement left Iraq owing major creditor nations (notably Russia, Japan, France and Germany) only $8,400m., with repayments rescheduled over some 20 years. The Iraqi Government has now signed bilateral agreements with all the 'Paris Club' members, including Russia. In February 2008 the latter cancelled $12,000m. in principal and arrears in exchange for access to Iraq's upstream oil sector and participation in infrastructural projects.

The 'Paris Club' agreement serves as a benchmark for enhanced debt relief from Gulf Arab governments and other creditors. Agreements have also been concluded with 11 non-'Paris Club' creditors. In 2007 Saudi Arabia and China agreed to cancel US $12,000m. and $4,000m., respectively, of Iraq's outstanding loans. In July 2008 the UAE also wrote off $7,000m. to help Baghdad with reconstruction. The total debt to non-'Paris Club' official creditors is reported at $76,800m., of which rescheduling terms have been reached for $6,900m. More than 85% of unscheduled debt is owed to the Gulf countries (principally Saudi Arabia and Kuwait) and China. Most of Iraq's commercial debt was also successfully renegotiated during 2004–06, leaving Iraq with an outstanding debt of $5,200m. by the end of 2007. In January 2006 Western banks, industrial suppliers and construction firms agreed to cancel over four-fifths of the $21,900m. debts owed to them in exchange for partial repayments. The old debt was transformed (with an 87% discount) into 20-year bonds worth $2,790m., bearing the name of the Republic of Iraq and guaranteed by the Iraqi Government; the return on the bonds—tradeable on global debt markets—is 5.8% a year.

As a result of debt relief, debt-servicing obligations had fallen from 32.5% of exports in 2004 to an estimated 4.6% in 2010. The IMF commented that 'without substantial debt relief, Iraq has no prospect of restoring its creditworthiness and of regaining access to private capital to finance future growth'. According to the central bank, Iraq's total external debt amounted to some US $87,700m. (equivalent to 106.7% of GDP) in 2010. Meanwhile, Iraq's international liabilities for war damages (to Iran and Kuwait) remain substantial, with claims amounting to as much as $352,500m.

The Interim Government pledged to pursue a prudent fiscal policy, representing a clear departure from past practices of chronic deficit financing. Yet, in a war-torn country, fiscal stimulus is a powerful instrument to restart economic activity and public services. In October 2003 the full-year budget for 2004, the first of the post-Saddam Hussein era, was published, detailing revenues of ID 19,258,800m. and expenditures of ID 20,145,100m. Oil export receipts of ID 18,000,000m. (US $11,900m.) dominated official reserves, while expenditures were distributed among government ministries, the largest beneficiary being the Ministry of Finance (ID 15,816,700m.). The budget deficit of ID 886,300m. was to be covered by funds remaining in the oil-for-food programme accounts. The budget report also revealed that $1,700m. of funds belonging to the former regime in US banks were to be unfrozen and used to pay salaries and pensions and to fund reconstruction projects.

According to government figures, recurrent expenditures and revenues were projected at US $23,842m. (95% of GDP) and $19,500m. (including oil earnings of $17,100m.), respectively, for 2005. About $14,500m. was to be spent on goods and services and subsidies, and overall expenditure on wages and pensions was expected to total $3,700m. The Ministry of Oil's budget was to rise from $3,100m. in 2004 to $4,300m. in 2005, with the aim of expanding production capacity. Outside the oil sector, public investment was projected at $6,100m. (an increase of 42% compared with 2004), assuming increased disbursements of donor aid.

The 2006 budget projected an overall government deficit of ID 5,619,000m., based on total revenues of ID 60,316,000m. (including grants) and recurrent/capital spending of ID 65,935,000m. Oil export receipts comprised around 90% of total state revenues (excluding grants). Public investment and security-related spending were set at ID 15,900,000m. and ID 8,000,000m., respectively. The fiscal deficit (9% of GDP) was to be covered by dipping into the remaining resources in the Development Fund for Iraq (DFI), together with some project-financing and the likely disbursement of a World Bank loan.

The 2007 budget projected total spending at US $41,000m.—the most ambitious since the pre-2004 era—of which $3,500m. was allocated to the petroleum sector. Revenues were predicted at $34,000m. Oil revenues were based on slightly higher export volumes of 1.7m. b/d (from 1.5m. b/d in 2006). The budget envisaged a modest increase in current spending (notably wages and pensions) and higher public investment, as well as outlays on the social safety net and national security. The Government predicted a fiscal deficit of ID 10,200,000m.

The 2008 budget envisaged a deficit of 8.5% of GDP—based on oil exports averaging 1.7m. b/d and a conservative price of US $57 per barrel—with total government revenue and expenditure pegged at $42,400m. and $48,400m., respectively. A sum of $13,000m. was allocated for capital projects, supplemented by $4,000m. carried over from 2007, plus $2,000m. in discretionary allocations, bringing the total development budget to $19,000m. Spending on security and food subsidies was set at $9,000m. and $3,300m., respectively. In fact, Iraq recorded only a modest budget deficit in 2008 (equivalent to 1.2% of GDP). Higher than expected oil revenues enabled greater capital spending.

Public finances showed healthy surpluses over 2005–08, thanks to high international oil prices, inflows of foreign aid and grants, and shortfalls in actual investment spending—owing to a combination of political, security and administrative difficulties. Ballooning oil revenues and a low rate of execution of the capital budget underpinned the fiscal position. The balance in the DFI reached US $23,500m. by the end of September 2008, up 85% from the end of 2007.

The Iraqi parliament passed a revised US $58,600m. budget for 2009 in March of that year, slashed from the $80,000m. proposed in November 2008, reflecting waning oil prices. It envisaged cuts in recurrent spending and adjusting investment to implementation capacity. However, it still provided for an increase in capital spending compared with expected 2008 out-turns, and a rise in security expenditure. A deficit of about $20,000m. (24% of GDP) was projected. This deficit was covered mainly by extracting resources from the DFI and by mobilizing domestic resources through the issuance of treasury bills.

The 2010 budget deficit was estimated at ID 10,000,000m. (equivalent to about 10.8% of GDP), which was significantly below initial projections, partly owing to delays in the execution of the investment budget. The budget aimed to contain recurrent spending in order to allow for higher investment outlays. In this regard, Iraq imposed freezes on public sector wage bills, following a large wage increase in 2008, which had been carried over into 2009. In addition, net hiring of non-security personnel in 2010 was to be limited to new teachers and doctors, until the civil service census was completed. Generalized transfers, in particular to state-owned enterprises, were to be sharply reduced, reflecting expected improvements in the financial position of many public enterprises.

At the same time, recurrent spending was to be capped at ID 62,900,000m. and capital investment expenditure was envisaged to total ID 25,800,000m., with a strong focus on electricity, water and sanitation, health and agriculture. Non-essential spending was again contained during 2011 in order to provide much-needed resources for public services, social safety net and security outlays, while remaining consistent with medium-term fiscal sustainability. The IMF estimated fiscal surplus in 2011 at 7.4% of GDP, reflecting higher than expected oil revenues of US $83,000m., and total government gross debt at 87% of GDP, down markedly from a high of 212.8% of GDP in 2006. The 2012 federal budget (predicted on exports of 2.6m. b/d at a price of $85 a barrel) envisaged current and capital spending at $100,500m. Investment projects and security forces were to receive $31,700m. and $14,600m., respectively, during the year. The 2013 budget envisaged increased expenditure of $118,600m. and projected a fiscal deficit of some $16,170m.

Iraq proposes to transform and modernize its public financial management system. Under the advice of the IMF and the World Bank, in late 2009 Iraq adopted a three-year plan, which focused specifically on budget preparation, execution and reporting; cash management; public procurement; and the accounting framework. Moreover, it has made some progress in developing a medium-term tax reform strategy with the aim of streamlining the tax system, broadening and diversifying the tax base, and increasing revenue collection. As a first step, a mobile phone tax was introduced in 2008. The authorities also intend to introduce a sales tax at some point in the future as a precursor for a value-added tax (VAT), and are considering the reduction of a number of income tax brackets.

Under the former regime, the (old) Iraqi dinar was the legal tender, comprising two types of co-circulating banknotes: the 'Saddam' dinar, issued by the CBI from 1990 onwards, and the 'Swiss' dinar, issued between 1979 and 1989, which circulated after 1989 in the northern Kurdish Autonomous Region only. On 15 October 2003 the CPA, advised by USAID and the US Department of the Treasury, introduced a new, fully convertible currency, the new Iraqi dinar, replacing both the Swiss dinar (at ID 1 = 150 Swiss dinars) and the Saddam dinar (at par). A large-scale currency operation involved shipping and distributing about ID 6,100,000m. of new dinars into Iraq and destroying the old currency. The new unit has six denominations of banknote instead of two, and has improved the efficiency of transactions, as well as monetarily reunifying the country. That, in turn, has revived commercial activity, despite turbulent conditions.

Furthermore, the printing of the new dinar is strictly controlled by the CBI, which operates a de facto peg to the US dollar. The framework is underpinned by the prohibition on net lending to the Government (which ensures that the money supply can only expand through increases in foreign exchange reserves), by timely actions in adjusting CBI interest rates and by holding daily CBI auctions of hard currencies. Since its introduction, the new Iraqi dinar has appreciated vis-à-vis the US dollar, from ID 2,000 = US $1 in October 2003 to around ID 1,170 = $1 by the end of December 2011. The dinar strengthened to ID 1,165 = $1 by mid-2013. A stable currency, supported by rising international liquidity (see Foreign Trade) has capped inflation, as well as assisting in the de-dollarization of the economy. With the rate of inflation remaining in low single-figure digits along with sustained exchange rate stability, the CBI has kept its policy interest rate unchanged at 6.0%, after having lowered it from 7.0% in early 2010.

The fulfilment of the donors' pledges made at the International Donors' Conference on Reconstruction in Iraq held in October 2003 in Madrid, Spain, will determine the pace of reconstruction efforts over the medium term. Total pledges of US $33,750m. in grants and low-interest loans for the period 2003–07 fell well short of the $56,000m. target. Excluding US donations, the total amount raised was just $13,000m., of which Japan pledged $5,000m., Saudi Arabia $1,000m. and the United Kingdom $900m. The World Bank and the UN subsequently established an International Reconstruction Fund Facility for Iraq (IRFFI) to channel donors' money into priority infrastructure projects. The IRFFI has two trust funds: the UN Development Group Iraq Trust Fund and the World Bank Iraq Trust Fund.

Meanwhile, the international financial institutions continue to play a role in supporting reconstruction efforts. The World Bank has provided almost US $500m. for 19 emergency projects, including education, health clinics, irrigation and drainage, the first such lending in 30 years. Furthermore, Iraq became eligible in late 2004 for concessional World Bank loans under the International Development Association (IDA). Since then, the IDA has approved five projects totalling $514.5m. for the roads, electricity, water and education sectors. In 2010 net official development assistance (ODA) to Iraq totalled $2,791m. (compared with $9,880m. in 2008), according to the Development Assistance Committee of the Organisation for Economic Co-operation and Development. ODA to Iraq had totalled just $100.8m. in 2000. Major donors in 2010 were the USA ($1,623m.), Japan ($144m.), the EU institutions ($54m.), Germany ($37m.), and the United Kingdom ($31m.).

In 2012 Iraq's fledgling banking system comprised seven state-owned banks, the three largest being Rafidain Bank, Rashid Bank and Trade Bank of Iraq (TBI), and 36 small private banks (including seven Islamic organizations) formed in the early to mid-2000s, the majority of which have shares listed on the Iraq Stock Exchange (ISX). Rafidain Bank (founded in 1941) and Rashid Bank (founded in 1988) have extensive branch networks and control about 70%–80% of banking sector assets. However, the two 'monolithic' banks (especially Rafidain) hold the bulk of (unpaid) sovereign debts and letters of credit, so international trade finance business is closed to Iraqi state banks. Only the TBI enjoys a monopoly issuing letters of credit (LCs) to public enterprises. The country's oldest banks are the Agricultural Co-operative Bank and the Industrial Bank, established in 1936 and 1940, respectively, to provide medium- and long-term loans to farmers and public and private industrial companies. The Real Estate Bank (founded in 1949) provides credits for housing, construction and tourism projects. Compared with other countries in the region, financial intermediation is weak, indicating that some of Iraq's provinces remain essentially a 'cash-based' economy with a thriving black market. Banks with SWIFT (Society for Worldwide Interbank Financial Telecommunications) connections remain confined to a few major cities, while the payments system until recently was largely manual. Corporate banking services at present are negligible, according to the Iraqi National Investment Commission. Personal banking and other services taken for granted elsewhere in the world, including cheque books, credit cards, savings products and mortgages, are only available to a tiny section of the population located in the major cities. Total deposits in 2010 amounted to ID 55,000,000m. The average asset-to-GDP ratio of 73% in 2011 fell below the regional average of 130% as a whole, although Iraqi banks are highly liquid: deposits and foreign assets at the CBI were reported at 63% of total assets.

In September 2003 the CPA issued a new banking law to bring the legal framework for banking into line with global standards. The main aim was to foster confidence in the system by establishing a safer, sound, competitive and accessible banking system. It provided for independence and accountability and prohibited the CBI from extending credit to the Government. The law also established a nine-member governing board for the CBI, comprising the governor, two deputy governors, three senior managers and three full-time external directors. The first meeting of the board, under the governorship of Dr Sinan al-Shibibi, took place in August 2004. The CBI—one of the first Arab monetary authorities—assumed responsibility for monetary and exchange rate policy. It approved the creation of a lender-of-last-resort facility, plus an overnight standing credit and deposit facility. The CBI made progress in improving its accounting and governance structures during 2008–10. To ensure the success of ongoing financial reforms, the CBI was seeking resident advisers with international experience in a broad range of areas such as information technology, banking supervision and reserve management.

Iraq has made concerted efforts further to develop banking supervision practices in line with best global practices. Commercial banks have been instructed to conform their accounting norms to the International Financial Reporting Standards (IFRS) and to prepare a set of financial soundness indicators that could be used by the CBI to monitor sectoral developments. Iraq has also reconciled almost all the outstanding suspense accounts and CBI intra-branch accounts, and established a register of outstanding off-balance sheet commitments (letters of credit and guarantees). In July 2010 the CBI completed the process of becoming IFRS compliant.

Furthermore, Iraq is in the process of conducting a full assessment of the banking supervision department. It has also completed a set of prudential regulations for commercial banks, including those related to minimum capital requirements, liquidity risk and anti-money-laundering. Concurrently, the financial services industry underwent a process of consolidation spurred by higher capital adequacy requirements. In October 2010 local commercial banks were instructed by the CBI to increase their capital base in two stages: US $85m. by mid-2011 and $128m. by mid-2012. By 30 June 2013 all operating banks were required to meet a proposed minimum capital threshold of ID 250,000 ($214m.). The intention of the CBI is to encourage consolidation within the sector by reducing the number of banks by one-third and create smaller but stronger banks that provide a full range of retail and corporate banking services.

Helped by the multilateral agencies, Iraq has developed a restructuring strategy for state-owned banks. The first important step involves finalizing the operational and financial audits of Rafidain and Rashid banks. In this regard, the foreign liabilities incurred by both banks on behalf of the previous regime and the large suspense accounts are being removed from balance sheets. Once their balance sheets are cleared of bad debts and are restructured, the core capital of Rafidain and Rashid banks will be raised to ID 500,000m. and ID 400,000m., respectively. Furthermore, their operational restructuring envisages a new organizational structure, comprising business units (retail, corporate and investment banking); risk management units; and governance, control and support units. The financial restructuring of Rafidain and Rashid banks represents an important step towards establishing the conditions for the banking system to extend credit to the private sector. The Board Supreme Audit has also completed the financial and operational audits for the three specialized state-owned banks. Iraq's banking law—outlined in CPA Order No. 94, issued in June 2004—permits foreign participation in several forms: wholly foreign-owned banks; joint venture banks with one or more foreign or local partners; subsidiaries; and foreign ownership of shares in local banks. Income and corporate taxes were capped at 15%.

The CBI has awarded licences to a number of foreign banks allowing them to operate in Iraq: the British-based HSBC and Standard Chartered; the National Bank of Kuwait, Burgan Bank and Commercial Bank of Kuwait; Bank Melli Iran; the Bahrain-based United Gulf Bank, Al-Ahli United Bank of Bahrain and Arab Banking Corporation; Jordan's Capital Bank (formerly Export and Finance Bank of Jordan), Arab Bank of Jordan and Housing Bank for Trade & Finance Jordan; Lebanon-based Bank Audi and Byblos Bank; and Qatar National Bank (QNB).

However, foreign banks have shown more interest in investing in private Iraqi banks rather than setting up new institutions, possibly in consequence of continuing sectarian violence in major cities. The National Bank of Kuwait has a majority ownership stake (75%) in the Credit Bank of Iraq, and the Jordanian Capital Bank bought a 49% equity in the National Bank of Iraq (subsequently increased to 59%). The Bank of Baghdad, the country's largest private bank, boosted its capital to ID 30,000m. (US $20m.) thanks to foreign funds from United Gulf Bank. HSBC has acquired a 70% stake in Dar el-Salaam Investment Bank (which has 14 branches and employs 450 staff), pledging to provide financial and technical support (including investing in computerized payment systems and cash machines) and underwriting loans for local businesses. In 2005 a group of investors, with the help of QNB, launched a new institution, al-Mansour Bank (capitalized at ID 50,000m.), of which QNB holds a 60% equity. Al-Ahli Bank of Bahrain owns a 49% stake in the Commercial Bank of Iraq. Standard Chartered has maintained indirect links by offering external training programmes for Iraqi bankers.

More than 100 additional companies were listed on the ISX during 2011, and a new electronic trading system was installed in 2009. Bank stocks comprise about 75% of the bourse weightings. Foreign companies are allowed to trade directly on the exchange. The ISX's market capitalization was reported at less than US $4,000m. in July 2011. Levels of FDI and private capital flows are modest, but are increasing. Inward (net) FDI in 2012 amounted to $2,000m., compared with $1,716m. in 2011, according to the UN Conference on Trade and Development's *World Investment Report 2013*. FDI inward stock was reported at $12,616m. in 2012. The IMF anticipates an upturn in FDI over the medium term, to $5,882m. and to $7,806m. by 2013 and 2015, respectively.

The Government is attempting to improve the country's investment regime under extremely difficult conditions. The Investment Law (approved in October 2006) aims to open the economy to foreign capital with a strong emphasis on attracting expatriate Iraqi overseas investments. The Law established a National Commission for Investment (a 'one-stop shop' for investors), attached to the Prime Minister's office and headed by a Chairman with the rank of Minister, who is responsible for overseeing and executing Iraq's FDI policy. Furthermore, there are investment commissions at the regional level. The legislation opened up all sectors of the economy (including the fledgling Securities Market), with the exception of the hydrocarbons industry. Foreign investors are allowed 100% ownership of Iraqi assets, and repatriation of capital and profits and enjoy 'equal' legal standing with local firms, except in owning land. However, under a new law proposed by the Government in late 2009, foreign investors would be permitted to purchase land for housing projects. Moreover, the Government is offering 50-year leases for projects in other sectors, coupled with a 15-year exemption from all taxes and fees if projects are at least 50% locally owned. The largely stable and investor-friendly Kurdistan region is expected to receive the lion's share of future FDI compared with other regions. Arab Gulf investors have expressed interest in housing, industrial and agricultural projects. Saudi investors are reportedly planning to invest US $500m. in three large Iraqi projects.

FOREIGN TRADE

Crude petroleum exports remain the bedrock of Iraq's economy, amounting on average to 98% of exports and government revenue. Despite the interruption in trade caused by the US-led invasion, the CBI estimated the value of total exports and imports in 2003 at US $10,082m. and $10,063m., respectively, increasing to $17,810m. in exports and $21,302m. in imports in 2004. In 2005 total exports and imports were estimated by the IMF at $23,500m. and $24,900m., respectively. In 2006 the value of exports was $30,300m., while that of imports was estimated at $24,100m. The 2007 figures show exports and imports reaching $38,700m. and $26,700m., respectively. Iraq's current account surplus in 2008 rose to $11,048m. (equivalent to 13% of GDP), as exports reached $62,013m. and imports totalled $40,813m.

However, according to IMF estimates, Iraq recorded a trade deficit of US $7,329m. and a large deficit on the external current account—at over 26.0% of GDP—in 2009, with exports falling substantially to $38,439m., and imports increasing to $45,768m. Depleted oil export revenues presented a major challenge in view of the country's huge reconstruction and rehabilitation spending needs. The average oil export price in 2009 was $57 per barrel, well below the average export price of $92 per barrel in 2008. With oil exports averaging 1.88m. b/d (below an original target of 2m. b/d), oil export receipts were estimated at $38,243m. in 2009. In 2010 Iraq's trade balance returned to registering a surplus, of $10,300m., as strong oil prices boosted export revenue to $52,800m. and imports fell slightly to $42,500m. However, the current account on the balance of payments still recorded a deficit of $1,400m. (1.8% of GDP), mainly owing to large outflows on services and higher interest payments. In 2011 Iraq's current account showed a surplus of $9,100m., based on total exports and imports of $80,800m. and $66,500m., respectively. In 2012 the IMF estimated a current account surplus of $14,900m. (7.0% of GDP), based on total exports and imports $94,100m. and $62,600m., respectively, over the year. The CBI is rapidly building up its foreign exchange reserves, which totalled US $7,902m. at the end of 2004, $12,024m. at the end of 2005, $19,655m. at the end of 2006 and $19,655m. at the end of 2007, up steeply from a low of $3,000m. in December 2003. The IMF estimated gross foreign reserves at $50,200m. at the end of 2008 (equivalent to 12 months of imports of goods and services). However, foreign reserves had fallen to $44,337m. at the end of December 2009—reflecting the drawdown of the Government's deposits with the CBI—before recovering to reach $50,632m. at the end of 2010. In addition, Iraqi deposits at Western banks reporting to the Bank for International Settlements at the end of 2011 totalled $4,725m. Gross reserves held in the CBI were estimated at $70,300m. at the end of 2012, up from $61,100m. in 2011, according to the IMF. Looking ahead, foreign exchange earnings from oil exports were expected to increase substantially over the medium and long term (provided that the security situation continues to improve) as existing oilfields are rehabilitated and new fields come online.

According to the IMF's *Direction of Trade Statistics*, Iraq's principal export markets in 2011 were the USA (accounting for 23.3% of the total value of exports), China (14.0%), South Korea (12.2%), Japan (5.0%), the Netherlands (4.5%) and Italy (4.0%). On the import side, the six main sources were Turkey (providing 25.0% of total imports), Syria (18.0%), China (11.5%), the USA (7.3%), South Korea (4.6%) and Germany (3.6%).

The authorities are committed to free trade policies and an open exchange system. In September 2003 tariffs were lowered to a universal 5% with none on food, pharmaceuticals, books and other humanitarian imports. However, Iraq is currently planning to adopt a new customs law which will establish a transparent and efficient tariff system with varied levels of tariffs being imposed on different products and fewer exemptions. In February 2004 Iraq was granted observer status in the World Trade Organization (WTO). Negotiations are under way for Iraq to join the WTO, and a series of bilateral meetings on market access for goods and services with member countries started in 2007. However, the violence of the post-Saddam era is preventing the development of Iraq's non-oil sectors, which stand to benefit from future WTO membership in terms of increased FDI and technological transfers, as well as access to new markets.

Statistical Survey

Sources (unless otherwise indicated): Central Organization for Statistics and Information Technology (COSIT), Ministry of Planning and Development Co-operation, 929/29/6 Arrasat al-Hindiya, Baghdad; tel. and fax (1) 885-3653; e-mail ministry@mopdc-iraq.org; internet cosit.gov.iq; Central Bank of Iraq, POB 64, al-Rashid St, Baghdad; tel. (1) 816-5170; fax (1) 816-6802; e-mail cbi@cbi.iq; internet www.cbi.iq.

Area and Population

AREA, POPULATION AND DENSITY

Area (sq km)	434,128*
Population (census results)	
17 October 1987	16,335,199
17 October 1997	
Males	10,987,252
Females	11,058,992
Total	22,046,244
Population (UN estimates at mid-year)†	
2011	31,837,014
2012	32,778,033
2013	33,765,232
Density (per sq km) at mid-2013	77.8

* 167,618 sq miles. This figure excludes 924 sq km (357 sq miles) of territorial waters and also the Neutral Zone, of which Iraq's share is 3,522 sq km (1,360 sq miles). The Zone lies between Iraq and Saudi Arabia, and is administered jointly by the two countries. Nomads move freely through it, but there are no permanent inhabitants.

† Source: UN, *World Population Prospects: The 2012 Revision*.

2011 (official estimate): Total population 33,330,512 (males 16,758,448, females 16,572,064).

POPULATION BY AGE AND SEX
(UN estimates at mid–2013)

	Males	Females	Total
0–14	6,955,643	6,577,173	13,532,816
15–64	9,635,653	9,516,787	19,152,440
65 and over	477,973	602,003	1,079,976
Total	17,069,269	16,695,963	33,765,232

Source: UN, *World Population Prospects: The 2012 Revision*.

GOVERNORATES
(official population estimates at 2011)

	Area (sq km)*	Population	Density (per sq km)
Nineveh	35,899	3,270,422	91.1
Salah al-Din	26,175	1,408,174	53.8
Al-Ta'meem (Kirkuk)	10,282	1,395,614	135.7
Diyala	19,076	1,443,173	75.7
Baghdad	734	7,055,196	9,612.0
Al-Anbar (Anbar)	138,501	1,561,407	11.3
Babylon	6,468	1,820,673	281.5
Karbala	5,034	1,066,567	211.9
Al-Najaf (Najaf)	28,824	1,285,484	44.6
Al-Qadisiya	8,153	1,134,314	139.1
Al-Muthanna	51,740	719,069	13.9
Thi-Qar	12,900	1,836,181	142.3
Wasit	17,153	1,210,591	70.6
Maysan	16,072	971,448	60.4
Al-Basrah (Basra)	19,070	2,531,997	132.8
Kurdish Autonomous Region			
D'hok	6,553	1,128,745	172.2
Irbil (Arbil)	14,471	1,612,693	111.4
Al-Sulaimaniya (Sulaimaniya)	17,023	1,878,764	110.4
Total	434,128	33,330,512	76.8

* Excluding territorial waters (924 sq km).

PRINCIPAL TOWNS
(population at 1987 census)

Baghdad (capital)	3,841,268	Al-Sulaimaniya (Sulaimaniya)	364,096
Al-Mawsil (Mosul)	664,221	Al-Najaf (Najaf)	309,010
Irbil (Arbil)	485,968	Karbala	296,705
Kirkuk	418,624	Al-Hillah (Hilla)	268,834
Al-Basrah (Basra)	406,296	Al-Nasiriyah (Nasiriya)	265,937

Source: UN, *Demographic Yearbook*.

Mid-2011 (incl. suburbs, UN estimate): Baghdad 6,035,580 (Source: UN, *World Urbanization Prospects: The 2011 Revision*).

BIRTHS AND DEATHS
(annual averages, UN estimates)

	1995–2000	2000–05	2005–10
Birth rate (per 1,000)	36.4	35.2	33.3
Death rate (per 1,000)	5.1	5.1	5.6

Source: UN, *World Population Prospects: The 2012 Revision*.

Registered marriages: 249,430 in 2009; 245,022 in 2010.

Life expectancy (years at birth): 69.0 (males 65.9; females 72.2) in 2011 (Source: World Bank, World Development Indicators database).

EMPLOYMENT
(labour force survey, '000)

	2006	2007	2008
Agriculture, hunting and forestry	1,925.7	1,066.2	1,759.9
Fishing	22.8	10.0	21.7
Mining and quarrying	43.4	84.4	32.4
Manufacturing	376.3	522.3	369.4
Electricity, gas and water	76.6	130.5	161.6
Construction	665.0	797.2	823.5
Wholesale and retail trade; repair of motor vehicles, motorcycles and personal and household goods	961.8	1,117.6	1,167.2
Hotels and restaurants	52.9	105.4	62.6
Transport, storage and communications	616.5	707.5	608.1
Financial intermediation	26.9	26.4	20.8
Real estate, renting and business activities	40.6	285.8	35.1
Public administration and defence; compulsory social security	727.3	677.6	1,003.3
Education	556.1	612.9	686.7
Health and social work	146.2	196.8	218.2
Community, social and personal services	312.7	520.8	618.5
Households with employed persons	1.5	—	9.7
Extra-territorial organizations and bodies	4.7	—	7.3
Sub-total	6,557.2	6,861.4	7,606.1
Activities not adequately defined	—	255.3	—
Total employed	6,557.2	7,116.7	7,606.1

Source: ILO.

Mid-2013 (estimates in '000): Agriculture, etc. 420; Total labour force 9,004 (Source: FAO).

Health and Welfare

KEY INDICATORS

Total fertility rate (children per woman, 2011)	4.6
Under-5 mortality rate (per 1,000 live births, 2011)	38
HIV/AIDS (% of persons aged 15–49, 2003)	<0.1
Physicians (per 1,000 head, 2009)	0.7
Hospital beds (per 1,000 head, 2010)	1.3
Health expenditure (2010): US $ per head (PPP)	346
Health expenditure (2010): % of GDP	8.5
Health expenditure (2010): public (% of total)	81.2
Access to water (% of persons, 2011)	85
Access to sanitation (% of persons, 2011)	84
Total carbon dioxide emissions ('000 metric tons, 2009)	109,038.2
Carbon dioxide emissions per head (metric tons, 2009)	3.5
Human Development Index (2012): ranking	131
Human Development Index (2012): value	0.590

For sources and definitions, see explanatory note on p. vi.

Agriculture

PRINCIPAL CROPS
('000 metric tons)

	2009	2010	2011
Wheat	1,700	2,749	2,809
Rice, paddy	173	156	235
Barley	502	1,137	820
Maize	238	267	336
Potatoes	223	205	557
Sugar cane	6	13	11
Chick peas	0.7	0.8	0.9
Tomatoes	913	1,013	1,060
Cauliflowers and broccoli	37	26	25
Pumpkins, squash and gourds	132	145	165
Cucumbers and gherkins	421	432	496
Aubergines (Eggplants)	396	387	452
Onions, dry	46	45	90
Watermelons	327	304	340
Canteloupes and other melons	185	177	161
Grapes	195	213	227
Oranges	102	98	91
Tangerines, mandarins, clementines and satsumas	4	4	4
Apples	37	40	46
Apricots	18	19	21
Peaches and nectarines	2	2	2
Plums	9	10	10
Dates	507	567	619

Aggregate production ('000 metric tons, may include official, semi-official or estimated data): Total cereals 2,650 in 2009, 4,362 in 2010, 4,270 in 2011; Total roots and tubers 223 in 2009, 205 in 2010, 557 in 2011; Total vegetables (incl. melons) 3,476 in 2009, 3,532 in 2010, 3,851 in 2011; Total fruits (excl. melons) 969 in 2009, 1,054 in 2010, 1,127 in 2011.

Source: FAO.

LIVESTOCK
('000 head, year ending September)

	2009*	2010	2011*
Horses	48	48	49
Asses*	380	380	380
Mules*	11	11	11
Cattle	1,557†	1,578†	1,600
Buffaloes	286†	295†	300
Camels	58†	60†	62
Sheep	7,945†	8,000*	8,200
Goats	1,475	1,519	1,560
Chickens*	27,000	34,000	38,000

* FAO estimate(s).
† Unofficial figure.

Source: FAO.

LIVESTOCK PRODUCTS
('000 metric tons)

	2009	2010	2011
Cattle meat*	47.5	50.0	52.0
Buffalo meat*	0.8	0.9	0.9
Sheep meat*	40.0	44.1	45.1
Goat meat*	11.2	11.6	12.0
Chicken meat	34.1	52.8	87.2
Cows' milk	178.0*	182.0*	185.5
Buffaloes' milk	23.0*	23.8*	27.2
Sheep's milk	60.0*	58.9*	55.8
Goats' milk*	18.0	18.4	18.8
Hen eggs	35.3	46.3	50.9
Wool, greasy*	17.0	17.2	17.0
Cattle and buffalo hides*	3.5	3.6	3.7

* FAO estimate(s).

Source: FAO.

Forestry

ROUNDWOOD REMOVALS
('000 cubic metres, excl. bark)

	1996*	1997*	1998
Sawlogs, veneer logs and logs for sleepers	20.0	20.0	25.0
Other industrial wood	30.0	30.0	34.0
Fuel wood	49.3	110.0	118.0
Total	99.3	161.0	177.0

* FAO estimates.

1999–2011: Annual production assumed to be unchanged from 1998 (FAO estimates).

Source: FAO.

SAWNWOOD PRODUCTION
('000 cubic metres, incl. railway sleepers)

	1996	1997	1998
Total (all broadleaved)	8	8	12

1999–2011: Annual production as in 1998 (FAO estimates).

Source: FAO.

Fishing

('000 metric tons, live weight)

	2009	2010	2011
Capture	28.2	19.3	31.5
Cyprinids (incl. Common carp)	10.0	1.2	10.5
Freshwater siluroids	2.7	3.0	1.1
Other freshwater fishes	9.6	8.0	3.6
Marine fishes	0.9	1.7	0.2
Aquaculture	18.7	20.3	20.3*
Common carp	15.2	16.8	16.8*
Total catch	46.9	39.6	51.8*

* FAO estimate.

Source: FAO.

Mining

('000 metric tons unless otherwise indicated)

	2009	2010	2011
Crude petroleum	119,984	121,447	136,936
Natural gas (million cu m)*	16,577	16,885	18,692
Ammonia (nitrogen content)	30	126	143
Sulphur†	20	20	20
Salt (unrefined)‡	113	102	136

* Figures refer to gross production.
† Figures refer to native production and by-products of petroleum and natural gas processing.
‡ Estimated figures.

2012: Crude petroleum 152,449.

Sources: BP, *Statistical Review of World Energy*; US Geological Survey.

Industry

SELECTED PRODUCTS
('000 metric tons unless otherwise indicated)

	2007	2008	2009
Naphtha	364	483	464
Motor spirit (petrol)	2,212	2,937	2,822
Kerosene	739	981	943
Jet fuel	409	543	522
Gas-diesel (distillate fuel) oil	4,995	6,633	6,373
Residual fuel oils	5,595	7,430	7,138
Paraffin wax	65	86	83
Petroleum bitumen (asphalt)	340	451	433
Liquefied petroleum gas:			
from natural gas plants	918	954	976
from petroleum refineries	121	161	155
Cement*†	4,500	6,453	7,000
Electric energy (million kWh)	33,183	36,779	46,063

* Source: US Geological Survey.
† Estimated figures.

Cement ('000 metric tons, estimates): 8,000 in 2010; 10,000 in 2011.

Source (unless otherwise indicated): UN Industrial Commodity Statistics Database.

Finance

CURRENCY AND EXCHANGE RATES

Monetary Units
1,000 fils = 20 dirhams = 1 new Iraqi dinar (ID).

Sterling, Dollar and Euro Equivalents (31 May 2013)
£1 sterling = 1,774.0 Iraqi dinars;
US $1 = 1,166.0 Iraqi dinars;
€1 = 1,516.5 Iraqi dinars;
10,000 Iraqi dinars = £5.64 = $8.58 = €6.59.

Average Exchange rate (Iraqi dinars per US $)
2010 1,170.00
2011 1,170.00
2012 1,166.17

Note: Following the overthrow of the regime of Saddam Hussain in 2003, the new Coalition Provisional Authority established an exchange rate of US $1 = 1,400 dinars. A new dinar currency, the new Iraqi dinar (ID), was introduced on 15 October to replace both the 'Swiss' dinar (at ID 1 = 150 'Swiss' dinars), the currency in use in the Kurdish autonomous regions of northern Iraq since 1991, and the 'Saddam' dinar (at par), the official currency of the rest of Iraq. The new currency was to be fully convertible.

BUDGET
(ID '000 million)

Revenue	2009*	2010†	2011†
Revenues	52,400	64,700	79,900
Crude petroleum export revenues	45,600	58,600	71,900
Grants	2,300	1,600	1,400
Total	54,700	66,400	81,300

Expenditure‡	2009*	2010†	2011†
Current expenditure	57,500	57,200	64,000
Salaries and pensions	27,800	30,000	32,200
Goods and services	14,300	11,100	12,300
Transfers	12,700	12,100	14,200
Capital expenditure	16,700	19,500	33,100
Non-petroleum	14,100	15,700	25,700
Petroleum	2,700	3,800	7,100
Total	71,400	66,400	97,000

* Estimates.
† Budget projections.
‡ Including deduction for returned letters of credit totalling 2,800 in 2009; 200 in 2010; 0 in 2011.

Source: IMF, *Iraq: Second Review Under the Stand-By Arrangement, Requests for Waiver of Applicability, Extension of the Arrangement, and Rephasing of Access—Staff Report; Press Release on the Executive Board Discussion; and Statement by the Executive Director for Iraq* (March 2011).

INTERNATIONAL RESERVES
(US $ million at 31 December)

	2010	2011	2012
Gold (national valuation)	266.0	296.9	1,593.6
IMF special drawing rights	1,773.9	1,743.8	1,724.4
Reserve position in IMF	263.5	262.7	263.0
Foreign exchange	48,339.6	58,737.9	66,746.1
Total	50,643.0	61,041.3	70,327.1

Source: IMF, *International Financial Statistics*.

MONEY SUPPLY
(ID '000 million at 31 December)

	2009	2010	2011
Currency outside depository corporations	21,775.7	24,342.2	28,296.0
Transferable deposits	18,618.0	30,039.2	37,991.9
Other deposits	6,397.6	7,011.6	7,810.1
Broad money	46,791.2	61,393.1	74,098.0

Source: IMF, *International Financial Statistics*.

COST OF LIVING
(Consumer Price Index; base: 2000 = 100)

	2010	2011	2012
Food (incl. non-alcoholic beverages)	330.1	340.1	362.3
All items (incl. others)	660.2	697.4	739.4

Source: ILO.

NATIONAL ACCOUNTS

National Income and Product
(ID '000 million at current prices, provisional estimates)

	2004	2005	2006
Compensation of employees	7,866.1	10,394.6	16,573.7
Operating surplus	33,857.9	45,296.7	67,543.7
Domestic factor incomes	41,723.9	55,691.2	84,117.4
Consumption of fixed capital	6,234.6	8,308.9	11,470.6
Gross domestic product (GDP) at factor cost	47,958.6	64,000.1	95,588.0
Indirect taxes (net)	−10,909.3	−14,009.4	−15,128.5
GDP in purchasers' values	37,049.3	49,990.7	80,459.4
Net factor income from abroad*	76.2	1,089.0	1,314.1
Gross national product (GNP)	37,125.5	51,079.7	81,773.6
Less Consumption of fixed capital	6,234.6	8,308.9	11,470.6
National income in market prices	30,890.8	42,770.8	70,303.0

* Figures obtained as residuals.

Gross Domestic Product by Economic Activity
(ID '000 million at current prices, provisional estimates)

	2004	2005	2006
Agriculture, hunting, forestry and fishing	3,539.4	4,248.8	5,569.0
Mining and quarrying	30,543.0	39,366.3	53,030.9
Crude petroleum	30,496.0	39,316.0	n.a.
Manufacturing	770.9	1,220.9	1,473.2
Electricity and water	263.3	393.1	779.4
Construction	468.3	2,932.4	3,449.7
Trade, restaurants and hotels	3,070.5	4,083.5	6,350.0
Transport, storage and communications	3,687.7	4,911.3	6,742.9
Finance, insurance and real estate	663.0	931.4	7,945.8
Government, community, social and personal services	5,200.4	6,139.9	10,726.2
Sub-total	48,206.5	64,227.6	96,067.2
Less Imputed bank service charge	248.0	227.5	479.2
GDP at factor cost	47,958.5	64,000.1	95,588.0
Indirect taxes / *Less* Subsidies	−10,909.3	−14,009.4	−15,128.5
GDP in market prices	37,049.3	49,990.7	80,459.4

2008 (ID '000 million at current prices): Agriculture, hunting, forestry and fishing 5,716.8; Mining and quarrying 86,867.1; Manufacturing 2,331.8; Construction 5,972.7; Electricity and water 1,307.9; Transport, storage and communications 12,030.9; Trade, restaurants and hotels 10,078.1; Finance, insurance and real estate 12,970.2; Government, community, social and personal services 19,394.5; *Sub-total* 156,670.1; *Less* Imputed bank service charge 687.8; *Gross domestic product at factor cost* 155,982.3.

2009 (ID '000 million at current prices): Agriculture, hunting, forestry and fishing 6,132.7; Mining and quarrying 56,654.0; Manufacturing 3,369.4; Construction 7,066.1; Electricity and water 1,686.1; Transport, storage and communications 14,185.9; Trade, restaurants and hotels 11,486.6; Finance, insurance and real estate 14,547.0; Government, community, social and personal services 25,031.3; *Sub-total* 140,159.1; *Less* Imputed bank service charge 828.9; *Gross domestic product at factor cost* 139,330.2.

2010 (ID '000 million at current prices): Agriculture, hunting, forestry and fishing 8,657.4; Mining and quarrying 74,357.2; Manufacturing 3,916.6; Construction 11,061.6; Electricity and water 1,979.8; Transport, storage and communications 19,415.2; Trade, restaurants and hotels 14,940.2; Finance, insurance and real estate 16,310.7; Government, community, social and personal services 27,459.4; *Sub-total* 178,098.0; *Less* Imputed bank service charge 1,089.3; *Gross domestic product at factor cost* 177,008.6.

BALANCE OF PAYMENTS
(US $ million)

	2009	2010	2011
Exports of goods	39,429.3	51,760.3	79,683.6
Imports of goods	−35,284.8	−37,328.0	−40,632.5
Balance on goods	4,144.5	14,432.3	39,051.1
Exports of services	2,193.4	2,833.6	2,822.5
Imports of services	−8,563.1	−9,863.5	−11,080.0
Balance on goods and services	−2,225.2	7,402.4	30,793.6
Primary income received	3,412.2	2,079.9	1,091.0
Primary income paid	−317.1	−486.7	−1,292.2
Balance on goods, services and primary income	869.9	8,995.6	30,592.4
Secondary income received	221.4	240.8	367.4
Secondary income paid	−2,243.1	−2,748.1	−4,757.1
Current balance	−1,151.8	6,488.3	26,202.7
Capital account (net)	10.2	25.3	11.1
Direct investment assets	−71.9	−124.9	−366.0
Direct investment liabilities	1,598.3	1,396.2	1,396.2
Portfolio investment assets	3,646.3	727.1	−6,572.1
Portfolio investment liabilities	2.9	56.5	94.3
Other investment assets	−5,362.4	5,310.4	−8,226.4
Other investment liabilities	3,270.4	337.8	573.8
Net errors and omissions	−7,787.4	−9,150.6	−3,194.0
Reserves and related items	−5,845.4	5,066.1	9,919.6

Source: IMF, *International Financial Statistics*.

External Trade

PRINCIPAL COMMODITIES
(US $ million)

Imports c.i.f.	2009	2010	2011
Food and live animals	2,076	2,371	2,581
Beverages and tobacco	500	571	622
Crude materials (inedible) except fuels	692	790	860
Mineral fuels, lubricants, etc.	3,767	4,304	4,685
Animal and vegetable oils and fats	2,460	2,811	3,059
Chemicals	2,575	2,942	3,203
Basic manufactures	4,381	5,006	5,450
Machinery and transport equipment	14,798	16,907	18,404
Miscellaneous manufactured articles	6,073	6,939	7,553
Total (incl. others)	38,437	43,915	47,803

Exports c.i.f.	2009	2010	2011
Food and live animals	110	145	223
Crude materials (inedible) except fuels	59	78	120
Mineral fuels, lubricants, etc.	39,131	51,376	79,083
Chemicals	4	5	8
Basic manufactures	20	26	40
Machinery and transport equipment	95	124	191
Total (incl. others)	39,427	51,764	79,681

PRINCIPAL TRADING PARTNERS
(US $ million)

Imports c.i.f.	1988	1989	1990
Australia	153.4	196.2	108.7
Austria	n.a.	1.1	50.9
Belgium-Luxembourg	57.6	68.2	68.3
Brazil	346.0	416.4	139.5
Canada	169.9	225.1	150.4
China, People's Republic	99.2	148.0	157.9
France	278.0	410.4	278.3
Germany	322.3	459.6	389.4
India	32.3	65.2	57.5
Indonesia	38.9	122.7	104.9
Ireland	150.4	144.9	31.6
Italy	129.6	285.1	194.0
Japan	533.0	621.1	397.2
Jordan	164.3	210.0	220.3
Korea, Republic	98.5	123.9	149.4
Netherlands	111.6	102.6	93.8
Romania	113.3	91.1	30.1
Saudi Arabia	37.2	96.5	62.5
Spain	43.4	129.0	40.5
Sri Lanka	50.1	33.5	52.3
Sweden	63.0	40.6	64.8
Switzerland	65.7	94.4	126.6
Thailand	22.3	59.2	68.9
Turkey	874.7	408.9	196.0
USSR	70.7	75.7	77.9
United Kingdom	394.6	448.5	322.1
USA	979.3	1,001.7	658.4
Yugoslavia	154.5	182.0	123.1
Total (incl. others)	5,960.0	6,956.2	4,833.9

Exports f.o.b.	1988	1989	1990*
Belgium-Luxembourg	147.5	249.6	n.a.
Brazil	1,002.8	1,197.2	n.a.
France	517.4	623.9	0.8
Germany	122.0	76.9	1.7
Greece	192.5	189.4	0.3
India	293.0	438.8	14.7
Italy	687.1	549.7	10.6
Japan	712.1	117.1	0.1
Jordan	28.4	25.2	101.6
Netherlands	152.9	532.3	0.2
Portugal	120.8	125.8	n.a.
Spain	370.0	575.7	0.7
Turkey	1,052.6	1,331.0	83.5
USSR	835.7	1,331.7	8.9
United Kingdom	293.1	167.0	4.4
USA	1,458.9	2,290.8	0.2
Yugoslavia	425.4	342.0	10.4
Total (incl. others)	10,268.3	12,333.7	392.0

* Excluding exports of most petroleum products.

Source: UN, *International Trade Statistics Yearbook*.

2009 (US $ million): *Imports by regions:* Arab nations 14,068; North and South America 5,001; European Union 3,348; Other Europe 9,475; Asia 5,104; Other countries 1,441; Total imports 38,437. *Exports by region:* Arab nations 871; North and South America 19,571; European Union 10,310; Other Europe 1,124; Asia 5,047; Other countries 2,504; Total exports 39,427.

2010 (US $ million): *Imports by regions:* Arab nations 10,399; North and South America 5,248; European Union 5,885; Other Europe 13,253; Asia 8,432; Other countries 698; Total imports 43,915. *Exports by region:* Arab nations 1,155; North and South America 15,886; European Union 11,155; Other Europe 1,289; Asia 21,953; Other countries 326; Total exports 51,764.

2011 (US $ million): *Imports by regions:* Arab nations 11,903; North and South America 4,101; European Union 4,881; Other Europe 13,925; Asia 12,615; Other countries 378; Total imports 47,803. *Exports by region:* Arab nations 2,853; North and South America 24,024; European Union 13,801; Other Europe 2,279; Asia 36,310; Other countries 414; Total exports 79,681.

Transport

RAILWAYS
(traffic)

	2008	2009	2010
Passengers carried ('000)	107.0	219.8	212.3
Freight carried ('000 tons)	432.0	644.0	995.0
Passenger-km (million)	53.7	102.6	99.7
Freight ton-km (million)	121.0	170.0	249.0

ROAD TRAFFIC
(estimates, '000 motor vehicles in use)

	1995	1996
Passenger cars	770.1	773.0
Buses and coaches	50.9	51.4
Lorries and vans	269.9	272.5
Road tractors	37.2	37.2

2006: Passenger cars 784,794; Buses and coaches 112,113; Vans and lorries 1,345,361; *Total* 2,242,269.

Source: IRF, *World Road Statistics*.

SHIPPING

Flag Registered Fleet
(at 31 December)

	2010	2011	2012
Number of vessels	78	78	78
Total displacement ('000 grt)	149.4	149.4	128.0

Source: Lloyd's List Intelligence (www.lloydslistintelligence.com).

CIVIL AVIATION
(revenue traffic on scheduled services)

	1991	1992	1994*
Kilometres flown (million)	0	0	0
Passengers carried ('000)	28	53	31
Passenger-km (million)	17	35	20
Freight ton-km (million)	0	3	2

* Figures for 1993 unavailable.

Source: UN, *Statistical Yearbook*.

Passengers carried: 89,297 in 2010; 88,774 in 2011 (Source: World Bank, World Development Indicators database).

Tourism

ARRIVALS AT FRONTIERS OF VISITORS FROM ABROAD*

Country of nationality	2008	2009	2010
India	6,031	13,876	13,860
Iran	840,362	1,161,541	1,413,792
Lebanon	129	1,916	4,466
Pakistan	5,771	18,004	13,815
Total (incl. others)	863,657	1,261,921	1,517,766

* Including same-day visitors.

Tourism receipts (incl. passenger transport, US $ million): 186 in 2005; 170 in 2006; 555 in 2007.

Source: World Tourism Organization.

Communications Media

	2010	2011	2012
Telephones ('000 main lines in use)	1,720.6	1,794.0	1,871.0
Mobile cellular telephones ('000 subscribers)	23,264	25,519	26,756
Internet subscribers ('000)	0.3	n.a.	n.a.
Broadband subscribers ('000)	100	n.a.	n.a.

Source: International Telecommunication Union.

Education

(2010/11 unless otherwise indicated)

	Institutions	Teachers	Students
Pre-primary	648	5,475	141,158
Primary	14,048	263,412	4,864,096
Secondary:			
academic	5,472	136,446	1,953,766
vocational	294	12,464	56,169
Teacher training	78	3,063	22,047
Higher*	65	14,700	240,000†

* 2002/03.
† Figure for undergraduates only.

Sources: Ministries of Education and Higher Education.

Pupil-teacher ratio (primary education, UNESCO estimate): 17.0 in 2006/07 (Source: UNESCO Institute for Statistics).

Adult literacy rate (UNESCO estimates): 78.2% (males 86.0%; females 70.6%) in 2010 (Source: UNESCO Institute for Statistics).

Directory

As a result of the US-led military campaign to oust the regime of Saddam Hussain in early 2003, and the ensuing insurgency, buildings occupied by a number of government ministries and other institutions were reported to have been damaged or destroyed.

The Constitution

On 15 November 2003 the Coalition Provisional Authority, established following the overthrow of the regime of Saddam Hussain that April, and the Governing Council, inaugurated in July, agreed on a timetable for the restoration of full Iraqi sovereignty, the drafting of a permanent constitution and the holding of free national elections. The Governing Council signed a Transitional Administrative Law (TAL) on 8 March 2004, which outlined a new timetable for the establishment of sovereign, elected organs of government. The basic tenets of the TAL were to define the structures of a transitional government and procedures for electing members of the Transitional National Assembly (TNA); guarantee basic rights for all Iraqis, including freedom of speech and the press; and respect the Islamic identity of the Iraqi majority and guarantee religious plurality. The TAL was to expire once a permanent, constitutionally elected government had been established.

Following national elections to the 275-member TNA, held on 30 January 2005, the elected members of this transitional legislature approved the text of a draft Constitution, which was ratified by the Iraqi people in a national referendum on 15 October (with the endorsement of 78.6% of the votes cast). National elections for a permanent legislature, the Council of Representatives, took place on 15 December, with members to serve a four-year term.

The Government

HEAD OF STATE

President: Jalal Talabani (assumed office 7 April 2005, re-elected by the Council of Representatives 22 April 2006 and 11 November 2010).

Vice-Presidents: Tariq al-Hashimi, Khudhair al-Khuzai.

COUNCIL OF MINISTERS
(September 2013)

Prime Minister and Acting Minister of the Interior: Nuri Kamal (Jawad) al-Maliki.

Deputy Prime Minister for Economic Affairs: Dr Rozh Nuri Shawais.

Deputy Prime Minister for Energy Affairs: Hussein al-Shahristani.

Deputy Prime Minister: Saleh al-Mutlaq.

Minister of Agriculture: Ezz al-Din Ahmad Hussein al-Dawla.

Minister of Communications and Minister of State for Provincial Affairs: Torhan Mudher Hassan al-Mufti.

Minister of Construction and Housing: Muhammad Saheb al-Darraji.

Minister of Culture and Acting Minister of Defence: Saadoun al-Dulaimi.

Minister of Displacement and Migration: Dindar Najman Shafiq Duski.

Minister of Education: (vacant).

Minister of Electricity: Abd al-Karim Aftan al-Jumaili.

Minister of the Environment: Sarkoun Sliwa.

Minister of Foreign Affairs: Hoshyar al-Zibari.

Minister of Health: Majid Hamad Amin.

Minister of Higher Education and Scientific Research: Ali al-Adib.

Minister of Human Rights: Muhammad Shayyaa al-Sudani.

Minister of Industry and Minerals: Ahmad Nasser al-Dali.

Minister of Justice: Hassan al-Shummari.

Minister of Labour and Social Affairs: Nassar al-Rubai.

Minister of Municipalities and Public Works: Adel Mhoder al-Radhi.

Minister of Oil: Abd al-Karim al-Luaibi.

Minister of Planning and Acting Minister of Finance: Ali Yousuf Abd al-Nabi al-Shukri.

Minister of Science and Technology: (vacant).

Minister of Trade: Khairallah Hassan Babakr Muhammad.

Minister of Transportation: Amir Hadi al-Amiri.

Minister of Tourism and Antiquities: Liwa Sumaysim.

Minister of Water Resources: Muhannad Salman al-Saadi.

Minister of Youth and Sports: Jasim Muhammad Ja'far.

Minister of State for Civil Society Affairs: Dakhil Qassim.

Minister of State for Council of Representatives Affairs: Safa al-Din Muhammad al-Safi.

Minister of State for Foreign Affairs: Ali al-Sajri.

Minister of State for National Reconciliation: Amer Hassan al-Khuzai.

Minister of State for Tribal Affairs: Jamal al-Batikh.

Minister of State and Government Spokesperson: Ali al-Dabbagh.

Minister of State for Women's Affairs: Ibtihal al-Zaidi.

Acting Minister of State for National Security: Falih al-Fayyad.

Ministers of State: Diyaa Najem al-Asadi, Salah Muzahim Darwish, Yassin Hassan Muhammad, Hassan al-Mutairi, Abd al-Sahib Qahraman, Hassan al-Radi, Bushra Hussein Saleh.

MINISTRIES

Ministry of Agriculture: Khulafa St, Khullani Sq., Baghdad; tel. (1) 887-3251; e-mail minis_of_agr@moagr.org; internet www.moagr.com.

Ministry of Civil Society Affairs: Baghdad.

Ministry of Communications: Baghdad; tel. (1) 717-9440; e-mail iraqimoc@iraqimoc.net; internet www.moc.gov.iq.

Ministry of Construction and Housing: Baghdad; e-mail moch@moch.gov.iq; internet www.moch.gov.iq.

Ministry of Culture: POB 624, Qaba bin Nafi Sq., Sadoun St, Baghdad; tel. (1) 538-3171.

Ministry of Defence: Baghdad; e-mail webmaster@mod.iraqiaf.org.

Ministry of Displacement and Migration: Baghdad; tel. (1) 537-0842; fax (1) 537-2497.

Ministry of Economic Affairs: Baghdad.

Ministry of Education: Saad State Enterprises Bldg, nr the Convention Centre, Baghdad; tel. (1) 883-2571; e-mail general@moedu.gov.iq; internet www.moedu.gov.iq.

Ministry of Electricity: Baghdad; e-mail infocen@moelc.gov.iq; internet www.moelc.gov.iq.

Ministry of Energy Affairs: Baghdad.

Ministry of the Environment: POB 10026, Baghdad; e-mail enviro_center@yahoo.com; internet www.moen.gov.iq.

Ministry of Finance: Khulafa St, nr al-Russafi Sq., Baghdad; tel. (1) 887-4871; e-mail iraqmof@mof.gov.iq; internet www.mof.gov.iq.

Ministry of Foreign Affairs: opp. State Organization for Roads and Bridges, Karradat Mariam, Baghdad; tel. (1) 537-0091; e-mail press@iraqmfamail.com; internet www.mofa.gov.iq.

Ministry of Health: Baghdad; e-mail hedmoh@moh.gov.iq; internet www.moh.gov.iq.

Ministry of Higher Education and Scientific Research: 52 Rusafa St, Baghdad; tel. and fax (1) 280-6315; e-mail info@mohesr.gov.iq; internet www.mohesr.gov.iq.

Ministry of Human Rights: Baghdad; e-mail minister1@humanrights.gov.iq; internet www.humanrights.gov.iq.

Ministry of Industry and Minerals: POB 5815, Baghdad; tel. (1) 816-2006; e-mail admin@industry.gov.iq; internet www.industry.gov.iq.

Ministry of the Interior: Baghdad; tel. (1) 817-3101; e-mail media@moi.gov.iq; internet www.moi.gov.iq.

Ministry of Justice: Baghdad; fax (1) 537-2269; internet www.moj.gov.iq.

Ministry of Labour and Social Affairs: Baghdad; e-mail info@molsa.gov.iq; internet www.molsa.gov.iq.

Ministry of Municipalities and Public Works: Baghdad; e-mail info@mmpw.gov.iq; internet www.mmpw.gov.iq.

Ministry of National Reconciliation: Baghdad.

Ministry of Oil: Oil Complex Bldg, Port Said St, Baghdad; tel. (1) 817-7000; e-mail minister.office@oil.gov.iq; internet www.oil.gov.iq.

Ministry of Planning: 929/29/6 Arrasat al-Hindiya, Baghdad; tel. (1) 778-3899; e-mail ministry@mopdc-iraq.org; internet www.mop-iraq.org.

Ministry of Science and Technology: Baghdad; internet www.most.gov.iq.

Ministry of State for Council of Representatives Affairs: Baghdad.

Ministry of State for National Security: North Gate, Baghdad; tel. (1) 888-9071.

Ministry of State for Provincial Affairs: Baghdad.

Ministry of State for Tribal Affairs: Baghdad.

Ministry of State for Women's Affairs: Baghdad.

Ministry of Tourism and Antiquities: Baghdad.

Ministry of Trade: POB 5833, Khullani Sq., Baghdad; tel. (1) 887-2681; fax (1) 790-1907; e-mail motcenter@motiraq.org; internet www.mot.gov.iq.

Ministry of Transportation: nr Martyr's Monument, Karradat Dakhil, Baghdad; tel. (1) 776-6041; e-mail mt_office@motrans.gov.iq; internet www.motrans.gov.iq.

Ministry of Water Resources: Palestine St, Baghdad; tel. (1) 772-0240; fax (1) 774-0672; e-mail waterresmin@yahoo.co.uk; internet www.mowr.gov.iq.

Ministry of Youth and Sports: Baghdad; internet www.moys.gov.iq.

Legislature

Council of Representatives

Baghdad International Zone Convention Center, Baghdad; e-mail press@parliament.iq; internet www.parliament.iq.

Elections to the Council of Representatives were held on 7 March 2010. The rate of participation by eligible voters was recorded at 62.4%. According to final results (including compensatory seats) published by the Independent High Electoral Commission (IHEC) on 26 March, the Iraqi National Movement, led by former interim Prime Minister Dr Ayad Allawi, with 91 seats, emerged as the largest group in the 325-seat legislature. The State of Law coalition of incumbent Prime Minister Nuri al-Maliki won 89 seats. The Iraqi National Alliance obtained 70 seats and the Kurdistan Alliance 43 seats. Meanwhile, the Kurdish Movement for Change won eight seats, the Iraqi Accord six, the Kurdistan Islamic Union List and the Iraqi Unity Coalition each four, and the Islamic Group of Kurdistan two. Of the remaining eight seats, five were reserved for Christian parties and one each for the Sabian, Shebek and Yazidi communities. (On 1 June the declared outcome was ratified by the Higher Judicial Council, following a manual recount of the votes cast in the capital, Baghdad.)

Speaker: OSAMA AL-NUJAIFI.

Kurdish Autonomous Region

A 15-article accord signed by the Iraqi Government and Kurdish leaders in 1970 provided for: the creation of a unified autonomous area for the Kurdish population, comprising the administrative departments of al-Sulaimaniya (Sulaimaniya), D'hok and Irbil (Arbil), and the Kurdish sector of the city of Kirkuk; and the establishment of a 50-member Kurdish Legislative Council. Following the recapture of Kuwait from Iraqi forces by a multinational military coalition in early 1991, renewed negotiations between the Iraqi Government (under Saddam Hussain) and Kurdish groups stalled over the status of Kirkuk, and in October 1991 the Government effectively severed all economic and administrative support to the region. In May 1992 the Kurdish Iraqi Front (KIF), an alliance of several Kurdish factions—including the two largest, the Patriotic Union of Kurdistan (PUK) and the Kurdistan Democratic Party (KDP)—established in 1988, organized elections to a new 105-member Iraqi Kurdistan National Assembly. However, by September 1996 bitter factional disputes had led to the effective disintegration of the KIF, and prompted the Government to reassert full Iraqi sovereignty over the Kurdish areas. At a meeting in Washington, DC, USA, in September 1998, representatives of the PUK and the KDP reached a formal peace agreement, which provided for a unified regional administration, the sharing of local revenues and co-operation in implementing the UN-sponsored 'oil-for-food' programme. In December 1999 the KDP announced the composition of a new 25-member coalition administration (comprising the KDP, the Iraqi Communist Party, the Assyrian Movement, the Independent Workers' Party of Kurdistan, the Islamic Union and independents) for the areas under its control, principally the departments of Arbil and D'hok. Municipal elections (to select 571 officials) were conducted in the KDP-administered region in May 2001; according to official KDP sources, KDP candidates received 81% of votes cast. Negotiations between representatives of the KDP and the PUK for the full implementation of the Washington accord were held during 2002, and resulted in the resumption of a transitional joint session of the Iraqi Kurdistan National Assembly in October. The autonomous regions retained their status following the removal of the regime of Saddam Hussain in early 2003, but the status of Kirkuk remained highly controversial.

THE GOVERNMENT OF THE KURDISH AUTONOMOUS REGION

President: MASOUD BARZANI.

THE CABINET
(September 2013)

A coalition Government comprising the Kurdistan Democratic Party (KDP), the Patriotic Union of Kurdistan (PUK), the Kurdistan Islamic Movement, Turkmen representatives, the Kurdistan Communist Party and independents.

Prime Minister: NECHIRVAN IDRIS BARZANI.

Deputy Prime Minister: IMAD AHMAD SAYFOUR.

Minister of Agriculture and Water Resources: SERWAN BABAN.

Minister of Culture and Youth: KAWA MAHMOUD SHAKIR.

Minister of Education: ASMAT MUHAMMAD KHALID.

Minister of Electricity: Yasin Sheikh Abu Bakir Muhammad Mawati.

Minister of Endowment and Religious Affairs: Kamil Ali Aziz.

Minister of Finance and the Economy: Bayiz Saeed Muhammad Talabani.

Minister of Health: Rekawt Hama Rasheed.

Minister of Higher Education and Scientific Research: Ali Saeed.

Minister of Housing and Reconstruction: Kamaran Ahmad Abdullah.

Minister of Justice: Sherwan Haidari.

Minister for the Interior: Abd al-Karim Sultan Sinjari.

Minister of Labour and Social Affairs: Asos Najib Abdullah.

Minister of Martyrs and Anfal Affairs: Sabah Ahmad Muhammad.

Minister of Municipalities and Tourism: Dilshad Shahab.

Minister of Natural Resources: Abdullah Abd al-Rahman Abdullah.

Minister of Peshmerga Affairs: Jafar Mustafa Ali.

Minister of Planning: Ali Sindi.

Minister of Trade and Industry: Sinan Abd al-Khalq Ahmad Chalabi.

Minister of Transport and Communications: Jonson Siyaoosh.

The President of the Divan of the Council of Ministers, the Secretary of the Cabinet, the Chief of Staff of the Presidency, the Head of the Department of Foreign Relations and the Chairman of the Investment Board also have full ministerial status.

LEGISLATURE

Iraqi Kurdistan Parliament

Erbil (Hewlêr) Kurdistan, Iraq; e-mail office@perleman.org; internet www.perleman.org.

In May 1992 negotiations with the Iraqi Government over the full implementation of the 1970 accord on Kurdish regional autonomy having stalled, the KIF unilaterally organized elections to a 105-member Iraqi Kurdistan National Assembly, in which almost the entire electorate of 1.1m. participated. The KDP and the PUK were the only parties to achieve representation in the new Assembly, and subsequently agreed to share seats equally (50 seats each—five having been reserved for two Assyrian Christian parties). However, the subsequent disintegration of the KIF and prolonged armed conflict between elements of the KDP and the PUK prevented the Assembly from becoming properly instituted. Relations between the KDP and the PUK improved following the Washington, DC, agreement of September 1998, and on 8 September 2002 representatives of the two parties signed an agreement providing for the inauguration of a transitional joint parliamentary session (with representation based on the results of the May 1992 elections) before the end of the year. On 4 October 2002 a joint session of the Iraqi Kurdistan National Assembly was convened for the first time since 1996. Following the removal of the regime of Saddam Hussain by US-led forces in early 2003, elections to a new Iraqi Kurdistan National Assembly took place on 30 January 2005, concurrently with elections to the Transitional National Assembly. The Kurdistan Democratic List won 104 of the 111 seats. On 12 June the new Kurdish legislature voted unanimously to appoint Masoud Barzani, leader of the KDP, to the post of President of the Kurdish Autonomous Region. The Government, led by Barzani, assumed office on 7 May 2006, and represented the region's first unified Cabinet. Prior to a unification agreement signed in January 2006, Sulaimaniya had been governed by the PUK, while Arbil and D'hok were administered by the KDP. In February 2009 the Iraqi Kurdistan National Assembly was renamed the Iraqi Kurdistan Parliament. A draft Constitution for the Kurdish Autonomous Region, which included territorial claims to Kirkuk and other disputed regions, was approved by the Iraqi Kurdistan National Assembly on 24 June 2009. However, a planned referendum on the draft Constitution was subsequently postponed, owing to opposition from the Independent High Electoral Commission and the Iraqi parliament. At elections to the Iraqi Kurdistan Parliament held on 25 July, the Kurdistani List, which comprised the PUK and the KDP, secured 59 of the 111 seats in the legislature. The significant reduction in the two main parties' majority was largely due to the success of the Movement for Change (Gorran), which received 25 seats; the group had been established in 2006 by former members of the PUK, and campaigned on a pro-reform and anti-corruption platform. An alliance of Islamist and left-wing parties, the Service and Reform List, won 13 seats. The Islamic Movement in Iraqi Kurdistan took two seats, and the Freedom and Social Justice List one seat. The remaining 11 seats were reserved for representatives of various minority groups. Meanwhile, in a concurrent election for the regional presidency, Barzani was re-elected with 69.6% of the valid votes cast.

Speaker: Dr Arslan Baiz.

Election, 25 July 2009

	Seats
Kurdistani List (PUK and KDP)	59
Movement for Change (Gorran)*	25
Service and Reform List†	13
Islamic Movement in Iraqi Kurdistan	2
Freedom and Social Justice List	1
Minority Groups	11
Total	111

* Established in 2006 by former members of the PUK.

† Comprises the Kurdistan Islamic Union, Islamic Group in Kurdistan, Kurdistan Socialist Democratic Party and Future Party.

Election Commission

Independent High Electoral Commission (IHEC): POB 55074, Baghdad; tel. (1) 743-2519; e-mail inquiries@ihec.iq; internet www.ihec-iq.com; f. 2004 as Independent Electoral Comm. of Iraq by fmr Coalition Provisional Authority; renamed as above 2007; Chair. Sarbast Rasheed.

Political Organizations

Following the removal from power of the Baathist regime, restrictions were effectively lifted on opposition political organizations that were either previously declared illegal, forced to operate clandestinely within Iraq or were based abroad. Some 306 political parties were reported to have participated in the election to the Council of Representatives held on 7 March 2010.

Arab Baath Socialist Party: revolutionary Arab socialist movement founded in Damascus, Syria, in 1947; governed Iraq during 1968–2003 as principal constituent of ruling coalition, the Nat. Progressive Front (NPF); the NPF was removed from power by US-led forces in May 2003, whereupon membership of the Baath Party was declared illegal and former party mems were barred from govt and military posts; subsequently thought to be involved in insurgent activities in Iraq; in Feb. 2008 new legislation was ratified permitting certain former Baathists to be reinstated to official posts; in Jan. 2007, following the execution of former Iraqi President Saddam Hussain, former Vice-President Izzat Ibrahim al-Douri was named as the party's new leader.

Assyrian Democratic Movement (Zowaa Dimuqrataya Aturaya—Zowaa): e-mail info@zowaa.org; internet www.zowaa.org; f. 1979; seeks recognition of Assyrian rights within framework of democratic national govt; Sec.-Gen. Younadam Yousuf Kanna.

Assyrian Socialist Party: Baghdad; e-mail gaboatouraya@yahoo.co.uk; internet asp2.no.sapo.pt; f. 2002 (refounded); advocates the establishment of an Assyrian nation.

Constitutional Party: Baghdad; f. 2004; Shi'ite; contested the March 2010 legislative election as part of the Iraqi Unity Coalition; Founder and Leader Jawad al-Bulani.

Al-Ezediah Movement for Progress and Reform: Yazidi grouping; Leader Amin Farhan Jejo.

Independent Democratic Gathering: f. 2003; seeks a secular and democratic govt of Iraq; contested March 2010 legislative election as part of the State of Law alliance; Leader Mahdi al-Hafez.

Iraqi Accord (Jabhat al-Tawafuq al-Iraqiya): f. 2005 as the Iraqi Accord Front; reformed to contest the March 2010 legislative elections; mainly Sunni; secular; coalition of the Iraqi Islamic Party and the Nat. Gathering of the People of Iraq.

Iraqi Communist Party (ICP): Baghdad; e-mail info@iraqicp.com; internet www.iraqicp.com; f. 1934; became legally recognized in July 1973 on formation of NPF; left NPF March 1979; First Sec. Hamid Majid Moussa.

Iraqi Constitutional Movement: Baghdad; f. 1993; fmrly Constitutional Monarchy Movement; contested March 2010 legislative election as part of Iraqi Nat. Alliance.

Iraqi Front for National Dialogue (Hewar National Iraqi Front): f. 2005 as breakaway party from Iraqi Nat. Dialogue Council; coalition of minor Sunni parties; contested the March 2010 legislative election as part of the Iraqi Nat. Movement list, although al-Mutlaq was himself banned from participating by the Justice and Accountability Comm; Founder and Leader Saleh al-Mutlaq.

Iraqi Islamic Party (IIP) (al-Hizb al-Islami al-'Iraqi): e-mail iraqiparty@iraqiparty.com; internet www.iraqiparty.com; f. 1960; Sunni; branch of the Muslim Brotherhood; contested March 2010 legislative election as part of the Iraqi Accord list; Sec.-Gen. IYAD AL-SAMARRAI.

Iraqi National Accord (INA): e-mail wifaq_ina@hotmail.com; internet www.wifaq.com; f. 1990; contested March 2010 legislative election as mem. of Iraqi Nat. Movement; Founder and Sec.-Gen. Dr AYAD ALLAWI .

Iraqi National Alliance: list of mainly Shi'ite parties, incl. the ISCI, the Sadr II Movement, the Iraqi Nat. Congress, the Nat. Reform Movement and the Islamic Virtue Party, which contested the March 2010 legislative elections as a single coalition.

Iraqi National Congress (INC): e-mail info@inciraq.com; internet inciraq.com; f. 1992 in London, United Kingdom, as a multi-party coalition supported by the US Govt; following the removal of the regime of Saddam Hussain, the INC moved to Baghdad and was transformed into a distinct political party; formed Nat. Congress Coalition before 2005 legislative elections, at which it failed to win any seats; contested March 2010 election as part of the Iraqi Nat. Alliance; Leader AHMAD CHALABI.

Iraqi National Foundation Congress (INFC): Baghdad; f. 2004; multi-party coalition incl. Nasserites, pre-Saddam Hussain era Baathists, Kurds, Christians, Sunnis and Shi'ites; seeks secular govt of national unity; opposed to presence of US-led coalition in Iraq, and consequently boycotted the electoral process initiated by the coalition; led by 25-mem. secretariat; Gen. Sec. Sheikh JAWAD AL-KHALISI.

Iraqi National Movement (Iraqiya): secular electoral list formed to contest the March 2010 legislative election, comprising a no. of political orgs, incl. the INA, the Iraqi Front for Nat. Dialogue, the Renewal List and Iraqis; Leader Dr AYAD ALLAWI.

Iraqis (Iraqiyun): f. 2004; moderate; includes both Sunnis and Shi'ites; contested March 2010 legislative election as part of Iraqi National Movement list; Leader Sheikh GHAZI MASHAL AJIL AL-YAWAR.

Iraqi Turkmen Front (Irak Türkmen Cephesi): Arbil; internet www.kerkuk.net; f. 1995; coalition of Turkmen groups; seeks autonomy for Turkmen areas in Iraq and recognition of Turkmen as one of main ethnic groups in Iraq, and supports establishment of multi-party democratic system in Iraq; contests status of Kirkuk with Kurds; Leader ERŞAT SALIH; Sec.-Gen. YUNUS BAYRAKTAR.

Iraqi Unity Coalition: f. 2009 to contest the March 2010 legislative election; electoral alliance comprising 38 parties, incl. the Constitutional Party and the Iraqi Awakening Conference.

Islamic Dawa Party (Hizb al-Da'wa al-Islamiya): Baghdad; e-mail info@islamicdawaparty.org; internet www.islamicdawaparty.org; f. 1957 in Najaf; banned 1980; fmrly based in Tehran, Iran, and London, United Kingdom; re-established in Baghdad 2003; contested March 2010 legislative election as part of State of Law coalition; predominantly Shi'ite, but with Sunni mems; advocates govt centred on the principles of Islam; Gen. Sec. NURI KAMAL (JAWAD) AL-MALIKI.

Islamic Group of Kurdistan (Komaleh Islami): Khurmal; f. 2001; splinter group of IMIK; moderate Islamist, aligned with the PUK; contested March 2010 legislative election independently; Founder and Leader Mullah ALI BAPIR.

Islamic Movement in Iraqi Kurdistan (IMIK): Halabja; e-mail bzotnawa@yahoo.com; f. 1987; Islamist movement seeking to obtain greater legal rights for Iraqi Kurds; Founder and Leader Sheikh UTHMAN ABD AL-AZIZ.

Islamic Supreme Council of Iraq (ISCI): Najaf; e-mail info@almejlis.org; internet www.almejlis.org; f. 1982 as the Supreme Council for the Islamic Revolution in Iraq; name changed as above in 2007; Shi'ite; seeks govt based on principle of *wilayat-e-faqih* (guardianship of the jurisprudent); armed faction, the Badr Organization (fmrly Badr Brigade), assisted coalition forces in Iraq after the removal of Saddam Hussain's regime; contested March 2010 legislative election as part of the Iraqi Nat. Alliance; Leader AMMAR AL-HAKIM.

Islamic Virtue Party (Hizb al-Fadhila al-Islamiya—IVP): Basra; Shi'ite; an offshoot of the Sadrist movement; follows the spiritual leadership of Ayatollah al-Sayyid Muhammad al-Ya'qubi; contested March 2010 legislative election as part of Iraqi Nat. Alliance; Sec.-Gen. ABD AL-RAHIM AHMAD ALI AL-HASINI.

Kurdistan Alliance List (Democratic Patriotic Alliance of Kurdistan—DPAK): f. 2004 as a coalition of the PUK, the KDP and smaller Kurdish parties to contest Jan. 2005 legislative elections; participated in March 2010 legislative election as a two-party coalition of the PUK and the KDP; the PUK and the KDP formed a separate electoral list, the Kurdistan List, to contest elections to the Iraqi Kurdistan National Assembly in July 2009.

Kurdistan Democratic Party (KDP): European Office (Germany), 10749 Berlin, POB 301516; tel. (30) 79743741; fax (30) 79743746; e-mail party@kdp.se; internet www.kdp.se; f. 1946; seeks to protect Kurdish rights and promote Kurdish culture and interests through regional political and legislative autonomy, as part of a federative republic; see also Kurdistan Alliance List; Pres. MASOUD BARZANI; Vice-Pres. NECHIRVAN BARZANI.

Kurdistan Islamic Union (Yakgrtui Islami Kurdistan): e-mail info@kurdiu.org; internet kurdiu.org; f. 1991; seeks establishment of an Islamic state in Iraq that recognizes the rights of Kurds; branch of the Muslim Brotherhood; contested July 2009 elections to the Iraqi Kurdistan National Assembly as part of the Service and Reform List; participated in the March 2010 legislative election independently; Sec.-Gen. MUHAMMAD FARAJ.

Kurdistan Socialist Democratic Party (KSDP): Sulaimaniya; e-mail info@psdkurdistan.org; internet www.psdkurdistan.com; f. 1994; splinter group of the KDP, aligned with the PUK; contested July 2009 elections to the Iraqi Kurdistan National Assembly as part of the Service and Reform List; Sec.-Gen. MUHAMMAD HAJI MAHMOUD.

Kurdistan Toilers Party (Hizbi Zahmatkeshani Kurdistan): f. 1985; advocates a federal Iraq; closely associated with the KSDP; contested July 2009 elections to the Iraqi Kurdistan Nat. Assembly as part of the Social Justice and Freedom List; Sec.-Gen. BALEN ABDULLAH.

Movement for Change (Gorran): e-mail info@gorran.net; internet www.gorran.org; f. 2006; established by fmr members of the PUK; advocates political and economic reform, anti-corruption measures and the independence of the judiciary; advocates a federal Iraq; contested July 2009 elections to the Iraqi Kurdistan Nat. Assembly as the Change List; contested the March 2010 legislative election independently; Leader NAWSHIRWAN MUSTAFA.

National Gathering of the People of Iraq: f. 2004 as the Iraqi People's Conference; name changed in 2009; Sunni; contested March 2010 legislative elections as part of the Iraqi Accord; Leader KHALED AL-BARAA.

National Rafidain List: e-mail info@alrafedainlist.com; internet www.alrafedainlist.com; f. 2004; Assyrian-Christian list headed by the Assyrian Democratic Movement; Leader YOUNADAM KANA.

National Reform Movement: f. 2008 by fmr mems of Islamic Dawa Party; Shi'ite; contested March 2010 legislative election as part of Iraqi Nat. Alliance; Leader IBRAHIM AL-JA'FARI.

National Tribal Gathering: f. 2007; Sunni; participated in March 2010 election as mem. of the Iraqi Accord list; Leader OMAR AL-HAYKAL.

Patriotic Union of Kurdistan (PUK): European Office (Germany), 10502 Berlin, POB 210213; tel. (30) 34097850; fax (30) 34097849; e-mail puk@puk.org; internet www.puk.org; f. 1975; seeks to protect and promote Kurdish rights and interests through self-determination; see also Kurdistan Alliance List; Pres. JALAL TALABANI.

Reconciliation and Liberation Bloc (Kutla al-Musalaha wa't-Tahrir): Mosul; f. 1995 in Jordan as Iraqi Homeland Party (Hizb al-Watan al-Iraqi); moved to Damascus, Syria, and to Mosul in 2003; liberal, secular Sunni; advocates withdrawal of coalition troops and partial rehabilitation of mems of the former Baathist regime; publishes *Al-Ittijah al-Akhar* newspaper; Leader MISH'AN AL-JUBURI.

Renewal List (Tajdeed): f. 2009 by Vice-Pres. Tariq al-Hashimi, following his resignation from the IIP; Sunni; contested March 2010 legislative election as part of the Iraqi Nat. Movement list; Leader TARIQ AL-HASHIMI.

Sadr II Movement (Jamaat al-Sadr al-Thani): Najaf; f. 2003; Shi'ite; opposes presence of US-led coalition in Iraq; mems of the Movement participated in the March 2010 legislative election as part of the Iraqi Nat. Alliance; military wing is Imam al-Mahdi Army; Leader Hojatoleslam MUQTADA AL-SADR.

Service and Reform List: alliance of Islamist and left-wing parties formed prior to the July 2009 elections to the Iraqi Kurdistan Nat. Assembly, comprising the Islamic Group of Kurdistan, the Kurdistan Islamic Union, the Kurdistan Socialist Democratic Party and the Future Party.

State of Law (Dawlat al-Kanoon): f. prior to 2009 provincial elections; contested March 2010 legislative election as a predominantly Shi'a alliance of parties and independent candidates, incl. the Islamic Dawa Party, the Independent Arab Movement and the Anbar Salvation Nat. Front.

Major militant groups that have launched attacks against Iraqis and the US-led coalition include: **Fedayeen Saddam** (Saddam's Martyrs; f. 1995 by mems of the former Baathist regime; paramilitary group); **Ansar al-Islam** (f. 1998; splinter group of IMIK; Islamist; suspected of having links with al-Qa'ida); **Hezbollah** (Shi'ite Marsh Arab; Leader ABD AL-KARIM MAHMOUD MOHAMMEDAWI—'ABU HATEM'); **Ansar al-Sunnah** (f. 2003 by mems of Ansar al-Islam; Islamist); **Imam al-Mahdi Army** (armed wing of the Sadr II Movement—Jamaat al-Sadr al-Thani); **Base of Holy War in Mesopotamia** (Tanzim Qa'idat al-Jihad fi Bilad al-Rafidain; Sunni insurgent network, also known as al-Qa'ida in Iraq; Leader AL-NASSER LIDEEN ALLAH ABU SULEIMAN, who was reported to have been killed in Feb. 2011); **Islamic State of Iraq** (Dawlat al-Iraq al-Islamiyya; network of Sunni insurgent groups; suspected of links with al-Qa'ida in Iraq; Leader ABU BAKR AL-BAGHDADI AL-HUSSEINI AL-QURASHI).

Diplomatic Representation

EMBASSIES IN IRAQ

Algeria: Hay al-Mansour, Baghdad; tel. (1) 543-4137; fax (1) 542-5829; Ambassador ABD AL-QADIR BIN SHA'A.

Australia: International Zone, Baghdad; tel. (1) 538-2103; e-mail austemb.baghdad@dfat.gov.au; internet www.iraq.embassy.gov.au; Ambassador LYNDALL SACHS.

Bahrain: 41/6/605 Hay al-Mutanabi, Baghdad; tel. (1) 580-8306; fax (1) 541-2027; e-mail baghdad.mission@mofa.gove.bh; internet www.mofa.gov.bh/baghdad; Ambassador SALAH AL-MALIKI.

Bangladesh: 6/14/929 Hay Babel, Baghdad; tel. (1) 719-0068; fax (1) 718-6045; Ambassador MUHAMMAD KAMAL EL-DIN.

Bulgaria: 12/25/624 al-Ameriya, Baghdad; tel. (1) 556-8197; fax (1) 556-4182; e-mail embassy.baghdad@mfa.bg; Ambassador VALERI RATCHEV.

Canada: International Zone, Baghdad; Chargé d'affaires STEPHANIE DUHAIME.

China, People's Republic: POB 2386, al-Jadryaa Post Office, Baghdad; tel. 7901912315 (mobile); e-mail chinaemb_iq@mfa.gov.cn; internet iq.chineseembassy.org; Ambassador NI JIAN.

Czech Republic: POB 27124, 37/11/601 Hay al-Mansour, Baghdad; tel. (1) 542-4868; fax (1) 214-2621; e-mail baghdad@embassy.mzv.cz; internet www.mzv.cz/baghdad; Ambassador ALEXANDR LANGER.

Egypt: 103/11/601 Hay al-Mansour, Baghdad; tel. (1) 543-0572; fax (1) 556-6346; e-mail egypt@uruklink.net; Ambassador SHERIF KAMAL SHAHIN.

France: POB 118, 7/55/102 Abu Nawas, Baghdad; tel. (964) 718-1996; fax (964) 718-1997; e-mail info@ambafrance-iq.org; internet www.ambafrance-iq.org; Ambassador DENYS GAUER.

Germany: POB 2036, Hay al-Mansour, Baghdad; tel. (1) 543-1470; fax (1) 543-5840; e-mail info@bagdad.diplo.de; internet www.bagdad.diplo.de; Ambassador BRITA WAGENER.

Greece: 63/31/913, Jadriyah University Sq., Hay Babel, Baghdad; tel. (1) 778-2273; e-mail gremb.bag@mfa.gr; Ambassador MIRKORIOZ KARAVOTHIAS.

Holy See: Apostolic Nunciature, POB 2090, 904/2/46 Saadoun St, Baghdad; tel. (1) 719-5183; e-mail nuntiusiraq@yahoo.com; Apostolic Nuncio Most Rev. GIORGIO LINGUA (Titular Archbishop of Tuscania).

India: POB 4114, 6/25/306 Hay al-Maghrib, Adhamiya, Baghdad; tel. (1) 422-2016; fax (1) 422-9549; e-mail eoibaghdad@yahoo.com; Ambassador SURESH K. REDDY.

Iran: POB 39095, Salehiya, Karadeh Maryam, Baghdad; tel. (1) 884-3033; fax (1) 537-5636; Ambassador HASSAN DANAFAR.

Italy: International Zone, Baghdad; tel. (1) 425-0720; e-mail ambasciata.baghdad@esteri.it; internet www.ambbaghdad.esteri.it/ambasciata_baghdad; Ambassador MASSIMO MAROTTI.

Japan: International Zone, Baghdad; tel. (1) 776-6791; e-mail azza_fh@yahoo.com; internet www.iraq.emb-japan.go.jp; Ambassador MASATO TAKAOKA.

Jordan: POB 6314, 145/49/617 Hay al-Andalus, Baghdad; tel. (1) 541-2892; fax (1) 541-2009; e-mail jordan@uruklink.net; Ambassador MUHAMMAD QARAAN.

Korea, Republic: POB 2387, Alwiya, Baghdad; e-mail kembiraq@mofat.go.kr; internet irq.mofat.go.kr; Ambassador KIM HYUN-MYUNG.

Kuwait: Baghdad; Ambassador GHASSAN YOUSEF AL-ZAWAWI.

Lebanon: Bldg 51, al-Askari St, 116 al-Sarafiya Area, Baghdad; tel. (1) 414-2711; fax (1) 885-6731; e-mail lebembbaghadad@yahoo.com; Chargé d'affaires NAWAF SHARIF HAZZA.

Netherlands: POB 2064, 7/15/215 International Zone, Baghdad; tel. (1) 778-2571; fax (1) 776-3513; e-mail bag@minbuza.nl; internet iraq.nlembassy.org; Ambassador JEANNETTE SEPPEN.

Pakistan: 14/7/609 Hay al-Mansour, Baghdad; fax (1) 542-8707; e-mail pakembbag@yahoo.com; Ambassador SHAH M. JAMAL.

Philippines: POB 3236, 4/22/915 Hay al-Jamiyah, al-Jadriya, Baghdad; tel. (1) 788-9761; fax (1) 719-3228; e-mail baghdad.pe@dfa.gov.ph; Chargé d'affaires a.i. MARLOWE A. MIRANDA.

Poland: 38/75 Karadat Mariam International Zone, Baghdad; tel. (1) 719-0297; fax (1) 719-0296; e-mail bagdad.amb.sekretariat@msz.gov.pl; internet www.bagdad.msz.gov.pl; Ambassador LECH STEFANIAK.

Romania: POB 2571, Arassat al-Hindia St, 452A/31/929 Hay Babel, Baghdad; tel. (1) 778-2860 fax (1) 778-7553; e-mail bagdad@mae.ro; Ambassador IACOB PRADA.

Russia: 4/5/605 Hay al-Mutanabi, Baghdad; tel. and fax (1) 541-4749; e-mail rusiraq@mail.ru; Ambassador ILYA MORGUNOV.

Serbia: POB 2061, 16/35/923 Hay Babel, Baghdad; tel. (1) 778-7887; fax (1) 778-0489; e-mail embsrbag@yahoo.com; internet www.baghdad.mfa.rs; Ambassador RADISAV PETROVIĆ.

Slovakia: 94/28/923 Hay Babel, Baghdad; tel. (1) 776-7367; fax (1) 776-7368; Ambassador MILOSLAV NAD.

Spain: POB 2072, 50/1/609 al-Mansour, Baghdad; e-mail emb.bagdad@maec.es; Ambassador JOSÉ TURPÍN MOLINA.

Sweden: POB 3475, Karadat Mariam, Baghdad; tel. 7801987450 (mobile); e-mail ambassaden.bagdad@foreign.ministry.se; internet www.swedenabroad.com/baghdad; Ambassador JÖRGEN LINDSTRÖM.

Syria: Hay al-Mansour, Baghdad; Ambassador SATTAM JAD'AN AL-DANDAH.

Tunisia: 1/49/617 Hay al-Andalus, Baghdad; tel. (1) 542-4569; Ambassador (vacant).

Turkey: POB 14001, 2/8 Waziriya, Baghdad; tel. (312) 218-6010; fax (312) 218-6110; e-mail embassy.baghdad@mfa.gov.tr; internet www.baghdad.emb.mfa.gov.tr; Ambassador YUNUS DEMIRER.

Ukraine: POB 15192, 50/1/609 al-Mansour, al-Yarmouk, Baghdad; tel. 7904167152 (mobile); fax 543-9849; e-mail emb_iq@mfa.gov.ua; internet iraq.mfa.gov.ua; Ambassador ANATOLII MARYNETS.

United Arab Emirates: 81/34/611 Hay al-Andalus (al-Daoudi), Baghdad; tel. (1) 543-9174, fax (1) 543-9093; Ambassador ABDULLAH IBRAHIM AL-SHEHHI.

United Kingdom: International Zone, Baghdad; e-mail britishconsulbaghdad@yahoo.co.uk; tel. 7901926280 (mobile); internet www.gov.uk/government/world/iraq; Ambassador SIMON COLLIS.

USA: Al-Kindi St, International Zone, Baghdad; e-mail baghdadirc@state.gov; internet iraq.usembassy.gov; Ambassador ROBERT STEPHEN BEECROFT.

Yemen: 4/36/904 Hay al-Wahada, Baghdad; tel. (1) 718-6682; fax (1) 717-2318; Ambassador ZAID HASSAN AL-WARITH.

Judicial System

Supreme Iraqi Criminal Tribunal: Following the ousting of the Baath regime, the judicial system was subject to a process of review and de-Baathification. In June 2003 the former Coalition Provisional Authority (CPA) established a **Judicial Review Committee**, the task of which was to review and repair the material status of the courts and to assess personnel. In December the Governing Council created the **Iraqi Special Tribune**, in order to bring to trial those senior members of the former regime accused of war crimes, crimes against humanity and genocide. The statute of the Tribune was amended by the former Transitional National Assembly in October 2005, when it was renamed the **Supreme Iraqi Criminal Tribunal**.

Central Criminal Court of Iraq: Consists of an **Investigative Court** and a **Trial Court**. It was created by the CPA in July 2003 as the senior court in Iraq, with jurisdiction over all crimes committed in the country since 19 March 2003. With a few exceptions, the application of justice was to be based upon the 1969 Penal Code of Iraq and the 1971 Criminal Proceedings Code of Iraq.

Higher Judicial Council: tel. (1) 538-4406; fax (1) 537-2267; e-mail iraqinfocenter@yahoo.com; internet www.iraqja.iq; Pres. HASSAN IBRAHIM HUSSEIN HUMAIRI.

Religion

ISLAM

About 95% of the population are Muslims, some 60% of whom are of the Shi'ite sect. The Arabs of northern Iraq, the Bedouins, the Kurds, the Turkomans and some of the inhabitants of Baghdad and Basra are mainly of the Sunni sect, while the remaining Arabs south of the Diyali are Shi'a.

CHRISTIANITY

There are Christian communities in all the principal towns of Iraq, but their main villages lie mostly in the Mosul district. The Christians of Iraq comprise three groups: the free Churches, including the Nestorian, Gregorian and Syrian Orthodox; the churches known as Uniate, since they are in union with the Roman Catholic Church, including the Armenian Uniates, Syrian Uniates and Chaldeans; mixed bodies of Protestant converts, New Chaldeans and Orthodox Armenians. There are estimated to be 500,000–700,000 Christians of various denominations in Iraq; however, there has been an exodus to neighbouring countries such as Syria and Jordan since the mid-2000s, as a result of the ongoing sectarian conflict.

The Assyrian Church

Assyrian Christians, an ancient sect having sympathies with Nestorian beliefs, were forced to leave their mountainous homeland in northern Kurdistan in the early part of the 20th century. The estimated 550,000 members of the Apostolic Catholic Assyrian Church of the East are now exiles, mainly in Iraq (about 50,000 adherents), Syria, Lebanon and the USA. Their leader is the Catholicos Patriarch, His Holiness MAR DINKHA IV.

The Orthodox Churches

Armenian Apostolic Church: Diocese of the Armenian Church of Iraq, POB 2280, al-Jadriya, Tayaran Sq., Baghdad; tel. (1) 815-1856; fax (1) 815-1857; e-mail iraqitem@yahoo.com; internet www.iraqitem.org; f. 1639; Primate Archbishop AVAK ASADOURIAN; 13 churches (four in Baghdad); 18,419 mems.

Syrian Orthodox Church: Syrian Orthodox Archbishopric, POB 843, al-Seenah St, Baghdad; tel. (1) 719-6320; fax (1) 719-7583; Archbishop of Baghdad and Basra SEVERIUS JAMIL HAWA; 12,000 adherents in Iraq.

The Greek Orthodox Church is also represented in Iraq.

The Roman Catholic Church

Armenian Rite

Archbishop of Baghdad: Most Rev. EMMANUEL DABBAGHIAN, 27/903 Archevêché Arménien Catholique, POB 2344, Karrada Sharkiya, Baghdad; tel. (1) 719-2461; e-mail dabbaghianemm@hotmail.com.

Chaldean Rite

Iraq comprises the patriarchate of Babylon, five archdioceses (including the patriarchal see of Baghdad) and five dioceses (all of which are suffragan to the patriarchate). Altogether, the Patriarch has jurisdiction over 21 archdioceses and dioceses in Iraq, Egypt, Iran, Lebanon, Syria, Turkey and the USA, and the Patriarchal Vicariate of Jerusalem.

Patriarch of Babylon of the Chaldeans: Cardinal EMMANUEL III DELLY, POB 6112, Patriarcat Chaldéen Catholique, al-Mansour, Baghdad; tel. (1) 537-9164; fax (1) 537-8556; e-mail info@st-addayyahoo.com.

Archbishop of Arbil: Most Rev. BASHAR WARDA, Archevêché Catholique Chaldéen, Ainkawa, Arbil; tel. (665) 225-0009.

Archbishop of Baghdad: the Patriarch of Babylon (q.v.).

Archbishop of Basra: Most Rev. IMAD AZIZ AL-BANNA, Archevêché Chaldéen, POB 217, Ashar-Basra; tel. (40) 613427; e-mail efather2006@yahoo.com.

Archbishop of Kirkuk: Most Rev. LOUIS SAKO, Archevêché Chaldéen, POB 490, Kirkuk; tel. (50) 220525; fax (50) 213978; e-mail luis_sako2@yahoo.com.

Archbishop of Mosul: Most Rev. EMIL SHIMOUN NONA, Archevêché Chaldéen, POB 757, Mayassa, Mosul; tel. (60) 815831; fax (60) 816742; e-mail archdioceseofmossul@yahoo.com.

Latin Rite

The archdiocese of Baghdad is directly responsible to the Holy See.

Archbishop of Baghdad: Most Rev. JEAN BENJAMIN SLEIMAN, Archevêché Latin, POB 35130, Hay al-Wahda—Mahallat 904, rue 8, Immeuble 44, 12906 Baghdad; tel. (1) 719-9537; fax (1) 717-2471; e-mail jbsleiman@yahoo.com.

Melkite Rite

The Greek-Melkite Patriarch of Antioch (GRÉGOIRE III LAHAM) is resident in Damascus, Syria.

Patriarchal Exarchate of Iraq: Exarchat Patriarchal Grec-Melkite, Karradat IN 903/10/50, Baghdad; tel. (1) 719-1082; 100 adherents (2006); Exarch Patriarchal (vacant).

Syrian Rite

Iraq comprises two archdioceses and the Patriarchal Exarchate of Basra.

Archbishop of Baghdad: Most Rev. ATHANASE MATTI SHABA MATOKA, Archevêché Syrien Catholique, 903/2/1 Baghdad; tel. (1) 719-1850; fax (1) 719-0166; e-mail mattishaba@yahoo.com.

Archbishop of Mosul: Most Rev. BOUTROS MOSHE, Archevêché Syrien Catholique, Hosh al-Khan, Mosul; tel. (60) 762160; fax (60) 771439; e-mail syrcam2003@yahoo.com.

The Anglican Communion

Within the Episcopal Church in Jerusalem and the Middle East, Iraq forms part of the diocese of Cyprus and the Gulf. Expatriate congregations in Iraq meet at St George's Church, Baghdad. The Bishop in Cyprus and the Gulf is resident in Cyprus.

JUDAISM

A tiny Jewish community, numbering only eight people in late 2008, remains in Baghdad.

OTHERS

About 550,000 Yazidis and a smaller number of Sabians and Shebeks reside in Iraq.

Sabian Community: al-Nasiriyah (Nasiriya); 20,000 adherents; Mandeans, mostly in Nasiriya; Head Sheikh DAKHIL.

Yazidis: Ainsifni; Leader TASHIN SAID ALI.

The Press

Since the overthrow of the regime of Saddam Hussain by US-led coalition forces in early 2003, the number of publications has proliferated: by the end of 2003 an estimated 250 newspapers and periodicals were in circulation, although only some 100 of these were reportedly still being published in 2008. Many newspapers are affiliated with political or religious organizations; however, the daily *Al-Sabah* is controlled by the Iraqi Government, with coalition backing. Security issues have resulted in severe distribution problems, and some newspaper offices have either relocated or chosen to publish online-only editions following threats being issued against journalists by militant groups, militias and security forces. A selection of publications is given below.

DAILIES

Al-Adala (Justice): Baghdad; e-mail aliisadik@yahoo.com; internet www.aladalanews.net; f. 2004; twice weekly; Arabic; organ of the Islamic Supreme Council of Iraq; publ. by the Al-Adala Group for Press, Printing and Publishing; Owner Dr ADIL ABD AL-MAHDI.

Baghdad: al-Zeitoun St, al-Harthiya, Baghdad; e-mail baghdadwifaq@yahoo.com; f. 1991; organ of the Iraqi Nat. Accord; Publr AYAD ALLAWI.

Al-Bayan (The Manifesto): Baghdad; f. 2003; Arabic; organ of Islamic Dawa Party; Man. Editor SADIQ AL-RIKABI.

Dar al-Salam (House of Peace): Baghdad; Arabic; organ of Iraqi Islamic Party.

Al-Dustur (The Constitution): Baghdad; f. 2003; Arabic; politics; independent; publ. by Al-Dustur Press, Publishing and Distribution House; Chair. BASIM AL-SHEIKH; Editor-in-Chief ALI AL-SHARQI.

Al-Jarida (The Newspaper): Baghdad; f. 2003; Arabic; organ of the Iraqi Arab Socialist Movement; Editor Prof. QAYS AL-AZZAWI.

Kul al-Iraq (All Iraq): Baghdad; e-mail info@kululiraq.com; internet www.kululiraq.com; f. 2003; Arabic; independent; Editor-in-Chief Dr ABBAS AL-SIRAF.

Al-Mada: 41/1 Abu Nuwas St, Baghdad; fax (1) 881-3256; e-mail fakhri_kareem@almadapaper.com; internet www.almadapaper.com; f. 2004; Arabic; independent; publ. by Al-Mada Foundation for Media, Culture and Arts; Editor-in-Chief FAKHRI KARIM.

Al-Mannarah (Minarets): Basra; tel. (40) 315758; e-mail almannarah@almannarah.com; internet www.almannarah.com; Arabic; publ. by South Press, Printing and Publishing Corpn; Editor-in-Chief Dr KHALAF AL-MANSHADI.

Al-Mashriq: Baghdad; internet www.al-mashriq.net; f. 2004; Arabic; independent; publ. by Al-Mashriq Institution for Media and Cultural Investments; circ. 25,000.

Al-Mutamar (Congress): Baghdad; e-mail almutamer@yahoo.com; internet www.inciraq.com/index_paper.php; f. 1993; Arabic; publ. by Iraqi Nat. Congress; Editor-in-Chief LUAY BALDAWI.

Al-Sabah: Baghdad; e-mail sabah@alsabaah.com; internet www.alsabaah.com; f. 2003; Arabic and English; state-controlled; publ. by the Iraqi Media Network; Deputy Editor-in-Chief ADNAN SHERKHAN.

Al-Sabah al-Jadid (New Morning): Baghdad; e-mail info@newsabah.com; internet www.newsabah.com; f. 2004; Arabic; independent; Editor-in-Chief ISMAIL ZAYER.

Sawt al-Iraq (Voice of Iraq): Baghdad; e-mail admin@sotaliraq.com; internet www.sotaliraq.com; online only; Arabic; independent.

Al-Taakhi (Brotherhood): e-mail badirkhansindi@yahoo.com; internet www.taakhinews.org; f. 1967; Kurdish and Arabic; organ of the Kurdistan Democratic Party (KDP); publ. by Al-Taakhi Publishing and Printing House; Editor-in-Chief Dr BADIRKHAN SINDI; circ. 20,000 (Baghdad).

Tariq al-Sha'ab (People's Path): Saadoun St, Baghdad; e-mail altareeq_1934@yahoo.com; internet www.iraqcp.org; f. 1974; Arabic and English; organ of the Iraqi Communist Party; Editor ABD AL-RAZZAK AL-SAFI.

Xebat: Arbil; e-mail info@xebat.net; internet www.xebat.net; f. 1959; Arabic and Kurdish; organ of the KDP; Editor-in-Chief NAZHAD AZIZ SURME.

Al-Zaman (Time): Baghdad; tel. (1) 717-7587; e-mail postmaster@azzaman.com; internet www.azzaman.com; f. 1997 in the United Kingdom, f. 2003 in Baghdad; Arabic, with some news translated into English; Editor-in-Chief SAAD AL-BAZZAZ.

WEEKLIES

Al-Ahali (The People): Baghdad; e-mail info@ahali-iraq.net; internet www.ahali-iraq.net; Arabic; politics; Editor HAVAL ZAKHOUBI.

Alif Baa al-Iraq: Baghdad; Arabic and English; general, social and political affairs.

Habazbuz fi Zaman al-Awlamah (Habazbuz in the Age of Globalization): Baghdad; f. 2003; Arabic; satirical; Editor ISHTAR AL-YASIRI.

Iraq Today: Baghdad; f. 2003; English; current affairs; Founder and Editor-in-Chief HUSSAIN SINJARI.

Al-Iraq al-Yawm (Iraq Today): Baghdad; e-mail iraqtoday@iraqtoday.net; Arabic and English; Editor ISRA SHAKIR.

Al-Ittihad (Union): Baghdad and Sulaimaniya; tel. (1) 543-8954; e-mail alitthad@alitthad.com; internet www.alitthad.com; Arabic and Kurdish; publ. by the Patriotic Union of Kurdistan; Editor ABD AL-HADI; circ. 30,000 (Baghdad).

Al-Ittijah al-Akhar (The Other Direction): Baghdad; tel. (1) 776-3334; fax (1) 776-3332; e-mail alitijahalakhar@yahoo.com; internet www.alitijahalakhar.com; Arabic; organ of Reconciliation and Liberation Bloc; Chair. and Editor MISHAAN AL-JUBOURI.

Kurdish Globe: Salah al-Din Highway, Pirzeen, Arbil; tel. (66) 2526792; e-mail info@kurdishglobe.net; internet www.kurdishglobe.net; f. 2005; English; Kurdish news and issues; Exec. Editor JAWAD QADIR; circ. 40,000.

Majallati: POB 8041, Children's Culture House, Baghdad; Arabic; children's newspaper; Editor-in-Chief Dr SHAFIQ AL-MAHDI.

Al-Muajaha (The Witness): 6/41/901, Karrada Dakhil, Baghdad; e-mail almuajaha@riseup.net; f. 2003; Arabic and English; current affairs; independent; Editor RAMZI MAJID JARRAR.

Al-Nahda (Renaissance): Basra; f. 2003; Arabic; organ of the Independent Democratic Gathering; Publr ADNAN PACHACHI.

Regay Kurdistan: Arbil; e-mail dwalapere@regaykurdistan.com; internet www.regaykurdistan.com; Arabic and Kurdish; organ of the Iraqi and Kurdistan Communist Parties; Editor-in-Chief HANDREN AHMAD.

Al-Sina'i (The Industrialist): Baghdad; Arabic; general; publ. by the Nat. Industrialist Coalition; Editor-in-Chief Dr ZAYD ABD AL-MAJID BILAL.

Al-Waqai al-Iraqiya (Official Gazette of the Republic of Iraq): Ministry of Justice, Baghdad; tel. (1) 537-2023; e-mail Hashim_Jaffar_alsaieg@yahoo.com; f. 1922; Arabic and English; Dir HASHIM N. JAFFAR; circ. 5,000.

PERIODICALS

Hawlati: e-mail hawlati2000@yahoo.com; internet www.hawlati.info; f. 2001; fortnightly; Kurdish, Arabic and English; independent, privately owned; mainly Kurdish politics; Publr TARIQ FATIH; Editor KAMAL RAOUF.

Majallat al-Majma' al-'Ilmi al-Iraqi (Journal of the Academy of Sciences): POB 4023, Waziriya, Baghdad; tel. (1) 422-4202; fax (1) 422-2066; e-mail iraqacademy@yahoo.com; internet www.iraqacademy.iq; f. 1950; quarterly; Arabic; scholarly magazine on Arabic Islamic culture; Editor-in-Chief Prof. Dr AHMAD MATLOUB.

Al-Sa'ah (The Hour): Baghdad; twice weekly; Arabic; organ of the Iraqi Unified Nat. Movement; Publr AHMAD AL-KUBAYSI; Editor NI'MA ABD AL-RAZZAQ.

Sawt al-Talaba (Voice of the Students): Baghdad; fortnightly; Arabic; publ. by New Iraq Youth and Students' Org; Editor MUSTAFA AL-HAYIM.

NEWS AGENCIES

Aswat al-Iraq (Voices of Iraq): e-mail aswat.info@gmail.com; internet www.aswataliraq.info; f. 2004; Arabic, English and Kurdish; independent news agency with contributions from Iraqi correspondents and three Iraqi newspapers; Editor-in-Chief ZUHAIR AL-JEZAIRI.

National Iraqi News Agency: Baghdad; tel. (1) 719-3459; e-mail news@ninanews.com; internet www.ninanews.com; f. 2005; Arabic and English; independent; Chair. Dr FARID AYAR; Man. Dir ABD AL-MUHSEN HUSSAIN JAWAD.

PRESS ORGANIZATION

Iraqi Union for Journalists: POB 14101, nr al-Resafah Bldg, al-Waziriya, Baghdad; tel. (1) 537-0762; fax (1) 422-6011; e-mail iraqiju@yahoo.com; Chair. MUAID AL-LAMI.

Publishers

Afaq Arabiya Publishing House: POB 4032, Adamiya, Baghdad; tel. (1) 443-6044; fax (1) 444-8760; publr of literary monthlies, periodicals and cultural books; Chair. Dr MOHSIN AL-MUSAWI.

Dar al-Ma'mun for Translation and Publishing: POB 24015, Karradat Mariam, Baghdad; tel. (1) 538-3171; publr of newspapers and magazines.

Al-Hurriyah Printing Establishment: Karantina, Sarrafiya, Baghdad; f. 1970.

Al-Jamaheer Press House: POB 491, Sarrafiya, Baghdad; tel. (1) 416-9341; fax (1) 416-1875; f. 1963; publr of a number of newspapers and magazines; Pres. SAAD QASSEM HAMMOUDI.

Kurdish Culture and Publishing House: Baghdad; f. 1976.

Al-Ma'arif Ltd: Mutanabi St, Baghdad; f. 1929; publishes periodicals and books in Arabic, Kurdish, Turkish, French and English.

Al-Mada Foundation for Media, Culture and Arts: 141 Abu Nuwas St, Baghdad; tel. 7702799999 (mobile); e-mail info@almadapaper.net; internet www.almadapaper.net; f. 1994; Dir FAKHRI KARIM.

Al-Muthanna Library: POB 14019, Mutanabi St, Baghdad; tel. 770-3649664 (mobile); e-mail mail@almuthannabooks.com; internet www.almuthannabooks.com; f. 1936; booksellers and publrs of books and monographs in Arabic and oriental languages; Propr ANAS AL-RAJAB; Dir IBRAHIM AL-RAJAB.

Al-Nahdah: Mutanabi St, Baghdad; tel. (1) 416-2689; e-mail yehya_azawy@yahoo.com; politics, Arab affairs.

National House for Publishing, Distribution and Advertising: POB 624, al-Jumhuriya St, Baghdad; tel. (1) 425-1846; f. 1972; publishes books on politics, economics, education, agriculture, sociology, commerce and science in Arabic and other Middle Eastern languages; Dir-Gen. M. A. ASKAR.

Al-Thawra Printing and Publishing House: POB 2009, Aqaba bin Nafi's Sq., Baghdad; tel. (1) 719-6161; f. 1970; Chair. (vacant).

PUBLISHERS' ASSOCIATION

Iraqi Publishers' Association: Baghdad; tel. (1) 416-9279; fax (1) 416-7584; e-mail al_nasheren@yahoo.com; Chair. Dr ABD AL-WAHAB AL-RADI.

Broadcasting and Communications

REGULATORY AUTHORITY

Communications and Media Commission (CMC): POB 2044, Hay Babel, al-Masbah, Baghdad; tel. (1) 718-0009; fax (1) 719-5839; e-mail enqiries@cmc.iq; internet www.cmc.iq; f. 2004 by fmr Coalition Provisional Authority; independent telecoms and media regulator; responsibilities include the award and management of telecommunications licences, broadcasting, media and information services, as well as spectrum allocation and management; CEO SAFAA RABEE.

TELECOMMUNICATIONS

Under the former Baathist regime, the Iraqi Telecommunications and Posts Co was the sole provider of telecommunications and postal services. Following the removal from power of Saddam Hussain, in 2003 the Coalition Provisional Authority issued three short-term licences for the provision of mobile telephone services to stimulate competition in the sector. Asiacell, led by the Iraqi Kurdish Asiacell Co for Telecommunication Ltd, was awarded the licence for the northern region; the licence for Baghdad and the central region was won by Orascom Telecom Iraq Corpn (Iraqna), led by Orascom Telecom of Egypt; and Atheer Telecom Iraq (MTC Atheer), led by the Mobile Telecommunications Co of Kuwait, won the licence for Basra and the southern region. In August 2007 Asiacell, Korek Telecom Ltd and MTC Atheer (which subsequently acquired 100% of Iraqna shares and was renamed Zain) won the auction launched by the Government for three new national licences to provide mobile telephone services over a 15-year period; Iraqna withdrew from the bidding process.

Asiacell: Headquarters Bldg, Sulaimaniya; e-mail customercare@asiacell.com; internet www.asiacell.com; f. 1999; 51% owned by Asiacell Co for Telecommunication Ltd, 40% by Wataniya Telecom (Kuwait) and 9% owned by United Gulf Bank (Bahrain); 6.0m. subscribers (Dec. 2008); Chair. of Bd FAROUK MUSTAFA RASOUL.

Iraqi Telecommunications and Posts Co (ITPC): POB 2450, Abu Nuwas St, Baghdad; tel. (1) 718-0400; fax (1) 718-2125; state-owned; Dir-Gen. KASSIM AL-HASSANI.

Korek Telecom Ltd: Kurdistan St, Pirmam, Arbil; tel. (66) 243-3455; e-mail info@korektel.com; internet korektel.com; f. 2001; 1.5m. subscribers (Dec. 2007); CEO HUMAM AMARA.

Zain: Basra; e-mail info@iq.zain.com; internet www.zain.com; f. 2003 as MTC Atheer, a subsidiary of Mobile Telecommunications Co (Kuwait); acquired Iraqna Co for Mobile Phone Services Ltd (operated by Orascom Telecom Holding—Egypt) in Dec. 2007; name changed to above in Jan. 2008; 9.7m. subscribers (Dec. 2008); CEO EMAD MAKIYA.

BROADCASTING

The **Iraqi Media Network (IMN)** was established by the former Coalition Provisional Authority (CPA) to replace the Ministry of Information following the ousting of the former regime. The IMN established new television and both FM and AM radio stations. In January 2004 the CPA announced that a consortium led by the US-based Harris Corpn had been awarded the contract to take over from the IMN the control of 18 television channels, two radio stations and the *Al-Sabah* daily newspaper.

Iraqi Media Network (IMN): Baghdad; e-mail info@imn.iq; internet www.imn.iq; f. 2003.

Al-Iraqiya Television: Baghdad; internet www.imn.iq/pages/iraqia-tv; terrestrial and satellite television.

Iraq Media Network—Southern Region: internet www.imnsr.com.

Republic of Iraq Radio: Baghdad; e-mail rir.info@iraqimedianet.net; internet www.imn.iq/pages/radio-iraqia.

Radio

Radio Dijla: House 3, Hay al-Jamia Zone 635/52, Baghdad; tel. (1) 555-8787; e-mail post@radiodijla.com; internet www.radiodijla.com; f. 2004; privately owned; first talk radio station to be established in post-invasion Iraq; also broadcasts music programmes; Founder Dr AHMAD AL-RIKABI.

Voice of Iraq: Baghdad; e-mail admin@voiraq.com; internet www.voiraq.com; f. 2003; privately owned AM radio station; broadcasts music, news and current affairs programmes in Arabic, Turkmen and English.

Television

Al-Sharqiya: 10/13/52 Karrada Kharj, Baghdad; tel. (88216) 6775-1380 (satellite); e-mail alsharqiya@alsharqiya.com; internet www.alsharqiya.com; f. 2004; privately owned; independent; broadcasts news and entertainment programming 24 hours a day terrestrially and via satellite; Founder SAAD AL-BAZZAZ; Dir ALAA AL-DAHAN.

Alsumaria TV: Beirut, Lebanon; tel. and fax 9614533344 (mobile); e-mail communication-department@alsumaria.tv; internet www.alsumaria.tv; f. 2004; privately owned, independent satellite network; broadcasts news, entertainment and educational programming 24 hours a day; currently operates from temporary offices in Lebanon.

Finance

(cap. = capital; res = reserves; dep. = deposits; brs = branches; m. = million; amounts in Iraqi dinars, unless otherwise stated)

All banks and insurance companies in Iraq, including all foreign companies, were nationalized in July 1964. The assets of foreign companies were taken over by the state. In May 1991 the Government announced its decision to end the state's monopoly in banking, and during 1992–2000 17 private banks were established; however, they were prohibited by the former regime from conducting international transactions. Following the establishment of the Coalition Provisional Authority in 2003, efforts were made to reform the state-owned Rafidain and Rashid Banks, and in October the Central Bank allowed private banks to begin processing international transactions. In January 2004 the Central Bank of Iraq announced that three foreign banks—HSBC and Standard Chartered (both of the United Kingdom), and the National Bank of Kuwait—had been awarded licences to operate in Iraq, the first such licences awarded for 40 years. A further five foreign banks had also been granted licences by mid-2005. There were six public sector and 37 private sector banks operating in Iraq in 2011.

BANKING

Central Bank

Central Bank of Iraq (CBI): POB 64, al-Rashid St, Baghdad; tel. (1) 816-5170; fax (1) 816-6802; e-mail cbi@cbi.iq; internet www.cbi.iq; f. 1947 as Nat. Bank of Iraq; name changed as above 1956; has the sole right of note issue; cap. 100,000m., res 246,026m., dep. 28,479,125m. (Dec. 2009); Gov. ABD AL-BASET TURKI (acting); 4 brs.

State-owned Commercial Banks

Rafidain Bank: POB 11360, Banks St, Baghdad; tel. (1) 816-0287; fax (1) 816-5035; e-mail emailcenter9@yahoo.com; internet www.rafidain-bank.org; f. 1941; cap. 25,000m., res 49,730m., dep. 22,638,963m. (Dec. 2007); Dir-Gen. HABIB ZIA ALCKHEON; 147 brs in Iraq, 8 brs abroad.

Rashid Bank: al-Rashid St, Baghdad; tel. (1) 885-3411; fax (1) 882-6201; e-mail natbank@uruklink.net; internet www.rasheedbank.gov.iq; f. 1988; cap. 2,000m., res 6,024m., dep. 815,522m. (Dec. 2001); total assets US $750m. (2003); Chair. KADHIM M. NASHOOR; 161 brs.

Private Commercial Banks

Babylon Bank: al-Amara St, Baghdad; tel. (1) 717-3686; fax (1) 719-1014; e-mail info@babylonbank-iq.com; internet www.babylonbank-iq.com; f. 1999; cap. and res 31,310m., total assets 89,981m. (Dec. 2007); Chair. ABD AL-RAZZAQ AL-MANSOUR; Gen. Dir TARIQ ABD AL-BAKI ABOUD; 6 brs.

Bank of Baghdad: POB 3192, al-Karada St, Alwiya, Baghdad; tel. (1) 717-5007; fax (1) 717-5006; internet www.bankofbaghdad.org; f. 1992; 50.6% stake owned by Burgan Bank (Kuwait); cap. 100,000m., res 5,118m., dep. 804,688m. (Dec. 2010); Chair. IMAD ISMAEL SHARIF; Man. Dir ADNAN AL-CHALABI; 5 brs.

Commercial Bank of Iraq PSC (CBIQ): Saadoun St, Alwiya, Baghdad; tel. (1) 740-5583; fax (1) 718-4312; e-mail cb.iraq@ahliunited.com; internet www.ahliunited.com/bh_aub_cbiq.html; f. 1992; Ahli United Bank BSC (Bahrain) acquired 49% stake in Dec. 2005; cap. US $60m., dep. $59.6m., total assets $124.3m. (2006); Chair. FAHAD AL-RAJAAN; CEO and Man. Dir ADEL A. AL-LABBAN; 10 brs.

Credit Bank of Iraq: POB 3420, Saadoun St, Alwiya, Baghdad; tel. (1) 718-2198; fax (1) 717-0156; e-mail creditbkiq@yahoo.com; f. 1998; 75% owned by Nat. Bank of Kuwait SAK, 10% by World Bank's Int. Finance Corpn and 15% by private investors; cap. 1,250m., res 528m., dep. 16,376.9m. (Dec. 2002); Chair. HIKMET H. KUBBA; Man. Dir FOUAD M. MUSTAFA; 12 brs.

Gulf Commercial Bank: POB 3101, nr Baghdad Hotel, Saadoun St, Alwiya, Baghdad; tel. (1) 719-8534; fax (1) 778-8251; e-mail admn@gulfbankiraq.com; f. 2000; cap. 37,500m. (Jan. 2009); Chair. ABU TALIB HASHIM; 14 brs.

National Bank of Iraq (al-Ahli al-Iraqi Bank): Saadoun St, nr Firdos Sq., Baghdad 11194; tel. (1) 717-7735; fax (6) 569-5942; e-mail Info@nbirq.com; internet www.nbirq.com; f. 1995; 59% owned by Capital Bank of Jordan; Chair. TALAL FANAR AL-FAISAL; 4 brs.

Sumer Commercial Bank: POB 3876, Hay al-Riad, Section 908, St 16, Baghdad; tel. (1) 719-6472; internet www.sumerbankiq.com; cap. 10,200m., res 531m., dep. 7,500m. (Aug. 2005); Chair. KHALIL KHAIRALLAH S. AL-JUMAILI; Man. Dir FOUAD HAMZA AL-SAEED; 9 brs.

Specialized Banks

Agricultural Co-operative Bank of Iraq: POB 2421, al-Rashid St, Baghdad; tel. (1) 886-4768; fax (1) 886-5047; e-mail agriculturalcoopbank@yahoo.com; internet www.agriculturalbank.gov.iq; f. 1936; state-owned; Dir-Gen. MUHAMMAD H. AL-KHAFAJI; 32 brs.

Basra International Bank for Investment: Watani St, Ashar, Basra; tel. (40) 616955; internet www.basrahbank.net; cap. 55,000m., res 10,320m., dep. 110,850m. (Dec. 2007); Chair. HUSSEIN GHALIB KUBBA; Man. Dir HASSAN GHALIB KUBBA; 12 brs.

Dar el-Salaam Investment Bank: POB 3067, al-Saadoun Park 103/41/3, Alwiya, Baghdad; tel. (1) 719-6488; e-mail info@desiraq.com; internet www.desiraq.com; f. 1999; 70.1% share acquired by HSBC (United Kingdom) in 2005; total assets 35,562m. (Aug. 2005); 14 brs.

Economy Bank for Investment and Finance (EBIF): 14 Ramadan St, al-Mansour Sq., Baghdad; tel. (1) 298-7712; fax (1) 298-7713; e-mail info@economybankiraq.com; internet www.economybankiraq.com; f. 1997; CEO HOUSSAM OBEID ALI; 23 brs.

Industrial Bank of Iraq: POB 5825, al-Sinak, Baghdad; tel. (1) 887-2181; fax (1) 888-3047; e-mail bank2004@maktoob.com; f. 1940;

state-owned; total assets US $34.7m. (2003); Dir-Gen. BASSIMA ABD AL-HADDI AL-DHAHIR; 9 brs.

Investment Bank of Iraq: POB 3724, 902/2/27 Hay al-Wahda, Alwiya, Baghdad; tel. (1) 719-9042; fax (1) 719-8505; e-mail chairman@ibi-bankiraq.com; internet www.ibi-bankiraq.com; f. 1993; cap. 75,020m., res 4,978m., dep. 139,014m. (Dec. 2010); Chair. THAMIR RESOUKI ABD AL-WAHAB AL-SHEIKHLY; Gen. Man. HAMZA DAWOUD SALMAN HALBOUN; 18 brs.

Iraqi Islamic Bank for Investment and Development: 609/18/67, al-Mansour, Baghdad; tel. (1) 416-4939; fax (1) 414-0697; e-mail info@iraqiislamicb.com; internet www.iraqiislamicb.com; f. 1992; Chair. Dr TARIQ KHALAF AL-ABDULLAH.

Iraqi Middle East Investment Bank: POB 10379, Bldg 65, Hay Babel, 929 Arasat al-Hindiya, Baghdad; tel. (1) 717-5545; e-mail cendep@iraqimdlestbank.com; internet www.iraqinet.net/com/3/mdlestbank.htm; f. 1993; cap. 66,000m., res 9,901m., dep. 463,328m. (Dec. 2010); Man. Dir M. F. AL-ALOOSI; Exec. Man. SUDAD A. AZIZ; 19 brs.

Kurdistan International Bank for Investment and Development: 70 Abd al-Salam Barzani St, Arbil; tel. (66) 223-0822; fax (66) 253-1369; e-mail info@kibid.com; internet www.kibid.com; f. 2005; private bank; cap. 100,000m., res 27,256m., dep. 324,315m. (Dec. 2010); Chair. SALAR MUSTAFA HAKIM; 4 brs.

Mosul Bank for Development and Investment: POB 1292, al-Markaz St, Mosul; tel. (60) 813-090; fax (60) 815-411; e-mail mosul_bank@yahoo.com; internet www.mosulbank.com.

Real Estate Bank of Iraq: POB 8118, 29/222 Haifa St, Baghdad; tel. (1) 885-3212; fax (1) 884-0980; e-mail estatebank194@yahoo.com; internet www.reb-iraq.com; f. 1949; state-owned; gives loans to assist the building industry; acquired the Co-operative Bank in 1970; total assets US $10m. (2003); Dir-Gen. ABD AL-RAZZAQ AZIZ; 25 brs.

United Bank for Investment: 906/14/69, al-Wathiq Sq., Hay al-Wehda, Baghdad; tel. (1) 888-112; e-mail unitedbank2004@yahoo.com; internet www.unitedbank–iq.net; f. 1995; Chair. IBRAHIM HASSAN AL-BADRI; Man. Dir ZIAD ABBAS HASHEM; 8 brs.

Warka Bank for Investment and Finance: POB 3559, 902/14/50, Hay al-Wehda, Baghdad; tel. (1) 717-4970; fax (1) 717-9555; e-mail info@warka-bank-iq.com; internet www.warka-bank.com; f. 1999; private bank; cap. 24,000m. (2006); Chair. and CEO SAAD SAADOUN AL-BUNNIA; 130 brs.

Trade Bank

Trade Bank of Iraq (TBI): POB 28445, Bldg 20, St 1, 608 al-Yarmouk District, Baghdad; tel. (1) 543-3561; fax (1) 543-3560; e-mail info@tbiraq.com; internet www.tbiraq.com; f. 2003 by fmr Coalition Provisional Authority to facilitate Iraq's exports of goods and services and the country's reconstruction; independent of Cen. Bank of Iraq; cap. US $427m., res $3m., dep. $13,321m. (Dec. 2010); Chair. HAMDIYAH MAHMOOD FARAJ AL-JAFF; 7 brs.

INSURANCE

Iraqi Insurance Diwan: Ministry of Finance, 147/6/47 Hay al-Eloom, Baghdad; tel. (1) 416-8030; e-mail IraqiInsuranceDiwan@iraqinsurance.org; internet www.iraqinsurance.org; f. 2005 as independent regulator for the insurance sector.

Ahlia Insurance Co: al-Tahreeat Sq., Baghdad; tel. (790) 4565829 (mobile); e-mail info@aic-iraq.com; internet www.aic-iraq.com; f. 2001; privately owned; general, marine, engineering, motor, health and life insurance; Chair. SAADOUN KUBBA; Gen. Man. SAADOUN M. KHAMIS AL-RUBAI.

Al-Hamra'a Insurance Co: POB 10491, Karrada, Baghdad; tel. (1) 717-7573; fax (1) 717-7574; e-mail info@alhamraains.com; internet www.alhamraains.com; f. 2001; private co; general and life insurance; CEO Dr YASIR RAOOF.

Iraq Insurance Co: POB 989, Khaled bin al-Walid St, Aqaba bin Nafi Sq., Baghdad; tel. (1) 719-2185; fax (1) 719-2606; state-owned; life, fire, accident and marine insurance.

Iraq Reinsurance Co: POB 297, Aqaba bin Nafi Sq., Khalid bin al-Waleed St, Baghdad; tel. (1) 719-5131; fax (1) 719-1497; e-mail iraqre@yahoo.com; f. 1960; state-owned; transacts reinsurance business on the international market; Chair. and Gen. Man. SAID ABBAS M. A. MIRZA.

National Insurance Co: POB 248, National Insurance Co Bldg, al-Khullani St, Baghdad; tel. (1) 885-3026; fax (1) 886-1486; f. 1950; state-owned; cap. 20m.; all types of general and life insurance, reinsurance and investment; Chair. and Gen. Man. MUHAMMAD HUSSAIN JAAFAR ABBAS.

STOCK EXCHANGE

Iraq Stock Exchange (ISX): Baghdad; tel. (1) 717-4484; e-mail Info-isx@isx-iq.net; internet www.isx-iq.net; f. 2004, following the closure of the fmr Baghdad Stock Exchange by the Coalition Provisional Authority in March 2003; 84 cos listed in Oct. 2013; CEO TAHA AHMAD ABD AL-SALAM.

Trade and Industry

DEVELOPMENT ORGANIZATION

Iraq Foreign Investment Board: e-mail info@ishtargate.org; internet www.ishtargate.org; seeks to attract inward private sector investment into Iraq and to stimulate domestic capital resources for growth and innovation, as well as promote Iraqi businesses; Senior Advisor WILLIAM C. DAHM.

CHAMBERS OF COMMERCE

Federation of Iraqi Chambers of Commerce: POB 3388, Saadoun St, Alwiya, Baghdad; tel. (1) 717-1798; fax (1) 719-2479; e-mail ficcbaghdad@yahoo.com; internet www.ficciraqbag.org; f. 1969; all 18 Iraqi chambers of commerce are affiliated to the Federation; Chair. JAAFAR AL-HAMADANI.

Arbil Chamber of Commerce and Industry: Chamber of Commerce and Industry Bldg, Aras St, Arbil; tel. (66) 2222014; e-mail erbilchamberofcommerce@yahoo.com; internet www.erbilchamber.org; f. 1966; Chair. DARA JALIL KHAYAT.

Baghdad Chamber of Commerce: POB 5015, al-Sanal, Baghdad; tel. (1) 880-220; fax (1) 816-3347; e-mail baghdad_chamber@yahoo.com; internet www.baghdadchamber.com; f. 1926; Chair. AMJAD ABD AL-KARIM AL-JUBURI.

Basra Chamber of Commerce: Manawi Pasha, Ashar, Basra; tel. (40) 614630; e-mail info@bcoc-iraq.net; internet www.bcoc-iraq.net; f. 1926; Chair. MAKKI HASSAN HAMADI AL-SUDANI.

Kirkuk Chamber of Commerce: Kirkuk; e-mail kirkukchamber@yahoo.com; f. 1957; Chair SABAH AL-DIN MUHAMMAD AL-SALIHI.

Mosul Chamber of Commerce: POB 35, Mosul; tel. (60) 774771; fax (60) 771359; e-mail mcc19262000@yahoo.com; Chair. MUKBIL SIDIQ AL-DABAGH.

Sulaimaniya Chamber of Commerce and Industry: Sulaimaniya; e-mail info@sulcci.com; internet www.sulcci.com; Chair. HASSAN BAQI HORAMI.

EMPLOYERS' ORGANIZATION

Iraqi Federation of Industries: 191/22/915 al-Zaweya, Karada, Baghdad; tel. (1) 778-3502; fax (1) 776-3041; e-mail info@fediraq.org; internet www.fediraq.org; f. 1956; 35,000 mems; Pres. HASHIM THANOUN AL-ATRAKCHI.

PETROLEUM AND GAS

Ministry of Oil: Oil Complex Bldg, Port Said St, Baghdad; tel. (1) 727-0710; e-mail oilministry@oil.gov.iq; internet www.oil.gov.iq; merged with INOC in 1987; affiliated cos: Oil Marketing Co, Oil Projects Co, Oil Exploration Co, Oil Products Distribution Co, Iraqi Oil Tankers Co, Gas Filling Co, Oil Pipelines Co, Iraqi Drilling Co, North Oil Co, South Oil Co, Missan Oil Co, North Refineries Co, Midland Refineries Co, South Refineries Co, North Gas Co, South Gas Co.

Iraq National Oil Co (INOC): POB 476, Khullani Sq., Baghdad; tel. (1) 887-1115; f. 1964; reorg. upon nationalization of Iraq's petroleum industry, and became solely responsible for exploration, production, transportation and marketing of Iraqi crude petroleum and petroleum products; merged with Ministry of Oil in 1987, and remained under its authority following the overthrow of the regime of Saddam Hussain in 2003; draft legislation providing for the reconstitution of INOC as an independent entity was approved by the Council of Ministers in July 2009; under the proposed reorganization, INOC would be responsible for the management and development of Iraq's petroleum industry and would assume control of the existing state-run oil and gas cos.

UTILITIES

Electricity

Electricity production in Iraq has been greatly diminished as a result of the US-led military campaign in 2003, subsequent looting and sabotage by Baathist loyalists, and disruptions in fuel supplies to power stations. Power outages are common, especially in Baghdad and the surrounding area, and the Government has resorted to power-rationing. With ongoing reconstruction of the means of generation, transmission and distribution, the Ministry of Electricity was achieving peak production levels of 6,750 MW by early 2009, supplying intermittent power for only 14 hours a day.

Water

The Ministry of Water Resources manages the supply of water throughout Iraq. Water resources are diminishing, and a large-scale investment programme is currently under way, which includes funding for new dam and irrigation projects, repairs to damaged facilities, and improvements in technology. Following years of neglect during the period of UN sanctions, infrastructure has also been damaged since the US-led military campaign in 2003, largely as a result of vandalism and looting. The Baghdad Water Authority is responsible for the management of water resources in the capital.

MAJOR COMPANIES

In June 2003, following the removal from power of the Baathist regime, it was reported that the 48 companies and enterprises controlled by the Ministry of Industry and Minerals were to start being privatized within the next year.

Al-Aftan Group: Bldg 49, St 19, 929, Hay Babel, al-Masbah, Baghdad; tel. (1) 718-0059; fax (1) 719-4823; e-mail alaa@alaftan.com; internet www.alaftan.com; 12 cos; engineering, construction, medical supplies, transport, general trading; some 3,500 employees.

Agmest Group: Karrada Kharij, Hay Babil POB 2489, Jodriah, Baghdad; tel. (1) 719-8822; fax (1) 717-3136; e-mail office2@agmest.com; internet www.agmest.com; f. 1989; nine cos; telecommunications, general trading, construction, engineering, pharmaceutical supplies; 1,120 employees.

Alousi Associates Technical Studies Bureau: Hasib Saleh Bldg, Nidhal St, Baghdad; tel. (1) 719-2833; e-mail faisal@alousi-associates.com; internet www.alousi-associates.com; f. 1974; architectural design and planning; offices in Cyprus and Singapore; Contact MAATH AL-ALOUSI.

American-Iraqi Solutions Group: APO AE 09348, Baghdad; e-mail info@aisgiraq.com; internet www.aisgiraq.com; 11 cos involved in reconstruction projects, incl. real estate, construction, security, travel, recruitment and investment; Contact STEVE FITZSIMONS; 60,000 employees.

Baghdad Co for Rehabilitation and Maintenance: 903/77/9, al-Karada, Baghdad; fax (1) 719-2924; e-mail baghdadboilers@gmail.com; internet www.baghdadcompany.com; jt venture with the Ministry of Industry and Minerals; power station construction, network transmission lines, water treatment; Man. Dir BASIL NAJI MAHMOUD.

Baghdad Factory for Furniture: Baghdad; tel. 7901-521066 (mobile); internet www.baghdadfurniture.com; f. 1996; under Ministry of Industry and Minerals supervision.

Al-Baqier Co: tel. 7704-435285 (mobile); e-mail mohamedbaqer@yahoo.com; internet www.albaqier.com; construction, electrical and mechanical contracting, general trading; Exec. Admin. MUHAMMAD BAQIER ISMAEL.

Basrah East Co Ltd: POB 2141, Basra; tel. (40) 640-691; fax (40) 623-919; e-mail info@basraheast.com; internet www.basraheast.com; civil, electrical and mechanical engineering, construction of oil and gas pipelines, water treatment, industrial equipment trading; Gen. Man. GHASSAN AL-JASIM.

Al-Burhan Group: Compound 20, Kindi St, Mahala 213, Baghdad; tel. (1) 541-1320; fax (1) 542-8603; e-mail info@alburhangroup.com; internet www.alburhangroup.com; offices in London (United Kingdom), Amman (Jordan) and Dubai (United Arab Emirates); construction, flour milling, railways, automobile manufacturing; Gen. Dir KUDHYER K. BURHAN; 1,900 employees.

Danube Group: POB 20166, Bldg 17, St 3, Karrada 929, Baghdad; tel. 7811-676666 (mobile); e-mail info@danube-co.com; internet www.danube-co.com; f. 1989; engineering, contracting, mine clearance, general trading.

Darin Co: Shaqlawa St, opp. Helena Center, Arbil; e-mail info@darincoltd.com; internet www.darincoltd.com; construction, flour production; Consultant Man. MALASHNI BASHIR SHANE; 200 employees.

Diala State Co for Electrical Industries: Baquba, Diala; tel. (1) 885-0755; fax (1) 886-4562; e-mail info@dialacompany.com; internet www.dialacompany.com; f. 1974; mfrs of electrical transformers, ceiling fans, optical fibre cables and steam irons; produces oxygen and argon gases.

Diamond Group: Bldg 35, St 3, al-Mansour, Baghdad; tel. (1) 542-7226; fax (6) 552-2790; e-mail info@diamond-grp.com; internet www.diamond-grp.com; 11 cos in a range of fields, incl. construction, port equipment, security, flight catering, oil and gas equipment supplies, medical and pharmaceutical supplies; offices in Jordan and the UAE; Pres. and CEO ZIYAD F. AL-SAFI.

Dijla Group: Tunis St, Nasser Sq., Baghdad; tel. (1) 718-6383; fax (1) 719-9380; e-mail dijlacoc@nol.com.jo; internet www.dijlagroup.com; offices in Jordan, Lebanon and Dubai (UAE); f. 1978; 13 cos; construction, real estate, import and export; Branch Man. AYAD R. FTIKHAN.

Dnana Group: Hay al-Wehda, beside al-Alowia Communication Centre, Baghdad; tel. (1) 719-8993; e-mail info@dnanaco.com; internet www.dnanaco.com; oil services, construction, tourism, general trading, transport, food manufacturing; Man. Dir KARIM HASSAN DNANA.

Eng. Sabah al-Shammery and Partners Group (SAPCO): POB 50300, 69/1/21, al-Mansour al-Maneerat St, Baghdad; tel. (1) 541-2787; fax (1) 541-8155; e-mail sapco_iraq@shammery.com; 16 cos; engineering, construction, general trading, transport, computer and oil services.

Al-Fadha'a Co Ltd: Bldg 18/1, St 43, 627, Hay al-Jamea, Baghdad; tel. (1) 556-4394; f. 2000; general trading, construction, water and wastewater services.

General Co for Vegetable Oils Industry: POB 2379, Baghdad; tel. (1) 718-2076; fax (1) 718-2356; e-mail info@vegoil-iraq.com; internet www.vegoil-iraq.com; f. 1970; state-owned.

Ghalib al-Saadi Group: 629/8/4 al-Rabee St, Baghdad; tel. (1) 556-0445; e-mail gm.ghalib@ghalibalsaadi.com; internet www.ghalibalsaadi.com; f. 1998; three cos; engineering, water treatment and maintenance; Gen. Dir GHALIB AL-SAADI.

Al-Ghodwa Group: POB 2610, al-Jadriya, Baghdad; tel. (1) 719-9973; fax (1) 718-8734; e-mail sales@alghodwagroup.com; internet www.alghodwagroup.com; f. 1997; general trading and contracting, importer of construction, oil and gas equipment; CEO SABAH I. GHAIDAN.

Al-Haitham Engineering Contracting Co: District 901, St 13, Bldg 75, al-Karada Dakhil, Abu Klam Bldg, Baghdad; tel. (1) 719-0995; fax (1) 719-0918; e-mail info@al-haitham.com; f. 1985; general construction, water and wastewater; Gen. Dir KHALID AZIZ AL-OBAIDY; Contact HISHAM A. AL-RAWI.

Hakkak Investment Group: al-Warqaa Trading Compound, Bldg 94, St 18, 929, al-Sharqiya, al-Karrada, Baghdad; tel. (1) 719-3220; fax (1) 718-6539; e-mail info@hakkakgroup.com; internet www.hakkakgroup.com; general trading, construction, telecommunications, transport.

Ibn Majid State Co for Heavy Engineering and Marine Industries: Basra; tel. (7801) 427-075; e-mail ibn_majidco@yahoo.com; internet www.ibnmajidco.com; f. 1990; 1,600 employees.

Iraq Projects Co Ltd (IPCO): Istiqlal St, Khora Bridge, Asharr, Basra; tel. 7901-906889 (mobile); e-mail management@ipco.net; internet www.ipco.net; construction and engineering services within the fields of communications, infrastructure, oil and gas and transport.

Iraqi Cement State Co: POB 2050, Jadryah, Baghdad; tel. (1) 773-6071; fax (1) 773-3625; f. 1936; Gen. Man. SALAM ABDULLAH.

Al-Mahara Productive Industries Co Ltd: Muhammad Asker Bldg, Quarter 123, St 53, Sheikh Omar, Bab al-Sheikh, Baghdad; tel. (1) 817-4016; fax (1) 816-1417; e-mail info@almahara.com; internet www.al-maharapic.com; f. 1971 as The Productive Industrial Factory; reorg. and renamed as above 1984; mfrs of metal equipment, incl. automobile parts, knives, moulds and machinery.

Al-Maysoon Trading Agencies Ltd: Offices 8 and 9, Bldg 9, St 25, Mahala 929, Hay Babel, Arassat al-Hindiya, Baghdad; tel. (1) 719-8960; fax (1) 719-8975; e-mail m.alameen@al-maysoon.com; internet www.al-maysoon.com; medical equipment suppliers; Consultant Eng. MUHAMMAD KARDI.

Al-Merjal General Contracting Co (MERGCC): Haddad Bldg, 2nd Floor, Attar St, Karrada al-Sharkia, Baghdad; tel. 7901-934343 (mobile); fax (1) 541-9043; e-mail baghdad@merjal.com; internet www.merjal.com; f. 1991; power plant construction; Man. Dir SABHAN J. GREAN.

Muhandis Inbehar Group (MIG): Nidhal St, al-Saadoun Park, 103/34/11, Baghdad; tel. (1) 717-7776; fax (1) 719-3313; e-mail info@migiraq.com; internet www.migcompanies.com; f. 2003; construction; consortium of 15 cos; Owners KHALID ALI AHMAD, WATHIQ ABD AL-JABBAR; 368 employees.

Nabeel Contracting Bureau: 2nd Floor, al-Saher Bldg, 14 Ramadan St, al-Mansour, Baghdad; tel. and fax (1) 543-8522; e-mail nabeel@nabeelcb.com; internet www.nabeelcb.com; engineering and construction of power plants, water treatment systems and gas turbine units; Technical Man. NABEEL KHALAF.

Nasser State Co for Mechanical Industries: Taji, Baghdad; tel. 7808-901925 (mobile); fax (1) 444-6668; e-mail info@nassr-mec.com; internet www.nassr-mec.com; f. 1984.

Al-Noaman Co: e-mail information@alnoamanco-iraq.com; internet www.alnoamanco-iraq.com; f. 1985; state-owned; mfrs of plastics, especially for irrigation systems.

Northern Cement State Co: POB 13, Mosul; tel. (60) 777180; fax (60) 777184; e-mail info@ncsc-iraq.com; internet www.ncsc-iraq.com; Gen. Man. HUSSAIN MOHSEN OBAID.

Pioneer Engineering Contracting Co (PCC): Bldg 17/1, St 23, Area 620, al-Safarat St, Baghdad; tel. (1) 556-9825; fax (1) 555-3488;

e-mail pcc@pcciraq.com; internet www.pcciraq.com; general construction, power stations, water treatment.

Pioneers Pharma: 301/3/9, al-Waziriya, Baghdad; tel. (1) 425-6664; e-mail mt@pioneerspharma.com; internet www.pioneerspharma .com; medical and pharmaceutical supplies; Man. Dir MUWAFFAQ TIKRITI.

Al-Qabas Group: tel. (1) 542-6229; fax (1) 541-2779; e-mail alqabasg@alqabasgroup.com; internet www.alqabasgroup.com; f. 1961; five cos; contracting, engineering, power and electricity services, general trading.

Al-Qarya Group: al-Mansour, Dawodi, Baghdad; tel. (1) 542-3886; e-mail info@alqaryagroup.com; internet www.alqaryagroup.com; f. 2001; construction, trading, information technology and telecommunications; Chair. and Man. Dir IMAD MAKKI.

Al-Qudrah Alfania Co: Bldg 17, St 57, Bab al-Sheikh, Baghdad; tel. (1) 817-4827; e-mail alqudraco@yahoo.com; internet www.alqudraco .com; mechanical and civil engineering, construction, water treatment.

Al-Rahmani Group: Hay al-Kindy, Baghdad; tel. (1) 541-4718; fax (1) 541-6967; e-mail sales@alrahmanigroup.com; internet www .alrahmanigroup.com; offices in Jordan and Dubai (UAE); transport, construction, import and export, oil and gas services, logistics.

Rowad Baghdad Construction Ltd: Zayouna, Baghdad; tel. 7901-343190 (mobile); e-mail info@rowadbaghdad.com; internet www.rowadbaghdad.com; f. 1985; civil and construction works.

Al-Sadda Group: tel. (780) 100-2279; fax (780) 100-2872; e-mail alshatyco@alsaddaco.com; internet www.alsaddaco.com; construction, electrical and communications projects, general trading; seven cos.

Saham Babil Co: 1st Floor, al-Fateh Bldg, al-Andalous Sq., al-Nidhal St, Baghdad; tel. (1) 717-5309; fax (1) 719-4173; e-mail contact@sahambabil.com; internet www.sahambabil.com; f. 1996; construction, general trading.

Salihi Group International: 9 Govt Circle, Nr Kirkuk Govt Capital, Kirkuk; tel. 7481–107600 (mobile); e-mail ako@salihi.net; internet www.salihi.net; f. 2003; construction; Chair. WARIA N. SALHI.

Al-Salman Group: Baghdad; tel. 7901-304126 (mobile); e-mail info@aalsalman-group.com; internet www.aalsalman-group.com; f. 1925; general trading, construction, real estate, marine, petroleum, media and security services; Chair. FARIS AL-SALMAN.

Al-Sameem Co: Baghdad; tel. (1) 817-7547; fax (1) 816-6216; e-mail info@alsameem.com; internet www.alsameem.com; f. 1990; construction, import and export; office in Jordan.

Al-Sawari State Co for Chemical Industries: POB 337, Baghdad; tel. 7901-281699 (mobile); e-mail alsawwar1@yahoo.com; internet www.alsawwary-iraq.com; f. 1994; Dir-Gen. RAISAN SADDAM HASSAN; 961 employees.

Southern Cement State Co: POB 9, Kufa; tel. (7801) 036-003; e-mail info@southern-cement.com; internet www.southern-cement .com; f. 1996; Gen. Man. Eng. NASSER AL-MADANI.

State Battery Manufacturing Co: POB 190, al-Waziriya, Baghdad; tel. (1) 425-5022; e-mail commerc_battery@yahoo.com; f. 1987; Dir-Gen. Eng. SALAM SAEED AHMED; 1,929 employees.

State Co for Automotive Industry (SCAI): POB 138, Iskandariya-Babylon; internet www.scaiiraq.net; f. 1976; specializes in assembling buses, trucks and semi-trailers.

State Co for Construction Industries: 931/27/2 Hay Babel, Baghdad; tel. 7901-374431 (mobile); f. 1987 by merger of state orgs for gypsum, asbestos, and the plastic and concrete industries; Dir ALI SALIM OMAR; 3,123 employees.

State Co for Cotton Industries: Khadimiya, Baghdad; e-mail dgoffice@cottonindiraq.com; internet www.cottonindiraq.com; f. 1964; 6,720 employees.

State Co for Dairy Industries: POB 21072, Abu Ghraib, Baghdad; tel. (1) 511-0923; fax (1) 511-0154; f. 1956; 1,251 employees.

State Co for Drinks and Mineral Water: POB 5689, Sara Khatoon Camp, Baghdad; POB 2108, al-Za'afaraniya, Baghdad; f. 1987 by merger of enterprises responsible for soft and alcoholic drinks.

State Co for Import and Export: POB 5642-5670, al-Nidal St, Baghdad; tel. (1) 719-0397; fax (1) 719-8732; f. 1987 to replace the five state orgs responsible to the Ministry of Trade for productive commodities, consumer commodities, grain and food products, exports and imports; Gen. Dir FOUZI H. AL-DHAHIR.

State Co for Leather Industries: Karrada Kharij, Baghdad; tel. (1) 778-5081; fax (1) 778-3828; e-mail info@jilood.com; f. 1976 by merger of State Co for Leather and Bata Co.

State Co for Petrochemical Industries (SCPI): POB 933, Khor al-Zubair, Basra; tel. (40) 610-840; e-mail scpibasrah@yahoo.com; internet www.pchem-iq.com; f. 1977; Dir-Gen. HUSSAIN M. AL-SHEMARY.

State Co for Refractories Industry: e-mail info@scir-iraq.com; internet www.scir-iraq.com; f. 1994.

State Co for the Sugar Industry: POB 42, Gizlani St, Mosul; f. 1987 by merger of sugar enterprises in Mosul and Sulaimaniya; 480 employees.

State Co for Textile Industries: POB 2, Hilla, nr Najaf; tel. (30) 243-200; fax (30) 242-627; e-mail infocenter@nasseg-hilla.com; internet www.nasseg-hilla.com; f. 1967.

State Co for Tire Industry: Najaf; tel. and fax (30) 222-399; e-mail sctib@yahoo.com; internet www.najaftyres.com; f. 1997.

State Co for Tobacco and Cigarettes: POB 10026, al-Habibiya, Baghdad; 2,246 employees.

State Co for Woollen Industries: POB 9114, Khadhumiya, Baghdad; 3,201 employees.

State Cos for Fertilizer (Northern and Southern Regions): POB 74, Khor al-Zubair Factories, Basra; internet www.iraqisscf .com; f. 1975; 4,276 employees.

Al-Sumood Co for Steel Industries: Baghdad; e-mail info_center@alsumood-steel.com; internet www.alsumood-steel .com; f. 1988; state-owned.

Sweer Co Contracting: POB 8095, Abu Ja'afar al-Mansour St, al-Mansour, Baghdad; tel. (1) 818-1196; fax (1) 817-7957; e-mail info@ sweerco.com; internet www.sweerco.com; mechanical and electrical contracting.

T. al-Shayei and Partner Co: Bldg 76/5, al-Rashid St, al-Sanak, Baghdad; tel. (1) 816-7942; fax (1) 556-2933; e-mail info@al-shayei .com; internet www.al-shayei.com; f. 1989; oil and chemical industry supplies, construction; Man. Dir TARIQ AL-SHAYEI.

Taha and Partners Group: Taha Group Bldg, Tunis St, Baghdad; tel. 7901-102707 (mobile); e-mail info@taha-partners.com; internet www.taha-partners.com; five cos; construction and printing; Gen. Man. WALID K. ISSA TAHA.

Technical United Oilfields Services and Supplies Co Ltd (TUOSSCO): al-Mansour, Baghdad; tel. (1) 541-1424; fax (1) 541-5493; e-mail tuossco_baghdad@tuossco.com; internet www.tuossco .com; f. 1992; suppliers of oil equipment and machinery; offices in Jordan and the UAE.

That Al-Sawary State Co for Chemical Industries: POB 337, Baghdad; tel. (1) 543-3701; e-mail alsawwary1@yahoo.com; internet www.alsawwary-iraq.com; f. 1994.

Uruk Group: POB 828, 25/35/222 Karradat Maryam, Baghdad; tel. (1) 538-0311; e-mail khalidjmk@urukgroup.com; internet www .urukgroup.com; f. 2003; construction, engineering and management; CEO and Gen. Man. JAFAR D. JAFAR.

Al-Wakeel International Co: al-Jeesr St, al-Samawah; tel. 7801-013252 (mobile); e-mail info@alwakeelint.com; internet www .alwakeelint.com; f. 2004; fmrly Al-Hadi Engineering Co; construction, contracting, civil and mechanical engineering, power supply; Dir AMAD AZIZ.

Al-Yaqut Group: Bldg 36, St 16, al-Yarmouk, 612, Baghdad; tel. 7901-909737 (mobile); e-mail info@al-yaqutgroup.com; internet www.al-yaqutgroup.com; f. 1988; import and export, construction consultancy; Gen. Man. SHATHA AL-ZUHAIRY.

ZamZam Group: POB 19184, Zayounah Post Office, Baghdad; tel. 7901-908175 (mobile); e-mail info@zamzam-group.com; internet www.zamzam-group.com; f. 1972; construction, engineering, hotels, general trading.

Zurafa Co: POB 6086, 39/6/605, al-Mansour, Baghdad; tel. (1) 543-0193; e-mail info@zurafacompany.com; internet www.octagoniraq .com/ZurafaCompany/Welcome.html; f. 2009; construction, general trading, consultancy; Man. Dir Dr RAID K. AL-SAIDI.

TRADE UNIONS

General Federation of Iraqi Workers (GFIW): POB 3049, Tahrir Sq., al-Rashid St, Baghdad; fax (1) 670-4200; e-mail abdullahmuhsin@iraqitradeunions.org; internet www .iraqitradeunions.org; f. 2005 by merger of Gen. Fed. of Trade Unions, Gen. Fed. of Trade Unions of Iraq (an offshoot of the former) and Iraqi Fed. of Workers' Trade Unions; covers all of Iraq's provinces except the three Kurdish Autonomous Regions; Pres. ALI RAHEEM ALI; Vice-Pres. HADI ALI LAFTA.

Iraqi Teachers' Union (ITU): al-Mansour, Baghdad; f. 2003; Pres. JASIM HUSSEIN MUHAMMAD AL-LAMI.

There are also unions of doctors, pharmacologists, jurists, writers, journalists, artists, engineers, electricity and railway workers.

Transport

RAILWAYS

In 2010 the total length of Iraqi railways was 2,025 route-km. A line covers the length of the country, from Rabia, on the Syrian border, via Mosul, to Baghdad (534 km), and from Baghdad to Basra and Umm Qasr (608 km), on the Persian (Arabian) Gulf. A 404-km line links Baghdad, via Radi and Haditha, to Husaibah, near the Iraqi–Syrian frontier. Baghdad is linked with Arbil, via Khanaqin and Kirkuk, and a 252-km line (designed to serve industrial projects along its route) runs from Kirkuk to Haditha, via Baiji (though this was rendered out of action in mid-2006, as a result of bombing by US forces). A 638-km line runs from Baghdad, via al-Qaim (on the Syrian border), to Akashat (with a 150-km line linking the Akashat phosphate mines and the fertilizer complex at al-Qaim). A regular international service between Baghdad and İstanbul, Turkey, was suspended following the US-led invasion in 2003; however, services on a section of the line, between Mosul and Gaziantep, resumed in early 2010. Passenger rail services between Mosul and Aleppo, Syria, resumed in August 2000 after an interruption of almost 20 years, but were closed again in 2004 after repeated insurgent attacks. Passenger rail services between Baghdad and Basra resumed in late 2007, and a Baghdad–Ramadi passenger service recommenced in May 2009. The railway system was due to be repaired and upgraded as part of the reconstruction of Iraq following the removal from power of Saddam Hussain's regime in 2003. Eventually, it was planned that the system would be divided, with the infrastructure being kept as a state asset, while operations were to be privatized. It was reported in 2006 that the Ministry of Transportation hoped to add an additional 2,300 km to the existing rail network, although concerns remained over funding. In May 2010 the Government announced that it had invited bids from eight short-listed foreign consortia for the contract to construct a 25-km, two-line metro system in Baghdad; the French company Alstom signed a memorandum of understanding to undertake the project in January 2011.

General Co for Railways: Ministry of Transportation, nr Martyr's Monument, Karradat Dakhil, Baghdad; e-mail iraqitransport@yahoo.com; internet www.scr.gov.iq.

Iraqi Republic Railways Co (IRRC): West Station, Baghdad; tel. (1) 537-0011; e-mail d1_g_office@iraqrailways.com; internet www.iraqrailways.com; f. 1914; Dir-Gen. RAFIL YUSSEF ABBAS.

ROADS

In 2010, according to estimates by the International Road Federation, Iraq's road network extended over 41,716 km, of which 1,006 km were highways, main or national roads, and 29,420 km were secondary or regional roads.

The most important roads are: Baghdad–Mosul–Tel Kotchuk (Syrian border), 521 km; Baghdad–Kirkuk–Arbil–Mosul–Zakho (border with Turkey), 544 km; Kirkuk–Sulaimaniya, 160 km; Baghdad–Hilla–Diwaniya–Nasiriya–Basra, 586 km; Baghdad–Kut–Nasiriya, 186 km; Baghdad–Ramadi–Rurba (border with Syria), 555 km; Baghdad–Kut–Umara–Basra–Safwan (border with Kuwait), 660 km; and Baghdad–Baqaba–Kanikien (border with Iran). Most sections of the six-lane, 1,264-km international Express Highway, linking Safwan (on the Kuwaiti border) with the Jordanian and Syrian borders, had been completed by June 1990. Studies have been completed for a second, 525-km Express Highway, linking Baghdad and Zakho on the Turkish border. A complex network of roads was constructed behind the war front with Iran in order to facilitate the movement of troops and supplies during the 1980–88 conflict. The road network was included in the US-led coalition's programme of reconstruction following the ousting of the Baathist regime in 2003.

Iraqi Land Transport Co: Baghdad; internet sclt.gov.iq; f. 1988 to replace State Org. for Land Transport; fleet of more than 1,000 large trucks; Dir-Gen. AYSAR AL-SAFI.

State Organization for Roads and Bridges: POB 917, Karradat Mariam, Karkh, Baghdad; tel. (1) 32141; responsible for road and bridge construction projects under the Ministry of Construction and Housing.

SHIPPING

The ports of Basra and Umm Qasr are usually the commercial gateway of Iraq. They are connected by various ocean routes with all parts of the world, and constitute the natural distribution centre for overseas supplies. The Iraqi State Enterprise for Maritime Transport maintains a regular service between Basra, the Persian (Arabian) Gulf and north European ports. There is also a port at Khor al-Zubair, which came into use in 1979.

For the inland waterways, there are 1,036 registered river craft, 48 motor vessels and 105 motorboats.

The port at Umm Qasr was heavily damaged during the early part of the US-led coalition's campaign to oust Saddam Hussain. A large-scale project to redevelop the port is under way. In July 2009 contracts to lease and develop new commercial berths at Umm Qasr were awarded to two foreign port operators. In February 2011 the UAE-based firm Gulftainer signed a US $150m. contract to construct and operate a dry port north of Umm Qasr. In August 2012 16 bids were received for the first phase in the construction of a new deep-sea port at Faw in Basra province. It was anticipated that the new $6,300m. facility would, upon completion, replace Umm Qasr as Iraq's main commercial port.

At 31 December 2012 Iraq's flag registered fleet totalled 78 vessels, with an aggregate displacement of 127,999 grt, of which two were fish carriers and six were general cargo ships.

Port and Regulatory Authorities

General Co of Iraqi Ports (IPA): Malik bin Dinar St, Basra; tel. (40) 041-3211; e-mail anmarbasrah@gmail.dom; internet scp.gov.iq; Dir-Gen. SALEH QADIR ABOUD.

State Enterprise for Iraqi Water Transport: POB 23016, Airport St, al-Furat Quarter, Baghdad; f. 1987, when State Org. for Iraqi Water Transport was abolished; responsible for the planning, supervision and control of six nat. water transportation enterprises, incl. General Co for Maritime Transport (see below).

Principal Shipping Companies

Arab Bridge Maritime Navigation Co: Aqaba, Jordan; tel. (3) 2092000; fax (3) 2092001; internet www.abmaritime.com.jo; f. 1987; jt venture by Egypt, Iraq and Jordan to improve economic co-operation; an expansion of the co established a ferry link between the ports of Aqaba, Jordan, and Nuweibeh, Egypt, in 1985; six vessels; cap. US $75m. (2010); Chair. Eng. OSAMA MUHAMMAD AL-SADER; Vice-Chairs. MOHANNAD SALMAN AL-QDAH, HISHAM OMAR AL-SARSAWI; Man. Dir HUSSEIN AL-SOUOB.

General Co for Maritime Transport: POB 13038, al-Jadiriya al-Hurriya Ave, Baghdad; Basra office: POB 766, 14 July St, Basra; tel. (1) 776-3201; e-mail watertrans@motrans.gov.iq; internet scmt.gov.iq; f. 1952 as State Enterprise for Maritime Transport; renamed as above 2009; Dir-Gen. SAMIR ABD AL-RAZZAQ.

Gulf Shipping Co: POB 471, Basra; tel. (40) 776-1945; fax (40) 776-0715; f. 1988; imports and exports goods to and from Iraq.

Al-Masar al-Iraqi Co LLC: Manawi Pasha St, nr Manawi Pasha Hotel, POB 85885, Basra; tel. 7704926113 (mobile); e-mail operation@iraqilogistic.com; internet www.iraqilogistic.com; provides a range of freight and shipping agency services.

CIVIL AVIATION

There are international airports at Baghdad, Basra and Mosul. Baghdad's airport, previously named Saddam International Airport, reopened in August 2000, after refurbishment necessitated by damage sustained during the war with the multinational force in 1991. However, international air links were virtually halted by the UN embargo imposed in 1990. Internal flights, connecting Baghdad to Basra and Mosul, recommenced in November 2000. In April 2003 the capital's airport was renamed Baghdad International Airport by US forces during their military campaign to oust the regime of Saddam Hussain. Following a programme of reconstruction, the airports at Baghdad and Basra were reopened to commercial flights from late 2003; Mosul International Airport reopened for civilian flights in December 2007. The expansion of Arbil International Airport (including the construction of a new passenger terminal and runway) was completed in mid-2010. In July 2008 Al-Hamza airport in Najaf (formerly a military airport) was inaugurated for civilian use, as increasing numbers of pilgrims were visiting the shrines of that holy city. Construction work on a new airport in Karbala, with a projected annual capacity of 30m. passengers, commenced in March 2010.

Iraq Civil Aviation Authority (ICAA): Baghdad; tel. 7901 448827 (mobile); fax (1) 543-0764; e-mail info@iraqcaa.com; internet www.iraqcaa.com; f. 1987; Dir-Gen. Capt. NASER HUSSEIN BANDAR.

Iraqi Airways Co: Baghdad International Airport, Baghdad; tel. (1) 537-2002; e-mail info@iraqiairways.co.uk; internet www.iraqiairways.co.uk; f. 1945; operates flights to other Arab countries, Iran, Turkey, Greece and Sweden; Dir-Gen. Capt. KIFAH HUSSEIN JABBAR.

Tourism

In 2010 (the last year for which statistics are available) some 1,517,766 tourists visited Iraq; tourist receipts in 2007 were estimated at US $555m. Arrivals of foreign nationals totalled 1.5m. in 2010. Following the US-led invasion of Iraq in 2003, the site housing the ruins of the ancient civilization of Babylon became part of a US military base; several other places of interest became military or refugee camps, and, amid the protracted period of conflict since 2003, tourists have been deterred from visiting the country's many cultural and religious sites. Nevertheless, in August 2006 the relatively peaceful Kurdish Autonomous Region launched a tourism campaign, with advertisements broadcast on US television. Since 2008 religious tourism has been growing, with increasing numbers of pilgrims using the newly renovated airport in Najaf (see Transport) to visit the Islamic holy shrines of both that city and nearby Karbala.

Iraq Tourism Board: POB 7783, Haifa St, Baghdad; tel. (1) 543-3912; Chair. HAMOUD MOHSEN AL-YACOUBI.

Defence

The US-led Coalition Provisional Authority (CPA) dissolved Iraq's armed forces and security organizations in place under Saddam Hussain in May 2003, following the ousting of the regime in the previous month. In August the CPA promulgated the establishment of the New Iraqi Army.

Chief of Staff of the Joint Armed Forces: Lt-Gen. BABAKIR SHAWKAT ZEBARI.

Commander of the Ground Forces: Lt-Gen. ALI GHAIDAN.

Commander of the Air Force: Lt-Gen. ANWAR HAMAD AMIN AHMAD.

Commander of the Navy: Rear Adm. MUHAMMAD JAWAD KADHAM.

Defence Budget (2013): ID 19,900,000m.

Total Armed Forces (as assessed at November 2012): 271,400: army 193,400; navy 3,600; air force 5,050; plus 69,350 support. In addition, there were 531,000 Ministry of Interior Forces, including 302,000 members of the Iraqi Police Service, 44,000 members of the Iraqi Federal police, 95,000 members of the Facilities Protection Service, 60,000 members of the Border Enforcement forces and 30,000 members of the Oil Police.

Education

After the establishment of the Republic in 1958, there was a marked expansion in education at all levels, and spending on education increased substantially. During the mid-1970s free education was established at all stages from pre-primary to higher, and private education was abolished; all existing private schools were transformed into state schools. However, military conflict and economic sanctions during the 1980s and 1990s undermined much of the progress made in education during the previous two decades. Primary education, beginning at six years of age, lasts for six years. Enrolment at primary schools of children in the relevant age-group had declined to 76% by 1995, but reportedly rose again, to 91%, in 2000/01. According to UNESCO estimates, in 2006/07 enrolment at primary schools included 88% of pupils in the relevant age-group. Secondary education, from 12 years of age and lasting for up to six years, is divided into two cycles of three years each. Enrolment at secondary schools in 2006/07 included some 43% of children in the appropriate age-group, according to UNESCO. Following the change of regime in Iraq in April 2003, a comprehensive reform of the country's education system was implemented. In the 2010/11 academic year there were estimated to be 19,814 primary and secondary schools in Iraq, with a total enrolment of 6,874,031 pupils. There are 43 technical institutes and colleges, two postgraduate commissions and 20 universities. In 2002/03 there were approximately 240,000 undergraduates attending institutions of higher education. In 2010 government expenditure on education amounted to US $4,310m., equivalent to 6.0% of total government spending.

Bibliography

General and Historical Context

Abdul-Jabar, Faleh. (Ed). *Ayatollahs, Sufis and Ideologues: State, Religion and Social Movements in Iraq*. London, Saqi Books, 2006.

The Shi'ite Movement in Iraq. London, Saqi Books, 2006.

Çetinsaya, Gökhan. *Ottoman Administration of Iraq, 1890–1908*. Abingdon, Routledge, 2006.

Franzén, Johan. *Red Star Over Iraq: Iraqi Communism Before Saddam*. New York, Columbia University Press, 2012.

Kent, Marian. *Oil and Empire: British Policy and Mesopotamian Oil, 1900–1920*. London, Macmillan, 1976.

Khoury, Dina Rizk. *Iraq in Wartime: Soldiering, Martyrdom, and Remembrance*. New York, Cambridge University Press, 2013.

Korn, David A. *Human Rights in Iraq*. New Haven, CT, Yale University Press, 1990.

Litvak, Meir. *Shi'i Scholars of Nineteenth-Century Iraq: The Ulama of Najaf and Karbala*. Cambridge, Cambridge University Press, 1998.

Lloyd, Seton. *Iraq*. Oxford Pamphlet in Indian Affairs, No. 13. Bombay, 1943.

Twin Rivers: *A Brief History of Iraq from the Earliest Times to the Present Day*. Oxford, 1943.

Foundations in the Dust. Oxford, 1949.

Longrigg, S. H. *Four Centuries of Modern Iraq*. Oxford, 1925.

Longrigg, S. H., and Stoakes, F. *Iraq*. London, Ernest Benn, 1958.

Mahdi, Kamil. A. *Iraq's Economic Predicament*. Reading, Ithaca Press, 2002.

Oil and Oil Policy in Iraq: Past and Present. Ann Arbor, MI, University of Michigan Press, 2007.

Al-Marashi, Ibrahim, and Salama, Sammy. *Iraq's Armed Forces: An Analytical History*. Abingdon, Routledge, 2009.

Al-Musawi, Muhsin J. *Reading Iraq: Culture and Power in Conflict*. London, I. B. Tauris, 2006.

Nakash, Yitzhak. *The Shi'is of Iraq*. Princeton, NJ, Princeton University Press, 1995.

Polk, William R. *Understanding Iraq: The Whole Sweep of Iraqi History from Genghis Khan's Mongols to the Ottoman Turks to the British Mandate to the American Occupation*. New York, HarperCollins, 2005.

Salter, Lord, assisted by Payton, S. W. *The Development of Iraq: A Plan of Action*. Baghdad, 1955.

Seierstad, Åsne. *A Hundred and One Days: A Baghdad Journal*. London, Virago, 2004.

Stark, Freya. *Baghdad Sketches*. London, John Murray, 1937.

Stevenson, Wendell. *The Weight of a Mustard Seed*. London, Atlantic Books, 2009.

Stewart, Desmond, and Haylock, John. *New Babylon: A Portrait of Iraq*. London, Collins, 1956.

Wien, Peter. *Iraqi Arab Nationalism: Authoritarian, Totalitarian and Pro-Fascist Inclinations, 1932–1941*. Abingdon, Routledge, 2006.

Contemporary Political History

Ali, Omar. *Crisis in The Arab Gulf: An Independent Iraqi View*. London, The European Group, 1994.

Allawi, Ali A. *The Occupation of Iraq: Winning the War, Losing the Peace*. New Haven, CT, Yale University Press, 2007.

Amnesty International. *Iraq: Victims of Systematic Repression*. London, 1999.

Anderson, Ewan W., and Rashidian, Khalil. *Iraq and the Continuing Middle East Crisis*. London, Printer Publishers, 1991.

Anderson, Liam, and Stansfield, Gareth. *The Future of Iraq: Dictatorship, Democracy or Division?* New York, Palgrave Macmillan, 2004.

Crisis in Kirkuk: The Ethnopolitics of Conflict and Compromise. Philadelphia, PA, University of Pennsylvania Press, 2009.

Arburish, Said. *Saddam Hussein: The Politics of Revenge*. London, Bloomsbury, 2000.

Arnove, Anthony (Ed.). *Iraq Under Siege: The Deadly Impact of Sanctions and War*. London, Pluto Press, 2000.

Barakat, Sultan. *Reconstructing Post-Saddam Iraq*. Abingdon, Routledge, 2006.

Baram, Amatzia. *Culture, History and Ideology in the Formation of Baathist Iraq, 1968–89*. Basingstoke, Macmillan, 1991.

Building towards Crisis: Saddam Husayn's Strategy for Survival. Washington, DC, Washington Institute for Near East Policy, 1998.

Batatu, Hanna. *The Old Social Classes and the Revolutionary Movements of Iraq*. Princeton, NJ, Princeton University Press, 1978.

Bengio, Ofra. *Saddam's World: Political Discourse in Iraq*. Oxford, Oxford University Press, 1998.

Bennis, Phyllis, and Moushabeck, Michael (Eds). *Beyond the Storm: A Gulf Crisis Reader*. Edinburgh, Canongate Press, 1992.

Blix, Hans. *Disarming Iraq: The Search for Weapons of Mass Destruction*. London, Bloomsbury, 2004.

Butler, Richard. *Saddam Defiant: The Threat of Weapons of Mass Destruction, and the Growing Crisis of Global Security*. London, Weidenfeld & Nicolson, 2000.

Chandrasekaran, Rajiv. *Imperial Life in the Emerald City: Inside Baghdad's Green Zone*. London, Bloomsbury, 2007.

Chehab, Zaki. *Iraq Ablaze: Inside the Insurgency*. London, I. B. Tauris, 2005.

Chubin, Shahram, and Tripp, Charles. *Iran and Iraq at War*. London, I. B. Tauris, 1988.

Cockburn, Andrew, and Cockburn, Patrick. *Out of the Ashes: The Resurrection of Saddam Hussein*. New York, HarperCollins, 1999.

Saddam Hussein: An American Obsession. London, Verso, 2002.

Cockburn, Patrick. *The Occupation: War and Resistance in Iraq*. London, Verso, 2006.

Muqtada: Muqtada Al-Sadr, the Shia Revival, and the Struggle for Iraq. New York, Scribner Book Company, 2008.

Cordesman, Anthony H. *The Iran–Iraq War and Western Security 1984–87*. London, Jane's Publishing Company, 1987.

Cortright, David, Millar, Alistair, and Lopez, George A. (contributing Ed. Gerber, Linda). *Smart Sanctions: Restructuring UN Policy in Iraq*. Policy Brief Series, Notre Dame and Goshen, IN, Joan B. Kroc Institute for International Peace Studies and Fourth Freedom Forum, 2001.

Danchev, Alex, and Macmillan, John (Eds). *The Iraq War and Democratic Politics*. London, Routledge, 2004.

Dann, Uriel. *Iraq under Qassem: A Political History 1958–63*. New York, Praeger, 1969.

Darwish, Adel, and Alexander, Gregory. *Unholy Babylon: The Secret History of Saddam's War*. London, Gollancz, 1991.

DeFronzo, James. *The Iraq War: Origins and Consequences*. Boulder, CO, Westview Press, 2009.

Dodge, Toby. *Inventing Iraq: The Failure of Nation Building and a History Denied*. London, C. Hurst & Co, 2003.

Iraq's Future: The Aftermath of Regime Change. Abingdon, Routledge, 2006.

Farouk-Sluglett, Marion, and Sluglett, Peter. *Iraq since 1958: From Revolution to Dictatorship*. London, I. B. Tauris, revised edn, 2001.

Fawn, Rick, and Hinnebusch, Raymond. *The Iraq War: Causes and Consequences*. Boulder, CO, Lynne Rienner Publishers, 2006.

Gittings, John (Ed.). *Beyond the Gulf War: The Middle East and the New World Order*. London, Catholic Institute for International Relations, 1991.

Graham-Brown, Sarah. *Sanctioning Saddam: The Politics of Intervention in Iraq*. Reading, Ithaca Press, 1999.

Haddad, Fanar. *Sectarianism in Iraq: Antagonistic Visions of Unity*. London, C. Hurst & Co, 2011.

Haj, Samira. *The Making of Iraq, 1900–1963: Capital, Power and Ideology*. New York, State University of New York Press, 1997.

Hallenberg, Jan, and Karlsson, Håkan (Eds). *The Iraq War: European Perspectives on Politics, Strategy and Operations*. Abingdon, Routledge, 2006.

Hashim, Ahmed S. *Iraq's Sunni Insurgency*. Abingdon, Routledge, 2009.

Heikal, Mohammed. *Illusions of Triumph: An Arab View of the Gulf War*. London, HarperCollins, 1992.

Henderson, Simon. *Instant Empire: Saddam's Ambition for Iraq*. San Francisco, CA, Mercury House, 1991.

Hiro, Dilip. *The Longest War: The Iran–Iraq Military Conflict*. London, Grafton, 1989.

Desert Shield to Desert Storm: The Second Gulf War. London, Routledge, 1992.

Neighbours, Not Friends: Iraq and Iran after the Gulf Wars. London, Routledge, 2001.

Iraq: A Report from the Inside. London, Granta Books, 2003.

Iraq: In the Eye of the Storm. New York, Thunder's Mouth Press, 2003.

Secrets and Lies: The Planning, Conduct and Aftermath of Blair and Bush's War. London, Politico's Publishing, 2005.

Secrets and Lies: Operation Iraqi Freedom and the Collapse of American Power in the Middle East. New York, Nation Books, 2005.

Hussein, Saddam. *Social and Foreign Affairs in Iraq (Routledge Revivals)*. Abingdon, Routledge, 2009. (First published 1979.)

Iraq: A Decade of Devastation. Middle East Report No. 215. Vol. 30, No. 2. Summer 2000.

Ismael, Tareq Y. *Iran and Iraq: Roots of Conflict*. Syracuse, NY, Syracuse University Press, 1983.

Karsh, Efraim. *The Iran–Iraq War: 1980–1988 (Essential Histories)*. Oxford, Osprey, 2002.

Karsh, Efraim, and Ravtsi, Inari. *Saddam Hussein: A Political Biography*. London, Brasseys, 1992.

Keegan, John. *The Iraq War*. London, Hutchinson, 2004.

Khadduri, Majid. *Independent Iraq 1932–58, A Study of Iraqi Politics*. Oxford, Oxford University Press, 2nd edn, 1960.

Republican Iraq: A Study in Iraqi Politics since the Revolution of 1958. Oxford, Oxford University Press, 1970.

Socialist Iraq: A Study in Iraqi Politics since 1968. Washington, DC, The Middle East Institute, 1978.

Khadduri, Majid, and Ghareeb, Edmund. *War in the Gulf 1990–91*. New York, Oxford University Press, 1997.

Kiely, Patrick, and Ryan, David. *America and Iraq: Policy-making, Intervention and Regional Politics*. Abingdon, Routledge, 2008.

Kienle, Eberhard. *Ba'th versus Ba'th: The Conflict between Iraq and Syria*. London, I. B. Tauris, 1990.

Kinsey, Christopher. *Private Contractors and the Reconstruction of Iraq: Transforming Military Logistics*. Abingdon, Routledge, 2009.

Iraq 1900–1950: A Political, Social and Economic History. London, 1953.

MacArthur, Brian (Ed.). *Despatches from the Gulf War*. London, Bloomsbury, 1991.

MacKey, Sandra. *The Reckoning: Iraq and the Legacy of Saddam Hussein*. New York, W. W. Norton & Co, 2002.

Mahnken, Thomas G., and Keaney, Thomas A. (Eds). *War in Iraq: Planning and Execution*. Abingdon, Routledge, 2007.

Makiya, Kanan. *Republic of Fear: The Politics of Modern Iraq*. Berkeley, CA, University of California Press, 2nd edn, 1998.

Malone, David M. *International Struggle over Iraq: Politics in the UN Security Council 1980–2005*. Oxford, Oxford University Press, 2006.

Al-Marayati, Abid A. *A Diplomatic History of Modern Iraq*. New York, Speller, 1961.

Mark, Phoebe. *The History of Modern Iraq*. London, Longman, 1983.

Mosallam, Mosallam Ali. *The Iraqi Invasion of Kuwait: Saddam Hussein, his State and International Politics*. London, I. B. Tauris, 1996.

Omaar, Rageh. *Revolution Day: The Human Story of the Battle for Iraq*. London, Viking, 2004.

Pelletiere, Stephen. *Iraq and the International Oil System: Why America Went to War in the Gulf*. Westport, CT, and London, Praeger, 2001.

Rahman, H. *The Making of the Gulf War: Origins of Kuwait's Long-standing Territorial Dispute with Iraq*. Reading, Ithaca Press, 1997.

Rear, Michael. *Intervention, Ethnic Conflict and State-Building in Iraq: A Paradigm for the Post-Colonial State*. Abingdon, Routledge, 2012.

Ritchie, Nick, and Rogers, Paul. *The Political Road to War with Iraq: Bush, 9/11 and the Drive to Overthrow Saddam*. Abingdon, Routledge, 2006.

Ritter, Scott. *Endgame: Solving the Iraq Problem—Once and For All*. New York, Simon & Schuster, 1999.

Rohde, Achim. *State-Society Relations in Baathist Iraq: Facing Dictatorship*. Abingdon, Routledge, 2010.

Salih, Khalid. *State-Making, Nation-Building and the Military: Iraq 1941–1958*. Göteborg, Göteborg University Press, 1996.

El-Sayed El-Shazly, Nadia. *The Gulf Tanker War: Iran and Iraq's Maritime Swordplay*. New York, St Martin's Press, 1998.

Schofield, R. *Kuwait and Iraq: Historical Claims and Territorial Disputes*. London, Royal Institute of International Affairs, 2nd edn, 1993.

Simons, Geoff. *Iraq Endgame: Surge, Suffering and the Politics of Denial*. London, Politico's Publishing, 2008.

Simpson, John. *From the House of War*. London, Hutchinson, 1991.

Springborg, Robert (Ed.). *Oil and Democracy in Iraq*. London, Saqi Books, 2007.

Steele, Jonathan. *Defeat: Why They Lost Iraq*. London, I. B. Tauris, 2007.

Sweeney, John. *Trading with the Enemy*. London, Pan Macmillan, 1993.

Thakur, Ramesh Chandra, and Sidhu, Waheguru Pal Singh. (Eds). *Iraq Crises and World Order*. United Nations University Press, 2006.

Tripp, Charles. *A History of Iraq*. Cambridge, Cambridge University Press, 2000.

Visser, Reidar, and Stansfield, Gareth. *An Iraq of its Regions: Cornerstones of a Federal Democracy?* New York, Columbia University Press, 2007.

Weller, Marc. *The Control and Monitoring of Iraqi Weaponry*. Cambridge, Cambridge University Press, 1995.

Minorities

Ahmad, Kamalmadhar. *Kurdistan During the First World War*. London, Saqi Books, 2001.

Arfa, Hassan. *The Kurds*. Oxford, Oxford University Press, 1966.

Badger, G. P. *The Nestorians and their Rituals*. 2 vols, London, 1888.

Bengio, Ofra. *The Kurds of Iraq: Building a State Within a State*. Boulder, CO, Lynne Rienner Publishers, 2012.

Blunt, A. T. N. *Bedouin Tribes of the Euphrates*. 2 vols, London, 1879.

Clark, Peter, and Nicholson, Emma. *The Iraqi Marshlands*. London, Politico's Publishing, 2002.

Cook, Helena. *The Safe Haven in Northern Iraq: International Responsibility for Iraqi Kurdistan*. Kurdistan Human Rights Project, 1995.

Damluji, S. *The Yezidis*. Baghdad, 1948 (in Arabic).

Field, H. *Arabs of Central Iraq: Their History, Ethnology, and Physical Characters*. Chicago, IL, 1935.

The Anthropology of Iraq. 4 vols, 1940, 1949, 1951, 1952. Chicago, IL, (first 2 vols), Cambridge, MA (last 2 vols).

Fuccaro, Nelida. *The Other Kurds: Yazidis in Colonial Iraq*. London and New York, I. B. Tauris, 1999.

Gat, Moshe. *The Jewish Exodus from Iraq 1948–1951*. London and Portland, OR, Frank Cass, 1997.

Kinnane, Dirk. *The Kurdish Problem*. Oxford, 1964.

The Kurds and Kurdistan. Oxford, 1965.

Luke, Sir H. C. *Mosul and its Minorities*. London, 1925.

McDowall, David. *A Modern History of the Kurds*. London, I. B. Tauris, 1995.

O'Ballance, Edgar. *The Kurdish Revolt 1961–1970*. London, Faber and Faber, 1974

O'Leary, Brendan, McGarry, John, and Salih, Kaled (Eds). *The Future of Kurdistan in Iraq*. Philadelphia, University of Pennsylvania Press, 2005.

Salim, S. M. *Marsh Dwellers of the Euphrates Delta*. New York, 1961.

Shiblak, Abbas. *Iraqi Jews: A History of Mass Exodus*. London, Saqi Books, 2005.

Short, Martin, and McDermott, Anthony. *The Kurds*. London, Minority Rights Group, 1975.

Spat, Eszter. *The Yezedis*. London, Saqi Books, 2006.

Stansfield, Gareth. *Iraqi Kurdistan: Political Development and Emergent Democracy*. London, Routledge, 2003.

Thesiger, Wilfred. *The Marsh Arabs*. London, 1964.

Van Bruinessen, Martin. *Agha, Sheikh and State. The Social and Political Structures of Kurdistan*. London, Zed Books, 1992.

ISRAEL

Physical and Social Geography

W. B. FISHER

The pre-1967 frontiers of Israel are defined by armistice agreements signed with neighbouring Arab states, and represent the stabilization of a military front as it existed in late 1948 and early 1949. These boundaries are thus, in many respects, fortuitous, and have little geographical basis. Indeed, prior to 1918, the whole area that is now partitioned between Syria, Israel, the Palestinian territories and Jordan formed part of the Ottoman Empire, and was spoken of as 'Syria'. Then, after 1918, came the establishment of the territories of Lebanon, Syria, Palestine and Transjordan—with the frontier between the last two lying, for the most part, along the Jordan river.

The present State of Israel is bounded on the north by Lebanon, on the north-east by Syria, on the east by Jordan and the Palestinian territory in the West Bank, and on the south and south-west by the Gulf of Aqaba and the Sinai Desert, occupied in 1967 and returned in April 1982 to Egyptian sovereignty. The so-called 'Gaza Strip', a small piece of territory some 40 km long, formed part of Palestine but was, under the Armistice Agreement of February 1949, then left under Egyptian control. Since May 1994 the Gaza Strip has been under the limited jurisdiction of the Palestinian (National) Authority (PA); however, Israel completed its disengagement from the territory in August–September 2005 (see History). The Gaza Strip will eventually—it is envisaged—form part of a single Palestinian entity, together with the Palestinian-controlled areas in the West Bank. The territories that were occupied after the war of June 1967 are not recognized as forming part of the State of Israel, although it seems unlikely that Israel will reverse its annexation of the Old City of Jerusalem. The geographical descriptions of these territories are, therefore, given in the supplementary section at the end of the chapter.

Owing to the nature of the frontiers, which partition natural geographical units, it is more convenient to discuss the geography of Israel partly in association with that of its neighbour, Jordan. The Jordan Valley itself is dealt with in the chapter on Jordan, but the uplands of Samaria-Judaea, from Jenin to Hebron, and including Jerusalem, which form a single unit, will be discussed below, although parts of this territory lie outside the frontiers of Israel.

PHYSICAL FEATURES

The physical geography of Israel is surprisingly complex and, though the area of the state is small, a considerable number of regions are easily distinguished. In the extreme north the hills of the Lebanon range continue without break, though of lower altitude, to form the uplands of Galilee, where the maximum height is just over 1,200 m. The Galilee hills fall away steeply on three sides: on the east to the well-defined Jordan Valley (see Jordan), on the west to a narrow coastal plain, and to the south at the Vale of Esdraelon or 'Emek Yezreel'. This latter is a rather irregular trough formed by subsidence along faults, with a flat floor and steep sides, and it runs inland from the Mediterranean south-eastwards to reach the Jordan Valley. At its western end the vale opens into the wide Bay of Acre, 25 km–30 km in breadth, but it narrows inland to only a few km before opening out once again where it joins the Jordan Valley. This lowland area has a very fertile soil and an annual rainfall of 400 mm, which is sufficient, with limited irrigation, for agriculture. Formerly highly malarial and largely uncultivated, the vale is now very productive. For centuries it has been a corridor of major importance linking the Mediterranean coast and Egypt with the interior of south-west Asia, and has thus been a passageway for ethnic, cultural and military invasions.

South of Esdraelon there is an upland plateau extending for about 150 km. This is a broad upfold of rock, consisting mainly of limestone and reaching 900 m in altitude. In the north, where there is a moderate rainfall, the plateau has been eroded into valleys, some of which are fertile, though less so than those of Esdraelon or Galilee. This district, centred on Jenin and Nablus, is the ancient country of Samaria, until 1967 part of Jordan. Further south rainfall is reduced and erosion is far less prominent; hence this second region, Judaea proper, stands out as a more strongly defined ridge, with far fewer streams and a barer open landscape of a more arid and dusty character. Jerusalem, Bethlehem and Hebron are the main towns. Towards the south-east rainfall becomes scarce and the Wilderness of Judaea, an area of semi-desert, unfolds. In the extreme south the height of the plateau begins to decline, passing finally into a second plateau only 300 m–450 m above sea level, but broader, and broken by occasional ranges of hills that reach 900 m in height. This is the Negev, a territory comprising nearly one-half of the total area of Israel, and bounded on the east by the lower Jordan Valley and on the west by the Sinai Desert. Agriculture, entirely dependent on irrigation, is carried on in a few places in the north, but for the most part the Negev consists of steppe or semi-desert. Irrigation schemes have been developed in those areas where soils are productive.

Between the uplands of Samaria-Judaea and the Mediterranean Sea there occurs a low-lying coastal plain that stretches southwards from Haifa as far as the Egyptian frontier at Gaza. In the north the plain is closely hemmed in by the spur of Mount Carmel (550 m), which almost reaches the sea; but the plain soon opens out to form a fertile lowland—the Plain of Sharon. Still further south the plain becomes broader again, but with a more arid climate and a sandier soil—this is the ancient Philistia. Ultimately the plain becomes quite arid, with loose sand dunes, and it merges into the Sinai Desert.

One other area remains to be mentioned—the Shephelah, which is a shallow upland basin lying in the foothills of the Judaean plateau, just east of the Plain of Sharon. This region, distinguished by a fertile soil and moister climate, is heavily cultivated, chiefly with cereals.

CLIMATE

Israel has the typical 'Mediterranean' cycle of hot, dry summers, when the temperature reaches 32°C–38°C, and mild, rainy winters. Altitude has a considerable effect, in that although snow may fall on the hills, it is not frequent on the lowlands. Several inches of snow may fall in Jerusalem in winter, whereas Upper Galilee may receive several feet. The valleys, especially Esdraelon and adjacent parts of the upper Jordan, lying below sea level, can become extremely hot (more than 40°C) and very humid.

Rainfall varies greatly from one part of Israel to another. Parts of Galilee receive over 1,000 mm annually, but the amount decreases rapidly southwards, until in the Negev and Plain of Gaza it is 250 mm or less. This is because the prevailing south-westerly winds blow off the sea to reach the north of Israel, but further south they come from Egypt, with only a short sea track, and therefore lack moisture.

PEOPLE AND LANGUAGE

At a census held in December 2008, the total population was recorded at 7,412,180 (males 3,663,910, females 3,748,270). By 31 December 2012, according to official estimates, this had increased to 7,981,400.

Under British mandatory rule there were three official languages in Palestine—Arabic, spoken by a majority of the inhabitants (all Arabs and a few Jews); Hebrew, the ancient language of the Jews; and English. This last was considered to be standard if doubt arose as to the meaning of translation from the other two. Since the establishment of the State of Israel the relative importance of the languages has changed. Hebrew is now dominant, Arabic has greatly declined following the flight of Arab refugees and English is also less important, though it remains the first foreign language of many Israelis.

Hebrew, prevalent in biblical days, was largely eclipsed after the dispersal of Jewish people by the Romans, and until fairly recently its use was largely restricted to scholarship, serious literature and religious observance. Most Jews of Eastern and Southern Europe did not employ Hebrew as their everyday speech, but spoke either Yiddish or Ladino, the former being a Jewish-German dialect current in East and Central Europe and the latter a form of Spanish. Immigrants into Israel since 1890, however, have been encouraged to use Hebrew in normal everyday speech, and Hebrew is now the living tongue of most Israeli Jews. The revival has been a potent agent in the unification of the Israeli Jewish people since, in addition to the two widely different forms of speech, Yiddish and Ladino, most Jewish immigrants spoke yet another language according to their country of origin, and the census of 1931 recorded more than 60 such languages in common usage within Palestine. Now, as the proportion of native-born Israelis increases, Hebrew is dominant and the use of other languages is diminishing.

It is only by a revival of Hebrew that the Jewish community has found a reasonable *modus vivendi*—yet this step was not easy, for some devout Jews opposed the use of Hebrew for secular speech. Furthermore, there was controversy as to the way in which Hebrew should be pronounced, although the Sephardic pronunciation was finally adopted.

History

Revised for this edition by DANA BLANDER

BEGINNINGS

For some Jews, the creation of the State of Israel in 1948 was the fulfilment of Biblical prophecy; to others, in this more secular age, Israel is a state won by political skill and force of arms in a world that denied Jews their legitimate national rights for nearly 2,000 years; either way, it is seen as the fulfilment of Jewish history.

The Jews trace their descent from Abraham, the first of the Patriarchs, who departed from Ur, the centre of the ancient Chaldean civilization, some time between 2300 and 2000 BC. Oral tradition, as recorded in the Old Testament (Hebrew Bible), states that he was instructed by God to leave Chaldea with his family and proceed to Canaan (Phoenicia), or Palestine, the land of the Philistines, where he would father a great nation that would play an important part in human history. The Old Testament was primarily concerned to establish the descent of the Jewish people from Abraham under the guidance of God, but, in so doing, it preserved the ancient history of the Jews.

The subsequent story of Abraham's sojourn in Sinai and return to Canaan, of his descendants' enslavement in Egypt, and their return under Moses and Joshua to the Promised Land, forms the bedrock of Jewish history. The experience of Judges and Kings, of the establishment of Jerusalem as the national capital and the building of the Temple, of the achievement of greatness under the kingdoms of David and Solomon, and then of division, destruction and captivity constitute the foundation stones of this identity.

Greek rule of Palestine, the replacement of Greece by Rome as the major regional power and periodic Jewish rebellions against the hegemon form the final chapters of this first era of the Jewish story. It ended with the suppression by Rome of the Bar-Kokhba revolt in AD 135, which put paid to Jewish hopes of renewed sovereignty. Jewish communities continued to exist, often persecuted, but united by religion and certain central themes: their belief in the oneness of God, His promise to Abraham, the promise of the 'return' and the Temple as the temple of all Jews. The scattered communities continued to look towards Jerusalem. To this day observant Jews face eastwards towards Jerusalem when they pray three times each day.

THE ZIONIST MOVEMENT

In the late 19th century Jews in Eastern Europe were second-class citizens, subject to persecution. In more liberal Western Europe, the situation was better. There Jews found themselves tempted by the attractions of assimilation and conversion. In 1881 a series of pogroms in Russia stirred the conscience of world Jewry, helping to catalyse a renewed national awareness.

Between 1881 and 1914 approximately 2m. Jews left Russia, the main destinations being Western Europe and the USA. Yet for a small minority, there could be only one destination: Palestine. The pogroms led directly to the formation in Russia of a movement called the Lovers of Zion (Hovevei Zion). A group of young Jews, mainly students, from Kharkov (Kharkiv), comprised the first immigrants to Palestine in 1882. Some called themselves Bilu—the Hebrew initials for 'House of Jacob, arise and let us go', from the Book of Isaiah. They issued a manifesto demanding a national home in Palestine. Theodor Herzl, a formerly assimilated Hungarian Jewish journalist who founded the modern Zionist movement, defined its aim specifically at the Basel Congress of 1897 (Documents on Palestine, see p. 56): 'Zionism', he said, 'strives to create for the Jewish people a home in Palestine secured by public law.' He wrote in his journal after the congress: 'At Basel I founded the state of the Jews . . . perhaps in five years, and certainly 50, everyone will know it.'

Herzl was concerned essentially with the creation of a safe refuge for the suffering communities of Eastern Europe, and thought that their migration and settlement could and should be financed by prosperous Jews. He considered other possible destinations as far apart as Uganda and Latin America, but even safe places could never have the same appeal to Jews as the Land of Israel/Palestine, sanctioned in their scriptures and 'promised' to them by God. Some of the Jews of Russia and Poland escaped persecution to make their own way to Palestine and became the earliest immigrant communities there.

When the Turkish Ottoman Empire was destroyed by Allied forces in the First World War, influential Zionists, notably Dr Chaim Weizmann, saw their opportunity to press the United Kingdom for a commitment to provide a national home for the Jewish people in Palestine. They secured the sympathy and support of the Prime Minister, David Lloyd-George, and the Foreign Secretary, Arthur Balfour. The resulting Balfour Declaration (Documents on Palestine, see p. 57), which was contained in a letter from Balfour to Lord Rothschild on behalf of the Zionist Federation, dated 2 November 1917, stated:

'His Majesty's Government view with favour the establishment in Palestine of a national home for the Jewish people, and will use their best endeavours to facilitate the achievement of this object, it being clearly understood that nothing shall be done which may prejudice the existing civil and religious rights of existing non-Jewish communities in Palestine, or the rights and political status of Jews in other countries.'

Herzl's first aim had thereby been achieved: the national home of the Jewish people had been 'secured by public law'; but major obstacles were still to be overcome. Most Zionists presumed that the entity would be a state, as did Lloyd-George and Balfour, but the Balfour Declaration only provided for 'a national home for the Jewish people' in Palestine. The rise of Jewish nationalism coincided with the rise of Arab nationalism. The 'Young Turks' revolt of 1908 imposed a policy of 'Turkification' on the Arab world and its embrace of nationalism was a reaction to this.

The end of the war brought the end of the Ottoman Empire and the division of its Arab dominions between the United Kingdom and France. Up until that point, it was difficult to determine where the actual borders of Palestine were located. Many referred to it as Southern Syria. The Mandate given to the United Kingdom also included Transjordan, the territory east of the river and beyond Amman. By the early 1920s pro-Zionist politicians such as Lloyd-George and Balfour had lost office. Lord Curzon, who became British Foreign Secretary, was much more predisposed towards the Arab cause. To serve as a balance to the granting of a national home in Palestine to the Jews, he detached Eastern Palestine and allotted it to the Amir Abdullah in 1921. (In 1946 it became the Kingdom of Jordan with the granting of full independence.)

Meanwhile, the Zionist leadership established institutions in Palestine, creating the infrastructure for a future Jewish state. These included a democratically elected Asephat HaNivcharim (Assembly of Representatives) of the Jewish community and the Histadrut (General Federation of Labour in Israel), the responsibilities of which extended far beyond those of a trade union (such as the provision of welfare support). The Zionist movement also formed its own military organizations in order to defend Jewish settlements against Arab attacks. The Haganah, which was established in the early 1920s and later had its own units of élite troops, the Palmach, were strengthened by those Jews who had fought on the side of the British during the war. Two smaller nationalist groups, opposed to the main leadership, the Irgun Tsvai Leumi and Lehi (the Stern Group), embarked on a policy of armed struggle against the British Mandate.

Arab nationalists bitterly opposed the Balfour Declaration and Jewish immigration, and advocated the prohibition of land sales to Jews. The United Kingdom would neither accede to their demands nor to Jewish claims to become a majority in Palestine, and there were intermittent outbreaks of violence, notably in 1920, 1921 and 1929, which brought the Arabs into conflict with the mandatory Government. In the 1930s the Jewish population almost tripled, from 46,000 in 1931 (17% of the total population) to 135,000 (30%) in 1935, and industry expanded. The influx of Jews fleeing from Nazi Germany coincided with the coming of age of a new educated élite. In 1936 there was an effective six-month general strike of the Arab population, followed by a large-scale rebellion that lasted until the outbreak of the Second World War. The strike was not very effective, however, since Arab workers could be replaced by Jewish workers. Jaffa port was closed and Tel-Aviv developed instead.

In response to the violence, the United Kingdom established the Peel Commission in 1937, which heard testimonies from both sides. The Jews wanted unrestricted immigration, while the Arabs wanted immediate independence and the closing of the gates to further Jewish immigration. The Commission published its findings in July. It advocated partition of the land. The mainstream Zionists accepted, but the Palestinian Arab leadership under the Mufti of Jerusalem rejected any such action. In 1939 another Commission issued yet another White Paper, which stated that the United Kingdom would not continue to develop the Jewish national home beyond the point already reached, and proposed that 75,000 more Jews should be admitted over five years after which time Jewish immigration would cease. Finally, it proposed that self-governing institutions should be established at the end of the five-year period. The United Kingdom, on the brink of war, believed its interests lay with the Arabs rather than the Jews, who already opposed Nazism. It was keen to secure its oil supplies, particularly the Kirkuk–Haifa pipeline, in the event of war.

THE BILTMORE PROGRAMME AND AFTER

When war did eventually come, the British impeded Jewish immigration from Nazi Europe, according to the tenets of the 1939 White Paper. During a visit to New York in 1942 by David Ben-Gurion, Chairman of the Jewish Agency Executive, an Extraordinary Zionist Conference was held at the Biltmore Hotel, which utterly rejected the White Paper and reformulated Zionist policy. The declaration of the conference (Documents on Palestine, see p. 62), issued on 11 May 1942, concluded as follows:

'The conference urges that the gates of Palestine be opened; that the Jewish Agency be vested with control of immigration into Palestine and with the necessary authority for building up the country, including the development of its unoccupied and uncultivated lands; and that Palestine be established as a Jewish Commonwealth integrated into the new structure of the democratic world.'

The Jewish population of Palestine, which had numbered 56,000 at the start of the Mandate, had risen to 608,000 by 1946 and was estimated to be 650,000 on the eve of the establishment of the State of Israel in 1948. The beleaguered mandatory authorities passed the problem on to the United Nations (UN, which had replaced the League of Nations) on 2 April 1947. On 29 November 1947, by 33 votes for and 13 against, with 10 abstentions, the UN General Assembly voted for the partition of Palestine into two states: one Jewish, one Arab. The Arab State was to comprise 4,500 sq miles, with 804,000 Arabs and 10,000 Jews; the Jewish State was to cover 5,500 sq miles, with 538,000 Jews and 397,000 Arabs. The plan divided Palestine into six principal parts, three of which, comprising 56% of the total area, were reserved for the Jewish State, and three (with the enclave of Jaffa), comprising 43% of the area, for the Arab state. It provided that Jerusalem would be an international zone administered by the UN as the holy city for Jews, Muslims and Christians. The Palestinian Arab leadership rejected the plan and, in the subsequent disorders, about 1,700 people were killed. In the first half of 1948 there was effectively a civil war between Arabs and Jews, and large numbers of Arabs fled or were expelled. The Palestinian leadership and the well-to-do were the first to leave, and Palestinian society effectively imploded as a result. The Jews were in a weak position militarily, but in April the Jewish forces launched a full-scale attack and, by the time the Mandate was terminated on 14 May, 300,000–400,000 Arabs had left their homes to become refugees in neighbouring Arab countries.

THE STATE ESTABLISHED

The Mandate was relinquished by the United Kingdom at 6 p.m. Washington, DC time on 14 May 1948; at 6.01 p.m. the State of Israel was officially declared by the Jewish authorities in Palestine; at 6.11 p.m. the USA accorded it recognition and immediately afterwards the USSR did likewise. A provisional Government was formed in Tel-Aviv the day before the Mandate ended, with Ben-Gurion as Prime Minister and other members of the Jewish Agency Executive in leading ministerial posts. On the same day neighbouring Arab countries invaded Israel, joining local forces in their war against the newly established state. The 1948 Arab–Israeli War, also known in Israel as the 'War of Independence', ended with Israeli territorial gains, although it was estimated that some 6,000 Jews were killed and many more were injured. During the War the Israeli leadership took steps to integrate the pre-state militias into a unified military force, the Israel Defence Forces (IDF).

The Constitution and electoral laws had already been prepared and the first general election was held in January 1949 for a single-chamber Knesset (parliament). The 120 deputies were elected by a closed-list proportional representation system, based on a single nation-wide district. This enabled several parties to gain representation, with Ben-Gurion's Labour Party (Mapai) in the majority but never predominant. As a result, government has usually been conducted by uneasy coalitions.

After the 1948 Arab–Israeli War, a further 200,000–300,000 Palestinian Arabs fled from the additional territory conquered by Israel, and over the coming year many left the Arab West Bank for the East Bank, or Transjordan. (In 1950 Abdullah held a referendum in which the West Bank Arabs agreed to be part of his kingdom, which then became known as Jordan.) The Israeli Government maintained the mandatory military control over 150,000 Arabs until 1966, mainly in the Galilee, which remained within its borders, but allowed Arabs to vote in the first Israeli election in 1949 and to be elected to the Knesset.

Israel was admitted to the UN, and secured eventual diplomatic recognition by the British. Israel's relations with the Arab states were governed by a series of armistice agreements reached in Rhodes, Greece, in 1949, which, in effect, established an uneasy truce without an Arab commitment to permanent peace. The Arabs continued to insist that the creation of Israel was a usurpation of Arab territory and rights. Defence policy therefore dominated Israel's political thinking and firmly established the principle that it would remain militarily superior to any combination of Arab states. The seeds of two different approaches in the ruling Labour Government were sowed at this time. Ben-Gurion, the Prime Minister, who was also Minister of Defence, favoured military retaliation, given the apparent absence of a basis for political rapprochement. Moshe Sharret, the Minister of Foreign Affairs, looked for any channel to create a dialogue with 'rejectionist' Arab regimes.

CHALLENGES OF NATION-BUILDING

Mass Immigration

The immediate tasks confronting the new state were clear: the development of permanent state institutions, the rebuilding of the economy and the attraction and absorption of new immigrants. Jewish immigration was, of course, a basic tenet of Zionism. However, the new state was also in dire need of manpower to populate its empty border areas, man its defence structures and help create a modern economy.

The newcomers came in waves. First, the Displaced Persons Camps housing Holocaust survivors in Europe arrived: 270,000 European Jews entered Israel during 1948–52. By 1950 some 50,000 Yemeni Jews had immigrated to Israel. The Jews of Iraq, one of the oldest of Diaspora communities, immigrated *en masse* to Israel in the first years of the 1950s, adding another 113,000 to the population. In a similar fashion, the greater part of the Jewish communities of Romania, Syria, Libya, Afghanistan and Egypt found their way to Israel in this period. By the end of 1956 the population of Israel, which was estimated in November 1948 at 712,000 residents, had more than doubled, to 1,667,000.

At first, immigrants were placed in abandoned Arab dwelling areas or former British barracks. When these had filled up, tent cities began to spring up, becoming natural breeding grounds for unemployment, poverty and alienation. To counteract this, the idea of the transit camp, or *'Ma'abara'*, was born. The idea of these settlements was to offer a temporary stopping point for immigrant families, in areas close to development towns, before they moved on to permanent living arrangements. By November 1951 a total of 127 *Ma'abarot* had been created. Immigration tailed off for a short time in the mid-1950s, before picking up again with the immigration of North African Jews. By May 1958 some 160,000 North Africans had arrived, and housing them presented a major problem. A third model of absorption was devised, whereby whole groups of immigrants were assigned to new 'development towns', mainly situated in the arid south of the country. Immigrants from North Africa and the Middle East, known for a while as the 'second Israel', would remain outside the mainstream channels of political and social influence for a considerable period, and their eventual entry into the political and social mainstream would have lasting, transforming effects on the country.

Reparations from Germany

The rapidly growing population, together with the economic consequences of the 1948 war, made austerity measures unavoidable in the 1950s. These factors also made external financial aid a necessity. US governmental assistance and loans, and support from Diaspora Jews helped, but the state remained in financial difficulties. The issue of German reparations to Israel was first raised in 1950 and immediately aroused strong emotions. Against widespread opposition, the Government argued that Germany had de facto acquired a huge quantity of Jewish assets after the war, which should rightfully be in the possession of the State of Israel. Initial contacts were therefore set up between the two countries and, in January 1951, the Knesset approved further negotiations. These would result in a pledge of US $820m. from Germany to Israel, and a structure dealing with claims for individual restitution. The treaty was ratified in March 1953. The reparations issue led to considerable domestic unrest in Israel, but the payments that resulted formed a crucial injection of funds into the Israeli economy.

INTERNAL DIVISIONS

The Arab Minority

After the conclusion of the 1948 war, an estimated 156,000 Arabs remained within the borders of the new State of Israel. They were concentrated in communities of their own, and in the mixed towns of Jerusalem, Jaffa, Haifa, Acre and Ramle. Nationality legislation enacted in 1952 laid down the conditions whereby the vast majority of these individuals were able to acquire Israeli citizenship over the next five years. While this enabled access to courts and public services, and afforded voting rights, in practice, Israel's Arabs suffered considerable hardship. The Provisional Government's Law and Administration Ordinance enabled the invoking of the Defence Emergency Regulations, originally brought in by the British in 1945 to combat Jewish paramilitary activity. This meant that the IDF co-opted government authority in the border defence areas where most Arabs lived, establishing military governorates over the population. Military courts in these areas possessed broad jurisdiction to try offences against the Emergency Regulations, often in closed session. Homes could be searched and individuals detained 'in the interest of public safety'. Travel and residency rights were limited.

In addition to the hardships associated with this regime (which continued until 1966), Israel's Arabs suffered further under the absentee property regulations. These effectively prevented Arabs who had left their property in the course of the 1948 war from returning to claim it. This included individuals who had remained within the borders of the State of Israel. Instead, the land and goods passed into the hands of the Custodian of Absentee Property. Despite moves from 1953 to compensate Arab citizens of Israel for lands lost, the sums offered were often inadequate, and the Absentee Property laws were a source of particular resentment for Arab Israelis.

Politically, Israel's Arabs suffered from the fact that almost the entire Palestinian Arab élite had fled in the course of the 1948 war. Lacking resources and political experience, Israel's Arabs nevertheless participated in large numbers in national elections from the outset. Even in 1949, 79.3% of registered Arab voters cast ballots. On the basis of local patronage, and via the Arab Labour lists it organized, Mapai enjoyed the support of the largest Arab voting bloc. This situation would persist until the 1970s.

It is undeniable that in the areas of education, health care and public welfare, the Arab position improved in the 1950s, and far outstripped the position of neighbouring Arab countries. (For example, the proportion of Arab girls attending school rose from 2% in 1949 to 40% by 1956.) However, Arab Israelis continued to identify themselves with the larger Arab collectivity, while noting the discrepancy between their own material situation and that of Jewish Israelis.

Religious-Secular Issues

Religious-state relations in Israel were founded on the basis of the consociational 'politics of accommodation'. The political leadership reached a series of compromises that formed a middle path between two approaches—the demand for Israel to be constituted as a religious state and the demand for the separation of religion and state. The ruling Mapai party adopted consociationalism primarily for pragmatic reasons. Ben-Gurion was also willing to make concessions because he believed that religion would eventually 'wither away' as Jews modernized. All these reasons underlay the establishment of the status quo, which has been a central element of the founding compromise regarding religious-state relations.

The core of the status quo, which was formally established in the pre-state period, fixed relations in four areas: the public status of the Sabbath; personal status, specifically the topic of marriage and divorce; Kashrut (dietary laws); and separate religious education. While the status quo was not maintained literally, it served as the guiding principle for adjudicating new circumstances and issues as they arose. In the realm of the Sabbath, agreement was reached that the weekly day of rest for Jews would be Saturday and that certain aspects of Halacha (Jewish Law) would have effect in the public realm. Thus, no public transport would operate on the Sabbath, while businesses, shops and recreational centres would be closed. In the realm of personal status, the Rabbinical Courts Act determined that marriage and divorce are performed only in accordance with Orthodox Halacha. This is the only case in which civil law is entirely based on religious law. This means that Israeli citizens can only get married in a religious ceremony. Ultra-Orthodox Jews were also exempted from military service; a measure that became increasingly contentious as the numbers choosing to continue studying in Yeshivot (religious schools) rather than serve in the army rose from 400 in 1948 to more than 55,000 in 2009.

The establishment of the status quo made possible the ongoing partnership (known as the 'historical alliance') between Mapai and the National Religious Party (NRP, formed by the union of the two pre-state religious Zionist organizations—Mizrachi and Hapoel Hamizrachi) in the first decades of Israel's existence. However, Mapai's relations with the ultra-Orthodox, non-Zionist Jewish communities were not as harmonious. While rejecting the modern Zionist ideology underlying the state, the ultra-Orthodox became involved in national politics, through the desire to protect their patronage system, education system and assets. They clashed with the Government in 1952, over the Defence Service Law, which would have rendered young women liable for a year's military service, or national service in a non-military framework. The ultra-Orthodox feared this possibility, and demonstrations and protests spread as far as Williamsburg and Brownsville in New York, USA, as well as throughout Jerusalem and Bnei Brak. The result was that the Government reached a private agreement with the national religious parties that in return for their support, the bill would be interpreted 'flexibly'. In practice, this allowed large numbers of Orthodox girls to avoid national service. A pattern was established of aggressive politicking by the ultra-Orthodox, to preserve and improve their position in a society whose basic values were alien to them.

ESCALATION OF CONFLICT, 1949–56

The Egyptian monarchy, disgraced by the defeat of 1948, was overthrown in 1952 by a group of 'Free Officers'. The new regime, dominated after 1954 by Col Gamal Abd al-Nasir (Nasser), adopted a creed of uncompromising Arab nationalism. The early 1950s saw frequent raids by bands of Palestinian *fedayeen* across the border with Jordan and from the Egyptian-controlled Gaza Strip. Israel's army, under the leadership of Moshe Dayan, responded to these raids with harsh counter-attacks led by commanders including Ariel Sharon. In the context of growing Egyptian–Israeli tension, Nasser began moves to establish an arms-purchasing relationship with the USSR. Nasser sealed the 'Czech' arms agreement in August 1955, by which he bartered cotton and took credits from the USSR for substantial quantities of arms and aircraft, which began to arrive promptly.

An Israeli raid on 28 February 1955 decimated the small Egyptian garrison at Gaza; the raid was carried out in order to deter Nasser from allowing Gaza to be used as a base for *fedayeen* activities, and led to the further deterioration of relations between the two countries.

SUEZ

On 26 July 1956 Nasser nationalized the Suez Canal Co, of which the United Kingdom and France were the principal shareholders (see the chapter on Egypt), and the two European powers prepared to retake control of it. In October Ben-Gurion entered into a secret pact with them by which Israel would invade the Sinai Peninsula and thus justify the United Kingdom and France intervening to keep the combatants apart. Israel's aim was to strike at Egypt before it had time to integrate the Soviet arms it had recently received.

In the subsequent war, launched on 29 October 1956, Israeli forces scored an impressive military victory, capturing the Gaza Strip and almost all of the Sinai area, including Sharm el-Sheikh, at the entrance to the Gulf of Aqaba. The forces withdrew from most of the Sinai Peninsula in January 1957, and from the Gaza Strip in March.

SOCIAL CONSOLIDATION AND GROWTH, 1960–70

The announcement of the capture of Nazi war criminal Adolf Eichmann, on 23 May 1960, and his subsequent trial, focused Israeli attention on the Holocaust. In the frenetic early days there had been little time to ponder such matters. Eichmann himself was convicted, and hanged on 31 May 1962, but the memories unearthed by the trial lingered. The Holocaust remained a presence for a new generation of Israeli Jews.

Large-scale immigration from North Africa and Eastern Europe continued throughout the first half of the 1960s. Israel's population reached 2,384,000 by 1967, making more effective exploitation of the country's natural resources a necessity. Although the population remained largely in the coastal plain area, the country's leadership considered that the reclaiming of the barren wastes of the Negev desert in the south represented a key national task. The barrier to the realization of this vision lay in Israel's scant water resources. By 1960 the blueprint was laid for a national irrigation scheme that Israeli leaders hoped would effectively address this problem.

The plan envisaged the intense utilization of ground water, reclamation of flood overflow and sewage, and the tapping of the full potential of the Yarkon and Kishon rivers. Central to the proposal, however, was the intention of tapping the waters of the Jordan river, and the construction of a national water carrier which would bring Jordan water to the Negev. This, it was clear, could only be carried out in the face of Arab opposition. Israel was concerned with tapping the resources of the upper part of the Jordan, into which most of the Galilee rainfall flowed. Jordan and Syria were convinced that the Israeli project would mean less water for them. Attempts to reach agreement quickly broke down, and the work of Israeli water engineers would be conducted under the threat, and sometimes the reality, of Syrian attempts at sabotage. Nevertheless, the construction of the National Water Carrier was completed by 1964. It consisted of a huge conduit, traversing two-thirds of the country, supplying 320m. cu m of water per year.

As a result of the efficient channelling of water resources, by 1967 140,000 acres of reclaimed Negev wasteland were under cultivation. The water supply also made possible the growth of the port of Eilat, on the southern tip of the Negev, and since, after 1956, the Straits of Tiran were open, the town could begin to play a crucial function as the stopping point for Israel's growing trade with the newly independent states of Africa. Exploitation of the mineral resources of the Negev also formed part of the growing infrastructure in Israel's south. Copper ore and potash began to be mined. Most importantly, throughout the decade new towns, inhabited for the most part by new immigrants, sprang up around the desert. Netivot, Dimona, Arad, Yerucham and Ashdod all date from this period. Some 250,000 new immigrants would make their homes in the Negev.

CHANGES IN POLITICS AND DIPLOMACY

Internal Politics

Mapai, Israel's Labour party, remained in power throughout the 1960s. As the largest party, it had been able to secure the most important ministerial positions and to dictate most policies. However, changes were afoot within the Labour establishment. A new generation of young technocrats, personified by former Chief of Staff Moshe Dayan and former Director-General of the Ministry of Defence Shimon Peres, championed by Ben-Gurion, came to the fore.

The re-eruption of wrangling over the so-called Lavon Affair (a labyrinthine scandal relating to clandestine operations in Egypt) led to new elections in 1961, from which Mapai emerged victorious but bruised, with its number of seats reduced from 47 to 42. Continued feuding in the party led to the final retirement of Ben-Gurion in June 1963, and his replacement as Prime Minister by Levi Eshkol. Ben-Gurion and his young allies later left Mapai to form the Rafi party, which did not achieve high levels of support. The parties of the centre and right, meanwhile, were gradually gaining ground. In 1961 the centrist liberals gained 17 seats, as did the rightist Herut. It was clear to the leaders of these parties that their best interests lay in coming together, to form a united anti-Labour list. After much negotiation, this was successfully achieved, with the foundation in 1964 of the Gahal bloc, under the leadership of former Irgun Tsvai Leumi commander Menachem Begin. Gahal would proceed to win 26 seats in the elections of 1965.

In 1965 Mapai established an electoral alliance with its old leftist rival, Ahdut Haavodah, creating the Maarach bloc. In 1968 Mapai, Ahdut Haavodah and Rafi merged to form the Israel Labour Party. Thus, by the end of the decade, Israel possessed the basic outline of a two-party system, with competing centre-left and centre-right blocs, although Labour continued to dominate Israeli politics until 1977.

Diplomacy

In the 1960s Israel attempted to broaden the circle of its diplomatic contacts, and break the attempt, led by Nasser's Egypt, to isolate it. France remained, as an Israeli diplomat put it, 'our one great friend'. However, French involvement in Algeria, the key motive behind French courtship of Israel, came to an end in 1960. Thenceforth, a slow, incremental change took place in the French attitude towards Israel. By the middle of the decade it was clear that the French connection could no longer be relied upon. Elsewhere in Europe, Israel maintained its ambiguous relationship with the Federal Republic of Germany. Under the table, German arms flowed into Israel. Prime Minister Eshkol directed diplomatic efforts towards building Israel's friendship with the USA. The Cold War was at its height, and the USSR had become the chief patron and armourer not only of Nasserite Egypt, but also of other Arab nationalist regimes in Syria and Iraq, which had emerged in the course of the 1950s. It was in this period, under Presidents Kennedy and Johnson, that the USA began to become an important arms supplier for Israel. Still, the USA fought shy of allying themselves too closely with an Israel still totally rejected by all Arab states. Israel did not lack friends and well-wishers in the West, but it did not yet possess what it most needed for its security: namely, a superpower patron to offset Russian support for its enemies.

Elsewhere, Israel tried to reach out to the developing world, offering its expertise in many areas directly relevant to the newly independent countries of Asia and Africa. The Israeli 'model' for the successful development of state institutions almost from scratch, and the efficient exploitation of natural resources, proved attractive to many of the countries of sub-Saharan Africa. Ghana was the first black African state to establish relations with Israel, in 1957, and by the mid-1960s Israel had diplomatic relations with all but one of the states of sub-Saharan Africa. Of 3,948 Israeli experts serving abroad in the period 1958–70, 3,483 were in Africa. They assisted in all areas, from architecture to health care, from drip-irrigation to military organization. In the UN, as a group, the African bloc often followed Egyptian leads and voted against Israel, but this did not affect the mutually beneficial relations these countries individually enjoyed with the Jewish State.

CONTINUED CONFLICT

There was a notable increase in Arab military strikes at Israel across the frontiers with Egypt, Jordan and Syria in the mid-1960s. Some Palestinian students in the Gulf states, including Yasser Arafat, formed a military organization called Fatah (the Palestine National Liberation Movement) in 1957. Their philosophy was non-ideological: quite simply, they demanded a return to pre-1948 Palestine. Israel was perceived as a colonialist state and society, and was equated with the Crusader states; Fatah believed in relentless war against Israel, and rejected all political compromises that would leave Israel in existence.

On 28 May 1964 a conference of traditionalist, pre-1948 notables established the Palestine Liberation Organization (PLO). The conference reconstituted itself as the Palestine National Council (PNC), effectively the ruling board of the PLO, and advocated military training for all Palestinians. The PLO charter sought a 'Palestine [that] is an Arab homeland tied by Arab nationalism to all the Arab countries which together compose the Arab homeland'. The charter also stressed Palestinian identity, specifically that 'Palestinian character was passed from father to son'.

Mutual accusations of frontier violations continued in the 1960s. President Nasser warned that he would have to activate the Egypt-Syria Joint Defence Agreement if Israel's aggression did not cease. In May 1967 King Hussein brought Jordan into the agreement and in that same month Nasser received information, which later proved to be unfounded, that Israeli troops were massing on the Syrian frontier. In response, Nasser ordered the withdrawal of the UN Emergency Force from the Gaza Strip, the Sinai Desert and Sharm el-Sheikh. U Thant, the Secretary-General of the UN, immediately complied, and Nasser then imposed a total blockade on Israeli shipping in the Straits of Tiran, although Israel had always made it plain that this would be considered a *casus belli*.

U Thant flew to Cairo on 22 May 1967 but, by that time, Nasser had already strengthened his forces in the Sinai and summoned his reserves. Israel, Jordan and Syria had also mobilized. Israel formed a national Government, introducing to the Cabinet one representative of each of the three opposition parties. Moshe Dayan, the leader of the 1956 Sinai campaign, was appointed Minister of Defence.

THE SIX-DAY WAR

Israel made its pre-emptive air strike in the early hours of 5 June 1967, when its armoured forces moved into Sinai. In an effort to prevent Jordan becoming involved, Eshkol sent King Hussein a message promising not to attack Jordan in the West Bank or in Jerusalem, if the King stayed out of the war. This effort failed. In the Six-Day War that followed, Israel achieved sweeping and comprehensive victory over the armed forces of Egypt, Jordan and Syria, capturing the West Bank, Sinai, Gaza Strip and Golan Heights.

In the course of the fighting, Israel gained control over the Old City of Jerusalem and access to the Western Wall, the outer wall of the Second Temple, which was a sacred place of worship for all Jews but to which they had been denied access since 1948. The city was immediately reunited, and effectively annexed. The UN General Assembly adopted a resolution on 4 July 1967, which urged the Israeli authorities to rescind all the measures taken, and to desist from any further action that would change the status of the holy city. Israel asserted from the outset that it would not countenance the return of the Old City of Jerusalem to Arab possession.

On 29 August 1967 Arab Heads of State began a summit conference in Khartoum, Sudan, at which they decided to seek a political settlement but not to make peace with or recognize Israel, nor to negotiate directly with it, and meanwhile 'to adopt necessary measures to strengthen military preparation to face all eventualities'. This became known as the 'three noes' summit. On 22 November, after many attempts, the UN Security Council agreed to Resolution 242 (Documents on Palestine, see p. 64), which stated that the establishment of a just and lasting peace in the Middle East should include the application of the following principles:

(i) withdrawal of Israeli armed forces from territories occupied in the recent conflict; and

(ii) termination of all claims or states of belligerency and respect for and acknowledgement of the sovereignty, territorial integrity, and political independence of every State in the area, and their right to live in peace within secure and recognized boundaries free from threats or acts of force. The Council affirmed also the necessity for (*a*) guaranteeing freedom of navigation through international waterways in the area, and (*b*) achieving a just settlement of the refugee problem.

The UN Secretary-General designated ambassador Gunnar Jarring of Sweden as Special Representative to assist the process of finding a peaceful settlement on this basis.

The essential ambiguity of the Resolution was contained in the phrase 'withdrawal ... from territories occupied ...' (which in the French translation became 'les territoires'), and the

Israeli Government contended that it meant an agreed withdrawal from some occupied territories 'to secure and recognized boundaries'. This was, in Israel's view, precluded by the Arab states' Khartoum Resolution and their insistence that Resolution 242 meant total withdrawal from the territories occupied in 1967. Furthermore, Israel insisted that it would only negotiate withdrawal directly with Egypt and the Arab states as part of a peace settlement and that the function of Jarring was to bring this about and not to initiate proposals of his own for a settlement.

UNEASY SECURITY

Meanwhile, Israel based its policy on retention of the Occupied Territories as warranty for its security. The 1967 defeat had severely damaged the USSR's prestige in the Arab world, and to repair its position it began immediately to restore the Egyptian armed forces, including the air force. Using powerful artillery installed by the USSR west of the Canal, Nasser began in 1968 a 'war of attrition' in order to force Israel to accept his terms. Relatively heavy casualties were inflicted on the Israeli troops, notably in July and October, and throughout the period Israel retaliated with air and artillery attacks, which forced Egypt to evacuate the Canal zone towns. Suez and its oil refineries were destroyed. The zone remained unsettled until 1970.

Israel's Prime Minister, Levi Eshkol, died on 26 February 1969, and was succeeded in the following month by Golda Meir, Minister of Foreign Affairs from 1956 to 1966 and a unifying figure within the Alignment, an alliance between the Israel Labour Party and Mapam.

In June 1970 US Secretary of State William Rogers announced an initiative designed 'to encourage the parties to stop shooting and start talking'. Nasser stunned Egypt and the Arab world with an unconditional acceptance of the Rogers plan and its related Canal zone 90-day cease-fire. King Hussein immediately associated Jordan with Nasser's acceptance. Israel accepted the Rogers plan on 7 August, prompting Gahal to withdraw from the Government. Israel complained that Egypt had broken the cease-fire agreement by moving SAM-III missile sites into the 30-mile wide 'standstill' area along the Canal.

President Nasser died suddenly on 28 September 1970, but President Sadat, who succeeded him, sustained his policy. Although he only agreed to extend the cease-fire for another 90 days, it continued indefinitely. The US effort was directed towards securing an interim agreement by which Israel would withdraw from the Suez Canal and allow it to be reopened. However, Israel, again on the basic principle of its security, would only consider a limited withdrawal and would not agree that Egyptian troops should cross the Canal, terms that Egypt refused. US–Israeli relations, vital to Israel, were uneasy during most of 1971 while the US Department of State pressed the Israeli Government to concede to terms of withdrawal from the Canal that were viewed as unacceptable. President Sadat gave the end of the year as a deadline for 'peace or war', but before the year was over Golda Meir secured a commitment to Israeli security from President Nixon firmer than any obtained in the past; the Rogers plan was thereby abandoned, but 1972 began without the threatened outbreak of war with Egypt.

Instead, there was a series of terrorist acts by various Palestinian groups, which in turn provoked punitive raids by Israeli forces. Israeli counter-insurgency measures eliminated Palestinian activity on the West Bank, although there was increased resistance in Gaza. By 1969 some 2,800 Palestinian fighters were in prison and 1,828 had been killed. Failure on the local level led to attempts to internationalize Palestinian military activity, and to the increased use of terrorism against civilians. On 23 July 1969 the Popular Front for the Liberation of Palestine (PFLP) hijacked and diverted a flight of the Israeli state airline, El Al, from Rome, Italy, to Tel-Aviv to Algiers, Algeria. The 'Black September' group, a faction of Fatah under Ali Hasan Salameh, emerged as the international terrorist wing of Fatah. The two groups organized attacks against Israelis and Diaspora Jews, such as the hijacking of a Sabena aircraft and an attack on the Olympic Village in Munich, Germany, in 1972. Israel initiated a campaign of reprisals, eliminating Fatah and PFLP representatives in: Paris, France; Rome; Nicosia, Cyprus; and Beirut, Lebanon.

THE OCCUPIED TERRITORIES

Nearly 1m. Arabs remained under Israeli occupation, including 70,000 in East (Arab) Jerusalem (which was annexed), who were treated as Israeli citizens. Following the 1967 war, there was a general integration of the Palestinian economy into that of Israel. Industrial and commercial expansion in Israel required Palestinian labourers, and there was greater employment and higher wages; it was no longer a peasant society. Women were more involved, were increasingly attending university, and there was a greater commitment to community work. Contact with Israel brought new ideas. Furthermore, there was a reaction against the pro-Jordanian traditionalist élite; Jordan still paid the salaries of judges, lawyers and teachers on the West Bank. In March 1972 the Israeli military authorities successfully held mayoral and municipal elections in the main Arab towns, despite threats of reprisals against any Arabs taking part.

Official government policy was that in a peace settlement substantial territories would be returned to the Arabs, but there was no clear consensus in the Government or the country as to what they would amount to, except to the extent that Israel should have 'secure frontiers'. A plan advanced by Deputy Prime Minister Yigal Allon, although not publicly approved by the Government, seemed to be in the process of de facto execution. He proposed that a chain of Israeli settlements should be established along the Jordan river (which was effectively being done), and a second chain along the road from Jerusalem to Jericho, in order to establish Israel's security. The rest of the West Bank and the main towns, except Jericho, would then be returned to Jordan, although the Golan Heights would remain under Israeli control. The virtue of the Allon plan for most Israelis was that it would absorb few Arabs, for the core of the dispute within Israel remained the question of demographic balance between Arabs and Jews.

THE YOM KIPPUR WAR

On 6 October 1973—the most important religious holiday in Israel, Yom Kippur (the Day of Atonement)—the fourth all-out Arab–Israeli war commenced when Egypt launched a successfully executed surprise attack across the Suez Canal, combined with a simultaneous Syrian strike on the Golan Heights. After initial setbacks, Israel succeeded in turning the tide on its adversaries, pushing the Syrians back to lines of defence around Damascus and thrusting across the Suez Canal into Egypt. The price, however, was a heavy one in lost lives and equipment.

A precarious cease-fire came into effect on 25 October 1973. This was followed by frantic US 'shuttle diplomacy' in the following months, which concluded with an agreement by Israel and Egypt concerning a disengagement of their forces on 18 January 1974. Israel now withdrew its forces to 20 miles from the Suez Canal, while the Egyptians substantially reduced their presence on the east side of the Canal. In the north, Israel and Syria agreed to withdraw their troops to lines on each side of the 1967 cease-fire line, and the ruined town of Quneitra, capital of the Golan Heights, was handed back to Syria.

Two important factors weakened Israel's position. In the last days of the war the Arab oil-producing states banned the supply of oil to the USA and the Netherlands, and reduced supplies to Western Europe. (The United Kingdom and France were exempted but, in fact, were unable to obtain their full supplies.) This, combined with steep increases in oil prices, which caused serious balance-of-payments problems for the European countries—although this had nothing to do with the war—led the European Community (EC, now European Union—EU) to issue a joint declaration in the Arabs' favour. Even more damaging to Israel was the confrontation that almost developed between the USSR and the USA when they both began delivering heavy supplies of war equipment to the Arabs and Israel, respectively.

The war had a profoundly disturbing effect on Israeli public opinion. Israel suffered huge losses: nearly 3,000 dead and missing. There was widespread dissatisfaction with the Government and a public debate ensued over the failure to anticipate the outbreak of war and the breakdown of military intelligence. There were mutual recriminations among the generals and Minister of Defence Dayan's popularity in the country slumped.

INTERNAL CHANGE, 1974–77

Elections of December 1973

In the general election of December 1973, there was a huge swing from the left to the right, particularly by the Mizrahi Jews, most of whom had arrived from North Africa in the 1950s. The Labour Alignment was once more elected as the strongest party, but the vote for Likud, an alliance of Herut and Liberal parties, increased by almost 50%, giving it 39 seats. None the less, Labour formed the Government and Golda Meir continued as Prime Minister. The report of the Agranat Commission into the causes of the 1973 war, however, led to her resignation. The Commission, which reported in April 1974, was perceived as being excessively lenient on the political leadership, in contrast to its harsh criticism of the military echelon, and this resulted in a public outcry. Meir resigned on 11 April. She was replaced by a relatively new face in Israeli politics, the Chief of Staff of the 1967 victory, and former ambassador to the USA, Itzhak Rabin. The new Israeli Government announced itself ready for territorial concessions in the quest for peace. A detailed map was devised by Minister of Foreign Affairs Yigal Allon, envisaging the ceding of most of the West Bank to Jordan. The plan found no echoes in the Arab world, however. Rather, the Arab states chose, in Rabat, Morocco, in 1974, to afford recognition to the PLO as the 'sole legitimate representative' of the Palestinian Arabs. This organization, a grouping of a number of different 'guerrilla' movements dominated by Yasser Arafat's Fatah, remained implacably opposed to the very existence of Israel, as its founding documents made clear. Israel was itself divided on the issue. Some Israelis remained opposed to the very idea of concessions in the Biblical heartlands of Judea and Samaria, and were determined that these areas should rightfully be settled by Jews as quickly as possible, to offset the possibility of any such concessions. A long tug-of-war between supporters and opponents of concessions now began, and soon came to constitute the essential source of division in Israeli politics.

During this period Israel's key strategic relationship—with the USA—was developed. The burgeoning US connection led to pressure from the USA on the USSR with regard to Soviet Jewry. Russian Jews were discriminated against, often harassed, and prevented from emigrating. The US pressure proved successful in the form of a gradual easing of emigration restrictions. Between 1969 and 1977 over 145,000 Soviet Jews (the majority of them highly qualified) arrived in Israel.

In the fight against Palestinian terrorism, Israel also scored successes. Most famous was the Entebbe operation of July 1976, in which an Israeli commando force succeeded in rescuing 100 hostages taken from an Air France jet and held by PFLP militants at Entebbe Airport, Uganda.

Despite these achievements, the Rabin Government of 1974–77 was to be the last in the unbroken line of Labour-dominated administrations. In May 1977 the country again went to the polls. The Labour Party was racked by the growing rivalry between Rabin and the man who replaced him at the helm, Shimon Peres, as well as by the scandals and fatigue of a party that had held uninterrupted office for nearly 30 years, and by the still-vivid memory of the Yom Kippur War. Against this background, Labour suffered a major setback, going from 51 seats to 32, losing most of its seats to a new, short-lived middle-class party called the Democratic Movement for Change (DMC). Likud increased its number of seats from 39 to 43—the largest single total. Begin was then able to form a coalition with the NRP, which broke its historic alliance with Labour, bringing to an end the long alliance between national religious Zionism and Labour. This was not simply a matter of pragmatism: religious Zionism had been undergoing a steady process of radicalization since 1967, reflected in the growing strength of elements pioneering Jewish settlement in the West Bank and Gaza among its younger adherents. No longer content to enter into pragmatic alliances in order to safeguard the status quo and their own sectoral interests, these young activists sought to play a leading role in what they regarded as a key national task: the building up of the Jewish presence in the recently captured territories, and particularly in the Biblically important areas of Judea and Samaria (the West Bank).

Menachem Begin accordingly set about forming Israel's first right-dominated cabinet, although it was partly counterbalanced by the centrist DMC. He appointed as Minister of Defence Ezer Weizman, who had commanded the air force in the 1967 war. Moshe Dayan, who had defected from the Labour Party, was given the foreign affairs portfolio. These two, together with Begin himself, formed the core policy-making group in the new Cabinet. Sharon, who was appointed as Minister of Agriculture, was the major force behind the establishment of dozens of settlements in the West Bank and Gaza Strip. The ultra-Orthodox parties joined the governing coalition for the first time since 1952, although they refrained from holding ministerial posts.

New Forces in Israeli Public Life

The victory of Menachem Begin's Likud bloc in the elections of 1977 was a watershed moment in the political life of Israel and became known as the mahapach (transformation). It ended nearly half a century of centre-left domination of Zionist and Israeli politics. Begin's victory was made possible by the coming to fruition of a number of processes of profound social change. Perhaps most significant of all was the very high level of support enjoyed by Likud among Jews of Asian (Sephardim) and North African origin (Mizrahim). At the beginning of the 1970s the emergence of a protest group referred to as the 'Black Panthers', whose members were young Mizrahim living in conditions of poverty, unemployment and crime, marked an attitudinal change among this ethnic group. They began expressing their feelings of being disregarded, excluded and discriminated against by the Israel of Mapai and the Labour Alignment, a feeling that was translated into the creation of a new alliance with Mapai's political rival, Likud.

The alliance was not only a pragmatic union of outsiders. Herut's language of respect for Jewish tradition and the unabashed assertion of Jewish power had a natural appeal for many Mizrahim. In 1977 the long crystallization of this process came together, making possible the achievement of power by Likud, but also, no less importantly, the clear integration of the Mizrahim into mainstream Israeli politics.

The mid-1970s were also marked by the growing radicalization and alienation of Israel's Arab population. Military government over the Arab Israelis ceased in 1966, but inequalities remained, and these, along with the presence of an educated and politically assertive younger generation, and a renewal of connections with the West Bank after 1967, led to an increasing process of 'Palestinization' in the identity of Arab citizens. This encompassed a declarative loyalty to the Palestinian cause, alongside a continued pragmatic engagement with Israeli society and institutions. The inherent dilemmas and contradictions in such a position would come to define the Arab Israeli experience. When six Arab citizens of Israel were killed during protests against land expropriation by the state on 'Land Day', 30 March 1976, this served to catalyse the move by Arab Israelis away from integration into Israel, and towards more open identification with their fellow Palestinians in the West Bank and Gaza Strip. The old clientelist politics of the Arab Israelis declined, to be replaced by competition for support primarily between the Communist Party (Rakah), the Israeli leftist lists (Mapam, Ratz and the Progressive List for Peace) and, over time, a number of Arab nationalist movements, the most well-known of which at this time was the Abna al-Balad (Sons of the Village) movement (which boycotted elections to the Knesset). The identity issue notwithstanding, however, the trend in the 1980s and 1990s would be towards progressively greater Arab involvement in the Israeli political system. The twin struggle of Arabs in Israel—for equal rights within Israel and against the Israeli occupation in the territories—continues to be the hallmark of the political discourse and activity of the Arab minority in Israel.

A religious Zionist group led by the extra-parliamentary group 'Gush Emunim' also started gaining political strength during this period. It was instrumental in the building of settlements in the occupied territories. The number of settlements established since 1967 had risen to 129 (114 in the West Bank) by 1985, and the number of Israeli settlers to 46,000 (42,500 in the West Bank), with Israel holding direct control of more than 50% of the 490,000 ha of land in the West Bank.

UNEXPECTED PEACE WITH EGYPT

Against widespread expectations, the new Likud Government established contacts with Egypt shortly after assuming office. President Sadat of Egypt visited Jerusalem in November 1977 and addressed the Knesset. Talks between Sadat and Begin continued, and finally an unexpected breakthrough occurred in September 1978 after talks at Camp David, USA, under the guidance of President Carter, when Begin and Sadat signed two agreements. The first provided for a five-year transitional period during which the inhabitants of the Israeli-occupied West Bank and Gaza would obtain full autonomy and self-government. The second agreement provided for the signing of a peace treaty between Egypt and Israel, which was signed on 26 March 1979. The treaty provided for a phased withdrawal from Sinai which was successfully completed on 25 April 1982. Diplomatic relations between Israel and Egypt were established on 26 January 1980.

Proposals for Palestinian autonomy provided for negotiations to be completed by 26 May 1980. However, that date passed without agreement, amid widely differing Israeli and Arab interpretations of the meaning of the term 'autonomy'. It became clear during the talks that Egypt and the Palestinians were considering 'autonomy' in terms of an independent Palestinian state, whereas Israel envisaged only some form of administrative self-government for the Palestinian Arabs in the West Bank.

BEGIN'S SECOND TERM

Begin's Government was beset by internal fissures. In the course of his first term, two of his most influential ministers, Moshe Dayan and Ezer Weizman, resigned over policy differences. The dire state of the economy, with rampant inflation, was the precipitating factor for new elections. When the country went to the polls in June 1981, the opposition Labour Party was confident of victory but against expectations, Begin won a second term. The tax-cutting policies of the new Minister of Finance, Yoram Aridor, together with Israel's successful attack on the Osiraq (Iraq) nuclear reactor, played an important role in Begin's victory.

Begin's majority was precarious, and his Government clashed with the US Administration over its annexation of the Golan Heights in December 1981, and with right-wing opponents over the evacuation of the Sinai settlements. The Sinai withdrawal nevertheless took place as planned, on 25 April 1982.

ADVANCE INTO LEBANON

Following the attempted assassination by members of the Palestinian Fatah Revolutionary Council, led by Sabri Khalil al-Banna ('Abu Nidal'), of Israel's ambassador to the United Kingdom, Shlomo Argov, Israel launched a large-scale offensive against PLO positions in Lebanon in June 1982, known as Operation Peace for Galilee (see the chapter on Lebanon). By the end of that month Israeli forces had advanced across Lebanon, pinning down 6,000 PLO fighters in West Beirut.

Intensive diplomatic efforts, hampered by repeated outbreaks of fighting, were made between June and August 1982 to find an acceptable basis for the supervised withdrawal of the trapped Palestinian and Syrian forces. With the help of a US envoy, Philip Habib, their evacuation began on 21 August and was completed by 1 September (estimates put the number of evacuees at 14,500–15,000).

Israeli forces remained in effective control of Beirut, although, under the terms of the evacuation agreement, an international peace-keeping force (predominantly comprising US, French and Italian troops) was stationed in various parts of the city until early September 1982. Despite US protests, Israeli forces moved into West Beirut again on 15 September, taking up positions around Palestinian refugee camps located in the Muslim sectors. In Israel itself, there were increasing protests against the Government's policies. On 17 September reports began to emerge of a massacre committed in the Sabra and Chatila camps by Israel's allies, the Maronite Christian Phalangist militias, who were ostensibly looking for Palestinian fighters. (The killings came shortly after the assassination of Maronite leader Bashir Gemayel.) The massacre provoked large demonstrations in Israel. Following public pressure, the Begin Government on 28 September initiated a full judicial inquiry, led by the Chief Justice of the Supreme Court, Itzhak Kahan. Published on 8 February 1983, the report of the inquiry placed actual responsibility for the massacre on Lebanese Phalangists, but concluded that Israel's political and military leaders bore indirect responsibility for the tragic events by failing properly to supervise the militiamen in the area. Begin was censured merely for showing indifference to reports reaching him of Phalangists entering the camps. As recommended by the inquiry commission, Ariel Sharon was removed as Minister of Defence (though he remained in the Government as Minister without Portfolio), to be replaced by the ambassador to the USA, Moshe Arens.

Direct talks between Israel and Lebanon for the withdrawal of foreign forces began on 28 December 1982. Progress was slow but a 12-article agreement, formulated by US Secretary of State Shultz and declaring the end of hostilities, was finally signed on 17 May 1983. Syria rejected the agreement and its forces held their positions in the Beqa'a valley, raising the possibility of open war with Israel, which, in turn, refused to withdraw while the Syrians remained. On the same day that Israel signed its agreement with Lebanon, it concluded another secret one with the USA which recognized Israel's right, despite the accord with Lebanon, to retaliate against terrorist attacks in Lebanon and to delay its withdrawal, beyond the date agreed in that accord (three months from the date of signing), if Syrian and PLO forces remained there. In July Israel, with its casualties from guerrilla attacks increasing, decided to redeploy its forces south of Beirut along the Awali river.

BEGIN'S RESIGNATION

Begin, distressed by the death of his wife in November 1982 and by the events in Lebanon, announced his resignation as Prime Minister and leader of the Likud bloc on 30 August 1983. Itzhak Shamir, the Minister of Foreign Affairs since 1980, was elected leader of Likud on 2 September 1983. Begin withheld his formal resignation until 15 September, while a period of political wrangling ensued to find a viable coalition government. Shamir was asked to form a government on 21 September, his Likud grouping having a theoretical majority of seven seats with the support of minority religious parties. Shamir pronounced his commitment to the Israeli presence in Lebanon, to the continuation of the West Bank settlement programme and to tackling the country's economic problems.

During the second half of 1983 a severe monetary crisis contributed to the declining popularity of the Government. The lack of a co-ordinated approach to the crisis led to the resignation, in October, of the Minister of Finance, Yoram Aridor, whose policies, diluted by the Cabinet, failed to prevent inflation from rising rapidly. The rigorously applied austerity measures of Aridor's successor, Yigal Cohen-Orgad, however, threatened to alienate elements of Shamir's fragile coalition, prompting concerns over the effects of reductions in social services and increases in food prices, and provoking growing labour unrest.

THE 1984 GENERAL ELECTION

Almost immediately upon taking office, Shamir was required to prepare his Likud Party for fresh elections. The defection of a small religious faction, the Tami party, over economic and social issues, gave Labour a majority in the Knesset to support its demand for early elections, which were then scheduled for 23 July 1984. The outcome of the elections was a stalemate: Labour secured 44 seats, Likud 41. Neither party proved able to forge a coalition enabling it to command at least 61 Knesset votes. Agreement was finally reached for the foundation of a national unity government, which would rest on the support of both major parties, and which would involve the rotation of the premiership, from Shimon Peres to Shamir, after a two-year period. The new government would be by definition a caretaker administration, unable to take major initiatives in either a leftward or rightward direction. Its component parties accounted for 97 of the 120 Knesset seats. It contained representatives of the two major party groupings (Labour and Likud); four religious parties (the NRP, Shas, Agudat Israel and Morasha); and the Shinui, Yahad and Ometz parties.

THE ISRAEL OCCUPATION OF SOUTHERN LEBANON

Following the withdrawal in September 1983 of Israeli forces in Lebanon to the Awali river, south of Beirut, a de facto partition of the country came into being. Israeli troops (reduced to some 10,000 by the end of 1983) faced about 50,000 Syrian troops and 2,000–4,000 Palestinian fighters entrenched in the Beqa‘a valley to the north. The 2,500 men of Maj. Sa'ad Haddad's Israeli-controlled, mainly Christian 'South Lebanon Army' (SLA), were employed to police the occupied area with the Israeli troops, and to combat attacks on the occupying forces. Militant Shi‘ite groups such as Hezbollah, which looked to Iran, began to operate during the early 1980s (see also the chapter on Lebanon). Although, after the withdrawal to the Awali river, the Israeli air force and navy were involved in attacks on Syrian targets in north Lebanon and against the PLO in the port of Tripoli (in November and December 1983), there were no serious land-based exchanges between Israeli and Syrian forces in Lebanon during the first half of 1984. Maj. Sa'ad Haddad died in December 1983 and Maj.-Gen. Antoine Lahad replaced him as leader of the SLA in March 1984. In the same month, under the influence of Syria, President Gemayel abrogated the 17 May 1983 peace agreement with Israel. The rising cost of involvement in Lebanon and the unpopularity of that policy at home disposed Israel at least to consider withdrawing. The official policy of the Shamir Government was that Syrian withdrawal from Lebanon was a precondition of Israeli withdrawal.

ISRAEL'S WITHDRAWAL FROM LEBANON

The Government of national unity pledged itself to withdrawing the IDF from Lebanon. Following the breakdown of talks with Lebanon, on 14 January 1985 the Israeli Cabinet voted to take unilateral steps towards withdrawal from that country. The Cabinet agreed a three-phase withdrawal plan whose final aim was the return of the IDF to the international border. The first phase took place in February and involved the evacuation of the IDF from the western occupied sector, around Sidon, to the Litani river area, around Nabatiyah. The Shi‘ites of southern Lebanon, antipathetic towards the PLO, had initially welcomed the IDF, but now they attacked it in retreat. Increasing attacks brought the Israeli death toll in Lebanon during the invasion and occupation to more than 650 by April. During March Israel accelerated the process of withdrawal. The second stage was completed with the evacuation of Tyre on 29 April.

On 4 April 1985 Israel released 750 Shi‘ite prisoners, detained as part of the 'Iron Fist' policy, from Ansar camp, prior to withdrawing from that part of western Lebanon. At the same time, some 1,200 Lebanese and Palestinian detainees were transferred to prisons in Israel. Then, on 20 May, 1,150 Lebanese and Palestinian prisoners were exchanged for three Israeli prisoners of war.

Israel announced the completion of the third and final stage of the withdrawal of the IDF, ahead of schedule, at the beginning of June 1985, though it was common knowledge that about 500 Israeli troops and advisers remained in Lebanon to support the SLA in patrolling the defensive buffer zone which formed a strip, 11 km–20 km wide, inside the border. Despite a continued Israeli presence in Lebanon, Syria withdrew 10,000 of its troops from the Beqa‘a valley at the end of June and the beginning of July, leaving fewer than 25,000 in the country. Attacks on the SLA-controlled 'security zone' were frequent, but the zone remained intact.

Israel was confronted by a more firmly entrenched enemy in the Shi‘ite community just across its northern border. After the final stage of the Israeli evacuation was completed, Shi‘ite guerrilla attacks on SLA and IDF forces continued.

THE FAILURE OF THE JORDANIAN-PALESTINIAN PEACE INITIATIVE

In 1984 Israel rejected a request by King Hussein of Jordan for a peace conference involving all the concerned parties in the Arab–Israeli conflict. In February 1985 King Hussein and Yasser Arafat established a combined Jordanian-Palestinian position on future peace talks, providing for a joint Jordanian-Palestinian delegation to such talks. Although Israel supported the involvement of the five permanent members of the UN Security Council in the peace process, it rejected the appeal for an international peace conference, which was reiterated in 1985 by King Hussein and President Mubarak of Egypt, and also their suggestion of preliminary talks between the USA, Egypt and a joint Jordanian-Palestinian delegation, if it contained PLO members. Israel was interested in direct talks only once an acceptable Palestinian delegation had been agreed. The major obstacle to progress at this time was the PLO's position regarding UN Security Council Resolution 242. The PLO consistently refused to accept this resolution as a basis for negotiations—because it referred only to a Palestinian refugee problem and not to the right of Palestinians to self-determination and a state of Palestine, and because it guaranteed Israel's right to live in peace and security. The PLO Executive Committee repudiated Resolution 242 again after the Amman agreement with Jordan.

In September 1985 three Israelis were murdered by terrorists in Larnaca, Cyprus. Israel held the PLO's élite Force 17 responsible, and, at the beginning of October, bombed the organization's headquarters in Tunis, Tunisia. Six days later an Italian cruise ship, the *Achille Lauro*, was hijacked in the eastern Mediterranean by members of the Palestine Liberation Front (PLF—one of two groups of that name, this being the pro-Arafat PLF, led by Muhammad 'Abu' Abbas). They killed a Jewish American passenger before surrendering to Egyptian authorities in Port Said. In December 17 people were killed when terrorists, believed to belong to the anti-Arafat Fatah Revolutionary Council, led by 'Abu Nidal', attacked passengers at the desks of El Al in Rome and Vienna (Austria) airports.

King Hussein, who had already prepared the ground for an alternative approach to the Palestinian question by initiating a rapprochement with Syria, formally severed political links with the PLO on 19 February 1986, 'until such time as their word becomes their bond'. After the collapse of the Jordanian-Palestinian peace initiative, Jordan resisted Israeli requests for direct talks excluding the PLO, and there was little prospect of an imminent revival of the peace process.

SHAMIR ASSUMES THE PREMIERSHIP

In accordance with the terms of the agreement under which the coalition Government of national unity was formed in September 1984, Peres and Shamir duly exchanged posts on 20 October when the new cabinet was approved by the Knesset.

In October 1986, using information supplied by Mordechai Vanunu, a former technician at Israel's nuclear research establishment at Dimona, the British *Sunday Times* newspaper claimed that Israel had succeeded in developing thermonuclear weapons and was stockpiling them at Dimona. Vanunu subsequently disappeared from London, United Kingdom, and at the end of October the Israeli authorities admitted that he was in their custody and would be tried for breaching national security. In March 1988 Vanunu was sentenced to 18 years' imprisonment.

ATTEMPTS TO REVIVE THE MIDDLE EAST PEACE PROCESS

Prime Minister Itzhak Shamir opposed the concept of an international peace conference involving the five permanent members of the Security Council, and instead proposed direct negotiations between Israel, Egypt, the USA and a joint Jordanian-Palestinian delegation, excluding the PLO. Although King Hussein resisted Shamir's advances, Jordan and Israel appeared to have a common interest in fostering a Palestinian constituency in the West Bank that was independent of the PLO and with which they could deal. In 1986, under the premiership of Shimon Peres (who promised to maintain the freeze on the building of new Jewish settlements in the West Bank), Israel revived a programme of limited Palestinian autonomy, with the appointment of Palestinian officials in municipal government, though this resulted in civil protests by pro-PLO Palestinians and the intimidation or assassination of Israeli appointees. In the less influential role of Minister of Foreign Affairs, Peres, without the knowledge of Shamir, conducted secret negotiations with King Hussein of Jordan in London and concluded 'the London Agreement'. This advocated an international conference to which the five permanent members of the Security Council and protagonists in the conflict were to be invited. The settlement of the conflict would be based on UN Resolutions 242 and 338 (Documents on Palestine, see p. 68). Negotiations would be conducted through bilateral committees, with the Palestinians forming part of the Jordanian delegation. The 'Agreement', however, was not acceptable to the Prime Minister. Peres failed to gain the approval of the 10-member Israeli 'inner' Cabinet for his plan, and his Labour bloc lacked the necessary support in the Knesset to force an early general election on the issue, or to be sure of being able to form a coalition government, thereafter, without Shamir's Likud bloc.

THE INTIFADA

The frequency of anti-Israeli demonstrations and violent incidents in the Occupied Territories increased during 1987, and a wave of violent protests against Israeli rule (the worst since Israel occupied the Territories in 1967) began in December. The rioting was precipitated by the deaths of four Palestinians on 8 December 1987, when the two vehicles in which they were travelling collided with an Israeli army truck at a military checkpoint in the Gaza Strip. The *intifada*, which probably began more as a spontaneous expression of accumulated frustration at 20 years of occupation, was soon being exploited and orchestrated by an underground leadership, the Unified National Leadership of the Uprising (UNLU), comprising elements from across the Palestinian political spectrum (the PLO, the Communist Party and Islamic Jihad). The UNLU organized strikes, the closure of shops and businesses, and other forms of civil disobedience, including the non-payment of taxes.

By mid-January 1988 up to 1,000 Palestinians had been arrested, and 24-hour curfews were in force around 12 or more refugee camps in the Gaza Strip and the West Bank, preventing the entry of food and supplies. The Israeli Cabinet repeatedly endorsed the security forces' 'iron fist' policy but was divided over the long-term solution to the Palestinian question. Shimon Peres, in contrast to Itzhak Shamir's Likud bloc (which considered the Occupied Territories to be non-negotiable), believed that only a political solution could end the uprising, and favoured a demilitarization of those areas and the removal of Jewish settlements prior to a negotiated agreement.

Most disturbing to the Israelis was the powerful new role being played in the uprising by militant Islamist groups, implacably opposed to Israel's existence. The most prominent of these was the Islamic Resistance Movement (Harakat al-Muqawama al-Islamiyya), known by its Arab acronym, Hamas, and founded as a radical incarnation of the Muslim Brotherhood. Hamas came into existence shortly after the outbreak of the *intifada* and its charter, published in August 1988, indicated that the group opposed a two-state solution and the right of the Jews to national self-determination.

THE SHULTZ PLAN

In February 1988 the US Secretary of State, George Shultz, embarked on a tour of Middle Eastern capitals, in an attempt to elicit support for a new peace initiative. The plan's failure to provide for PLO representation led to its rejection by the Arab states, while divisions within the Israeli Government precluded a coherent response from that quarter. This period saw the Occupied Territories sealed off from each other and from Israel, for the first time since 1967, and declared 'closed military areas'. For the Israeli public, the outbreak of the uprising came as a shock. The initial response was support for harsh measures. Over time, however, the increasing awareness that the population of the West Bank and Gaza could be neither absorbed nor permanently suppressed by Israel would lead to a new flexibility among the public, and a willingness to compromise, though not at the expense of endangering security.

JORDAN SEVERS ITS LINKS WITH THE WEST BANK

An Arab summit held in Algiers in June 1988 gave the PLO total control of the flow of funds into the Territories, with an initial sum of US $128m. and $34m. a month thereafter. On 28 July Jordan cancelled its Five-Year Development Plan for the West Bank and, on 31 July, King Hussein officially severed Jordan's legal and administrative links with the West Bank. The House of Representatives, in which deputies representing the West Bank held 30 of the 60 seats, was dissolved. While Jordan paid the salaries of civil servants and public sector employees, the PLO funded trade unions, social associations and the like; there were also housing loans and grants to educational institutions. Without the participation of Jordan, which had voluntarily withdrawn from the West Bank and renounced any pretension to represent the Palestinians, the PLO could make a stronger claim to be the sole legitimate representative of the Palestinian people. The movement's continued rejection of all UN resolutions recognizing Israel's right to exist, however, and its charter openly urging the destruction of the Jewish State, ruled out the organization as a negotiating partner as far as Israel was concerned.

NEW INITIATIVES BY THE PLO

The Palestine National Council met in Algiers in November 1988, and the PLO declared an independent Palestinian state (notionally on the West Bank) and endorsed UN Security Council Resolution 242. At a subsequent press conference in Geneva, Switzerland, Arafat announced his renunciation of 'individual, group and state terrorism'. Although the USA refused to accept the PLO proposals (because of their ambiguities), the apparent rejection of violence encouraged the US Government to open a dialogue with the PLO, implying a change in the direction of US-Israeli policy over Palestine. The United Kingdom and the USSR, among other countries, urged Israel to make a positive response to the PLO's new position.

1988 ELECTION

In the elections, Likud won 40 of the 120 seats in the Knesset, and Labour 39 seats. The religious parties won 18 seats, gaining potential significance in the formation of a government either by Likud or Labour. Initial attempts by Shamir, as the leader of the largest faction, to form a right-led government, rapidly ran aground, partly owing to the religious parties' demands concerning their monopoly on the definition of Judaism, which prompted an outcry from the Jewish Diaspora. Instead, Peres and the Labour Party eventually agreed to the formation in December of another Government of national unity under Shamir as Prime Minister, with Peres as Deputy Prime Minister and Minister of Finance.

The new Government took power against the background of a rapidly changing international situation, which would shortly transform Israel, both internally and in its relations with the Arab states. The USSR, which was the main supporter, both militarily and financially, of the Arab states and their policies, entered at the end of the 1980s into a process of disintegration which would unfold and run its course with remarkable rapidity. The collapse of the USSR freed for immigration the massive Soviet Jewish communities, which had long suffered from institutionalized anti-Semitism and discrimination. The disappearance of the USSR also removed any realistic chance for the forces of Arab rejectionism of achieving their ambition of attaining strategic military parity, and therefore posing a credible military threat to Israel. Furthermore, the removal of Soviet aid meant that such countries as Syria, in desperate need of help in developing their economic infrastructure, were forced to look westward, with all that that might imply in terms of participating in US-brokered attempts to bring about stable arrangements in the region. Israel thus ended the 1980s in an unprecedentedly advantageous position. Israel's deeply divided new Government of national unity, however, was to prove incapable of formulating a coherent policy response to this situation.

GROWING ULTRA-ORTHODOX INVOLVEMENT IN POLITICS

The central role played by ultra-Orthodox parties and leaders in the coalition negotiations following the 1988 elections cast light on the growing significance of the role played by the representatives of this community in Israeli politics. The community itself had undergone significant changes in its attitude towards the State of Israel and its institutions. The ultra-Orthodox streams in Judaism had not supported the Zionist movement and had played no role in the events leading to the creation of Israel. However, these communities had organized politically with considerable success, in order to guard their own interests in relation to Israel's central government. By the 1980s a considerable process of 'Israelization' had taken place within ultra-Orthodox communities, with the speaking of modern Hebrew increasingly widespread (originally, this had been discouraged, with Hebrew seen as a language of prayer and religious study only) and a growing sense of involvement in national life. This had implications for the political balance of power, due to their natural greater affinity with the Israeli right—which maintained a tradition of respect to Jewish practices—than with the left, which tended more towards assertive secularism, and a desire for the clear separation of religion and state. An additional important element of this process was the growing support among the ultra-Orthodox for an assertive, nationalist foreign policy, including the rejection of territorial concessions. Indeed, the so-called 'Hardalim'—ultra-Orthodox nationalists—would become a familiar and important part of the Israeli radical right in the 1990s, with a significant impact on political life in Israel.

Another significant aspect of ultra-Orthodoxy's growing engagement with Israeli politics was the birth in 1983 of the Shas party, a successful ultra-Orthodox Sephardi list. (Sephardim is the term originally used for Jews from the historic Spanish community and their descendants, but which in popular use is often expanded to include all Jews of non-European origin.) The Shas party was geared towards politically representing the attachment to tradition and sense of insult and rejection still felt by some sections of Israel's Mizrahim. It first stood in the 1984 elections, and, although it was not the first avowedly ethnic religious list, its impact was unprecedented. Shas gained four seats in 1984, increasing this to six in 1988. It would reach the height of its influence in the late 1990s, but from the outset, Shas was recognized as a unique political force in Israeli politics. Led by Sephardi graduates of religious seminaries run by Ashkenazim (Jews from communities in central, northern and eastern Europe and their descendants), the party managed to combine a unique image of religious observance and ethnic assertiveness, and a rapidly acquired reputation for political brinkmanship and negotiating skills. Its seemingly pragmatic attitude towards issues of territory proved crucial in this regard.

DIPLOMATIC IMPROVEMENTS AND MASS IMMIGRATION

In September 1989 Hungary became the first country of the Eastern bloc to restore diplomatic relations (severed in 1967) with Israel. In February 1990 Israel restored diplomatic relations with Poland and Czechoslovakia, and in May with Bulgaria. The Greek Government also formally recognized Israel in that month, becoming the last member state of the EC to do so. Simultaneously, non-European countries who had leaned towards the Soviets in the Cold War also began to re-establish contacts—Congo, for example, reopened its embassy in Israel in July 1991. More than 1m. immigrants arrived from Russia, Ukraine and other former Soviet republics. New methods of absorption were applied, in an attempt to avoid the mistakes of earlier periods. Whereas in the past there had been attempts to plan whole new communities in peripheral areas of the country and then transport an 'instant population' of newcomers, now immigrants would themselves choose their place of residence. After a six-month optional period of free Hebrew study and residence in an immigrant absorption centre, the newcomers would make their own way into Israeli society. To help them in this, each immigrant received a basket of rights, including help with housing rents, subsidized study and tax-free purchases.

The Russian immigration was augmented, in mid-1991, with the completion of the ingathering of Ethiopian Jewry that started in 1984 with Operation Moses. Since 1970, clandestinely, the Israeli authorities had helped 7,000 Ethiopian Jews to reach Israel. The exodus, by 1984, had reached dimensions too large to be attended to piecemeal. Thousands of Ethiopian Jews were trekking on foot across the desert to Sudan. Many were to die on the way and those who survived were interned by the Sudanese authorities. After US mediation, a large-scale Israeli airlift of these refugees began on 21 November. Some 8,000 Ethiopian Jews arrived in Israel this way. The airlift was halted after leaks and publicity placed the Sudanese Government in a potentially compromising situation vis-à-vis its Arab neighbours. The completion of the relocation of Ethiopian Jewry was therefore placed on hold until 1991, when, in a series of airlifts between 24 and 25 May, 14,000 Ethiopian Jews made their journey to Israel. The freeing of the Ethiopian Jews should also be seen in the context of diplomatic gains. During 1990–92 Israel regained almost completely the position it had held with the states of Africa prior to the Yom Kippur War, with Zambia, Nigeria, Angola and others all keen to restore full diplomatic relations.

HOPES IN THE DIPLOMATIC PROCESS

Shamir presented his own four-point proposals for peace when he visited Washington, DC, in April 1989. The proposals included free democratic elections in the West Bank and Gaza to elect delegates who could negotiate self-rule under Israeli authority, but only if the violence ceased. Although Palestinian activists dismissed these proposals as unacceptable because direct negotiations with the PLO were excluded, many observers felt that they offered a chance for talks to begin.

The USA was, by now, exerting pressure on the PLO to consider the Israeli plan for elections in the West Bank and Gaza, but in August 1989 Yasser Abd al-Rabbuh, a senior PLO spokesman, declared that 'the PLO does not consider, in any way, that elections can establish the basis for a political settlement'. In September President Mubarak of Egypt invited Israeli clarification on 10 points connected with Shamir's election plans and also offered to convene an Israeli-Palestinian meeting to discuss election details. Mubarak's 10-point plan was accepted by the Labour Party members of the 'inner' Cabinet, but was vetoed in October by the Likud ministers. In November the 'inner' Cabinet provisionally accepted a five-point initiative proposed by the US Secretary of State, James Baker, regarding a preliminary Israeli-Palestinian meeting to discuss the holding of elections in the West Bank and Gaza Strip, on condition that Israel would not be required to negotiate directly with a Palestinian delegation, and that the talks would be concerned only with Israel's election proposals. However, the PLO continued to demand a direct role in talks with Israel.

In July 1989 Israeli agents abducted Sheikh Obeid, a leading Shi'a Muslim, from a village in southern Lebanon, with the aim of securing the release of Israeli soldiers held by Hezbollah. Col William Higgins, a US hostage held by Hezbollah, was murdered in retaliation.

One obstacle to the progress of the peace negotiations was the question of whether residents of East Jerusalem should be allowed to participate in proposed elections in the Occupied Territories. On 28 February 1990 the USA suggested a compromise solution, which would allow East Jerusalem residents with second homes in the West Bank and some deported activists to stand in the elections.

LIKUD-LABOUR COALITION COLLAPSES AND THE RIGHT RETURNS TO POWER

On 11 March 1990 Shimon Peres and five Labour colleagues withdrew from a cabinet meeting in protest against further delays to a proposed vote on US plans for talks between an Israeli and a Palestinian delegation. Two days later Prime Minister Shamir dismissed Peres, the Labour leader and Minister of Finance, from the Government, prompting the resignation of all the Labour ministers. On 15 March a vote of no confidence was upheld against Prime Minister Shamir, the first such vote against an Israeli Government to have succeeded. Shamir was left in charge of a transitional administration. On 20 March President Chaim Herzog invited Peres to form a new coalition government after he had received assurances of support from Agudat Israel. A two-month period of political wrangling ensued, however, during which both Likud and Labour tried to establish a viable coalition government by soliciting the support of the minor religious parties.

By the end of April 1990 Peres acknowledged failure in his own attempts to form a new government. President Herzog accordingly invited Shamir to establish a new administration. On 8 June Itzhak Shamir announced the formation of a new Government, following the signing of a coalition agreement that gave him the support of 62 of the 120 members of the Knesset.

ISRAEL AND THE CONFLICT OVER KUWAIT

As crisis enveloped the Gulf region, following the occupation of Kuwait by Iraq in August 1990, there was support for Iraq both from Palestinians resident in the Occupied Territories and from the PLO.

Attacks on Israel by Iraqi Scud missiles, beginning on 18 January 1991, created the most serious threat to the integrity of the multinational force which had commenced hostilities against Iraq on 16–17 January. It was widely expected that Israel would retaliate immediately. Very low casualties and US diplomacy, supported by the installation in Israel of advanced US air-defence systems, succeeded in averting an immediate Israeli military response, although Israel vowed that it would, ultimately, retaliate for the attacks. By late February Iraq had launched 39 Scud missiles against Israel, killing two people and injuring more than 200. In response to the widespread support, expressed by ordinary Palestinians and in official PLO policy, for Iraqi President Saddam Hussain, the attitude of the Israeli Government hardened.

RENEWED ATTEMPTS TO CONVENE A PEACE CONFERENCE

Israel's greatest gain from the conflict over Kuwait had been the renewed goodwill of the USA: in February 1991 the US Secretary of State, James Baker, signed a guarantee for a US loan to Israel of US $400m. for the housing of immigrants. (Baker had previously refused to sign the guarantee, owing to his concern that the funds would be used to establish immigrant communities in the Occupied Territories.) However, it was clear that the USA would seek to use its increased influence in the Middle East to advance the Arab-Israeli peace process. The USA's efforts to initiate peace talks intensified in April, when Secretary of State Baker returned to the Middle East, visiting Israel, Egypt and Syria, in order to promote the idea of a regional peace conference. President Hafiz al-Assad of Syria agreed for the first time, following a meeting with Baker, to participate in direct negotiations with Israel at a regional conference, for which the terms of reference would be a comprehensive peace settlement based on UN Security Council Resolutions 242 and 338. The publicly stated positions of the Israeli and Syrian Governments, however, remained as far apart as ever. For its part, the US Government insisted that there were no preconditions for attending the peace conference, and that, with regard to the composition of the Jordanian-Palestinian delegation, only members of the PLO were excluded.

On 31 July 1991, at the conclusion of a summit meeting between US President George Bush and President of the USSR Mikhail Gorbachev, the two leaders announced their intention to act as joint chairmen of a Middle East peace conference which was scheduled to take place in October, and which representatives of the UN and the EC would attend in the capacity of observers. On 4 August the Israeli Cabinet formally agreed to attend a peace conference on the terms proposed by the USA and the USSR.

OTHER POST-WAR DEVELOPMENTS

A serious escalation of the conflict endemic to southern Lebanon occurred in February 1992, when Israeli armed forces advanced beyond Israel's 'security zone' to attack Hezbollah positions, and again in May, when the Israeli air force attacked Hezbollah villages to the north and west of the 'security zone', in response to attacks by Hezbollah units on positions occupied by the SLA.

On the diplomatic front, meanwhile, in April 1991 Prime Minister Shamir met the Soviet Prime Minister, Valentin Pavlov, in London. Full diplomatic relations with the USSR—followed by the establishment of relations with some of the newly independent, former Soviet republics—were formally re-established, after an interval of 24 years, in November; and in January 1992 Israel established diplomatic relations with the People's Republic of China for the first time.

NEGOTIATIONS AT AN IMPASSE

By March 1992, following an initial, 'symbolic' session of the conference, held in Madrid, Spain, in October 1991, four sessions of negotiations between Israeli, Syrian, Lebanese and Palestinian-Jordanian delegations had been held, but little progress had been achieved with regard to substantive issues, in particular the question of transitional Palestinian autonomy in the West Bank and Gaza Strip, pending discussions on the 'final status' of those territories. Five rounds of bilateral negotiations, between Israeli, Syrian, Lebanese and Palestinian-Jordanian delegations, were held in Washington, DC, in April 1992. In May the first multilateral negotiations between the parties to the Middle East peace conference commenced; however, the sessions were boycotted by Syria and Lebanon, which considered them futile until progress had been made in the bilateral negotiations. Various combinations of delegations attended meetings convened to discuss regional economic co-operation and arms control, the question of Palestinian refugees, water resources and environmental concerns. No substantive progress was made.

In February 1992 US Secretary of State James Baker demanded a complete halt to Israeli settlement in the Territories as a condition for the granting of US $10,000m. in US-guaranteed loans for the housing of Jewish immigrants from the former USSR. While the Israeli Government's refusal to freeze the construction of new settlements was regarded as provocative by all the other parties to the peace conference, and by the US Government, the right-wing minority members of Israel's governing coalition, who opposed any Israeli participation in the peace conference at all, threatened to withdraw from the coalition if funds were not made available for the settlement programme. In mid-January 1992 the majority was lost entirely when two right-wing, nationalist parties, Moledet and Tehiya (which together held five seats in the Knesset), withdrew from the coalition. A general election was subsequently scheduled to be held in June, and Itzhak Shamir remained the head of a transitional Government.

In late February 1992 Shamir was re-elected as leader of the Likud party. At the same time, former prime minister Itzhak Rabin was elected Chairman of the Labour Party, replacing Shimon Peres. Rabin's election was regarded as having improved Labour's prospects at the forthcoming general election, since he enjoyed more popular confidence than Peres with regard to issues affecting Israel's security.

A NEW LABOUR COALITION

In the general election held on 23 June 1992, the Labour Party won 44 seats in the Knesset and Likud 32. Meretz—an alliance of Ratz (Civil Rights and Peace Movement), Shinui and Mapam (the United Workers' Party), which had won 12 seats in the Knesset—confirmed its willingness to form a coalition government with the Labour Party on 24 June. The 'right bloc' (Likud, Tzomet, Moledet and Tehiya) and the religious parties that had allied themselves with Likud in the previous Knesset held 59 seats. Formally invited to form a government on 28 June, the Labour leader, Itzhak Rabin, was accordingly obliged to solicit support among certain religious parties. On 13 July Itzhak Rabin presented a new Government for approval by the Knesset. The new coalition, an alliance of Labour, Meretz and the ultra-Orthodox Jewish party, Shas, had a total of 62 seats in the 120-seat Knesset.

In 1992 the Israeli centre-left had thus secured its first clear electoral victory since 1974. It came about as a result of a number of factors: first, the former general Itzhak Rabin was able to convey a consensual, security-conscious image. In Labour election propaganda, an attempt was made to portray Rabin as the sober, statesman-like candidate, standing against the ideologues of Likud and their settler allies. This image enabled Labour to make some inroads into traditional areas of Likud support. Also, significantly, support for Labour among the new immigrants from the former USSR was high, reflecting their dissatisfaction with aspects of their absorption.

The 1992 elections were also significant because of the growing importance of Israeli Arab involvement in the system. For the first time, a Government was formed in Israel that had a blocking majority dependent on the votes of Arab Knesset members. The combined strength of Labour and the leftist Meretz list amounted to only 56 seats. In order to be able to govern, Labour was dependent on the votes of the five members of the Knesset representing lists dependent on Arab votes.

RENEWED NEGOTIATIONS

A sixth round of bilateral negotiations between Israeli, Syrian, Lebanese and Palestinian-Jordanian delegations, the first since the new Israeli Government had taken office, commenced in Washington, DC, in August 1992. Again, little progress was achieved on substantive issues. The Israeli delegation and the Palestinian component of the Palestinian-Jordanian delegation, for instance, were unable to agree terms for negotiating an initial, five-year period of Palestinian autonomy in the West Bank and Gaza Strip prior to a permanent settlement. Talks between the Israeli and the Syrian delegations remained deadlocked over the issue of the Golan Heights.

In spite of the hopes that had been expressed for the prospects of the peace process since the election of the Labour-led Israeli Government, October and November were marked by violent clashes between Palestinians and the Israeli security forces in the Occupied Territories. In November it was reported that, since 1987, 959 Palestinians, 543 alleged Palestinian 'collaborators' and 103 Israelis had died in the Palestinian *intifada*. The deportation of 400 Hamas members from the territories by Israel in December 1992 placed further strains on the beleaguered negotiating process. The *intifada*, meanwhile, sputtered on into its sixth year. In March 1993 the number of violent confrontations between Palestinians and the Israeli security forces in the Occupied Territories (especially in the Gaza Strip) increased to such an extent that, at the end of the month, the Israeli Cabinet responded by sealing off the West Bank and Gaza indefinitely. In late March the Knesset elected Ezer Weizman, leader of the Yahad political party, to replace Herzog as President of Israel in May 1993; Binyamin Netanyahu was elected leader of the opposition Likud in place of Shamir.

On 27 April 1993 the ninth round of bilateral negotiations in the Middle East peace process, which had been formally suspended in February, resumed in Washington, DC. The Palestinian delegation had reportedly only agreed to attend this round of talks following pressure from Arab governments. However, as previously, the talks achieved no progress on substantive issues. In particular, Israel and the Palestinian delegation were reported to have failed to agree on a statement of principles regarding Palestinian self-rule in the Occupied Territories. A 10th round of bilateral negotiations, held in Washington, DC, on 15 June–1 July, similarly concluded in deadlock.

ISRAEL IN THE 1990s: A CHANGING, DIVERSIFYING SOCIETY

Against the background of the peace process, and the hopes that it engendered, the early 1990s were a time of considerable internal change in Israel. On the one hand, many of the old ideological certainties were declining, in the face of growing individualism, materialism and Americanization. Here, the Israeli experience mirrored that of other Western democracies. Consumerism and openness to foreign influences went hand in hand with greater individualism, and an increasing scepticism towards political leadership.

This process reflected itself in manifold ways. In academia and artistic and cultural production, new and challenging voices were heard. So-called 'post-Zionist' academics challenged received wisdom regarding the birth of the state and the early period of Zionism. Historians such as Ilan Pappé and Avi Shlaim, sociologists such as Uri Ram, and others achieved prominence with their critical and iconoclastic analyses of Israeli society and history.

In 1992 two 'Basic Laws' concerning human rights were adopted by the Knesset. (In the absence of a written constitution, Israel developed a system of 'Basic Laws' on key matters.) This, coupled with the gradual expansion of the right to petition the High Court of Justice and the 'judicial activism' of the Supreme Court, especially the approach led by the future Supreme Court President Aharon Barak, precipitated the so-called 'judicial revolution', whereby the Supreme Court became more explicitly involved in everyday politics. Barak was accused by opponents of undermining the status of the Knesset.

Many observers also detected a growing 'fragmentation' of Israeli society, as separate ethnic and religious identities asserted themselves. Issues of lifestyle—the right of public non-observance of religious ritual, sale of non-kosher foodstuffs, and the ongoing, vexed question of 'Who is a Jew?'—acquired added prominence during this period. Partly, this was due to a prevailing sense of a winding-down in conflict from the 1993 period until the end of the decade. But it also related to broader social change, and to massive immigration to Israel from the former USSR. The newcomers were for the most part religiously non-observant, and the Jewish identity of some of them was open to question.

All of the above combined to transform the atmosphere of Israel in the 1990s, producing a less certain, less unified, but more open and dynamic, society.

UNEXPECTED BREAKTHROUGH IN THE PEACE PROCESS

In July 1993 Israeli armed forces mounted the most intensive air and artillery attacks on targets in Lebanon since 'Operation Peace for Galilee' in 1982. The offensive (Operation Accountability) was mounted in retaliation for attacks by Hezbollah fighters on settlements in northern Israel. On 13 September 1993 Israel and the PLO signed a declaration of principles on Palestinian self-rule in the Occupied Territories. The agreement, which entailed mutual recognition by Israel and the PLO, had been elaborated during a series of secret negotiations mediated by Norwegian diplomacy (and was therefore commonly known as the Oslo accords). The Declaration of Principles (Documents on Palestine, see p. 76) established a detailed timetable for Israel's disengagement from the Occupied Territories and stipulated that a permanent settlement of the Palestinian question should be in place by December 1998. From 13 October 1993 Palestinian authorities were to assume responsibility for education and culture, health, social welfare, direct taxation and tourism in the Gaza Strip and the Jericho area of the West Bank, and a transitional period of Palestinian self-rule was to begin on 13 December.

Rabin, in line with consensual Israeli thinking, had preferred to try to reach agreement with locally based Palestinians.

However, when these efforts failed to bear fruit, he had authorized an unofficial channel of communication with PLO officials via Knesset member Yossi Beilin. The Oslo accords were the product of the talks begun through this channel.

REACTION TO THE DECLARATION OF PRINCIPLES

While it was welcomed as a major breakthrough in the Middle East peace process, the Declaration of Principles was nevertheless regarded as only a tentative first step towards the resolution of the region's conflicts. Although the Israeli Prime Minister was able to obtain the ratification of the Declaration of Principles, and of Israel's recognition of the PLO, by the Knesset on 23 September 1993, there was widespread opposition to it from right-wing Israeli political groups. By the same token, the conclusion of the agreement aggravated divisions within the PLO and the wider Palestinian liberation movement. Hamas and Islamic Jihad denounced the Declaration of Principles as treason. King Hussein welcomed the accord and Jordan immediately agreed an agenda for direct talks with Israel, which was also ratified by the Knesset on 23 September. Lebanon, however, feared that the divisions that the Declaration of Principles had provoked among Palestinians might lead to renewed conflict in Lebanon. It remained unclear, too, whether Syria—which neither condemned nor welcomed the agreement—would continue to support those Palestinian groups opposed to the PLO's position.

In September 1993 the resignation of Aryeh Der'i as Minister of the Interior, following allegations of corruption, provoked the resignation of other Shas ministers from the Cabinet, thus reducing the governing coalition to an alliance between the Labour Party and Meretz (and the Government's majority in the Knesset to only two). However, in March 1994 the Labour Party and Shas were reported to have concluded a new coalition agreement.

BEGINNING OF PALESTINIAN SELF-RULE

On 6 October 1993 Itzhak Rabin and Yasser Arafat held their first meeting in the context of the Declaration of Principles in Cairo, where they agreed to begin talks on the implementation of the accord, and to establish general liaison, technical, economic and regional co-operation committees.

However, it proved impossible to finalize the details of Israel's military withdrawal from the Gaza Strip and Jericho by 13 December 1993. This failure cast doubt on the whole of the September agreement between Israel and the PLO. The main cause of the failure remained disagreement on security arrangements for border crossings between the Gaza Strip and Jericho and Jordan and Egypt. The PLO continued to insist that the border crossings should come under full, exclusive Palestinian control. Israel, however, opposed this claim since to grant it would imply at least a partial recognition of something resembling Palestinian sovereignty.

In February 1994 the PLO, together with the other Arab parties, withdrew from the peace process with Israel, following the murder, by a right-wing Jewish extremist, of some 30 Muslim worshippers in the Tomb of the Patriarch in Hebron (Al-Khalil) on the West Bank. Discussions between the PLO and Israel resumed in March, when the two sides signed an agreement on security in Hebron and the whole of the Occupied Territories. Israel agreed, among other things, to allow a team of international observers to monitor efforts to restore stability in Hebron.

On 4 May 1994 in Cairo, Israel and the PLO signed an agreement detailing arrangements for Palestinian self-rule in Gaza and Jericho (Documents on Palestine, see p. 79). The agreement provided for Israel's military withdrawal from Gaza and Jericho and the deployment there of a 9,000-strong Palestinian police force. A nominated Palestinian (National) Authority (PA) was to assume the responsibilities of the Israeli military administration in Gaza and Jericho, although Israeli authorities were to retain control in matters of external security and foreign affairs. Elections for a Palestinian Council, which, under the terms of the Declaration of Principles, were to have taken place in Gaza and the West Bank in July, were now postponed until October. Israel's military withdrawal from Gaza and Jericho was completed on 13 May, and on 17 May the PLO formally assumed control of the Israeli civil administration's departments there.

Arafat returned to Gaza City on 1 July 1994. In late August Israel and the PLO signed an agreement which extended the authority of the PA to include education, health, tourism, social welfare and taxation.

In September 1994 Morocco became the second Arab state to establish diplomatic relations with Israel, albeit at a low level. Tunisia did likewise on the following day.

PEACE WITH JORDAN

In July 1994 the Prime Ministers of Israel and Jordan signed a peace treaty in Washington, DC, that formally ended the state of war between them (Documents on Palestine, see p. 83). Bilateral relations had improved over the years, as demonstrated, for example, by the 'Open Bridges' policy adopted after the Six-Day War, but this relationship could only be formalized through an official public agreement once progress was made with the Palestinians.

ISLAMIST ATTACKS THREATEN PEACE PROCESS

Iran vehemently opposed the Arafat-Rabin discourse since it implied a two-state solution rather than an Islamic State of Palestine. Opposition to the Oslo process assisted in overcoming obstacles between Shi'a Iran and the Sunni Palestinian Islamists. The Islamist organizations, Hamas and Islamic Jihad, remained the most militant opponents of the Oslo accords and in late 1994 both groups escalated their campaigns of violence. On 9 October an Israeli soldier was kidnapped near Tel-Aviv by Hamas fighters, who subsequently demanded the release from Israeli gaols of their leader, Sheikh Ahmad Yassin, and other Palestinian prisoners in exchange for his life. Despite Palestinian action to detain some 300 Hamas members in the Gaza Strip, the kidnapped soldier was killed in the West Bank on 14 October during an abortive rescue attempt by the IDF. On 19 October an attack by a Hamas suicide bomber in Tel-Aviv, in which 22 people died, prompted Israel to close its borders with the West Bank and Gaza for an indefinite period.

Perhaps the most serious blow yet to the peace negotiations between Israel and the PLO was the suicide bombing at Beit Lid in Israel on 22 January 1995, in which 21 people—mostly Israeli soldiers—died and more than 60 were injured. Islamic Jihad claimed responsibility for the attack, which resulted in the Israeli Cabinet again sealing Israel's borders with the Occupied Territories, and postponing the planned release of some 5,500 Palestinian prisoners. Opinion polls published in Israel on 27 January revealed that the majority of Israeli citizens now opposed the peace process, while the majority of Palestinians favoured further suicide attacks against Israeli targets. The polls also revealed a drastic decline in support for the Israeli Labour Party. The leader of Likud, Binyamin Netanyahu, responding to public opinion, made an electoral promise to modify the peace negotiations, take tougher measures against suspected terrorists and abandon the promised return of more land occupied in 1967.

The latest events led to a decline in faith in the process also among Israel's security establishment, which increasingly came to doubt the PA's seriousness vis-à-vis the need to fight terrorism against Israelis. In this period, the demand for the construction of a barrier against terrorist infiltrations began to be heard emanating from senior members and former members of Israel's security echelon.

ISRAEL-SYRIA TALKS RESUME

In March 1995 it was announced that Israel and Syria had agreed to resume peace negotiations, which had been suspended since February 1994. The resumption of talks would initially involve the Israeli and Syrian ambassadors to the USA, meeting, at Syria's insistence, in the presence of US officials. At a later stage it was planned to introduce to the negotiations military technicians and, ultimately, the Syrian and Israeli Chiefs of Staff. Speculation that a breakthrough might shortly be achieved was subdued, however, in April, when the Syrian Vice-President made it clear that Syria had no intention of renouncing its demand that Israel should withdraw from the Golan Heights to the border pertaining before the June 1967 war. Nevertheless, on 24 May 1995 Syria and Israel concluded a 'framework understanding on security arrangements' which was intended to facilitate negotiations on security issues. At the end of the month Shimon Peres stated that Israel had proposed that its forces should withdraw from the Golan Heights over a four-year period. Syria, however, had insisted that the withdrawal should be effected over 18 months. Peace talks between Israel and Syria resumed in December 1995 in Maryland, USA, and a second round of US-mediated talks took place there in January 1996.

VIOLENCE PRECEDES AGREEMENT

In April 1995 two suicide bomb attacks in the Gaza Strip killed seven Israeli soldiers; Hamas and Islamic Jihad subsequently claimed responsibility for the attacks. Despite intensive negotiations, it proved impossible to conclude an agreement on the expansion of Palestinian self-rule in the West Bank by the target date of 1 July. On 21 August a suicide bombing of a bus in Jerusalem killed six people. Hamas again claimed responsibility for the attack, which raised the number of deaths in bombings over the previous 16 months to 77 and provoked demands from Israelis opposed to the Declaration of Principles that the talks should be suspended. The period since the signing of the Oslo accords had seen a sharp rise in terrorist attacks, leading a growing number of Israelis to question the wisdom of the policy of rapprochement with the PLO.

It was not until 28 September 1995 that the Israeli-Palestinian Interim Agreement on the West Bank and the Gaza Strip was finally signed by Israel and the PLO (Documents on Palestine, see p. 86). Its main provisions were the withdrawal of Israeli armed forces from a further six West Bank towns—Nablus (Nabulus), Ramallah (Ram Allah), Jenin (Janin), Tulkaram (Tulkarm), Kalkilya (Qalqilya) and Bethlehem (Beit Lahm)—and a partial redeployment away from the town of Hebron; Palestinian legislative elections to an 82-member Palestinian Council, and elections for a Palestinian Executive President; and the release, in three phases, of Palestinian prisoners detained by Israel. There were criticisms of the new agreement, many of which focused on the sheer complexity—and corresponding ambiguity—of the 400-page document. Right-wing Israelis also questioned the legitimacy of the agreement, which had been approved by only 61 votes to 59 in the Knesset, and only by inducing two right-of-centre Knesset members to vote for it by promising them ministerial posts.

RABIN'S ASSASSINATION AND ITS AFTERMATH

On 4 November 1995 Prime Minister Itzhak Rabin was assassinated while leaving a peace rally in Tel-Aviv. His assassin, Yigal Amir, was a young religious nationalist who opposed the peace process, and in particular Israeli withdrawal from the West Bank. While it was apparently an independent act, the assassination seemed certain further to marginalize those on the extreme right wing of Israeli politics who had advocated violence as a means of halting the implementation of the Oslo accords. The assassination also provoked criticism of Likud which, it was widely felt, had not sufficiently distanced itself from such extremist elements. Following the assassination, Shimon Peres, hitherto the Minister of Foreign Affairs, became acting Prime Minister. On 15 November, with the agreement of the opposition Likud, Peres was invited to form a new government. On 21 November the leaders of the outgoing coalition parties—Labour, Meretz and Yi'ud—signed a new coalition agreement, and Peres announced a new Cabinet, which was formally approved by the Knesset on the following day.

Israeli armed forces completed their withdrawal from the West Bank town of Jenin on 13 November 1995, and during December they withdrew from Tulkarm, Nablus, Qalqilya, Bethlehem and Ramallah. With regard to Hebron, Israel and the PA signed an agreement transferring jurisdiction in some 17 areas of civilian affairs from Israel to the PA.

Israel welcomed the decision of the Palestine National Council in late April 1996 to amend the Palestinian National Charter, or PLO Covenant (the constitution of the Palestinian resistance movement), thereby removing all clauses demanding the destruction of Israel. The Israeli Government had demanded that the Covenant be amended by 7 May 1996 as a precondition for its participation in the final stage of peace negotiations with the PLO.

SUICIDE BOMB ATTACKS RESUME

Palestinian legislative and presidential elections were held in January 1996. Subsequently, in February, Peres announced that elections to the Knesset and, for the first time, the direct election of the Prime Minister, would take place in May, which was as soon as electoral legislation allowed.

Meanwhile, in February and March 1996 suicide bombings in Jerusalem, Ashkelon and Tel-Aviv caused the deaths of more than 50 Israelis and led to a further suspension of the peace process. Following the attacks in Jerusalem and Ashkelon, Israel ordered the indefinite closure of the West Bank and Gaza, and demanded that the Palestinian authorities suppress the activities of Hamas and Islamic Jihad in the areas under their control.

The Lebanon front was also active. In April 1996, in response to a week of Hezbollah mortar attacks, Peres authorized the shelling of Hezbollah targets in southern Lebanon. The operation, code-named Grapes of Wrath, ended suddenly when Israeli shells hit a UN base at Qana, killing more than 100 Lebanese civilians sheltering there. (See also the chapter on Lebanon.)

LIKUD RETURNS TO POWER

The elections of May 1996 were the first to be held under the new electoral system, under the terms of which the Prime Minister was elected directly alongside the members of the Knesset. The Likud leader, Binyamin Netanyahu, gained a marginal and unexpected victory over Shimon Peres in the direct election of the Prime Minister, although his party, which prior to the elections had formed a formal alliance with the Tzomet party and Gesher, won only 32 seats. However, in mid-June Netanyahu signed a series of agreements with Shas, the NRP, Israel B'Aliyah, United Torah Judaism and the Third Way to form a coalition that would command the support of 66 deputies in the 120-member Knesset. The new split-voting system served to reduce the support commanded by the larger parties. Voters could now vote for their 'national' preference by choosing the left- or right-wing candidate for prime minister, and use their second vote to strengthen a religious or ethnic sectional bloc with which they identified.

IDF–PA CLASHES THREATEN PEACE PROCESS

Netanyahu and Arafat met, for the first time, at the Erez crossing point between Israel and Gaza, on 4 September 1996. At a press conference following the meeting, they confirmed their commitment to the implementation of the Interim Agreement. On 25 September violent confrontations began between Palestinian security forces, Palestinian civilians and the Israeli armed forces; at least 50 Palestinians and 18 Israelis were killed and hundreds wounded. The West Bank town of Ramallah was the initial point of confrontation, and the direct cause of the disturbances was attributed to the decision of the Israeli Government to open the north end of the Hasmonean tunnel which ran beneath the al-Aqsa Mosque in East Jerusalem. The violence was the most serious in the West Bank and Gaza since 1967. Subsequently, on 6 October 1996 it was announced that, following US mediation, Israel had agreed to resume negotiations on the partial withdrawal of its armed forces from Hebron. On 7 October, at the opening of the winter session of the Knesset, Netanyahu stated that once the question of the redeployment from Hebron had been settled, Israel would reopen its borders with the West Bank and Gaza—which had remained closed since February 1996—and move quickly towards seeking a settlement with the Palestinians.

HEBRON AGREEMENTS

In January 1997 Israel and the PA finally concluded an agreement on the withdrawal of Israeli armed forces from

Hebron. The principal terms of the US-brokered agreement were that Israeli forces should withdraw from 80% of the town of Hebron within 10 days, and that the first of three subsequent withdrawals from the West Bank should take place six weeks after the signing of the agreement, and the remaining two by August 1998.

The conclusion of the agreement marked the first significant progress in the peace process since Netanyahu's election as Prime Minister. However, renewed hopes for the future of the process appeared to be short-lived. The Israeli decision of February 1997 to proceed with the construction of 6,500 housing units at Har Homa in East Jerusalem attracted international criticism, but two UN Security Council resolutions, submitted during March, urging Israel to reconsider such plans were vetoed by the USA. Anti-Israeli sentiments intensified throughout the Arab world, but the Arab cause continued to be undermined by violent atrocities, including the massacre by a Jordanian soldier of seven Israeli schoolgirls in Naharayim, an enclave between Israel and Jordan, on 13 March. On 14 March King Hussein visited the families of the deceased to express his condolences. Israeli intransigence over Har Homa prompted the Palestinians to abandon the 'final status' talks. Riots erupted immediately, reaching a climax on 21 March when a bomb, planted by Hamas, exploded in a Tel-Aviv café, killing four people. Netanyahu accused Arafat of extending an invitation to Islamist activists to resume terrorist attacks, and the Israeli Cabinet immediately ordered a general closure of the West Bank and Gaza. At the end of the month the League of Arab States voted to resume their economic boycott of Israel, suspend moves to establish diplomatic relations with that country, and withdraw from multilateral peace talks. (Jordan, the PA and Egypt were excluded from the legislation owing to their binding bilateral agreements with Israel.) Demonstrations eventually subsided at the end of April, when the West Bank and Gaza were reopened. Despite further diplomatic efforts by USA's chief Middle East negotiator, Dennis Ross, there was no resumption of peace talks.

JERUSALEM BOMBS THWART HOPES FOR RENEWED TALKS

On 28 July 1997 both sides announced that peace talks were to be resumed in early August. However, on 30 July, the eve of a planned visit to Israel by Dennis Ross, two Hamas suicide bombers killed 14 civilians and wounded more than 150 others at a Jewish market in Jerusalem. The event effectively paralysed the peace process: Ross cancelled his visit and Israel immediately halted payment of tax revenues to the PA and closed the Gaza Strip and the West Bank. The sanctions provoked furious protest from Palestinians, as well as widespread international condemnation. Nevertheless, Binyamin Netanyahu insisted that restrictions would remain until the PA demonstrated a commitment to combat terrorism. Rather than condemning Palestinian political organizations, Arafat convened a two-day forum in August during which he publicly embraced Hamas leaders and urged them, together with Islamic Jihad, to unite with the Palestinian people against Israeli policies. On 26 August Hamas rejected a request from Palestinian leaders to suspend their attacks. Nevertheless, Israel relaxed its closure of the Palestinian areas on 1 September. Sanctions were reinforced on 4 September, however, after a triple suicide bombing took place in West Jerusalem, killing eight people (five Israelis and the bombers), and wounding more than 150 others. The bombing, followed one day later by the death of 12 Israeli commandos in Lebanon, prompted warnings from the Israeli Security Cabinet that possible military attacks on Palestinian and Arab territories might be launched.

ISRAELI CASUALTIES IN LEBANON

The deterioration in relations between Israel and the PA coincided with renewed hostilities in the north of the country, after Hezbollah launched their first major rocket attack for 16 months on civilians in the Israeli town of Kiryat Shmona in early August 1997. The barrage, in retaliation for attacks by Israeli commandos in which five Hezbollah members were killed, prompted further air-strikes against targets in southern Lebanon. Violence escalated and on 18 August the SLA shelled the Lebanese port of Sidon, killing at least six civilians.

FLUCTUATING RELATIONS WITH JORDAN

On 25 September 1997 two Israeli Mossad agents travelling on forged Canadian passports were detained in the Jordanian capital, Amman, in connection with the attempted assassination, by poisoning, of the local Hamas chief, Khalid Meshaal. In response to the incident, which caused severe embarrassment to the Israeli Government, Canada withdrew its ambassador to Tel-Aviv, while King Hussein of Jordan threatened to try the arrested men for murder and to sever diplomatic relations with Israel unless the Israeli authorities promptly supplied an antidote for the potentially lethal chemical agent used in the attack. The antidote was duly dispatched by Israel, and in late September frantic diplomatic efforts were undertaken to preserve cordial relations between the two countries. In early October the release from Israeli prisons of dozens of Arab detainees, including Sheikh Ahmad Yassin, a founder of Hamas, was thought to have been negotiated with the Jordanian authorities in exchange for the return of the two Mossad agents.

THE COALITION WEAKENED

In addition to the escalating security crisis in the region, Netanyahu also confronted increasing domestic difficulty in April 1997, after police recommended that he be charged with fraud and breach of trust following his appointment in January 1997 of an undistinguished lawyer, Roni Bar-On, as Attorney-General. Bar-On resigned within 12 hours of his appointment after it was alleged that his promotion had been made in order to facilitate a plea bargain for Aryeh Der'i, leader of Shas, who was facing separate corruption charges. There were suggestions that in return for Bar-On's appointment, Der'i had pledged Shas party support for the Cabinet's decision regarding the withdrawal from Hebron. In May Aryeh Der'i was indicted for obstruction of justice but Elyaqim Rubenstein, Bar-On's successor, ruled that, owing to lack of evidence, charges would not be brought against Netanyahu.

Evidence of further divisions within the coalition emerged at the end of December 1997, prior to the 1998 budget vote, effectively a demonstration of confidence in the Prime Minister. Although the budget was eventually approved, Netanyahu was left with a majority of only 61 to 59 after the withdrawal of Gesher, headed by David Levy, from the coalition. In October 1998 Ariel Sharon was appointed Minister of Foreign Affairs. Sharon's promotion was widely regarded as an attempt by Netanyahu to secure the support of settler groups and right-wing nationalists, since he was known to be opposed to redeployment from a further 13% of the West Bank. In June 1997 Ehud Barak, a former cabinet minister and chief of staff of the army, was elected as leader of the Labour Party.

On 4 March 1998 the Knesset re-elected Ezer Weizman as President for a further five-year term, by 63 votes to 49. Weizman defeated Shaul Amor, a Likud member of the Knesset whose candidacy had been sponsored by Netanyahu.

LIMITED POPULARITY SUSTAINED AND REDEPLOYMENT TALKS REACTIVATED

At the beginning of May 1998 Israeli and Palestinian leaders met US Secretary of State Madeleine Albright for separate talks in London, aimed at reactivating negotiations concerning redeployment. The discussions ended inconclusively but with a further invitation for Israeli and Palestinian delegations to visit Washington, DC, in mid-May for another round of talks with President Clinton and US officials. Once again, these talks concluded with no obvious sign of progress but not before Netanyahu had again demonstrated to the Clinton Administration the depth of support in the US Congress for his own Government and its uncompromising security agenda.

NO PROGRESS ON THE SYRIA TRACK

The possibility of a resumption of peace negotiations between Israel and Syria emerged after it was reported that the two countries had agreed to a French initiative to resume dialogue, based on an Israeli acceptance of the 'land-for-peace' formula and Syrian acceptance of Israel's security needs. However, prior to a visit to Paris by Syria's President Assad in mid-July 1998, Netanyahu apparently retracted his decision to accept the French initiative, reportedly owing to opposition from coalition partners. Later in July the Knesset gave preliminary approval to a bill that would require a majority vote in the Knesset and a referendum to be held prior to allowing an Israeli withdrawal from either the Golan Heights or Jerusalem. The legislation, which was fiercely denounced in Syria, was adopted in January 1999. The implementation of this law was conditioned upon additional legislation regarding referendums, which was finally approved in late 2010.

THE WYE RIVER MEMORANDUM

The Wye Plantation talks began on 15 October 1998, following a ceremonial meeting at the White House between President Clinton, Yasser Arafat and Binyamin Netanyahu. US negotiators at the intensive nine-day talks included Secretary of State Albright, Special Envoy Ross, and the Director of the US Central Intelligence Agency (CIA), George Tenet; President Clinton spent an estimated 70 hours in discussions. President Mubarak of Egypt and King Hussein of Jordan were kept informed of progress in the discussions, the latter playing a significant role as mediator. On 23 October Arafat and Netanyahu signed the Wye River Memorandum (Documents on Palestine, see p. 92) in the presence of President Clinton and King Hussein. In essence, the Memorandum outlined a three-month timetable for the implementation of earlier agreements, notably the Interim Agreement of 28 September 1995 and the Hebron Protocol of 15 January 1997. The signing of the agreement ended a 19-month deadlock in the Israeli-Palestinian track of the peace process, and was achieved in spite of a grenade attack carried out by Hamas on 19 October 1998 in Beersheba, in which at least 60 people were injured. Under the terms of the agreement (based on a 'land-for-security' exchange), Israel agreed to redeploy its troops from 13.1% of the West Bank (in three stages), while the Palestinians agreed to intensify measures to guarantee Israel's security by eradicating terrorist activity and revising the Palestinian National Charter. Both sides also agreed to the immediate resumption of 'final status' talks (originally scheduled to have begun in May 1996), with the aim of concluding a permanent agreement by 4 May 1999, and made commitments to refrain from taking any unilateral actions that would alter the status of the West Bank or Gaza.

IMPLEMENTATION OF THE FIRST STAGE OF WYE

On 17 November 1998 the Israeli Knesset ratified the Wye Memorandum by 75 votes to 19. Three days later the Israeli Government implemented the first stage of renewed redeployment from the West Bank, also releasing 250 Palestinian prisoners and signing a protocol allowing for the inauguration of an international airport at Gaza.

DISSOLUTION OF THE KNESSET

During December 1998 it became increasingly evident that divisions within Netanyahu's party and coalition over implementation of the Wye Memorandum were making effective government untenable. Attempts to rescue the coalition by offering to reappoint David Levy to the Government were frustrated when the Gesher leader refused the terms proposed by Netanyahu. On 21 December Netanyahu was forced to support an opposition motion demanding the dissolution of the Knesset and the organization of early elections to the legislature and premiership in mid-1999. A general election was subsequently scheduled for 17 May.

SUSPENSION OF PEACE PROCESS

There was considerable unrest in the West Bank and Gaza prior to a visit by President Clinton in December 1998. On 14 December Clinton attended a meeting of the PLO's Palestine National Council (PNC), at which the removal from the Palestinian National Charter of all clauses seeking Israel's destruction was reaffirmed. The US President also attended the formal inauguration of the new airport at Gaza. At a meeting between Clinton, Arafat and Netanyahu at the Erez checkpoint, Netanyahu reiterated accusations that the Palestinians had not adequately addressed their security commitments and announced that he would not release Palestinian prisoners considered to have 'blood on their hands'. Netanyahu also demanded that Arafat renounce his intention to unilaterally declare Palestinian statehood in May 1999. Arafat, for his part, conveyed his own security concerns and reasserted demands for a freeze on the construction of Jewish settlements in disputed territory. Following the meeting Netanyahu announced that the second phase of Israeli troop deployment envisaged by the Wye Memorandum, scheduled for 18 December 1998, would not be undertaken. On 20 December the Knesset voted to suspend implementation of the Memorandum. In late December Hamas leader Sheikh Ahmad Yassin was released from house arrest in Gaza. Yassin had been detained as part of a high-profile initiative by the PA security forces to subdue Hamas activists following a failed suicide bomb attack on settler schoolchildren in late October.

CONVICTION OF DER'I

In March 1999 the Shas party leader, Aryeh Der'i (a close associate of Prime Minister Netanyahu and an invaluable ally in the Likud-led coalition), was found guilty of bribery, fraud and breach of public trust by the Jerusalem District Court. Der'i immediately announced his intention to appeal to the Supreme Court against the verdict. Although on 15 April he was sentenced to four years' imprisonment and asked to pay a 250,000-shekel fine, the District Court ruled that Der'i's sentence would be suspended until after the outcome of his appeal, thus enabling the Shas leader to campaign for the 17 May general election. In mid-June, however, Der'i resigned as Chairman of Shas.

NEW LABOUR COALITION

By mid-May 1999 Ehud Barak and Binyamin Netanyahu were the only remaining candidates for the premiership, four nominated contestants having withdrawn their candidacy. Following a decision by Itzhak Mordechai to transfer his support to Barak, who in March had established the 'One Israel' movement (including Gesher and the moderate Meimad party), victory for the Labour leader appeared to be assured. On 17 May Barak was elected Prime Minister with 56.1% of the votes cast, compared with 43.9% for Netanyahu. In the elections to the Israeli Knesset, Barak's One Israel grouping secured 26 seats, while Likud's strength declined from 32 seats to 19. Shas, meanwhile, increased its representation from 10 to 17 seats. The newly elected Knesset contained 15 factions. Some 78.8% of Israel's 4.3m.-strong electorate were reported to have participated in the elections.

Netanyahu subsequently resigned from both the Knesset and the Likud leadership. In late May 1999 Ariel Sharon became Chairman of the Likud party; Sharon's position was confirmed following a party ballot on 3 September.

The election campaign had been bitter and divisive. Most observers believed that the election was lost by Netanyahu and Likud, rather than won by the One Israel movement. Netanyahu had become increasingly unpopular and had disappointed significant sections of his traditional support base, particularly right-wing nationalists and settler groups. Furthermore, many in Israel's business community attributed responsibility for the economic recession on his freezing of the peace process and his monetarist policies.

On 6 July 1999, after making full use of the 45 interim days allowed by law and following complex negotiations, Barak presented his Cabinet to the Knesset. He formed a broad-based coalition, with the Centre Party, Shas, Meretz, Israel B'Aliyah and the NRP taking ministerial positions (talks with Likud having collapsed). However, the most influential posts were reserved for himself (Barak was also appointed Minister of Defence) and for loyalists such as David Levy of Gesher, who became Minister of Foreign Affairs. Also in July the Speaker of the Palestinian Legislative Council (PLC), Ahmad Quray, was invited by Avraham Burg to address the Knesset—the first visit to the Israeli parliament by a leading Palestinian official.

GROWING DEMANDS FOR A WITHDRAWAL FROM LEBANON

Israel's occupation of southern Lebanon grew increasingly unpopular during early 1999. (Some 23 Israeli soldiers had been killed in Israel's 'security zone' during 1998.) On the night of 22–23 February 1999 three Israeli army officers were killed during fighting with Hezbollah guerrillas inside the zone. On 28 February Brig.-Gen. Erez Gerstein, the commander of the Israeli army's liaison unit with the SLA, was killed (together with three other Israelis) by a Hezbollah roadside bomb in the 'security zone': Gerstein was the most senior Israeli officer to be killed in Lebanon since the 1982 occupation. This loss was a particular blow to the morale of the Israeli army, which responded by launching its heaviest air bombardments against Lebanon since Operation Grapes of Wrath in 1996.

On 15 July 1999 the new Prime Minister Barak announced that he would propose to his Cabinet a unilateral withdrawal from Lebanon if no peace accord had been reached (in the context of an agreement with Syria over the Golan Heights) within one year.

NEGOTIATIONS ON THE SYRIAN AND PALESTINIAN TRACKS

When Ehud Barak won the Israeli elections in May 1999, he and President Assad of Syria exchanged words of mutual esteem unprecedented for an Israeli and a Syrian leader. Speaking at the inauguration of the new Israeli Cabinet on 6 July, Barak promised to negotiate a bilateral peace with Syria, based on UN Resolutions 242 and 338. Observers interpreted this as a signal to Syria of his intention to return most of the occupied Golan Heights in exchange for peace and normalized relations. Meanwhile, the first direct talks between Yasser Arafat and Prime Minister Barak were held at the Erez checkpoint in Gaza on 11 July 1999. By late July relations had deteriorated, after Barak expressed the desire to combine the Israeli land withdrawals agreed under the terms of the Wye Memorandum with 'final status' negotiations.

IMPLEMENTING THE SHARM EL-SHEIKH AGREEMENT

Subsequently, a revised Wye Memorandum was signed by Yasser Arafat and Ehud Barak in Sharm el-Sheikh, Egypt, on 4 September 1999. The revised memorandum repeated the appeal for the swift resumption of accelerated 'final status' negotiations, but, unlike the original Wye agreement, urged Israel and the PA to conclude a Framework Agreement on Permanent Status issues (or FAPS) by 13 February 2000 and a comprehensive 'final status' agreement by 13 September. Following the signing of the Sharm el-Sheikh Memorandum, Israel and the PA generally fulfilled their outstanding obligations, although frequently behind schedule. The amount of land slated for transfer to full and partial PA control was the same under Wye Two as under the original Wye agreement; however, the transfer was to take place in three stages instead of two. Israel was late in carrying out the first stage of the Sharm el-Sheikh redeployment. It turned over maps to the PA on 9 September 1999 and carried out the transfer of 7% of the West Bank from Area C to Area B on 10 September. However, the numerous pockets of land to come under PA control were sparsely populated, and no IDF forces or checkpoints were moved.

On 25 October 1999 a southern 'safe passage' for Palestinians travelling between Gaza and Hebron was finally opened, under the terms of the Wye Memorandum. On 15 November an additional 3% of the West Bank was supposed to be transferred from Area C to Area B, with an additional 2% moving from B to A. The third phase of redeployment was scheduled, on 20 January 2000, to see the transfer of an additional 1% of the territory from C to A status, while 5.1% was expected to be shifted from B to A status. On 11 November 1999 Israel presented the PA with the maps for the second stage of redeployment, but Arafat rejected them, claiming that the areas proposed were too sparsely populated and did not link existing areas of PA control. After three days of talks, held on 12–14 November, failed to produce a compromise, Israel postponed the second stage of redeployment.

LITTLE PROGRESS IN 'FINAL STATUS' NEGOTIATIONS

The focus shifted to 'final status' deliberations between Israel and the PA in September 1999. A symbolic opening ceremony was held at the Erez crossing on 13 September, the sixth anniversary of the Declaration of Principles of 1993. A few days later it was reported that Barak and Arafat had held a secret meeting to discuss an agenda for such talks. On 1 November 1999 US President Clinton held talks with Barak and Arafat in Oslo, during two days of ceremonies to commemorate the fourth anniversary of Itzhak Rabin's assassination. The talks sought to determine the best way to approach the 'final status' negotiations: Barak suggested that the USA convene a Camp David-style summit in January 2000. President Clinton agreed in principle, provided the two sides were near agreement, and promised to arrange regular visits to the region by US Special Envoy Dennis Ross and at least one by Secretary of State Albright before 2000.

Negotiations between Israel and the PA on 'final status' issues commenced on 8 November 1999 in the West Bank city of Ramallah. The first meeting was convened despite the explosion of three pipe bombs in the Israeli town of Netanya on 7 November, in which at least 33 people were injured. The teams met again in mid-November, but no progress was reported. Indeed, the regular meetings being held to negotiate a FAPS by the deadline of 13 February 2000 never appeared to move beyond discussing procedural issues and presenting maximalist opening positions. Moreover, interim talks (led by Oded Eran and, for the Palestinians, Saeb Erakat) were deadlocked over the implementation of the second stage of redeployment. In late November and early December 1999 Israel approved two plans to expand Jewish settlements in the West Bank, which convinced the PA that Israel was not negotiating in good faith. By the end of November interim talks had reached an impasse. The PA suspended 'final status' meetings, saying it would no longer discuss anything with Israel except settlements. On 21 December Barak and Arafat held private discussions in Ramallah (their first ever meeting on Palestinian territory), after which they announced their intention to resolve quickly the two most important outstanding interim obligations: the second stage of re-deployment and final prisoner releases.

The second stage of West Bank redeployment was implemented on 6–7 January 2000, when Israel transferred 2% of jointly controlled Area B to PA-controlled Area A and 3% of Israeli-controlled Area C to Area B, evacuating six IDF posts. By mid-February Area A represented 12.1% of the West Bank, Area B 26.9% and Area C 61%. On 16 January Israel postponed the implementation of the third stage of redeployment, planned for 20 January, on the pretext that Barak would not have a chance to review the redeployment maps until he returned from his negotiation round with Syria. Meanwhile, on 17 January as many as 20 people were wounded in a bomb explosion at Hadera, northern Israel, which appeared to have been perpetrated by Palestinian militants. Although the 10 January deadline passed without a draft FAPS, the USA was sufficiently satisfied with both sides' efforts to host a meeting in Washington, DC, on 20 January, at which Arafat, Clinton, and Albright discussed delays on the Palestinian track, and the USA urged the PA to push forward with the FAPS talks and continue to aim for the 13 February deadline.

The general optimism generated after September 1999 by the fulfilment of some of the interim obligations outlined in the Sharm el-Sheikh Memorandum had evaporated by early 2000. Indeed, the 'final status' talks between Israel and the PA appeared to be heading towards a stalemate. However, on 19 March the Israeli Cabinet approved the transfer of a further 6.1% of the West Bank. The redeployment took place two days later.

The future of the Palestinian political prisoners detained by Israel had always been central to any progress on the Israeli-Palestinian track. On 1 May 2000 a hunger strike was declared by 650–1,000 of the estimated 1,650 Palestinian political inmates held in Israeli gaols. Demonstrations in support of the prisoners' action began in the West Bank and Gaza on 10 May, and the unrest escalated dramatically on 15 May—the 52nd anniversary of the declaration of the State of Israel—on what was declared by Palestinians to be a 'day of rage'. Violent clashes between Israeli troops and Palestinian police in the West Bank led Barak to put on hold a decision by the Israeli Cabinet on 15 May to transfer the three Palestinian villages of Abu Dis, al-Azariyya and al-Sawahra to full PA control. The Israeli Knesset approved the transfer on the same day, by 56 votes to 48, with one abstention. Following the vote, the NRP (one of two coalition parties that had voted against the move) announced that it was leaving the Government. Religious, right-wing and Russian immigrant parties in Israel regarded the decision to transfer the three villages to PA control as evidence that Barak intended to give up part of East Jerusalem to the Palestinians. On 17 May the Knesset approved in preliminary reading a Likud Knesset member's bill to limit changes in Jerusalem's municipal boundaries and to ban the transfer of powers within them to a foreign element, which many of Barak's coalition partners had supported.

Meanwhile, on 6 September 1999 Israel's Supreme Court ruled that the use of 'physical force' by Shin Bet, the Israeli internal security agency, during the interrogation of suspects was illegal. The judgment invalidated a 1987 decision that allowed the use of 'moderate physical pressure' against those accused of plotting terrorist attacks against Israel (see the chapter on the Palestinian Territories). Moreover, on 8 March 2000 a landmark ruling by the Supreme Court made it illegal for the Government to allocate state-owned land for the exclusive purpose of constructing Jewish settlements, stating that it must not discriminate on the basis of religion, nationality or ethnicity.

ISRAELI-SYRIAN NEGOTIATIONS

On 15 December 1999 peace talks between Israel and Syria were inaugurated by President Bill Clinton in Washington, DC. At the welcoming ceremony, the Syrian Minister of Foreign Affairs, Farouk al-Shara', welcomed the talks but refused to shake hands with Barak. The two agreed to hold their first round of intensive negotiations on 3–10 January 2000 in Shepherdstown, West Virginia.

Subsequently, on 25 March 2000 President Clinton met President Assad in Geneva. There, Clinton informed Assad of the Israeli offer: full withdrawal from the Golan Heights on the basis of the pre-1967 border as the Syrians had demanded. Barak thought that there was room for flexibility, since this boundary was never properly demarcated following the armistice agreements following the 1948 war. In particular he wanted to correct the border on the north-eastern bank of the Sea of Galilee, where the Syrians had illegally occupied a narrow strip of land. This would allow Israel to retain full control over the Sea of Galilee as per the official 1923 international border. As compensation for this modification, Barak offered Assad the larger Hama enclave that was under Israeli control before 1967. Barak was also prepared to grant the Syrians fishing rights and to create a joint peace park in the north-eastern shore area. However, Assad rejected the offer outright.

The death of President Assad, on 10 June 2000, threw the Middle East peace process into further confusion. On 13 June six Arab members of the Knesset joined world leaders at Assad's funeral in Damascus, despite the absence of diplomatic relations between Israel and Syria. (The Israeli Government emphasized that the Knesset members were attending in a private capacity.) Assad's son, Bashar, was appointed President in his stead in July.

WITHDRAWAL FROM LEBANON

The collapse of peace talks with Syria and the mounting domestic pressure compelled Barak to fulfil his promise of a withdrawal from Lebanon by June 2000. Therefore, as Israel's ally, the SLA, began to collapse, Barak opted to pull Israeli forces out of Lebanon entirely in a very quickly executed operation that was completed on 24 May. However, neither Lebanon nor Syria was willing to guarantee that Hezbollah would cease its operations in southern Lebanon in the event of an Israeli withdrawal. Barak failed to achieve his aim of an orderly removal of troops conducted over several weeks and to be completed by 7 July, with an expanded UN peace-keeping force taking control of border areas. In the event, Israeli soldiers were driven out of Lebanon within 24 hours, in what was regarded by some observers as a humiliating rush for the border.

The withdrawal marked a change of strategy on the part of Israel, and most Israelis, considering that the cost of the occupation outweighed the benefits, were relieved to see their army leave southern Lebanon. Some 900 Israeli soldiers had died there since 1978. Hezbollah had lost 1,276 fighters since it began resistance operations in 1982, while many more Palestinians, Lebanese civilians and others also lost their lives in the conflict. Nevertheless, the success of Hezbollah strengthened the conviction among Palestinians in the West Bank and Gaza that violence was the only option that produced results. Meanwhile, it was unclear in mid-2000 whether Israel's war in southern Lebanon had completely ended. Hezbollah had always maintained that it would not lay down arms until Israel had also withdrawn from Shebaa Farms. This area close to the border was recognized by the international community as part of the area captured by Israel from Syria in 1967. As such, its future was to be decided within the framework of Israeli-Syrian negotiations. Hezbollah, however, chose to unilaterally ignore this distinction, declaring that the area was Lebanese territory occupied by Israel.

In mid-May 2000 the UN had some 4,515 troops in south Lebanon. On 23 May the Security Council endorsed a report by Secretary-General Kofi Annan on arrangements for the monitoring of Israel's withdrawal from Lebanon. Among the technical requirements was the need to identify a line to be adopted conforming to Lebanon's internationally recognized boundaries, for the purpose of confirming compliance with Resolution 425. In mid-June the UN Security Council formally confirmed that Israel had completed its withdrawal from Lebanon in compliance with UN Resolution 425.

The al-Aqsa *intifada*, which began in late September 2000, resulted in a renewed campaign by Hezbollah against Israel's armed forces. On 7 October three Israeli soldiers were kidnapped on the border with Lebanon by members of Hezbollah, which demanded the release of Palestinian prisoners held in Israeli gaols. One week later an Israeli army reservist was also captured by Hezbollah. Tensions escalated in November when an Israeli soldier was killed by a Hezbollah bomb in Shebaa Farms; Israel responded by launching air raids on suspected Hezbollah targets.

DOMESTIC TROUBLES

This period saw a number of revelations and accusations of corruption in high places in Israel. These included a police investigation into party funding for the 1999 elections, which resulted in a heavy fine being imposed upon the One Israel list of Prime Minister Barak. Police also recommended the indictment of former Prime Minister Binyamin Netanyahu and his wife Sarah on charges of fraud related to events that took place during Netanyahu's period as Prime Minister. President Ezer Weizman was also forced to resign amid revelations that he had been the recipient of large, undeclared cash 'gifts' from a French tycoon while serving as a member of the Knesset in the 1980s. Finally, on 8 March 2000 Minister of Transport Itzhak Mordechai took a leave of absence from the Government to face charges of sexual harassment. He was convicted of indecent assault against two women in March 2001.

In June 2000 Barak's Government nearly collapsed under the impact of a major crisis involving Shas, One Israel's largest coalition partner. Barak narrowly survived the crisis, but was left with an unstable Government that could sabotage his efforts to make peace with the Palestinians. After 10 days of political chaos, the four Shas ministers withdrew their resignations, after Barak capitulated to virtually all of the party's demands: extra cash injections for its religious schools, the legalization of its private radio network and a greater say for the party in the peace process. The return of Shas to the Government came with a heavy trade-off: the departure of the liberal and secular Meretz party.

On 9 July 2000, the eve of Barak's departure for Camp David, the three right-wing and religious parties in his coalition carried out their threat to leave the Government as a result of fears concerning Barak's readiness to concede Israeli territory to the PA. The resignation of six of his Cabinet ministers (from Shas, the NRP and Israel B'Aliyah, including party leader and Minister of the Interior Natan Sharansky) left Barak preparing to leave for a crucial summit meeting on the peace process with a seriously weakened Government. Moreover, Barak's Minister of Foreign Affairs, David Levy, refused to attend the Camp David talks, owing to disagreements regarding the peace process. After narrowly surviving a vote of no confidence brought to the Knesset by the Likud party, the Prime Minister pledged to pursue his policy regarding peace with the Palestinians. However, on 30 July the domestic situation worsened when Levy stated that he would resign unless Barak agreed to invite Likud to join his coalition. Meanwhile, on 12 July the former leader of Shas, Aryeh Der'i, was sentenced to three years' imprisonment, having been found guilty of bribery and fraud charges; he began his sentence in September.

In the presidential election held on 31 July 2000, Moshe Katsav of Likud unexpectedly defeated Barak's nominee, former Prime Minister Shimon Peres, by 63 votes to 57 in a second round of Knesset voting. Katsav was duly sworn in as the eighth President of Israel on 1 August, to serve a seven-year term. Only hours after the election, Barak survived another no confidence motion in the Knesset, thus preventing early parliamentary elections. Nevertheless, on 2 August it appeared as if early elections might be inevitable, when Levy resigned as Minister of Foreign Affairs in protest against recent concessions made to the Palestinians. On the same day the Prime Minister lost a vote giving preliminary approval for new elections. A minor reshuffle of the Cabinet was effected on 6 August, with certain ministers being allocated additional portfolios. On 10 August the Minister of Public Security, Shlomo Ben-Ami, was also appointed acting Minister of Foreign Affairs; he was confirmed in this post in November.

FAILURE OF THE CAMP DAVID SUMMIT

On 5 July 2000 Clinton invited both the Israelis and Palestinians to the presidential retreat of Camp David (the site of the 1978 Israeli-Egyptian peace agreement). The US President launched the summit on 11 July, and on the following day Barak and Arafat held a bilateral meeting without US mediation. With a news black-out effectively in force, there were few details regarding the progress of the talks. The US Administration described the discussions as 'tense', and reports indicated that differences remained very wide on the major issues of Jerusalem, Palestinian refugees, borders and Jewish settlements. On 13 July Arafat threatened to walk out of the talks owing to US bridging proposals that Palestinian officials regarded as too close to the Israeli position. However, Clinton withdrew the proposals and a crisis was averted. On 17 July US officials stated that talks had been intensified, while Clinton was scheduled to depart for a summit meeting of the Group of Eight industrialized nations (G8) in Okinawa, Japan, on 19 July. In the event, Clinton delayed his trip by one day to continue round-the-clock efforts to broker a peace agreement. On 19 July, shortly before his trip to Okinawa, Clinton presented the Israeli proposals to Arafat. While some dispute emerged as to the precise nature of the terms offered, the vast majority of those present agreed that Arafat was offered a Palestinian state in 92% of the West Bank and the entirety of the Gaza Strip, with seven or eight of the nine Arab neighbourhoods in Jerusalem included in the Palestinian state. This would have included Palestinian acquisition of the Muslim quarters. After deliberations, the Palestinian delegation announced that they rejected the offer and had no counter-offer. Moreover, Arafat went on to reject three proposals from Clinton concerning Jerusalem. Clinton told Arafat that he was leading his people and the region 'to a catastrophe'. The Israeli proposal was later caricatured by Palestinian spokesmen and their allies as Barak's 'so-called generous offer'.

However, these interpretations confused Barak's tactics for grand strategy, an error that stemmed from a failure to understand his position. During discussions within the Israeli team at Camp David, Barak stated that he was prepared to end up with the 'borders of 1967', with necessary changes. Barak viewed territory as Israel's main negotiating card and he held back on officially reaching a conclusion on this issue, in order to use it as a bargaining chip on other core matters of dispute, especially refugees.

The collapse of the Camp David talks also led to fears of renewed violence in the West Bank and Gaza. On 26 July 2000 Arafat and Barak returned to the Middle East—the Palestinian leader to a hero's welcome for refusing to yield on the issue of Palestinian claims to Jerusalem and the 'right of return', and his Israeli counterpart to criticism from both left- and right-wing parties. Israeli and Palestinian negotiators resumed discussions in an attempt to reactivate the peace process, as the PA faced growing international pressure to postpone a unilateral declaration of independence on 13 September. (Shortly before that date the Palestinian legislature voted to delay such a declaration for an indefinite period.)

RELATIONS WITH OTHER STATES

On 28 October 1999 Mauritania became the third member of the Arab League (after Egypt and Jordan) to establish full diplomatic relations with Israel, provoking protests in several Arab countries. On 12 January 2000 the Israeli Minister of Foreign Affairs, David Levy, undertook a four-day visit to Morocco, during which he held discussions with King Muhammad VI and other leading officials. It was announced that Israel and Morocco had agreed in principle to upgrade diplomatic relations to ambassadorial level, and to allow the Israeli national airline El Al to fly directly to Morocco. However, following a meeting of Arab leaders in Cairo on 21–22 October, Morocco declared that it had severed diplomatic relations with Israel, in protest against recent Israeli actions against Palestinians in the West Bank and Gaza. Tunisia also decided to close its liaison office in Tel-Aviv and the Israeli interests office in Tunis.

Meanwhile, in October 1999 Ehud Barak became the first Israeli Prime Minister to visit Turkey. During the visit Israel proposed to sell more military equipment to Turkey and to upgrade its tanks and aircraft. The Turkish leadership, for its part, was reported to have offered to mediate in negotiations between Israel and Syria. A major defence pact, worth some US $1,000m., was announced between Israel and Turkey in June 2000. King Abdullah of Jordan made his first visit to Israel in April of that year; the bilateral talks reportedly focused on water management.

President Jiang Zemin of the People's Republic of China met with Barak and other Israeli officials in April 2000. However, his visit to Israel was overshadowed by US dissatisfaction over a recent offer by Israel to sell military technology worth US $250m. to the Chinese Government, which resulted in threats, in June, by the US Congress to reduce military aid to Israel. The Israeli authorities, however, refused to cancel the contract until 12 July (the second day of the Camp David summit), by which time it had become clear to Barak that Israel could not afford to lose the US aid.

RENEWED VIOLENCE

The fall-out from the Camp David summit of July 2000 formed the background to a renewed uprising by Palestinians in the West Bank and Gaza Strip. As tensions grew in the region, Prime Minister Barak continued his efforts to forge a coalition government, making offers to almost every political party in the country. Barak's troubles were exacerbated when the Israeli Attorney-General announced on 27 September that he was dismissing the bribery and corruption case against former Likud Prime Minister Binyamin Netanyahu, owing to a lack of evidence, thereby clearing Netanyahu's way for a political comeback, should new elections be called. On the same day, as renewed Israeli-Palestinian peace talks were taking place in Virginia, USA, involving PA negotiators Saeb Erakat and Muhammad Dahlan, and Israeli Minister of Public Security and acting Minister of Foreign Affairs, Shlomo Ben-Ami, Israeli police in Jerusalem informed Muslim officials there of a request by the Likud leader, Ariel Sharon, to visit the Temple Mount/Haram al-Sharif compound in Jerusalem's Old City. Barak and Ben-Ami declined to intervene.

The visit duly went ahead, and it became the scene of confrontations between Palestinian youths and security forces. Demonstrations continued on 29 September 2000. The violence quickly spread throughout the West Bank. The Fatah Tanzim led the Palestinian attacks, with the compliance of Arafat. On 30 September the Arab Monitoring Committee, an informal umbrella representing Israel's more than 1m. Palestinian citizens, called a general strike in protest against the deaths of the seven Palestinians at the al-Aqsa Mosque compound the previous day. The first month of the al-Aqsa *intifada* witnessed armed Palestinian attacks on Jewish soldiers and civilians throughout the West Bank, and heavy Israeli military strikes against Palestinian targets. There was a lack of clarity to the Israeli response to the violence in this early period. On the one hand, mindful of the need to renew deterrence in the aftermath of the withdrawal from Lebanon, and to limit casualties, a swift, decisive response was required. On the other hand, the political echelon, while supporting these objectives, was keen to prevent violence from destroying prospects for negotiations, which militated towards support for a more restrained response.

In solidarity with the Palestinians in the Occupied Territories and exacerbated by long-held feelings of frustration and alienation, on 1 October 2000 demonstrations began to spread through Arab villages. There were violent clashes between Israeli Arab citizens and the Israeli security forces, resulting in the deaths of 13 Israeli Arabs. The events shocked both sides: the Jewish majority saw the riots as a betrayal by Israeli Arabs of the State of Israel, while the Israeli Arabs deplored the exaggerated use of force. Under pressure from the Arab sector, the Government approved the nomination of an inquiry commission, led by Supreme Court justice Theodor Or.

THE SHARM EL-SHEIKH SUMMIT

In an effort to reach a cease-fire, on 4 October 2000 US Secretary of State Madeleine Albright and the CIA Director, George Tenet, met with Arafat and Barak in Paris. UN Secretary-General Kofi Annan and French President Jacques Chirac attended some of the meetings, and both also met separately with Arafat and Barak. After 12 hours of heated talks, the sides reached a 'tentative' arrangement under which Barak agreed to withdraw Israeli troops to their positions held before 28 September and Arafat agreed to try to curb Palestinian protests. The USA had hoped that the Israeli and Palestinian leaders would sign a cease-fire or security co-operation agreement, but Arafat refused to do so unless the text also provided for an international inquiry into the violence, a demand rejected by Barak. Barak and Albright proposed as an alternative that Israel and the PA each investigate the actions of their own forces, with the CIA acting as arbitrator; Arafat rejected this as inadequate. Afterwards, Albright and Arafat left for Sharm el-Sheikh for further talks with Mubarak, but Barak returned to Israel. On 7 October, however, Palestinian crowds sacked Joseph's Tomb in Nablus (a shrine of religious significance to both Jews and Muslims) and destroyed a synagogue built close to the site. In retaliation, an historic mosque in Tiberias was vandalized. The Israeli authorities also ordered the closure of the Palestinian airport at Gaza. Barak called up IDF reserves and issued a 48-hour deadline for the PA to halt the violence; he also threatened to implement a 'sanctions package' that would include sealing off the West Bank and Gaza and suspending monetary transfers owed to the PA. Arafat's refusal to make a clear public announcement in Arabic demanding an end to violence coupled with his refusal to give an unambiguous order to the Tanzim following the talks pushed Barak in this direction. Following further attempts by international diplomats to defuse the situation, Barak extended his 48-hour deadline indefinitely on 9 October, in the interest of possible mediation, even though the clashes continued unabated in the West Bank and Gaza.

On 16–17 October 2000 an emergency summit meeting between Barak and Arafat was convened by US President Clinton and hosted by President Mubarak at Sharm el-Sheikh. The summit was the outcome of intense international diplomacy and was precipitated by the significant escalation of force used by Israel against Palestinian targets following the lynching of two Israeli army reservists by a Palestinian mob in Ramallah on 12 October.

With the violence escalating and the number of Palestinian deaths and casualties rising, Mubarak appealed to Arafat, Barak and Clinton to hold talks in Sharm el-Sheikh. After the intervention of UN Secretary-General Annan, Arafat and Barak reluctantly agreed to meet with Clinton, Mubarak, King Abdullah of Jordan and Javier Solana, the EU High Representative for the Common Foreign and Security Policy, on 16 October 2000. After more than 24 hours of nearly continuous talks, Clinton announced that Israel and the PA had agreed a fragile accord to: 'issue public statements unequivocally calling for an end of violence'; take steps to eliminate points of friction; commission an inquiry into the causes of the clashes; and explore the possibility of resuming talks. After much wrangling, the sides had agreed as a compromise that a committee charged with investigating the causes of the recent violence would be appointed by President Clinton in consultation with Israel, the PA and the UN; it would be led by an American but would include international members. In fulfilment of the agreement reached at Sharm el-Sheikh, Arafat issued a vague statement on 18 October urging individuals to do their utmost to avoid inciting violence. On the same day Israel lifted the internal closure of the West Bank and Gaza, withdrew tanks from Nablus, and reopened the borders with Egypt and Gaza airport. The PA, for its part, had reportedly rearrested all Hamas and Islamic Jihad members released since late September, plus others, including Hamas spokesman Abd al-Aziz al-Rantisi. Palestinian and Israel security officials also met to discuss how to reduce tensions. Despite these steps, the clashes escalated.

The Sharm el-Sheikh 'compromise' was rejected publicly at a Fatah-led march in Ramallah on 17 October 2000, and in a statement issued by the Palestinian National and Islamic Forces (PNIF), an umbrella movement made up of all the major Palestinian factions. Both Palestinian statements described the summit as a failure that did not meet the minimum expectations of Palestinians and appealed for a continuation of the 'people's peaceful uprising until sovereignty and independence are achieved'. Clashes continued and Barak formally suspended the peace process. He reimposed the internal closure, shut crossings into Egypt and Jordan, closed Gaza airport again, and resumed military strikes.

On 7 November 2000 the White House named the US-led investigative committee mandated at the Sharm el-Sheikh summit to investigate the causes of the Israeli–Palestinian clashes. The panel was to be chaired by former US senator George Mitchell. The Mitchell Committee began its investigations into the fighting in early December.

On 9 November 2000, just before Arafat's meeting with President Clinton, Israeli forces killed a senior Fatah commander, Hussein Abayyat, in Beit Sahur, tracking him by helicopter and shelling his car. Abayyat was the first victim of Israel's new policy of singling out for assassination leading Palestinian figures alleged to be orchestrators of 'terrorist' actions. The new type of killings, which Israeli officials described as 'focused assassinations', had claimed the lives of at least 10 local Palestinian leaders by the end of December. As Israeli–Palestinian clashes continued, by mid-November 2000 Israeli armed forces had tripled the number of troops in the West Bank and Gaza, reinforcing the economic blockade on Area A, and had secured control over movement along all major roads. The Israeli authorities also halted the payment of tax transfers owed to the PA.

NEW PREMIERSHIP ELECTION

In November 2000 Shas signed an agreement with Barak to provide him with a one-month 'safety net' against early elections, promising to vote as a bloc with Labour-One Israel on any no confidence motion. However, Barak was still unable to reach a deal on forming a government of national unity with the hardline Likud leader, Ariel Sharon, who insisted on having the power to veto all decisions relating to national security as part of a coalition deal. On 28 November Barak therefore announced that he would resign in order to seek early re-election to the premiership in 60 days. The Israeli Prime Minister stated that he wanted to prevent Israel from holding elections for both the premiership and the Knesset at a time of fragile national security. With a beleaguered and paralysed administration, Barak had few alternatives open to him: more than 70 members of the 120-member legislature were already committed to vote for the dissolution of the Knesset and early elections that would effectively end his term of office. It was Barak's failure to make good on his pledges to bring peace and domestic reform to Israel that was his undoing. The decisive factor was that in light of the renewed violence and the rejection of extensive Israeli concessions Israelis simply were no longer convinced that Arafat was a credible partner for negotiations.

Barak formally resigned as Prime Minister on 9 December 2000, and a prime ministerial election was scheduled for 6 February 2001. The Labour Party swiftly chose Barak, who remained the acting premier, as its candidate. On 19 December 2000 former Likud leader Binyamin Netanyahu withdrew from the contest. Netanyahu had urged the Knesset either to amend electoral legislation that prevents non-members from standing for election, or to vote for the Assembly's dissolution; however, the Knesset voted against its own dissolution and thus avoided a general election being held prior to the end of its term in May 2001. Barak's main challenger from the other side of the political spectrum was Likud's Sharon.

President Bill Clinton presented his latest proposals for resolving the Palestinian–Israeli conflict on 23 December 2000. The US peace initiative was more generous to the Palestinians than Clinton's offer at Camp David, and was endorsed by the Israeli Cabinet on 28 December, on condition that the Palestinians accepted the framework as well. Clinton proposed that the Palestinians should have a 'non-militarized' state covering 95% of an (undefined) West Bank and all of Gaza. The PA should also receive 3% of land from within Israel's 1967 borders to compensate for the 5% of the West Bank that Clinton believed Israel needed in order to annex the three Jewish settlements of Ma'aleh Adumim, Ariel and Gush Etzion. In East Jerusalem, the Palestinians would have sovereignty over all Arab neighbourhoods, while Israel would extend its sovereignty over the 11 Jewish settlements built within Jerusalem's annexed and enlarged city boundaries since 1967. The Old City of Jerusalem would be divided ethnically, with the Palestinians having sovereignty over the Muslim and Christian areas, and Israel gaining sovereignty over the Jewish quarter, the Western Wall and the access road through the Armenian Quarter. (In effect, Israel would have to hand over 85% of East Jerusalem.) However, Yasser Arafat gave a negative response to the Clinton initiative, demanding an explicit right of return, no international force in the Jordan Valley and no compromise on the Temple Mount.

With Clinton's presidential term coming to an end in the USA, on 5 January 2001 two authoritative Israeli opinion polls signalled a potentially devastating defeat for incumbent Prime Minister Barak. No sooner had Clinton bidden farewell to his various partners in the Oslo peace process than Arafat dispatched his senior negotiators to Taba, Egypt, to meet their Israeli counterparts in the hope of reaching an accord. The latest round of intensive talks, which began on 21 January but broke down without agreement six days later, evolved out of a CIA-drafted security plan presented to the two sides in Cairo on 10 January. The prospect of a Sharon victory had shaken the Palestinian leadership out of any pretence of not interfering in the Israeli election campaign.

SHARON'S GOVERNMENT OF NATIONAL UNITY

Ariel Sharon won the prime ministerial election of 6 February 2001 with a 25% margin of victory over Ehud Barak: Sharon won 62.4% of the total votes cast. The rate of voter participation was estimated at 62.3%. Arab parties in Israel—which had contributed significantly to Barak's election victory in 1999—urged their supporters to either boycott or abstain from the poll in reaction to the October 2000 violence. Sharon had railed against Barak for being 'soft': his election campaign slogan was 'Let the IDF win'. Sharon immediately set about constructing a government of national unity, but his Likud party could provide no more than 19 Knesset votes, clearly short of the majority the Prime Minister-elect needed to control the 120-member legislature. Barak, meanwhile, resigned the party leadership.

Labour's Central Committee voted on 26 February 2001 to enter into a coalition with Likud. Sharon's 26-member Government, which was dominated by Labour, Likud and Shas, but also included representatives from right-wing and religious parties, was presented for Knesset approval on 6 March and approved the following day. Sharon stated that what had been offered by his predecessor was no longer on the table, and that peace talks would not be resumed from where they stalled in January 2001. It was hard at this time to see how the Israeli–Palestinian conflict could become anything other than a long war of attrition. Sharon made it clear that he would not meet with Arafat during a trip to Washington, DC, on 19–20 March, when he held talks with new US President George W. Bush, who had been inaugurated on 20 January. Meanwhile, Israel continued its assassination of suspected Palestinian militant leaders.

On 15 April 2001 Israeli helicopter gunships bombed a Syrian radar station 35 km east of Beirut near the mountain town of Dahr al-Baydar, killing at least one Syrian soldier and wounding several others. The Israeli assault, the first against Syrian targets since 1996, was in retaliation for the killing by Hezbollah of an Israeli soldier in Shebaa Farms.

The Report of the Sharm el-Sheikh Fact-Finding Committee (the 'Mitchell Report') was officially released on 20 May 2001 (Documents on Palestine, see p. 96). The report failed to apportion blame for the recent Israeli–Palestinian violence; it described Sharon's visit to the Temple Mount/Haram al-Sharif compound in September 2000 as 'poorly timed' and 'provocative', but declared that this had not caused the violence. The Mitchell Committee also failed to accept that the PA leadership had orchestrated Palestinian violence following the failed Camp David talks, but demanded a greater effort by Palestinian leaders to prevent terrorist attacks on Israeli targets.

On 1 June 2001 20 Israelis were killed and scores wounded in a Palestinian suicide bombing at a beach-front disco in Tel-Aviv. (In mid-June another Israeli died as a result of injuries sustained in the attack.) The dramatic escalation of Israeli–Palestinian violence compelled the USA to increase its involvement in the conflict, attempting to broker a new round of talks from late May. On 5 June CIA Director George Tenet arrived in Israel, taking the Bush Administration a step further towards re-engagement in Arab-Israeli affairs. Tenet sought to consolidate the fragile cease-fire he had earlier helped to negotiate between Israel and the PA, and to implement the recommendations contained in the Mitchell Report. The Mitchell recommendations mapped out steps towards restoring the political process, ending the eight-month crisis and introducing confidence-building measures. By 12 June Tenet had persuaded Israel and the PA to agree the terms of an 'outline cease-fire deal'; however, violence between Israelis and Palestinians continued and the CIA-led talks were suspended.

Despite having begun to implement the cease-fire requirements to withdraw tanks from PA-controlled areas and to ease the economic blockade, in mid-June 2001 Israel was reported to be 'reassessing' the cease-fire following the killing by Palestinian gunmen of two Jewish settlers in the West Bank. On 22 June two Israeli soldiers were killed in a suicide bomb attack in the Gaza Strip. On 6 August Israel published a 'most wanted' list of seven Palestinians whom it held responsible for terrorist attacks against Israelis. Three days later a suicide bomber killed at least 15 Israelis at a restaurant in Jerusalem, leading the Israeli Government, on 10 August, to seize control of Orient House, the headquarters of the PA in East Jerusalem. In the second half of August Israeli armed forces on several occasions entered Palestinian-controlled towns in the West Bank, including Jenin, Hebron and Beit Jala, known centres of activity by Palestinian paramilitaries. Israeli tanks also entered a refugee camp in Gaza. Tensions increased on 27 August when the leader of the PFLP, Abu Ali Moustafa, was killed by Israeli security forces at the PFLP headquarters in Ramallah.

Meanwhile, in July 2001 the UN declared that it would allow Israeli and Lebanese officials to view a censored copy of a videocassette made by a UN peace-keeper in Lebanon, which Israel believed would give vital information relating to the three Israeli soldiers abducted by Hezbollah in October 2000. The UN had previously denied the existence of the tape.

The election for the Labour Party leadership proved inconclusive in early September 2001, when one of the two candidates, Minister of Defence Binyamin Ben-Eliezer, alleged that Knesset Speaker Avraham Burg (who had won a narrow victory) had engaged in vote-rigging. Ben-Eliezer initiated legal proceedings against the outcome of the ballot, and following a second election on 27 December was named as the new Labour leader (having received 51.2% of the votes cast).

At the end of September 2001 a report released by the State Comptroller raised doubts about the legality of certain donations made to Ariel Sharon and his campaign team in the approach to the premiership election. In early October the Attorney-General ordered a criminal investigation into the alleged violation of campaign funding regulations; the Prime Minister and his son, Omri (who had managed Sharon's campaign), were both questioned by police. In November Sharon was obliged to repay what had been found to be an illegal donation received by his campaign team.

In mid-October 2001 the right-wing National Union-Israel Beytenu bloc withdrew from Sharon's coalition, in protest against the Government's decision to withdraw Israeli troops from the West Bank town of Hebron and proposals to ease the blockade on the Palestinian territories; the bloc's representatives, Minister of National Infrastructure Avigdor Lieberman and Minister of Tourism Rechavam Ze'evi, both resigned from the Cabinet. Two days later (when the ministers' resignations were due to take effect) Ze'evi was assassinated at a hotel in East Jerusalem by a militant of the PFLP, which claimed that the killing was in revenge for the recent assassination of its leader. Ze'evi was the first Israeli cabinet minister to be killed by an Arab militant. Following his assassination, the National Union-Israel Beytenu bloc remained in the Government, with Lieberman retaining his post and Binyamin Elon subsequently being named as Minister of Tourism.

CONTINUED ESCALATION OF ISRAELI–PALESTINIAN HOSTILITIES

The second half of 2001 was marked by a continued and steady escalation of Israeli–Palestinian hostilities. The dynamics of the situation on the ground were altered after the massive suicide attacks on the World Trade Center in New York and the Pentagon in Washington, DC, on 11 September, in which some 3,000 people were killed. In the hope of invigorating the cease-fire and as a public relations move designed to help US coalition-building, US Secretary of Defense Donald Rumsfeld toured the Middle East in early October, and President Bush declared on 2 October that the creation of a Palestinian state 'has always been a part of our vision, so long as the right of Israel to exist is respected'. Although this marked the first explicit support for statehood by a Republican administration, the US Department of State denied any shift in official policy. Bush reiterated his support for a Palestinian state through negotiations on 11 October. However, with no new political initiatives on offer and no diplomatic progress in sight, Israeli–Palestinian clashes continued.

In late November 2001 the USA sent to the region its two special envoys to the Middle East, William Burns and Anthony Zinni, in an attempt to broker a new cease-fire. In early December the Israeli–Palestinian crisis witnessed a considerable escalation: in a single weekend (1–2 December) some 25 Israelis were killed, and scores wounded, in suicide bombings perpetrated by Palestinian militants in Haifa and Jerusalem. Sharon cut short his official visit to the USA and on his return to Israel convened an emergency Cabinet meeting, at which it was decided formally to declare the PA as an 'entity that supports terrorism'. (Labour ministers did not attend the vote.) Israel also launched heavy military strikes against Palestinian security targets in the Occupied Territories: two of Arafat's helicopters were destroyed in an Israeli raid on 3 December. The Government responded to a televised address by Arafat on 16 December, in which he ordered militant groups to end their armed campaign against Israelis and pledged to arrest the perpetrators of the violence, by demanding 'concrete action' from the PA. On 20 December Israeli armed forces staged a 'tactical' withdrawal from areas around Nablus and Ramallah to permit Arafat's security forces to arrest wanted Palestinian militants. However, Arafat remained confined to his headquarters in Ramallah after Israel imposed a travel ban on the Palestinian leader.

THE *KARINE A* AFFAIR

On 3 January 2002 Israeli naval commandos in the Red Sea captured a freighter, the *Karine A*, carrying some 50 metric tons of heavy weaponry from Iran destined for the PA. Among the arms seized were rockets and missiles capable of reaching Ben-Gurion International Airport and major Israeli cities from PA-controlled territory in the West Bank. Following the capture of official Palestinian documents by Israel later that year, it was later proven that the PA was directly involved in the smuggling. Subsequently, the USA accepted that there was 'convincing evidence' that Iran and Hezbollah were linked to the smuggling attempt.

ZINNI'S MEDIATION EFFORTS AND THE SAUDI PEACE PLAN

Anthony Zinni arrived in Israel on 14 March 2002 to seek implementation of a cease-fire under the terms of the Mitchell Committee. Zinni's visit followed the adoption by the UN Security Council, meeting on 12 March, of Resolution 1397 (Documents on Palestine, see p. 104), which for the first time affirmed the idea of a Palestinian state. The resolution, the first on the Middle East to be drafted by the USA for some 25 years, asserted the UN's 'vision of a region where two States, Israel and Palestine, live side by side within secure and recognized borders'.

Meanwhile, the summit meeting of the Arab League Council was held in the Lebanese capital on 27–28 March 2002. A principal consideration of the Beirut summit was a recent Saudi initiative. The Saudi proposals essentially reiterated the standard Arab position on the conflict, demanding a complete Israeli withdrawal from all land occupied since 1967, a 'just solution' to the refugee issue, and the establishment of a 'viable Palestinian state' with East Jerusalem as its capital. In return, the Arab nations would recognize the State of Israel and normalize diplomatic relations. The final declaration of the Arab League summit endorsed the Saudi initiative.

OPERATION DEFENSIVE SHIELD: FULL-SCALE INVASION OF WEST BANK POPULATION CENTRES

In early 2002 Israeli–Palestinian hostilities continued to escalate. By mid-March at least 1,065 Palestinians and 344 Israelis had been killed since the violence began in September 2000. During 2–3 March 2002 some 21 Israelis were killed in gun attacks in Gaza and the West Bank and a suicide bombing in Jerusalem; the attacks provoked a strong Israeli military response. On 11 March a major Israeli incursion into Ramallah took place. On 29 March Israel launched a large-scale offensive in the West Bank, in response to a series of suicide attacks by Palestinian militants and, more specifically, to a suicide bombing on 27 March that killed 29 Israelis who were celebrating the start of Passover in the coastal city of Netanya. Hamas claimed responsibility for the attack, which was the bloodiest since the outbreak of violence in September 2000. The goal of Israel's full-scale invasion of Palestinian cities in the West Bank was to eliminate the militant networks and seize weapons. Sharon was under intense pressure from right-wing members of his Cabinet to step up military action and oust Arafat.

On 30 March 2002 Israel began calling up thousands of army reservists and combat reserve units for a large-scale operation against the Palestinians. Israeli Army Radio reported that the mobilization would be the most significant call-up since just before the Gulf War in 1990. On 1 April 2002 Israeli tanks entered the town of Beitunya, near Ramallah, surrounding the Preventive Security compound of West Bank security chief Jibril Rajoub and causing widespread damage to the complex. Israeli tanks also entered the Palestinian town of Beit Jala, adjacent to Bethlehem, and Bethlehem itself, stopping some 500 yards from the Church of the Nativity (believed by Christians to be the birthplace of Jesus Christ). Earlier, dozens of Israeli tanks had rolled into the West Bank town of Qalqilya. Sharon announced that the operation would continue for weeks, if not longer. US Secretary of State Powell told reporters at a press briefing that he had received a commitment from Sharon that the operation would not bring any harm to Arafat himself.

The attack in Netanya represented the 'strategic attack' that led the Sharon Government to another turning-point in its relationship with the PA. Sharon now sought to expel Arafat from the area, publicly suggesting on 2 April 2002 that he should be sent into exile. However, although US Secretary of State Colin Powell stated that Israel had the right to 'self-defence', US officials urged Israel to show restraint. Meanwhile, Israeli forces clamped down on Palestinians in Ramallah, searching for gunmen and imposing a curfew. The military announced that it had arrested a total of 145 suspected Palestinian militants during the two-day operation, including more than 60 who were detained in Arafat's presidential compound.

On 2 April 2002 Israel widened its offensive by seizing more towns and cities in the West Bank. Prime Minister Ariel Sharon convened his 'inner' Security Cabinet to approve the next stage of Operation Defensive Shield. The next day some 300–400 Israeli tanks moved into the West Bank's largest city, Nablus, and encircled three adjacent refugee camps amid heavy fighting with Palestinian militiamen. Israel took control of several key cities and towns in the West Bank, stating that it was acting to eliminate the Palestinian terrorist infrastructure. Only two major West Bank towns—Hebron and Jericho—remained under Palestinian control. In the eight major Palestinian cities and towns under full Israeli control—Ramallah, Nablus, Qalqilya, Jenin, Salfeet, Tulkarm, Bethlehem and Beit Jala—tanks patrolled streets, enforcing strict curfews. Israeli troops had also laid siege to Jenin's refugee camp, battling with Palestinians who barricaded entrances and fought back with bombs and guns. Soldiers also encircled about 200 Palestinians in the Church of the Nativity in Bethlehem, among them militiamen (reportedly from Hamas, Islamic Jihad and the Tanzim), policemen, officials, clerics and church workers. On 2 April armed Palestinians had forced their way into the shrine while fleeing Israeli forces during prolonged gun battles near the church and adjacent Manger Square.

On 4 April 2002 the UN Security Council adopted a resolution (No. 1403) calling for both sides 'to move immediately to a meaningful cease-fire' and for 'the withdrawal of Israeli troops from Palestinian cities, including Ramallah'. The USA supported the resolution, but subsequently stated that Israel was not required to act until the PA agreed to a cease-fire. On 3 April Israel's ambassador to the UN, Yehuda Lancry, had declared that any new resolution must be balanced with a demand for Palestinians to end suicide attacks.

THE JENIN CONTROVERSY

The heaviest fighting between the Israeli army and Palestinian militias took place in the Jenin refugee camp, the home of some 13,000 Palestinian refugees. Dozens of Israeli tanks entered Jenin and surrounded the adjacent refugee camp early on 3 April 2002. Helicopters and tanks fired machine guns at Palestinians, who hurled grenades and fired on the Israeli troops with assault rifles. Initially Israeli commandos moved from house to house, under covering fire from the helicopters and tanks. On 9 April 13 Israeli army reservists were killed after entering a booby-trapped building in the refugee camp.

Palestinian spokesmen, echoed by a number of journalists, claimed at the time that Israel had committed a massacre of civilians in the camp. The figure of 500 fatalities was used by a Palestinian spokesmen speaking to US television network CNN on 17 April 2002. Such claims rapidly began to be scaled down, however, as evidence was not produced to support them. On 15 April Marwan Barghouthi, the West Bank Fatah leader who had turned the mainstream Tanzim from a civil guard into a major militia, was detained by an Israeli army operation in Ramallah. (Trial proceedings began on 5 September against Barghouthi; among the charges against him was one of heading the al-Aqsa Martyrs Brigades.) On 16 April Israel reopened Ketziot, a detention camp in the southern Israeli Negev desert, in order to hold some of the 4,000 Palestinians it had rounded up during Operation Defensive Shield. (Ketziot had held prisoners detained during the first Palestinian uprising of 1987–93.)

Meanwhile, on 9 April 2002 the USA made fresh demands for an Israeli withdrawal from PA-controlled areas, while Sharon vowed that the fight would continue until the Palestinian militias were crushed. Under pressure from President Bush, and with the impending arrival of US Secretary of State Powell, the Israeli army began withdrawing from Qalqilya and Tulkarm, but defied its closest political ally with raids on more Palestinian towns. On 11 April Powell arrived in Israel on a mission to forge a cease-fire. Powell met with both Sharon and Arafat and also visited Syria and Lebanon. However, his visit failed to secure a cease-fire; Sharon refused to promise a timetable for the withdrawal of Israeli troops from the West Bank, and Powell could not secure an unconditional pledge from Arafat to rein in Palestinian terror groups. Sharon indicated his desire for a regional conference that would include heads of states but exclude Arafat.

By mid-April 2002 events at the Jenin refugee camp had become the centre of a heated dispute. The UN Security Council voted unanimously to back a fact-finding mission to establish what had happened during the Israeli military assault on the Jenin camp. The Israelis asked that military and counter-terrorism experts be included in the panel. When this request was refused, Israel challenged the impartiality and military expertise of the team. The team was disbanded by UN Secretary-General Kofi Annan on 1 May.

In his report to the UN General Assembly on 30 July 2002, Annan related to the matter of the casualty figures in Jenin in the following terms: 'Palestinians had claimed that between 400 and 500 people had been killed, fighters and civilians together. They had also claimed a number of summary executions and the transfer of corpses to an unknown place outside the city of Jenin. The number of Palestinian fatalities, on the basis of bodies recovered to date, in Jenin and the refugee camp in this military operation, can be estimated at around 55. Of those, a number were civilians, four were women and two children. There were 23 Israeli fatalities in the fighting operations in Jenin.'

In any case, on 2 May 2002 Arafat was allowed to leave his compound and to move freely throughout the Palestinian areas of the West Bank and Gaza Strip, after agreeing to try the murderers of Israeli minister Rechavam Ze'evi.

SHARON'S DISMISSAL OF CABINET MINISTERS

On 20 May 2002 Ariel Sharon ordered the removal from the Cabinet of members of Shas and dismissed deputy ministers from another ultra-Orthodox party, United Torah Judaism, effectively expelling the two parties from his Government. The decision to remove the ministers came after the two parties failed to support the Government on an emergency economic package presented to the Knesset, which would have reduced benefits for the lowest echelons of Israeli society and which was defeated by 47 to 44 votes. (Israel's economy was in crisis partly because of the global economic downturn and partly as a result of the effects of almost 20 months of conflict with the Palestinians.) A fifth Shas minister, who was not a member of the Knesset, declared that he would resign in solidarity with his party colleagues. On 21 May 2002 the Chairman of Shas,

Eliyahu Yishai, announced that he was open to negotiating a new economic plan that would allow his party to remain in Sharon's coalition. However, in a letter to Shas's spiritual leader, Rabbi Ovadia Yosef, Sharon wrote that Shas would have to support the emergency economic plan in its second and third readings in the Knesset and respect government decisions that it had ignored in recent months. As a result of the dismissals, Sharon's Government thus commanded only 60 of the 120 seats in parliament, thereby losing its absolute majority, until 3 June, when Shas was brought back into the Cabinet.

REOCCUPATION OF WEST BANK CITIES AND BUSH'S PLAN FOR THE MIDDLE EAST

Following a new wave of suicide bombings, the Israeli military accelerated the construction of barriers on the outskirts of Palestinian towns and the Israeli Cabinet authorized the construction of a 'security fence' of thick coils of wire around East Jerusalem. Construction of the fence began in mid-June 2002. Later that month, after two suicide bombings in Jerusalem had killed at least 26 Israelis, the Israeli army began to reoccupy large sections of the West Bank.

On 24 June 2002 US President George W. Bush, in his long-awaited speech on the Middle East, set out his proposals for peace in the region. He appealed to the Palestinians to elect a 'new and different Palestinian leadership' and to adopt a new constitution with a fully empowered parliament, local government and an independent judiciary. The USA and its allies would help to organize multi-party local elections by the end of the year, with national elections to follow. Bush added that Palestinians should implement financial reforms, including the introduction of independent auditing to ensure 'honest enterprise'. In turn, the USA would increase the levels of humanitarian aid provided to the PA. After these steps were taken, Palestinians would be able to count on US support for a 'provisional state of Palestine', the final borders, capital and other aspects of sovereignty of which would be negotiated between Israel and the PA. The President's plan envisaged a peace settlement within three years. Bush urged Israel to withdraw its forces to positions it had held in the West Bank on 28 September 2000, and to stop building Jewish settlements in the West Bank and Gaza. He also pressed Israel to restore freedom of movement in the Palestinian areas so that civilians could resume work and normal life. Israeli officials praised Bush's speech but rejected the concept of a 'provisional Palestinian state', while PA officials insisted that Bush's appeal for the replacement of Arafat was unacceptable. Moreover, even before the presidential address, the US proposal for a 'provisional Palestinian state' had received a cool response in the Middle East.

FURTHER POLITICAL AND MILITARY DEVELOPMENTS

At the end of June 2002 Israeli forces began the removal of a small number of settler 'outposts' deemed to be illegal. Meanwhile, there were reports that a senior commander of Hamas's military wing had been killed by Israeli troops in Nablus. Israel alleged that the man was a prominent bomb-maker, who had been responsible for attacks such as the Passover bombing in Netanya. The UN again urged Israel to withdraw immediately from PA-controlled territory, referring to the serious humanitarian situation there. On 5 August the Israeli Minister of Defence, Binyamin Ben-Eliezer, held discussions with the PA Minister of the Interior, Abd al-Razzak Yahya, in an attempt to calm the situation. On 18 August Israel and the PA agreed to implement a security plan (termed the 'Gaza, Bethlehem First' plan) whereby Israel would withdraw from the Gaza Strip and Bethlehem in return for Palestinian security guarantees and a crackdown on militants. Israel began to withdraw its forces from Bethlehem on the following day; however, violence continued throughout the Territories and further talks were cancelled. The situation deteriorated further in mid-September, with two suicide bombings in Um al-Fahm and Tel-Aviv. Israeli forces entered Arafat's Ramallah compound once again on 19 September, and began the systematic destruction of buildings, in a stated attempt to force the surrender of some 20 Palestinian militants believed by the Israeli authorities to be sheltering there. A decision had been taken to 'isolate' the PA leader following the suicide attacks. Nevertheless, following considerable pressure from the US Administration, Israel agreed to withdraw its forces from the presidential compound on 29 September. The trial of Marwan Barghouthi, leader of the Fatah movement in the West Bank, accused of the murder of 26 Israelis, began in early October; Barghouthi was convicted of five counts of murder in May 2004 and was sentenced to life imprisonment in June. Meanwhile, there were further large-scale attacks by Palestinian militants in late June 2002: 14 Israelis were killed when a car bomb exploded next to a crowded bus in the town of Hadera, prompting an incursion by the Israeli army into Jenin.

At the end of October 2002 the Labour Party withdrew from Ariel Sharon's ruling coalition in connection with the party's opposition to the allocation of funds to Jewish settlements in the West Bank in the Government's 2003 budget, leaving Sharon to seek a new coalition with the largely pro-settlement nationalist and religious minority parties. Sharon was able to survive a no confidence vote in the Knesset in early November, but was ultimately unable to establish a new governing coalition, and was forced to call a general election, to be held in the last week of January 2003.

2003 ELECTIONS

In the run-up to the elections, the Government, and Likud in particular, were beset by controversy. The Deputy Minister of Infrastructure, Naomi Blumenthal, was dismissed for refusing to answer questions on alleged 'bribes for votes' during the party's recent internal elections, and reports in January 2003 suggested that Sharon was being investigated by the police over allegations that he had received US $1.5m. in illegal campaign funds from a South African businessman.

Meanwhile, the attacks by Palestinian militants continued. On 15 November 2002 12 Jewish settlers were killed by Islamic Jihad gunmen as they emerged from prayers at the Tomb of Patriarchs in Hebron. Hamas claimed responsibility after a suicide bomber killed 11 on a bus in Jerusalem on 21 November. On 28 November, the day on which primary elections for the leadership of the Likud party were due to take place (the elections were won convincingly by Sharon), Palestinian gunmen killed six Israelis at a polling station in the northern town of Beit Shean. However, the most significant attacks of the day took place in Mombasa, Kenya: a bomb exploded at an Israeli-owned hotel, killing 15 (including three Israelis), while at the airport surface-to-air missiles were unsuccessfully fired at an Israeli charter aeroplane bound for Tel-Aviv, with 271 passengers on board. Al-Qa'ida claimed responsibility for the attacks in a taped message sent to the Qatar-based satellite broadcaster Al Jazeera. The militants' campaign continued into 2003. On 5 January two suicide bombings in Tel-Aviv resulted in the deaths of more than 20 people.

In the elections of 28 January 2003, Likud won 29.4% of the vote and 38 seats in the Knesset; as the leader of Likud, the largest party in the Knesset, Ariel Sharon remained Prime Minister. Labour took 14.5% of the vote and 19 seats in the Knesset, with Shinui (12.3% of the vote and 15 seats) and Shas (8.2% of the vote and 11 seats) also significantly represented.

Sharon's victory was a sign of the public's approval for his security policies, which had significantly lowered the number of suicide attacks against Israeli civilians. The Labour opposition's appeal for some kind of a limited unilateral withdrawal from the West Bank and the speedy construction of a security fence had resonance with many Israelis, but Labour leader Amram Mitzna's appeal for negotiations with Arafat under fire with the aim of reaching a 'permanent status' peace agreement was viewed as unacceptable by the mainstream Israeli public. Against this background many traditional Labour voters switched their allegiance to Shinui, a secularist centre party that focused its agenda on countering the power and influence of the ultra-Orthodox parties.

Unable to persuade Labour to join the new coalition, Sharon was forced to look to the smaller parties to create a governing coalition. The new Cabinet comprised members of Likud, Shinui, led by Tommy Lapid, the NRP, National Union and

Israel B'Aliyah, the Russian immigrant party led by former Soviet dissident Natan Sharansky. Shaul Mofaz remained Minister of Defence and Binyamin Netanyahu was appointed Minister of Finance.

THE 'ROADMAP' PEACE PLAN

Inevitably, events in Israel and the Palestinian areas were overshadowed by the successful US-led campaign to oust the regime of Saddam Hussain in Iraq (see the chapter on Iraq). However, US President Bush had made it a condition of the war in Iraq that he would then turn his attention to helping effect a lasting peace in the Middle East through the implementation of the internationally sponsored peace plan known as the 'roadmap'. The implementation of the roadmap commenced at a time of heightened militant activity, countered by rapid Israeli responses. Fifteen Israelis were killed on 5 March 2003 in a suicide bomb attack on a bus in Haifa, and on 9 March a senior Hamas leader, Ibrahim al-Maqadma, was killed in an Israeli helicopter attack in Gaza City. On 29 April two Britons carried out a suicide bombing in Tel-Aviv, killing five at a popular café. This was the last major attack before President Bush presented the outline of the roadmap to both the Israeli and Palestinian administrations on 30 April (Documents on Palestine, see p. 104).

Drawn up by the Quartet group (comprising the USA, Russia, the UN and the EU), the roadmap was to consist of three distinct phases, due for completion by 2005–06, resulting in the complete withdrawal of Israeli forces from the West Bank and Gaza Strip and the establishment of an independent, sovereign state of Palestine. Phase one was primarily concerned with the ending of Palestinian militant action, the normalization of Palestinian life, and the creation of civil administrative and governmental institutions. The PA would promise to restrict the activities of militant groups based in the areas it governed, while Israel would withdraw from areas occupied since 2000 and dismantle settlements established since March 2001. The apex of this first phase would be unequivocal statements by both sides recognizing the other's right to statehood. Phase two would involve peace talks between Israel, Lebanon and Syria, leading to further talks establishing provisional Palestinian borders. Phase three would see the conclusion of the peace plan, a Palestinian state having been established, with issues such as Jerusalem, refugees and settlements having been resolved. This final phase would be based upon UN Security Council Resolutions 242, 338 and 1397, and would include as a prerequisite the recognition by all Arab states of Israel's right to exist.

There were initial objections from Israel. In early May 2003 Ariel Sharon insisted that he would recognize a Palestinian state only if the Palestinians abandoned the issue of the 'right to return' for Palestinian refugees, and he also refused to discuss, at least at that time, the issue of Jewish settlements. Indeed, it seemed as if a spate of suicide attacks on 18 and 19 May might undermine the roadmap altogether, but Sharon finally accepted the plan on 23 May, a decision contentiously accepted by the Israeli Cabinet two days later. This acceptance of the roadmap seemed to be enshrined in Ariel Sharon's unprecedented admission at the end of May that Israel was in occupation of the Palestinian areas. At the beginning of June Sharon met with the new Palestinian Prime Minister, Mahmud Abbas, and President Bush at Aqaba, Jordan. Bush urged the two parties to implement the roadmap.

A cease-fire began on 29 June 2003, providing Abbas with the opportunity to fulfil the PA's obligations under the roadmap. However, he proved unable to take forceful action against those Palestinian organizations continuing to conduct violence against Israel. Terrorist incidents had reportedly declined by 90%, but even during the two months when the cease-fire was in place the IDF thwarted 57 attempted terrorist attacks. In the field, the effective situation of war between the IDF and Palestinian Islamist organizations continued. Israeli forces killed a senior Islamic Jihad commander in Hebron on 14 August. On 19 August a suicide bomber killed some 20 Israelis on a bus in Jerusalem, an attack for which both Hamas and Islamic Jihad claimed responsibility. In retaliation, Israeli forces launched raids against members of both groups in the Gaza Strip and West Bank, during which Israeli helicopter gunships killed a senior Hamas leader in Gaza City, Ismail Abu Shanab. Hamas responded by firing a *Qassam-2* rocket, which landed near Ashkelon, some nine miles from the Gaza border. On 22 August Israel reimposed road-blocks on the main north–south highway in the Gaza Strip, a reversal of one of the earlier roadmap initiatives. The EU followed the USA in outlawing Hamas. In a speech to a closed session of the PLC in early September, Abbas told legislators that the Palestinians would only make progress on the roadmap if he were given the powers to implement rational policies. While Sharon could have offered much more to attempt to help Abbas, ultimately Abbas's failure was attributable to his inability to wrest effective control of the security services from Arafat. A few days later the Palestinian Prime Minister resigned after only four months in office and was replaced by Ahmad Quray, known as Abu Ala, the speaker of the PLC and a long-standing Arafat loyalist.

THE OR COMMISSION REPORT CASTS LIGHT ON THE POSITION OF ARAB ISRAELIS

The Or Commission's report into the killings of 13 Israeli Arabs and one Israeli Jew in the riots of October 2000 was released in September 2003. The police were severely criticized, with the report stating that they lacked 'a culture of reporting and full and true investigation when necessary'. They also apparently lacked a culture of learning from past experience and regarded Israeli Arabs as an 'enemy' element. Former Prime Minister Ehud Barak was criticized for failing to pay proper attention to the incidents and for not doing enough to calm the situation. The Minister of Public Security, Shlomo Ben-Ami, was deemed to have exhibited insufficient vigilance and to have failed in his post. The Or Report recommended that he should not serve in this post again.

The issuing of the report led to widespread discussion regarding the hitherto unknown depths of disaffection among Israel's Arab citizens, their growing radicalization and disappointment with the political process. Arab Israeli participation in the 2001 prime ministerial elections was very low. However, a 2005 opinion poll indicated that the longer-term trend was still towards demanding equality within Israeli society, rather than separation from it. According to the poll, conducted by Prof. Sammy Smooha, around 70% of Arab citizens of Israel accept Israel's continued existence as a democratic, Jewish state in which Jews and Arabs live side by side.

THE SEPARATION BARRIER

The British originally built a fence in the 1930s in the north of Israel to prevent the passage of Arab armed groups, which sought to attack civilians. In the current period, pressure grew on the Sharon Government from the Israeli public to construct a barrier as an effective security device in the absence of a viable diplomatic process. In the poll conducted by the Tel-Aviv University Peace Index in October 2003, 83% of respondents supported the construction of a separation barrier. The lowest rates of support were from the left-wing Meretz party and from the far-right National Union. National Union and settlers opposed the separation barrier because many settlements on the West Bank would lie outside its path. According to the Peace Index, in October 2003 some 63% believed that the route should follow the course determined by the Government; however, only 19% believed that it should follow the 'Green Line', which follows the border that had separated Israel and the West Bank before the 1967 war.

The first stage of the barrier ran between Salam and Elkana, east of Petach Tikva. The town of Hadera, which had been the target of numerous suicide bombings, had enjoyed a period of tranquillity since the erection of the northern part of the barrier. The Israelis argued that a similar fence around Gaza had been constructed in the context of an Israeli-Palestinian agreement in 1994, and had since ensured that virtually no bombers had come from Gaza. The planned route of the next section barrier deviated from the Green Line at sensitive areas, such as around Ben-Gurion airport where it was believed that hand-held weapons fired from the West Bank could bring down civilian aircraft. Israel proposed to control a ridge some three miles into the West Bank, near the settlement of Beit Arieh, in order to protect the airport from any such attempts.

In September 2003 the Israeli Cabinet approved the next stage of the barrier, which was estimated to cost US $1,000m., and was expected to enclose some 80% of the settlements and cut off 60,000 Palestinians. The Palestinians responded by drafting a UN Security Council resolution that barred Israel from extending the barrier. The Palestinians claimed that the construction of the barrier violated the UN Charter, Security Council resolutions and the Fourth Geneva Protocol. The USA vetoed the resolution, with the United Kingdom, Germany, Bulgaria and Cameroon all abstaining. The UN General Assembly formally voted by 144 to four, with 12 abstentions, to condemn the barrier as a violation of international law and demanded that its construction be halted. In response, Israel vowed to continue to build the barrier, which would lead to several West Bank towns such as Qibya, Beit Sira and Bir Nabala being surrounded by the barrier, isolating an estimated 70,000 Palestinians. The length of the 'border' would change from the 350 km of the Green Line of 1967 to 786 km, assuming that Sharon would wish to encapsulate Maaleh Adumim, near Jerusalem, and Kiriat Arba, near Hebron on the Israeli side. However, following negotiations with the USA, the route of the barrier was moved closer to the Green Line. The construction of other controversial parts of the barrier was frozen. Meanwhile, in June 2004 the Israeli Supreme Court ordered the Government to re-route 20 miles of the barrier to ease constrictions on Palestinian daily life.

In December 2003 the UN General Assembly approved a Palestinian-initiated resolution asking the International Court of Justice (ICJ) at The Hague, Netherlands, to issue an advisory opinion on the legal consequences of Israel's construction of the separation barrier. Ninety nations voted in favour, eight opposed and 74 abstained. In July 2004 a majority of the 15 judges at the ICJ, in a non-binding judgment, condemned the construction of the barrier and appealed for its dismantlement. Israeli officials noted that, in its 60-page report, the Court only mentioned the issue of terrorism twice. Prime Minister Sharon was at pains to state that the barrier did not mean a permanent border and that it could be removed if the two sides reached an agreement on a border in the future. Binyamin Netanyahu, Israel's Minister of Finance, stated that the barrier would pass through 12% of the West Bank and encapsulate 1% of Palestinians who live within the 'disputed territories'. The Peace Index of June 2004 showed that despite international condemnation of the barrier, 78% of Israelis now supported its construction, with 16% in opposition. Of those polled, 62% believed that the barrier had improved most Israelis' sense of security.

SHARON'S DISENGAGEMENT PLAN

In the 2003 election the Labour Party had proposed that Israel unilaterally withdraw from Gaza and parts of the West Bank, which would involve the dismantling of over 50 settlements. Nearly a year later Sharon and Likud Knesset member Ehud Olmert came out in support of a similar plan. These ideas gained the support of around one-half of the Israeli public. Proponents of the plan did not believe that there was a partner for peace on the Palestinian side. Against this background, the main rationale behind these plans was to protect Israel's identity as a democratic state with a Jewish majority. Without some sort of Israeli withdrawal, experts estimated that Jews would become a minority in Israel and the Palestinian territories combined within a decade.

The first version of this major new Israeli unilateral initiative was presented by Sharon at the Herzliya conference (an annual convention that focuses on security and foreign affairs issues, attended by members of various Israeli élites) on 18 December 2003. A week later US Administration officials gave approval to Sharon's ideas. While committed to a two-state solution and 'President Bush's vision', Sharon said that Israel had to react to the current stagnation and thereby improve the current reality. Since, he claimed, there was no Palestinian partner with whom to secure progress on a bilateral agreement, Israel had decided to act alone. The plan proposed withdrawal from the Gaza Strip, including all 17 settlements there, and from four settlements in the northern West Bank, namely Ganim, Kadim, Homesh and Sa-Nur. Israel would continue to deploy troops along the Philadelphi route, the border between Egypt and Gaza, and would continue to maintain control of the airspace and seaboard of the Gaza Strip. Israel reserved the right to self-defence, 'including [the] taking of preventative steps as well as responding with force against threats that emerge from this area'. Evacuated military installations and infrastructures would be transferred to an international body, possibly the World Bank, which would determine the value of the assets. In an exchange of letters between Bush and Sharon in April 2004, the US President endorsed the 'disengagement plan' and spoke about 'new realities on the ground'. He suggested that in the light of new major Israeli population centres, 'it would be unrealistic to expect that the outcome of final status negotiations will be a full and complete return to the armistice lines of 1949'. The evacuation of the settlements was scheduled to begin on 17 August 2005.

Although Sharon suffered a setback when 60% of members of his own Likud party rejected the disengagement plan in a referendum on 2 May 2004, he remained determined to see it through. However, Sharon faced strong opposition from within his coalition Government: Minister of Transport Avigdor Lieberman and Minister of Tourism Binyamin Elon (both members of National Union) were dismissed on 4 June for their opposition to the plan; and on 8 June the Minister of Construction and Housing, Efraim Eitam of the NRP, resigned, following a cabinet vote of 14 to seven in favour of Sharon's proposals. National Union's Knesset members subsequently withdrew from the ruling coalition, thus removing Sharon's parliamentary majority and forcing him into negotiations with the Labour Party.

In a breakdown of fatalities between 27 September 2000 and 23 March 2004, produced by the International Policy Institute for Counter-Terrorism at the Interdisciplinary Center in Herzliya, during the al-Aqsa *intifada* there had been 2,728 recorded Palestinian fatalities and 917 Israeli fatalities. Women comprised 4.5% of the Palestinian deaths and 31.1% of Israeli deaths. Some 55.3% of the Palestinian fatalities were non-combatants, compared with 78% among Israelis. This appeared to reflect the different foci of the two sides: the IDF claimed to target militants, whereas the victims of Palestinian suicide bombers were overwhelmingly civilians.

CONTINUED VIOLENCE, DEATH OF ARAFAT

Although the level of violence in Israel and the Palestinian territories began to decline from 2003, Israel, in the face of ongoing attacks, continued to enact its policy of 'targeted killings' of militants who had conducted operations within Israel itself. On 22 March 2004 the founder and spiritual leader of Hamas, Sheikh Ahmad Yassin, was killed in an Israeli helicopter gunship air-strike in the Gaza Strip. On 17 April Israeli forces also killed Sheikh Yassin's successor, Abd al-Aziz al-Rantisi, in a targeted air-strike in Gaza City. The violence took place against a backdrop of growing chaos in the Palestinian territories. In July clashes took place between PA security forces and gunmen of the al-Aqsa Martyrs Brigades. The members of the Brigades protested against plans for the amalgamation of Palestinian security agencies, but also the corruption of Arafat. On 17 July Ahmad Quray resigned his post as PA Prime Minister, citing growing lawlessness, poverty and a lack of progress in the diplomatic process with Israel as the reasons for his resignation.

On 31 August 2004 Hamas suicide bombers blew up two buses in the southern Israeli city of Beersheba, killing 16 people. The PA immediately condemned the bombing. Hamas spokesmen announced that the bombing was in revenge for the killing by Israel of Hamas leaders Yassin and al-Rantisi. The Hamas cell in Hebron was responsible for the attack, and was neutralized by Israeli security forces in the days that followed. Israelis were targeted for attack again a month later, when explosions ripped through the Hilton Hotel at the Red Sea resort of Taba, killing 36 people and wounding over 120. No group claimed responsibility for the attack, which resembled the 2002 bombing in Mombasa, Kenya, widely attributed to al-Qa'ida.

The ongoing stalemate in the conflict between Israelis and Palestinians was rocked by the death, on 11 November 2004, of Yasser Arafat. The Palestinian leader had reached the nadir of his influence in the months preceding his demise, when he had been increasingly attacked by the international community, criticized by his own people for the corruption of his rule and isolated by Israel in his Ramallah headquarters. Though Arafat left no obvious successor, a relatively orderly transition of power in the PA was facilitated. On 9 January 2005 Mahmud Abbas was victorious in elections to the chairmanship of the PA (see the chapter on the Palestinian Territories).

KNESSET APPROVES DISENGAGEMENT, LABOUR RETURNS TO GOVERNMENT

On 25 October 2004 the Knesset voted to approve the Disengagement Plan (Documents on Palestine). The vote was 67 for, seven against, with seven abstentions. On 2 November a law providing compensation for settlers to be displaced by the implementation of disengagement was also approved.

Political change was afoot, with the return of the Labour Party to the governing coalition, in response to the growing rightist campaign against the Disengagement Plan, and the departure of the centrist Shinui party from the Government. Shinui supporters were strongly in favour of unilateral disengagement, but the party had also run on a platform emphasizing opposition to religious coercion. They left the coalition after it became dependent on support from the ultra-Orthodox United Torah Judaism faction. Labour support for the Disengagement Plan was thus crucial. The new coalition deal was agreed upon on 17 December 2004, and the Government was narrowly approved by the Knesset on 10 January 2005. The extra-parliamentary campaign against the Disengagement Plan, meanwhile, was growing in strength. Some right-wing Israelis charged that unilateral withdrawal would be seen as a victory for the militant tactics employed by rejectionist Palestinian organizations. Others saw it as a betrayal of perceived Jewish national rights in the Land of Israel. Their demand was for the holding of a referendum on the Disengagement Plan, which they claimed had been approved without sufficient consultation of public sentiment. All available polls, however, at this stage indicated widespread public support for the plan.

CEASE-FIRE DECLARATION

The months that followed the election of Mahmud Abbas saw confidence-building measures from both sides. These included the release of security prisoners by Israel (500 were freed from custody on 21 February 2005) and Palestinian efforts to impose the authority of the PA security forces on the ground. A marked improvement in the atmosphere of relations between the sides was apparent in the weeks following the election of Abbas.

Meanwhile, the first high-level meeting between Palestinian and Israeli leaders since the outbreak of violence in 2000 took place at Sharm el-Sheikh in early February 2005. The meeting reflected the new hopes and possibilities brought about by the departure of Arafat from the scene. On 8 February, at the conclusion of the summit, a joint cease-fire declaration was issued by Prime Ministers Sharon and Abbas. The declaration promised a complete cessation of violence. The summit, which was hosted by Egyptian President Hosni Mubarak, also witnessed Egyptian and Jordanian decisions to return their ambassadors to Israel. (The ambassadors had been withdrawn at the outbreak of the violence in late 2000.)

Hamas and Islamic Jihad would not fully commit to the cease-fire, but Hamas pledged to refrain from further attacks on Israel and to 'consult' with the PA before carrying out what it referred to as 'retaliatory' actions. Islamic Jihad's continued commitment to violence, however, was demonstrated on 25 February 2005, when the organization carried out a bombing at a nightclub in Tel-Aviv; five Israelis were killed in the attack.

This period was characterized by Israeli demands for a crackdown by the Palestinian security forces on organizations such as Hamas and Islamic Jihad, and PA insistence that Israel accelerate the transfer of West Bank cities to its control. The PA maintained that drawing rejectionist forces into the political process would be most effective. This approach proved partially successful with the declaration on 18 March 2005 by 13 armed Palestinian factions of a cessation of attacks until the end of the year. They declared that the maintenance of the truce was conditional on Israel refraining from attacks and releasing 8,000 Palestinian prisoners. Israel welcomed the truce, while stressing that allowing a political role for armed factions would prevent real progress. The Israeli position remained that only the disarming of such groups as Hamas and Islamic Jihad could ensure lasting stability and a return to the negotiation process.

GROWING SUPPORT FOR HAMAS

Fatah and associated candidates were victorious in Palestinian municipal elections held on 5 May 2005. Nevertheless, considerable and unexpected gains were made by the candidates of the Hamas movement. Hamas won around 33% of the vote in the elections, compared with Fatah's 56%. Fear of the growing support for Hamas in the Palestinian areas may have played a role in the PA's decision to postpone PLC elections scheduled for July. The growing strength of the Islamists also presented a dilemma for Israel and the international community. Hamas gains in the municipal elections meant that the Islamists now held practical administrative power in certain areas, such as the West Bank city of Qalqilya.

NETANYAHU RESIGNS

On 7 August 2005, shortly before the Cabinet voted to authorize the first stage of the Disengagement Plan, Binyamin Netanyahu, who had consistently criticized the proposal, resigned as Minister of Finance. He condemned the Government for not having secured anything 'in return' for unilateral withdrawal, which he deemed to be harmful to the security of the country, and later warned that a planned port in Gaza could function as a 'terrorist base' and pose a direct threat to the region. Sharon, who asserted that neither the implementation of the Disengagement Plan, nor the state's economy, would be affected by the minister's resignation, appointed Ehud Olmert, Vice-Prime Minister and Minister of Industry, Trade and Labour, to replace Netanyahu in an acting capacity. Netanyahu announced subsequently that he intended to challenge Sharon for the leadership of Likud.

THE IMPLEMENTATION OF DISENGAGEMENT

Implementation of the Disengagement Plan began as scheduled on 15 August 2005. The Kissufim crossing was closed, making the Gaza Strip inaccessible to Israelis. During 15–17 August Israeli residents ready to leave Gaza of their own free will were afforded time to depart. The removal of settlers by force began on 17 August. A force of 14,000 from the IDF and the Israeli police was tasked with carrying out this mission. Despite anguished scenes, the evacuation of the Jewish residents of Gaza was not marred by any incidents of serious violence. By 22 August the evacuation was completed, with the peaceful departure of the last residents of Netzarim. Demolition crews responsible for destroying the residences of the settlers remained in the area.

The evacuation of the four West Bank settlements slated to be dismantled under the terms of the Disengagement Plan began on 23 August 2005. It had been anticipated that resistance here would be more intense. In the event, the mainly secular communities of Ganim and Kadim departed peacefully. At Sanur and Homesh, however, a group of around 2,000 demonstrators joined with residents in an attempt to stop the evacuation. After negotiation, the evacuation was completed without serious disruption. The evacuation of Sanur ended the first and most difficult phase of the disengagement—the removal of the civilian residents of the areas slated for dismantling. What remained was the demolition of houses and redeployment of military installations before the areas were handed over to the PA. The flag of Israel was lowered for the last time at Gaza Divisional Headquarters on 11 September.

The last IDF forces departed via the Kissufim crossing on the following day. On 22 September the IDF withdrew from Mevo Dotan, thereby completing the Plan.

LIKUD SPLITS, KADIMA ESTABLISHED

In the months following the disengagement, there was a growing sense that the ruling Likud party led by Sharon could no longer function as a unified body. The factor that precipitated the split was an attempt by Sharon to have two of his political allies—Zeev Boim and Roni Bar-On—appointed as ministers. The Knesset voted by 60 to 54 to reject the appointments. Likud members of the Knesset who had opposed the disengagement voted with the opposition. On the evening of 20 November 2005 Ariel Sharon announced that he had decided to leave Likud and found a new, centrist party, telling reporters: 'The Likud in its current constellation cannot lead Israel to its national goals ... Staying in the Likud means wasting time in political struggles instead of deeds on behalf of the country.' The split in Likud was a watershed moment in Israeli politics. Since its victory in the 1977 elections, the party had been out of power for only six years. The Disengagement Plan brought out the long-present tension in the party between security-minded hawks on the one hand, and ideological nationalists and more pragmatic forces on the other hand.

Meanwhile, the Chairman of the Histadrut trade union confederation, Amir Peretz, had replaced Shimon Peres as Chairman of the Labour Party in an internal ballot in mid-November 2005. In an attempt to force early legislative elections (scheduled for November 2006), Peretz secured the support of an absolute majority of Labour members at a party conference to withdraw his party from the Government. Eight Labour-Meimad ministers duly resigned their posts on 21 November 2005 (effective 23 November), including Peres. Sharon adopted the vacated portfolios on an interim basis, and additionally assumed Peres's responsibilities as Vice-Premier.

Sharon succeeded in taking 13 Likud members of the Knesset with him to his new party, Kadima (Forward), giving it the status of a Knesset faction. Subsequently, senior Labour party figures Shimon Peres, Haim Ramon and Dalia Itzik joined Kadima, along with Prof. Uriel Reichman, one of the founders of Shinui. These additions served to strengthen Kadima's centrist credentials. Binyamin Netanyahu was elected to replace Sharon as Chairman of Likud at an internal ballot in mid-December 2005. The Likud split made new elections in Israel inevitable, and the polls were duly brought forward to 28 March 2006. However, the new party headed by Sharon dominated in the opinion polls from the outset of campaigning.

SHARON DEPARTS THE STAGE

On 18 December 2005 Ariel Sharon was rushed to hospital after suffering a stroke. The Prime Minister was discharged from hospital two days later. However, on 4 January 2006 he suffered a second stroke, which left him in a coma from which he had not emerged by mid-2013. Vice-Prime Minister and Minister of Finance Ehud Olmert (who had been officially appointed to the latter post in November 2005) took over as acting Prime Minister following Sharon's incapacitation. The departure of Sharon from the political stage led to much political uncertainty in Israel. Although support for Kadima in the opinion polls initially remained steady, many analysts considered that the absence of Sharon at the helm would substantially reduce the new party's position.

Kadima became the only party represented in the Cabinet in mid-January 2006, after the four Likud ministers (including Minister of Foreign Affairs Silvan Shalom) resigned their posts at the request of Netanyahu, who wished to protest against the Government's policies and prepare the party list for the forthcoming elections. The Cabinet approved the reallocation of various portfolios among existing government members and the appointment of three new ministers. Notably, acting Prime Minister Ehud Olmert was appointed Minister of the Interior (he additionally held the industry, trade and labour, finance, and social affairs portfolios) and the Minister of Immigrant Absorption and of Justice, Tzipi Livni, was appointed Minister of Foreign Affairs. On the same day Olmert was appointed acting Chairman of Kadima.

HAMAS WINS THE PALESTINIAN ELECTIONS

Elections to the 132-seat PLC took place on 25 January 2006. The ruling Fatah movement was widely expected to win the highest proportion of votes, and the Change and Reform List, sponsored by the Islamist Hamas, was expected to make significant gains. However, in the event, Change and Reform unexpectedly won 74 of the 132 seats in the parliament, with 45% of the popular vote.

With the Israeli election campaign in full swing, it was expected that the Hamas victory would benefit the Israeli right. Opinion polls in Israel, however, did not register major changes in the days following the PLC elections. Yet the emergence of the Palestinian Islamists to the leading position in the PA was a moment of strategic importance. For the first time a significant rival had emerged to challenge Fatah's hegemony in the Palestinian national movement. Hamas remained openly opposed to Israel's right to exist, and, according to its founding document, was committed to the creation of an Islamic state in the area between the Jordan river and the Mediterranean Sea. The Israeli Government refused all contact with the new Hamas-led administration, until the group committed to existing agreements between Israelis and Palestinians, abandoned the use of terrorism, and accepted Israel's right to exist. Hamas remained defiant in all these areas, causing a deeper freeze in relations between the sides.

KADIMA WINS ISRAELI ELECTIONS

In the course of the election campaign, and contrary to expectations, acting Prime Minister Ehud Olmert announced his intention to carry out a second extensive Israeli unilateral withdrawal on the West Bank, should Kadima prove to be victorious. The Convergence Plan envisaged the setting of Israel's borders by 2010. Olmert did not lay out precise details, promising first to consult domestically and with the international community. However, Kadima made it clear that the plan would involve removing tens of settlements in the heart of the West Bank and the evacuation of tens of thousands of settlers, while retaining under Israeli control the three main settlement blocs and the Jordan Valley as Israel's security border. Kadima candidate and former settler leader Otniel Scheller also stated that convergence would include withdrawal from some Arab suburbs inside the municipal boundaries of Jerusalem. Many estimated that Olmert's plan would mean an Israeli withdrawal from over 90% of the West Bank.

The announcement of the Convergence Plan was significant, but did not succeed in turning the election campaign into a referendum on the issue of unilateralism. This was despite anguished scenes at the site of Amona in February 2006, when demonstrators sought to prevent the destruction of nine illegally built Jewish homes on the West Bank. Equally, however, the successful IDF incursion into a PA gaol in Jericho to capture PFLP leader Ahmad Saadat (who was believed to have planned the assassination of the former Israeli cabinet minister Rechavam Ze'evi in October 2001) before he was to be released in contravention of international commitments made by the PA failed to improve Kadima's standing in the polls in a sustained manner.

According to final official results released on 29 March 2006, Kadima secured the most seats (29), with which it would be able to form the next government. Labour-Meimad was second, with 19 seats. This was considered an achievement, albeit a modest one, since Amir Peretz had taken Labour in a new direction, campaigning almost exclusively on internal socio-economic issues. Likud suffered a very heavy defeat, winning only 12 seats. A significant and unexpected outcome of the elections was the high showing of the Pensioners' Party, which won seven seats. This party, founded by former senior security official Rafi Eitan, campaigned on a platform of bringing attention to the difficult plight confronted by many of Israel's elderly, following the reductions in benefits of recent years. The fact that such a single-issue party could do so well was widely seen as heralding the emergence of a new political atmosphere in Israel—at once more pragmatic on diplomatic matters, disenchanted and concerned with day-to-day issues and economic well-being.

The new Government formed under Prime Minister Ehud Olmert was dominated by the alliance of Kadima and Labour. The other coalition partners were the Pensioners' Party and Shas (which had taken 12 Knesset seats). Olmert failed in his bid to bring the rightist Israel Beytenu party (with 11 seats) into the Government, owing to that party's refusal to commit to government guidelines, including support for the Convergence Plan. The Knesset voted to approve the new Government on 4 May 2006. Amir Peretz was appointed Deputy Prime Minister and Minister of Defence, while Tzipi Livni adopted the foreign affairs portfolio along with the vice-premiership.

On the same day that the new Cabinet was sworn in, a Palestinian suicide bomber blew himself up in Tel-Aviv, killing himself and nine others. Hamas justified the attack (for which Islamic Jihad claimed responsibility) as an act of self-defence by the Palestinian people, while President Abbas condemned it, asserting that it was harmful to Palestinian interests. The Israeli Government decided not to implement any retaliatory attack on targets in the Palestinian territories.

Diplomatically, the Government's commitment to a strategy of unilateralism remained the key issue on the political agenda. Olmert spent the first months of his premiership attempting to ensure diplomatic support for the plan, visiting Washington, DC, London and Paris in order to explain the rationale behind his unilateralist strategy. Domestically, the key issues were the growing disorder in the PA territories (see the chapter on the Palestinian Territories) and its possible ramifications for the Convergence Plan. In particular, the continued launching of *Qassam* rockets from the Gaza Strip, with the tacit acquiescence of the Hamas-led PA, posed a significant challenge to the logic of unilateralism, an essential element of which was the ability of Israel to create a de facto 'balance of terror' with whoever was ruling on the other side.

CRISIS AND WAR, JULY–AUGUST 2006

In this regard, the violence that broke out in Gaza in late June 2006 (see the chapter on the Palestinian Territories), following the abduction of IDF soldier Corporal Gilad Shalit by Hamas militants, had grave implications for the strategy of unilateralism. The entry of the Lebanese Hezbollah organization into the circle of violence, and the subsequent outbreak of an all-out war between Israel and Hezbollah in July–August, led to the breakdown of the uneasy arrangements that had pertained on Israel's northern border since the Israeli unilateral withdrawal from southern Lebanon in May 2000. The war took Israelis by surprise, since they had assumed that high-intensity combat beyond the borders of Israel, the West Bank and Gaza was highly unlikely. It began with the kidnapping by Hezbollah militants of two Israeli soldiers and the killing of three others in a cross-border raid on 12 July 2006. The Hezbollah operation was accompanied by the firing of *Katyusha* rockets and mortar shells on Israeli border communities, prompting Israel to respond with air-strikes and artillery fire. This included the razing of targets in the southern Dahiyeh neighbourhood of Beirut, which was controlled by Hezbollah. The Israeli Government was keen to emphasize that it was not waging war against the pro-Western Lebanese Government of Fouad Siniora: on 16 July the Cabinet released a communiqué explaining that Israel was 'not fighting Lebanon but the terrorist element there, led by (Hezbollah Secretary-General Sheikh Hasan) Nasrallah and his cohorts, who have made Lebanon a hostage and created Syrian- and Iranian-sponsored terrorist enclaves of murder'.

Hezbollah bombardments, launched mainly in civilian areas of Israel, caused severe disruption. Hezbollah fired between 3,970 and 4,228 rockets in the course of the war. About 95% of these were 122 mm (4.8 in) *Katyusha* artillery rockets, which carried warheads of up to 30 kg (66 lb) and had a range of up to 30 km (19 miles). An estimated 23% of these rockets landed in built-up areas, which were primarily civilian. Many civilians, both in Israel's north and in southern Lebanon, were displaced by the fighting. Nevertheless, in an early military success, Israel succeeded in destroying Hezbollah's long-range rocket capability, thus preventing a greater loss of Israeli life.

Ground combat also took place in southern Lebanon. Israeli troops engaged Hezbollah in particularly intense combat in the towns of Bint Jbeil and Ayt al-Shab. Notable IDF actions also occurred in Ba'albek. However, despite the local successes of the IDF in the fighting, there was deep frustration at the apparent inability of the military to prevent the continued launching of *Katyushas* at civilian targets in northern Israel. This, coupled with the reports of insufficient preparation of reserve units and the sense that the governing echelons of Israel had no clear plan for the conduct of the war, led to deep public disquiet and concern as the war dragged on into August 2006.

The UN Security Council unanimously approved a cease-fire resolution on 11 August 2006. Resolution 1701 was approved by the Israeli and Lebanese Governments over the following days. In addition to calling for an immediate and full cessation of hostilities, the resolution authorized the deployment of the Lebanese army along Lebanon's southern border and the creation of a strengthened international force in the area. As with previous UN resolutions, it required that all armed groups in Lebanon disarm in order that the Government extend its sovereignty over the whole state. Resolution 1701 was endorsed as Israel increased the number of its forces in southern Lebanon. The IDF conducted a large-scale ground attack on the final day of the war, 14 August, which ended with heavy losses in the area of Wadi Saluki and elsewhere.

Overall, 119 Israeli troops were killed in the fighting, along with 43 civilians who died in Hezbollah bombardments. Around 1,000 Lebanese died, of whom 500–600 were thought to have been Hezbollah fighters. The war was celebrated as a strategic victory by many in the Arab world, who considered that Hezbollah, by avoiding destruction and inflicting heavy casualties against the IDF, had succeeded in severely puncturing Israel's deterrent image. There were those in Israel who were also deeply concerned, and in August 2006 a series of protests took place involving demobilized reserve IDF soldiers. The protesters demanded the resignation of Prime Minister Olmert and an inquiry into the conduct of the war. Olmert rejected demands for the appointment of a full state commission of inquiry; however, under public pressure, the Government eventually acceded to the creation of a committee of inquiry that would investigate the political and military leadership's conduct during and preceding the war.

UNILATERALISM DISCREDITED

For many Israelis, on both the left and the right, the events of mid-2006 discredited the strategy of unilateralism. In essence, it appeared that the flaw in this policy was its inability to create deterrence. Rather, unilateral withdrawals appeared to put wind in the sails of intransigent forces on the other side, who felt that it was their violent tactics that had forced an Israeli withdrawal. The sponsorship of Palestinian and Lebanese rejectionist groups by Iran and Syria made the situation yet more grave. It raised the possibility that any land from which Israel had unilaterally withdrawn would become open to the influence of these countries, with their anti-Israeli and anti-Western agenda. At least for the moment, the war in Lebanon had thus effectively removed the possibility of further unilateral withdrawals from the Israeli Government's agenda. This was openly acknowledged by the leaders of the ruling party, Kadima, in subsequent months. This gloomy turn of events did not, however, lead Israelis to re-embrace older political ideas.

The emergence of a centrist constituency broadly accepting Kadima's core contentions of the absence of a Palestinian partner and the infeasibility of the territorial status quo remained a salient fact of Israeli political life. Kadima and its unilateralist strategy in essence revealed the existence of this hitherto hidden consensus at the heart of Israeli political perceptions, breaking the stalemate between supporters and opponents of territorial compromise, which had dominated Israeli politics since 1967. However, the sense of renewed existential threat deriving from Iranian nuclear ambitions and from diminished deterrence after the Lebanon conflict of 2006 led to a rapid revival of the fortunes of Likud under Binyamin Netanyahu.

The coming to prominence of a new and more openly radical Islamist tone in Iran following the election of Mahmoud Ahmadinejad to the presidency in 2005 and the support offered by the Iranian Government to a host of organizations engaged in violence against Israel have combined to bring the issue of Iran to a place of prominence in Israeli political discussions. President Ahmadinejad proceeded openly to advocate the destruction of Israel, and thus internal Israeli policy discussion became overshadowed by this sense of growing regional threat. Netanyahu made the issue of Iran and its regime's ambitions the central element of his campaigning. He sought to place the threat of Iranian nuclear ambitions on the international agenda, simultaneously strengthening his position by doing so both within his party and in the eyes of the public. The result was a rapid return of Likud to the centre stage of Israeli politics, after the party's disastrous election result of March, when it had looked to be facing a historic eclipse.

THE WINOGRAD COMMISSION

In September 2006 Prime Minister Olmert approved the appointment of a commission of inquiry, headed by a retired judge, Dr Eliyahu Winograd, to investigate official conduct during the war. The Commission's investigations dealt not only with the conduct of the 2006 war in Lebanon itself, but also with the military's preparations in the preceding years. Members of the panel investigated a six-year period, from the date of Israel's unilateral withdrawal from southern Lebanon in May 2000.

The Winograd Commission issued its interim report (covering the period between May 2000 to mid-July 2006) on 30 April 2007. The report was harshly critical of the conduct of Olmert, Deputy Prime Minister and Minister of Defence Amir Peretz and Chief of Staff Lt-Gen. Dan Halutz. The Prime Minister was said to have shown 'a serious failure in exercising judgement, responsibility and prudence' during the early stages of the conflict. Following the publication of the interim report, there were demands for the resignation of both Olmert and Peretz (Halutz had already resigned on 17 January and was replaced in February by Lt-Gen. Gabi Ashkenazi). Despite the heated public response to the Winograd Commission's interim report, however, both Olmert and Peretz made clear that they had no intention of resigning, and both faced no real pressure from within their parties to do so. In Peretz's case, his conduct during the war was felt within Labour to have dealt a fatal blow to his chances of leadership of the party, but since the leadership elections were in any case due in June, it would serve little purpose to force Peretz's resignation two months earlier.

Olmert, after a few vulnerable days immediately following the issuing of the interim report, succeeded in rallying his party around him. This was despite Vice-Prime Minister and Minister of Foreign Affairs Tzipi Livni and coalition chairman Avigdor Yitzhaki urging him to resign; the latter himself resigned in protest against the Prime Minister's failure to do so. However, Olmert was aware that few within his party desired new elections, given that polls indicated that Kadima would suffer heavy losses. Olmert's cause was helped by the fact that the one figure who might genuinely have been able to rally support against him and to present herself as an alternative national leader—Livni—chose not to resign her post in the Cabinet, despite her earlier demands for Olmert to resign. Livni was widely criticized in the media for her perceived indecisiveness. Her decision enabled the Prime Minister to avoid a vote of no confidence within his party and simply to wait until public protests subsided. Despite a large demonstration on 3 May 2007 of around 100,000 people demanding Olmert's resignation, the public protest campaign rapidly faded. In late July the Commander-in-Chief of the Navy, Vice-Adm. David Ben Bashat, submitted his resignation.

INTERNAL DEVELOPMENTS

While Israel grappled with the urgent tasks imposed by conflict, the domestic scene remained as volatile as ever. On 7 February 2007 the Knesset approved the appointment of Prof. Daniel Friedmann as Israel's new Minister of Justice. This led to a storm of controversy, as senior members of Israel's judiciary expressed their disapproval of the appointment. Friedmann had been harshly critical of the Supreme Court and of its President, Dorit Beinisch, over the years in a number of articles in *Yedioth Ahronoth*. His criticisms centred on the system used for the appointment of judges in Israel, and on the appointment of Beinisch to head it. Defenders of the Supreme Court and its President alleged that Friedmann's criticisms contained a personal element: it was claimed that his closeness to Prof. Nili Cohen, an unsuccessful candidate for the Supreme Court presidency, lay behind his criticism of the court. Friedmann had also been harshly critical of Israel's rabbinical courts, which led to criticism of him from the Shas party and other religious elements. Moreover, in 2003 Friedmann had stood on the Knesset list for the fiercely secular Shinui party.

As Minister of Justice, Friedmann had been at the centre of a controversy over the rapid appointment of 15 new judges to Israel's rabbinical courts. Religious courts in Israel deal with significant issues, including those of marriage and divorce. Of the 15 new judges appointed by Friedmann, 12 were drawn from Israel's ultra-Orthodox communities, while three were religious Zionists. Since the ultra-Orthodox are associated with a far more stringent application of religious laws, the appointments led to an outcry from women's groups focusing on the issue of *agunot* (women whose husbands will not grant a divorce and who remain in marital limbo until the men agree to it). These groups feared that the appointment of the new judges would have a detrimental effect on women caught in this situation. More broadly, the appointments raised the whole vexed, unresolved issue of the role of religion in laws related to personal status in Israel.

This issue also came to prominence in a separate, but related, dispute over the issue of gay rights in Israel. The key issue was the holding of a Gay Pride parade in Jerusalem. The issue had first arisen in 2006, eventually being settled by a compromise, with the march organizers holding a rally at a closed venue instead. However, the dispute re-emerged in 2007, when gay activists made a new attempt to hold the parade. The background was that, while gay marriage was not legal in Israel, over recent years a number of laws had been adopted that afforded homosexuals certain protections. Thus, discrimination on the basis of sexual orientation in the workplace had been prohibited and the rights of homosexual partners had been partially regulated, in matters of common-law spouses, citizenship and economic rights. The issue of the Jerusalem demonstration was seen by gay activists and their supporters as one of freedom of speech. For their ultra-religious opponents, meanwhile, religious prohibitions on homosexuality formed the basis for their opposition. However, there were also those who argued that the gay activists' insistence on holding the march in Jerusalem was an unnecessary provocation, since it could have been held without problems in secular Tel-Aviv.

Both these controversies illustrate the extent to which Israel, though now refocused on the issues of the conflict, remains a society in which basic issues of definition remain unresolved. The competing claims of Jewish tradition, pluralism, equality before the law and the rights of particular communities have not yet been settled finally, and the contradictions which this produces continue to manifest themselves in Israeli public life.

PERETZ DEFEATED, BARAK RETURNS TO LABOUR LEADERSHIP

Primary elections in the Labour Party were scheduled for 29 May 2007. The two main contenders were Ehud Barak, the former Prime Minister and Chief of Staff, who had become a successful private businessman since leaving office in 2001, and former head of the security services, Ami Ayalon. Also standing in the primaries were Minister of Defence and party leader Amir Peretz, who was expected to lose, and two minor candidates, Ophir Pines-Paz and Danny Yatom. That the contest was between Barak and Ayalon testified to the extent that Israeli politics had changed as a result of the sense of renewed threat following the war between Israel and Hezbollah in Lebanon. When Peretz won the Labour leadership elections in 2005, his election had been seen as representing a new path for Labour, in which the party sought to become a

European-style social-democratic party. However, Barak and Ayalon, both generals who had grown up on collective settlements, were much more in the classic mould of Labour's leaders, drawn from the heart of the country's national security establishment. Barak based his campaign on the simple slogan that only he, with his centrist and security credentials, was capable of beating Netanyahu in an election. Ayalon, meanwhile, emphasized his reputation for integrity in a country weary of corruption scandals.

Barak won the first round of the leadership contest, winning 35.6% of the votes cast to Ayalon's 30.6%. This was not enough to prevent a run-off election, which took place on 13 June 2007. Barak was victorious, gaining 51.3% to Ayalon's 47.7%. Following Barak's victory, as had been expected, he assumed the post of Minister of Defence (in addition to becoming a Deputy Prime Minister) in the coalition Government. However, Barak made clear his view that Olmert should resign before the issuing of the final report of the Winograd Commission.

PRESIDENTIAL ELECTION

Another significant election in 2007 was that of veteran political leader Shimon Peres to the post of state President. The position had become available because of the disgrace of former President Moshe Katsav, who in October 2006 was arraigned on a series of scandals of a sexual nature and was forced to resign. Following Katsav's formal request to take a leave of absence, in January 2007 the Knesset voted to declare him 'temporarily incapacitated' for a three-month period while he contested the charges. The Speaker, Dalia Itzik, was named as acting President for this period, which was, in April, extended for a further three months, or until Katsav's term was scheduled to end in August. In June 2007 Katsav was reported to have agreed the terms of a plea bargain, according to which rape charges against him were to be withdrawn in exchange for him admitting to charges for lesser sexual offences involving two female employees; he was to receive a suspended prison sentence and pay a fine of NIS 50,000. In that month Katsav formally submitted his resignation, which entered effect in early July. The Supreme Court upheld the plea bargain in February 2008; however, in April Katsav decided that he would prefer to contest all the charges in court. In March 2009 Katsav was formally indicted on charges of rape, sexual assault, sexual harassment and the obstruction of justice. In March 2011 Katsav was convicted and sentenced to seven years' imprisonment. Although Katsav appealed to the Supreme Court, his request was rejected in November and he began serving his sentence the following month.

Meanwhile, in the presidential election of 2007, the 84-year-old Peres—whose political career dated back to before the founding of the State of Israel—stood against Reuben Rivlin of Likud and Colette Avital of Labour for the largely ceremonial post. At the first round of Knesset voting on 13 June, Peres won 58 votes, against 37 for Rivlin and 21 for Avital. Both of his challengers subsequently stood down, and Peres was elected by 86 votes. His presidential inauguration took place on 15 July, a few days after a reorganization of the Government had been effected. Changes to the composition of the Cabinet included the return of the former Minister of Justice, Haim Ramon, as Vice-Premier, and the replacement of Abraham Hirchson as Minister of Finance by Roni Bar-On, whose post as Minister of the Interior was given to Meir Sheetrit.

HAMAS SEIZES POWER IN GAZA

In mid-June 2007 the ongoing tension between Fatah and Hamas in the Palestinian territories erupted, as Hamas launched a successful coup in Gaza, defeating Fatah-led forces and taking over the President's residence and other key sites. The result was the de facto emergence of two rival seats of Palestinian power: a Fatah-led PA administration in the West Bank, and a Hamas-led entity of unclear status in the Gaza Strip. Israel, in co-operation with the USA and the international community, immediately recognized the Fatah-led administration. However, this development served to confirm the Israeli sense of a lack of a coherent partner for negotiation on the Palestinian side. There was support for the new administration led by the newly appointed Palestinian Prime Minister, Salam Fayyad, but little belief that its creation foresaw a return to a genuine negotiation process, or that it would succeed in pacifying the Iranian-backed Islamist forces on the rise among the Palestinians.

This sense of renewed threat, however, did not alter the deeper contours of the thinking of the Israeli public. The centrist consensus identified with the emergence of the Kadima party remained in existence, although Kadima itself was unlikely to remain the main beneficiary. This new Israeli political mood remained characterized by an absence of the political and ideological passion that had once formed such a noticeable part of Israeli society.

The core value of centrism remained the preservation of Israel as a Jewish and democratic state, which was understood primarily in demographic terms as the need to maintain a large Jewish majority. This was also the underlying consensual political value in Israel as a whole. The overwhelming majority of Jewish Israelis supported it as an expression of their national identity, their democratic values and as a mechanism for ensuring their physical security. Some 70% of Israeli Arabs also accepted a definition of Israel as a 'Jewish and democratic state, in which Jews and Arabs live together'. Centrists were willing in principle to make extensive compromises with regard to the 'peace process'; however, they were deeply sceptical that a 'permanent status' negotiated settlement could be achieved or that it could actually usher in peace or even greater stability. Thus, disenchanted pragmatism characterized the centre, and in turn this led to a greater desire to focus on social and economic issues. The eclipse of the unilateralist idea did not lead to the adoption by the Israeli centre of an alternative strategy for stability. Rather, the mood of uncertainty in Israel militated more towards scepticism about any great plan for peace—and a preference for the cautious management of the conflict, in co-operation with the secular Palestinian leadership where possible. The stable management of stalemate formed the centrepiece of the large, centrist consensus in Israel.

THE ANNAPOLIS PEACE MEETING AND ITS AFTERMATH

Prime Minister Ehud Olmert held discussions with the Palestinian President, Mahmud Abbas, in the West Bank town of Jericho on 6 August 2007—the first talks to be convened between Israeli and Palestinian leaders on Palestinian territory since May 2000. The two leaders held further talks on 'fundamental issues' later in that month and again in early September 2007. On 16 August Israel and the USA signed a memorandum of understanding concerning the provision to the Jewish state of some US $30,000m. of military assistance during the period of 2008–18. On 5 September 2007 Israel's Supreme Court issued a ruling that the route of a further section of the 'security fence' along Israel's boundary with the West Bank should be altered in order to improve the living conditions of Palestinians residing at that location. Israel released another 57 Palestinian prisoners to the West Bank and 29 to the Gaza Strip at the start of October. (A reported 255 Palestinian security prisoners—mainly from Fatah—had been released from Israeli gaols in July, as a gesture of 'goodwill' to the Palestinian President.) Towards the end of October, however, the Israeli Government responded to the launching of rockets into south-western Israel by Palestinian militants from the Gaza Strip by confirming a policy of reducing fuel and electricity supplies to Gaza, which it now classified as a 'hostile entity'.

Following a series of preparatory meetings between US officials and Israeli and Palestinian delegations in the preceding weeks, an international peace meeting intended officially to relaunch the Middle East peace process was held under US auspices in Annapolis, Maryland on 27 November 2007. Members of the international Quartet group and the Arab League attended the talks, and Syria notably sent a low-level delegation. At the close of the meeting US President Bush read a statement of Joint Understanding on Negotiations (Documents on Palestine, see p. 109) between Olmert and Abbas, who both expressed their commitment to achieving a final settlement of the outstanding issues of contention between

Israelis and Palestinians by the end of 2008. In order to succeed in this effort finally to effect a two-state solution to the Israeli–Palestinian conflict, it was revealed that: an Israeli-Palestinian steering committee would oversee 'vigorous, ongoing and continuous' negotiations between the two sides; the Israeli and Palestinian leaders would continue to meet on a fortnightly basis; and both Israel and the PA would comply with their obligations as agreed under the terms of the road-map signed in 2003. However, Palestinians were angered in early December 2007 when an Israeli ministry issued tenders for more than 300 new housing units at the Har Homa settlement in East Jerusalem. The US Secretary of State, Condoleezza Rice, had warned Israel that expanding Jewish settlements on the West Bank threatened to undermine recent progress in the peace process. Moreover, Olmert appeared to indicate that Israel would not be required to conclude a peace treaty with the PA by the end of 2008 if it considered that the Palestinians had not met their security obligations.

Although Hamas responded to the Annapolis peace meeting by pledging that Palestinian 'resistance' to Israeli occupation would continue, the Israeli authorities proceeded with the release of a further 429 Palestinian prisoners (none of whom had been involved in attacks against Israelis) at this time as a renewed gesture of support for President Abbas. Also in early December 2007 a court in Jerusalem sentenced a PFLP militant to a term of life imprisonment, after he was convicted of having assassinated the Minister of Tourism, Rechavam Ze'evi, in Jerusalem in October 2001, as well as being involved in other attacks against Israeli citizens. (The detainee had been serving a sentence for the crime at a West Bank prison; however, when Western supervisors withdrew from the Jericho gaol and Israeli forces entered it in 2006, he was handed over to the Israeli legal system.) In the second week of December 2007 Israeli forces conducted a series of air-strikes against militants in the Gaza Strip, as well as sending tanks into the southern part of the Strip in an attempt to prevent the continuing rocket fire against Sderot in northern Israel.

Following a Palestinian rocket assault against Ashkelon in early January 2008, Israel intensified its military offensive in the Gaza Strip. In response to international criticism regarding the number of Palestinians killed during the offensive, Israeli officials claimed that militants were deliberately firing on Israeli troops from civilian areas. In the second week of January US President Bush undertook a three-day visit to Israel and the West Bank, where he held discussions with both Olmert and Abbas. While assuring Israelis that he understood their security concerns, Bush also asserted that a future Palestinian state should be contiguous territory and not a 'Swiss cheese' of separate cantons. The US leader again urged Israel to cease the expansion of existing Jewish settlements in the West Bank and to remove illegal outposts, as well as stating that the PA must dismantle militant groups. President Bush also surprised some commentators by issuing a firm statement urging Israel to withdraw from Arab territory that its forces had occupied in 1967. In mid-January 2008 Israel imposed virtually a complete blockade on the Gaza Strip, which again prompted vehement international criticism: the Israeli response to Palestinian violence targeted at its citizens was widely viewed as collective punishment of the people of Gaza for the actions of a small number of militants. Amid concerns about a potential humanitarian crisis in Gaza, the Israeli Prime Minister subsequently agreed to allow food, medicine and necessary fuel to be supplied to Palestinians in Gaza.

Also in mid-January 2008 Olmert's governing coalition suffered a serious reverse, when the Deputy Prime Minister and Minister of Strategic Affairs, Avigdor Lieberman, announced that his party, the right-wing Israel Beytenu, was to withdraw its members in protest against the Prime Minister's policy of engaging in peace negotiations with the PA. This left Olmert with a reduced majority in the Knesset.

FINAL REPORT OF THE WINOGRAD COMMISSION

The long-awaited final report of the Winograd Commission was issued on 30 January 2008. Although the Commission described Israel's ground offensive in Lebanon in mid-2006 as a 'serious failure' in both military and political terms—noting the lack of any clear strategy prior to initiating the 34-day campaign against Hezbollah—it assessed Prime Minister Olmert to have acted 'in the sincere interest of Israel' in ordering the military action. Many observers expressed intense surprise at the lack of any serious personal criticism aimed at Olmert, particularly after he had ordered Israeli armed forces to undertake a large-scale ground offensive in southern Lebanon only hours before an agreed cease-fire was scheduled to take effect; 33 Israeli soldiers had died during this final stage of the war. It was notable that the Winograd Commission acknowledged Israel's failure to secure an obvious military victory as a result of its conflict with Hezbollah. Thus, although Olmert initially survived the aftermath of the report's publication, it was widely acknowledged that he had been weakened by the Commission's findings, especially at a time when he was already under investigation for alleged corrupt practices.

ISRAELI–PALESTINIAN RELATIONS DETERIORATE

Meanwhile, in the third week of January 2008 thousands of Palestinians entered Egypt from Gaza in search of food and other essential supplies, after Hamas militants had breached the border separating the two territories. When, in early February, an Israeli woman died in a suicide bombing in the southern town of Dimona, the Government implied that the Gazan perpetrator of the attack must have entered Israel via Egypt as a direct result of the border having been breached. A representative of the al-Aqsa Martyrs Brigades initially claimed responsibility for the suicide bombing—the first in Israel for more than a year—although there was some confusion about this claim after Hamas stated that militants of its organization had carried out the attack from Hebron in the West Bank. Amid an obvious stalling of bilateral peace negotiations as Israeli officials even threatened a full-scale military invasion of Gaza, the Israeli Prime Minister announced that, in his view, the status of Jerusalem would be the final 'core issue' to be negotiated by the two parties. A number of Palestinian politicians asserted that the issue of how to divide the city could not be postponed until the end of the peace process.

Israeli–Palestinian relations witnessed a new low-point in early March 2008. Eight students died, and several others were wounded, in a shooting at a Jewish religious college in Jerusalem believed to have been perpetrated by a Palestinian resident of East Jerusalem; the gunman was immediately shot dead by an off-duty Israeli soldier. Once again, the issue of whether ultimate responsibility for the shooting could be attributed to Hamas was unclear: a spokesman for the militant group appeared to claim, and later deny, its involvement in the attack, which represented the worst such incident to take place in Jerusalem since 2004. The Israeli Government affirmed that it would pursue peace negotiations with its Palestinian counterpart, despite the sudden upsurge in violence. However, the likelihood of a swift breakthrough in the peace process was again impeded when, shortly after the Jerusalem shooting, Olmert approved a controversial plan to construct a further 330 homes for Jewish settlers in the West Bank. Moreover, in mid-March 2008 the Israeli premier insisted that his Government would continue with its policy of settlement expansion in East Jerusalem. In early June the Israeli Government announced that it was to build another estimated 900 new Jewish homes in East Jerusalem, provoking predictable criticism from the international community.

Following several violent incidents in previous weeks, in mid-June 2008 a truce was agreed between Israel and Hamas representatives in the Gaza Strip, after lengthy negotiations had been conducted by Egyptian mediators. Israel was to end its economic blockade of the Strip and cease military action in the territory, on condition that Hamas militants and those of other Palestinian groups ceased their cross-border attacks on Israeli targets. Yet towards the end of the month Israeli officials complained of a 'grave violation' of the cease-fire by Palestinian militants who had launched a rocket attack against the town of Sderot, and closed its border crossings with Gaza. The rocket attack was alleged to have been carried out by Islamic Jihad in retaliation for an Israeli military raid in the West Bank, which caused two Palestinian deaths. Hamas spokesmen asserted in early July that, since Israel was not abiding by terms of the recent truce, it had suspended bilateral negotiations concerning a proposed prisoner exchange involving the release of Corporal Shalit—the Israeli soldier kidnapped in mid-2006.

ALLEGATIONS AGAINST EHUD OLMERT

In January 2007 police had begun investigations into the role played by Ehud Olmert in the privatization of Bank Leumi le-Israel in 2005, when the Prime Minister held the finance portfolio in Ariel Sharon's Government; it was alleged that Olmert had promoted the interests of two foreign businessmen in the sale of a controlling stake in the bank. In April 2007 the State Comptroller recommended that the Prime Minister face a criminal investigation into allegations that he arranged investment opportunities for an associate when he served as Minister of Industry, Trade and Labour. Olmert faced a new police investigation into his personal dealings in September: it was alleged that, while serving as mayor of Jerusalem, Olmert had acquired a property in the city at a price significantly below its market value, in exchange for the accelerated provision of building permits to the property developer involved. The Prime Minister's Office strenuously denied the claims. In November the police recommended that there was insufficient evidence to launch criminal proceedings against Olmert in the case concerning the Bank Leumi privatization.

However, in early May 2008 the Israeli police began questioning Olmert with regard to the alleged receipt of US $150,000 in donations from a US businessman to support Olmert's campaign for both elections for the mayoralty of Jerusalem and the Likud leadership during a 15-year period before he assumed the premiership in 2006. The Prime Minister subsequently admitted that he had received the donations, but insisted that these had not been for personal gain. While already reportedly being urged by his Vice-Prime Minister and Minister of Foreign Affairs, Tzipi Livni, to stand down, Olmert faced increasing pressure to tender his resignation following the announcement by Barak in early June 2008 that he would vote in favour of a dissolution of the Knesset in order for legislative elections to be held unless Kadima began the process of electing his successor as party leader. However, in late June, after Olmert asserted that primary elections for the party leadership (which he would not be contesting) would be held by 25 September, Barak's Labour Party voted against an opposition motion to dissolve parliament. The police investigation into Olmert's financial donations was reportedly widened in early July, when investigators stated that they intended to examine allegations that the Israeli premier had been involved in 'serious fraud and other offences'. Olmert announced his resignation on 30 July and agreed to relinquish the leadership of the Kadima party in September. However, the case concerning the privatization of Bank Leumi le-Israel was abandoned in December owing to a lack of evidence, and in March 2009 the investigation into the purchase by Olmert of a Jerusalem property was also terminated. None the less, in late August an indictment was filed against Olmert for fraud, receiving something by deceit in aggravated circumstances, tax evasion, breach of trust and falsification of official documents; it was the first time in Israeli history that a former Prime Minister had been indicted. In March 2011 18 high-ranking officials, including Olmert, were indicted in the 'Holyland affair' involving the approval of a real-estate project in Jerusalem during Olmert's tenure as Mayor of that city. As the Holyland trial began, the verdict in the former trial was given in July 2012. The court cleared Olmert of the major corruption charges, but found him guilty of breach of trust. Since these allegations had prompted Olmert's resignation in 2008, many observers suggested he had been a victim of injustice. Fierce criticism was also levelled against law authorities that their miscalculations had caused the unnecessary resignation of an acting Prime Minister.

PRISONER EXCHANGE WITH HEZBOLLAH

In early June 2008 Hezbollah returned to Israel the remains of five soldiers killed during their conflict of mid-2006, in exchange for the release to Lebanon of a man who had spent six years in Israeli detention after having been convicted of spying for the militant Shi'ite organization. This exchange, which had been brokered by the International Committee of the Red Cross, followed the exchange of a Lebanese prisoner and Israeli remains in October 2007. At the end of June 2008 the Israeli Cabinet agreed to exchange five Lebanese detainees for the bodies of the two Israeli soldiers whose abduction had sparked the recent conflict (having previously expressed hopes that the two men were alive); the exchange took place in mid-July, and also included the release by Israel of five Palestinian prisoners. It was reported in mid-2008 that the Israeli Government had offered to hold bilateral discussions with its Lebanese counterpart with a view to resolving all outstanding issues, while indirect peace talks with the Syrian regime, brokered by Turkish mediators, were also said to be under way in İstanbul. The Israeli Prime Minister was reported to have declared in late May that Israel was prepared 'to make substantial concessions to Syria that will be quite painful', although the Israeli authorities were swift to deny claims made by the Syrian Ministry of Foreign Affairs that Israel had agreed to a withdrawal from the Golan Heights prior to direct discussions being held.

Some optimism was expressed as far as Israeli–Palestinian relations were concerned, after the Israeli Government released almost 200 Palestinian prisoners in late August 2008 as a gesture of 'goodwill' to PA President Mahmud Abbas. The list included two of the longest-serving Palestinian detainees, who—contrary to Israel's usual policy of not freeing those with 'blood on their hands'—had been responsible for the deaths of two Israeli citizens in the 1970s. Earlier in that month Prime Minister Olmert was reported to have proposed a new peace plan whereby Israel would, *inter alia*, offer Palestinians 93% of the West Bank, provided that Abbas's security forces regained control of the Gaza Strip from Hamas.

LIVNI WINS KADIMA LEADERSHIP CONTEST BUT FAILS TO FORM COALITION GOVERNMENT

On 17 September 2008 Vice-Prime Minister and Minister of Foreign Affairs Livni narrowly defeated main rival Minister of Transport Shaul Mofaz in elections for the leadership of the ruling Kadima party, attracting 43.1% of the vote, compared with 42.0% for Mofaz. Livni was given a presidential mandate to form a new coalition government within 42 days of her selection. However, concerted negotiations with Kadima's coalition partners failed to result in concord. On 24 October Shas pulled out of talks, citing Livni's refusal to acquiesce to its two principal demands—that child welfare funding be increased and peace negotiations with the PA not be resumed at the current time. Consequently, Livni was unable to secure the required majority of at least 61 legislators, forcing her to announce her failure to form a new government on 26 October and recommend to President Peres that new elections be called, which were subsequently set for 10 February 2009. In the mean time, the Government remained unchanged, with Olmert continuing as Prime Minister on an interim basis.

OPERATION CAST LEAD, DECEMBER 2008–JANUARY 2009

Following Hamas rocket and mortar attacks upon Israeli territory, the IDF launched a military offensive in the Gaza Strip, codenamed Operation Cast Lead, on 27 December 2008. A week of aerial bombings ensued, during which Hamas bases and police headquarters and training facilities were targeted, although extensive damage was also caused to civilian infrastructure. An Israeli ground invasion was launched on 3 January 2009 and continued until 18 January, with the IDF completing its withdrawal on 21 January. Widespread international censure greeted the Israeli offensive, particularly with regard to the high number of reported civilian casualties. According to the Palestinian Centre for Human Rights, 1,434 Palestinians were killed during the three weeks of fighting, of whom some 906 were non-combatants, including 121 women and 288 children, while the Israeli Defence Intelligence Research Department contended that the total number of fatalities stood at 1,116, of whom between 295 and 460 were non-combatants, including 49 women and 89 children. Estimates by international human rights organizations appeared to support the higher figures cited by the Palestinians. Thirteen Israelis were reported to have been killed, of whom three were civilians. According to the UN, more than 50,000 residential homes, 800 industrial properties, 200 schools, 39 mosques and two churches were destroyed or damaged during Operation Cast Lead. Media stations also came under fire, and, despite a ruling on 29 December 2008 by the Israeli Supreme Court that foreign journalists must be allowed to enter the Gaza Strip whenever the main border-crossing was open, members of the international press were denied access to the enclave during the conflict, as they had been since November 2008.

In early May 2009 UN Secretary-General Ban Ki-Moon published his summary of the findings of a UN inquiry into nine incidents during Operation Cast Lead that had involved UN property and/or personnel. As well as attributing the responsibility for all but two of the incidents—one of which was blamed on Palestinian militants and the other of which remained unresolved—the inquiry found that white phosphorus shells had been used by the IDF in civilian areas, an activity prohibited under the terms of the Geneva Convention of 1980. Ban Ki-Moon also stipulated that the Israeli Government should provide US $11m. to compensate the UN for the damage caused to property, which had included the bombing of a UN-run school in which many civilians, including a large number of children, were sheltering from the fighting. In June 2009 UN investigators arrived in Gaza to commence a fact-finding mission, which included an unprecedented public hearing to obtain the testimony of Palestinian casualties of the war. Israel refused to co-operate with the team of investigators, protesting that the mission would be biased, despite the fact that it was headed by the esteemed South African judge Richard Goldstone. The EU, Canada, Switzerland, Japan and several other Western countries also boycotted the mission. The mission's report was published on 15 September. The report concluded that both the Israeli armed forces and the Palestinian militants appeared to have committed war crimes during the conflict, and outlined evidence of possible crimes against humanity committed by both sides. The most serious allegations against the Israeli operation included: the launching of a disproportionate offensive, which aimed to 'punish, humiliate and terrorize' the civilian population of Gaza; the targeting of civilian infrastructure, including schools, hospitals, factories, and water and sewage facilities; and the use of inappropriate armaments, including white phosphorous. On the Palestinian side, the report highlighted indiscriminate rocket attacks against Israel; the possible use of 'human shields' by militants in Gaza; and arbitrary arrests and extra-judicial executions carried out by the authorities in both Gaza and the West Bank. Furthermore, the report proposed that the authorities in Israel and Gaza should conduct fully independent inquiries into the findings within six months. Failure to comply with this proposal would result in the referral of the report's findings to the UN Security Council for further investigation. The Israeli authorities, who had refused to co-operate with the investigation, firmly rejected the report and labelled it as 'propaganda' and 'biased'. While the Hamas leadership denied the report's claims in so far as it applied to their own conduct, they supported its referral to the Security Council. The Human Rights Council endorsed the Gaza report in mid-October, and in early November the UN General Assembly endorsed a resolution demanding that Israel conduct an investigation into allegations that its forces had committed war crimes. In February 2010 the UN Secretary-General confirmed that Israel had submitted a formal response to the Goldstone report.

NETANYAHU RETURNS AS PRIME MINISTER

The early general election, held on 10 February 2009, was a tightly contested affair, with Kadima securing 28 seats with 22.47% of the votes and Likud-Ahi garnering 27 (21.61%). Israel Beytenu obtained 15 seats, while the Israel Labour Party and Shas won 13 and 11 seats, respectively. Despite Kadima winning the most seats, on 20 February President Peres requested Binyamin Netanyahu to form a new government; it was widely considered more likely that Netanyahu would be able to form a coalition government within the stipulated 42-day window, given that right-leaning parties (who would be likely to support Likud) had won more seats than centre-left parties (who might be expected to support Kadima). On 20 March Netanyahu was given a two-week extension in which to complete the coalition talks; on 30 March the new Prime Minister informed Peres that he had done so, having persuaded Israel Beytenu, Jewish Home, the Labour Party and Shas to join the Likud-led coalition. The new Government was inaugurated on the following day, with United Torah Judaism joining the coalition on 1 April, increasing the Government's representation in the Knesset to 74 seats.

OBAMA ADMINISTRATION ATTEMPTS TO RENEW IMPETUS IN MIDDLE EAST PEACE PROCESS

In mid-May 2009 Netanyahu visited Washington, DC, for his first meeting with US President Barack Obama, whose inauguration in January had fostered hopes of new momentum for the Middle East peace process. In a joint press conference following lengthy discussions, the two heads of state stressed rather different issues to which they attached importance vis-à-vis the Israeli–Palestinian impasse, prompting concerns that divisions between the long-standing allies would hamper efforts to move forward with the peace process. Obama repeatedly reiterated his commitment to the two-state solution propagated by the 2007 Annapolis summit, while the hardline Netanyahu stated that he was willing to resume direct peace negotiations immediately but notably refused to endorse the notion of a fully sovereign Palestinian state and instead advocated a drive for 'economic peace', whereby an improvement in the Palestinian economy would lead to greater stability and an improved security condition. The Israeli Prime Minister also warned that Iran's nuclear programme rather than the Israeli–Palestinian conflict posed the principal threat to peace in the Middle East.

In June 2009, shortly after an address to the international Muslim community by President Obama (see the chapter on Egypt), Netanyahu appeared to effect a *volte-face*, explicitly endorsing for the first time the notion of an independent Palestinian state. Netanyahu continued to reject a right of return for Palestinian refugees, arguing that this would compromise 'Israel's continued existence as the state of the Jewish people', and declared that the Jewish settlements in the West Bank would remain and expand in line with natural population growth.

In July 2009 the US Special Envoy for Middle East Peace, George Mitchell, travelled to Israel for a meeting with President Peres. In a joint statement to the press, Mitchell acknowledged that Israel had 'taken meaningful action in the West Bank, which we hope can be sustained and expanded', and that the Palestinians, in turn, had 'made significant strides in improving their security forces'. Mitchell stressed the need for the Israeli Government to tackle 'difficult issues' such as the Jewish settlements and outposts, and to effect further changes to improve economic conditions in the Palestinian territories.

Meanwhile, in May 2009 the head of the CIA, Leon Panetta, arrived in Israel to meet with Netanyahu and Deputy Prime Minister and Minister of Defence Ehud Barak to seek assurances that Israel would not launch an impromptu military attack on Iran without offering prior warning to the Obama Administration. Netanyahu and Barak were reported to have satisfied Panetta that such a scenario would not unfold. Secretary of State Hillary Clinton's announcement in mid-July that the USA was to extend its 'defence umbrella' across the region to defend its allies in the Middle East from a possible nuclear attack in the future from Iran was met by strong censure from the Israeli Deputy Prime Minister and Minister of Intelligence and Atomic Energy, Dan Meridor, who asserted that it signalled a disquieting US submission to the prospect of a nuclear-armed Iran.

Following the formation of Netanyahu's Government at the end of March 2009, the Syrian Government declared its interest in resuming peace talks, on the condition that discussions be focused on a complete Israeli withdrawal from the Golan Heights. Minister of Foreign Affairs Lieberman dismissed the value of reopening dialogue with Syria in mid-April in an interview with *The Jerusalem Post*, asserting: 'We don't see any goodwill from the Syrian side...'. However, just a few days later, Lieberman stated during a live broadcast on Israel Radio that he would be happy to reopen negotiations with Syria immediately, provided that no conditions were stipulated. Some analysts speculated that the focus of the Israeli Government might in future shift to the pursuit of a peace accord with Syria, an ally of Iran, as a means of furthering the isolation of the latter.

In April 2009 Lieberman was questioned by Israeli police as part of an ongoing investigation into allegations of corruption. The police recommended in early August that Lieberman should face a number of charges, including fraud, bribery and breach of the public trust, in relation to the allegations. Lieberman insisted that the charges were baseless and declared that he would resign if he were to be indicted. In May 2010 the police formally recommended that Lieberman be charged with 'breach of trust', along with a former Israeli ambassador to Belarus, Zeev Ben Aryeh. In April 2011 the State Prosecutor's Office issued a statement confirming that it would proceed with charges against Lieberman of fraud, money laundering, breach of trust and witness tampering. Pre-indictment hearings began in mid-January 2012 and concluded the following month. However, by September the Attorney-General, Yehuda Weinstein, had yet to announce whether Lieberman would indeed be charged.

CONTROVERSY OVER WEST BANK SETTLEMENTS

The prospects for a revival of peace talks were undermined in early September 2009 when the Ministry of Defence announced that approval had been granted for the construction of 455 new housing units in Jewish settlements in the West Bank. Observers noted that the decision was in all probability intended to placate pro-settlement elements within the governing coalition and Likud. Intensive efforts on the part of Mitchell to foster an agreement on settlements, during September, were unsuccessful. It was reported that Netanyahu was proposing a temporary moratorium on new housing units in the West Bank, but this was deemed inadequate by the Palestinian negotiators, who continued to demand a complete cessation of all settlement construction in the West Bank and East Jerusalem. President Obama hosted a tripartite meeting involving Netanyahu and Abbas, their first face-to-face discussions of Netanyahu's premiership, during a session of the UN General Assembly in New York on 22 September. However, all parties admitted that the meeting did not signal the resumption of negotiations and was of limited significance. The US position on settlements appeared to have softened on 31 October, when Secretary of State Hillary Clinton, during a visit to Jerusalem, praised Netanyahu's proposals on restraining settlement activity, describing his proposed concessions as 'unprecedented'. Clinton had met with Abbas earlier that day in Abu Dhabi, United Arab Emirates (UAE), where he had again rejected a resumption of talks based on a partial suspension of settlement activity.

In December 2009 Netanyahu formally announced the imposition of a 10-month moratorium on settlement construction in the West Bank. However, the initiative was to apply only to private homes and excluded up to 3,000 housing units that were already under construction or for which permission had already been granted. Crucially, the moratorium did not apply to settlements within East Jerusalem, which Netanyahu described as part of Israel's 'sovereign capital'. The issue of settlements continued to hamper relations between Israel and the Palestinian Authority in early 2010. In February it was revealed by the Israeli Ministry of Defence that construction work had continued in some 29 settlements in the West Bank, despite the moratorium on settlement-building activity. In the following month the approval of two further developments appeared to damage relations with the US Administration. In early March the Ministry of Defence announced the approval of an application to build up to 112 new homes at an Israeli settlement near Bethlehem, and two days later it was revealed that the Government had approved plans to construct 1,600 homes at the Ramat Shlomo settlement in East Jerusalem. The announcement coincided with a visit to Israel by the US Vice-President, Joseph Biden, who criticized the decision and claimed that the announcement would undermine efforts by the USA to foster the peace process. Netanyahu insisted that the decision had been made without his prior knowledge and denied that it would precipitate a crisis in relations with the USA, while reiterating his support for settlement-building in East Jerusalem. Relations appeared to decline further later that month after the postponement of a scheduled visit to Israel by George Mitchell. Also in March Netanyahu travelled to Washington, DC, for an official visit, during which he held talks with President Obama; however, no progress was reported on the issue of settlement-building.

In November 2009 it was announced that Israeli forces in the Mediterranean Sea had intercepted a cargo ship en route to Syria, the *Francop*, which Israel claimed was carrying a large consignment of Iranian-made weapons destined for Hezbollah militants in Lebanon, and in April 2010 President Shimon Peres provoked controversy by accusing Syria of clandestinely supplying Hezbollah with long-range Scud missiles; both the Syrian Government and Hezbollah denied the allegations.

In early 2010 relations with several other Western allies, including the United Kingdom and France, were strained after allegations of Israeli involvement in the assassination of a senior member of Hamas in Dubai, UAE. Following the death of Mahmoud al-Mabhouh on 19 January, the Dubai authorities issued details of 11 individuals suspected of carrying out the assassination, all of whom had travelled to the emirate using false British, Australian, Irish, French and German passports. Hamas accused the Israeli intelligence service, Mossad, of involvement in al-Mabhouh's death; nevertheless, the Israeli Government insisted that there was no proof that its intelligence service had been involved in the killing. In February two Palestinians were arrested in Amman, Jordan, and extradited to Dubai, and later that month the police authorities in the emirate announced details of 15 further suspects in the case. Also in that month the British Secretary of State for Foreign and Commonwealth Affairs, David Miliband, summoned the Israeli ambassador in London to the Foreign and Commonwealth Office to discuss the use of counterfeit British passports by 12 of those sought in connection with the killing. In March Miliband announced in the British House of Commons the expulsion of a diplomat from the Israeli embassy in London, asserting that there were 'compelling reasons to believe Israel was responsible for the misuse of the British passports'.

Relations between Israel and Turkey, which had been tense since January 2010 after a diplomatic dispute over a perceived insult against the Turkish ambassador to Israel by Deputy Minister of Foreign Affairs Danny Ayalon, deteriorated still further in May–June. On 31 May some nine Turkish citizens were killed in confrontations between pro-Palestinian activists and Israeli special forces who boarded a ship, the MV *Mavi Marmara,* bound for the Gaza Strip. The ship had been chartered as part of a flotilla of vessels attempting to break the Israeli blockade of Gaza. Following the incident, relations between Israel and Turkey deteriorated severely. The Turkish Prime Minister, Recep Tayyip Erdoğan, recalled the Turkish ambassador to Israel, and demanded the establishment of an international inquiry to investigate the incident, while accusing Israel of carrying out an act of 'state terror'. Netanyahu responded by insisting that Israeli troops had acted in self-defence after being attacked by the activists on board the ship. Separate inquiries into the incident were subsequently formed by the UN Human Rights Council and by Ban Ki-Moon; the latter inquiry, which met for the first time in August, was to be jointly chaired by former Prime Minister of New Zealand Sir Geoffrey Palmer and former Colombian President Alvaro Uribe Vélez, as well as representatives from Israel and Turkey. The two countries, for their part, also formed inquiries into the incident. In June it was reported that the Israeli Minister of Industry, Trade and Labour, Binyamin Ben-Eliezer, had held a meeting with the Turkish Minister of Foreign Affairs, Prof. Dr Ahmet Davutoğlu, in an attempt to resolve the dispute. However, by late 2010 concerns remained that the incident had inflicted lasting damage to the hitherto cordial relationship between the two countries. Relations worsened following the publication on 2 September 2011 of the Palmer inquiry's report. The report criticized the conduct of both countries over the incident and urged their respective Governments to do more to prevent such incidents from occurring in the future. The report found that 'Israel's decision to board the vessels with such substantial force at a great distance from the blockade zone and with no final warning immediately prior to the boarding was excessive and unreasonable', while stating that the blockade of Gaza 'was imposed as a legitimate security measure in order to prevent weapons from entering Gaza by sea and its implementation complied with the requirements of international law.' Citing Turkey's dissatisfaction with the report's findings and the refusal of the Israeli Government to issue a formal apology, Davutoğlu announced that Turkey would downgrade its diplomatic relations with Israel to the level of second secretary, expelling both the Israeli ambassador and his deputy, while withdrawing the country's remaining senior diplomats from its embassy in Tel-Aviv. Military co-operation between the two countries was also suspended. Nevertheless, diplomatic relations were renewed in March 2013 after the Israeli Government issued an apology for the incident and agreed to compensate the families of the victims.

STALEMATE IN ISRAELI–PALESTINIAN NEGOTIATIONS

Following months of so-called 'shuttle' diplomacy by George Mitchell and members of the Obama Administration, Netanyahu and Abbas agreed to hold direct discussions, the first such meeting since December 2008. On 2 September 2010 the two leaders arrived in the USA and commenced a first session of talks, at which a further round was scheduled. The second round of talks duly began on 14 September at Sharm el-Sheikh. However, the Israeli moratorium on settlement-building, which was due to expire at the end of that month, divided the two parties. Abbas demanded that the moratorium be extended before an agreement to continue talks could be reached; however, Netanyahu insisted that the 'freeze' was a temporary measure and would be lifted upon its expiry. Following the expiry of the 'freeze' on 26 September, the PA suspended its involvement in the peace process, stating that it would resume talks only when Israel had agreed to end settlement construction and its blockade of Gaza. Reports in mid-October that construction work had commenced on more than 600 new homes in Israeli settlements in the West Bank were duly cited by the PA as evidence that the Israeli Government was 'not serious' about the peace process. Tensions were exacerbated in mid-2011 following the 'unity agreement' signed by representatives of the major Palestinian political factions in Cairo in May (see the chapter on the Palestinian Territories). These tensions increased further in September after Abbas gave a speech to the UN General Assembly seeking formal recognition of Palestine as an independent state on the basis of its pre-1967 borders and with East Jerusalem as its capital at a meeting of the UN General Assembly later that month. The Israeli Government criticized the measures as damaging to the peace process. The stalemate in relations between Israel and the PA continued into 2012, with no breakthrough or any new initiatives. Meanwhile, on the Gaza front, Israel reached an agreement with Hamas for the release of Gilad Shalit. In an new escalation of violence in March, over the course of a week, some 300 missiles were fired towards Israel's southern cities, interrupting orderly life; however, the lack of casualties also demonstrated the effectiveness of the 'Iron Dome' anti-missile defence system.

INTERNAL DIVISIONS WITHIN LABOUR

Labour's participation in the right-wing governing coalition created internal tensions. Some Labour ministers openly criticized government policies and suggested that the party should consider leaving the Government. On 17 January 2011 Ehud Barak resigned as Chairman of the Labour Party and formed a new group, Ha'atzmaut (Independence), along with four other Labour Knesset members. The remaining Labour ministers withdrew from the coalition Government. On 19 January a renewed coalition agreement, which included Ha'atzmaut, received parliamentary approval. The new Government included four members of Ha'atzmaut; Barak retained the posts of Deputy Prime Minister and Minister of Defence. Shelly Yachimovich was elected as Labour Party chairperson in September.

SOCIAL PROTESTS

Meanwhile, from mid-July 2011 a wave of protests erupted across Israel, mainly in response to the rising cost of housing and other key living expenses. Demonstrators erected tents along the main streets of Tel-Aviv and were soon joined by other protest groups from various ideological streams. The demonstrations spread to numerous cities throughout the country, and the protesters' agenda gradually widened to include demands for the reinstatement of the welfare state and the cessation of privatization. In response, Prime Minister Netanyahu pledged to establish a committee of experts, under the chairmanship of Prof. Manuel Trajtenberg, to examine the issues raised by the protesters. Major rallies were held on 6 August and on 3 September in Tel-Aviv and other cities across the country, and, despite a court ruling that the encampment in Tel-Aviv must be dismantled, the protests continued into late September.

At the end of September 2011 the Trajtenberg Committee for Social and Economic Change submitted its recommendations, which included several reforms in the areas of taxation, housing, education and economic concentration. The Government adopted the majority of the recommendations and some were implemented: tax benefits for working parents of children under the age of three, and application of the free education law to the age of three. Critics claimed, however, that a fundamental change in priorities and economic policy was needed. Continued discontent with the Government's social and economic policies gave way to a further short wave of protests in mid-2012, some of which involved violent clashes between protesters and police.

RETURN OF GILAD SHALIT

On 18 October 2011 Hamas released Gilad Shalit from captivity after 1,941 days. Since his abduction in June 2006 Shalit had been a major issue in the Israel–Hamas conflict. During his captivity his family and supporters organized social protests to put pressure on the Government to negotiate his release. In exchange for Shalit's return, Israel released 1,027 Palestinian prisoners, some of whom had been convicted of terrorist activities. Although the majority of public opinion supported the exchange, some families who had been victims of terrorist attacks raised concerns that such actions might encourage terrorist responses.

CONTROVERSIAL LEGISLATION

The 18th Knesset, from 2009 onwards, debated numerous controversial bills, which were criticized by some observers as 'anti-democratic'. The aim of this legislation, according to its supporters, was to defend the identity of Israel as a Jewish State and to ensure the loyalty of its citizens. They also claimed that such laws were an expression of the Jewish majority will. However, the legislation was widely criticized for undermining democratic principles such as equality and freedom of speech. A controversial debate surrounded an initiative (that was not in fact written into law) to oblige new (non-Jewish) citizens to swear a 'loyalty oath' to Israel as a 'Jewish and Democratic State'. Another controversial initiative that was approved was the 'Nakba Law', which empowered the Minister of Finance to deny or reduce considerably funding to public institutes that supported events commemorating *al-Nakba* ('the catastrophe'—the Arabic term referring to the foundation of the State of Israel in 1948). Other laws also restricted the funding of non-governmental organizations—specifically human rights organizations that were supported by foreign governments and international institutions. Although some of the legislative initiatives were blocked by the opposition, and sometimes by the coalition and the Prime Minister himself (for example, a proposal to form a parliamentary commission of inquiry to investigate the activity of human rights organizations), other laws (such as that prohibiting a boycott on Israel) were approved by the Knesset owing to the support of a centre-right majority.

EARLY ELECTIONS END IN UNITY GOVERNMENT

Towards the end of 2011 the Netanyahu Government demonstrated a remarkable stability. The six-party coalition did not face any major internal challenges, and it seemed likely that it would complete its term to November 2013, becoming the first Government to do so since the 1980s. However, on 4 December 2011 Netanyahu decided to hold early primaries for the leadership of Likud. The move was immediately interpreted by politicians and political pundits as a pretext for calling early Knesset elections. Although Netanyahu denied any such intention, speculation concerning early elections spread. On 31 January 2012 Netanyahu's victory (75% to 25%) over the extreme-right candidate Moshe Feiglin in the Likud leadership primaries forced Kadima leader Tzipi Livni to proceed with leadership primaries in her own party. On 27 March, with 62% of the vote, Shaul Mofaz succeeded in ousting Livni. By the end of April the prospect of early elections seemed certain. A further signal came in the same month from the formation of a new party, Yesh Atid ('There is a future'), by Yair Lapid, a popular media figure. It was at this point, although reluctantly, that Netanyahu declared his readiness to call early elections. On 7 May the Cabinet approved the date of 4 September for legislative elections. The Knesset convened on the same day and approved a bill for early dissolution. However, the following day Netanyahu made the surprise announcement that Kadima would be joining the coalition and that the Government was prepared to complete its full term. The entry of Kadima into the Government created a large unity coalition that was supported by some 94 Knesset members, one of the largest majorities in Israel's history. Mofaz was nominated to the position of Vice-Prime Minister, although no other members of Kadima received ministerial posts. The two major goals of this new coalition, as prescribed by Netanyahu and Mofaz, were to legislate a new law regulating army conscription of ultra-Orthodox Jews (Tal Law) and to approve changes in the system of government such as raising the electoral threshold, granting the largest party the first right to form an administration and strengthening the government by demanding a super-majority for the approval of no confidence votes. The legislation of the Tal Law met with serious obstacles, not only owing to its rejection by ultra-Orthodox parties, which were opposed to the imposition of military service on Yeshiva students, but also to the right-wing parties' demand of including the Arabs' duty of civil service under the same equality initiative. Netanyahu dissolved the committee tasked with studying the issue shortly before the expected publishing of its recommendations, and a serious coalition crisis emerged. On 17 July Mofaz withdrew Kadima from the governing coalition, citing Netanyahu's decision to abandon the Tal Law, in favour of introducing gradual and more limited legislation on the issue of ultra-Orthodox military service. Following the end of the short-lived unity coalition, the Knesset announced that legislative elections would be held on 13 January 2013.

THE PERCEIVED IRANIAN THREAT AND THE 'ARAB SPRING'

The year 2012 was regarded by some as a crucial point in Iran's nuclear programme. It became a major issue in the political discourse of Israel and a controversial issue with respect to Israel's relations with the USA. In March Netanyahu visited Washington, DC, to discuss the perceived Iranian threat with President Obama. Although both sides agreed that it was important to restrict Iran's nuclear programme, they failed to agree on the measures to be taken to that end. While the USA and the international community favoured imposing further economic sanctions on Iran, certain Israeli political figures raised the possibility of a military strike against Iran's nuclear facilities, based on the assumption that the capacity for Iran to produce a nuclear weapon posed an existential threat to Israel. In May further rounds of talks were held in Baghdad, Iraq, between Iran, the so-called P5+1 (the five permanent members of the UN Security Council, plus Germany) and the International Atomic Energy Agency. The head of the Iranian delegation, Saeed Jalili, asked the P5+1 to recognize Iran's right to enrich uranium on its own territory; the request, however, was refused. According to a US official spokesperson, 'some common ground had been reached over the need to focus first on uranium enrichment at a level of 20%'. The Israeli Government criticized Iran's demands as 'buying time'. The various parties agreed to meet again in Moscow, Russia, in mid-June to hold further discussions. Meanwhile, in Israel the debate continued over the question of whether Iran's nuclear programme was in reality an existential threat to Israel, and whether a military strike would succeed in preventing Iran from enriching weapons-grade uranium. Meir Dagan, the former head of the Mossad, among others, expressed concerns that a military strike might not be beneficial for Israel, could cost many lives in counter-attacks, and would perhaps only delay Iran's nuclear programme, rather than terminate it. Public opinion, however, seemed to consider the Iranian threat as very serious, and by mid-2012 it was reported that the majority of the Israeli public supported a military strike against Iran's nuclear facilities.

Other events in the Middle East, known as the 'Arab spring', also posed a challenge to the position of Israel in the region. Throughout 2011 a wave of popular uprisings had deposed autocratic leaders in several Arab nations, including neighbouring Egypt. Although these popular movements were generally viewed world-wide as positive developments, some observers in Israel expressed concern that Islamist groups were emerging as leading political forces in those countries. The 'Arab spring' reached Egypt in January 2011, when thousands of protesters gathered in Tahrir Square in Cairo to demand the resignation of President Hosni Mubarak. The resignation of Mubarak in mid-February was troubling for Israel, which regarded its 1979 peace agreement with Egypt as one of its greatest diplomatic assets. The end of the Mubarak era signalled the beginning of a transition period characterized by uncertainty and instability. The political vacuum in Egypt allowed extremist groups to conduct anti-Israeli actions, including multiple attacks (a total of 15 by July 2012) against the pipeline supplying natural gas to Israel and Jordan, and the invasion of the Israeli Embassy in Cairo by anti-Israel protesters. Israeli concerns increased in June 2012, after the candidate of the Muslim Brotherhood, Muhammad Mursi, was elected as President of Egypt. However, the issue of Egyptian-Israeli relations was not an immediate priority for Mursi, as he was preoccupied with domestic political matters (see the chapter on Egypt). The Israeli authorities declined to comment on Mursi's ouster by the Egyptian armed forces on 3 July 2013.

OPERATION PILLAR OF DEFENCE

From June 2012 *Qassam* rockets were again launched into southern Israeli cities, and IDF forces were attacked near the Gaza border. On 14 November 'Operation Pillar of Defence' commenced with the assassination of Ahmad Jabari, the deputy head of the armed wing of Hamas. During the operation the Israeli air force launched attacks on Hamas's facilities and military bases in Gaza, as well as on tunnels used for smuggling goods into the Strip. About 1,500 rockets were fired into Israel, several of which landed in Tel-Aviv and Jerusalem (for the first time since the 1990–91 Gulf War), although the IDF's Iron Dome defence system achieved a high rate of successful interceptions (84%). Following international mediation, a cease-fire came into effect on 21 November 2012. Approximately 170 Palestinians and six Israelis lost their lives during the fighting. Violations of the cease-fire were subsequently reported by both sides.

THE 2013 ELECTIONS

A number of significant party political developments occurred during the pre-election period. Likud and Israel Beytenu declared they would contest the polls on a unified list. Livni announced the establishment of a new party, Hatnua (The Movement), which seven members of Kadima joined, together with other public figures such as former Labour leaders

Amram Mitzna and Amir Peretz. Aryeh Der'i was reinstated as leader of Shas, some 10 years after completing a three-year prison sentence for corruption, while Naftali Bennett, a former chief of staff to Netanyahu, was elected as the leader of Jewish Home. Barak, meanwhile, announced his retirement from political life.

At the general election, which took place on 22 January 2013, the joint Likud-Israel Beytenu list emerged victorious, winning 23.3% of the valid votes cast and 31 legislative seats, although this was a significant decline from the 43 seats that the two parties had controlled in the previous Knesset. Kadima also performed poorly, with its legislative representation decreasing dramatically, from 28 seats to just two. The new Knesset, comprising 12 parties and blocs, remained highly fragmented.

Although it was widely anticipated that Netanyahu would again become Prime Minister, he had to negotiate coalition agreements with two new political forces, Yesh Atid (19 seats) and Jewish Home (12 seats), which had formed an alliance after the election. Yesh Atid had become the second largest party in the Knesset after gaining in popularity by identifying with the social protest movement and promoting a socio-economic agenda centred on the demands of the middle class. Eventually, Netanyahu was able to form a coalition Government comprising Likud, Israel Beytenu, Yesh Atid, Jewish Home and Hatnua, which commanded the support of 68 Knesset members, excluding the ultra-Orthodox parties. The Labour Party (which had won 15 seats), Meretz–Yahad and the Arab parties constituted the rather weak opposition.

The first challenge confronting Netanyahu's Government was securing legislative approval of the budget. Yair Lapid, the new Minister of Finance, had to address the huge budgetary deficit. The budget he offered (which included higher taxes, reductions in child welfare payments and a modest decrease in the security budget) was harshly criticized by the opposition and the public. The Government was also challenged by the 'burden of equality' issue (the induction of ultra-Orthodox into military service). A ministerial commission was appointed to examine the issue, and it recommended that only 1,800 Yeshiva students (out of about 40,000) should be exempted from military service, with sanctions to be imposed upon those refusing to serve. Legislation based on these recommendations was approved on 23 July 2013. The ultra-Orthodox members of the Knesset condemned the new law, claiming that it would be disregarded by the ultra-Orthodox community. The Government's decision to allow the private sector to export Israel's natural gas also attracted considerable criticism. Consequently, the Government authorized the export of only 40% of the country's gas reserves, with the remainder reserved for domestic use. The long-term stability of the Government depended on the ability of Netanyahu to maintain a consensus among the coalition parties.

THE RESUMPTION OF NEGOTIATIONS WITH THE PALESTINIANS

On 29 November 2012 the UN General Assembly accepted the PA as an observer state. Although this announcement had no major practical consequences, Israel sanctioned the PA for this unilateral move towards independence.

In March 2013 President Obama held talks with representatives of Israel and the PA in an attempt to revive the faltering peace process. Owing to the efforts of John Kerry, the US Secretary of State, on 19 July it was announced that Israel and the Palestinians had agreed to renew the negotiations on a permanent status accord. The two delegations, headed by Livni and Saeb Erakat, respectively, met on 29 July in Washington, DC, for preliminary discussions. Within Netanyahu's coalition, the resumption of negotiations with the Palestinians provoked demands for a referendum on the issue. Netanyahu declared that any agreement with the Palestinians would be put to a referendum. Another controversial issue within Israel was the Government's decision in that month to release 104 Palestinian prisoners, some of whom were convicted terrorists.

ISRAEL AND THE SYRIAN CIVIL WAR

Although Israel was reluctant to intervene in Syria, which had been mired in a civil war since 2011, it remained concerned about the potential transportation of Iranian weapons via Syria to Hezbollah. Several attacks on weapons depots within Syria occurred during May–July 2013, and Syrian sources claimed that the Israeli air force was responsible. Israel denied any involvement, but emphasized that the transference of weapons to Hezbollah would not be tolerated.

Economy

Revised for this edition by RICHARD GERMAN and ELIZABETH TAYLOR

INTRODUCTION

The total area of the State of Israel, including East Jerusalem and the Golan sub-district, annexed by Israel in 1967 and 1981, respectively, amounts to 22,072 sq km, as compared with the 27,090 sq km area of Palestine under the British mandate. At the census of 4 November 1995 the population (including East Jerusalem and the Golan Heights) was 5,548,523. According to official estimates, by 31 December 2011 the population had increased to 7,836,600 (of whom 75.4% were Jews, 17.2% Muslims, 2.0% Christians, 1.7% Druze and 3.8% of no recorded affiliation); and by the end of December 2012 it had risen to 7,981,400. The population is heavily concentrated in the coastal strip, between Ashkelon and Naharia.

The main reason for the growth of the population has been Jewish immigration, accounting for 58% of the yearly increase between 1948 and 1977. Immigration up to 1948 totalled 482,857 persons, of whom nearly 90% came from Europe, North and South America and Oceania. The biggest wave of immigrants arrived within six years of the founding of the new state. These were refugees from post-war Europe, followed by Jews emigrating from the Arab states. Large numbers also came from North Africa as a result of political developments there. During 1955–64 more than 200,000 emigrated from Africa to Israel. Although immigration from Eastern Europe resumed in 1956, the overall number of arrivals declined in the 1960s, falling to 14,469 in 1967. The Six-Day War of 1967 sparked renewed immigration, with some 300,000 migrants arriving in the period up to the Yom Kippur War of 1973, around 70% of these from the USA and Europe. Following the latter conflict, immigration declined again, falling from 54,886 in 1973 to 12,599 in 1981; a rise to 19,981 in 1984 was attributable to the arrival of 7,800 Ethiopian Jews (Falashas). In 1988 new immigrants (13,034) were in fact outnumbered by Israelis emigrating from the country (18,900).

However, the collapse of communism in Eastern Europe in 1989 resulted in a renewed surge of migration, mainly from the disintegrating USSR (especially the Russian Federation). The number of immigrants totalled 199,516 in 1990. The rate slowed thereafter, but remained relatively high—immigrants numbered 70,919 in 1996, and 66,221 in 1997. By 31 December 1996 38.4% of Israel's Jewish population had been born abroad. These included 1,202,200 born in Europe, North and South America and Oceania, 327,100 in Africa and 249,900 in Asia. A new upward movement was registered in 1999, when immigrants numbered 76,766 (a 35% increase over the 1998 level), but the total decreased to 60,192 in 2000, 43,580 in 2001, 33,567 in 2002 and 23,268 in 2003. In 2004 numbers fell further, to 20,898, before rising slightly, to 21,180, in 2005. They subsequently declined again, to 19,269 in 2006, 18,131 in

2007 and 13,699 in 2008, before increasing to 14,572 in 2009, 16,633 in 2010 and 16,892 in 2011. There was a small decline, to 16,557, in 2012.

ECONOMIC GROWTH

Israel built a modern developed economy, making significant progress in the 1980s and 1990s as the proportion of gross domestic product (GDP) allocated to defence expenditure fell from a high of more than 40% in 1973 to 21.2% in 1985, and progressively to 8.9% in 1999. However, the second Palestinian uprising in the Occupied Territories from September 2000 resulted in renewed increases in the share allocated to defence. Israel has been assisted both by continuing substantial levels of official US military assistance and other aid, and by large financial donations from US and other Jewish communities abroad, which have been used in particular to assist the absorption of Jewish migrants into Israel. Also beneficial was the introduction in 1980 of the shekel as the official currency unit, in succession to the previous Israeli pound (or lira), after a period of rapid currency depreciation and rampant inflation. There followed an assault on the socialist structures and institutions that had dominated the economy since the state's foundation, and moves to eradicate the parallel 'black' economy, so that Israel would become better placed to compete with other world markets.

Israel's economic growth slowed sharply in 1996, to 4.6%, after averaging around 6% per year during the first half of the 1990s. In 1997 GDP increased, in real terms, by only 2.9%. The annual inflation rate, having fallen to 7% in 1997, rose to 8.6% in 1998, reflecting a sharp depreciation in the value of the currency in the second half of the year as the Bank of Israel (the central bank) cut base lending rates in response to the economic crises in the Far East and Russia. GDP growth slowed further in 1998, to only 2%, and real GDP per head actually fell by 0.4%. However, tight monetary policy and falling house prices reduced the inflation rate to 5.2% in 1999 and 1.1% in 2000. GDP growth edged up in 1999, to 3.0%, but GDP per head again declined, by 0.2%. Some progress was made with the privatization and liberalization programme implemented by the first administration of Binyamin Netanyahu (elected in 1996); however, the economic slowdown inhibited any substantial restructuring, as the authorities gave priority to curbing inflation and achieving macroeconomic stability.

Signs of recovery from recession emerged in 2000 under the new Government of Ehud Barak (elected in mid-1999). The first nine months of 2000 were characterized by rapid economic growth, led by increasing exports. However, an economic slowdown was reported in the fourth quarter, largely as a result of the renewed Palestinian uprising. Nevertheless, the rate of GDP growth for the year as a whole was 6.9%, while GDP per head increased by 3.4%, after two years of negative growth. Business sector growth accelerated to 7.4% in 2000 (from 2.0% in 1999), reflecting a rise in the output of high-technology industries, although growth rates in the traditional manufacturing and construction industries remained low. The low rate of inflation in 2000 was mainly attributable to the significant appreciation of the shekel, brought about by an unexpected surge in foreign direct investment (FDI).

The worsening Israeli–Palestinian conflict and the 11 September suicide attacks on the USA aggravated Israel's economic downturn in 2001, when a 50% slump in tourist arrivals contributed to a contraction in GDP—the first since 1953—of 0.6%. Reduced government revenues and increased military and security spending in 2001 produced a widening budget deficit and a fall in GDP per head. The slowdown in economic activity continued during 2002, as the impact of the deteriorating security situation spread to the whole economy and demand declined steeply. GDP contracted by 0.7%, and business sector GDP fell by 3.1%. The average rate of inflation, at 5.6%, exceeded the upper limit of the 3% target rate, and high interest rates exacerbated the slowdown in private consumption and investment. Following elections in January 2003, the new Government of Ariel Sharon (first elected in 2001) was forced to make substantial spending cuts to the budget to reach its 2003 deficit target, introducing an austerity package reflecting higher military spending at the expense of the public sector. In 2003 the rate of inflation declined to 0.7%, a consequence of tight monetary policy and the appreciation of the shekel against the US dollar. Led by a growth in both exports and private consumption, real GDP grew by 1.5% in 2003 and by 4.9% in 2004. Israel's economic recovery accelerated during 2005. In the IMF's assessment, this reflected a favourable global economic environment, an improvement in the security situation, prudent macroeconomic policies and structural reform aimed at boosting competition and efficiency. Real GDP again grew by 4.9%, the exchange rate was broadly stable, and unemployment, although high, continued to fall.

Despite some contraction in real terms in the third quarter of 2006, the worst economic expectations prior to that year's conflict with the Lebanese militant organization Hezbollah failed to materialize. Although the cost of the war amounted to approximately NIS 4,000m., GDP grew by 5.8% during 2006. Moreover, the exchange rate remained stable, reflecting foreign investor confidence. The high growth rate was accompanied by an improvement in the current account of the balance of payments (in surplus equal to 4.9% of GDP), an increase in the number of employed persons and a lower unemployment rate, and a high volume of FDI (US $14,200m.). Meanwhile, the impact of economic expansion and a sharp rise in government revenues meant that the budget deficit of the central Government fell to 0.9% of GDP in 2006.

The growth in GDP (by 5.9%) and employment, particularly in the business sector, continued during 2007. Reflecting this economic improvement, the Organisation for Economic Co-operation and Development (OECD) invited Israel to begin the process of applying for membership, and Israel's credit rating was raised by the international credit rating agencies Fitch Ratings and Standard & Poor's. (Israel formally acceded to OECD in September 2010.) However, the inflation rate rose by 3.4% in 2007, thereby exceeding the upper limit of the target range (of 1%–3% a year). This acceleration was caused by the significant increase in world fuel and food prices, as well as by the expansion of domestic demand, prompting the Bank of Israel to raise the interest rate three times between August 2007 and January 2008.

Having experienced five years of high growth, Israel's economy suffered a reversal in the second half of 2008, as the international credit crisis provoked a global economic downturn. Although GDP increased by an average of 4.1% for the year as a whole, it contracted in the fourth quarter (and again, by an annual rate of 3.6%, in the first quarter of 2009), reflecting steep declines in exports, tax revenues and private consumption. The fall in fiscal revenue led to an increase in the budget deficit to 2.4% of GDP for 2008. Meanwhile, the inflation rate, which reached a high of 5.5% in September 2008, began to decline sharply, and the Bank of Israel reduced the interest rate several times to reach an unprecedented low level of 0.5% by April 2009.

Although the credit crisis led to upheaval in Israel's financial sector, its effects were moderate compared with other small open economies. The relative strength of the sector reflected Israel's conservative banking practices, with comprehensive regulation and transparency, and an implicit government guarantee to support the banks, which bolstered confidence. Furthermore, the period of negative growth was short-lived, with the economy starting to recover from the second quarter of 2009, although GDP grew by only 1.1% in 2009 as a whole. Annual inflation during the year averaged 3.9%, and the Bank of Israel raised the interest rate on three separate occasions between August 2009 and March 2010, the rate reaching 1.25% in the latter month. Meanwhile, in December 2009 the IMF issued a generally positive assessment of Israel's economy, but voiced concern about the size of the fiscal deficit and the prevailing level of public debt.

GDP grew by 5.0% in 2010, underlining Israel's recovery from the global economic downturn and reflecting, according to the IMF, 'the fruit of decisive policies and strengthened macrofinancial policy frameworks'. There were rapid increases in fixed investment, exports and private consumption, a rise in employment, and a marked decline in the budget deficit from 5.1% of GDP in 2009 to 3.8% in 2010. The debt-to-GDP ratio also fell, from 79.5% in 2009 to 76.1% in 2010. However, inflationary pressures from domestic factors, particularly rising housing prices and rents, as well as global price increases for energy and commodities, prompted the Bank of Israel to raise the interest rate to 2% by December 2010, and to 3.25% by June 2011.

Economic momentum was maintained in 2011, with growth of 4.6% led by robust private consumption and buoyant business investment. However, the global slowdown meant that there was a deceleration in the second half of the year. The rate of unemployment declined to an annual average of 5.6% (from 6.7% at the end of 2010), its lowest level since 1983, while the budget deficit decreased to 3.3% of GDP (although still above target) and the debt-to-GDP ratio again contracted, to 74.2%. The deceleration in growth was accompanied by a reduction in inflation, to 2.2%, from 2.7% in the previous year. With the global and domestic economy slowing, the Bank of Israel began monetary easing from September 2011, reducing the interest rate in stages from 3.25% to 2.5% by February 2012. The Government's fiscal policy and the rising cost of housing and basic consumer goods and services prompted considerable social protest in mid-2011, in response to which the Government instituted changes to its tax policy and increased support for working families based on the recommendations of the Trajtenberg Committee (see Budget, Investment and Finance). At the same time, continuing political turmoil across much of the neighbouring Arab world heightened concerns regarding Israel's existing economic and trading links and their longer-term viability.

GDP growth in 2012 slowed to 3.1%, according to the Central Bureau of Statistics, although this performance still compared favourably with that of other developed economies in the challenging global circumstances. Exports, which account for about 40% of GDP, struggled in the context of the sluggishness in Israel's main overseas markets, particularly in Europe, and the country recorded a small current account deficit for the year as a whole—the first since 2003. Nevertheless, FDI inflows remained high in 2012, at US $10,400m.; industrial production grew by 3.7%, led by a surge in high-technology output; and annual inflation remained subdued, at 1.6%. The Bank of Israel made further cuts in the benchmark interest rate in 2012, to 1.75%; and then, in May 2013, an unscheduled cut in the rate, to 1.5%, in an effort to protect the export sector in view of the continued appreciation of the shekel, was swiftly followed by a further cut, to 1.25%. Meanwhile, in April 2013 the new coalition Government under Binyamin Netanyahu approved draft legislation for the establishment of a sovereign wealth fund to invest state revenue from Israel's prospective natural gas production.

AGRICULTURE

The agricultural sector is relatively small, employing only 42,600 of the employed labour force of 3.02m. in 2011. None the less, Israeli agriculture has attracted a great deal of international attention, and, more than any other sector of the economy, has been the focus of ideological pressure. For centuries, Jews in the diaspora were barred from owning land, and the Zionist movement therefore saw land settlement as one of its chief objectives. Since the establishment of the State of Israel, government agricultural policy has centred chiefly on the attainment of self-sufficiency in foodstuffs, in view of military considerations and Israel's possible isolation from its principal foreign food supplies; the saving of foreign exchange through import substitution and the promotion of agricultural exports; and the absorption of the large numbers of immigrants into the agricultural sector. In line with these objectives, the promotion of mixed farming and of co-operative farming settlements has also been an important element in government policy.

Cultivation has undergone a profound transformation into modern intensive irrigated husbandry. A special feature of Israel's agriculture is its co-operative settlements, which have been developed to meet the special needs and challenges encountered by a farming community new both to its surroundings and its profession. While there are a number of different forms of co-operative settlements, all are derived from two basic types: the *moshav* and the *kibbutz*. The *moshav* is a co-operative smallholders' village. Individual farms in any one village are of equal size. Each farmer is responsible for his or her own farm, but economic and social security is guaranteed by the co-operative structure of the village, which handles the marketing of produce, purchases farm and household equipment, and provides credit and many other services. At the end of December 2011 a total of 295,300 people inhabited *moshavim* and collective *moshavim*.

The *kibbutz* is a unique form of collective settlement developed in Israel. It is based on common ownership of resources and on the pooling of labour, income and expenditure. Every member is expected to work to the best of his or her ability; he or she is paid no wages, but is supplied by the *kibbutz* with all necessary goods and services. The *kibbutz* is based on voluntary action and mutual liability, on equal rights for all members, and assumes for them full material responsibility. At the end of December 2011 a total of 149,100 people inhabited *kibbutzim*. The large co-operatives are heavily subsidized, although the introduction of structural reforms in the agricultural sector (which included the abolition of production quotas for major categories) opened the market to wider competition from individual units that receive fewer subsidies.

During the years following the establishment of the State of Israel a large-scale expansion of the area under cultivation took place. This arose from the heavy influx of migrants and the recultivation and rehabilitation of land from which Arabs had been forced to flee. By 2011 the cultivated area included 1,339,700 dunums (1 dunum = 1,000 sq m) of field crops, an estimated 717,300 dunums of vegetables, potatoes and melons, 813,600 dunums of citrus and other fruit plantations, and 1,057,000 dunums of planted forest area.

The main factor limiting agricultural development is the availability not of land, but of water. Further development of the sector would involve intensifying the yield of existing land and the reuse of treated waste water to preserve fresh water essential for household consumption. Consumption of water totalled 1,919m. cu m in 2010, of which about 57% was attributable to agriculture, 36% to domestic households, and 7% to industry. The state-owned Mekorot (Israel National Water Co) supplies about two-thirds of Israel's fresh water. In 2004 the Government announced a restructuring of Mekorot to divide it into a cluster of companies separating the supply operations (a natural monopoly) and all the other operations in competitive sectors. The Government also established a special Water Administration, headed by a Water Commissioner, with statutory powers to control and regulate both the supply and the consumption of water.

The Water Administration has been charged with, among other tasks, the implementation of the national water project. The purpose of this project is to convey a substantial part of the waters of the Jordan river and of other water sources from the north to southern Judaea and the Negev, to store excess supplies of water from winter to summer and from periods of heavy rainfall to periods of drought, and to serve as a regulator between the various regional water supply systems. To provide a long-term national solution to water shortage problems, the Government in 2002 approved the installation of a series of coastal desalination plants. The Ashkelon facility, which is the largest of the series, was inaugurated in 2005. In that year Israel, Jordan and the Palestinian (National) Authority announced that they had agreed terms regarding a feasibility study for a proposed 180-km Dead Sea–Red Sea canal, to arrest the alarming water losses from the former and increase fresh supplies to the three territories. The study was to investigate the technical aspects and social and environmental impact of the scheme in a process overseen by the World Bank. In January 2013 the Bank released a draft report declaring the project viable from engineering, environmental and economic standpoints.

According to official estimates, agricultural production in 2011 was valued at NIS 28,401.4m. Field crops accounted for NIS 1,762.0m.; vegetables, potatoes and melons NIS 6,110.9m.; citrus and other fruit NIS 6,449.5m.; flowers and garden plants NIS 957.7m.; and livestock and other products NIS 11,297.8m. Estimated output of vegetables, potatoes and melons in 2011 was 2,292,700 metric tons, while that of citrus and other fruit was 1,250,100 tons. Wheat production suffered badly in 1999–2000, when severe drought conditions caused the Government to declare an official emergency and to impose a 40% reduction in water allocation to farmers. Production recovered to reach an estimated 200,800 tons in 2005, but has since fluctuated from 131,200 tons in 2006, to 158,900 tons in 2007, 75,700 tons in 2008, 133,000 tons in 2009, 112,300 tons in 2010 and 122,000 tons in 2011.

Cultivation of citrus fruit is one of the oldest and most important agricultural activities, and produces the main export crop. However, export levels have generally been declining over the last two decades. Some 461,900 metric tons were exported in 1990, but by 2003 the figure had decreased to 120,100 tons. Higher levels have been recorded more recently—reaching 178,000 tons in 2007, 172,000 tons in 2008, 174,500 tons in 2009 and 179,400 tons in 2010, before declining again, to 155,000 tons, in 2011. The Citrus Marketing Board of Israel supervises all aspects of the growing and marketing of the fruit, particularly exports. In 2011 flower and garden plant exports earned US $106.0m. Agricultural exports overall were valued at $1,380.6m. in that year, up from $1,326.8m. in 2010.

MINERALS

The Petroleum Law of 1952 has regulated the conditions for the granting of licences for petroleum-prospecting, having divided the country into petroleum districts and fixed a basic royalty of 12.5%. Petroleum was discovered in 1955 at the Heletz-Bror field on the coastal plain, and later at Kokhav, Brur and Negba, but these finds were not of the order to permit commercial production. From the time of the 1967 war to the 1975 Disengagement Agreement with Egypt, Israel was able to exploit the petroleum resources of the occupied Sinai; and, during 1978–79, those of the Suez Gulf (Alma fields), from which one-quarter of Israeli requirements were produced until the area was returned to Egypt in 1979. In July 1988 the Israeli Government awarded an offshore oil-prospecting concession of 7,000 sq km, about 16 km from Israel's southern Mediterranean coast, to Negev Joint Venture, a consortium of local and foreign companies. The consortium invested US $25.5m. in test drilling over a three-year period from 1988, without substantive results. Although such oil exploration in Israel has not proven very successful in the past, drilling has more recently been stepped up. In May 2004 Givat Olam Oil Exploration Co reported the discovery of up to 980m. barrels of oil near Kfar Sava, north of Tel-Aviv, although only about 20% of these reserves were thought to be extractable.

Israel has potentially huge recoverable oil shale reserves (sedimentary rock containing organic material from which liquid fuel may be extracted), mainly located in the northern Negev desert near the Dead Sea. Some estimates have suggested that the country could possess the third largest deposit of oil shale, after the USA and the People's Republic of China.

Pending significant production from recent gas discoveries, Israel has continued to import some 90% of its energy needs. Most of its crude petroleum requirements have traditionally been imported under long-term contracts from Egypt, Mexico and Norway, with the remainder bought on the international 'spot' market. More recently, Israel has stepped up its imports from Russia and the Central Asian states in the Caspian Sea region. Most imported crude petroleum is refined at the Haifa and Ashdod oil refineries. In 2004 the Government announced plans to privatize the two refineries, dividing the existing state monopoly operated by Oil Refineries Ltd into two competing entities. The Ashdod refinery was sold privately in 2006, while that of Haifa was made public on the Tel-Aviv Stock Exchange the following year.

Israel has sought to raise the share of natural gas among its energy sources, for economic, environmental and security reasons, and has developed its supply options, notably Egyptian imports and domestic offshore reserves. Offshore exploration for natural gas has been encouraging. In late 1999 and early 2000 both the US-Israeli Yam Thetis consortium and BG International announced significant discoveries in the Med Yavne offshore concession, 20 km off Ashkelon, where proven reserves of 40,000m. cu m were claimed by Yam Thetis for its Noah and Mary fields; while BG International stated that test drilling in its Or-1 well indicated reserves of 3,000m. cu m. In 2002 the Ministry of National Infrastructure signed an 11-year contract with the Yam Thetis consortium to supply gas to the state-owned Israel Electric Corpn (IEC), and this agreement was subsequently augmented by a further deal in 2006. In 2004 the Ministry of National Infrastructure granted the state-owned Israel National Gas Lines a licence for the construction and operation of a natural gas distribution grid.

In 2005 the Governments of Egypt and Israel signed a memorandum of understanding whereby the Israeli-Egyptian consortium East Mediterranean Gas (EMG) would export gas from Egypt to Israel for 15 years, with the possibility of a five-year extension. The agreement was implemented in 2008, with liquid natural gas being pumped from el-Arish on Egypt's Sinai peninsula to Ashkelon in Israel via a 100-km undersea pipeline. In April 2011, however the Egyptian Government announced that it intended to review gas export agreements with other countries, including Israel, amid accusations that the deposed Egyptian regime of Hosni Mubarak had improperly negotiated the sale of gas at preferential prices. Later that month supplies to Israel were disrupted by an armed attack on a gas pipeline in North Sinai, Egypt, and subsequent attacks on gas installations in Sinai continued to impede exports. In April 2012 Egypt's state-owned gas company, the Egyptian Natural Gas Holding Co, cancelled the supply contract with Israel, complaining that it had not been paid by EMG. Israel denied the claim, and warned Egypt that it was violating an economic provision of the 1979 peace treaty.

In January 2009 a US-Israeli consortium led by Nobel Energy announced the discovery of a major gasfield, Tamar, in the Mediterranean off the coast of Haifa. Then, in late 2010 the production potential of an even larger field, Leviathan, also offshore to the west of Haifa, was confirmed by the Nobel consortium. The Tamar field came on stream at the end of March 2013, and the Leviathan field is expected to commence production in 2017. In April 2012 an inter-ministerial committee, established under the director-general of the Ministry of Energy and Water Resources, Shaul Tzemach, to consider how Israel's new gas reserves should be managed, delivered an interim report for public debate. It recommended that the guiding principle should be to meet domestic gas needs before exporting the commodity. The final report of the Tzemach Committee was published in August. Earlier, the Government had approved an 'excess profit tax' on the production of natural gas (see Budget, Investment and Finance).

Israel has met about one-third of its energy requirements through coal imports. A fourth coal-fired power station, at Ashkelon, was completed in 2001, and a fifth 1,200-MW plant received government approval in 2002.

The Dead Sea, which contains potash, bromides, magnesium and other salts in high concentration, is the country's chief source of mineral wealth. The potash works on the southern shore of the Dead Sea are owned by Dead Sea Works Ltd. The works are linked by road to Beersheba, from where a railway runs northward. Phosphates are mined at Oron in the Negev, and in the Arava. An estimated 3.1m. metric tons of phosphate rock was produced in 2011.

INDUSTRY, MANUFACTURING AND CONSTRUCTION

Israel's industry was originally developed to supply such basic commodities as soap, vegetable oil and margarine, bread, ice, farm implements, printing and electricity. It used raw materials available locally to produce citrus juices and other citrus by-products, canned fruit and vegetables, cement, glass and bricks. In order to save foreign exchange, imports of manufactured goods were curtailed, thus giving local industry the opportunity of adding local labour value to semi-manufactures imported from abroad. Although most of Israel's industrial production is still for domestic consumption, the value of manufacturing exports (including diamonds) in 2011 was US $62,441.4m. (from total exports worth $67,802.2m.).

Israel's principal industrial export is cut and polished diamonds, most of the expertise for the finishing of which was supplied by immigrants from Belgium and the Netherlands. In 2011 Israel exported US $16,689.1m.-worth of cut diamonds, and it continues to be one of the world's largest traders.

The high-technology electronics industry specializes in equipment for military and communications purposes, and in computer and internet software in Israel's so-called 'Silicon Wadi'. The rapid advance of Israel's information technology (IT) sector attracted substantial investment by US corporations, estimated at more than US $14,000m. by 2000. Large US acquisitions at that time included Intel's $1,600m. buy-out of DSPC Communications in 1999, and Lucent Technologies' $4,500m. purchase of Chromatis networks in 2000. Subsequent recession, economic uncertainty over the Palestinian uprising and the events of 11 September 2001 in the USA dampened further foreign investment in Israel's IT sector until 2006, when the US computer company Hewlett-Packard announced its purchase of Israel's Mercury Interactive Corpn for $4,500m.

Once the leading sector in Israel, construction, with affiliated industries (cement, wood, glass and ceramics), accounts for about 5.0% of GDP. According to official estimates, during 2011 there were 8.9m. sq m of building area completed, and 11.2m. sq m on which building was started.

In 2011 there were 11,130 manufacturing establishments, which engaged a total of 365,000 employees. Of these, 486 engaged between 100 and 300 workers, and 182 more than 300. Some 144,000 were employed in the latter category. At the other end of the scale, 4,713 establishments engaged four or fewer workers, and 2,202 between five and nine.

The 1996 Electricity Industry Law revoked the state-owned IEC's exclusive right to generate electricity, setting a goal of up to 20% of generating capacity to be allocated to independent power producers. In the following year the Government also announced plans to establish a natural gas infrastructure in Israel—converting its oil- and diesel-fired generators to natural gas, with the aim of generating 50% of its electricity from gas. In 2005 new regulations were adopted that opened the electricity market to competition. The regulations allowed private power producers to build power plants and sell electricity direct to end users, rather than to the IEC. The first large-scale private combined-cycle power plant, located at Mishor Rotem, commenced operations at the end of June 2013, with a capacity of 440 MW. Israel's installed generating capacity at the end of 2011 was 12,759 MW. Output during 2011 totalled 57,145m. kWh, compared with 56,102m. kWh in 2010.

Israel is a world leader in solar technology research; the country's first solar power facility, in the Negev desert, became operational in August 2008.

TRANSPORT AND COMMUNICATIONS

Since 1948 Israel has operated its own international air carrier, El Al Israel Airlines. In 1997 the Government announced plans to privatize the airline by the end of 1998. However, opposition to privatization from staff unions, the Government's reluctance to push through the measure and significant reductions in the airline's activities delayed further progress until 2003, when the Government offered a 97% stake in the company, valued at US $113m., on the Tel-Aviv Stock Exchange. The state and El Al employees would retain just over one-half of the company after the flotation until options were converted. El Al's privatization was completed in December 2004, when the Government ceded control of the company to Knafaim-Arkia Holdings. Meanwhile, in 2000 the Government approved funding arrangements for the Airports Authority to complete a third terminal at Ben-Gurion International Airport near Tel-Aviv, at a total cost of $558m., and to enable the airport to handle up to 12m. passengers a year. There were 42,745 commercial aircraft landings in Israel in 2011, carrying 12.34m. passengers and 287,762 metric tons of freight. In April 2013 the Government signed an 'open skies' agreement with the European Union (EU), liberalizing air traffic between Israel and EU destinations.

Israel's merchant navy has been contracting, while its passenger fleet has been practically abolished. According to official figures, there were 58 vessels registered under the Israeli flag at 31 December 2011. In the north, the port of Haifa and its Kishon harbour extension provide Israel's main port facilities. The south is served by the port at the head of the Gulf of Aqaba, and mainly by the deep-water port of Hayovel at Ashdod, some 50 km south of Tel-Aviv. The amount of cargo loaded at seaports in 2011 totalled 19,415 metric tons, while the amount unloaded (including traffic between Israeli ports) was 25,101 tons. In September 2009 the Government approved a privatization plan for the ports, including an initial 15% share of the equity in Haifa and Ashdod ports, which commenced in early 2010. In April 2011 the Government announced its intention to sell 100% of the equity in the Eilat Port Company, and the Knesset (parliament) approved the privatization plan in May 2012. In November 2012 Papo Maritime Ltd, the sole bidder, was awarded the franchise for the port's operations for a 15-year period.

The total length of the country's railway network was 1,079 km in 2011. During that year traffic comprised 35.9m. passengers and 6.2m. metric tons of freight. In 2004 Israel Railways, converting into a public corporation, received an allocation of NIS 20,000m. to complete the national railway network, including the upgrading of existing railway tracks as well as the construction of new lines. However, this was superseded by a revised state budget for railway development of NIS 25,900m. for the period 2006–11, which was approved by the Government in 2006. In February 2010 the Government approved plans for further expansion of the network over the period to 2020, at a projected cost of NIS 27,500m. In 1996 a state-owned company was established to plan and promote the construction of a mass transportation system in Tel-Aviv, including a light railway. The concession for the light railway was signed with Metro Transportation Solution in 2007. In 2002 the Jerusalem municipal authorities awarded the contract for the construction and operation of a 14-km light railway in the city on a 30-year build-operate-transfer basis to the CityPass consortium. The Jerusalem light railway commenced passenger services in August 2011, and was fully operational by the end of the year. Funding for an extension of this first line, to add some 22 km to the existing route in two years, was approved in June 2013; earlier in the year plans had been announced for an additional extension of the light railway.

Roads are the chief means of transport. In 2011 there were 18,566 km of paved roads, of which 10,374 km were urban, 6,569 km were non-urban and 1,623 km were access roads. In 2011 there were 2,164,885 private vehicles, 15,382 buses and coaches, and 347,980 trucks registered. The first privatized bus lines came into operation in 1997. The Egged Transport Co-operative is Israel's largest bus transit company.

The privatization of Bezeq Israel Telecom, the state-owned telecommunications company, which had previously had a monopoly over the domestic market, was completed in 2005, when the state's remaining shares in the company were sold to the private Apax-Saban-Arkin group for NIS 4,237m.

TOURISM

The decline in the number of tourists entering Israel from 1973 continued until 1976, but increased thereafter, to reach almost 1.2m. in 1980. In 1982 the industry slumped again because of the war in Lebanon, labour disputes at El Al and less favourable exchange rates for tourists. There was then a fluctuating recovery from 1984, until Iraq's invasion of Kuwait in August 1990 and the ensuing crisis in the Persian (Arabian) Gulf region. The sector revived again in 1992, when 1.5m. tourist arrivals were recorded. By 1995 arrivals totalled 2.2m., an increase of 20% on the previous year's figure. In 1996 tourism again slowed, with approximately 2.1m. arrivals. This trend continued in 1997 and 1998, when arrivals dipped to 2.01m. and 1.94m., respectively. In 1999, however, tourist numbers recovered sharply, to 2.3m.

Although arrivals continued to expand strongly in the first nine months of 2000, the second Palestinian uprising from September produced a dramatic slump in the fourth quarter, with the result that arrivals for the year as a whole were only 4% up on 1999, at 2.42m. In 2001 the negative impact on tourism was aggravated by the 11 September suicide attacks in the USA, resulting in a 50% fall in arrivals (1.20m.) compared with 2000. Just 861,900 arrivals were recorded in 2002. Official sources estimated that the political tensions prior to the renewed conflict in Iraq led to a sharp fall in visitors in early 2003. Nevertheless, there was a recovery in tourism in 2003 as a whole, with arrivals increasing to 1,063,400. Arrivals were up significantly in 2004, to 1,505,606, and again in 2005, reaching 1,902,787. They then slowed to 1,825,200 in 2006, before rising again to 2,067,900 in 2007 and 2,559,600 in 2008. Having declined to 2,321,400 in 2009, arrivals rose significantly in 2010, to 2,803,100; and there was further expansion in 2011 and 2012, to 2,820,200 and 2,885,900, respectively. At the end of 2011 Israel had 338 tourist hotels, with a total of 47,578 rooms.

BUDGET, INVESTMENT AND FINANCE

There has been a substantial and long-standing deficit in the operations of the state budget. As approved by the Knesset in December 1999, the 2000 budget provided for expenditure of NIS 227,400m. and a deficit of NIS 10,400m.—envisaging that government expenditure as a proportion of GDP would fall from 46.3% in 1999 to 45.5%, and government debt from 107% to 105% of GDP. The Government declared its intention to amend the Deficit Reduction Law 'to create a new and binding trajectory in which the total government deficit (not including allocation of credit) should not exceed 2.5% of GDP in 2000 and should decline by no less than 0.25% year-on-year in 2001–02'.

The total government deficit in 2000 (excluding net allocation of credit) was NIS 2,800m. (0.6% of GDP); this resulted from three quarters in which there was a surplus, and a final quarter in which there was a large deficit as a result of security-related events. The deficit for 2000 was lower than the target set in the budget Deficit Reduction Law by 3% of GDP (i.e. NIS 13,000m.) and also 2.8% of GDP lower than the deficit in 1999. Budget revenue totalled NIS 177,269m., while total expenditure was NIS 178,367m. The state budget for 2001, approved by the Knesset in March of that year, provided for expenditure of NIS 245,813m. and a deficit of NIS 8,400m., equivalent to 1.75% of GDP. However, the need for increased spending on security provisions, in the context of the Palestinian uprising, and the first fall in overall GDP since 1953 (of 0.6%) resulted in the actual 2001 budget deficit rising to NIS 21,300m., representing 4.6% of GDP.

In light of the continuing Israeli–Palestinian conflict and the world economic downturn caused by the September 2001 suicide attacks in the USA, the Government was forced to revise its original spending plans. As adopted by the Knesset in February 2002, the budget provided for expenditure of NIS 248,000m. and a deficit equivalent to 3% of GDP. However, further fiscal deterioration and continuing contraction in overall GDP forced the Government to introduce a controversial economic austerity package, which, as finally adopted by the Knesset in May, included reductions in social welfare and other spending totalling NIS 6,000m. as well as tax increases of NIS 3,000m., including the raising of value-added tax (VAT). The revised target was a budget deficit in 2002 of 3.9% of GDP, to be followed by a deficit of 3.5% of GDP in 2003. Although the deficit reduction measures were politically difficult and socially unpopular, the Government achieved the revised target of 3.9% of GDP in 2002. Effective from January 2003, the Government introduced tax reforms, including a decrease in direct taxes on earned income and the introduction of capital gains tax on domestic traded securities and interest income and income of Israeli residents from overseas.

The 2003 budget was approved by the Knesset, although disagreements over funding for the Jewish settlements led to the collapse of the governing coalition in November 2002. The budget provided for expenditure of NIS 214,505m. and a reduction in the deficit equivalent to 3% of GDP. In the first two months of 2003, given the security implications of then likely military conflict in Iraq, the deficit widened to 6% of GDP, and the new Government was forced to introduce a further emergency economic recovery plan in March. The budget adjustment included reductions in public sector salaries and the workforce, a decrease in pension benefits, and an acceleration of the privatization programme. Despite public protests and the threat of a general strike, the Knesset approved the plan in May, voting to remove NIS 10,000m. from the public sector budget. In June the USA approved a US $10,000m. package of loan guarantees and defence aid, conditional on the ratification of the plan. Meanwhile, the Israeli Government raised $750m. in what it described as the largest independent bond offering ever made by the State of Israel on the international markets. The proceeds would be used to pay off old debt and lower the pressure on the local capital market to finance the budget deficit. Notwithstanding budgetary adjustments, the deficit reached 5.6% of GDP in 2003. The 2004 budget provided for expenditure of NIS 215,095m., based on 2.5% growth and a deficit target of 4% of GDP. It was approved by the Knesset in January 2004, despite protests over large reductions in both social services and defence expenditure. The Minister of Finance's proposals, particularly over pension reforms, triggered protests and a round of industrial disputes. In March the Government raised $500m. in an issue of 10-year bonds. According to the Bank of Israel, total government debt at the end of 2004 was NIS 539,000m., a rise of 2.3% from the 2003 level.

From January 2005 the maximum total tax rate in Israel (including income tax, health tax and national insurance contributions) was reduced to 49%, reflecting the Ministry of Finance's belief in the importance of tax cuts in stimulating growth. In March the long-delayed 2005 state budget was finally approved by the Knesset. Parliamentary approval of the NIS 221,890m. budget also paved the way for the implementation of the Government's controversial plan to disengage from the Gaza Strip (see History). Total government debt at the end of 2005 was NIS 552,000m., a nominal rise of 2.1% from the 2004 level. The debt increase in 2005 was the lowest (with the exception of 2000) for 10 years, reflecting the Government's reduced need for financing owing to the sharp reduction in the budget deficit, together with a marked increase in the proceeds of privatization.

The state budget proposal for 2006, which was not approved by the Knesset until June, totalled NIS 271,400m.—the budget plan targeting a deficit of NIS 17,200m., or 3.0% of GDP. Government expenditures were projected at NIS 231,800m., and revenues at NIS 217,200m. Gross state budget expenditure for 2007 (including revenue-dependent expenditure) was NIS 295,425m., and included extensive privatization proposals. This was approved by the Knesset in January 2007. The 2008 budget was adopted by the Knesset in December 2007, forecasting a deficit of 1.6% of GDP and expenditure growth of 1.7%. Income from taxes was expected to reach NIS 192,000m. and total income (excluding credit) NIS 237,000m.

Government approval of a two-year state budget for 2009 and 2010 was delayed until May 2009. This followed several months of political paralysis that eventually led to parliamentary elections in February and prolonged negotiations before a new coalition administration took office under Binyamin Netanyahu in March. In light of the economic recession and a sharp decline in tax revenues, the Government raised the budget deficit ceiling specified by law to 6.0% of GDP in 2009 and 5.5% in 2010, and resolved that the maximum rate of annual increase of public expenditure would be about 3.0% over the two years. The budget also allowed for a 1% increase in VAT, and for VAT to be levied on fruit and vegetables for the first time. The budget eventually received parliamentary approval in July 2009, although the Government subsequently agreed to increase the spending allocations for health and defence. The adoption of the two-year budget to absorb short-term fiscal stress was commended by the IMF in an appraisal of the Israeli economy conducted by the Fund in December 2009.

The draft two-year state budget for 2011 and 2012 was approved by the Knesset in December 2010. The spending package, which increased expenditure on education and employment programmes, was projected at NIS 348,185m. for 2011 and NIS 365,916m. for 2012, including debt-servicing, and envisaged budget deficits of 3% of GDP in 2011 and 2% in 2012. However, in the context of the slowing Israeli economy and an uncertain global environment, the Ministry of Finance subsequently admitted that its 2012 budget assumptions on state revenue were mistakenly optimistic, prompting reductions in its projections.

In late 2011 the Government had approved an 'excess profit tax' on the production of natural gas. To maximize the benefits of the new gas discoveries for the Israeli economy, the revenues from the tax would be deposited into a sovereign wealth fund (draft legislation for the establishment of which was approved by the Government in April 2013), which would invest the proceeds abroad and allocate a sum derived from its profits to the state budget each year. The Government also approved many of the taxation proposals formulated by the Trajtenberg Committee (which had been formed, under the chairmanship of economist Prof. Manuel Trajtenberg, in response to the nation-wide social protests in mid-2011), and new tax legislation was in turn adopted by the Knesset in December. Reflecting the need for fiscal tightening as well as greater social equality, the legislation increased tax rates on higher incomes, lowered them at middle-income levels, and cancelled a scheduled programme of gradual reductions in personal and corporate tax.

Following the Knesset elections in January 2013—which had been called partly owing to fears that the budget would not be approved by the previous legislature—protracted political negotiations until March on the composition of a new coalition government delayed the formulation of the next budget. A declining revenue trend had increased the budget deficit to 4.2% in 2012, and it continued to widen in the first quarter of 2013. In response, the new Minister of Finance, Yair Lapid, drafted an austerity budget for the period from August 2013 to the end of 2014. This provided for expenditure cuts (of at least NIS 25,000m.), to include defence spending, and for increases in personal and corporate taxes (expected to bring in some NIS 13,400m.) that would have a significant impact on the middle classes. The draft was adopted by the Government in mid-May, and received the Knesset's approval at the end of July. Meanwhile, the rate of VAT was increased from 17% to 18% with effect from the beginning of June.

Between 1986 and 1996 the Israeli Government sold part or all of its shareholding in 79 companies. In 1997 a total of $2,463m. was generated from privatization; this amount included $2,156m. from sales in the banking sector and $194m. from the sale of Israel Chemicals. In 1998 proceeds from privatization totalled $1,128m. In 2000 total government holdings continued to decline; privatization proceeds totalled $682m., which included the sale of the Government's remaining stake in Bank Hapoalim. Privatization revenue in 2002 amounted to NIS 400m., mainly from the sale of the Government's controlling stake in Bank Leumi. Israel's two oil refineries, at Ashdod and Haifa, were privatized in July 2006 and February 2007, respectively. The Ashdod facility was purchased in a private sale by the Israeli fuel retailer Paz Oil Co for about NIS 3,250m., while the Haifa refinery was sold on the Tel-Aviv Stock Exchange, raising NIS 6,400m.

In April 1998 foreign exchange restrictions were removed, in order to increase competition in the financial services sector and encourage foreign investment in Israel's economy. The Israeli Securities Authority adopted a dual listing regulation, allowing for securities traded on the US stock exchanges to trade on the Tel-Aviv exchange without additional regulatory requirements. The Bank of Israel reported a steady increase in overall foreign investment from US $694m. in 1994 (after the Oslo Agreement was signed) to $3,276m. in 1997 and $11,400m. in 2000. FDI slumped to $4,000m. in 2001, but increased to $6,200m. by 2005. In 2006 inflows rose sharply to reach $15,300m., boosted by the sale of an 80% stake in Iscar Metalworking for $4,000m. to US investor Warren Buffett, and the $4,500m. purchase of Israel's Mercury Interactive Corpn by US computer firm Hewlett-Packard. FDI totalled $8,800m. in 2007 and $10,900m. in 2008. However, it fell significantly in 2009, to $3,900m., in the wake of the global economic downturn. There was a subsequent improvement, with inward investment reaching $11,400m. in 2011, more than double the amount in the previous year, and FDI remained relatively high in 2012, at $10,400m.

Israel possesses a highly developed banking system, comprising the Bank of Israel, commercial banks, mortgage banks and other financial institutions. The three largest commercial banks are Bank Leumi, Bank Hapoalim and Israel Discount Bank. Their subsidiaries are represented all over the world. Long-term credits are granted by mortgage banks, the Israel Agricultural Bank, the Industrial Development Bank and the Maritime Bank. The function of the Bank of Israel is to issue currency (and commemorative coins), to accept deposits from banking institutions and extend temporary advances to the Government, to act as the Government's sole fiscal and banking agent, and to manage the public debt. Its Governor supervises the liquidity position of the commercial banks, and regulates the volume of bank advances. New legislation relating to the powers of the Bank of Israel was approved in March 2010, providing for the establishment of a six-member Monetary Policy Committee and ending the Governor's sole control over monetary policy.

The Supervisor of Banks took regulatory steps during 2003 to strengthen banks' monitoring and risk-management systems, in order to improve their ability to assess and manage operational, liquidity and credit risks, and in March 2012 issued a draft directive raising capital requirement levels. All Israeli banks were obliged to raise their core capital ratios to 9% by 2015, while Bank Leumi and Bank Hapoalim were required to reach 10% by 2017.

FOREIGN TRADE AND BALANCE OF PAYMENTS

Israel recorded a deficit on the current account of the balance of payments (goods, services, income and transfers) in each of the years 1990–97. The deficit increased to a record US $6,646m. in 1996, but was reduced to $5,014m. in 1997. Israel's foreign currency reserves, held by the Bank of Israel, stood at $20,600m. at the end of 1997. At the end of 1999 they totalled $22,515m., while Israel's foreign assets totalled $52,170m., compared with $43,024m. at the end of 1998.

The value of Israel's merchandise exports increased from US $22,974m. in 1998 to $25,577m. in 1999. Meanwhile, imports of goods (valued f.o.b.) increased from $26,315m. in 1998 to $30,041m. in 1999. In that year the trade deficit was $4,464m. and the current account deficit $3,277m., although the overall balance of payments showed a surplus of $9m. In 2000 the trade deficit fell to $3,089m., from imports of $34,036m. and exports of $30,947m. The current account deficit decreased to $1,974m., following a sharp increase in exports of services to $15,181m., resulting from the contribution of start-up companies. As a result of economic recession, merchandise imports fell in 2001 to $30,942m. and exports to $27,678m., giving a trade deficit of $3,264m. and a current account deficit of $1,852m. As a result of the deepening recession, the trade deficit increased to $3,684m. from imports of $31,219m. and exports of $27,535m. in 2002. The current account deficit stood at $1,544m. Foreign currency reserves stood at $23,700m. in December 2002. In 2003 the current account was close to balance; IMF data indicated that imports of goods reached $32,333m. and exports increased to $30,099m.

According to official Israeli statistics, imports in 2004 totalled US $40,969m., and exports reached $38,618m. By 2007 imports totalled $56,623m. and exports $54,092m, and these levels increased further in 2008, to $65,173.2m. and $61,339.1m. respectively. In 2009, however, there was a general trade depression, as exports declined to $47,935.5m. and imports to $47,368.2m. A subsequent recovery then saw exports reach $58,416m. in 2010, and imports $59,199m., resulting in a small deficit. Exports in 2011 and 2012 totalled $58,132.1m. and $53,973.0m., respectively, while the trade deficit widened as imports increased sharply, to $72,747.1m. and then $72,270.4m. The USA was the principal market in 2012, followed by Hong Kong, the United Kingdom, Belgium, China and India. The USA was also the principal source of imports in that year; other important suppliers were China, Germany, Switzerland, Belgium and the Netherlands. Foreign exchange reserves stood at $28,460m. at the end of 2007, but increased annually thereafter to reach $75,906m. by the end of 2012.

Israel's foreign trade is mainly focused on the EU and North America. In 1995 Israel concluded a free trade agreement with the EU regarding financial services, government procurement, co-operation in research and development, additional agricultural products and an improvement in Israel's access to European markets in the high-technology sector. An association agreement between the EU and Israel entered into force on 1 June 2000.

Statistical Survey

Source (unless otherwise indicated): Central Bureau of Statistics, POB 13015, Hakirya, Romema, Jerusalem 91130; tel. 2-6592037; fax 2-6521340; e-mail yael@cbs.gov.il; internet www.cbs.gov.il.

Area and Population

AREA, POPULATION AND DENSITY

Area (sq km)	
Land	21,643
Inland water	429
Total	22,072*
Population (*de jure*; census results)†	
4 November 1995	5,548,523
27 December 2008	
Males	3,663,910
Females	3,748,270
Total	7,412,180
Population (*de jure*; official estimates at 31 December)†	
2010	7,695,100
2011	7,836,600
2012	7,981,400
Density (per sq km) at 31 December 2012	368.8§

* 8,522 sq miles. Area includes East Jerusalem, annexed by Israel in June 1967, and the Golan sub-district (1,154 sq km), annexed by Israel in December 1981.

† Including the population of East Jerusalem and Israeli residents in certain other areas under Israeli military occupation since June 1967. Figures also include non-Jews in the Golan sub-district, an Israeli-occupied area of Syrian territory. Census results exclude adjustment for under-enumeration.

§ Land area only.

POPULATION BY AGE AND SEX

('000, official population estimates at 31 December 2011)

	Males	Females	Total
0–14	1,133.4	1,073.5	2,206.9
15–64	2,392.0	2,433.2	4,825.2
65 and over	349.4	455.1	804.5
Total	3,874.8	3,961.8	7,836.6

POPULATION BY RELIGION

(31 December 2011)

	Number	%
Jews	5,907,500	75.4
Muslims	1,354,300	17.3
Christians*	155,100	2.0
Druze	129,800	1.7
Unclassified†	289,900	3.7
Total	7,836,600	100.0

* Including Arab Christians.

† Including Lebanese not classified by religion.

DISTRICTS

(31 December 2011)

	Area (sq km)*	Population (rounded)†	Density (per sq km)
Jerusalem‡	653	968,800	1,483.6
Northern§	4,473	1,304,600	291.7
Haifa	866	926,700	1,070.1
Central	1,294	1,894,400	1,464.0
Tel-Aviv	172	1,295,000	7,529.1
Southern	14,185	1,121,600	79.1
Total	21,643	7,836,600	362.1

* Excluding lakes, with a total area of 429 sq km.

† Components exclude, but total includes, Israelis residing in Jewish localities in the West Bank totalling some 325,500 at 31 December 2011.

‡ Including East Jerusalem, annexed by Israel in June 1967.

§ Including the Golan sub-district (area 1,154 sq km, population an estimated 43,100 at 31 December 2011), annexed by Israel in December 1981.

PRINCIPAL TOWNS

(population at 31 December 2011)

Jerusalem (capital)*	804,400	Beersheba	196,300
Tel-Aviv—Jaffa	404,800	Netanya	189,700
Haifa	270,300	Holon	182,600
Rishon LeZiyyon	232,400	Bene Beraq	163,300
Ashdod	212,300	Ramat-Gan	148,000
Petach-Tikva	210,400	Bat Yam	128,200

* The Israeli Government has designated the city of Jerusalem (including East Jerusalem, annexed by Israel in June 1967) as the country's capital, although this is not recognized by the UN.

BIRTHS, MARRIAGES AND DEATHS*

	Registered live births		Registered marriages		Registered deaths†	
	Number	Rate (per 1,000)	Number	Rate (per 1,000)	Number	Rate (per 1,000)
2005	143,913	20.8	41,029	5.9	39,038	5.6
2006	148,170	21.0	44,685	6.3	38,765‡	5.5‡
2007	151,679	21.1	46,448	6.5	40,081	5.6
2008	156,923	21.5	50,038	6.8	39,484	5.4
2009	161,042	21.5	48,997	6.5	38,812	5.2
2010	166,255	21.8	47,855	6.2	39,613	5.2
2011	166,296	21.4	n.a.	n.a.	40,843	5.3
2012	170,940	21.6	n.a.	n.a.	41,854	5.2

* Including East Jerusalem.

† Including deaths abroad of Israelis residing outside of Israel less than one year.

‡ Excluding 116 deaths of military personnel resulting from hostilities with militant factions based in Lebanon.

Note: From 2006 data include marriages involving a spouse not resident in Israel and those in which spouses may be of different religions.

Life expectancy (years at birth): 81.8 (males 80.0; females 83.6) in 2011 (Source: World Bank, World Development Indicators database).

IMMIGRATION*

	2009	2010	2011
Immigrants on immigrant visas	12,099	13,678	14,332
Immigrants on tourist visas†	2,473	2,955	2,560
Total	14,572	16,633	16,892

* Excluding immigrating citizens (5,077 in 2009; 4,805 in 2010; 3,317 in 2011) and Israeli residents returning from abroad.

† Figures refer to tourists who changed their status to immigrants or potential immigrants.

2012: Total immigrants: 16,557.

ECONOMICALLY ACTIVE POPULATION

(sample surveys, '000 persons aged 15 years and over, excluding armed forces)*

	2010	2011	2012
Agriculture, hunting, forestry and fishing	47.8	42.6	39.6
Industry†	416.7	417.4	411.2
Electricity, gas and water supply	20.3	22.9	29.1
Construction	157.4	162.5	150.3
Wholesale and retail trade; repair of motor vehicles, motorcycles and personal and household goods	388.5	402.3	398.0
Hotels and restaurants	134.7	139.5	144.6
Transport, storage and communications	191.2	196.6	304.8
Financial intermediation	116.1	118.7	116.4
Real estate, renting and business activities	429.2	429.2	393.9
Public administration and defence; compulsory social security	134.6	146.3	342.5

—continued	2010	2011	2012
Education	367.5	385.4	417.2
Health and social work	303.7	306.8	326.9
Other community, social and personal service activities	147.2	154.2	148.4
Private households with employed persons	55.3	55.3	60.8
Extra-territorial organizations and bodies	2.3	2.5	1.5
Sub-total	2,907.9	2,979.1	3,285.2
Not classifiable by economic activity	25.8	45.6	73.7
Total employed	2,938.2	3,024.7	3,359.0
Unemployed	208.9	179.5	247.1
Total labour force	3,147.1	3,204.2	3,606.0
Males	1,664.3	1,698.8	1,917.8
Females	1,482.8	1,505.4	1,688.3

* Figures are estimated independently, so the totals may not be the sum of the component parts.

† Comprising mining and quarrying, and manufacturing.

Health and Welfare

KEY INDICATORS

Total fertility rate (children per woman, 2011)	2.9
Under-5 mortality rate (per 1,000 live births, 2011)	4
HIV/AIDS (% of persons aged 15–49, 2011)	0.2
Physicians (per 1,000 head, 2010)	3.7
Hospital beds (per 1,000 head, 2010)	3.5
Health expenditure (2010): US $ per head (PPP)	2,041
Health expenditure (2010): % of GDP	7.7
Health expenditure (2010): public (% of total)	61.7
Total carbon dioxide emissions ('000 metric tons, 2009)	67,216.1
Carbon dioxide emissions per head (metric tons, 2009)	9.0
Human Development Index (2012): ranking	16
Human Development Index (2012): value	0.900

For sources and definitions, see explanatory note on p. vi.

Agriculture

PRINCIPAL CROPS
('000 metric tons)

	2009	2010	2011
Wheat	133.0	112.3	122.0
Maize	81.1	86.5	96.4
Potatoes	608.8	548.7	621.1
Olives	30.5	73.5	66.0
Cabbages and other brassicas	56.8	52.4	57.7
Lettuce and chicory	36.3	28.7	32.2
Tomatoes	454.8	446.6	411.0
Cucumbers and gherkins	117.3	115.8	105.4
Aubergines (Eggplants)	46.4	45.3	46.1
Chillies and peppers, green	202.3	204.0	226.1
Onions, dry	75.3	83.3	91.8
Carrots and turnips	233.1	234.3	289.3
Watermelons	111.2	107.3	100.6
Cantaloupes and other melons	39.3	41.5	41.5
Bananas	93.5	112.7	101.3
Oranges	136.1	134.8	90.5
Tangerines, mandarins, clementines and satsumas	130.0	152.2	130.6
Grapefruit and pomelos	249.4	204.4	183.7
Apples	114.7	131.5	119.2
Peaches and nectarines	80.1	65.8	54.2
Grapes	91.2	95.1	89.5
Avocados	85.0	69.5	75.3

Aggregate production ('000 metric tons, may include official, semi-official or estimated data): Total cereals 257.0 in 2009, 241.1 in 2010, 257.7 in 2011; Total roots and tubers 641.1 in 2009, 568.7 in 2010, 641.3 in 2011; Total vegetables (incl. melons) 1,620.0 in 2009, 1,584.2 in 2010, 1,663.5 in 2011; Total fruits (excl. melons) 1,319.3 in 2009, 1,284.5 in 2010, 1,178.2 in 2011.

Source: FAO.

LIVESTOCK
('000 head, year ending September)

	2009	2010	2011*
Cattle	400	430	450
Pigs	224	224	224
Sheep	430	445	450
Goats	91	100	102
Chickens	41,095	42,599	43,500
Geese and guinea fowls*	1,000	1,000	1,050
Turkeys	3,396	3,800	3,900
Ducks*	200	200	200

* FAO estimates.

Source: FAO.

LIVESTOCK PRODUCTS
('000 metric tons)

	2009	2010	2011*
Cattle meat	104.0	108.1	112.0
Sheep meat*	6.0	6.2	6.3
Pig meat	19.6	18.9	19.0
Chicken meat	436.0	450.0	454.0
Goose and guinea fowl meat*	3.5	3.8	3.9
Turkey meat	92.0	90.0	91.3
Cows' milk	1,276.7	1,292.1	1,292.1
Sheep's milk	18.9	16.8	16.8
Goats' milk	21.8	23.4	23.4
Hen eggs	100.8	102.5	102.5
Honey	3.0	2.5	2.5

* FAO estimates.

Source: FAO.

Forestry

ROUNDWOOD REMOVALS
('000 cubic metres, excl. bark)

	1999*	2000†	2001†
Sawlogs, veneer logs and logs for sleepers	36	28	11
Pulpwood	32	22	7
Other industrial wood	32	22	7
Fuel wood	13	8	2
Total	113	81	27

* FAO estimates.

† Unofficial figures.

2002–11: Figures assumed to be unchanged from 2001 (FAO estimates).

Source: FAO.

Fishing

(metric tons, live weight)

	2009	2010	2011
Capture	2,712	2,588	2,650*
Carps, barbels, etc.	294	294	258
Aquaculture*	19,177	19,895	20,107
Common carp	5,892	5,629	5,840
Tilapias	7,789	7,662	7,390
Gilthead seabream	1,072	1,240	1,440
Flathead grey mullet	2,048*	2,125	2,169
Total catch*	21,889	22,483	22,757

* FAO estimate(s).

Source: FAO.

Mining

('000 metric tons unless otherwise indicated)

	2009	2010	2011
Crude petroleum ('000 barrels)	14.7	12.4	12.0*
Natural gas (million cu m)	2,825	3,234	4,300*
Phosphate rock†	2,697	3,135	3,105
Potash salts‡	1,900	2,080	2,100*
Salt (unrefined, marketed)	357	421	430*
Gypsum	9.2	99.7	100.0*
Bromine (elemental)	128	185	202

* Estimate.

† Figures refer to beneficiated production; the phosphoric acid content (in '000 metric tons) was: 740 in 2009; 860 in 2010 (estimate); 850 in 2011 (estimate).

‡ Figures refer to K_2O content.

Source: US Geological Survey.

Industry

SELECTED PRODUCTS

('000 metric tons unless otherwise indicated)

	2009	2010	2011
Wine*	4.8	5.0	5.0
Sulphuric acid†	520	630	630
Cement	4,759	5,139	5,200
Electric energy (million kWh)	53,179	56,102	57,145

* FAO estimates.

† Sulphuric content; US Geological Survey estimates.

Sources: mainly FAO; US Geological Survey.

Finance

CURRENCY AND EXCHANGE RATES

Monetary Units

100 agorot (singular: agora) = 1 new sheqel (plural: sheqalim) or shekel (NIS).

Sterling, Dollar and Euro Equivalents (31 May 2013)

£1 sterling = NIS 5.603;
US $1 = NIS 3.683;
€1 = NIS 4.790;
NIS 100 = £17.85 = $27.15 = €20.88.

Average Exchange Rate (NIS per US $)

2010 3.7390
2011 3.5781
2012 3.8559

STATE BUDGET*

(NIS million)

Revenue and grants†	2008	2009‡	2010‡
Current receipts	215,233	225,235	234,195
Taxes and compulsory payments	184,842	173,890	184,435
Income and property taxes	95,715	84,800	85,100
Taxes on expenditure	89,127	89,090	99,335
Interest, royalties, etc.	5,090	5,668	5,154
Transfer from loans and capital account receipts	25,301	45,677	44,607
Receipts from loans and capital account	81,031	91,318	91,093
Collection of principal	6,879	5,479	5,231
Miscellaneous	1,471	244	112
Privatization	1,752	298	500
Domestic loans	82,283	104,920	102,950
Loans and grants from overseas	13,947	26,056	26,907
Less Transfer to current receipts	25,301	45,677	44,607
Total	296,265	316,553	325,288

Expenditure§	2008	2009‡	2010‡
Civilian consumption	52,118	59,194	63,200
Domestic	33,853	36,291	39,101
Defence consumption	56,528	48,934	53,769
Transfer and support payments	83,690	87,941	87,463
Investments and credit granting	14,568	18,547	17,418
Interest payments and credit subsidies	33,137	35,673	38,039
Miscellaneous	6,964	7,423	7,523
Reserves	—	4,811	5,143
Debt repayment (principal)	62,835	68,343	69,245
Less Revenue-dependent expenditure	13,576	14,313	16,513
Total	296,265	316,553	325,288

* Excluding Bank of Israel.

† Revenue includes grants received from abroad (NIS million): 10,037 in 2008; 8,640 in 2009 (forecast); 9,900 in 2010 (forecast).

‡ Forecasts.

§ Expenditure includes the central Government's credit issuance (NIS million): 1,947 in 2008; 3,488 in 2009 (forecast); 2,504 in 2010 (forecast).

2011 (forecasts): *Revenue:* Current receipts 247,117 (Income and property taxes 103,500, Taxes on expenditure 111,489, Interest, royalties, etc. 6,449, Transfer from loans and capital account receipts 25,679); Receipts from loans and capital account 101,069 (Collection of principal 6,375, Miscellaneous 222, Privatization 3,813, Domestic loans 99,629, Loans and grants from overseas 16,709, *Less* Transfer to current receipts 25,679); Total revenue 348,185 (incl. grants 8,709). *Expenditure:* Civilian consumption 67,383 (Domestic 42,447); Defence consumption 54,094; Transfer and support payments 96,943; Investments and credit granting 19,895; Interest payments and credit subsidies 36,838; Miscellaneous 8,428; Reserves 6,268; Debt repayment (principal) 76,989; *Less* Revenue-dependent expenditure 18,652; Total expenditure 348,185 (incl. government credit issuance 2,478).

2012 (forecasts): *Revenue:* Current receipts 258,805 (Income and property taxes 111,800, Taxes on expenditure 122,026, Interest, royalties, etc. 6,539, Transfer from loans and capital account receipts 18,440); Receipts from loans and capital account 107,111 (Collection of principal 6,059, Miscellaneous 222, Privatization 1,813, Domestic loans 99,786, Loans and grants from overseas 17,672, *Less* Transfer to current receipts 18,440); Total revenue 365,916 (incl. grants 8,672); *Expenditure:* Civilian consumption 70,292 (Domestic 44,008); Defence consumption 55,627; Transfer and support payments 101,283; Investments and credit granting 20,983; Interest payments and credit subsidies 38,577; Miscellaneous 9,097; Reserves 7,870; Debt repayment (principal) 81,259; *Less* Revenue-dependent expenditure 19,072; Total expenditure 365,916 (incl. government credit issuance 2,673).

Source: Ministry of Finance, Budget Division.

INTERNATIONAL RESERVES

(excluding gold, US $ million at 31 December)

	2010	2011	2012
IMF special drawing rights	1,323.4	1,269.5	1,276.7
Reserve position in IMF	319.0	552.6	591.0
Foreign exchange	69,265.0	73,052.0	74,040.0
Total	70,907.3	74,874.1	75,907.6

Source: IMF, *International Financial Statistics*.

MONEY SUPPLY

(NIS million at 31 December)

	2007	2008	2009
Currency outside banks	24,021	30,180	35,606
Demand deposits at deposit money banks	52,766	61,564	87,493
Total money (incl. others)	76,948	95,507	127,510

2010: Demand deposits at deposit money banks 88,144.

2011: Demand deposits at deposit money banks 88,978.

Source: IMF, *International Financial Statistics*.

COST OF LIVING

(Consumer Price Index, annual averages; base: 2000 = 100)

	2010	2011	2012
Food	138.6	143.4	144.4
All items (incl. others)	123.6	127.9	130.1

Source: ILO.

NATIONAL ACCOUNTS

(NIS million at current prices)

National Income and Product

	2010	2011	2012
Gross domestic product in market prices	813,938	871,827	928,348
Net income paid abroad	–19,064	–20,163	–29,124
Gross national income (GNI)	794,874	851,664	899,224
Less Consumption of fixed capital	96,134	101,448	111,162
Net national income	698,740	750,215	788,062

Expenditure on the Gross Domestic Product

	2010	2011	2012
Final consumption expenditure	675,612	722,092	760,283
Private	476,772	510,994	534,364
General government	198,840	211,098	225,919
Changes in inventories	–18,033	–9,520	1,271
Gross fixed capital formation	137,903	163,365	177,074
Total domestic expenditure	795,482	875,937	938,628
Exports of goods and services	302,758	325,499	347,442
Less Imports of goods and services	284,302	329,609	357,723
GDP in market prices	813,938	871,827	928,348

Gross Domestic Product by Economic Activity

	2010	2011	2012
Agriculture, hunting, forestry and fishing	14,460	14,714	14,864
Manufacturing, mining and quarrying	104,224	105,638	111,349
Electricity, gas and water supply	12,599	13,875	15,568
Construction	39,059	44,719	48,921
Wholesale, retail trade, repair of motor vehicles, motorcycles and personal and household goods; hotels and restaurants	74,952	79,234	83,430
Transport, storage and communications	49,571	53,460	54,215
Financial intermediation; real estate, renting and business activities	208,454	214,048	243,899
Public administration and community services*	126,133	134,690	143,634
Housing services	98,360	106,818	114,206
Other community, social and personal services	16,932	19,122	20,203
Sub-total	744,744	786,318	850,289
Less Imputed bank service charge	26,563	16,557	26,200
Net taxes on products	95,748	101,673	104,259
Statistical discrepancy	9	393	0
GDP in market prices	813,938	871,827	928,348

* Including non-profit institutions serving households.

BALANCE OF PAYMENTS

(US $ million)

	2010	2011	2012
Exports of goods	56,386.1	64,184.7	61,453.2
Imports of goods	–58,085.3	–72,026.3	–71,937.7
Balance on goods	–1,699.2	–7,841.6	–9,944.5
Exports of services	24,348.2	26,839.1	29,673.1
Imports of services	–17,829.7	–19,407.6	–20,512.7
Balance on goods and services	4,819.3	–410.1	–784.1
Primary income received	6,292.2	7,293.1	7,162.6
Primary income paid	–11,427.9	–12,233.4	–14,714.1
Balance on goods, services and primary income	–316.4	–5,350.4	–8,335.6
Secondary income received	9,480.9	9,932.9	9,317.6
Secondary income paid	–1,055.2	–1,200.6	–1,180.2
Current balance	8,109.3	3,381.9	–198.2
Capital account (net)	982.7	1,234.0	672.6
Direct investment assets	–9,088.1	–3,308.7	–3,177.3
Direct investment liabilities	5,509.6	11,080.5	10,414.1
Portfolio investment assets	–9,370.2	–3,075.1	–7,076.9
Portfolio investment liabilities	8,592.1	–7,686.4	–3,434.9
Financial derivatives and employee stock options (net)	29.7	–12.3	297.5
Other investment assets	1,469.0	–903.7	1,321.8
Other investment liabilities	3,691.2	1,349.7	–6,099.6
Net errors and omissions	1,756.9	869.1	7,194.1
Reserves and related items	11,682.2	2,929.0	–86.8

Source: IMF, *International Financial Statistics*.

External Trade

PRINCIPAL COMMODITIES

(US $ million)

Imports c.i.f.	2010	2011	2012
Food and live animals	3,457.8	4,356.3	4,242.0
Mineral fuels, lubricants, etc.	10,441.2	13,635.9	16,078.8
Petroleum, petroleum products, etc.	8,700.0	11,709.4	14,309.0
Chemicals and related products	6,843.9	7,961.4	8,344.3
Basic manufactures	14,477.6	18,041.5	15,179.8
Non-metallic mineral manufactures	9,126.9	11,589.0	9,113.7
Machinery and transport equipment	16,751.0	21,146.7	21,039.6
General industrial machinery, equipment and parts	1,974.9	2,403.2	2,722.1
Machinery for particular industries	968.9	2893.1	2,172.3
Office machines and automatic data-processing machines	1,844.5	1,937.5	1,842.8
Telecommunications and sound equipment	2,259.9	2,751.8	2,320.8
Other electrical machinery, apparatus, etc.	3,822.2	4,455.9	4,974.5
Road vehicles and parts	4,383.4	4,824.0	4,206.6
Miscellaneous manufactured articles	5,175.8	6,082.1	6,175.1
Total (incl. others)	59,199.4	73,536.2	73,121.4

Exports f.o.b.	2010	2011	2012
Food and live animals	1726.1	1925.8	1,944.7
Mineral fuels, lubricants and related products	2796.1	4046.6	3,257.9
Chemicals and related products	13,477.6	15,398.0	14,735.9
Organic chemicals	1,481.7	1,891.6	2,026.0
Medical and pharmaceutical products	6,475.2	7,083.1	6,598.9
Basic manufactures	19,568.2	24,105.4	20,755.7
Non-metallic mineral manufactures	16,696.3	20,991.0	17,884.4
Machinery and transport equipment	14,710.9	15,013.2	15,404.2
Telecommunications and sound equipment	3,424.2	3,202.2	3,002.4
Other electrical machinery, apparatus, etc.	5,395.3	5,691.1	6,085.9
Road vehicles and other transport equipment and parts	2,294.0	2,131.3	1,903.6
Miscellaneous manufactured articles	4,876.6	5,873.2	5,760.6
Professional, scientific and controlling instruments, etc.	2,354.8	2,849.7	2,806.7
Total (incl. others)	58,415.9	67,802.2	63,145.3

PRINCIPAL TRADING PARTNERS
(US $ million)*

Imports (excl. military goods) c.i.f.	2010	2011	2012
Belgium-Luxembourg	3,576.4	4,465.0	3,544.9
China, People's Republic	4,736.8	5,450.5	5,322.2
Cyprus	152.6	318.9	964.7
France	1,517.2	1,625.5	1,646.2
Germany	3,678.8	4,566.5	4,621.8
Hong Kong	1,398.6	1,856.2	1,563.9
India	1,845.6	2,154.5	1,936.2
Italy	2,425.8	3,055.9	2,779.5
Ireland	519.5	994.5	1,006.0
Japan	1,779.6	2,402.1	1,727.3
Korea, Republic	1,100.7	1,607.7	1,663.0
Netherlands	2,102.1	2,761.5	2,746.9
Russia	784.6	1,052.9	819.4
Singapore	702.8	794.5	773.4
Spain	975.4	1,183.4	1,201.9
Switzerland-Liechtenstein	3,220.2	3,970.2	4,055.4
Taiwan	709.1	761.5	782.1
Turkey	1,800.1	2,171.1	2,082.7
United Kingdom	2,246.4	2,776.7	2,598.1
USA	6,701.0	8,706.7	9,398.7
Total (incl. others)	59,199.4	73,536.2	73,121.4

Exports f.o.b.	2010	2011	2012
Belgium-Luxembourg	3,116.8	3,767.5	2,929.7
Brazil	934.8	892.6	1,138.7
Canada	749.5	807.1	767.7
China, People's Republic	2,046.8	2,718.3	2,758.2
Cyprus	755.6	937.4	905.1
France	1,266.5	1,542.0	1,450.9
Germany	1,701.4	1,950.0	1,638.9
Hong Kong	3,915.2	5,339.1	4,882.8
India	2,890.4	3,036.4	2,495.3
Italy	1,253.2	1,390.5	1,164.3
Japan	657.2	900.8	831.8
Korea, Republic	850.3	724.1	704.8
Malaysia	798.0	717.2	763.3
Netherlands	1,818.0	2,160.6	2,248.6
Russia	818.2	954.3	1,053.1

Exports f.o.b.—*continued*	2010	2011	2012
Spain	1,031.8	984.2	1,039.1
Switzerland-Liechtenstein	1,047.5	1,438.4	1,133.0
Taiwan	726.2	776.6	699.4
Turkey	1,310.7	1,855.7	1,421.4
United Kingdom	2,268.1	3,424.7	3,588.7
USA	18,488.2	19,432.4	17,561.7
Total (incl. others)	58,415.9	67,802.2	63,145.3

* Imports by country of purchase; exports by country of destination.

Transport

RAILWAYS
(traffic)

	2010	2011	2012
Passengers carried ('000 journeys)	35,877	35,930	40,511
Passenger-km (million)	1,986	1,927	2,133
Freight carried ('000 metric tons)	7,023	6,229	6,265
Freight ton-km (million)	1,062	1,099	1,011

ROAD TRAFFIC
(motor vehicles in use at 31 December)

	2010	2011	2012
Private passenger cars	2,053,248	2,164,385	2,246,053
Taxis	18,878	19,020	19,222
Minibuses	15,026	14,848	14,492
Buses and coaches	14,762	15,382	15,625
Lorries, vans and road tractors	347,152	347,980	341,859
Special service vehicles	4,118	4,318	4,433
Motorcycles and mopeds	113,007	117,254	119,295

SHIPPING

Flag Registered Fleet
(at 31 December)

	2010	2011	2012
Number of vessels	38	37	38
Displacement ('000 grt)	292.1	318.6	272.0

Source: Lloyd's List Intelligence (www.lloydslistintelligence.com).

International Sea-borne Freight Traffic
('000 metric tons)

	2010	2011	2012
Goods loaded	19,270	19,554	19,401
Goods unloaded*	24,142	25,392	26,947

* Including traffic between Israeli ports.

CIVIL AVIATION
(traffic on scheduled services)

	2007	2008	2009
Kilometres flown (million)	111	104	103
Passengers carried ('000)	4,663	4,627	4,606
Passenger-km (million)	18,180	17,404	17,251
Total ton-km (million)	3,099	2,683	2,362

Source: UN, *Statistical Yearbook*.

Passengers carried ('000): 5,085 in 2010; 5,313 in 2011 (Source: World Bank, World Development Indicators database).

Tourism

TOURIST ARRIVALS
('000)*

Country of residence	2009	2010	2011
Canada	59.5	70.2	64.4
France	254.0	274.1	269.5
Germany	139.8	171.5	171.0
Italy	116.5	150.2	113.3
Netherlands	44.5	53.4	58.7
Poland	53.8	69.5	60.4
Russia	231.4	318.7	353.4
Spain	49.0	59.7	51.0
Ukraine	46.5	55.3	106.8
United Kingdom	163.5	168.8	168.0
USA	538.0	605.1	581.0
Total (incl. others)	2,321.4	2,803.1	2,820.2

* Excluding arrivals of Israeli nationals residing abroad.

Tourism receipts (US $ million, excl. passenger transport): 3,741 in 2009; 4,768 in 2010; 4,849 in 2011 (provisional) (Source: World Tourism Organization).

Communications Media

	2010	2011	2012
Telephones ('000 main lines in use)	3,408	3,500	3,594
Mobile cellular telephones ('000 subscribers)	9,111	9,200	9,225
Broadband subscribers ('000)	1,762	1,879	1,711

Internet subscribers ('000): 1,714.0 in 2008.

Source: International Telecommunication Union.

Education

(2011/12 unless otherwise indicated, provisional figures)

	Schools	Pupils	Teachers
Hebrew			
Kindergarten	n.a.	394,635	15,930
Primary schools	2,153	670,631	58,050
Special needs	198	10,635	n.a.
Intermediate schools*	502	183,414	24,489
Secondary schools†	1,394	470,765	62,081
Vocational schools‡	112	23,485	n.a.
Teacher training colleges	56‡	33,893‡	5,359§
Arab			
Kindergarten	n.a.	95,520	3,380
Primary schools	562	251,621	20,001
Special needs	58	3,334	n.a.
Intermediate schools*	138	70,463	5,195
Secondary schools†	355	159,861	14,414
Vocational schools‡	24	4,376	n.a.
Teacher training colleges	4‡	2,827‡	491§

* 2007/08 provisional data.
† 2010/11 provisional data.
‡ 2008/09 provisional data.
§ 2006/07 data.

Pupil-teacher ratio (primary education, UNESCO estimate): 13.1 in 2008/09 (Source: UNESCO Institute for Statistics).

Adult literacy rate (UNESCO estimates): 96.9% (males 98.3%; females 95.6%) in 2003 (Source: UN Development Programme, *Human Development Report*).

Directory

The Constitution

There is no written constitution. In June 1950 the Knesset (parliament) voted to adopt a state constitution by evolution over an unspecified period. A number of laws, including the Law of Return (1950), the Nationality Law (1952), the State President (Tenure) Law (1952), the Education Law (1953) and the 'Yad-va-Shem' Memorial Law (1953), are considered as incorporated into the state Constitution. Other constitutional laws are: the Law and Administration Ordinance (1948), the Knesset Election Law (1951), the Law of Equal Rights for Women (1951), the Judges Act (1953), the National Service and National Insurance Acts (1953), and the Basic Law (the Knesset—1958). The provisions of constitutional legislation that affect the main organs of government are summarized below:

THE PRESIDENT

The President is elected by the Knesset for a maximum of one seven-year term.

Ten or more Knesset members may propose a candidate for the Presidency.

Voting will be by secret ballot.

The President may not leave the country without the consent of the Government.

The President may resign by submitting his resignation in writing to the Speaker.

The President may be relieved of his duties by the Knesset for misdemeanour.

The Knesset is entitled to decide by a two-thirds' majority that the President is too incapacitated owing to ill health to fulfil his duties permanently.

The Speaker of the Knesset will act for the President when the President leaves the country, or when he cannot perform his duties owing to ill health.

THE KNESSET

The Knesset is the parliament of the state. There are 120 members. It is elected by general, national, direct, equal, secret and proportional elections.

Every Israeli national of 18 years or over shall have the right to vote in elections to the Knesset unless a court has deprived him of that right by virtue of any law.

Every Israeli national of 21 and over shall have the right to be elected to the Knesset unless a court has deprived him of that right by virtue of any law.

The following shall not be candidates: the President of the State; the two Chief Rabbis; a judge (shofet) in office; a judge (dayan) of a religious court; the State Comptroller; the Chief of the General Staff of the Defence Army of Israel; rabbis and ministers of other religions in office; senior state employees and senior army officers of such ranks and in such functions as shall be determined by law.

The term of office of the Knesset shall be four years.

The elections to the Knesset shall take place on the third Tuesday of the month of Marcheshvan in the year in which the tenure of the outgoing Knesset ends.

Election day shall be a day of rest, but transport and other public services shall function normally.

Results of the elections shall be published within 14 days.

The Knesset shall elect from among its members a Chairman (Speaker) and Vice-Chairman.

The Knesset shall elect from among its members permanent committees, and may elect committees for specific matters.

The Knesset may appoint commissions of inquiry to investigate matters designated by the Knesset.

The Knesset shall hold two sessions a year; one of them shall open within four weeks after the Feast of the Tabernacles, the other within four weeks after Independence Day; the aggregate duration of the two sessions shall not be less than eight months.

The outgoing Knesset shall continue to hold office until the convening of the incoming Knesset.

The members of the Knesset shall receive a remuneration as provided by law.

THE GOVERNMENT

The Government shall tender its resignation to the President immediately after his election, but shall continue with its duties until the formation of a new government. After consultation with representatives of the parties in the Knesset, the President shall charge one of the members with the formation of a government. The Government shall be composed of a Prime Minister (elected on a party basis from 2003) and a number of ministers from among the Knesset members or from outside the Knesset. After it has been chosen, the Government shall appear before the Knesset and shall be considered as formed after having received a vote of confidence. Within seven days of receiving a vote of confidence, the Prime Minister and the other ministers shall swear allegiance to the State of Israel and its Laws and undertake to carry out the decisions of the Knesset.

The Government

HEAD OF STATE

President: SHIMON PERES (took office 15 July 2007).

THE CABINET

(September 2013)

A coalition of Likud, Israel Beytenu, Yesh Atid, Jewish Home and Hatnua.

Prime Minister, Minister of Foreign Affairs and Minister of Public Diplomacy and Diaspora Affairs: BINYAMIN NETANYAHU (Likud).

Minister for Senior Citizens: URI ORBACH (Jewish Home).

Minister of Strategic Affairs, Minister of Intelligence and Minister Responsible for International Relations: YUVAL STEINITZ (Likud).

Minister of Defence: MOSHE YA'ALON (Likud).

Minister of Interior: GIDEON SA'AR (Likud).

Minister of Finance: YAIR LAPID (Yesh Atid).

Minister of Health: YAEL GERMAN (Yesh Atid).

Minister of Home Front Defence and Minister of Communications: GILAD ERDAN (Likud).

Minister of Industry, Trade and Labour, Minister of Religious Services and Minister for Jerusalem and the Diaspora: NAFTALI BENNETT (Jewish Home).

Minister of Immigrant Absorption: SOFA LANDVER (Israel Beytenu).

Minister of Energy and Water Resources, Minister of Regional Co-operation and Minister for the Development of the Negev and Galilee: SILVAN SHALOM (Likud).

Minister of Welfare and Social Services: MEIR COHEN (Yesh Atid).

Minister of Public Security: YITZHAK AHARONOVITCH (Israel Beytenu).

Minister of Environmental Protection: AMIR PERETZ (Hatnua).

Minister of Justice: TZIPI LIVNI (Hatnua).

Minister of Housing and Construction: URI YEHUDA ARIEL (Jewish Home).

Minister of Transport, National Infrastructures and Road Safety: YISRAEL KATZ (Likud).

Minister of Agriculture and Rural Development: YAIR SHAMIR (Israel Beytenu).

Minister of Tourism: UZI LANDAU (Israel Beytenu).

Minister of Education: SHAI PIRON (Yesh Atid).

Minister of Science and Technology: YAAKOV PERRY (Yesh Atid).

Minister of Culture and Sport: LIMOR LIVNAT (Likud).

Note: The Prime Minister automatically assumes responsibility for any portfolio which becomes vacant, until a permanent or acting minister is appointed.

MINISTRIES

Office of the President: 3 Hanassi St, Jerusalem 92188; tel. 2-6707211; fax 2-5887225; e-mail president@president.gov.il; internet www.president.gov.il.

Office of the Prime Minister: POB 187, 3 Kaplan St, Kiryat Ben-Gurion, Jerusalem 91950; tel. 2-6705555; fax 2-5664838; e-mail pm_eng@pmo.gov.il; internet www.pmo.gov.il.

Ministry of Agriculture and Rural Development: POB 50200, Agricultural Centre, Beit Dagan 50250; tel. 3-9485555; fax 3-9485858; e-mail pniot@moag.gov.il; internet www.moag.gov.il.

Ministry of Communications: 23 Jaffa St, Jerusalem 91999; tel. 2-6706301; fax 2-6240029; e-mail dovrut@moc.gov.il; internet www.moc.gov.il.

Ministry of Culture and Sport: POB 49100, Kiryat Hamemshala, Hamizrachit, Bldg 3, Jerusalem 91490; tel. 2-5411110; e-mail ministerts@most.gov.il; internet www.mcs.gov.il.

Ministry of Defence: Kirya, Tel-Aviv 64734; tel. 3-6975540; fax 3-6976711; e-mail pniot@mod.gov.il; internet www.mod.gov.il.

Ministry for the Development of the Negev and Galilee: 8 Shaul Hamelech Blvd, Tel-Aviv 64733; tel. 3-6060700; fax 3-6958414; e-mail hilap@pmo.gov.il; internet www.vpmo.gov.il.

Ministry of Education: POB 292, 34 Shivtei Israel St, Jerusalem 91911; tel. 2-5602222; fax 2-5602223; e-mail info@education.gov.il; internet www.education.gov.il.

Ministry of Energy and Water Resources: POB 36148, 216 Yaffo St, Jerusalem 91360; tel. 2-5006780; fax 2-5006720; e-mail pniot@energy.gov.il; internet www.energy.gov.il.

Ministry of Environmental Protection: POB 34033, 5 Kanfei Nesharim St, Givat Shaul, Jerusalem 95464; tel. 2-6495802; fax 2-6495892; e-mail pniot@environment.gov.il; internet www.environment.gov.il.

Ministry of Finance: POB 13195, 1 Kaplan St, Kiryat Ben-Gurion, Jerusalem 91030; tel. 2-5317111; fax 2-5637891; e-mail webmaster@mof.gov.il; internet www.mof.gov.il.

Ministry of Foreign Affairs: 9 Yitzhak Rabin Blvd, Kiryat Ben-Gurion, Jerusalem 91950; tel. 2-5303111; fax 2-5303367; e-mail pniot@mfa.gov.il; internet www.mfa.gov.il.

Ministry of Health: POB 1176, 2 Ben-Tabai St, Jerusalem 91010; tel. 2-5081222; fax 2-6787982; e-mail pniot@moh.health.gov.il; internet www.health.gov.il.

Ministry of Home Front Defence: Jerusalem; tel. 3-6977155; fax 3-6976990.

Ministry of Housing and Construction: POB 18110, Kiryat Hamemshala (East), Jerusalem 91180; tel. 2-5847551; fax 2-5847530; e-mail sar@moch.gov.il; internet www.moch.gov.il.

Ministry of Immigrant Absorption: 6 Ester Hamalka St. Tel Aviv; tel. 3-5209127; fax 3-5209161; e-mail sar@moia.gov.il; internet www.moia.gov.il.

Ministry of Industry, Trade and Labour: 5 Bank of Israel St, Jerusalem 91009; tel. 2-6662252; fax 2-6662908; e-mail dover@moit.gov.il; internet www.moit.gov.il.

Ministry of Intelligence: Jerusalem; tel. 2-6705360; fax 2-6703377.

Ministry of Interior: POB 6158, Kiryat Ben-Gurion, Jerusalem 91061; tel. 2-6701400; fax 2-566376; e-mail meda@moin.gov.il; internet www.moin.gov.il.

Ministry of Jerusalem Affairs and the Diaspora: Jerusalem; tel. 2-6587100; fax 2-6587118; e-mail yaels@it.pmo.gov.il.

Ministry of Justice: POB 49029, 29 Salahadin St, Jerusalem 91010; tel. 2-6466533; fax 2-6287757; e-mail pniot@justice.gov.il; internet www.justice.gov.il.

Ministry of Public Security: POB 18182, Bldg 3, Kiryat Hamemshala (East), Jerusalem 91181; tel. 2-5309999; fax 2-5847872; e-mail sar@mops.gov.il; internet www.mops.gov.il.

Ministry of Regional Co-operation: Jerusalem.

Ministry of Religious Services: POB 13059, 7 Kanfei Nesharim St, Jerusalem 95464; tel. 2-5311385; fax 2-5311310; e-mail keren@dat.gov.il; internet www.dat.gov.il.

Ministry of Science and Technology: POB 49100, Kiryat Hamemshala, Hamizrachit, Bldg 3, Jerusalem 91490; tel. 2-5411101; fax 2-5811613; e-mail minister@most.gov.il; internet www.most.gov.il.

Ministry of Senior Citizens: Jerusalem.

Ministry of Social Affairs and Social Services: POB 915, 2 Kaplan St, Kiryat Ben-Gurion, Jerusalem 91008; tel. 2-6752523; fax 2-5666385; e-mail sar@molsa.gov.il; internet www.molsa.gov.il.

Ministry of Strategic Affairs: Jerusalem; tel. 2-6773750; fax 2-6517299.

Ministry of Tourism: POB 1018, 5 Bank of Israel St, Jerusalem 91009; tel. 2-6664331; fax 2-6514629; e-mail sarb@tourism.gov.il; internet www.tourism.gov.il.

Ministry of Transport, National Infrastructures and Road Safety: POB 867, Government Complex, 5 Bank of Israel St, Jerusalem 91008; tel. 2-6663333; fax 2-6663195; e-mail sar@mot.gov.il; internet www.mot.gov.il.

GOVERNMENT AGENCY

The Jewish Agency for Israel

POB 92, 48 King George St, Jerusalem 91000; tel. 2-6202222; fax 2-6202303; e-mail pniyottzibor@jafi.org; internet www.jewishagency.org.

f. 1929; reconstituted in 1971 as a partnership between the World Zionist Organization and the fund-raising bodies United Israel Appeal, Inc (USA) and Keren Hayesod.

Organization: The governing bodies are: the Assembly, which determines basic policy; the Board of Governors, which sets policy for the Agency between Assembly meetings; and the Executive, responsible for the day-to-day running of the Agency.

Chairman of Executive: NATAN SHARANSKY.

Chairman of Board of Governors: JAMES S. TISCH.

Director-General: ALAN HOFFMANN.

CEO and President of Jewish Agency International Development: MISHA GALPERIN.

Functions: According to the Agreement of 1971, the Jewish Agency undertakes the immigration and absorption of immigrants in Israel, including: absorption in agricultural settlement and immigrant housing; social welfare and health services in connection with immigrants; education, youth care and training; and neighbourhood rehabilitation through project renewal.

Legislature

Knesset

Kiryat Ben-Gurion, Jerusalem 91950; tel. 2-6753665; fax 2-6753566; e-mail mshenkar@knesset.gov.il; internet www.knesset.gov.il.

Speaker: YULI-YOEL EDELSTEIN.

General Election, 22 January 2013

Party	Valid votes cast	% of valid votes	Seats
Likud Israel Beytenu*	885,163	23.34	31
Yesh Atid	543,458	14.33	19
Israel Labour Party	432,118	11.39	15
Jewish Home	345,985	9.12	12
Shas	331,868	8.75	11
United Torah Judaism	195,892	5.16	7
Hatnua	189,167	4.99	6
Meretz–Yahad	172,403	4.55	6
United Arab List	138,450	3.65	4
Hadash	113,439	2.99	4
Balad	97,030	2.56	3
Kadima	78,974	2.08	2
Others	268,795	7.09	0
Total	3,792,742†	100.00	120

* Likud and Israel Beytenu contested the election on a joint list.
† Excluding 40,904 invalid votes.

Election Commission

Central Elections Committee: Knesset, Kiryat Ben-Gurion, Jerusalem 91950; tel. 2-6753407; e-mail doverd@knesset.gov.il; internet www.bchirot.gov.il; independent; Supreme Court elects a Justice as Chair; each parliamentary group nominates representatives to the Cttee in proportion to the group's level of representation in the Knesset; Chair. Justice ELYAKIM RUBENSTEIN; Dir-Gen. ORLY ADAS.

Political Organizations

Agudat Israel (Union of Israel): POB 513, Jerusalem; tel. 2-5385251; fax 2-5385145; f. 1912; mainly Ashkenazi ultra-Orthodox Jews; stands for introduction of laws and institutions based on Jewish religious law (the Torah); contested 2009 legislative elections as part of the United Torah Judaism list (with Degel Hatorah).

Arab Movement for Renewal (Tnua'a Aravit le'Hitkadshut—Ta'al): Jerusalem; tel. 2-6753333; fax 2-6753927; e-mail atibi@knesset.gov.il; f. 1996 following split from Balad; contested March 2006 and Feb. 2009 legislative elections on joint list with United Arab List; Leader Dr AHMAD TIBI.

Balad (National Democratic Assembly): POB 2248, Nazareth Industrial Zone, Nazareth 16000; tel. 4-6455070; fax 4-6463457; e-mail balad@zahav.net.il; f. 1999; united Arab party; Leader Dr JAMAL ZAHALKA.

Communist Party of Israel (Miflagah Kommonistit Yisraelit—Maki): POB 26205, 5 Hess St, Tel-Aviv 61261; tel. 3-6293944; fax 3-6297263; e-mail info@maki.org.il; internet www.maki.org.il; f. 1948; Jewish-Arab party descended from the Socialist Workers' Party of Palestine (f. 1919); renamed Communist Party of Palestine 1921, Jewish and Arab sections split 1945, reunited as Communist Party of Israel (Maki) 1948; further split 1965: pro-Soviet predominantly Arab anti-Zionist group formed New Communist Party of Israel (Rakah) 1965, while predominantly Jewish bloc retained name Maki; Rakah joined with other leftist orgs as Hadash 1977; name changed to Maki 1989, as the dominant component of Hadash (q.v.); Gen. Sec. MUHAMMAD NAFA'H.

Degel Hatorah (Flag of the Torah): 103 Rehov Beit Vegan, Jerusalem; tel. 2-6438106; fax 2-6418967; f. 1988 by Lithuanian Jews as breakaway faction from Agudat Israel; mainly Ashkenazi ultra-Orthodox (Haredi) Jews; contested 2009 legislative elections as part of the United Torah Judaism list (with Agudat Israel).

Hadash (Hachazit Hademokratit Leshalom Uleshivyon—Democratic Front for Peace and Equality): POB 26205, Tel-Aviv 61261; tel. 3-6293944; fax 3-6297263; e-mail info@hadash.org.il; internet hadash.org.il; f. 1977 by merger of the New Communist Party of Israel (Rakah) with other leftist groups; party list, the principal component of which is the Communist Party of Israel (q.v.); Jewish-Arab membership; aims for a socialist system in Israel and a lasting peace between Israel, Arab countries and the Palestinian Arab people; favours full implementation of UN Security Council Resolutions 242 and 338, Israeli withdrawal from all Arab territories occupied since 1967, formation of a Palestinian Arab state in the West Bank and Gaza Strip (with East Jerusalem as its capital), recognition of national rights of State of Israel and Palestinian people, democratic rights and defence of working-class interests, and demands an end to discrimination against Arab minority in Israel and against oriental Jewish communities; Chair. MUHAMMAD BARAKEH.

Hatnua (The Movement): Tel-Aviv; internet www.hatnua.org.il; f. 2012; centrist; supports revival of peace talks with the Palestinian (National) Authority based on a two-state solution, increase to the minimum wage, environmental sustainability, extension of national service to all citizens; Leader TZIPI LIVNI.

Israel Beytenu (Israel Is Our Home/Nash dom Izrail): 78 Yirmiyahu St, Jerusalem 94467; tel. 2-5012999; fax 2-5377188; e-mail gdv7191@hotmail.com; internet www.beytenu.org.il; f. 1999; right-wing immigrant party; joined Nat. Union in 2000, but left to contest March 2006 and Feb. 2009 legislative elections alone; contested 2013 elections on joint list with Likud; seeks resolution of the Israeli–Palestinian conflict through the exchange of territory and population with the Palestinians, incl. the transfer of Arab Israelis to territory under Palestinian control; membership largely drawn from fmr USSR; 18,000 mems (2006); Leader AVIGDOR LIEBERMAN.

Israel Labour Party (Mifleget HaAvoda HaYisraelit): POB 62033, Tel-Aviv 61620; tel. 3-6899444; fax 3-6899420; e-mail inter@havoda.org.il; internet www.havoda.org.il; f. 1968 as a merger of the three Labour groups, Mapai, Rafi and Achdut Ha'avoda; Am Ehad (One Nation) merged with Labour in 2004; a Zionist democratic socialist party; Chair. SHELLY YACHIMOVITCH; Sec.-Gen. YECHIEL BAR.

Jewish Home (HaBayit HaYehudi): Jerusalem; internet baityehudi.org.il; f. 2008 by merger of Nat. Religious Party (NRP; f. 1956), Moledet and Tekuma; however, Moledet and some Tekuma mems subsequently withdrew from new party; right-wing nationalist, Zionist; opposes further Israeli withdrawals from the West Bank and the creation of a Palestinian state; favours strengthening of the state and system of religious education; Leader NAFTALI BENNETT.

Kadima (Forward): Petach Tikva, Tel-Aviv; tel. 3-9788000; fax 3-9788020; e-mail dovrutkadima@gmail.com; internet www.kadima.org.il; f. 2005; liberal party formed as a breakaway faction from Likud by fmr party Chairman Ariel Sharon; aims to pursue a peace agreement with the Palestinians in accordance with the 'roadmap' peace plan, and to establish Israel's permanent borders, if necessary unilaterally; seeks to combat economic and social problems; Leader SHAUL MOFAZ.

Likud (Consolidation): 38 Rehov King George, Tel-Aviv 61231; tel. 3-5630666; fax 3-5282901; internet www.likud.org.il; f. Sept. 1973; fmrly a parliamentary bloc of Herut (f. 1948), the Liberal Party of Israel (f. 1961), Laam (For the Nation—f. 1976), Ahdut, Tami (f. 1981; joined Likud in June 1987) and an ind. faction led by Itzhak Modai (f. 1990), which formed the nucleus of a new Party for the Advancement of the Zionist Idea; Herut and the Liberal Party formally merged in Aug. 1988 to form the Likud-Nat. Liberal Movement; Israel B'Aliyah merged with Likud in 2003; contested Feb. 2009 legislative elections on joint list with Ahi (right-wing nationalist; Leader EFRAIM EITAM); contested 2013 elections on joint list with Israel Beytenu; aims: territorial integrity; absorption of newcomers; a social order based on freedom and justice, elimination of poverty and want; economic devt and environmental reforms to improve living standards; Chair. BINYAMIN NETANYAHU.

Meimad: POB 53139, 19 Yad Harutzim St, Jerusalem 91533; tel. 2-6725134; fax 2-6725051; f. 1988; moderate democratic Jewish party; ended alliance with Israel Labour Party and joined list with Green

Movement (HaTnuah Hayeruka—f. 2008) prior to Feb. 2009 legislative elections, at which it failed to achieve representation in the Knesset; Leader Rabbi MICHAEL MELCHIOR.

Meretz (Social Democratic Party of Israel): Beit Amot Mishpat, 8th Shaul Hamelech Blvd, Tel-Aviv 64733; tel. 3-6098998; fax 3-6961728; e-mail siatmeretz@knesset.gov.il; internet www.meretz.org.il; f. 2003 as Yahad (Together—Social Democratic Israel) from a merger of Meretz (f. 1992; an alliance of Ratz, Shinui and the United Workers' Party) and Shahar (f. 2002; a breakaway faction of the Israel Labour Party); name changed to above in 2005; formed joint list with New Movement (Hatnua Hahadasha) prior to Feb. 2009 legislative elections; Jewish-Arab social democratic party; stands for: civil rights; welfarism; Palestinian self-determination and a return to the 1967 borders, with minor adjustments; a divided Jerusalem, but no right of return for Palestinian refugees to Israel; separation of religion from the state; Chair. ZAHAVA GAL-ON.

Moledet (Homeland): 14 Yehuda Halevi St, Tel-Aviv; tel. 3-654580; e-mail moledet@moledet.org.il; internet www.m-moledet.org.il; f. 1988; right-wing nationalist party; aims include the expulsion ('transfer') of Palestinians living in the West Bank and Gaza Strip; united with Tehiya—Zionist Revival Movement in June 1994 as the Moledet—the Eretz Israel Faithful and the Tehiya; contested Feb. 2009 legislative elections as part of the Nat. Union; Chair. URI BANK.

National Union (Haichud Haleumi): e-mail info@leumi.org.il; f. 1999 as right-wing coalition comprising Herut, Moledet and Tekuma parties; contested March 2006 legislative elections on joint list with Nat. Religious Party, but stood alone (comprising Moledet, Hatikva, Eretz Yisrael Shelanu and fmr Tekuma mems) in Feb. 2009 elections; believes in a 'Greater Israel'; opposed to further withdrawals from the Occupied Territories; stated aim of joint list was the creation of an Israeli society based on the spiritual and social values of Judaism and the retention of an undivided Israel; Leader YAAKOV DOV KATZ.

Pensioners' Party (Gimla'ey Yisrael LaKneset—Gil) (Pensioners of Israel to the Knesset—Age): 100 Ha' Hashmonaim, Tel-Aviv; tel. 3-5611900; fax 3-5611909; e-mail info@gimlaim.org.il; internet www.gimlaim.org.il; stands for pensioners' rights; failed to achieve representation in the Knesset at 2013 legislative elections; Leader RAFI EITAN.

Shas (Sephardic Torah Guardians): POB 34263, Jerusalem 91341; tel. 3-579776; e-mail p@shass.org.il; internet shas.org.il; f. 1984 by splinter groups from Agudat Israel; ultra-Orthodox Sephardic party; Spiritual Leader Rabbi OVADIA YOSEF; Chair. ARYEH DER'I.

United Arab List (Reshima Aravit Me'uchedet—Ra'am): Jerusalem; tel. 9-7997088; fax 9-7996295; e-mail media.amc@gmail.com; internet www.a-m-c.org; f. 1996 by merger of the Arab Democratic Party and individuals from the Islamic Movement and Nat. Unity Front (left-wing Arab parties); supports establishment of a Palestinian state, with East Jerusalem as its capital, and equality for all Israeli citizens; contested March 2006 and Feb. 2009 legislative elections on joint list with Arab Movement for Renewal; Chair. AHMAD TIBI.

United Torah Judaism (Yahadut Hatorah): f. prior to 1992 election; electoral list of four minor ultra-Orthodox parties (Moria, Degel Hatorah, Poale Agudat Israel and Agudat Israel) established to overcome the increase in election threshold from 1% to 1.5% and to seek to counter the rising influence of the secular Russian vote; contested 2003 election composed of Degel Hatorah and Agudat Israel, into which constituent parties it split in early 2005; two parties reunited in late 2005 and contested March 2006 and Feb. 2009 legislative elections together; represents Ashkenazi ultra-Orthodox Jews and advocates the application of religious precepts in all areas of life and government; Chair., Parliamentary Group ISRAEL EICHLER.

Yesh Atid (There's a Future): Tel-Aviv; e-mail s_yeshatid@knesset.gov.il; internet en.yeshatid.org.il; f. 2012; proposes reduction in the size of the Cabinet, reform of the education system, expansion of mandatory national service to include all citizens, increase in housing provision; Founder and Leader YAIR LAPID.

Diplomatic Representation

EMBASSIES IN ISRAEL

Albania: 54/26 Pinkas St, Tel-Aviv 62261; tel. 3-5465866; fax 3-5444545; e-mail embassy.telaviv@mfa.gov.al; Ambassador BUJAR SKENDO.

Angola: 14 Simtat Beit Hashoeva St, Tel-Aviv; tel. 3-6912093; fax 3-6912094; e-mail embangi@zahav.net.il; internet www.angolaembassy.org.il; Ambassador JOSÉ JOÃO MANUEL.

Argentina: 85 Medinat Hayehudim St, 3rd Floor, Herzliya Pituach 46120; tel. 9-9702744; fax 9-9702748; e-mail embarg@netvision.net.il; Ambassador CARLOS FAUSTINO GARCÍA.

Australia: POB 29108, Discount Bank Tower, 28th Floor, 23 Yehuda Halevi St, Tel-Aviv 65136; tel. 3-6935000; fax 3-6935002; e-mail telaviv.embassy@dfat.org.au; internet www.israel.embassy.gov.au; Ambassador DEVANAND NOEL (DAVE) SHARMA.

Austria: Sason Hogi Tower, 12 Abba Hillel St, 4th Floor, Ramat-Gan 52506; tel. 3-6120924; fax 3-7510716; e-mail tel-aviv-ob@bmeia.gv.at; internet www.aussenministerium.at/telaviv; Ambassador Dr FRANZ JOSEF KUGLITSCH.

Belarus: POB 11129, 3 Reines St, Tel-Aviv 64381; tel. 3-5231069; fax 3-5231273; e-mail israel@mfa.gov.by; internet www.israel.mfa.gov.by; Chargé d'affaires a.i. SERGEY KOZLOV.

Belgium: 12 Abba Hillel St, 15th Floor, Ramat-Gan 52506; tel. 3-6138130; fax 3-6138160; e-mail telaviv@diplobel.fed.be; internet www.diplomatie.be/telaviv; Ambassador JOHN CORNET D'ELZIUS.

Bosnia and Herzegovina: Yachin Bldg, 10th Floor, 2 Kaplan St, Tel-Aviv; tel. 3-6124499; fax 3-6124488; e-mail embtelaviv@bezeqint.net; Ambassador BRANKO KESIC.

Brazil: 23 Yehuda Halevi St, 30th Floor, Tel-Aviv 65136; tel. 3-7971500; fax 3-6916060; e-mail brasemb.telaviv@itamaraty.gov.br; internet telaviv.itamaraty.gov.br; Ambassador MARIA ELISA BERENGUER.

Bulgaria: 21 Leonardo da Vinci St, Tel-Aviv 64733; tel. 3-6961379; fax 3-6961430; e-mail embassy.telaviv@mfa.bg; internet www.mfa.bg/en/118; Ambassador DIMITAR MIHAILOV.

Cameroon: 28 Moshe Sharet St, Ramat-Gan 52425; tel. 3-5298401; fax 3-6370583; e-mail activ50@yahoo.fr; Ambassador HENRI ETOUNDI ESSOMBA.

Canada: POB 9442, 3/5 Nirim St, Tel-Aviv 67060; tel. 3-6363300; fax 3-6363380; e-mail taviv@international.gc.ca; internet international.gc.ca/missions/israel; Ambassador PAUL HUNT.

Chile: 34 Habarzel St, Bldg B, Floor 1, Ramat Hahayal, Tel-Aviv 69710; tel. 3-5102751; fax 3-5100102; e-mail echileil@inter.net.il; internet chileabroad.gov.cl/israel; Ambassador JORGE MONTERO FIGUEROA.

China, People's Republic: POB 6067, 222 Ben Yehuda St, Tel-Aviv 61060; tel. 3-5442638; fax 3-5467251; e-mail chinaemb_il@mfa.gov.cn; internet il.china-embassy.org; Ambassador GAO YANPING.

Colombia: Hogi Sason Bldg, 8th Floor, Abba Hillel St, Ramat-Gan 12; tel. 3-6953384; fax 3-6957847; e-mail emcolis@netvision.net.il; Ambassador Dr FERNANDO ALZATE DONOSO.

Congo, Democratic Republic: 1 Rachel St, 2nd Floor, Tel-Aviv 64584; tel. 3-5248306; fax 3-5292623; e-mail ambardc_il@yahoo.fr; Chargé d'affaires a.i. KIMBOKO MA MAKENGO.

Congo, Republic: POB 12504, 9 Maskit St, Herzliya Pituach 46120; tel. 9-9577130; fax 9-9577216; e-mail guy_itoua@yahoo.fr; Chargé d'affaires a.i. JEAN MARIE NGAKALA.

Costa Rica: Paz Tower, 5-7 Shoham St, 6th Floor, Ramat-Gan 52521; tel. 3-6135061; fax 3-6134779; e-mail emcri@netvision.net.il; Ambassador RODRIGO X. CARRERAS.

Côte d'Ivoire: South Africa Bldg, 12 Menachim Begin St, Ramat-Gan 52521; tel. 3-6126677; fax 3-6126688; e-mail ambacita@netvision.net.il; Ambassador JEAN-BAPTISTE GOMIS.

Croatia: 2 Weizman St, Migdal Amot, Tel-Aviv 64239; tel. 3-6403000; fax 3-6438503; e-mail croemb.israel@mvep.hr; Ambassador PJER ŠIMUNOVIĆ.

Cyprus: Top Tower, 14th Floor, Dizengoff Centre, 50 Dizengoff St, Tel-Aviv 64322; tel. 3-5250212; fax 3-6290535; e-mail ambassador@cyprusembassytelaviv.com; internet www.mfa.gov.cy/embassytelaviv; Ambassador DIMITRIS HATZIARGYROU.

Czech Republic: POB 16361, 23 Zeitlin St, Tel-Aviv; tel. 3-6918282; fax 3-6918286; e-mail telaviv@embassy.mzv.cz; internet www.mzv.cz/telaviv; Ambassador TOMÁŠ POJAR.

Denmark: POB 21080, Museum Tower, 11th Floor, 4 Berkowitz St, Tel-Aviv 61210; tel. 3-6085850; fax 3-6085851; e-mail tlvamb@um.dk; internet www.ambtelaviv.um.dk; Ambassador JESPER VAHR.

Dominican Republic: Beit Ackerstein, 3rd Floor, 103 Medinat Hayehudim St, Herzliya Pitauch 46766; tel. 9-9515529; fax 9-9515528; e-mail embajdom@netvision.net.il; Ambassador ALEXANDER DE LA ROSA.

Ecuador: POB 34002, Asia House, 5th Floor, 4 Weizman St, Tel-Aviv 64239; tel. 3-6958764; fax 3-6913604; e-mail eecuisrael@mmrree.gov.ec; Ambassador GUILLERMO BASSANTE RAMÍREZ.

Egypt: 54 Basel St, Tel-Aviv 62744; tel. 3-5464151; fax 3-5441615; e-mail egypem.ta@zahav.net.il; internet www.mfa.gov.eg/english/embassies/Egyptian_Embassy_TelAviv/Pages/default.aspx; Ambassador ATEF SALEM EL-AHL.

El Salvador: 6 Hamada St, 4th Floor, Herzliya Pituach 46733; tel. 9-9556237; fax 9-9556603; e-mail embassy@el-salvador.org.il; internet www.el-salvador.org.il; Ambassador SUZANA GUN DE HASENSON.

Eritrea: 1 Twin Towers, 33 Jabotinsky St, 11th Floor, Ramat-Gan 52511; tel. 3-6120039; fax 3-5750133; Ambassador TESFAMARIAM TEKESTE.

Estonia: POB 7166, 24th Floor, Menachem Begin Rd 125, 44 Kaplan St, HaYovel Tower, Tel-Aviv 61071; tel. 3-7103910; fax 3-7103919; e-mail embassy.telaviv@mfa.ee; internet www.telaviv.vm.ee; Ambassador MALLE TALVET-MUSTONEN.

Ethiopia: Bldg B, Floor 8B, 48 Darech Menachem Begin St, Tel-Aviv 66184; tel. 3-6397831; fax 3-6397837; e-mail info@ethioemb.org.il; internet www.ethioemb.org.il; Ambassador HELAWE YOSEF.

Finland: POB 39666, Canion Ramat Aviv, 9th Floor, 40 Einstein St, Tel-Aviv 61396; tel. 3-7456600; fax 3-7440314; e-mail sanomat.tel@formin.fi; internet www.finland.org.il; Ambassador LEENA-KAISA MIKKOLA.

France: 112 Tayelet Herbert Samuel, Tel-Aviv 63572; tel. 3-5208300; fax 3-5208340; e-mail diplomatie@ambafrance-il.org; internet www.ambafrance-il.org; Ambassador CHRISTOPHE BIGOT.

Georgia: 3 Daniel Frisch St, Tel-Aviv 64731; tel. 3-6093207; fax 3-6093205; e-mail israel.emb@mfa.gov.ge; internet israel.mfa.gov.ge; Ambassador ARCHIL KEKELIA.

Germany: POB 16038, 3 Daniel Frisch St, 19th Floor, Tel-Aviv 64731; tel. 3-6931313; fax 3-6969217; e-mail info@tel-aviv.diplo.de; internet www.tel-aviv.diplo.de; Ambassador ANDREAS MICHAELIS.

Ghana: 12 Abba Hillel St, 7th Floor, Ramat-Gan 52506; tel. 3-5766000; fax 3-7520827; e-mail chancery@ghanaemb.co.il; internet www.ghanaembassy.co.il; Ambassador ERNEST SOWATEY LOMOTEY.

Greece: POB 64731, 3 Daniel Frisch St, Tel-Aviv; tel. 3-6953060; fax 3-6951329; e-mail gremb.tlv@mfa.gr; internet www.mfa.gr/telaviv; Ambassador SPYRIDON LAMPRIDIS.

Guatemala: Beit Ackerstein, 4th Floor, 103 Medinat Hayehudim St, Herzliya Pituach 46766; tel. 9-9568707; fax 9-9518506; e-mail embguate@netvision.net.il; Ambassador ALFREDO VASQUEZ RIVERA.

Holy See: 1 Netiv Hamazalot, Old Jaffa 68037; tel. 2-6835658; fax 2-6835659; e-mail vatge@netvision.net.il; Apostolic Nuncio Most Rev. GIUSEPPE LAZZAROTTO (Titular Archbishop of Numana).

Honduras: Aharon Karon St, 3 Rishon le Zion 75262; tel. 3-9642092; fax 9-9577457; e-mail honduras@netvision.net.il; Ambassador JOSÉ ISAIAS BARAHONA HERRERA.

Hungary: POB 21095, 18 Pinkas St, Tel-Aviv 62661; tel. 3-5466985; fax 3-5467018; e-mail mission.tlv@kum.hu; internet www.mfa.gov.hu/emb/telaviv; Ambassador ZOLTÁN SZENTGYÖRGYI.

India: POB 3368, 140 Hayarkon St, Tel-Aviv 61033; tel. 3-5291999; fax 3-5291953; e-mail indemtel@indembassy.co.il; internet www.indembassy.co.il; Ambassador JAIDEEP SARKAR.

Ireland: The Tower, 17th Floor, 3 Daniel Frisch St, Tel-Aviv 64731; tel. 3-6964166; fax 3-6964160; e-mail telavivembassy@dfa.ie; internet www.embassyofireland.co.il; Ambassador BREIFNE O'REILLY.

Italy: Trade Tower, 25 Hamered St, Tel-Aviv 68125; tel. 3-5104004; fax 3-5100235; e-mail info.telaviv@esteri.it; internet www.ambtelaviv.esteri.it; Ambassador FRANCESCO MARIA TALÒ.

Japan: Museum Tower, 19th and 20th Floors, 4 Berkowitz St, Tel-Aviv 64238; tel. 3-6957293; fax 3-6910516; e-mail info@tl.mofa.go.jp; internet www.israel.emb-japan.go.jp; Ambassador HIDEO SATO.

Jordan: 14 Abba Hillel, Ramat-Gan 52506; tel. 3-7517722; fax 3-7517712; Ambassador WALID OBAIDAT.

Kazakhstan: 52A Hayarkon St, Tel-Aviv 63432; tel. 3-5163411; fax 3-5163437; e-mail tel-aviv@mfa.kz; internet www.kazakhemb.org.il; Ambassador BOLAT NURGALIYEV.

Kenya: 15 Aba Hillel Silver St, Ramat-Gan 52136; tel. 3-5754633; fax 3-5754788; e-mail kenya7@netvision.net; Ambassador Lt-Gen. AUGUSTIONO NJOROGE.

Korea, Republic: 4 Hasadna'ot St, 3rd Floor, Herzliya Pituach 46278; tel. 9-9510318; fax 9-9569853; e-mail israel@mofat.go.kr; internet isr.mofat.go.kr; Ambassador KIM IL-SOO.

Latvia: Amot Investments Tower, 15th Floor, 2 Weizman St, Tel-Aviv 64239; tel. 3-7775800; fax 3-6953101; e-mail embassy.israel@mfa.gov.lv; internet www.mfa.gov.lv/en/israel/; Ambassador VILCĀNS ANDRIS.

Lithuania: Amot Mishpat Bldg, 8 Shaul Ha Meleh, Tel-Aviv 64733; tel. 3-6958685; fax 3-6958691; e-mail amb.il@urm.lt; internet il.mfa.lt; Ambassador DARIUS DEGUTIS.

Macedonia, former Yugoslav republic: Paz Tower, 9th Floor, 5 Shoham St, Ramat-Gan 52136; tel. 3-7154900; fax 3-6124789; e-mail telaviv@mfa.gov.mk; internet www.missions.gov.mk/telaviv; Ambassador PETAR JOVANOVSKI.

Mexico: Trade Tower, 5th Floor, 25 Hamered St, Tel-Aviv 68125; tel. 3-5163938; fax 3-5163711; e-mail communication1@embamex.org.il; internet www.sre.gob.mx/israel; Ambassador FEDERICO SALAS.

Moldova: 38 Rembrandt St, Tel-Aviv 64045; tel. 3-5231000; fax 3-5233000; e-mail moldova@barak.net.il; internet www.israel.mfa.md; Chargé d'affaires a.i. ANATOL VANGHELI.

Myanmar: Textile Centre, 12th Floor, 2 Kaufman St, Tel-Aviv 68012; tel. 3-5170760; fax 3-5163512; e-mail myanmar@zahav.net.il; internet www.metelaviv.co.il; Ambassador MYO AYE.

Nepal: Textile Centre, 7th Floor, 2 Kaufman St, Tel-Aviv 68012; tel. 3-5100111; fax 3-5167965; e-mail nepal.embassy@012.net.il; internet www.nepalembassy-israel.org; Ambassador PRAHLAD KUMAR PRASAI.

Netherlands: Beit Oz, 13th Floor, 14 Abba Hillel St, Ramat-Gan 52506; tel. 3-7540777; fax 3-7540751; e-mail nlgovtel@012.net.il; internet www.netherlands-embassy.co.il; Ambassador CASPAR VELDKAMP.

Nigeria: POB 3339, 34 Gordon St, Tel-Aviv 61030; tel. 3-5222144; fax 3-5248991; e-mail support@nigerianembassy.co.il; internet www.nigerianembassy.co.il; Ambassador DAVID OLADIPO OBASA.

Norway: POB 17575, Canion Ramat Aviv, 13th Floor, 40 Einstein St, Tel-Aviv 69101; tel. 3-7441490; fax 3-7441498; e-mail emb.telaviv@mfa.no; internet www.norway.org.il; Ambassador SVEIN SEVJE.

Panama: 10/3 Hei Be'Iyar St, Kikar Hamedina, Tel-Aviv 62998; tel. 3-6956711; fax 3-6910045; Ambassador HECTOR APARICIO.

Peru: 60 Medinat Hayehudim St, Entrance B, 2nd Floor, Herzliya Pituach 46766; tel. 9-9578835; fax 9-9568495; e-mail emperu@012.net.il; Ambassador JOSÉ LUIS SALINAS MONTES.

Philippines: 18 Bnei Dan St, Tel-Aviv 62260; tel. 3-6010500; fax 3-6041038; e-mail filembis@netvision.net.il; internet www.philippine-embassy.org.il; Ambassador GENEROSO DE GUZMAN CALONGE.

Poland: 16 Soutine St, Tel-Aviv 64684; tel. 3-7253111; fax 3-5237806; e-mail telaviv.amb.sekretariat@msz.gov.pl; internet www.telawiw.msz.gov.pl; Ambassador JACEK CHODOROWICZ.

Portugal: 3 Daniel Frisch St, 12th Floor, Tel-Aviv 64731; tel. 3-6956373; fax 3-6956366; e-mail eptel@012.net.il; Ambassador MIGUEL DE ALMEIDA E SOUSA.

Romania: 24 Adam Hacohen St, Tel-Aviv 64585; tel. 3-5229472; fax 3-5247379; e-mail office_romania@bezeqint.net; internet telaviv.mae.ro; Ambassador EDWARD IOSIPER.

Russia: 120 Hayarkon St, Tel-Aviv 63573; tel. 3-5290691; fax 3-5101093; e-mail consul@russianembassy.org.il; internet russianembassy.org.il; Ambassador SERGEY YA. YAKOVLEV.

Serbia: 10 Bodenheimer St, Tel-Aviv 62008; tel. 3-6045535; fax 3-6049456; e-mail srbambil@netvision.net.il; internet serbiaembassy-il.org; Ambassador ZORAN BASARABA.

Slovakia: POB 6459, 37 Jabotinsky St, Tel-Aviv 62287; tel. 3-5449119; fax 3-5449144; e-mail slovemb1@barak.net.il; Ambassador RADOVAN JAVORČIK.

Slovenia: POB 23245, Top Tower, 19th Floor, 50 Dizengoff St, Tel-Aviv 64332; tel. 3-6293563; fax 3-5282214; e-mail vta@gov.si; internet telaviv.veleposlanistvo.si; Ambassador ALENKA SUHADOLNIK.

South Africa: POB 7138, Sason Hogi Tower, 17th Floor, 12 Abba Hilel Silver St, Ramat-Gan 52520; tel. 3-5252566; fax 3-5253230; e-mail info@saemb.org.il; internet www.safis.co.il; Ambassador SISA NGOMBANE.

Spain: Dubnov Tower, 18th Floor, 3 Daniel Frisch St, Tel-Aviv 64731; tel. 3-6958875; fax 3-6965217; e-mail emb.telaviv@maec.es; Ambassador FERNANDO CARDERERA SOLER.

Sri Lanka: 4 Jean Jaurès St, Tel-Aviv 63412; tel. 3-5277635; fax 3-5277634; e-mail srilanka@013.net; Ambassador SARATH DEVESENA WIJESINGHE.

Sweden: Asia House, 4 Weizman St, Tel-Aviv 64239; tel. 3-7180000; fax 3-7180005; e-mail ambassaden.tel-aviv@ gov.se; internet www.swedenabroad.com/telaviv; Ambassador CARL MAGNUS NESSER.

Switzerland: POB 6068, 228 Hayarkon St, Tel-Aviv 6106001; tel. 3-5464455; fax 3-5464408; e-mail tel.vertretung@eda.admin.ch; internet www.eda.admin.ch/telaviv; Ambassador ANDREAS BAUM.

Thailand: Mercazim Bldg 2001, 1 Abba Eban Blvd, Herzliya Pituach 46120; tel. 9-9548412; fax 9-9548417; e-mail thaisr@netvision.co.il; internet www.thaiembassy.org/telaviv; Ambassador JURK BOON-LONG.

Turkey: 202 Hayarkon St, Tel-Aviv 63405; tel. 3-35241101; fax 3-5241390; e-mail turkemb.telaviv@mfa.gov.tr; relations downgraded since Sept. 2011; Chargé d'affaires a.i. DOĞAN FERHAT IŞIK.

Ukraine: 50 Yirmiyahu St, Tel-Aviv 62594; tel. 3-6040242; fax 3-6042512; e-mail emb_il@mfa.gov.ua; internet www.mfa.gov.ua/israel; Ambassador HENNADII NADOLENKO.

United Kingdom: 192 Hayarkon St, Tel-Aviv 63405; tel. 3-7251222; fax 3-5278574; e-mail webmaster.telaviv@fco.gov.uk; internet ukinisrael.fco.gov.uk; Ambassador MATTHEW GOULD.

USA: 71 Hayarkon St, Tel-Aviv 63903; tel. 3-5197575; fax 3-5108093; e-mail nivtelaviv@state.gov; internet israel.usembassy.gov; Ambassador DANIEL B. SHAPIRO.

Uruguay: G.R.A.P. Bldg, 1st Floor, 4 Shenkar St, Industrial Zone, Herzliya Pituach 46725; tel. 9-9569611; fax 9-9515881; e-mail secretaria@emburuguay.co.il; Ambassador BERNARDO GREIVER.

Uzbekistan: 31 Moshe Sharet St, Ramat-Gan 52413; tel. 3-6722371; fax 3-6722621; e-mail admindep@uzbembassy.org.il; internet www.uzbembassy.org.il; Ambassador OYBEK I. ESHONOV.

Viet Nam: Asia Bldg, 4th Floor, 4 Weizman St, Tel-Aviv; tel. 3-6966304; fax 3-6966243; e-mail vnembassy.il@mofa.gov.vn; internet www.vietnamembassy-israel.org; Ambassador TA DUY CHINH.

Judicial System

The law of Israel is composed of the enactments of the Knesset and, to a lesser extent, of the acts, orders-in-council and ordinances that remain from the period of the British Mandate in Palestine (1922–48). The pre-1948 law has largely been replaced, amended or reorganized, in the interests of codification, by Israeli legislation. This legislation generally follows a very similar pattern to that operating in England and the USA. However, there is no jury system.

The Supreme Court: Sha'arei Mishpat St, Kiryat David Ben-Gurion, Jerusalem 91950; tel. 2-6759666; fax 2-6759648; e-mail marcia@supreme.court.gov.il; internet www.court.gov.il; This is the highest judicial authority in the state. It has jurisdiction as an Appellate Court over appeals from the District Courts in all matters, both civil and criminal (sitting as a Court of Civil Appeal or as a Court of Criminal Appeal). In addition, it is a Court of First Instance (sitting as the High Court of Justice) in actions against governmental authorities, and in matters in which it considers it necessary to grant relief in the interests of justice and which are not within the jurisdiction of any other court or tribunal. The High Court's exclusive power to issue orders in the nature of *habeas corpus, mandamus*, prohibition and *certiorari* enables the court to review the legality of, and redress grievances against, acts of administrative authorities of all kinds; Pres. ASHER D. GRUNIS.

District Courts: There are five District Courts (Jerusalem, Tel-Aviv, Haifa, Beersheba, Nazareth). They have residual jurisdiction as Courts of First Instance over all civil and criminal matters not within the jurisdiction of a Magistrates' Court (e.g. civil claims exceeding NIS 1m.), all matters not within the exclusive jurisdiction of any other tribunal, and matters within the concurrent jurisdiction of any other tribunal so long as such tribunal does not deal with them. In addition, the District Courts have appellate jurisdiction over appeals from judgments and decisions of Magistrates' Courts and judgments of Municipal Courts and various administrative tribunals.

Magistrates' Courts: There are 29 Magistrates' Courts, having criminal jurisdiction to try contraventions, misdemeanours and certain felonies, and civil jurisdiction to try actions concerning possession or use of immovable property, or the partition thereof, whatever may be the value of the subject matter of the action, and other civil claims not exceeding NIS 1m.

Labour Courts: Established in 1969. Regional Labour Courts in Jerusalem, Tel-Aviv, Haifa, Beersheba and Nazareth, composed of judges and representatives of the public; a National Labour Court in Jerusalem; the Courts have jurisdiction over all matters arising out of the relationship between employer and employee or parties to a collective labour agreement, and matters concerning the National Insurance Law and the Labour Law and Rules.

Religious Courts: The Religious Courts are the courts of the recognized religious communities. They have jurisdiction over certain defined matters of personal status concerning members of their respective communities. Where any action of personal status involves persons of different religious communities, the President of the Supreme Court decides which Court will decide the matter. Whenever a question arises as to whether or not a case is one of personal status within the exclusive jurisdiction of a Religious Court, the matter must be referred to a Special Tribunal composed of two Justices of the Supreme Court and the President of the highest court of the religious community concerned in Israel. The judgments of the Religious Courts are executed by the process and offices of the Civil Courts. Neither these Courts nor the Civil Courts have jurisdiction to dissolve the marriage of a foreign subject; Jewish Rabbinical Courts have exclusive jurisdiction over matters of marriage and divorce of Jews in Israel who are Israeli citizens or residents. In all other matters of personal status they have concurrent jurisdiction with the District Courts; Muslim Religious Courts have exclusive jurisdiction over matters of marriage and divorce of Muslims who are not foreigners, or who are foreigners subject by their national law to the jurisdiction of Muslim Religious Courts in such matters. In all other matters of personal status they have concurrent jurisdiction with the District Courts; Christian Religious Courts have exclusive jurisdiction over matters of marriage and divorce of members of their communities who are not foreigners. In all other matters of personal status they have concurrent jurisdiction with the District Courts; Druze Courts, established in 1963, have exclusive jurisdiction over matters of marriage and divorce of Druze in Israel, who are Israeli citizens or residents, and concurrent jurisdiction with the District Courts over all other matters of personal status of Druze.

Attorney-General: YEHUDA WEINSTEIN.

Religion

JUDAISM

Judaism, the religion of the Jews, is the faith of the majority of Israel's inhabitants. On 31 December 2011 Judaism's adherents totalled 5,907,500, equivalent to 75.4% of the country's population. Its basis is a belief in an ethical monotheism.

There are two main Jewish communities: the Ashkenazim and the Sephardim. The former are the Jews from Eastern, Central or Northern Europe, while the latter originate from the Balkan countries, North Africa and the Middle East.

There is also a community of Ethiopian Jews, the majority of whom have been airlifted to Israel from Ethiopia at various times since the fall of Emperor Haile Selassie in 1974.

The supreme religious authority is vested in the Chief Rabbinate, which consists of the Ashkenazi and Sephardi Chief Rabbis and the Supreme Rabbinical Council. It makes decisions on interpretation of the Jewish law, and supervises the Rabbinical Courts. There are eight regional Rabbinical Courts, and a Rabbinical Court of Appeal presided over by the two Chief Rabbis.

According to the Rabbinical Courts Jurisdiction Law of 1953, marriage and divorce among Jews in Israel are exclusively within the jurisdiction of the Rabbinical Courts. Provided that all the parties concerned agree, other matters of personal status can also be decided by the Rabbinical Courts.

There are over 170 Religious Councils, which maintain religious services and supply religious needs, and about 400 religious committees with similar functions in smaller settlements. Their expenses are borne jointly by the state and the local authorities. The Religious Councils are under the administrative control of the Ministry of Religious Services. In all matters of religion, the Religious Councils are subject to the authority of the Chief Rabbinate. There are 365 officially appointed rabbis. The total number of synagogues is about 7,000, most of which are organized within the framework of the Union of Israel Synagogues.

Head of the Ashkenazi Community: The Chief Rabbi YONA METZGER.

Head of the Sephardic Community: The Chief Rabbi SHLOMO AMAR, Jerusalem; tel. 2-5313131.

Two Jewish sects still loyal to their distinctive customs are:

The Karaites: a sect which recognizes only the Jewish written law and not the oral law of the Mishna and Talmud. The community of about 12,000, many of whom live in or near Ramla, has been augmented by immigration from Egypt.

The Samaritans: an ancient sect mentioned in 2 Kings xvii, 24. They recognize only the Torah. The community in Israel numbers about 500; about one-half of this number live in Holon, where a Samaritan synagogue has been built, and the remainder, including the High Priest, live in Nablus, near Mt Gerazim, which is sacred to the Samaritans.

ISLAM

The Muslims in Israel belong principally to the Sunni sect of Islam, and are divided among the four rites: the Shafe'i, the Hanbali, the Hanafi and the Maliki. Before June 1967 they numbered approximately 175,000; in 1971 some 343,900. On 31 December 2011 the total Muslim population of Israel was 1,354,300, equivalent to 17.3% of the country's population.

Mufti of Jerusalem: POB 17412, Jerusalem; tel. 2-283528; Sheikh MUHAMMAD AHMAD HUSSEIN (also Chair. Supreme Muslim Council for Jerusalem); appointed by the Palestinian (National) Authority (PA).

There was also a total of 129,800 Druzes in Israel at 31 December 2011. The official spiritual leader of the Druze community in Israel is Sheikh MUWAFAK TARIF, but his leadership is not widely recognized.

CHRISTIANITY

The total Christian population of Israel (including East Jerusalem) at 31 December 2011 was 155,100.

United Christian Council in Israel: POB 116, Jerusalem 91000; tel. and fax 2-6259012; e-mail ucci@ucci.net; internet www.ucci.net; f. 1956; member of World Evangelical Alliance; over 30 mems (evangelical churches and social and educational insts); Chair. Rev. CHARLES KOPP.

The Roman Catholic Church

Armenian Rite

The Armenian Catholic Patriarch of Cilicia is resident in Beirut, Lebanon.

Patriarchal Exarchate of Jerusalem and Amman: POB 19546, 36 Via Dolorosa, Jerusalem 91190; tel. 2-6284262; fax 2-6272123; e-mail acpejerusalem@yahoo.com; f. 1885; Exarch Patriarchal Mgr RAPHAEL FRANÇOIS MINASSIAN.

Chaldean Rite

The Chaldean Patriarch of Babylon is resident in Baghdad, Iraq.

Patriarchal Exarchate of Jerusalem: Chaldean Patriarchal Vicariate, POB 20108, 7 Chaldean St, Saad and Said Quarter, Jerusalem 91200; tel. 2-6844519; fax 2-6274614; e-mail kolin-p@zahav.net.il; Exarch Patriarchal Mgr MICHEL KASSARJI.

Latin Rite

The Patriarchate of Jerusalem covers Palestine, Jordan and Cyprus.

Bishops' Conference: Conférence des Evêques Latins dans les Régions Arabes, Notre Dame of Jerusalem Center, POB 20531, Jerusalem 91204; tel. 2-6288554; fax 2-6288555; e-mail evcat@palnet.com; f. 1967; Pres. His Beatitude FOUAD TWAL (Patriarch of Jerusalem).

Patriarchate of Jerusalem: Latin Patriarchate of Jerusalem, POB 14152, Jerusalem 91141; tel. 2-6282323; fax 2-6271652; e-mail chancellery@latinpat.org; internet www.lpj.org; Patriarch His Beatitude FOUAD TWAL; Auxiliary Bishop of Jerusalem WILLIAM SHOMALI; Vicar-General for Israel GIACINTO-BOULOS MARCUZZO (Titular Bishop of Emmaus Nicopolis); Vicariat Patriarcal Latin, Street 6191/3, Nazareth 16100; tel. 4-6554075; fax 4-6452416; e-mail latinpat@rannet.com.

Maronite Rite

The Maronite community is under the jurisdiction of the Maronite Patriarch of Antioch (resident in Lebanon).

Patriarchal Exarchate of Jerusalem: Maronite Patriarchal Exarchate, POB 14219, 25 Maronite Convent St, Jaffa Gate, Jerusalem 91141; tel. 2-6282158; fax 2-6272821; Exarch Patriarchal Mgr PAUL NABIL SAYAH (also the Maronite Archbishop of Haifa).

Melkite Rite

The Greek-Melkite Patriarch of Antioch and all the East, of Alexandria and of Jerusalem (GRÉGOIRE III LAHAM) is resident in Damascus, Syria.

Patriarchal Vicariate of Jerusalem

Patriarcat Grec-Melkite Catholique, POB 14130, Porte de Jaffa, Jerusalem 91141; tel. 2-6282023; fax 2-6289606; e-mail gcpjer@p-ol.com; Protosyncellus Archim. Archbishop GEORGES MICHEL BAKAR.

Archbishop of Akka (Acre): ELIAS CHACOUR, Archevêché Grec-Catholique, POB 9450, 33 Hagefen St, 31094 Haifa; tel. 4-8508105; fax 4-8508106; e-mail chacoure@netvision.net.il.

Syrian Rite

The Syrian Catholic Patriarch of Antioch is resident in Beirut, Lebanon.

Patriarchal Exarchate of Jerusalem: Vicariat Patriarcal Syrien Catholique, POB 19787, 6 Chaldean St, Jerusalem 91197; tel. 2-6282657; fax 2-6284217; e-mail st_thomas@bezeqint.net; Exarch Patriarchal Mgr GRÉGOIRE PIERRE MELKI.

The Armenian Apostolic (Orthodox) Church

Patriarch of Jerusalem: Archbishop NOURHAN MANOUGIAN, Armenian Patriarchate of St James, POB 14235, Jerusalem; tel. 2-6264853; fax 2-6264862; e-mail webmaster@armenian-patriarchate.org; internet www.armenian-patriarchate.org.

The Greek Orthodox Church

The Patriarchate of Jerusalem includes Israel, the Occupied Territories, Jordan, Kuwait, Saudi Arabia and the United Arab Emirates.

Patriarch of Jerusalem: THEOPHILOS III, POB 14518, Jerusalem 91145; tel. 2-6274941; fax 2-6282048; e-mail secretariat@jerusalem-patriarchate.info; internet www.jerusalem-patriarchate.info.

The Anglican Communion

Episcopal Diocese of Jerusalem and the Middle East: POB 19122, St George's Cathedral Close, Jerusalem 91191; tel. 2-6271670; fax 2-6273847; e-mail info@j-diocese.org; internet www.j-diocese.org; Bishop The Rt Rev. SUHEIL DAWANI (Anglican Bishop in Jerusalem).

Other Christian Churches

Other denominations include the Coptic Orthodox Church, the Russian Orthodox Church, the Ethiopian Orthodox Church, the Romanian Orthodox Church, the Baptist Church, the Lutheran Church and the Church of Scotland.

The Press

Tel-Aviv is the main publishing centre. Largely for economic reasons, no significant local press has developed away from the main cities; hence all newspapers have tended to regard themselves as national. Friday editions, issued on Sabbath eve, are increased to as much as twice the normal size by special weekend supplements, and experience a considerable rise in circulation. No newspapers appear on Saturday.

Most of the daily papers are in Hebrew, and others appear in Arabic, English, Russian, Polish, Hungarian, Yiddish, French and German. The total daily circulation is 500,000–600,000 copies, or 21 papers per hundred people, although most citizens read more than one daily paper.

Most Hebrew morning dailies have strong political or religious affiliations, and the majority of newspapers depend on subsidies from political parties, religious organizations or public funds. The limiting effect on freedom of commentary entailed by this party press system has provoked repeated criticism. There are around 400 other newspapers and magazines, including some 50 weekly and 150 fortnightly; over 250 of them are in Hebrew, the remainder in 11 other languages.

Ha'aretz is the most widely read of the morning papers, exceeded only by the popular afternoon press, *Ma'ariv* and *Yedioth Ahronoth*. *The Jerusalem Post* gives detailed news coverage in English.

DAILIES

Calcalist (Economist): Tel-Aviv; internet www.calcalist.co.il; f. 2008; Hebrew; business; publ. by Yedioth Ahronoth Group; Founder and Publr YOEL ESTERON; CEO STEVE SCHUMACHER.

Globes: POB 5126, Rishon le Zion 75150; tel. 3-9538611; fax 3-9525971; e-mail mailbox@globes.co.il; internet www.globes.co.il; f. 1983; evening; Hebrew; business and economics; owned by the Monitin Group; CEO EITAN MADMON; Editor-in-Chief HAGGAI GOLAN; circ. 45,000.

Ha'aretz (The Land): 21 Schocken St, Tel-Aviv 61001; tel. 3-5121212; fax 3-6810012; e-mail contact@haaretz.co.il; internet www.haaretz.co.il; f. 1919; morning; Hebrew and English; liberal; independent; 25% stake acquired by M. DuMont Schauberg (Germany) in 2006; Man. Dir RAMI GUEZ; Editor-in-Chief ALUF BENN; Publr AMOS SCHOCKEN; circ. 72,000 (weekdays), 100,000 (Fri.).

Hamodia (The Informer): POB 1306, 5 Yehudah Hamacabi St, Jerusalem 91012; tel. 2-5389255; fax 2-5003384; e-mail english@hamodia.co.il; internet www.hamodia.com; f. 1950; morning; Hebrew, English and French edns; Orthodox; organ of Agudat Israel; Editor HAIM MOSHE KNOPF; international circ. 250,000.

Israel HaYom (Israel Today): 2 Hashlosha St, Tel-Aviv; e-mail hayom@israelhayom.co.il; internet israelhayom.co.il; f. 2007; free daily publ. Sun.–Thur; Hebrew; Publr ASHER BAHARAV; Editor-in-Chief AMOS REGEV; CEO ZIPPI KOREN; circ. 255,000.

Israel Nachrichten (News of Israel): POB 28397, Tel-Aviv 61283; tel. 3-5372059; fax 3-5376166; e-mail info@israelnachrichten.de; f. 1935 as Neueste Nachrichten, renamed as above 1948; morning; German; Editor HELGA MÜLLER-GAZMAWE; circ. 1,500.

Israel Post: 15 HaAchim MeSalvita, Tel-Aviv; f. 2007 as Metro Israel; free daily; afternoon; Hebrew; publ. by Metro Israel Ltd; Co-owners ELI AZUR, DAVID WEISMAN; Editor-in-Chief GOLAN BAR-YOSEF.

Al-Itihad (Unity): POB 104, Haifa; tel. 4-8666301; fax 4-8641407; e-mail aletihad@bezeqint.net; internet www.aljabha.org; f. 1944; Arabic; organ of Hadash; Editor-in-Chief AIDA TOUMA-SLIMAN; circ. 60,000.

The Jerusalem Post: POB 81, The Jerusalem Post Bldg, Romema, Jerusalem 91000; tel. 2-5315666; fax 2-5389527; e-mail feedback@jpost.com; internet www.jpost.com; f. 1932 as The Palestine Post, renamed as above 1950; morning; English; independent; CEO RONIT HASIN-HOCHMAN; Editor-in-Chief STEVE LINDE; circ. 15,000 (weekdays), 40,000 (weekend edn); there is also a weekly international edn (circ. 70,000), and a weekly French edn.

Ma'ariv (Evening Prayer): 2 Carlebach St, Tel-Aviv 61200; tel. 3-5632111; fax 3-5610614; internet www.nrg.co.il; f. 1948; mid-morning; Hebrew; independent; publ. by Modiin Publishing House; Editor-in-Chief YOAV TZUR; circ. 150,000 (weekdays), 250,000 (weekends).

Nasha strana (Our Country): 52 Harakeret St, Tel-Aviv 67770; tel. 3-370011; fax 3-5371921; f. 1970; morning; Russian; Editor S. HIMMELFARB; circ. 35,000.

Novosti nedeli (The Week's News): 15 Ha-Ahim Mi-Slavita St, Tel-Aviv; tel. 3-6242225; fax 3-6242227; Russian; Editor-in-Chief DMITRII LODYZHENSKII.

Al-Quds (Jerusalem): POB 19788, Jerusalem; tel. 2-6272663; fax 2-6272657; e-mail hani@alquds.com; internet www.alquds.com; f. 1968; Arabic; Founder and Publr MAHMOUD ABU ZALAF; Gen. Man. Dr MARWAN ABU ZALAF; circ. 55,000.

Viata Noastra: 49 Tchlenor St, Tel-Aviv 66048; tel. 3-5372059; fax 3-6877142; e-mail viatanoastra2001@yahoo.com; internet viatanoastra.1colony.com; f. 1950; morning; Romanian; Editor NANDO MARIO VARGA; circ. 30,000.

Yated Ne'eman: POB 328, Bnei Brak; tel. 3-6170800; fax 3-6170801; e-mail let-edit@yatedneman.co.il; f. 1986; morning; Hebrew; religious; Editors Rabbi ITZHAK ROTH, Rabbi NOSSON ZE'EV GROSSMAN; circ. 25,000.

Yedioth Ahronoth (The Latest News): 2 Yehuda and Noah Mozes St, Tel-Aviv 61000; tel. and fax 3-6082222; e-mail service@y-i.co.il; internet www.ynet.co.il; f. 1939; evening; Hebrew; independent; Editor-in-Chief SHILO DE BEER; circ. 350,000, Fri. 600,000.

WEEKLIES AND FORTNIGHTLIES

Akhbar al-Naqab (News of the Negev): POB 426, Rahat 85357; tel. 8-9919202; fax 8-9917070; e-mail akhbar@akhbarna.com; internet www.akhbarna.com; f. 1988; weekly; Arabic; educational and social issues concerning the Negev Bedouins; Editor-in-Chief MUHAMMAD YOUNIS.

Aurora: Aurora Ltd, POB 57416, Tel-Aviv 61573; tel. 3-5625216; fax 3-5625082; e-mail aurora@aurora-israel.co.il; internet www.aurora-israel.co.il; f. 1963; weekly; Spanish; Editor-in-Chief ARIE AVIDOR; Director MARIO WAINSTEIN; circ. 20,000.

Bamahane (In the Camp): Military POB 1013, Tel-Aviv; f. 1948; illustrated weekly of the Israel Defence Forces; Hebrew; Editor-in-Chief YONI SHANFELD; circ. 70,000.

B'Sheva: Petach Tikva; internet www.inn.co.il/Besheva; f. 2002; Hebrew; religious Zionist newspaper, distributed freely in religious communities; owned by Arutz Sheva (Channel Seven) media network; Editor EMANUEL SHILO; circ. 140,000.

Etgar (The Challenge): POB 35252, Ha'aliyah St, 2nd Floor, Tel-Aviv 61351; tel. 3-5373268; fax 3-5373269; e-mail nirhanitzoz.org.il; internet www.etgar.info; twice weekly; Hebrew; publ. by Hanitzotz Publishing House; Editor NATHAN YALIN-MOR.

InformationWeek: POB 1161, 13 Yad Harutzim St, Tel-Aviv 61116; tel. 3-6385858; fax 3-6889207; e-mail world@pc.co.il; internet www.pc.co.il; weekly; Hebrew and English; Man. Dirs DAHLIA PELED, PELI PELED; Editor-in-Chief PELI PELED.

The Jerusalem Post International Edition: POB 81, Romema, Jerusalem 91000; tel. 2-5315666; fax 2-5389527; e-mail liat@jpost.com; internet www.jpost.co.il; f. 1959; weekly; English; overseas edn of *The Jerusalem Post* (q.v.); circ. 70,000 to 106 countries; Editor LIAT COLLINS.

Jerusalem Report: POB 1805, Jerusalem 91017; tel. 2-5315440; fax 2-5379489; e-mail jrep@jreport.co.il; internet www.jrep.com; f. 1990; bi-weekly; English; publ. under umbrella of *The Jerusalem Post*; Editor-in-Chief EETTA PRINCE-GIBSON.

Laisha (For Women): POB 28122, 35 Bnei Brak St, Tel-Aviv 66021; tel. 3-6386977; fax 3-6386933; e-mail laisha@laisha.co.il; internet laisha.co.il; f. 1949; Hebrew; women's magazine; Editor-in-Chief MIRIAM NOFECH-MOSES; circ. 100,000.

My Tour-Il Magazine: Tourist Guide Communications Ltd, POB 53333, Tel-Aviv 61533; tel. 3-6486611; fax 3-6486622; e-mail ilan777@gmail.com; internet www.mytour-il.co.il; f. 1994; weekly; Hebrew and English; Publr and Editor ILAN SHCHORI; circ. 50,000.

Reshumot: Ministry of Justice, POB 1087, 29 Rehov Salahadin, Jerusalem 91010; f. 1948; Hebrew, Arabic and English; official govt gazette.

Al-Sabar: POB 2647, Nazareth 16126; tel. 4-6462156; fax 4-6462152; e-mail alsabar.mag@gmail.com; internet www.alsabar-mag.com; publ. by the Org. for Democratic Action; Arabic; political and cultural Israeli-Palestinian affairs.

Vesti (News): 2 Homa U'Migdal, Tel-Aviv 67771; tel. 3-6383444; fax 3-6383440; f. 1992publ. Sun.–ThurRussian; Editor-in-Chief SERGEI PODRAZHANSKII.

OTHER PERIODICALS

Bitaon Heyl Ha'avir (Israel Air Force Magazine): Military POB 01560, Zahal; tel. 3-6067729; fax 3-6067735; e-mail iaf@inter.net.il; internet www.iaf.org.il; f. 1948; bi-monthly; Hebrew and English; Dep. Editor U. ETSION; Editor-in-Chief MERAV HALPERIN; circ. 30,000.

Al-Bushra (Good News): POB 6228, Haifa 31061; tel. 4-8385002; fax 4-8371612; f. 1935; monthly; Arabic; organ of the Ahmadiyya movement; Editor MUSA ASA'AD O'DEH.

Challenge: POB 35252, Tel-Aviv 61351; tel. 3-5373268; fax 3-5373269; e-mail oda@netvision.net.il; internet www.challenge-mag.com; f. 1989; magazine on the Israeli–Palestinian conflict, publ. by Hanitzotz Publishing House; online only; English; Editor-in-Chief RONI BEN EFRAT; Editor STEPHEN LANGFUR.

Diamond Intelligence Briefs: POB 3442, Ramat-Gan 52136; tel. 3-5750196; fax 3-5754829; e-mail office@tacy.co.il; internet www.diamondintelligence.com; f. 1985; English; Publr CHAIM EVEN-ZOHAR.

Eastern Mediterranean Tourism/Travel: Israel Travel News Ltd, POB 3251, Tel-Aviv 61032; tel. 3-5251646; fax 3-5251605; e-mail office@itn.co.il; internet www.itn.co.il; f. 1979; monthly; English; Editor GERRY AROHOW; circ. 20,000.

Hamizrah Hehadash (The New East): Israel Oriental Society, The Hebrew University, Mount Scopus, Jerusalem 91905; tel. 2-5883633; e-mail ios49@hotmail.com; f. 1949; annual of the Israel Oriental Society; Middle Eastern, Asian and African Affairs; Hebrew with English summary; Editors HAIM GERBER, ELIE PODEH; circ. 1,500–2,000.

Harefuah (Medicine): POB 3566, 2 Twin Towers, 35 Jabotinsky St, Ramat-Gan 52136; tel. 3-6100444; fax 3-5753303; e-mail tguvot@ima.org.il; internet www.ima.org.il/harefuah; f. 1920; monthly journal of the Israel Medical Asscn; Hebrew with English summaries; also publishes *Israel Medical Asscn Journal*; Editor Prof. YEHUDA SHOENFELD; circ. 16,000.

Hed Hachinuch (Echoes of Education): 2 Tashach St, Tel-Aviv 62093; tel. 3-6091819; fax 3-6094521; e-mail hed@itu.org.il; internet www.itu.org.il; f. 1926; monthly; Hebrew; also publishes Arabic edn; educational; publ. by the Israel Teachers Union; Editor DALIA LACHMAN; circ. 40,000.

Hed Hagan (Echoes of Kindergarten): 8 Ben Saruk St, Tel-Aviv 62969; tel. 3-6922958; e-mail hedhagan@morim.org.il; internet www.itu.org.il; f. 1935; quarterly; Hebrew; early education issues; publ. by the Israel Teachers Union; Editor ILANA MALCHI; circ. 9,000.

Historia: POB 4179, Jerusalem 91041; tel. 2-5650444; fax 2-6712388; e-mail shazar@shazar.org.il; internet www.shazar.org.il/historia.htm; f. 1998; bi-annual; Hebrew, with English summaries; general history; publ. by the Historical Society of Israel; Editors Prof. YITZHAK HEN, Prof. ISRAEL SHATZMAN, Prof. GIDEON SHELACH; circ. 1,000.

Israel Environment Bulletin: Ministry of Environmental Protection, POB 34033, 5 Kanfei Nesharim St, Givat Shaul, Jerusalem 95464; tel. 2-6553777; fax 2-6535934; e-mail shoshana@environment.gov.il; internet www.environment.gov.il; f. 1973; bi-annual; English; environmental policy, legislation and news; Editor SHOSHANA GABBAY; circ. 3,500.

Israel Exploration Journal: POB 7041, 5 Avida St, Jerusalem 91070; tel. 2-6257991; fax 2-6247772; e-mail ies@vms.huji.ac.il; internet israelexplorationsociety.huji.ac.il/iej.htm; f. 1950; bi-annual; English; general and biblical archaeology, ancient history and historical geography of Israel and the Holy Land; Editors SHMUEL AHITUV, AMIHAI MAZAR; circ. 2,500.

Israel Journal of Chemistry: POB 34299, Jerusalem 91341; tel. 2-6522226; fax 2-6522277; e-mail info@israelsciencejournals.com; internet www.sciencefromisrael.com; f. 1951; quarterly; English; publ. by Science from Israel; Editor Prof. HAIM LEVANON.

Israel Journal of Earth Sciences: POB 34299, Jerusalem 91341; tel. 2-6522226; fax 2-6522277; e-mail info@israelsciencejournals.com; internet www.sciencefromisrael.com; f. 1951; quarterly; English; publ. by Science from Israel; Editor-in-Chief Y. ENZEL.

Israel Journal of Ecology and Evolution: POB 34299, Jerusalem 91341; tel. 2-6522226; fax 2-6522277; e-mail info@israelsciencejournals.com; internet www.sciencefromisrael.com; f. 1951 as *Israel Journal of Zoology*; name changed in 2006; quarterly; English; publ. by Science from Israel; Editors LEON BLAUSTEIN, BURT P. KOTLER.

Israel Journal of Mathematics: The Hebrew University Magnes Press, POB 39099, Jerusalem 91390; tel. 2-6586656; fax 2-5633370; e-mail iton@math.huji.ac.il; internet www.ma.huji.ac.il/~ijmath; f. 1951; bi-monthly; English; Editor-in-Chief NATI LINIAL.

Israel Journal of Plant Sciences: POB 34299, Jerusalem 91341; tel. 2-6522226; fax 2-6522277; e-mail info@israelsciencejournals.com; internet www.sciencefromisrael.com; f. 1951 as *Israel Journal* *of Botany*; quarterly; English; publ. by Science from Israel; Editor-in-Chief EFRAIM LEWINSOHN.

Israel Journal of Psychiatry and Related Sciences: Gefen Publishing House Ltd, 6 Hatzvi St, Jerusalem 94386; tel. 2-5380247; fax 2-5388423; e-mail ijp@gefenpublishing.com; f. 1963; quarterly; English; Editor-in-Chief Dr DAVID GREENBERG.

Israel Journal of Veterinary Medicine: POB 22, Ra'nana 43100; tel. 9-7419929; fax 9-7431778; e-mail ivma@zahav.net.il; internet www.ijvm.org.il; f. 1943; fmrly *Refuah Veterinarith*; quarterly of the Israel Veterinary Medical Asscn; English; Editor-in-Chief TREVOR WANER.

Israel Law Review: Israel Law Review Asscn, Faculty of Law, Hebrew University of Jerusalem, Mt Scopus, Jerusalem 91905; tel. 2-5881156; fax 2-5819371; e-mail ilr@savion.huji.ac.il; internet law .huji.ac.il/eng/pirsumim.asp; f. 1966; 3 a year; English; Editors-in-Chief Sir NIGEL RODLEY, YUVAL SHANY.

Israel Medical Asscn Journal (IMAJ): POB 3604, 2 Twin Towers, 11th Floor, 35 Jabotinsky St, Ramat-Gan 52136; tel. 3-6100418; fax 3-7519673; e-mail imaj@ima.org.il; internet www.ima.org.il/imaj; f. 1999; monthly English-language journal of the Israel Medical Asscn; also publishes *Harefuah*; Editor-in-Chief Prof. YEHUDA SHOENFELD.

Journal d'Analyse Mathématique: The Hebrew University Magnes Press, POB 39099, Jerusalem 91390; tel. 2-6586656; fax 2-5633370; e-mail magnes@vms.huji.ac.il; internet www.ma.huji.ac.il/ jdm; f. 1955; 3 vols a year; French; Exec. Editor A. LINDEN.

Leshonenu: Academy of the Hebrew Language, Givat Ram Campus, Jerusalem 91904; tel. 2-6493555; fax 2-5617065; e-mail ivrit@ hebrew-academy.org.il; internet hebrew-academy.huji.ac.il; f. 1929; quarterly; Hebrew; for the study of the Hebrew language and cognate subjects; Editor MOSHE BAR-ASHER.

Leshonenu La'am: Academy of the Hebrew Language, Givat Ram Campus, Jerusalem 91904; tel. 2-6493555; fax 2-5617065; e-mail ivrit@heberw-academy.org.il; internet hebrew-academy.huji.ac.il; f. 1945; quarterly; Hebrew; popular Hebrew philology; Editor MOSHE FLORENTIN.

Lilac: Nazareth; f. 2000 for Christian and Muslim Arab women in the region; monthly; Arabic; Israel's first magazine for Arab women; Founder and Editor-in-Chief YARA MASHOUR.

MB-Yakinton (Yakinton): POB 1480, Tel-Aviv 61014; tel. 3-5164461; fax 3-5164435; e-mail info@irgun-jeckes.org; internet www.irgun-jeckes.org; f. 1932; 8 a year; monthly journal of the Irgun Jotsei Merkaz Europa (Asscn of Israelis of Central European Origin); Hebrew and German; Editor MICHA LIMOR.

Moznaim (Balance): POB 7098, Tel-Aviv; tel. 3-6953256; fax 3-6919681; f. 1929; monthly; Hebrew; literature and culture; publ. by Hebrew Writers Asscn; Editors ASHER REICH, AZRIEL KAUFMAN; circ. 2,500.

News from Within: POB 31417, Jerusalem 91313; tel. 2-6241159; fax 2-6253151; e-mail bryan@alt-info.org; internet www .alternativenews.org; monthly; joint Israeli-Palestinian publ; political, economic, social and cultural; publ. by the Alternative Information Centre.

PC Plus: PC Media, POB 11438, 13 Yad Harutzim St, Tel-Aviv 61114; tel. 3-6385810; fax 3-6889207; e-mail editor@pc.co.il; internet www.pc.co.il; f. 1992; monthly; Hebrew; information on personal computers; CEO and Man. Editor DAHLIA PELED; CEO and Editor-in-Chief PELI PELED; circ. 23,000.

Proche-Orient Chrétien: St Anne's Church, POB 19079, Jerusalem 91190; tel. 2-6281992; fax 2-6280764; e-mail mafrpoc@steanne .org; f. 1951; quarterly on churches and religion in the Middle East; publ. in asscn with St Joseph University, Beirut, Lebanon; French; circ. 1,000.

Terra Santa: POB 14038, Jaffa Gate, Jerusalem 91142; tel. 2-6272692; fax 2-6286417; e-mail cicts@netmedia.net.il; internet www.cicts.org; f. 1973; bi-monthly; publ. by the Christian Information Centre, which is sponsored by the Custody of the Holy Land (the official custodians of the Holy Shrines); Italian, Spanish, French, English and Arabic edns publ. in Jerusalem by the Franciscan Printing Press, German edn in Munich, Maltese edn in Valletta; Dir Fr JERZY KRAJ.

WIZO Review: Women's International Zionist Organization, 38 Sderot David Hamelech Blvd, Tel-Aviv 64237; tel. 3-6923805; fax 3-6923801; e-mail wreview@wizo.org; internet www.wizo.org; f. 1926; English (3 a year); Man. Editor INGRID ROCKBERGER; Asst Editor ZOHAR FRIEDMAN; circ. 6,000.

NEWS AGENCY

Jewish Telegraphic Agency (JTA): Mideast Bureau, Jerusalem Post Bldg, Romema, Jerusalem 91000; tel. 2-610579; fax 2-536635; e-mail info@jta.org; internet www.jta.org; Man. Editor URIEL HEILMAN.

PRESS ASSOCIATIONS

Daily Newspaper Publishers' Asscn of Israel: POB 51202, 74 Petach Tikva Rd, Tel-Aviv 61200; fax 3-5617938; safeguards professional interests and maintains standards, supplies newsprint to dailies; negotiates with trade unions; mems all daily papers; affiliated to International Federation of Newspaper Publishers; Pres. SHABTAI HIMMELFARB; Gen. Sec. BETZALEL EYAL.

Foreign Press Asscn: Beit Sokolov, 4 Kaplan St, Tel-Aviv 64734; tel. 3-6916143; fax 3-6961548; e-mail fpa@netvision.net.il; internet www.fpa.org.il; f. 1957; represents journalists employed by international news orgs who report from Israel, the West Bank and the Gaza Strip; private, non-profit org.; almost 500 mems from 30 countries; Dep. Chair. GWEN ACKERMAN.

Israel Association of Periodical Press (IAPP): 17 Keilat Venezia St, Tel-Aviv 69400; tel. 3-6449851; fax 3-6449852; e-mail iapp@zahav .net.il; internet www.iapp.co.il; f. 1962; 600 mems; Chair. JOSEPH FRENKEL.

Israel Press Council: Beit Sokolov, 4 Kaplan St, Tel-Aviv; tel. 3-6951437; fax 3-6951145; e-mail moaza@m-i.org.il; internet www.m-i .org.il; f. 1963; deals with matters of common interest to the Press such as drafting the code of professional ethics, which is binding on all journalists; Chair. ORNA LIN; Gen. Sec. AVI WEINBERG.

National Federation of Israeli Journalists (NFIJ): POB 585, 37 Hillet St, Jerusalem 91004; tel. 2-6254351; fax 3-6254353; e-mail office@jaj.org.il; internet www.jaj.org.il; affiliated to International Federation of Journalists; Chair. AHIA HIKA GINOSAR.

Publishers

Achiasaf Publishing House Ltd: 3, Bney Binyamin St, Netanya 4201959; tel. 9-8851390; fax 9-8851391; e-mail info@achiasaf.co.il; internet www.achiasaf.co.il; f. 1937; general; Pres. MATAN ACHIASAF.

Am Oved Publishers Ltd: 22 Mazeh St, Tel-Aviv 65213; tel. 3-6288500; fax 3-6298911; e-mail info@am-oved.co.il; internet www .am-oved.co.il; f. 1942; fiction, non-fiction, reference books, school and university textbooks, children's books, poetry, classics, science fiction; Man. Dir YAAKOV BREY.

Amihai Publishing House Ltd: POB 8448, 19 Yad Harutzim St, Netanya Darom 42505; tel. 9-8859099; fax 9-8853464; e-mail ami1000@bezeqint.net; internet www.amichaibooks.co.il; f. 1948; fiction, general science, linguistics, languages, arts; Dir ITZHAK ORON.

Arabic Publishing House: 93 Arlozorof St, Tel-Aviv; tel. 3-6921674; f. 1960; established by the Histadrut; periodicals and books; Gen. Man. GHASSAN MUKLASHI.

Ariel Publishing House: POB 3328, Jerusalem 91033; tel. 2-6434540; fax 2-6436164; e-mail elysch@netvision.net.il; internet www.arielp.co.il; f. 1976; history, archaeology, religion, geography, folklore; CEO ELY SCHILLER.

Astrolog Publishing House: POB 1231, Hod Hasharon 45111; tel. 3-9190957; fax 3-9190958; e-mail abooks@netvision.net.il; f. 1994; general non-fiction, religion, alternative medicine; Man. Dir SARA BEN-MORDECHAI.

Carta, The Israel Map and Publishing Co Ltd: POB 2500, 18 Ha'uman St, Industrial Area, Talpiot, Jerusalem 91024; tel. 2-6783355; fax 2-6782373; e-mail carta@carta.co.il; internet www .carta-jerusalem.com; f. 1958; the principal cartographic publr; Pres. and CEO SHAY HAUSMAN.

Eliner Library—The World Zionist Organization: POB 10615, Jerusalem 91104; tel. 2-6202137; fax 2-6202792; e-mail eliner@wzo .org.il; internet www.eliner.co.il; f. 1945; education, Jewish philosophy, studies in the Bible, children's books publ. in Hebrew, English, French, Spanish, German, Swedish and Portuguese, Hebrew teaching material; Dir of Publication Division ORIT AVITAL.

Gefen Publishing House Ltd: 6 Hatzvi St, Jerusalem 94386; tel. 2-5380247; fax 2-5388423; e-mail info@gefenpublishing.com; internet www.israelbooks.com; f. 1981; largest publr of English-language books in Israel; also publishes wide range of fiction and non-fiction; Publr ILAN GREENFIELD.

Globes Publishers: POB 5126, Rishon le Zion 75150; tel. 3-9538611; fax 3-9525971; e-mail mailbox@globes.co.il; internet www.globes.co.il; business, finance, technology, law, marketing; CEO EITAN MADMON; Editor-in-Chief HAGGAI GOLAN.

Gvanim: POB 11138, 29 Bar-Kochba St, Tel-Aviv 61111; tel. 3-5281044; fax 3-6202032; e-mail traklinm@zahav.net.il; f. 1992; poetry, belles lettres, fiction; Man. Dir MARITZA ROSMAN.

Hakibbutz Hameuchad—Sifriat Poalim Publishing Group: POB 1432, Bnei Brak, Tel-Aviv 51114; tel. 3-5785810; fax 3-5785811; e-mail info@kibutz-poalim.co.il; internet www.kibutz-poalim.co.il; f. 1939 as Hakibbutz Hameuchad Publishing House Ltd; subsequently merged with Sifriat Poalim; general; Gen. Dir UZI SHAVIT.

Hanitzotz Publishing House: POB 35252, Tel-Aviv 61351; tel. 3-5373268; fax 3-5373269; e-mail oda@netvision.net.il; internet www.hanitzotz.com; f. 1985; 'progressive' booklets and publications, incl. the periodicals *Challenge* (in English), *Etgar* (Hebrew), and *Al-Sabar* (Arabic); also produces documentary films on human and workers' rights; Contact RONI BEN EFRAT.

The Hebrew University Magnes Press: The Hebrew University, The Sherman Bldg for Research Management, POB 39099, Givat Ram, Jerusalem 91390; tel. 2-6586656; fax 2-5660341; e-mail info@magnespress.co.il; internet www.magnespress.co.il; f. 1929; academic books and journals on many subjects, incl. biblical, classical and Jewish studies, social sciences, language, literature, art, history and geography; Dir HAI TSABAR.

Hed Arzi (Ma'ariv) Publishing Ltd: 3A Yoni Netanyahu St, Or-Yehuda, Tel-Aviv 60376; tel. 3-5383333; fax 3-6343205; e-mail shimoni@hed-arzi.co.il; f. 1954 as Sifriat-Ma'ariv Ltd; later known as Ma'ariv Book Guild Ltd; general; Man. Dir ELI SHIMONI.

Hod-Ami—Computer Books Ltd: POB 6108, Herzliya 46160; tel. 9-9564716; fax 9-9571582; e-mail info@hod-ami.co.il; internet www.hod-ami.co.il; f. 1984; information technology, management; translations from English into Hebrew and Arabic; CEO ITZHAK AMIHUD.

Jerusalem Center for Public Affairs: 13 Tel Hai St, Jerusalem 92107; tel. 2-5619281; fax 2-5619112; e-mail info@jcpa.org; internet www.jcpa.org; f. 1976; Jewish political tradition; publishes *Jerusalem Viewpoints*, *Jerusalem Issue Brief*, *Jewish Political Studies Review* and other books; Pres. DORE GOLD; Chair. Dr MANFRED GERSTENFELD.

The Jerusalem Publishing House: 2B HaGai St, Beit Hakerem, Jerusalem 96262; tel. 2-6537966; fax 2-6537988; e-mail mh2@017.net.il; internet jerpub.com; f. 1966; biblical research, history, encyclopedias, archaeology, arts of the Holy Land, cookbooks, guidebooks, economics, politics; CEO MOSHE HELLER; Man. Editor RACHEL GILON.

Jewish History Publications (Israel 1961) Ltd: POB 1232, 29 Jabotinsky St, Jerusalem 92141; tel. 2-5632310; f. 1961; encyclopedias, World History of the Jewish People series.

Keter Publishing House Ltd: POB 7145, Givat Shaul B, Jerusalem 91071; tel. 2-6557822; fax 2-6536811; e-mail info@keterbooks.co.il; internet www.keterbooks.co.il; f. 1959; original and translated works of fiction, encyclopedias, non-fiction, guidebooks and children's books; publishing imprints: Israel Program for Scientific Translations, Keter Books, Domino, Shikmona, Encyclopedia Judaica; Man. Dir YIPHTACH DEKEL.

Kinneret Zmora-Bitan Dvir Publishing House: 10 Hataasiya St, Or-Yehuda 60210; tel. 3-6344977; fax 3-6340953; internet www.kinbooks.co.il; f. 2002 following merger between Kinneret and Zmora Bitan-Dvir publishing houses; adult and children's fiction and non-fiction, history, science, sociology, psychology, current affairs and politics, dictionaries, architecture, travel; Man. Dir YORAM ROZ.

MAP-Mapping and Publishing Ltd (Tel-Aviv Books): POB 56024, 17 Tchernikhovski St, Tel-Aviv 61560; tel. 3-6210500; fax 3-5257725; e-mail info@mapa.co.il; internet www.mapa.co.il; f. 1985; maps, atlases, travel guides, textbooks, reference books; Man. Dir HEZI LEVY.

Ministry of Defence Publishing House: POB 916, Yaakov Dori Rd, Kiryat Ono 55108; tel. 3-7380738; fax 3-7380645; e-mail minuy@inter.net.il; f. 1958; military literature, Judaism, history and geography of Israel; Dir JOSEPH PERLOVITZ.

M. Mizrachi Publishing House Ltd: 67 Levinsky St, Tel-Aviv 66855; tel. 3-6870936; fax 3-6888185; e-mail mizrahi.co@jmail.com; f. 1960; children's books, fiction, history, medicine, science; Dirs MEIR MIZRACHI, ISRAEL MIZRACHI.

Mosad Harav Kook: POB 642, 1 Maimon St, Jerusalem 91006; tel. 2-6526231; fax 2-6526968; e-mail mosad-haravkook@neto.bezeqint.net; f. 1937; editions of classical works, Torah and Jewish studies; Dir Rabbi YOSEF MOVSHOVITZ.

Otsar Hamoreh: c/o Israel Teachers Union, 8 Ben Saruk, Tel-Aviv 62969; tel. 3-6922983; fax 3-6922988; f. 1951; educational; Man. Dir JOSEPH SALOMAN.

People and Computers Ltd: POB 11438, 53 Derech Asholom St, Givatayim 53454; tel. 3-7330733; fax 3-7330703; e-mail info@pc.co.il; internet www.pc.co.il; information technology; Editor-in-Chief and CEO PELI PELED; Man. Editor and CEO DAHLIA PELED.

Rodney Franklin Agency: POB 37727, 53 Mazeh St, Tel-Aviv 65789; tel. 3-5600724; fax 3-5600479; e-mail rodneyf@netvision.net.il; internet www.rodneyagency.com; f. 1974; exclusive representative of various British, other European and US publrs; e-marketing services for academic and professional journal publrs in 15 countries; Dir RODNEY FRANKLIN.

Rubin Mass Ltd: POB 990, 7 Ha-Ayin-Het St, Jerusalem 91009; tel. 2-6277863; fax 2-6277864; e-mail rmass@barak.net.il; internet www.rubinmass.com; f. 1927; Hebraica, Judaica, export of all Israeli books and periodicals; Man. OREN MASS.

Schocken Publishing House Ltd: POB 57188, 24 Nathan Yelin Mor St, Tel-Aviv 61571; tel. 3-5610130; fax 3-5622668; e-mail gila_g@haaretz.co.il; internet www.schocken.co.il; f. 1938; general; Publr RACHELI EDELMAN.

Science from Israel—A Division of LPP Ltd: POB 34299, Merkaz Sapir 6/36, Givat Shaul, Jerusalem 91341; tel. 2-6522226; fax 2-6522277; e-mail elcya@bezeqint.net; internet www.sciencefromisrael.com; fmrly Laser Pages Publishing Ltd; scientific journals.

Shalem Press: POB 8787, 13 Yehoshua Bin-Nun St, Jerusalem 93102; tel. 2-5605586; fax 2-5605565; e-mail shalempress@shalem.org.il; internet www.shalempress.co.il; f. 1994; economics, political science, history, philosophy, cultural issues; Pres. DANIEL POLISAR.

Sinai Publishing: 24 Rambam St, Tel-Aviv 65813; tel. 3-5163672; fax 3-5176783; e-mail sinaipub@zahav.net.il; internet www.sinaibooks.com; f. 1853; Hebrew books and religious articles; Dir MOSHE SCHLESINGER.

Steinhart-Katzir: POB 8333, Netanya 42505; tel. 9-8854770; fax 9-8854771; e-mail mail@haolam.co.il; internet www.haolam.co.il; f. 1991; travel; Man. Dir OHAD SHARAV.

Tcherikover Publishers Ltd: 12 Hasharon St, Tel-Aviv 66185; tel. 3-6396099; fax 3-6874729; e-mail barkay@inter.net.il; education, psychology, economics, psychiatry, literature, literary criticism, essays, history, geography, criminology, art, languages, management; Man. Editor S. TCHERIKOVER.

Yachdav United Publishers Co Ltd: POB 20123, 29 Carlebach St, Tel-Aviv 67132; tel. 3-5614121; fax 3-5611996; e-mail info@tbpai.co.il; f. 1960; educational; Chair. EPHRAIM BEN-DOR; Exec. Dir AMNON BEN-SHMUEL.

Yavneh Publishing House Ltd: POB 4781, 4 Mazeh St, Tel-Aviv 65213; tel. 3-6297856; fax 3-6293638; e-mail publishing@yavneh.co.il; internet www.yavneh.co.il; f. 1932; general; Man. Dir NIRA PREISKEL.

Yedioth Ahronoth Books: POB 53494, 10 Kehilat Venezia, Tel-Aviv 61534; tel. 3-7683333; fax 3-7683300; e-mail info@ybook.co.il; internet www.ybook.co.il; f. 1952; non-fiction, politics, Judaism, health, music, dance, fiction, education; Man. Dir DOV EICHENWALD.

S. Zack: 31 Beit Hadfus St, Jerusalem 95483; tel. 2-6537760; fax 2-6514005; e-mail zackmt@bezeqint.net; internet www.zack.co.il; f. 1935; fiction, science, philosophy, Judaism, children's books, educational and reference books, dictionaries, languages; Dir MICHAEL ZACK.

PUBLISHERS' ASSOCIATION

The Book Publishers' Association of Israel: POB 20123, 29 Carlebach St, Tel-Aviv 67132; tel. 3-5614121; fax 3-5611996; e-mail info@tbpai.co.il; internet www.tbpai.co.il; f. 1939; mems: 84 publishing firms; Chair. YARON SADAN; Man. Dir AMNON BEN-SHMUEL.

Broadcasting and Communications

TELECOMMUNICATIONS

013 Netvision: Cibel Industrial Park, 15 Hamelacha St, Rosh Ha'ayin 48091; tel. 3-9001100; fax 3-9001113; e-mail service@netvision013.net.il; internet www.013netvision.net.il; f. 2007 after merger with 013 Barak and GlobCall; CEO RICHARD HUNTER.

Bezeq—The Israel Telecommunication Corpn Ltd: Azrieli Center 2, Tel-Aviv 61620; tel. 3-6262600; fax 3-6262609; e-mail dover@bezeq.co.il; internet www.bezeq.co.il; f. 1984; privatized in May 2005; launched own cellular network, Pelephone Communications Ltd, in 1986; total assets NIS 15,156m. (Dec. 2007); CEO AVI GABBAY; Chair. SHAUL ELOVITCH.

Pelephone Communications Ltd: 33 Hagvura St, Givatayim, Tel-Aviv 53483; tel. 3-5728881; fax 3-5728111; internet www.pelephone.co.il; f. 1986; launched Esc brand in 2003; 2.4m. subscribers (2006); CEO GIL SHARON.

Cellcom Israel: POB 4060, 10 Hagavish St, Netanya 42140; tel. 529990052 (mobile); fax 529989700; e-mail investors@cellcom.co.il; internet www.cellcom.co.il; f. 1994; mobile telecommunications operator; 3.3m. subscribers (Sept. 2009); Chair. AMI EREL; Pres. and CEO NIR SZTERN.

ECI Telecom Ltd: POB 3038, 30 Hasivim St, Petach-Tikva, Tel-Aviv 49133; tel. 3-9266555; fax 3-9266444; e-mail web.inquiries@ecitele.com; internet www.ecitele.com; f. 1961; Pres. and CEO RAFI MAOR.

Partner Communications Co Ltd: POB 435, 8 Amal St, Afeq Industrial Park, Rosh Ha'ayin 48103; tel. 54-7814888; fax 54-7814999; e-mail deborah.margalit@orange.co.il; internet www.orange.co.il; f. 1999; provides mobile telecommunications and Wi-Fi internet services under the Orange brand name; represents about one-third of the mobile-cellular market in Israel; Chair. CANNING FOK; CEO DAVID AVNER.

Vocal Tec Communications Ltd (Vocal Tec): 14 Beni Ga'on St, Bldg B2-Rakefet, Netanya 42504; tel. 9-9703888; fax 9-9558175; e-mail info@vocaltec.com; internet www.vocaltec.com; carrier services and telecommunications infrastructure; revenues US $6.1m. (2008); Chair. ILAN ROSEN; Pres. and CEO DANIEL BORISLOW.

BROADCASTING

In 1986 the Government approved the establishment of a commercial radio and television network to be run in competition with the state system.

Radio

Israel Broadcasting Authority (IBA) (Radio): POB 28080, 161 Jaffa Rd, Jerusalem 94342; tel. 2-5015555; e-mail dover@iba.org.il; internet www.iba.org.il; f. 1948state-owned station in Jerusalem with additional studios in Tel-Aviv and Haifa; broadcasts six programmes for local and overseas listeners on medium-wave, shortwave and VHF/FM in 16 languages: Hebrew, Arabic, English, Yiddish, Ladino, Romanian, Hungarian, Moghrabi, Farsi, French, Russian, Bukharian, Georgian, Portuguese, Spanish and Amharic; Chair. AMIR GILAT; Dir-Gen. YONI BEN-MENACHEM.

Galei Zahal: MPOB, Zahal; tel. 3-5126666; fax 3-5126760; e-mail glz@galatz.co.il; f. 1950; Israel Defence Force broadcasting station, Tel-Aviv, with studios in Jerusalem; broadcasts 24-hour news, current affairs, music and cultural programmes in Hebrew on FM, medium and short waves; Dir ITZHAK TUNIK.

Kol Israel (The Voice of Israel): POB 1082, 21 Heleni Hamalka, Jerusalem 91010; tel. 1-599509510; e-mail radiodirector@iba.org.il; internet www.iba.org.il/kolisrael; broadcasts music, news and multilingual programmes within Israel and overseas on short wave, AM and FM stereo, in 15 languages, incl. Hebrew, Arabic, French, English, Spanish, Ladino, Russian, Yiddish, Romanian, Hungarian, Amharic and Georgian; Dir SHMUEL BEN-ZVI; Gen. Dir YONI BEN-MENACHEM.

Television

Israel Broadcasting Authority (IBA) (Television): 161 Jaffa Rd, Jerusalem; tel. 2-5301333; fax 2-292944; internet www.iba.org .ilbroadcasts began in 1968; station in Jerusalem with additional studios in Tel-Aviv; one colour network (VHF with UHF available in all areas); one satellite channel; broadcasts in Hebrew, Arabic and English; Chair. AMIR GILAT; Dir-Gen. YONI BEN-MENACHEM.

The Council of Cable TV and Satellite Broadcasting: 23 Jaffa Rd, Jerusalem 91999; tel. 2-6702210; fax 2-6702273; e-mail inbard@moc.gov.il; f. 1982; Chair. NITZAN CHEN.

Israel Educational Television: Ministry of Education, 14 Klausner St, Tel-Aviv 69011; tel. 3-646227; fax 3-6466164; e-mail webmaster@ietv.gov.il; internet www.ietv.gov.il; f. 1966 by Hanadiv (Rothschild Memorial Group) as Instructional Television Trust; began transmission in 1966; school programmes form an integral part of the syllabus in a wide range of subjects; also adult education; Dir-Gen. ELDAD KOBLENTZ; Dir of Engineering SHLOMO KASIF.

Second Authority for Television and Radio: POB 3445, 20 Beit Hadfus St, Jerusalem 95464; tel. 2-6556222; fax 2-6556287; e-mail rashut@rashut2.org.il; internet www.rashut2.org.il; f. 1991; responsible for providing broadcasts through two principal television channels, Channel 2 and Channel 10, and some 14 radio stations; Chair. NURIT DABUSH.

Finance

(cap. = capital; res = reserves; dep. = deposits; m. = million; brs = branches; amounts in shekels)

BANKING

Central Bank

Bank of Israel: POB 780, Bank of Israel Bldg, Kiryat Ben-Gurion, Jerusalem 91007; tel. 2-6552211; fax 2-6528805; e-mail webmaster@bankisrael.gov.il; internet www.bankisrael.gov.il; f. 1954 as Cen. Bank of the State of Israel; cap. 60m., res 3,925m., dep. 212,688m. (Dec. 2009); Gov. Prof. STANLEY FISCHER; 1 br.

Principal Commercial Banks

Arab-Israel Bank Ltd: POB 207, 48 Bar Yehuda St, Tel Hanan, Nesher 36601; tel. 4-8205222; fax 4-8205250; e-mail aravi@bll.co.il; internet www.bank-aravi-israeli.co.il; res 344m., dep. 4,463m., total assets 5,160m. (Dec. 2010); subsidiary of Bank Leumi le-Israel BM; Chair. SHMUEL ZUSMAN; Gen. Man. ITZHAK EYAL.

Bank Hapoalim: 50 Rothschild Blvd, Tel-Aviv 61000; tel. 3-5673333; fax 3-5607028; e-mail international@bnhp.co.il; internet www.bankhapoalim.co.il; f. 1921 as Workers' Bank; name changed as above 1961; mergers into the above: American-Israel Bank in 1999, Maritime Bank of Israel in 2003, Mishkan-Hapoalim Mortgage Bank and Israel Continental Bank in 2004; privatized in June 2000; cap. 8,066m., res 408m., dep. 264,503m. (Dec. 2011); Chair. YAIR SEROUSSI; Pres. and CEO ZION KENAN; 325 brs in Israel and 10 brs abroad.

Bank of Jerusalem Ltd: POB 2255, 2 Herbert Samuel St, Jerusalem 91022; tel. 2-6706018; fax 2-6234043; e-mail webmaster@bankjerusalem.co.il; internet www.bankjerusalem.co.il; private bank; cap. 127m., res 86m., dep. 9,141m. (Dec. 2011); Chair. JONATHAN IRONI; CEO PAZ URI; 14 brs.

Bank Leumi le-Israel BM: 34 Yehuda Halevi St, Tel-Aviv 65546; tel. 3-5148111; fax 3-5148656; e-mail pniot@bll.co.il; internet www .bankleumi.co.il; f. 1902 as Anglo-Palestine Co; renamed Anglo-Palestine Bank 1930; reincorporated as above 1951; 34.78% state-owned; cap. 7,059m., res 909m., dep. 284,979m. (Dec. 2011); Chair. DAVID BRODET; 242 brs in Israel and 2 abroad.

Bank Otsar Ha-Hayal Ltd: POB 52136, 11 Menachem Begin St, Ramat-Gan 52136; tel. 3-7556000; fax 3-7556007; e-mail ozfrndep@netvision.net.il; internet www.bankotsar.co.il; f. 1946; 68% owned by First Int. Bank of Israel, 24% by Hever Veterans & Pensions Ltd, 8% by Provident Fund of the Employees of IAILTD; dep. 11,214.8m., total assets 13,638m. (Dec. 2008); Chair. SMADAR BARBER-TSADIK; Gen. Man. ISRAEL TRAU.

First International Bank of Israel Ltd (FIBI): 42 Rothschild Blvd, Tel-Aviv 66883; tel. 3-5196111; fax 3-5100316; e-mail zucker .d@fibi.co.il; internet www.fibi.co.il; f. 1972 by merger between Foreign Trade Bank Ltd and Export Bank Ltd; cap. 927m., res −16m., dep. 82,519m. (Dec. 2010); Chair. RONI HIZKIYAHU; CEO SMADAR BARBER-TSADIK; 182 brs in Israel and abroad (incl. subsidiaries).

Israel Discount Bank Ltd: POB 456, 27–31 Yehuda Halevi St, Tel-Aviv 61003; tel. 3-5145555; fax 3-5146954; e-mail intidb@discountbank.co.il; internet www.discountbank.co.il; f. 1935; name changed as above in 1957; 20% state-owned; dep. 151,187m., total assets 182,248m. (Dec. 2008); Chair. Dr JOSEPH BACHAR; Pres. and CEO REUVEN SPIEGEL; 126 brs in Israel and abroad.

Mercantile Discount Bank Ltd: POB 1292, 103 Allenby Rd, Tel-Aviv 61012; tel. 3-7105550; fax 3-7105532; e-mail fec@mdb.co.il; internet www.mercantile.co.il; f. 1971 as Barclays Discount Bank Ltd, to take over (from Jan. 1972) the Israel brs of Barclays Bank Int. Ltd; Barclays Bank PLC, one of the joint owners, sold its total shareholding to the remaining owner, Israel Discount Bank Ltd, in Feb. 1993, and name changed as above that April; Mercantile Bank of Israel Ltd became branch of the above in March 1997; cap. 51m., res 185m., dep. 19,151m. (Dec. 2010); Chair. Dr JOSEPH BACHAR; Pres. and CEO REUVEN SPIEGEL; 66 brs.

Mizrahi Tefahot Bank Ltd: POB 3450, 7 Jabotinsky St, Ramat-Gan 52136; tel. 3-7559468; fax 3-6234819; e-mail lernerh@umtb.co.il; internet www.mizrahi-tefahot.co.il; f. 1923 as Mizrahi Bank Ltd; mergers into the above: Hapoel Hamizrahi Bank Ltd, as United Mizrahi Bank Ltd; Finance and Trade Bank Ltd in 1990; Tefahot Israel Mortgage Bank Ltd in 2005, when name changed as above; Adanim Mortgage Bank merged into above bank in 2009; cap. 2,058m., res 63m., dep. 130,300m. (Dec. 2012); Chair. MOSHE VIDMAN; Pres. and CEO ELDAD FRESHER; 166 brs.

UBank Ltd: POB 677, 38 Rothschild Blvd, Tel-Aviv 61006; tel. 3-5645353; fax 3-5645285; e-mail gsteiger@u-bank.net; internet www .u-bank.net; f. 1934 as Palestine Credit Utility Bank Ltd; renamed Israel General Bank Ltd 1964; ownership transferred to Investec Bank Ltd (South Africa) 1996; name changed to Investec Clali Bank Ltd 1999, and to Investec Bank (Israel) Ltd 2001; control of bank transferred to First Int. Bank of Israel 2004 and name changed as above 2005; cap. 60m., res 338m., dep. 6,089m. (Dec. 2010); Chair. YORAM SIRKIS; CEO BENNY RON; 8 brs.

Union Bank of Israel Ltd: 6–8 Ahuzat Bayit St, Tel-Aviv 65143; tel. 3-5191222; fax 3-5191344; e-mail info@ubi.co.il; internet www .ubi.co.il; f. 1951; cap. 952m., res 21m., dep. 32,198m. (Dec. 2011); Chair. ZEEV ABELES; Pres. and CEO HAIM FREILICHMAN; 35 brs.

Mortgage Banks

Discount Mortgage Bank Ltd: POB 2844, 16–18 Simtat Beit Hashoeva, Tel-Aviv 61027; tel. 3-5643311; fax 3-5661704; e-mail contact@discountbank.net; internet www.discountbank.net; f. 1959; subsidiary of Israel Discount Bank Ltd; total assets 10,355m. (Dec. 2005); Chair. SHLOMO ZOHAR; Pres. and CEO GIORA OFFER; 3 brs.

Leumi Mortgage Bank Ltd: POB 69, 31–37 Montefiore St, Tel-Aviv 65201; tel. 3-5648444; fax 3-5648334; f. 1921 as Gen. Mortgage Bank Ltd; subsidiary of Bank Leumi le-Israel BM; res 2,567m., dep. 48,605m., total assets 56,532m. (Dec. 2011); Chair. AVI ZELDMAN; Gen. Man. R. ZABAG; 9 brs.

STOCK EXCHANGE

The Tel-Aviv Stock Exchange: 54 Ahad Ha'am St, Tel-Aviv 65202; tel. 3-5677411; fax 3-5105379; e-mail info@tase.co.il; internet tase.co.il; f. 1953; Chair. SAUL BRONFELD; CEO ESTER LEVANON.

INSURANCE

The Israel Insurance Asscn lists 14 member companies; a selection of these are listed below, as are some non-members.

Clal Insurance Enterprise Holdings Ltd: POB 326, 46 Petach Tikva Rd, Tel-Aviv 66184; tel. 3-6387777; fax 3-6387676; e-mail avigdork@clal-ins.co.il; internet www.clalbit.co.il; f. 1962; 55% owned by IDB Group, 10% by Bank Hapoalim and 35% by the public; insurance, pensions and finance; Chair. KAPLAN AVIGDOR.

Dikla Insurance Co Ltd: 1 Ben Gurion Rd, BSR-2 Tower, Bnei Brak 51201; tel. 3-6145555; fax 3-6145566; internet www.dikla.co.il; f. 1976; health and long-term care insurance; Chair. YAIR HAMBURGER.

Eliahu Insurance Co Ltd: 2 Ibn Gvirol St, Tel-Aviv 64077; tel. 3-6920911; fax 3-6952117; e-mail gad.nussbaum@eliahu.com; internet www.eliahu.co.il; f. 1966; Chair. SHLOMO ELIAHU; Man. Dir OFER ELIAHU.

Harel Insurance Investments and Financial Services Ltd: Tel-Aviv; tel. 3-7547000; e-mail infonet@harel-group.co.il; internet www.harel-group.co.il; f. 1935 as Hamishmar Insurance Service; Harel est. 1975, became Harel Hamishmar Investments Ltd 1982, Harel Insurance Investments Ltd 1998 and current name adopted 2007; 39.9% owned by Hamburger family, 20.2% by Sampoerna Capital; Chair. GIDEON HAMBURGER.

Menorah Mivtachim Insurance Co Ltd: POB 927, 15 Allenby St, Tel-Aviv 61008; tel. 3-7107777; fax 3-7107402; e-mail anat-by@bezeqint.net; internet www.menoramivt.co.il; f. 1935; Chair. MENACHEM GUREWITZ; Gen. Man. SHABTAI ENGEL.

Migdal Insurance Co Ltd: POB 37633, 26 Sa'adiya Ga'on St, Tel-Aviv 67135; tel. 3-5637637; fax 3-9295189; e-mail marketing@migdal-group.co.il; internet www.migdal.co.il; 70% owned by Generali Group; 10% by Bank Leumi and 20% by the public; f. 1934; Chair. AHARON FOGEL; CEO YONEL COHEN.

Phoenix Insurance Co Ltd: 53 Derech Hashalom St, Givatayim 53454; tel. 3-7332222; fax 3-5735151; e-mail ir@fnx.co.il; internet www.fnx.co.il; f. 1949; controlled by Delek Group; Pres. and CEO EYAL LAPIDOT.

Trade and Industry

DEVELOPMENT ORGANIZATIONS

Galilee Development Authority: POB 2511, Acco 24316; tel. 4-9552426; fax 4-9552440; e-mail judith@galil.gov.il; internet www.galilee.gov.il; f. 1993; statutory authority responsible for the social and economic devt of the Galilee region; Man. Dir MOSHE DAVIDOVITZ.

Jerusalem Development Authority (JDA): 2 Safra Sq., Jerusalem 91322; tel. 2-6297627; e-mail moty@jda.gov.il; internet www.jda.gov.il; f. 1988; statutory authority responsible for the economic devt of Jerusalem; CEO MOTY HAZAN.

Negev Development Authority: Negev; e-mail negev_de@netvision.net.il; internet www.negev.co.il; f. 1991; statutory authority responsible for the economic and social devt of the Negev region, and co-ordination between govt offices; Chair SHMUEL RIFMAN.

CHAMBERS OF COMMERCE

Federation of Israeli Chambers of Commerce: POB 20027, 84 Ha' Hashmonaim St, Tel-Aviv 67132; tel. 3-5631020; fax 3-5619027; e-mail chamber@chamber.org.il; internet www.chamber.org.il; co-ordinates the Tel-Aviv, Jerusalem, Haifa, Nazareth and Beersheba Chambers of Commerce; Pres. URIEL LYNN.

Israel Federation of Bi-National Chambers of Commerce and Industry with and in Israel: POB 50196, 29 Hamered St, Tel-Aviv 61500; tel. 3-5177737; fax 3-5142881; e-mail felixk@export.gov.il; Chair. JAIME ARON; Man. Dir FELIX KIPPER.

Beersheba Chamber of Commerce: POB 5278, 7 Hamuktar St, Beersheba 84152; tel. 8-6234222; fax 8-6234899; e-mail chamber7@zahav.net.il; internet www.negev-chamber.org.il.

Chamber of Commerce and Industry of Haifa and the North: POB 33176, 53 Ha'atzmaut Rd, Haifa 31331; tel. 4-8302100; fax 4-8645428; e-mail main@haifachamber.org.il; internet www.haifachamber.com; f. 1921; 850 mems; Pres. GAD SCHAFFER; Man. Dir DOV MAROM.

Israel-British Chamber of Commerce: POB 50321, Industry House, 13th Floor, 29 Hamered St, Tel-Aviv 61502; tel. 3-5109424; fax 3-5109540; e-mail info@ibcc.co.il; internet www.ibcc.co.il; f. 1951; 350 mems; annual bilateral trade of more than US $3,000m; Chair. LEN JUDES; Exec. Dir FELIX KIPPER.

Jerusalem Chamber of Commerce: POB 2083, Jerusalem 91020; tel. 2-6254333; fax 2-6254335; e-mail jerccom@inter.net.il; internet www.jerccom.co.il; f. 1908; 200 mems; Pres. NAHUM WISSMANN.

INDUSTRIAL AND TRADE ASSOCIATIONS

Agricultural Export Co (AGREXCO): POB 2061, 121 Ha'Hashmonaim St, Tel-Aviv 61206; tel. 3-5630940; fax 3-5630988; e-mail info@agrexco.com; internet www.agrexco.co.il; state-owned agricultural marketing org.; CEO SHLOMO TIROSH.

The Centre for International Agricultural Development Cooperation (CINADCO): POB 30, Beit Dagan 50250; tel. 3-9485760; fax 3-9485761; e-mail cinadco@moag.gov.il; internet www.cinadco.moag.gov.il; shares agricultural experience through the integration of research and project devt; runs specialized training courses, advisory missions and feasibility projects in Israel and abroad, incl. those in co-operation with developing countries; Dir OMAR ZEIDAN (acting).

Citrus Marketing Board of Israel: POB 54, Beit Dagan 50280; tel. 3-9595654; fax 3-9501495; e-mail info@jaffa.co.il; internet www.jaffa.co.il; f. 1941; central co-ordinating body of citrus growers and exporters in Israel; represents the citrus industry in international orgs; licenses private exporters; controls the quality of fruit; has responsibility for Jaffa trademarks; mounts advertising and promotion campaigns for Jaffa citrus fruit world-wide; carries out research and devt of new varieties of citrus and environmentally friendly fruit.

Fruit Board of Israel: POB 20117, 119 Rehov Ha' Hashmonaim, Tel-Aviv 61200; tel. 3-5632929; fax 3-5614672; e-mail fruits@fruit.org.il; internet www.fruit.org.il.

Israel Dairy Board (IDB): POB 15578, 46 Derech Ha'macabim, Rishon le Zion 75054; tel. 3-9564750; fax 3-9564766; e-mail office@is-d-b.co.il; internet www.israeldairy.com; regulates dairy-farming and the dairy industry; implements govt policy on the planning of milk production and marketing; Man. Dir SHYKE DRORI.

Israel Diamond Exchange Ltd: 3 Jabotinsky Rd, Ramat-Gan 52130; tel. 3-5760300; fax 3-5750652; e-mail ella@isde.co.il; internet www.isde.co.il; f. 1937; production, export, import and finance facilities; exports: polished diamonds US $6,610m., rough diamonds $2,701m. (2006); Pres. and Chair. AVI PAZ; Man. Dir YAIR COHEN-PRIVA.

Israel Export and International Co-operation Institute: POB 50084, 29 Hamered St, Tel-Aviv 68125; tel. 3-5142900; fax 3-5162810; e-mail galit@export.gov.il; internet www.export.gov.il; f. 1958; jt venture between the state and private sectors; Dir-Gen. AVI HEFETZ.

The Israeli Cotton Board: POB 384, Herzlia B 46103; tel. 9-9604000; fax 9-9604030; e-mail cotton@cotton.co.il; internet www.cotton.co.il; f. 1956 as the Israel Cotton Production and Marketing Board.

Kibbutz Industries' Asscn: POB 40012, 13 Leonardo da Vinci St, Tel-Aviv 61400; tel. 3-6955413; fax 3-6951464; e-mail kia@kia.co.il; internet www.kia.co.il; f. 1962; liaison office for marketing and export of the goods produced by Israel's kibbutzim; Chair. JONATHAN MELAMED; Man. Dir AMOS RABIN.

Manufacturers' Asscn of Israel: POB 50022, Industry House, 29 Hamered St, Tel-Aviv 61500; tel. 3-5198832; fax 3-5103154; e-mail leor@industry.org.il; internet www.industry.org.il; 1,700 mem. enterprises employing nearly 85% of industrial workers in Israel; Dir LEOR APPELBAUM; Pres. SHRAGA BROSH.

National Federation of Israeli Journalists: POB 585, Beit Agron, 37 Hillet St, Jerusalem 91004; tel. 2-6254351; fax 3-6254353; e-mail office@jaj.org.il; Chair. AHIYA GENOSAR.

Plants Production and Marketing Board: 46 Derech Ha'macabim, Rishon le Zion 75359; tel. 3-9595666; fax 3-9502211; e-mail plants@plants.org.il; internet www.plants.org.il.

UTILITIES

Israel Electric Corporation Ltd (IEC): POB 58003, Halechi 17, Bnei-Brak IT School, Haifa 1200; tel. 3-6174944; fax 3-6174922; e-mail ucgia@iec.co.il; internet www.iec.co.il; state-owned; total assets US $21,065m. (Dec. 2009); Chair. YIFTAH RON TAL; Pres. and CEO ELI GLIKMAN.

Mekorot (Israel National Water Co): POB 2012, 9 Lincoln St, Tel-Aviv 61201; tel. 3-6230555; fax 3-6230833; e-mail m-doveret@mekorot.co.il; internet www.mekorot.co.il; f. 1937; state-owned; sales more than US $700m. (2006); Chair. ALEX WIZNITZER; CEO SHIMON BEN HAMO.

MAJOR INVESTMENT HOLDING COMPANIES

Delek Group: POB 8464, 7 Giborei Israel St, Netanya 42504; tel. 9-8638444; fax 9-8854955; e-mail contact@delek.co.il; internet www

.delek-group.com; f. 1951; est. as Israel Fuel Corpn; energy, infrastructure, financial services, automotive import and retail distribution; Chair. GABRIEL LAST; CEO and Pres. ASAF BARTFELD.

Elco Holdings Ltd: 21 Shaul Hamelech Blvd, Tel-Aviv 64367; tel. 3-6939696; fax 3-6939689; internet www.elco.co.il; f. 1949; controls five business units: Electra Ltd, Electra Real Estate Ltd, Electra Consumer Products Ltd, Airwell Airconditioning B.V. and Elco Landmark Residential Holdings LLC; revenue US $1,766m. (2009); Chair. GEORG SALKIND.

Israel Corpn: POB 20456, Millenium Tower, 23 Aranha St, Tel-Aviv 61204; tel. 3-6844500; fax 3-6844570; e-mail IR@israelcorp.com; internet israelcorp.com; f. 1968; privatized in 1999; 55% owned by Ofer Group (Israel); chemicals, fertilizers, energy, transportation and shipping; sales US $12,498m. (2009); Chair. AMIR ELSTEIN.

Koor Industries Ltd: Azrieli Center, Triangle Tower, Tel-Aviv 67023; tel. 3-6075111; fax 3-6075110; e-mail info@koor.com; internet www.koor.com; investments in telecommunications, defence electronics, agrochemicals and venture capital; 76.5% owned by IDB Group (Israel); revenue NIS 2,860m. (2009); Chair. AMRI EREL; CEO RAANAN COHEN.

MAJOR COMPANIES

Alon Holdings Blue Square—Israel Ltd: 2 Amal St, Afek Industrial Park, Rosh Ha'ayin 48092; tel. 3-9282222; e-mail sherut@bsi.co.il; internet www.bsi.co.il; retail group; 72.7% owned by Alon Retail (Israel); operates 195 supermarkets under five brands; revenue US $1,039.7m.; CEO DAVID WIESSMAN; 7,000 employees.

Elbit Systems Ltd: POB 539, Advanced Technical Centre, Haifa 31053; tel. 4-8315315; fax 4-8550002; e-mail marketing@elbitsystems.com; internet www.elbitsystems.com; f. 1996; state-owned; defence electronics co engaged in wide range of defence-related programmes world-wide; acquired Tadiran Communications (Israel's leading mfr of civil and military communications technology) in 2008; total revenue US $2,888.6m. (2012); Chair. of Bd MICHAEL FEDERMANN; Pres. and CEO BEZHALEL MACHLIS; 12,100 employees.

Israel Aerospace Industries Ltd (IAI): Ben-Gurion International Airport, Tel-Aviv 70100; tel. 3-9353111; fax 3-9353131; e-mail corpmkg@iai.co.il; internet www.iai.co.il; f. 1953; 100% state-owned; designers and mfrs of military and civil aerospace; Chair. DOV BAHARAV; Pres. and CEO JOSEPH WEISS; 14,700 employees.

Israel Chemicals Ltd: Millenium Tower, 23 Aranha St, Tel-Aviv 61070; tel. 3-6844400; fax 3-6844444; e-mail contact@icl-group.com; internet www.icl-group.com; f. 1968; produces fertilizer, other chemicals and supplies phosphate products; revenue US $6,700m. (2013); Chair. of Bd NIR GILAD; Pres. and CEO STEFAN BORGAS; 12,000 employees (2013).

Israel Military Industries Ltd (IMI): POB 1044, Ramat Hasharon 47100; tel. 3-5485619; fax 3-5486125; e-mail imimrktg@imi-israel.com; internet www.imi-israel.com; f. 1933; govt-owned; designs and manufactures land, air and naval combat systems; turnover US $661.8m. (2012); Chair. of the Bd Gen. (retd) UDI ADAM; Pres. and CEO AVI FELDER; 3,200 employees.

Makhteshim Agan Industries Ltd (MA Industries): Golan St, Airport City 70151; tel. 3-2321000; fax 3-2321074; e-mail office@ma-industries.com; internet www.ma-industries.com; generic mfr and distributor of crop protection products; 60% owned by China National Chemical Corpn (People's Republic of China), 40% by Koor Industries Ltd; revenue US $803.3m. (2013); Chair. of the Bd YANG XINGQIANG; Pres. and CEO EREZ VIGODMAN.

Perrigo Israel Pharmaceuticals Ltd: 29 Lehi St, Bene Beraq 51200; tel. 3-5773700; fax 3-5773500; e-mail perrigo.israel@perrigo.co.il; internet www.perrigo-pharma.co.il; mfrs of over-the-counter and prescription drugs; subsidiary of Perrigo (USA); Pres. JOSEPH C. PAPA; 900 employees.

Rafael Advanced Defense Systems Ltd: POB 2250, Haifa 31021; tel. 4-8794444; fax 4-8794681; e-mail amitz@rafael.co.il; internet www.rafael.co.il; f. 2002; fmrly owned by the Ministry of Defence; designs and manufactures defence systems for air, land, sea and space applications; Chair. Brig.-Gen. (retd) YITZHAK GAT; 6,500 employees.

Scailex Corporation Ltd: 48 Ben-Zion Galis St, Segula Industrial Park, Petach Tikva 49277; tel. 3-9057730; fax 3-9300424; e-mail contact_us@scailex.com; internet www.scailex.com; f. 1968 as Scitex Corpn; present name adopted 2005; CEO YAHEL SHACHAR.

Soltam Systems Ltd: POB 13, Yokneam 20692; tel. 4-9896282; fax 4-9892045; e-mail headoffice@soltam.com; military manufacturer; owned by Elbit Systems; CEO GIDEON ARAZI; Pres. Col DAVID MARSIANO.

Strauss Group Ltd: 49 HaSivim St, Petach-Tikva 49517; tel. 3-6752111; fax 3-6752256; e-mail service@strauss-group.com; internet www.strauss-group.com; f. 2004 by merger of Strauss and Elite Industries Ltd; adopted present name 2007; produces, markets and distributes variety of food and drink products; operates in Israel and abroad; Chair. OFRA STRAUSS-LAHAT; Group CEO GADI LESIN; CEO, Israel ZION BALAS; 14,000 employees.

Teva Pharmaceutical Industries Ltd: 5 Basel St, Petach Tikva 49131; tel. 3-9267267; fax 3-9234050; internet www.tevapharm.com; f. 1944; pharmaceuticals; Chair. Dr PHILIP FROST; Pres. and CEO Dr JEREMY M. LEVIN; 46,000 employees world-wide (2013).

The Histadrut

Histadrut (General Federation of Labour in Israel): 93 Arlozorof St, Tel-Aviv 62098; tel. 3-6921511; fax 3-6921512; e-mail avitals@histadrut.org.il; internet www.histadrut.org.il; f. 1920; Chair. OFER EINI.

The Histadrut is the largest labour organization in Israel. It strives to ensure the social security, welfare and rights of workers, and to assist in their professional advancement, while endeavouring to reduce the divisions in Israeli society. Membership of the Histadrut is voluntary, and open to all men and women of 18 years of age and above who live on the earnings of their own labour without exploiting the work of others. These include the self-employed and professionals, as well as housewives, students, pensioners and the unemployed. Workers' interests are protected through a number of occupational and professional unions affiliated to the Histadrut (see below). The organization operates courses for trade unionists and new immigrants, as well as apprenticeship classes. It maintains an Institute for Social and Economic Issues and the International Institute, one of the largest centres of leadership training in Israel, for students from Africa, Asia, Latin America and Eastern Europe, which includes the Levinson Centre for Adult Education and the Jewish-Arab Institute for Regional Co-operation. Attached to the Histadrut is Na'amat, a women's organization which promotes changes in legislation, operates a network of legal service bureaux and vocational training courses, and runs counselling centres for the treatment and prevention of domestic violence; women joining the Histadrut automatically become members of Na'amat.

ORGANIZATION

In 2006 the Histadrut had a membership of 700,000. In addition, over 100,000 young people under 18 years of age belong to the Organization of Working and Student Youth, HaNoar HaOved VeHalomed, a direct affiliate of the Histadrut.

All members take part in elections to the Histadrut Convention (Veida), which elects the General Council (Moetsa) and the Executive Committee (Vaad Hapoel). The latter elects the 41-member Executive Bureau (Vaada Merakezet), which is responsible for day-to-day implementation of policy. The Executive Committee also elects the Secretary-General, who acts as its chairman as well as head of the organization as a whole and chairman of the Executive Bureau. Nearly all political parties are represented on the Histadrut Executive Committee.

The Executive Committee has the following departments: Trade Union, Organization and Labour Councils, Education and Culture, Social Security, Industrial Democracy, Students, Youth and Sports, Consumer Protection, Administration, Finance and International.

TRADE UNION ACTIVITIES

Collective agreements with employers fix wage scales, which are linked with the retail price index; provide for social benefits, including paid sick leave and employers' contributions to sick and pension and provident funds; and regulate dismissals. Dismissal compensation is regulated by law. The Histadrut actively promotes productivity through labour management boards and the National Productivity Institute, and supports incentive pay schemes.

There are unions for the following groups: clerical workers, building workers, teachers, engineers, agricultural workers, technicians, textile workers, printing workers, diamond workers, metal workers, food and bakery workers, wood workers, government employees, seamen, nurses, civilian employees of the armed forces, actors, musicians and variety artists, social workers, watchmen, cinema technicians, institutional and school staff, pharmacy employees, medical laboratory workers, X-ray technicians, physiotherapists, social scientists, microbiologists, psychologists, salaried lawyers, pharmacists, physicians, occupational therapists, truck and taxi drivers, hotel and restaurant workers, workers in Histadrut-owned industry, garment, shoe and leather workers, plastic and rubber workers, editors of periodicals, painters and sculptors, and industrial workers.

Histadrut Trade Union Department: Chair. DANIEL AVI NISSENKORN.

OTHER TRADE UNIONS

Histadrut Haovdim Haleumit (National Labour Federation): 23 Sprintzak St, Tel-Aviv 64738; tel. 3-6958351; fax 3-6961753; e-mail nol@netvision.net.il; f. 1934; Chair. YOAV SIMCHI; 220,000 mems.

Histadrut Hapoel Hamizrachi (National Religious Workers' Party): 166 Ibn Gvirol St, Tel-Aviv 62023; tel. 3-5442151; fax 3-5468942; 150,000 mems in 85 settlements and 15 kibbutzim.

Histadrut Poale Agudat Israel (Agudat Israel Workers' Organization): POB 11044, 64 Frishman St, Tel-Aviv; tel. 3-5242126; fax 3-5230689; 33,000 mems in 16 settlements and 8 educational insts.

Transport

RAILWAYS

In 2011 Israel's active railway network, including sidings, comprised an estimated 1,079 km of track. Freight traffic consists mainly of grain, phosphates, potash, containers, petroleum and building materials. A rail route serves Haifa and Ashdod ports on the Mediterranean Sea, while a combined rail-road service extends to Eilat port on the Red Sea. Passenger services operate between the main towns: Nahariya, Haifa, Tel-Aviv and Jerusalem. Construction of a high-speed rail link between Jerusalem and Tel-Aviv commenced in 2001. However, owing to technical and financial difficulties, completion of the project was not expected before 2017. The first line of a light railway network intended to ease traffic congestion in Jerusalem was inaugurated in August 2011. The project was a source of considerable controversy owing to the incorporation within the network of disputed Jewish developments in East Jerusalem.

Israel Railways (IR): POB 18085, Central Station, Tel-Aviv 61180; tel. 3-5774000; fax 3-6937443; e-mail pniyot@rail.co.il; internet www.rail.co.il; f. 2003 as an ind. govt-owned corpn; prior to that date IR had operated as a unit of the Ports and Railways Authority; CEO Boaz Zafrir.

Underground Railway

Haifa Underground Funicular Railway: 122 Hanassi Ave, Haifa 34633; tel. 4-8376861; fax 4-8376875; e-mail orna@carmelit.com; internet www.carmelit.com; opened 1959; 2 km in operation.

ROADS

In 2010 there were 18,470 km of roads, of which 447 km were motorways, 6,068 km were highways, main or national roads and 11,955 km were other roads.

Ministry of Transport, National Infrastructures and Road Safety: see The Government—Ministries.

Egged Bus Co-operative: POB 43, Egged Bldg, Airport City 70150; tel. 3-9142000; fax 3-9142237; internet www.egged.co.il; f. 1933; operates 2,980 bus routes throughout Israel; Chair. Gideon Mizrachi.

SHIPPING

At 31 December 2012 Israel's flag registered fleet consisted of 38 vessels, with a combined aggregate displacement of 271,992 grt, of which one was a fish carrier and four were general cargo ships.

Haifa and Ashdod are the main ports in Israel. The former is a natural harbour, enclosed by two main breakwaters and dredged to 45 ft below mean sea level. Haifa handled 24.0m. metric tons of cargo and 1.4m. 20-ft equivalent units (TEUs) in 2012. The deep-water port at Ashdod was completed in 1965. A new NIS 3,000m. container terminal, Eitan Port, was inaugurated at Ashdod in 2005. Ashdod handled 19.5m. tons of cargo and 1.2m. TEUs in 2012. In 2009 the Government approved proposals to sell minority stakes in the Haifa and Ashdod port companies. The three-stage privatization process commenced in early 2010, with 15% of the shares in each company to be sold via a public offering.

The port of Eilat, Israel's gateway to the Red Sea, has storage facilities for crude petroleum. It is a natural harbour, operated from a wharf. In April 2011 the Government announced its intention fully to privatize the Eilat Port Company. The plan was approved by the Knesset in May 2012.

Port Authority and Companies

Israel Ports Development and Assets Co Ltd (IPC): POB 20121, 74 Menachem Begin Rd, Tel-Aviv 61201; tel. 3-5657060; fax 3-5622281; e-mail dovf@israports.co.il; internet www.israports.co.il; f. 1961 as the Israel Ports Authority (PRA); the IPC was established by legislation in 2005 as part of the Israeli Port Reform Program, whereby the PRA was abolished and replaced by four govt-owned cos: the IPC as owner and developer of port and infrastructure, and three port-operating cos responsible for handling cargo in each of Israel's three commercial seaports; responsible for devt and management of Israel's port infrastructure on behalf of the Govt and carries out some of the largest infrastructure projects in the country; CEO Shlomo Brieman.

Ashdod Port Co Ltd: POB 9001, Ashdod 77191; tel. 8-8517605; fax 8-8517632; e-mail igalbz@ashdodport.co.il; internet www.ashdodport.co.il; provides full range of freight and passenger services; f. 1965; CEO Shuki Sagis.

Haifa Port Co Ltd: Haifa; tel. 4-8518365; fax 4-8672872; internet www.haifaport.co.il; 6.5-km dock, 10.5m–14m draught; f. 1933; CEO Mendi Zaltzman.

Principal Shipping Companies

Ofer Shipping Group: POB 15090, 9 Andre Saharov St, Matam Park, Haifa 31905; tel. 4-8610610; fax 4-8501515; e-mail mail@oferg.com; internet www.oferg.com; f. 1956 as shipping agency, Mediterranean Seaways; part of the Ofer Group; runs cargo and container services; Chair. Udi Angel.

ZIM Integrated Shipping Services Ltd: POB 1723, 9 Andrei Sakharov St, MATAM Park, Haifa 31016; tel. 4-8652111; fax 4-8652956; e-mail shats.avner@il.zim.com; internet www.zim.co.il; f. 1945; 100% owned by the Israel Corpn; international integrated transportation system providing door-to-door services around the world; operates about 100 vessels; estimated 2m. TEUs of cargo carried in 2006; Chair. of Bd Nir Gilad; Pres. and CEO Rafi Danieli.

CIVIL AVIATION

The principal airport is Ben-Gurion International Airport, situated about 15 km from the centre of Tel-Aviv. Limited international services also operate from Ovda Airport in the Negev Desert. The busiest domestic airports are located at Eilat, Haifa, Rosh Pina and Sde Dov (Tel-Aviv). In 2011 the Government approved a proposal to build a new international airport with a capacity of 1.5m. passengers at Timna, north of Eilat, at a projected cost of NIS 1,700m. Construction of the airport, which was to replace the existing airports at Eilat and Ovda, was expected to be completed in 2014.

Israel Airports Authority: POB 137, Ben-Gurion Airport, Tel-Aviv 70100; tel. 3-9752386; fax 3-9752387; internet www.iaa.gov.il; f. 1977; Chair. Eli Ovadia.

El Al Israel Airlines Ltd: 32 Ben-Yehuda St, Tel-Aviv; tel. 3-9771111; fax 3-6292312; e-mail customer@elal.co.il; internet www.elal.co.il; f. 1948; over 40% owned by Knafaim-Arkia Holdings Ltd; about 31% state-owned; regular services to many European cities, as well as to destinations in North America, Africa and Asia; direct flights to Brazil, with connecting flights to other South American destinations, launched in early 2009; Chair. of Bd Amikam Cohen; Pres. and CEO Gen. (retd) Eliezer Shkedi.

Arkia Israeli Airlines Ltd: POB 39301, Dov Airport, Tel-Aviv 61392; tel. 3-6902210; fax 3-6903311; e-mail customer.service@arkia.co.il; internet www.arkia.co.il; f. 1980 by merger of Kanaf-Arkia Airlines and Aviation Services; scheduled passenger services linking Tel-Aviv, Jerusalem, Haifa, Eilat, Rosh Pina, Kiryat Shmona and Yotveta; charter services to many European destinations, Turkey and Jordan; CEO Gad Tepper.

Israir Airlines: POB 26444, 23 Ben Yehuda St, Tel-Aviv 63806; tel. 3-7954038; fax 3-7954051; e-mail israir@israir.co.il; internet www.israir.co.il; f. 1996; domestic flights between Tel-Aviv and Eilat, and international flights to destinations in Europe and the USA; Pres. and CEO David Kaminitz.

Tourism

Israel possesses a wealth of antiquities and cultural attractions, in particular the historic and religious sites of Jerusalem. The country has a varied landscape, with a Mediterranean coastline, as well as desert and mountain terrain. The Red Sea resort of Eilat has become an important centre for diving holidays, while many tourists visit the treatment spas of the Dead Sea. In 2011 an estimated 2,820,200 tourists visited Israel, compared with some 2,803,100 the previous year. Tourism receipts, including passenger transport, in 2011 totalled US $4,849m.

Ministry of Tourism: See The Government—Ministries; Dir-Gen. Noaz Bar Nir.

Defence

The General Staff: This consists of the Chiefs of the General Staff, Personnel, Technology and Logistics, Intelligence, Operations, and Plans and Policy Branches of the Defence Forces, the Commanders-in-Chief of the Air Force and the Navy, and the officers commanding the four Territorial Commands (Northern, Central, Southern and Home Front). It is headed by the Chief of Staff of the Armed Forces.

Chief of Staff of the Armed Forces: Lt-Gen. Binyamin (Benny) Gantz.

Chief of Ground Forces Command: Maj.-Gen. Guy Zur.

Commander-in-Chief of the Air Force: Maj.-Gen. Amir Eshel.

Commander-in-Chief of the Navy: Maj.-Gen. Ram Rothberg.

Defence Budget (2012): NIS 60,000m.

Military Service (Jewish and Druze population only; Christians, Circassians and Muslims may volunteer): Officers are conscripted for regular service of 48 months, men 36 months, women 24 months. Annual training as reservists thereafter, to age 40 for men (54 for some specialists), 38 (or marriage/pregnancy) for women.

Total Armed Forces (as assessed at November 2012): 176,500: army 133,000 (107,000 conscripts); navy 9,500 (2,500 conscripts); air force 34,000. Reserves 465,000.

Paramilitary Forces (as assessed at November 2012): est. 8,000.

Education

Israel has high standards of literacy and advanced educational services. Free, compulsory education is provided for all children between five and 15 years of age. Following the recommendations of a committee set up in 2011 to investigate ways to improve socio-economic conditions within Israel, the Government announced that pre-primary education for children aged three and four years in public institutions would be provided free of charge. The changes entered into effect in August 2012, at the beginning of the new academic year. Primary education is provided for all those between five and 10 years of age. There is also secondary, vocational and agricultural education. Post-primary education comprises two cycles of three years. According to UNESCO estimates, enrolment at primary schools in 2008/09 included 97% of pupils in the relevant age group, while 98% of pupils in the appropriate age group were enrolled at secondary schools. There are six universities, as well as the Technion (Israel Institute of Technology) in Haifa and the Weizmann Institute of Science in Rehovot. In 2010 general government expenditure on education totalled NIS 55,015m. (some 15.9% of total spending).

OCCUPIED TERRITORIES

THE GOLAN HEIGHTS

LOCATION AND CLIMATE

The Golan Heights, a mountainous plateau that formed most of Syria's Quneitra Province (1,710 sq km) and parts of Dar'a Province, was occupied by Israel after the Arab–Israeli War of June 1967. Following the Disengagement Agreement of 1974, Israel continued to occupy some 70% of the territory (1,176 sq km), valued for its strategic position and abundant water resources (the headwaters of the Jordan river have their source on the slopes of Mount Hermon). The average height of the Golan is approximately 1,200 m above sea level in the northern region and about 300 m above sea level in the southern region, near Lake Tiberias (the Sea of Galilee). Rainfall ranges from about 1,000 mm per year in the north to less than 600 mm per year in the southern region.

DEMOGRAPHY

As a consequence of the Israeli occupation, an estimated 93% of the ethnically diverse Syrian population of 147,613, distributed across 163 villages and towns and 108 individual farms, was expelled. The majority were Arab Sunni Muslims, but the population also included Alawite and Druze minorities and some Circassians, Turkmen, Armenians and Kurds. Approximately 9,000 Palestinian refugees from the 1948 Arab–Israeli War also inhabited the area. At the time of the occupation, the Golan was a predominantly agricultural province, 64% of the labour force being employed in agriculture. Only one-fifth of the population resided in the administrative centres. By 1991 the Golan Heights had a Jewish population of about 12,000 living in 21 Jewish settlements (four new settlements had been created by the end of 1992), and a predominantly Druze population of some 16,000 living in the only six remaining villages, of which Majd al-Shams is by far the largest. According to official figures, at the end of 2011 the Golan Heights had a total population of 43,100, of whom 18,700 were Jews, 2,300 were Muslims and 21,000 Druze.

ADMINISTRATION

Prior to the Israeli occupation, the Golan Heights were incorporated by Syria into a provincial administration of which the city of Quneitra, with a population at the time of 27,378, was the capital. The Disengagement Agreement that was mediated by US Secretary of State Henry Kissinger in 1974 (after the 1973 Arab–Israeli War) provided for the withdrawal of Israeli forces from Quneitra. Before withdrawal, however, Israeli army engineers destroyed the city. In December 1981 the Israeli Knesset enacted the Golan Annexation Law, whereby Israeli civilian legislation was extended to the territory of Golan, now under the administrative jurisdiction of the Commissioner for the Northern District of Israel. The Arab-Druze community of the Golan responded immediately by declaring a strike and appealed to the UN Secretary-General to force Israel to rescind the annexation decision. At the seventh round of multilateral talks between Israeli and Arab delegations in Washington, DC, USA, in August 1992, the Israeli Government of Itzhak Rabin for the first time accepted that UN Security Council Resolution 242, adopted in 1967, applied to the Golan Heights. In January 1999 the Knesset approved legislation stating that any transfer of land under Israeli sovereignty (referring to the Golan Heights and East Jerusalem) must be approved by both an absolute majority of Knesset members and by the Israeli electorate at a national referendum. Following the election of Ehud Barak as Israel's Prime Minister in May 1999, peace negotiations between Israel and Syria were resumed in December. However, in January 2000 the talks were postponed indefinitely after Syria demanded a written commitment from Israel to withdraw from the Golan Heights. In July 2001 Israel's recently elected premier, Ariel Sharon, stated that he would be prepared to resume peace talks with Syria, but Sharon also declared that the Israeli occupation of the Golan was 'irreversible'.

Syrian President Bashar al-Assad claimed in March 2007 that Syrian representatives had been conducting secret, unofficial discussions with Israeli officials during recent years. Despite official denials of any such talks, in July a spokesman for the Israeli Ministry of Foreign Affairs confirmed that messages had been relayed between Israel and Syria by third parties for some time. Tensions between Israel and Syria worsened in September, after Israel carried out an air-strike on a military installation 'deep within' Syrian territory. Both countries confirmed in May 2008 that indirect negotiations aimed at concluding a 'comprehensive peace' were being held through Turkish intermediaries in İstanbul. By the second week of August four rounds of the Turkish-mediated discussions had taken place, although no significant progress had apparently been reached as far as resolving the principal outstanding issues was concerned. Despite subsequent claims by President Assad that Israel and Syria were within 'touching distance' of reaching a peace deal, a fifth round of talks, scheduled for September, was delayed owing to the political uncertainty in Israel following Olmert's resignation as premier. Moreover, President Assad apparently responded to Israel's large-scale military offensive against Hamas targets in the Gaza Strip between December and January 2009 by formally suspending the indirect discussions with Israel.

The inauguration, in March 2009, of a new Israeli Government under Prime Minister Binyamin Netanyahu of Likud, with the right-wing Israel Beytenu leader, Avigdor Lieberman, being appointed as Minister of Foreign Affairs, was widely perceived as an obstacle to hopes of a resumption of bilateral negotiations: both have declared their opposition to the surrender of the Golan Heights as part of any Israeli-Syrian peace agreement. In November the Knesset approved legislation stating that any Israeli withdrawal from the Golan Heights would require the prior endorsement of Israeli voters in a national referendum. Hopes of further progress towards a resumption of direct negotiations were put on hold as a result of the popular uprising that emerged in Syria (q.v.) from early 2011, with the Syrian Government's attention focused primarily on quelling increasing levels of civil unrest. In May Israeli troops clashed with hundreds of pro-Palestinian protesters who had broken through a security fence to enter the Golan Heights from Syria. Syrian state media reported in the following month that 12 Palestinians and two Syrians had been killed when Israeli soldiers opened fire at another group of protesters attempting to enter the Golan Heights from across the Syrian border; according to hospital reports, some 225 others were injured in the incident. The Israeli authorities accused the Assad regime of orchestrating the violence as a means of diverting international attention from the harsh measures employed by Syrian government forces against opposition activists. From late 2012, with the Syrian domestic unrest having descended into civil conflict, fears increased that the violence could spill over into the Golan Heights. In November a campaign by Syria against opposition fighters located near the border resulted in mortar shells landing close to Israeli army posts in the north of the territory, prompting retaliatory attacks on Syrian government positions by Israeli troops. Netanyahu responded by asserting that Israel would defend its borders and those citizens living in the Golan Heights. The Syrian Government, for its part, pledged to prevent any accidental shelling of the Israeli-controlled areas. In a report published at the end of June 2013, UN Secretary-General Ban Ki-Moon recommended that the UN Disengagement Observer Force (UNDOF) be expanded and that it be given additional self-defence capabilities. Earlier in that year there had been two separate instances in which UNDOF troops had been abducted by Syrian militant groups, while in early June Austria had announced the withdrawal of its troops from UNDOF (representing one-third of the total), citing concerns over their security.

EAST JERUSALEM

LOCATION

Greater Jerusalem includes: Israeli West Jerusalem (99% Jewish); the Old City and Mount of Olives; East Jerusalem (the Palestinian residential and commercial centre); Arab villages declared to be part of Jerusalem by Israel in 1967; and Jewish neighbourhoods constructed since 1967, either on land expropriated from Arab villages or in areas requisitioned as 'government land'. Although the area of the Greater Jerusalem district is 627 sq km, the Old City of Jerusalem covers just 1 sq km.

DEMOGRAPHY

In June 1993 the Deputy Mayor of Jerusalem, Avraham Kahila, declared that the city now had 'a majority of Jews', based on population forecasts that estimated the Jewish population at 158,000 and the Arab population at 155,000. For the Israeli administration this signified the achievement of a long-term objective. Immediately prior to the 1967 Arab–Israeli War, East Jerusalem and its Arab environs had an Arab population of approximately 70,000, and a small Jewish population in the old Jewish quarter of the city. By contrast, Israeli West Jerusalem had a Jewish population of 196,000. As a result of this imbalance, in the Greater Jerusalem district as a whole the Jewish population was in the majority even prior to the occupation of the whole city in 1967. Israeli policy following the occupation of East Jerusalem and the West Bank consisted of encircling the eastern sector of the city with Jewish settlements. In contrast to the more politically sensitive siting of Jewish settlements in the old Arab quarter of Jerusalem, the Government of Itzhak Rabin concentrated on the outer circle of settlement building. Official statistics for the end of 2011 reported that Greater Jerusalem had a total population of 968,800, of whom 650,000 were Jews, 291,100 were Muslims and 15,300 were Christians. The Jerusalem Institute for Israel Studies (JIIS) estimated in August 2007 that the growth rate for the Arab population of Greater Jerusalem was almost double that of the Jewish population. According to the JIIS, if this trend continued, the city's population would have a Jewish-Arab ratio of 60:40 by 2020, and of 50:50 by 2035. In May 2007 the mayor of Jerusalem, Uri Lupolianski, suggested easing the restrictions on family reunification for the estimated 10,000 Christian Arabs in Jerusalem, in order to prevent a further decline in their number.

The Old City, within the walls of which are found the ancient quarters of the Jews, Christians, Muslims and Armenians, is predominantly Arab. According to JIIS, the Old City had a total population of 40,607 in 2010.

ADMINISTRATION

Until the 1967 Arab–Israeli War, Jerusalem had been divided into the new city of West Jerusalem—captured by Jewish forces in 1948—and the old city, East Jerusalem, which was part of Jordan. Israel's victory in 1967, however, reunited the city under Israeli control. Two weeks after the fighting had ended, on 28 June, Israeli law was applied to East Jerusalem and the municipal boundaries were extended by 45 km (28 miles). Jerusalem had effectively been annexed. Israeli officials, however, still refer to the 'reunification' of Jerusalem.

Immediately following the occupation, all electricity, water and telephone grids in West Jerusalem were extended to the east. Roads were widened and cleared, and the Arab population immediately in front of the 'Wailing Wall' was forcibly evicted. Arabs living in East Jerusalem became 'permanent residents' and could apply for Israeli citizenship if they wished (in contrast to Arabs in the West Bank and Gaza Strip). However, few chose to do so. None the less, issued with identity cards (excluding the estimated 25,000 Arabs from the West Bank and Gaza living illegally in the city), the Arab residents were taxed by the Israeli authorities, and their businesses and banks became subject to Israeli laws and business regulations. Now controlling approximately one-half of all land in East Jerusalem and the surrounding Palestinian villages (previously communally, or privately, owned by Palestinians), the Israeli authorities allowed Arabs to construct buildings on only 10%–15% of the land in the city, and East Jerusalem's commercial district has been limited to three streets.

Since the 1993 signing of the Declaration of Principles on Palestinian Self-Rule, the future status of Jerusalem and the continuing expansion of Jewish settlements in East Jerusalem have emerged as two of the most crucial issues affecting the peace process. In May 1999 the Israeli Government announced its refusal to grant Israeli citizenship to several hundred Arabs living in East Jerusalem, regardless of their compliance with the conditions stipulated under the Citizenship Law. In October, however, Israel ended its policy of revoking the right of Palestinians to reside in Jerusalem if they had spent more than seven years outside the city. Moreover, the Israeli Government announced in March 2000 that Palestinian residents of Jerusalem whose identity cards had been revoked could apply for their restoration.

At the Camp David talks held between Israel and the Palestinian (National) Authority (PA) in July 2000, the issue of who would have sovereignty over East Jerusalem in a future 'permanent status' agreement proved to be the principal obstacle to the achievement of a peace deal. It was reported that the Israeli Government had offered the PA municipal autonomy over certain areas of East Jerusalem (including access to the Islamic holy sites), although sovereignty would remain in Israeli hands; the proposals were rejected by PA President Yasser Arafat. In September the holy sites of East Jerusalem were the initial focal point of a renewed uprising by Palestinians against the Israeli authorities, which became known as the al-Aqsa *intifada* (after Jerusalem's al-Aqsa Mosque). Although the publication of the internationally sponsored 'roadmap' peace plan in April 2003 offered directions for talks on the Jerusalem issue, the resumption of attacks by Palestinian militants against Israeli citizens in mid-2003 and Israeli counter-strikes against Palestinian targets, made any such discussions untenable at that time.

Following a lengthy period during which all negotiations between Israel and the PA were effectively stalled, owing to the continued Israeli–Palestinian violence as well as political instability in the Palestinian territories, some optimism was expressed in August 2007 when the Israeli Prime Minister, Ehud Olmert, held direct talks with the PA President, Mahmud Abbas, in the West Bank town of Jericho in preparation for an international Middle East peace conference, which was convened in Annapolis, Maryland, USA, in November. The US Administration of President George W. Bush declared its intention that a permanent Israeli-Palestinian settlement, including the establishment of a Palestinian state, could be reached by the end of the year. However, an increase in attacks being perpetrated by Palestinian militants from the Gaza Strip into northern Israel from January 2008, and a consequent military campaign by Israeli forces in Gaza, resulted in a stalling of negotiations. In February the Israeli Prime Minister angered Palestinians by declaring that talks concerning the final status of Jerusalem, and the key Palestinian demand that East Jerusalem become their capital, would be the last 'core issue' on the agenda to be negotiated by the two parties. Moreover, the Israeli Government continued to issue tenders for hundreds of new housing units at Jewish settlements in East Jerusalem and the West Bank, thereby contravening its obligations under the terms of the roadmap. Relations between Israelis and Palestinians worsened considerably in December, when the Israeli military initiated its month-long campaign against Hamas militants in Gaza.

Following the inauguration of Barack Obama as US President in January 2009, a series of senior-level summits between US envoys and Israeli and other Middle Eastern leaders took place. However, the Obama Administration's demand for a temporary halt to Israel's settlement-building programme, as a precondition for the resumption of the peace process, remained an obstacle to further progress. In December the Israeli Government announced the imposition of a 10-month moratorium on settlement-building in the West Bank; however, building activity in East Jerusalem was exempted. In a speech to the American Israel Public Affairs Committee in Washington, DC, USA, in March 2010, Netanyahu asserted that the settlements were an 'integral and inextricable' part of the city and that building activity in all areas of Jerusalem would continue. Following the expiry in September of the temporary ban on Israeli settlement-building, the PA suspended its involvement in the peace process, stating that it would resume talks only when the Israeli Government had agreed to end both settlement construction and the blockade of Gaza. In August 2011 the Israeli Government approved plans for the construction of 1,600 new homes at Ramat Shlomo, announced in March 2010, and the following month indicated its intention to authorize the construction of a brand new settlement at Givat Hamatos, to the south of Jerusalem; the settlement was to incorporate some 2,600 homes. The announcements came amid increased tensions between Israel and the PA, following the announcement by Abbas that the PA would seek full membership in the UN at the annual meeting of the UN General Assembly scheduled to be held in September. Abbas duly presented the application on 23 September. Following the PA's acceptance at the end of October as a full member of UNESCO, the Israeli Government announced that it was to accelerate the construction of around 2,000 new homes in East Jerusalem and the West Bank. Further plans for expansion at the Har Homa and Pisgat Ze'ev settlements were published in January and April 2012. In October the Israeli Government gave its final approval to plans for 797 new homes at Gilo. Following the UN General Assembly's decision in November to upgrade the PA's status in the organization to that of a non-member observer state, Netanyahu announced his Government's intention to accelerate plans for the construction of some 3,000 new homes in the so-called E-1 area between Jerusalem and the Ma'ale Adumim settlement to the east of the city. The Israeli general election held in January 2013 was characterized by the success of the centrist Yesh Atid party and the pro-settlement Jewish Home party; upon the appointment of a new Cabinet in early March the latter was allocated responsibility for the Jerusalem affairs and housing portfolios. During a visit to Jerusalem in March, President Obama appealed for Israel to resume negotiations with the PA. Following subsequent repeated visits to the region by the newly appointed US Secretary of State, John F. Kerry, preliminary talks were held in Washington, DC, on 29 July between Israel's chief negotiator, Minister of Justice Tzipi Livni, and her PA counterpart, Saeb Erakat. The stated aim of the latest round of talks was for both parties to reach a limited agreement within nine months. Further discussions, moderated by President Obama's Special Envoy for Israeli-Palestinian Negotiations, Martin Indyk, took place in Jerusalem and Jericho in August. However, no progress was reported.

Bibliography

General and Historical Context

Abu-Baker, Khawla, and Rabinowitz, Dan. *Coffins on Our Shoulders: The Experience of the Palestinian Citizens of Israel*. Berkeley, CA, University of California Press, 2005.

Allon, Yigal. *The Making of Israel's Army*. London, Vallentine, Mitchell, 1970.

Atashe, Zeidan. *Druze and Jews in Israel: A Shared Destiny?* Eastbourne, Sussex Academic Press, 1995.

Bentwich, Norman. *Fulfilment in the Promised Land 1917–37*. London, 1938.

Judea Lives Again. London, 1944.

Israel Resurgent. Ernest Benn, 1960.

Israel, Two Fateful Years 1967–69. London, Elek, 1970.

Bermant, Chaim. *Israel*. London, Thames and Hudson, 1967.

Bethell, Nicholas. *The Palestine Triangle: The Struggle Between the British, the Jews and the Arabs, 1935–48*. London, André Deutsch, 1979.

Black, Ian, and Morris, Benny. *Israel's Secret Wars: History of Israel's Intelligence Services*. New York, Grove Weidenfeld, 1992.

Cattan, Henry. *Palestine, the Arabs and Israel*. London, Longmans Green, 1969.

The Palestine Question. London, Croom Helm; New York, Methuen, 1987.

Cohen, Mark R., and Udovitch, Abraham L. *Jews among Arabs: Contacts and Boundaries*. Princeton, NJ, The Darwin Press, 1994.

Cohen, Michael J. *Palestine, Retreat from the Mandate: The Making of British Policy*. London, Elek, 1978.

Crossman, R. H. S. *Palestine Mission*. London, 1947.

A Nation Reborn. London, Hamish Hamilton, 1960.

Davis, Moshe (Ed.). *Israel: Its Role in Civilisation*. New York, 1956.

Dayan, Shmuel. *The Promised Land*. London, 1961.

Dershowitz, Alan. *The Case for Israel*. Indianapolis, IN, John Wiley & Sons, 2004.

Dumper, Michael (Ed.). *Arab-Israeli Conflict*. Abingdon, Routledge, 2009.

El-Eini, Roza I. M. *Mandated Landscape: British Imperial Rule in Palestine, 1929–1948*. Abingdon, Routledge, 2006.

Ellis, Mark H. *Beyond Innocence and Redemption: Confronting the Holocaust and Israeli Power*. San Francisco, CA, Harper and Row, 1990.

Esco Foundation for Palestine. *Palestine: A Study of Jewish, Arab and British Policies*. 2 vols, New Haven, CT, 1947.

Ezrahi, Yaron. *Rubber Bullets: Power and Conscience in Modern Israel*. New York, Farrar Strauss Giroux, 1997.

Gilbert, Martin. *Israel: A History* (revised edn). London, Black Swan, 2008.

Glueck, Nelson. *The River Jordan*. Philadelphia, PA, 1946.

Rivers in the Desert: A History of the Negev. London, 1959.

Grinberg, Lev Luis. *Politics and Violence in Israel/Palestine: Democracy versus Military Rule*. Abingdon, Routledge, 2009.

Heller, Joseph. *The Stern Gang: Ideology, Politics and Terror 1940–49*. London, Frank Cass, 1995.

Hersh, Seymour. *The Samson Option: Israel, America and the Bomb*. London, Faber and Faber, 1991.

Jiryis, Sabri. *The Arabs in Israel*. Beirut, Institute for Palestine Studies, 1968.

Khalidi, Walid. *From Haven to Conquest: Readings in Zionism and the Palestine Problem until 1948*. Beirut, Institute for Palestine Studies, 1971.

Koestler, Arthur. *Thieves in the Night*. New York and London, 1946.

Promise and Fulfilment: Palestine, 1917–1949. London, 1949.

The Thirteenth Tribe. London, Random House, 1976.

Lochery, N. *View From the Fence: The Arab–Israeli Conflict from the Present to its Roots*. New York, Continuum, 2005.

Lorch, N. *The Edge of the Sword: Israel's War of Independence 1947–49*. New York, Putnam, 1961.

Louër, Laurence. *Les citoyens arabes d'Israël*. Paris, Balland, 2003.

To Be An Arab In Israel. London, C. Hurst and Co, 2006.

Marlowe, John. *The Seat of Pilate, An Account of the Palestine Mandate*. London, Cresset, 1959; Philadelphia, PA, Dufour, 1958.

Marmorstein, Emile. *Heaven at Bay: The Jewish Kulturkampf in the Holy Land*. Oxford, Oxford University Press, 1969.

Parfitt, Tudor (Ed.). *Israel and Ishmael: Studies in Muslim–Jewish Relations*. London, RoutledgeCurzon, 1999.

Parkes, J. W. *The Emergence of the Jewish Problem, 1878–1939*. Oxford, 1946.

A History of Palestine from AD 135 to Modern Times. London, Gollancz, 1949.

End of Exile. New York, 1954.

Whose Land? A History of the Peoples of Palestine. Harmondsworth, Pelican, 1970.

Patai, R. *Israel Between East and West*. Philadelphia, PA, 1953.

Culture and Conflict. New York, 1962.

Rabinovich, Itamar, and Reinharz, Jehuda (Eds). *Israel in the Middle East: Documents and Readings on Society, Politics, and Foreign Relations, pre-1948 to the Present*. Waltham, MA, Brandeis University Press, 2007.

Raviv, Dan, and Melman, Yossi. *Every Spy a Prince: The Complete History of Israel's Intelligence Community*. Boston, MA, Houghton Mifflin, 1990.

Royal Institute of International Affairs. *Great Britain and Palestine 1915–45*. London, 1946.

Sachar, Howard M. *The Peoples of Israel*. New York, 1962.

Safran, Alexandre. *Israël et ses racines*. Paris, Editions Albin Michel, 2001.

Schwarz, Tanya. *Ethiopian Jewish Immigrants in Israel*. London, RoutledgeCurzon, 1999.

Sheffer, Gabriel, and Barak, Oren (Eds). *Militarism and Israeli Society*. Bloomington, IN, Indiana University Press, 2010.

Shipler, David K. *Arab and Jew: Wounded Spirits in a Promised Land*. London, Bloomsbury, 1987.

Shlaim, Avi. *Israel and Palestine: Reflections, Revisions, Refutations*. London, Verso, 2009.

Stendel, Ori. *The Arabs in Israel*. Eastbourne, Sussex Academic Press, 1996.

Summerfield, Daniel. *From Falashas to Ethiopian Jews*. London, RoutledgeCurzon, 1999.

Zander, Walter. *Israel and the Holy Places of Christendom*. Weidenfeld and Nicolson, 1972.

Contemporary Political History

Achcar, Gilbert, and Warschawski, Michel. *The 33-Day War: Israel's War on Hezbollah in Lebanon and Its Aftermath*. London, Saqi Books, 2007.

Alimi, Eitan Y. *Israeli Politics and the First Palestinian Intifada: Political Opportunities, Framing Processes and Contentious Politics*. Abingdon, Routledge, 2009.

Arian, Asher. *Politics in Israel: The Second Republic* (2nd edn). Washington, DC, CQ Press, 2004.

Avi-hai, Avraham. *Ben Gurion, State Builder*. Israel Universities Press, 1974.

Badi, Joseph. *Fundamental Laws of the State of Israel*. New York, 1961.

Barari, Hassan. A. *Israeli Politics and the Middle East Peace Process, 1988–2002*. London, RoutledgeCurzon, 2004.

Bar-Zohar, Michael. *Ben-Gurion: A Biography*. London, Weidenfeld and Nicolson, 1978.

Bengio, Ofra. *The Turkish-Israeli Relationship: Changing Ties of Middle Eastern Outsiders*. Basingstoke, Palgrave Macmillan, 2010.

Ben Gurion, D. *Rebirth and Destiny of Israel*. New York, 1954.

Israel: A Personal History. London, New English Library, 1972.

Ben-Porat, Guy, et al. *Israel Since 1980*. Cambridge, Cambridge University Press, 2009.

Ben-Zvi, Abraham. *The United States and Israel: The Limits of the Special Relationship*. New York, Columbia University Press, 1993.

Berger, Earl. *The Covenant and the Sword, Arab-Israeli Relations 1948–56*. Toronto, University of Toronto Press, 1965.

Bishara, Marwan. *Palestine/Israel: Peace or Apartheid. Prospects for Resolving the Conflict*. London, Zed Books, 2001.

Bowen, Jeremy. *Six Days: How the 1967 War Shaped the Middle East*. London, Simon & Schuster, 2003.

Bregman, Ahron. *A History of Israel*. New York, Palgrave Macmillan, 2003.

Cohen, Amichai, and Cohen, Stuart. *Israel's National Security Law: Political Dynamics and Historical Development*. Abingdon, Routledge, 2011.

Cohen, Avner. *Israel and the Bomb*. New York, Columbia University Press, 1998.

Cohen, Yoel. *The Whistleblower of Dimona: Israel, Vanunu, and the Bomb*. New York, Holmes and Meier, 2003.

Davis, Uri. *Israel: An Apartheid State*. London, Zed Press, 1987.

De Gaury, Gerald. *The New State of Israel*. New York, 1952.

Dieckhoff, Alain (Ed.) (trans. Shread, Carolyn). *The Routledge Handbook of Modern Israel*. Abingdon, Routledge, 2013.

Doron, Gideon, Naor, Arye, and Meydani, Assaf (Eds). *Law and Government in Israel*. Abingdon, Routledge, 2010.

Draper, T. *Israel and World Politics: Roots of the Third Arab–Israeli War*. London, Secker and Warburg, 1968.

Eban, Abba. *The Voice of Israel*. New York, Horizon Press, 1957.

The Story of Modern Israel. London, Weidenfeld and Nicolson, 1973.

Edelman, Maurice. *Ben Gurion, a Political Biography*. London, Hodder and Stoughton, 1964.

Enderlin, Charles. *Le rêve brisé, histoire de l'échec du processus de paix au Proche-Orient, 1995–2002*. Paris, Editions Fayard, 2002.

Faris, Hani A. (Ed.). *The Failure of the Two-State Solution: The Prospects of One State in the Israel-Palestine Conflict*. London, I.B. Tauris, 2013.

Finkelstein, Norman G. *Image and Reality of the Israel–Palestine Conflict*. London and New York, Verso, 1995.

Frankel, William. *Israel Observed: An Anatomy of the State*. London, Thames and Hudson, 1980.

Fraser, T. G. *The Arab–Israeli Conflict*. London, Palgrave Macmillan, 2004.

Freedman, Robert O. (Ed.). *Contemporary Israel: Domestic Politics, Foreign Policy, and Security Challenges*. Boulder, CO, Westview Press, 2008.

Gabbay, Rony E. *A Political Study of the Arab–Jewish Conflict, the Arab Refugee Problem*. Geneva and Paris, 1959.

Gerstenfeld, Manfred, Rynhold, Jonathan, and Shmeul, Samuel. (Eds). *Israel at the Polls 2006*. Abingdon, Routledge, 2006.

Gerstenfeld, Manfred, Sandler, Shmuel, and Frisch, Hillel (Eds). *Israel at the Polls 2009*. Abingdon, Routledge, 2010.

Gilboa, Eytan, and Inba, Efraim (Eds). *US-Israeli Relations in a New Era: Issues and Challenges after 9/11*. Abingdon, Routledge, 2008.

Gluska, Ami. *The Israeli Military and the Origins of the 1967 War: Government, Armed Forces and Defence Policy 1963–67*. Abingdon, Routledge, 2009.

Green, Stephen. *Taking Sides: America and Israel in the Middle East, 1948–1967*. London, Faber and Faber, 1984.

Living by the Sword: America and Israel in the Middle East, 1968–1987. London, Faber and Faber, 1988.

Al-Haj, Majid, and Rosenfeld, Henry. *Arab Local Government in Israel*. Boulder, CO, San Francisco, CA, and London, Westview Press, 1990.

Hazony, Yoram. *The Jewish State: The Struggle for Israel's Soul*. New York, Basic Books, 2000.

Hollis, Rosemary. *Israel on the Brink of Decision: Division, Unity and Cross-currents in the Israeli Body Politic*. London, Research Institute for the Study of Conflict and Terrorism, 1990.

Howard, M., and Hunter, R. *Israel and the Arab World*. Beirut, Institute for Palestine Studies.

Janowsky, Oscar I. *Foundations of Israel: Emergence of a Welfare State*. Princeton, Anvil Nostrand Co, 1959.

Jones, Clive, and Catignani, Sergio (Eds). *Israel and Hizbollah: An Asymmetric Conflict in Historical and Comparative Perspective*. Abingdon, Routledge, 2009.

Jones, Clive, and Murphy, Emma C. *Israel: Challenges to Identity, Democracy and the State*. London, Routledge, 2001.

Kader, Razzak Abdel. *The Arab–Jewish Conflict*. 1961.

Karsh, Efraim. *Peace in the Middle East: The Challenge for Israel*. London, Frank Cass, 1994.

(Ed.). *Israel: The First Hundred Years, Vol. 1. Israel's Transition from Community to State*. London, Frank Cass, 2000.

(Ed.). *Israel: The First Hundred Years, Vol. 2. From War to Peace?* London, Frank Cass, 2000.

(Ed.). *Israel: The First Hundred Years, Vol. 3. Israeli Politics and Society since 1948. Problems of Collective Identity*. London, Frank Cass, 2001.

Karsh, Efraim, and Miller, Rory (Eds). *Israel at Sixty: Rethinking the Birth of the Jewish State*. Abingdon, Routledge, 2008.

Karsh, Efraim, Kerr, Michael, and Miller, Rory (Eds). *Conflict, Diplomacy and Society in Israeli-Lebanese Relations*. Abingdon, Routledge, 2010.

Kaye, Dalia Dassa. *Beyond the Handshake: Multilateral Co-operation in the Arab-Israeli Peace Process, 1991–96*. New York, Columbia University Press, 2001.

Kimche, Jon. *Palestine or Israel*. London, Secker and Warburg, 1973.

Kober, Avi. *Israel's Wars of Attrition: Attrition Challenges to Democratic States*. Abingdon, Routledge, 2009.

Kraines, O. *Government and Politics in Israel*. London, Allen and Unwin, 1961.

La Guardia, Anton. *Holy Land, Unholy War. Israelis and Palestinians*. London, John Murray, 2001.

Landau, Jacob M. *The Arabs in Israel*. London, Oxford University Press, 1969.

Laqueur, Walter. *The Road to War, 1967*. London, Weidenfeld and Nicolson, 1968.

The Israel-Arab Reader. London, Weidenfeld and Nicolson, 1969.

Lazin, A., and Mahler, G. S. *Israel in the Nineties: Development and Conflict*. University Press of Florida, 1996.

Levran, Aharon. *Israeli Strategy after Desert Storm: Lessons of the Second Gulf War*. London, Frank Cass, 1997.

Likhovski, Eliahu S. *Israel's Parliament: The Law of the Knesset*. Oxford, Clarendon Press, 1971.

Lucas, Noah. *The Modern History of Israel*. London, Weidenfeld and Nicolson, 1974–75.

Mazie, Steven V. *Israel's Higher Law: Religion and Liberal Democracy in the Jewish State*. Lanham, MD, Lexington Books, 2006.

McDonald, James G. *My Mission in Israel 1948–1951*. New York, Simon & Schuster, 1951.

McDowall, David. *Palestine and Israel: The Uprising and Beyond*. London, I. B. Tauris, 1989.

Medding, Peter Y. *Mapai in Israel: Political Organization and Government in a New Society*. Cambridge, Cambridge University Press, 2010.

Meir, Golda. *This is our Strength*. New York, 1963.

Merhav, Peretz. *The Israeli Left: History, Problems, Documents*. Tantivy Press, 1981.

Mollov, M. Ben, Rynhold, Jonathan, and Sandler, Shmuel (Eds). *Israel at the Polls 2003 (Israel History, Politics and Society)*. Abingdon, Routledge, 2005.

Morris, Benny. *1948: A History of the First Arab–Israeli War*. New Haven, CT, Yale University Press, 2008.

Netanyahu, Binyamin. *A Durable Peace: Israel and Its Place Among the Nations*. New York, Warner Books, 2000.

Nusseibeh, Sari, and Heller, Mark A. *No Trumpets, No Drums: A Two-State Settlement of the Israeli–Palestinian Conflict*. London, I. B. Tauris, 1992.

O'Ballance, E. *The Arab–Israeli War*. New York, Praeger, 1957.

The Third Arab–Israeli War. London, Faber and Faber, 1972.

Oren, Michael B. *Six Days of War: June 1967 and the Making of the Modern Middle East*. Oxford University Press, 2002.

Oz, Amos. *In the Land of Israel*. London, Chatto and Windus, 1983.

Pappé, Ilan. *The Forgotten Palestinians: A History of the Palestinians in Israel*. New Haven, CT, Yale University Press, 2011.

Peleg, Ilan, and Waxman, Dov. *Israel's Palestinians: The Conflict Within*. Cambridge, Cambridge University Press, 2011.

Penslar, Derek. *Israel in History: The Jewish State in Comparative Perspective*. Abingdon, Routledge, 2006.

Peretz, Don. *Israel and the Palestine Arabs*. Washington, DC, The Middle East Institute, 1958.

Intifada. Oxford, Westview Press, 1990.

Perlmutter, Amos. *Military and Politics in Israel, 1948–1967*. 2nd edn, London, Frank Cass, 1977.

Politics and the Military in Israel, 1967–1976. London, Frank Cass, 1977.

The Times and Life of Menachem Begin. New York, Doubleday, 1987.

Petras, James. *The Power of Israel in the United States*. Atlanta, GA, Clarity Press, 2006.

Polakow-Rubenstein, Sasha. *The Unspoken Alliance: Israel's Secret Relationship with Apartheid South Africa*. New York, Pantheon, 2010.

Rabin, Yitzhak. *The Rabin Memoirs*. London, Weidenfeld and Nicolson, 1979.

Rabinovich, Itamar. *Waging Peace: Israel and the Arabs, 1948–2003*. Princeton University Press, 2004.

Rodinson, Maxime. *Israel and the Arabs*. Harmondsworth, Penguin Books, 1968; New York, Pantheon, 1969.

Rothstein, Robert L., Ma'oz, Moshe, and Shikaki, Khalil (Eds). *The Israeli-Palestinian Peace Process: Oslo and the Lessons of Failure*. Sussex Academic Press, 2002.

Rubin, Barry. *Israel: An Introduction*. New Haven, CT, Yale University Press, 2012.

Sachar, Howard M. *A History of Israel:* Vol. I: *From the Rise of Zionism to Our Time;* Vol. II: *From the Aftermath of the Yom Kippur War*. Corby, Oxford University Press, 1987.

Samuel, The Hon. Edwin. *Problems of Government in the State of Israel*. Jerusalem, 1956.

Savir, Uri. *The Process: 1,100 Days that Changed the Middle East*. London, Random House, 1998.

Schiff, Ze'ev, and Ya'ari, Ehud. *Israel's Lebanon War*. New York, NY, Simon & Schuster, 1984.

Intifada: The Palestinian Uprising—Israel's Third Front. London, Simon & Schuster, 1990.

Segev, Tom. *One Palestine, Complete: Jews and Arabs Under the British Mandate*. New York, Metropolitan Books/Henry Holt & Co, 2000.

Seikaly, May. *Haifa: Transformation of an Arab Society, 1918–1939*. London, I B. Tauris, 2001.

Shahak, Israel. *Open Secrets: Israeli Foreign and Nuclear Policies*. London, Pluto Press, 1997.

Shahak, Israel, and Mezvinsky, Norton. *Jewish Fundamentalism in Israel*. London, Pluto Press, 2004

Sharabi, Hisham B. *Palestine and Israel: The Lethal Dilemma*. New York, Van Nostrand Reinhold, 1969.

Shindler, Colin. *Ploughshares into Swords? Israelis and Jews in the Shadow of the Intifada*. London, I. B. Tauris, 1992.

The Land Beyond Promise. Israel, Likud, and the Zionist Dream. London, I. B. Tauris, 2001.

A Modern History of Israel. Cambridge, Cambridge University Press, 2008.

Spyer, Jonathan. *The Transforming Fire: The Rise of the Israel-Islamist Conflict*. New York, Continuum, 2011.

Stein, Leslie. *The Making of Modern Israel: 1948–1967*. Cambridge, Polity Press, 2009.

Sykes, Christopher. *Crossroads to Israel*. London, Collins, 1965.

Teveth, Shabtai. *Ben-Gurion*. Boston, Houghton Mifflin, 1987.

Timerman, Jacob. *The Longest War*. London, Chatto and Windus, 1982.

Weizman, Ezer. *The Battle for Peace*. New York, Bantam Books, 1981.

Yakobson, Alexander, and Rubinstein, Amnon. *Israel and the Family of Nations: The Jewish Nation-State and Human Rights*. Abingdon, Routledge, 2008.

Zionism

Avishai, Bernard. *The Tragedy of Zionism*. Farrar Strauss Giroux, 1986.

Avnery, Uri. *Israel without Zionists*. London, Collier-Macmillan, 1969.

Bein, Alex. *Theodor Herzl*. London, East and West Library, 1957.

Cohen, Israel. *A Short History of Zionism*. London, Frederick Muller, 1951.

Engle, Anita. *The Nili Spies*. London, Frank Cass, 1997.

Fisch, Harold. *The Zionist Revolution: A New Perspective*. London, Weidenfeld and Nicolson, 1978.

Frankl, Oscar Benjamin. *Theodor Herzl: The Jew and Man*. New York, 1949.

Herzl, Theodor. *The Jewish State: An Attempt at a Modern Solution of the Jewish Question* (trans.). New York, Dover Publications, 1989.

Huneidi, Sahar. *A Broken Trust: Herbert Samuel, Zionism and the Palestinians*. London, I. B. Tauris, 2001.

Laqueur, Walter. *A History of Zionism*. London, Weidenfeld and Nicolson, 1972.

Lowenthal, Marvin (Ed. and trans.). *Diaries of Theodor Herzl*. New York, Grosset and Dunlap, 1965.

Mandel, Daniel. *H. V. Evatt and the Establishment of Israel: The Undercover Zionist*. London, Taylor and Francis, 2004.

O'Brien, Conor Cruise. *The Siege: The Saga of Israel and Zionism*. London, Weidenfeld and Nicolson, 1986.

Prior, Michael. *Zionism and the State of Israel: A Moral Inquiry*. London, Routledge, 1999.

Rose, Norman. *Chaim Weizmann*. London, Weidenfeld and Nicolson, 1987.

Rubinstein, Amnon. *From Herzl to Rabin: The Changing Image of Zionism*. New York, Holmes and Meier, 2001.

Schama, Simon. *Two Rothschilds and the Land of Israel*. London, Collins, 1978.

Schechtman, J. *Rebel and Statesman: The Jabotinsky Story*. New York, Thomas Yoseloff, 1956.

Shindler, Colin. *The Triumph of Military Zionism: Nationalism and the Origins of the Israeli Right*. London, I. B. Tauris, 2006.

Sober, Moshe. *Beyond the Jewish State: Confessions of a former Zionist*. Toronto, Summerhill Press, 1990.

Stein, Leonard, and Yogev, Gedilia (Eds). *The Letters and Papers of Chaim Weizmann; Volume I 1885–1902*. Oxford University Press, 1968.

Vital, David. *The Origins of Zionism*. Oxford University Press, 1975, reissued 1980.

Weisgal, Meyer, and Carmichael, Joel. *Chaim Weizmann—a Biography by Several Hands*. London, Weidenfeld and Nicolson, 1962.

Weizmann, Dr Chaim. *The Jewish People and Palestine*. London, 1939.

Trial and Error: The Autobiography of Chaim Weizmann. London, Hamish Hamilton, 1949; New York, Schocken, 1966.

Economy

Aharoni, Yair. *The Israeli Economy: Dreams and Realities*. London, Routledge, 1991.

Haidar, Aziz. *On The Margins: The Arab Population in the Israeli Economy*. Hurst and Co, 1997.

Maman, Daniel, and Rosenhek, Zeev. *The Israeli Central Bank: Political Economy, Global Logics and Local Actors*. Abingdon, Routledge, 2011.

Senor, Dan, and Singer, Saul. *Start-Up Nation: The Story of Israel's Economic Miracle*. New York, Twelve Books, 2009.

Shatil, J. *L'économie collective du kibboutz israëlien*. Paris, Les Editions de Minuit, 1960.

Official Publications

Annual Yearbook of the Government of Israel.

Government Survey of Palestine. 2 vols, 1945–46, Jerusalem. Supplement, July 1947, Jerusalem.

Jewish Agency for Palestine. Documents Submitted to General Assembly of UN, relating to the National Home, 1947.

The Jewish Plan for Palestine. Jerusalem, 1947.

Statistical Survey of the Middle East. 1944.

Report of the Anglo-American Committee of Enquiry. Lausanne, 1946.

Report of the Palestine Partition Commission, 1938. Cmd 5854, London.

Report of the Palestine Royal Commission, 1937. Cmd 5479, London.

Report of the UN Economic Survey Mission for the Middle East. December 1949, United Nations, Lake Success, NY; HM Stationery Office.

Report to the United Nations General Assembly by the UN Special Committee on Palestine. Geneva, 1947.

Statement of Policy by His Majesty's Government in the United Kingdom. Cmd 3692, London, 1930; Cmd 5893, London, 1938; Cmd 6019, London, 1939; Cmd 6180, London, 1940.

Statistical Abstract of Israel. Central Bureau of Statistics, annual.

Occupied Territories

Armstrong, Karen. *A History of Jerusalem: One City, Three Faiths*. London, HarperCollins, 1997.

El-Assal, Riah Abu (Bishop of Jerusalem). *Caught In Between: The Extraordinary Story of an Arab Palestinian Christian Israeli*. London, SPCK, 1999.

Cattan, Henry. *Jerusalem*. London, Saqi Books, 2000.

Dumper, Michael. *The Politics of Jerusalem since 1967*. New York, Columbia University Press, 1997.

Friedland, Roger, and Hecht, Richard. *To Rule Jerusalem*. Cambridge University Press, 1997.

Goldhill, Simon. *The Temple of Jerusalem*. London, Profile Books, 2006.

Klein, Menachem. *Jerusalem: The Contested City*. London, C. Hurst and Co, 2001.

Kollek, Teddy, and Pearlman, Moshe. *Jerusalem, Sacred City of Mankind*. London, Weidenfeld and Nicolson, 1968.

Lundquist, John M. *The Temple of Jerusalem: Past, Present, and Future*. New York, Praeger, 2007.

Wasserstein, Bernard. *Divided Jerusalem: The Struggle for the Holy City*. London, Profile Books, 2001.

JORDAN

Physical and Social Geography

W. B. FISHER

The Hashemite Kingdom of Jordan (previously Transjordan) came officially into existence under its present name in 1947 and was enlarged in 1950 to include the districts of Samaria and part of Judaea that had previously formed part of Arab Palestine. The country is bounded on the north by Syria, on the north-east by Iraq, on the east and south by Saudi Arabia, and on the west by Israel and the Palestinian territory in the West Bank. The total area of Jordan is 88,794 sq km (34,284 sq miles). The territory west of the Jordan river (the West Bank)—some 5,633 sq km (2,175 sq miles)—was occupied by Israel in June 1967, but since May 1994 the Palestinian (National) Authority has assumed jurisdiction for civil affairs in some areas. (Jordan severed all legal and administrative links with the territory in July 1988.) According to the census of October 2004, the population of Jordan stood at 5,103,639, compared with 4,139,458 at the census of December 1994. According to official estimates, the population had increased to 6,388,000 by December 2012, giving a population density of 71.9 per sq km.

At 1 January 2013, there were 2,034,641 Palestinian refugees registered with the UN Relief and Works Agency for Palestine Refugees in the Near East (UNRWA) in Jordan. Following the outbreak of conflict in Syria between Government forces and groups opposed to the rule of President Bashar al-Assad during 2011, a significant number of Syrians have fled that country, many of whom have entered Jordan. By September 2013, some 523,607 Syrian refugees were registered with the Office of the UN High Commissioner for Refugees (UNHCR) in Jordan. In July the Jordanian Government had estimated the total number of Syrian refugees in the country at 600,000.

PHYSICAL FEATURES

The greater part of the State of Jordan consists of a plateau lying some 700 m–1,000 m above sea level, which forms the north-western corner of the great plateau of Arabia (see the chapter on Saudi Arabia). There are no natural topographical frontiers between Jordan and its neighbours Syria, Iraq and Saudi Arabia, and the plateau continues unbroken into all three countries, with the artificial frontier boundaries drawn as straight lines between defined points. Along its western edge, facing the Jordan Valley, the plateau is uptilted to give a line of hills that rise 300 m–700 m above plateau level. An old river course, the Wadi Sirhan, now almost dry with only occasional wells, fractures the plateau surface on the south-east and continues into Saudi Arabia.

The Jordanian plateau consists of a core or table of ancient rocks, covered by layers of newer rock (chiefly limestone) lying almost horizontally. In a few places (e.g. on the southern edge of the Jordan Valley) these old rocks are exposed at the surface. On its western side the plateau has been fractured and dislocated by the development of strongly marked tear faults that run from the Red Sea via the Gulf of Aqaba northwards to Lebanon and Syria. The narrow zone between the faults has sunk, to give the well-known Jordan rift valley, which is bordered both on the east and west by steep-sided walls, especially in the south near the Dead Sea, where the drop is often precipitous. The valley has a maximum width of 22 km and is now thought to have been produced by lateral shearing of two continental plates that on the east have been displaced by about 80 km.

The floor of the Jordan Valley varies considerably in level. At its northern end it is just above sea level; the surface of Lake Tiberias (the Sea of Galilee) is 209 m below sea level, with the deepest part of the lake over 200 m lower still. The greatest depth of the valley is at the Dead Sea (surface 400 m below sea level, maximum depth 396 m).

Dislocation of the rock strata in the region of the Jordan Valley has had two further effects: first, earth tremors are still frequent along the valley; and second, considerable quantities of lava have welled up, forming enormous sheets that cover wide expanses of territory in the State of Jordan and southern Syria, and produce a desolate, forbidding landscape. One small lava flow, by forming a natural dam across the Jordan Valley, has impounded the waters to form Lake Tiberias.

The Jordan river rises just inside the frontiers of Syria and Lebanon—a recurrent source of dispute between the two countries and Israel. The river is 251 km (156 miles) long, and after first flowing for 96 km in Israel, it lies within Jordanian territory for the remaining 152 km. Its main tributary, the Yarmouk, is 40 km long, and close to its junction with the Jordan forms the boundary between the State of Jordan, Israel and Syria. A few kilometres from its source, the Jordan river used to open into Lake Huleh, a shallow, marsh-fringed expanse of water that was previously a breeding ground of malaria, but which has now been drained. Lake Tiberias, also, like the former Huleh, in Israel, covers an area of 316 sq km and measures 22 km from north to south, and 26 km from east to west. Outflowing river water from the lake is used for the generation of hydroelectricity.

The river then flows through the barren, inhospitable country of its middle and lower valley, very little of which is actually, or potentially, cultivable, and finally enters the Dead Sea. This lake is 65 km long and 16 km wide. Owing to the very high air temperatures at most seasons of the year, evaporation from the lake is intense, and has been estimated as equivalent to 8.5m. metric tons of water per day. At the surface the Dead Sea water contains about 250 g of dissolved salts per litre, and at a depth of 110 m the water is chemically saturated (i.e. holds its maximum possible content). Magnesium chloride is the most abundant mineral, with sodium chloride next in importance, but commercial interest centres on the less abundant potash and bromide salts.

Climatically, Jordan shows close affinity to its neighbours. Summers are hot, especially on the plateau and in the Jordan Valley, where temperatures of up to 49°C have been recorded. Winters are fairly cold, and on the plateau frost and some snow are usual, though not in the lower Jordan Valley. The significant element of the climate of Jordan is rainfall. In the higher parts (i.e. the uplands of Samaria and Judaea and the hills overlooking the eastern Jordan Valley) 380 mm–630 mm of rainfall occurs annually, enough for agriculture; but elsewhere as little as 200 mm or less may fall, and pastoral nomadism is the only possible way of life. Only about 25% of the total area of Jordan is sufficiently humid for cultivation.

PEOPLE, LANGUAGE AND RELIGION

Arabic is spoken everywhere, except in a few villages inhabited by Circassians, who settled in Jordan as refugees during the 19th and 20th centuries AD. Over 90% of the population are Sunni Muslims, and King Abdullah can trace unbroken descent from the Prophet Muhammad. There is a Christian minority, as well as smaller numbers of Shi‘a Muslims.

History

Revised by CHRISTOPHER PHILLIPS

Jordan, as an independent state, was a 20th-century development. Before then it was seldom more than a rugged and backward appendage to more powerful kingdoms and empires, and indeed never existed alone. In biblical times the area was covered roughly by Gilead, Ammon, Moab and Edom, and the western portions formed for a time part of the Kingdom of Israel. During the sixth century BC the Arabian tribe of the Nabateans established their capital at Petra in the south and continued to preserve their independence when, during the fourth and third centuries, the northern half was incorporated into the Seleucid province of Syria. It was under Seleucid rule that cities such as Philadelphia (the modern Amman) and Gerasa (now Jarash or Jerash) rose to prominence. During the first century BC the Nabateans extended their rule over the greater part of present-day Jordan and Syria; they then began to recede before the advance of Rome, and in AD 105–06 Petra was incorporated into the Roman Empire. The lands east of the Jordan shared in a brief blaze of glory under the Palmyrene sovereigns Odenathus (Udaynath) and Zenobia (al-Zabba') in the middle of the third century AD, and during the fifth and sixth centuries formed part of the dominions of the Christian Ghassanid dynasty, vassals of the Byzantine Empire. Finally, after 50 years of anarchy in which Byzantine, Persian and local rulers intervened, Transjordania was conquered by the Arabs and absorbed into the Islamic empire.

For centuries nothing more was heard of the country; it was administered as a part of Syria, and as such was generally governed from Egypt. From the beginning of the 16th century it was included in the Ottoman *vilayet* (administrative district) of Damascus, and remained in a condition of stagnation until the outbreak of the First World War in 1914. The area was included in the zone of influence allocated to the United Kingdom under the Sykes-Picot agreement of May 1916 (Documents on Palestine, see p. 56), and Zionists held that it also came within the area designated as a Jewish National Home in the promise contained in the Balfour Declaration of November 1917 (Documents on Palestine, see p. 57). Apart from these somewhat remote political events, the tide of war did not reach Jordanian territory until the capture of al-Aqabah (Aqaba) by the Arab armies under Faisal, the third son of King Hussein of the Hedjaz, in July 1917. A year later, in September 1918, they shared in the final push north by capturing Amman and Deraa.

The end of the war thus found a large area, which included almost the whole of present-day Jordan, in Arab hands under the leadership of Faisal. To begin with, the territory to the east of the Jordan river was not looked on as a separate unit. Faisal, with the assistance of British officers and Arab nationalists, established an autonomous government in Damascus, a step encouraged by the Anglo-French Declaration of 7 November 1918, favouring the establishment of indigenous governments in Syria and Iraq. Arab demands, however, as expressed by Faisal at the Paris Peace Conference in France in January 1919, went a good deal further in claiming independence throughout the Arab world. This represented a challenge to French claims in the Near East, and when, in March 1920, the General Syrian Congress in Damascus declared the independence of Syria and Iraq, with Faisal and Abdullah, Hussein's second son, as kings, the decisions were denounced by France and the United Kingdom. In the following month the San Remo Conference awarded the Palestine Mandate to the United Kingdom, and thus separated it effectively from Syria proper, which fell within the French share. Faisal was forced out of Damascus by the French in July and left the country.

THE KINGDOM OF TRANSJORDAN

The position of Transjordania was not altogether clear under the new dispensation. After the withdrawal of Faisal, the British High Commissioner informed a meeting of notables at al-Salt that the British Government favoured self-government for the territory, with British advisers. At the Cairo (Egypt) conference of March 1921, which was attended by Abdullah, Winston Churchill (the new British Secretary of State for the Colonies), T. E. Lawrence ('Lawrence of Arabia') and Sir Herbert Samuel (British High Commissioner for Palestine), it was recommended that Faisal should be proclaimed King of Iraq, while Abdullah was persuaded to stand down in his favour by the promise of an Arab administration in Transjordania. He had in fact been in effective control in Amman since his arrival the previous winter, ostensibly to organize an uprising against the French in Syria. This project he now abandoned, and in April 1921 he was officially recognized as de facto ruler of Transjordan. The final draft of the Palestine Mandate confirmed by the Council of the League of Nations in July 1922 contained a clause giving the Mandatory Power considerable latitude in the administration of the territory east of the Jordan (Documents on Palestine, see p. 59).

Like much of the post-war boundary delineation, the borders of the new state were somewhat arbitrary. Although they lay mainly in desert areas, they frequently cut across tribal areas and grazing grounds, with small respect for tradition. Of the 300,000–400,000 inhabitants, only about one-fifth were town dwellers, and these were confined to four small cities ranging in population from 10,000 to 30,000. Nevertheless, Transjordan's early years were destined to be comparatively peaceful. On 15 May 1923 the United Kingdom formally recognized Transjordan as an independent constitutional state under the rule of the Amir Abdullah with British tutelage, and with the aid of a British subsidy it was possible to make some slow progress towards development and modernization.

The Amir Abdullah very nearly became involved in the fall of his father, King Hussein, in 1924. It was in Amman on 5 March 1924, that the latter was proclaimed Caliph, and during the subsequent fighting with Ibn Sa'ud Wahhabi troops penetrated into Transjordanian territory. They subsequently withdrew to the south, and in June 1925, after the abdication of Hussein's eldest son, Ali, Abdullah formally incorporated Ma'an and Aqaba within his dominions. The move was not disputed by the new ruler of the Hedjaz and Najd, and thereafter the southern frontier of Transjordan remained unaltered.

INDEPENDENCE

In February 1928 a treaty was signed with the United Kingdom granting a further measure of independence, though reserving for the advice of a British Resident such matters as financial policy and foreign relations. The same treaty provided for a Constitution, and this was duly promulgated in April 1928, the first Legislative Council meeting one year later. In January 1934 a supplementary agreement was added permitting Transjordan to appoint consular representatives in Arab countries, and in May 1939 the United Kingdom agreed to the conversion of the Legislative Council into a regular Cabinet with ministers in charge of specified departments. The outbreak of the Second World War delayed further advances towards independence, but this was finally achieved, in name at least, by the Treaty of London of 22 March 1946. On 25 May 1946 Abdullah was proclaimed King and a new Constitution replaced that of 1928.

In March 1948 the United Kingdom agreed to the signing of a new treaty in which virtually the only restrictive clauses related to military and defence matters. The United Kingdom was to have certain peacetime military privileges, including the maintenance of airfields and communications, transit facilities and co-ordination of training methods. It was also to provide economic and social aid.

Transjordan had not, however, waited for independence before making its weight felt in Arab affairs in the Middle East. It had not been active before the war, its first appearance on the international scene being in May 1939, when Transjordanian delegates were invited to the Round Table Conference on Palestine in London, United Kingdom. Transjordan took part in the preliminary discussions during 1943 and 1944 that finally led to the formation of the League of Arab States (the

Arab League) in March 1945, and was one of the original members of that organization.

ATTITUDES TOWARDS THE ESTABLISHMENT OF ISRAEL

On 14–15 May 1948 British troops were withdrawn to the port of Haifa as a preliminary to the final evacuation of Palestine, the State of Israel was proclaimed, and Arab armies entered the former Palestinian territory from all sides. Those from Transjordan played a significant part in the fighting, and by the time that major hostilities ceased in July they had succeeded in occupying a considerable area. The suspicion now inevitably arose that Abdullah was prepared to accept a *fait accompli* and to negotiate with the Israeli authorities for a formal recognition of the existing military boundaries. Moreover, whereas the other Arab countries refused to accept any other move that implied a tacit recognition of the status quo—such as the resettlement of refugees—Transjordan seemed to be following a different line. In September 1948 the 'All Palestine Government' was formed in the Gaza Strip, then occupied by Egyptian forces. Transjordan replied by proclaiming Abdullah as King of Arab Palestine (and Jordan) in December. In April 1949 the country's name was changed to Jordan and three Palestinians were included in the Cabinet. In the mean time, armistices were being signed by all the Arab countries, including Jordan, and on 31 January 1949 Jordan was finally recognized by the USA.

On the three major problems confronting the Arab states in their dispute with Israel, Jordan continued to differ openly with its colleagues. It refused to agree to the internationalization of Jerusalem, it initiated plans for the resettlement of the Palestinian refugees, and it showed a disposition to accept as permanent the armistice frontiers. In April 1950 elections were held in Jordan and Arab Palestine, the results of which encouraged Abdullah formally to annex the latter territory on 24 April 1950. This step was immediately recognized by the United Kingdom. Jordan signed a four-point agreement with the USA in March 1951. Although there remained constant friction between Jordan and Israel, the unified opposition of the Arab states to the new Jewish state seemed to have ended, and inter-Arab differences were gaining the upper hand.

ABDULLAH ASSASSINATED

On 20 July 1951 King Abdullah was assassinated in Jerusalem. Evidence that emerged at the trial of those implicated in the plot revealed that the murder had been partly motivated by opposition to Abdullah's 'Greater Syria' policy—the union of Transjordan, Syria and Palestine, as a step towards the final unification of the 'Fertile Crescent' by the inclusion of Iraq—and it was significant that Egypt refused to extradite some of those convicted. However, the background to the assassination also included Abdullah's alleged tacit alliance with the Israelis. Nevertheless, the stability of the young Jordanian state revealed itself in the calm in which the King's eldest son, Talal, succeeded to the throne, and the peaceful elections held shortly afterwards.

In January 1952 a new Constitution was promulgated. Even more significant, perhaps, was the dignity with which, only one year after his accession, King Talal, whose mental condition had long been a cause for anxiety, abdicated in favour of his son, Hussein—still a minor. In foreign policy Talal had shown some signs of rejecting his father's ideas in favour of a rapprochement with Syria and Egypt, one example being Jordan's signature of the Arab Collective Security Pact, which it had failed to join in mid-1950.

This policy was continued during the early reign of his son, King Hussein, notably by the conclusion of an economic and financial agreement with Syria in February 1953, and a joint scheme for the construction of a dam across the Yarmouk river to supply irrigation and hydroelectric power. One problem that became pressing in 1954 was the elaborate US-sponsored scheme for the sharing of the Jordan waters between Jordan, Iraq, Syria and Israel, which could make no progress in the absence of political agreement.

During December 1954 a financial aid agreement was signed with the United Kingdom, and the opportunity was taken to discuss the revision of the Anglo-Jordanian Treaty of 1948. Agreement over this was not possible owing to British insistence that any new pact should fit into a general Middle East defence system. In May 1955 Premier Abu'l-Huda was replaced by Sa'id al-Mufti, while an exchange of state visits with King Sa'ud hinted at a rapprochement with Saudi Arabia. Nevertheless, in November Jordan declared its unwillingness to adhere either to the Egyptian-Syrian-Saudi Arabian bloc or to the Baghdad Pact.

DISMISSAL OF GLUBB PASHA

On 15 December 1955 Sa'id al-Mufti resigned and was replaced by Hazza al-Majali. The following day there were violent demonstrations in Amman, and on 20 December Ibrahim Hashim became Prime Minister, to be succeeded on 9 January 1956 by Samir Rifai. In February the new Prime Minister visited Syria, Lebanon, Iraq, Egypt and Saudi Arabia, and shortly after his return the Egyptian-Syrian-Saudi Arabian bloc offered to replace the British financial subsidy to Jordan; however, the latter was not in fact withdrawn, and King Hussein and the Jordanian Government evidently felt that they had moved far enough in one direction, and committed themselves to a policy of strict neutrality. In April, however, the King and the Prime Minister paid a visit to the Syrian President in Damascus, and in May Lt-Col Ali Abu Nuwar, generally regarded as the leader of the movement to eliminate foreign influence from the Jordanian army and government, was appointed as Commander-in-Chief of the Jordanian armed forces. This coincided with the reappointment of Sa'id al-Mufti as Prime Minister. During the same period discussions culminated in agreements for military co-operation between Jordan and Syria, Lebanon and Egypt, and in July Jordan and Syria formed an economic union. At the beginning of the same month al-Mufti was replaced by Ibrahim Hashim.

RELATIONS WITH ISRAEL AND WITH THE OTHER ARAB STATES

Meanwhile, relations with Israel, including the problem of the Arab refugees, the use of Jordan waters, the definition of the frontier and the status of Jerusalem, continued to provide a cause for anxiety. Tension between Jordan and Israel was further increased after the Israeli, British and French military action in Egypt during the Suez Crisis of 1956. The crisis made a hero of Egyptian President Lt-Col Gamal Abd al-Nasir (Nasser), whose anti-imperialist Arab nationalism was popular among the Jordanian public. A new Cabinet, headed by Sulayman Nabulsi, had taken office in October, and new elections were followed by the opening of negotiations for the abrogation of the Anglo-Jordanian Treaty of 1948, and the substitution of financial aid from the Arab countries, notably Saudi Arabia, Egypt and Syria. As a result of subsequent political developments, however, the shares due from Egypt and Syria were not paid. On 13 March 1957 an Anglo-Jordanian agreement was signed abrogating the 1948 treaty, and by 2 July the last British troops had left.

By 1957, amid the increasing popularity of President Nasser across the region, Hussein sought to consolidate his rule. Nabulsi's evident leanings towards the USSR led to his breach with King Hussein and his resignation on 10 April; he was subsequently succeeded by Ibrahim Hashim. All political parties were then suppressed, and plans to establish diplomatic relations with the USSR were dropped. Gen. Ali Abu Nuwar was removed from the post of Commander-in-Chief, and the USA announced its determination to preserve Jordan's independence—a policy underlined by a major air-lift of arms to Amman in September in response to Syria's alignment with the USSR. In May Syrian troops serving under the joint Syro-Egypto-Jordanian command were withdrawn from Jordanian territory at Jordan's request, and in June there was a partial rupture of diplomatic relations with Egypt.

When Egypt and Syria announced at the beginning of February 1958 that they were to unite as the United Arab Republic (UAR), King Hussein acted quickly to prevent being overshadowed by the new state, which had met with considerable popular acclaim. On 14 February the kingdoms of Jordan and Iraq, ruled by Hussein's cousin, King Faisal II, were merged into a federal union, to be called the Arab Federation. Samir Rifai became Prime Minister of Jordan in May, on the resignation of Ibrahim Hashim, who took up the position of vice-premier in the new dual kingdom. This new Federation proved abortive when, in July, the Iraqi military overthrew the monarchy and Faisal was murdered. Fearing that Jordan would follow Iraq on the path to revolution, King Hussein requested help from his allies and British troops were flown to Amman from Cyprus later that month. By the beginning of November the threat had been contained and all troops withdrawn, under UN auspices, and in the two years that followed Jordan enjoyed a period of comparative peace. Hazza al-Majali succeeded Rifai as Prime Minister on 6 May 1959. Firm measures were taken against communism and subversive activities, and collaboration with the West was, if anything, encouraged by the country's isolation between Iraq, Israel and the two halves of the UAR.

Relations with Jordan's Arab neighbours continued to be uneasy, although diplomatic relations with the UAR, broken off in July 1958, were resumed in August 1959. Incidents on the Syrian border were almost as frequent as those on the Israeli border, and there were no signs of a rapprochement with the new Republican regime in Iraq. In January 1960 both the King and the Prime Minister condemned the Arab leaders' approach to the Palestine problem, and in February Jordanian citizenship was offered to all Arab refugees who applied for it. There was little change in the general position that Jordan wished for formal recognition of its absorption of the Palestinian territory west of the Jordan, while the UAR and other Arab countries favoured the establishment of an independent Palestine Arab government.

On 29 August 1960 Jordanian Prime Minister Hazza al-Majali was assassinated; he was succeeded by several premiers during the next five years. In April 1965 a constitutional uncertainty was resolved, with the nomination of the King's brother Hassan as Crown Prince; the King's own children were thus excluded from the succession to the throne at this time.

Meanwhile, in September 1963 the creation of a unified 'Palestinian entity' was approved by the Council of the Arab League, despite opposition from the Jordanian Government, which regarded the proposal as a threat to Jordan's sovereignty over the West Bank. The first congress of Palestinian Arab groups was held in the Jordanian sector of Jerusalem in May–June 1964, when the participants unanimously agreed to form the Palestine Liberation Organization (PLO) as 'the only legitimate spokesman for all matters concerning the Palestinian people'. The PLO was to be financed by the Arab League and was to recruit military units, from among refugees, to constitute a Palestine Liberation Army (PLA). From the outset, King Hussein refused to allow the PLA to train forces in Jordan or the PLO to levy taxes from Palestinian refugees in his country.

THE 1967 WAR

During the latter part of 1966 Jordan's deteriorating foreign relations were exacerbated by the widening breach with Syria. Charges and counter-charges of plots to subvert each other's governments were made, and, while the UAR (from which Syria had seceded in September 1961) and the USSR supported Syria, Jordan looked to Saudi Arabia and the USA for backing.

As the prospect of war with Israel drew nearer (see the chapters on Israel and the Palestinian Territories), King Hussein resolved his differences with Egypt, and personally flew to Cairo to sign a defence agreement. Jordanian troops, together with those of the UAR, Iraq and Saudi Arabia, went into action immediately on the outbreak of hostilities in June 1967. By the end of the Six-Day War, however, all Jordanian territory west of the Jordan river had been occupied by Israeli troops, and a steady stream of West Bank Jordanians began to cross the river to the East Bank. These estimated 150,000–250,000 persons swelled Jordan's refugee population and presented the Government with intractable social and economic problems.

In August 1967 King Hussein formed a nine-man Consultative Council, composed of former premiers and politicians of varying sympathies, to meet weekly and to participate in the 'responsibility of power'. Later a Senate was formed, consisting of 15 representatives from the inhabitants of the West Bank area and 15 from eastern Jordan. Several changes of government took place and the King took over personal command of the country's armed forces.

THE GUERRILLA CHALLENGE AND CIVIL WAR

The instability in Amman after the 1967 war was reflected in the short life of Jordanian cabinets—it became rare for one to remain unchanged for more than three months. A careful balance had to be struck between the Palestinians and the King's traditional supporters. Thus, in the new Cabinet announced after the June 1970 crisis (see below), Palestinians were given more of the key ministries, including the interior portfolio. Abd al-Munem Rifai, Jordan's senior diplomat, became Prime Minister for the second time.

The main factor in Jordan's internal politics between June 1967 and 1971 was the rivalry between the Government and Palestinian guerrilla organizations, principally Fatah (the Palestine National Liberation Movement), which from 1968 was led by Yasser Arafat, the Chairman of the PLO. These organizations gradually assumed effective control of the refugee camps and commanded widespread support among the Palestinian majority of Jordan's population. They also received armaments and training assistance from other Arab countries, particularly Syria, and finance from the oil-rich states bordering the Persian (Arabian) Gulf. The *fedayeen* ('martyrs') Palestinian liberation movement virtually became a state within a state, and its popularity and influence represented a challenge to the Government, while its actions attracted Israeli reprisals that did serious damage to the East Bank, now the only fertile part of Jordan, and generally reduced the possibilities of a peace settlement on which Jordan's long-term future depended.

A major confrontation between the two forces occurred in November 1968, after massive demonstrations in Amman on the anniversary of the Balfour Declaration. Extensive street fighting broke out between guerrillas and the army, and for a short period a civil war seemed possible, but both sides soon backed down. Similar confrontations followed in February and June 1970, and on both occasions the Government was forced to yield to Palestinian pressures. King Hussein and Arafat (whose own position was threatened by the rise of small extremist groups in Jordan) concluded an agreement redefining their respective spheres of influence. The guerrillas appeared to have granted little or nothing, but Hussein was forced to dismiss his Commander-in-Chief and a cabinet minister, both relatives. These were regarded as the leaders of the anti-*fedayeen* faction, which remained strong among the Bedouin sheikhs. Despite the accord, the tension between the Government and the guerrillas continued, aggravated by opposition to the Government's concessions from intransigent army officers.

A new and dangerous stage in relations between the two sides in Jordan was reached in July 1970 with the acceptance by the Government of the US peace proposals for the Middle East. The guerrilla groups, with few exceptions, rejected these, and, as the cease-fire between Egypt and Israel came into operation on 7 August, it was clear that the Jordanian Government was preparing for a full-scale confrontation with them.

Bitter fighting between government and guerrilla forces broke out at the end of August 1970. On 16 September a military Cabinet was formed under Brig. Muhammad Daoud—in any case, martial law had been in force since the end of the June 1967 war—and Field Marshal Habis Majali was appointed Commander-in-Chief, in place of Lt-Gen. Mashour Haditha, who had been sympathetic to the commandos.

In the latter half of September 1970 the fighting escalated into full civil war, with thousands of deaths and injuries. Scores of civilians were killed when the Jordanian army attacked refugee camps. The guerrillas claimed full control in the north, aided by Syrian forces and, it was later revealed, three battalions of the PLA sent back by President Nasser from the Suez front. The Arab states generally appealed for an end to the fighting. On the government side, talks were held with the USA about direct military assistance. In the event, such a dangerous widening of the Palestinian confrontation was avoided by the scale of the casualties in Jordan and by the diplomacy of Arab Heads of State (reinforced by President Nasser's reported threat to intervene on the guerrillas' behalf), who prevailed upon King Hussein and Yasser Arafat to sign an agreement in Cairo on 27 September, ending the war. The previous day a civilian Cabinet had been restored under Ahmad Toukan. Five military members were retained.

A definitive accord, very favourable to the militant organizations, was signed by Hussein and Arafat on 13 October 1970 in Amman, but this proved to be simply the beginning of a phase of sporadic warfare between the two parties, punctuated by new agreements, during which the commandos were gradually forced out of Amman and driven from their positions in the north back towards the Syrian frontier. At the end of October a new Government, still containing three army officers, was formed under Wasfi al-Tal. By January 1971 army moves against the Palestinian guerrillas had become much more blatant, and Egypt, Syria and Algeria all issued strong protests against the Jordanian Government's attempt to 'liquidate' the militant movements. However, all but two brigades of Iraqi troops were withdrawn from Jordan.

By April 1971 the Jordanian Government seemed strong enough to set a deadline for the guerrillas' withdrawal of their remaining men and heavy armaments from the capital. On 13 July a major government attack began on the guerrillas entrenched in the Jerash-Ajloun area, which lasted for four days. The Government claimed that all the bases had been destroyed and that 2,300 of the 2,500 guerrillas in them had been captured. Most of the Palestinians taken prisoner by the Jordanian authorities were released a few days later.

The 'solution' (in King Hussein's words) of the guerrilla 'problem' provoked strong reaction from other Arab governments: Iraq and Syria closed their borders with Jordan; Algeria suspended diplomatic relations; and Egypt, Libya, Sudan and both Yemens voiced public criticism. Relations with Syria deteriorated fastest of all, although normal trading and diplomatic relations were restored by February 1972.

Meanwhile, on 28 November 1971 Wasfi al-Tal, the Prime Minister and Minister of Defence, was assassinated by members of a Palestinian guerrilla group, the Black September organization (formed after the expulsion of the PLO from Jordan in September 1970).

THE 'UNITED ARAB KINGDOM' PLAN

Following the defeat of the Palestinian guerrillas in July 1971, Hussein sought to strengthen his political position. In August he announced the creation of a tribal council—a body of sheikhs or other notables, appointed by him and chaired by the Crown Prince—which was to deal with the affairs of tribal areas. A month later the formation of the Jordanian National Union was announced. This (renamed the Arab National Union in March 1972) was to be Jordan's only legal political organization. It was not a party in the usual sense; proponents of 'imported ideologies' were debarred from membership; the King became president, and the Crown Prince vice-president, and appointed the 36 members of the Supreme Executive Committee.

However, the King's boldest political move, and an obvious attempt to regain his standing in the eyes of Palestinians, was his unfolding of plans for a 'United Arab Kingdom' in March 1972. This kingdom was to federate a Jordanian region, with Amman as its capital and also federal capital, and a Palestinian region, with Jerusalem as its capital. Each region was to be virtually autonomous, although the King would rule both and there would be a federal Council of Ministers.

Outside Jordan there was almost universal criticism of this plan from interested parties—Israel, the Palestinian organizations and Egypt—which in the following month broke off diplomatic relations. Jordan's isolation in the Arab world had never been more complete. Throughout the rest of 1972 and the first half of 1973, however, Hussein continued to adhere to his plan, while insisting that peace with Israel could be arrived at only within the framework of UN Security Council Resolution 242 of November 1967 (Documents on Palestine, see p. 64).

The internal security of Jordan was threatened in November 1972 by an attempted military coup in Amman by Maj. Rafeh Hindawi; however, the coup was thwarted. In February 1973 Abu Daoud, one of the leaders of Fatah, and 16 other guerrillas were arrested on charges of infiltrating into Jordan for the purpose of subversive activities. The latter affair took place while King Hussein was on a visit to the USA requesting defence and financial aid. On his return, he commuted the death sentences passed on the guerrillas by a Jordanian military court and previously confirmed by himself, to life imprisonment. In May Hussein's Prime Minister, Ahmad Lauzi, resigned for health reasons and a new Government was formed under Zaid Rifai, son of former premier Samir Rifai and a known opponent of the Palestinian guerrillas.

In September 1973 Hussein attended a 'reconciliation summit' with President Col Anwar Sadat of Egypt and President Lt-Gen. Hafiz al-Assad of Syria. This was Jordan's first official contact with the two states since they had broken off diplomatic relations, and they were restored after the summit. The meeting was condemned by Fatah, Libya and Iraq, but Jordan regained some stature in the Arab world after Hussein's general amnesty for all political prisoners; among those released was Abu Daoud.

During most of 1974 King Hussein's policy towards the PLO and the status of the West Bank was somewhat ambiguous. He continued to try to preserve the West Bank as part of his kingdom despite strong pressure from other Arab states and the increasing influence of the PLO. In September, after a meeting between Egypt, Syria and the PLO expressing support for the PLO as the 'only legitimate representative of the Palestinian people', Jordan refused to participate in further Middle East peace talks. However, in October at the Arab Summit Conference at Rabat (Documents on Palestine, see p. 68), representatives of 20 Arab heads of state unanimously recognized the PLO as the sole legitimate representative of the Palestinians and its right to establish a national authority over any liberated Palestinian territory. Effectively ceding Jordan's claim to represent the Palestinians and reincorporate the West Bank, when recaptured, into the Hashemite kingdom, Hussein reluctantly assented to the resolution.

JORDAN AFTER THE RABAT SUMMIT

Following the Rabat Conference, Hussein was given more extensive powers in revisions to the Jordanian Constitution approved by the National Assembly in November 1974. He was allowed to rule without the National Assembly for one year, and to reorganize his kingdom in order to lessen the numbers of Palestinians in the executive and legislative branches of government, his 1972 plan for a United Arab Kingdom now being wholly defunct. The National Assembly was dissolved and a new Government formed in November 1974, with Zaid Rifai remaining Prime Minister. Palestinian representation was decreased, and the question of citizenship of the estimated 800,000 Palestinians on the East Bank became contentious. Elections in Jordan were postponed in March 1975, and when the National Assembly was briefly reconvened in February 1976, a constitutional amendment was enacted to suspend elections indefinitely.

In November 1977 President Sadat of Egypt visited Israel, and Jordan, unlike Syria, was anxious not to condemn Sadat's peace initiative, but did not want to destroy its relationship with Syria, which had been improving since the Rabat Summit. King Hussein, therefore, remained uncommitted and attempted to act as a conciliator between Egypt on the one hand and the 'rejectionist' states (Algeria, Libya, Iraq, Syria and the People's Democratic Republic of Yemen—PDRY) on the other.

After the signing of the Israeli-Egyptian peace treaty on 26 March 1979 (Documents on Palestine, see p. 71), Jordan was the first Arab country still having diplomatic relations with Egypt to sever them. In subsequent months, however, Jordan's hostility to Egypt subsided, and was replaced by the souring of relations with Syria, which had accused Jordan of harbouring anti-Syrian groups. Their policies also diverged in respect of the Iran–Iraq War, in which Syria supported Iran, and Jordan Iraq. The dispute escalated, prompting a build-up of Syrian and Jordanian troops on the frontier in December 1980. Tensions were heightened in February 1981 when the Jordanian chargé d'affaires in the Lebanese capital, Beirut, was abducted (allegedly by Syrians), and Jordan responded by abrogating a six-year economic and customs agreement with Syria.

In January 1984 the Jordanian Cabinet resigned, and a new one, containing a higher proportion of Palestinians and with Ahmad Ubeidat as Prime Minister, took office. With a view to recovering something from the West Bank before Jewish settlement there produced a de facto extension of Israel, on 5 January King Hussein dissolved the National Consultative Council (which had been appointed by royal decree in April 1978, four years after the suspension of the National Assembly) and reconvened the National Assembly for its first session since 1967.

Israel allowed the surviving West Bank deputies to attend the reconvened House of Representatives (the lower house), which unanimously approved constitutional amendments enabling elections to the House to be held in the East Bank alone, but giving itself the right to elect deputies from the West Bank, without whom the House would have been inquorate. The first elections in Jordan for 17 years, and the first in which women were allowed to vote, took place on 12 March 1984 (although political parties were still banned).

The nucleus of a moderate body of Arab opinion on the Palestinian question gave the impression of being formed around Jordan and the PLO leader, Yasser Arafat, with whom King Hussein had been holding discussions on the matter, with likely support to come from Saudi Arabia, Egypt and the Gulf states. The opposition to these developments of other Arab groups was reaffirmed when the Jordanian embassy in Tripoli, Libya, was burnt down in February 1984. Jordan responded by severing diplomatic relations with Libya. Sporadic attacks on Jordanian diplomats, principally in Europe, continued into 1985, responsibility for which was claimed by various extremist Arab and Islamist groups. Jordan suspected Syria and Libya of being behind these attacks.

Meanwhile, Hussein, frustrated by the unwillingness of the USA to use its influence with Israel to freeze Jewish settlement of the West Bank and unable to buy arms from the USA, began to look to the USSR for diplomatic backing in solving the problem of Palestinian autonomy and for armaments with which to defend his country. In January 1985 Jordan purchased an air defence system from the USSR, having already made an agreement to buy French anti-aircraft missiles in September 1984. In June 1985, following the repeated failure of the Administration of US President Ronald Reagan to secure approval to supply Jordan with arms, US Secretary of State George Shultz offered King Hussein extra economic aid of US $250m. as a token of US support for his efforts to achieve a peace settlement between the Arabs and Israel. The US Senate authorized the aid, to be spread over 27 months.

Ahmad Ubeidat resigned as Prime Minister in April 1985. On 5 April a new Cabinet was sworn in and Zaid Rifai was reappointed Prime Minister following a nine-year hiatus.

JOINT JORDANIAN-PALESTINIAN PEACE PROPOSALS

In September 1984, to the dissatisfaction of radical Arab states, Jordan re-established diplomatic relations with Egypt.

On 23 February 1985, in Amman, King Hussein and Yasser Arafat announced the terms of a joint Jordanian-Palestinian agreement on the framework for a peace settlement in the Middle East, which the two leaders had finalized on 11 February. It held that peace talks should take the form of an international conference including the five permanent members of the UN Security Council and all parties to the conflict, including the PLO, representing the Palestinian people in a joint Jordanian-Palestinian delegation. The Palestinian people would in future exercise their right to self-determination in the context of a proposed confederated state of Jordan and Palestine. However, the PLO subsequently adopted a new position on the status of the Palestinian representation at future peace talks, which, it said, should be within a united Arab, not merely a Jordanian-Palestinian, delegation. Syria, Libya and the rebel PLO factions predictably rejected the Amman agreement.

Israel rejected a four-stage plan proposed by Hussein in May 1985 intended to lead to direct negotiations between Israel and a Jordanian-Palestinian delegation. Instead, Israel proposed enlisting the support of the permanent members of the UN Security Council for direct talks between Israel and a joint Jordanian-Palestinian delegation including 'authentic Palestinian representatives' from the Occupied Territories who were not members of the PLO or the Palestine National Council (PNC). In July Israel rejected a list of seven Palestinians, five of whom were members of the PLO loyal to Arafat or had links with the PNC, whom King Hussein had presented to the USA as candidates for inclusion in a joint Jordanian-Palestinian delegation to hold preliminary talks with the USA. The Israeli Prime Minister, Shimon Peres, later conceded that two of the seven fulfilled his requirements.

In November 1985 King Hussein admitted that Jordan had, unwittingly, been a base for the Sunni fundamentalist Muslim Brotherhood in its attempts to overthrow Syria's President Assad, but stated that members of the group would no longer receive shelter there. The Prime Ministers of the two countries met in Damascus in November and agreed on the need for 'joint Arab action' to achieve peace in the Middle East. At previous talks in Saudi Arabia in October, Jordan and Syria had rejected 'partial and unilateral' solutions and affirmed their adherence to the Fez plan, omitting all mention of the Jordanian-Palestinian peace initiative. President Assad and King Hussein confirmed the improved state of Syrian-Jordanian relations when they met in Damascus in December.

At the end of October 1985 the Israeli press published a document, drawn up by the Israeli Prime Minister's office, which purported to summarize the state of negotiations between Israel and Jordan. The document suggested the establishment of an interim Israeli-Jordanian condominium of the West Bank, granting a form of Palestinian autonomy, and recorded mutual agreement on the need for an international forum for peace talks. Israel would consent to the participation of the USSR in such a forum (on the condition that it re-established diplomatic relations with Israel), and of Syria, but not of the PLO, on whose involvement King Hussein still insisted.

Given Yasser Arafat's persistent refusal to accept UN Security Council Resolutions 242 and 338 (Documents on Palestine, see p. 68) as the basis for peace talks, the demise of the Jordanian-Palestinian peace initiative had been forecast for some time. In February 1986 King Hussein publicly severed political links with the PLO 'until such time as their word becomes their bond, characterized by commitment, credibility and constancy'. Arafat was ordered to close his main PLO offices in Jordan by the beginning of April, and a number of Fatah officials, loyal to Arafat, were expelled. King Hussein made efforts to strengthen Jordanian influence and create a Palestinian constituency in the Occupied Territories, independent of Arafat's PLO, including: the approval of a draft law by the House of Representatives in March, increasing the number of seats in the House from 60 to 142 (71 seats each for the East and West Bank), thereby providing for greater West Bank Palestinian representation in the House; and the introduction, in August, with Israeli support, of a US $1,300m. five-year development plan for the West Bank and Gaza.

ARAB LEAGUE SUMMIT IN AMMAN

During 1987 King Hussein pursued his efforts, begun in 1986, to reconcile Syria and Iraq, with the wider aim of securing Arab unity. He was instrumental in arranging the first full summit meeting of the Arab League (excluding Egyptian representation) for eight years, which took place in Amman in November, principally to discuss the Iran–Iraq War. In September Jordan had restored diplomatic relations with Libya, which had modified its support for Iran and now urged a cease-fire. The Arab summit meeting unanimously adopted a resolution of solidarity with Iraq, which condemned Iran for its occupation of Arab territory and for prolonging the war. King Hussein's appeal for Egypt to be restored to membership of the League was successfully resisted by Syria and Libya, but nine Arab states re-established diplomatic relations with Egypt soon after the summit, and these were followed by Tunisia in January 1988 and by the PDRY in February. The resumption of co-operation between Jordan and the PLO was also announced.

THE PALESTINIAN *INTIFADA* AND DISENGAGEMENT FROM THE WEST BANK

In December 1987 Palestinians began a violent uprising (*intifada*) against Israeli occupation of the West Bank and Gaza Strip. Despite intensive and often brutal security measures, Israel was unable to suppress the revolt. Public demonstrations in Jordan in support of the *intifada* were muted, mainly owing to security precautions taken by the authorities to prevent unrest. In April 1988 the Palestinian extremist group Black September claimed responsibility for a series of bomb attacks in Amman, which, it said, were directed against the 'client Zionist regime in Jordan'.

The intensity of the *intifada*, the world-wide condemnation of Israeli security tactics and revulsion at the degrading conditions in which many Palestinians were forced to live in the Occupied Territories alerted the international community to the need for a revival of efforts to secure an Arab-Israeli peace agreement. An extraordinary summit meeting of the Arab League was held in Algiers, Algeria, in June 1988 to discuss the continuing *intifada* and the Arab–Israeli conflict in general. Addressing the summit, King Hussein gave his support to the *intifada* and disclaimed any ambition to restore Jordanian rule in the West Bank. He insisted that the PLO must represent the Palestinians at any future peace conference, and repeatedly stressed the PLO's status as 'the sole legitimate representative of the Palestinian people'. The final communiqué of the summit, which hailed the 'heroic' Palestinian uprising, endorsed the Palestinians' right to self-determination and the establishment of an independent Palestinian state in the West Bank, and insisted on PLO participation in future peace talks.

The effect of the *intifada* had been to increase international support for Palestinian national rights, to heighten Palestinian aspirations to statehood and to reinforce support for the PLO as the Palestinians' representative in achieving it. From King Hussein's point of view, the *intifada* had created a new set of conditions in which Jordan could no longer realistically present itself as an alternative to the PLO. The King's subsequent actions were entirely consistent with his acknowledgement of the new realities, yet they were still greeted with surprise.

In July 1988 Jordan cancelled its US $1,300m. development plan for the West Bank, which had been opposed by the PLO since its launch in 1986. Then, two days later, King Hussein severed Jordan's legal and administrative links with the West Bank, dissolving the lower house of the Jordanian parliament (the House of Representatives), where Palestinian representatives for the West Bank occupied 30 of the 60 seats. The King explained that his actions were taken in accordance with the PLO's wishes and with the resolutions of the Rabat and Fez Arab summits in 1974 and 1982, and the positions adopted at the recent Algiers summit, which recognized the PLO as 'the sole legitimate representative of the Palestinian people'. The move was generally welcomed by the Palestinians in the West Bank. According to the Jordanian Government, Palestinians residing there were no longer considered to be Jordanian citizens; they were still entitled to hold a Jordanian passport, but this would, in future, only have the status of a 'travel document'.

On 15 November 1988 the PNC proclaimed the establishment of an independent State of Palestine and, for the first time, endorsed UN Security Council Resolution 242 as a basis for a Middle East peace settlement, thus implicitly recognizing Israel. Jordan and 60 other countries recognized the new state. In December Yasser Arafat addressed a special session of the UN General Assembly in Geneva, Switzerland, where he renounced violence on behalf of the PLO. Subsequently, the USA opened a dialogue with the PLO, and it appeared that Israel too would have to negotiate directly with the PLO if it sought a solution to the Palestinian question.

In April 1989 rioting in several Jordanian cities following the Government's imposition of significant price rises on basic goods and services led to the resignation of the Prime Minister and his Cabinet. Later that month Field Marshal Sharif Zaid ibn Shaker, who had been Commander-in-Chief of the Jordanian armed forces between 1976 and 1988, was appointed Prime Minister, at the head of a new 24-member Cabinet. While King Hussein refused to make any concessions regarding the price increases, he announced that a general election would be held for the first time since 1967.

TOWARDS DEMOCRACY

A general election to the 80-seat House of Representatives took place on 8 November 1989 and was contested by 647 candidates, mostly independents, as the ban on political parties (in force since 1963) remained. However, the Muslim Brotherhood was able to present candidates for election, owing to its legal status as a charity rather than a political party. At the election, in which 63% of the electorate voted, the Muslim Brotherhood won 20 seats, while independent Islamists (who supported the Muslim Brotherhood) won a further 14 seats. Palestinian or Arab nationalists won an estimated seven seats and 'leftist' candidates won four. The remainder were won by candidates who were broadly considered to be pro-Government. The strength of support for the opposition candidates was regarded as surprising, especially since a disproportionately large number of seats had been assigned to rural areas, from which the Government had traditionally drawn most support.

In December 1989 Mudar Badran was appointed Prime Minister by King Hussein. (Badran had served as Prime Minister twice previously, during 1976–79 and 1980–84.) Included in the new Cabinet were three independent Muslim deputies and three 'leftists', all of whom were regarded as members of the opposition. The Government received a vote of confidence from the House of Representatives in January 1990. The Prime Minister affirmed continuing support for prevailing austerity measures, and at the end of January announced the abolition of the 1954 anti-communism law.

Following the 1989 election, King Hussein, under increasing pressure to initiate constitutional reform, promised to allow political parties more freedom and to tighten controls on corruption. In April 1990 he appointed a 60-member Royal Commission to draft a National Charter that would regulate political life in Jordan. In October a National Islamic Bloc was formed by more than one-half of the deputies in the House of Representatives.

On 9 June 1991 the National Charter was endorsed by the King and leading political figures. Among other things, the Charter revoked the ban on Jordanian political parties in return for their allegiance to the monarchy. On 19 June the King accepted the resignation of the Government headed by Mudar Badran and appointed a new Cabinet, with former Minister of Foreign Affairs Taher al-Masri as Prime Minister. Al-Masri was Jordan's first Palestinian-born Prime Minister and, in spite of his support for Iraqi President Saddam Hussain during the 1990–91 Gulf crisis, was known for his liberal, pro-Western views. Badran's resignation was attributed to the King's disapproval of his sympathy for the Muslim Brotherhood, which had urged that *Shari'a* (Islamic) law should govern the new National Charter and whose members were again excluded from the Cabinet. The new Government obtained a parliamentary vote of confidence on 18 July.

On 7 July 1991 the King issued a decree repealing the provisions of martial law, which had been in force since 1967, reportedly at the request of the new Prime Minister, who sought to continue the progress towards greater political freedom and democracy.

JORDAN'S POSITION IN THE GULF CRISIS

Even before the Iraqi invasion of Kuwait on 2 August 1990, Jordan's economy was in severe difficulties. Of all the Arab states affected, Jordan was probably the nation that was most likely to suffer from the effects of the conflict and the imposition of economic sanctions against Iraq, as stipulated by UN

Security Council Resolution 661 of 6 August. The loss of remittances from thousands of Jordanian workers who returned, destitute, from Iraq and Kuwait; the increased cost of importing petroleum products (almost all of Jordan's oil had been imported from Iraq); the threatened loss of as much as one-quarter of the country's exports and its transit trade with Iraq and Kuwait; the sudden decline in activity at the Red Sea port of Aqaba, as a result of the naval blockade; the enormous cost of humanitarian aid to refugees fleeing the conflict through its territory: all these were potentially disastrous for Jordan, which was embroiled in events beyond its control.

Following Iraq's invasion of Kuwait, the Palestinians and the PLO supported Iraq. Officially, Jordan, in its own interests, remained neutral in the conflict. King Hussein 'regretted', but did not condemn, the action of Saddam Hussain in invading Kuwait, and Jordanian public opinion was solidly pro-Iraq for the duration of the crisis. Arab League ministers, attending a meeting of the Organization of the Islamic Conference (now Organization of Islamic Cooperation—OIC) in Cairo on 3 August 1990, issued a statement, opposed by Jordan, condemning the invasion and demanding Iraq's immediate and unconditional withdrawal. At the emergency summit meeting of the Arab League, held in Cairo on 10 August, Jordan abstained in a vote to denounce the annexation of Kuwait and to advocate the deployment of a pan-Arab force to defend Saudi Arabia and neighbouring states from invasion by Iraqi armed forces. King Hussein welcomed Saddam Hussain's proposal, on 12 August, to link Iraq's occupation of Kuwait with the continued Israeli occupations, and he held talks with the Iraqi leader in the Iraqi capital, Baghdad, on the following day. Another Arab League meeting in Cairo (30–31 August) was boycotted by Jordan and other Arab nations that supported Iraq. King Hussein persistently argued in favour of an Arab solution to the crisis and opposed the deployment of a multinational armed force in the Gulf region.

In the West, which had always regarded King Hussein as one of its chief allies in the region, there was much criticism of the King's pro-Iraq stance, though this was tempered with acknowledgement of the extremely difficult position in which he found himself. Talks in the USA between the King and President George H. W. Bush, at Kennebunkport, Maine, on 16 August 1990, resulted in promises of US financial assistance in return for Jordanian observance of the economic embargo imposed on Iraq. A report by a UN envoy in October estimated that the crisis would cost Jordan some 30% of its gross domestic product (GDP) in 1990 and as much as 50% in 1991. As a result of the conflict, Jordan was temporarily overwhelmed by an influx of refugees.

King Hussein invested considerable personal effort in the search for a peaceful solution to the crisis, visiting London, Paris and Washington, DC, USA. In late August 1990 he arrived in Libya at the start of a peace mission among Arab leaders. He continued to advocate an Arab solution to the crisis and, in a televised message to the US Congress and people in September, urged the immediate withdrawal of the multinational force from the Gulf region. Following talks in Baghdad with Saddam Hussain in December, the King proposed a peace plan linking the Iraqi–Kuwait dispute and the Arab–Israeli conflict.

The King's diplomatic efforts continued into 1991, when he embarked, in January, on a fresh tour of European capitals in a final attempt to avert war in the Gulf region. Diplomatic ties with Iran, severed in 1981 after the start of the Iran–Iraq War, were resumed in mid-January 1991.

Following the outbreak of hostilities between Iraq and a US-led multinational force on 16 January 1991, the Jordanian Government condemned the bombardment of Iraq. Large-scale anti-Western and anti-Israeli demonstrations occurred throughout Jordan, where overwhelming popular support for Iraq was expressed. Sentiments were further aroused when air attacks on goods vehicles on the Baghdad–al-Ruweishid highway in late January killed at least six Jordanian civilians. Jordan had been entirely dependent on Iraqi oil owing to the suspension of Saudi Arabian supplies in September 1990. Now these consignments were halted and Jordan, which introduced petrol-rationing in February, was obliged to obtain more expensive supplies from Syria and Yemen. Oil imports from Iraq were eventually resumed in April 1991.

In a televised address in February 1991, King Hussein paid tribute to the people and armed forces of Iraq, describing them as victims of this 'savage and large-scale war'. The speech was condemned by the US Administration, which accused Jordan of abandoning its neutrality and threatened to review its economic aid. In March the US Congress approved legislation cancelling a US $57m. aid programme. The law was signed by President Bush in April. However, the effects were offset, to some extent, by the announcement of a $450m. Japanese concessionary loan. As the multinational force launched a ground offensive to liberate Kuwait on 24 February, Prime Minister Badran announced that the conflict had at that point cost Jordan some $8,000m.

In March 1991, following the liberation of Kuwait and the end of hostilities between Iraq and the multinational force, King Hussein, in a televised address to the nation, advocated regional reconciliation. Later that month he travelled to Damascus for talks with President Assad, and subsequently sought to improve relations with the West.

THE MADRID CONFERENCE OF 1991–94

In July 1991 King Hussein announced his intention to accept an invitation to Jordan to attend a Middle East peace conference sponsored by the USA and the USSR. It was hoped that the conference would be attended by delegations from Israel, Egypt, Syria and Lebanon, and by a joint Jordanian-Palestinian delegation, and that it would thus become the first occasion when Israel, the Palestinians and the Arab nations would participate in direct negotiations. The Jordanian House of Representatives opposed the plan, however, demanding Israeli withdrawal from the Occupied Territories and East Jerusalem as a precondition for Jordan's attendance, and rejecting Israel's insistence that neither Palestinians from East Jerusalem nor overt supporters of the PLO should be allowed to attend. In October King Hussein confirmed that a Jordanian delegation would attend the conference, while the Central Council of the PLO approved the formation of a joint Jordanian-Palestinian delegation.

The opening session of the historic conference, convened within the framework of UN Security Council Resolutions 242 and 338, and chaired by US President Bush and the Soviet President, Mikhail Gorbachev, was held in Madrid, Spain, during 30 October–1 November 1991. Subsequent negotiations in Washington, DC, and Moscow, Russia, between the Israeli and the joint Jordanian-Palestinian delegations remained deadlocked, with regard to substantive issues. However, secret talks between the PLO and the Israeli Government in Oslo, Norway, which had begun early in 1993, led to an agreement, in August of that year, on a Declaration of Principles, which involved a degree of Palestinian self-government in the Occupied Territories. The Declaration of Principles (Documents on Palestine, see p. 76) was signed in Washington, DC, on 13 September 1993. News of the agreement apparently came as a surprise to King Hussein, who had not been informed that negotiations were taking place in Oslo, and the agreement reportedly caused grave embarrassment to the Palestinian negotiators in Washington, DC. Despite the King's initial irritation at the Israeli-PLO accord, which presented a socio-economic as well as a political challenge for Jordan, he quickly accepted the Declaration of Principles. On 14 September Jordan and Israel concluded a 'common agenda' for subsequent bilateral negotiations, which aimed to achieve 'a just, lasting and comprehensive peace' between the Arab states, the Palestinians and Israel. Jordan and Israel agreed to respect each other's security and to discuss future co-operation on territorial and economic issues. The signing of the agenda was publicized as being the first agreement between an Arab state and Israel since the peace accord between Egypt and Israel in 1979; King Hussein, however, stressed that it was not a peace agreement but an outline of topics to be discussed at future talks. Much of the agenda had already been agreed in 1992, but an official signing had been delayed because of Palestinian objections.

At the beginning of 1994 King Hussein publicly criticized Arafat because Jordan had not been continuously advised about the progress of talks between the PLO and Israel concerning the implementation of Palestinian self-rule in Gaza and Jericho and economic co-operation. There was a relatively subdued reaction from the Jordanian Government to the Cairo Agreement (Documents on Palestine, see p. 79) signed by Israel and the PLO on 4 May. Arafat visited Amman the day after the signing to brief King Hussein on the agreement, but the King remained disillusioned by Arafat's failure to liaise with Jordan in the peace process.

Following a secret meeting in November 1993 between King Hussein and Shimon Peres, the Israeli Minister of Foreign Affairs, there was optimism in Israeli government circles that Jordan would soon sign a formal peace agreement with Israel. Jordan, together with Syria and Lebanon, withdrew temporarily from the current round of bilateral talks with Israel in Washington, DC, immediately after the Hebron massacre in February 1994 (see the chapter on Israel), although the gesture appeared to be largely symbolic and aimed at appeasing public anger at the incident. The King firmly rejected demands made by Islamist deputies for Jordan to withdraw permanently from the peace talks.

THE PEACE TREATY WITH ISRAEL

In mid-1994 the peace process received a new impetus, after King Hussein unexpectedly decided to proceed unilaterally with talks with Israel. After secret talks between the King and the Israeli Prime Minister, Itzhak Rabin, in London in May, negotiations resumed at a meeting of the Jordanian-Israeli-US Trilateral Commission, held in June in Washington, DC. At the meeting Jordan and Israel agreed to hold future bilateral talks in their countries, and to establish joint sub-commissions on boundary demarcation, security, and water and environmental issues. These sub-commissions began work in July, at a meeting on the Jordanian–Israeli border.

At a ceremony at the White House on 25 July 1994 King Hussein and Prime Minister Rabin signed the 'Washington Declaration', ending the state of war that had existed between Jordan and Israel since 1948, but stopping short of a full peace treaty. After years of secret meetings, it was the first time that King Hussein had publicly met with an Israeli Prime Minister. In Jordan, opposition to the Declaration was limited, although Islamists declared 'a day of sadness and mourning'.

From Gaza, PLO Chairman Arafat sent his congratulations to Jordanian leaders on the Declaration. However, Palestinian leaders were angered by a statement in the document endorsing the special role of King Hussein as guardian of the Muslim holy places in Jerusalem. They argued that it undermined the Palestinian claim to sovereignty over Jerusalem, and that it contradicted the Israeli-PLO Declaration of Principles, which stated that the final status of Jerusalem would be determined by negotiation between Israel and the PLO.

Bilateral talks between Jordanian and Israeli delegations continued in August and September 1994. In mid-October, despite reports that problems remained over border demarcation and water resource allocation, Rabin visited Amman, and agreement was reached on a final peace treaty between the two countries. On 26 October the Treaty (Documents on Palestine, see p. 83) was formally signed at a ceremony held on the Jordanian–Israeli border, Jordan thus becoming only the second Arab state (after Egypt) to conclude a peace treaty with Israel. The Treaty was adopted by both houses of the Jordanian National Assembly, and ratified by King Hussein on 9 November. As agreed in the Treaty, full diplomatic relations between Jordan and Israel were established in late November (although ambassadors were not exchanged until April 1995). Also in November the Jordanian–Israeli border was opened to citizens of the two countries, and Israeli troops began withdrawing from some 340 sq km of land occupied since the 1967 war.

Following an Islamist-led demonstration against the Peace Treaty in Amman by some 5,000 people, the Jordanian Government banned all public meetings. The Islamic Action Front (IAF—Jabhat al-Amal al-Islami—the political arm of the Muslim Brotherhood movement, formed in 1992 immediately upon the legalization of political parties in Jordan) and its allies continued to oppose the Treaty and began a campaign in the National Assembly against the normalization of relations with Israel. They attempted to prevent the repeal of legislation limiting relations with Israel, including a law (adopted in 1973) prohibiting land sales to Israelis, a 1958 law imposing a total economic boycott of Israel, and legislation from 1953 outlawing trade between the two states.

Initially, the Peace Treaty did little to improve relations with the Palestinian leadership. The reaffirmation of King Hussein's special role as guardian of the Muslim holy places in East Jerusalem was criticized by the PLO leadership. In September 1994 the Palestinian (National) Authority (PA) had claimed responsibility for all Islamic institutions in East Jerusalem, the West Bank and Gaza Strip. In response, Jordan had agreed to relinquish its rights over sites in the West Bank and Gaza, but it refused to renounce its guardianship over the holy shrines of East Jerusalem. A compromise was reached on the issue in January 1995, when a bilateral accord was signed. The Palestinians agreed to recognize the Jordanian-Israeli Peace Treaty, thus implying de facto recognition of Jordanian rights over the Jerusalem shrines, at least until the city came under Palestinian sovereignty. In return, Jordan reaffirmed its support for Palestinian autonomy and for the future creation of a Palestinian state, with East Jerusalem as its capital. The accord also covered economic, cultural and administrative affairs, and included an agreement to use the Jordanian currency in the Palestinian territories.

POLITICAL REFORM AND MULTI-PARTY ELECTIONS

On 6 October 1991 an alliance of 49 deputies in the House of Representatives, from the Muslim Brotherhood, the 'constitutional bloc', the 'Democratic Alliance' and some independent Islamist deputies, signed a petition in protest against the terms of Jordan's participation in the Middle East peace conference. They urged the resignation of the Government, and in November Taher al-Masri resigned as Prime Minister, having lost the confidence of the House. The King appointed his cousin, Sharif Zaid ibn Shaker, who had led a transitional government in 1989, as Prime Minister, and a new, broader-based Government received a vote of confidence in December. The Muslim Brotherhood was again excluded from the Cabinet.

In June 1992 an extraordinary session of the House of Representatives was convened in order to debate new laws regarding political parties and the press. In July the House adopted new legislation whereby, subject to certain conditions, political parties were formally legalized, in preparation for the country's first multi-party elections since 1956, which were to be held by November 1993. The new legislation was approved by royal decree in August 1992, and by March 1993 nine political parties had received government approval.

In May 1993 King Hussein appointed a new Cabinet, in which Dr Abd al-Salam al-Majali, the leader of the Jordanian delegation to the Middle East peace conference, replaced Sharif Zaid ibn Shaker as Prime Minister. The new Government was regarded as a transitional administration, pending the country's first multi-party election.

At the beginning of August 1993 King Hussein unexpectedly dissolved the House of Representatives, provoking criticism from some politicians who had expected the House to debate proposed changes to the country's electoral law. Changes in voting procedures for the forthcoming general election were subsequently announced by the King in mid-August. Voters were to be allowed to cast one vote only, rather than a number equal to that of the number of candidates contesting a given constituency, as before.

The King decided to hold the elections on 8 November 1993. The election campaign went smoothly and peacefully. Some 820,000 Jordanians (52% of eligible voters and 68% of registered voters) participated in the poll. However, the independent New Jordan Research Centre estimated that 70% of Jordanians of Palestinian origin abstained, apparently because they felt excluded from the political system and because the prevailing system of electoral districts favoured areas dominated by East Bankers.

The political parties, which had been legal for less than a year, had little time to organize and amass public support. Domestic issues, such as unemployment and public services, were the main focus in the electoral campaign. Of the 80 deputies returned, 45 were independents. With the traditions of tribalism deeply rooted in the customs of the country, they won largely because of their tribal affiliations and personal influence.

The IAF won 16 seats at the 1993 election, the largest number of any political party, but six fewer than in the 1989 elections. This reversal was largely thought to result from the new electoral law that embodied the 'one man, one vote' principle. Indeed, the new law was widely interpreted as an attempt to weaken the IAF. Others felt that the Islamists had misjudged the mood of the country and had not devoted enough attention in their campaign to basic issues related to the impact of the economic recession on the lives of ordinary Jordanians. Of the other political parties, leftists and Arab nationalists won eight seats, while five conservative and right-of-centre parties claimed a total of 14 seats. Only 14 of the 80 new deputies were of Palestinian origin. Among the new deputies was the first woman to be elected to the Assembly, Toujan al-Faisal, who won one of the seats reserved for the Circassian minority.

Soon after the election a number of political groupings were formed in addition to the IAF. The Progressive Democratic Coalition, consisting of liberal deputies and leftist and Arab nationalists, claimed the support of 22 deputies; the National Action Front (NAF) and the Jordan Action Front (JAF), both groupings of conservative parties and their allies, claimed 18 and nine seats, respectively. However, the IAF remained the largest single political organization in the country. Some deputies saw the emergence of parliamentary blocs as the first step in a move towards the formation of larger political parties.

Former Prime Minister Taher al-Masri, widely regarded as the most influential Palestinian in Jordanian politics, was elected Speaker of the House of Representatives on 23 November 1993. Dr Abd al-Salam al-Majali remained Prime Minister and his new Government won a vote of confidence in December.

In another cautious move towards democratization, in March 1994 the National Assembly approved legislation to allow municipal elections in Greater Amman, home to some two-fifths of the country's population. The Government, no doubt concerned about the strength of Palestinian and Islamist opposition in the capital, had originally proposed that only one-half of the municipal council should be elected, but this was increased to two-thirds by the National Assembly. The remaining one-third of the council, together with the mayor, was to continue to be appointed by the Government.

In June 1994 Prime Minister al-Majali announced a major cabinet reorganization. There were no changes in the key portfolios, but 18 new appointments were made to the 31-member Cabinet. Among the new ministers were deputies from the three main political groupings in the lower house, the NAF, the Jordanian National Alliance and the Progressive Democratic Coalition, but none was selected from the IAF. However, one well-known Islamist activist, Abd al-Baki Jammu, was included in the new Government.

There was a further extensive reorganization of the Government in January 1995, following the dismissal of al-Majali as Prime Minister. He was replaced by Sharif Zaid ibn Shaker, who had served as Prime Minister in 1989 and 1991–93, and was a close ally and a cousin of the King. Only seven ministers from the previous administration retained their portfolios in the new Government. At the same time, Taher al-Masri resigned as Speaker of the House of Representatives, and was replaced by Saad Hayel Srour, who represented one of the northern Bedouin constituencies. The new Government comfortably won a vote of confidence in January 1995.

Two new political blocs emerged in the National Assembly in early 1995. The Independent National Action Front, with 17 deputies, was formed by a merger of the NAF and the bloc of independent deputies in the Assembly. Al-Masri formed a second new grouping of some 15 liberal and independent Islamist deputies. In June the authorities arrested six members of an illegal Islamist organization, the Islamic Renewal Group, believed to be active among Jordanians who had returned from Kuwait after the Iraqi invasion of 1990, and claimed to have found weapons and explosives that were to be used in attacks against US interests in Jordan. In municipal elections held nation-wide for the first time in July 1995 Islamist and left-wing groups failed to gain significant popular support, most elected candidates being largely pro-Government or independent. The IAF attributed its poor performance to a low level of voter participation and alleged government harassment of its members during the campaign. In November King Hussein warned that the country's professional organizations, several of which strongly opposed the normalization of relations with Israel, were becoming too involved in national politics and that this was against the interest of their members. In December Leith Shbeilat, head of the Jordan Engineers' Association and an outspoken Islamist critic of the regime, was arrested and later gaoled for three years, a move regarded by some observers as an attempt to intimidate supporters of the 'anti-normalization' movement.

KABARITI APPOINTED PRIME MINISTER

In February 1996 King Hussein appointed the Minister of Foreign Affairs, Abd al-Karim al-Kabariti, as Prime Minister. The King was believed to have clashed with Kabariti's predecessor, Sharif Zaid ibn Shaker, on the pace of normalization with Israel and the severing of ties with Iraq. Kabariti's appointment was followed by the most radical reorganization of the Government for many years. He appointed a new Cabinet in which the majority of ministers took office for the first time. Twenty-two of the 31 members were deputies in the House of Representatives, strengthening the new administration's democratic credentials. The King hoped that the new Government would work towards 'full and comprehensive change'. In March Kabariti's new administration easily won a vote of confidence in the House of Representatives. The Prime Minister emphasized the need to promote pluralism and democracy. He also outlined plans to reform the Ministry of the Interior and the system of government appointments in order to combat nepotism and corruption, which had become an important political issue in recent years. Kabariti retained the foreign affairs portfolio and was known to be a strong supporter of the King's new policy on Iraq and of strengthening ties with Israel.

The popularity of Kabariti's Government was short-lived. In August 1996 fierce rioting erupted in the south of the country after the Government more than doubled the price of bread. The price rise was part of an IMF-sponsored austerity plan to remove the subsidies that stabilized food prices. About one-third of Jordan's population were believed to be living below the poverty line, and many people feared that the rise in the price of bread, the country's staple food, would lead to increases in the prices of all foodstuffs. The rioting quickly spread to other parts of the country, including the poor suburbs of Amman. King Hussein suspended the legislature and deployed élite units of the army to re-establish control in al-Karak (Kerak), the scene of the most severe rioting. The army quickly regained control over the town, which was placed under curfew, and some 190 people were reportedly arrested. King Hussein did not hold his Prime Minister responsible for the riots. It therefore came as a surprise when the King dismissed Kabariti on 19 March 1997 and again appointed Abd al-Salam al-Majali to the premiership.

The new Prime Minister appointed a 23-member Cabinet consisting mainly of technocrats; he retained five ministers from the previous administration, including Dr Abdullah al-Nusur, an East Banker, promoted to Deputy Prime Minister, and Dr Jawad al-Anani, a Palestinian and former Minister of Labour and Industry, who also became a Deputy Prime Minister, with special responsibility for development matters. The new Government's primary task was to supervise the forthcoming legislative elections. In preparation for the elections, the National Assembly voted to continue the 'one man, one vote' system adopted for the 1993 elections. The King also urged the Government to eliminate corruption in public office, to alleviate unemployment and to modify the education system to the needs of society.

In May 1997, following increasing media criticism of a number of government policies, several amendments were made to legislation governing the press, prompting strong protests from editors, journalists, professional associations and opposition groups. The amendments included a considerable increase in the minimum capital that weekly journals were required to raise as a precondition for publishing, an extension of the range of prohibited subjects to include the armed forces and the security services, and a substantial rise in the fines that could be levied for contravening press legislation. Also in May nine centre parties, including al-Ahd (Pledge) and the Jordan National Party, announced that they had united to form the National Constitutional Party (NCP), which became the country's largest political grouping. The formation of the NCP, together with the establishment in 1996 of the Unionist Arab Democratic Party (a coalition of three leftist parties), reduced the total number of political parties from 24 to 14. A further political grouping subsequently emerged; the progressive alliance included a number of eminent political figures (among them two former prime ministers, Ahmad Ubeidat and Taher al-Masri, and a former parliamentary speaker, Sulayman Arar). In June King Hussein appointed his close associate and adviser, Zaid Rifai, as Speaker of the Senate.

THE 1997 ELECTIONS AND 1998 GOVERNMENT

In July 1997 the Muslim Brotherhood declared that it would boycott the forthcoming parliamentary elections, which, King Hussein had announced, were to proceed in November, as scheduled. This decision appeared to reflect growing disillusionment with the role of the National Assembly, which was perceived to have little or no influence over important political and economic decisions in the country. The IAF endorsed the Muslim Brotherhood's decision by a large majority. The IAF, together with nine smaller leftist and nationalist parties, had demanded changes in the electoral legislation, arguing that the existing 'one man, one vote' system favoured candidates with strong tribal affiliations over those representing 'ideological' parties; however, King Hussein and al-Majali refused to make any concessions. In September the Government suspended some 13 weekly newspapers for three months (effectively during the electoral period) for failing to comply with the amendments to the press regulations that had been introduced in May.

The elections on 4 November 1997, which were boycotted by many parties, professional associations and respected political figures, attracted little popular enthusiasm. An estimated 55% of the registered electorate participated, with a voter turn-out of only 26% in parts of Amman. There were widespread allegations of electoral malpractice, and in a number of regions the security forces were obliged to intervene to suppress clashes between rival candidates and their supporters. Deputies with tribal affiliations dominated the new parliament. The NCP, which some sections of the press referred to as the 'party of the regime', won only two seats. Saad Hayel Srour was re-elected Speaker of the House of Representatives. Zaid Rifai was retained as Speaker of the Senate. Political figures critical of the Government were completely absent from the upper house. King Hussein confirmed the appointment of al-Majali to the office of Prime Minister.

In January 1998 the High Court ruled that the amendments to the press laws introduced in May 1997 were unconstitutional and that actions taken by the Government under the amendments were thus invalid. The authorities reluctantly agreed to accept the ruling, and several newspapers that had been banned resumed publishing in March. The country's Chief Justice, Farouq al-Kailani, claimed that, owing to his role in the High Court ruling on the press legislation, the Government had forced him to resign.

During the increase in tension between the USA and Iraq in early 1998 (see below) there was widespread support among Jordanians for Iraq. The authorities, however, decided to ban all pro-Iraqi demonstrations and urged the press to adopt the official government policy on the situation. When a grouping of Islamists, leftists and nationalists opposed to US policy in the Middle East attempted to hold a large rally in Amman in mid-February, the police quickly dispersed the meeting, and a number of leading government opponents were assaulted during the disturbances. Later in February there were violent clashes in the southern town of Ma'an when members of the security forces intervened to prevent a pro-Iraqi demonstration; the security forces subsequently denied responsibility for the death of one of the demonstrators. The Minister of the Interior, Nadhir Rashid, claimed that the riots in Ma'an had been instigated by the outspoken Islamist, Leith Shbeilat, who had addressed a meeting in the town that day, and stated that he would be put on trial for his involvement in the disturbances. Supporters of Shbeilat, however, insisted that he had left Ma'an before the violence erupted and was arrested on his return to Amman. Shbeilat was sentenced to nine months' imprisonment, but King Hussein ordered his release later in the year.

In early 1998 al-Majali announced a cabinet reorganization, in which five new ministers were appointed, notably Dr Bassam al-Umush, a member of the Muslim Brotherhood who had been suspended from the movement in 1997. Dr Fayez al-Tarawneh, hitherto Minister of Foreign Affairs, became Chief of the Royal Court, traditionally a move towards the premiership, with Jawad al-Anani assuming the foreign affairs portfolio. Rashid, who had been criticized for the suppression of the pro-Iraqi demonstrations by the security forces, retained his portfolio.

In August 1998 King Hussein (who was undergoing medical treatment in the USA—see below) appointed Fayez al-Tarawneh to the office of Prime Minister, replacing Abd al-Salam al-Majali. Al-Majali's removal was largely attributed to the criticism that the Government had attracted over the continuing water crisis in Amman. Later in August a new Cabinet, which included 10 new ministers, was installed; al-Anani replaced al-Tarawneh as Chief of the Royal Court. In December Abd al-Hadi al-Majali was appointed as Speaker of the House of Representatives.

DEATH OF KING HUSSEIN

In July 1998 King Hussein began to undergo treatment in the USA for lymphatic cancer. In August he issued a royal decree transferring responsibility for certain executive duties, including the appointment of ministers, to his brother, Crown Prince Hassan. On King Hussein's return to Jordan on 19 January 1999, amid considerable public celebration and government assurances that his health had been restored, the King prompted renewed speculation about the royal succession by appointing Crown Prince Hassan as his 'deputy' (a position believed to involve limited authority). On 24 January King Hussein issued a royal decree naming his eldest son, Abdullah, as Crown Prince of Jordan. It was reported that a letter had been conveyed from King Hussein to Crown Prince Hassan, who had been regent since 1965, in which the King had expressed his dissatisfaction with his brother's handling of Jordanian affairs during his six-month absence, in particular his attempts to interfere in military affairs. King Hussein had also accused his brother's supporters of slandering his immediate family, prompting speculation that serious divisions had emerged within the royal family.

In late January 1999 King Hussein left Jordan for emergency treatment in the USA, following a rapid deterioration in his health. However, King Hussein returned to Amman on 5 February, and was pronounced dead two days later. Hussein had been the Middle East's longest-serving ruler, controlling the fortunes of Jordan for the greater part of its modern history, during which time the country was transformed from an essentially artificial creation with few resources into a modern state. The funeral of King Hussein, held in Amman on 8 February, was attended by more than 50 heads of state or government, including US President Bill Clinton, Israeli Prime Minister Binyamin Netanyahu and Syria's President Assad.

On 7 February 1999, a few hours after King Hussein's death, the newly appointed Crown Prince was sworn in as King Abdullah ibn al-Hussein of Jordan. After formal education in the United Kingdom and the USA, Abdullah had embarked on a military career, becoming Commander of Special Forces with the rank of major-general. Abdullah was reported to have good relations with members of the political establishment in the Gulf states and the USA. However, although King Abdullah's many connections were seen as advantageous, some commentators expressed concern that the new monarch lacked political experience at a time when Jordan faced serious problems both at home and abroad. Soon after his father's death, the new King made a televised address to the nation, appealing for Jordanian unity and pledging to continue his father's policies. He subsequently named his half-brother, and the youngest son of King Hussein, Prince Hamzeh ibn al-Hussein, as the new Crown Prince of Jordan (apparently in accordance with the wishes of the late King).

KING ABDULLAH TAKES CONTROL

Before the official 40-day period of mourning for King Hussein had ended, the new King made a number of key changes at the Royal Palace and in the military high command and also appointed a new Government. In late February 1999 four senior army officers, who were believed to have pledged their loyalty to Prince Hassan shortly before King Hussein's death, were removed from their posts. In mid-March Prince Hassan was appointed to head the Higher Council of Science and Technology, while King Hussein's widow, Queen Noor, became head of the new King Hussein Foundation. While these appointments helped to preserve their elevated status, it was clear that henceforth both were expected to confine their activities to these well-defined roles, and had been excluded from positions of power. On 21 March King Abdullah issued a royal decree naming his wife, Rania Yassin, a Palestinian, whose family originated from the West Bank, as the Queen of Jordan. Also in March Jawad al-Anani, Chief of the Royal Court and a close associate of Prince Hassan, was replaced by former Prime Minister Abd al-Karim al-Kabariti, while Adnan Abu Odeh, an aide to King Hussein for many years, returned to the Palace as an adviser. Later in the year King Abdullah appointed his half-brother, Prince Ali, the son of King Hussein and his third wife, Queen Alia, to head a special force responsible for protecting the King.

On 4 March 1999 King Abdullah appointed a new 24-member Cabinet, with Abd al-Raouf al-Rawabdeh replacing Fayez al-Tarawneh as Prime Minister. The former Deputy Prime Minister and mayor of Amman was widely considered to be an experienced politician capable of implementing an effective reform programme. Al-Rawabdeh's Cabinet contained eight ministers from the outgoing administration, including the three key portfolios of the interior, finance and foreign affairs. However, several ministers regarded as loyal to Prince Hassan were replaced, although the respected Minister of Finance, Michel Marto, also a protégé of Prince Hassan, retained his post. In his letter of appointment to the new Prime Minister, King Abdullah prescribed 'fundamental reforms', including the strengthening of the rule of law and further democratization; he also urged al-Rawabdeh to address the serious problems of poverty and unemployment.

The Government won a vote of confidence from the National Assembly in April 1999. Those who voted against the Government were left-wing and Islamist deputies, who criticized the new administration for having failed to make provision for political reform in its publicized programme, in particular with regard to the electoral and press laws. However, opposition groups were willing to express cautious loyalty to the new King. The Muslim Brotherhood immediately sought an audience with King Abdullah, emphasizing the organization's strong links with the monarchy while continuing to press for changes to the electoral law. The Muslim Brotherhood also appealed for an open dialogue with the Government, and its political wing, the IAF, indicated that it would participate in municipal elections scheduled for July 1999 (despite having boycotted the 1997 parliamentary elections). However, the IAF did not join the Popular Participation Bloc, a new grouping of 13 leftist, Baathist and pan-Arab parties formed in May 1999 to contest the municipal elections, owing to a lack of agreement over the quotas of candidates to be fielded by each party.

In April 1999 all censorship of Arab and foreign newspapers and magazines was removed, as was censorship of imported audio and video cassettes. Amendments to the controversial Press and Publications Law (which had imposed a number of restrictions on journalists) were approved by the National Assembly in September, although critics of the legislation remained dissatisfied. Meanwhile, in late March King Abdullah released almost 500 prisoners as part of a recent amnesty law, while the Government also ended the security surveillance imposed on Leith Shbeilat. However, accusations of human rights abuses in Jordan continued in 1999. In its annual report, released in April, the Arab Human Rights Organization in Jordan criticized the Government for a 'considerable increase' in human rights violations, including the arrest of journalists and harsh treatment of prisoners held in detention centres.

On 14–15 July 1999 municipal elections were conducted throughout Jordan. Independent and tribal candidates gained the most seats in the elections, while Islamists too were successful in their traditional urban strongholds of Al-Zarqa (Zarqa), Irbid, Al-Rusayfah (Russeifa) and Tafilah. The IAF also won five of the 20 elected seats on the Great Amman Municipality, and at the national level 70 of its 100 candidates were successful. The local elections marked the return of the IAF to the formal political process. Later in 1999 the Prime Minister agreed to consider changes to the electoral system proposed by the Muslim Brotherhood, which, together with several other opposition groups that had sought electoral reforms before the 1997 poll, suggested increasing the number of seats in the House of Representatives from 80 to 120. The country would be divided into 80 electoral districts and voters would each cast two votes, one for their chosen candidate and the second for a political party list. Those parties securing the highest share of the vote would be allocated the additional 40 seats. Some political groupings, however, were unhappy with these proposals, fearing that they would result in the Islamists re-establishing their dominant position in the lower house. On 18 July 1999 King Abdullah issued a royal decree appointing Lt-Gen. Muhammad Yousuf al-Malkawi as Chairman of the Joint Chiefs of Staff, replacing Field Marshal Abd al-Hafez Mar'i al-Ka'ahinah, who became the King's own military adviser.

Relations between the Jordanian Government and the Muslim Brotherhood were strained in August 1999, when the security forces closed down the Amman offices of the Palestinian Islamic Resistance Movement (Hamas), following claims by the Ministry of the Interior that the offices were being used for illegal political activities by non-Jordanian groups. The authorities alleged that Hamas had organized military camps and created weapons dumps across the country. The home of Khalid Meshaal, head of Hamas's political bureau, was also raided, while some 15 Hamas officials were detained and arrest warrants were issued for a further five of the group's leaders. In September three of the five (including Meshaal and the Hamas spokesman, Ibrahim Ghosheh) were arrested by Jordanian security forces on their return to Amman from Iran, on charges of involvement in illicit political activities and the illegal possession of firearms. More serious charges relating to the possession of weapons for illegal use and the planning of military operations—which could carry the death penalty—were brought against Meshaal and Ghosheh in October. In early November another senior Hamas representative was arrested, amid reports that the organization had rejected an offer by the Government to release the detained activists, provided that they agreed to cease all political activity and that their leaders left the country. However, later in the month the Jordanian authorities released some 24 Hamas officials, including four leaders who were immediately expelled to Qatar.

In January 2000 Abd al-Karim al-Kabariti resigned as Chief of the Royal Court, less than a year after his appointment, and was replaced by former Prime Minister Fayez al-Tarawneh (who had held the same post during 1998). Although citing unspecified 'political and personal reasons', Kabariti—seen as the most prominent of the 'liberal reformists' among Jordan's political élite—was reported to have been frustrated by repeated clashes with al-Rawabdeh and by the resistance mounted by the traditionalist 'old guard' to his efforts to promote a 'reformist' agenda. Liberal reformists, who sought to introduce greater freedom, to reduce official bureaucracy and to promote political equality for Jordan's Palestinian population, saw the departure of Kabariti as a major defeat, especially as there had been widespread speculation that King Abdullah would replace al-Rawabdeh given his failure to address the urgent economic crisis. Some observers argued that the conflict between the liberal reformists and the 'old guard' had become the major feature of political life during the first year of the King's reign.

In December 1999 16 suspected terrorists (including Jordanians, an Iraqi and an Algerian) were arrested on charges of plotting attacks against US and Israeli tourist targets in Jordan. In September 2000 six of the militants were sentenced to death, having been convicted of the manufacture of explosives, membership of an illegal organization and fraud; 16 were sentenced to terms of imprisonment ranging from seven years to life, while the remaining six were acquitted. Meanwhile, another large group of Islamist militants from the northern town of Irbid was arrested later in December 1999. Opposition circles argued that the authorities' clampdown on Islamist groups supporting an armed struggle against Israel was serving the interests of the USA and Israel rather than that of Jordan. In July 2000 another group of suspected militant Islamists was detained by the authorities, on suspicion of plotting sabotage in the country; the arrests were believed to be linked to a recent warning that the US embassy in Amman was about to be targeted by Islamist fundamentalists. Four of the defendants were sentenced to death in September.

In January 2000 the four Hamas leaders who had, in November 1999, been expelled to Qatar—among them Meshaal and Ghosheh—filed an appeal with the Higher Court of Justice, on the grounds that their expulsion was unconstitutional. However, the appeal was rejected in June. Ghosheh strongly criticized the Muslim Brotherhood for failing to support them during the crisis and for abandoning the campaign to 'liberate Palestine' (although Hamas's spiritual leader, Sheikh Ahmad Yassin, praised the role played by the Muslim Brotherhood). Some sources claimed that one of the Government's objectives in taking action against Hamas was to cause a rift between the Palestinian resistance movement and the Muslim Brotherhood. Ghosheh provoked considerable controversy in mid-June 2001 when he returned to Amman, claiming that he was doing so with the backing of the Hamas leadership. However, he was forbidden by the Jordanian authorities to enter the country. At the end of June Jordan's Ministry of Information announced that Ghosheh would be permitted to enter the country, after he agreed to cease his activities on behalf of Hamas.

Meanwhile, in January 2000 allegations of corruption were made against Prime Minister al-Rawabdeh. Only days before the cabinet reorganization, al-Rawabdeh and his son Issam were accused publicly by an independent parliamentary deputy of having demanded a JD 15m. (US $20m.) bribe from an Arab Gulf investor, in return for securing official approval to build a planned tourism complex in Jordan. In mid-February the parliamentary committee charged with examining the allegations—the first time that a Jordanian premier had been subject to a public investigation on corruption charges—cleared both the Prime Minister and his son of any misdemeanour, owing to a lack of evidence, and Issam al-Rawabdeh subsequently filed a libel suit against the deputy. Later that month Rima Khalaf al-Hunaidi resigned as Deputy Prime Minister and Minister of Planning, following alleged differences with the Prime Minister over the implementation of economic reforms.

Despite strong backing from King Abdullah and Queen Rania, as well as the Chief Islamic Justice, Sheikh Izzedin al-Khatib al-Tamimi, government efforts to repeal an article in the penal code relating to so-called 'honour killings' were twice rejected by the House of Representatives with a large majority, in late 1999 and early 2000. The Government wished to abolish Article 340, under which those found guilty of murdering female relatives in the name of 'family honour' were protected, and to impose tough punishment for such crimes. Opponents in the lower house argued that such changes would encourage adultery and accelerate the decline in the country's moral values that, they considered, had taken place as a result of the normalization of relations with Israel. In February some 6,000 protesters marched to the National Assembly building and then to the Prime Minister's office demanding that parliament revoke the article related to 'honour killings'. It was the largest public demonstration in Amman for some years and was led by King Abdullah's half-brother, Prince Ali, and the King's cousin and adviser on tribal affairs, Prince Ghazi bin Muhammad.

In early April 2000 a political adviser to the King, Adnan Abu Odeh, resigned, citing the widespread controversy caused by his plans to reform legislation concerning Jordanians of Palestinian origin. He was replaced by Samir Rifai, grandson of the former Prime Minister of the same name and son of Senate Speaker Zaid Rifai, who was to remain the Secretary-General of the Royal Court, in August. Meanwhile, in mid-April a significant number of deputies in the House of Representatives, including senior figures such as Speaker al-Majali and the Chairman of the Economic and Finance Committee, Ali Abu al-Ragheb, appealed to King Abdullah to dismiss the Government for failing to introduce political and economic reforms and for violating public freedoms. They also urged the King to form a 'parliamentary government' composed of deputies. At the same time opposition parties accused the Government of employing excessive force to quell dissent. King Abdullah responded by expressing his confidence in premier al-Rawabdeh.

Nevertheless, on 18 June 2000 King Abdullah dismissed the conservative al-Rawabdeh and named Ali Abu al-Ragheb as Jordan's new Prime Minister. Al-Ragheb, a former Minister of Industry and Trade, was a prominent member of the Consultative Economic Council established by the King to increase government initiatives regarding development. On 19 June al-Ragheb appointed a new 29-member Cabinet, which was reported to include nine Palestinian ministers and three with 'Islamist leanings'. Among the objectives for the new Government, as outlined by King Abdullah, were to: ensure national unity through the principle of equal opportunities for all Jordanian citizens, both East Bankers and Palestinians; end nepotism in public office; and draft modern electoral legislation to pave the way for completely free parliamentary elections scheduled for late 2001. He also placed great emphasis on accelerating the implementation of IMF-sponsored economic reforms. Meanwhile, the IAF decided, in late June 2000, to freeze the membership of one of its leading members, Abd al-Rahim al-Akour, after he joined the Government as the Minister of Municipal, Rural and Environmental Affairs.

BREAKDOWN IN RELATIONS WITH IRAQ

In early August 1995 King Hussein granted political asylum to Hussain Kamel al-Majid, his brother Saddam Kamel and their wives after they fled from Baghdad to Amman. Hussain and Saddam Kamel had been senior figures in the Iraqi regime and were married to daughters of Saddam Hussain, the Iraqi President. Their defection marked a sharp deterioration in relations between Jordan and Iraq. At a press conference shortly after arriving in Jordan, Hussain Kamel appealed for the removal of Saddam Hussain and spoke of his hopes of leading an Iraqi opposition movement to rescue Iraqis from their worsening plight. Later that month King Hussein delivered a speech in which he praised Hussain Kamel as a great patriot and strongly criticized the Iraqi leader. In response, Iraq denounced Hussain Kamel as a traitor and a US agent, but carefully avoided attacks on King Hussein. Despite the political rupture, economic co-operation continued, with Iraq remaining Jordan's main source of oil supplies. Jordan continued to provide Iraq with a vitally important link with the outside world. In October King Hussein renewed his attack on the Iraqi regime, denouncing the presidential election there as a farce. He also established contact with Iraqi opposition groups in London, and promoted the idea of holding a congress in Amman to bring the different factions together in order to discuss political change in Iraq. However, the proposed congress drew criticism, especially from Syria, and the idea was abandoned In any case, his support for Hussain Kamel was short-lived. It quickly became clear that Kamel had few supporters in Iraq, while his appeals to the Iraqi opposition-in-exile were firmly rejected. By the end of 1995 his presence in

Jordan had become something of an embarrassment. When Hussain Kamel and his brother decided to return to Iraq in February 1996, after hearing that they had been pardoned, rumours circulated that the Jordanian authorities may have encouraged them in their decision. Nevertheless, the brutal murder of the two men by order of Saddam Hussain only days after their return was strongly condemned by Jordan.

In April 1996, after US aircraft were stationed at Azraq to enforce the air exclusion zone in southern Iraq, the Jordanian Government insisted that it would not permit the country to be used as a base for attacks against Iraq. Nevertheless, King Hussein met with Iraqi opposition leaders in London in March and gave permission for the Iraqi National Accord (INA) to open an office in Amman. There was another high-level defection from Iraq when Gen. Nizar Kazraji, a former Chief of Staff of the Iraqi army, arrived in Jordan and associated himself with the INA. In late March, amid speculation that Iraqi agents operating in Jordan might be seeking to target Jordanians, the first expulsion of an Iraqi diplomat from Jordan occurred. In retaliation, Iraq expelled a Jordanian diplomat.

Relations with Iraq improved slightly in December 1996, when the Iraqi Ministers of Trade and of Foreign Affairs held talks in Amman with senior Jordanian officials, marking a resumption in high-level bilateral contacts. King Hussein had reportedly been opposed to any relaxation of sanctions against Saddam Hussain's regime, but, after Iraq accepted UN Security Council Resolution 986 allowing the country to sell limited quantities of oil in order to purchase food and medicine, he was willing to adopt a less confrontational stance to protect Jordan's economic interests. The INA was allowed to keep its office in Amman, despite reports that the group had been infiltrated by Iraqi agents, but Jordan repeatedly asserted that it would not be used as a base for operations against the Iraqi regime.

Meanwhile, the Jordanian Government voiced concern over US missile attacks against Iraq, while the Jordanian National Assembly strongly condemned the US action. Despite Jordan's close alliance with the US Administration, the authorities reiterated that they would not allow Jordanian territory or airspace to be used for air-strikes against Iraq, but they urged the Iraqi Government to comply with all UN resolutions and allow UN weapons inspectors access to all suspect sites. Jordanian support for the Arab League's efforts to resolve the crisis by diplomatic means contributed to an improvement in relations with some other Arab states, notably Egypt. Although relations with Iraq remained uneasy, economic co-operation continued, and in February 1998 the two countries renewed the 1991 oil agreement. Most ordinary Jordanians remained strongly pro-Iraqi and, although they were strictly controlled by the Jordanian authorities, public demonstrations were allowed in protest against US and British air-strikes against Iraq in December 1998. The Jordanian Government also strongly condemned the attacks. At the end of December an emergency meeting of the Arab Parliamentary Union was held in Amman at which Crown Prince Hassan, acting as regent in the absence of King Hussein, appealed for the lifting of sanctions against Iraq. However, comments made by Hassan regarding the need for greater democracy in Iraq, and his demands for the release of all Kuwaiti prisoners of war held there, angered the Iraqi delegation. In early 1999 the Jordanian National Assembly voted to end the embargo imposed on Iraq by the UN.

Following King Hussein's death in February 1999, King Abdullah made efforts to improve bilateral relations with Iraq and publicly expressed his concern for the plight of the Iraqi people. In January 2000 the two countries renewed their annual trade protocol. Under the new oil agreement, one-half of the crude petroleum and derivatives supplied to Jordan by Iraq would be free of charge, while the annual trade protocol (in place since 1990) was increased in value from US $200m. to $300m. In November al-Ragheb undertook an official visit to Iraq, and the two countries agreed to increase the value of their trade agreement from $300m. in 2000 to $450m. in 2001.

RELATIONS WITH OTHER ARAB STATES

Jordan's new policy on Iraq was welcomed by Saudi Arabia and relations between the two countries continued to improve. Full diplomatic relations were restored with the appointment of a new Saudi ambassador to Jordan in November 1995. In January 1996 the Saudi Minister of Foreign Affairs visited Jordan and offered to resume supplies of some 40,000 barrels per day (b/d) of crude petroleum (cut off in September 1990). The normalization of relations with Saudi Arabia was sealed in August 1996 by a visit by King Hussein and a senior delegation to Riyadh, the Saudi capital. Both leaders agreed to strengthen bilateral relations, and agreements were concluded on the employment of Jordanians in Saudi Arabia and on resuming Jordanian agricultural exports to the kingdom.

While relations with other Gulf states improved in the mid-1990s, relations with Kuwait remained uneasy. However, in June 1997 the Kuwaiti Minister of Foreign Affairs declared that Kuwait was prepared to normalize relations with Jordan, Sudan and Yemen, the three Arab states that it had accused of supporting Iraq during the Gulf crisis. In the following month the Kuwaiti Government indicated that it favoured a faster normalization of relations with Jordan, but emphasized that the Jordanian press would have to modify its strongly critical attitude towards Kuwait. In March 1999 Jordan's embassy in Kuwait was reopened, following the restoration of full diplomatic relations between the two countries (which had been severed after Iraq's 1990 invasion of Kuwait), and later Kuwait began issuing visas to Jordanians.

Jordan's policy towards Iraq caused disquiet in Egypt and Syria, which feared that it could lead to a new, US-backed strategic reorientation in the region. The King had talks with Egypt's President Muhammad Hosni Mubarak in Washington, DC, in September 1995 during the signing of the Israeli-Palestinian Interim Agreement on the West Bank and the Gaza Strip (Documents on Palestine, see p. 86), and in December President Mubarak visited Amman. The two leaders issued a joint statement in which they emphasized the need to ensure the unity of Iraq and to allow the Iraqi people to decide their own future.

During the second half of 1997 there were indications that King Hussein wished to achieve an improvement in relations with Syria. The King praised President Assad, but also urged the Syrian Government to reciprocate by ceasing to support some Jordanian opposition parties and professional associations. For their part, the Jordanian authorities ordered the head of the Syrian branch of the Muslim Brotherhood's information office in Amman to leave the country. However, by the end of 1998 bilateral relations had deteriorated once again. Nevertheless, on the death of King Hussein in February 1999, the Syrian Government immediately announced three days of official mourning and President Assad attended the King's funeral at the head of a high-level Syrian delegation. Some commentators suggested that Assad's presence there marked a clear indication to the new King that Syria wished to improve relations with its southern neighbour and that closer links might offer an alternative to Jordan's current reliance on good relations with Israel and the USA. In April King Abdullah made his first official visit to Syria.

In July 1999, following the election of a new Israeli Prime Minister (see below), King Abdullah made an unannounced visit to Syria, amid Jordanian concerns that any peace agreement concluded by Israel and Syria could damage the Palestinians' position and effectively isolate them in future peace negotiations. In August the joint Jordanian-Syrian Higher Committee began talks in Amman. The meeting resulted in a bilateral agreement that officials hoped might double the volume of trade between the two countries. Later in the month Syria agreed to allow the free circulation of Jordanian newspapers and publications, ending a 10-year ban.

In September 1999 King Abdullah made an official visit to Lebanon—the first by a Jordanian monarch since 1965—where he held discussions with senior Lebanese officials regarding the Middle East peace process, as well as other bilateral issues. In June 2000 the King attended the funeral of President Assad in Damascus. Syria confirmed in November that it had upgraded its diplomatic representation in Jordan to ambassadorial status, and the Syrian state airline resumed regular flights to Amman after a break of more than 20 years. Moreover, the Syrian leadership announced in January 2001 that all Jordanian prisoners held in Syria would soon be released.

RELATIONS WITH ISRAEL AND THE PA

In May 1995 the Government banned a conference (organized by the IAF) to oppose the normalization of relations with Israel, claiming that it posed a threat to national security and to Jordan's image. In June Israel began to pipe 30m. cu m of drinking water per year from Lake Tiberias (the Sea of Galilee) to Jordan as agreed in the 1994 peace treaty. The project aimed to help Jordan overcome a growing shortage of drinking water and was promoted by the Jordanian authorities as one of the dividends of the peace process. However, there was some embarrassment when Israel indicated that the flow of water to Jordan could not be guaranteed in the event of shortages in Israel owing to drought. Opposition within many sections of Jordanian society to the peace treaty with Israel continued. In July 1995, under the terms of the peace treaty, Jordan finally annulled laws banning Jordanians from having contact with, doing business with, or selling land to Israelis, but only after several weeks of angry debate in the House of Representatives. After the assassination of the Israeli Prime Minister, Itzhak Rabin, in November, King Hussein made his first visit to Jerusalem since 1967 in order to attend the funeral, at which he delivered an emotional oration. Clearly shocked by Rabin's murder, the King emphasized the need to continue the peace process. In December 1995 Jordan expelled an Iranian diplomat, amid speculation that he may have been involved in planning an attack on Israeli tourists visiting the country. In order to strengthen bilateral relations, Shimon Peres, the new Israeli Prime Minister, visited Jordan in December, and King Hussein made a state visit to Israel in January 1996. A transport agreement was signed in January establishing direct road and air links between the two countries. The King and senior government officials condemned a spate of suicide bomb attacks carried out in Israel during February and repeatedly criticized the actions of Hamas militants.

After the surprise victory of Likud in the Israeli elections of May 1996, and the creation of a new right-wing Israeli Government, King Hussein declared that the implications of this did not worry him. He was the only Arab leader to have met Prime Minister Binyamin Netanyahu when he led the Israeli opposition and had maintained contacts with the Likud leader for some two years. An Israeli source indicated that the new Prime Minister expected the process of normalization with Jordan to continue. After his discussions with Netanyahu in Washington, DC, in October, the King attempted to persuade the Israeli Prime Minister to adopt a more constructive position on the redeployment of Israeli forces on the West Bank, set out in the Declaration of Principles but not yet implemented. As the peace process appeared to be expiring, protests against the normalization of relations with Israel intensified and succeeded in delaying the opening of the first Israeli trade fair in Amman by several weeks. The eventual opening of the fair, in January 1997, was attended by a demonstration organized by a 'national committee' consisting of political parties and trade unions, in which more than 2,500 Jordanians participated. In that month King Hussein intervened to support US efforts to secure an agreement between Israel and the PA on the issue of redeployment outlined in the Declaration of Principles. The King apparently persuaded Yasser Arafat to compromise on the timing of the second redeployment of Israeli forces from rural areas in the West Bank in order not to jeopardize the deal already made on Hebron. Israel's rapid redeployment of most of its forces from Hebron was welcomed by the Jordanian Government, and the release of three Jordanian prisoners held in Israel also helped to reduce tensions.

In February 1997 Prime Minister Netanyahu visited Amman to discuss bilateral relations, but his decision to continue with the construction of a large new Jewish settlement at Jabal Abu Ghunaim (Har Homa), on the outskirts of Jerusalem, plunged bilateral relations into a new crisis: the completed Har Homa project would result in Arab East Jerusalem becoming virtually surrounded by Jewish settlements, thereby prejudicing the future status of the city, which was due to be discussed during 'final status' negotiations between Israel and the PA. After the visit, in an exchange of letters, King Hussein stated that Netanyahu's policies threatened to destroy the peace process and could lead to violence. Shortly afterwards Crown Prince Hassan cancelled a visit to Israel. On 13 March, two days after the publication of the King's outspoken letter, a Jordanian soldier opened fire on a party of Israeli schoolgirls at Nayarayim, on the border with Jordan, killing seven of the girls and wounding six others. King Hussein and Crown Prince Hassan immediately expressed their sorrow and distress at the killings and promised a full investigation. Three days after the attack the King, together with Prime Minister Netanyahu, visited the relatives of the deceased to offer their condolences. A military court later sentenced Ahmad al-Daqamseh, the perpetrator of the attack, to 25 years' imprisonment.

Despite the increasing strain on bilateral relations, an agreement was reached in May 1997 on the transfer of drinking water from Israel to Jordan, following talks between King Hussein and Netanyahu in Aqaba. In August the two countries signed an accord to divert international flights from the heavily congested airport serving Israel's Red Sea resort at Eilat to nearby Aqaba airport in Jordan. In July Israel's Chief of Staff, Lt-Gen. Amnon Lipkin-Shahak, visited Jordan, the first official visit by the head of Israel's armed forces to an Arab country. The two countries were reported to have extended their co-operation in the fields of security and intelligence. However, the attempted assassination of Khalid Meshaal, the head of the political bureau of Hamas, in Amman in September by agents of the Israeli secret service, Mossad, created further bilateral tensions. King Hussein demanded and secured the release of Sheikh Ahmad Yassin, the spiritual leader of Hamas, and a number of other Palestinians who had been imprisoned in Israel, in exchange for the return of the two Mossad agents. King Hussein reportedly threatened to suspend diplomatic relations if the Israeli authorities failed to meet his demands. Following the attack on Meshaal, there were few high-level political contacts between Jordan and Israel for some months, although economic co-operation continued. In March 1998 Ariel Sharon, the Israeli Minister of National Infrastructure, and the senior Israeli responsible for relations with Jordan, visited Amman, followed by the Israeli Minister of Trade and Industry. Also in March a high-level Jordanian delegation, led by Crown Prince Hassan, visited Israel to hold talks with Netanyahu and the Israeli Minister of Defence, Itzhak Mordechai. Shortly afterwards, however, Ariel Sharon angered the Jordanian authorities by stating, in an Israeli news broadcast, that Israel was still determined to kill Meshaal. Abdullah al-Nusur, then the acting premier, condemned the statement and reminded Israel that Meshaal was a Jordanian national. Sharon subsequently wrote to Crown Prince Hassan, claiming that his comments had been misinterpreted and insisting that he respected Jordan's sovereignty.

In October 1998, while undergoing treatment for cancer in the USA, King Hussein attended the US-sponsored peace talks between Israel and the PA at Wye Plantation in the US state of Maryland. His participation was crucial in securing the two sides' agreement to the Wye Memorandum. Following the death of King Hussein in February 1999 numerous tributes were paid to the late monarch by prominent Israeli politicians and statesmen. President Ezer Weizman, who referred to the King as one of the great leaders of the 20th century, headed a large Israeli delegation, including Prime Minister Netanyahu, at Hussein's funeral.

Jordan's new ruler, King Abdullah, immediately assured Israel that he was committed to continuing his father's support for the Middle East peace process. In July 1999 King Abdullah held talks with the new Israeli Prime Minister, Ehud Barak, reportedly concerning ways to revive the peace process. As bilateral relations showed signs of improvement, in August the new Israeli Minister of Foreign Affairs, David Levy, made his first visit to Jordan since his appointment, and there were talks between Jordanian ministers and their Israeli counterparts on advancing co-operation in the fields of transport, tourism and telecommunications as proposed under the terms of the 1994 peace treaty.

King Abdullah welcomed the unexpected reactivation of the stalled Wye Memorandum following the signing of the Sharm el-Sheikh Memorandum, or Wye Two accords (Documents on

Palestine, see p. 94), by Yasser Arafat and Ehud Barak in Egypt on 4 September 1999. However, relations became strained in October when a Jordanian parliamentary delegation visiting the West Bank town of Hebron received verbal abuse from right-wing Israeli settlers and Israeli soldiers failed to intervene. The incident was aggravated by Israel's initial reluctance to issue an apology, as demanded by the Jordanian Government. Meanwhile, the anti-normalization campaign in Jordan continued, although it was weakened by internal divisions. In February 2000 King Abdullah postponed a scheduled visit to Israel; Jordanian officials stated that the King sought greater progress in the Middle East peace process prior to holding talks with the Israeli Prime Minister, but the principal reason for the postponement appeared to be Israel's recent launching of air-strikes against infrastructural targets in Lebanon, an action that King Abdullah strongly condemned. The King did not make his first visit to Israel until April of that year, when he held brief discussions with Ehud Barak at Eilat in an attempt to revive the peace process and to resolve bilateral issues, especially regarding water management.

As the Jordanian leadership became increasingly critical of the Netanyahu Government, its relations with the PA improved. At his meeting with Yasser Arafat in Aqaba in June 1996, King Hussein emphasized that under no circumstances would Jordan seek to replace the Palestinian leadership in negotiations with Israel over the 'final status' of the West Bank. When King Hussein visited Washington, DC, in the same month, the Jordanian Minister of Information stressed that Jordan's role was to assist Israeli-Palestinian discussions and not to supplant the PA. Arafat visited Amman in December, when the Jordanian leadership reiterated its full support for Palestinian independence. In November the two sides had reached agreement over the controversial issue of responsibility for the holy sites in East Jerusalem. It was agreed that Jordan would retain formal jurisdiction over the sites until the 'final status' talks between Israel and the Palestinians had been successfully completed. The management of the sites, however, would be transferred from Jordan's Ministry of Awqaf (Religious Endowments) and Islamic Affairs to the PA.

The eighth conference of the OIC, which took place in Tehran, the Iranian capital, in December 1997, unanimously recognized Jordan's role in preserving Jerusalem's Muslim identity. Following King Hussein's death in February 1999, King Abdullah appeared content to leave the issue of Jerusalem's future status to PA negotiators rather than to emphasize the special role of the Hashemites in the city. Indeed, some commentators argued that the new King did not share his father's preoccupation with the West Bank and East Jerusalem and preferred to focus on Jordan's role within the global economy. The Jordanian Government's crackdown on the Palestinian Islamist Hamas in August was interpreted as a move to support the PA in its talks with Israel concerning a reactivation of the peace process. Jordan was also reported to be involved in moves to bring about reconciliation between Yasser Arafat and PLO dissidents based in Damascus, notably the Democratic Front for the Liberation of Palestine. Despite pressure from Israel and the USA, King Abdullah refused to discuss the issue of confederation until the Palestinians had achieved statehood and future relations with Jordan could be negotiated between their respective governments.

The sensitive question of Jordan's Palestinian population came to the fore in late 1999 as Israel and the PA agreed to resume 'final status' negotiations. In October King Abdullah visited the country's largest Palestinian refugee camp at al-Baqa'a, where he pledged to cement national unity and equality among all Jordanians. Prior to the Camp David (Maryland, USA) summit held between Israel and the PA in July 2000, Jordan's new Prime Minister, Ali Abu al-Ragheb, informed the National Assembly that his Government would refuse to absorb any more refugees or immigrants and would support the right of return for Palestinian refugees.

IMPACT OF THE AL-AQSA UPRISING ON THE JORDANIAN-ISRAELI TRACK

The official Jordanian position with regard to the collapse of the Israeli-Palestinian peace process following the eruption of the al-Aqsa *intifada* by Palestinians in September 2000 was that Jordan would better serve the Palestinians by maintaining diplomatic relations with Israel, although as a symbolic protest Jordan decided on 7 October not to dispatch its newly appointed ambassador to Israel. The Jordanian Government generally distanced itself from the Israeli–Palestinian conflict to the extent possible; however, at US President Clinton's request and Egyptian President Mubarak's invitation, King Abdullah participated in the talks held between Ehud Barak and Yasser Arafat at Sharm el-Sheikh, Egypt, on 16–17 October. In the weeks between the failure of the Camp David talks and the outbreak of the *intifada*, King Abdullah met with Barak three times, and reiterated the fact that Jordan would not accept Israeli or international sovereignty over the Islamic holy sites in East Jerusalem. One explanation for Jordan's initially low profile with regard to the crisis in the West Bank and Gaza was its eagerness to conclude a free trade agreement with the USA before President Clinton's departure from office at the beginning of 2001. The final round of negotiations relating to the treaty opened on 12 September, and the final text, which was to be submitted to the US Congress for approval, was signed by Abdullah and Clinton on 24 October. Under the free trade agreement, Jordan and the USA were to phase out all customs duties over a 10-year period. On the same day as the accord was signed, Jordanian security forces used considerable violence to suppress a long-planned march by the country's professional associations in support of Palestinian refugees. Even before the outbreak of the al-Aqsa *intifada*, anti-Israeli and anti-normalization demonstrations had been common in Jordan, led by both the trade unions and the Muslim Brotherhood. Moreover, many Jordanians had reportedly been angered by King Abdullah's decision to proceed with the signing of a trade agreement with the USA at all.

Popular Jordanian outrage in support of the Palestinians was expressed in sharp contrast with the country's official position. Jordan is home to the single largest Palestinian refugee population, estimated at 1,999,466 at January 2011, according to the United Nations Relief and Works Agency for Palestine Refugees in the Near East (UNRWA). Immediately following the violent events in East Jerusalem in September 2000, anti-Israeli protests erupted across the kingdom. Tensions culminated on 6 October with an 'anti-normalization' rally in the capital that was attended by 30,000 Palestinian East Bankers and Jordanians—the largest demonstration in Jordan since the Gulf War of 1991. Jordanian police, fearing that the crowd would march on the Israeli embassy, as they had attempted to do earlier in the week, fired tear gas to disperse them. In Amman's al-Baqa'a refugee camp, police opened fire with live ammunition on 2,000 Palestinians, killing one and injuring 50. On the same day King Abdullah banned public demonstrations and several protesters were arrested. However, following Israel's shelling of Palestinian targets in the West Bank and Gaza on 12 October 2000, the Jordanian Government permitted a rally in Amman, sponsored by the opposition parties, which was attended by 8,000 people.

On 19 November 2000 the Israeli Vice-Consul, Yoram Havivian, was injured when a gunman fired on his car in Amman, reawakening fears that the uprising in the Occupied Territories might spread to Jordan. Two previously unknown groups, the Jordanian Islamic Resistance Movement for Struggle and the Group of the Holy Warrior Ahmad al-Daqamsah (named after the Jordanian soldier who had killed seven Israeli schoolgirls three years earlier), claimed responsibility for the attack. As the Jordanian Government became increasingly nervous at the prospect of the al-Aqsa *intifada* spilling over into Jordan, Jordanian officials confirmed that the kingdom was working hard with Egypt and the PA to find a formula 'for ending the bloodshed' in the West Bank and Gaza Strip. The Jordanian Government was also eager for the unrest in the Occupied Territories to end for economic reasons. There was, for example, a major drop in tourism, Jordan's second largest source of foreign currency, after the outbreak of the al-Aqsa *intifada*.

Other than the economic losses blamed on the violence in the West Bank and Gaza, the Government had other worries that were heightened by the al-Aqsa *intifada*. The banning of all public demonstrations failed to solve the country's 'security problem'. Widespread demands for the closure of the Israeli embassy and the severing of all ties with Israel continued to be declared at rallies held behind closed doors. The impact of two shooting incidents against Israeli diplomats, a second attack having occurred on 5 December 2000, prompted the Israeli embassy to send families of its staff back to Israel. The Government condemned the incidents. Further pressure was brought to bear on the Government on 13 December when 14 deputies in the House of Representatives tabled a motion for an open debate to review Jordan's peace treaty with Israel. Their principal motive appeared to be to use the issue as a campaign platform for re-election amid the substantial increase in anti-Israeli and anti-US sentiment. The anti-normalization campaign led by the powerful professional syndicates was certainly strengthened by the unrest. In November 2000 the syndicates finally published their blacklist of Jordanian 'normalizers' with Israel, apparently sensing that the Government would not make good its pre-uprising warnings to take legal action against them for 'infringing civil liberties' of individuals. Meanwhile, there were protests in Ma'an in southern Jordan—a city with few Palestinians, but which had in recent years been at the forefront of protests against price increases of basic commodities—demanding the release of local people detained in connection with earlier anti-Israeli demonstrations. Hundreds of protesters, grouped in what they called the Islamic and Popular Forces in Ma'an, began an indefinite sit-in on 10 December, also demanding the severing of ties with Israel and serious government action to combat corruption and nepotism.

The traditional political antagonism between the Government and the country's powerful professional syndicates, which represent some 130,000 members, moved towards a climax on 27 January 2001, when the authorities broke into the homes of prominent members of the associations' joint Anti-Normalization Committee before dawn and arrested seven of them, including the Islamist President of the Committee, Ali Abu al-Sukkar. (However, all the trade unionists were released on bail, pending trial, in February.) The syndicates' committee had directly challenged the Government by proceeding, on 22 January, with the publication of a list of 68 companies, two private schools, a hotel, and various businessmen, artists and journalists alleged to have links with Israel. The syndicates had delayed the publication for two years to avoid confrontation with the Government, which had threatened to take legal action. Jordan's House of Representatives demanded a special session on 4 February to debate the possibility of introducing legislation to curb significantly the syndicates' political activity. The lower house was dominated by tribal and pro-establishment figures, and the majority of deputies joined forces with the Government against the unions. Earlier, Prime Minister Ali Abu al-Ragheb had decided to delay drafting a new election law, even though parliamentary polls were due to be held in November. Officials indicated that there would be no significant change to the current voting system or the configuration of constituency boundaries—which served in effect to under-represent Jordanians of Palestinian origin, who were concentrated in and around Amman—until their long-term fate was determined in negotiations with Israel.

ARAB LEAGUE SUMMIT IN AMMAN

In late February 2001 King Abdullah met US Secretary of State Colin Powell in Amman and urged him to press for an end to Israel's closure of the Palestinian enclaves, to resume the US Administration's central role in the peace process and lift all US sanctions on Iraq. Increasing Jordanian involvement in the Palestinian–Israeli crisis was reflected in the hosting of the Arab League summit in Amman in March. The overall aim of the summit was to re-establish greater co-ordination between the Arab states and to express solidarity with the Palestinian cause. The fact that the summit met at all amounted to a victory for the majority of Arab states that sought unity and reconciliation it was the first annual gathering since the Arab world was divided by Iraq's invasion of Kuwait in August 1990, and the discussions were dominated by reconciliation efforts.

Although approaches to Israel among the Arab states differed, Jordan remained committed to the Oslo peace process. Confirming the US $1,000m. fund established by the Arab 'emergency' summit in Cairo of October 2000 in support of the *intifada*, the Amman summit agreed to transfer $40m. per month to the PA. While the Arab states were more politically united than they had been a year earlier, they failed to devise a policy to meet the very serious challenges they faced from Israel and the USA.

Although Jordan and Egypt, the two Arab countries that had signed peace treaties with Israel, would not implement a formal severance of diplomatic relations, both countries refused to return their ambassadors to Tel-Aviv, Israel, and declared that there would be no new diplomatic contacts or commercial deals with Israel until it ended its campaign of repression against the Palestinians. The final communiqué of the summit, the 'Amman Declaration', reiterated the need for Arab countries to present a united front and demanded once again the withdrawal of Israeli armed forces from all occupied land.

LEGISLATIVE ELECTIONS POSTPONED UNTIL 2002

In April 2001 King Abdullah exercised his constitutional right to extend the current term of the House of Representatives by two years. Parliamentary elections had been due to be held in November. However, observers noted that the ongoing Israeli–Palestinian conflict had significantly affected Jordan's already difficult economic and political situation, and that the King had acted in order to prevent a serious challenge to his Government being mounted by Islamist opposition parties, which had declared their intention to participate fully in the forthcoming elections (having boycotted the 1997 poll) and which were highly critical of the Government's failure to take a firmer stance against Israel. In June King Abdullah ordered the dissolution of the House of Representatives and carried out a reorganization of the al-Ragheb Government. Eleven new ministers were appointed to the Cabinet, although the key ministerial portfolios remained unchanged. On the following day King Abdullah informed the Government that it had one month in which to formulate a new electoral law.

The new electoral legislation duly drafted by the Government was ratified by King Abdullah in July 2001. The principal changes to the existing law were a reorganization of electoral boundaries (the number of constituencies was to rise from 21 to 44) in order to increase the number of seats in the House of Representatives from 80 to 104, and a reduction in the voting age from 19 to 18. Although the Muslim Brotherhood had pressed for an increase in the number of deputies sitting in the lower house, the failure of the Government to reintroduce a system of electoral lists (which had existed prior to 1997) resulted in a threat by the Muslim Brotherhood to boycott the legislative elections. Two days later it was announced that the November elections would be postponed. In August 2001 legislation was enacted imposing a ban on public gatherings and demonstrations. In November King Abdullah appointed a new 40-member Senate upon the expiry of its term.

JORDAN FEARS LOSING OIL SUPPLY FROM IRAQ

By mid-2001 Jordan, battered economically by almost 10 months of Israeli–Palestinian conflict, was braced for another blow to its economy. As the first likely economic casualty should the US-driven 'smart' sanctions against Iraq proceed, Jordan was confronted by the risk of losing its entire oil supply from Iraq, as well as its main export market in the region. Under the proposed new sanctions regime, although civilian trade with Iraq would be relaxed, border checks for military or dual-use goods would be tightened. This would place extra responsibility on Iraq's neighbours in general and on Jordan in particular, as the Iraqi President, Saddam Hussain, threatened to cease trading with any country that helped to implement the new sanctions regime. Jordan's oil agreement with Iraq accounted for about one-third of Jordan's exports, and thousands of Jordanians depended on it for their livelihood. Meanwhile, in June 2001 the state airline, Royal Jordanian, resumed scheduled flights to Iraq for the first time since 1990. Discussions were held between senior Jordanian and Iraqi officials during early 2002; in January the two countries renewed their oil protocol and also agreed to the creation of a free trade zone.

King Abdullah was unequivocal in his condemnation of the September 2001 suicide attacks against New York and Washington, DC, for which the USA held the al-Qa'ida organization of the Saudi-born militant Islamist Osama bin Laden principally responsible; the King swiftly affirmed his country's preparedness to join the USA's proposed international 'coalition against terror'. However, Jordan was anxious that any US-led military offensive against alleged terrorist targets must avoid attacks against Arab countries, notably Iraq. King Abdullah, who travelled to Washington, DC, in late September to sign the bilateral trade agreement, was the first Arab leader to meet US President George W. Bush after the suicide attacks; the bilateral trade accord was fully implemented in December.

SECURITY TRIALS AND DISPATCH OF TROOPS TO AFGHANISTAN

In the aftermath of the September 2001 attacks in the USA, the Jordanian authorities ushered in new restrictions on the press, apparently as the Government's latest weapon in its struggle against political dissent. Moreover, by late 2001 security trials had become frequent in Jordan, all of which involved radical Islamists. Over the years hundreds of political activists, often referred to as 'terrorists', had been in and out of prison, and of military courts, on charges of seeking to topple the Hashemite regime, plotting 'terrorist activities' and 'destabilizing the security' of the country. In recent years the threat to the Hashemite regime has been perceived as stemming from radical and militant Islamism. In October 2001 King Abdullah issued a royal decree amending Jordan's penal code in order to strengthen counter-terrorism measures.

Jordan moved swiftly to restrict manifestations of opposition to the US-led military campaign against suspected al-Qa'ida bases and the fundamentalist Islamist Taliban regime in Afghanistan from October 2001. Jordanian troops were even sent on a 'humanitarian mission' to the war-ravaged city of Mazar-i-Sharif in northern Afghanistan. One of the most controversial of several 'temporary laws' introduced by the Government since the dissolution of the House of Representatives in June 2001 was the rapid amendment in mid-November of the Armed Forces Law, after the Government decided to contribute to peace-keeping forces in Afghanistan. The 1964 Law was amended to provide legal cover for the deployment of Jordanian troops abroad, thus frustrating opposition plans to file a suit against the Government for violating Article 3 of the Constitution, which prohibits placing the life of Jordanian citizens in danger. (Jordan had apparently been in violation of its Constitution since 1989, when it began sending troops abroad, with 22,000 troops serving in 16 countries as part of UN peace-keeping operations.) However, the decision to send Jordanian troops to Afghanistan was heavily criticized by opposition parties as offering 'unconditional support' for the US-led war in Afghanistan.

CABINET REORGANIZATION FOLLOWED BY RIOTS IN MA'AN

In mid-January 2002 Prime Minister Ali Abu al-Ragheb again submitted the resignation of his Government, but was asked by King Abdullah to form a new administration capable of initiating economic and social reforms prior to parliamentary elections. On 14 January a new 27-member Cabinet was announced. However, the only significant changes were a new Minister of Foreign Affairs, Dr Marwan al-Muasher, who had served as Jordan's ambassador to both the USA and Israel, and a new Minister of the Interior, Qaftan al-Majali, who had formerly been Secretary-General of the same ministry. The change of Government was largely symbolic, and was apparently designed to show that the regime was serious about holding parliamentary elections in 2002, after postponing them indefinitely in November 2001. The King, whose dissolution of parliament had been followed by a series of controversial and often restrictive 'provisional laws', stated that 'short-lived and unexpected circumstances have brought about the absence of parliamentary life in Jordan', clearly referring to the Palestinian *intifada*. Both the King and Prime Minister al-Ragheb confirmed that elections were to be held later in the year. It was not clear, however, whether the biggest and most influential opposition party, the Muslim Brotherhood's IAF, which led 25 other opposition groups, intended to abandon its boycott of the electoral process, which had been undertaken in 1997 in protest against the 'temporary' elections law that the Islamists, as well as other leftists and pan-Arab nationalists, saw as guaranteeing legislative seats for tribal and pro-establishment figures. Although the number of parliamentary seats was raised from 80 to 104, the distribution of seats maintained the same ratio despite demands to increase the number according to demography rather than geography. Islamist leaders asserted that they would require a 'neutral government' to oversee free and fair elections if they were to abandon their boycott.

On 21 January 2002 a large number of people took to the streets of Ma'an, in another expression of rage after a local youth, Sulayman Ahmad al-Fanatseh, died in police custody. There were allegations of police brutality, although the authorities insisted that the boy had died of natural causes. The riots and violent confrontations with the police lasted for two days and resulted in the death of a policeman who was shot by unknown gunmen. Although the new Minister of the Interior denied reports that al-Fanatseh had been detained for political or religious reasons, Islamist activists accused the authorities of using the unrest as a pretext to detain local Islamists and further to harass and stifle the Islamist opposition. The violent riots appeared to stem from dissatisfaction with poverty and high unemployment. Following the unrest, the Government announced that two investigations had been launched to determine the causes of both the adolescent's death and the subsequent riots.

WIDESPREAD PROTESTS AGAINST US AND ISRAELI POLICIES

Since the outbreak of the al-Aqsa *intifada* in September 2000, Jordanian police had frequently clashed with Islamist groups that took to the streets after the Muslim Friday prayers to protest against Israeli policies. In 2000 and 2001 Jordan had imposed tough laws banning demonstrations after public sympathy with the Palestinian uprising produced the largest street protests in Jordan in more than a decade. However, on rare occasions the Government disregarded the demonstrations or allowed them to proceed in a gesture to public opinion.

In March 2002 the bloodiest violence yet in the almost 18-month Israeli–Palestinian confrontation sparked a new round of demonstrations and mass street protests in Jordan. The Jordanian authorities were swift to block opposition-led protests and demonstrations, on the grounds that these had not been authorized in advance. The authorities cited concerns that demonstrations might be used by opposition parties to challenge official intolerance towards public displays of anti-Israeli and anti-US sentiments.

Public anger within Jordan was further fuelled by Israel's reoccupation of Palestinian-controlled population centres in the West Bank from late March 2002, provoking mass street protests in Jordanian cities, with many unlicensed rallies often ending after considerable use of force by Jordanian riot police, who resorted to tear gas, water cannons and beatings. On 30 March, in the Palestinian refugee camp of al-Baqa'a, home to about 120,000 refugees, thousands of youths and supporters of PA President Yasser Arafat took to the streets inside the camp in a show of solidarity. However, demands for the Jordanian Government to sever diplomatic ties with Israel were not heeded.

The Jordanian Government remained in a critical situation, caught between its dependence on its close relationship with the USA and its own public's anti-Israeli and anti-US sentiment. Undermining Israel's attempt to 'isolate' Arafat, Minister of Foreign Affairs Marwan al-Muasher met with the

Palestinian leader at his Ramallah headquarters in April 2002. In May Prime Minister al-Ragheb and al-Muasher met Arafat in Ramallah to discuss the stalled political process. Al-Ragheb and al-Muasher also briefed Arafat on the outcome of talks that had taken place in Washington, DC, earlier in May between King Abdullah and US President Bush.

STALLING ON PARLIAMENTARY ELECTIONS

In May 2002 Prime Minister al-Ragheb stated that his Government had finalized plans for 'free and transparent elections', but added that only King Abdullah had the constitutional right to call elections. The Jordanian Constitution gave the King the right to postpone elections indefinitely, but he tended to rely on his Government and advisers for recommendations prior to issuing decrees. Initially, when the Government decided to delay parliamentary elections, it cited 'procedural considerations', which it finally resolved. However, the Government failed to provide justification for the continued delay, as stipulated by the Constitution: 'extraordinary circumstances', mainly 'regional tensions' such as the Palestinian *intifada* and Israel's campaign in the West Bank, as well as US President Bush's threat to attack Iraq, were the reasons cited by Jordanian officials for failing to hold parliamentary elections in November 2001. In August 2002 King Abdullah announced that legislative elections would be postponed until 2003, owing to the continuing instability in the region.

'JORDAN FIRST'

In late 2002 Jordan found itself contending with the continuing Israeli military presence in the West Bank and Gaza on the one hand, and the US insistence on pursuing 'regime change' in Iraq on the other. Palestinians, including refugees and citizens of Palestinian origin, were in a majority in Jordan, while Iraq was Jordan's only supplier of petroleum and a major trading partner. Being caught in the middle of two regional crises, the Jordanian Government sought to escape the regional turbulence by adopting the slogan 'Jordan First'. This was part of an official campaign launched in October, which sought ways to rally a sceptical public behind government policies on both Iraq and the Palestinian territories. The Government, in the absence of a parliament, acted both as policy-maker and legislator; it had a monopoly on media control in the kingdom. Public rallies and demonstrations in support of the Palestinians and Iraqis were banned in the name of the 'national interest'. Given its clear dependence on financial support from the USA, the Jordanian Government sought a diplomatic approach to the Israeli military presence in the Occupied Territories. King Abdullah's quest for Jordanians to put aside their differences and unite around a common national identity touched on several critical issues facing the kingdom, the most important of which was the unresolved status of millions of Palestinian refugees in the country.

The same 'Jordan First' campaign carried a strong message for the Islamist opposition parties and independent professional organizations, which remained highly critical of Jordanian policies towards Israel and the USA. In early October 2002 the Jordanian authorities had arrested three anti-Israeli activists from the Anti-Normalization Committee, including its Secretary-General, Ali Abu al-Sukkar. The three were charged by the State Security Court with belonging to an illegal organization and distributing anti-normalization leaflets, officially described as 'harming the national economy'. The Government continued to urge the associations to stay out of politics, and its actions were interpreted in Jordan as a further attempt to muzzle the opposition, which had been increasingly critical of the authorities' stance towards Israel. In late November the Government announced that it had received a judicial decision proscribing the Anti-Normalization Committee of the country's 14 professional associations, thereby allowing the Government to dissolve them. The following day Prime Minister al-Ragheb summoned the associations' leaders to his office to inform them that the High Court's Special Bureau for the Interpretation of Law had found the Anti-Normalization Committee 'in violation of the associations law'. However, the Chairman of the Jordanian Bar Association, Salah al-Armuti, pointed out on 1 December that the Special Bureau's decision on dissolving the associations' anti-normalization bodies was not yet final or effective, adding that a committee had been formed to study the legality of the verdict.

RENEWED CLASHES IN MA'AN

On 10 November 2002 the impoverished southern town of Ma'an erupted into violence again, when special police units occupied the town in a week-long operation that resulted in the deaths of three civilians and two police officers, and the arrests of dozens of people whom the authorities described as 'armed gang members', led by Muhammad Shalabi, also known as Abu Sayyaf. The assassination in Amman of a US diplomat, Laurence Foley of the US Agency for International Development (USAID), on 28 October by an unidentified gunman, was the apparent pretext for the operation in Ma'an and an opportunity for the Jordanian authorities to take firmer action against Islamist opponents in the country. Unnamed Jordanian officials stated that the operation was aimed at putting behind bars 'suspects and extremist individuals' who might attempt acts of sabotage amid a tense domestic situation in the event of a US-led military campaign against the regime of Saddam Hussain in Iraq. The Islamists in particular described the campaign in Ma'an as part of the authorities' attempts to curry favour with the US Administration in its 'war on terror'. On 13 November the Jordanian Government declared the area an 'arms-free zone', having seized a large quantity of weapons. The Government proclaimed that all weapons licences were revoked and asked residents to obtain new ones from the Ministry of the Interior. The residents of Ma'an are tribal and have traditionally carried weapons. Since the 1989 riots—which had broken out in Ma'an after the Government dramatically increased fuel prices, and which eventually spilled across the kingdom—and the Ma'an bread riots of 1996, the Government had sought to disarm the south, including Ma'an. The Islamist opposition parties, led by the IAF, criticized the Government, warning of 'an escalation in the situation and a widening of the repercussions' that could endanger national security.

FEMALE REPRESENTATION IN PARLIAMENT

On 9 February 2003 King Abdullah endorsed amendments to the provisional parliamentary law—approved by the Government during the suspension of the House of Representatives—which allocated six seats to women for the first time in the country's history by raising the number of seats in the lower house from 104 to 110 (with effect from the next election). The new provisional law was criticized both by women's groups, which wanted a quota of at least 20% of representatives in the legislature, and the Islamist parties, which had rejected any quota for women or other sections of the population. The Islamists, as well as some secular opposition leaders, maintained that quotas for Bedouin, Circassian and Christian communities were undemocratic. Meanwhile, the continued Israeli presence in the West Bank and Gaza and the growing threat of a US-led military campaign in Iraq were deemed by the Government to make the holding of legislative elections too risky. However, on 24 February King Abdullah issued a royal decree ordering elections to the House of Representatives to be held in early 2003; three days later the Prime Minister announced that the date of the poll would be 17 June.

THE IMPACT OF THE IRAQ CRISIS

Throughout late 2002 and early 2003 Jordan was seriously affected by the Iraq crisis, in political, security, economic and psychological terms. As early as 22 November 2002, the USA authorized the departure from Jordan of its non-essential embassy personnel and diplomatic dependants. This move followed the murder a month earlier of Laurence Foley, a senior embassy employee (see Renewed Clashes in Ma'an). In January 2003 a Jordanian military court upheld a guilty verdict and death sentence against a Jordanian-American, Raed Hijazi, who had been convicted of planning to launch poison gas attacks on US and Israeli targets in Jordan three years earlier.

Jordan was also directly affected by the Iraq crisis principally owing to the level of its trade with neighbouring Iraq. The country imported 100,000 b/d of Iraqi oil—100% of its oil requirements—under the UN-approved 'oil-for-food' agreement. Moreover, according to a statement made by al-Ragheb in January 2003, 20% of Jordanian exports went to Iraq. However, the real figure was thought to be much higher: a considerable quantity of Jordanian goods heading for Iraq was reputedly shipped via Turkey and then across the border into the autonomous Kurdish zone where import duty was only 5%, compared with the 10% charged by the Iraqis on the Jordanian border.

By early February 2003 Jordan had braced itself for an imminent US-led invasion of Iraq. Officially, Jordan repeatedly stated its opposition to a US-led intervention, and insisted that its territory and airspace would not be used by US forces. Jordan supposedly claimed 'neutrality' in the conflict between the coalition forces and the Iraqi regime, but in reality Jordanian officials made it clear that the Government was not prepared to 'get on the wrong side' of the USA as it had done during the Gulf War of 1991, since Jordan could not afford to pay the 'heavy price'. Moreover, the Government stated in late January 2003 that it was preparing to receive three *Patriot* anti-missile batteries from the USA. In 2002 Jordan had received a total of US $460m. in aid from the US Administration, including $200m. in military assistance. In early March 2003 Jordan formally acknowledged that 'several hundred' US troops—a figure that later turned out to be several thousand—were in the kingdom, after having persistently denied their presence. The Government insisted that the troops were there to train their Jordanian counterparts in the use of the three *Patriot* anti-missile batteries provided by the USA in February.

Throughout the Iraq crisis, oil supplies remained a major concern for Jordan. While Iraq promised to continue supplying Jordan with petroleum at discounted prices even during the conflict, the USA vowed to maintain the same terms of supply after its takeover of Iraq's oil wells in early 2003. On 10–11 March Marwan al-Muasher visited Kuwait to receive pledges that the emirate would provide the country with oil should supplies from Iraq be disrupted, although there were no guarantees that Kuwaiti prices would be on the same terms. At the same time al-Ragheb declared that Jordan possessed sufficient oil supplies to last for three months, but warned that fuel prices would rise if oil supplies from Iraq were disrupted. As a result of the Iraq crisis and concerns over oil supplies, the Jordanian public reacted with 'panic buying' of fuel and foodstuffs.

On the domestic front, the potential for unrest during the crisis was evident. However, the Government remained determined to stifle any opposition to its broad alliance with the USA over the impending war. The political parties and institutions of civil society were faced with a provisional public assembly law, approved in 2001, which banned all demonstrations without prior permission from the Government and gave the authorities the right to use force to dissolve protests. Although opposition parties found it difficult to confront these restrictions, the authorities, in view of the mass anti-war demonstrations in the West and the Arab world, seemed somewhat embarrassed and were forced to issue permits for a few rallies to be held in Amman in February 2003, although with a heavy security presence. Protesters at a massive demonstration organized by a coalition of 14 opposition parties on 15 March demanded the expulsion of US troops stationed in eastern Jordan. On 31 March around 95 prominent figures, including former Prime Ministers, former Chiefs of the Royal Court and former intelligence chiefs, petitioned King Abdullah, demanding that Jordan declare the war in Iraq to be 'illegal'.

Another potential problem that the Jordanian Government was anxious to avoid was the influx of a large number of Iraqi refugees. Jordan agreed to set up two refugee camps in Ruwaished—one for Iraqi refugees and the other a transit camp for third-country nationals—after having insisted initially that it would not permit Iraqi refugees to enter Jordanian territory. The UN and international relief agencies persuaded Jordan to participate in the humanitarian efforts by providing funds and staff to establish and manage camps. Jordan also agreed to become a transit route for international relief supplies into Iraq via the port of Aqaba.

Despite the Hashemite regime's secret co-operation with the US-led coalition, the fall of Baghdad to coalition forces on 9 April 2003 outraged the Jordanian public. In mid-April 99 prominent Jordanians (including former Prime Ministers and other former senior officials) sent a petition to King Abdullah, demanding that the Jordanian Government condemn the US-led invasion of Iraq. At about the same time the IAF endorsed a *fatwa* (Islamic edict) decreeing that it was a 'great sin' to allow US-led forces to use Jordanian territory. The King reacted by saying that the petition by prominent Jordanian figures represented Jordanian pluralism, which allows society to express its views freely. He again denied that US troops had launched an attack on Iraq from Jordan. However, the almost universal sentiment in Jordan was a fear that the whole Arab world might be under threat if the USA's actions did not stop in Baghdad. Among Jordanian officials the fear of a 'domino effect' on the stability of Arab regimes in the Middle East was also a prime concern. However, Jordanian officials made no secret of their fear that Jordan could be sandwiched between two foreign 'occupations'—Israeli and US—and of the repercussions that this would have on Jordan's social, economic and political stability. The official public reaction to the collapse of Saddam Hussain's regime was an insistence that the Iraqi people be allowed to choose their government without foreign interference and that Iraq's territorial integrity be maintained, a view that was expressed by Minister of Foreign Affairs al-Muasher to US Secretary of State Colin Powell in their meeting on 10 April. Jordan's precarious position was encapsulated by the bombing of the Jordanian embassy in Baghdad on 7 August by unknown assailants, in which at least 10 people were killed, and which was interpreted by many as a 'revenge' attack for Jordan's official stance during the conflict.

The US-led invasion of Iraq and the subsequent collapse of the Baath regime took place against the background of widening divisions within the Arab League and US threats to take similar action against Syria and Iran. The lack of supplies of petroleum to Jordan and the chaos, instability and humanitarian crisis in Iraq were now of major concern to Jordan. The supply of Iraqi oil had ceased on the first day of the conflict in March 2003. On 5 May the Government announced that it was raising the price of petroleum derivatives by 4%–8%, the third such increase in three months. Jordan had managed to bring in alternative supplies from Saudi Arabia, Kuwait and the United Arab Emirates (UAE), believed to be supplied 'free of charge' according to temporary arrangements that were to last until the end of June. On 12 May al-Muasher declared that Jordan could not afford to buy oil at international prices 'overnight without a severe jolt to the economy'. He stated that Jordan was conducting negotiations with the USA and the UN about an alternative arrangement, pointing out that the oil grants from Iraq were worth some US $600m. annually. Jordan also received an additional $70m. in economic assistance from the USA to cover the losses to its economy as a result of the conflict in Iraq.

On 4 June 2003 a summit meeting to begin implementing the 'roadmap' peace plan, which was published on 30 April (Documents on Palestine, see p. 104), was held in Aqaba. It was hosted by King Abdullah and attended by US President Bush, Israeli premier Ariel Sharon and the recently appointed Palestinian Prime Minister, Mahmud Abbas.

PARLIAMENTARY ELECTIONS

Jordan's long-awaited parliamentary elections were finally held on 17 June 2003. Representatives of tribes and families loyal to the Hashemite dynasty won more than two-thirds of the 110 contested seats in the House of Representatives, according to the Ministry of the Interior, while the leading opposition party, the IAF, which had boycotted the last elections in October 1997, won only 17 seats. Six female deputies took seats in the lower house under the new system, which introduced extra seats especially for women. The election result meant that opinion hostile to Jordan's peace treaty with Israel would be represented in the new parliament, but it also meant that the urban middle and professional classes were still being marginalized in favour of tribal leaders and, to a lesser extent, Islamist groups, a process that did not bode well for the future of democratization in Jordan. Furthermore, there were allegations of vote-rigging and of violations of the Elections Law, as well as claims that the Government had interfered in the elections. A royal decree issued on 25 June 2003 urged the newly elected House of Representatives to convene in an extraordinary session starting on 15 July. A new 28-member Cabinet was announced on 21 July, and included eight new ministers.

The new administration of al-Ragheb proved to be short-lived, however; following considerable criticism of the Government over the slow pace of reform and accusations of corruption, the Prime Minister resigned on 21 October 2003. On 25 October King Abdullah inaugurated a new, reduced 21-member Cabinet under Prime Minister Faisal al-Fayez, who had served as Minister of the Royal Court in the previous administration. Al-Fayez was also named as the Minister of Defence. The appointment of three female ministers preceded that of an expanded 55-member Senate on 17 November, in accordance with constitutional guidelines that membership of the Senate must be no larger than one-half that of the House of Representatives.

RELATIONS WITH ISRAEL AND ABDULLAH'S SECRET TALKS WITH SHARON

Despite their strained relations, on 9 March 2004 Jordan and Israel broke new ground by establishing a joint science and technology centre, the first major 'educational' venture since the signing of the peace treaty. The 'Bridging the Rift' Centre was to be built over the next five years on 150 acres of desert land straddling the Israeli–Jordanian border.

Throughout the second half of 2003 and the first half of 2004 relations between Israel and Jordan were at a low ebb. The strained relationship between the two countries formed the background to King Abdullah's secret visit to the Negev desert ranch of Ariel Sharon on 18 March 2004 for talks focusing on Israel's 'separation barrier' in the West Bank (see the chapters on Israel and the Palestinian Territories), of which Jordan was critical. Jordan was concerned that Palestinian refugees would be pushed into Jordan by the barrier, thereby upsetting the country's delicate demographic balance. Such concerns had prompted Jordan earlier in the year to argue against Israel's West Bank 'separation barrier' in hearings before the International Court of Justice (ICJ) in The Hague, Netherlands. The barrier, about one-third of which had been completed, had already disrupted the lives of tens of thousands of Palestinians. Abdullah was also reported to have discussed with Sharon the Israeli premier's 'disengagement plan' for Gaza. According to the Jordanian news agency, Petra, King Abdullah told the Israeli Prime Minister that an Israeli withdrawal from Gaza had to be the beginning of a 'comprehensive Israeli withdrawal' and not a tactical move to transfer Gaza settlers to the West Bank.

FLUCTUATING RELATIONS WITH THE USA

Many Jordanian citizens continued to question their Government's relationship with the USA, which they accused of siding with Ariel Sharon's actions against the Palestinians. King Abdullah, in particular, came under pressure at home to demonstrate that his close ties with the USA could further Arab positions on the Palestinian question as well as on the US-led occupation of Iraq. A rift emerged between the 'neo-conservative' Bush Administration—which was closely allied with the hardline Israeli policies of Sharon—and its 'moderate' Arab allies over President Bush's pro-Israeli statement on Jewish settlements of April 2004. The US policies towards the Israeli–Palestinian conflict further exacerbated the already tense relations between the USA and the Arab world with regard to the presence of US forces in Iraq. Although the Jordanian regime remained strongly tied to the USA, a rift between the two was exposed in mid-April, when King Abdullah cancelled a scheduled meeting with President Bush in protest against the USA's 'shift' in Middle East policy. Jordanian Minister of Foreign Affairs al-Muasher met his US counterpart, Colin Powell, on 20 April in Washington, DC. Following the meeting, al-Muasher said that Powell had 'made it clear that Washington supports the creation of an independent Palestinian state as called for by the roadmap'.

King Abdullah had flown to the USA for talks with US businessmen to promote investment in his kingdom on 14 April 2004, the same day that Bush met Sharon in the White House and announced the shift in US policy that had made it difficult for the King to meet the President without making some protest. However, it was not until Israeli forces killed the new leader of Hamas, Dr Abd al-Aziz al-Rantisi, in Gaza on 18 April, that the King appeared to have decided that it would be unwise to proceed with the discussions. (President Bush was widely viewed as having granted tacit approval for such an assassination, and White House officials had subsequently insisted that Israel was acting in 'self-defence'.) On 18 April King Abdullah said in statements from the USA that the assassination of al-Rantisi was a 'heinous crime that proves Israel is not serious about achieving peace'. Prime Minister al-Fayez cut short his visit to the USA and returned to Jordan on the day of the assassination. Furthermore, King Abdullah, who had planned to meet Bush to discuss the roadmap peace plan, found no point in proceeding with the meeting after it became clear that Bush had in effect given up on the plan. Abdullah's palace officials reported that the King was outraged that Bush had ignored a letter sent by him on 8 April, in which he insisted that a unilateral Israeli withdrawal from Gaza should be in line with the roadmap, and not an alternative to it.

The apparent snub to Bush came amid Arab anger with the USA for having endorsed an Israeli proposal to withdraw unilaterally from the Gaza Strip and parts of the West Bank, but to keep large Jewish settlement blocs in the West Bank. Palestinian leaders, in particular, attacked the US Administration for having undermined a future negotiated settlement. Clearly, King Abdullah did not want to be linked to a US-Israeli political agenda, especially after the King had already been embarrassed a month earlier by visiting Sharon's ranch.

However, in May 2004 King Abdullah met with President Bush in Washington, DC. At the meeting the US President made a point of apologizing to the Jordanian King for the humiliation that had reportedly been inflicted on Iraqi prisoners by certain US soldiers. Bush proceeded to declare that the USA would continue to pursue trade and investment opportunities with Jordan, and would assist the country's social and economic transformation programme to ensure its future prosperity. Bush added that 'all final status issues [between Israel and the Palestinians] must be negotiated between the parties in accordance with UN Security Council Resolutions 242 and 338'.

At his White House press conference with President Bush in May 2004, King Abdullah spoke about the urgent need to stabilize Iraq. Apparently, King Abdullah also believed that, if the Bush Administration hoped to defuse the Iraqi resistance, it should move quickly to give the country's Sunni minority a greater stake in the new Iraq. On 1 July, following the installation of the US-backed Interim Government in Baghdad, King Abdullah announced that his country would be willing to send Jordanian troops to Iraq.

CRACKDOWN ON ANTI-US MOSQUE SERMONS

The most significant challenge for the pro-US Hashemite regime during the second half of 2004 was containing growing popular anger at the US-led occupation of Iraq and general discontent with continued Israeli military attacks against Palestinians in the Occupied Territories. King Abdullah, while continuing to steer the regime close to the USA, acted to boost the security presence throughout the country, giving more power to his security services to crack down on anti-US sentiments. Consequently, September witnessed a major confrontation between the Muslim Brotherhood and the Jordanian authorities. On 8 September the security forces launched a large-scale operation against anti-US mosque sermons by clerics and members of the Muslim Brotherhood movement and the IAF, marking an end to decades of relatively peaceful co-existence, and at times close co-operation, between the influential Islamist movement and the Hashemite regime. Nine prominent Muslim Brotherhood *imams* and leaders were detained on charges of preaching sermons in mosques without prior permission from the Ministry of Awqaf, Islamic Affairs and Holy Places. The security forces also raided the homes of several senior members of the Brotherhood, including deputies in the House of Representatives and former ministers. Most detainees were released after signing pledges not to preach in mosques without official licences.

The leadership of the IAF condemned the harassment of its leaders and accused Prime Minister Faisal al-Fayez of supporting US-led action in Iraq and acting on US instructions to curb mosque activities. The leader of the Muslim Brotherhood in Jordan, Muhammad al-Dhunaybat, went further by warning of the dangerous consequences of the crackdown and the possibility that some members of the movement would be driven underground. Yet, the Brotherhood's strategy never appealed for toppling the regime; it had always advocated gradual reform and eschewed political violence. In fact, for many years both the Jordanian authorities and the Brotherhood had treated political sermons in mosques as a way of 'letting off steam' and discouraging Islamist activists from resorting to underground activities. In September 2004 the regime clearly sought to send a strong signal against anti-US preaching in mosques. However, both the regime and the IAF ultimately preferred a return to non-confrontational politics. The confrontation was quickly defused: on 12 September Prime Minister al-Fayez reached an agreement with the leaders of the IAF to release all detainees and allow *imams* to return to their mosques, in exchange for their commitment to abide by the 'preaching and guidance law' that regulated mosque activities. Throughout late 2004, however, the Muslim Brotherhood continued to speak out against the US-led occupation of Iraq, and against the regime's unpopular policies towards Israel.

UNITING PRO-REGIME PARTIES

In October 2004, inspired by the regime, 11 pro-establishment political parties in the country decided to merge, forming a new umbrella grouping called the Jordanian National Movement (JNM). The new political grouping was aimed at: first, uniting all the pro-regime forces in the country and providing support for the Government, with its often unpopular policies towards Iraq, Israel and the USA; and second, confronting the opposition bloc, consisting of 14 Islamist, pan-Arab nationalist and left-wing parties. The leaders of the JNM included prominent former government and security officials, as well as tribal leaders.

Later in October 2004, after several weeks of consultation and following the formation of the JNM, al-Fayez announced his first cabinet reorganization since coming to power a year earlier, bringing in 10 new ministers. King Abdullah had asked al-Fayez to form a new Cabinet that would focus on tackling unemployment and poverty, as well as social and economic reforms. The reorganization left a number of pro-Western ministers in office. Minister of Foreign Affairs Marwan al-Muasher became Deputy Prime Minister, with a new portfolio responsible for reducing a bloated civil service. Al-Muasher was replaced as Minister of Foreign Affairs by Hani Mulki, former ambassador to Egypt and a key figure in the negotiation of the Jordanian-Israeli peace treaty. However, the new ministers were largely technocrats and, overall, Jordan's domestic and foreign policies remained the domain of King Abdullah.

JORDAN'S PALESTINIANS MOURN YASSER ARAFAT

Following the death of Yasser Arafat in a Paris hospital in November 2004, Palestinians in Jordan grieved over the loss of their long-time leader. The Jordanian Government declared 40 days of mourning and black flags were raised alongside the Palestinian and Jordanian flag at half mast in the country's 13 crowded Palestinian refugee camps, in which more than 1.7m. people resided. A statement by the Royal Court said that King Abdullah mourned the passing of Arafat, describing the man as having dedicated his life 'in the firm defence of the just Palestinian cause'.

ABDULLAH STRIPS HAMZEH OF THE TITLE 'CROWN PRINCE'

On 28 November 2004 King Abdullah stripped his 24-year-old half-brother Prince Hamzeh of the title of 'Crown Prince' and heir to the Hashemite throne, in a move that surprised many observers. Hamzeh had been named Crown Prince in February 1999 by Abdullah himself upon the death of King Hussein. The King, who has four brothers and six sisters, refrained from naming a new heir to the throne, but was widely expected to name his eldest son, the then 10-year-old Hussein, as heir, in accordance with the Constitution.

NEW CABINET OF ADNAN BADRAN

On 5 April 2005 King Abdullah accepted the resignation of the al-Fayez Government and asked Adnan Badran, a former Minister of Higher Education and Minister of Agriculture, to form a new cabinet, amid claims of royal disapproval of the outgoing 'failing Cabinet'. It had been reported that the King was dissatisfied with the Government over several issues, including the slow pace of economic reforms and the failure of a Jordanian peace initiative at the Arab League summit in Algiers on 22 March; the summit had rejected Jordan's proposal for peace with Israel without Israel relinquishing all the territories it had occupied in 1967. The stated objective of the new Cabinet, inaugurated on 7 April 2005, was to push forward with accelerated privatization in an effort to make the kingdom more attractive to foreign investors. However, the Jordanian economy continued to be very vulnerable to external shocks and regional unrest, and rates of poverty and unemployment remained high. Meanwhile, in February 2005, Jordan had returned its ambassador to Israel after a four-year absence following the outbreak of the Palestinian uprising in September 2000.

A diplomatic row with Iraq after a suicide bombing in Hillah, south of Baghdad, on 28 February 2005, which killed 125 people, was also thought to have displeased the King: he believed that his Cabinet had failed to act decisively when a Jordanian citizen, Raed Mansur al-Banna, was accused by Iraq of involvement in the attack. One of the stated priorities of the Cabinet was a continuation of a recent improvement of relations with the new Iraqi Government, following the Hillah crisis. As part of steps to defuse the diplomatic row between the countries, on 21 March 2005 Jordan had sent its chief envoy to Iraq back to Baghdad, and the following day Iraq had returned its ambassador to Amman.

A further reorganization of the Cabinet effected in July 2005 involved eight new ministerial appointments. A new Senate was appointed by King Abdullah in November of that year.

CLOSE PARTNERSHIP WITH THE USA AND ISLAMIC MILITANCY

Throughout 2005 Jordan continued to face the deteriorating conditions in its eastern neighbour, Iraq, and continued Palestinian–Israeli confrontation across its western border. With the growing anti-US insurgency in Iraq, the Jordanian regime was forced to devote increasing efforts to combating what it described as 'Islamic militancy'. It also tried to project an image of a peaceful country seeking political stability and economic development. Domestically, the Jordanian authorities continued to crack down on Islamic clerics preaching anti-US sermons in mosques.

The decision of King Abdullah to support the continued US-led military operations in Iraq marked the regime as an enemy for some Jordanians, especially Islamists. However, the same security alliance led to some economic benefits for the country, including the provision of about US $450m. of economic and military aid from the USA annually. Some 500,000 wealthy Iraqis had fled to Jordan with their savings, and Amman had become a service centre for organizations and businesses involved in the pacification and 'reconstruction' of Iraq. Jordan's once faltering economy was booming as a result, growing by more than 7% in 2005. Nevertheless, the economic benefits did not filter through to the majority of the population. This uneven distribution of the economic boom and the disparity in wealth was fuelling some social unrest, which was increasingly becoming a focus for radical Islam.

Also, crucially, since the invasion of Iraq in 2003 King Abdullah had allowed US special forces to establish bases on Jordanian territory. Employees of Western private security companies and contractors involved in Iraqi reconstruction projects used Jordan as a base for their operations in Iraq. The Jordanian military was training Iraqi security forces, and Jordanian companies had contracts to provide services to the Iraqi administration such as refurbishing helicopters and training soldiers. Moreover, since the attacks of 11 September 2001 on New York and Washington, DC, Jordan's General Intelligence Department (GID), had become one of the USA's most effective allied 'counter-terrorism' agencies in the region. The GID's intelligence partnership with the US Central Intelligence Agency (CIA) grew even closer with the continuing US operations in Iraq, and CIA technical personnel became 'embedded' at GID headquarters in Amman. In 2005 and early 2006 the GID and the CIA aggressively hunted the followers of Abu Musab al-Zarqawi, a Jordanian militant and the leader of the Tanzim Qa'idat al-Jihad fi Bilad al-Rafidain (Base of Holy War in Mesopotamia, also known as 'al-Qa'ida in Iraq')—an organization that did not exist before the invasion of Iraq. In April 2004 al-Zarqawi had been sentenced to death *in absentia* by a Jordanian court after being convicted of the murder of US diplomat Laurence Foley in 2002. On 17 October 2004 Jordan's State Security Court had indicted al-Zarqawi and 12 other Jordanians for plotting an attack on the GID, the Prime Minister's office and the US embassy in Amman in April of that year.

On 9 November 2005 a triple suicide bombing in three major Western tourist hotels in Amman killed 59 people and wounded around 100. The suicide bombers were clearly targeting the increasing US security and political partnership with the Jordanian regime: all three hotels were popular with US and European diplomats and businessmen involved in Iraq. One of them, the Radisson SAS, was also popular with Israeli tourists, and had been the target of an allegedly foiled al-Qa'ida plot. However, although large numbers of Americans and Europeans were close to the explosion at the Grand Hyatt hotel, most of the victims of the suicide bombing were Jordanians, many at a wedding celebration. Al-Qa'ida in Iraq claimed responsibility for the hotel blasts. Its Iraqi-style *modus operandi* was familiar: powerful explosions targeting hotels used by Westerners. An audio message, purportedly from al-Zarqawi and posted on a website often used by insurgents in Iraq, defended the triple hotel bombings in Amman, but maintained that the group had intended to target US and Israeli intelligence agents and had not meant to hit wedding party guests at the Radisson SAS, which had suffered the worst of the three attacks. Further evidence of the link between the Iraqi insurgency and the Amman blasts emerged after the Jordanian authorities named three Iraqi suicide bombers, as well as an alleged fourth bomber, Sajida al-Rishawi (also Iraqi), who had failed to detonate her explosives and was shown on Jordanian television making an apparent confession. In September 2006, having subsequently claimed that her confession had been extracted under torture, al-Rishawi was convicted of direct involvement in the November 2005 attacks and was sentenced to death. Following an unsuccessful appeal, in January 2007 the original verdict was upheld by the Court of Cassation. A further six people, including at least one other Iraqi woman, were convicted *in absentia* and were also sentenced to death for their part in the Amman bombings.

King Abdullah condemned the attacks as 'criminal acts committed by a deviant and misleading bunch', and declared that they would not sway Jordan from continuing its battle against terrorism. Al-Zarqawi had appeared to enjoy certain sympathy in some sections of Jordanian society, but the deaths of so many Jordanian civilians seemed to have eroded that sympathy very sharply. Jordanians expressed a widespread sentiment in the country that they were caught in a conflict created by others and were stuck between US and British policies in Iraq and the indiscriminate methods of al-Zarqawi. On 10 November 2005 crowds of Jordanians took to the streets of Amman in protest against the bombings. Eight days later some 100,000 people marched through Amman in a mass demonstration of anger.

A NEW PRIME MINISTER AND THE REGIME'S 'WAR' ON RADICAL ISLAM

Two weeks after the Amman blasts, on 24 November 2005, King Abdullah appointed a new Prime Minister, Dr Marouf al-Bakhit, a retired army major-general, to replace the outgoing Adnan Badran. Badran was criticized in Jordan for having failed to implement an agenda of political and economic reforms. Al-Bakhit was closely associated with Jordanian policies towards Israel: he was the head of a state committee that oversaw the implementation of the peace treaty that Jordan signed with Israel in 1994 and also served as Jordan's ambassador to Israel until the attacks of 9 November 2005, when he was hurriedly called back to Amman and appointed national security adviser in a shake-up that was interpreted by some observers to be the outcome of the Amman blasts. The King's appointment of al-Bakhit, as well as other senior cabinet appointments of the same period, appeared to signal the Hashemite's new determination to give influence back to figures from the Jordanian security and military establishment, away from the young and liberal reformers who had risen to power in recent years but whose reputation had been tarnished by allegations of corruption.

The Cabinet's security priorities were reflected in the King's letter of appointment to the new Prime Minister, which urged firm action against 'Muslim extremists', particularly the so-called Muslim *takfiris*, those who believed that the Hashemite state, and indeed contemporary Jordanian society, had reverted to a state of unbelief (*kufr*), and who therefore considered it legitimate to mount a rebellion against the state. The King appealed for a 'relentless war on all the *takfiri* schools, which embrace extremism, backwardness, isolation and darkness and are fed on the ignorance and naiveté of simple people'. He added that *fatwas* issued by *takfiri* schools constituted a major threat to Jordanian society and that the November 2005 attacks increased Jordan's determination to pursue its political and economic reform agenda. Following the November blasts, security was tightened around the capital and roadblocks were established around Western hotels and embassies. Nevertheless, the security situation in the country remained tense.

A growing authoritarianism of the Hashemite regime was witnessed in 2005 and early 2006. Political repression in Jordan was on the increase, partly in response to intense public opposition to the regime's close political alliance and military co-operation with the USA, as the Bush Administration intensified its military operations against the Iraqi insurgency. The Hashemite monarchy had tolerated some semblance of a parliamentary democracy in which moderate Islamists participated, but any hopes for greater openness and media freedoms under King Abdullah had been dashed. Human rights organizations, in particular, accused the regime of cracking down on the media and on the right of free speech and public assembly. Jordan's security services, with authority to track both internal and external security threats, continued to take firm action against the political critics of King Abdullah's authoritarian policies, and those seeking peaceful political change in the country were also suppressed. The security services denied passports to citizens on national security grounds, and students applying to universities required a good behaviour certificate from the security services, according to the US Department of State human rights report of 2005. On 23 November a Brussels (Belgium)-based think tank, the International Crisis Group, concluded that long-promised political reforms were vital if Jordan wanted to prevent further violent attacks.

HUMAN RIGHTS ABUSES AND SECURITY PRISONERS' RIOTS

In 2005–06 human rights organizations also reported on the growing population of political prisoners and the expansion of the network of detention centres in the country. On 28 February 2006 clashes broke out at Juwaida prison in Amman, where

Islamist activists were being held. When police attempted to remove two detainees sentenced to death for the murder of Laurence Foley in 2002, the prisoners rebelled, fearing that the two men were being taken away to be executed. The inmates had also demanded new trials in civil courts for those who had been convicted and sentenced by military tribunals. When prison officials rejected their demands, the detainees closed the prison's main gates. Subsequently, a hostage crisis at the prison developed when prisoners took seven police hostages, including the head of the prison service. At the same time security detainees at two other prisons, Suwaiqa and Qafqafa, also rioted in response to the developments at Juwaida. However, on 1 March 2006 the crisis at Juwaida was brought to an end through negotiations and after the release of the police hostages. In return for freeing the hostages, the detainees were told that they would not be punished.

Yet, Jordan continued to face repeated allegations by human rights organizations of ill-treatment and torture in its security prisons. Apparently, the torture methods included sleep deprivation, beatings on the soles of the feet, prolonged suspension with ropes in contorted positions and extended solitary confinement. Even the US Department of State, while praising Jordan for combating terrorism in one report published in 2005, accused it of human rights abuses (including the physical and verbal abuse of detainees by the secret services) in another. However, experts on US-Jordanian relations observed that the Jordanian Government generally received 'a free pass' from the US Administration with regard to human rights because Jordan remained central to the 'war on terror' and US-led operations in Iraq, politically, militarily and strategically.

THE DEATH OF AL-ZARQAWI IN IRAQ

On 7 June 2006 al-Zarqawi was killed by a US air-strike outside Baquba, north-east of Baghdad. Public opinion polls conducted shortly after his death showed that 59% of Jordanians considered him to have been a terrorist and only 15% thought him a martyr. Moreover, four Islamist parliamentarians in Jordan faced charges of inciting sectarianism after visiting al-Zarqawi's family to deliver condolences. There was a precedent for returning the bodies of major figures to their families in the Iraq conflict, including the bodies of Saddam Hussain's two sons. However, the fate of al-Zarqawi's body continued to trouble both the US and Jordanian authorities. The Jordanian authorities announced that he would not be buried in Jordan under any circumstances because of the Amman suicide bombings. However, on 2 July Iraq's national security adviser, Muwaffaq al-Rubaie, stated that al-Zarqawi's body had been handed over by the US military and buried at a secret location in the country, thus thwarting demands by al-Zarqawi's relatives and some Jordanian Islamists for his body to be repatriated to Jordan.

ECONOMIC CO-OPERATION WITH ISRAEL AND TENSE RELATIONS WITH THE HAMAS-LED PALESTINIAN ADMINISTRATION

Since the Israeli-Jordanian treaty of 1994, Israel had viewed Jordan as a security partner and a bridge to other Arab countries. In particular, Israel saw the prospect of close economic and trade ties with this Arab state as an important step towards easing its regional isolation in the Middle East. The Jordanian regime, on the other hand, saw its economic relations with Israel as part of its wider ties with, and economic dependence on, the USA. The growing economic ties with Israel were evident in June 2006, when the two countries agreed on a number of joint projects, including the construction of a new international airport in the Gulf of Aqaba to serve international carriers. The airport was to have two terminals—one Jordanian and the other Israeli—and would be located in southern Jordan just across the border from Eilat. This and other projects were discussed at a meeting between Israel's Deputy Prime Minister Shimon Peres and King Abdullah on 21 June in Petra. Further meetings between Israeli and Jordanian officials were scheduled to finalize the project. Abdullah and Peres also discussed other joint economic projects, including the establishment of free trade zones and Israeli-Jordanian co-operation in quarry exploration, mainly copper-mining. They also agreed on plans for the Dead Sea–Red Sea project, which involved the construction of a 180-km canal to channel water from the Red Sea to prevent water evaporation of the Dead Sea. This project had many opponents, headed by international environmental organizations, who argued that the canal would damage the environment and destroy the Dead Sea completely by allowing an inflow of water that has a different chemical composition. However, it was announced in June 2007 that a number of firms had been commissioned to carry out feasibility studies on the proposed canal.

One day after Peres's meeting with King Abdullah, on 22 June 2006 Abdullah hosted an informal meeting—the first in a year—for Israeli Prime Minister Ehud Olmert and Palestinian President Mahmud Abbas in Petra. Abbas had long urged Israel to resume peace talks, but Olmert dismissed Abbas's appeals, insisting that the new Hamas-led Palestinian administration must first recognize Israel's right to exist. (Hamas had secured the largest share of the vote of any party in Palestinian legislative elections in January 2006, and had formed an administration, in which the group represented the sole faction, in March.) Instead of restarting peace talks, Olmert announced his unilateral plans to finalize Israel's border with the Palestinians, with the aim of carving up large chunks of the West Bank. The Petra meeting came amid intense Israeli bombardments of the Gaza Strip, with one Israeli air-strike killing two Palestinian civilians and wounding more than seven others, including children, in Khan Younis. Israeli forces had killed more than 20 Palestinian civilians, many of them children, in air-strikes in the previous days.

In sharp contrast to its growing economic co-operation with Israel, Jordan discreetly backed US-led efforts to isolate the Hamas administration unless it recognized Israel and halted attacks on Israeli settlers. This anti-Hamas strategy became evident in April 2006 when the Jordanian authorities accused the Palestinian militant groups of storing weapons on Jordanian territory. The Jordanian authorities also cancelled a visit by Palestinian Minister of Foreign Affairs Dr Mahmud al-Zahhar to Jordan, as part of a tour of Arab states to raise funds for the PA after the USA and European Union (EU) cut aid to the administration following Hamas's election victory. Hamas officials responded by strongly denying the Jordanian accusations and criticizing the Hashemite regime's decision to cancel the minister's visit.

On 23 November 2006 Prime Minister Marouf al-Bakhit effected a cabinet reorganization, the stated aim of which was to bolster the Government's programme of economic and political reform. The reorganization comprised nine changes, including the appointment of Muhammad al-Oran, formerly a member of the opposition, as Minister of Political Development, and that of Salem Khaza'leh, hitherto Minister of Public State Development, as the new Minister of Industry and Trade. Sherif al-Zohbi, former custodian of the industry and trade portfolio, became Minister of Justice.

THE IMPACT OF IRAQ'S CIVIL WAR AND JORDAN'S IRAQI REFUGEE CRISIS

The escalating violence and civil war in Iraq continued to dominate Jordan's foreign, regional and domestic security policies throughout 2006–07. The Iraq crisis provided proof that Jordan was not immune to the fall-out of the anti-US insurgency and sectarian civil war next door. In 2004 King Abdullah had coined a controversial phrase that continued to resonate throughout the region: there was, the King pronounced, a 'Shi'a crescent' that went from Iran to Lebanon, passing through Baghdad, where a Shi'a-dominated regime had been consolidated in recent years. This 'Shi'a crescent' was fuelling a new sectarian brand of politics with destabilizing consequences for the entire region. However, while the Jordanian regime was deeply concerned about the spread and deepening of sectarianism in Iraq, in the second half of 2006 and first half of 2007 King Abdullah stated repeatedly that the critical issue in the region remained the Israeli–Palestinian conflict. On 26 November 2006 the King warned that 'three civil wars' could break out in the area unless the conflicts in the Palestinian territories, Iraq and Lebanon were brought under control. 'Palestine is the core', he told the USA's ABC television network. On 29 November King Abdullah hosted both US President George Bush and Iraqi Prime Minister Nuri Kamal (Jawad) al-Maliki for talks in Amman against a backdrop of escalating sectarian violence in Iraq.

While the Arab world was deeply divided over the execution by hanging of Saddam Hussain by the Maliki Government on 31 December 2006, with the region's satellite television channels reflecting the divisions between Iraqi Shi'a and Sunni populations, in Jordan protesters from both Islamist and left-wing parties and the Palestinian Fatah movement held rallies at the Palestinian refugee camp of al-Baqa'a, on the outskirts of Amman. Statements were read describing Saddam as a 'martyr'. Moreover, a group of Iraqi Baathists in Jordan calling itself the 'Baghdad's Citizens Gathering' pledged allegiance to Saddam's fugitive deputy, the former Vice-President of Iraq's Revolutionary Command Council, Izzat Ibrahim, and called him the 'legitimate president of Iraq'.

Throughout 2006–07 the Jordanian intelligence service continued its efforts to seek to neutralize, suppress or wipe out *jihadist* and *takfiri* groups in the kingdom. On 7 March 2007 three Jordanian men appeared in the state security court in Amman, having been accused of plotting to assassinate US President Bush during a state visit to the country in November 2006. All three were accused of embracing militant *takfiri* ideologies that regarded supporters of the regime as infidels. The men faced charges of conspiracy to carry out terrorist acts and of plotting to bomb the US and Danish embassies in Amman.

More crucially, throughout 2006–07, as a result of the escalating sectarian conflict in Iraq, a severe refugee problem was developing in Jordan, which was reeling from an estimated 750,000 Iraqi refugees who had fled there since the 2003 invasion, making Jordan the largest concentration of Iraqis anywhere except Syria. Initially, wealthier Iraqis left for Jordan. However, as Iraq descended into chaos, poorer Iraqis crossed the Jordanian and Syrian borders in increasing numbers, contributing to societal and economic strains. The Iraqi refugees represented a huge number of immigrants for a small and resource-poor country with a population of just 5.6m. Furthermore, refugees had always been a sensitive issue in Jordan, which absorbed hundreds of thousands of Palestinians in 1948, 1967 and again in 1990, when those living in Kuwait were expelled to Jordan. Yet, partly owing to Jordanian hospitality and social tolerance, very few Iraqi refugees were deported from the country. Nevertheless, economic pressures on Jordan were growing. With high unemployment and 14% of Jordanians living in poverty, the cost of housing in Amman had doubled in the past year alone. The influx of Iraqis was putting a massive strain on the Jordanian economy, precipitating inflation and overburdening social services. Consequently, Jordan (as well as Syria) began taking measures to close its borders to refugees, with which Jordanian officials stated they could no longer cope.

THE CASE OF ABU QATADA AND THE RISK OF TORTURE IN JORDAN

On 26 February 2007 a British Special Immigration Appeals Commission (SIAC) dismissed an appeal by radical Muslim preacher Omar Mahmoud Muhammad Othman (Abu Qatada) against the British Government's attempt to deport him to his native Jordan, where he had been convicted *in absentia* of involvement in a number of terrorist attacks. Jordan was one of a number of countries with which the United Kingdom had agreed a memorandum of understanding (MOU)—signed by the two sides on 10 August 2005—promising that transferred persons would not be mistreated on their return. However, Abu Qatada's lawyers argued that the agreement with Jordan did not guarantee his safety. Furthermore, in 2005 the US-based non-governmental organization (NGO) Human Rights Watch argued that the United Kingdom could not deport security suspects to Jordan without violating the international prohibition against sending persons to countries where they faced a serious risk of torture. As Joe Stork, Deputy Director of Human Rights Watch's Middle East division, added: 'Jordan's General Intelligence Department, prisons and ordinary police stations all have known records of abuse'.

Jordan and the United Kingdom were also parties to the UN Convention against Torture and Other Cruel, Inhuman or Degrading Treatment or Punishment, which prohibited torture and the transfer, return or expulsion of persons to countries where there were substantial grounds for believing that they would be in danger of being subjected to torture. Under international law, the prohibition against torture was absolute and could not be waived under any circumstances. The London appeal by Abu Qatada thus tested the British Government's use of its MOU with Jordan. SIAC's ruling had in effect given a backing to the British policy of seeking to deport terror suspects to Jordan. SIAC accepted that senior members of the Jordanian GID had 'sanctioned or turned a blind eye' to torture in the past, but added that the GID would be aware of the risks of ill-treating Abu Qatada. The Commission said that: 'If he were to be tortured or ill-treated, there probably would be a considerable outcry in Jordan, regardless of any MOU. The likely inflaming of Palestinian and extremist or anti-Western feelings would be destabilising for the government.' However, the international human rights organization Amnesty International reacted by stating that it was 'profoundly concerned' by the ruling, and Abu Qatada's legal team sought leave to appeal SIAC's ruling.

REVIVING THE 'JORDANIAN OPTION'

In interviews with the Western press in March 2007, King Abdullah stated that creation of a Palestinian state in the West Bank and Gaza was becoming less likely because of the continued construction of Jewish settlements in these territories and the separation barrier in the West Bank. Rather than a state, he commented, the Palestinians would be left with 'Swiss cheese'—a fragmented territory riddled with holes: 'Physically there may not be a chance for a future Palestinian state . . . This is why the urgency is now'.

Perhaps echoing these comments, in early 2007 the so-called 'Jordanian option' was revived in semi-official Jordanian circles. Press reports were circulating that former premier Abd al-Salam al-Majali—a close ally of the royal family and an architect of the 1994 peace treaty between Jordan and Israel—was floating the notion of a confederation of the West Bank and Jordan. In mid-May 2007 the Israeli daily *Ma'ariv* reported that King Abdullah had drawn up a new initiative to solve the Palestinian question based on the historic confederation scheme of Jordan and Palestine. According to *Ma'ariv*, the King's envoys, such as al-Majali, were sent to Israel to explore this option. The newspaper quoted the envoys as proposing to the Israeli officials that, since they claimed that there was 'nobody to talk to on the Palestinian side' and 'nothing tangible to discuss', they could talk to the Jordanians, with the participation of representatives of the Palestinian President. The new initiative appealed for the establishment of a united Hashemite-Palestinian kingdom, to be termed the 'Palestinian-Jordanian United Kingdom', with the Jordanian King presiding over the two autonomous states. Under the King would be a Prime Minister, a Chairman of the Palestinian state and another of the Jordanian state. *Ma'ariv* did not exclude the possibility that the initiative could be a test aimed at reviving the paralysed peace process and at diverting deep public concern in Jordan over the US involvement in Iraq. However, the Israeli newspaper pointed out that several obstacles stood in the way of the new Jordanian initiative, including the stipulation that it should be implemented after securing complete Israeli approval of the Arab peace initiative, which was readopted by the Arab leaders at their summit in Riyadh at the end of March 2007.

Jordan still retained custodianship of the Muslim holy shrines in Jerusalem. In February 2007 violent clashes at Jerusalem's al-Aqsa Mosque resulted in the deaths of some 40 Palestinians and injuries to many Israeli police officers. Palestinian worshippers were protesting against Israeli renovation work nearby. The immediate trigger for the protests was a decision by the Israeli authorities to begin digging up the stone ramp used for access to the Muslim Mughrabi Gate. The Israeli archaeological excavations reignited repeated claims by local Muslim leaders that digging around the compound was threatening the foundations of the al-Aqsa Mosque, Islam's third holiest shrine. The compound, in religious and political terms, is the most sensitive site in the Israeli–Palestinian conflict, and the heavily policed walk on the compound by Ariel Sharon in September 2000 had precipitated the second Palestinian *intifada*. King Abdullah described the new Israeli excavations as a 'blatant violation' and a 'dangerous escalation'.

THE CRISIS OF IRAQI REFUGEES IN JORDAN

The displacement crisis caused by the US-led invasion of Iraq in 2003 and Iraq's subsequent sectarian conflict reached catastrophic proportions in 2007–08. Over 2m. Iraqis were refugees in the Middle East, the majority of them living in difficult conditions in Jordan and Syria. Their unresolved plight and their largely unmet needs constituted a humanitarian crisis. Furthermore, the refugees' presence in Jordan, where most of them were struggling to survive, had a major impact on the country. Jordan's geographic location thrust the country into the position of hosting a disproportionately large number of Iraqi refugees: according to a survey released by Fafo (a Norwegian-based research organization) in November 2007, between 450,000 and 500,000 Iraqis were estimated to be living in Jordan—largely concentrated in the capital, Amman. However, Jordanian officials privately maintained that the country was hosting a larger number, of between 700,000 and 800,000.

The Jordanian authorities were committed to non-refoulement until peace was achieved in Iraq. In the mean time, the Iraqis were described as 'guests'—rather than acknowledged 'refugees' for whom the Jordanian state took responsibility. In contrast, the Office of the UN High Commissioner for Refugees (UNHCR) deemed the Iraqis to be *prima facie* refugees.

Moreover, in 2007–08 access to Jordan remained restricted for Iraqi refugees. Already in 2006 Jordan was excluding single men and boys, aged between 17 and 35, from entering the country. Subsequently, the authorities began insisting that Iraqis should produce a newly issued passport, which, in practice, very few could obtain. Finally, in 2007 the border with Iraq was closed, other than for exceptional cases; the border remained closed in 2008. At the same time, Jordan had no specific provisions for allowing entry to individuals fleeing human rights abuses in Iraq—despite its obligation to respect the principle of non-refoulement under customary international law and as a party to both the UN International Covenant on Civil and Political Rights and the Convention against Torture. However, Jordan had signed an MOU with UNHCR in 1998, and the Government repeatedly affirmed its commitment to non-refoulement. The Government defended its policies as being flexible and responsive to humanitarian and security considerations.

The massive presence of Iraqi refugees in Jordan affected local residents both negatively and positively. In 2005–06 the Ministry of Industry and Trade recorded 4,616 registered Iraqi enterprises in Jordan, and some US $300,000m. in Iraqi investment. However, Jordanian citizens were often quick to blame the Iraqis for rising prices of real estate, rent and food; for overcrowded schools and health facilities; and for shortages of electricity and water. In reality, the Iraqi refugees were neither the sole cause of the rising prices, nor were they a net drain on Jordan's economy. Nevertheless, resources and services normally available to Jordanian citizens were seriously stretched. In February 2008 the Jordanian authorities announced that they would exempt Iraqis from accumulated fines if they decided to return home or travel to a third country, but that those who wanted to stay had until 17 April to pay 50% of their dues and change their status, or risk never being accepted for residency. In April a one-month extension was announced to this arrangement. On 1 May Jordan introduced additional restrictions on, and new visa requirements for, Iraqis. These requirements obliged Iraqis to apply for visas in Iraq, before travelling to Jordan.

Since the majority of Iraqis in Jordan did not have any legal status, they lived in a constant state of insecurity. According to a 2007 Fafo survey, of the poorest group of Iraqis that it had interviewed, only 22% had a valid residence permit. Many Iraqi refugees—including those registered with UNHCR—did not meet the criteria for obtaining a residence permit. Furthermore, some of the displaced from Iraq were Palestinian refugees who had lived in Iraq for several decades. The Jordanian authorities were reported to be holding scores of Palestinians from Iraq at the al-Ruweished camp. Some of these—who had in the past held official Jordanian documents—were trying to apply for Jordanian citizenship, but they were told that each application would cost US $5,000. Furthermore, other foreigners entering Jordan, who did not invest in economic enterprises, were required to show they were able to support themselves in order to obtain and renew residence permits. This meant that they were required to deposit JD 100,000 (about $150,000) in a Jordanian bank, and had to maintain a sufficient balance (about JD 50,000) to earn interest.

A large number of UN agencies, as well as local and international NGOs, were based in Jordan and worked with Iraqi refugees. In March 2008 an international NGO, the International Rescue Committee's Commission on Iraqi Refugees, reported on the worsening crisis of the Iraqi refugees in Jordan (and Syria) and sought ways to expedite international aid. 'Neither the US nor the rest of the world is paying sufficient heed to the crisis', the report stated, adding that help offered by the USA and other international and regional donors was paltry and half-hearted. The Commission found that the conditions of the hundreds of thousands of Iraqi refugees in Jordan (and Syria) were bleak and growing worse by the day. Most refugees lived in dilapidated and congested apartments in poor urban centres. Many were running out of money and could no longer cover basic needs, like rent and food. Some were getting sick or suffered chronic illnesses, but had limited access to medical care.

Officially, most Iraqi refugees in Jordan were not permitted to work and many were facing increasing impoverishment. According to a 2007 survey, the majority of them lived on savings or money transfers; 42% received such money transfers from Iraq. Yet this left the refugees vulnerable to destitution when savings ran out or if the situation in Iraq deteriorated and stopped the flow of support. Some Iraqis in Jordan were reported to work illegally, while others had work permits. According to NGO sources, those working were reported to be vulnerable to low pay, exploitation and arbitrary dismissals.

In 2007–08 24,000 Iraqi refugee children, including those without legal status, were given access to education in Jordan. Education was one significant area in which Jordan had substantially benefited from donor aid to support its overburdened system. In 2007–08 UNHCR raised US $11.2m. to educate Iraqi children in Jordan. The UN and aid agencies praised the Government's decision, and more money followed: in December 2007 the EU gave about $39m. to Jordan to support education for Iraqi refugees over three years; at the same time USAID provided another $8m. The United Nations Children's Fund (UNICEF) also paid school fees for more than 9,000 children.

DOMESTIC POLITICS AND ECONOMIC PRIORITIES

On 19 August 2007 King Abdullah issued a decree dissolving the House of Representatives in advance of legislative elections; the date of the polls was subsequently announced as 20 November. Meanwhile, municipal elections were held in July 2007 to select representatives to 93 councils throughout the country and one-half of the members of the Greater Amman Municipality. This was the first time that local elections had been conducted since the adoption of a new Municipalities Law earlier in the year. Changes to the legislation included the introduction of a quota of 20% of the 965 municipal seats being reserved for women. However, the IAF dramatically withdrew its candidates shortly after voting had begun, accusing the Jordanian authorities of committing electoral fraud and amid complaints that no more than 50% of the seats in the Greater Amman Municipality were elective.

On 22 November 2007 King Abdullah appointed Nader al-Dahabi as the country's new Prime Minister, charging him with forming a government that would prioritize the promotion of economic development. Al-Dahabi, a former Minister of Transport and a prominent technocrat, succeeded Marouf al-Bakhit, who had headed the Government since November 2005, and who had tendered his resignation in the wake of the parliamentary elections of 20 November 2007, in which loyalist candidates won a landslide victory and the Islamist opposition alleged electoral malpractice after suffering a major reverse. The polling resulted in pro-regime loyalists winning a majority in the 110-seat parliament, while the Islamist opposition took only six seats—11 fewer than they had held in the previous parliament elected in 2003. The IAF, Jordan's largest political party, had suffered its most severe parliamentary setback in two decades. The new House of Deputies consisted mainly of regime loyalists: businessmen, retired army officers and tribal leaders. Also on 22 November 2007 the King appointed a senior economist and close confidant, Bassem Awadallah, as Chief of the Royal Court.

A supporter of economic liberalization, al-Dahabi was expected to embrace the King's reform plan and nurture the regime's close ties with the USA. On 16 December 2007 the House of Deputies granted the new Government a vote of confidence. In February 2008 the Speaker of the House of Deputies, Abd al-Hadi al-Majali, praised the King's house-building initiative, which was designed to provide a wider segment of Jordanian society with affordable housing, at a time when the economic situation was very difficult. Under the plan, entitled 'Decent Homes for Decent Living', which was designed to alleviate the soaring housing prices in the country, 100,000 houses would be built in the northern, central and southern parts of Jordan over the next five years.

It was reported at the end of June 2008 that Jordan's inflation rate had reached a new high as increases in fuel prices and the effects of a poor harvest had combined with global inflationary pressures to push prices upwards. Almost all of Jordan's oil was imported from Iraq, although no longer at the extremely favourable prices that existed before the US-led invasion of 2003. From 2007 the Government was engaged in a process of gradual reduction of state subsidies on fuel and food. This policy was aimed at reducing the kingdom's spiralling budget deficit. However, it also had the effect of further increasing the financial hardship being experienced by ordinary Jordanians. The resulting price rises sparked protests from opposition deputies, and some observers commented that they would lead to discontent and social unrest. In response, the Government opted to delay the subsidy reductions on liquid petroleum gas, used for domestic heating and cooking, and to increase public sector wages.

In late June 2008 the Jordanian daily *Ad-Dustour* quoted a government source to the effect that Jordan had received additional foreign financial aid worth US $360m., including $300.8m. from Saudi Arabia and $59m. from other countries. The foreign aid, which covered part of extraordinary state expenses, valued at $700m., would help in settling government financial liabilities and covering soaring expenses, such as subsidies for fuel, enabling the authorities to postpone further liberalization of gas prices, as well as increasing monthly salaries for government employees. Other sums earmarked by foreign countries for aiding the kingdom were estimated at $621m., and were being delivered in stages from the donors. Official Jordanian figures showed that foreign financial aid to the kingdom between 2004 and 2007 amounted to $2,610m.

PARLIAMENT ENDORSES POLITICAL PARTIES LAW

The Jordanian parliament had endorsed the controversial Political Parties Law in 2007, amid protests from opposition parties that feared that the legislation would lead to the dissolution of many opposition groupings. Apparently, 12 out of 36 existing political parties, including the IAF, had rectified their status under the new law by the mid-April 2008 deadline. In April the Ministry of the Interior revoked the licences of 24 political parties for failing to meet the requirements of the new law, which stipulated that a party must have a minimum of 500 founding members from at least five different governorates. Five parties that failed to meet the requirements of the controversial new law dissolved themselves voluntarily—Al-Fajr, the Jordanian Arab Constitutional Front Party, Al-Ahd, the Ajial, and the Justice and Development Party. The Communist Workers Party of Jordan merged with Jordan's Communist Party owing to its relatively small membership base. Political parties had been given a one-year grace period to meet the new requirements, but many were confronted by serious challenges in meeting the new criteria, including the difficulty of recruiting in rural areas. In an official statement, the regime announced that, to encourage 'political life' in the country, the Government had added an article to the new law that provided official funding to political parties.

ABU QATADA'S APPEAL AGAINST DEPORTATION TO JORDAN

On 9 April 2008 Abu Qatada won an appeal against deportation from the United Kingdom to Jordan. The British Court of Appeal stated that SIAC had misdirected itself in law over the issue of any evidence obtained by torture. The Court was concerned that evidence allegedly obtained under torture could form part of a future trial in Jordan. The latter was one of a number of countries with which the United Kingdom had signed an MOU in 2005, which British ministers said would ensure that any deported terrorism suspects would not face torture or ill-treatment on return. The British Foreign and Commonwealth Office had obtained assurances from Jordan that suspects sent back would not be tortured. The British Home Office responded by saying that it would challenge the ruling of the Court of Appeal.

REGIONAL RELATIONS

Throughout 2007–08 the Jordanian regime continued to maintain cordial relations with Israel. In April 2008 Israeli Prime Minister Ehud Olmert made a surprise visit to Amman and held talks with King Abdullah concerning the Middle East peace process. The two leaders reportedly discussed ways to make progress towards the objectives set at the previous November's Annapolis conference in the USA. The conference was designed to relaunch Israeli-Palestinian peace negotiations, which had shown little visible sign of progress. Olmert's visit to Jordan, his second since January 2008, came a week after the King discussed the peace process with US President George Bush in Washington, DC. On the popular level, however, many Jordanians remained highly critical of Jordan's relations with Israel.

On 12 June 2008 Iraqi Prime Minister Nuri al-Maliki arrived in Amman on a two-day official visit. He urged the Jordanian Government to return its ambassador to Iraq. Following a 2003 attack against Jordan's embassy in Baghdad, which had left up to 19 people dead, Jordan had recalled its ambassador and downgraded diplomatic relations with Iraq. In mid-June 2008 King Abdullah promised al-Maliki that he would send an ambassador to Baghdad and work to improve relations with his neighbours. Apparently, this improvement came after the Iraqi Government announced that it would consider a discounted oil deal for Jordan. At the end of June Jordan appointed Nayef al-Zaidan, former chargé d'affaires in Tehran, as the country's new ambassador to Iraq.

Al-Maliki's visit was reciprocated in August 2008, when King Abdullah met the Iraqi Prime Minister in Baghdad to discuss relations between the two states. The visit was the first by an Arab head of state to Iraq since the US-led invasion of 2003.

Jordan's relations with Iran remained tense and indeed continued to deteriorate in early 2009. Closely allied to the USA and its policies in the Middle East, the Jordanian regime remained critical of Iran and its support for those who 'opposed the peace process' in the Middle East. In February, following remarks by a senior Iranian cleric in which he had referred to Bahrain as the 14th province of Iran, King Abdullah made a point of visiting Bahrain to express Jordan's support. On the issue of nuclear proliferation, however, Jordan remained cautious and the regime feared that an attack on Iran by the USA or Israel would inflame domestic opinion, with a potential surge of public outrage similar to the one that engulfed the whole region following the invasion of Iraq in 2003.

On 6 July 2009 the international press freedom organization Reporters Sans Frontières published a statement on its website condemning the Jordanian Government's closure of the Amman bureaux of two Iranian satellite TV stations, Al-Alam and Press TV, in the previous month. However, on 7 July the Jordanian Government denied claims that the closures were politically motivated, citing the expiry of permits allowing the two stations to operate in Jordan.

KING ABDULLAH APPOINTS HIS SON AS CROWN PRINCE

Meanwhile, on 2 July 2009 King Abdullah issued a royal decree appointing his 15-year-old eldest son, Prince Hussein, as Crown Prince. Abdullah had effectively removed his half-brother, Prince Hamzeh, from the post in November 2004. Despite accusations that the decision contravened the wishes of Abdullah's father, King Hussein, the Royal Court insisted that the decision to appoint Prince Hussein as Crown Prince had the full support of the country's political and military establishment.

THE IMPACT OF THE GLOBAL ECONOMIC DOWNTURN

In 2009 the global economic crisis took its toll on the Jordanian economy, affecting the majority of the inhabitants and not just the lower levels of society. There were potential long-term negative consequences for strategic national projects in the fields of water and energy. The influx of Iraqi refugees, which was estimated at 750,000, had increased the Jordanian population by 15%–20%. In the long term the country's reliance on foreign sources of energy and the lack of indigenous water were potentially of major consequence for political and economic stability. Jordan's mounting national debt was reportedly over US $11,000m. and the rate of unemployment close to 30%. Jordan's economy was further hurt by high inflation, of over 9%, driven by high international oil and food prices and the global financial crisis.

In July 2009 the Minister of Finance, Bassem al-Salem, confirmed that the economic situation was expected to be difficult in 2009. Earlier the Government had introduced a number of legislative proposals to revitalize the economy, including amendments to the law on income tax, designed to prevent Jordan from sliding into deeper recession. The year 2009 was characterized by serious economic decline, one immediate consequence of which was increased social unrest in the country. One example was the protest in Palestinian refugee camps at the reduction in financial resources of the UNRWA. In April some 7,000–10,000 UNRWA workers in Jordan held a one-day strike, which affected more than 200 schools and health centres in the 10 official Palestinian refugee camps located in Jordan. A further three-day strike was held the following month. At January 2011 some 350,899 registered refugees were accommodated in the 10 camps (17.7% of the total number of Palestinian refugees registered with UNRWA in Jordan).

In 2008–09 King Abdullah had continued to accelerate 'economic reform' and re-structuring through the privatization of major government-owned enterprises and the reduction of the public sector; state fuel subsidies were eliminated, and barley subsidies were scheduled to be phased out. However, the King's neo-liberal economic policy was not without its critics. In September 2008, as pressures on the Palace mounted, the King's closest adviser and a leading proponent of economic reform, Bassem Awadallah, resigned from office. The economic downturn led to a delay in the implementation of some of these reforms as the Government sought to shield the economy from some of the worst effects of the recession. The private sector has been reluctant to become involved in public service provision, ensuring that Jordan's bloated public sector continues to be a key employer and a drain on the Government's coffers.

DISSOLUTION OF PARLIAMENT AND NEW ELECTORAL LEGISLATION

In November 2009 King Abdullah unexpectedly dissolved parliament only two years into its four-year term. According to the Constitution, a new parliament must be formed within four months of dissolution. However, in a royal decree issued in December, the King postponed legislative elections indefinitely, pending the formulation by the Cabinet of new electoral legislation. On the following day Prime Minister al-Dahabi submitted the resignation of his Government and Abdullah announced the appointment of Samir Rifai, son of Zaid Rifai, as Prime Minister-designate. In the following week Abdullah approved the formation of a new Cabinet led by Samir Rifai, who was confirmed as Prime Minister and Minister of Defence; 15 members of the outgoing administration were retained in the new Cabinet. The task of overseeing the drafting of a new electoral law was specifically charged to the new Deputy Prime Minister and Minister of State, Rajai Muasher. Zaid Rifai submitted his resignation as Speaker of the Senate, thus averting concerns about the constitutionality of two close relatives heading the upper legislative chamber and the Cabinet, respectively. Shortly thereafter the King appointed a new Senate, with former Prime Minister Taher al-Masri as Speaker. Fresh legislative elections were eventually scheduled for November 2010, with the Government to rule by emergency law in the mean time.

After much deliberation, the new electoral law was announced in May 2010, disappointing many opposition figures on account of its limited scope. There were some notable changes, however: the quota reserved for female legislators was doubled from six to 12 seats, and nine and three seats, respectively, were henceforth to be reserved for Jordan's Christian and Circassian minorities. The law also expanded the total number of legislators from 110 to 120, including four new seats in traditionally under-represented urban and Palestinian-dominated areas in Amman, Irbid and Zarqa.

However, reformists were frustrated by the retention of the 'one person, one vote' electoral system, adopted in 1993, as it tended to foster tribalism rather than promoting party politics. This favouring of tribal leaders over national political parties was seen as a means of helping the regime to mitigate the popularity of the IAF. Similarly, the law's reordering of the current electoral districts into electoral 'zones'—each broken down into sub-districts in which voters would be able to choose any candidate in any sub-district within their zone—did little to counter the traditional disproportionality of electoral districts; critics of the Government argued that the new electoral structure still favoured the regime's traditional rural Trans-jordanian allies at the expense of the largely urban Palestinian population. Opposition figures were quick to highlight that the new law ignored not only the recommendations made by Jordanian NGOs and political parties but also those of the 2005 National Agenda Commission, established by King Abdullah, which had appealed for a gradual phasing out of tribalism in favour of greater national proportional representation. The selection of Rajai Muasher, a vocal critic of electoral reform, as arbiter of the new law was cited by many as the principal reason for the disappointing outcome.

DIVISIONS IN THE IAF

As the Hashemite regime continued its attempts to marginalize the IAF, the party was becoming increasingly divided. While moderates in the organization wished to focus largely on domestic issues, leaving the Palestinian issue to be dealt with by Hamas, hardliners sought closer ties with Hamas and a more confrontational stance with the Jordanian Government. The hardliners had seemed to be in the ascendency in May 2010 when a leading member, Ali Abu al-Sakkar, was elected as President of the IAF's Shura (Advisory) Council; a dispute during polling had led to many moderates walking out of the election hall, and these divisions were also evident during the election, in July, for the position of party General Secretary. However, after heated debates between the two camps, a compromise was reached whereby each faction's leading candidate—hardliner Zaki Bani Irshid and moderate Salim Falahat—withdrew from the contest in order to allow Hamza

Mansour, a moderate who was acceptable to the hardliners, to be duly elected.

Mansour's first major challenge on assuming office was to oversee the debate within the divided IAF regarding how best to respond to the new electoral law. While the party was opposed to the continuation under the new legislation of the process of manipulating district boundaries, which, it argued, represented a targeted attempt to hamper their electoral performance, the creation of four new seats in winnable areas (Amman, Irbid and Zarqa) was likely to serve as a powerful incentive to participate in the forthcoming election in order to increase the party's parliamentary representation. However, the hardliners retained significant influence, and directed the divided party towards a boycott of the poll.

STRAINED RELATIONS WITH ISRAEL

The return to the Israeli premiership of Binyamin Netanyahu in February 2009 resulted in a marked decline in Jordan's relations with its western neighbour. Netanyahu's Likud party, in coalition with the right-wing Israel Beytenu, pursued an unapologetically confrontational stance against the Palestinians, maintaining its blockade of the Gaza Strip and continuing settlement expansion, particularly in East Jerusalem. (For further details, see the chapter on Israel.) As a result, King Abdullah came under increasing domestic pressure to intervene on behalf of the Palestinians.

In 2010 King Abdullah made several statements to international audiences that attested to the increased tension in the relationship. In an interview published in April in the US daily newspaper *The Wall Street Journal*, he stated that Jordanian-Israeli relations were 'at an all bottom low'. At the Arab League summit in Sirte, Libya, in March, Abdullah had warned Israel against wasting its 'last opportunity' to make peace with the Palestinians and described its attempts to change the demographic character of East Jerusalem as 'illegal', 'illegitimate' and 'a violation of international and humanitarian law'. Meeting with Catherine Ashton, the EU High Representative for Foreign Affairs and Security Policy, in the same month, Abdullah urged the international community to take action on the 'red line' of Jerusalem, citing his historic role as guardian of the city's holy places.

A further cause of disagreement between Jordan and Israel has been the former's pursuit of nuclear power. Large deposits of uranium have been found in Jordan and the Government was keen to attract external assistance for the development of civilian nuclear facilities within the kingdom. However, King Abdullah complained of 'underhanded' Israeli actions intended to deter Jordan's potential international partners, notably France and the Republic of Korea (South Korea), from providing their expertise and technology to the Hashemite kingdom.

INCREASED TRANSJORDANIAN–PALESTINIAN TENSIONS

Diminishing hopes for the achievement of peace between Israelis and Palestinians resulted in a heightening of tensions between Jordanians of Palestinian origin and those with Transjordanian roots. The continued expansion of Jewish settlements in the West Bank reignited fears that Israel might try to transplant Jordan with an alternative Palestinian homeland, a prospect that was a source of considerable concern to Transjordanian nationalists who sought to limit the size and political influence of Jordan's existing Palestinian population. Intermittent hostility between the two factions within Jordan during previous decades became more pronounced following the return to power of Netanyahu, who had supported the old Likud slogan 'Jordan is Palestine'.

In May 2010 Jordan's National Committee of Military Veterans, which traditionally comprised loyal Transjordanian nationalists, published a petition criticizing the monarchy and the Palestinian population in the kingdom. The 60 former army officers lambasted King Abdullah's economic liberalization programme, which had in many cases benefited the (predominantly Palestinian) Jordanian business class, and condemned the appointment of Palestinians to key government posts, implying the involvement of Queen Rania in this process. The petition went on to demand the disenfranchisement of Jordan's Palestinians; the implementation of genuine political reform and anti-corruption measures; a strengthening of the military against Israel; and a formalization within the Constitution of the 1988 disengagement from the West Bank, in order to prevent Israel from reviving a 'Jordanian option' to the Palestinian question.

Suggestions that the Government was discreetly trying to appease Transjordanian nationalists were fuelled in February 2010 when Human Rights Watch published a report in which it claimed that over 2,700 Jordanians of Palestinian origin had had their citizenship removed between 2004 and 2008. Many of these Palestinians had returned to Jordan from Kuwait in 1991 after the 1988 disengagement, a loophole that enabled officials to strip them of their citizenship, rendering them unable to gain employment, buy property or vote. Government officials described this as an 'adjustment to circumstances' intended to help Palestinians preserve their identity in the face of Israeli plans to empty the West Bank; however, Human Rights Watch branded the process 'patently unfair' and 'a violation of human rights'.

RELATIONS WITH THE OBAMA ADMINISTRATION

In April 2009 King Abdullah became the first Arab leader to visit US President Barack Obama in Washington, DC, following the latter's inauguration in January of that year. Obama's election had kindled considerable hope that the new US Administration would adopt a more even-handed approach to the Middle East peace process than that engendered by the outgoing Bush Administration. However, initial hopes that Obama could break the diplomatic deadlock faded before long. Although Abdullah welcomed Obama's address to the Muslim world in Cairo in June, in which the US President pledged 'to seek a new beginning between the USA and Muslims' in order to achieve a relationship 'based upon mutual interest and mutual respect', the US Administration proved unable to pressure Netanyahu into halting settlement expansion and fully engaging with the Palestinians.

Relations with the USA were strained in January 2010 after a Jordanian man killed seven CIA agents in a suicide bomb attack in Afghanistan. It subsequently transpired that Humam Khalil Abu Mulal al-Balawi had been recruited by the Jordanian intelligence services to inform on al-Qa'ida in Afghanistan but had proved to be a double agent. Although the incident was a source of severe embarrassment to Jordan, as well as prompting many questions in the USA about the country's close relationship with the Jordanian intelligence services, it did not appear to have permanently damaged bilateral relations. In April of that year Abdullah again met with President Obama, at the Nuclear Security Summit in Washington, DC, during which they discussed the Middle East peace process, the US-led military campaign in Afghanistan and the need to pressure Iran to uphold its international obligations with regard to its development of nuclear technology.

ISRAELI-PALESTINIAN TALKS COLLAPSE

King Abdullah's support for President Obama's peace efforts was rewarded in September 2010, when he was invited to Washington, DC, alongside Egyptian President Hosni Mubarak, to take part in the US-brokered direct peace talks between Israeli Prime Minister Binyamin Netanyahu and Palestinian President Mahmud Abbas. Abdullah had been a leading advocate of such direct talks, and had reportedly played a role in persuading the Palestinians to take part. The Jordanian public, however, was sceptical, and the King's efforts received little support. The IAF, which opposed the 1994 Jordan-Israel peace treaty, led opposition to the talks and organized demonstrations against them. During several rounds of negotiations, first in Washington, DC, and then in the Egyptian resort of Sharm el-Sheikh, basic principles were agreed, but little detail was delivered. On 26 September 2010 a 10-month moratorium on Israeli settlement construction in the West Bank expired. Abbas had pledged to withdraw from the talks if the Israelis did not extend the settlement freeze. US diplomats failed in their efforts to persuade Netanyahu to extend the moratorium, even by a few months, despite offering a generous US $3,000m. military aid package, and Abbas declared a halt to the talks, a move backed by the Arab League. In spite of subsequent efforts to revive the freeze, and therefore the talks, Obama and his Secretary of State, Hillary Clinton, were unable to pressure the Israelis into action.

THE 2010 PARLIAMENTARY ELECTIONS

On 9 November 2010 legislative elections were held, one year after King Abdullah had controversially dismissed the previous parliament. Although a new electoral law had been announced in May, it retained the unpopular 'one person, one vote' system, which favoured tribal candidates loyal to the regime over organized parties, and few expected the new parliament to vary greatly from the old. On election day itself there were a few incidents of violence, notably in Jerash and Kerak, but overall voting proceeded smoothly. For the first time, international monitors were invited to observe the polls, with representatives from the EU and the USA reporting that they were satisfied with the fairness of the process. Some 53% of eligible Jordanians turned out to vote, a 6% decrease compared with the 2007 polls, with particularly poor showings in Amman (34%) and Zarqa (36%).

One reason for the low level of participation, especially in urban areas, was the refusal by the IAF to take part, having urged its supporters to boycott the elections. In August 2010, shortly after the election of Hamza Mansour as IAF General Secretary and the tilt towards hardliners in the party, the decision had been made to oppose the November elections. However, the IAF had suggested that it might reconsider if the Government agreed to initiate a process of political reform, including reviewing the electoral law yet again and appointing an independent body to conduct the elections. When these offers were largely ignored, Mansour had reiterated the IAF's past claims that the 2007 elections had been fraudulent and reasserted the group's decision to boycott the upcoming ballot. Consequently, as well as reducing the overall turn-out, particularly in the urban areas from which the IAF drew its core support, the boycott ensured that the November 2010 polls returned no members of the main opposition party to parliament. Seven Islamists defied the boycott and stood as independent candidates, but only one, Ahmad Qudah, won a seat.

The results, when they were announced, produced few surprises. With the IAF not participating, the vast majority of elected deputies were independents from loyalist tribal backgrounds. Although 70% of the representatives were new to parliament, they continued the traditional pattern of previous, uncritical legislatures. One of the few breakthroughs was the election of a female deputy, Reem Badran, daughter of former Prime Minister Mudar Badran. While 12 seats in the House of Representatives were reserved for women by law, Badran was the first woman to win a parliamentary seat in open competition with male candidates. In accordance with custom, Prime Minister Rifai offered his resignation after the election, only to be reappointed soon afterwards as the head of a Cabinet that retained 19 members of the previous Government. In December 2010 Rifai won a record vote of confidence from members of parliament, with 111 out of 119 deputies voting in his favour.

JORDAN AND THE 'ARAB SPRING'

Jordanian anti-Government unrest took a markedly different shape and tone to that in North Africa, being more modest in terms of size and the protesters' demands. While the several million demonstrators who gathered in Cairo's Tahrir Square in January and February 2011 demanded the resignation of President Mubarak, Jordanian protesters, who rarely congregated in numbers above 10,000, levelled their criticism at the Government rather than King Abdullah. The protests were initially small and divided. Inspired by events in Tunisia, a coalition of leftist political groups and the Professional Associations organized a modest rally on 14 January. The demonstration was opposed by the IAF, which arranged its own anti-Government protests two days later. These divisions were discarded a week later as momentum grew, and 5,000 people attended a protest in central Amman on 21 January, this time endorsed by the IAF. In contrast to Egypt, where the security forces clashed violently with protesters, these early demonstrations were characterized by their peaceful, non-violent nature, and the police earned praise for their hands-off approach. On the following Friday (28 January), which emerged as the main day of protest each week, unrest spread beyond Amman, with 3,500 demonstrators gathering in the capital and a further 2,500 in six other cities. Protesters demanded the resignation of the unpopular Prime Minister, Samir Rifai, and urged the Government to take action against rising unemployment and prices.

Complicating matters for the King and his Government was the composition of the protests. Alongside the usual opposition forces, notably the IAF, leftist groups and the Professional Associations, were some traditionally loyal Transjordanians, including members of the National Committee of Military Veterans. Tensions were further escalated when 36 members of leading Transjordanian tribes, core supporters of the Hashemite monarchy, sent King Abdullah a letter in February 2011 alleging that his ethnically Palestinian wife, Queen Rania, was interfering in politics and using her position to enrich her family and place Palestinians in influential positions. Although another petition signed by 3,000 tribal leaders was later sent, denouncing the letter and pledging loyalty to the monarchy, King Abdullah's regime faced criticism on two fronts: from the pro-democracy protesters, many of whom were of Palestinian origin, and from his traditional supporters among the Transjordanians.

Initially, the Government sought to placate protesters with economic measures. Two economic packages were announced in January 2011 that reduced tax on petrol, increased subsidies on gas and some food, and raised public sector salaries. This meant abandoning earlier attempts to reduce the country's fiscal deficit, and subsequently led to a revision of the 2011 budget, making Jordan even more reliant on foreign grants. However, these measures did little to reduce the protests. The fate of both the Tunisian and Egyptian Presidents prompted King Abdullah to act fast to neutralize any threat to his regime. On 1 February he dismissed Samir Rifai and appointed a new Government, led by Marouf al-Bakhit, Prime Minister in 2005–07. Al-Bakhit's appointment was immediately criticized by the IAF, citing the corruption and the allegedly fraudulent elections that took place under his previous premiership. Al-Bakhit had been previously appointed as Prime Minister during the aftermath of the 2005 Amman bombings and, as a former head of national security, was seen by Abdullah as a premier able to manage a crisis. Moreover, his appointment appeased the Transjordanian opposition, which preferred al-Bakhit's Transjordanian origins, being a member of the loyalist al-Abbadi tribe, to Rifai's Palestinian background. (The National Committee of Military Veterans, for example, immediately suspended its opposition activities after al-Bakhit's appointment.)

In appointing a new Prime Minister, King Abdullah also appeared to be responding to popular pro-democracy demands, charging al-Bakhit with initiating a real 'political reform process'. The King reiterated his commitment to reform during various public meetings and speeches, and highlighted his, admittedly lacklustre, past attempts to institute political changes, such as the 2005 National Agenda and the 2007 Political Parties Law. In March 2011 he established a 'National Dialogue Committee' under the leadership of the Senate Speaker and former Prime Minister, Taher al-Masri, to recommend swift reform measures. In particular, he targeted the unpopular 'one person, one vote' electoral law for amendment, which had only been revised in 2010. However, the leftist opposition and the IAF criticized the National Dialogue Committee for its limited scope and its pro-regime composition, and opposed al-Bakhit's role as the head of a reforming Government, given his poor credentials in this regard. They appealed instead for a transfer of some of the King's powers to the National Assembly, in accordance with the original 1952 Constitution, before King Hussein had amended it.

THE NEW GOVERNMENT STRUGGLES

Despite the appointment of a new Government and the promise of political reform, the protesters remained dissatisfied.

Throughout February and March 2011 protests continued, demanding a faster pace of reform from the new Government. On 18 February these demonstrations turned violent for the first time when pro-regime supporters attacked a peaceful protest, perhaps inspired by similar events in Egypt, where pro-Mubarak gangs had beaten demonstrators. No deaths were caused and the Government was quick to denounce the violence, opening an inquiry into the event. The violence did little to stem the protests, and the following demonstration on 25 February attracted 10,000 people to the centre of Amman, the largest so far. The pattern of regular Friday protests continued throughout early 2011, although the regime rarely looked seriously threatened, as the number of protesters fluctuated and never reached the volumes seen in Tunisia or Egypt.

On 24 March 2011 the first protest-related death was reported. A youth-led reform group, labelling itself 'the Youth of March 24', organized a sit-in at the Interior Ministry Circle in Amman, which was then attacked by pro-regime groups. The security forces intervened, although there were suggestions that they sided with the pro-regime supporters and used violence against members of March 24; 62 civilians and 58 police officers were reportedly injured, and Khairi Saad Jamil later died from his wounds. More violence followed on 15 April, when a group of Salafist Islamist extremists took to the streets of Zarqa. The Salafists, who had not been involved in the previous anti-Government protests and were quite separate from the mainstream Islamists, the IAF, demanded the release of their imprisoned relatives. After their demonstration, several pro-regime supporters attacked the Salafists, leading the security forces to intervene once again. In the violence that followed, the security forces alleged that armed Salafists had attacked and injured 80 police officers.

Although such incidents remained rare, they increased the pressure on the al-Bakhit Government to accelerate reforms. Yet, the new administration was already mired in controversy. The climate of increased political openness resulting from the unrest precipitated criticism of the Government, and allegations of corruption were made against several cabinet ministers. In May 2011 Hussein Mjalli, the Minister of Justice, and Yassin Husban, the Minister of Health, both resigned after a public outcry over the release from gaol of a corrupt businessman, Khalid Shahin, who had been permitted by the two ministries to travel abroad for medical treatment. Shortly afterwards, Prime Minister al-Bakhit was named in a corruption case involving the award of a casino licence during his previous term as premier. Although al-Bakhit was subsequently exonerated, with blame placed instead on the former Minister of Tourism and Antiquities, who was alleged to have negotiated the deal without full cabinet approval, the case increased public anger against the Prime Minister, who, many alleged, had been treated too favourably by the inquiry. Compounding matters for the embattled Government, the Minister of State for Media Affairs and Communications, Taher Odwan, resigned in June in protest against new press and publications, anti-corruption, and penal laws, which he claimed would limit freedom of expression.

AL-BAKHIT FAILS TO DELIVER ON REFORM

In July 2011 al-Bakhit reorganized his Cabinet in an attempt to restore public confidence in his administration. Notably, the Minister of the Interior, Saad Hayel Srour, who was widely disliked for his willingness to use force against protesters, as well as for his role in the Shahin corruption case, was replaced by Mazen al-Saket. However, those expecting new, reformist appointments were disappointed. The new Minister of State for Media Affairs and Communications, Abdullah Abu Rumman, was a former official media censor and was thus considered unlikely to take a liberal stance regarding freedom of speech. Meanwhile, in June the National Dialogue Committee released its long-awaited recommendations on reforming the electoral law. However, the modest amendments proposed prompted increased criticism of al-Bakhit's Government. Rather than replacing the unpopular 'one person, one vote' system, the Committee recommended keeping it in place at governorate level for 115 parliamentary seats, but introducing an additional 15 seats that would be contested at national level. The IAF, which had raised its profile and overcome previous divisions by playing a leading role in the emerging opposition movement, described the recommendations as 'an insult'.

Reformers were further frustrated in August 2011 when the Royal Committee on Constitutional Review (RCCR) presented its recommendations. Jordan's Constitution, although nominally democratic, had been repeatedly altered by King Hussein to strengthen the position of the monarch at the expense of the elected parliament. Although the 42 amendments recommended by the RCCR made an attempt to empower parliament, as demanded by the opposition, most were disappointed by the limited scope and ambition of the proposals. Concessions included the end of military trials for civilians, the outlawing of torture, greater accountability for ministers and a guarantee of independence for the judiciary. However, significant power remained in the hands of the monarch. Although the duration of time in which the King was permitted to rule without a parliament was reduced from two years to four months, the legislature was denied the right to appoint the Prime Minister (a key opposition demand), with that power being retained by the King. Despite opposition complaints that the creation of the RCCR had been just another strategy to avoid genuine reform, the recommendations were approved by parliament with some amendments. These included further curbs on the power of the Prime Minister and the Cabinet, but little was done to alter the power balance between parliament and the crown. With the House of Representatives still composed of mostly loyalist deputies elected by the unsatisfactory 2010 elections and with the Senate appointed by the King, the approval of the modest amendments proposed by the RCCR—itself an appointed body dominated by regime loyalists—was not surprising.

Opposition to al-Bakhit's Government grew during mid-2011, with various pro-reform public demonstrations taking place. Among the most significant was a sit-in protest held in central Amman in July that deteriorated into violence. According to claims by the Center for Defending Freedom of Journalists, which had helped to organize the protests, the security forces and regime loyalists had deliberately targeted peaceful demonstrators. Charges of corruption had damaged al-Bakhit's credibility, and his popularity declined further in September when he forced the Governor of the Central Bank of Jordan, Faris Sharaf, to resign. Sharaf had been critical of al-Bakhit's loose spending policies, arguing that they would hamper much-needed economic growth. In response, Al-Bakhit demanded Sharaf's resignation, and, when he refused to stand down, the Prime Minister, showing an authoritarian side, ordered the security forces to surround the Central Bank until the Governor capitulated. Although Sharaf was eventually succeeded by his deputy, the ramifications for al-Bakhit were greater than he had anticipated. The relative independence of the Central Bank from political interference had long been one of Jordan's attractions to foreign investors, and many politicians criticized the Prime Minister for compromising that image. Among the most vocal was Sharaf's mother, Leila, a well-respected political figure in her own right, who resigned from the Senate in protest, denouncing the Government as 'corrupt'.

The Prime Minister's position eventually became untenable when he lost the support of a large number of parliamentary deputies in October 2011. While concerns had been raised regarding his handling of the Faris Sharaf affair, as well as a proposed new anti-corruption law that many interpreted as a thinly veiled attempt to silence the press, it was al-Bakhit's performance on municipal electoral reform that eventually prompted the parliamentarians to withdraw their support. In that month, following demonstrations against al-Bakhit's attempts to restructure municipal boundaries in preparation for new local elections, 70 deputies wrote a letter to the Royal Court criticizing the Prime Minister's actions. King Abdullah was unusually swift to acquiesce to public and parliamentary opinion, replacing al-Bakhit as Prime Minister with the former Chief of the Royal Court, Awn Khasawneh, in late October.

ECONOMY UNDERMINED BY REGIONAL AND LOCAL UNREST

The invitation to join the Cooperation Council for the Arab States of the Gulf (GCC) was particularly welcomed by Jordan given the economic difficulties that the 'Arab spring' unrest had caused, including a general decline in tourism and foreign investment across the region. GCC membership, if granted, was expected to open new markets for Jordanian goods and provide Jordanian workers with unlimited access to the Gulf, and should also lead to a much-needed increase in aid and grants from the wealthier member states. While Jordan's economy had suffered far less than those states undergoing major political change such as Egypt or Syria, real GDP growth in 2011 was disappointing. Furthermore, trade with Syria, a key commercial partner, seriously declined due to the political crisis in that country, leading to a further decrease in economic activity in Jordan. Matters were made worse in November when the international ratings agency Standard & Poor's downgraded Jordan's credit rating, citing the country's negative economic and political outlook, a move that discouraged foreign investment.

With unemployment rising owing to the weak economy, potentially swelling the numbers of opposition protesters on the streets, Jordan's leaders increased spending in an effort to retain support. In July 2011 King Abdullah launched a US $210m. fund to create jobs and improve services, and in August announced that all civil service and military employees would receive a JD 100 payment to help with costs during the Muslim holy month of Ramadan. Yet, with public finances under strain owing to the sluggish economy, these budget increases made Jordan ever more reliant on aid from abroad. Fortunately, the unrest elsewhere in the region incentivized both the USA and Saudi Arabia to provide additional support to the Jordanian regime. Saudi Arabia granted Jordan $400m. in June, while USAID agreed in September to provide $359m. for various projects. By the end of the year Jordan had been promised over $1,440m. in grants, more than twice the amount received during a typical year, reflecting the nervousness of its international allies after the turmoil of the 'Arab spring'.

THE SHORT-LIVED PREMIERSHIP OF AWN KHASAWNEH

On 24 October 2011 King Abdullah appointed Awn Khasawneh as Prime Minister, charging him with reviving the reform process, which had stalled under al-Bakhit. Khasawneh, who had served as a legal adviser during the 1994 peace treaty negotiations with Israel and as a judge at the International Court of Justice in The Hague, Netherlands, was regarded by many in the political establishment as an outsider, untainted by the corruption scandals that had undermined al-Bakhit's term in office. He also enjoyed a reputation for honesty and a good relationship with the opposition IAF, and he impressed many on assuming office by stating that, if political reform was to be accomplished, many of the measures introduced by his predecessor would need to be revisited. The new Cabinet was ostensibly selected to revive public confidence in King Abdullah's reform process, with several new appointments and only four ministers from the previous administration retaining their portfolios. One of the new premier's first actions was to postpone the December municipal elections, which had ultimately led to al-Bakhit's dismissal, stating that the issue of municipal borders needed to be reconsidered before elections could take place. A new municipalities law was promised, with elections to be held within six months of its approval. Khasawneh's fresh approach swiftly earned him the nickname 'The Reformer' in segments of the Jordanian press.

However, the new Prime Minister failed in a bid to co-opt the largest opposition group, the IAF, into his new Government. On assuming office, Khasawneh adopted a conciliatory tone towards Jordan's Islamists, stating in the US magazine *Newsweek* that he felt that the Muslim Brotherhood had been 'unfairly demonized' in the past. However, while this goodwill ensured that IAF leader Hamza Mansour was more receptive to Khasawneh than he had been to al-Bakhit, an invitation to join the new Cabinet was still refused. Mansour demanded further democratic constitutional reforms as a precondition to the IAF joining any government. The general air of cordiality between the opposition and the new Government was tested in December 2011 when regime loyalists clashed with Islamist demonstrators in the northern town of Mafraq. The IAF's local headquarters were set alight, prompting Mansour strongly to criticize the police.

Khasawneh's attempts to satisfy both the IAF and the conservative reformist instincts of parliament and the Royal Court were hindered in March 2012 when his Cabinet submitted a much-anticipated new electoral law. The legislation largely reflected the recommendations of the National Dialogue Committee from June 2011, increasing the number of parliamentary seats to 138, three of which would be reserved for women and 15 determined by proportional representation. The remaining 120 seats would be elected on a constituency basis. There would be 45 constituencies, and each voter would receive two votes locally, as well as a third vote to determine which parties would be allocated the 15 extra seats. However, the law stipulated that no one party could win more than five of the 15 additional seats. Moreover, the majority of seats were still to be voted on locally, which tended to favour loyalist candidates rather than the national opposition parties. Not surprisingly, the IAF condemned the new law, denouncing it as only a slightly amended version of the existing 'one person, one vote' system that for years had returned loyal local deputies at the expense of the IAF.

King Abdullah's efforts to present Jordan as a beacon of steady reform amid the regional chaos brought about by the 'Arab spring' were seriously undermined on 26 April 2012 when, while on a trip to Turkey, Khasawneh unexpectedly resigned as Prime Minister. Reports suggested that he had become increasingly frustrated with trying to balance the demands of the opposition with those of the conservative elements of parliament. The debates over the electoral law proved to be the decisive factor, when parliamentarians denounced the very modest amendments to the electoral system as promoting Islamism. Some members even proposed a bill that would ban any party with a religious basis, a move clearly aimed at the IAF. Other reports claimed that Khasawneh was frustrated with the King, who had used the Prime Minister as a buffer to deflect any criticism away from himself. The slow progress of the reforms was due more to the conservative nature of Abdullah's loyalists in parliament than to reluctance on behalf of Khasawneh, yet the King publicly expressed his disappointment in the premier for the delays. Abdullah selected Fayez al-Tarawneh, who had previously held the post during 1998–99, as the new Prime Minister. Al-Tarawneh was regarded as an establishment figure, and, consequently, was not expected to be able to win the support of the IAF or oversee a viable reform process.

IMPROVED RELATIONS WITH HAMAS

One of Khasawneh's achievements in office was the successful rapprochement with Hamas, which had been expelled from Jordan in 1999. At that time, Jordan had recently made peace with Israel, which dismissed Hamas as a terrorist group and an obstacle to the resolution of the Israeli–Palestinian conflict, prompting the Hamas leadership led by Khalid Meshaal to seek refuge in Syria. However, with the Syrian regime fighting an uprising partly led by Sunni Islamists politically closer to Hamas than the secularist, Baathist, Alawi-dominated Government in Damascus, Meshaal found himself looking for a new base of operations by late 2011. Moreover, with the Muslim Brotherhood triumphing in elections in Egypt and the Islamist al-Nahdah party assuming power in post-revolution Tunisia, the reality that Islamist groups such as Hamas would no longer be regional pariahs was recognized by the Jordanian Government. As such, it was arranged for Meshaal to make his first visit to Amman in 12 years during November. Although this was subsequently cancelled, Meshaal did eventually travel to Jordan to meet King Abdullah in January 2012, alongside Qatar's heir apparent, Sheikh Tamim bin Hamad Al Thani. According to media reports, Qatar was keen to sponsor Hamas's attempts to reinvent itself as a peaceful Islamist party and had offered Jordan up to US $1,000m. a year and free supplies of gas in return for hosting the organization. At mid-2013 the future of the Hamas leadership, which had completely withdrawn from Damascus, remained unclear. However, Jordan would be keen to continue what it regarded as its traditional role of mediating between Israel and the Palestinians were any talks to resume, while balancing the desires of its large Palestinian population, its influential East Bank Jordanian population and its international allies, upon whom it was increasingly reliant for economic survival.

THE IMPACT OF THE SYRIAN CIVIL WAR

Syria's descent into civil war from 2011 had major ramifications in Jordan. The Syrian uprising, instigated by an initially peaceful movement protesting against the authoritarian regime of President Bashar al-Assad, soon became a bloody, and often sectarian, civil war. By mid-2013 more than 100,000 people were reported to have been killed, while over 4m. people had been displaced, of whom 1.7m had fled abroad. The uprising began in the southern Syrian city of Dar'a, close to the Jordanian border, the inhabitants of which shared tribal links, family ties and regular trade with northern Jordan, particularly with the town of Ramtha. Consequently, the first refugees to flee the Dar'a fighting had reason to head to Jordan. As the violence intensified, the number of registered refugees in Jordan increased, swelling from a relatively modest 25,000 in early 2012 to nearly 500,000 by mid-2013. The Jordanian Government claimed that the actual total was even higher, given that many middle-class Syrians chose to live in Amman rather than register with border officials.

While refugees initially lived with relatives or were housed by local charities, the sudden upsurge in numbers in mid-2012 prompted the Jordanian Government to construct a purpose-built refugee camp, with space for 60,000 residents, in Zaatari near Mafraq in July. Within months it had exceeded its capacity, and by mid-2013 it was home to an estimated 140,000 residents—making it Jordan's fourth-largest city. Two more camps were subsequently constructed near Zarqa, but both the Jordanian authorities and the various international charities administering the camps, led by UNHCR, admitted to being overwhelmed. Some international aid was provided, including US $200m. from the USA, but several Gulf states were criticized for failing to deliver large sums that they had pledged at a high-profile donor conference in Kuwait in January 2013. King Abdullah estimated that the refugees cost the Jordanian Government $550m. annually. Perhaps unsurprisingly, the cramped conditions, poor sanitation and lack of medical resources led to outbreaks of typhoid and hepatitis in the camps, as well as prompting some low-level rioting in April 2013.

The Syrian conflict had a severe impact on the Jordanian economy. The inflow of refugees stretched public health and education services, strained already-scarce water and electricity resources, pushed up house prices and contributed to major inflationary pressures. Moreover, the refugees presented a pool of cheap labour, thus depriving a significant number of Jordanian workers of income. This prompted growing levels of resentment among the traditionally sympathetic Jordanian population, with opinion polls suggesting that 65% favoured closing Jordan's borders to new arrivals while 80% thought that refugees should be confined to camps. Trade was also negatively impacted. Although Jordan had initially asked for an exception to Arab League economic sanctions on Syria, the intensification in violence in the latter country eventually deterred Jordanian truck drivers from driving through Syrian territory in any case, severing Jordan's agricultural traders from key markets in Syria, Lebanon and Turkey.

The Syrian conflict also presented a challenge to Jordan's leaders on a political level. The IAF backed Syria's opposition, arranging demonstrations outside the Syrian embassy and appealing to the Jordanian Government to withdraw its ambassador from Damascus. Although this move was resisted by King Abdullah, in contrast to the approach adopted by most Western and Arab nations, he did urge President Assad to step down in November 2011, becoming the first Arab leader to do so. At first, the King attempted to balance the different challenges that the Syria crisis posed. On the one hand, a large segment of his population and his major international allies (the USA, and the Gulf monarchies) wanted to see Assad removed from power. However, at the same time, a vocal minority within Jordan continued to support the Syrian regime, and there were clashes between pro- and anti-Assad demonstrators in Amman in 2011.

Since the beginning of the uprising in Syria, the Jordanian leadership had feared that it would descend into a protracted civil war, which had indeed happened by mid-2013. One concern was that the *jihadist* groups among the anti-Assad militant forces might turn their attention to Jordan, either directly or via Jordanian allies. This fear seemed vindicated in October 2012 when a group of 11 Jordanians with alleged links to al-Qa'ida in Iraq were arrested by Jordan's GID for plotting major terror attacks in Jordan using weapons acquired in Syria. Another fear was that Jordan would be directly dragged into the fighting, with the national army on several occasions drawn into skirmishes with Syrian troops as it protected fleeing refugees. Though reluctant to allow Syrian rebels to use its territory to launch attacks, it was reported in April 2013 that the Jordanian Government was allowing Saudi Arabia to supply weapons to its rebel allies from Jordan, in exchange for much-needed aid to the value of US $1,200m. The CIA was also reported to be training some rebels in Jordanian territory, and 200 US troops were also dispatched to Jordan to boost security. In June it was announced that US *Patriot* missile launchers and F-16 fighter aircraft were to be deployed to Jordan to counter the threat posed to the kingdom by the Syrian conflict. Assad had previously vowed, in April, that Jordan would be consumed by 'fire' for supporting his opponents.

ECONOMIC PROBLEMS CONTINUE

In the face of regional unrest, Jordan's economy continued to stutter, exacerbating political and social unrest. Despite more optimistic predictions, GDP grew by only 2.7% in 2012, representing only a marginal increase from the 2.6% growth recorded in 2011 and still falling far short of the levels needed to provide sufficient jobs for Jordan's young and growing population. While the IMF agreed to lend a record US $2,000m. in August 2012, this did little to tackle Jordan's expanding deficit. In November, in accordance with IMF requirements, fuel subsidies were removed. This had been attempted before, in 2008, but they had been reintroduced in 2011 to stave off potential unrest in the wake of the 'Arab spring'. Despite the guarantee to poorer families of compensatory cash payments, the decision prompted widespread protests and even led to a violent confrontation between legislators in parliament in March 2013. Although the removal of fuel subsidies appeased the IMF, Jordan entered 2013 expecting more social unrest and diminished economic activity as a result of the measure. The disbursement, in February 2013, by Saudi Arabia of $200m.-worth of aid for development projects in Jordan (following the delivery, in November 2012, of $125m.-worth of Saudi aid) did little to alleviate such concerns.

THE 2013 PARLIAMENTARY ELECTIONS

In an attempt to head off growing opposition and to emphasize his commitment to the faltering reform process, King Abdullah dissolved parliament on 5 October 2012 and called a general election, two years earlier than required. As is constitutionally demanded, Fayez Tarawneh tendered the resignation of his Government in advance of the poll. The King appointed Abdullah Ensour, widely seen as more independent and reformist than Tarawneh, as the new premier. However, Ensour faced similar problems to those encountered by fellow reformer Awn Kasawneh a few months previously. The final, royally approved, version of the new electoral law failed to satisfy large swathes of the opposition, who continued to regard it as a mere revision of the much-despised 'one person, one vote' system. Although the final version of the legislation provided for a quota of 15 parliamentary seats to be reserved for women and 27 seats to be chosen through party lists, the remaining 108 seats were still to be decided in a first-past-the-post local election in gerrymandered constituency boundaries heavily favouring independents who supported the King. Acting upon previous threats, the IAF announced that it was to boycott the poll and urged its supporters to do likewise; despite various attempts, Ensour and the King were unable to dissuade the IAF from pursuing this course of action.

The general election eventually took place on 23 January 2013, having been delayed in an attempt to maximize voter registration. Without the participation of the largest opposition grouping, the credibility of the elections was compromised and serious doubt was cast over the validity of the reform process. None the less, the turn-out of 56% prompted the Palace to claim that the majority of Jordanians had ignored the IAF's call to boycott the poll. However, the opposition retorted that such a turn-out, with only 2.28m. voters having registered, was by no means a strong endorsement. One institution to benefit from the process was the newly created Independent Election Commission (IEC), which won widespread praise for its transparent and efficient management of the poll. EU observers declared that, despite some reports of vote-buying incidents, there were no reports of 'intimidation or harassment of voters'.

Aided by the new electoral law, independents and tribal representatives loyal to King Abdullah were reported to have secured around three-quarters of the total number of votes. Although a newly created 'moderate' Islamist grouping, the Islamic Centrist Party (ICP), emerged with the highest number of seats (16 in total—13 district and three party-list seats), it failed to form a government as it hoped, with its candidate for the position of Speaker of the House of Representatives, Muhammad al-Haj, defeated by the King's candidate, Saad Hayel Srour, by 80 votes to 62. Following the publication of the election results, on 9 March 2013 the King invited Ensour to form a new government. The expectation was that, as promised as part of Abdullah's reform agenda, the new Government would have a far closer relationship with parliament than previous administrations had done. However, despite a lengthy consultation process with parliament, Ensour's 19-member Cabinet, which was inaugurated on 30 March, did not include a single parliamentarian. Contrary to the Palace's claims of pursuing a reform agenda, the 2013 elections and the Cabinet formed in its aftermath were of a very similar nature to those formed long before the 'Arab spring'.

INCREASING OPPOSITION AND CIVIL UNREST

Both before and after the 2013 general election opposition to King Abdullah's rule steadily increased, sometimes spilling over into violence. The IAF and other opponents of the Government—known as 'Hirak'—were rarely able to attract the kind of mass support that had destabilized the respective regimes in Egypt and Syria. One large IAF rally in Amman in September 2012 was expected to be attended by some 50,000 demonstrators, yet barely attracted 15,000 in the end. On the other hand, the opposition forces remained persistent and consistent, engendering fears of prolonged destabilization if not regime change. Exacerbating matters were the Palace's own authoritarian tendencies. Along with the failure to offer an empowered parliament in the 2013 elections, there has been a steady increase in censorship. Particularly controversial was a new press law introduced in September 2012 that required all online media to register with local authorities. This surprised many as Jordan was reputed to have the most-free internet access in the Arab world and King Abdullah himself often claimed that the internet would be the key to Jordan's future economic prosperity. However, many within the opposition argued that the new law was intended to enforce the same kind of restrictions on online news media as seen in Jordan's press, as a means of curbing their activity.

A sign of the increased pressure faced by the Palace was an increase in violence among tribal youth in southern Jordan during the first half of 2013. Jordan's East Bank tribes have traditionally been solid supporters of the Hashemite monarchy, although some had surprisingly been prominent in the early 'Arab spring'-inspired demonstrations of 2011. However, the new generation of East Bankers increasingly shared the frustrations of their fellow youth elsewhere in Jordan, at the lack of job opportunities and the inability of their elders to challenge the Government on the matter. Tensions spilled over into violence on several university campuses in tribally dominated regions in mid-2013. In April four people were killed during clashes at Al-Hussein Bin Talal University in Ma'an and a further death was reported following riots at Mutah University in Kerak. Sporadic violence continued, with riots erupting in Ma'an at the beginning of June in response to allegations of police brutality, and a further fatality reported amid fresh clashes at Mutah University in July, prompting the indefinite suspension of classes at the University. While parliamentarians sought to focus on the issue of campus security, many commentators highlighted the fact that much of the violence was the result of clashes between pro- and anti-Government tribe members. With such tensions exacerbating ongoing economic concerns, at mid-2013 King Abdullah was facing the prospect of losing key elements of his traditional support base.

Economy

Revised for this edition by RICHARD GERMAN and ELIZABETH TAYLOR

INTRODUCTION

Disrupted by wars between the Arab states and Israel from 1948, Jordan's vulnerable economy was again adversely affected by the Gulf crisis and hostilities of 1990–91. However, this dislocation of established patterns of trade, aid and labour migration failed to produce the predicted sustained downturn, and a recovery was under way by 1992. Jordanian economic planning then had to take account of the implications of the peace agreement between Israel and the Palestine Liberation Organization (PLO) reached in September 1993 and the Jordan-Israel treaty of October 1994 (although by 1998 it was widely acknowledged that Jordan was deriving only limited economic benefit from the peace dividend).

In the 1948–49 Arab–Israeli War, Jordan acquired some 5,600 sq km of new territory, and the country's population increased more than threefold. Before the war the population was perhaps 400,000. Those living on the West Bank of the Jordan river in the territory acquired in 1948 numbered well over 800,000. This territory was occupied by Israel in 1967, and perhaps 350,000 of the inhabitants fled to non-occupied Jordan. Jordan's 1979 census gave a total population for the East Bank of 2.1m., which implied an annual growth rate between 1961 and 1979 of 4.8% (with natural increase accounting for 3.8% and immigration for 1.0%). The population was officially estimated to have risen to 2.8m. by the end of 1986, to 4.1m. by 1994, to 5.1m. by 2004 and to 6.4m. by the end of 2012. The absorption of the refugees of 1948 and of 1967 caused problems that were accentuated by ethnic, cultural and religious differences. Jordanians before 1948 were mainly Bedouin and mostly engaged in pastoral, and even nomadic, activities. They therefore had little in common with the Palestinians, many of whom established themselves in Jordan as traders and professionals. At January 2013 there were 2,034,641 Palestinian refugees registered with the UN Relief and Works Agency for Palestine Refugees in the Near East (UNRWA) in Jordan.

The occupation of the West Bank by Israel in 1967 resulted in the loss not only of productive agricultural land, but also of an important element of Jordan's tourism industry and consequent foreign exchange earnings. Some of the more immediate problems caused by the war were met by aid from Arab countries, but the country's long-term economic future obviously depended on the evolution of the Arab–Israeli dispute and of regional relations generally. Nevertheless, Jordan enjoyed sustained economic growth from the mid-1970s into the early 1980s: gross domestic product (GDP) expanded, in real terms, at an average annual rate of more than 8%. The growth rate slowed markedly, however, to 5.6% in 1982, 2.5% in 1983 and 0.8% in 1984. In 1981 Jordan recorded its first current account deficit for five years, and it continued to record deficits in 1982–85. These shortfalls, combined with Jordan's customary trade deficit (generally in excess of US $2,000m. per year during the 1980s), obliged the Government to obtain new foreign development loans, which, in turn, assisted a partial recovery of GDP growth to 2.7% in 1985, 2.4% in 1986 and 1.9% in 1987. The current account balance, having recorded a small surplus in 1986, again showed deficits in 1987 and 1988, respectively. The Government agreed a five-year structural adjustment programme with the IMF, aiming, by 1993, to bring inflation down, reduce the budget deficit and eliminate the current account deficit.

This relatively positive economic scenario was then undermined by the onset of the 1990–91 Gulf crisis. At the time of Iraq's occupation of Kuwait, in August 1990, Iraq was Jordan's principal trading partner, taking at least 23% of Jordan's exports and supplying more than 80% of its petroleum. Adherence to the UN sanctions against Iraq, imposed by Security Council Resolution 661, therefore threatened the whole basis of Jordan's economy, forcing the Government to find alternative suppliers and also to introduce petrol rationing (see Mining and Minerals). Meanwhile, remittances from Jordanians working in the Gulf states dwindled as many workers returned to Jordan, raising the level of unemployment and putting an additional strain on health and education budgets.

Following a new agreement with the IMF in October 1991 (envisaging a seven-year economic reform programme) and the provision of external emergency aid, Jordan experienced an unexpectedly strong recovery in 1992, with GDP increasing by 10.1% in real terms. The return of some 300,000 Palestinians, expelled by Kuwait in 1991, meanwhile brought new capital resources into Jordan.

By 1993, while acknowledging that serious structural problems remained, Jordanian ministers and business leaders were generally optimistic about the prospects for continued progress in meeting IMF economic targets. The Fund subsequently extended substantial new assistance to support the process of structural reform, while Jordan's main creditors negotiated debt rescheduling arrangements. In addition, a new Economic and Social Development Plan, drafted for the period 1993–97, provided for a major extension of the private sector through the privatization of state enterprises. Its objectives were redefined under a further Five-Year Plan for 1999–2003, and in a Plan for Social and Economic Transformation published in late 2001.

Despite deteriorating regional security from September 2000 and the international economic downturn after the September 2001 attacks on the USA, Jordan recorded GDP growth of 4.9% in 2001 and 5.7% in 2002. The war in Iraq caused growth in 2003 to slow to 4.1%, mainly owing to the disruption of Jordanian exports to Iraq and the negative effects of the conflict on tourism and transport. GDP growth in 2004 increased significantly, to 8.4%. The fiscal position strengthened, reflecting buoyant tax revenues and tight budgetary management.

Jordan's economy continued to grow briskly, with real GDP increasing by 7.2% in 2005. This robust performance was maintained through 2006, despite the rapid increase in international oil prices. According to official figures, GDP growth was 6.4% for the year, reflecting strong domestic private consumption and investment. Core inflation was well contained, although headline inflation reached 6.3%, stemming mainly from rising prices for fuel and imported foods. The current account deficit narrowed, financed by record levels of long-term private capital inflows from foreign investments in banking, mining, telecommunications and real estate. Higher tax revenue receipts, larger foreign grants (particularly from Saudi Arabia) and the Government's decision substantially to lower domestic fuel subsidies meant that the fiscal situation also improved.

The economy again performed well in 2007, despite the challenging external environment, with GDP growing by 7.8%, according to the Central Bank of Jordan (CBJ), and unemployment declining marginally, from 14% to 13.1%. Foreign direct investment (FDI) and portfolio inflows remained strong, and international reserves increased. However, rapidly rising international prices for vital food and fuel imports put increasing pressure on the fiscal and external accounts from the middle of the year, and there was a widening of the external current account deficit. In response to these imbalances, the Government removed fuel subsidies from February 2008. It also put in place a new monthly fuel price adjustment mechanism in an effort to reduce the vulnerability of the budget to international oil price movements. At the same time, compensatory measures were introduced with the aim of offsetting public opposition to the removal of the subsidies, including an increase in public sector salaries and pensions, as well as an expansion of social safety net transfers. An immediate effect of ending fuel subsidies was a sharp rise in inflation, while the reintroduction in March of gas and barley subsidies, together with the cost of the compensatory measures, caused the Government to introduce supplementary budgets (see Budget, Investment and Finance).

According to CBJ data, GDP growth in 2008 was 7.2%, and the rate of unemployment declined to 12.7%. Inflation was high, averaging 14.9% for the year, but, having risen sharply until September, it subsequently decreased quickly in tandem with reductions in global fuel and food prices. Lower commodity prices also helped narrow the current account deficit, to an estimated 12% of GDP over the year. The relatively strong annual performance nevertheless masked a considerable economic slowdown in the last quarter of 2008. To maintain confidence and support in the domestic money market, in October of that year the CBJ announced a full guarantee of all bank deposits until the end of 2009. It also lowered banks' reserve requirements, and reduced interest rates. The Government, meanwhile, announced a modest JD 156m. stimulus package in January 2009, to help cushion the economy against the downturn. However, the global financial crisis caused GDP growth to slow to 5.5% in 2009, according to the CBJ. Jordan's fiscal position deteriorated sharply in 2009 as domestic revenues declined and public spending increased. The unemployment rate increased slightly, to 12.9%. In November the Government extended the guarantee on bank deposits for another year, to the end of 2010, as lending remained subdued. Inflation was marginally negative, following the sharp escalation in 2008.

Despite some reductions in public expenditure, the budget deficit (which at the end of 2009 was equivalent to some 9% of GDP) continued to pose a serious challenge to the Government in 2010. In June the Government announced a new set of measures intended to increase revenues, including higher taxes on luxury items, coffee, gas and cellular phone use. A slow recovery in domestic economic activity led to GDP growth of 2.3% in 2010 (although annual inflation rose to 5%, reflecting higher commodity prices), and the budget deficit declined to 5.6% of GDP. In early 2011 the political landscape was thrown into disarray by widespread popular protests, inspired by unrest in Tunisia and Egypt but underpinned by domestic economic grievances. The Government introduced some conciliatory measures aimed at quelling the disturbances, but increased subsidies and social spending commitments exacerbated pressures on Jordan's fiscal and external imbalances. Despite a record inflow of foreign grants (totalling JD 1,200m.), particularly from Saudi Arabia, the budget deficit widened to just over 6% of GDP. Meanwhile, in the context of continuing domestic and regional political uncertainty and the weak global economy, GDP growth remained sluggish, at 2.6%. Annual inflation averaged 4.4%.

A similar low level of growth, at 2.7%, was recorded in 2012, while inflation averaged 4.8%. Nevertheless, an IMF assessment, in December, of Jordan's economic performance during that year was positive, despite the continuing challenges confronting the country in terms of high food and energy prices; disruption in gas imports from Egypt; the adverse impact of regional and domestic political instability on tourism, remittances and FDI; and a growing burden of refugees (more than 300,000 by the end of the year) from the conflict in Syria. In early 2012 the Government had announced a three-year fiscal reform strategy to reduce the budget deficit, involving the abolition of tax exemptions and reductions in public expenditure and commodity subsidies, and in May it introduced new austerity measures, including reductions in the operational and capital expenditure of public institutions, an extension of the sales tax, and an increase in industrial electricity prices. In August the IMF approved a three-year US $2,000m. stand-by loan arrangement in phased support, subject to regular reviews, for the economic strategy to 2015. In a further significant initiative to counter the fiscal deficit (which, excluding grants, reached 9.7% of GDP in 2012), the Government announced in November the complete removal of fuel subsidies, although the impact was to be offset by compensatory payments channelled to poorer households. The IMF forecast that GDP growth would pick up slightly in 2013, to 3.3%, but cautioned that there would be a dampening impact on domestic demand because of the fuel subsidy removal (which also caused a spike in inflation, to 7.6% year-on-year in March) and restraints on investment reflecting earlier cuts in capital spending.

AGRICULTURE AND WATER SUPPLY

The major disruption to the agriculture sector caused by the loss of the relatively fertile West Bank in the 1967 war, and subsequent events on the East Bank, was later compounded by severe drought conditions between 1974 and 1979. In the 1980s, however, major investment in irrigation, particularly in the Jordan Valley, began to show results, and agricultural output increased by an average of 6% per year. The sector also retained an average 10% share of GDP through the decade, although this proportion began to decrease markedly thereafter, representing 2.8% by 2012. Meanwhile, migration away from the sector also began to reduce its importance as an employer within the economy.

A contrast can be drawn between the rain-fed upland zone (comprising about 90% of the cultivable land) and the irrigated Jordan Valley, which since 1973 has been subject to its own development plan. The productivity of the latter was far higher. The Jordan Valley, with its more favourable subtropical climate and available water, has been intensively exploited by small farmers, who have obtained huge increases in output (particularly of fruit and vegetables). The development of irrigation in the Jordan Valley began in 1958, but installations were severely damaged by Israeli bombardment in 1967 and repairs were not carried out until after the 1970–71 civil war. The first stage of the Jordan Valley Development Plan, funded by a variety of foreign aid organizations, was completed at the end of 1979. Irrigation projects centred mainly on the extension of the East Ghor canal and the Zarqa river complex. The King Talal dam was constructed in 1972–78; the East Ghor canal extended in 1975–78; and the Zarqa Triangle Irrigation Project completed in 1978. Other irrigation works included the Hisban Kafrein project, constructed in 1976–78, and the North-East Ghor complex. Projects undertaken in the second stage of the Plan included the raising of the King Talal dam, the construction of the Wadi al-Arab dam (to increase the irrigated area between Wadi al-Arab, Yarmouk river and Jordan Valley), the further extension of the East Ghor canal, and the irrigation of 4,700 ha in the Southern Ghor. The Water Authority of Jordan was, meanwhile, established in 1984.

One of the major schemes for the 1980s was to have been the construction of a dam and an associated hydroelectric power station on the Yarmouk river. The project, initially deferred, was revived in 1988 as the al-Wahda ('Unity') dam and hydroelectric scheme, a joint Jordanian-Syrian venture to store water for drinking, irrigation and electricity generation. After protracted delays, in 2003 the two countries signed an agreement whereby Turkish contractor Özaltın Construction Co would build the dam at a total cost of JD 61.7m. (US $86.9m.), to be financed by Jordan with loans from the Abu Dhabi Development Fund and the Arab Fund for Economic and Social Development (AFESD). Construction began in 2004 and the dam was completed in 2011. Another major project has been the 325-km pipeline to bring 100m. cu m of high-quality water per year to Amman from the Disi aquifer in the south of the country. In 2007 Gama Energy of Turkey was awarded the contract to construct the pipeline, on a build-operate-transfer (BOT) basis. By early 2013 33 of a total of 55 wells for pumping water from the aquifer had been drilled, although the project's progress was being impeded by insecurity in the south of the country around Ma'an.

In 2005 Jordan, Israel and the Palestinian (National) Authority (PA) announced plans for feasibility and environmental assessment studies for a proposed 180-km Dead Sea–Red Sea canal—a conveyance and desalination project formulated to arrest the alarming water losses from the Dead Sea and to increase fresh supplies to the three territories. The proposed scheme was to be overseen by the World Bank, and in 2008 French company Coyne et Bellier was selected to carry out the feasibility study, while the British firm Environmental Resources Management was awarded the contract for the environmental assessment. In January 2013 the World Bank released a draft report declaring the project viable from engineering, environmental and economic standpoints. Meanwhile, at the end of 2009 Jordan had launched its own Red Sea Water Project, which, according to the Government, would constitute part of the longer-term Dead Sea–Red Sea scheme. Overseen by the Jordan Red Sea Co (a private company under government authority), the project originally envisaged the construction of desalination plants with a combined production capacity of 930m. cu m of fresh water per year, as well as a number of real estate, housing and tourism developments. In 2011 the Ministry of Water and Irrigation shortlisted six firms for the construction of the first phase of the project; however, the selection process was not completed, and in November 2012 the Government announced that it was scaling down the scheme because of feasibility and financial obstacles.

Cereals, fruit and vegetables are the mainstays of Jordan's agriculture. Production levels vary widely, depending on the prevailing weather conditions. In 1999 the worst drought for decades resulted in an exceedingly low cereal harvest. Annual production levels have continued to fluctuate considerably, particularly for cereals.

MINING AND MINERALS

In a country short of natural resources, Jordan's mineral wealth lies predominantly in its phosphate reserves, which provide its main export commodity. The mining and marketing of phosphate is handled by the Jordan Phosphate Mines Co (JPMC), the country's largest mining and industrial employer. The expansion of the phosphate industry has been a major element in successive Development Plans. Quantities of uranium (see below) and vanadium are known to be mixed in with the phosphate reserves. There are also known deposits of good-quality copper ore at Wadi al-Arab, and potash in the Dead Sea. Other minerals include gypsum, manganese ore, abundant quantities of glass sand, and the clays and feldspar required for manufacturing ceramics.

JPMC operates three phosphate mines at Shidiya, Hassa and Abiad. In the longer term, the industry is focused on the major, low-cost mine at Shidiya, near Ma'an, in the south-east, which started production in 1988. In 2011 JPMC produced a record 7.6m. tons of rock phosphate, up from 6.5m. tons in 2010.

A 50% limit on foreign ownership of Jordanian mining companies was removed in early 2001, and in June that year the Government announced a target date of late 2002 for the privatization of JPMC. However, protracted delays meant that the sale of 37% of the Government's shares (to the Brunei Investment Agency) was not achieved until 2006. The Jordan Investment Trust (Jordinvest), the Government's investment arm, retained a 25.6% share in JPMC.

In March 2010 JPMC signed a 30-year agreement with the Aqaba Development Corpn (ADC—see also Transport and Communications) to build and operate a new phosphate terminal at the port. On completion, the US $240m. terminal was to have an average annual handling capacity of about 4m. metric tons.

The Arab Potash Co Ltd (APC) was formed in 1956 as one of the earliest Arab joint ventures. Reconstituted in 1983, the company produced about 487,000 metric tons of potash in 1984, its first full year of commercial operation. In 1990 the APC recorded its first profit (of JD 39.6m.). By 1996 the annual capacity of the APC's Ghor al-Safi extraction plant on the Dead Sea totalled 1.8m. tons. In 2002 the Government initiated the sale of one-half of its total 52% stake in the APC: the 26% shareholding was purchased by Canada's PotashCorp, for some JD 123m., in 2003. In that year total output amounted to 1.96m. tons, and total exports (mainly to India and the People's Republic of China) totalled JD 144.8m. Nevertheless, in 2004 the APC announced a JD 55.9m. loss for 2003; this was attributed to exceptional factors, including the liquidation of its Jordan Safi Salt Co subsidiary. Annual potash production declined from 1.9m. tons in 2004 to 1.7m. tons in 2006, but rose to 1.8m. tons in 2007 and further, to 2.0m. tons, in 2008. Output decreased to 1.1m. tons in 2009, before rising sharply again, to 2.1m. tons in 2010 and 2.26m. tons in 2011. In late 2010 the APC opened a new facility, with an annual capacity of 500,000 tons, at its Dead Sea works. Jordan's main potash export markets in 2009 were India, Indonesia, Malaysia and China.

Industries allied to phosphate production form an important part of Jordan's industrial base. JPMC operates a 'downstream' fertilizer and chemicals plant at Aqaba, which began production in 1982. The original project, managed by the Jordan Fertilizer Industries Co (JFIC), included an aluminium fluoride facility which entered production in 1984. In 1986 JPMC bought the JFIC (which had accumulated losses of JD 40.3m. by the end of 1985, owing to a slump in world fertilizer prices) for JD 60m. After a further loss of JD 1.3m. at the Aqaba plant in 1992, JPMC centred any future 'downstream' development plans on joint ventures with foreign partners that would provide investment funds and guarantee long-term export markets. The Indo-Jordan Chemicals Co (a joint venture with India's Southern Petrochemical Industries Co and Saudi Arabia's Arab Investment Co) opened a phosphoric acid plant at Shidiya in 1997. During 2007 JPMC concluded agreements with the Jordan Arab Fertilizer and Chemicals Co and Venture Capital Bank of Bahrain for the construction of a US $65m. industrial facility at its Abiad mine (to produce sulphuric acid, potassium sulphate, phosphoric acid and calcium chloride); with Mitsubishi Corpn of Japan for a $300m. fertilizer complex at the Shidiya mine; and with the Indian Farmers Fertilizer Corpn for a $625m. phosphoric acid plant, which was officially launched at Shidiya in March 2010 and was scheduled to begin commercial production during 2013.

A joint Jordanian-French mining company reported in late 2011 that it had found significant reserves of uranium in its exploration concession area in central Jordan. There were other known uranium reserves in the region south of Amman and also near the border with Iraq.

Jordan is almost wholly dependent on imports of crude petroleum for its energy needs, having no significant resources of its own. During the 1980s the cost of imported oil declined in relative terms, owing to reductions in world prices and to the availability of Iraqi oil at preferential prices. The deferment, in 1985, of plans to construct a pipeline to convey crude petroleum from Iraq to Aqaba contributed to the decision to renew an agreement to receive Saudi Arabian crude petroleum, via the Trans-Arabian Pipeline (Tapline), at Jordan's only oil refinery at Zarqa. Originally constructed in the 1940s as the principal means of exporting Saudi oil to the West via Jordan and the port of Haifa, the Tapline had been diverted to Sidon, Lebanon, following the creation of the State of Israel in 1948, but had been used exclusively to transport oil to Jordan after the closure of the Lebanese section in 1983. At the outbreak of the Gulf crisis in August 1990, Jordan was importing more than 80% of its oil requirements from Iraq, with almost all the remainder coming from Saudi Arabia. When, following the Iraqi invasion of Kuwait, Jordan announced its acceptance of the UN trade embargo on Iraq, Saudi Arabia pledged to supply at least one-half of Jordan's oil needs through Tapline. However, Jordan's reluctance to apply the UN embargo resulted in Saudi Arabia's suspension of all oil supplies to Jordan in September (the official reason given was non-payment of outstanding bills of US $46m.). Jordan accordingly became entirely dependent on Iraqi supplies by road tanker, which rose to some 60,000 barrels per day (b/d) by January 1991. The start of hostilities then resulted in the virtual cessation of such supplies, forcing Jordan to impose petrol rationing and to conclude emergency agreements to import oil from Yemen and Syria (at a higher price than the preferential rate charged by Iraq). It was announced in April 1991 that Iraqi supplies to Jordan would be resumed, but the after-effects of the war in Iraq inhibited normal trade for some time. (See Foreign Trade and Balance of Payments for the subsequent development of the Iraqi-Jordanian oil trade.)

In 1995 the Government approved the establishment of a National Petroleum Co (NPC), to be owned by the Jordan Investment Corpn. The company would function as an independent entity, and would be free to co-operate with foreign oil companies. In 1999 the NPC was divided into two separate entities, the Petra Drilling Co being established as a commercial enterprise that would be privatized to take better advantage of local and regional contract opportunities, while the NPC would concentrate on gas production and exploration.

The Jordanian authorities have continued to promote petroleum exploration. International oil companies with which exploration and production-sharing arrangements have been concluded since 1996 include Anadarko Petroleum Corpn and Trans Global Resources (both of the USA), Star Petroleum of the United Kingdom, Black Rock Petroleum of Australia, Dauntless Oil of Canada, and India's Universal Energy. In early 2012 the Jordanian Government commenced negotiations with Korea Global Energy Corpn of the Republic of Korea (South Korea) on an agreement to develop a potentially significant petroleum discovery in the Wadi al-Arab region.

In 2004 the Government approved a wide-ranging Energy Master Plan to modernize the kingdom's entire energy sector through the injection of about US $3,000m. of public and private sector capital over 10–15 years. Integral to the plan was the planned $700m. upgrading of the Zarqa refinery, owned by the Jordan Petroleum Refining Co (JPRC), to receive natural gas from Egypt via a new pipeline, and the privatization of JPRC, the monopoly rights of which to supply refined products within Jordan expired in 2008.

In an attempt to reduce petroleum imports, increasing attention has being given to the possibility of exploiting the estimated 40,000m. metric tons of oil shale deposits (containing about 4,000m. tons of oil) in southern Jordan. In early 2008 the Ministry of Energy and Mineral Resources launched a licensing round for exploration in the Attarat Umm Ghudran field in central Jordan. In May 2009 Jordan's National Resources Authority (NRA) signed a US $425m. agreement with the Royal Dutch Shell Group for the extraction of deep-lying oil shale deposits. The exploration phase of the deal will involve drilling in a 22,000-sq km concession in the north-east and south of the country. The NRA also signed memorandums of understanding (MOUs) and preliminary agreements with several other international energy companies for the possible development of shallow oil shale resources.

In April 2013 Jordan and Iraq signed an agreement to build a 1,700-km crude oil pipeline, with an 850,000 b/d capacity, from the southern oilfields around Basra (Iraq) to Aqaba in Jordan for export purposes, with the potential for substantial transit revenue for the Jordanian Government on the pipeline's envisaged inauguration in 2017.

The discovery of reserves of natural gas at locations around al-Risha in north-eastern Jordan in 1987 and 1988 encouraged speculation that the deposits would be sufficient to satisfy a significant proportion of Jordan's future energy requirements. By 1989 gas from the new discoveries was fuelling a 60-MW electricity generating plant at al-Risha. Total generating capacity at the plant was doubled to 120 MW in 1993–94, and by the late 1990s about 10%–13% of Jordan's national electricity supply was generated there. The results of a review of the al-Risha gasfield, completed in 2000, were generally disappointing, effectively ending hopes of a major increase in domestic gas production in the short term. The NPC none the less expressed confidence in the field's potential, and in 2002 entered into a joint venture with Golden Spike of Indonesia for the further exploration of the southern part of al-Risha.

In 2001 Jordan concluded an agreement with Egypt for the supply of Egyptian gas via a proposed high-capacity export pipeline. Deliveries began in 2003, at an initial rate of 1,100m. cu m per year. In the longer term, it was envisaged that the pipeline would carry 10,000m. cu m per year of gas from Egypt, to be used by Jordan to develop new industrial capacity in the north of the country. The construction of the Jordanian portion of the transmission pipeline, from Aqaba in the south to the Rehab power plant in the north, began in 2004, and the US $300m. project became operational in 2006. In December 2011 Jordan and Egypt concluded a new price agreement for Egyptian gas. However, supplies were unreliable throughout 2011 and again in 2012 because of political instability in Egypt and frequent attacks on the pipeline in Sinai. Shortfalls forced Jordan to import more expensive fuel for its power plants (adding to the country's budget deficit concerns), and prompted the opening of negotiations in early 2012 with Qatar on alternative supplies—although Egypt pledged to maintain future supplies under a new agreement signed at the end of that year.

ELECTRICITY

A link between the Egyptian and Jordanian electricity grids (the first phase of a regional interconnection project supported by the AFESD) was completed in 1999, and a link between the Jordanian and Syrian grids was inaugurated in 2001. In January 1999 the state-owned National Electric Power Co (NEPCO) was divided into three separate companies (for generation, transmission and distribution) under the 1996 Electricity Law, which also provided for an industry regulatory body and for the encouragement of private sector participation in future power generation projects. The name NEPCO was retained by the transmission company, which was to remain in state ownership, whereas the generating company (Central Electricity Generating Co—CEGCO) and the distribution company (Electricity Distribution Co—EDCO) were both included in privatization plans announced by the Government in 2000. The Government launched the process to privatize CEGCO, EDCO and the Irbid District Electricity Co (IDECO) in 2004. The sale of the Government's CEGCO shareholding was finally completed in mid-2007, when Energy Arabia, a joint venture including Amman-based JD Energy as the majority shareholder, bought the 51% stake. Later the same year a Jordanian-Gulf state company, Kingdom Electricity, bought 100% of EDCO and 55.4% of IDECO.

The three largest power stations are at Aqaba (650 MW), Zarqa (400 MW) and Rehab (360 MW). The conversion of these power plants to combined-cycle technology, to enable them to use Egyptian gas, has been a priority for the Government. The contract for the Aqaba plant conversion was awarded to Alstom of France, and Doosan of South Korea was selected for the Rehab conversion in 2003. In 1999 the Belgian company Tractebel began negotiations with the Jordanian Government for a BOT contract to develop Jordan's first independent power project (IPP) at Kherbet al-Samra, near Amman. After three years of talks, however, Tractebel announced in 2002 that it was withdrawing, and the planned IPP was abandoned. Black & Veatch of the USA and Turkey's Gama subsequently undertook construction of the combined-cycle plant on an engineering, procurement and construction (EPC) basis. In a second attempt to involve the private sector in power generation, the Government launched a tender process in 2005 for a combined-cycle power plant at Almanakher, near Amman. This IPP plant was to be supplied by pipeline with Egyptian natural gas, and would be required to supply up to 400 MW of electricity to the Almanakher area. The project concession was awarded in 2006 to the US-based AES Corpn and Japan's Mitsui & Co, and in 2007 South's Doosan was selected for the EPC contract to build the plant; the facility was inaugurated in November 2009. In 2007 the Government invited bids to build a combined-cycle IPP facility at al-Qatranah on a BOT basis. Korea Electric Power Corpn (Kepco) and Saudi Arabia's Xenel Industries were subsequently awarded the contract for the 380-MW plant. In September 2012 a consortium of Kepco, Japan's Mitsubishi Corpn and Finland's Wärtsilä signed a power purchase agreement for the construction and operation of a 600-MW diesel engine power plant in the eastern part of Amman, again on an IPP basis. Later in the year an agreement for a fourth IPP project was then signed with AES Corpn and Mitsui & Co. This fuel-fired diesel engine facility was to be located at Almanakher, next to the existing power plant.

The Jordanian authorities have studied the commercial viability of large-scale electricity generation from renewable resources, including wind power, biogas and solar energy, with the aim of deriving 10% of total energy needs from renewables by 2020. In late 2009 an Italian-Jordanian joint venture announced plans for a solar energy plant in the Ma'an area, and in mid-2011 an agreement was reached between Petra Solar of the USA and Kingdom Electricity to build a 50-MW plant at Al-Tafilah. Plans for another solar power venture, involving Saudi Arabia's ACWA Power International and CEGCO, were advancing by late 2011, with a number of foreign engineering and construction companies having applied for prequalification for the project. A civil nuclear power programme to meet the country's growing energy needs was also under preparation, for which in 2007 the Jordanian parliament approved legislation concerning developmental and regulatory foundations. The Jordan Atomic Energy Commission (JAEC) subsequently sought bids to carry out a site study (including seismic and environmental assessment) for the first nuclear power plant, to be located east of Aqaba, and by late 2011 it was assessing technical and financial tenders from three foreign companies. The JAEC meanwhile signed nuclear co-operation agreements with several countries, including China, France, Japan, Russia and the USA. In March 2010 the Government signed an agreement with a South Korean consortium, comprising the Korean Atomic Energy Research Institute and Daewoo Engineering and Construction Co Ltd, for the construction of a research reactor.

The repeated disruption of cheap Egyptian gas supplies in 2011–12, as a result of which NEPCO was forced to import more expensive fuels, led to serious financial difficulties for the state-owned company. In response, the Government proposed the introduction of a general rise in electricity prices with effect from July 2013. In June, however, following parliamentary opposition, the Prime Minister gave an assurance that the increase would not be applied to domestic consumers until early 2014, and that it would be limited in scope.

OTHER INDUSTRIES

Manufacturing industry is concentrated around Amman. The majority of factories produce clothing, consumer goods or food products, but the major industrial income has traditionally derived from the three heavier industries—phosphate extraction and petroleum-refining (see Mining and Minerals) and also cement manufacture. Manufacturing contributed about 16.5% of overall GDP in 2012.

In an effort to boost Jordan's role as an entrepôt, several free trade zones have been established. In 1997 the Government agreed that the Aqaba region should be fully converted into a free trade zone, offering special incentives for the development of manufacturing and service industries in addition to existing free trade facilities. The 375-sq km Aqaba Special Economic Zone (ASEZ) was inaugurated in 2001, including within its boundary a population of 70,000, an established sea port and airport installations, Jordan's largest power station, and some of the country's principal mineral-processing facilities. In 2006 the Jordanian authorities announced plans for the further development of the ASEZ, at a cost of US $1,000m., having in the previous month inaugurated the zone's Saraya Aqaba investment project (see Tourism). Also in 2006 King Abdullah announced the launch of a $750m. special development zone in al-Mafraq governorate, as the first of several such plans for areas around the country with relatively high levels of poverty and unemployment. With targeted investment in industry, logistics and services, housing and transport, the zone was expected to create 13,000 jobs by 2015.

Increasing demand for residential and commercial property, partly generated by Iraq-related activity and the substantial number of Iraqis now settled in Jordan, boosted the construction industry. In 2008 it was announced that the Government would give private sector property developers swathes of land to start a JD 5,000m. public housing programme: it was planned to build 120,000 residential properties over six years, for limited-income Jordanians, civil servants and armed forces personnel. Jordan's largest property and tourism project to date, the US $10,000m. Marsa Zayed development, at Aqaba port, was launched in May 2010. The three-phase scheme was being undertaken by the United Arab Emirates' (UAE) Al-Maabar real estate company. In 2011 the number of construction projects reached almost 31,000, but the sector was marked by a slowdown over the year, reflecting both negative investor sentiment towards the region as a whole and a tightening of the Government's capital spending. In 2012 the construction sector accounted for 4.4% of GDP.

In 2008 China's Hebei Zhongxing Automobile Co Ltd opened Jordan's first car assembly plant at Umm al-Rasas, south of Amman. Production at the US $30m. plant, a joint venture with the local firm Ayass Motors, was projected to increase from 6,250 vehicles in the first year to 24,000 in the third, with capital investment rising to $50m. by the end of the fifth year of operation.

Qualifying Industrial Zone (QIZ) terms, first designated in 1997, have attracted considerable foreign investment. To be eligible for QIZ status, companies are required to have a Jordanian and Israeli manufacturer, each contributing a minimum of 20% of total production costs; alternatively, Jordanian and Israeli manufacturers must contribute specified proportions of the content of goods produced in order to qualify for duty-free access to US markets. The Jordan Gateway Projects Co (a joint venture with Israeli interests) qualified as a QIZ in 1999 to develop a new zone on both the Jordanian and Israeli-occupied banks of the Jordan river. Other QIZ ventures included the Kerak, Al-Hassan and Ma'an Industrial Estates, under the aegis of the Jordan Industrial Estates Corpn. By the end of 2006 QIZs hosted more than 50 companies, drawn from over a dozen different countries.

In 2000 Jordan's House of Representatives approved a privatization law giving the Government the option of retaining a 'golden share' in any privatized entity. By 2005 some 66 public assets had been transferred to the private sector, generating about US $1,300m. in sale proceeds and $850m. in associated investments.

TRANSPORT AND COMMUNICATIONS

Jordan's only seaport is situated at Aqaba, on the country's 20-km Red Sea coastline. Cargo-handling facilities expanded rapidly during the 1980s, an important factor being the re-routing through Aqaba of much Iraqi trade when the Iran–Iraq War of 1980–88 severely dislocated trade through Iraq's own Gulf outlets. Aqaba's transit trade was then severely affected by the imposition of UN sanctions against Iraq from August 1990. Iraqi exports via the port ceased entirely. The estimated reduction in Aqaba's Iraq-bound imports was about 3.5m. tons per year, while up to 2.85m. tons of transit cargo for countries other than Iraq were being re-routed to non-Jordanian ports by shippers who did not wish to suffer the delays and inconveniences of UN monitoring of Aqaba-bound cargoes. For the same reason, some shippers were also routing part of Jordan's own import trade via Mediterranean ports in Syria and Lebanon. In the mid-1990s Jordan's port authorities implemented wide-ranging reductions in handling fees to stimulate the growth of transit trade, and by 2001 Aqaba was used by 2,673 vessels and handled a total cargo volume of 13.04m. tons. In 2004 the Netherlands-based APM Terminals signed a contract with the ADC to manage and upgrade the port's container terminal. The first phase of berth expansion was completed in early 2013.

The Jordanian section of the narrow-gauge Hedjaz railway runs from the Syrian border, via Amman and Ma'an, to the Saudi border. A 115-km link to a phosphate export terminal at Aqaba was added in the 1970s. The Aqaba Railways Corpn (ARC) was established in 1972 to manage the rail transport of rock phosphate and related products. Freight (mainly phosphates) accounts for virtually all of Jordan's rail traffic. An express rail link between Amman and the Syrian capital, Damascus (using a section of the Hedjaz railway), was launched in 1999. Also in 1999 the Government signed a 25-year management and operation agreement for the ARC with a US-led consortium, which undertook to invest US $130m. to connect the existing railway network with JPMC's Shidiya mine, situated near the border with Saudi Arabia. Long-standing plans to construct a light rail link between Amman and Zarqa were finally abandoned in March 2011 in favour of a rapid bus transport system. In May it was announced that the Ministry of Transport had received expressions of interest from a number of international financial institutions (including the European Investment Bank, the Islamic Development Bank and the World Bank) and from Jordan's regional allies to fund a national railway project. The $3,000m. project, involving the construction of new links from Aqaba to Amman and Zarqa, and then on to Syria, Iraq and Saudi Arabia, aimed to transform Jordan into a centre for regional trade and commerce. In the same month Jordan and Iraq signed a memorandum of understanding for the building of new track from Aqaba port to the Iraqi capital, Baghdad. In 2010 Egis Rail of France was awarded a feasibility/design contract for the development of an underground railway system in Amman.

The Jordanian road system centres on the main north–south desert highway from Amman to Aqaba, and interlinks with a number of major international transit routes. In 1997 the Government announced plans to privatize the Public Transportation Corpn (responsible for bus services in Amman). However, accumulated losses led to its liquidation in 1998, with private companies taking over the operation of its routes.

The national airline, Royal Jordanian, operates passenger and freight services from Queen Alia International Airport at Zizya, 40 km south of Amman. In 2007 the company became the region's first national airline to complete the transition from state-owned business to privatized enterprise, with a successful initial public offering (IPO) that resulted in 71% of its shares being sold to local, regional and international investors. Also in 2007 Airport International Group, a Jordanian consortium, was selected to modernize, expand and operate the Queen Alia International Airport under a 25-year concession. The construction of a third terminal, completed and inaugurated in March 2013, is helping increase airport capacity, in phases, to 12m. passengers annually. Jordan Aviation (JATE) was established in 2000 as Jordan's first privately owned chartered airline, with initial operations, from 2001, focusing chiefly on charter operations to Red Sea tourist resorts. JATE commenced scheduled regional operations from Aqaba in 2005.

A telecommunications law enacted in 1995 provided for the licensing of private sector competitors to the state-owned Jordan Telecommunications Corpn. During 1996 private companies were granted licences to develop new mobile communications, data communications and public payphone systems, although the state enterprise remained the sole provider of basic fixed-line services. From 1997 the Telecommunications Corpn was restructured as the JTC (now Jordan Telecom Group), with a share capital of JD 250m., and advisers were appointed to organize the proposed sale of part of the company's equity to the private sector. In 2000 Jordan signed an agreement whereby a consortium led by France Télécom obtained a 40% stake in the JTC for US $508m., with a further 8% being acquired by the Social Security Corpn for $102m. and 1% being allocated to the JTC staff fund, so that the Government retained a 51% majority stake. Its monopoly on fixed-line services was scheduled to expire at the end of 2004 (see below). In 2002 10.5% of the Government's equity in the JTC was sold through an IPO, raising some JD 60m. The transaction was Jordan's first divestment via an IPO on the Amman Stock Exchange (ASE).

Jordan's second mobile cellular telephone network licence was awarded in 1998 to the JTC. Its subsidiary, MobileCom, launched its service in 2000, in competition with the private operator Fastlink (then owned by Motorola), previously the monopoly-holder. Industry analysts subsequently suggested that the Government had foregone potential revenue of US $150m. by not putting licence out to tender (for which Fastlink had argued). In February 2002 the arrangement of a JD 60m. loan to MobileCom to finance the expansion of its mobile network was reported to be the largest loan by local banks to date for a private sector project in Jordan.

In 2004 the Telecommunications Regulatory Commission (TRC) granted Jordan's third mobile telephone licence to Umniah Telecommunications and Technologies Co (a joint venture including Kuwait's Alghanim Group and China's Huawei Technologies). In that year the Government approved the licensing process proposed by the TRC for opening up the fixed-line network to competition from January 2005 and ending the monopoly of Jordan Telecom; and in August 2005 Fastlink (later rebranded as Zain) secured a licence to provide services through its subsidiary company, Pella. France Télécom had meanwhile confirmed its intention to increase its stake in Jordan Telecom, and in March 2006 it became the majority shareholder with the purchase of an additional 11% from the Government. In June that year the Government confirmed that it would sell its remaining 41.5% stake in Jordan Telecom on the following terms: 3% to the staff and retirees of the armed forces; 5% to the Social Security Corpn; 20% between the Bahrain-based Gulf Finance House and the Kuwaiti Al Nour Co; a further 11% to France Télécom; and 2.5% for sale exclusively to Jordanians through the ASE. In the same month the Bahrain Telecommunications Co (BATELCO) agreed to buy a 96% stake in Umniah, Jordan's fastest growing mobile operator, for US $415m. In August 2009 Jordan Telecom was granted a 15-year licence by the TRC to become Jordan's first provider of 3G (third generation) mobile telecommunications services.

TOURISM

Following the disruption of the 1967 war and its aftermath, tourism recovered during the 1970s and 1980s. However, the Gulf crisis from August 1990 effectively ended all tourism until the latter part of 1991. A principal aim of government tourism development policy for the 1990s was to provide a varied range of attractions in different parts of the country, while taking steps to prevent the overdevelopment of Petra—its most popular tourist site, included on UNESCO's World Heritage List. Peace with Israel greatly enhanced Jordan's appeal to overseas tourists, while the opening of the border prompted a significant influx of Israeli tourists from late 1994 onwards. Income from tourism in 1995 was estimated at JD 568m., and total visitor numbers exceeded 1m. An estimated 100,000 Israelis visited Jordan in that year, while tourist arrivals from Japan and South Korea began to feature significantly in statistics for the first time. The re-emergence of regional political tensions in 1996 led to a significant decline in visitor numbers, with some hotels reporting occupancy rates as low as 10% at some points in that year. Nevertheless, the Ministry of Tourism and Antiquities pursued an expansion of tourist facilities, and in 1997 the Government announced the establishment of a new Jordan Tourism Board as a public-private venture to promote Jordan as a tourist destination.

Tourist arrivals in 1999 totalled 1,357,822, generating estimated revenue of JD 564m. Petra attracted over 420,000 visitors that year (more than double the number in 1994). The deterioration in Israeli–Palestinian relations from September 2000 and the September 2001 terrorist attacks on the USA had an adverse effect on bookings and revenue, but tourist arrivals recovered to reach a reported 6.7m. by 2006, generating JD 1,640m. (more than 10% of Jordan's GDP). The official figures showed a steady flow of tourist traffic from all regions in that year, although the most notable increases were in visitors from Europe, the USA and Arab countries. Tourist arrivals totalled some 6.5m. in 2007, 7.1m. in 2008 and just under 7.1m. in 2009. Visitor numbers rose sharply in 2010, to 8.2m., and revenue from tourism increased to JD 2,423m., but regional political turmoil, initially inspired by the unrest in Tunisia and Egypt, prompted a significant decline in tourist arrivals in 2011 and 2012, to 6.8m. and 6.3m. respectively. A new five-year National Tourism Strategy was announced in 2011, with the aim of increasing Jordan's annual tourism receipts to JD 4,200m. by 2015.

BUDGET, INVESTMENT AND FINANCE

Jordan adopted development plans from 1962 onwards, but targets had rarely been met by the end of the 1980s. From the early 1990s the Government sought, in accordance with IMF prescriptions, to reduce Jordan's persistent budget deficit.

The 1992 budget proposals reflected the terms of an IMF agreement reached in 1991, with government subsidies being reduced and new consumption taxes imposed. Of the structural reform measures proposed in the 1993 budget, price increases on selected oil products were implemented in June. However, a new sales tax, intended to supersede existing consumption taxes, was deferred following strong protests from private businesses. The 'London Club' of commercial creditors signed a debt rescheduling agreement in December, covering US $740m. in principal and $150m. in interest owed by the Jordan Government. Meanwhile, a new Economic and Social Development Plan was introduced for 1993–97, allotting a major role to the private sector through the disposal of stakes in government-owned concerns. The deferred sales tax finally secured parliamentary approval in May 1994, and took effect in July. Its adoption paved the way for the IMF to announce its formal approval of a three-year, SDR 127.8m. Extended Fund Facility (EFF) to support the next stage of the Government's structural adjustment programme. The IMF agreement also smoothed negotiations with the 'Paris Club' of official creditors, culminating in an agreement in June to reschedule $1,215m. of debt repayments over 20 years. (World Bank statistics for 1992 had given Jordan's total debt as $6,914m.) The IMF augmented Jordan's EFF allocation by SDR 25m. in September, and by a further SDR 36.5m. in February 1995.

In 1996 the IMF approved a Jordanian request for new credits totalling SDR 200.8m. to support the Government's economic and structural reform programme for 1996–98. This new EFF arrangement replaced the previous arrangement approved in 1994, which the IMF regarded as broadly successful. The Government's economic targets for the period to 1998 included: average GDP growth of at least 6% per annum; achievement of low inflation rates similar to those in industrialized countries; a reduction in the current account deficit to less than 3% of GDP; the accumulation of sufficient gross official reserves to cover about three months' expenditure on imports; and the reduction of the budget deficit to no more than 2.5% of GDP by 1998. The ongoing process of structural reform was to include further reductions in public subsidies and a wide-ranging privatization programme.

Jordan's 1997 budget provided for total spending of JD 1,753m. and total revenue of JD 1,651m., leaving a surplus of JD 102m. In February 1997 the IMF increased the total amount of credit available to Jordan under the 1996–98 EFF by SDR 37.2m., to SDR 238m. (US $330.5m.). The 'Paris Club' had meanwhile agreed in 1996 to reschedule $308m. of Jordanian official debt ($250m. of principal and $58m. of interest) falling due between July 1996 and May 1997, and further agreed in 1997 to reschedule $450m. due between June 1997 and September 1999. In September 1997 the USA agreed to cancel $63.4m. of debt, following two earlier agreements under which $1,100m. had been cancelled. Jordan's total foreign debt at the end of 1997 was $6,469.7m. (81.7% of GDP), of which about $4,000m. was owed to bilateral creditors. The 1998 budget provided for expenditure of JD 1,950m. and a net deficit (after aid receipts) of only JD 37m., although the out-turn was a deficit of 6% of GDP.

In April 1999 the IMF approved loans totalling SDR 161.98m. (US $220m.) to support the Government's economic and structural reform programme for 1999–2001. The loans were divided between a Compensatory and Contingency Financing Facility of SDR 34.1m. ($46m.) to offset a shortfall in exports, and a new EFF credit of SDR 127.88m. ($162m.). The new EFF programme targeted GDP growth of 2% in 1999, rising to 2.5% in 2001 and 3.5% in 2002, and a strengthening of reserves to $1,191m. by the end of 1999 and $1,691m. by 2001. The dinar would continue to be pegged to the US dollar at its prevailing rate (709–711 fils). The IMF recommended a faster pace of structural reform in 1999, and identified as major targets the reform of the tax system and the introduction of a new banking law to improve regulation and supervision and establish a deposit insurance scheme. A further Five-Year Plan for the period 1999–2003 focused on encouraging greater co-operation between the public and private sectors. In May 1999 the 'Paris Club' agreed to reschedule $800m. of Jordan's debt-service payments due between March 1999 and April 2002. The repayment period would be 20 years. Further disbursements of the EFF credit were made by the IMF in July 2000 and August

2001, and were completed in April 2002 with the release of the final SDR 60.89m. ($77m.).

Jordan's 1999 budget provided for total spending of JD 2,160m., 5% higher than the revised 1998 figure. Most of the increase was to come in the capital expenditure budget, which was expected to reach JD 477m. Current spending was expected to rise by only 3.8%. Total revenues, including aid, were forecast at JD 1,925m., 9% higher than the revised 1998 figure. The projected JD 435m. budget deficit would be part-financed by aid. Partly because of an increase in sales tax, from 10% to 13%, the out-turn for 1999 was a deficit of 3.5% of GDP, which was regarded as satisfactory progress compared with the 1998 out-turn. At the end of 1999 Jordan's total external debt stood at JD 5,186m. (US $7,409m.), equivalent to 96.4% of GDP (compared with $7,066m. at the end of 1998). The budget for 2000 originally provided for a deficit of 7% of GDP on projected expenditure of JD 2,210m., despite a 25% reduction in capital spending. In March 2000 the Government imposed a freeze on job creation in the public sector for the remainder of the year, the share of state expenditure absorbed by civil service salaries being estimated at about 40%. The out-turn was a budget deficit contained to 4.7% of GDP.

The 2001 budget, providing for expenditure of JD 2,300m., incorporated a projected deficit of JD 380m. before foreign aid. As originally drafted, the budget included capital spending totalling JD 470m., while the original revenue projections included up to JD 80m. from planned increases in prices for oil products in 2001. Implementation of these price increases was, however, deferred after they were opposed by parliamentary deputies, who recommended that the Government should instead make an equivalent downward adjustment in its capital spending plans. There was a satisfactory reduction in the budget deficit, to 3.7% of GDP, achieved by expenditure restraint to offset revenue shortfalls in the second half of the year. The shortfalls resulted from initial problems arising from the extension of the sales tax to the retail sector, disappointing revenues from phosphate and potash exports, and a decline in tourism. The lower fiscal deficit helped to reduce net public debt from 96% to 94% of GDP by the end of 2001, when the CBJ's net usable reserves stood at US $2,600m.

The 2002 budget, which provided for expenditure of JD 2,350m., incorporated measures to reduce unemployment and poverty levels, while at the same time aiming for a further reduction in the fiscal deficit. However, the simultaneous inauguration of a four-year Plan for Social and Economic Transformation, envisaging annual expenditure of JD 250m.–JD 275m. in the period 2002–05, was expected by the IMF to result in a small increase in the budget deficit in 2002, to 4.1% of GDP, although net public debt was projected to decline to 88% of GDP.

After delivering a generally favourable report on Jordan's economic performance, in July 2002 the IMF approved a new two-year stand-by credit of SDR 85.28m. (about US $113m.). As part of the agreement, the Government pledged the immediate reduction of state subsidies on basic commodities, including fuel oil, gas and flour. In the same month the 'Paris Club' again agreed to reschedule $1,200m. of Jordan's debts, representing the country's principal and interest payments due from 1 May 2002 until the end of 2007. In January 2003 the World Bank approved a new country assistance strategy for Jordan, including a $305m. loan package, to help counter unemployment and poverty. Government expenditure under the 2003 budget was forecast to reach JD 2,441m., while total state revenues, including foreign aid, were predicted to rise to JD 2,125m., increasing the budget deficit to 4.3% of GDP. As in previous years, grants from donor countries (JD 322m. in 2003) were expected to reduce the budget shortfall to some degree. Jordan's total external debt rose by about 7.6% in 2002, to reach $8,108m.—equivalent to some 83.8% of gross national income (GNI). External debt in 2003 was $8,337m., equivalent to 81.1% of GNI.

The 2004 budget envisaged a fiscal squeeze to cushion the effect on Jordan's economy of the loss of cheap Iraqi oil since the start of the US-led military campaign in 2003 that had ousted the regime of Saddam Hussain. The budget projected an increase in expenditure to JD 2,670m. and forecast revenue of JD 2,377m., leaving a budget deficit of JD 293m., equivalent to about 3.9% of GDP. In February 2005 the House of Representatives endorsed the JD 3,300m. state budget for 2005 (which forecast a deficit equivalent to 3.3% of GDP), while at the same time urging more economic self-reliance and less dependence on foreign aid (which constituted 53% of the expected revenues for the year). At the end of 2004 Jordan's external debt stood at US $8,175m., equivalent to 69.8% of GNI.

In 2006 the budget deficit (including foreign aid grants) reached JD 449m. or 4.5% of GDP, reflecting total revenues of JD 3,453m. (domestic revenue of JD 3,131m. and JD 322m. in grants) and total expenditure of JD 3,902m. Net outstanding public debt (domestic and external) at the end of the year stood at JD 7,350m., representing 72.8% of GDP (compared with 83.2% in 2005). Jordan's outstanding external debt at the end of 2006 totalled JD 5,186.5m. (51.4% of GDP), compared with JD 5,056.7m. at the end of 2005.

The draft budget for 2007 envisaged a reduced deficit (including grants) of JD 380m., equivalent to 3.4% of GDP. Total revenues were forecast at JD 3,954m., including JD 3,380m. in domestic revenue and JD 574m. in grants. Total expenditure was budgeted to rise to JD 4,334m., with capital spending set to increase by 32% compared with the previous year, to JD 1,014m. However, in April and September 2007, confronted with rising public employee wage and pension costs and the increasing international prices of imported goods (especially oil and cereals), the Government issued two supplements to the budget, totalling JD 578m. In addition, foreign grants fell short of the budget estimate by JD 228m., increasing pressure on the deficit. This was partly offset by a rise in domestic revenues, and re-estimated figures for 2007 indicated that the budget deficit would not exceed JD 616m., or 5.4% of GDP, according to the Minister of Finance.

Under the draft budget for 2008, total revenues were forecast at JD 4,501m., including JD 4,061m. in domestic revenue and JD 440m. in grants. Total expenditure was estimated at JD 5,225m., comprising current expenditure of JD 4,101m. and capital spending of JD 1,124m. As a result, the deficit was forecast at JD 724m., or 5.6% of GDP. Excluding grants, the deficit was estimated at JD 1,164m., or 9.1% of GDP. Again, the Government had to issue supplements to the budget during 2008, reflecting the strain caused by the cost of compensatory payments to offset the negative impact on disposable income of fuel price rises and the reversal of the lifting of cooking oil and fodder subsidies. Jordan's external debt at the end of 2008 decreased to JD 3,640.2m., from JD 5,253.3m. a year earlier.

The draft budget for 2009 forecast expenditure of JD 6,160m. and revenue of JD 5,470m., with a resulting deficit of about JD 690m. In the context of the global economic downturn, however, the Minister of Finance announced in April 2009 that revenue in the first quarter of the year was 10% less than had been envisaged in the budget, and that he expected the deficit to reach JD 1,100m. over the year. In December, in response to the rising fiscal deficit and increased public borrowing, the Government approved a provisional austerity budget for 2010. This envisaged a reduction in revenue and expenditure to JD 4,770m. and JD 5,460m., respectively, resulting in a projected deficit of JD 690m (including foreign grants—forecast at JD 330m.). In March 2010 the Government approved a JD 160m. supplementary budget to offset a decline in tax revenue. External debt, meanwhile, increased to JD 3,869.2m. in 2009.

In December 2010 the Government presented the 2011 draft budget to parliament. Overall revenue was estimated at JD 5,180m. (including JD 300m. in foreign grants), and expenditure was forecast to rise to JD 6,240m., with a projected deficit of JD 1,060m. (equivalent to 5% of GDP). However, these plans were derailed by the civil unrest that broke out in January 2011, in response to which the Government announced economic measures costing JD 460m. in an effort to counter the grievances of the demonstrators. These included fuel tax concessions, the maintenance of a subsidy on gas cylinders, and pension and public sector salary increases. In March the new Government presented a revised budget to parliament, projecting total revenue (including foreign grants) at JD 5,208m. and expenditure at JD 6,369m., with a higher budget deficit of JD 1,160m. (5.5% of GDP).

The 2012 draft budget, presented in December 2011, envisaged a reduced deficit of 4.6% of GDP. Expenditure was projected at JD 6,800m., and revenue was set at JD 5,800m. Foreign grants were expected to decline to JD 870m., from the record 2011 inflow figure of JD 1,200m. Commodity subsidies were estimated to have cost JD 2,300m. in 2011, prompting the Minister of Finance to announce in January 2012 that a new system of targeted cash payments to low- and medium-income households would replace existing universal subsidies. The IMF estimated that Jordan's public debt rose to 64.6% of GDP in 2011, compared with 57.1% in 2009 and 61.1% in 2010.

In December 2012 the Government approved a JD 7,456m. draft budget for 2013—with an estimated deficit of JD 2,160m. (equivalent to 8.9% of GDP) without foreign grants, or JD 1,300m. (5.4% of GDP) after foreign assistance. The budget set current spending about 2% lower than in 2012, at JD 6,210m., with the remaining JD 1,246m. to be allocated for significantly higher capital expenditure. Revenue was projected at JD 6,146m., including JD 850m. in foreign grants.

Jordan's strong banking sector weathered the worst of the 2008–09 global financial crisis, and has since managed to maintain profitability despite the slowdown in economic growth and increased domestic and regional political uncertainty. Total bank deposits reached JD 29,919m. in 2012 (deposit interest rates having been raised in May and again in December) and banks' average capital adequacy ratios were well above the 12% requirement of the CBJ.

In 1997 the authorities abolished exchange control restrictions, allowing the free movement of currency for the first time in Jordan since 1989. A new investment law introduced at the end of 1995 permitted foreign investors to buy shares on the Amman stock market without applying for government permission, although a limit of 50% was set on the proportion of an existing listed company's shares that could be owned by foreign interests. In the case of companies with shares that were being publicly floated for the first time, foreign buyers could purchase holdings of up to 100% with the Government's permission (which was required for any bid for foreign ownership of more than 50% of a newly floated company's shares). The minimum level for foreign investment through the stock market was reduced from JD 5,000 to JD 1,000, while the minimum level for direct foreign investment in Jordan was set at JD 50,000. A limit of 25% was imposed on foreign participation in local printing and publishing companies (previously prohibited under Jordanian law). In 1997 the Higher Council for Investment recommended that the 50% ceiling on foreign ownership of shares should be abolished in selected sectors (including banking and insurance), in order to encourage sustained foreign interest after the Government abolished a 15% tax on capitalized reserves. The 1997 Securities Law divided stock exchange activity between three bodies: the Jordan Securities Commission (an independent regulatory body); the Depository & Transfer Centre, to settle and clear stock; and the privately run ASE. Net foreign investment in the market reached US $174.9m. in 1998 (from $80.4m. in 1997), and non-Jordanian ownership stood at 44% (from 38%). Turnover on the market rose by 32% in 1998, to $653m., and total market capitalization at the end of that year was $5,842m. In 1999, however, ASE turnover decreased by 16%, to $549m., and a 1.6% contraction in the ASE index resulted in total market capitalization declining to $5,780m. at the end of 1999. Negative factors included the damage to Jordan's manufacturing industry caused by the continuing UN embargo against Iraq, and high domestic interest rates.

In 2000 the ASE suffered further reductions in turnover (to US $472m.) and market capitalization (to $4,950m.). There was a net outflow of $16.6m. of foreign funds in that year (compared with a net inflow of $21.8m. in 1999), leaving foreign shareholders with 41% of the market. In 2001 the ASE share index rose by 30%, buoyed in part by a strong financial performance by the banking sector. The exchange's market capitalization rose to JD 5,029m. in 2002 (from JD 4,477m. in 2001), and the trading volume increased by around 42%. Non-Jordanian share-ownership decreased to 37.4% (from 38.5% in 2001). In 2003, having slumped in early February to their lowest levels for more than a year, reflecting pessimism about developments with regard to Iraq, share prices on the exchange recovered to reach record levels by the end of June. The exchange continued to perform strongly in 2004. The ASE index increased by 62.4% compared with 2003, and there was unprecedented growth in trading activity (trading volume doubling to reach JD 3,800m.). Approximately 1,300m. shares changed hands during 2004, representing a rise of 33% compared with 2003. In addition, the exchange's market capitalization also rose by 67.8% during 2004, from JD 7,773m. to JD 13,034m. The exchange consistently reached new highs during 2005, with the ASE index increasing by 92.9% compared with 2004. Total trading volume reached JD 16,871m. (a 345% increase on the 2004 figure), and the number of shares traded during the year rose by almost 93%, to 2,582m. Market capitalization more than doubled during 2005, reaching JD 26,660m. at the end of the year. In 2006 the trading value, at JD 14,200m., was down by 16%. However, the volume of shares traded increased by 59%, and the number of transactions by 44%. Market capitalization totalled JD 21,100m., 21% lower than at the end of 2005. In 2007 the trading value decreased again, to JD 12,348m., but there were modest rises in the volume of shares traded and the number of transactions. Market capitalization increased to JD 29,214.2m. The trading value in 2008 rose sharply, to JD 20,318m., although market capitalization decreased to JD 25,406.3m. The number of shares traded reached 5,542.3m. In 2009 the trading value declined markedly, to JD 9,665.3m., and market capitalization again contracted, to JD 22,526,9m. The number of shares traded rose to 6,022.5m.; and the number of listed companies continued to increase, reaching 272 (up from 262 in 2008, 245 in 2007 and 227 in 2006). In 2010 the trading value decreased further, to JD 6,690.0m., and market capitalization declined again, to JD 21,858.2m. The number of shares traded rose to 6,988.8m., and the number of listed companies increased to 277. Reflecting the more difficult economic climate, there was a broader ASE decline in 2011 and 2012: the number of listed companies decreased to 247 in 2011 and 243 in 2012; market capitalization contracted to JD 19,272.7m. and JD 19,141m., respectively; traded shares fell to 4,072.3m. and 2,384.1m.; and trading value declined to JD 2,850m. and JD 1,978.8m.

In November 2010 the Government finalized its first, and over-subscribed, bond issue on the international market, raising US $750m.

FOREIGN TRADE AND BALANCE OF PAYMENTS

By 1990 Iraq's position as Jordan's main trading partner (and supplier of more than 80% of its petroleum) made it inevitable that the UN sanctions imposed after the Iraqi occupation of Kuwait in August would be fulfilled only with reluctance by Jordan. Transit trade with Iraq through the port of Aqaba collapsed, and the outbreak of war in January 1991 resulted in the virtual cessation of Iraqi oil deliveries. Following the end of hostilities, Iraq declared in April that it wished to resume normal trade with Jordan, which it proposed to make its main channel to the outside world (although a restoration of full bilateral trading links depended on removal of the UN embargo). Jordan's oil import requirement was subsequently supplied by road from Iraq under a bilateral arrangement that was deemed by Jordan to fall outside UN sanctions because it involved no financial transfers. Just over one-half of the supply was free of charge, while the remainder was counted as a repayment of Iraqi debt to Jordan. The agreement, which was understood to cover 55,000 b/d of crude petroleum in 1993, was informally monitored by UN sanctions administrators, but did not have the formal approval of the UN sanctions committee. Following widespread reports that there was a growing barter element (mainly involving the supply of Jordanian food to Iraq) in this trade, the USA began to exert pressure on Jordan to contribute 30% of the value of its oil imports to the UN-administered compensation fund for claims arising out of the Iraqi invasion of Kuwait. (This was the percentage levy that the UN intended to impose on UN-supervised oil exports from Iraq under a scheme that Iraq had so far declined to implement.) Iraq continued to supply all of Jordan's oil imports in 1994 and 1995.

In 1995 Jordan's balance of payments recorded a visible trade deficit of US $1,518.2m. and an overall current account deficit of $258.6m. The trade deficit widened to JD 1,753m. in 1996 (from imports of JD 3,041.6m. and exports of JD 1,288.2m.), contributing to a current account deficit of JD 157.4m. and an overall balance of payments deficit of JD 248.3m. In 1997 exports of JD 1,301.4m. and imports of JD 2,906.5m. produced a trade deficit of JD 1,605.1m., although the current account showed a small surplus of JD 20.8m. and the overall balance of payments a surplus of JD 193.9m. The current account remained in narrow surplus, of JD 15.5m., in 1998, when the trade deficit was JD 1,434.5m. (from imports of JD 2,712.4m. and exports of JD 1,277.9m.), but the overall balance of payments showed a deficit of JD 84.1m. In 1999 the overall balance showed a surplus of JD 441.3m., and the current account a surplus of JD 287.1m., owing in part to a narrowing of the trade deficit to JD 1,323.7m. (from imports of JD 2,622.5m. and exports of JD 1,298.8m.). In 2000 Jordan's trade deficit was JD 1,898.6m. (imports of JD 3,245.2m. and exports of JD 1,346.6m.), while the current account was in surplus by JD 15.5m.

In 2001, despite regional instability and the world economic downturn after the 11 September attacks on the mainland USA, Jordan's exports increased to JD 1,625.7m. by value; imports increased at a lower rate, to JD 3,407.3m., so that the trade deficit decreased to JD 1,781.6m., while the current account surplus rose to JD 20.8m. The balance of payments strengthened markedly in 2002. Exports grew by around 19.6%, amounting to JD 1,945m., while imports rose by only 2.3% to reach JD 3,531.5m. by value. The export surge appeared to justify the Government's efforts to liberalize Jordan's trade regime and to increase access to foreign markets. (Jordan had acceded to the World Trade Organization in 2000, and had entered into a number of trading agreements—see below). Despite the disruption caused by the war in Iraq, exports grew by 8.2% in 2003—although this performance was partly offset by import growth of 10.8%, owing to an increase in domestic demand and higher oil imports. The current account balance registered a large surplus in 2003, reported by the IMF to be 11.6% (after grants) of GDP. Jordanian exports in 2005 were valued at an estimated JD 3,049.6m. (up from JD 2,753.0m. in 2004), while imports increased sharply, to JD 7,442.9m. (from JD 5,799.2m. the previous year), resulting in a deficit of JD 4,393.3m. Foreign exchange reserves were US $5,250m. at the end of 2005, compared with $5,265m. at the end of 2004. Exports in 2007 increased in value to JD 4,063.6m. (from JD 3,689.9m. in 2006), while imports rose to JD 9,722.1m. (from JD 8,187.7m.), resulting in a sharp rise in the trade deficit to JD 5,658.5m. Reserves of foreign exchange increased to $6,870m. at the end of 2007, from $6,100m. in 2006. In 2008 exports rose to JD 5,633.0m., while imports increased to JD 12,060.9m., giving a deficit of JD 6,427.9m. The global economic downturn meant that exports and imports both declined in 2009, falling to JD 4,526.3m. and JD 8,975.1m., respectively, resulting in a narrowing of the deficit to JD 4,448.8m. None the less, foreign exchange reserves increased from $7,750m. in 2008 to $10,900m. in 2009. In 2010 exports increased to JD 4,990.1m. and imports to JD 9,711.9m., while reserves declined to JD 8,679.1m. CBJ data indicated that the trade deficit widened again in 2011, with imports valued at JD 11,549.1m. and exports at JD 5,654.0m., while reserves contracted to JD 7,448.8m. The current account deficit rose sharply in 2011, to the equivalent of 12% of GDP, and again in 2012, to 18%, reflecting volatile energy prices and declining expatriate remittances and tourism receipts in the uncertain global economic and regional political environment. Exports decreased to JD 5,598.7m. in 2012, while imports rose to JD 13,047.5m., resulting in a deficit of JD 7,448.8m.; foreign exchange reserves fell sharply, to JD 4,702.5m.

Under a bilateral trade protocol signed by Jordan and Iraq for 1997, Iraqi petroleum supplies to Jordan were to total 25m. barrels of crude petroleum and 7m. barrels of refined products. Jordanian exports to Iraq were to include humanitarian supplies within the framework of the UN 'oil-for-food' programme, which had come into operation in December 1996. The protocol for 1998 provided for the supply of 4.8m. metric tons of Iraqi petroleum and petroleum products, in exchange for Jordanian goods valued at US $255m. The 1999 protocol similarly provided for 4.8m. tons of Iraqi crude petroleum (50% provided free of charge) for Jordanian goods worth $200m. (the value reduced in line with the prevailing decline in world oil prices at that time). In 2000 Jordan's trade protocol with Iraq was worth $300m. There was an upward revision of the value of oil supplied by Iraq (reflecting the upturn in market prices), although Jordan's internal oil product prices for end users were held unchanged (necessitating reductions in other areas of government spending). The 2001 trade protocol was worth $450m., with Iraq undertaking to supply Jordan with 5m. tons of crude petroleum and products. Government plans to increase oil product prices for Jordanian end users in 2001 were postponed, following strong opposition in the Jordanian parliament. The protocol was renewed in December 2002, but ceased following the US-led military campaign to oust the Iraqi regime from March 2003. After the start of hostilities, Saudi Arabia, Kuwait and the UAE agreed to support Jordan with short-term oil supplies (Saudi Arabia providing 50,000 b/d, and Kuwait and the UAE 25,000 b/d each). Saudi Arabia agreed to extend this oil grant for a further year from April 2004. The value of Jordan's exports to Iraq recovered strongly thereafter.

In 1998 Jordan and Egypt signed an agreement providing for the establishment of a free trade zone by 2005. Jordan and Algeria ratified a 1997 trade agreement in 1999, exempting each other's agricultural and industrial products from customs duties. In 2004 Jordan, Egypt, Morocco and Tunisia signed a free trade agreement, regarded as an important step towards the envisaged creation of a Euro-Mediterranean free trade area by the end of 2010. However, all four countries have since joined the Greater Arab Free Trade Area, thus superseding the 2004 agreement.

A free trade agreement between Jordan and the USA entered effect in December 2001, providing for the elimination of all bilateral tariff and other trade restrictions over a 10-year period. Jordanian exports to the USA increased to 12.2% of overall exports in 2001, and 19% in 2002. This surge continued, with exports rising to JD 470.0m. in 2003, JD 724.0m. in 2004 and JD 798.1m. in 2005. Exports to the USA totalled JD 923.6m. in 2006, but fell to JD 879.8m. in 2007. Jordan's trade surplus with the USA in that year decreased by 37%, from US $798m. to $501m., reflecting a decline in exports from QIZs (see Other Industries) and higher imports of US goods. There was a marked decline in exports to the USA in 2008, to JD 743.0m., and again in 2009, to JD 619.3m.; but exports recovered somewhat in 2010, to JD 659.2m., and in 2011 they recovered to a value of JD 738.7m.

In 1997 Jordan and the European Union (EU) initialled an association agreement, providing for the progressive liberalization of trading arrangements over a 12-year period. The agreement came into effect on 1 January 2000. In 2004 the European Commission approved the first EU-Jordan Action Plan, under which Jordan would receive increased financial support in return for progress in economic, political and social reforms. The Plan would also extend trade relations to cover agriculture and the service sector, and was intended to simplify customs procedures. In May 2010 the EU and Jordan signed a new financial assistance package, worth €223m., covering the period 2011–13, in support of further economic and social reforms.

Statistical Survey

Source: Department of Statistics, POB 2015, Amman 11181; tel. (6) 5300700; fax (6) 5300710; e-mail stat@dos.gov.jo; internet www.dos.gov.jo.

Area and Population

AREA, POPULATION AND DENSITY

Area (sq km)	88,794*
Population (census results)	
10 December 1994	4,139,458
1 October 2004	
Males	2,626,287
Females	2,477,352
Total	5,103,639
Population (official estimates at 31 December)	
2010	6,113,000
2011	6,249,000
2012	6,388,000
Density (per sq km) at 31 December 2012	71.9

* 34,284 sq miles.

POPULATION BY AGE AND SEX

(estimated population at 31 December 2012)

	Males	Females	Total
0–14	1,223,055	1,159,270	2,382,325
15–64	1,962,900	1,831,475	3,794,375
65 and over	107,045	104,255	211,300
Total	3,293,000	3,095,000	6,388,000

Note: Figures are rounded to nearest five persons.

GOVERNORATES

(estimated population at 31 December 2012)

	Area (sq km)	Population	Density (per sq km)
Amman	7,579	2,473,400	326.3
Irbid	1,572	1,137,100	723.3
Al-Zarqa (Zarqa)	4,761	951,800	199.9
Al-Balqa	1,120	428,000	382.1
Al-Mafraq	26,551	300,300	11.3
Al-Karak (Kerak)	3,495	249,100	71.3
Jarash (Jerash)	410	191,700	467.6
Madaba	940	159,700	169.9
Ajloun	420	146,900	349.8
Al-Aqabah (Aqaba)	6,905	139,200	20.2
Ma'an	32,832	121,400	3.7
Al-Tafilah	2,209	89,400	40.5
Total	88,794	6,388,000	71.9

Note: Population figures are rounded to nearest 100 persons.

PRINCIPAL TOWNS

(population at 2004 census)

Amman (capital)	1,036,330	Wadi al-Sir	122,032
Al-Zarqa (Zarqa)	395,227	Tila' al-Ali (Tla' El-Ali)	113,197
Irbid	250,645	Khuraybat as-Suq (Khraibet Essoq)	84,975
Al-Rusayfah (Russeifa)	227,735	Al-Aqabah (Aqaba)	80,059
Al-Quwaysimah	135,500		

Mid-2011 (incl. suburbs, UN estimate): Amman 1,178,650 (Source: UN, *World Urbanization Prospects: The 2011 Revision*).

BIRTHS, MARRIAGES AND DEATHS*

	Registered live births		Registered marriages		Registered deaths	
	Number	Rate (per 1,000)	Number	Rate (per 1,000)	Number	Rate (per 1,000)
2004	150,248	28.1	53,754	10.0	17,011	3.2
2005	152,276	27.8	56,418	10.3	17,883	3.3
2006	162,972	29.1	59,335	10.6	20,397	3.6
2007	185,011	32.3	60,548	10.6	20,924	3.7
2008	181,328	31.0	60,922	10.4	19,403	3.3
2009	179,872	30.1	63,389	10.6	20,251	3.4
2010	183,948	30.1	62,107	10.2	21,550	3.5
2011	178,435	28.6	64,665	10.3	21,730	3.5

* Data are tabulated by year of registration rather than by year of occurrence. Registration of births and marriages is reported to be complete, but death registration is incomplete. Figures exclude foreigners, but include registered Palestinian refugees.

Life expectancy (years at birth): 73.4 (males 72.0; females 74.9) in 2011 (Source: World Bank, World Development Indicators database).

EMPLOYMENT

(economic survey at October, public and private sectors, excl. armed forces)

	2009	2010	2011
Mining and quarrying	8,626	8,520	8,600
Manufacturing	182,769	188,015	186,517
Electricity, gas and water	13,442	15,878	14,255
Construction	51,177	46,105	50,130
Wholesale and retail trade; repair of motor vehicles and motorcycles and personal and household goods	208,304	210,318	214,079
Hotels and restaurants	39,680	40,908	44,917
Transport, storage and communications	33,832	36,354	38,069
Financial intermediation	26,944	29,041	31,282
Real estate, renting and business activities	47,157	46,641	49,464
Public administration and compulsory social security	104,078	104,431	107,142
Education	165,294	170,384	181,940
Health and social work	55,682	57,879	59,647
Other community, social and personal service activities	25,288	23,241	26,055
Total employed	962,272	977,714	1,012,096
Males	742,631	752,121	779,466
Females	219,641	225,593	232,630

Note: Figures are assumed to exclude data for those engaged in agriculture and fishing—according to FAO estimates some 107,000 of a total economically active population of 1,929,000 were engaged in the sector at mid-2013. Figures include foreign nationals employed in Jordan, numbering 126,369 in 2009; 121,726 in 2010; 111,721 in 2011.

Health and Welfare

KEY INDICATORS

Total fertility rate (children per woman, 2011)	3.0
Under-5 mortality rate (per 1,000 live births, 2011)	21
HIV/AIDS (% of persons aged 15–49, 2007)	<0.2
Physicians (per 1,000 head, 2009)	2.4
Hospital beds (per 1,000 head, 2010)	1.8
Health expenditure (2010): US $ per head (PPP)	493
Health expenditure (2010): % of GDP	8.3
Health expenditure (2010): Public (% of total)	67.6
Access to water (% of persons, 2011)	96
Access to sanitation (% of persons, 2011)	98
Total carbon dioxide emissions ('000 metric tons, 2009)	22,548.4
Carbon dioxide emissions per head (metric tons, 2009)	3.8
Human Development Index (2012): ranking	100
Human Development Index (2012): value	0.700

For sources and definitions, see explanatory note on p. vi.

Agriculture

PRINCIPAL CROPS
('000 metric tons)

	2009	2010	2011
Wheat	12.5	22.1	19.8
Barley	17.1	10.7	29.3
Maize	19.8	29.0	16.5
Potatoes	118.7	174.9	216.5
Olives	140.7	171.7	131.8
Cabbages and other brassicas	25.4	20.3	22.1
Lettuce and chicory	39.8	48.2	40.4
Tomatoes	654.3	737.3	777.8
Cauliflowers and broccoli	80.3	54.7	62.5
Pumpkins, squash and gourds	59.3	69.7	93.1
Cucumbers and gherkins	137.7	176.2	227.6
Aubergines (Eggplants)	106.8	104.7	117.0
Chillies and peppers, green	43.7	55.1	63.7
Onions and shallots, green	8.9	3.5	1.1
Onions, dry	28.8	15.8	40.8
Beans, green	5.6	8.2	8.5
Okra	6.2	6.8	8.6
Watermelons	106.5	153.1	121.8
Cantaloupes and other melons	17.0	31.1	38.6
Bananas	43.8	43.8	48.3
Grapefruit and pomelos	8.1	8.4	7.6
Oranges	42.8	43.0	38.7
Tangerines, mandarins, clementines and satsumas	32.5	38.3	34.1
Lemons and limes	21.8	28.8	26.4
Apples	31.1	28.8	39.7
Peaches and nectarines	31.4	20.8	26.9
Grapes	34.4	29.7	38.4

Aggregate production ('000 metric tons, may include official, semi-official or estimated data): Total cereals 60.9 in 2009, 87.3 in 2010, 83.0 in 2011; Total roots and tubers 118.7 in 2009, 174.9 in 2010, 216.5 in 2011; Total vegetables (incl. melons) 1,421.9 in 2009, 1,609.7 in 2010, 1,749.6 in 2011; Total fruits (excl. melons) 288.4 in 2009, 289.6 in 2010, 319.7 in 2011.

Source: FAO.

LIVESTOCK
('000 head, year ending September)

	2009	2010	2011
Horses	3	2	2*
Asses*	10	10	10
Mules*	1.5	1.5	1.5
Cattle	64.5	65.4	67.6
Camels	13†	13†	12*
Sheep	2,070.9	2,175.7	2,264.6
Goats	919.7	751.7	752.2
Chickens*	27,000	25,000	26,000

* FAO estimate(s).
† Unofficial figure.

Source: FAO.

LIVESTOCK PRODUCTS
('000 metric tons)

	2009	2010	2011
Cattle meat	13.3	12.3	17.8
Sheep meat	20.3	17.7	12.1
Goat meat	5.0	4.0	5.1
Chicken meat	152.8	187.5	190.5
Cows' milk	244.6	215.0	238.6
Sheep's milk	56.0	58.6*	57.9
Goats' milk	18.8	15.8	10.5
Hen eggs	45.9	69.3	69.3
Wool, greasy†	2.8	2.8	2.8

* Unofficial figure.
† FAO estimates.

Source: FAO.

Forestry

ROUNDWOOD REMOVALS
('000 cubic metres, excluding bark, FAO estimates)

	2009	2010	2011
Industrial wood	4	4	4
Fuel wood	294	302	310
Total	298	306	314

Source: FAO.

Fishing

(metric tons, live weight)

	2009	2010	2011
Capture	569	486	500
Freshwater fishes	350	350	350
Tunas	131	93	102
Aquaculture (Tilapias)	440	541	575
Common carp	230	259	404
Total catch	1,009	1,027	1,075

Source: FAO.

Mining

('000 metric tons unless otherwise indicated)

	2009	2010	2011
Crude petroleum ('000 barrels)	9.4	8.9	7.2
Phosphate rock	5,282	6,529	7,643
Potash salts*	1,120	2,141	2,259
Bromine	69	329	148
Gypsum	304	292	255

* Figures refer to the K_2O content.

Source: US Geological Survey.

Industry

SELECTED PRODUCTS
(42-gallon barrels unless otherwise indicated)

	2009	2010	2011
Asphalt	1,171	914	648
Phosphatic fertilizers ('000 metric tons)	721	812	824
Cement ('000 metric tons)	3,876	5,000	6,000
Liquefied petroleum gas	1,235	985	958
Motor spirit (petrol)	7,566	7,029	6,810
Kerosene	625	654	448
Jet fuels	2,444	2,717	2,721
Distillate fuel oils	8,750	6,739	7,684
Electricity (million kWh)	14,272	14,777	14,647

Sources: mainly US Geological Survey.

Finance

CURRENCY AND EXCHANGE RATES

Monetary Units
1,000 fils = 1 Jordanian dinar (JD).

Sterling, Dollar and Euro Equivalents (31 May 2013)
£1 sterling = JD 1.080;
US $1 = 710 fils;
€1 = JD 0.923;
JD 10 = £9.26 = $14.08 = €10.83.

Exchange Rate: An official mid-point rate of US $1 = 709 fils (JD1 = $1.4104) has been maintained since October 1995.

BUDGET
(JD million)*

Revenue†	2011	2012‡	2013§
Taxation	3,062.2	3,351.4	3,770.0
Taxes on income and profits	667.4	688.4	765.0
Corporations	519.6	556.6	613.0
Individuals	78.8	64.4	71.0
Taxes on domestic transactions	2,033.2	2,274.8	2,610.0
General sales tax	2,033.2	2,274.8	2,610.0
Taxes on foreign trade	287.0	285.0	285.0
Other revenue	1,116.0	1,351.7	1,502.0
Fees	599.5	682.0	806.9
Interest and profits	216.0	304.4	311.6
Repayment	43.8	28.8	40.0
Pensions	20.7	24.3	24.0
Total	4,198.8	4,727.4	5,296.0

Expenditure	2011	2012‡	2013§
Current	5,739.5	6,186.2	6,210.1
Wages and salaries	950.2	1,109.0	1,201.7
Purchases of goods and services	265.4	236.2	256.1
Interest payments	429.5	582.7	800.0
Domestic	333.9	482.9	628.0
Foreign	95.6	99.9	172.0
Food and oil subsidies	796.5	887.0	225.0
Pensions	861.9	982.3	1,068.0
Defence and security	1,797.7	1,744.8	1,767.2
Capital	1,057.1	675.9	1,245.6
Total	6,796.6	6,862.1	7,455.7

* Figures represent a consolidation of the Current, Capital and Development Plan Budgets of the central Government. The data exclude the operations of the Health Security Fund and of other government agencies with individual budgets.
† Excluding foreign grants received (JD million): 1,215.0 in 2011; 327.1 in 2012 (preliminary); 850.0 in 2013 (budget figure).
‡ Preliminary.
§ Budget figures.

Source: Ministry of Finance, Amman.

INTERNATIONAL RESERVES
(US $ million at 31 December)

	2009	2010	2011
Gold (national valuation)	450.5	589.3	637.7
IMF special drawing rights	230.0	225.8	224.8
Reserve position in the IMF	0.5	0.5	0.5
Foreign exchange	11,458.8	12,830.5	11,241.9
Total	12,139.8	13,646.1	12,105.0

2012: IMF special drawing rights 220.3; Reserve position in the IMF 0.5.

Source: IMF, *International Financial Statistics*.

MONEY SUPPLY
(JD million at 31 December)

	2010	2011	2012
Currency outside banks	2,843.7	3,019.3	3,215.0
Demand deposits at commercial banks	3,657.2	4,206.3	3,934.5
Total money (incl. others)	6,504.4	7,228.0	7,152.1

Source: IMF, *International Financial Statistics*.

COST OF LIVING
(Consumer Price Index; base: 2006 = 100)

	2010	2011	2012
Food (incl. beverages)	137.7	143.4	150.0
Clothing (incl. footwear)	122.9	130.5	136.7
Housing	118.6	123.1	127.4
Other goods and services	114.4	120.2	127.0
All items	124.5	130.0	136.0

NATIONAL ACCOUNTS
(JD million at current prices)

Expenditure on the Gross Domestic Product

	2007	2008*	2009*
Government final consumption expenditure	2,499.4	3,363.6	3,699.5
Private final consumption expenditure	10,512.3	12,403.0	12,688.4
Changes in stocks	337.8	318.7	193.7
Gross fixed capital formation	3,334.1	4,342.9	4,254.2
Total domestic expenditure	16,683.6	20,428.2	20,835.8
Exports of goods and services	6,579.4	8,811.2	7,758.6
Less Imports of goods and services	11,131.6	13,646.0	11,682.2
GDP in purchasers' values	12,131.4	15,593.4	16,912.2
GDP in constant 1994 prices	8,629.0	9,252.1	9,759.9

* Preliminary.

GDP in constant 1994 prices (preliminary estimates): 9,985.5 in 2010; 10,243.8 in 2011; 10,515.3 in 2012.

Gross Domestic Product by Economic Activity
(preliminary estimates)

	2010	2011	2012
Agriculture, hunting, forestry and fishing	560.9	598.3	604.5
Mining and quarrying	621.8	803.5	723.5
Manufacturing	3,146.1	3,485.3	3,633.4
Electricity and water	380.0	417.5	482.8
Construction	896.2	888.0	961.7
Wholesale and retail trade, restaurants and hotels	1,723.9	1,845.3	2,055.8
Transport, storage and communications	2,285.2	2,426.1	2,637.4
Finance, insurance, real estate and business services	3,135.3	3,483.9	3,838.4
Public administration, defence, and social security	3,735.4	4,121.3	4,485.6
Other services	822.0	854.3	951.8
Sub-total	17,306.8	18,923.5	20,375.0
Less Imputed bank service charge	889.6	935.8	1,076.9
GDP in basic prices	16,417.2	17,987.7	19,298.2
Taxes on products (net)	2,344.8	2,488.9	2,667.3
GDP in purchasers' values	18,762.0	20,476.6	21,965.5

BALANCE OF PAYMENTS
(US $ million)

	2009	2010	2011
Exports of goods	6,375.1	7,028.3	8,006.3
Imports of goods	−12,641.1	−13,822.4	−16,825.6
Balance on goods	−6,266.0	−6,794.1	−8,819.3
Exports of services	4,554.2	5,600.0	5,138.5
Imports of services	−3,817.6	−4,419.0	−4,475.5
Balance on goods and services	−5,529.4	−5,613.1	−8,156.3
Primary income received	1,092.9	1,010.8	795.4
Primary income paid	−585.6	−1,102.0	−975.1
Balance on goods, services and primary income	−5,022.2	−5,704.2	−8,336.1
Secondary income received	4,433.8	4,372.5	5,365.5
Secondary income paid	−655.4	−550.4	−499.7
Current balance	−1,243.7	−1,882.1	−3,470.3
Capital account (net)	0.6	0.3	—
Direct investment assets	−72.4	−28.5	−30.8
Direct investment liabilities	2,413.1	1,650.8	1,469.0
Portfolio investment assets	−600.0	41.0	282.5
Portfolio investment liabilities	−29.6	729.6	11.1
Other investment assets	1,503.4	−1,228.7	−522.5
Other investment liabilities	763.5	1,422.0	468.5
Net errors and omissions	392.7	755.4	140.0
Reserves and related items	3,127.5	1,459.8	−1,652.6

Source: IMF, *International Financial Statistics*.

External Trade

PRINCIPAL COMMODITIES
(distribution by HS, JD million)

Imports c.i.f.	2010	2011	2012
Food, beverages and tobacco	1,927.6	2,369.2	2,587.5
Live animals and animal products	426.3	496.1	599.0
Vegetable products	742.5	986.2	1,025.0
Prepared foodstuffs; beverages, spirits and vinegar; tobacco and manufactured tobacco substitutes	665.9	738.5	815.8
Mineral products	2,503.7	3,775.4	4,725.9
Chemicals and related products	913.1	1,049.7	1,089.1
Plastics, rubbers, and articles thereof	449.9	536.5	617.7
Textiles and textile articles	615.4	701.3	758.0
Base metals and articles thereof	951.8	1,037.9	1,093.4
Machinery and mechanical appliances	1,577.1	1,624.0	1,565.9
Vehicles, aircraft, vessels and associated transport equipment	929.0	795.2	850.8
Total (incl. others)	11,050.1	13,440.2	14,733.7

Exports f.o.b.	2010	2011	2012
Food, beverages and tobacco	799.2	880.6	979.4
Live animals and animal products	152.3	168.8	192.1
Vegetable products	391.0	455.4	497.2
Prepared foodstuffs; beverages, spirits and vinegar; tobacco and manufactured tobacco substitutes	247.0	257.1	272.7
Mineral products	330.6	489.0	488.4
Chemicals and related products	1,242.0	1,765.4	1,679.7
Plastics, rubbers, and articles thereof	135.7	171.9	229.1
Textiles and textile articles	683.2	764.4	813.8
Pearls; precious or semi-precious stones; precious metals	233.5	273.0	182.3
Base metals and articles thereof	338.4	363.2	287.3
Machinery and mechanical appliances	400.9	451.1	409.0
Vehicles, aircraft, vessels and associated transport equipment	131.1	123.8	113.8
Total (incl. others)	4,990.1	5,684.6	5,599.5

PRINCIPAL TRADING PARTNERS
(countries of consignment, JD million)

Imports c.i.f.	2010	2011	2012
Argentina	117.4	173.7	233.3
Brazil	131.6	147.3	180.4
China, People's Republic	1,188.6	1,317.4	1,416.4
Egypt	492.9	535.0	560.5
France	246.6	264.2	265.7
Germany	729.0	607.5	575.2
India	275.3	360.2	506.8
Iraq	165.6	220.0	230.8
Italy	379.3	688.5	658.6
Japan	343.5	259.0	277.5
Korea, Republic	461.9	435.9	406.3
Malaysia	136.4	104.6	105.7
Netherlands	126.0	126.2	115.6
Romania	68.6	136.3	119.1
Russia	178.2	513.1	450.3
Saudi Arabia	2,164.4	2,968.7	3,469.7
Spain	85.1	163.5	137.0
Syria	267.2	268.4	171.3
Taiwan	127.7	178.5	194.4
Turkey	397.2	393.5	568.9
Ukraine	186.0	146.2	356.8
United Arab Emirates	286.0	504.9	418.8
United Kingdom	189.4	212.9	183.2
USA	615.6	861.4	977.5
Total (incl. others)	11,050.1	13,440.2	14,733.7

Exports f.o.b.	2010	2011	2012
Algeria	90.7	90.1	93.5
China, People's Republic	80.3	144.5	134.1
Egypt	101.9	89.2	93.6
Ethiopia	70.8	69.0	22.5
India	552.2	649.0	515.3
Indonesia	105.9	157.1	192.7
Iraq	800.8	862.2	868.3
Israel	74.8	80.5	89.0
Kuwait	64.0	102.0	74.9
Lebanon	164.2	238.3	208.6

Exports f.o.b.—*continued*	2010	2011	2012
Malaysia	50.7	80.0	46.7
Qatar	69.8	66.3	82.8
Saudi Arabia	475.4	482.9	547.9
Sudan	61.3	59.4	45.9
Switzerland	99.9	57.2	21.0
Syria	182.5	203.6	156.1
Turkey	43.2	69.7	93.9
United Arab Emirates	210.6	205.6	224.0
USA	659.2	738.7	799.0
Total (incl. others)	4,990.1	5,684.6	5,599.5

Transport

RAILWAYS
(traffic, million)

	2008	2009	2010
Passenger-km	0.4	0.9	1.3
Freight ton-km	448	439	344

Source: IRF, *World Road Statistics*.

ROAD TRAFFIC
(motor vehicles in use at 31 December)

	2008	2009	2010
Passenger cars	601,312	673,125	742,149
Buses	17,521	18,143	18,902
Lorries and vans	240,869	227,582	236,526
Motorcycles	3,845	3,489	4,079

Source: IRF, *World Road Statistics*.

2011 (licensed vehicles in use): Passenger cars 670,808; Buses 2,739; Vans and trucks 158,886; Tankers 1,050; Trailers 26,588, Others 46,724; *Total vehicles* 906,795.

SHIPPING

Flag Registered Fleet
(at 31 December)

	2010	2011	2012
Number of vessels	22	21	23
Displacement ('000 grt)	231.3	200.8	79.8

Source: Lloyd's List Intelligence (www.lloydslistintelligence.com).

International Sea-borne Freight Traffic
('000 metric tons)

	2009	2010	2011
Goods loaded	6,970	9,631	10,862
Goods unloaded	8,302	8,796	10,208

CIVIL AVIATION
(traffic on scheduled services)

	2007	2008	2009
Kilometres flown (million)	54	55	56
Passengers carried ('000)	2,288	2,355	2,324
Passenger-km (million)	6,446	6,400	6,363
Total ton-km (million)	756	719	687

Source: UN, *Statistical Yearbook*.

Passengers carried ('000): 2,972 in 2010; 3,123 in 2011 (Source: World Bank, World Development Indicators database).

Tourism

ARRIVALS BY NATIONALITY
('000)*

	2010	2011	2012
Egypt	379.8	326.5	353.8
Iraq	254.3	292.1	373.1
Israel	244.3	211.9	203.7
Lebanon	186.1	108.6	65.9
Palestinian Territories	393.5	441.6	470.2
Saudi Arabia	1,337.4	1,074.2	1,144.1
Syria	2,382.6	1,903.7	1,190.2
Turkey	171.3	156.0	46.1
USA	181.7	156.6	159.4
Total (incl. others)	8,247.1	6,812.4	6,314.3

* Including pilgrims and excursionists (same-day visitors).

Source: Ministry of Tourism and Antiquities, Amman.

Tourism receipts (US $ million, excl. passenger transport): 2,911 in 2009; 3,585 in 2010; 3,000 in 2011 (provisional) (Source: World Tourism Organisation).

Communications Media

	2010	2011	2012
Telephones ('000 main lines in use)	485.5	465.4	434.4
Mobile cellular telephones ('000 subscribers)	6,620.0	7,482.6	8,984.3
Internet subscribers ('000)	248.3	208.1	n.a.
Broadband subscribers ('000)	195.8	199.9	193.6

Source: International Telecommunication Union.

Education

(2009/10 unless otherwise indicated)

	Schools	Teachers	Pupils
Pre-primary	1,248*	5,381	99,168
Primary	2,877*	39,441†	819,601
Secondary: general	1,002*	30,426†	685,883
Secondary: vocational	40*	2,759‡	23,830
Higher	22*	10,024	252,446§
of which universities‖	20	3,982	89,010

* 2003/04 figure.
† 2002/03 figure.
‡ 2007/08 figure.
§ 2010/11 figure.
‖ 1996/97 figures.

Source: partly UNESCO Institute for Statistics.

Pupil-teacher ratio (primary education, UNESCO estimate): 19.9 in 2002/03 (Source: UNESCO Institute for Statistics).

Adult literacy rate (UNESCO estimates): 92.6% (males 95.8%; females 89.2%) in 2010 (Source: UNESCO Institute for Statistics).

Directory

The Constitution

The revised Constitution was approved by King Talal I on 1 January 1952.

The Hashemite Kingdom of Jordan is an independent, indivisible sovereign state. Its official religion is Islam; its official language Arabic.

RIGHTS OF THE INDIVIDUAL

There is to be no discrimination between Jordanians on account of race, religion or language. Work, education and equal opportunities shall be afforded to all as far as is possible. The freedom of the individual is guaranteed, as are his dwelling and property. No Jordanian shall be exiled. Labour shall be made compulsory only in a national emergency, or as a result of a conviction; conditions, hours worked and allowances are under the protection of the state.

The Press, and all opinions, are free, except under martial law. Societies can be formed, within the law. Schools may be established freely, but they must follow a recognized curriculum and educational policy. Elementary education is free and compulsory. All religions are tolerated. Every Jordanian is eligible for public office, and choices are to be made by merit only. Power belongs to the people.

THE LEGISLATIVE POWER

Legislative power is vested in the National Assembly and the King. The National Assembly consists of two houses: the Senate and the House of Representatives.

THE SENATE

The number of Senators is one-half of the number of members of the House of Representatives. Senators must be unrelated to the King, over 40, and are chosen from present and past Prime Ministers and Ministers, past Ambassadors or Ministers Plenipotentiary, past Presidents of the House of Representatives, past Presidents and members of the Court of Cassation and of the Civil and *Shari'a* Courts of Appeal, retired officers of the rank of General and above, former members of the House of Representatives who have been elected twice to that House, etc. They may not hold public office. Senators are appointed for four years. They may be reappointed. The President of the Senate is appointed for two years.

THE HOUSE OF REPRESENTATIVES

The members of the House of Representatives are elected by secret ballot in a general direct election and retain their mandate for four years. General elections take place during the four months preceding the end of the term. The President of the House is elected by secret ballot each year by the Representatives. Representatives must be Jordanians of over 30, they must have a clean record, no active business interests, and are debarred from public office. Close relatives of the King are not eligible. If the House of Representatives is dissolved, the new House shall assemble in extraordinary session not more than four months after the date of dissolution. The new House cannot be dissolved for the same reason as the last.

GENERAL PROVISIONS FOR THE NATIONAL ASSEMBLY

The King summons the National Assembly to its ordinary session on 1 November each year. This date can be postponed by the King for two months, or he can dissolve the Assembly before the end of its three-month session. Alternatively, he can extend the session up to a total period of six months. Each session is opened by a speech from the throne.

Decisions in the House of Representatives and the Senate are made by a majority vote. The quorum is two-thirds of the total number of members in each House. When the voting concerns the Constitution, or confidence in the Council of Ministers, 'the votes shall be taken by calling the members by name in a loud voice'. Sessions are public, though secret sessions can be held at the request of the Government or of five members. Complete freedom of speech, within the rules of either House, is allowed.

The Prime Minister places proposals before the House of Representatives; if accepted there, they are referred to the Senate and finally sent to the King for confirmation. If one house rejects a law while the other accepts it, a joint session of the House of Representatives and the Senate is called, and a decision made by a two-thirds majority. If the King withholds his approval from a law, he returns it to the Assembly within six months with the reasons for his dissent; a joint session of the Houses then makes a decision, and if the law is accepted by this decision it is promulgated. The Budget is submitted to the National Assembly one month before the beginning of the financial year.

THE KING

The throne of the Hashemite Kingdom devolves by male descent in the dynasty of King Abdullah ibn al-Hussein. The King attains his majority on his eighteenth lunar year; if the throne is inherited by a minor, the powers of the King are exercised by a Regent or a Council of Regency. If the King, through illness or absence, cannot perform his duties, his powers are given to a Deputy, or to a Council of the Throne. This Deputy, or Council, may be appointed by *Iradas* (decrees) by the King, or, if he is incapable, by the Council of Ministers.

On his accession, the King takes the oath to respect and observe the provisions of the Constitution and to be loyal to the nation. As Head of State he is immune from all liability or responsibility. He approves laws and promulgates them. He declares war, concludes peace and signs treaties; treaties, however, must be approved by the National Assembly. The King is Commander-in-Chief of the navy, the army and the air force. He orders the holding of elections; convenes, inaugurates, adjourns and prorogues the House of Representatives. The Prime Minister is appointed by him, as are the President and members of the Senate. Military and civil ranks are also granted, or withdrawn, by the King. No death sentence is carried out until he has confirmed it.

MINISTERS

The Council of Ministers consists of the Prime Minister, President of the Council, and of his ministers. Ministers are forbidden to become members of any company, to receive a salary from any company, or to participate in any financial act of trade. The Council of Ministers is entrusted with the conduct of all affairs of state, internal and external.

The Council of Ministers is responsible to the House of Representatives for matters of general policy. Ministers may speak in either House, and, if they are members of one House, they may also vote in that House. Votes of confidence in the Council are cast in the House of Representatives, and decided by a two-thirds' majority. If a vote of no confidence is returned, the ministers are bound to resign. Every newly formed Council of Ministers must present its programme to the House of Representatives and ask for a vote of confidence. The House of Representatives can impeach ministers, as it impeaches its own members.

AMENDMENTS

Two amendments were passed in November 1974 giving the King the right to dissolve the Senate or to take away membership from any of its members, and to postpone general elections for a period not to exceed a year, if there are circumstances in which the Council of Ministers feels that it is impossible to hold elections. A further amendment in February 1976 enabled the King to postpone elections indefinitely. In January 1984 two amendments were passed, allowing elections 'in any part of the country where it is possible to hold them' (effectively, only the East Bank) and empowering the National Assembly to elect deputies from the Israeli-held West Bank. In February 2003 the King ratified legislation according to which six seats in the House of Representatives were, from the next general election, to be reserved for women.

The Government

HEAD OF STATE

King: King ABDULLAH IBN AL-HUSSEIN (succeeded to the throne on 7 February 1999).

CABINET

(September 2013)

Prime Minister and Minister of Defence: ABDULLAH ENSOUR.

Minister of Higher Education and Scientific Research: Dr AMIN MAHMOUD.

Minister of Foreign and Expatriates Affairs: NASSER JUDEH.

Minister of the Interior: HUSSEIN HAZAA MAJALI.

Minister of Education: Dr MUHAMMAD THNEIBAT.

Minister of Industry, Trade and Supply: Dr HATEM HAFIZ AL-HALAWANI.

Minister of Water and Irrigation: Dr HAZEM AL-NASSER.

Minister of Agriculture: Dr AKIF AL-ZU'BI.

Minister of the Environment: TAHER AL-SHAKHSHIR.

Minister of Finance: Dr UMAYYA TOUQAN.

Minister of Public Sector Development: Dr KHLEIF AL-KHAWALDEH.

Minister of Awqaf (Religious Endowments) and Islamic Affairs: Dr HAYEL ABD AL-HAFIZ DAWOOD.

Minister of Labour and Minister of Tourism and Antiquities: NIDAL MARDI QATAMIN.

Minister of State for Prime Ministry Affairs: Dr AHMAD ZEYADAT.

Minister of Justice: Dr BASSAM SAMIR AL-TALHOUNI.

Minister of Municipal Affairs: WALID AL-MASRI.

Minister of Public Works and Housing: SAMI HALASEH.

Minister of Planning and International Co-operation: Dr IBRAHIM SAIF.

Minister of State for Media Affairs and Communications: Dr MUHAMMAD HUSSEIN MOMANI.

Minister of Social Development: REEM MAMDOUH ABU HASSAN.

Minister of State: SALAMEH AL-NEIMAT.

Minister of Health: Dr ALI AL-NAHLEH HIASAT.

Minister of Energy and Mineral Resources: Dr MUHAMMAD HAMAD.

Minister of Political and Parliamentary Affairs: KHALID AL-KALALDEH.

Minister of Culture: Dr LANA MAMKEGH.

Minister of Transport: HASHEM AL-MASAEED.

Minister of Information and Communications Technology: Dr AZZAM TALAL SLEIT.

Note: The Head of Intelligence and the Governor of the Central Bank also have full ministerial status.

MINISTRIES

The Prime Ministry of Jordan: POB 80, Amman 11180; tel. (6) 4641211; fax (6) 4642520; e-mail info@pm.gov.jo; internet www.pm.gov.jo.

Ministry of Agriculture: POB 2099, Amman; tel. (6) 5686151; fax (6) 5686310; e-mail agri@moa.gov.jo; internet www.moa.gov.jo.

Ministry of Awqaf (Religious Endowments) and Islamic Affairs: POB 659, Amman; tel. (6) 5666141; fax (6) 5602254; e-mail info@awqaf.gov.jo; internet www.awqaf.gov.jo.

Ministry of Culture: POB 6140, Amman; tel. (6) 5696218; fax (6) 5696598; e-mail info@culture.gov.jo; internet www.culture.gov.jo.

Ministry of Defence: POB 80, Amman; tel. (6) 4641211; fax (6) 4642520; e-mail info@jaf.mil.jo; internet www.jaf.mil.jo.

Ministry of Education: POB 1646, Amman 11118; tel. (6) 5607181; fax (6) 5666019; e-mail moe@moe.gov.jo; internet www.moe.gov.jo.

Ministry of Energy and Mineral Resources: POB 2310, Amman; tel. (6) 5803060; fax (6) 5865714; e-mail memr@memr.gov.jo; internet www.memr.gov.jo.

Ministry of the Environment: Amman; tel. (6) 5560113; fax (6) 5560288; e-mail info@moenv.gov.jo; internet www.moenv.gov.jo.

Ministry of Finance: POB 85, King Hussein St, Amman 11118; tel. (6) 4636321; fax (6) 4618527; e-mail info@mof.gov.jo; internet www.mof.gov.jo.

Ministry of Foreign and Expatriates Affairs: POB 35217, Amman 11180; tel. (6) 5735150; fax (6) 5735163; e-mail inquiry@mfa.gov.jo; internet www.mfa.gov.jo.

Ministry of Health: POB 86, Amman 11118; tel. (6) 5200230; fax (6) 5689177; e-mail info@moh.gov.jo; internet www.moh.gov.jo.

Ministry of Higher Education and Scientific Research: POB 35262, Amman 11180; tel. (6) 5347671; fax (6) 5349079; e-mail mohe@mohe.gov.jo; internet www.mohe.gov.jo.

Ministry of Industry, Trade and Supply: POB 2019, 11181 Amman; tel. (6) 5629030; fax (6) 5684692; e-mail info@mit.gov.jo; internet www.mit.gov.jo.

Ministry of Information and Communications Technology: POB 9903, Amman 11191; tel. (6) 5805700; fax (6) 5861059; e-mail moict@moict.gov.jo; internet www.moict.gov.jo.

Ministry of the Interior: POB 100, Amman; tel. (6) 5691141; fax (6) 5606908; e-mail info@moi.gov.jo; internet www.moi.gov.jo.

Ministry of Justice: POB 6040, Amman 11118; tel. (6) 4603630; fax (6) 4643197; e-mail feedback@moj.gov.jo; internet www.moj.gov.jo.

Ministry of Labour: POB 8160, Amman 11118; tel. (6) 5802666; fax (6) 5855072; e-mail info@mol.gov.jo; internet www.mol.gov.jo.

Ministry of Municipal Affairs: POB 1799, Amman 11118; tel. (6) 4641393; fax (6) 4640404; e-mail mma3@nic.net.jo; internet www.mma.gov.jo.

Ministry of Planning and International Co-operation: POB 555, Amman 11118; tel. (6) 4644466; fax (6) 4642247; e-mail mop@mop.gov.jo; internet www.mop.gov.jo.

Ministry of Political and Parliamentary Affairs: POB 841367, Amman 11180; tel. (6) 5695216; fax (6) 5686582; e-mail info@mopd.gov.jo; internet www.mopd.gov.jo.

Ministry of Public Sector Development: POB 3575, Amman 11821; tel. (6) 5695216; fax (6) 5686282; e-mail info@mopsd.gov.jo; internet www.mopsd.gov.jo.

Ministry of Public Works and Housing: POB 1220, Amman 11118; tel. (6) 5803838; fax (6) 5857590; e-mail mpwh@mpwh.gov.jo; internet www.mpwh.gov.jo.

Ministry of Social Development: POB 6720, Amman 11118; tel. (6) 5679327; fax (6) 5679961; e-mail contact@mosd.gov.jo; internet www.mosd.gov.jo.

Ministry of Tourism and Antiquities: POB 224, Amman 11118; tel. (6) 4603360; fax (6) 4648465; e-mail contacts@mota.gov.jo; internet www.mota.gov.jo.

Ministry of Transport: POB 35214, Amman 11180; tel. (6) 5518111; fax (6) 5527233; e-mail info@mot.gov.jo; internet www.mot.gov.jo.

Ministry of Water and Irrigation: POB 2412, Amman 11181; tel. (6) 5652265; fax (6) 5652287; e-mail admin@mwi.gov.jo; internet www.mwi.gov.jo.

Legislature

Majlis al-Umma (National Assembly)

Senate

POB 72, Amman 11101; tel. (6) 5664121; fax (6) 5689313; e-mail info@senate.jo; internet www.senate.jo.

The Senate (House of Notables) consists of 60 members, appointed by the King. The current Senate was appointed on 25 October 2011.

Speaker: TAHER AL-MASRI.

House of Representatives

POB 72, Amman 11118; tel. (6) 5635200; fax (6) 5685970; e-mail info@representatives.jo; internet www.representatives.jo.

Speaker: SAAD HAYEL SROUR.

General Election, 23 January 2013

Party/Group	Seats
Independents and tribal representatives	108
Islamic Centrist Party	3
Nation Party	2
National Current Party	2
National Union	2
Stronger Jordan	1
Other parties	17
Total	150*

* In accordance with the terms of electoral legislation approved in July 2012, 27 seats were allocated to political parties, while a further 15 seats were reserved for female candidates.

Election Commission

Independent Election Commission: POB 375, Tlaa al-Ali Area, Musa Saket Rd, Next to Chief Justice Bldg, Jordan 11953; tel. (6) 5607406; fax (6) 5607423; e-mail info@entikhabat.jo; internet www.entikhabat.jo; f. 2012; comprises Board of Commissioners and Executive apparatus; Chair. ABDELILAH AL-KHATIB.

Political Organizations

With the exception of the officially sanctioned Jordanian National Union (1971–76), political parties were effectively banned for most of the reign of King Hussein. However, in June 1991 a National Charter, one feature of which was the legalization of political parties, was formally endorsed. In August 1992 legislation allowing the formation of political parties was approved by royal decree, and by March 1993 nine parties had received official recognition. New amendments to the political parties law, approved by parliament in March 2007, required parties to have 500 founding members drawn from five different governorates with equal representation, and compelled parties to grant the Government access to their accounts; the reform also provided for public funding for political parties. Parties were given a period of one year to meet the new requirements or face dissolution. By April 2008 12 out of the 36 existing political parties had rectified their status; all other parties were dissolved, while two new parties were licensed. A number of parties were expected to launch lawsuits contesting their dissolution.

Arab Islamic Democratic Party (Dua'a): POB 104, Amman 11941; tel. and fax (6) 5514443; e-mail info@duaa-jo.com; f. 1993; moderate Islamist party; Founder YOUSUF ABU BAKR.

Higher Co-ordination Committee for Opposition Parties: Amman; opposition bloc currently consisting of 7 leftist, pan-Arab and Islamist parties: Baath Arab Progressive Party, Jordanian Arab Socialist Baath Party, Islamic Action Front, Jordanian Communist Party, Jordan People's Democratic Party (HASHD), National Movement for Direct Democracy and Jordanian Democratic Popular Unity Party (leftist).

Hizb-ut-Tahrir al-Islami (Party of Islamic Liberation): e-mail info@hizb-ut-tahrir.org; internet www.hizb-ut-tahrir.org; f. 1953; transnational org. prohibited in Jordan and many other countries; aims to establish Islamic caliphate throughout the world; denies claims that it is a militant group; Leader in Jordan RAMZI SAWALHAH.

Islamic Action Front (Jabhat al-Amal al-Islami—IAF): POB 925310, Abdali, Amman 11110; tel. (6) 5696985; fax (6) 5696987; e-mail info@jabha.net; internet www.jabha.net; f. 1992; seeks implementation of *Shari'a* (Islamic law) and preservation of the *Umma* (Islamic community); mem. of Higher Co-ordination Committee for Opposition Parties; Sec.-Gen. HAMZA MANSOUR.

Islamic Centrist Party (Hizb al-Wasat al-Islami): POB 2149, Haswa Bldg, 3rd Floor, Amman 11941; tel. and fax (6) 5353966; e-mail alwasaat@yahoo.com; internet www.wasatparty.org; f. 2001 by fmr mems of Islamic Action Front and Muslim Brotherhood; Sec.-Gen. Dr MUHAMMAD AHMAD AL-HAJ.

Jordan People's Democratic Party (Hizb al-Shaab al-Dimuqrati—HASHD): POB 9966, Amman 11191; tel. (6) 5691451; fax (6) 5686857; e-mail ahali@go.com.jo; internet www.hashd-ahali.org.jo; f. 1989; leftist party, which seeks to establish legal and institutional processes to protect the people, instigate economic, social, democratic and agricultural reform, and organize, unify and protect the working classes; supports the Palestinian cause; mem. of Higher Co-ordination Cttee for Opposition Parties; Sec.-Gen. ABLA ABU ULBAH.

Jordanian Arab Socialist Baath Party (Hizb al-Baath al-Arabi al-Ishtiraki al-Urduni): POB 8383, Amman; tel. (6) 4658618; fax (6) 4658617; f. 1993; promotes pan-Arabism; mem. of Higher Co-ordination Cttee for Opposition Parties; Sec.-Gen. AKRAM AL-HOMSI.

Jordanian Communist Party: POB 2349, Amman; tel. and fax (6) 4624939; e-mail jcp@nets.com.jo; internet www.jocp.org; f. 1951; merged with Communist Workers Party of Jordan 2008; Sec.-Gen. Dr MUNIR HAMARNEH.

Jordanian Democratic Popular Unity Party: POB 922110, Amman; tel. (6) 5692301; fax (6) 5692302; e-mail wihdaparty@gmail.com; internet www.wihda.org; f. 1990; publishes *Nida'a al-Watan* newspaper; Sec.-Gen. SAEED THIYAB.

National Constitutional Party (Al-Hizb al-Watani al-Dusturi—NCP): POB 1825237, Amman 11118; tel. (6) 5696256; fax (6) 5686248; f. 1997 by merger of 9 parties; Pres. ABD AL-HADI AL-MAJALI; Sec.-Gen. AHMAD SHUNNAQ.

National Current Party: Amman; f. 2009; seeks to promote the cause of national unity through the reform of political institutions; pro-monarchy; Sec.-Gen. ABDUL HADI MAJALI.

National Movement for Direct Democracy: POB 922478, Amman 11192; tel. (6) 5652125; fax (6) 5639925; f. 1997; Sec.-Gen. MUHAMMAD AL-QAQ.

Stronger Jordan (Urdun Aqwa): Amman; f. 2013; list formed to contest Jan. 2013 parliamentary elections; Leader ROLA AL-FARRA HROUB.

Other licensed parties include: Baath Arab Progressive Party, Al-Hayat, Jordan National Party, Mission Party (Hizb al-Risala) and the Unified Jordanian Front.

Diplomatic Representation

EMBASSIES IN JORDAN

Algeria: POB 830375, Amman 11183; tel. (6) 4641271; fax (6) 4616552; e-mail ambalg@go.com.jo; Ambassador MUHAMMAD QUWAR.

Australia: POB 35201, 41 Kayed al-Armouti St, Abdoun, Amman 11180; tel. (6) 5807000; fax (6) 5807001; e-mail amman.austremb@dfat.gov.au; internet www.jordan.embassy.gov.au; Ambassador HEIDI VENAMORE.

Austria: POB 830795, Jabal Amman, Amman 11183; tel. (6) 4601101; fax (6) 4612725; e-mail amman-ob@bmeia.gv.at; internet www.bmeia.gv.at/en/embassy/amman.html; Ambassador ASTRID HARZ.

Azerbaijan: POB 851894, 13 al-Awabed St, al-Kursi, Amman 11185; tel. (6) 5935525; fax (6) 5932826; e-mail amman@mission.mfa.gov.az; internet www.azembassyjo.org; Ambassador SABIR AGHABAYOV.

Bahrain: POB 5220, Faris al-Khoury St, Shmeisani, Amman 11183; tel. (6) 5664148; fax (6) 5664190; e-mail bahemb@maktoob.com; internet www.mofa.gov.bh/amman; Ambassador NASSER RASHID AL-KAABI.

Bangladesh: POB 5685, 10 Muzdalifa St, al-Rabieh, Amman 11183; tel. (6) 5529192; fax (6) 5529194; e-mail embangl@wanadoo.jo; internet www.bdembassyjordan.com; Ambassador FAZLUL KARIM.

Belgium: POB 942, 17 Sa'ad Jumah St, Jabal Amman, Amman 11118; tel. (6) 4655730; fax (6) 4655740; e-mail amman@diplobel.fed.be; internet www.diplomatie.be/amman; Ambassador THOMAS BAEKELANDT.

Bosnia and Herzegovina: POB 850836, 67 Said al-Mufti St, Amman 11185; tel. (6) 5856921; fax (6) 5856923; e-mail embjoamm@wanadoo.jo; Ambassador DARKO ZELENIKA.

Brazil: POB 5497, Amman 11183; tel. (6) 5923941; fax (6) 5931098; e-mail jorbrem@wanadoo.jo; Ambassador RENATE STILLE.

Brunei: POB 851752, Amman 11185; tel. (6) 5928021; fax (6) 5928024; e-mail amman.jordan@mfa.gov.bn; Chargé d'affaires a.i. MOHAMMAD SALIMIN BIN Haji MOHD DAUD.

Bulgaria: POB 950578, 7 al-Mousel St, Amman 11195; tel. (6) 5529392; fax (6) 5539393; e-mail embassy.amman@mfa.bg; internet www.mfa.bg/embassies/jordan; Chargé d'affaires a.i. ALEXANDER KOVACHEV.

Canada: POB 815403, Amman 11180; tel. (6) 5203300; fax (6) 5203396; e-mail amman@international.gc.ca; internet www.canadainternational.gc.ca/jordan-jordanie; Ambassador MARK GWOZDECKY.

Chile: POB 830663, 28 Hussein Abu Ragheb St, Abdoun, Amman 11183; tel. (6) 5923360; fax (6) 5924263; e-mail echile@batelco.jo; internet chileabroad.gov.cl/jordania; Ambassador VICTOR FERNANDO VARELA PALMA.

China, People's Republic: POB 7365, 9 Jakarta St, Amman 11118; tel. (6) 5516136; fax (6) 5518713; e-mail chinaemb_jo@hotmail.com; internet jo.china-embassy.org; Ambassador YUE XIAOYONG.

Cyprus: POB 5525, Bldg 233, Wadi Sakra St, Amman 11183; tel. (6) 5657143; fax (6) 5657895; e-mail info@cyprusembassyamman.org; Ambassador CHARALAMBOS HADJISAVVAS.

Czech Republic: POB 2213, 34 Halab St, Abdoun, Amman 11181; tel. (6) 5927051; fax (6) 5927053; e-mail amman@embassy.mzv.cz; internet www.mzv.cz/amman; Ambassador IVANA HOLOUBKOVÁ.

Egypt: POB 35178, 14 Riyad el-Mefleh St, Amman 11180; tel. (6) 5605202; fax (6) 5604082; e-mail eg.emb_amman@mfa.gov.eg; Ambassador KHALED THARWAT.

France: POB 5348, Amman 11183; tel. (6) 4604630; fax (6) 4604638; e-mail cad.amman-amba@diplomatie.fr; internet www.ambafrance-jo.org; Ambassador CAROLINE DUMAS.

Georgia: POB 851903, 31 Odeh Abu Tayeh, Shmeisani, Amman 11185; tel. (6) 5603793; fax (6) 5603819; e-mail geoemb@orange.jo; internet www.jordan.mfa.gov.ge; Ambassador ZURAB ERISTAVI.

Germany: POB 183, 25 Benghazi St, Jabal Amman 11118; tel. (6) 5901170; fax (6) 5901282; e-mail info@amman.diplo.de; internet www.amman.diplo.de; Ambassador RALPH TARRAF.

Greece: POB 35069, 7 Suleiman Youssef Sukkar St, Amman 11180; tel. (6) 5922724; fax (6) 5927622; e-mail gremb.amn@mfa.gr; internet www.mfa.gr/amman; Ambassador MARIA LUIZA MARINAKI.

Holy See: POB 142916, 14 Anton al-Naber St, Amman 11814; tel. (6) 5929934; fax (6) 5929931; e-mail nuntiusjordan@gmail.com; Apostolic Nuncio Most Rev. Archbishop GIORGIO LINGUA.

Hungary: POB 3441, 23 Yaqoub Ammari St, Abdoun, Amman 11181; tel. (6) 5925614; fax (6) 5930836; e-mail mission.amm@kum.hu; internet www.mfa.gov.hu/emb/amman; Ambassador Dr BÉLA JUNGBERT.

India: POB 2168, Amr bin Masadah St, Jabal Amman, 1st Circle, Amman 11181; tel. (6) 4622098; fax (6) 4659540; e-mail amb.amman@mea.gov.in; internet indembassy-amman.org; Ambassador RADHA RANJAN DASH.

Indonesia: POB 811784, 13 Ali Seedo al-Kurdi St, Sweifieh, Amman 11181; tel. (6) 5528912; fax (6) 5528380; e-mail amman96@go.com.jo; internet www.kemlu.go.id/amman; Ambassador TEGUH WARDOYO.

Iran: POB 173, Amman 11118; tel. (6) 4641281; fax (6) 4641383; e-mail pub-rel@iranembassyjordan.org; Ambassador MOSTAFA MOSLEH-ZADEH.

Iraq: POB 2025, Amman; tel. (6) 4623175; fax (6) 4619172; e-mail amaemb@mofaml.gov.iq; internet www.mofamission.gov.iq/amn; Ambassador Dr JAWAD HADI ABBAS.

Israel: POB 95866, 47 Maysaloon St, Dahiat al-Rabieh, Amman 11195; tel. (6) 5503500; fax (6) 5503579; e-mail embassy@amman.mfa.gov.il; internet amman.mfa.gov.il; Ambassador DANNY NEVO.

Italy: POB 9800, Jabal al-Weibdeh, 5 Hafiz Ibrahim St, Amman 11191; tel. (6) 4638185; fax (6) 4659730; e-mail info.amman@esteri.it; internet www.ambamman.esteri.it; Ambassador PATRIZIO FONDI.

Japan: POB 2835, Fa'eq Halazon St, Zahran, Abdun Shamali, Amman 11181; tel. (6) 5932005; fax (6) 5931006; e-mail mail@embjapan.org.jo; internet www.jordan.emb-japan.go.jp; Ambassador JUNICHI KOSUGE.

Kazakhstan: Abu Bakir al-Banany St, Amman; tel. (6) 5927953; fax (6) 5927952; e-mail kazemb@orange.jo; Ambassador BOLAT S. SARSENBAYEV.

Korea, Democratic People's Republic: POB 799, Amman; tel. (6) 4417614; fax (6) 4424735; e-mail dprk-embv@scs-net.org; Ambassador RI SI HONG.

Korea, Republic: POB 3060, Bahjat Homsi St, Amman 11181; tel. (6) 5930745; fax (6) 5930280; e-mail jordan@mofat.go.kr; internet jor.mofat.go.kr; Ambassador SHIN HYUN-SUK.

Kuwait: POB 2107, Amman 11181; tel. (6) 5675135; fax (6) 5681971; e-mail q8@kuwaitembassyamman.org; Ambassador Dr HAMAD SALEH DUAIJ.

Lebanon: POB 811779, Amman 11181; tel. and fax (6) 5929111; Ambassador MICHELIN PAZ.

Libya: POB 2987, Amman; tel. (6) 5693101; fax (6) 5693404; Ambassador (vacant).

Malaysia: POB 5351, Tayser Na'na'ah St, off Umawiyyeen St, Abdoun, Amman 11183; tel. (6) 5902400; fax (6) 5934343; e-mail malamman@kln.gov.my; Ambassador Datuk ABD MALEK ABDUL AZIZ.

Mauritania: POB 851594, Saleh Zakee St, Villa 19, Sweifiyeh, Amman 11185; tel. (6) 5855146; fax (6) 5855148; e-mail muritanyaembassy_amman1@hotmail.com; Ambassador ELY OULD AHMEDOU.

Morocco: POB 2175, Amman 11183; tel. (6) 5680591; fax (6) 5680253; e-mail ambmaroc@batelco.jo; Ambassador HASSAN ABD AL-KHALIQ.

Netherlands: POB 941361, 3 Abu Bakr Siraj al-Din St, Amman 11194; tel. (6) 5902200; fax (6) 5930161; e-mail amm-info@minbuza.nl; internet jordan.nlembassy.org; Ambassador PIET DE KLERK.

Norway: POB 830510, 25 Damascus St, Amman 11183; tel. (6) 5931646; fax (6) 5931650; e-mail emb.amman@mfa.no; internet www.norway.jo; Ambassador PETTER ØLBERG.

Oman: POB 20192, Amman 11110; tel. (6) 5686155; fax (6) 5689404; e-mail amman@mofa.gov.om; Ambassador MUSALLAM BEN BAKHIT AL-BARAMI.

Pakistan: POB 1232, al-Akhtal St, Jabal al-Weibdeh, Amman 11118; tel. (6) 4622787; fax (6) 4611633; e-mail parepamman@gmail.com; internet www.embassyofpakistanjordan.com; Ambassador Lt-Gen. AHSAN AZHAR HAYAT.

Philippines: POB 925207, 5 Salem al-Batarseh St, Amman 11190; tel. (6) 5923748; fax (6) 5923744; e-mail ammanpe@dfa.gov.ph; internet www.philembassy-amman.net; Ambassador OLIVIA V. PALALA.

Poland: POB 942050, Amman 11194; tel. (6) 5512593; fax (6) 5512595; e-mail info@amman.polemb.net; internet www.amman.polemb.net; Ambassador KRZYSZTOF BOJKO.

Qatar: POB 5098, Bldg 38, Hajj Hassan St, Amman 11183; tel. (6) 5902300; fax (6) 5902301; e-mail amman@mofa.gov.qa; internet www.qatarembassy-jo.net; Ambassador ZAYED BIN SAEED AL-KHAYARIN.

Romania: POB 2869, 35 Madina Munawwara St, Amman 11181; tel. (6) 5813423; fax (6) 5812521; e-mail roemb@orange.jo; internet amman.mae.ro; Ambassador BOGDAN FILIP.

Russia: POB 2187, 22 Zahran St, 3rd Circle, Amman 11181; tel. (6) 4641158; fax (6) 4647448; e-mail rusembjo@mail.ru; internet www.jordan.mid.ru; Ambassador ALEKSANDR KALUGIN.

Saudi Arabia: POB 2133, Zahrat al-Talhoni Bldg, Jabal Amman, Amman 11183; tel. (6) 5924154; fax (6) 5921154; e-mail joemb@mofa.gov.sa; Ambassador FAHD BIN ABD AL-MIHSIN AL-ZAID.

South Africa: POB 851508, Sweifiyeh, Amman 11185; tel. (6) 5921194; fax (6) 5920080; e-mail saembjor@index.com.jo; Ambassador MOLEFE SAMUEL TSELE.

Spain: Zahran St, POB 454, Jabal Amman, Amman 11118; tel. (6) 4614166; fax (6) 4614173; e-mail emb.amman@maec.es; internet www.exteriores.gob.es/embajadas/amman; Ambassador SANTIAGO CABANAS ANSORENA.

Sri Lanka: POB 830731, al-Madina al-Munawara St, Amman 11183; tel. (6) 5820611; fax (6) 5820615; e-mail lankaembjo@orange.jo; Ambassador GAMINI RAJAPAKSE.

Sudan: POB 3305, Bayader Wadi al-Seer, 7th Circle, Musa Irsheed al-Taib St, Amman 11181; tel. (6) 5854500; fax (6) 5854501; e-mail sudani@nets.com.jo; Ambassador MUHAMMAD OSMAN MUHAMMAD SAEED.

Sweden: POB 830536, 20 Abd al-Majid al-Adwan St, Abdoun, Amman 11183; tel. (6) 5901300; fax (6) 5930179; e-mail ambassaden.amman@gov.se; internet www.swedenabroad.com/amman; Ambassador HELENA RIETZ.

Switzerland: POB 5341, 19 Ibrahim Ayoub St, 4th Circle, Amman 11183; tel. (6) 5931416; fax (6) 5930685; e-mail amm.vertretung@eda.admin.ch; internet www.eda.admin.ch/amman; Ambassador MICHAEL WINZAP.

Syria: POB 1733, Amman 11118; tel. (6) 5920684; fax (6) 5920635; Ambassador Gen. BAHJAT SULEIMAN.

Thailand: POB 144329, 33 al-Hashemeen St, Dirghabar-Abdoun, Amman 11814; tel. (6) 5923300; fax (6) 5923311; e-mail thaiembassy.amman@gmail.com; internet www.thaiembassy.org/amman; Ambassador PIRIYA KHEMPON.

Tunisia: POB 17185, Amman 11195; tel. (6) 5922743; fax (6) 5922769; e-mail atamman@go.com.jo; Ambassador AFIFAH MALLAH.

Turkey: POB 2062, 31 Abbas Mahmoud al-Aqqad St, Amman 11181; tel. (6) 5002325; fax (6) 4612353; e-mail embassy.amman@mfa.gov.tr; internet amman.emb.mfa.gov.tr; Ambassador SEDAT ÖNAL.

Ukraine: POB 5244, 6 al-Umouma St, al-Sahl, Amman; tel. (6) 5922402; fax (6) 5922408; e-mail emb_jo@mfa.gov.ua; internet www.mfa.gov.ua/jordan; Ambassador SERGIY PASKO.

United Arab Emirates: POB 2623, Bldg 65, 5th Circle, Boumedienne St, Amman 11181; tel. (6) 5934780; fax (6) 5932666; e-mail amman@mofa.gov.ae; internet www.uae-embassy.ae/embassies/jo; Ambassador Dr ABDULLAH NASIR SULTAN AL-AMERI.

United Kingdom: POB 87, Abdoun, Amman 11118; tel. (6) 5909200; fax (6) 5909279; e-mail amman.enquiries@fco.gov.uk; internet ukinjordan.fco.gov.uk; Ambassador PETER MILLETT.

USA: POB 354, Umawiyyeen St, Abdoun, Amman 11118; tel. (6) 5906000; fax (6) 5920133; e-mail webmasterjordan@state.gov; internet jordan.usembassy.gov; Ambassador STUART E. JONES.

Yemen: POB 3085, Prince Hashem bin Al-Hussain St, Amman 11181; tel. (6) 5923771; fax (6) 5923773; Ambassador SHAYA MOHSIN ZINDANI.

Judicial System

With the exception of matters of purely personal nature concerning members of non-Muslim communities, the law of Jordan was based on Islamic Law for both civil and criminal matters. During the days of the Ottoman Empire certain aspects of Continental law, especially French commercial law and civil and criminal procedure, were introduced. Owing to British occupation of Palestine and Transjordan from 1917 to 1948, the Palestine territory has adopted, either by statute or case law, much of the English common law. Since the annexation of the non-occupied part of Palestine and the formation of the Hashemite Kingdom of Jordan, there has been a continuous effort to unify the law. A Constitutional Court was formally inaugurated on 7 October 2012, to replace the Higher Council for the Interpretation of the Constitution.

Constitutional Court: f. 2012; The Constitutional Court, established by royal decree in October 2012, retains the authority to decide 'the constitutionality of laws and regulations in force and issue its judgements in the name of the King'. It also 'has the right to interpret the provisions of the Constitution if requested, either by virtue of a decision of the Council of Ministers or by a resolution taken by the Senate or the Chamber of Deputies passed by an absolute majority.' The court comprised nine members, including the President, appointed by the King; Pres. TAHER HIKMAT.

Court of Cassation (Supreme Court): The Court of Cassation consists of seven judges, who sit in full panel for exceptionally important cases. In most appeals, however, only five members sit to hear the case. All cases involving amounts of more than JD 100 may be reviewed by this Court, as well as cases involving lesser amounts and those that cannot be monetarily valued. However, for the latter types of cases, review is available only by leave of the Court of Appeal, or, upon refusal by the Court of Appeal, by leave of the President of the Court of Cassation. In addition to these functions as final and Supreme Court of Appeal, the Court of Cassation also sits as High Court of Justice to hear applications in the nature of habeas corpus, mandamus and certiorari dealing with complaints of a citizen against abuse of governmental authority; Pres. HISHAM TAL.

Courts of Appeal: There are three Courts of Appeal, each of which is composed of three judges, whether for hearing of appeals or for dealing with Magistrates Courts' judgments in chambers. Jurisdiction of the three Courts is geographical, with one each in Amman, Irbid and Ma'an. Appellate review of the Courts of Appeal extends to judgments rendered in the Courts of First Instance, the Magistrates' Courts and Religious Courts.

Courts of First Instance: The Courts of First Instance are courts of general jurisdiction in all matters civil and criminal except those specifically allocated to the Magistrates' Courts. Three judges sit in all felony trials, while only two judges sit for misdemeanour and civil cases. Each of the 11 Courts of First Instance also exercises appellate jurisdiction in cases involving judgments of less than JD 20 and fines of less than JD 10, rendered by the Magistrates' Courts.

Magistrates' Courts: There are 17 Magistrates' Courts, which exercise jurisdiction in civil cases involving no more than JD 250 and in criminal cases involving maximum fines of JD 100 or maximum imprisonment of one year.

Religious Courts: There are two types of religious court: the *Shari'a* Courts (Muslims); and the Ecclesiastical Courts (Eastern Orthodox, Greek Melkite, Roman Catholic and Protestant). Jurisdiction extends to personal (family) matters, such as marriage, divorce, alimony, inheritance, guardianship, wills, interdiction and, for the Muslim community, the constitution of *Awqaf* (Religious Endowments). When a dispute involves persons of different religious communities, the Civil Courts have jurisdiction in the matter unless the parties agree to submit to the jurisdiction of one or the other of the Religious Courts involved; Each *Shari'a* (Muslim) Court consists of one judge (*Qadi*), while most of the Ecclesiastical (Christian) Courts are normally composed of three judges, who are usually clerics. *Shari'a* Courts apply the doctrines of Islamic Law, based on the Koran and the *Hadith* (Precepts of Muhammad), while the Ecclesiastical Courts base their law on various aspects of Canon Law. In the event of conflict between any two Religious Courts or between a Religious Court and a Civil Court, a Special Tribunal of three judges is appointed by the President of the Court of Cassation, to decide which court shall have jurisdiction. Upon the advice of experts on the law of the various communities, this Special Tribunal decides on the venue for the case at hand; Chief of Islamic Justice AHMAD HILAYEL; Dir of *Shari'a* Courts Sheikh ISSAM ABD AL-RAZZAQ ARABIYYAT.

Religion

Over 90% of the population are Sunni Muslims, and the King can trace unbroken descent from the Prophet Muhammad. There is a Christian minority, living mainly in the towns, and there are smaller numbers of non-Sunni Muslims.

ISLAM

Chief of Islamic Justice and Imam of the Royal Court: AHMAD HILAYEL.

Grand Mufti of the Hashemite Kingdom of Jordan: Sheikh ABD AL-KARIM KHASAWNEH.

CHRISTIANITY

The Roman Catholic Church

Chaldean Rite

The Chaldean Patriarch of Babylon is resident in Baghdad, Iraq.

Chaldean Patriarchal Vicariate in Jordan: Jabal al-Wabdeh, POB 910833, Amman 11191; tel. and fax (6) 4629061; e-mail raymovicariate66@hotmail.com; internet www.chaldeanjordan.org; f. 2002; Patriarchal Exarch Rev. RAYMOND MOUSSALLI.

Latin Rite

Jordan forms part of the Patriarchate of Jerusalem (see the chapter on Israel).

Vicar-General for Transjordan: Most Rev. SELIM SAYEGH (Titular Bishop of Aquae in Proconsulari), Latin Vicariate, POB 851379, Sweifiyeh, Amman 11185; tel. (6) 5929546; fax (6) 5920548; e-mail regina-pacis2000@yahoo.com.

Maronite Rite

The Maronite community in Jordan is under the jurisdiction of the Maronite Patriarch of Antioch (resident in Lebanon).

Patriarchal Exarchate of Jordan: Mgr PAUL NABIL SAYAH, St Charbel's Parish, Amman; tel. (6) 4202558; fax (6) 4202559; e-mail stcharbelparish@yahoo.com.

Melkite Rite

Jordan forms part of the Greek-Melkite archdiocese of Petra (Wadi Musa) and Philadelphia (Amman).

Archbishop of Petra and Philadelphia: Most Rev. YASSER AYYACH, Archevêché Grec-Melkite Catholique, POB 2435, Jabal Amman 11181; tel. and fax (6) 5866673; e-mail fryaser@yahoo.com.

Syrian Rite

The Syrian Catholic Patriarch of Antioch is resident in Beirut, Lebanon.

Patriarchal Exarchate of Jerusalem (Palestine and Jordan): Mont Achrafieh, POB 510393, Rue Barto, Amman; e-mail st_thomas@bezeqint.net; Exarch Patriarchal Mgr GRÉGOIRE PIERRE MELKI (Titular Bishop of Batne of the Syrians).

The Anglican Communion

Within the Episcopal Church in Jerusalem and the Middle East, Jordan forms part of the diocese of Jerusalem. The President Bishop of the Church is the Bishop in Cyprus and the Gulf (see the chapter on Cyprus).

Other Christian Churches

The Coptic Orthodox Church, the Greek Orthodox Church (Patriarchate of Jerusalem) and the Evangelical Lutheran Church in Jordan are also active.

The Press

DAILIES

Al-Anbat: POB 962556, Amman 11192; tel. (6) 5200100; fax (6) 5200113; e-mail info@alanbat.net; internet www.alanbat.net; f. 2005; independent; Arabic; political; Man. Editor MAZEN AL-KHATIB.

Al-Arab al-Yawm (Arabs Today): POB 962198, Queen Rania St, Amman 11196; tel. (6) 5683333; fax (6) 5620552; e-mail mail@alarab-alyawm.com.jo; internet www.alarabalyawm.net; f. 1997; Arabic; Chief Editor FAHED AL-KHITAN.

Al-Diyar (The Homeland): Al-Fanar Complex, Queen Rania Al-Abdullah St, Amman; tel. (6) 5166588; f. 2004; Arabic; Chair. of Bd MAHMOUD KHARABSHEH.

Ad-Dustour (The Constitution): POB 591, Amman 11118; tel. (6) 5608000; fax (6) 5667170; e-mail dustour@addustour.com.jo; internet www.addustour.com; f. 1967; Arabic; publ. by the Jordan Press and Publishing Co Ltd; owns commercial printing facilities; Chair. KAMEL AL-SHARIF; Chief Editor MUHAMMAD HASSAN TAL; circ. 70,000.

Al-Ghad (Tomorrow): POB 3535, Amman 11821; tel. (6) 5544000; fax (6) 5544055; e-mail editorial@alghad.jo; internet www.alghad.jo; f. 2004; independent; Arabic; Editor-in-Chief MOUSA BARHOUMEH.

The Jordan Times: POB 6710, Queen Rania Al-Abdullah St, Amman 11118; tel. (6) 5600800; fax (6) 5696183; e-mail jotimes@jpf.com.jo; internet www.jordantimes.com; f. 1975; English; publ. by Jordan Press Foundation; Editor-in-Chief SAMIR BARHOUM; circ. 15,000.

Al-Rai (Opinion): POB 6710, Queen Rania Al-Abdullah St, Amman 11118; tel. (6) 5667171; fax (6) 5676581; e-mail info@jpf.com.jo; internet www.alrai.com; f. 1971; morning; independent; Arabic; publ. by Jordan Press Foundation; Chair. AHMAD ABD AL-FATTAH; Editor-in-Chief ABD AL-WAHAB ZGHEILAT; circ. 90,000.

Al-Sabeel (The Path): POB 213545, Amman 11121; tel. (6) 5692852; fax (6) 5692854; e-mail assabeel@assabeel.net; internet www.assabeel.net; f. 1993; fmrly weekly; became daily publ. 2009; Arabic; Islamist; Editor-in-Chief ATEF GOLANI.

WEEKLIES

Al-Ahali (The People): POB 9966, Amman 11191; tel. (6) 5691452; fax (6) 5686857; e-mail ahali@go.com.jo; internet www.hashd-ahali.org.jo; f. 1990; Arabic; publ. by the Jordan People's Democratic Party; Editor-in-Chief SALEM NAHHAS; circ. 5,000.

Akhbar al-Usbou (News of the Week): POB 605, Amman; tel. (6) 5677881; fax (6) 5677882; f. 1959; Arabic; economic, social, political; Chief Editor and Publr ABD AL-HAFIZ MUHAMMAD; circ. 50,000.

Al-Hadath: POB 961167, Amman 11196; tel. (6) 5160824; fax (6) 5160810; e-mail info@al-hadath.com; internet www.al-hadath.com; Arabic; general news; Man. Editor FATEH MANSOUR.

Al-Haqeqa al-Duwalia (Fact International): POB 712678, Amman 11171; tel. (6) 5828292; fax (6) 5816646; e-mail info@factjo.com; internet www.factjo.com; f. 1996; independent; Arabic and English; aims to promote moderate image of Islam and to counter conflicts within the faith; Editor-in-Chief HILMI AL-ASMAR.

Al-Liwa' (The Standard): POB 3067, 2nd Circle, Jabal Amman 11181; tel. (6) 5642770; fax (6) 5656324; e-mail info@al-liwa.com; internet www.al-liwa.com; f. 1972; Arabic; Editor-in-Chief HASSAN AL-TAL; circ. 15,000.

Al-Majd (The Glory): POB 926856, Amman 11190; tel. (6) 5530553; fax (6) 5530352; e-mail almajd@almajd.net; internet www.almajd

.net; f. 1994; Arabic; political; Editor-in-Chief FAHID NIMER; circ. 8,000.

Shihan: POB 96-654, Amman; tel. (6) 5603585; fax (6) 5696183; Arabic; Editor-in-Chief (vacant); circ. 60,000.

The Star: POB 591, Queen Rania St, Amman 11118; tel. (6) 5653325; fax (6) 5697415; e-mail star@addustour.com.jo; internet www.star.com.jo; f. 1966; English; political, economic, social and cultural; publ. by the Jordan Press and Publishing Co; Editor-in-Chief MAHA AL-SHARIF; circ. 12,430.

PERIODICALS

Anty Magazine: POB 3024, Amman 11181; tel. (6) 5820058; fax (6) 5855892; e-mail chiefeditor@anty.jo; internet www.anty.jo; monthly; Arabic; publ. by Front Row Publishing and Media Services; fashion, culture and current affairs from a professional woman's perspective; Chief Editor SAHAR ALOUL; circ. 20,000.

Hatem: POB 6710, Queen Rania St, Amman 11118; tel. (6) 5600800; fax (6) 5676581; e-mail info@jpf.com.jo; children's; publ. by Jordan Press Foundation.

Huda El-Islam (The Right Way of Islam): POB 659, Amman; tel. (6) 5666141; f. 1956; monthly; Arabic; scientific and literary; publ. by the Ministry of Awqaf (Religious Endowments) and Islamic Affairs; Editor Dr AHMAD MUHAMMAD HULAYYEL.

Jordan: POB 224, Amman; e-mail webmaster@jordanembassyus.org; internet www.jordanembassyus.org/new/newsletter.shtml; f. 1969; quarterly; publ. by Jordan Information Bureau, Embassy of Jordan, Washington, DC, USA; 3 a year; Editor-in-Chief MERISSA KHURMA; circ. 100,000.

Jordan Business: POB 3024, Amman 11181; tel. (6) 5820058; fax (6) 5855892; e-mail info@frontrow.jo; internet www.jordan-business.net; monthly; English; publ. by Front Row Publishing and Media Services; circ. 10,000.

Jordan Today: Media Services International, POB 9313, Amman 11191; tel. (6) 652380; fax (6) 648298; e-mail star@arabia.com; internet www.jordantoday.com.jo; f. 1995; monthly; English; tourism, culture and entertainment; Editor-in-Chief ZEID NASSER; circ. 10,000.

Military Magazine: Army Headquarters, Amman; f. 1955; quarterly; dealing with military and literary subjects; publ. by Armed Forces.

Royal Wings: POB 3024, Amman 11181; tel. (6) 5820058; fax (6) 5855892; e-mail info@frontrow.jo; internet www.frontrow.jo; bi-monthly; Arabic and English; magazine for Royal Jordanian Airline; publ. by Front Row Publishing and Media Services; Man. Dir USAMA FARAJ; circ. 40,000.

Skin: POB 940166, ICCB Centre, Queen Rania Abdullah St, Amman 11194; tel. (6) 5163357; fax (6) 5163257; e-mail amer@neareastmedia.com; internet www.skin-online.com; f. 2006; quarterly; English; publ. by Near East Media Iraq; art, design, fashion, photography, film and music; Editor-in-Chief TARIQ AL-BITAR.

NEWS AGENCY

Jordan News Agency (PETRA): POB 6845, Amman 11118; tel. (6) 5609700; fax (6) 5682478; e-mail petra@petra.gov.jo; internet www.petra.gov.jo; f. 1965; independent entity since 2004; previously controlled by Ministry of Information prior to its disbandment in 2001; Chair. Dr MUHAMMAD HUSSEIN MOMANI (Minister of State for Media Affairs and Communications); Dir-Gen. RAMADAN AL-RAWASHDEH.

PRESS ASSOCIATION

Jordan Press Association (JPA): POB 8876, Abbas Mahmoud al-Aqqad St, Jabal Amman, 2nd Circle, Amman 18888; tel. (6) 5372005; fax (6) 5372003; e-mail info@jpa.jo; internet www.jpa.jo; f. 1953; Pres. ABD AL-WAHAB ZGHEILAT.

Publishers

Alfaris Publishing and Distribution Co: POB 9157, Amman 11191; tel. (6) 5605432; fax (6) 5685501; e-mail mkayyali@airpbooks.com; internet www.airpbooks.com; f. 1989; Dir MAHER SAID KAYYALI.

Aram Studies Publishing and Distribution House: POB 997, Amman 11941; tel. (6) 835015; fax (6) 835079; art, finance, health, management, science, business; Gen. Dir SALEH ABOUSBA.

Dar al-Manhal Publishers and Distributors: POB 926428, Amman 11190; tel. (6) 5698308; fax (6) 5639185; e-mail info@dmanhal.com; internet www.dmanhal.com; f. 1990; children's and educational publs; Exec. Man. KHALED BILBEISI.

Dar al-Nafa'es: POB 927511, al-Abdali, Amman 11190; tel. (6) 5693940; fax (6) 5693941; e-mail alnafaes@hotmail.com; internet www.al-nafaes.com; f. 1990; education, Islamic; CEO SUFYAN OMAR AL-ASHQR.

Dar al-Thaqafa: Amman 11118; tel. (6) 4646361; fax (6) 4610291; e-mail info@daralthaqafa.com; internet www.daralthaqafa.com; f. 1984; academic publr, specializes in law; Man. Editor KHALID MAHMOUD GABR.

Al Faridah for Specialized Publications: POB 1223, Amman 11821; tel. (6) 5630430; fax (6) 5630440; e-mail info@alfaridah.com.jo; internet www.alfaridah.com.jo; f. 2003; publr of magazines incl. *Layalina*, *Ahlan!*, *JO*, *Viva*, *Venture*; Editors-in-Chief RANIA OMEISH, SHIRENE RIFAI; Man. Dir QAIS ELIAS.

Front Row Publishing and Media Services: POB 3024, Muhammad Baseem Khammash St, Villa 3, Amman 11181; tel. (6) 5820058; fax (6) 5855892; e-mail info@frontrow.jo; internet www.frontrow.jo; f. 1997; publr of magazines incl. *Jordan Business*, *Living Well*, *Home*, *Royal Wings*; CEO IYAD SHEHADEH.

Jordan Book Centre Co Ltd: POB 301, al-Jubeiha, Amman 11941; tel. (6) 5151882; fax (6) 5152016; e-mail jbc@go.com.jo; internet www.JBC.com.jo; f. 1982; fiction, business, economics, computer science, medicine, engineering, general non-fiction; Man. Dir J. J. SHARBAIN.

Jordan Distribution Agency: POB 3371, Amman 11181; tel. (6) 5358855; fax (6) 5337733; e-mail jda@aramex.com; f. 1951; history; subsidiary of Aramex; Chair. FADI GHANDOUR; Gen. Man. WADIE SAYEGH.

Jordan House for Publication: POB 1121, Basman St, Amman; tel. (6) 24224; fax (6) 51062; f. 1952; medicine, nursing, dentistry; Man. Dir MURSI AL-ASHKAR.

Jordan Press and Publishing Co Ltd: POB 591, Amman 11118; tel. (6) 5608000; fax (6) 5667170; e-mail info@addustour.com.jo; internet www.addustour.com; f. 1967 by *Al-Manar* and *Falastin* dailies; publishes *Ad-Dustour* (daily), *Ad-Dustour Sport* (weekly) and *The Star* (English weekly); Chair. AMIN MASHAQBEH; Gen. Man. SAMER RAJOUB.

Jordan Press Foundation: POB 6710, Amman 11118; tel. (6) 5667171; fax (6) 5661242; e-mail info@jpf.com.jo; internet www.alrai.com; f. 1971; publishes *Al-Rai* (daily), *The Jordan Times* (daily) and *Hatem* (monthly); Chair. ALI AYED; Editor SAMIR HIYARI.

Al-Tanwir al-Ilmi (Scientific Enlightenment Publishing House): POB 4237, al-Mahatta, Amman 11131; tel. and fax (6) 4899619; e-mail taisir@yahoo.com; internet www.icieparis.net; f. 1990; affiliated with the Int. Centre for Innovation in Education; education, engineering, philosophy, science, sociology; Gen. Dir Prof. Dr TAISIR SUBHI YAMIN.

Broadcasting and Communications

TELECOMMUNICATIONS

Jordan Mobile Telephone Services Co (Zain Jordan): POB 940821, 8th Circle, King Abdullah II St, Amman 11194; tel. (6) 5803000; fax (6) 5828200; e-mail info@jo.zain.com; internet www.jo.zain.com; f. 1994 as Jordan Mobile Telephone Services Co (JMTS—Fastlink); merged with Mobile Telecommunications Co (MTC—Kuwait) 2003, corpn renamed Zain Group 2007; Zain Jordan merged with PalTel (Palestinian Territories) in 2009; private co; has operated Jordan's first mobile telecommunications network since 1995; CEO, Levant Region and CEO, Jordan Dr ABD AL-MALEK JABER.

Jordan Telecom Group (Orange Jordan): POB 1689, Amman 11118; tel. (6) 4606666; fax (6) 4639200; e-mail info@jordantelecomgroup.jo; internet www.jordantelecomgroup.jo; f. 1971; fmrly Jordan Telecommunications Corpn, Jordan Telecommunications Co and Jordan Telecom; current name adopted in Feb. 2006 following integration of the following cos' operations into a single management structure: Jordan Telecom, MobileCom (mobile cellular telecommunications services), Wanadoo (internet services) and e-Dimension (information technology); in 2007 Jordan Telecom, MobileCom and Wanadoo were all rebranded as Orange Jordan; 30.5% govt-owned, 69.5% privately owned: France Télécom SA, France, 51.0%; Social Security Corpn 12.4%; 6.1% of shares listed on Amman Stock Exchange; assets JD 664.8m., revenue JD 397.9m. (2007); CEO NAYLA KHAWAM.

Petra Jordanian Mobile Telecommunications: POB 941477, Amman 11194; tel. (6) 5630090; fax (6) 5630098; e-mail business@orange.jo; internet www.orange.jo; CEO NAYLA KHAWAM.

Umniah Mobile Company: POB 942481, Amman 11194; tel. (6) 5005000; fax (6) 5622772; e-mail contact@umniah.com; internet www.umniah.com; awarded contract for Jordan's third GSM licence in 2004; commenced operations in June 2005; first provider of wireless broadband internet services in Jordan; subsidiary of Alghanim Group (Kuwait); 96% owned by Bahrain Telecommunications Co; CEO JOSEPH HANANIA.

Regulatory Authority

Telecommunications Regulatory Commission (TRC): POB 850967, Amman 11185; tel. (6) 5501120; fax (6) 5863641; e-mail trc@trc.gov.jo; internet www.trc.gov.jo; f. 1995; Chair. and CEO MUHAMMAD AL-TAANI.

BROADCASTING

A new Audio Visual Media Law, enacted in 2002, allowed for the establishment of private broadcasters in Jordan for the first time. By 2007 16 new radio licences had been awarded. Jordan's first licensed independent television channel, Al-Ghad TV (ATV), was officially launched in August 2007; however, the channel was taken off-air before it began broadcasting, owing to a dispute over the terms of its licence. In 2008 ATV was purchased by Arab Telemedia Group and plans were announced for the launch of a two-channel network. By mid-2013 ATV had yet to begin broadcasting.

Regulatory Authority

Audio Visual Commission (AVC): POB 142515, Amman 11814; tel. (6) 5560378; fax (6) 5535093; e-mail avc@nic.net.jo; internet www.avc.gov.jo; f. 2002; Dir-Gen. HUSSAIN BANI-HANI.

Radio and Television

Jordan Radio and Television Corporation (JRTV): POB 1041, Amman; tel. (6) 773111; fax (6) 751503; e-mail general@jrtv.gov.jo; internet www.jrtv.jo; f. 1968; state broadcaster; operates 4 TV channels and 6 radio channels broadcasting programmes in Arabic, English and French; advertising accepted; Chair. Dr MUHAMMAD HUSSEIN MOMANI (Minister of State for Media Affairs and Communications); Dir-Gen. BAYAN AL-TAL; Dir of Radio Administration MAZEN AL-MAJALI; Dir of Television Administration HALA ZUREIQAT.

Radio Al-Balad: POB 20513, Amman 11118; tel. (6) 4645486; fax (6) 4630238; internet www.ammannet.net; f. 2000 as internet radio station AmmanNet; began broadcasting as an FM radio station 2005, renamed as above 2008; news, politics and community broadcasts; Gen. Man. SAWSAN ZAIDAH.

Sawt al-Madina (SAM): POB 1171, Amman 1953; tel. (6) 5500006; fax (6) 5500009; e-mail fateen@al-baddad.com; internet www.al-baddad.com; f. 2006; owned by Al-Baddad Media and Communications; radio station broadcasting news and politics programmes; Group Gen. Man. FATEEN H. AL-BADDAD.

Other independent radio stations include Mazaj FM, Amin FM, Al-Hayat FM, Rotana FM Jordan and Radio Fann FM.

Finance

(cap. = capital; p.u. = paid up; dep. = deposits; m. = million; res = reserves; br.(s) = branch(es); amounts in Jordanian dinars unless otherwise indicated)

BANKING

Central Bank

Central Bank of Jordan: POB 37, King Hussein St, Amman 11118; tel. (6) 4630301; fax (6) 4638889; e-mail info@cbj.gov.jo; internet www.cbj.gov.jo; f. 1964; cap. 18.0m., res 279.3m., dep. 5,610.2m. (Dec. 2008); Gov. and Chair. ZIAD FARIZ; 2 brs.

National Banks

Arab Bank PLC: POB 950545, Shmeisani, Amman 11195; tel. (6) 5607231; fax (6) 5606793; e-mail corpcomm@arabbank.com.jo; internet www.arabbank.com; f. 1930; cap. US $776m., res $6,541m., dep. $36,043m. (Dec. 2011); Chair. SABIH AL-MASRI; CEO NEMEH SABBAGH; 84 brs in Jordan, 99 brs abroad.

Bank of Jordan PLC: POB 2140, Shmeisani, Amman 11181; tel. (6) 5696277; fax (6) 5696291; e-mail boj@bankofjordan.com.jo; internet www.bankofjordan.com; f. 1960; cap. 100m., res 81m., dep. 1,688m. (Dec. 2010); Chair. and Gen. Man. TAWFIK SHAKER FAKHOURI; 77 brs and offices.

Cairo Amman Bank: POB 950661, Cairo Amman Bank Bldg, Wadi Saqra St, Amman 11195; tel. (6) 4616910; fax (6) 4642890; e-mail info@cab.jo; internet www.cab.jo; f. 1960; cap. 100m., res 69m., dep. 1,512m. (Dec. 2010); Chair. and CEO KHALED AL-MASRI; 63 brs in Jordan, 18 brs in the West Bank.

Capital Bank of Jordan: POB 941283, Issam Ajlouni St, Amman 11194; tel. (6) 5100200; fax (6) 5692062; e-mail info@capitalbank.jo; internet www.capitalbank.jo; f. 1996 as Export and Finance Bank; name changed as above 2006; cap. 150m., res 18m., dep. 1,114m. (Dec. 2010); Chair. BASSEM KHALIL SALEM AL-SALEM; Gen. Man. HAYTHAM KAMHIYAH.

Jordan Ahli Bank: POB 3103, Queen Noor St, Shmeisani, Amman 11181; tel. (6) 5622282; fax (6) 5622281; e-mail info@ahlibank.com.jo; internet www.ahli.com; f. 1955 as Jordan Nat. Bank; name changed as above 2006; cap. 110m., res 94m., dep. 2,237m. (Dec. 2010); Chair. RAJAI MUASHER; CEO and Gen. Man. MARWAN AWAD; 46 brs in Jordan, 6 brs abroad.

Jordan Commercial Bank: POB 9989, Yakoub Sarrouf St, Shmeisani, Amman 11191; tel. (6) 5603931; fax (6) 5603989; e-mail jcb@jcbank.com.jo; internet www.jcbank.com.jo; f. 1977 as Jordan Gulf Bank; name changed as above 2004; cap. 80m., res 11m., dep. 644m. (Dec. 2010); Chair. MICHEL AL-SAYEGH; CEO and Gen. Man. Dr JAWAD AL-HADID; 23 brs in Jordan, 3 brs in West Bank.

Jordan Islamic Bank: POB 926225, Shmeisani, Amman 11190; tel. (6) 5677377; fax (6) 5666326; e-mail jib@islamicbank.com.jo; internet www.jordanislamicbank.com; f. 1978; fmrly Jordan Islamic Bank for Finance and Investment current name adopted Oct. 2009; cap. 100m., res 56m., dep. 2,635m. (Dec. 2011); Chair. ADNAN AHMAD YOUSUF; Vice-Chair. and Gen. Man. MUSA ABD AL-AZIZ SHIHADEH; 59 brs.

Jordan Kuwait Bank: POB 9776, Abdali, Amman 11191; tel. (6) 5629400; fax (6) 5695604; e-mail webmaster@jkbank.com.jo; internet www.jordan-kuwait-bank.com; f. 1976; cap. US $141m., res $207m., dep. $2,373m. (Dec. 2010); Chair. and CEO ABD AL-KARIM AL-KABARITI; Dir-Gen. MUHAMMAD YASSER M. AL-ASMAR; 43 brs.

Société Générale de Banque-Jordanie: POB 560, 30 Prince Shaker bin Zeid St, Shmeisani, Amman 11118; tel. (6) 500300; fax (6) 5693410; e-mail sgbj.webmaster@socgen.com; internet www.sgbj.com.jo; f. 1965 as Middle East Investment Bank; became part of the Société Générale Group (France) 2000; name changed as above 2003; cap. 40m., res 5m., dep. 270m. (Dec. 2010); Chair. HASSAN MANGO; Gen. Man. NADIM ABAOUAT; 16 brs.

Specialized Credit Institutions

Agricultural Credit Corporation: POB 77, Amman 11118; tel. (6) 5661105; fax (6) 5668365; e-mail adminacc@go.com.jo; internet www.acc.gov.jo; f. 1959; cap. 24m., res 12.4m., total assets 125.1m. (Dec. 2000); Chair. Dr AKIF AL-ZU'BI (Minister of Agriculture); Vice-Chair. and Dir-Gen. TAWFIQ HABASHNEH; 22 brs.

Arab Jordan Investment Bank: POB 8797, Arab Jordan Investment Bank Bldg, Shmeisani, Amman 11121; tel. (6) 5607126; fax (6) 5681482; e-mail info@ajib.com; internet www.ajib.com; f. 1978; cap. 100m., res 16m., dep. 781m. (Dec. 2011); Chair. ABD AL-KADER AL-QADI; CEO HANI AL-QADI; 8 brs in Jordan, 2 brs abroad.

Bank al Etihad: POB 35104, Prince Shaker Ben Zeid St, Shmeisani, Amman 11180; tel. (6) 5607011; fax (6) 5666149; e-mail corporate@bankaletihad.com; internet www.bankaletihad.com; f. 1978 as Arab Finance Corpn; name changed to Union Bank for Savings and Investment 1991; name changed as above 2011; cap. 100m., res 112m., dep. 1,254m. (Dec. 2010); Chair. ISAM SALFITI; Gen. Man. NADIA AL-SAEED 22 brs.

Cities and Villages Development Bank (CVDB): POB 1572, Amman 11118; tel. (6) 5682691; fax (6) 5668153; e-mail cvdb100@hotmail.com; internet www.mma.gov.jo/Eng/Bank.aspx; f. 1979; 30% state-owned; cap. 50m. (Dec. 2002); Chair. ALI GHAZAWI; Gen. Man. Dr IBRAHIM AL-SOUR; 10 brs.

Housing Bank for Trade and Finance (HBTF): POB 7693, Parliament St, Amman 11118; tel. (6) 5005555; fax (6) 5690207; e-mail info@hbtf.com.jo; internet www.hbtf.com; f. 1973; cap. 355m., res 1,476m., dep. 6,667m. (Dec. 2012); Chair. Dr MICHEL MARTO; Gen. Man. OMAR MALHAS; 116 brs.

INVESTBANK: Issam Ajlouni St, Shmeisani, Amman; tel. (6) 5665145; fax (6) 5681410; e-mail info@investbank.jo; internet www.investbank.jo; f. 1982 as Jordan Investment and Finance Corpn; name changed 2009; cap. 77m., res 20m., dep. 542m. (Dec. 2010); Chair. BISHER M. JARDANEH; CEO MUNTASER DAWWAS; 9 brs.

Jordan Dubai Islamic Bank: POB 1982, al-Kuliah al-Elmiah, Amman 11118; tel. (6) 4602200; fax (6) 4647821; e-mail idb@indevbank.com.jo; internet www.jdib.jo; f. 1965 as Industrial Devt Bank; current name adopted Jan. 2010; cap. 89m., res 22m., dep. 219m. (Dec. 2011); Chair. ISMAIL TAHBOUB; CEO SAMI HUSSAM AL-AFGHANI; 7 brs.

STOCK EXCHANGE

Amman Stock Exchange (ASE): POB 212466, Arjan, nr Ministry of the Interior, Amman 11121; tel. (6) 5664109; fax (6) 5664071; e-mail info@ase.com.jo; internet www.exchange.jo; f. 1978 as Amman Financial Market; name changed as above 1999; 247 listed cos (2011); Chair. MUHAMMAD MALALLAH; CEO JALIL TARIF.

INSURANCE

At the end of 2008 there were 29 companies operating in the insurance sector in Jordan.

Jordan Insurance Co Ltd (JIC): POB 279, Company's Bldg, 3rd Circle, Jabal Amman, Amman 11118; tel. (6) 4634161; fax (6) 4637905; e-mail allinsure@jicjo.com; internet www.jicjo.com;

f. 1951; cap. 30m. (Dec. 2006); Chair. OTHMAN BDEIR; Man. Dir IMAD ABD AL-KHALEQ; 7 brs (3 in Jordan, 3 in the United Arab Emirates and 1 in Kuwait).

Middle East Insurance Co Ltd (MEICO): POB 1802, al-Kindi St, Um Uthanina, 5th Circle, Jabal Amman, Amman 11118; tel. (6) 5527100; fax (6) 5527801; e-mail info@meico.com.jo; internet www.meico.com.jo; f. 1962; cap. p.u. 18.0m., total assets 66,285.0m. (Dec. 2007); Chair. SAMIR KAWAR; Gen. Man. Dr RAJAI SWEIS; 13 brs.

National Insurance Co: POB 6156-2938, Sayed Qotub St, Shmeisani, Amman 11118; tel. (6) 5671169; fax (6) 5684900; e-mail natinsur@go.com.jo; f. 1965 as above; name changed to National Ahlia Insurance Co in 1986, following merger with Ahlia Insurance Co (f. 1975); reverted to original name July 2007; cap. 2m.; Chair. MUSTAFA ABU GOURA; Gen. Man. GHALEB ABU-GOURA.

Social Security Corporation: POB 926031, Amman 11110; tel. (6) 5501880; fax (6) 5501888; e-mail webmaster@ssc.gov.jo; internet www.ssc.gov.jo; f. 1978; regulates and implements a social security system, incl. the provision of health insurance, life insurance and unemployment benefit, funded by both voluntary and employer contributions; Dir-Gen. Dr MAEN NSOUR.

United Insurance Co Ltd: POB 7521, United Insurance Bldg, King Hussein St, Amman; tel. (6) 4648513; fax (6) 4629417; e-mail uic@united.com.jo; internet www.united.com.jo; f. 1972; all types of insurance; cap. p.u. 8m.; Chair. RAOUF ABU JABER; Gen. Man. IMAD AL-HAJI.

Insurance Federation

Jordan Insurance Federation (JOIF): POB 1990, Amman 11118; tel. (6) 5689266; fax (6) 5689510; internet www.joif.org; f. 1989 to replace the Jordan Assn for Insurance Cos (f. 1956); regulatory and management authority; Chair. JAWAD HADID; Sec.-Gen. MAHER AL-HUSAIN.

Trade and Industry

GOVERNMENT AGENCIES

Jordan Atomic Energy Commission: POB 70, Amman 11934; tel. (6) 5230978; fax (6) 5231017; internet www.jaec.gov.jo; f. 2007; devt of civil nuclear energy programme; Chair. Dr KHALED TOUKAN.

Natural Resources Authority: POB 7, Amman 11118; tel. (6) 5504390; fax (6) 5811866; e-mail dirgen@nra.gov.jo; internet www.nra.gov.jo; f. 1965; supervision and devt of mineral and non-nuclear energy resources; Dir-Gen. Dr MAHER HIJAZIN.

DEVELOPMENT ORGANIZATIONS

Aqaba Development Corporation (ADC): POB 2680, Chamber of Commerce Bldg, Aqaba 77110; tel. (3) 2039100; fax (3) 2039110; e-mail info@adc.jo; internet www.adc.jo; f. 2004 by Aqaba Special Economic Zone Authority and Govt of Jordan; devt and strategic management of infrastructure, industry, trade, transport, real estate, tourism and education within Aqaba Special Economic Zone; CEO MUHAMMAD SALEM TURK.

Development Zones Commission (DZC): POB 141277, Amman 11814; tel. (6) 3001300; e-mail info@dzc.jo; internet www.dzc.jo; f. 2008; responsible for creating, developing and monitoring the 3 development zones within Jordan; Chief Commr BILAL BASHIR.

Jordan Enterprise Development Corporation (JEDCO): POB 7704, Amman 11118; tel. (6) 5603507; fax (6) 5684568; e-mail jedco@jedco.gov.jo; internet www.jedco.gov.jo; f. 2003 to replace Jordan Export Devt and Commercial Centres Corpn; devt and promotion of industry, trade and exports; Chair. HATEM HAFIZ AL-HALAWANI (Minister of Industry, Trade and Supply); CEO YARUB AL-QUDAH.

Jordan Investment Board (JIB): POB 893, Amman 11821; tel. (6) 5608400; fax (6) 5608416; e-mail info@jib.com.jo; internet www.jordaninvestment.com; f. 1995; CEO Dr MAEN NSOUR.

Jordan Valley Authority (JVA): POB 2769, Amman 11183; tel. (6) 5689400; fax (6) 5689916; e-mail jva_complain@mwi.gov.jo; internet www.jva.gov.jo; f. 1973 as Jordan Valley Comm.; renamed as above 1977; govt org. responsible for the integrated social and economic devt of the Jordan Valley, with particular emphasis on the utilization and management of water resources; responsible for construction of several major irrigation, hydroelectric and municipal water projects; other projects include housing, schools and rural roads, and the devt of tourism infrastructure; Sec.-Gen. MUSA AL-JAMA'ANI.

CHAMBERS OF COMMERCE AND INDUSTRY

Amman Chamber of Commerce: POB 287, Amman 11118; tel. (6) 5666151; fax 5666155; e-mail info@ammanchamber.org.jo; internet www.ammanchamber.org.jo; f. 1923; more than 42,500 regd mems (2008); Chair. RIAD SAIFI; Dir-Gen. MUHANNAD ATTAR.

Amman Chamber of Industry: POB 1800, Amman 11118; tel. (6) 5643001; fax (6) 5647852; e-mail aci@aci.org.jo; internet www.aci.org.jo; f. 1962; approx. 7,500 regd industrial cos (2007); Chair. Dr HATEM H. HALAWANI.

Aqaba Chamber of Commerce: POB 12, Aqaba 77110; tel. (3) 2012229; fax (3) 2013070; e-mail info@aqabacc.com; internet www.aqabacc.com; f. 1965; Chair. NAEL AL-KABARITI; Sec.-Gen. MAHMOUD FRAIH.

Jordan Chamber of Commerce: POB 7029, Amman 11118; tel. (6) 5665492; fax (6) 5685997; e-mail info@jocc.org.jo; internet www.jocc.org.jo; f. 1955 as Fed. of the Jordanian Chambers of Commerce; renamed as above in 2003; intended to promote co-operation between the various chambers of commerce in Jordan, and to consolidate and co-ordinate the capabilities of each; Chair. HAIDAR MURAD; Sec.-Gen. AMIN AL-HUSSEINI.

Jordan Chamber of Industry: POB 811986, Amman 11181; tel. (6) 4642649; fax (6) 4643719; e-mail jci@jci.org.jo; internet www.jci.org.jo; promotes competitiveness in the industrial sector and co-operation between the various chambers of industry in Jordan; Chair. Dr HATEM H. HALAWANI; Dir-Gen. ZAKI M. AYOUBI.

Professional Associations Council (PAC): Professional Associations Complex, Amman; rep. body for 14 professional asscns; Pres. TAHER SHAKHSHIR.

PETROLEUM AND GAS

Jordan Oil Shale Co: c/o Royal Dutch Shell plc, Carel van Bylandtlaan 30, 2596 HR The Hague, The Netherlands; e-mail webmaster@josco.jo; internet www.josco.jo; f. 2009; wholly owned subsidiary of Royal Dutch Shell plc (Netherlands/United Kingdom); exploration and exploitation of oil shale deposits.

Jordan Oil Shale Energy Co: POB 962497, Amman 11196; tel. (6) 5157064; fax (6) 5157046; e-mail info@joseco.com.jo; internet www.joseco.com.jo; f. 2007; state-owned; promotion and devt of oil shale projects; Chair. MAJED KHALIFA.

National Petroleum Co PLC: POB 3503, Amman 11821; tel. (6) 5548888; fax (6) 5536912; e-mail management@npc.com.jo; internet www.npc.com.jo; f. 1995; petroleum and natural gas exploration and production; signed partnership agreement with BP (United Kingdom) for devt of Risha gasfield 2009; Chair. Dr ABD AL-RAZZAQ AL NUSUR.

UTILITIES

Electricity

Electricity Regulatory Commission: POB 1865, Amman 11821; tel. (6) 5805000; fax (6) 5805003; e-mail webmaster@erc.gov.jo; internet www.erc.gov.jo; f. 2001; regulatory authority; Chief Commr SULEIMAN HAFEZ; Chair. HISHAM KHATIB.

Central Electricity Generating Company (CEGCO): POB 2564, Amman 11953; tel. (6) 5340008; fax (6) 5340800; e-mail cegco@cegco.com.jo; internet www.cegco.com.jo; part-privatized in Sept. 2007; 51% owned by ENARA Energy Arabia, 40% by Govt and 9% by Social Security Corpn; electricity generation; Dir-Gen. ABD AL-FATTAH AL-NSOUR.

Electricity Distribution Company (EDCO): POB 2310, Orthodox St, 7th Circle, Jabal Amman, Amman; tel. (6) 5858615; fax (6) 5818336; e-mail info@edco.jo; internet www.edco.jo; f. 1999; privatized in Nov. 2007; wholly owned by Kingdom Electricity, a jt venture between Jordan, Kuwait and the United Arab Emirates; electricity distribution for southern, eastern and Jordan Valley regions; Dir-Gen. MUHAMMAD AMIN FREIHAT.

Irbid District Electricity Company (IDECO): POB 46, Amman; tel. (6) 7201500; fax (6) 7245495; e-mail ideco@wanadoo.jo; internet www.ideco.com.jo; f. 1957; 55.4% stake acquired by Kingdom Electricity (see EDCO) in Nov. 2007; electricity generation, transmission and distribution for northern regions; Chair. MUHAMMAD ABU HAMMOUR; Gen. Man. Eng. AHMAD THAINAT.

Jordanian Electric Power Company (JEPCO): POB 618, Amman 11118; tel. (6) 5503600; fax (6) 5503619; e-mail jepco@go.com.jo; internet www.jepco.com.jo; f. 1938; privately owned; electricity distribution for Amman, al-Salt, al-Zarqa and Madaba; Chair. ISSAM BDEIR; Gen. Man. MARWAN BUSHNAQ.

National Electric Power Company (NEPCO): POB 2310, Amman 11118; tel. (6) 5858615; fax (6) 5818336; e-mail info@nepco.com.jo; internet www.nepco.com.jo; f. 1996; fmrly Jordan Electricity Authority; electricity transmission; govt-owned; Chair. Dr ABD AL-RAZZAQ AL-NSOUR; Dir-Gen. Dr GHALEB AL-MAABRAH.

Water

Jordan Water Company (Miyahuna): POB 922918, Amman 11192; tel. (6) 5666111; fax (6) 5682642; internet www.miyahuna.com.jo; f. 2007; owned by Water Authority of Jordan; operates as an independent commercial entity; management of water and sewage services in Amman; CEO Eng. KAMAL AL-ZOUBI; Chair. Eng. MUNIR OWAIS.

Water Authority of Jordan (WAJ): POB 2412, Amman 11183; tel. (6) 5680100; fax (6) 5679143; e-mail administrator@waj.gov.jo; internet www.waj.gov.jo; f. 1984; govt-owned; scheduled for privatization; Sec.-Gen. Eng. MUNIR OWAIS.

MAJOR COMPANIES

Adnan Sha'lan & Co: POB 1428, King Hussein St, Amman 11118; tel. (6) 4894442; fax (6) 4894441; f. 1953; mfrs of paints, glues, refrigerators, gas cookers, dairy products and cosmetics; cap. US $3m.; Chair. ADNAN SHA'LAN; Man. Dir FAWEZ SHA'LAN; 400 employees.

Agricultural Marketing and Processing Co of Jordan (AMPCO): POB 7314, Bldg 22, Abd Al-Rahim Wakid St, Amman 11118; tel. (6) 5691961; fax (6) 5687155; e-mail info@ampcojordan.com; internet www.ampcojordan.com; f. 1984; govt-owned; Chair. Dr ABD AL-HADI ALAWEEN; Dir-Gen. ABD AL-HAMID AL-KAYED.

Arab Centre for Pharmaceuticals and Chemicals (ACPC): POB 22, 22 King Abdullah II Industrial City, Sahab 11512; tel. (6) 4022470; fax (6) 4022473; e-mail info@acpc.com.jo; internet www.acpc.com.jo; f. 1984; mfrs of pharmaceuticals and chemicals; cap. JD 5m. (1998); Man. Dir ATA AL-NAZER; 280 employees.

Arab Investment and International Trade Co Ltd: POB 94, Sahab Old Rd, al-Raqim, Amman 11591; tel. (6) 4161191; fax (6) 4161504; e-mail aiit@go.com.jo; f. 1978; mfrs of toiletries; sales JD 3.6m. (1998); cap. p.u. JD 5m. (1999); Chair. ABD AL-MALIK SAID; Gen. Man. Eng. MUHAMMAD S. ABU SALAH; 170 employees.

Arab Pharmaceutical Manufacturing Co Ltd (APM): POB 42, Amman 19110; tel. (6) 5802200; fax (6) 5802203; e-mail info@apm.com.jo; internet www.apm.com.jo; f. 1964; mfrs of pharmaceuticals; sales JD 30m. (1999); cap. p.u. JD 18m.; owned by Hikma; Chair. ANIS MOASHER; Man. Dir ISSAM HAMDI SAKET; 850 employees.

Arab Potash Co Ltd (APC): POB 1470, Amman 11118; tel. (6) 5200520; fax (6) 5200080; e-mail info@arabpotash.com; internet www.arabpotash.com; f. 1956; production of potash, with a by-product of salt; production 1.8m. tons, sales 1.7m. tons (1999); 27.7% owned by PotashCorp (Canada), 26.9% owned by Jordan Investment Corpn (through the Govt of Jordan), 19.9% owned by Arab Mining Co (Jordan), 25.9% owned by various other investors; Chair. JAMAL A. AL-SARAYRAH; Gen. Man. WILLIAM LAWRENCE FLAHR (acting); 2,316 employees.

Elba House Co WLL: POB 3449, Amman 11181; tel. (6) 5300600; fax (6) 5300624; e-mail info@elbahouse.com; internet www.elbahouse.com; f. 1976; mfrs of prefabricated buildings, caravans, steel structures, vehicle bodies and construction plants; Pres. and Dir-Gen. USAMA MUSA KHOURY; Chair. ZUHAIR MUSA KHOURY; 1,000 employees.

General Investment Co Ltd: POB 312, Abujaber Bldg, Prince Muhammad St, Amman 11118; tel. (6) 4625161; fax (6) 4657679; e-mail gic@go.com.jo; f. 1986 by merger of Jordan Brewery Co Ltd (f. 1955) and its subsidiary Gen. Investment Co Ltd; producers of beer, non-alcoholic malt beverages, soft drinks and alcohol for medical purposes; investment and real estate brokers; sales US $12m. (2001); cap. US $14m. (2002); Chair. Dr RAOUF ABUJABER; Gen. Man. MARWAN ABUJABER.

Hikma Pharmaceuticals Ltd: POB 182400, 11118 Amman; tel. (6) 5802900; fax (6) 5817102; e-mail jordan@hikma.com; internet www.hikma.com; f. 1978; mfrs of over 360 pharmaceutical products; CEO SAID DARWAZAH; Chair. SAMIH DARWAZAH.

Industrial, Commercial and Agricultural Co Ltd (ICA): POB 6066, Amman 11118; tel. (6) 5533201; fax (6) 5548389; e-mail icacontactus@ica-jo.com; internet www.ica-jo.com; f. 1961; industrial, commercial and agricultural investment; operates factories producing (under licence) soap, detergents, toiletries, paints, biscuits, ice-cream and containers; sales JD 21.5m., cap. p.u. JD 9m. (1999); Chair. and Man. Dir MUHAMMAD A. ABU HASSAN; 550 employees.

International Contracting and Investment Co: POB 19170, Amman; tel. (6) 5666133; f. 1977; building and civil construction; cap. p.u. JD 4m.; Chair. FAKHRY ABU SHAKRA; Vice-Pres. HASSAN SHIHABI; 176 employees.

Jordan Cement Factories Co Ltd: POB 930019, Abd al-Rahim Al-Wakid St, Amman 11193; tel. (6) 5600600; fax (6) 5600639; e-mail cement@go.com.jo; f. 1951; merged with South Cement Co 1985; annual production at two works 3.1m. tons (1995); 50.2% owned by Lafarge SA, France; Chair. LOUIS CHAVIN; CEO TAWFIQ A. TABARA; 607 employees (2012).

Jordan Petroleum Refinery Co (JPRC): POB 1097, Amman 11118; tel. (6) 4630151; fax (6) 4657939; e-mail addewan@jopetrol.com.jo; internet www.jopetrol.com.jo; f. 1956; petroleum refining and distribution of refined petroleum products (lube oil blending and canning; mfr of LPG cylinders); production 4.3m. tons, sales 4.7m. tons (JD 1,600m.), profits JD 6.0m. (2006); privatized in 2004; Chair. WALEED METHCAL ASFOUR; 3,577 employees.

Jordan Pharmaceutical Manufacturing Co (JPM): POB 94, Naour 11710; tel. (6) 5727207; fax (6) 5727641; e-mail jpm@go.com.jo; internet www.jpm.com.jo; f. 1978; manufacturer of generic pharmaceutical products, natural medicines and diagnostic products; Chair. SALEH AL-SHANTEER; Gen. Dir ADNAN A. H. BADWAN.

Jordan Phosphate Mines Co Ltd (JPMC): POB 30, 5 al-Shareef al-Radi St Shmeisani, Amman 11118; tel. (6) 5607141; fax (6) 5682290; e-mail webmaster@jpmc.com.jo; internet jordanphosphate.com; f. 1930; production and export of rock phosphate; absorbed Jordan Fertilizer Industries Co; 25.6% state-owned; 37.0% share bought by Brunei Investment Agency in 2006; 3 mines in operation; one mine dormant; production 7m. metric tons per year; exports approx. 4.5m. tons per year to 20 countries world-wide; CEO EMAD AL-MADADHA.

Jordan Steel: POB 35165, Amman 11180; tel. (6) 4619380; fax (6) 4619384; e-mail info@jordansteelplc.com; internet www.jordansteelplc.com; f. 1993; mfrs of steel bars, steel billets and wire mesh; cap p.u. JD 35m.; Chair. MUDAR MUHAMMAD BADRAN.

Metal Industries Co Ltd (Metalco): POB 143109, Amman Industrial Estate, Amman 11814; tel. (6) 5562153; fax (6) 5562175; e-mail export@metalco.com; internet www.metalco.com; f. 1965; mfrs of steel panel radiators and boilers; Chair. Eng. M. A. JARDANEH; Gen. Man. LUAY M. JARDANEH.

TRADE UNION

The General Federation of Jordanian Trade Unions: POB 1065, Amman; tel. (6) 5675533; fax (6) 5687911; e-mail khyasat@rja.com.jo; f. 1954; 17 affiliated unions; 200,000 mems; mem. of Arab Trade Unions Confed; Pres. MAZEN MA'AYTEH.

Transport

RAILWAYS

The Hedjaz–Jordan Railway crosses the Syrian border and enters Jordanian territory south of Dar'a. It runs for approximately 366 km to Naqb Ishtar, passing through Zarqa, Amman, Qatrana and Ma'an. An express rail link between Amman and Damascus was inaugurated in 1999. In 2008 a feasibility study concerning the upgrade and revival of the entire Hedjaz Railway was launched by the Governments of Jordan, Saudi Arabia and Syria. Formerly a division of the Hedjaz–Jordan Railway, the Aqaba Railway was established as a separate entity in 1972; it retains close links with the Hedjaz, but there is no regular through traffic between Aqaba and Amman. It comprises 292 km of 1,050-mm gauge track and is used solely for the transportation of minerals from three phosphate mines to Aqaba port.

In 2008 the Government announced that it was seeking up to US $6,000m. in foreign investment in order to implement a major railway development plan. The proposals included a north–south line of more than 500 km linking the Red Sea port of Aqaba with Amman, Zarqa and Irbid in the north, and would connect the network with systems in Syria, Iraq and Saudi Arabia. An international advisory team for the project was appointed in 2009. Plans to build and operate a 26-km light rail link between Amman and Zarqa were abandoned in 2011, owing to concerns over funding. In 2010 the total length of Jordanian railways was 294 route-km.

Aqaba Railways Corporation (ARC): POB 50, Ma'an; tel. (3) 2132114; fax (3) 2131861; e-mail arc@go.com.jo; internet www.arc.gov.jo; f. 1975; length of track 292 km (1,050-mm gauge); privately owned; Dir-Gen. HUSSEIN KRISHAN.

Jordan Hedjaz Railways: POB 4448, Amman 11131; tel. (6) 4895414; fax (6) 4894117; e-mail mkhazaleh@jh-railway.com; internet www.jh-railway.com; f. 1952 as Hedjaz–Jordan Railway; administered by the Ministry of Transport; length of track 496 km (1,050-mm gauge); Chair. Dr LINA SHABIB (Minister of Transport); Dir-Gen. MAHMOUD KHAZALEH.

ROADS

Amman is linked by road with all parts of the kingdom and with neighbouring countries. All cities and most towns are connected by a two-lane, paved road system. In addition, several thousand kilometres of tracks make all villages accessible to motor transport. In 2010 there was a total road network of 7,100 km, of which 2,878 km were highways, main or national roads, 1,733 km were secondary or regional roads and 2,489 km were of other roads.

Jordanian-Syrian Land Transport Co: POB 20686, Amman 11118; tel. (6) 4711545; fax (6) 4711517; e-mail josyco@josyco.com.jo; f. 1975; jt venture between Govts of Jordan and Syria; transports goods between ports in Jordan and Syria; operates 210 heavy-duty trailers; underwent restructuring in 2010; Dir-Gen. JAMIL ALI MUJAHID.

SHIPPING

The port of Aqaba, Jordan's only outlet to the sea, consists of a main port, container port (540 m in length) and industrial port, with 25 modern and specialized berths. It has 761,300 sq m of open and contained storage area. There is a ferry link between Aqaba and the Egyptian port of Nuweibeh. In 2008 the Government initiated a tendering process for a US $700m. project to relocate Aqaba's main port to the southern industrial zone. The new development, to be supervised by the Aqaba Development Corporation, was to significantly increase overall capacity, comprising a general cargo terminal with roll-on roll-off (ro-ro) facilities, a dedicated grain terminal and a new ferry terminal. Once vacated, the existing port site was to be redeveloped as a major new commercial, residential and tourism centre.

At 31 December 2012 Jordan's flag registered fleet totalled 23 vessels, with an aggregate displacement of 79,839 grt, of which three were general cargo ships.

Port Authorities

Aqaba Container Terminal (ACT): POB 1944, King Hussein bin Talal St, Aqaba 77110; tel. (3) 2091111; fax (3) 2039133; e-mail customerservice@act.com.jo; internet www.act.com.jo; CEO SOREN HANSEN.

Aqaba Ports Corporation: POB 115, Aqaba 77110; tel. (3) 2014031; fax (3) 2016204; e-mail info@aqabaports.gov.jo; internet www.aqabaports.com; f. 1952 as Aqaba Port Authority; name changed as above 1978; Dir-Gen. AWAD AL-MAAYTAH.

Principal Shipping Companies

Amman Shipping & Trading Co Ltd (ASTCO): POB 213083, 5th Floor, Blk A, Aqqad Bldg, Gardens St, Amman 11121; tel. (6) 5514620; fax (6) 5532324; e-mail sts@albitar.com; internet www.1stjordan.net/astco/index.html; f. 1990.

Arab Bridge Maritime Co: POB 989, Aqaba; tel. (3) 2092000; fax (3) 2092001; e-mail info@abmaritime.com.jo; internet www.abmaritime.com.jo; f. 1985; jt venture by Egypt, Iraq and Jordan; commercial shipping of passengers, vehicles and cargo between Aqaba and the Egyptian port of Nuweibeh; Man. Dir HUSSEIN AL-SOUOB.

T. Gargour & Fils (TGF): POB 419, 1st Floor, Bldg No. 233, Arar St, Wadi Saqra, Amman 11118; tel. (6) 4626611; fax (6) 4622425; e-mail tgf@tgf.com.jo; internet www.tgf.com.jo; f. 1928; shipping agents and owners; CEO Dr DUREID MAHASNEH.

Jordan National Shipping Lines Co Ltd (JNSL): POB 5406, Bldg No. 51, Wadi Saqra St, Amman 11183; POB 557, Aqaba; tel. (6) 5511500; fax (6) 5511501; e-mail jnslamman@jnslgroup.com; internet www.jnslgroup.com; f. 1976; 75% govt-owned; service from Antwerp (Netherlands), Bremen (Germany) and Tilbury (United Kingdom) to Aqaba; daily passenger ferry service to Egypt; land transportation to various regional destinations; Chair. AHMAD ARMOUSH.

Amin Kawar & Sons Co WLL: POB 222, 24 Abd al-Hamid Sharaf St, Shmeisani, Amman 11118; tel. (6) 5609500; fax (6) 5698322; e-mail kawar@kawar.com.jo; internet www.kawar.com; chartering, forwarding and shipping line agents; Chair. TAWFIQ KAWAR; CEO RUDAIN T. KAWAR; Pres. KARIM KAWAR.

Naouri Group: Um Uthaina, Saad Bin Abi Waqqas St, Bldg No. 30, Amman 11118; tel. (6) 5777901; fax (6) 5777911; e-mail info@naouri.com; internet www.naouri.com; f. 1994; operates several cos in shipping sector incl. Ammon Shipping and Transport, Salam Shipping and Forwarding, Kareem Logistics; Chair. IBRAHIM NAOURI.

Orient Shipping Co Ltd: Jordan Insurance Bldg, Bldg (A), 3rd Floor, POB 207, Amman 11118; tel. (6) 4641695; fax (6) 4651567; e-mail orship@orientshipping.jo; internet www.orientshipping.jo; f. 1965; shipping agency.

Petra Navigation and International Trading Co Ltd: POB 942502, Amman 11194; tel. (6) 5607021; fax (6) 5601362; e-mail info@petra.jo; internet www.petra.jo; f. 1977; general cargo, ro-ro and passenger ferries; Chair. AHMAD ARMOUSH; Man. Dir ANWAR SBEIH.

Red Sea Shipping Agency Co: POB 1248, 24 Sharif Abd al-Hamid Sharaf St, Shmeisani, Amman 11118; tel. (6) 5609501; fax (6) 5688241; e-mail rss@rssa.com.jo; internet www.redseashipping.com.jo; f. 1955.

Salam International Transport and Trading Co: POB 212955, Salam Trading Center, Arar St, Wadi Saqra, 11121; tel. (6) 5654510; fax (6) 5697014; e-mail tdajani@aagroup.jo; internet www.sittcogroup.com; f. 1996; publicly listed; diversified shipping, logistics, and oil and gas group; CEO TAREK DAJANI.

PIPELINES

Two oil pipelines cross Jordan. The former Iraq Petroleum Co pipeline, carrying petroleum from the oilfields in Iraq to Israel's Mediterranean port of Haifa, has not operated since 1967. The 1,717-km (1,067-mile) Trans-Arabian Pipeline (Tapline) carries petroleum from the oilfields of Dhahran in Saudi Arabia to Sidon on the Mediterranean seaboard in Lebanon. Tapline traverses Jordan for a distance of 177 km (110 miles) and has frequently been cut by hostile action. Confronted with the challenge of meeting rising oil demands, the Jordanian Government has been considering plans to rehabilitate disused sections of Tapline, at an estimated cost of US $200m.–$300m., since early 2005. In April 2013 the Governments of Jordan and Iraq signed an agreement for the construction of a US $18,000m., 1,700-km double pipeline to transport oil and natural gas from Basra province in Iraq to Aqaba.

CIVIL AVIATION

There are three international airports, two serving Amman and one in Aqaba. A 25-year concession to expand and operate Queen Alia International Airport at Zizya, 40 km south of Amman, including the construction of a new terminal building, was awarded to an international consortium, Airport International Group, in May 2007. The new terminal was officially opened in March 2013, increasing the airport's potential annual capacity to approximately 12m. passengers.

Jordan Civil Aviation Regulatory Commission (CARC): POB 7547, Amman 11110; tel. (6) 4892282; fax (6) 4891653; e-mail info@carc.gov.jo; internet www.carc.jo; f. 2007, to replace Civil Aviation Authority (f. 1950); Chief Commr and CEO Capt. MUHAMMAD AMIN AL-QURAN.

Aqaba Airports Co: POB 2662, King Hussein International Airport, Special Economic Zone, Aqaba 77110; tel. (3) 2034010; e-mail info@aac.jo; internet www.aac.jo; f. 2007; Dir MUNIR ASAD.

Jordan Aviation (JATE): POB 922358, Amman 11192; tel. (6) 5501760; fax (6) 5525761; e-mail info@jordanaviation.jo; internet www.jordanaviation.jo; f. 2000; first privately owned airline in Jordan; operates regional and international charter and scheduled flights; Chair. and CEO Capt. MUHAMMAD AL-KHASHMAN.

Royal Jordanian Airline: POB 302, Housing Bank Commercial Centre, Queen Noor St, Amman 11118; tel. (6) 5202000; fax (6) 5672527; e-mail AMMDDRJ@rj.com; internet www.rj.com; f. 1963; privatized in 2007; regional and international scheduled and charter services; Chair. NASSER A. LOZI; Pres. and CEO HUSSEIN H. DABBAS.

Royal Wings Co Ltd: POB 314018, Amman 11134; tel. (6) 5803340; fax (6) 5803344; e-mail info@royalwings.com.jo; internet www.royalwings.com.jo; f. 1996; subsidiary of Royal Jordanian Airline; operates regional and domestic scheduled and charter services; Man. Dir ABD AL-QADER KAILANI.

Tourism

The ancient cities of Jarash (Jerash) and Petra, and Jordan's proximity to biblical sites, have encouraged tourism. The development of Jordan's Dead Sea coast is currently under way; owing to the Sea's mineral-rich waters, the growth of curative tourism is anticipated. The Red Sea port of Aqaba is also undergoing a major programme of development, with a view to becoming a centre for water sports, diving and beach holidays. Since the creation of the Wadi Rum Protected Area in 1998 tourism in this desert region is promoted on the basis of its unique ecosystem, landscape and the traditional culture of its Bedouin inhabitants. The National Tourism Strategy (NTS) 2004–10 set out ambitious targets that included doubling the figures for foreign visitors and tourism-related income and jobs. (By 2008 the sector appeared already to have achieved the goal of doubling income.) However, political turmoil in the Middle East and North Africa contributed to a decline in visitors and revenue in 2011. According to data from the Ministry of Tourism and Antiquities, the number of foreign visitors to Jordan declined by 17.2%, to 6.8m., while income from tourism also declined, to JD 2,130m. Visitor numbers declined further, to 6.3m., in 2012, although receipts increased slightly to JD 2,456m.

Ministry of Tourism and Antiquities: see Ministries; Sec.-Gen. FAROUK AL-HADIDI.

Jordan Tourism Board (JTB): POB 830688, Amman 11183; tel. (6) 5678444; fax (6) 5678295; e-mail info@visitjordan.com; internet www.visitjordan.com; f. 1997; Man. Dir NAYEF AL-FAYEZ.

Defence

Supreme Commander of the Armed Forces: King ABDULLAH IBN AL-HUSSEIN.

Chairman of the Joint Chiefs of Staff: Lt-Gen. MESHAAL MUHAMMAD AL-ZABEN.

Commander of the Royal Jordanian Air Force: Maj.-Gen. MALEK AL-HABASHNEH.

Defence Budget (2012): JD 1,030m.

Total Armed Forces (as assessed at November 2012): 100,500: army 88,000; navy est. 500; air force 12,000. Reserves 65,000 (army 60,000, joint 5,000).

Paramilitary Forces (as assessed at November 2012): 10,000.

Education

Primary education, beginning at six years of age, is free and compulsory. This 10-year preparatory cycle is followed by a two-year secondary cycle. The UN Relief and Works Agency (UNRWA) provides educational facilities and services for Palestinian refugees. According to UNESCO estimates, in 2009/10 primary enrolment included 91% of children in the relevant age-group; in the same year secondary enrolment included 86% of children in the relevant age-group. There were 10,024 teachers and 246,928 students in higher education in 2009/10. Education in Jordan was provided at 5,167 schools and 22 institutions of higher education in 2003/04. The budget for central Government spending in 2012 allocated JD 738.5m. (11.1% of total current expenditure) to education.

Bibliography

Abdullah of Transjordan, King. *Memoirs* (trans. G. Khuri, ed. P. Graves). London and New York, Jonathan Cape, 1950.

Abidi, A. H. H. *Jordan, a Political Study 1948–1957*. Delhi, Asia Publishing House, 1966.

Abu Nowar, Maan. *The Struggle for Independence 1939–1947. A History of the Hashemite Kingdom of Jordan*. Reading, Ithaca Press, 1999.

The Jordanian–Israeli War, 1948–51: A History of the Hashemite Kingdom of Jordan. Reading, Ithaca Press, 2002.

The Development of Trans-Jordan 1929–1939: A History of the Hashemite Kingdom of Jordan. Reading, Ithaca Press, 2005.

Alon, Yoav. *The Making of Jordan: Tribes, Colonialism and the Modern State*. London, I. B. Tauris, 2009.

Anderson, Betty S. *Nationalist Voices in Jordan: The Street and the State*. Austin, TX, University of Texas Press, 2005.

Ashton, Nigel. *King Hussein of Jordan: A Political Life*. New Haven, CT, Yale University Press, 2008.

Blackwell, Stephen. *British Military Intervention and the Struggle for Jordan: King Hussein, Nasser and the Middle East Crisis, 1955-1958*. Abingdon, Routledge, 2009.

Bligh, Alexander. *The Political Legacy of King Hussein*. Brighton, Sussex Academic Press, 2002.

Boulby, Marion. *The Muslim Brotherhood and the Kings of Jordan 1945–1993*. Atlanta, GA, Scholars Press, 1999.

Dann, Uriel. *King Hussein and the Challenge of Arab Radicalism: Jordan, 1955–1967*. Oxford, Oxford University Press, 1991.

Day, Arthur. *East Bank, West Bank*. New York, Council on Foreign Relations, 1986.

Dearden, Ann. *Jordan*. London, Hale, 1958.

Glubb, John B. *The Story of the Arab Legion*. London, Hodder and Stoughton, 1948.

A Soldier with the Arabs. London, Hodder and Stoughton, 1957.

Britain and the Arabs: A Study of Fifty Years 1908–1958. London, Hodder and Stoughton, 1959.

War in the Desert. London, Hodder and Stoughton, 1960.

The Middle East Crisis—A Personal Interpretation. London, Hodder and Stoughton, 1967.

Syria, Lebanon, Jordan. London, Thames and Hudson, 1967.

Peace in the Holy Land. London, Hodder and Stoughton, 1971.

Habib, Randa. *Hussein and Abdullah: Inside the Jordanian Royal Family*. London, Saqi Books, 2010.

Hussein, His Majesty King. *Uneasy Lies the Head*. New York, Random House, 1962.

Ma guerre avec Israël. Paris, Albin Michel, 1968.

Mon métier de roi. Paris, Laffont, 1975.

Joffé, George (Ed.) *Jordan in Transition 1990–2000*. London, C. Hurst & Co, 2001.

Johnston, Charles. *The Brink of Jordan*. London, Hamish Hamilton, 1972.

Joyce, Miriam. *Anglo-American Support for Jordan: The Career of King Hussein*. New York, Palgrave Macmillan, 2008.

Kandeel, Amal A. *Jordan's Struggle for Survival: War in the Middle East and Arab Economies' Underdevelopment*. London, Pluto Press, 2008.

Knowles, Warwick. *Jordan Since 1989: A Study in Political Economy*. London, I. B. Tauris, 2005.

Konikof, A. *Transjordan: An Economic Survey*. 2nd edn, Jerusalem, 1946.

Layne, Linda. *Home and Homeland: The Dialogues of Tribal and National Identities in Jordan*. Chichester, Princeton University Press, 1994.

Legrand, Vincent. *Prise de décision en politique étrangère et géopolitique: Le triangle «Jordanie-Palestine-Israël» et la décision jordanienne de désengagement de Cisjordanie (1988)*. Bern, Peter Lang Verlagsgruppe, 2009.

Lowi, Miriam R. *Water and Power: The Politics of a Scarce Resource in the Jordan River Basin*. Cambridge, Cambridge University Press, 1994.

Lucas, Russell E. *Institutions and the Politics of Survival in Jordan: Domestic Responses to External Challenges, 1988–2001*. Albany, NY, State University of New York, 2005.

Luke, Sir Harry C., and Keith-Roach, E. *The Handbook of Palestine and Transjordan*. London, Macmillan, 1934.

Lunt, James. *Hussein of Jordan*. London, Macmillan, 1989.

Lyautey, Pierre. *La Jordanie Nouvelle*. Paris, Juillard, 1966.

Marashdeh, Omar. *The Jordanian Economy*. Amman, Al-Jawal Corpn, 1996.

Massad, Joseph A. *Colonial Effects: The Making of National Identity in Jordan*. New York, Columbia University Press, 2001.

Milton-Edwards, Beverley, and Hinchliffe, Peter. *Jordan: A Hashemite Legacy*. London, Routledge, 2001, 2nd edn, 2009.

Mishal, Shaul. *West Bank/East Bank: The Palestinians in Jordan 1949–67*. New Haven, CT, and London, Yale University Press, 1978.

Moaddel, Mansoor. *Jordanian Exceptionalism*. Basingstoke, Palgrave, 2001.

Morris, James. *The Hashemite Kings*. London, Faber, 1959.

Al-O'ran, Mutayyam. *Jordanian-Israeli Relations: The Peacebuilding Experience*. Abingdon, Routledge, 2009.

Patai, R. *The Kingdom of Jordan*. Princeton, NJ, Princeton University Press, 1958.

Peake, F. G. *History of Jordan and Its Tribes*. Oxford, OH, University of Miami Press, 1958.

Piro, Timothy J. *The Political Economy of Market Reform in Jordan*. Lanham, MD, Rowan and Littlefield, 1998.

Robins, Philip. *A History of Jordan*. Cambridge, Cambridge University Press, 2004.

Rogan, Eugene L., and Tell, Tariq (Eds). *Village, Steppe and State: The Social Origins of Modern Jordan*. London, British Academic Press, 1994.

Ryan, Curtis R. *Inter-Arab Alliances: Regime Security and Jordanian Foreign Policy*. Gainesville, FL, University Press of Florida, 2008.

Salibi, Kamal. *The Modern History of Jordan*. London, I. B. Tauris, 1999.

Sanger, Richard H. *Where the Jordan Flows*. Washington, DC, Middle East Institute, 1965.

Shlaim, Avi. *Collusion Across the Jordan*. Oxford, Oxford University Press, 1988.

Lion of Jordan: The Life of King Hussein in War and Peace. London, Allen Lane, 2007.

Shwadran, B. *Jordan: A State of Tension*. New York, Council for Middle Eastern Affairs, 1959.

Snow, Peter. *Hussein: A Biography*. London, Barrie and Jenkins, 1972.

Sosland, Jeffrey K. *Cooperating Rivals: The Riparian Politics of the Jordan River Basin*. Albany, NY, State University of New York Press, 2008.

Sparrow, Gerald. *Hussein of Jordan (The Authorized Biography)*. London, Harrap, 1961.

Modern Jordan. Sydney, Allen & Unwin, 1961.

Tal, Nachman. *Radical Islam in Egypt and Jordan*. Brighton, Sussex Academic, 2005.

Toukan, Baha Uddin. *A Short History of Transjordan*. London, Luzac & Co, 1945.

Vatikiotis, P. J. *Politics and the Military in Jordan 1921–57*. New York, Praeger, 1967.

Wilson, Rodney (Ed.). *Politics and Economy in Jordan*. London, Routledge, 1991.

KUWAIT

Physical and Social Geography

Kuwait lies at the head of the Persian (Arabian) Gulf, bordering Iraq and Saudi Arabia. The area of the State of Kuwait is 17,818 sq km (6,880 sq miles), including the Kuwaiti share of the Neutral or Partitioned Zone (see below) but without taking into account the increase in territory resulting from the adjustment to the border with Iraq that came into effect in January 1993.

Although, for some time, the Gulf was thought to extend much further north, geological evidence suggests that the coastline has remained broadly at its present position, while the immense bodies of silt brought down by the Tigris and Euphrates cause irregular down-warping at the head of the Gulf. Local variation in the coastline is therefore likely, with possible changes since ancient times. The development of Kuwait owed much to its zone of slightly higher, firmer ground (giving access from the Gulf inland to Iraq) and to its reasonably good and sheltered harbour, away from nearby sandbanks and coral reefs.

The territory of Kuwait is mainly flat desert with a few oases. An annual rainfall of 1 cm–37 cm falls almost entirely between November and April, and there is a spring 'flush' of grass. Summer shade temperature may reach 49°C (120°F), although in January, the coldest month, temperatures range between −2.8°C and 28.3°C (27°F–85°F), with a rare frost. There is little inland drinking water, and supplies are largely distilled from sea water and brought by pipeline from the Shatt al-Arab waterway, which runs into the Gulf.

According to census results, the population of Kuwait increased from 206,473 in February 1957 to 1,357,952 by April 1980 and to 1,697,301 by April 1985. It was estimated that in 1991, following the war to end the Iraqi occupation, the population had declined to only 1.2m., mainly as a result of the departure of a large proportion of the former non-Kuwaiti residents, who had previously formed a majority of the inhabitants (see below). The census of April 1995 recorded a total population of 1,575,570, including 653,616 Kuwaiti nationals. The population at the census of April 2005 was 2,193,651. By the end of 2012 the population had increased to 3,823,728, according to official estimates based on new methodology used by the Public Authority for Civil Information.

According to official estimates, at the end of 2012 Jaleeb al-Shuyukh was the largest town in Kuwait, with 285,019 inhabitants. Other sizeable localities were Salmiya (population 262,594) and Farwaniya (221,492). However, these settlements are contiguous with the capital, Kuwait City, and are sometimes described as suburbs. Indeed, UN estimates—which includes suburbs—put the capital's population at 2.4m. in 2011.

Apart from the distinction between Kuwaiti citizens and immigrants, Kuwaiti nationals can be divided into six groups. These groups reflect the tribal origins of Kuwaiti society. The first tribe of settlers, the Anaiza (led by the Sabah family), and later settlers, including the Bahar, Hamad and Babtain families, originated in the Nejd (central Arabia). Another group, the Kenaat (including the Mutawa family and its offshoot, the Saleh), came to Kuwait from Iraq, and remain distinct from the Nejdi families. There are also a few large families of Persian (Iranian) origin, including the Behbanis. The remaining citizens may be described as 'new Kuwaitis'; a few are former Palestinians, although most are Bedouin who have been granted second-class citizenship. The majority of Kuwaitis (including the ruling family) are Sunni Muslims, but most of the Persian families belong to the Shi'a sect. They, together with other Persians, comprise an estimated 25% of all Kuwaiti citizens. About 30% of the total population are thought to be Shi'ites.

Immediately to the south of Kuwait, along the Gulf, is a Neutral/Partitioned Zone of 5,700 sq km, which is divided between Kuwait and Saudi Arabia. Each country administers its own half as an integral part of the state. However, the oil wealth of the whole Zone remains undivided, and production from the onshore concessions in the Neutral/Partitioned Zone is normally shared equally between the two states.

History

Revised for this edition by JILL CRYSTAL

The establishment of the present city of Kuwait is usually dated to the beginning of the 18th century, when a number of families of the Anaiza tribe migrated from the interior to the Arabian shore of the Gulf. The foundation of the present al-Sabah ruling dynasty dates from about 1756, when the settlers of Kuwait took the protection of a sheikh against other tribal threats, and in order to administer their affairs, provide them with security, and represent them in their dealings with the Ottoman rulers of Iraq. The town prospered, and in 1765 it was estimated to contain some 10,000 inhabitants, possessing 800 vessels, engaged in trading, fishing and pearling.

Between 1775 and 1779, during the Persian occupation of Basra, the British East India Company moved the southern terminal of its overland Basra–Aleppo mail route to Kuwait, and much Basra trade was diverted there. This temporary relocation was repeated in 1793 and again in 1821–22, and many merchant families migrated from Basra to Kuwait. At around the same time Kuwait was repeatedly threatened by raids from the Wahhabis—puritanical Islamist tribesmen from central Arabia—and the need for protection led to closer contacts with the East India Company. Conflict between British and Arab fleets over control of the sea trade caused a decline in prosperity during the early years of the 19th century, but trade later expanded again under British Indian ascendancy. The growth of production in the region and the expansion of trade in the second half of the century brought renewed prosperity.

Although Kuwait was not under direct Ottoman administration, the Sheikh of Kuwait recognized a general Ottoman suzerainty over his sheikhdom by the payment of tribute and the acceptance of the title *Qa'immaqam* (District Officer) under the supervision of the Ottoman *Vali* (Provincial Governor) of Basra in 1871. The reign of Sheikh Mubarak al-Sabah (1896–1915) was notable for the increase of British Indian dominance over Kuwait. Mubarak 'the Great', as he is known today, feared that the Ottomans would bring Kuwait under direct administration, and in 1899, in return for British protection, he signed an agreement with the British Government of India not to cede, mortgage or otherwise dispose of parts of his territories to anyone except the British Government, nor enter into any relationship with a foreign government without British consent. In that year the British Government of India appointed Hajji Ali bin Mulla Ghulam Riza, a prominent local merchant with connections to Britain, as its political agent in Kuwait. In 1904 the Government replaced Hajji Ali with a British political agent, Capt. Stuart Knox. In 1909 the British and Ottoman Governments discussed proposals which, although never ratified because of the outbreak of the First World War (1914–18), in practice secured the status of Kuwait as a British protectorate (to remain thus until 1961).

Sheikh Mubarak died in 1915 and was succeeded by his eldest son, Sheikh Jaber, founder of the al-Jaber branch of the ruling family. Sheikh Jaber died just two years later. He was succeeded by his brother, Sheikh Salim (founder of the al-Salim branch of the family), beginning a pattern of succession—the alternating appointment of rulers from the al-Salim and al-Jaber branches of the ruling family—that continued until 2006. Sheikh Salim incurred British censure during the First World War, when he attempted to sell supplies to the Ottomans in Syria. Sheikh Salim died in 1921 and was succeeded by his nephew, Sheikh Ahmad al-Jaber. Sheikh Ahmad, in stark contrast to his predecessors, was long-lived. His 29-year reign witnessed the collapse of Gulf pearling income during the Great Depression and the introduction of less expensive Japanese cultured pearls to the world market, which together destroyed the market for Gulf pearls. Kuwait was able to adjust to those shocks by benefiting from the growth of Iraqi trade and through payments received for oil exploration. By 1937 Kuwait was a relatively prosperous mercantile community, with a population of about 75,000. There were strong civic demands for representation within Kuwait, and, under King Ghazi, the newly independent kingdom of Iraq was seeking the port city's integration and the end of British protection for Kuwait. Some of these demands were echoed within Kuwait itself, reflecting conflict between the established merchant families and the al-Sabah, particularly during the short-lived period of an elected representative assembly in the late 1930s.

The foundations of Kuwait's petroleum industry were laid during the 1930s. A joint concession was granted in 1934 to the Gulf Oil Corporation of the USA and the Anglo-Persian Oil Company of Great Britain, which together formed the Kuwait Oil Company Limited. Deep drilling started in 1936, and was just beginning to show promising results when the Second World War began in 1939. The oil wells were plugged in 1942 and drilling was suspended until the end of the war in 1945.

THE MODERN STATE

After the war the petroleum industry in Kuwait was revived on an extensive scale (see Economy), and within a few years the town of Kuwait had developed from a traditional dhow port to a thriving modern commercial city, supported by the revenues of the petroleum industry. In 1950 Sheikh Ahmad al-Jaber al-Sabah died and was succeeded by Sheikh Abdullah al-Salim al-Sabah (from the al-Salim branch of the al-Sabah), whose policies focused on the use of petroleum revenues to improve public welfare. In 1951 he inaugurated a programme of public works and educational and medical developments, which transformed Kuwait into a territory with a modern infrastructure and a high level of consumption for the indigenous population. The relationship between the ruling al-Sabah family and the traditional merchant élite and general Kuwaiti population began to change. Instead of the original two-way dependence between the Sheikh and the merchant élite—with the Sheikh providing representation with powers outside Kuwait and a measure of internal security, in return for a limited ability to tax local merchant activity—the Sheikh now became the main economic provider for the population, in addition to holding a much wider political, security, administrative and judicial role. Consequently, the Sheikh came also to rely more on his family than on building alliances with the merchant élite and with other sections of the population. Being a small, wealthy entity in a turbulent region, many Kuwaitis seemed to accept their dependence on the ruling family as the price of a privileged economic position. Thus, domestic opposition was muted, despite the increased education of the population.

Kuwait gradually built up comprehensive welfare services, which are for the most part free of charge—at least to native Kuwaitis. Education is provided completely free of charge. The health service is largely free, and a heavily subsidized housing programme has provided accommodation for many residents who are classified as poor. For a time, the state sector virtually guaranteed well-paid employment and retirement pensions to Kuwaiti citizens, while making minimal tax demands upon them. Citizens were also given advantageous positions in business, and for several decades the scale of petroleum revenues enabled the Government to guarantee widespread benefits, including huge subsidies on water, electricity and consumer products, while the ruling family continued to enjoy its own special privileges. However, the financial viability of these benefits and privileges has increasingly become a matter for debate, as the need for Kuwait to diversify away from dependence upon oil revenues has intensified.

The 1899 agreement under which the United Kingdom assumed responsibility for the conduct of Kuwait's foreign policy was terminated in 1961; Kuwait became an independent state on 19 June, although it remained under British protection until 1971. The ruling Sheikh took the title of Amir, and Kuwait was admitted to the League of Arab States (the Arab League).

Iraq, under the leadership of Gen. Abd al-Karim Kassem (President in 1958–63), did not recognize Kuwait's independence and revived a long-standing claim to sovereignty over the territory. British troops landed in Kuwait in order to deter Iraq from taking military action in support of its claim. The Arab League met in July 1961 and agreed that an Arab League force should be provided to replace the British troops as a guarantor of Kuwait's independence. This force, composed of contingents from Saudi Arabia, Jordan, the United Arab Republic (UAR) and Sudan, arrived in Kuwait in September. The UAR contingent was withdrawn in December, and those of Jordan, Saudi Arabia and Sudan before the end of February 1963, following the bloody coup by members of the Baath Party that overthrew Gen. Kassem.

In December 1961, for the first time in Kuwait's history, an election was held to choose 20 members of a Constituent Assembly (the other members being ministers). This Assembly drafted a new Constitution under which a National Assembly (Majlis al-Umma) of 50 members was elected in January 1963, and the first session was held, with Sheikh Sabah al-Salim al-Sabah, brother of the Amir and heir apparent, as the Prime Minister of a new Council of Ministers.

With the Baath Party now in power, in October 1963 the Iraqi Government announced its decision to recognize Kuwait's complete independence, in an attempt to dispel the tense atmosphere between the two countries. Kuwait was thought to have made a substantial grant to Iraq at this juncture.

In January 1965 a constitutional crisis, reflecting the friction between the ruling house and the National Assembly, resulted in the formation of a strengthened Council of Ministers under Crown Prince Sheikh Sabah. In November Sheikh Abdullah died and was succeeded by Sheikh Sabah, whose post of Prime Minister was assumed by another member of the ruling family, Sheikh Jaber al-Ahmad al-Jaber al-Sabah, who became heir apparent in May 1966.

Kuwait adopted a neutral role in inter-Arab conflicts during 1966 and 1967. It declared its support for the Arab countries in the June 1967 war with Israel, and joined in the oil embargo imposed against the USA and the United Kingdom. The Government donated KD 25m. to the Arab war effort. At the Khartoum Conference in September Kuwait joined Saudi Arabia and Libya in offering financial aid to Egypt and Jordan, to help their economies to recover from the 1967 war.

In 1968 the United Kingdom announced that the agreement of June 1961—whereby the British had undertaken to give military assistance to Kuwait if requested—would be terminated by 1971. This followed an earlier announcement that the United Kingdom would withdraw all troops from the Gulf region by the end of that year.

During the 1960s the Kuwaiti leadership's policies led to some redistribution of income, through the use of petroleum revenues in public expenditure and through the land compensation scheme. None the less, popular discontent over corruption and inefficiency in public services, as well as the manipulation of the press and the National Assembly, persisted.

In response to public opinion, the ruling family permitted the assembly elections of January 1971 to be held on the basis of a free vote, although women, illiterate males, members of the police and military, and all non-Kuwaitis were excluded. There was a lively election campaign, with 184 candidates contesting the 50 seats, despite the absence of political parties, which remained illegal. Several members and supporters of the Arab Nationalist Movement (founded in the 1950s by Dr George Habash—later leader of the Popular Front for the Liberation of Palestine) were elected. This radical group, led by Dr Ahmad al-Khatib, was generally regarded as the principal opposition to the Government.

After the 1971 elections the Crown Prince was reappointed Prime Minister and formed a new Council of Ministers. The representation of the ruling family was reduced from five to three; and, for the first time, the Council of Ministers included two ministers drawn from the elected members of the National Assembly.

In August 1976 the Amir, Sheikh Sabah al-Salim al-Sabah, suspended the National Assembly on the grounds that, among other things, it had been delaying legislation. A committee was ordered to be formed to review the Constitution. The episode highlighted the strength of political patronage and the limitations of Kuwait's democracy. The Kuwaiti rulers were determined to insulate the state from the popular nationalist trend that was still thriving in the Arab region.

Sheikh Sabah died on 31 December 1977; he was succeeded by his cousin, Crown Prince Sheikh Jaber al-Ahmad al-Jaber al-Sabah (from the al-Jaber branch of the family). Sheikh Saad al-Abdullah al-Salim al-Sabah (from the al-Salim branch) became Crown Prince and Prime Minister. Both the Amir and the Prime Minister publicly reaffirmed the Government's intention to reconvene the National Assembly and to restore democratic government by August 1980. In response to increasing public pressure, a 50-member committee was established in early 1980 to consider constitutional amendments and a revised form of legislature. Following its recommendations, an Amiri decree provided for the election of a new assembly before the end of February 1981. Despite the uncertainty generated by the Iran–Iraq War (1980–88), the election campaign proceeded, with 448 candidates contesting the 50 seats. The franchise was limited to 90,000 'first-class' Kuwaiti citizens, and, of these, fewer than one-half (or about 3% of the population) registered to vote. A conservative assembly was returned, including 23 tribal leaders, sympathetic to the ruling sheikhs, and 13 young technocrats. The radical Arab nationalists, the fiercest opposition to the Government in the previous assembly, failed to win any seats, while the Shi'a minority's representation was reduced to four seats. However, five Sunni Islamist fundamentalists were elected. The Crown Prince was subsequently reappointed Prime Minister, forming a new 15-member Council of Ministers in which the ruling family retained the major posts.

EXTERNAL RELATIONS, 1973–81

Despite recognition by Iraq in 1963, Kuwait's borders, including those with Iraq, remained unsettled. Of all the Gulf states, Kuwait has been the most vulnerable to regional disruption. In March 1973 Iraqi troops and tanks occupied a Kuwaiti outpost at Samtah, on the border with Iraq. Iraq later withdrew its troops, but a source of potential dispute remained over Iraq's territorial claim on Bubiyan Island and its desire to have secure access to the deep waters of the Gulf. Along with other Gulf states, Kuwait allocated larger sums for the expansion of its armed forces after 1973, and it established its own navy. Legislation to introduce conscription was approved in 1975, but it was generally accepted that Kuwait's security could not be guaranteed through its own armed strength. (Conscription was eventually abolished in 2001, only to be reintroduced in 2011.) Nevertheless, military purchases continued at a high level and substantially increased in the 1990s, largely for the political purpose of cementing relations with arms-supplying powers.

During the first two decades of Kuwait's independence, the country sought to project a distinct foreign policy, and attempted to enhance its security by broadening its international relations—including relations with the communist states, with non-aligned countries and across the Arab world. A new direction in Kuwaiti foreign policy was taken from May 1981, when Kuwait, with Saudi Arabia, the United Arab Emirates (UAE), Qatar, Oman and Bahrain, founded the Cooperation Council for the Arab States of the Gulf (the Gulf Cooperation Council—GCC). By encouraging economic and social integration, it was hoped that the GCC would increase the security of the small oil-producing states of the Gulf. Subsequently, the heads and key officials of the GCC states met regularly, but the cement of the alliance was the perceived common threats, as well as the rulers' alliances with the USA and the United Kingdom. From the 1990s a more positive regional integration agenda started to make slow progress, with some co-ordination of trade policies and with the resolution of border disputes among the member states themselves. Steps towards establishing a degree of internal consultation and representation mechanisms also improved relations between the ruling families of the Gulf. Nevertheless, the northern states of Kuwait and Bahrain remained more closely aligned with Saudi Arabian policy than did the other Gulf states.

THE IRAN–IRAQ WAR, 1980–88

Kuwait's regional security position began to change with the sequence of events that started with the Iranian Revolution of 1979 and with the war between Iran and Iraq, which began in September 1980. In that war, Kuwait supported Iraq, granting access to its strategic ports, and, with Saudi Arabia, exporting up to 310,000 barrels per day (b/d) of petroleum (250,000 b/d from the Neutral Zone and the remainder from Saudi Arabia) on Iraq's behalf, and contributing to the substantial financial aid, which by the end of the war, in 1988, was thought to have reached US $40,000m. (donated by both Kuwait and Saudi Arabia, as well as other Gulf states, mainly the UAE).

The potential threat of a rising domestic opposition from Kuwait's Shi'a minority, coupled with the authorities' suspicion that a number of bomb attacks had been directed by Iran in retaliation for Kuwaiti support of Iraq in the Iran–Iraq War, gave rise to increasing concerns for the country's security. As a result of the bombings, more than 600 Iranian workers were deported from Kuwait in early 1984.

In May 1984 two Kuwaiti and several Saudi Arabian tankers were bombed in a series of attacks by unidentified aircraft on shipping in the Gulf. Although both Iran and Iraq were known to have been firing at shipping, Iran was blamed for the attacks on Kuwaiti tankers. The bombings were seen as a warning to Kuwait to reduce its aid to Iraq and to put pressure on Iraq to desist from attacking tankers carrying Iranian oil. Concern arose as to whether the GCC countries could defend themselves unaided, and at the GCC summit conference in November the member states agreed to form a joint military force, capable of rapid deployment and aimed at combating any spread of the Iran–Iraq War.

Kuwait's attempts to mediate in the Iran–Iraq War in 1984 were hampered by Iran's increasing suspicion about the result of outstanding border disputes between Iraq and Kuwait. Iran believed that Kuwait was about to transfer three strategically important islands (Bubiyan, Warba and Failaka) to Iraq. In January 1985, however, Kuwait announced plans to build its own military bases on Bubiyan and Warba, and two months later Bubiyan was declared an out-of-bounds war zone. Kuwaiti forces were put on alert in February 1986, when Iranian forces crossed the Shatt al-Arab waterway and captured the Iraqi port of Faw, near Kuwait's north-eastern border. Iran pledged that Kuwait would not become embroiled in its war with Iraq provided that it maintained its military neutrality.

Between October 1986 and April 1987 Iranian forces attacked merchant ships sailing to and from Kuwait and seized cargoes, in reprisal for loading petroleum sold on Iraq's behalf and for the use of Kuwait's ports for Iraqi imports. In an attempt to deter Iranian attacks in the Gulf, Kuwait re-registered most of its fleet of oil tankers under the flags of the USA, Liberia, the USSR and the United Kingdom. Kuwait received help from the USA and Saudi Arabia in clearing mines from the channel leading to its main oil-loading facilities at Mina al-Ahmadi. France, the United Kingdom and other European states later also joined minesweeping operations.

Six Iranian diplomats were expelled from Kuwait in September 1987, following Iranian attacks on Kuwaiti installations. Kuwait's main offshore oil-loading terminal was closed between October and December, after an Iranian missile attack in which three workers were injured. A summit meeting of the GCC in December urged the UN Security Council to enforce its Resolution 598, which ordered a cease-fire to be observed in the Iran–Iraq War, and approved a pact to increase security co-operation between the member states.

Two Kuwaiti soldiers were wounded in March 1988, as Iranian and Kuwaiti armed forces clashed for the first time during the Iran–Iraq War when three Iranian gunboats attacked Bubiyan Island, situated 25 km from the southern coast of Iraq. In the following month an Iranian missile landed at al-Wafra oilfield, 80 km south of Kuwait City. The launching of the missile was believed to represent an Iranian warning to Kuwait for allegedly permitting Iraqi armed forces to use Bubiyan Island to recapture the Iranian-occupied Faw peninsula.

The cease-fire in the Iran–Iraq War in August 1988 brought a revival of economic growth in Kuwait. Relations between Kuwait and Iran improved, while co-operation with Iraq also appeared to increase.

INTERNAL UNREST AND SUSPENSION OF THE NATIONAL ASSEMBLY, 1985–90

In May 1985 an Iraqi member of the banned opposition Hizb al-Da'wa al-Islamiyya (Islamic Da'wa Party—by 2004 one of Iraq's dominant political groups) attempted to assassinate the Amir of Kuwait with a car bomb. In June 1986 four simultaneous explosions occurred at Kuwait's main oil export refinery at Mina al-Ahmadi. A hitherto unknown organization, the 'Arab Revolutionaries Group', later claimed responsibility for the attacks, which had been intended to force Kuwait to reduce its petroleum output.

In 1985 and 1986 almost 27,000 expatriates, many of whom were Iranian, were deported, and concern about Iranian influence over the Shi'a minority (about 30% of the population) led to severe measures to curb political agitation. In June 1987 six Kuwaiti Shi'a Muslims were sentenced to death for their part in sabotaging oil installations and plotting against the Government. There were further explosions in May and July. In June 1989 22 people accused of plotting to overthrow the ruling family were sentenced to prison terms of up to 15 years.

The tension in and surrounding Kuwait was reflected in the general political atmosphere. Although the traditional Arab nationalist opposition was dealt a severe blow by the dissolution of the National Assembly in 1976, political demands came to be more explicitly expressed on the basis of religious and tribal alliances represented within the new National Assembly. In July 1986, following 15 months of increasing confrontation with the National Assembly, the Amir dissolved the Assembly for a second time, and suspended relevant articles of the Constitution. A new Government, also with Crown Prince Sheikh Saad al-Abdullah al-Salim al-Sabah as Prime Minister, was appointed and given greater powers of censorship, including the right to close down newspapers for up to two years.

In December 1989 a number of former members of the National Assembly launched a campaign to restore the Assembly. In January 1990 the Amir appealed for political dialogue, and in March the Prime Minister declared that he would welcome the restoration of an elected legislature. However, the Government was only prepared to permit a partly elected body with severely limited powers, which the opposition rejected and urged all parties to boycott. On 10 June 62% of the electorate voted at a general election for 50 members of this new and distinct National Council. The Council was to be an interim body, and its members were to hold office for four years. It comprised 75 members, of whom 25 were appointed by the Amir. The Kuwaiti Government resigned following the election. The Amir reappointed the Crown Prince, Sheikh Saad al-Abdullah al-Salim al-Sabah, as Prime Minister, and a subsequent government reorganization resulted in 10 new appointments to the Council of Ministers. Only three ministers not belonging to the al-Sabah family retained their posts, while the new members were technocrats with no previous experience of government. The Council of Ministers was believed to have been reorganized in an attempt to satisfy domestic demands for new government policies. However, the fact that the al-Sabah family retained the majority of important ministerial positions, and that restoration of the National Assembly did not seem a realistic prospect, undermined the attempt to placate critics of the Government.

IRAQ'S INVASION OF KUWAIT: THE GULF CRISIS, 1990–91

In July 1990 President Saddam Hussain of Iraq publicly criticized unnamed states for exceeding the petroleum production quotas that had been established by the Organization of the Petroleum Exporting Countries (OPEC) in May in order to increase international prices. He accused Kuwait of having 'stolen' US $2,400m.-worth of Iraqi oil reserves from a field that straddles the unresolved border. The Iraqi Minister of Foreign Affairs, Tareq Aziz, declared that Kuwait should not only cancel Iraq's war debt, but also compensate it for losses of revenue incurred during the war with Iran and as a result of Kuwait's overproduction of oil, to which he attributed a decline in prices. Later in July Iraq began to deploy armed forces on the Kuwait–Iraq border, immediately before a meeting of the OPEC ministerial council in Geneva, Switzerland. At the meeting the minimum reference price for petroleum was increased, as Iraq had demanded. On 31 July representatives of Kuwait and Iraq conferred in Jeddah, Saudi Arabia, in an attempt to resolve the dispute, but the negotiations collapsed. A number of differing accounts have been offered of Kuwait's willingness at the Jeddah meeting to compromise on Iraq's financial claims.

On 2 August 1990 Iraq invaded Kuwait with 100,000 troops. The Iraqi Government claimed that its forces entered Kuwait at the invitation of insurgents who had overthrown the Kuwaiti Government, but there was no evidence to support this. The Amir and other members of the Government escaped to Saudi Arabia, along with many Kuwaiti citizens. The immediate response of the UN Security Council to the invasion of Kuwait was to adopt a series of resolutions that condemned the action, demanded the immediate and unconditional withdrawal of Iraqi forces from Kuwait, and appealed for a negotiated settlement of the conflict. A comprehensive economic blockade was also imposed on Iraq and Kuwait. Immediately after the invasion, the USA and the members of the European Community (EC, now European Union—EU) froze all Kuwaiti assets to prevent their transfer by an Iraqi-imposed regime.

On 7 August 1990 President George Bush ordered the deployment of US troops and aircraft in Saudi Arabia, with the declared aim of securing the country's borders with Kuwait in the event of an Iraqi attack. A number of European governments, together with some members of the Arab League, agreed to provide military support for the US forces. On 8 August the Iraqi Government announced the formal annexation of Kuwait, and at the end of the month most of Kuwait was officially declared to be the 19th governorate of Iraq, while a northern strip was incorporated into Basra governorate. Successive diplomatic efforts failed to achieve a peaceful solution to the crisis.

Following the Iraqi invasion, there were widespread reports of looting in Kuwait City. Some installations were completely dismantled and removed to Iraq. There were also frequent reports of serious human rights violations as Iraqi forces searched for Kuwaiti resistance fighters and Westerners in hiding. By October 1990 an estimated 430,000 Iraqi troops had been deployed in southern Iraq and Kuwait. Kuwait's population was estimated to have decreased from approximately 2m., prior to the invasion, to about 700,000, of whom Kuwaitis constituted an estimated 300,000 and Palestinians 200,000, while the remainder comprised other Arab expatriate workers, Asians, and stateless *bidoun*.

In October 1990 a conference was held in Jeddah, where the exiled Crown Prince and Prime Minister of Kuwait, Sheikh Saad al-Abdullah al-Salim al-Sabah, addressed approximately 1,000 Kuwaiti citizens, including members of the dissolved National Assembly. He agreed to establish committees to advise the Government on political, social and financial matters, and pledged that, after the liberation of Kuwait, the country's constitution and legislature would be restored, and that free elections would be held. This was seen as a necessary concession to maintain national unity, particularly given the emerging divide between Kuwait's wealthier citizens, most of whom were now living in exile, and those who remained in Kuwait.

In November 1990 the UN Security Council adopted a resolution that authorized the use of 'all necessary means' to liberate Kuwait. Iraq was given until 15 January 1991 to begin to implement the 10 resolutions that had so far been adopted, including that stipulating unconditional withdrawal from Kuwait. In the interim period, a massive build-up of around 600,000 US troops, along with further substantial forces from a coalition of more than 30 states, was assembled in Saudi Arabia and in other parts of the region in preparation for a military campaign against Iraq. Unsuccessful diplomatic attempts were made to avert a military confrontation between the multinational and Iraqi forces. On 17 January 1991 the UN-backed, US-led multinational force launched its military campaign with an intensive aerial bombardment of Iraq, with the aim of disabling that country's economic and military infrastructure. Soviet attempts to mediate were deemed unacceptable by the USA and its allies, as they proposed that a cease-fire should be declared before Iraq began to withdraw from Kuwait. On 24 February US-led ground forces entered Kuwait, encountering little effective Iraqi opposition. Within three days the Iraqi Government had agreed to accept all resolutions of the UN Security Council concerning Kuwait, and on 28 February the US Government announced a suspension of military operations—but not before Iraqi troops and fleeing civilians were bombarded by US aircraft at Mutla Ridge, north of Kuwait City, resulting in heavy casualties. In March the UN Security Council set out the terms for a permanent cease-fire. These included the release of all allied prisoners of war and of Kuwaitis who had been detained as potential hostages. They also required Iraq to repeal all laws and decrees concerning the annexation of Kuwait. Iraq promptly announced its compliance with these conditions. Another resolution, adopted in April, provided for the establishment of a demilitarized zone, supervised by the UN Iraq-Kuwait Observer Mission (UNIKOM), between the two countries. The UNIKOM mandate was subsequently renewed at six-monthly intervals until the mission ended in October 2003.

POLITICAL DEVELOPMENTS AND HUMAN RIGHTS AFTER THE IRAQI WITHDRAWAL, 1991–92

In mid-January 1991 a conference in Jeddah was attended by members of the Kuwaiti Government-in-exile and opposition delegates. Islamist and Arab nationalist groups had collaborated in forming a 'National Constitutional Front' to press for an immediate return of parliamentary and press freedom, while the more radical elements in the movement demanded the resignation of the al-Sabah family from all important positions in the Government and the establishment of a constitutional monarchy. In February, despite the expression of discontent among the exiled Kuwaiti community, the Kuwaiti Government-in-exile excluded the possibility of early elections after Kuwait had been liberated, on the grounds that the need to rebuild and repopulate the country took precedence. The opposition parties were further frustrated by the stated aim of the UN resolutions to reinstate Kuwait's 'legitimate' government prior to the invasion by Iraq, namely the al-Sabah family. In late February the Amir decreed that martial law would be enforced in Kuwait for the subsequent three months. The decree was contested by some members of Kuwait's opposition-in-exile, who expressed the need for the legislature to reconvene before any such decision could be made. In early March the opposition groups in exile made public their intention to form a coalition against the Government of the al-Sabah family. In the same month the Amir announced the formation of a committee to administer martial law and to supervise the state's security internally and abroad. The committee's domestic objectives were to identify people who had collaborated with Iraq, to prevent the formation of vigilante groups, and to identify civilians brought by the Iraqi authorities to settle in the emirate. The Prime Minister and other members of the exiled Government returned to Kuwait on 4 March, followed by the Amir 10 days later. The country was in a condition of instability, largely because the destruction of infrastructure and the emigration of most of the non-national work-force had led to a collapse in services. Departing Iraqi forces had set fire to over 600 oil wells as they retreated; these fires burned for nearly a year. Bitter resentment was felt by Kuwaiti citizens against members of the Palestinian community in particular, who were suspected of having collaborated with Iraq; human rights groups documented the use of torture by the Kuwaiti security forces against suspected collaborators. Later in March the Government announced that elections would take place within six to 12 months, following the return of Kuwaiti exiles and the compilation of a new electoral roll. The Government also declared its intention to reduce the number of foreign workers in Kuwait. On 20 March the Council of Ministers resigned, apparently in response to public discontent at the Government's failure to restore supplies of electricity, water and food. On 20 April the formation of a new Council of Ministers by the Crown Prince was announced. Although several technocrats were appointed to important positions within the Council, the major portfolios—foreign affairs, defence and the interior—were all retained by members of the al-Sabah family. Members of opposition groups immediately denounced the new Council of Ministers as unrepresentative.

There were reports in May 1991 that 900 people were under investigation in connection with crimes committed during the Iraqi occupation. In late May the human rights organization Amnesty International alleged that trials were being conducted in Kuwait without the provision of adequate defence counsel, and that, in some cases, torture had been used to extract confessions from defendants. In the same month the Prime Minister admitted that the abduction and torture of non-Kuwaiti nationals resident in Kuwait was taking place, and promised that the matter would be investigated. It was reported in June that 29 of a total of 200 defendants in trials for alleged collaboration during the occupation of Kuwait had been sentenced to death. The sentences were condemned by international human rights organizations as having resulted from the abuse of the judicial system. On 26 June, however, the Government repealed martial law and quashed all of the death sentences that had been imposed in earlier trials. Subsequent trials of those accused of collaboration were referred to civilian courts.

Also in June 1991 the Amir formally decreed that elections to a new National Assembly would be held in October 1992, and he ordered the National Council (which had held its first session in July 1990) to reconvene in preparation on 9 July 1991. However, the announcement failed to satisfy some opposition groups, which continued to demand the immediate introduction of democracy in Kuwait, and an end to the dominance of the al-Sabah family.

By July 1991 the Kuwaiti population had declined to an estimated 600,000 since August 1990. The Palestinian population, which had totalled 400,000 prior to the Iraqi invasion, was estimated to have declined to 80,000. Large-scale expulsions of Palestinians continued in August with airlifts to Jordan. International human rights organizations were critical of the continued deportation of non-Kuwaiti nationals, citing the 1949 Fourth Geneva Convention, which prohibits such action against civilians who are justified in fearing persecution for their political or religious beliefs.

The first half of 1992 was characterized by an unprecedented breakdown of law and order in Kuwait, with regular shootings and other incidents of violence. Many of these were directed against expatriates, especially Palestinians. There were widespread allegations that the Government was using the shootings, and the fear of further conflict with Iraq, as a pretext to restrict the press and opposition meetings. However, disaffection with the performance of the ruling family and Kuwait's traditional business élite was not allowed to evolve into a political challenge, and the dominance of Kuwait's pre-war institutions was re-established with a more prominent role for the National Assembly and the business class. The restoration of élite politics prevented the rise of a new opposition movement from within the poorer sections of the Kuwaiti population, who had been politicized by their experience of war and occupation.

US PROTECTION AND US FORCES IN KUWAIT

In June 1991, with British and US armed forces scheduled to leave Kuwait in July and September, respectively, the Minister of Defence declared that an agreement had been reached for their replacement by a united Arab force, to comprise contingents from the GCC states, Egypt and Syria. In September, however, it was announced that US armed forces would remain in the country for several more months, owing to the slow progress made in rebuilding the Kuwaiti security forces. The Arab alliance of the six GCC states, Egypt and Syria, known as the Damascus Declaration, never materialized, and the USA continued to play the predominant direct military role in the region. When the bulk of US armed forces withdrew from Iraq in 1991, they left behind vast quantities of military equipment for Kuwait under the Excess Defence Articles programme, providing a foundation for the post-occupation Kuwaiti Land Forces.

In September 1991 the Kuwaiti Minister of Defence signed a 10-year defence pact with the USA; another agreement was signed with the United Kingdom in February 1992; and one with France in August 1992 (which was amended and renewed in October 2009). The agreement with the USA included provisions for the stockpiling of US military equipment in Kuwait, the use of Kuwaiti ports by US troops, and joint training exercises; the pact was renewed for a further 10 years in early 2001, and Kuwait continued to spend considerable sums on facilities and infrastructure for US troops (in addition to an annual payment of US $35m. made in lieu of the cost of stationing US military personnel). The cost to Kuwait of maintaining the US troops had increased to an annual sum of $474m. by 2000, in addition to the financial contribution that Kuwait made to the US-led military campaign to remove the Iraqi regime in early 2003.

The agreements with major powers and the US military presence, supported by a 10-year programme of Kuwaiti military expenditure at times exceeding 12% of annual gross domestic product, became the cornerstone of Kuwait's security strategy. In 2010 there were about 15,000 US soldiers stationed in Kuwait. In addition, regional alliances such as the GCC defence pact (see The Iran–Iraq War, 1980–88) remained useful in providing political support for the main strategy. Following the 2003 conflict in Iraq, a wider regional defence pact became possible, but the opportunities for co-operation between states were overshadowed by the growing US military presence in the region and the continuing violence in Iraq. After the attacks on the US mainland of 11 September 2001, the USA paid far greater attention to its own domestic security and to its declared 'war on terror' than to national and regional aspects of security in the countries of the Middle East. There was, meanwhile, a growing US dominance of large-scale state-funded business contracts, stimulated by post-war reconstruction requirements, both in Kuwait after 1991 and in Iraq after 2003. US dominance increasingly edged out its minor allies, with British equipment purchases apparently being cancelled in mid-2004 at the same time as the Kuwaiti Government was contemplating further purchases of US military aircraft. In January 2011 Kuwait signed a US $145m. missile deal with the USA to supply Patriot missiles for Kuwait's armed forces.

WAR COMPENSATION AND MISSING KUWAITIS

The UN Compensation Commission (UNCC), the Geneva-based body established to consider claims for compensation arising from the 1990–91 Gulf crisis, approved the first disbursements in May 1994. The rate of payments increased rapidly following the implementation in December 1996 of UN Security Council Resolution 986 (the 'oil-for-food' arrangement), and by mid-2004 about US $18,400m. had been paid—a very substantial penalty against a sanctioned and impoverished Iraq, and the equivalent of almost two-thirds of the total value of merchandise received by Iraq during the years of the oil-for-food arrangement. Nearly all individual claimants, both Kuwaitis and expatriates who had been living in Iraq and Kuwait at the time of the conflict, have been compensated. (Some claimants have been remunerated twice: once through claims made by their own government; and a second time by the same claim being presented through the Government of Kuwait.) Major corporate payments commenced in late 2000; these included controversial claims for supposed lost potential profits, in addition to claims for loss of assets.

Earlier, in June 2000 a controversial Kuwaiti claim for US $21,000m. to compensate for oil revenue lost as a result of the Iraqi occupation brought the issue of the major corporate claims to the fore. The UNCC initially postponed a decision, and Russia and France meanwhile urged a full review of the underlying principles and operations of the Commission. Russia also called for an immediate reduction of the proportion of Iraqi oil revenues deducted for the purposes of compensation from 30% to 20%. The claims, initially totalling more than $350,000m., plus interest, were a continuing source of tension between Iraq and Kuwait. In September 2000 the governing council of the UNCC (which comprises the 15 member states of the UN Security Council) approved a reduced Kuwaiti oil claim of $15,900m., while the UN Security Council reduced the proportion of Iraqi oil revenues set aside for compensation purposes from 30% to 25%. An oil analyst writing in the specialist journal *Middle East Economic Survey* criticized the award as being exaggerated by $12,500m. In mid-2001 the UNCC began considering a Kuwait Investment Authority (KIA) claim of $86,000m., mostly for assumed lost interest earnings. In a deposition issued in June 2003, the UNCC rejected all but $1,500m. of the claim, leaving some $69,200m. of environmental losses as the largest part of unresolved Kuwaiti claims. These were gradually resolved until the UNCC completed its deliberations in June 2005.

Of the last batch of claims, US $50,000m. of alleged environmental losses were almost entirely rejected; in part, this can be taken as a reflection of the uncompromising nature of Kuwaiti official attitudes to the issue of compensation demands. In total, the UNCC awarded $52,500m. of compensation against Iraq, of which $33,000m. remained to be paid; the figures were large given the size of the Kuwaiti economy at the time of the Iraqi invasion. Meanwhile, Kuwait continued to receive substantial payments from Iraqi petroleum sales, but the proportion of Iraqi petroleum revenues set aside for compensation was reduced from 25% to 5% under UN Security Council Resolution 1483 of May 2003. Following the conflict in Iraq in 2003, Kuwait made an additional demand, of $1,200m., from Iraqi Airways as compensation for 10 Kuwaiti Airways aircraft that it had appropriated during the 1990–91 occupation. In May 2010 Kuwait forced Iraqi Airways into bankruptcy, after making several attempts to seize the company's aircraft overseas.

The establishment of an Iraqi regime that was amicable towards the USA and that sought good relations with Kuwait raised a major issue for the Kuwaiti Government with regard to its compensation claims. Many Iraqis considered their country's debt from the Iran–Iraq War to have accumulated as a result of a Kuwaiti alliance with the Saddam Hussain regime acting against the interests of the Iraqi people, who, together with the Iranians, bore the brunt of a regional war to defend the regimes of privileged minorities in the Gulf. However, this view was not shared by Kuwaiti politicians, and the Kuwaiti Government staked its claims for repayment and advanced them alongside the 'Paris Club' of official creditors. The UN compensation claims remained outside this framework, and Kuwait expressed disappointment that the proportion of Iraqi oil revenue allocated to compensation was reduced. Iraq, for its part, demanded a review of exaggerated claims and, in view of the country's dire economic and humanitarian situation, a further reduction of payments to only a nominal figure. In November 2004 a deal was reached between the Iraqi Interim Government and the Paris Club that stipulated an immediate reduction of Iraqi debt by 30%, rising to 80% following Iraq's implementation of an IMF-imposed policy programme. Some countries agreed to go beyond the 80% figure and to cancel all their debt. Kuwait, which had indicated its willingness to support the Paris Club arrangements, was not moved to follow with reductions or debt cancellations, and the Kuwaiti position remained intransigent. In June 2009 Iraqi members of parliament urged a halt to reparation payments to Kuwait over the 1990 occupation, with some wanting the country to compensate Iraq for its role in the US-led 2003 invasion. Iraq's Prime Minister, Nuri al-Maliki, reiterated the Iraqi parliamentarians' call during a visit to the UN headquarters in New York, USA, in July 2009. Al-Maliki's request received backing from the UN Secretary-General, Ban Ki-Moon, and the US and British Governments. The Iraqi deputies also demanded the cancellation of US $15,000m. of debt owed to Kuwait from the Saddam Hussain era, and that the borders between the two countries be renegotiated. These calls sparked an angry response from Kuwait. During a visit to Kuwait in August, the Speaker of the Iraqi Council of Representatives, Ayad al-Samarrai, proposed a compromise whereby Iraq's payments to Kuwait would be reinvested in the Iraqi economy. In March 2012 Kuwait and Iraq reached an agreement to resolve the outstanding airways debt, which included creation of a joint Iraqi-Kuwaiti airline group. However, the rest of the wider debt remained a matter of contention. Iraq continued to pay 5% of its annual oil and gas revenues to Kuwait, and it was estimated the debt would be discharged in 2015.

The Kuwait National Committee for Missing People and Prisoners of War stated in 1994 that 625 Kuwaiti residents, including more than 300 Kuwaiti nationals, were still missing in Iraq. From mid-1996 Iraqi and Kuwaiti officials held meetings in their mutual border area to discuss the fate of those not accounted for. The meetings were conducted in closed sessions under the auspices of the International Committee of the Red Cross (ICRC), and were attended by observers from the USA, the United Kingdom and France. Although Iraq stated that it was not holding any Kuwaiti nationals, in late 1997 Kuwait claimed to be in possession of documentation, submitted to the ICRC by Iraq, relating to 126 Kuwaiti prisoners of war whose whereabouts remained unknown. The Iraqi authorities claimed to have lost contact with the captives during the allied bombardment and the subsequent opposition uprising in Iraq in 1991. In July 1998 delegations from both countries met in Geneva for 'highly confidential' discussions on this issue. Iraq withdrew from a subsequent meeting scheduled for January 1999, following Kuwait's support for renewed US-British bombings of targets in Iraq in December 1998. The Iraqi Government also demanded that the whereabouts of more than 1,000 Iraqi citizens allegedly missing in Kuwait since 1991 should be included in any negotiations on this issue, and that representatives of states that had no missing persons should not take part in the negotiations. The Iraqi Government claimed to have released all detainees from Iraqi gaols in October 2002, but no Kuwaitis were among them. After the removal of Saddam Hussain's Government in April 2003 and the conclusion of chaotic exhumations from mass graves, a number of bodies were identified as those of missing Kuwaitis. In 2006 a joint Kuwaiti-Iraqi committee was established to investigate all missing person cases. By August 2009 the committee had identified the remains of 236 missing Kuwaitis from the 1990–91 war and returned them to their families.

Since 1991 the Kuwaiti Government has been pressing Iraq for the return of the Kuwait National Archives, containing tens of thousands of official documents removed during the 1990–91 Iraqi occupation. In May 2002 Iraq informed the UN that it intended to return the documents, and some were duly handed over in October of that year. However, it subsequently became apparent that not all of the archives had been returned, and Kuwait has been demanding the restoration of the remaining documents ever since.

THE KUWAIT–IRAQ BORDER: ONGOING PROBLEMS

The UN Iraq-Kuwait Boundary Demarcation Commission adjudged on 16 April 1992 that the border should be set 570 m to the north of the position existing at that time. This had the effect of awarding part of the port of Umm Qasr and several of the Rumaila oil wells to Kuwait. The decision was controversial, as Kuwait had never laid claim to that territory. The first Demarcation Commission Chairman resigned in apparent disagreement with the decision, and Iraq initially rejected the validity of the settlement.

In August 1992, after a dispute between the Iraqi Government and weapons inspectors (operating in Iraq under the 1991 cease-fire arrangements outlined in UN Security Council Resolution 687), the USA deployed missiles in Kuwait, and some 7,500 US troops participated in a military exercise in the emirate. At the end of the month the UN Security Council adopted a resolution guaranteeing the new land frontier between Kuwait and Iraq. Demarcation was to take place before the end of the year, and the new border was to come into force on 15 January 1993. However, in the week leading up to this deadline Iraqi forces made several incursions into disputed territory, during which they recovered armaments left behind at the end of the Gulf crisis. At the same time, as US aircraft led air attacks against Iraq, more than 1,000 US troops were dispatched to Kuwait. Following the deadline for enforcement of the border, Iraqi operatives began to dismantle installations on what had been declared Kuwaiti territory. Nevertheless, the USA deployed further missiles in Kuwait, and in early February the UN Security Council agreed to strengthen UNIKOM by approving the dispatch of armed troops (in addition to the existing unarmed personnel in the force) to patrol the Kuwaiti border with Iraq. In the same month Kuwait and Russia signed a memorandum of understanding leading to a defence pact between the two countries.

In March 1993 the UN Iraq-Kuwait Boundary Demarcation Commission announced that it had completed demarcation of the maritime border between the two countries along the median line of the Khor Abdullah waterway. The UN demarcation placed the shipping lane to Iraq's only deep-water port at Umm Qasr inside Kuwaiti territorial waters, thus enabling Kuwait to cut off Iraq's access to the Gulf by closing Kuwaiti waters to Iraqi shipping if it so desired. In May Kuwait announced that construction was to begin of a trench, to be protected by mines and a wall of sand, along the entire length of the land border. Allegations by Kuwait of Iraqi violations of the border intensified during the second half of 1993, and there were reports of exchanges of fire in the border region. In November it was reported that some 300 Iraqi civilians had crossed the border in the Umm Qasr region to protest against the digging of the trench, while Iraqi troops were reported to have attacked a border post. These incursions coincided with the beginning of the evacuation, under UN supervision, of Iraqi nationals and property from the Kuwaiti side of the new border. In November a 775-strong armed UNIKOM reinforcement was deployed in northern Kuwait, with authorization (in specific circumstances) to use its weapons to assist the unarmed force already in the demilitarized zone. During the 1990s there were few incidents involving UNIKOM itself, although there were numerous minor confrontations on the heavily reinforced Kuwaiti border, and in Gulf waters, between Kuwaiti troops and Iraqi refugees, potential migrants, smugglers and fishermen. In early 2001, as the USA and the United Kingdom maintained air activity, including the bombardment of Iraqi targets, Iraq formally demanded that UNIKOM log aerial activity above the demilitarized zone. The UN response was that UNIKOM was not technically equipped for the task, and in early 2003 UNIKOM stepped aside as US and British troops invaded Iraq from Kuwaiti territory in order to oust the regime of Saddam Hussain from power. The UN mission was terminated in October of that year.

Following the US-led occupation of Iraq in 2003 and the overthrow of the regime of Saddam Hussain, the border settlement again became problematic. With Iraqi government institutions largely paralysed, Kuwait unilaterally commenced the installation of a permanent physical barrier along the demarcated border. In mid-2005 construction reached the town of Umm Qasr, and many local people witnessed their private land and civilian facilities being cut off behind the Kuwaiti barrier. This led to mass protests in the town and a degree of disquiet elsewhere in both Iraq and Kuwait. The weak Iraqi Interim Government formed in May 2004 was anxious not to allow a new source of tension to develop, and therefore attempted to settle the issue by acquiring adequate Kuwaiti compensation for Iraqi farmers and others affected by the new border demarcation. Kuwaiti officials, for their part, appeared to be unconcerned that the barrier might have strayed beyond the increased bounds of Kuwaiti territory. In this, as in many other issues, Kuwait was pressing its advantage in a time of Iraq's weakness under occupation. There were reports of dramatic decreases in oil-well pressure on the Iraqi side of shared fields, raising suspicion that Kuwait had unilaterally increased its oil extraction from these fields. In 2006 Kuwait and Iraq reached an agreement whereby Kuwait could create a border fence and no-man's-land to separate the two countries, and pay compensation to Iraqi farmers who lost land because of this. Construction of the fence proceeded slowly. A violent clash between Kuwaiti security forces and Iraqis occurred along the border in mid-2005, and a shooting incident in August 2006 resulted in Kuwaiti protests to the Iraqi authorities. During a state visit to Kuwait in June 2008 the Iraqi Prime Minister, Nuri al-Maliki, announced that Iraq's border dispute with Kuwait had been settled. In June 2009, however, members of the Iraqi Council of Representatives called for the maritime border as demarcated by the UN in 1993 to be renegotiated. Kuwait expressed an interest in writing off a significant portion of Iraq's remaining war reparations to Kuwait, in return for Iraqi recognition of the UN-defined borders (Saddam Hussain's Government had granted them official recognition in 1994, but this endorsement had been abandoned by subsequent Iraqi administrations).

In January 2011 a Kuwaiti coastguard was killed in a shoot-out with Iraqi fishermen who had strayed into Kuwaiti waters. In April of that year Kuwait commenced construction of a new, US $1,100m. port, called Mubarak al-Kabir Port, on the east coast of Bubiyan Island. The Iraqi Government notified Kuwait in the following month that it objected to the port, which is situated directly opposite Iraq's Faw peninsula (only some 10 km away, across the mouth of the Shatt al-Arab). Here, the Iraqi Government planned to commence building a massive new port complex (with 100 berths), at a cost of $60,000m., along the entire length of the peninsula. The Iraqi authorities feared that the new Kuwaiti port would interfere with the operations of this Faw Grand Port, since the shipping lanes of the two countries would overlap and the increased levels of maritime traffic would lead to serious congestion in what is already a crowded waterway, making it more difficult for vessels to reach both Faw Grand Port and Umm Qasr Port. There were also concerns that waves created by the increased shipping would interrupt construction at Faw Grand Port on a daily basis. The fact that Kuwait has hundreds of miles of coastline yet chose to build a large new port in this location led many Iraqis to conclude that the project was an attempt by Kuwait to restrict Iraq's access to the Gulf. Iraqi protests over the new Kuwaiti port intensified in mid-2011, but Kuwait continued to dismiss the objections. In July militants in the Iraqi capital launched a rocket attack on the International Zone (more commonly known by its original name, the Green Zone), hitting the Kuwaiti embassy. While it was unclear whether this was an intentional act of retaliation for Kuwait's intransigence regarding the port, or simply an indiscriminate attack on the Green Zone, the Kuwaiti National Assembly demanded the recall of Kuwait's ambassador to Iraq and the expulsion of the Iraqi ambassador in Kuwait. The Kuwaiti Government subsequently recalled its ambassador and embassy staff from Baghdad, ostensibly for the summer holiday and the forthcoming month of Ramadan. In August the Iraqi Shi'a militant group Kata'ib Hezbollah announced that it would attack Mubarak al-Kabir Port, and the South Korean consortium undertaking its construction, if the Kuwaiti Government pressed ahead with the scheme. Kuwait dispatched security forces to defend the construction site, and demanded that the Iraqi Government prevent Kata'ib Hezbollah from launching an attack. Later in August Kuwait hosted an Iraqi technical delegation at Mubarak al-Kabir Port, in an effort to demonstrate that activity there would in no way impinge on Iraq's shipping lanes. The Kuwaiti Government hoped that the delegation's report to the Iraqi Government would offer some reassurance and silence Iraqi protests.

In April 2012, following a visit to Iraq by Kuwait's Amir, the two countries came to an agreement on land and maritime borders, and established a joint commission to oversee its implementation. The agreement included the creation of a 500-m no-man's-land on each side. Kuwait also agreed to build up to 15 homes for Iraqi farmers living close to the border. In June 2013 Kuwait's Prime Minister visited Iraq, at a time of growing sectarian violence there, to signal continuing improved bilateral relations.

ELECTIONS AND POLITICAL LIFE, 1992–2013

Following the end of the Iraqi occupation, Kuwait resumed its quasi-democratic political life. The Government revoked pre-publication censorship of written media in January 1992, but retained the right to close publications responsible for 'objectionable' articles. Only 'first-class' Kuwaiti male citizens, who numbered about 81,400 (just under 15% of the total, predominantly non-national adult population), were eligible to vote in the elections to the National Assembly in October that year. The Minister of Justice and Legal Affairs excluded the possibility of foreign observers monitoring the elections. A total of 280 candidates, many affiliated with one of several quasi-political organizations, stood for election. Groups of women staged protests against their exclusion from the political process. Anti-Government candidates, in particular representatives of Islamist groups, secured 31 of the Assembly's 50 seats, and several of those elected had been members of the legislature dissolved in 1986. The Prime Minister submitted the resignation of his Government, and subsequently named a new administration. The revised Council of Ministers included six members of the new National Assembly. Among these was Ali Ahmad al-Baghli, the new Minister of Oil and a critic of the economic policy of the previous Government; members of the Assembly were also given responsibility for education, Islamic affairs and justice. However, the ruling family retained control of the 'sovereign' ministries: defence, foreign affairs and the interior.

In January 1993, in an attempt to curb financial corruption, the Assembly adopted a law requiring state companies and investment organizations to produce accounts for the Auditor-General, who was in turn required to pass them on to a commission of members of the Assembly. The law also provided for harsher penalties for the misuse of public funds. In February a delegation of members of the Assembly travelled to the United Kingdom to investigate allegations that millions of dollars had been embezzled via the Kuwait Investment Office (KIO) in London. In March the Assembly voted to rescind a law of secrecy, which had been regarded as a legal mechanism to facilitate corruption. In the same month there were reports of criticism from members of the Assembly after the Government estimated defence spending for 1992/93 at US $6,200m. In August 1993 the Prime Minister submitted a proposal to the National Assembly whereby future budgets would, for the first time, contain details of purchases of defence equipment.

In January 1994 the National Assembly abrogated an earlier decree requiring that, in the case of legal proceedings, government ministers be tried by a special court. Sheikh Ali al-Khalifah al-Sabah, a former Minister of Finance and of Oil, and Abd al-Fattah al-Bader, a former Chairman of the Kuwait Oil Tanker Co, were among five people brought to trial in connection with alleged embezzlement from the company; hearings were subsequently adjourned, and legal proceedings continued into 1996. Meanwhile, in November 1995 a criminal court had ruled that the trial of the former minister would be held in a special court for cases involving ministers, despite the National Assembly's earlier ruling. In July 1996 three of the four former executives tried by the criminal court were found guilty of corruption, receiving prison sentences of between 15 and 40 years. In addition, they were ordered to repay the embezzled funds, together with fines totalling more than US $100m. The fourth defendant, a British national, was acquitted. The charges against the former oil and finance minister were later withdrawn—it was ruled that the correct procedures had not been followed to bring the case to trial. In August 1999 a senior official of the KIO, Sheikh Fahd Muhammad al-Sabah, was convicted *in absentia* by the High Court in London of a $460m. fraud against the KIO's Spanish subsidiary. Two other senior officials were also convicted. It was announced in 2000 that the KIO's head office would be transferred to Kuwait. The Future Generations Fund was held by the KIO in order to provide future investment income mainly from public assets held outside Kuwait and in order to guard against the eventual decline in oil revenues. At one point in the late 1980s it was boasted that income from these funds had exceeded oil revenues. Such major corruption in the management of these funds was, therefore, a highly sensitive political issue. The dramatic rise in oil prices and revenues following the US-led occupation of Iraq brought the management of the fund under particular scrutiny—especially as government spending had been cautious, and surpluses were mounting at a time when public services were perceived to be deteriorating.

Government attempts to pursue an agenda of economic reform encountered opposition in the National Assembly and within the ruling family. In April 1994 the Government resigned, and a new administration was named. It was subsequently announced that the new Government would persevere with economic reforms, including privatization. Relations between the Government and the National Assembly became increasingly strained during late 1994 and early 1995, not least because of the discord apparent between the Prime Minister, Crown Prince Sheikh Saad al-Abdullah al-Salim al-Sabah, and the then Speaker of the National Assembly, Ahmad Abd al-Aziz al-Saadoun, who sought a government composed only of elected members. (In Kuwait cabinet members, whether elected or not, vote in parliament.) A potential constitutional crisis developed in early 1995 with regard to the interpretation of Article 71 of the Constitution. Article 71 regulates the Amir's power to rule by decree during parliamentary recesses or when the Assembly is dissolved for new elections: the National Assembly is obliged to endorse all such legislation when it reconvenes. The Assembly argued that the Article did not apply to the 1976–81 or 1986–92 periods, when the Assembly was closed unconstitutionally by the Amir. Following these periods, a political agreement was reached with the Amir whereby the Assembly would review the Amiri decrees, rejecting, approving or amending the legislation as it saw fit. In February 1995, however, the Constitutional Court had overruled the National Assembly's rejection of a 1986 decree that allowed the Government to close down newspapers; in the following month the Government exercised its right to do so, temporarily suspending publication of the *Al-Anbaa* newspaper. In April 1995 the Government referred Article 71 to the Constitutional Court for interpretation in the light of the ruling on press censorship. If the Court were to rule in the Government's favour, the authority of the Assembly would effectively be threatened, as the Amir could force through controversial legislation by dissolving and subsequently reconvening the Assembly. The Assembly protested by suspending consideration of more than 200 Amiri decrees until late May, when the Government withdrew its request for the interpretation of the Article.

In June 1995 the National Assembly approved legislation designed to increase the size of the electorate by amending the 1959 nationality law to allow sons of naturalized Kuwaitis to vote. In the following month the Assembly approved a bill reducing the minimum period after which naturalized Kuwaitis become eligible to vote from 30 years to 20 years. In July 1996 the Ministry of the Interior announced that a recorded total electorate of 107,169 was eligible to vote in the forthcoming elections to the National Assembly. Pro-Government candidates were the most successful at the polls, which took place in October, securing an estimated 19 of the 50 legislative seats. A number of small demonstrations, organized and attended by women, in support of demands for female enfranchisement took place in the days preceding voting. Following the elections, Sheikh Saad al-Abdullah al-Salim al-Sabah was reappointed Prime Minister. He subsequently announced the composition of the Council of Ministers, which included four new members.

In June 1997 an assassination attempt was made on Abdullah al-Nibari, an opposition member of the National Assembly and a former Chairman of the Committee for the Protection of Public Funds. One of the five men charged in connection with the offence was discovered to be related to the Minister of Finance, Nasir al-Rodhan. Responding to suggestions that he should resign, al-Rodhan insisted that he had had no knowledge of the attack and was therefore under no obligation to stand down. In November an incendiary bomb attack destroyed al-Nibari's office. It was widely believed that a conspiracy linked to state corruption lay behind the attacks on al-Nibari, and these suspicions exacerbated tensions between the Government and the National Assembly. Later that month al-Rodhan was reported to have tendered his resignation, although the Prime Minister apparently asked him to remain in office.

Further tension between the Government and the National Assembly became apparent in early 1998, when a motion expressing no confidence in the Minister of Information, Sa'ud Nasir al-Sabah, was brought before the legislature, following his decision to allow allegedly anti-Islamic publications to be displayed at the previous year's Kuwait Book Fair. In March, however, two days before the vote was scheduled to take place in the National Assembly, the Council of Ministers resigned. The Crown Prince again formed a new Government. Sa'ud Nasir al-Sabah was transferred to the Ministry of Oil, while Nasir al-Rodhan retained the post of Deputy Prime Minister and became Minister of State for Cabinet Affairs. The reorganization apparently frustrated the opposition's attempts to seek scrutiny of certain ministers concerning decisions taken in their previous posts. Four new appointments were made, including Sheikh Ali Salim al-Sabah as Minister of Finance and Communications, bringing to six the number of members of the ruling family in the Council of Ministers. The portfolios of defence, foreign affairs and the interior were unchanged.

The National Assembly continued close monitoring of defence contracts and other matters concerning public services—including the alleged loss of KD 300m. as a result of speculation in stock options by the Public Institution for Social Security. In May 1998 the National Assembly approved a bill requiring public officials to declare their finances, in order to aid transparency and to facilitate moves to counter corruption. In June there was evidence that the authorities were seeking further to restrict the freedom of the press. The Government brought legal proceedings for religious defamation against the independent *Al-Qabas* newspaper; the paper was closed for one week, and its editor-in-chief received a six-month prison sentence. In the same month meetings involving the Speaker of the National Assembly, the Amir and the Government averted an imminent confrontation over the cross-examination of the Minister of the Interior on matters relating to crime and the narcotics trade, although underlying problems remained unresolved. The National Assembly had thus begun to assert its authority across a range of issues, and had claimed an increasing share of decision-making powers in areas previously considered—through its dominance of the Government and through the ultimate constitutional authority of the Amir—the preserve of the ruling family.

In April 1999 a confrontation between the National Assembly and the Government, arising from widespread consternation among Islamist assembly members over errors that had appeared in copies of the Koran printed and distributed by the Ministry of Justice and of Awqaf (Religious Endowments) and Islamic Affairs, prompted the Amir to dissolve the National Assembly. During the interval between the dissolution and the election of a new National Assembly in July, the Government introduced substantial legislation by means of Amiri decrees (legislation that would require approval by the incoming Assembly). Some 60 decrees were issued, including legislation to accelerate privatization and to open up the economy to foreign investment. Other decrees included provision for reductions in subsidies and social spending, and measures to rationalize the labour market. The Government considered the new legislation to be crucial to the successful diversification of the economy, enhancement of the private sector and reform of the labour market. However, liberal members of the new National Assembly blocked the decrees on constitutional grounds.

Among the most significant decrees was one proposing the extension of the franchise and eligibility to seek public office to women, for which women's groups had campaigned since the 1960s. Liberal members of the National Assembly, while sympathetic in principle, objected to the decrees on constitutional grounds, and the measure on women's political participation was defeated by an alliance of conservatives and liberals in November 1999. Liberals did, however, introduce an identical bill that would permit the enfranchisement of women, and for the first time in the Assembly's history, the issue was openly debated. The proposal was, however, defeated. Female activists continued to press for an end to the exclusion of women from the political process, and raised the matter, without success, in the Constitutional Court.

At the July 1999 legislative elections, government supporters retained only 12 of the 50 seats in the legislature (compared with 18 in 1996), behind Islamist candidates, with 20 seats, and liberals, with 14 seats. Independent candidates secured the remaining four seats. A new Council of Ministers, selected and headed by the Crown Prince, was subsequently formed. Members of the ruling family retained control of the most important portfolios (including Sheikh Sabah al-Ahmad al-Jaber al-Sabah, who remained Deputy Prime Minister and Minister of Foreign Affairs), although a number of new, liberal members were also appointed (most notably to the finance portfolio), thus seemingly improving the chances of securing approval for the economic reform programme. Several portfolios were merged, and a new post of Minister of State for Foreign Affairs was created. Jasem al-Kharafi was elected Speaker of the National Assembly, replacing the more populist and opposition-leaning Ahmad al-Saadoun.

In January 2001 the Government submitted its resignation, amid growing disagreements among its members. These apparently stemmed from rivalry between two branches of the ruling family, the al-Salim and al-Jaber: the former headed by the Crown Prince and Prime Minister, Sheikh Saad al-Abdullah al-Salim al-Sabah; and the latter by the Amir, Sheikh Jaber al-Ahmad al-Jaber al-Sabah, and his brother Sheikh Sabah al-Ahmad al-Jaber al-Sabah, the increasingly dominant First Deputy Prime Minister and Minister of Foreign Affairs. After two weeks of discussions, the Amir appointed a new Council of Ministers in which both Sheikh Saad and Sheikh Sabah retained their former positions.

Great uncertainty over the future political leadership of Kuwait resulted from the hospitalization of the Amir in September 2001, following a cerebral haemorrhage which incapacitated him until January 2002. While the Amir subsequently recovered to maintain a light schedule of duties, the Crown Prince's own health continued to deteriorate, and Sheikh Sabah in effect became acting Prime Minister. The Amir's illness focused attention on a situation in which the three most senior members of the ruling family were in various degrees of failing health. There followed frank discussion of the possibility of redefining the role of the ruling family and of restructuring its responsibilities.

Significant political reforms were finally introduced after legislative elections in July 2003. The election campaign was overshadowed by the US-led military campaign in Iraq, which was largely conducted from Kuwaiti territory. The war itself was not an election issue, not because Kuwait was unanimous on the subject, but because of the clear incapacity of Kuwait to affect US policies and its dependence upon the USA. The elections were, rather, fought over the issue of patronage. Opposition political groups—both liberals and moderate Islamists—lost ground, while gains were made by independents and a small group of Salafi Islamists. The independents were perceived to be aligned with the Government, although that did not mean that the Government's agenda of market reform, privatization and foreign investment in petroleum operations would necessarily gain wide support. Opposition to this agenda was widespread, and was expected to continue to some extent in the National Assembly. Voter turn-out in the elections was very low, at 45% of the 6% of the total population who formed the electorate. Indeed, the pattern of the gains and losses in the polls pointed to widespread disaffection with the entire political process, and the new Government was faced with a mounting volume of work and no clear mandate for taking difficult and unpopular decisions.

The unexpected results of the 2003 elections, at which some long-standing political figures from both the liberal and Islamist blocks lost their seats, or were nearly ousted, gave impetus to proposals for electoral reform intended to rejuvenate the political process. The constituency system then in force was seen to have encouraged the rise of a fragmented personal style of politics, in which large numbers of candidates competed through a narrow personal and family following and through promises to individuals, rather than on general principles and public discourse. Few votes were needed to gain seats, which were usually campaigned for without reference to national programmes. Moreover, the process was open to corruption, vote-buying and other irregularities, such as fictitious changes of voters' addresses. These factors appeared to have led to declining voter participation.

Following the elections, the Crown Prince relinquished the position of Prime Minister. The appointment of Sheikh Sabah as his replacement brought an unprecedented separation of the post of Prime Minister and the position of Crown Prince, and provided some encouragement to reformists after their heavy electoral losses. The most significant change in the new Council of Ministers (although proving only temporary) was the merger of the oil and the electricity and water portfolios to form the Ministry of Energy, headed by Sheikh Ahmad al-Fahd al-Ahmad al-Sabah. With Sheikhs Ahmad al-Fahd al-Ahmad and Muhammad Sabah al-Salim al-Sabah as members (the latter as Minister of Foreign Affairs), the Council of Ministers now included two of the main new generation of al-Sabahs, who expected promotion as the older leadership made way.

In mid-2004 the National Assembly first discussed the introduction of reforms that would reduce the number of constituencies, thereby requiring successful candidates to have a wider appeal among voters. Another radical change under way was the emergence of political groups such as the Islamist-leaning Justice and Peace and the liberal-leaning Justice and Development, both of which were formed in December that year.

In May 2005 the National Assembly finally approved a bill giving women the right to vote, stand for election and take high public office, after the Amir lent his full support to the measure. The recent extension of the franchise to women in Qatar, Bahrain and Oman was a factor, highlighting Kuwait's failure to modernize its institutions of state. A less ambitious bill to permit women to participate in municipal elections had failed to obtain a majority just two weeks earlier. Kuwait's first female minister, Dr Massouma al-Mubarak, was subsequently appointed (as Minister of Planning and Minister of State for Administrative Development Affairs). Discriminatory legislation governing areas such as women's employment, access to subsidized housing and ability to extend visas to a foreign husband continued to be debated, but enfranchisement was a major political transformation. Women took part in national elections for the first time in June 2006, both as voters and as candidates. A total of 27 women (out of 249 candidates) stood for election, although none secured a seat. In the May 2008 elections 28 women stood as candidates—most on a platform of issues such as the elimination of discriminatory laws, and the protection and expansion of women's political rights. Again, none won a seat. It was not until 2009 that the first women, Massouma al-Mubarak, Aseel al-Awadhi and Salwa al-Jassar (all professors at Kuwait University) and Rola Dashti, were elected to the National Assembly. All four had doctorates from universities in the USA. Their election marked a major victory for civil rights and for liberal reform in general in Kuwait, indicating a shift in the public mood. In October of that year Kuwait's Constitutional Court ruled that Kuwaiti women need not wear a *hijab* (headscarf) to vote or sit in the National Assembly, overturning legislation introduced by conservative Islamist deputies in 2005. It also ruled women had the right to obtain passports without the approval of their husband, thus amending the 1962 Constitution. The Court's rulings constituted a major defeat for conservative Islamists, who had sought to counter the women's rights agenda.

Meanwhile, the increasingly poor health of both the Amir and the Crown Prince motivated the activation of an al-Sabah family council, as well as wider discussion of the succession process. In late 2005 disputes within the ruling family erupted into the open, and there were demands for a more direct leadership role for the ruling family through an advisory panel. A statement in support of Sheikh Sabah, read out on behalf of the ailing Sheikh Jaber, raised tensions even further as its authenticity was called into question. At the same time, parliamentarians were pushing for more extensive political reform, and by the end of the year the left-leaning National Democratic Alliance and the Popular Action Bloc were together leading the campaign for electoral reform.

On 15 January 2006 the Amir, Sheikh Jaber al-Ahmad al-Sabah, died, leaving an ailing Crown Prince who was physically incapable of discharging the duties of Amir. Sheikh Saad al-Abdullah al-Salim al-Sabah was initially unwilling to abdicate, but on 24 January the Prime Minister and de facto ruler of Kuwait, Sheikh Sabah, convened the National Assembly and forced the abdication of Sheikh Saad on medical grounds. Sheikh Sabah was then chosen as Amir by the same Assembly. This unprecedented event was seen by some Kuwaitis as a historic shift towards constitutional monarchy democracy in Kuwait, because of the direct involvement of the National Assembly in the succession process. The accession of Sheikh Sabah was followed by the announcement that the former First Deputy Prime Minister and Minister of the Interior and of Defence, Sheikh Nawwaf al-Ahmad al-Jaber al-Sabah, was to become the new Crown Prince. Subsequently, the Amir's nephew, Sheikh Nasser al-Muhammad al-Ahmad al-Sabah, was appointed Prime Minister. These appointments consolidated the highest offices within the al-Jaber branch of the ruling family—and particularly in the hands of another elderly Amir—while keeping most of the younger al-Sabah from the highest political echelons.

The new Amir responded to demands for political reform by apparently reneging on an initial undertaking to reduce the number of constituencies from 25 to five. When members of the National Assembly expressed their intention to question the new Prime Minister on the matter, the Amir dissolved the Assembly and called new elections for the end of June 2006, based on the old system. However, the Amir's seeming bid to curb the demands for change failed, as reform became the main election issue. A group of 29 deputies formed an Alliance for Change that mitigated the usual antagonisms among Islamist, liberal, leftist and populist tendencies, instead concentrating on electoral reform and fighting corruption. The Alliance duly won 34 seats in the National Assembly, and the electoral constituency reform received legislative approval three weeks later. The new Government, subsequently formed by Sheikh Nasser, complied with the momentum for electoral reform, but it was thought unlikely that a more radical political reform would have an easy passage. The manner in which the Government secured the election of its preferred candidate, Jasem al-Kharafi, as Speaker of the National Assembly—by exercising the right of appointed ministers to vote in the Assembly—signalled its resolve in answer to the new legislature. A majority of elected members had favoured the opposition Popular Action Bloc leader and erstwhile Speaker, Ahmad al-Saadoun. Overall, Kuwait's politics had been seen to become more polarized in the run-up to the elections.

The Council of Ministers resigned in March 2007, after eight months in office, to prevent a vote of no confidence against the former Minister of Health, Sheikh Ahmad Abdullah al-Sabah, in the context of corruption allegations. The successor administration retained most of the key ministers (excluding Sheikh Ahmad) in the same posts; Dr Massouma al-Mubarak—who had been appointed to the Council of Ministers in June 2005 as Kuwait's first female minister—became Minister of Health. In June 2007 the Minister of Oil, Sheikh Ali Jarrah al-Sabah, and the Minister of Communications and Minister of State for National Assembly Affairs, Sharida al-Mu'ushirji, both resigned, days before they were due to appear before a special meeting of the National Assembly convened to question them about corruption. A no-confidence vote was the expected outcome of the session. In August al-Mubarak resigned as Minister of Health, following allegations of government mismanagement in the wake of a devastating fire at Jahra Hospital in which two patients died; the Minister of Information, Abdullah Saud al-Muhailbi, assumed the post in an acting capacity. In October the Prime Minister reorganized the Council of Ministers, in an effort to avoid a crisis with the National Assembly, naming four new ministers and making changes to five other portfolios. In the following month, however, the newly appointed Minister of Oil, Bader Mishari al-Humaidhi, resigned, in order to avoid appearing before a special session of the National Assembly that was to question him about accusations of corruption and his refusal to publish estimates of the country's oil reserves (feared to be only one-half of the figure claimed by the minister).

There followed further allegations of corruption against public figures in early 2008. Three (Deputy Prime Minister and Minister of State for Cabinet Affairs Faisal Muhammad al-Hajji Bukhadour; Minister of Health Abdullah Abd al-Rahman al-Taweel; and a former Minister of Communications) were subsequently summoned for questioning; however the entire Council of Ministers tendered its resignation in March, protesting that the deteriorating relationship between the Government and the Islamist-dominated National Assembly was causing gridlock in the legislative process. The unpopularity of the Prime Minister, Sheikh Nasser, and his policies with the majority of deputies was cited as a main reason for the impasse. The Amir responded by dissolving the National Assembly and calling elections for May. The elections were to be the first since the adoption into law of the new, five-constituency system in July 2006. The old system of 25 constituencies (in force since 1980) had encouraged voting along tribal or sectarian lines which, in recent years, had undermined national unity. Under the new system, each citizen was granted a maximum of four votes in each constituency, and candidates were required to obtain a greater number of votes in order to win. The new arrangement was intended to stem the problem of vote-buying. The main election issue was Kuwait's rapidly increasing rate of inflation, which had risen from 1.8% in 2005 to 11.4% in 2008, despite the delinking of the Kuwaiti dinar from the US dollar in the previous year. In April the Electoral Commission announced that candidates known to have been chosen in the popular, albeit illegal, tribal primaries would be prevented from standing for election. In the following month Kuwaiti police detained a number of men from the al-Mutair tribe who were accused of holding such primaries. Thousands of people from the al-Mutair tribe protested outside the police station where the detainees were held.

In total, 200,499 women and 161,185 men turned out to vote in the May 2008 elections—representing 59.4% of the eligible electorate. Islamists fared better in the polls than they had in 2006: Sunni Islamists secured 21 seats, the Popular Action Bloc won four seats, and other Shi'a candidates took five seats. Liberals and their allies won seven seats, and independent candidates 13. As in 2006, none of the female candidates was elected. Sheikh Nasser subsequently formed a new Council of Ministers—his fourth since assuming the post of Prime Minister in 2006—including two women.

In September 2008 the Amir issued a statement intended to end persistent speculation that the new National Assembly might again be dissolved because of the continuing opposition of Islamist and Popular Action Bloc deputies to the Government's legislative programme. In November three Salafi deputies demanded that the Prime Minister should submit to parliamentary interpellation and a no confidence vote. Although Sheikh Nasser commanded much sympathy within the National Assembly in this instance, and would have easily survived a motion of no confidence, he chose instead to submit the resignation of his Government. The Amir rejected the idea of holding fresh elections, and invited Sheikh Nasser to form a new administration. The Council of Ministers that the Prime Minister subsequently appointed in December included only two new members. The Minister of Oil and of Electricity and Water in the previous Government, Muhammad al-Olaim, from the moderate Islamic Constitutional Movement (the Kuwaiti branch of the Muslim Brotherhood), was not reappointed, since the organization refused to participate in the new Council of Ministers. The Deputy Prime Minister and Minister of Foreign Affairs, Sheikh Muhammad Sabah al-Salim al-Sabah, assumed the oil portfolio on a temporary basis until a new minister could be appointed; the electricity and water portfolio was allocated to Nabil bin Salamah, who also assumed responsibility for communications. The General Secretary of the National Assembly, Roudhan al-Roudhan (an independent deputy), was appointed Minister of Health, replacing Ali Muhammad al-Barrak. The limited extent of the reorganization prompted a walkout by a group of 12 National Assembly members. By early 2009 the Government and National Assembly were once again in deadlock. Many saw the crisis as the result of an alliance between Islamist deputies and conservatives within the al-Salim branch of the ruling family, who opposed the Government's reforms. It was also a result of a fundamental tension in Kuwait's political system: while the composition of the National Assembly (at this time conservative, largely Islamist) is determined by free elections, the Council of Ministers, members of which are eligible to vote in the Assembly, is appointed by the Prime Minister. As the National Assembly has the constitutional right to question ministers and dismiss them through a vote of no confidence, the deputies are able to use this mechanism to prevent the Council of Ministers from advancing its legislative (latterly more reformist) programme.

In March 2009, after National Assembly members again asked to question the Prime Minister and hold a no confidence vote, the Prime Minister and the Council of Ministers resigned once again. This time, the Amir chose to dissolve the Assembly, accusing deputies of abusing their constitutional right to question ministers. Elections—the third in three years—were subsequently held in May. There were 196 candidates, including 16 women; only 36 outgoing deputies stood for re-election. Turn-out was slightly reduced, at 58%. A large gain for the liberals, including four women—Kuwait's first female deputies—apparently reflected voters' increasing exasperation with the Islamists' obstructionism. Sheikh Nasser was subsequently reappointed as Prime Minister. His new Council of Ministers included few changes, the main (and most controversial) one being the return to government of Sheikh Ahmad Abdullah al-Sabah as Minister of Oil and of Information. Another notable appointment was that of Muhammad Mohsen al-Busairi (a member of the Islamic Constitutional Movement) as Minister of Communications and Minister of State for National Assembly Affairs. The Prime Minister also replaced the Minister of Education and of Higher Education, Nouriya al-Subeeh, with another liberal woman, Dr Moudhi Abd al-Aziz al-Homoud, despite objections from Islamist deputies.

At the opening session of the new National Assembly the Amir pleaded for the legislature and the executive to 'set aside previous conflicts, start with a clean slate, and adopt a new political approach to end years of development process suspension'. None the less, three Islamist deputies raised objections at the decision of al-Homoud and two of the female deputies to leave their heads uncovered within the assembly building. Two Popular Action Bloc deputies also submitted a request to question the Minister of the Interior, Sheikh Jaber Khalid al-Jaber al-Sabah. This was seen as retaliation for Sheikh Jaber's attempt to prevent illegal tribal primaries for the selection of candidates for elections. (Tribal members account for about half the deputies.) Sheikh Jaber survived the subsequent vote of no confidence. The conservatives no longer commanded a majority in the Assembly, making it theoretically easier for the Prime Minister to push through liberal reforms.

In December 2009 Prime Minister Sheikh Nasser agreed for the first time to answer questions in a closed session of the National Assembly about alleged corruption. After the questioning, 10 deputies submitted a motion of no confidence, which the Prime Minister survived by a vote of 35 to 13, with one abstention. The Minister of Interior, Sheikh Jaber, also survived a motion of no confidence by 26 votes to 18, with five abstentions. A further attempt to question the Prime Minister in June 2010, this time concerning alleged negligence in his duties, was cancelled after National Assembly deputies were unable to agree on whether this should be in a public or private session.

In late 2009 a prominent former editor of the conservative *Al-Watan* newspaper, Muhammad Abd al-Qader al-Jassem, publicly criticized the Prime Minister's governance of the country, and demanded his resignation. Sheikh Nasser filed a private lawsuit against al-Jassem for slander. Al-Jassem was arrested in December and detained for 12 days. In April 2010 he was sentenced to six months' imprisonment and fined US $17,500, but the sentence was suspended following an appeal. In May al-Jassem was arrested again, this time on charges of defaming the ruling family and Government, undermining the Amir's status, spreading false information and damaging Kuwait's national interests. He was released on bail in June, following pressure from several leading international human rights organizations. Al-Jassem told the press that the accusations against him were politically motivated, and that he was being punished for expressing his views. At that time, five similar lawsuits were pending against al-Jassem for criticizing the Prime Minister, three of which had been filed by Sheikh Nasser and two by the Ministry of Information. In November al-Jassem was sentenced to one year's imprisonment for defaming the Prime Minister, but he was released on appeal after two months; 17 other charges remained against him.

Meanwhile, the Prime Minister also filed a lawsuit against the head of the liberal National Democratic Alliance, Khaled al-Fadalah, accusing him of money-laundering. In June 2010 al-Fadalah was sentenced to three months' imprisonment and fined US $516, although he was released on appeal after 10 days. At a press conference in July, the Prime Minister and Minister of Information stated that public criticism of the Amir, the Prime Minister, government ministers and countries with which Kuwait had close relations undermined 'national unity', and that the Government intended to amend the press and publications law accordingly. In response, the French-based non-governmental organization Reporters Without Borders demoted Kuwait in its annual Worldwide Press Freedom Index from 60th place in 2009 (the highest in the Arab world) to 87th in 2010 (although still the second highest of the Arab countries, behind Lebanon). In February 2011, under pressure from a growing number of deputies in the National Assembly, the Amir ordered that the 600 lawsuits filed by the Ministry of Information against the local media and other government critics be abandoned.

In February 2010 the National Assembly finally approved the Prime Minister's US $129,000m. five-year development plan, which had long been delayed by conservative opposition. The plan, which took effect in April, envisaged the development of Kuwait into a regional trade and financial centre, with the construction of a $77,000m. business hub at Subiya, linked to the capital by a new causeway; a new container port on Bubiyan Island; a 518-km railway network (part of a wider GCC railway project); and a 171-km metro system. Provision was made for the establishment of a Capital Market Authority; and the plan also aimed to expanding the role of the private sector in developing the country's infrastructure and diversifying the national economy, both of which had hitherto been state-dominated.

KUWAIT AND THE 'ARAB SPRING'

Kuwait was thus already in a state of political mobilization as what came to be known as the 'Arab spring' spread across the region. In December 2010 Sheikh Nasser alienated many by attempting to deprive an Islamist deputy, Faisal al-Muslim, of his parliamentary immunity, in order to file a lawsuit against him for having accused the Prime Minister of corruption. Parliamentary immunity is a fundamental constitutional safeguard of Kuwait's democracy, and the Prime Minister's action prompted the establishment of a constitutional defence coalition comprising half the deputies in the National Assembly. A popular movement was formed to demand Sheikh Nasser's removal from office, and five people were injured when security forces intervened, on the orders of the Prime Minister, to quell a public protest in Kuwait City. A vote of no confidence was subsequently held in the National Assembly in late December, with 22 deputies opposing the Prime Minister, 25 supporting him, and one abstaining. This was the second motion of no confidence against Sheikh Nasser in just over a year.

In January 2011 Sheikh Nasser was questioned by deputies in the National Assembly over the police action in the previous month. Furthermore, the Deputy Prime Minister and Minister of the Interior, Sheikh Jaber Khalid al-Jaber al-Sabah, was forced to resign following reports that police had tortured to death a Kuwaiti citizen, Muhammad Ghazzai al-Mutairi. The Amir replaced Sheikh Jaber with Sheikh Ahmad Homoud al-Jaber al-Sabah, a senior member of the ruling family who had previously served as Minister of the Interior in 1991–92 and as Minister of Defence in 1994. In March 2011 18 police officers and two civilians were tried for the illegal detention, torture and murder of al-Mutairi. In the same month there was a renewal of demands by opposition deputies and political activists for the Prime Minister to step down. In one incident, around 1,000 youths occupied a car park in front of a government building in Kuwait City, demanding the resignation of Sheikh Nasser and six members of the Council of Ministers on grounds of corruption, ineffectiveness and violation of the Constitution. Opposition deputies filed a request for the Prime Minister and three other government ministers to appear before the National Assembly. A political crisis ensued, resulting in the resignation of the Prime Minister and the Government at the end of March in order to avoid questioning in the Assembly.

Kuwait also witnessed major protests by the *bidoun* in February and March 2011. *Bidoun* (meaning 'without'; short for *bidoun jinsiyya*, 'without nationality') are stateless Arabs with no acknowledged nationality documents. The Kuwaiti *bidoun* have long lived in Kuwait. Many were once well integrated into Kuwaiti society, often working in the police and military before 1990. They are permitted access to some state resources, but the Government rejects their claim to Kuwaiti citizenship. The Government argues that most *bidoun* came from Iraq in the 1930s–60s, with a few more settling in Kuwait during the Iraqi occupation of 1990–91. The Kuwaiti *bidoun* currently number as many as 120,000. Tens of thousands more were exiled to Iraq after the 1990–91 conflict. Formerly, Kuwait officially counted the *bidoun* as part of its indigenous population, but after the Iraqi occupation the division between the al-Sabah rulers who fled the country and the poorer sections of the population who endured the war and occupation widened. The al-Sabah tended to exploit their state power—and the abstruse, multi-layered definition of Kuwaiti nationality—to re-establish their political control. The Government's denial of identity and rights to the *bidoun* became an instrument for exercising power over society. The issue of the *bidoun* remains controversial in Kuwaiti politics, and protests and unrest in some *bidoun*-majority areas have occurred intermittently. In 2000 the government had adopted a law granting a small number of *bidoun* the opportunity to acquire citizenship and its associated privileges: namely, access to government housing, health care, education and jobs; the right officially to register births, deaths and marriages; and the right to possess a driving licence and a standard passport. The legislation, which in effect forced thousands of non-eligible *bidoun* into deeper poverty, was extremely unpopular with the *bidoun*, prompting widespread protests in the *bidoun*-majority city of al-Jahra (north-west of Kuwait City). In early 2001 about 1,000 *bidoun* were granted Kuwaiti citizenship, but protests continued by those whose claims were not recognized, with the protesters attempting to bring their case to international attention. The Government promised to address the situation more fully in 2003. The rights of the *bidoun* also featured in the recommendations of a major reform petition, announced in September of that year, that had support from liberal, Islamist and some government circles. In April 2006 another piecemeal measure to manage the issue of the *bidoun* was introduced, offering identity cards to 13,000 individuals and giving the newly recognized residents some basic access to social services and protection. The measure did not satisfy campaigners, including the National Assembly's Human Rights Committee. The National Assembly elected in June that year established a new parliamentary committee for *bidoun* affairs, with the aim of alleviating what were regarded as inhumane government practices. In December 2009 a National Assembly session that was due to approve a draft law granting full civil and social rights to some 100,000–120,000 *bidoun* living in Kuwait was cancelled when only five ministers and 26 deputies attended (two fewer than the required quorum). In April 2010, during a visit to Kuwait, the UN High Commissioner for Human Rights, Navanethem Pillay, urged the Government to resolve the *bidoun* issue. Later that year the Government established the Central System for Remedying the Status of Illegal Residents (CSRSIR), in an attempt to find a solution to the problem by establishing who was, and who was not, entitled to citizenship.

With the 'Arab spring', the *bidoun*, unable to access the parliamentary system, took to the streets. In February 2011 more than 1,000 *bidoun* joined a three-day protest in al-Jahra and other locations, demanding that the Government address their grievances. Security forces broke up the protests using batons, smoke bombs, tear gas and water cannon, and made several arrests. The First Deputy Prime Minister and Minister of the Interior, Sheikh Ahmad Homoud al-Jaber al-Sabah, informed the *bidoun* that the CSRSIR was studying their files, but cautioned that citizenship could only be granted in accordance with Kuwaiti law, and that only those who could prove their entitlement to Kuwaiti citizenship would receive it. A number of deputies responded to the protests by submitting a bill to the National Assembly that would grant the *bidoun* basic civil rights (such as access to free education, medical care and jobs), but the Government did not permit debate of the proposals. In March, when the Government's decision was made public, further protests broke out in al-Jahra, involving some 500 people. The security forces dispersed the protesters with tear gas, and again made arrests. Protests continued, and in January 2012 the Ministry of the Interior issued a statement banning all rallies and protests by *bidoun*.

Foreign workers also engaged the 'Arab spring'—albeit, fearing deportation, to a lesser degree. Kuwait has always had an uneasy relationship with its large expatriate population. In the aftermath of the Iraqi occupation, the Kuwaiti government vowed to reduce the number of foreign workers substantially, but it was ultimately unable to do so. Expatriates again now comprise the majority of the population. There have been recurring protests over the decades, generally by the lowest-paid foreign workers, who are typically from South Asia. Such demonstrators (or their leaders) are usually deported, with their removal being followed by modest reforms. For example, in April 2010 Kuwait introduced a minimum wage of KD 60 per month for labourers. However, this wage did not apply to Kuwait's 560,000 domestic workers (including maids, cooks and drivers), who represent some 25% of Kuwait's foreign labour force. Domestic workers in Kuwait are not entitled to a weekly rest day, a limit on their working hours, or a set minimum wage, and those who flee abusive employers are arrested and deported. While some legal protections for foreign workers do exist (although few for domestic workers), foreigners attempting to exercise those rights can be easily deported. In June 2013 the Government began implementing a pilot plan in al-Jahra to ban expatriates from attending public hospitals in the morning, with the goal of eventually extending the ban to other facilities.

By 2011, meanwhile, unrest had spread among Kuwaiti nationals as well. In April the Amir asked Sheikh Nasser to form a new government—his seventh in seven years. The Prime Minister reappointed five of six ministers to whom the opposition had earlier objected. Opposition deputies again filed a petition to question Sheikh Nasser, but the Government submitted a request to the National Assembly to postpone the questioning by a year while it referred the matter to the Constitutional Court; the Assembly subsequently approved this request. As a result of the growing frustration with the Prime Minister and his Government, political activists and opposition deputies called for a 'Day of Rage' rally to be held in Safat Square, outside the National Assembly building, in late May. The Government arranged a heavy security presence in anticipation of the event, and the protest passed without incident. In November 2011 more than 50,000 protesters took to the streets—with some briefly taking over the National Assembly building—to demand the ouster of the Prime Minister on grounds of corruption. This followed the Government's successful efforts to block a further request by some members of the National Assembly to summon Sheikh Nasser for questioning. While Kuwaitis did not echo the call of revolutionaries elsewhere in the region for the overthrow of the regime, many did demand movement toward a constitutional monarchy. The protests led, in late November, to the resignation of the Prime Minister and his Government, and in early December the Amir again dissolved the National Assembly.

The parliamentary elections that ensued on 2 February 2012 resulted in a decisive victory for the opposition, and produced a loose alliance between Sunni Islamist and tribal deputies—with the Sunni Islamists winning 14 seats and tribal candidates (about half of whom were also Islamists) taking 21 seats.

Liberal candidates performed poorly, and none of the 23 female candidates was elected. The number of Shi'a deputies, who are generally pro-Government, fell from nine to seven. Ahmad al-Saadoun was subsequently elected as the parliament's Speaker. A predictably fiery clash between the National Assembly and the Government emerged in the following months—beginning with the opposition deputies' demand for half the ministerial positions in Sheikh Nasser's new Government, and rejection of the counter-offer of four portfolios. The Minister of Finance resigned in May, after pressure from the National Assembly; and the Minister of Social Affairs and Labour resigned in June, following efforts by the legislature to question him over work permits.

With the inauguration of the new National Assembly, Islamist issues moved to the forefront of Kuwaiti politics. In March 2012 a court suspended publication of the *al-Dar* newspaper for three months for allegedly fomenting sectarian strife. In the same month the authorities arrested a Shi'a, Hamad al-Naqi, for allegedly insulting the Prophet Muhammad and his wife via a social-networking website (he claimed his account had been hacked). In June he was convicted and sentenced to 10 years' imprisonment. In May the National Assembly approved legislation imposing the death penalty for persons convicted of blasphemy. In the same month the Amir blocked a proposal by 31 deputies requiring that all legislation should conform to *Shari'a* law.

In mid-June 2012 these political tensions escalated into crisis, when the Government, invoking Article 106 of the Constitution, announced it would suspend the National Assembly for a month. (The suspension would thus abut Ramadan, during which period the National Assembly is typically closed.) The Government's action occurred a day before the Minister of Interior, Sheikh Ahmad Homoud al-Jaber al-Sabah, was due to appear before parliament for questioning. Although Kuwaiti rulers had previously dissolved the National Assembly seven times (twice unconstitutionally), this was the first suspension of parliament in Kuwait's history. Two days after the suspension was announced, the Constitutional Court—ruling on a challenge to the decree that had dissolved parliament in December 2011—took an unprecedented and still more dramatic action, declaring the February 2012 election void and ordering the reinstatement of the National Assembly previously elected in 2009. However, more than half the members of the restored parliament immediately resigned, in protest against the decision. A new election was subsequently scheduled for 1 December 2012.

In October 2012 the Amir issued a decree allowing voters to cast ballots for just one candidate (as reformed in 2006, the electoral system had allowed each voter to choose a maximum of four candidates). Opposition groups argued against the unilateral nature of the decree and its timing (just six weeks before the elections), and expressed concern that the restriction would inhibit their ability to form coalitions. Hundreds of thousands of Kuwaitis protested in a 'March of Dignity', said to be the largest demonstration in Kuwait's history. The opposition's appeal for a boycott resulted in a significantly low turnout, of 43%, at the elections. A notable outcome of voting was that Shi'a representation increased from seven seats to 17. Three women were elected. This new Assembly proved no less confrontational, and several ministers resigned in May 2013 rather than submit to parliamentary questioning.

In June 2013 the Constitutional Court rejected an opposition challenge to the one voter, one vote decree. However, it again ordered the dissolution of the National Assembly on procedural grounds. This forced new elections, which were initially scheduled for 25 July, but subsequently adjusted to 27 July. Voting was thus to take place within Ramadan, in which period formal politics typically halts in Kuwait. While some voters, including many Islamists, continued the boycott, others did not. The brief coalition of Islamists, tribal members, and liberals that had mobilized large numbers of demonstrators had by now collapsed. Voter turnout was recorded at 52.5% (above the rate recorded in the December 2012 elections, but still below historical levels). More than one-half those elected were new to parliament. Tribal candidates won 10 seats, after tribal leaders from the Ajman, Mutair, and Awazim tribes publicly called on members to vote. Liberals, who had boycotted the previous election, won three seats. Shi'a Islamists won only eight seats, down from 17 at the previous election. Meanwhile, two women (one Shi'a, one liberal) were also elected. Following the election, the Amir reappointed Sheikh Jaber al-Mubarak al-Sabah as Prime Minister, and a new Government was sworn into office on 4 August. Most notably, Sheikh Muhammad Khalid al-Sabah became Deputy Prime Minister and Minister of the Interior, Sheikh Khalid al-Jarrah al-Sabah Deputy Prime Minister and Minister of Defence, and Sheikh Salem Abd al-Aziz al-Saud al-Sabah Deputy Prime Minister and Minister of Finance. Mustafa al-Shamali, the Minister of Finance in the outgoing government, was appointed as Minister of Oil.

As public unrest grew, and in the context of the 'Arab spring', Kuwait's rulers responded with increasing harshness, focusing in particular on social media. In June 2013 a Kuwaiti woman, Huda al-Ajami, was sentenced to 11 years' imprisonment for posting messages deemed insulting to the Amir and to a religious sect. This followed the sentencing of nine Kuwaiti men in the course of the previous year for views expressed via social media sites. In May 2013, meanwhile, an appeals court overturned a five-year sentence against an opposition activist, former National Assembly deputy Mussallam al-Barrak, for 'undermining the ruling Amir' in remarks made at a rally in October 2012.

EXTERNAL RELATIONS, 1993–2013

Following the Gulf War, Kuwait continued to urge the GCC states to maintain an uncompromising stance towards Iraq, and to persist in a full enforcement of the UN sanctions regime. None the less, between 1998 and 2001 Iraq's regional isolation was easing, and it appeared that Kuwait was itself becoming more isolated in Arab and Islamic diplomatic circles. In 1993 Kuwait announced it was willing to restore relations with Arab states that had supported Iraq during the Gulf War, with the exception of Jordan and the leadership of the Palestine Liberation Organization (PLO). Relations between Kuwait and Jordan began to improve from 1996. In 1997–98 Kuwait pardoned and released Jordanians imprisoned in 1991 for collaboration with the Iraqi forces. Ministerial visits between Kuwait and Jordan were resumed in June 1998. In March 1999 the Jordanian embassy in Kuwait, which had been closed in 1990, was reopened. Later, Jordan's King Abdullah visited Kuwait; he returned for a second visit following the Arab League summit held in Amman in March 2001, which accorded him the task of trying to find common ground between Iraq and Kuwait.

At a meeting of GCC ministers responsible for foreign affairs in Riyadh, Saudi Arabia, in June 1998, extreme concern was expressed at a statement made by the Vice-Chairman of Iraq's Revolutionary Command Council dismissing the terms of the UN resolution that had demarcated the boundary between Iraq and Kuwait following the 1990–91 Gulf crisis. Similar concern was expressed by GCC foreign ministers in September 2000, in response to repeated Iraqi statements denouncing Kuwait and Saudi Arabia for permitting US and British aircraft to use their airspace and facilities to maintain attacks on Iraq. During the same period Kuwaiti military units were active in intercepting small commercial vessels destined for and sailing from Iraqi ports.

At the same time, the Kuwaiti Government declared its support for a diplomatic solution to the rapid escalation of tensions between the inspectors from United Nations Special Commission (UNSCOM) and the Iraqi authorities during 1998. Kuwait indicated that it would not be used as a base for a US-led attack on Iraq to enforce the UNSCOM mandate, but US and British air-strikes against strategic Iraqi installations were launched for this purpose from the Gulf in late 1998 with full logistical support from Kuwait. The US military presence in Kuwait continued to expand.

During the first half of 1998 there was a discernible change in the tone of Kuwaiti foreign policy, with the First Deputy Prime Minister and Minister of Foreign Affairs declaring that Kuwait no longer opposed Iraqi participation in Arab summit meetings; in May the Kuwaiti Red Crescent offered to send humanitarian supplies to Iraq. Subsequently, the National Assembly hosted a seminar that discussed the future of

Iraqi-Kuwaiti relations, with the participation of Iraqis opposed to the then Iraqi Government. While Kuwait's policy towards relations with Saddam Hussain's Government had not changed, there was for a time an implicit recognition that Kuwait could not rely solely and indefinitely on the defence umbrella provided by the USA. The shift in Kuwait's policy tone continued, with Minister of Foreign Affairs Sabah al-Ahmad al-Jaber al-Sabah declaring, at the Arab League summit conference in Amman, Jordan, in March 2001, that sanctions against Iraq should be revoked. This position was in line with official and popular regional sentiment, but it did not satisfy the Iraqi Government, which wanted Arab countries to declare that they would break UN sanctions and prevent the USA from attacking Iraq from neighbouring territories. Iraq, which had since 1998 been emerging from its diplomatic isolation, failed to gain practical Arab League support for its position, while Kuwait avoided being itself isolated. The new Kuwaiti position was usually prefaced with the stipulation that Iraq should comply with all pertinent UN resolutions, but the general perception that Iraq should be rehabilitated was gathering support in the Arab world, conditioned by heightened concerns about the humanitarian cost to Iraqi civilians of maintaining the sanctions regime, by mounting opposition to continuing US and British air-strikes inside Iraq, and by renewed Arab unity in support of a second Palestinian *intifada* against Israeli occupation after September 2000. Attempts to repair relations between the Palestinian leadership and the Kuwaiti Government were under way before the Palestinian *intifada* began, and a meeting between the President of the Palestinian (National) Authority (PA), Yasser Arafat, and the Kuwaiti Minister of Foreign Affairs had already taken place. However, Kuwait's relations with the Palestinian leadership remained cool, and Kuwait was the only Arab state not to be represented at the funeral of Yasser Arafat in November 2004. Nevertheless, relations appeared likely to improve after the PA Prime Minister, Mahmud Abbas, on a landmark visit to the emirate in December, apologized for the stance that the PLO had taken during Iraq's invasion of Kuwait. Following the Amir's attendance at the Organization of the Islamic Conference summit meeting in Tehran, Iran, in November 1997, several Iranian ministers visited Kuwait, and proposals for joint naval exercises with Iran were made, indicating a significant improvement in relations with that country. In July 2000 Kuwait and Saudi Arabia agreed the demarcation of their maritime borders, and Kuwait entered negotiations with Iran on delimiting their respective rights to the continental shelf. The talks had been convened following Kuwaiti and Saudi Arabian protests at Iran's decision to commence drilling for gas in a disputed offshore area. However, by mid-2013 the dispute remained unresolved.

General opposition to the hosting of US and other Western forces in the region increased from the late 1990s; one way in which this opposition manifested itself was the perpetrating of attacks of increasing violence against US targets both within the region and elsewhere. In Kuwait itself, in November 2000 six Kuwaitis were arrested on suspicion of planning bomb attacks on US forces stationed in the country.

Following the September 2001 attacks on the USA, the Kuwaiti Government expressed its readiness to take immediate action against individuals and groups suspected of involvement with those held responsible for the attacks. (The Kuwaiti-born spokesman for al-Qa'ida, Sulayman Abu Ghaith, was divested of his Kuwaiti citizenship.) In October the Government established a Supreme Council for Charity Work, a task of which was to expose charities being used to support al-Qa'ida or foster other proscribed activities; a number of branches of a Kuwaiti charitable organization were suspected by the US authorities of involvement in activities in support of militant Islamists. Kuwait expressed solidarity with the USA, and continued to facilitate the US military build-up in the region. Subsequently, US government officials visited the country and enlisted full Kuwaiti support for US President George W. Bush's declared 'war on terror'. US military units in Kuwait were reinforced, and the Kuwaiti Government intensified defence procurement negotiations with Western states. The dramatic rise in world prices for petroleum after 1999 facilitated an increase in military expenditure, although the Kuwaiti National Assembly continued to scrutinize military purchases. The growing US military activity in the region altered the relationship of the US Administration with the countries of the Gulf. The smaller GCC states entered into more extensive direct military and political relations with the USA at a time when the latter's relations with Saudi Arabia were coming under strain. Although regular GCC meetings and co-ordination continued, their political and military aspects were now subject to greater influence from US strategists. Saudi Arabia and the other large Arab states consequently lost influence in regional relations, a development that only intensified following the US-led military intervention in Iraq in 2003.

Kuwait followed a policy that was complementary to the US position, but fell short of a commitment of troops. Formally, the Government, in common with other Arab states, expressed opposition to bilateral US-British action, but this position was not reflected in any apparent tension with the USA. At the Arab League summit held in Beirut, Lebanon, in March 2002, Arab leaders reiterated their opposition to any US-led military campaign in Iraq. The head of the Iraqi delegation, Izzat Ibrahim al-Duri, Vice-President of the Revolutionary Command Council, thanked delegates for opposing US threats against Iraq and announced that Iraq would henceforth agree to respect the sovereignty of Kuwait, and guarantee its independence, stability and security within its internationally recognized borders. The other Arab states expressed the hope that Iraq and Kuwait would now begin to co-operate to resolve the outstanding issues between them.

The US-led military occupation of Iraq from 2003 to 2011 provided considerable opportunities for Kuwaiti enterprises north of the border. Kuwait found itself ideally placed within the US business- and military-service network in the region, and its facilities became crucial to developments deeper into Iraq. Some Kuwaiti firms, particularly those in the trade, construction and transport sectors, were able to benefit hugely, especially from servicing the ongoing US military activity in Iraq. Kuwaiti companies were awarded major service and supply contracts for the US military, including a US $3,300m. contract won by Kuwait's Public Warehousing Company, announced in February 2005, to supply subsistence items. A further contract, worth as much as $14,000m., stimulated an unprecedented rise of almost 4% in the overall Kuwait Stock Exchange (KSE) index, thereby contributing to the dramatic upward movement of the exchange and a general sense of euphoria and expectation of rapid windfall gains. However, the euphoria transmuted into gloom as the KSE, along with other Gulf markets, began in late 2005 to experience a reversal in the enormous advances achieved in the previous few years. By March 2006 investors were demonstrating outside the Kuwaiti National Assembly to demand action in support of the stock market; the KIA intervened to purchase stock, averting the need for a formal market adjustment. Kuwaiti companies were also awarded major shares in the mobile telecommunications contracts in the initial round of tenders in Iraq, and Kuwaiti finance interests were thought to be speculating in Iraq's real estate markets.

In July 2007, in an effort to gain support against Iran and strengthen regional security, the USA announced a US $20,000m. package of military aid and arms sales to Kuwait and the five other GCC states. In December of that year President Mahmoud Ahmadinejad described Iran's ties with Kuwait as 'good and cordial'. While Kuwait continued to oppose a military strike against Iran, it did support the UN's demands that Iran disclose the details of its nuclear programme and open its nuclear facilities to inspectors of the International Atomic Energy Agency (IAEA). In November 2010, however, as a result of Iran's persistent refusal to open its facilities to IAEA inspectors, Kuwait agreed to comply with UN sanctions on Iran designed to limit its nuclear programme.

Relations between Kuwait and Iraq continued to improve following the departure of US forces from Iraq in 2011. The resumption of diplomatic relations between the two countries had been announced in mid-2004, and a committee of the major Kuwaiti government departments with responsibility for financial claims and relations with Iraq established. Following a visit by Iraqi Prime Minister Nuri al-Maliki to Kuwait in

April 2007, the Kuwaiti Government announced its desire for Iraqi and Kuwaiti diplomatic missions to reopen concurrently as soon as possible. In November, during a visit to Kuwait, Iraqi President Jalal Talabani announced that Iraq had 'agreed with our Kuwaiti brothers to enhance political, economic, and cultural relationships'. Political ties between Kuwait and Iraq were strengthened when, in October 2008, Lt-Gen. Ali Muhammad al-Momen took up the post of Kuwaiti ambassador in Baghdad. In April 2010 Muhammad Hussain Bahr al-Ulum was appointed as Iraq's ambassador to Kuwait. In January 2011 Sheikh Nasser al-Muhammad al-Ahmad al-Sabah made a visit to Baghdad—becoming the first Kuwaiti Prime Minister to visit Iraq since 1989. During his visit it was agreed that a Kuwait-Iraq joint committee would be formed, chaired by the countries' respective premiers, to discuss all outstanding matters between them, including war reparations and the border issue. The committee held its first meeting in March in Kuwait City, and a second meeting in Baghdad in May. In 2012 the two countries settled their long-standing border dispute, following a visit by the Kuwaiti Amir to Iraq (see The Kuwait–Iraq Border). None the less, a large number of US forces remained in Kuwait in the aftermath of the Iraq War.

Rising sectarian tension in the region prompted the Kuwaiti Government to move closer to its GCC allies. In March 2011, during the crackdown on protests in Bahrain, Kuwait offered to mediate between the pro-democracy activists and the Bahraini Government. Although the leading Bahraini opposition party, the Wefaq National Islamic Society, accepted the offer, the Bahraini Government publicly denied that any such approach had been made, while privately rebuking Kuwait for interfering in Bahraini affairs. In May that year, after initially declining to participate, Kuwait sent a small coastguard reinforcement to join the predominantly Saudi Arabian GCC Peninsula Shield Force that had entered Bahrain in March to put down the protests. The suppression of Bahrain's pro-democracy movement was viewed very critically by liberal and Shi'a Kuwaitis. Kuwait's ambassador to Bhutan, for example, publicly criticized the intervention of the Peninsula Shield Force. While clearly in the GCC 'camp', Kuwait appeared more actively to resist the increasingly sectarian framing of regional conflict. It continued to work towards improving relations with Iraq, and did not witness a high level of sectarian tension domestically—although in late 2010 sectarian tension increased between Kuwait's Shi'a and Sunnis after inflammatory remarks were exchanged by activists on both sides. In response, the Government banned sectarian rallies, and the Amir appealed for national unity in an effort to defuse the situation.

In March 2011 Kuwait agreed to send medical and logistical aid to the rebels fighting the forces of Muammar al-Qaddafi in Libya. However, unlike Qatar and the UAE, it did not commit fighter aircraft (see the chapter on Libya). In July of that year Kuwait donated US $50m. to the Libyan opposition National Transitional Council.

As sectarian tension grew regionally, Kuwait retained a relationship with Iran. In 2006 President Ahmadinejad had made an official visit to Kuwait to discuss issues including gas and water exports to Kuwait, as well as the two countries' shared maritime fields. The visit came at a time of rising international tension as a result of claims, particularly by the USA, that Iran's nuclear programme was not intended for peaceful purposes (see the chapter on Iran). The Kuwaiti Government opposed a military strike carried out against Iran, and was unwilling to permit US forces to use Kuwait as a base of operations for such an attack. In February 2007 the Deputy Prime Minister and Minister of Foreign Affairs, Sheikh Muhammad Sabah al-Salim al-Sabah, paid an official visit to Tehran and held talks with the Iranian President about Iran's nuclear programme and regional security. He announced Kuwait's support for Iran's nuclear programme, believing it to be peaceful, and stated that the stand-off between the USA and Iran could only be resolved by negotiation. In June, following a four-day visit to Kuwait by the Speaker of the Iranian parliament, the Kuwaiti Government announced its intention to extend its bilateral ties with Iran. During the same month the mayors of Kuwait City and Esfahan, Iran, signed an agreement twinning the two cities. However, the spirit of closer co-operation was marred by an assault on a Kuwaiti diplomat in Tehran soon afterwards. Sheikh Muhammad announced that the incident constituted an attack on Kuwait itself, and demanded a written apology. In January 2008 Sheikh Muhammad attended the first meeting of the Kuwait-Iran Economic Commission in Tehran, where he met with both his Iranian counterpart and President Ahmadinejad. Both ministers proclaimed Kuwaiti-Iranian relations to be 'excellent', and spoke of their desire to strengthen bilateral ties in all fields. At the end of the two-day meeting, the ministers signed a treaty to eliminate double taxation, and announced that a bilateral agreement for Iran to provide Kuwait with water and natural gas would shortly be signed.

In November 2009 Kuwait's Prime Minister visited Tehran for talks with President Ahmadinejad about ways to strengthen bilateral ties. This was the first Kuwaiti prime ministerial visit to Iran since the fall of the Shah in 1979. In May 2010, however, the discovery and arrest of an alleged Iranian-led 'spy cell' of six men and one woman in Kuwait provoked a further dispute between the two countries, and deputies of the National Assembly immediately called for the expulsion of the Iranian ambassador. Later that month the Iranian ambassador returned to Tehran, having completed his tour of duty, but Tehran chose not to replace him (a move that was widely interpreted as a form of protest over the spying accusations). At the end of the trial of the seven accused, which took place in a closed court during August 2010–March 2011, two Iranians and a Kuwaiti national were sentenced to death; a Syrian man and a Kuwaiti *bidoun* were sentenced to life imprisonment; and an Iranian man and woman were acquitted. The three men who were condemned to death and the Syrian national had all been serving in the Kuwaiti army at the time of their arrest, while the *bidoun* had previously served in the Kuwaiti army. Iran continued to insist that the accusations were false. In April 2011 the Kuwaiti Government recalled its ambassador in Tehran and expelled three Iranian diplomats from Kuwait. Iran, in turn, expelled three Kuwaiti diplomats over the following weeks. In May the Iranian Minister of Foreign Affairs visited Kuwait in an attempt to improve relations. During his visit he announced that the two countries had agreed to exchange ambassadors again; the envoys were in place by late May. However, also in late May, it was reported that an alleged joint Iranian-Hezbollah 'spy ring' had been discovered in Kuwait. Kuwait, in common with the other GCC states, welcomed the election of Hassan Rouhani to the Iranian presidency in June 2013.

The 'Arab spring' prompted the Kuwaiti Government to re-examine issues of radical Islam and sectarian conflict. The influence of Islamists in Kuwaiti politics and society, which had been growing steadily in the 1990s, increased sharply following the US-led invasion of Iraq in 2003. For the most part, Kuwaiti Islamists and nationalists followed the path of political opposition to US policy, or acquiesced in their Government's increasingly close ties with the USA. However, radical opposition to the Government and to the presence of US forces has been persistent and at times militant. The initial build-up of US and British forces in Kuwait from mid-2002, in preparation for the invasion of Iraq, was disrupted by a series of low-level attacks against US forces by Kuwaitis who objected to war being conducted from their country. In October of that year US troops were attacked while training at Failaka Island; the assailants managed to kill one US marine and wound another before they were themselves killed. Attacks continued sporadically, including one on US forces in December 2003.

Economy

Revised for this edition by RICHARD GERMAN and ELIZABETH TAYLOR

INTRODUCTION

Kuwait is a relatively small, arid country with a severe climate. Fresh water is scarce, and agriculture limited. However, the discovery of extremely rich deposits of petroleum transformed the economy and has given the country a high level of material prosperity. Kuwait's population increased from approximately 200,000 in 1957 to 1,697,301 in 1985, of whom only 40% were Kuwaiti nationals; the remainder were mainly immigrant workers and their families. At mid-1990 the population was estimated to be 2.1m., of whom 1.5m. were non-Kuwaiti nationals (based on the definition of citizenship in use in 1992). A year later, following the Gulf conflict, it had declined to 1.2m. Census results for April 2005 recorded a total population of 2.2m. (of whom 39.2% were Kuwaiti nationals). By mid-2006 the population had risen to 3.1m., the marked increase being attributed to a new methodology applied by the Public Authority for Civil Information (PACI). At mid-2012, according to PACI estimates, the total population stood at 3.8m. (of whom 1.2m. were Kuwaiti nationals).

In 1987 the Government had initiated a five-year plan to reduce the number of expatriates in the Kuwaiti workforce. Taking advantage of the displacement caused by the Iraqi invasion in 1990, the Government subsequently announced its intention to restrict the level of non-Kuwaiti residents to less than 50% of the pre-crisis total. Kuwait subsequently attracted censure for its use of deportation and for its treatment of expatriate groups, especially Palestinians, within the country. In March 1994 it was officially reported that a total of 34,000 persons had been deported from Kuwait since June 1991.

The immediate costs of the military operation to liberate Kuwait (about US $22,000m.) and of rebuilding the country's infrastructure (some $20,000m.) were, in large part, met by liquidating about one-half of Kuwait's overseas investment portfolio (including about one-half of the Future Generations Fund—FGF—see Investment) and by external borrowing totalling $5,500m. In 2000 the Government sought to encourage further foreign investment in the economy through the limited participation of foreign companies in the petroleum sector and the introduction of measures to allow foreign nationals to invest on the Kuwait Stock Exchange (KSE). On 1 January 2003 Kuwait pegged the dinar to the US dollar (see Banking).

Kuwait's gross domestic product (GDP) fluctuated during 1980–89, declining by an average of 0.7% per year. More severe contractions in 1990 and 1991 were brought about by the disruption of the Iraqi invasion. However, GDP recovered towards the end of the decade, rising to KD 9,060m. by 1997. The sharp decline in international petroleum prices in 1998 resulted in a decrease in GDP, to KD 7,742m., although it increased again, to KD 8,884m. in 1999 and KD 11,357m. in 2000. GDP declined to KD 10,446m. in 1991, before increasing to KD 10,691m. in 2002 and KD 12,441m. in 2003. An IMF assessment of the Kuwaiti economy in May 2005 identified a strong macroeconomic performance in both 2003 and 2004, mainly reflecting sharply higher petroleum prices and production, and also the renewal of trade relations with Iraq following the 2003 war. After low levels of growth in 2000–02, the economy grew by 17.3% in 2003, driven by the petroleum and gas sector. More moderate increases were recorded in 2004 and 2005. Reflecting higher world petroleum prices, the economy grew by 6.3% in 2006, despite a collapse in regional stock market prices early in the year (see Capital Market). According to IMF estimates, GDP grew by 4.6% in 2007, while significantly higher global petroleum prices increased budget revenues and consequently improved the fiscal balance. In 2006/07 a surplus of KD 5,202.9m. was recorded, equivalent to 16.3% of GDP. However, higher rates of growth and increased revenues also increased inflationary pressure. Consumer prices rose by an average of 3.0% in 2006 and by 5.5% in 2007.

GDP growth in 2008 was estimated by the IMF at 6.4%, but inflation reached about 11% by mid-year, driven by increases in international food prices. The Government announced measures to offset the rising prices, including raising food subsidies, but its primary policy concern switched from controlling inflation to managing the effects of a deepening global financial crisis and a sharp decrease in the price of petroleum in the latter half of 2008. Furthermore, intensifying tensions between the Government and National Assembly, which had delayed the implementation of economic reforms and major sectoral projects, culminated in the dissolution of the National Assembly in March 2009 and the holding of early elections in May. Observers considered that it was vital for the new executive and legislature to reach a working compromise if the country was to avoid further economic stagnation, although a US $5,200m. economic stimulus package (also termed the financial stability law) was approved by Amiri decree in April following the dissolution of the National Assembly.

The IMF projected a contraction in GDP, in real terms, for 2009, to reflect lower petroleum production and weak activity in the financial and construction sectors. However, an apparent improvement from the end of the year in the relationship between the Government and National Assembly heralded the introduction of some progressive economic measures and overdue reforms. In February 2010 the Assembly formally approved the Government's new development plan for 2010/11–13/14 (the first for almost 25 years—see also Public Finance). In May 2010 a controversial privatization bill narrowly passed its final reading in the Assembly, paving the way for the sale of state-owned non-oil assets (although the Government was to hold a so-called 'golden share' in privatized entities). The Assembly also approved legislation establishing a Capital Market Authority to regulate the stock market. (Despite being one of the oldest and largest stock markets in the region, the Kuwait exchange was the only bourse without an independent watchdog.) Meanwhile, public-private partnerships (PPPs), regarded as integral to the new development plan, were to be facilitated by the Partnerships Technical Bureau (PTB), established in 2009.

According to Kuwait's Central Statistical Bureau, real GDP contracted by 7.8% in 2009—the weakest performance among the members of the Cooperation Council for the Arab States of the Gulf (Gulf Cooperation Council—GCC)— but improved in 2010, driven by exports and private consumption. Kuwait was less troubled by the regional unrest in the first half of 2011 than were other petroleum exporters, but, as in other GCC countries, the Government increased expenditure to offset social tensions. In January 2011, to mark the 50th anniversary of independence, the Amir assigned a cash grant of KD 1,000 and 13 months of free vouchers for essential food items to all Kuwaitis (covering the period from February 2011 to March 2012). The Government also announced a large pay rise for the military.

According to an IMF review published in June 2012, Kuwait's GDP growth in 2011 was estimated at around 8.3%. In April 2013, however, this figure was revised down, to 6.3%, by the Central Statistical Bureau, which also issued revised data for the years 2006-10 that indicated generally weaker economic growth than had previously been reported. In 2011, according to the IMF, higher oil revenues resulted in increases in the current account and fiscal surpluses to 41% and 30% of GDP, respectively. Growth in non-oil economic activity was moderate, according to the IMF, at an estimated 4.5%, while inflation increased marginally, from 4% in 2010 to nearly 4.8% in 2011. The IMF noted, however, that rising public sector wage and pension costs were increasing pressure on the public finances in the medium term, and that, despite recording strong fiscal and external surpluses for 13 consecutive years, Kuwait fared 'relatively low in international comparisons as regards the quality of its infrastructure, health, and education, when compared with countries with similar

GDP per capita level'. In addition, as ongoing political tensions and legislative bottlenecks continued to hamper economic policy-making and the implementation of key capital projects, the IMF stated that the 'overarching issue for Kuwait is the ability of the government and parliament to push an agenda that improves the investment climate and promotes sustainable and inclusive growth'. According to the *Middle East Economic Digest*, the Kuwaiti Government awarded projects to the value of US $10,400m. in 2011, a significant decline compared with $14,800m. in 2010, from pending projects of some $115,000m.

With the election of a new National Assembly in December 2012, there were initial hopes of progress on economic reform. Infrastructure projects such as the Subiya causeway (see Transport and Communications) and a new petroleum refinery and power station at al-Zour (see Petroleum and Natural Gas, and Electricity) were approved, and in January 2013 the Public Authority for Housing Welfare was looking to appoint advisers for the development of major housing projects. The Government also introduced new legislation intended to improve the business environment (Kuwait having fallen to 82nd place in the World Bank's *Doing Business 2013* survey), and in March the Assembly approved a KD 2,000m. fund to support small and medium-sized enterprises. However, populist measures put forward during the election campaign—including the cancellation of interest on citizens' debts and support for higher public sector salaries and benefits—were likely to exert upward pressure on overall spending at the expense of growth-promoting capital expenditure. In May the IMF advised that the Government should consider funding investment projects through debt issuance, rather than relying on petroleum revenue, which would also provide a buffer against oil price fluctuations and support the Central Bank's monetary policy. As a result of its sizeable budget surpluses, Kuwait has had one of the lowest levels of general government debt among the GCC countries. However, the IMF warned that rapidly rising public expenditure could overtake the Government's income from hydrocarbons by 2017. The IMF meanwhile estimated real GDP growth at 6.6% in 2012, but projected a much lower figure of 1.1% for 2013.

Following another dissolution of the National Assembly in June 2013, the potential political volatility again threatened to stall further public investment and economic reform.

PETROLEUM AND NATURAL GAS

Kuwait's proven recoverable reserves of petroleum were estimated at 101,500m. barrels at the end of 2012, and the petroleum sector remains the most important contributor to the country's GDP. Income from petroleum sales has been channelled mainly to five areas: industrial diversification, the development of substantial social service provision, the creation of the FGF, overseas investment, and aid to poorer countries through the Kuwait Fund for Arab Economic Development (KFAED).

In 1938 the Kuwait Oil Co (KOC), operated jointly by the Anglo-Persian Oil Co (subsequently British Petroleum Co PLC—BP) and the Gulf Oil Corpn, discovered a large oilfield at Burgan, about 40 km south of the town of Kuwait. The Second World War delayed development until after 1945, but by 1956 Kuwait's annual production had increased to 54m. metric tons, at that time the largest in the Middle East. Further fields were discovered, notably at Raudhatain, north of Kuwait, and annual production had reached over 148m. tons by 1972. To handle this vast production, a huge tanker port was constructed at Mina al-Ahmadi, not far from the Burgan field. Kuwait was the first Arab petroleum-producing state to achieve complete control of its own output, buying out Gulf Oil and BP in March 1975 for approximately £32m.

Kuwait was also the first within the Organization of the Petroleum Exporting Countries (OPEC) to restrict petroleum production for reasons of conservation. Until December 1976, when Kuwait (together with 10 other OPEC countries) decided to raise petroleum prices by 10% (compared with a 5% increase by Saudi Arabia and the United Arab Emirates—UAE), the country was generally regarded as moderate with regard to oil pricing. Subsequently it became increasingly 'hawkish', and during 1979–80 Kuwait was one of the first to set still higher prices every time that Saudi Arabia raised its prices in an attempt to achieve some kind of parity within OPEC. From 1972 Kuwait's annual petroleum production was around 3.0%–4.5% of world petroleum output. After 1982 the oil glut and the implementation of OPEC quota allocations led to greater fluctuations in output (although, in common with most OPEC members, Kuwait tended to exceed its quotas).

Meanwhile, the petroleum industry was reorganized in 1980, when the Kuwait Petroleum Corpn (KPC) was established to co-ordinate the four companies involved: KOC, the Kuwait National Petroleum Co (KNPC), the Petrochemical Industries Co (PIC) and the Kuwait Oil Tanker Co (KOTC). This led to the centralization of oil sales and improved Kuwait's market competitiveness. (By the early 1990s KPC was the 12th largest petroleum company in the world, and the sale of KPC stocks of oil was vital in supporting the Kuwaiti community in exile during the Iraqi occupation.)

In August 1990 Kuwait's OPEC production quota was fixed at 1.5m. barrels per day (b/d), but the invasion by Iraq meant that output averaged 1.065m. b/d for that year. Following liberation from Iraqi occupation in February 1991, it was estimated that 800 of the country's 950 oil wells had been damaged, some 600 having been set alight by Iraqi troops shortly before their retreat. The rehabilitation of the petroleum sector became the Government's highest economic priority, and Kuwait argued persistently within OPEC for a rise in the production ceiling and an increase in the country's quota, in order to offset losses and finance reconstruction. By June about 140 of the burning wells had been capped, and by late July onshore production of crude petroleum had resumed at a level of 115,000 b/d, while offshore production from fields in the Neutral/Partitioned Zone was estimated at 70,000 b/d. Exports of petroleum had also resumed by late July. By mid-1992 production exceeded 1m. b/d, and output was projected to reach 1.5m. b/d by 1993 and 2m. b/d thereafter. In June 1993 a meeting of OPEC oil ministers was obliged to exempt Kuwait from an agreement on production quotas, effectively allowing it to increase production to 2m. b/d in the third quarter of that year. In September this allocation was confirmed for a further six-month period. Kuwait rejected suggestions that it was seriously jeopardizing its reserves by forcing such a rapid rise in output. Meanwhile, the major work of repairing infrastructure had been completed. By 1997 capacity was 2.4m. b/d, and in November of that year Kuwait's OPEC quota was 2.19m. b/d. In March 1998, however, in response to declining world prices (and in conjunction with other major petroleum producers), output was reduced by 125,000 b/d. Another downward adjustment was made in July; and from April 1999 a further reduction in OPEC quotas meant that Kuwait's production quota was cut by 144,000 b/d, to 1.836m. b/d.

Petroleum prices improved dramatically in the second half of 1999, and at OPEC meetings in March and June 2000 Kuwait's production quota was increased to 1.98m. b/d and 2.037m. b/d, respectively. Petroleum prices remained at a high level thereafter, but entered a period of instability with the international crisis that followed the suicide attacks on the US mainland in September 2001. Average output was 2.20m. b/d in 1999 and 2.17m. b/d in 2000. In 2001 two further reductions in Kuwait's OPEC production quota were agreed—the second, to 1.7m. b/d, being effective from January 2002. With effect from 1 February 2003, Kuwait's production quota was raised to 1.97m. b/d. Petroleum prices increased strongly in late 2002 and early 2003, reflecting uncertainty regarding supplies in the event of a US-led military campaign in Iraq. Amid further significant increases in prices during 2004, from August Kuwait's production quota was increased to 2.09m. b/d, and further rises, to 2.17m. b/d and 2.21m. b/d, respectively, took effect from November 2004 and March 2005. The quota was increased again, to 2.25m. b/d, from July 2005. Average production during 2005 was 2.69m. b/d, according to industry sources. OPEC reduced Kuwait's quota by 100,000 b/d from November 2006 and by 42,000 b/d from February 2007, stating that supplies were well in excess of actual demand. Average production was 2.74m. b/d in 2006 and 2.66m. b/d in 2007. Output increased to 2.79m. b/d in 2008, although OPEC reduced members' quotas from November, and again from January 2009, in response to a sharp decline in prices in the wake of the global financial crisis and ensuing economic downturn. Production in 2009 decreased to 2.51m. b/d, reflecting further reductions to OPEC quotas, but increased marginally, to 2.54m. b/d, in 2010. In 2011 Kuwait's average production increased to 2.88m. b/d (considerably above its official quota of 2.2m. b/d), reaching 3m. b/d in November, to compensate for market shortages resulting from disruption in Libya. Output again increased significantly in 2012, to 3.13m. b/d.

A major feature of the Government's petroleum development plans has been the Project Kuwait initiative, intended to facilitate foreign investment in the oil sector as part of a long-term programme to expand Kuwait's production capacity. First formulated in 1997, the scheme envisaged a significant increase in petroleum production with the assistance of international oil companies under operating services agreements. However, with Kuwait's Constitution barring foreign ownership of the country's natural resources, the plan has remained controversial and projects have been subject to political delay. In February 2010 the Amir approved the establishment of a Supreme Petroleum Council (SPC), which was to serve as the industry's highest decision-making authority. In November KPC announced plans to invest US $90,000m. in the period to 2015, with the aim of increasing production capacity to 3.5m. b/d by 2015 and to 4m. b/d by 2020. The programme would include the construction of a new refinery and the upgrading of existing ones, expenditure on petroleum investments overseas, improvements to the tanker fleet, and the launching of major petrochemical projects. Meanwhile, it was reported that KOC had conducted a study revealing an increase in crude petroleum reserves of 12,000m. barrels from the Burgan field, and that in 2010 the company had awarded contracts worth more than $11,000m. to foreign companies. Also in 2010 Kuwait and Iraq began talks on the development of oilfields straddling their border.

There are three oil refineries in Kuwait: at Mina al-Ahmadi (the largest), built in 1946; at Mina al-Abdullah, built in 1958; and at Shuaiba, completed in 1969. The refineries were badly damaged during the Iraqi occupation, but resumed operations following repair work in the early 1990s. An explosion at Shuaiba in 2006 led to a partial shutdown of the facility, putting pressure on the Government to hasten construction of a planned new US $15,000m. refinery to be sited at al-Zour. However, the tender process was twice cancelled, in 2007 and in 2009. In June 2010 a parliamentary committee approved a bill allowing shareholding companies to build oil refineries, and in June 2011 the SPC authorized construction of the 615,000-b/d al-Zour facility. The SPC also approved proposals to upgrade the Mina al-Ahmadi and Mina al-Abdullah refineries. In early 2012 KNPC invited companies to submit pre-qualification applications for the new refinery and the upgrade projects, and in December it signed a project management consultancy contract for the al-Zour facility with the international engineering company AMEC. The Swiss-based firm Foster Wheeler was awarded the consultancy contract for the upgrade projects. In May 2013 KNPC signed a further agreement with Daelim Industrial of the Republic of Korea (South Korea) for the expansion of sulphur processing facilities at the Mina al-Ahmadi refinery.

Mina al-Ahmadi port is the country's main oil export outlet. Kuwait also has oil export terminals at Mina al-Abdullah, Shuaiba and Mina Saud, with a new terminal planned for Bubiyan island to handle increased production from the northern fields (see also Transport and Communications).

A further development in Kuwait's petroleum industry has been the expansion of upstream and downstream interests overseas. Upstream, Kuwait has acquired equity interests in production concessions in several countries through the Kuwait Foreign Petroleum Exploration Co (KUFPEC), which was established in 1981 as a subsidiary of KPC. Downstream, KPC and Kuwait Petroleum International (KPI, established in 1983) have been acquiring facilities for the overseas distribution, marketing and retail of Kuwait's refined products since the 1980s. By 2008 these facilities included refineries in the Netherlands and Italy, and petrol stations across Western Europe. Furthermore, Kuwait has been keen to acquire downstream assets and develop joint venture arrangements in high-growth markets in Asia, particularly the People's Republic of China. In March 2011 China gave KPC formal approval to build a US $9,000m. oil refinery and petrochemical facility in Guangdong Province, in a joint venture with the China Petroleum and Chemical Corpn.

Kuwait produced 14,500m. cu m of natural gas in 2012, with reserves at the end of that year estimated at 1,800,000m. cu m. Output has previously been limited by the absence of any known reserves independent of petroleum. Much of the gas produced has been flared to facilitate oil production, or reinjected to maximize petroleum output by maintaining pressure in the reservoir. In 2006 KOC announced a major non-associated gas discovery, as well as up to 13,000m. barrels of light oil, in two fields in the north of the country. However, since the gas discoveries would not cover all of Kuwait's requirements, plans remained under consideration for the import of gas either through pipelines from Iraq (subject to security factors) and Iran (with which an agreement was reached in 2008), and through liquefied natural gas (LNG) shipment (deals with Qatar and a subsidiary of the Shell Group were signed in the first half of 2009). In November 2008 UAE-based Petrofac International won a contract worth US $544m. to build a major pipeline to transport gas from Kuwait's northern fields to a fractionation plant at the Mina al-Ahmadi refinery. In June 2010 KOC awarded a $900m. contract to Daelim Industrial to build a fourth gas production line at Mina al-Ahmadi.

The development of the non-associated gas reserves to meet urgent domestic needs has proved problematic. In February 2010 KOC signed a new enhanced technical services agreement with Shell for development of the Jurassic gasfields. The accord, which linked fees to output levels, marked a turning point for foreign involvement in sector projects, where difficulties in negotiating agreements have traditionally proved a deterrent. In April of that year KPC signed supply agreements with Shell and Vitol of Switzerland to import LNG to Kuwait in order to help meet demand during peak periods in 2010–13. In June 2011 the Kuwait Energy Co signed two 20-year gas development and production service contracts for the Siba and Mansuriya fields in Iraq (the first time that a Kuwaiti company had become involved in Iraq's energy sector since the 1990 invasion). In the same month KOC awarded Italy's Saipem a US $900m. contract to build a gas booster station in western Kuwait. In 2011 Al-Khafji Joint Operations Co, a joint venture between KPC and Saudi Aramco, began to develop the offshore Dorra field of non-associated gas, despite long-standing disagreements with Iran over the field's ownership.

In March 2013 KOC announced that it had identified a commercially viable shale gas deposit and was conducting studies into the viability of extraction.

INDUSTRY

Although petroleum-related activities contribute the overwhelming proportion of Kuwait's total industrial output, the Government has tried to foster other industries in order to diversify the economy and to provide alternative sources of employment. The major branch of manufacturing has been the production of building materials and related projects such as aluminium extrusion. Fertilizer manufacturers also have a substantial production capacity, mainly in the form of urea and ammonia products.

Unlike its neighbours, Kuwait hesitated to undertake heavy industrial projects, concerned both for their viability and for the excess of foreign labour that they would involve. Instead, it favoured joint projects with Bahrain, Saudi Arabia and other Gulf countries. In 1996 the local Kuwait Industries Co applied for a licence to establish a 900,000-metric-tons-per-year alumina factory to supply producers in the UAE and Bahrain. In the same year the US company Raytheon Corpn secured approval to build a 230,000-tons-per-year aluminium smelter with foreign and local partners. Both projects were estimated to cost about US $1,000m.

The construction industry has benefited from extensive infrastructural development since the early 1970s. During that decade major projects were carried out by foreign contractors, but in 1981 the National Housing Authority announced that 80% of future housing contracts would be awarded to local firms. In other sectors of construction, however, foreign companies continued to dominate. The economic recession of the mid-1980s damaged the industry, and the collapse of petroleum prices in 1986 exacerbated the situation. In 1988, however, there was a distinct recovery, particularly in the private residential sector, where expansion was stimulated by the availability of cheap bank credits, as well as the completion of highway improvements in suburban Kuwait. In the aftermath of the 1990–91 Iraqi occupation, the Kuwaiti Government worked with international construction companies, in particular US firms, to rebuild the emirate's infrastructure. By early 2005 several major infrastructure projects (such as a proposed US $3,300m. tourist complex on Failaka island) and lower-profile construction schemes (including the $320m. Mahaboola residential and luxury resort development) were being planned, with private investment playing a key role. In 2006 the Government was presented with the master plan for the KD 25,000m. Madinat al-Hareer new city scheme—the largest construction project in the region to date. This envisaged a new city to be developed over a 25-year period on the Subiya peninsula, the centrepiece of which would be a 1,000-m tower (by far the world's tallest). However, it was reported in early 2011 that Kuwait Municipality had signed an agreement with Canada's Malone Given Parsons to redesign the master plan. Another major construction project, Sabah al-Ahmad Future City, scheduled for completion in 2015, was expected to include more than 9,000 housing units for Kuwaiti nationals. The waiting list for government-subsidized housing in Kuwait had grown to more than 100,000 by 2013, and in March the Government announced plans to build 174,000 new houses and three separate urban centres by 2020.

In the petrochemicals sector, KPC and the Dow Chemical Co announced plans in 2007 for a joint venture to develop a major polyethylene complex. However, the Government withdrew from the venture in December 2008, following parliamentary opposition and in response to the decline in the petrochemicals market with the onset of the global economic downturn. In May 2012 a ruling by the International Court of Arbitration of the International Chamber of Commerce awarded Dow US $2,160m. in compensation for the cancellation of the project. In March 2013 a further ruling by the Court set the total then owed by the Petroleum Industries Co (PIC—the KPC subsidiary responsible for the contract) at $2,480m., to include interest and costs; and in May Dow announced that it had received a cash settlement of $2,190m. from PIC.

ELECTRICITY

Kuwait's industrial and demographic growth have necessitated great increases in power generation. By the end of 1987 the country's power stations had a total installed capacity of 5,230 MW. Another power station, with an installed capacity of 2,511 MW, came into full production at al-Zour South in 1988. Substantial damage to power facilities resulted from the Iraqi occupation; al-Zour South was the least affected. At mid-1993 installed generating capacity remained 30% below the pre-invasion level of 7,100 MW, although Shuaiba North was the only station not to have resumed operations. By 2000, following the completion of a new, 2,400-MW plant at Subiya, Kuwait's total installed capacity had increased to 9,298 MW. In 2005 Germany's Siemens completed the construction of the 1,000-MW al-Zour South gas turbine power plant. Two new power projects—al-Zour North (2,400 MW) and al-Zour South II (1,000 MW)—were also planned. The contract for the installation of a new 300/132-kV Green Zone West substation near Kuwait City was awarded to Siemens in 2006. Mitsubishi of Japan was awarded the contract for the new Qurain West substation.

In mid-2006 Kuwait suffered widespread electricity and water shortages. It became apparent that deficiencies in the network had reduced the power available for transmission, and that Kuwait's outdated tender regulations had also deterred the development of additional generating facilities. In early 2007 the Government announced that it would increase total installed capacity by an additional 8,000 MW (5,000 MW from conventional supplies and the remainder from emergency sources). Contracts worth US $1,000m. were awarded to Alghanim International Contracting and Trading for the fast-track installation of nearly 1,000 MW of emergency capacity at three existing plants. A further contract was awarded to Kharafi National. Meanwhile, work on the al-Zour North facility and a new 1,500-MW plant at Subiya was to be retendered, and the conversion of the al-Zour South plant was to go ahead despite limited contractor interest. In May 2007, as further power cuts were reported, the Government invited bids to upgrade the Doha East power and desalination plants, and a consortium led by Mitsui was awarded a US $1,270m. contract to redevelop the Shuaiba North power facility. The new tender for the Subiya power plant was issued in early 2009: the $2,650m. contract was awarded later in the year to a consortium comprising the US-based General Electric and South Korea's Hyundai Heavy Industries. In March 2010 a consortium of international consultants was appointed to advise the PTB on the procurement of Kuwait's first independent water and power project—a 1,500-MW plant to be located at al-Zour. Since the electricity sector had traditionally been closed to private developers, the progress of this project was deemed an important test case for foreign investment in the country, and for other power schemes that had been subject to delay or revision. In mid-2010, with power consumption approaching peak production capacity, the Government announced that the construction of the Subiya power plant would be expedited to provide some extra capacity by mid-2011 and full capacity in 2012. The Government also approved the proposed independent power project at al-Zour North. Although the plan was rejected by the National Assembly in June 2012, following accusations of irregularities in the tendering process, a contract was none the less awarded to a consortium led by GDF SUEZ Energy International in January 2013.

In June 2010 the Ministry of Electricity and Water announced plans to build a US $650m. solar power plant with a capacity of 1,250 MW, to be located in the Abdali area, as part of its public-private partnership development programme. Also in 2010 the Government signed agreements with France, the USA, Japan and Russia on nuclear co-operation, and stated its intention to build four nuclear power plants by 2022, each with a capacity of 1,000 MW. However, following the nuclear accident at Fukushima, Japan, in 2011, the Government announced that it would abandon the pursuit of civil nuclear power.

TRANSPORT AND COMMUNICATIONS

In 2008 the Directorate-General of Civil Aviation announced plans for the expansion and modernization of Kuwait International Airport, which had first opened in 1980. The project, which includes the construction of a new airport terminal, will in its first phase increase handling capacity to 13m. passengers per year, and allows for an increase to 25m. passengers annually; future development would achieve annual passenger handling capacity of 55m.

Kuwait Airways Corpn (KAC) is the national airline. In 2005 a private commercial airline, Jazeera Airways, was awarded a licence to start services. KAC had long been scheduled for privatization, and in January 2008 the National Assembly approved a law providing for its transformation into a private company. In July 2011 the first phase of the delayed sale was launched, with investors invited to bid for a 35% stake in the company. However, the sale was postponed in October that year, as the KAC privatization committee recommended that the company first be restructured. In January 2013 the National Assembly approved a new plan providing for a name change to Kuwait Airways Co, and for the 35% sale to private shareholders within three years.

In April 2012 Kuwait and Iraq agreed to resume direct flights for the first time since the 1990–91 Gulf crisis.

The KOTC was fully nationalized in 1979. Kuwait's two main container ports are at Shuwaikh and Shuaiba. Despite the severe damage caused by the Iraqi occupation, Shuaiba port resumed operations in March 1991. In 2007 the Kuwait Ports Authority awarded a contract for dredging work in the redevelopment of Shuwaikh port to Gulf Dredging and Contracting Development. Meanwhile, the Ministry of Public Works signed a contract with the China Harbour Engineering consortium to start the first phase of the Bubiyan island seaport development and to build the road and bridge access to the island. This project formed part of the Government's plan to develop the island into a free zone with an oil terminal. In 2010 a US $1,140m. contract for the construction of a container terminal and surrounding infrastructure on Bubiyan was awarded to South Korea's Hyundai Engineering and the local Kharafi Group, and construction work on the new Mubarak al-Kabir Port began in early 2011. However, Iraq's concerns that its access to shipping routes would be adversely affected by the new port, which is sited directly opposite its Faw peninsula, provoked some tension in 2011–12.

At the end of 2012 Kuwait's merchant fleet numbered 155 vessels, with a total displacement of 2,479,500 gross registered tons.

Plans for the construction of a regional north–south railway network connecting Kuwait with other members of the GCC have progressed, with completion of the project envisaged by 2017. The tender for the Subiya causeway, to stretch across the Gulf from Kuwait City to Subiya, was again delayed in 2006 after environmental issues and planning changes forced revisions to the design. Following the approval of the new development plan in early 2010 (see Introduction), there was evidence of some progress in the tendering of long-awaited projects. The bidding process was reopened for the causeway, and construction of the proposed metro system on a build-operate-transfer basis came under review. In February 2011 the Ministry of Public Works launched the Jahra Road Development Project in western Kuwait, as part of the effort to improve the country's motorway network. In October 2012 the Ministry approved the award of the long-awaited contract for the Subiya causeway to the Hyundai consortium of South Korea.

In 2005 there were two mobile phone companies operating in the country—National Mobile Telecommunications Co (Wataniya Telecom—formed in 1999) and Zain Kuwait (formerly the Mobile Telecommunications Co—MTC). In 2006 the Government and National Assembly approved the establishment of a third mobile phone operator, and, following an initial public offering, VIVA launched operations in December 2008. Wataniya's majority owner is Qatar Telecommunications Corpn, while VIVA is 26% owned by Saudi Telecom. In mid-2010 India's Bharti Airtel acquired Zain's African assets in a US $9,000m. deal. In late 2011 the Saudi Kingdom Holding Co and Bahrain Telecommunications Co withdrew from negotiations to acquire a joint shareholding in Zain's Saudi subsidiary. In October 2012 the Kuwait Investment Authority (KIA) sold its 24% stake in Wataniya to Qatar Telecommunications. In June 2013, shortly before its dissolution, the National Assembly approved a draft law to establish an independent telecommunications commission to oversee the sector and regulate mobile, landline and broadband services.

AGRICULTURE AND FISHERIES

The scarcity of water in Kuwait means that little grain is produced and most of the country's food has to be imported. Efforts have been made to increase the area under vegetable production, and a considerable amount has been invested in the development of methods of using treated effluent for irrigation purposes. The Government has also encouraged animal husbandry, the main activity of the Bedouin before the development of the oilfields. Nevertheless, by 2010 agriculture and fishing contributed only about 0.3% of Kuwait's GDP, the principal agricultural crops being tomatoes, cucumbers and gherkins, potatoes, aubergines and dates. In 2011, according to FAO data, there were an estimated 35,000 cattle, 470,000 sheep, 178,000 goats and 33.0m. poultry.

Fishing, particularly of prawns and shrimps, is widely practised. A 20-year plan to develop the industry was announced in 1987, when local production was sufficient to satisfy only 25% of domestic demand. The total catch in 2011 was estimated at 4,860 metric tons.

FOREIGN TRADE

Kuwait's foreign trade is dominated by exports of crude petroleum and petroleum products, which generally account for more than 90% of the value of export earnings each year. According to the IMF, total export earnings in 1990, the year of the Iraqi invasion, fell to KD 2,031.4m. (of which petroleum accounted for KD 1,842.0m.), from KD 3,378.0m. in 1989, and in 1991 the total exports slumped to KD 309.4m. The conflict left Kuwait's petroleum production facilities severely damaged, and it was not possible to resume exports approaching pre-war levels in 1991. Export revenue recovered to KD 1,931.1m. in 1992, with the petroleum sector contributing KD 1,824.9m. (94.5% of the total). By 1997 total export earnings had increased to KD 4,314.3m., of which petroleum accounted for KD 4,085.4m. Fluctuations in the price of petroleum were more than offset by an improvement in market conditions by 2003. The ongoing rise in petroleum prices and a sharp increase in trade with Iraq led to exports valued at KD 8,428.1m. in 2004 (petroleum accounting for KD 7,861.1m.), KD 13,101.6m. in 2005 (KD 12,392.6m. from petroleum) and KD 16,166.7m. (KD 15,430.7m. from petroleum) in 2006. Reflecting even higher global oil prices, exports increased to KD 17,688.7m. (KD 16,845.7m. from petroleum) in 2007 and to KD 23,362.4m. (KD 22,200.1m. from petroleum) in 2008. The sharp reduction in world oil prices (and associated OPEC quota reductions), meant that export earnings declined by more than 30% in 2009, to KD 14,871m. (KD 13,415m. from petroleum). However, exports subsequently recovered to KD 19,195m. in 2010, and reached KD 28,556m. (KD 26,689m. from petroleum) in 2011. Imports increased to KD 6,061.5m. in 2007 and further to KD 6,678.7m. in 2008, before contracting to KD 5,852m. in 2009, following a decline in domestic demand. The value of imports increased to KD 6,428m. in 2010, and to KD 6,972m. in 2011. According to the Central Bank, the current account surplus widened significantly in 2012, to reach KD 22,174m.—equivalent to almost 50% of 2011 GDP. Exports rose to KD 33,389m., reflecting buoyant petroleum sales, while imports fell to KD 6,289m.

A Greater Arab Free Trade Area initiative implemented within GCC countries became effective in January 2005, eliminating import duties (further to the introduction of a 5% common external tariff in early 2003). As part of increased efforts to foster trade relations outside the region, the GCC states agreed to negotiate free trade agreements on a collective basis with foreign countries and unions.

BANKING

Although Kuwait's banking sector flourished in the early 1980s, the collapse of the Souk al-Manakh in 1982 (see Capital Market), the uncertainties caused by the Iran–Iraq War and the problems associated with the declining price of oil led to severe difficulties in the middle part of that decade. In 1985, as the banks suffered a burgeoning debt crisis, the National Bank of Kuwait (NBK—the country's largest) was the only bank to record a year-on-year increase in net profits. A series of measures approved by the Government in 1986 facilitated a rescue programme whereby debtors would repay as much as they could afford and the Government would pay the remainder of the debt. By 1989 the majority of the commercial banks in Kuwait remained dependent on this scheme for debt-restructuring.

Following the Iraqi invasion of Kuwait in 1990, all Kuwaiti bank deposits were frozen, paralysing the operations of the country's banks. The Bank of England allowed individuals and organizations from Kuwait to operate in the United Kingdom, but all of the banks had to seek permission from the Bank of England to pay out Kuwait-controlled assets.

After liberation NBK was the only bank in a position to participate in the reconstruction process, although Kuwaiti banks did recommence domestic operations. In March 1991 some branches of banks began to reopen, mainly to distribute the Government's cash grant to Kuwaiti citizens who had remained in the country during the occupation. In the following month an Amiri decree instructed the banks to cancel debts totalling US $4,900m., thereby clearing the debts of 180,000 people. As a result, many local bad debts that had been incurred in the stock market crisis of the mid-1980s were cancelled. In 1992 it was announced that the Government was to buy the entire domestic loan portfolio of the domestic banking system, covering credits to residents worth $20,400m. In 2001, as part of its programme of economic liberalization, the Government approved bills that would permit foreign banks to own controlling interests in Kuwaiti financial institutions, and that would reduce taxation on net profits paid by foreign companies operating in Kuwait from 55% to 25%. In 2002 a Secretariat-General of Economic Reforms was formed. In 2004 the Central Bank approved legislation that would allow foreign banks to open branches in Kuwait.

From January 2003 Kuwait pegged the dinar to the US dollar, as part of the GCC plan to create a single currency. However, having revalued the dinar by 1% against the dollar in May 2006, in March 2007 the Central Bank again revalued the currency by 0.37%, abandoning the dollar peg mechanism and instead pegging the dinar to a weighted basket of (undisclosed) international currencies. According to the Central Bank, the change of policy was made in response to higher inflation arising from the weakness of the US dollar against most other major currencies. The depreciation of the dollar against the euro and sterling had led to a substantial weakening of the dinar against those currencies. In the following month the Central Bank also announced a reduction in interest rates, in an effort to curb excessive currency speculation. The economic convergence criteria for a monetary union were agreed at a GCC summit in Abu Dhabi, UAE, in December 2005, and in January 2008 the GCC launched its common market. An accord on Gulf Monetary Union was signed in June 2009 by Bahrain, Kuwait, Qatar and Saudi Arabia (Oman and the UAE had previously withdrawn from the proposed monetary union), and was approved by the 30th meeting of the GCC Supreme Council, held in Kuwait in December. (Kuwait's National Assembly had meanwhile ratified the agreement in the same month.)

The Government took several measures to preserve banking stability in the wake of the global financial crisis that began in 2008, including the lowering of interest rates, large liquidity injections, a guarantee by the authorities of customer deposits at local banks, and a bank recapitalization plan. According to the IMF, the banking sector remained generally sound, but risks associated with banks' exposure to asset markets and distressed investment companies had emerged. Kuwait's banks generally maintained a relatively good level of profitability in 2008. However, Gulf Bank (the country's third largest bank) was forced to reveal losses of US $1,400m., mostly from derivative trading. In late 2008 the Central Bank halted trading in Gulf Bank and ordered a rescue plan, with shareholders providing 68% of new capital and the KIA offering the rest. The Government's economic stimulus package (the financial stability law) of April 2009 included measures to support the financial system and to promote bank lending to the economy (with the state guaranteeing 50% of any loans).

It was clear from results posted by domestic banks for 2009 that the need to increase provisions against non-performing loans had reduced profitability. In contrast to Gulf Bank's difficulties, NBK was a notably strong performer, recording a 4% increase in profits in 2009; its activities included the purchase of a controlling stake in Boubyan Bank, with the aim of acquiring a strong Islamic banking franchise in the domestic market. In February 2010, in response to decreasing inflationary pressures in 2009, the Central Bank reduced its discount rate to 2.5%, in order to increase monetary supply and promote private sector activity. Although the economic stimulus package had protected banks against large-scale default and had strengthened their balance sheets, members of the National Assembly argued that it had not ameliorated the situation of indebted individuals. In early 2010 the Government rejected a controversial bill, already approved by the Assembly, that would have required the purchase by the Government of consumer loan portfolios from the banks, the rescheduling of loans and the cancellation of interest payments. Instead, the Government proposed to increase the capital of the insolvency fund to assist those citizens who were struggling to repay loans. According to the IMF, which supported the Government's stance, the profits of local banks increased by about 70% in 2010, owing to a decline in loan loss provisions, and capitalization strengthened further. However, the IMF did have concerns about the concentration of loan portfolios in areas such as property. Following Central Bank instructions, banks continued their precautionary provisioning policies in 2010 to cover potentially risky exposures. The sector remained generally profitable in 2011, and banks' equity prices fell by only 5%—a much lower drop compared with the overall index. Following criticism from the IMF for weakness in financial monitoring, the Government adopted draft anti-corruption legislation in September 2011 that related to money-laundering and financial disclosure. In early 2012 the Central Bank introduced new lending rules to allow banks further to boost their liquidity and lending capability in support of economic development projects.

In October 2012 the Central Bank reduced its discount rate to 2%, with the aim of both stimulating economic growth in the non-oil sectors of the economy and supporting the competitiveness of the currency. In April 2013 the National Assembly approved a bill to cancel consumer loan portfolios taken out by Kuwaitis between January 2002 and April 2008, despite the Government's rejection of similar legislation in 2010 (see above). The measure established a state-financed Family Fund to purchase the loans from traditional banks, waive the interest and reschedule repayments. With 47,000 eligible Kuwaitis, the Ministry of Finance considered that implementation of the debt relief plan would cost KD 744m. Government officials and economists continued to voice concerns about the long-term sustainability of the scheme, but National Assembly members justified such action on the grounds that the Central Bank had not been sufficiently strict with regard to lending practices before 2008.

CAPITAL MARKET

In 1952 Kuwait had established what became, prior to the Iraqi invasion in 1990, the world's 12th largest stock exchange. The amount of capital holders seeking investment outlets in Kuwait, and the innate entrepreneurial spirit of locals, generally pushed the prices of shares far above their real value. In 1978, in an attempt to stem this trend, the Government sanctioned the reduction in nominal value of shares to one dinar, a move that resulted in a split of share values to 10%–13% of their previous value and thus broadened the base of the market.

Alongside the official stock market, the unofficial Souk al-Manakh also developed. After 1978 many Kuwaitis had invested in Iraq, and, as a result of the Iran–Iraq War, a severe cash-flow crisis emerged in Kuwait. In 1982 the ensuing liquidity shortage was particularly severe for the Souk al-Manakh. The unofficial market had been based on the use of post-dated cheques and the hope of continuously rising share prices. The system collapsed, as smaller creditors presented their post-dated cheques prematurely (perfectly legal under Kuwaiti law) at a time when many dealers were unable to pay. The collapse of the Souk al-Manakh initiated a major crisis in Kuwait's financial system, the impact of which was felt for several years.

Government measures to alleviate the crisis involved the immediate formation of the Kuwait Clearing Co to register and process all cheques involved, and the establishment of a KD 500m. fund to protect, and pay, the smaller debtors whose investors were bankrupt. In 1983 the Government urged the settlement of debts at the market price at the time of transaction, and set a maximum premium of 25% on post-dated cheques. It also appointed an arbitration panel to revalue the debts of the 17 leading dealers in the Souk al-Manakh. These accounted for about US $78,000m., or 82% of the estimated total of outstanding debts at the time of the crisis, and the dealers' assets were valued at between 20% and 30% of their liabilities. A new investment company was established, with capital of KD 300m. (in which the Government had a 40% share), to convert the debtors' non-liquid assets into payment for the creditors. In 1984 the Government announced further financial measures to resolve the crisis, including the division of assets into three categories. Bonds to repay creditors were issued, and, of the 254 people referred to receivership, 88 were declared bankrupt, three restored their solvency, and 163 reached agreements with their creditors.

The Souk al-Manakh was closed in November 1984, and trading in shares was thereafter restricted to the official stock exchange and to a parallel market that it operated. To avoid a repetition of the Souk al-Manakh crisis, measures were introduced to limit the activities of brokers on the official market. Before being allowed on the floor, brokers were required to pay a registration fee and provide a guarantee for KD 1m., and a percentage of brokers' commissions had to be paid to the exchange. By January 1985 creditors who had been owed money by Souk al-Manakh defaulters had received cash and bonds totalling KD 759m., accounting for about three-quarters of the net debts. At the end of 1987, however, 17% of the debts resulting from the collapse of the Souk al-Manakh remained outstanding.

The Government bore the brunt of the crisis, and was forced to inject large sums into the banking system to restore liquidity. In late 1985 the Minister of Finance and Economy made the following recommendations: 33 companies should be dissolved; a number of the remaining 47 companies should be merged; and, on behalf of the Government, the Kuwait Investment Co was to purchase the companies that closed; additionally, companies registered in the Gulf but falling outside the jurisdiction of Kuwait were urged to comply with the recommendations. At this time, 24 of the 36 companies that had closed and were under consideration for purchase by the Government had incurred losses exceeding 50% of the paid-up capital invested in them. It was estimated that the scheme had cost the Government approximately KD 121m. by mid-1986. In 1989 it was reported that stock market activity was disappointing, and that measures to deregulate the stock market to some extent were to be introduced before the end of the year in the hope that a reduction in restrictions would encourage investors. It was also announced that the Souk al-Manakh stock exchange was to be reopened in June of that year, to allow trading in companies that had failed to meet the minimum capital requirements of the official stock exchange.

From 1988 the Government permitted citizens of all GCC member states to purchase shares on the KSE. (Previously only Kuwaiti citizens had been permitted to do so.) The exchange was opened to international firms for the first time in 1992. In 1995 the KSE became the most active share market in the Arab world. Strong corporate earnings, excess liquidity and the privatization policy launched by the KIA maintained the buoyancy of the stock market, and in mid-1997 it was reported that the average market price of shares had increased by some 30% since the start of the year. The privatization programme had begun in 1994, and by early 1997 the KIA had sold shares to the value of KD 653m. It was announced at that time that a further KD 1,000m. worth of shares were available for sale at current prices. By early 1999, however, the stock market was in decline, as a result of the regional economic downturn, the absence of reforms to reduce the budget deficit, and poor company results for 1998; and in November 1999 it reached its lowest level since 1996. In 1998, meanwhile, legislation was adopted further rescheduling debts arising from the collapse of the Souk al-Manakh in 1982, and in 2000 a draft law was approved allowing foreign investment on the stock exchange; combined with the higher level of petroleum prices, this was expected to lead to a recovery in share values. By 2002, according to Central Bank figures, the value of traded shares reached KD 6,681.1m., and this increased markedly in 2003, to KD 16,253m. A decline in 2004, to KD 15,275.8m., was followed in 2005 by a dramatic rise, to KD 28,422.1m.

In February 2006 a regional stock market collapse was reflected in a decline in the KSE's performance index, which contracted by 10% in the first two financial quarters of the year. Although the exchange demonstrated comparative resilience in response to the crisis, which had a more devastating effect on neighbouring Gulf economies, the total value of shares traded fell, in line with the contraction in the market, to KD 17,280m. in 2006. In response, the KSE tightened its listing requirements, stipulating that shareholding companies must have paid-up capital of at least KD 10m. and have reported profits for two consecutive years exceeding 7.5% of the paid-up capital.

The KSE contracted sharply following the collapse of the US investment bank Lehman Brothers in September 2008. Trading was temporarily suspended, in an effort to curb the market decline and protect investors, and the Government instructed the KIA to establish a fund to invest in the KSE with an initial capital of some US $5,500m. Two investment companies—Global Investment House (GIH) and Investment Dar—defaulted on debt obligations in December 2008, and in April 2009 the KSE suspended trading in the shares of 36 listed companies (mostly investment companies, which had been most affected by the decline in the market) because of their failure to publish 2008 results within the maximum time limit. In December 2009 GIH agreed a debt restructuring deal with its creditors worth $1,700m. In June 2010 the Central Bank introduced tighter regulation of the sector in order to improve liquidity and leverage, including limiting the size of debts and foreign exposure in relation to capital. Earlier, in February, a Capital Market Law was approved by the National Assembly. This provided for the establishment of an independent Capital Market Authority (CMA), charged with regulating the KSE, ensuring transparency and preventing illegal practices. The financial situation of many investment companies remained precarious throughout 2010, as they continued to report significant losses (although at a lower level than in 2009) originating mostly from holdings in equities and property. The debt restructuring of some companies remained unresolved, and by mid-2010 two more investment firms—Gulfinvest International and Kuwait Finance and Investment Co—had defaulted. According to the Central Bank, the value of shares traded in 2010 declined to KD 12,526m., from KD 21,829m. in 2009. The KSE index fell further in early 2011, as a result of the unrest across the Middle East and North Africa, and in July it dropped to its lowest level since September 2004 in response to warnings by the Central Bank Governor of imbalances in the economy.

From mid-2011 investment companies were required to have separate licences for their lending and investment operations, as the Central Bank sought to eliminate regulatory overlap with the CMA. Companies involved in financing would henceforth be regulated by the Central Bank, while those dealing with investments and asset management would be overseen by the CMA. The latter continued in early 2012 to introduce measures designed to improve regulation, including restrictions on the concentration of investments in single entities and new procedures for company acquisitions. During 2012, with the assistance of HSBC Bank, plans to privatize the KSE progressed (with 50% to be sold in an initial public offering and 50% to be sold to listed companies), although there were reports by the end of the year that potential legal obstacles might delay completion. In May, meanwhile, the KSE inaugurated a new trading system and new index (Kuwait-15).

An IMF report in the first half of 2012 noted that the operations of investment companies continued to have financial stability implications, and that the resolution of their problems remained critical to improving investor confidence and growth in the financial sector. While there had been some initial progress in the restructuring of investment companies in 2009–10, the sector had suffered renewed setbacks because of adverse market conditions in 2011 and the re-emergence of global liquidity strains. In December 2011 GIH was forced to enter its second round of debt restructuring in two years; and in December 2012 it signed agreements with creditors on payments to the value of US $1,700m.

In December 2012 the Government introduced a new companies law that aimed to encourage investment. The legislation included the creation of a 'one-stop' process for the incorporation and licensing of new companies, as well as tougher corporate governance rules. Further measures in June 2013 provided for the establishment of an independent authority to promote investment opportunities.

PUBLIC FINANCE

The cumulative costs to the Kuwaiti Government of the 1990–91 Gulf crisis inevitably increased its budget deficits. By the end of July 1991 the cost to Kuwait of paying the expenses of Kuwaitis living abroad during the Iraqi occupation, and of financing Operation Desert Storm, had increased to US $22,000m. A further $6,000m.–$7,000m. was spent after liberation on stabilization measures, such as the cancellation of personal debts and cash grants to nationals who remained in Kuwait during the Iraqi occupation. The Government stated that it had no intention of making large-scale sales of investments to create revenue, but it was nevertheless reported in mid-1993 that the value of Kuwait's overseas investments had more than halved in the previous three years (see also Investment). At the end of 1991 a $5,500m. international loan to Kuwait was announced, together with export credit facilities worth the same amount with France, Japan, the Netherlands, the United Kingdom and the USA. Kuwait began repayments on the international loan in 1996.

In 1994 the National Assembly approved KD 3,500m. in extraordinary defence spending for 1992–2004, and the Government announced its intention to eliminate the budget deficit by 2000. Proposals to reduce the deficit included: an increase in customs fees; the imposition of a direct tax on commercial and industrial profits; welfare reforms; the gradual withdrawal of subsidies on public services; the ending of protectionism; and privatization through the divestment of public utilities. Such measures, coupled with increasing oil prices, did indeed result in surpluses from the 1999/2000 fiscal year.

A new fiscal year was introduced from 1 April 2001, replacing the 1 July to 30 June period. Revenues soon began to increase significantly as a result of the rising world oil prices. The budget for the 2006/07 financial year projected a deficit of KD 2,346.3m., based on a customarily conservative oil price of US $36 per barrel. However, the actual general budget that year recorded a surplus of KD 5,202.9m.—despite an increase in expenditure of 50.2% compared with the previous year. Total revenue was KD 15,509.3m., with total expenditure at KD 10,306.4m. In May 2006, meanwhile, the Ministry of Finance proposed the introduction of a flat rate of 10% income tax on both Kuwaitis and non-nationals working in the state; and the Government approved a draft law to reduce the 55% corporate tax levy imposed on the profits of foreign firms operating locally to 15%. The 2007/08 budget projected a deficit of KD 3,069.7m., again based on an oil price of $36 per barrel. Total expenditure was forecast at KD 11,300m., with revenue decreasing to KD 8,320.3m., reflecting an anticipated decline in international oil prices. By mid-2008, however, the petroleum price had risen to more than $140 per barrel (it peaked at $147 in July), and the budget surplus reached 40% of GDP in that year. The 2008/09 budget projected revenues of KD 12,700m. and expenditure of KD 18,970m., based on an average petroleum price of $50 a barrel.

For 2009/10, rather than follow an expansionary policy to stimulate the sluggish economy during the global downturn, the Government drafted a contractionary budget with a projected sharp decline in oil revenue based on a lower average price of US $35 per barrel. It envisaged total expenditure decreasing to KD 12,116m. and total revenue of KD 8,075m., leaving a KD 5,000m. deficit after mandatory transfers to the FGF. In April 2009, however, the Government announced its KD 1,500m. economic stimulus package to free up frozen credit markets, part-guarantee loans and extend selective assistance to the struggling investment sector.

The draft budget for 2010/11 projected increased expenditure of KD 16,300m., reversing the previous fiscal contraction. Revenue was projected to rise to KD 9,720m., based on a still-conservative petroleum price assumption of US $43 per barrel. The Government approved an allocation of KD 4,780m. for capital investment in 2010/11, as part of its new development plan to promote economic expansion and improve infrastructure. The development plan, which was approved by the National Assembly in January 2010, was to cover the period from 2010/11–2013/14, and was the first such plan to be published since 1986. It provided for estimated spending of KD 30,000m., with the aim of diversifying the economy away from oil, increasing the role of the private sector and streamlining bureaucracy. The plan envisaged the implementation of some long-delayed projects, such as the Madinat al-Hareer business hub, the Bubiyan port development, and a rail and metro system; as well as additional spending for new cities, for infrastructure and for social services—particularly within the health and education sectors. It also aimed to increase petroleum production capacity and modernize existing facilities. An extensive role for the private sector (through the privatization of existing public assets and a series of PPPs) was anticipated.

The IMF welcomed the proposed role of the private sector in the implementation of the development plan. It estimated the Government's contribution to the cost of the plan at US $55,000m., which was expected to be matched by the private sector. The IMF also considered that the containment of public sector wages and benefits was needed to encourage greater participation by Kuwaitis in the private sector and would contribute to long-term fiscal sustainability. It was estimated that Kuwaitis made up less than 10% of the private sector workforce in 2010 (given the attraction of generous public sector benefits and salaries), and the Government reportedly introduced a minimum wage for the private sector in an attempt to improve the balance. The IMF, meanwhile, expressed approval of the planned introduction of a value-added tax (VAT) from 2013, in conjunction with the other GCC countries. It also advised that the Government, while considering the introduction of a comprehensive income tax system, should prioritize the implementation of corporate, rather than personal, tax because the VAT already provided for a broad-based taxation of the population.

Preliminary figures indicated that the budget surplus for 2010/11 reached KD 6,500m. (even with the Amir's cash transfer to Kuwaiti citizens in January 2011—see Introduction), although subsequent figures from the Ministry of Finance in mid-2011 revised the figure downwards, to KD 5,300m. The draft budget for 2011/12 was approved by the Government in January 2011, projecting expenditure of KD 17,900m. and revenue of KD 13,400m., based on a still-conservative oil price assumption of $60 per barrel. The Government subsequently proposed budget amendments to raise spending by KD 1,800m., mainly for wage and benefit increases. However, the National Assembly rejected this proposal and instead approved revised expenditure in June of KD 19,435m. for 2011/12. In the event, the Government posted a record budget surplus of KD 13,200m. in 2011/12, driven by high petroleum prices. Although there had been a rise in current expenditure following the increase in public sector wages, political disagreement between parliament and the Government had continued to delay decision-making on the implementation of many capital expenditure plans.

In January 2012 the Government referred the draft budget for 2012/13 for approval by the Supreme Council for Planning and Development. It envisaged expenditure of KD 22,000m. and revenue of KD 14,000m., based on a marginally higher oil price assumption of $65 per barrel. However, actual spending was subsequently expected to increase, following widespread industrial action by public sector workers from late 2011, which resulted in pledges of substantial wage and benefit rises. In April 2012 the National Assembly rejected the proposed annual development plan for 2012/13 (separate from the budget), on the grounds that the Government had failed to meet its spending commitments in the previous two fiscal years. Parliamentary deputies described the plan as unrealistic, and criticized the Government for its failure to progress major projects that would attract foreign investment. The draft budget for 2012/13 was approved by decree in October 2012, with a marginal downward revision of expenditure. Having been urged by the Central Bank to reduce current spending and prioritize capital investment to support economic growth, in February 2013 the Government announced that KD 5,400m. would be allocated to the 2013/14 tranche of the development plan for infrastructure development in the power and water sectors, as well as for upgrading transport, energy, health and education services. In the following month the National Assembly approved a KD 2,000m. fund to support small and medium-sized companies, as part of efforts to diversify the economy away from dependence on petroleum.

INVESTMENT

Kuwait's main priorities in the allocation of its revenue from petroleum has been the development of its own economy and the provision, through the investment of surplus funds, of an income for its citizens in the future when the oil wells have run dry. In the mid-1970s, in addition to the general reserve, the Government established the FGF, to which, by law, at least 10% of total revenue was to be added annually. In September 2012 the Government increased the annual allocation to 25%, effective from 2012/13. This followed warnings from the IMF that Kuwait could struggle to pass on its oil wealth for future generations if it did not exercise fiscal consolidation.

Kuwait had a budget surplus for some years before 1973, and therefore developed an investment strategy considerably earlier than did other petroleum-producing countries. This strategy was implemented with the establishment of the Kuwait Investment Office (KIO) in the 1950s, the aim of which was to provide for its future generations by investing part of the Government's share of profits from the petroleum industry. The KIO, based in London, United Kingdom, handled much of the nation's investment in Europe and elsewhere.

In 1993 the dealings of the KIO were the subject of an inquiry by a commission comprising members of the new National Assembly. It was alleged that officials of the KIO had lost US $5,000m. in Spain since 1986, of which some $1,000m. had been embezzled through the collapsed Grupo Torras company. In mid-1993 it was reported that legal proceedings were being prepared against former KIO officials in the United Kingdom and Spain. A series of legislative measures in 1993 attempted to ensure greater accountability from state investment organizations and to increase penalties for the misuse of public funds. In 1999 a court in the United Kingdom found three former senior managers of the KIO guilty, *in absentia*, of embezzling some $500m. from Grupo Torras.

Kuwaiti private investment is substantial, and is predominantly in real estate and high-yielding equities. Although this investment is concentrated in the USA, Europe and Japan, Kuwaitis have shown an interest in investment in other non-Arab countries in Asia, Africa and South America, as well as in the Arab world. From August 1990 until July 1991 Kuwait's sole sources of income were earnings from its international financial investments and profits from Kuwait Petroleum International, which operates Kuwaiti petroleum companies in Europe and Asia. It was estimated that Kuwait's international investments in August 1990 were worth as much as US $100,000m., comprising the FGF and the General Reserve Fund. The rate of return on these investments was estimated at 5% per year. Although the Kuwaiti Government refused to disclose any details concerning the sale of assets to fund its activities during the 1990–91 Gulf crisis, it was estimated in mid-1993 that the value of Kuwait's overseas investments had more than halved since August 1990. Following the liberation of Kuwait, the Government indicated that it did not envisage the sale of large-scale investments, especially of important strategic assets such as its interests in Daimler-Benz, Hoechst, Metallgesellschaft, Hogg Robinson, HSBC UK and BP. By 2010, in addition to KIA assets, Kuwait's cross-border private sector investments were estimated at over $5,000m., with the majority held in the GCC states.

After its own development, Kuwait's next priority has been that of the rest of the Arab and Islamic world, and then of developing countries more widely. It pioneered foreign aid in the Arab world, setting up the KFAED in 1961 and later extending operations to Africa and Asia. At the end of the 2011/12 fiscal year the total number of loans extended by the KFAED since its establishment was 815, with a cumulative value of some KD 4,752m. Of the total loans by value, 55.6% were to Arab countries. The Arab Fund for Economic and Social Development is based in Kuwait; and Kuwait is a member of various Arab, Islamic and OPEC aid organizations, notably the Islamic Development Bank, the Arab Bank for Economic Development in Africa (BADEA) and the OPEC Fund for International Development. It has also contributed to IMF and World Bank facilities.

Statistical Survey

Sources (unless otherwise stated): Economic Research Department, Central Bank of Kuwait, POB 526, 13006 Safat, Kuwait City; tel. 22403257; fax 22440887; e-mail cbk@cbk.gov.kw; internet www.cbk.gov.kw; Central Statistical Bureau, Arabian Gulf St, Sharq, Kuwait City; tel. 22428200; fax 2430470; e-mail ppd@cso.gov.kw; internet www.csb.gov.kw.

Area and Population

AREA, POPULATION AND DENSITY

Area (sq km)	17,818*
Population (census results)†	
20 April 2005‡	
Males	1,300,347
Females	893,304
Total	2,193,651
21 April 2011 (preliminary)§	3,065,850
Population (official estimate at 31 December)	
2012	3,823,728
Density (per sq km) at 31 December 2012	214.6

* 6,880 sq miles.

† Figures include Kuwaiti nationals abroad.

‡ Excluding adjustment for underenumeration; the total population at the 2005 census comprised 860,324 Kuwaiti nationals (425,279 males, 435,045 females) and 1,333,327 non-Kuwaitis (875,068 males, 458,259 females).

§ Comprising 1,089,969 Kuwaitis and 1,975,881 non-Kuwaitis.

POPULATION BY AGE AND SEX
(UN estimates at mid-2013)

	Males	Females	Total
0–14	425,202	408,272	833,474
15–64	1,544,895	913,628	2,458,523
65 and over	43,840	32,738	76,578
Total	2,013,937	1,354,638	3,368,575

Source: UN, *World Population Prospects: The 2012 Revision*.

GOVERNORATES
(official population estimates at 31 December 2012)

Governorate	Area (sq km)*	Population	Density (per sq km)
Capital	199.8	517,786	2,591.5
Hawalli	368.4	835,110	5,633.2
Mubarak al-Kabir		229,804	
Farwaniya		1,010,369	
Al-Jahra	11,230.2	478,189	42.6
Al-Ahmadi	5,119.6	747,365	146.0
Total	16,918.0	3,818,623†	225.7

* Excluding the islands of Bubiyan and Warba (combined area 900 sq km).

† Excluding population of areas not officially demarcated (estimated at 5,105 persons).

PRINCIPAL TOWNS
(official population estimates at 31 December 2012)

Jaleeb al-Shuyukh	285,019	Fahaheel	90,632
Salmiya	262,594	Mahbula	85,593
Farwaniya	221,492	Subah Alsalim	82,168
Hawalli	185,535	Salwa	79,724
Khitan	137,385	Sabahiya	79,545
Munkaf	108,667	Jabriya	73,311

BIRTHS AND DEATHS
(annual averages, UN estimates)

	1995–2000	2000–05	2005–10
Crude birth rate (per 1,000)	25.4	21.2	21.7
Crude death rate (per 1,000)	3.1	3.1	3.1

Source: UN, *World Population Prospects: The 2012 Revision*.

Births: 56,503 in 2009; 57,533 in 2010; 58,198 in 2011.

Marriages: 14,526 in 2009; 13,993 in 2010; 19,860 in 2011.

Deaths: 5,935 in 2009; 5,448 in 2010; 5,339 in 2011.

Life expectancy (years at birth): 74.7 (males 73.8; females 75.7) in 2011 (Source: World Bank, World Development Indicators database).

ECONOMICALLY ACTIVE POPULATION
('000 persons aged 15 years and over, mid-2011)

	Kuwaitis	Non-Kuwaitis	Total
Agriculture, hunting and fishing	0.4	41.4	41.8
Mining and quarrying	4.9	2.1	7.1
Manufacturing	9.0	112.7	121.6
Electricity, gas and water	13.1	2.0	15.1
Construction	10.9	175.8	186.8
Wholesale and retail trade	14.5	331.2	345.7
Transport, storage and communications	9.3	59.9	69.1
Finance, insurance, real estate and business services	19.3	95.7	114.9
Public administration	270.6	764.0	1,034.6
Sub-total	352.0	1,584.9	1,936.7
Activities not adequately defined	37.9	252.8	290.7
Total labour force	389.7	1,837.7	2,227.4

Note: Totals may not be equal to the sum of components, owing to rounding.

Source: IMF, *Kuwait: Selected Issues and Statistical Appendix* (June 2012).

Health and Welfare

KEY INDICATORS

Total fertility rate (children per woman, 2011)	2.3
Under-5 mortality rate (per 1,000 live births, 2011)	13
HIV/AIDS (% of persons aged 15–49, 1994)	<0.2
Physicians (per 1,000 head, 2009)	1.8
Hospital beds (per 1,000 head, 2009)	2.0
Health expenditure (2010): US $ per head (PPP)	1,133
Health expenditure (2010): % of GDP	2.6
Health expenditure (2010): public (% of total)	80.4
Access to water (% of persons, 2011)	99
Total carbon dioxide emissions ('000 metric tons, 2009)	80,204.6
Carbon dioxide emissions per head (metric tons, 2009)	30.3
Human Development Index (2012): ranking	54
Human Development Index (2012): value	0.790

For sources and definitions, see explanatory note on p. vi.

Agriculture

PRINCIPAL CROPS
('000 metric tons)

	2009	2010	2011*
Potatoes	34.0	36.8	44.6
Cabbages and other brassicas	16.6	15.1	13.7
Lettuce	11.3	12.8	12.3
Tomatoes	74.4	73.7	71.3
Cauliflowers and broccoli	17.9	16.8	22.1
Pumpkins, squash and gourds	10.3	12.2	12.5
Cucumbers and gherkins	44.5	48.7	53.1
Aubergines (Eggplants)	26.7	25.0	25.0
Chillies and peppers, green	16.4	16.3	16.3
Onions, dry	15.6	18.6	19.7
Dates	29.8	32.6	33.6

* FAO estimates.

Aggregate production ('000 metric tons, may include official, semi-official or estimated data): Total cereals 14.2 in 2009, 21.4 in 2010–11; Total roots and tubers 34.0 in 2009, 36.8 in 2010, 44.6 in 2011; Total vegetables (incl. melons) 290.6 in 2009, 298.5 in 2010, 321.4 in 2011; Total fruits (excl. melons) 32.2 in 2009, 35.2 in 2010, 36.5 in 2011.

Source: FAO.

LIVESTOCK
('000 head, year ending September)

	2009	2010	2011
Cattle	35.8	35.7	35.0*
Camels	10.4	10.3	11.0*
Sheep	455	462	470*
Goats	145.0†	181.6	178.7
Chickens	40,902	30,559	32,000*

* FAO estimate.

† Unofficial figure.

Source: FAO.

LIVESTOCK PRODUCTS
('000 metric tons)

	2009	2010	2011*
Cattle meat*	2.5	2.6	2.6
Sheep meat*	37.5	35.7	35.7
Chicken meat*	41.3	39.9	39.0
Cows' milk	40.1	55.2	55.2
Goats' milk*	3.5	4.2	4.2
Hen eggs	35.0	40.0	40.0

* FAO estimates.

Source: FAO.

Fishing

(metric tons, live weight)

	2008	2009	2010*
Capture	3,979	4,707	4,500
Hilsa shad	84	110	110
Mullets	22	53	50
Groupers	140	147	150
Grunts and sweetlips	119	121	130
Croakers and drums	54	57	60
Yellowfin seabream	299	382	350
Indo-Pacific king mackerel	57	120	100
Carangids	39	54	60
Natantian decapods	1,807	1,754	1,700
Silver pomfret	115	268	220
Aquaculture*	360	360	360
Nile tilapia*	300	300	300
Total catch*	4,339	5,067	4,860

* FAO estimates.

2011: Figures assumed to be unchanged from 2010 (FAO estimates).

Source: FAO.

Mining

	2010	2011	2012
Crude petroleum ('000 metric tons)	122,689	140,041	152,494
Natural gas (million cu m)	11,730	12,950	14,540

Source: BP, *Statistical Review of World Energy*.

Industry

SELECTED PRODUCTS
('000 metric tons unless otherwise stated)

	2009	2010	2011
Bran and flour	340.2	336.2	355.1
Sulphur (by-product)*	800	820	830
Chlorine	24.5	21.8	21.4
Caustic soda (Sodium hydroxide)	36.9	35.5	40.2
Salt*	13.0	14.0	15.0
Nitrogenous fertilizers*†	450	340	460
Motor spirit (petrol) (million barrels)*‡	20	22	23
Kerosene (million barrels)*‡	60	68	66
Gas-diesel (distillate fuel) oils (million barrels)*‡	80	85	94
Residual fuel oils (mazout—million barrels)*‡	69	68	70
Quicklime*	45	50	50
Cement*	2,000	2,000	2,250
Electric energy (million kWh)‡	53,218	57,082	57,457

* Source: US Geological Survey; estimates.
† Production in terms of nitrogen.
‡ Including an equal share of production with Saudi Arabia from the Neutral (Partitioned) Zone.

Finance

CURRENCY AND EXCHANGE RATES

Monetary Units
1,000 fils = 10 dirhams = 1 Kuwaiti dinar (KD).

Sterling, Dollar and Euro Equivalents (31 May 2012)
£1 sterling = 434.89 fils;
US $1 = 285.85 fils;
€1 = 371.77 fils;
10 Kuwaiti dinars = £22.99 = $34.98 = €26.89.

Average Exchange Rate (fils per US $)
2010 286.6
2011 276.0
2012 279.9

From 1 January 2003 the official exchange rate was fixed within the range of US $1 = 289 fils to $1 = 310 fils (KD 1 = $3.4602 to KD 1 = $3.2258), but this 'peg' to the US dollar was abandoned in May 2007 in favour of a basket of currencies including the pound sterling, the euro and the yen.

GENERAL BUDGET
(KD million, year ending 30 June)

Revenue	2009/10	2010/11	2011/12
Tax revenue	296.4	320.1	326.1
International trade and transactions	190.8	218.4	222.9
Non-tax revenue	17,391.6	21,181.9	29,910.0
Oil revenue	16,584.9	19,947.4	28,569.6
Total operating revenue of government enterprises	566.3	566.6	576.7
Total	17,687.9	21,502.0	30,236.1

Expenditure	2009/10	2010/11	2011/12
Current expenditure	8,095.0	11,329.2	11,097.4
Land acquisitions	10.1	3.6	21.0
Capital expenditure	226.5	152.9	147.0
Construction expenditure	1,071.2	1,684.5	1,631.0
Other expenditure	1,847.8	3,050.8	4,111.1
Total	11,250.7	16,221.0	17,007.4

2012/13: *Revenue:* Oil revenue 12,768.2; Other receipts 1,164.2; Total revenue 13,932.4. *Expenditure:* Wages and salaries 5,146.0; Requirements of goods and services 4,169.0; Transport and equipment 477.0; Construction and land acquisition 2,162.0; Miscellaneous expenditure and transfer payments 9,286.0; Total expenditure 21,240.0.

INTERNATIONAL RESERVES
(US $ million at 31 December)

	2010	2011	2012
Gold (national valuation)	n.a.	113.9	112.8
IMF special drawing rights	2,222.9	2,219.0	2,222.4
Reserve position in IMF	390.8	654.7	699.2
Foreign exchange	18,623.0	22,921.4	25,964.1
Total	21,236.7*	25,909.0	28,998.5

* Excluding data for gold, which was not available.

Source: IMF, *International Financial Statistics*.

MONEY SUPPLY
(KD million at 31 December)

	2010	2011	2012
Currency outside depository corporations	842.9	1,024.6	1,120.7
Transferable deposits	5,285.1	6,304.2	6,889.2
Other deposits	19,506.2	20,495.3	21,530.8
Broad money	25,634.2	27,824.2	29,540.7

Source: IMF, *International Financial Statistics*.

COST OF LIVING
(Consumer Price Index; base: 2000 = 100)

	2010	2011	2012
Food	162.1	177.7	187.6
Beverages and tobacco	167.9	163.6	173.8
Clothing and footwear	151.7	157.0	163.2
Housing	143.8	149.2	151.4
Transport and communication	113.4	115.8	118.5
Education and medical care	155.0	161.1	165.0
All items (incl. others)	141.5	148.2	152.5

NATIONAL ACCOUNTS
(KD million at current prices)

Expenditure on the Gross Domestic Product

	2009	2010	2011
Government final consumption expenditure	5,635.5	5,946.6	6,719.8
Private final consumption expenditure	10,215.9	9,444.5	10,125.4
Increase in stocks } Gross fixed capital formation }	5,478.9	6,964.1	6,921.1
Total domestic expenditure	21,330.3	22,355.2	23,766.3
Exports of goods and services	18,125.0	22,055.0	31,578.0
Less Imports of goods and services	8,959.0	10,041.0	10,935.0
GDP in purchasers' values	30,496.2	34,369.2	44,409.3
GDP at constant 2000 prices	18,882.3	21,040.1	n.a.

Gross Domestic Product by Economic Activity

	2009	2010	2011
Agriculture, hunting, forestry and fishing	80.0	80.0	85.5
Mining and quarrying	15,059.9	18,483.9	27,575.4
Manufacturing	1,562.0	1,933.0	2,058.7
Electricity, gas and water	432.1	510.1	587.3
Construction	583.0	730.2	774.5
Trade	1,154.0	1,273.5	1,335.1
Restaurants and hotels	259.4	272.4	288.0
Transport, storage and communications	2,741.3	2,405.6	2,539.3
Finance, insurance, real estate and business services	5,058.7	4,649.8	4,444.3
Community, social and personal services	5,091.8	5,583.9	6,287.3
Sub-total	32,022.1	35,922.4	45,975.4
Import duties	196.8	211.5	206.4
Less Imputed bank service charges	–1,722.7	–1,764.7	–1,772.5
GDP in purchasers' values	30,496.2	34,369.2	44,409.3

BALANCE OF PAYMENTS
(US $ million)

	2009	2010	2011
Exports of goods f.o.b.	54,422.9	67,630.7	104,290.4
Imports of goods f.o.b.	–18,528.7	–20,067.9	–21,957.8
Balance on goods	35,894.3	47,562.8	82,332.6
Exports of services	11,570.7	9,323.9	10,193.4
Imports of services	–13,742.6	–14,962.0	–17,736.5
Balance on goods and services	33,722.4	41,924.7	74,789.6
Primary income received	8,861.3	10,620.0	11,417.9
Primary income paid	–1,178.3	–1,199.5	–321.3
Balance on goods, services and primary income	41,405.4	51,345.1	85,886.1
Secondary income paid	–13,021.6	–13,051.8	–15,124.5
Current balance	28,383.8	38,293.4	70,761.6
Capital account (net)	1,007.0	2,120.7	3,513.0
Direct investment assets	–8,581.8	–5,065.3	–8,728.0
Direct investment liabilities	1,113.6	318.7	399.9
Portfolio investment assets	–8,674.2	–17,021.8	–9,619.0
Portfolio investment liabilities	480.2	152.9	1,053.8
Financial derivatives and employee stock options (net)	–47.9	–24.9	66.8
Other investment assets	2,911.1	–17,573.0	–43,515.4
Other investment liabilities	–13,727.8	–7,225.5	–2,179.3
Net errors and omissions	894.8	6,635.6	–7,282.2
Reserves and related items	3,758.6	610.8	4,471.3

Source: IMF, *International Financial Statistics*.

External Trade

PRINCIPAL COMMODITIES
(KD million)

Imports c.i.f.	2008	2009	2010
Food and live animals	880	830	949
Chemicals and related products	558	558	653
Basic manufactures	1,482	952	1,103
Machinery and transport equipment	2,721	2,298	2,766
Miscellaneous manufactured articles	758	806	762
Total (incl. others)	6,679	5,723	6,499

Exports f.o.b.*	2008	2009	2010
Food and live animals	48	48	63
Crude materials, inedible, excl. fuels	39	40	39
Chemicals and related products	585	766	803
Basic manufactures	117	98	135
Machinery and transport equipment	438	433	250
Miscellaneous manufactured articles	37	59	68
Total (incl. others)	1,281	1,456	1,371

* Excluding petroleum exports (KD million): 22,200 in 2008; 14,073 in 2009; 17,711 in 2010.

2011: Total imports 7,012; Total exports 28,185 (petroleum 26,689, non-petroleum 1,496).

2012: Total imports 7,245; Total exports 33,180 (petroleum 31,608, non-petroleum 1,572).

PRINCIPAL TRADING PARTNERS
(KD million)*

Imports c.i.f.	2009	2010	2011
Australia	127.9	152.7	183.5
Brazil	78.2	74.1	100.9
Canada	50.0	78.4	72.5
China, People's Repub.	707.0	812.2	1,024.7
France (incl. Monaco)	160.4	153.1	153.3
Germany	445.7	475.0	457.6
India	315.5	369.2	412.2
Iran	35.3	31.2	29.0
Italy	261.2	307.1	265.9
Japan	419.4	517.0	458.4
Korea, Repub.	247.7	293.2	263.7
Malaysia	60.5	70.5	81.0
Netherlands	92.9	85.2	91.9
Saudi Arabia	346.8	344.3	398.0
Spain	59.7	66.5	63.9
Switzerland-Liechtenstein	91.8	143.6	109.9
Syria	32.3	28.4	23.1
Taiwan	106.7	55.3	60.6
Thailand	142.4	101.8	109.2
Turkey	76.3	137.0	115.6
United Arab Emirates	249.7	289.4	442.3
United Kingdom	188.4	200.0	186.6
USA	635.3	743.6	741.7
Total (incl. others)	5,852.2	6,498.6	6,938.1

Exports f.o.b.†	2009	2010	2011
Bahrain	41.2	29.7	22.9
Belgium-Luxembourg	5.1	3.6	14.8
China, People's Repub.	326.4	194.4	229.1
Egypt	23.3	19.3	16.5
India	94.4	118.5	176.3
Indonesia	41.8	58.1	35.2
Iran	26.8	32.2	22.7
Japan	2.1	1.6	1.5
Jordan	64.8	50.3	31.5
Korea, Repub.	3.4	25.5	52.1
Lebanon	13.4	13.7	13.7
Malaysia	10.1	38.1	29.4
Oman	18.9	24.1	22.8
Pakistan	37.0	44.6	68.2
Philippines	3.9	2.9	2.8
Qatar	42.3	36.0	39.3
Saudi Arabia	127.0	140.4	190.0
Spain	8.0	7.7	0.7
Syria	26.2	22.5	11.7
Taiwan	1.1	9.8	1.2
Turkey	65.9	37.4	62.9
United Arab Emirates	168.5	173.9	189.3
USA	51.8	49.4	51.8
Total (incl. others)	1,456.0	1,370.9	2,834.0

* Imports by country of production; exports by country of last consignment.
† Excluding petroleum exports.

Transport

ROAD TRAFFIC
(motor vehicles in use at 31 December)

	2009	2010
Passenger cars	1,150,840	1,202,704
Buses and coaches	24,759	25,668
Motorcycles and mopeds	7,664	8,765

Source: IRF, *World Road Statistics*.

SHIPPING

Flag Registered Fleet
(at 31 December)

	2010	2011	2012
Number of vessels	148	155	155
Displacement ('000 grt)	1,957.8	2,392.9	2,479.5

Source: Lloyd's List Intelligence (www.lloydslistintelligence.com).

International Sea-borne Freight Traffic
('000 metric tons)*

	1988	1989	1990
Goods loaded	61,778	69,097	51,400
Goods unloaded	7,123	7,015	4,522

* Including Kuwait's share of traffic in the Neutral (Partitioned) Zone.

Source: UN, *Monthly Bulletin of Statistics*.

Goods loaded ('000 metric tons): 89,945 in 1997.

Goods unloaded ('000 metric tons): 6,049 in 1997.

CIVIL AVIATION
(traffic on scheduled services)

	2007	2008	2009
Kilometres flown (million)	42	43	44
Passengers carried ('000)	2,660	2,524	2,597
Passenger-km (million)	7,721	7,368	7,670
Total ton-km (million)	967	945	976

Source: UN, *Statistical Yearbook*.

Passengers carried ('000): 4,050 in 2010; 3,482 in 2011 (Source: World Bank, World Development Indicators database).

Tourism

VISITOR ARRIVALS BY COUNTRY OF ORIGIN
(incl. excursionists)

	2008	2009	2010
Bahrain	112,910	125,962	122,192
Bangladesh	93,585	104,757	102,390
Egypt	532,753	540,708	569,452
India	673,671	733,117	751,059
Iran	90,839	89,219	81,136
Lebanon	117,055	119,998	117,686
Pakistan	214,427	219,502	228,028
Philippines	117,812	130,417	135,182
Saudi Arabia	1,425,049	1,613,460	1,708,661
Sri Lanka	90,896	95,250	99,330
Syria	304,605	306,561	307,949
Total (incl. others)	4,735,910	5,087,781	5,207,785

Tourism receipts (US $ million, excl. passenger transport): 354 in 2009; 241 in 2010; 199 in 2011 (provisional).

Source: World Tourism Organization.

Communications Media

	2010	2011	2012
Telephones ('000 main lines in use)	519.4	514.7	510.0
Mobile cellular telephones ('000 subscribers)	3,979.1	4,934.2	5,526.0
Broadband subscribers ('000)	46	47	47

Internet users ('000): 1,100 in 2009.

Source: International Telecommunication Union.

Education

(state-controlled schools, 2011/12)

			Students		
	Schools	Teachers	Males	Females	Total
Kindergarten	201	5,755	22,876	21,867	44,743
Primary	253	21,520	70,707	65,171	135,878
Intermediate	204	17,404	55,180	52,436	107,616
Secondary	136	12,363	39,233	29,803	69,036
Religious institutes	9	699	1,059	1,649	2,708
Special training institutes	29	1,285	663	1,031	1,694

Private education (2011/12): 105 kindergarten schools (1,888 teachers, 37,433 students); 132 primary schools (5,204 teachers, 94,260 students); 133 intermediate schools (3,065 teachers, 57,743 students); 105 secondary schools (2,872 teachers, 34,832 students).

Pupil-teacher ratio (primary education, UNESCO estimate): 8.6 in 2010/11 (Source: UNESCO Institute for Statistics).

Adult literacy rate (UNESCO estimates): 93.9% (males 95.0%; females 91.8%) in 2008 (Source: UNESCO Institute for Statistics).

Directory

The Constitution

The principal provisions of the Constitution, promulgated on 16 November 1962, are set out below. On 29 August 1976 the Amir suspended four articles of the Constitution dealing with the National Assembly, the Majlis al-Umma. On 24 August 1980 the Amir issued a decree ordering the establishment of an elected legislature before the end of February 1981. The new Majlis was elected on 23 February, and fresh legislative elections followed on 20 February 1985. The Majlis was dissolved by Amiri decree in July 1986, and some sections of the Constitution, including the stipulation that new elections should be held within two months of dissolving the legislature (see below), were suspended. A new Majlis was elected on 5 October 1992 and convened on 20 October. In 2005 the Majlis approved legislation allowing women to vote in and stand as candidates for parliamentary and local elections.

SOVEREIGNTY

Kuwait is an independent sovereign Arab State; its sovereignty may not be surrendered, and no part of its territory may be relinquished. Offensive war is prohibited by the Constitution.

Succession as Amir is restricted to heirs of the late Mubarak al-Sabah, and an Heir Apparent must be appointed within one year of the accession of a new Amir.

EXECUTIVE AUTHORITY

Executive power is vested in the Amir, who exercises it through the Council of Ministers. The Amir will appoint the Prime Minister 'after the traditional consultations', and will appoint and dismiss ministers on the recommendation of the Prime Minister. Ministers need not be members of the Majlis al-Umma, although all ministers who are not members of parliament assume membership ex officio in the legislature for the duration of office. The Amir also formulates laws, which shall not be effective unless published in the *Official Gazette*. The Amir establishes public institutions. All decrees issued in these respects shall be conveyed to the Majlis. No law is issued unless it is approved by the Majlis.

LEGISLATURE

A National Assembly, the Majlis al-Umma, of 50 members is elected for a four-year term by all natural-born Kuwaitis over the age of 21 years, except servicemen and police, who may not vote. (Unelected cabinet ministers also sit in the Majlis, bringing the total membership to around 65.) Candidates for election must possess the franchise, be over 30 years of age and literate. The Majlis will convene for at least eight months in any year, and new elections shall be held within two months of the last dissolution of the outgoing legislature.

Restrictions on the commercial activities of ministers include an injunction forbidding them to sell property to the Government.

The Amir may ask for reconsideration of a bill that has been approved by the Majlis and sent to him for ratification, but the bill would automatically become law if it were subsequently adopted by a two-thirds' majority at the next sitting, or by a simple majority at a subsequent sitting. The Amir may declare martial law, but only with the approval of the legislature.

The Majlis may adopt a vote of no confidence in a minister, in which case the minister must resign. Such a vote is not permissible in the case of the Prime Minister, but the legislature may approach the Amir on the matter, and the Amir shall then either dismiss the Prime Minister or dissolve the Majlis.

CIVIL SERVICE

Entry to the civil service is confined to Kuwaiti citizens.

PUBLIC LIBERTIES

Kuwaitis are equal before the law in prestige, rights and duties. Individual freedom is guaranteed. No one shall be seized, arrested or exiled except within the rules of law.

No punishment shall be administered except for an act or abstaining from an act considered a crime in accordance with a law applicable at the time of committing it, and no penalty shall be imposed more severe than that which could have been imposed at the time of committing the crime.

Freedom of opinion is guaranteed to everyone, and each has the right to express himself through speech, writing or other means within the limits of the law.

The press is free within the limits of the law, and it should not be suppressed except in accordance with the dictates of law.

Freedom of performing religious rites is protected by the State according to prevailing customs, provided it does not violate the public order and morality.

Trade unions will be permitted and property must be respected. An owner is not banned from managing his property except within the boundaries of law. No property should be taken from anyone, except within the prerogatives of law, unless a just compensation be given.

Houses may not be entered, except in cases provided by law. Every Kuwaiti has freedom of movement and choice of place of residence within the State. This right shall not be controlled except in cases stipulated by law.

Every person has the right to education and freedom to choose his type of work. Freedom to form peaceful societies is guaranteed within the limits of law.

The Government

HEAD OF STATE

Amir of Kuwait: His Highness Sheikh SABAH AL-AHMAD AL-JABER AL-SABAH (acceded 29 January 2006).

COUNCIL OF MINISTERS
(September 2013)

Prime Minister: Sheikh JABER MUBARAK AL-HAMAD AL-SABAH.

Deputy Prime Minister and Minister of Foreign Affairs: Sheikh SABAH AL-KHALID AL-HAMAD AL-SABAH.

Deputy Prime Minister and Minister of the Interior: Sheikh MUHAMMAD KHALID AL-AHMAD AL-SABAH.

Deputy Prime Minister, Minister of Oil: MUSTAFA JASSEM AL-SHAMALI.

Deputy Prime Minister and Minister of Finance: Sheikh SALIM ABD AL-AZIZ AL-SAUD AL-SABAH.

Deputy Prime Minister and Minister of Defence: Lt-Gen. Sheikh KHALID AL-JARRAH AL-SABAH.

Minister of Commerce and Industry: ANAS KHALID AL-SALEH.

Minister of Social Affairs and Labour: THEKRA AYED AL-RASHIDI.

Minister of State for Planning and Development Affairs and Minister of State for National Assembly Affairs: Dr ROLA ABDULLAH DASHTI.

Minister of State for Housing Affairs and Minister of State for Municipality Affairs: SALIM MUTHAYAB AHMAD AL-UTHAINA.

Minister of Information and Minister of State for Youth Affairs: Sheikh SALMAN SABAH SALIM AL-HUMOUD AL-SABAH.

Minister of Justice and Minister of Awqaf (Religious Endowments) and Islamic Affairs: SHARIDA ABDULLAH AL-MOUSHARJI.

Minister of Electricity and Water and Minister of Public Works: ABD AL-AZIZ ABD AL-LATIF AL-IBRAHIM.

Minister of Communications: ISSA AHMAD AL-KANDARI.

Minister of State for Cabinet Affairs and Minister of Health: Sheikh MUHAMMAD ABDULLAH AL-MUBARAK AL-SABAH.

Minister of Education and Higher Education: Dr NAYIF FALAH AL-HAJRAF.

MINISTRIES

Diwan of the Prime Minister: POB 1397, 13014 Kuwait City; tel. 22000000; fax 22223150; e-mail contact@pm.gov.kw; internet www.pm.gov.kw.

Ministry of Awqaf (Religious Endowments) and Islamic Affairs: POB 13, 13001 Safat, Kuwait City; tel. 22487225; internet www.islam.gov.kw.

Ministry of Commerce and Industry: POB 2944, 13030 Safat, Kuwait City; tel. 2248000; fax 22424411; e-mail admin@moci.gov.kw; internet www.moci.gov.kw.

Ministry of Communications: POB 15, 13001 Safat, Kuwait City; tel. 24840606; fax 24814448; internet www.moc.kw.

Ministry of Defence: POB 1170, 13012 Safat, Kuwait City; tel. 24848300; fax 24846059; e-mail mod_info@mod.gov.kw; internet www.mod.gov.kw.

Ministry of Education: POB 7, 13001 Safat, Hilali St, Kuwait City; tel. 24839452; fax 22423676; e-mail webmaster@moe.edu.kw; internet www.moe.edu.kw.

Ministry of Electricity and Water: POB 12, South al-Sourra St, Ministries Area, Al Assimah, 13001 Safat, Kuwait City; tel. 25371000; fax 25371420; internet www.mew.gov.kw.

Ministry of Finance: POB 9, 13001 Safat, al-Morkab St, Ministries Complex, Kuwait City; tel. 22480000; fax 22404025; e-mail webmaster@mof.gov.kw; internet www.mof.gov.kw.

Ministry of Foreign Affairs: POB 3, 13001 Safat, Gulf St, Kuwait City; tel. 22425141; fax 22420429; e-mail mofa.site@mofa.gov.kw; internet www.mofa.gov.kw.

Ministry of Health: POB 5, 13001 Safat, Arabian Gulf St, Kuwait City; tel. 24863840; fax 24863485; e-mail health@moh.gov.kw; internet www.moh.gov.kw.

Ministry of Higher Education: tel. 24925177; fax 24925260; e-mail info_minister@mohe.edu.kw; internet www.mohe.edu.kw.

Ministry of Information: POB 193, 13002 Safat, al-Sour St, Kuwait City; tel. 22415301; fax 22418605; e-mail info@moinfo.gov .kw; internet www.moinfo.gov.kw.

Ministry of the Interior: POB 11, 13001 Safat, Kuwait City; tel. 22430500; fax 24348821; e-mail contact@moi.gov.kw; internet www .moi.gov.kw.

Ministry of Justice: POB 6, 13001 Safat, al-Morkab St, Ministries Complex, Kuwait City; tel. 22486218; fax 22442257; e-mail info@moj .gov.kw; internet www.moj.gov.kw.

Ministry of Oil: POB 5077, 13051 Safat, Kuwait City; tel. 22406990; e-mail alnaft@moo.gov.kw; internet www.moo.gov.kw.

Ministry of Planning and Development Affairs: POB 15, 13001 Safat, Kuwait City; tel. 22428200; fax 22430403; e-mail info@mop .gov.kw.

Ministry of Public Works: POB 8, 13001 Safat, Kuwait City; tel. 25385520; fax 25380829; e-mail undersecretary@mpw.gov.kw; internet www.mpw.gov.kw.

Ministry of Social Affairs and Labour: POB 563, 13006 Safat, Kuwait City; tel. 22480000; fax 22419877; internet www.mosal.gov .kw.

Legislature

Majlis al-Umma
(National Assembly)

POB 716, Safat 13008; tel. 22436336; fax 22436331; e-mail kwt-ipu-grp@majlesalommah.net; internet www.kna.kw.

Speaker: MARZOUQ AL-GHANIM.

Elections to the 50-seat National Assembly took place more than one year early on 2 February 2012, following the dissolution of the legislature by Sheikh Sabah in December 2011 (precipitated by a dispute between the Government and parliament over allegations of corruption and public protests against the Government). Sunni Islamists opposed to the Government won 23 seats; liberals and their allies secured nine; Shi‘a Islamists took seven; and the remaining seats were won by independent candidates. On 20 June 2012 the National Assembly was dissolved and the Assembly members elected in 2009 reinstated, following a ruling by the Constitutional Court that declared the results of the February 2012 elections to be null and void. However, more than one-half of those reinstated members immediately resigned their seats in protest against the decision. The restored Assembly was itself dissolved by Amiri decree on 7 October, and early elections were subsequently scheduled for 1 December. Despite a boycott organized by leading opponents of the Government and ongoing anti-Government protests, the election took place as scheduled. Shi‘a Islamist candidates secured 17 seats (compared with just seven at the February 2012 election), while Sunni Islamists won four seats (compared with 23 in February).

The Assembly was again dissolved in mid-June 2013, after the Constitutional Court upheld changes to the electoral law decreed by the Amir in October 2012. Early elections were scheduled for 25 July 2013, but were subsequently postponed by two days. According to the final results of the elections, which were held on 27 July, candidates representing tribal areas secured 24 of the Assembly's 50 seats. Shi‘a Islamist candidates won just eight seats, while Sunni Islamists took seven. Liberals and their allies were reported to have won five seats, while the remainder went to independent candidates, some of whom represented the *bidoun*. Voter turn-out was recorded at 52.5%. The new Assembly was on 6 August.

Political Organizations

Political parties are not permitted in Kuwait. However, several quasi-political organizations are in existence. Among those that have been represented in the Majlis since 1992 are:

Islamic Constitutional Movement (Hadas): internet www.icmkw .org; f. 1991; Sunni Muslim; political arm of the Muslim Brotherhood; Sec.-Gen. NASSER AL-SANE.

Islamic Salafi Alliance: Sunni Muslim; Sec.-Gen. ALI AL-OMAIR (acting).

Justice and Peace Alliance: Shi‘a Muslim; Leader HASSAN NASIR.

Kuwait Democratic Forum: internet www.alminbarkw.org; f. 1991; loose assen of secular, liberal and Arab nationalist groups; campaigned for the extension of voting rights to women; Sec.-Gen. YOUSUF AL-SHAYJI.

National Action Bloc: liberal, nationalist.

National Democratic Alliance (NDA): f. 1997; secular, liberal; Sec.-Gen. KHALED AL-KHALED.

National Islamic Alliance: Shi‘a Muslim; Leader HUSSAIN AL-MATOUQ.

Popular Action Bloc: loose assen of nationalists and Shi‘a Muslims; Leader AHMAD AL-SAADOUN.

Diplomatic Representation

EMBASSIES IN KUWAIT

Afghanistan: POB 33186, 73452 Rawdah, Block 6, Surra St, Across Surra Co-op Society House 16, Kuwait City; tel. 25329461; fax 25326274; e-mail afg_emb_kuw@hotmail.com; Ambassador Dr ASADULLAH HANIF BALKHI.

Algeria: POB 578, 13006 Safat, Istiqlal St, Kuwait City; tel. 24820791; fax 24820853; e-mail ambalgkt@qualitynet.net; internet www.algerianembassy-kuwait.com; Ambassador KHAMISI ARIF.

Argentina: POB 3788, 40188 Mishref, Kuwait City; tel. 25379211; fax 25379212; e-mail ekuwa@mrecic.gov.ar; Ambassador JORGE OMAR ANTONIO BIGA.

Armenia: Jabriya District, Blk 8, St 3, Villa 8, Kuwait City; tel. 25322175; fax 25314656; e-mail embassy.kuwait@mfa.am; internet kuwait.mfa.am; Ambassador FADEY CHARCHOGHLYAN.

Australia: Dar al-Awadi Bldg (Level 12), Ahmad al-Jaber St, Sharq, Kuwait City; tel. 22322422; fax 22322430; e-mail austemb.kuwait@ dfat.gov.au; internet www.kuwait.embassy.gov.au; Ambassador ROBERT TYSON.

Austria: POB 15013, Daiyah, Ahmed Shawki St, House 10, 35451 Kuwait City; tel. 22552532; fax 22563052; e-mail kuwait-ob@bmaa .gv.at; internet www.bmeia.gv.at/botschaft/kuwait; Ambassador ULRICH FRANK.

Azerbaijan: al-Yarmouk, Block 2, Villa 15, Kuwait City; tel. 25355247; fax 25355246; e-mail embazerbaijan@yahoo.com; internet www.azerembassy-kuwait.org; Ambassador TURAL RZAYEV.

Bahrain: POB 196, al-Surrah, Plot 5, al-Surrah Rd, Villa 27, Kuwait City; tel. 25318530; fax 25330882; e-mail Kuwait.mission@mofa.gov .bh; internet www.mofa.gov.bh/kuwait; Ambassador Sheikh KHALIFA BIN HAMAD AL KHALIFA.

Bangladesh: House 11, St 29, Blk 2, Khaldiya, Kuwait City; tel. 24913219; fax 24913205; e-mail ambassador.kuwait@mofa.gov.bd; internet kuwait.mofa.gov.bd; Ambassador SYED SHAHED REZA.

Belgium: POB 3280, Bayan, Blk 13, St 4, Villa 8, Safat, 13033 Kuwait City; tel. 25384582; fax 25384583; e-mail kuwait@diplobel .fed.be; internet www.diplomatie.be/kuwait; Ambassador DAMIEN ANGELET.

Bhutan: POB 1510, 13016 Safat, Adailiya-Block 3, Issa Abd al-Rahman al-Assoussi St, Jadda 32, Villa 7, Kuwait City; tel. 22516640; fax 22516550; e-mail bhutankuwait@hotmail.com; Ambassador Dasho TASHI PHUNTSOG.

Bosnia and Herzegovina: Bayan, Blk 5, Rd 2, St 5, Villa 18, Kuwait City; tel. 25392637; fax 25392106; Ambassador SENAHID BRISTRIĆ.

Brazil: POB 39761, 73058 Nuzha, Blk 1, St 116, House 47, Kuwait City; tel. 25378561; fax 25378560; e-mail embassy@brazil.org.kw; internet www.brazil.org.kw; Ambassador ROBERTO ABDALLA.

Bulgaria: POB 12090, 71651 Shamiya, Jabriya, Area 11, St 107 and St 1, Kuwait City; tel. 25314458; fax 25321453; e-mail Embassy .Kuwait@mfa.bg; internet www.mfa.bg/embassies/kuwait; Ambassador ALEXANDAR OLSHEVSKI.

Canada: POB 25281, 13113 Safat, Daiyah, Blk 4, al-Mutawakkel St, Villa 24, Kuwait City; tel. 22563025; fax 22560173; e-mail kwait@ international.gc.ca; internet www.canadainternational.gc.ca/ kuwait-koweit; Ambassador DOUGLAS GEORGE.

China, People's Republic: POB 2346, 13024 Safat, Yarmouk, Sheikh Ahmad al-Jaber Bldgs 4 & 5, St 1, Villa 82, Kuwait City; tel. 25333340; fax 25333341; e-mail chinakwt@hotmail.com; internet kw.chineseembassy.org; Ambassador CUI JIANCHUN.

Czech Republic: Nuzha, Blk 3, St 34, House 13, Kuwait City; tel. 22529018; fax 22529021; e-mail kuwait@embassy.mzv.cz; internet www.mzv.cz/kuwait; Ambassador MARTIN VÁVRA.

Egypt: POB 11252, 35153 Dasmah, Istiqlal St, Kuwait City; tel. 22519955; fax 22563877; e-mail embassy.kuwait@mfa.gov.eg; Ambassador ABD AL-KARIM SULEIMAN.

Eritrea: POB 53016, 73015 Nuzha, Jabriya, Block 9, St 21, House 9, Kuwait City; tel. 25317427; fax 26631304; Ambassador MOHAMMED OMAR MAHMOUD.

Ethiopia: POB 939, 45710 Safat, Jabriya, Block 10, St 107, Villa 30, Kuwait City; tel. 25330128; fax 25331179; e-mail ethiokwt@qualitynet.net; Ambassador IBRAHIM DHEERE.

France: POB 1037, 13011 Safat, Mansouriah, Blk 1, St 13, Villa 24, Kuwait City; tel. 22582020; fax 22571058; e-mail cad.koweit-amba@diplomatie.gouv.fr; Ambassador NADA YAFI.

Georgia: Qurtoba, Blk 2, Area 1, Ave 3, Villa 6, Kuwait City; tel. 25352909; fax 25354707; e-mail kuwait.emb@mfa.gov.ge; internet www.kuwait.mfa.gov.ge; Ambassador EKATERIN MEIERING-MIKADZE.

Germany: POB 805, 13009 Safat, Dahiya Abdullah al-Salem, Area 1, Ave 14, Branch of al-Yousef St, Villa 13, Kuwait City; tel. 22520827; fax 22520763; e-mail info@kuwait.diplo.de; internet www.kuwait.diplo.de; Ambassador FRANK M. MANN.

Greece: POB 23812, 13099 Safat, Khaldiya, Block 4, St 44, House 4, Kuwait City; tel. 24817100; fax 24817103; e-mail gremb.kuw@mfa.gr; Ambassador KONSTANTINOS DRAKAKIS.

Holy See: POB 29724, 13158 Safat, Kuwait City; tel. 25337767; fax 25327776; e-mail nuntiuskuwait@gmail.com; Apostolic Nuncio Most Rev. Archbishop PETAR RAJIC (Titular Archbishop of Sarsenterum).

Hungary: POB 23955, 13100 Safat, Bayan, Blk 13, St 30, Villa 381, Kuwait City; tel. 25379351; fax 25379350; e-mail mission.kwi@mfa.gov.hu; internet www.mfa.gov.hu/emb/kuwait; Ambassador FERENC CSILLAG.

India: POB 1450, 13015 Safat, Diplomatic Enclave, Arabian Gulf St, Kuwait City; tel. 22530600; fax 22546958; e-mail contact@indembkwt.org; internet www.indembkwt.org; Ambassador SATISH C. MEHTA.

Indonesia: POB 21560, 13076 Safat, Kaifan, Blk 6, al-Andalus St, House 29, Kuwait City; tel. 24839927; fax 24819250; e-mail unitkom@kbrikuwait.org; internet kuwaitcity.kemlu.go.id; Ambassador FERRY ADAMHAR.

Iran: POB 4686, 13047 Safat, Daiyah, Embassies Area, Block B, Kuwait City; tel. 22560694; fax 22529868; e-mail iranembassy@hotmail.com; Ambassador RUHOLLAH QAHREMANI CHABOK.

Iraq: Kuwait City; e-mail kuwemb@iraqmfamail.com; Ambassador MUHAMMAD HUSSAIN BAHR AL-ULUM.

Italy: POB 4453, 13045 Safat, Jabriya, Blk 9, St 1, Villa 84, Kuwait City; tel. 25356010; fax 25356030; e-mail ambasciata.alkuwait@esteri.it; internet www.ambalkuwait.esteri.it; Ambassador FABRIZIO NICOLETTI.

Japan: POB 2304, 13024 Safat, Plot 57, Blk 7A, Diplomatic Zone, Mishref, Kuwait City; tel. 25309400; fax 25309401; e-mail info@embjp-kw.org; internet www.kw.emb-japan.go.jp; Ambassador YASUYOSHI KOMIZO.

Jordan: POB 39891, 73059 Kuwait City; tel. 22533261; fax 22533270; e-mail kujor@qualitynet.net; Ambassador MUHAMMAD AL-KAYED.

Korea, Republic: POB 4272, 13043 Safat, Plot 6, Blk 7A, Diplomatic Zone 2, Mishref, Kuwait City; tel. 25378621; fax 25378628; e-mail kuwait@mofat.go.kr; internet kwt.mofat.go.kr; Ambassador KIM KYUNG-SIK.

Lebanon: POB 253, 13003 Safat, Da'Yiah Diplomatic Area, Plot 6, Kuwait City; tel. 22562103; fax 22571682; e-mail lebembassy@lebanonembassy.org.kw; internet www.lebanonembassy.org.kw; Ambassador Dr KHADIR HILWE.

Libya: POB 21460, 13075 Safat, 27 Istiqlal St, Kuwait City; tel. 22575183; fax 22575182; Ambassador Dr MUHAMMAD SALEM EMAISH.

Malaysia: POB 4105, 13042 Safat, Daiya, Diplomatic Enclave, Area 5, Yemen St, Plot 5, Kuwait City; tel. 22550394; fax 22550384; e-mail malkuwait@kln.gov.my; internet www.kln.gov.my/perwakilan/kuwait; Ambassador Dato' ADNAN Haji OTHMAN.

Mongolia: Block 8, St 806, Villa 161, al-Zahra Area, Kuwait City; tel. 25216551; fax 25216557; e-mail kuwait@mfat.gov.mn; Ambassador SODNOMYN ENKHBAT.

Morocco: Yarmouk, Blk 2, St 2, Villa 14, Kuwait City; tel. 25312980; fax 25317423; e-mail ambkow@yahoo.fr; Ambassador YAHYA BANANI.

Netherlands: Blk 6, St 11, House 7, Jabriya, Kuwait City; tel. 25312650; fax 25326334; e-mail kwe@minbuza.nl; internet www.netherlandsembassy.gov.kw; Ambassador NICOLAAS BEETS.

Niger: POB 44451, 32059 Hawalli, Salwa Block 12, St 6, Villa 183, Kuwait City; tel. 25652943; fax 25640478; Ambassador ABDOULKARIMOU SEINI.

Nigeria: POB 6432, 32039 Hawalli, Surra, Area 1, St 14, House 24, Kuwait City; tel. 18278813; fax 18278896; Ambassador HARUNA GARBA.

Oman: POB 21975, 13080 Safat, al-Odeilia Block 3, St 3, Villa 25, Kuwait City; tel. 22561956; fax 22561963; e-mail kuwait@mofa.gov.om; Ambassador Sheikh SALIM BIN SUHAIL AL-MA'ASHANI.

Pakistan: POB 988, 13010 Safat, Jabriya, Police Station Rd, St 101, Plot 5, Blk 11, Villa 46, Kuwait City; tel. 25327649; fax 25327648; e-mail parepkwt@yahoo.com; internet www.mofa.gov.pk/kuwait; Ambassador SAYED ABRAR HUSSAIN.

Philippines: POB 26288, 13123 Safat, Blk 6, Villa 153, Nouman Bin Basher St, corner Damascus St, Faiha, Kuwait City; tel. 22528422; fax 22511805; e-mail kuwaitpe@philembassykuwait.gov.kw; internet www.philembassykuwait.gov.kw; Ambassador SHULAN O. PRIMAVERA.

Poland: POB 5066, 13051 Safat, Jabriya, Blk 7, St 3, Villa 20, Kuwait City; tel. 25311571; fax 25311576; e-mail kuwejt.amb.sekretariat@msz.gov.pl; internet www.kuwejt.polemb.net; Ambassador JANUSZ SZWEDO.

Qatar: POB 1825, 13019 Safat, Diiyah, Istiqlal St, Kuwait City; tel. 22523107; fax 22513604; e-mail kuwait@mofa.gov.qa; Ambassador ABD AL-AZIZ BIN SAAD AL-FEHAID.

Romania: POB 13574, 35152 Dasmah, Keifan, Area 4, Moona St, House 34, Kuwait City; tel. 24845079; fax 24848929; e-mail ambsa@kems.net; Ambassador VASILE SOFINETI.

Russia: POB 1765, Safat, Daya Diplomatic Area, Plot 17, Blk 5, Kuwait City; tel. 22560427; fax 22524969; e-mail rusposkuw@mail.ru; internet www.kuwait.mid.ru; Ambassador ALEKSANDR KINSHCHAK.

Saudi Arabia: POB 20498, 13065 Safat, Istiqlal St, Kuwait City; tel. 22550021; fax 22551858; Ambassador ABD AL-AZIZ AL-FAYEZ.

Senegal: POB 23892, 13099 Safat, Rawdah, Block 3, St 35, Villa 9, Kuwait City; tel. 22573477; fax 22542044; e-mail senegal_embassy@yahoo.com; Ambassador ABDOU LAHAD MBACKE.

Serbia: POB 20511, 13066 Safat, Surra, Blk 5, St 1, Villa 71, Kuwait City; tel. 25327548; fax 25327568; e-mail embrskw@qualitynet.net; internet kuwait.mfa.gov.rs; Ambassador MIHAILO BRKIĆ.

Somalia: POB 22766, 13088 Safat, Bayan, St 1, Block 7, Villa 25, Kuwait City; tel. 25394795; fax 25394829; e-mail webmaster@somaligov.net; internet www.kuwait.somaligov.net; Ambassador Dr ABDUL KHADIR AMIN SHEIKH ABUBAKER.

South Africa: POB 2262, 40173 Mishref, Salwa Block 10, St 1, Villa 91, Unit 3, Kuwait City; tel. 25617988; fax 25617917; e-mail kuwait.political@dirco.gov.za; Ambassador DELAREY VAN TONDER.

Spain: POB 22207, 13083 Safat, Surra, Block 3, St 14, Bldg 19, Kuwait City; tel. 25325827; fax 25325826; e-mail emb.kuwait@mae.es; Ambassador ÁNGEL LOSADA FERNÁNDEZ.

Sri Lanka: POB 44650, Jabriya, Blk 10, St 107, Bldg 1, Kuwait City; tel. 25339140; fax 25339154; e-mail lankaemb@qualitynet.net; internet www.slembkwt.org; Ambassador C. A. H. M. WIJERATNE.

Switzerland: POB 23954, 13100 Safat, Qortuba, Blk 2, St 1, House 122, Kuwait City; tel. 25340172; fax 25340176; e-mail kow.vertretung@eda.admin.ch; internet www.eda.admin.ch/kuwait; Ambassador ETIENNE THÉVOZ.

Syria: POB 25600, 13116 Safat, Kuwait City; tel. 25396560; fax 25396509; Ambassador (vacant).

Thailand: POB 66647, 43757 Bayan, Blk 6, St 8, Villa 1, Jabriya, Kuwait City; tel. 25317530; fax 25317532; e-mail thaiemkw@kems.net; internet www.thaiembassy.org/kuwait; Ambassador SURASAK CHUASUKONTHIP.

Tunisia: POB 5976, 13060 Safat, Nuzha, Plot 2, Nuzha St, Villa 45, Kuwait City; tel. 2542144; fax 2528995; e-mail tunemrku@ncc.moc.kw; Ambassador MUSTAPHA BAHIA.

Turkey: POB 20627, 13067 Safat, Blk 5, Plot 16, Istiqlal St, Kuwait City; tel. 22277400; fax 22560653; e-mail embassy.kuwait@mfa.gov.tr; internet kuwait.emb.mfa.gov.tr; Ambassador MURAT TAMER.

Ukraine: POB 7588, 32096 Hawalli, Jabriya, Blk 10, St 6, House 5, Kuwait City; tel. 25318507; fax 25318508; e-mail emb_kw@mfa.gov.ua; internet www.mfa.gov.ua/kuwait; Ambassador VOLODYMYR TOLKACH.

United Arab Emirates: POB 1828, 13019 Safat, Blk 5, Yemen St, Bldg 7, Kuwait City; tel. 22528544; fax 22526382; e-mail kuwait@mofa.gov.ae; internet uae-embassy.ae/Embassies/kw; Ambassador ALI AHMAD BIN SHUKR AL-ZA'ABI.

United Kingdom: POB 2, 13001 Safat, Arabian Gulf St, Kuwait City; tel. 22594320; fax 22594339; e-mail kuwait.generalenquiries@fco.gov.uk; internet ukinkuwait.fco.gov.uk; Ambassador FRANCIS RAYMOND (FRANK) BAKER.

USA: POB 77, 13001 Safat, Bayan, al-Masjed al-Aqsa St, Plot 14, Block 14, Kuwait City; tel. 22591001; fax 25380282; e-mail paskuwaitm@state.gov; internet kuwait.usembassy.gov; Ambassador MATTHEW H. TUELLER.

Uzbekistan: Mishref, Blk 2, St 5, Villa 18A, Kuwait City; Ambassador ABDURAFIK A. HOSHIMOV.

Venezuela: POB 24440, 13105 Safat, Block 5, St 7, Area 356, Surra, Kuwait City; tel. 25324367; fax 25324368; e-mail embavene@qualitynet.net; Ambassador ELOY FERNÁNDEZ AZUAJE.

Yemen: POB 7182, al-Jabriya St, Kuwait City; tel. 25349416; fax 25349415; Ambassador KHALED SHEIKH.

Zimbabwe: POB 36484, 24755 Salmiya, Kuwait City; tel. 25620845; fax 25621491; e-mail zimkuwait@hotmail.com; Ambassador MARK GREY MARONGWE.

Judicial System

Constitutional Court: Comprises five judges. Interprets the provisions of the Constitution; considers disputes regarding the constitutionality of legislation, decrees and rules; has jurisdiction in challenges relating to the election of members, or eligibility for election, to the Majlis al-Umma.

Court of Cassation: Comprises five judges. Is competent to consider the legality of verdicts of the Court of Appeal and State Security Court; Chief Justice FAISAL AL-MOURSHID.

Court of Appeal: Comprises three judges. Considers verdicts of the Court of First Instance; Chief Justice RASHED AL-HAMMAD.

Court of First Instance: Comprises the following divisions: Civil and Commercial (one judge), Personal Status Affairs (one judge), Lease (three judges), Labour (one judge), Crime (three judges), Administrative Disputes (three judges), Appeal (three judges), Challenged Misdemeanours (three judges); Chief Justice MUHAMMAD AL-SAKHOBY.

Summary Courts: Each governorate has a Summary Court, comprising one or more divisions. The courts have jurisdiction in the following areas: Civil and Commercial, Urgent Cases, Lease, Misdemeanours. The verdict in each case is delivered by one judge.

There is also a **Traffic Court**, with one presiding judge.

Prosecutor-General: DHARAR AL-AS'OUSI.

Religion

ISLAM

The majority of Kuwaitis are Muslims of the Sunni or Shi'a sects. The Shi'a community comprises about 30% of the total.

CHRISTIANITY

The Roman Catholic Church

Latin Rite

For ecclesiastical purposes, Kuwait forms part of the Apostolic Vicariate of Northern Arabia.

Vicar Apostolic: CAMILLO BALLIN (Titular Bishop of Arna), Bishop's House, POB 25362, Rd 4603, House 137/125, Blk 946, Awali, Bahrain; tel. (+973) 39504488; fax 22420297; e-mail mail@camilloballin.com; internet www.avona.org.

Melkite Rite

Exarch Patriarchal: Rev. BOUTROS GHARIB, Vicariat Patriarchal Greek-Melkite, POB 1205, Salwa Block 12, St 6, House 58, 22013 Salmiya, Kuwait City; tel. and fax 25652802; e-mail greekcatholickuwait@yahoo.com.

Syrian Rite

The Syrian Catholic Patriarch of Antioch is resident in Beirut, Lebanon. The Patriarchal Exarchate of Basra and the Gulf is based in Basra, Iraq.

The Anglican Communion

Within the Episcopal Church in Jerusalem and the Middle East, Kuwait forms part of the diocese of Cyprus and the Gulf. The Anglican congregation in Kuwait is entirely expatriate. The Bishop in Cyprus and the Gulf is resident in Cyprus, while the Archdeacon in the Gulf is resident in Bahrain.

Other Christian Churches

National Evangelical Church in Kuwait: POB 80, 13001 Safat, Kuwait City; tel. 22407195; fax 22431087; e-mail elc@ncc.moc.kw; Rev. NABIL ATTALLAH (pastor of the Arabic-language congregation), Rev. JERRY A. ZANDSTRA (senior pastor of the English-speaking congregation); an independent Protestant Church founded by the Reformed Church in America; services in Arabic, English, Korean, Malayalam and other Indian languages; combined weekly congregation of some 20,000.

The Armenian, Greek, Coptic and Syrian Orthodox Churches are also represented in Kuwait.

The Press

Freedom of the press and publishing is guaranteed in the Constitution, although press censorship was in force between mid-1986 and early 1992 (when journalists adopted a voluntary code of practice). In February 1995 a ruling by the Constitutional Court effectively endorsed the Government's right to suspend publication of newspapers; however, legislation passed in 2006 rendered this illegal without a court order. The Government provides financial support to newspapers and magazines.

DAILIES

Al-Anbaa (The News): POB 23915, 13100 Safat, Kuwait City; tel. 24830322; fax 24832647; e-mail editorial@alanba.com.kw; internet www.alanba.com.kw; f. 1976; Arabic; general; Editor-in-Chief BIBI KHALID AL-MARZOOQ; circ. 85,000.

Arab Times: POB 2270, Airport Road, Shuwaikh, 13023 Safat, Kuwait City; tel. 24849144; fax 24818267; e-mail arabtimes@arabtimesonline.com; internet www.arabtimesonline.com; f. 1977; English; political and financial; no Fri. edn; Editor-in-Chief AHMAD ABD AL-AZIZ AL-JARALLAH; Man. Editor MISHAL AL-JARALLAH; circ. 41,922.

Al-Jarida (The Newspaper): POB 29846, 13159 Safat, Kuwait City; tel. 22257036; fax 22257035; e-mail info@aljarida.com; internet www.aljarida.com; f. 2007; Arabic; affiliated with the Nat. Democratic Alliance; Editor-in-Chief KHALID HILAL AL-MUTAIRI.

Kuwait Times: POB 1301, 13014 Safat, Kuwait City; tel. 24833199; fax 24835621; e-mail info@kuwaittimes.net; internet www.kuwaittimes.net; f. 1961; English, Malayalam and Urdu; political; Editor-in-Chief ABD AL-RAHMAN ALYAN; circ. 32,000.

Al-Qabas (Firebrand): POB 21800, 13078 Safat, Kuwait City; tel. 24812822; fax 24834355; e-mail info@alqabas.com.kw; internet www.alqabas.com.kw; f. 1972; Arabic; independent; Gen. Man. FOUZAN AL-FARES; Editor-in-Chief WALEED ABD AL-LATIF AL-NISF; circ. 60,000.

Al-Ra'i al-'Aam (Public Opinion): POB 761, 13008 Safat, Kuwait City; tel. 24817777; fax 24838352; e-mail editor@alraialaam.com; internet www.alraialaam.com; f. 1961; Arabic; political, social and cultural; Editor-in-Chief YOUSUF AL-JALAHMA; circ. 101,500.

Al-Seyassah (Policy): POB 2270, Shuwaikh, Kuwait City; tel. 24813566; fax 24846905; internet www.al-seyassah.com; f. 1965; Arabic; political and financial; Editor-in-Chief AHMAD ABD AL-AZIZ AL-JARALLAH; circ. 70,000.

Al-Watan (The Homeland): POB 1142, 13012 Safat, Kuwait City; tel. 24840950; fax 24818481; e-mail alwatan@alwatan.com.kw; internet www.alwatan.com.kw; f. 1962; Arabic; political; Editor-in-Chief Sheikh KHALIFA ALI AL-KHALIFA AL-SABAH; Gen. Man. DINA AL-MALLAK; circ. 91,726.

WEEKLIES AND PERIODICALS

Al-Balagh (Communiqué): POB 4558, 13046 Safat, Kuwait City; tel. 24818820; fax 24812735; e-mail albalagh5@yahoo.com; internet www.al-balagh.com; f. 1969; weekly; Arabic; general, political and Islamic affairs; Editor-in-Chief ABD AL-RAHMAN RASHID AL-WALAYATI; circ. 29,000.

Byzance: Kuwait City; f. 2007; bi-monthly; Arabic and French; lifestyle magazine, incl. features on fashion, jewellery, furniture and art; Man. Editor JEAN-PIERRE GUEIRARD; Exec. Editor-in-Chief ANTOINE DAHER.

Al-Dakhiliya (The Interior): POB 71655, 12500 Shamiah, Kuwait City; tel. 22410091; fax 22410609; e-mail moipr@qualitynet.net; monthly; Arabic; official reports, transactions and proceedings; publ. by Public Relations Dept, Ministry of the Interior; Editor-in-Chief Lt-Col AHMAD A. AL-SHARQAWI.

Dalal Magazine: POB 6000, 13060 Safat, Kuwait City; tel. 24832098; fax 24832039; internet www.dalal-kw.com; f. 1997; monthly; Arabic; family affairs, beauty, fashion; Editor-in-Chief AHMAD YOUSUF BEHBEHANI.

Friday Times: POB 1301, 13014 Safat, Kuwait City; tel. 24833199; fax 24835627; e-mail info@kuwaittimes.net; internet www.kuwaittimes.net; f. 2005; weekend edn of *Kuwait Times*.

Al-Hadaf (The Objective): POB 2270, 13023 Safat, Kuwait City; tel. 24813566; fax 24816042; internet www.al-seyassah.com/alhadaf; f. 1964; weekly; Arabic; social and cultural; Editor-in-Chief AHMAD ABD AL-AZIZ AL-JARALLAH; circ. 268,904.

Al-Iqtisadi al-Kuwaiti (Kuwaiti Economist): POB 775, 13008 Safat, Kuwait City; tel. 1805580; fax 22404110; e-mail kcci@kcci.org.kw; internet www.kcci.org.kw; f. 1960; monthly; Arabic; commerce, trade and economics; publ. by Kuwait Chamber of Commerce and Industry; Editor MAJED B. JAMALUDDIN; circ. 6,000.

Journal of the Gulf and Arabian Peninsula Studies: POB 17073, 72451 Khaldiya, Kuwait University, Kuwait City; tel. 24833215; fax 24833705; e-mail jotgaaps@kuc01.kuniv.edu.kw;

internet pubcouncil.kuniv.edu.kw/jgaps; f. 1975; quarterly; Arabic and English; publ. by Academic Publication Council of Kuwait Univ; Editor-in-Chief Dr FATIMA HUSSAIN ABD AL-RAZZAQ.

Al-Khaleej Business Magazine: POB 25725, 13118 Safat, Kuwait City; tel. 22433765; e-mail aljabriya@gulfweb.com; Editor-in-Chief AHMAD ISMAIL BEHBEHANI.

Kuwait Medical Journal (KMJ): POB 1202, 13013 Safat, Kuwait City; tel. 25316023; fax 25317972; e-mail kmj@kma.org.kw; internet www.kma.org.kw/KMJ; f. 1967; quarterly; English; publ. by the Kuwait Medical Asscn; original articles, review articles, case reports, short communications, letters to the editor and book reviews; Editor-in-Chief Prof. FOUAD ABDULLAH M. HASSAN; circ. 5,000.

Kuwait al-Youm (Kuwait Today): POB 193, 13002 Safat, Kuwait City; tel. 24842167; fax 24831044; e-mail info@ipd.gov.kw; internet www.ipd.gov.kw; f. 1954; weekly; Arabic; statistics, Amiri decrees, laws, govt announcements, decisions, invitations for tenders, etc.; publ. by the Ministry of Information; circ. 5,000.

Al-Kuwaiti (The Kuwaiti): Information Dept, POB 9758, 61008 Ahmadi, Kuwait City; tel. 23981076; fax 23983661; e-mail kocinfo@kockw.com; f. 1961; monthly journal of the Kuwait Oil Co; Arabic; Editor-in-Chief KHALED AL-KHAMEES; circ. 6,500.

The Kuwaiti Digest: Information Dept, POB 9758, 61008 Ahmadi, Kuwait City; tel. 23981076; fax 23983661; e-mail kocinfo@kockw.com; f. 1972; quarterly journal of Kuwait Oil Co; English; Editor-in-Chief KHALED AL-KHAMEES; circ. 7,000.

Al-Majaless (Meetings): POB 5605, 13057 Safat, Kuwait City; tel. 24841178; fax 24847126; e-mail qasem@almajaless.com; weekly; Arabic; current affairs; Editor-in-Chief QASIM ABD AL-QADIR; circ. 60,206.

Mejallat al-Kuwait (Kuwait Magazine): POB 193, 13002 Safat, Kuwait City; tel. 22415300; fax 22419642; f. 1961; monthly; Arabic; illustrated magazine; science, arts and literature; publ. by the Ministry of Information.

Mirat al-Umma (Mirror of the Nation): POB 1142, 13012 Safat, Kuwait City; tel. 24837212; fax 24838671; weekly; Arabic; Editor-in-Chief MUHAMMAD AL-JASSEM; circ. 79,500.

Al-Nahdha (The Renaissance): POB 695, 13007 Safat, Kuwait City; tel. 24813133; fax 24849298; f. 1967; weekly; Arabic; social and political; Editor-in-Chief THAMER AL-SALAH; circ. 170,000.

Osrati (My Family): POB 2995, 13030 Safat, Kuwait City; tel. 24813233; fax 24838933; e-mail info@osratimag.com; internet www.osratimag.com; f. 1964; weekly; Arabic; women's magazine; publ. by Fahad al-Marzouk Establishment; Editor GHANIMA F. AL-MARZOUK; circ. 10,500.

Al-Talia (The Ascendant): POB 1082, 13011 Safat, Kuwait City; tel. 24831200; fax 24840471; f. 1962; weekly; Arabic; politics and literature; Editor AHMAD YOUSUF AL-NAFISI; circ. 10,000.

Al-Yaqza (The Awakening): POB 6000, 13060 Safat, Kuwait City; tel. 24831318; fax 24832039; internet www.alyaqza.com; f. 1966; weekly; Arabic; political, economic, social and general; Editor-in-Chief AHMAD YOUSUF BEHBEHANI; circ. 91,340.

NEWS AGENCY

Kuwait News Agency (KUNA): POB 24063, 13101 Safat, Kuwait City; tel. 24834546; fax 24813424; e-mail kuna@kuna.net.kw; internet www.kuna.net.kw; f. 1979; public corporate body; independent; also publishes research digests on topics of common and special interest; Chair. and Dir-Gen. Sheikh MUBARAK AL-DUAIJ AL-SABAH.

PRESS ASSOCIATION

Kuwait Journalists Association: POB 5454, 13055 Safat, Kuwait City; tel. 24843351; fax 24842874; e-mail kja@kja-kw.com; internet www.kja-kw.com; Chair. AHMAD YOUSUF BEHBEHANI.

Publishers

Al-Abraj Translation and Publishing Co WLL: POB 26177, 13122 Safat, Kuwait City; tel. 22442310; fax 22407024; Man. Dir Dr TARIQ ABDULLAH.

Dar al-Seyassah Publishing, Printing and Distribution Co: POB 2270, 13023 Safat, Kuwait City; tel. 24813566; fax 24833628; internet www.dar-al-seyassah.com; publ. *Arab Times*, *Al-Seyassah* and *Al-Hadaf*.

Gulf Centre Publishing and Publicity: POB 2722, 13028 Safat, Kuwait City; tel. 22402760; fax 22458833; Propr HAMZA ISMAIL ESSLAH.

Kuwait National Advertising and Publishing Co (KNAPCO): POB 2268, Safat 13023, Kuwait City; tel. 25745770; fax 25745779; e-mail support@knapco.com; internet www.knapco.com; f. 1995; publ. annual commercial business directory, *Teledymag*; Founder NAWAF ABD AL-RAZAK.

Kuwait Publishing House Co: POB 1446, 13015 Safat, Kuwait City; tel. 22449686; fax 22436956; e-mail info@kuwaitpocketguide.com; f. 1970; Dir ESAM AS'AD ABU AL-FARAJ.

Kuwait United Co for Advertising, Publishing and Distribution WLL: POB 29359, 13153 Safat, Kuwait City; tel. 24817111; fax 24817797.

Al-Talia Printing and Publishing Co: POB 1082, Airport Rd, Shuwaikh, 13011 Safat, Kuwait City; tel. 24840470; fax 24815611; Man. AHMAD YOUSUF AL-NAFISI.

GOVERNMENT PUBLISHING HOUSE

Ministry of Information: see Ministries.

Broadcasting and Communications

TELECOMMUNICATIONS

National Mobile Telecommunications Co KSC (Wataniya Telecom): POB 613, 13007 Safat, Kuwait City; tel. 65805555; fax 22423369; e-mail info@wataniya.com; internet www.wataniya.com; f. 1999; Qatar Telecommunications Corpn (Q-Tel) acquired 51% stake 2007; Chair. and Man. Dir Sheikh ABDULLAH BIN MUHAMMAD BIN SAUD AL THANI; CEO and Gen. Man. Dr BASSAM HANNOUN.

VIVA: POB 181, Salmiya 22002, Kuwait City; tel. 55670000; fax 55676666; e-mail info@viva.com.kw; internet www.viva.com.kw; f. 2008; mobile cellular communications; commercial brand of Kuwait Telecom Co; Chair. ADEL MUHAMMAD AL-ROUMI; CEO NAJEEB AL-AWADI.

Zain Kuwait: POB 22244, 13083 Safat, Kuwait City; tel. 24644444; fax 24641111; e-mail info.kw@zain.com; internet www.kw.zain.com; f. 1983 as Mobile Telecommunications Co; in Sept. 2007 began operating under new global brand, Zain; group operates in 24 countries in the Middle East and Africa; 1.8m. subscribers in Kuwait, 69.5m. total group subscribers (30 June 2009); Chair. ASAAD AL-BANWAN; CEO SCOTT GEGENHEIMER.

BROADCASTING

Radio

Radio of the State of Kuwait: POB 397, 13004 Safat, Kuwait City; tel. 22423774; fax 22456660; e-mail info@moinfo.gov.kw; internet www.moinfo.gov.kw; f. 1951; broadcasts daily in Arabic, Farsi, English and Urdu, some in stereo; Dir of Radio Dr ABD AL-AZIZ ALI MANSOUR; Dir of Radio Programmes ABD AL-RAHMAN HADI.

Television

Kuwait Television: POB 193, 13002 Safat, Kuwait City; tel. 22415301; fax 22438403; e-mail info@moinfo.gov.kw; internet www.moinfo.gov.kw; f. 1961; transmission began privately in Kuwait in 1957; transmits in Arabic; colour television service began in 1973; has a total of five channels; Head of News Broadcasting MUHAMMAD AL-KAHTANI.

Al-Rai: Kuwait City; tel. 24817777; fax 24953002; e-mail alraitv@alrai.tv; internet www.alrai.tv; f. 2004; first private satellite television station in Kuwait; admin. offices in Kuwait and transmission facilities in Dubai (United Arab Emirates); owned by Al-Rai Media Group.

Finance

(cap. = capital; res = reserves; dep. = deposits; m. = million; br(s) = branch(es); amounts in Kuwaiti dinars, unless otherwise stated)

BANKING

Central Bank

Central Bank of Kuwait: POB 526, 13006 Safat, Abdullah al-Salem St, Kuwait City; tel. 22449200; fax 22464887; e-mail cbk@cbk.gov.kw; internet www.cbk.gov.kw; f. 1969; cap. 5m., res 562m., dep. 3,369m. (March 2010); Governor Dr MUHAMMAD AL-HASHEL.

National Banks

Al-Ahli Bank of Kuwait KSC (ABK): POB 1387, 13014 Safat, Ahmad al-Jaber St, Kuwait City; tel. 22400900; fax 22424557; e-mail marketing@abkuwait.com; internet www.eahli.com/abk; f. 1967; wholly owned by private Kuwaiti interests; cap. 144m., res 266m., dep. 2,525m. (Dec. 2011); Chair. AHMAD YOUSUF BEHBEHANI; Dep. Chair. and Man. Dir ALI HILAL AL-MUTAIRI; 25 domestic brs and 2 foreign brs.

Ahli United Bank KSC (BKME): POB 71, 13001 Safat, Joint Banking Centre, East Tower, Darwazat Abd al-Razzak, Kuwait City; tel. 22459771; fax 22461430; e-mail hayakom@bkme.com.kw; internet www.bkme.com; f. 1971; fmrly Bank of Kuwait and the Middle East KSC; current name adopted in April 2010 after acquiring Kuwaiti brs of British Bank of the Middle East; 75% owned by Ahli United Bank (Bahrain); cap. 112m., res 69m., dep. 2,312m. (Dec. 2011); Chair. and Man. Dir HAMAD ABD AL-MOHSEN AL-MARZOUQ; 26 brs.

BBK: POB 24396, 13104 Safat, Ahmad al-Jaber St, Kuwait City; tel. 22417140; fax 22440937; e-mail bbkp@batelco.com.bh; internet www.bbkonline.com; f. 1971 as Bank of Bahrain and Kuwait BSC; name changed as above in 2005; dep. BD 1,756.4m. (Dec. 2009); Chair. MURAD ALI MURAD; Chief Exec. ABD AL-KARIM AHMAD BUCHEERI.

Boubyan Bank KSC: POB 25507, 13116 Safat, Kuwait City; tel. 22325000; fax 22454263; e-mail info@bankboubyan.com; internet www.bankboubyan.com; f. 2004; cap. 174m., res 63m., dep. 1,282m. (Dec. 2011); Chair. and Man. Dir ADEL ABD AL-WAHAB AL-MAJID.

Burgan Bank SAK: POB 5389, 12170 Safat, Abd al-Haih al-Ahmad St, Kuwait City; tel. 22439000; fax 22461148; e-mail info@burgan.com; internet www.burgan.com; f. 1975; 33.9% owned by Kuwait Projects Co (Holding), Safat; cap. 147m., res 229m., dep. 3,737m. (Dec. 2011); Chair. MAJID EISA AL-AJEEL; CEO EDUARDO EGUREN LINSEN; 20 brs.

Commercial Bank of Kuwait SAK: POB 2861, 13029 Safat, Mubarak al-Kabir St, Kuwait City; tel. 22411001; fax 22464870; e-mail cbkinq@cbk.com; internet www.cbk.com; f. 1960 by Amiri decree; cap. 127m., res 289m., dep. 3,140m. (Dec. 2011); Chair. and Man. Dir ALI MOUSA M. AL-MOUSA; CEO NUHAD KALIM SALIBA; 51 brs.

Gulf Bank KSC: POB 3200, 13032 Safat, Mubarak al-Kabir St, Kuwait City; tel. 22449501; fax 22445212; e-mail customerservice@gulfbank.com.kw; internet www.e-gulfbank.com; f. 1960; cap. 250m., res 171m., dep. 4,183m. (Dec. 2011); Chair. MAHMOUD ABD AL-KHALEQ AL-NOURI; CEO and Chief Gen. Man. MICHEL ACCAD; 52 brs.

Industrial Bank of Kuwait KSC (IBK): POB 3146, 13032 Safat, Joint Banking Centre, Darwazzat Abd al-Razaq, Commercial Area 9, Kuwait City; tel. 22457661; fax 22406595; e-mail ibk@ibkuwt.com; internet www.ibkuwt.com; 31.4% state-owned; f. 1973; cap. 20m., res 172m., dep. 133m. (Dec. 2011); Chair. and Man. Dir ABD AL-MOHSEN YOUSUF AL-HANIF; Gen. Man. ALI ABD AL-NABI KHAJA.

Kuwait Finance House KSC (KFH): POB 24989, 13110 Safat, Abdullah al-Mubarak St, Kuwait City; tel. 22445050; fax 22455135; e-mail kfh@kfh.com; internet www.kfh.com; f. 1977; 45% state-owned; Islamic banking and investment co; cap. 268m., res 943m., dep. 8,927m. (Dec. 2011); Chair. SAMIR YACOUB AL-NAFISI; Chief Exec. MUHAMMAD SULAYMAN AL-OMAR; 44 brs.

Kuwait International Bank (KIB): POB 22822, 13089 Safat, West Tower, Joint Banking Centre, Mubarak al-Kabir St, Kuwait City; tel. 22458177; fax 22462516; e-mail contact@kib.com.kw; internet www.kib.com.kw; f. 1973 as Kuwait Real Estate Bank KSC; name changed as above upon conversion into an Islamic bank in 2007; wholly owned by private Kuwaiti interests; cap. 103m., res 85m., dep. 699m. (Dec. 2011); Chair. MUHAMMAD JARRAH AL-SABAH; CEO LOAI MAQAMIS (acting); 11 brs.

National Bank of Kuwait SAK (NBK): POB 95, 13001 Safat, Abdullah al-Ahmad St, Kuwait City; tel. 22422011; fax 22462469; e-mail webmaster@nbk.com; internet www.nbk.com; f. 1952; cap. 395m., res 1,199m., dep. 11,109m. (Dec. 2011); Chair. MUHAMMAD ABD AL-RAHMAN AL-BAHAR; CEO IBRAHIM S. DABDOUB; 66 brs in Kuwait, 44 brs abroad.

INSURANCE

Al-Ahleia Insurance Co SAK: POB 1602, Ahmad al-Jaber St, 13017 Safat, Kuwait City; tel. 1888444; fax 22416495; e-mail aic@alahleia.com; internet www.alahleia.com; f. 1962; all forms of insurance; cap. 15.6m. (July 2007); Chair. and Man. Dir SULAYMAN HAMAD MUHAMMAD AL-DALALI.

Arab Commercial Enterprises WLL (Kuwait): POB 2474, 13025 Safat, Kuwait City; tel. 22413854; fax 22409450; e-mail acekwt@ace-ins.com; f. 1952; Man. SALIM ABOU HAIDAR.

First Takaful Insurance Co (FTIC): Abdullah al-Mubarak St, Alenma'a Tower, POB 5713, 13058 Safat, Kuwait City; tel. 21880055; fax 22444599; e-mail info@firsttakaful.com; internet www.firsttakaful.com; f. 2000; Islamic insurance; Chair. and Man. Dir KHALIL IBRAHIM MUHAMMAD AL-SHAMI; 5 brs.

Gulf Insurance Co KSC: POB 1040, 13011 Safat, Ahmad al-Jaber St, Kuwait City; tel. 1802080; fax 22961998; e-mail contacts@gig.com.kw; internet www.gulfins.com.kw; f. 1962; cap. 18.7m. (2012); all forms of insurance; Chair. FARKAD ABDULLAH AL-SANEA; CEO and Man. Dir KHALED SAOUD AL-HASSAN.

Al-Ittihad al-Watani Insurance Co for the Near East SAL: 4th Floor, Bahman Bldg, Ahmad al-Jaber St, POB 781, 13008 Safat, Kuwait City; tel. 22420390; fax 22420366; e-mail webmaster@alittihadalwatani.com.lb; Man. JOSEPH ZACCOUR.

Kuwait Insurance Co SAK (KIC): POB 769, 13008 Safat, Abdullah al-Salem St, Kuwait City; tel. 1884433; fax 22428530; e-mail info@kic-kw.com; internet www.kic-kw.com; f. 1960; cap. US $64.6m.; all life and non-life insurance; Chair. MUHAMMAD SALEH BEHBEHANI; Gen. Man. Dr ALI HAMAD AL-BAHAR.

Kuwait Reinsurance Co KSCC: POB 21929, 13080 Safat, Kuwait City; tel. 22432011; fax 22427823; e-mail kuwaitre@kuwaitre.com; internet www.kuwaitre.com; f. 1972; cap. 10.0m., total assets 59.3m. (2006); Chair. FAHED AL-IBRAHIM; Gen. Man. AMIR AL-MUHANNA.

Mohd Saleh Behbehani & Co: POB 341, 13004 Safat, Kuwait City; tel. 24721670; fax 24760070; e-mail msrybco@qualitynet.net; f. 1963; Pres. MUHAMMAD SALEH YOUSUF BEHBEHANI.

New India Assurance Co: 19th Floor, Behbehani Bldg, Jaber al-Mubarak St, Sharq, POB 370, 13004 Safat, Kuwait City; tel. 22404258; fax 22412089; e-mail newindia@qualitynet.net; f. 1919; Man. Dr G. VENKATAIAH.

The Oriental Insurance Co Ltd: Burj Jassim, 9th floor, Al Soor St, Kuwait City; tel. 22960500; fax 22960499; e-mail insurance@almullagroup.com; internet www.orientalinsurance.org.in; f. 1947; Man. ANIL KUMAR PARASHER.

Sumitomo Marine & Fire Insurance Co (Kuwait Agency): POB 3458, 13035 Safat, Kuwait City; tel. 22433087; fax 22430853; Contact ABDULLAH BOUDROS.

Warba Insurance Co SAK: POB 24282, 13103 Safat, Kuwait City; tel. 22445140; fax 22466131; e-mail warba@warbaonline.com; internet www.warbaonline.com; f. 1976; cap. 7.7m. (2002), total assets 80.1m. (Dec. 2005); all forms of insurance; Chair. ANWAR JAWAD KHAMSEEN; Man. Dir TAWFIK SHAMLAN AL-BAHAR; 3 brs.

Wethaq Takaful Insurance Co: Khaled bin al-Waleed St, City Tower, Kuwait City; tel. 21866662; fax 22491280; f. 2000; Islamic insurance; Chair. ABDULLAH YOUSUF AL-SAIF; Gen. Man. MAJID Y. AL-ALI.

STOCK EXCHANGE

Kuwait Stock Exchange (KSE): POB 22235, 13083 Safat, Mubarak al-Kabir St, Kuwait City; tel. 22992000; fax 22420779; e-mail webmaster@kuwaitse.com; internet www.kuwaitse.com; f. 1983; 226 cos and one mutual fund listed (Aug. 2009); Dir-Gen. SALEH MUBARAK AL-FALAH.

Markets Association

Kuwait Financial Markets Association (KFMA): 6th Floor, Deema Bldg, POB 25228, 13113 Safat, Block 3, St 64, Kuwait City; tel. 22498560; fax 22498561; e-mail kfma@kfma.org.kw; internet www.kfma.org.kw; f. 1977; represents treasury, financial and capital markets and their mems; Pres. AQEEL NASSER HABIB; Sec.-Gen. FERAS FAISAL AL-KANDARY.

Trade and Industry

GOVERNMENT AGENCY

Kuwait Investment Authority (KIA): POB 64, 13001 Safat, Kuwait City; tel. 22485600; fax 22454059; e-mail information@kia.gov.kw; internet www.kia.gov.kw; oversees the Kuwait Investment Office (London, United Kingdom); sovereign wealth fund; responsible for the Kuwaiti General Reserve; Chair. MUSTAFA AL-SHAMALI (Deputy Prime Minister and Minister of Finance); Man. Dir BADER MUHAMMAD AL-SAAD.

DEVELOPMENT ORGANIZATIONS

Arab Planning Institute (API): POB 5834, 13059 Safat, Kuwait City; tel. 24843130; fax 24842935; e-mail api@api.org.kw; internet www.arab-api.org; f. 1966; 15 Arab mem. states; publishes *Journal of Development and Economic Policies* (twice-yearly) and proceedings of seminars and discussion group meetings, offers research, training programmes and advisory services; Dir-Gen. BADER MALALLAH.

Industrial and Financial Investments Co (IFIC): POB 26019, 13121 Safat, Joint Banking Complex, 8th Floor, Industrial Bank Bldg, Derwaza Abd al-Razak, Kuwait City; tel. 22429073; fax 22448850; e-mail ific@ific.net; internet www.ific.net; f. 1983; privatized in 1996; invests directly in industry; Chair. and Man. Dir Dr TALEB AHMAD ALI.

Kuwait Fund for Arab Economic Development (KFAED): POB 2921, 13030 Safat, cnr Mubarak al-Kabir St and al-Hilali St, Kuwait City; tel. 22999000; fax 22999090; e-mail info@kuwait-fund.org; internet www.kuwait-fund.org; f. 1961; cap. KD 2,000m.; state-owned; provides and administers financial and technical assistance to developing countries; Chair. Sheikh SABAH AL-KHALID AL-HAMAD AL-SABAH (Deputy Prime Minister and Minister of Foreign Affairs); Dir-Gen. ABD AL-WAHAB A. AL-BADER.

Kuwait International Investment Co SAK (KIIC): POB 22792, 13088 Safat, al-Salhiya Commercial Complex, Kuwait City; tel. 22438273; fax 22454931; 30% state-owned; domestic real estate and share markets; Chair. and Man. Dir JASEM MUHAMMAD AL-BAHAR.

Kuwait Investment Co SAK (KIC): POB 1005, 13011 Safat, 5th Floor, al-Manakh Bldg, Mubarak al-Kabir St, Kuwait City; tel. 65888852; fax 22444896; e-mail info@kic.com.kw; internet www.kic.com.kw; f. 1981; 88% state-owned, 12% owned by private Kuwaiti interests; cap. KD 50.0m. (2002); international banking and investment; Chair. and Man. Dir BADER NASSER AL-SUBAIEE.

Kuwait Planning Board: POB 15, 13001 Safat, Kuwait City; tel. 22428200; fax 22414734; f. 1962; supervises long-term devt plans; through its Central Statistical Office publishes information on Kuwait's economic activity; Dir-Gen. AHMAD ALI AL-DUAIJ.

Mega Projects Agency (MPA): c/o Ministry of Public Works, POB 8, 13001 Safat, Kuwait City; tel. 25385520; fax 25385234; e-mail hmansour@mpa.gov.kw; f. 2005; supervises the progress of Failaka and Bubiyan island devts; Chair. BADER AL-HUMAIDI.

Public Authority for Industry (PAI): POB 4690, 13047 Safat, Kuwait City; POB 10033, Shuaiba; tel. 25302222; fax 25302190; e-mail indust@pai.gov.kw; internet www.pai.gov.kw; f. 1997; successor to Shuaiba Area Authority (f. 1964); develops, promotes and supervises industry in Kuwait; CEO ANAS KHALID AL-SALEH (Minister of Commerce and Industry); Gen. Man. ALI FAHAD AL-MUDHAF.

CHAMBER OF COMMERCE

Kuwait Chamber of Commerce and Industry: POB 775, 13008 Safat, Commercial Area 9, al-Shuhadaa St, Kuwait City; tel. 1805580; fax 22404110; e-mail kcci@kcci.org.kw; internet www.kuwaitchamber.org.kw; f. 1959; 36,000 mems; Chair. ALI MUHAMMAD THUNAYAN AL-GHANIM; Dir-Gen. RABAH AL-RABAH.

STATE HYDROCARBONS COMPANIES

Supreme Petroleum Council (SPC): Kuwait City; f. 1974; highest energy decision-making body, responsible for national oil policy; Chair. Sheikh JABER MUBARAK AL-HAMAD AL-SABAH (Prime Minister).

Kuwait Petroleum Corpn (KPC): POB 26565, 13126 Safat, al-Salhiya Commercial Complex, Fahed al-Salem St, Kuwait City; tel. 22455455; fax 22467159; e-mail info@kpc.com.kw; internet www.kpc.com.kw; f. 1980; co-ordinating org. to manage the petroleum industry; Chair. MUSTAFA AL-SHIMALI (Deputy Prime Minister, Minister of Oil); CEO NIZAR AL-ADASANI; subsidiaries include:

Kuwait Aviation Fuelling Co KSC (KAFCO): POB 1654, 13017 Safat, Kuwait City; tel. 24378500; fax 24378505; e-mail airfuel@kafco.com; internet www.kafco.com; f. 1963; Chair. FOUAD AL-ABBASI; Man. Dir ASAAD AHMAD AL-SAAD; 200 employees.

Kuwait Foreign Petroleum Exploration Co KSC (KUFPEC): POB 5291, 13053 Safat, Kuwait City; tel. 1836000; fax 24921818; internet www.kufpec.com; f. 1981; state-owned; overseas oil and gas exploration and devt; Chair. SANAD AL-SANAD; Man. Dir Sheikh NAWAF SAUD AL-SABAH; 169 employees.

Kuwait Gulf Oil Co KSC (KGOC): POB 9919, Ahmadi 61010; tel. 25454254; e-mail info@kgoc.com; internet www.kgoc.com; f. 2002 to take over Kuwait's interest in the Neutral (Partitioned) Zone's offshore operator, Khafji Joint Operations, and all of Kuwait's other offshore exploration and production activities; Chair. MUHAMMAD SAYYID ABD AL-WAHAB; Man. Dir ALI AL-SHEMMERI.

Kuwait National Petroleum Co KSC (KNPC): POB 70, 13001 Safat, Ali al-Salem St, Kuwait City; tel. 23989900; fax 23986188; internet www.knpc.com.kw; f. 1960; oil refining, production of liquefied petroleum gas, and domestic marketing and distribution of petroleum by-products; Chair. ASSAD AL-SAAD; Man. Dir MUHAMMAD AL-MUTAIRI; 5,611 employees.

Kuwait Oil Co KSC (KOC): POB 9758, 61008 Ahmadi; tel. 23983661; fax 23984971; e-mail kocinfo@kockw.com; internet www.kockw.com; f. 1934; state-owned; Chair. NABIL BOURESLI; Man. Dir HASHIM HASHIM; 4,815 employees.

Kuwait Petroleum International (Q8): POB 1819, 13019 Safat, Kuwait City; tel. 22332800; fax 22332776; e-mail info-kuwait@q8.com; internet www.q8.com; marketing division of KPC; controls 4,000 petrol retail stations in Europe, and European refineries with capacity of 235,000 b/d; Man. Dir BAKHIT AL-RASHIDI.

UTILITIES

The Government planned to create regulatory bodies for each of Kuwait's utilities, with a view to facilitating their privatization.

Ministry of Electricity and Water: see Ministries; provides subsidized services throughout Kuwait.

MAJOR COMPANIES

Aerated Concrete Industries Co KSC (ACICO): POB 24079, 13101 Safat, Kuwait City; tel. 1888811; fax 22422103; e-mail info@acico.com.kw; internet www.acico.com.kw; f. 1990; state-owned; cement, concrete, construction, etc.; Chair. ABD AL-AZIZ AHMAD AL-AYOUB; 1,700 employees.

Agility Logistics: POB 25418, 13115 Safat, Kuwait City; tel. 1809222; fax 24673098; e-mail press@agilitylogistics.com; internet www.agilitylogistics.com; f. 1979; logistics; Chair. and Man. Dir TAREK SULTAN; 32,000 employees world-wide.

Alghanim Industries: POB 223, 13003 Safat, Kuwait City; tel. 24843988; fax 22440306; e-mail impactinfo@alghanim.com; internet www.alghanim.com; f. 1932; trading, contracting, manufacturing, shipping, travel and financial services; Pres. SAMIR M. KASEM; CEO OMAR K. ALGHANIM; 12,000 employees.

Boubyan Petrochemical Co KSC: POB 2383, 13024 Safat, Kuwait City; tel. 22446684; fax 22414100; e-mail info@boubyan.com; internet www.boubyan.com; f. 1995; cap. KD 48.5m. (Aug. 2010); manufacture, import and distribution of petrochemical products; Chair. MARZOUK A. AL-GHANIM; 220 employees.

Contracting and Marine Services Co SAK (CMS): POB 22853, 13089 Safat, Kuwait City; tel. 22410270; fax 22442602; e-mail cms@qualitynet.net; f. 1973; associated with Nat. Industries Group; marine construction works and services; cap. KD 17.9m. (2009); Chair. and Man. Dir FAISAL IBRAHIM AL-NASIR AL-HAJRI; 12 employees.

Efad Real Estate: POB 616, 13007 Safat, Kuwait City; tel. 22427060; fax 22405093; e-mail info@efadholding.com; internet www.efadre.com; 12 subsidiaries, incl. Investment Dar; operates in real estate, contracting, general trading, hospitality, engineering, transportation and logistics, IT, investment banking; CEO REZAM MUHAMMAD AL-ROUMI; Gen. Man. KHALED BADER AL-ROUMI.

Gulf Cable and Electrical Industries Co KSC: POB 1196, 13012 Safat, Kuwait City; tel. 24645500; fax 24675305; e-mail info@gulfcable.com; internet www.gulfcable.com; f. 1975; cap. KD 20.9m., sales KD 71.1m. (2009); manufacture of cables and electrical equipment; Chair. and Man. Dir BADER NASER AL-KHARAFI; 441 employees.

Independent Petroleum Group SAK (IPG): POB 24027, 13101 Safat, Kuwait City; tel. 22276222; fax 22276100; e-mail general@ipg.com.kw; internet www.ipg.com.kw; f. 1976; cap. KD 10.9m., sales KD 275.0m. (2002); industrial, commercial and consulting role in hydrocarbons industry; Chair. KHALAF AHMAD AL-KHALAF; Man. Dir WALID JABER HADID; 46 employees.

Kuwait Aluminium Co KSC: POB 5335, 13054 Safat, al-Rai Industrial Area, Plot 1636, St No. 13, Kuwait City; tel. 24734000; fax 24710475; e-mail kalu@qualitynet.net; internet www.kuwaitaluminium.com; f. 1968; sales about KD 1.5m., cap. p.u. KD 2m.; design, manufacture, erection and maintenance of aluminium and glass works for construction industry; Chair. NASSER NAKI; 200 employees.

Kuwait Cement Co KSC: Cement House Bldg, al-Shuhada St/Khalid ibn al-Walid St, al-Sawaba, Kuwait City; tel. 22401700; fax 22432956; e-mail alcement@kuwaitcement.com; internet www.kuwaitcement.com; f. 1968; 32.4% govt-owned; planned privatization postponed indefinitely in late 2001; manufacture and marketing of cement; cap. KD 55.8m., sales KD 61.8m. (2009); Chair. and Man. Dir. RASHID ABD AL-AZIZ AL-RASHID; 462 employees.

Kuwait Food Co (Americana) SAK: POB 5087, 13051 Safat, Kuwait City; tel. 24815900; fax 24815914; e-mail headoffice@americanaf.com; internet www.americana-group.com; f. 1964; cap. KD 40.2m., sales KD 334.4m. (2009); chain of restaurants, meat industry, bakery plant for oriental sweets and English cakes; Chair. and Gen. Man. MARZOUK NASSER AL-KHARAFI; 15,000 employees.

Kuwait Livestock Transport and Trading Co KSC (KLTT): POB 23727, 13098 Safat, Kuwait City; tel. 22434185; fax 22402109; e-mail faisal@kltt.com.kw; internet www.kltt.com.kw; f. 1973; trade in livestock and livestock products; Chair. and Man. Dir FAISAL ABDULLAH AL-KHAZAM; 571 employees.

Kuwait Pipe Industries and Oil Services Co KSC (KPIOS): POB 3416, 13035 Safat, Kuwait City; tel. 24675622; fax 24675897; e-mail kpios@kpios.com; internet www.kpios.com; f. 1966; 16.6% govt-owned; mfrs of various pipes, tanks and coatings; cap. KD 22.5m., sales KD 36.5m. (2009); Chair. ADEL MUHAMMAD RIDA BEHBEHANI; CEO TALAL M. AL-QAHTANI; 322 employees.

Kuwait Portland Cement Co KSC: POB 42191, 70652 Shuwaikh, Kuwait City; tel. 24835615; fax 24846152; e-mail fatma@portland.com.kw; internet www.kpckuwait.weebly.com; f. 1976; cap. KD 7.2m., sales KD 17.0m. (2002); imports, exports and trades in construction materials; Chair. KHALID ABDULLAH AL-SAGAR; Gen. Man. KHALIFA HUMOUD AL-GHANIM; 122 employees.

Kuwait Projects Co KSC (KIPCO): POB 23982, 13100 Safat, Kuwait City; tel. 1805885; fax 22435790; e-mail kipco@kipco.com; internet www.kipco.com; f. 1975; investment holding co; operates in the financial services and media and technology sectors; Chair Sheikh HAMAD SABAH AL-AHMAD AL-SABAH.

Kuwait United Poultry KSC (KUPCO): POB 1236, 13013 Safat, Kuwait City; tel. and fax 248196500; e-mail info@kupco.net; internet www.kupco.net; f. 1974; cap. KD 11.5m. (2009); breeding and distribution of poultry and poultry products; Chair. KHALED SULAYMAN ALI AL-ALI; Man. Dir AZARA FALEH AL-HUSSINE; 700 employees.

Mushrif Trading and Constructing Co KSCC: POB 32514, 25556 Rumaithya, Kuwait City; tel. 24766172; fax 24741423; e-mail info@mushrif.com; internet www.mushrif.com; f. 1968; part of Al-Wazzan Trading Group; construction; Chair. FAISAL BELHOUL; CEO MOHSEN DEHGHANI; 2,500 employees.

Packaging and Plastic Industries Co: POB 10044, 65451 Shuaiba, Kuwait City; tel. 22435841; fax 22435839; f. 1974; sales KD 6.5m. (2000); production of polypropylene woven bags for packaging fertilizers, polyethylene agricultural sheets, co-extruded flexible film packaging; Gen. Man. MAZEN A. KHOURSHEED; 167 employees.

United Fisheries of Kuwait KSC: POB 22044, 13081 Safat, Kuwait City; tel. 24950101; fax 24950240; e-mail info@ufkonline.com; internet www.ufkonline.com; f. 1972; cap. KD 15.4m., sales KD 7.7m. (2001); production, export and import of frozen fish and shrimps; CEO KHALED AL-SAYEGH; 463 employees.

United Industries Co KSC (UIC): POB 25821, 13119 Safat, Kuwait City; tel. 22953000; fax 22423486; e-mail uic@uickw.com; internet www.uickw.com; f. 1979; member of Kuwait Projects Co (KIPCO); cap. 24.7m. (2009); Chair. Sheikh SABAH MUHAMMAD ABD AL-AZIZ AL-SABAH; 36 employees.

TRADE UNIONS

Federation of Petroleum and Petrochemical Workers: Kuwait City; f. 1965; Chair. JASEM ABD AL-WAHAB AL-TOURA.

KOC Workers Union: Kuwait City; f. 1964; Chair. HAMAD SAWYAN.

Kuwait Trade Union Federation (KTUF): POB 5185, 13052 Safat, Kuwait City; tel. 25636389; fax 25627159; e-mail ktuf@hotmail.com; internet www.ktuf.org; f. 1967; central authority to which all trade unions are affiliated; Pres. FAIEZ ALI AL-MUTAIRI; Gen. Sec. FARES AL-SAWAGH AL-AZEMI.

Transport

RAILWAYS

There are currently no railways in Kuwait. However, plans for a 518-km national rail network, which would be linked to a regional rail network, connecting Kuwait with member countries of the Cooperation Council for the Arab States of the Gulf (or Gulf Cooperation Council—GCC), were announced in 2008. Construction work on the first phase of a four-line, 171-km metro system in Kuwait City were expected to begin before the end of 2013. The project, the total cost of which was estimated at US $7,000m., was scheduled to commence operations in 2016.

ROADS

In 2010 the total road network was estimated at 6,608 km. Roads in the towns are metalled, and the most important are motorways or dual carriageways. There are metalled roads linking Kuwait City to Ahmadi, Mina al-Ahmadi and other centres of population in Kuwait, and to the Iraqi and Saudi Arabian borders. A 72-km Subiya–Jahra highway and a ring-road at Sabah al-Ahmad City are currently under construction; work on a 42-km, six-lane Nawaseeb Highway was expected to be completed in 2013. In late 2012 a US $3,700m. design-and-build contract for a causeway linking Kuwait City with Madinat al-Hareer (Silk City—a new development under construction in Subiya) was awarded to Hyundai Engineering and Construction Co of the Republic of Korea (South Korea).

Kuwait Public Transport Co SAK (KPTC): POB 375, 13004 Safat, Murghab, Safat Sq., Kuwait City; tel. 22328501; fax 22328870; e-mail info@kptc.com.kw; internet www.kptc.com.kw; f. 1962; state-owned; provides internal bus service; regular service to Mecca, Saudi Arabia; Chair. and Man. Dir MAHMOUD A. AL-NOURI.

SHIPPING

Kuwait has three commercial seaports. The largest, Shuwaikh, situated about 3 km from Kuwait City, comprises 21 deep-water berths, with a total length of 4 km, three shallow-water berths and three basins for small craft, each with a depth of 3.35 m. Shuaiba Commercial Port, 56 km south of Kuwait City, comprises 20 berths with a total length of 4 km. Since 2003 the port has been used by the US Army as a base for supplying its troops in Iraq. Expansion plans were announced in 2009. Doha, the smallest port, has 20 small berths, each 100 m long. An oil port at Mina al-Ahmadi, 40 km south of Kuwait City, comprises 12 tanker berths, one bitumen-carrier berth, two LPG export berths and bunkering facilities, and is able to load more than 2m. barrels of oil per day.

Plans for the privatization of Kuwait's ports were under development in the late 2000s. In 2010 a contract for the construction of a new US $1,200m. international port at Bubiyan island was awarded to Hyundai Engineering and Construction Co. The Mubarak al-Kabir port was expected to commence operations in 2016.

At 31 December 2012 Kuwait's flag registered fleet numbered 155 vessels, with a total displacement of 2,479,501 grt, of which two were bulk carriers, one was a fish carrier, four were gas tankers and two were general cargo ships.

Port Authority

Kuwait Ports Authority: POB 3874, 13039 Safat, Kuwait City; tel. 24812622; fax 24819714; e-mail info@kpa.gov.kw; internet www.kpa.gov.kw; f. 1977; Dir-Gen. Dr SABER JABER AL-ALI AL-SABAH.

Principal Shipping Companies

Arab Maritime Petroleum Transport Co (AMPTC): POB 22525, 13086 Safat, Kuwait City; tel. 24959400; fax 24842996; e-mail amptc.kuwait@amptc.net; internet www.amptc.net; f. 1973; six crude petroleum tankers, four LPG carriers and one product carrier; owned by Algeria, Bahrain, Egypt, Iraq, Kuwait, Libya, Qatar, Saudi Arabia and the UAE; Gen. Man. SULAYMAN I. AL-BASSAM.

Heavy Engineering Industries and Shipbuilding Co (Heisco): POB 21998, 13080 Safat, Kuwait City; tel. 24835488; fax 24830291; e-mail heisco@heisco.com; internet www.heisco.com; f. 1974 as Kuwait Shipbuilding and Repairyard Co; name changed as above in 2003; ship repairs and engineering services, underwater services, maintenance of refineries, power stations and storage tanks; maintains floating dock for vessels up to 35,000 dwt; synchrolift for vessels up to 5,000 dwt with transfer yard; seven repair jetties up to 550 m in length and floating workshop for vessels lying at anchor; Chair. JUHAIL MUHAMMAD AL-JUHAIL.

KGL Ports Int. Co (KGL PI): POB 42438, Shuwaikh 70655; tel. 22245155; fax 22245166; e-mail info@kglpi.com; internet www.kglpi.com; f. 2004; subsidiary of Kuwait and Gulf Link Transport Co; port management and stevedoring; operates Shuaiba Commercial Port Container Terminal; also operations and management contracts with ports in United Arab Emirates and Saudi Arabia; Chair. and Man. Dir FADHEL AL-BAGHLI; CEO ALLAN ROSENBERG.

Kuwait Maritime Transport Co KSC (KMTC): POB 22595, 13086 Safat, Nafisi and Khatrash Bldg, Jaber al-Mubarak St, Kuwait City; tel. 22449974; fax 22420513; f. 1981; Chair. YOUSUF AL-MAJID.

Kuwait Oil Tanker Co SAK (KOTC): POB 810, 13009 Safat, Shuwaikh Administrative Sector (P), Gamal Abdel Nasser St, Kuwait City; tel. 24625050; fax 24913597; e-mail nakilat@kotc.com.kw; internet www.kotc.com.kw; f. 1957; state-owned; operates eight crude oil tankers, 11 product tankers and five LPG vessels; sole tanker agents for Mina al-Ahmadi, Shuaiba and Mina al-Abdullah and agents for other ports; LPG filling and distribution; Chair. and Man. Dir NABIL M. BOURISLI.

United Arab Shipping Co SAG (UASC): POB 20722, 13068 Safat, UASC Bldg, Old Airport Rd, Beside Zain Bldg, Kuwait City; tel. 24848190; fax 24831263; e-mail gencom.uasackwt@uasc.net; internet www.uasc.net; f. 1976; nat shipping co of six Arabian Gulf countries; services between Europe, Far East, Mediterranean ports, Japan and east coast of USA and South America, and ports of participant states on Persian (Arabian) Gulf and Red Sea; operates 42 vessels; subsidiary cos include: United Arab Shipping Agencies Co (Kuwait), Arab Transport Co (Aratrans), United Arab Chartering Ltd (United Kingdom), Middle East Container Repair Co (UAE), Arabian Chemicals Carriers (Saudi Arabia), United Arab Agencies Inc (USA) and United Arab Shipping Agencies Co (Saudi Arabia); Chair. OTHMAN IBRAHIM AL-ISSA; Pres. and CEO JØRN HINGE.

CIVIL AVIATION

Kuwait International Airport opened in 1980, and by 2011 handled 8.5m. passengers, compared with 3.8m. in 2001. The airport is undergoing a major programme of expansion: the first phase of the project was to expand the airport's annual capacity to 20m. passengers and to modernize facilities, with a further final phase of development intended to achieve passenger capacity of 55m.

Directorate-General of Civil Aviation (DGCA): POB 17, 13001 Safat, Kuwait City; tel. 24744256; fax 24744396; e-mail president@dgca.gov.kw; internet www.dgca.gov.kw; Pres. FAWAZ AL-FARAH; Dir-Gen. Eng. BADER BOUTAIBAN.

Jazeera Airways: POB 29288, 13153 Safat, Kuwait City; e-mail helpdesk@jazeeraairways.com; internet www.jazeeraairways.com; f. 2005; low-cost airline owned by Boodai Group; serves 26 destinations in the Middle East, North Africa, Europe and Asia; Chair. MARWAN BOODAI; CEO STEFAN PICHLER.

Kuwait Airways Corpn (KAC): POB 394, Kuwait International Airport, 13004 Safat, Kuwait City; tel. 22248560; fax 22441304; e-mail kwi@kuwaitairways.com; internet www.kuwait-airways.com; f. 1954; scheduled and charter passenger and cargo services to the Arabian peninsula, Asia, Africa, the USA and Europe; scheduled for privatization; Chair. and Man. Dir HAMAD A. LATIF AL-FALAH.

Tourism

Attractions for visitors include the Kuwait Towers leisure and reservoir complex, the Entertainment City theme park, the Kuwait Zoological Garden in Omariya and the Khiran Resort tourist village near the border with Saudi Arabia, as well as extensive facilities for sailing and other water sports. In 2010 foreign tourist arrivals totalled some 5.2m. According to provisional data, tourism receipts (excluding passenger transport) of US $199m. were recorded in 2011.

Department of Tourism: Ministry of Information, Tourism Affairs, POB 193, 13002 Safat, al-Sour St, Kuwait City; tel. 22457591; fax 22401540; e-mail tourism_kw@media.gov.kw.

Kuwait Tourism Services Co: POB 21774, 13078 Safat, Kuwait City; tel. 2451734; fax 2451731; e-mail ktsc@qualitynet.net; internet www.ktsc-q8.com; f. 1997; Chair. KHALID AL-DUWAISAN.

Touristic Enterprises Co (TEC): POB 23310, 13094 Safat, Kuwait City; tel. 24965555; fax 24965055; e-mail info@tec.com.kw; internet www.kuwaittourism.com; f. 1976; 92% state-owned; manages 23 tourist facilities; Chair. BADER AL-BAHAR; Vice-Chair. SHAKER AL-OTHMAN.

Defence

Chief of Staff of Armed Forces: Lt-Gen. KHALID AL-JARRAH AL-SABAH.

Defence Budget (2012): KD 1,280m.

Military Service: voluntary.

Total Armed Forces (as assessed at November 2012): 15,500: army 11,000; navy est. 2,000 (including 500 coast guards); air force 2,500. Reserves 23,700.

Paramilitary Forces (as assessed at November 2012): est. 7,100 (national guard est. 6,600; coast guard 500).

Education

Compulsory education for children between six and 14 years of age was introduced in 1966–67. However, many children spend two years prior to this in a kindergarten, and go on to complete their general education at the age of 18 years. It is government policy to provide free education to all Kuwaiti children from kindergarten stage to university. In 2011/12 a total of 357,273 pupils attended 794 government schools (201 kindergarten, 253 primary, 204 intermediate and 136 secondary). In 2011/12 a total of 224,268 pupils attended 475 private schools (105 kindergarten, 132 primary, 133 intermediate and 105 secondary).

Primary education lasts for five years between the ages of six and 10, after which the pupils move on to an intermediate school for another four years. Secondary education, which is optional and lasts between the ages of 14 and 18, is given mainly in general schools. There are also commercial institutes, a Faculty of Technological Studies, a health institute, religious institutes (with intermediate and secondary stages) and 11 institutes for handicapped children. In 2008/09 enrolment at primary schools was equivalent to 95% of children in the relevant age-group, while at secondary schools the rate was equivalent to 90% of children in the relevant age-group.

Scholarships are granted to students to pursue courses not offered by Kuwait University. Such scholarships are mainly used to study in Egypt, Lebanon, the United Kingdom and the USA. There are also pupils from Arab, African and Asian states studying in Kuwait schools on scholarships provided by the Kuwaiti Government. Kuwait University had about 20,000 students in 2006, and also provides scholarships for a number of Arab, Asian and African students. In May 1996 the Majlis approved a draft law to regulate students' behaviour, dress and activities, with regard to observance of the teachings of *Shari'a* (Islamic) law, and to eradicate co-educational classes at Kuwait University over a five-year period. A KD 1,000m. project to build a new university campus and to gather the institution's dispersed facilities onto one site was expected to be completed by 2025. In 2008/09 an estimated 61,920 students were enrolled in tertiary education. Expenditure on education by the central Government in 2010/11 totalled KD 1,441m. (12.0% of total expenditure).

Bibliography

Bacik, Gökhan. *Hybrid Sovereignty in the Arab Middle East: the Cases of Kuwait, Jordan and Iraq*. Basingstoke, Palgrave Macmillan, 2008.

Boghardt, Lori Plotkin. *Kuwait Amid War, Peace and Revolution: 1979–1991 and New Challenges*. Basingstoke, Palgrave Macmillan, 2006.

Boutros-Ghali, Boutros (Ed.). *The United Nations and the Iraq–Kuwait Conflict, 1990–96* (UN Blue Books Series, V. 9). New York, United Nations Publications, 1996.

Browne, M. A. (Ed.). *Iraq–Kuwait: United Nations Security Council Resolution Texts, 1992–2002*. Hauppauge, NY, Nova Science, 2003.

Casey, Michael S. *The History of Kuwait*. Westport CT, Greenwood Press, 2007.

Chisholm, A. H. T. *The First Kuwait Oil Concession: A Record of the Negotiations 1911–1934*. London, Frank Cass, 1975.

Cordesman, Anthony H. *Kuwait*. Boulder, CO, Westview Press, 1997.

Daniels, John. *Kuwait Journey*. Luton, White Crescent Press, 1972.

al-Dekhauel, Abdulkarim. *Kuwait: Oil, State and Political Legitimation*. London, Ithaca Press, 2000.

Dickson, H. R. P. *Kuwait and her Neighbours*. London, Allen and Unwin, 1956.

Fandy, Mamoun. *Kuwait and a New Concept of International Politics*. Basingstoke, Palgrave Macmillan, 2003.

Finnie, David. *Shifting Lines in the Sand*. London, I. B. Tauris, 1992.

Gardiner, Stephen, and Cook, Ian. *Kuwait: The Making of a City*. London, Longman, 1983.

Hakima, Abu A. M. *The Modern History of Kuwait: 1750–1966*. St Ives, The Westerham Press, 1983.

Hassan, Hamdi A. *The Iraqi Invasion of Kuwait: Religion, Identity and Otherness in the Analysis of War and Conflict*. London, Pluto Press, 1999.

al-Hijji, Yacoub Yusuf. *Kuwait and the Sea: A Brief Social and Economic History* (trans.). London, Arabian Publishing, 2010.

International Bank for Reconstruction and Development. *The Economic Development of Kuwait*. Baltimore, MD, Johns Hopkins Press, 1965.

Joyce, Miriam. *Kuwait, 1945–1996: An Anglo-American Perspective*. London, Frank Cass, 1999.

Khouja, M. W., and Sadler, P. G. *The Energy of Kuwait: Development and Role in International Finance*. London, Macmillan, 1978.

Kuwait Oil Co Ltd. *The Story of Kuwait*. London, Kuwait Oil Co Ltd., 1963.

El Mallakh, Ragaei. *Economic Development and Regional Co-operation: Kuwait*. Chicago, IL, University of Chicago Press, 1968.

Marlowe, John. *The Persian Gulf in the 20th Century*. London, Cresset Press, 1962.

Al-Mdaires, Falah Abdullah. *Islamic Extremism in Kuwait: From the Muslim Brotherhood to Al-Qaeda and Other Islamic Political Groups*. Abingdon, Routledge, 2010.

Mezerik, Avraham G. *The Kuwait–Iraq Dispute, 1961*. New York, International Review Service, 1961.

Al-Mughni, Haya. *Women in Kuwait: The Politics of Gender*. London, Saqi Books, 2001.

Panaspornprasit, Chookiat. *US–Kuwaiti Relations, 1961–1992: An Uneasy Relationship*. Abingdon, Routledge, 2005.

Rahman, H. *The Making of the Gulf War*. Reading, Garnet, 1997.

Rizzo, Helen M. *Islam, Democracy and the Status of Women: The Case of Kuwait*. Abingdon, Routledge, 2005.

Rush, Alan. *Al-Sabah History and Genealogy of Kuwait's Ruling Family 1752–1987.* London, Ithaca Press, 1987.

Saldanha, J. A. *The Persian Gulf: Administration Reports 1873–1957.* London, Archive Editions, 1986.

The Persian Gulf Precis 1903–1908. London, Archive Editions, 1986.

Sandwick, John A. *The Gulf Co-operation Council: Moderation and Stability in an Interdependent World*. London, Mansell Publishing Ltd, 1987.

Slot, Ben J. (Ed.) *Kuwait: The Growth of a Historic Identity*. London, Arabian Publishing Ltd, 2003.

Tetreault, Mary Ann. *Stories of Democracy: Politics and Society in Contemporary Kuwait*. New York, Columbia University Press, 2000.

Winstone, H. V. F., and Freeth, Zahra. *Kuwait: Prospect and Reality*. London, Allen and Unwin, 1972.

LEBANON

Physical and Social Geography

W. B. FISHER

The creation, after 1918, of the modern state of Lebanon, first under French mandatory rule and then as an independent territory, was designed to recognize the nationalist aspirations of a number of Christian groups that had lived for many centuries under Muslim rule along the coast of the eastern Mediterranean and in the hills immediately adjacent. At least as early as the 16th century AD there had been particularist Christian feeling that ultimately resulted in the granting of autonomy, though not independence, to Christians living in the territory of 'Mount Lebanon', which geographically was the hill region immediately inland and extending some 30 km–45 km north and south of Beirut. The territory of Mount Lebanon was later expanded, owing to French interest, into the much larger area of 'Greater Lebanon' with frontiers running along the crest of the Anti-Lebanon mountains, and reaching the sea some miles north of Tripoli to form the boundary with Syria. In the south there is a frontier with Israel, running inland from the promontory of Ras al-Naqoura to the head of the Jordan Valley. In drawing the frontiers so as to give a measure of geographical unity to the new state, which now occupies an area of 10,452 sq km (4,036 sq miles), large non-Christian elements of Muslims and Druzes were included, so that today the Christians of Lebanon form less than 40% (and possibly as little as 30%) of the total population, which was officially estimated at 3,759,137 in 2007. By mid-2013 the population had increased to 4,821,970, according to UN estimates.

PHYSICAL FEATURES

Structurally, Lebanon consists of an enormous simple upfold of rocks that runs parallel to the coast. There is, first, a very narrow and broken flat coastal strip—hardly a true plain—then the land rises steeply to a series of imposing crests and ridges. The highest crest of all is Qurnet al-Sauda, just over 3,000 m high, lying south-east of Tripoli; Mount Sannin, north-east of Beirut, is over 2,700 m high. A few miles east of the summits there is a precipitous drop along a sharp line to a broad, trough-like valley, known as the Beqa'a (Biqa), about 16 km wide and some 110 km–130 km long. The eastern side of the Beqa'a is formed by the Anti-Lebanon mountains, which rise to 2,800 m, and their southern continuation, the Hermon Range, of about the same height. The floor of the Beqa'a valley, though much below the level of the surrounding mountain ranges, lies in places at 1,000 m above sea level, with a low divide in the region of Ba'albek. Two rivers rise in the Beqa'a—the Orontes, which flows northwards into Syria and the Gharb depression, ultimately reaching the Mediterranean through the Turkish territory of Antioch; and the Litani (Leontes) river. This latter river flows southwards, and then, at a short distance from the Israeli frontier, makes a sudden bend westwards and plunges through the Lebanon mountains by a deep gorge.

There exists in Lebanon an unusual feature of geological structure not present in either of the adjacent regions of Syria and Israel. This is the occurrence of a layer of non-porous rocks within the upfold forming the Lebanon mountains; and, because of this layer, water is forced to the surface in considerable quantities, producing large springs at the unusually high level of 1,200 m–1,500 m. Some of the springs have a flow of several thousand cu ft per second and emerge as small rivers; hence the western flanks of the Lebanon mountains, unlike those nearby in Syria and Israel, are relatively well watered and cultivation is possible up to a height of 1,200 m or 1,500 m.

With its great contrasts of relief, and the configuration of the main ranges, which lie across the path of the prevailing westerly winds, there is a wide variety in climatic conditions. The coastal lowlands are moderately hot in summer, and warm in winter, with complete absence of frost. Yet only 10 km or so away in the hills there is a heavy winter snowfall, and the higher hills are covered from December to May, giving the unusual vista for the Middle East of snow-clad peaks. From this the name Lebanon (*laban* —Aramaic for 'white') is said to originate. The Beqa'a has a moderately cold winter with some frost and snow, and a distinctly hot summer, as it is shut off from the tempering effect of the sea.

Rainfall is generally abundant but it decreases rapidly towards the east, so that the Beqa'a and Anti-Lebanon are definitely drier than the west. On the coast, between 750 mm and 1,000 mm fall annually, with up to 1,250 mm in the mountains; but only 380 mm in the Beqa'a. As almost all of this annual total falls between October and April (there are three months of complete aridity each summer), rain is extremely heavy while it lasts, and storms of surprising intensity sometimes occur. Another remarkable feature is the extremely high humidity of the coastal region during summer, when no rain falls.

ECONOMIC LIFE

The occurrence of high mountains near the sea, and the relatively abundant supplies of spring water, had a significant influence on economic development within Lebanon. Owing to the successive levels of terrain, an unusually wide range of crops can be grown, from bananas and pineapples on the hot, damp coastlands, olives, vines and figs on the lowest foothills, cereals, apricots and peaches on the middle slopes, to apples and potatoes on the highest levels. These last are the rarest crops and, with the growing market in the oilfield areas of Arabia and the Persian (Arabian) Gulf, they are sold for the highest price. Export of fruit is therefore important. In addition, abundant natural water led to the development of pine-woods and evergreen groves, which add greatly to the already considerable scenic beauty of the western hill country. Prior to the prolonged civil conflict in Lebanon during 1975–90 (see History), there was an important tourist trade in the small hill villages, some of which have casinos, luxury hotels and cinemas. The greatest activity was during the summer months, when wealthy Middle Easterners and others arrived; but there was a smaller winter sports season, when skiing was pursued.

In addition, the geographical situation of Lebanon, as a 'façade' to the inland territories of Syria, Jordan, and even northern Iraq and southern Turkey, enabled the Lebanese ports to act as the commercial outlet for a very wide region. The importance of Beirut as a commercial centre was due in large part to the fact that Lebanon was a free market. More than one-half of the volume of Lebanon's former trade was transit traffic, and Lebanon used to handle most of the trade of Jordan. Byblos claims to be the oldest port in the world; Tyre and Sidon were long world famous, and the latter was reviving as the Mediterranean terminal of the Tapline (Trans-Arabian Pipeline) from Saudi Arabia until the Lebanese branch of the pipeline was closed at the end of 1983. Another ancient centre, Tripoli, was also a terminal of the pipeline from Iraq. Beirut is now, however, the leading town of the country, and contains more than one-half of the total population, including many displaced persons. Although local resources are not in general very great (there are no minerals or important raw materials in Lebanon), the city in normal times lived by commercial activity on a surprising scale, developed by the ingenuity and opportunism of its merchant class.

Beirut, of recent years, came to serve as a financial and holiday centre for the less attractive but oil-rich parts of the Middle East. Transfer of financial credit from the Middle East to Zürich (Switzerland), Paris (France), London (United Kingdom), New York (USA) and Tokyo (Japan); a trade in gold and diamonds; and some connection with the narcotics trade of the Middle East—all these gave the city a very special function. Strenuous efforts began in 1977 to bring about reconstruction and redevelopment, assisted by loans from abroad. During 1980 a large contribution of 'front-line aid' was made by members of the League of Arab States (Arab League), and this showed signs of producing significant economic recovery. However, the abrupt intensification of military activity in 1981–82, the effects of the subsequent Israeli invasion and the prolonged sectarian conflict negated these hopes. Production declined because of damage and disruption; the south was virtually disconnected from the remainder of the Lebanese state until Israeli forces withdrew to just inside the border in June 1985; such was the extent of factional division within the country that, in the early years of the recent civil conflict, the Government's authority was barely felt outside Beirut; by the late 1980s, if not before, even the capital had effectively lapsed into anarchy; and the impossibility of controlling customs and tax collection caused a substantial reduction in government income. At least until the consequences of renewed violence between Israel and the Palestinians began to be felt in Lebanon, the economic situation appeared more favourable following the withdrawal of Israeli forces from southern Lebanon in May 2000. Moreover, some of the country's tourist trade started to be revived. However, Lebanon entered a further period of instability and economic disruption in July 2006, after Israel responded to a cross-border raid by Hezbollah militants in which two Israeli soldiers were abducted and several others killed by launching a major military offensive against Hezbollah positions in southern Lebanon, imposing a complete blockade of the country (see History). Reconstruction costs in the aftermath of the month-long conflict were considerable, since Beirut Rafiq Hariri International Airport and many of Lebanon's roads, bridges and other infrastructure were destroyed. Following the Doha Agreement of May 2008 (see History), there was a marked recovery in several sectors of the economy, including tourism, banking and construction. However, the descent of neighbouring Syria into civil conflict, and the collapse of the Lebanese Government in early 2013, prompted fears of renewed instability.

LANGUAGE

Arabic is current throughout the whole country. French is probably still the leading European language in use in Lebanon (although English is tending to replace it), and some of the higher schools and one university teach bprincipally in this language. In addition, Aramaic is used by some religious sects, but only for ritual—there are no Aramaic-speaking villages, unlike in Syria.

History

Revised for this edition by ADHAM SAOULI

PRE-MODERN TIMES

In the ancient world Lebanon was exploited for its forests and mineral wealth, but its mountainous character prevented any complete subjugation to outside authority. In the seventh century AD the Arab conquerors of Syria tried to assert greater control, but met with resistance from the indigenous Christian inhabitants, and from this time the 'Mountain' began to assume its historic function of providing a refuge for racial and religious minorities. While the Maronite Christians remained the predominant group in the north, by the 11th century Muslim groups, notably the Shi'a, together with the Druze, had begun to establish themselves in the south.

After the Ottoman conquest in the early 16th century the privileges of the amirs of Lebanon were confirmed, and in the early 17th century Lebanon enjoyed considerable prosperity. However, conflicts with the Ottoman rulers were not infrequent. The Turkish pashas of Damascus, Tripoli and Sidon tried to exercise indirect control by fomenting the family rivalries and religious differences that marked the course of Lebanese politics, while the Lebanese amirs tried to maintain and develop their power by setting one Turkish pasha against another and by bribing officials in İstanbul whenever expedient. The age of the Lebanese amirs came to an end in the early 19th century after Bashir II sided openly with Muhammad Ali of Egypt when he invaded Syria. Bashir was sent into exile and the Ottomans assumed direct control of the 'Mountain', appointing two officials—one Druze and the other Maronite—to rule there under the supervision of the pashas of Sidon and Beirut.

During this period of direct rule the Ottomans further aggravated mistrust between the Druze and Maronites as the only means of maintaining their control over Lebanon. It was also a time of social and economic discontent. In 1858 the Maronite peasantry revolted, destroying the feudal privileges of their aristocracy and facilitating the creation of a system of independent smallholdings. The Druze aristocracy, fearing similar discontent among their own Maronite peasantry, made a series of attacks on the Maronites of northern Lebanon in 1860. Turkish indifference to these massacres prompted French intervention and in 1864 the promulgation of an organic statute for Lebanon, which became an autonomous province under a non-Lebanese Ottoman Christian governor, appointed by the Sultan and approved by the European Great Powers, assisted by an elected administrative council. The period from 1864 to 1914 was one of increasing prosperity, especially among the Christians, who also played an important role in the revival of Arab literature and Arab national feeling during the last years of the 19th century.

THE FRENCH MANDATE

The First World War (1914–18) led to the collapse of the Ottoman Empire and the military occupation of its Syrian provinces by British and French troops. After the end of the war the League of Nations decreed that Greater Syria was to be partitioned into two French mandates, Lebanon and Syria, in order to prepare them for self-government and eventual independence. In 1920 the French Mandatory authorities established the Republic of Greater Lebanon by annexing to Mount Lebanon, the former autonomous province of the Ottoman Empire, the areas around it including Tripoli, Sidon, Tyre and Beirut. In the new republic the French ensured that the Maronite Christians, who had sought French protection against their Ottoman rulers as early as the 17th century, formed the largest religious community and would therefore dominate the new state politically and economically. Yet the enlargement of Lebanon incorporated into the new state large numbers of Muslims and Christians who would have preferred to remain part of Syria and who were deeply attached to the Arab world. Many of these people felt little allegiance to their new country and, like their Syrian neighbours, deeply resented what the French had done. Muslim opinion was divided between those who wished to see Lebanon reunited with the Arab world and those who wished to build a new Lebanon in partnership with their Christian compatriots. The Maronites were also divided between those who felt that Lebanon should not turn its back on the Arab world, and those who regarded Lebanon as a Christian homeland belonging to the same Mediterranean world as France. The latter regarded the Muslims as a potential danger to what they believed to be the 'Christian' state of Lebanon. In 1943 France reluctantly granted Lebanon independence, and an agreement between

France and the Lebanese Republic in 1946 provided for the withdrawal of French troops.

THE EARLY YEARS OF INDEPENDENCE

Like other Arab states, Lebanon was at war with the new State of Israel from May 1948, but signed an armistice agreement in March 1949 following negotiations under UN auspices. The first wave of Palestinian refugees arrived in Lebanon during the war. The failure of the Arab armies led to widespread disillusionment among peoples throughout the Arab world, and in Lebanon this feeling combined with considerable economic difficulties to cause political unrest and the resignation of the first President, Sheikh Bishara el-Khoury (1943–52), who had held office since independence. The new President, Camille Chamoun, allied Lebanon with the West by accepting the 'Eisenhower Doctrine' under which the USA offered economic and military aid to states seeking protection against 'International Communism'. His action effectively broke the terms of an unwritten 'national pact', agreed between leaders of the Christian and Muslim communities at independence and under which they agreed to give up their aspirations to align Lebanon to the West or to the Arab world. This was a time when enthusiasm for the new Arab nationalism of President Gamal Abd al-Nasir (Nasser) of Egypt was proving extremely attractive to many Lebanese Muslims. This tended to make Christians nervous, especially after the emergence of the United Arab Republic of Egypt and Syria and propaganda from Cairo and Damascus for the return to Syria of those predominantly Muslim areas that had been joined to the old Lebanon under the French mandate. Sporadic outbreaks of violence by critics of Chamoun's pro-Western policies escalated into a widespread insurrection in early 1958. In response, Chamoun called on the USA for assistance, and some 10,000 US troops were dispatched to the Beirut area.

In September 1958 Gen. Fouad Chehab, the Commander-in-Chief of the Lebanese army, succeeded Chamoun as President, a choice supported by both sides in the conflict. He at once invited Rashid Karami, the leader of the insurgents at Tripoli, to become Prime Minister and concluded an agreement for the withdrawal of US troops by the end of October. Chehab succeeded in achieving a measure of reconciliation, but was unable to reform the political system or build a strong public sector. Political parties in a real sense did not exist, apart from the Maronite Phalangist Party (Phalanges Libanaises, or Al-Kataeb), founded by Pierre Gemayel in 1936 and modelled on European fascism. Most parties simply represented the supporters of the different personalities who derived their influence from positions of privilege or commercial power.

The political élite combined to defeat Chehab's attempt to develop state institutions that would provide Lebanon with a strong central government because they did not wish to lose their independent power bases. Yet by this time the demographic balance upon which the whole political system was based was changing. Under the unwritten national pact of 1943 the highest offices of state were to be shared out between the different religious communities, according to their numerical strengths. When the Lebanese Republic was created, Christians, of whom Maronites were the largest community, outnumbered Muslims. Under the national pact the President would always be a Maronite, the Prime Minister a Sunni Muslim, and the President of the National Assembly a Shi'a Muslim. Other administrative posts would be distributed on the same basis. Although no population census had been held since 1932, by the 1970s it was clear to everyone that there were more Muslim than Christian Lebanese. Christian (especially Maronite) domination in political and economic life could no longer be justified, and Muslim demands for a greater share of political power became more insistent. However, the Muslim political leaders were comfortably ensconced in the political establishment and were out of touch with the poorer members of their community. Discontent was intensified by the tremendous disparity in wealth that emerged in the 1950s and 1960s. Lebanon's role as the West's main gateway to the Arab world brought wealth to the banking and services sector, but did nothing to promote economic development in rural areas.

The Government of Sulayman Franjiya, elected President in 1970, was more corrupt and partisan than any of its predecessors. The Druze leader Kamal Joumblatt emerged as the principal leader of the left, rallying around him the various small leftist parties. He established friendly relations with the Palestinians, whose armed presence in Lebanon had become a point of dispute between the different Lebanese political groups.

THE PALESTINIAN FACTOR

The basic problems underlying the Lebanese situation were aggravated after 1967 by a new influx of Palestinian refugees after the Israeli occupation of Gaza and the West Bank, and by the growing strength of the Palestinian guerrilla organizations which began to launch attacks against Israel from their military bases in southern Lebanon, provoking Israeli reprisals. In October 1969 violent clashes between Palestinian guerrillas and the Lebanese army, which was attempting to restrict their activities, threatened Lebanon's fragile political system and brought down the Government. In November Gen. Bustani, the Lebanese army chief, and Yasser Arafat, Chairman of the Palestine Liberation Organization (PLO), negotiated an agreement in Cairo with the help of President Nasser of Egypt. Under the so-called 'Cairo Agreement' Lebanon made important concessions to the PLO. The Palestinian guerrillas were given complete control over their military bases in southern Lebanon and also the right to administer and maintain law and order in the refugee camps, where most of the 250,000–300,000 Palestinians in Lebanon lived. The residents of the camps had complained bitterly about harassment from the Lebanese police and army intelligence services. The agreement legalized the uneasy existence of a Palestinian state-within-a-state in Lebanon, highlighted the weakness of the Lebanese Government and further aggravated the deep divisions within Lebanese society. Many Lebanese, especially the poorer Muslims, Sunni and Shi'a, were sympathetic to the Arab solidarity and revolutionary aspirations represented by the Palestinian resistance. They supported the Palestinian struggle, hoping for their assistance in bringing about changes in the Lebanese state that would give them a fairer share of wealth and power. The Lebanese right feared that the Palestinian resistance was undermining the character of the Lebanese state, the institutions and power structure of which they wished to preserve. The Lebanese Government, meanwhile, was afraid that if it set the Lebanese army against the Palestinians, it would provoke open revolt. The agreement did not bring an end to clashes between the Lebanese army and Palestinian guerrillas. Guerrilla attacks against Israel increased, especially after Jordan expelled the Palestinian resistance groups in 1971 and the PLO transferred its headquarters to Beirut; in turn, Israeli commandos began to attack Palestinian guerrilla training camps in Lebanon and to assassinate Palestinian guerrilla leaders at their homes in Beirut. Lebanon was not directly involved in the October 1973 Arab–Israeli War, but continued to suffer Israeli reprisals, with the villages of southern Lebanon bearing the brunt of Israeli raids. These attacks drove large numbers of poor Lebanese, mainly Shi'a Muslims, to swell the shifting population living in shanty towns and refugee camps around Beirut, where the radical and left-wing groups rapidly acquired supporters.

CIVIL WAR, 1975–76: THE SYRIANS ENTER LEBANON

The growing strength of the Palestinian guerrillas in Lebanon was an important factor in the outbreak of civil war in 1975. By the early 1970s right-wing Christians, under the leadership of Pierre Gemayel, stepped up the arming and training of private militia forces and prepared to take on themselves the task of expelling the Palestinians. The arming of private militias alarmed Lebanese Muslims and reformists, who began to create their own rival militias. Among the Shi'a Muslim community, Imam Sheikh Sayed Moussa al-Sadr rallied support against the Lebanese Government, which was unable or unwilling to protect his people against Israeli reprisals. The Shi'a militia, Amal, was formed in 1975 and quickly became the largest armed group in Lebanon. By the mid-1970s the country was divided between two large coalitions: the Lebanese Front, a Maronite Christian alliance between the private armies of the rival Gemayel, Chamoun and Franjiya families, who wanted to retain the existing political system, favoured links with the West and opposed direct Lebanese involvement in the Arab–Israeli conflict; and the Lebanese National Movement (LNM), which was mainly Muslim and consisted of a loose coalition of mostly small left-wing parties which demanded a more representative political system, closer links with the Arab world and a more active role for Lebanon in the conflict with Israel. The LNM was led by Kamal Joumblatt, of the Druze-dominated Parti Socialiste Progressiste (PSP), and enjoyed PLO support.

A reprisal attack by the Phalangists, the dominant faction within the Lebanese Front, in April 1975—in which 27 Palestinians were massacred—is usually recognized as the event that sparked off the civil war. In less than six months the fighting between rival militias had spread across the capital and to other parts of the country. The army later disintegrated as Muslim units expelled their Christian officers and joined the LNM, while many Christian units joined the Maronites. The militias controlled Beirut, which was soon effectively partitioned and the prosperous business district looted by all-comers. The conflict was characterized by extreme brutality and savagery on both sides. Once it had begun, non-combatant civilians and moderates and liberals on both sides felt compelled to remain loyal to their own religious communities for fear of their lives.

At first the militias of the Lebanese Front, especially the Phalangists, took the offensive, but their attacks on Tell al-Zaatar and other Palestinian refugee camps brought the full weight of the well-armed PLO forces against them in support of the LNM. With the support of the PLO, the LNM made important advances against the Lebanese Front, despite covert military support to the Maronites from Israel, and they were soon controlling nearly two-thirds of the country, and had the upper hand in the war. However, in May 1976 Syria, which had tried unsuccessfully to mediate in the conflict, sent troops into Lebanon against the Palestinians and their Lebanese allies, whom it had previously supported. Syria feared that if the PLO and LNM were victorious it would be unable to control them and their victory would inevitably provoke an Israeli intervention, with the possibility of a new confrontation between Syria and Israel. Having been rescued by the Syrians, the Christian militias began a new offensive against Muslim and Palestinian areas during which they finally overran Tell al-Zaatar, killing over 2,000 of its inhabitants. The Palestinians were forced to retreat from Beirut to their bases in the south. It was not until October that a lasting cease-fire came into effect and, at a summit meeting of the League of Arab States (Arab League) in Riyadh, Saudi Arabia, President Hafiz al-Assad of Syria, the new Lebanese President, Elias Sarkis, and PLO Chairman Yasser Arafat reached an agreement to end the war. A 30,000-strong Arab Deterrent Force (ADF), made up largely of Syrian troops, was established to keep the peace and a disengagement committee set up in an attempt to implement the 1969 Cairo Agreement between the Lebanese Government and the Palestinian guerrillas. An estimated 60,000 people, mainly civilians, had been killed in the fighting and some 100,000 injured.

Syrian troops, who occupied part of Beirut and much of the northern and eastern part of the country, soon found themselves hated by all sides and targets of attack. The Lebanese alliances of the first years of the civil war quickly fragmented. The assassination of Kamal Joumblatt in 1977, widely believed to have been instigated by Syria, deprived the left wing of its principal leader, and there were clashes between Palestinians, the Shi‘a Amal movement and the other small parties. Meanwhile, former President Sulayman Franjiya withdrew his militia from the Lebanese Front, while the Phalangist militia, led by Bashir Gemayel, forcibly integrated the smaller Christian militias into a strong, disciplined army, the Lebanese Forces (LF), which continued to receive supplies and discreet support from Israel, and sought the removal of Syrian forces from Lebanon.

ISRAEL'S 1982 INVASION OF LEBANON

Southern Lebanon became the scene of renewed fighting during 1977, with Syria once again allied with the Palestinians, who launched raids across the border into Israel, provoking Israeli reprisals. In March 1978, after Palestinian guerrillas carried out a raid near Tel-Aviv, killing 35 Israelis, the Israel Defence Forces (IDF) invaded and occupied southern Lebanon as far as the Litani river. On this occasion, international pressure forced the Israelis to withdraw. On 19 March the UN Security Council adopted Resolution 425, demanding that Israel cease its military action against Lebanese territorial integrity and withdraw its forces from Lebanese territory forthwith. A peace-keeping force, the UN Interim Force in Lebanon (UNIFIL), was created and given the task of assisting in the restoration of peace and Lebanese government authority in the south. The Israelis completed their withdrawal in June, but before UNIFIL could deploy its troops, the Israelis handed over their positions along Lebanon's southern border to units of the right-wing, mainly Christian militia of Maj. Saad Haddad, which were organized and armed by Israel. UNIFIL was therefore unable to patrol the actual border (as its instructions demanded) and was forced to deploy its forces further north, placing its units in a highly vulnerable position between the Haddad militia in the south and PLO fighters to the north. The UNIFIL troops, which numbered some 6,000, came under constant attack from the Haddad militia. Clashes between Israeli and PLO forces continued, and two weeks of particularly heavy fighting in the summer of 1981 was only brought to an end by US mediation.

An uneasy cease-fire prevailed, but the Israeli Government of Menachem Begin remained concerned about the strength of PLO forces in southern Lebanon. In early June 1982, after the attempted assassination of Israel's ambassador in London by a Palestinian gunman, the Israeli air force made a series of attacks against PLO positions in southern Lebanon and in Beirut, to which the Palestinians responded by shelling settlements in northern Israel. The PLO's response provided Prime Minister Begin and his Minister of Defence, Ariel Sharon, with the pretext to go to war, and on 6 June some 80,000 Israeli troops and 1,240 tanks crossed the border into southern Lebanon. They cut straight through the zone patrolled by UNIFIL and within two days had advanced 40 km into Lebanon, forcing the PLO to pull back its forces so that they were no longer capable of shelling Israel's northern settlements. However, the rapid campaign, code-named 'Operation Peace in Galilee', had failed to destroy the PLO's fire-power.

Although Begin and Sharon had insisted that the sole aim of the invasion was to ensure that the PLO's artillery could no longer threaten northern Israel, the IDF continued to advance towards Beirut and into the Beqa‘a valley, where they clashed with occupying Syrian forces. The Israeli air force destroyed Syria's missile installations in the Beqa‘a valley and almost one-quarter of Syria's fighter planes, giving Israel undisputed control over Lebanese airspace. By the time a cease-fire had been agreed with Syria on 11 June 1982, Israeli forces had entered the eastern and southern suburbs of the Lebanese capital and within days began a two-month-long siege of Beirut's western suburbs, where the PLO had its headquarters. The militias of the LNM, in particular the Sunni Murabitoun and the Shi‘a Amal, fought alongside the PLO in the south and later in Beirut. The Phalangists, on the other hand, welcomed the invasion and, during the siege of west Beirut, their militia and Maj. Haddad's forces acted as auxiliaries for the Israelis. It emerged that Ariel Sharon had more ambitious objectives than securing the defence of Israel's northern settlements. He wanted to install a friendly government in Lebanon, dominated by the Christian Maronites, and to crush the PLO so that it would no longer pose a threat to the Jewish state. Also, by crippling the PLO's organizational base in Lebanon, Sharon hoped to weaken or eliminate its influence over the Palestinians in the occupied West Bank and Gaza Strip, enabling the Israelis to impose their own version of the autonomy plan set out in the 1978 Camp David accords.

Israel's relentless bombardment of west Beirut, which had a devastating effect on the civilian population, finally came to an end on 21 August 1982, when the PLO and Israel accepted a US proposal for the withdrawal of Palestinian guerrillas from

Lebanon supervised by a multinational peace-keeping force. The evacuation of PLO forces was completed by 1 September and, following the election of Bashir Gemayel, the leader of the LF, as Lebanese President on 23 August, Israel appeared to have achieved its major objectives in Lebanon. However, three weeks later Bashir Gemayel was assassinated, the Israeli army moved into west Beirut and, with the apparent collusion of the Israelis, Phalangist militiamen entered the now defenceless Palestinian refugee camps of Sabra and Chatila on the outskirts and killed more than 2,000 people.

After the massacre in Sabra and Chatila, the multinational force, which had supervised the PLO evacuation, returned to Beirut to protect the Palestinian camps. Israeli forces withdrew from Beirut, but only as far as the airport, just south of the city, from where they consolidated their hold on the southern half of the country. In May 1983 the new Lebanese President, Amin Gemayel, elder brother of Bashir, was persuaded by the USA to sign a peace treaty with Israel, providing for the withdrawal of all foreign forces from Lebanon. Syria, which still controlled much of the north and east of the country, had not been party to the agreement and refused to accept it. President Amin Gemayel's Government, despite US support, was in control of only a small area of central Lebanon, and even there was often unable to assert its authority.

ISRAEL WITHDRAWS ITS FORCES FROM LEBANON

In July 1983 Israel, faced with mounting casualties, began unilaterally to pull back its forces and to reduce the number of troops deployed in Lebanon. In the wake of the departing Israelis, fighting between rival Lebanese militias, particularly the Phalangists and the Druze, intensified. The 5,800-strong multinational force (composed mainly of French, Italian and US troops) gradually abandoned its neutral peace-keeping role, and came under attack from Muslim militias and suicide bombers suspicious of its support for a Christian-led Government. The force's position became increasingly untenable and in early 1984 the USA and its allies decided to withdraw their troops from Beirut.

After the departure of the foreign troops who had supported his Government, President Amin Gemayel was forced to turn to Syria for support, and in March 1984 he abrogated the 1983 peace treaty with Israel in return for Syrian guarantees of internal security. At talks in Damascus in April 1984, President Assad approved plans for a Government of National Unity, giving equal representation to Christians and Muslims. Gemayel chose veteran politician Rashid Karami as the new Prime Minister, at the head of a Cabinet that included the leaders of all Lebanon's main religious groups. With Beirut still divided along the so-called 'Green Line' into Christian- and Muslim-controlled areas, the Lebanese army failed to gain control of the city and sporadic violence continued. Efforts to gain agreement on constitutional reform to reflect the majority status of Lebanon's Muslims made little progress.

Israel, faced with the financial burden of keeping a force in Lebanon and with its troops increasingly the target of attacks by Lebanese resistance groups, pledged in September 1984 to withdraw from Lebanon. In January 1985 the Israeli Cabinet voted to take unilateral steps towards a complete withdrawal, which was carried out in three stages and completed in June. Israel, however, left a buffer zone 10 km–20 km wide north of the international border, controlled by the former Haddad militia now reconstituted as the South Lebanon Army (SLA—supported by several hundred Israeli troops), which cut across the area patrolled by UNIFIL. The harsh policies adopted by the Israelis during their occupation of southern Lebanon created bitter hostility among the region's Shi'a Muslims and prompted the emergence of a resistance group that was to prove a more dangerous enemy than the PLO, Hezbollah. Created in the early 1980s by a group of Shi'a clerics united by radical and activist Shi'ism, Hezbollah's immediate aim was to end Israel's occupation of southern Lebanon, but its political programme also called for the destruction of the State of Israel, the creation of an Iranian-style Islamic Republic of Lebanon, and opposition to the Arab-Israeli peace process. Hezbollah's ideology was strongly anti-Western and it received vital financial support and arms from Iran. Contingents of Iran's Revolutionary Guards were also sent to Lebanon and co-operated closely with Hezbollah guerrillas. During the 1980s groups linked to Hezbollah carried out a number of violent attacks on Western targets in Lebanon, including a suicide bomb attack against the US embassy in Beirut in April 1983 (in which 241 US marines were killed), and were responsible for most of the Westerners abducted and held hostage in Lebanon during this period.

THE RESURGENCE OF THE PLO AND THE 'WAR OF THE CAMPS'

In the wake of the Israeli withdrawal, fighting was renewed between Christian and Muslim militias along the 'Green Line' dividing eastern and west Beirut. At the same time, in Christian east Beirut street battles were fought between pro- and anti-Gemayel factions, and in west Beirut fierce fighting erupted as the Shi'a Amal militia and their Druze allies tried to crush the Sunni Murabitoun militia and its Palestinian allies and prevent the revival of the pro-Arafat PLO force in Beirut. As Israeli forces had withdrawn, an estimated 5,000 Palestinian guerrillas had returned to Lebanon, and the PLO, under Chairman Arafat, was attempting to re-establish its power base there. Syria was strongly opposed to the PLO revival in Lebanon because the presence of Palestinian guerrillas loyal to Arafat challenged its own hegemony over the country and efforts to bring the Palestinian resistance movement under Syrian control. Amal also wanted to prevent the PLO from re-establishing itself in Lebanon, fearing that this would provoke new Israeli reprisal raids and challenge its own control over southern Lebanon.

In May 1985 Amal forces (with Syrian encouragement and assistance) began a savage assault on Palestinian refugee camps in southern Beirut, mainly Sabra, Chatila and Bourj el-Barajneh, where PLO guerrillas were based, but failed to subdue stubborn Palestinian resistance and an uneasy cease-fire was arranged after several weeks of fighting. From May 1986 the so-called 'war of the camps' erupted again—with major exchanges between Amal and PLO forces—and spread from Beirut to southern Lebanon, where Palestinian camps in and around Tyre and Sidon were besieged by Amal and cut off from access to food and medical supplies. Formerly rival pro-Syria and pro-Arafat Palestinian factions united to defend the camps and protect the refugees, while Sunni and Druze militias continued to lend discreet support to the Palestinians. There was serious fighting in June between Sunni forces and Amal, and shelling reduced large parts of the camps to rubble.

In February 1987, after fierce fighting occurred in west Beirut between Amal forces and an alliance of Druze, Murabitoun and communist militias, Muslim leaders appealed for Syrian intervention. Subsequently, some 7,500 Syrian troops were deployed in west Beirut and succeeded in enforcing a cease-fire in the central and northern districts. By April a Syrian-supervised cease-fire was agreed at all the embattled Palestinian refugee camps in Beirut; the siege of Chatila and Bourj el-Barajneh was suspended to allow supplies to be taken into the camps. However, in Sidon fighting was renewed between Amal and Palestinian Arafat loyalists and some 150 Syrian troops were deployed around Sidon in mid-April. In May the Lebanese National Assembly voted to annul the 1969 Cairo Agreement, which defined and regulated the PLO's activities and legitimized its presence in Lebanon. In June 1987 Prime Minister Karami, a firm ally of Syria, who had been instrumental in the deployment of Syrian troops in Beirut, was assassinated and, although it was unclear who was responsible, the Muslim community considered the Christian section of the divided Lebanese army and the Christian LF to be the leading suspects.

Although the most intense fighting between Amal and PLO guerrillas had ended, the camps remained effectively under siege, apparently under the supervision of Syrian troops, and freedom of movement in and out was confined to women and children. On 16 January 1988, avowedly as a gesture of support for the *intifada* (uprising) by Palestinians in the Israeli-occupied West Bank and Gaza Strip, which had begun a month earlier, Nabih Berri, the leader of Amal, announced an end to the siege of the camps in Beirut and southern Lebanon.

However, Syrian troops took over the checkpoints around the camps and Palestinian men were still unable to move freely. More than 2,500 people had died in the 'war of the camps', hundreds of refugees were wounded and many reduced to starvation. By June Arafat loyalists had lost control over their last stronghold in Beirut and were evacuated to Ain el-Hilweh camp near Sidon.

Having withdrawn from the Palestinian camps, Amal turned its forces against its rival, Hezbollah, and sporadic fighting occurred between the two militias in Beirut and southern Lebanon for control over areas of Shi'a population. In May 1988 Syrian troops encircled the southern suburbs of Beirut to enforce a Syrian- and Iranian-mediated cease-fire agreement between Amal and Hezbollah.

CONSTITUTIONAL CRISIS: TWO GOVERNMENTS CLAIM LEGITIMACY

As Amin Gemayel prepared to step down as President at the end of his term of office in September 1988, there was intense political manoeuvring to find a candidate acceptable to both Christians and Muslims. Consultations between Syria and the USA sought to agree a compromise candidate acceptable to the majority of Lebanese, but Christian army and LF leaders rejected any candidate imposed upon Lebanon by foreign powers. Two attempts in the National Assembly to elect a new President failed to achieve a quorum. Only minutes before Gemayel's term of office expired on 22 September, and in accordance with his constitutional privileges, he appointed a six-member interim military government with Gen. Michel Aoun (the Maronite Christian Commander-in-Chief of the Lebanese army) as Prime Minister to rule until a new President was elected. Muslims refused to recognize the interim military administration and announced that Sunni Muslim Dr Selim al-Hoss, who had been acting Prime Minister since Karami's assassination in June 1987, was the legitimate ruler of Lebanon in the absence of a President. Lebanon was plunged into a new constitutional crisis, with two Governments (one Christian, in east Beirut, and one predominantly Muslim, in west Beirut) claiming legitimacy. Syria, for its part, refused to recognize Gen. Aoun's Government. Of Lebanon's central institutions, only the central bank remained intact, and it continued to make funds available to both Governments for basic supplies of food and fuel. In November 1988 Gen. Aoun was dismissed as Commander-in-Chief by the Minister of Defence in the al-Hoss Government, but since he retained the loyalty of large sections of the military, he remained its de facto leader.

In March 1989 violent clashes erupted in Beirut between Christian and Muslim forces positioned on either side of the 'Green Line'. Throughout most of April Aoun's forces and Syrian troops exchanged artillery fire and by the end of the month almost 300 people had been killed. Despite Aoun's claim that he had a popular mandate for his attempt to expel Syrian forces from Lebanon, 23 Christian members of the National Assembly demanded an immediate cease-fire and appealed to the Arab League, the UN and European Economic Community (EEC, now European Union—EU) to intervene to end the fighting. The situation was further complicated as Iraq, traditionally hostile to Syria, had become the principal supplier of weapons to Gen. Aoun and the Lebanese army. In September the Arab League's Tripartite Committee (consisting of King Hassan of Morocco, King Fahd of Saudi Arabia and President Chadli of Algeria) resumed its efforts to bring peace to Lebanon, proposing the establishment of a Lebanese security committee, under the auspices of the League's Assistant Secretary-General, to supervise the cease-fire, and a meeting of the Lebanese National Assembly in September to discuss a 'charter of national reconciliation' drafted by the Arab League. Unlike the League's previous peace proposal, the new plan made no appeal for the withdrawal of Syrian troops and was thus welcomed by the Syrian Government. Gen. Aoun rejected the proposal for an exclusively Lebanese security committee, arguing that since Syrian forces were directly involved in the conflict, Syria should be represented on any committee established to supervise the truce. However, owing to his diplomatic isolation, Aoun subsequently relented and the cease-fire accordingly took effect from 23 September.

THE TA'IF AGREEMENT

In October 1989 the charter of reconciliation, drafted by the Tripartite Arab Committee, was endorsed by 58 of the 62 deputies of the Lebanese National Assembly, meeting in Ta'if, Saudi Arabia. With regard to political reform, the charter provided for the transfer of executive power from the presidency to a cabinet, with portfolios divided equally among Christian and Muslim ministers. The appointment of the Prime Minister would remain the prerogative of the President, but would be exercised in consultation with the members and President of the National Assembly. The charter further provided for an increase in the number of seats in the Assembly from 99 to 108, to be divided equally among Christian and Muslim deputies. Following the endorsement of the charter, the election of a President and the formation of a new government, all Lebanese and non-Lebanese militias were to be disbanded within six months, while the Internal Security Forces were to be strengthened. For a maximum period of two years the Syrian army would then assist the new government in implementing a security plan. The section dealing with Syria's role in Lebanon was the result of prior agreement between the Tripartite Committee and Syria, and Lebanese deputies were prohibited from altering it. The agreement had, to a large extent, been facilitated by the co-operation of Lebanon's Maronite leaders, most notably Georges Saadé, the leader of the Phalangist Party, who had played an important role in the Ta'if negotiations. Its endorsement by the National Assembly, however, was immediately denounced by Gen. Aoun as a betrayal of Lebanese sovereignty.

Under the terms of an annex to the Ta'if agreement on 5 November 1989, the National Assembly, meeting in the northern town of Qlaiaat, unanimously endorsed the agreement and elected René Mouawad, a Maronite Christian deputy and former Minister of Education and Arts, as President. In response, Gen. Aoun declared the National Assembly dissolved and the presidential election unconstitutional. On 13 November President Mouawad invited al-Hoss to form a 'government of national reconciliation'. However, Maronite leaders were reluctant to participate in such an administration and thus openly oppose Gen. Aoun. On 22 November, only 17 days after his election, President Mouawad was assassinated in a bomb explosion. Two days later, in the town of Shtaura, 52 deputies of the National Assembly convened and elected Elias Hrawi as the new President. At the same session deputies voted to extend the Assembly's term of office until the end of 1994. A new Government was formed by al-Hoss and, following a meeting of the new Cabinet on 28 November 1989, it was announced that Aoun had again been dismissed as Commander-in-Chief of the Lebanese army and that Gen. Emile Lahoud had been appointed in his place.

At the end of January 1990 intense fighting broke out between Gen. Aoun's forces and the LF for control of the Christian enclave, precipitated by the refusal of LF leader Samir Geagea to reject the Ta'if agreement. By March more than 800 people had been killed in Christian sectarian fighting. In April Geagea announced his recognition of the al-Hoss Government, formally accepting the Ta'if agreement, and in June Georges Saadé, appointed Minister of Post and Telecommunications in November 1989, assumed his duties.

THE 1990–91 GULF CRISIS: SYRIA GRANTED FREEDOM OF ACTION IN LEBANON

The crisis in the Gulf region, which was precipitated by Iraq's invasion of Kuwait in August 1990, had important repercussions for Lebanon. Syria was effectively granted freedom of action in Lebanon, in return for its participation in the US-led multinational force deployed against Iraq, and received assurances of US support for its continued dominance in Lebanon. On 28 September units of the Lebanese army loyal to the al-Hoss Government imposed an economic blockade on the areas of Beirut controlled by Gen. Aoun, and on 13 October Syrian forces commenced a military assault against the presidential palace at Baabda and other strategic areas under Aoun's control. In a clear breach of the 'Red Lines' agreement between Syria and Israel, which regulated the parameters within which each country could operate in Lebanon, the Syrian air force shelled the presidential palace. The fact that Israel did not retaliate in response to such a breach of the agreement reflected the USA's support of the Syrian offensive. Aoun's forces were completely defeated, and the areas under his control overrun. During the fighting Aoun took refuge in the French embassy, and the French Government subsequently offered him and his family political asylum. The Lebanese Government, however, refused to allow Aoun to depart for France and sought to put him on trial for embezzlement of funds and crimes against the state.

On 21 August 1990 the National Assembly amended the Constitution to incorporate the political reforms agreed at Ta'if. Executive power was effectively transferred to the Lebanese Cabinet. The main beneficiary of the changes was the office of Prime Minister, which became the head of government, speaking in its name, implementing its policies and co-ordinating the various ministries. In the event of a vacancy in the office of President, the Cabinet, under the chairmanship of the Prime Minister, would assume the privileges and responsibilities of the presidency. In December a new Government of national unity was formed under Omar Karami, the first since the amendment of the Constitution. The new Prime Minister enjoyed exclusive Syrian support. The 30-member Cabinet included various militia and party leaders as well as traditional political figures, and ministerial posts were divided equally between Muslims and Christians. The new Government proceeded to implement the four-point programme that it had presented to the National Assembly, aiming to extend its authority over the whole of Lebanon; to disband the militias; to formalize Lebanon's 'special relations' with Syria; and to appoint deputies to the vacant seats in the National Assembly and fill senior military and civilian posts.

In March 1991 a full session of the Cabinet approved plans to dissolve all Lebanese and non-Lebanese militias, but not surprisingly the larger militias viewed their disbandment with little enthusiasm. However, strong regional and international pressure ultimately compelled Lebanon's major militias to comply with the Government's order, and army units were deployed in areas previously controlled by the LF and the PSP. Apprehension remained, none the less, with regard to armed groups that had refused to disband. Arafat's 6,000-strong Fatah group, based in Sidon, refused to surrender its weapons on the grounds that it did not constitute a militia, but rather, a 'resistance movement' or, even, the regular Palestinian army. The Government, for its part, refused to negotiate an accord similar to the one signed in Cairo in 1969, and after much pressure the PLO finally declared that it would not impede the deployment of Lebanese troops in the south of the country. The 2,000-strong Iranian Revolutionary Guards, based in Ba'albek in the Beqa'a valley, insisted that they did not constitute a militia within Lebanon, and that their withdrawal could take place only following a decision by the Iranian Government, made in consultation with Syria. The 5,000-strong Iranian-backed Hezbollah, meanwhile, agreed to dismantle its military structures in Beirut, but insisted on maintaining units in the Beqa'a valley and in southern Lebanon in order to continue the struggle against Israel's occupation. The 3,000-strong Israeli-backed SLA rejected any suggestion that it should disarm or that Israel was ready to comply with the appeals of the Lebanese Government for the implementation of UN Security Council Resolution 425, which demanded the unconditional withdrawal of Israeli forces from Lebanon.

In May 1991 Lebanon and Syria signed a treaty of 'fraternity, co-operation and co-ordination' proceeding from the stipulations of the Ta'if agreement. The treaty declared that Syria and Lebanon had 'distinctive brotherly relations' based on their geographic propinquity, similar history, common belonging, shared destiny and common interests, and specified the executive mechanism by which these relations were to be managed and developed. The most important of these was the Higher Council, comprising the Presidents of Lebanon and Syria, their Prime Ministers, Deputy Prime Ministers and the presiding officers of their respective legislatures. The Higher Council assumed responsibility for the co-ordination and co-operation of the two states in political, economic, security, military and other spheres. Its decisions were to be binding, albeit within the constitutional and legal frameworks of both countries. In September 1991 Lebanon and Syria formally concluded a security agreement, as envisaged in the bilateral accord, which permitted Lebanon and Syria to seek mutual military assistance in the event of a challenge to the stability of either country. In October President Hrawi travelled to Damascus for the first session of the Lebanese-Syrian Higher Council. In March 1992 Syrian forces began to withdraw from Beirut, in preparation for their redeployment in eastern Lebanon by September (in accordance with the Ta'if agreement).

In May 1991 the National Assembly approved an amendment to Lebanon's electoral law, allowing the exceptional appointment of 40 deputies, 31 to seats that had become vacant since the last elections in 1972 and nine to the new seats created under the Ta'if agreement. The 40 deputies were selected from a list of 384 candidates by the President, the Prime Minister and the President of the National Assembly, in close consultation with Syria, and all except four (representing the Phalangist Party and LF) enjoyed close relations with the Syrian Government. Hezbollah and the new 'Aounist' grouping remained unrepresented in the National Assembly. At the end of May, following a decision that some 20,000 militia members would be incorporated in state structures, the Government began to compile a list of militia members who would be enrolled into the state's security and administrative structures, and to establish a schedule and locations for their rehabilitation. The decision stipulated that equal numbers of Muslims and Christians would be assimilated, among them 6,500 members of the LF, 2,800 members of Amal and 2,800 members of the PSP. The remainder would be absorbed from other militias. All were to undergo retraining courses, lasting up to six months, before being assigned to employment in the service of the state. In August the National Assembly approved a general amnesty for crimes committed during the civil war. Under the terms of a presidential pardon, Gen. Aoun was finally allowed to leave the French embassy compound and depart for exile in France. A condition of his exile was that he remained abroad for at least five years and refrained from political activities during that time.

In February 1991 Lebanese army battalions were deployed in the south of the country, for the first time since the Israeli invasion of 1978, in the wake of a serious escalation in Palestinian guerrilla operations in the south and consequent Israeli retaliation. However, the inadequacy of the army's capabilities in relation to the size of the area that it was supposed to patrol meant that its deployment was largely symbolic. In June Israel launched fierce attacks on Palestinian bases in southern Lebanon. The following month the Lebanese army began to deploy in and around Sidon, where it initially encountered some armed resistance from pro-Arafat guerrillas. Meanwhile, Hezbollah fighters continued their attacks against Israel's self-declared 'security zone' and their rocket attacks against settlements in Israel itself. The Syrian authorities believed that these attacks could be used to force Israel not only to abandon its security zone in southern Lebanon, but also to withdraw from Syria's Golan Heights, occupied since 1967. (It is widely accepted that Syria used its control over supplies of Iranian arms to Hezbollah to step up or reduce pressure on the Israeli Government in the context of the Middle East peace process.) In February 1992 the Israeli air force assassinated Sheikh Abbas Moussawi, Hezbollah's Secretary-General. After Hezbollah fighters retaliated, Israeli forces advanced beyond the security zone to attack Hezbollah positions. Serious escalations of the conflict between Hezbollah fighters, the SLA and Israeli armed forces occurred in October and November. In December, in response to the deaths in the Occupied Territories of five members of the Israeli security forces, and to the abduction and murder by the Islamic Resistance Movement (Hamas) of an Israeli border police officer, the Israeli Cabinet ordered the deportation to Lebanon of more than 400 alleged Palestinian supporters of Hamas. Owing to the Lebanese Government's refusal to co-operate in this action, the deportees were stranded in the territory between Israel's security zone and Lebanon proper.

1992 LEGISLATIVE ELECTIONS: HARIRI BECOMES PRIME MINISTER

During the early months of 1992 Lebanon's economic situation worsened dramatically, and general strikes took place in April and May. On 6 May Karami and his Cabinet were forced to resign, amid widespread allegations of corruption and incompetence within the Government. Rashid Solh was appointed Prime Minister (he previously held the post during 1974–75), but his Cabinet, which included 15 of its predecessor's members, was regarded as insufficiently distinctive to modify the widespread perception of Lebanon as a Syrian protectorate. In addition to efforts to alleviate the economic crisis, a principal task of the new Lebanese Government was to prepare the country for its first legislative elections since 1972. On 16 July 1992 the National Assembly approved a new electoral law whereby the number of seats in the Assembly was raised from 108 (as stipulated in the Ta'if agreement) to 128, to be equally divided between Christian and Muslim deputies. By August it was clear that most Maronite Christian groups, in particular the Phalangist Party, would not present candidates. In July Syria had indicated that its troops would not withdraw to the Beqa'a valley until the process of constitutional reform was complete, in accordance with its interpretation of the Ta'if agreement. Christian groups maintained that fair elections could not take place until the Syrian armed forces had withdrawn. As the Lebanese Prime Minister and Cabinet had been chosen in close consultation with the Syrian leadership, the Government continued to invoke the inability of the Lebanese army to guarantee the country's security in the absence of Syrian forces; the position of Christian ministers in the Cabinet thus appeared more compromised than ever. Voting in the elections took place as planned in three phases: the first on 23 August in North Lebanon and the Beqa'a, where participation was described as high in Muslim areas and very low in Christian ones; the second on 30 August in Beirut and Mount Lebanon, characterized by low participation especially in Christian areas; and the third on 6 September in the South and al-Nabatiyah al-Tahta (Nabatiyah). Hezbollah, which moved from the political fringe to participate in the elections as a political party, won all the seats that it contested. There were widespread allegations of electoral malpractice both during and after the polling, prompting the resignation of Hussain al-Hussaini, the President of the National Assembly, who was replaced in October by Nabih Berri, leader of Amal.

On 22 October 1992 Rafiq Hariri, a multimillionaire businessman with dual Lebanese-Saudi Arabian nationality, was invited by President Hrawi to form a government. The new 30-member Cabinet included many technocrats, and offices were not, as previously, distributed on an entirely confessional basis.

In March 1994 the National Assembly approved legislation instituting the death penalty for what were termed 'politically motivated' murders. Shortly afterwards the Phalangist LF was proscribed, on the grounds that the organization had promoted the establishment of a Christian enclave and hence, the country's partition. In the following month the LF leader, Samir Geagea, was arrested and with several associates subsequently charged in connection with the murder in October 1990 of Dany Chamoun, the son of former President Camille Chamoun and leader of the right-wing Maronite Parti National Libéral (PNL). In September 1994 it was reported that the LF had temporarily relieved Geagea of the organization's leadership, and that it had revoked Geagea's recognition of the Ta'if agreement. The LF command was also said to have countermanded Geagea's formal dissolution, in 1991, of the organization's militia status. In June 1995 Geagea and a co-defendant were convicted of instigating Chamoun's murder, and were sentenced to death, although the sentences were immediately commuted to life imprisonment. Geagea later received a further three life sentences for ordering the assassination of a Maronite rival in 1990, for orchestrating the murder of Prime Minister Rashid Karami in 1987 and for an assassination attempt on Deputy Prime Minister and Minister of the Interior Michel Murr in 1991.

In May 1995 Hariri resigned as Prime Minister, but was subsequently persuaded by the President to remain in office and was reappointed on 21 May. It was reported that Hariri had resigned as a result of a dispute concerning the Constitution. Hariri had reportedly sought to amend the Constitution in order to allow President Hrawi to serve a second term of office, which Hariri believed was necessary to guarantee stability during the early phase of economic reconstruction. In October the Assembly voted to amend Article 49 of the Constitution, thereby extending Hrawi's mandate for a further three years.

1996 LEGISLATIVE ELECTIONS: HARIRI REAPPOINTED PRIME MINISTER

In June 1996 the Cabinet approved a new electoral law in preparation for the legislative elections scheduled to begin in August. Under the new legislation, the Beqa'a valley was reunified as a single electoral area, having been divided into three areas for the 1992 legislative elections. In the forthcoming elections the 128 seats of the National Assembly were to be divided among the country's five governorates: Beirut (19), the Beqa'a valley (23), the South and Nabatiyah (23), the North (28) and Mount Lebanon (35). Leading Christians continued to criticize the new electoral legislation for its division of Mount Lebanon, the Maronite heartland, into five electoral constituencies, thereby effectively dividing the Maronite vote, to the advantage of other communities such as the Druze. In August 1996 the Constitutional Court decided that the amendments to the electoral law approved in July were unconstitutional. The National Assembly subsequently approved an amendment to the new electoral law, which retained the controversial division of Mount Lebanon governorate, but stated that this was an exceptional measure to be employed solely for the 1996 elections.

In the first round of voting in the legislative elections, which took place in Mount Lebanon on 18 August 1996, supporters of the Hariri Government achieved a comprehensive victory, winning 32 of the 35 seats. The second round of voting on 25 August was held in the North and, by contrast, opposition candidates reportedly enjoyed greater success. The third round of voting on 1 September took place in the Beirut governorate, where candidates contesting the election on the list headed by the Prime Minister secured 14 of the 19 seats. However, prominent opponents of the Government also took seats in Beirut. On 8 September the fourth round of voting was held in the South and Nabatiyah, and Hezbollah retained all four of its seats, having entered into an electoral alliance with Amal. The Amal-Hezbollah bloc, together with parties counted as their supporters, were reported to have won all of the 23 seats in the South. In the previous rounds of voting Hezbollah had lost two of the eight seats it had held in the outgoing National Assembly. Prior to the fifth round of voting, to be held in the Beqa'a valley, it was reported that Syria had redeployed some 12,000 of its estimated 30,000 troops in Lebanon to the eastern part of the Beqa'a valley. There was speculation that the redeployment had been made for fear of Israeli attacks. In the final round of voting on 16 September 1996, the Amal-Hezbollah alliance won 22 of the governorate's 23 seats. Average voter participation in all five governorates was 45%, a marked improvement on the 32% recorded in 1992.

In October 1996 Rafiq Hariri was appointed for his third term as Prime Minister and Nabih Berri was re-elected President of the National Assembly. In the new Cabinet, named in November following consultations with the Syrian leadership, the distribution of portfolios among the various Lebanese interests remained largely unchanged. The new Government's statement of policy emphasized a continuation of economic recovery efforts, and made reference to controversial proposals to prohibit public demonstrations, and to close private radio and television stations. The partial implementation of this last measure had already provoked considerable controversy. In September the Government had announced a ban on political broadcasts by about 150 radio and 50 television stations, and ordered the closure of these stations by the end of November.

The issue of the broadcast media again provoked controversy in the second half of 1997. In September the authorities began to close down unlicensed broadcasters, and two people were killed when security forces opened fire on members of the radical Islamic Unification Movement (Tawhid Islami), who were attempting to prevent the closure of a private station in Tripoli. In December the Minister of the Interior prohibited a televised broadcast (by a private satellite company) from France by Gen. Aoun, on the grounds that such transmissions were undermining national security. In January 1998 the Government announced a ban on the broadcast of all news and political programmes by privately owned satellite channels, after a company owned by prominent Maronite interests transmitted an interview with a National Assembly deputy who was an outspoken critic of the Government. It was stated that, henceforth, the stations in question (including a company owned by Hariri) would be authorized only to transmit news bulletins prepared by the state-controlled Télé-Liban.

Voting in Lebanon's first municipal elections since 1963 took place in four rounds in May–June 1998. At the first round in Mount Lebanon governorate, Hezbollah won convincing victories in Beirut's southern suburbs, despite an attempt by Hariri and Berri to moderate the influence of the opposition by supporting joint lists of candidates; right-wing organizations opposed to the Government, including Dory Chamoun's PNL, which had boycotted the 1992 and 1996 legislative elections, also took control of several councils. At the second round in North Lebanon, efforts failed to achieve a communal balance in Tripoli, where a council comprising 23 Muslims and only one Christian was elected; elsewhere in the governorate there was notable success for candidates loyal to former LF leader, Samir Geagea. However, a joint list of candidates supported by Hariri and Berri did win control of the Beirut council at the third round. Candidates endorsed by Hariri won seats in Sidon, while Berri's Amal gained overall control of Tyre. In the final round of voting, in the Beqa'a valley, Hezbollah candidates were largely defeated by their pro-Syrian secular rivals and by members of the governorate's leading families. Other than in Beirut, the rate of participation by voters at all stages was high, at about 70%, and most political groups expressed satisfaction at the conduct and outcome of the polls.

'OPERATION GRAPES OF WRATH'

On 25 July 1993 Israeli forces launched their heaviest artillery and air attacks on targets in southern Lebanon since the 1982 invasion, with the declared aim of eradicating the threat posed by Hezbollah and Palestinian guerrillas and, moreover, of creating a flow of refugees so as to compel the Lebanese and Syrian authorities to take action to curb Hezbollah and the Palestinians. According to Lebanese figures, Israel's so-called 'Operation Accountability' displaced some 300,000 civilians towards the north and resulted in 128 (mainly civilian) fatalities. What was termed a cease-fire 'understanding' (brokered by the USA) entered into effect at the end of July 1993, ending the week-long Israeli campaign. Yet this proved short-lived, and mutual offensives continued in subsequent months. In June 1994 Israeli forces mounted an air attack on an alleged Hezbollah training camp in the Beqa'a valley close to the Syrian border and in October attacked the southern town of Nabatiyah. Hezbollah responded with rocket attacks on targets in Israel, and the conflict in and around the security zone escalated.

In April 1996 Israel launched massive combined air and artillery strikes against southern Lebanon, the Beqa'a valley and, for the first time since the 1982 invasion, against targets in the southern suburbs of Beirut. The declared aim of Israel's campaign, code-named 'Operation Grapes of Wrath', was to defeat Hezbollah, which had earlier fired rockets into settlements in northern Israel, wounding several people and causing widespread panic among the civilian population, in retaliation for attacks on Lebanese civilians by Israeli troops. The operation resulted in the displacement of some 400,000 Lebanese, who were forced to flee north to escape the shelling. During the campaign the IDF not only targeted suspected Hezbollah bases, but also attacked the Damour power station near Beirut and the city's international airport; most significantly, Israeli shells hit a UN base at Qana, near the port of Tyre, killing over 100 Lebanese civilians who had taken shelter there and wounding many others, including troops serving with UNIFIL. A UN investigation into the tragedy rejected Israel's claim that the attack was the result of technical and procedural errors. The attack on Qana brought international condemnation of Israel and led to diplomatic efforts, notably by the USA and France, to bring about a cease-fire.

After over two weeks of fighting a cease-fire 'understanding' was reached between Israel and Hezbollah, effectively a compromise confining the conflict to the security zone and recognizing both Hezbollah's right to resist Israeli occupation and Israel's right to self-defence. Hezbollah agreed that it would not launch attacks from near civilian areas, and Israel promised to refrain from attacking civilian targets. The 'understanding' also led to the establishment in June of an Israel-Lebanon Monitoring Group (ILMG), comprising Israel, Lebanon, Syria, France and the USA, to supervise the cease-fire. Refugees began returning to southern Lebanon, where whole villages and much infrastructure had been destroyed by Israeli shelling. Many observers maintained that 'Operation Grapes of Wrath' had been launched by the Israeli Prime Minister, Shimon Peres, primarily to show that he was tough on security in the run-up to Israeli elections. If so, the exercise backfired; Hezbollah was undefeated and its standing in Lebanon enhanced.

ISRAEL 'ADOPTS' UN RESOLUTION 425, BUT DEMANDS LEBANESE GUARANTEES

Within weeks of the cease-fire 'understanding' of April 1996, there were renewed clashes between Hezbollah fighters and Israeli troops in the security zone, and numerous complaints were made to the ILMG by both sides throughout 1996–97. In June 1997 Lebanon welcomed the UN General Assembly's adoption of a resolution demanding that Israel should pay US $1.7m. in damages for the shelling of the UN base at Qana in April 1996. Violence continued to escalate in August 1997, following the deaths of two civilians in a bomb explosion in Jezzine, an SLA stronghold north of the security zone. In reprisal, the SLA launched an artillery attack on Sidon, killing at least six civilians. Hezbollah, in turn, violated the cease-fire 'understanding' with rocket attacks into northern Israel, prompting the IDF to direct its most intensive air-strikes against Hezbollah and the Popular Front for the Liberation of Palestine–General Command (PFLP—GC) since 'Operation Grapes of Wrath'. In late August, following the death of an Amal commander in a car bomb in central Beirut, four Amal fighters and four members of the Israeli security forces died in clashes on the edge of the security zone. Twelve members of an élite Israeli commando unit were killed in September after Amal fighters and the Lebanese army foiled an Israeli operation, apparently against an Amal base, south of Sidon. Later in the month there was intense fighting within the security zone; among those killed was a son of Hezbollah's Secretary-General, Sheikh Hasan Nasrallah.

Rising Israeli casualties as a result of the occupation of southern Lebanon prompted a vocal campaign within Israel for a unilateral withdrawal from the security zone. At the beginning of April 1998 Israel's 'inner' Security Cabinet voted to adopt UN Security Council Resolution 425 of March 1978, but with the stipulation that Lebanon provide guarantees for the security of Israel's northern border. While welcoming the proposed departure from its territory, Lebanon emphasized that Resolution 425 demanded an unconditional withdrawal, and stated that neither would it be able to guarantee Israel's immunity from attack, nor would it be prepared to deploy the Lebanese army in southern Lebanon for this purpose. Furthermore, Lebanon could not support the continued presence there of the SLA. Israel's demand that Hezbollah be disarmed prior to any Israeli withdrawal was, moreover, unacceptable not only to Lebanon but also to Syria, which continued to regard its support for the resistance in southern Lebanon as essential leverage in its efforts to secure a parallel Israeli withdrawal from the Golan Heights.

Clashes persisted in southern Lebanon following Israel's 'adoption' of Resolution 425, amid continuing protests of violations of the 1996 cease-fire understanding. There were serious exchanges in December 1998, when 13 civilians were injured by Hezbollah rocket attacks on northern Israel, launched in reprisal for an Israeli air-strike on southern Lebanon in which eight civilians were killed. Israel subsequently issued a formal apology for the incident, and both assaults were condemned by the ILMG.

In early January 1999 Israel's Security Cabinet voted to respond to future Hezbollah offensives by targeting infrastructure in central and northern Lebanon, thereby extending the conflict beyond suspected guerrilla bases in the south. Hezbollah intensified its campaign of resistance in the months preceding the Israeli elections scheduled for 17 May 1999. In February it was reported that Israeli forces had responded by annexing the village of Arnoun, on the edge of the security zone. Hostilities escalated, and at the end of the month hundreds of Lebanese students stormed Arnoun in protest at the annexation, apparently forcing its release from Israeli control. Israeli forces, however, re-annexed the village in April. Meanwhile, in February Brig.-Gen. Erez Gerstein, the commander of the Israeli army's liaison unit with the SLA, was killed in an ambush by Hezbollah in the security zone; Gerstein was the most senior member of the Israeli command to be killed in Lebanon since the 1982 invasion. Israel retaliated by launching intensive air attacks on selected Hezbollah targets, while warning of full-scale land, air and sea offensives across Lebanon. In April 1999 Israel's Minister of Defence, Moshe Arens, announced that 80% of Israel's army posts in southern Lebanon had been transferred to the SLA and that further transfers were imminent, thus enabling additional Israeli troops to withdraw from the security zone. Nevertheless, there was a sharp escalation of fighting as the date of the Israeli elections approached.

GEN. LAHOUD ELECTED PRESIDENT

Towards the end of 1998 the issue of President Hrawi's succession dominated political debate as his mandate neared completion. The Commander-in-Chief of the Armed Forces, Gen. Emile Lahoud, was increasingly suggested as a suitable successor. Moreover, despite Lahoud's reputation as a nationalist, his candidacy was fully endorsed by Syria. For Lahoud to be appointed, an exceptional amendment was necessary to Article 49 of the Constitution—which required that senior civil servants, such as Lahoud, resign from their posts two years prior to seeking political office—and on 13 October the National Assembly was convened and overwhelmingly endorsed the amendment bill. Lahoud was duly elected President on 15 October with the approval of all 118 National Assembly deputies present at the ballot, although Druze leader Walid Joumblatt and his supporters boycotted the meeting.

It was announced at the end of November 1998 that Hariri had unexpectedly declined Lahoud's invitation to form a new government. Hariri attributed his effective resignation from the post that he had held for over six years to what he regarded as a violation of constitutional procedures by Lahoud in appropriating powers not granted to the presidency under the Ta'if agreement. The accord specified that the appointment of a Prime Minister should be made following consultation with deputies, rather than directly by the President, and while 83 deputies favoured Hariri's retention, 31 deputies had delegated their right to endorse the premier to Lahoud. The election of Lahoud was widely believed to signal the beginning of a new era in which the President, rather than the Prime Minister, would play the central role in the political hierarchy and act as the principal channel of communication between the Lebanese establishment and the Syrian presidency.

In December 1998 Dr Selim al-Hoss, who had headed four Governments during the civil war, was named as the new Prime Minister. A new, streamlined 16-member Cabinet was appointed, containing only two ministers from the previous administration. The appointment of several 'reformists', together with the exclusion of representatives of the various 'confessional' blocs and former militia leaders was said to illustrate al-Hoss's declared commitment to a comprehensive programme of reconstruction under his leadership; Hezbollah declined to participate in the new Government. Later in December the newly promoted Gen. Michel Suleiman (a Maronite Christian) was appointed head of the armed forces to succeed Lahoud. The incoming Government also revoked the five-year ban on the holding of public demonstrations.

One of the first acts of the al-Hoss Government was to implement an uncompromising initiative to eradicate state corruption and inefficient use of public resources. The judiciary was granted powers to investigate a number of political scandals and to bring both current and former high-ranking officials to trial. In January 1999 a total of 19 senior civil servants and leading officials were removed from their posts at the initiative of the new Prime Minister and the recommendation of the Civil Service Council. Four other officials also lost their jobs in the first stage of an ambitious project to reform a state bureaucracy, which numbered more than 230,000. The majority of those dismissed owed their positions to either Hariri, former President Hrawi or former minister Walid Joumblatt, although it was Hariri's supporters who suffered more from the new reforms.

In June 1999 the state-run National News Agency published a strong verbal assault on Hariri, reportedly originating from anonymous 'ministerial sources', in which the former Prime Minister was accused of corruption, of seeking to undermine the Government in order to facilitate his return to power, and even of collusion with Israel. Al-Hoss, however, vehemently denied that his Government was responsible for the anti-Hariri statement, or indeed, that it had any prior knowledge of it.

ISRAEL WITHDRAWS ITS FORCES FROM THE 'SECURITY ZONE'

The incoming Israeli Prime Minister, Ehud Barak, had made a pre-election pledge to bring about an Israeli withdrawal from southern Lebanon by July 2000. After the victory of Barak's Labour-led One Israel coalition, Hezbollah began to concentrate its efforts on forcing Israel out of Lebanon and seeking to dismantle the demoralized SLA. On 31 May 1999 the SLA commander, Gen. Antoine Lahad, announced that the SLA command had decided to withdraw unilaterally from the enclave of Jezzine, in the north-east of the security zone. The withdrawal of SLA forces was reportedly completed by 3 June, when Lebanese Internal Security Forces officially took control in the town. The Lebanese army had refused to take control of Jezzine on the grounds that this would effectively provide Israel with security guarantees in southern Lebanon prior to any comprehensive regional peace deal being concluded between Israel and Syria. The Lebanese authorities claimed that the withdrawal from Jezzine was a victory for Lebanon's resistance movement led by Hezbollah, which had intensified its operations around the town in recent weeks. Clashes between Israeli forces and Hezbollah continued throughout the month.

On the night of 24 June 1999, as Barak was conducting delicate negotiations to form a new government, Binyamin Netanyahu, who was still technically the Israeli Prime Minister, ordered a series of air-strikes against infrastructure targets in central and southern Lebanon—the heaviest aerial bombardment since 'Operation Grapes of Wrath' in 1996. Barak was reportedly not informed about the strikes, which destroyed two power plants in Beirut, a telecommunications centre and bridges connecting southern Lebanon with the rest of the country, and which killed at least eight civilians. The Israeli air-strikes followed a cross-border rocket attack on the northern Israeli town of Kiryat Shmona, which killed two civilians. The Lebanese Prime Minister described the Israeli air-strikes as a 'deliberate, barbaric' act, and they were also condemned by the USA and the EU. In June 1999 UNIFIL accused Hezbollah of encouraging attacks on UN positions near the 'security zone' by using UNIFIL outposts to launch attacks on Israel and the SLA.

With the formation of a new Israeli Government in July 1999, a period of intense diplomatic activity on all tracks of the Middle East peace process ensued. As the prospect of Israel and the Palestinian (National) Authority (PA) entering 'final status' peace negotiations increased, the issue of the estimated 350,000 Palestinian refugees in Lebanon assumed particular importance. Following an announcement by Barak that the refugees would under no circumstances be permitted to return to Israel and that 'a solution should be found in the countries where they are living', Lebanese officials increasingly reiterated their rejection of the notion of permanent settlement of Palestinian refugees in Lebanon. Although in January 1999 the Lebanese authorities had agreed to upgrade the status of travel documents issued to Palestinians residing in Lebanon, thereby allowing them to be treated as holders of Lebanese passports, President Lahoud demanded that any permanent peace agreement would have to guarantee the right of Palestinians to return home. He subsequently initiated legislation to prevent Palestinian refugees in Lebanon from being granted Lebanese citizenship.

In southern Lebanon violent clashes continued. In May 1999 a senior Fatah official and his wife were killed by unidentified gunmen in Sidon, an attack apparently perpetrated by members of the PLO opposed to Fatah's willingness to negotiate with Israel. A few days later a car bomb exploded in southern Lebanon, seriously wounding another Fatah official and leading to fears of a renewed cycle of violence between rival Palestinian factions operating in Lebanon. In December the Israeli Government issued an apology to the Lebanese authorities after an attack by its forces in which at least 15 Lebanese school children were injured. The incident came amid an escalation in Hezbollah operations following the announcement of the resumption of Israeli-Syrian peace negotiations. In order to facilitate progress in the talks, an 'understanding in principle' was reportedly reached between Israel and Syria to curb the fighting in southern Lebanon. However, in January 2000 the informal cease-fire ended when a senior SLA commander was killed; the deaths of another three Israeli soldiers at the end of the month led Israel to declare that peace talks with Syria could resume only if Syria took action to restrain Hezbollah.

On 5 March 2000 the Israeli Cabinet voted unanimously to withdraw its forces from southern Lebanon by July, even if no peace agreement had been reached between Israel and Syria. In April Israel released 13 Lebanese prisoners who had been held without trial for more than a decade as 'bargaining counters' for Israeli soldiers missing in Lebanon. On 17 April Israel gave the UN official notification that it intended to withdraw its forces from southern Lebanon 'in one phase' by 7 July, leading the Lebanese Prime Minister to talk of a 'resounding victory for Lebanon'. At the end of April the Lebanese Government stated for the first time that it would accept a UN peace-keeping force in southern Lebanon after the Israeli withdrawal.

Israel's Security Cabinet voted on 23 May 2000 to accelerate the withdrawal of its remaining troops in Lebanon, after Hezbollah forces had taken control of about one-third of the security zone following the evacuation of the SLA outposts previously transferred to the militia by the Israeli army. Whereas the withdrawal had been expected to take place on 1 June, it was completed on 24 May, amid considerable chaos and almost six weeks ahead of Barak's original deadline. On 23 May, as the withdrawal was taking place, Lebanese citizens stormed the notorious al-Khiam prison in Israel's former 'security zone' and released around 144 Lebanese prisoners, several of whom had been detained there for many years.

On 18 June 2000 the UN Security Council endorsed the verification of Secretary-General Kofi Annan that the Israeli withdrawal had been completed, although Hezbollah maintained that Israel was still required to depart from territory known as Shebaa Farms and to release all Lebanese prisoners. The disputed Shebaa Farms area is situated on the Israeli side of the line of withdrawal, as demarcated by the UN and known as the 'Blue Line'. Israel argues that the sovereignty of Shebaa Farms is an issue with Syria, not Lebanon, and insists on retaining control of the area until a peace settlement has been agreed with Damascus. Lebanon and Syria, however, maintain that Shebaa Farms is Lebanese territory. (The UN has maintained that Shebaa Farms is part of territory captured by Israel from Syria, and as such must be considered under the Israeli-Syrian track of the Middle East peace process.) At the end of July a limited contingent of UNIFIL troops began to redeploy close to the Lebanese border with Israel, to fill the vacuum created by the departure of Israeli forces. At the same time the UN Security Council voted to extend UNIFIL's mandate until the end of January 2001. In early August 2000 Lebanon's own army returned to southern Lebanon, with the exception of the border areas; a Joint Security Force of some 1,000 Lebanese troops and Internal Security Forces were reported to have entered the territory on 9 August, with responsibility for the provision of general security. However, the area close to the Blue Line remained under the control of Hezbollah, and there were numerous reports of stone-throwing by Lebanese at the heavily fortified Israeli outposts. Continuing tension had discouraged most of the civilian population from returning to the territory.

Meanwhile, in June 2000 the Lebanese authorities initiated military court proceedings (some *in absentia*) against more than 2,500 former SLA militants, on charges of having collaborated with Israel during the occupation of southern Lebanon. The trial attracted strong criticism from human rights organizations. Reports stated that 2,041 alleged collaborators had been convicted by January 2001.

THE 2000 LEGISLATIVE ELECTIONS

Elections to the National Assembly took place in two rounds on 27 August (Mount Lebanon and North Lebanon) and 3 September 2000 (Beirut, the Beqa'a valley, Nabatiyah and the South). For the first time since 1972 Lebanese citizens in the former Israeli-occupied zone of southern Lebanon participated in the poll. Voting patterns in the first round swiftly indicated a rejection of al-Hoss's premiership, as the Druze leader Walid Joumblatt (one of former premier Rafiq Hariri's staunchest allies) secured an overwhelming victory in Mount Lebanon governorate. Furthermore, while Deputy Prime Minister Michel Murr retained his seat in the Maronite Metn district (north-east of Beirut), the election there of Pierre Gemayel, son of Amin Gemayel, was regarded as a considerable reverse for President Lahoud. Turn-out by voters was estimated at 51% of the registered electorate. Once again, the opposition Christian parties boycotted the elections in order to highlight their hostility to Syria's dominant influence over Lebanese political life. At the second round of voting, with a period of political 'cohabitation' between Lahoud and Hariri already appearing likely, the former Prime Minister's Al-Karamah (Dignity) list proceeded to secure 18 of the 19 assembly seats in Beirut (the remaining seat being won by a Hezbollah candidate); al-Hoss lost his own seat in the legislature. In the south an alliance of Hezbollah and Amal candidates took all the governorate's 23 seats, while Hezbollah enjoyed similar successes in the Beqa'a. Independent monitors reported numerous examples of voting irregularities during the elections. Shortly before voting in the first round began, Syria's new President, Bashar al-Assad, had visited Beirut for talks with key figures in Lebanese political affairs, indicating that he was unlikely to alter his late father's role as power-broker in Lebanon. However, the decisive rejection of the Syrian-backed Government of al-Hoss prompted speculation that there might be some redefinition of Syrian influence in Lebanese politics. This was considered all the more probable given the electoral successes for Joumblatt, who appeared to make common cause with Maronite supporters of Amin Gemayel and the imprisoned Geagea in demanding the withdrawal of Syrian forces. Debate about Syria's role in Lebanon had become more intense later in September when thousands of Lebanese, many brandishing portraits of Geagea and Gen. Aoun, greeted Cardinal Sfeir (head of the Maronite Church and leader of the anti-Syrian campaign) on his return from a visit to the USA. In response to this event, numerous Shi'a and Sunni Muslim religious and political figures strongly defended the Syrian presence. The controversy deepened when, later in September, Maronite bishops issued a statement demanding the complete withdrawal of the Syrian army from Lebanon. Following the legislative elections, several editorials in the Syrian state press declared that Damascus would not interfere in the choice of Lebanon's new Prime Minister.

Despite accusations that Rafiq Hariri had spent some US $50m. on his election campaign, the decisive defeat of the al-Hoss administration was attributed primarily to its failure to address the country's economic problems during its two years in office. During the campaign Hariri and his allies were able to exploit widespread popular disillusionment with the previous Government's performance, even though the economic crisis it had to grapple with was largely the result of the over-ambitious development schemes introduced under Hariri's first administration (1992–98). The election result was widely regarded as a defeat for President Lahoud. Before the vote the President had indicated both publicly and in private that he was opposed to Hariri's resuming the premiership. Moreover, as Lahoud was the principal channel through which Damascus exerted its political influence over Lebanon, his comments were also seen as representing Syria's position. The result of the vote, however, left President Lahoud with little alternative but to appoint Rafiq Hariri as Lebanon's new Prime Minister. Unofficial reports stated that as many as 106 of the 128 deputies in the National Assembly had expressed their support for Hariri during private talks with the President. Nevertheless, in the new administration Hariri was not to enjoy the dominant position that he had during his previous terms of office. Before his appointment Hariri had reportedly come to an informal agreement with Lahoud under which Hariri would take charge of economic policy, while the President would control defence and security issues.

The composition of the newly expanded 30-member Cabinet, announced in October 2000, reflected this power-sharing arrangement between the President and the Prime Minister, as well as the traditional practice of dividing portfolios among the main religious communities. Only four ministers remained from the previous Government. Hariri's appointments included Issam Fares as Deputy Prime Minister, Fouad Siniora as Minister of Finance and Samir Jisr as Minister of Justice. The appointment of one of Hariri's allies to the justice portfolio and of his former justice minister, Bahij Tabara, as a Minister of State without portfolio was interpreted by some as an attempt to exonerate a number of the new Prime Minister's associates—notably the new Minister of Finance—who had been charged with corruption by the al-Hoss administration. Appointments made by President Lahoud included that of his son-in-law, Elias Murr, who replaced his father, Michel Murr, as Minister of the Interior and of Municipal and Rural Affairs. Syria ensured that a number of its loyal supporters remained in the Cabinet: Najib Miqati as Minister of Public Works and Transport, Sulayman Franjiya as Minister of Public Health, and Ali Kanso, leader of the Lebanese branch of the Syrian Baath Party, as Minister of Labour. At the last minute Hezbollah—which now had 12 deputies in the Assembly as part of the Resistance and Development list—declined to participate in the new Government. In November Hariri defeated a motion of no confidence, instigated by a group of pro-Syrian deputies who had questioned his past criticism of Syria's continued military presence in Lebanon.

Soon after the new Lebanese Government was announced, there were indications that tensions between Prime Minister Hariri and President Lahoud were re-emerging. At the end of 2000 Hariri claimed that the security services, which are controlled by the President, were tapping his telephone conversations with Nabih Berri. In January 2001, after Hariri reportedly invited the former Christian militia leader, Gen. Aoun, to return to Lebanon from exile in France and gave guarantees that he would not be arrested, President Lahoud, acting through the security services, over-ruled the Prime Minister and insisted that Aoun would be put on trial if he returned. However, there were signs that Prime Minister Hariri had secured support from both President Lahoud and Berri for his ambitious programme of economic reforms (see Economy).

VIOLENCE ON SOUTHERN BORDER INCREASES

The Middle East entered a period of crisis in September 2000, when Palestinians in the West Bank and Gaza resumed their *intifada* against Israel. The uprising provided a pretext for Hezbollah to step up its militant campaign against Israel. The organization expressed strong support for the Palestinians, urging them to continue their struggle against the Israeli state, but its leadership refrained from offering direct military assistance to the Palestinians. Hezbollah launched a number of small-scale attacks on Israeli positions in Shebaa Farms, and on 7 October Hezbollah militants captured three Israeli soldiers on patrol there, demanding that Israel release dozens of Palestinian prisoners and 19 Lebanese being held in Israeli gaols. On 12 October UN Secretary-General Kofi Annan visited Beirut for talks regarding the soldiers' release. In the following week, however, Israel confirmed that a senior Israeli businessman and army reservist had been kidnapped in Switzerland, apparently by Hezbollah (who claimed that the officer was working for Israeli intelligence). It was unclear whether the Syrian leadership was encouraging Hezbollah's latest campaign against Israel, although some commentators felt that Syria was unlikely to support any activities that might result in renewed Israeli attacks against Lebanon. There were those who argued that since the death of President Hafiz al-Assad and the Israeli withdrawal from southern Lebanon, Syrian influence over Hezbollah had declined, and that Damascus might no longer be able to restrain Hezbollah fighters from provoking Israel.

In November 2000 Kofi Annan urged the Lebanese Government to take effective military control of the whole of southern Lebanon and deplored the fact that in practice Hezbollah still controlled the Blue Line. UNIFIL commanders met on 21 November to draw up contingency plans that would reduce the peace-keeping force from seven full-strength battalions to two, and eventually to one 'truce supervision' battalion. The threat of reducing the size of UNIFIL was seen as an attempt by the UN to force the Lebanese army to deploy troops along the southern border. However, Lebanon's position remained that it would not deploy its forces along the border until Israel had concluded peace agreements with both Lebanon and Syria. It was assumed that Beirut, under pressure from Damascus, would not extend its control over the border region until Israel returned the Golan Heights to Syria. At this time the Israelis were reported to be constructing a new concrete border fence. At the end of November an Israeli soldier was killed and two others wounded by an explosive device planted inside the disputed Shebaa Farms area; the operation was interpreted as a signal from Hezbollah that it could strike at Israeli forces south of the Blue Line and even within Israel itself. In retaliation, Israel used helicopter gunships to attack suspected Hezbollah bases in southern Lebanon—the first Israeli air-strikes on Lebanon since the Israeli withdrawal in May. There were reports in December that since the Israeli withdrawal at least 12 Lebanese demonstrators had been killed by Israeli troops during incidents along the border.

In January 2001, following complaints from the UN, Israel was reported to have stopped construction work on a section of its concrete security fence near the village of Ghajar (just north of the UN-delineated border and thus inside Lebanese territory). Later that month the UN Security Council reiterated its demand that both Israel and Lebanon end the numerous violations of the Blue Line. The Security Council also voted for a further six-month extension of UNIFIL's mandate in Lebanon and announced that from July 2001 the operational strength of UNIFIL was to be reduced. Meanwhile, in January two PFLP—GC guerrillas were killed while attempting to infiltrate Shebaa Farms, in the first operation by Palestinian guerrillas since the Israeli withdrawal from southern Lebanon. The operation was condemned by Prime Minister Hariri, who declared that Lebanon would not permit such activities and that Palestinians who wanted to fight against Israel should join the *intifada*. In February, after the assassination of Massoud Ayyad, an officer in Arafat's presidential guard (Force 17), Israel claimed that Ayyad was an agent of Hezbollah, and accused Hezbollah of direct involvement in the violence in the West Bank and Gaza. Israeli sources alleged that Hezbollah was attempting to unite Palestinian groups 'under its umbrella', that the movement organized military training sessions in Lebanon and was trying to smuggle weapons into areas controlled by the PA. Hezbollah was accused of trying to enlist Palestinians into its ranks, and it was claimed that the organization was considering operations within the 'Green Line', that is, within Israel's pre-1967 borders. However, Nasrallah strongly denied that his organization was involved in the Palestinian *intifada*, and several commentators argued that while Hezbollah was offering strong political support to the Palestinians, it was not in the movement's interest to become directly involved in the Israeli–Palestinian conflict. In February 2001 Hezbollah fighters killed an Israeli soldier in a missile attack against an Israeli army patrol in Shebaa Farms. Israel responded by shelling targets in southern Lebanon. The UN, France and the USA condemned the attack by Hezbollah, and the US Department of State urged the Lebanese Government to deploy its troops along the frontier with Israel. The attack proved particularly embarrassing for premier Hariri as it came the day after he had publicly assured President Jacques Chirac of France that there would be 'no provocation of Israel from our side because we seek security and peace'. Hariri had apparently failed to persuade the Hezbollah leadership to co-ordinate its operations with the state, although Nasrallah informed the Lebanese press that his movement would try to co-operate with the Prime Minister, and stressed that Israel, and not Hariri, was Hezbollah's prime target. In February and March a number of clashes occurred between Hezbollah and UNIFIL units when Hezbollah fighters prevented the UN peace-keepers from establishing new positions in the border area. Increasingly frustrated at the problems they faced in their role as peace-keepers, UNIFIL announced that it would reduce the size of its force from an estimated 5,700 troops to some 4,500 (the number of personnel deployed prior to the Israeli withdrawal).

On assuming the Israeli premiership in March 2001, the Likud leader Ariel Sharon declared that he wanted 'realistic political relations and a true peace' with Lebanon and Syria, based on formal peace treaties (as Israel had signed with Egypt and Jordan). In response to the formation of the Sharon Government, Prime Minister Hariri declared that Lebanon and other Arab states wanted to make peace on condition that they regained the territories occupied by Israel in 1967, and on condition that the Israeli Government respected international laws, UN resolutions and human rights. However, the Lebanese press was less restrained and, reviving memories of the early 1980s, some newspapers declared that the return to power in Israel of the man whom they held responsible for the massacre of Palestinians in the Sabra and Chatila refugee camps in September 1982 (when Sharon was Israel's Minister of Defence) would again plunge the region into war.

ISRAEL ATTACKS SYRIAN BASES IN LEBANON

In April 2001, after a further attack by Hezbollah on Israeli military positions in Shebaa Farms in which an Israeli soldier was killed, Israel responded by bombarding targets in southern Lebanon. Two days later the Israeli air force attacked and destroyed a Syrian radar station at Dahr al-Baydar, 45 km east of Beirut, killing at least one Syrian soldier, according to a statement from Damascus. An Israeli spokesman stated that the raid by his country's forces—the first military action by Israel against Syrian troops since 1996—was designed to send a clear message that the new Israeli Government headed by Ariel Sharon held Syria and Lebanon responsible for Hezbollah's actions, and that they would suffer reprisals for the organization's 'anti-Israeli' activities. President Lahoud described the Israeli air-strike as a dangerous development that revealed once again the 'murderous methods' of Prime Minister Sharon and that could lead to a wider Middle Eastern conflict. Prime Minister Hariri warned of an Israeli plan to extend the 'zone of instability' in the region and called for action by the international community to contain this dangerous escalation of violence.

In April 2001, on a visit to Washington, DC, USA, for talks with US President George W. Bush, US Secretary of State Colin Powell and US National Security Advisor Condoleezza Rice, the Lebanese Prime Minister called on the Bush Administration to play a more active role in advancing the Middle East peace process. Hariri also met the UN Secretary-General, Kofi Annan, during his visit to the USA. Both Powell and Annan were reported to have emphasized the importance of reducing the level of violence in the region before the international community could address questions of economic development. Hariri insisted, however, that the USA was not making the release of some US $20m. in economic aid to Lebanon conditional on the deployment of Lebanese armed forces along the southern border. At the end of April the French Minister of Foreign Affairs, Hubert Védrine, visited Beirut and Damascus to explore the basis for restarting Middle East peace negotiations. In Beirut he was informed by President Lahoud that Lebanon would not deploy its troops in the south of the country because such an action would be interpreted as ratifying the frontier delimited by the UN—the Blue Line—which Lebanon contested and where a number of problems remained unresolved, notably the issue of Shebaa Farms. Lahoud again denounced the 'aggressive policy' of Israel's Prime Minister, Ariel Sharon, and invited the EU, and particularly France, to play an active role in saving the peace process. The Lebanese authorities also stressed that Hezbollah's activities against Israeli forces in Shebaa Farms area were 'legitimate'.

In May 2001, during his first official visit to France since assuming office, President Lahoud called on the international community to revise its policies in order to force Israel to resume peace negotiations, and again urged the EU to play a more active role in reviving peace talks. President Chirac, for his part, stated that in order to prevent the escalating violence between Israel and the Palestinians from spreading to Lebanon, the Lebanese state must re-establish its authority in the south by deploying its troops in the border zone. In June UNIFIL announced that it had already dismantled 152 of its positions in the former Israeli security zone and was planning to establish new ones along the actual border between Lebanon and Israel, in preparation for the final establishment of the international border. By the end of July the UNIFIL force was to be reduced to some 4,500 troops, with further reductions to 2,000 troops by July 2002. The Lebanese Government stated that it wished to see the peace-keeping force maintained at 4,500 troops, and criticized proposals by the UN Secretary-General to consider downgrading UNIFIL to the status of an observer mission.

The UN revealed in June 2001 that it had in its possession a video-cassette which had reportedly been filmed by a member of the UNIFIL force 18 hours after the kidnapping of the three Israeli soldiers by Hezbollah in October 2000. The cassette was reported to show two UN vehicles—containing UN uniforms, arms and explosives—that were apparently used by Hezbollah in the abduction of the Israeli soldiers. Israeli television, which had obtained some pictures from the tape, demanded to know why UN officials had refused to hand over the video-cassette to the Israeli authorities as it could provide valuable evidence concerning the kidnapping. There were reports that Israeli security forces suspected that UN peace-keepers had turned a blind eye to preparations for the Hezbollah operation and may even have witnessed the abductions. There was also speculation that the UN had refused to hand over the cassette because it feared that any Israeli reprisals against the men pictured in the tape, who may or may not have been directly involved in the kidnapping, would compromise the organization's neutrality. The results of an internal UN investigation into the incident were published in August 2001. The report concluded that UN officials were not guilty of any conspiracy or malice, but noted several 'lapses in judgment and failures in communication', which had prevented the existence of the video-cassette from coming to light more promptly after the abduction of the Israeli soldiers. Some months later reports indicated that the matter had been resolved and that Israeli officials, including a senior intelligence officer, had viewed the cassette together with two other tapes held by the UN also relating to the abduction of the three Israeli soldiers. In November the IDF's Chief Rabbi declared that the three kidnapped soldiers were officially dead, an announcement dismissed by Hezbollah as an attempt to elicit information about the men.

In July 2001 Israeli air forces attacked a Syrian radar station in Lebanon's Beqa'a valley, in response to a Hezbollah operation in Shebaa Farms during which at least one Israeli soldier was wounded. Up to three Syrian soldiers and a Lebanese conscript were reportedly injured in the retaliatory attack. The Israeli administration stated that the Syrian authorities were preventing the deployment of the Lebanese army on the frontier and were allowing Hezbollah to re-arm. Later in July the UN Security Council voted to extend UNIFIL's mandate in Lebanon until 31 January 2002. The UN also confirmed a reduction in the number of UNIFIL troops from 4,500 to 3,600 and the nominal downgrading of their peace-keeping mission to an 'observer mission'. The observer mission's mandate was extended for a further six months on 31 January 2002, and on

31 July. By the end of 2002 the strength of the force had been reduced to some 2,000 troops. A new UN resolution approved in January 2003 extended UNIFIL's mandate until 31 July, and it was subsequently renewed at six-monthly intervals.

In January 2002 Israel seized a freighter, the *Karine A*, in the Red Sea, carrying a cargo of arms that the Israelis claimed had been purchased by the PA from Iran using Hezbollah as an intermediary. The Palestinian leadership, Hezbollah and Iran denied any involvement in the affair. Independent sources suggested that PLO officials had probably been engaged in the arms trade and that Hezbollah and Iran may have been involved. In March Nasrallah admitted that a number of Hezbollah members had been arrested by the Jordanian authorities earlier in the year while attempting to smuggle weapons from Jordan to Palestinian fighters in the West Bank. Hezbollah also appeared to have allowed at least two Palestinian guerrillas to travel from Lebanon to carry out an ambush in northern Israel in which the guerrillas were killed along with several Israelis. From late 2001 Hezbollah had been markedly less hostile towards Yasser Arafat and the PA.

In January 2002 Hezbollah began firing large-calibre anti-aircraft artillery across the border into Israel in retaliation for continued incursions by Israeli military aircraft into Lebanese airspace. In March, when Israel announced that it was reducing its 'reconnaissance' flights over Lebanon, Hezbollah described it as an 'Arab victory'. Meanwhile, Israel resumed construction work on a fence around the southern edge of Ghajar. In late March and early April, as Israeli forces began a major offensive in Palestinian-controlled territories in the West Bank, Hezbollah increased its cross-border attacks using anti-tank missiles and mortars, wounding several Israeli soldiers. The Hezbollah attacks were the most intensive since the Israeli withdrawal from southern Lebanon in May 2000. Reports also suggested that Hezbollah had given permission for militants from radical Palestinian groups to fire on Israeli settlements from inside Lebanon. However, in a speech in April 2002 Nasrallah insisted that there was no intention of opening up a 'second front' against Israel.

LEBANON AND THE 'WAR ON TERROR'

Most of Lebanon's political and religious leaders condemned the suicide attacks on New York and Washington, DC on 11 September 2001, and Prime Minister Hariri stated that Lebanon would support US retaliation 'if the evidence was clear'. Lebanon subsequently signed UN Security Council Resolution 1373, which was adopted to combat international terrorism. Some days after the attacks Hezbollah issued a statement in which it expressed regret at the killing of innocent people anywhere in the world, but urged caution, arguing that the US Administration would use the resulting fear and panic to practise 'all manner of aggression and terrorism under the pretext of fighting aggression and terrorism'. The statement declared that the Lebanese had been the victims of repeated Zionist massacres that the US Administration had refused to condemn. Druze leader Walid Joumblatt, who had at first categorically condemned the 11 September attacks, later described Osama bin Laden (the presumed instigator of the attacks) as an 'invention' of US intelligence services and suggested that these agencies might have been involved in the attacks. In the wake of the suicide attacks the ninth Francophone summit, which was to have been held in Beirut on 16–19 October, was postponed. This was the first time that an Arab capital had been selected as the venue for a Francophone summit, and, with delegates from 55 countries, it would have been the most important international event held in Beirut since the end of the civil war. Hezbollah denounced the subsequent US bombing campaign against Afghanistan, and Nasrallah declared that it was not permissible for any Islamic state, ruler or political organization to extend any assistance to the USA in its war against a Muslim country or group. He accused the USA of using the 11 September attacks as a pretext to wage war on its opponents and establish military bases around the world.

Hezbollah did not appear on the first US list of terrorist groups associated with bin Laden whose assets were to be frozen. Asbat al-Ansar, with both Palestinian and Lebanese members based in the Ain el-Hilweh refugee camp in Sidon, was the only Lebanese group included on the list, which was published at the end of September 2001. At a press conference Asbat al-Ansar's leadership immediately denied any links with bin Laden's al-Qa'ida organization. However, the USA subsequently included Hezbollah on an updated list of terrorist organizations along with Hamas, Islamic Jihad and the PFLP—GC. Nasrallah asserted that the US Administration was acting under pressure from Israel, and accused the USA of waging war 'against every Muslim who refuses to bow to it'. A member of Hezbollah, Imad Mughniyeh, was one of three Lebanese nationals included on a list issued by the US Federal Bureau of Investigation (FBI) of its 22 'most wanted' terrorists. In November the Lebanese Cabinet refused a US request to freeze Hezbollah's assets, stating that it was a resistance movement not a terrorist organization and arguing that resistance to Israel was legitimate so long as Israel occupied Arab lands. Shortly afterwards the US National Security Advisor, Condoleezza Rice, declared that Lebanon would not secure the international financial assistance it required for its economic recovery if it did not comply with the US Administration's demands. In December Rice urged Lebanon and Syria to dismantle Hezbollah's military wing, while the US ambassador to Beirut insisted that Hezbollah was an organization that carried out terrorist acts and was capable of staging them on a global scale.

Hezbollah was not included on the EU's list of 'terrorist' groups and individuals, released in December 2001: its omission appeared to have been the result of a late intervention by France. The United Kingdom, for its part, made a distinction between Hezbollah's domestic organization, which was deemed legitimate, and its external security organization, which was condemned as a terrorist group because of its attacks against Israeli interests abroad. In June 2002, after negotiations lasting six years (which had been officially concluded in January), Lebanon signed a Euro-Mediterranean Association Agreement with the EU. Romano Prodi, the President of the European Commission, stated that by signing the agreement, which awaited ratification, Lebanon clearly indicated its commitment to the values shared by the EU on democracy, human rights, economic liberalization and regional security. The EU promised to support Lebanon's application for membership of the World Trade Organization.

In March 2002 Syria and Lebanon issued a joint communiqué, after a brief state visit to Beirut by Syrian President Bashar al-Assad, in response to the peace plan proposed by Crown Prince Abdullah of Saudi Arabia to end the Arab–Israeli conflict. While supporting the principle of an exchange of land for peace, the joint statement by Presidents Assad and Lahoud drew attention to the right of return of Palestinian refugees—Lebanon in particular continued to reject the notion of the permanent settlement of some 200,000 Palestinian refugees in Lebanon—and the dismantling of Jewish settlements established in the Occupied Territories. This was Bashar al-Assad's first official visit to Lebanon since he assumed the presidency and the first by a Syrian President to the presidential palace at Baabda. At the end of March the Beirut summit meeting of the Arab League Conference (the first to be held in Lebanon since 1956) unanimously endorsed the Saudi peace plan. Arab leaders offered to normalize relations with Israel in return for an Israeli withdrawal from Arab territories occupied since 1967 (including the Syrian Golan Heights and Shebaa Farms), the establishment of a Palestinian state with East Jerusalem as its capital, and a 'just and negotiated solution' to the refugee problem. They also expressed their opposition to any US military attack against Iraq. Yasser Arafat (who was not permitted by the Israeli authorities to leave the West Bank) had been scheduled to address the summit by video link from his headquarters in Ramallah, but at the last minute the Lebanese authorities refused to allow the live transmission of his speech. The Saudi delegation denounced the Lebanese action (for which no real explanation was given) as 'inexplicable and unpardonable'. Addressing a crowd of some 200,000 people, Hezbollah's Secretary-General, Nasrallah, condemned any normalization of relations with Israel. Earlier, Hezbollah had rejected the Saudi peace plan and had called on the Arab leaders to send weapons to the Palestinians so that they could continue their resistance to Israeli rule.

Israel's military offensive into Palestinian-controlled areas in the West Bank, from March 2002, was condemned by all Lebanese political parties and all religious communities. Hezbollah stated that it could not ignore what was happening in the West Bank and that it was determined to continue the struggle for the liberation of those parts of Lebanon still occupied by Israel. Throughout the Israeli reoccupation of Palestinian-administered population centres in the West Bank, Hezbollah carried out almost daily attacks on Israeli positions in the border region. At the end of March demonstrations were held in Palestinian refugee camps across Lebanon, and for the first time in many years the authorities allowed several hundred Palestinians to hold a demonstration in the heart of west Beirut to express support for Arafat, although the protest was closely monitored by the Internal Security Forces.

MOUNTING OPPOSITION TO SYRIAN PRESENCE

Pressure for Syria to withdraw its troops from Lebanon and to relinquish its dominant role in the country's internal affairs—which had been growing since the Israeli withdrawal from southern Lebanon in May 2000 and the death of Syria's President Hafiz Assad in June—continued to mount after the Lebanese elections. It was particularly significant that Walid Joumblatt, the Druze leader and a long-standing ally of Syria, in late 2000 joined the Christian opposition in demanding a 'reassessment' of Lebanon's relationship with Syria. Joumblatt's statement provoked disquiet in Damascus, where there were fears that the anti-Syrian movement in Lebanon might spread beyond the Maronite community and begin to acquire a wider nationalist dimension. Meanwhile, in November the Shi'a leader and National Assembly President, Nabih Berri, provoked criticism from Damascus when, on a visit to Cardinal Sfeir, Berri announced that Syria would redeploy its troops from Lebanon 'in the near future'. Although Berri's meeting with the Cardinal had been made at Syria's request, Berri appeared to have exceeded his instructions by referring to the redeployment of Syrian troops. These developments were interpreted by some commentators as further evidence of divisions within the Syrian leadership over its policy on Lebanon. Syria's new President, Bashar al-Assad, had responded to mounting anti-Syrian feeling in Lebanon by seeking a rapprochement with the Maronite community, a policy that had been opposed by some of his advisers. In December Syria began the release of Lebanese political prisoners held in its gaols, many of them supporters of Gen. Aoun. At the end of the year there were reports from Damascus that President Assad was examining proposals to pull back all Syrian troops currently in Lebanon to the Beqa'a valley, but that he would only contemplate a complete withdrawal of Syrian forces within the context of a comprehensive Middle East peace settlement.

The controversy regarding Syria's presence in Lebanon provoked inter-communal tensions, and even violence, in the early part of 2001. In March, on the 12th anniversary of Gen. Aoun's attempt to expel Syrian forces from Lebanon, several thousand students staged protests at university campuses across Beirut, and the Lebanese army and security forces intervened to prevent the protesters from marching on a Syrian military position outside the capital. The debate became more acrimonious at the end of March when some 100,000 Lebanese Christians greeted Cardinal Sfeir on his return from the USA, where he had called for an end to Syrian tutelage. The crowds that lined the road from Beirut to Bkerké—the seat of the patriarch—again brandished portraits of Geagea, Bashir Gemayel and Gen. Aoun. Strong criticism of Cardinal Sfeir from senior Sunni clerics raised fears of renewed sectarian conflict within Lebanon. At the beginning of April former premier Selim al-Hoss established a National Action Front that called for an 'equitable relationship between the state of Lebanon and Syria to stop one from interfering in the domestic affairs of the other'. Later in the month several supporters of a militant pro-Syrian faction, the Ahbache, had demonstrated in west Beirut against the 'agents' who opposed Syria's involvement in Lebanon. On the previous day a parcel bomb had wounded three members of the family of PSP deputy Akram Chehayeb. The leader of the PSP, Walid Joumblatt, immediately declared that if the aim was to terrorize the Druze community, then such actions would achieve nothing, insisting that what was required was dialogue. In a move to ease the tensions, President Lahoud received Joumblatt—their first meeting for six months. Meanwhile, Sulayman Franjiya, the Minister of Public Health and a Christian with very close links with Syria, visited Cardinal Sfeir. The Cardinal adopted a more moderate tone, calling for 'narrow' but 'transparent' links with Damascus based on harmony and a sincere commitment to respect treaties. This message was repeated a day later when President Lahoud visited the Maronite patriarch. At the same time Cardinal Sfeir received an invitation from the Greek Catholic patriarch, whose seat is in Damascus, to visit Syria in May to take part in celebrations to greet the leader of the Roman Catholic Church, Pope John Paul II. However, in May the Cardinal announced that he would not attend the papal celebrations, owing to Lebanese public opinion and concerns that his visit might be exploited by Syria.

LEBANESE PRISONERS HELD IN SYRIA

In January 2001 the Lebanese Government set up a commission to examine the sensitive issue of Lebanese prisoners held in Syria. The commission was to be chaired by a minister and to include representatives of Lebanon's legal system, military intelligence, and internal and national security. For two years, until the release of some 46 Lebanese and eight Palestinians by Syria in December 2000, the authorities in Beirut had denied that any Lebanese were imprisoned in Syria. Faced with official indifference, the families of the Lebanese citizens detained in Syria had set up a committee to campaign for their release. The committee reported that Syria had released 168 Lebanese prisoners in two groups since 1998 and estimated that some 263 Lebanese remained in Syrian gaols. The London-based human rights organization Amnesty International put the figure at 228. During the official visit of President Bashar al-Assad to France in June 2001 the movement Solida (Soutien aux Libanais Détenus Arbitrairement) appealed to the Syrian President to stop the practice of forced disappearances from Lebanese territory and the secret detention of Lebanese nationals in Syria, and asked him to return the bodies of those detainees who had died in detention to their families or at least produce a list of those who had died.

SYRIAN WITHDRAWAL FROM BEIRUT FAILS TO EASE TENSIONS

In June 2001 Syria began to withdraw its armed forces from Beirut and its southern and eastern suburbs, and from Mount Lebanon; many of the troops were redeployed in the Beqa'a valley. During 14–19 June an estimated 6,000–10,000 Syrian troops were withdrawn from more than 12 major bases and several smaller positions in and around the Lebanese capital, most of them in largely Christian areas and near government buildings (including the presidential palace at Baabda and the defence ministry in Yarza). The redeployment from Greater Beirut was believed by some to be intended to reduce pressure from Lebanese Christians for a full Syrian withdrawal from the country, and to demonstrate a return to Lebanese sovereignty in the capital. Other analysts, however, speculated that the movement of Syrian forces to the Beqa'a valley demonstrated Syrian fears of a possible new confrontation with Israel. Cardinal Sfeir expressed his satisfaction at the redeployment, but noted that there was a long road to travel before relations between Lebanon and Syria could achieve a new 'equilibrium'. Walid Joumblatt stated that the redeployment was the first step in improving Lebanese-Syrian relations. However, some commentators saw the withdrawal as partial and merely symbolic—Syria retained 15 bases in strategic areas in Beirut, including the airport—and noted that Syria's intelligence services remained vigilant and omnipresent in Lebanon.

The Maronite patriarch, Cardinal Sfeir, visited the Chouf mountain region of Lebanon on 3–5 August 2001 to hold landmark discussions with Joumblatt, in order to demonstrate a new era of 'reconciliation' between the Maronite and Druze communities. Joumblatt also visited several Christian towns in the south of Lebanon in the following week. However, two days after Sfeir's visit to the Chouf, the Lebanese army intelligence service (which is largely pro-Syrian) implemented a crackdown on Maronite Christians who were again vociferously demanding a complete Syrian withdrawal from Lebanon. According to Joumblatt, the authorities' action was largely due to Syria's dislike of the recent Maronite-Druze reconciliation. On 7 August as many as 250 Christians—most of whom were members of the prohibited LF or supporters of Gen. Aoun's Free National Current (FNC) movement—were arrested on charges of involvement in 'illegal gatherings' and of seeking to destabilize and partition the country. It was unclear whether President Lahoud had ordered army intelligence officers to carry out the arrests, but reports stated that the Hariri Government had not been consulted. Both Christian and Muslim deputies condemned the detentions as 'unconstitutional'. The mass arrest of Christian opposition activists led to clashes between the Lebanese police and protesters demonstrating against the growing influence of the military in the country. The authorities made further arrests, this time including activists of the PNL. Two leading Lebanese journalists were also detained, on charges of having contacts with Israel. A few days after the clampdown, a military court began trial proceedings against more than 20 Christian activists who had taken part in the anti-Syrian protests. By 20 August it was reported that the vast majority of those arrested for their role in the disturbances had been released or tried on more minor charges (leading to a maximum of 45 days' imprisonment). However, it was reported that those LF members accused of conspiracy with Israel remained in detention.

The political crisis facing Rafiq Hariri increased during the latter part of August 2001. In mid-August the National Assembly passed legislation giving greater powers to President Lahoud. At the end of the month Hariri held talks with the President over the consequences of the recent security crackdown; the Prime Minister pledged to continue in office, despite being angered by the military's failure to consult him prior to its campaign of arrests. In September Maronite bishops again issued a strong criticism of Syria's domination of Lebanese affairs. It was reported at this time that up to seven Syrians had been killed in Lebanon during the past month.

In October 2001 Karim Pakradoumi, former lawyer to LF leader Samir Geagea, won a decisive victory in elections for the leadership of the Phalange party, now only a shadow of its former strength. Since his return to Lebanon in 2000 former President Amin Gemayel, son of the Phalange's founder, Pierre Gemayel, had sought to take control of the party, promising to restore its influence, but in the end his supporters boycotted the leadership elections. In November 2001 the Internal Security Forces entered the Université Saint-Joseph in Beirut and dismantled a display erected by anti-Syrian students—which included Lebanese flags hung with black ribbons to symbolize Lebanon's loss of independence. They also prevented students from joining an anti-Syrian demonstration by mainly right-wing student groups at the Lebanese University campus. Although the State Prosecutor upheld the actions of the security forces, the Minister of the Interior condemned them and reprimanded three of its officers. In December, after months of wrangling within the ruling troika over appointments to the civil service, it was announced that agreement had been reached on some 171 posts, with 66 divided among Christian communities and the remainder allocated to Muslims. These appointments, especially senior posts such as directors-general of ministries, form an important part of the country's elaborate patronage system, and disputes over their distribution intensified as President, Prime Minister and National Assembly President each sought to use them to extend their authority and influence within the political system. Hariri was reported to have successfully placed his own supporters in a number of key posts, notably those of head of the Council for Development and Reconstruction and of Electricité du Liban. The remaining civil service appointments were finally agreed by January 2002, when a new head of the National Security Fund was appointed.

At the end of January 2002 Elie Hobeika, former head of the LF, was killed when a car bomb exploded close to his home in a Beirut suburb. Hobeika's murder was the first high-profile political assassination for over a decade. Although Hobeika had many enemies, most Lebanese politicians, including government ministers, held Israel responsible for the assassination: many believed that it was a 'targeted killing' because Hobeika had agreed to testify against Israeli Prime Minister Ariel Sharon, whose role in the 1982 Sabra and Chatila massacres was the subject of legal proceedings brought before a court in Brussels, Belgium, by several survivors of the massacres. (The complaint against Sharon was judged inadmissible by the Court of Appeal in Brussels in June 2002.) Both Sharon and Israeli Minister of Foreign Affairs Shimon Peres dismissed accusations of any Israeli involvement in Hobeika's murder. As head of the LF's intelligence section in 1982, Hobeika was widely accused of 'overseeing' the massacres of Palestinians at Sabra and Chatila. He had later abandoned his Israeli patrons and made peace with Damascus. After the end of the civil war he served in three governments, but lost his seat in the National Assembly at the 2000 elections. While Israeli agents remained the prime suspect for the killing, there were also suggestions that the assassination could have been the work of Palestinians or rival Christian groups, notably those linked to Samir Geagea. In January 2002 the LF held its first official meeting since being banned in 1994, in what the party asserted was the first step in relaunching the party and restoring its legal status.

Leaders of anti-Syrian factions, including the Maronite patriarch, broadly welcomed the official visit to Beirut by President Bashar al-Assad and his senior ministers in March 2002. While pointing out that it was a useful 'first step', they continued to demand an end to Syria's dominant role in Lebanon's internal affairs. In April Syria announced that it was redeploying a further 20,000 troops based in Lebanon. It was expected that most of the units withdrawn from central Lebanon would be redeployed in the Beqa'a valley, with others returning to Syria. Some analysts interpreted the move as a sign that Syria was prepared to allow Lebanon greater autonomy in some areas while retaining tight control over security issues and foreign affairs. Others suggested that, by concentrating its forces in the Beqa'a valley, Syria was adopting a more defensive position in case of an attack by Israel.

Jihad Jibril, the head of the PFLP—GC's military operations and son of the group's leader, was killed by a car bomb in west Beirut in May 2002. The Lebanese security forces attributed his murder to inter-Palestinian rivalries, while the PFLP—GC initially accused the Israeli secret service, Mossad, and then the Jordanian secret services. Israel categorically rejected any involvement in the incident, even though in recent months the PFLP—GC had been involved in a number of successful attacks across the Lebanese border into Israel and claimed to have been actively engaged in smuggling arms into the West Bank. There were also claims that Jibril's murder might have been the work of right-wing Lebanese Christians who regarded the PFLP—GC as Syrian agents in Lebanon.

In August 2002 two people were killed in the worst factional fighting at the Ain el-Hilweh Palestinian refugee camp for several years. Tensions escalated following the arrest of an Islamist militant the previous month (accused of killing three Lebanese army intelligence officers) by the Lebanese army aided by Fatah. Violent clashes between the Lebanese army and Palestinian militants occurred at the normally relatively calm al-Jalil refugee camp, near Ba'albek, in September, which left one soldier and three Palestinians dead. Lebanese soldiers had entered the camp in search of a wanted man and removed a cache of armaments from offices of the Fatah Revolutionary Council, an organization founded by the militant leader Abu Nidal, who was found dead in Baghdad, Iraq, in August.

In September 2002 the Minister of the Interior closed down the main Christian opposition television station, Murr Television, and its owner, Gabriel Murr, was later stripped of his seat in the National Assembly. The following month Ghazi Kenaan, who had been head of Syrian military intelligence in Lebanon for some 20 years, and in effect Syria's pro-consul in Lebanon, retired and was replaced by Syria's long-serving military intelligence chief in Beirut, Rustom Ghazaleh. Also in

October Beirut hosted the ninth Francophone summit, which was attended by some 35 heads of state. It was the first major international meeting to be held in Lebanon since the civil war.

POLITICAL INFIGHTING BETWEEN LAHOUD AND HARIRI INTENSIFIES

The Paris II conference held in France in November 2002 provided additional financial aid to Lebanon, but on the understanding that important economic reforms were implemented. However, the Government's 2003 austerity budget met with stiff opposition in the National Assembly in January, although it was eventually passed into law largely unchanged. Continued disagreements in the Cabinet led to the resignation of Prime Minister Rafiq Hariri and his Government in April. Following consultations with members of the National Assembly, President Lahoud asked Hariri to form a new administration. In the new 30-member Cabinet, 16 portfolios changed hands and 11 new ministers were appointed. The major change at senior ministerial level was the appointment of Jean Obeid, a pro-Syrian Christian, as Minister of Foreign Affairs and Immigrants, in place of Mahmoud Hammoud who moved to the Ministry of Defence. The most noteworthy among the new faces in the Cabinet was Karim Pakradouni, a leader of the Phalangist Party, who became Minister for Administrative Reform. The Phalangist Party, formerly opposed to Syria's role in Lebanon, had in recent years adopted a more pro-Syrian stance. Elias Murr, Lahoud's son-in-law, returned as the Minister of the Interior and Municipalities and Fouad Siniora retained the finance portfolio. The new Government won a vote of confidence in the National Assembly, with those deputies voting against mainly being Christians opposed to Syria's role in Lebanon. Hezbollah's deputies were among those who abstained.

Hariri's new Government appeared to be weaker and more divided than its predecessor. The deepening power struggle between the President and the Prime Minister, each with very different political and economic agendas, prevented effective policy-making. In July 2003 Hariri stated that political infighting was delaying major development and reconstruction projects, but expressed hope that the dispute with Lahoud and his political allies, especially over privatization, could be overcome. However, during the following months a number of Hariri's important economic reform measures were held up by the President's allies. The 2004 budget was only approved after the Prime Minister made numerous compromises and direct intervention by Damascus prevented the political process from collapsing completely.

Tensions between President and Prime Minister over economic policy and their poor personal relations intensified as Lahoud began to seek Syrian support to prolong his period of office, which was due to expire in November 2004. An extension to Lahoud's term of office was strongly opposed by Hariri and his supporters, who feared that this would firmly establish Lahoud as the country's dominant political personality. The Prime Minister clearly hoped to see a new President elected who would not obstruct his reform programme and would allow him to resume the dominant political position that he himself had enjoyed for most of the 1990s. Both leaders visited Damascus to press their case with the Syrian leadership. In November 2003 President Lahoud held talks with Syrian President Bashar al-Assad, his first visit to Syria since the death of Assad's father in 2000, and agreed to reactivate the 1991 friendship and co-operation treaty. Hariri met the Syrian President in October 2003 and again in December, but appeared to have been told that he had to co-operate with Lahoud in order to retain the premiership. Meanwhile, Lahoud was reported to have called for the appointment of a Prime Minister who would support his re-election bid. However, during the early months of 2004 some observers argued that the political balance had shifted in Hariri's favour and that foreign and domestic considerations might persuade Damascus not to support an extension of Lahoud's mandate. PSP leader Walid Joumblatt was reported to have changed sides and was now supporting Hariri, who also had the backing of the President of the National Assembly, Shi'a leader Nabih Berri. The Maronite Patriarch, Cardinal Sfeir, outspoken in his demands for Lebanese sovereignty, was also opposed to Lahoud continuing as President.

Earlier, in June 2003 the news studios of the Al-Mustaqbal (Future) television station and Al-Sharq (East) Radio in Beirut, both owned by Hariri, were destroyed by a rocket attack. The Minister of the Interior and Municipalities later blamed Palestinian Islamists of Asbat al-Ansar, based in the Ain el-Hilweh refugee camp, for the attack. In December Tahsin Khayyat, the owner of NTV, a strong critic of Prime Minister Hariri, was arrested and briefly detained by military intelligence on suspicion of collaborating with Israel and damaging the country's relations with friendly countries, notably Saudi Arabia. Shortly afterwards the Government banned the station from reporting news and politics for 48 hours, provoking accusations from opposition groups that the Government was trying to silence the media.

In May 2003 Muhammad Khatami became the first Iranian President to visit Lebanon since the Iranian Revolution in 1979. He was met at the airport by President Lahoud, Prime Minister Hariri, members of the Cabinet and, in a departure from protocol, Sheikh Naim Kassem, Hezbollah's deputy leader. Tens of thousands of Lebanese Shi'a Muslims turned out to welcome Khatami as he drove through the streets of Beirut. Lahoud praised Iran's support for Lebanon's efforts to reclaim lands occupied by Israel, and stated that Iranian support for the Lebanese resistance had enabled Lebanon to recover its southern territories from Israeli occupation. He declared that Khatami's visit would strengthen support for Lebanon as a centre of resistance against Israel.

US Secretary of State Colin Powell visited Beirut in May 2003 to promote the US-backed 'roadmap' for a permanent settlement of the Israeli–Palestinian conflict, which had been published in April. Both Lebanon and Syria had criticized the plan and expressed the wish that it should also include efforts to settle their dispute with Israel. Powell stated that the USA was committed to a comprehensive Middle East settlement that would include the interests of Lebanon and Syria. On the sensitive issue of Palestinian refugees in Lebanon, Prime Minister Hariri stated that they could not be allowed to settle permanently in Lebanon as this would create several economic and social problems. In his talks with Lebanese leaders, Powell stated that the USA supported an independent and prosperous Lebanon, free of all foreign forces, adding that Lebanon could be a model for democracy and free trade in the region. The Lebanese, however, disagreed with the USA over calls for Syria to withdraw its troops from Lebanon.

In October and November 2003 the US Congress approved the Syria Accountability Act and the associated Lebanese Sovereignty Restoration Act by a large majority. In the build-up to the US-led military campaign in Iraq, the Bush Administration had blocked the legislation, but later, frustrated by Syria's continuing support for Palestinian and Lebanese militant groups opposed to Israel, President Bush signed the bills into law in December. The new legislation allowed the US President to impose sanctions against Syria if it did not cease assisting militant groups such as Hamas, Islamic Jihad and Hezbollah, prevent extremists from crossing its border to attack US-led forces in Iraq, abandon its alleged weapons of mass destruction programmes and withdraw its forces from Lebanon. It classified Syrian forces as an occupation army exerting undue influence on the Lebanese Government and undermining its independence, and stated that the USA should only provide humanitarian and educational assistance to the people of Lebanon, through appropriate private non-governmental organizations and international organizations, until the Government of Lebanon asserted sovereignty and control over all its territory and achieved full independence. The legislation was strongly condemned by the Lebanese leadership. President Lahoud stated that the laws demonstrated a 'disgraceful bias' towards Israel, while Prime Minister Hariri declared that the USA and Israel wanted to punish Syria and Lebanon for their stance on the Palestinian cause. Although the Syrian military presence remained a divisive issue in Lebanon, only Gen. Aoun publicly expressed support for the legislation. In September, in a statement to a US Congressional panel studying the bills, Aoun had declared that Syria had played the role of both 'arsonist and firefighter' in Lebanon since 1976 and that any Lebanese who dared to expose or resist Syria's hegemony was simply eliminated.

President Bush did not immediately impose any sanctions on Syria (the two countries had limited trade relations) and appointed a new US ambassador to Damascus. Nevertheless, in March 2004 Colin Powell again urged Syria to withdraw its troops from Lebanon and give Beirut 'full sovereignty'. A US Department of State spokesman reportedly stated that the old arguments for Syria's presence in Lebanon were now obsolete, while the US National Security Advisor, Condoleezza Rice, demanded that Lebanon's forthcoming presidential election take place without meddling from abroad, a clear reference to Syria. In an interview, Syria's Minister of Foreign Affairs insisted that Syria had no control over Lebanese politics and that those seeking to press this idea were trying to create a rift between the two countries. President Lahoud declared that Syrian troops were a stabilizing factor for Lebanon and the region, while Druze leader Walid Joumblatt stated that the Syrian presence was important amid regional disputes and accused the Bush Administration of interfering in Lebanese affairs. Gen. Aoun, however, declared that US pressure on Syria to withdraw from Lebanon proved that the Lebanese issue was once again back on the international agenda, reiterating that the Syrian presence in Lebanon was illegal and that the country should be liberated. Some sources suggested that US attempts to put pressure on Syria might make it more difficult for the Syrian leadership to support a new mandate for President Lahoud because of his unquestioned loyalty to Damascus. In May the USA imposed economic sanctions against Syria, ostensibly for its support for armed opposition to the US-led coalition forces in Iraq. US officials specifically called on Syria to withdraw its troops from Lebanon. The main impact of the sanctions, which excluded US exports of food and medicine, was expected to be political rather than economic.

In April 2004 some 2,000 Palestinians from the Ain el-Hilweh refugee camp near Sidon protested at US 'massacres' in Fallujah and Najaf in Iraq, and demanded the killing of US troops. Lebanon's senior Shi'a religious leader, Sheikh Muhammad Hussain Fadlallah, compared 'the brutal American massacres against the Iraqi people' with Israeli attacks on Palestinians in the West Bank and Gaza; Hezbollah stated that it was the right and duty of Iraqis to fight the US-led occupation of Iraq, but was careful not to express support for radical Shi'a cleric Muqtada al-Sadr, whose militia had begun launching attacks against US forces in Iraq. In an interview with a local newspaper, Hezbollah's Deputy Secretary-General denied that the organization had an Iraqi branch and played down al-Sadr's recent declaration that he was the 'striking hand' of Hezbollah and Hamas in Iraq. US intelligence sources had claimed that Hezbollah, with Iranian support, was providing assistance to al-Sadr's militia, and sections of the Israeli press reported that Hezbollah and Hamas had opened offices in Iraq and were infiltrating their supporters and recruiting Iraqis.

At the end of April 2004 Nayla Mouawad, widow of René Mouawad, who was assassinated in 1989 shortly after assuming the presidency, announced that she would run for President in November 2004—the first time that a Lebanese woman had been a presidential candidate. Mouawad, a member of the Lebanese parliament, stated that although she was not against Syria, she would campaign against Syrian control of political life in Lebanon and wanted to mobilize public opinion to show Syria that the Lebanese people wanted a President 'made in Lebanon'. Later, Boutros Harb, a leading member of the main Christian opposition group, the Qornet Shehwan Gathering, and Robert Ghanem, a pro-Syrian deputy representing the Beqa'a valley and a former minister, also announced that they would stand as candidates.

At the end of May 2004 rioting broke out in the mainly Shi'a southern suburbs of Beirut during a strike called by the Confédération Générale des Travailleurs du Liban to protest against the Government's economic policies and specifically to demand lower petrol prices. A small demonstration quickly grew in size, to involve some 2,000 people. Soldiers from the Lebanese army fired on protesters, who threw stones and blocked roads with burning tyres, killing five and wounding more than 30; dozens more were arrested. Rioters also set fire to a Ministry of Labour building in the southern suburbs. It was the worst civil unrest in the country for more than a decade. There were further protests the following day involving hundreds of demonstrators, but the soldiers kept their distance. In the months previous to this Lebanon had experienced a series of mainly peaceful strikes, amid growing popular discontent with the Government's management of the economy. President Lahoud called for calm and, while acknowledging that there were serious economic difficulties, stated that rioting was unacceptable and merely aggravated the difficulties. Hezbollah, the dominant political force in the southern suburbs, condemned the shootings, and its leaders were reported to be consulting with the authorities and other parties about the unrest. The local press reported that Syrian officials had met with various Lebanese groups to try to prevent further clashes.

LAHOUD'S TERM OF OFFICE EXTENDED FOR THREE YEARS

In August 2004 President Lahoud formally announced that he wished to remain in office for a second term, and on 28 August the Cabinet endorsed a draft amendment to the Constitution extending his term of office for a further three years, to November 2007. Premier Hariri was reported to have been summoned to Damascus and told by President Assad that re-electing Lahoud was a priority and that regional circumstances, in particular US pressure on Syria, the turmoil in Iraq and the Arab–Israeli conflict, dictated it. Syria's supporters stated that Damascus had compromised by accepting a three-year extension rather than a full second term of six years. Three ministers voted against the decision, to which there was widespread opposition within the country and abroad. Many Muslim politicians and religious leaders had joined their Christian counterparts in voicing opposition to the proposed amendment. Hezbollah's parliamentary bloc, Loyalty to the Resistance, however, supported the amendment, stating that Lahoud had played a fundamental role in supporting resistance to Israel.

In September 2004, the day before the National Assembly voted on the amendment, the UN Security Council approved a resolution (No. 1559) introduced by the USA and France and co-sponsored by Germany and the United Kingdom, aimed at putting pressure on Lebanon to reject the extension to Lahoud's term of office. The resolution called for the immediate withdrawal of Syrian forces from Lebanon, strict respect for Lebanon's sovereignty, territorial integrity, unity and political independence, and support for free and fair elections without foreign interference. Both Syria and Lebanon rejected the resolution as interference in Lebanon's internal affairs.

When the National Assembly voted on the amendment, Lahoud's supporters nevertheless secured more than two-thirds of the requisite votes, with 96 out of the 125 deputies present voting in favour and only 29 against. Four cabinet ministers (three of whom were members of Walid Joumblatt's PSP) resigned in protest at the extension of Lahoud's term of office. Presidential candidates Boutros Harb and Nayla Mouawad both condemned and rejected the amendment, which was also opposed by the Qornet Shehwan Gathering, the mainly Maronite group opposed to Syria's dominant role in Lebanon. The US Department of State accused Syria of threatening members of the National Assembly in order to secure a vote in favour of the amendment. Following the vote, Lahoud adopted a conciliatory stance offering to work with his opponents to put the past behind them.

In October 2004 UN Secretary-General Kofi Annan reported to the Security Council that Syria had not withdrawn its forces from Lebanon as required under Resolution 1559 and stated that he had requested a timetable from Damascus for its full implementation. He told the Security Council that the request to disband and disarm all Lebanese and non-Lebanese militias, also included in Resolution 1559, had not been carried out, and he had asked for a similar timetable. The USA and France continued to urge Syria to withdraw its remaining forces from Lebanon.

HARIRI RESIGNS; KARAMI APPOINTED PREMIER

In October 2004 Hariri resigned from the premiership, dissolved his Cabinet, and announced that he would not be a candidate to form a new government. He gave no official reason for his resignation, but it was widely believed to be the result of differences with Lahoud over Syria's influence in Lebanese politics. Some 28 parliamentary deputies declared that they would not take part in talks with Lahoud on forming a new government. After consultations with deputies, Lahoud chose pro-Syrian, veteran politician Omar Karami as premier, who pledged not to be swayed by US and domestic criticism that he was too close to Damascus. Karami formed a new Cabinet entirely composed of pro-Syrian politicians; he stated that he had called for a government of national unity and had invited all factions to take part, but several had declined in protest at Syrian influence. Among the senior appointments were Sulayman Franjiya, as Minister of the Interior and Municipalities, Mahmoud Hammoud, outgoing Minister of Defence, as Minister of Foreign Affairs and Emigrants, and multimillionaire businessman and close ally of Lahoud, Issam Fares, who retained the post of Deputy Prime Minister. For the first time since independence, two women were included in the new Cabinet: Leila Solh as Minister of Industry and Oil, and Wafaa Hamza as Minister of State.

In December 2004 opposition groups from different religions and political affiliations announced their first united platform since the civil war, demanding that Syria stay out of Lebanese legislative elections scheduled for May 2005 and redeploy its troops near the border. They called for the resignation of Karami's pro-Syrian Government and the appointment of a neutral cabinet to oversee elections under a new, modern and democratic electoral law that would ensure fairness. Demands were also made for: the release of Samir Geagea; the return from exile of Gen. Aoun; and a ban on Syrian security agencies and their Lebanese auxiliaries from interfering in Lebanon's political life, particularly in the election process.

Mahmud Abbas, the new PLO Chairman, and Ahmad Quray, the PA Prime Minister, visited Beirut in December 2004, whereupon they held separate talks with Lahoud, Karami and Berri—it was the first visit by senior PLO officials since 1982. They also visited the Rashidiyah refugee camp in southern Lebanon and promised not to forget the Palestinian refugees or their right to return to their former homes. After the talks Abbas stated that Lebanese-Palestinian relations had 'turned a positive page' and that the Lebanese authorities had promised to ease the situation in the Palestinian refugee camps.

ASSASSINATION OF HARIRI

On 14 February 2005 former Prime Minister Rafiq Hariri was killed in a huge bomb explosion in central Beirut. Seven of his bodyguards who were travelling with him in a convoy of vehicles were among 14 others killed, while some 135 people were injured in the powerful blast. It was the single most violent incident since the end of the civil war and plunged the country into a serious political crisis. The Lebanese army was immediately placed on a state of alert, while the Lebanese press voiced fears about the destabilization of the country and a new international intervention. An unknown Islamist group, the Group for Victory and Jihad in Greater Syria, claimed to have carried out the assassination because of Hariri's close association with the Saudi Arabian regime. However, the Lebanese opposition promptly issued a communiqué accusing the Lebanese authorities and their Syrian masters of responsibility and called for an international commission of inquiry. Demonstrations took place across the country accusing Syria of responsibility, and in Hariri's home town of Sidon demonstrators attacked Syrian workers. The USA stopped short of directly accusing Syria, but withdrew its ambassador from Damascus and reiterated its demand for the withdrawal of Syrian troops from Lebanon, insisting that they were a factor in the country's destabilization. Syria strongly denied any involvement and President Assad denounced 'this terrible, criminal act'. The Syrian Vice-President, who visited Hariri's family to offer his condolences, blamed Israel. Following his resignation from the premiership, Hariri had joined the opposition in demanding the withdrawal of Syrian forces from Lebanon. Tensions had continued to mount between the opposition and the Government, and in October 2004 former Minister of Economy and Trade Marwan Hamadeh (one of the four ministers who had recently resigned in protest at the extension of Lahoud's term of office) had been seriously wounded, and his driver killed, in a car bombing. The Hariri family insisted that they did not want a state funeral but a ceremony for the people, stating that members of the Lebanese Government should not attend. Several hundred thousand people attended Hariri's funeral on 16 February 2005, including former opponents, and thousands of mourners chanted anti-Syrian slogans.

SYRIA WITHDRAWS ITS TROOPS FROM LEBANON

At the end of February 2005, after some 25,000 people demonstrated outside the National Assembly against Syria's role in Lebanon, Karami suddenly resigned as Prime Minister, along with the entire Cabinet, asserting that he was doing so in the interest of the country. Demonstrations continued in Beirut by protesters who voiced demands for the withdrawal from Lebanon of all Syrian troops and numerous intelligence agents, and for free elections. In Karami's home town of Tripoli, however, demonstrators took to the streets in support of the former Prime Minister, and there were violent clashes with opponents. In early March President Assad announced in the Syrian People's Assembly that Syrian troops would withdraw first to the Beqa'a valley and then to the Syrian border, but gave no timetable. President Lahoud then held talks with the Syrian President in Damascus where it was agreed that Syrian troops were to be pulled back to the Beqa'a valley and border region by the end of March and that discussions would follow about a timetable for their withdrawal to Syria. The following day, 8 March, an estimated 500,000 people, mainly Shi'a, from the southern suburbs, took part in a peaceful pro-Syrian demonstration in Beirut organized by Hezbollah. Shortly afterwards President Lahoud, following consultations with parliamentary blocs, reappointed Karami to the premiership and asked him to form a new government. Karami urged the opposition to join him in a government of national unity, but his reappointment was strongly criticized by opposition leaders, who reiterated calls for a neutral and impartial transitional government.

On 12 March 2005 President Assad held talks with UN Special Co-ordinator for the Middle East peace process Terje Rød-Larsen and promised to withdraw all 14,000 Syrian troops and an estimated 3,000–4,000 intelligence agents from Lebanon to conform with the terms of Resolution 1559. The first phase of the withdrawal to the Beqa'a valley was to be completed by the end of March; however, no date was given for the second phase, which involved the complete withdrawal of Syrian troops from Lebanon. Rød-Larsen also met President Lahoud, who stressed the need for scheduled parliamentary elections to proceed peacefully, and Nabih Berri and opposition figures. Another large pro-Syrian demonstration to protest against Resolution 1559, involving 200,000–300,000 people, took place in Nabatiyah, southern Lebanon, on 13 March; it was organized by Hezbollah and Amal, factions of the various Islamist movements, and pro-Syrian secular parties. The following day hundreds of thousands of anti-Syrian protesters converged on Martyrs Square in Beirut as the opposition sought to regain the initiative.

Meanwhile, Lebanese army sources stated that some 4,000 Syrian troops had already returned home. By mid-March 2005 Syrian troops had withdrawn from positions in northern and central Lebanon and those remaining in the country had been redeployed in the Beqa'a valley. On 16 March Syrian intelligence agents abandoned their head office in Beirut, the last remnant of Syria's military presence in the capital, and shut down their offices in Halba, Qoubaiyat and Tripoli. In late March a further 2,000 Syrian troops were reported to have left the eastern Beqa'a valley for Syria, reducing Syria's military presence in Lebanon to 8,000, its lowest level for three decades. At the beginning of April, after another meeting with President Assad in Damascus, Rød-Larsen stated that Syria had agreed to withdraw all its troops and intelligence officers from Lebanon by 30 April. The Syrian Minister of Foreign Affairs added that the close ties between Syria and Lebanon could not be annulled by the withdrawal of Syrian troops or 'by incitement for the purpose of breaking Syrian–Lebanese relations'. Syria completed final troop withdrawals by 26 April. In late May a UN team verified the full withdrawal of Syrian troops, but could not confirm that all Syrian intelligence officers had left the country.

During the second half of March 2005 three bombs exploded, two in Christian neighbourhoods in Beirut and another in the mainly Christian port of Jounieh, north of the capital, in which three people were killed. There was a fourth explosion on 1 April in a commercial centre in the mountain resort of Brumana near Beirut, an opposition stronghold, in which several people were injured and there was heavy material damage. After the first car bomb President Lahoud cancelled plans to attend the Arab League summit in Algiers, Algeria, pledged to fight the violence, and called for dialogue between opposition and pro-Syrian parties. Many opposition politicians held the pro-Syrian Lebanese security services responsible for the attacks, accusing them of seeking to revive sectarian conflict, and there was speculation that the attacks were aimed at creating instability in order to justify the continued Syrian military presence. Phalangist Party leader, Karim Pakradouni, however, claimed that the attacks aimed to justify the deployment of international troops in Lebanon and pointed the finger at those external forces who supported UN Resolution 1559.

A UN report on the assassination of Hariri released in late March 2005 did not make specific accusations, but concluded that Syria had created a climate of tension in which the assassination occurred. It criticized the Lebanese authorities for gross negligence and probably criminal actions during the investigation. The UN investigating team had received testimony that President Assad had threatened Hariri and Walid Joumblatt with physical harm. Kofi Annan supported its recommendation for an independent commission with wide-reaching powers to establish the truth. Syria denied that its influence had created tension and blamed UN Resolution 1559 for 'polarising the Lebanese people'. After initially dismissing the UN report, the Lebanese Government agreed to accept a UN commission of inquiry into Hariri's murder.

NAJIB MIQATI FORMS NEW GOVERNMENT

At the end of March 2005 Prime Minister-designate Karami announced that he would step down, having failed to persuade the opposition to join a government of national unity. Pro-Syrian politicians, however, asked him to stay on and he agreed to continue to try to form an administration. The opposition accused Karami of adopting delaying tactics to prevent parliamentary elections, scheduled for May, from taking place. By mid-April all Karami's efforts to form a new government had reached an impasse and he resigned. After consultations, President Lahoud named a moderate pro-Syrian millionaire businessman and deputy, Najib Miqati, as Prime Minister, a choice supported by opposition deputies and some ardent supporters of Syria. Miqati thanked the opposition for its support and declared that he would be a 'symbol of moderation and national unity'. Four days later he announced the appointment of a small Cabinet of only 14 members and declared that, as a demonstration of the new administration's neutrality, none of them would stand in the forthcoming legislative elections. Hassan al-Sabaa, a retired General Security officer, was named as Minister of the Interior, Khalid Qabbani, Minister of Justice, Mahmoud Hammoud remained Minister of Foreign Affairs and Emigrants, and Elias Murr, Lahoud's son-in-law, became Deputy Prime Minister and Minister of Defence. Miqati stated that his new 'unity Government' had three priorities: to hold parliamentary elections by 29 May; to follow up on the international investigation into Hariri's assassination; and to revive the flagging economy. The new Government, which won a vote of confidence in the National Assembly at the end of April, swiftly appointed a new Prosecutor-General and replaced three senior security chiefs who had 'stepped down', including the police commander and the head of military intelligence. In May Gen. Aoun, leader of the Free Patriotic Movement (FPM), was allowed to return to Lebanon after years in exile in France. Addressing tens of thousands of his supporters who gathered in Martyrs Square in Beirut to welcome him, Gen. Aoun pleaded for a secular Lebanon. The day before, two people had been killed in another explosion in Jounieh.

2005 LEGISLATIVE ELECTIONS

Elections for a new National Assembly began as scheduled on 29 May 2005; they were to be conducted in four stages, according to the existing electoral law introduced in 2000. Many Christians argued that this system favoured Syria's allies, but demands for a new electoral law dividing the country into smaller constituencies had been rejected by the Government. In the first round of voting in the Beirut region, the anti-Syrian opposition Future Movement, led by Rafiq Hariri's son, Saad, who had succeeded his father as leader of Lebanon's Sunni Muslim community, allied with Druze leader Walid Joumblatt's PSP and some right-wing Christian groups, won a sweeping victory, taking all 19 seats, nine of which were uncontested, as rival candidates had withdrawn before the election. Official figures put voter turn-out at 28%, slightly lower than in 2000; turn-out was lower in Christian than Muslim districts. Four days later a car bomb exploded in a Christian district of Beirut, killing Dr Samir Kassir, a prominent journalist and vocal critic of Syria's role in Lebanon. The opposition blamed remnants of Syria's intelligence services for the murder and reiterated calls for the immediate resignation of President Lahoud. The second round of voting took place on 5 June in southern Lebanon, where an alliance of pro-Syrian Amal and Hezbollah secured all 23 seats in this mainly Shi'a-populated region by a wide margin; six seats were uncontested. Voter turn-out was estimated at 45%, but only 10%–12% in some Christian areas; prominent local politicians and Gen. Aoun's FPM had called on Christians to boycott the election.

Unofficial estimates of turn-out in the third round of voting on 12 June 2005 were 54% in Mount Lebanon and 49% in the Beqa'a valley. In the run-up to voting, fierce competition had been reported between candidates from the numerous lists competing for 35 seats in Mount Lebanon and 23 seats in the Beqa'a; only two seats were uncontested. In an unexpected development, Gen. Aoun (who had made last-minute alliances with pro-Syrian factions declaring that his feud with Damascus was over now that Syrian troops had withdrawn from Lebanon) and his allies won 21 seats. Gen. Aoun's surprise victory was a setback for Hariri and his allies, who secured 25 seats but had hoped to gain more in order to command a majority in the new Assembly. In the final round in North Lebanon on 19 June, however, Hariri and his allies swept to victory, gaining all 28 seats and decisively defeating Gen. Aoun's allies; turn-out, according to official sources, was 49%. When the Minister of the Interior and Municipalities, Hassan al-Sabaa, announced the final results of the elections he confirmed that Hariri's Future Movement had obtained 72 seats in the new Assembly, a clear majority; Amal and Hezbollah 35 seats; and Gen. Aoun and his allies 21 seats. Al-Sabaa insisted that, although there had been some minor complaints, polling had taken place in a calm atmosphere and voters had been free from any pressure or interference. International observers expressed general satisfaction with the voting process. Miqati and his Cabinet resigned after the elections, but continued in a caretaker capacity.

Two days after the final round of voting, a car bomb exploded in Beirut, killing George Hawi, former Secretary-General of the Parti Communiste Libanais. The anti-Syrian alliance again blamed Syrian agents and their allies in the Lebanese security services for the murder of another politician who had spoken out against Syria's role in Lebanon. The US State Department asserted that there was no doubt that agents of the Syrian security services remained in Lebanon and exercised a negative influence.

FOUAD SINIORA FORMS NEW GOVERNMENT

At the end of June 2005 the new National Assembly re-elected Nabih Berri, a loyal ally of Syria, as President of the Assembly by a comfortable majority. Two days later President Lahoud, after consultations, appointed Fouad Siniora, a member of

Saad Hariri's Future Movement, as Prime Minister and asked him to form a new government. Siniora, a close ally of the late Rafiq Hariri and Minister of Finance in all five of his administrations, won the support of 126 of the 128 members of the National Assembly.

Efforts to form a government of national unity, however, failed after disagreements over the portfolios to be allocated to Gen. Aoun's group. Eventually, after three weeks of political wrangling, Siniora announced a new, 24-member Cabinet including parliamentarians and technocrats. Only Gen. Aoun's group was not represented. Aoun had stated that he would not take part in the government and would lead the main opposition in the Assembly. Of the eight ministers close to Syria, three were allies of President Lahoud: Elias Murr, his son-in-law, who retained the defence portfolio; Charles Rizq, appointed to the sensitive post of Minister of Justice; and Ya'coub al-Sarraf, who became Minister of the Environment. The five Shi'a ministers, appointed with the agreement of Amal and Hezbollah, included Fawzi Salloukh, a career diplomat, to the key post of Minister of Foreign Affairs and Emigrants, Tarrad Hamadeh, who retained the Ministry of Labour, and Muhammad Fneish of Hezbollah, who was appointed Minister of Energy and Water. This was the first time that a member of Hezbollah had participated in the Government. The US State Department immediately declared that it would have no dealings with Fneish, but insisted that his appointment would not prevent the US Administration from conducting relations with the new administration as a whole. Among the 16 new ministers, several had no previous experience in government; they included two key appointments: Jihad Azour as Minister of Finance, and Sami Haddad as Minister of Economy and Trade, both of whom had worked for international organizations.

Only days before the new Government was announced, Minister of Defence Murr was slightly wounded and two others were killed in a powerful explosion in a Beirut suburb. Shortly after the formation of the new Government, a large car bomb exploded in a busy street in a Christian neighbourhood of Beirut, wounding 12 people. The explosion occurred only hours after the US Secretary of State, Condoleezza Rice, had visited the area. During her unscheduled visit to Beirut to express US support for the new Government, Rice warned Syria to end its interference in Lebanese politics. Earlier, the National Assembly pardoned former LF warlord, Samir Geagea, who was serving a life sentence for murder. He subsequently announced his intention to re-enter politics. Although officially banned, the LF achieved parliamentary representation for the first time as part of Hariri's anti-Syrian alliance.

UN COMMISSION OF INQUIRY INTO HARIRI'S ASSASSINATION

In April 2005 the UN Security Council approved Resolution 1595, establishing the UN International Independent Investigation Commission (UNIIIC) to investigate the assassination of Rafiq Hariri. UNIIIC began its work in June, headed by a highly experienced German judge, Detlev Mehlis, assisted by a team of 30 investigators. In August, acting on the recommendation of Mehlis, the Lebanese police arrested four of Lebanon's most senior intelligence and security chiefs, including the head of the Presidential Guard and one of Lahoud's closest advisers, who were charged with participation in the planning of Hariri's murder. Shortly before the report was published, the Syrian Minister of the Interior, Ghazi Kenaan, who had been the powerful head of Syrian military intelligence in Lebanon during 1982–2002, was found dead in his office in Damascus (see the chapter on Syria). According to official Syrian sources, Kenaan had committed suicide. However, as Kenaan had been one of several high-ranking Syrian officials interviewed by Mehlis in September 2005, rumours circulated that he may have been assassinated.

UNIIIC presented its preliminary report to the Security Council in October 2005. Mehlis's report stated that there was 'converging evidence' that high-ranking members of the Syrian and Lebanese security and intelligence services were involved in the assassination, and accused Syria of failing to co-operate with the inquiry and providing misleading information. Mehlis praised the Lebanese authorities for their assistance and co-operation in the investigation, which had taken statements from over 400 witnesses and suspects, consulted 60,000 documents, used forensic evidence and had access to intercepted telephone conversations immediately before and after the assassination. He also disclosed that there had been a number of 'credible' threats against him and his team of international investigators. An earlier draft version of the report released to the press included the names of members of President Assad's inner circle, among them his brother and brother-in-law, who, according to a witness statement, had attended meetings at the presidential palace in Damascus to discuss the planning of the assassination. Officially, however, the draft had been released in error and the names did not appear in the final version of the report. Mehlis strongly denied that the names were removed because of 'outside pressure'.

The Lebanese Cabinet stated that it considered the report to be an important step towards reaching the complete truth, and expressed its gratitude to the UN for agreeing to extend UNIIIC's mandate to 15 December 2005. President Lahoud also welcomed the report, and his advisers were keen to emphasize that it contained no accusations against the President, who would continue in his post. Amal and Hezbollah issued a joint statement criticizing the report. This stated that uncovering the truth would require further investigation based on tangible evidence and facts and away from political exploitation. It opposed any demands for sanctions to be imposed on Syria. The Syrian authorities immediately denounced the report as a biased political document whose objective was to put pressure on Syria in the interests of the USA, and accused investigators of ignoring testimony given by Syrian officials or distorting their content.

In response to the report, in October 2005 the UN Security Council unanimously adopted a resolution (No. 1636) demanding full co-operation from Syria without reservations or conditions in the next phase of the investigation, insisting that Damascus detain and make available for questioning any Syrian officials named as suspects by the inquiry. It also authorized the imposition of a travel ban and the freezing of assets of any suspects, including Syrian officials, identified by either the Lebanese Government or UNIIIC. In November President Assad stated that Syria would co-operate with UNIIIC, but implied that it was a plot to weaken his country. Assad accused Lebanon of serving as a platform against Syria and moving towards an accord with Israel. He also made a vitriolic attack on Prime Minister Siniora, describing him as 'a slave who takes order from a slave', a reference to Siniora's close relations with Saad Hariri. It was not until December and after extensive negotiations that Syria finally agreed to allow UN investigators to interview in Vienna, Austria, five senior Syrian intelligence officers as suspects in the case.

In his final report submitted to the UN Secretary-General in mid-December 2005, Mehlis reaffirmed his earlier conclusions that senior members of the Syrian and Lebanese security and intelligence services were implicated in Hariri's assassination, and accused Damascus of having been slow to co-operate with the inquiry. The report cited evidence that Syria had destroyed important documents relating to its intelligence operations in Lebanon and had threatened a key witness, and that a senior Syrian official had supplied arms and ammunition to individuals in Lebanon to stage attacks in order to create public disorder. Mehlis demanded full and unconditional co-operation from Syria in the future.

The day before Mehlis presented his report, Gebran Tueni, managing editor of the *An-Nahar* newspaper and a member of the National Assembly, was killed by a roadside bomb, in the latest in a series of attacks on prominent Lebanese figures, most of them known for their opposition to Syria. Tens of thousands of Lebanese converged on Martyrs Square in Beirut on the day of Tueni's funeral, turning the occasion into an anti-Syrian protest and demanding the removal of President Lahoud. The President was denounced as the head of the 'Syrian-Lebanese security system' that continued to maintain its grip on Lebanon despite the withdrawal of Syrian troops. The Lebanese Government, which had already asked the UN to extend UNIIIC's mandate by a further six months, now called for its mandate to be extended to include subsequent political killings and for the creation of an international court to try those responsible for Hariri's murder. In response, five ministers representing Amal and Hezbollah suspended their participation in the Government, stating that they had reservations about the creation of an international tribunal and were opposed to the broadening of the UN investigation to include other murders. Hezbollah's Secretary-General later stated that Israel had good reason to kill anti-Syrian figures in order to weaken the 'resistance' in Lebanon and create discord between Lebanon and Syria. The five ministers only ended their boycott of cabinet meetings in February 2006, after receiving political reassurances from the Prime Minister.

In December 2005 the UN Security Council adopted a resolution (No. 1644) renewing and strengthening UNIIIC's mandate, and asked the Secretary-General to help Lebanon identify the assistance it needed to set up an international tribunal to try those accused of Hariri's murder. It expressed deep concern at the commission's assessment of Syria's co-operation, and demanded that Damascus respond unambiguously and immediately to the needs of the UN inquiry. Later that month Abd al-Halim Khaddam, a close confidant of the Assad family for some two decades who had relinquished his position as Syrian Vice-President in June and gone into exile, gave a series of interviews in which he praised Mehlis's investigation and confirmed the involvement of several members of the Syrian and Lebanese intelligence services in Hariri's assassination. Khaddam accused the circle around President Lahoud, the security agencies and certain Lebanese figures of plotting against Hariri and was especially critical of Rustom Ghazaleh, former head of Syrian military intelligence in Lebanon, insisting that he was part of the circle that turned Bashar al-Assad against Hariri. Mehlis interviewed Khaddam in Paris in January 2006.

On 14 February 2006 hundreds of thousands of Lebanese—1m., according to some estimates—from all parts of the country and from all communities, took part in a mass demonstration in Martyrs Square in the centre of Beirut to mark the anniversary of Rafiq Hariri's death. Despite death threats, Saad Hariri returned to Lebanon from six months' self-imposed exile to address the meeting. Shortly afterwards deputies of the anti-Syrian alliance led by Hariri, Joumblatt and Geagea signed a petition demanding Lahoud's resignation before 14 March, but this did not have the two-thirds' majority required, as neither Aoun's bloc nor Amal/Hezbollah would support Lahoud's removal. Indeed, at the beginning of February Aoun's FPM and Hezbollah had signed a co-operation agreement in which both parties made concessions—Aoun on the disarming of Hezbollah, and Hezbollah on the establishment of formal diplomatic relations between Lebanon and Syria. It appeared to confirm Aoun's break with the anti-Syrian majority, and some commentators argued that the agreement was linked to Aoun's own aspirations to contest the Lebanese presidency in the future.

At the end of February 2006 US Secretary of State Condoleezza Rice visited Beirut, amid heavy security. She met Cardinal Sfeir, Prime Minister Siniora, Nabih Berri, Hariri and Joumblatt, but not President Lahoud, and invited Syria to co-operate fully with UNIIIC. Earlier, Rice had stated that the Middle East was menaced by a network composed of Iran, Syria and Hezbollah with the objective of destabilizing the region; Lebanon was the country most at risk from this network.

Belgian judge Serge Brammertz, who had taken over from Mehlis as head of UNIIIC at the beginning of 2006, made his first visit to Damascus in February of that year, where he met the new Syrian Minister of Foreign Affairs, Walid Mouallem. Before he stepped down 'for family reasons', Mehlis had asked to interview President Assad, after allegations were made that he had threatened Hariri in the months leading up to the assassination, but Syria had refused to agree to the direct questioning of the President by UN investigators and the inquiry had reached an impasse. In a report to the UN Security Council in March, Brammertz stated that he had concluded a joint agreement with Syria on the form that co-operation with Damascus would take and that both President Assad and Farouk al-Shara', the former Minister of Foreign Affairs, now Vice-President, had agreed to meet investigators in April. Later in March the UN Secretary-General, in his report to the Security Council, recommended the establishment of a tribunal composed of Lebanese and international judges sitting outside Lebanon to try those charged with the assassination of Rafiq Hariri. The Security Council unanimously adopted a resolution giving the Secretary-General powers to conclude an agreement with the Lebanese Government for the establishment of this international tribunal. At the end of April Judge Brammertz held meetings in Damascus with President Assad and Vice-President al-Shara'. Assad continued to deny Syrian involvement in Hariri's murder. He insisted that if Syrian officials were implicated in the assassination they must be tried in Syria and handing them over to an international tribunal would depend on 'the procedure chosen by the UN'.

Meanwhile, after numerous meetings held by leaders of the main Lebanese political groupings to attempt to resolve their differences within a framework of national dialogue, it was announced that agreement had been reached on three issues: opposition to all armed Palestinian presences outside the refugee camps; the need to establish friendly relations with Syria based on confidence and mutual respect with diplomatic relations at ambassadorial level; and recognition that Shebaa Farms was part of Lebanon. Two thorny questions remained: regarding the removal of Lahoud and the disarming of Hezbollah. In March 2006 Terje Rød-Larsen, now the UN Special Envoy responsible for the implementation of UN Security Council Resolution 1559, praised the Lebanese Government for launching the 'historic' national dialogue and told reporters that he was satisfied with the first results of the discussions, notably the agreement of all the participants on delimiting the frontier with Syria and establishing formal diplomatic relations with Damascus. He called on Syria to respond positively and furthermore to take urgent action to prevent the movement of weapons across the border into Lebanon. He made an urgent appeal for the dismantling and disarming of all Lebanese and foreign militias and called on all parties in a position to influence Hezbollah and other militias to support the full application of Resolution 1559. In April, during a visit to the USA, Siniora stated that a timetable had been set to disarm Palestinians (mainly the PFLP—GC) outside the refugee camps within six months. With reference to the refugee camps, he insisted that they were on Lebanese soil and that every part of Lebanon should be under the authority of the Lebanese state. For the first time in 15 years, Lebanese officials had entered the camps and held discussions on all relevant matters. In May Abbas Zaki, the first PLO envoy to Lebanon in 13 years, officially opened the PLO's office in Beirut.

After a further meeting of Lebanese political leaders at the beginning of April 2006 it was announced that further discussions would be held at the end of the month, a decision that suggested that the talks had reached an impasse, notably on the resignation or dismissal of Lahoud, who continued to express his determination to complete his mandate. Before the Arab League summit in Khartoum, Sudan, in March 2006 some 71 deputies from the parliamentary majority had sent an open letter to Arab leaders asking them not to have any contact with Lahoud because he 'lacked legitimacy'.

In May 2006 the UN Security Council adopted Resolution 1680, which encouraged Syria to respond positively to Lebanon's request to delimit their common frontier, in particular those zones where there was uncertainty or dispute, and establish full diplomatic relations. The resolution stated that such measures would constitute a significant step towards affirming the sovereignty, territorial integrity and political independence of Lebanon, improve relations between the two countries and contribute positively to the stability of the region. It called on all states and parties concerned—a reference to Iran and Hezbollah—to co-operate fully with the Lebanese Government and the Security Council to carry out all the recommendations of the earlier resolution (No. 1559) of September 2004. It also praised the Lebanese Government for taking measures to prevent the entry of weapons into Lebanese territory and called on Damascus to take similar measures. Resolution 1680 was proposed by France, the USA and the United Kingdom; the People's Republic of China and Russia abstained in the vote. Syria immediately denounced the resolution (as did Hezbollah) as an intolerable interference in its internal affairs and in the bilateral relations between states.

Meanwhile, some 300 Lebanese and Syrian intellectuals signed the Beirut-Damascus Declaration, distributed in the Lebanese capital on 11 May 2006. It called for respect for the sovereignty and independence of Lebanon and Syria in the context of transparent and formalized relations, and insisted that Syria unequivocally recognize the independence of Lebanon by delimiting frontiers and by the exchange of ambassadors. In the following week the Syrian authorities arrested 12 human rights activists, opponents of the Assad regime, who had signed the declaration.

At the end of May 2006 the Lebanese National Assembly rejected by a large majority warrants issued by a Syrian military court at the beginning of the month against Walid Joumblatt, Marwan Hamadeh, the Minister of Telecommunications, and Fares Khachan, a journalist, for remarks hostile to the Syrian regime, insisting that they were an insult to the dignity of parliament and the Lebanese people. Deputies belonging to Amal and Hezbollah abstained, but those belonging to Gen. Aoun's bloc voted in favour of the motion. Hamadeh stated that the vote revealed a new solidity between all activists of 14 March 2005 (the anti-Syrian alliance) and was significant for the next round of national dialogue talks.

In his second report, submitted to the UN Secretary-General in June 2006, Brammertz stated that the investigation was so complex that a one-year extension to UNIIIC's mandate was essential. The Security Council unanimously approved this request at a meeting later that month. The chief investigator reported that important progress had been made in understanding the circumstances of Hariri's assassination, the links between those who planned and executed the attack, and their motives. On the whole, co-operation from Syria with regard to demands for information and documents had been satisfactory, but the total and unconditional co-operation of the Syrian authorities remained crucial to the investigation. The report also suggested that a link was possible between the assassination of Hariri and 14 other attacks carried out in Lebanon against anti-Syrian personalities since October 2004, but only limited progress had been made on these dossiers as a result of insufficient technical support.

TENSIONS CONTINUE ALONG THE SOUTHERN BORDER

Meanwhile, Hezbollah continued sporadic attacks against Israeli targets along the southern border with Israel. Some sources argued that, while Hezbollah was keen to promote its active role in resistance to Israel, both Syria and Iran had placed strict limits on the group's military activities. In August 2002 an attack was launched against the Israeli army in the disputed Shebaa Farms area, prompting Israeli counter-attacks on Hezbollah positions in southern Lebanon, accompanied by the usual warnings to Lebanon and Syria to curb the activities of Hezbollah militants. Shebaa Farms was again targeted by Hezbollah artillery in January 2003; however, there were no Israeli casualties. The US-led coalition's military action in Iraq in March increased tensions along the southern border and provoked a number of demonstrations, some of them violent. In August a prominent member of Hezbollah, Ali Hussein Saleh, was killed when a car bomb exploded in Beirut. Both the Lebanese Government and Hezbollah blamed Israel, which denied any involvement. (Saleh was known to have taken part in operations against Israeli forces prior to their withdrawal in 2000.) In retaliation, Hezbollah bombarded the northern Israeli village of Tayr Harfa, killing a 16-year-old boy. Israel countered by sending aircraft deep into Lebanon, where they conducted low-level flights over Beirut. In October Lebanon condemned an Israeli attack on a training camp of the Palestinian group Islamic Jihad in Syria carried out in retaliation for a suicide bombing in Haifa—the first direct Israeli attack on Syria since the October 1973 war. The Lebanese military stated that eight Israeli warplanes had violated Lebanese airspace, but it was not clear whether it was these aircraft that carried out the attack in Syria. The Syria Accountability Act and the associated Lebanese Sovereignty Restoration Act, signed by President Bush in December 2003, reflected in part the US Administration's growing frustration with Syria's continuing support for Hezbollah. The legislation accused Syria of preventing Lebanon from deploying its troops in southern Lebanon and stated that it held Syria responsible for Hezbollah's attacks on Shebaa Farms and civilian targets in Israel. Furthermore, the legislation stated that the Lebanese Government should deploy its forces in the south, evict Hezbollah and enter into 'serious' negotiations with Israel.

In January 2004, under the terms of a deal mediated by Germany, Israel released 400 Palestinian prisoners, together with 23 Lebanese and 12 other Arab militants, in exchange for the release of the kidnapped Israeli businessman held by Hezbollah since 2000. The deal also included an exchange of bodies of soldiers and militants between the two sides, and Israel agreed to provide details of 24 Lebanese who disappeared during Israel's 1982 invasion and to hand over maps of landmines planted in southern Lebanon. A parliamentary delegation from Iran visited Beirut to take part in ceremonies to receive the Lebanese prisoners. The prisoner release was seen as a major propaganda coup for Hezbollah in the Arab world, bolstering its reputation, especially in the West Bank and Gaza where jubilant crowds, many waving Hezbollah flags, greeted the released Palestinians. Hezbollah's Secretary-General vowed to take more Israelis hostage and insisted that while there were detainees in prison, daily Israeli violations and a continuing Israeli threat to Lebanon, Hezbollah still had a role to play. The Israeli Prime Minister, Ariel Sharon, warned that his country would not allow any terrorist group to turn kidnapping and ransom into a system. Meanwhile, the UN Secretary-General reported an 'upsurge' in violence on the border during the previous six months, with regular violations of Lebanese airspace by Israeli planes, and anti-aircraft fire from Hezbollah positions into Israel. For some months Hezbollah had also been planting bombs close to the border, and at the end of January 2004 its fighters fired on an Israeli bulldozer that had entered Lebanese territory while clearing a bomb, killing an Israeli soldier.

In a television interview in February 2004, the Israeli Chief of Staff, Lt-Gen. Moshe Ya'alon, declared that a great deal of Palestinian 'terrorism' was currently originating in Lebanon and Syria. He also maintained that Hezbollah provided instruction and encouragement, and attempted to smuggle sophisticated Iranian-made weapons and experts into the Palestinian areas. In March a Hamas delegation held talks with Hezbollah's Secretary-General about the possible Israeli withdrawal from the Gaza Strip and insisted that resistance to occupation was a necessity and must persist. In retaliation for Israel's assassination of Sheikh Ahmad Yassin, the spiritual leader of Hamas, at the end of March, Hezbollah attacked Israeli troops in Shebaa Farms. Israel responded with artillery fire, and Israeli warplanes attacked suspected Hezbollah positions in the area. Sections of the Israeli press suggested that, following Yassin's assassination, Hamas would become more dependent on assistance from Hezbollah for operational activities and for funding, and warned of the possibility of a deeper alliance between Hamas, Hezbollah and Iran.

In a radio interview in April 2004, Israel's Chief of Staff stated that progress was being made in the second phase of the prisoner exchange with Hezbollah. It was hoped to obtain significant information about the fate of Ron Arad, an Israeli pilot shot down over Lebanon in 1986, in exchange for the release by Israel of several Lebanese detainees and dozens of Palestinians belonging to Hamas, Fatah and Islamic Jihad. Nevertheless, in May 2004 Israel attacked Hezbollah positions, claiming that militants had fired on Israeli planes. Shortly afterwards Hezbollah militants attacked an Israeli patrol in the Shebaa Farms area, killing one soldier and wounding seven others. In retaliation, Israeli planes attacked suspected Hezbollah positions, but no casualties were reported. Hezbollah claimed that the Israeli patrol had crossed the Blue Line into Lebanese territory, but Israel insisted that its troops were patrolling the border area inside Israel. Lebanon's Minister of Foreign Affairs and Emigrants held Israel responsible for the escalation of violence along the border.

In June 2004 Israel attacked a suspected position of the PFLP—GC in Naameh, near Beirut—the first raid near the Lebanese capital since May 2000—and claimed that it was in response to an attack by Palestinian militants against an Israeli vessel in Israel's territorial waters. No casualties were reported and the PFLP—GC insisted that Israel had targeted one of its centres for medical and social services. Israel's Deputy Minister of Defence, in an interview on state radio, declared that the attack was a clear warning to the Lebanese Government that it must prevent its territory from being used as a base for terrorist attacks against the Jewish state. In response, the Lebanese Government lodged a formal protest concerning the attack with the UN Secretary-General. Meanwhile, tensions mounted in the Shebaa Farms as Hezbollah militants and the Israeli army exchanged fire.

In October 2004 Israeli intelligence sources claimed that Hezbollah, backed by Iran, controlled numerous cells in the Palestinian territories that had carried out deadly attacks on Israelis. In an interview in November, Israeli premier Sharon claimed that some 80% of all terrorist activity in the northern West Bank was directed and financed by Hezbollah or the Iranians. He claimed that Hezbollah had close links with Fatah Tanzim cells in parts of the West Bank and Gaza and was encouraging, financing and providing operational expertise for their attacks. Israeli intelligence sources also claimed that Hezbollah had been actively recruiting 'terrorists' among Israel's Arab population for some years.

Hezbollah claimed in November 2004 to have successfully sent an unmanned drone over northern Israel for the first time, in response to Israel's repeated violation of Lebanese airspace. The IDF confirmed that a drone entered Israeli airspace and flew over the northern city of Nahariya, but that it crashed into the sea as it returned to Lebanon. The Israeli Chief of Staff stated that the drone, reported to be one of eight supplied by Iran, was capable of carrying an explosive device, and that Iranian military experts from the Revolutionary Guards had been directly involved in preparing and launching it. Hezbollah threatened further flights, and in response in December Israel installed *Patriot* missiles in the Haifa Bay area to intercept them. In April 2005 Hezbollah flew another unmanned drone over northern Israel. Meanwhile, after Yasser Arafat's death in November 2004, Israel claimed that Hezbollah had stepped up its involvement with Palestinian groups, and began intensive lobbying to persuade the EU to add Hezbollah to its list of terrorist organizations, but with little success.

In January 2005, after Hezbollah fighters attacked an Israeli military convoy in the Shebaa Farms area, killing an Israeli soldier, a new round of heavy artillery exchanges took place along the border, and Israeli helicopters and warplanes attacked Hezbollah positions in southern Lebanon. In April Hezbollah's deputy leader stated in an interview that his movement was ready for talks with other Lebanese groups on the future of its fighters, but only after the issue of the disputed Shebaa Farms had been settled. Later that month Lebanon's new Prime Minister, Najib Miqati, rejected international demands for the disarming of Hezbollah. Addressing the UN Security Council in May on the implementation of Resolution 1559, UN envoy Terje Rød-Larsen stated that dialogue between the UN and some relevant parties over disbanding and disarming all Lebanese and non-Lebanese militias was expected to intensify in the coming months. He declared that more must be done to ensure the return of effective governmental authority throughout the south of Lebanon, including the deployment of additional armed forces along the Blue Line.

New clashes occurred in the Shebaa Farms area in June 2005, in which an Israeli soldier was killed. In a report in July the UN Secretary-General stated that, with continued attacks along the Blue Line, the situation in southern Lebanon remained volatile. He recommended that UN peace-keepers, whose mandate was due to expire at the end of July, should remain in the area for another six months. In November, after several months of relative calm along the southern border, violent clashes again took place between Hezbollah fighters and Israeli forces in Shebaa Farms, with reports of a number of fatalities on both sides. UNIFIL called on both parties to exercise maximum restraint and asked Israel to cease all violations of Lebanese airspace. In December a number of rockets launched from southern Lebanon caused serious material damage in the northern Israeli town of Kiryat Shmona. In response, Israel attacked a Palestinian base south of Beirut. The Lebanese authorities condemned both the rocket attacks and the Israeli response and stated that they were investigating who was responsible for the attacks and would punish them. (Hezbollah had immediately denied responsibility for the attacks.) A few days later al-Qa'ida in Iraq claimed responsibility for rocket attacks on northern Israel from Lebanon. If the claim was true, it would represent the first time that the organization led by Abu Mussab al-Zarqawi (see the chapters on Iraq and Jordan) had involved itself in Lebanese affairs.

In February 2006 Hezbollah fighters attacked an Israeli position in the Shebaa Farms, wounding one Israeli soldier, after a young Lebanese shepherd was killed by Israeli artillery fire. In March UN envoy Terje Rød-Larsen stated that an eventual accord between Lebanon and Syria would not guarantee Israel's withdrawal from the Shebaa Farms. In a televised interview, the Lebanese Minister of Foreign Affairs and Emigrants, Fawzi Salloukh, challenged Rød-Larsen's statement that the Blue Line was the border between Lebanon and Israel, and insisted that Lebanon considered it as the 'line of withdrawal' rather than an internationally recognized border because Israel had not demarcated its borders. Hezbollah's deputy leader insisted that Lebanon's southern border included three points beyond the Blue Line in addition to the Shebaa Farms and stated that the UN should not interfere in this matter. Meanwhile, Lebanese sources reported repeated violations of Lebanese airspace by Israeli helicopters and warplanes between March and May.

Towards the end of May 2006 a senior member of the Palestinian group, Islamic Jihad, and his brother were killed by a car bomb in the southern city of Saida. The head of Islamic Jihad in Lebanon immediately accused Israel of carrying out the bombing and threatened reprisals. The Israeli army denied any involvement in the attack. Two days later, after a rocket attack from southern Lebanon on a military base in northern Israel in which an Israeli soldier was wounded, Israeli jets attacked two PFLP—GC bases in Lebanon, leaving one Palestinian dead and five wounded. The leader of Islamic Jihad in Lebanon denied that his group was responsible for the rocket attacks, but admitted that it was co-ordinating its operations against Israel with Hezbollah.

The Israeli Prime Minister, Ehud Olmert, warned Palestinians in Lebanon that Israel would use all means to respond to terrorists who attempted to attack the people of northern Israel, and called on Lebanon to implement UN Resolution 1559, impose its sovereignty over southern Lebanon and to deploy its own military units along the border with Israel. The Israeli army announced that it had placed its artillery and fighter planes on full alert along the northern border. Lebanese police sources stated that Israeli planes had also carried out air-strikes against targets in the hills of southern Lebanon, resulting in several injuries. Hezbollah claimed that one of its militants had been killed in these raids. Meanwhile, Israeli sources claimed that there were stockpiles of some 12,000 rockets in southern Lebanon, including very long-range rockets controlled by the Iranian Revolutionary Guards, and asserted that other weapons used by Hezbollah, such as the *Katyushas*, were only fired with Iranian permission and that their deployment was 'co-ordinated with the Iranians'.

In June 2006 the Lebanese army issued a statement that an investigation had identified a terrorist network—taking instructions from and equipped by the Israeli intelligence agency, Mossad—that was responsible for a number of assassinations (including the son of the PFLP—GC leader in 2002) and several explosions in Lebanon since 1999.

ISRAELI OFFENSIVE AGAINST LEBANON

On 12 July 2006 Hezbollah fighters crossed into Israel and, in a carefully planned operation, attacked an Israeli army border patrol, killing three soldiers and kidnapping two. A further five soldiers died in an attempt to rescue the kidnapped soldiers. Simultaneously, Hezbollah militants in southern Lebanon launched rockets across the border at the town of Shlomi and outposts in the Shebaa Farms. Israel immediately began an intensive and sustained offensive by land, sea and air against Hezbollah positions in southern Lebanon, targeting its communications and command headquarters in the southern suburbs of Beirut and its training camps and logistics centres in the Beqa'a valley. The Israeli air force, flying numerous missions, attacked and put out of action Beirut's international airport and bombed the main highway linking Beirut to Damascus; a blockade of Lebanon was imposed by land, sea and air. Numerous roads and bridges, especially in the south, were targeted, as well as telecommunications equipment and a major power station south of Beirut. The Israeli Chief of Staff, Lt-Gen. Dan Halutz, stated that Israeli Special Forces were operating inside Lebanon, and later declared that limited ground forces had entered Lebanon in order to destroy Hezbollah fortifications in the border region, where they met with fierce resistance and sustained casualties.

In July 2006 Israel called up thousands of reservists, but rejected any extension of the ground offensive and pledged to intensify its air-strikes to defeat Hezbollah. Lt-Gen. Halutz stated that enormous damage had been inflicted on Hezbollah's military capacity, but that the organization was still capable of firing rockets into Israel. Soon after the Israeli offensive began, Hezbollah launched rocket attacks against military positions and settlements in northern Israel, including Haifa, Israel's third largest city, located some 25 km from the border with Lebanon, and one of its missiles hit an Israeli gunboat off the Lebanese coast. At the end of July a new type of missile hit the town of Afoula, 15 km south of Haifa and over 50 km from the border, Hezbollah's deepest strike into Israeli territory. By the beginning of August Hezbollah had fired more than 3,000 rockets into Israel (compared with 10 over the previous six years).

Hezbollah Secretary-General Nasrallah declared that the attack on Afoula represented a new stage in the conflict, and threatened to launch missiles against cities in central Israel. He insisted that the party's command structure had not been damaged by Israeli air-strikes against the southern suburbs of Beirut, that its rocket capacity and warehouses in the south remained intact and that not a single rocket launcher had been destroyed. Hezbollah claimed to have repelled a number of incursions by Israeli ground forces, destroying a number of tanks and other heavy equipment. Hezbollah's television station, Al-Manar, was bombed, but continued broadcasting with virtually no interruptions from a safe site.

In a press conference on 12 July 2006, the Israeli Prime Minister stated that the kidnapping of his country's two soldiers was not a terrorist attack, but the action of a sovereign state that had attacked Israel for no reason and without provocation. He held Lebanon responsible and stated that it would bear the consequences of its actions. Israel had no intention of negotiating with Hezbollah, which Olmert insisted was 'an instrument of Iran', and rejected a request for a cease-fire by the Lebanese Government made through the UN. As rockets were launched against Haifa, the IDF declared that Israel would have to continue the operation in Lebanon until Hezbollah was unable to carry out its missile attacks. The Lebanese Government issued a statement claiming that it had no prior knowledge of the Hezbollah operation, and did not take responsibility or credit for what had happened. It strongly condemned the Israeli aggression, which targeted vital installations and civilians, and urged the international community to intervene to find a rapid solution. Nasrallah praised the 'heroic *mujahidin*' for the kidnapping operation, stated that the two abducted soldiers were safe, and demanded indirect negotiations and a prisoner exchange. As the Israeli attacks intensified, he declared open war on Israel 'to Haifa and beyond'. Amal announced a general mobilization and the establishment of a joint operations room with Hezbollah.

From the outset, the conflict resulted in mounting civilian casualties, especially on the Lebanese side. The Israeli army insisted that Hezbollah fighters operated out of villages and towns in southern Lebanon and that their rocket launchers were stored in the basements of houses and apartment blocks. It called on all the civilian population living south of the Litani river to evacuate the region; however, some did not have the means to travel north and others were afraid to make the journey because Israel had warned that it would attack any truck or commercial vehicle travelling south of the Litani river since Hezbollah was using trucks to move rockets and missiles. By the end of July 2006 numerous villages in the border region had been reduced to rubble under constant Israeli artillery bombardment and air-strikes. In a single incident on 30 July, 28 civilians—more than one-half of them children—who were sheltering in the basement of a house in Qana, near Tyre, were killed by Israeli air-strikes on the village.

A few days earlier a well-marked UN observer post at Khiam on the Israel–Lebanon border was shelled by the Israelis, killing four unarmed peace monitors. The UN Secretary-General stated that the attack was 'apparently deliberate', an allegation strongly denied by Israel. Humanitarian relief was unable to reach many villages to provide assistance, and the exact number of those killed and injured in the border region was unclear. Even in major towns such as Tyre food supplies, fuel and medical supplies were running out. The southern, mainly Shi'a suburbs of Beirut, where Hezbollah's headquarters are located, also sustained considerable damage as a result of repeated Israeli air-strikes, forcing the civilian population to flee their homes and seek refuge elsewhere in the city or in the mountains. By the end of July 2006 independent estimates suggested that at least 750 Lebanese had been killed thus far in the conflict, most of them civilians, with hundreds more wounded; in Israel 51 people had been killed—18 of these civilians killed by rocket attacks—and many more had been wounded. Hezbollah announced the deaths of 32 of its fighters and six belonging to Amal; the Israeli Chief of Staff stated that hundreds of Hezbollah 'terrorists' had been killed. The Lebanese authorities were faced with an estimated 800,000 to 1m. displaced people from the southern region and southern suburbs of Beirut, while a major international operation was launched to evacuate thousands of foreign nationals from Lebanon who were desperate to escape the Israeli bombardment. Syria reported that it was sheltering 100,000 Lebanese refugees. The cost of the destruction of vital infrastructure, public facilities and residential buildings in Lebanon was estimated at US $2,500m.

Mounting civilian casualties and extensive destruction of vital infrastructure in Lebanon provoked widespread criticism of Israel within the international community for a military offensive that was condemned as 'disproportionate'. There were repeated calls for an immediate cessation of hostilities, but little concrete action, largely because the US Administration was reluctant to demand an immediate halt to the Israeli offensive. It was not until 26 July 2006, after two weeks of fighting, that an international conference was convened in Rome, Italy, to discuss the crisis. At the meeting Prime Minister Siniora put forward a plan beginning with an immediate cease-fire, and including: an exchange of prisoners; placing the disputed Shebaa Farms under UN control; deploying the Lebanese army in southern Lebanon; and strengthening UNIFIL. Hezbollah had reservations on some issues, but expressed support for the plan. The meeting, however, stopped short of calling for an immediate cease-fire, although there was support for some of the Lebanese proposals, and the idea of creating a new international peace force to be deployed in southern Lebanon was discussed. The Israeli Minister of Justice insisted that the Rome meeting and the USA's refusal to support an immediate truce had given Israel the 'green light' to continue its operations against Hezbollah until the organization was removed from southern Lebanon and disarmed. A State Department spokesman categorically rejected this assertion. Shortly afterwards US President Bush and the British Prime Minister, Tony Blair, meeting in Washington, DC, agreed on the need for a UN Security Council resolution to halt the violence and supported the idea of the deployment of a multinational stabilization force in southern Lebanon. The Lebanese authorities continued to express reservations about the deployment of a new international force, and National Assembly President Berri declared that, if such a force was established, it should be deployed on the Israeli side of the border because it was Lebanon that needed protection from Israel. When the US Secretary of State made her second visit to the region at the end of July, the Lebanese Prime Minister declined to meet her, but in talks in Jerusalem Rice displayed a new sense of urgency, calling for a cease-fire 'as soon as possible', in a matter of days. Olmert, however, insisted that the Israeli offensive would continue until a strong international force was deployed in southern Lebanon, and declared that the fighting could continue for several weeks.

During the first week of August 2006, as the USA and France tried to agree a draft resolution calling for a cease-fire that could be brought before the UN Security Council, the fighting intensified, further impeding the delivery of urgently needed humanitarian relief supplies to Lebanon's civilian population. The IDF stepped up its ground offensive, deploying some 10,000 troops in the border region, supported by air-strikes, which met with fierce resistance from Hezbollah fighters. The Israeli air force also attacked targets in the Beqa'a valley close to the Syrian frontier and shelled a suburban area near Beirut's international airport, while Israeli commandos carried out a raid on the Hezbollah stronghold of Ba'albek, in the Beqa'a valley, more than 80 km from Israel's northern border. Hezbollah fired a barrage of missiles into northern Israel—over 200 in a single day, the largest number since the conflict began—and Nasrallah threatened to strike Tel-Aviv if Israel continued to attack Beirut; a senior Iranian source indicated that Hezbollah possessed *Zelzal-2* missiles made in Iran that were capable of hitting targets anywhere in Israel. The following day Hezbollah missiles hit the town of Hadera, 40 km north of Tel-Aviv. In response, Israeli forces began to push deeper into Lebanon to extend the buffer zone, against continued Hezbollah resistance, and the Israeli Minister of Defence, Amir Peretz, stated that troops should prepare to advance as far north as the Litani river.

On 5 August 2006, after intense negotiations, France and the USA finally agreed on the text of a draft resolution to submit to the UN Security Council, and on 11 August the Security Council adopted Resolution 1701, which had been unanimously approved. Implemented on 14 August, it called for: a full, immediate cessation of violence; strict respect by all for the sovereignty and integrity of Israel and Lebanon; delimitation of the frontiers of Lebanon, in particular in sectors that were disputed or uncertain, including Shebaa Farms; and the deployment of an international force in Lebanon subject to Israel and Lebanon accepting in principle the elements of a long-term solution. An Israeli government spokesman stated that the resolution was 'very important', but indicated that Israel would have to know full details before giving its opinion, more especially as the document was still liable to be modified. The Israeli army would continue its operations in Lebanon until the resolution came into force. Meanwhile, Hezbollah's representative in the Lebanese Cabinet, the Minister of Energy and Water, Muhammad Fneish, declared that his party would respect the cease-fire so long as all Israeli troops withdrew from Lebanon. The resolution was endorsed by the Lebanese Government on 12 August and by the Israeli Government on 13 August. However, both sides continued military operations, resulting in significant loss of life, right up until the deadline on the morning of 14 August, raising serious questions about the commitment of either party to ending the hostilities.

Israel lifted its restrictions on air travel into and out of Lebanon, as well as its naval blockade, in early September 2006, thereby formalizing the end of the conflict. In the same month Amnesty International accused Hezbollah of having committed war crimes during the fighting by deliberately targeting Israeli civilians in its air-strikes. The findings of an official UN investigation into the conflict were published in November, and asserted that Israeli forces had fired artillery shells containing white phosphorus, an incendiary substance the use of which against civilians, or against legitimate military targets within residential areas, is banned under the terms of the Geneva Convention. The Israeli Government adamantly refuted the claim, insisting that the shells had been aimed exclusively at military targets in open ground.

Lebanon's Higher Relief Council reported that about 1,190 Lebanese civilians had been killed during the conflict and a further 4,410 injured. The Israeli Ministry of Foreign Affairs estimated that 119 Israeli troops and 43 Israeli civilians had died in the fighting, and 530 Hezbollah members had also been killed. Despite an official end to the hostilities, unexploded cluster bombs still rendered parts of southern Lebanon uninhabitable, and at the end of 2006 it was estimated that approximately 200,000 Lebanese who fled the violence had yet to return to their homes (although many of these were able to do so during 2007).

EVENTS IN THE AFTERMATH OF THE ISRAEL–HEZBOLLAH CONFLICT

In October 2006 Nasrallah demanded that Hezbollah be allocated one-third of the seats in an expanded national unity government, prompting accusations that he was attempting to attain the right of veto in order to protect the Syrian Government from prosecution in the ongoing investigation into the assassination of Rafiq Hariri. Nasrallah's demands were ignored, however, and in the following month five ministers—two members of Hezbollah and three from its ally, Amal—resigned from the Cabinet, thereby removing any Shi'a presence from the Government. A sixth resignation, that of a Christian pro-Syrian minister, followed soon afterwards. The assassination later in November of Pierre Gemayel, the Minister of Industry since 2005, rendered the political situation even more unstable. Gemayel was shot dead in his car in a suburb of Beirut, and many Lebanese leaders were quick to blame Syria for his murder. Since the Lebanese Constitution decrees that any government in which one-third of the ministers have vacated their posts must automatically be dissolved, Gemayel's assassination meant that, should just one further minister resign, it would force the collapse of the Government.

In December 2006 thousands of demonstrators gathered in Beirut and erected tents in the capital's main square, besieging government buildings and proclaiming that the Cabinet was now constitutionally invalid. When the protests, aimed at pressurizing the Government into resigning, had failed to achieve any tangible results by late January 2007, the opposition intensified its efforts and called for a general strike, which brought commercial districts of the capital to a virtual standstill; at least three people were killed during clashes between protesters and the authorities. The security forces appeared to do little to remove the road blockades that were in place, leading to allegations that the police and the army were colluding with the opposition to bring about the Government's collapse. Nevertheless, the strike had a minimal effect on the resolve of the Government, which remained in place, despite the continuing efforts of those participating in the sit-in protest and the rapid intensification of sectarian violence. The presence of two separate Lebanese delegations at the annual summit meeting of the Arab League, held in Saudi Arabia in March 2007, symbolized the endemic divisions threatening the country's future stability.

Meanwhile, a disagreement between pro-Government Sunni and anti-Government Shi'a students at Beirut Arab University in January 2007 escalated into violent clashes that spilled out onto the streets; up to four people were killed and more than 150 were injured. The incident further fuelled concerns that Lebanon was about to spiral into full-scale sectarian conflict again, fears that appeared to be shared by the Government, which responded to the latest violence by imposing an overnight curfew in Beirut—the first of its kind in a decade. In February two bombs were detonated on commuter buses travelling through Ein Alaq, a village to the north-east of Beirut, killing three people. The attacks, which took place on the eve of the second anniversary of Hariri's assassination, were widely considered to have been timed so as to deter people from travelling to Beirut to attend a rally to mark the occasion; however, amid tight security, tens of thousands of people congregated on the following day to honour their former leader. In March Hassan al-Sabaa, who had retracted his resignation as Minister of the Interior and Municipalities in November 2006, announced that four Syrian members of Fatah al-Islam—a militant Islamist Palestinian group, inspired by al-Qa'ida and alleged by the Lebanese authorities to be supported by Syria—had been arrested on suspicion of involvement in the bus explosions in Ein Alaq.

In March 2007 UNIIIC released its latest report into the assassination of Rafiq Hariri, in which again it claimed to have made considerable progress in acquiring further evidence, but declined to give specific details. UNIIIC's mandate was extended to 15 June 2008. (On 2 June 2008 it was extended again, to 31 December.) Also in March 2007 recently appointed UN Secretary-General Ban Ki-Moon issued his report on the implementation of UN Security Council Resolution 1701, in which he rebuked both Israel and Lebanon for failing to adhere to all of its terms. However, he praised both sides' overall commitment to maintaining the cease-fire.

A copy of the interim report of Israel's Winograd Commission, a government-appointed commission of inquiry into Israel's military campaign in Lebanon, was made public at the end of April 2007. This preliminary report, which focused specifically on the period between Israel's withdrawal from southern Lebanon in 2000 to mid-July 2006, contained severe criticism of prominent Israeli government officials, notably Prime Minister Olmert, Minister of Defence Amir Peretz and the Chief of Staff of the Armed Forces during the conflict, Lt-Gen. Dan Halutz (who had resigned in January 2007). Olmert was accused of having initiated the military action against Hezbollah 'hastily' and without due consideration for the likely outcome and repercussions of such action, while Halutz was deemed to have provided inadequate information to the Prime Minister and Minister of Defence regarding the shortcomings of the Israeli armed forces. Nasrallah welcomed the findings of the Commission (for further details, see the chapter on Israel) and acknowledged the level of self-criticism that Israel had demonstrated, conceding that this was worthy of 'respect'.

At the end of May 2007 the UN Security Council adopted Resolution 1757, authorizing the formation of an international tribunal to try suspects in Hariri's assassination. The Special Tribunal for Lebanon was to comprise 11 independent judges, of whom seven were to be international judges and four were to be Lebanese; should a second trial chamber be created, there were to be nine international and five Lebanese judges. For security reasons, the tribunal would not be based in Lebanon itself, and in August it was reported that the Netherlands was close to reaching an agreement with the UN to allow the tribunal to be hosted by The Hague, Netherlands. While the creation of the tribunal was welcomed by the Siniora Government, the Hezbollah-led opposition was quick to challenge its validity. Nasrallah insisted that any such tribunal not approved by the Lebanese legislature was illegitimate, suggesting that the new body would be unable to rely on the co-operation of Hezbollah should no agreement concerning its establishment be reached between the opposition and the Government.

In mid-June 2007 Walid Eido, a prominent anti-Syrian legislator and member of Saad Hariri's Future Movement, was killed along with nine other people, including Eido's son, in a car bombing in Beirut. Once again, suspicions were immediately raised regarding Syria's involvement; however, Syrian officials vehemently denied the allegations. A few days later, following a request by Prime Minister Siniora, the UN Security Council announced that UNIIIC was to assist with the investigation into Eido's assassination. By-elections to select replacements for Eido, in Beirut's second district, and for Pierre Gemayel, in the Metn district, were held in August. The former seat was won comfortably by the pro-Government Muhammad Amin Itani, of the Future Movement, while the latter was secured by pro-Syrian Camille Khoury, of the FPM, in a very tight contest against his closest rival, former President Amin Gemayel. Khoury's victory was a considerable reverse for the Lebanese leadership, which had hoped to fill both seats with supporters of Siniora; since the assassination of Eido had reduced the number of pro-Government legislators to 68, the loss of just three more seats, for whatever reason, would result in the loss of the Siniora administration's majority quorum.

Meanwhile, the latest UNIIIC report (the sixth compiled during the tenure of Serge Brammertz) was released in mid-July 2007. The report asserted that a 'number of persons' had now been identified who might have been involved in Hariri's assassination, and stated that Syria and other states had continued to provide a 'mostly positive response' to UNIIIC's requests for co-operation and information. Also in July Lebanese investigators concluded that Fatah al-Islam had been responsible for the killing of Pierre Gemayel. In the previous month two UN armoured vehicles travelling between the villages of Marjayoun and Khaim, close to the Israeli border, were hit by a roadside bomb; six UN personnel were killed in the incident. In August the UN Security Council voted to extend the mandate of UNIFIL by another year. At 31 July 2008 UNIFIL had a strength of 12,334 military personnel, supported by some 333 international civilian and 627 local civilian staff. Its mandate was extended again, until 31 August 2009, by a UN Security Council vote on 28 August 2008. Meanwhile, the 10th UNIIIC report, and the first to be published since the appointment in early 2008 of Daniel Bellemare in place of Brammertz, was issued in March of that year. In this report the UN body revealed that the evidence it had examined thus far indicated that a network of people was behind Hariri's murder, without mentioning specific individuals. In early April Bellemare asked the UN Security Council for a further six months to investigate the crime.

A 105-day siege of the Nahr al-Bared refugee camp in Tripoli was finally concluded at the beginning of September 2007, when the Lebanese army seized control from Islamist militants. The siege had begun in late May, after members of Fatah al-Islam had fled to the camp having conducted a bank robbery in the town of Amioun, south of Tripoli. In the ensuing weeks more than 300 people were believed to have been killed in fierce clashes between the army and militants within the camp, which forced an estimated 40,000 Palestinian refugees to flee in order escape the violence. Fatah al-Islam's leader—Shaker al-Abassi, who had been sentenced to death *in absentia* in April 2004 for the murder in 2002 of a US diplomat, Laurence Foley (see the chapter on Jordan)—was reported to have been killed in the closing stages of the fighting; however, subsequent DNA tests carried out on the body thought to have been that of al-Abassi proved negative. The Syrian Government commended the efforts of the Lebanese army in ending the siege, and continued to deny ongoing claims that it in any way supported or condoned the activities of Fatah al-Islam. In March 2008 al-Abassi was charged with incitement to murder, in connection with the bus explosions at Ein Alaq in February 2007.

FAILURE TO ELECT A NEW PRESIDENT

With the scheduled expiry, in November 2007, of Lahoud's presidential term, the attention of the Government and the opposition in the preceding months came increasingly to focus on the election of his successor. The first session of the National Assembly to elect a new President was duly arranged for 25 September. The ambiguity of the Lebanese Constitution meant that, in the event of political divisions between the two camps preventing agreement on a common candidate, the likely eventuality remained deeply uncertain. According to the Constitution, if a new President was not elected by 23 November, then Siniora and his Cabinet would automatically assume executive control. However, the Constitution also authorizes the President to decree the resignation of the Cabinet, allowing Lahoud, should he choose, to appoint a new, opposition cabinet, which would almost certainly elect a pro-Syrian, anti-Government President. Lebanon experienced a further political assassination in late September, just six days before the scheduled presidential election, when Antoine Ghanem, a Christian Phalangist legislator, was killed in a car bombing in a predominantly Christian district of Beirut. Five others died in the explosion, for which Syrian officials were again obliged to deny claims of involvement by certain Lebanese leaders. With the Government and opposition unwilling to co-operate in order to elect a new President, the National Assembly failed to achieve the requisite two-thirds' quorum of members on 25 September owing to an opposition boycott; a second vote was thus scheduled for 23 October.

Following mediation by German diplomats and representatives of the International Committee of the Red Cross, Hezbollah and Israel carried out a limited exchange of prisoners and bodies in October 2007—the first such exchange between the two sides since their conflict of the previous year. However, the two Israeli soldiers whose abduction by Hezbollah militants in July 2006 had apparently provoked the conflict were not included in the arrangement. In January 2008 Nasrallah alleged that Hezbollah was holding the remains of a number of Israeli troops killed during the 2006 conflict. Indeed, the remains of several Israeli soldiers were handed over to Israel at the start of June 2008, when the Israeli authorities returned a Lebanese civilian who had served a six-year prison term for espionage. On 29 June the Israeli Cabinet controversially voted to exchange the bodies of the two soldiers abducted by Hezbollah in July 2006 (who it now transpired were certainly dead) for five Lebanese detainees.

The second postponement of the scheduled ballot to elect a successor to President Lahoud was announced by Berri on 22 October 2007, the day before the vote was to take place; a new date of 12 November was declared. In early October US President Bush had warned the Syrian Government not to interfere in Lebanon's internal affairs, since it was a boycott of the National Assembly by pro-Syrian opposition members that had rendered the parliament inquorate. Thus began a seven-month period during which no fewer than 17 further postponements of the presidential election were ordered, owing to a failure by the opposing factions to agree first on a mutually acceptable candidate, and then on the exact nature of administration to be formed after a new President had been elected. When the parliamentary session scheduled for 23 November—at the end of which Lahoud's term of office expired—was postponed until 30 November, it meant that Lahoud was obliged to leave office without a successor having been appointed. Under the terms of the Constitution, therefore, presidential duties were assumed by the Siniora Government in an acting capacity, although, shortly before the expiry of his mandate, Lahoud had issued a statement asserting that, owing to conditions being present for a 'state of emergency', he would hand over responsibility for the country's security to the armed forces. (He and other representatives of the pro-Syrian opposition refused to recognize the legitimacy of the Government following the ministerial resignations of November 2006.) Yet Lahoud's stance was firmly rejected by the Prime Minister, who insisted that no Head of State could call a state of emergency without the approval of the Cabinet. This represented the first time that Lebanon had been without a President since the civil war ended in 1990.

Although the Commander-in-Chief of the Army, Gen. Michel Suleiman (a Maronite Christian), was chosen as a 'compromise candidate' acceptable to both pro-Government and pro-opposition politicians towards the end of November 2007, disagreements remained as to how to amend the Constitution in order to permit Suleiman, as a serving senior state official, to assume the office of Head of State. Amid a flurry of international and regional diplomatic meetings, the ministers responsible for the foreign affairs of Arab League member states, meeting in Cairo, Egypt, in January 2008, approved details of a plan intended to bring to an end Lebanon's presidential vacuum. The three-phase proposals included the election of Suleiman as President, establishment of a Lebanese government of national unity (where Suleiman would have the deciding vote in any dispute) and approval of new electoral legislation. It was reported that the Arab League plan had received the support of both the Lebanese and Syrian administrations, but that Hezbollah and its principal allies continued to demand that they receive at least one-third of government portfolios in any new cabinet, thus granting them the right to veto important decisions. Following a 19th postponement of the National Assembly session to elect a President on 13 May, a new date of 10 June was set. In early April, meanwhile, Suleiman had announced his intention to retire from his military post in August, three months in advance of the scheduled date.

In December 2007 Brig.-Gen. François al-Hajj, the army's head of operations, was killed, along with three other people, in a car bomb attack in east Beirut. Observers noted the significance of the fact that al-Hajj had been widely expected to be promoted to Commander-in-Chief of the Army should Suleiman be elected as Lahoud's successor. It was, however, unclear as to which group had carried out the assassination, with Syria, Israel and the militant group Fatah al-Islam all being accused by various parties of responsibility for the blast. An explosion apparently aimed at US embassy officials in mid-January 2008 resulted in the deaths of four Lebanese bystanders. There was a further wave of unrest in the principally Shi'a suburbs of southern Beirut in late January, which had been precipitated by popular frustration over power shortages; seven protesters were reported to have died in the ensuing clashes with security forces. A group of army officers was detained and charged by the authorities in February, amid criticism of the military's handling of the protests. Towards the end of January, meanwhile, Capt. Wissam Eid, a senior member of the police team charged with investigating the recent bombings and assassinations, was himself killed in another car bomb attack in a suburb of the capital; Eid's driver and up to 10 others also died in the explosion. In February Imad Mughniyeh, one of Hezbollah's most senior militants, was killed in a car bombing in the Syrian capital. Hezbollah representatives immediately blamed Israel for Mughniyeh's death; however, Israeli officials rejected such claims. Mughniyeh had been implicated in a number of high-profile kidnappings of Western journalists, military personnel and religious envoys in Lebanon during the 1980s, and his funeral in Beirut attracted significant levels of support from Hezbollah members.

The Winograd Commission published the final results of its investigation into Israel's military campaign in Lebanon of July–August 2006 on 30 January 2008. Although the Commission described Israel's ground offensive in Lebanon as a 'serious failure' in both military and political terms—a large-scale offensive, in which 33 Israeli soldiers died, notably having been ordered in southern Lebanon only hours before an agreed cease-fire was scheduled to take effect—Prime Minister Olmert was judged to have acted 'in the sincere interest of Israel' in ordering the military action.

Lebanon's political situation deteriorated rapidly in early May 2008, when a decision taken by the Government to shut down a private telecommunications network controlled by Hezbollah and to remove the security chief at Beirut International Airport (where Hezbollah was accused of using surveillance equipment to spy on pro-Government politicians), who was a Hezbollah loyalist, prompted fierce clashes between members of the Shi'a opposition group and government loyalists. Moreover, a general strike called by the opposition in protest against price increases and to demand higher salaries descended into violence. As Nasrallah called the Government's actions against his organization a 'declaration of war', gunmen from Hezbollah and its allies besieged the Beirut offices of the media controlled by the Future Movement's Saad Hariri, while major roads were blocked. Observers noted that west Beirut was now effectively controlled by militants of the Hezbollah-led opposition. After several days of violent clashes, which spread to other cities such as Tripoli, an estimated 80 people had been killed, and some 200 wounded, in Lebanon's worst period of unrest since the civil war. However, by mid-May the Government and army claimed to have regained control, and, following mediation by the Arab League, the Cabinet voted to revoke the measures that had provoked the recent violence—an outcome widely viewed as a demonstration of Hezbollah's growing military strength and influence. This positive development meant that the lengthy sit-in by demonstrators in the centre of Beirut came to an end and businesses that had been closed during the months of paralysis began to resume trading.

GEN. MICHEL SULEIMAN BECOMES HEAD OF STATE

On 21 May 2008 18 months of conflict between the Lebanese Government on one side and Hezbollah and its allies on the other were apparently brought to an end through the signing of the Doha Agreement. The agreement was named after the Qatari capital, where—following effective mediation by the Qatari leadership under the auspices of the Arab League—the two sides finally agreed to seek to put aside their differences in order to restore national unity. The Doha Agreement encompassed: the election of a new President; formation of a national unity government, which would involve power-sharing with Hezbollah; and introduction of a new electoral law. A few days after the signing of the unity accord, Fouad Siniora was chosen by the National Assembly to remain as Prime Minister. Yet, notwithstanding the election of a new President and formation of a 30-member national unity Cabinet on 11 July (the administration consisted of 16 ministers of the Western-supported majority coalition, 11 linked to Hezbollah and its allies, and three appointed by President

Suleiman), the security situation in Lebanon remained uneasy as the summer of 2008 progressed. Heavy fighting between supporters of the Government and pro-opposition activists was reported in the eastern Beqa'a valley and Tripoli, resulting in a significant number of fatalities. The new Siniora Government secured a vote of confidence in the National Assembly on 12 August, and thus would administer the country until the holding of fresh legislative elections in 2009. On 30 August 2008 Brig.-Gen. Jean Kahwaji was chosen as Michel Suleiman's successor as Commander-in-Chief of the Army.

A landmark agreement was reached between Lebanon and Syria in mid-July 2008, when the two countries announced that they were to enter into diplomatic relations and open embassies in one another's capitals for the first time since they had achieved independence in 1943 and 1945, respectively. Following the agreement to resume ties, it was revealed that the work of a committee to demarcate the Lebanese–Syrian border and to investigate the issue of missing persons since Lebanon's civil war would be resumed. The Lebanese Cabinet formally adopted a resolution to establish diplomatic relations with Syria on 22 August 2008.

LEBANON AND SYRIA ESTABLISH DIPLOMATIC RELATIONS

Syria formally recognized Lebanon's independence on 13 October 2008 and opened its first embassy in Beirut in December. On 24 March 2009 President Suleiman accepted the credentials of Ali Abd al-Karim Ali as the first ambassador of Syria to Lebanon. Earlier that month Lebanon had opened its first embassy in Damascus, appointing Michel el-Khoury as ambassador. Syria's formal recognition of Lebanon was seen as a victory by Syria's adversaries in Lebanon, particularly the March 14 Alliance, led by Saad Hariri's Future Movement. It was hoped that relations between the two countries would now follow a state-to-state channel and would limit Syria's interference in Lebanon.

Before the diplomatic exchange took place, Syria ensured that the Lebanese domestic balance of power had been, if not directly to its own advantage, then at least conducive to its own interests. The election of President Suleiman, probably Syria's preferred candidate, and Gen. Michel Aoun's alliance with Hezbollah, brought relief to Syria. When Gen. Aoun visited Syria in early December 2008, he was given a 'presidential' welcome. Syria hoped that through Aoun it could mend its relations with Lebanon's Christians and, hence, would have the backing of two main communities in Lebanon: the Shi'a and Maronites.

Improved Lebanese–Syrian relations brought relative stability to Lebanon, although political assassinations continued. On 10 September 2008 a car bomb in a village to the east of Beirut killed Salah Aridi, an associate of Talal Arslan, a Druze leader and member of the pro-Syria opposition. However, this did not prevent rival political leaders from holding their first 'national reconciliation' round meeting, under the auspices of President Suleiman, on 16 September. It was hoped that the meetings would increase dialogue among the warring factions and provide a forum in which to discuss key issues including: an electoral law for legislative elections scheduled for June 2009; a defence strategy, ostensibly to increase ties between the military wing of Hezbollah and the state; and a means to establish political calm after years of sectarian agitation.

In November 2008 the Lebanese authorities announced that three people had been arrested on suspicion of espionage on behalf of Israel. By late May 2009 a total of 18 Lebanese citizens had been charged with participating in an alleged network of spies, including several security service personnel. It was reported that a total of 30 people had been detained in connection with the allegations; two others were thought to have fled across the border to Israel. The Lebanese authorities complained to the UN that Israel had violated the UN-mandated cease-fire along the Lebanese–Israeli border. Lebanon accused Israel of managing a spy network in Lebanon and of using its military units along the border to facilitate the suspects' escape into Israel.

THE SPECIAL TRIBUNAL FOR LEBANON OPENS

On 1 March 2009 the Special Tribunal for Lebanon formally opened in The Hague, with a mandate to prosecute the individuals responsible for the killing of Lebanon's former Prime Minister Rafiq Hariri. The main suspects for the murder at that time were four generals who formed the locus of the security apparatuses of the former pro-Syrian regime in Lebanon: Chief of General Security Maj.-Gen. Jamil al-Sayyid; former Chief of Police Maj.-Gen. Ali Hajj; former Military Intelligence Chief Brig.-Gen. Raymond Azar; and Republican Guard Commander Gen. Mustafa Hamdan.

However, on 29 April 2009 the four suspects were freed on orders of the international court. The tribunal declared that evidence against them 'was not sufficiently credible to request maintenance in detention of those persons'. Saad Hariri accepted the order and commended the tribunal for its 'seriousness'; journalists and politicians of the opposition called for a reform of the Lebanese legal system in the wake of its 'failure' to order the release of the prisoners before the international tribunal's decision.

JUNE 2009 PARLIAMENTARY ELECTIONS: THE CAMPAIGN

By April 2009 most political groups and leaders in Lebanon were concentrating on campaigning for legislative elections, which had been scheduled for June. The March 14 Alliance's main leaders and parties included: for the Sunnis, Saad Hariri (Future Movement); for the Druze, Walid Joumblatt (PSP); and for the Christians, the Lebanese Forces Party, Amin Gemayel's Al-Kataeb (formerly the Phalange Party) and other leading individuals such as Dory Chamoun and Michel Mawad. The main political figures of the opposition March 8 Alliance included: for the Shi'a, Hezbollah and Amal; for the Christians, Gen. Aoun (FPM) and Sulayman Franjiya (El-Marada Movement); for the Sunnis, former Prime Minister Omar Karami; and for the Druze, Talal Arslan and Wiam Wahab.

Although each camp had a cross-sectarian following, the general contours of the divisions remained sectarian: the backbone of the March 14 Alliance was formed from the majority of Sunnis, the majority of Druze and a minority (at least according to the results of the 2005 elections) of Christians; on the other hand, the opposition was composed of the vast majority of Shi'a, the majority of Christians (70% voted for the FPM in 2005), and the minority parties in the Druze community.

The elections attracted both Arab and international attention. In a sign of concern over a possible Hezbollah victory in the elections, the US Administration sent clear signals of support to its political allies in Lebanon. In April 2009 the US Secretary of State, Hillary Clinton, visited Lebanon and made it clear that the USA would 'continue to support the voices of moderation in Lebanon'. In late May US Vice-President Joseph Biden became the highest-ranking American official to visit Lebanon in decades. Stating US policy towards Lebanon, Biden declared that: 'The USA will evaluate the shape of its assistance program based on the policies of the new Government'. In a clear message to Gen. Aoun and his FPM, Biden called on 'those who think about standing with the spoilers of peace not to miss this opportunity to walk away'. During his visit, Biden had a private meeting with the March 14 Alliance.

Although Syria remained silent during the electoral campaign, its principal regional ally and Hezbollah's main supporter, Iran, appeared to be backing the opposition. Divisions on a regional level made the Lebanese elections pivotal: the victor, it was believed, would shape Lebanon's foreign policy. Consequently, money flowed into Lebanon from external sources, prompting media reports that the election campaign was among the most expensive per caput world-wide.

Domestically, political divisions were heightened during the electoral campaign. As the majority of Sunni and Shi'a Muslims would vote for the Future Movement, and Hezbollah and Amal, respectively, the main competition took place over the Christian vote. The March 14 Alliance aimed to defeat the FPM and, accordingly, weaken their main ally, Hezbollah. The opposition aimed, at least, to preserve Gen. Aoun's majority vote within the Christian community and, thus, drive the opposition towards victory. During the campaign, Christian factions within the March 14 Alliance accused Aoun of being a political subordinate of Hezbollah, of taking the Christian community away from its historical pro-Western stance, and of contributing to Hezbollah's control of Lebanon. In its turn, the FPM accused its Christian competitors of being the political subordinates of Saad Hariri, of seeking to isolate Lebanon's Christians from their compatriots (especially Hezbollah and its Shi'a supporters) and the Arab region (especially Syria, which, according to the FPM, had now left Lebanon), and of hindering economic and political reform.

Political divisions within the Christian community heightened during the campaign leading Cardinal Sfeir to issue an appeal to undecided Christian voters a day before the elections. Sfeir warned that if the opposition won, Lebanon's sovereignty and its Arab identity would be threatened. The FPM accused him of supporting one Christian faction against another.

THE MARCH 14 ALLIANCE RETAINS ITS PARLIAMENTARY MAJORITY

The parliamentary elections took place on 7 June 2009. Voter turn-out was recorded at 55% and polling took place in a calm atmosphere. To the surprise of many, the March 14 Alliance emerged victorious and was able to retain its majority in parliament. The results, which did not significantly differ from those of the 2005 elections, showed that the March 14 Alliance had secured 71 seats in the 128-seat legislature, while the opposition won 57 seats. Of the seats won by the March 14 Alliance, the Future Movement and its allies took 30, and the PSP and its allies 10; the Lebanese Forces Party and Al-Kataeb each won five seats, while the remaining seats went to smaller parties and independents. Of the opposition, Hezbollah and Amal took 12 and 11 seats, respectively, the FPM and its allies in the Reform and Change Bloc obtained 27 seats, and the remainder went to smaller parties and independents. Hezbollah and its allies in the opposition accepted the election results and conceded defeat.

The election results did not alter the balance of power in Lebanon, nor did they alter the sectarian basis of support for each of the main parties. The elections showed that in the Shi'a community Amal and Hezbollah won around 95% of the vote; in the Sunni community, the Future Movement took around 75% of the vote, with the rest going to the opposition; in the Druze community, Walid Joumblatt's PSP claimed 75%; while in the Christian community, Gen. Aoun's FPM continued to represent the majority of voters, winning 20 seats, compared with five each for Al-Kataeb and the Lebanese Forces Party (Aoun's party won in eight of the 11 Christian-majority districts).

The nature of Lebanon's 'consociational democracy'—the power-sharing system under which the various confessional groups are guaranteed a level of representation in the Government—inhibits the ability of the parliamentary majority to rule and for the minority to oppose. The need to bring representatives of all—or the main—sectarian communities into government limits the freedom of choice of the Prime Minister in appointing its members. The unlikely alternative would leave the Shi'a and the majority of Christians devoid of power, which could restrain the workings of any government. The opposition's defeat in the legislative elections did not prevent the re-election of Nabih Berri, leader of the Shi'a Amal, as President of the National Assembly for a fifth term in late June 2009.

On 27 June 2009 President Suleiman, following a constitutional consultation with Lebanese deputies, appointed Saad Hariri as Prime Minister-designate. Some 86 deputies nominated Hariri for the post. The opposition, with the exception of Amal, refused to support Hariri, rather preferring to wait to negotiate the formation of the new government. Hariri indicated that he would seek to form a government of national unity. The opposition's main aim was to hold veto power—at least one-third of the seats—in the new government. It was hoped that regional developments, particularly US overtures to Syria and Iran and an apparent thaw in relations between Syria and Saudi Arabia, might facilitate the coalition discussions.

Following negotiations with the leaders of the March 8 Alliance (including Nasrallah and Gen. Aoun) regarding the formation of a national unity coalition, in late July 2009 Hariri announced that an agreement had been reached on the number of cabinet posts allocated to each group. Under the terms of the deal, the March 14 Alliance would receive 15 seats and the March 8 Alliance 10 seats; the remaining five members would be nominated by President Suleiman. However, in August Joumblatt announced the withdrawal from the March 14 Alliance of his PSP, claiming that his participation in the alliance had been solely for electoral purposes. Moreover, the talks appeared to have reached an impasse owing to a dispute between the March 14 Alliance and Aoun over the allocation of seats to the FPM. In early September Suleiman urged the negotiating parties to form a cabinet by the end of that month to ensure continued political stability. On 10 September Hariri submitted his resignation as Prime Minister-designate after his proposed cabinet line-up was rejected by Nasrallah and Aoun, but he was reappointed to the post by Suleiman in the following week.

HARIRI FORMS A NATIONAL UNITY GOVERNMENT

In November 2009, some five months after the parliamentary elections, Saad Hariri finally succeeded in forming a national unity government. As agreed in July, the new 30-member Cabinet comprised 15 members of the March 14 Alliance, 10 members of the March 8 Alliance (of which only two were members of Hezbollah) and five appointed by President Suleiman; of the 15 positions allocated to the March 14 Alliance, three were awarded to the now disassociated PSP. In effect, the opposition, along with the President, held veto power over Hariri's electoral majority, being able to disrupt the required number for a quorum or to obstruct decisions requiring approval by a two-thirds' majority.

In December 2009 the new Government endorsed Hezbollah's right to maintain its arsenal of weapons, despite expressions of reservation from five ministers from Al-Kataeb and the Lebanese Forces Party. The new Government's decision to accept both Hezbollah's request to legitimize its resistance to Israel and Gen. Aoun's request to choose his own ministers reflected a new phase in Lebanese, and regional, power balance. In light of the Hariri family's links to Saudi Arabia and the long-standing influence of Syria within Lebanese domestic politics, the improvement in relations between those two countries—following considerable diplomatic tension in the wake of the US-led invasion of Iraq in 2003 and the assassination of Rafiq Hariri in 2005—paved the way for relative stability in Lebanon, resulting in the formation of the Government and the dispersal of the March 14 Alliance. The contours dividing the March 8 and March 14 Alliances, however, became more blurred.

AMELIORATION IN RELATIONS WITH SYRIA

Amid this changing political landscape, Prime Minister Saad Hariri made an official visit to Syria in December 2009, marking a significant turning-point in Lebanese-Syrian relations nearly five years after the assassination of Hariri's father, for which many in Lebanon still blamed Syria. The visit reflected a shift in the orientation of the main parties of the March 14 Alliance, with Al-Kataeb and the Lebanese Forces Party the only remaining vocal opposition to Syria in Lebanon.

This politics of necessity continued to dictate the behaviour of Lebanon's influential leaders and parties, and a similar shift away from anti-Syrian rhetoric was evident in the PSP, whose leader, Walid Joumblatt, made efforts significantly to improve his relations with Syria's allies in Lebanon, particularly Hezbollah, while at the same time becoming increasingly critical of the March 14 Alliance. Joumblatt underscored Lebanon's strong ties with Syria, Hezbollah's right to resist Israel, and the detrimental effect of Israeli threats, generally perceived in the Arab world to be backed by the US Government, against Lebanon and Syria. In a televised interview in March 2010 Joumblatt issued a public apology for the 'indecent comments' that he made in the past about the Syrian regime and its leader, with whom he met during a visit to Syria in the following month. There was further evidence of the normalization of ties between Lebanon and Syria in August: during an interview with the London-based daily *Asharq al-Awsat*, Saad Hariri apologized for having accused the Syrian Government of involvement in the assassination of his father in 2005, stating that 'deceitful witnesses' had misled the Special Tribunal in an attempt to damage relations between the two countries.

THE PALESTINIAN REFUGEE SITUATION

In June–July 2010 the issue of Palestinian refugees resurfaced after Joumblatt appealed for the 400,000 Palestinians living in 12 refugee camps in Lebanon to be granted basic civil rights. Joumblatt's suggestion threatened to polarize the country's religious factions. While most Lebanese political parties were opposed to the naturalization of Palestinians in Lebanon since this would annul their right of return to their homeland, some feared that affording the Palestinians civil rights would ultimately disrupt the sectarian and demographic balance in Lebanon itself. Traditionally, most Lebanese Christians have objected to such a proposal on account of such fears, while Muslims have tended to demonstrate a more lenient approach. In the latest crisis, Christian parties—from both the March 14 Alliance and the opposition—joined forces to oppose the move. The Christian Maronite Church insisted that the granting of rights to the Palestinians should only be sanctioned in exchange for certain concessions, such as the disarmament of Palestinian militias active in Lebanon.

As the prospect of naturalization remained highly contentious, a series of proposals were debated in an attempt to find a means of granting the Palestinian refugees certain civil rights without contributing to their full integration into Lebanese society. For many Lebanese, the source of the problem was the failure of Israel to accept responsibility for the refugees, preventing them from returning to their homes. Nevertheless, the various political factions achieved a measure of general consensus, and in August 2010 the National Assembly approved heavily-amended legislation allowing limited rights to Palestinians in the labour market. Under the terms of the legislation, Palestinians resident in Lebanon would be entitled to work legally in some areas of the private sector and to contribute and claim to the state social security fund. However, the law was criticized by many observers, as Palestinians would remain excluded from public sector employment, in addition to jobs in the private sector for which membership of a Lebanese professional syndicate is compulsory.

HEZBOLLAH AND THE SPECIAL TRIBUNAL FOR LEBANON

In August 2010 Hezbollah began a campaign to discredit the Special Tribunal for Lebanon, following several leaks to the media, especially a report published by German newspaper *Der Spiegel*, which indicated that Hezbollah had organized the assassination of Rafiq Hariri. Hezbollah claimed that the Tribunal's verdict was 'politicized', and represented an attempt by the USA and Israel to delegitimize their enemies in the Middle East, especially Hezbollah and Syria. To counter the possibility of being accused by the Tribunal of killing Hariri and to defuse any potential tension this might cause, Hezbollah began to play a role in the investigation, in an effort to deflect attention from its own members. In August Sheikh Nasrallah, in a televised press conference, presented material that apparently demonstrated Israeli involvement in the assassination.

A few months later, amid the political tensions between Hezbollah and Prime Minister Saad Hariri, further reports on the issue, which were broadcast on a Lebanese television channel, disclosed audiotapes of Hariri's testimony before UN investigators. In another audiotape, Hariri was recorded meeting Zuheir al-Sadiq (who is now known as the 'false witness' in the investigation), in the presence of the chief UN investigator, Gerhard Lehman; Hariri and his aides demanded that al-Sadiq provide evidence of Syria's involvement in Rafiq Hariri's murder. Hezbollah used this material to discredit the Special Tribunal and to accuse it of both corruption and politicization.

THE COLLAPSE OF THE HARIRI GOVERNMENT

In January 2011, as Prime Minister Hariri was about to meet US President Barack Obama, the 10 ministers of the March 8 coalition resigned from the Government. Later the same day one of the five ministers nominated by President Suleiman also resigned, thus causing the automatic dissolution of the residual Government of mainly March 14 coalition representatives (under the terms of the Constitution, the Government must resign if more than one-third of its members withdraw). The collapse of Hariri's administration represented the culmination of divisions in Lebanon over the Special Tribunal for Lebanon and its likely indictment of Hezbollah members.

These divisions had paralyzed Hariri's administration, which was intended to be a 'national consensus government'. While the participation of the March 14 Alliance had provided legitimacy for the Government, the March 8 Alliance refused any collaboration with the UN tribunal. Attempts by regional states (Turkey, Qatar, Saudi Arabia and Syria) to mediate a solution between the rival Lebanese movements over the tribunal proved unsuccessful. Hezbollah refused the whole principle of the tribunal and its right to level accusations against the movement, while the March 14 Alliance believed that, at least, the tribunal might deter future political assassinations in Lebanon and, at best, would bring the criminals to trial. Within these divisions, questions of power in Lebanon and the region were clearly manifested. Hezbollah's demand that 'false witnesses' stand trial in Lebanon was rejected by the March 14 Alliance, which believed that the issue of 'false witnesses' should be decided by the UN tribunal. At a regional level, the collapse of the Hariri Government reflected shifts in the balance of regional power from the USA to Syria. The failure to reach a Saudi-Syrian agreement over Lebanon led Syria and its allies to oust the Government in anticipation of forming a pro-Syrian administration. This was made possible owing to the policy realignment made by Druze and PSP leader Joumblatt several months earlier, when he established closer relations with Syria and Hezbollah, resulting in the March 8 Alliance securing a majority in the National Assembly.

In January 2011 the new parliamentary majority named former Prime Minister Najib Miqati as the favoured candidate for the premiership. The nomination of Miqati was unexpected for many, but unpleasantly so for the March 14 Alliance. Miqati had contested elections with Saad Hariri, but was always a central figure in Lebanese politics, refusing to be affiliated with either the March 8 or 14 Alliances. For the March 8 Alliance, especially Hezbollah, Miqati represented a moderate Sunni-elected deputy, who could bring with him another two Sunni deputies and, hence, increase the size of the new majority. On the part of Miqati, who had strong relations with both Syria and Saudi Arabia, his acceptance of the nomination was to fill a gap in a largely divided country.

Miqati's acceptance of the premiership, however, prompted the March 14 Alliance to accuse Hezbollah of orchestrating a 'constitutional coup', and to organize a series of protests, some of which became violent, in mainly Sunni towns. Miqati subsequently began to form an administration, first appealing to the March 14 Alliance to join a new national consensus government. When the group refused, he commenced the establishment of a government with a majority from the March 8 Alliance.

NEW COALITION GOVERNMENT AND UN TRIBUNAL INDICTMENTS

After five months of negotiations among the members of the March 8 Alliance, Aoun's FPM parliamentary group and the newly nominated Prime Minister Miqati, a 30-member Government, which represented the new majority in parliament, was formed in June 2011. Notably, Shi'a Muslims comprised five members of the new administration, compared with six previously; instead, Nabih Berri, a Shi'a leader, decided to grant the sixth Shi'a post to a Sunni ally, Faisal Kareme. The FPM was allowed to appoint 10 ministers of the 15 allocated to Christians, Aoun declaring this to be a victory for his movement. Hezbollah received two ministerial posts.

In July 2011 the Government narrowly secured a vote of confidence in the National Assembly, with 68 votes of the 128 cast. The parliamentary session included a heated debate centring on the UN Special Tribunal for Lebanon and Hezbollah weapons. The March 14 Alliance deputies withdrew from voting, and members of the coalition, including its leader, Hariri, labelled the administration the 'Hezbollah Government'. Hariri reiterated accusations that Sheikh Nasrallah and Syrian President Assad were responsible for overthrowing his own Government.

A few days before the new Government received its parliamentary vote of confidence, the Special Tribunal for Lebanon presented its indictments to the Lebanese authorities. A leaked copy of the officially embargoed document revealed that four significant members of Hezbollah were accused of being involved in the assassination of Rafiq Hariri. The Lebanese Government was given 30 days to arrest and extradite the suspects. Nasrallah, appearing in another televised conference, declared that Hezbollah would never hand over any of its members to a tribunal that his movement considered to be an 'American and Israeli tool'. During the speech Nasrallah accused some investigators and other advisers to the Prosecutor-General of having connections to the US Central Intelligence Agency (CIA) and to Israel, providing footage as evidence of these claims, and accused others of 'financial and moral corruption'. The Lebanese Government, on the other hand, affirmed that it would continue to respect international law and the UN resolutions, especially the one related to the UN tribunal.

LEBANON AND THE ARAB UPRISINGS

Popular political uprisings in both Tunisia and Egypt in early 2011 succeeded in overthrowing the rulers of those countries, precipitating similar protests in other Arab countries. In Lebanon, the uprisings were attractive for some civil society groups, which held a series of protests calling for the 'toppling of the sectarian system'. After a few weeks, however, the momentum of these protests began to weaken. The country's sectarian divisions and the loyalty of different groups to their sectarian leaders proved to be the principle constraints on the emergence of a national revolution.

The revolutionary protests in Syria, however, provoked intense controversy. For Hezbollah, which was supportive of the popular uprisings in the Arab world, the Syrian revolution generated a dilemma. On the one hand, Hezbollah was in alliance with the Syrian regime. On the other hand, the authoritarian nature of that regime, which by April 2011 was in a bloody confrontation with the protesters, could not be easily justified. In the midst of the uprising, Hezbollah was accused of giving military support to the Syrian Government, an accusation that it denied. Another issue for Hezbollah centred on the uprising in Bahrain. In this case, Hezbollah was clear in its condemnation of the repression of the peaceful protests, leading the Bahraini regime to condemn Hezbollah as a 'terrorist' organization, and indeed to expel a number of Lebanese citizens whom it accused of having links with Hezbollah.

The response of the March 14 Alliance to the Syrian crisis was more ambivalent. The Syrian regime had accused some members of the Alliance's Future Movement of intervening in Syria in support of some 'terrorist' groups during the uprising; Future Movement refuted these allegations. Hariri declared that he supported the right of the Syrian people to revolt against authoritarianism, but failed to condemn the regime outright. Christian members of the March 14 Alliance were more cautious. The prospects of the establishment of an Islamist regime in Syria, and the potential threat this could have on Syria's Christian minority, made many members less enthusiastic about regime change.

For many in Lebanon, there was a fear of a spillover effect of the Syrian crisis on Lebanon. Indeed, several anti-Syrian regime protests took place in some Sunni towns of north Lebanon. In general, however, especially at government level, most Lebanese factions were cautious in their response to the Syrian crisis.

LEBANON, ISRAEL AND CYPRUS: OIL DISAGREEMENTS

There has been much recent discussion in relation to the discovery of large quantities of oil and gas reserves in the Levant basin, which comprises territory of Israel, Lebanon, Syria and Cyprus. Israel has begun to explore the possibilities of extracting gas. In turn, Lebanon and Cyprus took rapid action to demarcate their maritime spheres. In August 2010 the Lebanese legislature approved a bill allowing exploration for gas and oil in Lebanon's waters. The main difficulty, however, is that Lebanon and Israel have no demarcated maritime boundaries, and the Lebanese Government has requested UN assistance in determining the current borders. For both Israel and Lebanon, the offshore gas and oil resources are of strategic importance.

In July 2011 the Lebanese Government announced that it would submit a complaint before the UN in response to a map relating to its demarcated area that Israel had submitted to the UN. The document conflicted with Lebanon's own map, which it had submitted in the previous August. The newly appointed Lebanese Minister of Foreign Affairs and Emigrants, Adnan Mansour, declared that the Israeli map constituted an act of 'aggression' on Lebanese sovereignty. If the dispute is not resolved according to international law and under the supervision of the UN, the natural resources located in the Levant basin could become another focus of contention between Lebanon and Israel.

LEBANON AND THE SYRIA CRISIS

By the end of 2011 the uprising in Syria and the violent reaction of its regime signalled a danger of the country deteriorating into a prolonged civil conflict. The domestic impasse was exacerbated by divisions at a regional level between, on the one hand, pro-US states such as Saudi Arabia and Qatar, and, on the other hand, Iran, Hezbollah and the Iraqi Government of Prime Minister Nuri Kamal al-Maliki. Internationally, Russia and China constrained any attempts at a UN-backed resolution to oust Syrian President Assad from power. Amid the regional and international polarization of power, fears mounted in Lebanon, which was divided between supporters and opponents of the Syrian regime, that the Syrian crisis might spill over to Lebanon. Lebanon's response to the crisis took two forms: a government-driven formal approach and an informal response by different political forces.

The Government of Prime Minister Miqati, conscious of Lebanon's geographical proximity and historical ties to Syria, and, most importantly, of the Lebanese political divisions regarding the Syrian regime, decided to pursue a policy of 'disassociation' in relation to the Syria crisis. The policy supported the Syrian people's political aspirations, Assad's stated reform agenda and a political solution to the crisis. Most significantly, however, it rejected any international intervention in Syria, especially the use of Lebanon as a base for such an incursion. In October 2011 Lebanon abstained from voting at the UN Security Council on a resolution that condemned the Syrian regime. In November Lebanon again abstained from voting on a resolution, initiated at an Arab League summit, which aimed to impose economic sanctions on Syria. In February 2012 Lebanon was one of 15 countries to abstain from voting at the UN General Assembly on a resolution condemning the Syrian Government and calling for Assad's removal from power.

The 'disassociation' policy contributed to the establishment of Lebanon's neutral stance in the Arab world and prevented the country from descending into chaos. Beyond the formal policy, however, Lebanon's different sectarian and political groups forcefully advanced their claims in support of or in opposition to Assad's regime. Hezbollah, the dominant political force in the Shi'a community, expressed its support for Assad and his political reform agenda. It urged both the Syrian regime and the opposition Free Syrian Army (FSA) to cease hostilities and engage in political dialogue as the only viable solution to end the crisis in Syria. Hezbollah's stance reflected its strategic interest in the survival of the Assad regime, which, as Nasrallah confirmed in July 2012, was crucial in Hezbollah's war with Israel.

Another main supporter of an ordered political reform in Syria was Aoun, who was in alliance with Hezbollah and who represented the majority of the Christians in the National Assembly. Aoun, supported by the main Christian churches—especially the Maronite church led by Patriach Cardinal Béchara Boutros Raï—feared that the collapse of Assad's secular regime would lead to chaos in Syria and to the possible political domination of Islamic movements, especially the Syrian Muslim Brotherhood. In the absence of any protection, most Lebanese and Syrian Christians feared their displacement and forced migration from Syria should chaos ensue—a concern that was informed by the experience of many Christians in post-invasion Iraq.

On the other hand, the Syrian crisis—and the broader political uprisings in the Arab world, which resulted in several Islamic groups either coming to power or becoming politically salient—encouraged Sunni Islamic movements to organize and express opposition to the Syrian regime. On an almost weekly basis, these groups, which included a number of mainstream Sunni movements (such as the Al-Jama'a al-Islamiya) and several other Salafi factions, demonstrated against the Syrian regime in Tripoli, in northern Lebanon. Some also denounced Hezbollah's stance towards Syria. These demonstrations in several instances led to political and violent clashes with pro-Syrian groups, especially with the Alawite supporters of the regime. In June 2012, in fighting reminiscent of the 1975–1990 civil war in Lebanon, more than 10 were killed and 30 were injured as the violence between the two opposing groups spread in Tripoli. In these clashes, the Lebanese army attempted with limited success to curb both factions. Pro-Assad forces accused the Islamists of smuggling weapons to Syria and of aiming to turn northern Lebanon into a secure base for forces to intervene against the regime in Syria. In turn, the Islamists and other anti-Syrian secular politicians alleged that Hezbollah was supporting the Syrian regime's campaign of repression. In 2011 Sheikh Ahmad Assir, a Sunni cleric based in Sidon, became politically salient in his vocal opposition of Assad and Hezbollah. His opponents accused him of being a 'Qatari tool', who aimed to establish a Sunni movement as a counterweight to Hezbollah. His main accusations targeted Hezbollah, which he claimed should relinquish its arms to the Lebanese state. In June his supporters occupied one of the main streets, which connects Sidon to both Beirut and the South, to demonstrate against Hezbollah.

Generally, in Lebanon the Sunnis had become the political opponents of the Syrian regime following the assassination of Rafiq Hariri, which Syria was initially accused of organizing. Saad Hariri's March 14 Alliance had initially been restrained in relation to the Syrian crisis; however, by the end of 2011 it had become more vocal in opposition to Assad and in support of the Syrian uprising. The March 14 Alliance's main strategic gamble was for Assad to be ousted and for a friendlier regime to be established in Syria. This, as their Saudi and US patrons envisioned, would isolate Iran and would significantly weaken Hezbollah, their main domestic adversary.

In May 2012, in a clear indication of the interlocking of Syrian and Lebanese politics, 11 Lebanese (Shi'a) pilgrims were kidnapped in the Syrian city of Aleppo while returning to Lebanon from Iran. The Syrian kidnappers hinted that the group were members of Hezbollah, which, however, denied the claim. The abduction prompted the families and supporters of the pilgrims to stage protests in demand of their release. In some cases, Syrian workers were attacked. Although the aims of the kidnappers were unclear, on several occasions they denounced Hezbollah's stance towards (and alleged role in) Syria. Following the mediation of the Turkish Government (which was believed to have connections with the Syrian opposition), one of the 11 pilgrims was released in August and another in September.

By mid-2012 Lebanon's political climate had become largely conditioned by the Syrian crisis. While the Government attempted to preserve the minimal political order and stability, different political forces were cautiously examining the political and military developments in Syria. One main threat to Lebanon was posed not only by a political spillover from Syria, but also by the physical inflow of Syrian refugees into the largely divided country. When Syrian security officials were killed in Damascus in July, more than 15,000 Syrian civilians crossed the border to take refuge in Lebanon. In addition, throughout the crisis the Syrian army has been crossing the Lebanese border in attempts to pursue the Syrian rebels, who, according to the claims of the Syrian Government, have established bases in border towns in the north and Beqa'a regions of Lebanon.

DISAGREEMENTS WITHIN THE COALITION GOVERNMENT

In June 2012 disagreements between the ministers of Aoun's FPM and the Shi'a Amal movement became public. Although both were allies of Hezbollah, each party had a different political agenda. The FPM's purpose in joining the Government and holding a main share of its posts was to enact political and economic reform. Unlike other political groupings in Lebanon, the FPM relies on its domestic constituency to support its political agenda, which largely aims at the reintegration of Christians in the state—the FPM regarding this as fundamental to support for the Christian minority—and at reforms to put Lebanon on the right political and economic path. However, the FPM's political agenda was constrained by the existence of several factions within the Lebanese Government, not least Amal, which played a major role in the former administrations of Rafiq Hariri that were considered by the FPM to be corrupt. In June the FPM suspended its participation in the Government and National Assembly, in protest at a proposed law to employ part-time workers in the Electricité du Liban public company. The legislation, which had been proposed by Berri, the National Assembly President and leader of Amal, was intended to give full employment to protesting workers. The FPM rejected the legislation for both legal and sectarian reasons, with the main concern that, as most of the workers were Muslims, it would exacerbate an already deficient balance in Lebanese public institutions in favour of Muslims. Amid this crisis, Hezbollah aimed to bridge the differences between its two main allies. While the FPM resumed participation in the Government, it subsequently resorted to public demonstration against Berri's actions. Christian forces of the March 14 Alliance joined with the FPM in opposition to Berri's proposed law.

Although major tensions existed between both allies and different factions of the ruling coalition, most parties agreed that the Government should be preserved. For Hezbollah and others, the Lebanese Government had at least kept some order in a particularly unstable time and region. The opposition, headed by the March 14 Alliance and in the absence of its leader, Saad Hariri (who left Lebanon after the collapse of his administration), had aimed to weaken the Government, but implicitly accepted the security-preserving purposes it now served, at least until the outcome of the Syrian crisis became clearer.

DEMONSTRATIONS AND STATE WEAKNESS

Mistrust in public institutions, especially the judiciary and the military and security agencies, which political rivals accused one another of politicizing and influencing, also exacerbated the general agitation. In May 2012 a Sunni cleric and another man (both of whom were supporters of the March 14 Alliance and who had been accused of supporting the Syrian uprising) were shot dead by army troops at a checkpoint in north Lebanon. The incident, which led to widespread demonstrations and violence in Sunni areas of Lebanon, increased the divisions. The March 14 Alliance demanded that the officers be placed on trial, while the FPM opposed their prosecution as it would weaken the morale of the army and incapacitate its ability to restrain the growing violence in the military. In opposition to protests in the north, the FPM organized a campaign of demonstrations in support of the army in Lebanon.

THE SYRIAN CIVIL WAR AND LEBANON

By mid-2012 it had become clear that the Syrian revolt, which started as a civil uprising against the Assad regime, had degenerated into a civil war. Syria was divided between the

Syrian army and its paramilitary forces on the one hand and the FSA and Islamist armed organizations on the other hand. Just as the Syrian war polarized regional and international forces, it threatened to have the same effect on Lebanon.

Islamist Lebanese groups began to talk about an 'Islamic spring' in the region. Salafist groups in Tripoli and Sidon protested against the Syrian regime and campaigned for support of the Syrian rebels. The March 14 Alliance, led by Hariri's Future Movement, initiated a media campaign against the Syrian regime and its Lebanese allies, particularly Hezbollah, which was accused of involvement in the Syrian civil war. The March 8 Alliance, on the other hand, continued to express support for the Assad regime. In the midst of these opposing stances, the Lebanese Government continued formally to pursue a policy of 'disassociation'.

A major turning point occurred, however, when Hezbollah publicly acknowledged its involvement in the Syrian war. In September 2012, when Nasrallah was asked if his organization was involved in the Syrian war he answered that 'until now' the movement had not participated in the war. However, in June 2013, Nasrallah admitted his group's involvement. During the intervening period between these two statements the media had recorded the return of the bodies of militants killed in Syria, but prior to this point Hezbollah had denied any involvement.

Hezbollah justified its involvement in the Syrian civil war on three levels. First, it argued that Hezbollah militants were in Syria to protect religious shrines, such as the Sayyida Zainab Mosque in Damascus, against potential attacks by Salafist groups. Second, Hezbollah justified its participation as a means to protect (Shi'a) Lebanese citizens who live in Syrian regions close to the Lebanese border. Lastly, Hezbollah argued that it was involved in a 'pre-emptive' war against Islamist terrorist groups, who might, if successful in Syria, turn against the Shi'a and Christian populations in Lebanon.

With the direct military assistance of Hezbollah, in June 2013 the Syrian army captured the strategic city of Qusayr, which links Damascus to the Syrian coast, where the vast majority of Alawite supporters of the regime live. The capture of the city (during which it was estimated that more than 200 Hezbollah militants were killed) prevented the isolation of the regime in Damascus and provided Hezbollah with a 'protection belt' across the Lebanese–Syrian border, effectively severing any links between Syrian Islamists and their brethren in Lebanon. Furthermore, control of Qusayr provided a springboard for military control of northern areas, such as Homs.

For Hezbollah's Lebanese adversaries, the group's participation in the Syrian conflict was held up as proof that Hezbollah's behaviour is dictated by Iran rather than by Lebanese interests. Accordingly, many, including Lebanese President Michel Suleiman, opposed Hezbollah's involvement and demanded that the group limit its military activities to resistance against Israel. In response, Hezbollah insisted that its involvement in Syria was to protect the furtherance of its fight against Israel.

Following the seizure of Qusayr, Saudi Arabia and Egypt (under the presidency of Muhammad Mursi of the Muslim Brotherhood), Turkey, and the USA all condemned Hezbollah's involvement in Syria. Furthermore, the member states of the Cooperation Council for the Arab States of the Gulf (Gulf Cooperation Council—GCC, see p. 1348) announced their intention to expel Hezbollah members from their territory.

Another major spillover from the Syrian war was the flow of refugees into the country. By September 2013 the Office of the UN High Commissioner for Refugees had registered more than 654,000 Syrian refugees in Lebanon. However, the Lebanese Government believed that the actual numbers were much higher, estimating that a total of around 1m. Syrians were living in Lebanon at March of that year. This situation, among other things, exacerbated the already difficult economic conditions prevailing in Lebanon. In July the Lebanese Minister of the Interior and Municipalities, requested financial help from external donors and the UN to cope with the rising numbers of Syrian refugees, emphasizing that the refugees would aggravate Lebanon's already foundering social, economic and security situation.

POLITICAL AND SECURITY INSTABILITY

The Syrian crisis has weakened Lebanon's fragile political situation. Since the uprising erupted in Syria, the pro-Syrian regime Alawites of the Jabal Mohsen district of Tripoli have been in intermittent conflict against the pro-opposition Islamist Sunni residents of the city's Bab al-Tibbanneh district. The Government and several political figures in Tripoli have failed to bring the hostilities to an end. In one particularly violent episode in May 2013, 10 people were killed and more than 70 injured after one night of sectarian violence.

In October 2012 Brig.-Gen. Wissam al-Hassan, chief of the Intelligence Bureau of the Internal Security Forces (a security organ dominated by the Future Movement) was assassinated in Achrafieh, a Christian area of Beirut. The huge car bomb killed seven others and injured 78. The March 14 Alliance accused the Syrians of killing al-Hassan, while others attributed blame to Hezbollah. It was claimed by some that al-Hassan had been targeted owing to his role in the unveiling of a Syrian plot to aggravate the security situation in Tripoli. (Michel Samaha, a Lebanese politician with close links to the Syrian regime, was arrested in August on charges of planning attacks in northern Lebanon and of transferring explosives from Syria.) Others claimed that al-Hassan had been targeted as a result of his alleged involvement in supporting the Syrian rebels.

Whatever the case, the killing of al-Hassan undermined the standing of the March 14 Alliance, especially its Sunni constituency, as well as trust in the state and other security organs. Many Lebanese Sunnis feared that Hezbollah's aim was to control the Lebanese state. Ahmed al-Assir, a Sunni cleric, based in the southern city of Sidon, publicly held forth this view. He also accused Hezbollah of being part of an Iranian plot to control Lebanon, of seeking to support the Syrian regime against the vast majority of (Sunni) Syrians, and of aiming to isolate Lebanon's Sunni population. Al-Assir demanded that Hezbollah surrender its weapons. He accused Sunni figures, especially Saad Hariri, who had been away from Lebanon since the Syrian uprising began, of failing to rein in Hezbollah. Al-Assir aimed to mobilize Sunni forces. As part of his protest, the Sunni cleric organized the blockade of roads, notably the strategic roads from Beirut to the south of the country, and demanded that Hezbollah and its allies close their offices in Sidon. Hezbollah, on the other hand, did not react to al-Assir's provocations, preferring to keep the army and other security bodies as a shield between itself and al-Assir. In June 2013 armed supporters of al-Assir made the fatal mistake of attacking an army checkpoint in Sidon; al-Assir had previously accused the Lebanese army of surrendering to Hezbollah's political interests. The subsequent death of 10 soldiers prompted the army to retaliate against al-Assir and his armed group. Following two days of fighting, during which another 16 Lebanese soldiers were killed, al-Assir fled into hiding. The March 14 Alliance condemned al-Assir's attack on the army, while also accusing Hezbollah of aiding the army in its attack on al-Assir's premises.

The assassination of al-Hassan and the defeat of al-Assir aggravated the Sunni–Shi'a division in Lebanon. In the Beqa'a region, intermittent clashes took place between Shi'a and Sunni villages (especially Irsal). In the Hermel region, Syrian rebels fired missiles on Shi'a-populated villages, while Syrian warplanes also targeted villages for allegedly supporting the rebels. In August 2013 Syrian warplanes bombed areas on the Lebanese–Syrian border, killing nine in the Syrian town of Yabroud. In other instances, several convoys—believed to be for Hezbollah and on their way to Syria—were targeted in the Beqa'a region.

In May 2013 missiles were fired on Chiah, an area populated by Shi'a Muslims and controlled by Hezbollah and its Shi'a partner Amal. The attack came one day after Nasrallah publicly justified his party's involvement in Syria. Threats made by the Syrian opposition to target Hezbollah targets in Lebanon increased after the declaration of Hezbollah's military involvement in Syria. As a result, Hezbollah introduced heightened security measures in the southern suburbs of Beirut, where it has a strong influence. In July, however, a bomb exploded in the heart of Hezbollah's stronghold in the city, causing many injuries but no deaths. Hezbollah accused Israel and its 'allies' in the region of orchestrating the attack, but claimed that such action would not lead it to change its policy. Although the March 14 Alliance condemned the attack, its members continued to hold Hezbollah responsible for drawing Lebanon into the Syrian war.

In August 2013 gunmen ambushed a bus in Beirut and kidnapped two of its passengers, both of whom were Turkish citizens. The kidnappers demanded that the Turkish authorities employ their influence to free the nine remaining (Shi'a) Lebanese pilgrims who were still being held hostage in Syria (see Lebanon and the Syria Crisis). The families of the Lebanese hostages denied responsibility for the abduction of the Turks, but welcomed the kidnapping as a potential route towards freeing their family members.

POLITICAL DIVISIONS AND INSTITUTIONAL PARALYSIS

The political polarization in Lebanon paralysed the country's political institutions. The crisis in Syria led to varying reactions from the Government. While publicly maintaining a policy of 'disassociation', the actual views of its various members reflected the divisions within Lebanon. Although the March 8 Alliance (including Minister of Foreign Affairs and Emigrants Adnan Mansour) and the FPM sided with the Syrian regime, Joumblatt expressed clear opposition to Assad. Prime Minister Miqati, on the other hand, upheld a neutral stance.

At a domestic level, the FPM's agenda of political and economic reform clashed with Amal's hesitancy about political change. The FPM also disagreed with its close ally Hezbollah over priorities. Whilst Hezbollah prioritized its war with Israel and its involvement in Syria, the FPM wished to focus on internal affairs. Hezbollah's aim of maintaining a minimum level of stability in Lebanon and of avoiding any major disagreements with its main Shi'a partner, Amal, and with Joumblatt, clashed with the FPM's aims to initiate political and economic change—particularly to boost the numbers and status of the Christians in the state, both of which had decreased since 1992.

In the face of the vast opposition to the Government—especially given the fact that many Sunnis questioned the administration's very legitimacy—its capacity to resolve security and political questions was considerably weakened. In the absence of political support from the Sunni community, the Government failed to curb the violent clashes in Tripoli or, at least until the army intervened, to stop al-Assir from blocking roads and occupying public places. Accordingly, public trust in the state diminished. This was vividly illustrated in July 2013, when Minister of the Interior and Municipalities Marwan Charbel was physically attacked by angry local residents as he visited the scene of a bomb explosion in Beirut's southern suburb of Dahiyeh. The kidnapping of the Turkish pilots in the following month also reflected the absence of trust in the Government—and the state as a whole—for their failure to help in the release of the Lebanese pilgrims being held hostage in Syria.

Following months of political deadlock caused by disagreements between the March 8 Alliance and the March 14 Alliance and divisions within the Government regarding amendments to the electoral law (with each block attempting to introduce changes that would give them a majority in the future parliament), Prime Minister Miqati tendered his resignation on 22 March 2013. The apparent trigger for this decision came when Miqati failed to convince the March 8 Alliance and the FPM to extend the tenure of the General Director of Lebanon's Internal Security Forces, Ashraf Rifi, who had close ties with the Future Movement. Some believed, however, that Miqati's resignation could have had deeper causes. Under Saudi and Western pressure, and against the background of growing condemnation of Hezbollah's involvement in Syria, Miqati might have felt that it was time to stand down. Domestic pressure, particularly from his own Sunni constituency, which portrayed Miqati as a Hezbollah premier, had increased following the assassination of al-Hassan in October 2012.

On 6 April 2013 Tammam Salam, a Beiruti legislator and son of former Prime Minister Saeb Salam, was named as Prime Minister-designate, having comfortably won a vote of confidence in the National Assembly the previous day. Salam was selected to form a 'national interest' government, to reconcile the deep divisions in Lebanon, and to insulate the country from the war in Syria. However, by September Salam had still not been able to form a government. Although the March 8 Alliance had nominated Salam, it regarded him as being overly close to Saudi Arabia and the West. Conversely, the March 14 Alliance believed that Salam was its nominee and, together with Saudi Arabia, it hoped that a government under his leadership would weaken Hezbollah and limit Iran's influence in the country.

The Future Movement refused Hezbollah's further participation in government, arguing that a non-political/technocratic government would be better for Lebanon; furthermore, they argued that the Lebanese Government should not provide any legitimacy for Hezbollah's involvement in the Syrian war. Hezbollah and its allies, on the other hand, asserted that Lebanon needed a national unity government that represented all factions in accordance with their parliamentary representation. Participating in government had become a priority for Hezbollah since the Syrian withdrawal from Lebanon in 2005; it became even more crucial after the EU designated Hezbollah's 'military wing' as 'terrorist' in July 2013. Hezbollah refuted the designation, arguing that the movement had no separate political and military branches.

As a sign of its exasperation with the political and security situation in Lebanon, and in the absence of agreement on a new electoral law and a government to oversee the electoral process, the Lebanese parliament agreed to postpone the elections, which were scheduled to be held in June 2013, until November 2014.

In July 2013, in a further indication of the increasing political turmoil within Lebanon, the Minister of National Defence, Faviz Ghosn, unilaterally extended the tenure of the Commander-in Chief of the Army, Gen. Jean Kahwaji, for two years to prevent the emergence of a power vacuum at the head of the armed forces. Ghosn made this decision after political infighting led to failure to agree on whether parliament should convene to extend the mandate of the military chief (as would take place under normal circumstances). The refusal of the FPM's Gen. Aoun to recognize the extension of Gen. Kahwaji's term prompted Berri to announce the collapse of the March 8 Alliance in the arena of internal issues. Berri stressed, however, that with regard to strategic and external issues the Alliance remained intact.

Economy

Revised for this edition by RICHARD GERMAN and ELIZABETH TAYLOR

INTRODUCTION

Lebanon's prosperity and position as the Middle East's leading centre for trade and financial services were blighted by the civil war that erupted in 1975 and the ensuing regional political and military ramifications. Prospects of an economic revival were raised after the war ended in 1990, paving the way for sustained reconstruction based on foreign aid. Lebanon then experienced levels of annual gross domestic product (GDP) growth averaging 6.5%, in real terms, before further destabilizing Israeli military action in 1996 contributed to a decline in inward investment. In recession, the economy contracted by 1% in 1999 and by 0.5% in 2000. GDP began to recover in 2002, increasing by almost 3%, then by 5% in 2003 and 6% in 2004. The growth rate then declined, to an estimated 1%, in 2005, reflecting political tensions prompted by the assassination in February of former Prime Minister Rafiq Hariri. Economic progress was further impeded in the wake of the disruption wrought by the Israeli military offensive against Hezbollah in July–August 2006, which resulted in a contraction of GDP. In 2007 growth recovered strongly to 7.5%, according to the IMF. However, an ambitious economic reform programme, presented to the Paris III donor conference in January of that year, was hampered by continuing security incidents and a political stalemate that paralysed legislative activity until the election in May 2008 of a new President and an agreement reached between the rival factions to form a national unity government. This Government oversaw further impressive GDP growth in 2008, estimated officially at 9.3%, as the financial sector was largely insulated from the global financial crisis, which unfolded in the second half of that year. Further political uncertainty followed the June 2009 parliamentary elections until a new national unity Government, including members of the Western-backed March 14 Alliance and the opposition March 8 Alliance, was eventually formed in November (see History). The economy nevertheless continued to perform well, and this momentum—driven by construction, tourism, retail trade and financial services, despite the global downturn—was carried over into 2010. However, political turbulence in 2011 again cast a shadow over the economic outlook, as the national unity Government collapsed in January, prompting a five-month stalemate before the endorsement of a new administration. Political and sectarian unrest erupted across much of the Middle East and North Africa region during 2011, and the turmoil persisted into 2012, particularly in neighbouring Syria where the descent into civil war exacerbated the existing tensions in Lebanon. Further destabilization at home, which precipitated a government collapse in March 2013 (see History), compounded this uncertain political backdrop, which in turn had a dampening impact on Lebanon's economic performance and prospects for structural reform.

In December 1991, after the end of the civil war, the World Bank sponsored a meeting in Paris, France, of potential donors to Lebanon. Following the meeting, it was confirmed that up to US $700m. in concessionary loans and grants had been pledged for the 1992–94 period. There was a further increase in foreign aid following legislative elections in 1992 and the appointment of a new Government under Hariri, reflecting increased international confidence in Lebanon's stability. In 1993 the World Bank agreed a grant of $175m. for infrastructure reconstruction, but stressed the need for the Government to bring state finances, particularly the budget deficit, under control. Meanwhile, the Government drew up an emergency reconstruction plan, covering 1992–95, which was to form part of a longer-term development programme, Horizon 2000, encompassing transport, housing, sanitation and health care schemes. During 1993 and 1994 there was a further influx of development aid from governments and lending agencies, and private capital began to return on a large scale (the IMF having estimated in 1991 that between $10,000m. and $15,000m. was held abroad by expatriates). In early 1995, according to the Council for Development and Reconstruction (CDR—created in 1977 as the main co-ordinator of reconstruction efforts), the total contribution of funds by donors to the Lebanese economic recovery programme amounted to $1,900m., principally from the European Union (EU), the World Bank, Saudi Arabia, Kuwait, the Arab Fund for Economic and Social Development, and Italy.

The Israeli attack on southern Lebanon and the capital, Beirut, in April 1996 (which cost an estimated US $500m. in damage and disruption to business) and the election of a right-wing Government in Israel in May depressed investor confidence. After the cease-fire agreement between Hezbollah and Israel, Prime Minister Hariri announced that his Government needed to raise $5,000m. for reconstruction during the period 1997–2001. In December 1996, at a meeting in Washington, DC, USA, attended by representatives from around 30 countries and many international organizations, the Lebanese Government claimed to have received pledges of $3,200m. However, the unravelling of the Middle East peace process then jeopardized Lebanon's plans to re-establish Beirut as a regional services centre.

In an attempt to restructure Lebanon's public debt, and so reduce the cost of debt-servicing, some US $2,000m. was borrowed on international capital markets between mid-1998 and February 1999. The Government of Selim al-Hoss, which took office in December 1998, proposed further such borrowing in order to increase the proportion of public debt denominated in foreign currency. Al-Hoss also pledged to implement administrative reforms, to reduce the burdensome public sector payroll, counter corruption in public life and improve fiscal discipline. The elimination of monopolies was meanwhile identified as a priority, and the private sector promoted as having a fundamental role in job creation. In February 1999 the World Bank agreed to disburse some $600m. in concessionary loans over a three-year period for reconstruction projects and in budgetary support.

The withdrawal of Israeli troops from southern Lebanon in May 2000 raised hopes that reconstruction of the economy could progress in earnest. In July the Government approached donor nations for more than US $6,500m. in aid for development projects, some $1,300m. of which was to go towards rehabilitating the damage caused to the economy during 22 years of Israeli occupation. The reincorporation of former Israeli-controlled areas into the south meant that Lebanon was once again—at least in principle—a fully integrated political and economic entity. During 2000 there were positive signs of recovery—new motorways were under construction in the north and south of the country; the Investment Development Authority of Lebanon (established in 1994) began attracting funds for projects in southern Lebanon; many more franchise outlets for Western companies opened in the larger cities; cellular networks and other telecommunications systems seemed set to expand; inflation remained low; and a surplus was recorded on the balance of payments. However, political weakness and divisions within the al-Hoss Government prevented his administration from carrying out many of its pledges on the economy. Rafiq Hariri, who was reappointed Prime Minister in October 2000, committed his administration to reducing taxes, easing capital spending controls and promoting free trade, arguing that in the medium-to-long term such measures would lead to an increase in economic activity, higher revenues and greater stability. The Government quickly introduced an 'open skies' policy to encourage more foreign airlines to use Beirut's newly expanded international airport, proposed sweeping tariff reductions, pledged to reduce private companies' contributions to the state social security system by up to 10%, and highlighted the importance of proceeding with the long-delayed privatization programme to reduce the burden of unprofitable state companies and generate revenues to help lower public debt. While the local business community generally welcomed the new Government's strategy, some commentators expressed doubts about Lebanon's ability to re-establish its role as a leading business and services centre amid increasing regional competition, or to offset the enduring negative images stemming from the years of political instability and conflict.

At a meeting in Paris in February 2001 (subsequently known as the Paris I donor conference), the international financial community expressed support for the economic strategy of the Hariri Government. The meeting was attended by officials from the World Bank and the European Investment Bank, the French Minister of Economy and Finance, and the President of the European Commission, together with premier Hariri and his economy and finance ministers. Some €500m. (US $458m.) was allocated to Lebanon unconditionally through the EU's Mennonite Economic Development Associates programme (30% as a gift and the remainder as long-term loans at preferential rates). In addition to the meeting in Paris, Hariri also made visits to Iran, Saudi Arabia and other Gulf states, and Japan, in an effort to secure investment or aid. Kuwait subsequently agreed to double its deposit in the central bank to $200m. and Saudi Arabia agreed to extend its deposit of $500m. at the central bank for a further three years. These funds were used to support the Lebanese pound. In the early months of 2002 several Gulf states also announced loans on generous terms for infrastructure and development projects.

In December 2001 the National Assembly finally approved the law introducing a value-added tax (VAT), a central feature of Hariri's fiscal reform programme. VAT was set at 10%, and an estimated 10,000 companies with a turnover of more than £L500,000m. were required to register. Items exempt from the new tax included fresh foods, medical supplies and services, books and newspapers, public transport, and banking and financial services. The Ministry of Finance estimated that the new tax would generate £L750,000m. a year in extra revenue. At the same time the Government made further tariff reductions and Hariri introduced legislation to remove import monopolies, a move that provoked strong opposition from those companies affected and their political allies. In June 2002 Lebanon signed a Euro-Mediterranean Association Agreement and an interim accord with the EU, a development that, it was hoped, would lead to EU aid and technical assistance and an increase in private foreign investment.

At the Paris II donor conference in November 2002, donors agreed to finance US $4,300m. of Lebanon's debt, on the understanding that important economic reforms were carried through. While these commitments provided initial security for the Hariri Government against domestic criticism, the 2003 budget proposals provoked stiff opposition in parliament. The proposals included increased taxation, a reduction in public sector spending and more privatization. Although the budget was eventually approved largely unchanged despite bitter parliamentary debate, the Government resigned in April 2003. (However, Hariri subsequently formed a new administration.) The 2004 budget proposals similarly provoked opposition, prompting a general strike in October 2003, called by the Confédération Générale des Travailleurs du Liban (CGTL), over freezes in public sector salaries and fears about the welfare system. Moreover, there continued to be scant progress in the planned privatization of several major state-owned interests, notably Electricité du Liban (EDL), Middle East Airlines (MEA) and the telecommunications network.

The Lebanese authorities were generally considered to have dealt successfully with the upheaval surrounding Hariri's assassination in February 2005, preventing devastating effects on the economy. Nevertheless, GDP growth was estimated at only 1% in 2005. According to the IMF, the detrimental consequences of the assassination included significant deposit withdrawals and a sharp rise in dollarization, which caused international reserves to decrease by some US $2,000m. in the first quarter of 2005 as well as a decline in public and private demand. However, a resumption of deposit inflows and implementation of financial stabilization measures helped the economy to recover by mid-2005 as export growth remained steady.

In June 2005 Fouad Siniora, who had served as Minister of Finance in Hariri's administrations, was appointed Prime Minister, and pledged to revitalize the economic reform programme. In the same month it was reported that international donors were discussing the possibility of another conference to reschedule Lebanon's debt repayment in exchange for a comprehensive fiscal adjustment programme. Although scheduled to have taken place in mid-2006, the conference was delayed owing to political deadlock between the Government and opposition, and was further delayed by the Israeli military intervention in Lebanon in July–August, which caused severe damage to infrastructure, population displacement as well as casualties, and the disruption of economic activity.

Following the hostilities, an early recovery plan, in which US $940m. was pledged to Lebanon by a number of international bodies and aid organizations, was agreed at a meeting in Stockholm, Sweden, at the end of August 2006. The Paris III donor conference finally convened in January 2007 despite opposition attempts to derail the Government's proposed reform agenda. Prime Minister Siniora presented a medium-term structural and fiscal reform package to increase economic growth and reduce Lebanon's debt levels (gross public debt having reached 178% of GDP by the end of 2006). In turn, the Government secured up to $7,600m. in aid commitments from international donors. However, reflecting the ensuing political paralysis, disbursements were slower than expected (59% of pledges having been mobilized by the end of March 2008) and the Government was prevented from advancing urgent structural reforms. Nevertheless, there was an improvement in fiscal performance in 2007 as revenues increased and expenditure was contained, and from May 2008 there was a more constructive political atmosphere following the agreement in that month to form a national unity government. GDP growth in 2008 reached a record 9.3% (up from 7.5% in 2007), and prudent financial policies and strict oversight of the banking system strengthened the economy's ability to weather the onset of the global recession in the second half of the year. Despite further political stalemate in 2009, the economy remained buoyant, with GDP growth of 8.5% in that year. Nevertheless, underlying economic vulnerabilities and contentious policy issues remained—particularly fiscal reform (promised at the Paris III conference) to reduce the high public debt-to-GDP ratio, privatization of the telecommunications network, and restructuring of the loss-making and heavily state-subsidized electricity sector. Although further growth of about 7% was recorded in 2010, there was a marked slowdown in economic activity in most sectors in 2011; GDP increased by only about 1.5% in that year, according to the IMF, as the volatile domestic and regional political situation fuelled uncertainty and further undermined the prospects for structural economic reform. Amid Lebanon's mostly poor annual economic indicators during 2012, GDP growth in that year remained constant, at about 1.5%, according to the IMF, and a similar figure was projected for 2013. Government attention was increasingly focused on the unstable political climate and sectarian rivalry, although the central bank in January 2013 launched a $1,470m. stimulus programme, which was to provide cheap loans at capped interest rates in support of housing projects, small and medium-sized enterprises, energy conservation and research and development, in an effort to revive economic activity.

AGRICULTURE

Of the total area of the country, about 52% consists of mountain, swamp or desert, and a further 7% of forest. Up to 40% is considered cultivable. The coastal strip enjoys a Mediterranean climate and is exceedingly fertile, producing mainly olives, citrus fruits and bananas. Many of the steep valleys leading up from the coastal plain are terraced and very productive in olives and soft fruit. In the Zahleh and Shtaura regions there are vineyards, while cotton and onions are grown in the hinterland of Tripoli. The main cereal-growing district is the Beqa'a, the fertile valley between the Lebanon and the Anti-Lebanon ranges, to the north of which lies the source of the river Orontes. The Litani river also flows southwards through the Beqa'a before turning west near Marjayoun to flow into the Mediterranean just north of Tyre. This valley is particularly fertile and cotton is grown there. The agricultural sector's contribution to GDP declined during the civil war, owing to depopulation of the countryside and a reduction in public and private investment. By 2011 it accounted for about

6.3% of GDP, according to the Council for Development and Reconstruction (CDR).

In 2002 the Kuwait Fund for Arab Economic Development agreed a loan of US $65m. to the CDR to finance the first phase of the Litani River Authority Conveyor 800 project, utilizing water from the Litani River for agricultural and domestic purposes in the southern and eastern parts of the country. The project, which was originally conceived in the 1950s, would be carried out in four phases at a total cost of $260m., the aim being to construct a 56-km water transport system from Lake Qaraoun to supply 90 villages with drinking water and to irrigate 15,000 ha of agricultural land. In December 2010 the World Bank approved a $370m. project to supply water to the Greater Beirut area, and at the end of 2011 the CDR invited contractors to issue tenders for work to build a tunnel and pipeline for the scheme.

INDUSTRY AND ENERGY

With its lack of raw materials and dependency on imported petroleum, Lebanese industry has traditionally centred on small business activity. The civil war and Israeli invasions had a dramatic impact on the sector, particularly textile manufacturing. The Israeli occupation of southern Lebanon also posed serious problems for industrialists, who had to compete with a large influx of Israeli goods entering the country. This not only meant that local goods were competing with cheaper Israeli items, but it also led to problems between Lebanon and its Arab neighbours, which suspected that Israeli goods were being exported to them via Lebanon and imposed an embargo on some Lebanese products. Other factors that hampered industrial development through the 1980s were the shortage of skilled workers (owing to emigration to the Gulf), ageing machinery, and the weak and damaged infrastructure. Following the end of the fighting in 1991, the value of industrial exports began to recover, although the Hariri Government, upon taking office in 1992, was criticized for giving the industrial sector a low priority in its investment plans and for implementing monetary policies that prevented the expansion of industrial production. The GDP of the industrial sector (including manufacturing, construction and power) decreased by an estimated average of 0.8% per year in 1995–2004, although manufacturing GDP was estimated to have increased at an average annual rate of 1.3% over the same period.

Investment in construction had initially been the main engine of economic recovery after the end of the civil war as large amounts of public and private capital financed major infrastructure projects and numerous residential and commercial developments. However, the sector declined sharply from 1996, and by 1999 apartments and offices valued at US $8,000m. remained unsold. Moreover, in 2003 construction firms warned of further problems because of the Government's decision to close all quarries, as a result of long-running concerns about the environmental impact of illegal quarrying. Industrial and commercial infrastructure suffered considerable damage during Israeli air-strikes in July–August 2006. Nevertheless, the construction sector subsequently performed strongly, buoyed by development of the tourism industry, with continued growth throughout 2009 and 2010 despite the negative effects of the global economic downturn. However, in 2011 and 2012 there was a fall in construction permits and real-estate sales transactions, reflecting increasing concern over the threat posed to the security situation by the Syrian civil war.

Lebanon has been in the process of converting its electricity generating plants from oil to gas. To help meet the demand for gas, a pipeline to deliver supplies from Banias in Syria to the Deir al-Ammar-Beddawi power plant (near Tripoli) in northern Lebanon was completed in March 2005. Plans to construct a second gas pipeline extending to its Zahrani power station (near Sidon, in the south of the country) were suspended owing to the renewed conflict with Israel in July–August 2006. In April 2007 the Government signed an agreement with Egypt providing for the future supply of Egyptian gas by pipeline via Syria, and in October 2009 deliveries to the Deir al-Ammar-Beddawi plant began. In 2010 Israel discovered significant recoverable quantities of natural gas in an offshore field bordering Lebanese waters. The find prompted the Lebanese Government to sign survey agreements with Norwegian and French companies during 2011 and to approve draft legislation in January 2012 that provided for the establishment of a regulatory authority to oversee offshore exploration and production. In the wake of promising survey results, in April 2013 several major international energy companies, including ExxonMobil, Shell, Chevron and Total, submitted bids for exploration contracts in up to 10 offshore blocks. The caretaker Government officially launched the first licensing round in May, and in the following month the companies nominated the blocks for which they wished to bid. The first licence was expected to have been awarded by early 2014.

EDL, the state-owned public utility operated under the Ministry of Energy and Water and Ministry of Finance, controls most electricity generation, transmission and distribution. Lebanon's generating capacity in 1990 totalled 515 MW, with thermal stations accounting for 465 MW and hydroelectric plants for 50 MW. With the end of the civil war, and in order to satisfy the projected rise in demand through the 1990s, EDL outlined plans in 1991 for a series of projects to rehabilitate and expand existing power facilities and establish new ones. Construction of two 450-MW combined-cycle power stations at Zahrani and at Beddawi was completed in 1998, although by mid-1999 both had a capacity of only 200 MW, largely because of inadequate transmission. Another two 77-MW gas turbine stations had been completed at Tyre and Ba'albek in June 1996. The Government also began a US $300m. plan to expand and upgrade the electricity grid, including the construction of several substations linked to the four new power plants. Production by EDL increased by almost 50% in 1996, by 11.6% in 1997 and by 7.7% in 1998, although it was estimated at that time that significant power generation was being lost owing to outdated equipment and earlier damage to the network during the civil war. Generating capacity in 1998 totalled 2,315 MW, with thermal stations accounting for 1,886 MW, hydraulic plants for 226 MW and gas turbines for 163 MW. In June 1999 Israeli bombing again damaged Beirut's electricity infrastructure with attacks on two power stations at Bsalim and Jamhour. Other power stations were damaged in further raids in February and May 2000, and the network was unable to satisfy peak demand during the summer months. By October, however, the Jamhour power station had been restored, and in November ABB High Voltage Technologies was awarded a contract to repair damaged equipment and upgrade the Bsalim substation. Repairing such damage was a serious burden to EDL, which also faced the rising cost of fuel imports. In 2000 the company was unable to fund sufficient fuel imports to meet demand and as a result the country faced a growing number of power cuts.

EDL has been a major drain on state fiscal resources. A parliamentary report in early 2001 stated that the company received revenues for only 55% of electricity output—30% of output was used by consumers who failed to pay and 15% of power was lost in transmission. While the utility spent £L750,000m. annually on oil purchases alone, it received revenues from consumers of only £L600,000m. Higher tariffs and better collection rates were needed to make the company profitable. In March 2001 it was announced that BNP Paribas of France had been appointed financial adviser to the Government for a three-stage privatization of EDL. However, serious doubts were raised as to whether anyone would be interested in investing in a company with such chronic problems and requiring urgent reforms. Following the infrastructure damage resulting from the Israeli offensive in July–August 2006, the focus shifted to strengthening the capacity of the electricity sector and reducing company losses, with the involvement of private finance where feasible. EDL's financial problems nevertheless continued to mount in the wake of government paralysis and soaring international petroleum prices. In 2008 the Ministry of Finance made transfers amounting to US $1,612m. to the company to offset huge losses, re-emphasizing the urgent need for restructuring. The state subsidy to EDL decreased to $1,500m. in 2009 (representing an estimated 13% of total government expenditure) and $1,190m. in 2010, but frequent power shortages to consumers continued, underlining the need for substantial investment in new power plants. Subsequent domestic and regional political instability further delayed plans to restructure EDL, although the National Assembly approved a five-year $5,000m. investment programme in September 2011 intended to boost electricity generation. In April 2013 the caretaker Government signed a $470m. contract with Greek firm J&P-AVAX for the construction of a new 540-MW power plant at Deir al-Ammar. Also in early 2013 the Government concluded a $370m. three-year agreement with Turkish company Karadeniz Holding for the deployment to the Lebanese coast off Beirut of two power-generating ships, which were to be linked to the national grid in an effort to ease electricity shortages.

EXTERNAL TRADE AND BALANCE OF PAYMENTS

In February 1998 it was reported that Lebanon and Syria had agreed gradually to abolish customs tariffs, reducing them by 25% annually from 1999. In 1998 there was a trade deficit of US $6,344m. (exports $716m., imports $7,060m.), and for the first time in several years the overall balance of payments recorded a deficit, of $487m. In 1999 the trade deficit declined to $5,528m. (exports $679m., imports $6,206m.), but with net invisibles, transfers and capital flows of $6,249m., Lebanon recorded a surplus of $2,611m. on the balance of payments. In 2000 the trade deficit remained virtually unchanged at $5,510m. (exports rose to $718m. and imports to $6,228m.). Net transfers and capital flows, however, decreased to $5,231m. (down 16% on 1999) giving a deficit of $289m. on the balance of payments. In 2001 the trade deficit rose to $6,402m. (exports rose by 24% to $889m. and imports by 17% to $7,291m.). Figures from the central bank indicated that non-trade inflows rose by only 0.7%, to $5,268m., leaving a balance of payments deficit of $1,146m. As earnings from tourism increased during the year, analysts suggested that there had been a decline in net capital inflows. The trade deficit was recorded at $5,339m. (exports $1,045m., imports $6,445m.) in 2002. In 2003 Lebanon recorded a trade deficit of $5,644m. (exports $1,524m., imports $7,168m.). This increased to $7,650m. (exports $1,747m., imports $9,397m.) in 2004. In 2005 it recorded a marginal decline, to $7,640m. (exports $1,880m., imports $9,340m.), which then decreased further, to $7,116m., in 2006 (exports $2,282m., imports $9,398m.) before rising sharply again in 2007, to $8,999m. (exports $2,816m., imports $11,815m.) and to $12,658m. in 2008 (with exports totalling $3,500m., but record imports of $16,100m.). Export earnings remained stable at $3,484m. in 2009, while the cost of imports increased marginally, to $16,242m., resulting in a visible trade deficit of $12,758m. In 2010 the value of exports and imports increased to $4,253m. and $17,964m., respectively, enlarging the deficit to $13,711m. There were further substantial shortfalls in 2011 and 2012, as exports rose slightly to $4,265m. and $4,483m., respectively, but imports increased sharply again, to $20,158m. in 2011, before rising further to $21,280m. in 2012.

Despite the July–August 2006 war and the ensuing political tensions, the balance of payments recorded a surplus of US $2,794m. in 2006, and continued to register surpluses in 2007 and 2008, of $2,037m. and $3,462m., respectively. In 2009 the central bank reported a greatly increased surplus of $7,899m., indicating that combined inflows of services, transfers and capital totalled about $20,700m. However, the surplus declined sharply to $3,300m. in 2010, and a deficit of $2,000m. was recorded in 2011. The value of net capital inflows fell by about 18% in 2011, to $13,900m., as the regional turmoil undermined the Lebanese financial sector generally, and tourism revenue in particular. The balance of payments deficit narrowed in 2012, to $1,540m., as capital inflows increased, by 10%, to $15,300m.

During the 1990s the Government was negotiating trade agreements that committed Lebanon to reducing tariffs. Lebanon hoped to sign a full Association Agreement with the EU as part of a European initiative to establish a Euro-Mediterranean Economic Area; sought membership of the World Trade Organization (WTO); entered into a customs union with Syria; and joined an Arab free trade agreement. (Lebanon was a founder member of the WTO's predecessor, the General Agreement on Tariffs and Trade—GATT, but declined to join the WTO initially, owing to its opposition to Israel's membership.) In November 2000 Rafiq Hariri's Government reversed tariff increases imposed by the previous al-Hoss administration and proceeded to make sweeping reductions to the country's customs duties, abolishing some duties completely. Customs formalities at the main ports were to be streamlined and all non-tariff trade barriers removed as additional measures to promote free trade and an open economy. Further reductions were made to import tariff rates in early 2002.

After almost six years of negotiations, in January 2002 Lebanon finally signed an Association Agreement with the EU, which entered into force in 2006, and as a result of which all bilateral tariffs and quotas were to be eradicated over a 12-year transitional period. According to EU data, trade between Lebanon and the Union increased at an average annual rate of 13.6% between 2008 and 2012; in the latter year, the EU was Lebanon's principal trading partner, accounting for 32% of total Lebanese trade.

Negotiations concerning Lebanon's entry to the WTO commenced in 1999. However, despite its observer status, at mid-2013 Lebanon had yet to satisfy all the requirements for full membership of the organization.

CURRENCY, DEBT AND FINANCE

The importance of Beirut as the commercial and financial centre of the Middle East derived, in the 1950s and onwards, from the lack of restrictions on the free movement of goods and capital, and from the transference of the Middle Eastern headquarters of many foreign concerns from Cairo, the Egyptian capital, to Beirut after 1952. Its dominance was subsequently further strengthened by the massive increases in surplus oil revenue earned by the producing states, much of which was channelled through Lebanon.

The resistance of the Lebanese pound to the pressures of the civil conflict was chiefly due to the absence of restrictions on withdrawals or foreign exchange transactions, to an increase in the supply of foreign currencies to finance the conflict, and to the pound's strong gold backing and the flow of remittances safeguarding the balance of payments. Shortly before the war, in October 1974, the pound had reached a record high value, standing at £L2.22 against the US dollar. It lost just over 30% of this value during the war in 1975–76, but quickly recovered to £L3 after the cease-fire. Although the Lebanese pound declined in value in the two months following the beginning of the Israeli invasion in June 1982, from £L5 to the US dollar to £L5.20, it had strengthened to £L4.11 to the dollar by November. However, the rapid erosion of its value from late 1983 onwards was a considerable psychological blow. In July 1983 the exchange rate stood at US $1 = £L4.15; by June 1984 it had dropped below $1 = £L6, and by March 1985 it stood at $1 = £L20, at that time its lowest ever level.

By July 1986 the Lebanese pound had depreciated to US $1 = £L38, a decline of about 50% since the end of 1985. This included an official devaluation of the pound by 16.35% against the US dollar in March 1986. The exchange rate fell below $1 = £L100 for the first time in February 1987 and continued to decline, reaching $1 = £L455 at the end of 1987 and $1 = £L530 at the end of 1988, following the failure to elect a new President in September of that year. During much of 1989 the exchange rate was stable, at about $1 = £L510, despite the violence of Gen. Michel Aoun's 'war of liberation' against Syria. With Aoun's acceptance of the League of Arab States (Arab League) peace plan in September, however, the pound strengthened, to $1 = £L460, and it appreciated further, to $1 = £L410, after the approval of the Ta'if agreement on 23 October and the election of President René Mouawad.

By January 1990, following President Mouawad's assassination, the pound had declined again, to US $1 = £L544. The continuing political deadlock between eastern and western Beirut, the inter-Christian fighting in eastern Beirut, and the impact of the crisis in the Gulf region from August all caused further deterioration in the value of the Lebanese pound. In September the average rate of exchange was $1 = £L1,080. Following the defeat of Gen. Aoun in October, the reunification of Beirut and the disbandment of the militias, the pound gained in strength. In January and February 1991 the exchange rate averaged $1 = £L1,000, but by the end of the year it had strengthened to about $1 = £L880. On 19 February 1992, however, the central bank resolved to cease its currency support operations, prompting a dramatic slide in the pound's value. By 5 May the exchange rate was $1 = £L1,600. The central bank claimed that it had withdrawn its support because the currency had become overvalued. It was widely believed, however, that the real reason was the central bank's concern over the Government's inability to reduce its deficit. Rising tensions in the prelude to the legislative elections held in mid-1992, and the implications of the Maronite boycott of the polls, gave rise to a further decline in the value of Lebanon's currency. On 21 July the exchange rate was $1 = £L2,050, and on 7 September it was almost $1 = £L2,800.

Post-electoral stability and the establishment of the Government of Rafiq Hariri caused the Lebanese currency to strengthen, and in 1993 the exchange rate averaged US $1 = £L1,741. The average rate then appreciated to $1 = £L1,680 in 1994, $1 = £L1,621 in 1995 and $1 = £L1,571 in 1996. In early 1997 the central bank announced that it would intervene in the exchange rate only when there was a rise or fall of £L10 against the dollar. Since September 1999 the rate has officially been maintained at $1 = £L1,507.5.

Excluding gold, Lebanon's official reserves declined from US $1,903m. to $672m. in 1984. They recovered to $1,074m. at the end of 1985, owing to new import controls and a net inflow of capital, but decreased to $488m. at the end of 1986, as imports began to rise again, and totalled only $368m. at the end of 1987. The appreciation of the Lebanese pound prompted a recovery and by the end of 1988 reserves stood at $978m. They exceeded $1,000m. for most of the first three quarters of 1989, but by the end of the year they had declined to $938m. After further reductions in the value of the pound, the value of reserves was only $659.9m. by the end of 1990. During 1991 the stabilization of the exchange rate, the growth in exports and an influx of private funds from expatriate Lebanese combined to produce an increase in reserves to $1,276m. by the end of the year, and by the end of 1993 they had reached $1,900m. There were further increases to $5,932m. in 1996, $5,976m. in 1997, $6,556m. in 1998 and $7,776m. in 1999. According to the central bank, foreign exchange reserves totalled $5,748m. in 2000, before decreasing to $4,361m. in 2001. Reserves rose again in 2002, to $5,070m., and increased further to $10,197m. in 2003, before declining to $9,494m. in 2004. Reserves rose again to $9,845m. in 2005 and $10,207m. in 2006, fell to $9,778m. in 2007, but increased sharply to $17,062m. in 2008, $25,660m. in 2009, $30,600m. in 2010, $33,700m. in 2011 and $36,800m. in 2012. The bank has maintained a high level of reserves to compensate for any capital flight in response to political and security developments and to uphold the currency peg to the dollar.

In May 1984 Lebanon's public debt amounted to £L35,529m. (US $2,250m.). However, by the end of 1987 it had risen to £L194,100m., of which £L127,200m. represented outstanding treasury bills. The Government had borrowed heavily from the central bank and commercial banks in order to meet anticipated budget deficits. At 31 October 1989 the debt totalled £L755,000m., and by March 1992 it had reportedly reached £L2,800,000m. Net total debt at the end of 1993 reached £L4,993,900m. Debt-servicing became a heavy burden on state finances, with interest payments totalling £L784,000m. in 1993 and £L1,488,000m. in 1994. The public debt continued to increase, despite warnings from independent financial organizations, and reached £L16,238,700m. by the end of 1996, equivalent to about 79% of that year's GDP. By the end of 1998 it amounted to £L25,826,300m. In April 1998 the Government converted part of the debt into foreign currency by borrowing on the Eurodollar market, in order to reduce debt-servicing obligations. Of total public debt at the end of 1998, £L19,543,800m. (75.7%) was domestic debt. External debt increased from $1,304.6m. at the end of 1995 to $1,856.0m. at the end of 1996. It then rose to $2,431.8m. at the end of 1997 and reached $4,166.1m. at the end of 1998. According to official figures, interest payments in 1995 totalled £L1,875,204m. (£L1,744,518m. on domestic debt and £L130,686m. on foreign debt), accounting for 32.0% of all government budgetary expenditure. The central bank reported that interest payments in 1996 totalled £L2,692,930m. (£L2,507,950m. on domestic debt and £L184,980m. on foreign debt), accounting for 37.2% of all budgetary spending. Payments increased to £L3,380,000m. (36.9% of total expenditure) in 1997 and £L3,214,000m. (41.1% of total expenditure) in 1998. Almost all of Lebanon's domestic debt was in the form of treasury bills. During the early months of 1997 interest rates on treasury bills declined steadily and there was an increase in the proportion of longer-term bills, easing the pressure somewhat on repayments. The central bank was continuing to issue new treasury bills, but was concentrating on those with longer maturities in order to restructure the domestic debt and make it more manageable. By the end of 1998 the share of long-term bonds in domestic debt had risen to 78%, from 54% two years previously.

By the end of October 2000 the central bank reported that public debt had risen by 17% since October 1999, to £L33,800,000m. (US $22,400m.), equivalent to 135% of GDP—the highest figure in the Middle East with the exception of Iraq. Net domestic debt rose to £L24,100,000m. by October 2000, compared with £L20,600,000m. in October 1999, with the foreign currency component rising from $5,500m. to $6,400m. over the same period (as the Government sold additional debt on the Eurobond market). By the end of 2000 the foreign currency component accounted for almost 29% of the total public debt. In its budget for 2000 the Government stated that it would continue to replace domestic debt with less expensive foreign debt, but indicated that it would not allow the foreign component to exceed one-third of the total debt. Interest payments on public sector debt rose sharply in 1999 and 2000, becoming the major charge on government resources. Interest payments on public debt in 2000 were equivalent to 97% of total government revenue and 40% of total expenditure. Debt stocks continued to rise as the Hariri Government borrowed heavily to fund the fiscal shortfall. Total public debt rose to £L34,440,000m. ($26,160m.) by September 2001, when it represented 154% of estimated GDP. By the end of 2001 total net public debt had increased by 16% year-on-year and was equivalent to 165% of estimated GDP. Debt-servicing costs rose by 3% year-on-year to £L4,312,000m. in 2001, which was equivalent to 48.6% of total spending (the largest single item of expenditure) and 93% of total revenue. Debt service expenditure in the 2002 budget was projected to rise by 4.7% to £L4,500,000m., equivalent to 47.7% of total expenditure. The Ministry of Finance issued $3,100m. in Eurobonds in 2001 (mostly placed with the local banks), and in October 2002 another $4,000m. was raised through the sale to local banks of zero-coupon, two-year Eurobonds, equivalent to 10% of the banks' deposit rate (the banks hold approximately 60% of the Government's debt). By the end of September 2001 the proportion of public debt denominated in foreign currency had risen to 36%, exceeding the one-third limit decreed in 2000.

In April 2002 Standard & Poor's announced that it had lowered its long-term ratings on Lebanon from B to B–, reflecting mounting concern over levels of public debt and the Government's ability to implement fiscal reform. In September 2004 the IMF noted that the manageability of Lebanon's debt was vulnerable to periods of low growth in the economy and to rises in global interest rates. Moreover, according to preliminary estimates from the IMF, by 2005 public debt had risen to US $38,507m., while net domestic debt was $19,609m. The foreign component of the debt stock was $18,899m., equivalent to 49.1% of the total. In June 2005 the US ambassador to Lebanon informed the country that it should not expect any international economic assistance until UN Resolution No. 1559, which was adopted in September 2004 and which called for the disarming of all militias, was fully implemented. In the wake of the severe impact of the renewed hostilities with Israel on Lebanon's fiscal situation, the level of public debt reached $40,000m. by the end of 2006. A further donor conference—Paris III—was subsequently convened in January 2007, at which the Government pledged to implement comprehensive financial reform in return for further international aid totalling $7,600m. The reform programme was subsequently constrained by political deadlock, but there was nevertheless a modest improvement in the public finances during 2007. According to Ministry of Finance figures, public debt rose to about $42,000m. but its ratio to GDP declined to 171% (from 178% in 2006), while the overall fiscal deficit improved compared with the previous year. This prompted international ratings agency Moody's Investors Services to change the outlook on Lebanon's sovereign ratings from negative to stable in March 2008. By the end of 2008 public debt stood at about $47,000m. (although the ratio to GDP had declined to 162%), 45% of which was in the form of foreign currency Eurobond issues. In March 2009 the Government improved the structure of the debt by completing a swap of $1,900m. of Eurobonds that were due to mature during the year for new, longer-term issues that were purchased mainly by local banks. In April Moody's Investors Service consequently upgraded Lebanon's government bond rating to reflect the improvement in the country's external liquidity and the willingness of the banking system to finance fiscal deficits. By the end of 2009 public debt had reached an estimated $51,100m., but the ratio to GDP again declined, to 148%. A more positive political outlook following the formation of the national unity Government in November prompted both Moody's and Standard & Poor's to upgrade further their respective ratings for Lebanon. The Ministry of Finance meanwhile raised fresh funds on the international Eurobond market with a $500m. issue in December 2009 and a further issue of $1,200m. in March 2010. The growth of public debt slowed in 2010, increasing by 3% to $52,600m., and there was a substantial decline, to 137%, in the ratio to GDP. The Ministry of Finance returned to the Eurobond market in November 2010 with a new $725m. dual-tranche offering (which was more than three times over-subscribed) and launched a further $1,000m. Eurobond in May 2011. In 2011 public debt again rose only marginally, by 2%, to $53,600m. while the ratio to GDP maintained a downward path to 133% (although it remained among the highest in the world). In April 2012 the Ministry of Finance issued a further $950m. dual-tranche Eurobond (which was again heavily over-subscribed) to replace existing maturing bonds. Public debt increased by 7.6% in 2012 to reach $57,700m.

In late 1991 the central bank ordered commercial banks to increase their capital and reduce their 'hard' currency loan exposure by restricting lending to 55% of their 'hard' currency deposits by September 1992. The banks were also instructed to make extra capital provisions for their head offices and for each branch. At the same time, the central bank informed commercial banks that they would be able to revalue their fixed assets. Their nominal value had remained constant for several years and had been rendered virtually meaningless by inflation. New banking and investment legislation required all Lebanese banks to meet the Bank for International Settlements' capital asset ratio of 8% by February 1995.

In 1996 commercial banks announced record profits, in some cases 50% higher than in 1995, achieved largely through the purchase of treasury bills issued by the central bank. However, with Lebanon experiencing mounting public debt and decelerating economic growth (owing to low levels of investment), the central bank attempted to make the banks less dependent on treasury bills for their income and to encourage them to lend more. At 31 December 1998 the commercial banks had total deposits to the value of £L46,113,004m. held for customers, of which 34.5% were held in local currency. Loans to the private sector in local currency were worth only £L2,073,501m., a mere 11.1% of all loans. Most lending was in foreign currency. In the first half of 1997 the Association of Banks in Lebanon reduced the interest rate on the Lebanese pound from 24% to 16%, and the central bank abolished the regulation requiring banks to hold at least 40% of their local currency deposits in treasury bills. In April the central bank also attempted to reduce the high cost of credit by introducing a programme to subsidize short- and medium-term loans by commercial banks to the private sector for productive projects. Independent financial analysts, however, argued that interest rates were still too high, and doubts were expressed that banks would find new investment outlets. It was argued that Lebanon was unlikely to re-establish itself as a major financial centre while there were more than 70 commercial banks. By January 2003 25 bank mergers had taken place since the introduction of banking consolidation legislation a decade earlier, reducing to 60 the number of banks. In September it was reported that the country's leading 20 banks accounted for 80%–85% of total assets.

By the end of the 1990s the fact that Lebanese banks had subscribed to almost three-quarters of treasury bill debt denominated in both Lebanese pounds and foreign currency provoked unease at their high exposure to government debt. With declining interest rates on government treasury bills, the main commercial banks began to devote more attention to developing their retail banking services—introducing services such as internet banking—and by the end of 2000 the number of credit and debit cards issued by banks was reported to have increased significantly. At September 2004 the total assets of Lebanon's five largest commercial banks were estimated at US $35,200m.—some 60.5% of total bank assets in the country. By the end of 2008 the number of active commercial banks in Lebanon had decreased further, to 53, and they experienced strong growth and high earnings during that year owing to a revival of domestic economic activity. Banking sector assets reached $101,862m. at the end of 2008, having increased from $88,853m. in 2007 and $78,855m. in 2006. Established conservative lending practices and high levels of capitalization enabled the sector to withstand the global financial crisis that erupted in the second half of 2008. The results for 2009 of some of Lebanon's leading banks indicated strong capital inflows, with significant increases in both deposits and profits. By the end of that year Lebanese banks had been awarded licences to operate in a number of Arab and North African countries, including Algeria, Bahrain, Egypt, Iraq, Jordan, Oman, Qatar, Saudi Arabia, Syria and the United Arab Emirates (UAE). The banking sector continued to perform robustly, as total assets reached $128,920m. in 2010 and $140,600m. in 2011, while private sector deposits increased to $115,700m. in 2011, compared with $107,230m. in the previous year. Total assets increased to $151,900m. in 2012, while private sector deposits reached $125,000m.

The Beirut Stock Exchange (BSE) reopened in September 1995, and trading began in January 1996 when three construction materials companies were listed. In 1997 the major real estate company, Solidère, moved from the secondary market, increasing total capitalization from an estimated US $1,800m. to $2,600m. The addition of several banks brought the number of companies listed on the exchange to 12. However, interest in the bourse failed to develop and the number of companies listed remained low. Operating losses of $70,000 were reported in 1999, compared with a profit of $330,000 in 1998. Trading volumes in 1999 contracted by 60%, compared with 1998, with turnover declining by 72.6% to $90.54m. The situation was aggravated by a dispute with Solidère—the shares of which represented more than one-third of all those traded—over transactions arranged by the real estate company outside the BSE. Average daily trading for most of 2000 was below $300,000. Hopes were expressed that the economic reform programme announced by Prime Minister Hariri at the end of 2000 would help to stimulate the market, with progress on privatization resulting in new listings. A decision in September 2000 by the Union of Arab Bourses—an organization bringing together stock markets across the Arab world—to move its headquarters from Cairo to Beirut was also expected to provide a boost to activity on the BSE. The Beirut bourse resumed trading in early August 2006, following its closure for a two-week period during the conflict with Israel that began in July. The combined value of the securities listed on the exchange had risen to $10,380m. by the end of 2008. Total market capitalization reached $12,800m. at the end of 2009, although there was a modest decline in the volume of shares traded during that year. Having risen sharply in 2010, the total trading volume underwent a 53% fall in 2011, while market capitalization also decreased, to $10,300m., compared with $12,700m. in 2010. In August 2011 the National Assembly finally approved a capital market law, first proposed in 2006, providing for the creation of an independent authority to regulate and supervise the market. The total trading volume fell by 28% in 2012, although market capitalization rose marginally, to $10,400m.

INFLATION

Long before the civil war, inflationary pressures had been one of Lebanon's most serious economic problems, and the years of conflict removed all vestiges of price restraint. By 1986 inflation was well over 100%, increasing to around 200% by the end of 1987 (with many basic consumer items registering a 300% increase). Demonstrations against poverty and the continuing civil upheaval became more frequent. Despite falling reserves of foreign exchange, the Government was reluctant to reduce state subsidies on basic commodities (which cost about US $100m. per year) for fear of provoking greater unrest. However, in September 1987 the subsidy on petroleum was substantially reduced with the result that the price of petrol more than doubled. Declines in standards of living prompted the CGTL, the country's leading independent labour union, to call a five-day general strike in November that year, which was generally supported in an unprecedented display of national unity. During 1987, according to official estimates, the consumer price index rose by 420%.

In 1988–92 the fall in the value of the Lebanese pound gave rise to further price increases. In two months, from mid-February 1992, the value of the currency declined by 65%, causing the price of food and that of many other commodities to double. Strikes and street demonstrations followed, culminating in the resignation, in May, of the Government led by Omar Karami. During 1992 the inflation rate was estimated to have averaged 100%. The stabilization of the exchange rate in 1992–93 resulted in lower inflation. In 1993 prices rose by about 10%. According to the Beirut Chamber of Commerce, the annual rate of inflation averaged 6.8% in 1994, 9.4% in 1995 and 6.1% in 1996. In early 1997 the Government declared that, although it was determined to boost economic growth, it was also committed to maintaining annual inflation at less than 10%. The annual rate of inflation averaged 24.0% in 1990–98; however, the rate averaged only 2.1% in 1997. According to Banque Audi, by December 1998 the annual rate of inflation was 2.9%, and in 1999 the annual average rate declined to 2%. Consumer prices decreased by an average of 0.9% in 2000, but increased by 1.3% in 2001 and by 4.3% in 2002. Following inflationary pressures attributable to the July–August war, inflation reached 5.6% in 2006. It then rose significantly, to 9.3%, in 2007, reflecting the world increases in petroleum and other commodity prices, before decreasing (according to official figures) to 5.5% in 2008 and 3.4% in 2009. Average inflation rates of 4.6% and 3.1% were recorded in 2010 and 2011, respectively—within the central bank's target range of below 5%; however, the rate increased sharply, to 10.1%, in 2012.

TOURISM

Beirut's hotels, its port and airport, as well as Lebanon's largest non-government employer, MEA (Middle East Airlines), were all severely affected by the civil conflict, which erupted just as tourism was beginning to recover from the effects of the October 1973 war. As the civil conflict progressed, the prosperous hotel district in the centre of Beirut became the scene of some of the fiercest fighting. The contribution of tourism to gross national product, which was 20% before 1975, declined to 7.4% in 1977. The cost of further damage sustained by Beirut's hotels during the Israeli invasion in 1982 was estimated at £L400m.

The Ministry of Tourism reported a significant rise in investment in hotel construction from the beginning of 1994 to the middle of 1996, with total investment for that period reported at US $325m. A number of leading pre-war hotels were refurbished and expanded, and new hotels built. Although the number of tourists visiting Lebanon, mainly Lebanese living abroad, increased after the end of the civil war, by 1996 hoteliers still reported very low occupancy rates. The Israeli attacks on southern Lebanon and Beirut in April of that year exacerbated the problem of diminished tourism levels, and a marketing campaign was launched by the Ministry of Trade and Industry in February 1997 to attract tourists from the Gulf states. According to the Ministry of Tourism, the number of tourist arrivals (excluding Syrian nationals) in 1997 was 557,568. Figures published by the World Tourism Organization indicated that the number of arrivals had risen steadily to 741,648 by 2000. The 'open skies' policy announced by the Government in November that year and continued improvements in the country's tourist infrastructure were meanwhile expected to boost the recovery of the sector in the longer term.

Despite concerns that the regional impact of the Israel–Palestinian crisis would undermine the revival of Lebanese tourism, figures for 2001 suggested that foreign tourist arrivals (excluding Syrian nationals, Palestinians and students) rose by 12.9%, compared with 2000, to reach 837,100. In 2002 there were an estimated 956,500 tourist arrivals, rising to some 1,015,800 in 2003, when receipts totalled an estimated US $6,782m. In 2004 arrivals reached 1,278,500, although receipts declined to $5,931m. Of total arrivals in 2004, according to the World Tourism Organization, 40.7% were from countries of the Middle East and 26.4% were from Europe. Tourist arrivals declined from 2005, deterred by violence and political uncertainty, but the political agreement reached between the Lebanese Government and opposition in May 2008 prompted optimism in the sector. Arrivals increased from 1.0m. in 2007 to 1.3m. in 2008 and further to nearly 1.9m. in 2009. In 2010 arrivals rose by 17% to a record level of 2.2m., but then fell sharply to about 1.7m. in 2011, and further to 1.4m. in 2012, owing to the regional unrest.

In April 2003 the World Bank approved a US $31.5m. loan to the Lebanese Government's Cultural Heritage and Urban Development project for the redevelopment of historic sites in Ba'albek, Byblos, Saida, Tripoli and Tyre. It was hoped that the loan would help local communities to benefit from the tourist market, as well as to combat the spread of modern urban development around the sites.

In July 2007 the Lebanese Ministry of Tourism signed a co-operation accord with the Saudi Arabian authorities that focused on joint investment planning in the tourism sector, and also signed an agreement to establish the Arab Tourism Bank, to be based in the Saudi city of Jeddah but with several branches planned for the Arab region.

TRANSPORT AND COMMUNICATIONS

Having incurred financial losses from the mid-1970s with the onset of the civil war, MEA faced further crises through the 1980s as the Israeli invasion in 1982 and Gen. Aoun's military action in 1989 against the Syrian presence in Lebanon caused prolonged closures of Beirut airport. In 1987 MEA also suffered from a dispute over the privately developed Halat airport, sited in Christian-held territory to the north of Beirut and intended to enable Christians to travel to and from the country without having to enter Muslim-controlled western Beirut. MEA remained over-staffed and inefficient, experiencing a decline in passenger numbers and recording operational losses through the 1990s. The company was bitterly opposed to the 'open skies' policy announced by the Hariri Government in November 2000, removing many restrictions in order to encourage more foreign airlines to use Beirut's expanded international airport. MEA, which had previously enjoyed considerable protection from competition, claimed that it would lose its market share to lower-cost carriers and might be plunged into bankruptcy. In May 2001 the Cabinet announced plans to privatize the airline and lay off 40% of its staff, prompting airline employees at Beirut International Airport to stage a one-day strike in protest. By mid-2002, despite rumours of interest from Air France, no foreign company had come forward as a strategic partner. However, in that year the airline reported an operating profit of US $8m. This was believed to have provided a reason for the Government to postpone further the airline's privatization. In 2005 it was reported that a restructuring programme had boosted the company's performance, with profits of at least $35m. in 2004. However, significant company losses were recorded in 2006 as a result of the renewed conflict with Israel, and a share offering of up to 25% in MEA that was to have been launched on the BSE the following year was shelved. The proposal was subsequently revived in early 2010, with the Governor of the central bank reportedly preparing a timetable for the share flotation, but in September the bank announced that an initial public offering would be postponed.

In 1994 a joint venture, comprising the German company Hochtief and Athens-based Consolidated Contractors International Co, won an estimated US $490m. contract to expand Beirut International Airport. By 2000 some 35 airlines were using the airport, where a new $400m. terminal had been opened. By 2004 the airport was handling some 3.3m. passengers, though this remained well below its capacity of 6m. Prime Minister Rafiq Hariri claimed that his 'open skies' initiative would lead to a substantial increase in passenger numbers. Following Hariri's assassination in February 2005, the airport was renamed Beirut Rafiq Hariri International Airport in his honour in May. In July 2006 Israeli air-strikes on the airport's runways forced it to close for a short period while repairs to the damaged infrastructure were carried out in the following month. By 2011 annual passenger numbers had reached nearly 5.7m.

During the early 1970s Beirut port suffered substantial congestion, mainly owing to the volume of goods bound for Saudi Arabia, Kuwait and Iraq, where petroleum revenues had boosted development expenditure. Subsequent efforts to reconstruct and modernize the port were subject to frequent disruptions, owing to the civil conflict. With the reunification of Beirut after the siege of 1982, a temporary strengthening of government authority began to ease the problem of illegal ports, of which at least 17 had begun operating as a result of the war. These ports imposed tariffs that were only a fraction of those payable at the official ports, and the official ports, for their part, were seriously affected by smuggling. Of particular significance was the appropriation by the Lebanese army, in March 1983, of the notorious fifth basin of Beirut port, which had been a valuable source of revenue for right-wing Lebanese militias for a number of years. According to some sources, it had accounted for 90% of the country's illegal trade. Import duties and airport and seaport charges, which had formerly accounted for more than 45% of government revenues, contributed less than 15% in 1983. Tripoli port remained under the control of pro-Syrian militias or was the scene of fierce fighting between rival groups, while Israeli forces continued to occupy the ports of Sidon and Tyre in the south. Fighting between rival militias intensified, however, and, after the withdrawal from Beirut of the multinational peace-keeping force in March 1984, the Government was unable to impose its authority over the operation of the ports. A brief expansion of government control took place during 1984, after the formation of an administration that was more representative of the country's diverse factions. This helped to increase customs revenues from the ports, but the improvement was short-lived. In February 1989 Gen. Aoun, the head of Lebanon's 'Christian Government', ousted the Lebanese Forces militia from the fifth basin of Beirut port and then, acting in the name of state legitimacy, moved to close illegal militia ports in the Muslim parts of the country, imposing an aerial and maritime blockade. Several weeks of bitter Christian–Muslim battles followed, and, during Gen. Aoun's 'war of liberation' against Syrian forces, ports were a major target. After a two-year closure, Beirut port reopened on 15 March 1992.

In late 1980 the CDR recommended to the Government that the concession for a new port at Sidon should be granted to Sidon businessman (and later Prime Minister) Rafiq Hariri for 30 years, and that he should set up a joint company with the CDR, with capital of £L250m. It was a controversial decision, because British consultants who had earlier prepared plans for Beirut port had said that, in a politically unified Lebanon, only two ports, Beirut and Tripoli, were needed, and that, if the south must have a port, then Tyre, further south, would be more suitable than Sidon. In 1985, however, Hariri's Paris-based company, Oger International, invited bids for the construction of the first phase of a new port at Sidon. The problem of illegal ports seemed, finally, to have been solved in May 1991, when, in an assertion of its authority, the new Government of national reconciliation disbanded the country's militias, and units of the Lebanese army were deployed in the ports. In May 1998 it was reported that bids were expected to be invited for the development of a new port in Sidon, requiring total projected investment of US $400m. The project, to be implemented in four stages, involved land reclamation, dredging, and the construction of two breakwaters and two berths. By 1999 the estimated cost of the project had increased to $530m., with infrastructure expected to cost $300m., and superstructure—to be carried out on a build-operate-transfer (BOT) basis—estimated at $230m.

In 1998 the Government appointed the Dubai Ports Authority to run Beirut port under a 20-year contract in order to improve efficiency. Work on the first phase of a plan to expand the port began in 2009 and was expected to be completed by the end of 2013. A second phase of the expansion was expected to commence shortly thereafter. Upon completion, the expansion would provide for an increase in the container terminal's total capacity to 2.1m. 20-foot equivalent units (TEUs). An increase in traffic at Beirut port as a result of the Syrian civil war—with the violence preventing access to overland transportation links—prompted the drafting of fresh plans, announced in June 2013, to modernize and expand the port; the project was to focus on accelerating the rate at which containers could be cleared through the port.

In 1994 plans were announced for a US $500m. scheme to rebuild Lebanon's coastal railway. The 170-km line links Tyre and Sidon in the south with Beirut and Tripoli in the north. The southern section of the line ceased operating in 1948, during the first Arab–Israeli War. Services on the section from Beirut to Tripoli stopped at the start of the Lebanese civil war. An east–west railway line from Beirut to the Syrian border also ceased operating during the civil war, and work began in 2004 on a project to reconstruct a section of the line.

In April 1983 the Ministry of Posts and Telecommunications confirmed that it intended to establish an autonomous body to administer the country's telephone and telecommunications services, as recommended by the World Bank. The deterioration of the telecommunications system during the civil war led many businesses to turn to private satellite communications systems. In addition, international links were being maintained via cellular telephone systems operating through Cyprus, while private telephone systems were also in use for internal communications. In 1993 a major telecommunications rehabilitation project was launched, involving the replacement of existing exchanges and the installation of more than 1m. lines. As part of this project, Siemens of Germany won an estimated US $40m. contract to install 420,000 new lines in and around Beirut, while the French company Alcatel began installing telephone exchanges with 270,000 new lines in the Beirut and Tripoli areas. Sweden's Ericsson was appointed to repair telephone-switching systems in the south, the Beqa'a valley and parts of Mount Lebanon.

The use of mobile phones has increased markedly in Lebanon. In 1997 two local companies, France-Télécom Mobile Liban (FTML) and Libancell, signed contracts with Ericsson and Siemens, respectively, to expand their network capacity. International consultants who were called in to advise the Government in subsequent negotiations recommended the introduction of licence agreements and suggested allowing an international operator to bid for a third cellular licence. In 2001 the Rafiq Hariri Government cancelled the BOT contracts of both Cellis (FTML's cellular operator) and Libancell, in order to prepare for the issue of two new Global System for Mobile Communications (GSM) licences by the end of the year. However, the issue was delayed because of a dispute over the level of compensation owed to FTML and Libancell and the proportion of profits owed to the Government under the original contracts. In April 2002 it was suggested, pending a full audit, that the Government could expect to pay the two companies a total of US $322m. for terminating their licences. Cabinet ministers were divided over the proposed sale. Some favoured allowing FTML and Libancell to continue to operate the licences until new tenders were issued, while others demanded that the companies transfer their equipment to the Ministry of Telecommunications immediately. The sharp downturn in the global telecommunications industry suggested that the sale might prove difficult, and in August the Government agreed to postpone the sale of the licences until January 2003. In March 2004 it was announced that the GSM licences had been awarded to Mobile Telecommunications Company (MTC) of Kuwait and Detecon of Germany (operating under four-year contracts in partnership with the Lebanese Government rather than owning the licences, with the revenues paid by the companies to the state, fewer management fees and expenses).

In 2005 plans were announced for the creation of a Telecommunications Regulatory Authority (TRA) to oversee the privatization of the industry, and also for the implementation of 2002 legislation enabling the incorporation of OGERO (the national fixed-line operator) and two departments of the Ministry of Telecommunications into a single operator, Liban Télécom, which was supposed to be partially privatized within two years of its establishment by the sale of a 40% stake in the company. These plans, and the proposed privatization of the two GSM licences and creation of a third mobile network, were delayed by the disruption caused by the conflict with Israel in 2006 and the subsequent governmental stalemate in Lebanon. However, the TRA was finally established in February 2007, and prospects for a resumption of preparations for liberalization of the sector improved following the new political alignment agreed in May 2008. The Government nevertheless announced in December 2008 that it would not go ahead with the privatization process until after the parliamentary elections scheduled for mid-2009, and in January awarded Egypt's Orascom Telecom and Kuwait's Zain Group one-year contracts to manage the two state-owned mobile networks. The contracts were subsequently extended, and in October 2010 the Minister of Telecommunications stated that privatization would not take place before the completion of a capital investment programme in the telecommunications infrastructure.

BUDGET

Poor budgetary predictions and persistent fiscal shortfalls have long been a feature of the Lebanese economy. In some years there was an alarming discrepancy between the budget proposals and the actual course of economic events, largely as a result of the political turbulence in the country and shortfalls in customs revenues. From the mid-1970s and through the 1980s, losses of revenue from taxation and customs duties, caused by the inability of the Government to impose taxes and the proliferation of illegal ports, deprived it of valuable income. From the early 1990s the Government of Rafiq Hariri began to assert greater fiscal authority. Actual revenues in 1993 totalled £L1,800,000m., (82% higher than in 1992), customs duties accounted for £L662,000m. (twice the 1992 figure), and income tax receipts, at £L126,000m., were three times the level of the previous year. However, debt-servicing continued to be the biggest spending category in the annual budget.

Projected expenditure in the 2000 budget was £L9,124,000m., with revenues at £L5,389,000m., giving a deficit of £L3,735,000m. In practice, the deficit was £L5,900,000m., following a sharp increase in expenditure and a decline in revenues. The 2000 deficit was the largest ever recorded, equivalent to 56% of expenditure and almost 24% of GDP. There was speculation that the Hariri Government, which assumed office again in October 2000, had held revenue over to the 2001 fiscal year and made allocations for 2001 expenditure in 2000, in order to show the outgoing al-Hoss administration's economic performance in a more unfavourable light. Interest payments on public debt in 2000 were equivalent to 97% of total government revenue and 40% of total expenditure. Before leaving office, the al-Hoss Government approved the 2001 budget, which forecast expenditure of £L8,900,000m. and revenue of £L5,730,000m., giving a deficit of £L3,170,000m., equivalent to 35.6% of expenditure.

The new Hariri Government produced its own budget for 2001 in January, but it was not approved by the National Assembly until June. Revenues were projected to rise to £L4,900,000m., a 9.6% increase from 2000, with expenditure declining to £L9,975,000m., a 4% decrease from 2000, giving a target deficit of £L5,075,000m., down 13.5% from 2000, but equivalent to 50.9% of expenditure and 20.3% of GDP. Debt-servicing was projected at £L4,300,000m., 43.1% of total expenditure. Official figures revealed that actual spending during 2001 declined to £L9,900,000m. while revenues decreased to £L4,650,000m., giving a total deficit of £L5,250,000m. (11% lower than 2000 and slightly below the projected figure). Nevertheless, the fiscal deficit was one of the largest in the world, equivalent to 20.2% of estimated GDP and 53% of expenditure. Debt-servicing accounted for 93% of total revenue and almost one-half of all fiscal expenditure. Analysts suggested that the reductions in public spending achieved in 2001 would be difficult to sustain. However, the decline in customs revenue that resulted from reductions in customs duties was partly offset by a 5.5% increase in tax revenue. The budget for 2002 projected revenues at £L5,500,000m., 12% higher than the target for 2001, and expenditure at £L9,375,000m., 5% lower than the target for 2001, giving a deficit of £L3,875,000m. (equivalent to 41.3% of expenditure). While sharp reductions in public spending were the main factor in lowering the budget deficit in 2001, in 2002 the emphasis was on a sharp increase in revenue to improve fiscal performance, notably revenues from VAT introduced from February 2002. In the 2003 budget, the Government reduced expenditure to £L8,600,000m. (a decrease of 8.3% from 2002) and increased revenue to £L6,475,000m. (an increase of 17.7% from 2002), leaving a proposed deficit of £L2,125,000m. (a decrease of 45% from 2002).

Expenditure in the 2004 budget totalled £L9,400,000m. and revenue £L6,400,000m., resulting in a budget deficit of £L3,000,000m. (an increase of 41.2% from 2003). Planned expenditure in 2005 was £L10,000,000m., while revenue was £L6,917,000m., leaving a deficit of £L3,083,000m. (an increase of 2.8% from 2004, representing 9.3% of GDP). As a result of the Paris III donor conference, the release of the 2007 draft budget was delayed until May of that year, but it anticipated revenues of £L7,675,000m. and expenditure of £L11,566,000m. (with notably higher military spending following the deployment of the Lebanese army in the south of the country after the conflict with Israel). The cost of debt-servicing remained the largest spending item in the budget. The 2008 budget proposal, presented to the National Assembly in November 2007, projected higher revenues, of £L8,368,000m., and lower expenditure, of £L11,465,000m. As a result, the budget deficit was forecast to decline from 11.3% of GDP to 8.2% and the total fiscal deficit to improve from 17% of GDP to 12%. In practice, the actual figures revealed that revenue in 2008 totalled £L10,553,000m. and expenditure reached £L14,957,000m.

The 2009 budget proposal, approved by the Cabinet in June of that year after months of political wrangling, forecast revenue of £L11,389,000m. and expenditure of £L16,304,000m., projecting a deficit of £L4,915,000m. Out-turn figures indicated that actual revenue for the year totalled £L12,705,000m. (the approximate 20% year-on-year increase being primarily attributable to higher tax revenues), while expenditure amounted to £L17,167,000m., resulting in a deficit of £L4,462,000m. Following the establishment of a new Government headed by Saad Hariri in November 2009, a draft budget for 2010 was prepared, which forecast revenue of £L12,880,000m. and expenditure of £L19,538,000m. The budget eventually secured cabinet approval in mid-June 2010, but the National Assembly failed to endorse it because of the prevailing political discord, which, as in previous years, undermined effective fiscal management. According to the Ministry of Finance, the actual out-turn figures for 2010 were slightly lower than those for the previous year, with revenue totalling £L12,684,000m. and expenditure £L17,047,000m., which narrowed the deficit to £L4,363,000m. A draft budget for 2011 was released by the Ministry of Finance in October 2010, which envisaged considerably higher revenue (£L15,100,100m.) but only a small rise in spending. However, given the collapse of the national unity Government in January 2011 and the delay until June in the formation of a new administration under Prime Minister Najib Miqati, no cabinet or parliamentary endorsement of the budget proposals was secured.

Actual revenue and expenditure for 2011 totalled £L13,352,773m. and £L16,022,347m., respectively, resulting in a reduced deficit of £L2,669,574m., which largely reflected the incorporation of previously withheld funds from the Ministry of Telecommunications. The ongoing political wrangling over Lebanon's public finances nevertheless continued in 2012. In October 2011 the new Minister of Finance announced draft budget proposals for the next year, including contentious VAT and other tax increases and an allocation of funding for the Special Tribunal for Lebanon (see History). Revenue was projected at £L15,500,000m. and expenditure at £L21,100,000m. However, the draft budget was rejected by the National Assembly in January 2012, with opposition March 14 Alliance deputies demanding expenditure revisions. Meanwhile, members of the March 8 Alliance pressed for a retroactive examination of state expenditure by the mainly March 14 administrations during 2006–11. The Minister of Finance subsequently issued a revised budget, which was designed to raise additional tax revenues; following a lengthy political impasse, the draft budget was finally approved by the Government in July 2012. The draft budget for 2013, initially presented to the Government in September 2012, was revised and resubmitted by the Minister of Finance in March 2013. Expenditure was forecast at about £L21,226,000m., with revenue projected at around £L16,000,000m. However, approval of the draft budget was likely to be delayed given the uncertain political and security conditions prevailing at mid-year.

Statistical Survey

Sources (unless otherwise stated): Central Administration for Statistics, Beirut; tel. (1) 373169; internet www.cas.gov.lb; Direction Générale des Douanes, Beirut.

Area and Population

AREA, POPULATION AND DENSITY

Area (sq km)	10,452*
Population (official estimate)	
15 November 1970†	
Males	1,080,015
Females	1,046,310
Total	2,126,325
Population (UN estimates at mid-year)‡	
2011	4,478,108
2012	4,647,077
2013	4,821,970
Density (per sq km) at mid-2013	461.3

* 4,036 sq miles.

† Figures are based on the results of a sample survey, excluding Palestinian refugees in camps. According to UNRWA, the total number of registered Palestinian refugees in Lebanon was around 441,000 at January 2013, although the actual resident number in refugee camps was estimated to be 240,000.

‡ Source: UN, *World Population Prospects: The 2012 Revision*.

2007 (official estimate): Total resident population 3,759,134 (males 1,857,659, females 1,901,475).

POPULATION BY AGE AND SEX
(UN estimates at mid-2013)

	Males	Females	Total
0–14	500,268	498,985	999,253
15–64	1,742,483	1,665,898	3,408,381
65 and over	207,405	206,931	414,336
Total	2,450,156	2,371,814	4,821,970

Source: UN, *World Population Prospects: The 2012 Revision*.

PRINCIPAL TOWNS
(population in 2003)*

Beirut (capital)	1,171,000	Jounieh	79,800
Tarabulus (Tripoli)	212,900	Zahle	76,600
Saida (Sidon)	149,000	Baabda	58,500
Sur (Tyre)	117,100	Ba'albak (Ba'albek)	29,800
Al-Nabatiyah al-Tahta (Nabatiyah)	89,400	Alayh	26,700

* Figures are rounded.

Source: Stefan Helders, *World Gazetteer* (internet www.world-gazetteer.com).

Mid-2011 (incl. suburbs, UN estimate): Beirut 2,022,350 (Source: UN, *World Urbanization Prospects: The 2011 Revision*).

BIRTHS, MARRIAGES AND DEATHS
(annual averages, UN estimates)

	1995–2000	2000–05	2005–10
Birth rate (per 1,000)	20.6	16.3	12.7
Death rate (per 1,000)	5.9	5.2	4.5

Source: UN, *World Population Prospects: The 2012 Revision*.

Live births (numbers registered, official estimates): 95,218 in 2010; 98,569 in 2011; 79,283 in 2012.

Marriages (numbers registered, official estimates): 41,758 in 2010; 42,500 in 2011; 32,577 in 2012.

Deaths (numbers registered, official estimates): 25,500 in 2010; 26,070 in 2011; 19,549 in 2012.

Life expectancy (years at birth): 72.6 (males 70.5; females 74.8) in 2011 (Source: World Bank, World Development Indicators database).

EMPLOYMENT
(ISIC major divisions)

	1975	1985*
Agriculture, hunting, forestry and fishing	147,724	103,400
Manufacturing	139,471	45,000
Electricity, gas and water	6,381	10,000
Construction	47,356	25,000
Trade, restaurants and hotels	129,716	78,000
Transport, storage and communications	45,529	20,500
Other services	227,921	171,000
Total	744,098	452,900

* Estimates.

1997 (provisional estimates at mid-year): Total employed 1,246,000; Unemployed 116,000; Total labour force 1,362,000.

2007 (household survey, persons aged 15 years and over): Total employed 1,033,572 (Agriculture and fishing 52,528, Unskilled 126,684, Skilled 188,168, Intermediate professions 108,051, Specialists 115,420, Office employees 84,269, Service sector workers and salespersons 131,950, General and corporate managers 132,761, Drivers 93,741). Note: Figures exclude members of the armed forces (84,224) and non-respondents (585).

Source: partly National Employment Office.

Mid-2013 ('000, estimates): Agriculture, etc. 24; Total labour force 1,611 (Source: FAO).

Health and Welfare

KEY INDICATORS

Total fertility rate (children per woman, 2011)	1.8
Under-5 mortality rate (per 1,000 live births, 2011)	9
HIV/AIDS (% of persons aged 15–49, 2011)	0.1
Physicians (per 1,000 head, 2009)	3.5
Hospital beds (per 1,000 head, 2009)	3.5
Health expenditure (2010): US $ per head (PPP)	872
Health expenditure (2010): % of GDP	6.2
Health expenditure (2010): public (% of total)	27.0
Access to sanitation (% of persons, 2011)	100
Total carbon dioxide emissions ('000 metric tons, 2009)	20,967.9
Carbon dioxide emissions per head (metric tons, 2009)	5.0
Human Development Index (2012): ranking	72
Human Development Index (2012): value	0.745

For sources and definitions, see explanatory note on p. vi.

Agriculture

PRINCIPAL CROPS
('000 metric tons)

	2009	2010*	2011*
Wheat	111	83†	90
Barley	30	24	24
Potatoes	425	260	275
Almonds, with shell*	34	28	40
Olives	87	90	91
Cabbages and other brassicas	49	50	46
Lettuce and chicory*	37	50	55
Tomatoes	195	310	315
Cauliflowers and broccoli	13	17	20
Pumpkins, squash and gourds*	31	26	25
Cucumbers and gherkins	87	163	170
Aubergines (Eggplants)	22	45	43
Onions, dry	87	90	91
Garlic	3	3	4
Beans, green	16	27	25
Carrots and turnips	6	4	4
Watermelons	53	74	70
Cantaloupes and other melons	14	21	22
Bananas	96	115	120
Oranges	177	130	110
Tangerines, mandarins, clementines and satsumas	31	28	23
Lemons and limes	121	85	80
Grapefruit and pomelos	17	8	7
Apples	138	140	150
Pears	36	22	20
Apricots	29	24	22
Sweet cherries	31	25	21
Peaches and nectarines	31	34	36
Plums and sloes	24	23	23
Strawberries	3	2	2
Grapes	108	90	89
Figs	6	9	9

* FAO estimates.
† Unofficial figure.

Aggregate production ('000 metric tons, may include official, semi-official or estimated data): Total cereals 147 in 2009, 113 in 2010, 121 in 2011; Total roots and tubers 426 in 2009, 261 in 2010, 276 in 2011; Total vegetables (incl. melons) 656 in 2009, 943 in 2010, 957 in 2011; Total fruits (excl. melons) 902 in 2009, 793 in 2010, 777 in 2011.

Source: FAO.

LIVESTOCK
('000 head, year ending September)

	2009	2010	2011*
Horses	4†	4†	4
Asses*	15	15	15
Mules*	5	5	5
Cattle	75	69	65
Pigs	8*	8	8
Sheep	372	265	255
Goats	430	404	400
Chickens*	37,500	37,000	38,000

* FAO estimate(s).
† Unofficial figure.

Source: FAO.

LIVESTOCK PRODUCTS
('000 metric tons)

	2009	2010	2011
Cattle meat*	67.7	69.3	68.6
Sheep meat*	13.4	9.5	10.5
Goat meat*	3.0	2.7	2.6
Pig meat*	0.8	0.8	0.8
Chicken meat*	129.9	129.2	131.0
Cows' milk	168.2	165.0*	165.0*
Sheep's milk	14.8	13.0*	13.0*
Goats' milk	21.7	32.0*	32.0*
Hen eggs	47.0†	47.0*	47.0*
Wool, greasy*	2.1	2.2	2.2

* FAO estimate(s).
† Unofficial figure.

Source: FAO.

Forestry

ROUNDWOOD REMOVALS
('000 cubic metres, excluding bark, FAO estimates)

	2009	2010	2011
Sawlogs, veneer logs and logs for sleepers*	7.2	7.2	7.2
Fuel wood	18.9	18.9	18.8
Total	26.1	26.0	26.0

* Assumed to be unchanged since 1992.

Source: FAO.

SAWNWOOD PRODUCTION
('000 cubic metres, including railway sleepers)

	1991	1992	1993
Total (all broadleaved)	10.9	9.1	9.1*

* FAO estimate.

1994–2011: Figures assumed to be unchanged from 1993 (FAO estimates).

Source: FAO.

Fishing

(metric tons, live weight)

	2004	2005	2006
Capture	3,866	3,798	3,811
Groupers and seabasses	245	250	252
Porgies and seabreams	365	370	371
Surmullets (Red mullets)	200	190	190
Barracudas	250	240	240
Mullets	360	365	360
Scorpionfishes	125	110	115
Carangids	400	380	383
Clupeoids	600	580	580
Tuna-like fishes	400	385	389
Mackerel-like fishes	300	320	322
Marine crustaceans	60	55	57
Aquaculture	790	803	803
Rainbow trout	700	708	708
Total catch	4,656	4,601	4,614

2007–11: Capture assumed to be unchanged from 2006 (FAO estimates).

Aquaculture (FAO estimates): 1,080 (Rainbow trout 1,000) in 2009; 1,180 (Rainbow trout 1,100) in 2010; 1,280 (Rainbow trout 1,200) in 2011.

Total catch (FAO estimates): 4,891 in 2009; 4,991 in 2010; 5,091 in 2011.

Source: FAO.

Mining

('000 metric tons, estimates)

	2009	2010	2011
Gypsum	100	105	105
Salt (unrefined)	20	20	20
Phosphoric acid	51	51	51

Source: US Geological Survey.

Industry

SELECTED PRODUCTS
('000 metric tons unless otherwise indicated)

	2009	2010	2011
Cigarettes (metric tons)	647.5	n.a.	454.0
Cement	4,897	5,227	5,550
Wine*	13	14	14
Electric energy (million kWh)	11,909	12,459	12,469

* FAO estimates (Source: FAO).

Flour and flour derivatives: 379 in 2007.

Bottled water and soda (million litres): 532 in 2008.

Electric energy (million kWh): 9,996 in 2012.

Finance

CURRENCY AND EXCHANGE RATES

Monetary Units:
100 piastres = 1 Lebanese pound (£L).

Sterling, Dollar and Euro Equivalents (31 May 2013):
£1 sterling = £L2,293.5;
US $1 = £L1,507.5;
€1 = £L1,960.7;
£L10,000 = £4.36 sterling = $6.63 = €5.10.

Exchange Rate: The official exchange rate has been maintained at US $1 = £L1,507.5 since September 1999.

BUDGET
(£L '000 million)

Revenue	2010	2011	2012
Tax revenue	9,976	9,885	10,187
Taxes on income, profits and capital gains	2,050	2,423	2,516
Taxes on property	1,088	1,144	1,193
Domestic taxes on goods and services	3,583	3,685	3,749
Taxes on international trade	2,802	2,179	2,251
Other taxes	453	454	478
Non-tax revenue	2,043	3,468	3,286
Income from public enterprises	1,382	2,679	2,530
Administrative fees and charges	535	570	587
Fines and confiscations	8	10	10
Other	118	208	159
Treasury revenue	666	718	691
Total	12,684	14,070	14,164

Expenditure	2010	2011	2012
Personnel costs	5,066	5,533	6,723
Salaries and wages	3,354	3,818	4,409
Interest payments and financial charges	5,893	5,655	5,457
Foreign debt principal repayment	324	379	295
Materials and supplies	277	329	305
External services	103	135	122
Various transfers	2,503	3,278	4,256
Acquisitions of land, buildings, for the construction of roads, ports, airports and water networks	1	1	18
Equipment	40	52	70
Construction in progress	467	402	486
Maintenance	129	186	180
Other expenditures (including unclassified and statistical discrepancy)	2,244	1,650	2,169
Total	17,047	17,600	20,081

Source: Ministry of Finance, Beirut.

INTERNATIONAL RESERVES
(US $ million at 31 December)

	2010	2011	2012
Gold (national valuation)	13,010.0	14,400.7	15,312.3
IMF special drawing rights	321.8	295.7	295.6
Reserve position in IMF	29.0	53.2	53.3
Foreign exchange	31,163.3	33,391.6	36,836.6
Total	44,524.1	48,141.2	52,497.8

Source: IMF, *International Financial Statistics*.

MONEY SUPPLY
(£L '000 million at 31 December)

	2010	2011	2012
Currency outside banks	2,712.9	2,891.0	3,213.2
Demand deposits at commercial banks	2,950.8	3,200.6	3,808.1
Total money (incl. others)	5,728.3	6,138.4	7,103.6

Source: IMF, *International Financial Statistics*.

COST OF LIVING
(Consumer Price Index for Beirut; December of each year; base: December 2007 = 100)

	2010	2011	2012
Food and non-alcoholic beverages	125.1	132.4	138.0
Alcoholic beverages and tobacco	108.6	121.0	131.1
Clothing and footwear	113.4	118.2	123.3
Water, electricity and gas	106.4	112.7	120.1
Housing	111.2	111.2	160.2
Health	103.9	107.2	106.9
Transport	124.6	121.3	124.1
All items (incl. others)	114.1	117.6	129.5

NATIONAL ACCOUNTS
(£L '000 million)

Expenditure on the Gross Domestic Product

	2008	2009	2010
Government final consumption expenditure	6,686	7,399	7,999
Private final consumption expenditure	38,018	41,215	44,672
Gross fixed capital formation } Changes in stocks }	13,810	18,114	18,986
Total domestic expenditure	58,514	66,728	71,657
Exports of goods and services	11,077	10,772	12,410
Less Imports of goods and services	24,244	25,265	28,102
GDP in purchasers' values	45,346	52,235	55,965

Gross Domestic Product by Economic Activity

	2007	2008	2009*
Agriculture, hunting, forestry and fishing	2,279	2,646	2,574
Manufacturing (including mining and quarrying)	3,325	3,545	3,947
Electricity, gas and water	–608	–1,341	–756
Construction	4,286	6,090	7,012
Wholesale and retail trade; repair of motor vehicles, motorcycles and personal and household goods	8,532	11,778	14,531
Hotels and restaurants	1,223	1,602	1,993
Transport, storage and communications	3,089	3,376	4,026
Financial intermediation	3,439	4,166	4,322
Real estate, renting and business activities	4,269	4,733	5,084
Government services	3,662	4,270	4,766
Education	3,509	3,837	4,105
Health	2,376	2,614	2,983
Other services	971	1,112	1,123
Sub-total	40,352	48,428	55,710
Less Financial intermediation services indirectly measured	2,579	3,084	3,061
GDP in purchasers' values	37,774	45,346	52,650

* Preliminary.

Note: Indirect taxes assumed to be distributed at origin.

2009 (revised figures): Agriculture, hunting, forestry and fishing 2,660; Manufacturing (including mining and quarrying) 3,982; Electricity, gas and water –867; Construction 7,018; Services 39,442 (Transport, storage and communications 3,426, Wholesale and retail trade and repair of motor vehicles, motorcycles and personal and household goods 14,658, Other market services 16,578, Government services 4,780); *GDP in purchasers' values* 52,235.

2010: Agriculture, hunting, forestry and fishing 2,650; Manufacturing (including mining and quarrying) 4,002; Electricity, gas and water –1,473; Construction 8,515; Services 42,271 (Transport, storage and communications 3,084, Wholesale and retail trade and repair of motor vehicles, motorcycles and personal and household goods 15,395, Other market services 18,721, Government services 5,071); *GDP in purchasers' values* 55,965.

Source: Presidency of the Council of Ministers, *Economic Accounts of Lebanon*.

BALANCE OF PAYMENTS
(US $ million)

	2009	2010	2011
Exports of goods	4,187.1	4,688.7	5,385.5
Imports of goods	–15,394.3	–17,187.8	–19,304.4
Balance on goods	–11,207.2	–12,499.0	–13,918.9
Exports of services	16,909.9	16,113.9	19,758.5
Imports of services	–14,042.7	–13,324.3	–12,989.4
Balance on goods and services	–8,340.0	–9,709.5	–7,149.7
Primary income received	2,040.2	1,448.1	1,615.9
Primary income paid	–2,268.3	–1,957.0	–1,200.6
Balance on goods, services and primary income	–8,568.1	–10,218.4	–6,734.4
Secondary income received	6,642.0	8,393.5	8,360.8
Secondary income paid	–4,814.9	–5,637.2	–5,789.7
Current balance	–6,740.9	–7,462.1	–4,163.3
Capital account (net)	18.0	267.9	165.0
Direct investment assets	–1,125.8	–486.7	–744.6
Direct investment liabilities	4,803.6	4,279.9	3,476.0
Portfolio investment assets	–825.9	–1,016.2	–687.9
Portfolio investment liabilities	2,690.5	–693.5	–1,141.4
Other investment assets	5,083.0	2,081.7	6,110.9
Other investment liabilities	8,075.0	388.6	3,924.2
Net errors and omissions	–3,042.1	5,699.8	–4,644.8
Reserves and related items	8,935.4	3,059.4	2,294.2

Source: IMF, *International Financial Statistics*.

External Trade

PRINCIPAL COMMODITIES
(£L '000 million)

Imports c.i.f.	2010	2011	2012
Live animals and animal products	1,306.0	1,307.6	1,243.0
Vegetable products	1,079.2	1,281.2	1,308.4
Prepared foodstuffs; beverages, spirits and vinegar; tobacco and manufactured substitutes	1,721.8	1,947.0	2,115.3
Mineral products	5,716.2	6,972.3	9,100.2
Products of chemical or allied industries	2,336.9	2,602.0	2,622.8
Plastics, rubber and articles thereof	966.2	1,062.1	1,148.7
Textiles and textile articles	1,059.8	1,060.0	1,133.5
Natural or cultured pearls, precious or semi-precious stones, precious metals and articles thereof; imitation jewellery; coin	1,747.8	3,229.2	2,390.4
Base metals and articles thereof	1,916.8	2,297.0	2,304.9
Machinery and mechanical appliances; electrical equipment; sound and television apparatus	3,271.3	3,212.1	3,126.1
Vehicles, aircraft, vessels and associated transport equipment	2,920.1	2,231.2	2,282.1
Total (incl. others)	27,089.5	30,398.7	32,090.0

Exports f.o.b.	2010	2011	2012
Vegetable products	232.4	242.2	258.2
Prepared foodstuffs; beverages, spirits and vinegar; tobacco and manufactured substitutes	488.9	572.8	591.4
Mineral products	84.1	52.3	198.7
Products of chemical or allied industries	467.5	578.6	516.5
Plastics, rubber and articles thereof	179.2	202.5	220.7
Paper and paperboard and articles thereof	356.7	326.6	274.8
Textiles and textile articles	162.5	194.7	175.6
Natural or cultured pearls, precious or semi-precious stones, precious metals and articles thereof; imitation jewellery; coin	1,671.9	2,250.3	2,600.5
Base metals and articles thereof	694.4	792.2	709.8
Machinery and mechanical appliances; electrical equipment; sound and television apparatus	1,118.6	782.9	721.3
Total (incl. others)	6,413.3	6,432.3	6,760.6

Source: Ministry of Finance, Lebanese Customs Administration, Beirut.

PRINCIPAL TRADING PARTNERS
(£L '000 million)

Imports c.i.f.	2010	2011	2012
Belgium	371.5	377.2	421.3
Brazil	402.7	459.3	455.5
China, People's Republic	2,470.0	2,449.1	2,672.6
Egypt	648.4	1,421.1	1,267.7
France	1,802.9	2,277.1	2,323.6
Germany	1,899.2	1,719.1	1,812.2
Italy	2,101.9	2,816.6	2,759.1
Japan	938.1	609.1	548.4
Korea, Republic	446.0	396.2	463.3
Kuwait	536.9	456.3	950.6
Netherlands	363.1	519.8	613.3
Romania	350.6	314.9	293.9
Russia	764.5	775.5	637.9
Saudi Arabia	613.2	801.7	638.8
Spain	462.9	510.2	642.4
Switzerland	843.0	1,499.1	765.7
Syria	511.8	467.7	401.4
Turkey	1,031.1	1,267.2	1,456.0
Ukraine	510.1	580.3	638.7
United Arab Emirates	557.4	896.0	627.8
United Kingdom	794.3	786.0	782.0
USA	2,878.8	3,001.2	3,582.3
Total (incl. others)	27,089.5	30,398.7	32,090.0

Exports f.o.b.	2010	2011	2012
Belgium	153.5	196.7	168.2
Egypt	303.1	102.0	132.9
France	524.3	86.5	90.0
Germany	73.7	68.2	52.0
Greece	49.9	41.8	44.2
Iran	60.3	19.9	7.5
Italy	46.2	55.4	55.3
Jordan	156.3	191.7	214.5
Korea, Republic	37.3	40.3	85.5
Kuwait	108.6	115.7	102.7
Netherlands	55.2	39.9	28.9
Nigeria	72.5	74.2	65.2
Qatar	124.7	120.4	128.9
Saudi Arabia	370.9	464.3	541.3
Spain	95.2	73.8	66.3
Switzerland	757.7	776.2	825.4
Syria	332.9	324.0	443.8
Turkey	347.7	416.2	237.0
United Arab Emirates	631.0	486.0	530.9
United Kingdom	73.4	92.2	67.3
USA	92.7	96.9	97.4
Total (incl. others)	6,413.3	6,432.3	6,760.6

Source: Ministry of Finance, Lebanese Customs Administration, Beirut.

Transport

ROAD TRAFFIC
(motor vehicles in use)

	1995	1996*	1997*
Passenger cars (incl. taxis)	1,197,521	1,217,000	1,299,398
Buses and coaches	5,514	5,640	6,833
Lorries and vans	79,222	81,000	85,242
Motorcycles and mopeds	53,317	54,450	61,471

* Estimates.

Source: IRF, *World Road Statistics*.

Passenger cars ('000, incl. taxis): 1,370.6 in 1999; 1,370.8 in 2000; 1,370.9 in 2001 (Source: UN, *Statistical Yearbook*).

SHIPPING

Flag Registered Fleet
(at 31 December)

	2010	2011	2012
Number of vessels	53	53	52
Total displacement ('000 grt)	136.4	146.4	151.8

Source: Lloyd's List Intelligence (www.lloydslistintelligence.com).

International Sea-borne Freight Traffic
('000 metric tons)

	2007	2008	2009
Goods loaded	891	841	669
Goods unloaded	4,426	4,906	5,641

CIVIL AVIATION
(traffic on scheduled services)

	2007	2008	2009
Kilometres flown (million)	27	29	30
Passengers carried ('000)	1,074	1,330	1,308
Passenger-km (million)	2,225	2,727	2,711
Total ton-km (million)	294	330	313

Source: UN, *Statistical Yearbook*.

2011: Passengers carried ('000) 2,000 (Source: World Bank, World Development Indicators database).

Tourism

FOREIGN TOURIST ARRIVALS
('000)*

Country of nationality	2008	2009	2010
Australia	40.9	62.1	58.2
Canada	66.8	87.1	88.0
Egypt	41.7	57.4	67.8
France	91.1	120.4	139.5
Germany	53.9	69.8	76.9
Iran	92.5	145.7	241.5
Iraq	72.8	101.6	129.8
Jordan	180.9	223.8	274.6
Kuwait	68.9	102.5	95.8
Philippines	28.0	39.4	41.2
Saudi Arabia	101.7	173.3	191.1
United Kingdom	38.1	50.0	60.2
USA	83.8	111.9	123.3
Total (incl. others)	1,332.5	1,844.1	2,168.0

* Figures exclude arrivals of Syrian nationals, Palestinians and students.

Total tourist arrivals ('000): 1,655 in 2011 (provisional).

Tourism receipts (US $ million, incl. passenger transport, unless otherwise indicated): 6,317 in 2008; 7,157 in 2009; 8,012 in 2010 (excl. passenger transport).

Source: World Tourism Organization.

Communications Media

	2010	2011	2012
Telephones ('000 main lines in use)	850.0	865.6	878.1
Mobile cellular telephones ('000 subscribers)	2,864.0	3,387.0	4,000.0
Broadband subscribers ('000)	198.0	210.0	500.0

Internet subscribers ('000): 468.5 in 2011.

Source: International Telecommunication Union.

Education

(2010/11 unless otherwise indicated)

	Institutions	Teachers	Students
Pre-primary	1,938*	10,144	154,168
Primary	2,160*	32,112	456,985
Secondary			
general	n.a.	31,365	326,777
vocational	275†	11,022	67,676
Higher	n.a.	26,025	216,851

* 1996/97 figure.

† 1994 figure.

Sources: UNESCO Institute for Statistics; Banque du Liban, *Annual Report*.

Pupil-teacher ratio (primary education, UNESCO estimates): 14.2 in 2010/11 (Source: UNESCO Institute for Statistics).

Adult literacy rate (UNESCO estimates): 89.6% (males 93.4%; females 86.0%) in 2007 (Source: UNESCO Institute for Statistics).

Directory

The Constitution

The Constitution was promulgated on 23 May 1926 and amended by the Constitutional Laws of 1927, 1929, 1943, 1947 and 1990.

According to the Constitution, the Republic of Lebanon is an independent and sovereign state, and no part of the territory may be alienated or ceded. Lebanon has no state religion. Arabic is the official language. Beirut is the capital.

All Lebanese are equal in the eyes of the law. Personal freedom and freedom of the press are guaranteed and protected. The religious communities are entitled to maintain their own schools, on condition that they conform to the general requirements relating to public instruction, as defined by the state. Dwellings are inviolable; rights of ownership are protected by law. Every Lebanese citizen over 21 is an elector and qualifies for the franchise.

LEGISLATIVE POWER

Legislative power is exercised by one house, the National Assembly, with 108 seats (raised, without amendment of the Constitution, to 128 in 1992), which are divided equally between Christians and Muslims. Members of the National Assembly must be over 25 years of age, in possession of their full political and civil rights, and literate. They are considered representative of the whole nation, and are not bound to follow directives from their constituencies. They can be suspended only by a two-thirds' majority of their fellow members. Secret ballot was introduced in a new election law of April 1960.

The National Assembly holds two sessions yearly, from the first Tuesday after 15 March to the end of May, and from the first Tuesday after 15 October to the end of the year. The normal term of the National Assembly is four years; general elections take place within 60 days before the end of this period. If the Assembly is dissolved before the end of its term, elections are held within three months of dissolution.

Voting in the Assembly is public—by acclamation, or by standing and sitting. A quorum of two-thirds and a majority vote is required for constitutional issues. The only exceptions to this occur when the Assembly becomes an electoral college, and chooses the President of the Republic or Secretaries to the National Assembly, or when the President is accused of treason or of violating the Constitution. In such cases voting is secret, and a two-thirds' majority is needed for a proposal to be adopted.

EXECUTIVE POWER

With the incorporation of the Ta'if agreement into the Lebanese Constitution in August 1990, executive power was effectively transferred from the presidency to the Cabinet. The President is elected for a term of six years and is not immediately re-eligible. He is responsible for the promulgation and execution of laws enacted by the National Assembly, but all presidential decisions (with the exception of those to appoint a Prime Minister or to accept the resignation of a government) require the co-signature of the Prime Minister, who is head of the Government, implementing its policies and speaking in its name. The President must receive the approval of the Cabinet before dismissing a minister or ratifying an international treaty. The ministers and the Prime Minister are chosen by the President of the Republic in consultation with the members and President of the National Assembly. They are not necessarily members of the National Assembly, although they are responsible to it and have access to its debates. The President of the Republic must be a Maronite Christian, and the Prime Minister a Sunni Muslim; the choice of the other ministers must reflect the level of representation of the communities in the Assembly.

Note: In October 1998 the National Assembly endorsed an exceptional amendment to Article 49 of the Constitution to enable the election of Gen. Emile Lahoud, then Commander-in-Chief of the Army, as President of the Republic: the Constitution requires that senior state officials relinquish their responsibilities two years prior to seeking public office. In September 2004 the National Assembly voted in favour of a constitutional amendment extending President Lahoud's term of office for a further three years.

The Government

HEAD OF STATE

President: Gen. MICHEL SULEIMAN (inaugurated 25 May 2008).

CABINET

(September 2013)

On 23 March 2013 the Prime Minister, Najib Miqati, tendered the resignation of his administration, citing disagreement among the constituent parties. The resignation followed the failure of the Government to agree the composition of a committee to supervise the conduct of legislative elections scheduled for June. President Michel Suleiman requested that Miqati remain in office until a new Cabinet could be formed. On 6 April Tammam Salam was appointed as Prime Minister-designate, having won a vote of confidence at the National Assembly the previous day. However, by September no progress had been made.

Prime Minister: NAJIB MIQATI.

Deputy Prime Minister: SAMIR MOQBEL.

Minister of the Interior and Municipalities: MARWAN CHARBEL.

Minister of Foreign Affairs and Emigrants: ADNAN MANSOUR.

Minister of Justice: SHAKIB QORTBAWI.

Minister of Industry: VREJ SABOUNJIAN.

Minister of Energy and Water: GEBRAN BASSIL.

Minister of Public Works and Transportation: GHAZI ARIDI.

Minister of Finance: MUHAMMAD SAFADI.

Minister of Economy and Trade: NICOLAS NAHHAS.

Minister of Education and Higher Education: HASSAN DIAB.

Minister of Culture: GABY LAYOUN.

Minister of Information: WALID AL-DAOUK.

Minister of Tourism: FADI ABBOUD.

Minister of Telecommunications: NICOLAS SEHNAWI.

Minister of Labour: SALIM JREISSATI.

Minister of Agriculture: HUSSEIN HAJJ HASSAN.

Minister of the Environment: Nazim al-Khoury.

Minister of National Defence: Fayiz Ghosn.

Minister of Public Health: Ali Hassan Khalil.

Minister of Social Affairs: Wael Abu Faour.

Minister of the Displaced: Alaa el-Din Terro.

Minister of Youth and Sports: Faisal Karami.

Minister of State for Administrative Reform: Muhammad Fneish.

Minister of State for Parliamentary Affairs: Nicolas Fattoush.

Ministers of State: Ali Qanso, Salim Karam, Ahmad Karami, Panos Manjian, Marwan Kheireddine.

MINISTRIES

Presidency of the Republic of Lebanon: Presidential Palace, Baabda, Beirut; tel. (5) 900900; fax (5) 900919; e-mail president_office@presidency.gov.lb; internet www.presidency.gov.lb.

Office of the President of the Council of Ministers: Grand Sérail, place Riad el-Solh, Beirut; tel. (1) 746800; fax (1) 746805; e-mail Conseilm@pcm.gov.lb; internet www.pcm.gov.lb.

Ministry of Agriculture: Embassies St, Bir Hassan, Beirut; tel. (1) 849600; fax (1) 849620; e-mail ministry@agriculture.gov.lb; internet www.agriculture.gov.lb.

Ministry of Culture: Immeuble Hatab, rue Madame Curie, Verdun, Beirut; tel. (1) 744250; fax (1) 756322; e-mail amalm@culture.gov.lb; internet www.culture.gov.lb.

Ministry of the Displaced: POB 9150, Minet el-Hosn, Starco Centre, Beirut; tel. (1) 366373; fax (1) 366087; e-mail modbeirut@hotmail.com; internet www.ministryofdisplaced.gov.lb.

Ministry of Economy and Trade: 5th Floor, Azarieh Bldg, rue Riad el-Solh, Hamra, Beirut; tel. (1) 982360; fax (1) 982293; e-mail Info@economy.gov.lb; internet www.economy.gov.lb.

Ministry of Education and Higher Education: Unesco Quarter, Habib Abi Chahla, Beirut; tel. (1) 772500; fax (1) 772529; e-mail info@higher-edu.gov.lb; internet www.higher-edu.gov.lb.

Ministry of Energy and Water: Beirut River Highway, Beirut; tel. (1) 565100; e-mail mew@terra.net.lb; internet www.energyandwater.gov.lb.

Ministry of the Environment: POB 11-2727, 7th and 8th Floors, Lazarieh Centre, Beirut; tel. (1) 976555; fax (1) 976530; e-mail webmaster@moe.gov.lb; internet www.moe.gov.lb.

Ministry of Finance: MOF Bldg, place Riad el-Solh, Beirut; tel. (1) 981001; fax (1) 981059; e-mail infocenter@finance.gov.lb; internet www.finance.gov.lb.

Ministry of Foreign Affairs and Emigrants: al-Sultana Bldg, al-Jnah, Sultan Ibrahim, Beirut; tel. (1) 840767; fax (1) 840924; e-mail director@emigrants.gov.lb; internet www.emigrants.gov.lb.

Ministry of Industry: Ministry of Industry and Petroleum Bldg, ave Sami Solh, Beirut; tel. (1) 423338; fax (1) 427112; e-mail ministry@industry.gov.lb; internet www.industry.gov.lb.

Ministry of Information: rue Hamra, Beirut; tel. (1) 754400; fax (1) 754776; internet www.ministryinfo.gov.lb.

Ministry of the Interior and Municipalities: Grand Sérail, place Riad el-Solh, Beirut; tel. (1) 754200; fax (1) 750084; e-mail info@moim.gov.lb; internet www.moim.gov.lb.

Ministry of Justice: rue Sami Solh, Beirut; tel. (1) 422112; fax (1) 427957; e-mail info@justice.gov.lb; internet www.justice.gov.lb.

Ministry of Labour: Shiah, Beirut; tel. (1) 556804; fax (1) 556806; e-mail mol@labor.gov.lb; internet www.labor.gov.lb.

Ministry of National Defence: Yarze, Beirut; tel. (5) 420000; fax (5) 951036; e-mail cmd@army.gov.lb; internet www.lebarmy.gov.lb.

Ministry of Public Health: Hussein Mansour Bldg, Museum St, Beirut; tel. (1) 615030; fax (1) 615773; e-mail info@moph.gov.lb; internet www.moph.gov.lb.

Ministry of Public Works and Transportation: Shiah, Beirut; tel. (5) 456482; fax (5) 455840.

Ministry of Social Affairs: rue Badro, Beirut; tel. (1) 611260; fax (1) 611246; e-mail info@socialaffairs.gov.lb; internet www.socialaffairs.gov.lb.

Ministry of State for Administrative Reform: 5th Floor, Immeuble Starco, rue Omar Daouk, place Minet el-Hosn 2020 3313, Beirut; tel. (1) 371510; fax (1) 371599; e-mail info@omsar.gov.lb; internet www.omsar.gov.lb.

Ministry of State for Parliamentary Affairs: Beirut.

Ministry of Telecommunications: Ministry of Telecom Bldg, 1st Floor, place Riad el-Solh, Beirut; tel. (1) 979319; fax (1) 979316; e-mail webmaster@mpt.gov.lb; internet www.mpt.gov.lb.

Ministry of Tourism: POB 11-5344, rue Banque du Liban 550, Beirut; tel. (1) 340940; fax (1) 340945; e-mail info@destinationlebanon.gov.lb; internet www.destinationlebanon.gov.lb.

Ministry of Youth and Sports: rue Sami Solh, Beirut; tel. (1) 425770; fax (1) 424387; e-mail minijes@cyberia.net.lb.

Legislature

Majlis al-Nuab
(National Assembly)

Place de l'Etoile, Beirut; tel. (1) 982047; fax (1) 982059; e-mail lp@lp.gov.lb; internet www.lp.gov.lb.

The equal distribution of seats among Christians and Muslims is determined by law, and the Cabinet must reflect the level of representation achieved by the various religious denominations within that principal division. Deputies of the same religious denomination do not necessarily share the same political or party allegiances. The distribution of seats is as follows: Maronite Catholics 34; Sunni Muslims 27; Shi'a Muslims 27; Greek Orthodox 14; Druzes 8; Greek-Melkite Catholics 8; Armenian Orthodox 5; Alawites 2; Armenian Catholics 1; Protestants 1; Others 1.

President: Nabih Berri.

General Election, 7 June 2009

Party list	Seats
March 14 Alliance*	71
March 8 Alliance†	57
Total	128

* Electoral list comprising the Future Movement, Parti socialiste progressiste, Lebanese Forces Party, Al-Kataeb, Democratic Left, Parti national libéral, Ramgavar Party, Al-Jama'a al-Islamiya and independents.

† Electoral list comprising Amal, Hezbollah, the Free Patriotic Movement, Armenian Revolutionary Federation, Syrian Social Nationalist Party, Al-Baath, Islamic Action Front, El-Marada Movement, Lebanese Democratic Party and independents.

Political Organizations

Amal (Hope—Afwaj al-Muqawamah al-Lubnaniyyah—Lebanese Resistance Detachments): e-mail info@amal-movement.com; internet www.amal-movement.com; f. 1975 as a politico-military organization; Shi'ite political party; contested 2009 legislative elections as part of March 8 Alliance; Leader Nabih Berri.

Armenian Revolutionary Federation (ARF) (Tashnag): rue Spears, Beirut; internet www.arfd.am; f. 1890; principal Armenian party; historically the dominant nationalist party in the independent Armenian Republic of Yerevan of 1917–21, prior to its becoming part of the USSR; socialist ideology; contested 2009 legislative elections as part of March 8 Alliance; Leader Hrant Markarian.

Al-Baath (Baath Arab Socialist Party): Beirut; f. 1948; local branch of secular pro-Syrian party with policy of Arab union; contested 2009 legislative elections as part of March 8 Alliance; Leader Fayez Shuker.

Bloc national libanais (Lebanese National Bloc): rue Pasteur, Gemmayze, Beirut; tel. (1) 584585; fax (1) 584591; e-mail ketleh@ketleh.org; internet www.ketleh.org; f. 1943; right-wing Lebanese party with policy of power-sharing between Christians and Muslims and the exclusion of the military from politics; Pres. Carlos Eddé.

Free Patriotic Movement (FPM) (Tayar al-Watani al-Horr): Beirut; tel. (3) 122858; e-mail info@tayyar.org; internet www.tayyar.org; aims to recover sovereignty and complete independence for Lebanon; majority of leaders and supporters are from the Christian community, although party is officially secular; largest party in the Change and Reform parliamentary bloc; contested 2009 legislative elections as part of March 8 Alliance; Leader Gen. Michel Aoun.

Future Movement (Tayar al-Mustaqbal): POB 123, Koraytem, Hamra, Beirut; tel. (3) 375442; fax (1) 375442; e-mail info@almustaqbal.org; internet www.almustaqbal.org; opposed to Syrian influence in Lebanese affairs; contested 2009 legislative elections as largest party of the March 14 Alliance; Leader Saad el-Din Hariri.

Hezbollah (Party of God): Beirut; e-mail info@moqawama.org; internet www.moqawama.org; f. 1982 by Iranian Revolutionary Guards who were sent to Lebanon; militant Shi'ite faction, which has become the leading organization of Lebanon's Shi'a community and a recognized political party; demands the withdrawal of Israeli forces from the occupied Shebaa Farms area of what it considers to be southern Lebanon (but which is designated by the UN as being part of Syria) and the release of all Lebanese prisoners from Israeli detention; contested 2009 legislative elections as part of March 8 Alliance; Chair. MUHAMMAD RA'D; Leader and Sec.-Gen. Sheikh HASAN NASRALLAH; Spiritual Leader Ayatollah MUHAMMAD HUSSAIN FADLALLAH.

Hizb-ut-Tahrir al-Islami (Party of Islamic Liberation): e-mail info@hizb-ut-tahrir.org; internet www.hizb-ut-tahrir.org; f. 1953; transnational org. granted a political parties licence in Lebanon in 2006; aims to establish Islamic caliphate throughout the world; denies claims that it is a militant group; Global Leader Sheikh ABU YASIN ATA IBN KHALIL ABU RASHTA, (Sheikh Ata Abu Rashta).

Al-Kataeb (Lebanese Social Democratic Party): POB 992, place Charles Hélou, Beirut; tel. (1) 584107; internet www.party.kataeb.org; f. 1936 as the Phalangist Party (Phalanges libanaises); nationalist, reformist, democratic social party; largest Maronite party, although is officially secular; contested 2009 legislative elections as part of March 14 Alliance; 100,000 mems; Pres. AMIN GEMAYEL.

Lebanese Democratic Party (LDP): Beirut; e-mail webmaster@ldparty.org; internet www.ldparty.org; f. 2001; contested 2009 legislative elections as part of March 8 Alliance; Leader TALAL ARSLAN; Sec.-Gen. WALID BARAKAT.

Lebanese Forces Party: Beirut; tel. and fax (9) 212989; e-mail contact@lebanese-forces.com; internet www.lebanese-forces.com; political successor to the **Lebanese Forces** (f. 1976; coalition of Maronite Christian militias); launched as political party in 1989; proscribed by the Government in 1994; resumed activities as a legal party in 2005; contested 2009 legislative elections as part of March 14 Alliance, securing five seats; Leader SAMIR GEAGEA.

Lebanese Option Gathering: POB 45-489, Hazmieh, Mar Takla, La Diva Bldg, Beirut; tel. (5) 957257; fax (5) 957357; e-mail lebaneseoption@lebaneseoption.org; internet lebaneseoption.org; f. 2007; aims to contest Hezbollah's monopoly over Shi'ite political representation in Lebanon, and to reform and develop the south of the country; Leader AHMAD AL-ASSAD.

El-Marada Movement: Zgharta; e-mail info@elmarada.org; internet elmarada.org; f. as the Marada Brigade, relaunched in 1996 as a political party; advocates Lebanese unity, sovereignty and independence; contested 2009 legislative elections as part of March 8 Alliance; Leader SULAYMAN FRANJIYA.

March 8 Alliance: contested 2009 legislative elections as an electoral bloc comprising Hezbollah, Amal, the Free Patriotic Movement, the Armenian Revolutionary Federation, the Syrian Social Nationalist Party, Al-Baath, the Islamic Action Front, the El-Marada Movement, the Lebanese Democratic Party and independents.

March 14 Alliance: contested 2009 legislative elections as an electoral bloc comprising Future Movement, Parti socialiste progressiste (PSP), the Lebanese Forces Party, Al-Kataeb and other smaller parties and independents; following disagreements over the formation of a new government, the PSP withdrew from the alliance in August 2009.

National Dialogue Party: POB 15-5060, Immeuble Marj el-Zouhour, 1st Floor, rue Donna Maria, Ras el-Nabeh, Beirut; tel. (1) 637000; fax (1) 6311234; e-mail info@alhiwar.com; internet www.alhiwar.com; f. 2004; advocates a comprehensive national dialogue to bring about political, social and judicial reforms; also seeks to target corruption and to ensure that the State has authority over the whole of Lebanon; Founder and Chair. FOUAD MUSTAFA MAKHZOUMI.

Parti communiste libanais (PCL) (Lebanese Communist Party): rue al-Bahatri, al-Watuat, Beirut; tel. and fax (1) 739615; e-mail lcparty@lcparty.org; internet www.lcparty.org; f. 1924; officially dissolved 1948–71; Marxist, with much support among intellectuals; Sec.-Gen. KHALID HADDADEH.

Parti national libéral (PNL) (Al-Wataniyin al-Ahrar): POB 165576, rue du Liban, Beirut; tel. (1) 338000; fax (1) 200335; e-mail ahrar@ahrar.org.lb; internet www.ahrar.org.lb; f. 1958; liberal reformist secular party, although has traditionally had a predominantly Maronite Christian membership; contested 2009 legislative elections as part of March 14 Alliance; Pres. DORY CHAMOUN.

Parti socialiste progressiste (PSP) (Al-Takadumi al-Ishteraki): POB 11-2893, Beirut 1107 2120; tel. (1) 309123; fax (1) 318119; e-mail internationalrelation@psp.org.lb; internet www.psp.org.lb; f. 1949; progressive party, advocates constitutional road to socialism and democracy; over 25,000 mems; mainly Druze support; contested 2009 legislative elections as part of March 14 Alliance; Pres. WALID JOUMBLATT; Sec.-Gen. SHARIF FAYAD.

Syrian Social Nationalist Party (al-Hizb al-Suri al-Qawmi al-Ijtima'i): internet www.ssnp.net; f. 1932 in Beirut; banned 1962–69; seeks creation of a 'Greater Syrian' state, incl. Lebanon, Syria, Iraq, Jordan, the Palestinian territories, Kuwait, Cyprus and parts of Egypt, Iran and Turkey; advocates separation of church and State, the redistribution of wealth and a strong military; supports Syrian involvement in Lebanese affairs; contested 2009 legislative elections as part of March 8 Alliance; Leader ASSAD HARDANE.

Al-Wa'ad (National Secular Democratic Party—Pledge): Beirut; f. 1986 by the late Elie Hobeika; pro-Syrian splinter group of Lebanese Forces; officially secular, although most supporters are Maronite Christians; aligned with March 8 Alliance; did not achieve parliamentary representation in June 2009 legislative elections; Leader JOSEPH HOBEIKA.

Other parties include the **Independent Nasserite Movement** (Murabitoun; Sunni Muslim Militia; Leader IBRAHIM QULAYAT) and the **Lebanese Popular Congress** (Pres. KAMAL SHATILA). The **Nasserite Popular Organization** and the **Arab Socialist Union** merged in January 1987, retaining the name of the former. The **Islamic Amal** is a breakaway group from Amal, based in Ba'albek (Leader HUSSEIN MOUSSAVI). **Islamic Jihad** is a pro-Iranian fundamentalist guerrilla group. The **Popular Liberation Army** (f. 1985 by the late MUSTAFA SAAD) is a Sunni Muslim faction, active in the south of Lebanon. **Tawhid Islami** (the Islamic Unification Movement; f. 1982; Sunni Muslim) and the **Arab Democratic Party** (or the Red Knights; Alawites; pro-Syrian; Leader ALI EID) are based in Tripoli.

Diplomatic Representation

EMBASSIES IN LEBANON

Algeria: POB 4794, face Hôtel Summerland, 1 rue Jnah, Sector 8, Beirut; tel. (1) 826712; fax (1) 826711; e-mail ambalbey@dm.nt.lb; Ambassador IBRAHIM BENAOUDA HASSI.

Argentina: Residence des Jardins, Immeuble Moutran, 2e étage, 161 rue Sursock, Achrafieh, Beirut; tel. (1) 210800; fax (1) 210802; e-mail elbno@mrecic.gov.ar; internet www.elbno.mrecic.gov.ar; Ambassador JOSÉ MAXWELL.

Armenia: rue Jasmin 28, Mtaileb, Beirut; tel. (4) 418860; fax (4) 402952; e-mail armlebanonembassy@mfa.am; Ambassador ASHOT KOCHARIAN.

Australia: Embassy Complex, Sérail Hill, Beirut; tel. (1) 960600; fax (1) 960601; e-mail austemle@dfat.gov.au; internet www.lebanon.embassy.gov.au; Ambassador LEX BARTLEM.

Austria: POB 11-3924, Immeuble Tabaris, 8e étage, 812 ave Charles Malek, Achrafieh, Beirut 2071 1606; tel. (1) 213017; fax (1) 217772; e-mail beirut-ob@bmeia.gv.at; internet www.bmeia.gv.at/en/embassy/beirut; Ambassador URSULA FAHRINGER.

Belgium: Bloc A, Immeuble Lazarie, 10e étage, rue Emir Béchir, Beirut; tel. (1) 976001; fax (1) 976007; e-mail beirut@diplobel.fed.be; internet www.diplomatie.be/beirut; Ambassador COLETTE TAQUET.

Brazil: POB 11-562, rue de l'Armée, Colline du Sérail, Beirut; tel. (1) 982161; fax (1) 982159; e-mail brasemb.beirute@itamaraty.gov.br; internet www.brazillebanon.org.lb; Ambassador PAULO ROBERTO CAMPOS TARRISSE DA FONTOURA.

Bulgaria: POB 11-6544, Sector 6, Mar-Takla, Hazmieh, Beirut; tel. (5) 452883; fax (5) 452892; e-mail embassy.beirut@mfa.bg; internet www.mfa.bg/embassies/lebanon; Chargé d'affaires PLAMEN TSOLOV.

Canada: POB 60163, Immeuble Coolrite, 1er et 2e étage, Autoroute Jal el-Dib 43, Beirut; tel. (4) 726700; fax (4) 710595; e-mail berut@international.gc.ca; internet www.lebanon.gc.ca; Ambassador HILARY CHILDS-ADAMS.

Chile: Nouvelle Naccache, Sector 2, rue 64, Immeuble Antoine Boukather, 1er étage, Beirut; tel. (4) 418670; fax (4) 418672; e-mail echilelb@dm.net.lb; internet chileabroad.gov.cl/libano; Ambassador JOSÉ MIGUEL MENCHACA.

China, People's Republic: POB 11-8227, 72 rue Nicolas Ibrahim Sursock, Ramlet el-Baida, Beirut 1107 2260; tel. (1) 856133; fax (1) 822492; e-mail chinaemb_lb@mfa.gov.cn; internet lb.china-embassy.org; Ambassador JIANG JIANG.

Colombia: Immeuble Mazda, 5e étage, Jal el-Dib, Beirut; tel. (4) 712646; fax (4) 712656; e-mail colombia@cyberia.net.lb; Ambassador RIDA MARIETTE ALJURE-SALAME.

Cuba: Center Farrania, 2e étage, rue Saïd Freiha, Mar-Takla, Hazmieh, Beirut 2901 6727; tel. (1) 459925; fax (1) 950070; e-mail libancub@cyberia.net.lb; internet www.cubadiplomatica.cu/libano; Ambassador RENÉ CEBALLO PRATS.

Cyprus: Immeuble M.N.C., 1er étage, rue Debbas, Achrafieh, Beirut; tel. (1) 326461; fax (1) 326471; e-mail info@cyprusembbeirut.org; internet www.cyprusembbeirut.org; Ambassador HOMER MAVROMMATIS.

Czech Republic: POB 40195, Baabda, Beirut; tel. (5) 929010; fax (5) 922120; e-mail beirut@embassy.mzv.cz; internet www.mzv.cz/beirut; Ambassador SVATOPLUK CUMBA.

Denmark: POB 11-5190, rue de l'Armée, Colline du Sérail, Beirut; tel. (1) 991001; fax (1) 991006; e-mail beyamb@um.dk; internet www.libanon.um.dk; Ambassador JAN TOP CHRISTENSEN.

Egypt: POB 5037, rue Dr Mohamad el-Bezri, Bir Hassan, Beirut; tel. (1) 825566; fax (1) 859988; Ambassador ASHRAF HAMDI.

France: rue de Damas, Beirut; tel. (1) 420000; fax (1) 420013; e-mail cad.beyrouth-amb@diplomatie.gouv.fr; internet www.ambafrance-lb.org; Ambassador PATRICE PAOLI.

Gabon: POB 11-1252, Riad el-Solh, Hadath, Beirut 1107 2080; tel. (5) 924649; fax (5) 924643; Ambassador SIMON NTOUTOUME EMANE.

Germany: POB 11-2820, Riad el-Solh, Beirut 1102 2110; tel. (4) 935000; fax (4) 935001; e-mail info@beirut.diplo.de; internet www.beirut.diplo.de; Ambassador CHRISTIAN CLAGES.

Greece: POB 11-0309, Immeuble Boukhater, rue des Ambassades, Nouvelle Naccache, Beirut; tel. (4) 418772; fax (4) 418774; e-mail gremb.bei@mfa.gr; internet www.mfa.gr/beirut; Ambassador AIKATERINI BOURA.

Holy See: POB 1061, Jounieh (Apostolic Nunciature); tel. (9) 263102; fax (9) 264488; e-mail naliban@terra.net.lb; Apostolic Nuncio Most Rev. GABRIELE GIORDANO CACCIA (Titular Archbishop of Sepino).

Hungary: POB 113-5259, Immeuble BAC, 9e étage, rue Justinien, Sanayeh, Beirut; tel. (1) 730083; fax (1) 741261; e-mail mission.bej@mfa.gov.hu; internet www.mfa.gov.hu/emb/beirut; Ambassador LÁSZLÓ VÁRADI.

India: POB 113-5240, 239 rue Ibrahim Abed el-Aal, Beirut; tel. (1) 741270; fax (1) 741283; e-mail amb.beirut@mea.gov.in; internet www.mea.gov.in/indian-mission.htm?123/Lebanon; Ambassador RAVI THAPAR.

Indonesia: POB 40007, ave Palais Presidential, rue 68, Secteur 3, Baabda, Beirut; tel. (5) 924682; fax (5) 924678; e-mail kbri@kbri-beirut.org; internet www.indonesianembassy.net; Ambassador ABDULLAH SYARWANI.

Iran: POB 5030, Bir Hassan, Beirut; tel. (1) 821224; fax (1) 821229; Ambassador GHANDAFAR RUKUN ABADI.

Iraq: Beirut; tel. (1) 453209; fax (1) 459850; e-mail brtemb@iraqmofamail.net; Ambassador RAAD AL-ALLOUSI.

Italy: POB 57, rue du Palais Présidentiel, Baabda, Beirut 2902 2633; tel. (5) 954955; fax (5) 959616; e-mail amba.beirut@esteri.it; internet www.ambbeirut.esteri.it; Ambassador GIUSEPPE MORABITO.

Japan: POB 11-3360, rue de l'Armée, Zkak al-Blat, Colline du Sérail, Beirut; tel. (1) 989751; fax (1) 989754; e-mail japanemb@japanemb.org.lb; internet www.lb.emb-japan.go.jp; Ambassador SEIICHI OTSUKA.

Jordan: POB 109, Beirut 5113; tel. (5) 922500; fax (5) 922502; e-mail joremb@dm.net.lb; Ambassador ZEID ZREIQAT.

Korea, Republic: POB 40-290, Diplomat Bldg 2F, Rue Palais Presidentiel, Baabda, Beirut; tel. (5) 953167; fax (5) 953170; e-mail lbkor@mofa.go.kr; internet lbn.mofa.go.kr; Ambassador KIM BYOUNG-GI.

Kuwait: POB 4580, Rond-point du Stade, Bir Hassan, Beirut; tel. (1) 756100; fax (1) 842220; e-mail info@kuwaitinfo.net; Ambassador ABD AL-AAL AL-QINAI.

Mexico: POB 70-1150, 1er étage, Immeuble Mansour 90, rue 53, Sector 2, New Naccache, Antélias, Beirut; tel. and fax (4) 418871; e-mail mail@embassyofmexicoinlebanon.org; internet www.embassyofmexicoinlebanon.org; Ambassador JORGE ÁLVAREZ FUENTES.

Morocco: Bir Hassan, Beirut; tel. (1) 859851; fax (1) 859839; e-mail sifmar@cyberia.net.lb; Ambassador ALI OUMLIL.

Netherlands: POB 167190, Netherlands Tower, ave Charles Malek, Achrafieh, Beirut 2073 0802; tel. (1) 211150; fax (1) 211173; e-mail bei@minbuza.nl; internet lebanon.nlembassy.org; Ambassador HESTER M.J. SOMSEN.

Norway: POB 113-7001, Immeuble Dimashki, rue Bliss, Ras Beirut, Hamra, Beirut 1103 2150; tel. (1) 960000; fax (1) 960099; e-mail emb.bey@mfa.no; internet www.norway-lebanon.org; Ambassador SVEIN AASS.

Pakistan: POB 135506, UNESCO Centre Crossroad, 8e étage, rue Saeb Salam, Immeuble 1, Verdun, Beirut; tel. (1) 790327; fax (1) 790471; e-mail pakemblb@gmail.com; internet www.mofa.gov.pk/lebanon; Ambassador RAANA RAHIM.

Paraguay: Immeuble La Rosa, Rez-de-chaussée, rue Farid Zeidan, Hazmieh, Mar Takla, Beirut; tel. and fax (1) 5458502; e-mail embaparlibano@hotmail.com; Ambassador HASSAN KHALIL DAY.

Philippines: POB 136631, rue Mar Geries, Immeuble W, Hadath, Baabda, Beirut; tel. (5) 953522; fax (5) 953521; e-mail beirut.pe@dfa.gov.ph; Ambassador LEAH M. BASINANG-RUIZ.

Poland: POB 40-215, Immeuble Khalifa, ave Président Sulayman Franjiya 52, Baabda, Beirut; tel. (5) 924591; fax (5) 924882; e-mail bejrut.amb.sekretariat@msz.gov.pl; internet www.bejrut.polemb.net; Ambassador WOJCIECH BOŻEK.

Qatar: POB 11-6717, Immeuble Deebs, 1er étage, Shouran, Beirut; tel. (1) 865271; fax (1) 810460; e-mail beirut@mofa.gov.qa; Ambassador SAAD BIN ALI AL-MUHANNADI.

Romania: route du Palais Présidentiel, Baabda, Beirut; tel. (5) 924848; fax (5) 924747; e-mail beirut@mae.ro; internet beirut.mae.ro; Chargé d'affaires a.i. CONSTANTIN BULEARCA.

Russia: POB 5220, rue Mar Elias el-Tineh, Wata Mseitbeh, Beirut; tel. (1) 300041; fax (1) 303837; e-mail rusembei@cyberia.net.lb; internet www.lebanon.mid.ru; Ambassador ALEKSANDR ZASYPKIN.

Saudi Arabia: POB 136144, Kuraitem, Beirut; tel. (1) 860242; fax (1) 860351; e-mail lbemb@mofa.gov.sa; Ambassador ALI BIN AWADH ASSERI.

Spain: POB 11-3039, Palais Chehab, Hadath Antounie, Beirut; tel. (5) 464120; fax (5) 464030; e-mail emb.beirut@maec.es; internet www.exteriores.gob.es/embajadas/beirut; Ambassador MILAGROS HERNANDO ECHEVARRÍA.

Sri Lanka: POB 175, Hazmieh, Beirut; tel. (5) 956031; fax (5) 956033; e-mail slemblbn@cyberia.net.lb; Ambassador RANJITH GUNARATHNA.

Sudan: POB 2504, Hamra, Beirut; tel. (1) 350057; fax (1) 353271; Ambassador AHMED HASSAN.

Switzerland: POB 11-172, Immeuble Bourj al-Ghazal, ave Fouad Chehab, Achrafieh, Beirut 1107 2020; tel. (1) 324129; fax (1) 324167; e-mail bey.vertretung@eda.admin.ch; internet www.eda.admin.ch/beirut; Ambassador RUTH FLINT.

Syria: rue Makdessi, Hamra, Beirut; Ambassador ALI ABD AL-KARIM ALI.

Tunisia: Mar-Takla, Hazmieh, Beirut; tel. (5) 457431; fax (5) 950434; Ambassador HATEM SAYEM.

Turkey: POB 70-666, zone II, rue 1, Rabieh, Beirut; tel. (4) 520929; fax (4) 407557; e-mail ambassade.beyrouth@mfa.gov.tr; internet beirut.emb.mfa.gov.tr; Ambassador SÜLEYMAN INAN OZYILDIZ.

Ukraine: POB 40268, rue Antoine El Rayes, Mount Lebanon, Casa Baabda, Beirut; tel. (5) 921975; fax (5) 921974; e-mail emb_lb@mfa.gov.ua; internet www.mfa.gov.ua/lebanon; Ambassador VOLODYMYR KOVAL.

United Arab Emirates: Ramla al-Bayda, Jnah, Beirut; tel. (1) 857000; fax (1) 857009; e-mail beirut@mofa.gov.ae; internet uae-embassy.ae/embassies/lb; Ambassador YOUSSEF ALI AL-ASSIMI.

United Kingdom: POB 11-471, Embassies Complex, rue de l'Armée, Colline du Sérail, Zkak al-Blat, Beirut; tel. (1) 960800; fax (1) 960855; e-mail chancery@cyberia.net.lb; internet ukinlebanon.fco.gov.uk; Ambassador TOM FLETCHER.

USA: POB 70-840, Antélias, Beirut; tel. (4) 542600; fax (4) 544136; e-mail beirutpd@state.gov; internet lebanon.usembassy.gov; Ambassador DAVID HALE.

Uruguay: POB 2051, Centre Stella Marris, 7e étage, rue Banque du Liban, Jounieh; tel. (9) 636529; fax (9) 636531; e-mail uruliban@dm.net.lb; internet www.embauruguaybeirut.org; Ambassador Dr MARTA INÉS PIZZANELLI.

Venezuela: POB 11-603, rue Amaret Chalhoub, Immeuble Baezevale House, 5e étage, Zalka, Beirut; tel. (1) 888701; fax (1) 900757; e-mail embajadora@embavenelibano.com; internet www.embavenelibano.com; Ambassador ZOED KARAM.

Yemen: Bir Hassan, Beirut; tel. (1) 852688; fax (1) 821610; Ambassador (vacant).

Judicial System

Law and justice in Lebanon are administered in accordance with the following codes, which are based upon modern theories of civil and criminal legislation:

Code de la Propriété (1930).

Code des Obligations et des Contrats (1932).

Code de Procédure Civile (1933).

Code Maritime (1947).

Code de Procédure Pénale (Code Ottoman Modifié).

Code Pénal (1943).

Code Pénal Militaire (1946).

Code d'Instruction Criminelle.

Courts of First Instance: Fifty-six courts, each consisting of a single judge, and dealing in the first instance with both civil and criminal cases; there are 17 such courts in Beirut and seven in Tripoli; Pres. Dr FADI ELIAS.

Courts of Appeal: Eleven courts, each consisting of three judges, including a President and a Public Prosecutor, and dealing with civil and criminal cases; there are five such courts in Beirut; First Pres. MAYSSAM NOUEIRI.

Courts of Cassation: Four courts, three dealing with civil and commercial cases and the fourth with criminal cases. A Court of Cassation, to be properly constituted, must have at least three judges, one being the President and the other two Councillors. If the Court of Cassation reverses the judgment of a lower court, it does not refer the case back but retries it itself; General Prosecutor of Cassation HATEM MADI.

State Consultative Council: deals with administrative cases; Pres. SHUKRI SADER.

Court of Justice: a special court consisting of a President and four judges, deals with matters affecting the security of the State; there is no appeal against its verdicts.

Constitutional Council: considers matters pertaining to the constitutionality of legislation; Pres. ISSAM SULEIMAN.

Higher Judicial Council: considers matters involving members of the executive branch; Pres. JEAN FAHED.

Military Court: competent to try crimes and misdemeanours involving the armed and security forces; Chief of the Military Court Brig. KHALIL IBRAHIM.

In addition, Islamic (*Shari'a*), Christian and Jewish religious courts deal with affairs of personal status (marriage, death, inheritance, etc.).

Religion

Of all the countries of the Middle East, Lebanon probably presents the closest juxtaposition of sects and peoples within a small territory. In 1994 it was estimated that 29%–32% of the population of Lebanon were Shi'a Muslims, 25%–28% Maronites, 16%–20% Sunni Muslims and 3.5% Druzes. The Maronites, a uniate sect of the Roman Catholic Church, inhabited the old territory of Mount Lebanon, i.e. immediately east of Beirut. In the south, towards the Israeli frontier, Shi'a villages are most common, while between the Shi'a and the Maronites live the Druzes (divided between the Yazbakis and the Joumblatis). The Beqa'a valley has many Greek Christians (both Roman Catholic and Orthodox), while the Tripoli area is mainly Sunni Muslim.

CHRISTIANITY

The Roman Catholic Church

Armenian Rite

Patriarchate of Cilicia: Patriarcat Arménien Catholique, rue de l'Hôpital orthodoxe, Jeitawi, Beirut 2078 5605; tel. (1) 570555; fax (1) 570563; e-mail nerbed19@magnarama.com; f. 1742; est. in Beirut since 1929; includes patriarchal diocese of Beirut, with an estimated 12,000 adherents (31 December 2007); Patriarch Most Rev. NERSES BEDROS XIX TARMOUNI; Protosyncellus Rt Rev. VARTAN ACHKARIAN (Titular Bishop of Tokat—Armenian Rite).

Chaldean Rite

Diocese of Beirut: Evêché Chaldéen de Beyrouth, POB 373, Hazmieh, Beirut; tel. (5) 457732; fax (5) 457731; e-mail chaldepiscopus@hotmail.com; an estimated 10,000 adherents (31 December 2007); Bishop of Beirut MICHEL KASSARJI.

Latin Rite

Apostolic Vicariate of Beirut: Vicariat Apostolique, POB 11-4224, Riad el-Solh, Beirut 1107 2160; tel. (9) 236101; fax (9) 236102; e-mail vicariatlat@hotmail.com; an estimated 15,000 adherents (31 December 2007); Vicar Apostolic PAUL DAHDAH (Titular Archbishop of Arae in Numidia).

Maronite Rite

Patriarchate of Antioch and all the East: Patriarcat Maronite, Bkerké; tel. (9) 915441; fax (9) 938844; e-mail jtawk@bkerke.org.lb; includes patriarchal dioceses of Jounieh, Sarba and Jobbé; the Maronite Church in Lebanon comprises four archdioceses and six dioceses; Patriarch Cardinal BÉCHARA BOUTROS RAÏ.

Archbishop of Antélias: Most Rev. JOSEPH MOHSEN BÉCHARA, Archevêché Maronite, POB 70400, Antélias; tel. (4) 410020; fax (4) 415872.

Archbishop of Beirut: Most Rev. PAUL YOUSUF MATAR, Archevêché Maronite, 10 rue Collège de la Sagesse, Achrafieh, Beirut; tel. (1) 561980; fax (1) 561930; e-mail maronitebeyrouth@yahoo.fr; also representative of the Holy See for Roman Catholics of the Coptic Rite in Lebanon.

Archbishop of Tripoli: Most Rev. GEORGES BOU-JAOUDÉ, Archevêché Maronite, POB 104, rue al-Moutran, Karm Sada, Tripoli; tel. (6) 624324; fax (6) 629393; e-mail rahmat@inco.com.lb.

Archbishop of Tyre: Most Rev. CHUCRALLAH-NABIL HAGE, Archevêché Maronite, Tyre; tel. (7) 740059; fax (7) 344891; e-mail abounacharbel@cyberia.net.lb.

Melkite Rite

Patriarch of Antioch: Patriarcat Grec-Melkite Catholique, POB 22249, 12 ave al-Zeitoon, Bab Charki, Damascus, Syria; tel. (11) 5441030; fax (11) 5417900; e-mail pat.melk@scs-net.org; internet www.pgc-lb.org; f. 1724; the Melkite Church in Lebanon comprises seven archdioceses, with an estimated 393,000 adherents (31 December 2009); Patriarch of Antioch and all the East, of Alexandria and of Jerusalem His Beatitude GREGORIOS III LAHAM.

Archbishop of Ba'albek: Most Rev. ELIAS RAHAL, Archevêché Grec-Catholique, Ba'albek; tel. (8) 370200; fax (8) 373986.

Archbishop of Baniyas: Most Rev. GEORGES NICOLAS HADDAD, Archevêché de Panéas, Jdeidet Marjeyoun; tel. and fax (3) 830007.

Archbishop of Beirut and Jbeil: CYRILLE SALIM BUSTROS, Archevêché Grec-Melkite-Catholique, POB 11-901, 655 rue de Damas, Beirut; tel. (1) 616104; fax (1) 616109; e-mail agmcb@terra.net.lb.

Archbishop of Saida (Sidon): Most Rev. ELIE BÉCHARA HADDAD, Archevêché Grec-Melkite-Catholique, POB 247, rue el-Moutran, Sidon; tel. (7) 720100; fax (7) 722055; e-mail mhaddad.saida@hotmail.com.

Archbishop of Tripoli: Most Rev. GEORGE RIASHI, Archevêché Grec-Catholique, POB 72, rue al-Kanaess, Tripoli; tel. (6) 431602; fax (6) 441716.

Archbishop of Tyre: Most Rev. GEORGES BAKOUNY, Archevêché Grec-Melkite-Catholique, POB 257, Tyre; tel. (7) 740015; fax (7) 349180; e-mail pbacouni@yahoo.com.

Archbishop of Zahleh and Furzol: Most Rev. ISSAM JOHN DARWISH, Archevêché Grec-Melkite-Catholique, Saidat el-Najat, Zahleh; tel. (8) 800333; fax (8) 822406; e-mail info@catholiczahle.org; internet www.catholiczahle.org.

Syrian Rite

Patriarchate of Antioch: Patriarcat Syrien Catholique d'Antioche, rue de Damas, POB 116–5087, Beirut 1106 2010; tel. (1) 615892; fax (1) 616573; e-mail psc_lb@yahoo.com; jurisdiction over about 150,000 Syrian Catholics in the Middle East; Patriarch Most Rev. IGNACE JOSEPH III YOUNAN; Protosyncellus Mgr GEORGES MASRI.

The Anglican Communion

Within the Episcopal Church in Jerusalem and the Middle East, Lebanon forms part of the diocese of Jerusalem (see the chapter on Israel).

Other Christian Groups

Armenian Apostolic Orthodox Church: Armenian Catholicosate of Cilicia, POB 70317, Antélias; tel. (4) 410001; fax (4) 419724; e-mail info@armenianorthodoxchurch.org; internet www.armenianorthodoxchurch.org; f. 301 AD in Armenia, re-established in 1293 in Cilicia (now in Turkey), transferred to Antélias, Lebanon, 1930; Leader His Holiness ARAM KESHISHIAN I (Catholicos of Cilicia); jurisdiction over an estimated 3.5m. adherents in Lebanon, Syria, Cyprus, Kuwait, Greece, Iran, Qatar, the United Arab Emirates, South America, the USA and Canada.

National Evangelical Synod of Syria and Lebanon: POB 70890, Antélias; tel. (4) 525030; fax (4) 411184; e-mail nessl@synod-sl.org; internet www.synod-sl.org; f. 1959; 20,000 adherents (2010); Gen. Sec. Rev. FADI DAGHER.

Patriarchate of Antioch and all the East (Greek Orthodox): Patriarcat Grec-Orthodoxe, POB 9, Damascus, Syria; tel. (11) 5424400; fax (11) 5424404; e-mail info@antiochpat.org; internet www.antiochpat.org; Patriarch His Beatitude IGNATIUS (HAZIM) IV.

Patriarchate of Antioch and all the East (Syrian Orthodox): Patriarcat Syrien Orthodoxe, Bab Toma, POB 22260, Damascus, Syria; tel. (11) 5951870; fax (11) 5951880; internet www.syrian-orthodox.com; Patriarch IGNATIUS ZAKKA I IWAS.

Supreme Council of the Evangelical Community in Syria and Lebanon: POB 70/1065, rue Rabieh 34, Antélias; tel. (4) 525036; fax (4) 405490; e-mail suprcoun@minero.net; Pres. Rev. Dr SALIM SAHIOUNY.

Union of the Armenian Evangelical Churches in the Near East: POB 11-377, Beirut; tel (1) 565628; fax (1) 565629; e-mail uaecne@cyberia.net.lb; f. 1846 in Turkey; comprises about 30 Armenian Evangelical Churches in Syria, Lebanon, Egypt, Cyprus, Greece, Iran, Turkey and Australia; Pres. Rev. MEGRDICH KARAGOEZIAN; Gen. Sec. SEBOUH TERZIAN.

ISLAM

Shi'a Muslims: Leader Imam Sheikh SAYED MOUSSA AL-SADR (went missing during visit to Libya in August 1978); Vice-Pres. of the Supreme Islamic Council of the Shi'a Community of Lebanon ABD AL-AMIR QABALAN; Beirut.

Sunni Muslims: Grand Mufti of Lebanon, Dar el-Fatwa, rue Ilewi Rushed, Beirut; tel. (1) 422340; Leader Sheikh Dr MUHAMMAD RASHID QABBANI.

Druzes: Supreme Spiritual Leader of the Druze Community, Beirut; tel. (1) 341116; Supreme Spiritual Leader Sheikh AL-AQL BAHJAT GHAITH; Political Leader WALID JOUMBLATT.

Alawites: a schism of Shi'ite Islam; there are an estimated 50,000 Alawites in northern Lebanon, in and around Tripoli.

JUDAISM

A small Jewish community, thought to number less than 100 people, remains in Lebanon.

Jewish Community: Pres. ISAAC ARAZI (Beirut).

The Press

DAILIES

Al-Akhbar (The News): POB 5963-113, Concorde Centre, 6th Floor, rue Verdun, Beirut; tel. (1) 759500; fax (1) 759597; internet www.al-akhbar.com; f. 2006; Arabic; independent; Editor-in-Chief IBRAHIM AL-AMIN.

Al-Anwar (Lights): c/o Dar Assayad, POB 11-1038, Hazmieh, Beirut; tel. (5) 456374; fax (5) 452700; e-mail info@alanwar.com; internet www.alanwar-leb.com; f. 1959; Arabic; independent; supplement, Sunday; cultural and social; publ. by Dar Assayad SAL; Editors-in-Chief MICHEL RAAD, RAFIK KHOURY; circ. 14,419.

Aztag: POB 80-860, Shaghzoyan Cultural Centre, Bourj Hammoud; tel. (1) 258526; fax (1) 258529; e-mail info@aztagdaily.com; internet www.aztagdaily.com; f. 1927; Armenian; Editor-in-Chief SHAHAN KANDAHARIAN; circ. 6,500.

Al-Balad: Beirut; tel. (1) 494694; fax (1) 494894; e-mail crm@albaladonline.com; internet albaladonline.com; Arabic; Chair. AHMAD BADRANI; Man. Editor GEORGE JABARA.

Al-Bayrak (The Standard): Immeuble Dimitri Trad, rue Issa Maalouf, Achrafieh, Beirut; tel. (1) 216393; fax (1) 338928; e-mail dalwl@dm.net.lb; internet www.albayrakonline.com; f. 1913; Arabic; publ. by Dar Alf Leila wa Leila Publishing House; politics and society; Editor-in-Chief MELHEM KARAM; circ. 10,000.

Daily Star: Markaziah Centre, 3rd Floor, Umm Gelias St, Beirut Central District, Beirut; tel. (1) 587277; fax (1) 561333; e-mail editorial@dailystar.com.lb; internet www.dailystar.com.lb; f. 1952; English; Publr SALMA EL-BISSAR; Editor-in-Chief NADIM LADKI; circ. 10,550.

Al-Diyar (The Homeland): al-Nahda Bldg, Yarze, Beirut; tel. (5) 923830; fax (5) 923773; e-mail info@addiyaronline.com; internet www.aldiyaronline.com; f. 1987; Arabic; Propr and Editor-in-Chief CHARLES AYYUB.

Al-Hayat (Life): POB 11-1242, rue Maarad, place Riad el-Solh, Beirut; tel. (1) 987990; fax (1) 983921; e-mail information@alhayat.com; internet www.daralhayat.com; f. 1946; Arabic; independent; Editor-in-Chief GHASSAN CHARBEL; circ. 196,800.

Al-Liwaa (The Standard): POB 11-2402, Beirut; tel. (1) 735745; fax (1) 735749; e-mail events@aliwaa.com.lb; internet www.aliwaa.com; f. 1963; Arabic; Propr ABD AL-GHANI SALAM; Editor SALAH SALAM; circ. 26,000.

Al-Mustaqbal: POB 14-5426, Beirut; tel. (1) 797770; fax (1) 869264; e-mail rnakib@almustaqbal.com.lb; internet www.almustaqbal.com.lb; f. 1999; Dir RAFIQ NAKIB; Editor-in-Chief HANI HAMMOUD; circ. 20,000.

An-Nahar (The Day): Immeuble An-Nahar, place des Martyrs, Marfa', Beirut 2014 5401; tel. (1) 994888; fax (1) 996777; e-mail webmaster@annahar.com.lb; internet www.annahar.com; f. 1933; Arabic; independent; publ. by Editions Dar an-Nahar SAL; Editor-in-Chief NAYLA TUENI; circ. 50,000.

L'Orient-Le Jour: POB 11-2488, Route de Damas, montée Fiyaddiyé, 200m après station Total, Beirut; tel. (5) 956444; fax (5) 957444; e-mail administration@lorientlejour.com; internet www.lorientlejour.com; f. 1970; by merger of two newspapers, *L'Orient* and *Le Jour*; French; independent; Pres. and CEO MICHEL EDDÉ; Editor-in-Chief NAGIB AOUN; circ. 23,000.

As-Safir: POB 113–5015, Immeuble as-Safir, rue Monimina, Hamra, Beirut 1103-2010; tel. and fax (1) 350001; fax (1) 743602; e-mail mail@assafir.com; internet www.assafir.com; f. 1974; Arabic; political; Publr and Editor-in-Chief TALAL SALMAN; circ. 45,000.

Zartonk: POB 11-617, rue Nahr Ibrahim, Beirut; tel. and fax (1) 566709; e-mail info@zartonkdaily.com; internet www.zartonkdaily.com; f. 1937; Armenian, Arabic and English; official organ of Armenian Liberal Democratic Party; Man. Editor BAROUYR H. AGHBASHIAN.

WEEKLIES

Achabaka (The Net): c/o Dar Assayad SAL, POB 11-1038, Said Freiha St, Hazmieh, Beirut; tel. (5) 453673; fax (5) 452700; e-mail info@dar-assayad.com; internet www.achabaka.com; f. 1956; Arabic; society and features; Founder SAID FREIHA; Editor ELHAM FREIHA; circ. 139,775.

Al-Anwar Supplement: c/o Dar Assayad, POB 11-1038, Hazmieh, Beirut; tel. (5) 450406; fax (5) 452700; e-mail info@alanwar.com; internet www.alanwar.com; cultural and social; every Sun.; supplement to daily *Al-Anwar*; Editor ISSAM FREIHA; circ. 90,000.

Assayad (The Hunter): c/o Dar Assayad, POB 11-1038, Hazmieh, Beirut; tel. (5) 450933; fax (5) 452700; e-mail assayad@inco.com.lb; internet www.al-sayad.com; f. 1943; Arabic; political and social; Editor-in-Chief MOUNIR NAJJAR; circ. 76,192.

Attamaddon: POB 90, Aljmizzat St, Tripoli; tel. (6) 441164; fax (6) 435252; e-mail info@attamaddon.com; internet www.attamaddon.com; f. 1972; political.

Al-Bayan: 5th Floor, Karim Centre, Tripoli; tel. and fax (6) 425555; e-mail info@albayanlebanon.com; internet albayanlebanon.com; political.

Ad-Dabbour: place du Musée, Beirut; tel. and fax (1) 616771; e-mail addabbour@yahoo.com; f. 1922; Arabic; CEO JOSEPH RICHARD MOUKARZEL; circ. 12,000.

L'Hebdo Magazine: POB 11-1404, Immeuble Sayegh, rue Sursock, Beirut; tel. (1) 202070; fax (1) 202663; e-mail info@ediori.com.lb; internet www.magazine.com.lb; f. 1956; French; political, economic and social; publ. by Editions Orientales SAL; Pres. CHARLES ABOU ADAL; Editor-in-Chief PAUL KHALIFEH; circ. 18,000.

Al-Hiwar (Dialogue): rue Donna Maria, Beirut; tel. (1) 637000; fax (1) 631282; e-mail info@alhiwar.info; internet www.alhiwar.info; f. 2000; Arabic; publ. by the National Dialogue Party; Chair. FOUAD MAKHZOUMI; Editor-in-Chief SAM MOUNASSA.

Al-Hurriya (Freedom): Beirut; e-mail info@alhourriah.org; internet www.alhourriah.org; f. 1960; Arabic; organ of the Democratic Front for the Liberation of Palestine; Editor DAOUD TALHAME; circ. 30,000.

Al-Intiqad: internet www.alintiqad.com; Arabic; political; organ of Hezbollah; Editor IBRAHIM MOUSSAWI.

Al-Kifah al-Arabi (The Arab Struggle): POB 5158-14, Immeuble Rouche-Shams, Beirut; tel. (1) 809300; fax (1) 808281; e-mail editor@kifaharabi.com; internet www.kifaharabi.com; f. 1974; Arabic; political, socialist, pan-Arab; Publr WALID HUSSEINI.

Massis: Immeuble Eglise Ste Croix des Arméniens Catholiques, rue Zoghbi, Zalka, Beirut; tel. (4) 715263; e-mail hebdomassis@sodetel.net.lb; internet www.armeniancatholic.org; f. 1947; Armenian; Catholic; Editor-in-Chief SARKIS NADJARIAN; circ. 2,500.

Al-Moharrer (The Liberator): POB 136702, rue Hamra, Beirut; tel. (1) 750516; fax (1) 750515; e-mail almoharrer@almoharrer.net; internet www.almoharrer.net; f. 1962; Arabic; circ. 87,000; Gen. Man. WALID ABOU ZAHR.

Monday Morning: POB 165612, Immeuble Dimitri Trad, rue Issa Maalouf, Achrafieh, Beirut; tel. (1) 200961; fax (1) 335079; e-mail info@mmorning.com; internet www.mmorning.com; f. 1971; political and social affairs; publ. by Dar Alf Leila wa Leila; circ. 15,000; Editor-in-Chief MELHEM KARAM.

Al-Nass (The People): POB 145583, ave Fouad Chehab, Beirut; tel. (3) 376185; fax (8) 376610; e-mail an-nass@live.com; f. 1959; Arabic; weekly news magazine; Editor-in-Chief HASSAN YAGHI; circ. 22,000.

Al-Ousbou' al-Arabi (Arab Week): POB 11-1404, Immeuble Sayegh, rue Sursock, Beirut; tel. (1) 202070; fax (1) 202752; e-mail info@arabweek.com.lb; internet www.arabweek.com.lb; f. 1959; Arabic; political and social; publ. by Editions Orientales SAL; Chair. and Editor-in-Chief CHARLES ABOU ADAL; circ. 88,407 (circulates throughout the Arab world).

La Revue du Liban (Lebanon Review): POB 165612, Immeuble Dimitri Trad, rue Issa Maalouf, Achrafieh, Beirut; tel. (1) 200961; fax (1) 338929; e-mail rdl@rdl.com.lb; internet www.rdl.com.lb; f. 1928; French; political, social, cultural; publ. by Dar Alf Leila wa Leila; Publr MELHEM KARAM; Gen. Man. MICHEL MISK; circ. 22,000.

Al-Shiraa (The Sail): POB 13-5250, Beirut; tel. (1) 703000; fax (1) 866050; e-mail alshiraa@alshiraa.com; internet www.alshiraa.com; Arabic; Chief Editor HASSAN SABRA; circ. 40,000.

OTHER SELECTED PERIODICALS

Alam Attijarat (Business World): Immeuble Strand, rue Hamra, Beirut; f. 1965; monthly; commercial; Editor (vacant); international circ. 17,500.

Al Computer, Communications and Electronics (ACCE): c/o Dar Assayad, POB 1038, Hazmieh, Beirut; tel. (5) 450935; fax (5) 452700; e-mail assayad@inco.com.lb; internet www.accemagazine.com; f. 1984; monthly; computer technology; publ. by Dar Assayad Int; Chief Editor Antoine Boutros; circ. 31,912 (Jan.–June 2006).

Arab Construction World: POB 13-5121, Chouran, Beirut 1102 2802; tel. (1) 352413; fax (1) 352419; e-mail info@acwmag.com; internet www.acwmag.com; f. 1983; monthly; English and Arabic; publ. by CPH World Media; Publr Fathi Chatila; Pres. and CEO Muhammad Rabih Chatila; circ. 10,100.

Arab Defence Journal: c/o Dar Assayad, POB 11-1038, Hazmieh, Beirut; tel. (5) 457261; fax (5) 452700; e-mail info@dar-assayad.com; internet www.arabdefencejournal.com; f. 1976; monthly; military; publ. by Dar Assayad Int; Editor-in-Chief Fawzi Abou Farhat; circ. 24,831 (July–Dec. 2005).

Arab Water World: POB 13-5121, Chouran, Beirut 1102-2802; tel. (1) 748333; fax (1) 352419; e-mail editorial@awwmag.com; internet www.awwmag.com; f. 1977; monthly; English and Arabic; publ. by CPH World Media; Pres., Publr and Editor-in-Chief Fathi Chatila; circ. 8,400.

The Arab World: POB 567, Jounieh; tel. and fax (9) 935096; e-mail info@naamanculture.com; internet www.naamanculture.com; f. 1985; 24 a yr; publ. by Dar Naamān lith-Thaqāfa (Maison Naaman pour la Culture); Editor Naji Naaman.

BusinessWeek Al-Arabiya: POB 11-4355, Beirut; tel. (1) 739777; fax (1) 749090; f. 2005; monthly; Arabic edn of US weekly business publ; publ. by InfoPro SA; distributed across 22 countries; Regional Dir Sylvie Gyuran.

Le Commerce du Levant: POB 45-332 Baabda, Route de Damas, Immeuble l'Orient-Le Jour, 3e étage, Hazmieh, Beirut; tel. (1) 952259; fax (1) 453644; e-mail redaction@lecommercedulevant.com; internet www.lecommercedulevant.com; f. 1929; monthly; French; commercial and financial; publ. by Société de la Presse Economique; Chief Editor Sibylle Rizk; circ. 15,000.

Déco: POB 11-1404, Immeuble Sayegh, rue Sursock, Beirut; tel. (1) 202070; fax (1) 202663; e-mail info@decomag.com.lb; internet www.decomag.com.lb; f. 2000; quarterly; French; architecture and interior design; publ. by Editions Orientales SAL; Pres. Charles Abou Adal; circ. 14,000.

Fairuz International: Dar Assayad, POB 11-1038, Hazmieh, Beirut; tel. (5) 456373; fax (5) 450609; e-mail assayad@inco.com.lb; internet www.darassayad.net; f. 1982; monthly; Arabic; for women; publ. by Dar Assayad Int; Chief Editor Elham Freiha; circ. 93,892 (July–Dec. 2005).

Al-Fares: c/o Dar Assayad, POB 11-1038, Hazmieh, Beirut; tel. (5) 450406; fax (5) 450609; e-mail assayad@inco.com.lb; internet www.alfaresmagazine.com; f. 1991; monthly; Arabic; men's interest; publ. by Dar Assayad Int; Chief Editor Elham Freiha; circ. 79,237 (July–Dec. 2005).

Al-Idari (The Manager): c/o Dar Assayad, POB 11-1038, Hazmieh, Beirut; tel. (5) 450406; fax (5) 450609; e-mail assayad@inco.com.lb; internet www.alidarimagazine.com; f. 1975; monthly; Arabic; business management, economics, finance and investment; publ. by Dar Assayad Int; Pres. Bassam Freiha; Gen. Man. Elham Freiha; circ. 31,867.

Lebanese and Arab Economy: POB 11-1801, Sanayeh, Beirut; tel. (1) 744160; fax (1) 353395; e-mail information@ccib.org.lb; internet www.ccib.org.lb; f. 1951; monthly; Arabic, English and French; publ. by Chamber of Commerce, Industry and Agriculture of Beirut and Mount Lebanon.

Lebanon Opportunities: c/o InfoPro sal, POB 11-4355, 2nd Floor, rue Hamra, Piccadilly Center, Beirut; tel. (1) 739777; fax (1) 749090; e-mail infopro@infopro.com.lb; internet www.opportunities.com.lb; monthly; English; real estate, business and general finance and economy; publ. by InfoPro SA; Publr and Editor-in-Chief Ramzi el-Hafez.

Al-Mar'a: POB 11-1404, Immeuble Sayegh, rue Sursock, Beirut; tel. (1) 202070; fax (1) 202663; e-mail info@almara.com.lb; internet www.almara.com.lb; f. 2000; monthly; Arabic; for women; publ. by Editions Orientales SAL; Dir Mouna Béchara; Chief Editor Paul Khalifeh; circ. 20,000.

MENA Health World: POB 13-5121, Chouran, Beirut 1102 2802; tel. (1) 748333; fax (1) 352419; e-mail editorial@mhwmag.net; internet www.mhwmag.net; f. 1986 as Arab Health World magazine, but publ. suspended in 1993; relaunched as above 2006; bi-monthly; English and Arabic; publ. by CPH World Media; Pres. and Publr Fathi Chatila; Editor-in-Chief Dr Rajaa Chatila Alayli.

Middle East Food: POB 13-5121, Chouran, Beirut 1102 2802; tel. (1) 352413; fax (1) 352419; e-mail content@mefmag.com; internet www.mefmag.com; f. 1985; monthly; publ. by CPH World Media; Pres. and CEO Muhammad Rabih Chatila; Editor-in-Chief Roula Hamdan; circ. 8,650.

Siyassa was Strategia (Politics and Strategy): POB 567, Jounieh; tel. and fax (9) 935096; e-mail naamanculture@lynx.net.lb; internet www.naamanculture.com; f. 1981; 36 a year; Arabic; publ. by Dar Naamān lith-Thaqāfa (Maison Naaman pour la Culture); Editor Naji Naaman.

Takarir Wa Khalfiyat (Background Reports): c/o Dar Assayad, POB 11-1038, Hazmieh, Beirut; tel. (5) 456374; fax (5) 452700; internet www.darassayad.net; f. 1976; monthly; Arabic; political and economic bulletin; publ. by Dar Assayad SAL; Editor-in-Chief Hassan el-Khoury.

Al-Tarik (The Road): Beirut; monthly; Arabic; cultural and theoretical; publ. by the Parti communiste libanais; circ. 5,000.

Travaux et Jours (Works and Days): Rectorat de l'Université Saint-Joseph, rue de Damas, Beirut; tel. (1) 421000; fax (1) 421005; e-mail travauxetjours@usj.edu.lb; internet www.usj.edu.lb; f. 1961; 2 a year; French; political, social and cultural; Editor Mounir Chamoun.

NEWS AGENCY

National News Agency (NNA): Hamra, Beirut; tel. (1) 754400; fax (1) 745776; e-mail akassas@nna-leb.gov.lb; internet www.nna-leb.gov.lb; state-owned; Dir Laure Sleiman; Chief Editor Ali Lahham.

PRESS ASSOCIATION

Lebanese Press Order: POB 3084, ave Saeb Salam, Beirut; tel. (1) 865519; fax (1) 865516; e-mail mail@pressorder.org; internet www.pressorder.org; f. 1911; 18 mems; Pres. Muhammad al-Baalbaki; Sec. Abd al-Karim el-Khalil.

Publishers

Dar al-Adab: POB 4123, Beirut; tel. (1) 795135; fax (1) 861633; e-mail d_aladab@cyberia.net.lb; internet www.adabmag.com; f. 1953; dictionaries, literary and general; Man. Aida Matraji Idriss; Editor-in-Chief Samah Idriss.

Arab Institute for Research and Publishing (Al-Mouasasah al-Arabiyah Lildirasat Walnashr): POB 11-5460, Beirut; tel. and fax (1) 751438; e-mail info@airpbooks.com; internet www.airpbooks.com; f. 1969; works in Arabic and English; Dir Maher Kayyali.

Arab Scientific Publishers BP: POB 13-5574, Immeuble Ein al-Tenah Reem, rue Sakiet al-Janzir, Beirut; tel. (1) 786233; fax (1) 786230; e-mail asp@asp.com.lb; internet www.asp.com.lb; computer science, biological sciences, cookery, travel, politics, fiction, children's; Pres. Bassam Chebaro.

Dar Assayad Group (SAL and International): POB 11-1038, Hazmieh, Beirut; tel. (5) 456376; fax (5) 452700; e-mail info@dar-assayad.com; internet www.dar-assayad.com; Dar Assayad SAL f. 1943; Dar Assayad Int. f. 1983 and provides publishing, advertising and distribution services; publishes in Arabic *Al-Anwar* (daily), *Assayad* (weekly), *Achabaka* (weekly), *Background Reports*, *Arab Defense Journal* (monthly), *Fairuz* (international monthly edition), *Al-Idari* (monthly), *Al Computer, Communications and Electronics* (monthly), *Al-Fares* (monthly); also publishes monthly background reports; has offices and correspondents in Arab countries and most parts of the world; Chair. Issam Freiha; CEO Bassam Freiha; Man. Dir Elham Freiha.

CPH World Media SARL: POB 13-5121, Chouran, Beirut 1102 2802; tel. (1) 352413; fax (1) 352419; e-mail marketing@cphworldmedia.com; internet www.cphworldmedia.com; f. 1977 as Chatila Publishing House; adopted present name 2008; magazine publishing, events and research; publishes *Arab Construction World* (monthly), *Arab Water World* (monthly), *MENA Health World* (monthly), *Middle East Food* (monthly); Pres. and Publr Fathi Chatila; CEO Muhammad Rabih Chatila.

Edition Française pour le Monde Arabe (EDIFRAMO): POB 113-6140, Immeuble Elissar, rue Bliss, Beirut; tel. (1) 862437; Man. Tahseen S. Khayat.

Editions Orientales SAL: POB 11-1404, Immeuble Sayegh, rue Sursock, Beirut; tel. (1) 202070; fax (1) 202663; e-mail info@ediori.com.lb; internet www.ediori.com.lb; political and social newspapers and magazines; Pres. and Editor-in-Chief Charles Abou Adal.

GeoProjects SARL: POB 113-5294, Immeuble Barakat, 13 rue Jeanne d'Arc, Beirut; tel. (1) 344236; fax (1) 342217; e-mail info@geo-publishers.com; internet www.geo-publishers.com; f. 1978; cartographers, researchers, school textbook publrs; Dir-Gen. Rida Ismail.

Dar el-Ilm Lilmalayin: POB 1085, Centre Metco, rue Mar Elias, Beirut 2045 8402; tel. (1) 306666; fax (1) 701657; e-mail info@malayin.com; internet www.malayin.com; f. 1945; dictionaries, encyclopaedias, reference books, textbooks, Islamic cultural books; CEO TAREF OSMAN.

InfoPro SARL: POB 11-4355, Centre Piccadilly, rue Hamra, Beirut; tel. (1) 739777; fax (1) 749090; e-mail infopro@infopro.com.lb; internet www.infopro.com.lb; f. 1997; information-based magazines, incl. *BusinessWeek Al-Arabiya* and *Lebanon Opportunities*, as well as reference books; Pres. RAMZI EL-HAFEZ.

Institute for Palestine Studies, Publishing and Research Organization (IPS): POB 11-7164, rue Anis Nsouli, Verdun, Beirut 1107 2230; tel. (1) 868387; fax (1) 814193; e-mail ipsbrt@palestine-studies.org; internet www.palestine-studies.org; f. 1963; independent non-profit Arab research org., which promotes better understanding of the Palestine problem and the Arab–Israeli conflict; publishes books, reprints, research papers, etc.; Chair. Dr TAREK MITRI; Gen. Dir MAHMOUD SOUEID.

The International Documentary Center of Arab Manuscripts: POB 2668, Immeuble Hanna, Ras Beirut, Beirut; e-mail alafaq@cyberia.net.lb; f. 1965; publishes and reproduces ancient and rare Arabic texts; Propr ZOUHAIR BAALBAKI.

Dar al-Kashaf: POB 11-2091, rue Assad Malhamee, Beirut; tel. (1) 249952; e-mail dakashaf4@yahoo.com; f. 1930; publrs of *Al-Kashaf* (Arab Youth Magazine), maps, atlases and business books; printers and distributors; Propr M. A. FATHALLAH.

Dar al-Kitab al-Lubnani: POB 11-8330, Beirut; tel. (1) 735731; fax (1) 351433; e-mail info@daralkitabalmasri.com; internet www.daralkitabalmasri.com; f. 1929; publr of books on Islamic studies, history, sciences and literature; Pres. and Gen. Dir Dr HASSAN EL-ZEIN.

Dar Alf Leila wa Leila: BP 165612, rue Issa Maalouf, Immeuble Dimitri Trad, Achrafieh, Beirut; tel. (1) 200961; fax (1) 338929; e-mail rdl@rdl.com.lb; internet www.rdl.com.lb; publishes *Al-Bayraq* (Arabic, daily), *Al-Hawadeth* (Arabic, weekly), *La Revue du Liban* (French, weekly), *Monday Morning* (English, weekly); Editor-in-Chief MELHEM KARAM.

Librairie du Liban Publishers: POB 11-9232, Beirut; tel. (9) 217944; fax (9) 217734; e-mail info@ldlp.com; internet www.ldlp.com; f. 1944; publr of children's books, dictionaries and reference books; distributor of books in English and French; Man. Dirs HABIB SAYEGH, PIERRE SAYEGH.

Dar al-Maaref Liban SARL: POB 2320, Riad el-Solh, Beirut; tel. (1) 931243; f. 1959; children's books and textbooks in Arabic; Man. Dir Dr FOUAD IBRAHIM; Gen. Man. JOSEPH NACHOU.

Dar al-Machreq SARL: POB 166778, Beirut 1100 2150; tel. (1) 202423; fax (1) 202424; e-mail info@darelmachreq.com; internet www.darelmachreq.com; f. 1848; religion, art, Arabic and Islamic literature, history, languages, science, philosophy, school books, dictionaries and periodicals; Man. Dir SALAH ABOUJAOUDE.

Dar Naamān lith-Thaqāfa (Maison Naaman pour la Culture): POB 567, Jounieh; tel. and fax (9) 935096; e-mail info@najinaaman.org; internet www.naamanculture.com; f. 1979; publishes *Mawsou'atul 'Alamil 'Arabiyyil Mu'asser* (Encyclopaedia of the Contemporary Arab World), *Mawsou'atul Waqa'e'il 'Arabiyya* (Encyclopaedia of Arab Events), and *Qitāboul A'lamil A'rabi* ; Propr NAJI NAAMAN; Exec. Man. MARCELLE AL-ASHKAR.

Editions Dar an-Nahar SAL: BP 11-226, Immeuble an-Nahar, rue Banque du Liban, Hamra, Beirut; tel. (1) 747620; fax (1) 747623; e-mail darannahar@darannahar.com; internet www.darannahar.com; f. 1967; pan-Arab publishing house; Pres. GHASSAN TUÉNI; Dir JANA TAMER.

Naufal Group SARL: POB 11-2161, Immeuble Naufal, rue Sourati, Beirut; tel. (1) 354898; fax (1) 354394; e-mail naufalgroup@terra.net.lb; f. 1970; encyclopaedias, fiction, children's books, history, law and literature; subsidiary cos: Macdonald Middle East Sarl, Les Editions Arabes; Man. Dir TONY NAUFAL.

Publitec Publications: POB 16-6142, Beirut; tel. (1) 495401; fax (1) 493330; e-mail info@whoswhointhearabworld.info; f. 1965; publishes *Who's Who in Lebanon* and *Who's Who in the Arab World* (both bi-annual); Pres. CHARLES GEDEON; Man. KRIKOR AYVAZIAN.

Rihani Printing and Publishing House: 13-5378, Beirut; tel. (1) 838281; fax (1) 868384; f. 1963; Propr ALBERT RIHANI; Man. DAOUD STEPHAN.

Sader Publishers: POB 55530, Immeuble Sader, Dekwaneh, Beirut; tel. (1) 488776; e-mail sader@saderpublishers.com; internet www.saderpublishers.com; f. 1863; legal publr; Chair. JOSEPH SADER.

Samir Éditeur: POB 175132, rue Gouraud Gemmayzé, Sin el-Fil, Beirut; tel. (1) 448181; fax (1) 482541; e-mail samir@samirediteur.com; internet www.samirediteur.com; children's books in Arabic, English and French.

World Book Publishing: POB 11-3176, 282 rue Emile Eddé, Sanayeh, Beirut; tel. (1) 349370; fax (1) 351226; e-mail info@wbpbooks.com; internet www.wbpbooks.com; f. 1926; literature, education, philosophy, current affairs, self-help, children's books; Chair. M. SAID EL-ZEIN; Man. Dir RAFIK EL-ZEIN.

Broadcasting and Communications

TELECOMMUNICATIONS

OGERO (Organisme de Gestion et d'Exploitation de l'ex Radio Orient): POB 11-1226, Bir Hassan, Beirut 1107 2070; tel. (1) 840000; fax (1) 826823; internet www.ogero.gov.lb; f. 1972; 100% state-owned; plans for the incorporation of OGERO and two depts of the Ministry of Telecommunications into a single operator, Liban Télécom, were announced in 2005; however, no progress has since been made; fixed-line operator.

In late 2008 it was announced that the planned privatization of Lebanon's two state-owned mobile telephone networks would be deferred until after the 2009 legislative elections. New management contracts to operate the Mobile Interim Company (MIC) networks until April 2010 were awarded with effect from February 2009 to Orascom Telecom Holding of Egypt (which was to operate the MIC1 network) and Zain Group of Kuwait (MIC2); those contracts have subsequently been extended on an annual basis.

Alfa: Palm Center, rond-point Chevrolet, Beirut; tel. (3) 391111; fax (3) 391109; e-mail customercare@alfamobile.com.lb; internet www.alfa.com.lb; managed by Orascom Telecom Holding (Egypt); operates the state-owned MIC1 mobile telephone network under licence; Chair. and CEO MARWAN HAYEK.

touch: POB 17-5051, Immeuble MTC Touch, ave Charles Helou, Beirut; tel. (3) 792000; e-mail info@mtc.com.lb; internet www.touch.com.lb; f. 2004 as MTC Touch; present name adopted 2012; managed by Zain Group (fmrly Mobile Telecommunications Co—Kuwait); operates the state-owned MIC2 mobile telephone network under licence; Gen. Man. CLAUDE BASSIL.

Regulatory Authority

Telecommunications Regulatory Authority (TRA): Marfaa Bldg 200, 2nd Floor, Beirut Central District, Beirut; tel. (1) 964300; fax (1) 964341; e-mail info@tra.gov.lb; internet www.tra.gov.lb; f. 2007; Chair. and CEO Dr IMAD HOBALLAH.

BROADCASTING

Radio

Radio Liban: rue Emile Edée, Sanayeh, Hamra, Beirut; tel. (1) 756185; fax (1) 347489; internet www.96-2.com; run by the Ministry of Information in conjunction with Radio France International; f. 1937; Arabic programmes broadcast on 98.1 FM and 98.5 FM; scheduled for privatization; Dir-Gen. FOUAD KABALAN HAMDAN; Dir of Programmes MICHÈLE DE FREIGE.

The Home Service broadcasts in Arabic on short wave, and the Foreign Service broadcasts in Portuguese, Armenian, Arabic, Spanish, French and English.

Television

Lebanese Broadcasting Corpn (LBC) Sat Ltd: POB 111, Zouk, Beirut 165853; tel. (9) 850850; fax (9) 850916; e-mail lbcsat@lbcsat.com.lb; internet www.lbcgroup.tv; f. 1985 as Lebanese Broadcasting Corpn Int. SAL; name changed 1996; operates satellite channel on Arabsat 2C, Arabsat 3A and Nilesat 102; programmes in Arabic, French and English; broadcasts to Lebanon, the Middle East, Europe, the USA and Australia; Chair. Sheikh PIERRE EL-DAHER.

Future Television (Al-Mustaqbal): POB 13-6052, White House, rue Spears, Sanayeh, Beirut; tel. (1) 355355; fax (1) 753434; e-mail future@future.com.lb; internet www.future.com.lb; f. 1993; privately owned; commercial; Gen. Man. NADIM AL-MONLA.

Al-Manar (Lighthouse): Bir Hassan, Beirut; tel. (1) 540440; fax (1) 553138; e-mail info@manartv.com.lb; internet www.almanar.com.lb; f. 1991; television station owned by Lebanese Communication Group; broadcasts to Arab and Muslim audiences world-wide; operates satellite channel since May 2000; partially controlled by Hezbollah; Chair. of Bd ABDALLAH KASSIR.

Murr Television: Naccache, Beirut; internet www.mtv.com.lb; f. 1991; closed down in 2002 for contravening electoral laws; relaunched April 2009; privately owned; CEO MICHEL EL-MURR.

Finance

(cap. = capital; dep. = deposits; res = reserves; m. = million; br(s) = branch(es); amounts in Lebanese pounds)

BANKING

Beirut was, for many years, the leading financial and commercial centre in the Middle East, but this role was destroyed by the civil conflict during 1975–90. To restore the city as a regional focus for investment banking has been a key element of the reconstruction plans of successive governments.

Central Bank

Banque du Liban: POB 11-5544, rue Masraf Loubnane, Beirut; tel. (1) 750000; fax (1) 747600; e-mail bdlfx@bdl.gov.lb; internet www.bdl.gov.lb; f. 1964 as successor in Lebanon to the Banque de Syrie et du Liban; cap. and res 3,342,331m., dep. 63,932,268m. (Dec. 2009); Gov. RIAD T. SALAMEH; 9 brs.

Principal Commercial Banks

Bank Audi SAL—Audi Saradar Group: POB 11-2560, Riad el-Solh, Beirut 1107 2808; tel. (1) 994000; fax (1) 990555; e-mail contactus@banqueaudi.com; internet www.banqueaudi.com; f. 1962 as Bank Audi; acquired Orient Credit Bank 1997 and Banque Nasr 1998; absorbed into Audi Saradar Group in 2004; cap. 455,440m., res 2,083,782m., dep. 38,066,066m. (Dec. 2011); Chair. and Gen. Man. RAYMOND W. AUDI; CEO SAMIR HANNA; 80 brs in Lebanon, 12 brs in Jordan.

Bank of Beirut SAL: POB 11-7354, Bank of Beirut SAL Bldg, Foch St, Beirut Central District, Beirut; tel. (1) 983999; fax (1) 972972; e-mail contactus@bankofbeirut.com; internet www.bankofbeirut.com.lb; f. 1973; acquired Transorient Bank 1999, Beirut Riyad Bank 2002; cap. 603,500m., res 491,519m., dep. 9,443,966m. (Dec. 2010); Chair. and Gen. Man. SALIM G. SFEIR; 46 brs.

BankMed SAL: POB 11-0348, Centre Groupe Méditerranée, 482 rue Clémenceau, Beirut 2022 9302; tel. (1) 373937; fax (1) 362706; internet www.bankmed.com.lb; f. 1944 as Banque Naaman et Soussou; name changed to Eastern Commercial Bank 1955, Banque de la Méditerranée SAL 1970 and as above 2006; acquired Allied Bank SAL in 2006; cap. 680,750m., res 478,488m., dep. 14,280,785m. (Dec. 2010); Chair. and Gen. Man. MUHAMMAD HARIRI; 51 brs.

Banque Bemo SAL: POB 16-6353, Immeuble Bemo, place Sassine, ave Elias Sarkis, Achrafieh, Beirut 1100 2120; tel. (1) 200505; fax (1) 217860; e-mail bemosal@dm.net.lb; internet www.bemobank.com; f. 1964 as Future Bank SAL; name changed to BEMO (Banque Européenne pour le Moyen-Orient) SAL 1994 and as above 2006; cap. 46,150m., res 59,815m., dep. 1,578,742m. (Dec. 2010); Chair. and Gen. Man. RIAD BECHARA OBEGI; Man. Dir and Gen. Man. SAMIH H. SAADEH; 9 brs in Lebanon, 1 br. in Cyprus.

Banque Libano-Française SAL: POB 11-0808, Tour Liberty, 5 rue de Rome, Beirut 1107 2804; tel. and fax (1) 791332; e-mail info@eblf.com; internet www.eblf.com; f. 1967; cap. 586,828m., res 392,458m., dep. 13,616,363m. (Dec. 2011); Chair. FARID RAPHAËL; 47 brs.

Banque Misr-Liban SAL: rue Riad el-Solh, Beirut 2011 9301; tel. (1) 986666; fax (1) 964296; e-mail mail@bml.com.lb; internet www.bml.com.lb; f. 1929 as Banque Misr Syrie Liban; name changed as above 1958; cap. 100,000m., res 29,425m., dep. 1,279,432m. (Dec. 2011); Chair. MUHAMMAD KAMAL EL-DIN BARAKAT; Exec. Gen. Man. HADI NAFFI; 14 brs.

BBAC (Bank of Beirut and the Arab Countries) SAL: POB 11-1536, Immeuble de la Banque, 250 rue Clémenceau, Riad el-Solh, Beirut 1107 2080; tel. (1) 360460; fax (1) 365200; e-mail contactus@bbac.com.lb; internet www.bbacbank.com; f. 1956; cap. 147,375m., res 192,566m., dep. 5,625,310m. (Dec. 2010); Chair. and Gen. Man. GHASSAN T. ASSAF; 37 domestic brs and 1 foreign rep. office.

BLC Bank SAL: POB 11-1126, BLC Bldg, Adlieh Intersection, Beirut 2064 5809; tel. and fax (1) 429000; e-mail info@blcbank.com; internet www.blcbank.com; f. 1950; 74.8% owned by Fransabank SAL; cap. 152,700m., res 149,087m., dep. 3,971,891m. (Dec. 2010); Chair. and Gen. Man. MAURICE SEHNAOUI; 35 brs.

BLOM Bank SAL: POB 11-1912, Immeuble BLOM Bank, rue Rachid Karameh, Verdun, Beirut 1107 2807; tel. (1) 743300; fax (1) 738946; e-mail blommail@blom.com.lb; internet www.blom.com.lb; f. 1951 as Banque du Liban et d'Outre-Mer; name changed as above 2000; cap. 282,000m., res 1,545,471m., dep. 30,933,706m. (Dec. 2011); Chair. and Gen. Man. SAAD AZHARI; 62 domestic brs and 11 foreign brs.

Byblos Bank SAL: POB 11-5605, ave Elias Sarkis, Achrafieh, Beirut 1107 2811; tel. (1) 335200; fax (1) 339436; e-mail byblosbk@byblosbank.com.lb; internet www.byblosbank.com; f. 1959; merged with Banque Beyrouth pour le Commerce SAL 1997; acquired Byblos Bank Europe SA 1998, Wedge Bank Middle East SAL 2001 and ABN AMRO Bank Lebanon 2002; cap. 689,113m., res 1,304,378m., dep 20,713,778m. (Dec. 2011) Chair. and Gen. Man. Dr FRANÇOIS S. BASSIL; 78 brs in Lebanon, 23 brs abroad.

Creditbank SAL: POB 16-5795, Immeuble Crédit Bancaire SAL, 680 blvd Bachir Gemayel, Achrafieh, Beirut 1100 2802; tel. (1) 501600; fax (1) 485245; e-mail info@creditbank.com.lb; internet www.creditbank.com.lb; f. 1981 as Crédit Bancaire SAL; name changed as above following merger with Crédit Lyonnais Liban SAL 2002; cap. 55,526m., res 99,477m., dep. 1,834,873m. (Dec. 2010); Chair. and Gen. Man. TAREK JOSEPH KHALIFÉ; 15 brs.

Crédit Libanais SAL: POB 16-6729, Centre Sofil, 5e étage, ave Charles Malek, Beirut 1100 2811; tel. (1) 200028; fax (1) 325713; e-mail info@creditlibanais.com.lb; internet www.creditlibanais.com.lb; f. 1961; cap. 250,000m., res 352,920m., dep. 8,564,329m. (Dec. 2010); Chair. and Gen. Man. Dr JOSEPH M. TORBEY; 57 brs in Lebanon, 2 brs abroad.

Fenicia Bank SAL: POB 113-6248, Immeuble Fenicia Bank, rue Foch, Beirut Central District, Beirut 1103 2110; tel. (1) 957800; e-mail info@feniciabank.com; internet www.bkawbank.com; f. 1959; as Bank of Kuwait and the Arab World SAL; name changed as above 2010; 74% owned by Achour Group, 15% by Maacaron Group, 10% by Merhi Group and 1% by Dr Cheaib; cap. 100,000m., res 17,258m., dep. 1,554,368m (Dec. 2010); Chair. and Gen. Man. ABD AL-RAZZAK ACHOUR; 14 brs in Lebanon.

First National Bank SAL: POB 11-0435, Immeuble 147, rue Allenby, Riad el-Solh, Beirut 2012 6004; tel. (1) 963000; fax (1) 973090; e-mail info@fnb.com.lb; internet www.fnb.com.lb; f. 1996; acquired Société Bancaire du Liban SAL 2002; cap. 137,605m., res 91,951m., dep. 2,922,936m. (Dec. 2009); Chair. RAMI REFAAT EL-NIMER; Gen. Man. ELIAS SALIM BAZ; 21 brs.

Fransabank SAL: POB 11-0393, rue Hamra, Riad el-Solh, Beirut 1107 2803; tel. (1) 745761; fax (1) 354572; e-mail fsb@fransabank.com; internet www.fransabank.com; f. 1921; acquired Banque Tohmé SAL 1993, Universal Bank SAL 1999, United Bank of Saudi and Lebanon SAL 2001 and Banque de la Beka'a SAL 2003; Banque de la Beka'a was subsequently sold to Bank of Sharjah Ltd (United Arab Emirates) in July 2007; cap. 438,500m., res 778,709m., dep. 15,612,755m. (Dec. 2010); Chair. ADNAN KASSAR; 63 brs.

IBL Bank SAL: POB 11-5292, Immeuble Ittihadiah, ave Charles Malek, Beirut 1107 2190; tel. (1) 200350; fax (1) 204505; e-mail info@ibl.com.lb; internet www.ibl.com.lb; f. 1961 as Intercontinental Bank of Lebanon SAL; cap. 151,657m., res 54,933m., dep. 4,456,678m. (Dec. 2010); Chair. and Gen. Man. SALIM Y. HABIB; 17 brs.

Jammal Trust Bank SAL: POB 11-5640, Immeuble Jammal, rue Verdun, Beirut; tel. (1) 781999; fax (1) 800361; e-mail services@jammalbank.com.lb; internet www.jammalbank.com.lb/home.html; f. 1963 as Investment Bank SAL; cap. 58,000m., res 22,869m., dep. 743,164m. (Dec. 2010); Chair. and Gen. Man. ANWAR A. AL-JAMMAL; 22 brs in Lebanon, 3 rep. offices abroad.

Lebanese Swiss Bank SAL: POB 11-9552, Immeuble Hoss, 6e étage, rue Emile Eddé, place Hamra, Ras Beirut, Beirut; tel. (1) 354501; fax (1) 346242; e-mail lbs@t-net.com.lb; internet www.lebaneseswissbank.com; f. 1962; cap. 70,000m., res 48,382m., dep. 1,265,653m. (Dec. 2010); Chair. and Gen. Man. Dr TANAL SABBAH; 14 brs.

Lebanon and Gulf Bank SAL: POB 11-3360, 124 Allenby St, Beirut Central District, Beirut; tel. (1) 965000; fax (1) 965199; e-mail info@lgb.com.lb internet www.lgb.com.lb; f. 1963 as Banque de Crédit Agricole; name changed as above 1980; cap. 106,000m., res 86,350m., dep. 2,526,227m. (Dec. 2010); Chair. and Gen. Man. ABD AL-HAFIZ MAHMOUD ITANI; 13 domestic brs, 1 foreign br.

MEAB SAL: POB 14-5958, Immeuble Hejeij, ave Adnan al-Hakim, Beirut 1105 2080; tel. (1) 826740; fax (1) 841190; e-mail meab@meabank.com; internet www.meabank.com; f. 1991 as Middle East and Africa Bank SAL; name changed as above 2003; cap. 41,000m., res 26,617m., dep. 1,144 214m. (Dec. 2010); Chair. and Gen. Man. KASSEM HEJEIJ; 6 brs.

Société Nouvelle de la Banque de Syrie et du Liban SAL (BSL): POB 11-957, rue Riad el-Solh, Beirut; tel. (1) 980080; fax (1) 980991; e-mail info@bsl.com.lb; internet www.bsl.com.lb; f. 1963; cap. 46,920m., res 64,676m., dep. 1,084,953m. (Dec. 2010); Chair. RAMSAY A. EL-KHOURI; Gen. Man. SÉLIM STÉPHAN; 17 brs.

Syrian Lebanese Commercial Bank SAL: SLCB Bldg, Makdessi St, Beirut; tel. (1) 741666; fax (1) 736629; e-mail hamra@slcbk.com; internet www.slcb.com.lb; f. 1974; cap. 132,000m., res 29,497m., dep. 137,097m. (Dec. 2010); Chair. ANTOINE FRANJIEH; 3 brs in Lebanon.

Development Bank

Audi Saradar Investment Bank SAL: POB 16-5110, Bank Audi Plaza, Omar al-Daouk St, Beirut; tel. (1) 994000; fax (1) 999406; e-mail contactus@asib.com; internet www.asib.com; f. 1974 as Investment and Finance Bank; name changed to Audi Investment Bank SAL 1996 and as above 2004; medium- and long-term loans, 100% from Lebanese sources; owned by Bank Audi SAL—Audi

Saradar Group; cap. 25,075m., res 164,154m., dep. 763,983m. (Dec. 2010); Chair. and Gen. Man. Dr MARWAN M. GHANDOUR; Gen. Man. RAMZI N. SALIBA.

Supervisory Body

Banking Control Commission of Lebanon: POB 11-5544, rue Masraf Loubnane, Beirut; tel. (1) 350167; fax (1) 750040; internet www.bccl.gov.lb; f. 1967; Chair. OSAMA MEKDASHI.

Banking Association

Association of Banks in Lebanon: POB 976, Gouraud St, Saifi, Beirut; tel. (1) 970500; e-mail abl@abl.org.lb; internet www.abl.org.lb; f. 1959; serves and promotes the interests of the banking community in Lebanon; mems: 64 banks and 7 foreign rep. offices; Chair. JOSEPH TORBEY.

STOCK EXCHANGE

Beirut Stock Exchange (BSE): POB 11-3552, Immeuble Azareih, 4e étage, Bloc O1, Beirut; tel. (1) 993555; fax (1) 993444; e-mail bse@bse.com.lb; internet www.bse.com.lb; f. 1920; recommenced trading in Jan. 1996; 10 cttee mems; Vice-Chair. GHALEB MAHMASSANI.

INSURANCE

About 80 insurance companies were registered in Lebanon in the late 1990s, although fewer than one-half of these were operational. An insurance law enacted in 1999 increased the required capital base for insurance firms and provided tax incentives for mergers within the sector.

Allianz SNA SAL: POB 16-6528, Immeuble Allianz SNA, Hazmieh, Beirut 1100 2130; tel. (1) 956600; fax (1) 956624; e-mail info@allianzsna.com; internet www.allianzsna.com; f. 1963 as Société Nationale d'Assurances SAL; renamed as above 2008; part of Allianz Group; cap. 13,264m. (2007); Chair. ANTOINE WAKIM; CEO XAVIER DENYS.

Arabia Insurance Co SAL: POB 11-2172, Arabia House, rue de Phénicie, Beirut; tel. (1) 363610; fax (1) 365139; e-mail arabia@arabia-ins.com.lb; internet www.arabiainsurance.com; f. 1944; cap. 51,000m.; Chair. WAHBÉ A. TAMARI; CEO FADY SHAMMAS.

Bankers Assurance SAL: POB 11-4293, 4th Floor, Immeuble Asseily, rue El Mir Bechir, Riad el-Solh Sq., Beirut; tel. (1) 962700; fax (1) 984004; e-mail mail@bankers-assurance.com; internet www.bankers-assurance.com; f. 1972; Chair. SABA NADER; Gen. Man. EUGÈNE S. NADER.

Commercial Insurance Co (Lebanon) SAL: POB 11-4351, Centre Starco, North Block, 9th Floor, Beirut; tel. (1) 373070; fax (1) 373071; e-mail comins@commercialinsurance.com.lb; internet www.commercialinsurance.com.lb; f. 1962; cap. 6,000m. (March 2006); Chair. MAX R. ZACCAR; 2 brs.

Compagnie Libanaise d'Assurances SAL: POB 3685, rue Riad el-Solh, Beirut; tel. (1) 868988; e-mail lebanese@sodetel.net.lb; internet www.lebaneseinsurance.com; f. 1951; cap. 22,500m.; Chair. PEDRO ABOUJAOUDÉ; Gen. Man. JIHAD SAKR.

Al-Ittihad al-Watani: POB 11-1270, Jisr al-Wati, Immeuble Al-Ittihad al-Watani, Beirut; tel. (1) 426480; fax (1) 426486; e-mail webmaster@alittihadalwatani.com.lb; internet www.alittihadalwatani.com.lb; f. 1947; cap. 20.6m. (2005); Chair. and Gen. Man. TANNOUS FEGHALI.

Libano-Suisse Insurance Co SAL: POB 11-3821, Immeuble Commerce and Finance, Beirut 1107 2150; tel. (1) 374900; fax (1) 368724; e-mail libano-suisse@libano-suisse.com; internet www.libano-suisse.com; f. 1959; Chair. MICHEL PIERRE PHARAON; Gen. Man. LUCIEN LETAYEF, Jr.

Al-Mashrek Insurance and Reinsurance SAL: POB 16-6154, Immeuble Al-Mashrek, Antélias Main Rd, Rabieh, Beirut 1100 2100; tel. (4) 408666; fax (4) 417688; e-mail almashrek@almashrek.com.lb; internet www.almashrek.com.lb; f. 1962; Chair. and CEO ABRAHAM MATOSSIAN.

'La Phénicienne' SAL: POB 11-5652, Immeuble Hanna Haddad, rue Amine Gemayel, Sioufi, Beirut; tel. (1) 425484; fax (1) 424532; e-mail phenicienne@sodetel.net.lb; f. 1964; cap. 3,167m.; Chair. and Gen. Man. CAROLE FÉGHALI CHAMOUN.

Insurance Association

Association des Compagnies d'Assurances au Liban: POB 45-237, Immeuble ACAL, Hazmieh, Beirut; tel. (5) 956957; fax (5) 458959; e-mail acal@acal.org.lb; internet www.acal.org.lb; f. 1971; Pres. ABRAHAM MATOSSIAN; Sec.-Gen. JAMIL HARB.

Trade and Industry

DEVELOPMENT ORGANIZATIONS

Council for Development and Reconstruction (CDR): POB 116-5351, Tallet el-Serail, Beirut; tel. (1) 980096; fax (1) 981252; e-mail general@cdr.gov.lb; internet www.cdr.gov.lb; f. 1977; an autonomous public institution reporting to the Cabinet, the CDR is charged with the co-ordination, planning and execution of Lebanon's public reconstruction programme; it plays a major role in attracting foreign funds; Pres. NABIL ADNAN EL-JISR.

Investment Development Authority of Lebanon (IDAL): POB 113-7251, Azarieh Tower, 4th Floor, Emir Bechir St, Riad el-Solh, Beirut; tel. (1) 983306; fax (1) 983302; e-mail invest@idal.com.lb; internet www.idal.com.lb; f. 1994; state-owned; Chair. and Gen. Man. NABIL ITANI.

Société Libanaise pour le Développement et la Reconstruction de Beyrouth (Solidere): POB 11-9493, 149 rue Saad Zaghoul, Beirut 2012-7305; tel. (1) 980650; fax (1) 980662; e-mail solidere@solidere.com.lb; internet www.solidere.com.lb; f. 1994; real estate co responsible for reconstruction of Beirut Central District after the civil war; Chair. NASSER CHAMMAA; Gen. Man. MOUNIR DOUAIDY.

CHAMBERS OF COMMERCE AND INDUSTRY

Federation of the Chambers of Commerce, Industry and Agriculture in Lebanon: POB 11-1801, Immeuble CCIAB, rue Justinien, Sanayeh, Beirut; tel. (1) 744702; fax (1) 349614; e-mail fccial@cci-fed.org.lb; internet www.cci-fed.org.lb; f. 1996; Pres. MUHAMMAD CHOUCAIR.

Chamber of Commerce, Industry and Agriculture of Beirut and Mount Lebanon: POB 11-1801, 1 rue Justinian, Sanayeh, Beirut; tel. (1) 353390; fax (1) 353395; e-mail information@ccib.org.lb; internet www.ccib.org.lb; f. 1898; 16,000 mems; Pres. MUHAMMAD CHOUCAIR.

Chamber of Commerce, Industry and Agriculture in Sidon and South Lebanon: POB 41, rue Maarouf Saad, Sidon; tel. (7) 720123; fax (7) 722986; e-mail chamber@ccias.org.lb; internet www.ccias.org.lb; f. 1933; Pres. MUHAMMAD SALEH.

Chamber of Commerce, Industry and Agriculture of Tripoli and North Lebanon: POB 47, rue Bechara Khoury, Tripoli; tel. (6) 627162; fax (6) 442042; e-mail abdallahg@cciat.org.lb; internet www.cciat.org.lb; Chair. ABDALLAH GHANDOUR.

Chamber of Commerce, Industry and Agriculture of Zahleh and Beqa'a: POB 100, Zahleh; tel. (8) 802602; fax (8) 800050; e-mail info@cciaz.org.lb; internet www.cciaz.org.lb; f. 1939; 2,500 mems; Pres. EDMOND JREISSATI.

EMPLOYERS' ASSOCIATION

Association of Lebanese Industrialists: POB 11-1520, Chamber of Commerce and Industry Bldg, 5e étage, rue Justinien, Sanayeh, Beirut; tel. (1) 350280; fax (1) 351167; e-mail ali@ali.org.lb; internet www.ali.org.lb; Pres. FADY ABBOUD; Gen. Man. SAAD S. OUEINI.

UTILITIES

Electricity

Electricité du Liban (EDL): POB 131, Immeuble de l'Electricité du Liban, 22 rue du Fleuve, Beirut; tel. (1) 442720; fax (1) 443828; e-mail info@edl.gov.lb; internet www.edl.gov.lb; f. 1954; state-owned; Chair. and Dir-Gen. KAMAL F. HAYEK.

Water

Legislation introduced in 2000 allowed for the merging of 21 water authorities into four new regional establishments for water exploitation—Beirut and the Mount of Lebanon; North Lebanon; South Lebanon; and the Beqa'a. Under the reorganization the new authorities were to operate under the supervision of the Ministry of Energy and Water.

The Water Establishment of Beirut and the Mount of Lebanon: Beirut; internet www.ebml.gov.lb; f. 2000.

The Water Establishment of North Lebanon: Tripoli; f. 2000; Chair. JAMAL KRAYYEM.

The Water Establishment of the Beqa'a: Zahleh; f. 2000; Gen. Dir JAMAL KRAYEM.

The Water Establishment of South Lebanon: Sidon; f. 2000; Chair. and Dir-Gen. Eng. AHMAD HASSAN NIZAM.

Litani River Authority: rue Bechara el-Khoury, Beirut; tel. (1) 666662; fax (1) 660476; e-mail litani@litani.gov.lb; internet www.litani.gov.lb; f. 1954; responsible for water resources management, irrigation, and the devt of dams and hydroelectric facilities.

MAJOR COMPANIES

Arabian Construction Co SAL: POB 114–5175, Bloc C, Gefinor, Ras Beirut; tel. (1) 355910; fax (1) 355917; e-mail beirut@accsal.com; internet www.accsal.com; f. 1971; construction of multi-storey buildings, hotels, houses, etc.; turnover US $1,400m. (2012); Chair. GHASSAN ABDALLAH AL-MEREHBI; Vice-Chair. ANAS MIKATI; 33,000 employees world-wide.

Château Ksara SAL: Immeuble Nakhle Hanna, ave Charles Malek, POB 16-6184, Beirut; tel. (1) 200715; fax (1) 200716; e-mail info@ksara.com.lb; internet www.ksara.com.lb; f. 1857; wines and spirits (incl. Ksarak); Chair. ZAFER CHAOUI; Man. Dir CHARLES GHOSTINE; 115 employees.

Consolidated Contractors International Co SAL (CCC): POB 11-2254, Bir Hassan, Nicolas Sursock St, Riad el-Solh, Beirut 1107-2100; tel. (1) 847777; fax (1) 856857; internet www.ccc.gr; general construction and engineering projects incl. infrastructure and heavy industry; subsidiary of Consolidated Contractors Co (Greece); revenue US $4.2m. (2012); Group Chair. HASSIB SABBAGH; Group Pres. SAID KHOURY; more than 130,000 employees (group total).

Contracting and Trading Co (CAT) Group: POB 11-1036, Immeuble CAT, rue al-Arz, Saifi, Beirut; tel. (1) 449910; fax (1) 448437; e-mail catgroup@catgroup.net; internet www.catgroup.net; main subsidiaries: Mothercat Ltd, CAT Int. Ltd, Contracting and Trading Co (CAT) Lebanon SAL; sales US $189m., total assets $166m. (2004); Pres. and CEO NASSER G. ISSA; 8,500 employees.

Filature Nationale de Coton SAL, Asseily & Cie: Immeuble Asseily, place Riad el-Solh, POB 11-4126, Beirut; tel. (1) 890610; production of textiles; Dir. G. ASSEILY.

Fonderies Ohannes H. Kassardjian SAL: POB 11-4150, Beirut; tel. (5) 462462; fax (5) 462948; e-mail contact@okfond.com; internet www.okfoundry.com; f. 1939; production of brass and gun-metal valves, ferrules, saddles and fittings for water-service house connections, cast-iron fittings for pipes, manhole covers and gratings, urban furniture, etc.; Pres. JOSEPH O. KASSARDJIAN; 250 employees.

Hamra Engineering SARL: POB 11-6040, Dekwaneh, Main St, Beirut; tel. and fax (1) 688747; fax (1) 688746; e-mail hameng@bignet.com.lb; internet www.hamengholdings.com; f. 1966; part of the Al-Hamra Group; civil, electrical and mechanical engineering; construction work on industrial projects, etc.; steel structures, offshore works; production and trading in building materials, etc.; Chair. HANNA AYOUB; Gen. Man. TONY HANANIA; 800 employees.

Industrial Development Co (INDEVCO) SAL: POB 11-2354, Tellat al-Ansafir, Ajaltoun, Beirut; tel. (9) 230130; fax (9) 235541; e-mail info@indevcogroup.com; internet www.indevcogroup.com; f. 1955; private co; mfrs of plastic and paper flexible packaging, corrugated containers, tissue rolls, personal hygiene products and other disposables; revenue over US $1,000m. (2007); Chair. CHAFIC FREM; CEO NEEMAT FREM; over 8,500 employees world-wide.

Karoun Dairies SAL: POB 11-9150, Immeuble Baghdassarian, Cité Industrielle, Bauchrieh, Beirut; tel. (1) 449470; fax (1) 497080; e-mail info@karoundairies.com; internet www.karoun.com; f. 1931; dairy products; Chair. and CEO ARA BAGHDASSARIAN.

Lahoud Engineering Co Ltd: POB 55366, Immeuble LEC, ave Charles de Gaulle, Sin el-Fil, Beirut; tel. (1) 513000; fax (1) 496540; e-mail lahoud@lahoud.com; internet www.lahoud.com; f. 1972; construction of industrial plants; Man. Dir SAMIR LAHOUD.

M1 Group: Immeuble Starco, Bloc B, rue Omar Daouk, Beirut 2020 3313; tel. (1) 356666; fax (1) 356635; e-mail pr@m1group.com; internet www.m1group.com; investment holding co with interests in various sectors, incl. oil & energy, real estate, retail and travel; CEO AZMI T. MIQATI.

Mothercat Ltd: POB 11-1036, Immeuble CAT, rue al-Arz, Saifi, Beirut; tel. (1) 449910; fax (1) 446931; f. 1994; civil, mechanical, electrical, pipeline, storage tanks and district cooling contractors; subsidiary of C.A.T. Holding SA (Luxembourg); sales US $250.6m. (2007); cap. $15.0m., total assets $272.0m.; CEO NASSER ISSA; 5,000 employees.

Société Nationale d'Entreprises: POB 11-7101, Beirut; tel. (1) 892805; fax (1) 892806; civil engineering incl. road construction and water contracting; Chair. JOSEPH KHOURY; 230 employees.

TRADE UNION FEDERATION

Confédération Générale des Travailleurs du Liban (CGTL): POB 4381, Beirut; f. 1958; 300,000 mems; only national labour centre in Lebanon and sole rep. of working classes; comprises 18 affiliated feds, incl. all 150 unions in Lebanon; Pres. GHASSAN GHOSN.

Transport

RAILWAYS

Office des Chemins de Fer et des Transports en Commun (OCFTC): POB 11-109, Gare St Michel, Nahr, Beirut; tel. (1) 587211; fax (1) 447007; since 1961 all railways in Lebanon have been state-owned; the original network of some 412 km is no longer functioning; however, in 2004 work began on a project to reconstruct a section of the railway network between Tripoli and the Syrian border; Dir-Gen. and Pres. RADWAN BOU NASSER EL-DIN.

ROADS

In 2005 Lebanon had an estimated 6,970 km of roads, of which some 170 km were motorways and 6,800 km were other roads. The two international motorways are the north–south coastal road and the road connecting Beirut with Damascus in Syria. Among the major roads are those crossing the Beqa'a and continuing south to Bent-Jbail and the Shtaura–Ba'albek road. It was reported that up to 80% of Lebanon's major roads, and almost all of its bridges, were destroyed as a result of the Israeli military offensive in mid-2006.

SHIPPING

In the 1990s a two-phase programme to rehabilitate and expand the port of Beirut commenced, involving the construction of an industrial free zone, a fifth basin and a major container terminal, at an estimated cost of US $1,000m.; the container terminal became operational in February 2005. A further extension to the container terminal, increasing total capacity at the port to 1.5m. TEUs, was due to open officially in November 2013. Tripoli, the northern Mediterranean terminus of the oil pipeline from Iraq, is also a busy port, with good equipment and facilities. Jounieh, north of Beirut, is Lebanon's third most important port. A new deep-water sea port was to be constructed south of Sidon. The reconstructed port of al-Naqoura, in what was then the 'security zone' along the border with Israel, was inaugurated in June 1987. Several ports were bombed by Israeli forces during the conflict of mid-2006.

At 31 December 2012 Lebanon's flag registered fleet totalled 52 vessels, with an aggregate displacement of 151,817 grt, of which two were bulk carriers and 17 were general cargo ships.

Port Authorities

Gestion et Exploitation du Port de Beyrouth: POB 1490, Beirut; tel. (1) 580211; fax (1) 585835; e-mail gepb@portdebeyrouth.com; internet www.portdebeyrouth.com; Pres., Dir-Gen. and Man. Dir HASSAN KAMEL KRAYTEM; Harbour Master MAROUN KHOURY.

Service d'Exploitation du Port de Tripoli: rond point Tripoli, rue Mina, Tripoli; tel. (6) 600413; fax (6) 220180; e-mail tport@terra.net.lb; f. 1959; Harbour Master MARWAN BAROUDI.

Principal Shipping Companies

Ademar Shipping Lines: POB 175-231, rue Shafaka, al-Medawar, Beirut; tel. and fax (1) 444100; fax (1) 444101; e-mail ademar@ademarlb.com; internet www.ademarlb.com; f. 1992.

Amin Kawar & Sons (Jordan): POB 11-4230, Beirut; tel. (1) 352525; fax (1) 353802; e-mail amkawar@travelkawar.com; internet www.kawar.com; f. 1963; Chair. TAWFIQ AMIN KAWAR; CEO RUDAIN KAWAR; Pres. KARIM KAWAR.

Beirut Cargo Center: Kurban Bldg, Corniche al-Nahr, Beirut; tel. (1) 585582; fax (1) 585580; e-mail bcc@bcc.com.lb; internet www.bcc.com.lb; f. 1993; air, sea and land freight forwarder; CEO JOSEPH HARB.

Consolidated Bulk Inc (CBI): POB 70-152, Centre St Elie, blk A, 6e étage, Antélias, Beirut; tel. (4) 410724; fax (4) 402842; e-mail info@bulkgroup.com; internet www.bulkgroup.com; f. 1993; Gen. Man. SAMI P. ZACCA.

Continental Shipping Agencies SARL: POB 17-5039, Immeuble Medawar, 5e étage, rue Saifi-Pasteur, Beirut; tel. (1) 567130; fax (1) 567132; e-mail info@csa-continental.com; internet www.csa-continental.com; f. 1991; member of The Lebanese Shipping Agents Syndicates and The Lebanese Shipping Association.

O. D. Debbas & Sons: POB 3, blvd Corniche du Fleuve, Achrafieh, Beirut; tel. (1) 585253; fax (1) 587135; e-mail oddebbas@oddebbas.com; internet www.oddebbas.com; f. 1892; Man. Dir OIDIH ELIE DEBBAS.

Freight Leader SARL: POB 175530, Immeuble Medawar, 5th Floor, rue Pasteur, Saifi, Beirut; tel. (1) 581870; fax (1) 564387; e-mail info@freightleader.com; internet www.freightleader.com; f. 2001; transportation services and logistics; Exec. Man. MOUSSA SALAMOUN.

Gezairi Ltd (GEZACHART): POB 11-1402, Immeuble Oseili, place Riad Solh, Beirut 2034 0716; tel. (1) 783783; fax (1) 784784; e-mail gezairi@gezairi.com; internet www.gezairi.com; f. 1945; ship management, chartering, brokerage; Pres. and CEO MONA BOUAZZA BAWARSHI.

Gulf Agency Co (Lebanon) Ltd: Immeuble Modern, 7e étage, rue el Arz, Beirut; tel. (1) 446189; fax (1) 446097; e-mail lebanon@gac.com; internet www.gac.com/lebanon; f. 1967; Man. Dir SIMON G. BEJJANI.

Lebanese Navigators Co SARL: POB 175179, Immeuble Pasteur 40, 1e étage, Achrafieh, Beirut; tel. (1) 570571; fax (1) 575730; e-mail navigators@navigators-lb.com; internet www.navigators-lb.com; Man. Dir ANTOINE MOUHAYAR.

Orient Shipping and Trading Co SARL: POB 11-2561, Immeuble Moumneh 72, rue Ain al-Mraisseh 54, Beirut; tel. (1) 364455; fax (1) 365570; e-mail ortship@inco.com.lb; internet orientgroup.net/lebanon.swf; Dirs ELIE ZAROUBY, EMILE ZAROUBY.

Ets Paul Adem: Centre Moucarri, 6e étage, autostrade Dora, Bourj Hammoud, Beirut; tel. (1) 244610; fax (1) 244612; e-mail padco@inco.com.lb; f. 1971; ship owners, operators, maritime agents, brokers, consultants; Gen. Man. PAUL ADEM.

G. Sahyouni & Co SARL: POB 17-5452, Mar Mikhael, Beirut 1104 2040; tel. (1) 257046; fax (1) 241317; e-mail postmaster@georgesahyouni.com; internet www.georgesahyouni.com; f. 1989; agents for Baltic Control Lebanon Ltd, SARL, and Lloyds; Man. Dir GEORGE SAHYOUNI.

CIVIL AVIATION

In late 2001 a major expansion project at Beirut International Airport was completed, at an estimated cost of US $600m.; facilities included a new terminal building and two new runways, increasing handling capacity to 6m. passengers a year. In May 2005 the airport was renamed Beirut Rafiq Hariri International Airport in honour of the former Prime Minister who had been killed in February of that year. The airport was targeted by Israeli armed forces in 2006, and was closed to commercial flights during the conflict between Israel and Hezbollah. Following extensive repairs to damaged runways and other infrastructure, the airport reopened to commercial operations in August. In 2009 some 5.0m. passengers used the airport.

MEA (Middle East Airlines, Air Liban SAL): POB 11-206, blvd de l'Aéroport, Beirut 1107 2801; tel. (1) 628888; fax (1) 629260; e-mail mikaouir@mea.com.lb; internet www.mea.com.lb; f. 1945; acquired Lebanese Int. Airways in 1969; regular services throughout Europe, the Middle East, N. and W. Africa, and the Far East; Chair. and Dir-Gen. MUHAMMAD A. EL-HOUT.

Trans-Mediterranean Airways SAL (TMA): POB 30-1001, Beirut Rafiq Hariri International Airport, Beirut; tel. (1) 629210; fax (1) 629219; e-mail cargo@tmacargo.com; internet www.tma.com.lb; f. 1953; cargo services covering Europe, the Middle East, Africa and the Far East; also provides handling, storage and maintenance services; CEO MAZEN BISSAT.

Tourism

Since the end of the civil conflict in 1990 Lebanon's scenic beauty, sunny climate and historic sites have once again attracted foreign visitors. The Government has chosen to concentrate its efforts on the promotion of cultural as well as conference and exhibition-based tourism, while the country is also being promoted as an 'eco-tourism' destination. Excluding Syrian visitors, the annual total of tourist arrivals increased from 177,503 in 1992 to some 1.28m. in 2004. The Lebanese tourism industry experienced a significant downturn in the aftermath of the conflict between Israel and Hezbollah in 2006. However, there was a marked revival in the sector following the Doha Agreement of May 2008, and by 2010 annual foreign tourist arrivals reached some 2.2m. Receipts from tourism totalled US $8,012m. in that year. According to provisional figures, tourist arrivals declined in 2011, to 1.7m., principally owing to the political instability in the region

Ministry of Tourism: see section on The Government—Ministries.

Defence

Commander-in-Chief of the Army: Gen. JEAN KAHWAJI.

Chief of Staff of Armed Forces: Maj.-Gen. WALID SALMAN.

Commander of the Air Force: Brig.-Gen. GHASSAN CHAHINE.

Commander of the Navy: Col JOSEPH GHADBAN (acting).

Director-General of State Security Forces: Maj.-Gen. GEORGES KARAA.

Defence Budget (2012): £L1,730,000m.

Total armed forces (as assessed at November 2012): 60,000: army 56,600; navy 1,800; air force 1,600.Paramilitary forces included an estimated 20,000 members of the Internal Security Force, attached to the Ministry of the Interior. Compulsory military service was formally abolished in February 2007. Hezbollah's active members numbered some 2,000, as assessed at November 2009.

Following conflict in Lebanon between Hezbollah and Israeli armed forces in July–August 2006, the UN Security Council unanimously adopted Resolution 1701, calling for a full cessation of hostilities, upon which Lebanon was to deploy government forces in southern Lebanon and the presence there of the UN Interim Force in Lebanon (UNIFIL) was to be expanded to a maximum authorized strength of 15,000 troops, while Israel was to commence the parallel withdrawal of all its forces from that region. A formal cease-fire entered into effect on 14 August. At the end of July 2012 there were 11,530 UNIFIL military personnel deployed in Lebanon.

Education

Education is compulsory for a period of nine years between six and 15 years of age. Primary education has been available free of charge in state schools since 1960, but private institutions still provide the main facilities for secondary and university education. Private schools enjoy almost complete autonomy, except for a certain number that receive government financial aid and are supervised by inspectors from the Ministry of Education and Higher Education. In the 2010 budget some £L1,293,000m. was allocated to the Ministry of Education and Higher Education (representing 5.9% of total budgetary expenditure).

Primary education begins at six years of age and lasts for six years, comprising two cycles of three years each. Secondary education, beginning at the age of 13, lasts for up to six years, comprising two cycles of three years each. Technical education is provided mainly at the National School of Arts and Crafts, which offers four-year courses in electronics, mechanics, architectural and industrial drawing, and other subjects. There are also public vocational schools providing courses for lower levels. In 2009/10 enrolment at primary schools included 92% of the relevant age-group, while the comparable rate for secondary schools was 75%. Higher education is provided by at least 14 institutions, including 12 universities, an arts academy and a school of theology. Some 216,851 students were enrolled in higher education institutes in 2010/11.

Bibliography

Abouchdid, E. E. *Thirty Years of Lebanon and Syria (1917–47)*. Beirut, Sader-Rihani Print. Co, 1948.

Achcar, Gilbert, and Warschawski, Michel. *The 33-day War: Israel's War on Hezbollah in Lebanon and its Aftermath*. London, Saqi Books, 2007.

Agwani, M. S. (Ed.). *The Lebanese Crisis, 1958: A Documentary Study*. London, Asia Publishing House, 1965.

Ajami, Fouad. *The Vanished Imam: Musa al-Sadr and the Shi'a of Lebanon*. London, I. B. Tauris; New York, Cornell University Press, 1986.

Alagha, Joseph. *The Shifts in Hizbullah's Ideology: Religious Ideology, Political Ideology, and Political Program*. Amsterdam, Amsterdam University Press, 2006.

Ammoun, Denise. *Histoire du Liban contemporain*. 2 Vols. Paris, Fayard, 1997 and 2005.

Attie, Caroline. *Struggle in the Levant: Lebanon in the 1950s*. London, I. B. Tauris, 2003.

Azani, Eitan. *Hezbollah: The Story of the Party of God*. Basingstoke, Palgrave Macmillan, 2008.

Barak, Oren. *The Lebanese Army: A National Institution in a Divided Society*. Albany, NY, State University of New York Press, 2009.

The Beirut Massacre: The Complete Kahan Commission Report. New York, Karz-Cohl, 1983.

Beydoun, Ahmad. *Le Liban. Itinéraires dans une guerre incivile*. Paris, Karthala and CERMOC, 1993.

Blanford, Nicholas. *Killing Mr Lebanon: The Assassination of Rafik Hariri and its Impact on the Middle East*. London, I. B. Tauris, 2006.

Bulloch, John. *Death of a Country: The Civil War in Lebanon*. London, Weidenfeld and Nicolson, 1977.

Final Conflict: The War in Lebanon. London, Century Publishing Co, 1983.

Burckhard, C. *Le Mandat Français en Syrie et au Liban*. Paris, 1925.

Catroux, G. *Dans la Bataille de Méditerranée*. Paris, Julliard, 1949.

Chamoun, C. *Les Mémoires de Camille Chamoun*. Beirut, 1949.

Chehabi, H. E. (Ed.). *Distant Relations: Iran and Lebanon in the Last 500 Years*. London, I. B. Tauris, 2006.

Dagher, Carole H. *Bring Down the Walls: Lebanon's Post-War Challenge*. New York, St Martin's Press, 1998.

Dib, Kamal. *Warlords and Merchants: The Lebanese Business and Political Establishment*. London, Ithaca Press, 2004.

El Khazen, Farid. *The Breakdown of the State in Lebanon, 1967–76*. Cambridge, MA, Harvard University Press, 2000.

Firro, Kais. *Inventing Lebanon: Nationalism and the State Under the Mandate*. London, I. B. Tauris, 2002.

Metamorphosis of the Nation (al-Umma): The Rise of Arabism and Minorities in Syria and Lebanon, 1850–1940. Eastbourne, Sussex Academic Press, 2009.

Fisk, Robert. *Pity the Nation: Lebanon at War*. London, André Deutsch, 1990; revised edn, Oxford Paperbacks, 2001.

Gaspard, Toufic K. *A Political Economy of Lebanon, 1948–2002: The Limits of Laizzez-faire*. Leiden, Brill, 2004.

Gaunson, A. B. *The Anglo-French Clash in Lebanon and Syria, 1940–45*. London, Macmillan, 1987.

Gilmour, David. *Lebanon: The Fractured Country*. London, Martin Robertson, 1983.

Gilsenan, Michael. *Lords of the Lebanese Marches: Violence and Narrative in an Arab Society*. London, I. B. Tauris, 1998.

Glass, Charles. *Tribes with Flags: A Journey Curtailed*. London, Secker and Warburg, 1990.

Haddad, J. *Fifty Years of Modern Syria and Lebanon*. Beirut, Dar-al-Hayat, 1950.

Haddad, Simon. *The Palestinian Impasse in Lebanon: The Politics of Refugee Integration*. Brighton, Sussex Academic Press, 2003.

Halawi, Majed. *A Lebanon Defied: Mosa al-Sadr and the Shi'a Community*. Oxford, Westview Press, 1993.

Harel, Amos, and Issacharoff, Avi. *34 Days: Israel, Hezbollah, and the War in Lebanon*. New York, NY, Palgrave Macmillan, 2008.

Harik, Iliya F. *Politics and Change in a Traditional Society—Lebanon 1711–1845*. Princeton, NJ, Princeton University Press, 1968.

Harik, Judith P. *Hezbollah: The Changing Face of Terrorism*. London, I. B. Tauris, 2004.

Hepburn, A. H. *Lebanon*. New York, Nelson Doubleday, 1966.

Hirst, David. *Beware of Small States: Lebanon, Battleground of the Middle East*. London, Faber and Faber, 2010.

Hitti, Philip K. *Lebanon in History*. London, Macmillan, 3rd edn, 1967.

Hollis, Rosemary, and Shehadi, Nadim (Eds). *Lebanon on Hold: Implications for Middle East Peace*. London, Royal Institute for International Affairs, 1996.

Hourani, Albert K. *Syria and Lebanon*. London, Oxford University Press, 1946.

Hovsepian, Nubar. *The War on Lebanon: A Reader*. Moreton-in-Marsh, Arris Books, 2007.

Hudson, Michael C. *The Precarious Republic: Political Modernization in the Lebanon*. New York, Random House, 1968.

Husayn, Abdul Rahim Abu. *The View from Istanbul: Ottoman Lebanon and the Druze Emirate*. London, I. B. Tauris, 2002.

Iskandar, Marwan. *Rafiq Hariri and the Fate of Lebanon*. London, Saqi Books, 2006.

Jaber, Hala. *Hezbollah*. London, Fourth Estate, 1997.

Johnson, Michael. *All Honourable Men: The Social Origins of War in Lebanon*. London, I. B. Tauris, 2001.

Jones, Clive, and Catignani, Sergio (Eds). *Israel and Hizbollah: An asymmetric conflict in historical and comparative perspective*. Abingdon, Routledge, 2009.

Kalawoun, Nasser M. *The Struggle for Lebanon. A Modern History of Lebanese-Egyptian Relations*. London, I. B. Tauris, 2000.

Kapeliouk, Amnon. *Sabra et Chatila: enquête sur un massacre*. Paris, Editions du Seuil, 1982.

Karsh, Efraim, Kerr, Michael, and Miller, Rory (Eds). *Conflict, Diplomacy and Society in Israeli-Lebanese Relations*. Abingdon, Routledge, 2010.

Kassir, Samir. *La guerre du Liban. De la dissension nationale au conflit régional*. Paris, Karthala and CERMOC, 1994.

Histoire de Beyrouth. Paris, Fayard, 2003.

Kerr, Michael. *Imposing Power-sharing: Conflict and Coexistence in Northern Ireland and Lebanon*. Dublin, Irish Academic Press, 2005.

Khalaf, S. *Civil and Uncivil Violence: The Internationalization of Communal Conflict in Lebanon*. New York, NY, Columbia University Press, 2002.

Klaushofer, Alex. *Paradise Divided: A Portrait of Lebanon*. Oxford, Signal Books, 2007.

LaTeef, Nelda. *Women of Lebanon: Interviews with Champions for Peace*. Jefferson, NC, McFarland and Co, 1997.

Lecerf, Marie-Ange. *Comprendre le Liban*. Paris, Karthala, 1988.

Llewellyn, Tim. *Spirit of the Phoenix: Beirut and the Story of Lebanon*. London, I. B. Tauris, 2010.

Longrigg, S. H. *Syria and Lebanon under French Mandate*. Oxford, Oxford University Press, 1958.

Mackey, Sandra. *Lebanon: A House Divided*. New York, W. W. Norton & Co, 2006.

Mirror of the Arab World: Lebanon in Conflict. New York, W. W. Norton & Co, 2008.

Makdisi, Samar. *Lessons of Lebanon: The Economics of War and Development*. London, I. B. Tauris, 2004.

Makdisi, Ussama. *The Culture of Sectarianism: Community, History and Violence in Nineteenth Century Ottoman Lebanon*. Berkeley, CA, University of California Press, 2000.

Mills, Arthur E. *Private Enterprise in Lebanon*. American University of Beirut, 1959.

Najem, Tom. *Lebanon: The Politics of a Penetrated Society*. Abingdon, Routledge, 2011.

Najjar, Alexandre. *The School of War*. London, Telegram Books, 2006.

Newman, Barbara, and Diaz, Tom. *Lightning Out of Lebanon: Hezbollah Terrorists on American Soil*. Novato, CA, Presidio Press, 2005.

Norton, Augustus Richard. *Hezbollah: A Short History*. Princeton, NJ, Princeton University Press, 2007.

O'Ballance, Edgar. *Civil War in Lebanon, 1975–1992*. New York, St Martin's Press, 1998.

Pellegrin, Paolo, Smith, Patti, and Anderson, Scott. *Double Blind: Lebanon Conflict 2006*. London, Trolley, 2007.

Picard, Elizabeth. *Lebanon: A Shattered Country*. New York and London, Holmes and Meier, revised edn, 2002.

Qassem, Naim. *Hizbullah: The Story from Within*. London, Saqi Books, 2005.

Qubain, Fahim I. *Crisis in Lebanon*. Washington, DC, Middle East Institute, 1961.

Rabil, Robert G. *Religion, National Identity, and Confessional Politics in Lebanon: The Challenge of Islamism*. New York, Palgrave Macmillan, 2011.

Randal, Jonathan. *The Tragedy of Lebanon*. London, Chatto and Windus, 1983.

Rougier, B. *Everyday Jihad: The Rise of Militant Islam among Palestinians in Lebanon*. Cambridge, MA, Harvard University Press, 2007.

Rubin, Barry. *Lebanon: Liberation, Conflict, and Crisis*. Basingstoke, Palgrave Macmillan, 2009.

Saad-Ghorayeb, Amal. *Hizbu'llah: Politics and Religion*. London, Pluto Press, 2001.

Safa, Elie. *L'Emigration Libanaise*. Beirut, Université Saint-Joseph, 1960.

Salam, Nawaf A. (Ed.). *Options for Lebanon*. London, I. B. Tauris, 2005.

Salem, Elie A. *Violence and Diplomacy in Lebanon*. London, I. B. Tauris, 1995.

Salibi, K. S. *The Modern History of Lebanon*. New York, Praeger, and London, Weidenfeld and Nicolson, 1964.

Cross Roads to Civil War: Lebanon 1958–76. New York, Caravan Books, 1976.

A House of Many Mansions: The History of Lebanon Reconsidered. London, I. B. Tauris, 2003.

Shaery-Eisenlohr, Roschanack. *Shi'ite Lebanon: Transnational Religion and the Making of National Identities*. New York, NY, Columbia University Press, 2008.

Shanahan, Rodger. *The Shi'a of Lebanon: Clans, Parties and Clerics*. London, I. B. Tauris, 2005.

Soueid, Mahmoud. *Israël au Liban. La fin de 30 ans d'occupation?* Paris, Revue d'études Palestiniennes, 2000.

Stewart, Desmond. *Trouble in Beirut*. London, Wingate, 1959.

Suleiman, M. W. *Political Parties in Lebanon*. Ithaca, NY, Cornell University Press, 1967.

Sykes, John. *The Mountain Arabs*. London, Hutchinson, 1968.

Traboulsi, Fawwaz. *A History of Modern Lebanon*. London, Pluto Press, 2007.

Vallaud, Pierre. *Le Liban au Bout du Fusil*. Paris, Librairie Hachette, 1976.

Wilson, Anna (Ed.). *Lebanon, Lebanon*. London, Saqi Books, 2006.

Young, Michael. *The Ghosts of Martyrs Square: An Eyewitness Account of Lebanon's Life Struggle*. New York, NY, Simon and Schuster, 2010.

Zamir, Meir. *The Foundation of Modern Lebanon*. London, Croom Helm, 1985.

Lebanon's Quest: The Road to Statehood 1926–1939. London, I. B. Tauris, 1998.

Ziadeh, Hanna. *Sectarianism and Inter-Communal Nation Building in Lebanon*. London, C. Hurst and Co, 2006.

Zisser, Eyal. *Lebanon: The Challenge of Independence*. London, I. B. Tauris, 2000.

LIBYA

Physical and Social Geography

W. B. FISHER

Libya is bounded on the north by the Mediterranean Sea, on the east by Egypt and Sudan, on the south and south-west by Chad and Niger, on the west by Algeria and on the north-west by Tunisia. The three component areas of Libya are Tripolitania, in the west; Cyrenaica, in the east; and the Fezzan, in the south—giving an approximate total for Libya of 1,775,500 sq km (685,524 sq miles). The independence of Libya was proclaimed in December 1951; before that date, following conquest by the Italians, Tripolitania and Cyrenaica had been ruled by a British administration (at first military, then civil), while the Fezzan had been administered by France. The revolutionary Government that came to power in September 1969 renamed the three regions: Tripolitania became known as the Western provinces, Cyrenaica the Eastern provinces, and the Fezzan the Southern provinces. Tarabulus (Tripoli) was formerly the administrative capital of the country, but under a decentralization programme announced in 1988 most government departments and the legislature were relocated to Sirte (Surt), while some departments were transferred to other principal towns. However, some departments were subsequently moved back to Tripoli. In August 2011 the National Transitional Council, which was widely recognized as the de facto governing body for Libya following the outbreak of conflict between opposition forces and those loyal to Muammar al-Qaddafi earlier that year (see History), issued an interim constitutional declaration, which re-established Tripoli as the country's capital.

PHYSICAL FEATURES

The whole of Libya may be said to form part of the vast plateau of North Africa, which extends from the Atlantic Ocean to the Red Sea; however, there are certain minor geographical features that give individuality to the three component areas of Libya. Tripolitania consists of a series of regions at different levels, rising in the main towards the south, and thus broadly comparable with a flight of steps. In the extreme north, along the Mediterranean coast, there is a low-lying coastal plain called the Jefara. This is succeeded inland by a line of hills, or rather a scarp edge, that has several distinguishing local names, but is usually alluded to merely as the Jebel. Here and there in the Jebel occurs evidence of former volcanic activity—old craters, and sheets of lava. The Jefara and adjacent parts of the Jebel are by far the most important parts of Tripolitania, since they are better watered and contain most of the population, together with Tripoli.

South of the Jebel there is an upland plateau—a desert landscape of sand, scrub and scattered irregular masses of stone. After several hundred kilometres the plateau gives way to a series of east–west running depressions, where artesian water, and hence oases, are found. These depressions make up the region of the Fezzan, which is merely a collection of oases on a fairly large scale, interspersed with areas of desert. In the extreme south the land rises considerably to form the mountains of the central Sahara, where some peaks reach 3,500 m in height.

Cyrenaica has a slightly different physical pattern. In the north, along the Mediterranean, there is an upland plateau that rises to 600 m in two very narrow steps, each only a few kilometres wide. This gives a bold, prominent coastline to much of Cyrenaica, and so there is a marked contrast with Tripolitania where the coast is low-lying, and in parts fringed by lagoons. The northern uplands of Cyrenaica are called the Jebel Akhdar (Green Mountain), and here, once again, are found the bulk of the population and the two main towns, Banghazi (Benghazi) and Darnah (Darna). On its western side the Jebel Akhdar drops fairly steeply to the shores of the Gulf of Sirte; on the east it falls more gradually, and is traceable as a series of ridges, about 100 m in altitude, that extend as far as the Egyptian frontier. This eastern district, consisting of low ridges aligned parallel to the coast, is known as Marmarica, and its chief town is Tubruq (Tobruk).

South of the Jebel Akhdar the land falls in elevation, producing an extensive lowland, which, except for its northern fringe, is mainly desert. Oases occur sporadically at Aujila (or Ojila), Jalo and Jaghbub in the north, and Jawf, Zighen and Kufra (the largest of all) in the south. These oases traditionally supported only a few thousand inhabitants and were less significant than those of the Fezzan, though some are now in petroleum-producing areas and, consequently, are increasing in importance. In the same region, and becoming more widespread towards the east, is the Sand Sea—an expanse of fine, mobile sand, easily lifted by the wind into dunes that can sometimes reach about 100 m in height and more than 150 km in length. Finally, in the far south of Cyrenaica, lie the central Saharan mountains—the Tibesti Ranges, continuous with those to the south of the Fezzan.

The climate of Libya is characterized chiefly by its aridity and by its wide variation in temperatures. Lacking mountain barriers, the country is subject to the climatic influence of both the Sahara and the Mediterranean Sea, and, as a result, there can be abrupt transitions in climatic conditions. In winter it can be fairly raw and cold in the north, with sleet and even light snow on the hills. In summer it is extremely hot in the Jefara of Tripolitania, reaching temperatures of 40°C–45°C. In the southern deserts, conditions are hotter still; Gharian has recorded temperatures in excess of 49°C. Several feet of snow can also fall here in winter. Northern Cyrenaica has a markedly cooler summer of 27°C–32°C, but with high air humidity near the coast. A special feature is the *ghibli*—a hot, very dry wind from the south that can raise temperatures in the north by 15°C or even 20°C in a few hours, sometimes resulting in temperatures of 20°C or 25°C in January. This sand-laden, dry wind (which can cause considerable crop damage) may blow at any time of the year, but spring and autumn are the usual seasons.

The hills of Tripolitania and Cyrenaica annually receive as much as 400 mm–500 mm of rainfall, but in the remainder of the country the rainfall is usually 200 mm or less. Once every five or six years there is a pronounced drought, sometimes lasting for two successive seasons.

ECONOMIC LIFE

Such conditions imposed severe restriction on all forms of economic activity. Although petroleum was discovered in considerable quantities in Libya, physical and climatic conditions made exploitation difficult and, until the closure of the Suez Canal in 1967, the remote situation of the country, away from the currents of international trade, was a further handicap. However, production of crude petroleum increased rapidly and proximity to southern and central Europe presented a considerable advantage over the costly Suez passage. The introduction of petroleum revenues transformed the economic situation of Libya. Extensive development was undertaken, with the aim of improving housing and of fostering industries to produce consumer goods. Roads, electricity, improved water supplies, telecommunications links and reorganized town planning were all targeted by development initiatives, and the construction of a number of sizeable industrial plants was approved.

In the better-watered areas of the Jefara and, to a smaller extent, in northern Cyrenaica, barley, wheat, olives and Mediterranean fruit are cultivated.

The Fezzan and the smaller oases in Cyrenaica are almost rainless, and cultivation depends entirely upon irrigation from wells. Millet is the chief crop, and there are several million date palms, which provide the bulk of the food. Small quantities of vegetables and fruit—figs, pomegranates, squashes, artichokes and tubers—are produced from gardens. Along the northern coast, and especially on the lower slopes of both the Tripolitanian Jebel and the Jebel Akhdar, vines are grown, though less so than formerly because of the prohibition of wine-making since independence.

Over much of Libya, pastoral nomadism, based on the rearing of sheep and goats (and some cattle and camels), is the only possible activity. In Cyrenaica nomads outnumbered the remainder of the population for many years, but in Tripolitania the main emphasis is on agriculture, although herding is still practised. Several industries have developed—petroleum refining, of course, plus some petrochemical activity, iron and steel production and some light industries. Overall, the scale of industrial activity is still small, but growing. Major efforts have been made to improve agriculture, with debatable success. One increasing difficulty is the exodus of rural workers to jobs in the developing towns, and foreign labour has had to be introduced on some rural development schemes. Another limitation is overuse of artesian water in the Jefara. In certain areas near the coast, the water table has fallen by 3 m–5 m per year, resulting in invasion of the aquifers by seawater.

PEOPLE AND LANGUAGE

The population of Libya, which at March 2010 was officially estimated at 6,100,000, seems to have been Berber in origin, i.e. connected with many of the present-day inhabitants of Morocco, Algeria and Tunisia. The establishment of Greek colonies, from about 650 BC onwards, and subsequent Roman rule seem to have had little effect on the population; but in the ninth and 10th centuries AD there were large-scale immigrations by Arabic-speaking tribes from the Najd of Arabia. This latter group is now entirely dominant, ethnically speaking, especially in Cyrenaica, of which it has been said that no other part of the world (central Arabia alone excepted) is more thoroughly Arab.

A few Berber elements do, however, survive, mainly in the south and west of Libya, while the long-continued traffic in Negro slaves (which came to an end in the 1940s) has left a visible influence on peoples throughout Libya and especially in the south.

Arabic, introduced by the 10th century invaders, is the one official language of Libya, but a few Tamazight-speaking Berber villages remain.

History

Revised for this edition by RONALD BRUCE ST JOHN

PRE-COLONIAL AND COLONIAL PERIODS

Both the Phoenicians and the Greeks colonized the coastlands of what is now called Libya before the area came under the control of Rome in 96 BC, inaugurating a period of great prosperity that lasted until the decline of the Roman Empire in the early fifth century AD. Arab invaders from the east swept across Libya in the mid-seventh century, and most of the Berber inhabitants were subsequently Islamized and Arabized. Urban life virtually disappeared and of the Libyan cities of antiquity only Tripoli survived. In the early 16th century Tripoli was captured by Spain, but in 1551 the city was seized by the expanding Ottoman Empire and Libya remained under Ottoman sovereignty until the early 20th century. For much of this time real power was exercised by professional soldiers, the Janissaries, and renegade adventurers from Greece, Italy and the Mediterranean islands in the name of the Ottoman Sultan. The activities of pirate corsairs expanded, attracting reprisals from the European naval powers. In 1835, probably owing to concerns about French expansion in Algeria and the British occupation of Malta, the Ottoman Sultan decided to bring Libya once more under direct rule. The years that followed were marked by corruption, oppression and revolts, and by the rise of the Sanusi religious brotherhood, which attracted many adherents, especially among the tribesmen of Cyrenaica.

In 1911 Italy declared war on Ottoman Turkey and with a large military force quickly occupied Tripoli and other coastal towns, although the invading troops met stiff resistance as they tried to press inland. In October 1912 the Sultan signed a peace treaty with Italy, under which he gave up his rights in Libya; however, he did not recognize Italian sovereignty. Instead, he granted Libyans 'full autonomy'. The Italians, who had already proclaimed their sovereignty over the country, ignored this provision and continued their military occupation. The outbreak of the First World War greatly weakened Italy's position, and the Sanusi, supplied with arms and ammunition by Turkey and its ally Germany, began to engage Italian forces, which by the end of the war held only Tripoli and a few other coastal towns. The Libyans continued to press for self-government and agreed to join forces under Said Muhammad Idris, the Sanusi leader, but negotiations with the Italians came to nothing. The advent of fascism in Italy in 1922 brought a new impetus to the Italian conquest of Libya. During the next decade Italian forces subdued first Tripolitania, then Fezzan and finally Cyrenaica in a series of ruthless military campaigns. This success was achieved by forcing the civilian population into concentration camps in order to deprive the Sanusi resistance of supplies and auxiliaries. Such a policy resulted in a heavy death toll among Libyans and caused bitterness that persists even into the 21st century.

INDEPENDENCE

During the Second World War Italian rule was overthrown by the Allied armies and Libya was placed under British and French military administration. However, its political future remained uncertain and in 1945 the Great Powers were unable to agree on a settlement. The USA favoured a UN Trusteeship, the USSR asked for the trusteeship of Tripolitania for itself and France recommended the return of all the Italian colonies to Italy. This was opposed by the United Kingdom, which had made pledges to its ally Muhammad Idris, the head of the Sanusi order, that Cyrenaica would never be returned to Italian rule. In the event, the UN took responsibility for Libya, and in 1949 the General Assembly voted in favour of independence, which was proclaimed in 1951 with Idris as King. Initially, the new kingdom had a cumbersome federal structure of government, but this was abolished in 1963 in favour of a unitary state.

During the first 10 years of independence Libya remained desperately poor and heavily dependent on foreign funds for its economic survival. In particular, Libya signed agreements under which the United Kingdom and the USA were allowed to maintain military bases in Libya in return for substantial economic aid. The discovery of petroleum in 1959 transformed Libya into a prosperous country, but also played an important part in unleashing social and political forces that within a decade were to expose the fragility of the monarchical regime.

These domestic developments coincided with the rise of political consciousness in the wider Arab world, and Libya's newly urbanized population was particularly receptive to political influences, especially from neighbouring Egypt. As Arab nationalism in the region grew, Libya, which remained a client state of the West, became more isolated, and divisions between the monarchy and the populace widened. There was widespread speculation that the monarchy would be overthrown; when a military coup took place on 1 September 1969, the only surprise was that the leaders were drawn from the junior rather than the senior officer ranks.

THE 1969 COUP: MUAMMAR AL-QADDAFI BECOMES LIBYAN LEADER

The military coup staged in Tripoli in 1969 was organized by young army officers led by a 27-year-old Captain, Muammar al-Qaddafi (who subsequently promoted himself to Colonel after the coup). In a matter of hours the young officers overthrew the Government and seized control of the state with relatively few arrests, virtually no fighting and no deaths being reported. King Idris refused to abdicate but accepted exile in Egypt, where he remained until his death in 1983.

Most of the new men of the revolution were from poor families from the interior who had joined the army because there were no other opportunities for them. Qaddafi himself was born in Sirte, in the desert that reaches to the coastline between Tripolitania and Cyrenaica, and he spent his formative years in the oasis town of Sabha in the Fezzan. From the outset supreme power lay with a 12-man Revolution Command Council (RCC), which proclaimed the Libyan Arab Republic. Its Chairman, Qaddafi, also became head of government and the Commander-in-Chief of the army. With his gift for communication with the Libyan people and a talent for conducting mass meetings, Qaddafi quickly established himself as chief spokesman and ideologist of the new regime.

Motivated by the principles of Arab nationalism, Libya's new leaders set to work with great enthusiasm and energy. Foreign businesses were nationalized, the property of all Jews and Italians still living in Libya was sequestered by the Government, and both communities were encouraged to leave. Furthermore, both the USA and the United Kingdom were required to close their military bases in Libya. Emphasis was placed on the Arabic language and a return to the fundamental precepts of Islam in everyday life. All street signs and public notices were to be in Arabic only, alcohol was forbidden and bars and nightclubs were closed.

In negotiations with the international oil companies operating in Libya, the new regime quickly achieved notable success, spearheading an early push for price increases by the Organization of the Petroleum Exporting Countries (OPEC). This allowed Libya to achieve continuous oil revenue growth, despite reducing production in order to conserve reserves. A large number of oil companies held concessions in Libya, including many small independent oil companies, some of which were heavily dependent on Libya for the bulk of their supplies. One of the leading independents, Occidental, obtained almost all its output from Libya. The independent operators were therefore extremely vulnerable, and in 1970–71 they gave in one after the other to pressure from the new regime for greater control over its hydrocarbon resources. This forced the major oil companies to follow suit for fear of losing their concessions. The Libyan Government subsequently acquired a 51% share in the Libyan operations of some of the oil companies and completely nationalized the holdings of others.

THE 'CULTURAL REVOLUTION' AND THE CREATION OF THE SOCIALIST PEOPLE'S LIBYAN ARAB JAMAHIRIYA

Despite the dominance of the new regime, Qaddafi's efforts to institutionalize his ideology and build a participatory political culture proved difficult. Firm control over the state's military and administrative apparatus was easily accomplished, and the early actions of the regime generated a degree of popular support and laid the foundations for Qaddafi's growing authority, primarily on account of his strong personal charisma. Nevertheless, as Qaddafi sought to extend his authority further, he encountered growing resistance from established interests, including bureaucrats, the tribal élite and the Westernized bourgeoisie. In April 1973, therefore, he launched the so-called 'Popular' or 'Cultural Revolution' to broaden his personal support base, as well as popular backing for his vision of a new revolutionary community. The 'Cultural Revolution' called for the destruction of imported ideologies, whether Eastern or Western, and the creation of a society based on the tenets of Islam. Officials and business executives who failed to show the required revolutionary fervour were dismissed, and books and magazines deemed to be offensive were destroyed. At the same time Qaddafi presented his 'third international theory', which claimed to be 'an alternative to capitalism, materialism and communist atheism'. Qaddafi's own personal leadership was firmly established by 1975, and with the first publication of his *Green Book* in 1975—a blueprint for the social and economic transformation of Libya—he emerged as the country's sole ideological authority. By the end of the 1970s a new political system had been established based on a 'popular democracy' organized through a series of assemblies and committees, from the grass-roots 'popular committees' through the 'basic people's congresses' and 'popular congresses' to the General People's Congress (GPC), a type of national assembly, the General People's Committee, corresponding to the cabinet, and the General Secretariat, the supreme political leadership, replacing the RCC. A separate network of 'revolutionary committees' responsible for political leadership within the popular committee structure was also created.

In March 1977 the official name of the country was changed to the Socialist People's Libyan Arab Jamahiriya (the prefix 'Great' was added in 1986), with power vested in the people through the GPC and the groups represented in it. However, although Qaddafi claimed that this system removed the barriers between people and leaders, the exercise of 'popular democracy' was firmly controlled from above. Recruitment to political office, major areas of policy-making and the actual implementation of policies were clearly determined by the leadership. Qaddafi appeared to have been genuine in his desire for popular participation in decision-making yet unwilling to accept 'popular' views that differed from his own. At the same time Qaddafi became convinced that a more radical transformation of the country along socialist lines was required. He was concerned that the state's ambitious development policies were transforming Libyans into a non-productive, dependent leisured class, and therefore set out to eliminate capitalism and build a new socialist society. Land was nationalized, no one was allowed to own more than one house, state-run supermarkets replaced private shops and demonetization eliminated many assets of the rich. Such measures, more radical than those attempted anywhere else in the Arab world, resulted in a massive levelling of the social structure. Those groups badly hit by the reforms, principally the upper and middle classes, were alienated and in some cases scarce skills were lost, making Libya more dependent on foreigners.

ARAB UNITY BY MERGER OR SUBVERSION

Foreign affairs remained one major area of policy always closely controlled by Qaddafi. When he came to power, the Arab world was more deeply divided than ever. Egypt had been defeated in the 1967 war with Israel, more Arab lands had been occupied and Arab ranks were in disarray. It was Qaddafi's deeply held belief that every reverse for the Arab cause arose from Arab disunity. The Arab world had to be united to win the battle for Palestine. Therefore, the vision of one Arab nation from the Gulf to the Atlantic, and opposition to Zionism and to its ally, Western imperialism, became the dominant themes of Libyan foreign relations.

Almost immediately Qaddafi suggested that Libya form an alliance with Egypt and Sudan in a revolutionary front to consolidate three 'progressive' revolutions. The Tripoli Charter linking the three countries was signed in December 1969. Qaddafi pressed for complete unity between the three states, but President Gamal Abd al-Nasir (Nasser) of Egypt was more cautious. After Nasser's death Egypt and Libya, now joined by Syria, created the Federation of Arab Republics on the principles of no negotiated peace with Israel and no abandoning support for the Palestinian cause. The federation had few practical consequences, and its shortcomings persuaded Qaddafi that something closer and stronger was needed.

In July 1972 Qaddafi appealed for an immediate merger of Egypt and Libya, and an agreement was signed to take effect in

September 1973. As the date for union drew nearer, Nasser's successor, Anwar Sadat, appeared to hesitate. Qaddafi became increasingly impatient and in July 1973 dispatched 40,000 Libyans towards Cairo, Egypt, on a 'unity march' designed to pressure Sadat into bringing about immediate fusion of the two countries. The marchers were turned back at the Egyptian frontier. Despite Egyptian suspicion of the Libyan revolution, the union came into effect in September but soon fell apart, wrecked by Qaddafi's opposition to Egypt's conduct of the October 1973 Arab–Israeli war.

When Egypt and Syria declared war on Israel in October 1973, Qaddafi, who had been the strongest supporter of the Palestinian movements, one of the chief paymasters of the *fedayeen* (martyrs or freedom fighters) and the leading advocate of war with Israel, was not consulted. He was deeply offended and refused to attend the Algiers (Algeria) meeting of Arab heads of state after the war, declaring that it would only ratify Arab capitulation.

Qaddafi's enthusiasm for Arab unity continued unabated, but the failure of political mergers led him to embark on a new course. His speeches attacked Arab leaders who blocked unity and failed to 'liberate' Palestine, and he spoke of providing Libyan aid for revolutionary movements and of the need for popular pressure on North African governments as a means of attaining Arab unity. For some time Libya had been providing money, arms and training for 'liberation' groups in Ireland, Eritrea, the Philippines, Rhodesia (now Zimbabwe), Portuguese Guinea (now Guinea-Bissau), Morocco and Chad, as well as providing aid for sympathetic countries such as Pakistan, Uganda, Zambia and Togo. Now it appeared that Libya was supporting subversion in Egypt and Sudan. Attempted coups in Egypt in April 1974 and in Sudan the following month were believed to have had Libyan support, and relations between Libya and other Arab states became increasingly hostile.

Relations with Egypt were not improved when, in November 1977, President Sadat launched his peace initiative with Israel. Qaddafi condemned Sadat's move and was a leading instigator of the Tripoli summit of 'rejectionist' states which formed a 'front of steadfastness and confrontation' against Israel in December. Meanwhile, relations with the mainstream Palestine Liberation Organization (PLO) became strained and Qaddafi accused the PLO Chairman, Yasser Arafat, of abandoning the armed struggle in favour of a strategy of diplomacy and moderation. For some time Libya had been supporting the 'rejectionist' wing of the Palestinian guerrilla movement, which was opposed to the concept of a possible negotiated settlement of the Arab–Israeli conflict, and it was not until early 1987 that Qaddafi was reconciled with Arafat and the PLO. After the Palestinian *intifada* (uprising) in the Israeli Occupied Territories began in December 1987, Qaddafi intensified his efforts to reconcile the opposing factions within the PLO, and in June 1988 he sent Libyan representatives to Lebanon to mediate in the conflict between Palestinian guerrillas loyal to Arafat and Fatah rebels.

In January 1984 Libya opposed a decision by the Organization of the Islamic Conference (OIC, now Organization of Islamic Cooperation) to readmit Egypt, and in November 1987 dissented from the decision of the League of Arab States (the Arab League) to remove the prohibition on diplomatic relations between member states and Egypt.

Qaddafi, who had been repeatedly accused of supporting plots to topple the Nimeri Government in Sudan, visited its capital, Khartoum, in May 1985 to endorse the new regime of Lt-Gen. Abd al-Rahman Swar al-Dahab, who had overthrown Nimeri in a bloodless coup the previous month. Qaddafi urged the rebels of the Sudan People's Liberation Army in southern Sudan, who had received Libyan support under Nimeri, to begin negotiations with the new Government. A military protocol was signed with Sudan in July, and Libya became Sudan's principal supplier of armaments. Following a military coup in Sudan in June 1989, Qaddafi discussed the possible merger of the two countries with the new Sudanese leader, Lt-Gen. Omar Hassan Ahmad al-Bashir, but little significant progress was made.

Following Iraq's invasion of Kuwait in August 1990 Libya voted against a motion put forward at an Arab League emergency summit meeting condemning the Iraqi action and advocating the deployment of a pan-Arab force for the defence of Saudi Arabia and other states from possible Iraqi aggression. Libya announced that its ports were at Iraq's disposal for the purpose of importing food supplies, and anti-war demonstrations took place in Libya when the US-led Operation Desert Storm began the liberation of Kuwait in January 1991. President Hosni Mubarak of Egypt was thought to have persuaded Qaddafi to exercise restraint during the war, and relations between Egypt and Libya continued to improve in its aftermath.

RELATIONS WITH LIBYA'S MAGHREB NEIGHBOURS

The coup that brought Qaddafi to power initially reorientated Libya away from the Maghreb, and in 1970 Libya withdrew from the Maghreb Permanent Consultative Committee. In 1971 relations with Morocco were severed after Libya prematurely gave its support to an unsuccessful attempt to overthrow King Hassan. After two failed attempts at union with Tunisia in 1972 and 1974, relations with Libya's western neighbour remained uneasy and often strained. Although Qaddafi strenuously denied Libyan involvement, a guerrilla raid on the Tunisian mining town of Gafsa in early 1980, with the presumed intent to incite a popular rebellion, was attributed to Libya.

There was widespread surprise when, in August 1984, Libya and Morocco signed a treaty of union creating the Arab-African Federation. It was an unlikely partnership given Morocco's pro-Western orientation. The union, which Qaddafi envisaged as the first step towards the creation of a politically united Great Arab Maghreb or Greater Maghreb, proved short-lived. Already angered by Qaddafi's announcement of a treaty between Libya and Iran, King Hassan abrogated the union in August 1986 following strong criticism by Qaddafi over his meeting in July with the Israeli Prime Minister, Shimon Peres.

Relations with Tunisia improved, and in April 1988 the two countries signed a co-operation pact encompassing political, economic, cultural and foreign relations. In June the leaders of Algeria, Morocco, Tunisia, Libya and Mauritania held a meeting in Algiers—the first of its kind since they had achieved independence—to discuss the prospects for 'a Maghreb without frontiers'. A Maghreb commission was created, which led to a treaty signed in February 1989 by the five countries proclaiming the formation of the Union du Maghreb arabe (UMA—Union of the Arab Maghreb). However, the union had few practical results owing to divisions between Algeria and Morocco over the Western Sahara, the Algerian civil war and UN sanctions against Libya.

QADDAFI'S AFRICAN POLICY

Like his appeal for Arab unity, Qaddafi's much publicized African policy formed part of his scheme to liberate Arab lands from Zionist aggression. He believed that Israel's presence in Africa threatened the Arab states through their own back door. Employing a policy of religious propaganda and promises of financial assistance and aid, Libya appealed to its black African, largely Muslim neighbours, to sever their diplomatic relations with Israel. This policy achieved some notable success, but it also drew Libya into a disastrous involvement with Idi Amin's brutal and repressive regime in Uganda and led to a costly military intervention in Chad, its neighbour to the south.

In 1973 Libya occupied the Aozou strip in northern Chad, basing its action on an unratified treaty of 1935 whereby Italy and France altered the frontiers between their two colonies. According to Libya, sovereignty over the strip passed to Italy and subsequently to Libya, when it achieved independence in 1951. The Government of Chad challenged these claims and referred the dispute to the Organization for African Unity (OAU, now the African Union—AU), which set up a committee of reconciliation, although Libya consistently refused to attend its sessions. For many years Libya had been supporting the predominantly Muslim Front de libération nationale du Tchad (FROLINAT) in its rebellion against the Chad Government, but in 1979, when the mainstream of FROLINAT severed their links with Libya over its annexation of the Aozou strip, Libyan army units invaded northern Chad.

During the 1980s an increasing number of Libyan troops were engaged in Chad and Libyan military aid was offered to first one faction and then another in a country caught up in a bitter civil war. As the Libyan army supported rebel forces in the north of Chad, France sent troops to help the beleaguered Government in the capital, N'Djamena. Despite an agreement between France and Libya providing for the evacuation of both countries' forces, Libya continued to support those rebel forces who had not declared allegiance to the Government in N'Djamena, while publicly denying any involvement in the fighting. However, in 1987 Libyan forces suffered heavy losses as forces loyal to the Chadian Government captured Libyan bases in the north and advanced into the Aozou strip. Libya responded by bombing towns in northern Chad and succeeded in recapturing Aozou. In September Libya and Chad agreed to observe a cease-fire proposed by the OAU, and in October 1988 diplomatic relations between the two countries were resumed. In August 1989 a peace accord was signed in Algiers, which provided for an end to fighting over the Aozou strip, the withdrawal of all forces from the disputed region and an agreement that both parties should attempt to resolve their dispute by means of a political settlement. In August 1990 Libya and Chad agreed to refer the dispute over the Aozou strip to the International Court of Justice (ICJ) in The Hague, Netherlands, which ruled against Libya's claim in February 1994. Libyan forces completed their withdrawal from the disputed region in May.

ATTEMPTS TO QUELL OPPOSITION AT HOME AND ABROAD

In February 1980 the third meeting of the revolutionary committees, responsible for ensuring the progress of the revolution at the popular level (and in practice for imposing Qaddafi's will on the people's committees), appealed for the 'physical liquidation' of opponents of the revolution who were living abroad and of 'elements obstructing change' inside Libya. An extensive anti-corruption campaign was launched in the same month, ostensibly to eradicate 'economic' crime. Between February and April more than 2,000 people were arrested, mainly on charges of bribery, to be tried by members of the revolutionary committees. However, the arrests of several senior military officers introduced political overtones. In April Qaddafi issued an ultimatum to Libyan exiles abroad to return to Libya by 10 June, beyond which date he could not undertake to protect them from the revenge of the revolutionary committees. According to the human rights organization Amnesty International (based in London, United Kingdom), Libya ordered the assassinations of at least 25 of its political opponents abroad between 1980 and 1987. The National Front for the Salvation of Libya (NFSL), formed in 1981 and led by Muhammad Yousuf Magariaf, was only one of several groups opposed to Qaddafi based abroad, which the Libyan leader accused foreign governments of nurturing.

Inside Libya, Qaddafi's opponents were active during 1984. In May as many as 20 commandos belonging to the NFSL attacked Qaddafi's residence in a heavily fortified barracks in the suburbs of Tripoli. According to the NFSL, 15 of its commandos were killed, but heavy casualties were inflicted on Libyan soldiers. The actions of Qaddafi's opponents were the signal for a wave of arrests of suspected dissidents in the first half of 1984, and several students were hanged.

RUMOURS OF AN ABORTIVE ARMY COUP AND INTERNAL DISSENT, 1993–99

During the second week of October 1993 rumours began to circulate in the Western media that a revolt by army units had been crushed by the Libyan air force, which had remained loyal to Qaddafi. There were unconfirmed reports that Libya had closed its borders and that after three days of unrest 2,000 people had been arrested and 12 officers executed. Qaddafi's second-in-command, Maj. Abd al-Salam Jalloud, was reported to have been placed under house arrest. There was speculation that the coup, described in the media as the most serious challenge to the Libyan leader since 1986, had arisen as a result of differences between Qaddafi and Jalloud over the handling of the Lockerbie crisis (see below) and that the armed forces divided along tribal lines. Throughout the Lockerbie affair, Jalloud, who belonged to the al-Magaraha tribe, was firmly opposed to surrendering the two suspects, both of whom were members of his tribe. Significantly, government changes at the end of January 1994 placed men known for their personal loyalty to Qaddafi in key positions, suggesting that, despite denying the existence of a plot to remove him from power, the Libyan leader felt the need to consolidate his leadership.

Libyan opposition groups in exile remained weak and divided and there was little evidence that they commanded significant support within the country. In October 1993 Muhammad Magariaf of the NFSL, Maj. Abd al-Moneim al-Houni of the Co-operation Bureau for Democratic and National Forces, and Mansour al-Kikhia of the Libyan National Alliance (LNA) met to discuss forming a united front against the Qaddafi regime. Abd al-Hamid al-Bakkush, the leader of the Libyan Liberation Organization, did not attend, and the meeting failed to resolve the differences between the various opposition groups.

In December 1993, when al-Kikhia, a former Secretary for Foreign Liaison and, since the early 1980s, leader of the opposition LNA, disappeared while attending a meeting of the Alliance in Cairo, it was widely assumed that he had been abducted by Libyan security agents. The affair proved particularly embarrassing as al-Kikhia had been living in the USA, had an American wife and had only agreed to attend the meeting in Cairo after receiving personal assurances from senior Egyptian officials about his safety there. The Libyan Secretariat for Foreign Liaison and Libya's representative to the Arab League both denied Libyan involvement in the affair, stating that al-Kikhia presented no threat to the Libyan Government. Qaddafi told Egyptian journalists that Libya was co-operating with the Egyptian authorities to discover what had happened. Both US President Bill Clinton and Dr Boutros Boutros-Ghali, the UN Secretary-General, appealed to President Mubarak of Egypt to investigate al-Kikhia's disappearance. However, Egyptian police admitted at the end of January 1994 that they had no information about al-Kikhia's whereabouts. In September 1997 a report by the US Central Intelligence Agency (CIA) alleged that al-Kikhia had been kidnapped by Egyptian agents while in Cairo and extradited to Libya, where he was murdered.

In March 1994 Libyan television broadcast 'confessions' by three army officers and a student, all members of the Warfallah tribe, who had been arrested in the Bani Walid region during the army revolt in October 1993. It was the first official acknowledgement of the attempted coup. The NFSL claimed that, after calls for the execution of the four men, demonstrations erupted in the Bani Walid region, where several protesters were arrested after setting fire to government buildings. At the beginning of 1996 it was reported that Qaddafi had overturned a court's ruling on 12 army officers of the Warfallah tribe accused of leading the abortive coup because the sentences were too lenient. According to one source, death sentences had been waived in order not to antagonize the Warfallah, who had threatened retaliation if the men were killed. Early in 1996 Qaddafi concentrated power within the armed forces in the hands of members of his own tribe, further alienating leaders of other tribes, who in the past had played key roles in internal security and foreign affairs.

In addition to reports of continued dissent within the armed forces and the destabilizing effects of tribal rivalries, some observers argued that the Islamist opposition was the most dangerous threat to the Qaddafi regime. Despite being subjected to harsh repressive measures by the security forces for some years, Islamist opposition to the regime, strongly rooted in Cyrenaica, appeared to have increased in strength, although little was known about the groups involved. In June 1995 there were a number of armed confrontations between police and Islamist militants in and around Benghazi. The regime blamed the unrest on 'extremist infiltrators' from Egypt and Sudan.There were reports of further clashes between the security services and Islamist militants in September 1995 in Benghazi, Darnah and al-Baida. In response to these incidents, thousands of Sudanese and Egyptian workers were expelled, the regime tightened its control over the country's mosques and hundreds of suspected Islamist militants were arrested. The regime also made moves to re-Islamize Libyan society, adopting laws based on the *Shari'a*.

In February 1996 it was reported that Islamist militants calling themselves the Jama'ah al-Islamiyah al-Muqatila (Libyan Militant Islamic Group—MIG) had attempted to assassinate Qaddafi in Sirte. After the assassination attempt security forces carried out further arrests of suspected Islamist militants. In March, following a mass escape from the al-Kuwaifiyya prison near Benghazi, during which police shot dead many of the prisoners, unrest erupted once again in and around Benghazi, Darnah and al-Baida, and there were reports of over 20 deaths in clashes between militants and the security forces. A number of other prison breakouts occurred at this time, as Abu Salim prison in particular became dangerously overcrowded owing to the security forces' crackdown on Islamists. In June the prisoners protested against the deteriorating conditions at the prison, in an uprising that was violently quashed by the authorities; it was reported that some 1,200 inmates had been killed.

Earlier, at the end of April 1996, the MIG issued a statement claiming to have killed 15 security officers in Sirte during the previous month, and to have seized weapons from police stations in Ras al-Hilal and al-Qubba. In May violent clashes were reported in Benghazi between security forces and supporters of a new opposition group, the Islamic Martyrs' Movement (IMM), which claimed responsibility for the assassinations of a number of high-ranking government officials. In June a third Islamist group, the Libya Islamic Group, claimed responsibility for the murders of eight police officers during an attack on a police training centre in Derna. Throughout the second half of 1996 there were reports of clashes between Islamist groups and government forces, especially in the eastern part of the country, where several hundred people were estimated to have been killed.

The threat from militant Islamist groups was accompanied by continued unrest within the armed forces and the alienation of tribal support for the regime. In July 1996 it was reported that an attempted coup organized by Col Khalifa Haftar, an officer who had taken part in the overthrow of the monarchy in 1969, had been quashed after fierce fighting in the Jebel Akhdar, near Darnah. In the same month bodyguards of Qaddafi's son Saadi opened fire on crowds at Tripoli's football stadium, after fans chanted anti-Government slogans following a decision by the referee that ruled in favour of a team sponsored by Saadi. In August another coup attempt was uncovered, involving some 45 army officers, and said to include members of the Libyan leader's own tribe, the Qadhafa. Three of the coup leaders were believed to have been executed. Tight security was maintained in and around Bani Walid, the home town of officers from the powerful Warfallah tribe purportedly accused of leading the abortive coup of 1993, who were put on trial at the Supreme Military Court in 1996. After being convicted of spying for the CIA and trying to overthrow the regime, six senior army officers and two civilians were executed in January 1997. The executions took place against the wishes of the leaders of the Warfallah tribe, and were strongly condemned by several exiled opposition groups.

In late 1996 there were reports that the two exiled opposition groups, the LNA and the NFSL, had once again agreed to cooperate to bring down the Qaddafi regime, and had rejected overtures from the Libyan leader to take part in negotiations. In January 1997 Muhammad al-Sanusi, the grandson of the late King Idris and the heir to the Libyan throne, who was living in exile in the United Kingdom, claimed to have received death threats from Qaddafi's agents. He later condemned the regime for threatening Libyan exiles and accused the security forces of having used chemical weapons in attacks against insurgents in the Jebel Akhdar in August 1996. A new secular opposition group, the Libyan Patriots Movement, emerged in January 1997. The group claimed to have supporters among the Libyan armed forces and announced its commitment to overthrowing the Qaddafi regime by force.

Following a major offensive against Islamist strongholds in the north-eastern part of the country in mid-1998, there were indications that the Islamist groups had been weakened militarily and were short of funds. In addition, reports in the Arab press suggested that Qaddafi's intelligence chief, Musa Kusa, had held talks with members of two Islamist groups—the MIG and the IMM—in order to persuade them to end their campaign of violence against the regime; the MIG, however, denied that the meeting had taken place.

ISLAMIST OPPOSITION IN THE 21ST CENTURY

Towards the end of the 1990s Libyan officials began to make conciliatory gestures to the opposition in exile, offering its members financial inducements if they agreed to return to Libya. While there were claims that some prominent opposition figures based in the USA were prepared to continue the dialogue, the London-based NFSL completely rejected any rapprochement with the Qaddafi regime. Unlike the Islamists, these groups were thought to have little or no support within Libya itself.

In June 2005 around 300 exiled Libyans met in London at a National Conference for the Libyan Opposition. The very fact that they managed to meet and, indeed, to issue a joint declaration at the close of the event was surprising, given that prior to the conference the opposition was notable only for its differences. At the same time demonstrations against Qaddafi were held in the Netherlands, Sweden and Switzerland. The London conference declaration urged the removal of Qaddafi and the resurrection of the country's 1951 Constitution. The opposition insisted that armed action was not envisaged and that it sought democratic change through peaceful means. A subsequent conference took place in London in early 2008, but few details emerged from its deliberations.

Conspicuous by its absence from both London events was the Muslim Brotherhood, the umbrella grouping for Libya's various Islamist organizations and associations, including the Libyan Islamic Group (LIG), the Libyan Islamic Fighting Group (LIFG) and the Libya Brothers. Rumours abounded at the time that the Muslim Brotherhood was in secret negotiations with the Government, through the Qaddafi International Foundation for Charity Associations (QICF—later the Qaddafi International Charity and Development Foundation), run by Qaddafi's son, Seif al-Islam, to secure the release of some of its members from Libyan gaols. A deal was apparently struck in return for the Muslim Brotherhood shunning links with other opposition groups and renouncing violence. These rumours appeared to have substance, when, in March 2006, 85 members of the group were released in an 'amnesty'.

Despite such reports, the regime continued to face threats from Islamist groups. In May 2007 the security forces launched an operation to round up suspected Islamist militants in the Benghazi area. The detentions appeared to have been a pre-emptive measure against Islamist mobilization, following the announcement earlier that year that the international terrorist al-Qa'ida network had established an organization, al-Qa'ida Organization in the Land of the Islamic Maghreb (AQIM), in neighbouring Algeria. Meanwhile, two of the LIFG's leaders, Abu-al-Layth al-Libi and Abu-Yahya al-Libi, were prominent in the core al-Qa'ida organization in Afghanistan (the former was reported to have been killed in a US airstrike in February 2008, and the latter to have been killed in a US drone attack in June 2012). The security operation around Benghazi also seemed to be designed to encourage the main body of Islamists to pursue its dialogue with the regime. The pre-emptive measure clearly identified a genuine threat since, in November 2007, just prior to his death, Abu-al-Layth al-Libi announced that the LIFG had joined AQIM.

However, in July 2009 it was reported that substantive talks between key members of the LIFG within Libya and the Libyan Government had been ongoing since late 2007. Brokered by LIFG members in exile, these discussions revolved around the LIFG renouncing violence and the overthrow of the Qaddafi regime in return for a wider amnesty that would see an estimated 250 of the organization's members released from gaol. In March 2009 the emir of the LIFG, Abu Abdullah al-Sadeq, wrote a letter from his prison cell stating that the leadership of the LIFG had pledged 'to renounce the method of military confrontation with the regime and to revise its literature and its past policies'. In July the LIFG renounced its affiliation to AQIM, and in the following month it published a *Book of Correctional Studies*, in which it denounced Salafism and the pursuit of violent *jihad* to achieve their Islamic goals. In September the LIFG issued a public apology, seeking forgiveness from Qaddafi for the violent actions that it had perpetrated against his regime in the 1990s. Later in September the Government appointed a judge to investigate the Abu Salim prison massacre, and in October 88 members of the LIFG were granted an early release from prison; three prominent LIFG leaders were among a further 214 prisoners released in March 2010. Further releases took place during late 2010 and by the end of the year almost all the members of the LIFG had been freed. However, there was still considerable anger among the victims' families, owing to the continuing failure of the commission set up to investigate the affair to publish any findings; instead, families were offered compensation on the condition that they dropped their claims to judicial redress. In February 2011 the Government arrested Fathi Terbil, the lawyer representing the families. His arrest proved to be one of the catalysts for the Libyan revolution, which began in earnest later that month (see Revolution and Civil War).

Islamists were active as individuals in the revolution that overthrew the Qaddafi regime; however, there is no evidence that Islamist bodies or groups played an organized role. Moreover, most Libyans displayed little interest, during or after the revolution, in an Islamist alternative to the non-ideological Libyan revolution. Moderate Islamist movements, coalitions, and associations have been active in post-Qaddafi Libya, but it is highly unlikely that the general Libyan public will embrace the message of more fundamental Islamist groups or jihadists. The Muslim Brotherhood announced the creation of the Justice and Construction Party (JCP) in March 2012, one of a number of Islamist parties and gatherings formed in early 2012. In elections for a General National Congress (GNC) in July, however, the JCP won only 17 of the 80 seats available to political parties.

The poor showing of the JCP and other Islamist parties in the July 2012 elections was due to a number of interrelated factors. Historically, the Libyan people have never shown any real appetite for radical Islam, as advocated by the Taliban, al-Qa'ida, or AQIM. Moreover, the Qaddafi regime had long suppressed all Islamist movements, especially the Muslim Brotherhood, which meant that there was little in the way of an organized base in Libya for the JCP to build upon. In recent years the Muslim Brotherhood had reached a political accommodation with the Qaddafi regime, and the terms of this pact were also widely criticized. In addition, Libyans in the post-Qaddafi era were highly suspicious of any potential effort by the Muslim Brotherhood or others to impose a new ideology or political agenda on them, and there was also concern that Islamist parties like the JCP could be influenced by outside forces. After 42 years of isolation under Qaddafi's rule, most Libyans longed for a more open socio-economic and political system and feared that Islamist politicians would again close them off from the outside world.

Nevertheless, militant Islamist elements continued to challenge sources of authority and sovereignty in Libya. In August 2012 Salafists attacked a Sufi mosque in Tripoli, razing it to the ground. In September an attack on the US consulate in Benghazi, which was believed to have been instigated by a radical Islamist group, resulted in the death of the US ambassador, J. Christopher Stevens, and three other Americans. In December a Coptic Christian building in Dafiniyya was attacked, resulting in the death of two Egyptians. Following the detention of scores of Coptic Christians in February 2013, the European Union (EU) issued a statement in March, expressing concern about religious freedom and rights in Libya. In March a Catholic priest was shot outside a Tripoli church, while a major Sufi shrine was destroyed by Salafists. In April Islamist militants attacked the French embassy in Tripoli, apparently in protest at the French military mission against *jihadists* in Mali. With lawless southern Libya becoming a haven for al-Qa'ida-affiliated fighters, unconfirmed reports in June 2013 suggested that the Lebanon-based Shi'ite Islamist group Hezbollah was also developing cells in Libya. Small in number and with only limited support among the general population, militant Islamist groups were nevertheless committed to the imposition of Islamic law throughout the country and at mid-2013 were taking advantage of the lawlessness prevailing in Libya to promote their political agenda by every means available to them.

THE OPPOSITION AND HUMAN RIGHTS

Human rights abuses were widespread in Qaddafi's Libya, particularly against those hostile to the regime. These were chronicled in a report on Libya by Amnesty International in 1998, which listed extensive human rights abuses, including the torture of Libyans suspected of non-violent opposition activities. After Amnesty International reported in September 2001 that Libya's longest serving political prisoner, Ahmad al-Zubayr Ahmad al-Sanusi, had been released after 31 years' incarceration, the organization expressed concern about hundreds of other political prisoners detained for more than 10 years without trial. In 2004 Qaddafi allowed Amnesty International into Libya for the first time. Following its inspection, he announced that the emergency laws imposed by the people's courts would be abolished and that, henceforth, Libya would adopt 'normal criminal law procedure'. Qaddafi announced that Libya would 'play a leading international role in defending human rights' and sign an international treaty banning torture. The visit came one year after Libya had been elected to chair the UN Commission on Human Rights, having been selected as Africa's candidate for the new body.

In May 2005 Qaddafi sanctioned a visit by US-based Human Rights Watch, which commended Libya for implementing some of Amnesty International's recommendations, including the abolition of the People's Prosecution Bureau—the so-called 'exceptional' court, in which due process was notoriously absent. Shortly after Human Rights Watch published its report, the Government claimed that it was prosecuting at least 48 security officials on charges of torture and was reforming the penal code to minimize the use of the death penalty. Nevertheless, an article by a senior member of Human Rights Watch published soon after the report stated that Libya remained a closed and tightly controlled society with no independent press or civil society, and no political groups that were not officially sanctioned; Libyans were not allowed to criticize the Government, the political system or the leader; torture remained a serious problem and the state security apparatus was pervasive; and cases of forced disappearances remained unresolved. Around the time of the Human Rights Watch visit, a prominent journalist, Daif al-Ghazal, was tortured and murdered, emphasizing the doubts about Libya's human rights record.

In May 2009 Amnesty International published a report on human rights in Libya. The report stated that continued violations of human rights in Libya 'cast a shadow over its improved international diplomatic standing'. It also asserted that basic human freedoms in the country, including those of expression, association and assembly, remained severely restricted. The report's findings were highlighted by two events that occurred at around the time of its publication. First, Ali Muhammed al-Fakheri, allegedly a senior paramilitary trainer for al-Qa'ida, was reported to have committed suicide in a Libyan prison. Although there was no proof otherwise, human rights groups raised concerns over the manner of his death. In a separate incident, another dissident, Fathi al-Jahmi, also died during incarceration. He had been in prison since 2002 for publicly demanding democracy in Libya and for urging the abrogation of Qaddafi's revolutionary ideology. Al-Jahmi's supporters had long-standing concerns over his treatment in prison, where he was allegedly denied medical treatment for serious ailments. According to official sources, he had been transferred to a hospital in Jordan after suffering a stroke and then lapsing into a coma. He never recovered and died two weeks later.

In a positive development in November 2009, a legal committee tasked with amending Libya's penal code announced that it would recommend that capital punishment be limited to just two crimes—premeditated murder and acts of terrorism;

previously, 21 crimes had carried the death penalty. The panel also suggested that the ban on civil society organizations was to be lifted, allowing Libyans for the first time to establish their own non-governmental organizations (NGOs).

In December 2009 the Government granted permission to Human Rights Watch to launch its annual human rights report on Libya at a public press conference in Tripoli. However, the meeting was disrupted by hardliners who shouted down members of the public who had come to speak out against the regime. The report, *Truth and Justice Can't Wait*, highlighted persistent human rights failings, including the continuing ban on political parties and pressure groups, detention of political prisoners and the lack of freedom of expression.

Libya's human rights credentials gained international legitimacy in May 2010, when the country was elected to the UN Human Rights Council. Although 30 international NGOs lobbied against its accession, the vote was considered a formality, as Libya had already secured its regional nomination unopposed. Libya's tenure was blighted by continued criticism from international NGOs, which formed a coalition to have Libya removed from the Council. They claimed that Libya had 'a notorious record as one of the world's worst violators of human rights'. Events soon overtook their campaign. After the outbreak of conflict in Libya in mid-February 2011, reports of serious human rights abuses by the regime's security forces began to emerge. By the end of the month all 192 members of the UN had voted unanimously to suspend Libya's membership of the UN Human Rights Council for 'gross and systematic violations of human rights'.

DOMESTIC REFORM

In 1988 Qaddafi embarked on a series of liberalizing economic and political reforms. This move stemmed from increasing domestic tensions, owing to a deteriorating economy and shortages of basic commodities, as well as widespread popular opposition to Libya's military involvement in Chad. Qaddafi was also under pressure from abroad to improve the image of his Government and ease his political isolation. In March Qaddafi began to encourage the reopening of private businesses, in recognition of the failure of the state-controlled supermarkets to satisfy the demand for even the most basic commodities, which had caused a thriving 'black market' to emerge. At the same time all prisoners (including foreigners), except those convicted of violent crimes or of conspiring with foreign powers, were released; Libyan citizens were guaranteed freedom of travel abroad; and the revolutionary committees were deprived of their powers of arrest and imprisonment, which had often been used indiscriminately and arbitrarily.

In June 1988 the GPC approved a charter of human rights, guaranteeing freedom of expression and condemning violence. Earlier in the year the GPC had created a people's court and a people's prosecution bureau to replace the 'revolutionary courts'. In August Qaddafi announced the abolition of the army and the police force. The army was to be replaced by a force of Jamahiri Guards, comprising conscripts and members of the existing army and police force, which would be supervised by 'people's defence committees' located in strategic areas. A new policy of decentralization was announced, and in September the decision was taken to relocate all but two of the secretariats of the General People's Committee (ministries) away from Tripoli, mostly to Sirte, Qaddafi's birthplace. Further reform was promised when, in January 1989, Qaddafi announced that all state institutions, including the state intelligence service and the official Libyan news agency, were to be abolished. Despite much official rhetoric, the practical consequences of these pronouncements proved limited and were non-existent as far as human rights were concerned.

QADDAFI'S DECENTRALIZATION OF GOVERNMENT

At the annual meeting of the GPC held in Sirte in March 2000, Qaddafi announced that most of the central government secretariats were being abolished and their functions devolved to the municipal and provincial levels. The move continued a decentralization policy introduced in the late 1980s, but was interpreted in part as a means of deflecting popular criticism away from central government by ensuring that any complaints would have to be dealt with by the relevant commune or provincial council. Significantly, however, the Libyan leader declared that the Secretariats for Foreign Liaison and International Co-operation, for Finance and for Justice and Public Security would be retained and that two new secretariats would be created (African Unity, and Information, Culture and Tourism), thus ensuring that key areas of government remained centralized. Policy on hydrocarbons was transferred to the National Oil Corporation (NOC) following the abolition of the energy secretariat, ensuring that this vital area also remained under central control. Continuity of hydrocarbon policy was ensured by the appointment of the former Secretary for Energy, Abdallah Salem al-Badri, as head of the NOC. A new and much smaller General People's Committee was formed, with Mubarak Abdallah al-Shamikh as Secretary (effectively Prime Minister). By the second half of 2000 practical implementation of the devolution process was reported to have made little progress.

In June 2003 another reorganization took place, amid press reports that Qaddafi had demanded the total privatization of key economic sectors, including the petroleum industry, arguing that the public sector was uncompetitive and had failed. Qaddafi called for key sectors to be run by companies formed by Libyan nationals who would be allowed to seek assistance from foreign experts. According to some sources, Dr Shokri Muhammad Ghanem, who had been appointed as Secretary of the General People's Committee in the reorganization, favoured economic openness and was keen to encourage greater foreign investment in Libya.

At the GPC meeting held in Sirte in March 2004, a reorganization of the General People's Committee was announced that appeared to strengthen the position of 'reformers' and gave the Libyan Government a more orthodox appearance. Ghanem retained his post as Secretary, indicating Qaddafi's continued commitment to reform. Five new secretariats were also created, relating to the portfolios of Energy (revived after having been abolished in 2000), National Security, Youth and Sport, Culture, and Training and Labour. New legislation was adopted to facilitate the transfer of state corporations to private management, to increase immigration controls and ban illegal immigration, and to promote the tourism sector.

Reports in the Arab press claimed that the government changes represented a victory for Seif al-Islam and his supporters over the uncompromising revolutionary committees opposed to the liberalization drive. In an interview with *Al-Hayat*, Seif al-Islam stated that Libya had to become an open, democratic state and that the Libyan people wanted development, democracy, human rights and freedoms. Seif al-Islam's subsequent announcement in August 2008 that he intended to withdraw from politics was widely viewed as political posturing and, indeed, his involvement in the wider political affairs of the country was confirmed in October 2009 when he was appointed General Co-ordinator of the People's Social Leadership Committees, a grouping of regional and tribal leaders. In May 2010 Seif al-Islam called for a new constitution, and publicly questioned the competence of the Government.

A further major reorganization of the GPC was announced in March 2006. Ghanem was replaced as Secretary by his Deputy, Dr al-Baghdadi Ali al-Mahmoudi, and was himself appointed as Chairman of the NOC. Some senior officials had strongly criticized Ghanem's pursuit of liberal economic policies, in particular the privatization of state-owned companies, the freezing of salaries and the removal of subsidies for a number of essential products. Al-Mahmoudi insisted that Ghanem's programme of reforms would continue; however, while he refrained from attacking the policies of his predecessor, he did little to support them. He also affirmed his commitment to opening the banking sector to investment from private and foreign banks.

In January 2006 it was reported that Qaddafi had given Seif al-Islam permission to proceed with a plan to permit privately owned newspapers and radio and television news organizations in the country. Seif al-Islam announced that preparations were under way to create a satellite television channel and contracts had been signed to distribute over 50 international and Arab publications in Libya without censorship. The Al-Ghad Foundation was duly set up and its various media organs gained notoriety for openly criticizing government officials and policies. Perhaps in an attempt to distance itself further from the Government, in May 2009 the Foundation announced plans to relocate its headquarters abroad, ostensibly to attract foreign investment. However, in the following month the Government abruptly announced that Al-Ghad was to be nationalized and placed under the control of the National Centre for Media Services, which was to redraft the group's editorial policy.

The weakening of Seif al-Islam's position was highlighted in December 2010, when the board of trustees of his charitable foundation, the Qaddafi International Charity and Development Foundation, announced that it would no longer include advocacy for political and human rights reform in Libya among its activities and would focus instead on aid and development work in Africa. Both the Foundation and Al-Ghad were the two vehicles through which Seif al-Islam promoted reform in Libya, and the curtailment of the domestic activities of both organizations pointed to the growing ascendancy of the hardliners.

CORRUPTION AND REFORM

Government corruption was a recurring theme from the 1990s, with Qaddafi himself the most vocal on the subject, consistently referring to it in public speeches, intimating that the lack of economic development in the country was due entirely to corruption. In November 2001 the People's Tribunal in Benghazi sentenced 47 senior officials of the Secretariat for Finance and of the Central Bank—all of whom had been convicted on corruption charges—to between one and 19 years' imprisonment. The Secretary for Finance, Abd al-Salam Burayni, and his immediate predecessor, Bait al-Mal, were among those convicted. In early 2006 Qaddafi launched an anti-corruption campaign, giving government officials a period of four months in which to declare their wealth. Despite a passionate speech against corruption by Qaddafi to the General Planning Council in November, and reports that the new measures had forced a number of officials to flee the country, the campaign appeared to lose momentum in the following months.

In March 2008 Qaddafi announced at the annual GPC meeting in Sirte his plan to abolish almost all of the government secretariats. Qaddafi also declared his intention to disburse the country's hydrocarbons revenues directly to the people. In his speech, he railed at the 'octopus' of government and stated that the 'administration had failed'. His proposals would effectively do away with the executive arm of government, with only some ministerial departments remaining (reportedly foreign affairs, defence, internal security and, according to some, justice and finance). A reorganization of the General Secretariat of the GPC and of the General People's Committee was also announced at the annual meeting. There was speculation that the new appointments mostly served to concentrate power more closely within the tight clique of Qaddafi's family and trusted friends—a trend that had become increasingly characteristic of the Libyan leader in the 2000s. On 1 September 2008, speaking on the 39th anniversary of his coming to power, Qaddafi reiterated his plans to dismantle the majority of secretariats and to redistribute oil revenues, stating that the reforms would come into effect at the beginning of 2009.

However, rather than implementing the proposed reforms directly, Qaddafi referred them to the Basic People's Congresses (BPCs). At the annual General People's Conference held in March 2009, the GPC rejected the proposed package of reforms, after the BPCs had themselves voted against it. The BPCs did not reject the scheme completely, saying that they endorsed it in principle, but 'supported the postponement of direct distribution (of oil revenue) until the relevant procedures have been completed', and in the interim 'supported continuing providing services through executive institutions'. Nevertheless, Qaddafi did effect a reorganization of the General People's Committee. Musa Kusa, hitherto the head of the Libyan intelligence service, was appointed as Secretary for Foreign Liaison and International Co-operation, while Abd al-Hafid Mahmoud Zlitni assumed responsibility for the newly merged Secretariat for Finance and Planning. Several other secretariats were also merged and the post of Secretary for Manpower, Training and Employment was abolished. In late January 2010 the number of secretariats was reduced from 12 to seven, in order to streamline the decision-making process, and Muhammad Aboulghasem al-Zwai, a former ambassador to the United Kingdom and to Morocco, was appointed as Secretary of the GPC.

WORSENING RELATIONS WITH THE WEST: LIBYA ACCUSED OF 'STATE-SPONSORED TERRORISM'

Qaddafi's policies in the Middle East and Africa and the actions of his people's bureaux in Europe and the USA increasingly antagonized Western governments during the late 1970s and 1980s. Early in 1984, following renewed official calls for Libyans to liquidate enemies of the revolution, seven bombs exploded in Manchester and London, in the United Kingdom. It was believed that these attacks were aimed at Libyan dissidents whom Qaddafi had recently accused the United Kingdom of harbouring. On 17 April, during a demonstration outside the Libyan people's bureau in London by Libyans opposed to Qaddafi's regime, a female police officer, Yvonne Fletcher, was killed and 11 people were wounded by shots fired from inside the bureau. A 10-day siege of the building ensued, during which the United Kingdom severed diplomatic relations with Libya and ordered Libyan diplomats to leave the country. Qaddafi denied responsibility for the murder of the police officer, but, after the United Kingdom broke off diplomatic relations, he was understood to have ordered so-called 'hit squads' to suspend their activities in Europe for fear of economic or other sanctions.

By the late 1970s relations with the USA had already become strained. In December 1979 a mob protesting against the presence in the USA of the exiled Shah of Iran sacked the US embassy in Tripoli, and it was closed in January 1980. As Libya drew closer to the Eastern Bloc by signing agreements with the USSR (already Libya's major arms supplier), Czechoslovakia, Poland, Bulgaria and Romania in the early 1980s, relations with the USA deteriorated further. When Ronald Reagan became US President in 1981, Qaddafi was quickly elevated to the status of 'international enemy number one' and the US campaign against Qaddafi moved swiftly from covert action to military confrontation. In August of that year US aircraft shot down two Soviet-made Libyan fighter planes over the Gulf of Sirte, which Libya claimed as its territorial waters, and in November Reagan alleged that Libya had sent a group to assassinate him. In March 1982 the USA announced that the US Navy's Sixth Fleet would exercise in the Gulf of Sirte, and in February 1983 US naval vessels moved into Libyan waters and US surveillance aircraft were spotted over the Libyan–Sudanese border after the discovery of an alleged Libyan coup plot against the Sudanese Government.

Details of a plan by the CIA to undermine the Qaddafi regime were revealed in the US press in November 1985. The following month the US Government accused Libya of harbouring and training members of the pro-Palestinian Fatah Revolutionary Council, led by Abu Nidal, who were believed to be responsible for simultaneous attacks on passengers at the departure desks of the Israeli airline, El Al, at Rome (Italy) and Vienna (Austria) airports on 27 December, and of being a centre for international terrorism. On 7 January 1986 President Reagan ordered the severance of all economic and commercial relations with Libya and, on the following day, he froze Libyan assets in the USA. He was unsuccessful, however, in persuading the USA's European allies to impose economic sanctions against Libya.

In December 1985 Qaddafi had drawn a notional 'line of death' across the north of the Gulf of Sirte, along latitude 32°30'N, which he warned US and other foreign vessels not to cross. In January 1986, ostensibly in the exercise of its right to navigation in the area under international law, the Sixth Fleet was deployed off the Libyan coast, although no US vessel was believed to have crossed the 'line of death'. On 24 March, the day after the Sixth Fleet had begun its fourth set of manoeuvres in the area since January (and the 18th since 1981), Libya fired recently installed Soviet SAM-5 missiles at US fighter aircraft flying over the Gulf of Sirte and inside the 'line of death'. In two retaliatory attacks on 24 and 25 March 1986, US fighter aircraft destroyed missile and radar facilities at Sirte and sank four Libyan patrol boats in the Gulf. On 15 April US F-111 bombers flying from bases in the United Kingdom, together with aircraft from the Sixth Fleet, bombed military installations (including the Aziziya barracks where Qaddafi and his family were living), airports, government buildings and suspected terrorist training camps and communications centres in Tripoli and Benghazi. Reliable estimates suggested that 39 people were killed, many of them civilians (reportedly including Qaddafi's adopted daughter), and almost 100 people were wounded. The US Administration justified the raids as 'self-defence' against 'state-sponsored terrorism' by the Libyan regime. In particular, it claimed to have proof that Libya was responsible for a bomb attack on a discotheque in West Berlin, Germany, on 5 April 1986, in which a US soldier and a Turkish woman were killed. There was little sympathy for Libya and most Arab countries confined themselves to verbal condemnation of the USA.

Conflict with the USA erupted again in January 1989, when US aircraft shot down two Libyan fighter aircraft in 'self-defence' over international waters in the Mediterranean. In March 1990 both the USA and the Federal Republic of Germany (West Germany) claimed that Libya had commenced production of mustard gas at a plant near Rabta, south of Tripoli. When a fire broke out at the plant during the same month, Libya accused those countries, together with Israel, of involvement in sabotage, allegations that all three countries denied. In September, following an official investigation, France alleged that Qaddafi, together with President Hafiz al-Assad of Syria and the leader of the Popular Front for the Liberation of Palestine, Ahmad Jibril, had been responsible for planning the bombing of a French Union des Transports Aériens (UTA) passenger aircraft over Niger in September 1989, in which 171 people were killed. In June 1991 a Libyan proposal aimed at restoring diplomatic relations with the United Kingdom was rejected by the British Foreign and Commonwealth Office, which stated that there could be no possibility of a resumption in relations until there was convincing evidence that Libya had renounced its support for groups engaged in international terrorism, including the Irish Republican Army (IRA), and was prepared to co-operate fully in bringing to justice those responsible for the death of Yvonne Fletcher. In an interview given in 1992 Qaddafi admitted that Libya had supplied arms and explosives to the IRA, but denied that IRA members had trained in Libya. He maintained that all links with the IRA had now been severed. However, relatives of victims of IRA violence believed to have been carried out with explosives supplied by Libya continued to pursue legal redress against the Libyan Government. In June 2010 they secured their aim, and Qaddafi agreed to pay US $2,000m. in compensation. However, in an attempt to prevent further claims against it, the Libyan Government refused to acknowledge specific liability.

THE LOCKERBIE AFFAIR AND THE IMPOSITION OF UN ECONOMIC SANCTIONS

In December 1988 all 259 people aboard a Pan Am Boeing 747, en route for New York, USA, died when the aircraft exploded over Lockerbie, Scotland. Eleven people in the village also died. The plane had been flying from Frankfurt-am-Main, Germany, where it was believed that a suitcase containing a bomb had been loaded on board. Investigations also revealed that this suitcase had arrived at Frankfurt on a flight from Malta, where an employee of Libyan Arab Airlines, Al-Amin Khalifa Fhimah, was stationed. On 13 November 1991 international warrants were issued for the arrest of Fhimah and the former security chief of the Libyan airline, Abd al-Baset al-Megrahi, accusing them both of responsibility for the bombing of the Pan Am aircraft; Libya denied any involvement in the bombing.

Libya resisted pressure for the extradition of the two Lockerbie suspects, and also for the arrest of four other Libyans sought by France in connection with the 1989 UTA airliner bombing, mounting a campaign among its Arab neighbours to enlist their support in countering the allegations. On 5 December 1991 the Arab League Council, meeting in Cairo, expressed solidarity with Libya and urged the avoidance of sanctions. However, on 26 December US President George Bush extended economic sanctions, which the USA had imposed on Libya in January 1986, for a further year. A unanimous resolution (No. 731), adopted by the UN Security Council on 21 January 1992, demanded the extradition of the Lockerbie suspects to the USA or the United Kingdom, as well as Libya's full co-operation with France's inquiry into the 1989 UTA airliner bombing.

On 31 March 1992 the UN Security Council adopted Resolution 748, imposing mandatory economic sanctions against Libya. From 15 April all civilian air links and arms trade with Libya were prohibited and its diplomatic representation abroad reduced. However, an embargo on the sale of Libyan petroleum was not imposed. Qaddafi responded with a threat to cut off oil supplies to, and withdraw all business from, those countries that complied with Resolution 748. Arab diplomats and the more pragmatic members of Qaddafi's circle urged a compromise, fearing that the imposition of further UN sanctions, particularly an embargo on the sale of petroleum, would be disastrous.

Despite the USA's efforts to secure a tightening of the economic embargo, the main European importers of Libyan petroleum, in particular Germany, Italy and Spain, remained firmly opposed to an oil embargo. In August 1993 the USA, the United Kingdom and France, increasingly frustrated at Qaddafi's defiance, issued an ultimatum to Libya stating that if the two suspects were not surrendered for trial by 1 October, they would propose a new UN Security Council resolution imposing tougher sanctions. When Libya failed to comply, on 11 November the Security Council adopted Resolution 883, which provided for the freezing of all Libyan assets abroad, with the exception of earnings from hydrocarbon exports, placed a ban on the sale to Libya of certain equipment for the 'downstream' oil and gas sectors, and placed further restrictions on Libyan civil aviation.

In June 1994 the ministers of foreign affairs of the OAU member states adopted a resolution urging the UN Security Council to revoke the sanctions that it had imposed on Libya. On the following day a member of the Palestinian Fatah Revolutionary Council, who was on trial in Lebanon (accused of the assassination of a Jordanian diplomat), claimed that the Council had been responsible for the Lockerbie bombing. At various times after February 1992, different parties had alleged that Iranian, Syrian and Palestinian agents—sometimes separately, sometimes in collaboration—had been responsible for the bombing. Nevertheless, the US and British authorities remained convinced that there was still sufficient evidence of Libyan involvement to continue to seek the extradition of the two Libyan suspects.

In April 1995 Qaddafi successfully defied UN sanctions by ordering a Libyan aircraft carrying 150 pilgrims to leave Tripoli for Jeddah in Saudi Arabia. The UN immediately condemned the Libyan action as a 'flagrant violation of the UN air embargo' and criticized Egypt and Saudi Arabia for their involvement. However, it rejected persistent US demands for stronger sanctions, including an oil embargo, and merely renewed existing sanctions. In June Qaddafi once again flouted UN sanctions by flying to Cairo to attend an Arab League summit, which urged the UN to lift sanctions against Libya, and appealed to the United Kingdom and the USA to accept an Arab proposal that the two Libyan suspects in the Lockerbie affair should be given a neutral and fair trial in The Hague, rather than the United Kingdom, but with Scottish judges in session and in accordance with Scottish law.

USA IMPOSES SECONDARY SANCTIONS

In July 1996 the USA increased its pressure on Libya when the US Congress unanimously approved the controversial Iran and Libya Sanctions Act (ILSA), which aimed to weaken further the Libyan economy as a penalty for that country's alleged support of international terrorism. The legislation had originally targeted only Iran, but had been amended to include Libya, and involved the imposition of sanctions on any non-US country investing more than US $40m. (subsequently revised to $20m.) in Iran or Libya in any one year. European governments protested vociferously against the legislation, and promptly lodged a protest with the World Trade Organization (WTO). European oil companies, particularly those of Italy and Spain, were heavily involved in the Libyan petroleum industry, and EU countries were, therefore, most likely to suffer as a result of the new sanctions. In April 1997 the EU and the USA reached a compromise: the US Administration promised to protect European companies from the adverse effects of the legislation, while in return the EU agreed to withdraw its complaint to the WTO regarding an earlier US law, the Helms-Burton Act, which imposed sanctions on non-US companies involved in business with Cuba.

Despite EU protests against the new US sanctions regime, relations between European countries and Libya remained strained. Nevertheless, Qaddafi tried to take advantage of the divisions between the USA and the EU by working to improve European relations, particularly with France. He praised France for its pursuit of an independent foreign policy and allowed the French judge investigating the 1989 bombing of the UTA airliner over Niger unprecedented access to Libyan evidence during his visit to Tripoli in July, which led to the judge's decision to try *in absentia* the Libyans suspected of the attack. A declaration by German authorities in October that clear evidence was available to prove the Libyan Government's direct involvement in the 1986 bomb attack on a Berlin discotheque, which provided a pretext for the US raids against Libya 10 days later, was also a major setback; it was announced that arrest warrants had been issued for the three Libyans believed to have been involved in the attack. In March 1997 Libya achieved a rare success in foreign policy when the Vatican resisted US pressure and established formal diplomatic relations with Libya.

In February 1997 the Ministerial Council of the OAU met in Tripoli for the first major meeting of the organization to be convened outside Addis Ababa, Ethiopia. The delegates called for an end to UN sanctions against Libya, and a committee of five ministers was established to mediate between Libya and the Western states in order to try to resolve the Lockerbie affair.

FURTHER DEVELOPMENTS IN THE LOCKERBIE AFFAIR

In July 1997 the Arab League, which had previously been criticized by Qaddafi for its lack of support, formally proposed that the two Libyan suspects in the Lockerbie affair be tried by Scottish judges under Scottish law in a neutral country. At an Arab League meeting in September the member states urged a relaxation of the air embargo on Libya and in October the President of South Africa, Nelson Mandela, visited Libya, despite US disapproval, and publicly expressed support for the proposals to hold a trial of the Lockerbie suspects in a third country. Later that month the United Kingdom requested that the UN send envoys to examine the Scottish legal system, and in December, following the renewal of sanctions by the UN in November, the UN issued a report concluding that the Libyan suspects would receive a fair trial under the Scottish system.

In April 1998 a representative for the families of the British victims of the Lockerbie bombing and a professor of Scottish law travelled to Libya, where they met Qaddafi. The Libyan leader was reported to have agreed to the trial of the two Libyan suspects in The Hague. At a meeting in Ouagadougou, Burkina Faso, in June, the OAU resolved that from September its members would cease to comply with UN sanctions against Libya unless the USA and the United Kingdom agreed to a trial being held in a neutral third country, and authorized flights to Libya on humanitarian, religious or diplomatic missions with immediate effect. In July a wide-ranging accord was signed in Rome, in which Italy expressed regrets for its colonial past, and which provided for joint infrastructure projects, especially in the energy sector. In October the two countries signed a further agreement on technical and scientific co-operation. France also appeared keen to improve relations with Libya, where French companies were actively seeking investment opportunities in the energy sector. France and Libya agreed that the six Libyans implicated in the 1989 UTA airliner bombing over Niger could be tried *in absentia*.

In August 1998 the USA and the United Kingdom, under mounting diplomatic pressure, sought to regain the initiative in the Lockerbie affair and agreed to a trial of the two Libyan suspects in the Netherlands before a panel of Scottish judges and in accordance with Scottish law. Soon after the offer was made the UN Security Council unanimously approved a resolution (No. 1192) allowing the lifting of UN sanctions against Libya as soon as the two suspects were surrendered for trial. Qaddafi gave a cautious welcome to the US and British proposal, and the Libyan Government appointed a new, high-level legal team to represent the two suspects, headed by a former Secretary for Foreign Liaison. During a British television broadcast in October, Qaddafi indicated that the two men might be guilty, but emphasized that the bombing had not been officially sanctioned and that the suspects may have been seeking their own revenge for the US air-strikes against Libya in 1986. By the time Kofi Annan, the UN Secretary-General, visited Libya in December, Qaddafi had agreed to a trial in the Netherlands under Scottish law.

In early March 1999 the six Libyans accused of the 1989 UTA bombing were found guilty *in absentia* after a three-day trial in Paris, France, and were sentenced to life imprisonment. The French authorities proceeded to issue international warrants for the arrest of the six men and demanded that the Libyan authorities should punish them. It appeared very unlikely that Libya would impose prison sentences on the men, who included Qaddafi's brother-in-law. In July 1999 Libya paid more than US $31m. in compensation to the families of the 70 people killed in the bombing of the French airliner.

In mid-March 1999, following further diplomatic efforts by South Africa, President Nelson Mandela, on a visit to Libya, announced that the Libyan authorities would release the two men accused of the Lockerbie bombing for trial by 6 April. The Libyan Government sent a letter to the UN Secretary-General soon after, guaranteeing to surrender the two suspects. On 5 April Fhimah and al-Megrahi arrived at Valkenburg airport in the Netherlands, accompanied by the UN's chief legal counsel, Hans Corell. With the surrender of the two suspects, the UN Security Council immediately suspended the sanctions imposed on Libya in 1992, but, under pressure from the USA, avoided a vote on whether to approve a permanent lifting of sanctions. On 9 July 2000 the Security Council issued a statement welcoming positive developments in Libya's co-operation with the UN, and reaffirmed its intention formally to revoke sanctions 'as soon as possible'. US sanctions against Libya—some of which dated from 1981—remained in place despite opposition from US business groups. In contrast, in September the EU removed most of its remaining sanctions against Libya, and Libya was invited to participate in the Euro-Mediterranean partnership programme initiated at Barcelona in 1995.

Several European countries moved quickly to strengthen political and economic links with Libya in the hope of gaining lucrative investment opportunities there. In December 1999 the Italian Prime Minister, Massimo D'Alema, became the first EU premier to visit Libya for more than eight years. During the visit the two countries issued a joint statement appealing for greater international co-operation to eradicate terrorism. In July the United Kingdom had announced that it was resuming full diplomatic relations with Libya after a rupture of 15 years. The decision followed a statement by Qaddafi in which he accepted Libya's 'general responsibility' for the murder of British police officer Yvonne Fletcher outside the Libyan people's bureau in London in 1984. Qaddafi expressed his 'deep regret' for the incident and offered to pay compensation to the woman's family. In November the British authorities confirmed that compensation (estimated at £250,000) had been paid, and a British ambassador arrived in Tripoli in the following month. British trade delegations visited Libya in July and October. Efforts by relatives of victims of the 1989 UTA airliner bombing to begin legal action against Qaddafi for complicity in the attack were not supported by the French Government, which considered the matter closed and was also anxious to strengthen links with Libya. In April 2000 Christian Pierret, Minister of State for Industry, became the first member of the French Government to visit Libya since sanctions had been suspended a year earlier. In September Libya won praise from the French and German Governments for its role in securing the release of 12 Western hostages held by the Abu Sayyaf rebel Muslim group on the island of Jolo in the southern Philippines. The Qaddafi regime denied claims that it had made ransom payments of US $12m. to secure the hostages' release, but admitted that a Libyan charitable foundation had offered to aid development projects in rebel-held areas.

In October 2000 the French Court of Appeal ruled that Qaddafi could be prosecuted in France for complicity in the 1989 UTA airliner bombing. On 13 March 2001 the Court of Cassation in Paris overturned the ruling, on the grounds that as head of state Qaddafi had immunity from such action. The families of victims of the bombing pledged to take their case to the European Court of Human Rights. In December 2000 Italy signed several agreements with Libya aimed at further improving political co-operation and increasing Italian investment.

However, Libya's relations with the EU suffered a reverse at the beginning of 2000. Although Libya had agreed to accept the terms for joining the Euro-Mediterranean partnership programme, it insisted that both Israel and the Palestinian (National) Authority (PA) should be excluded. This demand was unacceptable to the EU, and in January the President of the European Commission, Romano Prodi, withdrew an invitation to Qaddafi, originally made in December 1999, to visit Brussels, Belgium. In April 2000 the Libyan leader used his main speech to the EU-OAU summit in Cairo to castigate Africa's former colonizers. However, a private meeting with Prodi was described as more positive, and Libya was courted by several European leaders eager to capitalize on the country's rehabilitation. In October all EU member states supported a resolution proposed by Libya in the UN General Assembly criticizing unilateral sanctions, and in November Libya was invited to participate as an observer in the Euro-Mediterranean meeting of ministers responsible for foreign affairs in Marseille, France.

In February 2000 the US authorities had for the first time granted a visa to Libya's ambassador to the UN, enabling him to travel from the UN headquarters in New York to Washington, DC. A month later a group of officials of the US Department of State visited Libya to determine whether security arrangements were satisfactory for US citizens to travel there; a ban on Americans visiting Libya had been in place since 1981 and was renewed in November 1999. Although the US Government strenuously denied that it had any plans to lift unilateral sanctions, the visit angered the 'Lockerbie lobby' group of relatives of US victims of the 1988 bombing. In July 2000 the US Department of Defense stated that Libya was no longer engaged in acts of terrorism and that there was no evidence that it was pursuing a chemical weapons programme. Although the new Administration of President George W. Bush, which took office in early 2001, was regarded as more sympathetic to the US oil companies anxious to return to Libya, and the incoming Secretary of State, Colin Powell, had been critical of the use of US sanctions, an early lifting of the US embargo or the ban on US passport holders visiting Libya appeared unlikely.

Meanwhile, during a visit to Russia by the Libyan Secretary for Foreign Liaison and International Co-operation in July 2000, President Vladimir Putin called for a definitive end to UN sanctions. A month earlier Russia had indicated that it was resuming arms sales to Libya, with the first contracts reported to be worth US $100m. Other high-level political contacts followed.

THE LOCKERBIE TRIAL

The trial of the two Libyans accused of the Lockerbie bombing began on 3 May 2000. Fhimah and al-Megrahi were charged on three counts: murder; conspiracy to murder; and contravention of the 1982 Aviation Security Act. The prosecution alleged that the two accused were members of the Libyan intelligence service and had planted a bomb in a suitcase on an Air Malta flight which was then transferred to Pan Am flight 103 at Frankfurt. The two defendants pleaded not guilty, and their defence team alleged that a small Palestinian guerrilla group, the Popular Front for the Liberation of Palestine—General Command (PFLP—GC), acting as agents of the Iranian Government, had planted the bomb in revenge for the shooting down of an Iranian civilian airliner over the Gulf by a US warship in 1988. In August 2000 the United Kingdom and the USA released the text of a controversial letter from the UN Secretary-General to Qaddafi, written in February 1999 before the transfer of the two suspects, promising that they would not be used 'to undermine the Libyan regime'. Scottish legal officers insisted that these assurances would in no way inhibit the prosecution's case.

In November 2000, after 73 days of evidence and submissions from more than 230 witnesses, the prosecution concluded its case. Much of the evidence was highly circumstantial, and a number of key witnesses proved unreliable or offered testimonies that appeared to undermine the prosecution's case. The defence case began in December, when lawyers sought an adjournment to give them more time to gather new evidence, which they claimed was held by the Syrian Government and which purportedly implicated the Syrian-backed PFLP—GC and the obscure Palestinian Popular Struggle Front in the bombing. However, at the beginning of January 2001 the court was told that the Syrian authorities had refused to co-operate or hand over any documents. Lawyers for the defence subsequently announced that they did not intend to call the two defendants to give evidence, and concentrated instead on undermining the evidence presented by the prosecution's principal witness, Abd al-Majid Giaka, a Libyan double agent who had worked for both the Libyan intelligence services and the CIA.

On 31 January 2001 the three Scottish judges delivered their verdict. They unanimously found al-Megrahi guilty of the murder of 270 people and sentenced him to life imprisonment, with a recommendation that he serve a minimum of 20 years. However, Fhimah was acquitted, owing to a lack of evidence, and immediately freed. In an 82-page judgment, the judges accepted that al-Megrahi was a member of the Jamahiriya Security Organization (JSO—the Libyan intelligence services), 'occupying posts of fairly high rank', and, while they acknowledged their awareness of 'uncertainties and qualifications' in the case, they concluded that the evidence against him combined to form 'a real and convincing pattern' that left them with no reasonable doubt as to his guilt. The judges ruled out any involvement of the PFLP—GC and the Palestinian Popular Struggle Front in the bombing, stating that they inferred from the evidence that the planning and execution of the plot was of Libyan origin.

For many, al-Megrahi's conviction pointed clearly to Libyan state-sponsored terrorism and to the highest level in the Libyan leadership. Others continued to maintain that Libya had been made a convenient scapegoat by the West and remained convinced that suspicions should still focus on Iran, Syria and the PFLP—GC. British relatives of the victims stated that they intended to renew their campaign for a public inquiry into the atrocity, insisting that serious questions remained unanswered. A British government spokesman stated that the United Kingdom expected the Libyan authorities to take full responsibility for the actions of their official. US relatives pledged to pursue a civil case for damages from the Libyan Government. President Bush assured them that the US Administration would maintain sanctions against Libya until the Libyan authorities accepted responsibility for the bombing and agreed to compensate the families.

The day after the judgment was announced Qaddafi indicated that he would shortly reveal evidence that proved al-Megrahi's innocence. Four days later the Libyan leader made a long speech in Tripoli in which he repeated that Libya was not to blame for the bombing; however, he failed to produce the new evidence, claiming only that US and British investigators had planted evidence at Lockerbie to incriminate Libya. In March 2001 Libya's new ambassador to the United Kingdom, Muhammad Abu al-Qasim al-Zuai, stated that Libya would accept the verdict of al-Megrahi's appeal and would not interfere with the rebuilding of good relations with the United Kingdom. In July the US House of Representatives and the Senate voted overwhelmingly for a five-year extension to ILSA, with an option for the President to review terms of the sanctions provisions after three years.

RELATIONS WITH THE WEST AFTER THE LOCKERBIE VERDICT

Qaddafi immediately condemned the September 2001 suicide attacks on New York and Washington, DC, in the USA. He was swift to recall that, some six years earlier, he had issued a warrant for the arrest of Osama bin Laden, whom the USA held principally responsible for the attacks, and who, at that time, had been accused of financing a radical Islamist movement in Libya intending to assassinate the Libyan leader. Shortly after the attacks the MIG appeared on a list published by the US Federal Bureau of Investigation (FBI) of alleged terrorist organizations linked to the al-Qa'ida network whose assets were to be frozen. In October and again in January 2002 the US Assistant Secretary of State for Near Eastern Affairs, William Burns, met the head of Libyan intelligence services, Musa Kusa, in London. Kusa also held meetings with members of the CIA and the British security intelligence agency, MI5, regarding the combating of international terrorism. The Libyan team was reported to have provided US officials with information about the al-Qa'ida network, notably in the Philippines. The Libyans, for their part, requested co-operation in securing the extradition of Libyan militant Islamists living in Europe, particularly members of the MIG.

The 'war on terror' was one of the main topics discussed during a visit to Tripoli in October 2001 by the French Minister for Co-operation, Charles Josselin—the first visit by a French government minister since 1992. In February 2002 daily flights between Paris and Tripoli were resumed after a 14-year hiatus. Meanwhile, in November 2001 a German court sentenced a German woman, two Palestinians and a Libyan national to prison terms of 12–18 years' duration for carrying out a bomb attack on a West Berlin discotheque in April 1986. On the basis of new evidence from East German intelligence files, the prosecution stated that the Libyan intelligence services were implicated in the bombing, which was seen as a revenge attack for the sinking of two Libyan patrol boats in the Mediterranean by the US Navy a month earlier. The prosecution was, however, unable to prove that the Libyan leader had ordered or approved the attack.

Al-Megrahi's appeal began in January 2002 before a panel of five Scottish judges at Camp Zeist. At the centre of the appeal was new evidence from a former security guard at London's Heathrow Airport, who claimed that on the night that the Pan Am flight departed a door giving access to the loading area of Terminal 3 had been tampered with—suggesting that the bomb could have been planted in London and not in Malta, as the trial judges had concluded, thus casting doubt on the original judgment. On 16 March the five Scottish judges ruled that none of the grounds put forward by the defence was well founded, and al-Megrahi's appeal was unanimously rejected. He was immediately transferred to Barlinnie prison in Glasgow, Scotland, to serve his life sentence. Meanwhile, diplomatic contacts aimed at improving relations with the USA continued. US oil companies, which had assets exceeding US $2,000m. in Libya, lobbied the Administration of President George W. Bush, apparently concerned that unless relations improved Tripoli might terminate their concessions and allocate them to European companies. Nevertheless, relations remained strained. In late 2001 the US Department of State renewed the ban on US passport holders visiting Libya for another year, and cited Libya as one of the states it suspected of developing biological weapons. In March 2002 the US Administration named Libya as one of a number of potentially hostile states trying to establish a nuclear capability. In May John Bolton, the US Under-Secretary of State for Arms Control and International Security, condemned Libya, along with Syria and Cuba, for supporting terrorism and developing chemical and biological weapons.

In June 2002 former South African President Nelson Mandela visited al-Megrahi in prison in Glasgow to check on the conditions of his confinement. Following his visit, Mandela told a press conference that holding al-Megrahi in solitary confinement amounted to psychological persecution and argued that he should be allowed to serve the rest of his sentence in a Muslim country, suggesting Egypt, Tunisia or Morocco as possibilities. Mandela also stated that on the basis of the views of four African judges, who had monitored the proceedings at Camp Zeist on behalf of the OAU, the trial itself was flawed and that al-Megrahi should be given the opportunity to make a new appeal. In July Mandela met families of the British victims of the Lockerbie bombing to explain why he wanted al-Megrahi to serve his sentence in a Muslim country. At a press conference he stated that the relatives were not opposed to this suggestion and that both Tunisia and Egypt had offered to take al-Megrahi. However, US families of Lockerbie victims expressed anger at Mandela's proposal, claiming that al-Megrahi would be treated like a hero in a Muslim country.

In August 2002 Mike O'Brien, a minister in the British Foreign and Commonwealth Office, visited Libya for talks with Qaddafi; this was the first visit by a British government minister for some 20 years. After the meeting O'Brien stated that Libya was considering making an announcement whereby it accepted 'general responsibility' for the Lockerbie bombing, while the Secretary for Foreign Liaison declared that Libya was ready 'in principle' to take steps to compensate the relatives of victims. Qaddafi had also expressed his willingness to co-operate with the international community on issues such as weapons of mass destruction and the 'war on terror'. O'Brien welcomed these statements but emphasized that there had to be clear proof that the Libyan leader intended to fulfil his undertakings. He encouraged Libya to sign up to the International Chemical Weapons Convention and the International Atomic Energy Agency (IAEA)'s protocol on nuclear weapons and to allow UN inspectors into Libya. No reference was made to human rights issues. In September the British Prime Minister, Tony Blair, stated that he hoped Libya would become a 'fully fledged member of the international community' and that despite concerns relating to Libya's past he was prepared to extend the hand of partnership.

The French Minister of Foreign Affairs, Dominique de Villepin, visited Tripoli in October 2002 and reported that progress had been made regarding compensation for the families of victims of the 1989 UTA airliner bombing. Libya was ready to consider compensation for those French victims who had not already been compensated and to consider additional compensation as soon as a French court had ruled on this issue. Thus far Libya had paid some €32.5m., and families of 57 of the 171 victims (53 of whom were French nationals) had been compensated. It was reported that in Washington, DC, families of seven US victims had begun legal action in a federal court demanding US $3,000m. in damages from Libya. Before de Villepin's visit, families of French victims expressed their shock and indignation at the normalization of relations with Libya and at the forthcoming visit to Paris by the Libyan Secretary for Foreign Liaison and International Co-operation. On 22 October 2002 the first meeting of the Franco-Libyan Commission for 20 years took place in Paris, presided over by the two countries' ministers responsible for foreign affairs, a clear sign that bilateral relations were back on track.

It was reported in March 2003 that an agreement had been reached in London between Libyan, British and US negotiators under which Libya had taken responsibility for the actions of its officials in the Lockerbie affair and agreed to pay US $10m. in compensation to the family of each of the victims. Payment was to be made in three stages, with $4m. being paid to each family on the permanent lifting of UN sanctions; a further $4m. after the lifting of US sanctions; and the final $2m. when Libya was removed from the US list of countries deemed to support terrorism.

After long and protracted negotiations, on 16 August 2003 Libya finally delivered a letter to the President of the UN Security Council stating that it accepted responsibility for the actions of its officials in the Lockerbie bombing; agreed to pay compensation to the families of the victims; pledged co-operation in any further Lockerbie inquiry; and agreed to continue its co-operation in the 'war on terror' and to take practical measures to ensure that such co-operation was effective. The United Kingdom and the USA declared that they were prepared to allow the formal lifting of UN sanctions against Libya once the US $2,700m. in compensation had been transferred to the Bank for International Settlements. France, however, demanded a similar level of compensation for families of victims of the 1989 UTA bombing, who had received a mere $35m., and there were fears that France might veto the resolution unless Libya agreed to additional compensation. After intense negotiations between the United Kingdom, France and the USA, it was agreed to delay the vote on the draft resolution to allow more time for an agreement to be reached between the two groups representing families of the UTA victims and the Libyan authorities, who were holding talks in Tripoli. De Villepin stated that he was in favour of the formal lifting of UN sanctions but insisted that the principle of equity must be respected.

De Villepin announced on 11 September 2003 that a framework agreement had been reached between the relatives of the victims of the 1989 UTA bombing and the QICF providing for additional compensation, and that France had no objection to the UN Security Council vote taking place. No details were released regarding the level of compensation, however, and in a subsequent interview with French newspaper *Le Figaro*, Seif al-Islam stated that a special compensation fund would be established and managed by the two sides, which would receive contributions from French companies operating in Libya. On 12 September 2003 the Security Council voted formally to adopt Resolution 1506, which lifted the sanctions imposed against Libya; the USA and France abstained from the vote. Meanwhile, the Bush Administration confirmed that bilateral US sanctions would remain in place until Libya had addressed US concerns over its poor human rights record and lack of democratic institutions, its destructive role in perpetuating regional conflicts in Africa, and its continued pursuit of weapons of mass destruction and their related delivery systems.

In October 2003 Seif al-Islam Qaddafi appealed to President Jacques Chirac of France to lift the obstacles preventing the implementation of the framework agreement between the QICF and the families of victims of the UTA bombing. He stated that the Foundation would pay a maximum of US $1m. to each family and that the French had agreed to accept this offer. The victims' relatives, however, responded that the level of compensation proposed was unacceptable and that the framework accord was simply an agreement to pursue further negotiations. Shortly afterwards a Libyan delegation dispatched to Paris to negotiate with the families announced that talks had been suspended in the light of comments made by the French Ministry of Foreign Affairs. An agreement between Libya and France was finally signed in January 2004, according to which the Qaddafi International Foundation for Charitable Associations would pay $170m. in compensation to the families of victims in addition to the $35m. already paid. Nevertheless, Libya continued to deny any involvement in the UTA bombing; the Secretary for Foreign Liaison and International Co-operation, Abd al-Rahman Muhammad Shalgam, referred to the incident as a 'sad accident' and denied that his country had ever committed acts of terrorism.

Earlier, in June 2003 the Italian Prime Minister, Silvio Berlusconi, caused diplomatic embarrassment when he announced that Italy was close to signing an agreement with Libya that would allow Italian troops to patrol Libyan ports and Italian ships to sail in Libyan territorial waters, as part of a campaign to combat illegal immigration into Italy. Addressing the Italian Senate, he referred to the 'return' of Italian forces to Libya, a direct reference to the Italian colonial period. In return for Libyan co-operation, Italy, which assumed the presidency of the EU in July, promised the Libyan authorities that it would use its influence to persuade the EU to relax its arms embargo on Libya. The Libyan authorities, however, denied that any discussions with Italy had taken place and Libya's Secretary for Foreign Liaison and International Co-operation stated that his country would not allow such measures, although it was willing to co-operate in the curbing of illegal immigration, but not at the expense of its sovereignty. Meanwhile, Prodi discussed the matter at length with Qaddafi and emphasized the need for action through co-operation. The Libyan leader reportedly offered his full support to efforts to find an effective solution.

The Spanish Prime Minister, José María Aznar, arrived in Libya for talks with Qaddafi on 17 September 2003, thus becoming the first Western leader to visit the country since UN sanctions were imposed in 1992. Talks focused on Iraq and the Middle East peace process as well as Libya's role as a key transit point for illegal immigration from Africa to southern Europe. In December 2003 Qaddafi was invited to attend the first summit of heads of state and government of the 'Five plus Five' (the southern EU and Maghreb countries), held in Tunis, Tunisia. Prodi welcomed the fact that the lifting of UN sanctions had opened the way for an improvement in relations between Libya and Europe, but Qaddafi failed to respond. However, during talks between Prodi and Qaddafi at the extraordinary summit meeting of the AU in Sirte in February 2004, the Libyan leader stated that Libya was now ready to start working towards membership of the 'Euro-Med' trade and aid partnership. It was subsequently reported that Italy and the United Kingdom favoured the lifting of remaining EU sanctions against Libya, notably the arms embargo, but that Germany would continue to oppose this measure until Libya had agreed to pay compensation for the 1986 bombing in Berlin. Reports in September 2004 stated that Libya had agreed to pay US $35m. to compensate more than 150 non-US victims of the Berlin bombing.

LIBYA AGREES TO ABANDON WEAPONS OF MASS DESTRUCTION

On 19 December 2003 the United Kingdom and the USA announced that, after nine months of clandestine negotiations, Libya had agreed to disclose and destroy all its weapons of mass destruction, end all programmes to develop them and limit the range of its missiles to no more than 300 km. Libya would allow international inspectors to oversee the elimination of chemical, biological and nuclear weapons to ensure that the process was transparent and verifiable. The initiative for the talks evidently came from Qaddafi and was widely attributed to the 'Iraq effect'. US President Bush stated that the decision would allow Libya to begin the process of rejoining the community of nations and pledged that if Libya fulfilled its promises 'its good faith would be returned'. Within days a delegation from the IAEA had visited the country and in late December the Director-General of the IAEA, Muhammad el-Baradei, stated that after visits to four secret nuclear sites he could confirm that Libya had been in the very early stages of a weapons programme. In January 2004 the Secretary of the GPC, Shokri Muhammad Ghanem, stated that the USA should act quickly to reward Libya for abandoning its weapons of mass destruction programmes and warned that unless the USA lifted sanctions against Libya by 12 May, Libya would not be bound to pay the remaining US $6m. promised to each family of the Lockerbie victims. Ghanem also maintained that Libya wished to 'accelerate to the maximum' the dismantling of the weapons programmes so that President Bush could report to the US Congress that Qaddafi had fully and transparently destroyed or surrendered all illicit weapons. In a letter to US congressional leaders in early January 2004, President Bush had confirmed that US sanctions against Libya would remain in force despite recent 'positive developments'. Nevertheless, some economic restrictions were lifted by the USA in September.

In early February 2004 Silvio Berlusconi visited Tripoli for talks with Qaddafi. At the same time the USA announced that a US diplomat had been posted to Tripoli—the first for 25 years. In mid-February the Secretary for Foreign Liaison and International Co-operation, Abd al-Rahman Muhammad Shalgam, was invited to London, where he held talks with the British Prime Minister, Tony Blair, and the Secretary of State for Foreign and Commonwealth Affairs, Jack Straw. Both sides agreed to enhance co-operation in resolving the issue of the murder of British police officer Yvonne Fletcher outside the Libyan people's bureau in London in 1984. Libya had accepted 'general responsibility' for her murder but no one had been arrested. Blair agreed to visit Libya later in the year, while Straw stated that the United Kingdom was encouraging Libya to 'move forward' on human rights. British families of victims of the Lockerbie bombing stated that they felt 'let down' by the

British Government, which had failed to press Libya for more information on the bombing, and suggested that the United Kingdom and the USA wanted to ingratiate themselves with the Qaddafi regime in order to take advantage of developments within the Libyan petroleum industry.

Meanwhile, Dr Abdul Qadeer Khan, Pakistan's leading nuclear scientist responsible for developing Pakistan's nuclear bomb, admitted to selling nuclear expertise to a number of countries including Libya. Shortly afterwards it was reported in the US press that documents obtained from Libya contained proof that the People's Republic of China had played a key role in the transfer of nuclear technology to Pakistan in the early 1980s, and that technology from China had entered the international nuclear black market via the intermediary of Pakistan. Meanwhile, information leaked from a confidential IAEA report alleged that Libya had started a programme to develop nuclear weapons in the 1980s, beginning with exports to an unnamed nuclear weapons state in 1985 of uranium ore concentrate, which were then returned to Libya in the form of uranium compounds that could be used in the uranium enrichment process. Later, according to the report, Libyan scientists at the Tajura nuclear reactor succeeded in extracting small quantities of plutonium from uranium. From 1997 Libya began to procure parts and build centrifuges to enrich uranium and by 2002 was preparing to establish a plant to make those centrifuge components that could not be obtained from abroad. After his second visit to Libya in February 2004 el-Baradei praised the Libyan authorities for their co-operation and stated that Libya wished to develop a civil nuclear energy programme with the UN's assistance. Teams from the Organization for the Prohibition of Chemical Weapons subsequently visited Libya to oversee the dismantling of the country's chemical weapons programme. Libya had signed up to the international convention on the prohibition of chemical weapons in January 2004.

In February 2004, in a radio interview with the British Broadcasting Corporation (BBC), Ghanem caused controversy when he implied that Libya did not accept responsibility for the Lockerbie bombing, nor for the murder of Yvonne Fletcher. He stated that he did not see Libya's decision to pay compensation as an admission of guilt and that it had been done 'to buy peace with the West'. Following Ghanem's remarks, the United Kingdom announced that it had obtained assurances from Shalgam that Libya stood by the commitments it had made in relation to the Lockerbie bombing and the shooting of Fletcher. The USA, for its part, proceeded to lift the travel ban on US citizens visiting Libya, in place for 23 years, and stated that it would expand its diplomatic presence in Tripoli. The Bush Administration also announced that US oil companies operating in Libya before US sanctions were imposed would be allowed to begin negotiating their return, pending the lifting of sanctions. Some of the families of Lockerbie victims strongly criticized the decision.

In early March 2004 a delegation from the US Congress attended the GPC session in Sirte. In his address to the meeting, Senator Joe Biden of the Senate Committee on Foreign Relations urged Libyans to take the necessary steps to rejoin the community of nations. Later that month William Burns, US Assistant Secretary of State for Near East Affairs, held talks with Qaddafi—the highest level visit to Libya by a US official for more than 30 years. Shortly afterwards, Tony Blair became the first British Prime Minister to visit Libya since Qaddafi came to power. Blair acknowledged that his visit would be painful for some, especially the relatives of victims of the Lockerbie bombing, but commended Libya for the rapid progress that had been made in abandoning weapons of mass destruction and insisted that Libya could become an important partner in the fight against al-Qa'ida. The Libyan leader did not speak to reporters after their meeting, but Shalgam declared that Libya shared international concerns about al-Qa'ida. British officials announced that in time the United Kingdom would press for the EU's arms embargo to be lifted and would assist Libya in devising a new defence strategy. It was also announced that British police investigating the shooting of Yvonne Fletcher would visit Libya in April and hoped to talk directly to those suspected of involvement in her murder. At the same time the Royal Dutch Shell group announced an agreement, estimated to be worth US $1,000m., to develop Libya's gas resources, and BAE Systems, a major British aerospace and defence manufacturer, was reported to be about to sign a major deal with Libya on civil aviation.

It was announced in early April 2004 that the investigation into the shooting of Fletcher would be conducted under Libyan law and led jointly by a senior Libyan magistrate and a senior detective from London's Metropolitan Police. Witnesses would be summoned by the Libyan magistrate and questioned in the presence of British officers. The United Kingdom's Police Federation called for reassurances that the joint investigation would be 'independent and impartial'.

On 22 April 2004, the date by which the USA was required to have lifted US sanctions on Libya for the next tranche of compensation payments to be made to families of Lockerbie victims under the 2003 agreement, Libya announced that it had extended the deadline by three months. On the following day, however, the USA announced that it was lifting the majority of sanctions against Libya, including those imposed under ILSA; would no longer oppose Libya's accession to the WTO; and would work to rebuild diplomatic ties. The USA was to set up a liaison office in Tripoli as a step towards restoring normal diplomatic relations broken in 1981, and Libyan envoys would open a liaison office in Washington, DC. Certain US sanctions would remain in place while Libya continued to be designated a 'state sponsor of terrorism', and frozen Libyan assets valued at hundreds of millions of dollars would not be released. The USA's dialogue with Libya would continue to focus on issues of terrorism, human rights, political and economic modernization, and foreign policy in Africa. In June 2004 the USA formally re-established diplomatic relations with Libya when US Assistant Secretary of State William Burns opened a US liaison office in Tripoli. However, the US Department of State indicated that Libya would be closely monitored and would remain on the US list of countries supporting terrorism. In September President Bush issued a presidential executive order formally abolishing the US embargo against Libya and releasing frozen Libyan assets in the USA. Soon afterwards Qaddafi stated that although relations with the USA were good, there were still differences, notably on Iraq, and reiterated demands for the withdrawal of US troops, whose presence, he insisted, was a cause of the violence there.

In April 2004 Qaddafi made an official visit to Brussels at the invitation of European Commission President Prodi. It was his first visit to Europe for over 15 years. At a joint press conference Qaddafi stated that in the past Libya had led liberation movements in Africa and developing countries, but had now decided to lead the peace process all over the world. All states, including the USA, should follow its example and give up weapons of mass destruction. Libya wanted to be a bridge between Europe and Africa and to participate in reviving the Barcelona Process to bring peace and co-operation to the Mediterranean region. Qaddafi also urged the EU to help Libya and Algeria to control illegal immigration into Europe via North Africa. Prodi stated that his talks with Qaddafi had focused on Libya's joining the Barcelona Process, and after discussions with Germany and Bulgaria he was confident that issues between these countries and Libya could be solved 'within weeks'.

In July 2004 the Italian Minister of Internal Affairs, Giuseppe Pisanu, claimed in a speech to the Italian parliament that some 2m. African citizens were waiting in Libya to be smuggled into Europe via Italy. Libya claimed that, despite repeated requests, it had been unable to obtain planes, helicopters and sophisticated surveillance equipment owing to the EU embargo on equipment with dual military and civilian use. Consequently, Libya insisted that it could not effectively patrol its long land and maritime frontiers without international assistance. In August the Italian Minister of Foreign Affairs, Franco Frattini, stated that he was involved in strenuous diplomatic negotiations to seek to gain the EU's acquiescence to a partial lifting of its arms embargo. During a visit to Libya later that month by Frattini and Silvio Berlusconi, talks with Qaddafi focused on the problem of illegal immigration, with Berlusconi putting pressure on Libya to place stricter border controls on the country's northern coastline. In September, following the EU's announcement that it would lift the arms embargo and economic sanctions imposed on Libya since 1986 (a decision ratified by EU ministers of foreign affairs in October), Italy and Libya signed a new agreement on immigration. Pisanu stated that the lifting of the EU embargo would allow Italy to sell planes, boats, helicopters and jeeps to Libya to help the authorities combat the trafficking of illegal immigrants. The agreement also provided for joint patrols of Libya's coastline, the training of Libyan police by Italian officers, and the establishment of transit camps for immigrants on Libyan territory. In October Italy began deporting to Libya over 1,000 illegal immigrants who had recently arrived on the Italian island of Lampedusa. The UN High Commissioner for Refugees (UNHCR) expressed concern about the fate of illegal immigrants returned to Libya, pointing out that the country had not signed the Geneva Convention relating to the Status of Refugees.

Meanwhile, EU ministers responsible for foreign affairs stated that an improvement in human rights in Libya was an essential element for progress in relations with Europe and pointed to the serious obstacles to freedom of speech and association, credible reports of the torture of suspects, judicial errors and inhumane conditions of detention. They also underlined their opposition to the death penalty. In September 2004, after many years of difficult negotiations, an agreement was signed between the QICF and German lawyers representing German victims of the 1986 bomb attack on a Berlin discotheque, under which Libya was to pay US $35m. in compensation. In October 2004 Gerhard Schröder became the first German Chancellor to visit Libya. He welcomed the process of normalization in relations between Libya and the international community, and praised both the policy of openness and especially the decision to abandon weapons of mass destruction. The following month President Chirac became the first French head of state since 1951 to visit Tripoli, where he expressed his wish to begin afresh with Libya after years of tensions.

THE BULGARIAN MEDICAL STAFF HIV CASE

In early May 2004 EU officials expressed deep disquiet when six Bulgarian medical personnel (five nurses and a Palestinian-born doctor who was granted Bulgarian citizenship during his detention), who had been arrested in 1999 and charged with deliberately infecting several hundred Libyan children at a Benghazi hospital with blood products contaminated with the HIV virus, were convicted and sentenced to death by a Libyan court. Another Bulgarian and nine Libyans were acquitted of these charges but given sentences of between three and five years for trafficking in currency. At an international conference on AIDS held in Nigeria in May 2001, Qaddafi had declared that the Bulgarians were acting on the orders of Western intelligence services and demanded an international 'Lockerbie-style' trial. However, in the absence of any real motive for the alleged crimes, some observers argued that the Bulgarians had been made scapegoats by the Libyan authorities who were faced with a growing number of cases of HIV/AIDS in the country. Lawyers for the Bulgarians argued that their clients were being used to cover up inadequate sterilization of instruments at the paediatric hospital in Benghazi before the Bulgarian medics began working there. In mid-May 2004 the Libyan authorities prevented a further six medical personnel—five Bulgarian doctors and a nurse—from leaving the country. One of the doctors was accused of incorrect treatment of a patient, while three other doctors and the nurse were charged with negligence; the fifth doctor was a witness in a case against Libyan doctors. In late May, after a visit to Tripoli by the Bulgarian Minister of Foreign Affairs, Libya was reported to have refused to give any assurances that the death sentences against the original six Bulgarian medics would be cancelled on appeal. In January 2005 the state-run Jamahiriya News Agency reported that the GPC had appealed for the heaviest possible punishment for the medics. The European Commission, as well as the Bulgarian President, Georgi Parvanov, expressed deep concern; earlier, the EU had offered to provide assistance to the children infected with HIV in order to create conditions more favourable to the release of the medics.

In November 2005 the Supreme Court, which had been due to hear the final appeal of the six medics, postponed its proceedings and at the end of December ordered a retrial, a decision that angered some of the families of the children affected. President Parvanov welcomed the verdict but predicted that the nurses' release would come at a high price. A former Bulgarian government minister subsequently claimed that Libya had sought to exchange the nurses for Abd al-Baset al-Megrahi. In January 2006 an international fund to help the HIV-infected children was created and discussions began between Western officials and representatives of the families affected to determine the level of funding required. Bulgaria insisted that any financial settlement would constitute 'humanitarian aid', rather than an admission of its citizens' guilt. The retrial commenced in Tripoli in May, and it was finally announced in November that the jury would deliver its verdict in the following month.

Despite a wealth of genetic data that strongly suggested the children had already been infected with the HIV virus prior to the arrival in Libya of the accused in 1998, the judge upheld the original verdict and reinstated the six death sentences. The Libyan Government, despite widespread pressure to intervene, refused to be drawn on the issue, with Qaddafi insisting that the outcome of the trial was a purely juridical matter. In early 2007 the six medics were also charged with defamation, owing to their allegations that they had been tortured by Libyan officials during their detention and had thus been coerced into giving false confessions; however, this additional charge was dismissed by a Libyan court in May of that year. Meanwhile, in February 2007 the medics' lawyer filed a fresh appeal against the main convictions. The death sentences were upheld by the Supreme Court on 11 July, but on 17 July the High Judicial Council overturned this decision and commuted the death sentences to life imprisonment, after the families of those infected accepted a compensation deal reportedly worth US $1m. per child. Bulgaria formally requested that the medics be allowed to serve out their sentences on Bulgarian soil, and on 22 July Benita Ferrero-Waldner, the European Commissioner, responsible for External Relations and European Neighbourhood Policy, and Cécilia Sarkozy, the wife of French President Nicolas Sarkozy, arrived in Libya in order to procure the release of the detained medical staff into Bulgarian custody. Two days later all six medics were finally released from Libyan detention, and were transferred back to Bulgaria, whereupon they were pardoned immediately by President Parvanov. In August the Bulgarian Government announced its decision to waive Libya's debt of $56.6m., accrued during the Soviet era, and to divert the funds into providing both treatment for the children infected by HIV and compensation for their families. Meanwhile, both the EU and France denied having made any financial deals to procure the medics' release. In April 2013 a Dutch court ordered Libya to pay the Palestinian-born doctor, Ashraf al-Hajuj, €1m. in damages for his eight years' false imprisonment.

REVOLUTION AND CIVIL WAR

In January 2011 revolutions broke out in neighbouring Tunisia and Egypt, and the contagion quickly spread to Libya, with civil unrest erupting there later in the month. Initially, most observers believed that widespread fear of the Qaddafi regime would prevent the Libyan demonstrations from gaining momentum, allowing government forces to contain the violence. A heavy-handed government response to a demonstration in Benghazi on 17 February, a so-called 'day of rage', proved the tipping point, and from there the country rapidly descended into civil war. In the process, the focus of protests shifted from complaints about inadequate housing, social services and unemployment to demands for regime change. Fighting erupted throughout the country, especially in eastern Libya, but it soon became apparent that the rebel militias were ill equipped to take on the better-armed, better-organized government forces. The rebels were gradually forced back, leaving the road open to rebel-held Benghazi. As government troops advanced to the outskirts of the city, concern increased that the Qaddafi regime would take ruthless measures to crush the rebellion.

Alarm also spread throughout the international community, as it realized that it needed to act quickly in order to prevent large numbers of civilian casualties in Benghazi. In late February 2011 the UN Security Council unanimously adopted Resolution 1970, imposing sanctions on Qaddafi and his inner circle and calling on the International Criminal Court (ICC) to investigate government attacks on Libyan civilians. On 17 March the UN Security Council adopted Resolution 1973, imposing an air exclusion zone over Libya and authorizing member states to take 'all necessary measures' to protect civilians. One week later the North Atlantic Treaty Organization (NATO) agreed to enforce the UN-mandated air exclusion zone. Owing in part to the air support provided by NATO forces, rebel militias were able to halt the advance of government forces, forcing them to retreat from Benghazi. The jubilant rebels pursued the government forces, but their inexperience and lack of equipment thwarted major battlefield gains.

On the political front, Mustafa Muhammad Abd al-Jalil, who had served as Secretary for Justice under Qaddafi, announced on 26 February 2011 the establishment of the Transitional National Council of the Libyan Republic (subsequently National Transitional Council—NTC). The Council—which was largely staffed by technocrats from so-called Free Libya (the eastern part of the country) and senior defectors from the regime, including the former Secretary of Public Security, Gen. Abd al-Fattah Yunis, the former head of National Planning, Mahmoud Jibril, and Ali al-Essawi, a former Libyan ambassador to India—declared that it would draw up a new constitution that would allow for a free, democratic Libya. At the end of June the NTC proclaimed itself to be the sole legitimate representative of the Libyan people and by the end of September it had secured the official recognition of 94 countries.

As the fighting intensified, the NATO mission transgressed its original remit to protect Libyan civilians and began to target Qaddafi himself. Government circles in Europe openly admitted that there was no question of allowing Qaddafi to stay in power and that the unstated Western policy in Libya was regime change. In the process, NATO forces modified their tactics and started to target 'command and control' facilities in Tripoli. These were often buildings used by Qaddafi and his family, and uncorroborated reports suggested that Qaddafi narrowly avoided being killed a number of times.

As his regime slowly collapsed around him, Qaddafi became increasingly defiant, declaring that he would never leave Tripoli. At the end of March 2011 Musa Kusa, the Secretary for Foreign Liaison and International Co-operation and one of Qaddafi's closest lieutenants, fled to the United Kingdom. In late May eight senior army officers arrived in Rome, where they denounced Qaddafi, and a month later Shokri Ghanem, head of the NOC and a key reformist, appeared in Athens, Greece, announcing his defection. At the end of June the ICC issued arrest warrants for Muammar al-Qaddafi, Seif al-Islam and Abdullah al-Sanoussi, the head of intelligence. Meanwhile, after breaking the siege of Misurata, rebel forces made further advances on all fronts, encircling Tripoli.

In August 2011 foreign governments and observers expressed concerns regarding the stability and composition of the NTC. The assassination of the Commander-in-Chief of the so-called Free Libya Armed Forces, Yunis, precipitated a power struggle, leading to demands that the NTC form a new transitional government. However, with many competing interests, this was not achieved until November. In the interim, the NTC expanded the membership of its executive council in an effort to better represent all interests in Libya.

Militarily, the month of August marked the effective end of the Qaddafi regime. Early in August 2011 rebel forces consolidated their hold on Zlitan, and later in August they occupied Tripoli. Prolonged and bloody fighting continued in Qaddafi strongholds, such as Bani Walid, Sebha, and Sirte; however, for all intents and purposes, Qaddafi's rule had ended. In a futile effort to save himself and his family, Qaddafi proposed the formation of a transitional government, but this offer was immediately rejected by the rebels. At the end of August the Algerian Government confirmed that it had allowed members of Qaddafi's family, including his wife, his daughter, Aisha, and two of his sons, Muhammad and Hannibal, to cross the border into Algeria, citing humanitarian concerns. A third son, Seif al-Arab, was reported to have been killed in an air-strike in April, and a fourth son, Khamis, was believed to have been killed south-east of Tripoli at the end of August. In early September a fifth son, Saadi, fled into exile in Niger. Qaddafi himself was captured and killed outside Sirte on 20 October, together with another son, Muatassim. After being put on public display for several days, the bodies of both men were buried deep in the Sahara Desert in a secret location. Seif al-Islam Qaddafi was captured by rebel fighters near the town of Obari on 19 November and transferred to the western town of Zintan, where he was incarcerated, pending trial. On 17 January 2013 Seif al-Islam appeared in court for the first time, charged with involvement with an ICC delegation accused of 'carrying papers and other things related to the security of the state'.

Following the capture of Tripoli, the Chairman of the NTC, Abd al-Jalil, indicated that the Council would move its operations to the city, which had been declared as the capital in a Constitutional Declaration issued on 3 August 2011. In early September interim Prime Minister Mahmoud Jibril became the most senior NTC official to take up residence in Tripoli, while in mid-September Abd al-Jalil gave a televised address in the city's former Green Square—renamed Martyr's Square following Qaddafi's ouster—in which he outlined the plans for the transition to a multi-party democracy. On 16 September the UN General Assembly approved, by 117 votes to 17, a motion to accredit NTC-appointed representatives, effectively recognizing the NTC as the legitimate governing authority in Libya.

On 3 August 2011 the NTC released a Draft Constitutional Charter for the Transitional Stage, which outlined a workable political process leading to elections for a GNC in June 2012. Following the release of a draft election law in early February 2012, the NTC decided that of the 200 GNC seats 80 would be allocated to political parties while 120 would be reserved for independent candidates. In early March a conference of eastern leaders in Benghazi called for the adoption of a federal system similar to that which was in place in 1951–63. Bowing to federalist pressure, the NTC on 15 March 2012 amended the Draft Constitutional Charter to specify that the GNC would chose a 60-member constitutional committee based on the model of the 1951 constitutional committee, with 20 representatives each from Cyrenaica, Fezzan and Tripolitania. In an effort to reduce social cleavages and conflict, the NTC in late April 2012 banned ethnic, tribal and religious parties from participating in the GNC election; however, the ban was dropped in the following week, after protests by Islamist groups. On 5 July 2012, only two days before the scheduled GNC elections, the NTC announced a further amendment to the Draft Constitutional Charter, declaring that the GNC would now be responsible for overseeing a separate general election for a constitutional committee.

As the NTC and the interim Government appointed by it moved towards elections, they faced a number of challenges, including a lack of transparency, dialogue, legitimacy, and public confidence. Meetings were held behind closed doors with no minutes published, and both the NTC and the interim Government lacked a framework for dealing with recognized experts and interacting with a nascent civil society. A general lack of public confidence stemmed from their failure to address ongoing issues related to stabilizing security and establishing a framework for national reconciliation. The demobilization of the militias and their incorporation into a national army, police force, or security force remained an urgent requirement; however, little progress was made. Violent clashes between rival militias continued throughout the country, often reflecting tribal rivalries and the uncertain status of ethnic minorities. Border security was also a major problem with the return of heavily armed veterans of the Libyan army, racial bias against black Africans, and a refugee crisis contributing to widespread unrest throughout the region.

On 7 July 2012 general elections took place in Libya, for the first time in decades, to establish a 200-member GNC, which was to appoint a new interim government, oversee the drafting of a constitution, and supervise elections based on provisions in the new constitution. Widely commended by international observers as free and fair, the elections were doubly remarkable in that they took place only nine months after the fall of the Qaddafi regime and the Libyan electorate strongly supported moderate, mainstream parties, reversing a trend elsewhere in North Africa in favour of Islamist groups.

The National Forces Alliance (NFA), a coalition of political parties and civil society groups, won 39 of the 80 party seats. Headed by Mahmoud Jibril, who was unable to seek election since former members of the interim Government were barred from participating, the NFA was most often described in the Western press as a 'liberal' political party. In contrast, the NFA, recognizing the important role of Islam in Libyan society, presented itself to voters as a moderate Islamist movement. The JCP, the political arm of the Muslim Brotherhood, secured the second largest representation among political parties, with 17 seats. Collectively, moderate, mainstream parties, such as the NFA, won over 60% of the party seats in the GNC.

Election results for the 120 independent seats were not as clear-cut as those for the 80 party seats. Genuinely independent candidates and individual candidates with ties to parties other than the NFA won a majority of the GNC seats reserved for independents. As a result, they would have considerable influence over the policies of the new congress. With many of these independent candidates elected on the basis of local connections, tribal affiliation, or social standing, the composition of the GNC reflected the full extent to which politics in Libya tended to focus on local concerns and issues. On 8 August 2012 the GNC was inaugurated at a temporary chamber in the Tripoli Congress Centre. Abd al-Jalil formally announced the dissolution of the NTC, symbolically transferring its powers to the oldest member of the new legislature. On the following day Muhammad Yousuf Magariaf, the leader of the National Front Party, was elected as the Speaker of the GNC and de facto head of state.

On 12 September 2012 the GNC elected Mustafa Abu Shagur, Deputy Prime Minister in the outgoing administration of Abd al-Rahim al-Keib, as Prime Minister. Abu Shagur received 96 votes in the second round of voting, defeating Jibril who received 94 votes. On 7 October Prime Minister Abu Shagur was defeated in a vote of no confidence, and was subsequently replaced by Ali Zidan. At the inauguration ceremony for the new Government, Prime Minister Zidan announced that his administration's priorities would be restoring security and rebuilding the economy.

On 6 February 2013 the GNC upheld the earlier NTC decision that the constitutional committee would be elected in a general election as opposed to being appointed by the GNC, and it confirmed this decision on 9 April. In the interim the GNC approved a three-member committee representing Libya's three historical regions, Cyrenaica, Fezzan and Tripolitania, to draft an election law for the election of a 60-member constitutional committee consisting of 20 members each from Cyrenaica, Fezzan and Tripolitania. No timeline was set for the completion of the election law or the holding of the general election. On 5 May the GNC approved a political isolation law, which appeared to ban from government anyone linked to the Qaddafi regime, even those who had been actively involved in his removal from power. In response, Magariaf, who had been the Libyan ambassador to India until his defection from the Qaddafi regime in 1980, immediately resigned from his position as Speaker of the GNC. With the support of the JCP, the GNC elected Nuri Abu Sahmain, a political independent and member of the Amazigh (Berber) minority, to replace Magariaf on 25 June 2013.

Meanwhile, tensions between the Zidan Government and rebel militias continued, with the assassination of individuals tied to the Qaddafi regime and the current Government commonplace. The Government had taken some steps to rebuild the military and the police force, as well as to disband the militias; however, at mid-2013 progress towards the restoration of national security remained slow. Much also remained to be done with regard to the rebuilding of the economy, which in the post-war era remained highly dependent on oil and natural gas revenues, and hydrocarbon production was often disrupted by violence and by industrial action. Moreover, there was concern that the prevailing sense of entitlement would be conducive to widespread graft and corruption, undermining the policies required to foster an entrepreneurial spirit and bring much needed diversification to the economy.

RELATIONS WITH THE EU IMPROVE

On a visit to Tripoli in January 2006, the French Minister of Foreign Affairs, Philippe Douste-Blazy, praised the development in relations between the two countries and declared that France would provide treatment for the HIV-infected children. In March France and Libya signed an agreement to co-operate in the development of peaceful nuclear technology, the first such agreement since Libya abandoned its programme to develop weapons of mass destruction in 2003. A senior Libyan official praised the agreement as 'a qualitative leap in relations between the two countries'. In July 2007 France and Libya signed a deal providing for the sale to Libya of anti-tank missiles as part of a broader bilateral military agreement. The deal, which also provided for the sale of communications systems, was the first arms contract to be signed between Libya and a Western nation since the international arms embargo was lifted in 2004. Considerable anger greeted the news in France, where many linked the culmination of the deal with the release of the Bulgarian medics, in which the French presidency had played a central role; President Sarkozy firmly denied any correlation between the two events. Nevertheless, Sarkozy attracted further criticism when he invited the Libyan leader to Paris on a state visit. In his first trip to a major Western state since the imposition of sanctions, Qaddafi pitched his Bedouin tent in the French capital in December 2007 and spent five days signing contracts amounting to US $10,000m. Many senior French officials refused to meet the Libyan leader, including the Minister of Foreign and European Affairs, Bernard Kouchner—a long-term advocate for the protection of human rights. The French press was also critical of the trip, accusing President Sarkozy of subordinating public morals to the quest for commercial gain. From Paris, Qaddafi flew to Madrid, making his first ever trip to Spain, where he signed further commercial deals.

In October 2005 Libya signed a memorandum of understanding (MOU) with the British Government to allow the deportation of Libyan nationals held in the United Kingdom on suspicion of involvement in terrorist activities. The agreement included a written assurance from Libya that deportees would be treated in a humane manner. (British law forbids the deportation of foreign nationals to countries that it suspects of practising degrading or inhumane treatment.) Amnesty International responded by stating that, as torture and suspicious deaths in custody were still commonly reported in Libya, it would be misguided to assume that such an agreement would be honoured. In February 2006 the British Secretary of State for the Home Department, Charles Clarke, visited Tripoli for talks with Libyan officials, aimed at fostering greater co-operation on counter-terrorism and illegal immigration. In March 2007 Libya and the United Kingdom signed an MOU agreeing to enhance scientific and technical co-operation. In May Blair revisited Libya at the beginning of his last high-profile foreign visit as British premier prior to his planned resignation later that month. Upon his arrival in Tripoli, the outgoing Prime Minister met with Qaddafi, and the two leaders were reported to have signed an agreement pledging closer co-operation on defence matters. Blair hailed the former pariah of the West as a 'transformed' nation, and an example to Iran and other 'outcasts' in the international community.

In June 2007 the Scottish Criminal Cases Review Commission granted al-Megrahi the right to a second appeal, having identified six points during his 2001 trial that it believed might have constituted a miscarriage of justice. The decision was based on the contents of an 800-page report detailing the findings of an inquiry, lasting nearly four years, into the investigation and trial. A number of relatives of the victims of the bombing expressed doubts about the conviction of al-Megrahi, and the view that Iran or Syria might have been behind the incident was attracting increasing levels of support.

The EU sought to follow up on its success over negotiating the release of the Bulgarian medics by deepening its dialogue with Qaddafi. In February 2008 Ferrero-Waldner announced that the European Commission was looking to create a formal framework for the development of relations with Libya. To this end, she announced that the Commission would seek a 'negotiating mandate' from the 27 EU member states. According to Ferrero-Waldner, the framework would be built around EU support for Libya's economic and social reforms and would be aimed at the ultimate establishment of a free trade agreement. In particular, the EU hoped to secure significantly larger volumes of petroleum and gas from Libya; in return, Libya would gain greater access to the EU market for its goods—particularly fish and agricultural products. Libya's ongoing efforts to rebuild its tourist industry meant that the country was also eager to secure EU support and assistance for the restoration of its archaeological sites.

The renewed negotiations with Libya took place outside the EU's existing framework for relations with the southern Mediterranean countries, the Euro-Mediterranean Partnership, or Barcelona Process. Since the lifting of sanctions, the EU had tried to entice Libya into this scheme, but Qaddafi had shown continued reluctance, owing to the human rights and good governance conditions attached to membership. This was more forcefully expressed in June 2008, when Qaddafi derided plans by President Sarkozy to deepen economic ties between EU members and southern Mediterranean rim states with the launch of the Union for the Mediterranean. Officially inaugurated on 13 July, this initiative, which included all EU member states and nations bordering the Mediterranean Sea, was envisaged by Sarkozy as building upon the Barcelona Process. Qaddafi branded the initiative an 'insult to Arabs and Africans', and contended that the EU was 'taking us for fools'. In January 2009, following the Israeli incursion into Gaza, Qaddafi declared the Union defunct, stating that it had been 'killed by Israel's bombs'. Thereafter, Libya remained uninterested in full membership in a regional process with restrictive conditions, but continued negotiations with the EU for a less ambitious framework agreement, addressing issues such as border security, energy, immigration and trade.

The issue of illegal immigration was Libya's main point of contention with the EU and a number of European states—notably Italy. Despite considerable material and financial support from Europe, Libyan co-operation on the issue of illegal immigration had hitherto been erratic, at best. Matters appeared to improve towards the end of 2007, when the Libyan authorities introduced more stringent conditions for work permits for African labourers—thus making their entry into Libya more difficult. Increased patrols also led to a decline in the number of migrants attempting the sea crossing; however, the end result of this, according to a November 2007 report by the International Organization for Migration, was that over 2,000 migrants were stranded in Libya, unable either to reach Europe or to return home. Possibly for this reason, Qaddafi in May 2008 announced that he would no longer co-operate with the EU on immigration matters—despite claiming that it was due to the failure of Italy and other EU states to provide adequate support for the anti-migration programme—accusing European nations of 'deliberately' drowning illegal African migrants and claiming that the EU was 'waging a war against Africans'. In July relations between Libya and Italy appeared to improve when it was reported that the two countries had pledged to settle their outstanding disagreements. For his part, Berlusconi appealed for the immediate implementation of a December 2007 accord allowing for the establishment of joint marine patrols (in motor vessels supplied by the Italian navy) to help counter illegal immigration. This agreement came into force in May 2009, when the two countries commenced joint marine operations. Despite Italy's donation of three marine patrol boats, with the promise of three more, as well as a US $20m. contribution from the EU, Libya demanded that the EU also provide additional equipment, including boats, helicopters and trucks, valued at $1,000m. Qaddafi later increased his demands, calling on the EU to provide €5,000m. to stem illegal immigration. The EU responded in October 2010 committing to €50m. over a three-year period.

Overall, relations between Italy and Libya were further consolidated when Berlusconi in August 2008 apologized for the 'damage inflicted on Libya by Italy during the colonial era' and signed an agreement to invest US $5,000m. in Libya over the next 25 years as a form of compensation. The Friendship, Partnership and Co-operation Treaty was formally ratified during a visit to Libya by Berlusconi in March 2009. Under the deal, Italy was to disburse a total of $5,000m. to Libya, in annual instalments of $250m. until 2028. The money was to finance numerous infrastructure projects, which Italian companies were to carry out. In June 2009, further cementing the deal, Qaddafi visited Rome for the first time. During his trip he assured Italian companies that they would have priority access to a Libyan government investment scheme worth some €11,800m. He also promised special commercial benefits, which would give Italian firms an advantage over other foreign competitors and, acknowledging Italy's dependence on Libyan oil, guaranteed that Libya would not 'favour supplying gas and petrol to other countries if it is at Italy's expense'. At the end of 2010 the Italian oil and gas company Eni agreed to help Libya to build a port and related infrastructure along the Gulf of Sirte, as part of the 2008 agreement to invest in social projects.

As relations with Italy improved, those with Switzerland deteriorated. In July 2008 Hannibal Qaddafi, son of the Libyan leader, and his wife were arrested at a hotel in Geneva, Switzerland, and later charged with assaulting two members of their domestic staff. Although the case against them was dismissed when the charges were dropped, the Libyan Government responded angrily, claiming that their treatment was a serious case of 'abuse of Libyan diplomats'. In the immediate aftermath of the incident, Libya detained two Swiss nationals; stopped issuing visas to Swiss travellers; cancelled its oil exports to Switzerland; prohibited flights by Swissair into Tripoli; and threatened to remove all the money it held in Swiss bank accounts. Despite protracted discussions between officials of both countries, in April 2009 the Libyan Government filed a lawsuit against the civil authorities in Geneva for material damages suffered by Hannibal Qaddafi and his wife. Libya was reportedly prepared to drop the charges and normalize relations in return for a formal apology by the Swiss Federal Council. In August the President of the Swiss Confederation, Hans-Rudolf Merz, apologized for the arrests during a visit to Tripoli, in return for the release of the two Swiss citizens who had previously been refused permission to leave Libya. However, Merz was left embarrassed when Libya failed to honour its side of the bargain, resulting in a deepening of the diplomatic stand-off. As a consequence, the Swiss Government prohibited the entry into Switzerland of 188 Libyans, including Qaddafi, his family, and senior members of the regime. In retaliation, a Libyan court in December sentenced the two detained Swiss men to 16 months' imprisonment for overstaying their visas. Following a successful appeal, the conviction of one of the defendants was overturned in January 2010, and he was allowed to leave the country; the conviction of the second defendant was upheld, although his gaol term was reduced to four months. At the same time, the Libyan Government announced that it was suspending visas for citizens residing in those countries adhering to the EU's Schengen Agreement, effectively including 25 European countries in the dispute, in an apparent attempt to apply diplomatic pressure on Switzerland. Intense mediation, most notably by the Italians, finally resolved the impasse; the second Swiss detainee returned home in June 2010, and the two countries signed a formal accord agreeing to normalize relations.

In August 2009 it was reported that the Scottish Cabinet Secretary for Justice, Kenny MacAskill, was considering a request for the release of al-Megrahi on compassionate grounds after it was revealed that he was suffering from terminal prostate cancer. On 20 August MacAskill announced that al-Megrahi would be allowed to return to Libya; al-Megrahi had withdrawn an appeal against his conviction on the previous day. The celebrations that marked al-Megrahi's arrival in Tripoli and his subsequent meeting with Qaddafi provoked an angry reaction from the US Administration. It also prompted allegations that the British Government had secretly agreed to the release in order to secure commercial advantages for British companies in Libya. Both countries denied the allegations, but suspicions over al-Megrahi's release persisted as he survived well beyond the period that doctors had given him to live. Following the capture of Tripoli by NTC forces in August 2011, international media groups reported that al-Megrahi was in a coma, and he died in May 2012.

The speed with which the EU member states moved to condemn Qaddafi and offer support to the rebels reflected their deep ambivalence towards his regime prior to the outbreak of the civil war. The French Government, along with that of the United Kingdom, was instrumental in forging the military alliance against Qaddafi and both countries took a lead in the campaign. By late September 2011 all 27 EU member states had officially recognized the NTC as the legitimate governing authority in Libya, while the EU itself had held several rounds of discussions with the NTC leadership.

By establishing an air exclusion zone over Libya, individual European states, through NATO, undertook a key role in the success of the revolution; however, the EU has had only a limited role in post-Qaddafi Libya. The NATO intervention resurrected debates throughout the Arab world and Africa about the intentions of the Western powers in a region of considerable strategic importance. Consequently, the issue of the appropriate level and form of EU engagement dominated dialogue inside and outside Libya, as well as in Egypt and Tunisia, in regards to the pace and objectives of political transformation. In response, the EU and individual European countries have mostly limited their assistance to the NTC to the provision of training and equipment intended to enhance security, together with information, training, and support for democratic governance.

Areas of sustained EU interest in Libya include familiar ones, such as energy supply, illegal migration, investment and trade, and security concerns. Europe will remain the principal market for Libyan oil and gas, and EU member states are well placed to take advantage of commercial opportunities there. Immigration is an area of policy evolution as the new Libyan Government is more co-operative in restraining illegal immigration than was the Qaddafi regime. The EU and certain of its member states, notably France, are also well placed to assist Libya to secure its borders, suppress illegal trafficking, and reduce terrorist-related concerns through training, advanced equipment and co-ordinated strategies with neighbouring states. Following the July 2012 elections, EU High Representative for Foreign Affairs and Security Policy Catherine Ashton congratulated Libya on its successful conduct of the polls and indicated that the Union would continue to co-operate with a new government upon its appointment.

In October 2012 GNC Speaker Magariaf attended a meeting of the Western Mediterranean Forum (5+5 Dialogue), comprising Algeria, Libya, Mauritania, Morocco and Tunisia on the southern side of the Mediterranean, and France, Italy, Malta, Portugal and Spain on the northern side. In the first meeting of the group since the Arab Spring, and the first attended by heads of government or state in nine years, the Forum agreed to establish a humanitarian task force to combat illegal migration across the Mediterranean. At the end of November EU officials met with representatives of the Libyan Government to discuss the technical expertise, equipment and devices necessary for Libya to secure and manage its borders, and in mid-December the European Commission approved a €25m. package to support education, health care, security and rule of law reforms in Libya. The EU announced at the end of January 2013 that it was prepared to assist Libya in developing an integrated border management plan, and in mid-May that it would deploy a 110-member monitoring team, comprising European border security experts and costing €30.3m over two years. In late June the EU congratulated Nuri Abu Sahmain on his recent election as GNC Speaker and reiterated its commitment to assisting Libya in its democratic transition process. On the following day Libya applied to become a partner of the Organization for Security and Co-operation in Europe.

Individual European states, many of which have long-standing interests in Libya, moved quickly to re-establish bilateral diplomatic, economic, military and other ties. In November 2012 the British Government announced that it would not seek compensation from the Libyan Government for the cost of its intervention in the Libyan civil war, estimated at €200m., and in early December a large British trade mission, headed by Minister without Portfolio Kenneth Clarke, arrived in Tripoli. In mid-December Mahmoud Nacua, the new Libyan ambassador to the United Kingdom, presented his credentials to Queen Elizabeth II and paid tribute to Britain's support of Libya. In a surprise visit to Libya at the end of January 2013, British Prime Minister David Cameron pledged Britain's help in training Libyan security forces as part of broader European efforts to counter Islamist militancy in North Africa.

In February 2013 the Italian Government presented Libya with 20 armoured vehicles. Libyan media reported in late March that the Libyan Government planned to spend US $4,700m. over the coming year to upgrade the military. At the end of May Libyan officials asked Russian authorities to resume previously frozen arms contracts, and in mid-June Libya agreed to the purchase of 350 amphibious armoured vehicles from the Czech Republic for €38m.

THE USA RESTORES FULL DIPLOMATIC RELATIONS

In August 2005 Senator Richard Lugar, Chairman of the Senate Foreign Relations Committee, headed a senior US delegation on a visit to Libya for talks with Qaddafi. Shortly after the visit, Seif al-Islam Qaddafi declared that full diplomatic relations would be established with the USA within 'the next few days', and predicted that Libya would be removed from the US list of states deemed to sponsor terrorism before the end of that year. Officials from the US Department of State, however, urged caution and indicated that many issues remained unresolved. In December Ghanem contested that Libya should have been more generously rewarded by the USA in return for abandoning weapons of mass destruction but also noted a significant improvement in relations between the two countries. In February 2006 David Welch, the US Assistant Secretary of State for Near Eastern Affairs, declared that relations with Libya were 'improving slowly but surely' and that dialogue aimed at restoring normal relations was ongoing. The Assistant Secretary of State for African Affairs, Jendayi Frazer, on a visit to Tripoli in March to discuss prospects for bilateral co-operation, welcomed Libya's efforts to find a peaceful solution to the crisis in the Darfur region of Sudan. Later that month Qaddafi declared in an interview on Italian television that the 2003 invasion of Iraq had not been justified in view of that country's abandonment of weapons of mass destruction. Qaddafi insisted that the USA should withdraw its troops from the country and argued that Saddam Hussain remained the legal President of Iraq since he had been removed from office by occupation forces rather than by the Iraqi people. On 15 May 2006 the US Secretary of State, Condoleezza Rice, announced that the USA would re-establish full diplomatic relations with Libya, including the opening of an embassy in Tripoli. Libya was removed from the US list of states deemed to support terrorism and from the list of states that refuse to co-operate with US anti-terrorism activities at the end of June.

Despite Rice's announcement, ties failed to advance with any speed, owing to a continuing impasse over the final Lockerbie compensation payment. The first two instalments had been paid, according to the terms of the deal, in 2003 and 2004. However, in February 2005 Libya had withdrawn the remaining US $536m. from the holding account, arguing that the time limit on the deal had expired. Despite the USA finally removing Libya from the terrorism list in June 2006, Libya continued in its refusal to pay the outstanding balance, prompting the US Congress in June 2007 to block the release of funds requested by the Bush Administration to develop its ties with Libya. The US Government had requested $115.9m. to build an embassy in Tripoli and an additional $1.15m. to help Libya retrain weapons scientists to work on civilian projects and to promote democratic reforms in the country. In addition, some money was allocated to support US companies looking to do business in Libya. Further to blocking the funds, Congress also refused to confirm the nomination of Gene Cretz as US ambassador to Libya.

In April 2007 Qaddafi refused to meet the US Deputy Secretary of State, John Negroponte, when he visited Tripoli for talks on the Darfur crisis in Sudan. Despite Negroponte being the most senior US official to travel to Libya in over 50 years, Qaddafi's stance was understood to be a response to Rice's continued refusal to visit Libya until the Lockerbie reparations issue was settled. Relations improved in August when Welch visited Tripoli to prepare the ground for a forthcoming visit by Rice (see below), and in December the US Congress agreed to release the requisite funds to establish an embassy in Tripoli, although it refused to grant any additional Libya-related state support. As a result of this progress, in January 2008 Condoleezza Rice met with Shalgam in New York, making him the first Libyan minister responsible for foreign affairs to be officially invited to the USA in over three decades.

The rapprochement did not last long. Later in January 2008 President Bush signed into law a bill permitting the victims of state-sponsored terrorism to sue the foreign governments believed to be responsible and to have their assets in the USA seized. Although Bush sought to have Libya exempted from the law, Congress again proved awkward, refusing to ratify the presidential waiver. Ali Aujali, the Libyan ambassador to the USA, subsequently claimed that ties were becoming 'increasingly strained'. Following a meeting between representatives from the two countries in London in May, a joint statement declared the commitment of both parties to 'work together to resolve all outstanding claims in good faith'. This culminated in an announcement in August that Libyan and US officials had signed a deal in Tripoli agreeing to provide full compensation to all victims of bombings involving the two countries—although, notably, the agreement precluded any admission of fault by either state. Then, in a significant step, Rice visited Libya in September, the first US Secretary of State to do so since 1953. Following Libya's deposit in October 2008 of the final instalment of the Lockerbie compensation payments, in November Congress finally gave its approval for Gene Cretz, the US ambassador-designate, to take up his post in Tripoli. In May 2010 the two countries signed a Trade and Investment Framework Agreement, establishing a framework for the development of trade links and the resolution of outstanding disputes. Under the terms of the agreement, the two countries were to establish a US-Libya Council on Trade and Investment, designed to formalize and regularize bilateral trade-related contacts.

Following the online publication of large amounts of secret US Department of State correspondence by the WikiLeaks organization, Cretz was recalled after complaints by the Libyan Government. WikiLeaks exposed numerous cables written by Cretz to his superiors in Washington, DC, providing details about Qaddafi's private life. Following the outbreak of civil war, the Administration of President Barack Obama roundly condemned the Libyan leader. In mid-July 2011 the USA accepted the NTC as Libya's 'legitimate governing authority' and in September Cretz returned to his post upon the reopening of the US embassy in Tripoli.

Preoccupied with multiple commitments elsewhere and its own resource limitations, the USA sought a limited, support role in the NATO intervention; nevertheless, its participation was crucial, as it is the only country to possess certain technologies essential to the success of such a mission. Following the overthrow of the Qaddafi regime, the US Administration actively supported the political process which led to the elections in July 2012. Working through NGOs and the UN, the USA joined the EU in providing extensive support, training and materials prior to the July elections, focusing on creating a functioning legal system, developing an independent media and promoting women's rights. To support the NTC in the short term, while hydrocarbon production was being increased, it also encouraged and facilitated the return of Libyan assets seized abroad. US companies retained significant interests in the country's hydrocarbons industry, but the primary concern of the US Government was to avoid delivery disruptions to Europe that could compromise US supply sources elsewhere. In conjunction with EU efforts to establish border security, curtail arms-trafficking and limit illegal migration, the USA revisited regional initiatives, such as the US African Command (AFRICOM) and the Trans-Sahara Counterterrorism Partnership (TSCTP), which were opposed by the Qaddafi regime.

Bilateral relations were effectively put on hold following the death of US Ambassador J. Christopher Stevens and three other US consular employees on 11 September 2012, after an attack on the US consulate in Benghazi. The fatalities caused a political controversy in the USA, with the opposition Republican Party hoping to gain political advantage from the incident. In Libya, security concerns hampered for many months a thorough investigation into the parties responsible for the attack. During a visit to Libya in January 2013 by the US Under Secretary of Defense for Intelligence, Michael G. Vickers, Prime Minister Zidan professed Libya's wish to strengthen military ties with the USA, notably in modernizing the Libyan security forces, and to expand economic, trade and technical education co-operation, as well as to attract US support for civil society training and building up democracy. Later that month the Director of the FBI, Robert Mueller, visited Libya as part of an ongoing inquiry into the US consulate attack. In early June 2013 US officials and NATO representatives discussed the possibility of establishing a military training mission in Libya. Later that month the new US ambassador to Libya, Deborah K. Jones, arrived in Tripoli.

WIDER RELATIONS WITH THE ARAB STATES

Even though President Mubarak resisted Qaddafi's plans for Arab unity, relations between Libya and Egypt improved. Egypt firmly opposed the UN sanctions imposed on Libya and made strenuous diplomatic efforts to mediate between Libya and the West over the Lockerbie affair. Qaddafi's regime was seen as a bulwark against the spread of militant Islamist movements in the region, and offered the prospect of much-needed economic opportunities for Egypt, especially the employment of Egyptian manpower. For Libya, which had become increasingly isolated internationally through the efforts of the USA and the United Kingdom, Egypt served as a valuable intermediary with the outside world. The close relationship between the two countries survived the embarrassment resulting from the disappearance of Libyan opposition leader Mansour al-Kikhia in Cairo in December 1993 and Libya's strong condemnation of the Israel-PLO accord signed in September. Early in 1994 the Libyan press agency, JANA, declared that Libya and Egypt were continuing to co-operate in many areas and acknowledged Egyptian efforts to persuade the West to ease sanctions against Libya. At the end of 1994, Egypt's close relations with Libya provoked strong criticism from the US media. Egypt was accused of abusing US aid by defending a state involved in terrorism against the USA.

In November 1994 Libya supported Egypt's application to join the UMA; however, fresh political differences emerged during 1995, largely owing to Libya's outspoken opposition to the normalization of relations between a growing number of Arab states and Israel. Qaddafi was critical of Egypt's role in promoting economic co-operation between Israel and its Arab neighbours. Libya's expulsion of Egyptian workers during the second half of 1995 further soured relations. In January 1996 the Libyan leader agreed to halt the expulsion of Egyptian workers after Mubarak agreed to step up his mediation efforts on behalf of Libya. In March Qaddafi condemned the 'Summit of Peace-makers' held at Sharm el-Sheikh, Egypt, but carefully avoided any criticism of the host country. In May Qaddafi held talks in Cairo with Mubarak, but caused some embarrassment to his host by issuing a new threat to expel Palestinians living in Libya. In June the Libyan leader flew to Cairo, in violation of the UN air embargo, to attend the Arab League summit convened by Mubarak in response to the election of a right-wing Government in Israel. Several meetings took place between Qaddafi and Mubarak in the second half of 1996, and in December the Egyptian President made an official visit to Tripoli, at the head of a large delegation. At the end of 1996 Qaddafi announced that after liquidating a number of investments in Europe, Libya was to reinvest in Egypt, where its holdings were believed to total some US $440m.

Egypt had long been suspicious of Libya's close relations with Sudan, which supported Libyan opposition to the peace process and offered shelter to Islamist militants from Egypt. In April 1995 a Libyan delegation attended the Popular Arab and Islamic Conference in Khartoum, along with representatives of Islamist opposition groups from Algeria, Morocco and Tunisia. The meeting avoided any criticism of the Libyan Government's harsh repression of its Islamist opposition and appealed for the lifting of UN sanctions against Libya. In the second half of 1995 relations between Libya and Sudan deteriorated owing to Libya's expulsion of large numbers of Sudanese workers. Nevertheless, Sudanese President al-Bashir attended the 26th anniversary of the Libyan revolution in September 1995 as an honoured guest, and in January 1996 Abu Bakr Jaber Yunes, Co-ordinator of the General People's Committee for Defence, attended Sudan's celebrations of the 40th anniversary of its independence.

Although Libya joined the UMA and Qaddafi assumed the presidency of the organization for a period of six months on 1 January 1991, the Libyan leader appeared at this time to show little interest in further integration with his country's western neighbours and preferred to look east to Egypt. The union itself made little progress and few of the agreements adopted were ratified. At the sixth summit meeting, held in Tunis in April 1994, Libya, represented by Maj. Khoeldi al-Hamidi, threatened to leave the organization unless the other member states ceased to comply with the UN sanctions imposed against Libya. Of the UMA leaders, only the Algerian President, Liamine Zéroual, attended the celebrations marking the 25th anniversary of the Libyan revolution held in Tripoli in September 1994. At the beginning of 1995 Libya announced that it would not, in future, take over the presidency of the UMA nor chair any of its institutions. However, despite its threats to leave the organization, Libya continued to attend UMA meetings. In June the UMA expressed its solidarity with Libya by appealing for an end to UN sanctions. By the end of 1996 Libya had made some efforts to improve relations with its Maghreb neighbours and revive the UMA, largely in order to ensure their support for its efforts to obtain the lifting of UN sanctions.

Relations with Tunisia, often strained and sometimes hostile, improved after the imposition of UN sanctions. Libya came to depend increasingly on transit facilities through Tunisia as the air embargo imposed by the UN tightened. Tunisia profited greatly from this transit traffic, and remittances from the 20,000 Tunisians working in Libya represented another valuable source of foreign exchange. Despite Tunisia's strict implementation of UN sanctions and the large profits that it made out of its role as Libya's main transit route to Europe, relations remained cordial for most of 1995. In July Tunisia requested that the UN General Assembly lift sanctions against Libya, and Tunisia was among those countries that supported Libya's unsuccessful request to attend the EU summit in Barcelona, in November. During the second half of the year Tunisians were not included in the mass expulsion of foreign workers from Libya. However, relations deteriorated at the beginning of 1996 after Tunisia agreed to establish low-level diplomatic relations with Israel, a move that was sharply condemned by Libya. Relations were further soured in February, when Tunisia placed on trial an opposition leader, Muhammad Mouada of the Mouvement des Démocrates Socialistes. One of the charges against him was that he had links with the Libyan intelligence services. Relations improved in late 1996 when Qaddafi made two visits to Tunis and signed a number of bilateral co-operation agreements.

Despite misunderstandings with Algeria over Qaddafi's attitude towards the Front Islamique du Salut (FIS), the fundamentalist Islamist opposition in Algeria, Algeria continued to support Libya in the UN and the Arab League. In April 1995 Qaddafi visited Algeria for talks with President Liamine Zéroual. The talks were concluded with a joint statement reviewing bilateral and economic relations and urging the UN to end sanctions against Libya. Relations between the two countries increasingly focused on co-operation over security and the containment of Islamist militancy. In April 1996 the two countries signed a security agreement to co-operate in the struggle against the threat posed by militant Islamist groups, and shortly afterwards there was speculation that the Libyan authorities had handed over some 500 Algerian members of the FIS who had taken refuge in Libya. Relations became strained in January 1997 when it was announced that the FIS had asked Libya to mediate in their conflict with the Algerian authorities, since Libya had ostensibly broken off all links with the FIS in 1994 when Qaddafi had pledged to cease all support for the Islamist opposition in Algeria.

Morocco supported Libya in the UN by abstaining during the vote in the Security Council in November 1993 to impose tougher sanctions on Libya. After Libya criticized Morocco for its moves towards normalizing its relations with Israel, relations improved somewhat in 1995 when King Hassan, on a visit to Washington, DC, in March, urged the US Administration to re-examine its position on sanctions against Libya in the light of their impact on the Libyan people. During 1996 both countries appealed for a revival of the UMA.

In November 1995, after Mauritania had established diplomatic relations with Israel, Libya expelled some 10,000 Mauritanian workers, withdrew its ambassador to the country, severed economic links and threatened Mauritania's status as a member of the UMA and the Arab League. In March 1997, however, diplomatic relations between the two countries were restored, despite accusations by the Mauritanian authorities earlier in the year that Libya had maintained links with a number of opposition leaders, ostensibly for the purpose of destabilizing the Mauritanian regime.

In October 2000 Qaddafi embarked on a tour of the Arab world, visiting Jordan, Syria and Saudi Arabia, during which he presented a strategic proposal for Arab unity with Africa. At meetings in Jordan and Syria he declared that in the new world the Arabs were lost because they did not belong to any geographical grouping and that they 'must wake up from their long sleep and be part of the African space'. Qaddafi was due to end his tour by attending the Arab League summit in Cairo called in response to renewed violence between Israel and the Palestinians; however, after prematurely revealing the Egyptian draft of the final declaration of the summit, denouncing it as a betrayal and challenging Arab leaders 'to take steps that would satisfy the angry Arab masses', Qaddafi decided not to attend the summit. The Libyan leader also boycotted the OIC summit in November, on the grounds that it did not adopt a sufficiently tough stance on Israel and the Middle East peace process. The Arab League, at its meeting in Amman, Jordan, in March 2001, agreed to set up a committee to examine Qaddafi's proposal that the Arab states should join the new AU.

In March 2002 the Secretary-General of the Arab League, Amr Moussa, visited Tripoli after Qaddafi threatened to withdraw from the organization in protest against what he condemned as its ineptitude with regard to the Israeli–Palestinian conflict. Qaddafi also rejected the peace plan put forward by Crown Prince Abdullah ibn Abd al-Aziz Al Sa'ud of Saudi Arabia in June, which proposed full normalization of relations with Israel in exchange for Israeli withdrawal from all Arab territories occupied since 1967. The Libyan leader insisted on the return of all Palestinian refugees, the removal of all weapons of mass destruction from all countries in the region, and the organization of free elections under the auspices of the UN in Israel and the Palestinian territories. Qaddafi did not attend the Arab League's Beirut (Lebanon) summit; instead, the Libyan delegation was led by Dr Ali Abd al-Salam al-Turayki, the Secretary for African Unity, and Gen. Muhammad Qaddaf al-Dam, Qaddafi's cousin and close confidant. Nevertheless, Libya pledged US $50m. in assistance to the Palestinians. In October Libya again formally requested to withdraw from the Arab League because it was dissatisfied with the Arab stance on a range of issues, notably the Arab–Israeli conflict and the threat of a US-led military campaign in Iraq. Secretary-General Moussa made an urgent visit to Tripoli to defuse the crisis, and, after hectic diplomacy, Libya once again suspended its threat of withdrawal.

In November 2002 a British newspaper quoting diplomatic sources claimed that Iraqi President Saddam Hussain had paid US $3,500m. to Libyan banks so that his family and close associates would be given refuge in Libya in the event of a US-led attack against the Iraqi regime. The report was denied by Seif al-Islam Qaddafi, who stated that Iraq and the Hussain family were friends of Libya and thus an agreement of this kind was not necessary. There were angry exchanges between Libyan and Saudi Arabian officials at the Arab League summit in Sharm el-Sheikh in March 2003. Crown Prince Abdullah, the de facto Saudi ruler, took exception to comments made about Saudi Arabia in Muammar al-Qaddafi's speech, accused him of lying and left the meeting. Libya subsequently recalled its ambassador from Saudi Arabia, and Qaddafi again announced his determination to withdraw from the Arab League, stating that this time the decision to leave the organization was 'serious and official'. Nevertheless, at the end of the month Ali Abd al-Salam al-Turayki attended a meeting of Arab ministers responsible for foreign affairs in Cairo, where he was applauded when he congratulated the Iraqi people on their 'heroic' resistance to the US-led invasion. At the end of March Kuwait expelled Libya's chargé d'affaires and gave orders for the Libyan mission to be reduced to three diplomats after anti-war demonstrators attacked Kuwait's embassy in Tripoli.

After numerous Arab leaders contacted Qaddafi, Libyan television in May 2003 reported that the General Secretariat of the GPC had decided to postpone Libya's withdrawal from the Arab League so that further discussions could take place. In the following month Libya announced that it was preparing to close its embassy in Iraq but that its diplomats would return when a sovereign Iraqi government was installed. Also in June Qaddafi stated that the internationally sponsored roadmap for peace between Israel and the Palestinians (see the chapters on Israel and the Palestinian Territories) would not end the conflict and insisted that the so-called two-state solution was condemned to failure. He again appealed for the establishment of an Israeli-Palestinian state, under UN auspices, in which all ethnic and religious groups would be guaranteed political representation.

Libya closed its embassy in Beirut in September 2003, after the Speaker of the Lebanese Parliament, Nabih Berri, and Hezbollah leader Sheikh Hasan Nasrallah demanded that Qaddafi provide information about Imam Mousa al-Sadr, spiritual leader of Lebanon's Shi'a population, who had disappeared in Libya in 1978. Relations between Libya and Lebanon continued to deteriorate as Lebanon's Shi'a political leaders demanded that Qaddafi reveal al-Sadr's whereabouts. A report published in the Arab press in February 2004 stated that a group calling itself the 'Al-Sadr Brigades' had urged Hezbollah to kidnap Libyans in Lebanon and around the world in order to secure the release of the Imam. This case was also believed to have had a negative effect on Libya's relations with Iran. Thirty-five years later the family of al-Sadr complained in the Lebanese media that the NTC was not doing enough to investigate al-Sadr's disappearance.

Qaddafi attended the opening session of the Arab League heads of state summit held in Tunis on 22–23 May 2004 but left during the opening speeches. In a press conference Qaddafi stated that he was 'disgusted' by the summit's agenda, felt slighted that the League had ignored his repeated appeals for Israel and the Palestinian territories to be merged into a single, non-religious state, and again threatened to withdraw Libya from the organization. In June the US press reported allegations that in the second half of 2003 Qaddafi had ordered the assassination of Crown Prince Abdullah of Saudi Arabia, after their clash at the Arab League summit in March. The order for the assassination reportedly came from Libyan intelligence chief Musa Kusa and his deputy, Abdullah al-Senousi, and it was stated that several million US dollars had been spent by Libya to recruit Saudi militants to carry out the attack. Libyan sources close to Qaddafi also accused Saudi Arabia of financing Libyan opposition groups who had tried to kill the Libyan leader on at least two occasions. Seif al-Islam described the allegation as 'nonsense'. In December 2004 Saudi Arabia recalled its ambassador to Libya and expelled the Libyan ambassador to Saudi Arabia because of the alleged plot. Libya continued to deny the accusations, blaming 'hostile elements' for trying to poison relations with Saudi Arabia. In July 2005 Saudi Arabia rejected Libyan claims that it had orchestrated a recent meeting in London of Libya's exiled opposition groups. In December Ghanem stated that normal relations had been re-established with Saudi Arabia, and that Libya's ambassador had returned to the Saudi capital, Riyadh.

Libya's fraught relations with its fellow Arab League members were highlighted when it hosted the 2010 Arab League summit in Sirte in March. A significant number of Arab leaders failed to attend, including President Mubarak of Egypt, King Muhammad VI of Morocco, King Abdullah of Saudi Arabia, Sultan Qaboos bin Said al-Said of Oman, President Jalal Talabani of Iraq and President Gen. Michel Suleiman of Lebanon. The latter's absence was especially notable, as Libya and Lebanon had been mired in a diplomatic wrangle prior to the meeting. In a pointed snub at Lebanon, Suleiman's invitation to the summit was delivered to the Lebanese embassy in the Syrian capital, Damascus, insinuating that Lebanon remained under Syrian influence. Lebanon responded by refusing to dispatch senior representation to the summit, sending only its ambassador to Egypt, who was the lowest-ranking official present. In December 2003 Libya assumed the presidency of the UMA after the long-delayed heads of state summit due to have been held in Algiers that month was again postponed. Qaddafi announced that a new summit, at which the Western Sahara issue would be the priority, would be held in Libya following the Algerian presidential election in April 2004. At the end of August Qaddafi appealed to Egypt to turn away from the Middle East and join Libya in seeking an African destiny. He described the Arab League and the UMA as 'useless organizations'. In December Libya announced that it was relinquishing the chairmanship of the UMA because the organization had failed to achieve its goals; however, shortly afterwards it retracted the decision and declared that a heads of state summit would be held in Tripoli in January 2005 to revitalize the UMA. The proposed summit never took place. In August 2004 UMA member Mauritania had again accused Libya of involvement in an attempted military coup to overthrow the Mauritanian President, Col Maawiya Ould Sid'Ahmed Taya—an accusation that Libya strongly denied. After speculation that he might boycott the meeting, Qaddafi was the first Arab leader to arrive in Algiers for the Arab League summit in March. In his speech, he stressed the importance of international blocs and said that nation states were no longer viable. He appealed for the establishment of an Arab-African Union to include those Arabs who did not live in Africa and advised Iran to 'look for a bloc to join'. He reiterated his call for the establishment of one democratic state for both Palestinians and Jews and emphasized the right of return of Palestinian refugees. At the end of the Arab summit, Shalgam attended a meeting of UMA ministers responsible for foreign affairs, but the long-awaited summit of the UMA heads of state, scheduled to be held in Tripoli at the end of May, was postponed indefinitely after King Muhammad VI of Morocco announced that he would not be attending because of Algeria's stance on Western Sahara.

In November 2005 Qaddafi visited Tunis for the World Summit on the Information Society, where he held a meeting with President Zine al-Abidine Ben Ali of Tunisia and President Abdelaziz Bouteflika of Algeria to examine ways of strengthening co-operation and solidarity between Maghreb countries. In March 2006 Khalid Meshaal, the head of the Hamas political bureau, visited Libya for talks with Qaddafi. Following a visit to Libya in April by the Palestinian Minister of Foreign Affairs, Dr Mahmud Khalid al-Zahhar, Palestinian sources reported that Libya had offered regular financial aid to the new Hamas-led administration. In June the UMA ministers responsible for foreign affairs met in Tripoli and declared their support for plans to reinvigorate the institution. This desire to relaunch the UMA was reiterated in April 2008, during celebrations held in Tangier, Morocco, in honour of the 50th anniversary of the summit at which the idea of a union of Arab Maghreb states was first proposed. In spite of residual tension between Moroccan and Algerian officials, the event ended peacefully with renewed appeals for regional collaboration. In 2010 UMA officials decided to establish a Maghreb Customs Co-operation Council headquartered in Algiers and with a training centre in Casablanca, the most notable and concrete steps toward regional reconciliation in many years. In December 2012 Libya and Mauritania concluded an agreement aimed at reinforcing bilateral commercial ties. In early January 2013 Libya joined its UMA partners in creating an investment bank with capital of US $100m. to finance infrastructure projects in the region, and a few days later Libya, Algeria and Tunisia met in the western Libyan border town of Ghadames, whereupon they agreed to enhance border security in an effort to reduce the flow of illegal drugs and arms and the regional impact of organized crime. A deadly attack on the In Amenas gas complex in eastern Algeria in mid-January 2013 was reported to have been committed by Islamist terrorists who had trained in *jihadist* camps in southern Libya.

During a visit to Niger in late May the French Minister of Foreign Affairs, Laurent Fabius, urged African nations to make a concerted effort to tackle the growing Islamist threat in the deserts of southern Libya.

Prominent Libyan dissident Mansour al-Kikhia, who disappeared in Cairo in 1993, was finally laid to rest in early December 2012 after his body was found in a Libyan intelligence services morgue. In an effort to improve trade and manpower links between Egypt and Libya, in mid-December Egyptian President Muhammad Mursi agreed to build a new road to the Libyan border some 250 km south of the existing coastal border crossing at Musaid. In March 2013 the Libyan embassy in Cairo temporarily suspended operations after Egyptian demonstrators burned a Libyan flag in front of the embassy to protest against the death in prison of an Egyptian citizen detained by Libyan authorities for allegedly spreading Christianity in Libya. On the following day Egyptian police arrested three former Qaddafi loyalists (Gen. Ahmad Qaddaf al-Dam, a cousin and special envoy of Qaddafi, former Libyan ambassador to Egypt Ali Maria, and Muhammad Ibrahim Mansour, the brother of a Libyan spokesperson, Moussa Ibrahim) who had been living openly in Egypt despite being wanted for trial in Libya. Later in March media outlets reported that Libya had transferred US $2,000m. to the Egyptian central bank, a transation that some observers viewed as payment for the arrest of the three former Qaddafi officials. Prime Minister Zidan later commented that Libyan-Egyptian relations were 'much bigger than the current and passing issue of Ahmad Qaddaf al-Dam'. With Egypt suffering from fuel shortages, it was reported four days later that Libya planned to supply $1,200m. worth of crude oil to Egypt at world prices but on interest-free credit for one year. In April it was reported that Libya and Egypt had signed a military co-operation agreement pertaining to training, and combating illegal immigration, illicit fishing operations and drugs-trafficking.

In mid-February 2013 Prime Minister Zidan visited Turkey to award diplomas to 817 Libyan police graduates who had successfully completed a 30-month training programme at a training centre in the Turkish capital, Istanbul. Two days later, in a deal conditioned on Turkish firms completing suspended projects in Libya, Zidan announced that Libya would pay Turkish contractors US $10,000m., about one-half of what they were owed, with the remainder to be paid in two instalments upon completion of projects suspended during the civil war. In May Turkey officials indicated that Turkey was ready to provide greater support in boosting border security, stepping up military training and rebuilding military institutions.

In April 2013 Prime Minister Zidan denied accusations made by the President of Chad, Gen. Idriss Deby Itno, that Libya was training members of the opposition to carry out a coup in Chad, dismissing such claims as 'a practice of the old regime', a reference to Qaddafi's earlier interference in the internal affairs of African states. In May Libya, Sudan and Egypt agreed to work together to develop their border triangle, establish free trade zones and link electricity and alternative energy networks.

Speaking on the sidelines of an Arab summit in the Qatari capital, Doha, in March 2013, the Libyan Minister of Foreign Affairs and International Co-operation, Muhammad Imhamid Abd al-Aziz, appealed for the reform of the Arab League, stating that reform of the organization's procedures and rules was necessary to respond to new challenges in the Arab world. Three days later the final communiqué of the Arab summit supported Libyan efforts to recover stolen assets and rejected any form of outside interference in Libya's internal affairs. In June it was reported that an Arab League delegation had met with Abd al-Aziz in Tripoli to discuss Libya's security situation and offer assistance in the staging of elections for the 60-member constitutional committee and the building of an effective criminal justice system.

CHANGING RELATIONS WITH AFRICA

After some 30 years of promoting the virtues of Arab unity, Libya announced in October 1998 that it was downgrading its representation at the Arab League in Cairo, and in December the GPC abolished the Secretariat for Arab Unity. The official Libyan news agency emphasized that Libya belonged to the African continent, and from October the country's state-controlled radio station, 'Voice of the Greater Arab Homeland', changed its name to 'Voice of Africa'. Instead of his customary pan-Arab rhetoric, Qaddafi began to champion African self-determination, announcing that he wished Libya to become a 'black' country and urging Libyans to marry black Africans. The change reflected Qaddafi's growing frustration with Arab countries for not giving Libya stronger support on the Lockerbie issue, in marked contrast to the states of sub-Saharan Africa. For some time Libya had promoted closer relations with countries south of the Sahara, using financial assistance as an incentive, and in early 1998 initiated the Community of Sahel-Saharan States (CEN-SAD), comprising Burkina Faso, Chad, Mali, Niger and Sudan, in order to promote economic, social and cultural exchanges.

Libya's relations with Chad improved dramatically, after years of tension over the disputed Aozou strip. A number of bilateral agreements were signed, and at the beginning of May 1998 the Libyan leader made a much-publicized visit to N'Djamena. In his capacity as president of CEN-SAD, Qaddafi also attempted to mediate in a number of African disputes, even though most of these initiatives had more symbolic value than substance. In addition to mediating in the border dispute between Ethiopia and Eritrea, and between warring factions in Somalia, Sudan and Sierra Leone, Qaddafi was active in trying to end the war in the Democratic Republic of the Congo (DRC) between forces loyal to President Laurent Kabila and the rebel Rassemblement Congolais Démocratique, which was supported by Rwanda and Uganda. In April 1999 it was announced that Qaddafi had brokered a peace agreement between Kabila and President Yoweri Museveni of Uganda, which was intended to bring about a cease-fire, the deployment of an African peace-keeping force and the withdrawal of foreign troops from the DRC. Neither Rwanda nor the DRC rebels, however, were party to the agreement. At the end of May Libyan troops arrived in Uganda, and in June Qaddafi made a visit to Zambia, where he and President Frederick Chiluba arranged a meeting between the DRC President and the Rwandan-backed rebels. After visiting Zambia, the Libyan leader made a state visit to South Africa for the first time since the lifting of the UN sanctions against Libya.

The Libyan leader attended the OAU summit held in Algiers in July, and in September, on the occasion of the 30th anniversary of his seizure of power, he hosted an extraordinary OAU summit in Sirte. Qaddafi presented his vision of a 'United States of Africa' and demanded that Africa be given veto power in the UN Security Council. The Sirte Declaration, which was adopted by the 43 attending heads of state and government, appealed for the strengthening of the OAU, the establishment of a pan-African parliament, African monetary union and an African court of justice. Qaddafi's proposal for a United States of Africa was officially adopted at the OAU summit at Lomé, Togo, in July 2000, almost all the costs of which were met by Libya. However, the proposal for a United States of Africa required ratification by two-thirds of OAU members before implementation, and key states such as South Africa and Nigeria expressed their reservations, preferring a more cautious approach.

Meanwhile, the Libyan leader's African ambitions suffered a reverse in September 2000, when Libyans attacked black African migrant workers, reportedly killing more than 50 and forcing thousands of others to leave the country. African-owned businesses were destroyed and Niger's embassy in Tripoli was looted. It remained unclear exactly what triggered the violence, which began in Zuwara, west of Tripoli, but it quickly spread to other parts of the country. Qaddafi's charm offensive towards sub-Saharan Africa had proved unpopular with the majority of Libyans, who had become increasingly hostile to the presence of an estimated 1m. black African migrant workers in the country. Deep-rooted racism, fear that the migrants posed a threat to Libyan culture and were responsible for a range of social problems, such as crime, drugs and prostitution, and a widespread misperception that migrants competed with Libyans for low-paid jobs were among the factors apparently contributing to this hostility. Qaddafi later expressed regret at the violence and hinted that the attacks were aimed at undermining his efforts to promote African union.

In an attempt to improve relations with African states undermined by the September 2000 riots, Libya offered new trade, co-operation and aid agreements with its sub-Saharan neighbours and increased its efforts to mediate in African conflicts. In November Libya was host to a pan-African summit on the civil war in the DRC. However, Qaddafi's influence with the rival parties was clearly limited and the negotiations failed to make significant progress. At the beginning of March 2001 some 40 African heads of state were invited by the Libyan leader to a second summit meeting at Sirte. In place of Qaddafi's ambitious project for a United States of Africa, more modest plans were approved to replace the OAU with a new AU, incorporating a range of pan-African institutions, including a parliament, a central bank, an African monetary fund and a court of justice, but without supranational executive powers. The meeting also addressed the precarious state of the OAU's finances: Libya had already settled the arrears owed to the OAU by 10 member states, but several other states had still failed to pay their contributions. Some analysts expressed scepticism about the idea of an African parliament, pointing out that many African states were involved in armed conflicts with their neighbours, and questioning the democratic credentials of some potential members. Moreover, the proposal for equal representation was opposed by states such as Nigeria and Egypt, who were apparently concerned that if such an arrangement were adopted their regional influence would be diminished. Questions were also raised about the funding of the proposed African central bank, given the extent of the combined external debt of the sub-Saharan region.

In May 2001, following mediation by Qaddafi, Uganda and Sudan agreed to restore diplomatic relations, which had been severed in 1995. (Twelve years later the director of Sudan's National Intelligence and Security Services would accuse Qaddafi of being responsible for many of the internal and external crises that Sudan faced over the years, charging Qaddafi with having incited partisanship and strife instead of peace and reconciliation.) At the end of May 2001 Libya sent some 100 troops to support President Ange-Félix Patassé of the Central African Republic (CAR) after an attempted *coup d'état*, and in November dispatched another 80 soldiers to the CAR when there was another coup attempt. France was reported to have approved Libya's role as the new 'gendarme' in the CAR. In early 2002 the Libyan troops were reinforced by military personnel from Sudan and Djibouti as part of a CEN-SAD peace-keeping force. In October Libyan troops and military aircraft were engaged in fighting in the CAR's capital, Bangui, against forces loyal to rebel leader Gen. François Bozizé. The threat was repulsed, but in March 2003 the Patassé regime was overthrown and Gen. Bozizé seized power. Libyan troops had been withdrawn in December 2002 under pressure from France, and the overthrow of the Patassé regime was seen as a reverse for Qaddafi's influence in the Sahel region.

In June 2001 Libya agreed to supply Ghana with 30,000 barrels per day of oil, one-half of the country's requirements, on special concessionary terms with effect from August. After attending the OAU summit in Lusaka, Zambia, in July, Qaddafi visited Zimbabwe where he expressed strong support for the Government's programme of land seizures. During the visit Libya agreed to provide Zimbabwe with US $360m. to purchase petroleum products, with repayment to be made by exports of agricultural and mineral products to Libya. In January 2002 Libyan mediation helped to achieve a peace accord between the Government of Chad and the rebel Movement for Democracy and Justice operating out of the Tibesti mountains, which straddle Libya's southern border with Chad. Qaddafi's wide-ranging dealings with African states remained unpopular with many Libyans, who continued to blame social problems such as rising crime and the abuse of drugs on the country's African migrant workers.

In July 2002 Qaddafi travelled to Durban, South Africa, for the 38th and final summit of the OAU, which saw the formal creation of the new AU. While South African President Thabo Mbeki's speech focused on the need for democracy, good government, the eradication of corruption, respect for human rights and peace and stability, the Libyan leader addressed his comments to the West, declaring that those who wanted to assist Africa were welcome, but that those who insisted on imposing their conditions upon African states were not. He heralded the birth of the AU as his 'African dream'. During the summit Mbeki and numerous other African heads of state tried to persuade Qaddafi to abandon his hostility towards the New Partnership for Africa's Development (NEPAD), a contract between Africa and the international community under which, in exchange for aid and investment, the African states agreed to strive towards democracy and good governance. The Libyan leader criticized the programme for imposing a Western model of development on Africa and ignoring the continent's own traditions and religions. His views were supported especially by the poorest African states, which received Libyan aid. After the summit Qaddafi and his entourage visited Mozambique, Zimbabwe and Malawi. In November the South African press reported that the oil agreement between Libya and Zimbabwe had collapsed over mounting debts estimated at US $90m., and Libya's ambassador to Zimbabwe confirmed that the agreement had collapsed for commercial reasons. In May 2003, during a visit to Harare, Libya's Secretary for African Unity stated that Libya was keen to revive the oil agreement and that negotiations were taking place about resuming supplies. In June President Mugabe held talks in Tripoli in an attempt to revive the agreement.

In August 2002 Human Rights Watch criticized the appointment of Qaddafi to the steering group of NEPAD, stating that while the new initiative was committed to promoting human rights and good governance, Libya had a long record of human rights abuses. In January 2003, after the USA had taken the unprecedented step of demanding a vote on Libya's nomination, 33 of the 55 members of the UN Commission on Human Rights (UNCHR) voted in Libya's favour, 17 (including seven European countries) abstained and there were only three (including Canada and the USA) votes against Libya. Libya's Secretary for Foreign Liaison described the vote as a 'striking victory', which had 'restored the rights of oppressed people'. Libya's election provoked growing demands for reform, and some UN officials themselves voiced concern about the UNCHR's credibility. At the end of February 2004 Libya hosted an extraordinary meeting of the AU in Sirte. In his opening speech, Qaddafi launched an attack on 'the evils of European colonialism', but stated that a new phase of co-operation between Africans and Europeans had now begun, in order to combat poverty and achieve progress. He stated that Africa had the potential to be as strong as the USA or the EU and that this would benefit the whole world, as it would result in a balance of power leading to stability and peace. In March the chief prosecutor of the UN's recently established war crimes court for Sierra Leone revived controversy about human rights and the Libyan regime. He stated that Qaddafi must bear some responsibility for the civil unrest in West Africa, although he did not say whether the Libyan leader might be indicted for his involvement in Sierra Leone's civil war.

In October 2004 and again in May 2005 Libya hosted high-level summits on the Darfur crisis. The fifth ordinary summit of the AU was held in Sirte in July 2005. In his opening remarks Qaddafi stated that in order to tackle the big challenges of economic development and to fight poverty, African states needed to unite and become one country. The summit ended with appeals for a substantial increase in aid from the West and the cancellation of Africa's entire debt, despite comments by the Libyan leader that they should not 'beg' for money from rich states. In February 2006 Qaddafi helped to broker a peace accord between Sudan and Chad after President Idriss Deby Itno of Chad accused the Sudanese Government of supporting a rebel group that sought to overthrow his regime, and amid appeals for the deployment of a UN peace-keeping force in the Darfur region. The Libyan leader stated that it was vital to avoid outside interference in the peace process and condemned all armed rebel groups involved in the conflict. However, in January the UN had reported that Libya continued to supply arms and ammunition as well as financial and political support to rebel groups in the Darfur region, despite the imposition of a

UN embargo in 2004. On a visit to Mali in April 2006 Qaddafi appealed to the Tuareg tribes of the Sahel region to unite and form a 'Greater Sahara', a statement that caused disquiet among neighbouring countries, most notably Algeria and Niger. During a meeting in June with Malian President Amadou Toumani Touré, who was visiting Libya for the eighth CEN-SAD summit, Qaddafi condemned attacks by Tuareg rebels against three military bases in northern Mali in May, stating that they worked against the interests of the entire Sahel region. Questions were raised, most notably in the Algerian press, about Libya's role in the renewed violence in the region, as Libya had provided military training for Tuareg rebels, who had been active in Mali and Niger in the early 1990s, and in February 2006 had opened a consulate in Kidal in northern Mali.

In mid-2007 Qaddafi conducted a tour of West Africa, which included visits to Côte d'Ivoire, Guinea, Mali and Sierra Leone. The final leg of his tour was a visit in early July to the Ghanaian capital, Accra, for the ninth ordinary session of the AU, which was to focus on plans to establish a pan-African government. Qaddafi continued to champion the proposal, declaring on the eve of the summit that Africa must 'unite or die'. However, other AU heads of state and prominent figures were reluctant to allow the summit to afford primacy to the issue of continental unity, concerned that energy divested therein would result in the neglect of more pressing issues, such as the humanitarian crises in the Darfur region, Somalia and Zimbabwe. In the end, the attendant heads of state reached a largely non-committal agreement on the unity issue, pledging to establish a committee to consider the move towards a pan-African government, without determining any time-frame for this; Qaddafi was reported to have stormed out of the session when a majority of those present rejected his appeal for the immediate creation of a 'United States of Africa'. In July 2007 Libya played host to an international conference on Darfur, chaired by the AU and the UN, the intention of which was to facilitate the holding of talks between the Sudanese Government and rebel factions; a warning was issued to rebels that the UN Security Council would employ 'appropriate measures' against any group deemed to be obstructing the peace process.

In February 2009, at the annual AU heads of state summit meeting in Addis Ababa, Qaddafi was elected Chairman of the organization. He used the occasion to hector African leaders on the failings of African democracy, insisting that, as Chairman, he would prioritize the creation of a 'United States of Africa'. Indeed, his plan overshadowed the meeting's entire agenda, and discussions even continued into an unscheduled third day. However, the majority of the heads of state were opposed to full political union and only minor changes to existing AU institutions were agreed. At the subsequent AU summit in January 2010, Qaddafi defied the grouping's stipulation that the chairmanship should rotate annually by seeking re-election as Chairman for a second consecutive year. Despite gaining the support of a number of smaller African states, whose membership fees Qaddafi had paid, 53 other African countries voted instead for Malawi to assume the chairmanship, thwarting the Libyan leader's ambitions. During a bout of sectarian violence in Nigeria in March, Qaddafi provoked further consternation when he appealed for the country to be divided along confessional lines.

The African response to the revolution that broke out in Libya in January 2011 reflected the diplomatic support that the Qaddafi regime had generated in previous years, when many African states benefited considerably from Libyan aid and investment. In April, and again in July, the AU presented a peace plan to both sides, and South African President Jacob Zuma flew to Tripoli in order to persuade Qaddafi to accept it. Qaddafi did so, declaring that it was the only plan that he would countenance. However, the plan was rejected by both the rebels and the international coalition, as it would have allowed Qaddafi to remain in power during a transitional period. Despite the ouster of Qaddafi in late August, the AU did not formally recognize the NTC as the official representative authority of the Libyan people until 20 September, weeks after most European states, the USA, and several prominent African states, including Ethiopia, Ivory Coast, Nigeria and Senegal, had granted recognition. Reflecting the fears of many AU members that instability would follow the overthrow of the Qaddafi regime, Francisco Caetano José Madeira, the AU's special representative in charge of counter-terrorism, warned in June 2013 that Libya was becoming a prominent transit hub for terrorists.

The future role that post-Qaddafi Libya will play in Africa remains unclear. However, the disruption of regional alliances and the weakening of governments supported by the Qaddafi regime have set the stage for a policy reorientation away from the Sahel-Sahara sub-region upon which Qaddafi lavished financial aid in an effort to secure influence. Early policy shifts also suggest that the new Libya will turn towards North Africa and the Middle East, in addition to Europe, to the detriment of sub-Saharan Africa. Prime Minister Zidan summarized the ongoing reorientation of Libyan policy toward Africa at the opening of the extraordinary summit of CEN-SAD in mid-February 2013 when he declared that 'Libya intends to be actively involved in African affairs, but not in the interfering way of the Qaddafi regime'.

Economy

Revised for this edition by PHILIP McCRUM

INTRODUCTION

Libya has a total land area of 1,775,500 sq km (685,524 sq miles), about 95% of which is desert, with a relatively small population. According to the results of the latest census carried out in 2006, there were 5.7m. people in Libya, of whom 5.3m. were Libyans. This compares with a total population of 4.4m. at the time of the previous census in 1995. Until the country's petroleum resources began to be exploited, not more than 25% of the population lived in the towns. According to UN estimates, the urban population has risen dramatically, to 78% of the total in 2011, compared with less than 50% in 1970.

Petroleum has transformed Libya. In 1951 it was the poorest country in the world; in 2009 it was the highest ranking African nation in the UN's Human Development Index. Before the discovery of oil in commercial quantities in the 1950s, agriculture was the basis of the economy. By 1968, however, the petroleum industry accounted for 51% of gross domestic product (GDP), and since then the oil industry has retained its central role in the economy. At the end of 2010, prior to the outbreak of conflict (see History), it accounted for 90% of fiscal revenue and 96% of export earnings. However, it provided employment for less than 10% of the labour force. Although sanctions adversely affected the oil industry throughout the 1980s and 1990s, their gradual easing since 1999 has revived the sector's—and the economy's—fortunes. Nominal GDP had risen to just US $14,100m., from $7,800m., in the 20 years between 1979 and 1999. However, in the following decade to 2010 nominal GDP was estimated by the IMF to have increased more than five-fold, to over $76,600m. Although the 2011 conflict resulted in a significant contraction in the economy, equivalent to around 30% in real terms, the rapid recovery in oil production in the first half of 2012 produced a swift revival in the wider economy. After falling to $34,700 in 2011, nominal GDP rose sharply again, to $81,900, in 2012. The recovery could have been more pronounced if the slow pace of the political transition, which helped to perpetuate nation-wide insecurity, had not deterred investment.

THE STATE AND THE PRIVATE SECTOR

After the 1969 revolution, state intervention in the economy increased, in accordance with Muammar al-Qaddafi's ideas of 'Islamic socialism'. However, apart from the nationalization of distribution and marketing of petroleum in Libya in 1970, the Government refrained from directly taking over petroleum company assets until the dispute with British Petroleum (now BP) in 1971. In September 1978 and the first two months of 1979 a large number of private companies were taken over by workers' committees. Similarly, in 1979, all direct importing business was transferred to 62 public corporations, and the issuing of licences was stopped. In March 1981 it was announced that all licences for shops selling clothes, electrical goods, shoes, household appliances and spare parts were to be cancelled, and that by the end of the year all retail shops would have to close. Retail activity became controlled by state-administered supermarkets. The private sector was to be completely abolished by the end of 1981, to be replaced by people's economic committees.

These plans were not implemented according to schedule, and by the late 1980s Qaddafi was once again extolling the virtues of private enterprise, owing to the pressures placed on the state by international sanctions. In March and April 1988 Qaddafi introduced a series of economic and political liberalization measures. The state supermarket network, established in the early 1980s, was poorly organized and many basic commodities were usually unavailable, giving rise to a thriving black market. Consequently, private shops were encouraged to reopen, and Qaddafi adopted additional measures to dismantle obstacles to trade and tourism with Libya's neighbours, closing customs and immigration posts along the borders with Egypt and Tunisia. Thousands of Tunisians entered Libya in 1988 to work on Libyan farms, while a 'free zone' developed along the border where Libyans could purchase items that were scarce in their own country.

In September 1988 Qaddafi proposed an increase in 'privatization' and announced that Libyans would be able to import and export in complete freedom. Plans to remove subsidies on wheat, flour, sugar, tea and salt, announced in December, were never implemented. Nevertheless, further measures were adopted: a law was adopted in September 1992 formally authorizing the privatization of Libyan industries and permitting 'individuals or groups to exercise the liberal professions and to invest freely in the private sectors'.

The national debate on economic reform had, in 1992, been widened by Qaddafi to include the proposal that 50% of the state's oil revenues should be distributed directly to citizens, and that the 'very, very big octopus' of state administration should be cut back to a minimum by privatizing most educational and health care facilities, shutting down unprofitable state economic enterprises and devolving many defence responsibilities to local administrative units. Other leading figures, including the Governor of the Central Bank, spoke out strongly in favour of a more orthodox transition to a mixed economy.

However, in another reversal of policy, in 1996 the Government established 'purification committees' that were given the task of reinstating the ideals of the revolution. They forced the closure of privately owned shops that sold imported goods and reimposed trading and currency regulations in order to put a halt to trading activity. Many shopkeepers were imprisoned.

Nevertheless, these purification committees were themselves subsequently purged, after being accused of corruption. 'Normality' returned after this brief upheaval in 1999, with the suspension of UN sanctions. In June 2003 Qaddafi appealed for the wholesale privatization of the country's vital oil industry and other areas of the economy, citing the 'failure' of the public sector. In the same month the former Secretary for the Economy and Trade, Dr Shokri Muhammad Ghanem, was appointed Secretary of the General People's Committee and stated that his first priority was the liberalization of the Libyan economy. In late 2003 he announced that 360 state-owned companies in a variety of sectors—including steel, agriculture, petrochemicals and cement—would be privatized from 2004, and that Libya also planned to open a stock exchange.

In November 2004 Ghanem announced an economic reform programme that proposed substantial state subsidy reductions, offset by tax and interest rate cuts, and a doubling of the national minimum wage. Nevertheless, an IMF assessment of the Libyan economy released in March 2005 remained critical of the country's centralized and bureaucratic structures and its ad hoc and non-transparent approach to reform.

In March 2006 Ghanem was replaced as Secretary of the General People's Committee by the Deputy Secretary for Production, Dr al-Baghdadi Ali al-Mahmoudi. Since Ghanem had been an advocate of liberalization, many commentators regarded the personnel change as a reversal of the drive to reduce state control over the economy. However, Ghanem was transferred to the chairmanship of Libya's National Oil Corpn (NOC), indicating that the development of the oil sector was the Government's primary objective. The reorganization also involved the creation of several new secretariats, a development that was expected to assist the economic reform process. However, by mid-2006 only 66 small enterprises were reported to have been privatized, and it was announced that the divestment programme would be broadened to include sectors such as insurance, health and transport.

Having introduced a new labour law requiring companies to employ one Libyan national for each foreign worker, the General People's Committee in early 2007 announced proposals to cut 400,000 state jobs (mainly in health, education and the petroleum industry) as part of a drive to reduce and streamline the oversized public sector. Workers so affected were to be offered retraining or loans to start their own businesses. At the same time, the National Economic Development Board (NEDB) was launched to improve co-ordination between government departments, help foreign investors to negotiate the state bureaucracy, and facilitate rapid decision-making. Earlier, in November 2006, the GPC issued a decree requiring that foreign joint ventures have a minimum Libyan participation of 35%.

Qaddafi's announcement that he was to abolish most of the government secretariats in March 2008 further highlighted the haphazard approach to economic policy. Criticizing the state apparatus for its inefficiency and corruption, he announced that he would distribute the proceeds of oil directly to the people for them to spend as they wished (see History). However, at the annual General People's Congress (GPC) in March 2009, the so-called 'Wealth Distribution' programme was rejected, after having been overwhelmingly voted against in the earlier meetings of the local Basic People's Congresses.

In the budget for 2010 the Government allocated some LD 3,300m. over a three-year period in order to boost industrial output and create jobs. The plan dovetailed with the earlier announcement, in February 2010, of the establishment of the country's first free trade zone on the country's north-western coast. Part of the plan promoted the development of small and medium-sized enterprises (SMEs) and in March the Government announced the establishment of an SME Fund in order to give impetus to its aim of boosting private enterprise and entrepreneurship. In July the Government gave further indication of its intentions to liberalize the economy and to create a more transparent operating environment for the private sector and foreign companies in particular. It announced the introduction of 10 new laws, including an investment law, a commercial code, a free zone law and legislation for the regulation of the stock exchange. However, the state continued to exert considerable control over the economy. Later in the year the Government announced that its programme to distribute the country's oil wealth directly to its citizens was still ongoing. It claimed that since the start of the programme in 2006 some 230,000 families had each received between LD 30,000 and LD 50,000.

Following the overthrow of Qaddafi in August 2011 (see History), the interim National Transitional Council (NTC) that assumed power was confronted by too many security and social challenges to be able to implement any far-reaching economic policies during its brief tenure; in any case, the NTC argued that it was the responsibility of a democratically elected government to determine the future direction of economic policy. In mid-2012 the NTC, nevertheless, indicated its hope that the incoming elected administration would put the necessary business environment in place to encourage economic development, thereby implying that it understood the need for private sector investment in the non-oil economy. Prior to that, however, the interim Minister of Economy, Ahmad al-Koshli, introduced legislation governing the role of foreign companies operating in Libya. Under the new law, which was designed to attract higher levels of foreign investment, foreign companies were permitted to take a higher stake of up to 80% in joint ventures, and to create joint ventures as limited liability companies, while the range of sectors in which companies could set up a business without a local partner was widened. The legislation also reduced the cost of opening a representative office.

The official transfer of power to a popularly mandated Government in November 2012 did little to galvanize economic policy-making. Persistent instability ensured that the Government's focus remained firmly on imposing law and order. However, the new Government did introduce one significant measure: it prohibited the application of interest in all financial transactions, either between individuals and financial institutions, or between legal entities, including foreign companies, in accordance with Islamic law. Otherwise, the few public pronouncements that the Government made on the economy were directed at the oil sector. The Minister of Oil, Abd al-Bari al-Arusi made it clear that he intended to review a number of oil contracts, introduce new oil-related legislation, and hold another licensing round.

SANCTIONS AND THE ECONOMY

Throughout the 1970s and early 1980s relations between Libya and the USA deteriorated severely. In March 1982 US President Ronald Reagan banned imports of Libyan petroleum to the USA, and halted all exports to Libya other than food and medical supplies. Libya's perceived interference in the affairs of other nations (notably Chad) and its alleged association with international terrorism had further significant economic repercussions in January 1986, when President Reagan froze Libyan assets in the USA and banned all trade between the USA and Libya. However, the effectiveness of this action was vitiated by the unwillingness of Japan and Western European countries to institute a complementary economic boycott of Libya, and by the fact that assets worth some US $1,000m.–$2,000m. would have been surrendered to Libya by the US oil companies operating there if they had ceased operations immediately. These companies were given until 30 June to sell their assets to Libyan concerns, but only tenuous agreements had been reached by the time the deadline arrived. However, rather than punishing Libya, the sanctions had their greatest impact on the departing US oil companies, the withdrawal of which was of greater detriment to Libya's ability to market its petroleum than to actual levels of production, which were lower than capacity, owing to weak demand.

In January 1991 US sanctions were renewed for a further 12-month period, and in April the US Government published a list of 48 companies world-wide that it believed to be acting as agents or 'fronts' for Libyan nationals and which were therefore to be subject to the US sanctions; a supplementary list published in August 1991 added a further 12 companies to the total. According to the US Department of the Treasury, the mid-1993 value of Libyan assets frozen in the USA since 1986 was US $903m.

In addition to Libya's increasingly isolated international position, during the 1980s its economy was severely restricted by the effect of the low prices for petroleum consequent on the global oil glut. Revenue from sales of petroleum declined from US $22,000m. in 1980 to $5,000m. in 1988. Decreasing revenues caused serious cash flow problems and necessitated a major revision of the 1981–85 Development Plan. In 1980–89 GDP declined from $35,500m. to $23,000m.

Libya's economic relations with the West were further complicated during this period by allegations of official Libyan involvement in international terrorism (see History). Under Resolution 748, adopted by the UN Security Council on 31 March 1992, Libya was made subject to certain mandatory sanctions, in view of its failure to comply with Resolution 731 (of 21 January), requiring Libyan co-operation in bringing those responsible for the terrorist actions to justice. Effective from 15 April, the sanctions included an arms embargo and the severance of air transport links with Libya, but did not, at that time, encompass a general trade embargo or any moves against Libya's exports of petroleum. Prior to their imposition, the Libyan authorities took the precaution of transferring substantial Libyan assets from Western European to Middle Eastern banks.

In response to Libya's continuing non-compliance with Resolution 731, the Security Council extended the existing provisions of Resolution 748 for successive 120-day periods. The extension agreed in August 1993 was accompanied by a warning from three Council members (France, the United Kingdom and the USA) that they would seek to extend the scope of the sanctions if the situation remained deadlocked at the end of September 1993. Libyan claims that the country had suffered direct and indirect revenue losses totalling US $2,200m. during the first year of the sanctions regime were generally believed to be greatly exaggerated, the main reported trade effect of the sanctions being an increase in imports of priority items (including inputs for development projects) as a safeguard against the possibility of wider sanctions.

Following the August 1993 extension of UN Security Council Resolution 748 and the subsequent circulation by the USA, France and the United Kingdom of draft proposals for stronger international action against Libya, the Libyan Government increased its efforts to minimize its exposure to harsher sanctions. Libya's liquid assets overseas (estimated to total US $17,000m.), if not already located in financial 'safe havens', were constantly monitored to avoid unnecessary exposure to seizure. According to the Bank for International Settlements, Libya withdrew $2,800m. of its overseas deposits in the third quarter of 1993, including an estimated $430m. from Organisation for Economic Co-operation and Development countries. The functions and ownership structures of Libya's fixed assets overseas (which had an estimated worth of up to $4,000m.) were analysed to assess their exposure to sanctions, and a number of deals were struck with foreign (predominantly Italian) equity partners whereby Libya relinquished control of high-profile companies.

Security Council Resolution 883, which was approved in November 1993 and entered into effect on 1 December, called on UN member states to freeze all Libyan-controlled funds and financial resources abroad and to require the use of separate bank accounts for specified trade transactions; to prohibit the supply to Libya of specified items for use in the downstream oil and gas sector; to shut down overseas offices of Libyan Arab Airlines (LAA) and to ban the supply of civil aviation equipment and services and the renewal of aircraft insurance; and to reduce staffing levels at Libyan diplomatic missions.

The freeze on Libyan funds prohibited withdrawals from, but not payments into, existing overseas bank accounts. The new 'external' bank accounts specified by the resolution were to be set up to handle payments to foreign contractors and suppliers to the Libyan market, using revenue derived from Libyan exports of hydrocarbons and agricultural products. All transactions through such accounts had to be supported by evidence of compliance with the sanctions regulations. The petroleum and gas equipment specified in a detailed annex to Resolution 883 included pumps, loading equipment and various essential items of oil-refining equipment.

However, the complicated administrative arrangements under Resolution 883 meant that Libyan export revenues did not begin to reach the new 'external' accounts in overseas banks until mid-January 1994, delaying payments to many foreign contractors for some weeks. The UN Security Council renewed the terms of Resolution 883 for a further 120 days on 8 April.

In mid-1994 the sanctions appeared to have had no effect on the functioning of Libya's established oil and gas production facilities or the progress of development projects already under way when the sanctions were imposed. Many hydrocarbon facilities were not dependent on embargoed items, while others were fully supplied with stockpiled equipment. Some future projects had to be shelved for the duration of the current sanctions because they required embargoed items, but all were low-priority schemes for which no firm contracts had been awarded. There was, nevertheless, a marked decrease in the overall tempo of economic activity in Libya, and it was estimated that the country's GDP declined by 7% in both 1993 and 1994.

The UN sanctions remained in force in August 1995 on the same terms that applied in December 1993, the USA having failed to win UN Security Council backing for a proposal (tabled at the March and July 1995 sanctions reviews) to tighten them by imposing a total embargo on Libyan oil exports. European opposition to the US proposal had been strongest in Italy (which obtained 28% of its crude petroleum supplies from Libya). The US Government announced in April 1995 that it would examine the scope for further tightening of the USA's own unilateral sanctions against Libya.

Nevertheless, small increases in petroleum output in 1995 and 1996 demonstrated that the UN sanctions regime posed no significant threat to the implementation of its normal production schedules. Nor were there any reports of a slowdown in the pace of work on the 'Great Man-made River' project (GMR—see Power and Water), which accounted for a large proportion of government spending on economic development.

In January 1996 US President Bill Clinton extended the duration of all existing US sanctions against Libya. Some weeks earlier the US Senate had added Libya to a bill (previously applicable only to Iran) designed to inhibit hydrocarbons investments in these countries by non-US companies. Despite protests by the European Union (EU) regarding the 'extraterritoriality' of the draft legislation, the Iran and Libya Sanctions Act (ILSA) completed its passage through the US Congress in July and was signed into law by President Clinton on 5 August. It specified six forms of sanction available to the US Government: denial of access to US Export-Import Bank facilities; denial of export licences in respect of goods ordered from the USA; imposition of a ceiling of US $10m. per year on company loans from US financial institutions; withholding of permission to conduct primary dealings in US government bonds; exclusion from bidding for US government contracts; and exclusion from the US import market. A non-US company was liable to the imposition upon it of two of these sanctions (selected by the President) if it invested $40m. (later revised to $20m.) or more in the hydrocarbons industries of Libya or Iran in any one year, or if it violated current UN embargoes on Libya. However, the US President could decide to waive sanctions if a company's home country had 'agreed to undertake substantial measures, including economic sanctions' to prevent Libya or Iran from supporting terrorism or acquiring weapons of mass destruction, or if it had encouraged Libya to comply with UN Security Council Resolution 731 on the bringing to justice of terrorist suspects. The multilateral UN sanctions on Libya were renewed in 1996, 1997 and 1998. None the less, preliminary estimates of Libya's economic performance in 1996 indicated a return to positive GDP growth (at a rate of 3.5% per year) for the first time since the imposition of UN sanctions in 1992.

A relaxation in May 1998 of the threat of US sanctions against countries whose companies invested in Iran was widely seen in Europe as also applying to dealings with Libya, although substantial opposition was evident in the US Congress to ending the US ban on investment in the Libyan oil industry. Following talks between the Italian and Libyan ministers responsible for foreign affairs in the Italian capital, Rome, in July, the Italian Government declared that normalization of relations between the two countries would assist Libya to return to 'co-operation with the international community', while also asserting that Libyan adherence to UN resolutions would help the process. It was subsequently stated in Tripoli that Qaddafi had decreed that Italian companies should be 'given priority in all sectors' in the awarding of new government contracts.

The suspension of UN sanctions against Libya in April 1999 led to an immediate intensification of contacts with non-US companies wishing to restore or strengthen their business links with Libya. Bilateral US trade sanctions, however, were not suspended (other than to permit the export of foodstuffs and medicines to Libya), while the USA used its position in the UN Security Council to prevent the permanent lifting of the UN sanctions when they next fell due for review in July. In September the US Government permitted several US petroleum companies to inspect their Libyan assets. In the same month US wheat exporters resumed trade relations with the Libyan buying organization, which subsequently announced its first purchase of US wheat for 15 years. In contrast to the very slow thaw in US-Libyan economic relations, Libya's main non-US trading partners had by the end of 1999 made major efforts to achieve a full resumption of normal relations and to identify new investment opportunities in Libya. The 1999 oil price recovery was maintained in 2000, providing the Libyan Government with a strong revenue base to underpin a significant increase in infrastructural investment in its planning targets for 2001–05. By 2005 the rate of growth had increased significantly, with a real GDP increase of 9.9% recorded in that year, according to IMF figures.

Meanwhile, the contrast between US and non-US policies towards Libya sharpened in 2001, when the renewal of US sanctions in August coincided with a further strengthening of most European countries' economic relations with Libya, assisted by the conclusion of the Lockerbie bombing trial in January 2001 (see History) and the continuing buoyancy of petroleum prices. The Libyan Government's priority remained the lifting of US sanctions (in order that US oil companies could resume activities in Libya), to which end in April 2003 the Libyan Secretary for Foreign Liaison and International Co-operation, Abd al-Rahman Muhammad Shalgam, stated that his country had 'accepted civil responsibility for the actions of its officials in the Lockerbie affair', adding that full payment of compensation was conditional on the lifting of UN and US sanctions. In August the Libyan Government transferred US $2,700m. to the Bank for International Settlements, which would then make compensation payments to the families of the 270 Lockerbie victims. A draft resolution was presented to the UN Security Council shortly afterwards, resulting in the formal removal in September of UN sanctions, which had been suspended since 1999. However, any immediate lifting of US sanctions was ruled out by the US Administration of President George W. Bush.

Following Qaddafi's renunciation in December 2003 of Libya's weapons of mass destruction programme and his agreement to open the country's facilities to international inspection, British Prime Minister Tony Blair visited Tripoli in March 2004, opening up the prospect of new commercial opportunities for British oil companies. The following month the Bush Administration announced an easing of sanctions, allowing US companies to resume financial and commercial activities in Libya—including in the oil and gas sector—and in June the two countries restored diplomatic relations. The USA removed further economic sanctions in September, and announced that it was lifting the freeze on Libyan assets in the USA. In May 2006 the USA re-established full diplomatic relations with Libya, removing the country from its list of states that sponsor terrorism—a development that was expected to have a significant impact on the economy. In a further significant move, plans were announced in April 2007 for civil nuclear co-operation between the two countries.

According to IMF figures, the opening of Libya's economy boosted considerably its overall economic performance, with real GDP growth averaging 6.2% between 2000 (just after the easing of sanctions) and 2007 (just before the effects of the global economic downturn took hold). However, after slowing in 2008 to estimated growth of 2.7%, the economy contracted by almost 1% in 2009, following the impact of the global economic downturn. Economic performance only managed to recover briefly in 2010, before the conflict of 2011 resulted in an acute contraction of around 28%. From this very low base, the economy rebounded sharply in 2012, following the end of the conflict, with the IMF estimating that growth exceeded 100%.

AGRICULTURE AND FISHING

Agriculture dominated the economy until the discovery of oil, providing around 50% of employment up until the early 1970s. By 1997 agriculture and fishing accounted for an estimated 7% of GDP and 17% of employment. However, Central Bank figures indicated that the contribution of the sector had declined to 2.6% of GDP by 2010, and, according to the IMF, agriculture accounted for just 7.1% of employment by 2005. Post-conflict figures remain unavailable.

About 95% of Libya's land area is desert. Of the remainder, a high percentage is used for grazing; only 1.4% is arable, and 0.1% is irrigated. Since the 1980s the Government has continued to invest heavily in the massive GMR integrated water supply project to serve both urban and agricultural users (see Power and Water).

Despite its stated policies, the Qaddafi Government's financial commitment to the development of agriculture was erratic. In the mid-1970s agricultural development spending rose to as high as 30% of total budgetary expenditure, but by the mid-1980s the budgetary allocation had been reduced by more than one-half and the disbursement of allocated funds often fell short, sometimes by as much as one-third. As a result of the growing realization that the agricultural sector would never supply Libya with its food needs, let alone constitute a viable export base, government investment in the sector has gradually diminished.

Indeed, agricultural production was disappointing. Despite efforts to counter the effects of adverse climatic and soil conditions through irrigation schemes and a growth in the use of fertilizers, output has continued to fluctuate. The sector has also suffered from a lack of trained technicians and administrators and poor education among the farming communities. However, primarily it has been held back by inconsistently applied policies. Consequently, although gains in output have been made over the years, they have been limited, set against agricultural development in neighbouring countries. According to FAO, output of cereals increased from 82,458 metric tons in 1970 to 220,424 tons in 2011, while vegetable production rose from 196,534 tons to 979,020 over the same period. Similarly, annual production of fruits rose from 82,132 tons to 402,548 tons. Cereal production consists almost entirely of barley and wheat, while olives, dates and citrus constitute the bulk of fruit production. Dates are produced in oases in the south and on the coastal belt, while fruits and vegetables are grown mainly in the west of the country. Other important food crops include tomatoes, almonds, castor beans, groundnuts and potatoes. Esparto grass, which grows wild in the Jebel, is used for the manufacture of high-quality paper and banknotes, and was formerly Libya's most important article of export.

The limited nature of domestic production has seen Libya's import needs rise strongly. Libya imported 377,408 metric tons of cereals in 1970; by 2010, according to the FAO, this amount had risen to around 2.9m. tons. Likewise, the country's requirement for rice rose from 18,525 tons to 66,700 tons over the same period. In order to improve food security, in early 2010 the Libyan Government leased 100,000 ha of land in neighbouring Mali on which to grow crops for the domestic market. In 2009 a draft agreement was signed with the Ukrainian Government provisionally agreeing to a similar scheme with land in Ukraine.

Animal husbandry is set to remain the basis of farming in Libya until irrigation and reclamation measures really start to take effect. During the mid-1970s the breeding of cattle for dairy produce was expanded and livestock was imported on an increasing scale from a number of sources. There has also been a substantial expansion in camel and poultry numbers. In 2011 there were an estimated 197,000 cattle, 2.6m. goats, 7.1m. sheep and 57,000 camels in Libya. Meat production rose from 47,975 metric tons in 1970 to 172,156 tons in 2011.

The offshore waters abound in fish, especially tunny (tuna) and sardinellas, although fisheries of the former in the Mediterranean had collapsed by the early 2000s. Most of the fishing is done by Italians, Greeks or Maltese. Of special importance are the sponge beds along the wide continental shelf. These are exploited by foreign fishermen and divers, mainly Greeks from the Dodecanese. The 2001–05 Development Plan encouraged foreign investment in the fisheries sector. According to FAO estimates, total aquaculture production in 2011 was 240,000 metric tons.

MINING AND ENERGY

Non-hydrocarbon mineral resources in Libya include iron ore at Wadi al-Shati in the south of the country. Proposals to mine these reserves have appeared in official development plans since the mid-1970s, but remain unimplemented, owing to the major cost implications of the project, which included a requirement for a 900-km rail link to transport ore to the coastal region, where steel production has been developed using imported iron ore (see Industry and Manufacturing).

In early 2007 the National Bureau for Research and Development signed an exploration agreement with AREVA of France to mine uranium for civil nuclear purposes. In March 2008 Libya announced plans to build its first aluminium smelter; upon completion, originally anticipated in 2011, the smelter was to have a production capacity of 725,000 metric tons per year. However, the conflict in 2011 resulted in delays to the project.

That petroleum was present in both Tripolitania and Cyrenaica had long been suspected and, for several years after Libya became independent, a large number of the bigger oil companies carried out geological surveys of the country. In 1955 a petroleum law came into force setting up a petroleum commission, which was empowered to grant concessions on a 50:50 profit-sharing basis, with parts of each concession being handed back to the Government after a given period. Under this law, concessions were granted to many US companies and to British, French and other foreign groups.

Significant petroleum strikes were first made in 1957, and 10 years later Libya was already the fourth largest exporter in the world. The initial expansion of the industry was particularly rapid, owing to political stability, proximity to the Western European markets, and to the petroleum's lack of sulphur, which made it especially suitable for refining. The closure of the Suez Canal in 1967 was also an important factor in the growth of the industry. Production rose from 20,000 barrels per day (b/d) in 1962 to a peak of 3.3m. b/d in 1970, or 159.7m. metric tons in annual terms, equivalent to 13.6% of total Organization of the Petroleum Exporting Countries (OPEC) output and to 6.8% of world oil production. Output declined steadily to 71.3m. tons in 1975 (partly because of the reopening of the Suez Canal in 1974, as well as OPEC-imposed quotas), rising again to 100.7m. tons in 1979. Output fell in the 1980s, declining to 47.9m. tons in 1987, its lowest level since 1964. Production accelerated in 1990, as Libya took advantage of the rise in world petroleum prices caused by the 1990–91 Gulf crisis. Over the decade, production averaged 1.9m. b/d. The gradual dismantling of sanctions from 1999 onwards has not resulted in an increase in output—indeed, average output in 2000–09 declined to 1,590m. b/d; however, it opened up Libya's export market, and oil export revenues more than doubled from US $6,600m. in 1998 to $13,900m. in 2000. The subsequent rapid rise in oil prices led to a surge in oil export revenues; in 2008 export earnings reached $60,711m. However, owing to a slump in global demand and declining oil prices in 2009, oil export earnings fell markedly in that year, to $36,168m. A rally in oil prices in 2010 contributed to a rise in export revenues to around $46,523m., but earnings collapsed in 2011, after the conflict halted production and international sanctions reimposed on Libya blocked exports. According to OPEC, Libya's reserves currently stand at 46,420m. barrels.

In 1968 Libya set up the NOC in order to embed strong state participation in the oil sector. The NOC conducted extensive negotiations with the various petroleum producers in the early 1970s, with the result that, in 1973, the Libyan Government acquired a 51% share in the Libyan operations of the US companies Conoco/Marathon/Amerada Hess, Exxon, Mobil and Occidental, and the Italian company Agip, while it completely nationalized the holdings of American Overseas Petroleum (Amoseas), BP/Bunker Hunt, Shell, Texaco, California Asiatic and Atlantic Richfield. Most outstanding claims by the companies were settled in 1977, following arbitration.

In a restructuring of the management of state petroleum concerns in 1979, the NOC's operational responsibilities had been devolved to specialist subsidiary companies, leaving the NOC as a holding company responsible for strategic planning and supervision of the state oil sector. In March 1989 the Secretariat for Energy was revived, after a three-year period in which control of the oil industry had been ceded to the national companies. In mid-2006 the new Chairman of the NOC, Ghanem, initiated a major restructuring of the corporation, which was expected to include the sale of several of the NOC's affiliated oil services companies. Later that year a dispute purportedly over the terms of the contracts for the third licensing round led to the reclosure of the Secretariat for Energy, leaving the NOC responsible for energy policy. However, the Government introduced a further structural change in early 2007 with the establishment of a new body—the Council for Oil and Gas Affairs, comprising senior politicians—with overall authority for the sector.

Libya's moves to nationalize its oil resources were shortly followed by the enforced withdrawal of US petroleum companies from Libya in 1986. A three-year 'standstill period' officially expired at the end of June 1989, but continued to be observed by Libya as a means of exerting pressure for the repeal of US sanctions. Amid reports of renewed negotiations between Libya and the US companies, the Libyan Secretary for Energy confirmed, in March 1991, that the Government had no plans to sell the US companies' assets in Libya, adding that the companies were free to resume operations at any time.

International sanctions and the departure of the foreign oil majors resulted in a significant curtailment of exploration activity as well as development work on discovered fields. Moreover, the deficiencies in expertise and technology resulting from the withdrawal of US operators in 1986 (and compounded by the subsequent imposition of sanctions by the USA on Libya) were only partially compensated for by European, Canadian and Asian companies. Over the decade as a whole, only some 20% of current output was replaced by new proven reserves, while, as a result of poor state management, several established fields fell substantially below their theoretical production capacity.

Against this background, the Libyan authorities re-emphasized the need for an active exploration campaign, to which LD 200m. (US $700m.) was allocated in the NOC's 1991/92 budget. In particular, the Government was keen to evaluate the oil potential of parts of the country outside the Sirte basin in north-central Libya, where the commercial fields were grouped. There were two main areas of interest—Western Libya (formerly Tripolitania) and off shore. The Bouri offshore oilfield, situated some 125 km north-west of Tripoli, was brought into production in August 1988. New exploration concessions awarded to foreign oil companies in late 1990 and early 1991 included substantial offshore areas north-west of Tripoli. The NOC also signed deals to facilitate the exploitation of the Murzuk basin, in south-western Libya and prioritized water injection projects to increase output from certain established fields, in particular the giant Sarir field in the Sirte basin. It was officially claimed in 1994 that Libya was investing 23% of its oil revenues in petroleum exploration, production and development operations.

In February 1998 British operator Lasmo announced that a strike the previous year in the Murzuk basin, designated the Elephant field in block NC-174, was possibly the largest oil discovery in Libya since the mid-1980s, containing estimated reserves of over 500m. barrels. Following bureaucratic delays, production finally started from the field at a rate of 50,000 b/d in February 2004, operated by Italy's Eni energy group, which had acquired Lasmo in January 2001.

Following the lifting of sanctions, in 2000 the NOC sought bids for exploration and production-sharing rights in a new licensing round. Some 14 exploration blocks, divided into three packages, were included in the initial invitation for bids (which closed in January 2001), while a further 137 blocks (covering 835,000 sq km of hitherto unexplored territory) were available for subsequent licensing through a less formal bidding process with no closing date. The strong interest in the Libyan oil market was quickly dampened by the NOC's decision to delay the award of new exploration licences under the round until US companies were permitted to resume activities in Libya. The NOC not only was keen to bring the Oasis consortium (comprising Amerada Hess, Conoco, Occidental and Marathon) back into the market, but also wanted to put pressure on the US Administration to remove their unilateral sanctions, which were still in place. The NOC announced that their existing concessions, which were due to expire in 2005, would be reallocated to other companies if they did not resume operations by the end of 2002. In an attempt to head off this threat, in early 2002 the US Department of State authorized the Oasis companies to renegotiate their production agreements with the NOC, in order to expedite their return to Libya as soon as sanctions were lifted. In May and June 2003 European companies' frustrations over the slow progress in awarding Libyan oil concessions were finally eased by the signature of exploration and production sharing agreements (PSAs) between the NOC and Spain's Repsol, OMV of Austria and Germany's RWE-Dea, covering six blocks. A similar agreement, covering five onshore blocks in the Sirte and Murzuq basins, was signed by the NOC and a consortium comprising Australia's Woodside Energy, Repsol and Greece's Hellenic Petroleum in December.

With the Government planning to attract fresh investment in exploration in order to increase oil production to 2.1m. b/d by 2010, a new exploration and production licensing round—known as EPSA IV—was launched in September 2004. Bids for 15 exploration areas divided into 55 blocks were opened at the end of January 2005, with successful companies including Amerada Hess, ChevronTexaco of the USA, the Indian Oil Corpn, the United Arab Emirates (UAE)'s Liwa Energy, Algeria's SONATRACH, Verenex of Canada, Petrobras of Brazil, and Australia's Woodside. Nine concessions went to consortia involving Occidental, paving the way for it to resume operations in the country for the first time in 19 years. In a separate development, in December 2005 ConocoPhillips, Marathon Oil and Amerada Hess finalized an agreement with the Libyan Government that permitted them to resume their exploration and production activities in the country.

A second EPSA IV licensing round, postponed briefly as the NOC reviewed the terms of its contract structure, was launched in May 2005 for licences covering 17 areas divided into 44 blocks. Among companies securing rights to explore and develop Libya's oilfields in late 2005 were five Japanese firms—Nippon Oil, Mitsubishi Corpn, Japan Petroleum Exploration, Teikoku Oil and Inpex Oil—as well as the European firms BG (United Kingdom), Eni (Italy), Statoil (Norway) and Total (France).

In August 2006 the NOC launched the third licensing round on an open bid basis for 14 areas divided into 41 blocks in the main oil-producing basins, including Sirte, Ghadames and Kufra onshore and some offshore areas. The corporation selected 47 participants out of 70 applications from overseas oil companies, and agreements were signed in early 2007. Companies awarded concessions included Germany's Wintershall consortium in the Kufra basin; Russia's Tatneft and Gazprom, Japan's Impex consortium and the Chinese Petroleum Corpn in the Murzuq basin; and ExxonMobil and a consortium of PetroCanada and Repsol in the Sirte basin.

Rather than pushing for a fourth licensing round, in 2007 the NOC set about renegotiating bilateral exploration and production deals that it had agreed prior to the open licensing rounds, in order to secure better terms on the deals. These negotiations were conducted throughout 2008 and were deemed so successful that in January 2009 the NOC announced that it would undertake a review of its policies towards PSAs. A report released by the NOC indicated that it had earned an additional US $5,400m. in 2008 through its renegotiated deals with various oil companies, including Eni, PetroCanada, Occidental, Repsol and OMV. The NOC managed to raise its production share to up to 90%, giving it additional revenue of $2,400m. It also imposed up-front payments on the new contracts, collectively worth some $3,000m.

However, these tactics significantly reduced the profit margins of international oil companies (IOCs) and, in conjunction with continued uncertainty over Libya's energy policies, prompted some IOCs to re-evaluate their presence in Libya. The case of Verenex Energy, a Canadian operator, caused considerable consternation among the international oil community: in mid-2009 the Libyan Government blocked the sale of Verenex's Libyan assets to a Chinese company, instead forcing it to sell those assets to the NOC at a reduced price. The affair prompted the resignation of Ghanem as NOC Chairman, in apparent protest against the Government's handling of the case; however, he was reinstated in November. In addition to IOCs' growing concerns regarding political interference in the oil sector, many companies had little success in their exploration activities and in December Woodside of Australia announced that it was relinquishing its offshore concessions.

In the following month Chevron (as ChevronTexaco had been renamed) announced its withdrawal from Libya following the expiry of its five-year contract.

Following his reinstatement, Ghanem was clearly concerned at the IOCs' growing disillusionment and, in March 2010, he announced that the Government had prepared a new draft hydrocarbons law to replace existing legislation that dated back to 1955. It was hoped that the new legislation would engender greater clarity and certainty within the operating environment.

Upstream oil infrastructure—pipelines, storage terminals and refineries—remains antiquated, but sufficient for present production levels. Libya's five domestic oil refineries, with a combined processing capacity of about 380,000 b/d, are the 220,000-b/d Ras Lanouf export refinery on the Gulf of Sirte, which began production in 1985; the Azzawiya refinery in the north-west of the country, which opened in 1974 and has a capacity of 120,000 b/d; the Tobruk refinery, with a capacity of 20,000 b/d; the Brega refinery, the country's oldest, with a capacity of about 10,000 b/d; and the Sarir facility, also with 10,000 b/d of capacity. Additional infrastructure will be needed to meet future demand, and the NOC estimates that the sector needs investment of some US $30,000m. to take production up to the targeted capacity of 3m. b/d. In September 2009 the Government announced a $10,000m. oilfield development plan, which was to channel investment into 24 fields, with the aim of boosting output by a total of 775,000 b/d. However, the limited nature of recent discoveries by IOCs has forced the NOC to review the time frame of its ambitious expansion plans; in December Ghanem announced that the NOC did not expect oil output capacity to reach 3m. b/d until 2017.

Since Libya was unable to develop its infrastructure during the sanctions period, it set about awarding infrastructure-related contracts as soon as it could after the easing of sanctions. The Government itself also allocated a total of US $1,500m. for investment in the upgrading of pipelines and other oil industry infrastructure in 2001–05. In August 2002 the China National Petroleum Co won a £230m. contract to build twin oil and gas pipelines linking the Wafa field to Melita, near Tripoli. Tunisia and Libya signed an initial agreement in June 2003 to build new pipeline links between the two neighbours to carry crude and refined petroleum products. However, efforts to upgrade the Azzawiya refinery have met with numerous setbacks and after the collapse of successive deals, no progress has been made. According to the Government, the ongoing delay could potentially cost $2,000m. more than was originally budgeted. More encouragingly, however, in January 2008 the Government signed a deal worth $2,000m. with Al-Ghurair Investment of the UAE, to modernize Ras Lanouf.

Libya's proven reserves of natural gas at the end of 2012 were estimated at 1,500,000m. cu m, according to the *BP Statistical Review of World Energy 2013*, although the country's potential reserves may be considerably larger. Annual gas production had reached some 15,300m. cu m by 2007, increasing to 15,900m. cu m in 2008 and 2009, before declining slightly to 15,800m. cu m in 2010, and then falling to virtually nothing in 2011, after the conflict halted production activity.

Inaugurated in 1971, a liquefaction plant at Mersa Brega was the world's first scheme to convert flared gas into liquefied natural gas (LNG). Owing to technical issues, as well as sanctions, Libya was unable to exploit fully the sector's potential during the 1980s and 1990s, although it managed to undertake limited development during that period. However, following the easing of sanctions, Libya has sought to expand the industry rapidly. In particular, in 2002 the NOC activated a pre-existing sub-sea gas export scheme, by which Agip of Italy would transport 8,000m. cu m of gas per year from Libya to Italy. Libya has also started to develop its retail gas distribution in order to improve the domestic distribution of gas. In May 2009 Egypt's Taqa Arabia was awarded a €118m. (US $157m.) contract to build the infrastructure for a gas distribution network supplying 370,000 households in Tripoli, Benghazi and Misurata with natural gas.

Alongside these and numerous other upstream contracts, Libya has also put in place exploration and production agreements. Significant new gas discoveries by Hellenic Petroleum in the Sirte basin and by Repsol and Woodside in the Murzuq basin were reported in early 2007, and in May BP, returning to Libya after an absence of more than 30 years, signed a major US $900m. joint venture agreement with the Libya Investment Corpn to explore in the Ghadames basin and offshore Sirte. In July Libya launched a gas exploration licensing round for 41 blocks (19 on shore in Sirte, Ghadames, Murzuq and Cyrenaica, and 22 off shore). The results, announced in December, were disappointing. Deterred by the high exploration commitment against the low production share on offer, as well as the lack of gas infrastructure, only 12 of the 35 companies pre-selected submitted a final bid. Only six companies were awarded concessions: Algeria's state-owned oil company, Sonatrach, won four blocks, while Gazprom won three blocks. Other winners included RWE of Germany and Occidental Petroleum of the USA, the Anglo-Dutch Royal Dutch Shell and a Polish firm, Polskie Górnictwo Naftowe i Gazownictwo SA. They made significant concessions for their exploration rights; the average share won by the IOCs was around 13%. No bids were received for any of the five offshore concessions.

The outbreak of fighting and the onset of civil war in February 2011 drastically curtailed Libya's oil production. Output declined from around 1.6m. b/d in January to less than 200,000 b/d by April, and in May production had all but ceased. This was due in part to the rapid departure of skilled expatriate oil technicians, leaving only a skeleton local staff, but also because fighting in and around oil facilities disrupted production and distribution activity. During this period the Arabian Gulf Oil Co (AGOCO—a subsidiary of the NOC) announced its 'defection' from the NOC and the Government, giving the rebels in the east of the country control of the whole of the Sirte basin, which provides the bulk of Libya's oil. However, raids by pro-Government forces on remote facilities and pipelines meant that the rebels were unable to take advantage of their acquisition, while international sanctions imposed on Libya hampered their attempts to sell what oil they had in storage. By June rebels in the west of the country had cut off supplies to Tripoli from the Ghadames basin, leaving pro-Qaddafi forces increasingly short of supplies. In addition, heavy and protracted fighting around Zawia and Ras Lanouf had put a virtual stop to all downstream refining activity in the country. In early June the Qaddafi regime received another blow when Ghanem appeared suddenly in Athens, Greece, and announced his defection, a move that was seen as giving a considerable boost to the rebels' efforts to utilize their oil resources. In August forces loyal to the opposition NTC assumed de facto control of the country, having defeated Qaddafi's forces in Tripoli. Despite ongoing conflict in certain areas of the country, in late September limited production recommenced at Abu Attifel (operated by Mellitah Oil & Gas, a joint venture between the NOC and Eni), in the east of the country.

Initial estimates of the time frame over which Libya would be able to restore oil production to pre-war levels varied widely, but concern over the potential damage inflicted during the conflict led to the initial belief that it would take up to three years to revive the industry. However, these fears proved unfounded. Damage to oil facilities and related infrastructure was surprisingly light, and by the end of 2011 daily output had exceeded 1m. barrels. Averaged over the month of December, output rose to more than 500,000 b/d, from 227,000 b/d the previous month. By the end of April 2012 Libya was regularly producing just over 1.5m. b/d, although this level subsequently slowed slightly in May, when protests against the interim Government (see History) blockaded the headquarters of the AGOCO in Benghazi and the company was forced temporarily to reduce production as a result.

Although normal services resumed, Libya's upstream and downstream activities continued to be disrupted over the course of 2012 and 2013, both by insecurity and bouts of industrial action. Operations at both the Zawia and Ras Lanouf refineries were temporarily halted either by militant activity or industrial action by employees. Such activity continued well after the installation of the new Government; in May 2013 the Zueitina refinery, one of Libya's largest, was closed down for two days by local residents protesting at their lack of access to employment. The intermittent stoppages to production inevitably resulted in fluctuating output and obstructed further development of the industry. The Minister of Oil, Abd al-Bari al-Arusi, estimated that Libya had lost up to US $5,000m. in revenue, owing to the plant closures in the first five months of 2013 alone.

Nevertheless, the NOC managed to maintain a respectable level of output over the period; production in 2012 amounted to 485.1m. barrels of crude oil, equivalent to 1.33m. b/d. By April 2013 average daily output had risen to 1.66m. b/d. However, further strikes and forced closures of facilities in the following months resulted in oil production falling to below 1m. b/d by July, leading the Government to appeal to workers and militants that they were bankrupting the country.

The Government was keen to develop the industry further and in March 2013 a committee was established to review existing oil-related legislation, which was likely to include the division of upstream and downstream activity, an investigation into all pre-existing oil contracts along with a revision of the controversial EPSA IV agreement, and the launching of a new oil-licensing round by the end of 2013. By the end of July the committee was still in deliberation and the timetable for the licensing round was starting to appear over-ambitious.

INDUSTRY AND MANUFACTURING

Given its oil, the petrochemicals industry is one of Libya's largest. The NOC opened its first petrochemicals plants in September 1977 at Mersa Brega, with an initial production capacity of 1,000 metric tons per day of ammonia and 1,000 tons per day of ethanol. Capacity and product range were gradually expanded, and today Libya produces significant quantities of ammonia, urea and methanol, as well as ethylene and various by-products. The bulk of the activity is located around Mersa Brega and Ras Lanouf. In early 2007 the NOC announced that it would focus on downstream petrochemicals investment, offering investors a partnership in return for operating and upgrading facilities. In April the corporation and Dow Chemical of the USA disclosed plans for a joint venture to operate and expand the Ras Lanouf complex, including the construction of an ethane cracker and additional polyethylene and polypropylene plants. A second joint venture was subsequently agreed with Yara International to upgrade the ammonia and urea plants at Mersa Brega.

Although the development of a non-oil industrial manufacturing base was a key government priority in the 1970s, implementation was poor and little progress was made. This has also been the case since the lifting of sanctions, with the Government far more focused on the development of infrastructure than industry and manufacturing. Data released by the IMF in its October 2008 Article IV report showed that investment into manufacturing averaged around 4% of total investment in the five-year period between 2002 and 2006.

Other than petrochemicals, heavy industries that supported construction and that could benefit from Libya's abundance of gas experienced strong growth. During the 1980s a steelworks was constructed at Misurata, but it never reached full production capacity, producing an estimated 800,000 metric tons of steel annually by the early 1990s. The conflict of 2011 delayed development plans to boost liquid steel capacity to about 2m. tons per year. Production, which had been suspended for up to a year, began once again in June 2012, after conflict-related damage had been repaired and full power services restored. By mid-2013 the facility was producing around 1.3m. tons of liquid steel a year.

Libya has also continually expanded its production of cement. Production has only rarely caught up with domestic demand, and, as a consequence, in February 2005, in the country's largest initial public offering to date, the Government offered 40% of the state-owned Arab Cement Co (valued at about US $78m.) for sale to local and international firms to fund modernization and extra capacity. In June 2008 the Government signed a deal with the China National Building Material Company to build the country's eighth cement factory. Cement plants also suffered some damage during the war, and production was restored only gradually once the conflict had ended. However, industrial action halted output at the facilities owned by the Libyan Cement Company (LCC), as workers demanded compensation for wages lost during the fighting. The LCC met most of the strikers' demands, and work resumed after only a brief interruption. The LCC produces just under 3m. tons of cement annually, more than one-third of the country's total output.

An industrial expansion plan for 2010 laid out some specific targets. It aimed to set up 2,191 different industrial projects, which it envisaged would create 25,167 jobs. The bulk of the projects were in the food-processing sector, although projects producing construction materials, such as timber and bricks, also featured prominently. The plan offered incentives to encourage schemes to locate themselves in various regions of the country, in order to ensure adequate regional development. These plans, however, fell into abeyance during 2011 owing to the conflict. In its May 2013 Article IV report on Libya, the IMF urged the resumption of plans to develop the non-oil industry in order to support job creation efforts

POWER AND WATER

Power generation has been accorded a high priority in Libyan development planning. During the 1976–80 period US $3,195m. was spent on power schemes, and installed generating capacity rose from 879 MW in 1975 to 1,700 MW in 1979. However, with the deepening of sanctions during the 1980s, there were delays in power station construction schemes and installed capacity declined.

It was not until the easing of sanctions that expansion plans were revived. In 2001 the General Electricity Corpn of Libya (GECOL) stated that it planned to invest US $3,500m. to expand the country's installed generating capacity to 10,000 MW by 2010, of which 6,000 MW would be required to meet local peak demand in that year, with the remaining capacity to be used to produce electricity for export. At mid-2010 some 5,000 MW was estimated still to be under construction.

The main plant planned in this programme was the 1,200 MW–1,400 MW Gulf Steam power plant near Sirte. Other proposed schemes utilizing natural gas included the 660-MW Western Mountain power project, 280 km south-west of Tripoli; an 800-MW plant at Zuwara on the north-west coast; and a 1,400-MW facility to be located on the coast between Benghazi and Tripoli. Another plan was the expansion of the 450-MW Benghazi North power plant. In January 2002 Technoprom of Russia signed a US $600m. contract to undertake a 650-MW phase I expansion of the Tripoli West power station, for completion in 2005. It was envisaged that a further 650 MW would be installed in a second phase. Reports in July 2008 indicated that GECOL was planning to convert the Tripoli West plant into an independent power project; however, the project appeared to have stalled following demands by the Libyan Government that contractors submit lower bids. Meanwhile, in August 2003 Hyundai of South Korea won a $280m. contract for the expansion of the Azzawiya power plant west of Tripoli. By early 2005 installed generating capacity in Libya was estimated at 4,600 MW–4,700 MW. In mid-2005 GECOL was evaluating commercial bids from five international groups for an engineering, procurement and construction (EPC) contract for a new 750-MW gas-powered combined cycle power at Misurata. In March 2007 contracts were awarded to General Electric of the USA, to Doosan and Daewoo of South Korea, and to Archirodon of Greece for two steam-power projects at the Tripoli West and Al Khaleej plants, worth up to $1,400m. The deals were likely to be the first of many; at the end of 2007 the Secretary for Electricity, Water and Gas, Omran Ibrahim Abu Kraa, said that the Government had re-evaluated the country's power needs and that it needed to build an extra 7,000 MW of capacity, on top of current installed capacity, within the next five years. With the scale of development throughout the country having subsequently accelerated and expanded in scope, the Government subsequently revised its target, and by mid-2010 was aiming to add an additional 13,000 MW of new capacity by 2020.

However, these plans were halted by the civil war that broke out in early 2011. During the conflict, 300 electricity distribution stations, as well as 2,000 km of cable, oil pipelines to electricity-generating stations and fuel tanks were destroyed. The main power stations and numerous substations had also sustained damage. According to Muhammad Ali Ekhlat, the Deputy Minister of Electricity, by the end of June 2012 the Government had managed to repair more than 70% of the damage sustained in the conflict, but the network was still expected to have difficulty in meeting peak summer demand. He stated that demand in Libya was around 5,100 MW–5,200 MW in mid-2012 and could exceed 5,700 MW at the height of summer. Generation capacity at the end of June stood at 5,000 MW, and some towns, including Tripoli, continued to experience occasional blackouts. According to the Renewable Energy Authority of Libya (REAOL), demand for electricity was growing at around 7% a year. Residential electricity consumption accounts for about 30% of overall consumption, twice the amount used by industry. As a consequence, GECOL announced in early 2013 that it would be investing considerably more in the power generation sector, and under its revised demand forecasts, would aim to increase generating capacity to 20,000 MW by 2020.

Following a visit by the US Deputy Secretary of State to Tripoli in April 2007, it was announced that the USA was to assist Libya in the development of a civil nuclear generation programme. Libya has signed nuclear energy research and development deals with numerous other countries, including Argentina, Canada, Russia and Ukraine. The Libyan Nuclear Energy Corporation (NEC) was also reportedly in advanced negotiations with Areva of France to construct a nuclear reactor. In January 2010 the NEC announced that it was in the process of drawing up nuclear energy legislation in order to provide the regulatory framework for a nuclear programme.

Libya's most ambitious project is the GMR, first announced in 1983. Under the first stage of the irrigation and water supply project, the Dong Ah Construction Industrial Co, from South Korea, was contracted to build a man-made river, at a cost of US $3,300m., to carry 2m. cu m per day (cu m/d) of water along 2,000 km of pipeline from natural underground reservoirs at Tazerbo and Sarir, in the south-eastern Sahara desert, to Sirte and Benghazi and agricultural projects and towns on the Mediterranean coast, via Ajdabiya. A total of 270 wells were to be drilled in the Tazerbo and Sarir areas, with the aim of irrigating approximately 280,000 ha, on which some 37,000 model farms were to be established.

The US $5,300m. second stage of the GMR would eventually pipe 2m. cu m/d of water from Sawknah to Tripoli, a distance of 600 km. Three additional stages were planned, including the extension of the first phase southward to Kufra oasis (doubling its capacity to 4m. cu m/d) and the construction of pipelines to serve the north-eastern coastal town of Tobruk (from Ajdabiya) and to link the eastern and western systems of the first two stages along the coast (Tripoli–Sirte), thereby creating a national water grid. If all phases are completed, there will be a total of 4,040 km of pipeline, with a water-carrying capacity of 6m. cu m/d. The eventual cost of the GMR, including agricultural infrastructure, could be as high as $25,000m.

Despite numerous serious setbacks, and with 25% of the first phase still to be completed, the first phase of the GMR was inaugurated by Qaddafi in August 1991. Many other uncertainties prevailed including increasing evidence showing that the cost of using water supplied by the GMR for agriculture was commercially unviable. Furthermore, there was also a shortage of labour for the newly created agricultural land. As a consequence, in mid-1993 the Dong Ah Construction Industrial Co, which had thus far completed 33% of the engineering and 20% of the construction work on its phase II GMR contract, was instructed to modify certain pipeline routes and specifications in its future work schedule, in ways that indicated a shift of priorities away from agricultural development in favour of accelerating the supply of water to coastal towns.

By 1995 the GMR's phase I transmission system was supplying Benghazi with 500,000 cu m/d of water, and Tripoli received its first supplies of GMR water via the western (phase II) pipeline system in September 1996. Dong Ah was now employing 13,000 people on GMR works in Libya, including 2,500 at a plant manufacturing the world's largest pipes (4 m in diameter) and 4,000 involved in pipe-laying activities.

In all, the phase II project specification, as modified in 1993, involved a total of 1,287 km of pipeline (of which 85% had been manufactured and about 70% had been laid by the start of 1996), with a transmission capacity of 2.5m. cu m/d of water drawn from 484 desert wells. The US $310m. contract to drill the last 247 of these wells was awarded to Dong Ah in April 1996 for completion within two years. In the same month Qaddafi informed Dong Ah that it would be awarded the contracts to build phases III and IV of the GMR once designs were finalized.

However, by that stage, Dong Ah's parent company in South Korea was experiencing severe operational difficulties as a result of the Asian economic crisis. Dong Ah continued for a short while, but in November 2000, at which point the phase II works were reported to be about 90% complete, the South Korean company (which had debts of US $2,900m.) suspended work in Libya after filing for bankruptcy. Dong Ah subsequently claimed that it was owed $900m. for work on the GMR (including $350m. for unfinished construction work), while Libya stated in January 2001 that it would file a $3,000m. damages claim in respect of Dong Ah's suspension of work on the GMR. Reports indicated that some $700m. of phase II construction work had yet to be completed, as evidence emerged that the volume of water delivered via the GMR system had fallen to around 300,000 cu m/d (15% of phase I design capacity), owing to leakage from pipelines.

Despite these difficulties, an agreement was reached between the South Korean and Libyan Governments, by which Dong Ah would complete its contractual obligations with the assistance of the local Al-Nahr Co (ANC), itself a joint venture between Dong Ah and the GMR Authority. In April 2002 SNC Lavalin of Canada took over from Dong Ah as operator and manager of the Sarir factory, which manufactured most of the pipes for the GMR.

In December 2001 the Libyan Government selected Nippon Koei of Japan to provide design and consultancy services for phase III of the project. In April 2004 ANC was awarded the contract for the fourth phase to supply and install 620 km of pipeline to transfer water from an underground aquifer in the Ghadames region to the coast west of Tripoli. GMR tenders pending in mid-2005 included a US $500m. EPC contract (as part of phase III) to build a 380-km pipeline linking Kufra to the existing project pipeline at Sarir, and two tenders for extensions of the phase II pipeline network. Another tender for the Kufra-Tazerbo-Ajdabiya water system and pumping stations was issued in October 2006. Following the conflict, in January 2013 the new Government established a new Ministry of Water Resources, which was to bring a co-ordinated approach to the management of all the country's water issues, including waste water. The General Water Authority, the General Company of Desalination and the General Company for Water and Wastewater now all fall within its remit. It was only allocated a small budget of LD 268m. in the 2013 government budget, much of which was immediately spent on the establishment of an armed brigade to protect GMR infrastructure. The new Minister of Water Resources, Al-Hadi Suleiman Hinshir, estimated that the GMR was losing up to 250,000 cu m of water a day due to leakage, much of which was, in fact, due to illegal tapping of the pipelines.

Prior to the announcement of the GMR scheme in 1983, plans were announced for a desalination plant of 462,000 cu m/d, Tripoli 1, to provide Tripoli with drinking water. Plans for a further desalination plant of 150,000 cu m/d at Janzour, 20 km west of Tripoli, were also announced at the end of 1982. The site of Tripoli 1 was moved to Janzour in mid-1984. A water purification plant in Tobruk, with a daily capacity of 5,000 cu m for agricultural purposes (from 13,000 cu m of sewage), was inaugurated in April 1988. In 2001 three desalination plants, each with a capacity of 40,000 cu m/d, were under construction at Tobruk, Zuara and Sirte, while bidding was in progress for contracts for three further plants at Abutoraba (40,000 cu m/d), Tripoli (250,000 cu m/d) and Benghazi (150,000 cu m/d). (The contract for the Abutoraba project was awarded to Sidem of France in 2006.) Five more desalination projects (four of them extensions to existing plants), with a combined capacity of 140,000 cu m/d, were included in GECOL's US $900m. desalination expansion programme for 2000–10.

TRANSPORT AND COMMUNICATIONS

Rapid growth in the volume of imports led to severe congestion at the main ports of Tripoli and Benghazi in the 1970s, after which these and other Libyan ports underwent large-scale expansion. It was reported in 2001 that a total of 15m. metric tons of freight was being handled each year by 10 Libyan sea ports. At the end of 2012 Libya's flag-registered fleet consisted of 81 vessels, with a total displacement of 1,020,500 grt.

Libya's roads underwent significant expansion in the 1970s and early 1980s; the road from Tripoli to Sabha was opened at the end of 1983, providing 770 km of metalled surface. By 2001 Libya had an estimated total road network of 83,200 km, of which 57,200 km was paved. In early 2005 the Government was seeking bids from local and international contractors for the construction of five major coastal road projects. These plans were boosted by a deal concluded in August 2008, under which Italy agreed to pay for the construction of a 2,000-km coastal motorway stretching from Egypt to Tunisia. The scheme, with an estimated cost of US $4,700m., was part of a wider compensation settlement with Italy, related to its colonial era misdeeds.

There have been no railways in Libya since 1964, when the Benghazi–Barce line was abandoned. However, in 1998 plans were announced to construct 2,178 km of track running east to west along the coast and 992 km running north to south. Talks were subsequently opened with Tunisian and Egyptian officials regarding the feasibility of cross-border links to the proposed Libyan railway. A contract to lay an initial 191 km of track from Ras Ajdir on the Tunisian border to Tripoli and to install signalling and other facilities was awarded to China Civil Engineering Construction in March 2000. This work formed part of the first phase of the project, linking Sirte to Ras Ajdir, and in January 2003 manufacturers from the United Kingdom, France, Germany, Spain and Italy submitted bids for the provision of 100,000 metric tons of finished rails. Phase II would extend the coastal line east from Sirte to Benghazi, while phase III would further extend it from Benghazi to Musaid on the Egyptian border. However, confusion has surrounded the implementation of rail projects in Libya, with various schemes having been the victim of numerous policy reversals. This seemed to have been dispelled in February 2008, when the Libyan Government announced the signing of two contracts with the Chinese Civil Engineering Construction Corpn, worth US $3,200m., to build a 352-km line between Sirte and Misurata in the south and a second line linking Hicha and the south. In April Russian Railways OAO was awarded a contract for the construction of a 554-km railway between Sirte and Benghazi.

Following the suspension of UN sanctions in April 1999, regional and international airlines began to reintroduce services to Libya, while the new national carrier, Libyan Airlines (formed by the merger of LAA with another operator in 1989), opened discussions with other Middle East-based airlines with a view to leasing aircraft for international routes. The airline's fleet comprised just nine aircraft in 1999, compared with 35 (four of them leased) in the early 1990s. An agreement in principle was reached with Airbus Industrie in October 1999 to purchase 24 aircraft at such time as it became possible to proceed with such an order without contravening US trade sanctions. It was reported in April 2004 that BAE Systems of the United Kingdom was negotiating a series of agreements to modernize Libya's civil aviation infrastructure, and in June that year it was announced that the Government had allocated US $1,000m. to renovate Libyan Airlines, with plans to buy 22 short- and long-haul aircraft. Libya's first private airline, Buraq Air, signed a preliminary agreement in February 2005 to buy six 737-800 Boeing aircraft. In June 2007 Afriqiyah Airways confirmed its purchase of five Airbus A320 aircraft and signed a memorandum of understanding (MOU) to purchase six Airbus A350 aircraft; this followed the company's earlier order of 12 Airbus planes. In the same month Libyan Airlines also signed a new MOU with Airbus, which could see the carrier acquiring up to four A350s, four A330-200s and seven A320s.

Meanwhile, the General People's Committee approved contracts with companies from Brazil, France, Germany, Japan and Turkey to upgrade Tripoli International Airport, including the construction of an air terminal capable of handling 20m. passengers annually; following delays, the new terminal was not expected to open until 2012. A new airport has been proposed for Benghazi, and the development of tourist airports at Ghat, Ghadames and Sabha is also under way, although the status of all these projects remained uncertain in mid-2013, following the conflict of 2011.

As part of Libya's aim to create a comprehensive telecommunications network, in mid-1991 Swedish companies were awarded contracts for new installations in the south-west of the country; however, other parts of the programme, notably plans for 20 new exchanges and 182,000 extra lines in Tripoli and Benghazi, were not finalized until mid-1993.

According to the International Telecommunication Union, the number of telephone main lines increased from 59 per 1,000 people in 1995 to 172 per 1,000 in 2009. A mobile cellular telephone service was introduced in 1996, the number of subscribers reaching 779 per 1,000 people by 2009, when there were also 353,900 internet users in Libya. Zhongxing Technologies of the People's Republic of China signed a US $42m. contract with the state-owned General Post and Telecommunications Co (GPTC) in January 2004 to install a new GSM network covering major towns and cities in Libya. In December it was reported that the Government was tendering three contracts, worth a total of $1,000m., to modernize and upgrade the telecommunications system, including the installation of 1.5m. fixed lines and a 6,000-km optical fibre network. In the same month General People's Committee Secretary Ghanem ruled out any immediate plans to open up the GSM market to international operators Earlier, in September, a second GSM operator, Libyana Mobile Phone Co, had joined the incumbent provider in the local market, Al-Madar Al-Jadeed (both companies being owned by the GPTC). In 2006 the General Telecommunications Authority was established, reporting directly to the General People's Committee, and in early 2007 it was announced that Al-Madar and Libyana were to be privatized.

In January 2010 Ericsson of Sweden secured a contract to supply Libya with 'next generation' technology, which would allow users to access voice, television and internet services via a broadband internet connection. The service was to be provided by means of a fibre optic network, the installation of which Libya had contracted to the French firm Alcatel-Lucent in late 2009.

The civil war of 2011 damaged Libya's existing infrastructure to varying degrees, and also obstructed and delayed infrastructure development schemes that were ongoing at the time, such as the railway construction project. In an effort to restore confidence among contractors, however, the NTC stated that it would honour all contracts signed under the Qaddafi regime and would welcome back foreign investors to the country immediately after the conflict ended. This was supported by the swift restoration of key infrastructure services around the country. Although Tripoli airport was shelled during the war, it sustained only superficial damage and was reopened to international traffic in September. Similarly, Tripoli's sea port also reopened swiftly; a number of boats had been sunk in key water lanes, but they posed little obstruction, while the port itself had been relatively unscathed by the conflict.

The new Government quickly identified the country's infrastructure shortcomings as a major obstacle to domestic development and in early 2013 announced that it expected to invest up to US $140,000m. in key projects over the coming decade. These included the resumption of the airport upgrade scheme and, crucially, the immediate construction of some 200,000 new homes. The Government estimated that the country would face a housing shortage of up to 500,000 units by 2020.

TOURISM

Libyan initiatives to increase non-oil foreign currency earnings in the 1990s included plans for the development of a mass tourism industry. Despite the suspension of its international air links, the Government nevertheless announced its intention to invest US $1,700m. over the following five years 'to rehabilitate the tourism infrastructure'. In 1997 international consultants were appointed to draw up a plan for tourism development, which provided the blueprint for the development of the sector following the suspension of UN sanctions in 1999. In 1999 receipts from tourism totalled $28m. By 2005 this had risen more than 10-fold, to $301m., before declining to just $99m. in 2007. Tourist arrivals (including same-day visitors) totalled 999,343 in 2004.

In early 2001 the president of Libya's Tourism Investment and Promotion Board said that foreign investment of US $2,000m.–$3,000m. would be sought in the tourism sector during the 2001–05 Development Plan, with the aim of expanding the provision of hotel beds from 5,000 to more than 60,000 and increasing tourist arrivals to 1m. per year.

In June 2003 the Libyan authorities announced an ambitious US $7,000m. plan to develop the country's coastal infrastructure over five years to attract 3m. tourists each year. A contract for the first large-scale development under the plan was signed in April 2004 between Ldorado of the Netherlands and Tobruk municipality. Worth up to $2,000m., the scheme envisaged the construction of four tourist resorts with spas, golf courses, luxury hotels and shopping malls. Italy's Gruppo Norman signed a long-term concession agreement with the Libyan state-owned Farwa Tourism Co in December to develop and manage a coastal area and island near the Tunisian border as a tourist complex, with sufficient accommodation for up to 3,800 people. Several new tourism projects were announced during 2006, including the Andalus Tourist Centre and the Ghazala Tower luxury hotel in Tripoli.

In early 2007 the Secretariat for Tourism was abolished, to be replaced by a General Tourism Authority, and an agreement was concluded with a French company to develop tourist investment zones in the coastal regions of Sabratha (with important Roman archaeological sites) and Tobruk. In September Qaddafi's eldest son, Seif al-Islam, announced the establishment of the Green Mountain Conservation and Development Authority, which would oversee a huge conservation and sustainable development project in the Jebel Akhdar region. The project, the first phase of which was reported to be under way in 2009, would be the largest eco-project in the world, incorporating eco-tourism schemes, conservation projects as well as space for clean industries, relying on renewable energy. The scheme was part of a wider Government initiative to promote sustainable tourism.

Following the conflict, the Government has forged ties with the World Tourism Organisation (WTO) in order to help develop the sector. The WTO stated in mid-2013 that the sector has the potential of being the country's second highest revenue-earning industry after oil and gas and could be capable of generating 'hundreds of thousands' of jobs. However, the new Minister of Tourism, Ikram Abd al-Salam Bash Imam, announced that development would take time, owing to resource and skill constraints.

BUDGET, INVESTMENT AND FINANCE

Libya initiated its first five-year Development Plan in 1963/64, and they have been a feature of government budgeting ever since. While development budgets in the 1970s favoured agriculture, the 1981–85 plan was aimed at initiating structural change in the economy to reduce its dependence on petroleum. However, by 1983, owing to the abrupt reversal in Libya's petroleum revenues, the plan's targets were not being met, and major reassessments, involving substantial reductions in expenditure, had to be undertaken. The decline in government revenues curtailed budget expenditure throughout the 1980s and actual capital expenditure on development fell well below that budgeted.

Sanctions continued to take their toll on the public finances throughout the 1990s and although Libya received significant revenues from oil sales, in 1994 the Government indicated that 'several billion dollars' of cutbacks had been made to take account of the impact of UN sanctions. In 1996, however, the Government claimed that it had balanced the budget, by financing its deficit with drawdowns on its foreign reserves. It was the first time in many years that Libya had managed to avoid a deficit, a trend that was to continue to the end of the decade.

With the easing of sanctions from 1999, subsequent budgets placed greater emphasis on development expenditure, in order to rebuild Libya's dilapidated capital base. A new five-year Development Plan launched in 2001 called for total investment of US $35,000m., of which 60%–70% would come from the public sector, and the balance from foreign investment and the Libyan private sector. The main growth targets were an average 5% per year overall and an average of 6.2% per year for the non-hydrocarbons sector. Non-hydrocarbons industries identified for foreign participation included tourism, telecommunications, mining, fisheries, and road and railway development. The main areas of investment in the Plan were the hydrocarbons, power and water sectors, all of which had major expansion programmes in place in 2001.

Increased capital outlays were supported by a rise in oil receipts, which picked up considerably from 2002 onwards. On account of these significantly higher oil revenues, Libya moved into an era of strong fiscal surpluses. By 2007 Libya had built a surplus estimated at a huge 34% of GDP.

However, this rapid rise in liquidity exerted considerable upward pressure on consumer prices. Following a four-year period of deflation, ending in 2003, prices rose consistently each year, with annual average inflation reaching 10.3% in 2008. With the onset of the global economic downturn, inflationary pressures started to ease in early 2009, and by the end of the year annual average inflation had fallen to 2.4%. Expectations that inflation would rise again were prompted by the Government's 2010 budget, which projected a 32% increase in expenditure to an unprecedented high of LD 58,000m. The budget reflected the extent of the Government's development plans, with much of the outlay allocated to support capital projects. The Government also stated that it intended to allocate some LD 82,000m. to its capital budget over the course of the coming three years. However, these fears were not realized and consumer prices in 2010 were estimated to have remained stable, with inflation at around 2.5%. The outbreak of conflict in early 2011 exerted significant upward pressure on consumer prices, as basic goods became scarce. In addition, the shortage of local and foreign currency also helped to increase prices, as the value of the dinar declined. Although the production of official data was halted, anecdotal reports from both the rebel- and Government-held areas revealed that staples such as rice and cooking oil had doubled in price. Price pressures eased after the conflict ended and Libya's borders were reopened. Indeed, inflation was not the main concern for the Government, which aimed to resume spending quickly in order to recycle oil revenues as widely as possible. Its budget for 2012 was Libya's largest ever, with expenditure reaching LD 68,500m. Given the high oil price and the rapid recovery in production, the Government anticipated that it would be able to balance the budget with its oil receipts, which contributed around 95% of total fiscal revenue.

However, the numerous stoppages in production and the consequent decline in revenues, undermined the Government's ability to meet its budgetary commitments. The Government had set a lower budget for 2013, with expenditure of LD 66,900m., 2.4% less than in the previous year. The IMF had already highlighted the fiscal risks that the Government faced and urged swift subsidy reform; in June 2013 the Government announced that it would begin the implementation of a new plan to lift gradually subsidies on both food and fuel by August of that year.

Prior to the conflict, one of the contributory factors to the rapid rise in consumer prices was the weakness of the local banking system. Before the 1969 coup most Libyan banks were subsidiaries of foreign banks. However, among the first decrees issued by the Revolution Command Council was one that required 51% of the capital of all banks operating in Libya to be owned by Libyans; the majority of directors—including the chairman—of each bank had to be Libyan citizens. Under the monarchy the Government had followed a similar policy without compulsion, and a number of foreign banks had accordingly already 'Libyanized' themselves. In December 1970 all commercial banks were nationalized, with government participation set at 51%.

This policy was finally reversed in the years after the suspension of sanctions. As foreign firms returned to Libya, it was quite clear that Libya's banking system was archaic and highly conservative. Libya invited the World Bank to help modernize and upgrade banking systems and technology, and in July 2007 the Government concluded the sale of a minority (19%) stake in Sahara Bank, one of Libya's largest state banks, to France's BNP Paribas. Flush from this success, the Government then announced the sale of a second bank, Wahda Bank. This went through in February 2008, with the Jordan-based Arab Bank securing a 19% stake. Both strategic partners have the right to increase their stakes at a later stage to 51%. At the end of 2008 the authorities announced that they would sell off shares in two more banks—National Commercial Bank (NCB) and Gumhouria Bank—in 2009. Divestment of a 15% stake in the latter duly went ahead, although the privatization of the NCB was delayed. Meanwhile, in March a 40% stake in the United Bank for Commerce and Investment was sold to Ahli United Bank of Bahrain.

The concept of a privately run banking sector had been tested much earlier, when in March 1993 legislation was approved authorizing Libyan citizens and companies to establish privately owned commercial banks with a minimum capitalization of LD 10m. (US $37m.). Under the same law, Libyan nationals were permitted to apply to the Central Bank of Libya for authorization to hold foreign currency in local bank accounts and to make unrestricted use of such holdings. The heavily overvalued Libyan dinar was then being unofficially traded for convertible currencies at about one-sixth of its official exchange rate (which had been pegged to the IMF's special drawing right since 1986). Speaking in May 1993, Qaddafi said that he favoured a move towards full convertibility of the Libyan dinar at such time as 'there was adequate production' in the Libyan economy to prevent 'catastrophic' consequences.

In early November 1994 the Central Bank devalued the official exchange rate by 15.5%, from US $1 = LD 0.299 to $1 = LD 0.354, this being the fourth change in the official rate since 1992. The currency remained heavily overvalued, as its unofficial exchange rate was then about $1 = LD 3. Later the same month the Central Bank introduced a second-tier official rate of $1 = LD 1.019 'for use by local companies'. Also in November 1994 a consortium of seven local banks set up a new financial services company in Tripoli to meet the foreign currency requirements of travellers, using exchange rates 'set by supply and demand'. In early 1995 it was reported that a widening gap between official and unofficial exchange rates in Libya was pushing up the rate of price inflation, which, according to some estimates, was as high as 50%, compared with an estimated 15% in 1994. In late 1995 the unofficial exchange rate was reported to be averaging about $1 = LD 3.40. Price inflation affected mainly the growing range of 'non-essential' items whose importation was now handled by private sector companies with little or no access to foreign exchange at the official rate. The officially recorded rates of price inflation were 4.5% in 1994 and 6% in 1995.

In an address to the GPC in March 1997, Qaddafi acknowledged that the unofficial exchange rate at that time, of about US $1 = LD 3, represented a 'realistic' basis for foreign exchange transactions. However, the Central Bank's main official exchange rate was not devalued at that stage and it stood at $1 = LD 0.38 in September 1997. In October 1998 Qaddafi strongly urged traders and shopkeepers to reduce their prices and announced a country-wide campaign to maintain pressure for price cuts. In November the Central Bank's main official exchange rate was devalued to $1 = LD 0.45. The unofficial exchange rate stood at around $1 = LD 3.20 in early 1999, when it was estimated that one-fifth of all currency transactions were carried out on an unofficial basis. At the beginning of 2001 Libya's official exchange rate was $1 = LD 0.55, while the second-tier commercial exchange rate was $1 = LD 1.73; there was also a special exchange rate for government transactions. A further adjustment of the official rate to $1 = LD 0.64 was followed by a major devaluation of 50.3% with effect from 1 January 2002, setting the rate at $1 = LD 1.30, in what was described as the first step towards establishing a unified market-driven parity. Analysts expected the change to increase the competitiveness of the non-oil sector, to reduce the cost of most imports and to reduce the role of the black market in currency transactions. Finally, in June 2003 Libya unified the dinar exchange rate, signalling the end of the dual-rate system, as part of the Government's efforts to restructure the country's command economy. The dinar came under severe pressure after the outbreak of internal conflict and although local banks were reportedly still selling the dinar at the official rate of $1 = LD 1.25 in May 2010, the black market rate had risen to $1 = LD 3. A shortage of cash forced the Central Bank to reintroduce old notes and coinage and it limited cash withdrawals to LD 1,000 per person per month. The currency crisis prompted many Libyans to start buying gold, and as a result the local price of gold almost doubled, from LD 43 per g to LD 80 per g. By mid-2012 the dinar had stabilized at around $1 = LD 1.24, and the rate averaged $1 = LD 1.26 for that year, a level that it maintained throughout the first half of 2013.

Libya's strong oil revenues allowed it to develop a wide-ranging overseas aid programme, although many recipients, particularly Arab nations, had pledges withdrawn when their policies displeased Qaddafi. These donations enabled Libya to build strong links in sub-Saharan Africa, which in the post-sanctions era translated into wide-ranging investment projects throughout the continent. These overseas investments were channelled through the country's various investment vehicles, with the Libya-Africa Portfolio (LAP) managing the country's African assets. By 2009 the LAP was operating in 19 African countries and owned 30 hotels throughout the continent.

Libya's overseas investment programme originally gained momentum in 1977, when the Libyan Arab Foreign Bank (LAFB)—effectively the 'offshore' arm of the Central Bank of Libya, and a key institution in Libyan trade finance—bought a 15.2% stake in the equity of Fiat, the Italian motor car company, for US $400m. Until this purchase the LAFB had pursued a cautious and selective policy of putting Libyan capital into banking, hotels and tourism in many countries, as well as joint-stock ventures in agriculture, fishing and forestry projects in some African countries. Libya appeared to regard the Fiat purchase as the vanguard of its investment in industrial countries' manufacturing bases. Libya's holdings in Italy grew steadily over the years, and the country accrued interests in a whole range of industries and sectors, including sugar, steel, banking, telecommunications, oil construction, textiles and power. Its biggest investment in Italy was in the Unicredit bank, in which it held a 5% stake worth €1,500m.

In October 2007 Libya announced the establishment of a sovereign wealth fund—the Libyan Investment Authority (LIA)—which would manage all of Libya's overseas assets and acquisitions. It became the umbrella body under which the other investment vehicles (including the LAP) were collected and was estimated to have some US $40,000m. at its disposal. Each year it was to receive a proportion of the state's oil income. The LIA was to place a greater emphasis on portfolio investments managed by Western banks, as well as the international real estate market. It would also earmark funds for the development of the Libyan oil and gas industry. Taking advantage of the decline in global asset prices, the LIA announced in mid-2009 that it was opening an office in London, United Kingdom. However, in May 2011, during the ongoing civil war, documents came to light detailing the operations of the LIA, which showed that the organization managed its funds very poorly. A large proportion of these funds was held in cash in overnight deposits, thus losing value, while other monies were placed in high-risk derivatives, which recorded losses of around 8% over the year to the end of the first quarter of 2010. By that stage, the LIA's total assets had fallen by 4.5% on an annual basis, to $53,300m. Farhat Bengdara, the former Governor of the Central Bank, who also defected from the Qaddafi regime soon after the outbreak of the conflict, estimated that the LIA had lost some $2,000m. worth of assets in the first half of 2011 alone.

In 2006 it was announced that legislation to establish a stock exchange had been enacted. The Libyan Stock Market formally opened in March 2007; by the end of 2010 there were 25 companies listed on the exchange, with a total capitalization of US $1,300m.

One of the earliest laws adopted by the interim Government that was installed in November 2011 was Decree 46, which set out new regulations governing the financial system. The key clause in the Decree was one allowing the establishment of Islamic banks and the provision of financial services compliant with *Shari'a* law.

FOREIGN TRADE AND BALANCE OF PAYMENTS

Until production of petroleum began, Libya's exports consisted almost entirely of agricultural products, and its imports of manufactured goods. In 1960, for instance, imports were valued at LD 60.4m. and exports at LD 4.0m., leaving an adverse balance of LD 56.4m. (although LD 21m. of the total value of imports in 1960 was accounted for by goods imported for the account of the petroleum companies). Petroleum was first exported in late 1961, and by 1969, according to the IMF, imports totalled LD 241.3m. and exports LD 937.9m., of which LD 936.5m. was officially accounted for by crude petroleum. Although there were fluctuations within the overall trend, petroleum exports rose from LD 2,109.5m. in 1974 to LD 4,419.2m. in 1979, when they represented 99% of all Libyan exports by volume. The minute proportion of remaining exports were mainly hides and skins, groundnuts, almonds, metal scrap and re-exports.

Since petroleum has been exported, Libya's visible trade balance has normally shown substantial surpluses. There was a general trend of increasing surpluses during the 1970s, as output rose and prices reached record highs. However, this trend was reversed in the 1980s, as sanctions started to take their toll and output and exports declined. Prices also fell back during this period. Nevertheless, Libya managed to maintain a trade surplus for much of the decade and in 1989 exports totalled US $7,320m., surpassing imports of $6,460m. This pattern continued into the 1990s, with the trade surplus reaching $4,700m. in 1996. However, a drop in global oil prices forced a significant contraction in the surplus in 1998, when it narrowed sharply, to $471m.

Once sanctions were eased from 1999 onwards, Libya's oil export earnings started to pick up and more noticeably from 2002, when prices started to climb rapidly once again. Libya moved to liberalize its trade regime from 2005, reducing import monopolies and dismantling the highly convoluted import tariff structure. Although this let in a flood of imports, export revenues continued to surge and by 2006 had reached US $37,500m., an increase of more than five times the amount earned just a decade earlier in 1996. As a consequence, the trade surplus rose to more than 50% of GDP. It was estimated to have widened further in 2007 and 2008.

Libya's trade profile looked very different prior to the imposition of sanctions. In 1981 the USA was Libya's largest customer, taking 27.4% of Libyan exports by value. The other principal importers of Libyan oil were Italy (23.8%), West Germany (10.3%) and Spain (6.7%). The USA and Western Europe together accounted for almost 90% of total oil exports from Libya. However, in 1982 all imports of Libyan oil to the USA were banned. Similarly, Libyan imports from the USA fell by US $500m. from the level of $831m. in 1981. In January 1986, convinced of Libya's involvement in promoting international terrorism, President Reagan banned all trade between the USA and Libya. The USA succeeded in persuading some of its allies to reduce sharply their purchases of Libyan oil after the bombing of Tripoli and Benghazi in April 1986, but Italy, by far the largest customer for Libyan oil, actually increased its imports. The US embargo on bilateral trade with Libya reduced Libyan imports from the USA to $46.2m. in 1986, while Libyan exports to the USA amounted to a mere $1.6m. As Libyan debts accumulated under the sanctions regime, imports from Western European countries were also much reduced. Several countries, including India, Turkey and Uganda, accepted oil as payment for goods or debts owed to them by Libya.

However, given their own need for oil, Libya's Western European customers remained the mainstay of Libya's external trade. By 1999 Italy took 37.8% of Libya's exports by value and provided 18.3% of imports; the corresponding figures for Germany were 19.1% and 14.5%, respectively. By 2007 Italy had further cemented its bilateral trade relations with Libya, and had a 41% share of Libya's exports, which was more than the total imports of Libya's six next largest customers. Yet its share of imports had fallen to 12.6%, as China and the USA increased their share. These two countries became increasingly important importers of Libyan oil as well; since the dismantling of sanctions, the USA increased its share of Libya's exports from zero to just under 8% in four years, while China took 3%.

In contrast to its merchandise trade, Libya's non-merchandise (invisible) trade account has persistently run a deficit. Indeed, this has widened considerably since the suspension of sanctions, as repatriated profits by foreign companies and services costs associated with rising imports have increased significantly. However, given the scale of the trade surplus, the non-merchandise deficit has done little to offset it and Libya's current account surplus was in excess of 40% of GDP in 2008. By the end of 2010 this had narrowed to a still strong 20% of GDP. When civil war erupted in 2011, Libya's exports all but ceased, owing to the impact of fighting and the imposition of sanctions. These sanctions also hampered the importation of goods, with the result that basic goods began to be smuggled over Libya's land borders. Trade recovered rapidly in the aftermath of the conflict, and had normalized by mid-2012. Indeed, the more rapid recovery than expected of production ensured a swift return to strong export earnings, and by 2013 the IMF was anticipating that Libya would record a current account surplus of 26% of GDP.

Sanctions also froze Libya's stock of international reserves, which the country had been able to build up with its significant oil earnings. Indeed, the huge oil windfall in the boom years prior to 2008 pushed its stocks of reserves higher than ever, and by the end of 2009 Libya had accumulated over US $99,000m. of reserves, equivalent to an estimated 45 months of import cover. Expectations that Qaddafi had plundered the country's reserves in order to pay for the equipment and supplies needed to prosecute the war, as well as to ensure the continued support of his extensive patronage networks, proved largely unfounded, and at the end of 2011 the level of reserves was broadly unchanged from just prior to the conflict, amounting to $100,000m. By 2013 this had risen to over $140,000m., equivalent to 40 months of imports, according to the IMF.

Although Libya racked up considerable bilateral debt with trade partners during the sanctions period, its lack of access to international capital markets and international financial institutions forestalled any significant external borrowing. As a consequence, its levels of external debt have remained manageable and although precise data are hard to come by, Libya's total external debt was estimated at the end of 2009 to be around US $5,600m., equivalent to just 9.2% of GDP. In early June 2011 international partners that had given their support to the rebel movement in Libya pledged $1,300m. in aid.

Statistical Survey

Sources (unless otherwise stated): National Corporation for Information and Documentation; Census and Statistical Dept, Sharia Damascus 40, 2nd Floor, Tripoli; tel. (21) 3331731; Central Bank of Libya, POB 1103, Sharia al-Malik Seoud, Tripoli; tel. (21) 3333591; fax (21) 4441488; e-mail info@cbl.gov.ly; internet www.cbl.gov.ly.

Area and Population

AREA, POPULATION AND DENSITY

Area (sq km)	1,676,198*
Population (census results)†	
August 1995	4,404,986
August 2006	
Males	2,610,639
Females	2,687,513
Total	5,298,152
Population (UN estimates at mid-year)	
2011	6,103,235
2012	6,154,620
2013	6,201,523
Density (per sq km) at mid-2013	3.7

* 647,184 sq miles.
† Excluding non-Libyans: 409,326 in 1995 and 359,540 in 2006.

Sources: National Authority for Information and Authentication; UN, *World Population Prospects: The 2012 Revision*.

POPULATION BY AGE AND SEX
(UN estimates at mid-2013)

	Males	Females	Total
0–14	937,403	891,766	1,829,169
15–64	2,026,549	2,048,693	4,075,242
65 and over	137,379	159,733	297,112
Total	3,101,331	3,100,192	6,201,523

Source: UN, *World Population Prospects: The 2012 Revision*.

POPULATION BY REGION
(population at 2006 census)

	Area (sq km)	Population	Density (per sq km)
Al-Butnan	84,996	150,353	1.8
Banghazi (Benghazi)	11,372	622,148	54.7
Darnah (Darna)	31,511	155,402	4.9
Ghat	68,482	21,329	0.3
Al-Jabal al-Akhdar	11,429	192,689	16.9
Al-Jabal al-Gharbi	76,717	288,944	3.8
Al-Jifarah	2,666	422,999	158.7
Al-Jufrah	139,038	46,899	0.3
Al-Kufrah	433,611	42,769	0.1
Al-Marqab	6,796	410,187	60.4
Al-Marj	13,515	175,455	13.0
Marzuq	356,308	72,513	0.2
Misratah (Misurata)	29,172	511,628	17.5
Nalut	67,191	87,772	1.3
Al-Nuqat al-Khams	6,089	269,553	44.3
Sabha	17,066	119,038	7.0
Surt (Sirte)	86,399	131,786	1.5
Tarabulus (Tripoli)	835	997,065	1,194.1
Wadi al-Hayat	31,485	70,711	2.2
Wadi al-Shati	90,244	73,443	0.8
Al-Wahah	108,523	164,718	1.5
Al-Zawiyah (Zawia)	2,753	270,751	98.3
Total	1,676,198	5,298,152	3.2

Source: National Authority for Information and Authentication.

PRINCIPAL TOWNS
(population at census of 2006)

Tarabulus (Tripoli, the capital)	997,065	Al-Nuquat al-Khams	269,553
Banghazi (Benghazi)	622,148	Al-Jabal al-Akhdar	192,689
Misratah (Misurata)	511,628	Al-Marj	175,455
Al-Jifarah	422,999	Al-Wahah	164,718
Al-Marqab	410,187	Darnah (Darna)	155,402
Al-Jabal al-Gharbi	288,944	Al-Butnan	150,353
Al-Zawiyah (Zawia)	270,751	Surt (Sirte)	131,786

Source: National Authority for Information and Authentication.

BIRTHS, MARRIAGES AND DEATHS

	Registered live births		Registered marriages		Registered deaths	
	Number	Rate (per 1,000)	Number	Rate (per 1,000)	Number	Rate (per 1,000)
2004	119,633	23.5	39,105	7.6	15,765	3.1
2005	120,999	23.3	43,979	8.4	16,425	3.2
2006	124,541	23.2	47,219	8.8	17,975	3.4
2007	128,337	23.7	59,583	11.0	20,045	3.7
2008	132,826	24.1	65,326	11.9	21,481	3.9

Source: National Authority for Information and Authentication.

Life expectancy (years at birth): 75.0 (males 72.4; females 77.6) in 2011 (Source: World Bank, World Development Indicators database).

EMPLOYMENT
('000 persons)

	2007	2008	2009
Agriculture, forestry and fishing	40.8	74.0	77.7
Mining and quarrying	30.5	35.7	41.5
Manufacturing	66.2	65.6	65.2
Electricity, gas and water	37.1	44.2	50.3
Construction	34.7	34.9	36.3
Trade, restaurants and hotels	84.2	93.4	109.6
Transport and communications	65.8	66.0	66.0
Financing, insurance and real estate	40.7	48.2	57.1
Public administration	401.6	397.9	408.2
Education	462.4	456.4	459.7
Health services	79.6	77.0	75.4
Other services	32.8	32.8	30.6
Total	1,376.3	1,426.2	1,477.8

Mid-2013 ('000, estimates): Agriculture, etc. 60; Total labour force 2,354 (Source: FAO).

Health and Welfare

KEY INDICATORS

Total fertility rate (children per woman, 2011)	2.5
Under-5 mortality rate (per 1,000 live births, 2011)	16
HIV/AIDS (% of persons aged 15–49, 2003)	0.3
Physicians (per 1,000 head, 2009)	1.9
Hospital beds (per 1,000 head, 2009)	3.7
Health expenditure (2010): US $ per head (PPP)	573
Health expenditure (2010): % of GDP	3.0
Health expenditure (2010): public (% of total)	70.0
Access to water (% of persons, 2002)	72
Access to sanitation (% of persons, 2010)	97
Total carbon dioxide emissions ('000 metric tons, 2009)	62,874.4
Carbon dioxide emissions per head (metric tons, 2009)	10.0
Human Development Index (2012): ranking	64
Human Development Index (2012): value	0.769

For sources and definitions, see explanatory note on p. vi.

Agriculture

PRINCIPAL CROPS

('000 metric tons)

	2009	2010	2011
Wheat*	105	106	111
Barley*	101	102	98
Potatoes*	291	290	352
Broad beans, horse beans, dry*	2	2	1
Almonds, with shell*	29	30	38
Groundnuts, with shell†	26	22	17
Olives*	203	180	139
Tomatoes*	220	230	223
Pumpkins, squash and gourds*	32	33	34
Cucumbers and gherkins*	12	14	15
Chillies and peppers, green*	24	24	24
Onions and shallots, green*	59	50	54
Onions, dry*	186	195	206
Peas, green*	6	7	6
Carrots and turnips*	25	26	30
Watermelons*	225	245	243
Cantaloupes and other melons†	26	26	26
Oranges*	46	46	48
Tangerines, mandarins, etc.*	11	11	11
Lemons and limes*	17	18	18
Apples*	20	22	20
Apricots*	21	22	24
Peaches and nectarines*	11	12	13
Plums and sloes*	43	44	51
Grapes*	30	35	35
Figs*	10	11	10
Dates*	155	161	166

* FAO estimates.

† Unofficial figures.

Aggregate production ('000 metric tons, may include official, semi-official or estimated data): Total cereals 216 in 2009, 218 in 2010, 220 in 2011; Total roots and tubers 291 in 2009, 290 in 2010, 352 in 2011; Total vegetables (incl. melons) 912 in 2009, 947 in 2010, 979 in 2011; Total fruits (excl. melons) 370 in 2009, 386 in 2010, 403 in 2011.

Source: FAO.

LIVESTOCK

('000 head, year ending September)

	2009	2010	2011
Horses*	45	45	45
Asses*	29	29	29
Cattle	190†	195†	197*
Camels*	55	56	57
Sheep	6,700†	7,000†	7,100*
Goats	2,600†	2,700†	2,600*
Poultry*	27,000	33,000	34,000

* FAO estimate(s).

† Unofficial figure.

Source: FAO.

LIVESTOCK PRODUCTS

('000 metric tons, FAO estimates)

	2009	2010	2011
Cattle meat	9	9	8
Sheep meat	29	30	31
Goat meat	12	13	13
Chicken meat	125	129	124
Cows' milk	140	141	141
Sheep's milk	67	61	61
Goats' milk	18	19	19
Hen eggs	62	63	63
Wool, greasy	9	9	9

Source: FAO.

Forestry

ROUNDWOOD REMOVALS

('000 cubic metres, excl. bark, FAO estimates)

	2009	2010	2011
Sawlogs, veneer logs and logs for sleepers*	63	63	63
Other industrial wood	53	53	53
Fuel wood	939	952	964
Total	1,055	1,068	1,080

* Annual output assumed to be unchanged since 1978.

Source: FAO.

SAWNWOOD PRODUCTION

('000 cubic metres, incl. railway sleepers, FAO estimates)

	1976	1977	1978
Total (all broadleaved)*	9	21	31

* Annual output to 2011 assumed to be unchanged since 1978 (FAO estimates).

Source: FAO.

Fishing

(metric tons, live weight)

	2009	2010*	2011*
Capture	52,110	50,000	30,000
Groupers	990	950	570
Common pandora	7,200	6,950	4,200
Bogue	2,250	2,180	1,300
Surmullet	6,246	6,000	3,600
Jack and horse mackerels	2,817	2,720	1,650
Sardinellas	9,450	9,200	5,400
Dogfish sharks	7,596	7,300	4,400
Aquaculture*	240	240	240
Total catch (incl. others)*	52,350	50,240	30,240

* FAO estimates.

Source: FAO.

Mining

('000 metric tons unless otherwise indicated, estimates)

	2009	2010	2011
Salt	40	40	20
Gypsum (crude)	250	250	125

Source: US Geological Survey.

Crude petroleum (million barrels): 616.0 in 2010; 178.6 in 2011; 530.7 in 2012.

Natural gas (incl. flared, '000 million cu ft): 1,051,900 in 2008; 1,035,500 in 2009; 1,078,800 in 2010.

Industry

SELECTED PRODUCTS

('000 metric tons)

	2010	2011	2012
Jet fuels (incl. kerosene)	1,811	784	932
Motor spirit (petrol)	585	569	615
Naphthas (raw)	2,457	649	1,348
Gas-diesel (distillate fuel) oil	4,278	1,522	2,251
Residual fuel oils	7,103	2,242	3,123

Cement (hydraulic, '000 metric tons, estimates): 6,500 in 2009; 7,000 in 2010; 3,500 in 2011 (Source: US Geological Survey).

Electric energy (million kWh): 25,694 in 2007; 28,667 in 2008; 30,426 in 2009 (Source: UN Industrial Commodity Statistics Database).

Finance

CURRENCY AND EXCHANGE RATES

Monetary Units:
1,000 dirhams = 1 Libyan dinar (LD).

Sterling, Dollar and Euro Equivalents (30 April 2013):
£1 sterling = 1.9874 dinars;
US $1 = 1.2804 dinars;
€1 = 1.6737 dinars;
100 Libyan dinars = £50.32 = $78.10 = €59.75.

Average Exchange Rate (Libyan dinar per US $):
2010 1.2668
2011 1.2241
2012 1.2617

BUDGET

(LD million)

Revenue*	2010	2011†	2012†
Hydrocarbon budget allocation	55,713	20,293	71,491
Non-hydrocarbon	5,791	984	3,223
Non-hydrocarbon tax revenue	3,642	699	1,200
Taxes on income and profits	2,248	461	500
Taxes on international trade	1,394	238	700
Non-hydrocarbon non-tax revenue	2,149	285	2,023
Total	61,504	21,277	74,714

Expenditure‡	2010	2011†	2012†
Current	27,553	23,388	47,660
Expenditure on goods and services	8,151	2,780	17,333
Wages and salaries	11,383	14,800	18,924
Subsidies and other current transfers	8,019	4,414	11,400
Capital	24,279	3,503	5,500
Total	51,832	26,891	53,160

* Excluding grants received (LD million): 0 in 2010; 72 in 2011 (estimate); 0 in 2012 (estimate).
† Estimates.
‡ Excluding net lending (LD million): 1,280 in 2008; 1,000 in 2009 (estimate); 30 in 2010 (estimate).

2013 (projections): *Revenue:* Hydrocarbon revenue 83,575; Non-hydrocarbon revenue 4,101 (Tax revenue 1,650, Non-tax revenue 2,451); Total revenue 87,676. *Expenditure:* Current 50,070 (Goods and services 12,717, Wages and salaries 20,746, Subsidies and transfers 16,607); Capital 13,000; Total expenditure 63 070 (excl. net lending 1,500).

Source: IMF, *Libya: 2013 Article IV Consultation* (May 2013).

INTERNATIONAL RESERVES

(US $ million at 31 December)

	2010	2011	2012
Gold (national valuation)	194	158	158
IMF special drawing rights	2,473	2,471	2,480
Reserve position in IMF	372	454	455
Foreign exchange	96,800	101,872	117,984
Total	99,839	104,955	121,077

Source: IMF, *International Financial Statistics*.

MONEY SUPPLY

(LD million at 31 December)

	2010	2011	2012
Currency outside banks	7,609.0	14,840.1	13,397.0
Demand deposits at commercial banks	31,602.2	35,435.3	41,950.7
Total money (incl. others)	40,093.9	50,275.4	56,833.7

Source: IMF, *International Financial Statistics*.

COST OF LIVING

(Consumer Price Index; base 2003 = 100)

	2010	2011	2012
Personal services and others	132.3	162.4	162.9
Medical care	134.0	202.1	217.4
Recreation and education	105.3	110.4	121.9
Transport and communication	136.7	149.2	160.7
Clothing and shoes	106.8	120.8	141.1
Furniture	99.6	122.9	142.9
Housing	109.7	122.6	149.6
Food, beverages and tobacco	153.5	178.5	171.8
All items	129.8	150.4	159.6

NATIONAL ACCOUNTS

(LD million at current prices)

Expenditure on the Gross Domestic Product

	2009	2010	2011
Government final consumption expenditure	9,310.5	11,365.7	16,323.6
Private final consumption expenditure	26,964.7	32,758.4	13,133.5
Gross fixed capital formation	6,861.6	8,380.5	5,241.0
Changes in inventories	287.2	351.0	—
Total domestic expenditure	43,423.9	52,855.6	34,698.1
Exports of goods and services	50,139.0	62,314.3	20,189.3
Less Imports of goods and services	19,902.8	24,399.7	16,481.7
GDP in purchasers' values	73,660.1	90,770.3	38,405.8
GDP at constant 2005 prices	67,994.1	70,825.1	27,450.9

Source: UN National Accounts Main Aggregates Database.

Gross Domestic Product by Economic Activity

	2010	2011†	2012†
Agriculture, forestry and fishing	2,543.6	844.3	928.7
Mining and quarrying (incl. hydrocarbons)	60,969.8	22,332.2	76,932.3
Manufacturing	5,809.5	978.0	3,776.2
Electricity, gas and water	1,420.5	561.2	1,434.7
Construction	8,066.8	1,391.7	1,530.8
Trade, restaurants and hotels	4,607.5	2,923.1	4,875.3
Transport, storage and communications	4,432.1	3,317.7	3,553.3
Financial intermediation	1,262.0	745.9	1,066.7
Real estate, renting and business activities	6,636.4	4,546.7	5,819.8
Education and health, etc.*	316.5	126.9	253.2
Government, defence and mandatory social insurance	7,128.8	12,319.3	17,406.0
Other services	98.2	33.7	98.1
Sub-total	103,291.6	50,120.9	117,675.0
Less Financial intermediation services indirectly measured	753.4	436.0	—
Total	102,538.2	49,684.9	117,675.0

* Private sector only.
† Preliminary figures.

BALANCE OF PAYMENTS
(US $ million)

	2009	2010	2011
Exports of goods	37,055	48,935	12,986
Imports of goods	–22,002	–24,559	–11,200
Balance on goods	15,053	24,376	1,786
Exports of services	385	410	30
Imports of services	–5,063	–6,127	4,435
Balance on goods and services	10,375	18,659	–2,619
Primary income received	2,461	2,318	1,301
Primary income paid	–1,883	–2,348	–800
Balance on goods, services and primary income	10,953	18,629	–2,118
Secondary income (net)	–1,572	–1,828	–681
Current balance	9,381	16,801	–2,799
Direct investment assets	–1,165	–2,722	–257
Direct investment liabilities	1,371	1,784	200
Portfolio investment assets	–3,352	–4,396	–420
Other investment assets	–3,952	–4,889	1,472
Other investment liabilities	1,573	–116	277
Net errors and omissions	1,333	–2,292	687
Reserves and related items	5,188	4,170	–840

Source: IMF, *International Financial Statistics*.

External Trade

PRINCIPAL COMMODITIES
(LD million)

Imports c.i.f.	2009	2010
Food and live animals	1,663.9	2,320.4
Beverages and tobacco	72.8	101.0
Animal and vegetable oils and fats	72.2	82.1
Crude materials (inedible) except fuels	299.6	604.8
Mineral fuels and related materials	151.5	236.1
Chemical materials	1,056.6	1,287.4
Basic manufactures	3,229.7	4,818.8
Machinery and transport equipment	7,968.9	11,031.6
Miscellaneous products	1,540.8	1,894.1
Total	16,060.6	22,376.3

Exports f.o.b.*	2009	2010
Food and live animals	1.4	0.9
Crude materials (inedible) except fuel	1.2	0.8
Mineral fuels and related products	33,353.3	44,854.1
Chemicals and related products	562.2	989.0
Basic manufactures	151.9	351.4
Total (incl. others)	34,070.9	46,196.3

* Including re-exports.

PRINCIPAL TRADING PARTNERS
(LD million)

Imports c.i.f.	2009	2010
Brazil	96.5	541.5
China, People's Republic	1,949.7	2,183.4
Egypt	383.0	791.3
France (incl. Monaco)	300.8	1,117.2
Germany	779.0	1,523.2
Italy	1,157.9	2,106.6
Japan	598.1	895.3
Korea, Republic	1,467.9	2,060.8
Russia	203.1	290.7
Spain	178.3	296.2
Tunisia	711.9	487.1
Turkey	1,463.8	2,370.1
Ukraine	101.9	311.2
United Kingdom	438.1	711.4
USA	830.2	1,178.6
Total (incl. others)	16,060.6	22,376.3

Exports (incl. re-exports) f.o.b.	2009	2010
Brazil	1,140.5	249.9
Canada	721.1	287.9
China, People's Republic	3,811.6	4,319.4
Egypt	252.2	386.3
France (incl. Monaco)	4,091.0	7,178.7
Germany	2,358.3	1,182.4
Greece	1,216.3	2,059.7
India	584.7	638.8
Ireland	322.1	415.7
Italy	11,670.8	19,527.9
Netherlands	747.3	1,558.6
Portugal	543.6	748.8
Spain	2,637.7	4,264.7
Turkey	405.6	244.6
United Kingdom	1,297.1	494.7
USA	598.4	1,161.2
Total (incl. others)	34,070.9	46,196.3

Transport

ROAD TRAFFIC
(motor vehicles in use at 31 December)

	2000	2001
Passenger cars	549,600	552,700
Commercial vehicles	177,400	195,500

Buses and coaches: 1,424 in 1995; 1,490 in 1996.

Motorcycles and mopeds: 1,078 in 1995; 1,112 in 1996.

2007: Passenger cars 1,388,165; Buses and coaches 91,327; Vans and lorries 310,511; Motorcycles and mopeds 36,531.

Sources: IRF, *World Road Statistics*; UN, *Statistical Yearbook*.

SHIPPING

Flag Registered Fleet
(at 31 December)

	2010	2011	2012
Number of vessels	89	82	81
Total displacement ('000 grt)	1,052.0	1,024.3	1,020.5

Source: Lloyd's List Intelligence (www.lloydslistintelligence.com).

International Sea-borne Freight Traffic
(estimates, '000 metric tons)

	1991	1992	1993
Goods loaded	57,243	59,894	62,491
Goods unloaded	7,630	7,710	7,808

Source: UN Economic Commission for Africa, *African Statistical Yearbook*.

CIVIL AVIATION
(traffic on scheduled services)

	2007	2008	2009
Kilometres flown (million)	18	18	18
Passengers carried ('000)	1,204	1,214	1,147
Passenger-km (million)	1,579	1,597	1,521
Total ton-km (million)	140	148	142

Source: UN, *Statistical Yearbook*.

Passengers carried ('000): 2,431 in 2010; 1,896 in 2011 (Source: World Bank, World Development Indicators database).

Tourism

VISITOR ARRIVALS*

Country of origin	2002	2003	2004
Algeria	70,416	71,657	73,459
Egypt	354,189	429,220	441,230
Morocco	19,076	19,120	20,803
Tunisia	329,145	346,331	366,871
Total (incl. others)	857,952	957,896	999,343

* Including same-day visitors (excursionists).

Tourism receipts (US $ million, excl. passenger transport): 50 in 2009; 60 in 2010.

Source: World Tourism Organization.

Communications Media

	2010	2011	2012
Telephones ('000 main lines in use)	1,228.3	1,000.0	814.0
Mobile cellular telephones ('000 subscribers)	10,900.0	10,000.0	9,587.0
Broadband subscribers ('000)	72.8	70.0	67.3

Internet subscribers: 772,500 in 2009.

Source: International Telecommunication Union.

Education

(1995/96, unless otherwise indicated)

	Institutions	Teachers	Students
Primary and preparatory: general	2,733*	122,020	1,333,679
Primary and preparatory: vocational	168	n.a.	22,490
Secondary general	n.a.	17,668	170,573
Secondary teacher training	n.a.	2,760†	23,919
Secondary vocational	312	n.a.	109,074
Universities	13	n.a.	126,348

* 1993/94.

† 1992/93.

Source: partly UNESCO, *Statistical Yearbook*.

1998: 1,160,315 primary school students (Source: World Bank).

Students (UNESCO estimates, 2005/06 unless otherwise indicated): Pre-primary 22,246; Primary 755,338; Secondary 732,614; Tertiary 375,028 (2002/03) (Source: UNESCO Institute for Statistics).

Teachers (UNESCO estimates, 2005/06 unless otherwise indicated): Pre-primary 2,486; Primary 148,476; Secondary 152,338; Tertiary 15,711 (2002/03) (Source: UNESCO Institute for Statistics).

Adult literacy rate (UNESCO estimates): 89.2% (males 95.6%; females 82.7%) in 2010 (Source: UNESCO Institute for Statistics).

Directory

The Constitution

Following the capture of the capital, Tripoli, in August 2011 by forces loyal to the opposition National Transitional Council (NTC), all constitutional decrees approved during the rule of Muammar al-Qaddafi were suspended. A 37-article Constitutional Declaration had been published by the NTC on 3 August. The Declaration states that Libya is a independent democratic state, with Tripoli as its capital and Islam as its state religion. The country is to be organized as a multi-party democracy, with the principles of Islamic law (*Shari'a*) as the principal source of legislation. Under the terms of the Declaration, an interim government was to be installed no more than 30 days after the defeat of Qaddafi, and elections for a 200-member national assembly were to take place no more than 240 days after Qaddafi's ouster.

Elections to a 60-member committee tasked with drafting a new, permanent constitution were expected to be held by early 2014.

The Government

CABINET
(September 2013)

Prime Minister: Dr ALI ZIDAN.

First Deputy Prime Minister: ABD AL-SALAM AL-GHADI.

Second Deputy Prime Minister: (vacant).

Third Deputy Prime Minister: ABDUSSALAM AL-MEHDI AL-QADI.

Minister of Foreign Affairs and of International Co-operation: MUHAMMAD IMHAMID ABD AL-AZIZ.

Minister of Justice: SALAH BASHIR ABAJ MARGANI.

Minister of the Interior: SADIQ ABD AL-KARIM ABD AL-RAHMAN KRIM (ad interim).

Minister of Defence: ABDALLAH AL-THANI.

Minister of Oil: ABD AL-BARI ALI AL-HADI AL-ARUSI.
Minister of Health: NURIDEEN ABD AL-HAMID DAGMAN.
Minister of Finance: Dr AL-KILANI ABD AL-KARIM KILANI AL-JAZI.
Minister of the Economy: MUSTAFA MUHAMMAD ABUFUNAS.
Minister of Religious Affairs: ABD AL-SALAM MUHAMMAD ABUSAAD.
Minister of Water Resources: AL-HADI SULEIMAN HINSHIR.
Minister of Education: ALI OBAID.
Minister of Higher Education and Scientific Research: MUHAMMAD HASSAN ABUBAKER.
Minister of Culture and Civil Society: HABIB MUHAMMAD AL-AMIN.
Minister of Housing and Utilities: ALI HUSSEIN AL-SHARIF.
Minister of Agriculture: SALIH HAMID MAHJOUB.
Minister of Industry: SULAIMAN ALI AL-LATIF AL-FITURI.
Minister of Tourism: IKRAM ABD AL-SALAM BASH IMAM.
Minister of Social Affairs: KAMILA KHAMIS AL-MAZINI.
Minister of Labour and Retraining: MUHAMMAD FITOURI AHMAD SUALIM.
Minister of Transport: ABD AL-QADIR MUHAMMAD AHMAD AL-AYIB.
Minister of the Martyrs and Missing: ALI GADOUR.
Minister of Local Government: ABUBAKER AL-HADI MUHAMMAD.
Minister of Planning: MAHDI ATAHER GENIA.
Minister of Communications and Informatics: OSAMA ABDURAUF SIALA.
Minister of Sports and Youth: ABD AL-SALAM ABDULLAH GUAILA.
Minister of Information: YOUSEF MUHAMMAD SHERIF.
Minister of Electricity: ALI MUHAMMAD MUHAIRIQ.
Minister of State for the Wounded: RAMADAN ALI MANSOUR ZARMUH.

MINISTRIES

Office of the Prime Minister: Tripoli; internet www.pm.gov.ly.

Ministry of Agriculture: Tripoli; e-mail info@agriculture.gov.ly; internet www.agriculture.gov.ly.

Ministry of Communications: Tripoli; tel. (21) 3619011; fax (21) 3622452; e-mail info@cim.gov.ly; internet www.cim.gov.ly.

Ministry of Culture: Tripoli; internet culture.ly.

Ministry of Defence: Tripoli; tel. (21) 4800734; fax (21) 4800168; e-mail info@defense.gov.ly; internet www.defense.gov.ly.

Ministry of Economy: Tripoli; internet www.ect.gov.ly.

Ministry of Education: Tripoli; internet edu.gov.ly.

Ministry of Electricity: Tripoli.

Ministry of Finance: Tripoli.

Ministry of Foreign Affairs and International Co-operation: Tripoli; tel. (21) 3402121; internet www.foreign.gov.ly.

Ministry of Health: Tripoli; tel. (21) 4630704; fax (21) 4630704; internet www.health.gov.ly.

Ministry of Higher Education: Tripoli; tel. (21) 4630209; e-mail scholarship@edu.gov.ly; internet www.higheredu.gov.ly.

Ministry of Housing: Tripoli.

Ministry of Industry: Tripoli.

Ministry of Information: Tripoli.

Ministry of the Interior: Tripoli.

Ministry of Justice: Tripoli; tel. (21) 4808251; e-mail secretary@aladel.gov.ly; internet www.aladel.gov.ly.

Ministry of Labour and Retraining: Tripoli.

Ministry of Local Government: Tripoli.

Ministry of the Martyrs and Missing: Tripoli.

Ministry of Oil: Tripoli.

Ministry of Planning: Tripoli; tel. and fax (21) 4447372; internet www.planning.gov.ly.

Ministry of Religious Affairs: Tripoli.

Ministry of Social Affairs: Tripoli.

Ministry of Sports and Youth: Tripoli.

Ministry of State for the Wounded: Tripoli.

Ministry of Tourism: Tripoli.

Ministry of Transport: Tripoli; internet www.ctt.gov.ly.

Ministry of Water Resources: Tripoli.

Legislature

General National Congress
(Al-Mu'tamar al-Watani al-Amm)
Tripoli Congress Centre, Tripoli; tel. (21) 3622897; fax (21) 3622895; e-mail info@gnc.gov.ly; internet www.gnc.gov.ly.

President: NURI ALI ABU SAHMAIN.

Election, 7 July 2012

	Seats
National Forces Alliance (NFA)	39
Justice and Construction Party (JCP)	17
National Front Party	3
Union for Homeland	2
Wadi Al-Hayat Gathering	2
Central National Current	2
Others	15
Independents	120
Total	200*

* Of the 200 seats, 80 seats were allocated to party lists under a system of proportional representation, while the remaining 120 seats were reserved for individual candidates who were not affiliated to political organizations.

Political Organizations

In June 1971 the Arab Socialist Union (ASU) was established as the country's sole authorized political party. The General National Congress of the ASU held its first session in January 1976 and later became the General People's Congress. Following the ouster of Muammar al-Qaddafi, a number of new political organisations were formed, the most prominent among which have been listed below:

Central National Current: f. 2012.

Justice and Construction Party (JCP): f. 2012; Leader MUHAMMAD SAWAN.

National Forces Alliance (NFA): Tripoli; tel. (21) 4782593; e-mail info@nff.ly; f. 2012; comprises 58 political parties; Leader MAHMOUD JIBRIL; Sec.-Gen. SALAHEDDIN AL-BISHARI.

National Front Party: Tripoli; e-mail info@jabha.ly; internet www.jabha.ly; f. 2012; offshoot of National Front for the Salvation of Libya; Leader MUHAMMAD ALI ABDALLAH.

Union for Homeland: Tripoli; tel. (21) 4445315; fax (21) 4443805; e-mail info@ufh.ly; f. 2012; Leader ABDURRAHMAN SEWEHLI.

Wadi Al-Hayat Gathering: f. 2012.

Diplomatic Representation

EMBASSIES IN LIBYA

Afghanistan: POB 4245, Sharia Mozhar al-Aftes, Tripoli; tel. (21) 4841441; fax (21) 4841443; e-mail tripoli@afghanistan.mfa.net; Ambassador (vacant).

Algeria: Sharia Kairouan 12, Tripoli; tel. (21) 4440025; fax (21) 3334631; Ambassador ABDELHAMID BOUZAHER.

Argentina: POB 932, Gargaresh, Madina Syahia, Tripoli; tel. (21) 4771107; fax (21) 4782105; e-mail elbia@mrecic.gov.ar; Chargé d'affaires a.i. MAURICIO NINE.

Austria: POB 3207, Sharia Khalid ibn al-Walid, Garden City, Tripoli; tel. (21) 4443379; fax (21) 4440838; e-mail tripolis-ob@bmeia.gv.at; internet www.bmeia.gv.at/tripolis; Ambassador FRANZ HÖRLBERGER.

Bangladesh: POB 5086, Hi Damasq, Tripoli; tel. (21) 4911198; fax (21) 4906616; e-mail bdtripoli@yahoo.com; Ambassador (vacant).

Belarus: POB 1530, Tripoli; tel. (21) 3612555; fax (21) 3614298; e-mail libya@belembassy.org; internet libya.mfa.gov.by; Ambassador ANATOLY STEPUS.

Belgium: POB 91650, Jasmin St, Hay Andalus, Tripoli; tel. (21) 4782044; fax (21) 4782046; e-mail tripoli@diplobel.fed.be; internet www.diplomatie.be/tripoli; Ambassador ANDY DETAILLE.

Benin: POB 6676, Sharia Ghout al-Shaal, Tripoli; tel. (21) 4837663; fax (21) 834569; Ambassador LAFIA CHABI.

Bosnia and Herzegovina: POB 6946, Sharia Abd al-Melik bin Kutn, Tripoli; tel. (21) 4774327; fax (21) 4770652; Ambassador IBRAHIM EFENDIĆ.

Brazil: POB 2270, Sharia Ben Ashour, Tripoli; tel. (21) 3614894; fax (21) 3614895; e-mail brcastripoli@ittnet.net; Ambassador AFONSO CARBONAR.

Bulgaria: POB 2945, Sharia Medinat el-Hadaik-Muhammad Farid, Dahra, Tripoli; tel. (21) 3346630; fax (21) 3346633; e-mail embassy.tripoli@mfa.bg; internet www.mfa.bg/embassies/libya; Ambassador VENELIN LAZAROV.

Burkina Faso: POB 81902, Route de Gargaresh, Tripoli; tel. (21) 4771221; fax (21) 4778037; e-mail ambafasolibye@yahoo.fr; Ambassador YOUSSOUF SANGARE.

Burundi: POB 2817, Sharia Ras Hassan, Tripoli; tel. (21) 608848; Ambassador RAPHAËL BITARIHO.

Canada: POB 93392, al-Fateh Tower Post Office, Tripoli; tel. (21) 3351633; fax (21) 3351630; e-mail trpli@international.gc.ca; internet www.canadainternational.gc.ca/libya-libye; Ambassador MICHAEL GRANT.

Chad: POB 1078, Sharia Muhammad Mussadeq 25, Tripoli; tel. (21) 4443955; Ambassador DAOUSSA DÉBY.

China, People's Republic: POB 5329, Sharia Menstir, Andalus, Gargaresh, Tripoli; tel. (21) 4832914; fax (21) 4831877; e-mail chinaemb_ly@mfa.gov.cn; internet ly.china-embassy.org; Ambassador WANG WANGSHENG.

Croatia: Great al-Fatah Towers, Tower 2, 12th Floor, Rm 125, Tripoli; tel. (21) 3351097; fax (21) 3351486; e-mail tripoli@mvep.hr; Ambassador JOHN VEJNOVIĆ.

Cyprus: POB 3284, Wassayat Ebderi, Fashloum, Tripoli; tel. (21) 3622610; fax (21) 3622613; e-mail cyprusembassylibya@gmail.com; Ambassador PERICLES D. STIVAROS.

Czech Republic: POB 1097, Sharia Rewaifaa bin Thabet, Ben Ashour, Tripoli; tel. (21) 3615436; fax (21) 3615437; e-mail tripoli@embassy.mzv.cz; internet www.mzv.cz/tripoli; Ambassador JOSEF KOUTSKÝ.

Egypt: Sharia Omar el-Mokhtar, Tripoli; tel. and fax (21) 3339876; e-mail eg.emb_tripoli@mfa.gov.eg; Ambassador HESHAM ABD EL-WAHAB.

Equatorial Guinea: Tripoli.

Eritrea: POB 91279, Tripoli; tel. (21) 4773568; fax (21) 4780152; Ambassador ABDALLA MUSSA.

France: POB 312, Sharia Ben Khafaja, Hay Andalus, Tripoli; tel. (21) 4770452; fax (21) 4770450; e-mail tripoli-amba@diplomatie.gouv.fr; internet www.ambafrance-ly.org; Ambassador ANTOINE SIVAN.

Germany: POB 302, Sharia Hassan al-Mashai, Tripoli; tel. (21) 4448552; fax (21) 4448968; e-mail info@tripolis.diplo.de; internet www.tripolis.diplo.de; Ambassador RAINER EBERLE.

Ghana: POB 4169, Andalus 21A, nr Funduk Shati Gargaresh, Tripoli; tel. (21) 4772534; fax (21) 4773557; e-mail ghaemb@all-computers.com; Ambassador KODJO HODARI-OKAE.

Greece: POB 5147, Sharia Jalal Bayar 18, Tripoli; tel. (21) 3338563; fax (21) 4441907; e-mail gremb.tri@mfa.gr; internet www.mfa.gr/tripoli; Ambassador KYRIAKOS AMOIRIDIS.

Guinea: POB 10657, Hay Andalus, Tripoli; tel. (21) 4772793; fax (21) 4773441; e-mail magatte@lttnet.net; Ambassador ABDUL AZIZ SOUMAH.

Hungary: POB 4010, Sharia Talha Ben Abdullah, Tripoli; tel. (21) 3618218; fax (21) 3618220; e-mail missions.tpi@kum.hu; Ambassador Dr BÉLA MARTON.

India: POB 3150, Fashloom Area, Nafleen Area, Tripoli; tel. (21) 3409288; fax (21) 3409281; e-mail information@indianembassy.ly; internet indianembassy.ly; Ambassador ANIL TRIGUNAYAT.

Indonesia: POB 5921, Tripoli; tel. (21) 4842067; fax (21) 4842069; e-mail tripoli.kbri@deplu.go.id; internet tripoli.kemlu.go.id; Chargé d'affaires a.i. HERU PRAYITNO.

Iran: POB 6185, Tripoli; tel. (21) 3609552; fax (21) 3611674; e-mail iran_em_tripoli@hotmail.com; Ambassador HOSSEIN AKBARI.

Italy: POB 912, Sharia Vahran 1, Tripoli; tel. (21) 3334131; fax (21) 3331673; e-mail ambasciata.tripoli@esteri.it; internet www.ambtripoli.esteri.it; Ambassador GIUSEPPE BUCCINO GRIMALDI.

Japan: POB 3265, Sharia Jamal al-Din al-Waeli, Hay Andalus, Tripoli; tel. (21) 4781041; fax (21) 4781044; internet www.ly.emb-japan.go.jp; Ambassador TAKASHI ASHIKI.

Korea, Democratic People's Republic: Tripoli; Ambassador KIM TONG JE.

Korea, Republic: POB 4781, Abounawas Area, Sharia Gargaresh, Tripoli; tel. (21) 4831322; fax (21) 4831324; e-mail libya@mofat.go.kr; internet lby.mofat.go.kr; Ambassador CHO DAE-SIK.

Kuwait: POB 2225, Beit al-Mal Beach, Tripoli; tel. (21) 4440281; fax (21) 607053; Ambassador MUBARAK ABDULLAH AL-ADWANI.

Lebanon: POB 927, Malek Ben Auss, Al Noflyeen St, Tripoli; tel. (21) 3615744; fax (21) 3611740; e-mail emblebanon_ly@hotmail.com; Ambassador MUHAMMAD SKEINE.

Lesotho: POB 5771, Hay Andalus, Tripoli; tel. (21) 4840900; fax (21) 4840901; e-mail lesotho-tripoli@foreign.gov.ls; Ambassador MALEFETSANE MOHAFA.

Madagascar: POB 652, al-Maidan Zajeir, Tripoli; tel. (21) 3408257; fax (21) 3408256; e-mail ambamtri@yahoo.fr; Ambassador DIEUDONNÉ MARIE MICHEL RAZAFINDER SIMANIE.

Malaysia: POB 6309, Hay Andalus, Sharia Gargaresh, Tripoli; tel. (21) 4830854; fax (21) 4831496; e-mail maltripoli@kln.gov.my; internet kln.gov.my/web/lby_tripoli; Ambassador MUHAMMAD ZULKEPHLI BIN MUHAMMAD NOOR.

Mali: POB 2008, Sharia Jaraba Saniet Zarrouk, Tripoli; tel. (21) 4444924; Ambassador AMADOU TORÉ.

Malta: POB 2534, Sharia Ubei Ben Ka'ab, Tripoli; tel. (21) 3611181; fax (21) 3611180; e-mail maltaembassy.tripoli@gov.mt; Ambassador VICTOR CAMILLERI.

Mauritania: Sharia Aïssa el-Wakwak, Tripoli; tel. (21) 4443223; Ambassador (vacant).

Morocco: Sharia Ouahchi Ben Harb, Ave Ben Achour, Tripoli; tel. (21) 3617809; fax (21) 3614752; e-mail sifmatripo@hotmail.com; Ambassador MUHAMMAD BELAICH.

Netherlands: POB 3801, Sharia Jalal Bayar 20, Dahra, Tripoli; tel. (21) 4441549; fax (21) 4440386; e-mail tri@minbuza.nl; internet www.hollandembassy-libya.com; Ambassador ANTONIUS LANSINK.

Niger: POB 2251, Fachloun Area, Tripoli; tel. (21) 4443104; Ambassador AMADOU TIDJANI ALI.

Nigeria: POB 4417, Sharia Bashir al-Ibrahim, Tripoli; tel. (21) 4443038; e-mail ambassador@nigeriantripoli.org; internet www.nigeriantripoli.org; Ambassador ISA MUHAMMAD (recalled in March 2010).

Oman: Tripoli; tel. (21) 4772879; fax (21) 4773849; e-mail tripoli@mofa.gov.om; Ambassador Dr QASIM BIN MUHAMMAD BIN SALEM AL-SALEHI.

Pakistan: POB 2169, Sharia al-Jamei, Abu Zaid Dorda Area, Tripoli; tel. (21) 3610937; fax (21) 3600412; e-mail pareptripoli@gmail.com; Ambassador JAMIL AHMED KHAN.

Philippines: POB 12508, Km 7, Sharia Gargaresh, Abu Nawas, Hay Andalus, Tripoli; tel. (21) 4833966; fax (21) 4836158; e-mail tripoli.pe@dfa.gov.ph; Ambassador OSCAR G. ORCINE.

Poland: POB 519, Sharia Ben Ashour 61, Tripoli; tel. (21) 3608569; fax (21) 3615199; e-mail trypolis.amb.sekretariat@msz.gov.pl; internet www.trypolis.msz.gov.pl; Ambassador PIOTR T. CIEĆWIERZ.

Portugal: Zaid Bem Thabet, Sharia Ben Ashour, Tripoli; tel. (21) 3621352; fax (21) 3621351 Ambassador RUI NOGUEIRA LOPES ALEIXO.

Qatar: POB 6312, Libay, Tripoli; tel. (21) 4832431; fax (21) 4836660; e-mail tripoli@mofa.gov.qa; Ambassador Sheikh MUHAMMAD BIN NASSER BIN JASSIM AL THANI.

Romania: POB 5085, Sharia Ali bin Talib, Ben Ashour, Tripoli; tel. (21) 3615295; fax (21) 3607597; e-mail tripoli@mae.ro; Chargé d'affaires a.i. CRISTIAN MITITELU.

Russia: POB 4792, Sharia Mustapha Kamel, Tripoli; tel. (21) 3330545; fax (21) 4446673; e-mail embr@mail.ru; Ambassador IVAN MOLOTKOV.

Rwanda: POB 6677, Villa Ibrahim Musbah Missalati, Andalus, Tripoli; tel. (21) 72864; fax (21) 70317; Chargé d'affaires CHRISTOPHE HABIMANA.

Saudi Arabia: POB 2551, Sharia Kairouan 2, Tripoli; tel. (21) 3330485; fax (21) 4447180; e-mail lyemb@mofa.gov.sa; Ambassador MUHAMMAD MAHMOUD AL-ALI.

Senegal: POB 6392, el-Arabia Gotchalle 246/5, Gargaresh, Tripoli; tel. (21) 4836090; fax (21) 4838955; e-mail ambassene.tripoli@stcc.presidence.sn; Chargé d'affaires a.i. DIAME SARR.

Serbia: POB 1037, Abdalla Ben Salam St, Ben Ashour Area, Tripoli; tel. (21) 3623205; fax (21) 3623207; e-mail serbianembassy_tripoli@yahoo.com; internet www.tripoli.mfa.gov.rs; Ambassador OLIVER POTEZICA.

Sierra Leone: Tripoli; Ambassador Al-Haji ABUBAKARR JALLOH.

Slovakia: POB 5721, Km 3, Gargaresh, Hay Andalus, Tripoli; tel. (21) 4781388; fax (21) 4781387; e-mail slovembtrp@slovembtrp.com; Ambassador (vacant).

Spain: POB 2302, Sharia el-Amir Abd al-Kader al-Jazairi 36, Tripoli; tel. (21) 3620051; fax (21) 3620061; e-mail emb.tripoli@maec.es; internet www.maec.es/embajadas/tripoli; Ambassador JOSÉ RIERA SIQUIER.

Sudan: POB 1076, Sharia Gargaresh, Tripoli; tel. (21) 4775387; fax (21) 4774781; e-mail sudtripoli@hotmail.com; Ambassador Haj MAJED SUWAR.

Switzerland: POB 439, Sharia el-Moussawer Ben Maghzamah, off Sharia Ben Ashour, Tripoli; tel. (21) 3614118; fax (21) 3614238; e-mail tri.vertretung@eda.admin.ch; internet www.eda.admin.ch/tripoli; Ambassador MICHEL GOTTRET.

Syria: POB 4219, Sharia Muhammad Rashid Reda 4, Tripoli (Relations Office); tel. (21) 3331783; fax (21) 3339030; Ambassador HILAL AL-ATRASH.

Togo: POB 3420, Sharia Khaled ibn al-Walid, Tripoli; tel. (21) 4449565; fax (21) 3332423.

Tunisia: POB 613, Sharia el-Bashir Ibrahimi, Medinat el-Hadaik, Tripoli; tel. (21) 3331051; fax (21) 4447600; Ambassador RIDHA BOUKADI.

Turkey: POB 947, Sharia Zaviya Dahmani, Tripoli; tel. (21) 3401140; fax (21) 3401146; e-mail embassy.tripoli@mfa.gov.tr; internet tripoli.emb.mfa.gov.tr; Ambassador ALI KEMAL AYDIN.

Uganda: POB 80215, Ben Achour, Sharia Jaraba, Tripoli; tel. (21) 3603083; fax (21) 3634471; e-mail info@ugembassylibya.org; Ambassador MOSES KIWA SEBUNYA.

Ukraine: POB 4544, Sharia Dhil, Ben Ashour, Tripoli; tel. (21) 3608665; fax (21) 3608666; e-mail emb_ly@mfa.gov.ua; internet www.mfa.gov.ua/libya; Ambassador MYKOLA NAHORNYI.

United Kingdom: 24th Floor, Tripoli Towers (formerly Bourj al-Fateh), Tripoli; tel. (21) 3351084; fax (21) 3403648; e-mail tripoli.press@fco.gov.uk; internet ukinlibya.fco.gov.uk; Ambassador MICHAEL ARON.

USA: Sidi Slim Area, Sharia Wali al-Ahed, Tripoli; tel. (91) 2203239; e-mail tripolipao@state.gov; internet libya.usembassy.gov; Ambassador DEBORAH K. JONES.

Venezuela: POB 2584, Sharia Ben Ashour, Jamaa al-Sagaa Bridge, Tripoli; tel. (21) 3600408; fax (21) 3600407; e-mail embavenezlibia@hotmail.com; Ambassador AFIF TAJELDINE.

Viet Nam: POB 587, Sharia Gargaresh, Tripoli; tel. (21) 4901456; fax (21) 4901499; e-mail dsqvnlib@yahoo.com; internet www.vietnamembassy-libya.org; Ambassador DAO DUY TIEN.

Yemen: POB 4839, Sharia Ubei Ben Ka'ab 36, Tripoli; tel. (21) 607472; Ambassador AHMAD ABDULLAH AL-MAJIDI.

Judicial System

The judicial system under the rule of Muammar al-Qaddafi was composed, in order of seniority, of the Supreme Court, Courts of Appeal, and Courts of First Instance and Summary Courts.

Supreme Court: The judgments of the Supreme Court are final. It is composed of the President and several Justices. Its judgments are issued by circuits of at least three Justices (the quorum is three). The Court hears appeals from the Courts of Appeal in civil, penal, administrative and civil status matters; Chief Justice KAMAL DHAN.

Courts of Appeal: These courts settle appeals from Courts of First Instance; the quorum is three Justices. Each court of appeal has a court of assize.

Courts of First Instance and Summary Courts: These courts are first-stage courts in the Jamahiriya, and the cases heard in them are heard by one judge. Appeals against summary judgments are heard by the appellate court attached to the court of first instance, the quorum of which is three judges.

Attorney-General: ABD AL-AZIZ AL-HASAIRI.

Religion

ISLAM

The vast majority of Libyan Arabs follow Sunni Muslim rites, although Qaddafi rejected the Sunnah (i.e. the practice, course, way, manner or conduct of the Prophet Muhammad, as followed by Sunnis) as a basis for legislation.

Grand Mufti of Libya: Sheikh SADEQ AL-GHARIANI.

CHRISTIANITY

The Roman Catholic Church

Libya comprises three Apostolic Vicariates and one Apostolic Prefecture.

Apostolic Vicariate of Benghazi: POB 248, Benghazi; tel. and fax (61) 9081599; e-mail apostvicar@yahoo.com; Vicar Apostolic Mgr SYLVESTER CARMEL MAGRO (Titular Bishop of Salde).

Apostolic Vicariate of Tripoli: POB 365, Dahra, Tripoli; tel. (21) 3331863; fax (21) 3334696; e-mail bishoptripolibya@hotmail.com; internet www.catholicinlibya.com; Vicar Apostolic Mgr GIOVANNI INNOCENZO MARTINELLI (Titular Bishop of Tabuda).

The Anglican Communion

Within the Episcopal Church in Jerusalem and the Middle East, Libya forms part of the diocese of Egypt (q.v.).

Other Christian Churches

The Coptic Orthodox Church is represented in Libya.

The Press

Under the rule of Muammar al-Qaddafi, most newspapers and periodicals were published either by the Jamahiriya News Agency (JANA), by government secretariats, by the Press Service or by trade unions.

DAILIES

Al-Fajr al-Jadid (The New Dawn): POB 91291, Press Bldg, Sharia al-Jamahiriya, Tripoli; tel. (21) 3606393; fax (21) 3605728; e-mail info@alfajraljadeed.com; f. 1969; publ. by JANA; also publishes bi-monthly English version; Editor AOUN ABDULLAH MADI.

Al-Jamahiriya: POB 4814, Tripoli; tel. (21) 3605731; e-mail info@aljamahiria.com; f. 1980; Arabic; political.

Al-Shams: POB 82331, Al-Sahafa Bldg, Sharia al-Jamhouria, Tripoli; tel. (21) 4442524; fax (21) 609315; e-mail info@alshames.com; Editor MUHAMMAD M. IBRAHIM.

Az-Zahf al-Akhdar (The Green March): POB 14273, Al-Sahafa Bldg, Sharia al-Jamhouria, Tripoli; tel. (21) 4776890; fax (21) 4772502; e-mail info@azzahfalakhder.com; f. 1980; Editor-in-Chief HAMID ABU SALIM.

PERIODICALS

Al-Amal (Hope): POB 4845, Tripoli; e-mail info@alamalmag.com; internet www.alamalmag.com; monthly; social, for children; publ. by the Press Service.

Al-Daawa al-Islamia (Islamic Call): POB 2682, Sharia Sawani, Km 5, Tripoli; tel. (21) 4800294; fax (21) 4800293; f. 1980; weekly (Wed.); Arabic, English, French; cultural; publ. by the World Islamic Call Society; Eds MUHAMMAD IMHEMED AL-BALOUSHI, ABDULAHI MUHAMMAD ABD AL-JALEEL.

Economic Bulletin: POB 2303, Tripoli; tel. (21) 3337106; monthly; publ. by JANA.

Al-Jarida al-Rasmiya (The Official Newspaper): Tripoli; irregular; official state gazette.

Libyan Arab Republic Gazette: Tripoli; weekly; English.

Risalat al-Jihad (Holy War Letter): POB 2682, Tripoli; tel. (21) 3331021; f. 1983; monthly; Arabic, English, French; publ. by the World Islamic Call Society.

Scientific Bulletin: POB 2303, Tripoli; tel. (21) 3337106; monthly; publ. by JANA.

Al-Thaqafa al-Arabiya (Arab Culture): POB 4587, Tripoli; f. 1973; weekly; cultural; circ. 25,000.

The Tripoli Post: 32, 2nd Floor, Tripoli Tower, Tripoli; tel. and fax (21) 3351740; e-mail editor@tripolipost.com; internet www.tripolipost.com; f. 1999; weekly; English; privately owned; Editor-in-Chief Dr SAID LASWAD.

Al-Usbu al-Thaqafi (The Cultural Week): POB 4845, Tripoli; weekly.

Al-Watan al-Arabi al-Kabir (The Greater Arab Homeland): Tripoli; f. 1987.

Publishers

Al-Dar al-Arabia Lilkitab (Maison Arabe du Livre): POB 3185, Tripoli; tel. (21) 4447287; f. 1973 by Libya and Tunisia.

Al-Dar al-Hikma Publishing House: Tripoli; tel. (21) 3606571; fax (21) 3606610; e-mail info@elgabooks.com.

Al-Fatah University, General Administration of Libraries, Printing and Publications: POB 13543, Tripoli; tel. (21) 4628034; fax (21) 4625045; e-mail m.alfituri@hotmail.com; f. 1955; academic books.

General Co for Publishing, Advertising and Distribution: POB 921, Sirte (Surt); tel. (54) 63170; fax (54) 62100; general, educational and academic books in Arabic and other languages; makes and distributes advertisements throughout Libya.

Ghouma Publishing: POB 80092, Tripoli; tel. (21) 3630864; e-mail ghoumapub@hotmail.com; f. 1993; book publishing, distribution and art production; Gen. Man. MUSTAFA FETOURI.

Broadcasting and Communications

TELECOMMUNICATIONS

General Telecommunications Authority (GTA): POB 866, Sharia Zawia, Tripoli; e-mail info@gta.ly; internet www.gta.ly; f. 2006; supervisory body.

General Directorate of Posts and Telecommunications: POB 81686, Tripoli; tel. (21) 3604101; fax (21) 3604102; Dir-Gen. ABU ZAID JUMA AL-MANSURI.

General Post and Telecommunications Co (GPTC): POB 886, Sharia Zawia, Tripoli; tel. (21) 3617945; fax (21) 3619011; internet www.gptc.ly; f. 1984; operates and develops the postal and telecommunications networks; subsidiaries include Libyana Mobile Phone Co and Al-Madar Al-Jadeed (mobile cellular telecommunications operators), and Libya Telecom and Technology (internet service provider); Chair. (vacant).

Libyana Mobile Phone Co: POB 90071, Tripoli; tel. (21) 3406555; internet www.libyana.ly; f. 2004.

Al-Madar Al-Jadeed: Tripoli; internet www.almadar.ly; f. 1997; mobile telecommunications network operator; 1.2m. subscribers; Chief Exec. ABD AL-KHALEK BIN ASHOUR.

BROADCASTING

Radio

Great Socialist People's Libyan Arab Jamahiriya Broadcasting Corporation: POB 80237, Tripoli; tel. (21) 3402107; fax (21) 3403468; e-mail info@en.ljbc.net; internet www.ljbc.net; f. 1968; broadcasts in Arabic; additional satellite channel broadcast for 18 hours a day from 1982; Sec.-Gen. ABDULLAH MANSOUR.

Voice of Africa: POB 4677, Sharia al-Fateh, Tripoli; tel. (21) 4449209; fax (21) 4449875; f. 1973 as Voice of the Greater Arab Homeland; adopted current name in 1998; broadcasts in Arabic, French, English, Swahili and Hausa; Dir-Gen. ABDULLAH AL-MEGRI.

Television

People's Revolution Broadcasting TV: POB 80237, Tripoli; tel. (21) 3402107; fax (21) 3403468; e-mail info@en.ljbc.net; internet www.ljbc.net; f. 1957; broadcasts in Arabic; additional satellite channels broadcast for limited hours in English; Dir ABDULLAH MANSOUR.

Finance

(cap. = capital; res = reserves; dep. = deposits; m. = million; br(s) = branch(es); amounts in Libyan dinars, unless otherwise stated)

BANKING

The Libyan banking sector, hitherto highly state-controlled, was undergoing restructure in the late 2000s. Minority stakes in two state-owned commercial banks were sold to foreign banking interests in 2007–08. It was announced in early 2010 that the Central Bank of Libya (CBL) was to grant two licences to foreign banks for the creation of joint venture banking operations with Libyan investors. However, in August the CBL announced that it had decided to grant just one licence, to UniCredit (Italy); bids from two other European banks and three from the Gulf region were rejected.

Central Bank

Central Bank of Libya (CBL): POB 1103, Sharia al-Malik Seoud, Tripoli; tel. (21) 3333591; fax (21) 4441488; e-mail info@cbl.gov.ly; internet www.cbl.gov.ly; f. 1955 as Nat. Bank of Libya; name changed to Bank of Libya 1963, to Cen. Bank of Libya 1977; state-owned; bank of issue and central bank carrying govt accounts and operating exchange control; commercial operations transferred to Nat. Commercial Bank 1970; cap. 500m., res 909m., dep. 108,079m. (Dec. 2009); Gov. and Chair. SADDEK EL-KABER.

Other Banks

Alwafa Bank: POB 84212, Sharia Alfallah, Tripoli; tel. (21) 4815123; fax (21) 4801247; e-mail info@alwafabank.com; internet www.alwafabank.com; f. 2003; private bank; Chair. and Gen. Man. HADI M. GITELI.

Jumhouria Bank: POB 685, Sharia Omar el-Mokhtar, Tripoli; tel. and fax (21) 4442541; e-mail info@jbank.ly; internet www.jbank.ly; f. 1969 as successor to Barclays Bank Int. in Libya; originally known as Masraf al-Gumhouria; name changed as above 2000; merger with Umma Bank SAL completed mid-2008; cap. 1,000m., res 39m., dep. 19,817m. (Dec. 2009); Chair. MOSBAH MUHAMMAD EL-AKKARI; Gen. Man. AHMED OMAR RAJAB MUHAMMAD; 122 brs.

Libyan Foreign Bank: POB 2542, Tower 2, Dat al-Imad Complex, Tripoli; tel. (21) 3350155; fax (21) 3350164; e-mail it@lafbank.com; internet www.lafbank.com; f. 1972 as Libyan Arab Foreign Bank; present name adopted 2005; 'offshore' bank wholly owned by Cen. Bank of Libya; cap. US $2,000m., res $573m., dep. $10,166m. (Dec. 2009); Chair. Dr AHMED A. HODANA; Gen. Man. MUHAMMAD M. BEN YOUSUF.

National Commercial Bank SAL: POB 543, Aruba Ave, al-Baida; tel. (21) 3610306; fax (21) 3612267; e-mail ncbly@lttnet.net; internet www.ncb.ly; f. 1970 to take over commercial banking division of Cen. Bank (then Bank of Libya) and brs of Aruba Bank and Istiklal Bank; wholly owned by Cen. Bank; cap. 100m., res 4,685m., dep. 6,317m. (Dec. 2008); Chair. ABD AL-WAHAB MUKHTAR; Gen. Man. SULEIMAN AZZABI; 63 brs.

Sahara Bank SPI: POB 70, Sharia 1 September, Tripoli; tel. (21) 3340663; fax (21) 4443836; e-mail sahbankgm1@lttnet.net; internet saharabank.com.ly; f. 1964 to take over br. of Banco di Sicilia; the Govt sold a 19% stake to BNP Paribas (France) in July 2007; cap. and res 208.2m., total assets 1,951.8m. (March 2003); Chair. and Gen. Man. Dr ABD AL-LATIF ABD AL-HAFIZ EL-KIB; CEO CLAUDE RUFIN; 48 brs.

Wahda Bank: POB 452, Sharia Gamal Abd al-Nasser, Benghazi; tel. (61) 2224256; fax (21) 2224122; e-mail wahda@wahdabank.com; internet www.wahdabank.com; f. 1970 to take over Bank of North Africa, Commercial Bank SAL, Nahda Arabia Bank, Société Africaine de Banque SAL, and Kafila al-Ahly Bank; 19% stake acquired by Arab Bank PLC (Jordan) in February 2008; remainder owned by Cen. Bank of Libya; cap. 108m., res 115m., dep. 7,062m. (Dec. 2009); Chair. AHMAD R. ABD AL-AZIZ; 76 brs.

STOCK EXCHANGE

Libyan Stock Market: Sharia Omar el-Mokhtar, Tripoli; tel. (21) 3365026; fax (61) 9091097; e-mail info@lsm.gov.ly; internet www.lsm.ly; f. 2007; Sec. SULIMAN SALEM AL-SHOHOMIY.

INSURANCE

Libya Insurance Co: POB 80087, Aman Bldg, Sharia al-Taha, Tripoli; tel. (21) 4441499; fax (21) 4444176; e-mail infolt@libtamin.com; internet www.libtamin.com; f. 1964; merged with Al-Mukhtar Insurance Co in 1981; all classes of insurance; Man. ALI AMAR AL-RAGAYEE.

Trade and Industry

There are state trade and industrial organizations responsible for the running of industries at all levels, which supervise production, distribution and sales. There are also central bodies responsible for the power generation industry, agriculture, land reclamation and transport.

GOVERNMENT AGENCIES

Council for Oil and Gas Affairs: Tripoli; f. 2006; holds ultimate responsibility for all matters involving oil, gas and their by-products.

Great Man-made River Water Utilization Authority (GMRA): POB 7217, Benghazi; tel. (61) 2230392; fax (61) 2230393; e-mail info@gmrwua.com; internet www.gmrwua.com; supervises construction of pipeline carrying water to the Libyan coast from beneath the Sahara desert, to provide irrigation for agricultural projects; Sec. for the Great Man-made River Project ABD AL-MAJID AL-AOUD.

Libyan Investment Authority (LIA): Tripoli; e-mail info@lia.ly; internet www.lia.ly; f. 2006, operations commenced 2007; sovereign wealth fund managing state-allocated assets, including Oil Reserve Fund; Chair. Dr ABD AL-HAFID MAHMOUD ZLITNI.

National Economic Development Board (NEDB): Tripoli; internet www.nedb.ly; f. 2007; charged with the drafting and execution of reform campaigns, and the facilitation of decision-making and action on critical economic issues.

DEVELOPMENT ORGANIZATIONS

Arab Organization for Agricultural Development: POB 12898, Zohra, Tripoli; tel. and fax (21) 3619275; e-mail arabagri@lycos.com; internet www.aoad.org; responsible for agricultural devt projects.

General National Organization for Industrialization: Sharia San'a, Tripoli; tel. (21) 3334995; f. 1970; public org. responsible for the devt of industry.

Kufra and Sarir Authority: Council of Agricultural Development, Benghazi; f. 1972 to develop the Kufra oasis and Sarir area in south-eastern Libya.

CHAMBERS OF COMMERCE

Benghazi Chamber of Commerce, Trade, Industry and Agriculture: POB 208 and 1286, Benghazi; tel. (61) 3372319; fax (61) 3380761; f. 1956; Pres. Dr BADIA; Gen. Man. Dr TAREK TARBAGHIA; 150,000 mems.

Tripoli Chamber of Commerce and Industry: POB 2321, Sharia Najed 6–8, Tripoli; tel. (21) 3336855; fax (21) 3332655; f. 1952; Chair. MUHAMMAD KANOON; Dir-Gen. ABD AL-MONEM H. BURAWI; 30,000 mems.

UTILITIES

Electricity

General Electricity Company of Libya (GECOL): POB 668, Tripoli; tel. (21) 4445068; fax (21) 4447023; e-mail gecol@gecol.net; internet www.gecol.ly; Sec. of Management Cttee Eng. ABU AL-GHASSIM ONEAS.

STATE HYDROCARBONS COMPANIES

Until 1986 petroleum affairs in Libya were dealt with primarily by the Secretariat of the General People's Committee for Petroleum. This body was abolished in March 1986, and sole responsibility for the administration of the petroleum industry passed to the national companies that were already in existence. The Secretariat of the General People's Committee for Petroleum was re-established in March 1989 and incorporated into the new Secretariat for the General People's Committee for Energy in October 1992. This was dissolved in March 2000, and responsibility for local oil policy was transferred to the National Oil Corporation, under the supervision of the General People's Committee. From 1973 the Libyan Government entered into participation agreements with some of the foreign oil companies (concession holders), and nationalized others. It concluded 85%:15% production-sharing agreements with various oil companies.

National Oil Corporation (NOC): POB 2655, Sharia Bashier Sadawi, Tripoli; tel. (21) 3337141; fax (21) 3331390; e-mail info@noclibya.com; internet en.noclibya.com.ly; f. 1970 to: undertake jt ventures with foreign cos; build and operate refineries, storage tanks, petrochemical facilities, pipelines and tankers; take part in arranging specifications for local and imported petroleum products; participate in general planning of oil installations in Libya; market crude and refined petroleum and petrochemical products; and establish and operate oil terminals; Chair. and Dir-Gen. NURI BERRUIEN.

Arabian Gulf Oil Co (AGOCO): POB 263, Benghazi; tel. (61) 28931; fax (21) 49031; wholly owned subsidiary of the NOC; Chair. AHMAD MAJBRI.

Oilinvest International NV: Tripoli; f. 1988; wholly owned subsidiary of the NOC; Libya's foreign oil investment arm; Chair. and Gen. Man. AHMAD ABD AL-KARIM AHMAD.

Agip North Africa and Middle East Ltd—Libyan Branch: POB 346, Tripoli; tel. and fax (21) 3335135; Sec. of People's Cttee OMAR AL-SWEIFI.

Azzawiya Oil Refining Co (ARC): POB 6451, Tripoli; tel. (23) 610539; fax (23) 610543; e-mail infoazzawiya@azzawiyaoil.com; internet www.azzawiyaoil.com; f. 1976; Gen. Man. AL-MOAMARE A. SWEDAN.

Brega Oil Marketing Co: POB 402, Sharia Bashir al-Saidawi, Tripoli; tel. (21) 4440830; f. 1971; Chair. Dr DOKALI B. AL-MEGHARIEF.

International Oil Investments Co: Tripoli; f. 1988, with initial capital of US $500m. to acquire 'downstream' facilities abroad; Chair. MUHAMMAD AL-JAWAD.

National Drilling and Workover Co: POB 1454, 208 Sharia Omar Mukhtar, Tripoli; tel. (21) 3332411; f. 1986; Chair. IBRAHIM BAHI.

Ras Lanouf Oil and Gas Processing Co (RASCO): POB 1971, Ras Lanuf, Benghazi; tel. (21) 3605177; fax (21) 607924; f. 1978; Chair. ABULKASIM M. A. ZWARY.

Sirte Oil Co: POB 385, Marsa el-Brega, Tripoli; tel. (21) 607261; fax (21) 601487; internet www.soc.com.ly; f. 1955 as Esso Standard Libya, taken over by Sirte Oil Co 1982; absorbed Nat. Petrochemicals Co in Oct. 1990; exploration, production of crude petroleum, gas and petrochemicals, liquefaction of natural gas; Chair. ABD AL-BASET TAHER AL-REFAE.

Umm al-Jawaby Petroleum Co: POB 693, Tripoli; Chair. and Gen. Man. MUHAMMAD TENTTOUSH.

Waha Oil Co: POB 395, Tripoli; tel. (21) 3331116; fax (21) 3337169; e-mail infowaha@wahaoil.com; internet www.wahaoil.net; Chair. Dr BASHEER MUHAMMAD ELASHAHAB.

Zueitina Oil Co (ZOC): POB 2134, Tripoli; tel. (21) 3338011; fax (21) 3339109; e-mail info@zueitina-ly.com; f. 1986; Chair. of Management Cttee BASHIR BAZAZI.

TRADE UNIONS

General Federation of Producers' Trade Unions: POB 734, Sharia Istanbul 2, Tripoli; tel. (21) 4446011; f. 1952; affiliated to ITUC; Sec.-Gen. BASHIR IHWIJ; 17 trade unions with 700,000 mems.

General Union for Oil and Petrochemicals: Tripoli; Chair. MUHAMMAD MITHNANI.

Pan-African Federation of Petroleum Energy and Allied Workers: Tripoli; affiliated to the Organisation of African Trade Union Unity.

Transport

Department of Road Transport and Railways: POB 14527, Sharia al-Zawiyah, Tripoli; tel. and fax (21) 3605808; Dir-Gen. (Projects and Research) MUHAMMAD ABU ZIAN.

RAILWAYS

There are, at present, no railways in Libya. In 1998, however, the Government invited bids for the construction of a 3,170-km railway, comprising one branch, 2,178 km in length, running from north to south, and another, 992 km in length, running from east to west along the north coast. The railway may eventually be linked to other North African rail networks. Russian Railways OAO was awarded the contract to build a 554-km section of the network between Sirte and Benghazi in April 2008; construction work commenced in August. In 2008–09 a Chinese company was awarded contracts for a further three sections.

Railway Executive Board: POB 41758, Alkhoms, Tripoli; tel. (21) 3609486; fax (21) 626054; e-mail info@libyanrailways.com; oversees the planning and construction of railways; Sec. SAEED RASHID.

ROADS

The most important road is the 1,822-km national coast road from the Tunisian to the Egyptian border, passing through Tripoli and Benghazi. It has a second link between Barce and Lamluda, 141 km in length. Another national road runs from a point on the coastal road 120 km south of Misurata through Sabha to Ghat near the Algerian border (total length 1,250 km). There is a branch 247 km long running from Vaddan to Sirte. A 690-km road, connecting Tripoli and Sabha, and another 626 km long, from Ajdabiya in the north to Kufra in the south-east, were opened in 1983. The Tripoli–Ghat section (941 km) of the third, 1,352-km national road was opened in September 1984. There is a road crossing the desert from Sabha to the frontiers of Chad and Niger. As part of a wide-ranging agreement signed by Libya and Italy in August 2008, the latter agreed to fund construction of a new coastal motorway between the Tunisian and Egyptian borders. Construction work on the project commenced in mid-2009. In addition to the national highways, the west of Libya has about 1,200 km of paved and macadamized roads and the east about 500 km. All the towns and villages of Libya, including the desert oases, are accessible by motor vehicle. In 2001 Libya had an estimated total road network of 83,200 km, of which 57,200 km was paved.

SHIPPING

The principal ports are Tripoli, Benghazi, Mersa Brega, Misurata and al-Sider. Zueitina, Ras Lanuf, Mersa Hariga, Mersa Brega and al-Sider are mainly oil ports. A pipeline connects the Zelten oilfields with Mersa Brega. Another pipeline joins the Sarir oilfield with Mersa Hariga, and the port of Tobruk, and a pipeline from the Sarir field to Zueitina was opened in 1968. A port is being developed at Darnah, and plans were under way for the expansion of the port of Sirte. Libya also has the use of Tunisian port facilities at Sand Gabès, to alleviate congestion at Tripoli. At 31 December 2012 Libya's flag registered fleet consisted of 81 vessels, with a combined displacement of 1,020,450 grt, of which 12 were fish carriers, two were gas tankers and two were general cargo ships.

Principal Shipping Companies

General National Maritime Transport Co (GNMTC): POB 80173, el-Shaab Terminal, Tripoli; tel. and fax (21) 4843271; e-mail info@gnmtc.com; internet www.gnmtc.com; f. 1975 to handle all projects dealing with maritime trade; state-owned; Chair. Capt. ALI BELHAG AHMED.

Libya Shipping Agency: POB 4288, Abu Seta area, nr Abokmisha Mosque, Tripoli; tel. (21) 3402528; fax (21) 3403496; e-mail info@libyashipping.com; internet www.libyashipping.com; provides chartering, land transportation and customs clearance services; Gen. Man. IMAD FELLAH.

CIVIL AVIATION

There are four international airports: Tripoli International Airport, situated at Ben Gashir, 34 km (21 miles) from Tripoli; Benina Airport 19 km (12 miles) from Benghazi; Sabha Airport; and Misurata Airport. There are a further 10 regional airports. A US $800m. programme to improve the airport infrastructure and air traffic control network was approved in mid-2001. In the mid-2000s plans were announced for the upgrade and expansion of Tripoli International Airport, which were to include the construction of two new terminals, following which the airport's annual passenger capacity was expected to increase to some 20m., compared with 3m. in 2007. Work on the project commenced in September 2007 and was scheduled for completion by 2011. However, progress was halted owing to the outbreak of conflict in February of that year. In April 2012 the National Transitional Council formally regained control of Tripoli International Airport.

Civil Aviation Authority: Tripoli; tel. (21) 3605318; fax (21) 3605322; e-mail info@caa.ly; internet www.lycaa.org; Gen. Dir ABD AL-RAZZAK ZAATUT.

Afriqiyah Airways: 1st Floor, Waha Bldg, Sharia Omar al-Mokhtar, Tripoli; tel. (21) 4449734; fax (21) 4449128; e-mail customerservice@afriqiyah.aero; internet www.afriqiyah.aero; f. 2001; state-owned; flights to 29 destinations in Africa, Asia, Europe and the Middle East; Chair. Capt. SABRI SAAD ABDALLAH SHADI; CEO RAMMAH ETTIR.

Buraq Air: Tripoli International Airport, Tripoli; e-mail lias@buraqair.com; internet www.buraqair.com; f. 2001; first privately owned Libyan airline; scheduled international passenger and cargo flights to Egypt, Morocco, Syria and Turkey; domestic flights from Tripoli, Benghazi and Sabha; Chair. and Man. Dir Capt. MUHAMMAD A. BUBEIDA.

Libyan Airlines: POB 2555, Ben Fernas Bldg, Sharia Haiti, Tripoli; tel. (21) 3614102; fax (21) 3614815; e-mail i.alwani@ln.aero; internet www.libyanairlines.aero; f. 1964 as Kingdom of Libya Airlines; reorg. in 1975 as Libyan Arab Airline; present name adopted 2006; passenger and cargo services from Tripoli, Benghazi and Sabha to destinations in Europe, North Africa, the Middle East and Asia; domestic services throughout Libya; Chair. and CEO Capt. MUHAMMAD M. IBSEM.

Tourism

The principal attractions for visitors to Libya are Tripoli, with its beaches and annual International Fair, the ancient Roman towns of Sabratha, Leptis Magna and Cyrene, and historic oases. There were 999,343 visitor arrivals in 2004; in 2010 receipts from tourism totalled US $60m., excluding passenger transport.

General Board of Fairs: POB 891, Sharia Omar Mukhtar, Tripoli; tel. (21) 3332255; fax (21) 4448385; e-mail info@gbf.com.ly; internet gbf.com.ly; Head of Fairs GAMAL N. A. AL-AMOUSHI.

General Board of Tourism and Traditional Industries: POB 82063, Tripoli; tel. (21) 3334673; fax (21) 4445336; e-mail info@libyan-tourism.net; internet www.libyan-tourism.org; Chair. MUHAMMAD SEALNA.

Defence

The Libyan National Army was founded in 2011 by the National Transitional Council after the overthrow of Muammar al-Qaddafi's regime. A restructuring process continued in 2013.

Chief of Staff of Armed Forces: Gen. SALIM AL-GNAIDI.

Chief of Staff of Air Force: Brig. AHMED HABIB AL-MISMARI (acting).

Chief of Staff of Naval Force: Cdre HASSAN ALI BUSHNAK.

Estimated Defence Expenditure (2012): LD 3,770m.

Military Service: selective conscription; 1–2 years.

Total Armed Forces (as assessed at November 2010): 76,000: army 50,000, incl. (estimated) 25,000 conscripts; navy 8,000; air force 18,000.

People's Militia: (estimated) 40,000.

Education

Education is officially compulsory for nine years between six and 15 years of age. Primary education begins at the age of six and lasts for nine years. Secondary education, beginning at 15 years of age, lasts for a further three or four years. In 2005/06 some 755,338 students were enrolled in primary education. At the secondary level there were 732,614 students in the same year. The teaching of French was abolished in Libyan schools in 1983. Libya also has institutes for agricultural, technical and vocational training, of which there were 84 in 2004.

In 1958 the University of Libya opened in Benghazi with Faculties of Arts and Commerce, followed the next year by the Faculty of Science, near Tripoli. Faculties of Law, Agriculture, Engineering, Teacher Training, and Arabic Language and Islamic Studies have since been added to the University. In 1973 the University was divided into two parts, to form the Universities of Tripoli and Benghazi, later renamed Al-Fatah and Ghar Younis universities. The Faculty of Education at Al-Fatah University became Sabha University in 1983. There is a University of Technology (Bright Star) at Mersa Brega and the Al-Arab Medical University at Benghazi. In 1995 the number of public universities had reached 13. In 2002/03 some 375,028 students were enrolled in tertiary education. The Government's budget for 2012 allocated LD 4,600m. (equivalent to 6.7% of total spending) to the Ministry of Education.

Bibliography

Ahmida, Ali Abd al-Latif. *Forgotten Voices: Power and Agency in Colonial and Postcolonial Libya*. London, Routledge, revised edn, 2005.

The Making of Modern Libya: State Formation, Colonization and Resistance. Albany, NY, State University of New York Press, 2nd edn, 2011.

Allan, J. A. *Libya: The Experience of Oil*. London, Croom Helm, 1981.

Ansell, Meredith O., and al-Arif, Ibrahim M. *The Libyan Revolution*. London, Oleander Press, 1972.

Arnold, Guy. *The Maverick State: Qaddafi and the New World Order*. London, Cassell, 1997.

Baldinetti, Anna. *The Origins of the Libyan Nation: Colonial Legacy, Exile and the Emergence of a New Nation-State*. Abingdon, Routledge, 2009.

Berlardinalli, Arsenio. *La Ghibla*. Tripoli, 1935.

Blunsum, T. *Libya: The Country and its People*. London, Queen Anne Press, 1968.

Bowen, Wyn Q. *Libya and Nuclear Proliferation: Stepping Back from the Brink*. Abingdon, Routledge, 2006.

Cachia, Anthony J. *Libya under the Second Ottoman Occupation, 1835–1911*. Tripoli, 1945.

Chorin, Ethan. *Exit the Colonel: The Hidden History of the Libyan Revolution*. New York, PublicAffairs, 2012.

Colucci, Massimo. *Il Regime della Proprietà Fondiaria nell'Africa Italiana: Vol. I. Libia*. Bologna, 1942.

Davis, John. *Libyan Politics: Tribe and Revolution*. London, I. B. Tauris, 1987.

Deeb, Mary-Jane. *Libya's Foreign Policy in North Africa*. Boulder, CO, Westview Press, 1991.

Despois, Jean. *La Colonisation italienne en Libye; Problèmes et Méthodes*. Paris, Larose-Editeurs, 1935.

Dorsch, Monique, and Strunz, Herbert. *Libyen: Zurück auf die Weltbühne*. Frankfurt-am-Main, Peter Lang, 2000.

Epton, Nina. *Oasis Kingdom: The Libyan Story*. New York, 1953.

Evans-Pritchard, E. E. *The Sanusi of Cyrenaica*. London, 1949.

First, Ruth. *Libya: The Elusive Revolution*. London, Penguin, 1974.

Gurney, Judith. *Libya: The Political Economy of Oil*. Oxford, Oxford University Press, 1996.

Hajjaji, S. A. *The New Libya*. Tripoli, 1967.

Hehir, Aidan, and Murray, Robert (Eds). *Libya, the Responsibility to Protect and the Future of Humanitarian Intervention*. Basingstoke, Palgrave Macmillan, 2013.

Heseltine, Nigel. *From Libyan Sands to Chad*. London, Museum Press, 1960.

Hilsum, Lindsay. *Sandstorm: Libya in the Time of Revolution*. London, Faber and Faber, 2012.

Kawczynski, Daniel. *Seeking Gaddafi*. London, Dialogue, 2010.

Khadduri, Majid. *Modern Libya, a Study in Political Development*. Baltimore, MD, Johns Hopkins Press, 1963.

Khalidi, I. R. *Constitutional Developments in Libya*. Beirut, Khayat's Book Co-operative, 1956.

El-Kikhia, Mansour O. *Libya's Qaddafi: The Politics of Contradiction*. Berkeley, CA, University of California Press, 1997.

Kubbah, Abdul Amir Q. *Libya, its Oil Industry and Economic System*. Baghdad, Arab Petro-Economic Research Centre, 1964.

Layish, A. *Legal Documents on Libyan Tribal Society and the Process of Sedenterization: Part 1*. Wiesbaden, Harrassowirz Verlag, 1998.

Martel, André. *La Libye 1835–1990: Essai de géopolitique historique*. Paris, Presses Universitaires de France, 1991.

Martínez, Luís. (Ed.). 'La Libye après l'embargo', in *Monde Arabe Maghreb-Machrek*, La Documentation Française, Paris. Special issue, 170 (Oct.–Dec.) 2000.

The Libyan Paradox. London, C. Hurst & Co, 2006.

Micacchi, Rodolfo. *La Tripolitania sotto il dominio dei Caramanli*. Intra, 1936.

Murabet, Mohammed. *Tripolitania: the Country and its People*. Tripoli, 1952.

Norman, John. *Labour and Politics in Libya and Arab Africa*. New York, Bookman, 1965.

Obeidi, Amal. *Political Culture in Libya*. Richmond, Curzon, 2001.

Otman, Waniss, and Karlberg, Erling. *The Libyan Economy: Economic Diversification and International Repositioning*. Berlin, Springer-Verlag Berlin, 2007.

Ouannes, Moncef. *Militaires, élites et modernisation dans la Libye contemporaine*. Paris, L'Harmattan, 2009.

Pack, Jason (Ed.). *The 2011 Libyan Uprisings and the Struggle for the Post-Qadhafi Future*. Basingstoke, Palgrave Macmillan, 2013.

Pargeter, Alison. *Libya: The Rise and Fall of Qaddafi*. New Haven, CT, Yale University Press, 2012.

Péan, Pierre. *Manipulations Africaines*. Paris, Plon, 2001.

Pelt, Adrian. *Libyan Independence and the United Nations*. New Haven, CT, Yale University Press, 1970.

Pichou, Jean. *La Question de Libye dans le règlement de la paix*. Paris, 1945.

Pliez, Olivier. *La nouvelle Libye: Sociétés, espaces et géoplitique au lendemain de l'embargo*. Paris, Karthala, 2004.

Qaddafi, Muammar al-. *The Green Book*. 3 vols; Tripoli, 1976–79; Vol. I: 'The Solution of the Problem of Democracy', Vol. II: 'The Solution of the Economic Problem', Vol. III: 'The Social Basis of the Third Universal Theory'.

Rivlin, Benjamin. *The United Nations and the Italian Colonies*. New York, 1950.

Ronen, Yehudit. *Qaddafi's Libya in World Politics*. Boulder, CO, Lynne Rienner Publrs, 2008.

Roumani, Maurice M. *The Jews of Libya: Coexistence, Persecution, Resettlement*. Eastbourne, Sussex Academic Press, 2008.

Royal Institute of International Affairs. *The Italian Colonial Empire*. London, RIIA, 1940.

St John, Ronald Bruce. *Historical Dictionary of Libya*. African Historical Dictionaries Series, No. 33. Lanham, MD, 1998.

Libya and the United States. Two Centuries of Strife. Philadelphia, PA, University of Pennsylvania Press, 2002.

Libya: Continuity and Change. Abingdon, Routledge, 2011.

Libya: From Colony to Revolution. Oxford, Oneworld Publications, 2012.

Schlueter, Hans. *Index Libycus*. Boston, MA, G. K. Hall, 1972.

Simons, Geoff. *Libya and the West: From Independence to Lockerbie*. London, I. B. Tauris, 2004.

Simons, Geoff, and Dalyell, Tam. *Libya*. Basingstoke, Macmillan, 1996.

Steele-Greig, A. J. *History of Education in Tripolitania from the Time of the Ottoman Occupation to the Fifth Year under British Military Occupation*. Tripoli, 1948.

Terterov, Marat, and Wallace, Jonathan (Eds). *Doing Business with Libya*. London, Kogan Page, 2003.

Vandewalle, Dirk. *Libya Since Independence: Oil and State-Building*. Ithaca, NY, Cornell University Press, 1998.

(Ed.). *North Africa: Development and Reform in a Changing Global Economy*. New York, St Martin's Press, 1996.

(Ed.). *Qadhafi's Libya: 1969–1994*. London, Macmillan, 1996.

A History of Modern Libya. Cambridge, Cambridge University Press, 2006.

(Ed.). *Libya since 1969: Qadhafi's Revolution Revisited*. London, Palgrave Macmillan, 2008.

Villard, Henry S. *Libya: The New Arab Kingdom of North Africa*. Ithaca, NY, 1956.

Waddams, Frank C. *The Libyan Oil Industry*. London, Croom Helm, 1980.

Ward, Philip. *Touring Libya*. 3 vols; 1967–69.

Tripoli: Portrait of a City. 1970.

al-Werfalli, Mabroka. *Political Alienation in Libya: Assessing Citizens' Political Attitude and Behaviour*. Reading, Ithaca Press, 2011.

Williams, G. *Green Mountain: An Informal Guide to Cyrenaica and its Jebel Akhdar*. London, 1963.

Willimott, S. G., and Clarke, J. I. *Field Studies in Libya*. Durham, 1960.

Wright, John. *Libya: A Modern History*. London, Croom Helm, 1982.

The Emergence of Libya. London, Society for Libyan Studies, 2008.

MOROCCO

Physical and Social Geography

The Kingdom of Morocco is the westernmost of the three North African countries known to the Arabs as Jeziret al-Maghreb or 'Island of the West'. It occupies an area of 458,730 sq km (177,117 sq miles), excluding Western (formerly Spanish) Sahara (252,120 sq km), a disputed territory under Moroccan occupation. Morocco has an extensive coastline on both the Atlantic Ocean and the Mediterranean Sea. However, owing to its position and intervening mountain ranges, Morocco remained relatively isolated from the rest of the Maghreb and served as a refuge for descendants of the native Berber-speaking inhabitants of north-western Africa.

According to census results, the population at 2 September 1994 was 26,019,280. About 35% of the total were Berber-speaking peoples, living mainly in mountain villages, while the Arabic-speaking majority was concentrated in towns in the lowlands, particularly in Casablanca, Marrakesh, Fez and Rabat, the modern administrative capital. The census of September 2004 showed that the total population had increased to 29,680,069; Casablanca had a population of 2,936,874, Rabat 1,827,733, Marrakesh 1,063,415 and Fez 975,507. According to UN estimates, the total Moroccan population had increased to 33,008,150 by mid-2013.

PHYSICAL FEATURES

The physical geography of Morocco is dominated by the highest and most rugged ranges in the Atlas Mountain system of north-western Africa. They are the result of mountain-building in the Tertiary era, when sediment deposited beneath an ancestral Mediterranean Sea was uplifted, folded and fractured. The mountains remain geologically unstable and Morocco is liable to severe earthquakes.

In Morocco the Atlas Mountains form four distinct massifs, which are surrounded and partially separated by lowland plains and plateaux. In the north, the Rif Atlas comprise a rugged arc of mountains that rise steeply from the Mediterranean coast to heights of more than 2,200 m above sea level. There, limestone and sandstone ranges form an effective barrier to east–west communications. They are inhabited by Berber farming families who live in isolated mountain villages and have little contact with the Arabs of Tétouan (population 318,698 at the census of September 2004) and Tangier (756,964) at the north-western end of the Rif chain.

The Middle Atlas lie immediately south of the Rif, separated by the Col of Taza, a narrow gap that affords the only easy route between western Algeria and Atlantic Morocco. They rise to about 3,000 m and form a broad barrier between the two countries. They also function as a major drainage divide and are flanked by the basins of Morocco's two principal rivers, the Oum el-Rbia, which flows west to the Atlantic, and the Moulouya, which flows north-east to the Mediterranean. Much of the Middle Atlas consists of a limestone plateau dissected by river gorges and capped here and there by volcanic craters and lava flows. The semi-nomadic Berber tribes spend the winter in villages in the valleys and move to the higher slopes in summer to pasture their flocks.

To the south the Middle Atlas chain merges into the High Atlas, the most formidable of the mountain massifs, which rises to about 4,000 m and is heavily snow-clad in winter. The mountains extend from south-west to north-east, and rise precipitously from both the Atlantic lowland to the north and the desert plain of Saharan Morocco to the south. There are no easily accessible routes across the High Atlas, but numerous mountain tracks allow the exchange of goods by pack animal between Atlantic and Saharan Morocco. A considerable Berber population lives in the mountain valleys in compact, fortified villages.

The Anti-Atlas is the lowest and most southerly of the mountain massifs. Structurally it forms an elevated edge of the Saharan platform which was uplifted when the High Atlas was formed. It consists largely of crystalline rocks and is joined to the southern margin of the High Atlas by a mass of volcanic lava, which separates the valley of the river Sous, draining west to the Atlantic at Agadir, from that of the upper Draa, draining south-east towards the Sahara. On the southern side of the chain, barren slopes are trenched by gorges from which cultivated palm groves protrude.

Stretching inland from the Atlantic coast is an extensive area of lowland, enclosed on the north, east and south by the Rif, Middle and High Atlas. It consists of the Gharb plain and the wide valley of the River Sebou in the north, and of the plateaux and plains of the Meseta, the Tadla, the Rehamna, the Djebilet and the Haouz farther south. Most of the Arabic-speaking people of Morocco live in this region.

CLIMATE AND VEGETATION

Northern and central Morocco experience a 'Mediterranean' climate, with warm, wet winters and hot, dry summers, but to the south this gives way to semi-arid and eventually to desert conditions. In the Rif and the northern parts of the Middle Atlas mean annual rainfall exceeds 750 mm and the summer drought lasts only three months, but in the rest of the Middle Atlas, in the High Atlas and over the northern half of the Atlantic lowland rainfall is reduced to between 400 mm and 750 mm and the summer drought lasts for four months or more. During the summer intensely hot winds from the Sahara, known as the Sirocco or Chergui, occasionally cross the mountains and desiccate the lowland. Summer heat on the Atlantic coastal plain is tempered, however, by sea breezes.

Over the southern half of the Atlantic lowland and the Anti-Atlas semi-arid conditions prevail and rainfall decreases to 200 mm–400 mm per year, becoming very variable and generally insufficient for the regular cultivation of cereal crops without irrigation. East and south of the Atlas Mountains, which act as a barrier to rain-bearing winds from the Atlantic, rainfall is reduced still further and regular cultivation becomes entirely dependent on irrigation.

The chief contrast in the vegetation of Morocco is between the mountain massifs, which support forest or open woodland, and the surrounding lowlands, which tend to be covered only by scrub growth of low, drought-resistant bushes. The natural vegetation has been depleted, and in many places actually destroyed, by excessive cutting, burning and grazing. The middle and upper slopes of the mountains are often quite well wooded, with evergreen oak dominant at the lower and cedar at the higher elevations. The lowlands to the east and south of the Atlas Mountains support distinctive species of steppe and desert vegetation, among which esparto grass and the argan tree (which is unique to south-western Morocco) are conspicuous.

THE ANNEXED TERRITORY OF WESTERN SAHARA

After independence the Moroccan Government claimed a right to administer a large area of the western Sahara, including territory in Algeria and Mauritania, and the whole of Spanish Sahara. The claim was based on the extent of Moroccan rule in medieval times. The existence of considerable deposits of phosphates in Spanish Sahara and of iron ore in the Algeria–Morocco border region further encouraged Moroccan interest in expansion. After Spain's withdrawal from the Sahara in 1976, Morocco and Mauritania divided the former Spanish Sahara (now known as Western Sahara) between them, with Morocco annexing the northern part of the territory, including the phosphate mines of Bou Craa. In August 1979 Mauritania renounced its share, which was immediately annexed by Morocco and incorporated as a new province, Oued el-Dahab.

The current population of Western Sahara is of Moorish or mixed Arab-Berber descent with some negro admixture, who depend for their existence on herds of sheep, camels and goats which they move seasonally from one pasture to another. The main tribes are the R'gibat, Uld Delim, Izargien and Arosien. At the census of September 1994 the population of Western Sahara was 252,146; at the census of September 2004 it had increased to an estimated 417,000. The principal towns in the area are el-Aaiún, el-Smara (formerly Smara) and Dakhla (Villa Cisneros).

The relief of most of the area is gentle. The coast is backed by a wide alluvial plain overlain in the south by extensive sand dunes aligned from south-west to north-east and extending inland over 250 km (155 miles). Behind the coastal plain the land rises gradually to a plateau surface broken by sandstone ridges that reach 300 m in height. In the north-east, close to the Mauritanian frontier, isolated mountain ranges, such as the Massif de la Guelta, rise to over 600 m. There are no permanent streams and the only considerable valley is that of the Saguia el-Hamra which crosses the northernmost part of the area to reach the coast at el-Aaiún north of Cape Bojador. The whole region experiences an extreme desert climate. Nowhere does mean annual rainfall exceed 100 mm and over most of the territory it is less than 50 mm. Vegetation is restricted to scattered desert shrubs and occasional patches of coarse grass in most depressions. Along the coast, summer heat is tempered by air moving inland after it has been cooled over the waters of the cold Canaries current, which flows offshore from north to south.

History

Revised for this edition by NEIL PARTRICK

THE PRE-COLONIAL AND COLONIAL PERIODS

The Phoenicians and Carthaginians established trading posts on Morocco's coasts, and later the Romans took control of the north of the country, creating the province of Mauritanian Tingitana. By the eighth century AD Arab invaders from the east had conquered most of the country. The Berber tribes of Morocco quickly rallied to Islam, and new Arab invaders in the 11th and 12th centuries contributed greatly to Arabization, but significant segments of the population remained Berber speakers. In the 12th century a religious movement, the Almoravids, established control over Morocco and much of Algeria and also annexed Muslims lands in Spain, but their power rapidly declined. A new religious force, the Almohads, replaced them, conquering much of the Maghreb including Libya, and brought Muslim Spain under their control, but from the early 13th century their empire also began to decline. In the following centuries successive regimes strove to maintain their power in the face of tribal dissidence and the threat of foreign intervention, especially from the Spanish and Portuguese who were able to establish outposts along the Moroccan coasts. The dynasty of the Alaouites came to power in 1666 and has remained at least nominally in control to the present day. By the beginning of the 20th century Morocco was one of the few African states to remain independent, and competition among the great powers to control the country was increasing. In 1904 France and Spain concluded a secret agreement that divided Morocco into two zones of influence: a Spanish zone in the north and a French zone in the south. In 1912, after overcoming opposition from Germany, France established a protectorate over Morocco, and later in the year an agreement was signed with Spain over the limits of its zone in the north of the country. It was agreed that Tangier was to have an international regime, but this was not established until 1923.

The first French Resident-General, Gen. Hubert Lyautey, quickly established effective control over the plains and lower plateaux of Morocco from Fez to the Atlas mountains south of Marrakesh, but it was not until 1934 that the French established control over the Middle Atlas, the Tafilalt, the anti-Atlas and the deep south. A major rebellion against Spanish rule in the north during the 1920s, under the leadership of Abd al-Krim, had been crushed with the help of French troops. The pacification of Morocco strengthened the central authority, and the traditional distinction between *blad al-makhzen* (area controlled by the government) and the *blad al-siba* (area of dissidence), which had characterized the structure of government for centuries, disappeared.

INDEPENDENCE

By the early 1930s a Moroccan nationalist movement had emerged, but until the Second World War it remained a small movement that had to act clandestinely for much of the time. The Second World War gave a new impulse to the development of Moroccan nationalism, and in 1943 the Istiqlal (Independence) party was formed, demanding independence under the rule of Sultan Muhammad ibn Yousuf, who supported the nationalists and who exercised authority and leadership throughout Moroccan society. In the years following the Second World War the nationalist movement gained in strength and won growing international support. In August 1953 France moved to depose Muhammad ibn Yousuf, who was exiled to Madagascar, and replaced him as Sultan with another royal prince, Muhammad ibn Arafa. Urban violence continued, and with the outbreak of the Algerian war in 1954 the French Government urgently needed to find a settlement in Morocco. After a successful conference between French and Moroccan representatives in August 1955, ibn Arafa abdicated and ibn Yousuf returned from exile as the legitimate ruler. In March 1956 the French Government recognized the independence of Morocco. At the same time Spain relinquished its protectorate over northern Morocco, although it retained the enclaves of Ceuta and Melilla. The Spanish-controlled territories of Tarfaya and Ifni in the south became part of Morocco under agreements signed in 1958 and 1969, respectively. Tangier was restored to Morocco in 1956.

KING HASSAN REFUSES TO SHARE POWER

Muhammad ibn Yousuf, who had assumed the title of King Muhammad V after independence, died in 1961 and was succeeded by his son, Hassan II. The close association of the monarchy with the nationalist movement had strengthened the position of the King, who also enjoyed traditional religious authority as *amir al-mouminin* (Commander of the Faithful). Istiqlal remained the leading political party, but its efforts to curb the power of the monarchy had been hampered by internal divisions and a split in 1959 resulted in the creation of a breakaway party, the Union Nationale des Forces Populaires (UNFP), led by Mehdi Ben Barka. In 1962 a new Constitution—establishing a constitutional monarchy with the King as head of state, supported by an elected Parliament—was approved by referendum. In elections held to the new National Assembly in May the newly formed Front Pour la Défense des Institutions Constitutionnelles (FDIC), a coalition of monarchist parties, won the largest number of seats but failed to gain an overall majority. This situation gave rise to a period of ineffective government, and unemployment and rising prices led to riots in Rabat and Casablanca in 1965. The King responded by proclaiming a state of emergency, suspending parliament, and assuming full legislative and executive powers. After the 1963 elections repressive actions against the opposition Istiqlal and UNFP resulted in numerous arrests, and in October 1965 the UNFP leader, Ben Barka, disappeared in France and was presumed to have been assassinated. At a subsequent French trial Gen. Muhammad Oufkir, one of the King's closest supporters, was found guilty *in absentia* of complicity in Ben

Barka's disappearance. Parliamentary elections in 1970 were boycotted by Istiqlal and the UNFP.

In July 1971 a group of army officers attacked the King's summer palace at Skhirat, south of Rabat, but Hassan, together with Oufkir, escaped and with loyal forces foiled the attempted coup. Swift retribution followed, with a number of senior officers condemned and executed. A second attempt on Hassan's life was made in 1972. While returning from an official visit to France, the aircraft in which he was travelling was attacked above Kénitra by air force fighters. Although badly damaged, the King's aircraft managed to land at Rabat and Hassan again escaped unharmed. The attempted coup had apparently been planned by Oufkir, the King's erstwhile defender. Oufkir himself was found shot dead, and few believed the official version that he died by his own hand. Bomb attacks by armed groups in several cities in March 1973 prompted a series of arrests among leaders of the UNFP, some of whom were later executed; their trial had revealed widespread evidence of torture during police interrogation. Hassan quickly moved to regain control of the situation, reconstructing the security forces, dividing the opposition parties and using the Western Sahara issue to regain the political initiative and divert the army's attention away from domestic politics.

ANNEXATION OF WESTERN SAHARA

The independence agreement of 1956 did not define Morocco's precise boundaries. As the pre-protectorate nation also had no formal boundaries in the Sahara, the possibilities for territorial expansion were considerable. Prior to independence the Istiqlal party had envisaged the creation of a 'Greater Morocco', to include certain areas in south-western Algeria, the Spanish Sahara (the northern Saguia el-Hamra and the southern Río de Oro) and Mauritania, and Morocco reiterated these claims in the following years. In July 1962 Moroccan troops entered the region south of Colomb-Béchar in Algeria, a region never officially demarcated, and the Moroccan press also launched a strong campaign in support of Morocco's claims to the mineral-rich Tindouf area. In February 1964 an agreement was reached to establish a demilitarized zone, but a 1972 treaty on the demarcation of the joint border was not ratified by Morocco until 1989. Morocco abandoned its claim to Mauritania in 1969, and full diplomatic recognition and an exchange of ambassadors followed in 1970.

In 1974 Morocco stepped up its claims to the Spanish Sahara, where massive reserves of phosphates had been discovered and developed in the late 1960s. Its claim was essentially historical and based on the fact that in the past the people of the region had recognized the spiritual and temporal authority of the Sultan. Hassan's initiative was supported by all the country's political parties. After resisting UN demands for decolonization of the territory, in mid-1974 Spain declared its readiness to withdraw from its Saharan territories, and in October Morocco and Mauritania reached a secret agreement on the division of the territories and the joint exploitation of their important phosphate resources. A year later the International Court of Justice in The Hague, Netherlands, ruled in favour of self-determination for the people of Spanish Sahara. In response, King Hassan immediately ordered a march of 350,000 unarmed civilians to take possession of the Spanish territories. The so-called 'Green March' began in November, and the Spanish authorities allowed the marchers to progress a short distance across the border before halting their advance. Shortly afterwards, a tripartite accord was signed in Madrid, Spain, whereby the Spanish Government undertook to withdraw from Western Sahara (as the territory was redesignated) in early 1976 and transfer the territory to a joint Moroccan-Mauritanian administration. Algeria, however, opposed the agreement and increased its support for the Frente Popular para la Liberación de Saguia el-Hamra y Río de Oro (the Polisario Front), founded in 1973, which sought independence for Western Sahara. Moroccan troops swiftly occupied the territory and entered the capital, el-Aaiún, in early December 1975. They encountered fierce resistance from Polisario guerrillas, and many Sahrawis fled across the Algerian border to avoid the Moroccan advance. The last Spanish troops left in January 1976, and later that month there were clashes between Moroccan and Algerian troops within Western Sahara. The prospect of war between the two countries none the less receded, and Algeria contented itself with arming and training Polisario guerrillas and providing camps for civilian refugees. In February, in the Algerian capital, Algiers, Polisario proclaimed the Sahrawi Arab Democratic Republic (SADR), and in March Morocco severed diplomatic relations with Algeria.

In April 1976 Morocco and Mauritania reached agreement on the division of Western Sahara. The greater part of the territory, containing most of the known mineral wealth, was allotted to Morocco, which subsequently divided it into three provinces and absorbed these into the kingdom. By placing strong army garrisons in the territory's few scattered urban centres, the Moroccans were able to secure them against guerrilla attacks, but incursions by forces of the Polisario Front into the surrounding desert areas could not be prevented. Clashes between the Moroccan army and Polisario forces resulted in heavy casualties on both sides. Morocco also took increasing responsibility for the defence of the Mauritanian sector. France favoured the expansion of Moroccan, rather than Algerian, interests in this area, and on a number of occasions launched air attacks on Polisario forces. After a military coup in Mauritania in July 1978, Mauritania signed a peace treaty with Polisario, renouncing its territorial claims to Western Sahara. King Hassan immediately claimed the former Mauritanian sector and proclaimed it a province of Morocco. Polisario forces continued their attacks, some of these inside Morocco's original borders, and in 1980, with its military resources considerably stretched, Morocco resorted to defensive tactics, protecting a *triangle utile*, between el-Aaiún, Bou Craa and el-Smara, containing most of the population and the most important phosphate mines, by a line of defences, which were later extended to the southern border of the territory.

In November 1979 the UN General Assembly adopted a resolution confirming the legitimacy of the Polisario Front's struggle for independence, and a year later it urged Morocco to end its occupation of Western Sahara. At a summit meeting of the Organization of African Unity (OAU, now African Union—AU) in 1980 a majority of members approved the admission of the SADR, and Morocco subsequently withdrew from the organization—the first state to do so. By 1981 the SADR had been recognized by about 45 governments. After Morocco claimed that Polisario had shot down some of its aircraft using Soviet-built surface-to-air missiles, the USA agreed to triple its military aid to the kingdom, and in May 1982 the two countries signed a military co-operation accord providing for the establishment of US military aircraft bases on Moroccan territory in the event of crises in the Middle East or Africa.

GROWING SOCIAL AND POLITICAL UNREST

The Saharan takeover won King Hassan considerable domestic prestige and popularity, and in 1977 he felt sufficiently secure to hold national elections originally envisaged under the 1972 Constitution. With the exception of the UNFP, the opposition parties agreed to participate. Two-thirds of the new Chamber of Representatives were elected by universal suffrage, and one-third chosen by an electoral college. The election of the new chamber, in which independent pro-monarchy candidates won 141 of the 264 seats, ended some 12 years of direct rule.

Although there appeared to be solid support for the war effort among the Moroccan people, signs of social discontent did emerge, which could be partly attributed to the financial burden of the Western Sahara conflict. In 1979 there were numerous strikes by workers demanding higher wages, and in 1980 students went on strike to protest against decreased education spending. In June 1981 at least 66 people were killed in Casablanca during a general strike against reductions in food subsidies. Further unrest was aroused in October when constitutional changes, approved by referendum, extended the maximum period between parliamentary elections from four to six years. In January 1984 violent street protests erupted in several towns after the Government announced imminent increases in the prices of basic foodstuffs and in education fees. Troops intervened to quell the disturbances, opening fire on demonstrators. Unofficial estimates indicated that more than 100 civilians were killed in the riots and that almost 2,000 were detained, many of whom subsequently received prison sentences of up to 10 years.

In new parliamentary elections, eventually held in September 1984, the legislature was again controlled by centre-right parties. King Hassan named a new coalition Government of four centre-right parties, which did not include any members of Istiqlal or the Union Socialiste des Forces Populaires (USFP), which had been established in 1972 following a split in the UNFP. Meanwhile, the Government mounted a campaign against organizations deemed to pose a threat to internal security, particularly left-wing and Islamist movements. In the 1970s left-wing militancy had been the gravest threat to the regime, and Hassan had used his religious legitimacy to counter the rise of the left by appealing to religious elements in society. However, the tactics had backfired when Sheikh Abdessalam Yassine, founder and leader of the Islamist movement Al-Adl wal-Ihsan (Justice and Charity), accused the King of ruling illegitimately and not abiding by religious teachings. For this, he was arrested and confined in a psychiatric hospital for at least two years. During the 1980s Islamism began to grow to the detriment of left-wing movements. In 1982 Al-Adl wal-Ihsan was refused official registration, and in 1989 a total of 24 of its members were arrested for threatening state security. The conviction of 17 of the accused and the placing under house arrest of Sheikh Yassine provoked demonstrations and further arrests. In January 1990 the Government ordered the dissolution of Al-Adl wal-Ihsan, and arrested and imprisoned members of its executive committee. In May 1991 Al-Adl wal-Ihsan and other opposition groups participated in a rally in Casablanca in which some 100,000 demonstrators demanded measures to enshrine the sovereignty of the people and reduce the powers of the King.

Rising frustration at the country's socio-economic problems led to rioting in Fez and Rabat in December 1990 during a general strike; some 20 people were killed and more than 1,500 arrested. By the late 1980s concerns over human rights abuses, notably the question of political prisoners, attracted considerable international attention, despite the creation of a Conseil Consultatif Royal des Droits de l'Homme (CCDH) in May 1990.

EFFORTS FAIL TO DRAW THE OPPOSITION INTO GOVERNMENT

In June 1992 the Chamber of Deputies, in the absence of opposition parties which boycotted the session, adopted a new electoral law. The legislation reduced the minimum voting age to 20 years and the minimum age for candidates for election to 23 years. It also made provision for equal funding and media exposure for all parties. The opposition parties—Istiqlal, the USFP, the Parti de l'Avant-garde Démocratique Socialiste (PADS—a breakaway organization from the USFP) and the Parti du Progrès et du Socialisme (PPS)—had earlier formed a Bloc Démocratique, the expressed aims of which were: a minimum voting age of 18 years; a minimum age of 21 for candidates; a two-tier voting system; and the appointment of an independent chairman of a new electoral supervisory body. On 4 September a revised Constitution was endorsed at a national referendum: according to official results, 99.96% voted in favour of the amended document (the proportion increased to 100% in the main cities and in three of the four 'Saharan provinces'), with the rate of participation recorded at 97.3% of the 11.7m. registered voters. The opposition claimed that the result destroyed all credibility in the democratic process. The revised Constitution required the composition of the Government to reflect that of the Chamber of Deputies and to submit its programme to a vote in the legislature.

Despite protests over the results of the referendum, the Bloc Démocratique did participate in communal elections in October 1992. The loyalist Rassemblement National des Indépendants (RNI) became the party with the greatest representation in local government, winning 18.1% of the votes cast and 21.7% of the 22,282 seats contested. The 'independent' Sans Appartenance Politique list, which, despite its name, was loyal to the Government, obtained 13.8% of the votes cast, and the loyalist Union Constitutionnelle (UC) 13.4%. Istiqlal emerged as the most successful opposition party (with 12.5% of the votes cast), followed by the USFP. The opposition parties, however, failed to improve on their performance in the previous communal elections, despite contesting more seats, and complained of widespread malpractice by local authorities in favour of 'loyalist' parties.

Parliamentary elections finally proceeded in June 1993, the first for almost 10 years. The number of seats in the Chamber of Representatives was increased from 306 to 333: 222 members were to be elected by universal adult suffrage, and the remainder by local councils and professional organizations. The two main opposition parties, Istiqlal and the USFP, substantially increased their representation in the Chamber (to 91, from 57 in 1984) at this stage of the electoral process. The parties of the Bloc Démocratique won a total of 99 seats. The UC had been the largest single party at the 1984 election, with 55 seats, but now held only 27 seats in the new legislature. The Mouvement Populaire (MP) emerged with 33 seats, two more than in 1984. According to official figures, 62.8% of the electorate voted, but other observers suggested that the level of participation may have been lower. Despite reports of abuses by local officials, polling was generally judged to have been fairer than in previous elections, although the opposition parties complained of numerous irregularities. In the second stage of the elections, held in September 1993, the loyalist parties made significant gains, winning 79 of the 111 seats contested. The UC alone won 27 seats, making it the second largest party, after the USFP, in the new Chamber. The USFP and Istiqlal secured only 17 seats, and Abd al-Rahman el-Youssoufi, the USFP leader, resigned in protest against the attitude of the administration during the election. At the end of the second stage the five loyalist parties held 195 seats in the new Chamber and the Bloc Démocratique 120 seats, with independents holding the remaining 18 seats.

After the election it was reported that King Hassan had agreed that the USFP and Istiqlal, as the main components of the Bloc Démocratique, could form a government on condition that he appointed three principal ministers. After the two parties rejected the offer, in July 1994 King Hassan again appealed to the opposition to join a 'government of change and renewal', and in October he announced his intention to select a Prime Minister from the ranks of the opposition. However, talks between the palace and the opposition parties collapsed over the issue of the appointment of the Minister of State for the Interior and Information in the new government. Having failed to draw the opposition into government, in January 1995 King Hassan reappointed Abdellatif Filali, a member of his inner circle, as Prime Minister, and once again selected a Government from among the loyalist UC, MP and the Parti National Démocrate (PND). The other two main centre-right parties, the RNI and the Mouvement National Populaire (MNP), declined an offer to join the administration, but confirmed that they would continue to support the Government in parliament. Of the 35 cabinet posts, 20 were allocated to political parties. Yet, despite an attempt to give the political process greater legitimacy by drawing more than one-half of ministers from elected political parties, the King retained control of appointments to key ministries.

In a concession to the opposition, however, in June 1995 charges against Muhammad Basri, the former leader of the USFP who had lived in exile for some 28 years, were dismissed. El-Youssoufi, who had resigned as Secretary-General of the USFP in 1993, agreed to resume the post in July 1995.

UNIONS AND ISLAMISTS FLEX THEIR MUSCLES

The regime remained nervous of any challenge to its authority, and determined to act against organized labour movements, students and other dissenting groups. In June 1994 several unemployed graduates were given two-year prison sentences after holding an unauthorized demonstration to protest against corruption in local government. The penal code was also revised so that trade unionists involved in strike action over pay would be subject to prison sentences or fines.

In mid-1995 the Minister of Higher Education admitted publicly for the first time that Islamist militants were gaining strength among university students. The authorities announced their intention to continue to target the ringleaders, and also to encourage other student organizations in order to counter the Islamist threat. This time it was the turn of the left to function as a rampart against rising Islamism. In December Abdessalam Yassine, leader of Al-Adl wal-Ihsan, was released after spending six years under house arrest. A week later, after addressing worshippers at a mosque and denouncing certain aspects of government policy, he was placed once again under house arrest, although the authorities insisted that he was under 'police protection'.

This episode was regarded as illustrative of the Government's 'dual' attitude towards the Islamist opposition: a measure of tolerance was displayed towards the more moderate Islamist movements (although they were refused permission to form a political party), while armed Islamist groups were severely repressed. Although small extremist Islamist groups certainly existed and were supported in particular by young militants, since the 1980s the main currents of the Islamist movement had evolved towards an 'Islamism of compromise' with the Government. Islamist groups such as Al-Adl wal-Ihsan and Al-Islah wa Attajdid (Reform and Renewal) insisted that they wished to be integrated into the political system, rejecting violence and favouring the peaceful re-Islamization of society. They conducted a range of sociocultural activities, including charitable work, and sought to gain influence in trade unions and in major political parties such as the USFP and Istiqlal. Poor employment prospects (especially among young people), low pay, redundancies owing to the privatization of state companies, declining living standards and the consequences of a severe drought not only provided fertile ground for the Islamist movement but also led to widespread strike action. Although the Government attempted to promote dialogue between employers and workers, several trade unionists were imprisoned, and, amid allegations of police brutality, unions and human rights groups condemned the Government's repressive policy in labour disputes.

Renewed labour unrest culminated in a general strike in June 1996, during which there were serious clashes between demonstrators and the security forces. The strike was organized by the Union Générale des Travailleurs Marocains (UGTM) and the Confédération Démocratique du Travail (CDT), which urged the Government to increase the minimum wage and to establish a national fund for the unemployed. Fearing more violence, the Government made concessions, and in July concluded a new accord on labour relations with employers' associations and trade unions.

CONSTITUTIONAL CHANGES—1996

In August 1995 King Hassan announced plans to hold a referendum to decide whether to create a second parliamentary chamber. The referendum, held on 13 September 1996, confirmed overwhelming support for the new parliamentary system, whereby all members of the Chamber of Representatives would be directly elected and their term of office reduced from six to five years. A new upper house, the Chamber of Advisers, was to be established, and its members chosen by electoral colleges representing mainly local councils, with the remainder selected from professional associations and trade unions. The Chamber of Advisers would be competent to initiate legislation, issue 'warning' motions to the Government and, by a two-thirds' majority vote, force its resignation. Moroccan officials denied that the role of the new upper house was to neutralize the Chamber of Representatives. The USFP and Istiqlal, together with the PPS, gave a guarded welcome to the reforms, but the Organisation de l'Action Démocratique et Populaire (OADP), their partner in the Bloc Démocratique, condemned them.

After the referendum, the OADP split when a group of officials left to form the Parti Socialiste Démocratique (PSD). The Ministry of Information reported that 10.2m. people had voted in favour of the King's proposal, representing 99.6% of the votes cast. Some 83.0% of the electorate participated in the referendum. In early December 1996 the Government announced that it was beginning to reform electoral procedures in preparation for the forthcoming elections; a commission, on which all officially recognized political parties were allowed representation, commenced examining electoral lists to identify irregularities. Within days the commission had identified more than 400,000 voters whose names appeared twice on the electoral lists. In mid-December draft legislation was approved, providing for the establishment of elected councils in 16 new regions, including Western Sahara. Each regional council would be elected for a six-year period and would have responsibility for tax collection and the construction of schools and hospitals.

In February 1997 a total of 11 political parties, including five from the opposition, signed a political pact with Minister of State for the Interior Driss Basri, with the aim of 'strengthening the democratic regime based on the monarchy'. All the signatories agreed to abide by the law. The authorities conceded that they would treat all political parties equally and ban illegal practices. For their part, the political parties promised to mobilize their supporters in 'a positive spirit' and not to contest, in advance, the integrity of future voting. After lengthy negotiations, the authorities and the opposition parties agreed that new electoral lists would be prepared and a national commission established to oversee the elections. The scale of irregularities in previous elections was revealed when the Moroccan press published figures indicating that 4.5m. voter registrations out of an electorate of 12m. were unreliable. While the official media welcomed the pact with enthusiasm, some leading members of the opposition expressed caution. The Bloc Démocratique announced that it would present joint candidates in some 25,000 municipal districts. The 'loyalist' parties (including the UC, the MP and the PND), which held a majority of seats in the current Chamber of Representatives, also formed a common front, the Entente Nationale (or Wifaq), and adopted the same strategy. However, the small parties of the radical left felt excluded from the political process, as did the Islamists. Several radical Islamist groups demanded the right to form political parties and to contest the forthcoming elections. However, although Al Islah wa Attajdid acquired legal status in January 1997 as a result of its merger with the Mouvement Populaire Constitutionnelle et Démocratique (MPCD), the authorities rejected Al-Adl wal-Ihsan's claim for recognition as a political party.

THE 1997 LOCAL AND LEGISLATIVE ELECTIONS

The political pact signed in February 1997 had its first test at local elections held in June. A national commission, including members of political parties as well as government representatives, was established to monitor the election process. Despite some complaints of irregularities, the elections for 24,253 seats on municipal and commune councils were judged to have been relatively fair, with turn-out officially estimated at 75.0%. Although the opposition Bloc Démocratique achieved a much better result than in the 1992 elections, winning 31.7% of the seats, overall control of local councils was retained by the right-wing Entente Nationale and the centrist grouping led by the RNI, which took 30.3% and 26.4% of the seats, respectively. The MPCD refused to participate in the elections on the grounds that it was not represented on the national election commission; however, there were claims that the authorities had put pressure on the party to withdraw because they feared that there would be strong support for radical Islamists. None the less, Al Islah wa Attajdid presented a number of independent candidates. Prior to the elections, more than 100 left-wing activists, including 67 members of the PADS, were arrested for campaigning for a boycott of the electoral process. Some 26 PADS supporters were subsequently sentenced to short terms of imprisonment, having been found guilty of violating electoral and press codes.

In August 1997 King Hassan appointed a new Cabinet, primarily comprising technocrats. Legislation promulgated later in the month detailed the composition of the future bicameral parliament: the Chamber of Representatives would comprise 325 members, directly elected for a five-year term; the Chamber of Advisers would have 270 members, chosen by indirect election, of whom 162 would represent local authorities, 81 trade chambers and 27 employees' associations. In September the Assistant Secretary-General of Istiqlal stated that the parties of the Bloc Démocratique planned to present joint candidates in the legislative elections. However, observers noted that deep rivalries still existed between its two main parties, the USFP and Istiqlal. One of the Bloc's smaller parties, the PPS, which performed poorly in the local elections, lost 40 of its members in June when they established a rival Front des Forces Démocratiques (FFD).

Voting for the wholly elected Chamber of Representatives in the new bicameral parliament took place on 14 November 1997. The legislative elections were considered to have been fairer than previous polls, although some complaints were registered. Of the country's legalized political parties, only the extreme left-wing PADS boycotted the elections, but the rate of voter participation was officially estimated at only 58.3%. The Bloc Démocratique, which had been widely predicted to dominate the new Chamber, won only 102 of the 325 seats, 57 of which went to the USFP, while Istiqlal secured only 32 seats. The Entente Nationale secured 100 seats, one-half of which were won by the UC, and parties of the centre-right took 97 seats (including 46 obtained by the RNI). Right-wing and centre-right parties performed much better than in direct voting in the 1993 elections. The Bloc Démocratique won 34.3% of the vote, compared with 27.3% by the centre-right parties and 24.8% by the Entente Nationale. The MPCD, the PPS and the FFD each won nine seats.

Indirect elections for the new Chamber of Advisers took place on 5 December 1997. As predicted, the right and centre-right parties gained a dominant position in the upper house, winning 166 of the 270 seats. Centrist parties secured 90 seats, with the RNI emerging as the largest single party in the Chamber with 42 seats, while the Entente Nationale took 76 seats. The Bloc Démocratique obtained only 44 seats, of which 21 were won by Istiqlal. Smaller parties made significant gains, winning 33 seats, of which 13 went to the Parti de l'Action and 12 to the FFD. The new bicameral parliament met for the first time in January 1998.

KING HASSAN APPOINTS MOROCCO'S FIRST USFP-LED GOVERNMENT

With the three main political groupings holding roughly the same number of seats in the Chamber of Representatives, on 4 February 1998 King Hassan named Abd al-Rahman el-Youssoufi, the veteran leader of the USFP, as Prime Minister. In March el-Youssoufi formed a coalition Government in which 23 of the 41 members were from the USFP and its allies (14 from the USFP, six from Istiqlal and three from the PPS); three from two small opposition splinter parties, the FFD and the PSD; and nine from two centre-right parties (six from the RNI and three from the MNP). Although hailed as the country's first 'gouvernement d'alternance' in the transition to democracy, with opposition parties taking charge of key areas of economic and social policy, the ministers with responsibility for the interior, foreign affairs, justice, and religious endowments and Islamic affairs, together with the Secretary-General of the Government and the Minister-delegate in charge of the Administration of National Defence, were direct appointees of the King. Critics were swift to point out that not only the security services but also important networks of economic influence were outside the new premier's control, thus restricting his room to manoeuvre. King Hassan formally approved the new Cabinet, but warned the political parties represented in the Government that they had a duty to control their supporters in the interest of social stability.

Immediately on assuming the premiership, el-Youssoufi ordered all civil servants, cabinet ministers and legislators to disclose their wealth and private interests. The Minister of Justice, Omar Azzimane, began the enormous task of reforming the country's justice system, initiating disciplinary proceedings against some 30 magistrates, mainly on the grounds of corruption. By the end of the year nine judges had been dismissed, and others suspended. In a stated effort to root out corruption and promote transparency at local government level, the King approved the creation of 16 regional courts.

Some progress was also achieved on human rights, a personal priority of el-Youssoufi. Visiting Morocco in April 1998, the UN High Commissioner for Human Rights, Mary Robinson, signed a memorandum to open a North Africa and Middle East centre in Rabat to promote and protect human rights in the region; she stated that Rabat had been chosen as the location for the new centre because of Morocco's efforts to address human rights issues. In October King Hassan declared that it was his firm determination that all outstanding human rights issues should be resolved within six months. Shortly after the King's statement, the CCDH, the country's official multi-party human rights advisory council, reported that the commission investigating the fate of opponents of the regime who had 'disappeared' in the 1960s, 1970s and 1980s had examined 112 cases. Some 56 of these missing persons were confirmed dead, but no details were given of how they had died. Although the CCDH had examined the circumstances of 45 prisoners who had died in custody, its chairman stated that in certain cases it had been decided not to bring charges against those responsible. At the same time, the CCDH reported that having examined the cases of 48 'political' prisoners, some 28, many of them members of Al-Adl wal-Ihsan, had been released, but that the rest would remain in prison because they had been convicted of murder and sabotage. Independent human rights organizations, such as the Association Marocaine des Droits Humains (AMDH), criticized the CCDH for releasing so little information about the cases that it had examined and insisted that the files of those who had 'disappeared' or died could not be closed until those responsible were brought to trial. Particular concern was expressed that the CCDH had not considered two outstanding cases—those of the exiled dissident Abraham Serfaty and of Abdessalam Yassine, leader of Al-Adl wal-Ihsan, who remained under house arrest.

In April 1999 Muhammad Benaïssa, Morocco's outgoing ambassador to the USA, replaced Abdellatif Filali as Minister of Foreign Affairs and Co-operation. Filali had held the foreign affairs portfolio for 14 years, and no reason was given for his removal, although there was speculation that dissatisfaction with Filali's handling of recent talks on Western Sahara may have precipitated the change.

Towards the end of 1998 the PPS and the PSD, which had been co-operating within the legislature, announced their intention to merge. Meanwhile, the MPCD, which had been giving critical support to the el-Youssoufi Government, changed its name to the Parti de la Justice et du Développement (PJD), in order to differentiate itself from right and centre-right parties with similar names but very different policies.

THE DEATH OF KING HASSAN AND THE ACCESSION OF MUHAMMAD

King Hassan died of a heart attack on 23 July 1999. His eldest son, who succeeded him as Muhammad VI, announced his father's death to the nation on state television after members of the royal family, government ministers and senior members of the armed forces had made the oath of allegiance to the new monarch. Although Hassan had groomed his eldest son to succeed him, he had been reluctant to let Muhammad share power or play a role in the armed forces despite his status as a four-star general. Muhammad had been given no administrative responsibilities of any importance, and his public appearances had been largely ceremonial; indeed, Muhammad had apparently shown little interest in the preoccupations of government.

None the less, the new King immediately demonstrated his enthusiasm for change, and emerged as a strong advocate of reform and modernization. He rid the Royal Court of some of the most antiquated and traditional aspects of royal protocol, introducing a more informal style of interaction between the King, his advisers, elected politicians and visiting foreign officials.

In his first address following his accession, Muhammad pledged to support the multi-party system, the rule of law, and respect for human rights and individual liberties. He adopted a populist style very different from that of his late father, travelled widely throughout the kingdom (notably undertaking a 10-day visit to the isolated and impoverished northern Rif region, which had been virtually ignored by King Hassan), raised issues of social justice, pledged to help the poor and reduce unemployment, and spoke out on sensitive social issues such as the importance of equal rights for women. Shortly after his succession, the King granted an amnesty to thousands of prisoners and established an arbitration body to determine compensation for the families of political opponents who had 'disappeared' or those who had suffered arbitrary detention. In September 1999 the King granted permission for Abraham Serfaty, the country's most prominent dissident, to return from exile in France. Two months later the family of Mehdi Ben Barka, the Moroccan opposition leader murdered in Paris, France, in 1965, was allowed to return after spending 35 years in exile in Europe. Domestic and international human rights associations alike praised the new King for his actions.

In November 1999 the King abruptly dismissed the unpopular Minister of State for the Interior, Driss Basri, who had held the post for two decades and whose influence extended well beyond his portfolio. A month earlier the King had deprived Basri of responsibility for Western Sahara and for the Direction de Surveillance du Territoire. As the late King Hassan's closest adviser and loyal servant, Basri was closely identified with the repressive policies of the old regime. King Muhammad's decision was widely applauded, and was interpreted as a clear break with the past and a sign of his desire for a faster pace of political change. Basri was replaced by Ahmed Midaoui, a former chief of national security, and Fouad Ali el-Himma, Muhammad's *chef de cabinet*, became Secretary of State at the Ministry of the Interior. The ministry itself was to be reduced in size, with the armed forces assuming greater responsibility for national security. The King subsequently replaced more than one-half of the country's provincial governors, and several new appointments were made to the security establishment, ensuring that key posts were occupied by men loyal to the new monarch. A new generation of technocrats who had studied and worked abroad was brought back to Morocco to help the new King achieve his objectives of reform and modernization.

In September 2000 King Muhammad reorganized his Cabinet, reducing the number of ministerial portfolios from 43 to 33. The political composition of the administration, in which Prime Minister el-Youssoufi retained his post, remained largely unchanged. Most notable among the new appointments were those of two senior figures from Istiqlal: the party's leader, Abbas el-Fassi, was appointed Minister of Social Development, Solidarity, Employment and Vocational Training, while Muhammad Khalifa assumed the public sector and administrative reform portfolio. Shortly afterwards, elections were held for one-third of the seats in the Chamber of Advisers. The RNI won the largest number of seats, taking 14 of the 90 seats available.

In July 2001, in a speech marking the second anniversary of his accession, King Muhammad reaffirmed his commitment to establishing a modern democratic state founded on fundamental public freedoms and human rights, and to modernize the economy and combat poverty; he also expressed his desire to eliminate nepotism and corruption in the administration and to establish a new social contract between unions, employers and government. Furthermore, the King pledged to promote the country's different regional and cultural components, and announced the establishment of a royal institute to 'protect, revive and promote Berber culture' and explore ways of integrating Tamazight (the principal Berber language) into the education system. At a time of violent unrest among Berbers in neighbouring Algeria, the authorities evidently wished to establish a basis for the legitimate expression of the aspirations of Morocco's large Tamazight-speaking population.

In September 2001 King Muhammad replaced Ahmed Midaoui as Minister of the Interior with a technocrat, Driss Jettou. This was the first appointment to the interior portfolio from outside the security services for 40 years. No reason was given for the sudden redeployment of Midaoui, who became an adviser to the King, but he had been criticized in some circles for failing to change the political culture of the ministry under his control. Jettou's appointment was interpreted as an attempt to improve the image of the monarchy in advance of parliamentary elections, which the King announced would take place as scheduled in September 2002.

While modernizing and changing the style of the monarchy, King Muhammad insisted on exercising the powers vested in the monarchy under the Constitution, and left no doubt that—like his father—he intended to reign and rule. The King continued to dominate the political sphere, making appointments to all key posts and formulating political strategy. There was disquiet in some circles at the appearance of a number of senior army officers in prominent positions in the King's entourage. Furthermore, the King's enthusiasm and high-profile activities contrasted sharply with the style of the opposition-led Government, which appeared lethargic and was subject to increasing public criticism. Despite some achievements el-Youssoufi's administration had failed to adopt important measures, notably concerning labour relations and women's rights, and in a context of sharply deteriorating socio-economic conditions was viewed as weak on economic management.

In March 2001 the sixth congress of the USFP—the first for 12 years—highlighted serious dissent within the party. A large group of delegates and three members of the party's political bureau, including Muhammad Nouabir Amaoui, head of the CDT, boycotted the meeting. Amaoui claimed that there had been irregularities in the election of delegates and an attempt to marginalize those who did not subscribe to the official party line. The CDT was opposed to the party's participation in government while the monarchy retained what it considered to be 'quasi-absolute powers', and was critical of the USFP-led Government's economic policies. Members of the party's youth wing (the Jeunesse Socialiste) also boycotted what they described as a 'congress of apparatchiks', criticized the leadership for participating in government when all key initiatives came from the King, and demanded the establishment of a constitutional monarchy. In October dissidents announced the creation of a separate political party, the Parti de Congrès National Unioniste, and elected Abdelmajid Bouzoubaâ as its leader. Meanwhile, following dissent within the MNP, three leading party figures, including Ahmad Moussaoui, the Minister for Youth and Sport, were expelled from its political bureau.

THE KING MOVES TO REDRESS HUMAN RIGHTS GRIEVANCES

After Muhammad's accession, Moroccan civil society swiftly grew in confidence and became more vocal, pressing for further changes and reforms. Particularly active were the associations for the defence of human rights such as Justice and Truth, established in October 1999 by the victims of arbitrary detention. Despite the payment of some US $14m. in compensation to past victims of repression, human rights organizations insisted that there could be no reconciliation without justice and demanded that those responsible for human rights abuses should be brought to trial. However, their outspokenness eventually provoked tensions with the authorities and a demonstration organized by the AMDH to mark the 52nd anniversary of the Universal Declaration of Human Rights in December was violently suppressed by the security forces. A later demonstration planned by Justice and Truth in January 2001 was banned.

Despite the Government's discontent with the human rights groups' forcefulness, in April 2001 it nevertheless signed a co-operation agreement with Amnesty International to promote awareness of human rights issues among those who make and implement the law. Amnesty International recognized the Moroccan Government's efforts in giving independence to the official CCDH and in reviving the debate on the rights of women. Nevertheless, Amnesty International maintained that there were still 60 political prisoners held in Moroccan gaols and that some 450 missing persons remained unaccounted for, and also criticized the authorities for not bringing to justice officials responsible for human rights abuses, as well as for allowing some of those suspected of such abuses to remain in post.

In June 2001 it was reported that the Moroccan authorities had for the first time given permission for a French judge to carry out inquiries in Morocco into the disappearance of opposition leader Mehdi Ben Barka in Paris in 1965. This followed strong lobbying by the nine surviving members of Ben Barka's family upon their return from exile. At the end of June 2001 a former member of the Moroccan special services, Ahmed

Boukhari, purportedly confessed in an interview with the French daily *Le Monde* and the Moroccan weekly *Le Journal* that a unit of the Moroccan special services had kidnapped Ben Barka in Paris, where he had died under torture. In subsequent interviews, Boukhari, the first Moroccan secret service agent to speak out publicly about the 'dirty war' conducted against dissidents in the 1960s and 1970s, began naming those allegedly responsible. In August 2001 he was sentenced to three months' imprisonment on unrelated charges of fraud dating back to the early 1990s, and after being released was subsequently rearrested and imprisoned for 'defamation'.

Alongside its moves to own up to past human rights abuses, the Government also stepped up its campaign against corruption in public life. It was reported that some 74,000 corruption cases had been referred to the courts during 2000 and 2001, including 211 major cases, compared with only 105 during the previous two decades; however, progress in these cases was slow. In a survey carried out by Transparency Maroc, a non-governmental organization (NGO) campaigning against corruption, one-third of respondents reported that they experienced corruption on a daily basis, with security personnel in rural areas and local and regional government officials identified as the most corrupt.

As illustrated by the behaviour of the AMDH, the King's new liberal approach encouraged many to test the limits of the state's beneficence. Berber groups, long denied a voice, felt sufficiently confident to express their dissatisfaction at plans, announced in March 2000, for the introduction of courses in Berber language in schools and universities from September, insisting that they lacked proper preparation and were intended to fail. However, it was the press that was most notable for its attempts to push the new boundaries. In the atmosphere of greater liberty that prevailed following Basri's removal from office, sections of the independent press acted as a driving force for change. However, it quickly became apparent that comments on the monarchy, the army and Western Sahara remained subject to censure. In April the authorities banned two of the most outspoken and popular weekly magazines, *Le Journal* and its Arabic companion *Al-Sahifa*, after the former published an interview conducted in the USA between its editor, Aboubakr Jamai, and the Polisario leader and SADR 'President', Muhammad Abd al-Aziz. Shortly afterwards, three senior officials of the popular TV channel 2M were dismissed after the banning of *Le Journal* was reported on a news broadcast, and the Minister of Communications took charge of the channel. Meanwhile, Mustafa Alaoui, the director of the best-selling Arabic weekly, *Al-Ousbouaa al-Maghribia*, was sentenced to three months' detention, suspended from practising as a journalist for three years and ordered to pay 1m. dirhams in damages after the magazine published allegations of corruption involving the Minister of Foreign Affairs and Co-operation, Muhammad Benaïssa. Khalid Mechbal, the editor of *Achamal*, received a six-month suspended sentence, was banned from journalism for one year and was ordered to pay damages of 100,000 dirhams for covering the same story. There was particular concern that the two men were sentenced not under the press code but under the penal code. In May 2000, however, the King granted the two men a royal amnesty, and the magazines banned a month earlier were allowed to resume publication. Nevertheless, Reporters sans frontières, an international NGO concerned with press freedom, claimed that during the first half of the year seven newspapers had been banned by the authorities.

In November 2000 the authorities expelled the bureau chief of Agence France-Presse in Morocco for 'hostile conduct'. In December *Le Journal*, *Al-Sahifa* and another popular French-language weekly, *Demain*, were proscribed indefinitely by the Government after they published a letter written in 1974 by Muhammad Basri, claiming that leading personalities in the USFP had been implicated in the 1972 failed military coup against King Hassan. The affair provoked a significant political crisis as, according to the official history of the USFP, the party had always used non-violent methods to oppose King Hassan's authoritarian regime. If the contents of the letter were to be believed, its leaders had collaborated not only with those elements in the military intent on overthrowing King Hassan by force, but also with the coup's leader, Gen. Oufkir, held responsible for the death of Mehdi Ben Barka in 1965.

El-Youssoufi insisted that the ban had been imposed not because of the reproduction of the letter but because the three weeklies had consistently attacked the monarchy and the army, and endangered the transition to democracy. In January 2001 Jamai claimed that el-Youssoufi's action exposed the growing influence of senior figures in the security apparatus opposed to greater democracy and their close alliance with the leadership of the USFP. After a wave of protests and the commencement by Jamai of a hunger strike, the Government announced that it would allow *Le Journal* to resume publication. At the beginning of March a court in Casablanca sentenced Jamai to three months' imprisonment and Ali Amar, the director-general of *Le Journal*, to two months' imprisonment, and ordered the payment of 2m. dirhams in damages. The two men had been charged with defamation after they approved a series of articles alleging financial irregularities related to the purchase of a new residence for the Moroccan ambassador to the USA at a time when Benaïssa held this post. The sentences were condemned by Reporters sans frontières. In November the editor-in-chief of *Demain* was sentenced to four months' imprisonment and fined for 'diffusion of false information', following an article that reported that one of the royal palaces might be sold to foreign interests. In December the authorities seized an issue of the magazine that carried the names of 45 people, some still holding official posts, alleged to have been responsible for human rights abuses during King Hassan's reign.

In March 2002 the lower house approved controversial new press legislation granting the courts, rather than the Prime Minister, authority to close down newspapers but retaining tough prison sentences for journalists whose writings offended the monarchy, the values of Islam or Morocco's 'territorial integrity'.

THE LEGISLATIVE ELECTION OF SEPTEMBER 2002

In March 2002 the parties represented in el-Youssoufi's coalition Government agreed important changes to the electoral system. These included abandoning the simple majority 'first-past-the-post' system, used since 1955, in favour of proportional representation. The Government insisted that the new system would reduce fraudulent practices and increase public confidence in the political system. At least 10% of the 325 seats in the lower house were to be reserved for women. The Ministry of the Interior was to redraw electoral boundaries, prepare new electoral rolls and issue millions of new identity cards. The draft legislation proposed stringent penalties for anyone attempting to interfere with the ballot or found guilty of offering or taking bribes to influence voting. The right-wing UC condemned the Government for rushing through changes to the electoral system only a few months before the next round of parliamentary elections, scheduled for 27 September. Al-Adl wal-Ihsan and the PADS both announced that they would boycott the poll.

The elections themselves were held in a relatively calm atmosphere, marred only by a few isolated violent incidents and occasional accusations of malpractice. The official results, announced on 1 October 2002, put the rate of participation at between 52% and 55% of the registered electorate, compared with 58.3% in 1997. Some sources, however, claimed that the level of abstention had been much higher, assessing turn-out at just 35%. The USFP enjoyed the greatest success, retaining 50 seats (down from 57 in 1997), while Istiqlal increased its representation from 32 in 1997 to 48. In third place was the PJD, which increased its number of seats from nine in 1997 to 42: this was a remarkable result, as the party had only presented candidates in 56 of the 91 constituencies. One of its leaders claimed that the party had wished to avoid a landslide victory and the resulting political consequences both at home and abroad, referring to 'the Algerian scenario'. It was speculated that advisers to the King persuaded the PJD to field candidates in a limited number of constituencies to allow the continuation of the process of democratization, which, with a PJD victory, could have been endangered.

The growing appeal of the PJD, however, was widely interpreted as a sign of protest against the failure of the mainstream parties to address the country's deep-seated social and economic problems. The centre-right RNI came fourth, with 41 seats (compared with 46 seats in 1997). Among the other parties, the main losers were the right-wing UC (16 seats, against 50 in 1997) and MP (27 seats, compared with 40 in 1997)—their past success had been widely attributed to support from the establishment—and the centre-right Mouvement Démocratique et Social (MDS), the representation of which declined from 32 seats to just seven. The centre-right MNP won 18 seats (compared with 19 in 1997), and the smaller left-wing parties slightly increased their representation—the PPS to 11 seats (from nine), the PSD to six (from five) and the FFD to 12 (from nine). Under the new electoral system, national lists reserved for female candidates ensured that 10% of deputies in the new 325-seat parliament would be women. In the event, 35 women were elected (compared with just two in 1997), the highest figure anywhere in the Arab world. As many had predicted, the new voting system produced a very fragmented lower house, and one unlikely to be able to assert itself against the dominant role of the palace.

The King had been expected to choose a new Prime Minister from the USFP leadership, as the party still held the largest number of seats in the new lower house. There was some surprise, therefore, when the King appointed Jettou to the post. Some commentators saw the decision as an extension of the King's policy of appointing so-called super-*walis* (regional governors) linked directly to the palace, and contested that, whereas King Hassan had ruled by manipulating the political parties, his son apparently sought to rule without them in the name of addressing urgent social and economic problems.

On 7 November 2002 a new Government was appointed, composed of six political parties: the USFP (eight ministers), Istiqlal (eight), the RNI (six), the MP (three), the PPS (two) and the MNP (two). (The PJD refused to participate in the new administration.) More than one-half of members were newcomers to government posts. The new Government included two leaders of political parties: Istiqlal's Secretary-General, Abbas el-Fassi, was promoted to the post of Minister of State without portfolio, and MP leader Mohand Laenser became Minister of Agriculture and Rural Development.

Following the elections, the USFP, together with five small parties—the PPS, the PSD, the Parti Al Ahd, the Union Démocratique and the FFD—announced that they would implement joint action within parliament and on other fronts 'to consolidate the regime founded on constitutional, democratic and social monarchy'. The right-wing UC and PND, with a combined total of 28 seats, declared that they would be forming a single bloc in the lower house, while the MDS urged its deputies to join a group to be formed with the MP and the MNP.

In October 2002 a group of young officers serving in Western Sahara, calling themselves the Comité d'Action des Officiers Libres des Forces Armées, issued a communiqué to the foreign press, under cover of anonymity, accusing certain senior officers of financial irregularities, which they claimed had resulted in a sharp deterioration in the living conditions of ordinary soldiers. They threatened to move to 'direct action', urging the King to retire senior commanders, to institute strict controls over the finances of army units, and to free and reintegrate officers condemned for denouncing corruption in their units. This was the first time that a 'free officers' movement had emerged in Morocco.

In December 2002 the King announced that the minimum age of eligibility to vote would be reduced from 20 years to 18, 'to bring new blood into the practice of democracy'. At the end of that month the new Government gave a commitment to cooperate with the CCDH on human rights issues, but a few days later Moroccan human rights organizations strongly condemned the authorities for what they claimed was a vast campaign of arrests since May, involving dozens of Moroccans and foreigners suspected of having links with Osama bin Laden's militant Islamist al-Qa'ida organization. It was alleged that the detainees had been tortured.

In October 2003 el-Youssoufi, who had remained Secretary-General of the USFP, announced that he was withdrawing from political life. A month later Muhammad el-Yazghi, Deputy First Secretary of the party since 1992 and currently Minister of Territorial Administration, Water Resources and the Environment, was elected party leader.

SUICIDE BOMBINGS IN CASABLANCA AND THE RISE OF ISLAMISM

The Islamist movement, the influence of which extended over wide sections of society, had started to become more visible since 2000, as both the officially recognized PJD and the unauthorized Al-Adl wal-Ihsan increased in prominence. In February of that year the leader of Al-Adl wal-Ihsan, Abdessalam Yassine, posted on his internet site an 18-page letter, addressed to King Muhammad, in which he launched a vitriolic attack on the reign of Hassan II. In it, he appealed to King Muhammad to relinquish his father's assets abroad—estimated at US $400m.—in order to pay off the national debt, and condemned the traditional ceremony of allegiance to the monarch (*baia*) as a sacrilegious abomination. Yassine also stated that the current political system was the principal reason for the backwardness of the country and that only genuine democratic reforms would save Morocco. In March Al-Adl wal-Ihsan, together with the PJD and the League of Ulama, organized a rally in Casablanca in which a reported 500,000 Islamists protested against a controversial programme of social reforms, proposed by the Secretary of State for Social Affairs, a principal outcome of which would be vastly to improve the social status and legal rights of Moroccan women. The proposals included allocating women one-third of all seats in parliament; raising the minimum age of marriage for women from 15 to 18 years; bans on polygamy and on 'repudiation' as a form of divorce; and equal rights for women under a divorce settlement. The plan was regarded by Islamists as a serious assault on the country's religious code of personal law. The protests forced the Government to establish a special panel to review the planned reforms, and a new law on personal statute was not promulgated until 2003, following the personal intervention of the King and the unexpected turnaround of Al-Adl wal-Ihsan.

In May 2001 Abdessalam Yassine was released from house arrest, although Al-Adl wal-Ihsan remained technically prohibited. At the same time the organization's newspaper was banned, as were marches planned near the border with Algeria. In June mosques, which had been ordered by Basri to close between prayers, were allowed to open from dawn to last prayers. However, the decision was quickly reversed by the Ministry of the Interior because of fears of the politicization of the mosques. In July security forces broke up a beach camp organized by Al-Adl wal-Ihsan at Mahdia, north of Rabat, arresting 49 Islamists. In December numerous Islamists were arrested when police dispersed peaceful demonstrations in the capital and in a number of other cities, organized to protest against the restrictions placed on Al-Adl wal-Ihsan's activities and to demand its recognition as a political party.

From August 2002 there were reports that the security forces had launched a campaign to target Islamist extremists, closing Islamist bookshops and seizing 'extremist' literature and audio-cassettes. The extent of extremist activities became all too apparent on the evening of 16 May 2003, when a series of suicide bomb attacks in central Casablanca targeted restaurants and hotels frequented by foreigners and a Jewish cultural centre; 45 people were killed, and 100 others injured. Six Europeans were among the dead, but most of the victims were Moroccans. Army units were immediately deployed outside major public buildings and the main hotels in the city. Some 30 arrests quickly followed, and the authorities announced that they had already identified the 12 suicide bombers, all of whom were Moroccans believed to be linked to a small extremist Islamist group, based in one of Casablanca's many shanty towns. The authorities insisted that the attacks had been orchestrated by an international terrorist network operating in Europe, possibly al-Qa'ida.

The Casablanca bombings were very similar to attacks perpetrated a few days before in Riyadh, Saudi Arabia, said to be the work of al-Qa'ida. Certain commentators referred to a recorded message issued some months before, attributed to

Osama bin Laden, in which Morocco was named as one of the Arab countries that Muslims must liberate from an 'apostate regime subservient to the USA'. However, some specialists emphasized that groups associated with al-Qa'ida recruit from among the underprivileged and marginalized strata of society and have local traditions. The attacks were viewed not only as a challenge to the Moroccan state but also to the traditional Islamist leadership of the PJD and Al-Adl wal-Ihsan, although the secular parties immediately directed blame at both movements for their politicized use of religion. At the end of May 2003 Prime Minister Jettou, with several government officials, led a march through Casablanca to condemn terrorism; 1m. people were estimated to have taken part. The PJD stayed away, and police were reported to have prevented members of Al-Adl wal-Ihsan from joining the demonstration. Leaders of several political parties accused the PJD of spreading radicalism among the country's youth, and there were some demands for the party and all Islamist organizations to be dissolved and banned.

Following the suicide bomb attacks in Casablanca, the Moroccan parliament swiftly approved uncompromising new anti-terrorism legislation (with the support of the PJD), giving the security forces increased powers. By July 2003 it was reported that more than 200 people had been arrested in connection with the attacks. Meanwhile, the trial began of the first 16 defendants, including three alleged suicide bombers who had survived the attacks and six people accused of preparing bomb attacks in Essaouira, Agadir and Marrakesh at the same time as those in Casablanca. In August four men, including two surviving suicide bombers, were sentenced to death for their part in the Casablanca attacks. Meanwhile, the Moroccan authorities issued international arrest warrants for several members of the extremist Groupe Islamique Combattant Marocain (GICM) living in Europe for their alleged involvement in the bombings, although the supporting evidence presented did not appear to be particularly strong.

In July 2003 a total of 10 of the 31 alleged members of a small radical group, Salafia Jihadia, who had been arrested during police operations against Islamist networks in mid-2002, were sentenced to death by a court in Casablanca, having been convicted of murder and attempted murder. Among those who received the death penalty were the group's leader, Youssef Fikri, who admitted at his trial to having killed 'enemies of God'. Eight of the accused received sentences of life imprisonment, and the remainder custodial sentences of 10–20 years. Salafia Jihadia was suspected of being involved in the suicide bomb attacks in Casablanca in May 2003.

During 2005 the King pardoned 285 Islamist prisoners who had been convicted under anti-terrorism legislation, including 164 members of Salafia Jihadia (who were released in November). Reports also suggested that death sentences imposed on a further 27 Islamists would be commuted to custodial terms. Ennassir, a support association for Islamist prisoners in Morocco, estimated that more than 2,000 Islamists were imprisoned in the country's gaols, the majority of whom were members of Salafia Jihadia and the GICM. In November police arrested 17 Islamists suspected of planning attacks on US and Jewish interests in Morocco and on the parliament building in Rabat. The group included two men who previously had been detained at the US military base at Guantánamo Bay, Cuba, and who had been deported to Morocco in August 2004. In December 2005 some 11 members of another group suspected of organizing terrorist acts were arrested in Casablanca. In May 2006 a total of 240 prisoners belonging to Salafia Jihadia began a month-long hunger strike in an attempt to force an appeal against their sentences. In late May and early June 500 Al-Adl wal-Ihsan activists were arrested, and materials produced to publicize the movement were seized in operations carried out by the security forces across the country. The Minister of the Interior asserted that the movement had 'placed itself outside the law and legitimate representative institutions' when it had announced a campaign to recruit new members, and emphasized that the actions of the security forces had been necessary to prevent the manipulation of Moroccan citizens. The threat from Islamist militants resurfaced in April 2007 when a number of attempts by suicide bombers to attack sensitive sites such as the US consulate in Casablanca were thwarted by the security forces. Some of the bombers chose to detonate their devices against themselves rather than face capture, while others were arrested during the planning stage of their operations.

In January 2008 some 50 Islamists belonging to the little-known Mehdi Partisans were imprisoned after having been found guilty of plotting bomb attacks and carrying out robberies. The following month the security forces announced that they had uncovered a large Islamist network, resulting in the arrest of 35 suspects and the discovery of a significant cache of arms. The suspected leader of the group was Abdelkader Belliraj, who ordinarily resided in Belgium. The Belgian media subsequently reported that Belliraj was on the payroll of the Belgian intelligence services as an informer, thus raising diplomatic tensions between the two countries. Among the other detainees were two senior members of a small Islamist party, al-Badil al-Hadari (Civilized Alternative). The party, which was accused of acting as a front for the militant Islamist network and for planning to assassinate government ministers and Moroccan Jews, was subsequently dissolved. However, in March the group filed a lawsuit challenging the dissolution order. In July 2009 Belliraj was convicted of 'disturbing the state's internal security and premeditated murder', and sentenced to life imprisonment. Some 30 other defendants received sentences of between two and 30 years' imprisonment.

In April 2008 Islamist prisoners incarcerated around the country held a one-day hunger strike in protest against prison conditions and their alleged mistreatment. A report by Agence France-Presse claimed that since the Casablanca bombings the security services had arrested more than 3,000 suspected militants and that up to 1,000 remained in prison.

Of particular concern to the authorities has been the spill-over effect of militancy from other countries in the region—especially Algeria. In late 2006 an Algerian Islamist group, the Groupe Salafiste Pour la Prédication et le Combat, announced that it was aligning itself with al-Qa'ida, changing its name in early 2007 to al-Qa'ida Organization in the Land of the Islamic Maghreb (AQIM). The new group stated that it wanted to spread its influence over the whole of North Africa. Attuned to the threat, in May 2008 Moroccan security forces arrested 11 people who were suspected of recruiting fighters on behalf of al-Qa'ida to join the insurgency in Iraq. Some of their number were also accused of planning attacks in Morocco, suggesting that AQIM was slowly gaining a foothold in the country. These concerns were reiterated in July, when police arrested a further 30 people suspected of recruiting jihadists to the Islamist cause.

Another 15 arrests took place in August 2008. The Government stated that its security operations were designed to be 'preventative' and that it was particularly concerned about the activities of Moroccans residing in Europe. As a consequence, during Ramadan (which fell during September that year), the Government sent Moroccan preachers abroad, mainly to France, to promote moderate spiritual guidance. Later that month, in a key speech, the King announced reforms to Islamic jurisprudence in Morocco. These included the restructuring of local *ulama* councils; the establishment of an *ulama* council for the Moroccan community in Europe; and the creation of a new and separate body with the power to issue *fatwas* (religious edicts). The Government's concerns over the involvement of Moroccan expatriates in militant activity was borne out in December, when a number of radical Moroccan Islamists were arrested in separate raids in Belgium and Italy. The security forces also remained active within Morocco. In April 2010 a total of 24 alleged members of AQIM, suspected of seeking to target Moroccan-based foreigners, were arrested, and arms and ammunition were seized. This action was followed in August with the arrest of an additional 18 suspected Islamic militants, who were believed to have been plotting to attack foreign targets in Morocco.

In April 2011 Morocco suffered another bomb attack, this time in Marrakesh. The explosives, which had been planted in a café popular with tourists, killed 17 people and injured 20 more. AQIM denied responsibility for the attack, which appeared to be the work of an independent Islamist group. A total of nine Moroccans were subsequently arrested in connection with the incident; the trial of the nine men on charges including forming a criminal group to commit terrorist acts, possession and manufacture of explosives, and premeditated murder, began at a court in Salé in June. In October Adel Othmani was convicted of participation in the bombing and sentenced to death; a second defendant was also convicted for his role in the attack and received a sentence of life imprisonment. The seven remaining defendants were sentenced to terms of imprisonment of between two and four years. In March 2012, however, an appeals court increased the second defendant's life sentence to one of death, while extending the seven other prison sentences to between six and 10 years. The court also confirmed Othmani's death sentence.

REFORM OF THE FAMILY CODE

The new liberal era ushered in by King Muhammad highlighted differences between moderates and conservatives, which were most noticeable over women's rights. After the King met representatives of women's groups in March 2001, he announced the establishment of a royal commission, headed by Driss Dahak, President of the Supreme Court, and including leading Islamic scholars and jurists, to revise the country's laws on personal rights and responsibilities. However, given the strength of opposition to proposals introduced in 2000 to give women greater rights, doubts were raised whether this latest commission would make any progress on this issue. Nevertheless, the King continued to show his commitment to greater rights for women by appointing women to posts of royal advisers, ambassadors and other senior public positions. In July 2001 the King appointed new *walis* without consulting premier el-Youssoufi, and in January 2002 he granted them extensive new powers to give their actions maximum efficiency. Some observers contended that the appointment of these US-style 'city managers' in the name of decentralization and regionalization had, in practice, strengthened the influence of the palace at the expense of the Government.

In a speech at the opening of parliament in early October 2003 King Muhammad announced the main outlines of a controversial new family code (*moudawana*). Under the new code, the family was to become the joint responsibility of both spouses, rather than just the father. A wife's obligation to obey her husband was to be replaced by equality between the two partners. A woman would no longer require the permission of her father or brother to marry, and the minimum age of marriage for girls was to be raised from 15 to 18 years. While there was to be no formal ban on polygamy, the practice would be made extremely difficult. Similarly, the act of repudiation would be restricted and would require legal authorization. If a couple separated, the mother would normally be granted guardianship of the children. The bill was adopted unanimously by both upper and lower chambers in January 2004. The King had made it clear that the legislature would not be permitted to change the basic principles incorporated in the new code but only to comment on legal procedures, and insisted that the new code must be implemented effectively. The new *moudawana* was seen as the most important of King Muhammad's reforms since taking the throne.

THE EQUITY AND RECONCILIATION COMMISSION

In January 2004 King Muhammad officially inaugurated an Equity and Reconciliation Commission (Instance Equité et Réconciliation—IER) to close the file on serious human rights violations committed between 1956 and 1999. Among the IER's aims were to establish a detailed schedule of the violations committed during this period, and to put forward recommendations to the King to ensure that they were never repeated. In December 2004 the IER organized the first of a series of public meetings, broadcast on national television and radio, at which victims of human rights abuses spoke about their experiences—this was the first time in any Arab country that victims had been given such a public platform. However, victims were obliged to agree not to name their torturers. The UN Commission on Human Rights expressed concern that it had been decided not to open criminal proceedings against those responsible for human rights abuses, and the AMDH condemned the fact that those responsible, including several still holding senior positions in the state apparatus, should benefit from impunity. For his part, the King insisted that the IER was not a tribunal, rather a forum for examining this page in the country's history.

The IER presented its final report to King Muhammad in November 2005. More than 17,000 individual cases were reviewed and over 9,000 victims received compensation as a result. Investigations had discovered the graves of over 600 'disappeared' political opponents who had died in illegal detention centres. The report drew attention to the state's role in past human rights abuses, and sought an official apology for the victims. The IER recommended reforms to the justice system, and emphasized the need to strengthen the latter's independence; it also stressed the importance of measures to ensure that no one responsible for human rights abuses should benefit from impunity. The Government reacted favourably to the recommendations, and indicated that it would examine how the state should officially acknowledge its responsibility for past acts. The King expressed his resolve to 'turn the page on those dark years'. None the less, Human Rights Watch regretted that the IER was only a consultative body and that no state institution was obliged to implement or even seriously consider its recommendations, and insisted that those involved in torture be brought to justice. In December the French judge investigating the disappearance of Ben Barka criticized the Moroccan authorities for their continued obstruction of his inquiries. Meanwhile, human rights activists reported that the Moroccan authorities had exhumed the remains of 100 people killed during riots in Casablanca in 1981 (at that time, 66 deaths had been officially reported), who had subsequently been buried in mass graves.

In January 2006 King Muhammad announced that the CCDH would be charged with implementing the IER's recommendations and insisted that state authorities would co-operate. The King also expressed sympathy for the families of victims, but stopped short of issuing a formal apology. In late January the Ministry of Justice announced that the security forces had arrested 31 police and penal administrators on charges of torture; they were to face prosecution under new legislation, approved by parliament in October 2005, outlawing torture. In May 2006 the CCDH and the Ministry of the Interior signed an agreement to co-operate as part of a national initiative to promote a 'culture of human rights' in education and training. Meanwhile, the CCDH continued the IER's work, locating the graves of a further 100 people who had 'disappeared' during King Hassan's reign. Despite the promise of change, the regressive anti-terrorism legislation has led to renewed claims of torture and unfair trials.

In a speech in August 2009, the King outlined plans for the 'in-depth, comprehensive reform of the judicial system', which included the establishment of an advisory panel to discuss the priority goals of the reform process: judicial independence; administration and efficiency; human resources and expertise; and corruption. The Ministry of Justice was charged with overseeing the implementation of the reforms, but little progress had been made by the time protests broke out in Morocco in early 2011, prompted by the revolutions that had occurred in Tunisia, Libya and Egypt. Among the protesters' demands was the call for an independent judiciary, to which the King subsequently responded in a package of constitutional reforms.

PUBLIC DISSENT AND THE FREEDOM OF EXPRESSION

Social depredation has long been a source of unrest in Morocco, with jobs—either the lack of them, or conditions within them—causing sporadic outbreaks of public disturbances. Upon his accession, King Muhammad inherited long-standing welfare and employment-related concerns. In 2000 employers' organizations demanded greater flexibility in the rules governing employment. There was mounting discontent among trade unions and employees over pay, and a general strike was only averted in April after the Government agreed to concessions, including a 10% increase in the minimum wage and further negotiations on the proposed new labour law. These concessions, enshrined in a 'social contract to establish social peace', failed to prevent renewed industrial action by some workers. Despite government pledges to accelerate the recruitment of graduates into the public sector, unemployed graduates continued to demonstrate, and in June violent clashes erupted in Rabat between police and protesters from the proscribed l'Association Nationale des Diplômés Chômeurs du Maroc (ANDCM). The Government defended its decision to use force on the grounds that the protest had been unauthorized.

In June 2003 the Court of Appeal upheld a four-year prison sentence imposed in the previous month on a journalist, Ali Lmrabet, for 'insulting the King' by publishing the annual budget for the royal household. Lmrabet had been on a hunger strike since May and had been hospitalized because of a sharp deterioration in his health. Lmrabet ended his hunger strike later in June. He was one of seven journalists pardoned by the King in January 2004.

Meanwhile, in June 2005 a court of appeal upheld a sentence forbidding Lmrabet from working as a journalist for 10 years after he challenged official policy on the Sahrawi refugees in Tindouf, and in July Nadia Yassine, spokesperson for Al-Adl wal-Ihsan, was put on trial for insulting the monarchy after she expressed her preference for a republican regime. The international publicity attracted by the case of Nadia Yassine prevented the courts from pursuing the matter further, although some restrictions were placed on her movements for a time. In December the Minister of Justice announced that he had set up a unit to monitor the press. Several journalists were subject to charges of defamation and very heavy fines after reporting on sensitive topics, exemplifying the limits that continued to be placed on freedom of expression. The practice of imposing heavy fines on newspapers and magazines had become an effective substitute for closing them down, as very rarely do these publications have the necessary resources to meet the cost.

In December 2006 Jamai was fined 3m. dirhams for libel, after publishing an article in *Le Journal* which alleged that the head of the European Strategic Intelligence and Security Center, Claude Moniquet, was biased in favour of the Moroccan Government's position on Western Sahara. After Moniquet launched proceedings against Jamai in a Moroccan court (a move supported by the Government), Jamai resigned and left the country to allow the magazine to continue publishing. However, the ruling was upheld in 2009 after he returned to Morocco, resulting in the magazine's bankruptcy. Meanwhile, in July 2007 the authorities arrested the editor of the magazine *Al-Watan al-An*, Abderrahim Ariri, for having published documents relating to national security matters. Ariri was later released, but a journalist for the publication, Mustapha Hormatallah, was sentenced to eight months' imprisonment.

Official sensitivity over press freedom was further demonstrated in February 2008, when a man who had created a false profile of the King's brother, Prince Moulay, on the social networking website Facebook was sentenced to three years' imprisonment for identity fraud. Although he was pardoned by the King a month later, both this incident and the earlier detention of Ariri indicate that the subjects of the royal family and Western Sahara continue to test Morocco's tolerance of press freedom. This view was reinforced by an incident in May, when the Government withdrew the broadcasting licence of the Qatar-based television network Al Jazeera, officially for technical and legal reasons. However, tellingly, the measure came after the network had interviewed human rights activists who had criticized the Government's policy towards Western Sahara. The Government had already been provoked by an earlier report broadcast by the channel, which suggested that a secret relationship existed between King Hassan's regime and Israel.

Unrest linked to unemployment and deteriorating standards of living emerged again in May 2008, when hundreds of youthful demonstrators took to the streets in Sidi Ifni, a port on Morocco's south-western coast. Organized by Attac Maroc, an anti-globalization movement, and the ANDCM, a group representing unemployed graduates, the protests succeeded in blockading the town's port for a week, before demonstrators were dispersed by riot police in early June. Al Jazeera reported that up to 10 demonstrators had been killed during the protests, although this was denied by the Government, which subsequently summoned the Al Jazeera reporter for questioning.

FURTHER POLITICAL REFORM AND THE EMERGENCE OF THE PAM

At the PJD's fifth congress, held in April 2004, Saâdeddine el-Othmani was elected Secretary-General. The election of Othmani, regarded as a moderate, was seen by some as marginalizing radical elements in the party. In October King Muhammad announced details of a bill designed to reform the regulation of political parties, notably imposing stringent rules concerning democratic practices and transparent financial management. The bill received parliamentary approval a year later. At the opening of parliament in October 2005 King Muhammad insisted that the new legislation would strengthen the political parties and allow them to play a major role in the development of a democratic society. However, critics claimed that the new law was designed to limit the right of association and to strengthen state control over political discourse. The law proscribed any party based on religion, ethnicity, language, or region, or that had the aim of impugning Islam, the monarchy or Morocco's territorial integrity.

Several political parties merged during 2005. In September the Parti de la Gauche Socialiste Unifiée—itself a coalition of small left-wing groups—and Fidélité à la Démocratie combined to form the Parti Socialiste Unifié (PSU). In December the PSD merged with the USFP, under the latter's name. In February 2006 the USFP and the PPS reaffirmed their commitment to the alliance with Istiqlal in the 'Koutla Démocratique' and to the presentation of a common programme for the 2007 legislative elections.

In February 2006 Chakib Benmoussa, a non-affiliate, was appointed as Minister of the Interior. In April Benmoussa began consultations with the main political parties regarding proposals to revise the electoral code, and in June the constituent parties of the governing coalition accepted a proposal to modify the proportional list system adopted in 2002. Most notably, the threshold required for a party to enter parliament was to be increased from 3% to 5%, an amendment likely to lead to a reduction in the number of parties represented in Parliament, and which could encourage further mergers and alliances. The quota of seats in the Chamber of Representatives reserved for female candidates remained unchanged at 10%; women's associations had previously demanded an increase to one-third of the total number of seats. Under the proposed amendments, the Ministry of the Interior would retain the responsibility of defining constituency boundaries. The PSU dismissed the proposed 5% threshold as 'undemocratic and unconstitutional', and protested against the exclusion of opposition parties from the discussions. Elections were conducted on 8 September 2006 to renew one-third of the seats in the Chamber of Advisers. The largest number of seats went to Istiqlal, which took 17 of the 90 seats that were contested.

Legislative elections were held on 7 September 2007. In accordance with a provision announced by King Muhammad in November 2005, for the first time in the country's history Moroccans resident abroad (numbering approximately 2.8m. in 2005) were eligible both to vote and to stand as candidates in the polls. Istiqlal emerged as the largest party in the Chamber of Representatives, with 10.7% of the vote and 52 seats. The PJD narrowly surpassed Istiqlal in the popular vote, achieving 10.9% of the valid votes cast; however, it only won 46 seats, four more than in the previous legislature. The discrepancy was attributed to the inequalities of the electoral system, which favoured rural, conservative constituencies over urban ones. The USFP relinquished 12 of its 50 seats, and was outperformed by both the MP and the RNI, which achieved 41 and 39 seats, respectively. Voter turn-out was reported as 37%, of whom 19% deposited blank or invalid ballots. In mid-September 2007 King Muhammad appointed Abbas el-Fassi, Secretary-General of Istiqlal, as Prime Minister. The new premier established a ruling four-party coalition, consisting of Istiqlal, the USFP, the PPS and the RNI, together with a number of independents. However, due to political differences, it took more than a month to agree a mutually acceptable 33-member Cabinet, which consisted mostly of technocrats. Although local analysts suggested that the balance within the Cabinet highlighted the weakness of the coalition, it was broadly agreed that policy continuity would be assured, with a resolution to the controversial question of Western Sahara high on the agenda. The Prime Minister was challenged by his first mini-crisis almost immediately upon assuming the post, when the leader and deputy leader of the USFP—Minister of State Muhammad el-Yazghi and Minister of Justice Abdelwahed Radi, respectively—were forced to resign. The two men, already under pressure following the party's poor election results, precipitated an internal argument after giving their support to a series of tax reduction measures proposed in the draft 2008 budget in November 2007. Most of the party's representatives in parliament opposed the measures, and, although the bill was eventually approved, the party forced the two members either to resign their party positions or their ministries; they both chose the former course of action.

The ruling coalition was also challenged by another emerging threat in the shape of a new political association, which was established in January 2008 by Fouad Ali el-Himma, a member of the Chamber of Representatives and former Minister of the Interior (as well as being a school friend of the King). The new group, the Mouvement Pour Tous les Démocrates (MTD), positioned itself to the left of the centre and was clearly acting as a pro-Government organization. Concerns were soon voiced that the MTD was just the latest disguise to be adopted by the so-called *makhzen*—the ruling cabal centred around the monarchy—in order that it might wield more direct influence over the political process.

Despite this scepticism, by the middle of 2008 the new group had consolidated its position and, having co-opted five other small parties (PND, Al Ahd, the Parti de l'Environnement et du Développement, the Alliance des Libertés and the Initiative Citoyenneté et Développement), announced in August that it was setting itself up as a political party, under the name Parti de l'Authenticité et de la Modernité (PAM). Between them, the five parties held 21 of the 325 seats in parliament. They were all dissolved and merged into the PAM, and were joined by 15 serving parliamentarians informally aligned with the PAM, giving the new party control of 11% of the seats in parliament. The PAM won another seat in a by-election in September, but differences quickly emerged within the broad coalition and the former leaders of the PND and the Parti de l'Environnement et du Développement announced their departure from the party. (In 2009 the two leaders founded new parties as a 'continuation' of their respective previous formations.) However, in late September 2008 the PAM announced that it had agreed a separate merger with the RNI, one of the country's main parties within the ruling coalition, effectively taking the PAM into government. Meanwhile, the USFP, struggling to regroup after the earlier resignations of its leaders and continued internal discord, elected Abdelwahed Radi as Secretary-General in November.

Much of the political focus in the early part of 2009 was on the PAM, as internal discord threatened to splinter the group. In February a former Minister of Health, Muhammad Cheikh Biadillah, was chosen as the party's first leader. However, less than a month later the former Secretary-General of Al Ahd announced his resignation from the PAM and the formation of a new party, Al Ahd Démocratique. In May, following simmering differences with the governing coalition, the PAM announced its withdrawal from the RNI, effectively denying the Government a majority in parliament. Despite these continual internal tensions, the PAM performed strongly in the municipal elections in mid-June, securing 21.7% of the seats and relegating Istiqlal (19.1%) into second place. The PJD only managed to take 5.5% of seats, coming seventh overall. The PAM further consolidated its position in October, when Biadillah was elected as President of the Chamber of Advisers. However, as protests took place in Morocco in early 2011 and demands for political reform increased, the PAM's proximity to the regime looked increasingly like a liability. In particular, Fouad el-Himma was widely perceived as an obstacle to political reform and perhaps in recognition of this, in May, he offered his resignation from the PAM, although the party rejected his offer.

In July 2009 King Muhammad announced a minor reorganization of the Government. Most notably, the leader of the MP, Mohand Laenser, joined the Cabinet as Minister of State, while party colleague Muhammad Ouzine became Secretary of State for Foreign Affairs and Co-operation. In January 2010 Chakib Benmoussa was replaced as Minister of the Interior by Taïb Cherkaoui, hitherto President of the Supreme Court, while Muhammad Naciri became the new Minister of Justice. In early April Radi was elected as President of the Chamber of Representatives.

PROTESTS AND CONSTITUTIONAL REFORM

The fervour for democratic political reform that swept across much of North Africa and parts of the wider Middle East in early 2011 inevitably gained traction in Morocco, fuelled by long-standing political and socio-economic disaffection. On 20 February protests took place in the main urban areas across the country, including Rabat, Casablanca, Marrakesh and Tangier. They brought together a whole range of diverse groups and interests, under the banner of the February 20th Movement for Change. They demanded constitutional reform and a shift in the structure of government from an absolute to a constitutional monarchy. The protesters were clear that they did not challenge the legitimacy of the King, but that they wanted sufficiently far-reaching reform to ensure a clear separation and balance of power. The demonstrations were peaceful and only attracted around 40,000 participants, which in part reflected the widespread support for King Muhammad VI, as well as public concerns over instability.

Although the protests failed to rouse the mass public support seen in Tunisia and Egypt, they were large enough to force the King into responding to the protesters' demands. In early March 2011 he announced that he would establish a constitutional reform committee, which would report in June, and on whose findings the public would vote in a referendum. However, the protesters claimed that the move did not go far enough, since the King retained control over the appointment of the committee and the scope of its deliberations. Their own demands had also become more specific: they wanted the Government to be dismissed and the *makhzen* to be dismantled, and also demanded that public officials be tried for corruption. As a result, more protests followed, although they failed to gain any real critical mass of public support. The King responded with further concessions: in mid-April he ordered the release of numerous political prisoners and later that month he raised public sector salaries and increased the minimum wage.

In early June 2011 the constitutional committee delivered its report and the referendum duly went ahead in the following month. The Government claimed that turn-out was 73.5% and stated that the proposed constitutional reforms were approved by 98.5% of voters. The uncorroborated figures raised doubt both domestically and internationally, but the Government argued that they were a vindication of the King's plans. In fact, the reforms did not go nearly as far as the protesters had demanded, and while they granted the Government executive power and gave wider legislative authority to parliament, the King still retained wide-ranging powers, allowing him to intervene in almost all areas of state. The February 20th Movement for Change staged another set of protests just after the referendum, but in recognition of the support for the King, their demands were more focused on corruption and human rights. Following much speculation regarding the likelihood of early legislative elections, in August Cherkaoui announced that polls would be held on 25 November.

THE 2011 LEGISLATIVE ELECTIONS

The PJD emerged as the strongest party in the Chamber of Representatives after the November 2011 polls, winning 107 of the 395 seats. Istiqlal obtained 60 seats, followed by the RNI with 52, the PAM with 47 and the USFP with 39. Having failed to secure an outright majority, the PJD was obliged to form a coalition Government that included the centre-right MP (which controlled 32 seats) and the socialist PPS (18 seats). PJD Secretary-General Abdelilah Benkirane was appointed as Prime Minister. Notably, the Minister of the Interior, MP leader Mohand Laenser, remained in office despite the change of government.

The voter participation rate was only 45%, although that was higher than the 37% recorded in 2007. The modest turn-out in

2011 partly reflected the assumption held by some Moroccans, including those younger voters sympathetic to the February 20th Movement who had urged a boycott, that government power would continue to be circumscribed in practice by the palace, and was also indicative of frustration with the assumed dominance of the old parties over the parliamentary process.

In theory, Benkirane could exploit the powers granted to the Chamber of Representatives under the new Constitution to ensure that his Government determined domestic policy, as opposed to the palace. In practice, however, the King's approval was still needed to advance policy. Authority over foreign affairs also remained with the King, who retained prerogative power. PJD officials spoke optimistically of restoring 'balance' in Morocco's relations with Europe but knew that they lacked the authority to effect this. The PJD did not directly oppose the ruling authorities, reflecting the party's philosophy, which was rooted in pragmatism and a rejection of the harder-line approach of other Moroccan Islamists, and was shaped by the experience of conflict in neighbouring Algeria between the state and militant Islamists in the 1990s. Indeed, in January 2012 the PJD reportedly accused supporters of the February 20th Movement of wanting to overthrow the monarchy.

Despite the greater authority that had ostensibly been bestowed upon the elected Government, the reform process continued to be criticized as inadequate by different sections of society. In May 2012 a number of judges publicly expressed their frustration at the perceived failure of the Government to carry out the judicial reforms promised by the King, while trade unions organized a mass demonstration in Casablanca to protest against the Government's failure to implement reforms. The February 20th Movement also had a tense relationship with the authorities. In March the detention of a February 20th activist in Beni Ayach prompted disturbances and further arrests, and in July the Movement led a 3,000-strong protest in the capital. For his part, Benkirane had had a periodically tense relationship with parts of the private sector, which he accused of colluding with certain private media outlets to undermine his Government and his relationship with the King.

At the opening session of the legislature in October 2012, King Muhammad gave a speech in which he urged parliament to encourage democratic reforms, including furthering the policy of regionalization and promoting judicial independence. Earlier that month an unauthorized protest by members of the judiciary took place in Rabat, at which they called for an end to official interference in judicial matters.

A broader mass protest took place in Rabat in March 2013. The march was supported by trade unionists, human rights activists, members of the February 20th Movement and representatives of civil society. Protesters called for economic and social reforms, and denounced the high level of unemployment and increased living costs, although some also demanded Benkirane's resignation. Unofficial reports put the number of demonstrators at 30,000, while police stated that around 3,000 people had attended. Further criticism followed in April, after the Government's deferred some 15,000m. dirhams in investment spending in an effort to address the public deficit.

In early May 2013 Istiqlal announced its intention to withdraw from the coalition Government, claiming that Benkirane had monopolized decision-making within the coalition and citing its disagreement with his economic policies, which, it claimed, had caused an increase in consumer prices. Following a subsequent intervention by King Muhammad, however, the party revoked its decision, citing a desire to maintain stability and to serve the interests of the country. Yet the coalition remained uneasy and in early July Istiqlal finally left the Government, citing irrevocable differences with the PJD. Five of Istiqlal's six ministers submitted their resignations to King Muhammad and these were accepted later that month. It was reported at that time that the Minister of National Education, Muhammad el-Ouafa, had refused to resign and was threatened with expulsion from the party. In the following months Benkirane held discussions with other leading parties to form a new coalition, and in early September it was reported that the RNI had agreed to participate.

UN PEACE PLAN FOR WESTERN SAHARA—1988

As fighting between Moroccan troops and Polisario forces continued, the UN and the OAU made a concerted effort to settle the conflict in Western Sahara. In August 1988 the UN Secretary-General announced that a detailed peace plan had been drafted. The plan contained proposals for a cease-fire and a referendum to determine the status of the territory, while a UN representative, with wide-ranging powers, and a 2,000-strong UN monitoring force were to oversee their implementation. Prior to the referendum, Morocco was to reduce its presence in Western Sahara from 100,000 to 25,000 troops, who would then be confined to barracks, while Polisario forces (totalling an estimated 8,000) were to withdraw to their bases. The referendum was to offer a choice between complete independence for the territory and its integration into Morocco; it was hoped that a further option would be added, offering a large measure of autonomy for the Sahrawi people under the Moroccan crown. Both Morocco and the Polisario Front formally accepted the UN peace plan, although both sides expressed reservations. However, the UN's expectation that a cease-fire could be secured within a month, and the referendum held within six months, proved wholly unrealistic.

In October 1988 the UN General Assembly agreed that direct talks should be held, to be followed by a cease-fire and a referendum. Morocco abstained in the voting, claiming that, since both sides had accepted the UN proposal for a cease-fire, there was no need for direct talks. Polisario stepped up their attacks, but King Hassan refused to 'negotiate with his own subjects' and announced his readiness to order his troops across international borders in pursuit of Polisario forces. Morocco, meanwhile, continued its massive development programme in Western Sahara, where Moroccan settlers, able to relocate as a result of attractive financial packages, now outnumbered the original inhabitants in the territory. It was not until April 1991 that the UN Security Council approved Resolution 690, authorizing the establishment of a UN Mission for the Referendum in Western Sahara (MINURSO), which was to implement the plan for a referendum of self-determination with a UN peace-keeping force to supervise the operation. The cease-fire came into effect on 6 September, and the deployment of MINURSO personnel began at el-Aaiún. Within two weeks each side had accused the other of violating the cease-fire, while disagreements over exactly who was entitled to vote resulted in the postponement of the referendum, originally scheduled for January 1992.

Indirect talks, under UN auspices, between the two sides in May 1992 proved inconclusive. In March 1993, adopting Resolution 809, the UN Security Council decreed that the referendum should take place before the end of the year, regardless of Polisario co-operation; that further efforts should be made to compile a satisfactory electoral list; and that the Secretary-General should undertake a new round of negotiations. Both Morocco and Polisario accepted the resolution, but as a result of continued disputes over the process of identification of voters, plans to hold the referendum were successively delayed. At intervals the Security Council voted to extend MINURSO's mandate on a short-term basis, but by the end of 1996 the operation's personnel in the territory had been reduced and the process of voter identification suspended.

In March 1997 the new UN Secretary-General, Kofi Annan, appointed former US Secretary of State James Baker as his personal envoy to Western Sahara. Between June and September Baker chaired a series of direct talks between the Moroccan Government and representatives of Polisario in Lisbon (Portugal), London (United Kingdom) and Houston, Texas (USA). Although Baker admitted that the talks had been difficult, in September a compromise agreement (often referred to as the Houston accords) was reached on the highly contentious issue of who would be eligible to vote in the long-delayed referendum, now scheduled to be held in December 1998. Baker appeared to have persuaded the Moroccan Government to accept a lower figure for the number of eligible voters than it had originally demanded. Agreement was also reached on the reduction of both sides' military forces in the disputed territory, on the repatriation of refugees, and on the release of detainees.

In spite of the agreement brokered by Baker in 1997, voter registration continued to be impeded by disputes, and the process had not been completed by 31 May 1998, the date set by the UN Secretary-General for finalizing electoral lists. The referendum was postponed yet again, and in December, following a visit to the region by Annan, the UN set out new proposals to clarify the process of identifying which Sahrawis were eligible to vote. A new date, December 1999, was set for the referendum. In January 1999 the UN warned Morocco that if it did not co-operate fully, MINURSO's mandate would not be renewed and the UN would withdraw from the region. Polisario, for its part, declared that if the referendum did not take place, the alternative was war. It was later announced that the referendum would be postponed until July 2000.

The death of King Hassan in July 1999 brought few changes in Morocco's uncompromising stance regarding Western Sahara. In September and October there were riots in el-Aaiún after police clashed with Sahrawis protesting against poor social and economic conditions in the territory. Local Sahrawis claimed that what had been peaceful protests had only become violent because Morocco's Minister of the Interior, Driss Basri, had ordered police to use harsh methods against the demonstrators. In response, Morocco's new ruler, King Muhammad, established a Royal Commission for Sahrawi Affairs and proposed the establishment of an elected assembly for the territory, which would enjoy some autonomy from central government, but would still be a full part of the kingdom. Polisario condemned these initiatives, claiming that Morocco was attempting unfairly to influence the population in its favour in advance of the forthcoming referendum.

AUTONOMY PLAN FOR WESTERN SAHARA

In December 1999 Annan conceded that the referendum was unlikely to take place before 2002, and early in 2000, amid growing frustration within the UN at the lack of progress in voter identification, he expressed doubts that the referendum would be held at all. Although more than 86,000 eligible voters had been identified, some 79,000 appeals had been lodged by those rejected under the first stage of the identification process, and by March that number had risen to 130,000. By encouraging these appeals, Morocco would be able to ensure further delays to the referendum timetable. In February the leader of Polisario warned that renewed hostilities were possible if the referendum were not held before the end of 2000. Annan also confirmed that the UN had made no provisions for enforcing the result of a referendum should one side refuse to accept it.

It was against this unhopeful background that the Secretary-General asked James Baker to resume his role as special envoy with a mandate to explore with the parties concerned 'all ways and means to achieve an early, durable and agreed solution to the dispute'. The UN's favoured option appeared to be autonomy for Western Sahara under Moroccan sovereignty, and there were reports that both the USA and France preferred to press for the widest possible autonomy for the disputed territory. However, a number of meetings in mid-2000 between Baker and representatives of the Moroccan Government and Polisario failed to make any progress, and neither side was prepared to discuss Baker's suggestion of an alternative political solution to the referendum plan. Indeed, Moroccan officials threatened their country's withdrawal from the process if all Sahrawis in the 'southern provinces', and not just those found eligible under the criteria set by the UN, were not allowed to vote in a referendum. At a further meeting chaired by Baker in September, Morocco indicated its willingness to begin talks on autonomy for Western Sahara. Prime Minister el-Youssoufi subsequently stated that his Government was looking at models of regionalization adopted by other countries and was preparing plans to allow the inhabitants of the territory to administer their own affairs, but Polisario continued to reject any alternative to the referendum, which it remained confident of winning. Nevertheless, Polisario suffered from declining diplomatic support in Africa, and there were reports of unrest among Sahrawi civilians under Polisario control.

In December 2000 Polisario released 201 Moroccan prisoners of war, taken captive in the mid-1970s, but, despite appeals from the International Committee of the Red Cross (ICRC), it refused to release almost 1,500 Moroccans still held in detention. Polisario claimed that 179 of its troops were being held by Morocco. In April 2001 the UN Security Council extended MINURSO's mandate for a further three months and reaffirmed its support for the UN settlement plan and referendum, while expressing the hope that the parties involved would try to agree a mutually acceptable political solution to the dispute. Annan reported with regret that no progress had been made in trying to overcome the obstacles to the UN peace plan, but some sources suggested that Baker had received a pledge from Morocco that it would agree to a substantial compromise on devolution of authority for all the inhabitants of the disputed territory. Polisario remained opposed to any agreement without a referendum, but its threat to resume hostilities if the referendum were abandoned seemed unlikely to be supported by Algeria, which was confronting its own domestic rebellion from Islamist groups.

In June 2001 the UN Security Council unanimously approved a compromise resolution encouraging Morocco and Polisario to discuss an autonomy plan for Western Sahara, proposed by Annan, but without abandoning the delayed referendum. The Security Council also extended MINURSO's mandate until the end of November. Under the terms of the autonomy proposal, the inhabitants of Western Sahara would have the right to elect their own legislative and executive bodies and to have control over areas of local government administration—including budget and taxation, law enforcement, internal security, local economy, infrastructure and social affairs—for a period of at least five years, during which Morocco would retain control over defence and foreign affairs. It also provided for the holding of a referendum on the final status of the territory within that five-year period. Questions were, however, raised as to why the long-delayed referendum could not proceed immediately if it were possible to hold transparent local elections in the territory. Some commentators argued that the UN, under pressure from the USA and France, had capitulated to Moroccan procrastination. Earlier in June it had been reported that Polisario had rejected a Moroccan plan for the autonomy of Western Sahara. Although the Moroccan proposals included the establishment of an elected local assembly for the territory, Sahrawis would be given control over only part of their affairs, notably in social and cultural areas, and would administer only 20% of government revenues from the territory, with Morocco remaining responsible for foreign affairs, defence and customs. Moreover, Western Sahara would be administered by a senior official appointed by the Moroccan Government.

Polisario categorically rejected the autonomy proposals, and continued to demand that the long-delayed referendum should proceed. King Muhammad, however, in an interview with the French daily *Le Figaro* in September 2001, stated that the Western Sahara issue had been settled and that members of the UN Security Council recognized the legitimacy of Moroccan sovereignty over 'our Sahara'. At the end of October the King made his first visit to the disputed territory since his accession; he was reported to have received an enthusiastic welcome from crowds in el-Aaiún. The Sahrawi Minister of Foreign Affairs condemned the visit as a flagrant violation of UN resolutions. Meanwhile, some commentators argued that Morocco's decision to withdraw its ambassador from Madrid at the end of October had been taken in part because of Morocco's displeasure at Spain's position on Western Sahara.

A veteran US diplomat, William Lacy Swing, took up his appointment as Special Representative of the UN Secretary-General and MINURSO Chief of Mission in December 2001. However, there were reports that the mission's staff in the territory was being reduced and that the work of voter identification had effectively ceased. Within the European Union (EU), only Spain now continued to uphold the original referendum plan. Although Algerian officials denied reports in the local press that President Abdelaziz Bouteflika had accepted the Baker plan at a meeting with US President George W. Bush in November, some commentators maintained that the price of Algeria's growing rapprochement with the West after the September suicide attacks on the mainland USA would be its abandonment of the Sahrawi cause.

Meanwhile, Polisario lodged a legal challenge at the UN when Morocco granted the first oil permits in Western Sahara, one to Kerr-McGee of the USA and another to TotalFinaElf (now Total) of France. In February 2002 the UN's legal counsellor stated that although the oil permits were not illegal per se, exploration work and production that was not in the interests of, or according to the wishes of, the Sahrawi people would represent a violation of the principles of international law. While the companies restrict their activities to geological evaluation they do not breach international law, but should they move to the exploration and production phase then the question of who benefits would arise. At the beginning of January Polisario released 115 Moroccan detainees who had been held for more than 20 years, angering the Moroccan authorities by highlighting the role played by the Spanish premier, José María Aznar, in their release. According to the ICRC, some 1,362 Moroccan prisoners of war were still held by Polisario in camps around Tindouf in Algeria. The Moroccan authorities insisted that they no longer held any Polisario supporters as prisoners.

In a new report to the UN Security Council in February 2002, Kofi Annan stated that the future of the peace process in Western Sahara was rather depressing, and that in his opinion there were only four options available: that the Security Council insist on proceeding with the long-delayed referendum on self-determination; that Western Sahara become a semi-autonomous province of Morocco—an option rejected by both Polisario and Algeria; that the UN end its peace mission in the disputed territory and withdraw its military observers, risking possible confrontation between Algeria and Morocco; and, the most controversial proposal, that Western Sahara be divided between Morocco and Polisario. However, the Secretary-General pointed out that while Algeria and Polisario might be willing to discuss this last option, Morocco was firmly opposed to it.

Meanwhile, Morocco's permanent representative to the UN attributed the partition plan to Algeria, claiming that the Algerian authorities wished to create a Sahrawi 'mini-state', under their protection, through which Algeria would acquire an outlet to the Atlantic. Algeria's representative at the UN denied advancing such a plan. On 26 February 2002 the UN Security Council adopted a resolution rejecting the option of a UN withdrawal from the disputed territory and setting a deadline of 30 April for the UN to decide which of the remaining three options should be pursued. On 27 February President Bouteflika made an unexpected visit to the Sahrawi refugee camps around Tindouf. Morocco described the visit, the first by an Algerian President, as 'provocative'. At the beginning of March King Muhammad made a two-day visit to Western Sahara, his third in four months, and convened a meeting of the Cabinet at the southern port of Dakhla. The visit, designed to reaffirm Moroccan sovereignty over Western Sahara, was similarly condemned by Polisario.

In late March 2002 MINURSO announced that Polisario had decided to allow UN military observers freedom of movement in areas controlled by their forces. According to the Moroccan authorities, restrictions on the movement of UN peace-keepers had been in force since January 2001. In late April and early May 2002 US diplomats tried unsuccessfully to persuade members of the Security Council to accept the autonomy option favoured by Morocco. Polisario had declared that if US efforts were successful it would demand the withdrawal of the UN troops from Western Sahara, a development that could lead to the renewal of hostilities between Polisario and Moroccan forces. The setback to US efforts demonstrated that Polisario could still count on some diplomatic support internationally. On 30 April the UN Security Council renewed MINURSO's mandate for a further three months. In May Polisario signed an agreement with Fusion Oil of Australia to undertake at its own cost a 16-month integrated study of all relevant geological and geophysical data available on 'Sahrawi territorial waters'. When completed, Fusion would be able to nominate up to three areas for future exploration licences, which would only come into effect within six months of the SADR's eventual admission to the UN.

At the end of July 2002 the UN Security Council met again to discuss the issue, but it remained deeply divided and was unable to agree on any of the options put forward by the Secretary-General in February. A resolution was adopted renewing MINURSO's mandate for a further six months and James Baker was invited to continue his efforts to seek a political solution to the dispute. Some UN sources, however, stated that it would be virtually impossible to find any common ground for the parties even to begin talking, and that Baker's room to manoeuvre was extremely limited: in six months' time the Security Council would encounter exactly the same problems.

The UN World Food Programme stated in August 2002 that by October it would have to make drastic reductions in the amount of food that it provided for some 155,000 Sahrawi refugees living in camps in Algeria. As the plight of the refugees had attracted little attention internationally, the agency found it extremely difficult to obtain regular contributions of food aid. The Office of the UN High Commissioner for Refugees (UNHCR) also declared that it was having difficulty funding its aid programme for Western Sahara, and drew attention to what it termed the 'enormous difficulties' experienced by Sahrawi refugees. However, at the beginning of October the High Commissioner for Refugees, Ruud Lubbers, stated that the 'shameful situation' of Sahrawi refugees was not the result of lack of assistance but lack of political solutions; he urged Morocco and Algeria to act to redress this. In an address to the UN General Assembly in September President Bouteflika reaffirmed Algeria's stance on Western Sahara, demanding the implementation of UN resolutions and the 1997 Houston accords. However, he stated that the issue should not obstruct the revival of the Union of the Arab Maghreb (Union du Maghreb Arabe—UMA) or Algeria's relations with Morocco, and expressed Algeria's readiness to engage in efforts to resolve the crisis.

BAKER PRESENTS REVISED PLAN

In mid-January 2003 James Baker visited Morocco to present new proposals to provide for a political solution to the Western Sahara conflict. At the end of the month Polisario rejected Baker's new proposals, stating that they were simply a new formulation of the plan to integrate Western Sahara into Morocco. In late January the UN Secretary-General, in a report to the Security Council, recommended a two-month technical extension of MINURSO's latest mandate, to allow time for the parties to examine Baker's new proposals. At the end of March the Security Council unanimously agreed to a further technical extension to MINURSO's mandate until 31 May.

At celebrations marking Polisario's 30th anniversary in late May 2003, the SADR 'President', Muhammad Abd al-Aziz, stated that Polisario had made fundamental concessions concerning the UN peace plan and would now accept all voters willing to participate in the referendum, provided that they were registered by MINURSO. However, Polisario reiterated that it had not ruled out the military option. At the end of May the UN Secretary-General urged Morocco, Polisario and Algeria to accept a new peace plan, which proposed immediate self-government for the territory for a period of four to five years, followed by a referendum providing all bona fide residents with an opportunity to determine the future for themselves. The Security Council approved the Secretary-General's proposals at the beginning of June. At the end of June Polisario, under strong pressure from Algeria, accepted the Baker plan as a basis for negotiation. Morocco, however, refused to accept any 'imposed decision' on Western Sahara.

On 31 July 2003 the UN Security Council unanimously adopted Resolution 1495 on Western Sahara. This supported the Baker plan and appealed to parties and states of the region to co-operate fully with the Secretary-General and his special envoy in working towards the implementation of the peace plan. MINURSO's mandate was extended to 31 October 2003. Negotiations on specific elements of the plan were expected to take place, in an attempt at progress towards implementation before the end of the year. However, given what was regarded as Morocco's intransigence, compounded by divisions within the Security Council, independent observers were not optimistic that significant progress would be made.

The resolution also demanded that Polisario release all remaining Moroccan prisoners of war, and appealed to Morocco and Polisario to co-operate with the ICRC to resolve the fate of persons unaccounted for since the beginning of the conflict. Shortly afterwards, Morocco stated that it was satisfied with Resolution 1495 because it accepted the basic principle that any solution to the problem should be negotiated and accepted by all parties. However, it reiterated its rejection of Baker's latest proposals, arguing that they drew inspiration from the 1991 settlement plan and moved away from the principle of a political solution. All Morocco's political parties reaffirmed their rejection of Baker's proposals and their support for Morocco's 'territorial integrity'. Addressing the UN General Assembly in New York, USA, in September 2003, King Muhammad stated that Morocco would co-operate with the UN to find a political solution to the Western Sahara dispute.

At the end of October 2003 the UN Security Council unanimously adopted Resolution 1513, extending the mandate of MINURSO until 31 January 2004. In a report to the Security Council, the Secretary-General urged Morocco to become actively engaged by accepting and implementing the peace plan. The Secretary-General welcomed the release of 243 Moroccan prisoners of war on 1 September 2003, and appealed to Polisario to ensure the immediate release of the remaining 914 prisoners of war. Morocco, for its part, responded angrily to Annan's suggestion that it should become actively engaged in implementing the Baker plan, accusing him of deliberately misinterpreting Resolution 1495 and deviating from the UN's neutral position. It argued that the Baker proposal was more a product of the original settlement plan than the quest for a 'third way' or political solution to the dispute, and that the extension of MINURSO's mandate should not be used to impose the plan but to open a dialogue under UN auspices so as to discuss a political and lasting solution to the Western Sahara dispute that respected Morocco's national sovereignty and territorial integrity. On a visit to Rabat in late October, US Assistant Secretary of State for Near East Affairs William Burns appealed for the opening of a dialogue between Morocco and Algeria on the Western Sahara issue. French President Jacques Chirac had reiterated France's support for Morocco's position on Western Sahara during his state visit in early October. Algeria's permanent representative to the UN, however, stated that Algeria had no intention of engaging in negotiations with Morocco on Western Sahara.

Polisario's Secretary-General announced in November 2003 that a further 300 Moroccan prisoners of war would be released for humanitarian reasons. Seif al-Islam Qaddafi attended the press conference and indicated that the decision to free the prisoners of war was at the request of his father, Libyan leader Muammar al-Qaddafi. Another 100 Moroccan prisoners of war were released in February 2004 through mediation by the UN and Qatar, and a further 100 prisoners were freed in May. According to Moroccan sources, some 400 Moroccan prisoners were still being held by Polisario.

In November 2003 the recently appointed MINURSO Chief of Mission, Peru's Alvaro de Soto, toured the region and held meetings with Moroccan, Algerian and Mauritanian officials as well as with Polisario. Morocco continued to declare that it remained committed to a peaceful settlement of the dispute in co-operation with the UN, but insisted that the international community had recognized the impracticality of implementing the 1991 settlement plan and that the only way forward was the so-called 'third way'. Some observers argued that Morocco feared that Polisario cadres would dominate the transitional local administration proposed under the Baker plan, leading to a pro-independence vote in the referendum. On a visit to Morocco in early December 2003, US Secretary of State Colin Powell declared that the parties had to find a solution through negotiations on the basis of the Baker plan. Yet, mindful that the loss of Western Sahara could bring down King Muhammad's regime, he stated that the USA was not seeking to impose a solution but would concentrate its efforts on promoting negotiations between Morocco and Algeria. However, Algeria insisted that Morocco should talk directly to Polisario under the auspices of the UN, emphasizing that the Security Council had recently renewed its support for the Sahrawi people's right to self-determination. In late December, after Libya assumed the presidency of the UMA, Col Qaddafi announced that the Western Sahara issue would be at the top of the agenda at the next summit meeting of heads of state, due to be held in Libya after the Algerian presidential election in April 2004.

At the end of January 2004, on the basis of recommendations from the Secretary-General, the UN Security Council agreed a three-month extension to MINURSO's mandate, in the hope that an agreement could be reached on the Baker plan by the end of April. Kofi Annan had indicated that he wanted a 'final response' from Morocco on the peace plan by that time. Meanwhile, Western Sahara had become an important transit point for illegal immigrants, especially from sub-Saharan Africa, seeking to enter Europe via Spain. As a result, Morocco began a joint maritime surveillance operation with Spain in the waters between Western Sahara and Spain's Canary Islands in February.

Shortly before the UN Security Council was due to meet at the end of April 2004 to discuss Western Sahara, Morocco's Minister of Communication and Government spokesman announced that Morocco had given its response to the UN on the Baker plan. He stressed that Morocco was seeking an agreed and lasting political solution, but insisted that it absolutely ruled out the independence option and the transitional period. It was willing to discuss other aspects of the plan and to negotiate on the basis of a lasting autonomy for Western Sahara (i.e. the devolution of some authority to the population of Morocco's 'southern provinces' within a framework that guaranteed Morocco's sovereignty and territorial unity). Morocco's Minister of Foreign Affairs and Co-operation expressed strong reservations about the Baker plan, but insisted that Morocco did not reject it 'either in part or parcel', while emphasizing that there were red lines that the plan could not cross. In his report to the Security Council, Kofi Annan stated that there were two options from which to choose: either to withdraw the peace-keeping force, or to seek once again to get the parties to work towards accepting and implementing the revised Baker plan. Annan reiterated his support for the second option, providing each side with some of what it wanted. On 29 April the UN Security Council unanimously adopted Resolution 1541, which extended MINURSO's mandate for another six months. Polisario and Algeria both welcomed the new resolution, emphasizing that it reiterated the Security Council's commitment to respect the Sahrawi people's right to self-determination. Morocco's permanent representative to the UN stated that it was now clear to the international community that dialogue between Algeria and Morocco was the only way to achieve progress in finding a political solution to the conflict.

On a visit to Morocco in mid-May 2004, William Burns stated that US efforts would be directed towards trying to strengthen bilateral relations between Morocco and Algeria in order to create an atmosphere favourable for a peaceful resolution of the Western Sahara dispute. At the end of May the new French Minister of Foreign Affairs, Michel Barnier, asserted that a rapprochement between Algeria and Morocco was necessary in order to resolve the issue. At the beginning of June a Spanish government delegation led by the Secretary of State for Foreign Affairs visited the Sahrawi refugee camps in Tindouf and held talks with Muhammad Abd al-Aziz and other Polisario officials. During the visit, the first by a Spanish government member, Polisario officials emphasized that Spain, as the former colonial power, had a historical responsibility in the long-running dispute. The minister stated that Spain wanted to encourage rapprochement and dialogue between the parties involved in the dispute.

BAKER RESIGNS AS PERSONAL ENVOY

In mid-June 2004 James Baker resigned from his post, frustrated by his failure as the personal envoy of the UN Secretary-General to break the political stalemate. Kofi Annan asked Alvaro de Soto to take over the role, with instructions to continue to seek a mutually acceptable political solution that would provide for the self-determination of the Sahrawi people.

On a visit to Algiers in July 2004, Michel Barnier appealed for a new effort towards a fundamental dialogue between

Algeria and Morocco to seek to resolve the Western Sahara dispute. In response, the Algerian Minister of State for Foreign Affairs stated that Algeria recognized the importance of moving forward to improve relations with Morocco but insisted that Western Sahara was a problem of decolonization that should be resolved by the UN. Shortly afterwards, Spain's new Prime Minister, José Luis Rodríguez Zapatero, on his first official visit to Algeria, stated that the UN should play a 'decisive role' in finding a lasting solution to the Western Sahara dispute but that he did not wish to be bound to a particular plan, 'be it called Baker or not'. He argued that a solution would only be effective if it were acceptable to all parties involved in the dispute. The Algerian press expressed suspicion that Spain had changed policy on Western Sahara and was now aligned with France in supporting Morocco's claims to sovereignty over the disputed territory.

In September 2004 South Africa recognized the SADR, and at the opening of the Pan-African Parliament of the AU President Thabo Mbeki declared that it was a matter of 'great shame and regret' that the issue of self-determination for the people of Western Sahara remained unresolved, and that every effort should be made to ensure that the Sahrawi people could enjoy this 'fundamental and inalienable right'. South Africa's recognition of the SADR was welcomed by Algeria. Kenya recognized the SADR in June 2005, a decision denounced by the Moroccan authorities; Morocco's ambassador to Kenya was immediately recalled. In October the UN Special Political and Decolonization Committee voted in favour of endorsing the Baker plan with 52 votes for and none against (there were, however, 89 abstentions). Morocco stated that the large number of abstentions indicated that the plan should be revised, whereas Polisario asserted that the vote was a 'categorical rejection of the colonialist policy of Morocco in Western Sahara'.

THE IMPASSE CONTINUES: UNREST ERUPTS

Reporting to the UN Security Council in late October 2004, Kofi Annan admitted that an agreement between the parties on the Baker plan appeared to be more distant than ever. However, on 29 October the Security Council unanimously adopted Resolution 1570 to extend MINURSO's mandate for a further six months, and reaffirmed its commitment to assist the parties in achieving a mutually acceptable political solution that would provide for the self-determination of the people of Western Sahara. It reiterated its appeal to the parties and states of the region to continue to co-operate fully with the UN to end the current impasse. Morocco argued that the new resolution clearly asked both sides to find an alternative political solution to the Baker plan, and insisted that a 'compromise' must take into account Morocco's inalienable right to preserve its territorial integrity. It announced that it was willing to enter UN-sponsored talks to formulate a suitable arrangement whereby the inhabitants of the region could manage their own affairs. Algeria strongly supported the resolution, stating that this stressed the validity of the Baker plan as the most suitable political solution and reaffirmed the right of the Sahrawi people to self-determination.

In an interview in November 2004, the Polisario leader, Muhammad Abd al-Aziz, stated that since the Zapatero Government had taken office Spain's position on Western Sahara had been 'ambiguous' and characterized by 'incomprehensible fluctuations', especially with regard to the Baker plan. He urged the Spanish authorities to clarify their position and lend full support to the referendum on self-determination. Later that month Abd al-Aziz held talks with Zapatero in Madrid, during which the Spanish premier expressed his willingness to work for a comprehensive agreement between Morocco and Polisario at UN headquarters; none the less, Zapatero emphasized that the key to a solution lay not with Spain but with the parties to the conflict, implicitly indicating that direct talks might be the only way forward. In December Abd al-Aziz accused Spain of encouraging Morocco's more intransigent stance, and spoke of a 'conspiracy' between the governments of Morocco, Spain and France against the Sahrawi people and international legality. In the same interview, the Polisario leader described the latest UN resolution on Western Sahara as a victory for the Sahrawi people, confirming their right to self-determination and independence and sending a clear message to Morocco to abide by international legality.

The SADR welcomed Total's decision in December 2004 to suspend all petroleum exploration in Western Sahara, and urged Kerr-McGee to do the same, warning that international companies should avoid the Moroccan Government's attempts to implicate them in its illegal occupation. At a meeting in London in May 2005, the SADR invited multinational oil companies to bid for exploration licences for 12 offshore blocks in the territory. In October the SADR warned Kerr-McGee and its partners not to commence offshore exploration in the disputed territory's waters, as the safety of their staff could not be guaranteed. In January 2006 the SADR announced that it was to invite bids for exploration licences for six onshore blocks in Western Sahara.

Meanwhile, in April 2005 the UN Security Council agreed a six-month extension of MINURSO's mandate and appealed to Morocco and Polisario to co-operate with the UN to end the continuing impasse. In May de Soto assumed a new UN post and was replaced in early August by Peter van Walsum of the Netherlands. Francesco Bastagli of Italy was appointed Special Representative of the Secretary-General and MINURSO's Chief of Mission. In August Polisario released the remaining 404 Moroccan prisoners of war (some of whom were reported to have been held for more than 20 years) in an operation supervised by Senator Richard Lugar, Chairman of the US Senate Foreign Relations Committee. Lugar urged the Governments of Morocco and Algeria to recommence talks and create a climate conducive to resolving the dispute. However, in October, following his first visit to the region, van Walsum concluded that the positions of the main parties in the dispute were 'quasi-irreconcilable'.

In May 2005 a large pro-independence demonstration in el-Aaiún led to violent clashes between protesters and Moroccan security forces that quickly spread to other towns. Around 30 youths were arrested during the disturbances, and 12 people were subsequently convicted of participating in the riots, each receiving prison sentences of between five and 20 years. The Moroccan security forces were accused of using disproportionate force during the demonstration. The protests continued, however, and by October there were reports of daily clashes between Sahrawi youths and police. In one of the clashes, a young Sahrawi died after allegedly being beaten. Polisario officials appealed for urgent UN intervention to protect Sahrawi civilians and guarantee their basic rights, and accused Morocco of increasing its security forces in the territory and of transforming el-Aaiún into a military camp. In December, as violence persisted, the Moroccan Minister of the Interior claimed that groups of youths were being manipulated by 'the enemies of our territorial integrity' to commit acts of vandalism and disturb public order. A number of foreign delegations on fact-finding missions were refused entry to the territory, and international human rights organizations expressed growing concern about the deteriorating situation in the territory, the imprisonment of local human rights activists and torture of detainees.

In a report to the UN Security Council in late October 2005, Annan acknowledged the ongoing impasse between the parties. In view of the continued instability in the territory, as well as the violation of the military accords and alleged human rights abuses by both sides, a further six-month extension to MINURSO's mandate was adopted by the Security Council, which was intended to enable van Walsum to conduct talks with Morocco and Polisario.

In November 2005 King Muhammad reiterated his desire to seek a negotiated political solution to the dispute that would grant autonomy to Western Sahara within the framework of Moroccan sovereignty. The Conseil Royal Consultative Pour les Affaires du Sahara (CORCAS)—a consultative body created by King Hassan in 1981, which had since become inactive—would be reconstituted to include a wider range of representatives, and would work actively for the development of the region.

In February 2006, at a ceremony to mark the 30th anniversary of the SADR, Abd al-Aziz reaffirmed Polisario's rejection of the proposal for autonomy, and the Algerian Government insisted that the revised Baker plan remained viable. During a six-day visit to Western Sahara in March King Muhammad pardoned 216 Sahrawi prisoners. Polisario described the visit as 'a provocation', and claimed that, despite a large police and military presence, pro-independence demonstrators had held protests against the visit in several areas of el-Aaiún. A local human rights organization reported that a number of Sahrawi political activists had been arrested before and during the visit.

CORCAS, composed of 140 members, held its first meeting in early April 2006. Its priorities were the development of the provinces and the addressing of social problems; creating a united front against Polisario; communicating with all the Sahrawi people; and elaborating its view on the form that autonomy, within the framework of Moroccan sovereignty, should take. Later in that month the President of CORCAS, Khalienna Ould Errachid, reiterated the view that self-determination would best be expressed through extensive autonomy within the framework of Moroccan sovereignty. Critics argued that CORCAS was undemocratic and unrepresentative. In late April, at the request of CORCAS, the King pardoned the remaining 46 Sahrawi political prisoners held in various Moroccan gaols. Polisario, however, insisted that 13 Sahrawi prisoners remained in prisons in el-Aaiún and Agadir. At a meeting held in Rabat in May CORCAS created five commissions dealing with social affairs and development; foreign affairs and co-operation; human rights, public freedoms and the defence of refugees in the camps around Tindouf; economic affairs; and information, communication and promotion of Hassaniya (a dialect spoken by Bedouin tribes in Mauritania and Western Sahara) culture. In April, meanwhile, at a meeting with the UN Secretary-General in New York, Abd al-Aziz reported his concerns about the violation of human rights in Western Sahara and expressed opposition to a Security Council resolution that served only to extend MINURSO's mandate.

ANNAN PROPOSES DIRECT TALKS

In a report to the UN Security Council in mid-April 2006, Annan referred to an earlier briefing by his personal envoy, who had pointed out that since Morocco had rejected the revised Baker plan in April 2004, no reference had been made to the plan in any subsequent Security Council resolution and that countries allied with Morocco had not used their influence to encourage a change of stance. As the Security Council was firm in its opinion that it could only consider a consensual solution to the Western Sahara question, the personal envoy could see no advantage in the formulation of a new plan, as Morocco was likely to reject any plan that did not rule out the prospect of independence. Neither could the UN endorse a plan that excluded a genuine referendum on Sahrawi self-determination. According to van Walsum, direct negotiations between Morocco and Polisario, without preconditions, were the sole remaining option. In his view, it should be made clear to the parties involved that the UN was taking a step back and that responsibility now rested with them. However, as the Security Council insisted that any solution must be reached within the framework of the UN and under its auspices, the Secretary-General urged the Security Council to invite Algeria and Mauritania to participate in the negotiations, and appealed to Security Council members that had previously supported Morocco's stance to do everything possible to ensure the success of the talks. As Polisario had reiterated its opposition to any proposal of autonomy under Moroccan sovereignty, the personal envoy had pointed out that negotiations 'without preconditions' meant that there was no requirement for Polisario to recognize Morocco's sovereignty before discussing the 'granting' of autonomy. A solution could only be achieved if the parties worked to seek a mutually acceptable compromise based on relevant principles of international law and current political imperatives. Annan noted that most countries had not put the Western Sahara high on their political agenda, and were reluctant to express a strong view on the issue owing to fears of damaging relations with Morocco or Algeria. The Secretary-General urged the Security Council and its individual member states 'to rise to the occasion and do all in their powers to help negotiations get off the ground', before the Western Sahara question became a threat to international peace and security. He recommended that MINURSO's mandate be extended for a further six months, but emphasized that it did not have the resources to address the growing unrest in the territory and allegations of human rights abuses. None the less, Annan announced that all parties had accepted a mission by the Office of the UN High Commissioner for Human Rights, which would visit the territory and Tindouf in May to conduct analysis.

Polisario immediately rejected these proposals as 'unacceptable and unfeasible', and threatened to resume its armed struggle if the report's recommendations were adopted. Algeria also rejected the report, stating that any negotiations should be between Morocco and Polisario and should concern the implementation of the revised Baker plan. A spokesman for the Moroccan Government stated that a final solution to the conflict required a change of attitude from Algeria, insisting that Polisario acted on the instructions of the Algerian Government. In late April 2006 the UN Security Council unanimously adopted Resolution 1675, which affirmed its commitment to finding a lasting solution to the dispute and extended MINURSO's mandate to 31 October. Polisario declared that the resolution represented 'an outstanding victory for the Sahrawi cause and for international legitimacy', in that it rejected the Secretary-General's report and confirmed the right of the Sahrawi people to self-determination and the commitment of the UN to the revised Baker plan. For its part, the Moroccan Ministry of Foreign Affairs and Co-operation also welcomed the resolution, stated that Morocco wished to continue with a series of internal negotiations, and urged other parties to join these negotiations.

Reports in the Moroccan press in late May 2006 suggested that a pro-Moroccan demonstration in the refugee camps near Tindouf had been violently suppressed by Polisario's security forces. Polisario denied the allegations, but independent sources stated that violent disturbances, resulting in numerous arrests, had taken place in one of the camps (although the majority of those detained were released after a few days).

In July 2006 Muhammad Benaïssa attended the AU summit meeting in Banjul, The Gambia. Morocco had withdrawn from the OAU in 1985 and had not applied to join the AU, which had replaced the OAU in 2002. The meeting declared that Western Sahara merited greater attention from the international community, and appealed for urgent action to allow the Sahrawi people to exercise their right to self-determination. Morocco's decision to send its Minister of Foreign Affairs and Co-operation to the meeting indicated a renewed diplomatic effort to defend the proposal for autonomy. In March 2007 Bouteflika stated forcefully that the Sahara issue would 'never constitute a *casus belli* between Algeria and Morocco'. Also, increased co-operation between the two countries in combating terrorism reduced tensions on the issue of Polisario and the fate of Western Sahara.

In this context, in April 2007 Morocco presented to the UN Security Council a comprehensive plan for autonomy in Western Sahara. Later that month the Security Council adopted Resolution 1754, which referred to Morocco's proposal in favourable terms and encouraged both sides to begin direct talks without preconditions. In June the new Secretary-General of the UN, Ban Ki-Moon, confirmed that both parties would attend talks, together with Algeria and Mauritania, at the invitation of the UN. The first round of negotiations, held in Manhasset, New York, in mid-June, yielded little in the way of agreement between the parties. At further talks in mid-August it was reported that both Morocco and Polisario agreed that the status quo was unacceptable and that the process of negotiations would continue. The new framework was given a boost when the EU called the talks 'substantive', and the USA endorsed the Moroccan view that 'meaningful autonomy is a promising and realistic way forward'. In a further UN Security Council resolution (No. 1783) adopted in October to extend the monitoring mandate of MINURSO, the Council welcomed Morocco's 'serious and credible' efforts to seek a resolution. However, Polisario stated that such international support for Morocco was only adding to its 'intransigence' in talks, and, exasperated by the slow pace of negotiations (which had faltered in late 2007), in December Polisario threatened to resume military operations if the talks failed to achieve what it considered to be reasonable progress. The third round of talks was eventually held in January 2008 in the USA; however, no tangible progress was made.

Western backing for Morocco's plan was further emphasized in April 2008, when van Walsum told the UN Security Council that an independent Western Sahara was 'not a realistic goal'. It was his belief that further talks should be based on two 'realities': that the UN would not force a referendum on Morocco, but nor would it recognize Moroccan sovereignty without an agreement. Van Walsum's statement clarified the UN Security Council's long-held position that sees it unwilling to impose a solution to the Western Sahara question. With the exception of an agreement to meet again, a fourth round of talks, held in March 2008, yielded little in the way of significant progress. Moreover, fresh uncertainty was generated in late August, when it was announced that van Walsum's mandate as Western Sahara envoy had not been renewed when it expired on 21 August.

In the mean time, Morocco appealed to Algeria to join the talks, since earlier negotiations had raised the possibility of allowing families who are split between Moroccan-administered Western Sahara and Sahrawi refugee camps in Algeria to travel by road to visit each other. Such an agreement could not be put in place without the co-operation of Algeria, which had been responsible for keeping the border closed since 1994. Indeed, in late March 2008 the Minister of the Interior, Chakib Benmoussa, told the Cabinet that any settlement would be 'impossible' in the absence of Algeria's 'total involvement'. Algeria, however, rebuffed Morocco's overtures, stating that any agreement must come as part of a wider deal to improve relations more broadly between the two countries. In November King Muhammad gave his annual address to mark the anniversary of the 'Green March'. He criticized Algeria for jeopardizing Maghreb unity and expressed his disappointment that Algeria had rejected Morocco's attempt to normalize relations, but reiterated appeals for the opening of their shared borders.

Hopes of a resolution received a boost in January 2009, when Christopher Ross, a former US diplomat, was appointed as the UN Secretary-General's personal envoy for Western Sahara. He visited Morocco in February, meeting King Muhammad and Morocco's Minister of Foreign Affairs and Co-operation, Taieb Fassi Fihri. Ross also travelled to Tindouf, where he met Abd al-Aziz, before heading to Algiers for talks with President Bouteflika. In mid-April Morocco accused Polisario of a 'serious and blatant' violation of the cease-fire agreement. It claimed that 1,400 Polisario supporters had crossed the border from Algeria into a closed military zone. Polisario dismissed Morocco's accusations, calling the group 'a huge peaceful demonstration'. On 30 April the UN Security Council adopted Resolution 1871, which extended the mandate of MINURSO for a further 12 months.

A fifth round of talks between representatives of the Government and Polisario finally took place in February 2010 in the USA, but they ended without agreement. In November 2009 the King had given a speech reiterating the Government's plan for autonomy for Western Sahara, under a new regionalization process that would devolve authority to Morocco's provinces. Many European states quietly supported this plan, and, during a visit to Morocco in that month, the US Secretary of State, Hillary Clinton, had intimated that the USA also endorsed the Government's policy of regional autonomy. However, Polisario continued to demand full independence and the redress of human rights grievances. This latter issue came to the fore at the end of April 2010, when the UN Security Council adopted Resolution 1920, extending the mandate of MINURSO for another year. Polisario criticized the Resolution for failing to address human rights abuses and threatened to withdraw from the cease-fire agreement in protest.

Talks resumed in October 2010, but they too foundered after just two days, as both sides were unable to agree a basic agenda for discussion. The following month Morocco was the subject of a European Parliament resolution that 'strongly' condemned the use of violence by the Moroccan security forces in the dismantling of a camp set up by Sahrawi protesters at Gdaim Izyk in early November, during which 11 people were killed, according to Moroccan official figures. (It was claimed by Polisario that 36 people had been killed.) Morocco called the resolution 'hasty and unbalanced', and Fassi Fihri subsequently appeared before the European Parliament's Committee for Foreign Affairs to rebut the 'politically driven' resolution. Further talks were held in December 2010 and in June and July 2011, although no progress was reported to have been made. MINURSO's mandate was extended by UN Security Council Resolutions 1979 and 2044, which were adopted in April 2011 and April 2012, respectively. In May 2012 Morocco blamed Ross for the failure of the talks, claiming that he was biased against Moroccan interests. Later that month a Moroccan news agency accused Polisario 'dissidents', allegedly aided by Spanish nationals, of being responsible for an attack on the Moroccan consulate in Palma de Mallorca, Spain. This issue also exacerbated tensions with Spain.

In June 2013 Wolfgang Weisbrod-Weber became Special Representative of the UN Secretary-General and MINURSO Chief of Mission, in place of Abd al-Aziz. Following intervention by Ban Ki-Moon, Ross resumed the role of mediator, and later that year made his first visit to Western Sahara. In early April 2013, in his annual report to the UN Security Council regarding Western Sahara, Ban noted that Ross had secured the continued commitment of both the Moroccan Government and Polisario, as well as neighbouring states, to remain engaged in the UN-sponsored effort. However, it had been agreed that to convene further informal talks in the near future would be futile, owing to the lack of compromise on the part of the negotiating parties. Resolution 2099 was adopted by the Security Council at the end of that month, thus extending MINURSO'S mandate for another year.

RELATIONS WITH THE USA

Morocco was swift to capitalize on the goodwill that it had generated in the USA by sending a small detachment of Moroccan troops to Saudi Arabia after Iraq's invasion of Kuwait in August 1990. It benefited from both bilateral aid and credits from US-dominated agencies, receiving more from the World Bank than any other country in the Middle East or North Africa. Morocco also appeared to have secured US support for its policy on Western Sahara. In return, it supported the US peace initiative in the Middle East and hosted a number of meetings with key representatives.

The Moroccan authorities strongly condemned the suicide attacks on New York and Washington, DC, of 11 September 2001, but many ordinary Moroccans held Osama bin Laden, the USA's prime suspect in the attacks, in the highest esteem for his defiance of the USA. In October 16 Moroccan *ulama* (religious scholars appointed by the Minister of Religious Endowments and Islamic Affairs) issued a *fatwa* condemning the Moroccan Government for taking part in a multi-faith ceremony held in Rabat's Roman Catholic cathedral shortly after the attacks and warning against any Moroccan participation in a US-led military alliance against a Muslim state or group. On two occasions the authorities banned a protest march planned by Al-Adl wal-Ihsan against the US-led air offensive against bases of al-Qa'ida and its Taliban hosts in Afghanistan. The Moroccan security services were, meanwhile, co-operating with the US Federal Bureau of Investigation (FBI) in tracking down alleged terrorists of Maghreb origin based in Europe.

In early April 2002, in response to the Israeli military incursions into Palestinian-controlled areas of the West Bank, US Secretary of State Colin Powell began a regional tour in Morocco. More than 1m. protesters, including Islamists as well as representatives of the main political parties, took to the streets of Rabat the day before Powell's visit to express solidarity with the Palestinian people. Nevertheless, King Muhammad made an official visit to Washington, DC, in late April, during which discussions focused on the crisis in the Middle East. The Western Sahara dispute was also discussed, and there were reports that progress had been made in negotiations on a free trade accord between Morocco and the USA. Moroccan secret service agents were reported to have taken part with the US Central Intelligence Agency (CIA) in interrogating detainees held in Guantánamo Bay and in analysing information provided by Abu Zoubeida, a senior figure in al-Qa'ida believed to have details of al-Qa'ida cells in Morocco, Tunisia and Libya. In June the Moroccan authorities announced that at the beginning of May they had arrested three Saudi nationals and a number of Moroccans who were alleged to be members of an Islamist cell, linked to al-Qa'ida, that had been preparing terrorist attacks on US and British warships in the Strait of Gibraltar, similar to the October 2000 attack against the USS *Cole* in Aden, Yemen. Morocco's Minister of the Interior attributed the success in discovering and dismantling this terrorist cell to close co-operation between Morocco's security services and their Saudi and US counterparts. In February 2003 the three Saudis were sentenced to 10 years' imprisonment, and five Moroccans received custodial sentences ranging between four months and one year. Also in February a young Moroccan, Mounir al-Motassadek, became the first person to be convicted in connection with the September 2001 attacks on the mainland USA, when a German court found him guilty of being an accessory to murder and of membership of a terrorist organization and sentenced him to 15 years in prison. The prosecution claimed that he had been a key member of the Hamburg cell responsible for the attacks. Al-Motassadek's conviction was quashed by the German Federal Criminal Court in March 2004. A retrial began in August, and in August 2005 al-Motassadek was acquitted of involvement in the September 2001 attacks; he was nevertheless convicted of belonging to a terrorist organization and sentenced to seven years' imprisonment.

In July 2002 mediation by Colin Powell helped to defuse a crisis between Morocco and Spain over the disputed islet of Perejil, and resulted in an accord between the two countries on this issue. In January 2003 thousands of people marched through the streets of Rabat to protest against a likely US-led war against the regime of Saddam Hussain in Iraq, denouncing the impotence of Arab governments in the face of US policy. Anti-war protests continued, and in early March, in the biggest protest march in the region since the Iraq crisis began, some 160,000 Moroccans marched in Casablanca to condemn 'US imperialist aggression' and pledge support for the Iraqi people. Islamist groups were active in organizing these demonstrations, but people from across the political spectrum took part, including leaders of the main political parties and even a number of cabinet ministers. After the USA and the United Kingdom began military operations in Iraq, there were almost daily protests, during which US and Israeli flags were burned. Following the commencement of hostilities, the Moroccan Government, which had appealed for diplomatic efforts through the UN to resolve the crisis, avoided open criticism of the USA but expressed 'profound disappointment' at the launching of the offensive.

The US Assistant Secretary of State, William Burns, visited Morocco in October 2003 as part of a tour of Maghreb countries. He announced that the USA had decided to quadruple non-military aid to Morocco to US $40m. from 2004 and to double military aid to $20m. During the visit Burns appealed for the opening of a dialogue between Morocco and Algeria on the Western Sahara issue. US Secretary of State Powell visited Morocco in December 2003, also as part of a tour of the Maghreb states. He reaffirmed US support for Morocco in its fight against terrorism and thanked the King for his efforts in supporting the internationally sponsored 'roadmap' for peace between Israel and the Palestinians. In March 2004 Morocco and the USA announced that they had concluded negotiations for a free trade agreement, only the second to be made by the USA with an Arab state; the agreement was approved by the US Senate in July, and President Bush signed legislation to implement the accord in August. The agreement entered into effect on 1 January 2006.

In November 2004 the Moroccan press reported that King Muhammad had sent a personal message to President Bush congratulating him on his re-election and expressing the desire to strengthen the strategic partnership between the two countries. Among many Moroccans, however, anti-US feelings remained strong. In November tens of thousands of demonstrators, mainly Islamists, marched in Rabat to protest against the continuing US-led military occupation of Iraq and to express support for the Palestinians. There were further anti-US demonstrations in December when Morocco hosted the first 'Forum of the Future', part of the USA's Greater Middle East Initiative to promote democracy and economic reform in the region, which was attended by finance and foreign ministers of the Group of Eight (G8) industrialized nations and Middle East and North African countries. In August 2005 it was reported that the USA had been involved in discreet but intense diplomatic efforts that helped to secure the release of the remaining Moroccan prisoners of war held by Polisario. In December the Moroccan authorities denied allegations that the CIA had transferred detainees suspected of involvement in terrorist activities to secret detention centres in Morocco, where they were subjected to torture.

In recent years support within US political circles for Morocco's position on Western Sahara has grown. This has chiefly arisen out of a growing belief that it is in the security interest of the USA to push for a resolution of the Western Sahara conflict and that meaningful autonomy, under Moroccan sovereignty, is the most feasible solution. The US Administration has become increasingly concerned over the emergence of AQIM, and believes that rapprochement between Algeria and Morocco will do much to counter the threat from AQIM. Relations with the USA remained firm following the political changes in Morocco, in part due to the King's ongoing control of foreign policy. Talks were conducted between Minister of Foreign Affairs and Co-operation Saâdeddine el-Othmani and US Secretary of State Clinton in Washington, DC, in March 2012, and defence and security co-operation was ongoing. However, relations were compromised somewhat in April 2013 after Morocco cancelled joint military exercises scheduled to take place that month. The decision followed a US proposal to expand the mandate of MINURSO to include the monitoring and investigation of human rights issues in Western Sahara.

RELATIONS WITH EUROPE

In February 1996 Morocco signed an economic association agreement with the EU, as part of the EU's plan for a 'Euro-Mediterranean partnership' leading to the gradual introduction of free trade in manufactured goods with the EU. When the European Parliament ratified the agreement in June, it insisted on the insertion of a clause allowing for the accord's suspension should concerns arise regarding the violation of human rights in Morocco. For some years the European Parliament had voiced doubts about Morocco's human rights record. Indeed, despite Morocco's desire for closer ties with Europe, its major trading partner, a number of problems, notably fisheries, illegal immigration and drugs-trafficking, remained sources of friction. Morocco also expressed concern that Eastern Europe rather than the countries of the southern Mediterranean had become the EU's main priority. Relations became strained at the end of 1999 when Morocco refused to renew its fisheries agreement with the EU, under which Morocco received annual compensation for allowing fishing boats from EU countries (mainly Spain) to operate in its territorial waters.

The dispute with Spain over Perejil in July 2002 put further strain on Morocco's relations with the EU. In September Benaïssa cancelled a visit to Brussels, Belgium, after the President of the European Commission, Romano Prodi, stated that he was too busy to meet him; Benaïssa considered that Prodi had come under pressure from Spain, although this was denied by the Commission. In November Benaïssa held talks in Brussels with Chris Patten, Commissioner for External Relations, in an attempt to improve relations with the EU. At a meeting of the EU-Morocco Association Council in Brussels in February 2003, Moroccan delegates appealed for 'advanced status' in the country's relationship with Europe in order that it might prepare for future co-operation beyond the creation of the free trade area in 2012.

In December 2003 King Muhammad attended the first 5+5 Dialogue Summit of the heads of state and government of the UMA and of France, Italy, Malta, Portugal and Spain, held in Tunis, the Tunisian capital. The meeting emphasized that EU enlargement should not be at the expense of the Maghreb states, and Prodi stated that priority should be given to strengthening co-operation between the EU and the Maghreb states. In December 1995 Morocco became the second country to sign an 'Open Skies' accord with the EU, allowing free access for Moroccan and EU member states' airlines to the airports of the other member countries.

In October 2008 Morocco and the EU finally signed an 'advanced status' agreement, building upon their 1996 Association Agreement. This integrated Morocco into an EU plan to create a 'common economic space' (along with other countries such as Norway, Liechtenstein and Iceland) in advance of the establishment of a wide-ranging free trade agreement. Morocco was expected to be invited to join various EU agencies, mainly in the defence and security sphere, including Europol and the European Air Security Agency.

In March 2010 the EU and Morocco held their first bilateral summit in Granada, Spain. The meeting focused on accelerating Morocco's progress on its 'advanced status', in anticipation of the establishment of an EU-Morocco Joint Parliamentary Committee and Morocco's accession to the Council of Europe's North-South Centre. Trade liberalization and regulatory convergence were also discussed. Furthermore, the EU agreed to increase aid 'substantially' to Morocco during 2011–13; Morocco received €654m. during 2007–10. Relations cooled briefly, however, following the European Parliament's censure of Morocco's treatment of Sahrawi protesters during the dismantling of the Gdaim Izyk camp in November 2010. In July 2013 a new common fisheries agreement was reached between the EU and Morocco, the previous accord having lapsed in 2011 (see Economy).

Morocco continued to rely on France for diplomatic support in the UN Security Council and within the EU. In July 1994 the new French President, Jacques Chirac, visited Morocco. This was his first foreign visit in his capacity as head of state. Chirac pledged to assist Morocco in combating Islamist extremism, and his administration subsequently further strengthened relations by assisting with Morocco's external debt and increasing project aid to the country. The Socialist administration of Prime Minister Lionel Jospin, which assumed office in France in May 1997, sought to demonstrate that Morocco remained an important partner in France's Mediterranean strategy. Visiting Morocco in March 1998, the French Minister of the Interior, Jean-Pierre Chevènement, emphasized the great importance that France attached to its relations with Morocco, which he referred to as a country 'firmly on the path of progress and modernization'. During Prime Minister el-Youssoufi's visit to Paris in October Morocco and France signed several co-operation agreements, and the French Government announced additional aid amounting to US $765m. as well as plans for a second debt swap agreement between the two countries.

King Muhammad's first official overseas visit was to Paris in March 2000. During the visit the French Government announced emergency aid worth 100m. French francs to help Morocco deal with the impact of the recent drought. The French Minister of Foreign Affairs, Hubert Védrine, and President Chirac visited Rabat in October and December 2001, respectively, as part of their tours of Maghreb capitals, and declared that there was full agreement with the Moroccan Government on the 'war on terror'. Moreover, the French President delighted his hosts by referring to Western Sahara as the 'southern provinces of Morocco'.

In March 2004 French security forces arrested a number of Moroccans living in the Paris area, believed to be members of a cell of the GICM, for their alleged involvement in the suicide bomb attacks in Casablanca in May 2003. In May 2004 France's new Minister of Foreign Affairs, Michel Barnier, visited Morocco for talks, which included the Middle East, especially the situation in Iraq, Maghreb integration and the latest developments in the Western Sahara dispute. Together with his Moroccan counterpart, Barnier opened the first partnership and guidance monitoring council.

In February 2006 the French Government reiterated its view that only direct political dialogue between Morocco and Algeria would allow a permanent solution to the Western Sahara conflict. In April President Chirac stated that France supported a political 'situation' in Western Sahara acceptable to the UN. In May a report in the Moroccan press claimed that France was to begin modernizing 27 of the Moroccan air force's *Mirage* F1 fighter planes under an agreement signed in October 2005, and that the French army was to deliver an advanced radar system for the monitoring of aircraft movements.

In July 2007, during a visit to the Maghreb shortly after his election as President of France, Nicolas Sarkozy reiterated that he was 'very satisfied' with the state of relations between France and Morocco. He expressed the wish that Morocco would take very seriously his proposal regarding the creation of a 'Mediterranean Union'. Morocco responded favourably to the initiative, envisaging for itself a leading role in the development of closer co-operation between the Mediterranean states.

In January 2008 Morocco hosted a meeting of UMA foreign ministers in preparation for President Sarkozy's summit for the Union for the Mediterranean (as it subsequently came to be known), to be held in July. Morocco also intensified its diplomatic activity in the months leading up to the summit, in an effort to demonstrate its desire to play a prominent role in the proceedings and ensure progress in ongoing discussions over the 'advanced status' agreement. In May a new think-tank focusing on EU-Maghreb co-operation was opened in Rabat, and in June, reflecting its strong backing, the Government convened a second large conference to discuss the forthcoming summit. Given his support for the initiative, there was some surprise that, when the Union for the Mediterranean was officially inaugurated in Paris on 13 July, King Muhammad did not attend, choosing instead to send his brother, Prince Moulay, as the country's representative.

Meanwhile, as part of his efforts to generate support for the Union for the Mediterranean, President Sarkozy had in October 2007 visited Morocco, where he announced that discussions between the two countries were under way to explore the possibility of France providing Morocco with nuclear technology for civilian use. Further progress was made in July 2010, when the two countries signed 11 co-operation agreements, worth €146m., including an accord on nuclear energy. At the signing ceremony, France also announced that it would increase its aid to Morocco for 2010–12, to €600m., to help the country in its modernization efforts.

Although Morocco and Spain signed a treaty of friendship in 1991 and Spain overtook France as the principal foreign investor in the kingdom, diplomatic relations became strained as a result of disputes over the EU fisheries accord, sovereignty of the Spanish enclaves of Ceuta and Melilla, the problem of illegal immigration into Spain from Morocco, and the situation of Moroccans working in Spain. In September 1994 Morocco criticized Spain at the UN General Assembly for its autonomy plans for Ceuta and Melilla, and, after the Spanish parliament gave final approval to the statutes of autonomy for the two enclaves in February 1995, Morocco intensified its diplomatic campaign to obtain sovereignty over the two territories. Spanish concern over illegal immigration from Morocco was one of the subjects discussed at a meeting between the Spanish and Moroccan interior ministers in Tangier in August 1998. However, after Morocco refused to renew the EU fisheries accord, which expired in December 1999, an agreement that largely affected Spanish fishing vessels, relations with Spain deteriorated sharply. Spain closed its ports to Moroccan vessels, and on a visit to Ceuta and Melilla in January 2000 Aznar described them as constant parts of Spain's future, emphasizing the 'Spanishness' of the two. In February a large number of people were injured during violence resulting from attacks on Moroccan migrant labourers at El Ejido in southern Spain. King Muhammad made an official visit to Spain in September, when it was agreed that the two countries would work together to settle their differences. Nevertheless, relations remained strained, particularly due to Morocco's lack of flexibility over the proposed new EU fisheries accord and attacks by angry Spanish fishermen on vehicles carrying Moroccan exports through Spanish ports.

In October 2001 Morocco took the unprecedented and unexpected step of recalling its ambassador to Spain for consultations, provoking a diplomatic crisis. The Moroccan Minister of Foreign Affairs and Co-operation stated that the Spanish Government was out of step with the EU on certain 'Moroccan national issues', a clear reference to Western Sahara, and criticized recent border controls introduced by the Spanish authorities for Moroccans entering the Spanish enclaves of Ceuta and Melilla. He stated that since the September suicide attacks in the USA, Spain had implied that there was a link between illegal immigration and terrorist networks (a number of Islamist cells active in Spain had recently been dismantled by Spanish police). The breakdown in April of talks on renewing the EU fisheries accord also contributed to strained relations between the two countries. A new disagreement erupted in December over maritime boundaries between the Spanish Canary Islands and Morocco's Atlantic coast after the Spanish Government granted petroleum exploration rights around the Canary Islands to a Spanish company, Repsol.

Relations deteriorated further in mid-July 2002 when a small detachment of Moroccan troops occupied the uninhabited rocky islet of Perejil (called Laila by Morocco), west of the Spanish enclave of Ceuta and close to the Moroccan coastline. Morocco claimed that it was establishing a surveillance post on the island as part of its campaign against illegal emigration and drugs-smuggling. Spain rejected this explanation, describing the Moroccan occupation as a 'serious incident'. The Spanish Government insisted that since 1990 there had been an agreement that neither Morocco nor Spain would occupy the island, whereas the Moroccan authorities claimed to have held full sovereignty over the island since 1956 and the end of the Spanish protectorate over northern Morocco, maintaining that Moroccan troops had been deployed there in the past when it was deemed necessary. Spain, which proceeded to reinforce its military presence in Ceuta and Melilla, stated that it did not make a formal claim to sovereignty over the island, but demanded the immediate evacuation of Moroccan troops from Perejil and a return to the *status quo ante* whereby neither Spain nor Morocco occupied the island permanently, a demand supported by the EU and the North Atlantic Treaty Organization (NATO). A week before Moroccan troops landed on Perejil, Morocco had protested to the Spanish ambassador after five Spanish warships approached the Moroccan coast near al-Hoceima during a naval exercise. Some analysts suggested that the occupation of Perejil was Morocco's response to this incident, while others believed that it was designed to draw international attention to Morocco's claims to Ceuta and Melilla and perhaps to put pressure on Spain to change its position with regard to Western Sahara. A few days later Spain's ambassador to Morocco was recalled for an indefinite period, and Spanish special forces intervened and removed Moroccan troops from Perejil without casualties on either side. While Spanish officials underlined the sensitivity of the situation, they insisted that Spanish troops would be withdrawn if King Muhammad gave assurances that his forces would not reoccupy the island. They also suggested joint use of the island in the campaign against drugs-trafficking. Morocco denounced the Spanish action as equivalent to a declaration of war, but maintained that it sought a diplomatic solution to the crisis.

Morocco's stance regarding Perejil was supported by all political parties and the Islamist organizations, and a number of popular demonstrations were held in northern Morocco to protest against the Spanish assault on Perejil. Both the League of Arab States (Arab League) and the Organization of the Islamic Conference (OIC—now Organization of Islamic Cooperation) expressed support for Morocco. Following mediation by the US Secretary of State, Colin Powell, Spanish forces withdrew from the island, and talks in Rabat between the Spanish Minister of Foreign Affairs, Ana Palacio, and her Moroccan counterpart towards the end of July 2002 (the first at this level since October 2001) resulted in an accord whereby both states agreed to return to the *status quo ante*. A meeting to discuss some of the other issues causing friction between the two countries was, however, cancelled by Morocco, which claimed that a Spanish military helicopter had landed on the disputed islet on the eve of the talks. The Moroccan Ministry of Foreign Affairs and Co-operation described the incident as an unacceptable violation of Morocco's airspace and territory. Talks finally proceeded in early December 2002, when the Moroccan Minister of Foreign Affairs and Co-operation met his Spanish counterpart in Madrid. Both sides agreed to normalize relations, although no date was set for the return of their respective ambassadors to their posts. All major bilateral issues had been discussed, and the Spanish foreign minister stated that she was 'very satisfied' with the meeting.

In late December 2002, following widespread oil pollution along the Galician coastline resulting from the sinking of the oil tanker *Prestige* in November, Morocco offered to allow 67 Spanish fishing vessels to operate in Moroccan territorial waters. The offer, made by King Muhammad himself, was welcomed by the Spanish Government as a clear sign of a change in attitude on the part of Morocco. However, some sections of the Spanish press argued that it was merely a tactical move to secure Spanish support at the UN for Morocco's position on Western Sahara. (Spain was due to become a non-permanent member of the UN Security Council in January 2003.)

In mid-January 2003 a Spanish delegation travelled to Rabat to set up three working groups on immigration, delimitation of territorial waters and political issues. Two other groups, on economic co-operation and the rapprochement of civil society, would be established at a later date. When the Moroccan and Spanish foreign ministers met in Agadir at the end of January, both countries announced the return of their ambassadors (this subsequently took place in February). The meeting was extremely cordial, but it was clear that Spain had not changed its position on Ceuta and Melilla or on Western Sahara. In April talks on Moroccans working in Spain took place in Rabat between the Moroccan Minister of the Interior and the Spanish interior ministry's delegate in charge of foreigners' affairs and immigration, and an agreement was reached on readmission procedures to Morocco for Moroccans illegally resident in Spain. A meeting of the Spanish and Moroccan premiers in Spain in June was stated to have been 'very positive'. In December the Moroccan and Spanish Prime Ministers met in Marrakesh, where they signed a new debt conversion agreement and pledged to strengthen co-operation in combating illegal immigration.

In March 2004, after a series of co-ordinated bomb attacks on commuter trains in Madrid, which killed more than 190 people and injured some 1,900, Spanish police arrested 18 men, most of them Moroccans. The Spanish security services suspected that the extremist GICM, which the Moroccan authorities believed to have been involved in the Casablanca bomb attacks in May 2003, was behind the Madrid attacks and had links with al-Qa'ida. A number of Islamist extremists were believed to have fled to Spain after the Casablanca attacks. Arrests of suspected GICM members also took place in France and Belgium. At the beginning of April a number of Moroccans, together with a Tunisian, Sarhane Ben Abdelmajid Fakhet—believed to be one of the organizers of the attacks—blew themselves up in an apartment in a Madrid suburb after being surrounded by Spanish special forces. King Muhammad and leaders of Morocco's political parties, including the Islamist PJD, immediately condemned the Madrid bomb attacks and expressed their solidarity with the Spanish people. Moroccan security experts quickly arrived in Spain to assist with the investigations. After the Spanish general election, which took place three days after the bombings, King Muhammad sent a message of congratulation to the leader of the Spanish Socialist Party and Prime Minister-elect, José Luis Rodríguez Zapatero, assuring him that Morocco was willing to co-operate fully with Spain against extremism and terrorism. Zapatero responded by stating that a priority of his foreign policy would be to begin a new era of good relations with Morocco. In late April, soon after becoming premier, Zapatero visited Morocco for talks with King Muhammad and Prime Minister Jettou. At a news conference Zapatero stated that it had been agreed to intensify co-operation in the fight against terrorism. On Western Sahara, the Spanish premier stated that Spain would adopt 'a constructive and positive position to reach a broad agreement on the issue'. The difficult question of illegal immigration was also reported to have been discussed during the visit. In May Spain's new Minister of Foreign Affairs stated that Spain would support the plan for the self-determination of the Sahrawi people based on all UN resolutions.

In October 2004 the Spanish Minister of Foreign Affairs and Co-operation held talks with King Muhammad in Tangier, and in an interview stated that a final solution to the Western Sahara conflict, acceptable to all parties, was vital for the Maghreb and for future relations between the Maghreb and EU. In December four Moroccan immigrants were arrested in the Spanish Canary Islands on suspicion of preparing a new logistical base for the GICM there, and three others were arrested on the Spanish mainland near Barcelona where they were alleged to have been attempting to obtain explosives. The Spanish Government's legalization of 'illegal' foreign workers in 2005 pleased the Moroccan authorities, as a significant number of these foreign workers were from Morocco and could now have legal status in Spain.

In January 2005 King Juan Carlos made a three-day official visit to Morocco, his first since 1979 and a clear sign of the marked improvement in bilateral relations. The Spanish King congratulated King Muhammad on a series of important political and social reforms, and stated that Spain advocated privileged links between Morocco and the EU. In June, however, relations became strained over Western Sahara after the Moroccan authorities refused to allow a number of Spanish delegations to enter the territory to carry out fact-finding missions after demonstrations in el-Aaiún and other towns. At a meeting in Madrid with his Moroccan counterpart in July, the Spanish premier spoke of the urgent need to find a political solution to the Western Sahara issue. He stated that Spain would try to contribute to resolving the conflict but that agreement had to be reached within the UN framework.

In September and early October 2005 hundreds of illegal immigrants, mostly from sub-Saharan Africa, made repeated attempts to breach security barriers that had been constructed to protect the borders between Morocco and Ceuta and Melilla. Violent clashes with the Moroccan security forces and the Spanish civil guard followed, in which 11 immigrants were killed (four were shot dead by Moroccan troops). Prime Ministers Jettou and Zapatero agreed to open an inquiry into the events. Morocco subsequently announced plans to increase police operations in areas surrounding the enclaves. Several European NGOs later accused the Moroccan authorities of abandoning illegal immigrants, apprehended following the assaults on Ceuta and Melilla, without food or water in the desert close to the borders with Algeria and Mauritania; the Government denied these allegations. Some 2,500 illegal immigrants were subsequently repatriated to sub-Saharan African countries. During talks in Rabat in early October the Spanish Minister of Foreign Affairs and Co-operation and his Moroccan counterpart agreed to increase bilateral co-operation and to study further measures to combat illegal immigration. Nevertheless, they insisted that illegal immigration was a problem that required close co-operation between all EU member states and the countries of the Maghreb and Africa. A Euro-Africa ministerial conference on illegal immigration was held in Rabat in July 2006. The Moroccan Government described a visit by Zapatero to Ceuta and Melilla in February as 'inopportune', and reiterated Morocco's territorial claim to the enclaves. Nonetheless, the Government later insisted that Zapatero's visit would not prejudice Morocco's excellent relations with Spain.

Tensions between the two countries flared up again in October 2006 when Spanish anti-terrorism judge Baltasar Garzón announced that he would convene an inquest into allegations of suspected Moroccan atrocities, including genocide, in Western Sahara. The following day a Spanish court handed down prison sentences to two Moroccans who had been convicted of carrying out the 2004 Madrid train bombings.

Relations were further strained in November 2007 when King Juan Carlos paid a visit to Ceuta and Melilla—the first of his reign. The visit drew fierce criticism from the Moroccan Government, with King Muhammad going so far as to say that the visit 'jeopardizes the future' of bilateral relations. As a result, Morocco recalled its ambassador to Spain. Meanwhile, Moroccan protesters staged demonstrations in the streets, brandishing placards declaring that 'Ceuta, Melilla and Western Sahara are Moroccan'. Following a visit by Zapatero to Rabat in January 2008, however, Morocco returned its ambassador to Spain, and, signalling a further rapprochement, in December a high-level Moroccan delegation visited Madrid and signed a three-year bilateral investment agreement worth €520m.

Relations deteriorated once again in November 2010 when Spain criticized Morocco over the deaths of protesters at the Gdaim Izyk protest camp. As a result, Morocco's Chamber of Representatives took the decision of referring the status of the Spanish enclaves of Ceuta and Mellila to the UN Special Committee on Decolonization. A mass demonstration took place in Casablanca protesting against Spanish 'interference'.

In June 2012 the visit of the Spanish crown prince, Felipe de Borbón, to a bilateral economic conference in Morocco helped to improve relations. However, Spain's willingness to raise contentious issues such as the Western Sahara question continued to strain ties, as did the attack on a Moroccan consulate in Spain in May of that year, which was allegedly carried out by elements formerly connected to Polisario. Ongoing official Spanish visits to disputed territories on and around the Moroccan coast for military and diplomatic purposes also undermined attempts at strengthening bilateral relations.

RELATIONS WITH MOROCCO'S MAGHREB NEIGHBOURS

Following the alliance of Algeria, Tunisia and Mauritania, through the Maghreb Fraternity and Co-operation Agreement of March 1983, and Mauritanian recognition of the SADR in February 1984, Morocco found itself isolated in the Maghreb. King Hassan found an unlikely ally in Muammar al-Qaddafi of Libya, and in August 1984 the two signed the Arab-African Federation Treaty at Oujda, which established a 'union of states' between their countries as the first step towards the creation of a Greater Arab Maghreb. Qaddafi was persuaded to end Libyan aid to Polisario. The union, however, proved short lived, and after disagreements on a number of issues King Hassan abrogated the Oujda Treaty in August 1987.

At a summit meeting of heads of state in Marrakesh in February 1989 the UMA was inaugurated, grouping Morocco with Algeria, Libya, Mauritania and Tunisia. The new body aimed to promote unity by allowing free movement of goods, services and labour, but the Western Sahara dispute, civil war in Algeria and UN sanctions against Libya prevented any real progress, with the result that by the mid-1990s the organization was virtually moribund. Subsequently, various efforts to revive the organization resulted in failure, largely because of strained relations between Morocco and Algeria. At a meeting of UMA foreign ministers, referring to the acutely sensitive issue of Western Sahara, Benaïssa stated that there was no question of Morocco sacrificing its 'national cause to build a Greater Maghreb'. Attending a meeting of UMA foreign ministers in Algiers in January 2003, Morocco's Minister of Foreign Affairs and Co-operation appealed for renewed efforts to overcome differences between members, but added that the strength of the UMA lay 'in the territorial integrity and strength of its individual states'. Plans to hold the long-delayed seventh heads of state summit of the UMA in Algiers in December were cancelled at the last minute when King Muhammad indicated that he would not attend. The presidency of the UMA passed to Libya, and Qaddafi announced that a new summit would be held in Libya after the Algerian presidential election in April 2004, when the Western Sahara issue would be at the top of the agenda. In June 2006 Benaïssa attended a meeting of UMA ministers responsible for foreign affairs in Tripoli, Libya, where the ministers reaffirmed their commitment to reviving the organization.

Relations with Algeria improved during 1992 while Muhammad Boudiaf, who had lived in exile in Morocco for more than 20 years, was Algerian head of state, but after Boudiaf's assassination relations quickly deteriorated; the frontier was closed, and Algerian supplies to the Polisario Front were resumed. In January 1993 there was a reconciliation, when ambassadors were exchanged and the border was reopened. However, relations deteriorated again in 1994, reaching their lowest ebb for many years. At his trial in Algiers, the alleged leader of the Algerian Groupe islamique armée (GIA) stated that, before his extradition from Morocco, senior Moroccan army officers had asked him to eliminate certain members of the Moroccan opposition living in Algeria, together with

Polisario Secretary-General Muhammad Abd al-Aziz. In August, after the murder of two Spanish tourists at Marrakesh, the Moroccan Ministry of the Interior issued a public statement alleging that two of the suspects were in the pay of the Algerian secret services. The Algerian Government strongly denied that it was sponsoring terrorism against its neighbour, and sealed the border with Morocco. By mid-September, however, the tension between the two countries had eased somewhat, and in a gesture of goodwill Algeria appointed a permanent ambassador to Morocco. However, the frontier remained closed and visa requirements for Algerian nationals continued to be enforced. Despite a meeting between the respective ministers responsible for the interior in late 1996, relations remained strained, with Algeria accusing Morocco of providing covert assistance to armed opposition groups in Algeria, and Morocco accusing Algeria of attempting to destabilize Morocco as preparations were made for the referendum on Western Sahara.

The election of Abdelaziz Bouteflika as President of Algeria in April 1999 raised hopes of a rapprochement. President Bouteflika attended the funeral of King Hassan in July, and met briefly with Morocco's new ruler. However, the improvement in relations with Algeria proved short-lived. In August Algeria again accused Morocco of providing a haven for its Islamist opponents. The long-awaited reopening of the land border between the two countries failed to take place, and the press embarked on a new round of mutual accusations. The continuing Western Sahara dispute and Algeria's support for Polisario continued to prevent any significant improvement in relations. In June 2003, however, the Moroccan Minister of Foreign Affairs visited Algiers for a comprehensive review of bilateral relations, and it was agreed to set up three commissions, to deal with political consultations, economic and social issues, and consular affairs. In September King Muhammad and President Bouteflika were reported to have held an unscheduled meeting at the UN headquarters in New York, at which it had been agreed to establish a joint task force to improve co-operation on issues such as illegal immigration and security. King Muhammad was one of the first leaders to congratulate President Bouteflika on his re-election in April 2004, and he expressed the hope that they could work together to create a better understanding and solidarity between their two countries. However, when Algeria failed to respond to Morocco's unilateral decision in July to abolish visa requirements imposed in 1994 on Algerians visiting Morocco, the Moroccan press accused President Bouteflika of 'slamming the door on reconciliation'. In October 2004 a new war of words erupted over Western Sahara.

King Muhammad attended the summit meeting of heads of state of the Arab League in Algiers in March 2005, his first visit to Algeria since his accession and the first visit by a Moroccan monarch since 1991. The King and President Bouteflika held a private meeting; although no details were given, the Algerian Minister of Foreign Affairs stated that this had helped to 'thaw' relations between the two countries. Morocco welcomed Algeria's decision in April 2005 to reciprocate and abolish visa requirements for Moroccans visiting Algeria. However, in May, just before the UMA heads of state summit was due to be held in Tripoli, King Muhammad announced that he would not be attending because of recent comments by President Bouteflika in which he reaffirmed Algeria's support for Polisario. The summit was postponed indefinitely. Nevertheless, celebrations to mark the 50th anniversary of the summit at which the idea of a union of Arab Maghreb states was first proposed, held in Tangier, in April 2008, hinted at an improvement in relations.

Following Polisario's release, in August 2005, of the remaining Moroccan prisoners of war, there were reports of a rapprochement between Morocco and Algeria. The Moroccan authorities welcomed a message from President Bouteflika to King Muhammad in which he expressed his determination to develop 'fraternal and privileged relations' between the two countries. However, following a series of attempts by illegal immigrants to enter the Spanish enclaves of Ceuta and Melilla in September and October, Morocco insisted that many of the immigrants involved had entered the country via Algeria and criticized the Algerian authorities for their failure to prevent the immigrants from crossing the border. In November Algeria rejected Morocco's proposal of autonomy for Western Sahara within the framework of Moroccan sovereignty, and reiterated its support for the Sahrawis' right to self-determination. Concerns over security related to the threat of terrorism led to an increase in the level of co-operation between Morocco and Algeria, as the start of direct talks over Western Sahara demonstrated.

In June 2007 King Muhammad announced that Morocco and Algeria had agreed to co-ordinate more closely on security matters, particularly over issues relating to the rise of radical Islamism in North Africa. However, this consensus failed to break either the ongoing deadlock over the border closure or the impasse over Western Sahara. In May 2008 Algeria rejected further overtures from Morocco to collaborate on either issue, in spite of Morocco's announcement that the Western Sahara problem was impossible to resolve without Algeria's involvement. None the less, there were indications of a rapprochement in mid-2010. Following the death of President Bouteflika's brother in July, a Moroccan delegation, including Minister of Foreign Affairs and Co-operation Taieb Fassi Fihri, travelled to Algiers to convey King Muhammad's condolences. Shortly afterwards, the King expressed his desire for 'reconciliation and solidarity' between the two countries in a personal message to Bouteflika acknowledging Algeria's Independence Day celebrations. In February 2012 the two countries signed a political consultation agreement.

Relations between Morocco and Tunisia improved following the overthrow of the Tunisian regime of Zine al-Abidine Ben Ali in January 2011. In part, this was a result of the concomitant political changes that were taking effect in both countries. Morocco's relations with Libya were also strengthened during that year following the collapse of the Libyan regime of Muammar al-Qaddafi, who had been distrusted in Morocco, and the subsequent move towards a more democratic polity. The political transformations improved bilateral relationships across the Maghreb, in turn prompting proposals to revitalize the UMA. However, Tunisia's republican tradition, Libya's nascent political development and the long-standing resistance among the Maghreb nations to fundamental compromises of national sovereignty could limit the prospects for a more meaningful union in the future.

King Muhammad's historic visit to Mauritania in September 2001, intended to inaugurate an era of improved relations between the two countries, was cut short as a result of the suicide attacks on New York and Washington, DC. In March 2002 it was reported that the land frontier between Morocco and Mauritania, closed for 23 years, would be reopened. In November 2005 Col Ely Ould Mohamed Vall, the new Mauritanian head of state, visited Morocco on the invitation of King Muhammad and signed three agreements on bilateral co-operation. He also noted a significant improvement in relations between the two countries. In April 2006 King Muhammad received the Mauritanian Prime Minister, Sidi Mohamed Ould Boubacar, for talks in Meknès.

RELATIONS WITH THE WIDER MIDDLE EAST

Morocco was the first Arab state to condemn Iraq's invasion of Kuwait in August 1990, and voted for the resolutions at the Arab League summit held in Cairo, Egypt, denouncing Iraq's action. King Hassan agreed to send 1,200 Moroccan troops to Saudi Arabia and a further 5,000 were stationed in Abu Dhabi, the United Arab Emirates (UAE). However, faced with strong pro-Iraqi feelings among the Moroccan people and hostility towards US military intervention in the region, the King quickly adopted a more neutral stance in the conflict and attempted to act as mediator in the dispute. Shortly before hostilities began King Hassan sent a letter to Saddam Hussain, urging him to accept the deployment of a North African military force in Kuwait to replace the Iraqi army and avoid conflict with the US-led multinational force. In January 1991 opposition parties appealed for the withdrawal of the Moroccan contingent, and all parties in parliament demanded a negotiated solution to the crisis. Several pro-Iraqi demonstrations took place despite a government ban on street protests. Shortly before hostilities began trade unionists were allowed to hold a

24-hour general strike to denounce war against Iraq. The Government also allowed the opposition parties to hold a march of solidarity with Iraq in Rabat, which the organizers claimed attracted 500,000 people. King Hassan stated that an agreement to send Moroccan troops to Saudi Arabia had been made before the Cairo summit, that their role was to be purely defensive, and that they were totally independent of coalition forces. The King further declared that, despite the Government's official position, 'our hearts are with our Iraqi brothers'.

In January 1992 Arab ministers responsible for foreign affairs met in Marrakesh to agree a common strategy for the forthcoming Moscow session of the Middle East peace talks. In October, just before the seventh round of talks (held in Washington, DC), King Hassan made his most extensive tour of the Middle East in 30 years, visiting Jordan, Syria, Saudi Arabia, the Gulf states and Egypt. In December 1994 Morocco hosted a summit meeting of the OIC at the request of Saudi Arabia; however, despite lengthy negotiations, King Hassan failed to bring about any reconciliation between Iraq and Saudi Arabia and Kuwait. King Hassan made an official visit to Egypt in May 1998 in order to strengthen bilateral relations. The King and President Hosni Mubarak signed a number of economic agreements, and, in a joint statement, expressed support for the Palestinian people and urged the USA to continue its efforts to revive the Middle East peace process. In July Morocco again hosted a meeting of the OIC's Al-Quds (Jerusalem) Committee, of which King Hassan was the Chairman, to discuss the stalled Middle East peace process.

In September 1993, following the mutual recognition and signature of a peace accord between Israel and the Palestine Liberation Organization, the Israeli Prime Minister, Itzhak Rabin, and the Minister of Foreign Affairs, Shimon Peres, visited Rabat for talks with King Hassan. Apart from Egypt, Morocco was the only Arab state to receive the two Israeli leaders. In October a group of Moroccan industrialists, including King Hassan's economic adviser, visited Israel to attend a business conference: this was the first official Moroccan delegation to visit the country. Commercial links developed rapidly, and tourism was expected to expand: the Moroccan-Jewish community constitutes more than 10% of the Israeli population, and large numbers visit their country of origin every year. After talks with King Hassan in June 1994, Shimon Peres announced that the two countries had agreed to establish telecommunications links and, at a later date, to establish 'representations of some kind'. In September, as the peace process gained momentum, Morocco and Israel agreed to open 'liaison offices' in Rabat and Tel-Aviv. King Hassan had maintained discreet contacts with Israeli leaders since the 1970s. The latest move towards a normalization of relations with Israel was criticized by the opposition parties, which urged caution until a comprehensive Middle East peace settlement had been achieved. In October 1994, during an historic appearance on Israeli television, King Hassan declared that the peace process would lead to the establishment of full diplomatic relations between Morocco and Israel, but carefully avoided stating when this would take place. He reiterated Morocco's stance on the restoration of Arab lands and rights, while insisting that the unconditional recognition of Israeli sovereignty within internationally agreed borders was essential. In early 1995 Morocco opened an economic bureau in Tel-Aviv, making it the third Arab state after Egypt and Jordan to have a representative office in Israel. However, King Hassan continued to stress that full normalization of relations between the two countries would only be achieved after the conclusion of a comprehensive Middle East peace settlement. In February 1996 an Israeli-Moroccan chamber of commerce was opened in Tel-Aviv.

In March 1997 the King organized a meeting in Rabat of the OIC's Jerusalem Committee. The committee demanded that the Israeli Government stop construction of the controversial Jewish settlement at Har Homa on the outskirts of Arab East Jerusalem, and appealed to Arab states that had begun to establish relations with Israel to reconsider these links. A threat by Morocco in April to close the Moroccan-based Bureau for Economic Development in the Middle East, established to promote economic relations between the Arab states and Israel, was withdrawn in May after US intervention. Morocco did not close its liaison office in Tel-Aviv despite King Hassan's continued refusal to have any contact with the Netanyahu administration. Along with most Arab League members, Morocco boycotted the fourth US-sponsored Middle East and North Africa Economic Conference held in Qatar in November, arguing that while the Middle East peace process remained deadlocked there was little to be gained from discussing economic co-operation with Israel. Nevertheless, commercial and business links between Morocco and Israel remained strong. In October 1998 Morocco refused to allow the Israeli Prime Minister to make a stop-over in Rabat after attending peace negotiations in the USA. In contrast, King Hassan extended a warm welcome to the Palestinian Executive President, Yasser Arafat, who made a short visit to the Moroccan capital on his return from the USA. In July 1999 the new Israeli Prime Minister, Ehud Barak, attended the funeral of King Hassan in Rabat.

In August 2000 King Muhammad chaired a meeting of the OIC's Jerusalem Committee, which reaffirmed that the city should be the capital of a Palestinian state. Shortly afterwards, the acting Israeli Minister of Foreign Affairs, Shlomo Ben-Ami, met with King Muhammad and his Moroccan counterpart in Agadir to discuss the Middle East peace process. Following renewed violence between Israel and the Palestinians in September–October, there was growing criticism within Morocco of the country's links with Israel. In late October Morocco closed Israel's liaison office in Rabat and its own interest section in Tel-Aviv. Earlier in the month 500,000 Moroccans had demonstrated in Rabat in support of the Palestinians—the largest protest march since the 1991 Gulf War. However, in December 2000 Israel's Deputy Prime Minister and Minister of Foreign Affairs, Shimon Peres, visited Rabat to discuss US peace proposals with King Muhammad, suggesting that Morocco was continuing its role as mediator between the Arab states and Israel.

There was widespread outrage in Morocco in response to the Israeli military offensive in Palestinian-controlled areas of the West Bank from March 2002. A national march in solidarity with the Palestinian people, which took place in Rabat in April, attracting more than 1m. people, was the biggest demonstration in the Arab world. Meanwhile, there were reports in the Moroccan press that an apparent resurgence of anti-Semitism since the onset of the second *intifada*, a renewed uprising by Palestinians against Israeli occupation, was causing disquiet among members of Morocco's Jewish community, who found themselves the target of verbal and physical assaults. The Moroccan authorities remained silent on this subject, but did arrest a number of radical imams for criticizing the Moroccan and other Arab governments' alleged quiescence with regard to the situation in the Palestinian Territories.

In July 2003 the Moroccan Minister of Foreign Affairs and Co-operation met his Israeli counterpart in London to express Morocco's support for the internationally sponsored roadmap for peace between Israel and the Palestinians. At the same time the Palestinian Prime Minister, Mahmud Abbas, made a short visit to Morocco while returning from talks with US officials in Washington, DC. Meanwhile, there were reports that King Muhammad had held a secret meeting in Tangier with Israel's Chief Sephardi Rabbi, Shlomo Amar, at which the rabbi had asked the King to continue to work for peace between Arabs and Israelis. In September, during a visit to the UN headquarters in New York, King Muhammad met the Israeli Foreign Minister and the Minister of External Affairs of the Palestinian (National) Authority. In March 2004 Morocco strongly condemned Israel's assassination of Sheikh Ahmad Yassin, the spiritual leader of the Islamic Resistance Movement (Hamas), and the apparent escalation of its military campaign against the Palestinian people, and reiterated its commitment to reviving the peace process. The Secretary-General of Morocco's Jewish community called Yassin's assassination a 'brutal act' of state terrorism, and pronounced that without a political solution there would only be terror and extremism.

In an interview with Israeli radio in March 2005, Israel's Vice-Premier, Shimon Peres, confirmed reports in the Israeli press that relations between Israel and Morocco were soon to be re-established and that he had been invited to make an official visit to Rabat. He added that relations with Morocco had already improved. In April Morocco's Minister of Agriculture, Rural Development and Maritime Fisheries denied reports that Morocco had trade links with Israel. In February 2006 King Muhammad received the new leader of the Israel Labour Party, Amir Peretz, who is of Moroccan origin, and in April the Palestinian President, Mahmud Abbas, visited Rabat for talks with King Muhammad. In early July Morocco condemned Israeli military incursions into the Gaza Strip and demanded the release of Palestinian ministers and members of parliament who had been arrested by the Israeli army. In July 2007 Benaïssa and the Israeli Vice-Prime Minister and Minister of Foreign Affairs, Tzipi Livni, held the first such official meeting for four years in order to discuss the Middle East peace process.

In January 2001 Prime Minister el-Youssoufi led a delegation of ministers and business representatives to Iran, with the aim of preparing for closer political relations. A number of commercial agreements were signed during the visit. (No senior Moroccan politician had visited Iran since the Islamic Revolution in 1979, and in 1981 Iran had severed diplomatic relations with Morocco after King Hassan allowed the deposed Shah to take refuge in Morocco.) In May 2003 the Iranian Minister of Foreign Affairs visited Rabat at the head of a high-ranking delegation, and at a meeting with his Moroccan counterpart there were appeals for closer economic, political and cultural ties between the two countries. In June 2006 Benaïssa visited the Iranian capital, Tehran, for talks with Iranian President Mahmoud Ahmadinejad, whereupon an agreement was concluded to create a joint political committee. However, relations took a sudden and unexpected turn for the worse in March 2009, when Morocco severed diplomatic relations with Iran following remarks made by a senior Iranian official, in which he appeared to claim Iranian sovereignty over Bahrain. Morocco's reaction to the incident took the international community by surprise, raising questions over whether there was more to the dispute than was made public. Relations had not improved by mid-2013, in part reflecting the King's ongoing control over foreign policy.

Increased ties with Saudi Arabia have been established since the accession of King Muhammad VI. In May 2007 Morocco and Saudi Arabia signed a co-operation accord that included a Saudi pledge of US $50m. to promote Morocco's development. This brought the total sum of Saudi aid to the kingdom to $170m. over eight years. As the regional turmoil of 2011 intensified, Morocco (and Jordan) received an unexpected invitation in May from Saudi Arabia's King Abdullah to join the Cooperation Council of the Arab States of the Gulf (Gulf Cooperation Council—GCC). The invitation, which was clearly designed to bring the Arab monarchies closer together and to close ranks against the democratizing forces within the region, provoked widespread bemusement in Morocco, and subsequent discussions over Morocco's membership proved tentative. After indications from the UAE and Kuwait that they opposed the inclusion of Morocco and Jordan in the GCC, and that they had not been consulted over King Abdullah's invitation, the Saudi Minister of Foreign Affairs, Prince Sa'ud al-Faisal Al Sa'ud, declared in December that the two countries' 'applications' would need further consideration in light of the EU's problems with sustaining Greece as a full member of the union. In January 2012 Kuwait proposed 'full integration' after two years of partnership with Morocco and Jordan. In the event, the GCC's pledge to provide dedicated funding to Morocco and Jordan seemed to replace the fading and barely formed 'commitment' to their GCC membership.

Economy

Revised for this edition by PHILIP McCRUM

By the early 1980s Morocco was in economic crisis. The fiscal deficit exceeded 12% of gross domestic product (GDP), the current account deficit on the balance of payments was over 10% of GDP, foreign reserves were depleted and the country was unable to service its external debt. With the support of the World Bank and the IMF, the Government introduced structural adjustment policies from 1984. Over the next five years Morocco made considerable progress as manufacturing exports expanded, the fiscal deficit was reduced, external debt was rescheduled and the current account deficit was cut, although problems in fiscal and public sector management remained. Between 1988 and 1990 new IMF and World Bank support arrangements were negotiated and debt-rescheduling agreements were reached with the 'Paris Club' of creditor governments and the 'London Club' of official creditors. The Government, meanwhile, made a commitment to a radical reform of the economy, creating a Ministry of Privatization in 1989 and enacting new privatization legislation from January 1990.

The debt-rescheduling cycle was forecast to end in 1993, by which date the dirham was to be made convertible and Morocco would return to international capital markets. In 1992 it was announced that the IMF had approved further credit in support of the Government's economic programme for the following year, aiming to promote investment, increase productivity, strengthen the budgetary position and reorientate credit towards the private sector. High priority was to be given to the development of the capital and financial markets, although social concern was also expressed about the high rates of infant mortality and illiteracy. Despite government claims that there had been a significant reduction in the gap between rich and poor, opposition parties argued that economic liberalization had widened the divide and a survey by the UN Development Programme and Morocco's Direction de la Statistique in 1993 estimated that almost one-quarter of the population lived below the poverty line.

In 1993 an IMF study concluded that Morocco's financial balances had been restored and the economy's structural weaknesses substantially resolved. Nevertheless, it stated that the economy still faced significant challenges to achieve higher sustainable growth. Under a five-year assistance agreement, beginning in 1995, Morocco was to receive US $1,350m. from the World Bank to help the country achieve stronger economic growth, reduce social disparities and carry out administrative reforms.

In 1994 Prime Minister Abd al-Latif Filali pledged to expedite an ambitious programme of privatization (see Industry). During 1994 receipts from the sale of state assets reached 3,700m. dirhams, and in 1995 the Government announced that the privatization schedule had been extended and that new companies would be added to the list, including those previously considered as 'strategic' and excluded from the programme. However, by the end of 1998 only 58 of 114 firms originally listed in 1993 had been sold. Despite some ministers being hostile to privatization on ideological grounds, the Government had little alternative but to continue the sale of state assets in order to help cover the budget deficit, although some of the enterprises that remained to be sold were considered unattractive to investors. A new privatization law was adopted in 1999 under which firms being considered for sale were to be examined on a case-by-case basis. The Government raised only one-half of the 2,000m. dirhams of revenues forecast from privatization during the 1998/99 fiscal year. However, in December 2000 the Government divested a 35% stake in Maroc Télécom for US $2,200m., and in mid-2003 it sold a substantial stake in the state tobacco monopoly, Régie des Tabacs du Maroc. In late 2004 the Government completed the sale of further interests in Maroc Télécom. In 2006 there were additional proceeds from the sale of the remaining stake in Régie des Tabacs du Maroc and of Société Marocaine du Thé et du Sucre.

Morocco's GDP has been heavily influenced by agricultural performance, which has been particularly erratic owing to the country's susceptibility to drought. GDP rose by 6.5% in 2001, reflecting a recovery in agricultural production, which increased by 27% after two years of contraction caused by severe drought. According to the IMF, GDP increased by 4.5% in 2002 as a result of a further rise in agricultural output and higher growth of 3.9% in the non-agricultural sector, despite a less favourable international environment.

Real GDP growth reached 6.1% in 2003, mainly as a result of an exceptionally good cereal harvest. Inflation was 1.2% and the external position showed a surplus on the current account. The IMF, however, noted that growth had been insufficient to reduce poverty and unemployment, and was still volatile owing to the dependency of the agricultural sector on rainfall. According to the central bank, Bank Al-Maghrib, growth reached 4.2% in 2004, with the inflation rate at about 1.5% and the budget deficit reaching 3.2% of GDP. In 2005 GDP growth contracted to 2.4%, according to the IMF, while inflation decreased further to 1.0%. This decline reflected a reduction in agricultural production as a result of drought conditions, a slowdown in industrial output and exports resulting from weak European demand, and increased competition in the textile sector following the abolition of the World Trade Organization (WTO) quota system. Real GDP growth of 8.0% was achieved in 2006, according to Bank Al-Maghrib, reflecting a strong agricultural performance and expansion of the construction and tourism sectors following the slowdown in 2005. Although the central bank maintained a prudent monetary policy, inflation increased to 3.3%, mainly due to higher energy prices.

To encourage the diversification of the economy and to raise productivity, a new strategy (termed Plan Emergence—see Industry) was announced in 2006; this aimed to raise real GDP by 1.6% per year, create an additional 440,000 jobs and halve the trade deficit by 2015. Nevertheless, GDP growth declined to an estimated 2.2% in 2007, due to another agricultural contraction. The Government's decision not to pass on higher international food prices to consumers moderated inflation during 2007, which was estimated to average 2.1%. According to the High Commission for Planning, growth increased again to 5.6% in 2008, due to a satisfactory harvest. Non-agricultural GDP decreased to 4.2% (from 6.5% in 2007), reflecting the deteriorating global economic environment from the second half of the year. Morocco was most vulnerable to the international downturn through its reliance on expatriate remittances, tourism income and textiles exports. Agricultural growth rose dramatically to 30.6% in 2009, offsetting the decline in non-agricultural growth, which slowed to just 1%, due to the impact of the economic downturn in Europe, Morocco's main export market. Overall growth decreased to 4.9%. These trends reversed in 2010, when adverse weather conditions resulted in a very poor harvest, causing a 7.5% decline in the agricultural sector. Conversely, non-agricultural activity picked up by 4.4%, allowing for an overall rise in real GDP of 3.7%.

A good cereal harvest in 2011 supported wider economic growth of 4.9%, underscoring the sector's continued importance to economic expansion. In the course of 2011 Morocco witnessed minor political turmoil, as the impact of wider regional turbulence prompted domestic protests. In general, however, domestic disturbances did little to disrupt economic performance during the year and non-agricultural economic activity also showed a moderate increase. Growth in the telecommunications and mining sectors both exceeded 9%, although the tourism sector fared less well, with numbers of visitors from the troubled EU economies falling markedly. With the EU economies remaining in recession in 2012, tourist arrivals stagnated, rising by just 0.4% over the year, a situation not helped by sporadic political protests in Morocco and wider regional instability. Morocco also suffered from a drought in 2012 and, as a result, agricultural output fell by 8.9%, slowing overall real GDP growth to just 2.7%. Non-agricultural GDP grew by 4.4%.

The average inflation rate, meanwhile, rose in 2008 to about 3.9%, causing some social unrest and prompting the Government to raise its subsidy budget. However, the contraction in GDP eased inflationary pressures in 2009 and consumer price growth decreased to just 1%, the level at which it remained during 2010, before easing marginally, to just 0.9%, in 2011. The slowing economy in 2012, in combination with the widespread subsidy system, kept consumer price inflation low. Despite a rise in imported food costs, inflation was recorded at 1.3% for the year.

Unemployment has remained an ongoing problem. In 1999, according to official figures, the rate was 22.1% in urban areas and 5.3% in rural areas (although independent sources insisted that the real level was much higher). In 2003 the Government introduced legislation to change the more restrictive aspects of the labour code. The following year the national unemployment rate contracted to 10.8% (from 11.9% in 2003, with the urban rate decreasing to 18.4% from 19.3%), but rose again slightly in 2005, to 11.1% (with the urban rate remaining at 18.4%). The labour force at that time numbered 10.8m., but it was increasing by an estimated 300,000 per year. In 2006 the level decreased significantly, to 9.7% (with the urban rate declining to 15.5%), before again rising slightly, to 9.8%, in 2007. The rate of unemployment eased marginally, to 9.6%, in 2008, before narrowing further in 2009, to 9.1%. At the end of 2010 the rate was unchanged, although large urban-rural discrepancies remained; unemployment stood at 13.7% in urban areas, compared with just 3.9% in rural areas. In mid-2011 the latest estimates showed that the rate was again largely unchanged, but the low level of rural unemployment serves to highlight the role that agriculture plays not just in directly supporting output, but also in providing an income for a large proportion of the population. The overall unemployment rate was little changed in 2012, settling at 9.0%. However, youth unemployment was recorded at more than double the overall level, rising to 18.6%.

AGRICULTURE AND FISHERIES

The principal crops are cereals (especially wheat, barley and maize), citrus fruit, as well as tomatoes, potatoes, olives, beans and chickpeas. Canary seed, cumin, coriander, linseed and almonds are also grown. Sugar beet and cane are cultivated on a large scale to substitute for imports; sugar is one of Morocco's principal food imports owing to the high level of domestic consumption. Climatic conditions cause substantial annual variations in agricultural output. These fluctuations, moreover, have a significant impact on the economy, affecting the level of GDP growth or decline and the rate of unemployment. By 2011 an estimated 40% of the working population were employed in agriculture, forestry and fishing; in 2012 the sector accounted for about 14% of GDP.

After successive years of drought and poor harvests, heavy rainfall led to an increased production of 4.6m. metric tons in 2001 and 5.3m. tons in 2002. The harvest then increased to 8.0m. tons in 2003, the highest level since 1996, with wheat production at 5.2m. tons and barley at 2.6m. tons. Aggregate production rose further in 2004, to a record 8.5m. tons, owing to favourable climatic conditions and larger areas coming under cultivation. However, output decreased sharply in the 2005 season, to 4.3m. tons, again as a result of below-average rainfall. Wheat production in the 2006 season increased to an estimated 6.3m. tons, but the total cereal harvest slumped in 2007, to about 2.5m. tons, after late rains damaged crops. This prompted the Government to launch a 10-year strategy—the Maroc Vert (Green Morocco) Plan—to modernize and diversify the agriculture sector, and to initiate a land-leasing programme to transfer arable, state-owned land to private investors in public partnership schemes. In 2007/08 cereal production recovered significantly, to 5.2m. tons, and, with exceptionally high rainfall, the harvest for the 2008/09 season rose markedly, to 10.2m. tons. The Government announced in April 2010 that it would lease an additional 30,000 ha of state-owned farmland, particularly land suitable for fruit production, to foreign or domestic investors, under the Maroc Vert Plan. In June the Government raised import tariffs for wheat to 135% in order to protect domestic production, but a sharp rise in international wheat prices forced the Government to suspend duties on soft wheat for the last quarter in order to ensure stability of supply in the domestic market. Morocco produced 3.8m. tons of soft wheat in 2010, a decline of 12% compared with the previous year's yield. Overall grain output reached 7.8m. tons in 2010, rising to 8.7m. tons in 2011. However, owing to the drought in 2012, the overall yield of cereals fell to 5.3m. tons.

Morocco has also been a major food exporter, particularly of citrus fruit (annual production of which in recent years has averaged about 1.2m. tons). The country exports approximately 40% of its citrus crop, of which about 70% goes to European Union (EU) countries. Under the terms of a free trade agreement with the EU, signed in February 1996, both parties agreed to increase trade in agricultural products. In February 2012 the agreement with the EU was expanded significantly, in an attempt to boost bilateral agricultural trade (see Balance of Payments and Trade).

Livestock numbers declined during the 1990s, and by 2008 they totalled approximately 27.0m. (mainly sheep, which numbered about 16.9m. in 2006). The numbers declined further, to 25.5m. in 2009 and 25.1m. in 2010. However, total numbers rose once again in 2011, to 26.9m.

Fishing has become increasingly important. In 2006 the total catch (mainly sardines) declined to 869,000 metric tons (from some 1,028,800 tons in 2005, according to FAO) following an 18% decrease in coastal fishing catches. Exports of fishery products amounted to 436,000 tons. To offset the decline in catches, the Government launched a new investment plan for the fishing sector under the 10-year agricultural strategy. The total catch increased in 2008, reaching 943,000 tons, and rose again to, 1,166,500 tons, in 2009. A slight decline, to 1,137,800 tons, was recorded in 2010. In 2011 the figures declined more significantly, with the total catch falling to 960,300 tons.

In 1988 Morocco signed a four-year agreement with the European Community (EC—now EU) that restricted EC vessels to a catch of 95,000 tons a year in Moroccan waters, in return for licence fees and compensation worth US $48.3m. annually. In May 1992 a new three-year accord came into force allowing 650 Spanish, 50 Portuguese and 36 other trawlers into Moroccan waters, in return for increased compensation of 102m. ECUs ($131m.). A further four-year agreement came into effect in December 1995. Catches by EU fishing vessels were to be reduced by up to 40% for certain species, and total compensation payments from the EU were set at $355m. over four years. Despite the EU fisheries accord, tensions over the mostly Spanish vessels fishing in Moroccan waters continued. The accord expired in November 1999, and in 2002 negotiations over a new agreement were suspended. In July 2005 Morocco and the EU finally signed a further four-year deal. With limited fishing rights in Moroccan territorial waters, the EU was restricted to catching a maximum of 60,000 tons of small, open-water fish using 119 fishing boats per year. In exchange, the EU paid Morocco $43m. annually. However, in December 2011 the European Parliament decided to abrogate the agreement, on the grounds that much of the fishing activity took place off the coast of Western Sahara, with parliamentarians expressing concerns that they were exploiting the resources of the disputed territory. Fishing in the maritime zone belonging to Western Sahara accounts for 50% of Morocco's total annual catch. The Moroccan authorities responded by ordering all EU fishing boats out of its waters with immediate effect. Although negotiations began again in 2012, they were hampered by differences over the long contentious issue of Western Sahara (see History). After a further 18-month hiatus, Morocco and the EU finally reached an agreement in July 2013, under which Morocco would receive €40m. annually in return for allowing 126 boats from 11 EU nations to fish in its waters.

MINING

With the exception of phosphate-mining and its derivatives, there was a progressive decline in the importance of the mining sector from the late 1980s. However, reflecting the Government's intention to upgrade the sector, parliament approved legislation in 2003 to establish the Office National des Hydrocarbures et des Mines (ONHYM) to replace the Bureau de Recherches et de Participation Minières (BRPM) and the Office National de Recherches et d'Exploitations Pétrolières (ONAREP). The new office was to be responsible for research and exploration, improving geological surveys, and managing the transportation system more efficiently.

The Office Chérifien des Phosphates (OCP) manages phosphate-mining as well as phosphoric acid and phosphate fertilizer production facilities. Morocco has about two-thirds of the world's known reserves of phosphate rock. Proven reserves are 10,600m. metric tons, and probable reserves some 57,200m. tons. Major deposits are located at Khouribga, Youssoufia and Ben Guerir. Morocco also controls production at Bou Craa in Western Sahara. By 1997 Morocco had become the world's leading exporter, overtaking the USA and accounting for almost one-third of world trade. The principal export markets by 2004 were the USA (taking 21.2%), Spain (14.2%), India (8.3%) and Mexico (7.9%). In 2005 production of phosphate rock totalled an estimated 27.3m. tons (up from 25.4m. tons in 2004) and exports 13.3m. tons (compared with 11.8m. tons in 2004). In 2006 an estimated 27.4m. tons were produced and 13.4m. tons exported. In 2007 production increased again, to about 28m. tons, with exports reaching 14.1m. tons. In 2008 production declined to 25m. tons, while exports also decreased, to 11m. tons. Exports declined considerably in 2009, to just 5.8m. tons, as external demand slumped, but recovered in 2010, rising to 10.2m. tons. The rise in exports coincided with a marked rise in the international price of phosphates, which boosted export revenues by over 100%. In October 2010 the OCP issued a bond of 2,000m. dirhams to support its expansion plans, under which it anticipates boosting phosphates output to around 50m. tons by 2020. By 2030 it is expected that Morocco will be producing between 80%–90% of total global demand. In 2011 exports fell slightly, to 9.4m tons. However, owing to the sharp rise in global prices, the value of phosphates exports rose by 44%, to 13.0m. dirhams.

Exploration for hydrocarbons in Morocco intensified following the creation of ONAREP in 1981. However, the collapse in oil prices in 1986 prompted many foreign oil companies to relinquish their onshore and offshore exploration interests. After a revised hydrocarbon law came into force in 1992, which included provisions to reduce the state's holding in concession contracts to a maximum of 25%, renewed efforts were made to attract foreign investment. In 1997 ONAREP announced the discovery in the Gharb region of reserves of some 300m. cu m of natural gas near Kénitra, with potential production of 75,000 cu m a day. Cabre Maroc of Canada also subsequently announced that several exploratory wells drilled in that region had produced low-sulphur gas.

In 2000 the discovery by a US firm of oil and gas reserves in the Talsint block in the north-east of the country close to the Algerian border encouraged several international companies to convert their reconnaissance licences for offshore blocks in southern Morocco into exploration licences. The following year the Government signed two controversial exploration agreements, both offshore, in the disputed Western Sahara region, which is believed to be potentially rich in oil reserves. These were with TotalFinaElf (now Total) of France for the Dakhla zone, and with the USA's Kerr-McGee (already holding six reconnaissance permits with partners on the Cap Draâ offshore field on the Atlantic coast) for an area in the Boujdor region, near the city of el-Aaiún. The Polisario Front, which is seeking independence for the Western Saharan region, protested against the contracts to the UN, which determined that Morocco would be in violation of international law if it allowed foreign firms to produce oil from the disputed territory without taking into account the interests of its inhabitants. Total was reported to have ceased all petroleum exploration in Western Sahara in late 2004. Political sensitivities over Western Sahara have for the most part deterred large oil companies from entering Morocco, and the country only attracted interest from small independent companies. However, high oil prices and a growing conviction within the industry that Morocco offered considerable offshore potential resulted in Chevron signing an exploration deal in January 2013.

Morocco has two oil refineries, at Mohammedia and Sidi Kacem. They were originally owned by Société Anonyme Marocaine de l'Industrie du Raffinage (SAMIR) and Société

Chérifienne des Pétroles (SCP), respectively. The Government began to sell its holdings in the two companies in 1996. In May 1997 a Saudi-owned company, Corral Petroleum Holdings, purchased majority stakes in both companies, and the two entities were subsequently merged in September 1999. In November 2002 the Mohammedia refinery, producing 80%–90% of the country's refined products, was badly damaged following a severe flood and massive fire. In June 2005 a rehabilitation and upgrading contract was awarded to a team of Italy's Snamprogetti and Turkey's Tekfen. In 2006 a consortium led by Terminals Ltd (United Arab Emirates—UAE) was awarded a 25-year concession to build and operate an international petroleum storage terminal at the port of Tangier. In 2007 the Government announced that it would build a US $3,000m. refinery at Jorf Lasfar.

In July 1992 Morocco and Spain signed a 25-year agreement to build the Maghreb–Europe gas pipeline, to run from Hassi R'Mel in Algeria, across Morocco and the Strait of Gibraltar to Spain. Despite concerns over the security situation in Algeria and rising tensions between Morocco and Algeria, work on the pipeline began formally in October 1994. The pipeline became operational in November 1996 when the first gas supplies were delivered to Spain, and a link to Portugal was completed in early 1997. In 2007 the Government announced that it was planning to build a liquefied natural gas (LNG) terminal, at an estimated cost of US $1,000m., as part of a drive to diversify energy supply, and a natural gas discovery was reported by Maghreb Petroleum Exploration. In early 2009 further discoveries were reported by Ireland's Circle Oil, at its Sebou concession in the Rharb basin, and by Repsol of Spain, off the Mediterranean coast in the Tangier-Larache concession. In May 2010 the Government announced plans to build an LNG terminal in the country, to facilitate the importation of greater quantities of LNG and to reduce dependence on Algeria (Morocco's sole source of LNG).

Coal production declined sharply through the 1990s. Most of Morocco's coal supplies (mainly for electricity generation) have been imported from South Africa and Poland. Output of iron ore, mainly from mines in the north-east of Morocco, totalled an estimated 8,400 metric tons (gross weight) in 2007 (compared with 8,100 tons in 2006 and 8,130 tons in 2005). Production is undertaken by the Société d'Exploitation des Mines du Rif. Other minerals produced include barytes, lead, copper, zinc, fluorspar and manganese. Total output of mineral products, excluding phosphates, was estimated to have exceeded 1.2m. tons in 2005, mainly resulting from an increase in extraction of fluorspar and of zinc following the opening of a deposit in the Marrakesh area.

The local holding company Omnium Nord Africain (ONA—now Société Nationale d'Investissement) bought interests in mining operations as part of the Government's privatization programme. In 1996 it acquired the cobalt mine at Bou Azzer operated by Compagnie de Tifnout Tiranimine, the Bleida copper mine operated by Société Minière du Bou Gaffer, and an interest in the el-Hammam fluorite mine operated by Société Anonyme d'Entreprises Minières. ONA acquired a further interest in the silver mine at Imiter, operated by Société Metallurgique d'Imiter, following the Government's sale of a 20% stake on the stock exchange in 1997. ONA's other interests have included Akka Gold Mining, responsible for exploiting gold-bearing deposits in the Iourim region in southern Morocco, and the Guemassa polymetallic mine in the High Atlas, which has produced zinc, lead and copper concentrates since 1992. ONA reorganized all its mining equity holdings within a new subsidiary, Managem, which was listed on the stock exchange in June 2000. Toro Energy of Australia signed an agreement with ONHYM in 2007 for exclusive uranium exploration rights over a concession of 4,000 sq km.

In mid-2013 the Government announced that it would increase investment in the non-phosphates mining industry to 4,000m. dirhams over the next 12 years, in an attempt to triple the sector's annual revenues to 15,000m. dirhams by 2025. The Government also expected the industry to support employment, with the number of jobs provided to double to 30,000.

INDUSTRY

In the 1980s the Government made particular efforts to promote industrial development, in order to reduce Morocco's dependence on agriculture and phosphate-mining, to create employment, and to reduce imports. Official policy was to promote export-orientated industry and to encourage private sector investment; this was supported by the World Bank. An investment code provided attractive incentives for both national and foreign investors (principally from France, Spain and Italy). Between 1993 and 1997 foreign funds accounted for 21% of investment in Moroccan industry but declined to 15% during 1998–2002. Regional investment centres (Centres de Formalités de Service), designed as 'one-stop shops' for foreign investors seeking to do business, were established in 2003. The industrial sector grew by 3.1% in 2004, compared with 3.5% in the previous year, and this slipped further, to 2.5%, in 2005, attributable to increased energy costs and the rise in the guaranteed minimum wage in the textile and foodstuffs sectors. According to the central bank's annual report for 2006, the manufacturing sector had contributed an average of 17% to GDP over the previous five years and 12% to national employment. By 2009 the manufacturing industry's contribution to GDP had decreased slightly, to 15.1%, due to the impact of the global economic downturn, declining further, to 14.9% in 2010 and 14.3% in 2011. The secondary sector as a whole (including mining, manufacturing, industry, oil refining, utilities and construction) accounted for 28.4% of GDP in 2009, down from 30.3% in 2008. By the end of 2010 it contributed 29.0% to GDP, falling further, to 28.0%, in 2011.

In 2006 the Government initiated a new industrial strategy—Plan Emergence—envisaging the modernization of traditional sectors, such as textiles, and the development of new sectors, including electronic components, information technology, automotive parts, aeronautics and crafts. Then, in the wake of the global financial crisis in the second half of 2008, the Government took further action to support local industry. In February 2009 it launched a revised development strategy—Plan Emergence II—to boost the performance of the manufacturing sector over a seven-year period. The strategy aims to continue to develop key new industries (particularly the manufacture of automobiles and electronics), help small and medium-sized enterprises to improve their competitiveness, extend work-force skills, and improve the overall business environment. It details measures to be taken by the Government and by enterprises, including the provision of financial aid, improved access to bank credit, tax incentives, vocational training, reducing bureaucracy, and the creation of more industrial zones for foreign investors.

The main industry, in terms of investment and foreign exchange earnings, is the processing of phosphates, which is undertaken by the state-controlled OCP. Other established industries include cement production, food-processing, textiles and chemicals. Manufacturing remains a relatively small sector. A number of state-owned industrial concerns were among the first to be offered for sale in the privatization programme in the early 1990s. Among these were the Ciment de l'Oriental (Cior) and Société Nationale d'Electrolyse et de Pétrochimie (SNEP). From the mid-1990s the privatization programme was expanded to incorporate some of the so-called strategic industries, including the country's two oil refineries (see Mining). The possibility of opening the key phosphate industry to private investment was also announced, and in 1996 a 30% stake in OCP's subsidiary, the Société Marocaine des Fertilisants (FERTIMA), was floated on the stock exchange. In late 1999 a 51% stake in FERTIMA was sold for 230m. dirhams. In 2000 the Société Marocaine de Constructions Automobiles (SOMACA) car assembly plant, the textiles firm Complexe Textile de Fès and the state tobacco company, Régie des Tabacs du Maroc, were listed for sale. The privatization programme had experienced its first reverse in February 1995, when the Government failed to find a buyer for SONASID (the national steel company); however, in 1996 a 35% share was floated on the stock exchange, and in October 1997 the state's remaining 62% holding was sold to a consortium of local financial institutions, notably the Société Nationale d'Investissement (SNI), and Marcial Ucin, a Spanish steel company. In 2003 the Government sold an 80% stake in Régie des tabacs du Maroc to Altadis, a French-Spanish company, for €1,292m. Altadis acquired the remaining interest in 2006. In 2005 ONA acquired four state-owned sugar-processing companies for US $150m., and in 2006 the Government sold the Société Marocaine du Thé et du Sucre to local private conglomerate Holmarcom for $61m. In April 2008 the local fertilizer producer, Charaf Corpn, bought a controlling stake in FERTIMA, its main competitor.

Following the conclusion of an EU association agreement in February 1996 (see Balance of Payments and Trade), the Ministry of Trade, Industry and Handicrafts published a report assessing that some 45,000m. dirhams (US $5,287m.) would be needed over the following five years if local industries were to survive competition from EU markets after the free trade accord became effective. Under the accord, Morocco agreed to phase out protective customs barriers on all its manufactured products over a 12-year period, with the most sensitive industries being given the longest time to adjust. In April the EU pledged ECU 450m. ($570m.) in grants to help Moroccan industries restructure to meet the challenge of European competition, with the aim of assisting them to modernize, expand and improve training. Morocco was also eligible to receive additional funds from 1999. During 1997 the Government embarked on a plan to provide financial assistance to small and medium-sized firms, which accounted for about 90% of Moroccan industry, in order to prepare them for increased competition from the EU after 2008. Companies would be offered long-term credits at preferential rates so that they could invest in new equipment and training. Under the terms of the EU association agreement, which came into effect in March 2000, customs duties and tariffs on goods not manufactured in Morocco were to be reduced by a maximum of 25% over four years, while those on goods manufactured in Morocco would remain unchanged for two years and from then on would be reduced by 10% annually.

Morocco has invested heavily in the 'downstream' phosphates industry, with processing plants in operation at Safi and Jorf Lasfar, producing phosphoric acid, fertilizers and sulphuric acid. In 1987 the value of exports of phosphate derivatives had surpassed that of phosphate rock for the first time, and by 1988 the combined value of phosphoric acid and fertilizers accounted for almost two-thirds of total exports of phosphates and phosphate derivatives. By 2004 phosphoric acid production reached 3.3m. metric tons, of which 2.2m. tons were exported. The Government intends further to capitalize on Morocco's phosphate resources by processing more at home rather than sending them for export, and by exploiting the fertilizers for domestic agricultural consumption. In May 2010 the OCP announced that it hoped to reduce the cost of phosphate production by up to 40%, to less than US $10 per ton, through the use of new extraction techniques. It was anticipated that these new procedures would also boost output to over 50m. tons a year, up from the current level of around 30m. tons a year, supported by a pipeline between the mines and the export-processing zone on the coast.

One of Morocco's major import-substitution industries is cement production. Lafarge Ciments (Maroc), a part-owned subsidiary of France's Lafarge, is the largest cement company, with an estimated market share of 40%. Other major companies in the country are Asment de Temara; Holcim Maroc; and Ciment du Maroc, which manages cement plants in Agadir and Safi and also has ready-mixed concrete and aggregates operations. In 1999 Ciment du Maroc acquired Société des Ciments de Marrakesh (Asmar) to become the second largest firm after the Lafarge group. A new plant, with a capacity of 960,000 metric tons per year, was opened by Lafarge at Tétouan in 2003. In December 2004 Holcim Maroc announced its intention to build a cement plant at Settat, with a capacity of 1.7m. tons per year (which came into operation in 2007). Ciment du Maroc and Italcementi both announced projects to construct new cement plants at Agadir. Overall annual production of cement reached 10.3m. tons in 2005 and 12.8m. tons by 2007. Domestic cement consumption rose by 10% in 2008, but then contracted by 3.4% in 2009, although the longer-term trends indicate further growth. Plans to increase production capacity were initiated in 2012, with Holcim Maroc looking to double its output of clinker.

The food-processing industry remains of considerable importance. It produces both for export and for domestic consumption. A large quantity of grain is processed into flour locally, but imported wheat is processed at a number of mills. There are also extensive sugar-processing facilities in the country. Other food industries include fruit and vegetable processing and canning—mainly for export—and fish-canning. This sector encountered restrictions on exports by the EC from 1986, when Spain and Portugal acceded to the Community. By 2004 the industry employed 24% of the industrial work-force and contributed 21% to exports. This level was largely unchanged by the end of 2010. The industry is supported generously by government subsidies, with the Government paying wheat millers the total difference between its reference price and import prices. However, in September 2012 the Government announced that it would henceforth only pay 85% of the difference, although it cut import duties on wheat at the same time.

Textiles were at the forefront of export-led industrial growth from the 1980s and in the late 1990s accounted for some 40% of total exports in processing industries. More recently, however, expansion has slowed. European firms invested strongly in Morocco in the 1990s. Nevertheless, rising labour costs led to fears that some European-owned textile plants could transfer their operations to Asia. There was also concern that the gradual reduction in customs duties and tariffs provided for under the EU association agreement might be particularly damaging for the textile industry, with cheap goods from outside the EU routed through Western Europe, flooding the local market. In 2000 manufacturers complained that their exports were being adversely affected by the overvaluation of the Moroccan dirham against the euro and by a 10% rise in the minimum wage. The industry was also considered vulnerable to widespread lay-offs and the loss of export markets when the WTO's Agreement on Textiles and Clothing expired on 1 January 2005. By 2004 the textile sector still accounted for around one-third of export earnings. However, exports from the knitwear and ready-made clothing branches to the European market were encountering increased competition, particularly from China and Turkey. Furthermore, a 17% decline in the value of textile exports during the first five months of 2005 prompted official forecasts that as much as 30% of the sector's jobs and 25% of its exports could be lost within five years. Nevertheless, textile exports seemed to benefit from the establishment of temporary EU quotas for Chinese exports in 2006, and rose by 16%, to 20,600m. dirhams, in that year, decreasing slightly, to 19,100m. dirhams, in 2008. Exports declined further in 2009, to 18,100m. dirhams, as the European economy contracted, before recovering slightly in 2010, to 18,041m. dirhams. Exports then increased in 2011, amounting to 18,259m. dirhams.

In the engineering sector, the car assembly market has largely been dominated by Renault Maroc and PSA Peugeot Citroën, both of which hold significant stakes in SOMACA. In 1999 Yamaha of Japan and its Moroccan partner, Marocaine Industrielle, Financière et Agricole (Mifa), announced the construction of a new factory to produce motorcycles for the local market. In 2003 Renault signed a memorandum of understanding for the purchase of the Government's 38% stake in SOMACA, planning to invest €22m. to modernize the plant by 2005. In 2005 Renault purchased a further stake in SOMACA from Italy's Fiat, thus increasing its holding to 54% (PSA Peugeot Citroën owns 20%). In 2007 Renault and Nissan of Japan announced joint plans to locate a car-manufacturing plant in Meloussa in the Tangier free zone, mainly serving the European export market and creating 6,000 jobs. The plant opened in February 2012, with an initial production capacity of 170,000 vehicles.

In 1998 the US information technology firm Microsoft announced that it was establishing its regional headquarters in Casablanca, and two other US companies, Compaq and Oracle, stated that they would co-operate in opening Moroccan-based subsidiaries. In January 2001 Boeing of the USA announced a joint venture agreement with Royal Air Maroc to build an electronics component plant at the Nouasser industrial complex. The plant opened in 2002. In April 2001 the Franco-Italian semi-conductor manufacturer

ST Microelectronics opened a new US $300m. assembly and test plant at Bouskoura.

The construction industry has seen strong growth since 1997 as a result of a government programme, backed by international funding agencies, to build cheap housing to replace slum dwellings. The Government is developing 5,000 ha of land in the Bouregreg valley near Rabat, and in 2005 signed an estimated US $2,000m. construction agreement with Emaar Properties and Dubai International Properties of the UAE. The phased project aimed to transform the Bouregreg valley into a new urban district. The sector suffered in 2009 as a result of the economic downturn, and throughout 2010 recovery was slow. However, government plans to spend heavily on infrastructure development, particularly social housing, supported by tax incentives, were expected to stimulate considerable growth in the sector in 2013 and beyond.

POWER AND WATER

Morocco's rising population and continued economic development has caused a rapid increase in demand for electricity, while severe droughts have exacerbated power shortages. The Government's most recent response to the rising demand has been the launch in early 2009 of a new national plan to raise capacity and diversify energy sources, through increased investment and a focus on renewable energy. Greater co-operation in civil nuclear technology, a return to coal use and the encouragement of petroleum exploration have also been proposed as ways to alleviate the country's dependence on imported energy supplies. A campaign to raise energy conservation awareness among the public was launched in June 2009, and in December the Government announced a US $9,000m. solar energy plan. The scheme seeks to produce 2,000 MW of electricity from 2020, equivalent to 14% of Morocco's projected electricity production in that year. In addition to reducing the country's dependence on energy imports, the project will also contribute to a decrease in carbon dioxide emissions. The solar plants will be located at five sites in the disputed Western Sahara region. The development of solar energy was further encouraged in late 2011, when Morocco was awarded loans totalling US $300m. by various World Bank agencies to construct a network of solar and wind power plants that will be able to supply Europe with energy. The first contract under the plan, worth $1,500m., was awarded in 2012 to an international consortium, ACWA Power Ouarzazate (made up of Saudi Arabia's ACWA Power International, Moroccan Agency for Solar Energy—MASEN and two Spanish firms, Aries IS and TSK EE), for the design, finance, construction, operation and maintenance of a 160 MW concentrated solar power plant.The first phase, the construction of the Noor 1 Concentrated Solar Power (CSP) Independent Power Project, was launched in May 2013.

In 1994 the Office National de l'Electricité (ONE) invited tenders to build and operate Morocco's first private power project, the Jorf Lasfar III and IV units. The US $1,600m. contract for the privatization and expansion project was awarded to ABB Asea Brown Boveri of Switzerland and CMS Energy Corpn of the USA in 1997. By 2001 the Jorf Lasfar III and IV units were operating with capacity of 1,400 MW. The Abu Dhabi National Energy Co (TAQA) acquired CMS Energy Corpn's interest in May 2007, and in 2009 signed a contract to expand Jorf Lasfar with two new coal-fired units. Delays to the expansion plans postponed their implementation, but in 2012 TAQA agreed project financing of some $1,400m. to increase production by a further 700 MW. In 2005 a 400-MW combined cycle power plant began operation in Tahaddart, near Tangier. The plant is linked to the Europe–Maghreb gas pipeline, and is owned by ONE (with 48%), Endesa of Spain (32%) and Siemens of Germany (20%). The construction of a 460-MW pumped-storage facility (pumping water into two artificial storage basins to power four hydro-electric turbines) was completed by Alstom of France at Afourer in the Beni Mellal region in 2004. In June 2008 ONE identified a site at Safi for a new coal-fired power plant, and also announced plans to build gas-fuelled plants at Mohammedia and Kénitra.

In 1998 a 400-kV undersea electricity link between Spain and Morocco (the first power link between North Africa and Europe) was inaugurated. The project was partially funded by the European Investment Bank, which also approved a €120m. loan in 2002 to finance a doubling of the capacity of the undersea link and terminals. Following a prime ministerial visit to Western Sahara in 1998, ONE announced a US $58m. investment programme in the disputed territory to expand the electricity grid, including a 21-MW power plant at Dakhla.

Morocco has also focused on alternative sources of power to generate electricity. In May 2000 a US $48m., 50-MW wind-driven power plant—the first in the Arab world—was inaugurated in Tétouan. The plant was built by a consortium of Electricité de France, Compagnie Financière de Paribas and Germa, which also agreed a 20-year contract to manage the facility. In January 2004 ONE launched a $3,400m. energy development plan, which aimed to provide 80% of rural areas with electricity by 2008, while increasing the share of renewable energy from 0.24% in 2003 to 10% by 2011. The plan also envisaged the construction of two wind power plants in Essaouira and Tangier, as well as a thermo-solar facility in Aïn Beni Mathar. In June 2010 the $300m., 140-MW Tangier plant was inaugurated by King Muhammad VI. The plant was reported to be the largest such facility in Africa. Meanwhile, during a state visit to Morocco in October 2007, President Nicolas Sarkozy of France stated that his country would assist Morocco with the development of a civil nuclear energy industry.

The Office National de l'Eau Potable (ONEP) invested some 18,600m. dirhams in the water sector during 2004–07, including 8,300m. dirhams for urban water supply, 6,400m. dirhams for rural supply and 4,000m. dirhams to expand sewage treatment capacity. The EU and World Bank approved further loans for water sector development in Morocco in 2006. In August 2009, as part of its seven-year energy plan announced in April, the Government promulgated the merger of ONEP and ONE. The Office National de l'Electricité et de l'Eau Potable (ONEE) was subsequently created in November 2011; it was hoped that the new grouping would result in long-term efficiency gains.

BALANCE OF PAYMENTS AND TRADE

Morocco's main sources of revenue are earnings from exports of phosphate rock and phosphate derivatives, agricultural products and manufactured goods, receipts from tourism, and workers' remittances from abroad. Expenditure is mainly on imports of capital equipment, food and crude petroleum.

Morocco's external transactions have been characterized since the early 1980s by a large annual merchandise trade deficit, which has tended to be offset by tourism earnings and expatriate remittances. The deficit continued to widen in 2005 as the value of exports rose to 99,265m. dirhams and that of imports reached 184,379m. dirhams. According to provisional data for 2006, the value of exports increased to 111,688m. dirhams and imports rose to 206,997m. dirhams. The trade deficit was 15.2% of GDP and the current account surplus declined to 0.1% of GDP. However, tourism receipts and financial transfers increased to 52,487.6m. dirhams and 47,859m. dirhams, respectively. Figures for 2007 indicated that the trade deficit widened substantially, to 39% of GDP, based on imports valued at 256,979m. dirhams and exports at 119,874m. dirhams. The 22% increase in import costs was a result of both high international food and fuel prices and poor domestic agricultural output. The current account recorded a small deficit of less than 1% of GDP. Tourism receipts increased to 58,538m. dirhams and expatriate remittances to 55,054m. dirhams. Foreign investment reached 37,400m. dirhams. The trade balance remained in deficit in 2008, with exports valued at 154,493m. dirhams and imports at 321,931m. dirhams. There was a surplus on the transfers and services account, although remittances from expatriates and tourism receipts both decreased slightly, to 53,041m. dirhams and 55,403m. dirhams, respectively. The current account deficit widened to about 5% of GDP. The trade balance narrowed slightly in 2009, to 133,300m. dirhams, a notable achievement given the state of the global economy. With the transfers and services accounts remaining in surplus and the income account in deficit, the overall current account deficit declined to 39,900m. dirhams, but remained static at 5% as a proportion of GDP. Strong exports of phosphates in 2010 again helped to narrow the trade deficit slightly, to 123,470m. dirhams, while a substantial rise in remittances boosted the non-merchandise account. As a result, the current account deficit narrowed to 33,200m. dirhams. However, by the end of 2011 it was clear that the downturn in Europe was exacting a heavy toll on Morocco's external position. The trade deficit had widened significantly, to 157,169m. dirhams, as export earnings slowed markedly. In addition, non-merchandise earnings also fell, and as a result the current account deficit almost doubled, to 64,648m. dirhams.

The EU remains Morocco's largest trading partner, accounting for more than one-half of all trade. The value of Moroccan exports to the EU reached 86,250m. dirhams in 2008, while imports from the region amounted to 159,812m. dirhams. Owing to the economic downturn in 2009, exports declined to 69,678m. dirhams and imports to 133,921m. dirhams in the following year. France constituted the largest source of goods, accounting for 15.0% of imports, while Spain provided 11.0%. France was also Morocco's largest export market, taking 20.0% of exports, followed by Spain (18.0%). By 2011 these ratios were largely unchanged.

Morocco's trade is likely to remain dependent on Europe, and, in view of this, Morocco has continually sought more favourable trade agreements (and twice made unsuccessful applications for full membership of the EC in the 1980s). A formal association accord with the EU was signed in February 1996, including an agreement for the eventual creation of a Euro-Mediterranean free trade zone. The accord came into effect in March 2000. Under the accord, customs duties and tariffs on manufactured goods not produced locally, together with raw materials and spare parts, were to be reduced by a maximum of 25% over four years. Tariffs on goods manufactured in Morocco would remain unchanged for two years and from then on would be reduced by 10% per year for 10 years. In early 2012 Morocco and the EU extended their long-standing agreement to cover a wider range of agricultural products. Under the revised arrangement, up to 70% of EU agricultural exports were to be permitted duty-free entry into Morocco by 2022. In return, all duty was to be lifted from 55% of Moroccan agricultural products with immediate effect, with a few minor exemptions. In an effort to consolidate relations with North African states following the outbreak of civil unrest across the Middle East and North Africa region in 2011, the EU and Morocco launched a fresh round of talks in 2013, with the intention of liberalizing further trade in services, improving market access and easing visa regulations.

During the 1990s Morocco's trade with the other Maghreb countries remained limited despite the creation in 1989 of the Union du Maghreb Arabe (Union of the Arab Maghreb—UMA) and numerous subsequent initiatives to encourage closer economic collaboration and integration. By 2005 the total value of imports from other UMA countries had reached 4,805m. dirhams; exports totalled 1,218m. dirhams. In 1999 Morocco and Tunisia agreed to end duties on a large number of industrial and commercial goods with immediate effect, and in June 2002 signed several co-operation accords aiming to increase the value of their bilateral trade to US $500m. annually.

From the late 1990s other trade accords were negotiated in an attempt to offset Morocco's dependence on Europe, including with China, Thailand and Senegal. In 2002 Morocco and Qatar agreed to explore co-operation in trade and investment and the creation of a bilateral free trade zone, while a free trade agreement with Turkey was concluded in 2004. In March 2004 the Moroccan authorities concluded a free trade agreement with the USA. Under the agreement, more than 95% of industrial tariff lines would become duty-free immediately, with the remainder phased out over nine years. Most ordinary agricultural tariffs would be phased out over 15 years, and a system of tariff-rate quotas for politically sensitive products, such as wheat, would be maintained. The agreement, which was approved by the US Senate in July and signed by President George W. Bush in August, contains a preference clause that prevents other countries from obtaining better agricultural access to the Moroccan market than the USA. It entered into force at the beginning of 2006. Morocco has been a member of the WTO since 1995.

TOURISM

The tourism industry has become an increasingly important source of foreign exchange (after phosphates and their derivatives, and workers' remittances). Major tourist complexes have been constructed at Casablanca, Agadir, Tangier and Restinga, near Tétouan.

In 2001 King Muhammad launched Morocco's Vision 2010, which set key objectives for the tourism sector. These included an annual increase of 15% in the number of tourists (including Moroccans resident abroad as well as foreign nationals) visiting the country, to reach 10m. by 2010; creating some 600,000 jobs in the sector; and a four-fold increase in tourism revenues. There were 2.4m. foreign visitors in 2001, and revenues increased despite the effects of the 11 September attacks in the USA, which caused a reduction in arrivals in the final quarter of the year. However, the effects were more keenly felt in 2002, coupled with the increased likelihood of US-led military action against the regime of Saddam Hussain in Iraq. There was a decrease to an estimated 2.2m. foreign visitors, and revenues contracted by 20%. Then, in May 2003 more than 40 people were killed in suicide bombings in Casablanca (see History). Numbers recovered to 3.0m. in 2004. Foreign arrivals increased to 3.3m. (1.3m. of which were from France) in 2005 and to 3.8m. in 2006 (1.5m. from France). Although a series of suicide bombings in Morocco in March and April 2007 briefly threatened another downturn, arrivals for that year reached 4.0m. (1.6m. from France). In 2008, despite an increase in arrivals between January and October, the annual total decreased to 4.2m., as the negative effects of the global financial crisis started to have an impact. In December 2008 the Government launched a new strategy—Cap 2009—to promote domestic tourism during the economic downturn and to target new markets, such as Russia and the Gulf region. In April 2009 the Government announced that the deadline for completion of the Vision 2010 plan was to be extended to 2016. In 2009 the number of tourist arrivals grew by around 7%; however, since the majority of these visitors were lower-spending expatriate Moroccans, tourism revenue declined by 6%. Tourism activity increased significantly in 2010, when some 9.3m. visitors travelled to Morocco, just below the target set in the Vision 2010 plan.

In 2011 the Government demonstrated its continued commitment to augmenting the tourism market by announcing a new 10-year tourism plan, Vision 2020. The plan anticipated increasing tourist arrivals to 18.6m, increasing bed capacity by an additional 200,000 beds and boosting annual tourism receipts to 140,000m. dirhams. It was hoped that this expansion would create a further 470,000 jobs in the sector. However, the Government's plans suffered a serious reverse in April 2011, when a bomb exploded in the centre of Marrakesh, killing 17 people, the majority of whom were French tourists. Tourist arrivals from France comprise 36% of the total and this event, combined with the regional political turmoil and the economic downturn in Europe, severely damaged the tourism industry. As a result, overnight stays by non-residents fell by 11%. Total tourist arrivals remained largely stagnant, at 9.3m., in that year. The persistent economic recession in the EU caused the number of tourist arrivals to remain at that level in 2012, but the sector showed signs of life in early 2013 and was boosted by Royal Air Maroc's decision to expand its fleet in order to improve air connections with Morocco.

TRANSPORT AND COMMUNICATIONS

With funding from the EU and the African Development Bank (AfDB), the Government launched a Transport Sector Reform Programme (TSRP) in 2004, to include the modernization of the transport infrastructure network, greater autonomy for the national regulating offices, privatization and the encouragement of private sector investment, and the strengthening of the merchant fleet.

Morocco's ports include Casablanca, Safi, Mohammedia, Agadir, Kénitra, Jorf Lasfar, Tan Tan along its Atlantic coast, and Nador (in the north-east) and Tangier (in the north-west) on the Mediterranean. Dakhla and el-Aaiún are in the disputed territory of Western Sahara. In 2004 the country's ports handled 61.5m. metric tons of cargo. Casablanca is the largest port, accounting for 40% of cargo. Mohammedia port specializes in oil, Agadir in fishing, Safi and Jorf Lasfar in minerals, Tangier in passenger transport, and Nador in the steel, mining and food-processing industries. Since 1985 the major ports have been controlled by the Office d'Exploitation des Ports (ODEP). In 1998 ODEP announced that it was planning to spend US $220m. on modernizing and expanding the country's port facilities during 1998–2002. In 2003 Bouygues Construction group of France was awarded a contract for the first phase of construction of a new port near Tangier. The port would be part of a wider development known as the Tangier-Mediterranean Project, comprising industrial and trade zones as well as the port itself. The port, to be sited about 35 km east of Tangier, would be equipped with oil, grain, general cargo and container terminals. The Tangier-Mediterranean Special Agency (TMSA) and the Jebel Ali Free Zone International (of the UAE) signed a 10-year co-operation agreement for the operation of Tangier-Mediterranean Project free zones in October 2004. In December a consortium led by Denmark's Maersk was awarded the 30-year concession to operate the first container terminal, construction contracts related to which were subsequently awarded to a consortium led by Belgium's Besix and to Société Maghrébienne de Génie Civil. In June 2006 a consortium led by the UAE's Horizon Terminals was awarded the 25-year concession to operate the oil terminal. In May 2007 the TMSA announced a $1,700m. plan to develop port facilities to the west of Tangier.

Meanwhile, to comply with international security and safety standards, ODEP was divided into two separate agencies—L'Agence Nationale des Ports as regulator and Société d'Exploitation des Ports as manager and operator—in December 2006. The national shipping company, the Compagnie Marocaine de Navigation (established in 1946), was sold to CMA CGM of France in January 2007 for $256m. Also in 2007 TMSA launched a project to extend the Tangier-Mediterranean port complex (known as TangMed II). TMSA awarded concessions for two new container terminals in the complex during 2008, and in June 2009 the Government gave its final approval for work to begin on the port extension. In April 2008 a direct shipping link between Morocco and Tunisia was inaugurated in order to accelerate shipments between the two countries and reduce the costs of using indirect routes via Europe. However, Moroccan-flagged shipping lines and ferry services appear to be struggling in an increasingly competitive environment. The country's leading ferry company, Comarit-Comanav, is in severe financial difficulty, while another, the International Maritime Transport Corporation, has mounting debts. Moves to liberalize the sector in 2007, which allowed foreign operators greater access to Moroccan ports, as well as greater competition from low-cost air carriers, has increased pressures on domestic shipping firms.

The railways are operated by the Office National des Chemins de Fer (ONCF). In 2002 the Government began to restructure the agency into a public company, with a view to eventual privatization. The ONCF offers local services between Casablanca, Rabat, Kénitra and el-Jadida, and some long-distance services to other major cities throughout the country. In 2007 it carried 26m. passengers and 36.5m. metric tons of cargo. During 2003 the Islamic Development Bank agreed to contribute US $65m. to a project to build a 45-km railway link between Tangier town and Tangier-Mediterranean port. Also, as part of an undertaking to upgrade the rail network, the ONCF appointed Italy's Ansaldobreda to conduct a feasibility study for improvements to the Casablanca–Marrakesh–Agadir rail link. Following more than 20 years of on-off consultations, the Governments of Morocco and Spain announced plans in 2003 to build a 39-km train tunnel link (27.7 km of which would be submarine) between their two countries. The tunnel would connect Punta Malabata in Morocco with Punta Paloma, to the west of Gibraltar. The TSRP envisaged the acquisition of multi-unit trains, and the doubling of the rail network to Fez, Settat and Jorf Lasfar. Construction work subsequently began on a number of projects, including the extension of the network to Tangier port and modernization of the Casablanca–Marrakesh main line. In 2006 the Government announced long-term plans to build high-speed rail links between Casablanca, Marrakesh, Agadir, Tangier and Oudja. Work finally began on the first stage of the project in late 2011, with the construction of a line linking Tangiers and Casablanca via Rabat, which was due to be completed in 2015. However, the scheme has attracted considerable criticism, owing to its high costs, with objectors maintaining that the funds could be better spent on basic services such as education, health and housing.

The Casablanca–Rabat highway was completed in 1986. The Rabat–Fez highway was completed in 1999, and opened in three phases (Fez–Meknès, Meknès–Khemisset, and Khemisset–Rabat). The Rabat–Kénitra section of the Rabat–Tangier highway was opened in 1995, the section to Larache in 1996, and the section to Asilah in 2002. In 1998 the Government announced that it was proceeding with the construction of a Mediterranean coastal highway linking Tangier with Saidia, near the border with Algeria. Much of the construction costs would be financed by the state, but certain stretches were to be privately financed on a build-operate-transfer basis. A 30-km section of the highway linking Tangier and Laksar S'ghir opened in May 2000. In 1998 work began on the construction of a motorway between Casablanca and Settat. In 1999 ADM, a public-private partnership, announced new investment of US $100m. to develop the country's road network, including highways linking Sidi el-Yamani to Tangier and Khemisset to Fez. During 2004 Autoroutes du Maroc (ADM) issued a tender for the construction of a 240-km highway between the southern tourist resorts of Marrakesh and Agadir; the Hassan II Fund was partly to finance the project by providing $166m. of the estimated $690m. cost. The Kuwait Fund for Arab Economic Development (KFAED), meanwhile, approved a $149m. loan to finance the construction of a 62-km section of highway linking Settat and Skhour Rhamna in the south, and another 28-km highway section between Tétouan and Fnideq in the north. The European Investment Bank (EIB) approved a €110m. loan to construct a section of motorway between Marrakesh and Settat. The KFAED was also co-funding a project to connect the port of Tangier to the national highway; the planned 54-km highway was scheduled to open for traffic by the time the new port of Tangier became operational. In 2005 the Government announced that ADM was to receive funding from the Hassan II Fund for a 320-km highway between Fez, Taza and Oujda. The $700m. project would extend the existing Rabat–Meknès–Fez road and form a major new east–west link. Under the TSRP, the Government planned to complete 1,500 km of highways by 2010, including the Tangier–Saidia, Tétouan–Fnideq, Settat–Marrakesh and Tangier-Mediterranean Port motorway projects. The Asilah–Tangier motorway was completed in 2005. In 2006 the Arab Fund for Economic and Social Development (AFESD) agreed to finance the Fez–Oujda highway and part-finance the project to link Marrakesh and Agadir. Between 1995 and 2005 the World Bank provided funding for a national programme to upgrade 10,000 km of rural roads. In 2006 the Bank approved a $60m. loan for a second national programme of rural road-building. The EIB similarly contributed to the project in late 2008, with a €60m. grant to build 700 km of roads in isolated areas. The second national programme aims to build 15,560 km of roads at the rate of 2,000 km each year.

The main international airports in Morocco are located in Casablanca, Marrakesh and Agadir. El-Aaiún in Western Sahara also has an airport. In 1992 the AfDB approved a loan of US $102m. to support plans by the Office National des Aéroports (ONDA) to upgrade the infrastructure of Morocco's airports. In 1998 ONDA began to implement long-standing plans for a new airport at Nador, in the north-east. In 1999 AFESD granted a loan worth $32.7m. to finance a project to further extend and modernize Casablanca's King Muhammad V airport. In 2001 the AfDB approved a loan to finance some of the project's foreign exchange costs, and ONDA launched the tender for the construction of a second runway. There were also plans for new terminal buildings, and a new ground control system to bring the airport in line with International Civil Aviation Organization standards, and in 2004 the local Société Générale des Travaux de Maroc won the contract to build a third terminal. The total number of passengers handled by Morocco's airports was forecast to rise from 6.8m. in 2001 to 27m. in 2020. Royal Air Maroc (RAM), which was formed in 1953, is the national airline, operating services to European and African countries, as well as to the USA. Tourism accounted for a significant proportion of passengers carried, although flights for business-related purposes were increasingly important. Total freight carried by air also continued to rise. In 1998 RAM signed a co-operation agreement with Spain's national carrier, Iberia. RAM also signed an agreement to operate joint flights with Gulf Air, and in 1999 became one of the first companies to begin regular flights to the newly opened Gaza International Airport. RAM has embarked on a programme to update and expand its fleet. Boeing agreed to supply 20 medium-range and three long-range aircraft by 2012 at a cost of $1,100m. The deregulation of the aviation sector, including the improvement of air access to prime tourist destinations and the end of RAM's monopoly, forms part of the Vision 2010 plan (see Tourism). Since February 2004 airlines may operate scheduled or charter flights to Morocco from any airport abroad. Previously, flagship carriers could only operate scheduled flights and charter firms could only fly foreign tourists to Morocco. In May of that year RAM created a subsidiary company, Atlas Blue, offering low-cost flights to domestic and European destinations. However, since the liberalization of the sector RAM has increasingly struggled against the foreign competition, and by mid-2011 the company was facing an uncertain future, amid growing losses. Earlier, in 2010, it shut down Atlas Blue, and by 2012 was aiming to implement an emergency recovery plan, under which the airline would undergo extensive restructuring. Although RAM escaped bankruptcy, as part of its restructuring it was forced to cut 20 routes. However, by 2013 it appeared to have overcome its difficulties and was looking to replace and expand its fleet.

In 2005 Morocco's airports handled 9.2m. passengers; of these, 7.1m. were international arrivals and 1.4m. were charter flight passengers. In April 2006 ONDA awarded the Swiss-based company SITA, a provider of information technology solutions to the aviation industry, a five-year contract to improve passenger flow through the country's main airports. Also in 2006 the Government and the EU signed an aviation agreement aiming to regulate the market in relation to competition, state-aid, and consumer and environmental protection. Following on from this agreement, a new low-cost domestic airline (Jet4you) was created and two low-cost European companies announced new services from Europe to Marrakesh, Fez and Agadir.

In 1997 the Chamber of Representatives adopted a new law heralding the liberalization of the fixed and mobile telecommunications sector. In 1998 the functions of the state-owned Office National des Postes et Télécommunications (ONPT) were divided between a new Agence Nationale de Réglementation des Télécommunications (ANRT), responsible for telecommunications regulation, and Itissalat al-Maghrib (Maroc Télécom), which was granted a monopoly of telecommunications services until 2001. With the approach of privatization, Maroc Télécom, valued at US $5,000m., took various measures to improve its competitiveness, including increasing the number of its mobile telephone subscribers. The sale of the second Global System for Mobile Communications (GSM) licence, originally planned for 1997, took place in July 1999 and generated $1,100m., more than twice the sum expected when the sale was planned. The 15-year licence was awarded to Médi Télécom (Méditel), a consortium led by Telefónica of Spain together with Portugal Telecom and Moroccan investors, which pledged to invest $660m. over the following four years. The network became operational in March 2000. In December the Government announced that a 35% stake in Maroc Télécom had been sold to Vivendi Universal (now Vivendi SA) of France for $2,200m. Having completed a contract for the expansion of the GSM network in the main northern cities, in 2001 Maroc Télécom signed a further agreement with US telecoms equipment supplier Motorola to expand its network infrastructure.

In November 2004 the Government sold a further 16% stake in Maroc Télécom to Vivendi-Universal for US $1,483m., giving the French group a 51% majority holding. More than $1,000m. was also raised from the sale of a further 14.9% stake in the company on the Casablanca and Paris stock exchanges in December. In 2005 and 2007 a further 17% of the company was sold, on these occasions to the public through an Initial Public Offering (IPO). In 2010 and 2011 the Government attempted to divest more of its remaining 30% of stock, putting a further 8% and 7%, respectively, out to IPO. However, on both occasions the Government subsequently cancelled the tenders, on the grounds that the market conditions were not quite right. Maroc Télécom faced further problems in 2013 when Vivendi announced that it was looking to sell its stake. The sale attracted numerous interested parties, but the lead bidder, Qatar Telecom, pulled out in June, leaving the field to Etisalat, the Abu Dhabi-based provider. However, negotiations were being drawn out over the value of the sale; Vivendi was asking for more than the US $5,500m.–$5,600m. valuation.

In early 2005 ANRT invited applications for three new types of telecommunications licence, covering the local network, with a maximum of two licences available for each region, two licences for the national system and two international licences. Companies bidding for the international licences were also to bid for at least one of the other contracts. In July that year Méditel was awarded the country's second fixed-line licence. In late 2005 ANRT completed the liberalization of fixed-line services by awarding a third licence to local operator Maroc Connect, controlled by ONA. In May 2006 ANRT launched the tender for the third GSM licence. To meet increased demand for access to broadband connections, in July Maroc Télécom and Alcatel of France signed a US $26m. contract to install a submarine cable network linking Asilah in north-west Morocco with Marseille in southern France. Also in July three domestic operators—Maroc Télécom, Méditel and Maroc Connect (since rebranded as Wana)—were awarded national 3G (third generation) licences. In 2007 the Government launched the sale of a further 4% stake in Maroc Télécom on the stock exchange (with Vivendi-Universal raising its holding to 53%). In 2008 Maroc Télécom commenced high-speed phone services using 3G technology in the major cities, and Wana also launched its 3G mobile service. In February 2009 ANRT awarded the licence for a second generation (2G) network to Wana, and in March Kuwait's Zain Group announced that it was to acquire a 31% stake in Wana. By the end of 2008 the number of subscribers in Morocco had risen by 13.9%, to 22.8m., according to ANRT. Maroc Télécom was the dominant operator, with a 63.4% share of the mobile telecommunications market. Méditel held a 34.7% share and Wana just 1.9%. In February 2010 the Government announced a new three-year plan to liberalize the sector further, designed to increase the number of mobile and fixed-line subscribers to 35m. and the number of internet subscribers to 2m. by 2013, promote competition, raise market penetration and reduce prices.

There is a nation-wide television network (Société Nationale de Radiodiffusion et de Télévision) and regional radio stations broadcasting in the Arabic, French and Berber languages. In 2002 the Government announced plans to end state control of television and radio, and to establish an independent regulatory authority. The High Audiovisual Communication Authority was established in October 2004 to take responsibility for the deregulation of services.

BANKING AND FINANCE

By the early 1980s Morocco's foreign debt had reached unmanageable proportions, necessitating difficult economic restructuring, extensive IMF and World Bank support, and the rescheduling of repayments to its international creditors over the rest of the decade. According to the Ministry of Finance, Morocco's external debt at the end of 1991 totalled US $21,000m., of which $10,600m. was outstanding to the 'Paris Club' of official creditors, $3,600m. to the 'London Club', $3,300m. to the World Bank, $1,600m. to the USA and $600m. to the IMF. However, Morocco's economic prospects improved significantly, when in late 1991 Saudi Arabia and other Gulf states agreed to cancel bilateral debts estimated at around $3,600m. In February 1992 the IMF approved a new standby credit to support the Government's economic programme from January 1992 to March 1993. At the end of this period the Government expected to be able to return to the international capital markets and to make no further demands on IMF resources. Also in February 'Paris Club' governments agreed to reschedule further official debt worth $1,500m., and in March the World Bank approved a $275m. structural adjustment loan. By May 1993 Morocco's external debt stood at $21,305m. Debt-service repayments in 1992 had increased to $3,000m., but were projected to decline from $2,848m. in 1993 to $2,126m. in 2000. In June 1993 the Ministry of Finance introduced new rules whereby Moroccan banks or private enterprises were allowed to raise credits with foreign financial institutions to finance imports of goods and services without prior authorization.

In 1992 Morocco became the major recipient of concessionary development financing from France, while Spain agreed to provide a new five-year credit programme worth US $1,056m. (under a credit line originally signed in 1988). The EU also agreed to lend Morocco a total of ECU 438m. in 1992–96, together with funds for structural adjustment and EIB loans for the Europe–Maghreb gas pipeline. In 1995 Spain renewed a credit line of $1,125m., as part of an economic and financial co-operation agreement. From 1996 Morocco signed a series of bilateral agreements under which France and Spain agreed to forgive or convert into equity Moroccan debt, and promised further aid and technical assistance. In 1998 the United Kingdom also agreed to make $42m. of 'Paris Club' debt available for conversion into equity. In December 1997 Morocco returned to international capital markets for the first time since 1981, when Commerzbank of Germany and Sumitomo Bank Ltd of Japan began arranging a five-year loan of $200m. The Euroloan was fully subscribed when it closed in February 1998. In April 2001 the Ministry of Finance announced a 5% devaluation in the dirham, a move regarded by some analysts as overdue and not large enough to have a significant effect on the economy. In June 2003 Morocco issued the kingdom's first euro-denominated sovereign bond (€400m.). Proceeds from the issue, postponed from 1998, were expected to refinance some of Morocco's more expensive debt. The Government stated that the issue was twice oversubscribed and was well received on the international markets, indicating undaunted investor confidence in the light of the May 2003 suicide bombings in Casablanca (see History).

In March 1998 Moody's Investors Service and Standard & Poor's awarded Morocco its first international credit ratings, a positive development that would help the Government to raise additional funds on the market. According to the Ministry of Finance, Morocco's foreign debt declined from US $18,000m. at the end of 1999 to $15,360m. at the end of 2000. The bulk of the debt was publicly guaranteed medium- and long-term debt, of which 38% was owed to bilateral official creditors, 31% to multilateral agencies and the remaining 31% to private creditors, mainly commercial banks. The IMF estimated Morocco's total external debt at $15,700m. in 2002, $16,800m. in 2003 and $16,600m. in 2004. As a percentage of GDP, it totalled 24.2% in 2005, 23.9% in 2006, 23.8% in 2007, 20.6% in 2008, 23.3% in 2009 and 24.8% in 2010. Foreign currency reserves stood at $18,770m. in 2006, $24,700m. in 2007, $22,024m. in 2008, $22,700m. in 2009 and $23,610 in 2010. By 2012, however, they had fallen to $17,535m.

Morocco's central bank, the Bank Al-Maghrib, is the sole issuer of currency; it holds and administers the state's foreign currency reserves, regulates the commercial banking sector, and advises the Government on financial policy. The financial sector has undergone a period of liberalization, reflected in reforms backed by a series of World Bank initiatives that began in the early 1990s. The main reforms have included the elimination of credit ceilings, interest rate liberalization, overhaul of the legislative framework governing lending institutions (under a 1993 banking law), gradual elimination of mandatory holdings of government securities, and the strengthening of prudential regulation of banks in accordance with international standards. A revised banking law and new central bank statutes were adopted in 2005, establishing the central bank's independence in monetary policy and clarifying its role in determining exchange rate policy in relation to that of the Ministry of Finance and Privatization. Bank Al-Maghrib was also given greater powers to supervise banks and to diversify its policy instruments to ensure efficient functioning of the money market. The new statutes prohibited the central bank from giving finance facilities to the Government and state-owned institutions.

By the end of 2004 there were 17 approved commercial banks, the largest of which were the Banque Marocaine de Commerce Extérieur (BMCE), Crédit du Maroc, Banque Centrale Populaire (BCP) and Attijariwafa Bank (established following the merger in that year of Wafabank and the Banque Commerciale du Maroc—BCM). Commercial banks are permitted to have foreign majority ownership. In June 1993 the Banco Exterior de España had become the first wholly owned foreign company authorized to open a subsidiary in Morocco since independence. In 1995 the Minister of Privatization sold most of the state's 50.4% holding in the BMCE. Some 14% of the bank's shares were offered for sale on the stock exchange, and another 26% were offered for sale by international tender. The new shareholders included the Royale Marocaine d'Assurances, United Kingdom-based Morgan Grenfell and Co, and Morgan Stanley of the USA. The last publicly owned shares in the BMCE were sold to the private sector in 1997. At the end of 2000 a parliamentary inquiry into the state-owned bank Crédit Immobilier et Hôtelier (CIH), which had debts totalling some 11,000m. dirhams, accused the bank's directors of poor management and widespread fraud and misappropriation of funds (see History).

From the beginning of 1999 the central bank authorized all Moroccan banks to invest up to 10% of their equity in the euro, which became the major currency for Morocco's external transactions in January 2002. Transactions would continue to be carried out in British sterling, Swiss francs, Danish krone and Norwegian krone, with separate rates for these currencies. In 2004 the BCM purchased 36.4% of the capital and 47.7% of the voting rights of Wafabank, as well as 70.5% of Wafa Assurance. The merger of the two banks created one of the largest banks in Africa—Attijariwafa Bank—with more than 1m. clients and 460 branches. In June of that year the BMCE signed an agreement with France's Crédit Industriel et Commercial (CIC), giving CIC a 10% stake in the BMCE for €72m. As part of the 2004 privatization programme, the Government raised US $86m. from the sale of its 20% shareholding in the BCP in an initial public offering; the issue was nine times oversubscribed. By late 2004 five 'offshore' banks were operational in Morocco (Tangier having become the kingdom's first 'offshore' banking zone in August 1991 with the intention of attracting major international banks). In 2005 the World Bank approved a $200m. loan to support a programme of reform in the financial sector, including the restructuring of two banks—CIH and Caisse Nationale de Crédit Agricole—and the introduction of new procedures for banks experiencing commercial difficulties. The sector received further multilateral support in 2011, when the AfDB agreed to lend Morocco €224m. to develop the sector by improving governance, widening access to financial services, and helping to diversify the range of products on offer.

In April 2007 the Spanish savings bank Caja de Ahorros del Mediterraneo acquired 5% of the capital of the BMCE. In late 2008 BCP bought a 50.1% stake in Upline Group, a large independent investment bank. Attijariwafa Bank, meanwhile, sought opportunities in Africa, acquiring 51% of the Banque Internationale of Mali in July 2008. In November it announced the acquisition of Crédit Agricole's retail banking assets in the Republic of Congo, Cameroon, Côte d'Ivoire and Senegal. Prudent management and modernization of the financial sector by Bank Al-Maghrib enabled the banking system to weather the international financial crisis. The central bank raised the capital adequacy ratio of banks and maintained a cautious monetary policy. Nevertheless, the economy slowed in response to declining external demand and foreign investment. Having raised its benchmark interest rate in September 2008 in an attempt to contain inflation, Bank Al-Maghrib reduced the rate in March 2009 (the first reduction in six years), in anticipation of price stagnation and a worsening global economic outlook. Continued liquidity constraints forced the bank to make two decreases in the reserve requirements during 2009, which stood at 8% by the end of the year, and were further reduced to 6% in April 2010. The banking sector proved resilient throughout the global financial crisis and by the end of 2009 had managed to reduce its portfolio of non-performing loans to 5.5%, down from 6% in 2008. In May 2011 the Government announced the sale of a 20% stake in the BCP, Morocco's largest bank, for 5,300m. dirhams. The Government was reportedly also seeking to sell a similar-sized stake in Attijariwafa Bank. In April 2012 the Government sold a further 5% tranche of BCP to a French co-operative bank, Groupe BPCE (Banques Populaires et les Caisses d'Epargne).

Meanwhile, plans to promote Morocco's position and status as a financial sector hub and gateway to West Africa progressed in 2012, with the inauguration of the Casablanca Financial City (CFC). In order to attract international interest, the Moroccan Government issued a decree which provided for tax concessions and clear legal and regulatory frameworks for companies setting up in the zone. By July 2012 six companies had joined the scheme and a further seven were reportedly due to follow suit.

The Government launched the first issue of a new privatization bond in January 1996. The bonds could be exchanged for shares in any of the companies to be privatized on the stock exchange in the following three years, and, to make the bonds attractive to the public, holders would be given priority access to shares in newly privatized companies. Individual investors were offered the majority of the bonds, while companies, especially investment funds, were offered the remainder. Some 1,700m. dirhams (US $200m.) were raised through the sale of the first issue, which was oversubscribed by 25%. The first test of the new bond came in March 1996, when the Government offered for sale on the stock exchange 25% of its stake in SAMIR. The offer was fully subscribed, with about three-quarters of the buyers using privatization bonds. A second tranche of bonds was issued in May, this time with one-half reserved for institutional investment. However, demand for the second issue was lower than for the first. At the end of 1998 the Government appeared to have decided to end the policy when it was announced that the Treasury would reimburse holders of existing bonds after they reached maturity.

In 1993 the volume of transactions on the stock exchange increased more than three-fold as a result of the privatization of state companies. A further major boost to stock exchange activity in 1994 was the issue of shares worth 1,500m. dirhams in ONA. Local companies turned increasingly to the stock market to raise capital through local share offers. In 1995 the General Tire and Rubber Co raised its capital by 20% in a stock market offering, becoming the first newly privatized company to do so. The Asian stock market crisis in 1997 had little impact on the stock exchange as only 5% of transactions involved foreign investors. That year the exchange began a campaign to attract new listings, especially from small and medium-sized firms. The results, however, were disappointing (partly owing to delays in the privatization programme), and the number of companies listed remained at around 50. Foreign participation remained very limited (around 10% of total capitalization), despite the absence of any restrictions. Two new indices were launched on the exchange in 2002—the Most Active Shares Index (MADEX), monitoring the 10 most liquid stocks on the exchange, and the Moroccan All-Share Index (MASI), replacing the benchmark Casablanca Stock Exchange (CSE) index covering all stocks listed. There were 53 companies listed in 2003, and market capitalization increased by 32.5%, to 115,500m. dirhams, in that year. In 2005 the volume of transactions reached 148,500m. dirhams. At the end of 2006 MADEX recorded annual gains of 77.7% and the volume of transactions increased to 166,400m. dirhams. There were 63 companies listed at that time. Following the sharp decline in the share values on the stock exchange in September 2008, there were rumours of market manipulation. An investigation by the regulator led to a series of recommendations, including changes to the exchange's management structure and personnel, and greater independence for the regulator. These were duly carried out in the course of 2009, although the index failed to recover as strongly as had been hoped. Also, in that year the total volume of shares traded declined by 40%, after a reduction of 60% in 2008, although the MASI and the MADEX indices only contracted by 1% and 3%, respectively. The performance of the indices improved in 2010, however; the MASI grew by 23% and the MADEX rose by 24%. The rally in the CSE was short-lived, however, and in 2011 both indices declined by 13%, with the downward trend continuing in early 2012. The Government was concerned that the poor performance of the exchange would affect its plans to develop the CFC and was considering ways of deepening the market's liquidity, such as by establishing a futures market and permitting transactions in foreign currency, as well as by developing the regulatory framework needed for a derivatives market. These plans gathered pace in early 2013, after the bourse registered its lowest trading levels for a number of years, with volumes on the CSE declining by 30%. MASI dropped by 19%. However, the Government's intentions received a huge setback in June 2013, when the Morgan Stanley Capital International (MSCI) Index downgraded the CSE from 'Emerging Market' status to 'Frontier' status. By the end of the second quarter the overall index had fallen by 7%, with a steeper decline expected following the downgrade.

BUDGET

During the 1980s the Government was obliged to make severe reductions in public expenditure in order to satisfy the terms of agreements made with the IMF, and throughout the 1990s sought to constrain a widening budget deficit. The 1999/2000 budget envisaged total expenditure of 125,300m. dirhams, excluding debt service payments, with revenues projected at 109,700m. dirhams, giving a deficit of 15,600m. dirhams (equivalent to 2.8% of GDP). In December 1999 the Government adopted a five-year social and economic plan to run from 2000–04, involving a total investment of some 520,000m. dirhams (US $50,600m.) designed to improve the country's infrastructure, strengthen business and create new jobs. Around two-thirds of the investment was to come from the public sector, and one-third from the private sector. Meanwhile, the Government announced that from 2001 the financial year would revert to January–December rather than from July–June. A six-month transitional budget was introduced to run from the end of the 1999/2000 fiscal year on 30 June 2000. The transitional budget envisaged GDP growth of 3% and forecast revenues at 74,880m. dirhams and expenditure at 79,650m. dirhams, resulting in a budget deficit of 4,770m. dirhams. However, severe drought and the Government's decision to raise the minimum wage by 10% meant that these projections would prove unrealistic. The budget for 2001 was approved by parliament in December 2000 and was based on GDP growth of 8%.

The draft budget for 2002 set revenue at 159,500m. dirhams and expenditure at 165,400m. dirhams. It was based on forecast growth of 4.5%, an inflation rate of 2.5% and an external current account deficit of 1% of GDP. The fiscal deficit (excluding privatization receipts) decreased significantly, to 4.7% of GDP in 2002 from 6.2% in 2001, as the Government's debt-to-GDP ratio declined from 48% in 2000 to 35% in 2002. Privatization revenues, initially projected at 12,500m. dirhams, decreased to 621m. dirhams as the sale of state tobacco interests and the remaining stake in Maroc Télécom failed to proceed in that year. The draft budget for 2003 forecast a deficit equivalent to 3% of GDP. Inflation was estimated to decrease to 2%. With the aim of improving public asset management systems in Morocco, the World Bank approved a US $45m. loan in mid-2003 to support public expenditure rationalization and efficiency, notably in the public education and health sectors. The fiscal deficit increased to 5.0% of GDP in 2003. This deterioration resulted from a higher wage bill, increased security-related spending after the Casablanca bombings in May, and weaker revenue performance on account of ongoing trade liberalization and tariff reductions on selected imports. The 2004 draft budget set expenditure at 141,800m. dirhams and revenue at 141,370m. dirhams, forecasting a deficit of 430m. dirhams (equivalent to 5.4% of GDP). Privatization receipts (including the sale of an additional government stake in Maroc Télécom) were expected to provide 2.7% of total revenues. Meanwhile, in October 2004 the Government inaugurated an $800m. programme to develop Morocco's 'southern provinces' (the territory of Western Sahara) by generating employment and improving housing. The programme was to run for five years with funding allocations of $188m. for housing and urban development, $177m. for fisheries, $256m. for water and environment, and $173m. for ports and infrastructure.

The 2005 draft budget set revenue at 185,920m. dirhams and expenditure at 186,630m. dirhams, envisaging a 3.0% growth in GDP and a budget deficit of 3.2%. The inflation rate was projected at 2.0%. According to IMF preliminary data, however, the budget deficit increased to 5.9% of GDP in 2005. The 2006 budget, adopted by parliament in November 2005, set revenue at 197,137m. dirhams and expenditure at 197,463m. dirhams. The deficit was projected at 4.1% of GDP. The draft budget for 2007 estimated real GDP growth of 7.3%–7.5% and a general budget deficit of 3.0% of GDP. It included a total subsidy bill of 10,000m. dirhams, including 5,800m. dirhams for fuel and 2,200m. dirhams for sugar. The 2008 draft budget was approved by parliament in December 2007, despite objections from some representatives to proposed tax reform measures reducing corporation tax and customs duties. The budget forecast a widening of the deficit to 3.4% of GDP, with an assumption of 6.8% GDP growth. Spending was projected to increase on security, social welfare, subsidies and infrastructure. In mid-2008 the Government reduced its growth forecast for the year to 6.2%, due to concerns about the global economy, and raised its inflation forecast to 2.7%–2.9%, compared with a previous projection of 2.0%. The subsidy budget was also increased, reflecting the surge in international commodity prices, although part of this rise was to be offset by grants from Saudi Arabia and the UAE.

The 2009 draft budget, approved at the end of 2008, projected a deficit equivalent to 2.9% of GDP (based on estimated revenues of 177,402m. dirhams and expenditure of 164,785m. dirhams) and a reduction in growth, amid fears of a lasting recession in the EU, Morocco's main export market. The focus of the budget was on development projects, with a large increase in government investment in education and training, health and housing, as well as an increase in salaries for public sector workers. The 2010 budget established some changes to the tax system, including the lowering of tax rates, the introduction of tax breaks and the simplification of the value-added tax structure. Projected revenues, at 168,913m. dirhams, were virtually unchanged from the previous budget, while expenditure was projected at 156,435m. dirhams. Overall, the budget projected a reduced deficit of around 1.6% of GDP. The high price of oil, which in 2010 forced a significant increase in the Government's subsidy bill, necessitated a revised budget, which set the forecast deficit at 4% of GDP. The proposed budget for 2011, based on the assumption of there being growth amounting to 5% of real GDP which would boost tax revenues, anticipated a slightly narrower deficit of 3.5% of GDP. However, a substantial increase in the wage bill and persistently high subsidies meant that the public accounts stayed in deficit. By mid-2011 the budget forecasts were under pressure, as increasing political tensions, prompted by unrest in the wider region, compelled the Government to raise salaries and deepen subsidies yet further. Indeed, the budget out-turn in 2011 showed that wages and subsidies comprised almost two-thirds of recurrent expenditure, representing an increase from less than 60% in the previous year. Both wages and subsidies continued to dominate the budget for 2012, which was aimed at alleviating social stresses. Some 32,500m. dirhams were allocated to the subsidy fund, representing a significant increase compared with the previous year's budget, but a decline against the 2011 out-turn. The wage bill showed a steady rise, as the Government agreed with the unions to raise both public sector salaries and the minimum wage. However, by the second quarter of 2012 it appeared evident that the Government had miscalculated its projected outlay; by the end of May the subsidy bill showed a 61% rise compared with the corresponding period of the previous year. Wages had risen by 17%, far higher than the anticipated 6% increase. The figures indicated that the Government would have great difficulty in achieving its budgeted deficit target for 2012, which stood at 5.0% of GDP. In fact, the deficit widened to 8.3% of GDP in 2012, although the 2013 budget projected a much reduced deficit of 4.7%. The Government expected to reduce the deficit through further subsidy reforms, a policy supported by the IMF, which extended a US $6,200m. precautionary credit line to Morocco in August 2012 and renewed it for two further years in July 2013.

Statistical Survey

Sources (unless otherwise stated): Haut Commissariat au Plan, Direction de la Statistique, rue Muhammad Belhassan el-Ouazzani, BP 178, Rabat 10001; tel. (53) 7773606; fax (53) 7773217; e-mail statguichet@statistic.gov.ma; internet www.hcp.ma; Bank Al-Maghrib, 277 ave Muhammad V, BP 445, Rabat; tel. (53) 7702626; fax (53) 7706667; e-mail webmaster@bkam.ma; internet www.bkam.ma.

Note: Unless otherwise indicated, the data exclude Western (formerly Spanish) Sahara, a disputed territory under Moroccan occupation.

Area and Population

AREA, POPULATION AND DENSITY

Area (sq km)	710,850*
Population (census results)†	
2 September 1994	26,019,280
2 September 2004	
Males	14,640,662
Females	15,039,407
Total	29,680,069
Population (UN estimates at mid-year)‡	
2011	32,059,424
2012	32,521,146
2013	33,008,150
Density (per sq km) at mid-2013	46.4

* 274,461 sq miles. This area includes the disputed territory of Western Sahara, which covers 252,120 sq km (97,344 sq miles).

† Including Western Sahara, with an estimated population of 417,000 at the 2004 census.

‡ Source: UN, *World Population Prospects: The 2012 Revision*.

POPULATION BY AGE AND SEX
(UN estimates at mid-2013)

	Males	Females	Total
0–14	4,711,793	4,481,924	9,193,717
15–64	10,889,590	11,282,147	22,171,737
65 and over	690,873	951,823	1,642,696
Total	16,292,256	16,715,894	33,008,150

Source: UN, *World Population Prospects: The 2012 Revision*.

REGIONS
(population at 2004 census)

	Population
Oued el-Dahab Lagouira*	73,067
El-Aaiún Boujdour*	245,562
Guelmim el-Semara†	425,211
Souss Massa-Draa	3,094,985
Gharb Chrarda Beni-Hsen	1,849,776
Chaouia Ouardigha	1,646,051
Marrakech Tensift al-Haou	3,088,338
Oriental	1,908,905
Grand Casablanca	3,615,903
Rabat Salé Zemmour Zaer	2,349,202
Doukkala Abda	1,978,189
Tadla Azilal	1,448,155
Meknès Tafilalet	2,125,608
Fès Boulemane	1,567,846
Taza al-Hoceima Taounate	1,803,051
Tanger Tétouan	2,460,220
Total	29,680,069

* Regions situated in Western Sahara.
† Region partly situated in Western Sahara.

PRINCIPAL TOWNS
(population at 2004 census)

Casablanca	2,936,874	Tétouan	318,698
Rabat (capital)*	1,827,733	Safi	282,227
Marrakech (Marrakesh)	1,063,415	Mohammedia	187,708
Fès (Fez)	975,507	El-Aaiún†	179,542
Agadir	815,032	Khouribga	165,976
Tanger (Tangier)	756,964	Beni-Mellal	162,341
Meknès	703,363	El-Jadida	143,419
Oujda	473,922	Taza	137,778
Kénitra	352,058		

* Including Salé and Temara.
† Town situated in Western Sahara.

Mid-2011 (incl. suburbs, UN estimate): Rabat 1,842,850 (Source: UN, *World Urbanization Prospects: The 2011 Revision*).

BIRTHS AND DEATHS
(annual averages, UN estimates)

	1995–2000	2000–05	2005–10
Birth rate (per 1,000)	23.7	20.9	20.1
Death rate (per 1,000)	6.1	6.1	6.3

Source: UN, *World Population Prospects: The 2012 Revision*.

Life expectancy (years at birth): 72.1 (males 69.9; females 74.5) in 2011 (Source: World Bank, World Development Indicators database).

ECONOMICALLY ACTIVE POPULATION
('000 persons aged 15 years and over)

	2009	2010	2011
Agriculture, hunting, forestry and fishing	4,311.3	4,188.1	4,179.0
Mining and quarrying	42.5	41.8	50.2
Manufacturing	1,190.9	1,182.7	1,148.4
Electricity, gas and water	45.5	42.9	37.3
Construction	967.6	1,029.1	1,059.0
Wholesale and retail trade; repairs	1,503.9	1,522.7	1,555.9
Hotels and restaurants	225.5	248.2	266.8
Transport, storage and communications	442.4	464.6	493.5
General administration and community services	1,042.5	1,005.1	1,020.4
Financial intermediation, real estate and business services	669.4	665.2	683.9
Sub-total	10,441.4	10,390.5	10,494.3
Activities not adequately defined	13.4	14.2	15.0
Total employed	10,454.8	10,404.7	10,509.3
Unemployed	1,029.4	1,037.1	1,028.3
Total labour force	11,484.1	11,441.8	11,537.6

2012 ('000): Total employed 10,511; Unemployed 1,038; Total labour force 11,549.

Health and Welfare

KEY INDICATORS

Total fertility rate (children per woman, 2011)	2.2
Under-5 mortality rate (per 1,000 live births, 2011)	33
HIV/AIDS (% of persons aged 15–49, 2011)	0.2
Physicians (per 1,000 head, 2009)	0.62
Hospital beds (per 1,000 head, 2009)	1.1
Health expenditure (2010): US $ per head (PPP)	257
Health expenditure (2010): % of GDP	5.4
Health expenditure (2010): public (% of total)	29.8
Access to water (% of persons, 2011)	82
Access to sanitation (% of persons, 2011)	70
Total carbon dioxide emissions ('000 metric tons, 2009)	48,815.1
Carbon dioxide emissions per head (metric tons, 2009)	1.5
Human Development Index (2012): ranking	130
Human Development Index (2012): value	0.591

For sources and definitions, see explanatory note on p. vi.

Agriculture

PRINCIPAL CROPS
('000 metric tons)

	2009	2010	2011
Wheat	6,371	4,876	3,400*
Rice, paddy	50	51	40
Barley	3,770	2,566	2,340*
Maize	205	279	200*
Potatoes	1,234	1,605	1,948†
Sugar cane	813	632	632†
Sugar beet	2,753	2,436	2,436†
Broad beans, dry	153	149	134†
Peas, dry	28	26	28†
Chick peas	52	57	62†
Lentils	23	28	31†
Almonds, with shell	115	102	131†
Groundnuts, with shell	52	50	45†
Olives	850	1,484	1,365†
Sunflower seeds	50	59	55*
Cabbages and other brassicas	39	65	59†
Artichokes	57	45	44†
Tomatoes	1,230	1,278	1,236†
Cauliflowers and broccoli	51	70	93†
Pumpkins, squash and gourds	238	208	212†
Cucumbers and gherkins	35	115	125†
Aubergines (Eggplants)	30	38	38†
Chillies and peppers, green	203	225	224†
Onions, dry	802	1,131	1,196†
Peas, green	144	140	123†
String beans†	90	160	157
Carrots and turnips	239	253	288†
Carobs†	20	20	20
Watermelons	747	453	449†
Cantaloupes and other melons	887	567	558†
Figs†	70	74	74
Grapes	338	316	317†
Dates	85	119	119†
Apples	423	506	506†
Pears	39	41	41†
Quinces	39	46	46†
Peaches and nectarines	87	93	93†
Plums and sloes	74	83	83†
Strawberries	355	141	141†
Oranges	715	849	850*
Tangerines, mandarins, clementines and satsumas	353	473	473†
Apricots	134	132	133†
Bananas†	240	280	290
Anise, badian, fennel and coriander†	23	29	29

* Unofficial figure.
† FAO estimate(s).

Aggregate production ('000 metric tons, may include official, semi-official or estimated data): Total cereals 10,444 in 2009, 7,834 in 2010, 6,039 in 2011; Total pulses 276 in 2009, 282 in 2010, 281 in 2011; Total roots and tubers 1,246 in 2009, 1,615 in 2010, 1,956 in 2011; Total vegetables (incl. melons) 5,256 in 2009, 5,487 in 2010, 5,657 in 2011; Total fruits (excl. melons) 3,088 in 2009, 3,292 in 2010, 3,307 in 2011.

Source: FAO.

LIVESTOCK
('000 head, year ending September)

	2009	2010	2011*
Cattle	2,788	2,896	2,900
Sheep	17,006	18,023	18,500
Goats	5,293	5,686	5,900
Camels*	50	52	55
Horses	147	155	160
Asses	963	955*	955
Mules	505	500*	500
Chickens*	165,000	170,000	175,000

* FAO estimate(s).

Source: FAO.

LIVESTOCK PRODUCTS
('000 metric tons)

	2009	2010	2011*
Cattle meat	190	192	200
Sheep meat	134	139	142
Goat meat	22	23	25
Chicken meat	490	560	591
Cows' milk	1,800	1,900	1,900
Sheep's milk*	33	38	38
Goats' milk*	40	58	58
Hen eggs*	200	230	230
Honey	3	4	4
Wool, greasy*	55	55	55

* FAO estimates.

Source: FAO.

Forestry

ROUNDWOOD REMOVALS
('000 cubic metres, excl. bark)

	2009	2010	2011
Sawlogs, veneer logs and logs for sleepers	190	113*	113*
Pulpwood	305	259	259*
Fuel wood*	6,802	6,786	6,762
Total*	7,297	7,158	7,134

* FAO estimate(s).

Source: FAO.

SAWNWOOD PRODUCTION
('000 cubic metres, incl. railway sleepers)

	1987*	1988	1989
Coniferous (softwood)	40	26*	43*
Broadleaved (hardwood)	40	27	40
Total	80	53	83

* FAO estimate(s).

1990–2011: Production assumed to be unchanged from 1989 (FAO estimates).

Source: FAO.

Fishing

('000 metric tons, live weight)

	2009	2010	2011
Capture	1,165.1	1,136.2	958.9
European pilchard (sardine)	790.6	771.5	504.0
Chub mackerel	83.8	76.0	121.3
Jack and horse mackerels	23.4	23.2	22.1
Octopuses	60.2	32.0	32.7
Aquaculture*	1.5	1.5	1.4
Total catch (incl. others)*	1,166.5	1,137.8	960.3

* FAO estimates.

Note: Figures exclude aquatic plants ('000 metric tons, all capture): 10.4 in 2009; 7.4 in 2010; 5.8 in 2011. Also excluded are corals (metric tons, all capture): 6.5 in 2009; 7.1 in 2010; 7.4 in 2011.

Source: FAO.

Mining

('000 metric tons)

	2009	2010	2011
Iron ore*	30.5	44.7	78.9
Copper concentrates*	42.1	53.3	43.0
Lead concentrates*	49.0	46.4	43.8
Manganese ore*	51.8	75.6	58.0
Zinc concentrates*	88.4	87.4	90.1
Phosphate rock†	18,307.0	26,603.0	28,052.0
Fluorspar (acid grade)	72.1	89.7	79.2
Barytes	586.9	572.4	769.5
Salt (unrefined)	310.4	503.4	720.8
Bentonite	84.1	110.7	97.1

* Figures refer to the gross weight of ores and concentrates.
† Including production in Western Sahara.

Source: Ministère de l'Energie, des Mines, de l'Eau et de l'Environnement.

Industry

SELECTED PRODUCTS
('000 metric tons unless otherwise indicated)

	2007	2008	2009
Wine*	37	35	29
Olive oil (crude)	75	95	112†
Motor spirit—petrol	365	404	313
Naphthas	596	455	335
Distillate fuel oils	1,996	1,819	1,385
Residual fuel oils	2,269	1,880	1,492
Jet fuel	292	262	257
Petroleum bitumen—asphalt	257	275	307
Liquefied petroleum gas ('000 barrels)	1,972	2,000	2,000
Cement	12,792	14,048	14,519
Carpets and rugs ('000 sq m)	226	n.a.	n.a.
Electric energy (million kWh)	19,670	20,345	21,191

* Estimated figures.
† Unofficial figure.

2010 (estimates unless otherwise indicated): Wine 33; Olive oil (crude) 148 (unofficial figure); Liquefied petroleum gas ('000 barrels) 2,000; Cement 14,000.

2011 (estimates unless otherwise indicated): Wine 33; Olive oil (crude) 130 (unofficial figure); Liquefied petroleum gas ('000 barrels) 2,000; Cement 14,000.

Sources: FAO, US Geological Survey, UN Industrial Commodity Statistics Database.

Finance

CURRENCY AND EXCHANGE RATES

Monetary Units:
100 centimes (santimat) = 1 Moroccan dirham.

Sterling, Dollar and Euro Equivalents (30 April 2013):
£1 sterling = 13.207 dirhams;
US $1 = 8.508 dirhams;
€1 = 11.122 dirhams;
100 Moroccan dirhams = £7.57 = $11.75 = €8.99.

Average Exchange Rate (dirhams per US $):
2010 8.417
2011 8.090
2012 8.628

GENERAL BUDGET
('000 million dirhams)

Revenue*†	2011	2012‡	2013‡
Tax revenue	191.0	202.6	212.5
Taxes on income and profits	68.4	72.6	76.2
Taxes on property	9.1	10.9	12.3
Taxes on goods and services	95.2	100.3	104.5
Taxes on international trade	13.7	13.9	14.5
Other tax revenues	4.7	4.9	4.9
Non-tax revenue	30.7	29.0	30.2
Total	221.7	231.6	242.7

Expenditure§	2011	2012‡	2013‡
Wages and salaries	99.4	106.2	110.6
Use of goods and services	20.2	23.6	30.2
Interest	18.2	20.2	22.4
Subsidies	48.8	52.3	40.0
Grants	29.1	29.8	32.3
Other expense	25.6	16.9	16.8
Total	241.4	249.0	252.3

* Excluding grants (million dirhams): 1.3 in 2011; 1.2 in 2012 (budget projection); 11.2 in 2013 (budget projection).
† Includes tariffs destined for food subsidies and road fund revenues.
‡ Projections.
§ Excluding net lending.

Source: IMF, *Morocco: 2012 Article IV Consultation and First Review Under the Two-Year Precautionary and Liquidity Line—Staff Report; Public Information Notice and Press Release on the Executive Board Discussion; and Statement by the Executive Director for Morocco* (April 2013).

INTERNATIONAL RESERVES
(US $ million at 31 December)

	2010	2011	2012
Gold (national valuation)	1,000	1,116	1,179
IMF special drawing rights	743	616	435
Reserve position in IMF	108	108	108
Foreign exchange	21,762	18,802	15,812
Total	23,613	20,642	17,534

Source: IMF, *International Financial Statistics*.

MONEY SUPPLY
(million dirhams at 31 December)

	2010	2011	2012
Currency outside depository corporations	144,660	158,288	163,641
Transferable deposits	366,450	393,110	410,899
Other deposits	322,311	329,675	339,009
Securities other than shares	21,996	30,480	36,051
Broad money	855,417	911,553	949,599

Source: IMF, *International Financial Statistics*.

COST OF LIVING
(Consumer Price Index for urban areas; base: 2006 = 100)

	2010	2011	2012
Food and non-alcoholic beverages	114.7	116.3	119.1
Alcoholic beverages and tobacco	108.3	108.3	108.5
Clothing and footwear	104.3	106.0	108.2
Shelter	104.3	104.8	105.3
Household equipment	106.2	107.1	107.2
All items (incl. others)	108.4	109.4	110.8

NATIONAL ACCOUNTS
(million dirhams at current prices)

Expenditure on the Gross Domestic Product

	2010	2011	2012*
Government final consumption expenditure	133,938	146,332	159,118
Private final consumption expenditure	437,547	472,938	494,499
Change in inventories	33,251	42,168	32,697
Gross fixed capital formation	234,407	246,394	259,680
Total domestic expenditure	839,143	907,832	945,994
Exports of goods and services	253,941	285,530	299,646
Less Imports of goods and services	329,053	390,755	417,471
GDP in purchasers' values	764,031	802,607	828,169

Gross Domestic Product by Economic Activity

	2010	2011	2012*
Agriculture, hunting and forestry	98,991	106,342	102,572
Fishing and aquaculture	6,543	8,524	8,003
Mining and quarrying	29,579	41,355	40,343
Manufacturing	105,250	114,338	120,694
Oil refining and energy products	2,799	1,960	1,692
Electricity and water	19,362	18,962	20,044
Construction	47,085	47,941	50,099
Commerce	72,815	76,977	79,824
Hotels and restaurants	19,446	18,852	19,745
Transport	27,480	28,424	30,030
Post and communications	23,065	22,473	21,329
Public administration and social security	62,600	69,611	74,830
Other services	172,707	186,660	199,197
Sub-total	687,722	742,419	768,402
Taxes, less subsidies, on imports	76,309	60,188	59,767
GDP in purchasers' values	764,031	802,607	828,169

* Provisional figures.

BALANCE OF PAYMENTS
(US $ million)

	2009	2010	2011
Exports of goods	9,166	12,309	15,946
Imports of goods	–28,027	–29,627	–37,333
Balance on goods	–18,861	–17,318	–21,387
Exports of services	14,833	14,736	15,899
Imports of services	–6,898	–7,372	–8,574
Balance on goods and services	–10,927	–9,953	–14,063
Primary income received	925	868	804
Primary income paid	–2,421	–2,110	–2,856
Balance on goods, services and primary income	–12,422	–11,196	–16,115
Secondary income received	7,278	7,240	8,071
Secondary income paid	–218	–254	–293
Current balance	–5,362	–4,209	–8,337
Direct investment assets	–479	–580	–248
Direct investment liabilities	1,970	1,241	2,521
Portfolio investment assets	–12	–22	–400
Portfolio investment liabilities	–4	132	166
Other investment assets	–56	880	–536
Other investment liabilities	63	–287	791
Net errors and omissions	–523	–167	–370
Reserves and related items	–4,404	–3,012	–6,413

Source: IMF, *International Financial Statistics*.

External Trade

PRINCIPAL COMMODITIES

(million dirhams)

Imports c.i.f.	2010	2011	2012*
Foodstuffs, beverages and tobacco	29,100	38,810	41,762
Wheat	7,397	11,639	12,067
Energy and lubricants	68,479	90,350	106,522
Crude petroleum	25,090	31,423	37,518
Crude products	15,915	22,542	22,967
Semi-finished products	62,772	76,483	77,041
Chemical products	8,788	11,139	11,638
Finished capital goods	63,915	66,313	71,120
Finished consumer products	55,753	61,427	64,961
Pharmaceutical products	4,554	4,907	4,613
Textile and cotton fabrics	6,611	7,733	7,839
Total (incl. others)	297,963	357,770	386,127

Exports f.o.b.	2010	2011	2012*
Foodstuffs, beverages and tobacco	26,796	28,644	30,428
Crustaceans and molluscs	4,564	5,486	5,790
Prepared and preserved fish	4,968	4,193	5,550
Energy and lubricants	1,589	4,558	7,318
Crude mineral products	14,322	19,400	19,303
Phosphates	8,984	12,610	13,308
Semi-finished products	43,397	53,960	52,245
Finished industrial capital goods	23,089	26,535	26,951
Electric wire and cable	13,693	16,570	14,810
Finished consumer products	35,145	38,090	44,898
Manufactured garments	17,801	18,134	19,148
Hosiery	6,973	7,742	8,039
Total (incl. others)	149,583	174,994	184,650

* Provisional figures.

PRINCIPAL TRADING PARTNERS

(million dirhams)*

Imports c.i.f.	2010	2011	2012†
Algeria	7,055	8,687	9,720
Belgium-Luxembourg	4,283	6,815	6,359
Brazil	6,443	8,412	8,735
Canada	1,867	2,941	3,887
China, People's Republic	24,993	23,313	25,585
France	46,379	50,989	47,832
Germany	13,706	16,013	18,443
India	4,876	4,760	4,377
Italy	17,729	18,568	18,934
Japan	3,766	3,363	5,631
Netherlands	5,195	5,893	5,748
Spain	31,603	39,267	50,876
United Kingdom	6,322	7,175	8,474
USA	20,981	28,984	24,598
Total (incl. others)	297,963	357,770	386,127

Exports f.o.b.	2010	2011	2012†
Algeria	1,163	1,899	1,815
Belgium-Luxembourg	3,985	3,501	3,455
Brazil	5,645	9,038	9,016
China, People's Republic	2,059	1,588	1,590
France	33,558	36,680	35,723
Germany	4,685	4,999	4,831
India	9,056	12,164	11,786
Italy	6,725	7,340	7,239
Netherlands	4,219	5,446	4,953
Spain	25,297	31,958	31,638
United Kingdom	4,341	4,889	4,398
USA	5,640	7,950	7,555
Total (incl. others)	149,583	174,994	184,650

* Imports by country of production; exports by country of last consignment.
† Provisional figures.

Transport

RAILWAYS

(traffic)*

	2009	2010	2011†
Passengers carried ('000)	29,599	30,910	33,879
Freight ('000 metric tons)	25,722	35,669	37,178

* Figures refer to principal railways only.
† Provisional.

2008: Passenger-km (million) 3,836; Freight ton-km (million) 4,985).

ROAD TRAFFIC

('000 motor vehicles in use at 31 December)

	1999	2000	2001
Passenger cars	1,161.9	1,211.1	1,253.0
Commercial vehicles	400.3	415.7	431.0

Motorcycles and scooters: 20,388 in 2000; 20,569 in 2001.

Passenger cars: 1,326,108 in 2003.

2007: Passenger cars 1,644,523; Buses and coaches 22,841; Vans and lorries 525,334; Motorcycles and mopeds 22,841.

2010: Passenger cars 1,976,172; Motorcycles and mopeds 31,353.

Sources: IRF, *World Road Statistics*; UN, *Statistical Yearbook*.

SHIPPING

Flag Registered Fleet

(at 31 December)

	2010	2011	2012
Number of vessels	412	409	409
Total displacement ('000 grt)	383.7	374.9	364.6

Source: Lloyd's List Intelligence (www.lloydslistintelligence.com).

International Sea-borne Freight Traffic

('000 metric tons)

	2009	2010*	2011*
Goods loaded	20,341	26,123	25,261
Goods unloaded	39,395	43,113	43,779

* Provisional figures.

CIVIL AVIATION

(traffic on scheduled services)

	2007	2008	2009
Kilometres flown (million)	120	110	111
Passengers carried ('000)	4,624	4,927	4,931
Passenger-km (million)	9,073	9,901	9,582
Total ton-km (million)	861	947	947

Source: UN, *Statistical Yearbook*.

2010: Aircraft movements 196,538; Passengers carried ('000) 15,499; Freight carried (metric tons) 55,558.

2011 (provisional): Aircraft movements 192,553; Passengers carried ('000) 15,802; Freight carried (metric tons) 55,297.

Tourism

FOREIGN TOURIST ARRIVALS*

Country of nationality	2009	2010	2011
France	1,699,201	1,827,453	1,775,983
Germany	174,384	205,417	219,667
Italy	177,915	233,224	211,408
Spain	642,817	726,540	693,255
United Kingdom	252,945	338,060	352,143
Other European countries	209,153	255,076	255,661
Maghreb countries	135,766	155,550	174,417
USA	121,144	135,376	130,427
Total (incl. others)	4,292,958	4,910,435	4,934,052

* Excluding Moroccans resident abroad (4,048,279 in 2009; 4,377,903 in 2010; 4,408,250 in 2011).

Cruise-ship passengers: 319,353 in 2009; 475,915 in 2010; 441,629 in 2011.

Receipts from tourism (US $ million, excl. passenger transport): 6,703 in 2010; 7,307 in 2011 (provisional) (Source: World Tourism Organization).

Communications Media

	2010	2011	2012
Telephones ('000 main lines in use)	3,749.4	3,566.1	3,279.1
Mobile cellular telephones ('000 subscribers)	31,982.3	36,553.9	39,016.3
Internet subscribers ('000)	500.5	591.6	n.a.
Broadband subscribers ('000)	498.7	589.0	681.6

Personal computers: 1,800,000 (57.0 per 1,000 persons) in 2008.

Source: International Telecommunication Union.

Education

(2011/12 unless otherwise indicated)

	Institutions	Teachers	Pupils/Students		
			Males	Females	Total
Pre-primary	33,577*	37,621	392,417	290,284	682,701
Primary	6,565†	155,481	2,106,223	1,910,711	4,016,934
public	5,940†	n.a.	1,834,611	1,666,144	3,500,755
private	625†	n.a.	271,612	244,567	516,179
Secondary (public and private)	1,664†	100,367‡	1,405,441	1,148,609	2,554,050
Tertiary	68*	19,598§	235,554‖	210,519‖	446,073‖

* 1997/98 figure.

† 1999/2000 figure.

‡ 2003/04 figure.

§ 2008/09 figure.

‖ 2009/10 figure.

Pupils/Students (2008/09): Primary 3,863,838 (public 3,492,312, private 371,526); Secondary 2,232,289 (public 2,103,768, private 128,521).

Teachers: Primary 144,722 in 2008/09.
Sources: Ministry of National Education; Ministry of Higher Education, Staff Training and Scientific Research; UNESCO Institute for Statistics.

Pupil-teacher ratio (primary education, UNESCO estimate): 25.8 in 2011/12 (Source: UNESCO Institute for Statistics).

Adult literacy rate (UNESCO estimates): 56.1% (males 68.9%, females 43.9%) in 2009 (Source: UNESCO Institute for Statistics).

Directory

The Constitution

The following is a summary of the main provisions of the Constitution, as approved in a national referendum on 1 July 2011.

PREAMBLE

The Kingdom of Morocco is founded on the principles of participation, pluralism and good governance, and is a sovereign Islamic state. Acknowledging its diverse heritage and peoples, the Kingdom aims to preserve its singular national identity and territorial integrity. It adheres to the principles, rights and obligations of those international organizations of which it is a member, reaffirms its respect for human rights as they are universally recognized, and works for the preservation of peace and security in the world.

GENERAL PRINCIPLES

Morocco is a constitutional, democratic, parliamentary and social monarchy. Sovereignty pertains to the nation and is exercised directly by means of the referendum and indirectly by the constitutional institutions. The territorial organization of the Kingdom is decentralized. All Moroccans are equal before the law, and all adults enjoy equal political rights including the franchise. Islam is the religion of the state, which guarantees freedom of worship for all. Arabic is the official language of the state. Tamazight also constitutes an official language. There shall be no one-party system.

LIBERTIES AND FUNDAMENTAL RIGHTS

Men and women enjoy, equally, the fundamental civil, economic, political, social, cultural and environmental rights as stipulated by the Constitution. The Kingdom of Morocco strives to achieve equality between men and women, and to fight against discrimination in all forms.

The right to life is the most fundamental right of all human beings, and is protected by the law. No person may be subject to treatment that is cruel, inhuman, degrading or otherwise damaging to their dignity. The use of torture, no matter by whom it is committed, is a crime punishable by law. Arbitrary or secret detention are crimes of the utmost severity and those responsible will be subject to the most severe punishment.

Freedoms of movement, opinion and speech and the rights of assembly and non-violent protest are guaranteed. The freedom of the press and the right of citizens to publish ideas and opinions are inviolable.

All Moroccans shall have equal access to social welfare, health care, education, housing, employment and water. The right to strike, and to private property, is guaranteed. All Moroccans contribute to the defence of the Kingdom and to public costs.

THE MONARCHY

The King, as Commander of the Faithful, ensures respect for Islam and guarantees freedom of worship for all. As head of state, supreme representative, symbol of the unity of the nation, he safeguards the Constitution and guarantees the durability and continuity of the state. The Crown of Morocco and its attendant constitutional rights shall be hereditary in the line of HM King Muhammad VI, and shall be transmitted to the oldest son, unless during his lifetime the King has appointed as his successor another of his sons. The person of the King is inviolable. The King appoints as Prime Minister the leader of the party with the largest representation in the Chamber of Representatives. Upon the Prime Minister's recommendation, the King appoints government ministers, and presides over the Council of Ministers. The King may, on his own initiative and after consultation with the head of government, dismiss one or more ministers. He shall promulgate adopted legislation within a 30-day period, and has the power to dissolve the Chamber of Representatives and/or the Chamber of Advisers. The sovereign is the Commander-in-Chief of the Armed Forces; makes appointments to civil and military posts; appoints Ambassadors; signs and ratifies treaties; presides over the Supreme Council of Security, the Supreme Council of the Magistracy, the Supreme Council of Education and the Supreme Council for National Reconstruction and Planning; and exercises the right of pardon. In cases of threat to the national territory or to the action of constitutional institutions, the King, having consulted the President of the Chamber of Representatives, the President of the Chamber of Advisers and the Chairman of the Constitutional Council, and after addressing the nation, has the right to declare a State of Emergency by royal decree. The State of Emergency shall not entail the dissolution of Parliament and shall be terminated by the same procedure followed in its proclamation. The fundamental liberties and rights as stipulated by the Constitution shall remain guaranteed under the State of Emergency.

LEGISLATURE

The legislature consists of a bicameral parliament: the Chamber of Representatives and the Chamber of Advisers. The Opposition is an integral component of both chambers. Members of the Chamber of Representatives are elected by direct universal suffrage for a five-year term. Members of the Chamber of Advisers, of whom there shall be no fewer than 90 and no more than 120, are elected for a six-year term. Three-fifths of the members of the Chamber of Advisers are elected by electoral colleges of local councils; the remainder are elected by electoral colleges representing chambers of commerce and trade unions. Deputies in both chambers shall not be arrested or convicted for opinions or votes expressed during the exercise of their functions, except if said opinion represents an attack on the system of monarchy, the religion of Islam or the person of the King. Parliament shall adopt legislation, which may be initiated by members of either chamber or by the Prime Minister. Draft legislation shall be examined consecutively by both parliamentary chambers. If the two chambers fail to agree on the draft legislation the Government may request that a bilateral commission propose a final draft for approval by the chambers. If the chambers do not then adopt the draft, the Government may submit the draft (modified, if need be) to the Chamber of Representatives. Henceforth the draft submitted can be definitively adopted only by absolute majority of the members of the Chamber of Representatives. Parliament holds its meetings during two sessions each year, commencing on the second Friday in October and the second Friday in April.

GOVERNMENT

The Government, composed of the Prime Minister and his Ministers, is responsible to the King and Parliament and ensures the execution of laws. After its appointment by the King, the Prime Minister must submit his Government's programme to a debate in each of the parliamentary chambers. The Government shall be sworn in to office only after having gained an absolute majority in a vote by the members of the Chamber of Representatives. The Prime Minister is empowered to initiate legislation and to exercise statutory powers except where these are reserved to the King. He is responsible for co-ordinating ministerial work.

RELATIONS BETWEEN THE AUTHORITIES

The King may request a second reading, by both Chambers of Parliament, of any draft bill or proposed law. In addition, he may submit proposed legislation to a referendum by decree; and dissolve either Chamber or both if a proposal that has been rejected is approved by referendum. He may also dissolve either Chamber by decree after consulting the President of the Constitutional Court, and addressing the nation, but the succeeding Chamber may not be dissolved within a year of its election, except in the absence of a governing majority. The head of government may also dissolve the Chamber of Representatives by decree, having consulted the King and the Presidents of the Chamber of Representatives and the Constitutional Court. The Chamber of Representatives may force the collective resignation of the Government either by refusing a vote of confidence or by adopting a censure motion. The election of the new Parliament or Chamber shall take place within two months of its dissolution. In the interim period the King shall exercise the legislative powers of Parliament, in addition to those conferred upon him by the Constitution. A censure motion must be signed by at least one-quarter of the Chamber's members, and shall be approved by the Chamber only by an absolute majority vote of its members. The Chamber of Advisers is competent to issue 'warning' motions to the Government and, by a two-thirds' majority, force its resignation.

JUDICIARY

The Judiciary is independent. Judges are appointed on the recommendation of the Supreme Council of the Magistracy presided over by the King.

THE CONSTITUTIONAL COURT

The Constitutional Court consists of 12 members, of whom six are appointed by the King, and six members appointed for the same period—three elected by a two-thirds' majority of each parliamentary chamber. The King appoints the Chairman from among the members of the Court. One-third of each category of the Council are renewed every three years. The Council is empowered to judge the validity of legislative elections and referendums, as well as that of organic laws and the rules of procedure of both parliamentary chambers, submitted to it.

REGIONS AND TERRITORIAL COLLECTIVITIES

The territorial collectivities of the Kingdom comprise the regions, governorships, provinces and communes. The governing Councils of the regions and communes are elected by universal suffrage.

THE HIGH AUDIT COUNCIL

The High Audit Council exercises the general supervision of the implementation of fiscal laws. It ensures the regularity of revenues and expenditure operations of the departments legally under its jurisdiction, as it assesses the management of the affairs thereof. It is competent to penalize any breach of the rules governing such operations. Regional audit councils exercise the supervision of the accounts of local assemblies and bodies, and the management of the affairs thereof.

THE ECONOMIC, SOCIAL AND ENVIRONMENTAL COUNCIL

An Economic, Social and Environmental Council shall be established to give its opinion on all matters of an economic, social or environmental nature. Its constitution, organization, prerogatives and rules of procedure shall be determined by an organic law.

GOOD GOVERNANCE

Public services shall be organized according to the principles of equal access for all citizens, of even coverage of the national territory and of continuity of provision. The bodies and organizations in charge of ensuring good governance are independent. The following institutions shall be established: a National Council for Human Rights; a Council for the Moroccan Community Abroad; a Council for Competition; National Institute for Financial Probity and the Prevention of Corruption; a Superior Council for Education, Professional Training and Scientific Research; a Consultative Council for the Family and Children; a Council for Youth Affairs and Associations. An independent Mediator shall defend citizens' rights in their interaction with public bodies, contribute to efforts to uphold the law and promote transparency in the administration of public affairs. All of the above institutions shall present a report to parliament annually.

REVISION OF THE CONSTITUTION

The King, the head of government, the Chamber of Representatives and the Chamber of Advisers are competent to initiate a revision of the Constitution. The King has the right to submit the revision project he initiates directly to a national referendum. A proposal for a revision by either parliamentary chamber shall be adopted only if it receives a two-thirds' majority vote by the chamber's members. Revision projects and proposals shall be submitted to the nation for referendum by royal decree; a revision of the Constitution shall be definitive after approval by referendum. Neither the state, system of monarchy, liberties and fundamental rights, nor the prescriptions related to the religion of Islam may be subject to a constitutional revision.

The Government

HEAD OF STATE

Monarch: HM King MUHAMMAD VI (acceded 23 July 1999).

CABINET

(September 2013)

A coalition of the Parti de la justice et du développement (PJD), Istiqlal, the Mouvement populaire (MP), the Parti du progrès et du socialisme (PPS) and independents (Ind.).

On 9 July 2013 the leader of Istiqlal announced the party's intention to withdraw from the governing coalition, citing disagreements with the PJD, principally over economic policy. Five of the party's six ministers duly submitted their resignations to King Muhammad VI the following day, and the King's formal acceptance was granted on 22 July. The ministers in question were, however, instructed to remain in post until a new Government could be formed. It was reported that the Minister of National Education, Muhammad el-Ouafa, had refused to resign from the Government.

Prime Minister: ABDELILAH BENKIRANE (PJD).

Minister of State: ABDELLAH BAHA (PJD).

Minister of the Interior: MOHAND LAENSER (MP).

Minister of Foreign Affairs and Co-operation: SAÂDEDDINE EL-OTHMANI (PJD).

Minister of Justice and Liberties: MUSTAFA RAMID (PJD).

Minister of Habous (Religious Endowments) and Islamic Affairs: AHMED TOUFIQ (Ind.).

Secretary-General of the Government: DRISS DAHAK (Ind.).

Minister of the Economy and Finance: NIZAR BARAKA (Istiqlal).

Minister of Housing, Town Planning and Development: MUHAMMAD NABIL BENABDELLAH (PPS).

Minister of Agriculture and Fisheries: AZIZ AKHANNOUCH (Ind.).

Minister of National Education: MUHAMMAD EL-OUAFA (Istiqlal).

Minister of Higher Education, Staff Training and Scientific Research: LAHCEN DAOUDI (PJD).

Minister of Youth and Sports: MUHAMMAD OUZZINE (MP).

Minister of Equipment and Transport: ABDELAZIZ RABBAH (PJD).

Minister of Health: EL-HOSSEIN EL-OUARDI (PPS).

Minister of Communication and Government Spokesperson: MUSTAPHA EL-KHALFI (PJD).

Minister of Energy, Mining, Water and the Environment: FOUAD DOUIRI (Istiqlal).

Minister of Employment and Vocational Training: ABDELOUAHED SOUHAIL (PPS).

Minister of Industry, Trade and New Technologies: ABDELKADER AÂMARA (PJD).

Minister of Tourism: LAHCEN HADDAD (MP).

Minister of Solidarity, Women, Family and Social Development: BASSIMA HAKKAOUI (PJD).

Minister of Culture: MUHAMMAD AMINE SBIHI (PPS).

Minister of Handicrafts: ABDESSAMAD QAIOUH (Istiqlal).

Minister in charge of Relations with Parliament and Civil Society: LAHBIB CHOUBANI (PJD).

Minister-delegate to the Prime Minister, in charge of the Administration of National Defence: ABDELLATIF LOUDIYI (Ind.).

Minister-delegate to the Prime Minister, in charge of Moroccans Resident Abroad: ABDELLATIF MAÂZOUZ (Istiqlal).

Minister-delegate to the Minister of the Interior: CHARKI DRAISS (Ind.).

Minister-delegate to the Minister of Foreign Affairs and Cooperation: YOUSSEF AMRANI (Istiqlal).

Minister-delegate to the Prime Minister, in charge of General Affairs and Governance: MUHAMMAD NAJIB BOULIF (PJD).

Minister-delegate to the Prime Minister, in charge of Civil Service and the Modernization of the Public Sector: ABDELÂDIM GUERROUJ (MP).

Minister-delegate to the Minister of the Economy and Finance, in Charge of the Budget: DRISS EL-AZAMI EL-IDRISSI (PJD).

MINISTRIES

Office of the Prime Minister: Palais Royal, Touarga, Rabat; tel. (53) 7219400; fax (53) 7768656; e-mail courrier@pm.gov.ma; internet www.pm.gov.ma.

Ministry in charge of the Administration of National Defence: Rabat.

Ministry of Agriculture and Fisheries: ave Muhammad V, Quartier Administratif, pl. Abdellah Chefchaouni, BP 607, Rabat; tel. (53) 7760933; fax (53) 7776411; internet www.agriculture.gov.ma.

Ministry of Civil Service and the Modernization of the Public Sector: Quartier Administratif, rue Ahmed Cherkaoui, Agdal, BP 1076, Rabat; tel. (53) 7773106; fax (53) 7778438; e-mail info@mmsp.gov.ma; internet www.mmsp.gov.ma.

Ministry of Communication: ave Allal el-Fassi, Madinat al-Irfane Souissi, 10000 Rabat; tel. (53) 7678112; fax (53) 7680178; e-mail ministre@mincom.gov.ma; internet www.mincom.gov.ma.

Ministry of Culture: 1 rue Ghandi, Rabat; tel. (53) 7209494; fax (53) 7209400; e-mail webmaster@minculture.gov.ma; internet www.minculture.gov.ma.

Ministry of the Economy and Finance: blvd Muhammad V, Quartier Administratif, Chellah, Rabat; tel. (53) 7677501; fax (53) 7677526; e-mail internet@finances.gov.ma; internet www.finances.gov.ma.

Ministry of Employment and Vocational Training: ave Muhammad V, Hassan, BP 5015, Rabat; tel. (53) 7760521; fax (53) 7750192; e-mail communication@emploi.gov.ma; internet www.emploi.gov.ma.

Ministry of Energy, Mining, Water and the Environment: rue Abou Marouane Essaadi, BP 6208, Agdal, Rabat; tel. (53) 7688857; fax (53) 7688863; e-mail dsi@mem.gov.ma; internet www.mem.gov.ma.

Ministry of Equipment and Transport: Quartier Administratif, Chellah, Rabat; tel. (53) 7684151; fax (53) 7764825; internet www.mtpnet.gov.ma.

Ministry of Foreign Affairs and Co-operation: ave Franklin Roosevelt, Rabat; tel. (53) 7761583; fax (53) 7765508; e-mail mail@maec.gov.ma; internet www.maec.gov.ma.

Ministry in charge of General Affairs and Governance: Quartier Administratif, Agdal, BP 412, Rabat; tel. (53) 7687300; fax (53) 7771697; e-mail sec-sg@affaires-generales.gov.ma; internet www.affaires-generales.gov.ma

Ministry of Habous (Religious Endowments) and Islamic Affairs: al-Mechouar Essaid, Rabat; tel. (53) 7766801; fax (53) 7666037; e-mail infos@islam-maroc.ma; internet www.habous.gov.ma

Ministry of Handicrafts: Rabat; internet www.artesnet.gov.ma.

Ministry of Health: 335 ave Muhammad V, Rabat; tel. (53) 7761121; fax (53) 7763895; e-mail information@sante.gov.ma; internet srvweb.sante.gov.ma.

Ministry of Higher Education, Staff Training and Scientific Research: rue Idriss Al Akbar-Hassan, BP 4500, Rabat; tel. (53) 7217501; fax (53) 7217547; internet www.enssup.gov.ma.

Ministry of Housing, Town Planning and Development: rues al-Jouaze and al-Joumaize, Hay Riad, Secteur 16, 10000 Rabat; tel. (53) 7577000; fax (53) 7577373; e-mail mhuae@mhuae.gov.ma; internet www.mhu.gov.ma.

Ministry of Industry, Trade and New Technologies: 1 ave el-Hassan, Rabat; tel. (53) 7761878; fax (53) 7766265; e-mail ministre@mcinet.gov.ma; internet www.mcinet.gov.ma.

Ministry of the Interior: Quartier Administratif, Chellah, Rabat; tel. (53) 7761868; fax (53) 7762056.

Ministry of Justice and Liberties: pl. Mamounia, Rabat; tel. (53) 7732941; fax (53) 7730772; e-mail kourout@justice.gov.ma; internet www.justice.gov.ma.

Ministry in charge of Moroccans Resident Abroad: 59 rue Moulouya, Agdal 10000, Rabat; tel. (53) 7737573; fax (53) 7770006; e-mail info@mcmre.gov.ma; internet www.marocainsdumonde.gov.ma

Ministry of National Education: Bab Rouah, Rabat; tel. (53) 7771822; fax (53) 7687255; internet www.men.gov.ma.

Ministry in charge of Relations with Parliament and Civil Society: Nouveau Quartier Administratif, Agdal, Rabat; tel. (53) 7775170; fax (53) 7777719; e-mail mirepa@mcrp.gov.ma; internet www.mcrp.gov.ma.

Ministry of Solidarity, Women, Family and Social Development: 47 ave ibn Sina, Agdal, Rabat; tel. (53) 7684060; fax (53) 7671967; e-mail mdsfs@mdsfs.ma; internet www.social.gov.ma.

Ministry of Tourism: Centre d'Affaires-Aile Sud, Lot 1 C17, ave Ennakhil-Hay Riad, Rabat; tel. (53) 7563729; fax (53) 7716923; e-mail webmaster@tourisme.gov.ma; internet www.tourisme.gov.ma

Ministry of Youth and Sports: ave ibn Sina, Agdal, Rabat; tel. (53) 7680028; e-mail masterweb@mjs.gov.ma; internet www.mjs.gov.ma.

Legislature

Majlis al-Nuab
(Chamber of Representatives)

POB 431, Rabat; tel. (53) 7760960; fax (53) 7767726; e-mail parlement@parlement.ma; internet www.parlement.ma.

President: KARIM GHELLAB.

General Election, 25 November 2011

	Seats
Parti de la justice et du développement (PJD)	107
Istiqlal	60
Rassemblement national des indépendants (RNI)	52
Parti de l'authenticité et de la modernité (PAM)	47
Union socialiste des forces populaires (USFP)	39
Mouvement populaire (MP)	32
Union constitutionnelle (UC)	23
Parti du progrès et du socialisme (PPS)	18
Parti travailliste (PT)	4
Mouvement démocratique et social (MDS)	2
Parti du renouveau et de l'équité (PRE)	2
Parti de l'environnement et du développement durable (PEDD)	2
Parti Al Ahd Démocratique	2
Others	5
Total	395*

* Of the total number of seats, 305 seats are reserved for candidates from local party lists, while the remaining 90 seats are allocated to candidates from national lists. Each party must allocate two-thirds of its share of those 90 seats to women and the remaining one-third to men under 40 years of age.

Majlis al-Mustasharin (Chamber of Advisers)

POB 432, Rabat; tel. (53) 7218304; fax (53) 7733192; e-mail info@conseiller.ma; internet www.conseiller.ma.

President: MUHAMMAD CHEIKH BIADILLAH.

Election, 5 December 1997*

	Seats
Rassemblement national des indépendants (RNI)	42
Mouvement démocratique et social (MDS)	33
Union constitutionnelle (UC)	28
Mouvement populaire (MP)	27
Parti national démocrate (PND)	21
Istiqlal	21
Union socialiste des forces populaires (USFP)	16
Mouvement national populaire (MNP)	15
Parti de l'action (PA)	13
Front des forces démocratiques (FFD)	12
Parti du progrès et du socialisme (PPS)	7
Parti socialiste démocratique (PSD)	4
Parti démocratique et de l'indépendance (PDI)	4
Trade unions	
Confédération démocratique du travail (CDT)	11
Union marocaine du travail (UMT)	8
Union générale des travailleurs du Maroc (UGTM)	3
Others	5
Total	270

* Of the chamber's 270 members, 162 were elected by local councils, 81 by chambers of commerce and 27 by trade unions. Further elections were held on 15 September 2000, 6 October 2003, 8 September 2006 and 3 October 2009. According to the provisions of the 2011 Constitution, the number of seats in the Chamber was to be reduced to no more than 120.

Political Organizations

Congrès national ittihadi (CNI): 209 blvd Strasbourg, Résidence C, 2ème étage, Casablanca; tel. and fax (52) 2447664; e-mail onittihadi@caramail.com; f. 2001 by dissident mems of USFP; Sec.-Gen. ABDESSALAM ELAZIZ.

Front des forces démocratiques (FFD): 13 ave Tariq ibn Ziad, Hassan, Rabat; tel. (53) 7661625; fax (53) 7660621; e-mail forces@menara.ma; internet www.ffd.ma; f. 1997 after split from PPS; Sec.-Gen. THAMI EL-KHYARI.

Istiqlal (Independence): 4 ave Ibn Toumert, Bab el-Had, 50020 Rabat; tel. (53) 7730951; fax (53) 7725417; e-mail p.istiqlal2009@hotmail.com; internet www.partistiqlal.org; f. 1944; aims to raise living standards and to confer equal rights on all; emphasizes the Moroccan claim to Western Sahara; Sec.-Gen. HAMID CHABAT.

Mouvement démocratique et social (MDS): 4 ave Imam Malik, route des Zaërs, Rabat; tel. (57) 7631552; fax (53) 7658253; f. 1996 as Mouvement national démocratique et social after split from Mouvement national populaire (MNP); adopted current name in Nov. 1996; Sec.-Gen. MAHMOUD ARCHANE.

Mouvement populaire (MP): 66 rue Patrice Lumumba, Rabat; tel. (53) 7766431; fax (53) 7767537; e-mail parti_mp@hotmail.fr; internet www.alharaka.ma; f. 1958; merged with the MNP and Union démocratique in 2006; liberal; Sec.-Gen. MOHAND LAENSER.

Parti de l'action (PA): 113 ave Allal Ben Abdallah, Rabat; tel. (53) 7206661; f. 1974; advocates democracy and progress; Sec.-Gen. MUHAMMAD EL-IDRISSI.

Parti Al Ahd Démocratique: 14 rue Idriss al-Akbar, rue Tafraout, Hassan, Rabat; tel. (53) 7204816; fax (53) 7204786; e-mail alhakika@iam.net.ma; f. 2002; Chair. NAJIB EL-OUAZZANI.

Parti de l'authenticité et de la modernité (PAM): internet www.pam.ma; f. 2008; Founder FOUAD ALI EL-HIMMA; Sec.-Gen. MUSTAPHA BAKKOURI.

Parti de l'avant-garde démocratique socialiste (PADS): 54 ave de la Résistance Océan, Rabat 10000; tel. and fax (53) 7200559; e-mail pads.pads@gmail.com; an offshoot of USFP; legalized in April 1992; Sec.-Gen. ABDERRAHMAN BENAMEUR.

Parti démocrate national (PDN): f. May 2009 by fmr members of Parti national démocrate, following that party's merger into PAM; Sec.-Gen. ABDULLAH KADIRI.

Parti démocratique et de l'indépendance (PDI): 9 Lalla Yakout, rue Araar, Apt 11, 2ème étage, blvd d'Anfa, Casablanca; tel. (52) 2200949; fax (52) 2200928; f. 1946; Sec.-Gen. ABDELWAHID MAÂCH.

Parti de l'environnement et du développement durable (PEDD): 3 rue Azilal, Hassan, Rabat; tel. and fax (53) 7670620; e-mail pedmaroc@menara.ma; internet www.pedmaroc.ma; f. 2002 as Parti de l'environnement et du développement; merged with PAM in 2008; relaunched as above in 2009; environmentalist; Pres. Dr AHMAD AL-ALAMI; Sec.-Gen. KARIM HRITANE.

Parti des forces citoyennes (PFC): 353 blvd Muhammad V, 9ème étage, Casablanca; tel. (52) 2400608; fax (52) 2400613; e-mail citoyennes@menara.ma; f. 2001; Sec.-Gen. ABDERRAHIM LAHJOUJI.

Parti de la justice et du développement (PJD): ave Abdelwahed Elmorakechi, rue Elyafrani, 4 les Orangers, Rabat; tel. (53) 7208862; fax (53) 7208854; e-mail info@pjd.ma; internet www.pjd.ma; f. 1967 as Mouvement populaire constitutionnel et démocratique; breakaway party from MP; formally absorbed mems of the Islamic asscn Al Islah wa Attajdid in June 1996; adopted current name in Oct. 1998; Sec.-Gen. ABDELILAH BENKIRANE.

Parti marocain libéral (PML): 114 ave Allal Ben Abdellah, 2ème étage, Rabat; tel. (53) 7733670; fax (53) 7733611; e-mail pml@menara.ma; f. 2002; Nat. Co-ordinator MUHAMMAD ZIANE.

Parti du progrès et du socialisme (PPS): 29 ave Muhammad VI, Youssoufia, Rabat; tel. (53) 7759464; fax (53) 7759476; e-mail sg@pps.maroc.org; internet www.ppsmaroc.com; f. 1974; successor to Parti communiste marocain (banned in 1952) and Parti de la libération et du socialisme (banned in 1969); left-wing; advocates modernization, social progress, nationalization and democracy; 35,000 mems; Sec.-Gen. MUHAMMAD NABIL BENABDELLAH.

Parti de la réforme et du développement (PRD): 34 ave Pasteur, Rabat; tel. and fax (53) 7703801; f. 2001 by fmr mems of RNI; Sec.-Gen. MUHAMMAD GOUMANI.

Parti de la renaissance et de la vertu: Bouznika; f. 2005; national democratic party based on the principles of Islam; Sec.-Gen. MUHAMMAD KHALIDI.

Parti du renouveau et de l'équité (PRE): 16 rue Sebou, Apt 5, Agdal, Rabat; tel. (53) 7777266; fax (53) 7777452; e-mail partipre@yahoo.fr; internet www.pre.ma; f. 2002; Pres. CHAKIR ACHEHBAR.

Parti socialiste unifié (PSU): 9 rue d'Agadir, Immeuble Maréchal Ameziane, Casablanca; tel. (52) 2485902; fax (52) 2278442; e-mail psumaroc@yahoo.fr; f. 2005 by merger of Parti de la gauche socialiste unifieé and Fidélité à la démocratie; Sec.-Gen. NABILA MOUNIB.

Parti travailliste (PT): 9 rue Ksar Essouk, Hassan, Rabat; f. 2005; centre-left; Sec.-Gen. ABDELKRIM BENATIQ.

Rassemblement national des indépendants (RNI): 6 rue Laos, ave Hassan II, Rabat; tel. (53) 7721420; fax (53) 7733824; internet www.rni.ma; f. 1978 from the pro-Govt independents' group that then formed the majority in the Chamber of Representatives; Pres. SALAHEDDINE MEZOUAR.

Union constitutionnelle (UC): 158 ave des Forces Armées Royales, Casablanca; tel. (52) 2441144; fax (52) 2441141; e-mail union_constit@menara.ma; f. 1983; 51-mem. Political Bureau; Sec.-Gen. MUHAMMAD ABIED.

Union Marocaine pour la démocratie (UMD): Rabat; f. 2006; Sec.-Gen. JAMAL MANDRI.

Union socialiste des forces populaires (USFP): 9 ave al-Araâr, Hay Riad, Rabat; tel. (53) 7565511; fax (53) 7565510; e-mail usfp@usfp.ma; internet www.usfp.ma; f. 1959 as Union nationale des forces populaires (UNFP); became USFP in 1974 after UNFP split into 2 separate entities; merged with Parti socialiste démocratique in 2005; democratic socialist and progressive party; 260,000 mems; First Sec. DRISS LACHGAR.

The following movement is not authorized as a political party by the Government, but is generally tolerated:

Al-Adl wal-Ihsan (Justice and Charity): internet www.aljamaa.net; advocates an Islamic state based on *Shari'a* law; rejects violence; Sec.-Gen. MUHAMMAD ABBADI.

The following group is active in the disputed territory of Western Sahara:

Frente Popular para la Liberación de Saguia el-Hamra y Río de Oro (Frente Polisario) (Polisario Front): BP 10, el-Mouradia, Algiers, Algeria; fax (2) 747206; e-mail dgmae@mail.wissal.dz; f. 1973 to gain independence for Western Sahara, first from Spain and then from Morocco and Mauritania; signed peace treaty with Mauritanian Govt in 1979; supported by Algerian Govt; in February 1976 proclaimed the Sahrawi Arab Democratic Republic (SADR); admitted as the 51st mem. of the OAU in Feb. 1982 and currently recognized by more than 75 countries world-wide; its main organs are a 33-mem. Nat. Secretariat, a 101-mem. Sahrawi Nat. Assembly (Parliament) and a 13-mem. Govt; Sec.-Gen. of the Polisario Front and Pres. of the SADR MUHAMMAD ABD AL-AZIZ; Prime Minister of the SADR ABDELKADER TALEB OUMAR.

Diplomatic Representation

EMBASSIES IN MOROCCO

Algeria: Angle ave Muhammad VI, Rue Ghiyata, Soulssi, BP 448, 10001 Rabat; tel. (537) 756931; fax (537) 756918; Ambassador AHMED BENYAMINA.

Angola: km 5, 53 Ahmed Rifaï, BP 1318, Souissi, Rabat; tel. (53) 7659239; fax (53) 7653703; e-mail amb.angola@menara.ma; internet www.embaixada-angola-marrocos.org; Ambassador (vacant).

Argentina: 4 ave Mehdi Ben Barka, Souissi, 10000 Rabat; tel. (53) 7755120; fax (53) 7755410; e-mail emarr@mrecic.gov.ar; Ambassador JOSÉ PEDRO PICO.

Austria: 2 rue Tiddas, BP 135, 10000 Rabat; tel. (53) 7761698; fax (53) 7765425; e-mail rabat-ob@bmeia.gv.at; internet www.aussenministerium.at/rabat; Ambassador Dr WOLFGANG ANGERHOLZER.

Azerbaijan: rue 3 Abu Hanifa, Aqdal, Rabat; tel. (53) 7671915; fax (53) 7671918; e-mail azembma@menara.ma; Ambassador TAREK ISMAEIL ALIEV.

Bahrain: rue Béni Hassan, km 6.5, route des Zaërs, Villa 318, POB 1470, Souissi, Rabat; tel. (53) 7633500; fax (53) 7630732; e-mail rabat.mission@mofa.gov.bh; Ambassador KHALID BIN SALMAN AL KHALIFA.

Bangladesh: 25 ave Tarek ibn Ziad, BP 1468, Rabat; tel. (53) 7766731; fax (53) 7766729; e-mail bangladoot@menara.ma; internet bangladeshembassy-morocco.webs.com; Ambassador NUR MUHAMMAD.

Belgium: 6 ave de Muhammad el-Fassi, Tour Hassan, Rabat; tel. (53) 7268060; fax (53) 7767003; e-mail rabat@diplobel.fed.be; internet www.diplomatie.be/rabat; Ambassador JEAN-LUC BODSON.

Benin: 30 ave Mehdi Ben Barka, BP 5187, Souissi, 10105 Rabat; tel. (53) 7754158; fax (53) 7754156; e-mail benin@menara.ma; Ambassador BIO TORO OROUGUIWA.

Brazil: 10 ave el-Jacaranda, Secteur 2, Hay Riad, 10000 Rabat; tel. (53) 7714613; fax (53) 7714808; e-mail ambassadedubresil@menara.ma; internet rabat.itamaraty.gov.br; Ambassador FREDERICO SALOMÃO DUQUE ESTRADA MEYER.

Bulgaria: 4 ave Ahmed el-Yazidi, BP 1301, 10000 Rabat; tel. (53) 7765477; fax (53) 7763201; e-mail embassy.rabat@mfa.bg; internet www.mfa.bg/embassies/morocco; Ambassador BORIANA SIMEONOVA.

Burkina Faso: 7 rue al-Bouziri, BP 6484, Agdal, 10101 Rabat; tel. (53) 7675512; fax (53) 7675517; e-mail ambfrba@smirt.net.ma; Ambassador YERO BOLY.

Cameroon: 20 rue du Rif, BP 1790, Souissi, Rabat; tel. (53) 7758818; fax (53) 7750540; e-mail ambacam@iam.net.com; Ambassador MOUHAMADOU YOUSSIFOU.

Canada: 13 bis rue Jaâfar al-Sadik, BP 709, Agdal, Rabat; tel. (53) 7687400; fax (53) 7687430; e-mail rabat@international.gc.ca; internet www.morocco.gc.ca; Ambassador SANDRA MCCARDELL.

Central African Republic: 65, rue 29 Youssoufia est-ext. de l'etat, BP 770, Agdal, 10000 Rabat; tel. (53) 7658970; fax (53) 7659216; e-mail centreafriquemaghreb1@menara.ma; Ambassador ISMAÏLA NIMAGA.

Chile: 35 ave Ahmed Balafrej, Souissi, Rabat; tel. (53) 7636065; fax (53) 7636067; e-mail echilema@mtds.com; Ambassador CARLOS CHARME SILVA.

China, People's Republic: 16 ave Ahmed Balafrej, 10000 Rabat; tel. (53) 7754056; fax (53) 7757519; e-mail chinaemb_ma@mfa.gov.cn; internet ma.china-embassy.org; Ambassador SUN SHUZHONG.

Congo, Democratic Republic: 34 ave de la Victoire, BP 553, 10000 Rabat; tel. (53) 7262280; fax (53)7207407; e-mail ambardcrabat60@yahoo.fr; Chargé d'affaires a.i. WAWA BAMIALY.

Congo, Republic: 197 ave Général Abdendi Britel, Souissi II, Rabat; tel. (53) 7659966; fax (53) 7659959; Ambassador VALENTIN OLLESSONGO.

Côte d'Ivoire: 21 rue de Tiddas, BP 192, 10001 Rabat; tel. (53) 7763151; fax (53) 7762792; e-mail ambcim@clam.net.ma; Ambassador IDRISSA TRAORE.

Croatia: 73 rue Marnissa, Souissi, Rabat; tel. (53) 7638824; fax (53) 7638827; e-mail croemb.rabat@mvpei.hr; Chargé d'affaires a.i. JASNA MILETA.

Czech Republic: Villa Merzaa, km 4.5, ave Muhammad VI, BP 410, rue Zankat Aït Melloul, Souissi, 10000 Rabat; tel. (53) 7755421; fax (53) 7754393; e-mail rabat@embassy.mzv.cz; internet www.mzv.cz/rabat; Ambassador MICHAELA FROŇKOVÁ.

Denmark: 14 rue Tiddas angle rue Roudana, Quartier Hassan, 10020 Rabat; tel. (53) 7665020; fax (53) 7665021; e-mail rbaamb@um.dk; internet www.rabat.um.dk; Ambassador MICHAEL LUND JEPPESEN.

Dominican Republic: 3 ave Mehdi Ben Barka, Secteur 6, Bloc E, Hay Riad, 10000 Rabat; tel. (53) 7715905; fax (53) 7715957; Ambassador FRANCISCO A. CARABALLO.

Egypt: 31 rue al-Jazair, 10000 Rabat; tel. (53) 7731833; fax (53) 7706821; e-mail embegypt@mtds.com; Ambassador ABU BAKR HEFNI.

Equatorial Guinea: ave President Roosevelt, angle rue d'Agadir 9, Rabat; tel. and fax (53) 7660337; Ambassador MANUEL BIBANG ASECO EYANG.

Finland: 145 rue Soufiane Ben Wahb, BP 590, 10002 Rabat; tel. (53) 7658775; fax (53) 7658904; e-mail sanomat.rab@formin.fi; internet www.finlande.ma; Ambassador CHRISTINA HARTTILA.

France: 1 rue Aguelmane Sidi Ali, BP 577, Agdal, 10190 Rabat; tel. (53) 7276600; fax (53) 7276711; internet www.ambafrance-ma.org; Ambassador CHARLES FRIES.

Gabon: 72 ave Mehdi Ben Barka, BP 10170, Souissi, 10105 Rabat; tel. (53) 7751950; fax (53) 7757550; e-mail chancellerie@ambagabon.ma; internet www.ambagabon.ma; Ambassador ABDOU RAZZAQ GUY KAMBOGO.

The Gambia: 11 rue Cadi Ben Hammadi Senhadji, Souissi, 10000 Rabat; tel. (53) 7638045; fax (53) 7752908; Ambassador LAMIN KABBA BAJO.

Germany: 7 Zankat Madnine, BP 235, 10000 Rabat; tel. (53) 7218600; fax (53) 706851; e-mail info@rabat.diplo.de; internet www.rabat.diplo.de; Ambassador MICHAEL WITTER.

Ghana: 27 rue Ghomara, La Pinede, Souissi, Rabat; tel. (53) 7757620; fax (53) 7757630; e-mail ghanaemb@menara.ma; Ambassador CLIFFORD AKOTEY.

Greece: km 5.5, ave Muhammad VI, Villa Chems, Souissi, 10000 Rabat; tel. (53) 7638964; fax (53) 7638990; e-mail gremb.rab@mfa.gr; internet www.mfa.gr/missionsabroad/morocco; Ambassador PLATON ALEXIS HADJIMICHALIS.

Guinea: 15 rue Hamzah, Agdal, 10000 Rabat; tel. and fax (53) 7674148; fax (53) 7675070; e-mail ambaguirabat@mae.gov.gn; Ambassador ABOUBACAR KABA.

Holy See: rue Béni M'tir, BP 1303, Souissi, Rabat (Apostolic Nunciature); tel. (53) 7772277; fax (53) 7756213; e-mail nuntius@iam.net.ma; Apostolic Nuncio Most Rev. ANTONIO SOZZO (Titular Archbishop of Concordia).

Hungary: route des Zaërs, 17 Zankat Aït Melloul, BP 5026, Souissi, Rabat; tel. (53) 7750757; fax (53) 7754123; e-mail mission.rba@kum.hu; internet www.mfa.gov.hu/emb/rabat; Ambassador JÁNOS PERÉNYI.

India: 88, rue Oulad Tidrarine, Souissi, Rabat; tel. (53) 7635801; fax (53) 7634733; e-mail amb.rabat@mea.gov.in; internet www.indianembassyrabat.com; Ambassador KRISHAN KUMAR.

Indonesia: 63 rue Béni Boufrah, km 6, route des Zaërs, BP 576, 10000 Rabat; tel. (53) 7757860; fax (53) 7757859; e-mail kbrirabat@iam.net.ma; internet www.indonesie.ma; Ambassador TOSARI WIDJAJA.

Iran: ave Imam Malik, rue Kadi Muhammad Achour, BP 490, Souissi, 10001 Rabat; tel. (53) 7752167; fax (53) 7659118; e-mail ambassadiran@gmail.com; Ambassador (vacant).

Iraq: 39 blvd Mehdi Ben Barka, 10100 Rabat; tel. (53) 7754466; fax (53) 7759749; e-mail rbtemb@iraqmofamail.net; Ambassador HAZEM AHMED MAHMOUD AL-YOUSOFI.

Italy: 2 rue Idriss al-Azhar, BP 111, 10001 Rabat; tel. (53) 7219730; fax (53) 7706882; e-mail ambassade.rabat@esteri.it; internet www.ambrabat.esteri.it; Chargé d'affaires a.i. MARCO ROMITI.

Japan: 39 ave Ahmed Balafrej, Souissi, 10170 Rabat; tel. (53) 7631782; fax (53) 7750078; e-mail amb-japon@fusion.net.ma; internet www.ma.emb-japan.go.jp; Ambassador TOSHINORI YANAGIYA.

Jordan: 65 Villa Wafaa Lodgement Militaire, Souissi II, Rabat; tel. (53) 7751125; fax (53) 7758722; e-mail jo.am@iam.net.ma; Ambassador ALI HASSAN EL-KAID.

Korea, Republic: 41 ave Mehdi Ben Barka, Souissi, 10100 Rabat; tel. (53) 7756791; fax (53) 7750189; e-mail morocco@mofat.go.kr; internet mar.mofat.go.kr; Ambassador LEE TAE-HO.

Kuwait: km 4.3, ave Imam Malik, Souissi, Rabat; tel. (53) 7631111; fax (53) 7753591; e-mail alrabat@mofa.gov.kw; Ambassador SHAMLAN ABD AL-AZIZ AL-ROUMI.

Lebanon: 114 ave Abd el-Malek Ben Marouane, Rabat; tel. (53) 7656949; fax (53) 7657195; Ambassador MUSTAPHA HAMDAN.

Liberia: 23 rue Qadi Ben Hamadi Senhaji, Souissi, Rabat; tel. and fax (53) 7638426; e-mail liberanmissioninrabat@yahoo.fr; Chargé d'affaires MORIEBA K. SANOE.

Libya: km 5.5, route de Zaërs, ave Imam Malik, Souissi, Rabat; tel. (53) 7631871; fax (53) 7631877; Ambassador ABUBAKR ALI SHAKLAWOON.

Malaysia: 17 ave Bir Kacem, Souissi, Rabat; tel. (53) 7658324; fax (53) 7658363; e-mail malrabat@kln.gov.my; internet www.kln.gov.my/perwakilan/rabat; Ambassador JAMAL BIN HASSAN.

Mali: 7 rue Thami Lamdouar, Souissi, Rabat; tel. (53) 7759121; fax (53) 7754742; Ambassador TOUMANI DJIMÉ DIALLO.

Mauritania: 6 rue Thami Lamdouar, BP 207, Souissi, 10000 Rabat; tel. (53) 7656678; fax (53) 7656680; e-mail ambarim-rabat@menara.com; internet www.ambarimrabat.ma; Ambassador MOHAMED OULD MAAOUYA.

Mexico: 6 rue Kadi Mohamed Brebri, BP 1789, Souissi, 10100 Rabat; tel. (53) 7631969; fax (53) 7631971; e-mail embamexmar@smirt.net.ma; internet embamex.sre.gob.mx/marruecos; Ambassador PORFIRIO THIERRY MUÑOZ-LEDO CHEVANNIER.

Netherlands: 40 rue de Tunis, BP 329, Hassan, 10001 Rabat; tel. (53) 7219600; fax (53) 7219665; e-mail rab@minbuza.nl; internet www.mfa.nl/rab; Ambassador RON STRIKKER.

Niger: 14 bis, rue Jabal al-Ayachi, Agdal, Rabat; tel. (53) 7674615; fax (53) 7674629; Ambassador ABDOULAYE MOUMOUNI DJERMAKOYE.

Nigeria: 70 ave Omar ibn al-Khattab, BP 347, Agdal, Rabat; tel. (53) 7671857; fax (53) 7672739; e-mail nigerianrabat@menara.ma; Ambassador ABDULLAH MUHAMMAD WALI.

Norway: 6 rue Beni Ritoune, BP 757, Agdal, Souissi, 10106 Rabat; tel. (53) 7664200; fax (53) 7664299; e-mail emb.rabat@mfa.no; internet www.norvege.ma; Ambassador FRED HARALD NOMME.

Oman: 21 rue Hamza, Agdal, 10000 Rabat; tel. (53) 7673788; fax (53) 7674567; Ambassador MOUSA HAMDAN MOUSA AL-TAEI.

Pakistan: 37 ave Ahmed Balafrej, Souissi, Rabat; tel. (53) 7631192; fax (53) 7631243; e-mail pareprabat@menara.ma; internet www.mofa.gov.pk/morocco/mission.aspx; Ambassador MUHAMMAD WAHEED UL-HASSAN.

Peru: 16 rue d'Ifrane, 10000 Rabat; tel. (53) 7723236; fax (53) 7702803; e-mail leprurabat@menara.ma; Ambassador CARLOS MANUEL VELASCO MENDIOLA.

Poland: 23 rue Oqbah, Agdal, BP 425, 10000 Rabat; tel. (53) 7771173; fax (53) 7775320; e-mail apologne@menara.ma; internet www.rabat.polemb.net; Ambassador WITOLD SPIRYDOWICZ.

Portugal: 5 rue Thami Lamdouar, Souissi, 10100 Rabat; tel. (53) 7756446; fax (53) 7756445; e-mail ambassade.portugal@menara.ma; Ambassador FRANCISCO MANUEL DA FONSECA XAVIER ESTEVES.

Qatar: 4 ave Tarik ibn Ziad, BP 1220, 10001 Rabat; tel. (53) 7765681; fax (53) 7765774; e-mail rabat@mofa.gov.qa; Ambassador ABDALLAH BIN FALLAH ABDALLAH AL-DAWSSARI.

Romania: 10 rue d'Ouezzane, Hassan, 10000 Rabat; tel. (53) 7724694; fax (53) 7700196; e-mail amb.roumanie@menara.ma; internet rabat.mae.ro; Ambassador SIMONA MARIANA IOAN.

Russia: km 4, ave Muhammad VI, Souissi, Rabat; tel. (53) 7753509; fax (53) 7753590; e-mail ambrusmaroc@inbox.ru; internet www.marocco.mid.ru; Ambassador (vacant).

Saudi Arabia: 322 ave Imam Malik, km 3.5, route des Zaërs, Rabat; tel. (53) 7657454; fax (53) 7639696; e-mail maemb@mofa.gov.sa; Ambassador Dr MUHAMMAD ABD AL-RAHMAN IBN ABD AL-AZIZ BACHAR.

Senegal: 17 rue Cadi Ben Hamadi Senhaji, Souissi, BP 365, 10000 Rabat; tel. (53) 7754171; fax (53) 7754149; e-mail ambassene@menara.ma; Ambassador AMADOU SOW.

Serbia: BP 5014, 23 ave Mehdi Ben Barka, Souissi, 10105 Rabat; tel. (53) 7752201; fax (53) 7753258; e-mail sermont@menara.ma; Ambassador STANISLAV STAKIĆ.

South Africa: 34 rue Saâdiens, Rabat; tel. (53) 7706760; fax (53) 7706756; e-mail sudaf@mtds.com; Ambassador J. VAN VOLLENHOVEN.

Spain: 3 rue Aïn Khalouiya, ave Muhammad VI, km 5.3, route des Zaërs, Souissi, 10000 Rabat; tel. (53) 7633900; fax (53) 7630600; e-mail emb.rabat@maec.es; internet www.maec.es/subwebs/embajadas/rabat; Ambassador ALBERTO JOSÉ NAVARRO GONZÁLEZ.

Sudan: 5 ave Ghomara, Souissi, 10000 Rabat; tel. (53) 7752863; fax (53) 7752865; e-mail sudanirab@menara.com; Ambassador TAYEB ALI AHMED.

Sweden: 159 ave Muhammad VI, BP 428, Souissi, 10001 Rabat; tel. (53) 7633210; fax (53) 7758048; e-mail ambassaden.rabat@gov.se; internet www.swedenabroad.com/rabat; Ambassador ANNA HAMMARGREN.

Switzerland: sq. de Berkane, BP 169, 10020 Rabat; tel. (53) 7268030; fax (53) 7268040; e-mail rab.vertretung@eda.admin.ch; internet www.eda.admin.ch/rabat; Ambassador LOUIS BERTRAND.

Syria: km 5.2, route des Zaërs, BP 5158, Souissi, Rabat; tel. (53) 7757521; fax (53) 7757522; e-mail syriaembassy@menara.ma; Ambassador (vacant).

Thailand: 33 ave Lalla Meriem, Souissi, 10170, Rabat; tel. (53) 7634603; fax (53) 7634607; e-mail thaima@menara.ma; internet www.thaiembassy.org/rabat; Ambassador KUNDALEE PRACHIMDHIT.

Tunisia: 6 ave de Fès et 1 rue d'Ifrane, 10000 Rabat; tel. (53) 7730636; fax (53) 7730637; Ambassador CHAFIK HAJJI.

Turkey: 7 ave Abdelkrim Benjelloun, 10010 Rabat; tel. (53) 7661522; fax (53) 7660476; e-mail ambassade.rabat@mfa.gov.tr; internet rabat.emb.mfa.gov.tr; Ambassador UĞUR ARINER.

Ukraine: 222, rue Mouaouya Ben Houdaig, Cité OLM, Souissi II, 10020 Rabat; tel. (53) 7657840; fax (53) 7754679; e-mail emb_ma@mfa.gov.ua; internet www.mfa.gov.ua/morocco; Ambassador YAROSLAV KOVAL.

United Arab Emirates: 11 ave des Alaouines, 10000 Rabat; tel. (53) 7702085; fax (53) 7724145; e-mail rabat@mofa.gov.ae; internet uae-embassy.ae/embassies/ma; Ambassador AL-ASRI SAID AHMAD AL-DAHIRI.

United Kingdom: 28 ave S. A. R. Sidi Muhammad, BP 45, Souissi, 10105 Rabat; tel. (53) 7633333; fax (53) 7758709; e-mail generalenquiries.rabat@fco.gov.uk; internet www.gov.uk/governemnt/world/morocco; Ambassador CLIVE ALDERTON.

USA: 2 ave de Muhammad el-Fassi, Rabat; tel. (53) 7762265; fax (53) 7765661; e-mail ircrabat@usembassy.ma; internet morocco.usembassy.gov; Chargé d'affaires a.i. MATTHEW LUSSENHOP.

Venezuela: 58 Lot OLM, Villa Yasmine, rue Capitaine Abdeslam el-Moudden el-Alami, Souissi, Rabat; tel. (53) 7650315; fax (53) 7650372; e-mail emvenez@menara.ma; Chargé d'affaires a.i. AHMED ABUSAID.

Yemen: ave Imam Malik, km 6.6, rue Beni Tajit, Quartier des Ambassadeurs, Souissi, Rabat; tel. (53) 7631220; fax (53) 7631267; e-mail yemen@menara.ma; Chargé d'affaires a.i. AHMAD MUHAMMAD SALEM HAIDRAH.

Judicial System

Supreme Court (Al-Majlis al-Aala): Hay Riad, Ave al-Nakhil, Rabat; tel. (53) 7714931; fax (53) 7715106; e-mail coursupreme@coursupreme.ma; internet www.coursupreme.ma; responsible for the interpretation of the law and regulates the jurisprudence of the courts and tribunals of the Kingdom. The Supreme Court sits at Rabat and is divided into 6 Chambers; First Pres. MUSTAPHA FARÈS.

Courts of Appeal: The 21 courts hear appeals from lower courts and also comprise a criminal division.

Courts of First Instance: The 65 courts pass judgment on offences punishable by up to five years' imprisonment. These courts also pass judgment, without possibility of appeal, in personal and civil cases involving up to 3,000 dirhams.

Communal and District Courts: composed of one judge, who is assisted by a clerk or secretary, and hear only civil and criminal cases.

Administrative Courts: The seven courts pass judgment, subject to appeal before the Supreme Court pending the establishment of administrative appeal courts, on litigation with government departments.

Commercial Courts: The nine courts pass judgment, without the possibility of appeal, on all commercial litigations involving up to 9,000 dirhams. They also pass judgment on claims involving more than 9,000 dirhams, which can be appealed against in the commercial appeal courts.

Permanent Royal Armed Forces' Court: tries offences committed by the armed forces and military officers.

Attorney-General: MUSTAPHA MEDDAH.

Religion

ISLAM

About 99% of Moroccans are Muslims (of whom about 90% are of the Sunni sect), and Islam is the state religion.

CHRISTIANITY

There are about 69,000 Christians, mostly Roman Catholics.

The Roman Catholic Church

Morocco (excluding the disputed territory of Western Sahara) comprises two archdioceses, directly responsible to the Holy See. The Moroccan archbishops participate in the Conférence Episcopale Régionale du Nord de l'Afrique (f. 1985).

Bishops' Conference: Conférence Episcopale Régionale du Nord de l'Afrique, 1 rue Hadj Muhammad Riffaï, BP 258, 10001 Rabat; tel. (53) 7709239; fax (53) 7706282; e-mail archev.rabat@wanadoo.net.ma; f. 1985; Pres. Most Rev. VINCENT LANDEL (Archbishop of Rabat).

Archbishop of Rabat: Most Rev. VINCENT LANDEL, Archevêché, 1 rue Hadj Muhammad Riffaï, BP 258, 10001 Rabat; tel. (53) 7709239; fax (53) 7706282; e-mail landel@wanadoo.net.ma.

Archbishop of Tangier: Most Rev. SANTIAGO AGRELO MARTÍNEZ, Archevêché, 55 rue Sidi Bouabid, BP 2116, 9000 Tangier; tel. (53) 9932762; fax (53) 9949117; e-mail agrelomar@hotmail.com.

Western Sahara comprises a single Apostolic Prefecture, with an estimated 80 Catholics (2007).

Prefect Apostolic of Western Sahara: Fr ACACIO VALBUENA RODRÍGUEZ, Misión Católica, BP 31, 70001 el-Aaiún; e-mail omisahara@menara.ma.

The Anglican Communion

Within the Church of England, Morocco forms part of the diocese of Gibraltar in Europe. There are Anglican churches in Casablanca and Tangier.

Protestant Church

Evangelical Church: 33 rue d'Azilal, 20000 Casablanca; tel. (52) 2302151; fax (52) 2444768; e-mail eeam@lesblancs.com; f. 1920; established in 8 towns; Pres. Pastor JEAN-LUC BLANC; 1,000 mems.

JUDAISM

It is estimated that there are fewer than 7,000 Jews in Morocco, of whom approximately 5,000 reside in Casablanca, with smaller communities in Rabat and other cities.

Conseil des Communautés Israélites du Maroc: 52 Béni Snassen, Souissi, Rabat; tel. (53) 222861; fax (53) 266953; Pres. SERGE BERDUGO.

The Press

DAILIES

Casablanca

Al-Ahdath al-Maghribia (Moroccan Events): 5 rue Saint-Emilion, Casablanca; tel. (52) 2443038; fax (52) 2442976; e-mail elberini@ahdath.info; f. 1998; Arabic; Dir MUHAMMAD EL-BERINI; circ. 19,811 (2008/09).

Assabah (The Morning): Groupe Ecomedia, 70 blvd al-Massira al-Khadra, Casablanca; tel. (52) 2953660; fax (52) 2364358; e-mail assabahcasa@leconomiste.com; internet www.assabah.press.ma; f. 2000; Arabic; sister publication of *l'Economiste* ; Pres. ABDELMOUNAÏM DILAMI; Dir-Gen. KHALID BELYAZID; circ. 71,935 (2008/09).

Assahra al-Maghribia: 17 rue Othman Ben Affan, Casablanca; tel. (52) 2489120; fax (52) 2203935; e-mail web.master@almaghribia.ma; internet www.almaghribia.ma; f. 1989; Arabic; Dir AHMED NACHATTI.

Aujourd'hui le Maroc: 213 Rond-Point d'Europe, 20490 Casablanca; tel. (52) 2262674; fax (52) 2262443; e-mail alm@aujourdhui.ma; internet www.aujourdhui.ma; f. 2001; French; Dir KHALIL HACHIMI IDRISSI; Editor-in-Chief OMAR DAHBI; circ. 5,435 (2008/09).

Al-Bayane (The Manifesto): 119 blvd Emile Zola, 8ème étage, BP 13152, Casablanca; tel. (52) 2307882; fax (52) 2308080; internet www.casanet.net.ma/albayane; f. 1971; Arabic and French; organ of the Parti du progrès et du socialisme; Dir ALLAL EL-MALEH; Editor AHMED ZAKI; circ. 2,364 (2008/09).

L'Economiste: Groupe Ecomedia, 70 blvd al-Massira al-Khadra, Casablanca; tel. (52) 2953600; fax (52) 2365926; e-mail info@leconomiste.com; internet www.leconomiste.com; f. 1991; French; Pres. ABDELMOUNAÏM DILAMI; Dir-Gen. KHALID BELYAZID; Editor-in-Chief NADIA SALAH; circ. 19,937 (2008/09).

Al-Ittihad al-Ichtiraki (Socialist Unity): 33 rue Amir Abdelkader, BP 2165, Casablanca; tel. (52) 2407385; fax (52) 2619405; e-mail ail@menara.ma; internet www.alittihad.press.ma; Arabic; f. 1983; organ of the Union socialiste des forces populaires; Dir ABD AL-HADI DATE; Editor MUSTAPHA LAÂRAKI; circ. 9,513 (2008).

Libération: 33 rue Amir Abdelkader, BP 2165, Casablanca; tel. (52) 2619400; fax (52) 2620972; e-mail liberation@usfp.ma; internet www.liberation.press.ma; f. 1964; French; organ of the Union socialiste des forces populaires; Dir ABDELHADI KHAÏRAT; circ. 2,719 (2008).

Al-Massae (The Evening): 10 ave des Forces Armées Royales, 2ème étage, Casablanca; tel. (52) 2275918; fax (52) 2275597; e-mail contact@almassae.press.ma; internet www.almassae.press.ma; f. 2006; Arabic; independent; Dir RACHID NINI; circ. 113,849 (2008/09).

Le Matin du Sahara et du Maghreb: 17 rue Othman Ben Affane, Casablanca; tel. (52) 2489100; fax (52) 2203048; e-mail m.jouahri@lematin.ma; internet www.lematin.ma; f. 1971; French; royalist; Dir-Gen. MUHAMMAD JOUAHRI; Editor-in-Chief ABDELHADI GADI; circ. 24,816 (2008/09).

Rissalat al-Oumma (The Message of the Nation): 152 ave des Forces Armées Royales, BP 20005, Casablanca; tel. (52) 2901925; fax (52) 2901926 Arabic; weekly edn in French; organ of the Union constitutionnelle; Dir MUHAMMAD TAMALDOU.

Rabat

Al-Alam (The Flag): ave Hassan II, Lot Vita, BP 141, Rabat; tel. (53) 7294832; fax (53) 7291784; e-mail alalam@alalam.ma; internet www.alalam.ma; f. 1946; Arabic; literary supplement on Sat; organ of the Istiqlal party; Dir ABD AL-JABBAR SUHEIMAT; Editor-in-Chief HASSAN ABDELKHALEK; circ. 10,274 (2008/09).

Annahar Al Maghribia (The Moroccan Day): 12 pl. des Alaouites, 2ème étage, Rabat; tel. (53) 7737568; fax (53) 7737547; e-mail annahar21@yahoo.fr; internet www.annahar.ma; f. 2002; Arabic; Dir and Editor-in-Chief ABD EL-HAKIM BADI; circ. 6,953 (2008).

Attajdid (Reform): 3 blvd al-Moukawama, BP 9173, Rabat; tel. (53) 7705854; fax (53) 7705852; e-mail attajdid@attajdid.ma; internet www.attajdid.ma; f. 1999; Arabic; associated with the Parti de la justice et du développement; Dir ABDELILAH BENKIRANE; circ. 2,903 (2008/09).

Al-Haraka (Progress): 66 rue Patrice Lumumba, BP 1317, Rabat; tel. (53) 7768667; fax (53) 7767537; e-mail harakamp@menara.ma; internet www.harakamp.ma; Arabic; organ of the Mouvement populaire; Dir ALI ALAOUI; circ. 1,002 (2008).

L'Opinion: ave Hassan II, Lot Vita, Rabat; tel. (53) 7293002; fax (53) 7292639; e-mail lopinion@lopinion.ma; internet www.lopinion.ma; f. 1962; French; organ of Istiqlal; Dir MUHAMMAD IDRISSI KAÏTOUNI; Editor-in-Chief JAMAL HAJJAM; circ. 18,347 (2008/09).

SELECTED PERIODICALS

Casablanca

actuel: 1 blvd Abdellatif Ben Kaddour, 20050 Casablanca; tel. (52) 2951815; fax (52) 2951814; e-mail courrier@actuel.ma; internet www.actuel.ma; f. 2009; weekly; French; publ. by Logique Presse; Dir and Editor HENRI LOIZEAU.

Al-Ayam (The Days): Espace Paquet, 508 rue Muhammad Smiha, Casablanca; tel. (52) 2442694; fax (52) 2441173; e-mail alayams75@yahoo.fr; f. 2001; Arabic; weekly; Editor NOUREDDINE MIFTAH; circ. 22,163 (2008).

CGEM Mag: 23 blvd Muhammad Abdou, Palmiers, 20340 Casablanca; tel. (52) 2997000; fax (52) 2983971; e-mail mustaphamoulay@cgem.ma; internet www.cgem.ma; monthly; French; organ of the Confédération Générale des Entreprises du Maroc; Dir MIRIEM BENSALAH-CHAQROUN; Editor-in-Chief MUSTAPHA MOULAY.

Challenge Hebdo: 58 ave des Forces Armées Royales, Tour des Habous, 13ème étage, Casablanca; tel. (52) 2548150; fax (52) 2318094; e-mail redaction@challengehebdo.com; internet www.challengehebdo.com; weekly; French; business; Dir ADIL LAHLOU; Editor-in-Chief KHALID TRITKI; circ. 8,410 (2008/09).

Construire: 744 rue Boukrâa (angle rue Ouled Said), Résidence Hanane Jassim I, Bourgogne, Casablanca; tel. (52) 2220271; fax (52) 2273627; e-mail nlleconstruire@yahoo.fr; internet www.nouvelleconstruire.com; f. 1940; weekly; French; building and architecture magazine; Dir ABDELKRIM TALAL.

Femmes du Maroc: Immeuble Zénith I, Lot Attaoufik, route de Nouaceur, Sidi Maârouf, Casablanca; tel. (52) 2973949; fax (52) 2973929; internet www.femmesdumaroc.com; monthly; French; lifestyle magazine for women; Dir AÏCHA ZAÏMI SAKHRI; Editor-in-Chief GÉRALDINE DULAT; circ. 12,029 (2008/09).

La Gazette du Maroc: ave des Forces Armées Royales, Tour des Habous, 13ème étage, Casablanca; tel. (52) 2548150; fax (52) 2318094; e-mail info@lagazettedumaroc.com; internet www.lagazettedumaroc.com; weekly; French; Dir KAMAL LAHLOU; Editor-in-Chief ABD AL-LATIF EL-AZIZI; circ. 8,969 (2008).

Le Journal Hebdomadaire: 61 ave des Forces Armées Royales, BP 20000, Casablanca; tel. (52) 2546670; fax (52) 2446185; e-mail courrier@lejournal-press.com; internet www.lejournal-press.com; weekly; French; news, politics, economics; Dir ALI AMAR; Editor-in-Chief ABOUBAKR JAMAÏ; circ. 11,895 (2008/09).

Maroc Hebdo International: 4 rue des Flamants, Casablanca; tel. (52) 2238176; fax (52) 2981346; e-mail mhi@maroc-hebdo.press.ma; internet www.maroc-hebdo.com; f. 1991; weekly; French; Editor-in-Chief MUHAMMAD SELHAMI; circ. 10,510 (2008).

Nissae min al-Maghrib (Women of Morocco): Immeuble Zénith I, Lot Attaoufik, route de Nouaceur, Sidi Maârouf, Casablanca; tel. (52) 2973949; fax (52) 2973929; e-mail y.guennoun@akwagroup.com; monthly; Arabic edn of *Femmes du Maroc*; Editor-in-Chief KHADIJA SAEIL; circ. 30,703 (2008/09).

La Nouvelle Tribune: 320 blvd Zerktouni, angle rue Bouardel, Casablanca; tel. (52) 2424670; fax (52) 2200031; e-mail courrier@lanouvelletribune.com; internet www.lanouvelletribune.com; f. 1996; weekly (Thur.); French; Dir FAHD YATA; circ. 6,741 (2007).

Parade: Immeuble Zénith I, Lot Attaoufik, route de Nouaceur, Sidi Maârouf, Casablanca; tel. (52) 2973949; fax (52) 2973929; e-mail y .guennoun@akwagroup.com; monthly; French; Editor-in-Chief MARIA DAIF; circ. 4,716 (2006).

Perspectives du Maghreb: 8 blvd Yacoub el Mansour, 31 Maârif, Casablanca; tel. (52) 2257844; fax (52) 2257738; e-mail popmedia@ menara.ma; f. 2005; monthly; French; circ. 6,531 (2007).

La Quinzaine du Maroc: 53 rue el-Bakri, Casablanca; tel. (52) 2440033; fax (52) 2440426; e-mail mauro@editionsmauro.ma; internet www.quinzainedumaroc.com; f. 1951; fortnightly; English and French; visitors' guide; Dir HUBERT MAURO.

Le Reporter: 1 Sahat al-Istiqlal, 2ème étage, 20000 Casablanca; tel. (52) 2541103; fax (52) 2541105; e-mail lereporter@gmail.com; internet www.lereporter.ma; f. 1998; weekly; French; Dir BAHIA AMRANI.

TelQuel: 28 ave des Forces Armées Royales, Casablanca; tel. (52) 2220951; fax (52) 2220563; e-mail courrier@telquel.info; internet www.telquel-online.com; f. 2001; weekly; French; Dir AHMED BENCHEMSI; Editor-in-Chief KARIM BOUKHARI; circ. 23,172 (2008/09).

Version Homme: ave des Forces Armées Royales, Tour des Habous, 13ème étage, Casablanca; tel. (52) 2450089; fax (52) 2442213; e-mail redaction@versionhomme.com; internet www.versionhomme.com; monthly; lifestyle magazine for men; Dir ADIL LAHLOU; circ. 6,051 (2008/09).

La Vie éco: 5 blvd Abdallah Ben Yacine, 20300 Casablanca; tel. (52) 2450555; fax (52) 2304542; e-mail vieeco@marocnet.net.ma; internet www.lavieeco.com; f. 1921; weekly; French; economics; Dir FADEL AGOUMI; Editor-in-Chief SAÂD BEN MANSOUR; circ. 16,426 (2008/09).

La Vie Touristique Africaine: 17 rue El Houcine Ben Ali, Casablanca; tel. (52) 2227643; fax (52) 2275319; e-mail vietouristique@ wanadoo.net.ma; internet www.vietouristique.com; fortnightly; French; tourist information; Dir AHMED ZEGHARI.

Al-Watan al-An (The Nation Now): 33 rue Muhammad Bahi, Casablanca; tel. (52) 2251295; fax (52) 2251325; e-mail alwatanpress@menara.ma; internet www.alwatan.press.ma; weekly; Arabic; news; Editor ABDERRAHIM ARIRI; circ. 5,982 (2008).

Rabat

Al-Alam al-Amazighi: Éditions Amazigh, 5 rue Dakar, BP 477, Rabat; tel. 66-1767073 (mobile); fax (53) 7727283; e-mail lemondeamazigh@hotmail.com; weekly; Berber.

Asdae (Echoes): 30 ave Okba, Rabat; tel. (53) 7773706; e-mail asdae@menara.ma; internet www.asdae.com; weekly; Arabic; Dir and Editor-in-Chief EL-HASSAN ARBAI; circ. 1,415 (2008/09).

Da'ouat al-Haqq (Call of the Truth): al-Michwar al-Said, Rabat; tel. (53) 7766851; e-mail direction_haq@habous.gov.ma; internet www .daouatalhaq.ma; publ. by Ministry of Habous (Religious Endowments) and Islamic Affairs; f. 1957; monthly; Arabic.

Al-Mountakhab (The Team): 42 bis rue de Madagascar, Rabat; tel. (53) 7201774; fax (53) 7201776; e-mail contact@almountakhab.com; internet www.almountakhab.com; f. 1986; fortnightly; Arabic; sport; Dir MUSTAFA BADRI; Editor-in-Chief BADREDDINE IDRISSI; circ. 25,137 (2008/09).

Al-Tadamoun (Solidarity): Apt 1, Immeuble 6, rue Aguensous, ave Hassan II, Les Orangers, BP 1740, Rabat; tel. (53) 7730961; fax (53) 7738851; e-mail amdh1@mtds.com; internet www.amdh.org.ma; monthly; Arabic; organ of the Association marocaine des droits humains; Dir ABD AL-MAJID SEMLALI EL-HASANI.

Tangier

Achamal 2000: 137 blvd Prince Héritier, 1, Tangier; tel. (53) 9940391; fax (53) 9944216; e-mail ashamal@menara.ma; weekly; Arabic; Editor-in-Chief KHALID MECHBAL; circ. 7,912 (2008/09).

Le Journal de Tanger: 7 bis, rue Omar Ben Abdelaziz, Tangier; tel. (53) 9943008; fax (53) 9945709; e-mail direct@lejournaldetanger .com; internet www.lejournaldetanger.com; f. 1904; weekly; French, English, Spanish and Arabic; Dir ABDELHAK BAKHAT; Editor-in-Chief MUHAMMAD ABOUABDILLAH; circ. 8,776 (2008/09).

NEWS AGENCY

Maghreb Arabe Presse (MAP): 122 ave Allal Ben Abdallah, BP 1049, 10000 Rabat; tel. (53) 7279464; fax (53) 7279465; e-mail mapweb@map.co.ma; internet www.map.ma; f. 1959; Arabic, French, English and Spanish; state-owned; Dir-Gen. KHALIL HACHIMI IDRISSI.

PRESS ASSOCIATIONS

Fédération Marocaine des Editeurs de Journaux (FMEJ): Groupe Ecomedia, 70 blvd al-Massira al-Khadra, Casablanca; tel. (52) 2953600; fax (52) 2365926; f. 2005; Pres. ABDELMOUNAIM DILAMI.

Organisme de Justification de la Diffusion (OJD Maroc): 4 rue des Flamants, Casablanca; tel. (52) 2238176; fax (52) 2981346; e-mail asmae@maroc-hebdo.press.ma; internet www.ojd.ma; f. 2004; compiles circ. statistics; Pres. AISSAM FATHYA; Dir ASMAE HASSANI.

Publishers

Afrique Orient: 159 bis blvd Yacoub el-Mansour, Casablanca; tel. (52) 2259813; fax (52) 2440080; f. 1983; sociology, philosophy and translations; Dir MUSTAPHA CHAJII.

Belvisi: 17 rue Abbas Ibnou Farnass, BP 8044, Casablanca; tel. (52) 2250973; fax (52) 2986258; f. 1986.

Dar el-Kitab: place de la Mosquée, Quartier des Habous, BP 4018, Casablanca; tel. (52) 2305419; fax (52) 3026630; f. 1948; Arabic and French; philosophy, history, Africana, general and social sciences; state-controlled; Dir BOUTALEB ABDOU ABD AL-HAY; Gen. Man. KHADIJA EL-KASSIMI.

Editions Le Fennec: 89B blvd d'Anfa, 14ème étage, Casablanca; tel. (52) 2209314; fax (52) 2277702; e-mail info@lefennec.com; internet www.lefennec.com; f. 1987; fiction, social sciences; Dir LAYLA B. CHAOUNI.

Editions La Porte: 281 blvd Muhammad V, BP 331, Rabat; tel. (53) 7709958; fax (53) 7706476; e-mail la_porte@meganet.net.ma; law, guides, economics, educational books.

Les Editions Maghrébines: Quartier Industriel, blvd E, N 15, Sin Sebaâ, Casablanca; tel. (52) 2351797; fax (52) 2357892; f. 1962; general non-fiction.

Les Editions Toubkal: Immeuble I. G. A, pl. de la Gare Voyageurs, Bélvèdere, 20300 Casablanca; tel. and fax (52) 22342323; e-mail contact@toubkal.ma; internet www.toubkal.ma; f. 1985; economy, history, social sciences, literature, educational books; Dir ABDELJALIL NADEM.

Malika Editions: 60 blvd Yacoub el-Mansour, 20100 Casablanca; tel. (52) 2235688; fax (52) 2251651; e-mail edmalika@connectcom.net .ma; internet www.malikaedition.com; art publications.

Tarik Editions: 321 route el-Jadida, 20390 Casablanca; tel. (52) 2259007; fax (52) 2232550; e-mail tarik.edition@gmail.com; internet www.tarikeditions.com; f. 2000; history and social sciences; Dir BICHR BENNANI.

Yomad: 4 rue Melouiya, Apt 7, Agdal, Rabat; tel. (53) 7686430; fax (53) 7686431; e-mail yomadeditions@yahoo.com; internet www .yomadeditions.net; f. 1998; children's literature; Dir NADIA ESSALMI.

GOVERNMENT PUBLISHING HOUSE

Imprimerie Officielle: ave Yacoub el-Mansour, Rabat-Chellah; tel. (53) 7765024; fax (53) 7765179.

Broadcasting and Communications

TELECOMMUNICATIONS

inwi: Lot la Colline II, Sidi Maârouf, 20190 Casablanca; tel. (52) 2900000; internet www.inwi.ma; f. 2009 as Wana following award of third GSM licence; mobile telephone and internet services launched Feb. 2010; Dir-Gen. FRÉDÉRIC DEBORD.

Itissalat al-Maghrib—Maroc Télécom: ave Annakhil Hay Riad, Rabat; tel. (53) 7719000; fax (53) 7714860; e-mail webmaster@iam .ma; internet www.iam.ma; f. 1998; privatized in 2004; Vivendi SA (France) holds a 53% stake; Chair. ABDESLAM AHIZOUNE.

Méditel: Twin Centre, angle blvd Zerktouni et blvd Massira al-Khadra, Casablanca; e-mail hassan.bouchachia@meditel.ma; internet www.meditel.ma; f. 1999; Caisse de Dépôt et de Gestion (CDG) and FinanceCom hold a 64.4% stake; provides national mobile telecommunications services; Dir-Gen. MUHAMMAD EL-MANDJRA; Chair. OTHMAN BENJELLOUN; 8.63m. subscribers (June 2009).

Regulatory Authority

Agence Nationale de Réglementation des Télécommunications (ANRT): Centre d'Affaires, blvd al-Riad, BP 2939, Hay Riad, 10100 Rabat; tel. (53) 7718400; fax (53) 7203862; e-mail com@anrt.ma; internet www.anrt.ma; f. 1998; Dir-Gen. AZDIR EL-MOUNTASSIR BILLAH.

BROADCASTING

Morocco can receive broadcasts from Spanish radio stations, and the main Spanish television channels can also be received in northern Morocco.

Radio

Radio Casablanca: c/o Loukt s.a.r.l, BP 16011, Casa Principal, 20001 Casablanca; e-mail i-rc@maroc.net; internet www.maroc.net/rc; f. 1996; Gen. Man. AMINE ZARY.

Radio Méditerranée Internationale: 3 rue M'sallah, BP 2055, 9000 Tangier; tel. (53) 9936363; fax (53) 9935755; e-mail medi1@medi1.com; internet www.medi1.com; Arabic and French; Man. Dir PIERRE CASALTA.

Voice of America Radio Station in Tangier: c/o US Consulate-General, chemin des Amoureux, Tangier.

Television

Société Nationale de Radiodiffusion et de Télévision: 1 rue el-Brihi, BP 1042, 1000 Rabat; tel. (53) 7685100; fax (53) 7733733; internet www.snrt.ma; govt station; transmission commenced 1962; 45 hours weekly; French and Arabic; carries commercial advertising; Dir-Gen. and Dir Television FAIÇAL LARAICHI.

SOREAD 2M: Société d'études et de réalisations audiovisuelles, km 7.3, route de Rabat, Aïn-Sebaâ, Casablanca; tel. (52) 2667373; fax (52) 2677856; e-mail portail@tv2m.co.ma; internet www.2m.tv; f. 1988; transmission commenced 1989; public television channel; owned by Moroccan Govt (72%) and by private national foreign concerns; broadcasting in French and Arabic; Man. Dir SAMI EL-JAI.

Finance

(cap. = capital; res = reserves; dep. = deposits; m. = million; br(s) = branch(es); amounts in dirhams)

BANKING

Central Bank

Bank Al-Maghrib: 277 ave Muhammad V, BP 445, Rabat; tel. (53) 7702626; fax (53) 7706667; e-mail webmaster@bkam.ma; internet www.bkam.ma; f. 1959 as Banque du Maroc; name changed as above in 1987; bank of issue; cap. 500m., res 5,033m., dep. 47,366m. (Dec. 2009); Gov. ABDELLATIF JOUAHRI; Gen. Man. ABDELLATIF FAOUZI; 20 brs.

Other Banks

Attijariwafa Bank: 2 blvd Moulay Youssef, BP 11141, 20000 Casablanca; tel. (52) 2298888; fax (52) 2294125; e-mail contact@attijariwafa.com; internet www.attijariwafabank.com; f. 2004 by merger between Banque Commerciale du Maroc SA and Wafabank; 33.2% owned by Groupe ONA, 14.6% by Grupo Santander (Spain); cap. 1,929m., res 4,152m., dep. 222,003m. (Dec. 2010); Pres. and Dir-Gen. MUHAMMAD EL-KETTANI.

Banque Centrale Populaire (Crédit Populaire du Maroc): 101 blvd Muhammad Zerktouni, BP 10622, 21100 Casablanca; tel. (52) 2202533; fax (52) 2229699; e-mail bcp@banquepopulairemorocco.ma; internet www.cpm.co.ma; f. 1961; 51% state-owned, 49% privately owned; merged with Société Marocaine de Dépot et Crédit in 2003; cap. 6,111m., res 12,605m., dep. 171,335m. (Dec. 2010); Pres. and Man. Dir MUHAMMAD BENCHAÂBOUNE; 530 brs.

Banque Marocaine du Commerce Extérieur SA (BMCE): 140 ave Hassan II, BP 13425, 20000 Casablanca; tel. (52) 2200325; fax (52) 2200512; e-mail communicationfinanciere@bmcebank.co.ma; internet www.bmcebank.ma; f. 1959; transferred to majority private ownership in 1995; cap. 1,719m., res 8,813m., dep. 149,906m. (Dec. 2011); Pres. and Dir-Gen. OTHMAN BENJELLOUN; 310 domestic brs and 3 brs abroad.

Banque Marocaine pour le Commerce et l'Industrie SA (BMCI): 26 pl. des Nations Unies, BP 15573, Casablanca; tel. (52) 22461000; fax (52) 22299406; e-mail adiba.lahbabi@africa.bnpparibas.com; internet www.bmci.ma; f. 1964; 65.05% owned by BNP Paribas (France); cap. 1,281m., res 5,625m., dep. 59,728m. (Dec. 2011); Chair. MOURAD CHERIF; 260 brs.

Citibank-Maghreb: Zénith Millenium, Immeuble 1, Lot Attaoufik, Sidi Maârouf, BP 13362, Casablanca; tel. (52) 2489600; fax (52) 2974197; f. 1967; cap. and res 194.0m., total assets 1,211.0m. (Dec. 2003); Pres. NUHAD SALIBA; 2 brs.

Crédit Agricole du Maroc SA: 29 rue Abou Faris al-Marini, BP 49, 10000 Rabat; tel. (53) 7208219; fax (53) 7445063; e-mail m_kettani@creditagricole.ma; internet www.creditagricole.ma; f. 1961 as Caisse Nationale de Crédit Agricole; became a limited co and adopted present name in 2003; 78% owned by Ministry of the Economy and Finance; cap. 2,820m., res –1,197m., dep. 60,843m. (Dec. 2009); Chair. TARIQ SIJILMASSI.

Crédit Immobilier et Hôtelier: 187 ave Hassan II, Casablanca; tel. (52) 2479000; fax (52) 2479363; e-mail info-client@cih.co.ma; internet www.cih.co.ma; f. 1920; transferred to majority private ownership in 1995; cap. 2,660m., res 5m., dep. 20,112m. (Dec. 2011); Pres. and CEO AHMAD RAHHOU; 91 brs.

Crédit du Maroc SA: 48–58 blvd Muhammad V, BP 13579, 20000 Casablanca; tel. (52) 2477477; fax (52) 2477127; e-mail mohammadine.menjra@ca-cdm.ma; internet www.cdm.co.ma; f. 1963 as Crédit Lyonnais Maroc; name changed as above in 1966; 52.6% owned by Crédit Agricole (France); cap. 2,586m., res 382m., dep. 40,014m. (Dec. 2011); Chair. PIERRE-LOUIS BOISSIERE; 264 domestic brs, 1 br. abroad.

Société Générale Marocaine de Banques SA: 55 blvd Abdelmoumen, BP 13090, 21100 Casablanca; tel. (52) 2438888; fax (52) 2234931; e-mail contact@sgmaroc.com; internet www.sgmaroc.com; f. 1962; cap. 2,050m., res 3,414m., dep. 54,878m. (Dec. 2010); Pres. ALBERT LE DIRAC'H; 300 brs.

STOCK EXCHANGE

Bourse de Casablanca: angle ave des Forces Armées Royales et rue Muhammad Errachid, Casablanca; tel. (52) 2452626; fax (52) 2452625; e-mail contact@casablanca-bourse.com; internet www.casablanca-bourse.com; f. 1929; Chair. AOMAR YIDAR; CEO K. HAJJI.

INSURANCE

Atlanta Assurances: 181 blvd d'Anfa, BP 13685, 20001 Casablanca; tel. (52) 2957676; fax (52) 2369812; e-mail info@atlanta.ma; internet www.atlanta.ma; f. 1947; cap. 591.6m.; Dir-Gen. MUHAMMAD HASSAN BENSALAH.

AXA Assurance Maroc: 120–122 ave Hassan II, 20000 Casablanca; tel. (52) 2889292 fax (52) 2889189; e-mail communication@axa.ma; internet www.axa.ma; cap. 900m.; Pres. and Dir-Gen. MICHEL HASCOET.

CNIA Saada Assurance: 216 blvd Muhammad Zerktouni, 20000 Casablanca; tel. (52) 2474040; fax (52) 2206081; internet www.cniasaada.ma; f. 2009 by merger of CNIA Assurance and Es-Saada; 53% owned by Groupe Saham; Pres. and Dir-Gen. MOULAY HAFID ELALAMY.

Compagnie d'Assurances et de Réassurances SANAD: 181 blvd d'Anfa, Tours Balzac, Casablanca; tel. (52) 2957878; fax (52) 2360406; e-mail webmaster@sanad.ma; internet www.sanad.ma; f. 1946; cap. 125m.; Chair. MUHAMMAD HASSAN BENSALAH; Dir-Gen. ABDELTIF TAHIRI.

La Marocaine Vie: 37 blvd Moulay Youssef, Casablanca; tel. (52) 2206320; fax (52) 2297307; f. 1978; 83% owned by Société Générale Marocaine de Banques SA; Pres. MARC DUVAL; Gen. Man. KARIM MOULTAKI.

Mutuelle Centrale Marocaine d'Assurances (MCMA): 16 rue Abou Inane, BP 27, Rabat; tel. (53) 7767800; fax (53) 7766440; f. 1968; part of the MAMDA-MCMA group; CEO HICHAM BELMRAH.

Mutuelle d'Assurances des Transporteurs Unis (MATU): 215 blvd Muhammad Zerktouni, Casablanca; tel. (52) 2954500; fax (52) 2367721; e-mail info@matu.ma; Pres. HADJ OMAR BENNOUNA; Dir-Gen. AHMAD MAZOUZ.

RMA Watanya: 83 ave des Forces Armées Royales, 20000 Casablanca; tel. (52) 2312163; fax (52) 2313137; e-mail contact@rmawatanya.com; internet www.rmawatanya.com; f. 2005 by merger of Al-Wataniya and La Royale Marocaine d'Assurances; cap. 1,774m.; Pres. OTHMAN BENJELLOUN.

Société Centrale de Réassurance (SCR): Tour Atlas, pl. Zallaqa, BP 13183, Casablanca; tel. (52) 2460400; fax (52) 2460460; e-mail scr@scrmaroc.com; internet www.scrmaroc.com; f. 1960; cap. 30m.; Chair. AHMAD ZINOUN; Man. Dir MUHAMMAD LARBI NALI.

Société Marocaine d'Assurance à l'Exportation (SMAEX): 24 rue Ali Abderrazak, BP 15953, Casablanca; tel. (52) 2982000; fax (52) 2252070; e-mail smaex@smaex.com; internet www.smaex.com; f. 1988; insurance for exporters in the public and private sectors; assistance for export promotion; Pres. and Dir-Gen. NEZHA LAHRICHI; Asst Dir-Gen. ABDERRAZZAK M'HAIMDAT.

WAFA Assurance: 1–3 blvd Abd al-Moumen, BP 13420, 20001 Casablanca; tel. (52) 2224575; fax (52) 2209103; e-mail webmaster@wafaassurance.com; internet www.attijariwafabank.com; subsidiary of Attijariwafa Bank; Pres. ABDELAZIZ ALAMI; CEO MUHAMMAD EL-KETTANI.

Zurich Assurances Maroc: 166 angle Zerktouni et rue Hafid Ibrahim, 20000 Casablanca; tel. (52) 22499808; fax (52) 22491733; e-mail customerservice@zurich.com; f. 1954; cap. 90m.; all kinds of insurance; Pres and Dir-Gen. BERTO FISLER.

Insurance Association

Fédération Marocaine des Sociétés d'Assurances et de Réassurances: 154 blvd d'Anfa, Casablanca; tel. (52) 2391850; fax (52) 2391854; e-mail contact@fmsar.ma; internet www.fmsar.org.ma; f. 1958; 15 mem. cos; Pres. MUHAMMAD HASSAN BENSALAH.

Trade and Industry

GOVERNMENT AGENCIES

Agence National pour la Promotion de Petite et Moyenne Entreprise (ANPME): 10 rue Gandhi, BP 211, 10001 Rabat; tel. (53) 7708460; fax (53) 7707695; e-mail info@anpme.ma; internet www.anpme.ma; f. 1973 as the Office pour le Développement Industriel; name changed as above in 2002; state agency to develop industry; Dir-Gen. LATIFA ECHIHABI.

Centre Marocain de Promotion des Exportations (CMPE): 23 rue Ibnou Majed el-Bahar, BP 10937, 20000 Casablanca; tel. (52) 2302210; fax (52) 2301793; e-mail info@marocexport.ma; internet www.cmpe.org.ma; f. 1980; state org. for promotion of exports; Man. Dir SAAD BEN ABDALLAH.

Direction des Entreprises Publiques et de la Privatisation (DEPP): rue Haj Ahmed Cherkaoui, Quartier Administratif, Agdal, Rabat; tel. (53) 7689303; fax (53) 7689347; e-mail talbi@depp.finances.gov.ma; part of the Ministry of the Economy and Finance; in charge of regulation, restructuring and privatization of state enterprises; Dir ABDELAZIZ TALBI.

Office National des Hydrocarbures et des Mines (ONHYM): 5 ave Moulay Hassan, BP 99, 10050 Rabat; tel. (53) 7239898; fax (53) 7709411; e-mail presse@onhym.com; internet www.onhym.com; f. 2003 to succeed Bureau de Recherches et de Participations Minières and Office National de Recherches et d'Exploitations Pétrolières; state agency conducting exploration, valorization and exploitation of hydrocarbons and mineral resources; Dir-Gen. AMINA BENKHADRA.

Société de Gestion des Terres Agricoles (SOGETA): 35 rue Daïet-Erroumi, BP 731, Agdal, Rabat; tel. (53) 7772778; fax (53) 7772765; f. 1973; oversees use of agricultural land; Man. Dir BACHIR SAOUD.

DEVELOPMENT ORGANIZATIONS

Caisse de Dépôt et de Gestion: pl. Moulay el-Hassan, BP 408, 10001 Rabat; tel. (53) 7669000; fax (53) 7763849; e-mail cdg@cdg.ma; internet www.cdg.ma; f. 1959; finances small-scale projects; Dir-Gen. ANASS ALAMI; Sec.-Gen. SAÏD LAFTIT.

Caisse Marocaine des Marchés (Marketing Fund): 101 blvd Abdelmoumen, 4e étage, 20100 Casablanca; tel. (52) 22472683; fax (52) 22472554; e-mail s.benbrahim@cmm.ma; internet www.cmm.ma; f. 1950; cap. 70m. dirhams.

Société de Développement Agricole (SODEA): ave Hadj Ahmed Cherkaoui, BP 6280, Rabat; tel. (53) 7677953; fax (53) 7771514; internet www.sodea.com; f. 1972; state agricultural devt org.; Man. Dir AHMED HAJJAJI.

Société Nationale d'Investissement (SNI): 60 rue d'Alger, BP 38, 20000 Casablanca; tel. (52) 2224102; fax (52) 2484303; f. 1966; transferred to majority private ownership in 1994; cap. 10,900m. dirhams; Pres. HASSAN BOUHEMOU; Sec.-Gen. SAÂD BENDIDI.

CHAMBERS OF COMMERCE

Fédération des Chambres Marocaines de Commerce, d'Industrie et de Services (FCMCIS): 6 rue Erfoud, BP 218, Hassan, Rabat; tel. (53) 7767078; fax (53) 7767896; e-mail fcmcis@menara.ma; internet www.fcmcis.ma; f. 1962; groups the 28 Chambers of Commerce and Industry; Pres. DRISS HOUAT; Dir-Gen. MUHAMMAD LARBI EL-HARRAS.

Chambre de Commerce, d'Industrie et de Services de la Wilaya de Rabat-Salé: 1 rue Gandhi, BP 131, Rabat; tel. (53) 7706444; fax (53) 7706768; e-mail info@rabat.cci.ma; internet www.ccirabat.ma; Pres. OMAR DERRAJI.

Chambre de Commerce, d'Industrie et de Services de la Wilaya du Grand Casablanca: 98 blvd Muhammad V, BP 423, Casablanca; tel. (52) 2264327; fax (52) 2268436; e-mail ccisc@ccisc.gov.ma; internet www.ccisc.gov.ma; Pres. HASSAN BERKANI.

INDUSTRIAL AND TRADE ASSOCIATIONS

Office National Interprofessionnel des Céréales et des Légumineuses (ONICL): 3 ave Moulay Hassan, BP 154, Rabat; tel. (53) 7217300; fax (53) 7709626; e-mail directeur@onicl.org.ma; internet www.onicl.org.ma; f. 1937; Dir-Gen. ABDELLATIF GUEDIRA.

Office National des Pêches: 15 rue Lieutenant Mahroud, BP 16243, 20300 Casablanca; tel. (52) 2242084; fax (52) 2242305; e-mail onp@onp.co.ma; internet www.onp.co.ma; f. 1969; state fishing org.; Man. Dir MAJID KAISSAR EL-GHAIB.

EMPLOYERS' ORGANIZATIONS

Association Marocaine des Exporteurs (ASMEX): 36B blvd Anfa, Casablanca; tel. (52) 2261033; fax (52) 2484191; e-mail asmex@asmex.org; internet www.asmex.org; f. 1982; Pres. ABDELLATIF BEN MADANI.

Association Marocaine des Industries du Textile et de l'Habillement (AMITH): 92 blvd Moulay Rachid, Casablanca; tel. (52) 2942086; fax (52) 2940587; e-mail amith@amith.org.ma; internet www.textile.ma; f. 1960; 850 mems; textiles, knitwear and ready-made garment mfrs; Pres. MUSTAPHA SAJID; Dir-Gen. MUHAMMAD TAZI.

Association des Producteurs d'Agrumes du Maroc (ASPAM): 283 blvd Zerktouni, Casablanca; tel. (52) 2363946; fax (52) 2364041; e-mail aspam@menara.ma; f. 1958; links Moroccan citrus growers; has its own processing plants; Pres. HASSAN LYOUSSI.

Association Professionnelle des Agents Maritimes, Consignataires de Navires, et Courtiers d'Affrètement du Maroc (APRAM): 219 blvd des Forces Armées Royales, 5ème étage, 20000 Casablanca; tel. (52) 2541112; fax (52) 2541415; e-mail apram@wanadoopro.ma; internet www.apram.ma; f. 1999; 37 mems; Pres. ABDELAZIZ MANTRACH.

Association Professionnelle des Cimentiers (APC): Villa APC, Lot Allaymoune 1, 476 Hay Almatar, Casablanca; tel. (52) 2936660; fax (52) 2904491; e-mail apc@menara.ma; internet www.apc.ma; 4 mems; cement mfrs; Pres. JEAN-MARIE SCHMITZ.

Confédération Générale des Entreprises du Maroc (CGEM): 23 blvd Muhammad Abdou, Quartier Palmiers, 20100 Casablanca; tel. (52) 2997000; fax (52) 2983971; e-mail cgem@cgem.ma; internet www.cgem.ma; 25 affiliated feds; Pres. MUHAMMAD HORANI.

UTILITIES

Electricity and Water

Office National de l'Eau Potable (ONEP): Station de Traitement ONEP, ave Muhammad Belhassan El Ouazzani, BP 10002 Rabat-Chellah, Rabat; tel. (53) 7759600; fax (53) 7759106; e-mail onepbo@onep.ma; internet www.onep.ma; f. 1972; responsible for drinking-water supply; Dir-Gen. ALI FASSI FIHRI.

Office National de l'Electricité (ONE): 65 rue Othman Ben Affan, BP 13498, 20001 Casablanca; tel. (52) 2668080; fax (52) 2220038; e-mail offelec@one.org.ma; internet www.one.org.ma; f. 1963; state electricity authority; Dir-Gen. ALI FASSI FIHRI.

Gas

Afriquia Gaz: 139 blvd Moulay Ismail, Aïn Sebaâ, 20700 Casablanca; tel. (52) 22639600; fax (52) 22639666; e-mail r.idrissi@akwagroup.com; internet www.afriquiagaz.com; f. 1992; Morocco's leading gas distributor; Pres. ALI WAKRIM; Dir-Gen. TAWFIK HAMOUMI.

MAJOR COMPANIES

Brasseries du Maroc: blvd Ahl Loghlam, BP 2660, Aïn Sebaâ, 20251 Casablanca; tel. (52) 2754646; fax (52) 2740792; e-mail gbm@gbm.ma; internet www.brasseries-maroc.com; f. 1919; distillery, brewery and producer of soft drinks; Chair. and Man. Dir PIERRE CASTEL; 2,000 employees.

Charbonnages du Maroc: Centre Minier, 60550 Jerada; tel. (5) 5821048; fax (5) 5821158; f. 1946; coal mining; Dir-Gen. BELNKADAN DRISS; 5,300 employees.

Chérifienne de Travaux Africains: blvd du Fourat, Casablanca; tel. (52) 2323317; fax (52) 2324746; f. 1960; building and civil engineering contractors; cap. 10m. dirhams; Dir-Gen. SERGE BERDUGO; 1,500 employees.

Compagnie Générale Immobilière (CGI): Espace Oudayas, ave Mehdi Ben Barka, BP 2177, Hay Riad, Rabat; tel. (53) 7239494; fax (53) 7563225; e-mail contact@cgi.ma; internet www.cgi.ma; f. 1960; real estate devt; cap. 1,840m. dirhams (2009); Dir-Gen. MUHAMMAD ALI GHANNAM.

Compagnie Marocaine des Hydrocarbures: angle rond Point des Sports et rue Point du Jour, blvd Abd al-Latif Benkaddour, BP 6180, Casablanca; tel. (52) 2424300; fax (52) 2207955; e-mail info@cmh.co.ma; internet www.cmh.co.ma; marketing of petroleum and oil products; cap. 33m. dirhams; CEO HASSAN AGZENAI.

Complexe Textile de Fès (COTEF): Quartier Industriel Sidi Brahim, route de Sefrou, BP 2267, 30000 Fez; tel. (52) 5641309; fax (52) 5641354; e-mail cotef@fesnet.net.ma; f. 1967; production of yarns and textiles; Pres. ALAMI TAZI; 1,100 employees.

COSUMAR: 8 rue el Mouatamid Ibnou Abbad, BP 3098, 20300 Casablanca; tel. (52) 5678300; fax (52) 2241071; internet www.cosumar.co.ma; f. 1967; sugar refining and trading; cap. 419m. dirhams; Pres. and Dir-Gen. MUHAMMAD FIRKAT; 3,300 employees.

Douja Promotion Group Addoha: km 7, autoroute de Rabat, Ain Sebaâ, 20600 Casablanca; tel. (52) 2679900; fax (52) 2351763; e-mail contact@groupeaddoha.com; internet www.groupeaddoha.com;

f. 1988; real estate devt; cap. 2,835m. dirhams (2009); Pres. and Dir-Gen. ANAS SEFRIOUI.

Les Grandes Marques et Conserveries Chérifiennes Réunies: 3 route el-Jadida, Lot Fadloullah, 1 Hay Erraha, 20200 Casablanca; tel. (52) 2777299; fax (52) 2984323; e-mail kav@lgmcindustries.com; internet www.lgmcindustries.com; f. 1946; fish and food processing and canning; cap. 16.2m. dirhams; Pres. MUHAMMAD EL-JAMALI; 1,685 employees.

Lafarge Ciments: 6 route de Mekka, Quartier les Crêtes, BP 7234, Casablanca; tel. (52) 2524972; fax (52) 2504446; internet www.lafarge.ma; f. 1928; mfrs of cement and building materials; cap. 1,746m. dirhams; Dir-Gen. SAÂD SEBBAR.

Manufacture Nationale Textile (MANATEX): 164 blvd de la Gironde, 20500 Casablanca; tel. (52) 2286655; fax (52) 2282530; f. 1957; mfrs of textiles and furnishings; Pres. OMAR KETTANI; 800 employees.

Office Chérifien des Phosphates (OCP): 2 rue al-Abtal, Hay Erraha, 20200 Casablanca; tel. (52) 2230025; fax (52) 2230635; e-mail contact@ocpgroup.ma; internet www.ocpgroup.ma; f. 1921; state co producing and marketing rock phosphates and derivatives; CEO MUSTAPHA TERRAB.

ONA: 60 rue d'Alger, BP 13657, 20001 Casablanca; tel. (52) 2224102; fax (52) 2299318; e-mail ona@ona.co.ma; internet www.ona.co.ma; f. 1919; fmrly Omnium Nord Africain; largest private co in Morocco; owns over 100 subsidiaries in food, mining, energy, distribution, telecommunications, real estate and insurance industries; cap. 1,700m. dirhams (2006); Chair. and CEO SAÂD BENDIDI; 120 employees.

Phosphates de Boucraa SA (PHOSBOUCRAA): Immeuble OCP, angle route d'el Jadida et blvd de la Grande Ceinture, 20200 Casablanca; tel. (52) 2230025; fax (52) 2230565; f. 1962; production and processing of phosphate rock; cap. 328m. dirhams; Dir MAOULAÏNINE MAOULAÏNINE; 3,000 employees.

Société d'Exploitation des Mines du Rif (SEFERIF): 30 Abou-Faris el-Marini, BP 436, Rabat; tel. (7) 7766350; nationalized 1967; open and underground mines produce iron ore for export and for the projected Nador iron and steel complex; Man. Dir MUHAMMAD HARRAK.

Société Marocaine de Constructions Automobiles (SOMACA): km 12, autoroute de Rabat, BP 2628, Ain Sebaâ, 20600 Casablanca; tel. (52) 2754848; fax (52) 2754822; f. 1959; assembly of motor vehicles; owned by Renault; Dir-Gen. FABRICE DELECROIX; 823 employees.

Société Nationale de Sidérurgie (SONASID): Twin Centre, angle blvd Zerktouni et blvd Massira al-Khadra, Tour A, 18ème étage, Casablanca; tel. (52) 2954100; fax (52) 2958643; e-mail l.bouchourl@sonasid.ma; internet www.sonasid.ma; f. 1974; mfrs of construction and building materials; cap. 390m. dirhams; transferred to private ownership in 1997; Dir-Gen. AYOUB AZAMI; 900 employees.

Société Nouvelle des Conduites d'Eau (SNCE): Résidence Kays Sahat Rabia, Al Adaouiya Agdal, 10000 Rabat; tel. (53) 7776714; fax (53) 7776674; f. 1961; manufacture of steel and cast-iron pipes and materials; cap. 156.8m. dirhams; Chair. KAMAL LARAQUI; Dir-Gen. ABDELJEBBAR LAHBABI; 3,000 employees.

TRADE UNIONS

Confédération Démocratique du Travail (CDT): 64 rue al-Mourtada, Quartier Palmier, BP 13576, Casablanca; tel. (52) 2994470; fax (52) 2994473; e-mail cdtmaroc@cdt.ma; internet www.cdt.ma; f. 1978; Sec.-Gen. NOUBIR EL-AMAOUI.

Fédération Démocratique du Travail (FDT): 12 rue Muhammad Diouri, Sidi Belyoute, Casablanca; tel. (52) 2446362; fax (52) 2446365; e-mail fdt@menara.ma; internet www.fdt.ma; f. 2003 by fmr mems of CDT associated with USFP; Sec.-Gen. ABD EL-HAMID FATIHI.

Union Générale des Travailleurs du Maroc (UGTM): 43 rue Mansour Eddahbi, blvd Allal Ben Abdellah, Rabat; tel. (53) 7702396; fax (53) 7736192; e-mail info@ugtm.ma; internet www.ugtm.ma; f. 1960; associated with Istiqlal; supported by unions not affiliated to UMT; Sec.-Gen. HAMID CHABAT.

Union Marocaine du Travail (UMT): Bourse du Travail, 232 ave des Forces Armées Royales, 20000 Casablanca; tel. (52) 2302292; fax (52) 2307854; f. 1955; left-wing; most unions are affiliated; Sec.-Gen. MILOUDI MOUKHARIK.

Union Nationale du Travail du Maroc (UNTM): 352 ave Muhammad V, Immeuble Saâda, Rabat; tel. (53) 7793196; fax (53) 7263546; f. 1976; Islamist, associated with the PJD; Sec.-Gen. MUHAMMAD YATIM.

Transport

Société Nationale des Transports et de la Logistique (SNTL): rue al-Fadila, Quartier Industriel, BP 114, Chellah, Rabat; tel. (53) 7289300; fax (53) 7797850; e-mail ahachemi@sntl.ma; internet www.sntl.ma; f. 1958; Dir-Gen. OUSSAMA LOUDGHIRI.

RAILWAYS

In 2010 the total length of Moroccan railways was 2,109 route-km. All services are nationalized. Plans for a four-line, 76-km tram system in Casablanca were approved in 2008; line 1, comprising 50 stations on a 29-km route, was inaugurated in December 2012. Meanwhile, a feasibility study into plans for a 39-km railway tunnel under the Strait of Gibraltar linking Morocco and Spain commenced in 2007; however, by mid-2013 the project had yet to receive formal approval. In December 2010 Morocco and France signed an agreement whereby France would provide rolling stock and equipment for the first African high-speed train link; the new line was scheduled to run between Casablanca and Tangier by the end of 2015, and subsequently to be extended to other major Moroccan cities.

Office National des Chemins de Fer (ONCF): 8 bis rue Abderrahmane el-Ghafiki, Rabat-Agdal; tel. (53) 7774747; fax (53) 7774480; e-mail ketary@oncf.ma; internet www.oncf.ma; f. 1963; administers all Morocco's railways; Dir-Gen. MUHAMMAD RABIE KHLIE.

ROADS

In 2010 there were 58,395 km of roads, of which 1,096 km were motorways, 11,364 km were highways, main or national roads, and 10,091 km were secondary or regional roads.

Autoroutes du Maroc (ADM): Hay Riad, Rabat; tel. (53) 7711056; fax (53) 7711059; e-mail naitbrahim.ismail@adm.co.ma; internet www.adm.co.ma; responsible for the construction and upkeep of Morocco's motorway network; Dir-Gen. OTMANE FASSI FIHRI.

Compagnie de Transports au Maroc (CTM—SA): km 13.5, autoroute Casablanca–Rabat, Casablanca; tel. (52) 2762100; fax (52) 2765428; internet www.ctm.ma; f. 1919; 18 agencies nationwide; privatized in 1993, with 40% of shares reserved for Moroccan citizens; Pres. and Dir-Gen. MUHAMMAD BOUDA.

SHIPPING

According to official figures, Morocco's ports handled 96m. metric tons of goods in 2011. The most important ports, in terms of the volume of goods handled, are Casablanca, Jorf Lasfar, Safi and Mohammedia. Tangier is the principal port for passenger services. The first phase of a new container port, Tangier-Med, which had an initial annual capacity of 3.5m. containers, became operational in 2007. Construction work on a second phase began in 2009, which was expected to increase capacity to 8.5m. containers per year on its completion in 2015. At 31 December 2012 Morocco's flag registered fleet consisted of 409 vessels, with a combined displacement of 364,598 grt, of which 297 were fish carriers and six were general cargo ships.

Port Authorities

Agence Nationale des Ports (ANP): f. 2006, following division of Office d'Exploitation des Ports; regulator of port activity; also responsible for development and maintenance of port facilities; Dir-Gen. MUHAMMAD JAMAL BENJELLOUN.

Société d'Exploitation des Ports (Marsa Maroc): 175 blvd Zerktouni, 20100 Casablanca; tel. (52) 2258258; fax (52) 2995217; internet www.sodep.co.ma; f. 2006, following division of Office d'Exploitation des Ports; responsible for management of port terminals and quayside facilities; Pres. MUHAMMAD ABDELJALIL.

Principal Shipping Companies

Agence Med SARL: 3 rue ibn Rochd, 90000 Tangier; tel. (53) 9935875; fax (53) 9933239; e-mail agencemed@menara.ma; f. 1904; owned by the Bland Group; also at Agadir, Casablanca, Jorf Lasfar, Nador and Safi; Operations Man. MUHAMMAD CHATT.

Compagnie Chérifienne d'Armement: 5 blvd Abdallah Ben Yacine, 21700 Casablanca; tel. (52) 2309455; fax (52) 2301186; f. 1929; regular services to Europe; Man. Dir MAX KADOCH.

Compagnie Marocaine d'Agences Maritimes (COMARINE): 45 ave des Forces Armées Royales, BP 60, 20000 Casablanca; tel. (52) 2548510; fax (52) 2548570; e-mail comarine@comarine.co.ma.

Compagnie Marocaine de Navigation (COMANAV): 7 blvd de la Résistance, BP 628, Casablanca 20300; tel. (52) 2303012; fax (52) 2302006; e-mail comanav@comanav.co.ma; internet www.comanav.ma; f. 1946 as Cie Franco-Chérifienne de Navigation; name changed as above in 1959; privatization pending; regular services to European, Middle Eastern and West African ports; tramping; Pres. and Dir-Gen. TOUFIQ IBRAHIMI; Sec.-Gen. MEHDI BELGHITI; 12 agencies.

Intercona: 6 rue Méditérranée, Edifici Coficom, Tangier 90000; tel. (53) 9945907; fax (53) 9945909; e-mail intercona-sa@menara.ma; internet intercona.com; f. 1943; shipping agent; Pres. VICENTE JORRO.

Limadet-ferry: 3 rue ibn Rochd, Tangier; tel. (53) 933639; fax (53) 937173; e-mail headoffice@limadet.com; f. 1966; daily services between Algeciras (Spain) and Tangier; Dir-Gen. RACHID BEN MANSOUR.

Société Marocaine de Navigation Atlas: 81 ave Houmane el-Fatouaki, 21000 Casablanca; tel. (52) 2224190; fax (52) 2200164; e-mail atlas@marbar.co.ma; f. 1976; Chair. HASSAN CHAMI; Man. Dir MUHAMMAD SLAOUI.

Voyages Paquet: 65 ave des Forces Armées Royales, 20000 Casablanca; tel. (52) 2761941; fax (52) 2442108; f. 1970; Pres. MUHAMMAD ELOUALI ELALAMI; Dir-Gen. NAÏMA BAKALI ELOUALI ELALAMI.

CIVIL AVIATION

The main international airports are at Casablanca (King Muhammad V), Rabat, Tangier, Marrakesh, Agadir Inezgane, Fez, Oujda, al-Hocima, el-Aaiún, Ouarzazate, Agadir al-Massira and Nador. The completion of a second runway at King Muhammad V airport was followed by the inauguration, in September 2007, of a second terminal, which increased the airport's annual passenger capacity from 5m. to 11m.

Jet4you: 4 Lot la Colline, Sidi Maarouf, 20270 Casablanca; fax (52) 2584228; internet www.jet4you.com; f. 2006; wholly owned by TUI Travel PLC (United Kingdom); low-cost airline; services to destinations in 5 European countries; CEO JAWAD ZIYAT.

Office National des Aéroports (ONDA): Siège Social Nouasseur, BP 8101, Casablanca; tel. (52) 2539040; fax (52) 2539901; e-mail onda@onda.ma; internet www.onda.ma; f. 1990; Dir-Gen. DALIL GUENDOUZ.

Royal Air Maroc (RAM): Aéroport de Casablanca-Anfa; tel. (52) 2912000; fax (52) 2912087; e-mail callcenter@royalairmaroc.com; internet www.royalairmaroc.com; f. 1953; 94.4% state-owned; scheduled for partial privatization; domestic flights and services to Western Europe, Scandinavia, the Americas, North and West Africa, the Middle East; Chair. and CEO DRISS BENHIMA.

Tourism

Tourism is Morocco's second main source of convertible currency. The country's tourist attractions include its sunny climate, ancient sites (notably the cities of Fez, Marrakesh, Meknès and Rabat) and spectacular scenery. There are popular holiday resorts on the Atlantic and Mediterranean coasts. In 2011 foreign tourist arrivals totalled 4.9m., compared with 1.6m. in 1996. Tourism receipts, excluding passenger transport, were estimated at US $7,307m. in 2011.

Office National Marocain du Tourisme: angle rue Oued el-Makhazine et rue Zalaga, BP 19, Agdal, Rabat; tel. (53) 7674013; fax (53) 7674015; e-mail contact@onmt.org.ma; internet www.tourisme-marocain.com/onmt; f. 1918; Dir-Gen. FATHIA BENNIS.

Defence

Commander-in-Chief of the Armed Forces: HM King MUHAMMAD VI.

Defence Budget (2012): 29,400m. dirhams.

Military Service: 18 months.

Total Armed Forces (as assessed at November 2012): 195,800 (army 175,000—including some 100,000 conscripts; navy 7,800—including 1,500 marines; air force 13,000). Reserves 150,000.

Paramilitary Forces (as assessed at November 2012): 50,000: royal guard 20,000; auxiliary force 30,000.

Education

Since independence in 1956, Morocco has tried to resolve a number of educational problems: a youthful and fast-growing population, an urgent need for skilled workers and executives, a great diversity of teaching methods between French, Spanish, Muslim and Moroccan government schools (syllabuses have been standardized since 1967), and, above all, a high degree of adult illiteracy. In recent years increasing attention has been given to education for girls. There are now a number of mixed and girls' schools, notably in urban areas.

In 2011/12 there were an estimated 4,016,934 pupils in primary schools. A decree of November 1963 made education compulsory for children between the ages of seven and 13 years, and this has now been applied in most urban areas; from September 2002 children were to be educated from six years of age. In 2010/11, according to UNESCO estimates, enrolment at primary level included 96% of the relevant age-group. Instruction is given in Arabic for the first two years and in Arabic and French for the next four years, with English as the first additional language. Teaching in the principal Berber language, Tamazight, began in primary schools in the 2003/04 academic year.

Secondary education, beginning at the age of 13, lasts for up to six years (comprising two cycles of three years), and in 2011/12 provided for an estimated 2,554,050 pupils. In 1988 the secondary school graduation examination, the *baccalauréat*, was replaced by a system of continuous assessment. Secondary enrolment in 2006/07 was equivalent to 56% of the relevant age-group. Under the 2009 budget, expenditure on education by the central Government was projected at 47,269m. dirhams (21.7% of total spending).

There are eight universities in Morocco, including the Islamic University of al-Quarawiyin at Fez (founded in 859), the Muhammad V University at Rabat (opened in 1957), and an English-language university, inaugurated at Ifrane in 1995. In addition, there are institutes of higher education in business studies, agriculture, mining, law, and statistics and advanced economics. In 2009/10 there were some 446,073 students enrolled in tertiary education.

Bibliography

Amin, Samir. *The Maghreb in the Modern World.* Harmondsworth, Penguin, 1971.

Ashford, D. E. *Political Change in Morocco.* Princeton, NJ, Princeton University Press, 1961.

Perspectives of a Moroccan Nationalist. New York, 1964.

Ayache, A. *Le Maroc.* Paris, Editions Sociales, 1956.

Baduel, Pierre-Robert. *Enjeux Sahariens.* Paris, CNRS, 1984.

Barbier, Maurice. *Le conflit du Sahara occidental.* Paris, L'Harmattan, 1982.

Barbour, Nevill. *Morocco.* London, Thames and Hudson, 1964.

Belal, Youssef. *Le cheikh et le calife: Sociologie religieuse de l'islam politique au Maroc.* Lyon, Éditions de l'ENS, 2011.

Ben Barka, Mehdi. *Problèmes de l'édification du Maroc et du Maghreb.* Paris, Plon, 1959.

Option Révolutionnaire en Maroc. Paris, Maspéro, 1966.

Bernard, Stephane. *Le Conflit Franco-Marocain 1943–1956*, 3 vols. Brussels, 1963; English translation, New Haven, CT, Yale University Press, 1968.

Berque, Jaques. *Le Maghreb entre deux guerres.* Paris, Edns du Seuil, 1962.

Boukhars, Anouar. *Politics in Morocco: Executive Monarchy and Enlightened Authoritarianism.* Abingdon, Routledge, 2010.

Charrad, Mounira M. *States and Women's Rights: The Making of Postcolonial Tunisia, Algeria and Morocco.* Berkeley, CA, University of California Press, 2000.

Cherkaoui, Mohamed. *Morocco and the Sahara: Social Bonds and Geopolitical Issues*, revised 2nd edn. Oxford, The Bardwell Press, 2007.

Cohen, M. I., and Hahn, Lorna. *Morocco: Old Land, New Nation.* New York, Praeger, 1964.

Cohen, Shana. *Searching for a Different Future: The Rise of a Global Middle Class in Morocco.* Durham, NC, Duke University Press, 2004.

Cohen, Shana, and Jaidi, Larabi. *Morocco: Globalization and its Consequences.* Abingdon, Routledge, 2006.

Daure-Serfaty, Christine. *Lettre du Maroc.* Paris, Stock, 2000.

Dawson, Carl. *EU Integration with North Africa: Trade Negotiations and Democracy Deficits in Morocco.* London, Tauris Academic Studies, 2009.

Eickelman, Dale F. *Moroccan Islam: Tradition and Society in a Pilgrimage Center.* Princeton, NJ, Princeton University Press, 1986.

Gershovich, Moshe. *French Military Rule in Morocco: Colonialism and its Consequences.* London and Portland, OR, Frank Cass, 2000.

Halstead, John P. *Rebirth of a Nation: The Origins and Rise of Moroccan Nationalism.* Cambridge, MA, Harvard University Press, 1967.

Hassan II, King of Morocco. *Le Défi.* Paris, Albin Michel, 1976.

Hodges, Tony. *Western Sahara: The Roots of a Desert War.* London, Croom Helm, 1983.

Historical Dictionary of Western Sahara. London, Scarecrow Press, 1982.

Horton, Brendon. *Morocco: Analysis and Reform of Foreign Policy.* Economic Development Institute of the World Bank, 1990.

Howe, Marvine. *Morocco: The Islamist Awakening and Other Challenges.* New York, Oxford University Press, 2005.

Hughes, Stephen O. *Morocco Under King Hassan.* Reading, Ithaca Press, 2006.

Julien, Charles-André. *Le Maroc face aux Impérialismes (1415–1956).* Paris, Editions Jeune Afrique, 1978.

Kaioua, Abdelkader, *Cassablanca: L'industrie et la ville, Tomes I et II.* Tours, France URBAMA, 1996.

Kay, Shirley. *Morocco.* London, Namara Publications, 1980.

Lacouture, J. and S. *Le Maroc à l'épreuve.* Paris, Edns du Seuil, 1958.

Landau, Rom. *The Moroccan Drama 1900–1955.* London, Hale, 1956.

Morocco Independent under Mohammed V. London, Allen & Unwin, 1961.

Hassan II, King of Morocco. London, Allen & Unwin, 1962.

The Moroccans: Yesterday and Today. London, Whitethorn Press, 1963.

Morocco. London, Allen & Unwin, 1967.

Layachi, Azzedine. *State, Society and Democracy in Morocco: The Limits of Associative Life.* Washington, DC, Georgetown University Center for Contemporary Arab Studies, 1998.

Le Tourneau, Roger. *Evolution politique de l'Afrique du Nord musulmane.* Paris, Armand Colin, 1962.

Marzok, Mokhtar Mohatar. *La contestation au Maroc à l'epreuve du politique: Le cas du Rif, 1980–2008.* Algiers, Editions Bouchène, 2009.

Maxwell, Gavin. *Lords of the Atlas.* London, Longmans, 1966.

Metcalf, John. *Morocco—An Economic Study.* New York, First National City Bank, 1966.

Middle East Report No. 218, Vol. 31 No. 1, Spring 2001. *Morocco in Transition.*

Mumson, Henry, Jr. *Religion and Power in Morocco.* London, Yale University Press, 1993.

El Ouali, Abdelhamid. *Saharan Conflict: Towards Territorial Autonomy as a Right to Democratic Self-Determination.* London, Stacey International, 2008.

Pennell, C. R. *Morocco since 1830: A History.* New York, New York University Press, 2001.

Morocco: From Empire to Independence. Oxford, Oneworld Publications, 2003.

Perrault, Gilles. *Notre Ami le Roi.* Paris, Editions Gallimard, 1991.

Porch, Douglas. *The Conquest of Morocco.* New York, Farrar Straus Giroux, 2005.

Robert, J. *La monarchie marocaine.* Paris, Librairie générale de droit et de jurisprudence, 1963.

Sater, James N. *Civil Society and Political Change in Morocco.* Abingdon, Routledge, 2007.

Morocco: Challenges to Tradition and Modernity. Abingdon, Routledge, 2009.

Slyomovics, Susan. *The Performance of Human Rights in Morocco.* Pennsylvania, PA, University of Pennsylvania Press, 2005.

Storm, Lise. *Democratization in Morocco: The Political Élite and Struggles for Power in the Post-independence State.* Abingdon, Routledge, 2007.

Thobhani, Akbarali. *Western Sahara since 1975 under Moroccan Administration: Social, Political and Economic Transformation.* Lewiston, NY, Edwin Mellen Press, 2002.

Thompson, Virginia, and Adloff, Richard. *The Western Saharans.* London, Croom Helm, Totowa, NJ, Barnes and Noble, 1980.

Tiano, André. *La politique économique et financière du Maroc indépendant.* Paris, Presses universitaires de France, 1963.

Tozy, Muhammad. *Monarchie et islam politique au Maroc.* Paris, Presse de Sciences-Po, 1999.

Tuquoi, J. P. *'Majesté, je dois beaucoup à votre père...': France–Maroc, une affaire de famille.* Paris, Albin Michel, 2006.

Vermeren, Pierre. *Le Maroc en transition.* Paris, La Découverte, 2001.

Waterbury, John. *The Commander of the Faithful. The Moroccan Political Élite.* London, Weidenfeld & Nicolson, 1970.

Wegner, Eva. *Islamist Opposition in Authoritarian Regimes: The Party of Justice and Development in Morocco.* Syracuse, NY, Syracuse University Press, 2011.

World Bank. *The Economic Development of Morocco.* Baltimore, MD, Johns Hopkins University Press, 1966.

Growing Faster, Finding Jobs: Choices for Morocco. 1997.

White, Gregory. *A Comparative Political Economy of Tunisia and Morocco: On the Outside of Europe Looking In.* Albany, NY, State University of New York Press, 2001.

Zartman, I. W. *Morocco: Problems of New Power.* New York, Atherton Press, 1964.

Zeghal, Malika. *Les islamistes marocains: Le défi à la monarchie.* Paris, Cahiers libres, 2005.

Islamism in Morocco: Religion, Authoritarianism, and Electoral Politics. Princeton, NJ, Markus Wiener Publishers, 2008.

OMAN

Geography

The Sultanate of Oman occupies the extreme east and south-east of the Arabian peninsula. It is bordered by the United Arab Emirates (UAE) to the north and west, by Saudi Arabia to the west, and by Yemen to the south-west. A detached area of Oman, separated from the rest of the country by UAE territory, lies at the tip of the Musandam peninsula, on the southern shore of the Strait of Hormuz. Oman is separated from Iran by the Gulf of Oman, and has a coastline of some 1,700 km (1,056 miles) on the Indian Ocean. The total area of the country is 309,500 sq km (119,500 sq miles). Disputes over the demarcation of Oman's frontiers often complicated the country's foreign relations in the past; however, in mid-1995 Oman completed the demarcation of its joint borders with both Yemen and Saudi Arabia (in May 1997 Oman and Yemen signed international border demarcation maps in Muscat), and in June 2002 it was reported that agreement had also been reached with the UAE on the demarcation of common international borders.

The first full census in Oman was held in 1993. Previous estimates of the country's population varied widely between official Omani figures and those of independent international organizations. The UN Population Division, basing its assessment on a mid-1965 figure of 571,000, estimated totals of 654,000 for mid-1970 and 984,000 for mid-1980. By 1990 the UN estimated that Oman's mid-year population had grown to 1,502,000. World Bank estimates indicated average annual population growth of 1.6% during 1996–2006. According to the census of December 2010, the population totalled 2,773,479, comprising 1,957,336 Omani nationals (70.6%) and 816,143 non-Omanis (29.4%), compared with a total of 2,340,815 at the 2003 census. By mid-2012, the population had increased to 3,623,001, according to official estimates.

At Muscat the mean annual rainfall is 100 mm and the mean temperature varies between 20°C and 43°C (69°F and 110°F). Rainfall on the hills of the interior is somewhat heavier, and the south-western province of Dhofar is the only part of Arabia to benefit from the summer monsoon.

Oman may be divided into nine topographical areas. The largest urban area in the country is the capital region, around Muscat. Although most of the country is arid, the al-Batinah plain, which lies between the Gulf of Oman and the Hajar al-Gharbi range of mountains, comprises a fertile coastal region, and is among the most densely populated areas of the country. Another such plain is found between Raysut and Salalah, on the south-west coast in the Dhofar region, which, in total, occupies one-third of the country's area and extends northwards into the Rub al-Khali, or 'empty quarter', on Oman's western border: a rainless, unrelieved wilderness of shifting sand, almost entirely without human habitation.

Irrigation has been developed in some parts of the country, including the Dhahira area, a semi-desert plain between the south-western Hajar mountains and the Rub al-Khali, which also provides clusters of cultivable land near the Dank and Ain *wadis* (river valleys) and the Buraini oasis. From Jebel al-Akhdar, at the southern tip of the Hajar al-Gharbi range, towards the desert in the south, lies the Interior, the country's central hill region and the most densely populated zone. The area has four main valleys, two of which (Halafein and Samail) provide the traditional route to Muscat.

The less hospitable regions are sparsely populated by groups of tribal settlers. The Hajar al-Gharbi, running parallel to the coast southwards from Oman's border with the UAE, is the home of the Rostaq, Awabi and Nakhe tribes. To the east of the Hajar range, the Sharqiya area extends south towards the Arabian Sea. It is an area of sandy plains and the home of the various Bani tribes. Musandam, separated from Oman by the UAE, is a mountainous area inhabited by the al-Shahouh tribes. Around the eastern coast of the Arabian Sea, the Barr al-Hekkman, a group of islands and salt-plains of 650 sq km (250 sq miles), is inhabited by fishing communities.

Following the creation of seven new governorates in October 2011, the Sultanate is divided into 11 governorates and five regions, subdivided into 61 *wilayat* (provinces), each under the jurisdiction of a *wali*, or provincial governor.

History

Revised for this edition by MARC VALERI

Oman was probably the land of Magan (mentioned in Sumerian tablets) with which cities such as Ur of the Chaldees traded in the third millennium BC. The territory of the modern province of Dhofar also produced frankincense in vast quantities, which was shipped to markets in Iraq, Syria, Egypt and the Mediterranean. Oman, at various times, came under the influence of the Himyaritic kingdoms of southern Arabia and of Iran, which are believed to have been responsible for the introduction of the *falaj* irrigation systems.

The tribal people of Oman come from two main ethnic stocks, the Qahtan, who migrated from southern Arabia, and the Nizar, who came in from the north. According to tradition, the first important invasion from southern Arabia was led by Malik bin Faham, after the final collapse of the Marib dam in Yemen in the second century AD. Oman was one of the first countries to be converted to Islam by Amr bin al-As, who later converted Egypt. Omanis of the tribe of al-Azd played an important part in the early days of Islam in Iraq. They subsequently embraced the Ibadi doctrine, which holds that the caliphate in Islam should not be hereditary or confined to any one family, and established their own independent Imamate in Oman in the eighth century. Subsequently, although subject to invasions by the Caliphate, Iranians and others, Inner Oman largely maintained its independence.

During the 10th century Sohar was one of the most important cities in Western Asia, while Omani mariners, together with those from Basra (Iraq) and other ports of the Persian (Arabian) Gulf, went as far afield as China. When the Portuguese arrived in 1507, on their way to India, Afonso de Albuquerque and his forces found the Omani seaport under the suzerainty of the King of Hormuz, himself of Omani stock. The towns of Qalhat, Quryat, Muscat and Sohar were already prosperous.

The Portuguese established themselves in the Omani ports, concentrating principally on Sohar and Muscat. British and Dutch traders followed in the wake of the Portuguese, though they did not establish themselves by force of arms in Oman. In 1650 the Imam Nasir bin Murshid of the Yaariba dynasty, who was also credited with a period of Omani renaissance during which learning flourished, effectively expelled the Portuguese from Muscat and the rest of Oman. The Omanis then extended their power, and by 1730 had conquered the Portuguese settlements on the east coast of Africa, including Mogadishu (now in Somalia), Mombasa (Kenya) and Zanzibar (now part of Tanzania). The country was, however, ravaged by civil war in the first half of the 18th century, when the authority of the Imam diminished. During this period the Iranians were summoned to assist one of the contenders for the Imamate, but they were subsequently ousted by Ahmad bin Said, who was elected Imam in 1749 and founded the al-Bu-Said dynasty, which still rules Oman. The country prospered under the new dynasty and its maritime influence revived.

Said bin Sultan ruled Oman from 1804 until 1856. While officially an independent state, Oman had been under informal British protection since 1829. Treaties providing for the establishment of consular relations were negotiated with the British in 1839 (there had been earlier treaties of friendship in 1798 and 1800), the USA in 1833 and France in 1844.

Said bin Sultan revived Omani interest in Zanzibar and, after having made it his capital in 1832, spent an increasing amount of his time there. He started the clove plantations, which later brought great wealth to the islands of Zanzibar and Pemba. As part of his imperial conquest, Said bin Sultan encouraged the settlement of Omani people on the eastern African coast, a process which did not cease until the mid-20th century. The 'return' of their descendants to Oman started after the 1964 revolution in Zanzibar, which put an end to the local al-Bu-Said dynasty. In 1829 Said claimed suzerainty over the region of Dhofar in south Arabia. The territory was eventually annexed to Oman in 1879. During Said's reign, Omani dominions expanded to their greatest extent, covering the whole north-western edge of the Indian Ocean, from contemporary Mozambique to Baluchistan.

The latter half of the 19th century was a difficult period for Oman. After Said's death, the inability of his sons to regulate the succession led, under British pressure, to the dismemberment of the Omani possessions into two political entities of Muscat and Zanzibar in 1861. Moreover, a series of treaties with Britain to curb the slave trade also brought about a decline in the local economy, as Muscat had been an important port for this lucrative traffic. Oman's ruler, Sultan Faisal bin Turki, had become dependent on British support by the 1900s; this was illustrated by the 1891 treaty, under which Faisal committed himself never to cede a part of his territory without British agreement. Oman's foreign affairs were managed from that time on by the United Kingdom, except for relations with the USA, France and (after 1947) India, but only after prior British approval. This arrangement continued until 1971, when the United Kingdom withdrew its military forces from the Gulf.

The economic difficulties, linked in people's minds to the British tutelage over Muscat, led to several tribal and religious insurrections towards the end of the 19th century, and in 1913 a new Imam was elected in the interior, in defiance of the Sultan who ruled from Muscat. This led to the expulsion of the Sultan's garrisons from Nizwa, Izki and Sumail. In 1920, an agreement was reached under the supervision of the British political agent between Sultan Taimur (who had ruled since Faisal's death in 1913) and the leaders of the Imamate. It provided for peace, free movement of persons between the interior and the coast, limitation of customs duties, and non-interference by the government of the Sultan in the internal affairs of the signatory tribes. A Treaty of Friendship with the United Kingdom, signed on 20 December 1951, recognized that the Sultanate, officially called Muscat and Oman, had certain rights, although in reality the British kept the upper hand over a divided and weakened territory.

The issue of petroleum resources severely disrupted the status quo. In 1949 Ibn Sa'ud awarded a concession to the Arabian American Oil Company (Aramco) south of Al-Buraymi oasis. In May 1954 Imam Muhammad al-Khalili, who had coexisted peacefully since 1920 with Sultan Said bin Taimur (who had succeeded his father in 1932) and had agreed to join forces with the Sultan to expel the Saudis from Al-Buraymi, died. The political line of the Imamate, led by the new Imam, Ghalib al-Hinai, changed in favour of a rapprochement with the Saudis. In the face of the Saudi-US threat, the British took the initiative, convinced that there was no alternative. In October 1955 the Trucial Oman Scouts, based in Abu Dhabi, launched a head-on attack on the Imamate, leading to its collapse. However, no strategy of development and political stabilization had been implemented by Sultan Said, except for the building of a road to the interior, to provide access to the Fahud oil wells. This led to the proclamation of the Imamate's swift rebirth in June 1957 in the Jebel Akhdar (the Green Mountain), north-west of Nizwa. The major interior towns once again flew the Imamate's flag, but the Trucial Oman Scouts, with the decisive support of the British Royal Air Force, regained control in January 1959. From then on, the Imamate resorted to intimidation (such as mines and sabotage) and the establishment of a government in exile, supported by the League of Arab States (Arab League), with offices in Cairo and Baghdad. Even though the 'question of Oman' was regularly discussed in UN commissions, the Imamate authorities in exile were slowly marginalized in the 1960s. The question was debated on several further occasions until, more than a year after Sultan Qaboos's accession, Oman (as Muscat and Oman was renamed in 1970) became a member of the UN in October 1971.

TRANSFORMATION UNDER QABOOS, 1970–82

From 1958 Sultan Said retired to Salalah, in the south of Oman. The features of his mode of government which emerged in the 1940s—deep suspicion towards the Omanis, aversion to social and economic reforms, and entrustment of the daily running of the country to foreign experts—were to be exacerbated. This evolution explains why, at the end of the 1960s, more than 50,000 Omanis had migrated to other Gulf emirates, where they sought better living conditions. Under the impulse of the revolution in Yemen, a Dhofar Liberation Front formed in 1965 became the Popular Front for the Liberation of the Occupied Arabian Gulf (PFLOAG) in 1968, and declared itself Marxist-Leninist. It wanted nothing short of the elimination of monarchy from Arabia and was backed by the People's Democratic Republic of Yemen (PDRY—formerly South Yemen), the People's Republic of China, the German Democratic Republic (East Germany), the USSR and Iraq. By early 1970, the Sultan's forces in Dhofar only controlled the Salalah plain and their remaining courses of action were limited to air raids on the positions controlled by the PFLOAG.

When the rebellion threatened to spread to northern Oman in 1970, the British had no other solution to counter this situation than a psychological blow—Sultan Said's forced abdication in favour of his son Qaboos on 23 July. This change enjoyed the support of the other Gulf rulers as well as the Shah of Iran, all of whom were worried by potential revolutionary contagion. In August 1970 Muscat and Oman became simply the Sultanate of Oman. Sultan Qaboos appointed his uncle, Tariq bin Taimur, as Prime Minister. Qaboos's unwillingness to question the strategic and economic British influence in Oman and his own inclination to personal power led to Tariq's resignation from his office in December 1971, since which time the Sultan has himself acted as Prime Minister. He holds the positions of Head of State, Chief of Staff of the Sultan's Armed Forces, Chairman of the Central Bank and (since the 1990s) Chairman of Financial Affairs. He also hold the posts of Minister of Foreign Affairs, Minister of Defence and Minister of Finance, although Ministers Responsible for Defence Affairs, for Foreign Affairs, and for Financial Affairs handle the day-to-day operations of these departments. After taking power, Sultan Qaboos effected a radical change of policy, as the authorities both increased defence expenditure to 50% of the state budget and decided to use part of the oil income (exploited since 1967) in pursuing development programmes in education, health, and agriculture. In addition, a number of prisoners were released and many Omanis returned from abroad.

The summer of 1972 represented the turning point of the conflict. Not only was the PFLOAG heavily defeated in the coastal town of Mirbat, but the year also witnessed a dramatic increase of foreign help to the Sultan, with the arrival of Iranian troops, in addition to more British personnel. The Sultan also received assistance from Jordan, Saudi Arabia, the United Arab Emirates (UAE), Pakistan and India. In 1974 PFLOAG's Omani and non-Omani branches separated: the Omani branch renaming itself the Popular Front for the Liberation of Oman (PFLO). In 1975 joint offensives by the Sultan's Armed Forces (SAF) and Iran were able to overcome the most secure of the rebel positions, although at a very heavy human and material cost. On 11 December 1975 Sultan Qaboos could proclaim the official end of the insurrection. Saudi Arabia helped to negotiate a cease-fire, and an amnesty was granted to Omani nationals who had been fighting for the PFLO. Nevertheless, small, well-equipped PFLO groups continued to fight fiercely for several years. In January 1977 Iran withdrew the majority of its forces from Dhofar. British forces also officially withdrew that year, but several hundred officers and non-commissioned officers (NCOs) seconded from the British armed forces, and former British officers and NCOs on private contract (as military and intelligence advisers), remained in the SAF. Many of these still serve in the SAF today. A renewal of the insurrection occurred in June 1978, when a party of British engineers was attacked in the Salalah region of Dhofar. However, the PFLO had little success in attracting adherents within Oman, despite the assassination, in 1979, of the Governor of Dhofar. In January 1981 Oman closed its border with the PDRY, and more British officers were seconded to the Omani forces as the frontier defences were put on alert.

DOMESTIC DEVELOPMENTS, 1981–2013

A 45-member Consultative Assembly (consisting of 17 representatives of the Government, 11 representatives of the private sector and 17 regional representatives—all appointed by the Sultan) was created in October 1981 in response to suggestions that Sultan Qaboos was not being made sufficiently aware of public opinion. In 1983 the Assembly's membership was expanded to 55, including 19 representatives of the Government. Its role, however, was confined to comment on economic and social development and recommendations on future policy. In November 1990 Sultan Qaboos announced that the Assembly was to be replaced by a new Consultative Council (Majlis al-Shura) from 1991. The Council was composed of 59 members, who would serve three-year terms of office, and a President, appointed by the Sultan. In April 21 prominent figures met to nominate three candidates for each of the country's *wilayat* (provinces). From these three, one was chosen by the Deputy Prime Minister for Legal Affairs, Sayyid Fahd bin Mahmoud al-Said. The final decision was taken by the ruler himself. Although the Council had no legislative power, ministers, except those linked to national sovereignty (Foreign Affairs, Defence, Finance, Interior, Oil) were obliged to present annual statements to it and to answer any questions addressed to them. Membership of the Council was increased to 80 in 1995, allowing constituencies of 30,000 or more inhabitants to have two seats. Women were permitted, for the first time, to be nominated as candidates in the capital area governorate (*muhafadha*). In early 1995 two women were appointed to the Council.

In mid-1994 the Omani Government was reported to be employing stringent measures to curb an apparent rise in Islamist militancy in the country. In August the security forces announced the arrest of more than 430 members of an allegedly foreign-sponsored Islamist organization. Among those arrested were two junior ministers, businessmen, university lecturers and soldiers. Some 150 people were tried before a special Security Court. In November several detainees were sentenced to death, having been found guilty of conspiracy to foment sedition; the Sultan subsequently commuted the death sentences to life imprisonment. A year later, the Sultan announced that he would grant royal pardons to every prisoner.

In November 1996 Sultan Qaboos issued a decree promulgating a Basic Statute of the State: a constitutional document defining, for the first time, the organs and guiding principles of the State. The Sultan of Oman, defined as 'the symbol of national unity' (Article 41), has all the prerogatives of executive and legislative power. He promulgates and ratifies laws, and can grant pardons and commute sentences. Article 41 explicitly states that respecting him is a duty and that his orders must be obeyed. Articles 44 to 55 establish that the Sultan will be helped and advised by the Council of Ministers, to which is given the task of implementing general state policies. Article 58 of the Statute provides for a Council of Oman (Majlis Oman), to be composed of the Consultative Council and a new State Council (Majlis al-Dawlah). The latter was to be appointed by the Sultan for three years from among prominent Omanis (including tribal leaders, businessmen, former senior military officers and ambassadors). In December a Defence Council was established by royal decree, comprising the Minister of the Royal Court, the heads of the branches of the armed and police forces, and the head of internal security (all officials who do not belong to the al-Said royal family). The process of succession to the Sultan, as defined by the Basic Statute, required the ruling family to choose a successor from within the family within three days, failing which the Defence Council would open a sealed letter containing the name of the Sultan's preferred successor.

In 1997 there were public signs of growing impatience with the slow pace of progress on political reform and economic development. In May civil disturbances were reported in al-Hajer, west of Muscat; troops were eventually deployed to end the demonstrations and disperse the crowds. University students also protested against the introduction of severe security measures on campus, which included a ban on public gatherings. Hitherto, such demonstrations had been virtually unknown in Oman, and it was widely believed that budget reductions and privatization plans had created anxiety about employment prospects among the younger generation.

Voting was organized in October 1997 to select candidates for appointment to the Consultative Council. The electorate amounted to 51,000 people (one for every 15 adults), 10% of whom were women. Women were also given the right to vote and to stand for election throughout Oman. Of a total of 736 candidates, 164 were chosen, from whose number the Sultan selected the 82 members of the new Council. The two female members of the outgoing Council were returned to office. A total of 541 candidates, including 21 women, contested the September 2000 election, in which 83 candidates, two of them women, were elected to the Council. The candidates with the highest numbers of votes were automatically elected, and the Sultan no longer intervened in a discretionary second round. Although the number of people eligible to vote was extended to some 150,000 (i.e. one adult in four), only 65% had registered their intention to vote, compared with some 90% at the previous election. From late 2000 the Government undertook measures aimed at reducing the number of expatriates in Oman's labour force, including the deportation of illegal immigrants, a process termed 'Omanization'. This need to reduce the labour force was also behind the Sultan's appeal in February 2005 for Omanis to have smaller families, claiming that 'a reasonable number of family members would find more job opportunities'.

Elections to the Consultative Council were held on 4 October 2003; voting rights (previously limited to prominent professionals, intellectuals and tribal chiefs) were for the first time granted to all Omani citizens over 21 years of age—a total of some 820,000 people. A total of 506 candidates, 15 of them women, stood for election to the 83-seat Council. Few changes to the composition of the Council resulted from the elections. While the electoral process was described by observers as fair and open, only 32% of Omani citizens had registered to vote. Critics of the elections claimed that tribal loyalties had guided the decision-making of most voters, resulting in a predictable set of results—a situation that was exacerbated by the lack of legislative power wielded by council members. Only two female candidates secured election to the Council. A royal decree adopted in October extended the term of office for members of both the Consultative Council and the State Council from three to four years. Meanwhile, in March 2003 Sultan Qaboos issued a decree establishing a Public Authority for Craft Industries. The President of the Authority, Sheikha Aisha bint Khalfan bin Jumiel al-Siyabiah, was given the rank of Minister, and thus became the first woman to be appointed to that level of government.

In March 2004 Sultan Qaboos issued a decree appointing Dr Rawya bint Saud bin Ahmad al-Busaidiyah as Minister of Higher Education (the first female to secure control of an Omani ministry). In June the Sultan created by royal decree a Ministry of Tourism; another woman, Rajha bint Abd al-Amir bin Ali, was allocated the new portfolio. A third woman was appointed to the Council of Ministers in October, when Dr

Sharifah bint Khalfan bin Nasser al-Yahiyaia was given the role of Minister of Social Development.

The following elections to the Consultative Council were held on 27 October 2007. Membership was increased from 83 to 84. The polls were contested by 632 candidates, including 21 women; however, none of those women won a seat. Of Omanis eligible to register 45% registered and 62.7% of those registered actually cast their vote. Thus only 28% of those eligible to vote cast their ballot. A new State Council, comprising 70 members, was appointed on 5 November.

A key element of the new regime's legitimization has rested on the nation-building process implemented since 1970, which links the country's economic and social development to the modernizing state (as the administrator of the oil rent), on the one hand, and to the person of the Sultan who embodies the state and has become the subject of a personality cult, on the other. By recreating a national identity within the framework of an omnipresent state and by unifying cultural and religious references, Qaboos has legitimized his paternalistic authority. The Sultan portrays himself as the embodiment of modern Oman in general and of the post-1970 renaissance (*nahda*) ideology in particular. However, since the early 2000s, Oman has faced a series of social and economic challenges which are calling into question the order established in the 1970s. The Omani population is one of the youngest in the world: in 2012 35% of Omani nationals were aged 15 years or under, and 49% were aged under 20 years. The arrival on the labour market of young, educated people coincides with an economy which remains extremely dependent on revenues from oil. There are ever increasing signs that growing sectors of society, particularly the younger generations, are reluctant to guarantee the perpetuation of a system in which they feel excluded from political and economic decisions that determine the future of their country.

In January 2005 it was announced that 'at least 100 suspected extremists' had been arrested over a plot to attack a festival coinciding with the start of the Id al-Adha celebration. When the case came to the State Security Court in April, 31 Islamist Ibadis were accused of membership of a 'banned organization' and of plotting the violent overthrow of the Government. During the trial the prosecution alleged that those arrested belonged to a 'secret organization' that, while nominally organizing pilgrimages and youth summer camps for the observant, concurrently ran an underground organization that sought to establish an Imamate in Oman. The defendants were sentenced to prison terms ranging from one to 20 years. A further 43 members of the military, including senior officers, were also found guilty in a second, secret trial held the following month. The Sultan pardoned all 74 men in June. In July a journalist and former member of the Consultative Council, Tayyibah al-Mawali, was tried and sentenced to 18 months' imprisonment for publicly criticizing human rights violations in Oman. In April 2009 Ali al-Zuwaidi, the moderator of a popular internet forum, received a one-month prison sentence for publishing a government directive that banned live radio phone-in programmes because they 'encouraged public criticism'.

Inspired by a wave of anti-regime demonstrations that had spread across the Middle East and North Africa region since December 2010, on 17 January 2011 around 200 people assembled in Muscat to protest against government corruption and economic hardship. This was followed in February by a series of nation-wide protests, each attended by several hundred people demonstrating against low salaries, high unemployment rate among Omanis and the Consultative Council's lack of legislative powers. There were no arrests during these initial protests. However, in response Sultan Qaboos increased the private sector minimum wage for nationals by 43%, introduced a financial support package for government employees, raised student allowances and reorganized the Council of Ministers.

In spite of these measures, further protests took place in Sohar in late February 2011, in which unemployed young people rallied against the lack of job opportunities. The security forces shot dead one protester. The protests prompted Sultan Qaboos to make further concessions, including the introduction of a job-seeker's allowance and the creation of 50,000 new jobs for Omanis. He also announced the establishment of a ministerial committee to examine the possibility of granting legislative powers to the Consultative Council. Nevertheless, protests continued in Sohar, and on 1 March demonstrators burned down a supermarket, clashing with riot police in the process. The protesters demanded that all long-serving ministers be put on trial for corruption. In an attempt to appease the protests, Sultan Qaboos dismissed two of his most unpopular ministers: the Minister of the Diwan of the Royal Court, Sayyid Ali bin Hamoud bin Ali al-Busaidi, and the Minister of the Royal Office, Gen. Ali bin Majid al-Maamari. They were replaced by Sayyid Khalid bin Hilal bin Saud al-Busaidi and Lt-Gen. Sultan bin Muhammad al-Numani, respectively.

In March 2011 there was an expansion of the unrest across the country. Many workers went on strike, and a growing number of protesters pitched tents outside government buildings. Sultan Qaboos responded on 7 March by dismissing 10 long-serving ministers suspected of corruption (one-third of his cabinet). He replaced them with younger politicians who had not held ministerial posts before, including five members of the elected Consultative Council: Saad bin Muhammad bin Said al-Mardhouf al-Saadi (Minister of Commerce and Industry), Muhammad bin Salim bin Said al-Toobi (Environment and Climate Affairs), Sheikh Muhammad bin Said bin Saif al-Kalbani (Social Development), Dr Fuad bin Jaafar bin Muhammad al-Sajwani (Agriculture and Fisheries), and Ahmad bin Abdullah bin Muhammad al-Shuhi (Regional Municipalities and Water Resources). The Ministry of National Economy was also abolished, its duties being redistributed among the other ministries. This was the largest cabinet reorganization in 40 years and met one of the protesters' key demands.

On 10 March 2011 a foreign ministerial meeting organized by the Cooperation Council for the Arab States of the Gulf (Gulf Cooperation Council—GCC, see p. 1348) was held to discuss the protests in Oman and Bahrain, and US $10,000m. in financial aid was pledged to each country, with the UAE providing Oman's allocation. The funds were intended to support government efforts to create jobs, build more housing and improve infrastructure. On 13 March Sultan Qaboos announced that the unpopular Inspector-General of Police and Customs, Lt-Gen. Malik bin Sulaiman al-Maamari, would be replaced by Maj.-Gen. Hassan bin Mohsen bin Shuraiqi. The prerogatives of the Public Prosecutor were expanded by royal decree, with all jurisdictions of the Inspector General of Police and Customs mentioned in the Public Prosecution Law to be assigned to the Public Prosecutor's office. Sultan Qaboos also increased the pensions of retired low-ranking civil servants by 50% and doubled the social security grant paid to certain vulnerable groups.

During April–May 2011 frustration grew over the slow pace of change, with the result that Friday after-prayer protests became a weekly event across the country. On 1 April around 300 protesters who had been camping for over a month at the Globe Roundabout in Sohar, which had become a focal point for the demonstrations, clashed with police, resulting in the death of one protester and the arrest of 50–60 others. Further Friday protests in Sohar were averted following the deployment of a large security force and the establishment of checkpoints throughout the city. Nevertheless, Friday protests continued in other cities during this time, with the overall number of arrests increasing after each event, which in turn resulted in more protests demanding the release of the growing number of imprisoned demonstrators. Several journalists and writers were harassed, jailed and tortured for criticizing the Government (for instance Ahmed al-Shizawi, for his participation in sit-ins in Muscat demanding political reform.) On 12 April two prominent democracy activists in Muscat, Saeed al-Hashimi and Basma al-Rajhia, were abducted by masked men and taken to a remote part of town where they were threatened and assaulted before being released. On 13 May police raided a protest camp outside the Consultative Council in Muscat, arresting 15–20 activists in the process. The same day, the sit-in of protesters in front of the office of Salalah's Governor was cleared by riot police backed by tanks and armed cars. During the same month Sultan Qaboos expanded the powers of the police, allowing them to arrest individuals without an arrest warrant from the public prosecution, and detain them for longer before bringing them to court. After four-and-a-half months of protests, during which time Qaboos had issued some 40 royal decrees, activists announced in July their intention to suspend their action during Ramadan. The Sultan did not address the population directly during the crisis, only government ministers spoke to the people, and it was they who attracted the bulk of the criticism for their alleged corruption.

In October 2011 1,133 candidates (including 77 women) stood in the elections to the Consultative Council. Sixty-one new members were elected, including a woman, Nema al-Busaidi, and three men who took part in the protests earlier in the year. Some 60% of eligible Omanis registered to vote and 76% of those registered voted. Thus 46% of eligible people cast their ballot. This higher turn-out than in 2007 was, perhaps, a reflection of Omanis' expectations that the Council would promote greater reform. However, voting was still primarily conducted along tribal, rather than political, lines. Candidates competed in their names only, because the regime outlaws political parties and platforms. It was forbidden to tackle any general topic (like the role of the religion in present society) or to campaign jointly with a candidate from another *wilaya*. Five days after the election, Sultan Qaboos issued a decree amending the Basic Statute in relation to the succession process. Chairmen of both the Consultative Council and State Council, along with three Supreme Court members and Defense Council members, are henceforth to confirm the appointment to the throne of the person designated by the former ruler in his letter to the Ruling Family Council. Another amendment to the Basic Statute granted the Consultative Council the ability to elect its own Chairman and to amend and propose laws. However, the Council's role remained largely consultative. It cannot address issues such as national security, oil, foreign relations or the structure of the political system. The initiative to establish a parliamentary committee in charge of security and foreign affairs by Consultative Council members was rejected by the Council of Ministers in June 2012. Moreover, the Consultative Council cannot question ministers of sovereign ministries and the opinion of the two chambers is not binding on the Government or on the Sultan, who can dissolve both chambers. At the opening session of the Council on 31 October, the Sultan made his first public address since the protests, promising to combat unemployment and corruption. The election campaign itself coincided with the trial of the editor-in-chief and reporter for the independent newspaper *al-Zaman* for publishing an article giving evidence of corruption in the Ministry of Justice. On 21 September the Primary Court sentenced both journalists to gaol for five months for insulting the Minister of Justice and his undersecretary, and ordered the closure of the newspaper for one month. The Appeal Court upheld the verdict in late December.

In October 2011 several articles of the Penal Law were amended by royal decree, including article 137 which states that anyone participating in a gathering of at least 10 persons, with an intent to affect the public system, can be punished with a gaol term of one month to one year. The same month, a royal decree announced the creation of municipal councils in all 11 governorates, composed of members representing provinces and elected by universal suffrage (all Omanis over 21 registered on the voting lists) for a four-year renewable term, in addition to ex-officio members representing ministries. Previously only Muscat governorate had a (fully-appointed) municipal council. Provinces with up to 30,000 inhabitants are represented in the local council by two members, while those having more than 30,000 but fewer than 60,000 have four representatives, and larger provinces have six representatives. All the municipal councils are chaired by the head of the governorate appointed by the Sultan. According to the Municipal Council Law promulgated on 26 October 2011, municipal councils enjoy advisory powers only. They provide opinions and recommendations on the development of systems and municipal services in the governorate (such as infrastructure, health, environment, local taxes). On 22 December 2012 Oman held its first ever municipal elections. At least 50 applications for candidacies submitted by individuals who took part in 2011–12 protests were rejected by the election committee 'on security reasons'. Of 1,475 candidates (including 46 women), 192 were elected, including four females. According to the Ministry of the Interior, turnout was low. Only 50.3% of the total 447,500 voters installed on the electronic identity card system (compared to 522,000 people registered for the previous year's Consultative Council elections) cast their vote.

In February 2012 Qaboos reorganized his cabinet for the third time in just over a year, removing two unpopular ministers—Sheikh Muhammad bin Abdullah bin Zahir al-Hinai (the Minister of Justice) and Hamad bin Muhammad bin Muhsin al-Rashdi (the Minister of Information)—and reassigning three others. Sheikh Abd al-Malik bin Abdullah bin Ali al-Khalili was appointed as the new Minister of Justice, Dr Abd al-Munem bin Mansour bin Said al-Hasni became the new Minister of Information and Ali bin Massoud bin Ali al-Sunaidi received the commerce portfolio.

Popular frustration with the slow pace of reform became evident in May–June 2012. Around 1,000 oil workers went on strike in May, demanding better pay and working conditions. On 25 May protests in Sohar and Liwa in support of Consultative Council member Talib al-Maamari, who faced calls from the Public Prosecutor for his parliamentary immunity to be lifted, following postings on the social networking website Facebook, resulted in clashes with police and arrests. In early June, the Government adopted a hard line: the Public Prosecutor, on the basis of the amended Penal Law criminalizing *lèse-majesté* and 'publication of false news, statements or rumours liable to undermine the prestige of the state', announced that anyone who publically criticized the Government would be charged with sedition. Between July and December 2012 more than 30 writers, human rights activists, lawyers and students—a number of whom were alleged to have been subjected to practices of mistreatment amounting to torture—were sentenced to gaol terms (from six to 18 months) on various charges related to illegal gathering, incitement to cause riot and defamation of the Sultan. A number of websites, blogs and Facebook accounts were closed. In January 2013 another journalist from *al-Zaman* was sentenced to one-year gaol term for *lèse-majesté*. However, in March and July 2013 Sultan Qaboos pardoned (and ordered the release of) all 50–60 individuals sentenced and imprisoned since 2011 for insulting him, or for violating the country's laws regarding online activity, including 14 activists from Sohar, who were serving terms of between 30 months and five years for their role in protests in the northern industrial port town. The Sultan also ordered those dismissed from private- and public-sector jobs after the 2011–12 protests to be reinstated. Meanwhile prominent blogger and human rights activist Saeed Jaddad was arrested again in July 2013, facing charges for 'undermining the status and prestige of the state', following his calls for political and social reforms, and contact with foreign human rights organizations. Another blogger, Sultan al-Saadi, who had been pardoned in March 2013, was again detained for three weeks in August 2013 for posts on the social networking site Twitter.

Despite these challenges to his legitimacy, the Sultan remains the only candidate for power, and much is made of his annual tours around the country to 'meet the people'. In October 2012, on the occasion of Id al-Adha, Sultan Qaboos visited Musandam and Sohar—his first visit to the towns since the beginning of the 2011 protests. In January 2013 he undertook another tour in the interior governorate, holding a symposium on the development of small and medium enterprises. However, these visits have become heavily choreographed, with the Sultan only meeting individuals who have been thoroughly vetted in advance. Moreover, his occupation of the most important government portfolios, coupled with the lack of a credible heir apparent, is increasingly regarded as potentially destabilizing. Unlike in other GCC monarchies, Sultan Qaboos has largely excluded his extended family from office. As of mid-2013, the Sultan had no children and had not publicly designated an heir. The fear remained that Oman could undergo considerable turmoil in the event of his sudden demise. There are four potential candidates to succeed him: Sayyid Asad bin Tariq al-Said (the Sultan's Personal Representative), Sayyid Haitham bin Tariq al-Said (the Minister of Heritage and Culture) and Sayyid Shihab bin Tariq al-Said (Adviser to the Sultan)—all three of whom are sons of former

Prime Minister Tariq bin Taimur—and, lastly, the Deputy Prime Minister, Sayyid Fahd bin Mahmoud al-Said. Speaking in July 2013, the Omani Minister Responsible for Foreign Affairs, Yousuf bin Alawi bin Abdullah said there was 'no power vacuum' in the country, but the process of appointing a Prime Minister to support Sultan Qaboos was a 'complex issue'. Despite the widespread public support for the expansion of the Consultative Council's role, the Sultan's refusal to appoint a Prime Minister in 2011 and his apparent intention to keep all executive and major legislative powers as his personal prerogative have only exacerbated popular anxiety.

FOREIGN RELATIONS UNDER QABOOS, 1970–2013

Oman's relations with other Arab states improved considerably following the accession of Sultan Qaboos in 1970. Omani dependence on British military force to suppress the revolts in Jebel Akhdar and Dhofar had been condemned by Egypt, Syria, Iraq and Saudi Arabia, among others, increasing Oman's isolation in the Arab world. However, since the 1970s both Kuwait and the UAE have supplied much-needed financial support to Oman, while diplomatic relations were established with Iraq, a former supporter of the PFLO. The establishment of economic and diplomatic links with Saudi Arabia was particularly significant. Oman's support for the Israeli-Egyptian peace treaty of 1979 threatened to damage relations with a number of members of the Arab League, but promised closer ties with the USA and with Egypt, which, at that time, undertook to respond to any request from Oman for military aid. Concern over regional security prompted Oman to join the GCC, which was founded in May 1981.

Oman has never lost its title of 'Britain's oldest friend on the Arabian Peninsula' (according to the words of a correspondent of *The Times* in 1974). The inescapable corollary of the desire to perpetuate an independent policy towards its regional neighbours has been that Oman has never been able—and has certainly not wanted—to question the strategic and economic privileged partnership with Britain and the USA. In July 2010 the British Parliamentary Under Secretary of State for Foreign and Commonwealth Affairs, Alistair Burt, and the Omani Minister Responsible for Foreign Affairs, Yousuf bin Alawi bin Abdullah, announced the creation of the United Kingdom–Oman Joint Working Group to further develop the strategic relationship.

After the United Kingdom withdrew the bulk of its forces from Masirah island in 1977 the USA demonstrated keen interest in the territory. In February 1980 Oman began negotiations with the USA concerning a defence alliance whereby, in exchange for US military and economic aid and a commitment to Oman's security, Oman would grant the USA use of port and airbase facilities in the Gulf (including Masirah island). The renewal of military co-operation agreements with Britain in 1985 and 1995 confirmed Oman's dependency on the USA and Britain. The outbreak of the Iran–Iraq War in September 1980 only served to underline Oman's strategic importance, particularly with regard to the Strait of Hormuz, a narrow waterway at the mouth of the Gulf, between Oman and Iran, through which approximately two-thirds of the world's sea-borne trade in crude petroleum passed at that time (this had decreased to one-third by 2013).

In 1981 the USA established a communications centre in Oman, and pledged more than US $300m. in 1981–85 to develop port and airport facilities in return for the right to stockpile supplies in Oman for possible use by the US Rapid Deployment Force. US forces were permitted to make landings in Oman during the Bright Star military exercises, held in the region in December 1981. In a preliminary attempt to coordinate the Gulf's own independent defence system, the GCC focused its attention on Oman, awarding a five-year defence grant to the country in July 1983 and holding joint military exercises there in October.

In September 1985 Oman established diplomatic relations with the USSR. The move was encouraged by the peaceful relations that had been maintained between Oman and the PDRY since the resumption of diplomatic contact in October 1982. However, US troops were allowed to use military bases in Oman only with the agreement of the Omani Government. The USA continued to make improvements to existing installations in the Sultanate, expanding fuel, ammunition, power and water facilities at Seeb airfield. In October 1988 Oman and the PDRY signed an agreement to increase co-operation in the sectors of trade and communications. The signing took place during the first visit to the Sultanate by a President of the PDRY since that country's independence in 1967.

After the invasion of Kuwait by Iraqi troops in August 1990, the Omani Government stated that the dispute should be resolved without the use of force. However, when it became clear that Iraq would not withdraw from Kuwait, Oman, together with the other members of the GCC, gave its support to the deployment of a US-led defensive force in Saudi Arabia. In November there was evidence that Oman had attempted to mediate in the crisis, when the Iraqi Minister of Foreign Affairs, Tareq Aziz, made the first official Iraqi visit to a GCC state, other than Kuwait, since the invasion.

In September 2001 Oman confirmed that joint Omani-British military exercises would take place despite the international tensions arising from the suicide attacks in the USA on 11 September. As elsewhere in the region, there was concern in Oman that US-led military action against the al-Qa'ida network of Osama bin Laden and the Taliban regime in Afghanistan should not be extended to target any Arab state. Street demonstrations were held in October by Omani students protesting against the war in Afghanistan. Meanwhile, during an official visit to Oman by the US Secretary of Defense, Donald Rumsfeld, in early October, it was reported that the USA was to supply Oman with 12 *F-16* fighter aircraft and other advanced weaponry, at a cost of some US $1,120m. The US military presence in Oman dramatically increased from a pre-2001 level of 200 personnel to more than 4,300 personnel in support of Operation Enduring Freedom in Afghanistan. In 2002 Oman opposed attempts by the USA, as part of its 'war on terror', to garner international support for an eventual offensive against the Iraqi regime of Saddam Hussain, and advocated a diplomatic solution to the escalating crisis. In March 2003, as the US-led forces began assaults on targets in Iraq, Sultan Qaboos appealed for a swift curtailment of the conflict, which he described as 'unjustified' and 'illegitimate'. There were frequent anti-war protests in Oman at this time. Despite the Sultan's opposition to the war in Iraq, he was a close military ally of the USA in all other respects. Oman hosted up to three US Air Force Expeditionary Wings (at Masirah island; Seeb, near Muscat; and Thumrait, near Salalah) supporting military operations in the GCC and Afghanistan, although the presence of these units was not commonly known in Oman. As at August 2013, only one Expeditionary Wing remained in Oman, at Thumrait. Defence and national security forces account for 24% of the state's expenditure, that is 9% of 2011's GDP—one of the world's highest rates. According to the Stockholm International Peace Research Institute, Oman registered a 51% increase in defence spending in 2012—the highest world-wide. In December 2012, during his second visit to Oman since taking office, British Prime Minister David Cameron met the Sultan and signed a $4,100m. contract for Oman to purchase 12 Typhoon and eight Hawk Advanced Jet Trainer aircraft from the British defence manufacturer BAE Systems. A $1,500m. deal with the US firm Raytheon for the acquisition of a ground-based air-defence system received formal approval from the Omani Government when US Secretary of State John Kerry flew to Oman in May 2013.

An agreement between Oman and the UAE on the demarcation of common international borders was reached in June 2002. (This agreement was later expanded and a final draft was signed in July 2008.) However, relations with the UAE deteriorated significantly in 2004, after the UAE Armed Forces, on the orders of the Crown Prince of Abu Dhabi, Sheikh Muhammad bin Zayed Al Nahyan (the Deputy Supreme Commander of the UAE Armed Forces), dismissed the large number of Omani soldiers that it employed. This was followed by increased tensions along the UAE–Omani border, symbolized by the UAE's construction of an extensive fence and border posts between Al-Ain (UAE) and Al-Buraymi. In January 2011 bilateral relations weakened further when the Omani security forces claimed that they had uncovered a UAE spy ring within the Omani Government and military; the UAE denied the allegations. However, there was little negative effect on Oman's relationship with its neighbours, as was demonstrated by GCC plans for an aid package worth more than US $10,000m. to help Oman cope with anti-government protests in March 2011, and also Oman's concomitant support for Saudi Arabia and the UAE's decision to send troops to Bahrain. In July 2011 Sultan Qaboos accepted an invitation from the UAE President, Sheikh Khalifa bin Zayed Al Nahyan, to visit Abu Dhabi. Sheikh Khalifa reciprocated in October when he attended the opening of the Royal Opera House in Muscat, and returned in April 2012 with Sheikh Muhammad to discuss bilateral co-operation. Sultan Qaboos travelled to Dubai on 23 October for talks with its ruler Sheikh Muhammad bin Rashid Al Maktoum.

Oman has expressed a particular desire to promote relations between the GCC states and Iran, and to support gradual political reform in the latter. Sultan Qaboos did not cease diplomatic relations with Tehran after the Islamic Revolution in 1979. He considered that he had no interest in presenting Iran as the sole source of regional tensions, as such an attitude would only hinder long-term stability and mutual co-operation. In early 1989 Oman adopted a more conciliatory policy towards the Islamic Republic of Iran (in November 1987 Oman had supported the Arab League's condemnation of Iran for prolonging hostilities with Iraq), and in March the two countries established an economic co-operation committee. However, Oman's support for Iran was conditional upon the latter's efforts to achieve political stability in the Gulf region. In March 1991 Oman hosted a meeting at which diplomatic relations between Saudi Arabia and Iran were restored. In September 1992 the Governments of Oman and Iran signed an agreement to increase trade and economic co-operation, in particular in the sectors of transport and shipping. Further bilateral discussions were conducted in June 1998, in an attempt to formulate a strategy to combat smuggling activities across the Strait of Hormuz; a memorandum of understanding (MOU) was signed to that end. As a result of these agreements, three ministerial-level forums were established: the Iran-Oman Joint Political Committee, the Iran-Oman Joint Economic Commission and the Iran-Oman Joint Military Conference. These forums have convened annually since the 1990s, and Iran now enjoys closer relations with Oman than with any other GCC state, with official visits at ministerial level and below between the two countries a regular, semi-monthly occurrence. In May 2006 Oman signed accords on oil and gas co-operation, allowing for Omani investment in Iran's oil and gas sector; the construction of a gas pipeline between Iran and Oman; the joint development of the Henjam/Bukha gasfield in the Strait of Hormuz; and the establishment of a joint oil company. Later that month the Iranian President, Mahmoud Ahmadinejad, paid a state visit to Oman, during which he appealed for the further strengthening of ties between the two countries. In 2007 President Ahmadinejad returned to Oman, signing an agreement on the joint development of the Henjam/Bukha gasfield. In 2008 the two countries signed an agreement to develop the Kish gasfield, 170 km west of Henjam, and to supply Oman with gas.

Oman's increasing dependence on Iran for gas has given the Government a particular interest in maintaining good relations with the Islamic Republic. At a joint press conference in December 2007, Yousuf bin Alawi and Iranian Minister of Foreign Affairs Manouchehr Mottaki announced the two countries' intention to increase bilateral trade to US $1,000m. a year. In April 2008 Oman sent a high-level delegation, led by Deputy Prime Minister Sayyid Fahd bin Mahmoud al-Said, to the Iranian capital, Tehran, to meet President Ahmadinejad. During the visit, Yousuf bin al-Alawi bin Abdullah described his country's relations with Iran as 'very good and satisfying'. In July 2009 Ahmadinejad described Omani-Iranian relations as 'exemplary and praiseworthy'. In the following month Sultan Qaboos and seven of his ministers paid a three-day state visit to Tehran to promote trade between the two countries and possibly dialogue with the West. This was his first visit to Iran since the overthrow of the Shah in 1979; it symbolized his pragmatic view that the Iranian Government in its current form was here to stay. In November Yousuf bin al-Alawi bin Abdullah described his country's relations with Iran as 'strategic'. In August 2010 Oman signed a defence co-operation agreement with Iran.

Oman also acted as mediator in securing the release of US nationals held by Iran, as well as Iranian nationals detained by Britain and the USA. In 2010 and 2011 Oman successfully negotiated the release of three US tourists arrested by the Iranian security forces for allegedly crossing into Iran illegally. The bail of $500,000 per person was reportedly paid by Oman. In 2013 Oman successfully mediated the release of Iranian diplomat Nasratallah Tajik, who had been held in the United Kingdom for nearly six years, and of an Iranian scientist, Mojtaba Attarodi, detained by US authorities on suspicion that he was a conduit for dual-use equipment destined for Iran's nuclear programme. These cases illustrated Oman's value to both the USA and Iran as a discreet and neutral intermediary. In an interview on a US television station in January 2012, Sultan Qaboos contended that Iran was not seeking conflict with the USA. Oman supports Iran's use of nuclear energy for peaceful purposes, rejecting US claims that Iran poses a threat to the wider Gulf region, and opposes the use of force against Iran. However, Oman does not support Iran's claims to sovereignty over Abu Musa and the Greater and Lesser Tunb islands (all of which are claimed by the UAE). Following the downgrading of diplomatic relations between Iran and the United Kingdom in November 2011, Oman has been representing Iran in the United Kingdom since June 2012.

In October 1992 Oman signed an agreement with Yemen (the Yemen Arab Republic—YAR—and the PDRY were unified in May 1990) to establish the demarcation of their border. The agreement was officially ratified in December. The efforts of Sultan Qaboos to mediate a settlement to the civil conflict in Yemen ended in disappointment when fighting broke out again between the two rival Yemeni factions in April 1994. In recognition of Sultan Qaboos's mediatory role, Oman was elected a non-permanent member of the UN Security Council for a two-year term commencing in January 1994. In June 1995 Oman and Yemen completed the demarcation of their joint border; in the following month Oman and Saudi Arabia officially demarcated their common border. In July 1996 Oman withdrew an estimated 15,000 troops from the last of the disputed territories on the Yemeni border, in accordance with the 1992 agreement. In May 1997 official representatives from both countries signed the international border demarcation maps at a ceremony in Muscat. It was also agreed to promote bilateral trade by building a new 245-km road linking the two countries. In September 1998, following a meeting of border officials from both countries, 12 economic co-operation accords were announced, as were plans for the establishment of a free trade zone; Saudi claims that the border agreement violated sovereign Saudi territory were rejected by both countries. In November 2011 Oman negotiated the release of three French hostages, who had been held by Yemeni tribesmen for five months. In May 2013 Oman was reported to have paid US $50m. to secure the release of three other European hostages (two Finnish and one Austrian) kidnapped in San'a in December 2012 and sold to members of al-Qa'ida.

In the 1990s Oman, which had only in 1988 recognized the existence of the Palestinian leadership, began to give financial aid to the Palestinian (National) Authority (PA), but also established relations with Israel in 1993. In April 1994 the Israeli Deputy Minister of Foreign Affairs, Yossi Beilin, participated in talks in Oman. This constituted the first official visit by an Israeli minister to a Gulf Arab state since Israel's declaration of independence in 1948. In September 1994, moreover, Oman and the other GCC member states announced the partial ending of their economic boycott of Israel. The Israeli Prime Minister, Itzhak Rabin, made an official visit to the Sultanate in November to discuss the Middle East peace process, and in February 1995 it was announced that low-level diplomatic relations were to be established between the two countries with the opening of interests sections, respectively, in Tel-Aviv and Muscat. In April 1996 bilateral relations were consolidated further by a two-day official visit to Oman by Shimon Peres, the new Israeli Prime Minister. Israel opened its trade office in Muscat in May 1996. Oman opened its trade office in Tel-Aviv in August, despite concerns that relations with Israel would be undermined by the uncompromising international stance adopted by the new Government of Binyamin Netanyahu in Israel. In April 1997, in accordance with an Arab League resolution adopted in March in protest against Israel's decision to construct a Jewish settlement in a disputed area of East Jerusalem, Oman suspended diplomatic links with Israel, officially resumed the economic boycott and withdrew from multilateral peace talks, although it did not close its trade office in Tel-Aviv. As the Middle East peace process faltered, Oman suspended all commercial and business activities with Israel, and two Israeli Ministry of Foreign Affairs officials were refused visas to enter Oman in order to find a permanent site for the Israeli diplomatic mission in Muscat.

In July 1997 the Omani Ministry of Foreign Affairs announced the opening of a representative office in the PA-administered city of Gaza, and, in an address to the UN General Assembly in October, Yousuf bin al-Alawi bin Abdullah urged UN members to encourage Israel to withdraw from the Golan Heights and southern Lebanon. In December Oman recalled its representative from its trade office in Tel-Aviv, but it did not close the office. In May 1998 Sultan Qaboos formally received the first Palestinian envoy to Oman, and in the following month Yasser Arafat, the President of the PA, visited Oman and met Qaboos during a tour of Arab states. In October 2000, after the start of the second *intifada* (uprising), Oman closed both its trade office in Tel-Aviv and the Israeli trade office in Muscat. While Oman has voiced its support for the 'roadmap', designed to introduce confidence-building measures between Israelis and Palestinians (see the chapters on Israel and the Palestinian Territories), it has yet to reopen its low-level diplomatic engagement with Israel. After the Palestinian legislative elections of January 2006, the victorious Islamic Resistance Movement (Hamas) sent a high-level delegation to Oman in April, after similar visits to the other GCC states, seeking financial support for its newly formed administration. Oman, along with the other GCC states, pledged to support Hamas.

Oman's relations with India have strengthened considerably since the 1990s. In 1995 the two countries established the India-Oman Joint Commission, a ministerial-level forum that meets every few years to facilitate closer economic ties. Sultan Qaboos paid his first state visit to India in April 1997, during which the two Governments signed a number of MOUs. In February 2002 the two countries established the Oman-India Strategic Consultation Group. In November 2005 the Omani and Indian navies held a joint exercise in Indian waters. In the following month Oman and India signed an MOU on defence co-operation—the first agreement of its type that India had signed with a GCC state. The memorandum provided for military exchanges, training, joint exercises, and the purchase of arms, ammunition and equipment for the SAF. In March 2006 Oman and India signed an agreement to establish the India-Oman Joint Military Co-operation Committee, to be headed by the Indian Minister of Defence and the Omani Undersecretary for Defence. Its purpose was to identify areas of co-operation, including the purchase and joint production of military equipment for the SAF. It was the first joint military committee that India had established with a Muslim state. In November 2008 Oman established a US $100m. Oman-India Investment Fund intended to promote Omani investment in India, which was launched during the visit of Indian Prime Minister Dr Manmohan Singh to Muscat. Oman has been actively involved in negotiations for a proposed India-GCC free trade agreement; however, by mid-2013 no such agreement had been signed. In January 2013, on the occasion of the visit of Indian Defence Secretary Shashikant Sharma to Muscat, Oman and India agreed to expand co-operation in fields ranging from maritime security and anti-piracy measures to joint training and combat exercises.

Oman also strengthened its economic ties with a number of Asian countries in the mid-2000s. By 2005 the Sultanate was the second largest supplier of petroleum to China, and by 2007 it was the sixth largest supplier of petroleum and second largest supplier of liquefied natural gas (LNG) to the Republic of Korea (South Korea). In September of that year the Deputy Prime Minister, Sayyid Fahd bin Mahmoud al-Said, paid official visits to both countries. Two months later the South Korean Prime Minister visited Oman to discuss the strengthening of economic ties. In February 2006 the Undersecretary for Foreign Affairs, Sayyid Badr bin Hamad al-Busaidi, visited Pakistan to promote economic ties and to discuss the problem of illegal Pakistani workers in Oman. During a second visit to Pakistan in April, he announced that Oman would invest US $100m. in development projects at the port of Gwadar (a former Omani enclave in southern Pakistan sold to the South Asian state in 1958). In December 2007 Vietnamese Deputy Prime Minister Nguyen Sinh Hung visited Oman to promote investment in Viet Nam. The two sides agreed that Oman would create a $1,000m. fund for investment in Viet Nam and that the two countries would establish a joint government committee on economic co-operation. Oman signed a free trade agreement with Singapore in 2009.

Economy

Revised for this edition by RICHARD GERMAN and ELIZABETH TAYLOR

INTRODUCTION

Oman's economy continues to be based largely on the hydrocarbons sector, although there has been significant progress towards non-oil industrial diversification in recent years. It also relies heavily on expatriate labour, in common with the economies of other member countries of the Cooperation Council for the Arab States of the Gulf (Gulf Cooperation Council—GCC). According to the 2010 census, the total population of Oman was 2,773,479, of whom 816,143 were non-Omanis. However, more recent data from the National Center for Statistics and Information have suggested that the expatriate figure might have been a substantial underestimate.

Oil was first produced commercially in 1967, but it was not until 1970, when Sultan Qaboos bin Said assumed power, that the income was invested in the country's economic development. Oman's economy has since expanded considerably under a prudent policy of avoiding external debt while developing both public and private sectors. While petroleum production remains the predominant feature of the economy, there has been increasing emphasis on the exploitation of the country's gas reserves for export (mainly as liquefied natural gas—LNG) and as the basis for energy-intensive industrial diversification.

Oman's economic growth since the mid-1960s has been rapid but uneven. Between 1965 and 1980, according to World Bank estimates, the country's gross domestic product (GDP) increased, in real terms, by 12.5% per year, one of the highest national growth rates in the world. The annual GDP growth rate then declined during the 1980s to an average of 6% in 1990–95 and 3.1% during 1998–2004. Real GDP grew by 2.7% in 1998, but contracted by 0.2% in 1999, when economic policy was tightened in response to the 1998 downturn in world oil prices. In 2000 it rose by an estimated 5.1%, owing mainly to growth of about 10% in the hydrocarbons sector, where a sustained recovery in petroleum prices coincided with the start of LNG exports in April to the Republic of Korea (South Korea—see Petroleum and Natural Gas). Following a 2.6% increase in 2002, GDP rose by 2.0% in 2003 and by an estimated 5.6% in 2004. According to the Central Bank, GDP growth reached 4.9% in 2005, 6.0% in 2006 and 7.7% in 2007, supported by high petroleum prices on the international markets and by rapid growth of the non-hydrocarbon sectors.

Oman's macroeconomic performance in 2008 remained robust, reflecting accelerated GDP growth of 12.8%, significant job creation, further progress on diversification, large fiscal and balance of payments surpluses, a comfortable level of foreign exchange reserves, and a resilient banking system. Although 2009 proved more challenging in the wake of the international financial crisis, which provoked a global downturn and sharp decline in world oil prices, the economy still grew by 1.1%, which, according to the IMF, reflected the Sultanate's 'prudent macroeconomic management of oil wealth, appropriate regulatory and supervisory policies, and implementation of structural reforms to enhance non-hydrocarbon growth'. The economy recovered in 2010 and official figures estimated GDP growth at 5.0%, driven by a revival in international oil prices and domestic demand. There was also a significant improvement in the fiscal balance, from a deficit of 1.2% of GDP in 2009 to a surplus of 6.2% in 2010. Despite adverse global conditions, the economy continued to gather momentum in 2011, with estimated growth of 5.5%, which was driven by higher oil prices and increased government spending. According to an IMF report, Oman's fiscal and external surpluses increased to 9.8% and 12.7% of GDP, respectively, in 2011, but the Fund warned that the economy remained vulnerable to oil price developments and that fiscal sustainability was a 'mounting challenge'. In the longer term, the report stated that the health of the economy depended on further diversification and that the problem of high unemployment among Omani nationals needed to be effectively addressed. The IMF estimated GDP growth in 2012 at 5.0% (although preliminary government estimates for the year indicated growth of 8.3%, including a 10.6% expansion of the non-oil economy). The Fund cited higher oil prices, increased petroleum production (due to new recovery technologies) and fiscal expansion as the main economic drivers. However, while the near- and medium-term outlook remained positive, with robust non-oil growth and moderate inflation, the IMF projected fiscal and external deficits, as recent initiatives, including government job creation measures and wage increases, had resulted in substantially higher expenditure between 2010 and 2012 and reduced the policy scope to respond to economic shocks and any sustained decrease in oil prices.

Annual inflation declined by an average of 0.5% in 1998–2005. The consumer price index increased by an estimated 0.4% in 1999, but declined by 1.2% in 2000, by 1.0% in 2001, by 0.7% in 2002 and by 0.3% in 2003. Although increases of 0.4% and 1.2% were registered for 2004 and 2005, respectively, the rate of inflation still remained significantly lower than the 2.3% averaged by advanced global economies in that year. However, the rate increased sharply to average 3.2% in 2006 and 5.5% in 2007, reflecting rising world food prices and the depreciation of the US dollar (to which the rial Omani has remained pegged at an official exchange rate of RO 1 = US $2.6008 since January 1986). In 2008 the rate of inflation rose sharply, to 12.4%, largely owing to high domestic demand and price increases in food and commodities on world markets. However, pressures abated in the second half of the year as petroleum prices declined markedly, and the inflation rate continued a steady deceleration in 2009, reaching 3.4%. The annual rate remained stable at 3.3% in 2010 and was again largely influenced by higher prices for imported food. The Central Bank warned of an upward trend in 2011 as inflation increased to 4% over the year. However, the rate declined to 2.9% in 2012, given the moderation in international food prices and the Government's subsidies on core goods and services.

Revenues from petroleum have been used to underpin a series of five-year development plans, starting in 1976. These plans have aimed to provide the country with necessary social amenities while investing further in the petroleum sector, but in recent years there has been a strong emphasis on diversification. The 1991–95 Plan imposed strict limits on projected external borrowing, and again emphasized economic diversification, which was to be achieved through the expansion of the private sector, and renewed focus on industry, agriculture and fisheries, mining, and services. In November 1994 an investment law was introduced to allow foreign nationals to own as much as 100% of 'projects contributing to the development of the national economy', particularly if they pertained to infrastructure. A new tax law was introduced in October 1996, reducing the rate of tax paid by Omani companies with 49% or less foreign ownership, as part of the Government's efforts to promote foreign investment and strengthen the role of the private sector in the economy. All companies working in industry, mining, fishing, tourism and agriculture would benefit from tax exemptions that previously applied only to firms that were entirely Omani-owned. In 1997 the Minister of Commerce and Industry announced that all new Omani companies would be required to offer 49% of their shares to foreign ownership, a move that was not welcomed by a number of the country's major trading families, who felt that this initiative would undermine their dominant position.

In the fifth Development Plan (1996–2000), emphasis was placed on the elimination of the budget deficit by 2000 through the reduction of public expenditure, the development of the non-petroleum sector and the expansion of the privatization programme. A policy of 'Omanization' of the work-force (to reduce the country's dependence on expatriate labour, thereby providing opportunities for Oman's rapidly expanding population) was given more impetus when, in June 1996, the Government stated that it would assume the full cost of training Omani nationals employed in the private sector and announced that a schedule of charges would be imposed on private sector companies employing foreign workers.

The Government's 2001–05 planning targets (the sixth Development Plan) included the creation of 100,000 new private sector employment opportunities for Omanis. It was also planned to increase state funding for their education and training, and to limit further the employment of expatriates in certain fields. The seventh Plan (2006–10) came into effect at the beginning of 2006, with the aim of accelerating economic diversification by increasing non-petroleum activities and further developing the Omanization programme. The sectors targeted for growth included tourism, manufacturing and fisheries, and the Government set an overall goal for annual growth of 7.5% in non-petroleum activities over the five-year period. In February 2009 the Government backtracked to some extent on its Omanization policy and partially reversed a decision announced in 2007 banning foreign workers from 15 specific professions (the restriction being lifted for eight of them). The programme was nevertheless set to continue, having already made a significant impact on Oman's labour market. According to the Central Bank, the growth of Omani employment in the private sector since 2001 had remained consistently higher than that in the public sector.

The eighth Development Plan (2011–15) was announced in January 2011. It envisaged total investment of RO 30,000m.—funded by higher oil revenue, based on an assumed average price of US $59 per barrel and average production of about 900,000 barrels per day (b/d)—and minimum annual GDP growth of 5% throughout the period. The drive for economic diversification would be maintained, with the aim of creating about 50,000 additional jobs annually, together with greater emphasis on infrastructure and social sector reforms.

AGRICULTURE AND FISHERIES

Much of the area under cultivation is planted with date palms. Other important crops include lemons, limes, mangoes, melons, bananas, papayas, tomatoes, onions and potatoes. Livestock-farming is practised extensively in Dhofar, which benefits from monsoon rains between June and September. Cattle are raised in the hills north of Salalah, and goats are reared in the Hajar mountains. Oman remains a leading livestock producer in the Arabian peninsula, with 1.75m. goats, 396,500 sheep, 339,500 cattle and 132,200 camels in 2011, according to FAO estimates. Although agriculture and fishing still provide employment for large numbers of Omanis, the sector accounts for only 1%–2% of annual GDP. However, by 2020 the Government expects agriculture to have increased its contribution to 3.1% of GDP and fishing to 2% of GDP, with targeted annual growth of at least 4.5% for agriculture and 5.6% for fishing.

The Oman Bank for Agriculture and Fisheries was established in 1981 to provide loans to farmers, with the intention of curbing rural-to-urban migration, and in the same year a state marketing authority, the Public Authority for Marketing Agricultural Produce (PAMAP), was set up with the aim of increasing domestic consumption of local products. During 1992–96 annual agricultural output rose from 784,200 metric tons to 1,181,800 tons, reflecting an expansion of modern techniques and intensification methods. As a result of an increase in production, the value of agricultural produce rose from RO 85.1m. in 1992 to RO 100.8m. in 1996, an average annual increase of some 4.6% (although below the 6.3% targeted in the 1991–95 Development Plan). Over the same period the value of agricultural exports increased from RO 31.8m. to RO 50.8m. In October 2000 the Government announced the closure of PAMAP (after an attempt to privatize it had failed), expressing confidence that with continuing state subsidies the farming industry was sufficiently mature to market itself.

Irrigation accounts for about 90% of the country's water consumption, and the rate of water usage by the agricultural sector has remained a matter of concern for the Government. By 2007 there were 25 groundwater-recharge dams and 58 small surface-storage dams across the Sultanate. Two dams across the Dayqah *wadi* (river valley)—the only significant stretch of permanently flowing water in Oman—were subsequently completed. There has also been increasing investment in desalination facilities to supply potable water to reduce the need to extract scarce groundwater reserves. In December 2011 the first stage of the Al-Najd Project for Agricultural Development was inaugurated. The scheme was to relocate grass farms from the Al-Batinah and Salalah regions to Al-Najd, with the aim of both increasing the production of animal fodder and rationalizing groundwater use.

Fishing is a traditional and growing industry off Oman's 1,700-km coastline. Fishing and fish-processing have been developed into an important export industry. Although large commercial trawlers have become increasingly important, the sector has remained dominated by independent fishermen using small vessels. During the late 1970s the annual catch was approximately 60,000 metric tons, and this rose steadily to reach about 165,000 tons by the late 1980s. An uneven decline in the 1990s, to about 106,000 tons in 1998, was attributable to overfishing and the depletion of breeding stock. Another negative factor was a decision by the European Union (EU) to suspend imports of fish from Oman in 1998 because of concerns over quality control. However, the introduction of measures to prevent further overfishing and the lifting of the EU ban resulted in an increase in the total catch to 120,400 tons in 2000, and by 2010 the figure had risen to 164,100 tons.

PETROLEUM AND NATURAL GAS

In 1937 Petroleum Concessions (Oman) Ltd, a subsidiary of the Iraq Petroleum Co, was granted a 75-year concession to explore for petroleum in Oman, extending over the whole area except for the district of Dhofar. A concession covering Dhofar was granted in 1953 to Dhofar Cities Service Petroleum Corpn. Petroleum was not discovered until the early 1960s, when deposits were found near Fahud, and commercial production began in 1967.

In 2012 oil and gas accounted for 52.2% of nominal GDP and 85.4% of government revenues. Proven oil and condensate reserves were estimated at 5,500m. barrels by the end of that year. Production is managed by Petroleum Development Oman (PDO), in which the Government holds a 60% share, while Royal Dutch Shell (the other major shareholder) has 34%. PDO was responsible for over 60% of Oman's daily oil output in 2012, the remainder being produced by a number of foreign concerns. PDO is heavily dependent on managerial and technical assistance from Shell, which operates most of Oman's main oilfields. The number of oil-producing fields in Oman stood at 162 in 2012. The key producers are the Yibal, Nimr, Fahud and Lekhwair fields; Yibal, situated in the north of the country, is Oman's largest producing oilfield. A north–south pipeline connects the oilfields to the port of Mina al-Fahal, near Muscat. Oman is neither a member of the Organization of the Petroleum Exporting Countries (OPEC), nor of the Organization of Arab Petroleum Exporting Countries, and is not, therefore, subject to controls on petroleum production and pricing, although it has generally respected OPEC's policies.

In April 2001 Denmark's Maersk Oil Oman obtained concession agreements for two exploration blocks in western Oman. New exploration and production-sharing agreements were also signed with Novus of Australia in October 2001, Hunt Oil of the USA in November and TotalFinaElf (now Total) of France in March 2002. In April, moreover, Novus took over an onshore concession relinquished by Occidental Petroleum Corpn of the USA, to become the biggest foreign operator in Oman in terms of acreage. In 2005 the Government announced that it had turned over the Mukhaizna oilfield in central Oman to a joint venture between Occidental and Liwa Energy of the United Arab Emirates (UAE). Further exploration and production-sharing agreements were signed with local and foreign oil companies, including Indago Petroleum of the United Kingdom and the Oman-based Taqah Oil Exploration Co, in June 2006 and with India's Reliance Industries and RAK Petroleum in 2007. In February 2009 the Government awarded an exploration concession to Epsilon Energy of Canada. In the same month the Sultanate's first offshore oilfield, 25 km from the coast of Musandam, came on stream with an initial flow of 10,000 b/d. Later that year four new exploration agreements were signed (with Ibson Energy of Canada, Harvest and Petrotel of the USA, and Petronas of Malaysia). In 2010 42 exploration wells were drilled by various companies in Oman (26 by PDO), resulting in several new discoveries, including in the Amal, Siah, Ghubar East and Bourj North fields. The production potential from these discoveries was estimated at 93m. barrels. Five onshore and offshore exploration agreements were signed in 2011—three with local Oman Oil Co Exploration and Production and Masirah Oil Limited, and two with Petrotel and Canada-based Allied Petroleum Exploration. During that year a further 41 exploration wells were drilled. Of these, 21 were drilled by PDO, resulting in new discoveries in four of them. In 2012 the Government signed two onshore exploration agreements—one with Hungary's MOL Oman Ltd and the other with the United Kingdom's Frontier Resources Oman—and also invited companies to participate in bid rounds for 12 onshore and offshore blocks, which were to be operated on a production-sharing basis. Another 41 wells were drilled during that year, including 18 by PDO. In March 2013 the Ministry of Oil and Gas signed a new exploration and production-sharing agreement with Petrotel for two blocks in Dhofar.

By 2001 Oman's average petroleum output stood at 961,000 b/d, but thereafter declined until 2007, by which time production had decreased to 710,000 b/d. However, reversing this trend, it then increased annually to reach 891,000 b/d in 2011 and 918,500 b/d in 2012, reflecting the discovery of new oilfields and the application of improved recovery techniques. Oil exports in 2012 totalled 279.8m. barrels, up from 269.4m. barrels in 2011, and, in view of the rise in oil prices during the year, the value of crude exports increased by 10.7% (to RO 11,795m.). The People's Republic of China remained the main importer of Omani crude supplies in 2012, followed by Japan and Taiwan.

In April 2002 PDO announced details of its 'Target 50' (T50) five-year plan for substantial investment in improved oil recovery (IOR) and enhanced oil recovery (EOR) programmes intended to increase the recovery rate from mature oilfields from 23% to 50% of their proven reserves. This planned investment was to include US $1,000m.–$2,000m. to be spent on steam injection technology, in order to boost production from the Mukhaizna field to 60,000 b/d–80,000 b/d by 2010, and $200m. to be spent on a similar project in the northern Qarn Alam field, where the oil is of very high viscosity. High-pressure gas injection to increase output from the Harweel field was also scheduled in four phases. It was estimated that the IOR and EOR investment would more than double Oman's average oil production costs, from $3–$4 per barrel to as much as $9 per barrel.

Oman's first petroleum refinery came into production at Mina al-Fahal, near Muscat, in 1982. Negotiations with international oil companies commenced in October 2000 for a long-term offtake agreement for products from a proposed refinery at Sohar (which would include propylene, liquefied petroleum gas, unleaded gasoline, low-sulphur gas oil, fuel oil and sulphur). Four bids were submitted in July 2002 for the contract to build the refinery, and in January 2003 the contract was awarded to a Japanese consortium. The 116,000-b/d refinery, completed at a cost of US $1,300m., commenced operations in 2006. The Oman Refinery Co was to operate and manage a 260-km pipeline linking the crude petroleum exporting terminal at Mina al-Fahal to the planned Sohar refinery. The engineering, procurement and construction (EPC) contract for the pipeline was awarded to a joint venture of Italy's Saipem and Greece's Consolidated Contractors Co in 2004. The refinery at Mina al-Fahal has since been upgraded to boost capacity to 106,000 b/d. In 2007 the Government merged the Oman Refinery Co and the Sohar Refinery Co into the Oman Refineries and Petrochemicals Co. In May 2009 Sohar Industrial Port Co (a joint venture between the Oman Government and the Netherlands' Port of Rotterdam Authority) signed a contract with Bahrain's Mashael Group for the construction of a $200m. refinery in the Sohar industrial zone to produce 30,000 b/d of bitumen. In June 2012 the Oman Oil Co and the UAE's International Petroleum Investment Co formed a joint venture to build and operate a new refinery and petrochemical complex at Duqm. In January 2013 it was reported that two state-owned investment companies planned to build and operate a new 200m.-barrel oil storage terminal at Ras Markaz in the south-east of the country. The project would include the construction of a pipeline linking the terminal with the northern pipeline network.

Oman's proven reserves of natural gas were estimated at 900,000m. cu m at the end of 2012. Gas production continued to rise annually, from 14,000m. cu m in 2001 to 27,100m. cu m in 2010, until 2011, when it slowed to 26,500m. cu m. However, output increased again in 2012, to 29,000m. cu m from 32 producing fields. Due to rising domestic consumption and long-term LNG export obligations, Oman's gas demand has outpaced its production capacity, prompting the Government to extend exploration, develop new gasfields, increase EOR applications and also to import gas supplies.

In February 1992 plans had been announced for massive investment in a project to produce LNG, to be implemented by Oman LNG, a consortium led by the Government (which had a 51% share), Shell, Total and various Japanese and South Korean companies. The liquefaction plant, with two gas trains, was subsequently constructed at Qalhat near Sur, on the coast 150 km south of the capital, by the Chiyoda Corpn of Japan and Foster Wheeler of the USA at a cost of US $2,250m., becoming Oman's largest single construction project to date. Production began in February 2000 at a rate of 6.6m. metric tons per year, and the first LNG exports were shipped in April to South Korea under a 25-year agreement with the Korea Gas Corpn for the supply of 4.1m. tons per year. By mid-2000 long-term sales and purchase agreements had also been concluded with Japan's Osaka Gas, for 0.7m. tons per year from 2000 to 2025, and with Enron of the USA for the supply of 1.6m. tons per year of LNG to India's Dabhol Power Co over 20 years, starting in February 2002.

The sudden collapse of Enron in December 2001 caused major difficulties for Oman LNG, since it forced Dabhol—in which Enron was a major shareholder—to cancel the LNG import agreement with Oman. However, in March 2002 Oman LNG concluded a five-year agreement with Royal Dutch Shell for the supply of 700,000 metric tons of LNG per year to that company's customers in Spain. A further agreement was negotiated in April whereby Gaz de France was to take nine spot tanker cargoes of LNG in 2002. Most crucially, in May an agreement was signed with Unión Fenosa (now Gas Natural Fenosa) of Spain providing for the annual export to Spain, by tanker, of 1.6m. tons of LNG over a period of 20 years, starting in 2006. An undertaking by Unión Fenosa to invest in a long-discussed 50% 'third train' expansion of the Qalhat plant's capacity, to about 10m. tons per year, lent new impetus to the US $700m. project, the EPC contract for which was awarded in January 2003 to Chiyoda-Foster Wheeler. In November Oman LNG signed an agreement to supply BP Gas Marketing of the United Kingdom with 3.6m. tons of LNG over a six-year period, beginning in 2004. Further long-term sales and purchase agreements for output from the third train were signed in 2004 with three Japanese companies—Itochu Corpn (which was to take 700,000 tons of LNG per year for 20 years from 2006), Mitsubishi Corpn (800,000 tons a year for 15 years, also from 2006) and Osaka Gas (800,000 tons a year for 17 years from 2009).

Plans were meanwhile in progress to drill new wells at three of the country's central gasfields, Barik, Saih Rawl and Saih Nihayda, in order to supply the amount of gas required by the Qalhat plant and other planned developments, amid industry concern that existing supplies were insufficient for expected requirements. In February 2004 Al-Hassan Engineering of Oman and India's Punj Lloyd were awarded the US $56m. contract to build a 48-inch diameter, 265-km long gas loop-line—with a total capacity of 5.0m. cu m/d—from central Oman to the third LNG train at Qalhat; the project was completed in 2005, and, in addition to the successful commissioning of a gas-processing facility at Saih Nihayda, PDO supply capacity to Omani gas-liquefaction plants was expanded by 30%.

In April 2009 the Government signed gas exploration and production-sharing concession agreements with three international companies—Petronas of Malaysia, US-based Harvest and BP. In February 2010 PDO announced the discovery of a new and potentially large gasfield near Fahud in the north of the Sultanate, and in June 2011 BP revealed plans to invest US $15,000m. in the development of the Khazzan and Makarem gasfields. A number of companies continued exploration activities in 2012 with notable results, particularly a major gas discovery in the Mabrouk field in northern Oman.

Given the shortfalls in its own production, in order to meet the burgeoning domestic demand and its LNG export commitments, Oman sought to import natural gas, principally from Qatar's North Field through the Dolphin Gas Project pipeline. The Omani Government signed a memorandum of understanding (MOU) with the Dolphin group in 1999 in acknowledgement of potential future demand for Qatari gas. The delivery of Qatari gas to Oman began in November 2008. Following protracted negotiations since 2006, Oman reportedly signed an initial contract in July 2011 to import additional natural gas supplies from Iran.

Within Oman, EPC contracts were awarded in May 2000 for two new gas pipeline projects, involving the construction of a 305-km line between Fahud and Sohar (awarded to India's Dodsal) and a 700-km line from Saih Rawl to Salalah (awarded to an Italian-led consortium). Completed in the latter half of 2002, the pipelines transport gas to feed industries at Sohar (see Industry and Power) and Salalah. The addition of the new pipelines more than doubled the total length of Oman's main gas-transportation and transmission network (excluding the supply lines serving the LNG plant), which was estimated to be around 800 km in 2001.

In November 2011 Oman became the 11th member of the Gas Exporting Countries Forum, a grouping of the world's leading gas producers.

INDUSTRY AND POWER

Before 1964 industry in Oman was confined to small traditional handicrafts, such as silversmithing, weaving and boatbuilding. The development of petroleum reserves generated activity in the construction sector, but it was not until the change of regime in 1970 that government investment in infrastructure projects and private spending on housing started a boom in construction. A large proportion of Oman's labour force in construction has been provided by immigrant workers from India and Pakistan.

The 1981–85 Development Plan aimed to quadruple industrial output, giving the industrial sector an average growth rate of 36.2% per year over the Plan's term. Development plans since 1986 have sought to diversify Oman's industrial base as a provision against an eventual exhaustion of hydrocarbon reserves. The 1996–2000 Plan envisaged the expansion of Oman's non-oil industrial sector in order to reduce dependence on petroleum revenues, with Sohar and Sur becoming the country's principal industrial centres. The 2001–05 Plan introduced strategies to encourage new economic and service sectors, boost exports and improve Oman's balance of trade. This was to be achieved through the supply of cheap Omani natural gas and other local raw materials to local industries, which was to encourage the development of information technology and telecommunications, and thus improve private sector productivity and increase the number of Omani nationals working in the industrial sector.

Development projects planned in the late 1990s in gas-intensive industries, including a fertilizer plant at Sur and an aluminium smelter and petrochemicals facility at Sohar, were initially delayed by declining commodity prices, investor caution and complicated financing arrangements. In 1997 Oman and India signed an agreement to construct a fertilizer plant at Sur, next to the Qalhat LNG complex (see Petroleum and Natural Gas). The plant, costing US $969m., was intended to produce ammonia and urea and have a capacity of 1.7m. metric tons per year. It was to be constructed and managed by the Oman-India Fertilizer Co (Omifco), in which the state-owned Oman Oil Co (OOC) would have a 50% stake and Indian partners the other 50%. Gas feedstock for the plant would be provided by PDO, and the Indian partners were to take most of the output. Difficulties arose in 1999 when the Indian authorities undertook a re-examination of the financial terms of the proposed venture, and one of the original Indian partners withdrew, blaming low fertilizer prices. However, in May 2000 the Indian Government approved new offtake proposals and in July 2002 financing arrangements were finalized with a view to enabling construction of the plant to start; the foundation stone was laid in October 2003 and production from the plant commenced with the first 15,000-ton shipment of ammonia in April 2005, followed by 25,465 tons of urea in June.

A US $2,500m. aluminium smelter and a $900m. petrochemicals complex proposed in the 1996–2000 Development Plan were to be sited at Sohar, north-east of Muscat. The smelter was intended to have a capacity of 480,000 metric tons per year, and the petrochemicals plant was projected to produce 450,000 tons per year of ethylene and 450,000 tons per year of polyethylene. Both plants would use gas feedstock from fields in central Oman, supplied via pipeline. Despite ongoing negotiations, however, financing arrangements for these projects remained unresolved, although in May 2003 it was reported that the OOC and the Abu Dhabi Water and Electricity Authority (ADWEA—based in the UAE) intended to form a 'special purpose company', which, together with an unnamed international investor, would develop the aluminium smelter. (The function of the OOC is to invest in hydrocarbon-related joint ventures in Oman and abroad. It is funded out of a State General Reserve Fund set up by the Government to receive the gross proceeds of 15,000 b/d of Oman's crude petroleum production.) In June 2004 Canada's Alcan signed an MOU to take a 20% stake in the project (with the OOC and ADWEA each holding 40%). In December 2005 Alcan announced that construction of the smelter, at a revised cost of $1,700m. and (scaled-down) planned capacity of 350,000 tons per year, would commence, and full production at the newly inaugurated plant was reached in April 2009.

A proposal in 2000 to add a polypropylene unit to the planned oil refinery at Sohar (see Petroleum and Natural Gas) was widely regarded as a substitute for the stalled ethylene/polyethylene project. Upon completion in September 2006, the new polypropylene plant had a production capacity of 340,000 metric tons per year. It was built and operated by Oman Polypropylene LLC (OPP), in which the OOC is the majority shareholder with 60%, together with the Gulf Investment Corpn (GIC) and South Korea's LG Engineering, each of which hold 20% stakes. The GIC acquired its interest from the OOC in June 2004, following the withdrawal of ABB Lummus of the Netherlands as an equity partner the previous April.

Plans for a 5,000-metric-tons-a-day methanol plant at Sohar, first announced in 2000, advanced in December 2003 with the signing of a joint venture agreement between the project's promoters—the Oman Methanol Holding Co (OMHC, a division of Oman's Omar Zawawi Establishment or Omzest Group), Germany's Ferrostaal and Methanol Holdings (Trinidad) Ltd (MHTL). MHTL had a 50% stake, OHMC 30% and Ferrostaal 20%. The first phase, costing US $400m., envisaged the construction of a 2,500-tons-a-day plant to be operational by the end of 2006. Construction began in that year of the Oman Formaldehyde Chemical Co LLC plant in Sohar's Industrial Port Area, with an expected production of 125 tons a day of urea formaldehyde, or 203 tons a day of aqueous formaldehyde. The joint venture, between OHMC and Manso Holding Co WLL (a subsidiary of Manso Group, Bahrain), represented a downstream offshoot of the methanol plant and was expected to double its output in the second phase of development. The expansion of Oman's petrochemicals sector was bolstered with the announcement in 2006 of an initiative by the Oman Aromatics Co (a joint investment venture of the OOC, Oman Refineries and Petrochemicals Co and LG International, holding 60%, 20% and 20% stakes, respectively) to construct a $1,600m. aromatics plant at Sohar, with work beginning in August of that year; production commenced in November 2009. It was hoped that this project would promote downstream development in the Sultanate and facilitate the shift in emphasis from crude petroleum and LNG industries to oil derivative production. Another methanol plant in the Salalah free zone (90% owned by the OOC and 10% by the Oman Energy Trading Co), with a production capacity of 3,000 tons per day, was commissioned in 2010 after it received its first natural gas feedstock piped from central Oman following an agreement with the Ministry of Oil and Gas. In late 2012 it was announced that the OOC was planning to invest $800m. in a new petrochemical plant in Sohar and also that Hanwha of South Korea had been awarded a contract to build a $500m. plant at Salalah.

In 2008 the Government signed agreements with a Brazilian mining company, Vale, involving the construction, from mid-2009, of an iron ore pelletizing and distribution plant in Sohar. Vale would supply the iron ore for the plant from its Brazilian mines, and the processed pellets would be exported to Middle Eastern and South-East Asian markets. The plant began production in April 2011. A new iron and steel plant in Sohar, operated by India-based Jindal Shadeed, started commercial operations in January 2011. It was announced in July 2012 that Sun Metals LLC, a locally incorporated firm established by a group of Indian-based investors, was to begin construction work on a new steel mill in Sur, which would have a production capacity of 1.2m. tons per year.

In November 2007 an agreement was signed for the establishment of a new sugar refinery at Sohar port. Beginning operations in 2010, with a capacity of 660,000 metric tons per year, the facility was built by the local Al Hafri Sugar Refinery Co and was among the largest in the Gulf region.

Alongside the major industrial projects under development, the Government has encouraged small-scale industries to locate to specially constructed industrial estates; in particular, it hoped to attract advanced technology companies. Government incentives to private industry have included interest-free loans and exemption from customs duties on imports of capital goods and raw materials. The first such industrial estate was established in 1985 at Rusayl, near Seeb International Airport (renamed Muscat International Airport in early 2008); others have since been established at Raysut (near Salalah), Sohar, Nizwa, Sur and al-Buraimi. As a result of the growing number of industries setting up in Sohar, in mid-2008 the Government announced the designation of a new Sohar special economic zone. The 45-sq km zone would be implemented by Sohar International Development Co, a joint venture between the Oman Government, India's Skil Infrastructure and the Port of Rotterdam Authority. In 2011 the Duqm Special Economic Zone Authority was established.

Geological surveys have been undertaken to locate mineral deposits other than petroleum and natural gas. Sizeable reserves of copper and chromite (chromium ore) have been found, as well as deposits of iron, gold and silver. Oman also has significant quantities of non-metallic minerals, particularly marble, gypsum and limestone (used in the production of cement). According to government figures, the Sultanate produced 554,800 metric tons of chromite, 103,600 tons of copper, 6.45m. tons of limestone, 1.1m. tons of marble and 1.9m. tons of gypsum in 2012.

The economic and industrial changes that have taken place in the country since 1970 have needed major increases in power and water supply. Total electricity generating capacity in Oman rose from 479 MW in 1981 to 2,303 MW in 2003, when a total of 50 power plants (46 diesel-based stations, three gas turbines and one combined-cycle plant) were in operation.

By the end of 2003 about 97% of Oman's populated areas were connected to mains electricity supplies. With demand for power growing by more than 5% a year, the Government planned to augment generating capacity to 3,260 MW by the end of the sixth five-year Development Plan. In March 2009 the Oman Power and Water Procurement Co issued a new forecast projecting that peak demand for electricity would rise from 3,031 MW in 2008 to 5,348 MW in 2015 and that demand for desalinated water would increase from 22,467m. gallons to 53,524m. gallons over the same period. The country would require between 2,420 MW and 3,470 MW of new power generation capacity and an extra 31m. gallons per day of new desalination capacity by 2015. In response, the Government announced in August 2009 that a US $7,800m. six-year investment programme was planned for the electricity and associated water sector in an effort to keep pace with spiralling demand.

Older power stations include those at Ghubrah (dating from 1976) and Rusayl (dating from 1984). Muscat's Manah generating plant (dating from 1996 and expanded in 2000 to 270 MW capacity) was the Gulf region's first independent power project (IPP). Financed entirely by private capital on 'build, own, operate, transfer' terms, it is operated by the United Power Co under a 20-year agreement with the Oman Government. Under 'fast-track' IPP contracts awarded in 2000, the 285-MW al-Kamil power plant at Sharqiya Sands was completed in the latter half of 2002, while a 427-MW power station (with 91,200 cu m per day of desalination capacity) commenced operations at Barqa in early 2003. Both projects had initial 100% foreign ownership (agreed in order to accelerate their implementation), but this was to be reduced to 65% within four years through share offerings on the Muscat Securities Market (MSM). In March 2001 a third 'fast-track' contract was concluded when Dhofar Power Co (whose 81% foreign ownership was subject to reduction to 65% in due course) won a 20-year concession to implement an integrated power project, entailing the construction and operation of a 200-MW gas-fired power station at Salalah and the acquisition of existing transmission and distribution infrastructure in the area (which the concession-holder undertook to expand to keep pace with the growth of local demand). The Salalah plant began operations in May 2003. A 140-MW power plant at Qarn Alam in southern Oman was inaugurated in mid-2004. In early 2003 the Government sought tenders from contractors for the development, construction and operation of a new independent water and power project (IWPP) to be located at Sohar (with capacity to generate some 500 MW and 30m. gallons a day). Belgium's Tractebel was awarded the concession in July 2004, with South Korea's Doosan as its nominated EPC contractor.

In April 2008 it was reported that the Government had approved proposals for an independent coal-fired power plant at Duqm, which would be the first such facility in the Gulf region. However, the Government subsequently reversed its policy on environmental grounds and in mid-2011 appointed a US consulting firm to conduct a study for a gas-fired IWPP facility instead. Also in mid-2011 the Oman Power and Water Procurement Co (OPWP) signed an agreement with a Japanese-led consortium for the construction of a new 2,000-MW independent power plant at Sur. Another major US $1,000m. IWPP at Salalah, developed on a build, own and operate basis by a joint venture comprising Oman Investment Co and Sembcorp Utilities of Singapore, was completed and ready for full commercial operation in mid-2012. Further gas-fired, combined cycle IPP facilities at Sohar and Barqa achieved full commercial operation in April 2013, adding almost 1,500 MW of power to Oman's existing capacity of 4,500 MW. Construction of the plants had begun in 2010, with a consortium of Siemens of Germany and South Korea's GS Engineering and Construction Corpn designated as the EPC contractor.

In June 2008 the Authority for Electricity Regulation (AER) published a comprehensive survey of Oman's renewable energy resources, which emphasized the extensive potential for harnessing solar power to meet the country's electricity needs. The Government floated a tender in April 2009 for a contract to advise the Public Authority for Energy and Water on the implementation of the Sultanate's first large-scale concentrated solar power project, and Australia's WorleyParsons was selected towards the end of the year. In April 2010 a short-list of six smaller proposed wind and solar projects was announced, two of which (one wind and one solar) were subsequently earmarked for immediate development. In January 2012 it was announced that a group of Swiss and German investors planned to develop a major solar power infrastructure project at Duqm, including a 400-MW plant.

In July 2004 a royal decree finally mandated the privatization of state-owned public utilities. The proposal envisaged the division of the Ministry of Housing, Electricity and Water's assets and functions between a number of separate companies responsible for power generation, transmission and distribution, some of which would be opened up to 65% private ownership (although the Ministry would retain ownership of smaller facilities serving rural areas). A state-owned power and water procurement company would be responsible for planning new capacity and awarding contracts, while a state-owned holding company would oversee the whole sector.

Tendering for the initial phase of a US $1,600m. regional electricity 'inter-exchange' grid connecting the GCC states was completed in 2006 by the GCC Interconnection Authority, allowing for production-sharing that would eliminate the need for discrete power plants and ultimately achieve regional self-sufficiency up to 2058. The first stage, connecting Qatar, Bahrain, Saudi Arabia and Kuwait, was inaugurated in the latter half of 2009, while work on the interconnection of the individual grids of the UAE and that of Oman was also completed in that year; the final stage involves the connection of the two grids.

Oman's renewable water resources per caput decreased from 4,000 cu m per year in 1960 to 1,133 cu m per year in 1990, and were projected to decline to 421 cu m per year by 2025. In 2000 the Sultanate had over 20 desalination plants, the combined capacity of which totalled 377,880 cu m per day; the Ghubrah power station accounted for 159,110 cu m per day of this capacity. At the beginning of 2002 the Government launched the first phase of the Sharqiya Sands scheme to supply fresh water to some 80,000 people in towns and villages to the south of Muscat. The al-Masarat scheme, inaugurated in 2002, supplies clean water to 115,000 people in the towns of Ibri, Yanqul and Dhank and surrounding villages (to the west of Muscat). The Muscat Wastewater project is a US $1,000m. scheme aiming to connect 90% of the capital's population to a sewerage network by 2017. The government-owned Oman Wastewater Services Co was formed in December 2002 to carry out the scheme. Construction work on the development's initial phase began in 2003, with the award of a contract to build a sewage treatment plant at Darsait. In January 2009 the first phase of the al-Dakhliya water supply project was inaugurated. On completion, the scheme is intended to supply water from the Barqa desalination plant on the coast to the expanding towns (including Nizwa) in the al-Dakhliya region. At the same time a project was launched in the eastern region of al-Sharqiya supplying water to the districts of Ibra and al-Qabil. The scheme included a 260-km pipeline, seven underground storage tanks and 16 tanker filling stations. In March 2010 a new, privately funded desalination plant in Sur was officially opened, and in March 2012 the second stage of a project to connect the Dayqah *wadi* (see Agriculture and Fisheries) to the water supply network serving Muscat and surrounding area was inaugurated. Also in 2012, a contract was awarded for the construction of a new desalination plant at Ghubrah.

TRANSPORT AND COMMUNICATIONS

Transport and other communications projects have been prioritized in successive five-year development plans. Port facilities were improved by the expansion of Salalah Port and Port Sultan Qaboos, and the development of Port Sohar. A new container terminal at Salalah Port, a key element in the development of southern Oman, was officially opened in December 1998, and by April 1999 the port had four berths with a total handling capacity of 2m. 20-ft equivalent units (TEU). Salalah Port Services (SPS) was formed by the Omani Government, Sea-Land of the USA and Maersk of Denmark to carry out the development and holds a 30-year concession to operate, manage and procure equipment for the container port.

In May 2000 SPS effectively became the port authority for Salalah, which had quickly established a major role, partly at the expense of Port Sultan Qaboos. SPS also formed a new company to manage a free trade zone at Salalah, extending 2 km beyond the existing port boundaries and funded mainly by the private sector. SPS announced in June 2004 that it was investing US $249m. in new port infrastructure to increase the port's capacity to 3m. TEUs a year.

Work commenced in 2000 on the first phase of a major expansion of port facilities at Sohar, which was designated in government development plans as a centre of hydrocarbon-based industrialization. The new facility was completed in 2004, managed by Sohar Industrial Port Co. Hutchison Port Holdings (Hong Kong), Steinweg Oman and the Omani Government subsequently collaborated on the 800,000-TEU Oman International Container Terminal at Sohar, completed in two phases in 2006–07, to serve the district's exporting industries. In mid-2011 the Ministry of Transport and Communications announced that all commercial cargo and container activities would be transferred to Sohar and that Port Sultan Qaboos would exclusively serve tourist traffic. In January 2013 Hutchison secured a further contract to build and operate a new 70-ha container terminal at Sohar, which would double the port's capacity to 1.5m. TEUs. Construction began in March, and its completion was envisaged in early 2014. In 2007 Oman's Ministry of National Economy invited foreign and local companies to bid for the contract to build a new dry-dock complex as part of ambitious expansion plans for Duqm Port, and in January 2008 a consortium of Oman's Galfar Engineering and Contracting and South Korea's Daewoo Engineering and Construction was selected. The dry dock was fully operational and officially inaugurated in June 2012.

Improvement of Oman's road network in 2000 included the award of contracts for some 700 km of new roads in the central region. In May 2005 construction began on the southern expressway, an ambitious 56-km partial ring road around Muscat at a cost of US $342m. (which opened in November 2010). In tandem with this project, the contracted construction firm Galfar Engineering and Contracting LLC began work in April 2006 on a RO 11m. 6-km central corridor linking principal residential districts in Muscat with the southern expressway. In February 2009 an 87-km coastal dual carriageway between Muscat and Sur was officially opened. In March the Ministry of Transport and Communications appointed Turkey's Bosphorus Technical Consulting Corpn to provide design and construction supervision services for a major 265-km carriageway scheme in Al-Batinah to enhance transport links between Muscat and Fujairah in the UAE. A RO 140m. construction contract for the first stage of the project was awarded in early 2012, again to Galfar Engineering and Contracting LLC. In April 2013 a contract for the second stage, which had earlier been awarded to a Malaysian-Omani venture, was cancelled and retendered by the Ministry of Transport and Communications, which confirmed the award of the third-stage contract to India's Simplex Infrastructures. In July Larsen and Toubro, an Indian conglomerate, won the contract for the fourth stage and was also declared the lowest bidder for the fifth and sixth stages.

It was reported in April 2008 that the Government was considering plans for the construction in phases of a coastal railway line to link Sohar, Muscat and Duqm. The contract to carry out an assessment of the proposed first phase, a 230-km line linking Sohar and Muscat, was awarded to a French contractor in February 2009. The project would be integral to the construction of a regional north–south railway network connecting the member states of the GCC. In 2012 a state-owned National Railway Co was established to develop and implement the planned network in Oman.

A major expansion programme at Seeb International Airport (now Muscat International Airport) was completed in 1985, and in the following year more than 1.4m. passengers passed through the airport. A further two-stage expansion plan envisaged an increase in capacity from to 6m. passengers per year by 2004 and to 10m. by 2010, at an estimated cost of US $500m. Oman's second largest airport, at Salalah, which was upgraded to receive cargo and passenger aircraft of all sizes, handled 184,000 passengers by 2003, and tenders for further expansion work were submitted in late 2010. Effective privatization of the two airports in October 2001, under a 25-year contract awarded to a consortium (led by BAA of the United Kingdom, and including an Omani company—the Suhail Bahwan Group), collapsed in October 2004 following financial disagreements, and the airports were returned to the Government's control. Under its seventh Development Plan (2006–10), focusing on infrastructural development and industrial diversification, the Government announced plans for the construction of three new regional airports located at Sohar (scheduled to be operational by 2013), Duqm and Ras Al Hadd. In March 2007 the Government increased its financial stake in Oman Air from 34% to 81% (with the aim of boosting services, particularly to encourage tourism), and in May withdrew from its part-ownership of Gulf Air (designating Oman Air as the national carrier). In 2008 Oman Air experienced a difficult trading year, citing high fuel bills during the first half of the year and the costs associated with upgrading its fleet. In response, in April 2009 the Government announced a large injection of working capital for the airline, increasing capital to RO 300m. from RO 50m. Also in early 2009, tendering started for the expansion of Muscat International Airport, involving the planned construction of a second runway, as well as a new terminal building and an air traffic control tower. The expanded airport would have the capacity to handle 12m. passengers per year, compared with 4m. in 2008. The contract for the construction of the new terminal was awarded in October 2010 to a consortium comprising Bechtel of the USA, Turkey's Enka and the local Bahwan Engineering Co. Despite a significant increase in passenger traffic and the inauguration of flights to new international destinations, Oman Air had another difficult trading year in 2009 in view of the global economic environment, and it was announced that its authorized capital would be increased to RO 500m.

During the 1990s Oman lagged behind the other Gulf states in telecommunications development, having in 1999 only 9.2 fixed telephone lines per 100 inhabitants and only 1.6 public telephones per 1,000 inhabitants. In July 1999 the Government announced the establishment of the Oman Telecommunications Co (Omantel), which replaced the General Telecommunications Organization as the country's sole provider of telecommunication services, in a first step towards eventual privatization. However, a sharp downturn in the global telecommunications industry in 2001–02 forced the Government, in May 2002, to postpone the sale of a stake in Omantel. The Government scaled back its initial plans to sell 40% of the company's shares, and instead proposed to sell 20% through an initial public offering, with a further 10% distributed among state pension funds; this took place in 2005. Meanwhile, a joint venture of Qatar Telecom, Denmark's TDC Mobile International and local Omani investors, known as Nawras, was awarded Oman's second Global Standard for Mobiles (GSM) licence by the regulatory authority, ending Omantel's mobile monopoly. The introduction of competition to the market precipitated a dramatic increase in the mobile subscriber base, which numbered 1.3m. in June 2006 (compared with 124,000 in 1999), of which Oman Mobile (the mobile telecommunications division of Omantel) had secured 1.0m. customers. In November 2008 the Telecommunications Regulatory Authority (established in 2002) awarded a second fixed-line licence to Nawras. In November 2009 the Government announced a new universal telecommunications service policy to extend coverage across the Sultanate. In July 2013 Connect Arabia International, owned by a consortium that included the United Kingdom's Virgin Group, was awarded a 15-year licence to provide telecommunication services in Oman, providing that it sold 40% of its shares through an initial public offering on the MSM within five years.

TOURISM

Following the issue of the first tourist visas in 1990, tourism is still in the relatively early stages of development in Oman. However, as the country strives to diversify its economy and reduce its reliance upon petroleum and gas reserves, government officials have identified tourism as a sector with potential for expansion. Oman's 2001–05 Development Plan considered tourism to be an important potential source of new employment opportunities, and set an annual growth target of 6.1%. The actual average annual growth rate was, however, considerably higher, at 9.9%. In June 2004 the Government established a new Ministry of Tourism, and in July Oman joined the World Tourism Organization. The new Ministry's mandate was to double tourism receipts by 2015 (to US $6,200m.) and to raise the contribution of tourism to GDP to 5% by 2020. The 2006–10 Plan maintained a priority focus on tourism, with a planned annual growth target of 7% and proposed investment of RO 777m., of which RO 214m. was to be funded by the state and RO 563m. by the private sector.

In February 2002 an Omani company, Zubair Enterprises, announced plans for a US $200m. resort complex to be located at Barr al-Jissah on the Gulf of Oman, some 12 km south of Muscat. A key component of the project was the proposed construction of a road link between Barr al-Jissah and Muscat. In February 2004 the Government (in partnership with Majid al-Futtaim Investments of Dubai) launched 'The Wave', comprising a 195-ha, $1,000m. resort and residential development occupying 7.3 km of beachfront west of Muscat. Muriya, a 70:30 joint venture between Oman Tourism Development Co, a wholly government-owned interest, and Orascom Hotels and Development (Egypt), envisaged the development of four tourism projects in Oman located at Qurum (Muscat), Salalah, Sifah and al-Soda, mainly comprising luxury hotels and associated activities. Other major development projects included the $779m. resort at Khasab, orchestrated by the local Majan Gulf Properties, and Al Medina al-Zarqa (Blue City)—a 32-sq km mixed-use coastal enterprise, valued at around $20,000m., at al-Sawadi. Blue City represented Oman's largest tourism and real estate project to date, but concerns over its viability led an international ratings agency to downgrade its credit rating in December 2008, and in March 2011 the Government intervened to take over the project's debt bonds. In October 2011 Muscat was selected as the Arab Tourism Capital for 2012.

BUDGET, INVESTMENT AND FINANCE

The targets of the 1976–80 Development Plan were relatively modest, concentrating on establishing a workable basis for light industry and agriculture. The Oman Development Bank was established in December 1977 to encourage private sector investment. The general aim of the 1981–85 Plan was to reduce economic dependence on petroleum, in favour of private sector industry. The Plan included development of tourism, education, health, welfare, housing and roads. In 1984 it was announced that total spending on projects undertaken during the 1981–85 Development Plan would total RO 1,800m., 28% more than was originally envisaged.

At the end of 1985 the 1986–90 Development Plan was approved, with proposed expenditure totalling RO 9,250m. (US $26,780m.). Early in 1986, however, proposed spending was reduced to RO 8,830m. as a result of decreasing oil prices. The revised total was based on an estimated average petroleum price of $20 per barrel. The subsequent decline in oil prices, to less than $10 per barrel in July, necessitated further revision of proposed expenditure. Although oil prices rose above $17 per barrel by the end of 1986, the Plan was postponed for re-evaluation. In January 1991 the Government announced the fourth Development Plan, covering the period 1991–95. It envisaged total expenditure of RO 9,450m., and the projected rate of annual GDP growth in the five years was about 6.3%. In April 1991 total development spending for the Plan period was reportedly budgeted at RO 2,107m. Of this, some RO 319m. was to be allocated to construction projects.

The 1996–2000 Development Plan envisaged the elimination of the budget deficit by 2000. However, after the 1998 budget had predicted a deficit of RO 295m. (based on proposed revenue of RO 2,012m. and expenditure of RO 2,307m.), declining international petroleum prices resulted in an actual budget deficit in 1998 of RO 375.3m., equivalent to 6.9% of GDP. The 1999 budget, announced by the Government in January and based on an average oil price of only US $9 per barrel, forecast a deficit of RO 631m. from revenue of RO 1,525m. ($3,961m.) and expenditure, reduced by 7%, of RO 2,156m. Non-oil income was forecast at RO 550m., the calculations including a range of new revenue-raising measures, in particular an increase in corporate taxes and taxes on luxury goods, and the introduction of higher customs duties. Increased oil revenue produced an effective fiscal surplus in 1999 equivalent to 1.8% of GDP, although the transfer of above-forecast oil revenues to the State General Reserve Fund (SGRF) resulted in a nominal budget deficit of RO 472.9m. (equivalent to 7.8% of GDP), based on actual revenue of RO 1,796.1m. and actual expenditure of RO 2,269.0m. The 2000 budget provided for total revenue of RO 2,091m. and total expenditure of RO 2,440m., 7.7% higher than actual spending in 1999. Out-turn figures for 2000 showed actual revenue of RO 2,289.9m. and actual expenditure of RO 2,656.2m., leaving a nominal budget deficit of RO 366.3m. Overall, there was an effective fiscal surplus equivalent to 9.8% of GDP in 2000. An average $12 excess of the actual oil export price over the budgeted price was large enough to prompt the Government to draw down some revenue from the SGRF to finance increased capital spending in the last quarter of 2000. The estimated balance in the SGRF at the end of 2000 was equivalent to about 20% of Oman's GDP.

The 2001–05 Development Plan envisaged a decrease in the nominal budget deficit to RO 138m. in 2005, when annual revenue was expected to be 5.1% greater, and expenditure 1.8% lower, than in 2001. The Plan set an overall target for economic growth of 3.5% per year, to be achieved primarily through average growth of 5.2% per year in non-oil activities (including new industries based on natural gas, the development of which would require RO 1,807m. of private investment). Of the Plan's overall investment target of RO 8,118m., some RO 3,746m. represented public sector investment (an increase of 20% compared with the corresponding target in the 1996–2000 Plan), leaving a total of RO 4,372m. to be invested by the private sector (an increase of 132% over the 1996–2000 target). The Plan envisaged stable export receipts over the period 2001–05, on the assumption that a decline in earnings from crude petroleum would be offset by growth in exports of LNG and other non-oil items. The target for labour market expansion in the 2001–05 plan period was 110,000 new employment opportunities for Omani nationals (compared with the previous Plan's target of 78,000 jobs), over 90% of them in the private sector. New jobs were to be created mainly through projected growth in tourism, manufacturing and construction activities. The public sector was to invest RO 35m. per year from 2001–05 in a human resources development programme, with the improvement and expansion of basic educational facilities receiving high priority.

Oman's 2001 budget provided for revenue of RO 2,495m. (including net oil revenue of RO 1,875m.) and expenditure of RO 2,812m., leaving a nominal budget deficit of RO 317m. The assumed oil export price in this budget was US $18 per barrel (compared with a 'floor' price of $22 per barrel currently used as a reference point by OPEC members). In the event, the oil export price remained at about the budgeted level in 2001, with the result that the actual budget deficit totalled some RO 320.4m. (about 4.2% of GDP). The Government's budget for 2002 was similar to the original 2001 projections, being again based on an assumed oil export price of $18 per barrel, and providing for total revenue of RO 2,490m. and expenditure of RO 2,870m., leaving a nominal budget deficit of RO 380m. Projected expenditure in 2002 included a 12% increase in capital investment, to RO 589m., most of it earmarked for civil projects (RO 280m.) and for works to enhance the sustainability of Oman's hydrocarbons production (RO 218m.). However, due to higher oil prices, the budgeted deficit in 2002 was transformed into an actual surplus of RO 70.0m. (0.9% of GDP).

The budget for 2003 forecast revenue and expenditure of RO 2,600m. and RO 3,000m., respectively, based on an assumed average oil price of US $20 per barrel—$2 per barrel higher than the estimate in 2002 and for the sixth Development Plan (2001–05). The anticipated deficit of RO 400m. was to be financed through borrowings of RO 300m. from domestic and external sources and a withdrawal of RO 100m. from the SGRF. Oil revenue was estimated to account for about 71% (RO 1,800m.) of total government revenue in 2003. Any increase in oil revenue resulting from an improvement in prices was to be used to reduce the actual budget deficit. Projected expenditure was 4.5% higher than the projected figure for 2002. The budget provided for an increase in development spending from RO 589m. in 2002 to RO 614m. in 2003. As in 2002, high oil prices resulted in a significant budget surplus for 2003, of RO 119.1m., despite declining oil output, according to Central Bank figures published in July 2004.

The budget for 2004, based on an oil price of US $21 per barrel, envisaged a deficit of RO 500m., based on total revenue of RO 2,925m. and expenditure of RO 3,425m. However, given the spiralling price of oil throughout the first half of 2004, such a deficit again seemed improbable. Increased current and capital expenditure was largely intended to reverse the decline in oil production through expensive enhanced oil recovery programmes (see Petroleum and Natural Gas). In January 2005 the Government announced an estimated RO 540m. deficit in its 2005 budget, based on total revenue of RO 3,140m. and expenditure of RO 3,680m. However, since petroleum prices remained stronger than the Government's cautious estimates, a surplus of RO 303m. was recorded.

The 2006–10 Development Plan focused on enhancing non-oil revenues, apprehending the decline in oil production and investing heavily in development projects oriented towards the diversification of economic activity, with a relatively even balance between public and private sector participation in the planned RO 13,000m. investment (to be divided 54% and 46%, respectively). The nominal budget deficit predicted for 2006 was RO 650m., with revenue expected to decline to RO 3,587m. (a decrease of 21.6% compared with 2005), and general expenditure predicted to increase by 15.1%, to RO 4,237m. Economic growth was set at a modest 3% per year, based on estimated oil prices of US $32 per barrel in 2006 (and an average price of $30 per barrel over the five-year period) and average oil production of 746,000 b/d, although considerable investment in oil and gas production and gas-based industries was expected to restore oil production to 827,000 b/d. Government investment in the human resources development programme totalled RO 44.7m. in 2005, while in 2006 expenditure on education was to increase by 21% and health care by 13%. Tourism and industrial construction projects, particularly at the Sohar industrial port complex, were expected to generate many new employment opportunities, with budgeted expenditure on development projects projected at RO 375m., a 14% increase on the previous year. The 2007 budget, based on an average oil price of $40 per barrel, forecast increased revenues of RO 4,500m. (despite declining petroleum production) and higher expenditure at RO 4,900m. However, the projected deficit was likely to be more than offset as the oil price continued to spiral upwards through the year. Meanwhile, many of the Government's spending plans in 2007 to improve the country's infrastructure suffered major setbacks as a result of 'Cyclone Gonu' in June.

According to the 2008 budget, presented in January, spending for the year was forecast at RO 5,800m., while revenues were estimated at RO 5,400m., resulting in a RO 400m. deficit based on a conservative oil price of US $45 per barrel. However, this price remained substantially lower than the unprecedented levels prevailing on international markets in the first seven months of 2008, and Oman went on to register a record budget surplus of almost RO 1,600m. for the year (the seventh consecutive year of surplus), according to provisional figures from the Central Bank. Total revenue for 2008 was almost RO 8,000m. and total expenditure was RO 6,400m. The 2009 budget, announced in January, was prepared against a backdrop of declining petroleum prices and a deepening global economic and trading recession. It again assumed an average oil price of $45 a barrel, but a slightly higher level of average crude production of 805,000 b/d. Revenues were forecast to total RO 5,614m., despite the decline in petroleum prices, while expenditure was estimated at RO 6,424m., giving a deficit of RO 810m. (5% of GDP), which would be financed mainly by drawing from the SGRF (RO 710m.) and through external borrowing (RO 100m.). However, according to Central Bank figures released in February 2010, the budget deficit for 2009 was RO 22m., substantially less than had been forecast.

The budget for 2010 was presented at the beginning of the year, at a time when the global economy was showing signs of a gradual, if fragile, recovery. It assumed a higher average oil price of US $50 per barrel and higher daily average oil production of 870,000 barrels. Revenues were projected to increase by 13.6% to RO 6,380m. and expenditure was expected to rise by 11.8% to RO 7,180m., resulting in a deficit of RO 800m. Net oil revenues for 2010 were estimated at RO 4,050m. compared with RO 3,522m. the previous year. Gas revenues were also expected to increase to RO 800m., from an estimated RO 670m. in 2009. Other government revenues were forecast to rise to an estimated RO 1,477m. from RO 1,355m. in the previous year. Current and investment expenditure under the 2010 budget were estimated to increase to RO 4,432m. and RO 2,218m., respectively. The growth in investment expenditure reflected the Government's policy objectives of improving public infrastructure and public services within the framework of the 2006–10 Development Plan.

The budget for 2011 was announced in January. Revenues and expenditure were forecast to rise to RO 7,280m. and RO 8,130m., respectively, resulting in a deficit of RO 850m. Net oil revenues for 2011 were budgeted at RO 4,956m. and gas revenues were projected to increase to RO 920m. Current and capital revenues were estimated at RO 1,404m. However, as a consequence of economic concessions made by the Government in the wake of protests and strikes in February and March, supplementary spending was expected to increase budget expenditure to about RO 9,100m. The provisions of the budget for 2012 were released in January. Assuming a higher average oil price of US $75 per barrel (compared with $58 in 2010) and higher daily average oil production of 915,000 barrels, total revenue was projected to rise sharply to RO 8,800m. and expenditure to RO 10,000m. Net oil revenues were forecast to increase to RO 6,100m. and gas revenues to RO 1,100m. Almost RO 2,000m. of budget expenditure was allocated to education, health and social welfare. The RO 1,200m. budget deficit was expected to be financed from reserves, loans, the issue of development bonds, and the actual fiscal surplus carried over from 2011. The budget for 2013 assumed an increased average oil price of $85 per barrel and daily average oil production of 930,000 barrels. Total revenue was projected to reach RO 11,155m., a 26.8% rise, with revenues from crude petroleum and gas accounting for 72% and 12%, respectively, of the total. Expenditure was forecast to increase by 29%, to RO 12,855m., with greater spending on education, social security, welfare and housing.

In comparison with some other countries in the region, Oman has a small banking sector. By December 2012 there were 16 commercial banks (seven local and nine foreign) operating in the Sultanate. The largest bank is BankMuscat; other locally incorporated institutions are the National Bank of Oman, Oman International Bank, Bank Sohar, Bank Dhofar (formerly Bank Dhofar al-Omani al-Fransi), Oman Arab Bank and Ahli Bank. At the end of 2012 there were also two government-owned specialized banks in operation (Oman Housing Bank and Oman Development Bank), six finance and leasing companies licensed by the Central Bank, and 46 money exchange establishments. In 2011 the Government licensed Oman's first Islamic banks—Bank Nizwa and Al Izz International Bank—in a move that had previously been resisted and that had set Oman apart from its GCC neighbours. Mergers have been officially encouraged since the 1990s to strengthen the banking sector. A merger between Bank Muscat and the Commercial Bank of Oman at the end of 2000 left the merged entity (since known as BankMuscat) with the country's largest branch network (comprising 95 branches) after the sale of 16 former Commercial Bank of Oman branches to Bank Dhofar al-Omani al-Fransi. In a further consolidation at the end of 2001, BankMuscat absorbed the Industrial Bank of Oman, the new entity being formally instituted on 1 January 2002. In April 2012 the United Kingdom's HSBC Middle East Bank announced its plan to merge its Oman operations with Oman International Bank under the new name of HSBC Bank Oman. The merger was formally approved by the Ministry of Commerce and Industry in June.

In 2001 total profits for all banks operating in Oman decreased by 41%, to RO 38m. This was mainly caused by the collapse of the Ali Redha Trading Group, in which local banks had an estimated RO 31m. exposure. Net profits of commercial banks almost doubled from RO 79.4m. in 2004 to RO 162.9m. in 2006, and then rose sharply again, to RO 213.7m., in 2007. The commercial banks' core capital and reserves stood at RO 1,800m. in 2008, and their capital adequacy ratio averaged 14.7% (considerably higher than the minimum regulatory requirement of 10%). Oman's banking sector proved resilient during the global downturn, owing to strong supervisory and regulatory frameworks and to liquidity support. Total assets of the commercial banks at the end of 2009 stood at RO 14,198.9m., compared with RO 13,778.4m. a year earlier, but net profits declined to RO 190.8m. from RO 234.1m. at the end of 2008. The banks' core capital and reserves reached RO 1,906.5m. in 2009, and their overall capital adequacy ratio remained secure at 15.5%. The banking sector continued to perform well in 2010 and 2011, consistent with the economic recovery. In 2010 commercial banks increased their profits to RO 247.7m., and their core capital and reserves rose to RO 2,100m. by the end of the year. The capital adequacy ratio averaged 15.8%, again comfortably higher than the (revised) minimum requirement of 12%. In 2011 core capital and reserves amounted to RO 2,300m., with the ratio averaging 15.9%, while banks' profits rose by 6.6% to RO 264m. The commercial banking sector strengthened further in 2012 due to robust growth in deposits and credit, with core capital and reserves reaching RO 2,700m. and the capital adequacy ratio averaging 16%.

In early 2007 the Central Bank announced that Oman was withdrawing its participation from the GCC's planned monetary union, stating that it believed that adopting a shared currency would hinder its development goals, particularly of meeting public debt convergence and budget deficit criteria. In January 2008 the GCC launched its common market.

In 1989 Oman's first stock exchange, the MSM, was opened, trading in shares in local companies with a potential total value of RO 250m. Oman's first investment fund open to non-GCC nationals was listed on the London (United Kingdom) and Muscat stock exchanges in March 1994. Subscriptions for the Oryx fund, launched to raise US $52m., closed in June. A second investment fund set up in 1994 was the UAE-Omani Joint Holding Co, with a capital of $78m. Both funds were fully subscribed. In March 1995 the stock exchanges of Muscat and Bahrain were formally linked. In November 1998 a new National Investment Fund (NIF) was established by royal decree to support the MSM by channelling RO 100m. ($260m.) from pension funds into the bourse. A new regulatory body, the Capital Market Authority (CMA), formally separated from the MSM in January 1999, in accordance with the capital market law promulgated in November 1998. The new authority was to supervise the MSM and guarantee investors' rights. In 1999 the World Bank's International Finance Corporation launched a stand-alone index for the MSM. In April 2000 the CMA introduced new MSM regulations aimed at protecting shareholders by requiring quoted companies to make quarterly disclosure of financial and other information relevant to their performance. In September 2001, moreover, the CMA introduced new company listing requirements intended to promote MSM transparency. In November 2000 the Government introduced a package of measures designed to stimulate the MSM, which had experienced a 31% decline in trading in the course of the year. In addition to offering incentives to encourage mergers between brokerage firms, the Government undertook to settle up to RO 14m. of negative equity in share trust accounts held by brokers on behalf of small investors, and to invest RO 50m. of public funds in shares traded on the MSM. In 2001 the CMA announced further regulatory initiatives intended to improve the operation of the MSM.

In March 1997 Oman had become the first GCC state to venture into the Eurobond market, with an issue that was heavily oversubscribed, and in February 1999 the Government secured a US $350m. five-year syndicated loan from a consortium of local and international banks.

FOREIGN TRADE AND BALANCE OF PAYMENTS

Oman's trade pattern has continued to reflect the dominance of petroleum in the economy, although, since the early 1990s, the Government's efforts at diversifying the economy have demonstrated a degree of success. Mainly as a result of a significant increase in revenue from oil and gas exports, Oman achieved a trade surplus of RO 1,127m. in 1999, from exports of RO 2,780m. (including RO 2,139m. from oil) and imports of RO 1,653m. A further surge in the value of exports in 2000, to RO 4,352m. (including RO 3,426m. from oil), and relatively flat imports of RO 1,766m. more than doubled the trade surplus, to RO 2,586m. Figures for 2001 showed a slight decrease in the value of exports, to RO 4,258m., and a rise in imports to RO 2,042m., yielding a trade surplus of RO 2,216m. In 2002 exports of RO 4,296m. (including RO 2,985m. from oil) and imports of RO 2,167m. resulted in a narrower surplus of RO 2,129m. The trade surplus remained at a similar level in 2003 (RO 2,147m., from exports of RO 4,487m., including RO 2,985m. from oil, and imports of RO 2,340m.). The narrowing trend persisted until 2004, but in 2005 witnessed a substantial reversal, with the surplus widening to RO 3,737.6m. (from exports of RO 7,186.9m. and imports of RO 3,449.3m.). According to the Ministry of National Economy, exports of RO 8,299.5m. and imports of RO 4,244.4m. in 2006 resulted in another increase in the trade surplus, to RO 4,055.1m. It then narrowed in 2007 to RO 3,344.2m. as exports reached RO 9,505.7m. but imports rose sharply, to RO 6,161.5m. The surplus reached RO 5,606.6m. in 2008—a 68.2% increase on the level the previous year—with exports valued at RO 14,502.9m. (RO 11,000m. from oil) and imports at RO 8,896.3m. (reflecting strong domestic demand and the investment needs of ongoing projects). Despite the rising contribution of non-oil exports to domestic economic activities, their value remained modest at 8.5% of GDP at the end of 2008. In 2009 the value of exports declined to RO 10,632.0m. and that of imports to RO 6,896.0m., resulting in a RO 3,736.0m. trade surplus. The surplus increased to RO 6,393.7m. in 2010 as the value of exports rose sharply to RO 14,073.2m., while imports expanded more modestly to RO 7,679.5m. In 2011 and 2012 the value of exports again increased markedly to reach RO 18,106.8m. and RO 20,047.2m., respectively, which, with imports valued at RO 9,235.2m. and RO 11,010.4m., resulted in record RO 8,871.6m. and RO 9,036.8m. surpluses. The UAE and Japan remained the two main sources of imports for Oman in 2012, supplying 25.7% and 13.5%, respectively, while the USA provided 5.9%. India was the main market for Oman's non-petroleum exports (taking 17.0%), followed by the UAE (15.3%) and China (8.1%).

The principal variable factors affecting Oman's balance of payments performance have been petroleum revenue and the level of remittances being transferred abroad by expatriates working in Oman. According to the Central Bank, the current account on the balance of payments registered a record surplus of more than RO 3,947m. (14.1% of GDP) in 2011, compared with RO 2,257m. (10.1% of GDP) in 2010. The overall payments surplus (current, capital and financial accounts combined) was RO 574m. in 2011, almost the same as in the previous year. Despite a slowdown in export growth, merchandise trade continued to dominate the balance of payments in 2012, when an overall surplus of RO 397m. was recorded. Foreign exchange reserves amounted to RO 5,248m. at the end of 2011, compared with RO 4,720m. in the previous year, but totalled RO 5,222m. at the end of 2012.

In June 1996 the World Trade Organization (WTO) agreed to establish a working party to negotiate terms of entry for Oman. The decision followed a commitment made by the Omani Undersecretary for Commerce and Industry to co-operate with other GCC countries (Oman's most important trading partners) in the promotion of liberal trade. In November 1999 Oman was a signatory of a GCC agreement to create a customs union in 2005, with common tariffs of 5.5% on basic goods and 7.5% on luxury items. Oman became the 139th member of the WTO in November 2000, having paved the way for its accession by introducing various measures, including bilateral trade agreements with key WTO members; new laws to protect intellectual property rights; new regulations on customs valuations and import fees; a lower maximum tax rate for branches of foreign companies (30% from 2001, compared with 50% previously); a higher ceiling for foreign participation in Omani businesses (70% from 2001, compared with 49% previously);

and the authorization, from 2003, of 100% foreign ownership of companies providing specified financial services (including banking, insurance and brokerage).

In July 2006 the US House of Representatives ratified a US-Oman free trade agreement that would effectively eliminate most levies on industrial and consumer goods and, it was hoped, encourage the establishment of US businesses within Oman and investment in the proliferation of industrial development projects at Sohar. The agreement came into force in January 2009.

Statistical Survey

Sources (unless otherwise stated): National Center for Statistics and Information, Supreme Council for Planning, POB 881, Muscat 100; tel. 24698900; fax 24698467; internet www.ncsi.gov.om; Central Bank of Oman, POB 1161, 44 Mutrah Commercial Centre, Ruwi 112; tel. 24777777; fax 24788995; e-mail cboccr@omantel.net.om; internet www.cbo-oman.org.

Area and Population

AREA, POPULATION AND DENSITY

Area (sq km)	309,500*
Population (census results)	
1 December 2003	2,340,815†
12 December 2010	
Males	1,612,411
Females	1,161,068
Total	2,773,479‡
Population (official estimates at mid-year)§	
2011	3,295,298
2012	3,623,001
Density (per sq km) at mid-2012	11.7

* 119,500 sq miles.

† Comprising 1,781,558 Omani nationals and 559,257 non-Omanis.

‡ Comprising approximately 1,957,336 Omani nationals and 816,143 non-Omanis. Note: The number of non-Omanis was believed to have been reduced significantly by the proximity of the census to the Christmas holiday season.

§ Estimates not adjusted to take account of the 2010 census.

POPULATION BY AGE AND SEX

(population estimates at mid-2011)

	Males	Females	Total
0–14	378,538	361,487	740,025
15–64	1,661,667	799,818	2,461,485
65 and over	50,678	43,110	93,788
Total	2,090,883	1,204,415	3,295,298

Estimates not adjusted to take account of results of the 2010 census.

ADMINISTRATIVE DIVISIONS

(population estimates at mid-2012)

	Area (sq km)*	Population†	Density (per sq km)
Muscat Governorate	3,900	1,093,360	280.3
Al-Batinah Region	12,500	921,330	73.7
Musandam Governorate	1,800	34,148	19.0
Al-Dhahira Region	44,000	170,584	3.9
Al-Dakhliya Region	31,900	368,027	11.5
Al-Sharqiya Region	36,400	464,195	12.8
Al-Wosta Region	79,700	36,391	0.5
Dhofar Governorate	99,300	346,046	3.5
Al-Buraymi Governorate	n.a.	89,564	n.a.
Total (incl. others)	309,500	3,623,001	11.7

* Figures for area are rounded, and totals may not be equal to the sum of components as a result; area data predate the creation, from al-Dhahira Region, of al-Buraymi Governorate in October 2006.

† Estimates not adjusted to take account of results of the 2010 census; total also includes 99,356 persons of unspecified location.

PRINCIPAL TOWNS

(population at 2010 census)

Al-Seeb	302 992	Ibri	116,416
Bawshar	192 235	Nizwa	84,528
Salalah	172 570	Al-Rustaq	79,720
Mutrah	150 124	Sur	64,988
Sohar	140 006	Al-Buraymi (Buraimi)	63,159

Muscat (capital): 27,216.

BIRTHS AND DEATHS

(Omani nationals only, official estimates)

	2010	2011	2012
Live births	59,903	67,922	67,251
Birth rate (per 1,000)	31.0	31.2	32.1
Deaths	6,444	7,667	6,647
Death rate (per 1,000)	3.3	3.3	3.2

Registered marriages: 25,768 (marriage rate 7.8 per 1,000) in 2011.

Life expectancy (years at birth, official figures): 75.4 (males 73.1, females 77.7) in 2011.

EMPLOYMENT

(persons aged 15 years and over, 2003 census)

	Omanis	Non-Omanis	Total
Agriculture and fishing	14,210	43,904	58,114
Mining and quarrying	11,998	8,117	20,115
Manufacturing	13,831	45,661	59,492
Electricity, gas and water	1,826	2,219	4,045
Construction	10,128	108,129	118,257
Trade, hotels and restaurants	24,999	84,158	109,157
Transport, storage and communications	17,202	10,472	27,674
Finance, insurance and real estate	12,657	12,543	25,200
Public administration and defence	144,699	18,043	162,742
Other community, social and personal services	54,923	83,299	138,222
Sub-total	306,473	416,545	723,018
Activities not adequately defined	5,973	7,633	13,606
Total employed	312,446	424,178	736,624
Males	258,655	364,337	622,992
Females	53,791	59,841	113,632

Mid-2013 (estimates in '000): Agriculture, etc. 321; Total labour force 1,193 (Source: FAO).

Health and Welfare

KEY INDICATORS

Total fertility rate (children per woman, 2011)	2.2
Under-5 mortality rate (per 1,000 live births, 2011)	9
HIV/AIDS (% of persons aged 15–49, 2009)	0.1
Physicians (per 1,000 head, 2008)	1.9
Hospital beds (per 1,000 head, 2009)	1.8
Health expenditure (2010): US $ per head (PPP)	591
Health expenditure (2010): % of GDP	2.7
Health expenditure (2010): public (% of total)	81.1
Access to water (% of persons, 2011)	92
Access to sanitation (% of persons, 2011)	97
Total carbon dioxide emissions ('000 metric tons, 2009)	41,143.7
Carbon dioxide emissions per head (metric tons, 2009)	15.2
Human Development Index (2012): ranking	84
Human Development Index (2012): value	0.731

For sources and definitions, see explanatory note on p. vi.

Agriculture

PRINCIPAL CROPS
('000 metric tons)

	2009	2010	2011
Sorghum	42.0	26.1	36.2
Potatoes	10.0	7.2	8.1
Tomatoes	74.0	82.2	53.7
Onions, dry	5.2	4.4	7.8
Watermelons	15.4	19.1	18.6
Bananas	29.0	56.7	61.6
Lemons and limes	6.4	6.4	6.5
Mangoes, mangosteens and guavas	10.2	10.2	8.9
Dates	259.0	276.4	268.0
Papayas	1.9	1.9	1.7

Aggregate production ('000 metric tons, may include official, semi-official or estimated data): Total cereals 47.0 in 2009, 31.7 in 2010, 42.5 in 2011; Total roots and tubers 10.0 in 2009, 7.2 in 2010; 8.1 in 2011; Total vegetables (incl. melons) 234.4 in 2009, 340.7 in 2010, 284.8 in 2011; Total fruits (excl. melons) 305.9 in 2009, 351.6 in 2010, 346.8 in 2011.

Source: FAO.

LIVESTOCK
('000 head, year ending September)

	2009	2010	2011
Asses*	28.5	28.5	28.5
Cattle	326	333	340
Camels	127	130	132
Sheep	381	389	396
Goats	1,685	1,719	1,754
Chickens*	4,300	4,390	4,450

* FAO estimates.

Source: FAO.

LIVESTOCK PRODUCTS
('000 metric tons)

	2009	2010	2011
Cattle meat*	5.2	5.3	5.6
Camel meat*	6.7	7.4	7.7
Sheep meat*	19.5	19.7	20.1
Goat meat*	14.5	15.0	15.7
Chicken meat*	5.9	5.9	6.0
Cows' milk	49.6	69.6	71.0
Sheep's milk*	4.1	4.2	4.3
Goats' milk*	71.9	100.6	100.8
Hen eggs	9.3	9.3	10.7

* FAO estimates.

Source: FAO.

Fishing

('000 metric tons, live weight)

	2009	2010	2011
Capture	158.6	163.9	158.6
Groupers	6.0	5.2	3.9
Emperors (Scavengers)	11.3	10.8	8.9
Porgies and seabreams	10.3	9.9	4.2
Hairtails and scabbardfishes	5.7	6.7	11.5
Demersal percomorphs	7.6	6.3	3.9
Indian oil sardine	36.6	32.1	27.9
Longtail tuna	8.1	8.6	10.2
Yellowfin tuna	7.0	3.2	2.0
Indian mackerel	11.0	10.1	8.0
Sharks, rays, skates, etc.	4.8	5.3	7.1
Cuttlefish and bobtail squids	6.6	9.8	7.5
Aquaculture	0.1	0.1	0.2
Total catch	158.7	164.1	158.8

Source: FAO.

Mining

('000 metric tons unless otherwise indicated)

	2009	2010	2011
Crude petroleum	40,300	42,900	44,100
Natural gas (million cu m)	24,760	27,100	26,520
Chromium	798.5	865.4	616.7
Gold (kg)	28	27	—
Marble	630.8	695.1	931.4
Salt	30.6	12.3	12.4
Gypsum	254.2	653.2	1,254.1

2012: Crude petroleum 45,800; Natural gas (million cu m) 28,960.

Sources: BP, *Statistical Review of World Energy*; US Geological Survey.

Industry

SELECTED PRODUCTS
('000 barrels, unless otherwise indicated, estimates)

	2009	2010	2011
Jet fuel and kerosene	5,840	4,599	4,891
Motor spirit (petrol)	18,396	16,242	23,250
Gas-diesel (distillate fuel) oils	13,396	11,132	15,804
Residual fuel oils	5,804	2,263	3,650
Electric energy (million kWh)	17,823	19,159	21,354

2012 (million kWh): Electric energy 25,018.

Source: mainly US Geological Survey.

Finance

CURRENCY AND EXCHANGE RATES

Monetary Units

1,000 baiza = 1 rial Omani (RO).

Sterling, Dollar and Euro Equivalents (31 May 2013)

£1 sterling = 585.0 baiza;
US $1 = 384.5 baiza;
€1 = 500.1 baiza;
10 rials Omani = £17.09 = $26.01 = €20.00.

Exchange Rate: Since January 1986 the official exchange rate has been fixed at US $1 = 384.5 baiza (1 rial Omani = $2.6008).

BUDGET

(RO million)

Revenue	2010	2011	2012*
Petroleum revenue (net)	5,470.1	7,798.4	10,437.1
Gas revenues	929.9	1,172.9	1,583.7
Other current revenue	1,464.2	1,596.5	2,033.7
Taxes and fees	707.6	728.5	909.9
Income tax on enterprises	272.6	281.9	353.3
Customs duties	179.6	161.2	250.1
Non-tax revenue	756.6	868.0	1,123.7
Surplus from public authorities	9.2	10.3	7.4
Income from government investments	379.9	512.0	775.2
Capital revenue	29.9	17.6	13.0
Capital repayments	22.4	39.3	12.8
Total	7,916.5	10,624.7	14,080.3

Expenditure	2010	2011	2012*
Current expenditure	4,791.3	6,103.8	8,772.6
Defence and national security	1,888.2	2,563.7	4,742.5
Civil ministries	2,613.5	3,186.9	3,503.2
Investment expenditure	2,596.8	2,959.5	2,886.5
Share of PDO expenditure†	613.5	624.3	659.9
Participation and subsidies	577.2	1,674.6	1,895.9
Total	7,965.3	10,737.9	13,555.0

* Provisional figures.

† Referring to the Government's share of current and capital expenditure by Petroleum Development Oman.

INTERNATIONAL RESERVES

(US $ million at 31 December)

	2010	2011	2012
Gold (national valuation)	0.9	1.0	1.0
IMF special drawing rights	285.8	268.8	270.3
Reserve position in IMF	67.2	113.3	115.4
Foreign exchange	12,671.3	13,983.2	14,014.4
Total	13,025.2	14,366.3	14,401.1

Source: IMF, *International Financial Statistics*.

MONEY SUPPLY

(RO million at 31 December)

	2010	2011	2012
Currency outside depository corporations	702.0	843.1	926.0
Transferable deposits	2,596.1	2,600.2	3,042.4
Other deposits	5,369.5	6,342.2	6,913.0
Securities other than shares	117.2	69.4	30.7
Broad money	8,784.8	9,854.9	10,912.0

Source: IMF, *International Financial Statistics*.

COST OF LIVING

(Consumer Price Index; base: 2000 = 100)

	2010	2011	2012
Food, beverages and tobacco	154.4	161.4	164.9
Textiles, clothing and footwear	104.5	105.2	108.0
Rent, electricity, water and fuel	134.3	138.0	141.0
All items (incl. others)	133.7	139.1	143.2

NATIONAL ACCOUNTS

(RO million in current prices)

Expenditure on the Gross Domestic Product

	2009	2010	2011*
Final consumption expenditure	10,876.4	11,625.0	12,703.1
General government	3,601.1	4,092.0	4,627.0
Households	7,254.7	7,520.1	8,054.1
Non-profit institutions serving households	20.6	12.9	22.1
Gross capital formation	4,698.2	5,477.4	6,250.1
Gross fixed capital formation	6,421.3	6,302.7	7,082.2
Changes in inventories	–1,723.2	–825.3	–832.1
Total domestic expenditure	15,574.6	17,102.4	18,953.2
Balance on goods and services	2,973.8	5,511.2	7,951.0
GDP in purchasers' values	18,548.4	22,613.6	26,904.2
GDP at constant 2000 prices	11,445.9	12,085.5	12,120.7

* Provisional figures.

Gross Domestic Product by Economic Activity

	2010	2011*	2012†
Agriculture and fishing	283.0	316.0	333.4
Mining and quarrying	10,480.1	14,239.9	15,779.1
Crude petroleum	9,526.6	13,117.9	14,548.6
Natural gas	861.8	1,022.7	1,129.1
Non-petroleum	91.7	99.3	101.4
Manufacturing	2,418.7	2,965.2	3,040.1
Electricity and water	271.0	322.2	369.6
Construction	1,313.7	1,390.1	1,455.9
Wholesale and retail trade	1,735.2	1,945.3	2,242.8
Hotels and restaurants	172.5	175.0	201.0
Transport, storage and communications	1,161.1	1,346.1	1,511.9
Financial intermediation	974.5	1,053.5	1,164.6
Real estate	984.2	1,043.9	1,113.8
Public administration and defence	1,604.5	1,861.6	2,422.6
Other community, social and personal services	1,629.0	1,708.8	1,978.9
Sub-total	23,042.1	28,367.6	31,613.7
Less Financial intermediation services indirectly measured	468.3	513.8	577.7
Gross value added in basic prices	22,573.8	27,853.8	31,036.0
Taxes on imports	39.8	–949.6	–1,002.4
GDP in purchasers' values	22,613.6	26,904.2	30,033.6

* Provisional figures.

† Preliminary figures.

Note: Totals may not be equal to the sum of components, owing to rounding.

BALANCE OF PAYMENTS

(US $ million)

	2010	2011	2012
Exports of goods	36,601	47,092	52,138
Imports of goods	–17,874	–21,498	–25,628
Balance on goods	18,726	25,594	26,510
Exports of services	1,899	2,148	2,874
Imports of services	–6,291	–7,066	–8,681
Balance on goods and services	14,334	20,676	20,702
Primary income received	869	697	939
Primary income paid	–3,628	–3,896	–5,243
Balance on goods, services and primary income	11,574	17,477	16,398
Secondary income paid	–5,704	–7,215	–8,086

—*continued*	2010	2011	2012
Current account	5,871	10,263	8,312
Capital account (net)	−65	−146	−86
Direct investment assets	−1,012	−572	−1,371
Direct investment liabilities	1,142	788	1,514
Portfolio investment assets	−284	−310	−710
Portfolio investment liabilities	571	−447	1,373
Other investment assets	−3,026	−7,376	−8,083
Other investment liabilities	−1,764	299	1,243
Net errors and omissions	65	−1,037	−1,157
Reserves and related items	1,499	1,462	1,036

Source: IMF, *International Financial Statistics*.

External Trade

PRINCIPAL COMMODITIES
(RO million)

Imports c.i.f. (distribution by HS)*	2010	2011	2012
Live animals and animal products	282.0	337.4	380.7
Prepared foodstuffs; beverages, spirits, vinegars; tobacco and related products	364.6	316.9	352.7
Mineral products	673.7	1,317.3	1,462.7
Chemicals and related products	597.8	667.5	857.9
Plastics, rubber, and articles thereof	279.7	333.4	359.3
Iron and steel; other base metals and articles thereof	880.6	1,095.9	1,402.6
Machinery and mechanical appliances; electrical equipment; parts thereof	1,572.2	1,941.9	1,988.0
Vehicles, aircraft, vessels and associated transport equipment	1,944.5	1,882.9	2,564.4
Total (incl. others)	7,603.3	9,081.8	10,811.3

Exports f.o.b.	2010	2011	2012
Petroleum and natural gas	9,703.3	12,826.0	13,966.8
Crude petroleum	8,007.7	10,659.6	11,795.0
Refined petroleum	519.4	697.1	557.1
Natural gas	1,176.2	1,469.3	1,614.7
Non-hydrocarbon exports	2,448.2	3,033.2	3,594.1
Live animals and animal products	160.3	173.4	175.6
Mineral products	612.7	422.1	1,001.8
Chemicals and related products	709.0	1,181.4	1,076.3
Plastics, rubber, and articles thereof	254.9	300.8	252.4
Iron and steel; other base metals and articles thereof	335.9	542.0	671.2
Total†	14,073.2	18,106.8	20,047.2

* Excluding unrecorded imports (RO million): 76.2 in 2010; 153.4 in 2011; 199.1 in 2012.

† Total also includes re-exports (RO million): 1,921.7 in 2010; 2,247.6 in 2011; 2,486.3 in 2012.

PRINCIPAL TRADING PARTNERS
(RO million)

Imports c.i.f.	2010	2011	2012
Australia	158.9	155.4	180.9
Bahrain	91.1	147.1	n.a.
Belgium	77.7	61.1	111.6
Brazil	58.7	240.7	457.8
China, People's Republic	368.0	420.8	540.1
France	172.3	148.6	161.0
Germany	279.6	315.4	349.5
India	344.0	437.6	592.4
Italy	124.0	169.9	212.3
Japan	1,271.6	1,148.0	1,455.9
Korea, Republic	256.2	350.2	398.2
Kuwait	103.3	76.7	n.a.
Malaysia	89.2	110.6	n.a.
Netherlands	78.5	105.6	123.1
Saudi Arabia	240.8	454.4	453.0
Singapore	107.1	63.3	69.1
Thailand	188.3	217.4	n.a.
United Arab Emirates	2,156.0	2,490.3	2,781.5
United Kingdom	171.4	177.8	201.6
USA	374.6	535.7	641.3
Total (incl. others)	7,603.3	9,081.8	10,811.3

Exports f.o.b.*	2010	2011	2012
China, People's Republic	276.8	566.0	726.0
Hong Kong	65.6	91.4	72.7
India	371.6	468.0	646.4
Indonesia	59.6	173.0	90.6
Iran	185.1	154.0	114.1
Iraq	63.2	64.0	286.3
Korea, Republic	88.5	85.0	45.1
Kuwait	26.6	128.3	66.6
Netherlands	28.9	88.1	89.6
Pakistan	72.0	152.1	217.8
Qatar	66.9	50.7	61.6
Saudi Arabia	265.5	388.6	509.4
Singapore	97.9	65.6	17.9
United Arab Emirates	1,626.4	1,338.6	1,539.1
United Kingdom	40.4	76.2	24.8
USA	118.5	129.1	233.2
Total (incl. others)	4,369.9	5,280.7	6,080.4

* Excluding petroleum exports.

Transport

ROAD TRAFFIC
(registered vehicles at 31 December)

	2001	2002	2003
Private cars	309,217	335,771	284,902
Taxis	20,901	23,639	23,761
Commercial	132,920	140,270	109,118
Government	27,788	29,175	14,861
Motorcycles	5,195	5,436	3,977
Diplomatic	1,274	1,386	561
Other	23,631	24,625	7,320
Total	520,926	560,302	444,500

2007 (registered vehicles at 31 December): Passenger cars 453,362; Buses 26,387; Vans and Lorries 113,341; Motorcycles and mopeds 6,297 (Source: IRF, *World Road Statistics*).

SHIPPING

Flag Registered Fleet
(at 31 December)

	2010	2011	2012
Number of vessels	43	46	47
Total displacement (grt)	48,545	51,284	52,164

Source: Lloyd's List Intelligence (www.lloydslistintelligence.com).

International Sea-borne Freight Traffic
('000 metric tons unless otherwise indicated)

	2010	2011	2012
Port Sultan Qaboos:			
Vessels entered (number)	1,858	4,792	4,013
Goods loaded	911	803	829
Goods unloaded	4,082	4,018	4,229
Salalah Port:			
Vessels entered (number)	1,639	1,103	924
Goods loaded	5,345	5,556	6,058
Goods unloaded	935	963	1,193
Mina al-Fahal Coastal Area			
Vessels entered (number)	456	382	n.a.
Petroleum loaded	37,250	37,331	n.a.
Petroleum products unloaded	1,518	1,515	n.a.

CIVIL AVIATION
(aircraft movements, passengers and cargo handled at Muscat International Airport)

	2010	2011	2012
International flights:			
flights (number)	60,467	61,441	65,649
passengers ('000)	5,196	5,865	6,818
goods handled (metric tons)	95,411	92,521	n.a.
Domestic flights:			
flights (number)	6,269	6,943	7,921
passengers ('000)	555	613	727
goods handled (metric tons)	1,284	1,400	n.a.

Tourism

FOREIGN TOURIST ARRIVALS*

Country of nationality	2008	2009	2010
Bahrain	13,363	15,759	9,567
Egypt	22,648	26,853	26,807
France	39,704	35,828	38,217
Germany	101,737	85,768	81,372
India	156,723	162,832	158,739
Italy	23,544	21,849	20,909
Kuwait	16,102	20,728	13,487
Netherlands	20,615	22,327	18,638
Pakistan	21,867	18,149	20,878
Saudi Arabia	24,177	25,312	17,550
Switzerland	24,423	25,366	23,898
United Arab Emirates	112,785	130,487	93,585
United Kingdom	122,723	100,671	81,677
USA	38,630	111,304	66,761
Total (incl. others)	1,378,078	1,279,678	1,048,052

* Figures refer to international arrivals at hotels and similar establishments.

Tourism receipts (US $ million, excl. passenger transport): 689 in 2009; 775 in 2010.

Source: World Tourism Organization.

Communications Media

	2010	2011	2012
Telephones ('000 main lines in use)	281.8	287.3	304.5
Mobile cellular telephones ('000 subscribers)	4,606.1	4,809.2	5,277.6
Internet subscribers ('000)	73.9	89.1	119.4*
Broadband subscribers ('000)	45.4	52.6	71.2

* Provisional.

Source: mainly International Telecommunication Union.

Education

(state schools; 2011/12, unless otherwise indicated)

	Institutions	Teachers	Pupils/Students Males	Pupils/Students Females	Pupils/Students Total
Pre-primary*	5	529	4,973	4,456	9,429
Basic†	855	38,650	184,137	182,136	366,273
General†:					
Grades 1–6	238	1,098	8,066	7,787	15,853
Grades 7–9		2,911	12,723	12,535	25,258
Grades 10–12		9,684	55,557	54,112	109,669
Higher‡§	34	1,608	12,282	11,004	23,286
University‖	1	1,181	8,371	8,123	16,494

* 2005/06.

† The Basic education system began to replace the General education system from 1998/99.

‡ Comprising six teacher-training colleges, the College of *Shari'a* and Law, five technical colleges, the Academy of Tourism and Catering, the College of Banking and Financial Studies, 16 institutes of health, and four vocational-training centres.

§ 2004/05.

‖ 2010/11.

Pupil-teacher ratio (primary education, UNESCO estimate): 11.8 in 2008/09 (Source: UNESCO Institute for Statistics).

Adult literacy rate (UNESCO estimates): 86.6% (males 90.0%; females 80.9%) in 2008 (Source: UNESCO Institute for Statistics).

Directory

The Constitution

The Basic Statute of the State was promulgated by royal decree on 6 November 1996, as Oman's first document defining the organs and guiding principles of the State. A series of amendments to the Basic Statute were promulgated by royal decree on 13 October 2011, most notably including changes to the jurisdiction and terms of the Majlis Oman (see below).

Chapter 1 defines the State and the system of government. Oman is defined as an Arab, Islamic and independent state with full sovereignty. Islamic law (*Shari'a*) is the basis for legislation. The official language is Arabic. The system of government is defined as Sultani (Royal), hereditary in the male descendants of Sayyid Turki bin Said bin Sultan. Article 6 determines the procedure whereby the Sultan is designated.

Chapter 2 defines the political, economic, social, cultural and security principles of the State. Article 11 (economic principles) includes the stipulation that 'All natural resources and revenues therefrom shall be the property of the State which will preserve and utilize them in the best manner taking into consideration the requirements of the State's security and the interests of the national economy'. The constructive and fruitful co-operation between public and private activity is stated to be the essence of the national economy. Public property is inviolable, and private ownership is safeguarded. Article 14 (security principles) provides for a Defence Council to preserve the safety and defence of the Sultanate.

Chapter 3 defines public rights and duties. Individual and collective freedoms are guaranteed within the limits of the law.

Chapter 4 concerns the Head of State, the Council of Ministers, Specialized Councils and financial affairs of the State. Article 41 defines the Sultan as Head of State and Supreme Commander of the Armed Forces. The article states that 'His person is inviolable. Respect for him is a duty and his command must be obeyed. He is the symbol of national unity and the guardian of its preservation and protection'. The Sultan presides over the Council of Ministers, or may appoint a person (Prime Minister) to preside on his behalf. Deputy Prime Ministers and other Ministers are appointed by the Sultan. The Council of Ministers and Specialized Councils assist the Sultan in implementing the general policy of the State.

Chapter 5 defines the jurisdiction, terms, sessions, rules of procedure, membership and regulation of the legislature. This states that the Majlis Oman (Council of Oman) shall consist of the Majlis al-Shura (Consultative Council) and the Majlis al-Dawlah (State Council). The Consultative Council shall consist of elected members representing all *wilayat* (provinces) of the Sultanate. All *wilayat* with a population of less than 30,000 shall be entitled to elect one representative to the Consultative Council and those with a population over 30,000 two representatives. The election of the Consultative Council members shall be conducted through general secret ballot and according to the provisions of the electoral law. Following the election of a new Consultative Council, its Chairman shall be elected by an absolute majority of the members. The State Council consists of a chairman and members not exceeding the total number of Consultative Council members, appointed by royal decree. Members of both Councils shall serve for a term of no more than four years. The government must submit draft legislation to the Council of Oman for amendment or approval prior to promulgation by the Sultan. The Council may propose draft legislation and refer it to the government for consideration.

Chapter 6 concerns the judiciary. Articles 59 and 60 state that the supremacy of the law shall be the basis of governance, and enshrine the dignity, integrity, impartiality and independence of the judiciary. Article 66 provides for a Supreme Council of the judiciary.

Chapter 7 defines the general provisions pertaining to the application of the Basic Statute.

The Government

HEAD OF STATE

Sultan: Qaboos bin Said al-Said (assumed power on 23 July 1970, after deposing his father).

COUNCIL OF MINISTERS

(September 2013)

Prime Minister and Minister of Foreign Affairs, Defence and Finance: Sultan Qaboos bin Said al-Said.

Deputy Prime Minister for the Council of Ministers: Sayyid Fahd bin Mahmoud al-Said.

Minister Responsible for Defence Affairs: Sayyid Badr bin Saud bin Hareb al-Busaidi.

Minister of Legal Affairs: Dr Abdullah bin Muhammad bin Said al-Saeedi.

Minister of Oil and Gas: Dr Muhammad bin Hamad bin Saif al-Rumhi.

Minister of Justice: Sheikh Abd al-Malik bin Abdullah bin Ali al-Khalili.

Minister Responsible for Financial Affairs: Darwish bin Ismail bin Ali al-Balushi.

Minister of Awqaf (Religious Endowments) and Religious Affairs: Sheikh Abdullah bin Muhammad bin Abdullah al-Salimi.

Minister Responsible for Foreign Affairs: Yousuf bin Alawi bin Abdullah.

Minister of Information: Dr Abd al-Munem bin Mansour bin Said al-Hasni.

Minister of Housing: Sheikh Saif bin Muhammad al-Shabibi.

Minister of Education: Madeeha bint Ahmad bin Nasir al-Shibaniyah.

Minister of Higher Education: Dr Rawya bint Saud bin Ahmad al-Busaidiyah.

Minister of Heritage and Culture: Sayyid Haitham bin Tariq al-Said.

Minister of Tourism: Ahmad bin Nasser bin Hamad al-Mehrzi.

Minister of Social Development: Sheikh Muhammad bin Said bin Saif al-Kalbani.

Minister of Manpower: Abdullah bin Nasser al-Bakri.

Minister of Sports Affairs: Saad bin Muhammad bin Said al-Mardhouf al-Saadi.

Minister of Transport and Communications: Ahmad bin Muhammad bin Salim al-Futaisi.

Minister of the Interior: Sayyid Hamoud bin Faisal bin Said al-Busaidi.

Minister of Commerce and Industry: Eng. Ali bin Massoud bin Ali al-Sunaidi.

Minister of Agriculture and Fisheries: Dr Fuad bin Jaafar bin Muhammad al-Sajwani.

Minister of Environment and Climate Affairs: Muhammad bin Salim bin Said al-Toobi.

Minister of Health: Dr Ahmad bin Muhammad bin Obaid al-Saeedi.

Minister of Regional Municipalities and Water Resources: Ahmad bin Abdullah bin Muhammad al-Shuhi.

Minister of the Civil Service: Sheikh Khalid bin Omar bin Said al-Marhoon.

Minister of State and Governor of Muscat: Sayyid Saud bin Hilal bin Hamad al-Busaidi.

Minister of State and Governor of Dhofar: Sayyid Muhammad bin Sultan bin Hamoud al-Busaidi.

Minister of the Diwan of the Royal Court: Sayyid Khalid bin Hilal bin Saud al-Busaidi.

Minister of the Royal Office: Lt-Gen. Sultan bin Muhammad al-Numani.

MINISTRIES

Diwan of the Royal Court: POB 632, Muscat 113; tel. 24738711; fax 24739427.

Ministry of Agriculture and Fisheries: POB 467, RB 100, Muscat; tel. 24696300; fax 24696271; e-mail infonet@maf.gov.om; internet www.maf.gov.om.

Ministry of Awqaf (Religious Endowments) and Religious Affairs: POB 3232, Ruwi 112; tel. 24696870; e-mail info@mara.gov.om; internet www.maraoman.net.

Ministry of the Civil Service: POB 3994, Ruwi 112; tel. 24696000; fax 24601365; internet www.mocs.gov.om.

Ministry of Commerce and Industry: POB 550, Muscat 113; tel. 24813500; fax 24817238; e-mail info@mocioman.gov.om; internet www.mocioman.gov.om.

Ministry of Defence: POB 113, Muscat 113; tel. 24312605; fax 24702521.

Ministry of Education: POB 3, Muscat 113; tel. 24775209; e-mail moe@moe.gov.om; internet www.moe.gov.om.

Ministry of Environment and Climate Affairs: POB 323, Muscat 100; tel. 24404805; fax 24603993.

Ministry of Finance: POB 506, Muscat 100; tel. 24738201; fax 24737028; e-mail info@mof.gov.om; internet www.mof.gov.om.

Ministry of Foreign Affairs: POB 252, Muscat 112; tel. 24699500; fax 24696141; e-mail info@mofa.gov.om; internet www.mofa.gov.om.

Ministry of Health: POB 393, Muscat 113; tel. 24602177; fax 24602647; e-mail webmaster@moh.gov.om; internet www.moh.gov.om.

Ministry of Heritage and Culture: POB 668, Muscat 113; tel. 24641300; fax 24641331; e-mail info@mhc.gov.om; internet www.mhc.gov.om.

Ministry of Higher Education: POB 82, Ruwi 112; tel. 24340999; fax 24340172; e-mail info_dept@mohe.gov.om; internet www.mohe.gov.om.

Ministry of Housing: POB 173, Ruwi 100; tel. 24601276; e-mail dept.infopr@housing.gov.om; internet eservices.housing.gov.om.

Ministry of Information: POB 600, Muscat 113; tel. 24603222; fax 24693770; e-mail omanet@omantel.net.om; internet www.omanet.om.

Ministry of the Interior: POB 127, Ruwi 112; tel. 24602244; fax 24696660; internet www.moi.gov.om.

Ministry of Justice: POB 354, Ruwi 112; tel. 24697699; fax 24607716; e-mail webmaster@moj.gov.om; internet www.moj.gov.om.

Ministry of Legal Affairs: POB 578, Ruwi 112; tel. 24605802; fax 24482309; e-mail inquiry@mola.gov.om; internet www.mola.gov.om.

Ministry of Manpower: POB 413, Muscat 113; tel. 24816739; fax 24816234; e-mail webmaster@manpower.gov.om; internet www.manpower.gov.om.

Ministry of Oil and Gas: POB 551, Muscat 100; tel. 24640555; fax 24691046; internet www.mog.gov.om.

Ministry of Regional Municipalities and Water Resources: POB 461, Muscat 112; tel. 24692550; fax 24694015; e-mail admin@mrmwr.gov.om; internet www.mrmwr.gov.om.

Ministry of the Royal Office: POB 2227, Ruwi 112; tel. 24600841.

Ministry of Social Development: Muscat; internet mosd.gov.om.

Ministry of Sports Affairs: POB 211, Muscat 113; tel. 24755240; fax 24704558; e-mail feedback@sportsoman.com; internet www.sportsoman.com.

Ministry of Tourism: Madinat al-Sultan Qaboos, POB 200, Muscat 115; tel. 24588700; fax 24588880; e-mail info@omantourism.gov.om; internet www.mot.gov.om.

Ministry of Transport and Communications: POB 684, Ruwi 112; tel. 24685000; fax 24685757; e-mail info@motc.gov.om; internet www.motc.gov.om.

MAJLIS OMAN
(Council of Oman)

Majlis al-Shura
(Consultative Council)

POB 981, 111 Muscat; tel. 24510444; fax 24510560; e-mail info@shura.om; internet www.shura.om.

President: Sheikh KHALID BIN HILAL BIN NASSER AL-MA'AWALI.

The Majlis al-Shura was established by royal decree in November 1991. Initially, members of the Majlis were appointed by the Sultan from among nominees selected at national polls, but from the September 2000 elections members were directly elected. Two representatives are elected in each *wilaya* (district) of more than 30,000 inhabitants, and one in each *wilaya* of fewer than 30,000 inhabitants. Members of the Majlis are appointed for a single four-year term of office. The Majlis elected in October 2011 comprised 84 members. The duties of the Majlis include the approval and amendment of all social and economic draft laws prior to their enactment by the Sultan; public service ministries are required to submit reports and answer questions regarding their performance, plans and achievements. A decree issued by Sultan Qaboos bin Said al-Said on 19 October 2011 granted members of both chambers of the Majlis Oman the right to propose draft legislation, while members of the Majlis al-Shura may issue a request to question government ministers. The President of the Majlis is elected by an absolute majority of its members.

Majlis al-Dawlah
(State Council)

POB 59, Muscat; tel. 24699677; fax 24698719; e-mail statecouncil@statecouncil.om.

President: Sheikh YAHYA BIN MAHFOUDH AL-MANTHERI.

The Majlis al-Dawlah was established in December 1997, in accordance with the terms of the Basic Statute of the State. Like the Majlis al-Shura, it is an advisory body, the function of which is to serve as a liaison between the Government and the people of Oman. Its members are appointed by the Sultan for a four-year term. A new Majlis al-Dawlah, comprising 70 members, was appointed on 1 November 2011.

Political Organizations

There are no political organizations in Oman.

Diplomatic Representation

EMBASSIES IN OMAN

Algeria: POB 216, Muscat 115; tel. 24694945; fax 24694419; e-mail afcongem@omantel.net.om; Ambassador MUHAMMAD YOUSFI.

Bahrain: al-Khuwair, POB 66, Madinat Qaboos; tel. 24605133; fax 24605072; e-mail muscat.mission@mofa.gov.bh; Ambassador MUHAMMAD BIN SALEH AL-SHEIKH ALI.

Bangladesh: St 664, Bldg 5903, POB 3959, Ruwi 112; tel. 24698660; fax 24698789; e-mail bangla@omantel.net.om; Ambassador NURUL ALAM CHOWDHURY.

Brazil: al-Khuwair, Villa 1424, Way 1521, POB 1149, Muscat; Ambassador MITZI GURGEL VALENTE DA COSTA.

Brunei: Shatti al-Qurum, St 3050, Villa 4062, POB 91, Ruwi 112; tel. 24603533; fax 24605910; e-mail kbopuni@omantel.net.om; Ambassador Dato' Seri Setia Dr Haji BESAR BIN Haji BAKAR.

China, People's Republic: House No. 1368, Shatti al-Qurum, POB 315, Muscat 112; tel. 24696698; fax 24602322; e-mail chinaemb_om@mfa.gov.cn; internet om.chineseembassy.org; Ambassador WU JIUHONG.

Egypt: Jamiat al-Dowal al-Arabiya St, Diplomatic City, al-Khuwair, POB 2252, Ruwi 112; tel. 24600411; fax 24603626; e-mail eg.emb_muscat@mfa.gov.eg; Ambassador AMR AHMAD ABD AL-MAJEED AL-ZAYAT.

France: Diplomatic City, al-Khuwair, POB 208, Madinat Qaboos 115; tel. 24681800; fax 24681843; e-mail diplofr1@omantel.net.om; internet www.ambafrance-om.org; Ambassador YVES OUDIN.

Germany: POB 128, Ruwi 112; tel. 24832482; fax 24835690; e-mail info@maskat.diplo.de; internet www.maskat.diplo.de; Ambassador HANS-CHRISTIAN FREIHERR VON REIBNITZ.

India: New Chancery Complex, Jamiat al-Dowal al-Arabiya St, al-Khuwair, POB 1727, Ruwi 112; tel. 24684500; fax 24698291; e-mail indiamct@omantel.net.om; internet www.indemb-oman.org; Ambassador J. S. MUKUL.

Iran: Diplomatic Area, Jamiat al-Dowal al-Arabiya St, POB 3155, Ruwi 112; tel. 24696944; fax 24696888; e-mail iranembassy@hotmail.com; internet www.iranembassy.gov.om; Ambassador ALI AKBAR SEBAWYEH.

Iraq: Shatti al-Qurum, Way 3015, House No. 1073, POB 262, Muscat 115; tel. 24603642; fax 24602026; e-mail musemb@iraqmofamail.net; Ambassador MUIZ KADIM SALMAN AL-NOAH.

Italy: Shatti al-Qurum, Way No. 3034, House No. 2697, POB 520, Ruwi 115; tel. 24693727; fax 24695161; e-mail ambasciata.mascate@esteri.it; internet www.ambmascate.esteri.it; Ambassador PAULA AMADI.

Japan: Shatti al-Qurum, Villa No. 760, Way No. 3011, Jamiat al-Dowal al-Arabiya St, POB 3511, Ruwi 112; tel. 24601028; fax 24698720; e-mail embjapan@omantel.net.om; internet www.oman.emb-japan.go.jp; Ambassador GEORGE HISAEDA.

Jordan: Diplomatic City, Arab League St, POB 70, al-Adhaiba 130; tel. 24692760; fax 24692762; e-mail embhkjom@omantel.net.om; Ambassador MITEB ZAIN.

Kenya: Muscat; Chargé d'affaires a.i. YABESH MONARI.

Korea, Republic: POB 377, Madinat Qaboos 115; tel. 24691490; fax 24691495; e-mail emboman@mofat.go.kr; internet omn.mofat.go.kr; Ambassador CHOE JONG-HYUN.

Kuwait: Diplomatic Area al-Khuwair, Arab League St, Blk 13, Bldg 58, POB 1798, Ruwi 112; tel. 24699626; fax 24604732; e-mail muscat@mofa.gov.kw; Ambassador FAHED HAJAR AL-MUTAIRI.

Lebanon: Shatti al-Qurum, Way No. 3019, Villa No. 1613, al-Harthy Complex, POB 67, Muscat 118; tel. 24695844; fax 24695633; e-mail lebanon1@omantel.net.om; Ambassador AFIF AYYUB.

Malaysia: Shatti al-Qurum, Villa No. 1611, Way No. 3019, POB 3939, Ruwi 112; tel. 24698329; fax 24605031; e-mail mwmuscat@omantel.net.om; internet www.kln.gov.my/web/omn_muscat; Ambassador Dato' RUSTUM BIN YAHAYA.

Morocco: Shatti al-Qurum, Villa No. 2443, Way No. 3030, POB 3125, Ruwi 112; tel. 24696152; fax 24601114; e-mail sifamamu@omantel.net.om; Ambassador NOURDINE BEN OMAR.

Netherlands: Shatti al-Qurum, Way No. 3017, Villa No. 1366, POB 3302, Ruwi 112; tel. 24603706; fax 24603778; e-mail mus@minbuza.nl; internet www.mfa.nl/mus; Ambassador STEFAN VAN WERSCH.

Pakistan: Way No. 2133, POB 1302, Madinat Qaboos, Ruwi 112; tel. 24603439; fax 24697462; e-mail parepmuscat@hotmail.com; internet www.mofa.gov.pk/oman; Ambassador (vacant).

Philippines: POB 420, Madinat Qaboos 115; tel. 24605140; fax 24605176; e-mail muscatpe@omantel.net.om; internet www.muscatpe.org; Ambassador JOSELITO A. JIMENO.

Qatar: Diplomatic City, Jamiat al-Dowal al-Arabiya St, al-Khuwair, POB 802, Muscat 113; tel. 24691152; fax 24691156; e-mail sad707@omantel.net.om; Ambassador ABDULLAH BIN MUHAMMAD BIN KHALID AL-KHATIR.

Russia: Shatti al-Qurum, Way No. 3032, Surfait Compound, POB 745, Ruwi 115; tel. 24602894; fax 24604189; e-mail rusoman@omantel.net.om; internet www.oman.mid.ru; Ambassador SERGEI N. PESKOV.

Saudi Arabia: Diplomatic City, Jamiat al-Dowal al-Arabiya St, POB 1411, Ruwi 112; tel. 24698780; fax 24607418; e-mail omemb@mofa.gov.sa; Ambassador ABD AL-AZIZ BIN SULAIMAN AL-TURKI.

Senegal: Muscat; tel. 24694139; fax 24694151; Ambassador AL-SHAIKH AL-TIJANI.

Somalia: Mumtaz St, Villa Hassan Jumaa Baker, POB 1767, Ruwi 112; tel. and fax 24697977; e-mail danjsiad@omantel.net.om; Ambassador HASSAN MOHAMED SYAAD BERI.

South Africa: al-Harthy Complex, POB 231, Muscat 118; tel. 24694791; fax 24694792; e-mail southae@omantel.net.om; Ambassador YUSEF SALOJI.

Spain: Shatti al-Qurum, Way No. 2834, House No. 2573, POB 3492, Ruwi 112; tel. 24691101; fax 24698969; e-mail emb.mascate@mae.es; internet www.exteriores.gob.es/embajadas/mascate; Ambassador José Luis Roselló Serra.

Sri Lanka: POB 95, Villa No. 701, Way No. 2114, PC 115, Madinat Qaboos; tel. 24697841; fax 24697336; e-mail lankaemb@omantel.net.om; Ambassador Madukande Asoka Kumara Girihagama.

Sudan: Diplomatic City, al-Khuwair, POB 3971, Ruwi 112; tel. 24697875; fax 24699065; e-mail suanimt@gto.net.om; Ambassador Awadh Muhammad Ahmed.

Syria: al-Ensharah St, Villa No. 2826, POB 85, Madinat Qaboos, Muscat 115; tel. 24697904; fax 24603895; e-mail syria@omantel.net.om; internet www.syrianembassy.gov.om; Ambassador Farouk Mahmoud Qaddour.

Thailand: Shatti al-Qurum, Villa No. 1339, Way No. 3017, POB 60, Ruwi 115; tel. 24602684; fax 24605714; e-mail thaimct@omantel.net.om; Ambassador Dr Pornchai Danvivathana.

Tunisia: al-Ensharah St, Way No. 1507, POB 220, Muscat 115; tel. and fax 24603486; Ambassador Tariq el-Adab.

Turkey: Shatti al-Qurum, Bldg No. 3270, St No. 3042, POB 47, Mutrah 115; tel. 24697050; fax 24697053; e-mail embassy.muscat@mfa.gov.tr; internet muscat.emb.mfa.gov.tr; Ambassador Kerem Ahmet Kiratli.

United Arab Emirates: Diplomatic City, al-Khuwair, POB 551, Muscat 111; tel. 24400000; fax 24602584; e-mail muscat@mofa.gov.ae; Ambassador Abd al-Redha Abdullah Khouri.

United Kingdom: POB 185, Mina al-Fahal 116; tel. 24609000; fax 24609010; e-mail enquiries.muscat@fco.gov.uk; internet ukinoman.fco.gov.uk; Ambassador James Bowden.

USA: Jamiat al-Dowal al-Arabiya St, POB 202, Madinat Qaboos, Muscat 115; tel. 24643400; fax 24643740; e-mail answersom@state.gov; internet oman.usembassy.gov; Ambassador Greta Holtz.

Yemen: Shatti al-Qurum, Area 258, Way No. 2840, Bldg No. 2981, POB 105, Madinat Qaboos 115; tel. 24600815; fax 24605008; e-mail yemenom@hotmail.com; Chargé d'affaires Nagi Hassan al-Awadhi.

Judicial System

Oman's Basic Statute guarantees the independence of the judiciary. The foundation for the legal system is *Shari'a* (Islamic law), which is the basis for family law, dealing with matters such as inheritance and divorce. Separate courts have been established to deal with commercial disputes and other matters to which *Shari'a* does not apply.

Courts of the First Instance are competent to try cases of criminal misdemeanour; serious crimes are tried by the Criminal Courts; the Court of Appeal is in Muscat. There are district courts throughout the country. Special courts deal with military crimes committed by members of the armed and security forces.

The Basic Statute provides for a Supreme Council to supervise the proper functioning of the courts.

An Administrative Court, to review the decisions of government bodies, was instituted in April 2001.

The office of Public Prosecutor was established in 1999, and the first such appointment was made in June 2001.

Religion

ISLAM

The majority of the population (estimated at 89.2% in 2001) are Muslims, of whom approximately three-quarters are of the Ibadi sect and about one-quarter are Sunni Muslims.

Grand Mufti of Oman: Sheikh Ahmad bin Hamad al-Khalili.

HINDUISM

According to 2001 estimates, 6.0% of the population are Hindus.

CHRISTIANITY

According to 2001 estimates, 2.9% of the population are Christians.

Protestantism

The Protestant Church in Oman: POB 1982, Ruwi 112; tel. 24702372; fax 24789943; e-mail pcomct@omantel.net.om; internet 76.12.38.165/occ2003/skur/history.htm; joint chaplaincy of the Anglican Church and the Reformed Church of America; four interdenominational churches in Oman, at Ruwi and Ghala in Muscat, at Sohar, and at Salalah; Senior Pastor Rev. Michael Peppin.

The Roman Catholic Church

A small number of adherents, mainly expatriates, form part of the Apostolic Vicariate of Southern Arabia. The Vicar Apostolic is resident in the United Arab Emirates.

The Press

Article 31 of Oman's Basic Statute guarantees the freedom of the press, printing and publishing, according to the terms and conditions specified by the law. Published matter 'leading to discord, harming the State's security or abusing human dignity or rights' is prohibited.

NEWSPAPERS

Oman: POB 3002, Ruwi 112; tel. 24699689; fax 24697443; e-mail editor@omandaily.com; internet www.omandaily.com; daily; Arabic; publ. by Oman Establishment for Press, News, Publication and Advertising; Editor-in-Chief Abdullah bin Nasser al-Rahbi; circ. 26,000.

Al-Shabiba (Youth): POB 2998, Ruwi 112; tel. 24814373; fax 24811722; e-mail editor@shabiba.com; internet www.shabiba.com; f. 1993; daily; Arabic; culture, leisure and sports; publ. by Muscat Press and Publishing House SAOC; Editor-in-Chief Ahmad bin Essa al-Zedjali; circ. 15,000.

Al-Watan (The Nation): POB 463, Muscat 113; tel. 24491919; fax 24491280; e-mail alwatan@omantel.net.om; internet www.alwatan.com; f. 1971; daily; Arabic; Editor-in-Chief Muhammad bin Sulayman al-Tai; circ. 40,000.

English Language

Oman Daily Observer: POB 3002, Ruwi 112; tel. 24699647; fax 24600362; e-mail editor@omanobserver.com; internet www.omanobserver.com; f. 1981; daily; publ. by Oman Establishment for Press, News, Publication and Advertising; Chair. Abdullah bin Nasser al-Rahbi; Editor Ibrahim bin Saif al-Hamdani; circ. 22,000.

Oman Tribune: POB 463, Muscat 113; tel. 24491919; fax 24498444; e-mail eomantribune@omantribune.com; internet www.omantribune.com; f. 2004; Chair. Muhammad bin Sulayman al-Tai; Editor-in-Chief Abd al-Hamid bin Sulayman al-Tai.

Times of Oman: POB 770, Ruwi 112; tel. 24811953; fax 24813153; e-mail online@timesofoman.com; internet www.timesofoman.com; f. 1975; daily; publ. by Muscat Press and Publishing House SAOC; Founder, Chair. and Editor-in-Chief Essa bin Muhammad al-Zedjali; Man. Dir Anis bin Essa al-Zedjali; circ. 34,000.

TheWeek: POB 2616, Ruwi 112, Muscat; tel. 24799388; fax 24793316; e-mail theweek@apexstuff.com; internet www.theweek.co.om; f. 2003; weekly; free; publ. by Apex Press and Publishing; CEO and Man. Editor Mohana Prabhakar; circ. 50,743 (copies per week).

PERIODICALS

Al-Ain al-Sahira (The Vigilant Eye): Royal Oman Police, POB 302, Mina' al-Fahl 116; tel. 24569270; fax 24567161; internet www.rop.gov.om; quarterly magazine of Royal Oman Police; Editor-in-Chief Col Abdullah bin Ali al-Harthi.

Alam Aliktisaad Wala'mal (AIWA) (World of Economy and Business): POB 3305, Ruwi 112; tel. 24700896; fax 24707939; e-mail avi@umsoman.com; f. 2007; monthly; Arabic; business magazine; publ. by United Press and Publishing LLC; Business Head Avi Titus.

Al-'Aqida (The Faith): POB 1001, Ruwi 112; tel. 24701000; fax 24709917; weekly illustrated magazine; Arabic; political; Editor Said al-Samhan al-Kathiri; circ. 10,000.

Business Today: POB 2616, Ruwi 112; tel. 24799388; fax 24793316; e-mail editorial@apexstuff.com; internet www.businesstoday.co.om; monthly; publ. by Apex Press and Publishing; Man. Editor Mohana Prabhakar.

The Commercial: POB 2002, Ruwi 112; tel. 24704022; fax 24795885; e-mail omanad@omantel.net.om; f. 1978; monthly; Arabic and English; business news; Man. Muhammad Ayoob; Chief Editor Ali bin Abdullah al-Kasbi; circ. 10,000.

Al-Ghorfa (The Chamber): POB 1400, Ruwi 112; tel. 24703082; fax 24708497; e-mail alghorfa@chamberoman.com; internet www.chamberoman.com; f. 1978; bi-monthly; English and Arabic; business; publ. by Oman Chamber of Commerce and Industry; Editor Hamood Hamad al-Mahrouq; circ. 10,500.

Al-Jarida al-Rasmiya (Official Gazette): POB 578, Ruwi 112; tel. 24605802; fax 24605697; f. 1972; fortnightly; publ. by Ministry of Legal Affairs.

Jund Oman (Soldiers of Oman): Ministry of Defence, POB 113, Muscat 113; tel. 24613615; fax 24613369; f. 1974; monthly; Arabic;

illustrated magazine of the Ministry of Defence; Supervisor Chief of Staff of the Sultan's Armed Forces.

Al-Mar'a (Woman): United Media Services, POB 3305, Ruwi 112; tel. 24700896; fax 24707939; e-mail almara@umsoman.com; internet www.almaraonline.com; monthly; Arabic and English; women's interest; publ. by United Press and Publishing LLC.

Al-Markazi (The Central): POB 1161, Ruwi 112; tel. 24702222; fax 24707913; e-mail cboccr@omantel.net.om; internet www.cbo-oman.org; f. 1975; bi-monthly economic magazine; Arabic and English; publ. by Cen. Bank of Oman; Editor-in-Chief HAIDER BIN ABD AL-REDHA AL-LAWATI.

Al-Nahda (The Renaissance): POB 979, Muscat 113; tel. 24563104; fax 24563106; weekly illustrated magazine; Arabic; political and social; Editor TALEB SAID AL-MEAWALY; circ. 10,000.

Nizwa: POB 855, 117 Wadi Kabir; tel. 24601608; fax 24694254; e-mail nizwa99@nizwa.com; internet www.nizwa.com; f. 1994; quarterly; Arabic; literary and cultural; publ. by Oman Establishment for Press, News, Publication and Advertising; Editor-in-Chief SAIF AL-RAHBI.

Oman Economic Review: POB 3305, Ruwi 112; tel. 24700896; fax 24707939; e-mail editor@oeronline.com; internet www.oeronline.com; f. 1998; monthly; English; business news; publ. by United Press and Publishing LLC; Editor-in-Chief Sayyid TARIK BIN SHABIB; circ. 25,000.

Oman Today: POB 2616, Ruwi 112; tel. 24799388; fax 24793316; e-mail editorial@apexstuff.com; internet www.omantoday.co.om; f. 1981; monthly; English; leisure and sports; publ. by Apex Press and Publishing; Man. Editor MOHANA PRABHAKAR; circ. 20,000.

Al-Omaniya (Omani Woman): POB 3303, Ruwi 112; tel. 24792700; fax 24707765; f. 1982; monthly; Arabic; Editor AIDA BINT SALIM AL-HUJRI; circ. 10,500.

Risalat al-Masjid (The Mosque Message): POB 6066, Muscat; tel. 24561178; fax 24560607; issued by Diwan of the Royal Court Protocol Dept (Schools and Mosques Section); Editor JOUMA BIN MUHAMMAD BIN SALEM AL-WAHAIBI.

Al-Usra (The Family): POB 440, Mutrah 114; tel. 24794922; fax 24795348; e-mail admeds@omantel.net.om; f. 1974; fortnightly; Arabic; socio-economic illustrated magazine; Chief Editor SADEK ABDOWANI; circ. 15,000.

NEWS AGENCY

Oman News Agency: Ministry of Information, POB 3659, Ruwi 112; tel. 24698891; fax 24699657; e-mail onaoman@omantel.net.om; internet www.omannews.gov.om; f. 1986; Dir-Gen. and Editor-in-Chief MAJID BIN MUHAMMAD BIN FARAJ AL-ROWAS.

Publishers

Apex Press and Publishing: POB 2616, Ruwi 112, Muscat; tel. 24799388; fax 24793316; e-mail editorial@apexstuff.com; internet www.apexstuff.com; f. 1980; art, history, trade directories, maps, leisure and business magazines, and guidebooks; publs incl. *TheWeek* (English weekly), *Business Today* (business monthly), *Oman Today* (leisure monthly); Pres. SALEH M. TALIB AL-ZAKWANI; Man. Editor MOHANA PRABHAKAR.

Muscat Press and Publishing House SAOC: POB 770, Ruwi 112; tel. 24811953; fax 24813153; publs incl. *Times of Oman* (English daily) and *Al-Shabiba* (Arabic daily); Chair. ESSA BIN MUHAMMAD AL-ZEDJALI; CEO AHMAD BIN ESSA AL-ZEDJALI.

National Publishing and Advertising LLC: POB 3112, Ruwi 112; tel. 24793098; fax 24708445; e-mail advertising@npaoman.com; internet www.npaoman.com; f. 1987; Man. ASHOK SUVARNA.

Oman Establishment for Press, News, Publication and Advertising (OEPNPA): POB 974, al-Qurum, Muscat 113; tel. 24649458; fax 24649469; f. 1996 as Oman Newspaper House; publs include *Oman* (Arabic daily), *Oman Daily Observer* (English language) and *Nizwa* (Arabic quarterly); three regional offices in Dhofar, Nizwa and Sohar; CEO ABDULLAH BIN NASSER AL-RAHBI; Editor-in-Chief FAHMI BIN KHALID AL-HARTHI.

United Press and Publishing LLC (UPP): POB 3305, Ruwi 112; tel. 24700896; fax 24707939; internet www.renaissanceoman.com; f. 1995; part of Renaissance Services SAOG; publishes *Alam Aliktisaad Wala'mal* (Arabic monthly) and *Oman Economic Review* (English monthly); Chief Exec. SANDEEP SEHGAL.

Broadcasting and Communications

TELECOMMUNICATIONS

Oman Telecommunications Company SAOC (Omantel): POB 789, Ruwi 112; tel. 24631417; fax 24697066; e-mail info@omantel.net.om; internet www.omantel.om; f. 1999 as successor to Gen. Telecommunications Org.; provider of fixed-line, mobile and internet services; held a monopoly on fixed-line services until 2008; 70% stake owned by the Government of Oman; Chair. Eng. SULTAN BIN HAMDOUN AL-HARTHI; CEO Dr AMER BIN AWADH AL-RAWAS.

Oman Mobile Telecommunications Company LLC (Oman Mobile): POB 694, al-Azaiba 130; tel. 24474000; e-mail enquiry@omanmobile.om; internet www.omanmobile.om; f. 2004; Chair. Eng. SULTAN BIN HAMDOUN AL-HARTHI.

Omani Qatari Telecommunications Co SAOC (Nawras): POB 874, Muscat 111; tel. 95011500 (mobile); fax 95011555; e-mail customerservice@nawras.om; internet www.nawras.om; f. 2004; awarded Oman's second mobile cellular telecommunications licence 2004; awarded Oman's second fixed-line licence 2008; jt venture between Qatar Telecommunications Corpn (Q-Tel), TDC A/S (Denmark) and several Omani investors; Chair. Sheikh SALIM BIN MUSTAHIL AL-MA'ASHANI; CEO ROSS CORMACK.

Regulatory Authority

Telecommunications Regulatory Authority: POB 579, Ruwi 112; tel. 24574300; fax 24565464; e-mail traoman@tra.gov.om; internet www.tra.gov.om; f. 2002 to oversee the privatization of Omantel and to set tariffs and regulate the sale of operating licences; Chair. MUHAMMAD BIN NASSER AL-KHUSAIBI.

BROADCASTING

The Law on Private Radio and Television Stations, enacted in 2004, provided for the establishment of private broadcasters for the first time.

Radio

Sultanate of Oman Radio: Ministry of Information, POB 600, Muscat 113; tel. 24602058; fax 24601393; e-mail omanet@omantel.net.om; internet www.oman-radio.gov.om; f. 1970; operates four services: General Arabic Channel, Al-Shabab Channel (youth service), English-language FM service, Holy Koran Channel; Dir-Gen. NASSER SULAYMAN AL-SAIBANI.

The first private radio licences were issued in 2005, and broadcasts began in 2007 with the launch of Hala FM (Arabic, entertainment and music) and Hi FM (English, entertainment and music). A third private station, Al-Wisal FM, began broadcasting in Arabic in 2008.

Television

Sultanate of Oman Television: Ministry of Information, POB 600, Muscat 113; tel. 24603222; fax 24605032; e-mail feedback_tv@oman-tv.gov.om; internet www.oman-tv.gov.om; began broadcasting in 1974; programmes broadcast via Arabsat and Nilesat satellite networks.

Finance

(cap. = capital; res = reserves; dep. = deposits; m. = million; brs = branches; amounts in rials Omani)

BANKING

At the end of March 2010 there were 17 commercial banks (seven local and 10 foreign) and two specialized banks, with a total network of 451 domestic branch offices operating throughout Oman.

Central Bank

Central Bank of Oman: POB 1161, 44 Mutrah Commercial Centre, Ruwi 112; tel. 24777777; fax 24788995; e-mail cboccr@omantel.net.om; internet www.cbo-oman.org; f. 1974; cap. 400m., res 774m., dep. 2,851m. (Dec. 2009); 100% state-owned; Dep. Chair. Dr ALI BIN MUHAMMAD BIN MOUSA; 2 brs.

Commercial Banks

Ahli Bank SAOG: POB 545, Mina al-Fahal 116; tel. 24577000; fax 24568001; e-mail info@ahlibank-oman.com; internet www.ahlibank-oman.com; f. 1997 as Alliance Housing Bank; renamed as above 2008; privately owned; cap. 80m., res 24m., dep. 696m. (Dec. 2011); Chair. HAMDAN ALI NASSER AL-HINAI; CEO ABD AL-AZIZ AL-BALUSHI; 12 brs.

Bank Dhofar SAOG: POB 1507, Ruwi 112; tel. 24790466; fax 24797246; e-mail info@bankdhofar.com; internet www.bankdhofar.com; f. 1990 as Bank Dhofar al-Omani al-Fransi SAOG; renamed as above in 2004 after merger with Majan Int. Bank SAOC; cap. 91m., res 115m., dep. 1,519m. (Dec. 2011); Chair. Eng. ABD AL-HAFIDH SALIM RAJAB AL-AUJAILI; CEO ANTHONY MAHONEY; 54 brs.

BankMuscat SAOG: POB 134, Ruwi 112; tel. 24768888; fax 24785572; e-mail banking@bkmuscat.com; internet www.bankmuscat.com; f. 1993 by merger as Bank Muscat Al-Ahli Al-Omani; renamed Bank Muscat Int. in 1998, and as above in 1999; merged with Commercial Bank of Oman Ltd SAOG in 2000 and with Industrial Bank of Oman in 2002; 88.8% owned by Omani shareholders; cap. 154m., res 562m., dep. 5,587m. (Dec. 2011); Chair. Sheikh KHALID BIN MUSTAHAIL AL-MASHANI; Chief Exec. ABD AL-RAZAK ALI ISSA; 129 brs in Oman, 2 brs abroad.

Bank Sohar SAOG: POB 44, Hay al-Mina, Muttrah 114; tel. 24730000; fax 24793972; e-mail info@banksohar.net; internet www.banksohar.net; f. 2007; 32.5% owned by Oman Govt, 12% by Al Ghadir Al Arabia LLC, 55.5% by various Omani shareholders; cap. 100m., res 4m., dep. 1,171m. (Dec. 2011); Chair. Sheikh Dr SALIM SAID AL-FANNAH AL-ARAIMI; CEO Dr MUHAMMAD ABD AL-AZIZ KALMOOR; 11 brs.

HSBC Bank Oman SAOG: POB 240, Ruwi 112; tel. 80074722; internet www.hsbc.co.om; merged with Oman International Bank SAOG in June 2012; Chair. SIMON COOPER.

National Bank of Oman SAOG (NBO): POB 751, Ruwi 112; tel. 24778000; fax 24778585; e-mail ask@nbo.co.om; internet www.nbo.co.om; f. 1973; 100% Omani-owned; cap. 108m., res 117m., dep. 1,611m. (Dec. 2011); Chair. OMAR HUSSAIN AL-FARDAN; CEO SALAAM BIN SAEED AL-SHAKSY; 64 brs in Oman, 6 brs abroad.

Oman Arab Bank SAOC: POB 2010, Ruwi 112; tel. 24706265; fax 24797736; e-mail mktoab@omantel.net.om; internet www.oman-arabbank.com; f. 1984; purchased Omani European Bank SAOG in 1994; 51% Omani-owned, 49% by Arab Bank PLC (Jordan); cap. 85m., res 54m., dep. 772m. (Dec. 2010); Chair. RASHAD MUHAMMAD AL-ZUBAIR; CEO ABD AL-QADER ASKALAN; 46 brs.

Development Banks

Oman Development Bank SAOC: POB 3077, Ruwi 112; tel. 24812507; fax 24813100; e-mail customer.care@odboman.net; internet www.odb.com.om; f. 1977; absorbed Oman Bank for Agriculture and Fisheries in 1997; provides finance for devt projects in industry, agriculture and fishing; state-owned; cap. 70m., res 8m., dep. 2m. (Dec. 2010); Chair. Sheikh YAQOOB BIN HAMAD AL-HARTHY; Gen. Man. SAMIR BIN BECHIR AL-SAID; 9 brs.

Oman Housing Bank SAOC: POB 2555, Ruwi 112; tel. 24704444; fax 24704071; e-mail ohb@ohb.co.om; internet www.ohb.co.om; f. 1977; long-term finance for housing devt; 100% state-owned; cap. 30m., res 55m., dep. 14m. (Dec. 2010); Gen. Man. ADNAN HAIDAR DARWISH AL-ZA'ABI; 9 brs.

STOCK EXCHANGE

Muscat Securities Market (MSM): POB 3265, Muscat 112; tel. 24823600; fax 24823706; e-mail info@msm.gov.om; internet www.msm.gov.om; 221 cos listed (Jan. 2009); f. 1989; Chair. HASSAN BIN ALI JAWAD AL-LAWATI; Dir-Gen. AHMAD SALEH AL-MARHOON.

Supervisory Body

Capital Market Authority (CMA): POB 3359, Ruwi 112; tel. 24823224; fax 24817471; e-mail info@cma.gov.om; internet www.cma.gov.om; f. 1998 to regulate capital market and insurance sector; Chair. Eng. ALI BIN MASSOUD BIN ALI AL-SUNAIDI (Minister of Commerce and Industry); Exec. Pres. YAHYA BIN SAID ABDULLAH AL-JABRI.

INSURANCE

In 2008 there were 23 licensed insurance companies operating in Oman. Of these, 11 were local firms and the remainder were branches of non-resident companies.

Al-Ahlia Insurance Co SAOG: POB 1463, Ruwi 112; tel. 24766800; fax 24797151; e-mail aaic@alahliaoman.com; internet www.alahliaoman.com; f. 1985; part of Royal and Sun Alliance Group (United Kingdom); cap. 6.0m., total assets 63.1m. (June 2008); Man. Dir LLOYD EAST; 23 brs.

Dhofar Insurance Co SAOG: POB 1002, Ruwi 112; tel. 24705305; fax 24793641; e-mail dhofar@dhofarinsurance.com; internet www.dhofarinsurance.com; f. 1989; cap. 20.0m. (Dec. 2007); Chair. Sheikh SALIM BIN MUBARAK AL-SHANFARI; Man. Dir and CEO TAHER T. AL-HERAKI.

Falcon Insurance Co SAOC: POB 2279, Ruwi 112; tel. 24660900; fax 24566476; e-mail info@falconinsurancesaoc.com; internet www.falconinsurancesaoc.com; f. 1977 as Al-Ittihad al-Watani; assoc. co of Al Anwar Holdings SAOG; cap. 5.4m.; Gen. Man. MICHAEL JAN WRIGHT.

Al Madina Insurance Co SAOC: POB 1805, Athaiba 130; tel. 24771888; fax 24771899; e-mail contact@amicoman.com; internet www.amicoman.com; f. 2006; cap. 10m. (Dec. 2006); CEO GAUTAM DATTA.

Muscat Insurance Co SAOC: POB 72, Ruwi 112; tel. 24478897; fax 24481847; e-mail info@muscatlife.com; internet www.omzest.com/mic.htm; f. 1995 as Muscat Insurance Co SAOG; restructured in 1999 as Muscat Nat. Holding Co SAOG (parent co), Muscat Insurance Co SAOC and Muscat Life Assurance Co SAOC; subsidiary of Omar Zawawi Establishment (OMZEST); Gen. Man. ANDREW M. WOODWARD.

National Life and General Insurance Co SAOC: POB 798, Wadi Kabir 117; tel. 24730999; fax 24795222; e-mail natlife@nlicgulf.com; internet www.nlicgulf.com; f. 1983; subsidiary of Oman Nat. Investment Corpn Holding SAOG; Gen. Man. S. VENKATACHALAM.

Oman Qatar Insurance Co SAOC: POB 3660, Ruwi 112; tel. 24700798; fax 24700815; e-mail contact@oqic.com; internet www.qatarinsurance.com/net_oman.htm; subsidiary of Qatar Insurance Co; CEO GEOFFREY BLOFELD.

Oman United Insurance Co SAOG: POB 1522, Ruwi 112; tel. 24477300; fax 24477334; e-mail info@omanutd.com; internet www.omanutd.com; f. 1985; cap. 10.0m., total assets 65.4m. (Dec. 2007); Chair. and CEO SAID SALIM BIN NASSIR AL-BUSAIDI.

Trade and Industry

GOVERNMENT AGENCY

The Public Authority for Investment Promotion and Export Development (PAIPED): POB 25, al-Wadi Kabir 117, Muscat; tel. 24623300; fax 24623331; e-mail info@paiped.com; internet www.paiped.com; f. 1996; promotes investment to Oman and the devt of non-oil Omani exports; Chair. Dr SALEM NASSER AL-ISMAILI.

CHAMBER OF COMMERCE

Oman Chamber of Commerce and Industry: POB 1400, Ruwi 112; tel. 24707674; fax 24708497; e-mail occi@chamberoman.com; internet www.chamberoman.com; f. 1973; Chair. KHALIL BIN ABDULLAH BIN MUHAMMAD AL-KHONJI; 142,881 mems (Sept. 2008).

STATE HYDROCARBONS COMPANIES

National Gas Co SAOG: POB 95, Rusayl 124; tel. 24446073; fax 24446307; e-mail info@nationalgasco.net; internet www.nationalgasco.net; f. 1979; bottling of LPG; Chair. Sheikh KHALID AHMAD SULTAN AL-HOSNI; CEO GOUTAM SEN; 158 employees.

Oman Gas Co SAOC (OGC): POB 799, al-Khuwair 133; tel. 24681600; fax 24681678; e-mail info@oman-gas.com.om; internet www.oman-gas.com.om; f. 2000; govt-owned (80% Ministry of Oil and Gas; 20% Oman Oil Co SAOC); operates gas network and builds pipelines to supply power plants and other industries in Oman; Chair. Dr MUHAMMAD BIN HAMAD BIN SAIF AL-RUMHI (Minister of Oil and Gas); CEO YOUSUF BIN MUHAMMAD AL-OJAILI.

Oman LNG LLC: POB 560, Mina al-Fahal 116; tel. 24609999; fax 24609900; e-mail info@omanlng.co.om; internet www.omanlng.com; f. 1994; 51% state-owned; Royal Dutch Shell 30%; manages 6.6m.-metric-tons-per-year LNG plant at Qalhat; manufacturing, shipping and marketing; Chair. NASSER BIN KHAMIS AL-JASHMI; CEO and Gen. Man. Dr BRIAN BUCKLEY; 225 employees.

Oman Oil Co SAOC (OOC): POB 261, Ruwi 118; tel. 24573100; fax 24573101; e-mail info@oman-oil.com; internet www.oman-oil.com; f. late 1980s to invest in foreign commercial enterprises and oil-trading operations; incorporated 1996; 100% state-owned; Chair. NASSIR BIN KHAMIS AL-JASHMI; CEO AHMAD AL-WAHAIBI.

Oman Refineries and Petroleum Industries Co SAOC (ORPIC): POB 3568, Ruwi 112; tel. 24561200; fax 24561384; internet orpic.om; f. 2010 after merger of Oman Refineries and Petrochemicals Co, Aromatics Oman and Oman Polypropylene; production of light petroleum products; 75% owned by Oman Govt, 25% by Oman Oil Co SAOC; Chair. Dr MUHAMMAD BIN HAMAD BIN SAIF AL-RUMHI (Minister of Oil and Gas); CEO Dr MUSAB AL-MAHRUQI; 1,600 employees.

Petroleum Development Oman LLC (PDO): POB 81, Muscat 113; tel. 24678111; fax 24677106; e-mail external-affairs@pdo.co.om; internet www.pdo.co.om; incorporated in Sultanate of Oman by royal decree as an LLC since 1980; 60% owned by Oman Govt, 34% by Royal Dutch Shell; exploration and production of crude petroleum and gas; crude petroleum production (2007) averaged 561,000 b/d from over 100 fields, linked by a pipeline system to terminal at Mina al-Fahal, near Muscat; gas production (2007) totalled 63.3m. cu m/d; Chair. Dr MUHAMMAD BIN HAMAD BIN SAIF AL-RUMHI (Minister of Oil and Gas); Man. Dir JOHN MALCOLM; 5,000 employees.

Qalhat LNG SAOC: POB 514, al-Khuwair 133; tel. 24574004; fax 24574090; e-mail info@qalhatlng.co.om; internet www.qalhatlng.com; f. 2003; production of LNG; 46.84% owned by Oman Govt, 36.80% by Oman LNG LLC, 16.36% by foreign investors; Chair. Sheikh AL-FADHIL BIN MUHAMMAD AL-HARTHY; CEO HARIB AL-KITANI.

UTILITIES

As part of its privatization programme, the Omani Government is divesting the utilities on a project-by-project basis. Private investors have already been found for several municipal wastewater projects, desalination plants and regional electricity providers.

Supervisory Body

Public Authority for Electricity and Water (PAEW): POB 1889, al-Azaiba 130; tel. 24611100; fax 24611133; e-mail dg-project@paew.gov.om; internet www.paew.gov.om; f. 2007 following restructuring of fmr Ministry of Housing, Electricity and Water; Chair. MUHAMMAD BIN ABDULLAH BIN MUHAMMAD AL-MAHROUQI.

Electricity

Authority for Electricity Regulation (AER): POB 954, al-Khuwair 133; tel. 24609700; fax 24609701; e-mail enquiries@aer-oman.org; internet www.aer-oman.org; f. 2004 to regulate and facilitate the privatization of the electricity and related water sector; Chair. Dr SALEH MUHAMMAD AL-ALAWI; Exec. Dir JOHN CUNEEN.

Electricity Holding Co SAOC (EHC): POB 850, Mina al-Fahal 116; tel. 24559200; fax 24559288; e-mail ehcoman@omantel.net.om; internet www.ehcoman.com; f. 2005; state-owned; established to hold Govt's ownership in 9 utility cos and to facilitate the commercial restructuring of the sector; Al-Rusail Power Co was privatized in 2007; of the remaining 8 successor cos, 6 are currently scheduled for privatization; Chair. MUHAMMAD BIN ABDULLAH BIN MUHAMMAD AL-MAHROUQI; CEO KARL MATACZ.

Principal subsidiaries of the EHC include:

Muscat Electricity Distribution Co SAOC (MEDC): POB 3732, al-Ghubrah 112; tel. 24588600; fax 24588666; e-mail medc@medcoman.com; internet www.medcoman.com; f. 2005; responsible for all distribution in the Governorate of Muscat; Chair. Eng. SALEH AL-FARSI; Gen. Man. Eng. ZAHIR AL-ABRI.

Oman Electricity Transmission Co SAOC (OETC): POB 1224, al-Hamriya 131; tel. 24573221; fax 24573222; e-mail info@omangrid.com; internet www.omangrid.com; f. 2003; owns and operates the Main Interconnected System, which covers the north of Oman and accounts for 90% of the Sultanate's electricity transmission; scheduled for privatization; Chair. Eng. SAIF ABDULLAH RASHID AL-SUMRY; Gen. Man. ALI AL-HADABI.

Oman Power and Water Procurement Co SAOC: POB 1388, Ruwi 112; e-mail vacancies@omanpwp.com; internet www.omanpwp.co.om; f. 2003; responsible for forecasting and managing the supply and demand of electricity and water; Chair. SAUD NASSIR AL-SHUKAILY; CEO BOB WHITELAW.

Other subsidiaries of the EHC are: Al-Ghubrah Power and Desalination Co, Majan Electricity Co, Mazoon Electricity Co, Rural Areas Electricity Co and Wadi Jizzi Power Co.

Water

Ministry of Regional Municipalities and Water Resources: (see The Government); assesses, manages, develops and conserves water resources.

Oman Power and Water Procurement Co SAOC: see Electricity.

Oman Wastewater Services Co SAOC (Haya Water): POB 1047, al-Khuwair 133; tel. 24590544; fax 24693418; e-mail customerservice@omanwsc.com; internet www.owsc.com.om; f. 2002; devt and operation of a wastewater system in the Governorate of Muscat; govt-owned; CEO OMAR KHALFAN AL-WAHAIBI.

MAJOR COMPANIES

Construction Materials Industries SAOG: POB 1791, Ruwi 112; tel. 24875044; e-mail cmioman@omantel.net.om; f. 1977; cap. RO 3m., sales RO 1.0m. (2001); manufacture and supply of calcium silicate bricks, paving and hydrated lime and limestone products; Chair. NIMER IBRAHIM AL-SEMNA; Gen. Man. ADIL MANSOUR AL-JUMA; 122 employees.

National Detergent Co SAOG: POB 3104, Ruwi 112; tel. 24493824; fax 24492145; e-mail ndcoman@omantel.net.om; internet www.ndcoman.com; f. 1980; cap. RO 1.7m., sales RO 12.4m. (2007); manufacture and marketing of detergents; Chair. ABD AL-HUSSAIN BIN BHACKER AL-LAWATI; Dir and Gen. Man. V. SUNDARESAN; 237 employees.

Oman Cement Co SAOG: POB 650, Ruwi 112; tel. 24437070; fax 24437777; e-mail admin@omancement.com; internet www.omancement.com; f. 1978; partially privatized in 1994; cap. RO 33.1m., sales RO 49.9m. (2007); development and production of cement; Chair. SAYYED QAHTAN YARUB AL-BUSAIDI; 362 employees.

Oman Chromite Co SAOG: POB 346, Tareef Sohar 321; tel. 26845115; fax 26845155; e-mail chromite@omantel.net.om; internet www.omanchromite.com; f. 1991; cap. and res US $7.78m., sales US $4.17m. (2006); production of chromite; Chair. AHMAD BIN MUHAMMAD AL-MUHAMMAD; Gen. Man. IBRAHIM MUBARAK AL-BULUSHI.

Oman Fisheries Co SAOG: POB 2900, Ruwi 112; tel. 24509500; fax 24597804; e-mail samak@omanfisheries.com; internet www.omanfisheries.com; f. 1980 as Oman Nat. Fisheries Co; renamed as above 1989; Oman Govt holds 24% share of capital; cap. RO 12.5m., sales RO 8.1m. (2007); responsible for commercial devt of fishing, processing and marketing of marine products; operates nine deep-sea trawlers, a processing and freezing plant, and an on-board fishmeal plant; Chair. SALIM BIN HAMAD BIN ALI AL-MASROUI; Gen. Man. MUHAMMAD ALAWI; 150 employees.

Oman Flour Mills Co SOAG: POB 566, Ruwi 112; tel. 24711155; fax 24714711; e-mail flour@omantel.net.om; internet www.omanflourmills.com; f. 1977; cap. RO 40.9m., sales RO 48.0m. (2008); 51% state-owned; produces 800 metric tons per day (t/d) of various flours and 1,100 t/d of animal feedstuffs; Chair. MANAL MUHAMMAD AL-ABDUWANI; CEO ALI AL-HABAJ; 208 employees.

Oman Mining Co LLC: POB 758, Muscat 113; tel. 24669420; fax 24669411; e-mail ominco@omantel.net.om; f. 1978; state-owned; cap. RO 25m.; devt of copper, gold and chromite mines; Chair. AHMAD BIN HASSAN AL-DHEEB; Gen. Man. ALI S. A. AL-WAILY; 383 employees.

Oman Refreshment Co Ltd SAOG: POB 30, Central Post Office, Seeb 111; tel. 24589100; fax 24589099; e-mail info@pepsioman.com; internet www.pepsioman.com; f. 1974; cap. RO 3.0m., sales RO 42.8m. (2009); bottling and distribution of soft drinks; Chair. BUTI OBAID AL-MULLA; Man. Dir Sheikh HAMOUD AHMED AL-HINAI; 700 employees.

Poly Products LLC: POB 2561, Ruwi 112; tel. 24446044; fax 24446046; e-mail info@rahaoman.com; internet www.rahaoman.com; f. 1979; sales US $40m. (2008); manufacture of flexible and rigid polyurethane foam and spring mattresses, divans and upholstered beds, sofas, sofa seats and polyester fibre; Man. Dir SAID AL-HINAI; Gen. Man. SAID ANWAR AHSAN; 500 employees.

Raysut Cement Co SAOG: POB 1020, Salalah 211; tel. 24219137; fax 24219291; e-mail raysut@raysutcement.com.om; internet www.raysutcement.com.om; f. 1982; cap. US $1,300m. (March 2008), sales $163.8m. (2007); production of cement; Chair. MUHAMMAD BIN ALAWI ALI MUQAIBEL; CEO MUHAMMAD AHMAD AL-DHEEB; 300 employees.

Shell Oman Marketing Co SAOG: POB 38, Mina al-Fahal 116; tel. 24570200; fax 24570164; e-mail somcsc@omantel.net.om; internet www.shell.com; f. 1997 by merger of Shell Marketing (Oman) Ltd and Oman Lubricants Co LLC; cap. and res RO 13.6m., sales RO 247.8m. (Dec. 2007); supply and marketing of petroleum products; Chair. Dr ANDREW WOOD; Man. Dir FAISAL KHAMIS AL-HASHAR; 210 employees.

Sohar Aluminium: POB 80, Sohar Industrial Estate, Sohar 327; tel. 26863000; fax 26883001; e-mail info@sohar-aluminium.com; internet www.sohar-aluminium.com; f. 2004 to undertake US $2,400m. Greenfield Aluminium Smelter project in Sohar; inaugurated April 2009; capacity of 370,000 metric tons of primary aluminium per year; Chair. AHMAD BIN SALIM AL-WAHAIBI; CEO HENK PAUW.

Yahya Construction LLC: POB 2282, Ruwi 112; tel. 24591366; fax 24591981; e-mail yacostgm@omantel.net.om; internet www.yahyacon.com; f. 1977 as Yahya Costain LLC; civil and building engineering, furniture manufacture and joinery; Chair. YAHYA MUHAMMAD NASIB; Gen. Man. TAJAMAL IQBAL JAMI; 576 employees.

Transport

RAILWAYS

There are no railways in Oman, although plans for a regional rail network, connecting Oman with member countries of the Cooperation Council for the Arab States of the Gulf (or Gulf Cooperation Council—GCC), were finalized in late 2009. A feasibility study into the proposed first phase of the Omani section of the GCC network, a 230-km line linking Sohar and Muscat, was carried out by a French contractor in 2009. Tenders for contracts to design and manage the Omani rail project were issued in April 2010. Construction work was scheduled to begin in late 2014, with completion expected by 2018.

ROADS

A network of adequate graded roads links all the main centres of population, and only a few mountain villages are inaccessible by off-road vehicles. In 2010 there were an estimated 59,363 km of roads, of which 1,791 km were dual carriageways and a further 28,903 km were asphalted roads. The eighth Development Plan (2011–15) provided for several large-scale road-building projects, including the third phase of a new 240-km Batinah coastal road linking Barka and Sohar with Khatmat Malaha on the border with the United Arab Emirates. A new 81-km dual carriageway linking Sohar with Buraimi, in north-eastern Oman, was inaugurated in January 2010.

Directorate-General of Roads: Ministry of Transport and Communications, POB 338, Ruwi 112; tel. 24697870; fax 24696817; e-mail dgroads@omantel.net.om; internet www.motc.gov.om/en/edgr/edgr.html; Dir-Gen. of Roads Sheikh MUHAMMAD BIN HILAL AL-KHALILI.

Oman National Transport Co SAOG (ONTC): POB 620, Muscat 113; tel. 24490046; fax 24490152; e-mail info@ontcoman.com; internet www.ontcoman.com; f. 1972; re-established in 1984; operates local, regional and long-distance bus services from Muscat; Chair. MAJID SAID SALIM AL-RUWAHI; Gen. Man. MAJID AL-MANDHRY.

SHIPPING

Port Sultan Qaboos (Mina Sultan Qaboos), at the entrance to the Persian (Arabian) Gulf, was built in 1974 to provide nine deep-water berths varying in length from 250 ft to 750 ft (76 m to 228 m), with draughts of up to 43 ft (13 m), and three berths for shallow-draught vessels drawing 12 ft to 16 ft (3.7 m to 4.9 m) of water. A total of 12 new berths have been opened, and two of the existing berths have been upgraded to a container terminal capable of handling 60 containers per hour. The port also has a 3,000-metric-ton-capacity cold store, which belongs to the Oman Fisheries Co. In the 1990s Port Sultan Qaboos underwent a further upgrade and expansion. A new terminal for passenger cruise ships was inaugurated in February 2010.

The oil terminal at Mina al-Fahal can also accommodate the largest super-tankers on offshore loading buoys. Similar facilities for the import of refined petroleum products exist at Mina al-Fahal. Salalah Port, formerly known as Mina Raysut, is Oman's largest transshipment terminal and serves as a major transshipment centre for the region. Salalah has been developed into an all-weather port, and, in addition to container facilities, has six deep-water berths with an annual capacity of 4.5m. 20-ft equivalent units; plans for the construction of three additional deep-water berths were announced in 2008. A major redevelopment of the port at Duqm, on the Gulf of Masirah, was announced in 2007. In 2008 the authorities announced that the project would be significantly expanded to provide: deep-water berths of 18 m; a deepened approach channel; breakwaters expanded to 7.7 km; a new dry dock for ships of up to 400,000 tons; and a new ship repair yard. The project was allocated an initial RO 700m. in government investment and was completed in March 2013.

At 31 December 2012 Oman's flag registered fleet totalled 47 vessels, with an aggregate displacement of 52,164 grt.

Port Authorities and Regulatory Body

Directorate-General of Ports and Maritime Affairs: POB 684, Ruwi 113; tel. 24685994; fax 24685992; e-mail dgpma@omantel.net.om; Dir-Gen. Eng. QASSIM AHMAD ABD AL-MOHSEN AL-SHIZAWI.

Port Services Corpn SAOG (PSC): POB 133, Muscat 113; tel. 24714000; fax 24714007; e-mail mktg@pscoman.com; internet www.pscoman.com; f. 1976; jointly owned by the Govt of Oman and private shareholders; responsible for management and operation of Port Sultan Qaboos; cap. RO 7.9m. (2007); CEO SAUD BIN AHMAD AL-NAHARI.

Salalah Port Services Co SAOG (SPS): POB 105, Muscat 118; tel. 24601003; fax 24600736; e-mail info@salalahport.com; internet www.portofsalalah.com; f. 1997; holds a 30-year concession to manage and develop Salalah Port; CEO PETER FORD.

Principal Shipping Companies

National Ferries Co SAOC: Jibroo, Blk 1, nr DHL, Muscat; tel. 24715252; fax 24711333; e-mail reservation@nfcoman.com; internet www.nfcoman.com; f. 2006; govt-owned; operates a high-speed, passenger and vehicle ferry service between Muscat and Khasab, on the Strait of Hormuz; Chair. MEHDI MUHAMMAD AL-ABDUWANI.

Oman Shipping Co SAOC (OSC): al-Harthy Complex, POB 104, Madinat Sultan Qaboos St, Muscat 118; tel. 24400900; fax 24400922; e-mail info@omanship.co.om; internet www.omanship.co.om; f. 2003; govt-owned (Ministry of Finance 80%, Oman Oil Co SAOC 20%); owns and operates a fleet of over 30 vessels; transportation of LNG, crude petroleum and petrochemical products; subsidiaries include: Oman Charter Co, Duqm Maritime Transportation Co, Liwa Maritime Transportation Co, Energy Spring LNG Carrier SA, Oasis LNG Carrier SA; Dep. Chair. AHMAD BIN MUHAMMAD BIN SALIM AL-FUTAISI (Minister of Transport and Communications); CEO NICHOLAS FISHER.

CIVIL AVIATION

Domestic and international flights operate from Muscat International Airport (known as Seeb International Airport prior to February 2008). In 2010 5.8m. passengers passed through the airport; a project designed to increase annual passenger capacity to 12m. was expected to be completed by 2014. Oman's second international airport, at Salalah, was completed in 1978; in 2010 455,000 passengers passed through the airport. Both Seeb and Salalah were effectively privatized in October 2001. Responsibility for the management and refurbishment of the airports passed to Oman Airports Management Co (OAMC), 75% of which was owned by foreign investors and 25% by the Omani Government; however, following the failure of the Government successfully to agree financial terms for the privatization and ongoing development of the airports with OAMC, the 25-year contract was cancelled in October 2004 and Seeb and Salalah airports were returned to state control. OAMC continues to manage and operate Oman's airports, but it is now a wholly government-owned entity. Plans for substantial development and expansion of both international airports to provide additional terminals and increase passenger-handling capacity were announced as part of the Government's seventh Development Plan in 2006. There are also airports at Sur, Masirah, Khasab and Diba, with six further airports planned for Sohar, Duqm, Ras Al Hadd, Adam, Haima and Shaleem. Three new private airfields, owned and operated by Petroleum Development Oman, were opened in 2008 at Marmul, Qarn Alam and Fahud.

Directorate-General of Civil Aviation Affairs: POB 1, CPO Muscat International Airport, Muscat 111; tel. 24519356; fax 24519880; e-mail hakeem@dgcam.gov.om; internet www.met.gov.om; Dir of Airports ABD AL-HAKEEM AMUR AL-KIYUMI.

Oman Air SAOC: POB 58, Muscat International Airport, Muscat 111; tel. 24531111; fax 24765121; e-mail wycallcenter@omanair.aero; internet www.omanair.aero/wy; f. 1993 as a subsidiary of Oman Aviation Services Co (f. 1981); whole corpn renamed Oman Air 2008; state-owned; cap. US $1,300m.; air-charter, maintenance, handling and catering; operators of Oman's domestic and international commercial airline; operates a fleet of 21 aircraft; carried over 2.3m. passengers in 2009; Chair. DARWISH BIN ISMAIL BIN ALI AL-BALUSHI (Minister Responsible for Financial Affairs); CEO WAYNE PEARCE.

Oman Airports Management Co SOAC: POB 1707, Muscat 111; tel. 24518030; fax 24518088; e-mail oamcinfo@omanairports.com; f. 2002; originally 75% owned by private investors; 100% owned by Oman Govt since 2004; operates Muscat International and Salalah airports; Chair. AHMAD BIN MUHAMMAD BIN SALIM AL-FUTAISI (Minister of Transport and Communications); CEO GEORGE BELLEW.

Tourism

Tourism, introduced in 1985, is strictly controlled. Oman's attractions, apart from the capital itself, include Nizwa, ancient capital of the interior, Dhofar, and the forts of Nakhl, Rustaq and al-Hazm. The country also possesses an attractive and clean environment, including around 1,700 km of sandy beaches. The tourism sector has been undergoing a period of intensive investment and development in recent years, overseen by the Oman Tourism Development Co (Omran). The emphasis has been on the development of extensive luxury resorts in areas of outstanding natural beauty. By 2011 there were 11,779 hotel rooms, with plans to increase this to 18,000 by 2015. In 2010 there were 1,048,052 visitor arrivals in Oman, and tourism receipts totalled US $775m. (excluding passenger transport).

Directorate-General of Tourism: Madinat al-Sultan Qaboos, POB 200, Muscat 115; tel. 24588700; fax 24588880; e-mail info@omantourism.gov.om; internet www.omantourism.gov.om; Dir-Gen. MUHAMMAD ALI SAID.

Oman Tourism Development Co (Omran): POB 479, Muttrah 114; tel. 24773700; fax 24793929; e-mail enquiries@omran.om; internet www.omran.om; f. 2005; CEO WAEL BIN AHMAD AL-LAWATI.

Defence

Chief of Staff of the Sultan's Armed Forces: Lt-Gen. AHMED BIN HARITH AL-NABHANI.

Commander of the Royal Army of Oman: Maj.-Gen. MATAR BIN SALIM AL-BALUSHI.

Commander of the Royal Air Force of Oman: Air Vice-Marshal MATAR BIN ALI AL-OBAIDANI.

Commander of the Royal Navy of Oman: Rear Adm. ABDULLAH KHAMIS AL-RAISI.

Commander of the Royal Guard of Oman: Maj.-Gen. KHALIFA BIN ABDULLAH AL-JUNAIBI.

Defence Budget (2012): RO 2,590m.

Total armed forces (as assessed at November 2012): 42,600: army 25,000; navy 4,200; air force 5,000; plus 2,000 expatriate personnel. There is a 6,400-strong Royal Guard.

Paramilitary forces: 4,400: tribal Home Guard (*Firqat*) 4,000; police coastguard 400.

Education

Great advances have been made in education since 1970, when Sultan Qaboos came to power. Although education is still not compulsory, it is provided free to Omani citizens from primary to tertiary level, and attendance has increased greatly. Primary education begins at six years of age and lasts for six years. The next level of education, divided into two equal stages (preparatory and secondary), lasts for a further six years. In 1998/99 a new system, comprising 10 years of basic education and two years of secondary education, was introduced in 17 schools; it was to be implemented gradually throughout the country. In 2011/12 there were 1,040 schools in the state sector, as well as 406 private kindergartens and schools regulated by the Ministry of Education. In total, 517,606 students were in state education and 71,274 in private education in 2011/12. As a proportion of the school-age population, the total enrolment at primary, preparatory and secondary schools increased from 25% (boys 36%; girls 14%) in 1975 to 76% (boys 78%; girls 74%) in 1997/98. Primary enrolment in 2008/09 included 94% of children in the relevant age-group, while secondary enrolment included 90% of children in the relevant age-group. In 2010 there were six teacher-training colleges, five vocational institutes, seven technical colleges and 16 institutes of health, together with the College of Shari'a and Law, the Academy of Tourism and Catering, and the College of Banking and Financial Studies. There are 26 private universities and technical colleges. Oman's first national university, named after Sultan Qaboos, was opened in late 1986, and had 16,494 students in 2010/11. In the 2012 budget, a total of RO 1,300m. was allocated to education, equivalent to 13% of total government expenditure.

Bibliography

Agius, Dionisius A. *Seafaring in the Arabian Gulf and Oman: People of the Dhow*. Abingdon, Routledge, 2009.

Akehurst, John. *We Won a War: The Campaign in Oman 1965–75*. London, Michael Russell, 1982.

Allen, Calvin H. *Oman: the Modernization of the Sultanate*. London, Croom Helm, 1987.

Allen, Calvin H., and Rigsbee, W. Lynn. *Oman Under Qaboos: From Coup to Constitution, 1970–1996*. London, Frank Cass, 2000.

Arkless, David C. *The Secret War: Dhofar 1971/72*. London, W. Kimber, 1988.

Badger, G. P. *The History of the Imams and Sayyids of Oman, by Salilbin-Razik, from AD 661 to 1856*. London, Hakluyt Society, 1871, reprint 1967.

Bailey, Ronald (Ed.). *Records of Oman 1867–1960*. Slough, Archive Editions, 1988 (12 vols).

Barrault, M. *Sultanate of Oman*. Paris, M. Hetier, 1994.

Beasant, John. *Oman: The True-life Drama and Intrigue of an Arab State*. Edinburgh, Mainstream, 2002.

Beasant, John, and Ling, Christopher. *Sultan in Arabia: A Private Life*. Edinburgh, Mainstream, 2004.

Bhacker, M. *Trade and Empire in Muscat and Zanzibar*. London, Routledge, 1992.

Clark, Sir Terence. *Underground to Overseas: The Story of Petroleum Development Oman*. London, Stacey International, 2008.

Clements, F. A. *Oman: A Bibliography*. Oxford, Clio Press, 2nd edn, 1994.

Eickelman, Christine. *Women and Community in Oman*. New York, New York University Press, 1984.

Ghubash, Hussein. *Oman: A Millennial Islamic Democracy*. London, Saqi Books, 2004.

Oman—The Islamic Democratic Tradition. Abingdon, Routledge, 2005.

Graz, Liesl. *The Omanis: Sentinels of the Gulf*. London, Longman, 1982.

Hawley, Donald. *Oman and its Renaissance*. London, Stacey International, 5th edn, 1995.

Hill, Ann, and Hill, Daryl. *The Sultanate of Oman: A Heritage*. London, Longman, 1977.

Joyce, Miriam. *The Sultanate of Oman*. Westport, CT, Praeger Publrs, 1995.

Kechichian, J. *Oman and the World*. Santa Monica, CA, RAND Corporation, 1997.

Kelly, J. B. *Eastern Arabia Frontiers*. London, Faber and Faber, 1964.

Great Britain and the Persian Gulf, 1793–1880. London, 1968.

Landen, R. G. *Oman Since 1856*. Princeton, NJ, Princeton University Press, 1967.

Manea, Elham. *Regional Politics in the Gulf: Saudi Arabia, Oman and Yemen*. London, Saqi Books, 2005.

Maurizi, Vincenzo. *History of Seyd Said*. Cambridge, Oleander Press, 1984.

Morris, James (now Jan). *Sultan in Oman*. London, Faber, 1957.

Nicolini, Beatrice. (Trans. Watson, Penelope-Jane). *Makran, Oman and Zanzibar: Three-Terminal Cultural Corridor in the Western Indian Ocean, 1799–1856*. Leiden, Brill Academic Publrs, 2004.

Oman Studies Bibliographic Info. Oman Studies Centre, Pforzheim, Germany.

Owtram, Francis. *A Modern History of Oman: Formation of the State Since 1920*. London, I. B. Tauris, 2004.

Peterson, J. E. *Oman in the Twentieth Century*. London, Croom Helm, 1978.

Oman's Insurgencies: The Sultanate's Struggle for Supremacy. London, Saqi Books, 2008.

Phillips, Wendell. *Unknown Oman*. London, Longman, 1966, reprint 1971.

Plekhanov, Sergey. *A Reformer on the Throne*. London, Trident Press, 2004.

Pridham, Brian R. (Ed.). *Oman: Economic, Social and Strategic Developments*. London, Croom Helm, 1987.

Rabi, Uzi. *The Emergence of States in a Tribal Society: Oman Under Sa'id Bin Taymur, 1932–1970*. Eastbourne, Sussex Academic Press, 2006.

al-Rawas, Isam. *Oman in Early Islamic History*. Reading, Ithaca Press, 2000.

Riphenburg, Carol J. *Oman*. Westport, CT, Praeger Publrs, 1998.

Risso, Patricia. *Oman and Muscat: An Early Modern History*. London, Croom Helm, 1986.

Shannon, Michael O. *Oman and Southeastern Arabia: A Bibliographic Survey*. Boston, MA, G. K. Hall, 1978.

Sirhan, Sirhan ibn Said ibn. *Annals of Oman*. Cambridge, Oleander Press, 1985.

Skeet, Ian. *Oman before 1970: The End of an Era*. London, Faber, 1985.

Oman: Politics and Development. London, Macmillan, 1992.

el-Solh, Raghid (Ed.). *Oman and the South-Eastern Shore of Arabia*. Reading, Ithaca Press, 1997.

Thesiger, Wilfred. *Arabian Sands*. London, Longman, 1959.

Townsend, John. *Oman: The Making of the Modern State*. London, Croom Helm, 1977.

Valeri, Marc. *Oman: Politics and Society in the Qaboos State*. London, C. Hurst & Co, 2009.

Vine, Peter. *The Heritage of Oman*. London, Immel, 1995.

Ward, Philip. *Travels in Oman: on the Track of the Early Explorers*. Cambridge, Oleander Press, 1986.

Wikan, U. *Behind the Veil in Arabia: Women in Oman*. London, The Johns Hopkins University Press, 1982.

Wilkinson, John C. *Water and Tribal Settlement in South-East Arabia*. Oxford, Oxford University Press, 1977.

The Imamate Tradition of Oman. Cambridge, Cambridge University Press, 1987.

al-Yousuf, Muhammad bin Musa. *Oil and the Transformation of Oman 1970–1995*. London, Stacey International, 1995.

PALESTINIAN TERRITORIES

Physical and Social Geography

The West Bank lies in western Asia, to the west of the Jordan river and the Dead Sea. To the north and south is the State of Israel, to the west the State of Israel and the Gaza Strip. The Israeli-Palestinian Interim Agreement on the West Bank and the Gaza Strip of September 1995 (Documents on Palestine, see p. 86) provides for the creation of a corridor, or 'safe passage', linking the Gaza Strip with the West Bank. A 'southern' safe passage between Hebron and Gaza was opened in October 1999 (although it has been closed since October 2000). Including East Jerusalem, the West Bank covers an area of 5,655 sq km (2,183 sq miles). The West Bank can be divided into three major sub-regions: the Mount Hebron massif, the peaks of which rise to between 700 m and 1,000 m above sea level; the Jerusalem mountains, which extend to the northernmost point of the Hebron-Bethlehem massif; and the Mount Samaria hills, the central section of which—the Nablus mountains—reaches heights of up to 800 m before descending to the northern Jenin hills, of between 300 m and 400 m. The eastern border of the West Bank is bounded by the valley of the Jordan river, leading to the Dead Sea (part of the Syrian–African rift valley), into which the Jordan drains. The latter is 400 m below sea level. Precipitation ranges between 600 mm and 800 mm on the massif and averages 200 mm in the Jordan valley; 36% of the area is classified as cultivable land, 32% grazing land, 27% desert or rocky ground and 5% natural forest. Apart from the urban centres of Bethlehem (Beit Lahm) and Hebron (al-Khalil) to the south, the majority of the Palestinian population is concentrated in the northern localities around Ramallah (Ram Allah), Nablus (Nabulus), Jenin (Janin) and Tulkarm. In November 1988 the Palestine National Council proclaimed Jerusalem as the capital of a newly declared independent State of Palestine. In fact, West Jerusalem has been the capital of the State of Israel since 1950. In 1967 East Jerusalem was formally annexed by the Israeli authorities, although the annexation has never been recognized by the UN (Occupied Territories, see p. 554). Under the terms of the Declaration of Principles on Palestinian Self-Rule, concluded by Israel and the Palestinians in September 1993 (Documents on Palestine, see p. 76), negotiations on the 'final status' of the city were scheduled to begin no later than the beginning of the third year of the five-year transitional period following the completion of Israel's withdrawal from the Gaza Strip and the Jericho (Ariha) area. However, despite the signing of the Wye Memorandum (Documents on Palestine, see p. 92) in October 1998, 'final status' negotiations did not commence until November 1999, and are currently stalled. The future of Jerusalem is probably the most bitterly contentious of all the issues subject to 'final status' talks, and, in the opinion of some observers, may elude agreement by negotiation. The Palestinian (National) Authority's administrative centre is in Ramallah.

The Gaza Strip, lying beside the Mediterranean Sea and Israel's border with Egypt, covers an area of 365 sq km (141 sq miles). Crossed only by two shallow valleys, the Gaza Strip is otherwise almost entirely flat, and has no surface water. Annual average rainfall is 300 mm. Gaza City is the main population centre and the centre of administration. Israel completed the implementation of its Disengagement Plan (Documents on Palestine, see p. 106), which involved principally the withdrawal of Israeli armed forces and settlers from the Gaza Strip, during August–September 2005 (see Recent History).

The language of the Palestinians in the West Bank and the Gaza Strip is Arabic. The majority of the Palestinian population are Muslims, with a Christian minority representing about 2% of the Palestinian population of the territories. This minority, in turn, represents about 45% of all Palestinian Christians. According to official estimates for mid-2013, the total population of the Palestinian territories was projected at 4,420,549.

Recent History

Revised by NIGEL PARSONS

Until the end of the 1948 Arab–Israeli War, the West Bank formed part of the British Mandate of Palestine, before becoming part of the Hashemite Kingdom of Jordan under the Armistice Agreement of 1949. It remained under Jordanian sovereignty, despite Israeli occupation in 1967, until King Hussein of Jordan formally relinquished legal and administrative control on 31 July 1988. Under Israeli military occupation, the West Bank was administered by a military government, which divided the territory into seven sub-districts. The Civil Administration (as it later became known) did not extend its jurisdiction to the many Jewish settlements that were established under the Israeli occupation; these remained subject to the Israeli legal and administrative system. The Interim Agreement of September 1995 divided the West Bank into three zones: Areas A, B and C. By October 2000 approximately 17.2% of the West Bank (Area A) was under sole Palestinian jurisdiction and security control, but Israel retained authority over movement into and out of the zone; about 23.8% of the West Bank (Area B) was under Israeli military control, with responsibility for civil administration and public order transferred to the Palestinian authorities; the remaining 59% of the territory (Area C) was under Israeli military occupation.

An administrative province under the British Mandate of Palestine, Gaza was transferred to Egypt after the 1949 armistice and remained under Egyptian administration until June 1967, when it was invaded and occupied by Israel. Following Israeli occupation, the Gaza Strip also became an 'administered territory'. Until the provisions of the Declaration of Principles on Palestinian Self-Rule (signed in 1993) began to take effect, the management of day-to-day affairs was the responsibility of the area's Israeli military commander. In 2001 an estimated 42% of the Gaza Strip was under Israeli control, including Jewish settlements, military bases, bypass roads and a 'buffer zone' along the border with Israel. However, under the terms of the Disengagement Plan (Documents on Palestine, see p. 106) formulated by the Government of Ariel Sharon, Israel implemented a unilateral withdrawal from the territory in mid-2005.

TOWARDS AN INDEPENDENT STATE

In accordance with the Declaration of Principles on Palestinian Self-Rule of 13 September 1993 (Documents on Palestine, see p. 76), and the Cairo Agreement on the Gaza Strip and Jericho of 4 May 1994 (Documents on Palestine, see p. 79), the Palestine Liberation Organization (PLO) assumed control of the Jericho area of the West Bank, and of the Gaza Strip on 17 May 1994. In November and December 1995, under the terms of the Israeli-Palestinian Interim Agreement on the

West Bank and the Gaza Strip (the third 'Oslo Accord'—a term referring to the role played by Norwegian diplomacy in their negotiation) signed by Israel and the PLO on 28 September 1995 (Documents on Palestine, see p. 86), Israeli armed forces withdrew from the West Bank towns of Nablus, Ramallah, Jenin, Tulkarm, Qalqilya and Bethlehem. In late December the PLO assumed responsibility in some 17 areas of civil administration in the town of Hebron. Under the terms of the Oslo Accords, the PLO was eventually to assume full responsibility for civil affairs in the 400 surrounding villages, but the Israeli armed forces were to retain freedom of movement to act against potential hostilities there. In Hebron Israel effected a partial withdrawal of its troops in January 1997, but retained responsibility for the security of some 400 Jewish settlers occupying about 15% of the town. Responsibility for security in the rest of Hebron (excluding access roads) passed to the Palestinian police force. Israel was to retain control over a large area of the West Bank (including Jewish settlements, rural areas, military installations, and the majority of junctions between Palestinian roads and those used by Israeli troops and settlers) until July 1997. Following the first phase of the redeployment and the holding, on its completion, of elections to a Palestinian Legislative Council (PLC) and for a Palestinian executive president, Israel was to effect a second redeployment from rural areas, to be completed in that month. The Israeli occupation was to be maintained in Jewish settlements, military installations, East Jerusalem and the Jewish settlements around Jerusalem until the conclusion of 'final status' negotiations between Israel and the Palestinians, scheduled for May 1999.

Subsequent postponements, and further negotiations within the context of the Oslo peace process, resulted in a new timetable for Israeli redeployment, which envisaged two phases, subsequent to the Hebron withdrawal, to be completed by October 1997 and August 1998. 'Final status' discussions on borders, the Jerusalem issue, Jewish settlements and Palestinian refugees were to commence within two months of the signing of the agreement on Hebron. As guarantor of the agreements, the USA undertook to obtain the release of some Palestinian prisoners, and to ensure that Israel continued to engage in negotiations for the establishment of a Palestinian airport in the Gaza Strip and for safe passage for Palestinians between the West Bank and Gaza. The USA also undertook to ensure that the Palestinian (National) Authority (PA—appointed in May 1994) would continue to combat terrorism, complete the revision of the Palestinian National Charter (or PLO Covenant), adopted in 1964 and amended in 1968 (Documents on Palestine, see p. 65), and consider Israeli requests to extradite Palestinians suspected of involvement in attacks perpetrated on Israeli territory. By July 1998, however, conflicting interpretations of the extent of both the phased and total final redeployment of Israeli armed forces (90% of the West Bank, according to the Palestinians; less than 50%, according to the Israelis) had resulted in a seemingly intractable impasse in the Oslo peace process. Those within the wider Palestinian movement who had never accepted the peace process argued that an essential weakness of the Oslo Accords was that they failed to stipulate the precise area of the territory over which the PA should assume control. The implementation of the Oslo Accords was further complicated by the election, in May 1996, of Binyamin Netanyahu as Israeli Prime Minister. Netanyahu formed a new coalition Government, in which his party, Likud, was the dominant force. Likud had never sought to conceal its opposition to the Oslo Accords negotiated by the previous Labour Government.

A significant paralysis of the peace process emerged from the decision of the Israeli Government, announced in February 1997, to begin the construction of a new Jewish settlement on Jabal Abu Ghunaim (Har Homa in Hebrew), near Beit Sahur. Construction in this area was particularly controversial because, if completed, the new settlement would make it impossible to reach East Jerusalem from the West Bank without crossing Israeli territory, thereby prejudicing 'final status' negotiations concerning Jerusalem. In response, the Palestinians withdrew from 'final status' talks that had been scheduled to commence on 17 March. The beginning of construction work at Jabal Abu Ghunaim on the following day provoked rioting among the Palestinian population and a resumption of attacks by the military wing of the Islamic Resistance Movement (Hamas) on Israeli civilian targets. The Israeli Cabinet responded by ordering a general closure of the Palestinian areas.

Both the Jabal Abu Ghunaim (Har Homa) construction and Israel's unilateral decision to redeploy its armed forces from only 9% of West Bank territory (announced in March 1997) were regarded by many observers as a vitiation of both the Oslo and the subsequent post-Hebron agreements. These were further undermined by the publication, in the Israeli daily newspaper *Ha'aretz*, of the results of a US study that claimed that more than 25% of Jewish settlers' homes in the Gaza Strip and the West Bank were uninhabited (a claim rejected by the Israeli Central Bureau of Statistics, which cited a figure of only 12%). The same newspaper later reported that Netanyahu's original plan, evolved within the framework of the Oslo Accords, eventually to relinquish 90% of the West Bank, had been revised in a new proposal—the so-called 'Allon plus' plan—to a 40% redeployment.

In June 1997 the US House of Representatives voted in favour of recognizing Jerusalem as the undivided capital of Israel and of transferring the US embassy to the city from Tel-Aviv. US President Bill Clinton was reported to have strongly disapproved of the vote, owing to its possible implications for the peace process. The decision coincided with violent clashes between Palestinian civilians and Israeli troops in Gaza and Hebron. On 28 July, following US mediation, the PA and the Israeli Government announced that peace talks were to be resumed in early August. However, on 30 July, on the eve of a scheduled visit by Dennis Ross, the US Special Co-ordinator to the Middle East, to reactivate the discussions, Hamas carried out a suicide bomb attack at a Jewish market in Jerusalem, in which 14 civilians were killed. Ross cancelled his visit, while the Israeli Government immediately halted the payment of tax revenues to the PA and closed the Gaza Strip and the West Bank. In the aftermath of the suicide bombing, the PA commenced a campaign to detain members of Hamas and another militant group, Islamic Jihad. In late August, however, President Yasser Arafat convened a Palestinian national dialogue conference in Gaza, in response to the Israelis' imposition of sanctions. On this occasion, representatives of Hamas, who had boycotted a similar conference held in the previous year, agreed to participate, on the condition that the Palestinian authorities would address the issue of the Hamas members whom they were holding in detention. During the conference Arafat publicly embraced Hamas leaders and urged them, and representatives of Islamic Jihad, to unite with the Palestinian people against Israeli policies. On 26 August Hamas rejected a request from Palestinian leaders to suspend their attacks on Israeli targets.

At the beginning of September 1997, in anticipation of a visit to the Middle East by the US Secretary of State, Madeleine Albright, the Israeli authorities relaxed the closure they had imposed on the West Bank and Gaza on 30 July. On 4 September, however, a further suicide bomb attack in Jerusalem, in which eight people died, led to the reimposition of Israeli sanctions. Hamas claimed responsibility for the attack, and the Israeli Prime Minister immediately renewed his demand that the PA should take effective action against the 'terrorist infrastructure'. During her visit in mid-September Albright reportedly stated that Israel should halt the construction of Jewish settlements on Arab lands, cease confiscations of land and the demolition of Arab dwellings, and end its policy of confiscating Palestinian identity documents. At the same time she endorsed Netanyahu's demand that the Palestinian leadership should take more effective measures to suppress the military wing of Hamas. Impatience within the US Administration at the Israeli Government's apparent provocation was demonstrated by Albright's criticism of Netanyahu's decision, announced in late September, to permit the construction of 300 new homes for Jewish settlers at Efrat in the West Bank.

On 28 September 1997 it was announced that, as a result of US diplomacy, Israeli and Palestinian officials had agreed to recommence negotiations in October. The first round of talks, scheduled to begin on 6 October, would reportedly focus on the outstanding issues of the Oslo Accords, in particular the opening of an airport and seaport facilities in the Gaza Strip, the establishment of a safe corridor linking Gaza with the West Bank, and the release of Palestinian prisoners from Israeli detention. A second round of talks was to commence on 13 October, at which the participants were to address the issues of security co-operation between the Palestinian and the Israeli authorities; the long-delayed redeployment of Israeli armed forces from the West Bank; Israeli expansion and construction of settlements; and questions pertaining to 'final status' negotiations.

There were reports in late September 1997 that the PA had closed some 16 institutions—mainly providers of social welfare services—with links to Hamas, and arrested 'scores' of its officials since the recent suicide bombing in Jerusalem. Hamas officials who remained at liberty, however, insisted that the organization's campaign against Israeli civilian targets would continue. In particular, the attempted assassination in the Jordanian capital, Amman, of Khalid Meshaal, the head of the Hamas political bureau in Jordan, provoked warnings of retaliation both before and after official confirmation that agents of the Israeli security service, Mossad, had been responsible for the attack. In order to secure the release of its agents by the Jordanian authorities, Israel was obliged, on 1 October, to free (together with other Arab political prisoners) Sheikh Ahmad Yassin, the founder and spiritual leader of Hamas, who had been sentenced to life imprisonment in Israel in 1989 for complicity in attacks on Israeli soldiers. As had been widely predicted, Israel's release of Sheikh Yassin into Jordanian custody was swiftly followed by his return, on 6 October 1997, to Gaza, where he received an enthusiastic welcome from the local population. The return of Sheikh Yassin prompted speculation concerning the possible benefits that the Palestinian leadership might derive from increased political co-operation with Hamas. However, it appeared in late October that Yassin, while prepared to promote Palestinian unity, would not approve the acceptance of even the original terms of the Oslo Accords.

On 7 October 1997 talks resumed between Palestinian and Israeli negotiators on the outstanding issues of the Oslo Accords, and on the following day the Palestinian President and the Israeli Prime Minister held their first meeting for eight months at the Erez checkpoint between Israel and the Gaza Strip. In December, following further US pressure, the Israeli Cabinet reportedly agreed in principle to withdraw troops from an unspecified area of West Bank territory. Some two weeks later, however, it remained uncertain whether Netanyahu would be able to persuade intransigent elements within his Government to endorse this decision. In early January 1998 Dennis Ross visited Israel in a further attempt to break the deadlock regarding the redeployment of Israeli armed forces from the West Bank. However, in the second week of January the Israeli Government declared that it would not conduct such a redeployment until the PA had fulfilled a series of conditions. Among these were requirements that: the Palestinian leadership should make a 'systematic and effective' effort to counter terrorism; it should reduce the strength of its security forces from 40,000 to 24,000; and the Palestinian National Charter should be revised to recognize explicitly Israel's right to exist. Palestinian officials maintained that these conditions had already been met when the agreement regarding the withdrawal of Israeli forces from Hebron was concluded one year earlier. There was further evidence of a hardening of the Israeli position prior to a summit meeting, scheduled to take place in Washington, DC, USA, in the third week of January. The Israeli Cabinet issued a communiqué detailing 'vital and national interests' in the West Bank that it was not prepared to relinquish: in total this amounted to some 60% of all West Bank territory, including that surrounding the Jerusalem region.

On 20 January 1998 President Clinton held discussions with the Israeli Prime Minister in Washington, DC. It was reported that the USA was seeking to persuade Israel to effect a second withdrawal of its armed forces from some 12% of the West Bank over a period of 80 days, in exchange for increased co-operation on security issues by the PA. On 25 January, however, Mahmud Abbas, the Secretary-General of the PLO Executive Committee, reported that direct contacts between the Palestinian delegation and the Israeli premier had collapsed.

In March 1998 it emerged that the USA planned to present new proposals regarding the withdrawal of Israeli armed forces at separate meetings between the US Secretary of State and Arafat and Netanyahu in Europe. On 26 March Ross arrived in Jerusalem in order to present details of the latest US initiative, which, it appeared, would involve an Israeli withdrawal from slightly more than 13% of West Bank territory, and a suspension of settlement construction in return for further efforts by the PA to combat Palestinian organizations engaged in campaigns of violence against Israeli targets. President Arafat sought an Israeli withdrawal from a further 30% of the West Bank, but there were indications that he might be prepared to accept an initial withdrawal from some 13% of the territory. However, it was evident that, even if a bilateral agreement could be reached, the issue of whether a subsequent withdrawal should take place prior to the commencement of 'final status' negotiations remained far more contentious. In any case, the Israeli Cabinet rejected the reported details of the new US initiative. At the end of March US Secretary of State Albright stated that the peace process was on the verge of collapse, and indicated that the USA was considering ending its involvement as a mediator.

Meanwhile, the European Union (EU) was seeking to play a greater role in the stalled Middle East peace process. On 20 April 1998 it was reported that, during a visit to Gaza City, the British Prime Minister, Tony Blair, had obtained the agreement of President Arafat to attend a conference in London, United Kingdom, based on the most recent US peace proposals. A summit meeting, hosted by Blair and attended by Netanyahu, Arafat and the US Secretary of State, took place in early May. At its conclusion Albright invited Netanyahu and Arafat to attend a summit meeting with US President Clinton in Washington, DC, on 12 May. The USA had reportedly proposed that the parties could proceed to 'final status' negotiations as soon as the scope of the next Israeli withdrawal from the West Bank had been agreed. However, the Israeli Government subsequently rejected the US initiative in advance of Clinton's direct participation.

In early June 1998 the details of the latest US initiative were unofficially disclosed in the Israeli press. Israel would have to agree to 'no significant expansion' of Jewish settlements and relinquish slightly more than 13% of West Bank territory over a period of 12 weeks, in exchange for increased Palestinian co-operation. The adoption by the Israeli Cabinet, in late June, of a plan to extend the boundaries of Jerusalem and construct homes there for a further 1m. people prompted incredulity at the US Department of State, and accusations by PA officials that the proposal amounted to a de facto annexation of territories that were officially subject to 'final status' talks.

On 7 July 1998 the UN General Assembly, in defiance of objections from the USA and Israel, approved a resolution, by a vote of 124–4, to upgrade the status of the PLO at the UN. The new provision allowed the PLO to participate in debates, to co-sponsor resolutions and to raise points of order during discussions on Middle Eastern affairs.

On 19–22 July 1998 Israeli and Palestinian delegations held direct negotiations for the first time since March 1997. They discussed the most recent US initiative to reactivate the peace process, but the proposal was deemed unacceptable by the Israelis. In late August Netanyahu was reported to have presented a compromise plan to his Cabinet, whereby Israel would effect a full redeployment from a further 10% of the West Bank and a partial withdrawal from 3% of the Judaean desert. Arafat cautiously welcomed the plan. In September Netanyahu and Arafat met at the White House in Washington, DC, and agreed to participate in a peace conference in the USA in the following month. The summit meeting, also attended by US President Clinton, began at the Wye Plantation, Maryland, on 15 October 1998 (see the chapter on Israel), and culminated in the signing, on 23 October, of the Wye Memorandum (Documents on Palestine, see p. 92), which was intended to facilitate the implementation of the Interim Agreement of September 1995.

Under the terms of the Wye Memorandum, which was to be implemented within three months of its signing, Israel was to transfer a further 13.1% of West Bank territory from exclusive Israeli control (Area C) to joint Israeli-Palestinian control (Area B). An additional 14% of the West Bank was to be transferred from joint Israeli-Palestinian control to exclusive Palestinian control (Area A). The Wye Memorandum also stipulated that: negotiations with regard to a third Israeli redeployment (under the terms of the Oslo Accords) should proceed concurrently with 'final status' talks; the PA should reinforce anti-terrorism measures under the supervision of the US Central Intelligence Agency (CIA); the strength of the Palestinian police force should be reduced by 25%; the Palestinian authorities should arrest 30 suspected terrorists; Israel should carry out the phased release of 750 Palestinian prisoners (including political detainees); the Palestine National Council (PNC) should annul those clauses of the PLO Covenant deemed to be anti-Israeli; Gaza International Airport should become operational, with an Israeli security presence; and an access corridor linking the West Bank to the Gaza Strip should be opened.

The Memorandum was endorsed by the Israeli Cabinet on 11 November 1998, and was approved by the Knesset (parliament) on 17 November. Three days later Israel redeployed its armed forces from about 500 sq km of the West Bank. Of this area, some 400 sq km came under exclusive Palestinian control for both civil and security affairs. In the remaining 100 sq km the PA assumed responsibility for civil affairs, while Israel retained control over security. At the same time Israel released some 250 Palestinian prisoners (although a majority were non-political detainees) and signed a protocol for the opening of Gaza International Airport. Israel retained the right to decide which airlines could use the airport, which was officially inaugurated by President Arafat on 24 November. However, implementation of the Wye Memorandum did not proceed smoothly, with mutual accusations of failure to observe its terms.

In the weeks prior to a visit to Israel and the Gaza Strip by the US President on 12–15 December 1998, violent clashes erupted in the West Bank between Palestinians and Israeli security forces. One cause of the unrest was a decision by the Israeli Cabinet to suspend other releases of Palestinian prisoners under the terms of the Wye Memorandum, and its insistence that Palestinians convicted of killing Israelis, together with members of Hamas and Islamic Jihad, would not be freed. On 14 December, meanwhile, in the presence of President Clinton, the PNC voted to annul articles of the Palestinian National Charter deemed to be anti-Israeli. While the Israeli Prime Minister welcomed the vote, he insisted that several other conditions had to be met before Israel would further implement its commitments under the Wye Memorandum. At a summit meeting between the US President, Netanyahu and Arafat at the Erez checkpoint on 15 December, Netanyahu reiterated Israel's stance regarding the release of Palestinian prisoners. He further demanded that the Palestinians should cease incitement to violence and formally relinquish plans unilaterally to declare Palestinian statehood on 4 May 1999, the original deadline as established by the Oslo Accords. At the conclusion of the meeting Netanyahu announced that Israel would not proceed with the second scheduled redeployment of its armed forces (under the Wye agreement) on 18 December 1998, claiming once again that the Palestinians had failed to honour their commitments. On 20 December the Israeli Cabinet voted to suspend implementation of the Wye Memorandum.

In late January 1999 President Arafat indicated that he might postpone a unilateral declaration of Palestinian statehood if he received certain assurances from Israel and the international community, particularly with regard to the question of settlement expansion. Besides remonstrances from the Israeli Government, he had been under intense pressure from the USA, EU states, Egypt and Jordan to delay any declaration, at least until after the Israeli elections, scheduled for 17 May. During a tour of several European countries the Palestinian leader was counselled by EU governments that a declaration of independence might well result in another victory in the Israeli elections for Netanyahu and those parties that rejected the Oslo peace process outright. As part of a further international mission of diplomacy, on 23 March 1999 Arafat met privately with President Clinton in Washington, DC. During the meeting the US President reportedly promised to press Israel for 'final status' negotiations to be commenced soon after the May elections. At a summit meeting in Berlin, Germany, on 26 March, EU leaders issued their firmest commitment to date to support the creation of an independent Palestinian state. The 'Berlin Declaration' appealed to Israel to conclude 'final status' talks with the Palestinians within one year, insisting that Israel's security would best be assured through the establishment of a viable Palestinian state.

As the deadline for a final decision regarding the 4 May 1999 declaration approached, it became increasingly apparent that Arafat would be forced to capitulate under the weight of both international and domestic opinion. In late April PLO chief negotiators Mahmud Abbas and Saeb Erakat (the Minister of Local Government) visited Washington, DC, in order to secure certain assurances from the USA in return for an extension of the Oslo deadline. On 27 April the Palestinian Central Council (PCC), together with Hamas representatives, met in Gaza for final discussions. On 29 April the Council announced a postponement of any declaration on statehood until after the Israeli elections. The announcement was welcomed by Israel, the USA, and EU and Arab states; however, Palestinians in the Occupied Territories held violent protests against the decision.

Palestinians extended a cautious welcome to Ehud Barak's victory over Netanyahu in the Israeli premiership elections of 17 May 1999. PA officials immediately urged Barak to break the deadlock in the Middle East peace process. However, in his victory address the new Israeli Prime Minister insisted that he would not offer the Palestinians any fundamental concessions. After the elections there was a Palestinian consensus that a halt to Israel's programme of settlement expansion in the Occupied Territories must be a precondition for any meaningful resumption of the peace process. On 3 June Palestinians in the West Bank declared a 'day of rage' against continuing settlement expansion there; the mass demonstrations, which were particularly violent in Hebron, followed an announcement in late May that the population of the West Bank's largest Jewish settlement, Ma'aleh Adumim, was to be expanded from 25,000 to 50,000 settlers.

The first direct meeting between Prime Minister Barak and President Arafat was held at the Erez checkpoint on 11 July 1999. Although both leaders repeated their commitment to restarting the peace process, Arafat was said to have been alarmed by Barak's apparent opposition to full implementation of the Wye Memorandum, his evasiveness on the issue of settlements and his seeming preoccupation with the Syrian track of the peace process. During the second meeting between the Israeli and Palestinian leaders on 27 July at Erez, Barak angered Palestinians by seeking to win Arafat's approval to postpone implementation of the Wye agreement until it could be combined with 'final status' negotiations (thereby implying a 15-month delay in further redeployments of Israeli armed forces). On 1 August Barak promised to bring forward the release of 250 Palestinian prisoners if Arafat agreed to a postponement. On the same day, however, talks between the Israeli and PA delegations broke down after Arafat rejected the Israeli position. Discussions were resumed in mid-August, when Israel agreed to pursue implementation of the Wye Memorandum, and on 4 September Barak and Arafat signed the Sharm el-Sheikh Memorandum or Wye Two accords (Documents on Palestine, see p. 94), in the presence of US Secretary of State Albright and President Muhammad Hosni Mubarak of Egypt. Under the terms of the Memorandum (which outlined a revised timetable for implementation of the outstanding provisions of the Wye agreement), on 9 September Israel released some 200 Palestinian 'security' prisoners; on the following day Israel effected the transfer of a further 7% of the West Bank to PA control.

'FINAL STATUS' NEGOTIATIONS WITH ISRAEL

A ceremonial opening of 'final status' talks between Israel and the PA took place at the Erez checkpoint on 13 September 1999; shortly afterwards details emerged of a secret meeting between the Israeli and Palestinian leaders to discuss an agenda for such talks. However, on 8 October the Palestinians' chief negotiator and Minister of Culture and Information, Yasser Abd al-Rabbuh, warned that the PA would boycott 'final status' talks unless Israel ended its programme of settlement expansion. In mid-October Barak, also under pressure from left-wing groups in Israel, responded by dismantling 12 'settlement outposts' in the West Bank, which he deemed to be illegal. Meanwhile, on 15 October Israel released a further 151 Palestinian prisoners, under the terms of Wye Two. The inauguration of the first 'safe passage' between the West Bank and Gaza Strip took place on 25 October. The opening had been delayed by almost a month owing to a dispute between Israel and the PA over security arrangements for the 44-km route, which linked the Erez checkpoint in Gaza to Hebron in the West Bank. Israel asserted that it would maintain almost complete control over the so-called 'southern' route, including decisions on which Palestinians would be permitted to use it.

'Final status' negotiations between Israel and the PA commenced in Ramallah on 8 November 1999, following a summit meeting held on 2 November in Oslo, Norway, between Arafat, Barak and US President Clinton. On the day before the talks opened, three bombs had exploded in northern Israel; the Israeli authorities claimed that Hamas was responsible. A further redeployment of Israeli troops from 5% of the West Bank, scheduled for 15 November, was postponed owing to disagreement over the areas to be transferred (see the chapter on Israel). Relations between the two sides worsened when on 6 December PA negotiators walked out of 'final status' talks after demanding that Israel should end immediately its policy of settlement expansion. The announcement came amid reports that settlement activity had intensified under Barak's premiership. On the following day the Israeli Prime Minister, apparently in response to US pressure, announced a halt to settlement construction while the negotiations regarding a Framework Agreement on Permanent Status (or FAPS) were proceeding. However, the PA continued to demand the complete cessation of Jewish settlement building. On 21 December Arafat held talks in Ramallah with Barak—the first Israeli premier to hold peace discussions in Palestinian territory.

On 6–7 January 2000 Israeli armed forces withdrew from a further 5% of the West Bank, under the terms of Wye Two; 2% of the land was transferred from partial Palestinian control (Area B) to complete Palestinian control (Area A), while 3% shifted from Israeli control (Area C) to Area B. However, Israel announced on 16 January that a third redeployment from 6.1% of the territory (scheduled to take place on 20 January) would be postponed by three weeks until Barak had returned from peace talks with Syria in the USA. The delay was apparently due to disagreements over Arab villages on the outskirts of Jerusalem. Meanwhile, the explosion of a bomb in northern Israel appeared to be a further attempt by Palestinian militants to disrupt the peace process.

The approval by the Israeli Cabinet of a withdrawal of its troops from only a sparsely populated area of the West Bank led Palestinian negotiators to break off the discussions in early February 2000. On 3 February peace talks held between Arafat and Barak at Erez broke down acrimoniously, after Arafat had reportedly been angered by an Israeli map showing the proposed redeployment from a further 6.1% of the West Bank. The map included none of the Arab villages situated near East Jerusalem (as Arafat had anticipated), but instead showed various pockets of land in the north and south of the territory. On 6 February the PA announced that it was suspending peace talks with Israel. Mediation by US Special Middle East Coordinator Dennis Ross later in that month failed to break the deadlock, and both sides acknowledged that the 13 February deadline to reach a framework agreement would elapse. On 2 March four members of Hamas's military wing were killed in the Israeli Arab town of Tayibbah by Israeli security forces, who claimed that the men were plotting suicide bombings inside Israel. 'Final status' talks resumed between Israel and the PA on 21 March, and on the same day the redeployment of Israeli troops from a further 6.1% of the West Bank was carried out, including villages near Ramallah, Hebron, Jericho and Jenin.

Meanwhile, in early February 2000 the summary of a report on the methods of interrogation used by the Israeli internal security service, Shin Bet, during the first Palestinian *intifada* or uprising (1987–93) was published for the first time. The report acknowledged that Palestinian detainees (and especially those in the Gaza Strip) had been 'systematically tortured' by members of Shin Bet.

On 15 February 2000 an 'historic' agreement was signed between the Vatican and the PLO, with the intention of strengthening relations between the Roman Catholic Church and a future Palestinian state. The Vatican reiterated its view that Jerusalem should be granted a special international status so that the rights of Christians, Jews and Muslims (especially the right of access to their holy sites) were protected. It also implicitly criticized Israel for its 'Judaization' of Arab East Jerusalem, its settlement expansion in and around the city, and its gradual expulsion of the city's Palestinian inhabitants. On 21 March Pope John Paul II commenced a five-day visit to Israel and the Palestinian self-rule areas. The Pope's visit, which the Vatican insisted was purely spiritual in nature, was accorded unprecedented importance by Palestinian and Israeli leaders. The pontiff paid a symbolic visit to Dheisheh refugee camp, south of Bethlehem. Speaking at the camp, which houses some 10,000 Palestinian refugees expelled from their homes in 1948, Pope John Paul II expressed his support for justice for the refugees and indicated that they had a 'natural right to a homeland'.

Following further discussions between Ehud Barak and Bill Clinton in Washington, DC, on 11 April 2000, it was announced that the Israeli premier had agreed to PA demands for a greater US presence in future Israeli-Palestinian negotiations. The third round of 'final status' negotiations opened at the Israeli port of Eilat on 30 April. Palestinian negotiators immediately complained of the recent Israeli plan to construct 174 new housing units at Ma'aleh Adumim. On 7 May Barak and Arafat held a crisis meeting in Ramallah, in the presence of Dennis Ross, to discuss 'sticking and interim phase issues'. The talks were unsuccessful, however, and led to a further suspension of the peace process. Barak had reportedly proposed the transfer to full PA control of three Palestinian villages (Abu Dis, al-Azariyya and al-Sawahra) bordering Jerusalem, on condition that the third West Bank redeployment be postponed. The Palestinians, meanwhile, agreed that the new 13 May deadline for reaching a FAPS would not be met.

On 15 May 2000 Yasser Abd al-Rabbuh resigned his post as Chief Negotiator after discovering that 'secret' informal talks between the PA and Israel had been proceeding in Stockholm, Sweden, without his knowledge. The establishment of an alternative negotiating channel appeared to reflect Israel's dissatisfaction with the progress being made through the official process. The Stockholm talks, which began in early May, were led by Ahmad Quray, Speaker of the PLC, and Shlomo Ben-Ami, the Israeli Minister for Public Security. According to Palestinian sources, the talks had been arranged by Arafat and Barak at their summit meeting in early May.

On 21 May 2000 Barak ordered the suspension of the Stockholm talks, following the worst outbreak of violence to occur in the West Bank and Gaza Strip since the rioting provoked by the Israeli decision to reopen the Hasmonean tunnel in Jerusalem in 1996. On 1 May 2000 as many as 1,000 of the 1,650 Palestinian prisoners held in Israeli gaols began a hunger strike. A few days later mass demonstrations were initiated by Palestinians throughout the self-rule areas in support of the prisoners. By 15 May, a date declared by Palestinians to be a 'day of rage' (marking *al-Nakba* or 'the Catastrophe'—the anniversary of the foundation of the State of Israel in 1948), the protests had escalated into extreme violence. By the time the clashes between stone-throwing Palestinians and the Israeli security forces subsided on 18 May 2000, seven Palestinians were reported to have been killed and about 1,000 injured; some 60 Israelis were also wounded. The Palestinian prisoners ended their hunger strike at the end of May.

For some time there had been signs that the 'hard core' of the PA leadership, including Arafat and his close aides (Mahmud Abbas, Ahmad Quray, Nabil Amr and Muhammad Dahlan), would be willing to reach a deal with Israel that compromised the PA's official position. There was a deep sense of anxiety among Palestinians that their unaccountable leadership—

which had agreed to go to Stockholm secretly without consulting even the PA's own Cabinet—would eventually make far-reaching concessions to Israel, compromising fundamental rights and aspirations in exchange for a nominal Palestinian state without any real substance. This concern was apparently what prompted Yasser Abd al-Rabbuh to resign and, along with the explosion of Palestinian anger in the streets of the West Bank and Gaza in May 2000, reflected growing popular Palestinian hostility to the direction in which 'final status' negotiations were moving. Israeli draft maps of a future Palestinian state were intersected with Jewish settlements and Israeli roads, and there was no sign of a peace plan for Jerusalem or of a solution to the problem of Palestinian refugees. However, this was not the only manifestation of PA internal dissent at the 'final status' talks with Israel. A number of Palestinian officials spoke out with unprecedented openness against Arafat's perceived autocracy, including the way in which he was handling the talks. The PA responded with more arrests (see Internal Affairs) and Arafat stepped up his campaign against critics of his administration, especially regarding the ongoing negotiations with Israel.

In late May 2000 Palestinians throughout the Occupied Territories reacted enthusiastically to Hezbollah's victory in hastening an Israeli withdrawal from southern Lebanon. At the popular level many people drew a comparison between the Lebanese victory and the Palestinians' rather different situation. In contrast, Arafat sought to play down Hezbollah's achievement, apparently to secure favour with the Israeli Government; the Palestinian President maintained in an interview with an Israeli television station that Israel's withdrawal from Lebanon had not been precipitated by Hezbollah resistance but by Barak's desire to implement UN Security Council Resolution 425 (see the chapter on Israel).

THE CAMP DAVID SUMMIT

US Secretary of State Albright began a tour of Israel and the Palestinian areas in early June 2000, in an attempt to reinvigorate the peace talks. The US Administration was seeking to increase its diplomatic efforts in preparation for hosting a summit meeting between Barak and Arafat prior to the expiry of President Clinton's term of office in the autumn. On 21 June it was reported that the PA had agreed to a delay in the latest Israeli withdrawal from the West Bank, scheduled to take place two days later. On 2 July the PCC convened and, after two days of talks, announced that the PLO would unilaterally declare statehood on or before 13 September, with Jerusalem as its capital.

On 11 July 2000 peace talks between Ehud Barak and Yasser Arafat were inaugurated by President Clinton at Camp David, Maryland, USA, in a renewed attempt to reach a FAPS. An official news blackout was imposed, and thus few details emerged about the discussions. However, on 13 July it was reported that Barak and Arafat had held their first talks in private. Nevertheless, despite round-the-clock diplomatic efforts, the talks failed to break the deadlock regarding future arrangements for Jerusalem; the PA refused to accept anything less than full Palestinian sovereignty over the city's Islamic holy sites (notably the Dome of the Rock and the al-Aqsa Mosque), with East Jerusalem as the capital of a Palestinian state. The Camp David summit ended, without agreement, on 25 July. Despite the failure of the summit, both sides, under the guidance of President Clinton, pledged to continue their diplomatic efforts and promised not to pursue 'unilateral actions' (apparently referring to Arafat's threat to declare Palestinian statehood). On his return to the Middle East Arafat was hailed by Palestinians as the 'hero of Jerusalem' for his refusal to grant concessions to Israel over the future of the city.

At the end of July 2000 the Palestinian leadership was angered by statements issued by President Clinton in which the US leader hinted at moving the US embassy from Tel-Aviv to Jerusalem. Amid growing international pressure, it emerged in August that Arafat had agreed, in principle, to a postponement of his declaration of Palestinian statehood. (The PCC announced on 10 September that it would postpone indefinitely such a declaration, although 15 November was reportedly designated as the target date.) Meanwhile, Israeli and PA negotiators continued to meet during August and September in the hope of achieving a breakthrough regarding the third redeployment of Israeli armed forces from the West Bank, as well as further prisoner releases. On 26 September Arafat and Barak held their first direct discussions since the Camp David summit. However, tensions between the two communities remained high, especially in Jerusalem, where several clashes were reported between Palestinians and the Israeli security forces.

RELATIONS WITH OTHER ARAB STATES

After Ehud Barak's electoral victory in May 1999, one of Arafat's principal concerns was the Israeli concentration of efforts on the Lebanese and, especially, Syrian tracks of the Middle East peace process. Any shift of focus away from Israeli-Palestinian talks was likely to leave the Palestinian leadership in an acutely vulnerable and isolated position. In June Arafat was reported to have accused both the Jordanian and Syrian leaders of having turned their backs on the PA. In August a political crisis developed after the Syrian Deputy Prime Minister and Minister of Defence, Maj.-Gen. Mustafa Tlass, allegedly made highly insulting remarks about Arafat—including a claim that Arafat had 'sold Jerusalem and the Arab nation' in peace deals concluded with Israel since 1993—leading to Palestinian demands for Tlass's resignation, and the issuing, by Fatah, of a death warrant against him. Following the resumption of the Israeli-Syrian track of the peace process in December 1999, US and Israeli officials sought to reassure Arafat that negotiations on the Palestinian track would not be sidelined. When President Hafiz al-Assad of Syria died on 10 June 2000, Arafat declared three days of mourning in the Palestinian self-rule areas for the man who had once accused him of making the 'peace of cowards' with Israel. On 13 June Arafat attended President Assad's funeral in Damascus, Syria, despite his poor relations with the Syrian regime.

Palestinians reacted to the death of King Hussein of Jordan on 7 February 1999 with great sorrow. (Of the kingdom's more than 4m. inhabitants, around 65% are believed to be of Palestinian origin.) Three days of mourning were declared in the Palestinian territories, while Arafat travelled to Amman to pay his last respects to the man he once called a 'Zionist agent', but later praised as 'the wise man of the Arabs'. Public grief was particularly apparent in the West Bank, which King Hussein had ruled for 15 years until June 1967. For Arafat, the death of Hussein was a political disaster; the King had frequently supported Arafat in times of crisis, especially when the peace process with Israel appeared to be on the verge of collapse. Hamas leaders also paid tribute to King Hussein, recalling his efforts in September 1997 to free Sheikh Ahmad Yassin from an Israeli gaol after the assassination attempt on Khalid Meshaal. Only days after Hussein's death, Arafat surprised many Jordanians by proposing the establishment of a Palestinian-Jordanian confederation. The proposal (which had been put forward as part of a peace initiative in 1985, but was subsequently rejected by King Hussein) was not welcomed in Jordan, where it was considered to be somewhat premature while the West Bank was still largely occupied by Israel.

INTERNAL AFFAIRS

Elections to a Palestinian Legislative Council (PLC) took place on 20 January 1996. Some 79% of the estimated 1m. eligible Palestinian voters were reported to have participated in the elections, returning 88 deputies to the 89-seat Council. (One seat was automatically reserved for the president of the PLC's executive body—the Palestinian President.) The election of a Palestinian Executive President was held at the same time. Yasser Arafat, who was opposed by one other candidate, Samiha Khalil, received 88.1% of the votes cast and took office as President on 12 February. Deputies returned to the PLC automatically became members of the PNC, the existing 483 members of which were subsequently permitted to return from exile by Israel. The PLC held its first session in Gaza City on 7 March, electing Ahmad Quray as Speaker.

On 22–24 April 1996 the PNC held its 21st session in Gaza City. At the meeting the PNC voted to amend the Palestinian National Charter by annulling all of the clauses that sought the destruction of the State of Israel. The PNC also voted to amend all clauses that were not in harmony with the agreement of mutual recognition concluded by Israel and the PLO in September 1993. On the final day of its meeting the PNC elected a new Executive Committee. In May 1996 it was reported that President Arafat had appointed the members of a Palestinian Cabinet. The appointments were approved by the PLC in July.

In April 1997 President Arafat's audit office reported the misappropriation by PA ministers of some US $326m. of public funds. PA General Prosecutor Khalid al-Qidra promptly resigned in response to the findings and was reportedly placed under house arrest in June. At the end of July a parliamentary committee, appointed by Arafat to conduct an inquiry into the affair, concluded that the Cabinet should be dissolved and some of its members prosecuted. In August the Cabinet submitted its resignation, but this was not accepted by Arafat until December. Arafat's long-awaited new Cabinet was announced on 5 August 1998 and was promptly denounced by all sides. Only one prominent minister of the former administration had been removed, many others assuming alternative responsibilities or becoming ministers of state without portfolios. (The size of the Cabinet was increased significantly by the appointment of a number of PLC members to minister-of-state status.) Despite the immediate resignations of the newly appointed Ministers of Higher Education (Hanan Ashrawi) and Agriculture (Abd al-Jawad Saleh), on 10 August the new administration was approved by the PLC. Although the Cabinet was criticized by officials of the principal international organizations granting funds to the PA, in November donors agreed to grant the PA more than $3,000m., to be disbursed over the next five years.

In addition to persistent allegations of corruption within the PA, President Arafat himself was frequently accused of autocracy. In March 1998 the PLC threatened to organize a vote of no confidence in Arafat's leadership, in protest against alleged corruption, the long delay in approval of the budget and the failure to hold local elections. The PLC renewed its threat in mid-1998 in an ultimatum to the President and the Cabinet, demanding that they respond to allegations of corruption and mismanagement and approve the budget proposals within two weeks. In September the PA chief negotiator at the peace talks and Minister of Local Government, Saeb Erakat, and the PA Minister of State for the Environment, Yousuf Abu Saffieh, were both persuaded by Arafat to withdraw their resignations, tendered in protest against alleged inefficiency and incompetence within the PA.

In March 1998 US officials reportedly confirmed that the CIA was assisting the Palestinian security forces in the spheres of espionage, information-gathering and interrogation. Later in the month the death, in mysterious circumstances, of Muhi al-Din Sharif, the second-highest ranking member of the military wing of Hamas, the Izz al-Din al-Qassam Brigades, prompted accusations by Hamas of PA collusion with Israeli security forces in his murder, and fears that a new wave of retributive bomb attacks would be unleashed against Israeli targets. However, a succession of conflicting accusations and confessions surrounding Sharif's murder (including a number which alleged that it was the result of an internal dispute among the organization's leadership) appeared to defuse the immediate tension. Meanwhile, it was reported that Hamas had become the dominant political force in Palestinian universities, where the organization claimed to command the allegiance of some 40% of students.

In August 1998 the Palestinian Ministry of the Interior dissolved the Palestinian Ahd Party, the Palestinian Labour Party, the Ahrar Party and the Popular Forces party, claiming that, as small individual entities that were unsuccessful in the previous legislative elections, the groups were not financially viable. According to a spokesman at the Ministry of the Interior, it was planned to merge small parties with similar ideologies.

Shortly after the signing of the Wye Memorandum, on 24 October 1998 the PA detained 11 journalists for attempting to obtain an interview with the spiritual leader of Hamas, Sheikh Ahmad Yassin (who was placed under house arrest on 29 October). On the same day the Palestinian authorities arrested outspoken al-Aqsa cleric Sheikh Hamid Bitawi and Islamic Jihad's chief spokesman for publicly criticizing the Wye agreement. In the weeks following the agreement there was a steady erosion of press freedom in the West Bank and Gaza: several radio and television stations, as well as press offices, were closed down by the PA, and journalists and cameramen were imprisoned for crimes ranging from 'endangering the national interest' to reporting 'illegal' demonstrations.

The PA's human rights record remained a major concern for Palestinians. In January 1999 the PLC approved a motion urging an end to political detention and the release of all those imprisoned on exclusively political charges. The PA responded by releasing 37 political prisoners (36 Islamists and one member of the Popular Front for the Liberation of Palestine—PFLP). However, on 24 January scores of detainees linked to Hamas and Islamic Jihad began a hunger strike in Jericho and Nablus, in protest against their continued detention without trial by the Palestinian authorities. During February thousands of Palestinians—mostly Hamas supporters—demonstrated in support of the detainees. On 6 February some 3,000 protesters marched to the PA headquarters, chanting slogans criticizing the PA's alleged 'subservience to Israel and the CIA'.

Also in February 1999 the Gaza-based chief of police, Ghazi al-Jabali, alleged that Hamas had received some US $35m. from Iran to carry out suicide bomb attacks against Israeli targets that would undermine the prospects of Israeli moderates and assist Netanyahu's May 1999 election campaign. Both Iranian and Hamas leaders vehemently denied the allegations. Relations between the PA and Hamas were further strained following the murder of a Palestinian intelligence officer in Rafah on 1 February. On 10 March a security agent and former member of Hamas's military wing was sentenced to death for the attack, while two accomplices received lengthy prison sentences. The verdict provoked serious clashes between Palestinian police and protesters in the Gaza Strip, during which two teenagers were shot dead by police.

Security surrounding Arafat was intensified in June 1999, after a group of Palestinian dissidents calling themselves 'the Free Officers and the Honest People of Palestine' released a statement in which they accused leading Palestinian officials of corruption and of collaboration with Israel, and indirectly threatened to assassinate the President. Nine arrests were made by the security forces following the issuing of the statement.

There was considerable criticism by Palestinian opposition groups of the Sharm el-Sheikh Memorandum signed with Israel on 4 September 1999. Palestinians in East Jerusalem observed a general strike in protest against the agreement, while dozens staged a sit-in at Orient House, the de facto headquarters of the Palestinian administration in East Jerusalem, to denounce concessions on the release of political prisoners. However, the PA continued to encourage meetings among opposition groups to seek agreement on a unified Palestinian position on 'final status' issues. On 1 August a Palestinian national dialogue had been held in Cairo, Egypt, with the participation of officials from Fatah and the PFLP. At the end of August representatives of nine political factions agreed on an agenda for a comprehensive national dialogue. Three meetings were held in the West Bank town of Ramallah to discuss the convening of such a dialogue. The first, hosted by the PLO Executive Committee on 31 August, was attended by the Arab Liberation Front (ALF), the Democratic Front for the Liberation of Palestine (DFLP), Fatah, the Palestinian Democratic Union (FIDA) and the PFLP. Hamas and Islamic Jihad both declined an invitation to attend; in late August the PA had arrested several suspected activists of these two organizations. The second meeting, on 14 September, was held among FIDA, the Palestinian People's Party (PPP) and the Palestinian Popular Struggle Front (PPSF). The third, on 12 October, was attended by all seven of the political organizations, as well as Hamas and the Palestine Liberation Front (PLF). The Damascus-based opposition groups held a similar meeting in late September.

In talks in Cairo on 22–23 August 1999, Yasser Arafat and the DFLP Secretary-General, Nayef Hawatmeh, agreed to set aside their differences and co-ordinate their positions on the 'final status' issues; it was their first meeting since 1993. The head of the PLO Political Department, Faruq Qaddumi, conducted further discussions with DFLP officials in Damascus on 2 November 1999. Meanwhile, it was reported in early September that the leader of the PFLP, George Habash, had decided to resign. (Habash resigned the leadership on 27 April 2000 and was replaced by his deputy, Abu Ali Moustafa, on 8 July.) On 28 September 1999 representatives of Fatah and the PFLP met in Amman. Although the two parties failed to reach an agreement on the PFLP's participation in 'final status' talks, they issued a joint statement appealing to all PLO factions to take part in an upcoming Central Council session to discuss organizational matters. Qaddumi continued discussions with PFLP leaders in Damascus on 2 November. At Arafat's request, on 16 September Israel agreed to allow the PFLP Deputy Secretary-General, Abu Ali Moustafa, to return to PA-controlled areas after more than 30 years in exile, in order to participate in reconciliation talks; he returned to the West Bank on 30 September. However, although the Israeli Government had also reportedly granted an entry permit to Nayef Hawatmeh of the DFLP on 25 October, Hawatmeh's right of return was rescinded on 29 October, after he stated in an interview that armed struggle was legitimate as long as Jewish settlements remained in the Occupied Territories. On 12 October the Israeli Supreme Court ruled that PLF head Muhammad 'Abu' Abbas was immune from trial in Israel for the 1985 *Achille Lauro* hijacking (see the chapter on Israel).

The Palestinian leadership continued to delay the PCC meeting that had been originally scheduled to take place in June 1999, after Barak's election victory in Israel. On 20 September the PA Minister of Planning and International Co-operation, Dr Nabil Shaath, stated that the PCC's constitution committee was still working on a preliminary draft. Once the draft was complete, it was to be submitted to the Palestinian leadership for review and possibly to a referendum. Revisions would then be made and a new draft submitted to legal experts for comment. On 10 October the Chief Justice of the High Court, Radwan al-Agha, abruptly ordered a number of PA judges to be transferred from their positions to posts in the West Bank, leading judges there to go on strike in protest against the decision. (In May lawyers and jurists in the West Bank and Gaza had staged a series of strikes and protests against the alleged 'virtual collapse of the Palestinian judicial system'.)

A series of protests staged during November 1999 prompted the Chairman of the PLC, Azmi Shuaybi, to criticize publicly the PA's lack of fiscal monitoring and accountability. Shuaybi claimed that the Administration was afraid of instituting a monitoring process because it 'would reveal the extent of public funds that are going missing'. He noted that the US $126m. that the Minister of Finance, Muhammad Zohdi al-Nashashibi, claimed to have transferred to various ministries could not be accounted for. Shuaybi added that a number of PA-run companies that received several million dollars in public funding did not report their profits to the PLC's budget committee, claiming to be private companies, yet at the same time did not pay taxes, claiming to be government enterprises. His report was followed on 27 November by a petition signed by 20 leading Palestinian academics, professionals and members of the PLC that not only accused the PA of corruption, mismanagement and abuse of power, but also implicated Arafat personally. Between 28 and 30 November PA security services arrested, interrogated or placed under house arrest 11 of the document's signatories; the other nine (all Fatah officials) were immune from prosecution because of their status as members of the PLC. At an emergency session, convened on 1 December by Arafat in Nablus, PLC members voted to condemn their nine colleagues for seeking to divide the Palestinian people, but did not act on Arafat's reported wish to deprive them of their immunity. Outside the meeting thousands of Arafat supporters marched in solidarity with the PA. Returning from the session, one of the nine PLC members who had signed the anti-corruption manifesto, Mouawiyyah al-Masri, was shot and wounded by unidentified gunmen. Another legislator was reportedly detained by the General Intelligence Service and severely beaten for participating in a sit-in supporting the signatories. Between 19 December and 6 January 2000 Arafat released the 11 detainees on bail. The PA's draconian reaction to the anti-corruption petition prompted international condemnation: statements in solidarity with the anti-corruption campaigners were signed by hundreds of Palestinians worldwide, and demonstrations were organized, including a rally of 5,000 protesters in Ramallah on 4 December. The DFLP, Hamas, Islamic Jihad and the PFLP also held a 'solidarity' meeting in Gaza on 29 November to condemn the PA response.

On 10 January 2000 the PA established a Higher Council for Development, to be chaired by Arafat. The Council's role would be to ensure the transparency of the public finance system: it would handle the general revenue administration, reporting all revenue collected into a single treasury account; oversee management of all commercial and investment operations of the PA; develop a privatization strategy; and oversee the handling of internal and external debt policy and the repayment of loans. The IMF and foreign donors praised the Council as a major step towards ending corruption and mismanagement. In mid-January Arafat ratified the Non-Governmental Organization (NGO) law, delineating the relationship between the PA and the Palestinian NGOs, which broadly welcomed the new legislation.

On 2–3 February 2000 the Central Council finally convened in Gaza with 96 of the 126 members attending. Participants represented the ALF, the DFLP, Fatah, FIDA, the PPP, the PPSF, the Islamic Salvation Party and the National Salvation Party. The PFLP presented its positions prior to the meeting but did not participate. Hamas also boycotted the session, although its spiritual leader, Sheikh Ahmad Yassin, attended as an observer. Invited but not attending were Islamic Jihad, the Popular Front for the Liberation of Palestine—General Command (PFLP—GC) and al-Saiqa. The Council's final communiqué urged Arafat to declare an independent Palestinian state by September at the latest, outlined consensus positions on interim and 'final status' issues, and appealed for the reactivation of dormant PLO committees. The DFLP accepted an invitation by the PLO to join the Palestinian delegation attending the Camp David talks with Israel during July, although many opposition organizations decried the summit.

It was announced on 3 April 2000 that a new PNC was to be established, including the PLO Executive Committee and other leading public figures; the new council's considerations were to include the issue of the Palestinian diaspora, of refugee camps in other Arab countries, and the possible participation of the Palestinians concerned in elections in those countries. In June there were reports that the first draft of the constitution for a Palestinian state was complete and had been submitted to the President for approval.

Fathi Barqawi, the chief news editor at the state-run Voice of Palestine radio station, was arrested in May 2000, after publicly criticizing the talks being conducted with Israel in Stockholm. During May and June a crackdown on the media was reported, including the closure of four television and two radio stations. Dozens of people were arrested, among them members of Fatah and eight leaders of the PFLP. In late June the police reportedly detained Arafat's adviser on refugee camp affairs, Abd al-Fattah Ghanayim, after he was said to have criticized the PA's 'secret' talks with Israel and corruption within the PA. In July a leading representative of Hamas, Abd al-Aziz al-Rantisi, was arrested by security forces in Gaza, on charges of defamation, incitement and sedition; he was accused of having threatened internal security by claiming that the PA negotiators who attended the Camp David summit with Israel were guilty of treason.

THE AL-AQSA UPRISING: THE FATAH TANZIM AND INTRA-PALESTINIAN CO-ORDINATION

In September 2000 the West Bank and Gaza became engulfed in the most serious violence seen in the territories for many years, as Palestinians demonstrated their frustration at the lack of progress in the peace process. On 28 September Ariel Sharon, leader of Israel's right-wing Likud party, visited Temple Mount/Haram al-Sharif in Jerusalem—the site of the al-Aqsa Mosque and the Dome of the Rock—flanked by Israeli security guards. Sharon's visit to the Islamic holy sites provoked violent protests by stone-throwing Palestinians, to which Israeli security forces responded with force. The clashes spread rapidly to other Palestinian towns; by the end of October more than 140 people had died—all but eight of them Palestinians—and thousands were reportedly wounded. The Palestinians received considerable international support and there were widespread protests in Arab capitals. Arafat and Barak visited Paris, France, on 4 October for discussions led by US Secretary of State Albright. However, no agreement was reached on the composition of an international commission of inquiry into the causes of the clashes. Arafat and Albright continued discussions at the Egyptian resort of Sharm el-Sheikh on the following day. The Israeli authorities subsequently closed the borders of the West Bank and Gaza. On 7 October the UN Security Council issued a resolution condemning the 'provocation carried out' at Temple Mount/Haram al-Sharif and the 'excessive use of force' employed by the Israeli security forces. Israeli officials, meanwhile, accused Arafat of failing to halt the violence, as members of his own organization, Fatah, joined Hamas and other militant groups in what swiftly became known as the 'al-Aqsa *intifada*'. In mid-October Israel launched rocket attacks against Arafat's headquarters in the territories, following the murder, on 12 October, of two Israeli army reservists by a Palestinian crowd in Ramallah.

In an attempt to prevent the latest Middle East crisis from developing into a major regional conflict, a US-brokered summit meeting between Barak and Arafat was convened on 16–17 October 2000 at Sharm el-Sheikh. President Clinton announced that Israel and the PA had agreed a 'truce' to halt the spiralling violence. The two sides were also said to have agreed on the establishment of a US-appointed committee to investigate the violence. (The five-member international commission of inquiry was appointed by Clinton in early November, to be chaired by former US senator George Mitchell.) Barak, meanwhile, insisted that Arafat re-arrest about 60 Islamist militants who had been released by the PA in early October. Amid renewed clashes in the Palestinian self-rule areas, the League of Arab States (the Arab League) held an emergency summit meeting in Cairo on 21–22 October and strongly condemned Israeli actions. Barak responded by announcing that Israel was calling a 'time-out' on the peace process.

The al-Aqsa *intifada* marked a new phase in the Palestinian struggle for independence. The leading political and military forces behind the revolt appeared to be grassroots cadres belonging to the backbone of Arafat's Fatah organization, the Tanzim. These consisted mainly of Fatah's 'inside' leadership, which emerged before and during the first *intifada*, and included fighters who had been members of the PA's myriad intelligence services. It was this legacy and role that increasingly bestowed on Fatah the contradictory function of being at once the military basis of the PA's government and also its most steadfast political opposition. The Tanzim were concerned by the PA's increasingly incompetent performance and the seepage of popular support away from Fatah, as well as the very terms of the Oslo process, whereby Palestinian national aspirations had been subject to a negotiating strategy based on US-led diplomacy and security co-operation with Israel. Fatah Tanzim leaders increasingly advocated other options aside from negotiation and diplomacy, including popular and armed resistance against Israeli military 'outposts' and Jewish settlements in order to augment the cost of the occupation to Israel. The new Palestinian uprising led to armed attacks being routinely deployed against Israeli soldiers, settlements and bypass roads in or near Palestinian areas throughout the Occupied Territories, including East Jerusalem. It was this armed dimension that most distinguished the al-Aqsa revolt from the first *intifada*.

A second dimension was the shifting of the Palestinian struggle away from the perceived tutelage of US diplomacy and Israeli hegemony to the forum of the UN and the Arab world. In particular, there was a reassertion of the principle that an end to the current conflict must be conditional upon Israel's full withdrawal from the territories occupied in 1967 (including East Jerusalem), the dismantlement of Jewish settlements and Israel's acknowledgement of the right of return of Palestinian refugees. The Israeli air-strikes of mid-October 2000 (see the chapter on Israel) resulted in an escalation of Palestinian outrage. Certainly, when Palestinian debate on the forthcoming Sharm el-Sheikh summit began, there was a groundswell of Palestinian anger towards Yasser Arafat that had not been seen previously. Hundreds of Palestinians immediately rallied in Gaza on 13 October to denounce the PA; the subsequent announcement of the Sharm el-Sheikh meeting was followed by another Gaza demonstration attended by thousands of Hamas supporters who urged Arafat not to attend the meeting. While the summit was taking place, during 16–17 October, Fatah and Hamas again organized demonstrations condemning Arafat's participation. When the 'cease-fire' arrangements between Israel and the PA were announced on 17 October, various organizations, including Fatah, Hamas, Islamic Jihad, the DFLP and the PFLP, denounced them and vowed to continue the *intifada*.

At the end of October 2000 there was an upsurge in violence against Israeli targets by militant Islamist groups opposed to the Oslo peace process. Israel responded by launching air-strikes against Fatah military targets in the Palestinian enclaves and announced a new policy of targeting leaders of militant Islamist organizations deemed to be involved in 'terrorist' actions. On 1 November Arafat and the Israeli Minister for Regional Co-operation, Shimon Peres, held crisis discussions in Gaza, at which they were reported to have agreed a 'cease-fire' based on the truce brokered at Sharm el-Sheikh in October; however, violence between Israelis and Palestinians intensified during November. Nevertheless, bilateral negotiations were resumed later in that month, partly as a result of Russian diplomatic efforts. At the end of November a partial peace plan, announced by the Israeli Government, was rejected by the PA.

Although the Palestinian demonstrations during the early days of the al-Aqsa *intifada* appeared to be spontaneous, within the first two weeks highly localized, though apparently unco-ordinated, leaderships did emerge in the West Bank and Gaza. While many of the local organizers were Fatah officials—most famously Marwan Barghouthi, who was said to attract considerable support among Palestinians in Ramallah and other parts of the West Bank, Fatah and the Tanzim, groups much vilified by Israel, seemed not to be operating on a mass scale. Claims that Fatah radiated instructions to the Palestinian masses ignored the divisions that existed within Fatah. Throughout the first two months of the al-Aqsa *intifada*, Arafat and the PA were in many ways non-present, neither organizing protests nor making a concerted effort to prevent them. Hamas and Islamic Jihad were similarly inactive as organizations. On 8 October 2000 Arafat met with the PLO Executive Committee and representatives of Hamas and Islamic Jihad to co-ordinate a joint response to Barak's threats to escalate military action. Arafat held similar meetings in November, but these seemed more directed towards gauging consensus and keeping Islamist groups within the fold than towards drafting battle plans.

However, an important dimension of the al-Aqsa *intifada* did emerge in the first few weeks, and was reflected in moves towards a national unity among all the Palestinian factions—including the non-PLO members Hamas and Islamic Jihad. Prior to the outbreak of the *intifada*, nationalist and Islamist groups had generally limited their joint discussions and co-operation efforts to achieving a broad consensus on fundamental issues: whether and how to continue the peace process, fundamental positions on 'final status' issues, and the timing of a declaration of Palestinian statehood. From late September 2000, however, this national unity was reflected in the formation of an umbrella movement comprising all the Palestinian factions—the Palestinian National and Islamic Forces (PNIF), which laid down a calendar of mass protests and actions. The PNIF included both members of the PLO and Hamas and Islamic Jihad. From its inception, the driving force behind the al-Aqsa revolt remained Arafat's Fatah movement and, in particular, its grassroots organization. However, the direction of the organization's policy remained determined by the decisions of local leaders rather than by orders 'from above'. The basic strategy behind Fatah's local leadership was expressed less by PA officials than by grassroots leaders such as Marwan Barghouthi in the West Bank and Saqr Habash. Modelling themselves on the final phase of Hezbollah's resistance in southern Lebanon, these two leaders described the al-Aqsa uprising as 'peaceful civilian' protests combined with 'new forms of military actions against soldiers and settlers in the Occupied Territories'. Moreover, the longer the revolt continued, the more the 'military actions' by Palestinians took precedence over peaceful ones, and stemmed in the view of many from the fractured, atomized geography that the Oslo Accords had imposed on the West Bank and Gaza.

A major element of the al-Aqsa *intifada* was the importance of unity between the contending 'nationalist' and 'Islamist' groupings within Palestinian politics. Although lending a certain religious imagery to the al-Aqsa *intifada*—due mainly to the role that Jerusalem's al-Aqsa Mosque had played in its ignition—the initial role of Hamas and Islamic Jihad in the uprising was merely supportive. The two groups did not challenge Fatah's leading role on either the political, diplomatic or military levels, and granted the PLO unprecedented legitimacy by attending, for the first time, sessions of its leadership and by joining the PNIF. In return for this alliance, the uprising saw the release of most Hamas and Islamic Jihad detainees from Palestinian gaols; this was the clearest evidence of the breakdown in the PA's security co-operation with Israel and the CIA. On 2 November 2000 a car bomb attack in West Jerusalem left two Israelis dead; on 22 November another car bomb exploded in the Israeli town of Hadera, killing another two civilians. Islamic Jihad claimed responsibility for the first attack, and the second bore a resemblance to Hamas's operations. The response to both attacks by Fatah and the PNIF as a whole was a resounding silence.

The encirclement of Palestinian towns by the Israeli army and the obstruction of roads in the West Bank and Gaza, combined with Israel's escalation of military reprisals against residential areas, added a new dynamic to the conflict. The larger demonstrations of the first few weeks of the Palestinian uprising—which led to clashes with the Israeli army at checkpoints and major crossings, particularly near Jewish settlements—became more difficult and more costly. Given the new situation, it was no coincidence that the PNIF, comprising all nationalist and Islamist parties but separate from the PA, began issuing its leaflets on 23 October 2000. The PNIF's weekly leaflets were generally appeals for non-violent demonstrations and co-ordinated social activities, such as olive-picking. However, they also urged Palestinians to organize themselves locally and suggested general strategies, such as focusing attacks on Israeli soldiers and settlers, which became standard after this period. By mid-November the PNIF was still a nascent body that was far from having well-delineated networks on the ground, though it heralded a new chapter in intra-Palestinian co-ordination.

Prior to the outbreak of the al-Aqsa *intifada* the PA had begun to place more emphasis on state-building activities. For example, on 27 August 2000 the Ministry of Local Government had begun planning elections for 350 villages and municipal councils in the West Bank and Gaza Strip. The PA had originally planned to hold local elections in June 1996, but Arafat had postponed them indefinitely and appointed Fatah loyalists as new council heads, replacing long-standing elected and popular figures. On 20 September 2000 the PA's Minister of Planning and International Co-operation, Dr Nabil Shaath, began forming a team to draft plans to transform the ministry into a foreign ministry, to appeal to foreign countries to upgrade the diplomatic status of PLO offices to that of embassies, and to otherwise standardize the Palestinian diplomatic network. PLC deputy Azmi Shuaybi announced on 28 September the formation of a new anti-corruption coalition (consisting of PLC members, intellectuals and representatives of leading institutions), aimed at promoting and enforcing the rule of law. After the al-Aqsa clashes erupted, however, the PA shifted to crisis management. The PCC was unable to meet in full session due to economic closures, demonstrations and Israel's revocation of VIP passes. PA ministries shifted from regular project work to monitoring the damage to their sectors caused by the Israeli blockade and by Israeli air-strikes and shelling.

In November 2000 PA officials began stating repeatedly that there could be no return to the old Oslo formula in which the promise of nominal 'statehood' was traded for very significant Palestinian concessions on issues like settlements, refugees and Jerusalem. Similarly, Arafat himself increasingly opted for the 'internationalization' of the diplomatic process. Like the majority of Palestinians, he wanted the Oslo process unshackled from what he deemed the pro-Israel bias imposed by the USA's monopoly of the negotiations, and balanced by the participation of countries like Egypt and Russia and international bodies such as the UN and EU. An offshoot of the same strategy was the public Palestinian appeal for 2,000 UN peacekeeping troops to be dispatched to Gaza and the West Bank in order to ensure protection for the Palestinian people.

By November–December 2000 the al-Aqsa *intifada* was rapidly escalating into armed combat between Israel and the Palestinians. One trend was the slow decline of popular Palestinian protests in deference to armed actions, usually in reaction to Israeli military attacks. A second trend was the clear shift in power within the Palestinian national leadership, with grassroots Fatah leaders such as Marwan Barghouthi becoming major players. Moreover, institutions such as the PLC and the PA ministries—which drew their authority from the Oslo Accords—effectively ceased to function or were relegated to the subsidiary role of service providers. In their stead, there was a revival in legitimacy and public loyalty towards the PLO and, above all, Fatah—the latter as a national liberation movement rather than as the 'ruling party of the PA'. This development enabled a new Palestinian unity, with Hamas openly participating in Fatah-dominated bodies like the PNIF, the 'field' organization that determined the time-scale and nature of *intifada* activities. Nevertheless, this 'unity' remained largely tentative. For example, there was a broad agreement among the PLO factions that resistance should be confined to the West Bank and Gaza Strip, since the strategic aim was to end the Israeli occupation on the basis of international legitimacy. It was less clear whether this consensus was shared by the Islamist groups. Arafat himself refused to consider the idea of a Palestinian national unity administration. As for the transformation of PA institutions into state institutions, the response was that the goal was not a formal declaration of statehood but to sustain the *intifada* to end the occupation.

In December 2000 a court in the West Bank town of Nablus passed a death sentence on a Palestinian who had been found guilty of collaborating with Israeli secret services in the assassination of a Hamas commander. This signalled a change in policy by the PA, which in January 2001 carried out the executions by firing squad of two alleged collaborators. In the same month Hisham Mekki, the Chairman of Palestinian Satellite Television, Director of the state broadcasting corporation and a close associate of Arafat, was killed by unidentified gunmen in Gaza. A militant Palestinian group, the al-Aqsa Martyrs Brigades, claimed responsibility for the attack, and accused Arafat of failing to end official corruption. Israel denied PA claims that Palestinian collaborators with Israel were behind the assassination.

In the run-up to the end of Bill Clinton's presidency in the USA in January 2001 and to the Israeli premiership election in February, a further round of peace negotiations opened in mid-December 2000. The outgoing US President was reported to have proposed a peace settlement that included plans for a future Palestinian state covering the Gaza Strip and around 95% of the West Bank, as well as granting Palestinian sovereignty over the Islamic holy sites in Jerusalem. However, the US proposals also required that the Palestinians renounce the right of return to Israel for 3.7m. refugees, which the PA deemed unacceptable. In late December the talks ended after two Israelis were killed by Palestinian bombings in Tel-Aviv and Gaza. Arafat travelled to Washington, DC, in early January 2001 to seek official clarification of the Clinton proposals, while Israel was said to have cautiously accepted the peace initiative as a basis for further discussions.

From its outbreak, there existed a rift between the 'field' leadership of the *intifada* and the PA. Several months into the uprising—and with the arrival of an Israeli Government under Ariel Sharon in early February 2001—the rift was beginning to show signs of political confusion and internal breakdown. Violent demonstrations by Palestinians in the Occupied Territories followed the election of Sharon, whom they held responsible for the massacre of Palestinian refugees in Lebanese camps in 1982 (at which time he was Israel's Minister of

Defence). The Palestinian authorities, under strong pressure from their European and Egyptian allies, had gone to inordinate lengths, if not to get Barak re-elected, then at least not to be blamed for bringing Sharon to power. This had been the main motivation for the PA to attend the Israeli-Palestinian negotiations, which began on 21 January 2001 in Taba, Egypt, since they apparently knew that no agreement would be reached. Indeed, the talks ended without settlement soon afterwards, following the killing of two Israeli civilians in the West Bank for which Hamas claimed responsibility. The drift into disarray and popular resentment was compounded by the absence of the PA in every public sphere except education and health and its apparent inability to alleviate Palestinian suffering. In Gaza there were simmering clashes between Palestinian refugees and the PA's Preventive Security Force (PSF), ostensibly over the arrest of a Hamas activist.

Arafat's problem was that the *intifada* on the ground refused to be halted. Most Palestinians viewed the 'Egyptian-Jordanian' plan with a combination of cynicism and indifference. A dynamic of action and reaction had developed between armed Palestinian resistance and the Israeli army that was now perilously close to being beyond control. On 17 April 2001, in response to a Palestinian mortar attack on the southern Israeli town of Sderot, the Israeli army moved tanks to the PA-controlled town of Beit Hanoun in the Gaza Strip. However, as was to occur frequently in the Palestinian territories in subsequent months, Israeli forces were soon withdrawn from the town. On 26 April four Fatah activists were killed in an explosion on Gaza's border with Egypt, including Raad Azzam, the leader of the Popular Resistance Committee (PRC), which had led the armed resistance and defence of southern Gaza since the start of the uprising. The Palestinian police chief based in Gaza, Ghazi al-Jabali, insisted that the four 'police officers' had been assassinated by a remote-controlled Israeli device. Palestinians responded by renewing mortar attacks on Gaza's Jewish settlements of Gush Qatif and Kfar Darom on 28–29 April. Convening a session of the PA's National Security Council (which represented all the Palestinian police and intelligence forces), on 29 April, Arafat appealed to his followers to curb all 'security breaches', especially the mortar attacks. According to Palestinian sources, he also disbanded the PRC, appealing to its members to return to their original security institutions. In addition, the Palestinian President arrested Hamas official Abd al-Aziz al-Rantisi, following a recent speech during which al-Rantisi urged Palestinians to reject the Egyptian-Jordanian initiative, while brandishing a Kalashnikov, as the 'only way to liberate Palestine'.

The PA leadership now seemed to view engagement in any diplomatic process—no matter how futile in practical terms—as a crucial part of the struggle for sheer survival that it was now reduced to waging. However, the PA needed something to show for the Palestinians' suffering and sacrifices, hence the authorities' insistence on the settlement-building moratorium as part of the 'cease-fire'. A moratorium was one of the components of the package that Israel's Government under Ariel Sharon categorically rejected. Instead, the Israeli Deputy Prime Minister and Minister of Foreign Affairs, Shimon Peres, proposed limited settlement expansion to encompass 'natural growth', which the PA interpreted as meaning a licence for Israel to accelerate the pace of settlement construction.

The PA agreed in early June 2001 to implement the recommendations contained in the report of the international fact-finding committee headed by George Mitchell (the 'Mitchell Committee'), which had been published on 20 May (Documents on Palestine, see p. 96). The report's recommendations included a freeze on Israeli settlement activity; a clear statement by the PA leadership demanding an end to the violent protests; an 'immediate and unconditional' end to the violence and the disengagement of forces by both sides; and the resumption of security co-operation. The report failed to support Palestinian demands for a UN peace-keeping force to be stationed in the West Bank and Gaza (a request which had been consistently rejected by the Israeli Government and which had been blocked by a US veto at the UN Security Council vote in March). On 12 June the PA also approved an extended 'cease-fire', negotiated by CIA Director George Tenet. The reaction of Hamas to the tentative cease-fire between Israel and the PA was rather conflictual. Hamas had claimed responsibility for a suicide bomb attack on a Tel-Aviv disco on 1 June which killed 21 Israelis. On 5 June a senior Hamas official in Gaza, Mahmud al-Zahhar, had stated that Hamas would attack Israelis 'everywhere, by all means', thereby casting doubt on the viability of the recent cease-fire. Al-Zahhar declared that earlier reports that Hamas was willing to abide by the truce were due to 'miscommunications' between the group's military and political wings. In early July both Islamic Jihad and Hamas formally declared an end to the cease-fire.

During August 2001 a number of Palestinians were sentenced to death and at least 100 others were detained by the authorities, on charges of having collaborated with Israeli security services in recent attacks on senior Hamas officials. Meanwhile, the PA rejected a request by the Israeli Government that it arrest seven alleged Islamist militants, who headed a 'most wanted' list of about 100 Palestinians. On 10 August, in response to a suicide bomb attack on a restaurant in central Jerusalem (in which at least 15 Israelis died), Israel ordered its forces to occupy a number of official PA buildings, including Orient House. On 14 August Israeli armed forces entered the town of Jenin in the West Bank; this was the first time that Israel had ordered its military into land that had been transferred to full PA control under the terms of the Oslo peace process initiated in 1993. PA officials described the Israeli action as a 'declaration of war'. On 27 August 2001 the leader of the PFLP, Abu Ali Moustafa, was assassinated by Israeli troops in the West Bank. Moustafa was the highest-ranking Palestinian official to be killed by Israel under its so-called policy of 'targeted killings'. (Ahmad Saadat later assumed the PFLP leadership.)

IMPROVEMENT IN RELATIONS WITH SYRIA

The expected reconciliation between Arafat and the Syrian leadership, under the impact of the al-Aqsa *intifada* and after some 20 years of estrangement, was achieved during sessions of the Arab League summit held in Amman in March 2001. Arafat met Syrian President Bashar al-Assad on the sidelines of the summit. President Assad demanded the liberation of all Palestinian territory occupied by Israel in 1967 (including East Jerusalem), the unconditional return of all 3.7m. Palestinian refugees to their homeland and the creation of an independent Palestinian state (with Jerusalem as its capital). The meeting indicated that the Palestinian leader had met Syria's condition that the PA commit itself to the borders of 4 June 1967. The two sides agreed on the 'unity of the tracks' in the peace process and pledged to co-ordinate and to maintain bilateral contacts.

THE *INTIFADA* IN THE AFTERMATH OF 11 SEPTEMBER 2001

The unprecedented scale of the suicide attacks launched by the Islamist al-Qa'ida organization against the World Trade Center in New York and the Pentagon in Washington, DC, on 11 September 2001 led to a further escalation of tensions between Israel and the PA. As the US Administration sought to gain support for an international 'coalition against terror', President George W. Bush placed considerable pressure on the two sides to end the fighting in the West Bank and Gaza. In mid-September Yasser Arafat, who had strongly condemned the attacks in the USA, announced that he had given militant Palestinian groups 'strict orders for a total cease-fire', while the Israeli Government agreed to withdraw from PA-controlled territory in the West Bank. However, Sharon prevented a planned meeting between Arafat and Shimon Peres from taking place, stating that Israel required 48 hours without violence prior to the convening of peace talks. On 26 September Arafat and Peres finally met in the Gaza Strip, in an attempt to consolidate the 'cease-fire' arrangements outlined in the Mitchell Report. However, retaliatory attacks soon resumed between Israelis and Palestinians. According to the Palestinian Red Crescent Society (PRCS), by the end of September 2001 at least 690 Palestinians had been killed and more than 16,000 injured since the start of the al-Aqsa *intifada* one year earlier. An estimated 170 Israelis had reportedly died as a result of the violence, and many more had been wounded. The

USA's launch of its 'war on terror' in the aftermath of the 11 September attacks appeared to encourage Israel to step up assaults on PA targets and ultimately to reoccupy six major Palestinian cities.

On 17 October 2001 PFLP militants assassinated Israeli Minister of Tourism Rechavam Ze'evi in East Jerusalem. In response, Israel escalated its military campaign in PA-controlled areas of the West Bank. Although Arafat denounced Ze'evi's murder, ordered Palestinian security forces to arrest the perpetrators and outlawed the armed wing of the PFLP, Sharon issued an ultimatum to the PA that they arrest and extradite Ze'evi's killers and other leading PFLP militants or face a harsh response.

The USA urged Sharon to show restraint. It still wanted Israel to resume talks with the PA and for the two sides to implement previous cease-fire agreements, which would facilitate US coalition-building for the 'war on terror' and the US-led military campaign in Afghanistan. In an attempt to revitalize the cease-fire arrangements, US Secretary of Defense Donald Rumsfeld toured the Middle East in early October 2001, and President Bush declared on 2 October that the creation of a Palestinian state 'has always been a part of our vision, so long as the right of Israel to exist is respected'. This public US support for a Palestinian state apparently angered Sharon, as did the fact that Rumsfeld had not come to Israel during his regional consultations on the 'war on terror'. Furthermore, the USA had not backed Israel's demand for the extradition of Ze'evi's assassins. Together with the EU and Russia, the USA continued to put pressure on both the PA and Israel to adhere to the cease-fire arrangement of 29 August, which had been mediated by the EU's High Representative for the Common Foreign and Security Policy, Javier Solana.

Sharon rejected personal appeals by President Bush and US Secretary of State Colin Powell to resume talks with the PA, on 18 October 2001 suspending all contacts with the PA, and giving the Israeli military the 'green light' to step up assassinations of Palestinian activists. Some right-wing Israeli politicians even demanded the expulsion of Arafat from the West Bank and Gaza. In mid-October Israel deployed helicopter gunships over Palestinian cities and moved troops to the outer fringes of Jenin. On 18 October Israeli forces reoccupied Jenin, Nablus and Ramallah, while Bethlehem and Beit Jala were taken on 19 October, and Qalqilya and Tulkarm on 20 October. The USA, on 22 October, condemned the Israeli invasion of PA-controlled cities in Area A as 'unacceptable', and demanded Israel's immediate withdrawal. Israel was forced to pull back from the cities, but its army continued to occupy large sectors of territory belonging to the PA and to carry out 'targeted killings' of senior members of Hamas. The violence continued throughout late 2001, and Arafat reportedly expressed his disappointment at the lack of international pressure on the Israeli Government. Mounting internal opposition to Arafat's policy of arresting Palestinian militants did little to strengthen his position in the Occupied Territories.

THE *KARINE A* AFFAIR

As the US special envoy, Anthony Zinni, returned to the region in an effort to broker an Israeli-Palestinian cease-fire, on 3 January 2002 Israeli naval commandos captured a freighter ship, the *Karine A*, in the Red Sea, which was alleged to be carrying 50 tons of heavy weaponry destined for the PA. The Israelis argued that the smuggling operation had been devised by the PA leadership and approved by Arafat. They also accused Iran of involvement. Although both the Palestinian authorities and Iran denied any responsibility, the Israeli interrogation of the ship's crew (including senior members of the PA's naval forces) apparently indicated direct PA involvement. The US Administration accepted the Israeli position regarding the *Karine A* affair, declaring that it had 'convincing evidence' proving that Iran and the Lebanese Hezbollah were linked to the smuggling operation.

For months after the seizure of the *Karine A*, US and Israeli intelligence officials continued to claim that the affair was part of a broader relationship and accused Arafat of personally forging an alliance with Iran that included imports of Iranian heavy weapons and millions of US dollars to Palestinian guerrilla organizations in the Occupied Territories. This PA-Iranian alliance, they claimed, was conceived at a secret meeting held in Moscow, Russia, in May 2001 between some of Arafat's senior aides and Iranian government officials. The meeting allegedly took place while Arafat was visiting Russian President Vladimir Putin. For their part, Palestinian spokesmen dismissed the claims and denied that Arafat had any prior knowledge of the *Karine A* shipment. They argued that the allegations were part of an attempt by Israel to justify its 'aggressive' military operations in the West Bank and Gaza Strip.

THE RISE OF THE AL-AQSA MARTYRS BRIGADES

The first three months of 2002 witnessed the rise of the al-Aqsa Martyrs Brigades, a militant offshoot of the mainstream Fatah Tanzim, which had been purposely built as a loose network of regional 'cells'. The Brigades pursued a campaign of gun attacks against Israeli soldiers at military road-blocks in the West Bank and Gaza, and dispatched suicide bombers deep into Israel. On 21 March, after suicide bombers from the al-Aqsa Martyrs Brigades killed three Israelis and wounded dozens more in West Jerusalem, the US Department of State branded the Palestinian militia a 'terrorist organization'.

On 27 January 2002 a volunteer for the PRCS in Ramallah became the first female suicide bomber. On 19 February the al-Aqsa Martyrs Brigades claimed joint responsibility for a raid on a West Bank checkpoint, in which six Israeli soldiers died. On 3 March 10 Israelis (most of them soldiers) were shot dead by a sniper from the Brigades at a West Bank checkpoint. The Brigades' success encouraged a belief that Israel could be driven out of the Occupied Territories, just as Hezbollah had forced Israeli troops from southern Lebanon. The doggedness of the Brigades also served as a counterpoint to Arafat's compromises and efforts to regain US approval by vowing to punish those responsible for the 21 March bombing and continuing discussions concerning a US-mediated cease-fire. The commanders of the al-Aqsa Martyrs Brigades answered to no higher authority and certainly not to Arafat, who made several attempts to disband the militia. This autonomy produced a curious hybrid: while the fighters remained part of the mainstream, secular Fatah movement, they adopted the strategies of radical Islamists. The Brigades' suicide bombings in early 2002 broke two Palestinian taboos: they defied Fatah's policy of confining the uprising to the West Bank and Gaza, and, for the first time, they employed women as suicide bombers. In late 2001 and early 2002, after Israel had deployed its air force, navy, tanks and ground forces against Palestinian refugee camps and cities in the biggest military offensive carried out by Israel in a generation, the al-Aqsa Martyrs Brigades decided to concentrate its attacks inside Israel itself. The Jerusalem bombing of 21 March, in particular, encapsulated the limits of Arafat's influence over his mainstream Fatah militia, let alone his radical Islamist opponents such as Hamas and Islamic Jihad.

THE RAMALLAH INCURSION OF MARCH 2002 AND ITS IMPACT ON PALESTINIAN INFRASTRUCTURE

Only after the Palestinians were beaten, Ariel Sharon reportedly stated in early March 2002, would negotiations be possible. According to a report by the human rights organization Amnesty International, the scale of Israeli attacks on Palestinian cities and refugee camps in the West Bank and Gaza was 'disproportionate and often reckless'. Amnesty estimated that in the six weeks from 1 March to mid-April more than 600 Palestinians had been killed and over 3,000 wounded by Israeli soldiers. A major escalation occurred on 11 March 2002, when the Israeli army entered Ramallah, the Palestinians' commercial and political hub in the West Bank, in what Israel said was part of a general sweep for activists and militants. The massive incursion involved some 150 tanks and was part of Israel's largest military offensive in the West Bank and Gaza Strip since the Israelis captured these territories in 1967. The incursion took place while US envoy Anthony Zinni was engaged in a renewed effort to broker a cease-fire between the two sides.

The Israelis' short-lived incursion into Ramallah resulted in huge damage to Palestinian infrastructure, affecting water and electricity supplies, the sewerage system and roads, and was estimated by PA officials as costing tens of millions of US dollars. Twelve Palestinians were also killed during the assault on Ramallah. On 16 March 2002 Israeli tanks withdrew from the West Bank city, ending their brief reoccupation of President Arafat's power base. The Israeli army, meanwhile, announced that its forces had left positions in two other West Bank cities but that they remained on the outskirts of Bethlehem, Nablus, Jenin and Hebron. Israeli forces also formed a cordon around Ramallah.

THE USA'S 'WAR ON TERROR' AND THE FAILURE OF US MEDIATION

Both Anthony Zinni and Israel demanded that Arafat should end the *intifada*, collect illegal weapons from militants and arrest those Palestinians wanted by Israel for 'terrorist' activities. However, the PA could not arrest the hundreds, or even thousands, of Palestinians who now participated in the regular attacks against the Israeli occupation. The reason for this was the shift in the nature of the *intifada* in recent months. While, in the initial months of the uprising, most of the attacks had been carried out by minority groups of Hamas and Islamic Jihad, now the *intifada* had apparently become the struggle of an entire nation. Deep-seated feelings of frustration, fury and desire for revenge against the Israeli state appeared to lead large numbers of Palestinian youths to volunteer as suicide bombers. PA officials used this argument to explain their demands for the lifting of the closures, for the removal of the roadblocks, and for the Israeli army's withdrawal to the positions it held prior to September 2000. Only then, according to Arafat and Palestinian officials, would it be possible to start to bring about calm among the Palestinian population.

As Zinni pressed ahead with cease-fire talks between the PA and Israel, the Bush Administration demanded a complete withdrawal of all Israeli forces from PA-controlled areas, stating that this would create a better environment for the US envoy to attempt to broker a truce. However, at the same time, both Israel and the USA continued to repeat their demand that Arafat 'must do more' to rein in Palestinian militants and halt attacks on Israelis. Zinni convened the joint Israeli-Palestinian security committee for discussions on how to move into the security plan prepared by CIA Director George Tenet.

The joint Israeli-Palestinian security committee met on 20 and 21 March 2002, with Zinni in attendance; however, no agreement was reached on the terms of a cease-fire. Representing the Palestinians in the meetings were Col Jibril Rajoub, the head of the PSF in the West Bank, and his Gaza counterpart, Muhammad Dahlan. Besides differences of opinion between Israel and the PA as to the length of time to be allocated to the Tenet cease-fire plan before the resumption of the diplomatic process, there was also disagreement over the arrest of Palestinian militants wanted by Israel. Israel demanded the arrests of those involved in past attacks against Israelis, but the Palestinians replied that they would only detain those who intended to launch future attacks.

Meanwhile, the PA continued to demand that Israel withdraw its troops to their positions as at September 2000, and lift all sieges and remove all checkpoints around Palestinian towns and villages, as stated by the Tenet plan; the Palestinians also demanded that international observers be placed in the Occupied Territories. PA representatives insisted that, despite the difficulties posed by the Tenet plan, they would do what was required, but only if they could prove to the Palestinian public that there would be an immediate response from Israel, and only if the security arrangements and consequent calm would result in a renewal of the political negotiations. Israel, on the other hand, wanted the Palestinians first to take a series of steps against militant groups, including arrests, dismantling the militias and collecting weapons.

ISRAELI REOCCUPATION OF PA-CONTROLLED AREAS

On 29 March 2002 Israel launched 'Operation Defensive Shield'—a large-scale military offensive in the West Bank in response to a series of suicide attacks by Palestinian militants and, more specifically, to a suicide bombing two days previously in Netanya (in which some 29 Israelis celebrating Passover died). This was the bloodiest attack since the start of the Palestinian uprising against Israeli occupation in September 2000. As part of its military campaign, Israeli forces broke into Arafat's presidential compound in Ramallah, where the Palestinian leader remained inside his office, effectively cut off from the rest of the city. Although Israel stated that it had no intention of harming Arafat personally, PA officials insisted that Arafat's life was in danger. On 1 April 2002 Israeli tanks entered the town of Betunya, near Ramallah, surrounding the PSF compound of West Bank security chief Jibril Rajoub and causing considerable damage to the complex. The PSF apparatus had been the strongest and most prominent of all PA forces on the West Bank.

Israeli tanks also entered Beit Jala, Bethlehem, Qalqilya, Salfeet, Tulkarm, Nablus and Jenin, patrolling the streets and enforcing strict curfews which confined hundreds of thousands of Palestinians to their homes. In addition, Israeli troops laid siege to Jenin's refugee camp, resulting in battles with Palestinian residents of the camp who retaliated with bombs and guns. Israeli soldiers also encircled hundreds of Palestinian gunmen who had barricaded themselves in Bethlehem's Church of the Nativity. Arafat, meanwhile, confined to his Ramallah headquarters, remained defiant, stating that he would prefer to die rather than be forced into exile.

It was apparent that Sharon now wanted to expel Arafat from the Territories, publicly suggesting on 2 April 2002 that he be exiled. However, although the US Administration offered Sharon tacit support for Israel's military operation in the West Bank, US officials were not prepared to allow the Israeli Government to expel the PA President, to destroy the PA or to completely retake the areas under nominal Palestinian control. Yet, the Israeli offensive prevented the PA from taking effective control of the security situation in the Palestinian self-rule areas because vital Palestinian installations, including its West Bank security headquarters, had been destroyed.

THE BATTLE FOR THE JENIN REFUGEE CAMP

The heaviest fighting between the Israeli army and Palestinian militias occurred in the refugee camp at Jenin, home to some 13,000 Palestinians. Israeli tanks had entered Jenin and surrounded the adjacent refugee camp on 3 April 2002, provoking fierce opposition from Palestinian gunmen. Many of the camp's inhabitants fled during the fighting and heavy bombardment by Israeli tanks and helicopters. The fighting in the Jenin camp lasted until 11 April. Palestinians subsequently estimated that more than 100 Palestinians had died as a result of the Israeli invasion of the camp. The UN's special envoy to the Middle East, Terje Rød-Larsen, was strongly critical of Israel's actions at Jenin. However, an exact tally of the number of fatalities was not possible because Israel initially barred reporters and medical personnel from the camp. After the siege of early April the Palestinians came to embrace Jenin as a symbol of wider resistance to the Israeli occupation.

THE ARREST OF MARWAN BARGHOUTHI

On 15 April 2002 Marwan Barghouthi, one of the most influential Fatah leaders in the West Bank, was detained by Israeli armed forces in Ramallah. Israel presented Barghouthi's detention as a major achievement of its reoccupation of the city, using it to counter strong international pressure against its military offensive in the West Bank. Israel accused Barghouthi of being the leader of the al-Aqsa Martyrs Brigades, despite the fact that he had never acknowledged a formal relationship with the group. In recent years Barghouthi had attained the status of a 'folk hero' among most young Palestinians. His fiery speeches and almost daily media interviews—including several that he had given to Israeli television in Hebrew—had made him a defining face of the

Palestinian *intifada*. Since September 2000 Barghouthi had at times appeared to disagree publicly with Arafat over the direction of the Palestinian uprising. However, Barghouthi's acumen—he never mentioned the Palestinian leader by name when criticizing his policies—and popularity had ensured his political survival. Trial proceedings against Barghouthi began on 5 September 2002.

ENDING THE STAND-OFFS IN RAMALLAH AND BETHLEHEM

The stand-off at the Church of the Nativity began on 2 April 2002, when Israel invaded Bethlehem and about 200 Palestinians (including militiamen, policemen, officials, clerics and church workers) sought refuge in the shrine. By 23 April Israeli forces had pulled back from most West Bank cities, but still surrounded Arafat's compound in Ramallah and the Bethlehem church. In Ramallah, Israel demanded that Arafat hand over five men suspected of involvement in the October 2001 assassination of Rechavam Ze'evi, as well as the alleged mastermind of the *Karine A* arms shipment to the PA. Although Arafat had initially refused this request, he now took pre-emptive legal action by putting the suspected assassins of Ze'evi on trial in a makeshift court, using Palestinian policemen in the Ramallah compound as judges. On 25 April 2002 the 'military field court' handed out gaol terms of between one and 18 years to four men convicted of involvement in Ze'evi's assassination. The sentences were ratified by Arafat. On 28 April the Israeli Cabinet approved a US proposal aimed at ending the siege of Arafat's compound. The US plan required US and British personnel to guard six Palestinians wanted by Israel, and, in turn, Arafat was allowed to leave his headquarters and to move freely in the Palestinian areas of the West Bank and Gaza. Finally, an accord based on proposals to offer militants wanted by Israel and stranded in the Church of the Nativity a choice of exile or trial in Israel, or transfer to the Gaza Strip, was devised, with US mediation. Arafat approved the dispatch of 13 Palestinians to Europe and of a further 26 to Gaza, despite strong Fatah and Hamas criticism of the agreement. On 12 May the 13 Palestinian militants were flown initially to Cyprus after leaving the Bethlehem church, on their way to permanent exile.

REOCCUPATION OF THE WEST BANK AND THE DETERIORATING HUMANITARIAN SITUATION

On 23 June 2002, after two suicide bombings in Jerusalem had killed some 26 Israelis, the Israeli military reinvaded all West Bank cities, keeping at least 600,000 Palestinians under effective house arrest with round-the-clock curfews and largely barring the media from covering its military operations. This military offensive encountered minimal Palestinian resistance and limited international criticism. Israeli tanks again surrounded Arafat's shell-damaged compound, with the President and his aides inside. As Israeli forces clamped down harder on security in the West Bank, Sharon pledged to widen the Israeli offensive against the Palestinians to the Gaza Strip. The reoccupation of the West Bank and the prolonged curfews imposed by Israel brought about a major humanitarian crisis for the Palestinians, with UN and aid agencies having trouble getting assistance to hundreds of thousands of Palestinians there.

GENERAL ELECTION AND PA REFORM ANTICIPATED

In mid-May 2002 Yasser Arafat decided to hold presidential and parliamentary elections within a year, which, according to PA officials, would be part of a broader reform package of the administration. Long-standing Palestinian complaints about widespread corruption and nepotism in the PA had intensified during the months of Israeli closures and invasions, which had severely disrupted everyday life. Previous attempts to reform the administration had led to few significant changes, with Arafat disregarding laws adopted by the PLC as well as decisions by the judiciary. However, despite widespread Palestinian dissatisfaction with the PA, Arafat continued to be seen as a symbol of the Palestinian people and was not expected to face a strong challenge for leadership. None the less, Israel's six-week reoccupation of the West Bank towns during April–May had strengthened a sense among many Palestinians that the PA was ineffective and unable to protect them against the Israeli military. Thus, Arafat may have decided to hold elections as a way of ensuring renewed legitimacy. PA officials emphasized that polling would be conducted on the condition that Israeli troops first withdrew to positions they had held before September 2000.

The elections would be the first time that Arafat faced voters since he was overwhelmingly elected as President of the PA in 1996. The parliament's list of demands was drafted by a committee of eight legislators from Arafat's Fatah movement, who had requested that a post of prime minister be created, with the premier to be in charge of day-to-day government operations. The planned reforms also urged a streamlining of the Palestinian security services. However, Abd al-Aziz al-Rantisi, leader of the Hamas movement, dismissed the planned administrative changes as merely cosmetic.

On 27 May 2002 Arafat, following strong demands for reform by ordinary Palestinians and Western governments alike, named a new Cabinet that included a new minister to oversee the security forces. Arafat streamlined his Cabinet from 31 to 21 ministers, and brought in several new faces. Most notably, he named Abd al-Razzak al-Yahya as the new Minister of the Interior. By appointing al-Yahya, a former PLO commander who had not held any high-profile positions in recent times, Arafat had bypassed more prominent figures. Dogged by accusations of widespread financial corruption in his administration, Arafat also named a new Minister of Finance, Dr Salam Fayyad, who had recently been employed by the IMF in Jerusalem and had urged greater financial accountability in the Palestinian administration.

PRESIDENT BUSH URGES THAT ARAFAT BE REPLACED

Despite the reorganization of the Palestinian Cabinet, Arafat remained under pressure from Europe and the USA to carry out wide-ranging 'reforms' of his administration. On 24 June 2002 President Bush, in a speech concerning the Middle East, set out the US Administration's plan for peace in the region. Bush appealed to the Palestinians to elect a 'new and different Palestinian leadership' and to adopt a new constitution with a fully empowered parliament, local-level governments and an independent judiciary. The USA and its partners would help to organize multi-party local elections by the end of the year, with national elections to follow. The President added that the PA should undertake an externally supervised overhaul of their security and police forces, dismantle 'terrorist groups', and implement financial reforms. In turn, the USA would increase humanitarian aid to the PA. Setting stringent conditions for the creation of a Palestinian state, President Bush stated that, after these steps were taken, the Palestinians would be able to count on US support for a 'provisional state of Palestine', with the final borders, capital and other aspects of sovereignty to be negotiated between Israel and the PA. Bush also appealed to Israel to withdraw its forces to positions it had held in the West Bank on 28 September 2000 and to cease building Jewish settlements in the West Bank and Gaza. Questions about the status of Jerusalem and the right of Palestinian refugees to return home would be dealt with during 'final status' negotiations.

Palestinian officials responded to the US President's speech by stating that the demand to replace Arafat was not acceptable. In late May 2002 84 Palestinian parties, organizations and leading figures had signed a statement demanding a refusal of aid from the US Administration because of its support for Israel.

ARAFAT'S DISMISSAL OF HIS WEST BANK SECURITY CHIEF

In early July 2002, while the Israeli army continued its offensive in the West Bank, Yasser Arafat dismissed his most powerful security chief, Jibril Rajoub, the commander of the PSF in the West Bank. Although Arafat's motives were unclear, Rajoub had evidently lost credibility following the Israeli military takeover of the PSF's headquarters in Betunya four months earlier. Moreover, several Palestinian leaders, including some of Arafat's closest aides, had insinuated that Rajoub had handed over Fatah and Hamas fighters to Israel. On 5 July a terse formal statement from the PA stated that Arafat had decided to 'relieve' Rajoub of his responsibilities and to appoint in his place Zuheir Manasra, a former governor of Jenin. On the same day three peaceful demonstrations were staged by PSF officers and employees in the West Bank in support of Rajoub's reinstatement. The following day several high-ranking PSF officers met Arafat in an effort to persuade him to reconsider Rajoub's position; it was reported that Arafat subsequently offered Rajoub a number of posts within the PA. Gen. Ghazi al-Jabali, the Palestinian police chief, was dismissed by Arafat in a similar fashion, also in early July, and his deputy, Col Salim Bardini, was nominated to replace him. The tumult of the al-Aqsa *intifada* prompted a period of sustained upheaval within the upper ranks of the PA's security forces, precipitating structural reform.

The entire Palestinian Cabinet resigned on 11 September 2002, in order to prevent a vote of no confidence being brought against it in the PLC. (On the same day Arafat had issued a decree setting 20 January 2003 as the date of the presidential and legislative elections.) Although a new cabinet was expected to be announced within two weeks, Arafat subsequently declared that he was unable to form a new administration while his compound in Ramallah was under Israeli occupation. Following a further Palestinian suicide bombing in Tel-Aviv, on 19 September 2002 Israel had ordered its troops into Ramallah and demolished Arafat's presidential buildings, where a number of 'wanted' militants were believed to be sheltering. Amid strong international pressure, Israeli forces redeployed to the outskirts of the Ramallah compound on 29 September. The incumbent Palestinian ministers were to remain in office pending the formation of a new cabinet.

THE DEBATE ON THE FUTURE OF THE AL-AQSA *INTIFADA* AND THE POWER STRUGGLE BETWEEN ARAFAT AND ABBAS

On 26 November 2002 the Secretary-General of the PLO's Executive Committee and Arafat's deputy, Mahmud Abbas, urged Palestinian militants fighting the Israeli occupation to halt suicide attacks in Israel 'to avoid giving Israel the pretext to reoccupy more Palestinian land'. Abbas (who had been the key PLO figure behind the secret talks with the Israelis in Oslo, which eventually led to the signing of the Declaration of Principles in 1993) had consistently criticized the use of arms by Palestinians during the al-Aqsa *intifada*. Meanwhile, a poll conducted by Birzeit University and released in late 2002 showed that almost two-thirds of Palestinians in the Occupied Territories disapproved of the way in which the *intifada* had evolved and supported immediate reform of the PA.

The power struggle between Arafat and Abbas dominated PA politics at this time. Both were co-founders of Fatah and the clash reflected the depth of the Palestinian crisis. Following the Oslo agreements, a kind of Palestinian mini-entity had come into being, consisting of several small enclaves on the West Bank and the Gaza Strip. However, the Palestinian national vision of 'a viable, independent and sovereign state in all the West Bank and Gaza Strip, including East Jerusalem' was far from being realized. Consequently, two different, and even contradictory, structures had emerged side by side in the West Bank and Gaza: a national liberation movement, defined by its assortment of militant groups and requiring direction, and a micro-entity in need of a transparent administration. Arafat remained the symbol of the national liberation movement, with his charisma and authoritarian leadership. Abbas, by nature a man of compromise and a diplomat, represented the second reality of small fragmented enclaves, surrounded by and dependent on Israel. Abbas had little influence over the Palestinians, but did have the support of the USA and Israel.

The conflict between the two leaders centred on diverging assessments of the al-Aqsa *intifada*. By mid-2003 some 2,500 Palestinians had been killed, some 10,000 disabled and injured, and the Palestinian economy debilitated. Abbas appealed for the cessation of the 'armed *intifada*' and maintained that the Palestinians could achieve more in negotiations with the USA and Israel. Relying on mainstream Israeli politicians such as former Labour Party minister Yossi Beilin in his assessment of the *intifada*, Abbas believed that the military confrontation with Israel undermined the Oslo process and harmed Palestinian interests.

Abbas's Palestinian critics (including Arafat loyalists) argued that the *intifada* had not failed; on the contrary, it had in their view achieved important results: first, the Israeli economy was in deep crisis; second, social and political cleavages within Israeli society had widened; third, Israel's image in the world had been severely harmed; fourth, Israeli security had worsened to the point where there was a conspicuously ubiquitous public security presence; and fifth, Israeli casualties were high. Palestinian supporters of the *intifada* believed that Israel would eventually be forced to accede to the minimum demands of the Palestinians: a viable independent state based on the 1967 borders, with Jerusalem as a shared capital between Palestine and Israel, in addition to the dismantlement of Jewish settlements and the achievement of a negotiated solution to the Palestinian refugee question. Moreover, Abbas's critics believed that his basic political assumptions were wrong: the Bush Administration would never pressurize Israel, which had a strong lobby presence in Washington, DC; Israel would never concede anything without being forced to do so; and Sharon would continue building settlements, while at the same time giving the appearance of negotiating.

THE NATIONAL DIALOGUE IN CAIRO

In late 2002 and early 2003 both the PA and the Fatah movement were facing a mounting challenge from Hamas, the armed wing of which, the Izz al-Din al-Qassam Brigades, spearheaded anti-Israeli attacks in the Occupied Territories, thus gaining increasing support among the Palestinians. By mid-2002 the Israeli army had destroyed the PA's security infrastructure in the West Bank, although the PA still maintained control in many areas in the Gaza Strip, which had been heavily targeted by the Israeli army but had not been reoccupied. The rise of Hamas provided the background for the Palestinian national dialogue in Cairo. In November representatives of Fatah and Hamas launched a new round of talks in Cairo, sponsored by President Hosni Mubarak, aimed at agreeing on a common Palestinian strategy in the face of escalating Israeli attacks and the reoccupation of Palestinian territories. The delegations to the Cairo talks were initially led by Fatah representative Zakaria al-Agha and Hamas politburo chief Khalid Meshaal.

Arafat himself had repeatedly appealed to all Palestinian factions to agree to halt suicide attacks within Israel and had voiced his condemnation of all attacks perpetrated against both Palestinian and Israeli civilians. However, the Cairo talks yielded little except a commitment to continue dialogue. Subsequently, PA Minister of External Affairs Dr Nabil Shaath elaborated by saying that Fatah would 'maintain its demands, namely a halt to all operations against civilians as a first step towards a cease-fire to allow Israel to pull back its forces from the territories to the September 2000 lines'. He stated that 'civilians' meant all unarmed Israelis 'including unarmed settlers' in the West Bank and Gaza Strip.

The national dialogue in Cairo was resumed in mid-January 2003 and involved 12 Palestinian factions, with delegates from across the political spectrum. However, the delegates failed to agree on an Egyptian draft proposal for a Palestinian-Israeli cease-fire that also upheld the right to resist Israeli occupation through civil disobedience. Delegates fell into three broad camps concerning the Egyptian proposal: those who accepted it unconditionally; those who only agreed to halting attacks against civilians inside Israel; and those who would only agree to halting attacks if Israel gave reciprocal guarantees to stop 'targeted killings' of leading Palestinian militants.

POSTPONEMENT OF ELECTIONS AND REFORM OF THE PA

In late 2002 PA officials began arguing that they had been hampered in their reforms, including the holding of elections, by the Israelis' reoccupation of the West Bank and their regular incursions into the Gaza Strip. In December PLC Speaker Ahmad Quray announced that it would not be practical to proceed with the presidential and legislative elections scheduled for 20 January 2003 until Israel withdrew from the reoccupied PA areas. PA officials argued that the Israeli blockades made it impossible for the Palestinian population to move around, crippling the economy and undermining hopes that voters could get to polling stations. In the mean time, the USA and Israel, which both demanded that the PA undertake sweeping 'democratic and security reforms', now requested that the Palestinian presidential election be delayed for fear that Arafat could win a new term as President.

In January 2003 the PCC met for the first time in two years to ratify the draft of a Palestinian constitution, including a clause establishing the post of prime minister—one of the conditions of the peace plan known as the 'roadmap', drafted by the Quartet group (comprising the USA, the EU, the UN and Russia). Meanwhile, the European Commission praised PA efforts to achieve transparency in its finances, while Israel claimed that money was being used to finance 'terrorism'. The PA's first complete budget, submitted by Minister of Finance Salam Fayyad to the PLC in December 2002, received widespread praise. In late January 2003 PA officials in Ramallah reacted with dismay to Ariel Sharon's re-election to the Israeli premiership.

THE ABBAS CABINET

On 14 February 2003 Arafat finally yielded to pressure from the EU, Israel and the USA, and announced that he would create a prime ministerial post as part of efforts to reform his administration. Mahmud Abbas was immediately considered the most likely candidate. Arafat, whose personal power was largely unchecked, made the announcement after a meeting with special representatives from the UN, Russia and the EU. However, the Palestinian President gave no indication as to when the new prime minister might be appointed, although al-Rabbuh stated that the PLC would convene on the issue. The new post's terms of reference were unclear, with Abbas refusing to accept what he called a 'ceremonial job'.

The power struggle between Arafat and Abbas continued throughout early 2003. In mid-April Abbas's efforts to form a new cabinet ran into trouble, when several leading PA figures and Arafat loyalists remained highly critical of Israeli and US pressure on the PA. On 22 April Abbas announced that talks with Arafat had broken down over the latter's refusal to accept his nomination of Muhammad Dahlan, who had long-term relations with both the USA and Israel, and who had clashed with Arafat while serving as the PA President's security chief.

Meanwhile, the USA, which firmly backed Abbas, declared that he had until midnight on 23 April 2003 to name a new cabinet or step aside, thereby jeopardizing the chances for the Quartet-sponsored roadmap, which US President George W. Bush had said he would release when Abbas had announced his cabinet. With world leaders urging him to back down, Arafat was forced to bow to key cabinet demands from Abbas. Dahlan was appointed a Minister of State for Security Affairs, while Abbas himself would become Prime Minister and Minister for the Interior. The new Cabinet marked a major victory for Abbas and a severe blow for Arafat, who had been struggling to maintain control of the key Palestinian security forces in the most serious challenge to his leadership for two decades. Yet, Abbas's appeals for a suspension of attacks on Israel angered radical Fatah and Islamist leaders. Hamas's political leader, Abd al-Aziz al-Rantisi, warned the new Cabinet not to take on the militants who had been fighting Israeli occupation. On 29 April the Cabinet comfortably won a vote of confidence in the PLC. Abbas had promised the Quartet that he would root out corruption, crack down on Palestinian militants and open the way for renewed peace talks with Israel.

THE ROADMAP PEACE PLAN

On 30 April 2003, four months after it had been finalized by the Quartet group, the roadmap to peace in the Middle East was formally placed on the diplomatic agenda and presented to the PA and Israel (Documents on Palestine, see p. 104). The presentation of the roadmap took place in Ramallah within hours of the swearing in of the new Palestinian Cabinet. The roadmap was the first major international diplomatic initiative in three years aimed at resuming negotiations between Israel and the Palestinians. The document urged an end to the Israeli–Palestinian conflict and the establishment of a Palestinian state by 2005. From the point of view of PA officials, the roadmap, at the very least, was supposed to create the diplomatic pressure necessary to end Israel's policy of 'creating facts on the ground' by its military actions in the West Bank and Gaza.

The roadmap focused upon a Palestinian renunciation of efforts to use force and 'terror' to change the status quo. The plan offered the option of the 'possible creation of an independent Palestinian state with provisional borders in 2005' and demanded a complete cessation of Israeli settlement expansion in the West Bank and Gaza and the evacuation of settlements established after March 2001. Under the terms of the roadmap, Israel was also required to end its prohibition on Palestinian travel on most roads in the Palestinian territories. The PA endorsed the roadmap almost immediately. Israel, however, rejected the demand for an effective settlement freeze, referring instead to a policy permitting the 'natural growth' of settlements. Israeli officials opposed the removal of the approximately 70 new settlement 'outposts' established since March 2001, and insisted that such measures would be implemented only 'following a continuous and comprehensive security calm'.

On 16 May 2003 Saeb Erakat handed in his resignation as Minister for Negotiation Affairs to Abbas without explanation; it came a day before a planned meeting between Abbas and Sharon. Erakat had previously led Palestinian teams in negotiations with Israel prior to the al-Aqsa *intifada* and had been considered closer to Arafat than to Abbas. While the Minister of State for Security Affairs, Muhammad Dahlan, and the PLC Speaker, Ahmad Quray, had been invited to join Abbas in his talks with Sharon, Erakat had not been invited and he appeared to have resigned in order to express his displeasure at this perceived snub. In late May Sharon's vague acceptance of the roadmap and the seemingly conflicting messages to the Palestinians and Israelis by the Bush Administration in the USA were cautiously welcomed by the PA. After the USA had, in late May, declared that it would consider 'fully and seriously' Israeli concerns relating to the roadmap, the Palestinian leadership emphasized the importance of implementing the roadmap without any change to its detail, and insisted that it should be dealt with as a 'package'.

THE AQABA SUMMIT

Soon after Israel had announced its qualified acceptance of the roadmap, President Bush declared that he was calling a three-way summit, to take place in Aqaba, Jordan, between himself, Sharon and Abbas in what would mark the US President's first major involvement in the Middle East peace process. Although the USA had been the senior partner in the Quartet group that had drafted the peace plan, Bush had been slow to engage in this process. His Administration had had no serious dialogue with the Palestinians for more than a year. Prior to the Aqaba summit, Abbas stated that he expected to reach an agreement with Hamas whereby the organization would halt its campaign of attacks against Israelis. Hamas had rejected the roadmap but its spokesman disclosed that the group was considering a temporary cease-fire. Since November 2002 Egypt had hosted several rounds of inter-Palestinian talks in a bid to stop attacks against Israelis, with Hamas and Islamic Jihad rejecting a truce unless Israel stopped its 'targeted killings' of Palestinian activists and withdrew its army from the West Bank and Gaza. Israel had earlier ruled out the prospect of a cease-fire agreement at this stage, stating that 'terrorist organizations would take advantage of it to rebuild their infrastructure.'

On 4 June 2003 the Aqaba summit formally launched the roadmap. Bush held separate meetings with the summit's host, King Abdullah, followed by discussions with Sharon and Abbas before the three-way summit began at King Abdullah's summer residence of Beit al-Bahr. Separate statements were issued after the talks, since the Israelis and Palestinians failed to agree on a joint communiqué.

On the same day Israeli forces pushed into the West Bank towns of Nablus and Jenin, prompting clashes with inhabitants that left several Palestinians injured. Israeli troops in Hebron demolished three houses owned by Palestinian fighters in the southern district and imposed a curfew on the area. More critically, however, the decision to target Hamas leader al-Rantisi for assassination on 10 June 2003 threatened to derail the efforts of Abbas to negotiate a cease-fire with Hamas representatives. From Sharon's perspective, Hamas had invited the assault on al-Rantisi with its deadly attack on Israeli soldiers in Gaza two days earlier, and he had never favoured the idea of Abbas negotiating a cease-fire with the militant group. Following the Aqaba summit, the Israeli policy of 'targeted assassination' of Hamas militants continued.

On 14 June 2003, after a particularly violent week in Israel and the Palestinian territories, there was a growing chorus of voices, led by UN Secretary-General Kofi Annan, demanding the deployment of an armed force of peace-keepers to keep the two sides apart and enable them to begin implementing the roadmap. Palestinians had long maintained that an international peace-keeping force could reduce tensions and end the curfews, roadblocks and travel restrictions that put severe constraints on life in the West Bank and Gaza. However, Israel remained vehemently opposed to such a force, stating that it would not relinquish control over its security to a third party. Meanwhile, on the same day Israel and the Palestinians resumed talks concerning the withdrawal of Israeli troops from parts of the Gaza Strip and Bethlehem. In late June Hamas and other militant organizations declared a cease-fire, which they said was conditional upon Israel ending its policy of killing Palestinian militants and upon the release of Palestinian prisoners.

Following the Aqaba summit, the Cabinet led by Mahmud Abbas continued to demand from Israel the removal of settlement outposts, the release of Palestinian tax revenues, the easing of movement around the Occupied Territories and the release of Palestinians detained in Israeli gaols without trial. Yet, Abbas appeared to have no power base among the Palestinians and little mandate from the Palestinian people to negotiate on their behalf. On 6 July 2003 the Israeli Cabinet 'reluctantly' agreed to free several hundred Palestinian prisoners, but Sharon ruled out releasing members of Hamas and Islamic Jihad involved in attacks on Israeli targets. Abbas, who had made the prison releases a key demand, pressed Sharon to free a number of prominent detainees, including Marwan Barghouthi, who was on trial in Israel, accused of perpetrating terrorism against Israeli citizens. Barghouthi had played a crucial role in persuading Hamas, Islamic Jihad and Fatah to agree to the cease-fire announced in late June. The Palestinian leadership stated that the prisoner releases would not only help to reinforce the truce but also shore up public support for the roadmap.

On 25 July 2003 President Bush received Abbas at the White House in Washington, DC, for the first time, in a visit designed to hasten the implementation of the roadmap and to reinforce Abbas's authority. The visit came at a critical time for Abbas, a month after he had coaxed Palestinian militants into ending their attacks on Israel; Abbas was also under pressure to demonstrate that the cease-fire had achieved concrete results for the Palestinians. During the meeting Bush appeared to side with Abbas on one key issue, the demand for a halt to construction of the 'security fence' that Israel was building along the length of the West Bank, which appeared effectively to annex areas of Palestinian land. At the same time, however, Bush was equivocal on a demand by Abbas for Israel to release substantial numbers of the 6,000 Palestinian prisoners it held.

By early June 2003 the number of people killed since the outbreak of the al-Aqsa *intifada* in September 2000 had risen to 3,278, including 2,476 Palestinians and 742 Israelis. In early May 2003 the UN Relief and Works Agency for Palestine Refugees in the Near East (UNRWA) reported that the total number of Palestinians made homeless by the Israeli military demolition campaign had risen to above 12,000 following a rapid acceleration of the demolition policy in Gaza during the first quarter of the year.

Mahmud Abbas resigned as Prime Minister at the beginning of September 2003; it was widely believed that his resignation was the culmination of his ongoing dispute with Arafat regarding ultimate authority over the Palestinian security apparatus. Arafat moved quickly to nominate Ahmad Quray, the Speaker of the PLC, as the new Prime Minister. Quray accepted the post shortly afterwards. Also in early September Saeb Erakat was reappointed as the Minister for Negotiation Affairs. In mid-September the USA vetoed a draft UN Security Council resolution condemning Israel's attempts to remove Arafat from power, stating that the resolution had failed to condemn adequately acts of violence by Palestinian militants.

NEW PALESTINIAN CABINET AND EGYPTIAN MEDIATION OF TRUCE NEGOTIATIONS

On 12 November 2003 Arafat inaugurated the long-awaited new Palestinian Cabinet, headed by Prime Minister Ahmad Quray. Quray immediately vowed to seek a cease-fire with Israel and to bring an end to the al-Aqsa *intifada*. In mid-November Egyptian intelligence chief Omar Suleiman held talks in Ramallah with Arafat and Quray, aimed at facilitating a new, durable and mutually accepted cease-fire. Both Suleiman and his PA hosts hoped that this time the cease-fire would hold, unlike the previous *hudna* (truce) unilaterally declared by the Palestinian resistance groups in June. On 18 November Suleiman also dispatched some of his aides to Gaza to meet with the leaders of local Fatah, Hamas and Islamic Jihad organizations to discuss the proposed truce.

Following this round of Egyptian mediation, Hamas's founder and spiritual leader Sheikh Ahmad Yassin publicly welcomed the Egyptian efforts, calling Egypt an 'older brother'. Yassin indicated that Hamas was willing in principle to accept a new cease-fire provided that Israel refrained from assassinating Palestinian leaders and al-Aqsa *intifada* activists, and ended its repeated incursions into Palestinian population centres in the Gaza Strip. The leaders of Hamas also demanded that Israel end its policy of demolishing Palestinian homes and destroying orchards and farms, and removed all travel restrictions throughout the West Bank and Gaza Strip. In response, both the Egyptian mediators and PA officials declared that Hamas's demands were reasonable, since no lasting cease-fire agreement would be sustained without ending Israeli 'targeted killings' of Palestinians.

However, the anticipated meeting between Sharon and Quray did not take place, despite renewed US pressure; both the PA and Israel blamed each other for not holding the meeting. In the period between 4 October 2003 and 31 January 2004 the Israeli army was reported to have killed 113 Palestinians, the majority of them civilians (including 25 children). In January Palestinian guerrillas and suicide bombers killed four Israeli soldiers, two settlers and 11 civilians. After a series of bloody incursions by the Israeli army into Palestinian population centres in Gaza which left scores of Palestinians dead or wounded, Hamas responded on 14 January by carrying out a suicide bombing against Israel at the Erez border crossing; three Israeli soldiers and a security guard were killed. On 28 January Israeli armed forces stormed the al-Zayton neighbourhood in central Gaza, killing at least eight Palestinians. Two weeks later, on 11 February, the Israeli army invaded the Shujaiya neighbourhood, to the east of Gaza. At least 15 Palestinians, including five civilians, were killed in the eight-hour incursion. The Israeli operation began as an undercover attempt to assassinate Sheikh Yassin.

More crucially, however, there were few signs that Israel was prepared to abandon its 'targeted killings' policy. On 25 December 2003 an Israeli helicopter gunship fired several missiles at a car travelling in the Sheikh Radwan neighbourhood of Gaza, killing five people. Among the victims was the head of Islamic Jihad's military wing. Israel also continued to demand that the PA dismantle the Palestinian 'terror organizations' and collect all illegal weapons; Sharon insisted on a 'total defeat' of the *intifada* as a *sine qua non* for the resumption of peace talks with the Palestinians. In late November 2003 PLC Speaker Rafiq al-Natsheh ruled out the possibility of any real breakthrough with Israel as long as Sharon stayed in power and the USA remained 'at Israel's beck and call'. Al-Natsheh, who stated that the PA was still committed to 'true peace and reconciliation' with Israel, dismissed Israel's purported willingness to reach a cease-fire with the Palestinians as 'tactical in nature and motivated by public relations considerations'. Hamas, on the other hand, realizing that a new truce with Israel was unrealistic, continued to advocate armed resistance.

THE RIGHT OF RETURN AND PALESTINIAN OPPOSITION TO THE GENEVA ACCORDS

On 1 December 2003 a group of Palestinian politicians and Israeli opposition figures signed and launched the 'Geneva Accords' (named after the Swiss city in which they were signed). The document, which had been concluded two months earlier by Palestinian and Israeli political figures such as Yasser Abd al-Rabbuh and Yossi Beilin, laid out a plan for a peace agreement between Israel and the Palestinians. The PA did not officially adopt the Geneva Accords, but the 50-member Palestinian delegation, which signed the document in their personal capacity, were closely associated with the PA and President Arafat. As the new initiative was being launched, thousands of Palestinians took to the streets in the Palestinian territories to protest against and condemn the 'treacherous document'. In the Gaza Strip, home to more than 800,000 refugees, thousands of angry Palestinians called Palestinian signatories to the document 'traitors' and accused them of 'striving to please the Americans and the Zionists at our people's expense'. Palestinian opposition and Islamist leaders were particularly angered by the renunciation of the right of return. In Gaza City itself, hundreds of political leaders representing major Palestinian political strata, including key PLO figures, denounced the Geneva Accords and urged Arafat to reject them outright.

Palestinian opposition to the Geneva declaration centred on the following: first, the perception that the document nullified the right of return, both as a collective national right and as an individual right, of Palestinians to their homeland; second, the perception that the document provided a Palestinian cover for the exclusive nature of the Israeli polity as a 'Jewish State', thus failing to recognize the rights of the 1.2m. Arab citizens of Israel to live in a democratic state for all its citizens; third, that it accepted the reconfiguration of Jerusalem based on Israeli annexation plans, and that it granted Palestinian legitimacy to Israeli 'colonial' processes that altered the Arab character of Jerusalem; fourth, that it permanently accepted the presence of the vast majority of Israeli settlements in the West Bank; fifth, that it provided a Palestinian endorsement of a truncated and demilitarized Palestinian entity devoid of real sovereignty; and finally, that it left open all Israeli claims to the West Bank's water resources and airspace.

Faced with strong public opposition to the Geneva Accords, Arafat found himself in an unenviable position for, while it was reported that he had encouraged the Palestinian signatories, he was reluctant to speak out openly in support of the document. Arafat reportedly called it 'a brave initiative that would push the peace process forward', but refused to adopt it officially. Earlier, on 22 November 2003, Arafat loyalist Rafiq al-Natsheh denied that the PA had endorsed the document. Al-Natsheh stated that any final peace agreement with Israel would have to be approved by the Palestinian people both at home and abroad through a referendum. Nevertheless, there was a general unanimity within Palestinian political circles that PA official Abd al-Rabbuh would not have dared sign the document had he not received a definite 'green light' from Arafat. The latter's public hesitation was the outcome of the overwhelming opposition among Palestinians to the agreement, especially those parts tacitly conceding the right of return. Arafat knew well that he would lose stature, even legitimacy, if he confronted the Palestinian masses with the abandonment of the principle of the right of return. Another reason explaining Arafat's equivocation was Sharon's 'total rejection' of the Accords on 1 December 2003, describing them as 'amounting to suicide' for the Jewish state.

PALESTINIAN REACTIONS TO SHARON'S GAZA PLAN AND UNILATERAL DESIGNS

In his 'Herzliya speech' on 18 December 2003, Prime Minister Sharon presented the plan that Israel officially dubbed as 'disengagement from the Palestinians'. He vowed to take far-reaching unilateral measures against the Palestinians if they did not meet Israeli conditions for 'peace' within the next six or nine months. He stated that Israel would tighten its already firm grip on the Palestinian population centres in the West Bank, complete the construction of the 'separation barrier' (or 'security fence') and eventually redeploy the Israeli army to new lines, all for the purpose of 'disengaging from the Palestinians'. Sharon's 'disengagement plan' also envisaged the 'evacuation of all Jewish settlers' from the Gaza Strip, of which there were some 7,000 in more than 70 settlements. The Israeli Ministry of the Interior, however, reported on 30 December a 16% increase in the number of West Bank and Gaza settlers since Sharon came to power.

Sharon's 'unilateral' designs inevitably elicited strong Palestinian reactions. The PA leadership declared that a more appropriate name for Sharon's plan should be 'suffocating the Palestinians', since the plan would encircle Palestinian population centres in the West Bank with the security fence and Israeli military watchtowers, checkpoints and roadblocks. Inevitably, Palestinian leaders and media strongly condemned the plan, calling it 'another Israeli ploy to steal more Palestinian land'. They thought that if Sharon's designs were implemented, at least 58% of the West Bank area would effectively become part of Israel: the State of Israel would be in control of 90% of historic Palestine (the land between the Mediterranean Sea and the river Jordan). The disjointed remaining 10% of historic Palestine would be left to the Palestinians, who would be enclosed in a series of isolated enclaves behind a security barrier.

Although PA premier Quray denounced Sharon's expansionist designs, at the same time, Palestinians expressed serious doubts about Sharon's actual willingness to carry out his plan, which required the 'relocation' of some 'small and isolated settlements'. Furthermore, so they claimed, the implementation of Sharon's designs, with all the accompanying upheaval of Palestinians' daily life, would undoubtedly precipitate fresh waves of violence, not only in Israel and the Palestinian enclaves but in the region as a whole. In effect, Palestinians viewed the Gaza disengagement plan as a bargaining chip to persuade the USA to agree to further construction in major settlement blocs in the West Bank.

ISRAELI ASSASSINATIONS OF HAMAS LEADERS YASSIN AND AL-RANTISI

On 22 March 2004 Sheikh Ahmad Yassin, the founder and spiritual leader of Hamas, was killed by Israeli forces in the Gaza Strip by rockets fired from an Israeli helicopter as he was leaving a mosque in Gaza City. Sheikh Yassin was the most prominent Palestinian leader to be killed since the outbreak of the al-Aqsa *intifada*. According to the Israeli daily *Ha'aretz*, the Israeli Security Cabinet took the decision to target Yassin following a double suicide bombing at the Ashdod port earlier in March, in which at least 10 Israelis were killed. Sharon, who personally oversaw the operation, brushed aside international condemnation and vowed to continue the war against Hamas.

As Hamas and other Palestinian resistance groups warned of an immediate upsurge in violence in the Middle East, an estimated 200,000 mourners poured onto the streets of Gaza for Yassin's funeral procession. Political leaders across the Arab world and beyond lined up to condemn Israel's action. Palestinian Prime Minister Quray considered it 'one of the biggest crimes that the Israeli Government has committed', while Arafat described the assassination as a 'barbaric' crime. Hamas itself responded by threatening, for the first time, revenge on the USA as well as Israel, claiming that US backing of Israel had made Yassin's assassination possible. The USA, however, denied any prior knowledge of the operation.

After the assassination of Yassin, his successor as leader of Hamas in the Gaza Strip, Dr Abd al-Aziz al-Rantisi, became a principal Israeli target. On 18 April 2004 al-Rantisi, his son and a bodyguard were also killed in an Israeli helicopter missile attack.

Meanwhile, on 29 January 2004 Israel released 400 Palestinian prisoners into the West Bank and Gaza Strip as part of a German-mediated prisoner swap agreement reached earlier in the week with Hezbollah. However, there were reportedly still as many as 7,500 Palestinian prisoners in Israeli gaols and detention centres, a large number of whom were interned without charge or trial. Many of the prisoners released were in fact college students from the Hebron region imprisoned for their affiliation with Islamist student blocs in local colleges.

THE TRIAL OF MARWAN BARGHOUTHI

On 20 May 2004 a Tel-Aviv court convicted imprisoned Fatah leader Marwan Barghouthi on five counts of murder and of commanding a 'terrorist organization', relating to Palestinian militant attacks on Israeli forces and settlers. Barghouthi, who was viewed by many Palestinians as a potential successor to Arafat, had always rejected Israel's right to try him, arguing that Israel was an occupying power and that the Palestinians were victims of a military occupation that dehumanized them and denied them basic human rights. During a court hearing in the previous year Barghouthi reportedly told Israeli prosecutors that resistance was not 'terror' but rather a personal, human and national duty upon the oppressed. The PA strongly denounced the conviction of Barghouthi, calling it 'illegal, immoral and unjust'. According to the Palestinian Human Rights Monitoring Group, from the outset of the al-Aqsa *intifada* to 5 February 2004, 2,826 Palestinians and 952 Israelis had been killed.

DEMOLITION OF PALESTINIAN HOUSES IN RAFAH, MAY–JUNE 2004

In late 2003 and early 2004 the Rafah area, a small strip of land at the southern edge of the Gaza Strip, remained a major point of Israeli–Palestinian confrontation. On 23 December 2003, just hours after two Israeli soldiers were killed by Islamic Jihad fighters outside a Jewish settlement in southern Gaza, Israeli forces attacked the Rafah refugee camp, killing 10 Palestinians. Rafah also became the target of a major military assault by the Israeli army during 17–20 May 2004, in which 43 Palestinians were killed, mostly civilians (among them nine children). On 19 May an Israeli helicopter gunship fired at a peaceful demonstration against Israel's campaign in Rafah, resulting in the deaths of some two dozen people. Israel declared that its operation in Rafah was in response to the killing of 13 of its troops at the hands of Palestinian militants, who had earlier deployed landmines against Israeli soldiers.

Following the escalation of the Rafah clashes, and the intensification of Israel's policy of demolishing houses along the Gaza–Sinai border, Egyptian intelligence chief Omar Suleiman returned on 25 May 2004 to hold extensive talks with Palestinian and Israeli leaders for the purpose of reactivating the cease-fire plan. His talks came as Israeli tanks were withdrawing from Rafah, ending a 10-day operation and home demolitions, in which dozens of Palestinian civilians were killed and hundreds of homes were destroyed. According to Israeli sources, Suleiman informed Israeli leaders of Egypt's willingness to play a more active role along the Rafah–Sinai borders in the event of an Israeli military withdrawal from Gaza. Suleiman also told Israeli leaders that if Israel carried out an 'honest and complete withdrawal from Gaza', Egypt would make serious efforts to maintain security on the borders and prevent the smuggling of weapons from Sinai to the Gaza Strip, a message that he later relayed to the Palestinian leadership. However, the Egyptian official made clear that his Government's commitments to that effect would be honoured only if Israel stopped all assassinations, incursions and attacks in Gaza.

Following the talks with Suleiman, the PA leadership restated its readiness to 'assume its responsibilities' in the Gaza Strip following the 'presumed' Israeli withdrawal. The PA also undertook to present a workable plan for the Gaza Strip, which would include the unification of Palestinian security agencies, as well as a readiness to prevent security violations. Suleiman reportedly proposed the formation of a committee, comprising the USA, Israel, Egypt and the PA, to oversee the implementation of the Gaza withdrawal plan. However, PA officials dismissed Sharon's purported willingness to negotiate with the PA as a 'public relations' exercise. The Israeli army was reportedly opposed to a staged withdrawal from Gaza, on the grounds that such an arrangement would invite attacks from Palestinian resistance fighters.

THE INTERNATIONAL COURT OF JUSTICE'S RULING ON THE 'SEPARATION BARRIER'

In December 2003 the UN General Assembly approved a resolution asking the International Court of Justice (ICJ) in The Hague, Netherlands, to consider the legality of the controversial 'separation barrier' that Israel was building inside the West Bank in an attempt to prevent Palestinian militants from infiltrating Israeli territory. (In October the UN General Assembly had adopted a resolution demanding that Israel halt construction of the barrier.) The Palestinians argued that the barrier, which cut into West Bank territory, was designed to redraw borders ahead of any future peace settlement. On 23 February 2004 the ICJ, which has the power to issue legal opinions but does not have any power to impose rulings or sanctions, began examining the barrier issue. On the same day thousands of Palestinians and international peace activists took to the streets throughout the West Bank and Gaza Strip to protest against its construction. Palestinian representatives argued that Israel's barrier made the creation of a viable Palestinian state impossible.

On 9 July 2004 the ICJ gave its long-awaited advisory opinion, ruling that Israel's separation barrier in the West Bank contravened international law; that it must be dismantled; and that compensation must be paid by Israel to the Palestinian owners of property confiscated for its construction. The ICJ found that the construction of the first 200 km of the planned 700-km barrier was causing widespread confiscation and destruction of Palestinian property, and the disruption of the lives of thousands of civilians. The ICJ decision branded Israel's vast concrete and steel barrier through the West Bank a political rather than a security measure. The court concluded that the barrier severely impeded the Palestinian right to self-determination, in breach of the Geneva Convention and international humanitarian law. It appealed to the UN to consider measures against Israel and stated that signatories to the Geneva Convention, such as the United Kingdom and the USA, were obliged to ensure that Israel upheld the ruling.

The Palestinian leadership hailed the ruling as a landmark judgment that could mobilize international opinion. Israel rejected the ruling, but on 20 July 2004 the UN General Assembly voted to demand that Israel comply with the ICJ ruling and remove the barrier. The United Kingdom backed the resolution, while the USA opposed it.

ONGOING CRISIS WITHIN FATAH

In February 2004 hundreds of low- and medium-ranking members resigned from Fatah in protest against the lack of political and organizational reform, corruption, and the leadership's enduring failure to challenge effectively the Israeli occupation. More than 350 activists signed the resignation letter delivered to President Arafat and Fatah's Central Committee. Fatah's constitution required leadership elections every five years, but none had been held since 1989 and many members were frustrated at what they saw as an entrenched leadership unwilling to surrender power. This chronic malaise created deep disenchantment among younger grass-roots members. Fatah was also plagued by its unclear and overlapping relationship with the PA, in which many Fatah leaders from the Central Committee and Revolutionary Council held key positions. Moreover, the uprising had greatly strained whatever semblance of ideological homogeneity Fatah had possessed. Some factions of the movement, particularly in the northern part of the West Bank, had effectively 'converted' to the Islamist camp, with many field guerrillas and activists joining, either formally or practically, Hamas and Islamic Jihad.

The internal Fatah crisis escalated in July 2004 amid rebellion in the Gaza Strip against PA corruption and incompetence, and a threat by Prime Minister Quray to bring down the administration if he were not given more powers. On 17 July, in a desperate attempt to stem growing anarchy in the Strip, Arafat dismissed two senior security commanders, Ghazi al-Jabali (national police chief) and Abd al-Razek al-Majajdeh (Commander of the General Security Services), declared a state of emergency, and sent loyal troops to protect government buildings. In a highly controversial move, the deeply unpopular Musa Arafat, the head of the Palestinian intelligence service and President Arafat's cousin, replaced al-Majajdeh. Furthermore, under Egyptian pressure, Arafat promised to amalgamate the overlapping groups of rival security forces in Gaza into a more coherent three-branched model. On 18 July Arafat rejected the 'resignation' of Quray, who stated that he was appalled at the chaos reigning in Gaza.

However, Fatah dissenters dismissed Arafat's 'reforms' as inadequate. They also criticized Quray for being part of the corrupt PA system. The al-Aqsa Martyrs Brigades directed their criticism against Musa Arafat, accusing him of personal corruption. On 18 July 2004 the head of the Gaza coastguard resigned in protest against the appointment of Musa Arafat, as did other security officials in Gaza; these resignations appeared to persuade the PA leader to change his mind, and on 20 July Quray agreed to stay in office as 'caretaker' Prime Minister. (Musa Arafat eventually retired in April 2005, but was assassinated by Palestinian gunmen in September at his home in Gaza City.)

REFRAMING GAZA

On 29 September 2004 the Israeli military launched 'Operation Days of Penitence', the most extensive incursion into the Gaza Strip since the beginning of the al-Aqsa *intifada* and the largest Israeli offensive within the Occupied Territories since the 2002 reoccupation of the West Bank. The backdrop for the incursion was Sharon's Gaza redeployment plan and the need to prevent Palestinian fighters from using northern Gaza as a launching pad for rocket attacks on Israeli border towns. Sharon rejected the concept of a Palestinian negotiating partner due to the territorial concessions that any negotiated agreement would entail. The Gaza redeployment plan became popular in Israel partly because the Labour Party had failed to conclude a viable agreement with the Palestinians under the framework of the Oslo Accords. The resulting four years of violent conflict saw a growing majority of the Israeli public prepared once again to consider 'unilateral disengagement'. In December 2004 the Labour Party, led by Shimon Peres, joined Likud in a unity Government committed to the Gaza redeployment plan.

From an Israeli point of view, the redeployment plan had the advantage of not relinquishing physical control of the Gaza Strip, while freezing any discussion on the peace process, the creation of a Palestinian state, refugees and borders. Although Sharon was determined to act unilaterally, his Government sought Palestinian partners in Gaza to implement the plan. Rather than seeking to scuttle Sharon's plan, former Gaza security chief Muhammad Dahlan, and his erstwhile patron Mahmud Abbas (who had succeeded Yasser Arafat in November 2004 as leader of the politically dominant Fatah movement), believed that redeployment could establish the basis for renewed international engagement leading to an Israeli-Palestinian settlement. Dahlan held that the ability of Fatah to ensure stability in the Gaza Strip in the wake of an eventual Israeli redeployment would both place it at the helm of the political system and mark it out as a 'reliable partner' for Israel and the international community. Dahlan's faction of Fatah contended for influence in the Gaza Strip with a rival grouping encompassing Hamas and a broad array of Islamist and nationalist militants. In contrast with Dahlan's faction, the radical trend saw Israeli redeployment, through the prism of Hezbollah's success in Lebanon, as vindication of the strategy of armed struggle to force Israel to withdraw under fire. Hamas's tactics had included bold attacks on Israeli positions and the launching of home-made missiles into Israel. Dahlan's strategy, on the other hand, was predicated on his ability to neutralize the radical Islamists and promote a Palestinian cease-fire. His other urgent priority had been to establish control over the Palestinian security forces and Fatah itself in Gaza.

ARAFAT'S DEATH

In mid-October 2004, after enduring prolonged ill health at his Ramallah headquarters (the *muqata'a*), Yasser Arafat fell seriously ill. On 25 October the Israeli Government granted Arafat permission to leave the *muqata'a* to visit a Ramallah hospital, but on 29 October he was flown with his wife to a military hospital in Paris, still conscious but unable to walk. The precise nature of his illness remained a mystery. Arafat's condition continued to deteriorate; according to hospital sources, the Palestinian leader had fallen into a deep, irreversible coma and was brain-dead.

Arafat's failing health left Palestinians in a state of political crisis. In Ramallah Palestinian security chiefs held an emergency meeting at the *muqata'a* to discuss how to handle the likely event of Arafat's imminent death. The PLO leadership in the West Bank agreed to cede more of Arafat's powers to Prime Minister Ahmad Quray. Quray and his Minister of Foreign Affairs, Dr Nabil Shaath, travelled to the Gaza Strip to press Palestinian factions there to avoid internal conflict during the crisis. After meeting representatives of all 13 Palestinian factions, including Hamas and Islamic Jihad, in Gaza City on 6–7 November 2004, Quray announced that agreement had been reached to avoid in-fighting. In the mean time, in Ramallah, former premier Mahmud Abbas was swiftly named by the Fatah Revolutionary Council as the new head of the PLO, while PLC Speaker Rawhi Fattouh was sworn in as caretaker President of the PA.

On 10 November 2004 Palestinian officials announced that Arafat was close to death after having suffered a brain haemorrhage. His death was announced on 11 November. Palestinians gave credence to rumours of poisoning by Mossad; however, this theory was ruled out following a PA investigation in 2005. Although the French authorities also initially ruled out this theory, they failed adequately to explain Arafat's illness and subsequent death. After the reported emergence of new evidence, which led his widow to initiate legal proceedings in France in July 2012, it was announced in late August that French prosecutors were to launch a murder inquiry into whether the former Palestinian leader had in fact died as a result of radioactive poisoning.

Arafat had previously stated that he wished to be interred at the Haram al-Sharif inside Jerusalem's Old City. However, Israel ruled this out and attempted to force a burial in the Gaza Strip, saying that it was making preparations for Arab leaders and foreign dignitaries to travel there without passing through Israel. However, Saeb Erakat of the PA announced that the burial would take place at the wrecked *muqata'a*, 'the symbol of the steadfastness of the Palestinian people, the President's place of siege'. On 12 November 2004, after a short funeral in Cairo attended by Arab leaders and world dignitaries, Arafat's body was buried in Ramallah. Some of the tens of thousands of Palestinians in attendance wore the black masks of Hamas or the al-Aqsa Martyrs Brigades, and carried guns or swords.

PRESIDENTIAL ELECTION

A presidential election was scheduled for 9 January 2005. Although the new head of the PLO, 69-year-old Mahmud Abbas, was favoured by Fatah's Central Committee, the family and political associates of the much younger Marwan Barghouthi declared that he was interested in contesting the presidency. The incarcerated Barghouthi had strong appeal on the Palestinian street as the former head of Fatah's Tanzim in the West Bank. He also had widespread support as one of a younger generation of leaders committed to political reform and had been at the forefront of the al-Aqsa *intifada*. In early December 2004 Barghouthi reversed his initial decision not to challenge Abbas, and unexpectedly threw open the Palestinian ballot by registering as an independent candidate just hours before the deadline. Barghouthi's break with Fatah, however, drew stiff criticism from allies and other Fatah reformers who argued that dividing the movement played into Israel's hands. Opinion polls in November and early December showed no clear favourite in the contest between Abbas and Barghouthi as the principal contenders out of some 10 candidates. On 12 December Barghouthi, under intense pressure, dropped out of the race. In an open letter from gaol, he remained critical of the Fatah leadership for apparently abandoning armed resistance, but indicated that he would support Abbas.

Mahmud Abbas won by a clear majority in the 9 January 2005 presidential election, which was restricted to Palestinians inside the West Bank and Gaza Strip; final results gave Abbas 62.5% of the vote, and his nearest rival, Mustafa Barghouthi, 19.5%. The Central Elections Commission (CEC) reported that 45.6% of the 1.8m. Palestinians who were eligible to vote had participated. The EU observer team asserted that the election represented 'a genuine effort to conduct a regular electoral process. However, the [Israeli] occupation and continuing violence, as well as restrictions on freedom of movement, meant that a truly free election was always going to be difficult to achieve.' UN Secretary-General Kofi Annan welcomed the news as 'a significant step in what is a historic democratic transition'. Hamas, which had boycotted the poll, declared that it would work with Abbas but complained of electoral irregularities.

Abbas was sworn in as PA President on 15 January 2005. He stated that he was extending the hand of peace to Israel and that he denounced violence. However, prior to the inauguration ceremony, Israel had severed ties with Abbas in response to an attack by Palestinian fighters on a Gaza cargo crossing in which six Israeli workers were killed, announcing that it would only renew contacts with him once he reined in the militants. In his first speech to the PLC as President in Ramallah, Abbas emphasized his commitment to democratic reforms and national unity. He identified his priorities as: national liberation; ending Israeli occupation and establishing a Palestinian state within the 1967 borders, with Jerusalem as its capital; and reaching a 'just and agreed solution to the refugee problem on the basis of international resolutions', including UN Resolution 194 of December 1948 and the resolution approved at the March 2002 Arab summit in Beirut, Lebanon. He also stressed his commitment to the roadmap as a 'matter of Palestinian national interest'. In return, he expected Israel to implement its obligations.

On 8 February 2005 Abbas met Israeli Prime Minister Sharon in the Red Sea resort of Sharm el-Sheikh, at a summit hosted by Egyptian President Hosni Mubarak. It was the Palestinian leader's first meeting with Sharon since succeeding Arafat. Abbas and Sharon agreed a cease-fire and pledged to 'end violence' after more than four years of confrontation. As part of the Sharm el-Sheikh deal, Israel agreed to hand over control of five West Bank towns to the PA within three weeks and to release 500 Palestinian political prisoners. The two sides also agreed to set up a number of joint committees, and their leaders reiterated that future negotiations would be conducted under the aegis of the roadmap. Hamas reacted to the summit by saying that, although it was not bound by the cease-fire declaration, it had no intention of being the first to break it.

NEW PALESTINIAN CABINET

On 23 February 2005 the PLC approved a new line-up of ministers proposed by Abbas, in a Cabinet in which 'technocrats' replaced several Arafat loyalists. The vote was a key test for Abbas. Initially, Prime Minister Ahmad Quray had proposed to the PLC a cabinet consisting largely of the ministers who had been in office under Arafat, but the PLC had rejected this. Fatah's Central Committee was forced to produce new candidates, to the delight of PA reformists. The new Cabinet, again headed by Quray, committed itself to reform. The most important new ministers were: Dr Nasser al-Kidwa, Arafat's nephew and for many years Palestinian Permanent Observer to the UN, who became Minister of Foreign Affairs; Muhammad Dahlan, Minister of Civil Affairs, whose job entailed dealing with Israel; and Maj.-Gen. Nasser Yousuf, Minister of the Interior and National Security. Yousuf's main role would be to reorganize the security forces and 'maintain the cease-fire'. Yousuf had been responsible for a crackdown on Hamas in 1997 following a spate of suicide bombs in Israel. Dr Nabil Shaath, the former Minister of Foreign Affairs, was appointed Deputy Prime Minister.

MUNICIPAL ELECTIONS: HAMAS'S ELECTORAL BREAKTHROUGH

Following Arafat's death, a series of elections was held: local elections in the West Bank (December 2004); the presidential poll (January 2005); local elections in Gaza and the remainder of the West Bank (May 2005); and finally legislative elections (January 2006). In conjunction with the unilateral Israeli withdrawal from Gaza in September 2005, these polls would do much to shape PA politics in the post-Arafat era.

The first municipal elections were held on 23 December 2004. The polls were well organized, and the diversity of parties and candidates gave voters a genuine choice. Palestinians in 26 West Bank towns and villages cast their votes, and according to the Minister of Local Government, Dr Khaled al-Qawasmi, 81% of the 144,000 eligible voters turned out to vote. Strong popular participation was thought to reflect the fact that candidates were drawn from local communities and hence were more accessible to voters. It was announced that Fatah had taken 136 seats (out of 306 council seats), representing 44.4% of the vote, closely followed by Hamas, with a total of 109 seats (35.6%). Independent candidates won 40 of the remaining seats, and 21 were split between representatives of local tribes and left-wing groups. Of the 887 local council candidates, one in six were women, all of whom won seats, partly due to a clause in the Palestinian electoral laws that stipulates that women candidates must constitute at least 16% of elected representatives.

Following the presidential election, held on 9 January 2005, polls were conducted on 5 May to elect municipal council representatives in both the West Bank and Gaza. There had been no municipal elections in Gaza since the end of the British Mandate in 1948; in recent years all the previous Gaza town officials had been Fatah appointees. Municipal elections had last been held in the West Bank in 1976. Some 3,000 Palestinian security officers ensured public order at the polling stations. Israel had informed the CEC that its army would not enter any of the areas where elections were scheduled to be held from 18.00 hours on the evening of 4 May until 06.00 hours on 6 May 2005. Nevertheless, voting in several localities in the northern part of the West Bank was disrupted by Israeli army incursions. One serious violation also occurred when a group of some 20 masked men stormed two polling stations in the West Bank village of Attarah and destroyed three ballot boxes as votes were being tallied. The CEC reported that 2,519 candidates (including 399 women) competed for 906 seats at 84 municipal councils in the two territories. There were 784 polling stations, 534 of which were in the West Bank and 250 in the Gaza Strip. More than 400,000 civilians were registered as eligible voters and 141 lists of candidates were presented. In practice, the voter registration lists were complemented by the civil registration lists, which meant that the actual figure of voters was much higher. Although officially Fatah won a majority of the seats (56%), Hamas took at least 33% and the PFLP received a large share of the remaining seats, with some seats going to independent candidates and left-wing factions. This meant that 45 out of 84 municipal councils had a majority of Fatah representatives, 23 had a majority of Hamas representatives and 16 had a majority from left and independent lists. However, Hamas's leader in Gaza, Dr Mahmud al-Zahhar, subsequently disputed the official results. According to him, Hamas had actually won 34 municipalities, including 11 municipalities that were officially categorized as independent candidates but were in practice Hamas affiliates. Apparently, these candidates had concealed their true identities as they feared persecution and arrest by Israel.

Hamas's full participation in the local elections and its declared intention to take part in the PLC elections appeared to represent a major victory for the democratic process in the

Palestinian territories. Moreover, Hamas and other militant groups had earlier committed themselves to a de facto cease-fire, in order to allow Abbas some negotiating power. If Hamas could translate its street popularity and municipal success into an effective political campaign, then institutional power would be within its reach. For Fatah, the local elections sent a clear signal that it could not afford to isolate itself from the electorate or take power for granted. The municipal elections also suggested that, despite the disproportionate international media attention given to the presidential election, the democratic priorities of the Palestinian people in the West Bank and Gaza centred on the local level. The impressive voter turn-out further suggested that legitimization of political power could be found at the grass-roots level of Palestinian civil society; however, the challenge remained to translate local democracy into national institutions such as the PLC and PA ministries.

PARLIAMENTARY ELECTIONS AND HAMAS'S LEGISLATIVE MAJORITY

In early May 2005 the CEC signalled its intention to postpone the parliamentary elections, scheduled for 17 July, for several months, ostensibly to allow time for further preparations. It was not entirely clear whether Abbas himself had originally sought the postponement. 'Democratic elections' were the cornerstone of the agreements he had signed with all the political factions in Cairo in March and a condition for the cease-fire. None the less, he appeared swayed by the advice given by the USA, the EU and Egypt: to defer all elections so that the PA could consolidate its rule in Gaza and 'win back' the popular support that was now flowing to Hamas. Fatah's electoral standing had been seriously damaged by a long history of corruption and inefficiency, especially during its exclusive control of the PA throughout its 11-year existence. Abbas issued a presidential decree on 3 June confirming the postponement, until further notice. The delay allowed Fatah to capitalize on Israel's withdrawal from the Gaza Strip, scheduled to take effect in mid-August.

The Palestinian public was largely hostile to the postponement, and the move increased the already heightened tensions between Fatah and Hamas as a result of the dispute over local election results. The situation degenerated into the worst period of fighting in the Occupied Territories since the Palestinian factions had committed themselves to a cease-fire in March 2005. This further undermined the Abbas regime's legitimacy, which had already been damaged by the apparent lack of diplomatic progress with Israel and the perceived inadequacy of the reform of the security forces and other PA institutions. In early June officers from PA Military Intelligence attacked the PLC building in Gaza City, closed roads in Rafah and briefly abducted a PA diplomat en route to Egypt. The officers feared that proposed reforms would deprive them of some of their privileges and autonomy. Meanwhile, on 5 June militiamen from Fatah's al-Aqsa Martyrs Brigades laid siege to the governor's house in Nablus in protest against the PA's failure to provide the Brigades with protection and salaries commensurate with their status as the 'armed resistance'. The Ministry of the Interior pacified the two revolts by effectively yielding to their demands. These challenges to law and order were exacerbated by other developments. Despite a court decision annulling election results in three Gaza municipalities where Hamas had won majorities, Hamas officials had taken up PA offices, creating a situation of de facto dual power. New elections were postponed indefinitely in order to defuse the tension.

The legislative elections were subsequently rescheduled for 25 January 2006. Hamas had earlier stated that, in return for acquiescing to the postponement of the poll, Abbas had promised an amendment to the election laws that could favour the Islamist movement. Hamas had wanted one-half of the legislators to be chosen on the basis of district constituencies and the other half on the basis of party lists. Apparently, Abbas had agreed to such a system in early 2005 when he brokered an informal Hamas cease-fire with Israel, but had subsequently stated that he would prefer all legislators to be chosen from party lists. Meanwhile, Palestinians in the Gaza Strip held large celebrations to mark the completion of the Israeli military's withdrawal from the territory on 12 September 2005.

Sixteen constituencies in the West Bank and Gaza Strip were scheduled to elect 132 deputies to the PLC. Under the new system, one-half of the 132 seats would be chosen by proportional representation, with the rest contested by individual candidates in a 'first-past-the-post' system. The Palestinian Elections Law stipulated that at least one woman should be among the first three names on any party list, at least one woman among the next four names, and at least one woman among each five names after that. Six seats were guaranteed to Palestinian Christian candidates. Palestinian residents in the West Bank, Gaza Strip and East Jerusalem were allowed to vote, and there were about 1.34m. eligible voters. The 100,000 eligible voters living in occupied East Jerusalem had their own special arrangements. Initially, Israel had threatened to ban voting there, but, after international pressure, it decided to allow Palestinian residents to vote through an 'absentee ballot' at five city post offices, as had happened in 1996. In reality, however, only 6,300 residents were allowed to vote in this way; the remainder had to travel outside the (Israeli-defined) city boundaries. Israel also refused to allow Hamas to campaign in Jerusalem.

Hamas ran an effective campaign centred on government corruption, under the title of the Change and Reform list, in order to avoid a ban on its direct participation. Hamas's manifesto combined an established social welfare programme and generally pragmatic Islamic principles with a 'pro-resistance' stance towards Israel. Conspicuous in its exclusion from the manifesto was Hamas's commitment, enshrined in its charter, to destroy Israel through *jihad* and replace it with an Islamic state; however, the manifesto did pledge to use any means necessary to defend the Palestinian nation and establish a state with Jerusalem as its capital.

Hamas won a majority in the new PLC, securing 74 of the 132 parliamentary seats and earning the right to form the next administration under President Abbas. Fatah, a dominant force in Palestinian politics since the late 1960s, suffered a historic defeat, emerging with 45 seats. The strategic failure of the Oslo process and a record of poor governance through the PA contributed to the defeat. Internal divisions also played a role, as a younger and more radical grouping (the 'new guard'), led by the gaoled Marwan Barghouthi, had registered its own list of candidates for the elections, although the group had agreed to rejoin a unified list shortly before the deadline for registration. A collection of nationalist, leftist and independent parties claimed the remainder of the seats.

Hamas's spectacular victory stunned the Israelis, their US allies and the EU. All three reacted by repeatedly stating that they would not work with or fund a PA that included Hamas, which they classified as a terrorist organization. Meeting on 30 January 2006, the Quartet group announced that financial assistance to a future Palestinian administration would depend on the extent to which Hamas as a partner fulfilled the following conditions: that it renounce violence; respect agreements approved under the Fatah regime; and recognize Israel's right to exist. Hamas rejected the conditions, asserting that the Quartet group should have demanded an end to Israeli 'occupation and aggression' and arguing that the Oslo process had not benefited the Palestinians. Following the inauguration of the new Cabinet, headed by Ismail Haniya, on 28 March, the USA and the EU declared the withdrawal of all direct aid to the PA until Hamas complied with the terms. Sanctions and a funding boycott resulted in Palestinian public revenues declining by 40%–50%.

Fatah adjusted poorly to forfeiting its dominant position in both the PLC and the PA. The Palestinian electorate's switch of support to Hamas was widely interpreted as a form of popular protest against Fatah's endemic corruption and authoritarianism. Competition for jobs and access to limited resources intensified after the elections, with occasional violent clashes between the armed militias and security forces. Fatah resisted attempts by Hamas to tempt it into an administration of national unity. Instead, Abbas tried to maintain his role determining Palestinian national policy and controlling the PA security services, although he still needed PLC approval for his budget and legislative proposals. Hamas's victory undermined Abbas's efforts to seek negotiations with Israel, with Hamas repeatedly refusing to recognize Israel and renounce violence. Abbas also publicly quarrelled with Hamas's Minister of the Interior over control of the security forces in Gaza.

Neighbouring Jordan backed international efforts to isolate and undermine the Hamas administration. In April 2006 the Jordanian authorities accused Hamas of stockpiling arms on Jordanian territory—allegations that Hamas officials denied—and cancelled a visit by the Palestinian Minister of Foreign Affairs, Dr Mahmud al-Zahhar, to Amman. In July the Jordanian Arab Bank turned back remittances intended for PLC members, saying that it was not prepared to deal with PLC members affiliated with Hamas.

THE 'PRISONERS' DOCUMENT'

On 27 June 2006 representatives of Fatah and Hamas agreed to a joint political platform, which contained implicit recognition of Israel's existence. The representatives approved a document drawn up in early May by a number of Palestinian political prisoners in Israeli gaols, led by Marwan Barghouthi and fellow prisoner Sheikh Abd al-Khaleq Natshe of Hamas. Setting out 18 points for a return to negotiations with Israel, the document demanded the creation of a Palestinian state, with Jerusalem as the capital, on all land occupied by Israel in 1967. It did not explicitly recognize Israel's right to the territories that it controlled prior to the 1967 war. Moreover, it did not renounce violence, as demanded by the Quartet group, but advocated that 'resistance' be limited to the Occupied Territories under a 'unified resistance front'. It also appealed for the formation of a national unity administration in which the major parliamentary blocs, especially Hamas and Fatah, but also other parties that supported the document's principles, would be represented. Israel was to recognize the Palestinian 'right of return' and release all Palestinian prisoners and detainees.

President Abbas seized on the prisoners' document and issued an ultimatum to Hamas to announce its recognition of Israel within 10 days or face a referendum on the matter. Hamas's senior leadership initially discounted the document as an untenable compromise on its own position regarding Israel, but came under intense Palestinian pressure to accept it, reinforced by the crippling economic sanctions imposed by foreign donors. Although Hamas had not been directly blamed for the economic hardships faced by Palestinians—for which the policies of Israel, the USA and the EU had been responsible—an opinion poll carried out by Birzeit University in late May showed that popular support for Hamas had declined from over 50% at the end of 2005 to 37%. A similar poll carried out in June revealed that 77% of Palestinians supported the prisoners' document. In late June Hamas endorsed the document and agreed in principle to a power-sharing administration with Fatah, committed to a negotiated two-state settlement and negotiations with Israel on the basis of an independent Palestinian state on territories occupied in 1967. Nevertheless, Hamas emphasized that its acceptance of the document did not constitute explicit recognition of Israel, while the group's military wing and its political leaders in exile continued to oppose the agreement, an opposition likely to complicate any attempt to implement it.

THE KIDNAP OF CORPORAL GILAD SHALIT

The Israeli Government of Ehud Olmert, formed in May 2006, adopted the former Cabinet's policy of insisting that the Hamas-led Palestinian administration recognize Israel's right to exist before it would allow peace negotiations to be restarted, and continued to advocate plans to annex large parts of the West Bank and fix Israel's border unilaterally. The Gaza Strip remained under siege; Gazan targets were routinely attacked; and Palestinian fighters fired home-made *Qassam* missiles into Israel in response, mainly towards the town of Sderot. Tensions escalated in June after shelling killed a family of Palestinians picnicking on a beach in northern Gaza. On 25 June eight Hamas fighters from Gaza launched a daring raid into Israel: after a fierce gun battle that left two dead on either side, an Israeli corporal, Gilad Shalit, was kidnapped and taken to Gaza. The Palestinian fighters stated that the kidnapping had been carried out in a bid to secure an exchange of prisoners. Israel reacted by shelling bridges and a power plant in the Strip, and by reinvading southern and northern Gaza. 'Operation Summer Rain' was ostensibly ordered to free Shalit. Water and electricity were cut off to one-half of the Strip and all supplies of food halted.

On 29 June 2006 Israel arrested 64 senior Palestinian officials, including one-third of the Palestinian Cabinet (eight Hamas ministers) and 20 other parliamentarians. The Palestinian Deputy Prime Minister, Dr Nasser al-Shaer, went into hiding to avoid capture, and an Israeli minister hinted that even Prime Minister Ismail Haniya would not be exempt from arrest or possible assassination. The Israeli Government's undeclared objective appeared to be the ousting of the democratically elected administration of Hamas. The next day an Israeli missile destroyed the offices of the Palestinian Ministry of the Interior and Civil Affairs in Gaza City. On 2 July another strike destroyed Haniya's office. On 6 July Israeli forces and Palestinian fighters fought a fierce battle, with reports of at least 25 Palestinian deaths, mostly civilian. In the period between late June and 23 July Israeli troops killed more than 160 Palestinians, the majority of whom were women and children, and injured hundreds more. Israel arrested a further member of the Hamas regime, Speaker of the PLC Aziz Duweik, on 5 August.

THE MECCA AGREEMENT AND 'COALITION GOVERNMENT'

In December 2006 the continuing political deadlock between the PA-dominated presidency and the Hamas administration compelled Abbas to call for the holding of early presidential and parliamentary elections. However, he lacked the authority to enforce such a demand; early elections held with the dissent of Hamas and other factions would have been politically unsustainable. Consequently, on 21 January 2007 Abbas met the head of Hamas's political bureau, Khalid Meshaal, in Damascus to discuss the formation of a 'coalition government'. However, no agreement was reached. On 6 February the two men embarked on another attempt to form a 'unity government', at a meeting hosted by King Abdullah of Saudi Arabia in the holy city of Mecca. Two days of intensive negotiations produced an agreement. The symbolism of holding the talks at Islam's holiest site seemed to have some effect, with the promise of US $1,000m. in Saudi aid acting as a further incentive. In the Gaza Strip, people took to the streets to cheer the signing of the deal, which had ended months of violence between Fatah and Hamas. The 'national unity Government' was formed in March, headed by Ismail Haniya of Hamas. Hamas received nine posts, while Fatah was allotted six and other smaller parties four. Independents were given responsibility for key portfolios. Dr Salam Fayyad, a respected technocrat, became the Minister of Finance—a position he had held previously during 2002–05. An independent PLC deputy, Dr Ziad Abu Amr, became Minister of Foreign Affairs, while Hani al-Qawasmi, technically an independent, became Minister of the Interior. For the long-suffering Palestinians, the real value of a 'national unity Government' was the expectation that international aid would be resumed. However, the West had demanded much more: Hamas still had to recognize Israel, renounce violence and formally accept existing agreements with Israel. This partially explained the USA's muted response to the Mecca agreement.

HAMAS TAKES CONTROL OF GAZA

Throughout the first half of 2007 growing Israeli and Western pressures had disastrous consequences for internal Palestinian affairs. Israel and the USA seemed determined to undermine the Hamas-led 'coalition Government', and they facilitated a marked increase in the military capability of the Fatah-controlled Special Presidential Guard. Gaza witnessed renewed internecine violence between Hamas and Fatah, while the PA remained largely incapable of governing the Strip.

Lawlessness and the proliferation of armed groups in the Strip extended to the spread of militant *salafism*, influenced by the al-Qa'ida network. This was exemplified by the kidnapping at gunpoint in Gaza City of a reporter for the British Broadcasting Corporation, Alan Johnston, on 12 March 2007. The Army of Islam, a *salafi*-type group centred around the powerful Dughmush clan, was held responsible and was also suspected of being behind the kidnappings of other foreigners in Gaza. The clan's activities were described by PA officials as being largely criminal, involving extortion, smuggling and arms-dealing. On 9 May the group issued an audio tape demanding the release of Muslim preacher Abu Qatada, who was held in prison in the United Kingdom on suspicion of being a key al-Qa'ida figure in Europe. On 4 July, following the military takeover of the Gaza Strip by Hamas, the Army of Islam was forced, under threat of military action from Hamas, to release Johnston, after 114 days in captivity.

Despite the formation of the national unity administration in March 2007, the power struggle between Hamas and Fatah in Gaza continued and the spectre of an open civil war was much in evidence. Fighting in Gaza continued to escalate, and around 80 Palestinians were killed in factional clashes between mid-May and mid-July. The immediate cause of friction was the struggle for control of the security services, but the conflict was not totally detached from the abysmal social and economic conditions in Gaza, exacerbated by international sanctions. The Strip had around 1.5m. Palestinians—mostly refugees from what became Israel in 1948—living in one of the most crowded regions in the world, with most people struggling on less than US $2 a day.

On 5 June 2007 gunmen from Hamas and Fatah fought each other in the Strip, while President Abbas himself warned that the Palestinians were now on the brink of civil war. On 11 June at least 13 Palestinians were killed in factional fighting in Gaza, three of whom died in a gun battle inside a hospital. In Gaza City government offices were fired upon and the killings became increasingly brutal. Heavy gun battles erupted in several locations in the Gaza Strip on 12 June, as better organized and better disciplined Hamas fighters captured positions from Fatah supporters. Hamas militants launched a successful attack on the headquarters of the Fatah-controlled security forces in northern Gaza. Hamas issued an ultimatum to Fatah supporters to abandon their posts in the Strip, prompting President Abbas to accuse Hamas of attempting to stage a military coup. In the mean time, the head of the Egyptian mediation team in the Strip, Lt-Col Burhan Hamad, announced that neither side had responded to his appeal to hold truce talks.

The Gaza battles were won decisively by Hamas. By 13 June 2007 hundreds of Fatah fighters had surrendered to Hamas, which systematically took control of security positions in the north and south of Gaza, leaving the main battle for the Strip's security and political nerve centre, in Gaza City, until last. At the same time, however, across the West Bank hundreds of Fatah gunmen stormed Hamas-controlled institutions, seeking revenge for the Islamist movement's takeover of the Strip. Dozens of terrified Fatah officials and fighters tried to flee the Strip via Israel and Egypt. Abbas dismissed Prime Minister Haniya and dissolved his 'unity Government'. Haniya, in a bid to consolidate control over the Strip, sought to reorganize the previously Fatah-dominated National Security Forces; he appointed a new security chief, Maj.-Gen. Said Fanouna. Hamas also accused Muhammad Dahlan, formerly the Fatah 'strongman' in Gaza (who had been in Cairo for medical treatment during most of the fighting), of attempting a coup against the Hamas leadership.

FATAH RETRENCHMENT IN THE WEST BANK AND THE EMERGENCY GOVERNMENT OF SALAM FAYYAD

Fatah continued to exercise influence in Palestinian cities of the Israeli-occupied West Bank, even though the PA remained without any real power in the territory. Yet, with two separate Palestinian administrations, the separation between the West Bank and Gaza was widening and consequently endangering further the prospect of future Palestinian political unity. Abbas continued to reject pleas from the Arab League to meet with Hamas's exiled leader in Syria, Khalid Meshaal. He refused to conduct dialogue with Hamas until the Islamist movement withdrew its forces from former Fatah positions in Gaza. To the delight of Western donors, Abbas installed former Minister of Finance Salam Fayyad as the new Prime Minister in Ramallah. Fayyad had worked at the World Bank in Washington, DC, in 1987–95 and had then served as the IMF's representative to the Palestinian territories until 2001.

Abbas was backed by the USA, the EU and most Arab regimes, and, in a major boost for the Palestinian President, the US consul-general in Jerusalem, Jacob Walles, announced that the US Administration would end its 15 months of sanctions once the new Palestinian administration was in place. Fayyad moved quickly to form an 'emergency government'. On 17 June 2007 his administration was sworn in at the presidential compound in Ramallah; it comprised 12 ministers, most of them from the West Bank. Fayyad himself held three portfolios: Prime Minister, Minister of Finance, and briefly Minister of Foreign Affairs (Riyad al-Maliki assumed the foreign affairs portfolio in July). The administration included two Christians and two women. Fayyad announced that his main priority was restoring law and order. Earlier, Abbas had signed a decree granting himself, as President, the power to make decisions without PLC approval (Hamas still held an elected majority in the PLC). A second decree issued by Abbas outlawed the paramilitary force of Hamas and other 'militias' linked to the Islamist group. In reality, however, the ban could not be enforced.

On 18 June 2007 the USA and the EU rewarded Abbas's 'West Bank government' by lifting their economic and political boycott of the Palestinian administration. On 24 June Israel also agreed to release some of the US $350m. in blocked tax revenues to Fayyad's administration. Palestinian officials, however, insisted that Israel owed the PA as much as $700m. The Israeli move was announced on the eve of a summit in Sharm el-Sheikh between Israeli Prime Minister Ehud Olmert, President Abbas, President Hosni Mubarak of Egypt and King Abdullah of Jordan. The meeting was aimed at bolstering the 'West Bank government' of Fayyad, leaving Hamas isolated in Gaza. On 4 July, three days after Israel began transferring $117m. of withheld Palestinian taxes to the 'West Bank government', thousands of Palestinian civil servants began receiving their first full salaries for 16 months. An estimated 170,000 employees on the PA's books had received only partial pay packets since March 2006. However, the Fayyad administration refused to pay civil servants hired by Hamas in Gaza.

On 27 November 2007 the Annapolis International Conference was held at the US Naval Academy in Annapolis, Maryland, and was attended by 40 leaders, including Abbas, Israeli Prime Minister Olmert and US President George W. Bush. The conference aimed ostensibly to relaunch serious negotiations between Israel and the PA for the first time in seven years, but was devised partly to strengthen the standing of Abbas (for further details, see the essay on Arab–Israeli Relations). In the event, Annapolis ended inconclusively. The six core issues at the heart of the conflict (the 'final status' issues—Jerusalem, refugees and their right of return, borders, settlements, water, and security) remained unresolved, and Israel and the PA had only agreed to hold new talks, which were to begin on 12 December. The Israeli Government appeared unwilling to make concessions on any of the fundamental questions, and the USA did not seem prepared to exert serious pressure on the Israelis. The Israeli Government continued its construction of the 'separation barrier' that sliced through Palestinian territory on the West Bank, and continued to expand Israeli settlements there.

Nevertheless, Abbas's position was strengthened through other developments. On 1 October 2007, as part of its strategy to support the PA President in his power struggle with Hamas, Israel freed 57 Palestinian prisoners, most of whom belonged to Abbas's Fatah movement; none belonged to Hamas. To bolster further the administration in the West Bank, Israel cracked down on charitable organizations associated with Hamas. On 17 December Israeli troops arrested 24 Hamas activists in Nablus and other West Bank cities. Many of those arrested were politicians and intellectuals rather than fighters. Among those rounded up was Ahmad al-Hajj Ali, a member of the PLC.

His arrest brought to 46 the number of Palestinian parliamentarians held in Israeli gaols. These raids and arrests came hours after some 200,000 Hamas supporters rallied in Gaza to celebrate the 20th anniversary of the Islamist movement's foundation. Addressing the rally, deposed Hamas premier Ismail Haniya told demonstrators that Hamas would pursue anti-occupation resistance as the only way to 'liberate Palestine'. At the same time a Hamas spokesman in Gaza, Fawzi Barhoum, accused Abbas and Fayyad of collaboration with Israel in tracking down Hamas fighters and politicians in the West Bank.

ISRAELI BLOCKADE OF THE GAZA STRIP

Following Hamas's seizure of the Strip in June 2007, Israel tightened its blockade of coastal Gaza; supplies of food, fuel and aid were strictly limited. In addition, Israel continued a series of military incursions and air-strikes in response to the firing of rockets and mortars into Israel. Egypt also sealed its border with Gaza after June 2007, reopening the border only occasionally on humanitarian grounds. In January 2008, under pressure from UN agencies and international human rights organizations, Israel agreed to allow humanitarian food and medical supplies to enter Gaza at the rate of 50 lorries a day. Following a 10-day embargo, Israel also agreed to deliver about 500,000 litres of diesel oil and petrol a day for vehicles, industry and power stations. Yet, this action fell short of meeting international demands or warding off a humanitarian crisis; electricity was still being cut for hours every day.

On 31 December 2007 hundreds of Palestinian pilgrims returning from Saudi Arabia to Gaza went on the rampage (smashing windows and setting fire to bedding) in temporary desert camps in northern Sinai, after the Egyptian authorities insisted that they return via Gaza border crossings controlled by the Israeli army. The Palestinian protesters demanded to enter Gaza via the Egyptian terminal at Rafah—the main Egyptian terminal through which the pilgrims had left for the *Hajj* (pilgrimage) in Mecca. The Rafah crossing had become Gaza's main gateway to the outside world. An elderly woman died during a scuffle between the protesting pilgrims and Egyptian policemen. Egypt had allowed a few thousand to leave via its Rafah crossing because it did not want to be accused of stopping Muslims making the *Hajj*. However, Egyptian President Hosni Mubarak had subsequently decided to yield to Israeli demands to send the pilgrims back via two Israeli-controlled crossings, Kerem Shalom and Erez. The Israeli army had intended to arrest Hamas activists among the returning pilgrims.

Hamas fighters blew up the Egypt–Gaza border wall on 23 January 2008 in a bid to end the siege of Gaza. Thousands of Gazans surged into the Egyptian territory in northern Sinai. The following day dozens of Egyptian police gathered at the border and directed traffic away from the smashed frontier wall, while the Egyptian Government sought to assure its US ally that it would soon reseal its border with Gaza. Egypt at this point was more interested in bringing Hamas and the West Bank administration together and was no longer pretending to boycott Hamas. However, the PA persisted in refusing to recognize the authority of Hamas in Gaza.

On 27 January 2008 President Abbas met Israeli Prime Minister Olmert in Jerusalem partly to discuss Hamas's demolition of the Gaza–Egyptian border fence and the collapse of their joint strategy of isolating Hamas. However, Israel was sceptical of the suggestion that the PA share control of the Rafah crossing with Egyptian and EU monitors, with Shlomo Dror, a spokesman for the Israeli Ministry of Defence, expressing his concern that Hamas would retain effective control of the crossing. On 3 February the Gaza border was finally sealed by Egyptian forces; the Rafah crossing would henceforth be opened occasionally on humanitarian grounds.

On 4 February 2008 a Palestinian suicide bomber blew himself up at a shopping centre in the southern desert town of Dimona, killing one Israeli. Hamas claimed responsibility for the bombing, the first Hamas militant attack inside Israel since 2004. On 8 February 2008 Israeli troops backed by tanks, helicopter gunships and warplanes killed seven Palestinians in a raid in the Strip. In Ramallah, the PLO Executive Committee, at a meeting chaired by President Abbas, issued a statement demanding that Israel halt its operation in Gaza. The statement also expressed its opposition to rocket fire being launched against Israel from Gaza. On 6 March an attack by a lone Palestinian gunmen on a Jewish religious college in Jerusalem killed eight students.

YEMENI MEDIATION

On 23 March 2008 Hamas and Fatah signed up to the 'San'a Declaration', a Yemeni-brokered agreement designed to reconcile the two rival factions. The statement was signed, after a week of talks, by Fatah's parliamentary leader, Azzam al-Ahmad, and Hamas leader Mousa Abu Marzuk. The Yemeni initiative envisaged new Palestinian elections, the creation of a 'government of national unity' and the restructuring of the security forces along national rather than factional lines. However, only hours after the signing of the agreement, an apparent dispute broke out over just what was included in the deal. Abbas's chief negotiator, Saeb Erakat, insisted that Hamas must agree to end its control of Gaza, allow the PA back into the Strip, accept the PLO 'obligations' towards the 1993 Oslo Accords and accept the principle of negotiation with Israel for a two-state solution. Meanwhile, Hamas demanded that Abbas restore the 'national unity government' led by Hamas's Ismail Haniya. Furthermore, Hamas argued that long-term peace depended not on endorsing the Oslo Accords, but on ending Israeli occupation of the West Bank, dismantling Jewish settlements and opening the crossing points into the Strip. The San'a Declaration demonstrated that the two sides were willing to engage in dialogue, but that there remained substantial differences between them.

EGYPTIAN-BROKERED HAMAS-ISRAEL TRUCE

Following months of indirect negotiations brokered by Egyptian intelligence officers, a preliminary six-month truce between Israel and Hamas came into effect on 19 June 2008. It was primarily aimed at bringing an end to fighting that had resulted in the deaths of more than 600 Palestinians, many of them civilians, and some 18 Israelis since the last Hamas-Israel cease-fire collapsed in April 2007. The terms required Hamas to halt attacks on Israel; the latter was to cease military incursions into the Gaza Strip. If the cessation of hostilities lasted for three days, Israel would then ease its blockade of Gaza, allowing vital supplies into the territory. If further progress were achieved in the Egyptian-mediated negotiations, Israel would then allow more commodities into Gaza and Egypt would open the Rafah crossing for two to three days per week. Moreover, a week after the cease-fire took hold, Egypt would host indirect negotiations between Hamas and Israeli representatives to broker a prisoner deal that would swap Gilad Shalit—captured by Palestinian fighters in mid-2006—for Palestinian prisoners being held in Israeli gaols. Hamas had earlier conditioned the release of Shalit on the freeing of 450 Palestinian prisoners, of whom Israel had publicly stated that it would release only 70.

However, the cease-fire deal reached in June 2008 in effect constituted no more than promises from both Hamas and Israel to Egypt. Consequently, on 26 June, barely a week into the cease-fire, Israel declared that its border crossings with Gaza would remain closed. This prompted Hamas spokesman Sami Abu Zuhri to accuse Israel of breaching the truce. He added that the commitment of Hamas to the deal hinged on Israel's lifting of the siege of Gaza and the opening of all the crossings. Israel claimed that it had reinstated the blockade on 25 June in response to rockets fired from Gaza by Islamic Jihad fighters, apparently in retaliation for the Israeli army's killing of an Islamic Jihad commander in the West Bank. Israel maintained that the truce covered only Gaza and not the West Bank. On 1 July Israel closed all its cargo crossings with Gaza, accusing Hamas of firing a rocket at southern Israel the previous night.

In the mean time, both Israel and the PA continued to combat the growing support for Hamas across the West Bank. On 7 July 2008 Israeli troops raided the offices of the Tadamun association, a Palestinian charity in Nablus with links to Hamas. Similar raids were carried out around Ramallah, Hebron and Qalqilya.

'OPERATION CAST LEAD'

On 27 December 2008 Israeli forces began a bombing campaign on the Gaza Strip, as part of 'Operation Cast Lead', the stated aim of which was to prevent further rocket attacks into Israel by Hamas militants. The scale and intensity of the Israeli attacks were unprecedented. More Palestinians were killed and more properties destroyed in the 22-day military campaign than in any previous Israeli offensive against Gaza; according to Amnesty International, some 1,400 Palestinians were killed and 5,000 injured. Palestinian human rights NGOs estimated that nearly two-thirds of those killed were civilians. Targeted institutions included police stations, schools, clinics, mosques, welfare organizations and the Islamic University of Gaza, as well as a range of media outlets. On 6 January 2009 Israeli shelling killed 46 people at the UN-operated al-Fakhoura school in the Jabalya refugee camp.

However, the aerial campaign failed to decapitate Hamas, defeat it militarily or even prevent the intensification of rocket-fire into Israel. Senior Hamas leader Nizar Rayyan was killed on 31 December 2008 during the bombing of a residential building, which also resulted in the deaths of over a dozen women and children. On 15 January 2009 Said Siam, the Minister of the Interior in the de facto Hamas administration, was assassinated when Israeli warplanes attacked his brother's home in Gaza City. Siam was thought to be Hamas's number three in Gaza, behind Ismail Haniya and the group's political chief in Gaza, Dr Mahmud al-Zahar. Nevertheless, the Damascus-based Khalid Meshaal remained de facto leader of Hamas. In April Meshaal was re-elected head of the political bureau in a secret vote conducted over several days. It was reported that some 50 senior members of Hamas inside and outside the Palestinian territories (including some of those in Israeli gaols) had taken part in the vote. There was no report of any significant challenge to Meshaal's leadership.

The Gaza campaign came ahead of an Israeli general election, scheduled for 10 February 2009. Israeli leaders seemed to believe that they could weaken Hamas militarily and transform the situation on the ground while boosting their electoral prospects and the fortunes of the Ramallah-based PA. The Gaza campaign also presented an opportunity to restore Israeli military prestige, much tarnished following the offensive against Hezbollah in 2006. In the Arab world, the 22-day campaign prompted pro-Palestinian demonstrations targeting Egyptian embassies in Beirut, Amman, and elsewhere in protest against Egypt's perceived complicity in the Israeli blockade of Gaza. The official Arab response was deeply divided, with Syria and Hezbollah urging a full Arab boycott of Israel. The PA issued tough statements condemning the Israeli attacks, while at the same time cracking down on anti-Israeli protests in the West Bank—partly in order to deflect attention from its support for the Israeli siege of Gaza and its desire that Hamas would finally be weakened by Israel.

FATAH-HAMAS MEDIATION IN CAIRO

Arab efforts to broker Fatah-Hamas reconciliation recommenced on 27 April 2009 in Cairo. Hamas was represented by Dr Mahmud al-Zahhar, while Dr Nabil Shaath, a senior Fatah leader, represented the PA. The talks focused on the formation of a transitional 'unity government', based on power-sharing, which would remain in place until the 2010 parliamentary elections.

The first round of unity talks, which had been arranged by Saudi Arabia in February 2007, had collapsed and the factions had reverted to internal fighting until Hamas seized full control of Gaza in June of that year. The second round of talks between the two factions began on 9 November 2008 under Egyptian auspices. Egyptian officials had produced proposals for an agreement, including the formation of a government of national unity, an end to the economic blockade, the reform of the security forces, and the holding of presidential and legislative elections. Hamas, for its part, had demanded an end to the blockade of Gaza and membership of a reformed PLO.

The legal mandate and term of President Mahmud Abbas was due to expire on 9 January 2009, but the prospect of a new presidential election being held seemed unlikely, leaving Abbas without democratic legitimacy. The work of the PLC had been frozen since 2006, and the Governments of Salam Fayyad in Ramallah and Ismail Haniya in Gaza both confronted isolation. Abbas's mandate topped the agenda of the Cairo negotiations in November 2008, and Hamas initially insisted on the illegality of an extension of his mandate. However, Hamas's subsequent concession for Abbas to keep his position beyond January 2009 only underscored the fact that the PA was on the verge of institutional breakdown.

By early April 2009 the third round of unity talks had broken down, mainly over the issue of the PA's previous accords with Israel. Egypt pressed for persevering with further such talks, arguing that an agreement was vital in order for the US $4,500m. of aid pledged by international donors to be paid out to help rebuild Gaza. Many donor countries refused to channel their aid through Hamas, insisting that disbursal of the money should be the responsibility of a unity government. The Quartet group continued to state that it would only deal with Hamas if the Islamist organization recognized Israel, accepted previous Israeli-PA agreements and laid down its arms. However, Ali Barakeh, a senior Hamas official based in Damascus, claimed that Fatah's co-operation with Israel and the USA represented the main obstacle to reconciliation.

The fourth round of power-sharing talks between Hamas and Fatah again ended without a deal, and the two factions agreed to resume negotiations on 16 May 2009. However, divisions remained on key issues such as the electoral system, reform of the Palestinian police and security services (including the role of Jordan and the USA in training), and possible Hamas participation in the PLO. The two sides also remained deeply suspicious of each other; the Cairo talks came just two weeks after Hamas had accused Fatah of attempting to assassinate one of its leaders in the West Bank. Further talks in October also failed to produce an agreement.

Throughout the first half of 2009 both the PA and Israel continued to detain senior Hamas figures on the West Bank. On 19 March the Israeli security forces arrested 10 leaders of Hamas in the West Bank, including Nasser al-Shaer, the Deputy Prime Minister and Minister of Education and Higher Education in the Government formed by Hamas in early 2006. Three others, including a member of the Legislative Council and a local mayor, were arrested in Ramallah, while a Hamas member of the PLC, Ayman Daraghmeh, was detained near Jenin. The arrests followed the failure of Egyptian-mediated negotiations between Hamas and Israel over a proposal for the release of Gilad Shalit in exchange for hundreds of Palestinians held in Israel. By late March 2009 more than 40 Hamas members of the PLC from the West Bank were imprisoned in Israel.

THE 13TH PA CABINET

In May 2009 the PA Cabinet was reorganized for the first time since the appointment of the 'emergency government' in 2007. Some 12 new ministers entered an expanded PA executive, most of whom were members of Fatah. Expansion allowed Abbas to retain the technocratic core of Fayyad's administration while placating restless elements within Fatah. Saeed Abu Ali, of Fatah, remained Minister of the Interior and was joined by a further eight Fatah ministers, including Issa Qaraqe as Minister of Detainees' Affairs and Muhammad Shtayyeh as Minister of Public Works. Fayyad remained Prime Minister and Minister of Finance. Representatives of three other PLO factions also entered the Cabinet: the DFLP, FIDA and the PPSF. They joined several independents, among them Dr Riyad al-Maliki (formerly of the PFLP), who had held the role of Minister of Foreign Affairs since July 2007.

PA SECURITY REFORM IN THE WEST BANK

The USA had been involved in training the PA's security forces since the 1990s. Following the Wye negotiations in 1998, the CIA increased its support for the PA, to bolster it against Hamas. However, in the post-Arafat, post-al-Aqsa *intifada* era, the scale and ambition of US involvement deepened considerably, increasing further following the electoral ascent of Hamas. The US 'security co-ordination' programme, headed by Lt-Gen. Keith Dayton, was launched by the Bush Administration in 2005 to help the PA to reform its security services.

In effect, Dayton was, controversially, given overall responsibility for the PA security forces. It was reported that the Dayton programme planned to train seven battalions totalling 4,700 troops, in addition to training and supplying equipment for an additional 15,000 troops. It was estimated that the total cost of the programme would reach US $1,300m., although by 2009 costs amounted to just $161m. However, overall US investment in training, arming and financing the PA's Presidential Guard and National Security Forces was thought to be much higher.

The Dayton programme helped to restructure, retrain and re-equip the PA's security forces, and close ties with PA commanders were established. Forces were reorganized into three main branches: police, intelligence and military. The primary goal was to provide the PA leadership with the capacity to contain resistance on the part of Hamas or other opposition factions; to that end, forces engaged in a series of offensives against members of Hamas across the West Bank. The PA claimed that the 'Dayton force' had made discoveries of arms and explosives across the West Bank, while President Abbas insisted that he had been the target of a Hamas assassination plot.

However, the Dayton initiative attracted criticism. The equipment used was vetted and approved by Israel, leaving the force largely under-resourced (but not underfunded). Israel had refused to allow body armour, which meant that recruits risked their lives in every operation. Some critics within the PA complained that the amount of funding the 'Dayton force' received was disproportionate compared with other sections of the PA, such as the neglected judicial system. The Dayton programme posed deeper questions about Palestinian national security. The PA had opted to embrace security co-operation with Israel, but it remained subject to Israeli influence, and as a result it ran the risk of further weakening the PA's standing with the public. The Dayton mission came under severe criticism from Hamas as a major barrier to the establishment of a Palestinian unity government and as an unjustified US intrusion into internal Palestinian affairs. The Dayton programme had already forced Hamas to seek support from regional powers in the Middle East to counter the US-sponsored security forces. In effect, the programme risked deepening internal divisions in the Palestinian territories.

THE SIXTH FATAH GENERAL CONFERENCE

Security sector reform facilitated an incremental re-extension of PA territorial reach. PA police returned to Nablus in late 2007, to Jenin and Hebron during 2008, and by mid-2009 were on patrol in Bethlehem as the city prepared to host the long-delayed sixth Fatah General Conference.

The conference was held on 4–11 August 2009, with over 2,300 delegates in attendance. Some 400 delegates from Gaza were prevented from travelling to the conference by Hamas in retaliation for PA detention of Hamas members in the West Bank. Abbas continued to eschew armed struggle, but did link the resumption of direct negotiations with Israel to a settlement freeze. The PA President was re-elected unopposed to the post of Fatah Chairman. Of the 18 members of the Central Committee, only five were re-elected.

Capitalizing on Fatah's organizational momentum, the PNC convened on 26–27 August 2009 in Ramallah, and six new members were added to the Executive Committee. Two of the new members were prominent figures within Fatah: Ahmad Quray and Saeb Erakat. They were joined by the first woman to take a seat on the Committee, Hanan Ashrawi.

PROGRESS UNDER FAYYAD

The bifurcation of the Palestinian territories persisted into 2010; with the absence of fresh elections or a restoration of national unity, Hamas continued to preside over the economically devastated Gaza Strip, but in the West Bank the uneasy partnership of Fayyad and Fatah steered in a different direction. Favoured by the West for his independence, technical expertise, commitment to reform and political moderation, the technocrat Fayyad stood apart from the established Palestinian political factions and culture. However, echoing the criticism of Abbas's expired presidency, Hamas could reasonably contest the legality of Fayyad's premiership, since the PLC, in which Hamas still enjoyed a technical majority, had not been afforded a vote on the appointment. Fayyad combined administrative competence with a surprising degree of nationalist combativeness, emerging as a political force in his own right.

Like Abbas, Fayyad eschewed armed struggle, instead focusing on the construction of political and economic infrastructure and systematic institutional capacity-building, to lay the foundations of an independent Palestinian state. The internal merit of Fayyad's constructive agenda attracted the attention of external parties such as the USA and the EU, while a peaceful method of implementation was more difficult for Israel to oppose forcibly. Launched in August 2009, the Fayyad plan, officially entitled 'Ending the Occupation, Establishing the State', proposed to create the basis for Palestinian independence by 2011. The risks inherent to this approach would become increasingly evident as the state itself failed to come into being. However, in the mean time PLO and PA officials set out to secure international support for the plan, although Israel objected to this new Palestinian unilateralism as a breach of the Oslo Accords.

In December 2009 Fayyad launched a PA boycott of settlement produce, sale of which was estimated to be worth up to US $200m. per year to the settler economy. In January 2010 Fayyad followed this up with a 'National Honour Fund', intended to replace settlement products with Palestinian goods and to strengthen Palestinian exporters. Subsequent measures during that year aimed to ban Palestinian labourers from working in the settlements, while making provision for their systematic reintegration into the national economy. Meanwhile, improvements in the PA's security forces in the West Bank expedited a modest reduction in Israeli military checkpoints and raids.

THE PROLONGED CRISIS OF THE ABBAS PRESIDENCY

In April 2009 the UN appointed South African judge Richard Goldstone to head an independent inquiry into alleged human rights violations committed during 'Operation Cast Lead'. On 15 September Goldstone published his report, in which he was heavily critical of the Israeli military campaign, but also careful to highlight Hamas's transgressions. Israel was censured for the use of disproportionate force and laying siege to the Strip, while Hamas was criticized for firing indiscriminately at civilian targets in southern Israel. Under US pressure, on 2 October Abbas backed down from an earlier plan to refer the report to the UN Human Rights Council, which in theory would have opened up the possibility of trials for war crimes and crimes against humanity at the International Criminal Court (ICC). The presidential *volte face* prompted a furious backlash from Gaza, and Abbas felt compelled to admit that this reversal in policy had been a mistake. Members of Fatah, the PA Cabinet and the PLO were deeply embarrassed, to the extent that the PLO undertook an internal inquiry into the decision-making process.

Reeling from the Goldstone affair and cognizant that his diplomatic strategy had failed to generate results, on 5 November 2009 Abbas revealed that he would not seek re-election to the presidency. The immediate consequences were limited, however, because elections under the prevailing conditions were simply not viable, on account of Hamas opposition and uncertainty over the Israeli position on a poll in East Jerusalem. The constitutional term of the PLC expired on 25 January 2010. Plans were announced in April for a fresh round of local elections in July, but the idea was abandoned owing to the inability of some Fatah branches to agree on a list of candidates, and the refusal by Hamas to permit the poll in Gaza or to participate in elections in the West Bank.

RESUMPTION OF DIRECT NEGOTIATIONS

While Fayyad's Government pursued the practicalities of state-building, which could—at least in part—be carried out independently of talks with Israel, the PLO had a remit to pursue negotiations, albeit in the context of the discredited

Oslo framework and subsequent attempts to resuscitate it. However, by late 2009 the Fatah leadership was proving to be uncharacteristically obdurate in resisting US pressure to return to bilateral negotiations. More than 15 years of attrition at the negotiating table seemed to have prompted a rethink among mainstream secular Palestinian nationalists. The re-election of Binyamin Netanyahu as Israeli Prime Minister in March 2009 was regarded as a further obstacle to a negotiated settlement. Mindful of the resolutions of the Sixth General Conference earlier in the year, the Fatah-led PLO began to hold out for a comprehensive Israeli settlement freeze and clarification of the purpose of negotiations, including assurances of statehood within 1967 borders subject to minor amendments. For Abbas and Fatah, this strategy promised to restore a measure of popular (if not yet electoral) legitimacy to a President and movement recently tarnished by constitutional crisis, the loss of Gaza, and an ambiguous response to 'Operation Cast Lead' and the Goldstone Report, while also putting pressure on Israel and the USA.

On 25 November 2009 Netanyahu yielded to US pressure and agreed to a limited 10-month settlement freeze. However, as with the roadmap, the Israeli Government appended a series of exceptions, including work on existing projects, public buildings, and the full range of construction under way in East Jerusalem. Consequently, Israel's settlement freeze failed to meet Abbas's preconditions for a resumption of direct negotiations. US-proposed 'proximity talks', whereby both parties agreed to negotiate separately with the USA rather than with each other, did finally commence in May 2010, and on 2 September direct negotiations between Abbas and Netanyahu began in Washington, DC, but with little fanfare or hope of substantial success. As the 30 September expiry date on the settlement freeze drew nearer, the external pressures on Abbas were expected to grow. However, the internal rewards resulting from adherence to nationalist principles were tangible; resuming talks too readily could erode Fatah's standing with the Palestinians once more, to the advantage of Hamas.

HAMAS AND GAZA, WITHIN AND WITHOUT

Largely isolated from the West Bank and subject to close surveillance by the authorities, local Fatah elements struggled to mount an effective challenge to Hamas in Gaza. However, an altogether different challenge arose in the form of a salafi insurrection in Rafah. A commitment to resistance had led Israel to designate Hamas-controlled Gaza as a 'hostile entity' since September 2007. However, for radical critics of Hamas, cease-fire arrangements in place since the end of 'Operation Cast Lead' and Hamas's efforts to prevent the launching of rockets into southern Israel brought this commitment into question. In mid-August 2009 an 'Islamic Emirate' was declared in Rafah by the Jund Ansar Allah, led by Abd al-Latif Musa. The group was one of a number of small *salafi* movements established amid Gaza's isolation and poverty. This direct challenge to Hamas was short-lived, however, and the 'Emirate' was quickly subjugated. Hamas's effective suppression of resistance in the Strip led to a period of relative calm for southern Israel, although this was interrupted in July 2010 by a rocket strike on the port of Ashkelon. Israel struck back at Hamas, even though it was thought that the Islamist movement was not responsible, echoing Israeli policy during the al-Aqsa *intifada*, when PA security forces were routinely attacked in reprisal for independent acts. In April 2011 alleged *salafis* kidnapped and murdered an Italian peace activist in Gaza, prompting Hamas security forces to track down and kill those responsible.

Meanwhile, on 19 January 2010 a leading figure from Hamas's military wing, Mahmoud al-Mabhouh, was assassinated in Dubai, United Arab Emirates (UAE). It was alleged by Dubai police that Israeli agents had carried out the killing, travelling on false or stolen third-country passports. Israel refused to comment on the assassination, but found itself exposed to official criticism and diplomatic censure from around the world.

Even more controversial than the assassination of al-Mabhouh were the events surrounding the so-called 'Gaza Freedom Flotilla' at the end of May 2010. The flotilla was organized by a group of humanitarian organizations in an attempt to breach the blockade of Gaza to bring aid and other supplies into the territory. The Israeli armed forces undertook to intercept the flotilla, and paratroopers boarded the lead ship, the MV *Mavi Marmara*. In the subsequent skirmish, nine activists—all of whom were Turkish citizens—were killed. The incident put tremendous strain on Israeli-Turkish relations (which were downgraded in August 2011) and prompted the formation of a UN panel of inquiry. Chaired by former New Zealand Prime Minister Sir Geoffrey Palmer, the panel published its findings in September 2011. Pro-Gaza activists were deeply disappointed to find the Israeli naval blockade deemed 'a legitimate security measure', but noted that the military's actions were found to be 'excessive and unreasonable', with the panel adding that 'non-violent options should have been used in the first instance'. Mindful of this diplomatic and public relations disaster, in mid-2011 Israel took a series of pre-emptive steps against a planned second flotilla, effectively neutralizing the initiative.

THE PLO, ISRAEL AND THE USA: STAGNANT NEGOTIATIONS

The PLO-Israeli negotiations briefly recommenced in September 2010, with the opening session in Washington, DC, followed by a further round in Sharm el-Sheikh and Jerusalem, but the momentum proved short-lived. Israel declined to extend the West Bank settlement freeze at the end of the month, and, consistent with the platform agreed by Fatah during its 2009 General Conference, the Palestinians withdrew from the talks. PLO officials directed unusually harsh criticism at the USA for its failure to secure an additional settlement freeze. This more resolute political stance resonated well with domestic constituents; local Fatah leaders understood that a clear policy, firmly adhered to, would help to bolster the movement's tentative but still precarious rehabilitation in the West Bank. The USA responded by announcing that it would continue to work towards a solution with both parties separately, although visits by US diplomats became less frequent, and US President Barack Obama's special envoy to the region, George Mitchell, finally resigned in May 2011.

In January 2011 the parameters of the PLO-Israeli negotiations were released into the public domain as the Qatari satellite television broadcaster Al Jazeera published a tranche of leaked Palestinian documents. Managed in conjunction with the British newspaper *The Guardian*, the publication of the so-called 'Palestine Papers' generated considerable controversy, but the extent to which they revealed much of real surprise was debatable. Evidence of compromise allowed Hamas to capitalize on the situation at Fatah's expense, but the impact appeared short-lived. The main institutional effect was the dissolution in March of the PLO's Negotiations Support Unit, identified as the source of the leak, and its replacement by a Negotiations Office.

While the US-sponsored negotiations stalled, Abbas escalated an international diplomatic campaign aimed at securing recognition, on a bilateral basis (in contrast to the unilateral declaration of independence issued in 1988), of a Palestinian state in the West Bank, the Gaza Strip and East Jerusalem. PLO diplomacy quickly registered a number of bilateral successes, including recognition from Brazil and a number of other Latin American states, and upgraded diplomatic relations with several European nations, while the PLO General Delegation to the USA was permitted to fly the Palestinian flag at its premises in Washington, DC. As the annual session of the UN General Assembly scheduled for September 2011 approached, Abbas announced that 122 nations already recognized a Palestinian state within the 1967 borders. To admit that state as a full member of the UN required a two-thirds' majority in the General Assembly, but first a recommendation from the Security Council was needed, and the USA predictably threatened to use its veto. (In February 2011 the USA had vetoed a draft resolution on the illegality of Israeli settlement construction in the West Bank and East Jerusalem, despite all 14 of the other Security Council members voting in favour.) Israel dismissed this initiative as a Palestinian attempt to delegitimize it amid plans for mass violence. The PLO retained the option of submitting an alternative resolution to the General Assembly, which would bypass the US veto, to upgrade the Permanent Observer Mission of Palestine to the UN to non-member observer state, comparable in status to the Holy See. Approval would require a simple majority among the UN's 193 member states and would result in important privileges being granted, including membership rights in UN agencies; the prospect of Palestinian leverage at the ICC was of particular concern to Israel. The Arab League supported a move to seek full UN membership for a Palestinian state. Despite confirmation by the US Administration that it would use its veto, Abbas duly submitted the application on 23 September. The President's uncharacteristically resolute stance was welcomed by many within the Palestinian territories. However, the application itself, even before it could meet the US veto, was shunted to the margins via a Committee on the Admission of New Members; it looked likely to remain there for some time.

FATAH POLITICS SINCE THE SIXTH GENERAL CONFERENCE

Fatah's Central Committee announced in December 2010 that it was suspending the membership of spokesman and former Gazan security chief Muhammad Dahlan, pending an internal investigation into charges of Dahlan conspiring against Abbas and establishing a heavily armed personal militia. Dahlan was regarded with suspicion by many Palestinians due to his perceived closeness to Israel and the USA. Popular opinion held that he was being punished for accusing Abbas's two sons, Tariq and Yasir, of accruing wealth improperly. Dahlan's organizational network and media interests were closed down, and in June 2011 it was reported (though disputed) that Dahlan had been expelled from Fatah altogether. Dahlan remained in exile in the UAE at mid-2013.

Away from the divisions in the higher echelons of the movement, local Fatah leaders focused on maintaining the momentum from the 2009 General Conference. Adhering to principle on the settlement freeze issue was popular with the public, but maintaining the organization itself required enthusiasm among the lower and middle ranks. The conference had produced mixed results in this respect: on the one hand, it had generated a great deal of activity and excitement, but, on the other hand, the limited number of seats available on the Revolutionary Council had left many aspirants disappointed and a corresponding decline in commitment ensued. In response, Fatah planned fresh elections at district and regional level; the movement hoped that this would keep internal political life healthy while also serving as preparation for proposed local council elections. The prospect of mobilizing behind the PLO at the UN offered another opportunity for action; both Abbas and, from prison, Marwan Barghouthi appealed for mass demonstrations. The full extent of local preparation was not immediately apparent, although Fatah leaders made it clear that support could be mobilized at short notice.

PALESTINIAN FACTIONAL POLITICS DURING THE 'ARAB SPRING'

In the short term, the 'Arab spring'—the series of anti-Government protests that spread throughout the Middle East and North Africa from December 2010—reversed the usual state of affairs in the region, as turmoil in neighbouring Arab states contrasted with relative calm in the Palestinian territories. Although the Fayyad Government formally resigned on 14 February 2011, the move was seen as a superficial attempt to mollify public opinion with little practical impact. However, the dramatic changes occurring near its borders inevitably crossed into the Palestinian factional landscape. In Egypt, the fall of long-standing President Hosni Mubarak at first seemed to benefit Hamas; Mubarak's ouster removed a stalwart opponent of political Islam and opened up the possibility of a much higher profile for the Muslim Brotherhood in politics and government. However, the Islamists' early optimism faded into uncertainty; the Egyptian military, at least initially, remained steadfast at the helm of a transitional administration, and the Brotherhood exercised its new-found freedom with caution. When a similar, but more violent, upheaval affected Syria, the Damascus-based Hamas leadership itself appeared exposed, particularly when the influential Egyptian cleric Sheikh Yusuf al-Qaradawi declared his support for the anti-Government protesters in late March. The Assad regime subsequently deployed Hamas chief Khalid Meshaal to bolster Syria's pro-Palestinian credentials, although the intervention sat uneasily with Syrian protesters and the Palestinian public.

The conjunction of PLO diplomacy, the destabilization of Syria and the lure of better relations with Egypt precipitated a fresh attempt at Palestinian national reconciliation. A surprise agreement between Fatah and Hamas, mediated by Egypt, was announced in late April 2011 and signed by Abbas and Meshaal on 4 May. The terms stipulated that a unity government, comprised of independents, be formed, with elections to the PLC and the presidency to follow within a year; the contentious issue of security arrangements was finessed in the short term as Egypt planned to send technical support to Gaza. However, implementation of the deal stalled when the two sides could not agree on who should serve as Prime Minister, with Hamas rejecting Abbas's choice of Fayyad. The process also exposed the lingering disagreements within the Hamas leadership, as the Gaza-based Mahmud al-Zahar expressed surprise at the April agreement brokered by Mousa Abu Marzuk on Meshaal's behalf. Like the earlier momentum, the subsequent stall owed much to regional events, specifically the end of a tentative rapprochement between Egypt and Iran, due to Saudi pressure on the former. In retaliation, Iran may have urged Hamas to distance itself from a reformed unity government, to deprive the Egyptian administration of its diplomatic success.

Meanwhile, Israel expressed its dissatisfaction with the Fatah-Hamas agreement by withholding tax receipts collected on the PA's behalf, forcing Fayyad temporarily to halve public sector salaries in July 2011, in an echo of the 2007 crisis. Palestinian officials also linked Israel's response to their leadership's diplomatic moves.

THE INTERNAL AND EXTERNAL BORDERS OF ISRAEL/PALESTINE

Conditions in the West Bank enclaves of Area A and Area B improved during the first half of 2011. The PA continued the construction of extensive new government offices in the Ramallah suburb of Masyun, the town assuming the appearance of state administrative (if not political) permanence. PA and NGO opportunities attracted migrants, prompting a construction boom. Reforms implemented by the Palestine Monetary Authority increased the availability of credit, encouraging consumption, and the PA was correspondingly able to accumulate limited tax revenues. However, pressure on Palestinians outside the urban enclaves increased: the Jordan Valley population struggled against restrictions on zoning and planning; military measures against Bedouin were intensified; and settler violence rose sharply.

In the mean time, Hamas continued its efforts to curb rocket attacks launched from the Gaza Strip, as the PA worked to limit Hamas's influence in the West Bank. None the less, there was an increase in violence around Gaza in early April 2011, after a rocket hit an Israeli school bus. Further south, the post-Mubarak Government in Egypt opened the Rafah crossing in late May. However, to the dissatisfaction of Hamas and residents in Gaza, it quickly became clear that the new transit procedures were merely a limited relaxation of existing restrictions. Meanwhile, lax security in Sinai led to a rise in the transfer of goods via the Rafah tunnels, with Israel expressing concern at an increased flow of arms, especially from eastern Libya (where a popular uprising was taking place against the regime of Libyan leader Muammar al-Qaddafi).

Online groups inspired by the 'Arab spring' demonstrations tried to mobilize support for protests at Israel's frontiers to mark the anniversary of *al-Nakba* in mid-May 2011. In the West Bank, turn-out at the Qalandiya checkpoint was limited, while Gazan protesters attempting to march to the Erez checkpoint were fired upon by Israeli troops. More significant were the protests at the Syrian and Lebanese borders, which apparently went ahead with the support of Syria and Hezbollah, respectively. In Syria, dozens of Palestinian refugees breached the border fence and crossed into the Golan Heights. In the south of Israel, near Eilat, a series of gun and bomb attacks perpetrated by suspected Palestinian militants on 18 August left eight Israelis dead and more than 30 wounded; five of the attackers were killed and several more Palestinians later died as the result of Israeli air-strikes on Gaza. The deaths of three Egyptian security personnel in Sinai during subsequent Israeli military action added to the strain on relations between the two increasingly unenthusiastic allies.

'STATE OF PALESTINE' ADMITTED TO UNESCO

The PLO's diplomatic initiative may have stalled at the UN Security Council in New York, but progress did extend to entry into UNESCO in Paris. 'The state of Palestine' secured a comfortable vote in favour of membership on 31 October 2011, and became the 189th state party to the World Heritage Convention in December. The proactive ambassador Elias Sanbar was recorded as the Permanent Delegate of Palestine to UNESCO from January 2012. Membership of UNESCO afforded the PA a new diplomatic tool: accession to the World Heritage Convention permitted nomination of sites of cultural or natural significance for inscription on the World Heritage List. During 2012 the PA successfully nominated the Church of the Nativity in Bethlehem and the associated Pilgrimage Route; 13 additional sites were put forward on a Tentative List for possible consideration 12 months later. They included the Jerusalem Southern Terraced Landscape, centred on the village of Battir, which had hoped to secure the original nomination on account of imminent danger from Israel's 'separation barrier'. Supporters of Battir chastised the Palestinian leadership for allegedly bowing to external intervention: the case was made that UNESCO protection of Battir, in Area C, might have been deemed more confrontational than the listing of an established international landmark in Area A. The PA, however, disputed that view. Independent of domestic politics, controversy at home was preceded by fallout abroad: Israeli-US objections to the admission of 'the state of Palestine' to UNESCO triggered another temporary freezing by Israel of customs revenue transfer to the PA during November 2011 and, in line with established congressional legislation, the withdrawal of US contributions to UNESCO's budget.

PALESTINIAN PRISONERS BEGIN HUNGER STRIKE

With the membership application to the UN under scrutiny by a sub-committee, the PLO's international diplomacy faded from the headlines; this process continued as Hamas and Israel agreed to exchange large numbers of Palestinian prisoners in return for kidnapped Israeli soldier Gilad Shalit. The agreement stipulated that a total of 1,027 Palestinian prisoners be released in exchange for Shalit. The initial release on 18 October 2011 included a tranche of 477 prisoners, the first of them being 27 women; some 40 Palestinians were released into exile overseas.

In 2012 Palestinian prisoners secured headlines for a second time, with a major cross-factional and lengthy hunger strike. Action initiated in February gained momentum from 17 April, when the Jerusalem-based prisoner support and rights association, Addameer, estimated that around 1,200 prisoners had launched a major strike; the number of participants subsequently rose by several hundred as protests peaked. Addameer reported that Israel held 4,706 political prisoners at mid-2012, of whom 285 were administrative detainees (a technical measure preceding the occupation through which suspects could be detained without charge or trial for up to six months and their detention renewed indefinitely); 18 administrative detainees were members of the PLC. The hunger strikers' demands included the restoration of family visiting rights for Gazan prisoners: suspended in the wake of Shalit's abduction, Israel had been expected to restore these rights upon the soldier's release but then demurred. Other complaints included the use of administrative detention and solitary confinement, as well as a ban on academic studies and access to books. Pressure on the Israel Prison Service (IPS) increased, as leading hunger strikers Bilal Diyab and Tahir Halahleh approached and then exceeded the recorded limit for endurance of a fast. On hunger strike for 77 days before reaching terms with IPS on 14 May, both prisoners were objecting to the prospective renewal of their terms in administrative detention; they were following the lead of Khader Adnan, an administrative detainee who had successfully forced the hand of the IPS with a 66-day hunger strike ending in mid-April. Israel was said to have agreed to multiple concessions: Palestinians claimed that administrative detainees would no longer have their terms renewed without the presentation of fresh evidence; there would be an end to long-term solitary confinement; and family visits for Gazans and West Bankers denied the right would be reinstated. Moreover, a number of other issues were reported to be under negotiation.

Keeping prisoners in the news, Akram Rikhawi undertook a 102-day fast, ending on 22 July 2012; he ultimately secured a revised release date on medical grounds. Rikhawi was preceded by renowned Palestinian footballer Mahmud Sarsak, who had been held in administrative detention for almost three years; Sarsak was ultimately released and permitted to return to Gaza after a 96-day hunger strike. Meanwhile, Israel released the remains of 91 Palestinians to the PA on 31 May 2012; some of the bodies had been held in Israeli custody for almost four decades.

FROM RAMALLAH: DEVELOPMENT UNDER OCCUPATION?

The PA had presided over a period of relative calm for much of the 'Arab spring', but the future remained unpredictable. The PA Cabinet in Ramallah was vulnerable on several levels. Israel retained the ability to sever the transfer of customs revenues at will. Initiatives at the UN prompted the latest freeze and reminded the Ramallah payroll of just how precarious was its ability to manage personal as well as institutional debt. Compounding structural vulnerability, the PA's fiscal position appeared even worse than usual. Redress was pursued in the form of increased taxation from early 2012, coupled with proposed early retirement for some longer-serving civil servants. Neither move was well received. During January national dialogue of sorts paved the way for an acceptable compromise, but the episode underlined the democratic deficit gnawing away at the core of Palestinian governance. Neither Fayyad nor Abbas had a valid electoral mandate. The PLC had been defunct since 2007. The PA continued to mediate military occupation. There was no cessation of settlement expansion in the West Bank; a decision in July 2012 by the UN Human Rights Council to launch an investigation into the matter received short shrift—Israel decreed that the mandated jurists be denied access to the area. There was still no resumption of peace negotiations between the PA and Israel, and independent diplomacy had stalled. PA authority might still be contested; the Governor of Jenin, Qadura Musa, died of a cardiac arrest after shots were fired outside home in early May. The uncivil side of the PA was clearly revealed at the end of June and beginning of July. Looking to reopen a line to Israel, Abbas extended an invitation to visit Ramallah to Shaul Mofaz, head of the Kadima list in the Knesset. Local residents recalled Mofaz as the tough Chief of Staff during 'Operation Defensive Shield', the campaign launched by the Israeli army in late March 2002 to put down the al-Aqsa *intifada*. The invitation prompted substantial public protest and was hastily rescinded. However, by now simmering discontent had spilled out onto the streets, and PA security forces responded with considerable violence.

NEW CABINET IN RAMALLAH

In an attempt to provide some fresh momentum to the PA in Ramallah, Abbas installed a new Cabinet on 16 May 2012, the first major government reorganization for three years. Ministers were tasked first and foremost with preparing the ground for local elections, due to have been held in 2009. The new Cabinet was composed of 23 ministers (in addition to the Prime Minister) and a Cabinet Secretary with ministerial rank; 11 of the ministers were new to their posts and a total of six portfolios were now held by women. The most significant change saw Fayyad, who remained as Prime Minister, relinquish the finance portfolio; he was replaced in that post by the independent academic and technocrat Nabil Qassis. Two primary issues drove the reorganization: the PA's looming financial crisis and the persistent failure to expedite reconciliation with Hamas. Rising indebtedness and a major shortfall in the PA's annual budget cost Fayyad the portfolio, despite his favour with Western donors. Besides the occupation and related limits on economic growth and tax collection, the PA had to deal with a reduction in donor aid compounded by a failure to meet pre-existing pledges. Hamas complained that the unilateral formation of a new PA Cabinet in the West Bank was in breach of the Doha agreement reached in February 2012 and had no electoral mandate; Abbas responded that longevity and attrition—including the resignation of two ministers charged with corruption—required that he act, while also pointing out that the Cabinet could be dissolved in an instant should national unity be realized.

HAMAS ON THE MOVE

The Palestinian polity remained divided at mid-2012: Fatah and Fayyad wrestled with one set of dilemmas, as well as each other, in Ramallah; Hamas remained dormant under repression throughout the West Bank but continued to rule in Gaza, from where it surveyed a rapidly changing neighbourhood. Building on the *rapprochement* of May 2011, inter-factional reconciliation took another tentative step forward during December and January 2012. By way of preparing the ground for elections, negotiations between the Damascus-based head of Hamas's political bureau, Khalid Meshaal, and Fatah's Abbas led to a public revision of tactics by the Islamists: Hamas would reserve the right to use force in defence, but otherwise turn away from armed struggle. The move did not sit well with some in the Gaza-based leadership; both Hamas premier Ismail Haniya and senior leader Mahmud al-Zahar contested the shift in policy. Fissures became apparent again following a more substantive step forward; the Doha agreement concluded on 6 February 2012 was signed by Abbas for Fatah, Meshaal for Hamas, and the Amir of Qatar, Sheikh Hamad bin Khalifa Al Thani.

Denied a secure base on Palestinian soil, events in the wider region afforded Meshaal a different perspective that would have been familiar to the historic PLO leadership; deteriorating conditions in host country Syria left him struggling to reconcile loyalty to the Assad regime with solidarity towards his Sunni brethren. Mindful of the spat with Qaradawi earlier in the crisis and encouraged by agitated supporters back home, Hamas's Damascus-based leadership declined to offer any further public support to the minority Alawi regime. The Damascus headquarters was eventually abandoned and the leadership team in exile dispersed: Meshaal joined Qaradawi in Doha during February 2012; Musa Abu Marzuk opted for Cairo; and other Hamas officials scattered across the region. The diminution of the alliance with Hamas was a clear setback for Syria's strategic ally, Iran, and as a result, Hamas forfeited substantial financial backing from Tehran. The distance between the two parties was underlined in March, when senior Hamas figures let it be known that in the event of an Israeli attack on Iran's nuclear facilities, the Islamist movement could not be expected to open up a southern front that did not serve Palestinian national interests. Regional upheaval appeared to undermine Meshaal's standing in the movement, but he continued to lead, holding meetings with King Abdullah of Jordan in late June and with Egypt's new President, Muhammad Mursi, in July. Meanwhile, a skirmish on the Israel–Egypt border on 18 June drew fresh attention to the security vacuum in Sinai and prompted a rare military escalation between Hamas and Israel: dozens of rockets were fired by Hamas militants in exchange for Israeli air-strikes being carried out on the Strip.

'OPERATION PILLAR OF DEFENSE'

In November 2012 Israel launched a series of heavy strikes on the Gaza Strip under the codename 'Operation Pillar of Defense'. The precise reason for this action was disputed, but the intensive bout of conflict that ensued appeared to be prompted by an incursion into the Gazan town of Khan Yunis by the Israeli Defense Forces on 8 November, in the course of which a Palestinian child was killed. Hamas responded by firing an anti-tank missile two days later; a fierce escalation in violence involving Israeli air-strikes and Palestinian rocket fire left over 170 Palestinians dead in an eight-day campaign briefly reminiscent of the 2008/09 assault codenamed 'Operation Cast Lead'. The most prominent Palestinian fatality occurred on 14 November with the targeted assassination of Ahmad al-Jabari, head of Hamas's military wing the Izz al-Din al-Qassam Brigades. Al-Jabari, a former Fatah activist, was alleged to have been on the brink of concluding a truce with Israel immediately prior to his assassination. In the event, the bout of hostilities that cost al-Jabari his life was brought to an end through Egyptian mediation. Israel reported five citizens amongst its dead, along with injuries to many more.

HAMAS GOVERNS GAZA

Beneath the ever-present threat of aerial assault, life continued in much the same vein in Gaza during 2012–13 as it had done since the schism of 2007. On the domestic front, two contrasting developments made headline news in this period. Internal to Hamas, Qatar-based political chief Khalid Meshaal crossed from Egypt via Rafah to make his first visit to the Palestinian territories in almost four decades; besides one short visit in the mid-1970s, Meshaal had been in exile from his home near Jerusalem since the 1967 Six-Day War. During his two-day visit in early December 2012 Meshaal paid his respects at the homes of prominent Hamas martyrs, including the group's spiritual guide and founder Sheikh Ahmad Yassin and the more recently assassinated al-Jabari. Meshaal then attended a rally to commemorate the 25th anniversary of the founding of Hamas during the early days of the first *intifada*. Logistical arrangements obliged Hamas to bring celebrations forward slightly from the official date of 14 December. Taking note, Fatah activists followed this with a huge demonstration of their own on 4 January 2013. The demonstration was organized to mark Fatah's 48th anniversary (and to recall the launch by Yasser Arafat of the armed struggle under the name of al-Asifa in 1965), and was attended by hundreds of thousands of Fatah supporters gathered in Gaza City's Saraya Square. That they were permitted to mobilize on this scale—the first time since 2007—was taken as evidence of goodwill as Fatah and Hamas negotiators navigated the treacherous route to national reconciliation.

On a regional level, the ouster of Egypt's elected, if controversial, President Muhammad Mursi on 3 July 2013 deprived Hamas of a kindred spirit at the helm in a major Arab state. Cairo's Muslim Brotherhood-led Government had overseen a modest extension of support for the Palestinians in Gaza: movement through the Rafah crossing had been eased and a visit—amid 'Operation Pillar of Defense'—from Prime Minister Hisham Qandil. Rafah's tunnels had long been a target of the Egyptian authorities, but following Mursi's removal from office, efforts to curb tunnel traffic were redoubled. Gaza was seemingly caught up in the Egyptian national goal of re-securing Sinai for the state. Matters deteriorated further when it was announced later in July that Mursi was under investigation for collusion with Hamas. The charge was levelled that during the internal upheaval in Egypt in January 2011 Mursi, together with other Muslim Brotherhood leaders and inmates, had escaped from Wadi al-Natrun prison with the assistance of Hamas (and Hezbollah). It was further alleged that Hamas had then joined Brotherhood forces in violent attacks on Egyptian security facilities in a campaign against the state. Hamas denied any such involvement and claimed that the allegations were the result of attempts by Fatah and the PA to besmirch its reputation in Egypt.

The apparent loss of Egyptian support compounded a fast-moving regional change of attitude towards Hamas: Egypt joined Syria and Iran on a lengthening list of states withdrawing support from the Islamist movement in Gaza. To make matters worse, sectarian fallout from the Syrian civil war put Hamas in opposition to Hezbollah, a previously valued, respected and potent ally. Further afield, Hamas leaders pondered the crises besetting Muslim Brotherhood affiliates in Libya and Tunisia; the 'Arab spring', it seemed, cut both ways. On an international level, Hamas officials responsible for foreign relations let it be known that several European states—Norway and Switzerland outside of the EU and, less visibly, a number within it—were attempting to encourage an alignment of Hamas policies with Quartet positions (essentially eschewing armed struggle, recognizing Israel and abiding by the Oslo accords). The disconnection between Hamas policy and Quartet conditions had long structured Gaza's isolation.

PALESTINE ACKNOWLEDGED AT THE UN

In lieu of meaningful negotiations, the PLO pursued an independent diplomatic campaign to secure an upgrade in status at the UN. Circumventing the US veto at the Security Council, focus fell on the General Assembly. Besides pressuring Israel and the USA, the vote to secure non-member state standing was one of the few means available to try and revive the fortunes of the secular-nationalist mainstream in Palestinian politics. The moment arrived on 29 November 2012, when 'the state of Palestine' was duly granted an upgrade to non-member observer status by the General Assembly. The pertinent UN document A/67/L.28 (2012) recounted a list of resolutions underpinning the decision, including: UN General Assembly (UNGA) Resolution 181 (1947), which sought to partition Palestine into separate, 'Independent Arab and Jewish States'; UN Security Council (UNSC) Resolution 242 (1967) calling on Israel to withdraw from 'territories occupied' (which included the West Bank and the Gaza Strip); UNSC Resolution 338 (1973), which reiterated that demand; UNGA Resolution 3236 and UNGA Resolution 3237 (1974), which respectively recognized the Palestinian people's right to self-determination and first granted the PLO observer status; and UNSC Resolution 1397 (2002), in which the USA signed up to 'a vision of a region where two States, Israel and Palestine, live side by side within secure and recognized borders'. The upgrade in UN standing of 2012 built on the decision one year earlier to admit 'the state of Palestine' as a full member of UNESCO.

A total of 138 members of the General Assembly cast their ballot in support of the upgrade; nine cast a vote against and 41 abstained. The minority against included Israel, North American allies Canada and the USA, Panama, plus a cluster of minor Pacific island states dependent on US aid (the Marshall Islands, Micronesia, Nauru and Palau). Among the European members, only the Czech Republic's centre-right and pro-USA Government cast one isolated ballot against the motion.

WEST BANK ADMINISTRATION IN CRISIS

Technical progress at the UN stubbornly refused to translate into substantive progress on the ground; in fact it would actually feed into a downward spiral. In lieu of an end to occupation, colonization and any prospect of sustainable development, economic stagnation and deepening fiscal crisis generated social tension that fuelled long-established political frustrations. Furthermore, in the moribund political environment overseen by the PA, this tension lacked any obvious procedural outlet. Local elections held unevenly across the West Bank in October 2012 generated limited renewal; the polls were banned by Hamas in the Gaza Strip and boycotted by the Islamists in the West Bank. Reflecting protest elsewhere in the Arab world, discontent surfaced, ostensibly in response to an increase in the cost of living. West Bank anger was compounded by an increase in the rate of value-added tax. Trade unions led a succession of strikes that did not spare PA institutions; reinforced by low-level Fatah mobilization, dissent rumbled on for months. Fleeting success at the UN then added to the stress: demonstrations drew renewed vigour towards the end of the year as Israel revisited the sanction earlier imposed for success at UNESCO. Customs revenues collected on the PA's behalf in accord with the Oslo-era Paris Protocol were suspended. Consequently, the PA proved unable to meet salary commitments and the anomie besetting the national project deepened. There was a resurgence of demonstrations during early 2013, with fresh mobilization behind the issue of prisoners. The immediate trigger was the death (following his alleged torture) of Palestinian detainee Arafat Jaradat in Israeli custody in February; fellow prisoners launched a mass hunger strike in protest.

Fiscal pressures and social unrest gradually eased over the following weeks; Israeli-held revenues and US aid were transferred, the PA drew on renewed liquidity and a semblance of calm resumed during April 2013. The relief had been timed to coincide with a brief visit to Ramallah by US President Barack Obama on 21 March. Following meetings in Israel the previous day, Obama met with Abbas at the presidential compound. During an ensuing press conference the US President said little to lift Palestinian spirits, particularly regarding the PLO's position that settlement construction needed to halt prior to any resumption of negotiations. This press conference was emblematic of a visit that generated little enthusiasm and a modicum of protest amongst a deeply jaded Palestinian public.

NEW PA PRIME MINISTER IN RAMALLAH

Deficits in representation, purpose and legitimacy continued seriously to erode the standing of the PA into 2013, with consequences for the executive. Buffeted by popular discontent, amid the evident failure to build a state, and undermined by Fatah, PA Prime Minister Salam Fayyad finally resigned on 13 April 2013. This was the second cabinet portfolio that Fayyad had relinquished in less than a year, having stepped down as Minister of Finance in May 2012. In early June President Abbas announced Fayyad's replacement to be the respected but politically inexperienced Dr Rami Hamdallah, an independent with a reputation for sound administration forged during his long tenure as president of the Nablus-based Al-Najah National University. However, on 20 June Hamdallah tendered his resignation just two weeks after being appointed. Surrounded by members of Fatah in cabinet, Hamdallah's political independence had appeared further compromised following the President's appointment of two Deputy Prime Ministers. Constitutionally, these appointments should have been the Prime Minister's prerogative. In lieu of an immediate replacement, Hamdallah acceded to the President's request to remain in the premiership on a caretaker basis. On 13 August Hamdallah accepted a request from Abbas to form a new government. That Government, the composition of which was the same as that appointed in June, duly took office on 19 September.

THE PLO AND ISRAEL NEGOTIATE NEGOTIATIONS

Mindful of the unsustainable status quo in the Palestinian territories and hopeful of a second-term foreign policy legacy in the Middle East, the Obama Administration, in the person of US Secretary of State John Kerry, put considerable energy into restarting PLO-Israeli negotiations. Months of intense diplomacy throughout the first half of 2013 culminated in a tentative revival of dialogue at the end of July. Kerry thus realized his immediate goal of simply getting the two sides to sit at the same table in Washington, DC. The event received little praise among Palestinians: initiated in Oslo some 20 years earlier, the process was now viewed with despair by many of its previous advocates and with hostility by its opponents, and was flatly rejected by much of the diaspora. At best, these factors represented an unpromising point of entry for a process that had seen no substantive negotiations since 2008 or preliminary talks of any sort since 2010. Agreement to hold even a preparatory meeting had required Kerry to navigate substantial (if familiar) obstacles: Palestinian insistence on agreed terms of reference that included the 1967 Green Line as a border and a time frame for negotiation with a prompt end point; Israeli insistence on fully negotiable borders, determined in part by ongoing settlement construction, and a time frame to accommodate this. A breakthrough of sorts was achieved when both sides accepted a nine-month time frame for a final status agreement; however, the question of where to start border talks remained unanswered. Bolstering the fragile legitimacy of the Palestinians' secular nationalist leadership, Israel agreed to release 104 long-term Palestinian prisoners in stages subject to progress in the talks. Kerry appointed former US ambassador to Tel Aviv Martin Indyk as the special envoy with the task of overseeing progress; preparatory meetings between the two sides were held in Washington on 30 July 2013 and negotiations resumed in Jerusalem on 14 August.

Economy

Revised for this edition by the editorial staff, with some previous material by NUR MASALHA

INTRODUCTION

Economic conditions in the Gaza Strip, the West Bank and East Jerusalem (Occupied Territories, see p. 554) have deteriorated significantly since the signing of the Declaration of Principles on Palestinian Self-Rule in September 1993. The dominant characteristic of these economies has been their dependence on Israeli markets and their consequent vulnerability to the closures imposed at various times by the Israeli authorities, mainly in response to attacks on Israeli civilians by members of militant Palestinian organizations. Israeli military offensives—most recently 'Operation Cast Lead' in December 2008–January 2009 (see Recent History)—have had profound effects on the macroeconomic and socioeconomic environment within the Palestinian territories.

In November 1998 an international airport was inaugurated at Gaza; however, the implementation of further measures to reduce the dependence of the Palestinian economy, such as the opening of seaport facilities in the Gaza Strip, has been halted by the prolonged delay in implementing the agreements finalized in Oslo, Norway, in 1993 (and thus known as the Oslo Accords). In October 1999 a 'southern' safe corridor between Gaza and Hebron in the West Bank was finally inaugurated. Despite this achievement, by mid-2013 the provision for a seaport at Gaza had still not been implemented, although in April 2000 a contract to construct the port was signed by the Palestinian (National) Authority (PA) and a Franco-Dutch consortium; moreover, the airport and safe passage were both closed by the Israeli authorities.

Perhaps the strongest link with the Israeli economy, and the one that proved the most difficult to break, was the employment that Palestinians found within the 'Green Line' (separating them from Israel), which provided many families with their livelihoods. In 1992 some 35% of the West Bank's and 45% of the Gazan labour force was employed in Israel, mainly in unskilled and semi-skilled occupations—especially in the construction industry. In 1993, following a series of attacks on Jews within Israel, the Israeli Prime Minister, Itzhak Rabin, ordered the closure of Israel's borders with the West Bank and Gaza, preventing an estimated 70,000 West Bank and some 50,000 Gazan Palestinians from travelling to work. Significantly, controls on cross-border movement were relaxed only after considerable pressure from Israeli employers; the 'reserve labour force' of some 100,000 unemployed Israelis had been reluctant to do the Palestinians' work, much of which was low paid and menial. However, as a result of the al-Aqsa *intifada* (uprising), which began in September 2000, by 2005 only an estimated 46,300 Palestinians were employed in Israel and the Jewish settlements—about 2% of the Israeli labour force, and an estimated 20,000 of whom were employed in the settlements—compared with some 124,000 previously. More than 5,000 Palestinian workers lost their jobs as a result of the Israeli disengagement from the Gaza Strip, which was completed in September 2005. The number of permits issued to Palestinians to work in Israel had decreased from around 30,000 prior to the al-Aqsa *intifada* to 2,000 by September 2001; by April 2005 it stood at around 20,000. In June 2004 the Israeli Government issued a decree to reduce significantly the number of Palestinians working in Israel by 2008, although by 2011 the Palestinian Central Bureau of Statistics (PCBS) estimated that some 10% of the employed labour force continued to work in Israel or the settlements. Furthermore, there were reported to be a significant number of Palestinians working illegally in Israel and the settlements, equal to or even exceeding the number of those to whom a permit had been granted. Since February 1996 Israel and East Jerusalem have been closed to most Palestinian residents of the West Bank and Gaza Strip. As the closures affect movement in both directions, the economy of East Jerusalem (see Occupied Territories), deprived of West Bank markets for its goods and services, has all but collapsed. Closures have had a similarly disruptive effect within the West Bank, since they restrict communications between Palestinian towns via Israeli-controlled Jewish areas of the West Bank. Such areas comprise most of the territory of the West Bank outside the Palestinian population centres.

THE ECONOMIC IMPACT OF THE AL-AQSA UPRISING AND HAMAS'S RISE TO POWER

Living standards among Palestinians in the West Bank and Gaza have deteriorated considerably as a result of the al-Aqsa *intifada*, and the subsequent closure by Israel of the Palestinian territories and Gaza International Airport. By the end of September 2004 the Palestinian Economic Council for Development and Reconstruction (PECDAR) estimated that the total monetary loss to the economy during the four years of the *intifada* and Israel's policy of closures and incursions was some US $19,900m. According to PECDAR, the closure of Gaza's airport has had a particularly serious impact on tourism and foreign investment in the Palestinian enclaves, resulting in losses of an estimated $392m. by the same month. However, agriculture, industry, construction, trade, tourism and social services have also been badly affected by the political situation in the region, suffering losses estimated to be in excess of $10,000m.

The military blockade first imposed on the Palestinian territories by Israel in immediate reaction to the al-Aqsa protests, on 28 September 2000, quickly hardened into a comprehensive siege of the Palestinian economy. After 9 October the movement of people and goods across the 'Green Line' dividing the West Bank from Israel was halted. Palestinian goods were subsequently denied passage through the West Bank border crossings with Jordan, Gaza's Rafah crossings with Egypt and Israeli transit facilities. Thousands of truck-loads of goods were impounded in Israeli ports. After 14 November the Israeli army imposed an almost complete internal closure on the territories. The economic blockade deprived the PA of the taxes on goods and salaries of those Palestinians employed in Israel. The PA also lost revenues from the commercial enterprises in which it held stakes; the most prominent of these was the Paris Casino in Jericho, which was closed in mid-October. The combination of unrest and closure brought the Palestinian economy to a near standstill. Some 125,000 workers—about one-quarter of the labour force—who carried out regular day-labour in Israel, lost their jobs. Another 60,000 within the Occupied Territories were prevented from reaching their workplace.

In the first months of the al-Aqsa *intifada*, the Palestinian economy was losing an estimated US $9m. per day, of which $3.5m. was lost wages. The total economic losses by the end of October 2001 roughly equalled losses during the first year of the original *intifada*, which began in 1987. Thousands of dunums of agricultural land in the West Bank and Gaza had been demolished and numerous Palestinian buildings either destroyed or occupied by the Israeli military. Moreover, facing the prospect of starvation, many Palestinians were forced to accept UN handouts. During late 2000 and early 2001 UN workers began distributing sacks of food to around 217,000 families throughout the territories; however, despite an international appeal, the shortage of funds meant that deliveries were restricted to three-monthly intervals.

The European Union (EU) sought to play an active role in the Palestinian–Israeli conflict, both politically and economically, but largely acted as a moral voice in support of Palestinian rights. On 8 November 2000 the EU approved an emergency payment of some US $23.3m. to the PA to enable it to meet its current expenses, such as the salaries of public sector employees. The payment was the first to be made from the EU's Special Cash Facility, a fund established in 1998 to provide refundable advances to the PA to cover current expenses at times of crisis. In December the organization pledged a further $57m. to the PA. In March 2001 the EU Commissioner for External Affairs, Chris Patten, warned Israeli leaders that their economic stronghold on the Palestinian territories must be lifted. Patten stated that the EU was urging Israeli Prime Minister Ariel Sharon to transfer £36m. in tax revenue, which Israel had withheld from the Palestinian administration.

In January 2001 the Palestinian Minister of Finance, Muhammad Zohdi al-Nashashibi, requested that Arab League states transfer more of the estimated US $1,000m. of funds pledged to the PA by Arab leaders at their extraordinary summit meeting held in Cairo, Egypt, in October 2000. Al-Nashashibi announced that the Palestinian economy had lost a staggering US $2,900m. since Israel ordered the closure of the West Bank on 9 October. The economy was in a state of paralysis, with the World Bank estimating that gross domestic product (GDP) had contracted by some 12% in 2001; productive activity had virtually ceased in much of the West Bank. Amid continued border closures, military incursions by Israel into Palestinian towns, and the destruction of much of the PA's infrastructure, the administration was effectively bankrupt.

The worsening economic and humanitarian situation in the Palestinian territories from the second half of 2002 caused much international concern. In January 2003 the UN Conference on Trade and Development reported that the Israeli blockade and closures over the past two years had pushed the Palestinian economy into such a stage of 'de-development' that as much as US $2,400m. had been drained out of the economy of the West Bank and the Gaza Strip, and that Israeli restrictions on travel had squeezed Palestinian manufacturing, construction and much of the public service sector. The prolonged occupation had also led to 'deep-seated structural weaknesses and imbalances' that would make it almost impossible for the PA to meet either domestic or international demands for reform.

In September 2003 Peter Hansen, Commissioner-General of the UN Relief and Works Agency (UNRWA) outlined the main points of the economic and humanitarian crisis in the Palestinian enclaves: unemployment had risen to 80% in some areas; approximately 60% of the population was living on an income below the UN's poverty threshold of US $2 per day; levels of acute malnutrition had reached 25%, with women and children the most acutely affected; and the vaccination rate had fallen to 85%. UNRWA delivered emergency relief to thousands of Palestinian refugees, but in 2003 it was reported that the Palestinians had received only $90m. of the $172m. sought from donors.

The PA's financial situation remained precarious. As a result of rising unemployment, reduced demand and Israel's withholding of taxes collected on the PA's behalf, monthly revenues dropped from US $91m. in late 2000 to $19m. in 2003. A collapse of the PA was avoided by donor budget support, which had totalled $1,100m. over the previous two years; 75% of this came from Arab countries. The resumption of revenue transfers by Israel was a positive development. With unemployment rising and incomes collapsing, more than 500,000 Palestinians became fully dependent on food aid. Donor disbursements as a whole doubled from pre-*intifada* levels to $929m. in 2001, and increased again in 2002, to just over $1,000m.

In February 2003 the PA called for US $1,500m. in aid to deal with the worsening humanitarian crisis in the West Bank and Gaza at talks in London, United Kingdom. The PA's plea for funds was issued after UNRWA had stated that it needed $94m. immediately for food purchases. Meanwhile, the World Bank warned that the Palestinian economy had shrunk to half its size in the previous two years, blaming Israeli closures as the 'proximate cause' thereof.

In December 2003 the UN released a summary of 'The Right to Food', a report on the Palestinian territories by the Special UN Rapporteur, Jean Ziegler. The report stated that between September 2000 and May 2003 Israeli forces had uprooted hundreds of thousands of olive, citrus and other fruit trees. Some 806 wells, 296 agricultural warehouses and 2,000 roads were also destroyed. The Palestinian Hydrology Group reported that between June 2002 and February 2003 some 42 water tankers and 9,128 Palestinian rooftop water tanks had been destroyed by the Israeli military. The international charity Oxfam reported that Israel had extracted more than 80% of the water from the West Bank aquifer, despite the fact that it was the Palestinians who were legally entitled to this water. Palestinians were also entitled to the Gaza aquifer and the water from the Jordan river; however, irrigated farmland along the river had been declared a closed military area that Palestinians were not permitted to use. Furthermore, statistics suggested that Israelis received and used five times more water than Palestinians. Meanwhile, a 2008 World Health Organization (WHO) report warned of increasing levels of sewage in public drinking water around the Gaza Strip. Low levels of rainfall in that year exacerbated the problem, but it is the pumping of untreated sewage into the sea, which then seeps back into the Gaza aquifer and its drinking water, that continues to be the main cause. The WHO report concluded that with Israel cutting all electricity and fuel supplies to Gaza, following the rise to power of the militant Islamic Resistance Movement (Hamas), the water and sanitation system in the area was on the brink of collapse, a situation exacerbated by damage caused during the Israeli military offensive in the Gaza Strip in December 2008–January 2009. A report published in June 2009 by the International Committee of the Red Cross contended that the dismal state of the water and sanitation services in the Gaza Strip 'raises the spectre of a major public health crisis', and the humanitarian organization urged the Israeli Government to lift import restrictions on cement, steel and other materials needed to rebuild houses and to maintain and upgrade vital infrastructure.

Optimism was expressed at the prospect of Israel's plan to withdraw its troops and remove Jewish settlements from the Gaza Strip, and to withdraw from four settlements in the West Bank, in August 2005 (see Recent History). It was hoped that this measure would improve Palestinian access to export markets. This, together with investment in skill development and the building of infrastructure (with the help of aid donors), could rejuvenate the private sector, analysts asserted. A further restriction on the Palestinian economy was lifted in November 2005, when the Rafah crossing between the Gaza Strip and Egypt was opened, reportedly significantly improving conditions for the Palestinian export market and opportunities for Palestinians to work abroad. However, the constant closure of the Karni crossing between the Gaza Strip and Israel was detrimental to the Palestinian economy, especially the food export sector. Moreover, the victory of the militant Hamas in the January 2006 Palestinian legislative elections led to an almost complete international boycott of the PA, which had severe effects on the Palestinian economy (see Aid and Economic Development). Following the capture of an Israeli soldier by Palestinian militants in June 2006 (see Recent History), Israel reoccupied parts of the Gaza Strip and placed severe restrictions on its links to the outside world. The escalation of political unrest between the Fatah and Hamas organizations in 2007, and in particular the seizure of control of the Gaza Strip by Hamas militants in June (see Recent History), had serious economic implications for the Palestinian territories. Israel's consequent isolation of the Gaza Strip exacerbated the situation for the population there, as did 'Operation Cast Lead'.

POPULATION

According to the results of the second census conducted by the PCBS, the Palestinian population of the West Bank and Gaza Strip totalled 3,698,257 (males 1,877,028; females 1,821,229) in December 2007. By mid-2013 the total population had increased to 4,420,549, according to PCBS estimates. The administrative capital, Ramallah, was home to an estimated 74,792 people at mid-2011, according to UN figures. The population of the West Bank and Gaza increased at an average annual rate of some 2.5% in 2002–11, according to the World Bank. The population of the Palestinian territories is very young, with some 40.1% of the population estimated to be aged under 14 years in 2013. Thus, education has been targeted as a key area of economic development.

LABOUR FORCE

According to ILO, the strength of the Palestinian labour force aged 15 years and over was 875,012 in 2008, while the rate of unemployment stood at 26.1%. An estimated 22.9% of the total labour force in the West Bank was unemployed in 2004, and the rate was 35.4% in the Gaza Strip; the World Bank asserted that unemployment in the Palestinian enclaves in that year was about two-and-a-half times greater than it had been prior to the start of the *intifada* in 2000. Unemployment in Gaza increased significantly following the installation of the Hamas-led administration in early 2006 and the subsequent trade blockades imposed on the territory. In 2008 the IMF cited average unemployment rates of 40% in Gaza and 19% in the West Bank, up from 30% and 18%, respectively, in 2007. Unemployment was reported to have risen further following the Israeli offensive in the Gaza Strip in December 2008–January 2009. According to the PCBS, the rate of unemployment for the Palestinian territories declined in 2010, to 23.7%, and again in 2011, to 20.9%. However, the rate increased again, to 23.0%, in 2012.

NATIONAL ACCOUNTS

In 1997, according to the PCBS, the gross national income (GNI) of the West Bank and Gaza Strip, measured in current prices, totalled US $4,906m. Net factor income from abroad comprised $625m. in wage income, mainly from Palestinian workers in Israel, and $108m. in net property income from abroad. GDP in market prices amounted to $4,173m. GDP at factor cost totalled 10,602m. new Israeli shekels in 1996. Of this total, private services (including trade, rental services and transport) contributed 38%, public services (including central and local government) 23%, industry (manufacturing, quarrying and the supply of utilities) 16%, agriculture and fishing 14%, and construction 9%. On the basis of these figures and surveys by the PCBS of the population in 1997, average GNI per head in the West Bank and Gaza Strip amounted to $1,779 in that year, while average GDP per head was $1,537. In 2003 the World Bank estimated that GNI in the Palestinian territories, measured at average 2001–03 prices, totalled $3,584m., equivalent to $1,060 per head. According to the World Bank, real GDP per head declined by 2.1% per year during 1995–2005. Per caput GNI, meanwhile, decreased by an average annual rate of 2.3% over the period 1996–2005. According to the PCBS, in 2003–07 GDP decreased by an average annual rate of 0.2%. The economy grew by 0.7% in 2007, but, taking the rise in population into account, actual incomes fell. A report published in July 2009 by the IMF Resident Representative in the West Bank and Gaza, Oussama Kanaan, indicated that real GDP per head had fallen by an annual average rate of 4% in 2006–08. According to PCBS figures, real GDP increased by 9.9% in 2011, while real GDP per caput growth was 6.2% in 2010 and an estimated 6.6% in 2011. However, the economic performance of the territories declined significantly in 2012, owing to a variety of external factors, including shortfalls in external aid and a concomitant increase in the public deficit. According to preliminary PCBS estimates, real GDP growth declined in 2012, to 5.8%, while per caput growth fell to just 2.7%.

CONSUMER PRICES

The annual rate of consumer price inflation in the West Bank and Gaza averaged 4.3% in 1996–2006. Annual inflation in the Palestinian economy averaged 2.8% in 2007, before increasing significantly in 2008, to 9.7%. The rate slowed considerably in 2009, to 2.8%, before increasing to 3.7% in 2010, according to PCBS figures. In 2011 the rate was recorded at 2.9%, falling marginally, to 2.8%, in 2012.

AGRICULTURE

According to the PCBS, the agriculture, forestry and fishing sector contributed 6.7% of GDP in the West Bank and Gaza Strip in 2011. PECDAR estimated losses to the agricultural sector as a result of the al-Aqsa *intifada* and Israel's closures and incursions to be US $884m., from the start of the *intifada* in September 2000 to September 2004. According to ILO, agriculture, hunting, forestry and fishing engaged an estimated 15.6% of the classified employed Palestinian labour force in 2008; by 2010 PCBS figures suggested that this rate had declined to 11.8%. The trade embargo imposed by Israel in June 2007 resulted in the near-total cessation of Palestinian exports. In November Israel announced that it would allow the export of some agricultural products from the Gaza Strip, but attacks on border crossings by alleged Palestinian militants prompted the Israeli Government to rescind this overture in early 2008. Previously, citrus fruits were the principal export crop, and horticulture also made a significant contribution to trade. Other important crops included tomatoes, cucumbers, olives, potatoes, aubergines and grapes. The livestock sector was also significant. Agro-industrial production was focused on the dairy and olive oil sectors. Although about one-half of Palestinian exports were derived from agricultural production, the sector remained orientated towards supplying local needs. Like other sectors of the economy, agricultural production and export trade were characterized by a high degree of dependence on Israel, and consequent vulnerability to Israeli border policy: some 60% of Gaza's agricultural production was exported via Israel as originating in Israel. One example was the lucrative, export-orientated production of carnations in Gaza. In 1994, of total production of 120m. flowers, only 2m. were exported directly to European markets, the remainder being distributed through Israel. Carnation production is also heavily reliant on water resources controlled by the Israeli authorities. In February 2009, at the request of the Dutch Government, Israel sanctioned the shipment of 25,000 carnations from Gaza, the first time that the export of flowers from the Palestinian territory had been permitted in over a year. Meanwhile, in June 2006 the Ministry of Agriculture reported that Palestinian agriculture had lost more than $1,200m. since the outbreak of the al-Aqsa *intifada*. In April 2009 former Minister of Agriculture Muhammad al-Aghaa claimed that the sector had lost $147m. as a result of the Israeli offensive in the Gaza Strip at the turn of the year.

Expansion of agricultural production in the West Bank and Gaza is severely limited by problems with irrigation. Traditionally, wells and cisterns have accounted for some 66% of all water consumed, highland springs for some 27% and surface run-off water and water purchased from the Israeli water utilities for the remainder. Some 75% of annual rainfall is lost to evaporation. Agriculture uses about 70% of water consumed in the West Bank, but only 4% of the total land area in the West Bank is irrigated, compared with 45% within Israel. In the mid-1990s Palestinian agricultural production consumed some 152m. cu m of water annually, compared with consumption (for the same purpose) of 56m. cu m by the approximately 120,000 Jewish settlers in the West Bank. In the Gaza Strip, irrigation of the important citrus crop has been affected by rising salinity in the groundwater supply. In central Gaza, groundwater salinity levels are three times as high as WHO's recommended safety level. The area also suffers from a water deficit, estimated at approximately 60m. cu m annually. Consumption per head is estimated at around 110 litres per day for drinking, washing and cleaning, far below WHO's recommended amount. Heavy tapping by Israeli wells and some 4,000 illegal Palestinian wells drains the aquifer in the Gaza Strip, and its water is heavily chlorinated and contains six times the level of nitrates that WHO deems safe for consumption. The US Agency for International Development (USAID) issued a request for proposals in March 2003 for a contract to design and build a major water carrier in the Gaza Strip. The project was postponed following the killing of three US citizens by Palestinian militants in Gaza in October; however, in September 2005 the US construction company Morganti was reported to be preparing to start work on the project, which would involve the construction of 137 km of pipeline, 11 storage reservoirs and six pumping stations. USAID was to provide US $66m. for the project. The carrier was to connect to reservoirs and wells in the Gaza Strip, as well as a planned $70m. desalination plant, which was also to be funded by USAID. However, as of mid-2013 plans for the project appeared to have stalled.

In 2008 a feasibility study got underway to evaluate the social and environmental impact of a proposed 180-km Dead Sea–Red Sea canal, intended to reduce the extremely high water losses from the PA and to increase fresh supplies to the PA, Israel and Jordan by as much as 800m. cu m annually. The study, jointly commissioned by the three territories, was ongoing in mid-2013; draft reports for public consultation were published in July, but the release of final reports was undetermined. The total cost of the scheme was projected at US $800m.

The fishing industry, formerly one of the Gaza Strip's most profitable activities, has been severely constricted by Israeli restrictions on the area in which Palestinian boats may fish. In August 2006, after Israel had begun an offensive in Gaza in late June (see Recent History), FAO expressed concern about further declining incomes in the fishing and farming sectors, following the imposition by Israel of severe restrictions on fishing and exports, fuel shortages, the destruction of thousands of square metres of agricultural land, the drop in international aid and declining cash incomes. The deteriorating conditions increased uncertainty throughout the agricultural sector (particularly in Gaza) during 2006–13. Previously imported items such as fertilizers were no longer readily available and demand for locally produced agricultural products declined, following the huge increase in food aid (which decreased domestic demand) and the trade embargo (which restricted access to foreign markets).

INDUSTRY

According to the PCBS, industry (mining and quarrying, manufacturing, electricity and water supply, and construction) contributed 23.2% of the GDP of the West Bank and Gaza Strip in 2011. PECDAR estimated losses to the sector owing to the al-Aqsa *intifada* and Israel's closures and incursions at US $2,003m., from the start of the *intifada* in September 2000 to September 2004. According to PCBS figures, the sector engaged 26.8% of the employed labour force in the West Bank and Gaza in 2010.

Mining and quarrying contributed 0.8% of the GDP of the West Bank and Gaza Strip in 2011, according to the PCBS; the sector accounted for 0.3% of the classified employed labour force in 2008, according to ILO. According to the PCBS, manufacturing contributed 12.3% of the GDP of the West Bank and Gaza in 2011. In 2008 some 12.7% of the classified employed labour force in the West Bank and Gaza Strip were employed in construction, according to ILO. However, the imposition of trade blockades in 2006 impeded the flow of raw materials required to sustain the manufacturing and construction sectors in the Gaza Strip. By mid-2007 conditions had worsened and firms in both sectors were forced to halt production as a consequence. The associated effect of the industrial collapse was a massive increase in unemployment, and some sources estimated that 63,000 workers in the manufacturing industry lost their jobs between June and August. However, ILO data for 2007 suggest that the proportion of the employed labour force engaged in manufacturing actually rose slightly from the previous year, to 12.3%, while the proportion engaged in construction declined modestly, to 10.9%. Meanwhile, UNRWA was forced to abandon construction of a number of key projects that it had initiated in Gaza, mainly related to the reconstruction effort and the provision of basic facilities. Total losses accrued in the construction sector were valued at some US $160m. in mid-2007. In late July 2009 it was reported that—at the behest of the UN Special Co-ordinator for the Middle East Peace Process, Robert Serry—the Israeli Government had authorized a lone shipment to the Gaza Strip of 130,000 metric tons of cement, together with other building materials, much needed for reconstruction efforts in the wake of the Israeli offensive at the start of the year. The shipment constituted the first such official transfer since before the military operation. In June 2010, following international criticism of Israel's continued blockade of Gaza after the interception of a Turkish-led convoy attempting to deliver humanitarian supplies and construction materials to Gaza (see chapter on Israel), the Israeli Government announced that it would ease restrictions on the transfer of goods into Gaza, instituting a list of prohibited goods which it believed to be for military use. According to PCBS figures, construction contributed 8.3% of the GDP of the West Bank and Gaza in 2011. The sector engaged 14.5% of the employed labour force in 2010.

The frequent closure of the West Bank and Gaza Strip by the Israeli authorities has prompted the development of free trade industrial zones on the Palestinian side of the boundaries separating Israel from the territories. Israeli and Palestinian enterprises can continue to take advantage of low-cost Palestinian labour at times of closure, and the zones also benefit from tax exemptions and export incentives. Small and medium-sized enterprises dominate production in the three Gazan and six West Bank industrial zones. At the Erez zone, adjacent to the crossing between Israel and the Gaza Strip, textile production has emerged as a significant industry. In January 1998 the World Bank announced a loan of US $10m. to the PA for the development of the Gaza Industrial Estate project; other donors included the International Finance Corporation and the European Investment Bank. However, between 2001 and 2005, with the devastating effects of the *intifada* and Israeli repercussions on the Palestinian economy, over one-half of the Estate's factories were closed. A new industrial zone was inaugurated in the West Bank in July 2009, and was expected to create over 2,000 jobs. A further two industrial zones, to be sponsored by Germany and Turkey, respectively, were planned for the West Bank in the short term. A Qatari-Palestinian joint project for the construction of a new, planned city in the West Bank was approved by the PA Cabinet in July 2009. Construction work on Rawabi, which was intended to provide homes for up to 40,000 residents and was situated some nine km north of Ramallah, commenced in January 2010; the first residents were expected to move into the city in early 2014.

ENERGY

According to the PCBS, electricity and water supply accounted for 1.9% of the GDP of the West Bank and Gaza Strip in 2011. Electricity and gas utilities together employed some 0.5% of the total classified employed Palestinian labour force in 2008, according to ILO. The Palestinian Energy Authority (PEA) was established in 1994 to develop the energy and power sectors. In addition to the Jerusalem District Electricity Co (JDECO—which supplies Jerusalem, Jericho, Bethlehem, Ramallah and al-Birah), the Palestine Electric Co (PEC) began operations in 1999. In Gaza the distribution of electric power supply is the responsibility of 16 municipalities and village councils, which mostly purchase electricity from the Israel Electric Corpn (IEC). In the West Bank, distribution is the responsibility of 252 municipalities and village councils, of which 110 purchase electricity from the IEC, 67 receive partial supplies from village generator systems, and 75 have no formal supplies. The PEC constructed a 140-MW power plant in Gaza, which commenced operations in 2002 and reached full capacity in 2004. However, at mid-2009 the plant was reported to be running only at half-capacity owing to the trade embargo blocking the transfer of necessary fuel and parts, and to damage sustained during an Israeli military attack in late June 2006 as part of its offensive in the Gaza Strip intended to secure the release of an Israeli soldier captured by Palestinian militants. It was expected that the plant would cost US $10m. to repair. Meanwhile, residents in the Gaza Strip were reportedly left with only eight hours of electricity per day. In late August 2007 thousands of Gazans were again left without electricity, after the EU withdrew payments for fuel supplies to Gaza's power plant, amid reports that the Hamas administration in Gaza planned to impose a tax on electricity bills. However, following assurances by leading Hamas officials that this was not the group's intention, the EU agreed to resume fuel payments, albeit on a provisional basis. The National Electric Co—created in 2000—plans to build a second power plant in the West Bank, and in early 2005 the PEC announced plans to construct a 1,000-MW independent power installation in the north of the Gaza Strip to provide West Bank and Israeli businesses with electricity.

In September 2000 production started at the Gaza Marine natural gas field, which had been discovered off the coast of the Gaza Strip in 1999. However, further production was stymied by the effects of the al-Aqsa *intifada* and, since 2007, the Israeli economic blockade on Gaza. The field contains an estimated 1,200,000m. cu ft of natural gas, which could be worth US $50m.–$100m. per year to the PA. The contract to develop the field was awarded to the British company BG Group plc, and in July 2005 agreement was reached between BG and the PA on a $400m. development plan for Gaza Marine. BG was assessing plans for the construction of a pipeline to transport natural gas from Gaza Marine to el-Arish in Egypt, from where it could be transported to Europe or North America. Under the proposed scheme, an estimated 1,200m. cu m of natural gas would be transported annually over a 50-year period. As well as helping the Palestinian territories to avoid an energy crisis, exploiting the field was expected to provide the PA with some $50m.–$70m. a year in revenues. However, by mid-2013 progress appeared to have stalled.

SERVICES

In 2011, according to the PCBS, the wholesale and retail trade sector contributed 17.5% of GDP; transport, storage and communications 9.2%; financial intermediation 4.0%; real estate, renting and business services 5.9%; and public administration and defence 16.7%. Some 61.7% of the employed labour force were engaged in the services sector in that year. According to ILO figures for 2008, of the classified employed labour force, 20.1% worked in wholesale and retail trade; 3.5% in hotels and restaurants; 5.8% in transport, storage and communications; 0.9% in financial intermediation; 18.3% in public administration and defence; 12.8% in education; and 4.9% in health and social work.

In February 1997 a stock exchange, the Palestine Exchange (PEX), was inaugurated. With an initial listing of 23 companies, the aim is to develop the PEX as the foundation of a Palestinian capital market and to facilitate the investment of expatriate funds. By mid-2013 49 companies were listed on the PEX, with a total market capitalization of around US $3,000m. According to the Palestine Monetary Authority, there were 19 banks (of which 10 were foreign) operating in the West Bank and Gaza at mid-2013.

In July 2004 the Arab Advisors Group issued a report in which it ranked the Palestinian telecommunications market as the most competitive in the Arab world, with private and foreign investors having a 100% share of its 2003 revenues. The acquisition by Kuwait's Mobile Telecommunications Co (Zain) of a 56.3% stake in Palestine Telecommunication Co (PalTel—the sole mobile and fixed-line provider in the Gaza Strip and the West Bank) was announced in May 2009. PalTel was subsequently merged with Zain Jordan; a combined, rebranded entity was launched later that year. Meanwhile, Wataniya Mobile, a joint venture between the Palestine Investment Fund and Kuwait's National Mobile Telecommunications Co (Wataniya), was awarded a mobile operator licence in September 2006 and had expected to commence operations by the end of 2008; however, following a dispute with the Israeli Government over the release of the necessary radio spectrum, the launch was delayed. Services finally commenced in the West Bank in November 2009.

EXTERNAL TRADE

Israel remains by far the largest market for goods and services from the West Bank. In 2011 trade with Israel represented some 86.0% of exports from, and 56.8% of imports to, the Palestinian territories. During 1988–90 exports of goods and services from the West Bank decreased at an average annual rate of 16%, and the overall trade deficit was aggravated by the 1990–91 crisis in the Persian (Arabian) Gulf region, when the closure of borders and reduced demand affected the export of agricultural goods and manufactures to Arab markets. In 2003, according to the PCBS, there was a deficit of US $198m. on the current account of the balance of payments. Imports were valued at $1,826m. and exports at $327m., producing a visible trade deficit of $1,499m. By 2008 the trade deficit had increased, to $2,908m. (from imports of $3,466m. and exports of $558m.). The current account in that year stood at $535m. In 2009 the trade deficit increased further, to $3,505m.: while the value of imports rose to $4,136m., the value of exports fell to $631m. There was a deficit of $713m. on the current account in that year. In 2010 the trade deficit increased again, to $3,653m.; although exports increased slightly to $666m., the value of imports also increased to $4,319m. By 2012 preliminary estimates indicated that the trade deficit had increased still further, to $4,884m., while the current account deficit had also expanded, to $2,815m. It had been hoped that, following the implementation of Israel's plan to disengage from the Gaza Strip in 2005, Palestinians in that territory would have improved access to export markets. However, Israeli restrictions on economic activity in the Gaza Strip and the military's reoccupation of and attacks on parts of the Gaza Strip in mid-2006 brought about the almost complete cessation of the Gazan export market. Following widespread international condemnation of 'Operation Cast Lead' in December 2008–January 2009, a slight relaxation of Israeli restrictions on Palestinian trade was discernible. In a July 2009 press statement, IMF Resident Representative in the West Bank and Gaza Kanaan reported that this, together with an improving security situation, had contributed to an amelioration of economic conditions in the West Bank. However, by late 2013 the outlook was less positive. IMF Resident Representative Udo Kock reported that the trade deficit was expected to grow still further in that year, owing to increased demand within the territories and declining growth in Israel, the territories' principal export market.

PUBLIC FINANCES

Sanctions imposed on the West Bank and Gaza Strip by the Israeli authorities in August 1997 included the partial suspension of transfers of tax revenues, which, according to data released by the Israeli Ministry of Foreign Affairs in July of that year, accounted for more than 60% of the PA's total revenues. One month after the border closures, according to the World Bank, losses in the Palestinian territories were reported to total US $4m.–$5m. per day, and tax and customs transfers suspended by the Israeli authorities amounted to $65m. The PA was reported to have been obliged to borrow heavily from local banks in order to pay the salaries of its 81,000 employees. Some funds were, in fact, released in August and September 1997, and Israel announced in October that it would release the balance of suspended transfers. Similarly, Israel withheld Palestinian customs and taxes following the commencement of the al-Aqsa *intifada* in September 2000. In July 2002, however, Israel resumed monthly payments of customs and taxes to the PA.

In January 1998 the PA drafted a Palestinian Development Plan for the period 1998–2000, envisaging investment expenditure of US $3,500m. The budget, expected to be completely financed by donor countries, was to allocate $1,690m. to infrastructure projects, $856m. to the public sector, $604m. to manufacturing and $304m. to private institutions. In 1998 the budget of the PA envisaged total revenues of $863.1m., while capital expenditure was projected at $204.7m. and current expenditure was forecast at $802.6m. In that year, according to the IMF, the PA recorded an overall budget deficit of $144.7m., equivalent to an estimated 3.4% of GDP. The 1999 budget forecast revenues totalling $1,589m. and total expenditure of $1,740m., projecting an increased deficit of $151m. In the 2000 budget, total revenues and total expenditure were both forecast at $1,386m.—the first time that the PA had expected a balanced budget. According to the Ministry of Finance, the 2002 budget of the PA recorded revenues of just $335m. and expenditure of $1,171m., leaving a deficit of $836m. The production of a transparent budget was one of the key reforms of the PA demanded by international observers and in January 2003 Dr Salam Fayyad, the PA Minister of Finance, released a provisional budget that drew widespread international praise for its accountability. The Ministry of Finance's revised estimates for the 2003 budget showed total revenue of $701m. (of which $442m. was to come from tax revenues collected by Israel) and total expenditure of $1,403.5m.—although the actual expenditure figure was significantly higher, at $11,404m. The 2004 budget provisionally estimated revenues at $806m. and expenditure at $1,596m., leaving a deficit of $790m.

In November 2003 the EU initiated an investigation into claims that EU funds intended for the PA had been channelled to a Palestinian militant group, the al-Aqsa Martyrs Brigades. An audit of the PA's finances carried out by the IMF in 2003 had estimated that in the period 1995–2000 nearly US $900m. had been diverted into accounts controlled by Yasser Arafat. Moreover, documents seized by Israeli forces during the reoccupation of Palestinian areas in 2001 reportedly revealed that some EU funds had been used by the al-Aqsa Martyrs Brigades. In late February 2004 Israeli soldiers raided banks in Ramallah in an operation to seize funds reputedly belonging to Palestinian militant groups. The Arab Bank and the Cairo-Amman Bank were among those raided, and it was later reported that nearly $9m. had been confiscated.

The PA depended heavily on foreign financing and Israeli tax and customs duties to fund its budget. In December 2004 the USA paid US $20m. of direct budgetary assistance to the PA in advance of the January 2005 presidential election. Some 63% of the 2004 budget revenue had been funded by taxes collected by Israel, while some 31% of the PA's 2005 budget had been funded externally. The decision of Israel and many international donors to cease funding the PA, following Hamas's victory at legislative elections in January 2006, seriously impeded the ability of the PA to find sufficient funds to support the public sector in the Palestinian territories. Some public sector workers received their salaries after the Minister of Foreign Affairs arrived in Gaza in June with $20m. garnered during a trip to various majority-Muslim countries. Also in June the Middle East Quartet group (comprising the UN, the USA, the EU and Russia) agreed to resume aid to the Palestinians (see Aid and Economic Development).

Meanwhile, in April 2006 the US Department of the Treasury Office forbade US businesses and citizens from contributing to the PA without official authorization. Commercial banks in the region that had previously disbursed credit to the PA were discouraged by counter-terrorism legislation from offering further assistance, while many of these lending institutions recalled existing loans. This increased the debt burden of the PA (which already risked defaulting on loans to the private sector) and exacerbated the fiscal shortfall. Previously, external budget financing had been directed into a single treasury account, a practice that had greatly improved fiscal transparency in the PA. However, the freeze on foreign credit blocked this channel of accountability and forced the PA to seek assistance from other sources. Indeed, there were suggestions in 2007 that Hamas was increasingly relying upon Iran to subsidize its operations in the Gaza Strip. Elsewhere, the PA's President, Mahmud Abbas, was leading a separate Fatah administration in the West Bank with support from the international community. Fatah attempts to oust the Hamas contingent from the PA culminated in June 2007 when the national unity administration was dissolved and a 30-day Emergency Cabinet was established in its place (see Recent History). President Abbas appointed a new Prime Minister, former Minister of Finance Fayyad, a move that prompted Israel to resume tax contributions to the West Bank, and funds of some US $350m. were expected to be released to the new administration incrementally. An initial payment of $117m. enabled the PA to pay the wages of thousands of public sector employees in the West Bank, most of whom had not received full salaries since April 2006.

According to the Ministry of Finance, total budgetary support in 2008 reached a record US $1,763m., sufficient to cover the recurrent deficit in that year and allow the repayment of all public sector wage arrears, as well as reducing private sector arrears and the PA's debt to commercial banks. The emergency situation in Gaza contributed to an increase in the PA's recurrent budget deficit from $1,493m. in 2008 to almost $1,641m. in 2009; however, total external budgetary support fell in 2009, to $1,355m. In 2010 the budget deficit declined to $1,056m., exceeding the target of $1,200m. set in the PA's budget for that year, while external budgetary support declined further, to $1,147m. In 2011 the budget deficit fell further, to $783m. External budgetary support also continued to decline, reaching $814m. in that year. However, partly owing to the fall in external budgetary support below expected levels, the IMF reported a shortfall of some $500m. in revenues, which caused the PA to fall into arrears in its domestic payments. In mid-September the World Bank issued a report, in which it forecast a budgetary shortfall of some $1,500m. for 2012. Earlier that month, following protests prompted by rising prices and ongoing high levels of unemployment in the Palestinian territories, Prime Minister Fayyad announced a series of measures intended to alleviate economic pressure on the population. Most notable among the measures announced were a reduction in the rate of VAT to 15%, reductions in fuel prices and cuts in expenditure for some PA departments.

Delays in payment of salaries to PA employees continued into 2013, while political turmoil prompted fears of a deepening of the PA's fiscal difficulties. A budget for that year was finally approved in April. It projected total public revenues of US $2,880m. and expenditure of $3,548m., with an overall deficit of some $1,400m. including development costs, to be covered by external support. However, in September the IMF projected that the total deficit would reach $1,700m. in that year, resulting in a budgetary shortfall of some $300m.

AID AND ECONOMIC DEVELOPMENT

Following the signing of the Declaration of Principles on Palestinian Self-Rule in September 1993, hopes were raised in the West Bank that future economic reconstruction would be financed from abroad. A World Bank report on the territories estimated that a 10-year programme to construct essential infrastructure and social facilities would cost US $3,000m. The Palestine Liberation Organization (PLO), with a more ambitious Palestine Development Programme, estimated that the reconstruction of the Palestinian economy during 1994–2000 would cost $11,600m. The planners expected to generate $2,000m. from domestic savings, and the remainder from external donors; however, it was unclear how much of the total would be allocated to the West Bank if the plan were to be implemented. Following the signing of the Declaration of Principles in 1993, international donors pledged to invest some $2,900m. in the Gaza Strip and the West Bank. However, only $1,348m. of the money pledged between 1994 and 1996 actually reached the Palestinian authorities, owing to the vicissitudes of the peace process and to donors' concerns about the accountability of the Palestinian institutions involved. In December 1997, following a meeting of the Consultative Group of donors (to the Palestinian authorities), held under the auspices of the World Bank, a three-year economic development plan, involving projected expenditure of some $2,600m., was approved. The scheme aimed to rehabilitate the Palestinian economy and to reduce dependence on Israel. The most substantial investments that the plan envisaged were to be made in infrastructure projects, including improvements to irrigation, road construction and waste disposal. Private sector projects, including agriculture and tourism, would also receive funds. The donor countries committed some $750m. of aid for 1998, which would help to finance projects during the initial year of the development plan. For 1999 donor countries pledged to commit aid worth some $770m., although by September only $174m. had been received. In May 1999 the PA requested an additional $40m. in emergency aid, following the 1998–99 drought.

In March 2002 Arab states pledged a further US $330m. in aid to the Palestinian authorities, and in the following month international donors agreed to grant $900m. to assist the PA in rebuilding vital infrastructure destroyed during Israel's military offensive known as 'Operation Defensive Shield', and a further $300m. as emergency relief. In May UNRWA assessed that, in addition to the $117m. that it had previously estimated as being necessary to fund its emergency programmes for 2002, some $70m. would be required to address the immediate humanitarian needs of Palestinians in the West Bank and Gaza arising from the recent Israeli military incursions into the Palestinian enclaves; however, in 2003 it was reported that of the $172m. sought from donors for emergency relief, only $90m. had been forthcoming. In July the US Department of State approved aid to the PA worth $20m. This was the first time that the US Government had given money directly to the PA.

In early 2000 the PA announced the creation of a Palestinian Investment Fund and a Higher Council for Development, the latter being charged with the preparation of a comprehensive privatization strategy by May.

According to a study by the World Bank, programmes operated by UNRWA form the basis of the social welfare system in the West Bank and Gaza Strip, since a significant proportion of the population in the territories is comprised of registered refugees. At 1 January 2013, according to UNRWA, there were 741,409 registered refugees in the West Bank and 1,203,135 in the Gaza Strip. A number of UNRWA's programmes are directed at particularly vulnerable groups, such as the aged and the physically disabled. Palestinians working for Israeli employers are required to participate in Israel's national social security scheme. However, taxes deducted from Palestinian workers finance only very limited benefits to Palestinians because residency in Israel is a prerequisite for most Israeli schemes.

Health services in the West Bank (excluding those areas where jurisdiction has been transferred to the PA) are provided by the Israeli Civil Administration, UNRWA, private voluntary organizations and private, profit-making organizations. Institutions operated by the Israeli Civil Administration in the West Bank derive from Jordanian systems. Until 1974, when a government health insurance scheme was introduced, residents of the West Bank were entitled to free health care from these facilities. Now only members of the government health insurance scheme may receive comprehensive care at government facilities without charge. Pre-natal care and preventive services are provided by the Civil Administration free of charge to all children under the age of three years. UNRWA has traditionally provided basic health care free of charge to refugees in the West Bank and Gaza. It has also reimbursed refugees for 60% of the cost of hospital treatment obtained outside the UNRWA system. UNRWA's budget for 2012/13 provided for about US $28m. to be spent on health programmes in the West Bank, and $27m. on those in the Gaza Strip. UNRWA provides its services through a network of 42 health centres in the West Bank, where some 843 health staff are employed. UNRWA also operates feeding centres, dental clinics, maternity centres and a 34-bed hospital. Twenty-two health centres in the Gaza Strip provide UNRWA services, with 1,037 health staff employed to care for refugees there. In 2012, according to the PCBS, there were 79 hospitals in the West Bank and Gaza Strip.

In May 2005 the PCBS reported on an assessment conducted in January–March of the economic conditions of Palestinian households. According to the report, 65.2% of Palestinian households had experienced a decrease in income during the al-Aqsa *intifada*. During the period of assessment, 66.7% of households surveyed were reportedly living below the poverty line, defined as an income of less than 1,934 new Israeli shekels during the three-month period for a household comprising two adults and four children. In the Gaza Strip, 84.1% of households were apparently living below the poverty line; in the West Bank, the figure was 57.9%. Some 34.8% of households in the Palestinian territories reported that they had received humanitarian assistance during the three months; however, more than twice that number (70.2%) asserted that they required such assistance. The main source of aid was UNRWA, which provided a reported 40.7% of assistance.

In January 2006 Israel halted payments of tax and customs duties to the PA, after Hamas' victory in that month's legislative elections. In February Israel transferred the tax and customs revenues, but announced that all payments to the PA would be halted once the Hamas-led administration had been appointed. At some US $50m. per month, tax revenues from Israel had been the PA's largest source of monthly income. Following the installation of the Hamas-led administration in March, the USA and the EU announced their withdrawal of direct aid to the PA. Every year since the PA had been established in 1994, the EU had donated an estimated $600m., and the USA some $400m. However, the USA promised to increase by over 50% the amount of humanitarian aid it donated to the Palestinians via agencies not linked to the administration, to $245m. The EU maintained that its direct humanitarian aid to Palestinians, which included annual donations from individual states of some $262m., would not be affected by its decision to withdraw direct aid to the PA. Meanwhile, the new Palestinian Cabinet held discussions with other majority-Muslim states with a view to obtaining future funding. Gulf states pledged aid to the PA of some $80m. and Iran some $50m.

Analysts predicted that the Palestinian people would suffer grave economic consequences if other donors did not compensate for the withdrawal of aid by the USA and the EU. Hamas asserted that the PA needed some US $115m. every month just to pay the wages of government workers, of which there were some 165,000, or about one-quarter of the population under the PA's control. Amid a rapidly escalating humanitarian crisis in the Gaza Strip and West Bank, in mid-June 2006 the Quartet group agreed to a plan, proposed by the EU, to resume aid to the Palestinians. Under the so-called Temporary International Mechanism (TIM), no funds would be transferred to the PA. It would support local health services, guarantee fuel supplies, and strive to meet the basic needs of Palestinians living in poverty. In the first of the three stages of the TIM's implementation, some $130m. was transferred to support the emergency provision of health services and utilities. In the second stage, funds were to be used to provide energy supplies in the territories. The third stage was a 'needs-based allowance programme', the aim of which was to create a 'social safety net'. The fund was to be managed by the World Bank and the EU in co-operation with President Abbas. In 2007 the EU committed a further €258m. to finance the second two stages of the TIM strategy.

The aid and humanitarian situation in Gaza further deteriorated as a result of the Israeli offensive launched therein in June 2006. By August, according to the UN Development Programme (UNDP), US $85m.-worth of its projects had been seriously impeded as a result of the Israeli campaign. None the less, in mid-2008 at a donor conference in Berlin, Germany, more than 40 countries pledged $242m. for security projects intended to further the progress towards a Palestinian state. The money was to be channelled to the PA. The pledge followed one of $7,400m. made by donors in December 2007, in the month after the attempted revival of the peace process at the Annapolis conference, in Maryland, USA. However, analysts remained concerned that dependence on charitable donations would not encourage entrepreneurship in the territories, so emphasis was placed on private sector development. The dilemma for the PA was that its economy, as the fifth most aid-dependent in the word, could not function without financial assistance, but this hindered private sector growth, which is crucial for the development of the economy as a whole. The authorities, therefore, urged donors to invest in local businesses, instead of making donations.

According to the Palestinian Ministry of Finance, the USA was the single largest bilateral donor in 2008, providing the PA with US $300m. during that year; Saudi Arabia was the next biggest donor, contributing $234m.-worth of aid. In March 2009 the US Administration pledged $900m. to help alleviate the PA's budgetary deficit and to aid reconstruction efforts in the wake of the Israeli offensive in the Gaza Strip at the turn of the year. Some $200m. of this sum was disbursed in July, with US Secretary of State Hillary Clinton insisting that none of the funds would reach Hamas.

Principally owing to its isolation from foreign markets as a result of the Israeli-imposed economic blockade, the Palestinian economy had remained largely unaffected by the global financial crisis that intensified in September 2008. However, there were concerns that deteriorating economic conditions in donor countries had affected the level of aid disbursement to the PA, amid reports that Arab states, in particular, had significantly reduced their financial assistance in 2010.

The PA suffered a shortfall of some US $200m. in external budgetary assistance for 2011, and was forced to delay wage payments to public sector workers. Following President Abbas' application for full membership of the UN in September (see History), it was revealed that the US House of Representatives Foreign Affairs Committee and the Senate Foreign Relations Committee had voted the previous month to freeze the transfer of US aid totalling some $200m., prompting fears of a severe financial crisis, despite the earlier announcement that Saudi Arabia would increase its contribution for 2011 by the same amount. According to the Palestinian Monetary Authority, total US budgetary assistance fell to just $51m. in 2011, compared with $223m. in 2010.

In March 2013, as part of its initiatives to restart direct negotiations between Israel and the PLO, the Obama Administration announced that it would release up to US $500m. of budgetary support for the PA. Israel also agreed to transfer previously blocked tax and customs revenues. However, the budgetary shortfall projected by the IMF in late 2013 would necessitate further external donor contributions of up to $300m.

Statistical Survey

Source (unless otherwise indicated): Palestinian Central Bureau of Statistics (PCBS), POB 1647, Ramallah; tel. (2) 2406340; fax (2) 2406343; e-mail diwan@pcbs.gov.ps; internet www.pcbs.gov.ps.

Note: Unless otherwise indicated, data include East Jerusalem, annexed by Israel in 1967.

Area and Population

AREA, POPULATION AND DENSITY

Area (sq km)	6,020*
Population (census of 9 December 1997)†	2,895,683
Population (census of December 2007)‡	
Males	1,877,028
Females	1,821,229
Total	3,698,257
Population (official projected estimates at mid-year)	
2011	4,168,860
2012	4,293,313
2013	4,420,549
Density (per sq km) at mid-2013	734.3

* 2,324 sq miles. The total comprises: West Bank 5,655 sq km (2,183 sq miles); Gaza Strip 365 sq km (141 sq miles).

† Figures include an estimate of 210,209 for East Jerusalem and an adjustment of 83,805 for estimated underenumeration. The total comprises 1,873,476 (males 951,693, females 921,783) in the West Bank (including East Jerusalem) and 1,022,207 (males 518,813, females 503,394) in the Gaza Strip. The data exclude Jewish settlers. According to official Israeli estimates, the population of Israelis residing in Jewish localities in the West Bank (excluding East Jerusalem) and Gaza Strip was 243,900 at 31 December 2004 (West Bank 235,700, Gaza Strip 8,200). The withdrawal of Israeli settlers residing in Jewish localities in the Gaza Strip was completed in September 2005.

‡ Includes population counted between 25 December 2007 and 8 January 2008, and estimates for underenumeration.

Note: Official projected estimates of a total world-wide Palestinian population of 10,094,565 at 31 December 2006 included 1,134,293 Palestinians resident in Israel and 2,799,440 resident in Jordan.

POPULATION BY AGE AND SEX

(official projected estimates at mid-2013)

	Males	Females	Total
0–14	904,352	866,778	1,771,130
15–64	1,286,172	1,234,801	2,520,973
65 and over	54,876	73,570	128,446
Total	2,245,400	2,175,149	4,420,549

GOVERNORATES

(official projected estimates at mid-2013)

	Area (sq km)	Population	Density (per sq km)
West Bank			
Janin (Jenin)	583	295,985	507.7
Tubas	402	60,582	150.7
Tulkarm	246	175,494	713.4
Qalqilya	166	105,330	634.5
Salfeet	204	67,641	331.6
Nabulus (Nablus)	605	364,333	602.2
Ram Allah (Ramallah) and Al-Birah	855	328,811	384.6
Al-Quds (Jerusalem)	345	404,165	1,171.5
Ariha (Jericho) and Al-Aghwar	593	49,390	83.3
Beit Lahm (Bethlehem)	659	204,929	311.0
Al-Khalil (Hebron)	997	662,452	664.4
Gaza Strip			
North Gaza	61	335,253	5,496.0
Gaza	74	588,033	7,946.4
Deir al-Balah	58	247,150	4,261.2
Khan Yunus (Khan Yunis)	108	320,835	2,970.7
Rafah	64	210,166	3,283.8
Total	6,020	4,420,549	734.3

PRINCIPAL LOCALITIES

(population at 2007 census, excluding Jewish settlers)

West Bank			
Al-Quds (Jerusalem)	225,416*	Al-Dhahiriya	28,776
Al-Khalil (Hebron)	163,146	Dura	28,268
Nabulus (Nablus)	126,132	Ram Allah (Ramallah)	27,460
Tulkarm	61,941	Beit Lahm (Bethlehem)	25,266
Janin (Jenin)	49,375	Halhul	22,128
Yattah (Yatta)	48,672	Al-Ram and Dahiyat al-Bareed	20,359
Qalqilya	41,739	Bani Na'im	20,084
Al-Birah	38,202		
Gaza Strip			
Ghazzah (Gaza)	449,477	Al-Nuseirat	60,627
Jabalyah (Jabalia)	165,169	Deir al-Balah	54,399
Rafah	156,515	Beit Hanoun	38,074
Khan Yunus (Khan Yunis)	142,613	Bani Suhaylah	31,688
Beit Lahya	64,437	Al-Maghazi Camp	22,612

* The figure refers only to the eastern sector of the city.

Mid-2011 (incl. suburbs, UN estimate): Ramallah 74,792 (Source: UN, *World Urbanization Prospects: The 2011 Revision*).

BIRTHS, MARRIAGES AND DEATHS

(West Bank only, official estimates unless otherwise indicated)*

	Live births		Marriages†		Deaths	
	Number	Rate (per 1,000)	Number	Rate (per 1,000)	Number	Rate (per 1,000)
2010	71,705	n.a.	20,185	8.0	6,253	n.a.
2011	68,197	30.1	20,165	7.8	6,562	4.1
2012	64,895	29.9	23,764	9.0	6,351	4.0

* Excluding Jewish settlers.

† Registered marriages.

Gaza Strip: Live births 50,127 (2007); Registered marriages 16,528 (10.1 per 1,000 persons, 2012); Deaths 4,483 (2007).

Life expectancy (years at birth, official estimates): 72.7 (males 74.1; females 71.3) in 2012.

ECONOMICALLY ACTIVE POPULATION

(persons aged 15 years and over)

	2006	2007	2008
Agriculture, hunting, forestry and fishing	107,024	103,721	86,447
Mining and quarrying	2,237	1,542	1,462
Manufacturing	80,543	81,964	n.a.
Electricity and gas	2,500	2,230	2,780
Construction	73,905	72,722	70,688
Wholesale and retail trade	114,662	116,408	111,537
Hotels and restaurants	13,492	13,407	19,599
Transport, storage and communications	38,242	37,404	32,046
Financial intermediation	4,503	4,214	4,916
Real estate, renting and business activities	11,217	11,380	n.a.
Public administration and defence	98,922	99,584	101,723
Education	67,704	68,034	71,114
Health and social work	24,400	24,525	27,265

—continued	2006	2007	2008
Services	19,426	20,594	19,189
Extra-territorial organizations and bodies	7,221	7,411	6,449
Households with employed persons	348	182	483
Sub-total	666,345	665,322	555,698
Unclassified	30	298	91,324
Total employed	666,375	665,620	647,022
Unemployed	206,150	183,689	227,990
Total labour force	872,525	849,309	875,012
Males	721,153	691,695	715,822
Females	151,372	157,615	159,192

Source: ILO.

Health and Welfare

KEY INDICATORS

Total fertility rate (children per woman, 2011)	3.3
Under-5 mortality rate (per 1,000 live births, 2005–06)	28.2
Physicians (per 1,000 head, 2009, official estimate)	1.9
Hospital beds (per 1,000 head, 2011, official estimate)	1.3
Access to water (% of persons, 2008)	91
Access to sanitation (% of persons, 2008)	89
Total carbon dioxide emissions ('000 metric tons, 2009)	2,163.5
Carbon dioxide emissions per head (metric tons, 2009)	0.6
Human Development Index (2012): ranking	110
Human Development Index (2012): value	0.670

For other sources and definitions, see explanatory note on p. vi.

Agriculture

PRINCIPAL CROPS
('000 metric tons, FAO estimates)

	2009	2010	2011
Wheat	30.0	17.0	17.8
Barley	9.8	6.0	5.8
Potatoes	69.5	40.0	48.6
Sweet potatoes	2.5	0.2	0.0
Olives	85.4	103.6	115.6
Cabbages and other brassicas	25.1	24.5	22.3
Tomatoes	222.4	204.8	198.2
Cauliflowers and broccoli	25.7	26.2	34.6
Cucumbers and gherkins	208.2	233.8	255.2
Aubergines (Eggplants)	57.4	48.0	47.9
Onions, dry	44.6	49.8	52.7
Watermelons	20.0	5.0	5.0
Grapes	55.4	55.2	55.3
Plums and sloes	9.5	8.9	10.3
Oranges	40.8	42.5	44.3
Tangerines, mandarins, clementines and satsumas	7.7	8.4	8.7
Lemons and limes	16.5	16.3	16.8
Grapefruit and pomelos	1.9	1.8	1.6
Bananas	5.5	5.5	5.6
Strawberries	3.4	3.3	3.4

Aggregate production ('000 metric tons, may include official, semi-official or estimated data): Total cereals 40.0 in 2009, 23.3 in 2010, 23.9 in 2011; Total roots and tubers 74.2 in 2009, 40.8 in 2010, 49.4 in 2011; Total vegetables (incl. melons) 735.1 in 2009, 695.4 in 2010, 728.5 in 2011; Total fruits (excl. melons) 171.1 in 2009, 171.7 in 2010, 178.0 in 2011.

Source: FAO.

LIVESTOCK
('000 head)

	2009	2010	2011
Cattle	28.3*	27.4*	30.0†
Sheep†	650.0	613.0	640.0
Goats	300.0*	219.4	200.0†
Chickens†	7,500	7,500	7,600

* Unofficial figure.
† FAO estimate(s).

Source: FAO.

LIVESTOCK PRODUCTS
('000 metric tons)

	2009	2010	2011
Cattle meat	4.3*	5.8*	6.0†
Chicken meat†	47.1	49.0	52.0
Goat meat†	4.9	4.3	4.3
Sheep meat†	11.3	10.7	10.7
Cows' milk†	95.0	98.3	98.3
Hen eggs†	39.7	40.5	40.5

* Unofficial figure.
† FAO estimate(s).

Source: FAO.

Fishing

GAZA STRIP
(metric tons, live weight)

	2009	2010	2011
Capture	1,525	1,699	1,318
Bogue	10	25	14
Jack and horse mackerels	57	82	86
Sardinellas	337	702	256
Chub mackerel	15	39	83
Cuttlefish and bobtail squids	17	8	5
Aquaculture	115	280	189
Total catch	1,640	1,979	1,507

Source: FAO.

Finance

CURRENCY AND EXCHANGE RATES

Monetary Units:
At present, there is no domestic Palestinian currency in use. The Israeli shekel, the Jordanian dinar and the US dollar all circulate within the West Bank and the Gaza Strip.

BUDGET OF THE PALESTINIAN AUTHORITY
(US $ million, estimates)

Revenue	2002	2003*	2004†
Domestic revenue	185	259	298
Revenue clearances‡	150	442	508
Total	335	701	806

Expenditure	2002	2003*	2004†
Central administration	141.8	128.0	109.2
Public security and order	310.4	392.1	433.9
Financial affairs	292.5	352.2	410.7
Foreign affairs	13.8	17.2	25.6
Economic development	35.8	39.8	43.1
Social services	340.5	432.9	526.6
Cultural and information services	25.4	29.2	32.8
Transport and communication services	10.4	12.1	14.2
Total	1,170.6	1,403.5	1,596.1

* Revised estimates.

† Provisional figures.

‡ Figures refer to an apportionment of an agreed pool of selected tax revenues arising as a result of the de facto customs union between Israel and the Palestinian territories. Israel is the collecting agent for these receipts and periodically makes transfers to the Palestinian Authority.

Source: Ministry of Finance, Ramallah.

2010 (US $ million): *Revenue:* Local taxes 707; Clearing 1,320; Total 2,027. *Expenditure and net lending:* Wages and salaries 1,550; Other current expenditure 1,370; Net lending 250; Total 3,170.

2011 (US $ million): *Revenue:* Local taxes 812; Clearing 1,442; Total 2,254. *Expenditure and net lending:* Wages and salaries 1,710; Other current expenditure 1,363; Net lending 160; Total 3,232.

2012 (US $ million): *Revenue:* Local taxes 812; Clearing 1,542; Total 2,354. *Expenditure and net lending:* Wages and salaries 1,793; Other current expenditure 1,290; Net lending 105; Total 3,188.

Source: Ministry of Finance, Palestinian National Authority.

COST OF LIVING

(Consumer Price Index; base: 2000 = 100)

	2010	2011	2012
Food	157.8	161.6	165.0
All items (incl. others)	148.4	152.7	157.0

Source: ILO.

NATIONAL ACCOUNTS*

(US $ million at current prices)

Expenditure on the Gross Domestic Product

	2010	2011	2012*
Final consumption expenditure	10,263.8	12,352.1	13,648.6
Households	7,868.5	9,094.3	10,141.6
Non-profit institutions serving households	356.2	337.4	399.0
General government	2,039.1	2,920.4	3,108.0
Gross capital formation	1,541.1	1,688.9	1,403.0
Gross fixed capital formation	1,445.3	2,020.6	1,834.0
Changes in inventories	95.8	−331.7	−431.0
Total domestic expenditure	11,804.9	14,041.0	15,051.6
Exports of goods and services	1,151.6	1,509.7	1,669.6
Less Imports of goods and services	4,625.9	5,775.4	6,466.6
GDP in purchasers' values	8,330.6	9,775.3	10,254.6

* Preliminary figures.

Gross Domestic Product by Economic Activity

	2009	2010	2011
Agriculture and fishing	373.8	430.3	575.1
Mining and quarrying	48.8	33.2	68.2
Manufacturing	670.2	849.0	1,061.6
Electricity and water supply	157.8	168.0	153.8
Construction	265.6	365.2	710.9
Wholesale and retail trade	1,013.5	1,326.7	1,507.7
Transport, storage and communications	616.4	681.8	790.9
Financial intermediation	270.8	307.4	341.2
Real estate, renting and business services	417.4	526.2	506.1
Community, social and personal services	28.3	34.9	42.3
Hotels and restaurants	98.7	126.7	72.2
Education	523.2	605.7	786.5
Health and social work	223.8	267.0	361.5
Public administration and defence	969.5	1,236.0	1,440.9
Households with employed persons	3.7	5.7	6.0
Other services	140.7	182.5	187.7
Sub-total	5,822.2	7,146.3	8,612.6
Less Financial intermediation services indirectly measured	202.7	236.2	236.2
Gross value added	5,619.5	6,910.1	8,376.4
Taxes on imports	1,100.1	1,420.5	1,398.9
GDP in purchasers' values	6,719.6	8,330.6	9,775.3

* Referring to the West Bank and Gaza Strip, but excluding that part of Jerusalem annexed in 1967.

BALANCE OF PAYMENTS

(US $ million, preliminary estimates)

	2010	2011	2012
Exports of goods f.o.b.	666.1	1,524.9	1,249.6
Imports of goods f.o.b.	−4,318.9	−6,188.3	−6,133.6
Trade balance	−3,652.8	−4,663.4	−4,884.0
Exports of services	830.7	686.3	649.0
Imports of services	−1,142.8	−948.1	−1,031.5
Balance on goods and services	−3,964.9	−4,925.2	−5,266.5
Other income received (net)	1,098.1	1,148.9	1,072.4
Balance on goods, services and income	−2,866.8	−3,776.3	−4,194.1
Current transfers (net)	2,175.9	1,346.7	1,379.4
Current balance	−690.9	−2,429.6	−2,814.8
Capital account (net)	846.1	438.9	297.9
Direct investment abroad (net)	103.0	250.9	246.1
Portfolio investment (net)	−453.4	86.2	44.0
Other investment (net)	341.0	1,739.8	2,410.0
Net errors and omissions	−109.6	−119.8	−17.2
Overall balance	36.4	−33.6	166.0

External Trade

PRINCIPAL COMMODITIES

(US $ million)

Imports c.i.f.	2009	2010	2011
Food and live animals	628.4	703.7	714.7
Beverages and tobacco	137.1	166.1	161.0
Crude materials (inedible) except fuels	36.8	39.3	78.1
Mineral fuels, lubricants, etc.	1,141.4	1,247.5	1,380.8
Animal and vegetable oils and fats	17.6	21.1	22.6
Chemicals and related products	294.3	353.2	352.3
Basic manufactures	553.5	651.0	699.7
Machinery and transport equipment	571.2	536.6	596.6
Miscellaneous manufactured articles	220.4	239.9	215.3
Total	3,600.8	3,958.5	4,221.1

Exports f.o.b.	2009	2010	2011
Food and live animals	61.3	79.4	105.2
Beverages and tobacco	22.0	24.0	30.1
Crude materials (inedible) except fuels	7.2	11.6	94.3
Mineral fuels, lubricants, etc.	2.7	1.5	1.6
Animal and vegetable oils and fats	14.6	15.8	19.9
Chemicals and related products	67.7	74.0	51.9
Basic manufactures	210.5	244.9	240.5
Machinery and transport equipment	30.0	33.0	30.8
Miscellaneous manufactured articles	102.2	91.2	145.3
Total	518.4	575.5	719.6

PRINCIPAL TRADING PARTNERS
(US $ million)

Imports c.i.f.	2009	2010	2011
China, People's Republic	161.8	181.3	194.1
France (incl. Monaco)	38.8	43.5	48.2
Germany	97.3	82.9	100.3
Israel	2,651.1	2,873.5	2,938.4
Italy	40.4	49.0	61.8
Jordan	48.1	67.4	90.0
Korea, Republic	50.5	29.7	46.9
Spain	33.5	39.9	56.1
Switzerland	—	37.3	40.4
Turkey	113.8	179.1	214.7
USA	40.4	41.9	39.9
Total (incl. others)	3,600.8	3,958.5	4,221.1

Exports f.o.b.	2009	2010	2011
Algeria	8.9	7.2	6.4
Israel	453.5	488.4	617.8
Jordan	28.9	31.2	38.9
Netherlands	0.8	3.0	4.6
Saudi Arabia	4.2	5.7	9.7
United Arab Emirates	—	11.7	8.8
USA	6.1	7.3	8.7
Total (incl. others)	518.4	575.5	719.6

Source: Trade Map-Trade Competitiveness Map, International Trade Centre, www.intracen.org/marketanalysis.

Transport

ROAD TRAFFIC
(registered motor vehicles holding Palestinian licence, 2011 unless otherwise indicated)

	West Bank	Gaza Strip*
Private cars	100,406	30,830
Taxis	8,706	2,841
Buses	1,533	615
Trucks and commercial cars	24,999	11,172
Motorcycles and mopeds	373	14,083
Tractors	1,246	738

* 2010 figures.

Tourism

ARRIVALS OF VISITORS AT HOTELS*

	2010	2011	2012
Total	577,383	510,435	575,495

* Including Palestinians.

2010: Total guest nights in hotels 1,285,661 (Palestinians 120,142; European Union members 512,637; Israelis 77,191; Asians 142,271).

2011: Total guest nights in hotels 1,254,496 (Palestinians 141,973; European Union members 469,135; Israelis 73,538; Asians 129,728)..

2012: Total guest nights in hotels 1,336,860 (Palestinians 174,330; European Union members 532,666; Israelis 112,443; Asians 120,587).

Communications Media

	2010	2011	2012
Telephones ('000 main lines in use)	360.4	382.7	406.0
Mobile cellular telephones ('000 subscribers)	2,603.6	2,885.0	3,041.0

Broadband subscribers: 55,600 in 2007.

Internet subscribers: 114,700 in 2009.

Source: International Telecommunication Union.

Education

(2011/12 unless otherwise indicated)

	Institutions	Teachers	Students
Pre-primary	862*	3,285†	63,007*
Primary	1,792	43,560† (Primary and Secondary)	980,213
Secondary	915		149,325
Higher:			
universities, etc.	11‡	6,861§ (universities and other)	213,973§
other	23‡		

* West Bank only.
† 2007/08.
‡ 2006/07.
§ 2010/11.

Pupil-teacher ratio (primary education, UNESCO estimate): 25.6 in 2010/11 (Source: UNESCO Institute for Statistics).

Adult literacy rate (persons aged 15 and over, UNESCO estimates): 94.9% (males 97.6%; females 92.2%) in 2010 (Source: UNESCO Institute for Statistics).

Directory

Administration

PALESTINIAN NATIONAL AUTHORITY

Appointed in May 1994, the Palestinian National Authority, generally known internationally as the Palestinian Authority (PA), has assumed some of the civil responsibilities formerly exercised by the Israeli Civil Administration in the Gaza Strip and parts of the West Bank.

Executive President: MAHMUD ABBAS (assumed office 15 January 2005).

CABINET
(September 2013)

The executive is formed by Fatah, the Democratic Front for the Liberation of Palestine, the Palestinian Democratic Union and independents.

Prime Minister: Dr RAMI HAMDALLAH.

Deputy Prime Minister: ZIAD ABU AMR.

Deputy Prime Minister for Economic Affairs: MUHAMMAD MUSTAFA.

Minister of Finance: SHUKRI BISHARA.

Minister of the Interior: SAID ABU ALI.

Minister of Foreign Affairs: Dr RIYAD NAJIB AL-MALIKI.

Minister of the Environment: YOUSEF ABU SAFIEH.

Minister of Local Government: SAID AL-KAWNI.

Minister of Tourism and Antiquities: ROLA MA'AIYA.

Minister of National Economy: JAWAD NAJI.

Minister of Education and Higher Education: ALI ABU ZUHRI.

Minister of Health: JAWAD AWAD.

Minister of Awqaf (Religious Endowments): MAHMUD SIDQI AL-HABBASH.

Minister of Transport: NABIL SAMAIDI.

Minister of Telecommunications and Information Technology: SAFA NASSER EL-DIN.

Minister of Detainees' Affairs: ISSA QARAQE.

Minister of Women's Affairs: RABIHA THIAB.

Minister of Social Affairs: KAMAL SHARAFI.

Minister of Justice: ALI MUHANNA.

Minister of Labour: Dr AHMAD AL-MAJDALANI.

Minister of Agriculture: WALID ASSAF.

Minister of Culture: SIHAM AL-BARGHOUTHI.

Minister of Public Works and Housing: MAHER GHANIM.

Minister of Jerusalem Affairs: ADNAN HUSSEINI.

Minister of State for Planning: MAHMOUD ABU RAMADAN.

MINISTRIES

Office of the President: Ramallah.

Ministry of Agriculture: POB 197, Ramallah; tel. (2) 2961080; fax (2) 2961212; e-mail moa@planet.edu.

Ministry of Awqaf (Religious Endowments): POB 17412, Jerusalem; tel. (2) 6282085; fax (2) 2986401.

Ministry of Culture: POB 147, Ramallah; tel. (2) 2986205; fax (2) 2986204; e-mail moc@moc.pna.ps.

Ministry of Detainees' Affairs: Ramallah; tel. (2) 2961713; internet www.mod.gov.ps.

Ministry of Education: POB 576, al-Masioun, Ramallah; POB 5285, al-Wihda St, Gaza; tel. (2) 2983200; fax (2) 2983222; e-mail moehe.p@gmail.com; internet www.moehe.gov.ps.

Ministry of Environment: Ramallah.

Ministry of Finance: POB 795, Sateh Marhaba, al-Birah/Ramallah; POB 4007, Gaza; tel. (2) 2825255; fax (2) 2848900; e-mail mof@mof.ps; internet www.mof.gov.ps.

Ministry of Foreign Affairs: POB 1336, Ramallah; tel. (2) 2405040; fax (2) 2403772; e-mail info@mofa-gov.ps; internet www.mofa.gov.ps.

Ministry of Health: POB 14, al-Mukhtar St, Nablus; POB 1035, Abu Khadra Center, Gaza; tel. (9) 2384772; fax (9) 2384777; e-mail moh@gov.ps; tel. (8) 2829173; fax (8) 2826295; internet www.moh.gov.ps.

Ministry of Higher Education: Ramallah.

Ministry of the Interior: Ramallah; tel. (2) 2429873; fax (2) 2429872.

Ministry of Jerusalem Affairs: POB 20479, Jerusalem; tel. (2) 6273330; fax (2) 6286820.

Ministry of Justice: POB 267, Ramallah; POB 1012, Gaza; tel. (2) 2987661; fax (2) 2974491; e-mail info@moj.gov.ps; internet www.moj.gov.ps.

Ministry of Labour: POB 350, al-Irsal St, Ramallah; tel. (2) 2982800; fax (2) 2982801; e-mail info@mol.gv.ps; internet www.mol.gov.ps.

Ministry of Local Government: POB 731, Albaloo, al-Birah/Ramallah; Gaza; tel. (2) 2401092; fax (2) 2401091; tel. (8) 2820272; fax (8) 2828474; e-mail info@molg.gov.ps; internet www.molg.pna.ps.

Ministry of National Economy: POB 1629, Umm al-Sharayet, Ramallah; POB 4023, Maqqusi Bldg, al-Nasser St, Gaza; tel. (2) 2981218; fax (2) 2981207; tel. (8) 2874146; fax (8) 2874145; e-mail info@met.gov.ps; internet www.met.gov.ps.

Ministry of State for Planning: POB 4557, al-Birah/Ramallah; POB 4017, Gaza; tel. (2) 2973010; fax (2) 2973012; tel. (8) 2828825; fax (8) 2830509; e-mail mop@gov.ps; internet www.mop-gov.ps.

Ministry of Public Works and Housing: Gaza; tel. (8) 2829232; fax (8) 2823653; e-mail mopgaza@palnet.com.

Ministry of Social Affairs: POB 3525, Ramallah; tel. (2) 2986181; fax (2) 2985239; e-mail msa@hally.net; internet www.mosa.gov.ps.

Ministry of Telecommunications and Information Technology: Ramallah; Gaza; tel. (2) 2829720; fax (2) 2829740; e-mail smadoukh@gov.ps; internet www.mtit.gov.ps.

Ministry of Tourism and Antiquities: POB 534, Manger St, Bethlehem; Gaza; tel. (2) 2741581; fax (2) 2743753; tel. (7) 2824866; fax (7) 2824856; e-mail mota@visit-palestine.com; internet www.dach.pna.ps.

Ministry of Transport: POB 399, Ramallah; tel. (2) 2986945; fax (2) 2986943.

Ministry of Women's Affairs: al-Birah/Ramallah; tel. (2) 2403315; e-mail contactus@mowa.ps; internet www.mowa.gov.ps.

President and Legislature

Presidential and legislative elections had been due to take place by 25 January 2010; however, the polls were postponed indefinitely owing to the ongoing dispute between the Palestinian (National) Authority Cabinet and the de facto Hamas administration in the Gaza Strip. Following the signature of a unity agreement by the main Palestinian factions in early May 2011, it had been expected that elections would take place later that year. However, by September 2013 no further progress had been made, and elections had yet to be scheduled.

PRESIDENT

Election, 9 January 2005

Candidates	Votes	%
Mahmud Abbas (Fatah)	501,448	62.52
Mustafa Barghouthi (Ind.)	156,227	19.48
Tayseer Khalid (DFLP)	26,848	3.35
Abd al-Halim al-Ashqar (Ind.)	22,171	2.76
Bassam el-Salhi (PPP)	21,429	2.67
Al-Said Baraka (Ind.)	10,406	1.30
Abd al-Karim Shbeir (Ind.)	5,717	0.71
Invalid votes	57,831	7.21
Total	802,077	100.00

Palestinian Legislative Council

e-mail info@plc.gov.ps; internet www.plc.gov.ps.

Speaker: Dr AZIZ DUWAIK.

General Election, 25 January 2006

Parties, Lists and Coalitions	Seats: Majority system	Seats: Proportional system	Seats: Total
Change and Reform*	29	45	74
Fatah	28	17	45
Martyr Abu Ali Moustafa†	3	0	3
The Third Way	2	0	2
The Alternative‡	2	0	2
Independent Palestine§	2	0	2
Independents	0	4	4
Total	66	66	132

* The Islamic Resistance Movement (Hamas) contested the elections as Change and Reform.

† The Popular Front for the Liberation of Palestine contested the elections as Martyr Abu Ali Moustafa.

‡ Electoral list comprising the Palestinian Democratic Union, the Coalition of the Democratic Front (representing the Democratic Front for the Liberation of Palestine) and the Palestinian People's Party.

§ Coalition comprising independents and representatives of the Palestinian National Initiative.

Election Commission

Central Elections Commission (CEC): POB 2319, Qasr al-Murjan Bldg, Al-Balou, nr Jawwal Circle, Ramallah; tel. (2) 2969700; fax (2) 2969712; e-mail info@elections.ps; internet www.elections.ps; f. 2002; independent; comprises 9 mems, appointed by the Exec. Pres. of the PA; Chair. Dr HANNA NASIR; Sec.-Gen. Dr RAMI HAMDALLAH.

Political Organizations

Alliance of Palestinian Forces: f. 1994; comprises representatives of the PLF, the PPSF, the PRCP and the PFLP—GC; opposes the Declaration of Principles on Palestinian Self-Rule signed by Israel and the PLO in September 1993, and subsequent agreements concluded within its framework (the 'Oslo Accords'). The PFLP and DFLP left the Alliance in 1996. The **Fatah Revolutionary Council**, headed by Sabri Khalil al-Banna, alias 'Abu Nidal', split from Fatah in 1973. Its headquarters were formerly in Baghdad, Iraq, but the office was closed down and its staff expelled from the country by the Iraqi authorities in November 1983; a new base was established in Damascus, Syria, in December. Al-Banna was readmitted to Iraq in 1984, having fled Syria. With 'Abu Musa' (whose rebel Fatah group is called **Al-Intifada** or 'Uprising'), Abu Nidal formed a joint rebel Fatah command in February 1985, and both had offices in Damascus until June 1987, when those of Abu Nidal were closed by the Syrian Government. Forces loyal to Abu Nidal surrendered to Fatah forces at the Rashidiyeh Palestinian refugee camp near Tyre, northern Lebanon, in 1990. Abu Nidal was reportedly found dead in Baghdad in August 2002.

Arab Liberation Front (ALF): Ramallah; internet alfpalestine .org; f. 1969; fmrly supported by Iraq's Arab Baath Socialist Party under the leadership of former President Saddam Hussain; member of the PLO; opposes Oslo Accords; Sec.-Gen. RAKAD SALIM (imprisoned in 2002).

Democratic Front for the Liberation of Palestine (DFLP) (Al-Jabha al-Dimuqratiyya li-Tahrir Filastin): Damascus, Syria; tel. (11) 4448993; fax (11) 4442380; Ramallah; tel. (2) 2954438; fax (2) 2980401; e-mail dflp-palestine@dflp-palestine.org; internet www .dflp-palestine.net; f. 1969 following split with PFLP; Marxist-Leninist; contested Jan. 2006 legislative elections on The Alternative electoral list as the Coalition of the Democratic Front; Sec.-Gen. NAIF HAWATMEH (Damascus).

Fatah (Harakat al-Tahrir al-Watani al-Filastin—Palestine National Liberation Movement): POB 1965, Ramallah; tel. (2) 2986892; fax (2) 2987947; e-mail fact@palnet.com; internet www .fateh.ps; f. 1957; militant group that became the single largest Palestinian org. and strongest faction in both the administration and Palestinian Legislative Council until the legislative elections of Jan. 2006; leadership is nominally shared by the members of the Cen. Cttee, who were elected at Fatah's Sixth Gen. Conference on 10 Aug. 2009; Chair. of Cen. Cttee MAHMUD ABBAS.

Islamic Jihad (Al-Jihad al-Islami): Damascus, Syria; f. 1979–80 by Palestinian students in Egypt; militant Islamist; opposed to the Oslo Accords; Sec.-Gen. RAMADAN ABDULLAH SHALLAH.

Islamic Resistance Movement (Hamas—Harakat al-Muqawama al-Islamiyya): Gaza; Damascus, Syria; f. 1987; originally welfare organization Mujama (f. 1973) led by the late Sheikh AHMAD YASSIN (killed by Israeli forces in March 2004); militant Islamist; opposes the Oslo Accords; following the killing by Israeli forces of Hamas's leader in the Gaza Strip, Abd al-Aziz al-Rantisi, in April 2004, the group announced that it was adopting a policy of 'collective leadership'; contested Jan. 2006 legislative elections as Change and Reform; Head of Political Bureau KHALID MESHAAL (Doha, Qatar); Gen. Commdr of military wing, Izz al-Din al-Qassam Brigades, MUHAMMAD DEIF (in hiding from the Israeli authorities since 1992, though presumed to be in Gaza).

Palestine Liberation Front (PLF): f. 1977 following split with PFLP—GC; the PLF split into three factions in the early 1980s, all of which retained the name PLF; one faction (Leader MUHAMMAD 'ABU' ABBAS) was based in Tunis, Tunisia, and Baghdad, Iraq, and remained nominally loyal to Yasser Arafat; the second faction (Leader TALAAT YAQOUB) belonged to the anti-Arafat National Salvation Front and opened offices in Damascus, Syria, and Libya; a third group derived from the PLF was reportedly formed by its Central Cttee Secretary, ABD AL-FATTAH GHANIM, in June 1986; the factions of Yaqoub and Ghanim were reconciled in early 1985; at the 18th session of the PNC a programme for the unification of the PLF was announced, with Yaqoub (died November 1988) named as Secretary-General and Abu Abbas appointed to the PLO Executive Committee, while unification talks were held. The merging of the two factions was announced in June 1987, with Abu Abbas becoming Deputy Secretary-General. Abu Abbas was apprehended by US-led coalition forces in Iraq in April 2003, and reportedly died of natural causes in March 2004 while still in US custody; Sec.-Gen. WASSEL ABU YUSUF.

Palestine Liberation Organization (PLO) (Munazzimat al-Tahrir al-Filastiniyya): Negotiations Affairs Dept, POB 4120, Ramallah; tel. (2) 2963741; fax (2) 2963740; internet www.nad-plo .org; f. 1964; the supreme organ of the PLO is the Palestine Nat. Council (PNC; Pres. SALIM AL-ZA'NUN), while the PLO Exec. Cttee (Chair. MAHMUD ABBAS; Sec.-Gen. FAROUK KADDOUMI) deals with day-to-day business. Fatah (the Palestine Nat. Liberation Movement) joined the PNC in 1968, and all the guerrilla orgs joined the Council in 1969. In 1973 the Palestinian Cen. Council (PCC; Chair. SALIM AL-ZA'NUN) was established to act as an intermediary between the PNC and the Exec. Cttee. The Council meets when the PNC is not in session and approves major policy decisions on its behalf; Chair. MAHMUD ABBAS.

Palestine Revolutionary Communist Party (PRCP) (Al-Hizb al-Shuyu'i al-Thawri al-Filastini): principally based in Lebanon; promotes armed struggle in order to achieve its aims; Sec.-Gen. ARABI AWAD.

Palestinian Democratic Union (FIDA): POB 247, Ramallah; tel. 2954072; fax (2) 2954071; e-mail info@fida.ps; internet www.fida.ps; f. 1990 following split from the DFLP; contested Jan. 2006 legislative elections on The Alternative electoral list; Leader YASSER ABD AL-RABBUH; Sec.-Gen. ZAHIRA KAMAL.

Palestinian National Initiative (Al-Mubadara): Ramallah; tel. (5) 9293006; e-mail almubadara@almubadara.org; internet www .almubadara.org; f. 2002; seeks peaceful resolution of conflict with Israel through establishment of an independent, unified, viable and democratic Palestinian state, with East Jerusalem as its capital; advocates reform of internal political structures, and aims to fight corruption and injustice, and to uphold citizens' rights; contested Jan. 2006 legislative elections as part of the Independent Palestine coalition; Sec.-Gen. Dr MUSTAFA BARGHOUTHI.

Palestinian People's Party (PPP) (Hezb al-Sha'ab): Ramallah; tel. (2) 2963593; fax (2) 2963592; e-mail info@ppp.ps; internet www .palpeople.org; f. 1921 as Palestine Communist Party; adopted current name in 1991; admitted to the PNC at its 18th session in 1987; contested Jan. 2006 legislative elections on The Alternative electoral list; Sec.-Gen. BASSAM EL-SALHI.

Palestinian Popular Struggle Front (PPSF) (Jabhat al-Nidal al-Sha'biyya al-Filastiniyya): f. 1967; has reportedly split into two factions which either support or oppose the PA; the pro-PA faction (Leader AHMAD AL-MAJDALANI) is based in the West Bank; the anti-PA faction (Leader KHALID ABD AL-MAJID) is based in Damascus, Syria.

Popular Front for the Liberation of Palestine (PFLP) (Al-Jabha al-Sha'biyya li-Tahrir Filastin): Damascus, Syria; internet www.pflp.ps; f. 1967; Marxist-Leninist; publr of *Democratic Palestine* (English; monthly); contested Jan. 2006 legislative elections as Martyr Abu Ali Moustafa; Sec.-Gen. AHMAD SAADAT (imprisoned in 2002).

Popular Front for the Liberation of Palestine—General Command (PFLP—GC): Damascus, Syria; internet www.palestinesons .com; f. 1968 following split from the PFLP; pro-Syrian; Leader AHMAD JIBRIL.

Popular Front for the Liberation of Palestine—National General Command: Amman, Jordan; split from the PFLP—GC in 1999; aims to co-operate with the PA; Leader ATIF YUNUS.

Al-Saiqa (Thunderbolt, or Vanguard of the Popular Liberation War): f. 1968; Syrian-backed; pan-Arab; opposed to the Oslo Accords; Sec.-Gen. ISSAM AL-QADI.

The formation of the **Right Movement for Championing the Palestinian People's Sons** by former members of Hamas was announced in April 1995. The movement, based in Gaza City, was reported to support the PA. The **Al-Aqsa Martyrs Brigades**, consisting of a number of Fatah-affiliated activists, emerged soon after the start of the al-Aqsa *intifada* in September 2000, and have carried out attacks against Israeli targets in Israel, the West Bank and Gaza Strip.

Diplomatic Representation

On 29 November 2012 an application to the UN General Assembly by the PLO (as Palestine) for non-member observer status was approved. Of the 193 member states, 138 voted in favour of the application, while nine voted against. A further 46 countries abstained from the vote or were absent.

Countries with which the PLO maintains diplomatic relations include:

Afghanistan, Albania, Algeria, Angola, Argentina, Austria, Azerbaijan, Bahrain, Bangladesh, Belarus, Benin, Bolivia, Bosnia and Herzegovina, Brazil, Brunei, Bulgaria, Burkina Faso, Cambodia, Cameroon, Chad, Chile, China (People's Rep.), Comoros, Congo (Rep.), Costa Rica, Côte d'Ivoire, Cuba, Cyprus, Djibouti, Dominican Republic, Ecuador, Egypt, El Salvador, Ethiopia, Gabon, The Gambia, Georgia, Ghana, Guinea, Guinea-Bissau, Guyana, the Holy See, Honduras, Hungary, India, Indonesia, Iran, Iraq, Jordan, Kazakhstan, Kenya, Korea (Dem. People's Rep.), Kuwait, Laos, Lebanon, Libya, Malawi, Malaysia, Maldives, Mali, Malta, Mauritania, Mauritius, Mongolia, Montenegro, Morocco, Mozambique, Namibia, Nicaragua, Niger, Nigeria, Norway, Oman, Pakistan, Paraguay, Peru, Philippines, Poland, Qatar, Romania, Russia, Saudi Arabia, Senegal, Serbia, Seychelles, Slovakia, Somalia, South Africa, Sri Lanka, Sudan, Syria, Swaziland, Sweden, Tajikistan, Tanzania, Tunisia, Turkey, Uganda, Uruguay, the United Arab Emirates, Uzbekistan, Vanuatu, Venezuela, Viet Nam, Yemen, Zambia and Zimbabwe.

The following states, while they do not recognize Palestine, allow the PLO to maintain a regional office: Australia, Belgium, Canada, Colombia, Denmark, Estonia, Finland, France, Germany, Greece, Iceland, Ireland, Korea (Rep.), Italy, Japan, Latvia, Lithuania, Luxembourg, Mexico, the Netherlands, New Zealand, Portugal, Slovenia, Spain, Switzerland, Syria and the United Kingdom.

Judicial System

In the Gaza Strip, the West Bank towns of Jericho, Nablus, Ramallah, Jenin, Tulkarm, Qalqilya, Bethlehem and Hebron, and in other, smaller population centres in the West Bank, the PA has assumed limited jurisdiction with regard to civil affairs. However, the situation is confused owing to the various and sometimes conflicting legal systems which have operated in the territories occupied by Israel in 1967: Israeli military and civilian law; Jordanian law; and acts, orders-in-council and ordinances that remain from the period of the British Mandate in Palestine. Religious and military courts have been established under the auspices of the PA.

Higher State Security Court: Gaza; f. 1995; decides on security crimes both inside and outside the PA's area of jurisdiction; and to implement all valid Palestinian laws, regulations, rules and orders in accordance with Article 69 of the Constitutional Law of the Gaza Strip of 5 March 1962.

General Prosecutor of the PA: AHMAD AL-MOGHANI.

Religion

The vast majority of Palestinians in the West Bank and Gaza are Muslims, while a small (and declining) minority are Christians of the Greek Orthodox and Roman Catholic rites.

ISLAM

The PA-appointed Grand Mufti of Jerusalem and the Palestinian Lands is the most senior Muslim cleric in the Palestinian territories.

Mufti of Jerusalem: Sheikh MUHAMMAD AHMAD HUSSEIN.

CHRISTIANITY

The Roman Catholic Church

Latin Rite

The Patriarchate of Jerusalem covers Israel and the Occupied Territories, the Palestinian territories, Jordan, and Cyprus.

Patriarchate of Jerusalem: Patriarcat Latin, POB 14152, Jerusalem 91141; tel. (2) 6282323; fax (2) 6271652; e-mail latinvic@latinpat.org; internet www.lpj.org; Patriarch His Beatitude Archbishop FOUAD TWAL; Vicar-General Emeritus for Jerusalem KAMAL HANNA BATHISH (Titular Bishop of Jericho); Vicar-General for Israel GIACINTO-BOULOS MARCUZZO (Titular Bishop of Emmaus Nicopolis).

Melkite Rite

The Greek-Melkite Patriarch of Antioch and all the East, of Alexandria, and of Jerusalem (GRÉGOIRE III LAHAM) is resident in Damascus, Syria.

Patriarchal Vicariate of Jerusalem: Patriarcat Grec-Melkite Catholique, POB 14130, Porte de Jaffa, Jerusalem 91141; tel. (2) 6282023; fax (2) 6289606; e-mail gcpjer@p-ol.com; about 3,300 adherents (31 December 2007); Protosyncellus Archim. Archbishop JOSEPH JULES ZEREY (Titular Archbishop of Damietta).

The Greek Orthodox Church

The Patriarchate of Jerusalem covers Israel and the Occupied Territories, the Palestinian territories, Jordan, Kuwait, the UAE, and Saudi Arabia.

Patriarchate of Jerusalem: POB 14518, Jerusalem 91145; tel. (2) 6274941; fax (2) 6282048; e-mail secretariat@jerusalem-patriarchate.info; internet www.jerusalem-patriarchate.info; Patriarch THEOPHILOS III.

The Press

NEWSPAPERS

Al-Ayyam: POB 1987, al-Ayyam St, Commercial Area, Ramallah; tel. (2) 2987341; fax (2) 2987342; e-mail info@al-ayyam.com; internet www.al-ayyam.ps; f. 1995; weekly; Arabic; publ. by Al-Ayyam Press, Printing, Publishing and Distribution Co; Editor-in-Chief AKRAM HANIYA.

Al-Ayyam al-Arabi: POB 1987, al-Ayyam St, Commercial Area, Ramallah; tel. 2-2987341; fax 2-2987342; e-mail info@al-ayyam.com; internet www.al-ayyam.com; f. 1995; daily; Arabic; publ. by Al-Ayyam Press, Printing, Publishing and Distribution Co; Editor-in-Chief AKRAM HANIYA.

Filastin al-Thawra (Palestine of the Revolution): fmrly publ. in Beirut, Lebanon, but resumed publication from Cyprus in November 1982; weekly newspaper of the PLO; Arabic.

Al-Hadaf (The Target): e-mail alhadaf@alhadafmagazine.com; internet www.alhadafmagazine.com; f. 1969 in Beirut, Lebanon; weekly; Arabic; organ of the Popular Front for the Liberation of Palestine.

Al-Hayat al-Jadidah: POB 1822, Ramallah; tel. (2) 2407251; fax (2) 2407250; e-mail info1@alhayat-j.com; internet www.alhayat-j.com; f. 1994; weekly; Arabic; Editor NADIL AMR.

Al-Hourriah (Liberation): POB 11488, Damascus, Syria; tel. (1) 6319455; fax (1) 6319125; e-mail hourriah@hotmail.com; internet www.alhourriah.org; Arabic; organ of the Democratic Front for the Liberation of Palestine; publ. in Beirut (Lebanon) and Damascus; Editor-in-Chief HAMADEH MU'TASIM.

Al-Istiqlal (Independence): al-Thawra St, Gaza City; e-mail alesteqlal@p-i-s.com; weekly; Arabic; organ of Islamic Jihad; Sec. TAWFIQ AL-SAYYID SALIM.

Palestine Times: POB 10355, London, NW2 3WH, United Kingdom; e-mail palestimes@ptimes.org; internet www.ptimes.org; f. 2006; monthly; English; privately owned; independent; Editor-in-Chief AHMAD KARMAWI; circ. 5,000.

Al-Quds (Jerusalem): POB 19788, Jerusalem; tel. (2) 5833501; fax (2) 5856937; e-mail info@alquds.com; internet www.alquds.com; Arabic; independent; pro-PA; supports peace negotiations; reportedly has largest circulation of all Palestinian newspapers; daily; Editor MAHER AL-ALAMI.

Al-Risala (Letter): Gaza City; weekly; Arabic; affiliated with the Islamic Resistance Movement (Hamas); Editor-in-Chief GHAZI HAMAD.

Al-Watan: Gaza City; weekly; Arabic; supports Hamas.

PERIODICALS

Filastin (Palestine): Gaza City; e-mail adel@falasteen.com; internet www.falasteen.com; f. 1994; weekly; Arabic; pro-Hamas, banned from publication and distribution in the West Bank; Editor-in-Chief MUSTAFA AL-SAWWAF.

The Jerusalem Times: POB 20185, 19 Nablus Rd, Jerusalem; tel. (2) 2961078; fax (2) 2961079; e-mail tjt@yahoo.com; internet www.jerusalemtimes.info; f. 1994; weekly; English; independent; Publr HANNA SINIORA; Man. Editor HALIMA ABU HANEYA.

Al-Karmel Magazine: POB 1887, Ramallah; tel. (2) 2965934; fax (2) 2987374; e-mail editor@alkarmel.org; internet www.alkarmel.org; f. 1981 in Beirut, Lebanon; literature; Editor-in-Chief HASAN KHADER.

Madar: Madar—al-Markaz al-Filastini lil-Dirasat al-Israiliyah, Ramallah; publ. by Madar—The Palestinian Centre for Israeli Studies; political; Editor SALMAN NATOUR.

Palestine Report: Jerusalem Media and Communications Centre, POB 25047, 7 Nablus Rd, Jerusalem 97300; tel. (2) 5838266; fax (2) 5836837; e-mail jmcc@jmcc.org; internet www.jmcc.org; f. 1990; weekly; English; current affairs; publ. by the Jerusalem Media and Communications Centre; Editor-in-Chief JOHARAH BAKER; Man. Dir OMAR KARMI.

The Youth Times: Orabi Bldg, 2 Ramallah St, Jerusalem; tel. (2) 2426280; fax (2) 2426281; e-mail pyalara@pyalara.org; internet www.pyalara.org; f. 1998; monthly; Arabic and English; publ. by the Palestinian Youth Association for Leadership and Rights Activation; Editor-in-Chief HANIA BITAR.

NEWS AGENCY

Wikalat Anbaa' Filastiniya (WAFA, Palestine News Agency): POB 5300, Gaza City; tel. (8) 2824036; fax (8) 2824046; e-mail edit@wafa.ps; internet www.wafa.ps; official PLO news agency; Editor ZIAD ABD AL-FATTAH.

Publishers

Al-Ayyam Press, Printing, Publishing and Distribution Co: POB 1987, Ramallah; tel. (2) 2987341; fax (2) 2987342; e-mail info@al-ayyam.com; internet www.al-ayyam.com; f. 1995; publishes *Al-Ayyam al-Arabi* daily newspaper, *Al-Ayyam* weekly newspaper, books and magazines.

Beit Al-Maqdes for Publishing and Distribution: Ramallah; history, politics, fiction, children's.

Centre for Palestine Research and Studies (CPRS): POB 132, Nablus; tel. (9) 2380383; fax (9) 2380384; f. 1993; history, politics, strategic studies and economics; Dir SAID KANAAN.

Ogarit Centre for Publishing and Distribution: Ramallah; non-fiction, children's.

Broadcasting and Communications

TELECOMMUNICATIONS

A monopoly on fixed-line services is held by the Palestine Telecommunications Co PLC (PalTel). However, a second mobile telephone licence was awarded to Wataniya Mobile in 2006.

Palestine Telecommunications Co PLC (PalTel): POB 1570, Nablus; tel. (9) 2390108; fax (9) 2350140; e-mail paltel@palnet.net; internet www.paltel.ps; f. 1995; following acquisition of 56% stake by Zain Kuwait in May 2009, PalTel was merged with Zain Jordan; provider of fixed-line, mobile (cellular) and internet services; Chair. SABIH T. MASRI; CEO AMMAR AKER.

Palestine Cellular Co (Jawwal): POB 3999, al-Birah/Ramallah; tel. (2) 2402440; fax (2) 2968636; e-mail atyourservice@jawwal.ps; internet www.jawwal.ps/index.php; f. 1999; wholly owned subsidiary of PalTel; 700,000 subscribers (May 2006), representing some 55% of the Palestinian mobile (cellular) telecommunications market; CEO AMMAR AKER.

Wataniya Mobile: POB 4236, al-Birah/Ramallah; tel. (2) 2415000; fax (2) 2423044; e-mail hanin.khoury@wataniya.ps; internet www.wataniya-palestine.com; launched in Nov. 2009; 48.45% owned by Wataniya Group (Kuwait), 36.55% owned by Palestine Investment Fund; Chair. MUHAMMAD MUSTAFA; CEO FAYEZ HUSSEINI.

BROADCASTING

Palestinian Broadcasting Co (PBC): POB 984, al-Birah/Ramallah; tel. (2) 2959894; fax (2) 2959893; e-mail pbcinfo@pbc.gov.ps; internet www.pbc.gov.ps/English/about_us.htm; f. 1994; state-controlled; Chair. BASEM ABU SUMAYA.

Sawt Filastin (Voice of Palestine): c/o Police HQ, Jericho; tel. (2) 921220; f. 1994; official radio station of the PA; broadcasts in Arabic from Jericho and Ramallah; Dir RADWAN ABU AYYASH.

Palestine Television: f. 1994; broadcasts from Ramallah and Gaza City; broadcasts online on JumpTV; Dir RADWAN ABU AYYASH.

Finance

(cap. = capital; p.u. = paid up; res = reserves; dep. = deposits; brs = branches; m. = million)

BANKING

The Palestine Monetary Authority (PMA) is the financial regulatory body in the Palestinian territories, and is expected to evolve into the Central Bank of Palestine. Three currencies circulate in the Palestinian economy—the Jordanian dinar, the Israeli shekel and the US dollar—and the PMA currently has no right of issue. According to the PMA, there were 17 banks operating in the West Bank and Gaza in early 2013.

Palestine Monetary Authority (PMA): POB 452, Nablus Rd, Ramallah; POB 4026, Nasrah St, Gaza; tel. (2) 2415250; fax (2) 2409922; tel. (8) 2407779; fax (8) 2409646; e-mail info@pma.ps; internet www.pma.ps; f. 1994; began licensing, inspection and supervision of the Palestinian and foreign commercial banks operating in the Gaza Strip and the Jericho enclave in the West Bank in July 1995; assumed responsibility for 13 banks in the Palestinian territories over which the Central Bank of Israel had hitherto exercised control in Dec. 1995; Gov. Dr JIHAD AL-WAZIR.

National Banks

Bank of Palestine PLC (BOP): POB 471, Court St, Ain Misbah, Ramallah; tel. (2) 2965010; fax (2) 2964703; e-mail info@bankofpalestine.com; internet www.bankofpalestine.com; f. 1960; cap. US $100m., res $42m., dep. $1,313m. (Dec. 2010); Gen. Man. Dr HANI HASHEM SHAWA; 31 brs and sub-brs in West Bank and Gaza.

Palestine Commercial Bank: POB 1799, Michael Tanous Bldg, Alawda St, Ramallah; tel. (2) 2979999; fax (2) 2979977; internet www.pcb.ps; f. 1992; as Commercial Bank of Palestine; name changed as above 2009; cap. US $35m. (May 2008); Pres. MAHMOUD ZUHDI MALHAS; 5 brs.

Palestine International Bank: al-Birah/Ramallah; tel. (2) 2983300; fax (2) 2983344; e-mail issam@ias.intranets.com; internet www.pibank.net; f. 1997; cap. US $20m.; Chair. OSAMA MUHAMMAD KHADIR; 4 brs.

Investment Banks

Arab Palestinian Investment Bank: POB 1260, al-Harji Bldg, Ramallah; tel. (2) 2987126; fax (2) 2987125; e-mail apibank@palnet.com; internet www.apibank.ps; f. 1996; Arab Bank of Jordan has a 51% share; cap. US $15m.; Dir ABD AL-MAJID SHOMAN; Gen. Man. BESHARA DABBAH.

Palestine Investment Bank PLC: POB 3675, al-Helal St, al-Birah/Ramallah; tel. (2) 2407880; fax (2) 2407887; e-mail info@pinvbank.com; internet www.pinvbank.com; f. 1995 by the PA; some shareholders based in Jordan and the Gulf states; cap. US $60m.; provides full commercial and investment banking services throughout the West Bank and Gaza; Chair. ABD AL-AZIZ ABU DAYYEH; 7 brs.

Al-Quds Bank for Development and Investment (Quds Bank): POB 2471, Ramallah; tel. (2) 2961750; fax (2) 2961754; e-mail quds@qudsbank.ps; internet www.alqudsbank.ps; f. 1995; merchant bank; cap. p.u. US $50m.; Gen. Man. AZZAM A. SHAWWA; 8 brs and 12 offices.

Islamic Banks

Arab Islamic Bank: POB 631, Nablus St, al-Birah/Ramallah; tel. (2) 2407060; fax (2) 2407065; e-mail aib@arabislamicbank.com; internet www.aibnk.com; f. 1995; cap. US $40m., res $9m., dep. $231m. (Dec. 2010); Chair. WALID T. FAKHOURI; Gen. Man. SAMI SAIDI; 8 brs.

Palestine Islamic Bank: POB 1244, Omar al-Mukhtar St, Gaza City; tel. (8) 2827360; fax (8) 2825269; e-mail info@islamicbank.ps; internet www.islamicbank.ps; f. 1996; Chair. MUHAMMED FAYEZ JABER ZAKARNEH.

STOCK EXCHANGE

Palestine Exchange (PEX): POB 128, 4th Floor, Amman St, Nablus; tel. (9) 2390999; fax (9) 2390998; e-mail pex@pex.ps; internet www.pex.ps; f. 1995; CEO AHMAD AWEIDAH.

INSURANCE

A very small insurance industry exists in the West Bank and Gaza.

Ahleia Insurance Group Ltd (AIG): POB 1214, al-Jalaa Tower, Remal, Gaza; tel. (8) 2824035; fax (8) 2824015; e-mail info@aig.ps; internet www.aig.ps; f. 1994; Chair. and CEO Dr MUHAMMAD AL-SABAWI; 11 brs.

Arab Insurance Establishment Co Ltd (AIE): POB 166, al-Qasr St, Nablus; tel. (9) 2341040; fax (9) 2341033; e-mail info@aie.com.ps; f. 1975; Chair. WALID ALOUL.

National Insurance Co: POB 1819, 34 Municipality St, al-Birah/Ramallah; tel. (2) 2983800; fax (2) 2407460; e-mail nic@nic-pal.com; internet www.nic-pal.com; f. 1992; Chair. MUHAMMAD MAHMOUD MASROUJI; Gen. Man. AZIZ MAHMOUD ABD AL-JAWAD; 8 brs.

DEVELOPMENT FINANCE ORGANIZATIONS

Arab Palestinian Investment Co Ltd: POB 2396, Kharaz Center, Yafa St, Industrial Zone, Ramallah; tel. (2) 2981060; fax (2) 2981065; e-mail apic@apic.com.jo; internet www.apic.ps; f. 1995; headquarters in Amman, Jordan; Chair. and CEO TAREK OMAR AGGAD.

Jerusalem Real Estate Investment Co: POB 1876, Ramallah; tel. (2) 2965215; fax (2) 2965217; e-mail jrei@palnet.com; f. 1996; Chair. AWNI ALSAKET.

Palestine Development & Investment Co (PADICO): POB 316, Nablus; tel. (9) 2384480; fax (9) 2384355; e-mail padico@padico.com; internet www.padico.com; f. 1993; 12 subsidiary and affiliate cos; Chair. MUNIB R. AL-MASRI; CEO Dr SAMIR HULILEH.

Palestine Real Estate Investment Co (Aqaria): POB 4049, Gaza; tel. (8) 2824815; fax (8) 2824845; e-mail aqaria@rannet.com; internet www.aqaria.com; f. 1994; Chair. NABIL SARAF; Vice-Chair. OMAR AL-ALAMI.

Palestinian Economic Council for Development and Reconstruction (PECDAR): POB 54910, Dahiyat al-Barid, Jerusalem; tel. (2) 2974300; fax (2) 2974331; e-mail info@pecdar.pna.net; internet www.pecdar.org; privately owned; Pres. Dr MUHAMMAD SHTAYYEH.

Trade and Industry

CHAMBERS OF COMMERCE

Federation of Chambers of Commerce, Industry and Agriculture: tel. (2) 2344923; fax (2) 2344924; e-mail fpccia@palnet.com; internet www.pal-chambers.org; f. 1989; 14 chambers, 32,000 mems.

Bethlehem Chamber of Commerce and Industry: POB 59, Bethlehem; tel. (2) 2742742; fax (2) 2764402; e-mail bcham@palnet.com; internet www.bethlehem-chamber.org; f. 1952; 2,800 mems; Chair. of Bd SAMIR HAZBOUN.

Gaza Chamber of Commerce, Industry and Agriculture: POB 33, Sabra Quarter, Gaza; tel. and fax (8) 2864588; e-mail gazacham@palnet.com; internet www.gazacham.ps; f. 1954; Chair. MUHAMMAD QUDWAH; Man. Dir BASSAM MORTAJA; 14,000 mems.

Hebron Chamber of Commerce and Industry: POB 272, Hebron; tel. (2) 2228218; fax (2) 2227490; e-mail ceo@hebroncci.org; internet www.hebroncci.org; f. 1953; Chair. M. GHAZI HERBAWI; 7,350 mems.

Jenin Chamber of Commerce, Industry and Agriculture: Jenin; tel. (4) 2501107; fax (4) 2503388; e-mail jencham@hally.net; internet www.pal-chambers.org/chambers/jenin.html; f. 1953; 3,800 mems.

Jericho Chamber of Commerce, Industry and Agriculture: POB 91, Jericho 00970; tel. (2) 2323313; fax (2) 2322394; e-mail jericho@pal-chambers.org; internet www.pal-chambers.org/chambers/jericho.html; f. 1953; 400 mems; Chair. HAJ MANSOUR SALAYMEH; Sec.-Gen. SELMI HAMAD.

Jerusalem Arab Chamber of Commerce and Industry: POB 19151, Jerusalem 91191; tel. (2) 2344923; fax (2) 2344914; e-mail chamber@jerusalemchamber.org; internet www.jerusalemchamber.org; f. 1936; 2,050 mems; Chair. AHMAD HASHEM ZUGHAYAR; Dir AZZAM ABU SAUD.

Nablus Chamber of Commerce and Industry: POB 35, Nablus; tel. (9) 2380335; fax (9) 2377605; e-mail nabluschamber@gmail.com; internet www.pal-chambers.org/chambers/nablus.html; f. 1943; Pres. MA'AZ NABULSI; Dir TAJ EL-DIN BITAR; 7,000 mems.

Palestinian-European Chamber of Commerce: Jerusalem; tel. (2) 894883; Chair. HANNA SINIORA.

Qalqilya Chamber of Commerce, Industry and Agriculture: POB 13, Qalqilya; tel. (9) 2941473; fax (9) 2940164; e-mail chamberq@hally.net; internet www.pal-chambers.org/chambers/qalqilya.html; f. 1972; 1,068 mems.

Ramallah Chamber of Commerce and Industry: POB 256, al-Birah/Ramallah; tel. (2) 2955052; fax (2) 2984691; e-mail ramallahcci@gmail.com; internet www.ramallahcci.org; f. 1950; Chair. KHALIL RIZEQ; Vice-Chair. MUHAMMAD ZEID; 3,566 mems.

Salfeet Chamber of Commerce, Industry and Agriculture: Salfeet; tel. and fax (9) 2515970; e-mail salfeetchamber@hotmail.com; internet www.pal-chambers.org/chambers/salfeet1.html; f. 1997; Chair. FOUAD AWAD.

Tulkarm Chamber of Commerce, Industry and Agriculture: POB 51, Tulkarm; tel. (9) 2671010; fax (9) 2675623; e-mail tulkarm@palnet.com; internet www.tulkarmchamber.org; f. 1945; 2,000 mems; Chair. SHUKRI AHMAD JALLAD.

TRADE AND INDUSTRIAL ORGANIZATIONS

Palestinian General Federation of Trade Unions (PGFTU): POB 1216, Nablus; tel. (9) 2385136; fax (9) 2384374; e-mail pgftu@pgftu.org; internet www.pgftu.org; f. 1965; Sec.-Gen. SHAHER SAED.

Union of Industrialists: POB 1296, Gaza; tel. (8) 2866222; fax (8) 2862013; Chair. MUHAMMAD YAZIJI.

UTILITIES

Electricity

Palestinian Energy Authority (PEA): POB 3591, Nablus St, al-Birah/Ramallah; POB 3041, Gaza; tel. (2) 2986190; fax (2) 2986191; tel. (8) 2821702; fax (8) 2824849; e-mail pea@palnet.com; internet pea-pal.tripod.com; f. 1994; Chair. Dr ABD AL-RAHMAN T. HAMAD.

Jerusalem District Electricity Co (JDECO): POB 19118, 15 Salah el-Din St, Jerusalem; tel. (2) 6269333; fax (2) 6282441; e-mail info@jdeco.net; internet www.jdeco.net; Gen. Man. HISHAM OMARI.

National Electric Co (NEC): West Bank; f. 2000.

Palestine Electric Co (PEC): POB 1336, Gaza; tel. (8) 2823800; fax (8) 2823297; e-mail info@pec-gpgc.com; internet www.pec-gpgc.com; f. 1999; 33% state-owned; Chair. SAID KHOURY; CEO WALID SALMAN.

Water

Palestinian Water Authority (PWA): POB 2174, Baghdad St, Ramallah; tel. (2) 2429022; fax (2) 2429341; e-mail pwa@pwa.ps; internet www.pwa.ps; f. 1995; Dir Dr SHADDAD AL-ATTILI.

Transport

ROADS

In 2006, according to estimates by the International Road Federation, the Palestinian territories had 5,147 km of paved roads, of which 535 km were highways or main roads, 438 km were secondary roads and 4,175 km were other roads.

CIVIL AVIATION

Palestinian Civil Aviation Authority (PCAA): Yasser Arafat International Airport, POB 4043, Rafah, Gaza; tel. and fax (8) 2827844; e-mail abuhalib@gaza-airport.org; internet www.gaza-airport.org; f. 1994; Gaza International Airport (renamed as above after Arafat's death in Nov. 2004) was formally inaugurated in November 1998 to operate services by Palestinian Airlines (its subsidiary), EgyptAir and Royal Jordanian Airline; Royal Air Maroc began to operate services to Amman (Jordan), Abu Dhabi and Dubai (both UAE), Cairo (Egypt), Doha (Qatar), Jeddah (Saudi Arabia), İstanbul (Turkey) and Larnaca (Cyprus), and intends to expand its network to Europe; the airport was closed by the Israeli authorities in February 2001 and the runway seriously damaged by Israeli air-strikes in late 2001 and early 2002; Dir-Gen. SALMAN ABU HALIB; Admin. Man. JAMAL AL-MASHHARAWI.

Palestinian Airlines: POB 4043, Gaza; tel. and fax (8) 2827844; e-mail commercial@palairlines.com; internet www.palairlines.com; f. 1994; state-owned; operates flights from el-Arish, Egypt, and Amman, Jordan; Dir-Gen. Capt. ZEYAD ALBADDA; Commercial. Dir YASSER IRQAYEQ.

Tourism

Although the tourism industry in the West Bank was virtually destroyed as a result of the 1967 Arab–Israeli War, by the late 1990s the sector was expanding significantly, with a number of hotels being opened or under construction. Much of the tourism in the West Bank centres around the historical and biblical sites of Jerusalem and Bethlehem. However, the renewed outbreak of Israeli–Palestinian conflict in the West Bank and Gaza Strip from late 2000, as well as the recent increase in inter-Palestinian violence, has generally prevented the recovery of the tourism industry.

Ministry of Tourism and Antiquities: See Administration.

NET—Near East Tourist Agency: POB 19015, 30 Mount of Olives Rd, Jerusalem 91190; tel. (2) 5328720; fax (2) 5328701; internet new.netours.com; f. 1964; CEO SAMI ABU DAYYEH; Man. STEVE USTIN.

Defence

Commander of the Palestinian National Security Forces: Maj.-Gen. NIDAL ABU DUKHAN.

Commander of the Interior Forces and the Civil Police: Maj.-Gen. HAZEM ATALLAH.

Commander of General Intelligence: Maj.-Gen. MAJID FARAJ.

Estimated Public Security and Order Budget (2004): US $433.9m.

Paramilitary Forces (as assessed at November 2012): Paramilitary forces in the Gaza Strip and in the areas of the West Bank where the PA has assumed responsibility for security totalled an estimated 56,000; however, figures for personnel strength in the various forces were impossible to confirm, owing to the uncertain situation in the Palestinian territories at that time. There is, *inter alia*, a Presidential Security Force, a Preventative Security Force, a Civil Defence Force and a Police Force. Units of the Palestine National Liberation Army (PNLA) have been garrisoned in various countries in the Middle East and North Africa; however, much of the PNLA's personnel strength has now been incorporated into the PA's various security forces.

Education

According to the World Bank, Palestinians are among the most highly educated of any Arab group. However, basic and secondary education facilities in the West Bank and Gaza Strip are described as poor. In the West Bank, the Jordanian education system is in operation. Services are provided by the Israeli Civil Administration, the UN Relief and Works Agency for Palestine Refugees in the Near East (UNRWA) and private, mainly charitable, organizations. Vocational education is offered by the Civil Administration and UNRWA. All university and most community college education is provided by private, voluntary organizations. There are 20 community and teacher training colleges in the West Bank, and six universities (including an open university). The Egyptian system of education operates in the Gaza Strip, where there are three universities and one teacher training college. Palestinian education has been severely disrupted since the first *intifada* (uprising) of 1987, and more recently as a result of the al-Aqsa *intifada*, which began in late 2000. Universities have played a major role in the political activities of the West Bank and Gaza, and were closed by the Israeli Civil Administration during 1987–1992.

Since May 1994 the PA has assumed responsibility for education in Gaza and parts of the West Bank. Some 980,213 pupils attended 1,792 primary institutions across the Palestinian territories in 2011/12, while 149,325 students were enrolled at 915 secondary institutions. In 2010/11 213,973 students attended universities or equivalent third-level institutions, while teachers numbered 6,861. In 2011/12 UNRWA operated 99 schools in the West Bank and 245 in the Gaza Strip, providing education to 51,695 pupils in the West Bank and to 225,098 pupils in Gaza. Education personnel in that year numbered 3,134 in the West Bank and 9,444 in Gaza. In addition, UNRWA operated four vocational training centres (two in the West Bank and two in Gaza). In 2009/10 UNRWA budgeted some US $187.1m. for expenditure on education in the Palestinian territories.

Bibliography

A very large literature on the Palestinian question exists and many of these works are included in the bibliography concluding the chapter on Israel. The following are mainly volumes which have appeared since the signing of the Declaration of Principles on Palestinian Self-Rule by Israel and the PLO in September 1993.

Abu-Amr, Ziad. *Islamic Fundamentalism in the West Bank and Gaza: Muslim Brotherhood and Islamic Jihad*. Bloomington, IN, Indiana University Press, 1995.

Abu Sharif, Bassam. *Arafat and the Dream of Palestine: An Insider's Account*. Basingstoke, Palgrave Macmillan, 2009.

Ahmed, Hisham. *Hamas: From Religious Salvation to Political Transformation—The Rise of Hamas in Palestinian Society*. Jerusalem, The Palestinian Academic Society for the Study of International Affairs, 1994.

Artz, Donna E. *Refugees into Citizens: Palestinians and the End of the Arab–Israeli Conflict*. New York, Council on Foreign Relations, 1997.

Aruri, Naseer. *The Obstruction of Peace: The US, Israel and the Palestinians*. Monroe, ME, Common Courage Press, 1995.

(Ed.). *Palestinian Refugees: The Right of Return*. London, Pluto Press, 2001.

Ashrawi, Hanan. *This Side of Peace*. London, Simon and Schuster, 1995.

Ateek, Naim, and Prior, Michael (Eds). *Holy Land, Hollow Jubilee: God, Justice and the Palestinians*. London, Melisende, 1999.

Baron, Xavier. *Les Palestiniens: Genèse d'une nation*. Paris, Editions du Seuil, 2000.

Bouillon, Markus. *The Peace Business: Money and Power in the Palestine-Israel Conflict*. London, I. B. Tauris, 2004.

Buchanan, Andrew S. *Peace with Justice: A History of the Israeli-Palestinian Declaration of Principles on Interim Self-Government Arrangements*. London, Macmillan, 2001.

Butt, Gerald. *Life at the Crossroads: A History of Gaza*. London, Rimal-Scorpion Cavendish, 1995.

Cattan, Henry. *The Palestine Question*. London, Saqi Books, 2000.

Chehab, Zaki. *Inside Hamas: The Untold Story of Militants, Martyrs and Spies*. London, I. B. Tauris, 2007.

Cohn-Sherbok, Prof. Dan, and El-Alami, Dawoud. *The Palestine–Israeli Conflict: A Beginner's Guide*. Oxford, Oneworld Publications, 2001.

Cubert, Harold M. *The PFLP's Changing Role in the Middle East*. London, Frank Cass, 1997.

Darweish, Marwan, and Rigby, Andrew. *Palestinians in Israel: Nationality and Citizenship*. University of Bradford, 1995.

Dolphin, Ray. *The West Bank Wall Unmaking Palestine*. London, Pluto Press, 2006.

Efrat, Elisha. *The West Bank and Gaza Strip: A Geography of Occupation and Disengagement*. Abingdon, Routledge, 2006.

Faris, Hani A. (Ed.). *The Failure of the Two-State Solution: The Prospects of One State in the Israel-Palestine Conflict*. London, I. B. Tauris, 2013.

Farsoun, Samih K. *Culture and Customs of the Palestinians*. Santa Barbara, CA, Greenwood Press, 2004.

Farsoun, Samih K., and Aruri, Naseer. *Palestine and the Palestinians: A Social and Political History*. Boulder, CO, Westview Press, 1997, 2nd edn, 2006.

Finkelstein, Norman J. *The Rise and Fall of Palestine*. Minneapolis, MN, University of Minnesota Press, 1997.

Gee, John. *Unequal Conflict: Palestinians and Israel*. London, Pluto Press, 1998.

Gelber, Yoav. *Palestine, 1948: War, Escape and the Emergence of the Palestinian Refugee Problem*. Brighton, Sussex Academic Press, 2001.

Ghanem, As'ad. *The Palestinian Regime: A 'Partial Democracy'*. Brighton, Sussex Academic Press, 2002.

Gunning, Jeroen. *Hamas in Politics: Democracy, Religion, Violence*. London, C. Hurst & Co, 2007.

Hanafi, Sari, and Tabar, Linda. *The Emergence of a Palestinian Globalized Elite: Donors, International Organizations and Local NGOs*. Institute for Palestine Studies, 2005.

Hilal, Jamil. *Where Now for Palestine? The Demise of the Two-State Solution*. London, Zed Books, 2007.

Hroub, Khaled. *Hamas: Political Thought and Practice*. Institute for Palestine Studies, 2000.

Hamas: A Beginner's Guide. London, Pluto Press, 2009.

Israeli, Raphael. *Dangers of a Palestinian State*. Jerusalem, Gefen Publishing House, 2002.

Palestinians Between Nationalism and Islam. Portland, OR, Vallentine Mitchell, 2008.

Jamal, Amal. *The Palestinian National Movement: Politics of Contention, 1967–2005*. Bllomington, IN, Indiana University Press, 2005.

Jones, Clive, and Pedahzur, Ami. (Eds). *Between Terrorism and Civil War: The Al-Aqsa Intifada*. Abingdon, Routledge, 2004.

Karmi, Ghada, and Cotran, Eugene (Eds). *The Palestinian Exodus, 1948–98*. Reading, Ithaca Press, 1999.

Khalidi, Rashid. *Palestinian Identity: The Construction of Modern National Consciousness*, revised edn. New York, Columbia University Press, 2010.

Khalili, Laleh. *Heroes and Martyrs of Palestine: The Politics of National Commemoration*. Cambridge, Cambridge University Press, 2007.

Khan, Mushtaq (Ed.). *State Formation in Palestine: Establishing Good Governance and Democracy Through Social Transformation*. London, RoutledgeCurzon, 2004.

Khatib, Ghassan. *Palestinian Politics and the Middle East Peace Process: Consensus and Competition in the Palestinian Negotiating Team*. Abingdon, Routledge, 2011.

Kimmerling, Baruch and Migdal, Joel S. *The Palestinian People: A History*. Cambridge, MA, Harvard University Press, 2003.

Klieman, Aharon. *Compromising Palestine: A Guide to Final Status Negotiations*. New York, Columbia University Press, 2000.

Kurz, Anat N. *Fatah and the Politics of Violence: The Institutionalization of a Popular Struggle*. Eastbourne, Sussex Academic Press, 2005.

Le More, Anne. *International Assistance to the Palestinians after Oslo: Political Guilt, Wasted Money*. Abingdon, Routledge, 2008.

Levenberg, Haim. *The Military Preparations of the Arab Community in Palestine 1945–48*. London, Frank Cass, 1993.

Lia, Brynjar. *Police Force without a State: A History of the Palestinian Security Forces in the West Bank and Gaza*. Reading, Ithaca Press, 2006.

Building Arafat's Police: The Politics of International Police Assistance in the Palestinian Territories After the Oslo Agreement. Reading, Ithaca Press, 2006.

Masalha, Nur (Ed.). *The Palestinians in Israel: Is Israel the State of All Its Citizens and 'Absentees'?* Haifa, Galilee Centre for Social Research, 1993.

A Land Without a People: Israel, Transfer and the Palestinians 1949–96. London, Faber and Faber, 1997.

(Ed.). *Catastrophe Remembered: Palestine, Israel and the Internal Refugees*. London, Zed Books, 2005.

Mattar, Philip. *Encyclopaedia of the Palestinians*. New York, Facts on File Inc, 2005.

Mazzawi, Musa. *Palestine and the Law*. Reading, Ithaca Press, 1997.

McDowall, David. *The Palestinians: The Road to Nationhood*. London, Minority Rights Publications, 1995.

Milton-Edwards, Beverley. *Islamic Politics in Palestine*. London, I. B. Tauris, 1996.

Milton-Edwards, Beverley, and Farrell, Stephen. *Hamas: The Islamic Resistance Movement*. Cambridge, Polity Press, 2010.

Neff, Donald. *Fallen Pillars: US Policy Towards Palestine and Israel, 1947–1994*. Institute for Palestine Studies, 1995.

Norman, Julie M. *The Second Palestinian Intifada: Civil Resistance*. Abingdon, Routledge, 2010.

O.K. Centrum für Gegenwartskunst Oberösterreich. *Remapping the Region: Culture and Politics in Israel/Palestine*. Vienna, Folio Verlag, 2004.

Pappe, Ilan. *A History of Modern Palestine: One Land, Two Peoples*. Cambridge, Cambridge University Press, 2004.

Parsons, Nigel. *The Politics of the Palestinian Authority: From Oslo to Al-Aqsa*. Abingdon, Routledge, 2006.

Peleg, Ilan. *Human Rights in the West Bank and Gaza: Legacy and Politics*. Syracuse, NY, Syracuse University Press, 1995.

Robinson, Glenn E. *Building a Palestinian State: The Incomplete Revolution*. Bloomington, IN, Indiana University Press, 1997.

Rogan, Eugene L. and Shlaim, Avi (Eds). *The War for Palestine: Rewriting the History of 1948*. Cambridge University Press, 2000.

Roy, Sara. *The Gaza Strip: The Political Economy of De-Development*. Institute for Palestine Studies, 1995.

Hamas and Civil Society in Gaza: Engaging the Islamist Social Sector. Princeton, NJ, Princeton University Press, 2011

Said, Edward W. *The Politics of Dispossession: The Struggle for Palestinian Self-Determination 1969–1994*. London, Chatto and Windus, 1994.

Peace and its Discontents. London, Vintage, 1995.

The End of the Peace Process: Oslo and After. New York, Granta Books, 2000.

Sayigh, Yezid. *Armed Struggle and the Search for State: The Palestinian National Movement, 1949–1993*. New York, NY, Oxford University Press, 1998.

Schanzer, Jonathan. *Hamas vs. Fatah: The Struggle For Palestine*. Basingstoke, Palgrave Macmillan, 2008.

Schiff, Benjamin N. *Refugees unto the Third Generation: UN Aid to Palestinians*. Syracuse, NY, Syracuse University Press, 1995.

Seliktar, Ofira. *Doomed to Failure?: The Politics and Intelligence of the Oslo Peace Process*. Santa Barbara, CA, Praeger, 2009.

Shachar, Nathan. *The Gaza Strip: Its History and Politics—From the Pharoahs to the Israeli Invasion of 2009*. Eastbourne, Sussex Academic Press, 2010.

Sherman, A. J. *Mandate Days: British Lives in Palestine, 1918–1948*. London, Thames and Hudson, 1997.

Tamimi, Azzam. *Hamas: Unwritten Chapters*. London, C. Hurst & Co, 2006.

Usher, Graham. *The Oslo Agreement: Palestine and the Struggle for Peace*. London, Pluto Press, 1995.

Wasserstein, Bernard. *Israel & Palestine: Why They Fight and Can They Stop?* London, Profile Books, 2004.

Zahlan, Rosemarie Said. *Palestine and the Gulf States: The Presence at the Table*. Abingdon, Routledge, 2009.

QATAR

Geography

The State of Qatar occupies a peninsula (roughly 160 km long, and between 55 km and 90 km wide), projecting northwards from the Arabian mainland, on the west coast of the Persian (Arabian) Gulf. Its western coastline joins onto the shores of Saudi Arabia, and to the east lie the United Arab Emirates and Oman. The total area is 11,493 sq km (4,437 sq miles), and at the census of 16 March 1986 the population was 369,079, of whom fewer than one-third were native Qataris. The census of March 1997 enumerated a total population of 522,023. About 60% of the total were concentrated in the capital, Doha, on the east coast. A total population of 744,029 was recorded at the census of March 2004, giving a population density of 64.7 persons per sq km. According to final results of the census held in October 2010, the population (including resident workers from abroad) reached 1,699,435, giving a significantly increased population density of 147.9 persons per sq km.

The climate of Qatar is hot and humid in summer, with temperatures reaching 44°C between July and September, and humidity exceeding 85%. There is some rain in winter, when temperatures range between 10°C and 20°C. Qatar is stony, sandy and barren; limited supplies of underground water are unsuitable for drinking or agriculture because of high mineral content. More than one-half of the water supply is now provided by seawater distillation processes.

History

DAVID ROBERTS

THE DEVELOPMENT OF MODERN QATAR

Though there is evidence of human activity on the Qatari peninsula dating back thousands of years, there is no meaningful historical record before the mid-18th century. Without a natural water supply and with the soil for agriculture, the Qatari peninsula was not an ideal location for a settled community, particularly as other nearby locations are regarded as more hospitable. Nevertheless, migratory routes of roaming Bedouins and sporadic settlements along the coasts appear to have been the norm and it is from these beginnings that the modern state of Qatar emerged.

In the 1760s large sections of the Bani Utub tribal confederation moved to Qatar from Kuwait. Initially, these groups attempted to settle in Bahrain—well-known for its rich pearling banks—but land there had been taken by tribes loyal to Persia. Therefore, the Bani Utub settled in Zubara (al-Zubara) on Qatar's west coast. This Bani Utub grouping included the Al Khalifa family, whose descendants now include the royal family of Bahrain.

At that time there were existing tribes on the Qatari peninsula. The Al Musallam, for example—though the records are far from complete—are thought to have been pre-eminent at that time. In turn, the Al Musallam paid a tribute to the much larger Bani Khalid confederation, whose notional area of control included the Qatari peninsula via the Al Musallam.

Either through initial conflict or through the sheer number of them arriving in Qatar, the Bani Utub (led by the Al Khalifa) came to dominate Qatar. Another section of the confederation—the Al Jalahimah—was relegated to second place in the pecking order, a situation that did not sit well with this group. Indeed, after having their demands for a greater share of profits dismissed by the Al Khalifa, the Al Jalahimah retreated to the south of Zubara. Though they were soon comprehensively defeated in battle, the threat persisted as the Al Jalahimah allied with a range of actors in an attempt to regain their prestige.

Indeed, this resort to seeking alliances was the central mode of operation on the peninsula. Like the Al Musallam, the Al Khalifa (and the other Bani Utub tribes) were not numerous enough to ensure their own survival. They, therefore, needed to come to arrangements with larger regional groupings (such as Persia, the Wahhabis from central Arabia, and the Sultan of Muscat) for a wider guarantee of protection.

This was not an academic desire to ensure a wider array of allies, but an immediate practical and perhaps existential need. A plague in 1773 and the subsequent blockage in 1775–79 of the great port of Basra diverted a substantial amount of maritime traffic to Zubara, which had recently become a working port. Zubara thus quickly became a rich settlement, and attracted wider attention. The Persians and their proxies in Bahrain attacked sporadically from 1777 onwards. With the assistance of other tribes in Qatar, the Al Khalifa managed to defend Zubara and themselves then attacked Bahrain, taking control of those islands during 1782–83, though they still ruled from Zubara for a time.

From the 1790s, the Qatari peninsula was subjected to repeated raids by Wahhabi tribesmen, often aided by the Al Jalahimah. By 1797 the Al Khalifa were forced to relocate to Bahrain, leaving the Qatari peninsula to the Wahhabis. Only two years later the Al Khalifa were attacked by the Sultan of Muscat's forces in Bahrain. After attempts to persuade Persian forces to protect them failed, the Al Khalifa ceded Bahrain to the Sultan in 1800. Displaced to the Wahhabi-controlled Qatar peninsula, the Al Khalifa reached an agreement with the Wahhabis and, with their support, having promised to promote a Wahhabi 'tribal commonwealth', regained control of Bahrain in 1802. However, the Al Khalifa grew to resent Wahhabi suzerainty shortly thereafter. After the United Kingdom refused in 1805 to help the Al Khalifa extract themselves from their agreements with the Wahhabis, they turned to the Sultan of Muscat for protection in 1811.

The Ottoman and British Empires became increasingly involved in this as the 19th century progressed. The Ottomans had maintained a presence in Qatar from the late 19th century, while the British, using their naval fleet and a series of agents stationed around the Persian (Arabian) Gulf region, corralled and persuaded various Gulf sheikhdoms into joining treaties to preserve the peace. Far from being an external imposition, this complemented existing arrangements that had existed in the region for centuries.

The United Kingdom's interest in the Gulf was primarily to maintain peace in the region and to protect its trading routes to India. When, therefore, in 1867, the Al Khalifa—who were still dominant in Qatar—joined with forces from Abu Dhabi to raid Qatar, explicitly breaking their treaty obligations to the United Kingdom, the British authorities reacted negatively. In 1868 the British Political Resident in the Gulf, Lt-Col Lewis Pelly, removed Muhammad bin Khalifa from power in Bahrain and demanded reparations. Meanwhile, Pelly met with Muhammad bin Thani, the representative of the people of Qatar, and signed a treaty with him. Though this treaty did not independently recognize Al Thani as the legitimate power in Qatar, for it still included provisions for the payment of tribute to the Al Khalifa, it is regarded as the de facto starting point of the Al Thani's rule. Muhammad Al Thani paid the tribute until 1872, when he signed an agreement with the Ottoman Empire for the stationing of its troops in Qatar, ending his reliance on the Al Khalifa.

Like all rulers in the region, the Al Thani resisted attempts at meaningful control and oversight by the Ottomans and ruled the east of the peninsula autonomously. The Ottoman presence in Qatar finally ended in 1915 and the following year Abdullah Al Thani signed an agreement with the United Kingdom. Abdullah was officially recognized as the ruler of Qatar, under the auspices of the wider British agreements in the Gulf. However, the whole of Qatar was still far from united. Tribes in the west retained their loyalty to the Al Khalifa, until a decisive final battle in 1937 when Zubara was captured and the peninsula was finally brought under a single ruler in Abdullah Al Thani. Nevertheless, the weakness of the Qatari state was evident until the late 1940s, when Saudi Arabian geologists with armed guards travelled into the centre of the peninsula, exploring for petroleum deposits. While this was conducted under the notion that roaming Al Murrah tribes in Qatar's interior were loyal to the Saudi King, Abd al-Aziz Al Sa'ud, it served as an example of the Al Thanis' continued lack of control over parts of Qatar's territory.

The discovery of petroleum deposits in Qatar in the late 1930s came too late for immediate exploitation, as the outbreak of World War II (1939–45) intervened. This came at a critical time for Qatar. Its existing economic difficulties were exacerbated by a decline in the market for pearls, the overrunning of fertile, rice-producing areas by warring troops in south-east Asia and the sinking of food-laden ships, which led to severe food shortages. Some estimates suggest that up to one-third of Qatar's population left during that period, leaving only 10,000 people living on the peninsula by the end of the Second World War. The eventual beginning of petroleum exports in 1949 was much needed.

The United Kingdom surprised its dependants in the Gulf in 1968, by announcing their intention to withdraw British forces from the region by 1971. Initial attempts by Qatar, Bahrain and the Trucial States (now the United Arab Emirates—UAE) to form a federation of Gulf Arab states failed, with Qatar's relations with Bahrain in particular hindering an agreement. Qatar became a fully independent nation state on 1 September 1971, and the ruler, Sheikh Ahmad Al Thani, took the title of Amir.

However, arguably the first ruler to concentrate meaningfully on state building was Sheikh Khalifa bin Hamad Al Thani, a cousin of Sheikh Ahmad, who proclaimed himself as Amir after a bloodless coup in February 1972. Sheikh Khalifa's first act was to attempt to create wider sources of legitimacy and support beyond the Al Thani family. He began with widespread programmes to build housing, create jobs, increase pension payments and social aid for ordinary Qataris, while he also promoted Qatar in foreign media outlets. Meanwhile, foreign archaeologists were invited to the country to uncover its history, as Sheikh Khalifa attempted to create a national identity. Embassies were opened and Qatar positioned itself as a donor of financial aid to developing countries.

Qatar's economy remained wholly reliant upon revenues from petroleum and thus the country's financial security ebbed and flowed with the its price on the international market. The 1970s were thus a period of great wealth for Qatar, but budget deficits were recorded for the first time in the 1980s, prompted by the fall of the price of petroleum. Though the world's largest gasfield was discovered in 1971, in the waters between Qatar and Iran, at that time gas was seen as merely a by-product of the discovery and processing of petroleum. It, therefore, was largely ignored until the early 1990s.

THE ACCESSION OF SHEIKH HAMAD

Just as Sheikh Ahmad had spent increasingly less time in Qatar towards the end of his rule, as did Sheikh Khalifa, producing the same result: Sheikh Khalifa was ousted by his son, the Deputy Amir, Heir Apparent, Minister of Defence and Commander-in-Chief of the Armed Forces, Sheikh Hamad bin Khalifa Al Thani, in a bloodless coup in June 1995. Sheikh Hamad had begun to build a power base of his own in the late 1980s, with Qatar's opening of diplomatic relations with the USSR and the People's Republic of China in 1988 being an indication of Hamad's influence on policy areas outside of his given remit. In all discernible matters of importance throughout the 1970s and much of the 1980s, Qatar under the leadership of Sheikh Khalifa resolutely followed Saudi Arabia's lead. To break with this trend in such an unusual and striking manner as to give diplomatic recognition to these two countries is an indication that new ideas were being implemented. Moreover, the opening of diplomatic relations with countries that were unpopular or with which Qatar previously no relations would soon come to be a hallmark of Sheikh Hamad's rule.

His ascent to power was further aided by a government reorganization in 1989. This represented the first large-scale change in government that been effected since independence. Sheikh Hamad's closest political ally, Sheikh Hamad bin Jassim Al Thani, crucially took responsibility for the municipalities portfolio. Meanwhile, Sheikh Hamad had begun to form 'Supreme Councils' under his direct control, with oversight of policy in key areas such as planning, education, and health. During the following years, these Councils would become a mechanism through which Sheikh Hamad and his allies could bypass the habitually bureaucratic and slow ministries, and develop policies after their own vision.

While changes were taking place within Qatar, external developments also had a profound effect. The Iraqi invasion of Kuwait in 1990 prompted particular concern. Much like Kuwait, Qatar was a small, intrinsically defenceless country. It was potentially exceedingly wealthy and was surrounded by larger countries with which it had historically been in conflict. For many influential people in Qatar, the analogies between the two were clear and concerning.

Qatar used this opportunity to guarantee its long—term security. Rejecting any would-be protection by Saudi Arabia, Sheikh Hamad, like others in the region at that time, turned to the USA. The shock of the Kuwait invasion negated sufficiently the intrinsic resentment of partnering closely with the USA, which until then (except in the case of Oman) precluded the Gulf states from seeking open, close relations with a country that was the main ally of Israel.

The breaking of Qatari–US relations in the late 1980s over Qatar's refusal to return illegally purchased missiles to the USA was overcome, and the first of a series of bilateral defence agreements was signed in June 1992. Part of this relationship included the expansion of the US military presence in Qatar. The Qatari Government invested around US $1,000m. in building and upgrading an air force base at al-Udaid, 30 km from the capital, Doha. Between al-Udaid and Camp al-Sayliyah, the two centres of US military activity in the country, Qatar was soon hosting one of the largest US pre-positioning bases in the world and a central hub of a key command centre for an entire regional force.

Qatar's arrangements with the USA came at a time when its relations with Saudi Arabia were markedly deteriorating. The exact point at which this began is impossible specifically to define, but it is notable that they appeared to decline as Sheikh Hamad's influence on Qatar increased. Partly it seems that Hamad had displeased the authorities in the Saudi capital, Riyadh, as he sought to carve an independent policy for Qatar and he increasingly avoided following the Saudi line. While there was something of a détente between Iran and the Arab Gulf states in the early 1990s, after Ali Akbar Hashemi Rafsanjani took office as President of Iran in 1989 and sought a more conciliatory relationship, Qatar took this even further, much to the Saudis' displeasure.

Relations between Qatar and Saudi Arabia declined still further in the early 1990s. The years 1992, 1993 and 1994 each were marked by border skirmishes between the two countries' forces. Moreover, during this time Qatar began to augment its relations with Israel, a policy opposed to that of Saudi Arabia. When, in June 1995, Sheikh Hamad replaced his father as Amir while Khalifa was out of the country, this proved to be a step too far. The young Heir Apparent had not only been leading an independent and controversial foreign policy, but he had now usurped his father, which was an unpopular move among conservative, monarchical neighbours. Sheikh Khalifa returned to the region after the coup and was received as the legitimate ruler by both the UAE and Saudi Arabia. At least two attempts were subsequently launched by Sheikh Khalifa to regain power, with, it was believed, the support of Saudi Arabia. However, these attempts failed and Saudi Arabia reluctantly gave its recognition to the new Amir, Sheikh Hamad. Saudi–Qatari relations were, however, difficult from there on. Indeed, after something of a 'cold war' between the two states, Saudi Arabia withdrew its ambassador from Doha in 2002. The ambassador's return after élite-level talks in 2008 signalled a new and more co-operative era in bilateral relations.

Qatar, a significantly smaller country than Saudi Arabia in traditional terms, understandably struggled to counter Saudi influence. However, the reanimation of an existing idea—to create a Qatar-based television news network—in 1996 was to prove to be a centrally important method through which Qatar not only burnished its image, but developed a way to counter Saudi Arabia's dominance of the region.

BURGEONING 'SOFT' POWER UNDER SHEIKH HAMAD'S RULE

Arguably the single most effective tool used to enhance Qatar's reputation was Al Jazeera. The broadcaster's antecedents went back into the early 1990s under the rule of Sheikh Khalifa, but it was in 1996 that Al Jazeera was finally launched. It was staffed by a cadre of Western-trained journalists, lending it a degree of credibility and a professional approach from the beginning.

Initially, the channel was small in scope, in the number of hours of programming, and in its reach. However, it was to grow rapidly through carefully managed planning and some fortune. One of the key restrictions initially limiting Al Jazeera's growth was the lack of a 'C-band' transponder, which would have allowed Al Jazeera to reach many more viewers. However, these transponders were limited in number and thus in short supply. In July 1997 a French-owned channel had its transponder removed owing to a technical error. Al Jazeera took it over, increased its on-air time to 17 hours per day and began to expand.

Al Jazeera first gained wider prominence in 1998 when it sold exclusive footage of Operation Desert Fox conducted by the USA in Iraq (see the chapter on Iraq) to a number of foreign channels. Early in 1999 Al Jazeera began 24-hour broadcasting and by 2000 it had become the pre-eminent Arab news broadcaster. The suicide attacks in New York and Washington, DC, USA in September 2001 and their aftermath increased Al Jazeera's notoriety outside the Middle East, as it broadcast video messages from Osama bin Laden, the leader of the Islamist militant group al-Qa'ida that was blamed for the attacks. However, despite the apparent disapproval of the USA, Al Jazeera continued to expand. An English-language channel, Al Jazeera English, was founded in 2006, in an attempt to compete in terms of depth and breadth of coverage with international rivals. In 2013 a new US-based channel, Al Jazeera America, began broadcasting.

It is difficult to grasp the importance and novelty of Al Jazeera in the Middle East from a outside perspective. The channel's programming amounted to little less than a revolution in the region's media. In contrast with the constricted and partisan state broadcasters, Al Jazeera offered criticism of government, talk-shows discussing subjects never broached in such a public manner, and interviews with opposition figures, all in a modern, vibrant setting. It can rightly be seen as the vanguard of Qatar's efforts to define itself as a modern state on the international stage.

Several countries in the region have complained to the Qatari Government about Al Jazeera's coverage at certain times. The complaints have included banning Al Jazeera from operating the countries in question, deporting journalists, expelling Qatari diplomats, and even cutting off diplomatic ties with Qatar altogether. In 1999, for example, the Algerian Government was alleged to have cut electricity supplies to that country's capital city, Algiers, in an attempt to prevent the inhabitants from watching the broadcast of a debate with anti-Government figures.

Qatar has consistently promoted the arts as ways to boost its 'soft' power and to establish itself as a hub for culture and art. The founding of The Museum of Islamic Art in Doha in 2008 and the hosting of an annual film festival in 2009–12 in conjunction with the New York-based Tribeca organization are only some of Qatar's endeavours to prove itself as a mature, cultured country.

Another aspect of Qatar's desire to increase its culturally-based 'soft' power is through sport. As the 2000s progressed in particular, Qatar became increasingly keen to host regional and global sporting events. From staging Asian and world championships in sports such as handball, wrestling, sailing and fencing, Qatar progressed to hosting large-scale events, including the Asian Games in 2006 and the Asian Cup association football tournament in 2011. Additionally, annual tournaments in tennis, golf, motor racing, and athletics all take place in the country. The biggest achievement of this strategy to date came in December 2010, when Qatar was awarded the right to host the world's second largest sporting tournament, the International Federation of Association Football (Fédération Internationale de Football Association—FIFA) World Cup in 2022.

Moreover, Qatar began to involve itself in international diplomacy under the leadership of Sheikh Hamad, particularly in the 2000s, with a range of mediation efforts throughout the Middle East and beyond in, for example, Yemen, the disputed territory of Western Sahara, the Sudanese region of Darfur, Ethiopia and Eritrea, and Somalia. Additionally, Qatar has hosted negotiations between the Lebanese militant organization Hezbollah and the Lebanese Government in 2008, and between the Palestinian political movements Hamas and Fatah in 2012. Qatar's active diplomacy became a hallmark of Sheikh Hamad's rule and was usually associated with his Prime Minister and Minister of Foreign Affairs, Sheikh Hamad bin Jassim.

Qatar's recent history has also been marked by financial generosity. The Government donated US $100m. to the US city of New Orleans in the aftermath of Hurricane Katrina in 2005, allegedly paid around $460m. to secure the release of a group of Bulgarian nurses and a Palestinian doctor held in Libya in 2007, and pledged at least $50m. to Hamas following its victory in the 2006 Palestinian legislative elections. Elsewhere, its munificence was often channelled through the Qatar Foundation, which was established in 1995 to fund community projects, scientific research and educational programmes in Qatar and abroad.

Qatar paid for these initiatives with revenues from the largest gas field in the world, the North Field. Qatar has been exporting petroleum since 1949, but is a relatively new entrant to the market for liquefied natural gas (LNG). The North Field was first discovered in 1971. However, it was not developed until the early 1990s due to political instability in the region and domestic indifference to the economic potential of gas.

Sheikh Hamad's political ascent in the late 1980s coincided with an upsurge in Qatar's interest in exploiting its natural gas reserves. Though discussions had been ongoing for more than a decade, Sheikh Hamad gave a new focus to the process. Despite a range of issues including the invasion of Kuwait scattering foreign workers, technical difficulties, and the withdrawal of the international hydrocarbons company BP from the programme in 1992, particularly with the help of Japanese customers guaranteeing demand and Japanese finance allowing Qatar to develop the necessary infrastructure, LNG eventually began production in 1997.

Qatar's vast reserves and growing demand, especially in east Asia and Europe, enabled it to become the world's largest producer of LNG after only one decade of its entrance into the market. Though petroleum continued to be a major source of revenues for Qatar, it was LNG that has transformed it, according to some per caput measurements, into the richest country in the world, and was the main facilitating factor that allowed Sheikh Hamad to pursue the policies that defined his rule.

It is possible to discern a range of motives for the pursuit of such expansionist policies. In supporting and hosting a variety of cultural events, Qatar is not only seeking to increase visitor numbers to aid economic diversification, but it is fundamentally advertising Qatar world-wide. In this, and its desire to host global sports events, Qatar seeks to promote itself as a modern and attractive state with which to do business. Indeed, one must not forget the regional competitive context. Abu Dhabi and Dubai (both UAE) are two exceedingly similar territories within the same region, and Qatar needs to find ways to differentiate itself from them, not just in order to compete for foreign direct investment (FDI), but so that Qataris can foster a distinct national identity among regional competitors with a similar tribal, cultural, social, political, and economic history.

Meanwhile, high-profile exercises in international diplomatic mediation, such as in Darfur and Lebanon, foster the notion of Qatar as a quasi-neutral, peace-promoting actor. The fact that Qatar is willing to deal with both Israel and Hezbollah, while also trying to establish relations with Iran, underlines this notion of neutrality.

There are also more security-orientated reasons as to why Qatar's has chosen to pursue such internationally directed actions. Qatar's colonial experiences offer today's leaders a bleak view of international relations. From its modern-day inception in the late 18th century, Qatar's leaders have found themselves in need of alliances for formal protection. The Al Khalifa of Bahrain, the Wahhabis of (Saudi) Arabia, the Persians, the Sultan of Muscat from modern-day Oman, the Ottoman Empire and the United Kingdom were all suzerains at one stage. However, those suzerains and alliances changed frequently: allies could become enemies within a short period of time. Leaders, therefore, had to be dextrous in international affairs.

Aside from the consistent vacillation of allies and rivals, it is worth highlighting the potential impact of the dissolution of the Ottoman Empire and the world-spanning British Empire as suzerains on future Qatari leaders. Having enjoyed the support of such large entities at one stage would have been comforting. Yet, these empires—just as Qatar's previous backers—eventually disappeared. Overall, therefore, Qatar's historical predicament in its international relations evokes the dictum that states have neither permanent friends nor allies, only permanent interests.

While, just as before, Qatar is largely reliant upon one key ally for its security under Sheikh Hamad (the USA), its policies have reduced this dependency to a significant degree. The fact that Qatar exports a significant proportion of the energy required by the United Kingdom, the Republic of Korea (South Korea), and Japan, among others, means that Qatar's continued prosperity is critical to these countries. Whether they hold formal defensive agreements with Qatar is almost irrelevant to their interests: given the dependence of many countries on Qatar's gas, they are highly likely to be supportive should Qatar come under threat.

Qatar is also courting support within the region, seeking to boost the popularity of the country by way of providing the Middle East's leading source of information, or playing to the often-cited 'Arab street' as some observers would put it. Given the continued popularity of Al Jazeera, this part of the plan appears to have been remarkably effective, despite increased competition and damage to its reputation after the recent popular uprisings in the Middle East and North Africa.

Qatar's ever-growing 'brand' also contributes to, if not solving, then at least assuaging some of the modern day challenges that confront it. For example, although Qatar has huge reserves of natural gas, it must nevertheless plan for the long-term viability of its economy. FDI is, therefore, vital. Qatar will need to seek investment in terms of finance, technology and skills to transform itself from a primarily single industry country into a diverse economy. At the same time, however, Saudi Arabia, Bahrain, Kuwait, and the UAE are in the same position and competing for that same investment. Whatever Qatar can do to increase its chances by using 'soft' power to augment its international image, it must. Seeking to make itself as attractive as possible to multi-national companies and their employees through the promotion of sporting events, museums and educational facilities is just one further step that it can take.

QATAR AND THE 'ARAB SPRING'

The fundamental trait of Qatar's foreign policy in the last 20 years—its desire to be regarded as neutral—was at odds with its prominent role in fostering the popular uprisings in the Middle East and North Africa in 2010–11, collectively known as the 'Arab spring'. First, in Libya in 2011 and now in Syria, Qatar supported the removal from power of those country's respective leaders, Muammar al-Qaddafi and President Bashar al-Assad. Qatari forces participated directly in the North Atlantic Treaty Organization (NATO) mission against Qaddafi in March–October 2011, and has since early 2012 been supplying aid to forces opposed to Assad's rule in Syria.

However, while Qatar's tactics changed during the 'Arab spring', the overall strategy stayed the same. The main aim of foreign policy has been to make Qatar as important as possible to as many international actors as possible. Previously, Qatar's relations with Libya and Egypt were insignificant. The revolutions of 2011 allowed a small, but prosperous state such as Qatar to contribute to effecting great changes in the region, many of which proved to be beneficial for Qatar's own geopolitical position. Specifically, the new Middle East that was created was more receptive to Qatar's overtures, compared with the entrenched powers in those countries with which, while there was sporadic engagement and co-operation, Qatar had no prospect of becoming long-term allies.

In Libya, Tunisia, and especially Egypt, Qatar directed its support largely via the local incarnation of the Muslim Brotherhood. Partly this was because exiles resident in Doha provided influential contacts with that organization. Also, given the coherence of the Muslim Brotherhood as a structured organization with popular support, it was regarded as an appropriate vehicle. Indeed, given the comparative lack of an opposition comprising secular, liberal and moderate politicians, Qatar had little choice but to support the Brotherhood if it wanted to take a leading role in the uprisings from the beginning.

While such a move may have bolstered Qatar's popularity among sections of the Arab world, supporting the Brotherhood was more of a tactic to allow Qatar to support the new Governments in those countries themselves. In the case of Egypt, Qatar became its most significant financial supporter prior to the removal from power of President Muhammad Mursi, a member of the Brotherhood, in July 2013. In April Qatar had agreed to increase its total financial aid to Egypt to some US $8,000m. This was not due to any kind of ideological affiliation with the Brotherhood, but because of the prestige which Egypt represents.

Previously, Qatar's relations with Egypt were strained. This was problematic for Qatar, particularly as it sought to involve itself in diplomatic affairs in which Egypt held considerable influence, such as Sudan and the League of Arab States (Arab League, see p. 1359). Indeed, according to a secret US diplomatic cable published by the WikiLeaks organization, in 2010 the Egyptian Minister of Foreign Affairs, Ahmad Aboul Gheit, had threatened to 'thwart every single initiative' proposed under Qatar's presidency of the Arab League. However, with the development of élite-to-élite relations following the removal of President Hosni Mubarak from power in February 2011 and with the credit that Qatar was building with its financial and diplomatic support of the new Egyptian leadership, it was a reasonable assumption that Qatar could expect greater co-operation in future.

Meanwhile, the importance of individual power and freedom of action is key to understanding the Syrian intervention, in light of the effect that this will have on Iran. Given that there is no empirical reason to believe that Iran's perceived threat to Qatar has dissipated, and, therefore, the principal reason for encouraging good relations remains, Qatar's bold actions in Syria appear to contradict its own interests. Many observers would contend that it is the Amir's personal belief that Qatar's long-term interaction with Iran has proved that Qatar poses no threat to Iran, and that it prefers to maintain cordial relations. Without a belief that Qatar would remain safe despite taking aggressive action against Iran's interests, it could not have intervened as forcefully as it has. It is contended that a decision of such significance could only feasibly come from the Amir, in conjunction with a small number of senior advisors.

This issue lies at the heart of Qatar's foreign policy success and its potential failures. The high level of personalization of Qatar's foreign policy has allowed an unusual, progressive policy to be followed in recent decades. The élite-led nature of the policy has allowed Qatar to make decisions quickly, while maintaining consistency by virtue of continuity among the members of that élite. Equally, however, the lack of institutionalization of foreign policy is potentially concerning in the long term. Without a large, dedicated team of professional diplomats and advisers, policymakers may struggle to cope with the vast increase in the number of decisions required now that Qatar has interests and representatives across the world. In a country where all important decisions are made at the highest level, Qatar's leaders could find themselves inundated. Moreover, the type of decisions that are required is also changing. While establishing relations in a part of the world where there was previously none is simple to enact, military conflicts are complex and difficult to manage.

Thus far Qatar's foreign policy has proved remarkably successful, though as the Arab uprisings evolved in 2012–13, Qatar seemed to be confronted by a number of difficulties. Overall, there have been setbacks, such as the failed attempt to mediate a political transition in Yemen in 2011, and the challenges to Qatar's allies in Egypt and Syria in mid-2013, but the fundamental goal of securing the state by diversifying sources of dependency has yielded results. That Qatar has been able to take advantage of the 'Arab spring' to advance its interests is potentially beneficial. Equally, however, that it has changed its tactics and overtly supported a particular group over others potentially complicates its future decisions. Qatar appears not only to be accruing enemies (for example, among supporters of President Assad in Syria), but its apparent support for the Muslim Brotherhood and its affiliates may prompt a backlash among that organization's opponents, and caused Qatar to lose influence to other Gulf states, particularly in Egypt. Qatar's decision to confirm its continued support for the Egyptian interim Government that replaced the Brotherhood-led administration in June could be regarded as its first response to such challenges.

QATAR UNDER SHEIKH TAMIM

In a surprise move, Sheikh Hamad abdicated as Amir on 25 June 2013, transferring power to his 33-year-old son and Heir Apparent, Sheikh Tamim bin Hamad Al Thani. Sheikh Tamim effected a substantial reorganization of the Council of Ministers on the following day, most notably replacing Sheikh Hamad bin Jassim as Prime Minister and Minister of Foreign Affairs. Sheikh Hamad bin Jassim was also replaced as CEO of the Qatar Investment Authority (of which the new Amir was Chairman) and as Chairman of Qatar's national airline. The changes appeared to mark a meaningful change in Qatar's leadership, as both Sheikh Hamad, as Amir, and Sheikh Hamad bin Jassim, as premier, had been pivotal in building Qatar's contemporary wealth and prestige. Sheikh Abdullah bin Nasser bin Khalifa Al Thani was appointed as Prime Minister and Minister of the Interior, while the foreign affairs portfolio was allocated to Khalid Muhammad al-Attiya. The former CEO of Qatar National Bank, Ali Sharif al-Emadi, became Minister of Finance.

The reasons behind the changes were difficult to discern. One explanation proposed by observers was that serious concerns for the health of Sheikh Hamad had prompted him to consider his future. Rather than leaving Qatar in an uncertain position following an abrupt end to his rule, it was decided to anticipate changes and act early. This would allow Sheikh Tamim a period to adapt to leadership, with Sheikh Hamad (who was awarded the title of Father Amir) in an advisory role, while also breaking a regional taboo in resigning in favour of a son, thus once more distinguishing Qatar from other Gulf states.

Under the rule of Sheikh Tamim, Qatar will necessarily change, potentially quite significantly. Indeed, without the dynamism and drive of the two Hamads, Qatar cannot but change. Sheikh Tamim, inculcated in Qatar's new values, was regarded as unlikely to pursue policies as controversial as those of his father.

If his father's rule was characterized by the establishment of modern institutions, Sheikh Tamim's may be defined by the completion of the process of establishing a modern state. He was, therefore, expected to oversee the consolidation of his father's reforms and the professionalization of government institutions, in place of the hitherto highly centralized and personal process of decision-making. Externally, meanwhile, without the experience of the former Prime Minister, Sheikh Hamad bin Jassim, and given the recent setbacks to Qatar's foreign policy in Syria and Egypt, Qatar was expected to take a more cautious approach to foreign affairs.

Economy

Revised for this edition by RICHARD GERMAN and ELIZABETH TAYLOR

INTRODUCTION

Qatar is a largely barren peninsula, with stony and sandy soil that is generally unsuitable for arable farming. There are numerous coastal saline flats, known as *sabkha*, and the only agricultural soils are found in small depressions in the centre of the country and towards the north. Traditionally, the Qatari economy was based on the nomadic farming of livestock, and on fishing and pearling. Significant reserves of petroleum were discovered in 1939, however, providing the basis for Qatar's transformation into one of the richest countries in the region by the 1970s.

The development of the modern Qatari economy has entailed high levels of labour immigration. In 2001 85.7% of the economically active population were non-Qataris, although of the 33,800 employees working in the government sector, 66.3% were Qataris. According to the March 2004 census, the overall population had risen to 744,029 from the 522,023 recorded at the time of the 1997 census, representing a rise of 42.5% and an average annual increase of 5.3% over the period (compared with 3.7% during 1986–97). This very rapid rate of expansion was largely attributed to the sustained influx of foreign workers. The economically active population at the time of the 2004 census was 437,561 (compared with the 1997 figure of 280,122), with non-Qataris constituting 88.5% of this figure. The General Secretariat for Development Planning assessed the mid-year population (including resident workers from abroad) at 1,041,734 in 2006, rising to 1,226,210 in 2007, 1,448,446 in 2008 and 1,638,829 in 2009. The population at the time of the April 2010 census was recorded at 1,699,435 (with males representing some 75.6% of the total, reflecting the large expatriate work-force), and by mid-2013 it was estimated at about 1,916,400.

In the 1980s, although still heavily reliant on revenue from petroleum, the Government sought to restructure and diversify the economy in anticipation of a future decline in crude petroleum output. As a result, a programme of industrialization, implemented from 1987, centred on ambitious plans for the development of the North Field, the world's largest single non-associated natural gas deposit (see Petroleum and Natural Gas), production from which began in September 1991.

Despite a significant increase in petroleum production in 1997 and 1998, and the first liquefied natural gas (LNG) exports from Qatar, the value of the oil and gas sector declined sharply in 1998 as a result of the decrease in petroleum export prices from late 1997. However, following a subsequent recovery in prices, the hydrocarbons sector grew by an estimated

53% in 1999 and 75% in 2000, producing growth in nominal gross domestic product (GDP) of 19% in 1999 and 35% in 2000, and real increases of 7% and 12%, respectively. There were strong surpluses on the current account of the balance of payments in both years. The moderation of world oil prices in 2001 resulted in a 1.8% contraction in GDP in nominal terms, but, with inflation remaining minimal, real growth of around 2% was achieved. Confidence was boosted further by the announcement in May 2002 that proven gas reserves in the North Field had been upwardly revised by 50%, representing an increase in the value of Qatar's gas reserves of around US $500,000m. As a result of increased exports of oil and gas and favourable oil prices, final figures for 2003 showed that nominal GDP grew by 19.8% (24.1% in the oil and gas sector and 14.1% in the non-oil sector). Such rapid economic growth enabled Qatar to reach the top ranks of the world's wealthiest countries in terms of per caput income, which stood at $31,897 in 2003. Nominal growth continued at a high rate of 24.8% in 2004 (with oil and gas contributing 62% of total GDP and the non-oil sector 38%).

According to official figures, real GDP increased by 6.1% in 2005 and by 12.2% in 2006, reflecting in particular strong growth in the LNG, construction and financial sectors. (Oil and gas contributed 57% of total GDP in the latter year.) The IMF reported real GDP growth of 18.0% in 2007. However, this economic expansion was accompanied by a continued upward trend in inflation, caused largely by increases in rent combined with higher construction costs and material shortages. Annual inflation averaged 11.8% in 2006, despite a 10% cap on rent increases announced in January of that year, rising to 13.8% in 2007.

According to the IMF, Qatar had the fastest growing economy among the countries of the Cooperation Council for the Arab States of the Gulf (the Gulf Cooperation Council—GCC) in 2008, and was well placed to weather the negative impact of the global financial crisis that developed in the second half of the year. Real growth was recorded at 17.7%, driven by expansion in hydrocarbons production and exports, but the annual inflation rate accelerated to 15.0% (owing to increases in commodity prices and rising rents) before decreasing later in the year. Although the difficult global economic climate prompted a sharp decline in international petroleum prices, Qatar maintained fixed revenues from its LNG export agreements (based on long-term contracts) and continued to press ahead with major development projects into 2010.

Meanwhile, the Government launched the Qatar National Vision 2030 in October 2008—a broad strategy for the future, promoting reduced dependence on hydrocarbons, focusing on human, social, economic and environmental development, and emphasizing planned and regulated growth. It also outlined the need for a reduction in the number of unskilled foreign workers, who constituted around 75% of the country's expatriate population.

Qatar remained the fastest-growing economy among the GCC states in 2009, according to IMF data; despite the depressed global environment, real GDP growth was 12.0%. The underlying strength of the economy continued to derive from petroleum and gas revenues (despite a significant reduction from the high levels experienced in 2008) and returns from the Qatar Investment Authority (QIA—the Government's sovereign wealth fund). However, there was also continuing growth in the non-hydrocarbon sector, while timely official intervention in the banking system (including equity injections and asset purchases) helped to limit the impact of the financial crisis. The Government pressed ahead with infrastructure projects, such as an expansion of Doha International Airport and the development of a national rail network, and with efforts to boost LNG production capacity (to a planned level of 77m. metric tons per year). Meanwhile, the fiscal surplus rose to 14.3% of GDP in 2009, from 10.4% of GDP in 2008, in spite of the steep decrease in international hydrocarbon prices, which dampened export revenues. In July 2010 international credit ratings agency Standard & Poor's raised Qatar's long-term sovereign rating to 'AA' from 'AA–', in order to reflect the country's strengthening fiscal and external balance sheets.

According to the IMF, Qatar weathered the global financial crisis 'exceptionally well, reflecting the quick and strong policy response by the authorities'. Enhanced LNG production capacity, the provision of support to the banking system (which ensured financial stability) and an increase in public spending helped to sustain high levels of growth, with real GDP increasing by 16.6% in 2010. In March 2011 the Government announced a new five-year National Development Strategy for 2011–16 as part of the Qatar National Vision 2030 (see Budget, Investment and Finance), aiming to promote growth in the non-hydrocarbon sector, enhance the role of the private sector, upgrade infrastructure to accommodate the needs of a fast-growing population and prepare for future investment commitments—including hosting the 2022 International Federation of Association Football (Fédération internationale de football association—FIFA) World Cup competition.

Qatar maintained its economic momentum in 2011 despite the challenging global environment, with large external current account and fiscal surpluses and continuing financial stability and banking profitability. The IMF recorded real GDP growth at 13.0% in that year. The Fund then projected a reduced rate of growth, of 6.6%, for 2012, as LNG production remained static due to a self-imposed moratorium on new projects (see Petroleum and Natural Gas). Nevertheless, significant investment in infrastructure projects, as the Government increasingly focused on economic diversification, was expected to sustain further robust growth in the non-hydrocarbons sector at between 9% and 10% beyond 2012. The Fund considered the principal risks to the economy to be lower hydrocarbon prices, tighter external financing conditions and potential disruption in the transportation of LNG (due to increased geopolitical tensions). At the same time, it welcomed the Government's commitment to making fiscal savings in order to protect the economy from external shocks, to saving for future generations and to fully financing the budget after 2020 from non-hydrocarbon revenues. As in 2011, inflation averaged around 2% in 2012.

AGRICULTURE AND FISHING

In 2011 the agriculture, hunting, forestry and fishing sector employed some 1.4% of the work-force, according to official figures. Qatar has to import nearly all of its food needs and, in order to facilitate security of supplies, has been seeking to purchase stakes in overseas farmland (in Australia and Sudan, for example) and agricultural companies through Hassad Foods, an investment vehicle established by the QIA in 2008. The Government is also pursuing a national food security programme, the primary objective of which is to increase domestic output by harnessing advanced technologies.

Most of the country's fishing is undertaken by the Qatar National Fishing Co, which was formed in 1966 and nationalized in 1980. According to FAO data, the total catch was 13,796 tons in 2010 and 13,021 tons in 2011.

PETROLEUM AND NATURAL GAS

The oil and gas sector is vital to Qatar's economy, accounting for some 58% of GDP in 2012. A significant milestone was reached in 2008 when gas production overtook petroleum output as the largest contributor to the economy, accounting for 32.3% of GDP that year. As part of its five-year plan for 2010–14, Qatar Petroleum (QP) announced that it would spend QR 111,700m. on the further development of the hydrocarbons sector.

At the end of 2012 Qatar's proven reserves of petroleum were estimated to be 23,900m. barrels. The first concession to explore for oil in Qatar was granted to the Anglo-Persian Oil Co in 1935, and was later transferred to Petroleum Development (Qatar) Ltd. Deposits were first discovered in Qatar in 1939, although exploration and production were delayed during the Second World War. By 1949 a pipeline had been constructed from the Dukhan oilfield, on the west coast, to Umm Said (also known as Mesaieed) in the east, where terminal facilities had also been built, and in December of that year the first shipment of Qatari petroleum was exported. In 1952 the Shell Co of Qatar acquired a concession to develop the entire continental shelf offshore area, and by 1960 petroleum had been discovered at Idd al-Shargi, 100 km to the east of Qatar. Soon afterwards, a second offshore oilfield was discovered, to the north-east of the first, at Maydan Mahzam, and in 1970 a third offshore field, Bul Hanine, was discovered nearby. In 1953 Petroleum Development (Qatar) Ltd was renamed the Qatar Petroleum Co, and by 1960 Qatar's onshore production had reached 60,360,000 barrels, compared with 800,000 barrels in 1949. Qatar was admitted to membership of the Organization of the Petroleum Exporting Countries (OPEC) in 1961. In 1969 Qatar and Abu Dhabi agreed to a joint production scheme for the al-Bunduq field, which straddles the border between Qatar and the United Arab Emirates (UAE).

Following Qatar's attainment of full independence in 1971, the petroleum industry was reorganized, and in 1972 the Qatar National Petroleum Co was created to supervise the country's oil operations. In 1974 the Qatar General Petroleum Corpn (QGPC) was established, and new participation agreements were signed with the foreign oil companies operating in the country to give the Government a 60% share of profits. In December 1974 the Government announced its intention to purchase the remaining 40% share in the ownership of QGPC and the Shell Co of Qatar. After lengthy negotiations, the state took over the assets and rights of QGPC in September 1976, and acquired those of the Shell Co of Qatar in February 1977.

Qatar's oil production varied considerably during the 1970s and the early 1980s, declining from 570,300 barrels per day (b/d) in 1973 to only 332,000 b/d in 1982. By July 1990 Qatar's OPEC quota had been raised from 300,000 b/d to 371,000 b/d. However, quotas were suspended following Iraq's invasion of Kuwait in August. Between August 1990 and February 1991 Qatari production averaged 420,000 b/d. After the liberation of Kuwait, Qatar's production quota was set by OPEC at 399,000 b/d and by the fourth quarter of 1993 it was 378,000 b/d. Total oil production (including natural gas liquids) averaged 568,000 b/d in 1996, rising sharply to record levels of 694,000 b/d in 1997 and 747,000 b/d in 1998. Qatar accepted a nominal OPEC production quota of 414,000 b/d from January 1998 while continuing to lobby (based on its financial needs as OPEC's smallest producer) for a substantial quota increase to a level closer to its actual output. When OPEC made a series of supply reductions in 1998–99 to counteract the decline in world petroleum prices, Qatar agreed to lower its actual output, adopting reference levels of 670,000 b/d from April 1998, 640,000 b/d from July and 593,000 b/d from April 1999; its formal OPEC quota remained unchanged at 414,000 b/d. Qatar's total oil production (including natural gas liquids) averaged 724,000 b/d in 1999.

Qatar's agreed reference level within the OPEC production quota system was raised four times in 2000, reaching 691,800 b/d from November, as OPEC took steps to moderate excessive upward price pressures in the world oil market. Qatar's actual output level in 2000 (including natural gas liquids, which were not subject to OPEC quotas) averaged 796,000 b/d, an increase of 9.9% over 1999. In 2001 OPEC quotas were progressively reduced in response to a softening of market conditions, and by January 2002 Qatar's agreed reference level was 562,000 b/d. Actual oil production in 2001 (including natural gas liquids) declined to 783,000 b/d, of which crude output was 681,000 b/d, significantly above the OPEC quota. As a result of OPEC's enforced output reductions in 2002, crude production declined by 5%, averaging 644,000 b/d, but in 2003 it increased by 10.9%, to 714,000 b/d. Qatar's agreed OPEC quota was steadily increased in 2004–05, reaching 726,000 b/d in July 2005; in November the quota was reduced to 691,000 b/d, and further to 676,000 b/d in February 2007. Oil output reached 1,449,000 b/d in 2008, but then declined to 1,416,000 b/d in 2009, before rising sharply to 1,676,000 b/d in 2010, 1,836,000 b/d in 2011 and 1,966,000 b/d in 2012. Although the Government's energy policy has become focused more on gas production and exports, it is taking measures to extend the life of its oilfields through enhanced oil recovery techniques, and is converting all production-sharing agreements with foreign partners into joint ventures.

In planning to increase Qatar's crude petroleum production capacity from around 800,000 b/d to 1.03m. b/d, QP (as QGPC was renamed in January 2001—see below) approved significant oilfield development programmes by several foreign oil companies in 2000–02. In 2003 QP and the Qatar Petroleum Development Co (a consortium led by Cosmo Oil) agreed to develop two small offshore oil deposits at al-Karkara and A-North. Also in 2003 the National Petroleum Construction Co of Abu Dhabi was awarded a major platform contract for the Idd al-Shargi field to provide additional capacity. In 2004 QP signed EPSAs with Anadarko Petroleum Corpn for an offshore block, located to the north of Qatar, and Denmark's Maersk Oil for an offshore concession located north-west of the al-Shaheen field. QP also signed an agreement with Japan Drilling Co to establish the first national drilling company in Qatar, to be named Gulf Drilling International (GDI). GDI was to be based on six rig operations, with an investment capital of US $258m. during the initial three years of the joint venture. A comprehensive development plan for the al-Shaheen field in December 2005 was to receive more than $5,000m. in government investment; in May 2006 Maersk Oil signed the first substantial construction contract of $150m. for the project, designed to increase production to more than 200,000 b/d from 2008–09. The second phase was completed in 2010, increasing production capacity to 525,000 b/d. Meanwhile, production started at the al-Karkara field. During 2008 QP awarded Germany's Wintershall an exploration licence for an offshore block located close to the North Field. Encouraged by the success of the al-Shaheen project, QP also initiated studies for the redevelopment of the older Maydan Mahzam and Bul Hanine offshore fields using enhanced petroleum recovery techniques. In September 2012 Maersk Oil started negotiations with QP to extend a production-sharing contract for the al-Shaheen field to 2030.

In January 2001 QGPC was renamed QP, notwithstanding its diversification over recent years into an ever-widening range of industries, including natural gas and petrochemicals. QP (with an authorized capital of QR 20,000m.) was a shareholder in 10 subsidiary or joint venture companies in Qatar, and an investor in eight other companies (including five Arab joint ventures based outside Qatar) at the start of 2001. As the controller of the natural gas resources central to the country's industrial development strategy, QP was the dominant force in planning the development of Qatar's industrial cities, and was notably responsible for 'fast-tracking' the finalization of an independent water and power project at Ras Laffan in 2001 (see Power and Water).

Qatar's first major refinery, at Umm Said, was commissioned in 1974 for the National Oil Distribution Co (NODCO), which had been founded in 1968 to manage the refining and distribution of oil products. (Formerly managed as a wholly owned subsidiary of QGPC, NODCO was fully merged into QGPC during 2000.) The first Umm Said refinery had an initial capacity of 6,200 b/d, which had increased to 12,000 b/d by 1977. In 1984 it was linked to a second refinery, with a capacity of 50,000 b/d, built on an adjacent site. In 1988 two new pipelines were constructed to carry light and heavy products from Umm Said to QGPC's export terminal. In June 1998 contracts were awarded to increase the total processing capacity of the Umm Said complex to 137,000 b/d. The new capacity was phased into production from late 2002. Also in 2002 QP, TotalFinaElf and ExxonMobil signed a joint venture agreement for the construction and operation of a 140,000-b/d condensate refinery at Ras Laffan; a consortium from the Republic of Korea (South Korea), led by GS Engineering and Construction, was awarded the US $600m. engineering, procurement and construction (EPC) contract for the project in April 2005, and the completed refinery came on stream in September 2009.

Qatar's total proven gas reserves amounted to some 25,100,000m. cu m at the end of 2012, equivalent to 13.4% of the world's reserves (only Iran and Russia having larger shares). Qatar's total output of natural gas was 157,000m. cu m in 2012, up from 145,300m. cu m in 2011. A moratorium on new gas export agreements has been imposed and will be reviewed on the basis of the results of studies of the North Field reserves to evaluate future expansion without damaging the reservoirs. At 105,400m. cu m in 2012, Qatar's exports of LNG provided 32% of the world's total LNG imports in that year, with over 60% shipped to the Asia Pacific region. (In 2006 Qatar had succeeded Indonesia as the world's largest exporter of LNG.)

The North Field was discovered in the 1970s, and subsequently assumed a central position in the Government's development plans. Prior to its inauguration in 1991, Qatar's gas output was drawn from a relatively small onshore deposit of non-associated gas (used mainly for power generation) and from the onshore and offshore oilfields. The first phase of Qatar's North Field Development Project (NFDP) was designed to produce a constant 22.6m. cu m per day of gas for domestic use, together with 1.65m. metric tons per year of liquefied petroleum gas (LPG) and condensate for export. In May 2002 the Government announced a major upward revision of natural gas reserves in the North Field.

The second NFDP phase involved the construction of an integrated LNG complex and associated export facilities at Ras Laffan, with an annual capacity of up to 6m. metric tons of LNG, of which 4m. tons were to be shipped to Japan under a 25-year agreement with Chubu Electric Power Co. Contracts for most of the 'downstream' construction work were signed in July 1993, when the shareholders in the Qatar Liquefied Gas Co (Qatargas) company that would operate the LNG plant were QGPC (65%), Mobil and France's Total (each 10%), Marubeni Corpn and Mitsui & Co (each 7.5%). Construction work on the liquefaction plant began in April 1994. A US $2,000m. 'downstream' financing package (funded by four Japanese and two European financial institutions) became available for disbursement in October 1995. A $570m. 'upstream' financing arrangement was syndicated in September 1996. Qatargas made its first condensate exports in that month, and dispatched its first LNG shipment to Japan in December. Qatargas signed two medium-term sales and purchase agreements in May 2001 to supply a total of 9.1m. tons of LNG to the Spanish group Gas Natural between 2001 and 2009.

By 2003 a project by Qatargas to relieve pressure on its three existing LNG trains (trains 1, 2 and 3) and construct two new trains (4 and 5), to add almost 10m. metric tons per year to Ras Laffan's capacity, was well advanced; Qatargas, in partnership with ExxonMobil, was working on the Qatargas II project (estimated to cost US $11,000m.) to export an estimated 15m. tons per year of LNG (with the addition of trains 4 and 5) to the British market. Total entered into an agreement in July 2006 whereby it acquired a 16.7% equity stake in the Qatargas II venture and was to purchase 5.2m. tons a year of LNG for distribution to destinations including new customers for Qatar's LNG in France, the United Kingdom and Mexico. Qatargas also signed a preliminary agreement with the US company ConocoPhillips for the development of Qatargas III—a $6,000m. scheme to export 7.5m. tons, via a new LNG train (train 6), to the USA. Société Générale of France was appointed financial adviser for Qatargas III. In July 2004 Qatargas and Spain's Gas Natural signed a 20-year agreement for the sale and purchase of 30m. tons of LNG beginning in 2005, as well as the extension to 2012 of the existing contracts signed in 2001. A joint venture of Japan's Chiyoda Corpn and Technip of France was meanwhile awarded the main plant contract worth more than $4,000m. for the construction of the 7.8m.-ton LNG trains 4 and 5. In February 2005 Shell signed a preliminary heads of agreement for a 30% stake in Qatargas IV—a $7,000m. project envisaging a single 7.8m.-ton LNG train (train 7) at Ras Laffan, the output of which was to be marketed in North America and Europe. In September Japan's Mitsui signed an agreement to acquire a 1.5% interest in Qatargas III, purchasing 10m. barrels of condensate per year for 13 years from 2010. In December 2005 a joint venture of Chiyoda and Technip was awarded the contract to build trains 6 and 7. In 2008 Qatargas IV agreed to supply LNG to the China National Offshore Oil Corpn (CNOOC) from 2009, to PetroChina from 2011, and to Dubai in the UAE (particularly for the summer months when air conditioning increases fuel consumption) for 15 years. Agreements with the two Chinese companies for additional supplies were later signed in November 2009. Train 4 of Qatargas II was officially inaugurated in March 2009, while train 5 started production in September, train 6 in November 2010 and train 7 in February 2011.

In a separate venture, the Ras Laffan Liquefied Natural Gas Co Ltd (RasGas) was established in 1992 as Qatar's second LNG project, the two major shareholders being QP and ExxonMobil. Two onshore liquefaction trains were initially constructed with the capacity to manufacture 6.6m. metric tons per year of LNG. The first train was completed in 1999 and loaded its first cargo in August of that year for the Korea Gas Corpn (KOGAS), with which a 25-year supply agreement had been signed in 1995. The second train became operational in 2000. Further long-term LNG supply agreements were arranged with Petronet of India in 1999 (for 7.5m. tons a year from 2004) and with Edison of Italy in 2001 (for 3.5m. tons a year, beginning in 2005). To increase production capacity, the RasGas II project was established in 2001 by QP and ExxonMobil for the construction of three more LNG trains (trains 3, 4 and 5).

In 2003 RasGas signed an agreement with the Chinese Petroleum Corpn (CPC) of Taiwan to supply 3m. tons of LNG per year for 25 years, starting from 2008. Also in 2003 the agreement with Edison was amended to increase the LNG supply to 4.7m. tons starting from 2007. QP and ExxonMobil then signed an agreement to purchase a 90% stake in the Edison Gas Adriatic LNG terminal project, located on the north-east coast of Italy. In October 2003 QP and ExxonMobil announced the establishment of RasGas III (a joint venture, with QP taking a 70% stake and ExxonMobil 30%), and an agreement was also signed for the supply of 15.6m. tons of LNG to the USA, with deliveries set to commence by 2010. Estimated to cost US $12,000m., the RasGas III project included the construction of a further two LNG trains (6 and 7), each with a capacity of 7.8m. tons. Siemens of Germany was named as the supplier of power distribution systems and compressor drives for the project in August 2006. The project was also to include a dedicated fleet of LNG vessels. In 2004 RasGas II contracted with Fluxys LNG of Belgium to supply 3.4m. tons from 2007, and with Florida Power and Light group for 6m. tons for the US market starting in 2008. The third RasGas LNG train was inaugurated in March 2004 (the EPC contract for which having been awarded to a consortium of Chiyoda Corpn, Mitsui and Italy's Snamprogetti); the fourth was completed in 2005, and a fifth inaugurated in 2007 (through the same consortium partners). According to RasGas, the commissioning of the fifth train, with (like the third and fourth trains) an annual capacity of 4.7m. tons, took Qatar's overall LNG production capacity to 30.7m. tons per year. In November 2004 KOGAS signed a short-term sales and purchase agreement to buy an additional 4m. tons of LNG per year. In May 2005 after several years of negotiation, the Governments of Qatar and Bahrain announced the signing of an agreement for Qatar to supply natural gas to Bahrain. Meanwhile, the onshore EPC contract for the RasGas III project was awarded to a joint venture of Chiyoda and Technip, and the offshore contract to J. Ray McDermott Middle East of the USA. Also in 2005 RasGas signed a contract with CPC to supply LNG to Taiwan for 25 years. The sixth RasGas train was inaugurated in October 2009, and the seventh came on stream in February 2010.

The inauguration of the final Qatargas train in February 2011 completed the country's LNG infrastructure expansion programme, bringing total production capacity to 77m. tons per year. However, Qatar's LNG export prospects and price expectations were constrained by a decrease in demand after the global economic downturn (from 2008), by a shale gas production boom in the USA and by the expansion of LNG ventures elsewhere (such as in Australia and Russia). This prompted Qatargas and RasGas to extend their marketing efforts, particularly in Asia, and in 2011–12 additional supply agreements were signed with customers in Japan, the People's Republic of China, India, Malaysia, South Korea, the United Kingdom and Argentina. Qatar has also sought to acquire stakes in projects abroad in order to compete with rival gas-exporting states. In November 2011 the Government opened talks with Russian gas company Novatek regarding the purchase of a stake in the Yamal LNG project in eastern Russia, and with the Greek Government to discuss the acquisition of holdings in three of Greece's energy companies. In June 2012 the QIA acquired a stake in Royal Dutch Shell, having earlier increased its holdings in France's Total and Xstrata, a British-Swiss mining group.

In March 1999 QGPC signed an outline agreement with the UAE Offsets Group (UOG) to develop and supply Qatari gas to the UAE and Oman via an undersea pipeline from Ras Laffan. In July 2000 a project development company, Dolphin Energy (DEL), was established by the UOG (51%), Total (24.5%) and Enron Corpn (24.5%) to conduct detailed negotiations with QGPC on the terms of a gas offtake agreement. In March 2001 QP (as QGPC had become) signed an agreement with the UOG setting out terms and conditions for the exploitation of two North Field blocks by DEL's 'upstream' partner (Total) and the construction and operation by Enron Corpn of a 350-km pipeline to the UAE, through which up to 56m. cu m per day of dry gas would be exported after extraction of condensate and related products at a treatment plant at Ras Laffan. Later extensions to the principal pipeline would link Oman into the network, facilitating the exchange of gas between the states, and ultimately envisaging connection to a future regional network for all the members of the GCC. The estimated cost of the Dolphin Gas Project was US $3,500m. The troubled Enron Corpn withdrew from the Dolphin project in May, obliging the remaining participants to reassess their development plans. In December 2003 the Dolphin group signed the final field development plan with QP. In January 2004 DEL awarded the first EPC package covering the onshore treatment plant and compression plant to Japan's JGC Corpn, with the platform package awarded to J. Ray McDermott and gas turbines to be supplied by Rolls Royce of the United Kingdom. It had been planned that the Dolphin pipeline would be operational by late 2006, but the project was beset by escalating costs, and Saudi Arabia's assertion that the marine pipeline breached territory demarcations further impeded progress. As a result, the first phase of the project was not completed until July 2007, when the pipeline supplied its first commercial delivery of gas to the UAE. The Dolphin project began to supply Oman in November 2008.

In May 2000 QGPC signed a development and production-sharing agreement (DPSA) with ExxonMobil for enhanced gas utilization (EGU) in a portion of the North Field (the al-Khaleej Gas Project), supplies from which would be variously used for power generation within Qatar, for processing into exportable liquid products (condensates, butane and propane) and for direct export via pipeline. In the first half of 2003 Chiyoda Corpn, Mitsui and Snamprogetti were awarded the EPC contract for the first phase of the project. In 2001 QP, ExxonMobil and Kuwait Petroleum Corpn signed a memorandum of understanding for the supply of gas from the al-Khaleej Gas Project through a 590-km submarine pipeline to transport up to 40m. cu m of dry gas per day from Ras Laffan to al-Zour in southern Kuwait. Qatari officials regarded the prospective pipelines to Kuwait and the UAE as the core of a future regional gas network, which would be extended to other states in the region in due course. In July 2006 QP and ExxonMobil announced the signing of a development plan and launch of the US $3,000m. second phase of the al-Khaleej project, expected to deliver more than 35.4m. cu m per day of North Field gas to domestic consumers, 15m. barrels per year of condensates, 1m. metric tons per year of propane, butane and plant condensate, and about 870,000 tons per year of ethane destined for the petrochemicals industry. The project came on stream in 2009. Also in that year QP awarded a licence to the CNOOC to explore for deep offshore gas, and in mid-2010 it signed a 30-year EPSA with the China National Petroleum Corpn, in partnership with Shell, covering an area bordering the North Field. A further 30-year EPSA, with JX Nippon Oil & Gas Exploration Corpn of Japan, was signed in May 2011. In late 2011 QP and ExxonMobil completed financing arrangements for the large-scale Barzan project (delayed since 2008 because of the global economic downturn), which would process gas from the North Field. Hyundai Heavy Industries Co of South Korea and the JGC Corpn were awarded construction contracts for the project's offshore and onshore facilities, respectively, and gas-processing operations were expected to commence in 2014.

Another intended use for output from Qatar's EGU project was as feedstock for the region's first gas-to-liquids (GTL) plants. Between June 1999 and May 2000 QGPC secured syndicated loans totalling US $1,200m. from a consortium of regional and international banks, primarily to finance its natural gas liquids development programme at Umm Said. In July 2001 QP (the majority partner) signed a 51:49 joint-venture agreement with the South African company Sasol Synfuels International to set up a GTL plant at Ras Laffan to produce 24,000 b/d of fuel, 9,000 b/d of naphtha and 1,000 b/d of LPG, using Sasol's slurry phase distillation process. The $675m. EPC contract was awarded to Technip-Coflexip for construction of the new ORYX GTL facility, and the syndication for the $700m. debt facility closed in the first half of 2003. In March 2004 QP and Sasol signed an agreement to expand production facilities to 100,000 b/d by 2010. QP and Exxon Mobil had previously announced a feasibility study for a 100,000-b/d GTL plant using ExxonMobil's advanced conversion process, and in July agreed plans to construct a $3,000m. plant at Ras Laffan (although this scheme was later discontinued). By mid-2004 four other major GTL projects were progressing jointly with Shell International Gas (which signed a development and production agreement for a $5,000m. plant to produce 140,000 b/d), Ivanhoe Energy of Canada, Conoco and Marathon. Also in 2004 ExxonMobil signed a DPSA for a $7,000m. plant to produce 154,000 b/d of GTL. The agreement was to run for 25 years from the start of production, which was scheduled for 2011. In 2005 SasolChevron concluded outline agreements for GTL projects worth $6,000m., including a 65,000-b/d expansion at the ORYX GTL plant (which became operational in June 2006) and a new GTL base oil facility (producing primary feedstock for high-quality lubricants). Royal Dutch Shell Group's integrated Pearl GTL project, based at Ras Laffan, was confirmed in July 2006, (despite escalating construction costs then estimated to have exceeded $10,000m.) with EPC contracts for both onshore and offshore development, totalling over $4,000m., awarded in August. Linde of Germany was granted a $900m. contract for eight air separation units to deliver 28,800 metric tons per day of oxygen; Chiyoda Corpn in collaboration with Hyundai Heavy Industries Co secured the largest contract, of $1,750m., for the construction of a feed gas processing plant with a capacity of 45.3m. cu m per day, while Japan's Toyo Engineering Corpn and Hyundai Engineering and Construction Co of South Korea won a $1,480m. contract for a liquid processing facility (incorporating a heavy paraffin converter, synthetic crude distiller and related product splitters). The first shipment from the Pearl GTL project was despatched in June 2011 and full capacity was achieved in October 2012.

MANUFACTURING AND INDUSTRY

Qatar's hydrocarbons-based industrialization strategy has centred on the development of 'downstream' processing facilities for oil and gas feedstocks, coupled with some diversification into heavy industry, using local gas as a low-cost fuel source. Three core schemes were initiated at Umm Said in the late 1970s and early 1980s: the Qatar Fertilizer Co (QAFCO), the Qatar Petrochemical Co (QAPCO) and the Qatar Steel Co (QASCO). In early 2003 the Government established a new holding company, Industries Qatar (IQ), with an authorized capital of QR 5,000m., and transferred QP's controlling shares in four subsidiaries—QAFCO, QAPCO, QASCO and Qatar Fuel Additives Co. QP held 85% of the company, and the remaining 15% of the shares were offered to Qatari nationals through an initial public offering (IPO) on the Doha Securities Market. The Government was to offer a further 15% of the equity since the IPO was heavily over-subscribed.

QAFCO was established in 1969 and had been owned jointly by QGPC/QP (75%) and Norsk Hydro of Norway (25%) since 1975. Production of fertilizers began in 1973, with gas feedstocks being supplied from the Dukhan field. The second plant, QAFCO II, was completed in 1979. The third plant, using non-associated gas supplied from the North Field and with a capacity of 1,500 metric tons per day of ammonia and 2,000 tons per day of urea, came into production in March 1997. In mid-2000 QAFCO announced plans to build a fourth plant with a capacity of 2,000 tons per day of ammonia and 3,500 tons per day of urea. The project was completed in 2004, at a cost of US $535m. QAFCO's total annual capacity was scheduled to rise to 2.8m. tons of urea and 2m. tons of ammonia. In 2006 QAFCO signed a preliminary agreement with Yara

International for a fifth plant at Umm Said (which came on stream in 2011), and in 2009 awarded a $610m. contract for a sixth plant to a consortium of Saipem of Italy and Hyundai of South Korea.

The petrochemicals facilities of QAPCO were commissioned at Umm Said during 1980 and 1981. The company was established in 1974. IQ owns 80% of the company, while the remaining capital is held by France's Total. QAPCO's manufacturing facilities consist of an ethylene plant with a designed annual capacity of 525,000 metric tons, two low-density polyethylene plants with a capacity of 360,000 tons, and a sulphur plant with a capacity of 70,000 tons. In 2003 QAPCO awarded the EPC contract for a linear alkyl benzene project to the South Korean company LG Engineering & Construction, and in March 2004 awarded Japan's JPC and US-based Stone Webster the EPC contract for the upgrade of its ethylene cracker to increase capacity by 200,000 tons per year.

In May 1996 QGPC signed a preliminary agreement with a group of European companies (Norsk Hydro, Elf Atochem and Enichem) for a project to produce an annual 175,000 metric tons of ethylene dichloride, 230,000 tons of vinyl chloride monomer and 290,000 tons of caustic soda, using ethylene feedstock supplied by QAPCO. Participation in the new venture, Qatar Vinyl Co (QVC), was subsequently finalized as follows: QAPCO 31.9%; Norsk Hydro 29.7%; QGPC 25.5%; and Elf Atochem 12.9%. The QVC plant, built at an estimated cost of US $700m., was inaugurated in June 2001. In May 1997 QGPC signed an outline agreement with Phillips Petroleum to develop a chemicals complex, which was to include a 500,000-tons-per-year ethylene cracker, 467,000 tons per year of polyethylene capacity and 47,000 tons per year of hexene-1 capacity. Feedstock would be supplied from a natural gas liquids plant at Umm Said. In August 1999 Qatar Chemical Co (Q-Chem, 51% owned by QGPC and 49% by Chevron Phillips Chemical Co) secured a $750m. project-financing loan from a group of 24 regional and international banks, enabling it to award contracts for construction of the new complex. The plant was inaugurated in 2003. In June 2001 Q-Chem's parent companies signed an agreement to develop a high-density polyethylene and olefins plant (Q-Chem II) at Umm Said; the plant began operating in November 2010. In 2002 Qatofin—a joint venture between QAPCO (63%), Atofina (36%) and QP (1%)—was formed to oversee the establishment of a linear low-density polyethylene plant, with a 450,000-tons-per-year capacity, also in Umm Said. In the same year Qatofin signed an agreement with Q-Chem and QP to establish a 1.3m.-tons-per-year ethylene cracker at Ras Laffan and a 120-km pipeline to transport the ethylene feedstock from there to Q-Chem II and Qatofin in Umm Said. In June 2004 QP and ExxonMobil signed a memorandum of intent to conduct a feasibility study for the project. In the first half of 2005 Technip of France was awarded the EPC contract for the $800m. ethylene cracker (which was inaugurated in May 2010) and Tekfen of Turkey was awarded the $120m. contract for the pipeline. QP, meanwhile, announced plans to build a new ethylene cracker/aromatics complex to be integrated into the existing Umm Said refinery. In November 2005 a team of Italy's Technimont and South Korea's Daewoo was awarded the EPC contract to build the Q-Chem II downstream units (a high-density polyethylene unit and an alpha olefins plant) at Umm Said.

In January 2010 QP and ExxonMobil signed an agreement to develop a new petrochemical complex in Ras Laffan at a projected cost of US $6,000m. The complex was to include a steam cracker (with an annual capacity of 1.6m. tons) and speciality polyethylene plants. In December 2011 QP and Shell agreed to build a $6,400m. monoethylene glycol plant at Ras Laffan, and in February 2012 QP announced a venture with QAPCO to establish another major petrochemical facility, also at Ras Laffan. The Government intended to invest $25,000m. in the petrochemical industry over an eight-year period to raise annual production to 23m. tons by 2020. In November 2012 QAPCO opened its third low-density polyethylene (LDPE) plant at Umm Said, increasing potential annual output to 700,000 tons and making Qatar one of the largest LDPE manufacturers in the Middle East. In the following month the Government established the Qatar Chemical and Petrochemical Marketing and Distribution Co (also known as Muntajat) to control Qatar's chemical and petrochemical trade world-wide.

QASCO began commercial production in 1978, processing imported iron ore and local scrap for export, mainly to Saudi Arabia, Kuwait and the UAE. The Government acquired the holdings of the original Japanese partners (a total of 30%) in May 1997. A contract was awarded in early 1995 for the supply and installation of a 140,000-tons-per-year rolling mill to raise reinforced steel bar capacity to 470,000 tons per year. A contract was then signed in May 1996 for the installation, over a period of 18 months, of an electric arc furnace with an annual output capacity of 500,000 tons of molten steel. In 2005 QASCO was pursuing an expansion programme intended to increase production capacity to 1.5m. tons annually. In 2005 Italy's Danieli Co, Austria's VOEST-Alpine Industrieanlagenbau (now Siemens VAI Metals Technologies) and Japan's Kobe Steel were awarded the three main EPC packages on the programme. In addition, QASCO and India's Essar Global also announced plans to build a large-scale greenfield steel plant at Umm Said, estimated to cost US $1,250m.Qatar National Cement Manufacturing Co (now Qatar National Cement Co—QNCC) was founded in 1965. A second state cement company, Gulf Cement Co, was launched in April 2006, with plans to construct a 5,000-tons-per-day plant at Umm Bab under a fast-tracking system in an attempt to address severe cement shortages in the country (a symptom of a boom in construction projects).

In December 2004 QP signed a heads of agreement with Norway's Hydro Aluminium to develop, as a joint venture, a US $3,000m. aluminium smelter, with an annual capacity of 585,000 metric tons, and a dedicated power plant at Ras Laffan. Qatar Aluminium Co (Qatalum—jointly owned by QP and Hydro) began exporting aluminium (making its first delivery to India) in December 2009, and the plant was officially inaugurated in April 2010.

Major real estate development projects initiated in 2005 and 2006 included the US $5,000m. Lusail scheme, launched by state-owned Qatari Diar Real Estate Investment, incorporating residential areas, commercial districts, and leisure and marina facilities; the $1,000m. Al Waab City development in Doha, with residential and business units, luxury hotel, retail outlets, and other amenities; The Gate, a mixed-use development in the business district of Doha, having two commercial office towers with a mall, entertainment area and basement car park; and the Doha City Centre expansion, entailing the construction of five hotel towers. In 2008 Barwa Real Estate announced the launch of the Urjuan project, a QR 35,000m. integrated city development to be located in al-Khawr (al-Khor) and offering more than 24,500 housing units. The development of Doha Festival City, a large retail and hospitality complex, was being undertaken by a consortium including the UAE-based Al Futtaim Group, the Qatar Islamic Bank (QIB), Aqar Real Estate Development and Investment, and a private Qatari investor. In June 2012 the consortium raised a $1,000m. loan to fund construction. Further major infrastructure projects were planned in advance of the 2022 FIFA World Cup tournament (see Tourism).

POWER AND WATER

In 2000 Qatar's public electricity supply system had around 1,863 MW of installed generating capacity, of which up to 132 MW was located at the Ras Abu Aboud power station, 620 MW at the Ras Abu Fontas 'A' power station, 609 MW at the Ras Abu Fontas 'B' power station and 503 MW at supporting stations (mainly located near Doha). Peak demand (in the months of July and August) exceeded total capacity by 100 MW or more at that time, necessitating some buying-in of electricity from generating plants operated by large industrial users. There had been more than US $25,000m. invested in the Qatari energy sector by the end of 2006, with a large proportion coming from foreign sources, and from ExxonMobil in particular. By 2007 Qatar's power-generating capacity exceeded 3,700 MW, compared with 1,500 MW in 1995, and was reported to have reached 9,000 MW by January 2011. In August 2007 the energy unit of General Electric Co (USA) and Doosan Heavy Industries (South Korea) won a $1,000m. contract to a construct a power plant in Umm Said industrial city, which was to supply electricity to Qatalum's aluminium smelting plant (see Manufacturing and Industry); the power plant was inaugurated in May 2010.

Qatar has one of the world's highest levels of domestic demand for water per caput of population, and one of the highest rates of dependency on desalination plants to provide drinking water. However, by early 2011 there was reported to be a substantial surplus in water production, with demand peaking at 200m. gallons per day, while total capacity at Qatar's water plants stood at 320m. gallons per day.

The central planning and supervisory authority for the power and water sectors, and the managing authority for the transmission and distribution networks, is the Qatar General Electricity and Water Corpn (Kahramaa), established in April 2000 to take over these roles from the Ministry of Electricity and Water (MEW). Kahramaa also took over the MEW's responsibility for operating the Ras Abu Fontas 'A' and Ras Abu Aboud power stations and their supporting stations. The Ras Abu Fontas 'B' power station remained under the management of Qatar Electricity and Water Co (QEWC).

Qatar's first independent water and power project (IWPP), with a capacity of 750 MW of electricity and 40m. gallons per day of desalinated water, went into full production in 2004 at Ras Laffan. A US company, AES Corpn, had initialled a power and water purchase agreement in May 2001 providing for the establishment of a new utility company to implement the IWPP on build-operate-transfer terms. The company was to be owned 55% by AES (which sold its share to QEWC in 2010), 25% by QEWC, 10% by Gulf Investment Corpn and 10% by QP (which was to supply the plant with natural gas and also with coolant from a sea-water circulation system currently under development for the benefit of new industries in Ras Laffan). Kahramaa was to be the sole buyer of the IWPP's electricity output (the bulk of which would be sold to industrial end-users). In October 2004 Qatar Power, a consortium led by QEWC in partnership with the United Kingdom's International Power and Japan's Chubu Electric Power Co, was awarded a second IWPP, to be located at Ras Laffan. Estimated to cost US $900m., it was to have capacity of 1,025 MW and 60m. gallons per day. The key project agreements, including the 25-year power and water purchase agreement, were signed with Kahramaa in March 2005. The plant became operational in 2008. Also in 2005 QEWC awarded a joint venture of GE Energy of the USA and Italy's Fisia Italimpianti the contract for the expansion of the Ras Abu Fontas 'B' plant. When fully commissioned, the new facility would provide an additional 567 MW of electricity and 30m. gallons per day of water. Kahramaa planned to build a third IWPP at Umm Said (referred to as 'Facility B') and had awarded Germany's Fichtner the consultancy contract. Qatar's foreign investment law enacted in October 2000 permitted up to 100% foreign ownership of power plants. Contracts for the Ras Laffan 'C' project, to be owned, managed and operated by the Ras Girtas Power Co (a joint venture between QP, QEWC, Suez Energy International of France and Mitsui of Japan), were signed in May 2008. Ras Laffan 'C' was inaugurated in May 2011, with power generation capacity of 2,730 MW and desalination capacity of 63m. gallons per day. During 2008 Qatar and France signed energy co-operation agreements, which included the development of civil nuclear power infrastructure as part of a strategy announced by the GCC countries in 2007 to help meet their increasing electricity demands.

The Government was also to expand the sewage system to connect with the more heavily populated areas. Drainage projects were to include the construction of pumping stations and effluent treatment systems. In June 2004 the French-Japanese joint venture Degremont/Marubeni was awarded the contract for the design, construction and 10-year operation of the Doha West sewage treatment plant expansion project. In March, meanwhile, Gulf Energy, a global consortium of energy consultants and investors including Abu Dhabi Investment House and Kuwait Investment Co, launched the US $2,600m. Energy City project, a pioneering development to establish Qatar as an integrated energy centre attracting the world's leading oil and gas companies. It was also to include the International Mercantile Exchange, a dedicated energy trading platform.

Tendering for the initial phase of a US $1,600m. regional electricity 'inter-exchange' grid, connecting the GCC states, was completed in 2006 by the GCC Interconnection Authority; it was planned that the network would allow for production-sharing, eliminate the need for discrete power plants and ultimately achieve regional self-sufficiency in electricity generation to 2058. Qatar's share of the $994.7m. investment for 2006–08 was reported to be $146.8m. The first stage, connecting Qatar, Bahrain, Saudi Arabia and Kuwait in the North Grid, was completed in early 2009; the South Grid, linking the individual grids in the UAE and Oman, was completed in July of that year. The final stage involved the interconnection of both sections.

In February 2013 Kahramaa outlined plans for a further upgrading of Qatar's power and water sectors over an eight–year period in order to meet increased demand. The company envisaged the construction of an additional two power stations to add a further 2,100 MW of capacity, together with new water pipelines measuring over 800 km and five new reservoirs. In May three state-controlled companies —Qatar Holding, Qatar Petroleum International and QEWC—jointly formed a new company, Nebras Power, to invest in power generation and water desalination projects abroad.

TRANSPORT AND COMMUNICATIONS

The Public Works Authority (PWA, also known as Ashghal) was established in 2004 to take over the country's infrastructure programme. It is an independent authority formed to facilitate the tendering and award of contracts and reduce bureaucratic constraints. The PWA's five-year plan envisaged the implementation of major infrastructure development projects with an overall budget allocation of QR 25,000m. Road projects accounted for the largest share, with a total allocation of QR 13,000m. In August 2006 a German consultancy firm, PTV, was appointed to prepare a comprehensive national transport plan by the Urban Planning and Development Authority. Covering infrastructural developments over a 20-year period, the Transportation Master Plan for Qatar was to consider the possibility of implementing a rail transit system and developing an Intelligent Transport System in addition to upgrading roads, traffic systems, bus networks and ensuring the development of a public transport system equipped to cope with Qatar's rapid urban development. The plan was delivered in late 2007.

The first contracts for a major port development project at Doha were awarded in 1993. Extensive dredging work on the 17-km port approach channel would serve the dual purpose of upgrading the maritime access facility and providing landfill material to create 360,000 sq m of new quayside space at the port and to fill some 3.55m. sq m of reclaimed land, which was designated as the site of a new international airport. Also under development at Doha was a new container terminal with two berths and a roll-on, roll-off (ro-ro) facility. At Ras Laffan major new port facilities for LNG and condensate carriers and ro-ro vessels were completed in 1995. The development plan for Ras Laffan proposed the linking of the port area to a 50-sq km industrial area surrounded by a buffer zone. In April 1996 Ras Laffan was officially designated an industrial city. In November 2005 a contract involving reclamation and dredging work and the construction of breakwaters was awarded to Royal Boskalis Westminster in partnership with Belgian dredging company Jan de Nul for the US $2,000m. scheme to build a new LNG harbour facility at Ras Laffan. Umm Said was granted industrial city status in December 1998, and subsequently announced plans to upgrade its port facilities to handle a projected growth in trade. In late 2004 the US-based company Bechtel produced a master plan for a new port east of the Doha Airport project on 500 ha of reclaimed land. The port was to be connected to the mainland by a bridge and have a free trade zone shared with the new airport. (The free trade zone was subsequently commissioned by the Government in early 2006.) In October 2007 the Amir, Sheikh Hamad bin Khalifa Al Thani, decreed that the new Doha port development, estimated to cost some $5,500m., would instead be located at Umm Said industrial city. In its first phase, the port was expected to have annual handling capacity of 2m. 20-ft equivalent units (TEUs), taking Qatar's overall container-handling capacity to 6m. TEUs by 2030. Doha's existing port was to be decommissioned on completion of the new port. In a step towards privatization, a shareholding company was established to manage and operate Qatar's ports for 15 years from January 2010 in place of the General Authority for Customs and Ports, although QP would continue to operate the ports handling hydrocarbon exports.

In February 2000 Qatar and Bahrain agreed to establish a committee to assess the feasibility of building a causeway between the two countries (see History), and approval for the project was granted by both Governments in 2004. As a purely traffic-serving development, the so-called Friendship Bridge—which, upon completion, would be the world's longest fixed link—would not have been viable, but proposals to incorporate electricity and gas pipelines and possible development of artificial islands along its length rendered the scheme more economically and diplomatically favourable. In May 2008 the contract to build the causeway was awarded to a consortium led by Qatari Diar and Vinci Construction. The project was later revised to include a railway link for passenger and freight services. Construction had been expected to begin in early 2009, but was delayed owing to financial difficulties and redesign work to accommodate the rail link. In April 2011 a QR 3,700m. contract was awarded to a joint venture of Qatari Diar and the Saudi Binladin Group for work on the Dukhan highway project in Doha, and in May 2012 Hyundai Engineering and Construction won the QR 3,500m. construction contract for the Lusail Expressway project in Doha. In June 2013 Ashghal announced contracts worth QR 7,200m. to build further expressways across the country.

A national railway system has been under development in consultation with Deutsche Bahn of Germany, which was appointed as an adviser in 2008. In November 2009 Qatari Diar and Deutsche Bahn signed an agreement to launch, as a joint venture, the Qatar Railways Development Co (QRDC), which was to build a 650-km network at a projected cost of US $25,000m. In addition to the proposed Qatar–Bahrain causeway line, the network would include an east coast link between Ras Laffan and Umm Said, a high-speed link from the New Doha International Airport through Doha city centre and on to the causeway, a link to a wider GCC rail network, and a Doha metro system. The project was formally launched in May 2011, with the Qatar Railways Co (Qatar Rail) being established by the QRDC to oversee development of the railway system. In June 2013 Qatar Rail awarded contracts worth QR 30,000m. to four consortiums for the first phase of the Doha Metro. The project includes the construction of four railway lines and an underground section in the centre of the capital; it will provide a link between football stadiums for the 2022 FIFA World Cup tournament, although it is not expected to be completed until 2026. The first line of the planned 300-km metro system is scheduled to open in 2019. Qatar Airways, originally established by Qatari business interests in 1993, embarked on an extensive restructuring programme in 1997, one outcome of which was to bring the company into 50% government and 50% Qatari private ownership. Having approved a plan for the construction of a new international airport at Doha, with a handling capacity of 12m. passengers annually, in January 2004 the Government appointed the US-based engineering firm Bechtel to project-manage the development. The new airport was to be built in three phases, mainly on reclaimed land to the east of the existing facility. Completion of all phases of the airport was scheduled for 2015. During the construction process, the old airport was to be expanded and refurbished, at a cost of US $140m., in order to increase its capacity for the interim period. The opening of the new international departure terminal was delayed in April 2013, reportedly owing to the airport's failure to meet new safety and security standards. Further delays later that year pushed back the opening until at lest early 2014. In June Qatar Airways placed an order for nine new Boeing aircraft.

The state-owned Qatar Telecommunications Corpn (Q-Tel), established in 1987, was for many years the sole provider of fixed, mobile, cable and internet telecommunications in Qatar. In 1998 Q-Tel was partially privatized, with 45% of its shares being sold for some US $650m. In 2000 it awarded a contract to the French company Alcatel to add 100,000 new lines to Q-Tel's GSM network, which had 81,500 existing subscribers at that time. Rapid growth in wireless communications saw subscriber numbers rise by 41% in 2003, to reach 376,535. In 2005 a joint venture between Q-Tel and Denmark's TDC Mobile International was awarded the second mobile telephone licence in Oman. Q-Tel had some 1.26m. mobile telephone subscribers in 2007, an increase of 37% from 2006. The company also had operating interests in 15 other countries by the end of 2007. A notable acquisition in that year was that of a 51% stake in the Kuwait-based National Mobile Telecommunications Company KSC (Wataniya Telecom). Meanwhile, in May 2005 an independent telecommunications regulator, the Supreme Council for Communications and Information Technology (ictQatar), was established as a prelude to the complete liberalization of the sector. In December 2007 ictQatar announced that the second mobile telecommunications licence, valued at $2,120m., would be awarded to a consortium of Qatar Foundation and the United Kingdom's Vodafone; the service under this licence commenced in March 2009, and 40% of shares in the new company were offered for public subscription in May. In April 2010 ictQatar announced that the same consortium had been selected to receive Qatar's second fixed telecommunications licence. The regulator stated that the issuing of the licence concluded the first major phase of deregulation of the telecommunications sector. In October 2010 Q-Tel launched a $500m. six-year bond and a $1,000m. 10-year bond. The success of these prompted the company to launch a third bond issue, worth $1,250m., in November to fund overseas acquisitions and to refinance its loans. In February 2013 Q-Tel was relaunched under the new brand name of Ooredoo.

In May 2010 Qatar signed a partnership agreement with Eutelsat Communications of France to invest in, and operate, its first satellite. It was intended to provide superior coverage across the Middle East, North Africa and Central Asia and was launched in August 2013.

TOURISM

Qatar had about 1.9m. tourist arrivals in 2010 (compared with only 732,500 in 2004), despite the relatively small scale of its tourism infrastructure, which was based largely on the market for business visitors. There was a 12% increase in tourist numbers in 2011, including a 50% rise in visitors from other GCC countries.

A new Qatar Tourism Authority was established in 2000. Qatar's foreign investment law of October 2000 permitted foreign ownership of hotels and tourism facilities, while hotel restaurants and selected clubs were permitted to sell alcohol to non-Muslims. In May 2004 the Government presented proposals to invest US $15,000m. in tourism projects, including beach resorts at al-Fareej and al-Mafjar, luxury hotels to add an additional 2,550 rooms, cultural projects, and international sports facilities. Work, meanwhile, commenced on two 'lifestyle cities': the 3.2m.-sq m Pearl of the Gulf Island, costing $2,000m., with 7,600 high-quality homes, three luxury hotels, four marinas, and a variety of community and entertainment areas; and the North Beach development, featuring resort hotels, two golf courses, villas and apartments. The Government's plan also included the development of the $2,500m. New Doha International Airport (see Transport and Communications). Cultural projects under the auspices of the National Council for Culture, Arts and Heritage included the Qatar National Library, the Museum of Islamic Arts (which opened in November 2008) and the redevelopment of Qatar's National Museum.

In November 2000 Qatar was awarded the right to host the 2006 Asian Games, having pledged to build a US $700m. Sports City (renamed the ASPIRE Zone in 2006), to the north of Doha. The country hosted the Asian Football Confederation's Asian Cup in January 2011, and in December 2010 was selected to stage the 2022 FIFA World Cup.

BUDGET, INVESTMENT AND FINANCE

Qatar's budgetary performance is very closely linked to international prices for oil and to production levels. The increases in petroleum revenue since the 1970s have generally resulted in large budget surpluses, enabling the country to pursue an extensive programme of industrial and infrastructural projects.

According to figures published by the Ministry of Finance, total revenue under the 2005/06 budget increased by 18% compared with the previous year, to QR 64,984m. Revenue from the oil and gas sector amounted to QR 43,616m., compared with QR 36,319m. in 2004/05. Development expenditure increased by more than 130%, to QR 18,072m., while overall expenditure increased by 40.8%, to QR 50,833m. Current expenditure in that year increased by 15.9%, to QR 32,761m., with expenditure on salaries and wages notably decreasing by 16.2%. The budget surplus achieved in 2005/06 was equivalent to 9.2% of GDP, compared with a surplus equivalent to 16.4% of GDP in the previous year. Preliminary data for 2006/07 indicated a 30.8% increase in total revenues, to QR 84,994m., with an increase of 25.9%, to QR 54,919m., in oil and gas revenues. Development spending contracted by 6.4%, to QR 16,912m., although overall expenditure increased by 30.5%, to QR 66,356m. Current expenditure increased by 50.9%, to QR 49,444m., and notably included a 94.8% increase in spending on salaries and wages. The budget surplus in that year was equivalent to 9.0% of GDP. According to figures published by the IMF, projected revenue in 2007/08 was QR 113,365m. (compared with a budgeted QR 72,457m.); hydrocarbons revenues were projected to increase substantially, to QR 73,640m. (the budgeted figure was QR 42,095m.), with oil contributing QR 62,858m. and LNG QR 10,782m. Development expenditure was projected to reach QR 27,310m. (compared with a budgeted QR 20,980m.), while overall expenditure was projected to total QR 84,053m. (compared with a budgeted QR 65,713m.). Within current expenditure of QR 56,743m. (QR 44,733m.), salaries and wages accounted for QR 17,864m. (QR 15,627m.). The 2008/09 budget projected total revenue of QR 103,300m. and total expenditure of QR 95,900m., based on an oil price of US $55 per barrel. After consecutive years of surplus, the 2009/10 budget projected a deficit of about 2% of GDP following the decline in oil prices, OPEC output reductions and the Government's commitment to maintain capital expenditures for major infrastructure projects. It projected total revenue to decline to QR 88,700m. and expenditure to decrease to QR 94,500m., based on an oil price of $40 per barrel. The budget allocated 40% of total expenditure for non-oil and gas development projects.

The 2010/11 budget projected an increase in expenditure to QR 117,900m., and revenue was set to rise to QR 127,500m., generating a surplus of about QR 10,000m. based on an increased oil price of US $55 per barrel. The Government allocated about 30% of budgetary expenditure for infrastructure development, 15% for education and 7% for health (including new hospitals and other health care facilities). Maintaining the Government's expansionary policy, the 2011/12 budget projected increased expenditure of QR 139,900m. and revenue of QR 162,500m. (still based on an oil price of $55 per barrel). Greater expenditure (41%) was allocated to public projects, including railway infrastructure development and the new Doha port and airport, while spending on education was to increase to QR 19,300m. and health care to QR 8,800m. The Government also allotted QR 5,200m. for housing loans to eligible Qatari nationals and for increased public sector salaries and allowances for Qatari workers. According to the IMF, the fiscal balance was set to record a surplus of 7.2% of GDP in 2011/12, despite additional post-budget capital spending and salary increases. The 2012/13 budget, issued in May 2012, projected a 26% expansion in revenue to QR 206,000m. and a 28% rise in expenditure to QR 178,000m., based on a higher, but still conservative, oil price of $65 per barrel. Major infrastructure and FIFA World Cup projects were allocated QR 62,000m., while QR 22,000m. was allotted to education and QR 14,000m. to health care. The overall fiscal surplus in 2011/12 was higher than expected, at 8.2% of GDP, because of strong hydrocarbon revenues; however, the budget for 2013/14 was again based on an oil price of $65 per barrel. It envisaged an 18% increase in expenditure, to QR 210,660m., and a 6% rise in revenue, to QR 218,000m. The surplus was expected to fall to around 1% of GDP. The IMF, meanwhile, welcomed the Government's adoption of a three-year budget framework to help shield government spending from revenue volatility and to enable the better utilization of resources.

In January 2010 the Government implemented a long-promised reduction, to 10%, in the rate of corporation tax, in accordance with a proposed flat tax across the GCC. In the following month investment legislation was amended to permit 100% foreign ownership of companies in sectors in which involvement had previously been restricted to 49%, including consultancy services, information technology, and services related to sports, culture and distribution. Most financial companies cannot be majority-owned by non-Qataris and remain heavily regulated. In June 2011 the Government introduced a withholding tax, which included a levy on payments made to non-residents without a permanent place of business in Qatar. The Government also planned to amend the law on commercial agencies in order to open up the market to fair competition.

In a report published in January 2008, the IMF estimated Qatar's total external debt, including that of commercial banks, at US $29,878m., equivalent to 56.7% of GDP, in 2006, compared with $20,422m. (48.1% of GDP) in 2005 and $15,011m. (47.3%) in 2004. Of this, government external debt was estimated at $3,387m. (equivalent to 6.4% of GDP) in 2006, compared with $3,743m. (8.8%) in 2005 and $4,017m. (12.7%) in 2004. These figures contrasted with total external debt equivalent to 81.7% of GDP in 2001, including government external debt equivalent to 25.7% of GDP. The cost of servicing the external debt declined from 25.1% of the value of exports of goods and services in 2001 to 7.4% in both 2005 and 2006. According to IMF projections, Qatar's total external debt was expected to increase to $40,243m. by the end of 2007 (equivalent to 61.1% of GDP), while government external debt would be reduced to $3,049m. (4.6% of GDP). The projected cost of debt-servicing in that year was 5.4% of the value of exports of goods and services. Total external debt was estimated by the IMF to have increased to $60,680m. by the end of 2008 and to $83,800m. by the end of 2009. It rose further in 2010, to $103,900m., as the Government took advantage of an improved external financing environment to issue several tranches of bonds. There was also a series of issues by government-owned corporations. In 2012 the Government established an independent Office for Management of Credit Policies and Debt, aiming to modernize cost-risk strategies, including those for government agencies, and to manage debt-servicing, interest rate, currency and liquidity risks. Total external debt (excluding banking debt) was estimated by the IMF at $102,000m. in 2012.In October 1993 the Qatar Monetary Authority was superseded by the Qatar Central Bank, which has supervisory powers over all banks, foreign exchange houses, investment companies and finance houses operating in Qatar. In August 1997 the central bank was empowered to license Qatar-based banks and finance companies to establish 'offshore' banking units, with effect from October. Bahrain had previously been the only GCC member state with an 'offshore' banking sector. In November the Qatar Industrial Development Bank, structured as a joint venture between the Qatar Government and local private sector interests (mainly banks and insurance companies), was inaugurated to provide concessionary loans to fund the fixed capital requirements of small and medium-sized industrial ventures. Plans were announced in January 2005 for the establishment of a new financial and business centre, the Qatar Financial Centre (QFC). The Qatar Financial Centre Authority was to operate the new centre, and an independent Qatar Financial Centre Regulatory Authority (QFCRA) was to supervise business conduct and grant licences. The QFCRA began receiving licence applications in May of that year. Corporations based in the QFC were to be entitled to 100% foreign ownership, full repatriation of profits and a three-year tax holiday. In March 2009 Qatar First Investment Bank became the first independent Islamic investment bank to be licensed by the QFC.

To promote credit growth in the wake of the international financial crisis, the central bank reduced its overnight deposit rate by 50 basis points in August 2010 to encourage banks to explore lending opportunities in the private sector rather than placing their deposits in the central bank. In April 2011 the central bank lowered its policy lending rate by 50 basis points in a further move to encourage banks to lend more. There were more reductions in the lending rate (by 50 points to 4.5%) and deposit rate (to 0.75% from 1%) in August, although stricter post-crisis credit guidelines on individual loan thresholds continued to subdue private sector credit growth. In March the Bank had opened a credit bureau to increase transparency, promote information sharing among banks and help to reduce investor risk aversion. In May 2012 the central bank introduced an inter-bank offered rate as an indicator of the cost of borrowing in the local wholesale banking market.

In August 2010 the central bank placed limits on the lending that conventional banks could offer through their Islamic branches. The measures also prohibited conventional banks from opening new Islamic branches and required that their *Shari'a* assets be limited to 15% of total assets. In February 2011 the central bank instructed all conventional banks to stop offering Islamic banking services by the end of the year, claiming that the overlapping nature of non-Islamic and Islamic activities at these banks had proved difficult to manage. The existing Islamic banks in Qatar, which held about 20% of total banking assets in 2010, were likely to benefit substantially from this decision. It was also anticipated that the new regulations might prompt conventional banks to invest more overseas, and in February 2011 QNB completed the acquisition of a majority share of Indonesia's Bank Kesawan. The International Bank of Qatar sold its Islamic banking retail operations to Barwa Bank in August and its *Shari'a*-compliant corporate portfolio to the QIB in December. Six conventional banks had discontinued or divested their Islamic banking operations by the start of 2012. Further extending its overseas interests, in 2012 QNB increased its stakes in the UAE's Commercial Bank International and Iraq's Mansour Bank, bought a 49% stake in Libya's Bank of Commerce and Development and, in December, also entered into an agreement with Société Générale to acquire its 77% stake in its Egyptian subsidiary. In the same month QNB became the first commercial bank in Qatar to launch a debt fund, enabling investment in debt securities that are directly issued by sovereign and corporate entities based in GCC countries.

The banking sector as a whole was not overexposed to the impact of the international financial crisis that took hold in the latter half of 2008, but was not unscathed by the recessionary after-effects. In an attempt to increase confidence in the banking system, the QIA was authorized in October 2008 to purchase stakes in the country's domestic banks, and this intervention was followed in March 2009 by the Government's offer to buy the listed investment portfolios of seven Qatari banks. The QIA also embarked on a strategy of acquiring interests in foreign banks, including Credit Suisse and the United Kingdom's Barclays Bank. According to the IMF in early 2009, the banking system remained sound and the liquidity position comfortable. To further support the banking sector, the Government bought the property loans of the local banks, worth QR 15,000m., in June 2009, and, through the QIA, bought additional 5% equity stakes in the banks for about US $2,000m. in December. In January 2011 the QIA announced that it would purchase a further 10% stake in the domestic banks in an effort to increase their capital bases. The IMF reported that Qatar's banking system remained well capitalized and profitable in 2012. The capital adequacy ratio of commercial banks rose from 16.1% in 2010 to 21.1% in June 2012, while non-performing loans declined from 2.0% to 1.7% over the same period.

In 2009–10 the QIA had continued to expand its non-bank overseas investments with several high-profile asset acquisitions, including stakes in German automobile firm Volkswagen, French nuclear energy company Areva, Canadian hotel chain Fairmont Raffles, the Harrods department store in London, United Kingdom, and the Brazilian subsidiary of Spain's Banco Santander. In June 2012 the QIA acquired a stake in Royal Dutch Shell, having earlier in the year increased its holdings in Total, Xstrata and Iberdrola (Spain's largest electricity supplier). Also in 2012 QIA took a 49% stake in AUX, a Brazilian gold mining company, for US $2,000m., and agreed to take a 20% stake, worth $1,400m., in the British airport operator BAA (now Heathrow Airport Holdings Ltd). Having previously made some investments in China, including a stake in funds partly owned by China's sovereign wealth fund, the QIA received a qualified foreign institutional investor licence to invest up to $1,000m in Chinese capital markets. The IMF estimated the value of QIA's assets at $175,000m. in 2012.

In May 1997 an official Doha Securities Market (DSM), supervised by the Ministry of Finance, Economy and Trade, began trading in the shares of 17 companies and banks. In May 1998 the Qatar Arabian Investment Co was launched with plans for its shares to be listed on the DSM—the first listing of a US dollar-denominated stock and the first open to non-Qatari investment. The market's start-up costs were funded by the Government, which planned to organize a series of share offers as part of a future privatization programme. In March 2000 the right to buy and sell the shares of DSM-listed companies was extended to nationals of all GCC member states. Electronic trading was implemented in 2002. Following a decree amending the provisions of the law regulating foreign investment, foreigners were allowed to trade on the DSM from April 2005. In June 2008 NYSE Euronext, the US-European stock exchange group, took a 25% stake in DSM in a transaction intended to boost business in the Middle East for both partners. However, as in the rest of the Gulf region, the DSM declined markedly in the wake of the global financial crisis in the latter half of 2008, losing 60% of its value by early 2009. In June 2009 the Government and NYSE Euronext launched a new stock exchange, the Qatar Exchange (QE), to replace the DSM. NYSE Euronext acquired a 20% stake in the QE, while a majority 80% share was retained by the state. In 2009 NYSE Euronext announced plans to launch a derivatives exchange in Qatar, while in March 2010 the authorities announced that national banks were to be permitted to trade in shares in order to boost liquidity. The QE was the best performing market in the GCC and wider Arab region during 2010 and 2011. In order to diversify away from equities on the QE and to redirect excess liquidity from the banking system, the Government listed short-term treasury bills on the exchange from December 2011, creating a secondary market in debt securities, while in March 2012 the QE introduced a market for small and medium-sized companies. In October 2012 IQ increased its foreign ownership limit to 12.25% from 7.5%, while in May 2013 QP announced plans to list four subsidiaries on the QE in line with government plans to encourage private sector investment. In June of that year Morgan Stanley Capital International (MSCI) declared that it would upgrade and reclassify the QE's index from 'frontier' to 'emerging market' status.

In early 2007 the Government announced that a unified regulatory authority for the financial services sector was to be established, comprising the QFCRA, the banking supervision department of the central bank and the Qatar Financial Markets Authority (QFMA—the regulator of the DSM). The new Qatar Financial Regulatory Authority would oversee all banking, insurance, securities, asset-management and other financial services activities. It was intended that this structure would result in increased transparency and efficiency, thus facilitating Qatar's efforts to secure increased levels of long-term investment, and render Doha more competitive among other financial centres in the region. A new law paving the way for the central bank to act as a single financial regulator was published in December 2012. It mandated the Bank to act as the supreme authority for framing policies for the regulation and supervision of all financial service providers, including banks, Islamic financial institutions, investment, insurance and finance companies, exchange houses and companies licensed by the QFC and the QFMA to conduct financial activities.

A 10-year Eurobond, worth US $1,000m., was issued by the Qatari authorities in May 1999. In June 2000 Qatar's second sovereign Eurobond issue raised $1,400m., making it possible for the Government to pay down some of its short-term debt. In December 1999 Qatar negotiated a so-called 'oil prepayment' facility with a group of international banks, effectively providing the Government with advance access to oil revenue. The facility was for $500m., repayable over five years. A further $250m., repayable over three years, was raised through a similar arrangement in early 2000. A $500m. sovereign loan, repayable over seven years, was arranged for Qatar in

November 2000 by the Japanese Sumitomo Bank, which had been the lead arranger for previous sovereign loans in 1994, 1995 and 1996, and a co-arranger of Qatar's most recent syndicated sovereign loan in 1997. In October 2003 the Government issued Qatar's first sovereign Islamic bond, worth $700m. The Government returned to the international bond market during 2009, raising $3,000m. in April and $7,000m. in November, to be used for contingency funding and infrastructure investment.

As part of an IMF-backed programme to develop a domestic bond market and provide new mechanisms to absorb excess liquidity in the banking sector, government bonds were issued in June 2010 (worth US $3,300m.) and in January 2011 ($13,700m.). During 2010 QNB completed a bond issue worth $1,500m. (believed to be one of the largest issues from a financial institution in the Middle East and North Africa region), the Commercial Bank of Qatar (CBQ) launched a Swiss franc-denominated bond issue (worth $283.6m.) and also approved a $5,000m. bond programme starting in 2011, and the QIB successfully issued its debut $750m. *sukuk* (*Shari'a*-compliant bond issue) in October. A bond issue by Qatari Diar in July 2010 raised $3,500m. In November 2011 the Government successfully issued a $5,000m. sovereign bond, which was the largest in the GCC in that year and was heavily over-subscribed despite the turbulent global market conditions. Local banks also utilized the international bond market to bolster their cash reserves; QNB raised $1,000m. in February 2012, Doha Bank secured $500m. in March and the CBQ issued a $500m. bond in April. In July the Government issued a $4,000m. Islamic bond and in September QP issued a $1,000m. Samurai bond (issued in Japan by a foreign institution). In March 2013 the central bank started issuing local currency-denominated government securities on a quarterly basis, with the aim of developing the domestic debt market and liquidity management.In December 1995 IMF statistics for Qatar indicated total official reserves of US $694m. and total foreign assets of $787m. However, it was confirmed by the Government in the following month that a substantial tranche of Qatar's reserves had remained under the control of the former Amir, Sheikh Khalifa, following his removal from office in June 1995. The sum involved was widely reported to be in the region of $3,000m. A settlement agreement was signed in February 1997 whereby Sheikh Khalifa was understood to have formally ceded control over disputed assets. By the end of 2010 Qatar Central Bank's total international reserves amounted to QR 113,262.3m., declining to QR 60,804.6m. by the end of 2011 following the imposition of restrictions on commercial bank deposits placed with the central bank. However, as the rate of investment outflows slowed, international reserves recovered to QR 120,348.1m. by the end of 2012.

FOREIGN TRADE AND BALANCE OF PAYMENTS

According to official figures, in 2002 exports increased by 1.5%, to QR 40,155m., while imports increased by 27%, to QR 15,743m., which narrowed the trade surplus by about 10%, to QR 24,412m. The current account recorded a surplus of QR 13,918m. In 2003 export earnings rose by 20% to reach QR 48,021m., including 51% from crude petroleum and 32% from LNG. Import spending totalled QR 17,826m. There was a current account surplus of QR 20,800m. and an overall balance of payments surplus of QR 16,100m. Figures for 2004 indicated export earnings of QR 61,505m., import spending of QR 17,561m., a current account surplus of QR 29,426m. and an overall balance of payments surplus of QR 14,294m. Qatar's exports have increased substantially, averaging a growth rate of 23% from 2000 to 2004. The principal export items in 2005 were mineral fuels and lubricants, accounting for 90.2% of the total value of goods exported in that year. The main import products in 2005 were machinery and transport equipment, and basic manufactures. There was an overall balance of payments surplus in 2005 of QR 15,683m., and a current account surplus of QR 25,710m., followed in 2006 by a trade surplus of QR 70,034m. and current account surplus of QR 34,430m. According to official figures, the trade surplus in 2007 reached QR 72,857m. Qatar's leading export partner in that year was Japan, receiving 40.6% of the total. The value of imports reached QR 80,097m., an increase of 33.8% compared with the previous year. The largest source of imports in 2007 was the USA, which represented 11.4% of the total. In September 2007 the QIA, which manages the nation's surplus revenues, announced that it intended to diversify the portfolio away from the weakening US dollar and instead to invest more heavily in East Asian countries, including Japan and China.

In 2008 the trade surplus increased to QR 108,388m. and the current account surplus reached QR 51,685m., reflecting the strong performance of LNG exports. In 2009 the value of exports contracted to QR 170,498m. as a result of the decline in petroleum prices, while that of imports decreased to QR 84,593m. resulting in a reduced trade surplus of QR 87,264m. Hydrocarbon exports represented about 76% of total exports. The current account surplus narrowed to QR 30,542m. The trade surplus increased in 2010 as the value of exports reached QR 264,992m. and imports QR 84,593m. The current account recorded a surplus of QR 86,622m. in that year, equivalent to 18.7% of GDP. According to preliminary official figures, in 2011 the value of exports rose considerably, to QR 410,456m., following an increase in oil prices. Meanwhile, imports declined, to QR 81,275m., prompting a preliminary current account surplus of some QR 189,200m. (or 30.0% of GDP). The surplus widened in 2012 by nearly 20%, to reach QR 224,171m., representing about 32% of GDP. The trade surplus also increased as the value of exports rose to QR 484,003m. (principally reflecting LNG sales growth) against imports of QR 112,065m.

GCC member states established a unified regional customs tariff in January 2003, and agreed to create a single market and currency no later than January 2010. The economic convergence criteria for the monetary union were agreed at a GCC summit in Abu Dhabi in December 2005, and the GCC common market was launched in January 2008. However, in May 2009 plans for the creation of a single currency were cast into uncertainty by the withdrawal from the scheme of the UAE. In June 2010 Qatar, Bahrain, Kuwait and Saudi Arabia signed an agreement reaffirming their commitment to establishing the monetary union.

Statistical Survey

Sources (unless otherwise stated): Dept of Economic Policies, Qatar Central Bank, POB 1234, Doha; tel. 4456456; fax 4413650; e-mail elzainys@qcb.gov.qa; internet www.qcb.gov.qa; Qatar Statistics Authority, POB 7283, Doha; tel. 4958888; fax 4839999; e-mail customer_services@planning.gov.qa; internet www.qsa.gov.qa.

Area and Population

AREA, POPULATION AND DENSITY

Area (sq km)	11,493*
Population (census results)†	
1 March 2004	744,029
20 April 2010	
Males	1,284,739
Females	414,696
Total	1,699,435
Population (official estimates at mid year)‡	
2011	1,732,717
2012	1,832,903
Density (per sq km) at mid-2012	159.5

* 4,437 sq miles.
† Including resident workers from abroad.
‡ Estimates not adjusted to take account of the 2010 census.

POPULATION BY AGE AND SEX
(population at 2010 census*)

	Males	Females	Total
0–14	119,140	113,444	232,584
15–64	1,157,450	295,584	1,453,034
65 and over	8,149	5,668	13,817
Total	1,284,739	414,696	1,699,435

* Including resident workers from abroad.

PRINCIPAL TOWNS
(population of municipalities at 2010 census)

Al Dawhah (Doha)	796,947	Umm Salal	60,509
Al-Rayyan	455,623	Al Daayen	43,176
Al-Khawr (Al-Khor)	193,983	Al-Shamal	7,975
Al-Wakrah	141,222		

BIRTHS, MARRIAGES AND DEATHS

	Registered live births		Registered marriages		Registered deaths	
	Number	Rate (per 1,000)	Number	Rate (per 1,000)	Number	Rate (per 1,000)
2004	13,190	17.5	2,649	3.5	1,341	1.8
2005	13,401	16.8	2,734	3.4	1,545	1.9
2006	14,120	16.8	3,019	3.6	1,750	2.1
2007	15,681	12.8	3,206	2.6	1,776	1.5
2008	17,210	11.9	3,235	2.2	1,942	1.3
2009	18,351	11.2	3,153	1.9	2,008	1.2
2010	19,504	11.2	2,977	1.7	1,970	1.1
2011	20,623	11.9	3,293	1.9	1,949	1.1

2012: Registered marriages 3,532 (marriage rate 1.9).

Life expectancy (years at birth): 78.2 (males 78.5; females 77.9) in 2011 (Source: World Bank, World Development Indicators database).

ECONOMICALLY ACTIVE POPULATION
(population aged 15 years and over, 2012)

	Qatari	Non-Qatari	Total
Agriculture, hunting, forestry and fishing	26	18,136	18,162
Mining and quarrying	7,738	75,373	83,111
Manufacturing	918	101,888	102,806
Electricity, gas and water	1,450	7,511	8,961
Construction	709	498,555	499,264
Wholesale and retail trade; repair of motor vehicles, motorcycles and personal and household goods	1,451	167,908	169,359
Hotels and restaurants	593	31,612	32,205
Transport and storage	1,466	36,809	38,275
Information and communications	2,403	9,055	11,458
Financial intermediation	2,802	8,656	11,458
Real estate, renting and business activities	669	8,665	9,334
Public administration	45,463	36,077	81,540
Professional, scientific and technical activities	301	25,232	25,533
Administrative and support service activities	718	40,729	41,447
Education	10,652	19,757	30,409
Health and social work	4,516	18,994	23,510
Arts, entertainment and recreation	828	6,936	7,764
Other community, social and personal service activities	89	4,924	5,013
Private households with employed persons	—	139,904	139,904
Extra-territorial organizations and bodies	21	1,659	1,680
Total employed	82,813	1,258,380	1,341,193
Unemployed	2,586	3,892	6,478
Total labour force	85,399	1,262,272	1,347,671
Males	56,488	1,118,610	1,175,098
Females	28,911	143,662	172,573

Health and Welfare

KEY INDICATORS

Total fertility rate (children per woman, 2011)	2.2
Under-5 mortality rate (per 1,000 live births, 2011)	8
Physicians (per 1,000 head, 2006)	2.8
Hospital beds (per 1,000 head, 2009)	1.2
Health expenditure (2010): US $ per head (PPP)	1,621
Health expenditure (2010): % of GDP	2.1
Health expenditure (2010): public (% of total)	77.5
Total carbon dioxide emissions ('000 metric tons, 2009)	70,344.1
Carbon dioxide emissions per head (metric tons, 2009)	44.0
Human Development Index (2012) ranking	36
Human Development Index (2012) value	0.834

For sources and definitions, see explanatory note on p. vi.

Agriculture

PRINCIPAL CROPS
('000 metric tons)

	2009	2010	2011
Barley	0.7	0.7	0.5
Cauliflowers and broccoli	1.6	2.1	1.4
Pumpkins, squash and gourds	0.4	0.6	0.4
Aubergines (Eggplants)	4.5	4.7	3.6
Chillies and peppers, green	0.8	1.0	0.9
Onions, dry	2.4	2.8	2.6
Tomatoes	12.6	12.8	10.7
Cantaloupes and other melons	2.9	2.1	1.8*
Dates	20.8	21.5	20.7

* FAO estimate.

Aggregate production ('000 metric tons, may include official, semi-official or estimated data): Total cereals 2.2 in 2009, 2.7 in 2010, 1.7 in 2011; Total fruits (excl. melons) 21.6 in 2009, 22.3 in 2010, 21.6 in 2011; Total vegetables (incl. melons) 45.7 in 2009, 48.4 in 2010, 47.9 in 2011.

Source: FAO.

LIVESTOCK
('000 head, year ending September)

	2009	2010	2011
Horses	6.1	6.0	5.8*
Cattle	11.1	11.4	10.1
Camels	47.3	51.5	61.7
Sheep	199.8	213.8	241.4
Goats	165.6	171.6	190.0
Chickens	6,800.0	7,300.0	8,000.0

* FAO estimate.

Source: FAO.

LIVESTOCK PRODUCTS
('000 metric tons)

	2009	2010	2011
Camel meat*	1.2	1.3	1.4
Sheep meat*	9.5	8.6	8.7
Chicken meat*	7.3	8.1	9.2
Cows' milk*	6.8	7.0	6.9
Camels' milk*	4.6	4.9	4.9
Goats' milk*	5.9	6.0	6.0
Hen eggs	4.3	4.5	5.0

* FAO estimates.

Source: FAO.

Fishing

(metric tons, live weight)

	2009	2010	2011
Capture	14,064	13,760	12,985
Groupers	1,318	1,335	1,292
Grunts and sweetlips	746	772	552
Emperors (Scavengers)	4,700	4,105	3,313
Narrow-barred Spanish mackerel	1,750	2,107	1,978
Aquaculture	36	36	36
Total catch	14,100	13,796	13,021

Source: FAO.

Mining

	2010	2011	2012
Crude petroleum ('000 metric tons)	72,131	78,206	83,346
Natural gas (million cu m)*	116,700	145,271	157,050

* Excluding gas flared or recycled.

Source: BP, *Statistical Review of World Energy*.

Industry

SELECTED PRODUCTS
('000 metric tons unless otherwise indicated)

	2004	2005	2006
Ammonia (for fertilizer)	1,737.2	2,133.8	2,170.2
Urea (for fertilizer)	2,238.7	2,978.8	2,908.9
Organic fertilizers	24.0	42.0	57.0
Cement	1,202.0	1,182.0	2,169.0
'Super' petrol (motor spirit—gasoline)	801.0	754.6	889.4
'Premium' petrol (motor spirit—gasoline)	857.9	901.7	1,004.7
Jet fuel (incl. kerosene)	957.7	905.5	1,087.1
Gas diesel (distillate fuel) oils	995.1	925.6	997.9
Residual fuel oils	250.7	418.3	614.6
Liquefied petroleum gas	127.6	131.0	217.0
Natural gas condensate	1,545.1	1,556.1	1,667.9
Butane	963.0	1,075.4	1,151.8
Propane	1,242.6	1,403.1	1,576.2
Electric energy (million kWh)	12,992.6	14,395.9	14,983.2

Electric energy (million kWh): 21,616 in 2008; 24,158 in 2009; 28,144 in 2010 (Source: UN Industrial Commodity Statistics Database).

Finance

CURRENCY AND EXCHANGE RATES

Monetary Units

100 dirhams = 1 Qatar riyal (QR).

Sterling, Dollar and Euro Equivalents (31 May 2013)

£1 sterling = 5.538 riyals;
US $1 = 3.640 riyals;
€1 = 4.734 riyals;
100 Qatar riyals = £18.06 = $27.47 = €21.12.

Average Exchange Rate

Note: Since June 1980 the official mid-point rate has been fixed at US $1 = QR 3.64.

BUDGET
(QR million, year ending 31 March)

Revenue	2009/10	2010/11	2011/12*
Petroleum and natural gas	82,807	96,849	153,198
Investments	53,881	36,090	25,764
Other	32,454	22,968	41,132
Total	169,142	155,907	220,094

Expenditure	2009/10	2010/11	2011/12*
Current expenditure	75,788	98,127	115,661
Wages and salaries	21,594	23,065	29,613
Interest payments	3,998	5,577	9,613
Supplies and services	8,082	15,188	11,586
Other	42,114	54,297	64,849
Development expenditure	39,246	44,243	50,091
Total	115,034	142,370	165,752

* Preliminary figures.

INTERNATIONAL RESERVES
(US $ million at 31 December)

	2010	2011	2012
Gold (national valuation)	566.5	626.1	668.3
IMF special drawing rights	413.2	412.5	413.2
Reserve position in IMF	96.0	144.6	151.3
Foreign exchange	30,111.6	15,641.3	31,956.5
Total	31,187.3	16,824.6	33,189.3

Source: IMF, *International Financial Statistics*.

MONEY SUPPLY
(QR million at 31 December)

	2010	2011	2012
Currency outside depository corporations	6,095	7,013	8,161
Transferable deposits	81,484	106,305	110,415
Other deposits	177,137	196,648	262,476
Broad money	264,716	309,966	381,053

Source: IMF, *International Financial Statistics*.

COST OF LIVING
(Consumer Price Index; base: 2007 = 100)

	2010	2011	2012
Food, beverages and tobacco	123.9	129.4	134.2
Clothing and footwear	105.2	113.3	116.5
Rent, fuel and energy	91.9	87.4	84.6
Transport and communication	107.2	114.1	116.7
All items (incl. others)	106.9	108.9	111.0

NATIONAL ACCOUNTS
(QR million at current prices)

Expenditure on the Gross Domestic Product

	2009	2010	2011*
Government final consumption expenditure	55,652	63,689	76,840
Private final consumption expenditure	68,623	73,646	79,906
Gross capital formation	152,946	143,011	183,873
Total domestic expenditure	277,221	280,346	340,619
Exports of goods and services	182,034	283,270	442,960
Less Imports of goods and services	103,269	108,171	159,405
GDP in purchasers' values	355,986	455,445	624,173
GDP at constant 2004 prices	243,492	68,623	321,074

Gross Domestic Product by Economic Activity

	2010	2011*	2012*
Agriculture and fishing	537	590	641
Mining and quarrying†	239,745	370,161	404,750
Manufacturing	40,832	56,742	68,906
Electricity, gas and water	2,113	2,351	2,637
Construction	27,500	28,339	30,967
Trade, restaurants and hotels	31,500	35,603	39,453
Transport and communications	18,069	20,993	23,397
Finance, insurance, real estate and business services	60,291	65,559	71,162
Government services	37,388	46,239	60,890
Social services	4,522	5,028	5,682
Other services	1,881	2,013	2,321
Sub-total	464,378	633,618	710,806
Import duties	3,793	3,920	4,345
Less Imputed bank service charge	12,726	13,365	14,806
GDP in purchasers' values	455,445	624,173	700,345

* Preliminary figures.
† Including services incidental to mining of petroleum and natural gas.

BALANCE OF PAYMENTS
(QR million)

	2010	2011*	2012*
Exports of goods f.o.b.	272,309	416,047	486,730
Imports of goods f.o.b.	–76,210	–98,010	–112,065
Trade balance	196,099	318,037	374,665
Exports of services	10,961	26,913	36,117
Imports of services	–31,961	–61,395	–87,019
Balance on goods and services	175,099	283,555	323,763
Other income received	8,698	22,445	23,726
Other income paid	–55,813	–70,752	–67,880
Balance on goods, services and income	127,984	235,248	279,609
Current transfers (net)	–41,362	–46,048	–52,711
Expatriates' remittances	–29,577	–37,543	–38,971
Current balance	86,622	189,200	226,898
Capital account (net)	–7,489	–13,121	–22,631
Financial account (net)	–31,379	–214,685	–139,371
Net errors and omissions	–3,361	–13,605	–6,366
Overall balance	44,393	–52,211	58,529

* Preliminary figures.

External Trade

PRINCIPAL COMMODITIES
(distribution by HS, QR million)

Imports	2010	2011*	2012*
Live animals and animal products	2,718.2	3,181.7	3,906.0
Mineral products	3,237.8	5185.3	4,785.1
Chemicals and related products	6,132.0	6,714.6	7,659.5
Iron and steel; other base metals and articles of base metal	10,976.4	8,852.9	10,460.8
Articles of iron and steel	6,180.4	5,069.3	5,979.2
Machinery and mechanical appliances; electrical equipment; parts thereof	27,744.4	22,423.1	24,355.5
Boilers, machinery, etc.	16,087.2	12,333.6	14,242.6
Electrical machinery and equipment; sound and television recorders and reproducers	11,657.2	10,089.4	10,112.9
Vehicles, vessels, aircraft and other transport equipment	13,278.9	13,066.0	18,135.7
Vehicles other than trains, vessels and air and spacecraft	9,010.5	8,529.0	14,156.8
Total (incl. others)	84,593.0	81,293.5	94,940.8

Exports†	2010	2011*	2012*
Mineral products	246,516.2	383,670.6	427,405.6
Mineral fuels and oils, and products thereof	245,822.8	382,269.7	425,976.8
Chemicals and related products	8,151.5	10,990.4	18,993.9
Plastics, rubber, and articles thereof	5,401.1	8,821.0	15,719.0
Plastics and articles thereof	5,400.3	8,821.0	15,718.7
Total (incl. others)	265,552.9	411,000.8	479,076.1

* Preliminary figures.
† Including re-exports (QR million): 7,317.8 in 2010; 5,590.8 in 2011 (preliminary); 4,989.0 in 2012 (preliminary).

PRINCIPAL TRADING PARTNERS
(QR million)

Imports	2010	2011*	2012*
Australia	1,309.2	1,844.3	2,635.3
Bahrain	1,986.6	1,796.7	1,620.6
Belgium	980.2	703.2	688.5
Brazil	1,443.7	1,949.4	1,521.0
China, People's Republic	7,658.2	7,843.4	9,274.2
Egypt	1,044.5	969.9	1,103.0
France	4,026.0	2,724.1	2,788.3
Germany	6,129.8	5,645.6	6,265.5
India	2,553.1	2,672.7	3,408.4
Italy	5,498.7	4,644.8	4,637.6
Japan	6,373.2	4,557.4	7,759.7
Korea, Republic	2,642.2	2,048.5	2,900.9
Malaysia	1,252.7	1,030.8	1,171.9
Oman	852.5	603.5	606.8
Saudi Arabia	4,441.1	4,257.7	4,437.2
Spain	927.6	1,089.4	1,106.4
Sweden	819.7	1,398.1	738.7
Switzerland	1,388.3	1,928.9	3,676.2
Thailand	1,349.9	1,375.5	1,921.1
Turkey	980.4	876.5	1,340.8
United Arab Emirates	5,795.6	6,567.2	7,410.0
United Kingdom	4,308.6	4,025.7	4,277.3
USA	9,980.7	9,314.9	10,432.8
Total (incl. others)	84,593.0	81,293.5	94,940.8

Exports†	2010	2011*	2012*
Belgium	4,819.8	7,173.2	6,183.8
China, People's Republic	8,054.3	16,253.2	24,653.6
France	4,224.9	6,221.2	5,530.0
India	23,235.6	39,420.0	53,191.5
Japan	78,162.7	108,711.7	134,064.8
Korea, Republic	43,758.2	73,273.5	89,675.7
New Zealand	1,519.5	2,750.4	1,306.4
Philippines	1,568.1	1,500.2	2,350.2
Saudi Arabia	2,266.6	2,004.3	3,882.1
Singapore	21,033.1	29,689.4	25,574.2
Spain	11,724.2	15,794.3	16,142.3
Taiwan	6,944.5	13,472.6	19,228.9
Thailand	7,903.1	8,772.1	9,479.8
Turkey	2,775.9	2,660.0	4,299.7
United Arab Emirates	13,379.1	14,297.4	20,602.0
United Kingdom	12,631.6	28,691.4	16,469.6
USA	2,743.0	3,711.9	3,794.3
Total (incl. others)	265,552.9	411,000.8	479,076.1

* Preliminary figures.
† Including re-exports (QR million): 7,317.8 in 2010; 5,590.8 in 2011 (preliminary); 4,989.0 in 2012 (preliminary).

Transport

ROAD TRAFFIC
(registered vehicles)

	2004	2005	2006
Private cars	265,609	293,355	337,056
Other private transport	114,115	126,541	148,436
Heavy equipment	11,162	13,262	17,438
Motorcycles and mopeds	4,420	4,698	5,048
Total (incl. others)	406,626	451,388	525,795

SHIPPING

Flag Registered Fleet
(at 31 December)

	2010	2011	2012
Number of vessels	146	152	152
Total displacement ('000 grt)	1,037.3	1,047.0	860.6

Source: Lloyd's List Intelligence (www.lloydslistintelligence.com).

INTERNATIONAL SEA-BORNE FREIGHT TRAFFIC
(2011)

	Traffic
Doha Port	
Vessels entered and cleared	1,188
Containers	534
Capacity ('000 grt)	19,792
Umm Said (Mesaieed) Port	
Vessels entered and cleared	2,112
Tankers	795
Containers	446
Capacity ('000 grt)	46,238
Halul Port	
Vessels entered and cleared	109
Tankers	109
Capacity ('000 grt)	15,783
Ras Laffan Port	
Vessels entered and cleared	1,944
Tankers	1,790
Capacity ('000 grt)	190,895
Total	
Vessels entered and cleared	5,353
Tankers	2,694
Containers	980
Capacity ('000 grt)	272,708

CIVIL AVIATION
(Doha International Airport)

	2004	2005	2006
Aircraft arrivals	49,614	60,828	67,472
Passenger arrivals ('000)*	2,790	3,654	4,424
Passengers in transit ('000)	1,589	2,185	4,573
Cargo and mail received (metric tons)	102,455	127,042	161,759
Cargo and mail dispatched (metric tons)	61,047	83,554	105,760

* Excluding private aircraft.

Aircraft arrivals: 50,603 in 2009; 59,088 in 2010; 68,734 in 2011.

Tourism

TOURIST ARRIVALS
(arrivals of non-resident tourists in hotels and similar establishments)

Region of residence	2008	2009	2010
Asia	216,742	264,550	298,395
Europe	329,059	406,725	730,034
Middle East	628,440	679,859	751,924
Total (incl. others)	1,404,850	1,658,569	1,866,471

Tourism receipts (US $ million, excl. passenger transport): 179 in 2009; 584 in 2010; 1,170 in 2011 (provisional).

Source: World Tourism Organization.

Communications Media

	2010	2011	2012
Telephones ('000 main lines in use)	270.0	309.0	327.0
Mobile cellular telephones ('000 in use)	2,186.4	2,302.3	2,600.0
Internet subscribers ('000)	150.4	167.4	n.a.
Broadband subscribers ('000)	142.0	163.0	159.0

Source: International Telecommunication Union.

Education

(2011/12)

	Institutions	Teachers	Students		
			Males	Females	Total
Private schools*	479	9,125	67,044	58,503	125,547
Pre-primary	225	2,361	18,570	16,686	35,256
Primary	111	4,048	31,340	27,261	58,601
Preparatory	79	1,457	9,911	8,615	18,526
General secondary	64	1,259	7,223	5,941	13,164
Independent schools†	246	12,447	45,221	48,784	94,005
Pre-primary	37	746	2,754	3,277	6,031
Primary	101	6,518	20,434	22,389	42,823
Preparatory	56	2,594	10,591	11,323	21,914
General secondary‡	52	2,589	11,442	11,795	23,237
Total	725	21,572	112,265	107,287	219,552
Pre-primary	262	3,107	21,324	19,963	41,287
Primary	212	10,566	51,774	49,650	101,424
Preparatory	135	4,051	20,502	19,938	40,440
General secondary‡	116	3,848	18,665	17,736	36,401
University of Qatar§	—	761	2,711	8,595	11,306

* Including the Qatar Foundation for Education, Science and Community Development (including the Qatar Academy and the Qatar Leadership Academy and Learning Centre) and the Academy for Sports Excellence (Aspire).

† Including Government schools.

‡ Including specialized secondary schools.

§ Including Qatar Community College.

Pupil-teacher ratio (primary education, UNESCO estimate): 11.3 in 2010/11 (Source: UNESCO Institute for Statistics).

Adult literacy rate (UNESCO estimates): 96.3% (males 96.5%; females 95.4%) in 2010 (Source: UNESCO Institute for Statistics).

Directory

The Constitution

According to the provisional Constitution adopted on 2 April 1970, executive power was vested in the Amir, as Head of State, and exercised by the Council of Ministers, appointed by the Head of State. The Amir was assisted by the appointed Advisory Council of 20 members (increased to 30 in 1975 and to 35 in 1988), whose term was extended for six years in 1975, for a further four years in 1978, and for further four-year terms in 1982, 1986, 1990, 1994 and 1998. Most recently, the Council's term was renewed for a further two years in July 2008. All fundamental democratic rights were guaranteed. In 1975 the Advisory Council was granted the power to summon individual ministers to answer questions on legislation before promulgation. In March 1999 elections took place, by universal adult suffrage, for a 29-member Central Municipal Council, which was to have a consultative role in the operations of the Ministry of Municipal Affairs and Agriculture. The Amir formally adopted a new Constitution following a referendum held on 29 April 2003. Under this Constitution, the Amir was to remain head of the executive, while a 45-member unicameral parliament, of which two-thirds was to be directly elected (the remainder being appointed by the Amir), was to have the powers to legislate, review the state budget, monitor government policy and hold ministers accountable for their actions. The parliament was to have a four-year mandate. Suffrage was to be extended to all citizens, including women, aged 18 years and above. Elections to the new legislature, after which the Advisory Council was to be abolished, were initially expected to be conducted in 2004; however, owing to alleged difficulties pertaining to the electoral roll, they were subsequently deferred, pending the introduction of a new electoral law. Such a law was adopted by the Advisory Council in May 2008, pending ratification by the Amir. The Constitution guarantees freedom of association, expression and religious affiliation, and provides for the establishment of an independent judiciary; however, it does not authorize political parties.

The Government

HEAD OF STATE

Amir and Commander-in-Chief of the Armed Forces: Sheikh TAMIM BIN HAMAD AL THANI (assumed power 25 June 2013).

COUNCIL OF MINISTERS

(September 2013)

Prime Minister and Minister of the Interior: Sheikh ABDULLAH BIN NASSER BIN KHALIFA AL THANI.

Deputy Prime Minister and Minister of State for Cabinet Affairs: AHMAD BIN ABDULLAH BIN ZAID AL-MAHMOUD.

Minister of Foreign Affairs: Dr KHALID BIN MUHAMMAD AL-ATTIYA.

Minister of State for Defence Affairs: Maj.-Gen. HAMAD BIN ALI AL-ATTIYA.

Minister of Municipal Affairs and Urban Planning: Sheikh ABD AL-RAHMAN BIN KHALIFA BIN ABD AL-AZIZ AL THANI.

Minister of Energy and Industry: MUHAMMAD SALEH AL-SADA.

Minister of Finance: ALI SHARIF AL-EMADI.

Minister of Culture, Arts and Heritage: Dr HAMAD BIN ABD AL-AZIZ AL-KAWARI.

Minister of Public Health: ABDULLAH BIN KHALID AL-QAHTANI.

Minister of Awqaf (Religious Endowments) and Islamic Affairs: Dr GHAITH BIN MUBARAK BIN IMRAN AL-KUWARI.

Minister of Youth and Sports: SALAH BIN GHANEM BIN NASSER AL-ALI.

Minister of Economy and Trade: Sheikh AHMAD BIN JASIM BIN MUHAMMAD AL THANI.

Minister of Justice: Dr HASSAN LAHDAN SAQR AL-MOHANNADI.

Minister of Administrative Development: Dr ISSA SAAD AL-JAFALI AL-NUAIMI.

Minister of Communication and Information Technology: Dr HESSA SULTAN AL-JABER.

Minister of Administrative Planning and Statistics: Dr SALEH MUHAMMAD SALEM AL-NABIT.

Minister of Education and Higher Education: MUHAMMAD ABD AL-WAHID ALI AL-HAMMADI.

Minister of Labour and Social Affairs: ABDULLAH SALEH MUBARAK AL-KHULAIFI.

Minister of the Environment: AHMAD AMR MUHAMMAD AL-HUMAIDI.

Minister of Transport: JASIM SAIF AHMAD AL-SULAITI.

MINISTRIES

Ministry of Awqaf (Religious Endowments) and Islamic Affairs: POB 422, Doha; tel. 44470777; fax 44470700; e-mail awqaf@awqaf.gov.qa; internet www.islam.gov.qa.

Ministry of Business and Trade: POB 1968, Doha; tel. 44945555; fax 44945000; e-mail mbt@mbt.gov.qa; internet www.mbt.gov.qa.

Ministry of Culture, Arts and Heritage: POB 23700, Doha; tel. 44022222; fax 44022212; e-mail info@moc.gov.qa; internet www.moc.gov.qa.

Ministry of Defence: Qatar Armed Forces, POB 37, Doha; tel. 44614111.

Ministry of Economy and Finance: POB 83, Doha; tel. 44461608; fax 44413617; e-mail qatfin@mof.gov.qa; internet www.mof.gov.qa.

Ministry of Education and Higher Education: POB 80, al-Waqf Tower, al-Dafna, Doha; tel. 44941111; fax 44941445; e-mail e.alhorr@moe.edu.qa; internet www.moe.edu.qa.

Ministry of Energy and Industry: POB 2599, Doha; tel. 44846444; fax 44832024; e-mail did@mei.gov.qa; internet www.mei.gov.qa.

Ministry of the Environment: POB 7634, Doha; tel. 44207777; fax 44207000; e-mail responsibility@moe.gov.qa; internet www.moe.gov.qa.

Ministry of Foreign Affairs: POB 250, Doha; tel. 44334334; fax 44324131; e-mail webmaster@mofa.gov.qa; internet www.mofa.gov.qa.

Ministry of the Interior: POB 115, Doha; tel. 44330000; fax 44322927; e-mail info@moi.gov.qa; internet www.moi.gov.qa.

Ministry of Justice: POB 917, Doha; tel. 44842222; fax 44832875; e-mail info@moj.gov.qa; internet www.moj.gov.qa.

Ministry of Labour: POB 36, Doha; tel. 44841111; fax 44841441; e-mail customerservice@mol.gov.qa; internet www.mol.gov.qa.

Ministry of Municipal Affairs and Urban Planning: POB 22332, Main Bldg, Corniche St, Doha; tel. 44413331; fax 44430239; e-mail info@baladiya.gov.qa; internet www.baladiya.gov.qa.

Ministry of Public Health: POB 42, Doha; tel. 44070000; fax 44446294; e-mail info@nha.org.qa; internet www.nha.org.qa.

Ministry of Social Affairs: POB 36, Doha; tel. 44841137; fax 44841959; e-mail mosa@mosa.gov.qa; internet www.mosa.gov.qa.

Advisory Council

POB 2034, Doha; tel. 44416292; fax 44221222; e-mail fahad@shura.gov.qa.

The Advisory or *Shura* Council was established in 1972, with 20 nominated members. It was expanded to 30 members in 1975, and to 35 members in 1988. Under the terms of the new Constitution, promulgated in 2003, the Advisory Council was to be replaced by a 45-member unicameral parliament, of which two-thirds of the members were to be directly elected.

Speaker: MUHAMMAD BIN MUBARAK AL-KHULAIFI.

Political Organizations

There are no political organizations in Qatar.

Diplomatic Representation

EMBASSIES IN QATAR

Afghanistan: POB 22104, Isteolal St, West Bay, Doha; tel. 44931511; fax 44932330; e-mail doha@afghanistan-mfa.net; Ambassador KHALID AHMAD ZEKRIYA.

Albania: POB 22659, Doha; tel. and fax 44953522; e-mail embassy.doha@mfa.gov.al; Ambassador RIDI KURTEZI.

Algeria: POB 2494, Doha; tel. 44838729; fax 44836072; Ambassador ABD AL-FATTAH ZAYYANI.

Azerbaijan: POB 23900, Doha; tel. 44932450; fax 44931755; e-mail azembassy@qatar.net.qa; Ambassador TOFIQ A. ABDULLAYEV.

Bahrain: al-Dafna St, Section 66, POB 24888, Doha; tel. 44839360; fax 44831018; e-mail doha.mission@mofa.gov.bh; Ambassador WAHEED MUBARAK ABDULLAH SAYYAR.

Bangladesh: POB 2080, 77 Mussab bin Omair St, Doha; tel. 44671927; fax 44671190; e-mail bdootqat@qatar.net.qa; internet www.bdembassydoha.com; Ambassador MUHAMMAD SHAHADAT HUSSAIN.

Belgium: POB 24418, al-Sanaa St, District 64, Doha; tel. 44931542; fax 44930151; e-mail doha@diplobel.fed.be; internet www.diplomatie.be/doha; Ambassador HERMAN MERCKX.

Benin: POB 24210, Doha; tel. 44930128; fax 44115713; e-mail ambabenin-doha@hotmail.com; Ambassador SAIDOU BAKU BUKHARI.

Bosnia and Herzegovina: POB 876, Doha; tel. 44113828; fax 44113234; e-mail ambasada@qatar.net.qa; internet www.bhembassyqatar.org; Ambassador NUDZEIM RECICA.

Brazil: POB 23122, Doha; tel. 44838227; fax 44838087; e-mail brasemb.doha@itamaraty.gov.br; internet doha.itamaraty.gov.br; Ambassador TADEU VALADARES.

Brunei: POB 22772, Doha; tel. 44831956; fax 44836798; e-mail bruemb@qatar.net.qa; Ambassador Haji NURUDDIN BIN Haji AHMAD.

China, People's Republic: POB 17200, Doha; tel. 44934203; fax 44934201; e-mail chinashi@qatar.net.qa; internet qa.china-embassy.org; Ambassador GAO YOUZHEN.

Cuba: POB 12017, Saha 76, New Dafna, West Bay Lagoon, Doha; tel. 44110713; fax 44110387; e-mail embacuba@qatar.net.qa; internet www.cubadiplomatica.cu/qatar; Ambassador ERNESTO D. PLASENCIA ESCALANTE.

Cyprus: POB 24482, 3 Saba Saha 12 St, District 63, West Bay, Doha; tel. 44934390; fax 44933087; e-mail kyprosdoha@qatar.net.qa; internet www.mfa.gov.cy/embassydoha; Ambassador CHARALAMBOS PANAYIDES.

Djibouti: POB 23796, Doha; tel. 44838461; fax 44839245; e-mail guarileh@gmail.com; Ambassador HASSAN MUMIN BARREH.

Dominican Republic: POB 23545, Doha; tel. 44113868; fax 44113267; e-mail info@domrepemb-qatar.com; internet www.domrepemb-qatar.com; Ambassador HUGO GUILIANI CURY.

Egypt: POB 2899, Doha; tel. 44832116; fax 44832196; e-mail eg.emb_doha@mfa.gov.eg; Ambassador MUHAMMAD MURSI AWAD.

El Salvador: POB 23031, Saha 72, Doha; tel. 44110195; fax 44110962; e-mail esvq@rree.gob.sv; Ambassador VICTOR MANUEL LAGOS PIZZATI.

Eritrea: POB 4309, D-Ring Rd 14, Doha; tel. 44667934; fax 44664139; Ambassador ALI IBRAHIM AHMED.

France: POB 2669, West Bay, Diplomatic Area, Doha; tel. 44021777; fax 44021701; e-mail ambadoha@qatar.net.qa; internet www.ambafrance-qa.org; Ambassador JEAN-CHRISTOPHE PEAUCELLE.

The Gambia: POB 12232, Doha; tel. 44657780; fax 44657391; Ambassador ANSUMANA JAMMEH.

Germany: POB 3064, 12 al-Jazeera al-Arabiya St, Doha; tel. 44082300; fax 44082333; e-mail germany@qatar.net.qa; internet www.doha.diplo.de; Ambassador ANGELIKA RENATE STORZ-CHAKARJI.

Hungary: POB 23525, Area 66, West Bay, Doha; tel. 44932531; fax 44932537; e-mail mission.doh@mfa.gov.hu; internet www.mfa.gov.hu/emb/doha; Ambassador Dr ISTVÁN ELTER.

India: POB 2788, Doha; tel. 44255777; fax 44670448; e-mail ambassadorindia@qatar.net.qa; internet www.indianembassy.gov.qa; Ambassador SANJIV ARORA.

Indonesia: POB 22375, al-Maheed St, Doha; tel. 44657945; fax 44657610; e-mail inemb@qatar.net.qa; internet www.kbridoha.com; Ambassador DEDDY SAIFUL AL-HADI.

Iran: POB 1633, Doha; tel. 44831951; fax 44831665; e-mail iranemb.doh@mfa.gov.ir; internet www.iranembassy.org.qa; Ambassador MUHAMMAD JAWAD ASAYESH ZARCHI.

Iraq: POB 1526, Doha; tel. 44216146; fax 44216152; e-mail dohemb@iraqmofamail.net; Ambassador Dr JAWAD AL-HINDAWI.

Italy: POB 4188, St 913, Plot 83, Villa 31, Doha; tel. 44831828; fax 44831909; e-mail ambasciata.doha@esteri.it; internet www.ambdoha.esteri.it; Ambassador GUIDO DE SANCTIS.

Japan: POB 2208, Diplomatic Area, West Bay, Doha; tel. 44840888; fax 44832178; e-mail eojqatar@dh.mofa.go.jp; internet www.qa.emb-japan.go.jp/en; Ambassador KENJIRO MONJI.

Jordan: POB 2366, Doha; tel. 44832202; fax 44832173; e-mail jordand@qatar.net.qa; internet www.jordanembassy.com.qa; Ambassador ZAHI MUHAMMAD AL-SEMADI.

Kazakhstan: POB 23513, Doha; tel. 44128015; fax 44128014; e-mail embassykz@qatar.net.qa; Ambassador AZAMAT R. BERDYBAI.

Kenya: POB 23091, West Bay, Zone 66, St 840, Doha; tel. 44931870; fax 44831730; e-mail Information@kenyaembassydoha.com; Ambassador GALMA MUKHE BORU.

Korea, Republic: POB 3727, Diplomatic Area, West Bay, Doha; tel. 44832238; fax 44833264; e-mail koemb_qa@mofat.go.kr; internet qat.mofat.go.kr; Ambassador CHUNG KEE-JONG.

Kuwait: POB 1177, Doha; tel. 44832111; fax 44832042; e-mail kuwaitembassy@qatar.net.qa; Ambassador MUTAB SALIH ALMTOTAH.

Lebanon: POB 2411, 63 United Nations St, al-Haditha Area, Doha; tel. 44933330; fax 44933331; e-mail embleb@qatar.net.qa; Ambassador HASSAN SAAD.

Libya: POB 574, Doha; tel. 44429546; fax 44429548; Ambassador ABD AL-MONSEF HAFIZ AL-BOURI.

Macedonia, former Yugoslav republic: POB 24262, Villa 54, al-Ithar St, Diplomatic Area, al-Dafna, Doha; tel. 44931374; fax 44831572; e-mail doha@mfa.gov.mk; Ambassador FUAD HASANOVIC.

Malaysia: POB 23760, Zone 66, Lusail St, West Bay, al-Dafna, Doha; tel. 44836463; fax 44836453; e-mail maldoha@kln.gov.my; internet www.kln.gov.my/perwakilan/doha; Ambassador AHMAD JAZRI BIN MUHAMMAD JOHAR.

Mauritania: POB 3132, Doha; tel. 44836003; fax 44836015; Ambassador SAYID AHMAD BAKAY OULD HAMADI.

Morocco: POB 3242, Doha; tel. 44831885; fax 44833416; e-mail moroccoe@qatar.net.qa; Ambassador EL MEKKI GAOUANE.

Nepal: POB 23002, St No. 810, Doha; tel. 44675681; fax 44675680; e-mail nembdoha@qatar.net.qa; internet www.nembdoha.org.qa; Ambassador Dr MAYA KUMARI SHARMA.

Netherlands: POB 23675, 6th Floor, al-Mirqab Tower, al-Dafna, Corniche, Doha; tel. 44954700; fax 44836340; e-mail doh@minbuza.nl; internet qatar.nlembassy.org; Ambassador YVETTE BURGHGRAEF VAN EECHOUD.

Oman: POB 1525, 41 Ibn al-Qassim St, Villa 7, Doha; tel. 44931514; fax 44932278; e-mail doha@mofa.gov.om; Ambassador MUHAMMAD BIN NASSER HAMAD AL-WIHAIBI.

Pakistan: POB 334, Diplomatic Area, Plot 30, West Bay, Doha; tel. 44832525; fax 44832227; e-mail parepqat@qatar.net.qa; internet www.pakmissiondoha.com; Ambassador MUHAMMAD SARFRAZ AHMAD KHANZADA.

Philippines: POB 24900, Doha; tel. 44831585; fax 44831595; e-mail doha.pe@dfa.gov.ph; Ambassador CRESCENTE RELACION.

Poland: POB 23380, al-Qutaifiya 66, St 519, Saha 49, West Bay, Doha; tel. 44113230; fax 44110307; e-mail doha.amb.sekretariat@msz.gov.pl; internet www.doha.polemb.net; Ambassador ROBERT ROSTEK.

Romania: POB 22511, Doha; tel. 44934848; fax 44934747; e-mail romamb@qatar.net.qa; internet doha.mae.ro; Chargé d'affaires a.i. CONSTANTIN DARIE.

Russia: POB 15404, Doha; tel. 44836231; fax 44836243; e-mail rusemb@qatar.net.qa; internet www.qatar.mid.ru; Chargé d'affaires a.i. DMITRII TROFIMOV.

Saudi Arabia: POB 1255, Doha; tel. 44832030; fax 44832720; Ambassador AHMAD BIN ALI AL-QAHTANI.

Senegal: Ibn Almoutas St, House 65, al-Dafna, Doha; tel. 44837644; fax 44838872; Ambassador ADAMA SARR.

Singapore: POB 24497, New West Bay Area, Doha; tel. 44128082; fax 44128180; e-mail singemb_doh@sgmfa.gov.sg; internet www.mfa.gov.sg/doha; Ambassador WONG KWOK PUN.

Somalia: POB 1948, Doha; tel. and fax 44935751; Ambassador OMAR IDRIS.

South Africa: POB 24744, Doha; tel. 44857111; fax 44835961; e-mail doha.consular@foreign.gov.za; Ambassador SAAD CACHALIA.

Spain: POB 24616, Lusail St, West Bay, Doha; tel. 44835886; fax 44835887; e-mail emb.doha@maec.es; Ambassador MARÍA DEL CARMEN DE LA PEÑA CORCUERA.

Sri Lanka: 4 al-Kharja St, POB 19075, Doha; tel. 44677627; fax 44674788; e-mail lankaemb@qatar.net.qa; internet www.slembassy-qatar.com; Ambassador JAYANTHA PALIPANE.

Sudan: POB 2999, Doha; tel. 44831474; fax 44833031; e-mail suemdoha@yahoo.com; Ambassador YASSIR KHALAF ALLAH KHADIR.

Syria: POB 1257, Doha; tel. 44831844; fax 44832139; Ambassador Dr RIAD ISMAT.

Thailand: POB 22474, Doha; tel. 44934426; fax 44930514; e-mail thaidoh@qatar.net.qa; internet www.thaiembassy.org/doha; Ambassador PANYARAK POOLTHUP.

Tunisia: POB 21185, Doha; tel. 44128188; fax 44128938; e-mail at.doha@qatar.net.qa; Ambassador MUHAMMAD MONDHER DHERIF.

Turkey: POB 1977, al-Istiqlal St, Doha; tel. 44951300; fax 44951320; e-mail embassy.doha@mfa.gov.tr; internet www.doha.emb.mfa.gov.tr; Ambassador HAKKI EMRE YUNT.

United Arab Emirates: POB 3099, 22 al-Markhiyah St, Diplomatic Area, Khalifa Northern Town, Doha; tel. 44838880; fax 44836186; e-mail doha@mofa.gov.ae; internet www.uae-embassy.ae/embassies/qa; Ambassador JUMA RASHID SAIF AL-DHAHERI.

United Kingdom: POB 3, West Bay, Doha; tel. 44962000; fax 44962086; e-mail embassy.qatar@fco.gov.uk; internet ukinqatar.fco.gov.uk; Ambassador MICHAEL O'NEILL.

Uruguay: POB 23237, Doha; tel. 44113833; fax 44113540; e-mail uruqatar@uruguayembassy.org.qa; Ambassador Dr JOSÉ LUIS REMEDI.

USA: POB 2399, 22nd February St, al-Luqta District, Doha; tel. 44966000; fax 44884298; e-mail pasdoha@state.gov; internet qatar.usembassy.gov; Ambassador SUSAN L. ZIADEH.

Venezuela: POB 24470, Doha; tel. 44932730; fax 44932729; e-mail embavencatar@gmail.com; internet www.embavenqatar.org; Ambassador JUAN ANTONIO HERNÁNDEZ.

Yemen: POB 3318, Doha; tel. 44432555; fax 44429400; Ambassador ABD AL-MALIK SAID.

Judicial System

The independence of the judiciary was guaranteed by the provisional Constitution and further augmented in the Constitution formally adopted by the Amir in April 2003. All aspects pertaining to the civil judiciary are supervised by the Ministry of Justice, which organizes courts of law through its affiliated departments. The *Shari'a* judiciary hears all cases of personal status relating to Muslims, other claim cases, doctrinal provision and crimes under its jurisdiction. Legislation adopted in 1999 unified all civil and *Shari'a* courts in one judicial body, and determined the jurisdictions of each type of court. The law also provided for the establishment of a court of cassation; this was to be competent to decide on appeals relating to issues of contravention, misapplication and misinterpretation of the law, and on disputes between courts regarding areas of jurisdiction. In addition, the law provided for the establishment of a supreme judiciary council, to be presided over by the head of the court of cassation and comprising, *inter alia*, the heads of the *Shari'a* and civil courts of appeal. The legislation came into effect in 2003. An Amiri decree published in June 2002 provided for the establishment of an independent public prosecution system. A Supreme Constitutional Court was established in 2008 to adjudicate on the constitutionality of laws and to arbitrate in disputes between different branches of the judiciary.

Presidency of Shari'a Courts: POB 232, Doha; tel. 44452222; Pres. Sheikh ABD AL-RAHMAN BIN ABDULLAH AL-MAHMOUD.

Public Prosecution Office: POB 705, Doha; tel. 4843333; fax 44843211; e-mail info@pp.gov.qa; internet www.pp.gov.qa; Attorney-Gen. Dr ALI BIN FITAIS AL-MERRI.

Supreme Judiciary Council: POB 9673, Doha; tel. 44859222; fax 44833939; e-mail sjc@sjc.gov.qa; internet www.sjc.gov.qa; f. 2003; Pres. MASOUD MUHAMMAD AL-AMRI.

Religion

The indigenous population are Muslims of the Sunni sect, most being of the strict Wahhabi persuasion. In March 2008 the first official Christian church (of the Roman Catholic branch) was consecrated in Doha; open worship among adherents of Christianity had previously been prohibited.

CHRISTIANITY

The Anglican Communion

Within the Episcopal Church in Jerusalem and the Middle East, Qatar forms part of the diocese of Cyprus and the Gulf. The Anglican congregation in Qatar is entirely expatriate. The Bishop in Cyprus and the Gulf is resident in Cyprus, while the Archdeacon in the Gulf is resident in Bahrain.

The Roman Catholic Church

An estimated 100,000 adherents in Qatar, mainly expatriates, form part of the Apostolic Vicariate of Northern Arabia. The Vicar Apostolic is resident in Bahrain.

The Press

NEWSPAPERS

Al-'Arab (The Arabs): POB 22612, Doha; tel. 44997333; fax 44997411; e-mail alarab@alarab.qa; internet www.alarab.qa; f. 1972; ceased publication in 1996, but recommenced following relaunch in Nov. 2007; daily; Arabic; publ. by Dar al-Ouroba Printing and Publishing; Editor-in-Chief Prof. AHMAD SAID AL-ROMAIHI.

Gulf Times: POB 2888, Doha; tel. 44350478; fax 44350474; e-mail edit@gulf-times.com; internet www.gulf-times.com; f. 1978; daily and weekly edns; English; political; publ. by Gulf Publishing and Printing Co; Man. Editor NEIL COOK; circ. 20,000 (daily).

The Peninsula: POB 3488, Doha; tel. 44557777; fax 44557746; e-mail editor@thepeninsulaqatar.com; internet www.thepeninsulaqatar.com; f. 1995; daily; English; political; publ. by Dar al-Sharq Printing, Publishing and Distribution; Chair. Sheikh THANI BIN ABDULLAH AL THANI; Man. Editor RACHEL MORRIS; circ. 8,000.

Qatar Tribune: POB 23493, Doha; tel. 44422077; fax 44416790; e-mail editor-in-chief@qatar-tribune.com; internet www.qatar-tribune.com; f. 2006; daily; English; Editor-in-Chief Dr HASSAN MUHAMMAD AL-ANSARI; circ. 10,000.

Al-Rayah (The Banner): POB 3464, Doha; tel. 44466636; fax 44320080; e-mail edit@raya.com; internet www.raya.com; f. 1979; daily and weekly edns; Arabic; political; publ. by Gulf Publishing and Printing Co; Editor NASSER AL-OTHMAN; circ. 25,000.

Al-Sharq (The Orient): POB 3488, Doha; tel. 44557702; fax 44557760; e-mail jaber.alharmi@gmail.com; internet www.al-sharq.com; f. 1985; daily; Arabic; political; publ. by Dar al-Sharq Printing, Publishing and Distribution; Editor-in-Chief JABER AL-HARAMI; Dep. Editor KHALED AL-JABER; circ. 45,018.

Al-Watan: POB 22345, Doha; tel. 44652244; fax 44654482; e-mail alwatan@qatar.net.qa; internet www.al-watan.com; f. 1995; daily; Arabic; political; publ. by Dar al-Watan Printing, Publishing and Distribution; Editor-in-Chief MUHAMMAD HAMAD AL-MERRI; circ. 25,000.

PERIODICALS

Glam: POB 3272, Doha; tel. 44672139; fax 44550982; e-mail contact@omsqatar.com; internet www.omsqatar.com/glam; monthly; English; fashion and lifestyle; publ. by Oryx Advertising Co; f. 2008; Editor-in-Chief YOUSUF JASSEM AL-DARWISH.

Al-Jawhara (The Jewel): POB 2531, Doha; tel. 44414575; fax 44671388; f. 1977; monthly; Arabic; magazine covering watches and jewellery; publ. by al-Ahd Establishment for Journalism, Printing and Publications Ltd; Editor-in-Chief ABDULLAH YOUSUF AL-HUSSAINI; circ. 8,000.

Al-Ouroba (Arabism): POB 663, Doha; tel. 44325874; fax 44429424; f. 1970; weekly; Arabic; political; publ. by Dar al-Ouroba Printing and Publishing; Editor-in-Chief YOUSUF NAAMA; circ. 12,000.

Qatar Al-Yom: POB 3272, Doha; tel. 44672139; fax 44550982; e-mail contact@omsqatar.com; internet www.omsqatar.com/qatar-al-yom; f. 2005; Arabic; news, business and lifestyle; publ. by Oryx Advertising Co; Editor-in-Chief YOUSUF JASSEM AL-DARWISH; circ. 22,000.

Qatar Today: POB 3272, Doha; tel. 44672139; fax 44550982; e-mail qtoday@omsqatar.com; internet www.omsqatar.com/qatar-today; f. 1978; monthly; English; news, business and lifestyle; publ. by Oryx Advertising Co; Editor-in-Chief YOUSUF JASSEM AL-DARWISH; circ. 27,000.

Al-Tarbiya (Education): POB 9865, Doha; tel. 44044596; fax 44044557; e-mail qnc@sec.gov.qa; f. 1971; quarterly; publ. by Qatar Nat. Comm. for Education, Culture and Science; Editor-in-Chief MUHAMMAD SIDDIQ; circ. 2,500.

Al-Tijara Wal A'amal: POB 272, Doha; tel. 44478042; fax 44478063; e-mail info@mashaheermedia.com; internet www.mashaheermedia.com; f. 2003; English; business and industry; publ. by Mashaheer Media Qatar.

Al-Ufuq: POB 3488, Doha; tel. 44602844; fax 44601294; e-mail alsharqpp@qatar.net.qa; f. 2002; monthly; Arabic; business; publ. by Dar al-Sharq Printing, Publishing and Distribution.

Al-Ummah: POB 893, Doha; tel. 44447300; fax 44447022; e-mail m_dirasat@islam.gov.qa; f. 1982; bi-monthly; Islamic thought and affairs, current cultural issues, book serializations.

Woman Today: POB 3272, Doha; tel. 44672139; fax 44550982; e-mail wtoday@omsqatar.com; internet www.omsqatar.com/woman-today; f. 2005; monthly; English; magazine aimed at working women; publ. by Oryx Advertising Co; Editor-in-Chief YOUSUF JASSEM AL-DARWISH; circ. 20,500.

NEWS AGENCY

Qatar News Agency (QNA): POB 3299, Doha; tel. 44450321; fax 44438316; e-mail info@qnaol.com; internet www.qnaol.net; f. 1975; affiliated to Ministry of Foreign Affairs; Dir and Editor-in-Chief AHMAD JASSIM AL-HUMAR.

Publishers

Ali bin Ali Media and Publishing: POB 75, Doha; tel. 44313245; fax 44411251; e-mail publishing@alibinali.com; internet www.abamediapublishing.com; part of Ali bin Ali Group; publrs of *Qatar Telephone Directory* and *Yellow Pages*; Chair. and Pres. ADEL ALI BIN ALI; Gen. Man. ANTOINE CHERFANE.

Bloomsbury Qatar Foundation Publishing: POB 5825, Villa 3, Qatar Education City, Doha; tel. 44542431; fax 44542438; e-mail bqfp@qf.org.qa; internet www.bqfp.com.qa; f. 2009; publr of fiction and non-fiction in English and Arabic, including educational, academic, reference and children's books; owned by the Qatar Foundation; Dir KATHY ROONEY.

Dar al-Sharq Printing, Publishing and Distribution: POB 3488, Doha; tel. 44557866; fax 44557871; e-mail alsharqpp@qatar.net.qa; internet www.al-sharq.com; publrs of *Al-Sharq* and *The Peninsula* newspapers, and *Al-Ufuq* magazine; distributor for various foreign newspapers; Gen. Man. ABD AL-LATIF AL-MAHMOUD.

Gulf Publishing and Printing Co: POB 533, Al Hilal Area, C Ring Rd, Doha; tel. 44350475; fax 44350474; e-mail gm@gulftimes.com; internet www.gulf-times.com; f. 1978; publrs of *Gulf Times* and *Al-Rayah*; Chair. ABDULLAH BIN KHALIFA AL-ATTIYA.

Oryx Advertising Co WLL: POB 3272, Doha; tel. 44550983; fax 44550982; e-mail info@omsqatar.com; internet www.omsqatar.com; f. 1973; publs include *Qatar Today*, *Qatar Al-Yom*, *Glam* and *T Qatar*; Publr and Editor-in-Chief YOUSUF JASSEM AL-DARWISH.

Qatar National Printing Press (QNPP): POB 355, Doha; tel. 44448452; fax 44449550; e-mail info@qnpp.net; internet www.qnpp.net; f. 1958; books, magazines, promotional materials, business forms, stationery, screenprinting, etc.; Gen. Man. JOSEPH DORLIAN.

Broadcasting and Communications

TELECOMMUNICATIONS

Supreme Council for Communications and Information Technology (ictQATAR): POB 23264, al-Mirqab Tower, al-Corniche St, Doha; tel. 44995333; fax 44935913; e-mail info@ict.gov.qa; internet www.ict.gov.qa; f. 2004 to oversee deregulation of telecommunications sector; Chair. HH Amir Sheikh TAMIM BIN HAMAD AL THANI; Sec.-Gen. (vacant).

Qatar Telecommunications Corpn—Qatar Telecom (Q-Tel): POB 217, Doha; tel. 44830000; fax 44476231; e-mail customer.service@qtel.com.qa; internet www.qtel.com.qa; f. 1987; majority state-owned; provides telecommunications services within Qatar; Chair. Sheikh ABDULLAH BIN MUHAMMAD AL THANI; CEO Dr NASSER MARAFIH.

Vodafone Qatar QSC: POB 74057, Unit 207, Level 2, Tech 2, Qatar Science & Technology Park, Doha; tel. 44096666; internet www.vodafone.qa; f. 2008; majority shareholders Vodafone Group PLC (United Kingdom) and Qatar Foundation for Education, Science and Community Devt; initial public offering for Qatari nationals of 40% of shares conducted in April 2009; awarded Qatar's second mobile telephone operating licence in June 2008; Chair. Sheikh ABD AL-RAHMAN BIN SAUD AL THANI; CEO KYLE WHITEHILL.

BROADCASTING

Regulatory Authority

Qatar Radio and Television Corpn (QRTC): POB 1414, Doha; tel. 44894444; fax 44882888; e-mail ksaid@rtc.gov.qa; f. 1997; autonomous authority reporting direct to the Council of Ministers; Dir-Gen. ABD AL-RAHMAN OBEIDAN.

Radio

Qatar Broadcasting Service (QBS): POB 3939, Doha; tel. 44894444; fax 44882888; f. 1968; govt service transmitting in Arabic, English, French and Urdu; programmes include Holy Quran Radio and Doha Music Radio; Dir ALI NASSER AL-KUBAISI.

Sout al-Khaleej: POB 1414, Doha; tel. 44888334; fax 44879999; e-mail info@soutalkhaleej.fm; internet www.soutalkhaleej.fm; f. 2002; Arabic arts broadcasting.

Television

Al Jazeera Satellite Network: POB 23123, Doha; tel. 44896044; fax 44873577; e-mail imr@aljazeera.net; internet www.aljazeera.net; f. 1996; 24-hr broadcasting of news and current affairs in Arabic; English-language service launched Nov. 2006; documentary channel launched Jan. 2007; Dir-Gen. (vacant); Chief Editor AHMAD SHEIKH.

Qatar Television Service (QTV): POB 1944, Doha; tel. 44894444; fax 44874170; f. 1970; operates 2 channels (of which 1 broadcasts in

English); 24-hr broadcasting; Dir MUHAMMAD AL-KUWARI; Asst Dir ABD AL-WAHAB MUHAMMAD AL-MUTAWA'A.

Finance

(cap. = capital; res = reserves; dep. = deposits; m. = million; brs = branches; amounts in Qatar riyals)

STATE FINANCIAL AUTHORITIES

In March 2005 the Government established the Qatar Financial Centre (QFC), which was intended to attract international financial institutions and multinational corporations to Qatar, 'to establish business operations in a best-in-class international environment'. The QFC comprised the QFC Authority and the QFC Regulatory Authority (QFCRA), as well as two legal bodies—the QFC Regulatory Tribunal and the QFC Civil and Commercial Court—which were charged with upholding the rule of law and ensuring the transparency of QFC transactions. In July 2007 plans were announced for the creation of a single, integrated, fully independent financial regulatory authority, which would merge the regulatory activities of the QFCRA, the Qatar Financial Markets Authority and the Qatar Central Bank, and oversee all banking, insurance, securities, asset management and other financial services.

Qatar Financial Centre Authority (QFCA): POB 23245, Doha; tel. 44967777; fax 44967676; e-mail info@qfc.com.qa; internet www.qfc.com.qa; f. 2005; charged with promoting Qatar as an attractive location for international banking, insurance and financial services; Chair. ALI SHARIF AL-EMADI (Minister of Finance); CEO SHASHANK SRIVASTAVA.

Qatar Financial Centre Regulatory Authority (QFCRA): POB 22989, Level 14, Qatar Financial Centre Tower, Doha; tel. 44956888; fax 44835031; e-mail info@qfcra.com; internet www.qfcra.com; f. 2005; charged with the regulation and supervision of a wide range of financial activities, incl. banking, insurance, asset management and financial advisory services; Chair. and CEO MICHAEL RYAN.

Qatar Financial Markets Authority (QFMA): POB 25552, Doha; tel. 44289999; fax 44441221; e-mail info@qfma.org.qa; internet www.qfma.org.qa; f. 2007 to supervise the stock exchange and securities industry; Chair. ALI SHARIF AL-EMADI (Minister of Finance); Chief Exec. NASSER AHMAD SHAIBI.

BANKING

Central Bank

Qatar Central Bank: POB 1234, Doha; tel. 44456456; fax 44414190; e-mail webmaster@qcb.gov.qa; internet www.qcb.gov.qa; f. 1966 as Qatar and Dubai Currency Bd; became Qatar Monetary Agency in 1973; renamed Qatar Cen. Bank in 1993; state-owned; cap. and res 9,982.5m., total assets 44,458.5m., currency in circulation 6,912.8m. (Dec. 2008); Gov. ABDULLAH BIN SAUD AL THANI.

Commercial Banks

Ahlibank QSC: POB 2309, Suhmin bin Hamad St, al-Sadd Area, Doha; tel. 44232222; fax 44232323; e-mail info@ahlibank.com.qa; internet www.ahlibank.com.qa; f. 1984 as Al-Ahli Bank of Qatar QSC; name changed as above in 2004; cap. 700m., res 1,689m., dep. 14,681m. (Dec. 2011); Chair. Sheikh FAISAL BIN ABD AL-AZIZ BIN JASIM AL THANI; CEO SALAH JASIM MURAD; 9 brs.

Commercial Bank of Qatar QSC (CBQ): POB 3232, Grand Hamad Ave, Doha; tel. 44900000; fax 44490070; e-mail info@cbq.com.qa; internet www.cbq.com.qa; f. 1975; cap. 2,474m., res 11,545m., dep. 46,374m. (Dec. 2011); Man. Dir HUSSAIN IBRAHIM AL-FARDAN; Group CEO ANDREW C. STEVENS; 23 brs.

Doha Bank: POB 3818, Grand Hamad Ave, Doha; tel. 44456600; fax 44410625; e-mail international@dohabank.com.qa; internet www.dohabank.com.qa; f. 1979; cap. 2,066m., res 4,807m., dep. 33,357m. (Dec. 2011); Chair. Sheikh FAHAD BIN MUHAMMAD BIN JABER AL THANI; Group CEO R. SEETHARAMAN; 35 brs in Qatar, 3 abroad.

International Bank of Qatar QSC (IBQ): POB 2001, Suhaim bin Hamad St, Doha; tel. 44473700; fax 44473745; e-mail qatarenq@ibq.com.qa; internet www.ibq.com.qa; f. 2000 as Grindlays Qatar Bank QSC; previously a branch of ANZ Grindlays Bank (f. 1956); name changed as above in 2004, after Nat. Bank of Kuwait SAK assumed management of the bank; announced plans to merge with Al-Khalij Commercial Bank in mid-2010; cap. 1,100m., res 2,791m., dep. 22,752m. (Dec. 2011); Chair. Sheikh HAMAD BIN JASIM BIN JABER AL THANI (Prime Minister and Minister of Foreign Affairs); Man. Dir GEORGE NASRA.

Al-Khalij Commercial Bank (QSC) (al-Khaliji): POB 28000, Doha; tel. 44996000; fax 44996020; e-mail info@alkhaliji.com; internet www.alkhaliji.com; f. 2007; announced plans to merge with Int. Bank of Qatar in mid-2010; cap. 3,600m., res 1,689m., dep. 16,175m. (Dec. 2011); Chair. and Man. Dir HAMAD BIN FAISAL BIN THANI AL THANI; Group CEO ROBIN MCCALL.

Masraf Al Rayan: POB 28888, Doha; tel. 44253333; fax 44253312; e-mail info@alrayan.com; internet www.alrayan.com; f. 2006; offers *Shari'a*-compliant banking services; cap. 7,500m., res 975m., dep. 46,263m. (Dec. 2011); Chair. and Man. Dir Dr HUSSAIN ALI AL-ABDULLA; Group CEO ADEL MUSTAFAWI; 5 brs.

Qatar Development Bank (QDB): POB 22789, Doha; tel. 44596666; fax 44350433; e-mail contact@qdb.org.qa; internet www.qidb.com.qa; f. 1996 as Qatar Industrial Devt Bank; inaugurated Oct. 1997; relaunched under above name in April 2007 with expanded capital provision to facilitate private sector involvement in national economic devt; state-owned; provides long-term low-interest industrial loans; finances wide range of industrial and social projects; broadened consultancy services following relaunch; cap. 2,900m., res 200m., dep. 555m. (Dec. 2010); Chair. Sheikh ABDULLAH BIN SA'UD AL THANI; CEO MANSOUR IBRAHIM AL-MAHMOUD.

Qatar First Investment Bank: POB 28028, Suhaim bin Hamad St, Doha; tel. 44483333; fax 44483560; e-mail information@qfib.com.qa; internet www.qfib.com.qa; f. 2008; offers *Shari'a* -compliant investment banking services; Chair. ABDULLA BIN FAHAD BIN GHORAB AL-MARRI; CEO EMAD MANSOUR.

Qatar International Islamic Bank: POB 664, Grand Hamad St, Doha; tel. 44385555; fax 44444101; e-mail qiibit@qiib.com.qa; internet www.qiib.com.qa; f. 1990; cap. 1,513m., res 3,279m., dep. 18,106m. (Dec. 2011); Chair. and Man. Dir KHALID BIN THANI BIN ABDULLAH AL THANI; CEO ABD AL-BASIT AL-SHAIBEI; 5 brs.

Qatar Islamic Bank SAQ (QIB): POB 559, Grand Hamad St, Doha; tel. 44409409; fax 44412700; e-mail info@qib.com.qa; internet www.qib.com.qa; f. 1982; cap. 2,362m., res 8,459m., dep. 41,087m. (Dec. 2011); Chair. Sheikh JASIM BIN HAMAD BIN JASIM BIN JABER AL THANI; CEO AHMAD MESHARI (acting); 25 brs.

Qatar National Bank SAQ: POB 1000, Doha; tel. 44407777; fax 44413753; e-mail ccsupport@qnb.com.qa; internet www.qnb.com.qa; f. 1964; owned 50% by Govt of Qatar and 50% by Qatari nationals; cap. 6,361m., res 28,689m., dep. 237,784m. (Dec. 2011); Chair. ALI SHARIF AL-EMADI (Minister of Finance); Group CEO ALI AHMAD AL-KUWARI (acting); 32 brs in Qatar, 3 abroad.

SOVEREIGN WEALTH FUND

Qatar Investment Authority (QIA): POB 23224, Doha; tel. 44995900; fax 44995991; e-mail info@qia.qa; internet www.qia.qa; f. 2005 to develop, invest and manage state reserve funds; Chair. Amir Sheikh TAMIM BIN HAMAD AL THANI; CEO AHMAD MUHAMMAD AHMAD AL-SAYED.

STOCK EXCHANGE

Qatar Exchange (QE): POB 22114, Grand Hamad St, Doha; tel. 44333666; fax 44319233; e-mail dsm@dsm.com.qa; internet www.dsm.com.qa; f. 2009 to replace fmr Doha Securities Market (f. 1997); 80% stake owned by Qatar Holding, 20% owned by NYSE Euronext; 42 cos listed in June 2009; Chair. Dr KHALID BIN MUHAMMAD AL-ATTIYA; CEO ANDRE WENT.

INSURANCE

Doha Insurance Co: POB 7171, Doha; tel. 44335000; fax 44657777; e-mail dohainsco@qatar.net.qa; internet www.dicqatar.com; f. 1999 as public shareholding co; cap. 127.2m., total assets 518.3m. (Dec. 2007); Chair. Sheikh NAWAF BIN NASSER BIN KHALID AL THANI; Gen. Man. BASSAM HUSSAIN.

Al-Khaleej Insurance and Reinsurance Co QSC (SAQ): POB 4555, Doha; tel. 44414151; fax 44430530; e-mail alkhalej@qatar.net.qa; internet www.alkhaleej.com; f. 1978; cap. and res 568.4m. (2007); all classes except life; Chair. ABDULLAH BIN MUHAMMAD JABER AL THANI; Gen. Man. KARAM AHMAD MAHMOUD.

Qatar General Insurance and Reinsurance Co SAQ: POB 4500, A Ring Rd, al-Asmakh Area, Doha; tel. 44282222; fax 44437302; e-mail qgirc-tec@qatar.net.qa; internet www.qgirco.com; f. 1979; total assets 1,729.7m. (2007); all classes; Chair. and Man. Dir Sheikh NASSER BIN ALI AL THANI; Gen. Man. GHAZI ABU NAHL.

Qatar Insurance Co SAQ: POB 666, Tamin St, West Bay, Doha; tel. 44962222; fax 44831569; e-mail qatarins@qic.com.qa; internet www.qatarinsurance.com; f. 1964; cap. 424.7m., total assets 5,860.7m. (Dec. 2007); all classes; the Govt has a majority share; Chair. and Man. Dir Sheikh KHALID BIN MUHAMMAD ALI AL THANI; Pres. and CEO KHALIFA A. AL-SUBAEY; brs in Qatar, Dubai and Abu Dhabi (UAE), Kuwait and Oman.

Qatar Insurance Services LLC (Qatarlyst): 6th Floor, QFC Tower, POB 23245, Doha; tel. 44968301; fax 44968310; e-mail enquiries@qatarlyst.com; internet www.qatarlyst.com; f. 2008 by the QFCA, with the aim of establishing Qatar as a regional hub for the insurance industry; launched internet-based insurance-trading and -processing service (Qatarlyst) June 2009; CEO KHALID AL-MUGHESIB; Chair. ABD AL-RAHMAN AHMAD AL-SHAIBI.

Qatar Islamic Insurance Co: POB 22676, Doha; tel. 44658888; fax 44550111; e-mail qiic@qatar.net.qa; internet www.qiic.net.qa; f. 1993; cap. 150.0m., res 137.0m. (Dec. 2007); Chair. Sheikh ABDULLAH BIN THANI AL THANI; Gen. Man. JASSIM A. AL-SADI.

Trade and Industry

DEVELOPMENT ORGANIZATIONS

Department of Industrial Development: POB 2599, Doha; tel. 44846444; fax 44832024; e-mail did@mei.gov.qa; a div. of the Ministry of Energy and Industry; conducts research, licensing, devt and supervision of new industrial projects; Dir-Gen. SAID MUBARAK AL-KUWAIRI.

General Secretariat for Development Planning: POB 1588, Doha; tel. 44958888; e-mail webmaster@planning.gov.qa; internet www.gsdp.gov.qa; f. 2006; responsible for co-ordination of the emirate's long-term devt strategy; monitors progress of Qatar's Nat. Vision 2030 and Nat. Devt Strategy; Sec.-Gen. Dr SALIH BIN MUHAMMAD AL-NABIT.

Public Works Authority (Ashghal): POB 22188, Doha; tel. 44950000; fax 44950999; e-mail info@ashghal.gov.qa; internet www.ashghal.com; f. 2004; responsible for the management and devt of public infrastructure projects; Chair. Sheikh ABD AL-RAHMAN BIN KHALIFA BIN ABD AL-AZIZ AL THANI (Minister of Municipal Affairs and Urban Planning); Pres. NASSER ALI ABDULLAH AL-MAWLAWI.

Urban Planning and Development Authority: POB 22423, Doha; tel. 44955549; fax 44955594; e-mail general@up.org.qa; internet www.up.org.qa; f. 2005; planning, co-ordination and management of urban devt projects; oversees devt of the Master Plan for the State of Qatar; Dir-Gen. ALI ABDULLAH AL-ABDULLAH.

CHAMBER OF COMMERCE

Qatar Chamber of Commerce and Industry: POB 402, Doha; tel. 44559111; fax 44661693; e-mail info@qcci.org; internet www.qcci.org; f. 1963; 17 elected mems; Chair. Sheikh KHALIFA BIN JASIM BIN MUHAMMAD AL THANI; Gen. Man. REMY ROWHANI.

STATE HYDROCARBONS COMPANIES

Qatar International Petroleum Marketing Co (Tasweeq): POB 24183, Doha; tel. 44976111; fax 44976276; e-mail info@tasweeq.com.qa; internet www.tasweeq.com.qa; f. 2007 to take sole responsibility for all exports of natural gas and oil products; wholly govt-owned; CEO ALI AL-HAMADI.

Qatar Petrochemical Co SAQ (QAPCO): POB 756, Doha; tel. 44242444; fax 44324700; e-mail information@qapco.com.qa; internet www.qapco.com.qa; f. 1974; 80% owned by Industries Qatar, 20% by Total Petrochemicals (France); total assets QR 5,090.7m. (2006); operation of petrochemical plant at Mesaieed; produced 549,928 metric tons of ethylene, 359,460 tons of low-density polyethylene, and 32,297 tons of solid sulphur in 2007; Chair. HAMAD RASHID AL-MOHANNADI; Gen. Man. MUHAMMAD YOUSUF AL-MULLA; 879 employees (2004).

Qatofin Co Ltd: POB 55013, Doha; tel. 44242555; fax 44325936; e-mail info@qatofin.com.qa; internet www.qatofin.com.qa; f. 2009; 63% owned by Qatar Petrochemical Co, 36% by Total and 1% by Qatar Petroleum; capacity to produce 450,000 metric tons of low-density polyethylene; Chair. HAMAD RASHID AL-MOHANNADI; Vice-Chair. MUHAMMAD YOUSUF AL-MULLA.

Qatar Petroleum (QP): POB 3212, Doha; tel. 44402000; fax 44831125; e-mail webmaster@qp.com.qa; internet www.qp.com.qa; f. 1974 as Qatar Gen. Petroleum Corpn (QGPC), name changed 2001; total assets QR 137,851m. (2006); sales QR 2,243m. (2006); oil production 850,000 b/d (2006); the State of Qatar's interest in cos active in petroleum and related industries has passed to QP; has responsibility for all phases of oil and gas industry both on shore and off shore, incl. exploration, drilling, production, refining, transport and storage, distribution, sale and export of oil, natural gas and other hydrocarbons; Oryx gas to liquids (GTL) plant became operational in 2006, with capacity for 34,000 b/d of GTL products; Chair. and Man. Dir MUHAMMAD SALEH AL-SADA (Minister of Energy and Industry); Dep. Chair. HAMAD RASHID AL-MOHANNADI; 5,500 employees.

Qatar Liquefied Gas Co (Qatargas): POB 22666, Doha; tel. 44736000; fax 44736666; e-mail infos@qatargas.com.qa; internet www.qatargas.com; f. 1984 to develop the North Field of unassociated gas; cap. QR 500m.; 65% owned by Qatar Petroleum, 10% each by ExxonMobil (USA) and Total, and 7.5% each by Marubeni Corpn and Mitsui & Co of Japan; production capacity 42m. metric tons of LNG; Chair. MUHAMMAD SALEH AL-SADA (Minister of Energy and Industry); CEO KHALID BIN KHALIFA AL THANI.

Ras Laffan LNG Co Ltd (RasGas): POB 24200, Doha; tel. 44738000; fax 44738480; e-mail site-admin@rasgas.com.qa; internet www.rasgas.com; f. 1993; 70% owned by Qatar Petroleum, 30% by ExxonMobil; operates five LNG trains, which had a production capacity of 20.7m. metric tons per year in 2007; CEO HAMAD RASHID AL-MOHANNADI.

Qatar Petroleum also wholly or partly owns: Industries Qatar (IQ) and its subsidiaries, Qatar Gas Transport Co (Nakilat), Gulf Helicopters Co Ltd (GHC), Qatar Vinyl Co (QVC), Qatar Chemical Co (Q-Chem), Qatar Clean Energy Co (QACENCO), Qatar Electricity and Water Co (QEWC), Qatar Shipping Co (Q-Ship), Arab Maritime Petroleum Transport Co (AMPTC), Arab Petroleum Pipelines Co (SUMED), Arab Shipbuilding and Repair Yard Co (ASRY), Arab Petroleum Services Co (APSC) and Arab Petroleum Investments Corpn (APICORP).

UTILITIES

Qatar General Electricity and Water Corpn (Kahramaa): POB 41, Doha; tel. 44845555; fax 44845496; e-mail kmcontact@km.com.qa; internet www.km.com.qa; f. 2000; state authority for planning, implementation, operation and maintenance of electricity and water sectors; Chair. ISSA HILAL AL-KUWARI.

Qatar Electricity and Water Co (QEWC): POB 22046, Doha; tel. 44858585; fax 44831116; e-mail welcome@qewc.com; internet www.qewc.com; f. 1990; 57% privately owned; devt and operation of power generation and water desalination facilities; Gen. Man. FAHAD HAMAD AL-MOHANNADI.

MAJOR INVESTMENT HOLDING COMPANIES

Qatar Intermediate Industries Holding Co Ltd (Qatar Holding): POB 28882, 37 Muhammad bin Thani St, bin Omran Area, al-Maha Bldg, Doha; tel. 44976454; fax 44293440; e-mail qh@qh.com.qa; internet www.qh.com.qa; f. 2005; wholly owned subsidiary of Qatar Petroleum; investment holding; Man. Dir and CEO MUHAMMAD KHALIFA TURKI AL-SOBAI.

Qatar Investment and Projects Development Holding Co (QIPCO Holding): POB 8612, Doha; tel. 44341112; fax 44341115; e-mail qipcoq@qatar.net.qa; internet www.qipcoqatar.com; f. 1999; privately owned; investment holding; subsidiaries in real estate devt and management, construction, oil and gas and services sectors; cap. QR 300m. (2009); Chair. and CEO Sheikh HAMAD BIN ABDULLAH BIN KHALIFA AL THANI; Man. Dir MUHAMMAD ALI AL-KUBAISI.

Qatari Diar Real Estate Investment Co: POB 23175, Lusail, Doha; tel. 44974444; fax 44974333; e-mail info@qataridiar.com; internet www.qataridiar.com; f. 2005; real estate investment holding, land acquisition and devt; owned by QIA and Govt. of Qatar; cap. US $1,000m. (2009); CEO GHANEM BIN SAAD AL-SAAD.

MAJOR COMPANIES

Aamal Co QSC: POB 22477, Doha; tel. 44864397; fax 44864324; e-mail info@aamal.com.qa; internet www.aamal.com.qa; f. 2001; property devt, industrial manufacturing, retail, managed services and pharmaceuticals; Chair. and CEO Sheikh FAISAL BIN QASSIM AL THANI; 3,000 employees.

AKC Contracting: POB 2760, Doha; tel. 44665576; fax 44665579; e-mail akcqatar@qatar.net.qa; f. 1975; building, plumbing, joinery, landscaping, etc.; Man. Dir ISSA A. R. AL-MANNAI; Gen. Man. JOHN W. FOX; 700 employees.

Arab-Qatari Co for Dairy Production: POB 8324, Doha; tel. 44601107; fax 44600516; e-mail ghadeerr@qatar.net.qa; f. 1985; cap. p.u. QR 58.4m.; production of dairy products, ice creams and fruit juices; Man. Dir SHAMSEDDIN HUSSAINI.

Arab-Qatari Co for Poultry Production: POB 3606, Doha; tel. 44729042; fax 44729028; 40% state-owned; 60% owned by Arab Livestock Devt Co; produces 7m. chickens, and 10m.–25m. eggs per year; Dir ISMAIL FAITI AL-ISMAIL.

Barwa Real Estate Co: POB 27777, Doha; tel. 44088888; fax 44998994; e-mail info@barwa.com.qa; internet www.barwa.com.qa; f. 2005; real estate devt; Chair. and Man. Dir GHANIM BIN SAAD AL-SAAD.

Ezdan Real Estate Co QSC: POB 23407, Doha; tel. 44620912; fax 44622023; internet www.ezdanqatar.com; f. 1960; real estate devt and trading; Chair. Sheikh THANI BIN ABDULLAH BIN THANI AL THANI.

Industries Qatar Co (IQ): POB 3212, Doha; tel. 44308681; fax 44308628; internet www.industriesqatar.com.qa; f. 2003 as part of the Govt's programme of privatization; 70% stake owned by Qatar Petroleum; controls Qatar Petrochemical Co, Qatar Fertilizer Co, Qatar Fuel Additives Co and Qatar Steel; Chair. MUHAMMAD BIN SALEH AL-SADA (Minister of Energy and Industry).

Kassem Darwish Fakhroo & Sons (KDS): POB 92, Doha; tel. 44422781; fax 44426378; e-mail kdsgroup@qatar.net.qa; internet www.darwish-group.com; f. 1911; corporate group est. 1971; electrical, mechanical and civil contractors, general trading, mfrs; Chair. KASSEM DARWISH FAKHROO; Man. Dir HASSAN DARWISH; 1,000 employees.

Mideast Constructors Ltd (MECON): POB 3325, Doha; tel. 44558888; fax 44439219; e-mail mecon@qatar.net.qa; f. 1975; mem. of the Mannai Group; sales QR 300m. (2001); mechanical and electrical instrumentation, heating, ventilating and air-conditioning, and civil engineering and contracting; Chair. KHALID AHMED MANNAI; Gen. Man. MICHAEL HERBERT; 1,650 employees.

National Industrial Gas Plants (NIGP): POB 1391, Doha; tel. 44689083; fax 44682764; e-mail info@mhalmanagroup.com; internet www.mhalmanagroup.com/ni_gas.htm; f. 1954; part of the Mohammed Hamad Al Mana Group; production of industrial gases (oxygen, carbon dioxide, nitrogen, argon and acetylene), liquid gases (oxygen, nitrogen and argon), and dry ice, hydrostatic pressure testing of high-pressure cylinders; Pres. M. H. AL-MANA; 125 employees.

Qatar Fertilizer Co SAQ (QAFCO): POB 50001, Umm Said (Mesaieed); tel. 44228888; fax 44770347; e-mail mktg@qafco.com; internet www.qafco.com; f. 1969; gross sales QR 6,119.5m., total assets QR 12,472m. (Dec. 2008); produced 2.18m. metric tons of ammonia and 3.0m. tons of urea in 2008; owned by QP (75%) and Norsk Hydro (Norway—25%); Chair. ABDULLAH H. SALATT; Man. Dir KHALIFA ABDULLAH AL-SUWAIDI; 852 employees.

Qatar Flour Mills Co SAQ: POB 1444, Doha; tel. 44415000; fax 44438137; e-mail qfmmgmt@qatar.net.qa; internet www.qatarflourmills.com; f. 1969; cap. QR 60.0m., sales QR 45.9m. (2000); produced 33,000 metric tons of flour and 11,500 tons of bran in 1993; Chair. Sheikh NASSER BIN MUHAMMAD BIN JABER AL THANI; Man. Dir Sheikh TALAL BIN MUHAMMAD BIN JABER AL THANI; 250 employees.

Qatar Industrial Manufacturing Co (QIMC): POB 16875, al-Corniche St, West Bay, Doha; tel. 44831199; fax 44837878; e-mail qimc@qimc.com.qa; internet www.qimc.com.qa; f. 1989 to establish domestic and international industrial ventures; 20% state-owned; cap. QR 300m., sales QR 253.0m. (2006); subsidiaries and associated cos include Qatar Nitrogen Co, Qatar Metal-Coating Co, National Paper Industries Co, Qatar Sand-Treatment Plant, Qatar Acids Co, National Food Co, Qatar Jet Fuel Co, Qatar-Saudi Gypsum Industries Co, Qatar Paving Stones; Chair. and Man. Dir Sheikh ABD AL-RAHMAN BIN MUHAMMAD JABER AL THANI; CEO ABD AL-RAHMAN AL-ANSARI.

Qatar National Cement Co SAQ (QNCC): POB 1333, Doha; tel. 44693800; fax 44693900; e-mail qatarcement@qatar.net.qa; internet www.qatarcement.com; f. 1965; cap. QR 491.01m., sales QR 989.63m. (2011); produced 3m. metric tons of cement products in 2008; Chair. and Man. Dir SALEM BUTTI AL-NAIMI; Gen. Man. MUHAMMAD ALI AL-SULAITI; 1,247 employees.

Qatar National Plastic Factory (Q-PLAST): POB 5615, Doha; tel. 44689977; fax 44689922; e-mail qnpf@qatar.net.qa; internet www.qatarnationalplasticfactory.com; f. 1977; production of polyethylene bags, film and UPVC pipes; Man. Dir ABD AL-AZIZ BIN MUHAMMAD AL-ATTIYA; Gen. Man. KHALID BIN MUHAMMAD AL-ATTIYA; 130 employees.

Qatar Steel Co (QASCO): POB 50090, Mesaieed; tel. 44778778; fax 44771424; e-mail webmaster@qatarsteel.com; internet www.qasco.com; the plant was completed in 1978 and produced some 800,000 metric tons of concrete-reinforcing steel bars in 2004; 100% govt-owned; Chair. YOUSUF HUSSAIN KEMAL; Dir and Gen. Man. Sheikh NASSER BIN HAMAD AL THANI; 1,250 employees.

Readymix Qatar LLC: POB 5007, Doha; tel. 44653070; fax 44651534; e-mail rmq@qatar.net.qa; f. 1978; production of ready-mixed concrete; Gen. Man. LOREN ZANIN; 1,500 employees.

Qatar Quarry Co LLC: POB 5007, Doha; tel. 44728162; fax 44651534; e-mail qquarry@qatar.net.qa; f. 1983; production of aggregates, road materials and armour rock; Gen. Man. LOREN ZANIN.

Transport

RAILWAYS

In 2009 the Qatar Railways Development Co (QRDC), a joint venture comprising Qatari Diar Real Estate Investment Co and Deutsche Bahn AG (Germany), was established to supervise the development of a national rail network, which would be linked to a regional rail network, connecting Qatar with member countries of the Cooperation Council for the Arab States of the Gulf (Gulf Cooperation Council—GCC). In 2011 QRDC established the Qatar Railways Co (Qatar Rail) to oversee the implementation of plans to develop a national rail network in Qatar. In February 2012 Qatar Rail awarded a US $535.4m. contract for work on a light rail network serving the new, planned city of Lusail to Qatari Diar Vinci Construction. The project, which eventually would comprise a 30-km, four-line network, was expected to be completed in 2016. Qatar Rail awarded three contracts in August 2012 for phase one of construction work on a planned 300-km, four-line metro system in Doha, the first line of which was due to be operational by 2019.

Qatar Railways Co (Qatar Rail): Qatar Rail Tower, 231 Suhaim bin Hamad St (C-Ring Rd), al-Sadd Area 38, POB 29988, Doha; tel. 44331111; fax 44331110; e-mail info@qr.com.qa; internet www.qr.com.qa; f. 2011; fully owned by Qatar Railways Development Co (QRDC); CEO SAAD AHMAD AL-MUHANNADI.

ROADS

The total road network in 2010 was estimated to be 9,830 km. A major upgrading of the national road network was planned for the first years of the 21st century. Work on the QR 8,000m., 13-phase Doha Expressway project, which involves the construction of a dual carriageway linking the north and south of the country and a Doha ring road, commenced in late 2007. A project to construct a causeway (the Friendship Bridge) linking Qatar with Bahrain was approved by both Governments in 2004. After protracted discussions and numerous delays, in May 2008 the contract to design and build the causeway, at a cost of some US $3,000m., was awarded to a France-based consortium. The decision, in late 2008, to incorporate a railway line into the project necessitated substantial design revisions that were expected to add up to $1,000m. to the cost of the causeway. Construction had yet to commence at late 2013.

SHIPPING

Doha Port has nine general cargo berths of 7.5 m–9.0 m depth. The total length of the berths is 1,699 m. In addition, there is a flour mill berth, and a container terminal (with a depth of 12.0 m and a length of 600 m) with a roll-on roll-off (ro-ro) berth at the north end currently under construction. Cold-storage facilities exist for cargo of up to 500 metric tons. The North Field gas project has increased the demand for shipping facilities. A major new industrial port was completed at Ras Laffan in 1995, providing facilities for LNG and condensate carriers and ro-ro vessels. Qatar Petroleum initiated a US $1,000m. expansion of Ras Laffan port in 2005. Further expansion plans at Ras Laffan, to accommodate the shipping requirements of the burgeoning LNG and associated industries, were finalized in 2008; completion of the project would render Ras Laffan the largest man-made harbour in the world, bounded by 26 km of breakwaters. In October 2007 Sheikh Hamad issued a decree announcing that the New Doha Port development would be located at Mesaieed industrial city. On completion of its first phase (scheduled for 2014), at a projected cost of some $5,500m., the port was expected to have annual handling capacity of 2m. 20-ft equivalent units (TEUs), with capacity projected to increase to 6m. TEUs by 2025. Capacity at Doha's existing port, which was to be decommissioned on completion of the new port, was 400,000 TEUs.

At 31 December 2012 Qatar's flag registered fleet totalled 152 vessels, with an aggregate displacement of 860,605 grt, of which three were bulk carriers, six were gas tankers and two were general cargo ships.

Port Authority

Customs and Ports General Authority (CPGA): POB 81, Doha; tel. and fax 44457457; e-mail comments@customs.gov.qa; internet www.customs.gov.qa; Chair. AHMAD ALI MUHAMMAD AL-MOHANNADI.

Principal Shipping Companies

Qatar Gas Transport Co Ltd (Nakilat): Royal Plaza, al-Sadd St, POB 22271, Doha; tel. 44998111; fax 44483111; e-mail info@qgtc.com.qa; internet www.nakilat.com.qa; f. 2004; 50% owned by founding shareholders and 50% owned by public; specializes in the shipment of LNG, LPG and petroleum products; owns 54 vessels; Chair. HAMAD RASHID AL-MOHANNADI; Man. Dir MUHAMMAD GHANNAM; 220 employees.

Qatar Navigation QSC: POB 153, 60 al-Tameen St, West Bay, Doha; tel. 44468666; fax 44468777; e-mail info@qatarnavigation.com; internet www.qatarnav.com; f. 1957 as Qatar Nat. Navigation and Transport Co Ltd; acquired Qatar Shipping Co in 2010; 100% owned by Qatari nationals; shipping agents, stevedoring, chandlers, forwarding, ship-owning, repair, construction, etc.; Chief Exec. KHALIFA BIN ALI AL-HITMI; Chair. and Man. Dir Sheikh ALI BIN JASSIM BIN MUHAMMAD AL THANI.

Qatar Shipping Co QSC (Q-Ship): POB 22180, al-Jazeera Tower, 61, Conference Center St, West Bay, Doha; tel. and fax 44191760; e-mail rahul@qship.com; internet www.qship.com; f. 1992; subsidiary of Qatar Navigation QSC; oil and bulk cargo shipping; wholly owns 7 vessels; Chair. and Man. Dir SALEM BIN BUTTI AL-NAIMI; CEO K. K. KOTHARI.

CIVIL AVIATION

A substantial redevelopment of Doha International Airport (to be known upon completion of the project as Hamad International Airport), 4 km to the east of the existing site, is currently under way. Phase one of the project, which was expected to cost some QR 9,500m., involved the construction of two runways and a new terminal building, and was intended to increase annual passenger-handling capacity to 24m. After delays to the original schedule, phase one was expected to be completed by April 2013. However, the opening was postponed until at least early 2014. Upon completion of the third, and final, phase of the expansion, scheduled for 2015, passenger-handling capacity was to reach 50m.

Civil Aviation Authority: POB 3000, Doha; tel. 44557333; fax 44557105; e-mail info@caa.gov.qa; internet www.caa.gov.qa; Chair. and Man. Dir ABD AL-AZIZ MUHAMMAD AL-NOAIMI.

Doha International Airport: POB 24659, Doha; tel. 44656666; fax 44622044; e-mail diainfo@qatarairways.com.qa; internet www.dohaairport.com; CEO AKBAR AL-BAKER.

Gulf Helicopters Co (GHC): POB 811, al-Areesh St, Ras Abu Aboud Rd, Doha; tel. 44333888; fax 44411004; e-mail enquiries@gulfhelicopters.com; internet www.gulfhelicopters.com; f. 1970; owned by Qatar Petroleum; owns a fleet of 32 helicopters; CEO MUHAMMAD AL-MOHANNADI.

Qatar Airways: POB 22550, Airport Rd, Doha; tel. 44496666; fax 44621792; e-mail infodesk@qatarairways.com; internet www.qatarairways.com; f. 1993; state-owned; services to more than 80 international destinations; operated a fleet of 87 aircraft at August 2010; planned fleet expansion to 110 aircraft by 2013; CEO AKBAR AL-BAKER.

Tourism

Since 2000 the tourism industry has been undergoing a programme of expansion and development, and Qatar's reputation as a venue for international conferences and sporting events has grown. The 15th Asian Games, held in Doha in December 2006, provided a substantial impetus for increased hotel construction from 2004. In December 2010 Qatar was awarded the right to host the 2022 International Federation of Association Football (Fédération internationale de football association—FIFA) World Cup, an event that was expected to promote extensive development of the country's tourism infrastructure. A new Museum of Islamic Art opened in Doha in 2008, and several other new museums and cultural establishments were planned. Notable tourist attractions outside the capital include the historic forts and archaeological sites at al-Zubarah, and the natural beauty of the Khor al-Udaid, or Inland Sea, region. There were 1.9m. tourist arrivals in 2010; receipts from tourism (excluding passenger transport) were provisionally estimated at US $1,170m. in 2011.

Qatar National Hotels Co: POB 2977, Doha; tel. 44237777; fax 44270707; internet www.qnhc.com; f. 1993; develops and manages hotels and other tourist facilities; govt-owned; Chair. Sheikh NAWAF BIN JASIM BIN JABER AL THANI; CEO JAN POUL N. DE BOER.

Qatar Tourism Authority (QTEA): POB 24624, Doha; tel. 44997499; fax 44991919; e-mail soha@qatartourism.gov.qa; internet www.qatartourism.gov.qa; f. 2000; affiliated with the Ministry of Business and Trade; Chair. AHMED ABDULLAH AL-NUAIMI; Head of Promotions SOHA MOUSSA.

Defence

Chief of Staff: Air Vice-Marshal GHANIM BIN SHAHEEN AL-GHANIM.

Defence Expenditure (2011): QR 12,600m.

Total armed forces (as assessed at November 2012): 11,800: army 8,500; navy 1,800 (incl. marine police); air force 1,500.

Education

All education within Qatar is provided free of charge, although it is not compulsory, and numerous scholarships are awarded for study overseas. In the academic year 2011/12 there were 94,005 students at pre-primary, primary, preparatory and secondary levels of government-funded, regular education in Qatar; there were 125,547 students in private schools in the same year. In that year there were 41,287 children enrolled in pre-primary education. Primary schooling begins at six years of age and lasts for six years. In 2009/10 state primary schools were attended by 12,204 pupils. The next level of education, beginning at 12 years of age, is divided between a three-year preparatory stage and a further three-year secondary stage, with a total of 18,912 pupils at government schools in 2009/10. In that year there were 136 independent schools, which were attended by 27,306 pupils at primary level and 35,609 at preparatory and secondary levels. There are specialized religious, industrial, commercial and technical secondary schools for boys; the technical school admitted its first students in 1999/2000, as did two scientific secondary schools (one for girls). According to UNESCO estimates, enrolment at primary schools in 2009/10 included 92% of children in the relevant age-group; the comparable ratio for secondary enrolment was 83%. The University of Qatar was established in 1977. In 2011/12 there were 11,306 students enrolled at the university (including Qatar Community College). The Qatar Foundation for Education, Science and Community Development, established in 1995, is involved in various programmes to develop educational and research facilities, including through partnerships with international institutions. Education City Qatar, the foundation's flagship project, which opened in October 2003, hosts branch campuses of five US universities and numerous other educational and research institutions. In 2011/12 government expenditure on education amounted to QR 6,040m., equivalent to 14% of total government spending.

Bibliography

al-Abdulla, Yousof Ibrahim. *A Study of Qatari-British Relations 1914–1945.* Orient Publishing and Translation, 1981.

al-Arayed, Jawal Salim. *A Line in the Sea: The Qatar Versus Bahrain Border Dispute in the World Court.* Berkeley, CA, North Atlantic Books, 2003.

Fromherz, Allen. *Qatar: A Modern History*. London, I. B. Tauris & Co, 2012.

Graham, Helga. *Arabian Time Machine: Self-Portrait of an Oil State.* London, Heinemann, 1978.

al-Mallakh, Ragaei. *Qatar, Energy and Development.* London, Croom Helm, 1985.

Miles, Hugh. *Al Jazeera: How Arab TV News Challenged the World.* London, Abacus, 2005.

Nab, Ibrahim Abu. *Qatar: A Story of State Building.* Ministry of Information, Qatar, 1977.

Nafi, Zuhair Ahmed. *Economic and Social Development in Qatar.* London and Dover, NH, Frances Pinter, 1983.

al-Nawawny, Muhammad, and Farag, Adel Iskander. *Al-Jazeera: How the Free Arab News Network Scooped the World and Changed the Middle East.* Boulder, CO, Westview Press, 2002.

al-Othman, Nasser. *With Their Bare Hands: The Story of the Oil Industry in Qatar.* London, Longman, 1984.

Rahman, Habibur. *The Emergence Of Qatar: The Turbulent Years 1627–1916.* London, Kegan Paul International, 2005.

Rahman, Habibur, al-Sulaiti, Mubarak E., and al-Jaber, Jassem. *The Changing Face of Qatar: From the Age of the Pearl to the 21st Century.* London, Kegan Paul International, 2007.

Seib, Philip (Ed.). *Al Jazeera English: Global News in a Changing World.* Basingstoke, Palgrave Macmillan, 2012.

Smith, Simon C. *Britain's Revival and Fall in the Gulf: Kuwait, Bahrain, Qatar, and the Trucial States, 1950-71.* London, Routledge, 2004.

For further titles of relevance to Qatar, see the Bibliography sections for Bahrain and the United Arab Emirates.

SAUDI ARABIA

Physical and Social Geography of the Arabian Peninsula

The Arabian peninsula is a distinct geographical unit, delimited on three sides by sea—on the east by the Persian (Arabian) Gulf and the Gulf of Oman, on the south by the Indian Ocean, and on the west by the Red Sea—while its remaining (northern) side is occupied by the deserts of Jordan and Iraq. This isolated territory, extending over some 2.5m. sq km (about 1m. sq miles), is divided politically into several states. The largest of these is Saudi Arabia, which occupies 2,240,000 sq km (864,869 sq miles); to the east and south lie much smaller territories where suzerainty and even actual frontiers are disputed in some instances. Along the shores of the Persian Gulf and the Gulf of Oman there are, beginning in the north, the State of Kuwait, with two adjacent zones of 'neutral' territory; then, after a stretch of Saudi Arabian coast, the islands of Bahrain and the Qatar peninsula, followed by the United Arab Emirates and the much larger Sultanate of Oman. Yemen occupies most of the southern coastline of the peninsula, and its south-western corner.

PHYSICAL FEATURES

Structurally, the whole of Arabia is a vast platform of ancient rocks, once continuous with north-east Africa. Subsequently, a series of great fissures opened, as a result of which a large trough, or rift valley, was formed and later occupied by the sea, to produce the Red Sea and Gulf of Aden. The Arabian platform is tilted, with its highest part in the extreme west, along the Red Sea, and it slopes gradually down from west to east. Thus the Red Sea coast is often bold and mountainous, whereas the Persian Gulf coast is flat, low-lying and fringed with extensive coral reefs which make it difficult to approach the shore in many places.

Dislocation of the rock strata in the west of Arabia has led to the upwelling of much lava, which has solidified into vast barren expanses, known as *harras*. Volcanic cones and flows are also prominent along the whole length of the western coast as far as Aden, where peaks rise to more than 3,000 m above sea level. The mountains reach their highest in the south, in Yemen, with summits at 4,000 m, and the lowest part of this mountain wall occurs roughly half-way along its course, in the region of Jeddah, Mecca and Medina. A principal reason for the location of these three Saudi Arabian towns is that they offer the easiest route inland from the coast, and one of the shortest routes across Arabia.

Further to the east the ancient platform is covered by relatively thin layers of younger rocks. Some of the strata have been eroded to form shallow depressions; others have proved more resistant, and now stand out as ridges. This central area, relieved by shallow vales and upstanding ridges and covered in many places by desert sand, is called the Najd, and is considered to be the homeland of the Wahhabi sect, which now rules the whole of Saudi Arabia. Further east, practically all the land lies well below 300 m in altitude, and both to the north and to the south are desert areas. The Nefud in the north has some wells, and even a slight rainfall, and therefore supports a few oasis cultivators and pastoral nomads. South of the Najd, however, lies the Rub al-Khali, or Empty Quarter, a rainless, unrelieved wilderness of shifting sand, too harsh for occupation even by nomads.

Most of the east coast of Arabia (al-Hasa) is low-lying, but an exception is the imposing ridge of the Jebel al-Akhdar ('Green Mountain') of Oman, which also produces a fjord-like coastline along the Gulf of Oman. Another feature is the large river valleys, or *wadis*, cut by river action during an earlier geological period, but in modern times almost, or entirely, dry and partially filled with sand. The largest is the Wadi Hadramout, which runs parallel to the southern coast for several hundred km; another is the Wadi Sirhan, which stretches north-westwards from the Nefud into Jordan.

CLIMATE

Owing to its land-locked nature, the winds reaching Arabia are generally dry, and almost all the area is arid. In the north there is a rainfall of 100 mm–200 mm annually; further south, except near the coast, even this fails. The higher parts of the west and south do, however, experience appreciable falls—rather sporadic in some parts, but copious and reliable in areas adjacent to the Red Sea.

As a result of aridity, and hence relatively cloudless skies, there are great extremes of temperature. The summer is overwhelmingly hot, with maximum temperatures of more than 50°C, which are intensified by the dark rocks, while in winter there can be general severe frost and even weeks of snow in the mountains. Another result of the wide variations in temperature is the prevalence of violent local winds. Also, near the coast, atmospheric humidity is particularly high, and the coasts of both the Red Sea and the Persian Gulf are notorious for their humidity. Average summer temperatures in Saudi Arabia's coastal regions range from 38°C to 49°C (100°F–120°F), sometimes reaching 54°C (129°F) in the interior, or falling to a minimum of 24°C (75.2°F) in Jeddah. The winters are mild, except in the mountains. Winter temperatures range from 8°C (46.4°F) to 30°C (86°F) in Riyadh, and reach a maximum of 33°C (91.4°F) in Jeddah.

Owing to the tilt of the strata eastwards, and their great elevation in the west, rain falling in the hills near the Red Sea apparently percolates gradually eastwards, to emerge as springs along the Persian Gulf coast. This phenomenon, borne out by the fact that the flow of water in the springs greatly exceeds the total rainfall in the same district, suggests that water may be present underground over much of the interior. Irrigation schemes to exploit these supplies have been developed, notably in the Najd at al-Kharj, but results have been fairly limited.

ECONOMIC LIFE

Over much of Arabia, life is based around oases. Many wells are used solely by nomads for watering their animals, but in some parts, more especially the south, there is regular cultivation. Yemen, in particular, has a well-developed agriculture, showing a gradation of crops according to altitude, with cereals, fruit, coffee and qat (a narcotic) as the chief products. Other agricultural districts are in Oman and in the large oases of the Hedjaz (including Medina and Mecca). However, conditions in Arabia are harsh, and the population depends partly on resources brought in from outside, such as revenues from pilgrims. A major change in the economy of Saudi Arabia and the Gulf states resulted from the exploitation of petroleum, the revenues from which transformed those states.

PEOPLE, LANGUAGE AND RELIGION

A recent result of the rapid economic growth in the petroleum-producing countries has been the influx of large numbers of expatriates from the developed countries of the Western world, and labourers from developing countries further east. At the national census of 2010, the population was recorded at 27,136,977, including some 8,429,401 foreign nationals. According to official estimates, the total population had reached 29,994,272 by mid-2013. The official language of Saudi Arabia is Arabic, which is spoken by almost all of the population.

As its borders enclose the holy cities of Mecca and Medina, Saudi Arabia is considered the centre of the Islamic faith. About 85% of Saudi Muslims belong to the Sunni sect of Islam, the remainder being Shi'a. Except in the Eastern region, Sunni rites prevail.

History

Revised for this edition by J. E. PETERSON; based on an earlier essay by GERD NONNEMAN

ANCIENT AND MEDIEVAL HISTORY

For the most part, Arabian history has been the account of small pockets of settled civilization, subsisting mainly on trade, in the midst of nomadic tribes. The earliest urban settlements developed in the south-west, where the flourishing Minaean kingdom is believed to have been established in the 12th century BC. This was followed by the Sabaean and Himyarite 'kingdoms' (loose federations of city states), which lasted until the sixth century AD. As an important trading station between east and west, southern Arabia was brought into early contact with the Persian and Roman empires, and thereby with Judaism, Zoroastrianism and, later, Christianity. However, the south Arabian principalities remained politically independent.

By the end of the sixth century the centre of power had shifted to the west coast, to the Hedjaz cities of al-Ta'if, Mecca and Yathrib (later known as Medina, or *'madinat al-nabi'*—city of the Prophet). While the southern regions fell under the control of the Sasanid rulers of Persia, the independent Hedjaz grew in importance as a trade route between the Byzantine Empire, Egypt and the East. From the fifth century Mecca was dominated by the tribe of Quraish. Meanwhile, the central deserts remained nomadic, and the inhospitable east coast remained, for the most part, under Persian influence.

The development of Arab-Islamic civilization from the seventh century, inspired by the Prophet Muhammad (the founder of Islam), proceeded, for the most part, outside the Arabian peninsula itself. The Islamic unification of the Near and Middle East reduced the importance of the Hedjaz as a trade route. Mecca retained a unique status as a centre of pilgrimage for the entire Islamic world, but Arabia as a whole, temporarily united under Muhammad and his successors, soon drifted back into disunity, starting with Yemen from the ninth century onwards. Mecca also had its semi-independent governors, though their proximity to Egypt made them more cautious in their attitude towards the Caliphs and the later rulers of that country, particularly the Fatimids of the 10th to 12th centuries.

THE OTTOMAN PERIOD

Arabia remained unsettled until the beginning of the 16th century, when much of the peninsula came under the nominal suzerainty of the Ottoman Sultans in İstanbul. Their control was never very strong, even in the Hedjaz, and in Oman and Yemen native imams once again exercised unfettered authority before the end of the century. More important for the future of the peninsula was the appearance of European merchant adventurers in the Indian Ocean and the Gulf. The Portuguese were the first to arrive, in the 16th century, and they were followed in the 17th and 18th centuries by the British, Dutch and French. By the beginning of the 19th century the United Kingdom had supplanted its European rivals and had established its influence firmly along the Gulf littoral and, to a lesser extent, along the southern coast of Arabia.

The political structure of Arabia was now beginning to develop along its modern lines. Yemen was already a virtually independent Imamate; Lahej broke away in the middle of the 18th century, only to lose Aden to the United Kingdom in 1839 and to become the nucleus of the Aden Protectorate. To the north of Yemen was the principality of the Asir, generally independent, though both countries were occupied by the Turks from 1850 until the outbreak in 1914 of the First World War. The Hedjaz continued to be a province of the Ottoman Empire. In 1793 the Sultanate of Oman was established with its capital at Muscat, and during the 19th century all the rulers and chieftains along the Gulf coast, including Oman, the sheikhdoms of the Trucial Coast, Bahrain and Kuwait, entered into 'exclusive' treaty relations with the British Government. The United Kingdom was principally concerned with preventing French, Russian and German penetration towards India, avoiding maritime warfare in Gulf shipping lanes, and suppressing the trade in slaves and weapons.

Meanwhile, the Najd, in the centre of Arabia, was the scene of another upheaval with religious inspirations. In the mid-1800s Muhammad ibn Abd al-Wahhab, the founder of the puritanical reforming *Muwahhidun* movement ('unitarians', referring to Allah's oneness), struck an alliance with the chief of the Sa'ud clan (in Arabic, *Al Sa'ud*), Muhammad ibn Sa'ud, pledging to support each other's respective spiritual and temporal-political leadership aims. By the beginning of the 19th century the alliance had grown so powerful that its followers were able to capture Karbala and Najaf in Iraq, Damascus in Syria, and Mecca and Medina in the Hedjaz: the greatest extent of what is now referred to as the first Saudi state. They were defeated by Muhammad Ali of Egypt, acting in the name of the Ottoman Sultan in 1811–18 and again in 1838, but the Al Sa'ud rebounded under the 'second Saudi state', ruling in the interior until 1890, when the rival Al Rashid clan, which had Ottoman support, seized control of Riyadh. The leadership of the Al Sa'ud sought refuge in Kuwait.

In 1901 Abd al-Aziz ibn Abd al-Rahman, the young son of the Al Sa'ud chief, set out from Kuwait to regain the family's former domains. In 1902, with only about 200 followers, Abd al-Aziz captured Riyadh, expelled the Rashidi dynasty and proclaimed himself ruler of the Najd. Having revived the alliance with the Wahhabi movement's leadership (the Al al-Sheikh, or 'family of the Sheikh'—viz. Muhammad ibn Abd al-Wahhab), he succeeded in consolidating control over the interior of Arabia, playing a cautious diplomatic game to avoid subjugation by Turkey by attempting to obtain an agreement with the United Kingdom, without as yet formally denying Ottoman suzerainty. Having restored the House of Sa'ud under what is now referred to as the 'third Saudi state', Abd al-Aziz was increasingly referred to as 'Ibn Sa'ud'. To strengthen his position, he fostered Wahhabi settlements, overseen by zealous activists, known as the Ikhwan (Brethren), throughout the territory under his control. The first Ikhwan settlement was founded in 1912, and about 100 more were established, spreading Wahhabi doctrines to communities in remote desert areas, over the next 15 years. This network was to prove a powerful instrument in later years. By the outbreak of the First World War, Abd al-Aziz was effectively the master of central Arabia but, critically, the Saudi domains had also become a Gulf power by the 1913 conquest of al-Hasa—thus forcing the United Kingdom to take Abd al-Aziz's approaches seriously.

ARABIA FROM THE FIRST WORLD WAR TO 1932

When Turkey entered the war on the side of Germany in October 1914, Arabia inevitably became a centre of intrigue. British influence was paramount along the eastern and southern coasts, where the various sheikhs and tribal chiefs from Kuwait to the Hadramout lost no time in severing their remaining connections with the Ottoman Empire. On the other hand, the Turks had faithful allies in Ibn Rashid of the Shammar, to the north of the Najd, and in Imam Yahya of Yemen. Abd al-Aziz attempted to balance nominal recognition of Ottoman suzerainty with a long-pursued alliance with Britain, playing on the mutual suspicions and interests of the latter, the Ottoman Porte, Russia and France. Yet the British initially remained tentative. In their search for an Arab ally against the Ottomans, they eventually opted for the Sharif of Mecca, Hussein, a member of the Hashimi family, which had ruled in Mecca since the 11th century AD, causing Abd al-Aziz to sign a secret treaty with the Ottomans in May 1914 in which he was recognized as the governor of Najd.

British military strategy consisted of a two-pronged offensive against the Turks from both Egypt and the Gulf. Opinions were divided on the extent to which use could be made of the Arab population. The Indian Government, while favouring the pretensions of Abd al-Aziz, opposed any suggestion of an Arab revolt. However, this was the scheme favoured by the Arab

Bureau in Cairo, Egypt, whose views eventually prevailed. They were alarmed at the Ottoman declaration of a *jihad* (holy war) and possible repercussions in Egypt and North Africa. Early negotiations with Arab nationalist movements in Syria and Egypt met with little success, but more progress was made when the British negotiators turned their attentions to Sharif Hussein. The support of such a religious dignitary would be an effective counter to Turkish claims. Hussein was inclined to favour the Allied cause, but it was only after he had elicited promises from the British in the Hussein-MacMahon correspondence (Documents on Palestine, see p. 56), which he believed would meet Arab nationalist aspirations, that he decided to move. On 5 June 1916 he proclaimed Arab independence and declared war on the Turks. In July 1917 the port of Aqaba was captured and the Hedjaz cleared of Turkish troops except for a beleaguered garrison in Medina.

Although two of Hussein's sons, Abdullah and Faisal, became Kings of the newly created states of Transjordan and Iraq in the aftermath of the war, in the Hedjaz itself Hussein's star was waning by comparison with that of Abd al-Aziz Al Sa'ud. Hussein also failed to impress the British Government in the post-war negotiations over the shape of the Middle East, leaving him without real support in the rivalry with Abd al-Aziz. In November 1921 the latter succeeded in supplanting the house of Ibn Rashid and annexing the Shammar, and a year later he was recognized by the Government of India as overlord of Ha'il, Shammar and Jawf. When, on 5 March 1924, Hussein laid claim to the title of Caliph, made vacant by the deposition of the Ottoman Sultan, his claims were not recognized, and Abd al-Aziz overran the Hedjaz in a campaign of a few months, captured Mecca and forced Hussein's abdication. Hussein's eldest son, Ali, continued to hold Jeddah for another year, but was then ousted, and on 8 January 1926 Abd al-Aziz Al Sa'ud was proclaimed King of the Hedjaz. In the 1927 Treaty of Jeddah, Britain recognized his absolute independence as King of the Hedjaz, and Sultan of Najd and its dependencies (the so-called Dual Kingdom). The more cosmopolitan Hedjaz was administered with some measure of local participation. Meanwhile, Abd al-Aziz had already proved to be a highly pragmatic politician—avoiding the problems of overreach that had helped to bring down the two previous 'Saudi states', and taking care to avoid clashes with Britain—even to the extent of suppressing those sections of the Ikhwan who were unwilling to compromise their missionary expansionism: he eventually defeated the last Ikhwan rebels in battle in 1929. He acknowledged the sons of his rival Hussein, Abdullah and Faisal, as rulers of Transjordan and Iraq, and also the special status of the British-protected sheikhdoms along the Gulf coast. The northern frontier of his domains was first established, under the coaxing and cajoling of Britain's High Commissioner, Sir Percy Cox, in the Treaty of Uqayr in 1922–23, which demarcated the boundaries with Iraq and Kuwait, and then by the Hadda and Bahra agreements of November 1925, which set the Mandate boundaries as the limit of his expansion.

THE KINGDOM OF SAUDI ARABIA

In 1932 Abd al-Aziz Al Sa'ud renamed his domains the 'Kingdom of Saudi Arabia'. In the years that followed, the new King's priority remained the unification and development of his country. The settlement policy that he had begun in 1912 was pursued vigorously and unruliness among the *bedouin* was suppressed. The border with Yemen was settled in Ta'if in 1934 after protracted negotiations and a brief war. Critical both to the King's rule and to his ambitions for the kingdom was the revenue from petroleum concessions, and eventually from petroleum. Indeed, amid the global and regional economic crisis of the early 1930s and in addition to the expense of the Yemen border war, the halting of British subsidies in 1924 seriously affected the Saudi treasury. Heavily in debt, and at the same time signalling that he was not to be taken for granted, in 1933 Abd al-Aziz awarded the concession to explore for oil in al-Hasa province not to the British-owned Iraqi Petroleum Company (IPC), but to Standard Oil of California (SOCAL), which easily outbid the British. Oil was discovered in March 1938.

The Second World War slowed the development of Saudi Arabia's oil sector and led to other economic damage. Pilgrimage traffic declined dramatically, and in April 1943 it became necessary to include Saudi Arabia as a beneficiary of Lend-Lease, the arrangement whereby the USA supplied equipment to allied countries. Recognition of both the country's difficulties and its strategic importance brought renewed British subsidies of £1m. a year from 1940.

Following the war, Saudi Arabia's production of crude petroleum increased steadily as new oilfields were developed. SOCAL and Texaco bought out the British and French IPC shareholders and established the Arabian-American Oil Company (Aramco). In October 1945 a petroleum refinery opened at Ras Tanura, and two years later work started on the Trans-Arabian Pipeline (Tapline), to connect the Arabian oilfields with ports on the coast of the Mediterranean Sea in Lebanon. Petroleum first reached the Lebanese port of Sidon on 2 December 1950. In the same month the Saudi Government and Aramco signed a new agreement providing for equal shares of the proceeds of petroleum sales. In 1956 a government-owned National Oil Co was formed to exploit areas not covered by the Aramco concession.

Saudi Arabia was a founder member of the League of Arab States (the Arab League), formed in 1945, and initially played a loyal and comparatively inconspicuous part. The Saudi King sent a small force to join the fight against Israel in 1948. When the solidarity of the Arab League began to weaken, it was natural that he should side with Egypt and Syria rather than with his old dynastic enemies, the rulers of Iraq and Jordan. Overall, the King's policy was one of cautious modernization at home, and the enhancement of Saudi Arabian prestige and influence in the Middle East and in world affairs generally.

AFTER ABD AL-AZIZ

On 9 November 1953 King Abd al-Aziz died at the age of 71, and was succeeded by Crown Prince Sa'ud ibn Abd al-Aziz, who had been appointed Prime Minister in the previous month. Another of the late King's sons, Faisal ibn Abd al-Aziz, replaced Sa'ud as Crown Prince and Prime Minister. The policy of strengthening the governmental machine and relying less on one-man rule, was continued by the formation of new ministries and a regular Council of Ministers. In March 1958, bowing to pressure from the royal family, King Sa'ud conferred on Crown Prince Faisal full powers over foreign, internal and economic affairs, with the professed aim of strengthening the machinery of government and of centralizing responsibilities. In December 1960, however, amid continuing frictions, the Crown Prince resigned as Prime Minister, and the King assumed the premiership himself. In the following month a high planning council, with a team of international experts, was formed to survey the country's resources.

Throughout his reign King Sa'ud regarded his role as that of a mediator between the conflicting national and foreign interests in the Arab Middle East. He refused to join either the United Arab Republic (UAR) or the rival Arab Federation. Relations with Egypt ranged from the mutual defence pacts between Egypt, Syria and Saudi Arabia in October 1955 (which Yemen and Jordan also signed a year later) to the open quarrel in March 1958 over an alleged plot to assassinate President Nasser. Subsequently, relations improved. The Saudi Government also played a leading role in bringing the Arab governments together after Egypt's nationalization of the Suez Canal in July 1956 and the Israeli, British and French military action in the Sinai peninsula in November, organizing an oil embargo against France and Britain. In 1961 Saudi Arabia supported the Syrians in their break with the UAR (Egypt), and, in general, relations with Nasser deteriorated.

In March 1964 King Sa'ud relinquished all real power over the affairs of the country to his brother, Crown Prince Faisal, who had again acted as Prime Minister intermittently during 1962, and continuously since mid-1963. In November 1964 Sa'ud was forced by family members to abdicate in favour of Faisal. Underlying this move were concerns over his management of both the economy and the country's foreign affairs. The new King retained the post of Prime Minister, appointed his half-brother, Khalid ibn Abd al-Aziz, as Crown Prince, and embarked on a programme of reform and economic development.

The 'Arab Cold War' intertwined again with Arabian politics when, in the civil war that erupted in Yemen in 1962, Egypt supported the republican side while Saudi Arabia assisted the royalists. Even though King Faisal concluded an agreement at Jeddah with President Nasser on a peace plan for Yemen in August 1965, the issue remained unresolved until Egypt withdrew its forces from Yemen in 1967: up until that point, Saudi relations with the Republican Government of Yemen, the UAR and the Arab League remained tense.

THE SIX-DAY WAR, AND AFTER

In the June 1967 Arab–Israeli war, Saudi forces collaborated with Jordanian and Iraqi forces in action against Israel. At a summit conference of Arab leaders held in Khartoum at the end of August 1967, Saudi Arabia agreed to provide £50m. of a total £135m. fund to assist Jordan and the UAR after the hostilities with Israel. An agreement was also concluded with President Nasser on the withdrawal of UAR and Saudi military support for the warring parties in Yemen. By way of recompense for these concessions, Saudi Arabia persuaded other Arab states that it was in their best interests to resume shipments of petroleum to Western countries—supplies had been suspended for political reasons after the war with Israel.

The internal political situation was disturbed by abortive coups in June and September 1969. Plans for both coups seem to have been discovered in advance, the only visible evidence being the arrests of numbers of army and air force officers. In Yemen the royalist cause, which the Saudi Government had strongly supported, was no longer a significant issue by 1970. Discussions between San'a representatives and Saudi officials took place in 1970, and the Yemen Arab Republic (YAR) was officially recognized in July of that year. Relations with the People's Republic of Southern Yemen (renamed in November of that year the People's Democratic Republic of Yemen—PDRY—following a radical Marxist coup in 1969) deteriorated. Saudi Arabia's superior air power brought an easy victory in a December 1969 border war.

REPERCUSSIONS OF THE 1973 OCTOBER WAR

When the Arab–Israeli war of October 1973 broke out and US aid to Israel continued, Saudi Arabia, despite its traditionally good relationship with the West, led a movement by all the Arab petroleum-producing countries to exert political pressure by means of cuts in petroleum production. Since there was no immediate response from the USA, on 20 October 1973 members of the Organization of Arab Petroleum Exporting Countries (OAPEC—of which Saudi Arabia is a member) placed an embargo on petroleum supplies to the USA and the Netherlands—regarded as excessively supportive of Israel—proclaiming that production would be progressively reduced until more balanced attitudes prevailed. Western states attempted to repair their links with the petroleum-producing countries, who were debating among themselves how far they should wield the so-called 'oil weapon' to achieve their ends.

As the possessor of 40% of the Middle East's petroleum reserves, and one-quarter of the world's, Saudi Arabia, together with Egypt, was at the very forefront of negotiations. However, it soon became apparent that the Saudis held different views from those of other producer nations (notably Libya, Algeria and Iran) on the extent to which their control of petroleum supplies could safely be used to put pressure on the West. While Riyadh feared the economic repercussions if this were taken too far, the more radical OAPEC members wanted to retain the embargo until a satisfactory outcome to the war was achieved. At a meeting in March 1974 Saudi Arabia pressed for a resumption of supplies to the USA and, when this was agreed, resisted any moves to increase prices any further.

In negotiations with consumer countries, the Saudis made it clear that the continued supply of petroleum was dependent not only on a change in attitudes towards Israel but also on assistance to Saudi Arabia itself in industrializing and diversifying its economy, in preparation for such time as reserves of petroleum would be depleted. The USA proved eager to satisfy these conditions, and an important economic and military co-operation agreement was signed in May 1974.

ASSASSINATION OF FAISAL, ACCESSION OF KHALID

On 25 March 1975 King Faisal was assassinated by one of his nephews, Faisal ibn Musa'id ibn Abd al-Aziz. There were fears of a conspiracy, but it soon became clear that the assassin had acted on his own initiative, possibly induced by radical Islamist sympathies for which his brother had previously been killed in a clash with the security forces. King Faisal was succeeded by his half-brother Khalid, who also became Prime Minister, and who appointed one of his brothers, Fahd ibn Abd al-Aziz (Minister of the Interior since 1962), as Crown Prince and First Deputy Prime Minister; Prince Nayef ibn Abd al-Aziz was appointed as the new Minister of the Interior.

No major change of policy followed Khalid's succession. He quickly announced that Saudi Arabia would follow the late King Faisal's policies of pursuing Islamic solidarity and the strengthening of Arab unity, and that Saudi Arabia's objectives remained 'the recovery of occupied Arab territories' and the 'liberation' of the eastern half of the city of Jerusalem from Israeli control. Khalid was supported by a consensus within the family, but had no strong personal interest in government, and it was, in fact, Crown Prince Fahd who proved to be the most significant influence.

Saudi Arabia supported President Anwar Sadat of Egypt, fearing the likely ascendancy of Egypt's political left if Sadat fell from power. When the Egyptian President visited Israel in November 1977, Saudi Arabia discreetly extended support for the Sadat peace initiative—his blueprint for peace with Israel. However, this position, was abandoned following the signing of the Egyptian-Israeli peace treaty in March 1979. At the Arab summit meeting held in April, Saudi Arabia aligned itself with the 'moderate' states in supporting the sanctions against Egypt that had been outlined at the Arab League meeting in the previous November. Nevertheless, flights between Egypt and Saudi Arabia continued, and there was no ban on the employment of Egyptian workers in Saudi Arabia.

In domestic affairs, the Saudi Government was content to allow social change to unfold gradually, although the country's vast petroleum wealth and its progress in development brought about a great improvement in communications, welfare services and the standard of living in general.

The stability of the kingdom and the hegemony of the royal family were abruptly challenged when some 250 armed 'traditionalist' dissidents seized and occupied the Grand Mosque at Mecca on 20 November 1979, the eve of the Islamic year AH 1400. The insurgents, led by Juhaiman ibn Saif al-Otaibi, attempted to force the estimated 50,000-strong congregation to recognize one of their number, Muhammad ibn Abdullah al-Qatami, as the Mahdi (the 'Guided One' of Islamic theological tradition—a prophet sent to replace corruption and evil with justice and law at the end of time). Al-Otaibi declared that the corruption, ostentation and 'Westernization' of the Al Sa'ud dynasty required this response. The Council of Senior Ulama (a body of senior Islamic scholars with far-reaching influence over religious and legal affairs) issued a special dispensation to the security forces to use arms to end the siege, which continued for two weeks; al-Qatami was one of 102 insurgents killed during the reclamation of the Mosque (with the unacknowledged assistance of French special forces), while al-Otaibi was among the 63 rebels executed following the siege.

SAUDI ARABIA IN THE 1980s AND THE ACCESSION OF FAHD

The siege of the Grand Mosque revealed a degree of popular unease in Saudi Arabia. Although the royal family retained a firm grip on power, the existing system entitled as many as 5,000 Saudi princes to royal privileges, and there was widely rumoured disenchantment with the royal family's conspicuous level of consumption and privilege. An eight-man committee, under the chairmanship of Minister of the Interior Prince Nayef, was appointed in March 1980 to draft a 200-article 'system of rule' based on Islamic principles. It was announced that a consultative assembly would be formed to act as an advisory body, although the assembly was not inaugurated until 1993 (see Domestic Challenges, 1991–95). However, Saudi Arabia's geopolitical position added to the unease. With the PDRY already in the Soviet sphere of influence, the YAR concluding an agreement to purchase armaments from the USSR in November 1979 and the Soviet invasion of Afghanistan in December, Saudi Arabia regarded itself as increasingly vulnerable. This sense of vulnerability was intensified by the Iranian Revolution in 1979, and the ideological threat this posed for the pro-Western monarchies in the region. Moreover, there was a particular fear that revolutionary Shi'a Iran would agitate Saudi Arabia's Shi'a minority—and riots did indeed take place in the Eastern region in late 1979. Saudi Arabia therefore supported Iraq in its war against Iran, launched in September 1980. When that offensive began to stagnate and threaten to end in a stalemate, Saudi Arabia combined large-scale material support for Iraq with intermittent overtures to Iran. The country also became involved, with the USA and Pakistan among others, in attempts to aid Afghan resistance against the Soviet Union. Defence spending became a major feature of Saudi Arabia's current expenditure, largely involving the purchase or loan of armaments and military equipment from the USA, the United Kingdom and France.

In May 1981, against the background of regional threats and while Iraq was engaged in the Iran–Iraq War, Saudi Arabia joined the five other Arab Gulf states in founding the Cooperation Council for the Arab States of the Gulf (Gulf Cooperation Council—GCC), formally pursuing economic co-operation but also with some emphasis on the formation of a military alliance and a collective security agreement.

Saudi Arabia became increasingly involved in trying to find a solution to the Arab–Israeli question and the issue of Palestinian autonomy. The basis of Saudi Arabia's policy on these issues was the eight-point 'Fahd Plan', first publicized by Crown Prince Fahd in August 1981. The plan (Documents on Palestine, see p. 73) caused concern in the rest of the Arab world because it implicitly recognized the legitimacy of Israel. The plan was due to be discussed at an Arab summit meeting in Morocco in November, but disagreement over its implications led to the summit breaking up in disarray.

Owing to King Khalid's ill health, Crown Prince Fahd already exercised considerable power. Thus, there was no real shift when Fahd acceded to the throne, following Khalid's sudden demise on 13 June 1982. King Fahd also became Prime Minister, and appointed a half-brother, Abdullah ibn Abd al-Aziz (Commander of the National Guard since 1962), as Crown Prince and First Deputy Prime Minister. The previous Saudi policy of positively seeking a solution to the Palestine question, inflamed still further by the Israeli invasion of Lebanon on 6 June 1982, was continued. The Saudi Government was unwilling to exercise the political influence over Syria (particularly concerning Lebanon) that Western countries assumed it to have, demonstrating clearly that its priority was Arab unity. In February 1984 Crown Prince Abdullah expressed support for the Syrian position in Lebanon, demanding the withdrawal of US marines from the area.

As the war between Iran and Iraq showed signs of escalating towards the end of 1983 and in early 1984, Saudi Arabia appeared to be in danger of becoming involved militarily. In April 1984 a Saudi Arabian merchant ship, a tanker loading at Iran's Kharg Island oil terminal, was struck by missiles from Iraqi fighter aircraft. In retaliatory actions in May, Iranian aircraft attacked two more tankers, one in Saudi waters. In response, Saudi Arabia approached the USA to request help in improving its defence systems.

Saudi Arabia announced the 'Peace Shield' defence programme in February 1985, which included major investment in a new computerized command, control and communication system. In June 1986 a controversial sale of military equipment was agreed between Saudi Arabia and the USA. Initially valued at US $3,000m., it was slashed by more than 90% following strong congressional opposition to the sale of 800 *Stinger* anti-aircraft missiles and 60 advanced fighter aircraft. Also in June another controversial agreement was signed between the two countries for the sale of five US-built AWACS aircraft, worth $8,600m. Saudi Arabia's co-operation became essential to the US naval convoys that began to escort reflagged Kuwaiti tankers through the Gulf in June, following an increase in attacks on shipping in the Gulf by Iran and Iraq during the year. In March 1988 the disclosure that Saudi Arabia had taken delivery of an unspecified number of Chinese medium-range missiles provoked threats by Israel of a pre-emptive strike on the missiles' base at al-Kharj. The USA subsequently warned Israel against taking such action, while in April King Fahd requested the replacement of the US ambassador, following his delivery of an official complaint against Saudi Arabia concerning the purchase of the missiles. In May the US Senate voted to ban sales of military equipment to any nation that had taken delivery of such missiles), unless the US President could certify that the country purchasing the missiles had no chemical, biological or nuclear warheads with which to equip them.

Following the refusal of the US Congress to supply military equipment to Saudi Arabia, in 1985 the kingdom signed the so-called al-Yamamah agreement with British Aerospace of the United Kingdom, valued at a record US $20,000m., for the supply of fighter-bomber aircraft, trainer aircraft, helicopters and mine-sweepers and the construction of two huge airbases in collaboration with Ballast Nedam of the Netherlands.

In early 1985, following a visit by the Saudi Minister of Foreign Affairs, Prince Sa'ud al-Faisal, to Iran, Ali Akbar Velayati, his Iranian counterpart, visited Riyadh in an attempt to improve relations. However, two bomb explosions in Riyadh, responsibility for which was claimed by the Iranian-based Islamic Jihad group, brought a downturn. Relations deteriorated further in 1987, following clashes on 31 July between Iranian pilgrims and Saudi security forces during the *Hajj* (the annual pilgrimage of Muslims to the holy city of Mecca). Denying rumours of shootings, Saudi Arabia reported that 402 people, of whom 275 were Iranians, were killed in a stampede caused by Iranian pilgrims, following unlawful demonstrations in support of Ayatollah Khomeini. Saudi Arabia severed diplomatic relations with Iran in April 1988.

In November 1987 Saudi Arabia resumed full diplomatic relations with Egypt, following an Arab League decision to permit member states to restore relations with Egypt at their own discretion.

Following the August 1988 cease-fire in the Iran–Iraq War, a major issue in Iranian-Saudi relations disappeared, and it was decreed that the Saudi official media would halt their campaign of attacks on that country. Nevertheless, in October that year four Saudi Shi'a Muslims, convicted of sabotaging a petrochemicals plant and collaborating with Iran, were executed; and in late 1988 and early 1989 two senior Saudi intelligence officers, posing as diplomats in an attempt to trace members of the pro-Iranian Shi'a group believed to be responsible for the sabotage, were assassinated in Turkey and Thailand.

Saudi Arabia, along with Sudan, recognized the Afghan *mujahidin* Government-in-exile, formed following the Soviet withdrawal, and, at a meeting of the Organization of the Islamic Conference (OIC, now Organization of Islamic Cooperation) in March 1988, it urged other countries to do likewise. Indeed, Saudi funds had been flowing to the *mujahidin* in the years prior to the withdrawal, often in co-ordination with the USA. By contrast, Saudi Arabia failed to send condolences upon the death of Ayatollah Khomeini in June 1989, illustrating the renewed deterioration in relations with Iran. Iranian pilgrims boycotted the *Hajj* for the third successive year in 1990, and Iran claimed that the Saudi Arabian Government opposed their participation. However, Saudi officials said that Iranian pilgrims were welcome on condition that Iran observed the allocated quota.

In March 1989 King Fahd signed a non-aggression pact with Iraq, a development apparently designed to ease concerns among conservative Arab Gulf states about Iraq's political ambitions following the war between Iran and Iraq. In April Saudi Arabia announced that it would help Iraq to rebuild the nuclear reactor that had been destroyed by Israel (see the chapter on Iraq), on condition that the installation be used for peaceful purposes. King Fahd's visit to Egypt in March 1989 was viewed as signifying the end of Egypt's isolation from the Arab world.

Defence remained a major concern. In March 1989 allegations surfaced that bribery had been used to secure the contracts between British Aerospace and Saudi Arabia. Saudi Arabia denied the allegations, stating that the sales were agreed by the two Governments without the use of intermediaries.

OPERATION DESERT SHIELD AND ITS IMPLICATIONS, 1990-91

Saudi Arabia's concern about its capacity to defend itself and its fears of Iraqi expansionism were substantiated in August 1990, when Iraq invaded Kuwait and proceeded to deploy armed forces along the Kuwaiti–Saudi border. King Fahd condemned the invasion and offered refuge to the Amir of Kuwait; Kuwait established a Government-in-exile at Ta'if. The King, encouraged by the USA, decided that he had no option but to invite—in accordance with Article 51 of the UN Charter—multinational armed forces to deter an attack by Iraq. Thus Operation Desert Shield was launched (see the chapters on Kuwait and Iraq). The Saudi leaders stressed Egyptian, Moroccan, Pakistani, Bangladeshi, Kuwaiti and Syrian participation in the multinational force, to counter accusations from within and outside the country that, by allowing the deployment of US forces in its defence, the regime had allowed itself to become an instrument of US strategic interests in the Gulf. Saudi Arabia stressed that the presence of the multinational defensive force was temporary.

There was a shift in the pattern of Saudi Arabia's foreign relations after the onset of the Gulf crisis in August 1990. The co-operation of the USSR, within the structures of the UN, was regarded as vital to the defence of Saudi Arabia, and in September Saudi Arabia and the USSR re-established diplomatic relations after a rupture lasting 50 years. Syria, aware of the diplomatic benefits that it could gain, committed forces to the defence of Saudi Arabia.

In mid-January 1991, following the failure of international diplomatic efforts to effect Iraq's withdrawal from Kuwait, the US-led multinational force launched a military campaign (Operation Desert Storm) to liberate Kuwait, as authorized by the UN Security Council's Resolution 678 of November 1990. As part of its response to the allied aerial bombardment, Iraq launched 35 *Scud* missiles against mainly urban targets in Saudi Arabia, and made similar attacks against Israel. Most of the missiles proved ineffective, although one of those that struck Saudi Arabia in February 1991 demolished a US barracks near Dhahran, killing 28 soldiers. Many Saudi installations, including desalination plants, were threatened by the release into the Gulf by Iraq of an estimated 4m. barrels of Kuwaiti petroleum, although the long-term effects of the spillage eventually proved less devastating than feared. In late January Iraqi forces entered Saudi Arabia, briefly occupying the town of Ras al-Khafji, close to Saudi Arabia's border with Kuwait, before being repelled by US, Saudi Arabian and Qatari units. Other Iraqi incursions in the same region were likewise repelled, and there was no further fighting on Saudi Arabian territory. In early February Iraq formally severed diplomatic relations with Saudi Arabia, and by the end of that month, when hostilities were suspended, Saudi Arabian casualties amounted to 26 killed and 10 missing.

Following the liberation of Kuwait in February 1991, the Kuwaiti Prime Minister and other members of his Government returned to Kuwait from Saudi Arabia in early March, followed subsequently by the Amir. Also in early March Saudi Arabia, the other members of the GCC, Egypt and Syria agreed to form an Arab peace-keeping force in the Gulf region, as part of a draft plan on security and economic co-operation. Later in the month the withdrawal of coalition forces from bases in Saudi Arabia began. The return to Iraq of an estimated 62,000 Iraqi prisoners of war, held in camps in Saudi Arabia, also commenced in March. In April Saudi Arabia announced its decision to give refuge to an estimated 50,000 Iraqis, many of whom had participated in an unsuccessful revolt against Saddam Hussain's regime in the previous month. In early May the GCC member states endorsed US proposals for an increased Western military presence in the Gulf region, as a deterrent to any future military aggression. Diplomatic relations between Saudi Arabia and Iran were re-established in late March 1991, and Iranian pilgrims resumed participation in the *Hajj*, their numbers regulated in accordance with Saudi Arabia's quota system.

DOMESTIC CHALLENGES, 1991–95

In February and May 1991 two petitions were presented to King Fahd appealing for more extensive Islamization in areas as diverse as the armed forces, the press and all administrative and educational systems. The first petition bore the signatures of as many as 100 senior Saudi religious dignitaries, including that of Sheikh Abd al-Aziz al-Baz, the most influential Saudi theologian. Following the second petition, the Government immediately sent security forces personnel to visit leading signatories, some of whom were forbidden to travel abroad. In June the Government's Higher Judicial Council issued a statement warning the signatories of the consequences of issuing any further criticism against the King. The existence of the Higher Judicial Council, within the Ministry of Justice, was considered to represent an institutional challenge to the judicial powers of the *ulama* (Islamic legal scholars) in Saudi Arabia. Reform of the judicial system was one of the principal aims of the petition, as it stipulated the establishment of a supreme judiciary council with the authority to implement Islamic laws, which would conflict with the powers of the existing Higher Judicial Council. Early 1992 brought instances of Islamist dissent and their suppression. The Minister of Justice ordered the deposition of Sheikh Abd al-Ubaykan, the President of Riyadh's main court, who had criticized government policies in his Friday sermons.

A royal decree issued in March 1992 announced the creation of a Consultative Council (Majlis al-Shura) within six months. Its members were to be selected by the King every four years, but were not to have any legislative powers. Two further decrees provided the framework for the creation of regional authorities and for a 'basic law of government', equivalent to a written constitution. However, in an interview in a Kuwaiti newspaper, King Fahd stated that Islam favoured 'the consultative system and openness between a ruler and his subjects', rather than free elections.

In a speech in December 1992 King Fahd warned religious leaders not to use public platforms to discuss secular matters. He also denounced the spread of Islamist fundamentalism. In May 1993 Saudi authorities disbanded the Committee for the Defence of Legitimate Rights (CDLR), established by a group of six prominent Islamic scholars and lawyers, less than two weeks after its formation. The six founders were dismissed from their positions, and their spokesman, Muhammad al-Mas'ari, was arrested. In the following month it was reported that an accommodation had been reached between the Saudi authorities and an opposition Shi'a organization, the Reform Movement, whereby members of that organization undertook to cease 'dissident' activities, in return for permission to return to Saudi Arabia and the release of a number of Shi'a Muslims held in detention there. In April 1994 members of the CDLR, including al-Mas'ari (who had recently been released from custody), relocated their organization to London, United Kingdom.

In August 1993 four royal decrees had defined the membership and administration of the new Consultative Council, and outlined new rules governing the composition and procedure of the Council of Ministers. The Consultative Council was to consist of 60 men selected by King Fahd from the educated and professional classes. It was to meet regularly in full session, and eight committees were to be established to review the activities of the Government. In relation to the Council of Ministers, King Fahd set fixed limits for the cabinet's term of office and that of each cabinet member. Many incumbent ministers had held the same portfolio since the mid-1970s.

In September 1993 a further decree concerned a provincial system of government, the last of the constitutional reforms promised in March 1992. The decree defined the nature of government for the 13 regions, as well as the rights and responsibilities of their governors, and created councils of officials and citizens for each region to monitor developments and to advise the Government. Each council was to meet four times a year under the chairmanship of its governor. By the end of 1993 both the Consultative Council and the regional councils had been inaugurated.

In September 1994 a demonstration was held in Buraidah in support of two arrested religious leaders who had been demanding the stricter enforcement of *Shari'a* (Islamic) law, leading to a number of further arrests. In October the King approved the creation of a Higher Council for Islamic Affairs, under the chairmanship of Prince Sultan ibn Abd al-Aziz, the Second Deputy Prime Minister and Minister of Defence and Civil Aviation, in what was widely interpreted as a measure to limit the influence of militant clerics and to diminish the authority of the powerful Council of Senior Ulama.

In 1995 an opposition activist, Abdullah Abd al-Rahman al-Hudhaif, was sentenced to 20 years' imprisonment for his part in an attack on a security officer and for maintaining links with the CDLR in London. He was later reported to have been executed. A further nine opposition activists were reported to have received prison sentences ranging from three to 18 years, and, according to the human rights organization Amnesty International, as many as 200 'political suspects' were in detention in the kingdom that year. The increase in the number of executions in Saudi Arabia during 1995—primarily for those convicted of drugs-smuggling or murder—provoked international criticism. Between January and October 1995 a total of 191 people received the death penalty, compared with 53 during the whole of 1994.

In 1995 King Fahd suffered a stroke which proved debilitating. Henceforth, he would be unable to fulfil his full official duties and many of these were assumed by his half-brother Crown Prince Abdullah. The King would increasingly leave the running of the country to him, although the Crown Prince's power remained restricted by the formal authority of the King and the power retained by Fahd's full brothers, Princes Sultan, Nayef and Salman.

DEVELOPMENTS IN FOREIGN RELATIONS, 1991–95

In mid-1992 there were signs of a rapprochement between Saudi Arabia and Jordan, as well as with the Palestine Liberation Organization (PLO). In January 1994 King Fahd met the leader of the PLO, Yasser Arafat, for the first time since the Gulf crisis and pledged US $100m. towards the reconstruction of the Gaza Strip and Jericho, the two sites for Palestinian interim self-rule agreed by Israel and the PLO in their 1993 Declaration of Principles (Documents on Palestine, see p. 76). In September 1994 Saudi Arabia, in common with the other GCC members, agreed to a partial removal of the economic boycott of Israel. In April 1995 Saudi Arabia became the first Arab country to recognize passports issued by the Palestinian (National) Authority (PA) for Palestinians in Gaza and Jericho. In June the Council of Ministers approved the import of goods made within the area controlled by the PA. In July Jordan's Minister of Foreign Affairs met his Saudi counterpart in Riyadh, the first high-level visit made by a Jordanian official since the Gulf crisis.

In September 1992 the Government sent a memorandum to the Government of Yemen in an attempt to expedite demarcation of the Saudi–Yemeni border, but progress was seriously impeded by the 1994 Yemeni civil war. The Saudi Government sympathized with the secessionists, and, following their defeat in July 1994, bilateral tensions increased; the two sides failed to renew the 1934 Ta'if agreement (renewable every 20 years), which delineated their de facto frontier. Following military clashes between the two sides, and intense mediation by Syria, a joint statement was issued in January 1995, in which Saudi Arabia and Yemen undertook to halt all military activity in the border area. The following month a memorandum of understanding between the two countries reaffirmed their commitment to the legitimacy of the Ta'if agreement and provided for the establishment of six joint committees to demarcate their land and sea borders and to develop economic and commercial ties. In March a joint Saudi-Yemeni military committee held its first meeting in Riyadh. In June President Saleh of Yemen visited the kingdom, accompanied by a high-ranking delegation. This was the first official Yemeni visit since February 1990.

At the end of September 1992 Qatar accused a Saudi military unit of attacking a border post at al-Khofous, killing two soldiers and capturing a third. In October Qatar suspended the 1965 border agreement with Saudi Arabia. However, in December 1992, following mediation by President Muhammad Hosni Mubarak of Egypt, the Qatari Amir, Sheikh Khalifa, signed an agreement with King Fahd to establish a committee that was to demarcate the border between the two states. Relations were further complicated by the 1995 coup in Qatar, during which Sheikh Hamad deposed his father, as Saudi Arabia took some time to recognize the change of premiership, and was subsequently suspected of supporting the former Amir. The new Amir's visit to King Fahd in August 1995 demonstrated an attempt to settle relations, but tension remained.

A significant breakthrough with Oman occurred when, in July 1995, officials from Saudi Arabia and Oman signed documents to demarcate their joint borders.

POLITICAL DEVELOPMENTS, 1995–2001

In November 1995 a car bomb exploded outside the offices of the Saudi Arabia National Guard in Riyadh (used temporarily by US civilian training personnel), killing seven foreign nationals. Responsibility was claimed by several organizations, including the Islamic Movement for Change, which earlier in the year had warned that it would initiate attacks if non-Muslim Western forces did not withdraw from the Gulf region. In April 1996 four Saudi nationals were charged with the attack and executed the following month; in their confessions they claimed to have been influenced by Islamist groups outside the kingdom.

In June 1996 19 US personnel were killed, and as many as 400 others—including 147 Saudi citizens—were injured, when an explosive device attached to a petroleum tanker was detonated outside a military housing complex in al-Khobar, near Dhahran. Saudi officials pledged increased security measures in the kingdom. Earlier in the year US officials had reportedly been critical of the Saudi authorities' investigation of the November 1995 attack, and of the swift execution of the alleged perpetrators. Some 40 Saudis were reported to have been arrested on suspicion of involvement in the 1996 bombing, but little information was forthcoming. US intelligence claimed evidence of Iranian involvement, possibly through Saudi Shi'a groups, although the Saudi Government consistently rejected those claims, declaring in 1998 that the perpetrators were Saudis acting independently.

Saudi-US relations had been placed under increasing strain as a result of the bomb attack and subsequent investigation. In June 1997 a Saudi citizen, Hani Abd al-Rahim al-Sayegh, was deported from Canada to the USA to face charges in connection with the June 1996 bombing. After initially determining that there was insufficient evidence to secure a conviction, in October 1999 the USA extradited him to Saudi Arabia, after the Saudi Arabian Minister of the Interior claimed to have further evidence. In January 2001 several Saudi nationals were arrested in connection with the bombing, and in June US investigators indicted 14 more individuals, although three of them were still at large in June 2002 when the Saudi authorities announced that sentences had been passed on a number of the detainees.

In June 2000 the Government announced the establishment of a new Council of the Royal Family, to be headed by Crown Prince Abdullah, appearing to reflect a view that more formal structures for consultation were required within a royal family that now included more than 6,000 princes. The new Council met for the first time in August. In the same month the Government continued its efforts to improve its human rights reputation by announcing that it would sign the UN Convention on the Elimination of All Forms of Discrimination against Women, although it would enter reservations regarding any section of the Convention that it deemed to violate *Shari'a* law. Some linked this announcement to the appointment of a Saudi woman, Thuraya Ahmad Obeid, to the post of Director of the UN Fund for Population Activities in October.

In September 2001 King Fahd appointed Prince Nawaf ibn Abd al-Aziz to replace Prince Turki al-Faisal ibn Abd al-Aziz as the head of the intelligence services. Prince Nawaf, known to be close to Crown Prince Abdullah, was seen as a transitional figure. There was speculation that the change was intended to head off controversy (not least in the USA) over Prince Turki's earlier contacts with the exiled Saudi-born dissident, Osama bin Laden, who was held responsible for the bombing of two US embassies in Africa in August 1998, and the Taliban—even though those links had formed part of a broader strategy to use them against the Soviet presence in Afghanistan and, subsequently, to contain them.

During 2001 a number of the younger members of the Saudi royal family, most notably Prince Talal ibn Abd al-Aziz, openly expressed support for the creation of an elected assembly in Saudi Arabia. Certainly, there was considerable Saudi interest in the democratic experiment under way in Bahrain during 2001 (see the chapter on Bahrain), but similar moves were not being considered seriously within the kingdom itself.

DEVELOPMENTS IN FOREIGN RELATIONS, 1995–2001

Normalization of relations was agreed between Saudi Arabia and Jordan in November 1995, and was consolidated by two meetings in Saudi Arabia the following year between King Hussein of Jordan and Crown Prince Abdullah.

Disagreement remained between Saudi Arabia and Yemen over the demarcation of their border. In December 1995 both sides denied that there had been further military clashes on the land border. In July 1996 they signed a border security agreement, but tensions persisted. In November 1997 armed clashes on the border resulted in the deaths of three Saudis and one Yemeni border guard. A Saudi memorandum to the UN stated that it did not recognize the 1992 border agreement between Yemen and Oman, and claimed parts of the area concerned as Saudi Arabian territory. A Yemeni memorandum to the Arab League rejected the claim. During June and July 1998 there were further clashes on land and around a group of disputed Red Sea islands. A joint military committee meeting was convened in early August, but made little progress.

Tension between Saudi Arabia and Qatar over the demarcation of their mutual border resurfaced in December 1995 when Qatar boycotted the closing session of the annual GCC summit. Nevertheless, in April 1996 Qatar and Saudi Arabia agreed to accelerate the completion of their border demarcation.

Relations with Iran, strained in early 1997 over allegations of Iranian involvement in the al-Khobar bombing, subsequently improved. In September Iran Air resumed flights to Saudi Arabia for the first time since the 1979 revolution. The installation of the new Government of President Khatami in Iran, in August 1997, facilitated further rapprochement; the new Iranian Minister of Foreign Affairs toured Saudi Arabia and other GCC states in November, and Crown Prince Abdullah attended the Conference of Heads of State of the OIC in Tehran in December. An Iranian delegation, led by former President Rafsanjani, began a 10-day visit to Saudi Arabia in February 1998. The formation of a joint ministerial committee for bilateral relations was announced at the end of the visit.

Saudi Arabia advocated a diplomatic solution to the heightening tension between the Iraqi authorities and weapons inspectors of the UN Special Commission (UNSCOM) in late 1999. Furthermore, when tension mounted again in late 1998, the kingdom asserted that it would not allow its territory to be used as a base for US-led air-strikes against Iraq, although it was widely believed that discreet support was given, including the use of its bases.

Relations with Afghanistan deteriorated during 1998, and in September Saudi Arabia withdrew its chargé d'affaires from that country and asked his Afghan counterpart to leave Saudi Arabia. This was widely attributed to the presence in Afghanistan of Osama bin Laden. Saudi Arabia had previously enjoyed good relations with Afghanistan, and was one of only three states to have recognized the Taliban Government. A Saudi request in October for bin Laden's extradition was denied.

In March 1999 Saudi Arabia held talks with Iran in an effort to mediate in its dispute with the United Arab Emirates (UAE) over the Tunb islands. Despite tensions between the GCC and Iran in that month, bilateral ties continued to improve, and in May the Iranian President made an official visit to Saudi Arabia—the first Iranian Head of State to do so since the revolution. During a visit to Tehran in April 2001 by the Saudi Minister of the Interior, Prince Nayef, a security agreement to combat crime, terrorism and drugs-trafficking was signed. The agreement pointedly excluded arrangements for extradition, despite US claims that Iran might have been involved in the 1996 al-Khobar bombing. Meanwhile, in October 2000, in a sign of an improvement in relations with Libya, Libyan leader Muammar al-Qaddafi made his first visit to Riyadh for 20 years, for 'consultations'.

As a result of Saudi Arabia's rapprochement with Iran, relations with the UAE deteriorated, and in March 1999 the UAE boycotted a meeting of GCC ministers responsible for petroleum production in protest against Saudi exploration of an oilfield in disputed territory prior to an agreement being reached. At the 21st GCC summit in December 2000 Saudi Arabia played a prominent role in its decision to increase the strength of the GCC's Rapid Defence Force (established in 1982) to 22,000.

During 2000 and into 2001 Saudi Arabia, allied with Kuwait, continued to oppose wider Arab initiatives to improve relations with Iraq. Saudi Arabia also supported the maintenance of full UN sanctions against Iraq. The Government did not condemn major US- and British-led air-strikes on Iraq in August 2000 and February 2001, and dismissed Iraqi appeals for an emergency summit meeting of Gulf states following the first wave of attacks. In June 2001 Saudi Arabia accused Iraq of launching 11 raids on Saudi border posts during the preceding months; Iraq denied the allegations.

The collapse of the Middle East peace process and the eruption of the al-Aqsa *intifada* from late September 2000 led to a more active Saudi role in wider Arab diplomatic initiatives. Saudi Arabia's priority was to support a unified Arab effort to revive the peace process while displaying solidarity with the Palestinians. While opposing appeals for all Arab states to terminate diplomatic relations with Israel, the kingdom started a fund-raising effort at home to assist the Palestinians. In November Saudi Arabia threatened to withdraw from a scheduled OIC summit in Qatar because the latter had refused to close the Israeli trade office in its capital, Doha. The threat was withdrawn following the formal closure of the office. At the March 2001 summit meeting of the Arab League in Amman, Jordan, Saudi Arabia joined with other states in agreeing to send emergency aid to the Palestinians and in condemning the USA's failure to support the dispatch of a UN-sponsored international observer force to Israel and the Palestinian territories. It also endorsed demands for senior Israeli public figures to face an international war crimes tribunal and for a feasibility study to be initiated regarding a revival of the Arab boycott of Israel.

In 2001 the Government urged the new US Administration of President George W. Bush to become more engaged in the peace process, and supported the recommendations of the Mitchell Report on the causes of the violence between Israel and the Palestinians. Saudi displeasure at US disengagement was demonstrated by the refusal of Crown Prince Abdullah to accept invitations to visit Washington, DC, for a meeting with President Bush. Tensions were exacerbated in June when the US authorities issued indictments against 13 Saudi nationals and one Lebanese national for complicity in the 1996 al-Khobar bombing. The Saudi authorities complained of lack of consultation and insisted that any trials should take place in Saudi Arabia.

DOMESTIC DEVELOPMENTS AFTER 11 SEPTEMBER 2001

Following the attacks on New York and Washington, DC, on 11 September 2001, in which up to 15 Saudi nationals were implicated, the authorities declared their determination to identify and apprehend sympathizers of Osama bin Laden (whose al-Qa'ida network was held by the USA to be principally responsible for the attacks) within Saudi Arabia and subsequently took action to freeze their financial assets. More than 40 Saudi nationals were detained in the USA following the attacks, including two members of the royal family, although they were subsequently released. Relations between the USA and Saudi Arabia were fraught with mutual recriminations, especially at the level of Congress and the media, although both President Bush and the Saudi Government attempted publicly to contain the damage. Nevertheless, a combination of Saudi irritation over the US approach and concern on both sides over potential hostile reactions to the visible presence of US troops in Saudi Arabia led to a scaling back of the overt use of Saudi bases. No missions were flown from US bases in Saudi Arabia during the US-led military campaign against the Taliban regime in Afghanistan, which began in October, although command-and-control facilities at Prince Sultan airbase were used. Dissident clerics within Saudi Arabia issued *fatwas* (religious edicts) threatening the excommunication of the royal family should it support the US-led offensive. In December the authorities requested that Saudi nationals detained by US military personnel following the overthrow of the Taliban regime (some of whom were subsequently transferred with other foreign nationals to the US military base at Guantánamo Bay, Cuba) be repatriated for trial. These requests were denied, but in June 2002 a Saudi delegation of interior and foreign ministry officials was allowed access to the Saudi prisoners (thought to number more than 100). In January 2002 it was announced that the Saudi Arabian Monetary Agency had been charged with drafting legislation to combat the laundering of illicit funds through the banking system. Prince Turki al-Faisal admitted that, in the past, the kingdom had been naïve in the way it had inadvertently allowed money collected in mosques for ostensibly charitable causes to be channelled to groups with terrorist links. Accordingly, from May 2003 the kingdom banned cash donations by worshippers in mosques and demanded that any future alms-giving be made by cheque, thereby allowing a money trail to be established and supervised.

In February 2003 the Saudi authorities announced that at least 90 nationals had been charged with having links to al-Qa'ida and would stand trial. A further 250 nationals were detained and under investigation.

The US-led attack on Iraq that began in March 2003 had significant consequences in Saudi Arabia, including an increase in anti-US feeling. In early May at least 19 suspected members of al-Qa'ida, 17 of whom were Saudis, were arrested in Riyadh in connection with an alleged plot to assassinate members of the royal family, including Prince Nayef and Prince Sultan. On 12 May Saudi Arabia was rocked by a series of co-ordinated suicide attacks on four residential housing compounds occupied by Western expatriates in Riyadh. Nine militants shot their way into the compounds before detonating their bombs. The death toll ultimately reached 34, including eight US nationals. The attackers appeared to be supporters of al-Qa'ida. The USA withdrew most of its diplomats from the country and criticized the Saudi authorities for failing adequately to respond to the threat of terrorism within Saudi Arabia. The Saudi leadership acknowledged the severity of the threat and pledged to take effective action against al-Qa'ida. However, the continuing difficulties faced by reformist elements within the Saudi royal family were demonstrated later in the month when pressure from conservative clerics led to the dismissal of Jamal Khashoggi, editor of *Al-Watan*, the kingdom's most liberal daily newspaper, which had campaigned strongly against religious extremism (he was subsequently appointed as Prince Turki al-Faisal's adviser).

In June 2003 the Saudi security services announced that 11 Saudis, one Iraqi national and one Sudanese national (all believed to be members of al-Qa'ida) had been arrested following an unsuccessful missile attack on the Prince Sultan airbase in May.

In August 2003 Crown Prince Abdullah announced that the kingdom was engaged in a 'decisive battle' against terrorism; throughout mid-2003 security forces intensified their campaign against militants. In June five suspected Islamist militants were killed in Mecca and seven others arrested; six were killed in the Qasim region later that month. Also in June some 1,000 Muslim clerics were suspended and ordered to undergo retraining aimed at eliminating Islamist militancy from the profession. On 1 July the Minister of the Interior announced that 124 people—some with alleged links to al-Qa'ida—had been arrested, including the supposed mastermind of the May attacks, Ali Abd al-Rahman al-Faqasi al-Ghamdi; 16 further al-Qa'ida suspects were arrested later in July. Three militants were killed in September, among them one suspected of the Riyadh bombings, who had also been linked by the US Federal Bureau of Investigation to threats of terrorism made against the USA.

By the end of 2003 some 200 Islamist militants with suspected links to al-Qa'ida had been arrested by the Saudi authorities, while a further 12 had been killed. Yet from late 2003 to mid-2004 militants engaged in a series of bloody attacks on individuals and targets associated with Saudi Arabia's oil and commercial infrastructure. In November 2003 an explosion at a residential compound in Riyadh killed 18 people, many of them Muslims, and shocked many throughout the kingdom and the wider Arab world. In April 2004 a suicide bombing by a shadowy Islamist group—the al-Haramain Brigade—on a Saudi security building in Riyadh left four people dead and a further 150 injured. In May gunmen in the Red Sea port of Yanbu killed one Saudi and five Western oil industry workers. On 29 May militants attacked two locations at al-Khobar. The attacks began at the headquarters of the Arab Petroleum Investments Corpn, where fatalities included a British senior executive. The militants then attacked the Oasis Compound, a housing complex for expatriate workers, taking more than 50 hostages, many of whom were killed. Despite an attempt by Saudi special forces to storm the compound three of the attackers managed to escape. Allegations that the militants had struck a deal with police officers sympathetic to al-Qa'ida were angrily denied by the authorities. While 200 people were eventually evacuated, the events resulted in the deaths of three Saudis and up to 19 expatriate workers.

In the 13 months up to the end of June 2004, more than 80 people were killed in terrorist-related incidents, of whom over 50 were foreign nationals. In April of that year the US State Department urged some 35,000 US citizens resident in Saudi Arabia to leave the kingdom. Realizing its dependence on expatriate labour to help maintain its oil infrastructure, as well as the need to convince sceptical allies of its commitment to fighting terrorism, Saudi Arabia made very visible efforts to find the perpetrators of these attacks. Soon after the al-Khobar attack, Abd al-Rahman Muhammad Yazji, one of the kingdom's most wanted militants, was killed by security forces near Mecca. At the same time on 23 June Crown Prince Abdullah announced that a dozen named individuals with alleged ties to al-Qa'ida would not face the death penalty if they surrendered to the security forces within one month. The Saudi authorities proved particularly keen to obtain the surrender of Saleh Muhammad al-Oufi, regarded by the Saudi intelligence services as the overall leader of al-Qa'ida in the kingdom following the death of Abd al-Aziz al-Muqrin in a police raid on 18 June. The death on 30 June of Sheikh Abdullah Muhammad Rashid Rushoud, regarded by many as the spiritual guide to al-Qa'ida in the kingdom, was seen as a serious blow to militants throughout Saudi Arabia.

In August 2004 one of the kingdom's most wanted al-Qa'ida militants, Faris al-Zahrani, was captured by the security forces in the southern city of Abha. By 2005 the main threat of the domestic al-Qa'ida in the Arabian Peninsula (AQAP) appeared to be contained, as a result not only of the security forces' successes but also of AQAP overreaching itself and of the Government's success in co-opting some of the militants while undermining their religious justifications. The result was that violent jihadists within the country lost popular support among Saudis themselves.

Even so, al-Qa'ida-inspired militants still possessed some ability to stage violent attacks in the kingdom. On 6 December 2004 Saudi insurgents attacked the US consulate in Jeddah, killing 12 people, although no US fatalities were incurred. This was followed by twin suicide bomb attacks against the Ministry of the Interior on 29 December—without casualties. In January 2005 it was announced that the head of the Saudi intelligence services, Prince Nawaf ibn Abd al-Aziz, had resigned on health grounds. In October, following Crown Prince Abdullah's accession to the throne in August (see Domestic Politics under

King Abdullah), Prince Muqrin ibn Abd al-Aziz was appointed as the new Director of General Intelligence. In an apparent attempt to strengthen the country's national security framework, newly crowned King Abdullah in the same month announced the formation of a National Security Council, including the Ministers of Defence, of the Interior and of Foreign Affairs, and with Prince Bandar ibn Sultan—until then the Saudi ambassador in Washington, DC—appointed as Secretary-General. Occasional attacks continued, but the authorities clearly now had the upper hand—illustrated in the killing of the reputed leader of al-Qa'ida in Saudi Arabia, Fahd Faraj al-Juweir, in February 2006.

Amid the changing environment brought about both by the 11 September 2001 attacks and by the upsurge of violence within the kingdom—and the associated conflicting demands for change from liberal and Islamist reformers and from the Government itself—other signs of reform were also in evidence. In March 2002 at least 14 schoolgirls died in a fire in Mecca after members of the religious police stopped them from fleeing a blazing school building because they were improperly dressed. The case provoked unprecedented criticism of the religious police in the Saudi media, and the department responsible for female education (whose Director was dismissed) was subsequently merged with the Ministry of Education. Official control over the national media was somewhat loosened during 2002.

In January 2003 the Consultative Council rejected a bill proposing to levy an income tax on foreigners working in Saudi Arabia. This represented an unprecedented show of independence and emboldened some members of the Council to call for increased powers. In the same month, a group of intellectuals gathered a wide coalition of 104 signatories for a respectful petition for constitutional reform, which was sent to the Crown Prince (who had earlier appealed for Arab governments to agree a new 'covenant' based on an agenda for political and economic reform) and other royals. A delegation was received by the Crown Prince in a friendly meeting, but the delay in actual reform following this meeting precipitated the issuing of a new petition in December, this time including a larger proportion of Islamists. It linked the recent violence with the presence of the USA and the absence of political participation, and demanded a timetable for constitutionalization. However, on this occasion the proposals found a less amicable reception; Minister of the Interior Prince Nayef stressed that continued demands for a constitutional monarchy would not be tolerated. In October the Crown Prince had overseen the establishment of a human rights association, but its members were hand-picked by the Government and its impact on the human rights situation had proved limited. When several campaigners then established their own human rights organization in March 2004, 12 of them were promptly arrested. While most were released after they undertook not to continue agitating, three were sentenced to several years' imprisonment in May 2005.

This was regarded as evidence that Crown Prince Abdullah's reformist inclinations remained constrained by others in the royal family. Such feeling persisted until his accession upon the death of King Fahd on 1 August 2005, after which the three detained intellectuals were promptly released. Meanwhile, the Crown Prince did press ahead with a number of initiatives. In particular, he championed the foundation of the National Dialogue Forum, designed to encourage debate concerning Saudi society, which would bring together representatives of sections of society that had not previously enjoyed such a forum for expression. Most particularly, younger people, women and Shi'a religious leaders would have freedom to become involved in the forum, a development that clashed with the views of many more conservative sections of the population and the *ulama*. The National Dialogue Forum's first session was held in June 2003, and a National Dialogue Centre was also subsequently established.

In 2004 elections were announced for one-half of the nearly 12,000 seats in the 178 municipal councils throughout the kingdom (the remaining seats were to be appointed). They were held over three rounds between 10 February and 21 April 2005. Women were denied participation on 'logistical' grounds, a decision regarded as a concession to conservatives. No group platforms or political parties were allowed, and it was clear that the councils would not have any real power over local issues. The best organized proved to be the moderately Islamist candidates: they scored a clear victory, overall, over those candidates who ran on a liberal political platform or espoused tribal values. Many of these Islamist candidates were known as the 'Golden List', since they had been approved by the kingdom's clerics in advance. There was also a sectarian cast to the results, particularly in the Eastern region. The councils were finally formed on 15 December 2005; since then they have not gained real power, effectiveness or respect.

In April 2005 the Consultative Council was sworn in with an expanded membership of 150. In the same month a major reform of the much-criticized judicial system was announced, involving the intended establishment of a Supreme Court and a network of appeal courts, commercial courts and labour courts.

FOREIGN RELATIONS AFTER 11 SEPTEMBER 2001

Under evident pressure from the USA, Saudi Arabia severed diplomatic relations with the Taliban regime in Afghanistan in late September 2001, in response to the attacks on New York and Washington, DC. The Saudi authorities emphasized that Osama bin Laden had long since been stripped of his Saudi citizenship. Crown Prince Abdullah visited Washington, DC, shortly after the attacks to express Saudi support for efforts to eliminate terrorism. However, Saudi Arabia warned against any 'vengeful' response to the atrocities, and attempted to influence the USA to avoid any action through its 'war on terror' that might lead to an escalation of the conflict between Israel and the Palestinians. When the US-led coalition embarked on a military intervention to overthrow the Taliban regime in Afghanistan in October, the Saudi authorities accepted the legitimacy of military action, but opposed the bombing of civilians, urging Osama bin Laden and the Taliban leader, Mullah Omar, to surrender and stand trial.

During October and November 2001 Saudi Arabia was the subject of considerable criticism in the US media for its alleged complicity in the emergence of global Islamist terror networks, but the ruling family vigorously defended the country's reputation and urged the US authorities to play a more active role in the resolution of the Israeli–Palestinian conflict. Media representations of Saudi Arabia were gradually modified as the US Administration sought to ensure that its 'war on terror' was not interpreted as a war on Islam. Yet relations came under renewed strain in August 2002 after a group representing 900 relatives of victims of the September 2001 attacks filed a civil suit in Washington, DC, against senior Saudi ministers and institutions (and the Government of Sudan) seeking compensation for their alleged funding of al-Qa'ida activities. Saudi investors reacted angrily to the suit, threatening in response to withdraw from the USA some US $750,000m. in Saudi investments. Substantial disinvestment had already occurred following the attacks of 11 September 2001 in order to avoid assets being frozen.

The Saudi Government welcomed President Bush's announcement in November 2001 that the USA supported the creation of a Palestinian state and would be launching a new diplomatic initiative to end the violence between Israelis and Palestinians. While continuing to play an active role in support of a revived Arab economic boycott of Israel, in February 2002 Crown Prince Abdullah put forward an outline proposal in which Arab relations with Israel would be fully 'normalized' in exchange for the creation of a Palestinian state based on pre-1967 borders: Israel was, for the first time, being offered full *de jure* and de facto recognition by the Arab world. The USA and European countries, as well as the Palestinian leadership, welcomed the proposal, and Israel's response was cautiously positive. In order to secure the agreement of Lebanon and Syria, Crown Prince Abdullah agreed to a reformulation whereby 'normal relations' would follow a 'comprehensive peace', explicitly involving Israeli withdrawal from the Golan Heights and Shebaa Farms; reference to a 'just solution' to the Palestinian right of return in accordance with UN General Assembly Resolution 194 was also added. The plan received UN support on 12 March 2002 in Security Council Resolution 1397, in which the Security Council explicitly endorsed the creation of a Palestinian state for the first time. The plan was unanimously approved by an Arab summit in Beirut, Lebanon, on 28 March.

The summit also opposed further allied military action against Iraq and saw Crown Prince Abdullah and the Vice-President of Iraq's Revolutionary Command Council, Izzat Ibrahim, publicly embrace. Abdullah expressed Saudi Arabia's opposition to the maintenance of UN sanctions against Iraq and reiterated its refusal to allow the use of US military bases for allied air-strikes against Iraq.

However, the Israeli military intervention in the West Bank from March 2002, and reports circulated by both the Israeli and US Governments detailing alleged Saudi financial support for Hamas and Islamic Jihad undermined the kingdom's diplomatic effort. On the other hand, the Saudi Government was increasingly critical of the suicide attacks, and, during a meeting between Crown Prince Abdullah and Presidents Mubarak of Egypt and Bashar al-Assad of Syria in Egypt in May, the participants rejected 'all forms of violence'. Still, there was little sign of concerted activity by the follow-up committee established at the Beirut summit. Saudi Arabia welcomed President Bush's acceptance of the principle of Palestinian statehood in his speech on the Middle East peace process in June, but criticized the US President's insistence on prior reform of Palestinian institutions and his effective repudiation of Yasser Arafat as a negotiating partner. Over the following months the USA continued to consult Saudi Arabia while developing its own peace plan in tandem with its main partners—the European Union, the UN and Russia (together known as the Quartet). Saudi Arabia became involved in Egyptian-led efforts to arrange talks between Palestinian factions during late 2002 in pursuit of a moratorium on attacks against civilians in Israel. Saudi Arabia was also represented at the January 2003 British-organized conference on Palestinian reform.

By late 2002 the growing crisis over Iraq was taking priority. In June it was reported that the Saudi authorities were considering the negotiation of a free trade agreement with Iraq. In September, following intense pressure from the US and British Governments, the Saudi Minister of Foreign Affairs suggested that the Saudi authorities might be prepared to approve the use of military bases in Saudi Arabia for a future US-led attack on Iraq, if the Iraqi authorities continued to reject UN resolutions demanding the unconditional return of UNSCOM weapons inspectors to Iraq, and if such a military undertaking were conducted under UN auspices. However, following the decision of Iraq to readmit UNSCOM inspectors in the same month, Saudi Arabia's position appeared to shift back again. Amid uncertainty over whether US military bases in Saudi Arabia would be available in the event of military action, the USA began upgrading its military facilities in Qatar from November 2002. In March 2003 Saudi Arabia joined other Arab states at the Arab League summit in Doha, Qatar, in agreeing that it would not participate in a US-led war against Saddam Hussain's regime in Iraq, arguing that the weapons inspectors needed more time to complete their work.

However, once hostilities commenced it was clear that Saudi Arabia had agreed to allow the USA and its allies the right to use the kingdom's airspace. Even so, the Saudi Minister of Foreign Affairs appealed for an immediate end to the fighting. On 30 April 2003, within days of the fall of Baghdad, US Secretary for Defense Donald Rumsfeld visited Riyadh to make a joint announcement with the Saudi authorities that all but 400 of the 5,000 US military personnel in Saudi Arabia were to be withdrawn by mid-2003. Those troops that remained would be based near Riyadh and would assist in training the Saudi military. Prince Sultan airbase was to be abandoned by US forces. This appeared to have been a mutually agreed move, arising from an awareness of the legitimacy questions the US presence posed for the Saudi regime.

The complications arising from the insurgency in Iraq—which involved significant numbers of Saudi nationals—and the aftermath of the Afghanistan operation, together with the associated detention of 124 Saudi nationals at the US military facility at Guantánamo Bay, further added to friction with the USA. Minister of Foreign Affairs Prince Sa'ud al-Faisal asserted that Riyadh was doing everything possible to secure the release of the Saudi detainees. In June 2004, during a visit to Turkey, the US President declared that his Administration would no longer condone regimes in the Middle East where 'stability was purchased at the price of liberty'. Nevertheless, Saudi Arabia and the USA remained keen to safeguard bilateral ties. In July, during a visit by US Secretary of State Colin Powell, Crown Prince Abdullah raised the possibility of Saudi Arabia taking a lead role in the formation of a Muslim security force for Iraq, to help the Iraqi people 'reclaim their sovereignty as quickly as possible'. During the same month Saudi Arabia and Iraq announced the restoration of diplomatic relations and expressed their intention to reopen their embassies in their respective capitals for the first time since 1990. (In fact, the Iraqi embassy in Riyadh would eventually reopen only in February 2007, while the Saudi embassy in Baghdad, despite ongoing discussions, remained closed as of late 2013.) The conflict in Iraq continued to be a source of concern for Saudi officials as many young Saudi men aspired to fight US-led coalition forces there. Saudi officials and liberals alike worried about the radicalizing effect of the Iraq imbroglio, and the consequences of such young men returning home.

In February 2005 Riyadh hosted an international conference aiming to establish a global centre for the study of counter-terrorism. Notwithstanding British and US scepticism, over 50 participating states announced the establishment of a 'task force', aiming to promote 'inter-agency co-operation and co-ordination on national, bilateral and regional levels to combat terrorism, money-laundering, weapons and explosives trafficking and drugs-smuggling'.

Other aspects of regional relations were pursued at the GCC summit in Muscat, Oman, in December 2001, with Saudi Arabia instrumental in concluding agreements to establish a Supreme Joint Defence Council and to work to achieve a single GCC currency by 2010. Crown Prince Abdullah acknowledged that the GCC had failed to fulfil expectations since its creation in 1981. At the December 2002 summit, Saudi Arabia supported a resolution appealing for a peaceful resolution to the crisis over Iraq, and Crown Prince Abdullah pledged to present his proposals to the Arab League summit in Doha in March 2003. However, the proposals were overshadowed at that summit by a major argument between Crown Prince Abdullah and Libyan leader Muammar al-Qaddafi, in which the latter accused King Fahd of being an agent of the USA. Relations deteriorated further when, in July 2004, allegations were made in the Saudi-owned pan-Arab daily *Asharq al-Awsat* concerning a Libyan plot to assassinate Crown Prince Abdullah. Saudi Arabia expelled the Libyan ambassador in December.

Friction within the GCC also re-emerged, on this occasion owing to the interconnection of trade policy with changes in US-Saudi relations effecting an apparently increasing reluctance on the part of the smaller GCC states to defer to Saudi leadership. Following the formal announcement of a GCC customs union from January 2003—a long-pursued milestone in GCC integration—actual implementation proceeded slowly and partially, as expected. Bahrain's decision to sign a bilateral free trade agreement with the USA in 2004 seemed to contradict the very concept of the customs union and the common external tariff that accompanied it. Saudi Arabia expressed its irritation and condemned bilateral deals as incompatible with the customs union. Crown Prince Abdullah refused to attend the 2004 GCC summit in December, and the Saudi oil subsidy to Bahrain appeared to have been reduced from 150,000 barrels per day (b/d) to 100,000 b/d in 2005. The USA actively pursued further bilateral deals with the other GCC states and, to Saudi Arabia's annoyance, found most of them willing to follow Bahrain's example. While Saudi Arabia from 2006 tried to adapt to this new reality, resentment clearly remained.

Meanwhile, relations between Saudi Arabia and Iran, which had improved considerably since 1997, were initially further strengthened following the 11 September 2001 terrorist attacks on New York and Washington, DC. It was only with the election of President Ahmadinejad in June 2005 that the situation between the two countries would again take a turn for the worse.

DOMESTIC POLITICS UNDER KING ABDULLAH

King Fahd's death was announced on 1 August 2005; he was succeeded by his half-brother, Crown Prince Abdullah, then aged 81. Prince Sultan ibn Abd al-Aziz Al Sa'ud, a full brother of King Fahd and then aged 77, was named the new Crown Prince and Deputy Prime Minister. King Abdullah assumed the role of Prime Minister. However, no replacement was named for the position of Second Deputy Prime Minister—which had in practice become synonymous with being next in line as Crown Prince. While this led to speculation that the succession might skip a generation, it remained most likely that the next in line after Sultan would be one of his full brothers—in particular, Minister of the Interior Prince Nayef (aged 71 in 2005), and the Governor of Riyadh, Prince Salman (68 that year).

In October 2006 King Abdullah announced that, upon the succession of Crown Prince Sultan as King, a new system would take effect to select future Kings and Crown Princes. A committee, to be called the Allegiance Institution, would be composed of sons and grandsons of King Abd al-Aziz, and chaired by the King's eldest son or grandson. The Basic Law of Government would be amended to that effect. Until this time, the King, at least formally, had the full prerogative to select the Crown Prince. Under the new system, the Allegiance Institution would have a say in the appointment of a Crown Prince suggested by the King. If the institution rejected the nominated Crown Prince, it would then vote for one of three princes nominated by the King. Under the new system, a new Crown Prince should be appointed within 30 days of the accession of a new King. Should neither the King nor the Crown Prince be considered fit to rule the country, five members of the institution would form a Transitory Ruling Council, which would assume responsibility for state affairs for a maximum period of one week. The Transitory Ruling Council would not enjoy prerogatives affecting state institutions, such as the power to dissolve the Government or the Consultative Council, and would not be able to amend the Basic Law of Government.

The appointment of Nayef in March 2009 as Second Deputy Prime Minister did not definitively end the uncertainty over the succession. Within the kingdom, some saw the appointment simply as a management decision to ensure continuity in government while Crown Prince Sultan was undergoing extended medical treatment abroad. Others assumed that it did in effect mean that Nayef would become the next Crown Prince.

What did become clear in the aftermath of the succession, was that King Abdullah was now somewhat less constrained in his pursuit of cautious reform. In education, the curriculum was checked for aspects that could inspire extremism and xenophobia. By May 2006 a major operation was under way to remove extremist books from libraries, and new school textbooks, promoting what was described in the Saudi press as a more moderate form of Islam, were introduced in 2008. The sixth session of the National Dialogue Forum in November 2006 focused on education and the need for reform. The King's convening of a major Islamic Dialogue Conference in Mecca in June 2008, and his co-hosting of an inter-faith conference with King Juan Carlos I of Spain in the following month, were further important indications in this direction—addressing directly the need to reduce Shi'a–Sunni tensions and to improve relations with non-Muslims, and doing so in the face of anti-Shi'a statements by several Saudi clerics.

In 2005 the Government authorized partial elections for the boards of regional chambers of commerce. Significantly, women were able to vote in all of these and to stand for election in Jeddah and the Eastern region (two women were voted onto the board of the Jeddah Chamber of Commerce). In December the one female candidate (among 72) in the first elections for the board of the Saudi National Agency for Engineers was elected. In the same month the Government established the Saudi Human Rights Agency; while as a government body this was probably the least significant of these developments, its official role of spreading awareness of human rights issues nevertheless illustrated the tentative shifts taking place under King Abdullah.

A further indication of this trend was the approval in May 2007 of new laws regarding the judiciary and the grievances courts, following the announcement in 2005 of a far-reaching reform of the judicial system. The new Judiciary Law called for the establishment of appeal courts, criminal courts and specialized courts. A Supreme Court was to be established in Riyadh and new appeals courts were planned for each of the kingdom's 13 regions. There were to be general courts to deal with all conflicts except labour, commercial and family disputes, and criminal courts to address crimes. Family and personal conflicts were to be handled by civil courts. The first signs of these changes being implemented appeared in 2008.

Expressions of reformist demands continued, including over the role of the religious police (the *Mutawwa'in*, under the control of the Committee for the Promotion of Virtue and Prevention of Vice), some of whose personnel were defendants in a court case from May 2007—the first of its kind—brought by a woman in a civil court over alleged excessive and unlawful behaviour. In July the religious police were formally stripped of their ability to detain people, in an order that included an explicit ban on extracting confessions and inspections of police offices to ensure that no one was being detained there.

Meanwhile, some prominent reformist critics remained banned from travel. Even so, the publication of an extensive report by the National Society for Human Rights in May 2007 was a significant event, lauded by some in the kingdom as representing a major shift in attitudes. The report, delivered to the Consultative Council, sketched the extent of a wide range of human rights problems, including domestic violence and violations of the rights of women, prisoners and workers, as well as injustices in law courts, discrimination against non-Saudis and forced confessions by detainees held by the religious police. In June the religious police announced a review following the criticisms. In a striking development, in May 2007 Prince Sultan announced plans to allocate one-third of government jobs to female candidates and to create additional job opportunities for women in other areas, although as of 2013 it remained unclear how this would be implemented.

In April 2007 the Ministry of the Interior announced that at least 172 suspected militants had been detained in various parts of the kingdom and seven armed militant cells dismantled. This was followed by the introduction of new regulations curbing the sale of industrial and agricultural chemicals that could be used to make explosives. In June Minister of the Interior Prince Nayef advised the country's clerics that they should discourage Saudis from going to fight in Iraq.

In November 2007 some 1,500 detainees were released after a re-education or de-radicalization programme, but the Saudi authorities arrested several hundred more suspected militants in 2008 and 2009. In October 2008 Prince Nayef announced that some 991 suspects had been charged, but several hundred remained in detention, suspected of links to al-Qa'ida. In July 2009 it was reported that 330 of the accused had been convicted on terrorism charges. In a high-profile report in August 2009, Human Rights Watch criticized the judicial process and treatment of these detainees. The trials of those convicted had been secret, summary and without normal access to legal counsel. Human Rights Watch criticized the very re-education programmes for which the Saudi authorities had been receiving praise in other quarters, as an inappropriate substitute for a proper judicial process and running counter to international human rights law. While concerns over the judicial and prison system, and over observance of human rights, remained very much alive both inside and outside the kingdom, this did not amount to serious opposition to the Government's overall strategy for containing Islamist violence.

On 27 August 2009 an attempt by a suicide bomber to assassinate Prince Muhammad ibn Nayef, in effect the head of the country's counter-terrorism effort and son of Minister of the Interior Prince Nayef, appeared to indicate a new focus on targeting the royal family directly. Although the Prince suffered only minor injuries, the episode focused minds even further on the nature of the threat, and the seemingly growing ability of AQAP to penetrate the kingdom's security—not least from across the porous border with Yemen, which was increasingly regarded as a haven for Saudi militants. The attacker was identified as a wanted terrorism suspect who had been based in Yemen, and who had apparently indicated that he wished to give himself up to Prince Muhammad. In March 2010 a further 133 militants said to have been acting on AQAP instructions from Yemen were arrested.

Meanwhile, more signs that the tentative reform process was genuine appeared in February 2009, when a number of changes in key positions in the Government and the legal system were announced. The Supreme Judicial Council's Chairman, Sheikh Salih ibn Muhammad al-Luhaidan, regarded by some as an obstacle to King Abdullah's judicial reform plans, was replaced by Dr Salih ibn Humayd, hitherto Chairman of the Consultative Council. The head of the Commission for the Promotion of Virtue and Prevention of Vice, Sheikh Ibrahim al-Ghaith, associated with the religious police's aggressive conduct, was replaced by Sheikh Abd al-Aziz al-Humayun, who immediately stressed the principle that 'a person is innocent until proven guilty'. The Council of Senior Ulama was expanded, introducing representatives of all four main Sunni legal schools (as opposed to the previous virtual monopoly of the Hanbali school)—although still leaving the Isma'ili and Shi'a schools unrepresented. Sheikh Abd al-Rahman ibn Abd al-Aziz al-Kolaya was appointed Chairman of the Supreme Court, while Muhammad ibn Fahd al-Dosari became President of the new Supreme Administrative Court.

Equally striking were the changes at the Ministry of Education. Not only did this bring the appointment of the first female minister, Noura bint Abdullah al-Fayez, as Deputy Minister for Girls' Education, but also that of Prince Faisal ibn Abdullah ibn Muhammad Al Sa'ud, the husband of King Abdullah's daughter Princess Adila and hitherto the deputy head of the General Intelligence Directorate, as the new Minister of Education.

The Minister of Labour, Dr Ghazi al-Gosaibi, confirmed in a media statement following this programme of changes in February 2009 that they reflected King Abdullah's intention to accelerate his intended reforms. This impression was reinforced when King Abdullah decided on a controversial project to codify the *Shari'a*, which was approved by the Council of Senior Ulama in April 2010. Also in the area of justice, a little-noted but important development was the approval of the new position of Public Defender in January, a measure intended to ensure proper access to defence.

On the political level, the appointment (to replace his father) in November 2009 of Prince Mansour ibn Mutaib ibn Abd al-Aziz Al Sa'ud, who had been prominent in guiding the process of the 2005 municipal elections and was seen as a reformist, as Minister of Municipal and Rural Affairs was interpreted by many observers as a further sign of Abdullah's intentions. Another unexpected development was a decree issued by King Abdullah in August 2010, which stipulated that henceforth only members of the Council of Senior Ulama would be permitted to issue formal *fatwas*, in an attempt to staunch an increasing flow of such edicts from other imams and religious scholars.

However, none of this meant that reform proceeded across the board, or that tensions and debates disappeared. In a flare-up of long-simmering tensions only weeks after the government reorganization in February, clashes between Shi'a protesters and the *Mutawwa'in* broke out in Medina over the issue of Shi'a visits to Baqi cemetery (on the anniversary of the Prophet Muhammad's death). Subsequent demonstrations in the Eastern region also led to clashes and arrests during February–March. These events triggered a report by Human Rights Watch in September, criticizing the overall treatment of the country's Shi'a population as 'systematic discrimination'. However, even this report recognized that under King Abdullah some positive gestures had been made, including the formation of the National Dialogue framework and a royal decree in March ordering the release of all those detained in the disturbances.

In March 2009 King Abdullah appointed his son Prince Mish'al as Governor of the southern region of Najran. Under the previous Governor, the region's mainly Isma'ili population had become increasingly restive over economic and religious discrimination. However, this contrasted with the treatment of the Shi'a in the Eastern region, where the Shi'a mosque in al-Khobar was seized in a heavy-handed operation in September.

FOREIGN RELATIONS UNDER KING ABDULLAH, 2005–10

Together with the deteriorating situation in neighbouring Iraq, Iran became a renewed source of concern in the wake of the election of Iranian President Mahmoud Ahmadinejad in June 2005, less than two months before Abdullah's formal accession to the throne. The election raised growing Saudi worries about Iran's regional and international posture, as well as about its nuclear programme. While Iranian officials continued to assert the programme's peaceful nature, 2005 and 2006 saw increasing expressions of concern among Saudi officials and commentators on three grounds: fears that even the suspicion of an Iranian nuclear weapons capability, regardless of the reality, would cause regional instability; fears of an armed US or Israeli response; and fears of the potential environmental dangers for the Arab side of the Gulf of even a peaceful nuclear programme. Saudi Arabia continued to oppose any suggestions of US military action and advocated continued diplomatic efforts to persuade Iran away from the pursuit of a military nuclear programme. Although from 2005 Saudi leaders and opinion-makers increasingly showed their irritation with Iran's attitude, the policy élite remained unsure about how best to address the problem; however, the option of US military action was, if anything, feared even more.

In this, as in a range of other issues, managing relations with the USA remained even more of a balancing act for Abdullah than for his predecessors. By the same token, the new King was seen by many as better equipped than Fahd had been to balance Saudi interests and the need to avoid being seen as subservient with the need to maintain the still crucial link with the USA.

Meanwhile, the country's long-standing ambition of gaining accession to the World Trade Organization was achieved after an agreement was finally reached with the USA in September 2005, leading to formal accession on 12 December. The House of Sa'ud also sought to shore up its ties with the US Administration. Crown Prince Abdullah enjoyed a warm welcome when he visited President Bush on his Texas ranch in May 2005, while the Bush Administration refused to pass comment on the reform process within Saudi Arabia. Nevertheless, Saudi Arabia felt itself targeted by President Bush's appeal in February 2006 for a sharp reduction in dependence on Middle East oil. Saudi officials, including Prince Turki al-Faisal who had moved from London to Washington, DC, as the kingdom's ambassador to the USA, expressed their surprise and strove to restrict the damage this statement might cause to relations.

Relations with the USA underwent a further test in July–August 2006, following Israel's sustained attack on Lebanon—wreaking huge destruction on the country's infrastructure and killing over 1,000 people, mainly civilians—ostensibly in response to the kidnapping of two Israeli soldiers by the Shi'a Hezbollah movement and the killing of several others. This followed extensive attacks on Gaza and the Islamist Hamas administration that had been elected there. Saudi Arabia, as a leading player in both the Muslim and Arab worlds, and with its claim to legitimacy resting in part on its protection of Muslim interests, could not afford to be seen as condoning the apparently unconditional support that Israel's actions had received from the USA, still a key Saudi ally. King Abdullah forcefully condemned Israel's actions, and Saudi Arabia implored the international community to act. At the same time, there was an ambivalence both in Saudi society and among the leadership: Hezbollah was a Shi'a group supported actively by Iran; for the Al Sa'ud this had implications of wider Shi'a agitation in the region—not least in response to events in Iraq—which might impact on the country's own Shi'a population. They also felt that Hezbollah had unnecessarily provided Israel with an excuse. In the Government's initial comments, disquiet over Israel's actions was mixed with concern about Hezbollah's motives. However, it soon became apparent that, as elsewhere in the Arab world, misgivings about the Shi'a were temporarily overwhelmed by anger at the Israeli (and, by implication, US) treatment of Lebanese and Palestinians, prompting the Government to adjust its own message. In August the Imam of the Grand Mosque in Mecca labelled the Israeli assault 'Zionist terrorism', and called for a war crimes trial. The episode provoked a further surge of anti-US feeling among the Saudi population, even though popular prejudice against the Shi'a at home remained. In an attempt to bolster its influence in Lebanon against that of Iran or Hezbollah, Saudi Arabia also signalled its readiness to donate large amounts of aid towards Lebanon's reconstruction, following the adoption of the cease-fire called for in UN Security Council Resolution 1701 in August.

Meanwhile, Saudi Arabia was paying increasing attention to relations with Asia, largely for economic reasons, but also as a demonstration that the country did not rely solely on the West. In April 2006 King Abdullah visited four Asian countries, namely the People's Republic of China (signing energy, defence and security deals with that country), India, Malaysia and Pakistan, during which Crown Prince Sultan explicitly emphasized Saudi Arabia's 'looking east' policy. This was followed over the following year by a series of reciprocal visits by Saudi and Asian officials, including the first visit in 27 years by a South Korean President, in March 2007.

In August 2006 a deal estimated to be worth over £4,000m. for the purchase of 72 Typhoon Eurofighter jets from the United Kingdom was tentatively agreed in another illustration of the kingdom's traditional pattern of diversifying its sources of arms supplies. Indeed, in the following January Crown Prince Sultan stated explicitly that Saudi Arabia did not want to depend on a single source for its defence requirements.

In July 2006 the US Administration approved the sale to Saudi Arabia of Black Hawk helicopters and other military equipment valued at more than US $6,000m., and announced plans for an additional sale of tanks and tank upgrades worth up to $2,900m. This was followed by the announcement in July 2007 of a mooted $20,000m. arms package for the GCC states over a 10-year period—part of a US attempt to increase the pressure on Iran and to reconcile the Arab Gulf Governments with, or reassure them about, US policy on Iraq and Iran.

Meanwhile, Saudi Arabia became increasingly concerned about developments in Iraq, and, apart from maintaining its own links with the country's Sunni tribal establishment, took an active part in attempts to bring various factions together. In a related effort, it hosted a major gathering of Sunni and Shi'a religious scholars from Iraq, under the auspices of the OIC and the International Islamic Fiqh Academy. The meeting issued a declaration on 21 October 2006, the 'Mecca Pact', which forbade killing between Sunnis and Shi'a. Strikingly, given traditional attitudes to Shi'ism in Saudi Arabia, the declaration said that the 'fundamental principles' of Islam 'apply equally to the Sunni and the Shi'a without exception'. It stated that the differences between the two schools of thought are 'merely differences of opinion and interpretation and not essential differences of faith'. The declaration received support from leading Muslim scholars world-wide.

However, Saudi concerns were heightened by talk in the USA of withdrawing its troops from Iraq before stability was assured. The Minister of Foreign Affairs in January 2007 requested clarification about the US position, while Prince Turki al-Faisal warned that limiting the number of US troops would be a mistake. Yet with an Arab audience in mind, in March King Abdullah branded the US presence in Iraq an 'illegitimate foreign occupation'. Saudi suspicions of Iraq's Shi'a Prime Minister, Nuri al-Maliki, and his alleged sectarian and pro-Iranian bias, further complicated relations, to the extent that Zalmay Khalilzad—US ambassador to the UN, and formerly the US ambassador to Iraq—accused Saudi Arabia in July of lending support to groups opposed to the Iraqi Government, an accusation vehemently denied in Riyadh. Indeed, Saudi Arabia and Iraq agreed to monitor the issuance of anti-Shi'a *fatwas* after a number were issued by Saudi clerics that could be construed as permitting the destruction of Shi'a shrines in Iraq.

The Saudi authorities also continued to apply pressure on the US Administration to restart a major peace initiative in the Arab–Israeli conflict. At an Arab League summit in Riyadh at the end of March 2007, the so-called Abdullah peace plan of 2002 was formally relaunched.

In 2007 there were two major instances of Saudi Arabia assuming an uncharacteristically proactive role. In February King Abdullah brought together the rival Palestinian factions Hamas and Fatah, which had been locked in a protracted dispute following Hamas's election victory and the subsequent boycott of Hamas and the PA by much of the international community. The King succeeded in extracting an agreement between the two sides meeting in Mecca, to end the violence and form a unity administration, while even obtaining a statement that Hamas would 'respect existing agreements'; this was widely assumed to refer to previous Israeli-Palestinian agreements, which Hamas had hitherto rejected. Even if a continuing international boycott left little room for the advancement of the peace process or a recovery of the economy, it was a striking example of Saudi assertiveness. After Hamas seized control of Gaza from Fatah in June 2007, Saudi Arabia again extended the offer of its services as a mediator, together with Egypt.

Similarly, Saudi Arabia played a key role in trying to ensure a return to stability in Lebanon in late 2006 and into 2007. Even while lending strong support to Prime Minister Fouad Siniora, the Saudi Government also attempted to bring Hezbollah into an accommodation—including a January 2007 visit by a senior Hezbollah delegation, during which the visitors were encouraged to be flexible about the planned UN tribunal on the assassination of former Lebanese Prime Minister Rafiq Hariri and to accept a compromise in the impasse with the Government. Even so, Saudi efforts ultimately proved less effectual than those of Qatar, which finally brokered a Lebanese power-sharing deal, the Doha Agreement, in May 2008 (see the chapter on Lebanon). Saudi leaders had, in the end, come to be seen as too close to the Lebanese Government and too critical of Hezbollah to act as an 'honest broker'.

Meanwhile, even while Saudi Arabia repeatedly expressed exasperation with Iranian posturing over that country's nuclear programme and pointed to Iran as exerting a nefarious influence in Iraq, the Saudi Government was also prepared to keep open active channels of communication with Iran, and continued to object to any US military solution to the nuclear dispute with that country. King Abdullah and Iranian President Ahmadinejad met in Riyadh in March 2007, discussing a wide range of regional issues and stating that they aimed to curb tensions between Sunni and Shi'ite Muslims. Even so, the announcement at the December 2006 GCC summit that the six Gulf states planned to develop a peaceful nuclear programme, followed by an approach to the International Atomic Energy Agency for help, may at least in part have been aimed at sending a signal about the proliferating effects Iran's stance might have. Yet it also annoyed the USA, with Secretary of State Condoleezza Rice questioning why Saudi Arabia needed nuclear energy. In any case, by 2008 it had become clear that Saudi Arabia, along with its GCC partners, was indeed serious about embarking on a peaceful nuclear energy programme.

Another show of Saudi independence was put on in February 2007, when Vladimir Putin became the first Russian President to make a state visit to Saudi Arabia. This came at a time when Russia was increasingly asserting its views and interests internationally and was incurring criticism from Western powers. The visit acquired added significance given Europe's rising concern over energy security and its dependence on Russian gas and Saudi Arabia's role as a key traditional reliable supplier of oil to the world economy.

The United Kingdom's Serious Fraud Office, in December 2006, abandoned a two-year investigation into the alleged use by BAE Systems (formerly British Aerospace) of a 'slush fund', from which illegal payments were said to have been made to Saudi royals in the context of the al-Yamamah arms contract first signed in 1985 (see Saudi Arabia in the 1980s and the Accession of Fahd). In the previous month Saudi Arabia had appealed for the investigation to be halted, hinting at diplomatic repercussions and threatening to cancel the contract to buy Eurofighter jets.

The British Government indicated that the move had been taken after Prime Minister Tony Blair, security service chiefs and the Saudi ambassador in London expressed concern that prolonging the investigation could cause 'serious damage' to relations with Saudi Arabia. BAE has since consistently denied any impropriety, as have Saudi officials, including Prince

Bandar, the former Saudi ambassador to the USA, who had been intimately involved in the negotiation of the 1985 deal, and was named in press reports in 2007 as having received large payments from BAE: all of these, the Prince insisted, were proper payments to accounts coming under the Ministry of Defence and Civil Aviation.

The Eurofighter deal was formally signed in September 2007, and in 2008 the purchase of a further 72 aircraft was discussed—with the kingdom aiming to double its fleet of Eurofighters (in replacement of its ageing Tornadoes) to 144.

However, focus on Saudi Arabia's role in the world oil market in 2008 rivalled the international attention provoked by the BAE/Typhoon case, as oil prices rose to unprecedented levels. Initially, Saudi Arabia denied repeated requests from the USA and other consuming countries to increase production—arguing that the real cause of the price rise was the weakening dollar, constraints in US refining capacity, and speculation—but in June Saudi concerns over an international economic downturn brought a change in direction. King Abdullah took direct control of policy by convening a major producer-consumer conference in Riyadh and by announcing a unilateral production increase of 200,000 b/d, risking a public split within the Organization of Petroleum Exporting Countries (OPEC). A further production increase to 9.7m. b/d followed, along with comments that Saudi Arabia was pushing ahead with capacity expansion to 12m. b/d. The announcements failed to bring about any immediate correction in prices—although wider global economic dynamics had by August caused a significant decrease in prices.

In 2009–10 the key foreign affairs issues for Saudi Arabia remained those with a direct impact on domestic and regional security—whether economic or political and strategic. While Riyadh hoped that Iran's President Ahmadinejad would fail in his attempt to be re-elected, his election victory in June 2009 and subsequent turmoil in Iran brought concern over the implications of that country's future nuclear and regional policies, but failed to change the dominant opinion that Iran must not be dealt with militarily. With Iraq, relations remained troubled. On the one hand, Saudi Arabia was intent on maintaining its links to and influence among Sunni groups in Iraq, especially some of the tribes; this was both a continuation of traditional Saudi links and a reflection of the kingdom's desire to retain some grip on Iraqi dynamics should things go wrong, not least in order to balance Iranian influence. Yet at the same time there was no wish to risk disintegration of the Iraqi state, with all the spill-over effects that this would have. The relationship was undoubtedly complicated by King Abdullah's personal distrust of Iraqi Prime Minister Nuri al-Maliki. Following the March 2010 Iraqi legislative elections, Saudi Arabia intimated its preference for the appointment to the premiership of Dr Ayad Allawi, whose cross-sectarian (but predominantly Sunni-supported) Iraqi National Movement bloc had won the largest number of seats. Al-Maliki's eventual continuation as Prime Minister did not ease relations.

On the Arab–Israeli front, Saudi Arabia's commitment to the peace process was reiterated, and the stance of the newly elected US President, Barack Obama, on the issue of Israeli settlements in the West Bank was received favourably. However, at the same time it was made clear that Saudi Arabia would not normalize relations with Israel in the absence of what it regarded as 'genuine progress'. This message was repeated during a visit to the USA by King Abdullah in June 2010.

Active regional diplomacy was also in evidence with King Abdullah's joint visit to Lebanon on 30 July 2010 with President Bashar al-Assad of Syria, in a clear attempt to defuse and pre-empt potential tensions within the Lebanese national unity Government, in light of the forthcoming verdict of the UN Special Tribunal created to investigate the 2005 assassination of Rafiq Hariri.

Another item on the agenda combined domestic and foreign concerns. The question of instability in Yemen, and that country's possible role as a breeding ground for violent Islamism allied with al-Qa'ida, became ever more acute from 2008 onwards, as the attack on Muhammad ibn Nayef, and the alleged Yemeni links of the 113 AQAP supporters arrested in 2010 illustrated. At the same time, the Saudi authorities were being pressed to consider accepting not only Saudi nationals who were being released from Guantánamo Bay, but also Yemeni citizens. This remained a question fraught with uncertainty, given the recognition in Saudi circles that it was by no means clear how the success achieved in the deradicalization programme with Saudi participants—in which families and kinship networks were very much integrated—could be replicated with Yemeni detainees for whom no such context was available. For the USA, on the other hand, releasing the detainees into Yemen itself seemed undesirable given the unsettled security environment in that country—including several escapes of high-value prisoners.

The concern with securing the border led not only to a longer-term intention to expand the partly completed border fence, but more immediately to the Saudi armed forces becoming directly involved in the conflict in Yemen's northern provinces. Concerned about the so-called Houthi uprising destabilizing the Government in San'a, and provoked by cross-border raids by some of the Yemeni rebels, Saudi armed forces for the first time attacked Houthi positions directly on 19 October 2009, intensifying their attacks in the course of the following month and devoting a 4,000-strong brigade to the conflict. This intervention seemed very much designed by Gen. Prince Khalid ibn Sultan, in what may have been a calculated move to increase his profile in Saudi succession politics. The declared aim was to create a buffer zone of several miles inside Yemeni territory, although Saudi troops returned to the Saudi side of the border. Subsequent regional and international concern, exemplified by the January 2010 meeting of the 'Friends of Yemen' group in London, matched a Saudi desire both to see the conflict settled and to support Yemen's economic rescue. Saudi Arabia later that year committed itself to investing US $1,000m. in the country over five years.

Meanwhile, an intra-GCC issue generated tension between Riyadh and Abu Dhabi in 2009. When a GCC agreement was announced in May 2009 to locate the Central Bank for the proposed GCC monetary area in Riyadh, it soon became clear that this went against the expectations of the UAE federal Government, which had long lobbied for the Bank to be located in Abu Dhabi. The UAE subsequently withdrew from preparations for the introduction of a common currency. King Abdullah appeared to be taken aback by this, and Saudi and GCC officials tried to engineer a compromise solution. Nevertheless, relations between Saudi Arabia and the increasingly assertive UAE became more fraught, with territorial disagreements over the Khor al-Udaid area in south-west Qatar resulting in a minor naval clash in March 2010, following which Saudi citizens were temporarily detained in Abu Dhabi. The 1974 agreement, which was meant to have settled the border, has again been questioned by the Government in Abu Dhabi, but Saudi Arabia has not shown any inclination to revisit it substantially (see the chapter on the UAE).

By contrast, relations with Qatar improved from 2009. In February 2010 Qatar's Amir, Sheikh Hamad, visited Riyadh, and later that month Prince Nayef travelled to Doha to co-chair the Qatari-Saudi co-ordination council with Qatar's Heir Apparent, Sheikh Tamim bin Hamad Al Thani. This followed the registration of the new Saudi–Qatari border agreement with the UN in June 2009 (to which the UAE had objected as contrary to its own 1969 agreement with Qatar). In May 2010 the Deputy Commander of the National Guard for Executive Affairs, King Abdullah's son Prince Mitab, visited Doha, and Sheikh Hamad announced the release of several Saudis who had been imprisoned for involvement in the 2006 coup attempt—making clear he did so in accordance with the wishes of King Abdullah. Meanwhile, relations with Bahrain were also strengthened by the beginning of work on a new pipeline intended to transport 350,000 b/d of crude petroleum to Bahrain's Sitra refinery, and an agreement to expand the King Fahd Causeway between the two countries to accommodate up to 100m. passengers per year.

DOMESTIC POLITICS FOLLOWING THE 'ARAB SPRING', 2011–13

King Abdullah's departure for medical treatment to the USA in November 2010 was followed less than two months later by the eruption of the 'Arab spring' of revolutionary protests in Middle East and North African states, bringing together two major issues affecting Saudi politics and foreign policy: intra-family politics and succession; and the question of reform. The King's medical condition—a slipped disc and associated blood clot—was treated with unprecedented openness, in contrast to the deterioration in Prince Sultan's health; consequently, the King's transfer of the administration of the nation's affairs to the incapacitated Crown Prince was a gesture devoid of meaning. As King Abdullah's hospital treatment in the USA was followed by extended recuperation in Morocco, questions over the succession continued and brought further intra-family positioning.

The popular uprising in Tunisia in January 2011 was watched with fascination both by the population and at least part of the royal family, as were the initial stages of the subsequent upheaval in Egypt. Certainly in the case of Tunisia there was widespread agreement that the people's cause was just, especially in view of the regime's apparent corruption. With regard to Egypt there was more ambivalence, President Mubarak being viewed as personally not so corrupt and as having had a credible military record. When it was announced in January that former Tunisian President Zine al-Abidine Ben Ali and his family had been granted asylum in Saudi Arabia, there was some consternation. The official stance was that the country had a tradition of extending hospitality, and that the move would ease the transition in Tunisia. Yet there were also comments that this was a personal instinctive reaction by Prince Nayef—then effectively in charge—in part because of his reported marriage to a member of the Ben Ali family. The Saudi regime generally seemed to acknowledge that the uprising was justified. Not so Nayef, although once the change of power in Tunisia was a fait accompli, the Saudi Government recognized the new interim administration.

Egypt was a different case: the King and senior princes had a long-standing personal and policy relationship with Mubarak. They supported the Egyptian President long after the USA had begun to pressurize him to resign, and expressed concern over potential chaos and violence in Egypt. Domestic repercussions did of course play a role in these responses, especially given the uncertainties engendered by the King's absence. At the same time, long-standing popular concerns over unemployment, and the renewed and badly managed flooding of Jeddah were bringing explicit criticism. In February 2011 a new political party, the Umma Islamic Party, was established, with five of its seven founding members being arrested soon afterwards. Prince Al-Walid ibn Talal, King Abdullah's nephew, significantly published an article in the *New York Times* in February, arguing for political reform.

It seems evident that King Abdullah's return in late February 2011 was hastened by the increasing concerns. Notably, among his welcoming party at the airport was the King of Bahrain, Hamad bin Isa Al Khalifa, who was subject to the strongest 'Arab spring'-related pressures among the Gulf monarchies (see Foreign Relations Following the 'Arab Spring', 2011–13). When some 120 intellectuals issued a web-based petition for reform (including a demand for a constitutional monarchy) in late February, the Saudi Government blocked websites carrying the document, but also promised to make all temporary contracts for government employees permanent. Shortly after Abdullah's return, a US $36,000m. package was announced including funding for new affordable housing, compensation for inflations, and unemployment benefits. Further concessions followed in March, with two months' extra salaries for employees, promises of better health care and housing promises, and a commitment of 60,000 new jobs at the Ministry of the Interior, as well as the establishment of an anti-corruption committee. While some of this addressed genuine grievances and needs, especially in housing and unemployment benefit, it was widely perceived as a very expensive interim measure which failed to deal with deeper concerns about governance.

Even so, a number of limited demonstrations in the Shi'a areas in late February and early March 2011 were easily contained, and were not replicated among the rest of the population: the announced 'Day of Rage' on 11 March, modelled on those in Tunisia and Egypt, proved insignificant. The Ministry of the Interior reiterated the ban on demonstrations, 'because these contradict the principles of *Shari'a* law and the values and norms of the Saudi society', while a reinforced security presence helped to pre-empt trouble.

Control was tightened further in May 2011, with amendments to the Press and Publications Law of 2000, prohibiting anything that 'violates Islamic law rulings, in conflict with national interests, affects the reputation or dignity of the Kingdom's grand mufti, members of the Council of Senior Ulama or state dignitaries, incites division between citizens, promotes crime or damages the country's public affairs'. The amendment also banned the publication without permission of details of investigations or trials. From February, the regulations on electronic publication also introduced fines for new websites that publish material deemed to offend against Islamic law or the country's security of economic interest.

At the same time, it was announced in April 2011 that the country's second municipal elections were to take place on 29 September. Women were again to be excluded from voting. Unlike the previous elections, when voters could vote for a number of candidates, this time they were to select a single candidate. In a surprising development, in a speech to mark the beginning of the annual meeting of the Consultative Council one week before the scheduled date for the elections, King Abdullah announced that women would be granted the right to participate in the Consultative Council from its next term and would be allowed to vote and to seek election at the third municipal elections, which were scheduled to take place in 2015.

In April 2011 the first full summary of the results of the campaign against al-Qa'ida in the country were released. The Ministry of the Interior announced that 11,527 people had been arrested since the start of the campaign, of whom a little over one-half (5,831) had been released after serving sentences for non-violent crimes; 5,696 remained in detention, of whom 1,612 were serving prison sentences, 603 were being tried, 934 were awaiting trial, and 616 were still under investigation.

In July 2011 the appointment was announced of King Abdullah's son, Prince Abd al-Aziz, as Deputy Minister of Foreign Affairs. More significantly, on 22 October Crown Prince Sultan died, and Prince Nayef was promptly confirmed as his successor. Prince Salman became the Minister of Defence, and Prince Sattam bin Abd al-Aziz replaced Salman as Governor of Riyadh. Speculation about the future direction of reforms under Nayef intensified due to the increased activity of the religious police after his elevation, but in mid-January 2012 King Abdullah demonstrated that he remained firmly in control by replacing the organization's head, Abd al-Aziz al-Humain, with a moderate, Abd al-Latif Al al-Sheikh.

On 16 June 2012 Nayef died unexpectedly from an unspecified illness while in Switzerland. Salman became Crown Prince (while retaining the defence portfolio), and his younger full brother, Ahmad (then aged 71), was appointed as Minister of the Interior. Once again, the new Crown Prince was selected by the most senior princes rather than by the Allegiance Institution. Salman was regarded by many within the kingdom as a pragmatic, hard-working traditionalist, and he was expected to be more accepting of the current reformist trends in the country than Nayef had been.

Succession remained one of the most important and urgent issues in the kingdom, particularly as rumours circulated of the poor health of both King Abdullah and Crown Prince Salman. Other sons of the late King Abd al-Aziz were not expected to succeed, even though some have been promoted to key positions. Among them, Prince Ahmad ibn Abd al-Aziz was appointed in June 2012 to succeed Prince Nayef as Minister of the Interior, and Prince Muqrin ibn Abd al-Aziz, after being replaced as head of the intelligence agency in July, became, first, an adviser to the king and then Second Deputy Prime Minister in February 2013.

Instead, indications were eagerly sought by international observers as to who would be the first king from the second or even third generation (after King Abd al-Aziz). One principal contender was deemed to be Prince Muhammad ibn Nayef, whose father had moved him into position as Deputy Minister of the Interior. Several sons of the late Crown Prince Sultan were also promoted: Prince Bandar (the long-standing ambassador to the USA) became the new head of the intelligence agency in July 2012, while Prince Salman bin Sultan was named as Deputy Minister of Defence in August 2013, replacing Prince Khalid, who, however, was left without a significant position. King Abdullah appointed his son Prince Mitab as Minister of the National Guard in June 2013. In what was widely believed to be a sign of displeasure over corruption and mismanagement of the Shi'a issue, Prince Muhammad ibn Fahd, a son of the late King Fahd, was removed from his long-standing post as Governor of the Eastern Province in early 2013 and replaced by Prince Sa'ud ibn Nayef.

Expectations of significant reform arising from King Abdullah's reign and the effects of the 'Arab spring' uprising were dampened. First, a radical cleric was jailed in April 2012 for 'incitement' and the King dismissed Sheikh Abd al-Muhsin al-Ubaykan as his adviser in May, after the latter criticized reforms to give women more freedom. Furthermore, the long-expected permission for women to drive vehicles was not realized.

In addition, the Saudi authorities kept a tight hold over the Shi'a population. Some eight Shi'a men were killed by police during demonstrations in Qatif, in the Eastern Province, in February–March 2012. The subsequent arrest of prominent Shi'a cleric and activist Nimr al-Nimr in the restive Eastern Province town of Awamiya on 8 July shocked the Shi'a community, partly because he was wounded while allegedly resisting the security forces. The arrest provoked more Shi'a demonstrations, during which two protesters were killed on the same day of the arrest. A few days later, the police station in Awamiya was attacked and a local man killed. The Government followed up with arrests and convictions in August and September for participation in demonstrations and arrested another Shi'a cleric. Also in September, three Shi'a were killed in Awamiya as police tried to arrest them. More attacks on government facilities took place in November and a protester was killed in December.

Rebel activities continued into 2013, with an attack on a prison in Awamiya in February. This was followed in March by the reported arrest of 16 Saudi Shi'a, as well as a Lebanese and an Iranian, on charges of spying for Iran. Another military confrontation took place in Awamiya in April and two more Shi'a were killed in June. A number of the 23 Shi'a accused by the Government of taking part in violence were tried and convicted in June and July, while the authorities announced that only nine of the group were still at large.

Another disquieting feature of 2012–13 was a heavy-handed government attitude towards critics of the regime. A number of activists were arrested after the outbreak of the 'Arab spring' uprising in 2011 and most of these remained in detention into 2013. One prominent critic, Muhammad al-Bajadi, was tried in secret and sentenced to four years in prison. Rare public demonstrations by both men and women took place in Riyadh, the Eastern Province and the Qasim region in September and November 2012, in protest against the continued detention of relatives who had been arrested as early as 2003. A group of women were briefly detained in Buraidah after another demonstration in January 2013, while 176 demonstrators were arrested in Qasim in March; more arrests followed in June.

Political critics, human rights activists, and social media commentators were also identified as targets. Among them, prominent writer Turki al-Hamad was arrested in December 2012 (although he was released six months later) and activists Muhammad Fahd al-Qahtani and Abdullah al-Hamad were sentenced to prison terms of 10 and 11 years, respectively, in March 2013. Large numbers of critical messages were posted on the social networking site Twitter after the sentencing, including one from reformist religious leader Sheikh Salman al-Awdah. The authorities then sentenced Abd al-Karim al-Khadr, a colleague of al-Qahtani and al-Hamad, to eight years' imprisonment in June. After publishing an open letter to the Government calling for reform, al-Awdah was warned in July that his popular television programme would be taken off air; a principal website owner, Raif Badawi, received a prison sentence in the same month. Harsh measures against religious non-conformists included the extradition from Malaysia in February 2012 of a Saudi accused of blasphemy and the charging of another with apostasy (a crime that is punishable by death in Saudi Arabia) in December.

Continuing high prices for crude oil prompted the Saudi Government to announce expanding budgets, with annual increases of almost 20%. The 2013 budget was set at expenditure of US $218,600m., not including defence spending, but was still expected to result in a surplus. Nevertheless, an IMF report in August 2012 warned the kingdom that spending should be reduced to preserve oil wealth for future generations.

FOREIGN RELATIONS FOLLOWING THE 'ARAB SPRING', 2011–13

Saudi Arabia's foreign relations in 2011–13 were largely shaped by the 'Arab spring', concerns about Iran's role in the Middle East, and the civil war in Syria. Regional policies were subject to the sudden impact of the Arab uprisings, although in the case of Yemen the reaction also stemmed from longer-term policies towards a problem of much longer standing.

In many respects, the resulting policy issues also deepened disagreement with the USA, causing some, including in Saudi Arabia, to start referring to a crisis in, and a recalibration of, US-Saudi relations. Whatever the disagreements, however, the underlying bond between the two states was illustrated by the US $60,000m. arms deal that US President Obama presented to Congress in October 2010, which included an allocation of $25,000m. to the National Guard. From the Saudi side, this was clearly intended to send a signal to Iran, but arguably also to ensure US support for the next decade or so.

Disagreement intensified when Saudi Arabia sent troops to give support to the Bahraini government during the protests in Bahrain in March 2011, as the main component of a GCC force: the USA had been among those trying to engineer a compromise solution in negotiations with the Bahraini Crown Prince and the opposition, and found these efforts curtailed by the Saudi-assisted operation (see the chapter on Bahrain). The Saudi leadership clearly viewed the situation in Bahrain—unlike the other Arab revolutions—as a potential Shi'a and Iranian-supported threat to the Sunni Arab monarchical systems. Saudi Arabia claimed that its troops were not directly involved in any crowd suppression, but their symbolic function was potent. In its position on Bahrain, of which this was the most explicit instance, the Saudi leadership went strongly counter to US (and British) advice and admonitions. At the same time, Saudi Arabia also announced a US $10,000m. support package for its fellow kingdom.

The emerging differences with the USA over regional policy, and the reduced trust in US support, seemed reflected in a further extension of the approach of seeking complementary security relationships. From March 2011 Saudi Arabia began discussions with other Muslim states (mainly Pakistan, Malaysia and Indonesia) regarding co-operation against the perceived Iranian (and Iranian-inspired) threats. While Prince Sa'ud al-Faisal visited Europe and the USA to explain the Bahrain intervention, Prince Bandar was sent to do the same in China, Pakistan, India and Malaysia. He also held discussions with the Pakistani military about possible backing, including in Bahrain.

In early April 2011 US Secretary of Defense Robert Gates visited Riyadh, in an apparent attempt to resolve or contain the rift. An article published in the *Washington Post* in May by an adviser to Prince Turki, arguing that the US-Saudi partnership was about to be 'recalibrated', was one instance of similar signals being emitted from Saudi Arabia. In part, this was also driven by disagreement on the question of whether to support the Palestinian request for a vote on statehood at the UN. As the September date for the vote became imminent, the USA made every effort to postpone it, suggesting that the Administration would be obliged to vote against the proposal. Saudi Arabia proved one of the more forceful advocates of supporting Palestinian aspirations, in view of the failure of the US-backed peace process. Even so, none of this represented quite as dramatic a reversal in the relationship as some suggested. Indeed, further confirmation of this came in the announcement in August that the USA and Saudi Arabia were to begin negotiations over a formal nuclear co-operation agreement, following the Memorandum of Understanding signed in 2008.

Meanwhile, some measure of understanding on Yemen had also been reached between Saudi Arabia and its GCC partners on the one hand, and the USA and the United Kingdom on the other, in the Friends of Yemen grouping, which had been established in early 2010 to support political reform and economic development in that country. However, Saudi strategy on Yemen remained somewhat disparate, especially with the effective disappearance from the political scene of Crown Prince Sultan, who had long dealt with Yemen, and also with King Abdullah's absence since November 2010. In early 2011 there was increased co-ordination within Saudi policy circles and with the GCC, prompted by the swift escalation of the Yemeni crisis. In April Saudi Arabia led the GCC in drafting and formally presenting a plan, endorsed by the USA and others, for transition from Yemeni President Ali Abdullah Saleh's rule. Saleh finally ceded the presidency to his Vice-President, Abd al-Rabbuh Mansur al-Hadi, in February 2012. Saudi Arabia continued thereafter to support the transition process.

Saudi reaction to the Libyan and Syrian upheavals from February 2011 was different again. Relations between Saudi Arabia and Libya had never been amicable. Thus, it was unsurprising that Saudi Arabia concurred with a GCC, and then Arab League, position supporting the Libyan rebels, and endorsing UN and NATO resolutions and action to protect civilians, although it did not play an active role.

In the case of Syria, where demonstrations had gathered pace much more slowly and the regime had a greater base of support, the Saudi Arabian Government was cautious and appealed for stability, while encouraging Syrian President Bashar al-Assad to respond to existing grievances. By August 2011, however, after repressive measures by the Syrian authorities had killed hundreds of protesters, King Abdullah urged the regime to 'stop the killing machine', and announced the withdrawal of the Saudi ambassador in Syria. During 2012 Saudi Arabia, alongside Qatar, became a forceful advocate of regime change in Syria and a supporter of the Syrian opposition, both bilaterally and in regional and international forums, including the GCC, the Arab League and the UN. Saudi equipment began reaching the Syrian rebels from early 2012. It was noteworthy that the approach to the Yemeni, Bahraini and Libyan crises showed a new vigour to common GCC action, as well as a more active international role. One other striking development within the GCC was the further improvement in relations with Qatar. Possibly under the implementation of a land-maritime border delimitation agreement of 2008–09, a border change was effected in late May 2011, with the south side of the Khor al-Udaid region apparently ceded to Qatar, presumably while retaining Saudi access rights to the Gulf. In July Qatar Airways received permission nearly to double its flights to the kingdom from 35 to 60, while the Qatar-based satellite television station Al Jazeera was for the first time given permission to open a bureau in Saudi Arabia; the establishment of a joint industrial zone and bank was to be discussed by the two countries in September.

One factor unifying the GCC (with the exception of Oman) was concern over Iran, particularly regarding the nuclear issue and the country's perceived interference in regional political and sectarian disputes. Tensions between Saudi Arabia and Iran reached a peak in September 2011 after the discovery of an alleged Iranian plot to assassinate the Saudi ambassador in Washington, DC. At the same time Saudi Arabia accused Iran of involvement in the disturbances in the Eastern region but provided little evidence to support this claim. These perceptions of Iran's role within the region largely shaped the Saudi Government's foreign policy decisions. Many observers regarded the appointment in February 2012 of Saudi Arabia's first (non-resident) ambassador to Iraq since the overthrow of the regime of Saddam Hussain in this context.

However, the limitations of Saudi Arabia's leverage over the GCC were underlined by the country's failure to make any substantive progress with its aim of granting GCC membership to Morocco and Jordan, and by the similar failure of the much-rumoured plan for Saudi-Bahraini unification at the May 2012 GCC summit.

As the situation in Syria worsened in 2013 and Iran became more involved there, Saudi Arabia increased its assistance to anti-regime forces. It had been reported in early 2012 that Saudi military equipment was being sent to the opposition Free Syrian Army via Jordan. A February 2013 report alleged that the kingdom had purchased large quantities of weaponry from Croatia and was supplying them to more nationalist and secular opposition forces, thereby aiming to prevent them from being used by jihadist groups. However, it was also widely believed that the Saudi Government was supporting Islamist groups, perhaps including Salafis, as well as the Free Syrian Army, with supply lines through Jordan, while Qatar was backing the Muslim Brotherhood from northern Syria. Saudi Arabia was reported to have begun sending anti-aircraft missiles to the Free Syrian Army from about April 2013.

Saudi Arabia's differences with Iran were not confined to the issue of Syria. On 15 August 2012 a virus erased critical files on some 30,000 computers belonging to Saudi Aramco, the world's largest oil company; Iran was suspected as the source of the virus. The Saudi Government also accused Iran of continuing to encourage dissent among the Shi'a population of the Eastern Province, and, in March 2013, of organizing an espionage group in the kingdom. It was believed that Russia's support for the Syrian regime prompted an unannounced visit to the Russian capital, Moscow, by head of the Saudi intelligence agency Prince Bandar in August. Reports that Saudi Arabia had offered Russia a significant agreement for the purchase of military equipment in return for withdrawing its support for the Assad regime was denied by the Russian Government.

Elsewhere, relations with Egypt were conflicted. Despite its support of President Mubarak until his removal, Saudi Arabia, along with other GCC states, agreed to provide financial support for Egypt, beginning with a sum of US $500m. The fragile relationship survived a brief April–May 2012 dispute, during which Saudi Arabia closed its embassy in Cairo. The Egyptian military's ouster of Muslim Brotherhood President Muhammad Mursi in July 2013 improved ties and later that month the Saudi Government pledged $5,000m. in aid, including a grant of $2,000m. and another $2,000m. in supplies of petroleum and natural gas.

Syria was a principal focus of discussions when US Secretary of State John F. Kerry visited Riyadh in March 2013. Following Saudi provision of arms to the rebels, the USA finally decided to supply some food and medicine, while continuing to ponder whether it should also send arms. The meetings with Saudi Minister of Foreign Affairs Prince Sa'ud al-Faisal also involved counter-terrorism strategy and policy on Iran's alleged drive for nuclear weapons. Normally cordial relations with the United Kingdom were troubled by British criticism of Saudi Arabia's decision to send troops to Bahrain in 2011 and by the decision in mid-2012 of the House of Commons Foreign Affairs Committee to open a review of bilateral relations.

Despite US-Saudi disagreement on matters such as the Israeli-Palestinian conflict and Syria, the US Administration announced in December 2011 that US $29,000m. worth of advanced *F-15* fighter aircraft would be sold to the kingdom. This followed an agreement on the sale of military helicopters. The two countries continued close co-operation in counter-terrorism affairs and the USA was permitted to operate a base inside Saudi Arabia for the use of unmanned aerial vehicles (or drones) against militants based in Yemen.

Economy

Revised for this edition by the editorial staff; based on an earlier essay by MOIN SIDDIQI

The economy of Saudi Arabia, the largest among the Arab countries and the powerhouse of the Persian (Arabian) Gulf, is dominated by petroleum, of which the country is by far the greatest producer within the Organization of the Petroleum Exporting Countries (OPEC). Saudi Arabia has received massive revenue from petroleum exports (particularly since the dramatic increase in international petroleum prices in 1973–74), which it has used, in part, to finance an ambitious programme of infrastructural development and modernization, as well as far-reaching programmes for health, social and educational purposes. Substantial budgetary allocations have also been made to the country's armed forces and to the purchase of sophisticated weaponry from abroad.

Conservative and strictly Islamic in orientation, the Saudi ruling family has consistently favoured a pro-Western, market-orientated economic strategy and has placed great reliance on Western and Japanese expertise for the development of the country's petroleum and other sectors. There remains a substantial expatriate contribution to the management of various economic sectors, although Saudi nationals have come increasingly to the fore, especially in the petroleum and gas industries. Throughout the economy, expatriates form the majority of the work-force. Emphasis has been placed, under recent development plans, on the promotion of 'downstream' oil industries, such as refining and petroleum derivatives, and progress has also been made in developing the country's non-oil industries.

The economy grew at a sluggish pace during 1980–99. Having achieved an average annual growth rate of 10.6% in the period 1968–80, Saudi Arabia's gross domestic product (GDP) declined, in real terms, at an average rate of 1.2% per year over the decade 1980–90, largely because petroleum output declined from a peak of almost 10m. barrels per day (b/d) in 1980 to 3.6m. b/d in 1985. Although production rose to more than 5m. b/d in 1988 and 1989, depressed international prices resulted in substantially reduced revenue, with adverse consequences for the current account and national budget, both of which moved into deficit. According to the IMF, real GDP growth expanded at an average annual rate of 1% during 1990–99, which lagged behind a population increase of around 2.7% per year. Overall, GDP totalled US $160,960m. in 1999, compared with $104,670m. in 1990. GDP per caput, which exceeded $16,000 in the early 1980s, fell sharply, to $7,497, by the end of 1999.

Fuelled by strong global petroleum markets, the Saudi economy in the early 21st century entered a new period of healthy economic growth, coupled with burgeoning 'twin surpluses' (the government budget and current account). In nominal terms, GDP rose at an average of 6.3% per year, owing to steady growth in both petroleum and non-oil output. In 2012 the kingdom's national output amounted to SR 2,666m. (US $675,000m.) equivalent to GDP per caput of $24,524, compared with $10,095 in 2006. The kingdom accounts for more than two-fifths of economic output of the six-member Cooperation Council for the Arab States of the Gulf (Gulf Cooperation Council—GCC).

The growth of the private sector (which contributed 58% of GDP in 2013), a sharp rise compared with 10.0% in the 1980s, represented a positive development. The IMF estimated average non-oil GDP growth at 7.8% per year during 2008–12, the most rapid expansion since 1982, reflecting brisk commercial activity. Rising capital expenditure and an improved business climate should further accelerate non-oil growth. A report by Saudi-based Jadwa Investment identified the manufacturing sector (led by petrochemicals) as the largest contributor to economic expansion in 2007–10, with estimated growth of 9.4%, followed by transport and communications (9.3%), banking and finance (8.1%) and construction (7.8%). Oil windfalls have fuelled private consumption and investment in recent years. Moreover, the non-oil economy has benefited from an expansionary fiscal stance and a number of mega-projects across the kingdom.

Although Saudi Arabia was not 'decoupled' from the global financial crisis, the effects were less severe than elsewhere, reflecting low manageable external (private) debt, and a strongly capitalized banking system (not reliant on external funding), as well as the Government's pledge to spend US $400,000m. over the medium term in order to bolster economic activity and diversify into new areas. Despite this, nominal GDP contracted by 21.7% in 2009 to SR 1,414m. ($377,000m.), with real GDP growth estimated at just 0.1%—its slowest rate since 2002. The petroleum sector's performance was dented by weaker crude prices, causing oil GDP to plunge by 7.8%, but the non-hydrocarbons sector grew at 3.5%. Official figures showed public and private sector growth at 4.4% and 3.5%, respectively. The best-performing sector of 2009 was transport and communications, which grew by 6.0%, followed by construction and electricity (3.9%), and the gas and water sector (3.4%). The industrial sector also expanded by 2.2%, as domestic demand remained strong. The wholesale, retail, restaurants and hotels sector grew by 2.0%, while finance, insurance and real estate expanded at a sluggish rate of 1.8%. The Saudi economy, amid the regional downturn, proved resilient by avoiding a recession. Real GDP growth was recorded at 7.4% in 2010, before increasing to 8.6% in 2011, driven mainly by higher petroleum output, as well as increased government consumption and investment. Growth declined in 2012, to 5.1%, and was projected by the IMF to decrease further, to 4.4%, in 2013.

Despite robust domestic demand and a high level of liquidity, until recently inflationary pressures remained subdued, largely owing to generous subsidies for essential goods and services and prudent monetary policy. The state provides implicit subsidies for gasoline, electricity and water utilities. Rises in the consumer price index averaged a paltry 1% per year over 2002–06. Inflation accelerated during 2007 to 4.1%, and reached an historical high of 9.9% (year-on-year) in 2008, fuelled by robust domestic demand, supply bottlenecks (especially in housing), rising import prices (mostly food) and soaring rents.

The Government has approved ad hoc measures to mitigate the effects of higher inflation, including providing a cost of living allowance for all state employees and pensioners, equivalent to 5.0% of their income for three years; increasing its social security contributions by 10.0%; and extending subsidies on basic commodities. In addition, the Government will pay 50% of fees for port handling, passport issuance, vehicle licensing, transfers of ownership and renewing the residence permits of domestic staff, again for a period of three years. The package includes measures to ensure fair competition and consumer protection, as well as preventing monopolistic practices. Inflation decreased significantly to 5.1%, 5.4% and 5.0%, respectively, in 2009, 2010 and 2011, according to the IMF, owing to lower import prices and rents, and less buoyant domestic demand. Inflation continued to decline in 2012, reaching 2.9%, but was expected to increase, to 4.0%, in 2013.

An upper-middle-income country, Saudi Arabia boasted among the best social indicators in the developing world in the early 21st century. Life expectancy equalled 74 years in 2011; 100% of the population had access to clean water and sanitation facilities. Higher spending on health care over many decades reduced the under-five mortality rate to nine deaths per 1,000 live births by 2011. Significant progress was reported in reducing illiteracy among Saudi nationals: according to UNESCO, the adult literacy rate in 2010 was 87%.

These gains notwithstanding, the kingdom still faces considerable demographic challenges, notably a burgeoning indigenous population (two-thirds of whom are under 30 years old), a rapidly growing labour force (an estimated 150,000 young nationals enter the labour market annually), high unemployment and immense pressure on housing, public services and utilities. An increasingly youthful population could pose political risks if job creation and provision of welfare services fall below general expectations. The unemployment rate among

Saudi nationals was above 10.0% in 2012, according to the Ministry of Economy and Planning, although private estimates put this figure much higher. The UN has projected that the total population could increase to 37m. and 50m. by 2025 and 2050, respectively. Consequently, massive public and private investments are needed, especially in the electricity and water sectors, in order to prevent bottlenecks within the Saudi economy in the coming decades. The combination of expected rapid population growth and a disproportionate reliance on oil exports—rendering the economy vulnerable to external shocks—requires continuous efforts towards diversification and the attraction of greater foreign direct investment (FDI) in non-oil sectors, which is regarded as key to future job creation.

POPULATION AND LABOUR FORCE

In mid-2013 the population of Saudi Arabia was estimated at 30.0m.; expatriates represented just under one-third of the total. By contrast, in 1971 the population was only 6m. The majority of non-nationals (estimated at 9.7m.) are from South Asia (especially Pakistan and India), South-East Asia, and the Middle East and North Africa. The Eastern region, Jeddah, Mecca and Riyadh contain about two-thirds of the kingdom's population. The Ministry of Economy and Planning projects a total population of 33m. in 2020. The structure of the indigenous population is also expected to witness a marked change in the coming years, with rising numbers of over-65s requiring higher social and health care spending for senior citizens. Around 70% of the population is under the age of 31—a legacy of the petroleum boom in the early 1980s—indicating the importance of job creation and total Saudi population is forecast to double by year 2050.

Youth unemployment rate stood at 28.2% at the end of 2011. The kingdom plans to create 3m. and 6m. new jobs for Saudi nationals in the private sector by 2015 and 2030, respectively, as part of the 'Nitaqat Initiative', which seeks to increase the number of nationals employed in the private sector. Total civilian employment in Saudi Arabia was 9.6m. in 2010, of which expatriate labour comprised over 80%, or 8.0m. The agriculture, industry and services (including the public administration) sectors accounted for 5%, 25% and 70%, respectively, in the first quarter of 2013. Expatriates were mostly employed in private companies, while jobs in the civil service, autonomous government institutions and parastatal organizations were reserved exclusively for Saudi nationals. Presently, as much as 90% of the indigenous work-force is employed by the state. According to the Ministry of Labour, non-nationals comprised 90% of the 6.9m. total work-force in the private sector in 2009. Expatriates earn a total of US $35,000m.–$40,000m. annually; in 2010 outflows of workers' remittances from Saudi Arabia were estimated at $27,069m. The Government is keen for the private sector to employ more Saudi citizens, thereby reducing the heavy reliance on expatriate contract labour.

From the beginning of 1996 the Government began to enforce quotas for the employment of Saudi citizens in various sectors of the economy, including certain types of manual and clerical work. The minimum Saudi element that the affected industries were required to employ varied from 5% to 40% of the company work-force. In July 1998 the Saudi Government restricted the duration of public sector employment contracts for expatriates to a maximum of 10 years in most categories of work, while a policy of 'Saudiization' of the work-force brought to 36 the total number of occupations to which expatriate access was restricted or denied. The Human Resources Development Fund, financed partly by more expensive expatriate work permits and visas, was launched in April 2002 to subsidize skills training for nationals. In 2004 the Fund subsidized over 20,000 individuals, in order to increase the employability of the indigenous labour force. In February 2003 the Minister of the Interior announced plans to reduce the number of expatriate workers and their dependants in the kingdom to 20% of the population by 2013. However, it was clear by early 2013 that this target had not been met, as expatriates were estimated to comprise some 32% of the total population.

DEVELOPMENT PLANS

Since 1970 the development of the Saudi economy has been guided by a series of five-year plans. The first Five-Year Plan (1970–75) was a relatively modest programme costing SR 56,223m., of which SR 32,762m. was allotted to economic and social development. However, after the rise in petroleum revenue in 1973–74 (see Petroleum), the Government found itself in possession of vast financial resources and determined to embark on a massive programme of industrialization and modernization. Hence the second Five-Year Plan (1975–80) provided for expenditure of SR 498,230m. (US $142,000m.).

A major feature of the second Plan was a project to increase industrial output, creating two new industrial cities, one at Jubail on the Gulf coast and the other at Yanbu on the Red Sea. Development of the two sites was to take 10 years and cost about US $70,000m. There were also plans to expand existing industrial and commercial sites, particularly at Dammam. The Government pursued the goals of the second Plan with great determination, and the results were, on the whole, successful. Although the main industrial projects fell behind schedule, infrastructure grew apace, endowing the country with the basic transport and communications facilities required by a modern industrial state.

As a consequence of this, the third Five-Year Plan (1980–85) was intended to shift the emphasis from infrastructure projects to the productive sectors, with particular importance accorded to agriculture and the aim of achieving 'food security' by being less dependent on imported foodstuffs. The Plan stressed the need for manpower training, to reduce reliance on foreign labour, and for Saudi private investors to be encouraged to play a more prominent role in the economy. Planned investment for the five-year period was set at SR 782,000m. (US $235,000m.), but this total did not include defence spending, the largest item of expenditure under the previous Plan.

The fourth Five-Year Plan (1985–90) envisaged total expenditure of SR 1,000,000m. at current prices, of which SR 500,000m. was allocated to development projects in the civilian sector. Four policy principles underpinned the Plan: greater operational efficiency; an emphasis on non-oil revenue-generating activities, particularly industry, agriculture and financial services; a campaign to develop private sector involvement and initiatives; and the need for further economic and social integration among the countries of the GCC. Within the details of the Plan, considerable emphasis was also given to raising desalination capacity, the expansion of irrigation and power facilities, a review of subsidies, the reduction of foreign labour, the development of new industrial estates and the expansion of health services. By mid-1988 the fourth Development Plan was widely considered to have fallen short of its targets, mainly as a result of the steep decline in oil revenue following the collapse in oil prices in 1986. The implementation of many projects, in particular those involving public utilities, had been delayed.

The fifth Five-Year Development Plan (1990–95) envisaged total expenditure of SR 753,000m. Owing to the crisis in the Gulf following the invasion of Kuwait by Iraq, Saudi Arabia increased military spending, and about 34% (SR 255,000m.) of total expenditure in the fifth Plan was to be allocated to defence. The six major themes of the Plan were the expansion of government revenue, in particular from non-oil sources; increased reliance on the private sector; further job opportunities and training for the Saudi Arabian labour force; import substitution and the promotion of exports; the diversification of economic activities into non-oil areas; and a balanced development of the regions. Under the fifth Plan, the encouragement of Saudi Arabian industry, notably in the construction sector, was to be reinforced by a ruling that at least 30% of the value of government contracts must be awarded to Saudi Arabian companies.

The sixth Development Plan, for the period 1995–2000, was designed to achieve average annual growth of 3.8%. Priority was to be given to: measures to balance the national budget by the end of the planning period (including reductions in direct and indirect price subsidies); the development of a privatization programme; increasing the proportion of Saudi nationals in the private sector work-force; and bringing about greater private sector participation in infrastructural and other development projects. However, the Plan was based on an overly optimistic estimate of petroleum prices and state revenue, and assumed the ability to sustain a high rate of growth in government investment. In the event, fluctuating petroleum prices resulted in lower than predicted revenue and consequently disrupted expenditure. Overall real GDP growth for the first three years of the Plan was recorded at 1.2% annually, with oil and non-oil sector growth of 1.6% and 1.0%, respectively. (The Plan had predicted annual oil sector growth of 3.8% and annual non-oil sector growth of 3.9%.)

The seventh Five-Year Plan (2000–05) aimed to create 817,000 new jobs for the indigenous work-force, mainly in the private sector. The Plan envisaged increased private investment, and higher growth for the private and non-oil sectors, with overall growth in real GDP averaging 3.2% per year. The Plan was reliant upon the success of economic reforms to encourage the participation of both domestic and foreign investors.

In August 1999 the Supreme Economic Council, headed by then Crown Prince Abdullah, was formed to advise upon and accelerate structural reforms. The main objectives of the Council were to attract private investments, including FDI, to promote privatization and to create jobs for Saudi nationals. The Council's membership comprises relevant government ministries, and it has a consultative committee of private sector representatives as well as academics and professional experts. The late King Fahd ibn Abd al-Aziz Al Sa'ud declared that 'the world is heading for globalization' and that 'it is no longer possible for [Saudi Arabia] to make slow progress'. Real GDP growth averaged 3.4% per year during the Seventh Plan, with nominal GDP rising from SR 603,600m. in 1999 to SR 714,900m. in 2004. The non-oil economy recorded an average annual growth of 3.9% and its share of total GDP rose to 73.5%. Gross fixed capital formation as a share of GDP grew slightly from 19.6% in 1999 to 20.5% by the end of 2004.

The eighth Five-Year Plan (2005–09) sought to achieve the objectives of the kingdom's long-term goals, notably 'a diversified and prosperous economy that ensures supply of rewarding job opportunities and economic welfare for all citizens, provision of good quality education and health care to the population', and assistance to enable 'manpower [to] acquire the necessary skills, while maintaining the kingdom's Islamic values and cultural heritages'. The underlying economic objectives were: fostering a climate for sustainable, vigorous GDP growth—a prerequisite for increased job creation; raising the private sector's contribution to national income; diversifying the Saudi economy and export base; and realizing balanced development in all regions of the kingdom.

The eighth Development Plan aimed to increase the value of real GDP from SR 714,900m. in 2004 to some SR 895,200m. by 2009 (at 1999 constant prices), representing an average annual growth rate of 4.6%. The petroleum sector and non-oil economy were projected to grow at 2.7% and 5.2% per year, respectively. The added value, generated by non-oil sectors, was expected to rise by almost 30% to SR 677,200m. by the end of 2009. It was anticipated that private sector growth would attain an average annual rate of 5.7%, with its contribution to GDP rising from SR 390,200m. in 2004 to SR 514,300m. by 2009 (at constant 1999 prices). As regards the hydrocarbons sector, the Plan envisaged its value added rising from SR 196,700m. in 2004 to SR 225,000m. by 2009 (at constant 1999 prices). The value of gross fixed capital formation was expected to increase by 10.7% per year (led by the oil sector) during the Plan period, to reach SR 243,900m. by 2009. It was hoped that such robust projected growth would boost the share of investment in GDP to 27.3% by the end of 2009. Concurrently, the Plan aimed to raise the national savings ratio to two-fifths of GDP by 2009 (from 39.8% in 2004). It was anticipated that higher private sector investment and economic diversification, along with an emphasis on educational training policies, would help to create 1.21m. new jobs during the eighth Plan and that the unemployment rate among Saudi nationals would decrease from 7.0% in 2004 to just 2.8% in 2009. The Plan envisaged government revenues of SR 1,323,700m. and spending on development projects in the civilian sector of SR 614,600m. over a five-year period.

The ninth Development Plan (2010–14) is the second in a series of long-term development strategies aimed at achieving a comprehensive socio-economic vision by 2024. Total spending is targeted to surge by 67.5% to SR 1,444,600m. (US $385,227m.) during this period, in which the authorities' main goals are achieving balanced regional development within the kingdom and poverty reduction; diversifying of the economic base; sustaining economic stability; boosting domestic and foreign investments; pursuing institutional and administrative reforms; approving the privatization programme; upgrading technological capability; and strengthening the infrastructure (especially power) and logistics basis.

The ninth Development Plan seeks to realize average annual real GDP growth of 5.2%, with economic output (in constant 2009 prices) expected to rise from SR 855,700m. (US $228,186m.) in 2009 to SR 1,101,200m. ($293,653m.) in 2014. The growth in GDP would boost GDP per caput income from SR 46,200 in 2009 to around SR 53,200 in 2014. Higher government investment will be reflected in the share of gross fixed capital formation to GDP, which is expected to rise from 26% in 2009 to 38.5% of GDP in 2014. The ninth Plan envisages a rapid increase in the proportion of the non-oil sector's contribution to GDP, which is projected to reach around 81.3% by 2014. During this period, the private sector is also expected to register vigorous growth of 38.5% up to 2014 and will remain dominated by financial, insurance, business and real estate services (estimated at 14.7% of GDP) and manufacturing industries (14% of GDP). The Plan also aims to raise generating capacity by 20.4 GW by 2014, when total installed capacity should reach about 72 GW.

The Government has placed strong emphasis on sectoral development, with highest contribution of more than 50% being allocated to Human Resources Development. The sector, which includes general education, higher education, technical and vocational training and science, technology and innovation, receives the highest share of spending totalling SR 731,500m. (US $195,006m.), representing an increase of 52.4% compared with the allocation under the eighth Plan. The ninth plan encourages the private sector to establish more schools and increase its share to 15% by 2014.

As part of its vision to develop a 'knowledge economy', the Government plans to build 25 new technological research institutes and facilities. Economic resources development witnessed the highest sector allocation growth, of 115.2%, under the ninth Plan. The allocation target includes achieving a growth rate of 6.6% for investment in agriculture, and increasing the storage capacity of dams to 2,500m. cu m and capacity of desalination plants to 2,070m. cu m by 2014. The Plan also aims to achieve an industrial sector growth rate of 7.2%, and the allocation of mineral manufacturing sites in the Jubail and Yanbu industrial cities and King Abdullah Economic City.

PETROLEUM

The origins of Saudi Arabia's oil power date back to the early 1930s. In 1933 a concession was granted to Standard Oil Co of California to explore for hydrocarbons reserves in the new desert kingdom. The operating company, the Arabian-American Oil Co (Aramco) began exploration in that year, and discovered crude oil in commercial quantities in 1938. The kingdom's first oil tanker sailed from the Gulf port of Ras Tanura in 1939. By 1945 four oilfields had been discovered, and the necessary facilities had been established to satisfy demands for crude petroleum and refined products. Other US companies gradually acquired shares in Aramco and by 1948 Standard Oil, Texaco and Exxon each owned a 30% share, with Mobil accounting for the remaining 10%. In November 1962 the Government created the General Petroleum and Mineral Organization (Petromin) as the instrument for increasing state participation in the petroleum and gas industries. In accordance with the action of other Arab petroleum-producing states, the Saudi Government acquired a 25% share in Aramco in January 1973. A 100% takeover of the company was agreed in 1980.

The expansion of Saudi Arabia's petroleum output in the 1960s and 1970s was spectacular. Production increased from about 62m. metric tons (equivalent to 1.3m. b/d) in 1960 to 178m. tons (3.8m. b/d) in 1970, and to 412m. tons (8.5m. b/d) in 1974. This growth in output was accompanied by rising prices for petroleum, culminating in the huge increases of October and December 1973, which almost quadrupled the price per barrel. The Government's petroleum revenue increased dramatically, from US $1,214m. in 1970 to $22,573m. in 1974.

In April 1989 Saudi Aramco was formed to take control of the nationalized Aramco assets. It is an independent enterprise with the right to establish companies and initiate projects. In addition, a new Supreme Oil Council was formed to take responsibility for the country's petroleum industry. The council's members included private businessmen as well as government ministers, and it was seen as an indication of the Government's desire to involve the private sector in the management of the economy. A new 12-member Supreme Council for Petroleum and Mineral Affairs was formed in January 2000 under the chairmanship of King Fahd. It was responsible for all policy relating to oil and gas affairs, including any agreements with international oil companies, and for general policy guidelines for Saudi Aramco.

The hydrocarbons industry forms the bedrock of the Saudi economy, providing a preliminary 47% of GDP and 75% of total state revenues in 2012. The stability of global energy markets rests heavily upon Saudi Arabia (the world's largest oil exporter), which acts as a 'swing producer' within OPEC, underpinned by a large excess production capacity, estimated at 4m. b/d (equivalent to the total output of the People's Republic of China). According to the *BP Statistical Review of World Energy 2013*, the country's total production (crude oil, natural gas liquids—NGLs and condensates) averaged 11.53m. b/d in 2012, representing 13.3% of the world's total (86.15m. b/d) and 30.8% of OPEC's aggregate of 37.41m. b/d.

The quality of Saudi petroleum ranges from medium-and-heavy 'sour' crude, containing higher sulphur levels and derived from offshore fields, to 'extra-lighter' grades (i.e. super light), mainly produced from onshore fields. An estimated 65% of total output is considered of light gravity. Most Saudi crude petroleum is exported from the Persian Gulf via the giant Abqaiq processing facility. Major export terminals are situated at Ras Tanura Facility, which can handle over 6m. b/d, Yanbu (4.5m. b/d), Ras al-Ju'aymah (3.6m. b/d) on the Gulf coast and Ras Tanura Port (2.5m. b/d). Combined, these terminals are capable of handling 16.6m. b/d. Saudi Aramco employs more than 5,000 armed guards to protect its petroleum installations from possible terrorist attacks.

The kingdom may hold as much as 1,200,000m. barrels of 'ultimately' recoverable oil. According to Saudi Aramco, original-oil-in-place is 735,000m. barrels, while incremental probable and possible reserves are about 103,000m. barrels. Proven oil reserves (including one-half of the Neutral/Partitioned Zone) as of the end of 2012 totalled 265,900m. barrels (15.9% of the world's total). The reserves-to-production (R/P) ratio was assessed by the *BP Statistical Review of World Energy 2013* at 63.0 years. The authorities claim that, through new discoveries and an aggressive exploration and development programme, provable reserves could reach more than 461,000m. barrels by 2025. That, in turn, would increase the kingdom's R/P ratio to over 100 years. The Paris-based International Energy Agency estimates that Saudi Arabia still has about 70 'undeveloped' oilfields, mainly in the Rub al-Khali (Empty Quarter) and the Red Sea basin, which could hold an estimated 100,000m. barrels of probable reserves. The method Aramco uses to estimate reserves is consistent with standards adopted by reputable professional agencies, notably the International Petroleum Congress, the Society of Petroleum Engineers and the American Society of Petroleum Geologists.

Although the kingdom has about 100 major oil- and gasfields, with 320 reservoirs (and 1,849 wells), more than two-thirds of proven reserves are deposited in eight 'ultra-giant' oilfields. These include Ghawar (with reserves of 70,000m. barrels), offshore Safaniya (35,000m. barrels), Manifa (22,800m. barrels), Abqaiq (17,000m. barrels), Shaybah (15,000m. barrels) and Khurais (16,800m. barrels). The Najd fields, south of Riyadh, contain about 30,000m. barrels of liquids and substantial natural gas reserves. The Ghawar oilfield (which, at 1,260 sq miles, is the world's largest) holds more than 80% of the total reserves of the Russian Federation (87,100m. barrels) and accounts for one-half of Saudi total output capacity.

Together with Kuwait, Saudi Arabia shares equal exploitation and production rights to 5,000m. barrels of proven reserves within the 6,200-sq m Neutral Zone, the total output of which was about 600,000 b/d in 2010. In February 2000 negotiations for the renewal of a concession in the Saudi portion of the Zone, which Japan's Arabian Oil Co (AOC) had operated for 40 years, ended without agreement. Saudi Arabia had stipulated Japan should undertake major investments, including a US $1,000m. railway project linking the Eastern region to northern areas and import more Saudi petroleum, as a precondition for extending AOC's drilling rights. Saudi Aramco subsequently established the Aramco Gulf Operations Co (AGO) to operate the concession. A planned upgrade and expansion of the Neutral Zone's fields by Al-Khafji Joint Operations—a joint venture between AGO and Kuwait Gulf Oil Co—was expected to increase total production to 1m. b/d.

The kingdom continues to play a constructive role in support of oil market stability. To this end, Saudi Aramco plans to invest US $129,000m. in new energy projects over the next five years, aimed at boosting crude oil, gas (including NGLs), refining and petrochemicals capacities, of which about $70,000m. would be spent by international and domestic joint ventures and the remaining $59,000m. on projects exclusively undertaken by Aramco. Total capital spending for 2009–13, the largest five-year programme in Aramco's history, represents one-quarter of Saudi GDP. Planned capacity increases would be facilitated by the following mega-projects: the Khurais extension (1.2m. b/d); Manifa (900,000 b/d); Abu Hadriya/Fadhili/Khursaniyah (500,000 b/d); Marjan/Safaniya/Zuluf (450,000 b/d); Shaybah (250,000 b/d); and Nuayyim (100,000 b/d). The Khurais project, estimated to cost $11,000m., was designed to involve the exploration and production of three fields, comprising Abu Jifan (2,600m. barrels), Khurais (22,800m. barrels) and Mazolij (1,400m. barrels).

The kingdom claimed a 'sustainable' production capacity of 12.5m. b/d in mid-2012. The possibility of raising long-term capacity to 15m. b/d within a decade was discussed at the Jeddah Energy Forum in June 2008. Saudi Aramco has identified another 2.5m. b/d for future projects, if required. The US Energy Information Administration estimated that Saudi production capacity should exceed 23m. b/d by 2025. Saudi Arabia is also the largest energy consumer in the Middle East and North Africa, especially in the area of transportation fuels. In 2012 domestic consumption totalled about 2.94m. b/d, up from 1.97m. b/d in 2005, reflecting robust industrial growth and subsidized fuel prices.

INDUSTRY, GAS AND MINING

Saudi Arabia has expended substantial oil revenue in financing major industrial projects under successive development plans (see Development Plans). The industrialization programme has focused on the construction of refineries and downstream industries to exploit Saudi Arabia's reserves of petroleum and natural gas. (According to the *BP Statistical Review of World Energy 2013*, Saudi Arabia had published proven gas reserves of 8,200,000m. cu m at the end of 2012, the sixth largest in the world, after Iran, Russia, Qatar, Turkmenistan and the USA).

The manufacturing sector, which represented a preliminary 10% of GDP in 2012, has received substantial capital investments over the decades. Invested capital in non-hydrocarbons sectors totalled SR 343,300m. (US $91,547m.) at the end of 2008, of which chemicals and plastics received almost three-fifths of the aggregate, according to the Saudi Industrial Property Authority. The chemicals/plastics industries generate 70% of non-oil exports. In early 2009 there were about 4,167 factories in operation, engaged in the manufacture of chemicals, plastics, rubber, wood products, paper and printing, fertilizers, steel, machine tools, equipment, finished metal goods, cement, building materials, ceramics, glass, textiles and garments, leather, food-processing and soft drinks. According to the World Bank, manufacturing value added in 2010 was $43,850m., up from $23,005m. in 2003.

The rapid expansion of the state-owned Saudi Basic Industries Corpn (SABIC), founded in 1976, has represented the most successful aspect of Saudi Arabia's diversification drive. SABIC, the Middle East's largest non-oil industrial enterprise, which had total assets of SR 332,780m. (US $88,741m.) at the end of 2011, accounts for 8.0% and 95%, respectively, of global and total Saudi production of petrochemicals. The company operates 17 major facilities, located at Jubail, Jeddah and Yanbu—12 factories for chemicals, four for fertilizers and one for metals. Eight of the 17 manufacturing affiliates are joint ventures with foreign companies and three are wholly SABIC-owned, while six are joint-venture partnerships with local and regional private investors. Production in 2011 totalled 69m. metric tons (up from 35m. tons in 2001) and net profits were reported at SR 29,240m.($7,797m.) on a total sales turnover of SR 189,900m. ($50,640m.). SABIC posted a net profit of SR 12,574m. ($3,353m.) for the first half of 2012, compared with SR 15,790m. ($4,211m.) during the first six months of 2011.

SABIC enjoys a competitive edge over most petrochemicals producers, reflecting its access to subsidized gas feedstock from Saudi Aramco at US $0.75 per million British thermal units. SABIC's ongoing and planned investments in capacity expansions are expected to total $25,000m. over the next five years and as much as $75,000m. by 2020. The company (employing over 33,000 people world-wide) intends to expand annual capacity—both at home and overseas—to 130m. metric tons, by 2020.

It is estimated that the kingdom's overall share of global petrochemicals output will be 20% by 2015, making it the world's third largest producer. SABIC is among global market leaders in the production of polyethylene, polypropylene and other advanced thermoplastics, ethylene-glycol, methanol and fertilizers. By the end of 2009 two new facilities—the Eastern Petrochemical Co and the Yanbu National Petrochemical Co (Yansab)—had started production. 'Jubail 11' and 'Yanbu 11' remain key to petrochemicals development over the medium term. Ethylene output capacity is projected to reach 13.5m. metric tons per year.

The petrochemicals sector has also attracted private investment in recent years. A milestone project is the Petro Rabigh joint venture between Saudi Aramco (37.5%) and Sumitomo Chemical Co of Japan (37.5%) to transform Aramco's Rabigh Refinery into a fully integrated petrochemical complex. The first phase of the US $10,000m. project came online in March 2009, and is designed to produce 18.4m. metric tons per year of benzene and high-quality fuels (including gasoline), 2.4m. tons a year of ethylene derivatives and 1.3m. tons a year of olefins, as well as a range of plastics, including linear low-density polyethylene and impact copolymer polypropylene. Aramco was to supply the project with feedstock amounting to 400,000 b/d of crude oil, 15,000 b/d of butane and 95m. cu ft per day of ethane.

In May 2007 Saudi Aramco and the USA's Dow Chemical Co signed a Memorandum of Understanding for a petrochemicals and plastics complex at Ras Tanura, with total investment likely to reach US $20,000m.–$26,000m. It was to have 25–30 downstream manufacturing units producing over 300 products. Aramco subsequently decided to move the project to the Jubail Industrial City, where it could be partially integrated with its planned new export refinery.

The US $10,000m. Saudi Kayan complex is another privately funded project, which started operations in 2010 with total output of 5.6m. metric tons per year, producing high-value added speciality products such as amines and polycarbonate. The Al-Rajhi Co is reportedly working on a $4,000m. polypropylene and ethylene glycol facility, in addition to a 50,000 tons per year benzene unit. The US-based ChevronPhillips is building 650,000 tons per year of styrene monomer capacity at Jubail, along with expanding its benzene, propylene and ethylbenzene units as part of a $1,000m. investment. The private sector petrochemicals capacity is forecast to reach 18m. tons a year by 2015, up from 4m. tons a year in 2007, underpinned by 40 new production lines.

The Saudi Iron and Steel Co (Hadeed), based in Jubail, is a joint venture of SABIC with Germany's Korf-Stahl. It exports iron products to South-East Asian countries and Japan. Saudi Arabia's steel output was 5.3m. metric tons in 2011, compared with 3.9m. tons in 2004, according to the World Steel Association. The Saudi steel producers, led by Hadeed, the Al-Tuwairqi Group and Al-Rajhi Steel Industries reported combined annual capacity of 8.4m. tons, but the kingdom faces a deficit of 3m.–4m. tons per year of reinforcing bars (rebar) used in the construction industry. SABIC aims to expand steel production to 17m. tons by 2020, from a current total of 5.5m. tons.

The building materials sector, particularly the cement industry, flourished in the early 21st century. Saudi Arabia's cement output in 2011 was 48.4m. metric tons (from 13 factories) out of a total capacity of more than 52m. tons. The two major producers were Saudi Cement Co and Yamama, with 5.5m. tons and 5.2m. tons of capacity, respectively. Over 95% of supply is used by the local market. If all announced expansion projects are commissioned, capacity should reach 65.7m. tons by 2015, according to local investment bank NCB Capital. It predicts domestic demand rising to 57.6m. tons by 2015, driven by mega-infrastructure development.

Saudi Arabia had nine refineries with a total capacity of 2.11m. b/d in 2011, two of which are joint ventures with international oil companies. Major refineries are Ras Tanura (550,000 b/d—the largest oil refinery in the Middle East), Saudi Aramco/ExxonMobil at Yanbu (400,000 b/d), Petromin/Shell at Jubail (400,000 b/d), Rabigh (400,000 b/d) and Yanbu (240,000 b/d). Aramco revealed plans for upgrading the Ras Tanura refinery, which entailed installing mixed xylene, cumene, isobutane and petroleum coke facilities, along with overhauls at five other refineries. The kingdom was building three grass-roots refineries which were expected to increase distillation capacity by 1.6m. b/d to 3.7m. b/d by the end of 2013. Saudi Aramco and France's Total and Aramco without a foreign partner (after the withdrawal of the USA's ConocoPhillips) are in the process of building 400,000 b/d export-orientated refineries at Jubail and Yanbu (each costing about US $10,000m). The Jubail refinery was scheduled to enter into production by the end of 2013, while Yanbu—on which Aramco has retained the right to use ConocoPhillips's technology—is due for completion by the end of 2014.

A third planned refinery, at Jizan in the south-west, will have a capacity of 400,000 b/d; its completion is not expected until 2016. In addition Aramco has revealed plans for a new facility at Ras Tanura, named the East Coast refinery, capable of processing 400,000 b/d of Arabian heavy crude. The new Saudi refineries will help to ease a global contraction in refining, which was largely responsible for the over-inflated crude oil prices of recent years. In total, Saudi Aramco's expansion plan for the refining sector, which is designed to integrate several new refineries with large petrochemicals complexes, is expected to cost as much as US $70,000m.

An important element of Saudi Arabia's overall product marketing strategy has been the acquisition by Saudi Aramco of refining interests in prime petroleum-importing countries. Aramco owns a 50% stake in the Motiva (Shell) refinery in the USA, which has a refining capacity of 740,000 b/d, and a 35% equity interest in the Republic of Korea (South Korea)'s largest refining company, Ssangyong Oil, which has a refining capacity of 525,000 b/d. Other joint ventures include a 42% holding in a Greek company, Motor Oil Hellas (with a refining capacity of 100,000 b/d); a 40% interest in the Philippine company Petron, which, through its 180,000-b/d Bataan refinery and its associated transportation and retailing network, supplies about two-fifths of the market for refined products in the Philippines; a 25% stake in China's 240,000-b/d Fujian refinery; and a 15% interest in Japan's 515,000-b/d Showa Shell refinery. Overall, the kingdom seeks to achieve a global refining capacity of 6.4m. b/d within five years, compared with a current total of 4.2m. b/d—equivalent to 4.7% of global refining capacity.

The exploitation and production of vast gas reserves is expected to stimulate the development of energy-intensive industries and to provide feedstock for new power and water desalination plants. About 60% of proven reserves (or 172,680m. cu ft) consists of associated gas (found in conjunction with crude petroleum), mainly from the onshore Ghawar oilfield and the offshore Safaniya and Zuluf fields. The Ghawar field alone holds one-third of total gas reserves. The deep Khuff reservoir contains the bulk of non-associated gas deposits. Of the remaining 115,120m. cu ft of non-associated natural gas, 75% has a higher sulphur content (i.e. comprising sour gas), thus leaving only 28,780m. cu ft of conventional gas deposits that are easy to process. The US Geological Survey estimated that Saudi Arabia could possess ultimately recoverable reserves of 19,000,000m. cu m—compared with the actual proven figure of 8,200,000 cu m.—which represents 4.4% of the world's total.

In November 2006 the Ministry of Petroleum and Mineral Resources and Saudi Aramco announced a US $9,000m. exploration and development strategy to add another 1,416,000m. cu m of non-associated gas resources by 2016. The plan involves drilling 307 new development wells (including over 70 exploration and delineation wells) in the Rub al-Khali, the Nefud basin, north of Riyadh, the Red Sea and the Gulf coast. Only 52 exploratory wells were drilled over 1996–2004, with an exploration success rate of 44%, according to Aramco. Domestic gas demand is projected at 14,500m. cu ft per day by 2030, up from 7,100m. cu ft a day in 2007. However, with annual demand surging by 7.0%–9.0%, the United Kingdom-based energy consultancy, Wood Mackenzie, expects total consumption to reach 15,000m. cu ft per day in 2025. At present, about 55% of gas output is consumed by the power and desalination sector, with the remaining 45% being used as feedstock for petrochemicals. Total gas production is predicted to reach 134,400m. cu m by 2020, compared with 102,800m. cu m in 2012, making Saudi Arabia the region's third largest natural gas producer after Iran (160,500m. cu m), and Qatar (157,000m. cu m), according to BP. The kingdom in 2012 was ranked as the world's eighth largest producer of natural gas.

A number of upstream projects are currently under way to boost gas production capacity over the medium term, thereby keeping pace with annual domestic gas demand growth of 6.0%. These include the Karan project, which was expected to yield 1,800m. cu ft per day of natural gas from 2013; the Wasit project with a nameplate capacity of 2,500m. cu ft per day by mid-2014; the 1,500m. cu ft per day Shaybah NGL venture; and 1,000m. cu ft per day from the Arabiyah gasfield, as well as 800m. cu ft per day from Hasbah gasfield, expected online within four years.

Strong domestic demand also underpinned a US $4,500m. expansion of the Master Gas System (MGS), which was completed in 1984. The MGS—the largest integrated gas gathering, processing and distribution system of its kind (fed entirely by non-associated gas)—is capable of delivering over 7,000m. cu ft per day of net sales gas to the industrial cities of Jubail and Yanbu. Moreover, it facilitates more than 1m. b/d for export by meeting domestic needs for fuel and feedstock with gas. Three processing plants have been built (at Berri, Shedgum and Uthmaniyah) to separate NGLs from methane, and two fractionation plants, at Ju'aymah on the Gulf coast and at Yanbu on the Red Sea, process the NGLs into ethane, liquefied petroleum gas and condensate.

There are currently seven gas-processing plants with a total production capacity of about 10,000m. cu ft per year, plus 1m. b/d of NGLs and about 2,700 tons of sulphur at Berri, Shedgum, Uthmaniyah and Hawiyah facilities. Saudi Aramco aims to process 15,500m. cu ft per day through additional plants and capacity expansion. Mega-projects are under way at Ju'aymah, Khurais, Khursaniyah, Hawiya and Yanbu. Gas is carried to Yanbu through the 1,200-km Trans-Arabian pipeline.

The kingdom also boasts substantial mineral deposits, mostly in the north, including copper, zinc, lead, iron ore, gold, silver, magnetite, limestone, colane, gypsum, marble, clay, bauxite, phosphate, tantalum, silica and some uranium. The Government has yet to explore fully the commercial viability of untapped mineral resources.

Estimated phosphate deposits of 400m. metric tons at al-Jalamid in the northern region are sufficient to mine 4.5m. tons per year of phosphate rock for over 50 years. Ghurayyah in the north-west region holds the world's largest single tantalum deposit, extending over 47 sq km, while gypsum deposits of about 33m. tons, graded between 83% and 90%, are found around the Red Sea basin and the Gulf of Aqaba. High-quality gypsum, ideal for manufacturing plaster, has been identified near Yanbu. In the Fursan mountain area (Western Province), significant marble deposits exist and silica deposits have been found near al-Jouf, Buraydad, Riyadh and Tabuk. About 1.9m. tons of new zinc deposits were recently discovered at Khnaiguiyah. The main open gold mines are situated at al-Amar, al-Duwayhi, al-Hajar, Bulghah and Sukhaybarat in the west of the kingdom.

Strategic control of the minerals sector is exercised by the Directorate-General of Mineral Resources. In 1997 the state-owned Ma'aden was established to take over existing state interests in the non-oil mining sector and to serve as a vehicle for future state mining ventures. The company is planning to invest SR 60,000m. (US $16,000m.) in projects to mine phosphate, bauxite, gold, and other base metals and minerals. Officials expected the nascent mining industry to expand by about 8.0% per year. Ma'aden is planning to develop one of the world's largest phosphate reserves in the northern region, in partnership with foreign investors, as well as to build a multi-billion dollar aluminium plant, located at Ras al-Khair on the south-east coast.

The fully integrated scheme (costing some US $10,800m.), based on the development of the 126m.-metric-ton al-Zabirah bauxite mine, will consist of a smelter producing 750,000 tons of aluminium annually, plus an alumina refinery with an initial capacity of 1.8m. tons per year. Ma'aden owns 75% of the joint venture with the USA-based Alcoa controlling the remaining 25% stake. The project is due onstream in 2014 and is expected to create 12,000 direct and indirect jobs, stimulate related industries and increase GDP by $30,000m. over 25 years. In Jazan region two large-scale aluminium production facilities are also being developed. According to the Saudi Arabian General Investment Authority (SAGIA), Saudi Arabia could produce 6.25m. tons per year if the 10 planned smelters and alumina refineries are commissioned. The sector is due to receive $15,000m. of investment in the coming years. Ma'aden also intends to boost annual gold output to 400,000 troy oz by 2015, from 150,000 oz currently, and to increase gold resources to 20m. oz by 2020, compared with 11m. oz in 2011. The Government opened the minerals sector to foreign mining companies under the 2004 Mining Law, which offers attractive incentives such as 100% foreign ownership, mining leases of 30 years, reduced tax rates of 20% and tax-free importation of machinery and equipment.

The non-oil industry associated with the new 'economic cities'—each focusing on different sectors—is expected to demonstrate vigorous growth over the medium to long term. Five of the cities have been officially launched: the King Abdullah Economic City in Mecca (light and heavy industry, and finance); the Prince Abd al-Aziz Bin Mosaed Economic City in Ha'il region (transport, logistical services and agribusiness); the Jazan Economic City in the south-west area (energy and labour-intensive industries); the Medina Knowledge Economic City (information technology and communications); and the Sudair Industrial City in Qassim region (telecommunications and electronics). Two other schemes are at the planning stage, namely the Tabouk Economic City and the Ras al-Zour Resource City in the Eastern region, with a focus on mining and mineral refining. SAGIA expects the industrial cities, with a projected total population of 4.5m., to contribute US $150,000m. to GDP and create 1.3m. jobs by 2020. The Saudi British Bank estimates the total cost of building these ambitious economic cities at $500,000m. SAGIA has introduced fiscal incentives and 100% foreign ownership rights to invest in various projects. The Government has approved a plan to increase the industrial sector's share of GDP to 20% by 2020, with the aim of achieving 8% annual growth in non-hydrocarbons industries over the next decade.

ELECTRICITY AND WATER

Saudi Arabia's electricity system has to satisfy rapidly growing urban and industrial demand, and also to supply power for small, widely scattered rural settlements. An increasing amount of electricity is produced in association with seawater desalination. Demand grew during the 1990s, and a major programme for the expansion of capacity was planned, coupled with a campaign to reduce wasteful consumption (accounting for an estimated 30% of current electricity usage). In November 1998 10 regional power companies (including the four Saudi

Consolidated Electric Cos—East, West, Central and South—which controlled 85% of the kingdom's power supplies) and six smaller regional power-generating companies were merged into the Saudi Electricity Co (SEC). A new higher structure of tariffs was introduced prior to the SEC's incorporation in April 2000 and the new company was mandated to collect tariffs more effectively. The Electricity and Co-generation Regulatory Authority was established in 2001.

The SEC, a joint-stock company co-owned by the Government, is now the largest electricity utility in the Middle East. In 2012 installed generating capacity totalled over 50,000 MW, an increase from 23,438 MW in 1999. Some 70% of the kingdom's electricity supply is fuelled by gas, while steam-powered facilities represent 15%. The remainder is accounted for by diesel (10%) and combined-cycle plants (5%). Saudi Arabia uses about 750,000 b/d of heavy crude to fire its power plants. SEC, which accounts for 85% of the kingdom's total capacity, spent US $25,100m. in 2007 on implementing various power-generation, transmission and distribution projects. About one-fifth of SEC's power stations (45) are over 25 years old.

With electricity demand rising by 7.0%–8.0% per year, the Government claims that the sector requires US $90,700m. of capital investment from both the public and private sectors in power-generation and transmission/distribution infrastructure by 2020, when total demand is forecast to reach 78,000 MW (from 46,000 MW in 2011). A report by Banque Saudi Fransi revealed that electricity generation alone requires investment of some SR 300,000m. ($80,000m.) over the next 15 years. According to official sources, additional power capacity of 27,000 MW to 30,000 MW is needed within the next two decades, while domestic oil usage by power stations could double to 1.5m. b/d by 2020. In common with other GCC member states, private power developers were expected to provide the bulk of the funding. In July 2002 the Supreme Economic Council passed a resolution setting out a framework for private sector participation in independent water and power projects (IWPPs).

The United Arab Emirates (UAE)-based daily *Gulf News* reported in 2008 that Saudi Arabia intended to establish 10 IWPPs by 2016, with total estimated investment costs of US $16,000m. The Government favoured a 60:40 equity-ownership model between private operators and the SEC or public bodies. The Water and Electricity Co, jointly owned by the SEC and the Saline Water Conversion Corpn (SWCC), was to buy the entire output from IWPPs under a 20-year purchase agreement. In September 2003 the SEC revealed plans for seven new electric power stations, four of which were also to produce desalinated water, to be located at al-Muzahimiyah, al-Qurayyat 2, Salboukh, Riyadh PP10, Rabigh 2, Yanbu 2 and Shuqaiq 2, with a total capacity of 14,575 MW. They were scheduled for completion between 2010 and 2017, and were to cost $7,476m. A Malaysian-led consortium has invested $6,700m. in a power and water desalination facility at Shuaiba on the Red Sea coast. The SEC also announced details of 10 transmission projects (costing about $2,000m.), involving the erection of 4,800 km of power lines. By 2015 15,000 MW of extra capacity was expected online, at an estimated cost of $20,000m.

The SEC has unveiled plans to add 20,000 MW of capacity by 2018 (costing US $80,000m.), in addition to 10,000 MW of new capacity arising from six independent power producer (IPP) projects, due for completion between 2013 and 2021. They include the 2,520-MW plant in Ras al-Zour, the Riyadh 2,000-MW PP11 plant, the 2,000-MW Qurayyah plant, the 1,200-MW Rabigh plant, a 1,000-MW plant in Dheba and an 800-MW plant in Shuqaiq. The total cost of these IPP projects is reported at $20,000m. According to the SEC, power generation, transmission and distribution sectors will absorb $46,000m., $30,000m., and $20,000m., respectively, of capital spending over the long term.

The Government has issued a royal decree establishing the 'King Abdullah City (complex) for Atomic and Renewable Energy' (KA-Care) for peaceful uses, while the kingdom was reported to be in negotiations with France regarding an agreement for co-operation in civil nuclear energy production. Saudi Arabia plans to commission 16 nuclear power reactors over the next 20 years at a cost of US $300,000m. The first two reactors would be built within a decade—with two following every year thereafter. It was anticipated that nuclear power and renewable energy would provide around one-half of the kingdom's power needs by 2030, when peak demand for electricity was projected to reach 120 GW. In June 2012 the kingdom also announced a $109,000m. scheme to install 41 GW of solar power capacity over the next two decades.

About one-fifth of the country remains unconnected to the national power grid and creating a unified national grid is estimated to require over 30,000 km of new power transmission lines. In 2004 the kingdom had about 250,000 km of transmission lines. According to the GCC Interconnection Authority, a regional inter-exchange electricity grid serving the six GCC states at an estimated cost of US $1,600m. was scheduled to be fully operational in 2011–12. The first phase of the project, linking Saudi Arabia, Kuwait, Bahrain and Qatar, was completed in early 2009, while the second phase, linking the individual grids of the UAE with that of Oman was completed in July of that year.

Besides power generation demand, Saudi Arabia will also require an additional 250m. gallons per day (g/d) of water over the next 20 years, according to local sources. Per caput demand for water is also growing by 7.0% annually. The SWCC projected that total domestic consumption of water would increase from currently 1,300 g/d to 1,700 g/d by 2031, 60% of which would be met through desalination. This change reflected the projected expansion of the industrial and agricultural sectors, as well as burgeoning population growth. The SWCC estimated that the funding needed to deal with the projected change could equal SR 160,000m. (US $42,667m.) over the same period. In addition, $23,000m. of new investment is required for building waste-water treatment plants over the next 20 years.

The SWCC is the world's largest producer of desalinated water, accounting for 24.5% of global output. From its 28 plants, the organization produces about 3.4m. cu m per day of water, equivalent to more than one-half of the country's daily requirements. It expects to invest SR 1,300m. for renovation of old water desalination plants, in addition to new desalination projects being implemented all over the kingdom. Several water transmission networks were under construction in 2006, and the total length of water pipelines was expected to reach more than 4,000 km during the eighth Development Plan.

AGRICULTURE AND FISHING

Agriculture (including forestry and fishing) contributed a preliminary 1.9% of GDP in 2012, and in 2013 the sector employed almost 573,000 people. Agricultural GDP increased by an average of 1.6% per year in 2002–11. Cultivation is confined to oases and to irrigated regions, which comprise only 2% of the total land area. About 39% of land is used for low-grade grazing. Watermelons, tomatoes, dates and grapes are produced in significant quantities.

The importance of developing the agricultural sector, requiring long-term investment of US $28,300m. as a means of reducing imports, has been emphasized by the Government. In 2009 agricultural projects accounted for nearly one-quarter of the kingdom's expected SR 181,000m. ($48,267m.) private sector investments, enhancing Saudi Arabia's status as a major player in the regional agribusiness. Food and agricultural products accounted for around 16.9% of total imports in 2011; the kingdom is currently the GCC's largest agricultural importer. The kingdom consumed almost 28m. metric tons of food in 2011, of which 80% was imported, according to the UAE-based Alpen Capital.

Saudi Arabia is subject to important natural limitations on the development of agriculture, principally the scarcity of water. Agriculture accounts for 85%–90% of water demand in the kingdom, which is met mostly by non-renewable groundwater reserves. The Government has initiated an ambitious programme to increase the country's water supply, including surveys for underground water resources, construction of dams, and irrigation and drainage networks, combined with distribution of fallow land, settlement of *bidoun* and the introduction of mechanization. The principal aim of the programme was to raise agricultural production to the level of near self-sufficiency in all foods. Consequently, budgetary allocations for the agricultural sector have increased considerably.

Wheat production totalled 1.4m. metric tons in 2011, compared with 1.7m. tons in 2008. The National Agricultural Development Co (NADEC), formed in 1981, is a major producer of fruit, open-field and greenhouse vegetables. NADEC also specializes in dairy farming and processing and has over 50,000 cattle on six dairy farms, as well as two dairy plants with a total production capacity of 1m. litres per day. The kingdom is 50% self-sufficient in poultry production, with the country ranking among the highest consumers of chicken per caput in the world, according to FAO. A major success has been achieved with dairy farming, using the most modern technical expertise from Sweden, Denmark and Ireland, and Saudi Arabia has some of the world's most efficient dairy farms. Although domestic milk consumption is relatively low, at 60 litres per caput per year, compared with 120 litres in Western Europe, an expanding, young population presents a future growth market for producers.

The fishing industry has grown in recent years, and in 2011 the total catch was estimated at 91,236 metric tons. New projects launched by the Saudi Fisheries Co in the past decade included a facility to convert fish to fodder, a processing factory and the purchase of shrimping vessels.

TRANSPORT, COMMUNICATIONS AND TOURISM

Until 1964 the only surfaced roads, besides those in the petroleum network, were in the Jeddah-Mecca-Medina area. Since then, roads have been given priority, and at the end of 2009 there were about 221,372 km of roads, of which 21.5% were paved. The government is spending SR 10,800m. (US $2,880m.) to support the construction of 284 road projects, including highways, secondary roads and branch roads. The biggest regional allocations are for 814 km, 432 km and 428 km of new roads in the Riyadh, Mecca and Asir regions, respectively. When completed, these projects will expand the size of the kingdom's road network by almost 17%. The Saudi Public Transport Co (the national bus operator) serves mainly inter-city routes. A causeway linking Bahrain with the Saudi mainland was opened in late 1986. It is open 24 hours per day, although trucks may only use it at off-peak times.

The main seaports are at Jeddah, Yanbu and Jizan on the Red Sea and at Dammam and Jubail on the Gulf. An estimated 12,000 vessels annually use Saudi Arabian ports, which in 2002 had a total of 183 organized and mechanized berths (137 at six commercial ports and 46 at two industrial ports). The volume of cargo (excluding crude petroleum) handled by Saudi ports in 2001 totalled 100.6m. metric tons (68.9m. tons of exports and 31.7m. tons of imports); by 2011 this had risen to 165m. tons. Containerized tariffs through the Saudi ports in 2011 were reported to amount to 9.0m. 20-ft equivalent units (TEUs), compared with 3.9m. TEUs in 2006. The Saudi Ports Authority plans to expand national container capacity to over 15m. TEUs by 2015.

Saudi Arabia is upgrading facilities at a number of major seaports, while developing two new cargo centres along the Red Sea coast. By far the kingdom's largest port, the Jeddah Islamic Port, which handles more than 70% of total container traffic, is due for a large-scale expansion, with this coming after its total capacity was doubled in late 2009 with the opening of a third terminal—Red Sea Gateway (costing US $450m.). Plans are under way to expand the port's cargo facilities by one-half, with a longer-term target of raising overall capacity from 6.5m. to 13m. containers by 2020. Saudi Arabia's existing ports handled over 154m. tons of freight in 2010, an increase of 8% compared with the previous year, according to the Saudi Ports Authority.

A programme was introduced in 1997 to 'commercialize' the operation of the main ports by offering 10-year operations, maintenance and management leases to private sector contractors, which would derive their income from stevedoring fees charged to port users and would pay a proportion of their income to the Saudi Ports Authority as royalties. In 1983 Saudi Arabia became the 40th member of the British-based International Maritime (now Mobile) Satellite Organization.

Vela International Marine (Vela), the shipping arm of Saudi Aramco, operates the world's sixth largest fleet of super oil-tankers, which in 2011 included 24 vessels classified as very large crude carriers (VLCCs) and four ultra-large crude carriers, as well as four product tankers and one Aframax class vessel. Vela transports an average of about 3m. b/d. Aramco also owns or leases oil storage facilities around the world, including in Rotterdam, Sidi Kerir (the Sumed pipeline terminal on Egypt's Mediterranean coast), South Korea, the Philippines, and the Caribbean.

The National Shipping Co of Saudi Arabia (Bahri) also operates a fleet of eight VLCCs and through its subsidiaries—National Chemical Carriers and Arabian Chemical Carriers—owns 14 chemical tankers, plus four container vessels, bringing the total to 26 vessels. Bahri is a public company, in which the Public Investment Fund (PIF) of the Saudi Government holds a 28% stake, while the remaining 72% is publicly traded. In June 2012 Saudi Aramco and Bahri signed a US $1,300m. agreement for the sale of Vela International Marine. The merger of the two companies would create the fourth largest fleet of VLCCs in the world and a total fleet of 77 vessels.

There are 36 commercial airports in the kingdom. The principal international airports are at Jeddah (King Abd al-Aziz), Dhahran (the Eastern Province International Airport and King Fahd International Airport) and Riyadh (King Khalid). More than 54m. passengers passed through Saudi Arabian international airports during 2011 (an increase of 12.4% on the previous year), according to data from the General Authority for Civil Aviation. Construction of a new passenger terminal building at King Abd-al Aziz International airport in Jeddah was expected to be completed by 2014, which will increase annual passenger capacity from currently 13m. to 30m. The capacity of King Khalid International airport is also being expanded from 14m. passengers to 24m. The Government operates the national carrier, Saudi Arabian Airlines (SAUDIA), which links important Saudi cities and operates regular flights to many foreign countries. SAUDIA controls 90% and 84%, respectively, of domestic and international traffic in the kingdom, according to the Centre of Asia Pacific Aviation. In June 2003 the Council of Ministers approved plans to open up the domestic aviation sector to competition. There are now two privately owned, low-cost carriers (Nas Air and Sama Airlines) competing with SAUDIA on both international and domestic destinations.

Saudi Arabia has the only rail system in the Arabian peninsula, with a total rail network of 2,400 km; in 2008 the Saudi Railways Organization carried some 337 passengers per km. The principal lines are a 570-km single-track railway that connects the port of Dammam, on the Gulf, with Riyadh, and a 322-km line, linking Riyadh with Hufuf, which was inaugurated in May 1985. Plans for a rapid expansion of the rail network are under way, centred on three major projects. The US $7,000m. Saudi Landbridge Project, launched in 2006, will provide west-east freight and passenger services between Jeddah and Dammam via Jubail and Riyadh. The $1,800m. contract for the first phase of the $6,000m., 444-km Haramain high-speed electrified railway to carry pilgrims travelling to Mecca and Medina, via Jeddah, was awarded to a consortium including China Railways Engineering Corpn and Alstom of France. The link will also transport commuters between the three cities. Meanwhile, work has started on the new, 2,400-km 'North-South' railway project (costing SR 20,000m. or $5,333m.), designed to link the kingdom's mineral extraction sites. In July 2013 three contracts were issued for the construction of a six-line metro system in Riyadh. A contract to build lines 1 and 2 went to a consortium led by Bechtel of the USA; line 3 was to be built by ArRiyadh New Mobility, a consortium led by Italian companies Ansaldo STS and Salini-Impregilo; and the three remaining lines by the FAST consortium, which included Spain's Fomento de Construcciones y Contratas. Construction work on the $22,500m. project was expected to begin in early 2014 and to be completed by 2018.

In the late 1980s Saudi Arabia established satellite transmission and reception stations, facilitating direct telephone dialling to most of the rest of the world. In 2012 there were about 4.8m. fixed telephone lines (an increase from 3.8m. lines in 2005). The number of mobile cellular telephone users in the kingdom had grown to 53m. in 2012.

In July 2002 the Saudi Communications and Information Technology Commission issued new legislation that provided a comprehensive framework for deregulation of the telecommunications sector by 2004. There are now four mobile phone providers—Saudi Telecommunications Co (STC—Saudi Telecom), the UAE-based Etihad Etisalat (operating locally under the brand name Mobily), Kuwait's Zain Group and Mobile Telecommunications Corpn. The STC's monopoly on the fixed-line sector was ended when the authorities awarded three licences to foreign operators—namely Bahrain Telecommunications Corpn (Batelco), Pacific Century CyberWorks of Hong Kong and Verizon Communications of the USA.

The number of internet users was estimated at 13.6m. (48.4% of the population) at the end of 2011 (an increase from 5.79m. users in 2008). In 2012 broadband subscribers numbered 2.0m. Saudi Arabia comprises nearly one-third of the regional telecommunications market. Under the current ninth Development Plan (2010–14), the Government has pledged to spend SR 112,500m. (US $30,000m.) on upgrading transportation infrastructure and communications networks.

The Government regards the tourism industry as a source of foreign exchange and job creation, and advertises abroad the kingdom's many archaeological and heritage sites. The Saudi Commission for Tourism and Antiquities (SCTA—formerly Supreme Commission for Tourism and Antiquities) is keen to promote adventure and sports tourism, targeting both Westerners and locals. The number of hotel rooms across major cities of Saudi Arabia is to be expanded from 95,000 to 150,000 by 2013. The SCTA hopes to attract an annual 6m. international tourists (excluding pilgrims) by 2025. Many facilities are, in fact, designed to induce Saudi nationals to take a holiday in their own country; an estimated 7.23m. Saudis spent a total of US $22,803m. on foreign travel (including business trips) during 2010.

According to provisional figures, tourism expenditure in the country totalled US $8,459m. in 2011, while the number of tourists reached 17.4m. Religious tourism, however, remains the main reason for overseas visitors to Saudi Arabia. In 2011 the Kingdom issued 9.5m. religious visas (up 11.3% from 2010), with *Umrah* visas rising by 1m. (from 2010), according to the Ministry of *Hajj*. Some 1.8m. foreign pilgrims arrived in Mecca during 2012 to perform the annual *Hajj*. The SCTA has set an ambitious target of attracting 88m. tourists by 2020, focusing on Muslim cultural history and business travel in particular.

FOREIGN TRADE AND INVESTMENT

Driven by the oil-related terms-of-trade gains, the kingdom's external account has improved markedly in recent years, reflected in perennial trade and current account surpluses. The merchandise trade surplus averaged US $166,335m. annually during 2004–11, while a substantial average surplus of $85,987m. was recorded on the current account of the balance of payments over the same period. The value of Saudi Arabia's exports more than doubled between 2004 ($125,998m.) and 2008 ($313,333m.). However, they declined by some 38.6% in 2009 to $192,600m. in tandem with lower oil prices, before recovering to $251,500m. and $365,000m., respectively, in 2010 and 2011. The value of exports increased further in 2012, reaching $388,400m. In cumulative terms, export revenues for the period 2004–11 were over $1,875,000m., according to the IMF, with oil exports accounting for 85%–90% of the total. In 2011 oil export revenues of $331,000m. represented 32.0% of the OPEC total. The five leading export markets in 2012 were Japan (with 13.2% of the aggregate), China (12.9%), the USA (13.4%), the Republic of Korea (South Korea—9.4%) and India (8.3%). The Asia-Pacific region received 60% of Saudi exports of petroleum, including refined oil, NGLs and petrochemical products.

The value of Saudi Arabia's imports increased from US $41,050m. in 2004 to $141,800m. in 2012. The kingdom's major suppliers in 2012 were China (accounting for 12.7% of total imports), the USA (13.5%), Germany (7.1%), Japan (6.7%) and South Korea (6.1%). Machinery and transportation equipment accounted for the largest share of imports (44.2%). Chemicals and base metals (22.0%) were the next largest imports. The depreciation of the US dollar against other major currencies since 2002 has increased the cost of the kingdom's main non-dollar imports, which are priced in Japanese yen, the euro and the British pound. In 2012 surpluses on the merchandise trade and current accounts increased, in accordance with strong oil prices and continued robust demand in Asia (led by China). A trade surplus of $246,570m. was recorded in that year, while the current account surplus reached $164,764m. (equivalent to 23.2% of GDP).

In June 1993 Saudi Arabia, which had held observer status to the General Agreement on Tariffs and Trade (GATT) since 1985, submitted an application for full membership. However, negotiations with GATT's successor body, the World Trade Organization (WTO), were prolonged. WTO membership became a major objective of the Saudi Government, and a number of liberalization measures were introduced in an apparent attempt to counter objections to WTO accession. In August 2003 the Government signed a trade agreement with the European Union that was intended to ease the kingdom's path towards membership of the WTO. The US Government insisted that a bilateral US-Saudi agreement was dependent on Saudi Arabia opening up its telecommunications and banking sectors to 100% foreign ownership. In December 2005 Saudi Arabia finally joined the WTO as its 149th member, after signing a bilateral trade accord with the USA. The Government was obliged to eliminate (in stages) non-tariff barriers deemed unfair under WTO rules, although it retained the right to block certain imports prohibited under *Shari'a* law, notably pork, alcohol and pornography. It was to phase out all export subsidies on agricultural products; reduce average tariffs on imported goods to 12.4% (agricultural) and 10.5% (industrial) towards the end of a 10-year implementation period; and abolish tariffs on personal computers, semiconductors and other information technology items by January 2008. Saudi Arabia has also agreed to allow 'duty-free' entry of pharmaceuticals and civil aircraft on accession, as well as to permit majority foreign equity stakes in the telecommunications and financial services industry. The Saudi Government has pledged not to participate in the boycott of Israel by the League of Arab States (Arab League), thus complying with the WTO stipulation of 'freer trade' and 'fairer competition' among the member states.

Since 2000 the kingdom has made great strides towards becoming more integrated into the global economy. In marked contrast with the previous three decades, during the early 21st century the country boasted the most liberal FDI regime in the Gulf region. SAGIA, formed in May 2000, acts as a 'one-stop shop' for global, regional and domestic investors, and has enhanced the kingdom's profile within the international investment community. New regulations permitted 100% foreign equity holding (compared with 49% previously) in most industries, including power generation, water desalination and petrochemicals; moreover, wholly foreign-owned businesses are able to qualify for tax breaks and soft loans from the Saudi Industrial Development Fund and can buy properties, except in the holy cities of Mecca and Medina. Furthermore, corporate taxes were reduced from 45% to 20% in most sectors (30% for the gas sector). The Government signed bilateral treaties with several countries to provide relief from double-taxation and is a member of the Multilateral Investment Guarantee Agency.

The 'Negative List' (banning FDI on strategic grounds) was shortened from 23 to 16. Besides upstream gas exploration and development, non-Saudi investors enjoy access to other sectors such as cellular phones, ICT, extractive mining, transportation, tourism, insurance, education, health care, printing, power transmission and distribution and pipeline services. Furthermore, from the end of 2008 foreigners were allowed to acquire a 75% stake in the insurance, wholesale and retail trade, and aviation and railway sectors (formerly 51%). For fixed-line and mobile phone companies, the foreign ownership ceiling was raised to 60%. The Supreme Economic Council is committed under WTO obligations to review those sectors closed to FDI, such as upstream real estate investment, recruitment and fisheries companies. Nevertheless, a few sectors—notably upstream oil exploration, drilling and production, defence and security, and media and publishing—remain closed to foreign investors.

The kingdom was the region's second largest FDI recipient (after Turkey), with net inflows of US $12,182m. in 2012, according to the *World Investment Report 2013* published by the UN Conference on Trade and Development. This figure represented a decline of some 25.3% compared with 2011, and was less than one-third of the total FDI inflow recorded in 2008. FDI inward stock in 2012 was estimated at $199,032m. By contrast, FDI inward stock in 2000 was reported at just $17,577m.

The Government also pursued reforms that facilitated the kingdom's accession to the WTO in December 2005. These measures included devising a new 'business-friendly' tax code, revising commercial laws, implementing intellectual property rights, reducing import tariffs and removing non-trade barriers, as well as liberalizing the financial services industry and strengthening insurance and capital market regulations and supervision. WTO membership was expected to improve longer-term growth prospects through increased FDI and non-oil exports. In its *Doing Business in 2013* report, the World Bank rated Saudi Arabia as the 22nd most competitive economy for doing business out of 183 (above several OECD countries including Japan, Switzerland, Belgium, France and Israel, among others). It was the highest ranked Middle Eastern country for undertaking business ventures.

FINANCE

The Saudi Arabian Monetary Agency (SAMA), the central bank, which was established in 1952, is responsible for the formulation of monetary policy, the management of official external assets and the supervision of commercial banks. SAMA is credited with preserving currency and price stability. The riyal has been pegged to the US dollar at $1 = SR 3.745 since June 1986. The current pegged exchange rate regime is expected to remain unchanged in the period leading to the GCC monetary union. Moreover, the main Saudi exports—crude petroleum and gas-based products such as methanol and ammonia-urea—are priced in US dollars.

SAMA boasts an exceptionally solid international liquidity position. Foreign exchange reserves (excluding gold) in April 2012 totalled US $587,687m. (the world's fourth largest), compared with $155,029m. in December 2005. Gold bullion holdings were reported by the World Gold Council at 10.4m. fine troy oz (up from 4.6m. oz). Furthermore, in April 2012 SAMA's aggregate foreign assets (mostly comprising US treasuries, British gilts and eurodollar deposits) were estimated at $582,203m., substantially higher than the $152,981m. recorded in December 2005. The IMF projected gross official reserves for the end of 2012 at $701,800m. Saudi Arabia is also a 'net creditor' to the global banking sector. According to the Bank for International Settlements, its net assets at OECD-based banks were $105,791m. in December 2011; gross deposits totalled $188,552m. Private flight capital, including both foreign direct and portfolio investments, remains substantial. 'Offshore' assets of some 80,000 high-net-worth individuals are estimated at between $600,000m. and $1,000,000m., equivalent to 193%–322% of GDP and among the world's highest capital-flight ratios.

In 2012 the banking and financial system consisted of 12 local commercial banks: six specialized credit institutions, namely the Saudi Industrial Development Fund—SIDF (which finances industrial projects); the Public Investment Fund—PIF (which finances large scale government and private industrial projects); TASNEE—formerly the National Industrialization Co, the Real Estate Development Fund—REDF (which finances individuals and corporate residential and commercial real estate); the Saudi Credit & Savings Bank—SCSB (which provides interest-free loans for small and emerging businesses and professions); and the Agricultural Development Fund—SADF (which finances farmers and agricultural projects). There were also 16 foreign banks (HSBC, JPMorgan Chase & Co, Deutsche Bank, BNP Paribas, Crédit Suisse Group, Barclays, Société Générale, National Bank of Kuwait, National Bank of Bahrain, Emirates Bank Group, Bank Muscat–Oman, Gulf International Bank, EFG Hermes Holdings, Bank Audi, National Bank of Pakistan and State Bank of India), and some 92 licensed investment houses, including local firms and joint ventures with foreign banks (notably Barclays Capital, Calyon, Credit Suisse, Goldman Sachs, UBS, Merrill Lynch and Morgan Stanley). Following the liberalization of the insurance sector in 2004, 29 insurance companies have received licences to operate in the kingdom. Previously, the only licensed operator was the Riyadh-based National Co for Co-operative Insurance. The kingdom's insurance penetration level as a percentage of GDP (1.5% in 2010) was among the lowest in the world. The life sector is also very small, although it has been growing at faster rates during recent years.

Banking is regulated under the Banking Control Law issued by royal decree in 1966. SAMA's regulatory framework is on a par with the Group of Ten (G10) nations' central banks. The IMF commended SAMA for effective supervision of the banking system, which has resulted in 'the development of well-managed, profitable and financially sound institutions'. SAMA has also effectively introduced global accounting and auditing norms (International Financial Reporting Standards and International Standards on Auditing) for banks and their auditors. Therefore, all banks must now comply with stringent guidelines on provisions against bad debts, and with international accounting standards. SAMA reported a non-performing loans (NPLs) ratio of only 3.0% in 2010. In August 2003 the Council of Ministers approved anti-money-laundering legislation designed to bring the kingdom into line with international banking practice. The move came just before the country's banking sector was scheduled to be evaluated by the Financial Action Task Force on Money Laundering.

The five principal banks, ranked by 2011 assets, were the NCB (US $ 80,314m.), Al-Rajhi Banking and Investment Corpn ($58,880m.), SAMBA Financial Group ($51,403m.), Riyad Bank Ltd ($48,233m.) and Banque Saudi Fransi ($37,459m.). The main three lenders (Al-Rajhi, NCB and SAMBA) announced record profits of $1,967m., $1,628m. and $1,147m., respectively, given healthy average returns of 3.3%, 2.0% and 2.2% on total assets, respectively, during the reporting year. By the end of April 2012 total banking assets had reached SR 1,499,000m. ($399,733m.), the region's second highest after the UAE.

Saudi banks have become more outward-looking and the most obvious example of this trend is the 55% Saudi-owned Saudi International Bank, which opened as a fully fledged merchant bank in London, United Kingdom, in March 1976. SAMA holds 50% of the capital, while the NCB and Riyad Bank have 25% each. The first wholly private Saudi bank abroad—Al-Saudi Banque—opened in Paris, France, in late 1976. Riyad Bank has a share in the Paris-based Union de Banques Arabes et Françaises, and in the Gulf Riyad Bank in Bahrain. The NCB has small stakes in European-Arab Holding and the Compagnie Arabe et Internationale d'Investissement, both based in Luxembourg, and in the Amman-based Arab-Jordanian Investment Bank, which opened in 1978. Gross foreign assets of Saudi banks were US $55,157m. in April 2012, compared with $24,360m. in December 2005.

Specialized credit institutions provide short-, medium- and long-term project finance: the SIDF, set up by the Government in 1974, is a major source. It grants low-interest loans to industrial enterprises for up to 50% of the total cost of a project (up to 80% in the case of electricity projects). The maximum tenure allowed for a SIDF loan—with an upper limit of SR 4,875m. (US $1,300m.)—was extended from 15 to 20 years, including five years' grace and repayments structured to match the project's projected cashflows. As of the end of 2007 the SIDF (managed by JPMorgan Chase & Co)—with a capital base of SR 20,000m. ($5,333m.)—approved business venture loans worth SR 66,800m. ($17,813m.) in support of 2,000-plus industrial projects. While the PIF, established in 1972, finances large-scale commercial and industrial projects in the public sector, in 1985 the NIC was established by private investors to encourage and plan development in the private sector.

In 1990 SAMA introduced an electronic trading system that enabled brokers at Saudi banks to trade online. The value of shares traded has risen steeply in recent years: in 2005 shares were being traded in 79 companies with a market capitalization of US $650,130m. (compared with $40,906m. in 1995). However, only 10 prime stocks, led by SABIC, the STC and the Al-Rajhi Banking and Investment Corpn, representing two-thirds of total capitalization and profits of all quoted companies, dominated trading. Reflecting buoyant corporate profits, excessive liquidity and 'offshore' capital repatriation, the benchmark Tadawul All-Share Index (TASI) recorded spectacular growth of 85% and 104% in 2004 and 2005, respectively. The Saudi Stock Exchange (Tadawul) was among the world's best performers of 2005.

However, the market suffered unprecedented volatility during 2006, which saw its value halved between highs of US $834,000m. (25 February) and lows of $400,000m. (11 May). Paper losses on the stock market in the first five months of 2006 were equivalent to the entire GDP of Saudi Arabia. By the end of 2006 the market value of shares was reported at $326,933m.—almost one-half of its 2005 level—as the TASI suffered a 52.5% slump during the year. The stock market rebounded in 2007, with the TASI soaring by 41%; the market value of shares recovered to $518,933m. However, the TASI followed global markets downwards, with the benchmark index of 127 listed stocks losing 56.5% during 2008. Total market capitalization was reported to be $318,737m. as of the end of 2009 (a rise of 29.2% compared with the previous year). A sustained recovery in share prices continued in 2010 as market value rose by 10.8% to $353,414m. However, foreign portfolio investment on the Saudi bourse remains modest, at about $4,000m. A total of 157 companies were listed by Tadawul at mid-2013 with overall market capitalization of $399,230m. The equity market is largely dominated by financial, petrochemical and telecommunications stocks.

The Capital Market Authority (CMA), the sole regulator for the Saudi capital markets, pledged to upgrade trading platforms for licensing of non-bank mutual funds in order to entice institutional investors and to establish an independent authority that would license financial analysts. The CMA also reduced trading commissions to 0.12% (from 0.15%) and abolished Thursday trading in an effort to curb speculative trading, which was regarded as largely responsible for the market's recent turbulence. Other measures to instill confidence and improve liquidity included restoring the 10% fluctuation limits, splitting stocks into smaller denominations and permitting foreigners (including expatriates) to invest directly on the Saudi stock exchange by using swap deals or exchange traded funds, which are tradeable index-linked financial products (foreign workers were previously restricted to mutual funds). However, expatriates are still excluded from participating in initial public offerings, which are reserved exclusively for Saudi nationals.

BUDGET

The Government's fiscal position has improved in the early 21st century, underpinned by higher-than-budgeted oil receipts and fiscal prudence. The state's huge oil windfalls were used to accumulate official external reserves, reduce public debt and fund extra spending on welfare, education, development projects and national security. Since 2000 the budget, with the exception of 2001, 2002 and 2009, has been in surplus every year, a significant turnaround from the chronic deficits of the 1990s. According to the Ministry of Finance, the final figures for 2005 and 2006 showed healthy surpluses of SR 214,000m. and SR 265,125m., respectively, compared with surpluses of SR 36,000m. during 2003 and SR 98,000m. in 2004. Official figures for 2001 and 2002 indicated deficits of SR 26,981m. and SR 20,500m., respectively, compared with a fiscal surplus of SR 22,743m. in 2000.

The 2007 budget envisaged total revenues of SR 400,125m. and expenditure of SR 379,875m., thus yielding a modest surplus of SR 20,250m. (US $5,400m.). In fact, in that year the kingdom posted its fourth largest surplus of SR 178,500m. ($47,600m.). In 2008 SAMA reported the largest surplus in the kingdom's history (SR 590,000m., or $157,333m.), equal to 33.5% of GDP, with the State's revenue and expenditure soaring to SR 1,100,000m. and SR 510,000m., respectively. In contrast, the 2009 fiscal account recorded a SR 45,000m. ($12,000m.) shortfall, with total spending and revenue at SR 550,000m. and SR 505,000m., respectively, although the deficit fell below the initial estimate of SR 65,000m. Despite revenue contraction, SR 25,000m. ($60,000m.) was allocated for capital spending in support of vital infrastructure projects such as schools, universities, hospitals, roads, railways and airports. An expansionary policy helped to mitigate the impact of the downturn. The 2010 budget envisaged a SR 70,000m. ($18,667m.) deficit based on an average oil price of $50 a barrel—with total expenditure and revenue predicted at SR 540,000m. and SR 470,000m., respectively, over the year. The 2010 fiscal account (despite higher-than-projected spending) actually recorded a healthy surplus—estimated by the IMF at 5.1% of GDP or SR 87,401m. ($23,307m.)—reflecting an increase in average oil price to more than $70 per barrel (compared with $53.5 in 2009).

In 2011 the Government unveiled another expansionary budget of SR 580,000m.—with revenues expected at SR 540,000m. (based on a conservative oil price forecast of US $60), thus resulting in a deficit of SR 40,000m. The budget provided for higher spending on education and vocational training (up 8.0%), health and social development (up 12.3%) and basic infrastructure (up 10.4%). These three sectors together comprised over two-fifths of total public expenditure. As a result of increasing oil revenues (with Saudi Arabian Light crude averaging US $107.8 per barrel), the Ministry of Finance estimated that actual 2011 revenues had reached SR 1,100,000m. while total expenditure rose to SR 804,000m. That, in turn, yielded a large surplus of SR 296,000m. ($78,933m.), equivalent to 13.2% of GDP, of which SR 250,000m. was channelled back into the Government's housing programme, with the remainder allocated for reducing the national debt. The 2012 budget placed an emphasis on capital spending (about 40% of the budget was allocated for socio-economic infrastructure projects across the kingdom). Based on a conservative oil price of US$70 per barrel, the Government predicted 2012 revenues at SR 702,000m. ($187,200m.) against total spending of SR 690,000m. ($184,000m.), thus yielding a modest fiscal surplus of $3,200m. (0.5%). Amid higher oil prices—averaging over $100 per barrel during 2012—both revenues and expenditure comfortably exceeded the allocations projected in the budget. Actual revenues were recorded at SR 1,247,000m. and expenditure at SR 917,100m. for that year, resulting in a surplus of SR 329,500m. (12.4% of GDP).

Gross domestic debt in 2012 constituted just 3.7% of GDP, a steep decline from the figure of 119% recorded in 1999. Debt-servicing costs are manageable, since four-fifths of aggregate debt comprises medium- or long-term liabilities and is owed to quasi-governmental entities.

Saudi Arabia is a major donor to mainly low-income Muslim countries in Asia and Africa; in particular, the kingdom makes significant contributions to the Heavily Indebted Poor Countries Debt Initiative, which was proposed by the World Bank and the IMF in 1996, and to the Exogenous Shocks Facility. Bilateral aid and debt relief have exceeded US $75,000m. over the past three decades. In 2010 net disbursement of official development assistance (ODA) provided by the Saudi Government was $3,480m.—making it the largest donor within the non-Development Assistance Committee (DAC) countries. Saudi Arabia's foreign aid flows averaged 1.0% of GDP in recent years, consistently exceeding the UN target of 0.7% of gross national income. Net ODA (excluding concessional loans) totalled $15,139m. during 2006–10, according to OECD figures, representing 44.0% of the total bilateral aid given by the non-DAC donors.

EDUCATION, HEALTH AND SOCIAL SECURITY

Education spending in Saudi Arabia has more than tripled in the past decade. The ninth Development Plan allocated SR 731,250m. (US $195,000m.) for increasing the capacity of primary, secondary and tertiary education in order to accommodate an extra 1.7m. students up until 2014. This was to involve—besides building new schools—the construction of 25, 28 and 50 technology colleges, technical institutes and industrial training centres, respectively. Around one-quarter of the

2012 budget (amounting to SR 168,600m. or $44,960m.) was allocated for 'education and training'— representing a 13.0% increase over 2011. The bulk of the funds were intended for the building of 742 new schools, 40 new colleges and to complete existing work on almost 3,000 ongoing projects.

The ninth Plan allocated SR 273,750m. (US $73,000m.) to improving the country's health care infrastructure. Funds were to be directed toward the construction of 117 new hospitals, 750 primary health care centres and 400 emergency centres across the kingdom. The largest projects being planned were two medical cities at Jeddah and Riyadh, costing an estimated SR 25,000m. ($6,666m.). Both projects—each with a total area of 1.3m. sq m—were to include three hospitals and related medical and residential facilities. Health care services remained a priority for the 2012 national budget, receiving 13.0% of the aggregate or SR 86,500m. (US $23,066m.). New projects unveiled in the budget included 17 hospitals and additional primary care centres. In 2011 22 hospitals were built that added 3,200 beds. Currently, some 130 hospitals are under construction, with a total capacity of 28,470 beds.

The demand for new homes is exceptionally high, reflecting rising population growth and economic prosperity; private developers believe that the kingdom requires investment of $53,300m. over the next two decades to build 1.5m. new housing units for lower- and medium-income families. According to the NCB, as much as $181,300m. of real estate investment is required to meet the expected demand for 1.3m. housing units by 2015. The five major cities—Jeddah, Mecca, Medina, Riyadh and the Eastern region conurbation of Dammam-Dhahran-al-Khobar—will require an additional 180,000 units per year over the medium term, based on estimates by the Ministry of Economy and Planning. The Ministry has suggested that demand will double by 2015 and has envisaged a shortage of 2m. homes by that year in the absence of new investment. Furthermore, a report by the Jeddah Municipality estimated that as many as 5m. new homes will be required across the kingdom by 2020.

A report by Banque Saudi Fransi indicated the need for 1.65m. new residential units by 2015, with the burgeoning middle class fuelling much of that demand. Against this background, King Abdullah in March 2011 announced a programme to build 500,000 low-cost public housing units by 2014 (costing SR 251,250m, or US $67,000m) in order to tackle the sector's chronic shortfall. This scheme is also intended to create demand for retail and commercial facilities to serve new residential developments. According to local estimates, however, even with 500,000 extra units, the country's housing stock expansion may not be sufficient to meet growing demand. The Real Estate Development Fund is expected to disburse about SR 25,125m. ($6,700m.) for low-cost housing schemes, while the Saudi Credit and Saving Bank is to receive SR 10,125m. ($2,700m.) to provide cheap mortgages to poorer households.

All adult Saudi Arabians, if not independently wealthy, are entitled to a plot of land and a loan of US $133,333 (up from $80,000 previously), with which to build a home. The residential segment was expected, in the long-term, to benefit from the implementation of new legislation governing the provision of mortgages, which entered into effect in July 2012. The mortgage market business could be huge, which would benefit Saudi banks. According to research by Credit Suisse, some 52% of Saudi households meet the affordability threshold for purchasing residential property, and 17% would be potential mortgage seekers. However, only 40% of Saudi nationals currently own their property.

Statistical Survey

Sources (unless otherwise indicated): Central Department of Statistics, Ministry of Economy and Planning, POB 358, University St, Riyadh 11182; tel. (1) 401-3333; fax (1) 401-9300; e-mail info@cds.gov.sa; internet www.cdsi.gov.sa; Saudi Arabian Monetary Agency, *Annual Report* and *Statistical Summary*.

Area and Population

AREA, POPULATION AND DENSITY

Area (sq km)	2,240,000*
Population (census results)	
15 September 2004	22,678,262
28 April 2010†	
Males	15,460,147
Females	11,676,830
Total	27,136,977
Population (official estimates at mid-year)	
2011	28,376,355
2012	29,195,895
2013‡	29,994,272
Density (per sq km) at mid-2013	13.4

* 864,869 sq miles.

† Of the total population at the 2010 census, 18,707,576 (males 9,527,173, females 9,180,403) were nationals of Saudi Arabia, while 8,429,401 (males 5,932,974, females 2,496,427) were foreign nationals.

‡ Population comprised of 20,271,058 Saudi nationals and 9,723,214 foreign nationals.

Saudi Arabia-Iraq Neutral Zone: The Najdi (Saudi Arabian) frontier with Iraq was defined in the Treaty of Mohammara in May 1922. Later a Neutral Zone of 7,044 sq km was established adjacent to the western tip of the Kuwait frontier. No military or permanent buildings were to be erected in the zone and the nomads of both countries were to have unimpeded access to its pastures and wells. A further agreement concerning the administration of this zone was signed between Iraq and Saudi Arabia in May 1938. In July 1975 Iraq and Saudi Arabia signed an agreement providing for an equal division of the diamond-shaped zone between the two countries, with the border following a straight line through the zone.

Saudi Arabia-Kuwait Neutral Zone: A Convention signed at Uqair in December 1922 fixed the Najdi (Saudi Arabian) boundary with Kuwait. The Convention also established a Neutral Zone of 5,770 sq km immediately to the south of Kuwait in which Saudi Arabia and Kuwait held equal rights. The final agreement on this matter was signed in 1963. Since 1966 the Neutral Zone, or Partitioned Zone as it is sometimes known, has been divided between the two countries and each administers its own half, in practice as an integral part of the state. However, the petroleum deposits in the Zone remain undivided and production from the onshore oil concessions in the Zone is shared equally between the two states' concessionaires.

POPULATION BY AGE AND SEX
(official demographic survey, 2007)

	Males	Females	Total
0–14	3,926,920	3,856,076	7,782,996
15–64	9,024,995	6,496,928	15,521,923
65 and over	349,254	326,661	675,915
Total	13,301,169	10,679,665	23,980,834

ADMINISTRATIVE REGIONS
(official population estimates at mid-2013)

Aseer	2,095,854	Makkah	7,688,609
Al-Baha	450,733	Najran	555,129
Eastern	4,533,841	Northern Borders	350,972
Ha'il	654,736	Qassim	1,337,563
Jazan	1,497,377	Riyadh	7,516,959
Al-Jouf	483,138	Tabouk	866,803
Al-Madinah	1,962,558	**Total**	29,994,272

PRINCIPAL TOWNS
(population at 2010 census)

Riyadh (royal capital)	5,188,286	Jubail	337,778
Jeddah (administrative capital)	3,430,697	Ha'il (Hayil)	310,897
Makkah (Mecca)	1,534,731	Naijran	298,288
Al-Madinah (Medina)	1,100,093	Hafar al-Batin	271,642
Dammam	903,312	Al-Thuqbah	238,066
Hufuf*	660,788	Abha	236,157
Al-Ta'if	579,970	Al-Saih	234,607
Tabouk	512,629	Yanbu	233,236
Buraidah	467,410	Al-Khubar	219,679
Khamis-Mushait	430,828		

* Includes population of Al-Mobarraz city.

BIRTHS AND DEATHS
(UN estimates, annual averages)

	1995–2000	2000–05	2005–10
Birth rate (per 1,000)	29.6	24.7	22.0
Death rate (per 1,000)	4.3	3.8	3.4

Source: UN, *World Population Prospects: The 2012 Revision*.

Crude birth rate (per 1,000): 23.3 in 2010; 22.9 in 2011; 22.5 in 2012.

Crude death rate (per 1,000): 3.9 in 2010–11; 3.8 in 2012.

Life expectancy (years at birth): 74.1 (males 73.0; females 75.2) in 2011 (Source: World Bank, World Development Indicators database).

ECONOMICALLY ACTIVE POPULATION
(persons aged 15 years and over, labour force survey, January–June 2013)

	Males	Females	Total
Agriculture, hunting, forestry and fishing	569,580	2,839	572,419
Mining and quarrying	113,534	1,093	114,627
Manufacturing	627,029	9,906	636,935
Electricity, gas and water	131,733	861	132,594
Construction	1,722,728	8,980	1,731,708
Wholesale and retail trade	1,567,707	20,558	1,588,265
Restaurants and hotels	248,858	4,001	252,859
Transport and communications	421,047	3,942	424,989
Financial intermediation	108,684	7,198	115,882
Real estate, renting and business activities	393,156	8,899	402,055
Public administration and defence	1,747,445	48,869	1,796,314
Education	709,622	534,297	1,243,919
Health and social work	363,003	143,806	506,809
Other community and personal services	177,498	14,668	192,166
Private households with employed persons	393,948	510,638	904,586
Extra-territorial organizations	9,658	—	9,658
Total employed	9,313,382	1,321,351	10,634,733
Unemployed	277,610	374,401	652,011
Total labour force	9,590,992	1,695,752	11,286,744

Health and Welfare

KEY INDICATORS

Total fertility rate (children per woman, 2011)	2.6
Under-5 mortality rate (per 1,000 live births, 2011)	9
Physicians (per 1,000 head, 2008)	0.9
Hospital beds (per 1,000 head, 2009)	2.2
Health expenditure (2010): US $ per head (PPP)	914
Health expenditure (2010): % of GDP	4.0
Health expenditure (2010): public (% of total)	66.0
Total carbon dioxide emissions ('000 metric tons, 2009)	432,772.0
Carbon dioxide emissions per head (metric tons, 2009)	16.1
Human Development Index (2012): ranking	57
Human Development Index (2012): value	0.782

For sources and definitions, see explanatory note on p. vi.

Agriculture

PRINCIPAL CROPS
('000 metric tons)

	2009	2010*	2011*
Wheat	1,152	1,300	1,364
Barley	20	18	17
Maize	161	182	182
Millet	8	9	10
Sorghum	244	275	327
Potatoes	444	490	594
Tomatoes	543	500	484
Pumpkins, squash and gourds	117	120	122
Cucumbers and gherkins	326	367	400
Aubergines (Eggplants)	57	56	56
Onions, dry	62	69	73
Carrots and turnips	49	47	54
Okra	61	56	58
Watermelons	338	296	294
Cantaloupes and other melons	211	194	191
Grapes	160	160	160
Dates	992	1,089	1,123

* FAO estimates.

Aggregate production ('000 metric tons, may include official, semi-official or estimated data): Total cereals 1,586 in 2009, 1,784 in 2010, 1,900 in 2011; Total roots and tubers 444 in 2009, 490 in 2010, 594 in 2011; Total vegetables (incl. melons) 2,240 2009, 2,236 in 2010, 2,439 in 2011; Total fruits (excl. melons) 1,619 in 2009, 1,744 in 2010, 1,842 in 2011.

Source: FAO.

LIVESTOCK
('000 head, year ending September)

	2009	2010	2011*
Asses*	100	100	100
Camels	230	230*	240
Cattle	424	404*	400
Sheep	5,886	5,245†	5,000
Goats	3,809	3,408†	3,200
Chickens*	146,000	146,000	147,000

* FAO estimate(s).
† Unofficial figure.

Source: FAO.

LIVESTOCK PRODUCTS
('000 metric tons)

	2009	2010	2011
Cattle meat*	31.6	44.0	43.6
Sheep meat*	64.0	63.0	61.0
Goat meat*	18.4	24.0	26.5
Chicken meat	570.0†	575.0†	580.0*
Camel meat*	42.0	43.0	44.0
Cows' milk	1,508.4	1,670.0*	1,670.0*
Sheep's milk*	68.0	66.9	66.9
Goats' milk*	65.0	75.0	75.0
Camels' milk*	80.5	97.8	97.8
Hen eggs	191.0	193.0*	193.0*
Wool, greasy*	9.0	10.5	10.5

* FAO estimate(s).
† Unofficial figure.

Source: FAO.

Fishing

(metric tons, live weight)

	2009	2010	2011
Capture	67,664	65,145	64,481
Pink ear emperors	2,990	2,460	3,126
Emperors (Scavengers)	4,386	4,224	3,741
Spinefeet (Rabbitfishes)	2,075	2,170	1,702
Narrow-barred Spanish mackerel	4,802	3,728	3,441
Indian mackerel	3,950	3,950	3,900
Green tiger prawns	9,083	7,571	6,354
Aquaculture*	26,120	26,374	26,755
Nile tilapia	3,837	3,382	3,400*
Indian white prawns	20,781	20,652	21,000*
Total catch*	93,784	91,519	91,236

* FAO estimate(s).

Source: FAO.

Mining

('000 metric tons unless otherwise indicated)

	2009	2010	2011
Crude petroleum (million barrels)*	2,987	2,980	3,399
Silver (kg)†	8,527	7,670	7,900‡
Gold (kg)†	4,857	4,476	4,611
Salt (unrefined)	1,640	1,800	1,800‡
Gypsum (crude)	2,000	2,100	2,300‡
Pozzolan	802	915	1,000‡

* Including 50% of the total output of the Neutral (Partitioned) Zone, shared with Kuwait (Source: Saudi Arabian Monetary Agency).
† Figures refer to the metal content of concentrate and bullion.
‡ Estimated figure.

2012: Crude petroleum 3,573 million barrels.

Source: mainly US Geological Survey.

Natural gas (excluding flared and recycled, million cu m): 87,660 in 2010; 92,260 in 2011; 102,800 in 2012 (Source: BP, *Statistical Review of World Energy*).

Industry

SELECTED PRODUCTS
(including 50% of the total output of the Neutral Zone; '000 barrels unless otherwise indicated)

	2010	2011	2012
Phosphatic fertilizers ('000 metric tons)*†	300	300†	n.a.
Motor spirit (petrol) and naphtha	208,770	204,706	210,069
Jet fuel and kerosene	58,112	60,738	63,802
Gas-diesel (distillate fuel) oils	231,212	229,397	234,122
Residual fuel oils	162,575	152,172	168,383
Petroleum bitumen (asphalt)	18,212	18,718	17,688
Liquefied petroleum gas	12,228	11,970	11,249
Cement ('000 metric tons)	42,300	48,000†	n.a.
Crude steel ('000 metric tons)	5,000	5,300†	n.a.
Electric energy (million kWh sold)	212,263	219,662	240,288

* Production in terms of phosphoric acid.
† Estimate(s).

Sources: Saudi Arabian Monetary Agency; US Geological Survey.

Finance

CURRENCY AND EXCHANGE RATES

Monetary Units:
100 halalah = 20 qurush = 1 Saudi riyal (SR).

Sterling, Dollar and Euro Equivalents (31 May 2013):
£1 sterling = 5.705 riyals;
US $1 = 3.750 riyals;
€1 = 4.877 riyals;
100 Saudi riyals = £17.53 = $26.67 = €20.50.

Exchange Rate: Since June 1986 the official mid-point rate has been fixed at US $1 = 3.75 riyals.

BUDGET ESTIMATES
(million riyals)

Revenue	2011	2012	2013
Petroleum revenues	468,000	621,000	727,000
Other revenues	72,000	81,000	102,000
Total	540,000	702,000	829,000

Expenditure	2011	2012	2013
Human resource development	148,307	167,970	203,147
Transport and communications	17,334	20,566	22,063
Economic resource development	32,938	41,152	46,696
Health and social development	52,447	61,284	70,938
Infrastructure development	8,918	10,525	11,702
Municipal services	21,201	25,460	31,729
Defence and security	181,991	211,867	251,325
Public administration and other government spending	93,820	107,551	119,948
Government lending institutions*	635	10,785	14,950
Local subsidies	22,410	32,840	47,502
Total	580,000	690,000	820,000

* Including transfers to the Saudi Fund for Development (SFD).

2011 (revised figures, million riyals): Total revenue 1,117,792 (Petroleum revenue 1,034,360, Other revenue 83,432); Total expenditure 826,700 (Current 550,500, Capital 276,200).

2012 (million riyals): Total revenue 1,247,398 (Petroleum revenue 1,144,818, Other revenue 102,580); Total expenditure 873,305 (Current 611,626, Capital 261,679).

INTERNATIONAL RESERVES
(US $ million in December)

	2010	2011	2012
Gold*	415	415	415
IMF special drawing rights	10,646	10,293	9,860
Reserve position in IMF	1,981	4,862	5,630
Foreign exchange	432,094	525,521	640,975
Total	445,136	541,091	656,879

* Valued at US $40 per troy oz at 31 December 2012.

Source: IMF, *International Financial Statistics*.

MONEY SUPPLY
('000 million riyals in December)

	2010	2011	2012
Currency outside banks	95.52	119.93	163.22
Demand deposits at commercial banks	530.39	641.51	754.35
Total money	625.91	761.44	917.57

Source: IMF, *International Financial Statistics*.

COST OF LIVING
(Consumer Price Index for all cities; base: 2007 = 100)

	2010	2011	2012
Food and beverages	120.8	127.1	132.9
Housing, fuel and water	129.2	143.9	148.7
Textiles and clothing (incl. footwear)	101.1	99.7	103.3
House furnishing	107.0	115.5	117.5
Medical care	103.3	103.4	105.6
Transport	99.7	103.1	108.3
Communications	97.7	92.0	92.1
Education	113.2	108.7	110.2
Recreation and culture	97.2	104.7	104.5
Miscellaneous goods and services	110.1	113.9	117.8
All items (incl. others)	114.7	119.0	122.4

NATIONAL ACCOUNTS
(million riyals at current prices)

Expenditure on the Gross Domestic Product

	2010	2011	2012*
Government final consumption expenditure	400,173	488,062	542,699
Private final consumption expenditure	639,417	681,761	749,073
Increase in stocks	123,426	103,607	92,735
Gross fixed capital formation	483,921	568,793	591,128
Total domestic expenditure	1,646,937	1,842,223	1,975,635
Exports of goods and services	981,867	1,410,841	1,497,824
Less Imports of goods and services	653,261	742,414	807,023
GDP in purchasers' values	1,975,543	2,510,650	2,666,436
GDP at constant 1999 prices	1,067,097	1,158,546	1,217,933

Gross Domestic Product by Economic Activity

	2010	2011	2012*
Agriculture, forestry and fishing	47,063	48,163	49,816
Mining and quarrying:			
crude petroleum and natural gas	813,147	1,206,751	1,242,333
other	8,081	8,767	9,368
Manufacturing:			
petroleum refining	63,771	64,216	66,873
other	154,400	187,787	201,597
Electricity, gas and water	26,281	28,285	30,076
Construction	90,780	107,021	118,192
Trade, restaurants and hotels	174,506	197,926	219,144
—continued			
Transport, storage and communications	101,205	115,272	124,279
Finance, insurance, real estate and business services:			
ownership of dwellings	88,276	96,715	105,431
other	94,328	98,339	108,047
Government services	280,863	312,308	344,464
Other community, social and personal services	37,768	41,892	45,969
Sub-total	1,980,469	2,513,442	2,665,588
Import duties	14,669	17,285	21,520
Less Imputed bank service charge	19,595	20,077	20,672
GDP in purchasers' values	1,975,543	2,510,650	2,666,436

* Preliminary.

BALANCE OF PAYMENTS
(US $ million)

	2010	2011	2012
Exports of goods	251,142.7	364,735.5	388,369.6
Imports of goods	–97,431.1	–119,960.7	–141,799.2
Balance on goods	153,711.5	244,774.8	246,570.4
Exports of services	10,688.5	11,488.7	11,049.9
Imports of services	–76,772.1	–78,016.6	–73,407.0
Balance on goods and services	87,628.0	178,246.9	184,213.3
Primary income received	18,171.5	19,765.7	23,647.5
Primary income paid	–11,127.6	–10,081.6	–12,658.9
Balance on goods, services and Primary income	94,671.9	187,931.0	195,201.9
Secondary income received	—	34.7	70.8
Secondary income paid	–27,920.9	–29,420.5	–30,509.1
Current balance	66,751.0	158,545.2	164,763.7
Direct investment assets	–3,906.8	–3,429.9	–4,401.5
Direct investment from liabilities	29,232.7	16,308.3	12,182.4
Portfolio investment assets	–16,656.9	–15,423.9	–4,093.4
Portfolio investment liabilities	1,502.7	–623.7	909.1
Other investment assets	–6,523.2	–7,249.5	–10,285.0
Other investment liabilities	–991.4	–3,993.9	–680.8
Net errors and omissions	–34,152.7	–48,075.2	–42,621.1
Reserves and related items	35,255.4	96,057.3	115,773.3

Source: IMF, *International Financial Statistics*.

External Trade

PRINCIPAL COMMODITIES
(distribution by SITC, million riyals)

Imports c.i.f.	2009	2010	2011
Food and live animals	47,114	55,825	64,844
Cereals and cereal preparations	15,115	17,275	18,599
Chemicals and related products	35,759	40,646	49,414
Medicinal and pharmaceutical products	12,184	12,865	14,384
Basic manufactures	61,246	74,009	95,938
Iron and steel	18,189	25,235	33,900
Non-ferrous metals	9,138	12,833	18,197
Machinery and transport equipment	163,437	169,925	205,094
Power generating machinery and equipment	16,654	12,543	15,534

Imports c.i.f.—*continued*	2009	2010	2011
Machinery specialized for particular industries	12,939	13,472	16,711
General industrial machinery equipment and parts	29,694	26,625	36,257
Telecommunications and sound recording and reproducing apparatus and equipment	16,326	18,231	27,874
Electrical machinery, apparatus, etc.	17,574	18,147	23,165
Road vehicles and parts	47,943	58,444	62,488
Miscellaneous manufactured articles	35,638	38,760	48,490
Total (incl. others)	358,290	400,736	493,449

Exports f.o.b.	2009	2010	2011
Mineral fuels, lubricants, etc.	611,469	807,183	1,191,089
Petroleum, petroleum products and related materials	591,774	780,742	1,160,424
Natural gas, manufactured	19,694	26,440	30,662
Chemicals and related products	52,600	82,005	114,995
Organic chemicals	18,754	27,914	45,518
Plastics in primary form	21,284	39,636	51,210
Basic manufactures	15,283	16,266	18,251
Machinery and transport equipment	23,580	17,818	20,607
Total (incl. others)	721,109	941,785	1,367,620

2012 (million riyals, provisional): *Imports:* Live animals and animal products 21,232; Vegetable products 31,324; Foodstuff, beverages and tobacco 24,609; Chemicals and related products 48,208; Textiles and related articles 18,065; Base metals and articles thereof 80,376; Machinery, mechanical appliances, electrical equipment and parts thereof 154,062; Transport equipment 103,544; Total (incl. others) 583,473. *Exports:* Mineral products 1,266,237; Chemical products 66,636; Plastic products 57,823; Total (incl. others and re-exports) 1,456,386.

PRINCIPAL TRADING PARTNERS
(million riyals)

Imports c.i.f.	2010	2011	2012*
Australia	6,216	6,567	8,199
Belgium	4,536	5,028	5,541
Brazil	11,699	14,222	11,810
Canada	5,467	6,067	8,574
China, People's Republic	46,851	64,829	74,195
Egypt	6,074	7,021	7,520
France (incl. Monaco)	16,395	18,178	18,603
Germany	31,032	33,964	41,367
India	15,116	16,191	19,581
Indonesia	4,291	5,407	7,301
Italy	12,682	17,290	17,484
Japan	29,957	31,065	38,989
Korea, Republic	17,789	29,076	35,467
Malaysia	4,439	6,129	5,840
Netherlands	4,582	5,534	6,274
Spain	4,735	5,655	6,984
Sweden	5,365	6,615	6,652
Switzerland (incl. Liechtenstein)	8,437	12,264	13,620
Thailand	8,753	10,149	12,707
Turkey	8,246	9,192	13,422
United Arab Emirates	14,190	20,426	24,495
United Kingdom	12,909	14,313	15,719
USA	52,749	61,943	78,770
Total (incl. others)	400,736	493,449	583,473

Exports (incl. re-exports)	2010	2011	2012*
Bahrain	29,849	36,935	39,121
Belgium	12,845	18,305	19,793
China, People's Republic	112,210	170,500	188,229
Egypt	9,625	10,696	10,498
France (incl. Monaco)	15,739	24,679	26,002
India	71,891	103,272	120,841
Indonesia	14,388	17,847	19,739
Italy	15,529	38,611	39,326
Japan	135,634	180,828	192,201
Jordan	12,849	16,816	19,404
Korea, Republic	682,63	92,431	137,392
Netherlands	12,730	31,667	33,298
Pakistan	12,298	16,323	12,932
Singapore	37,931	60,398	53,582
Spain	17,763	27,770	29,134
Taiwan	37,685	46,848	50,277
Thailand	17,924	24,641	27,123
Turkey	9,012	12,555	16,187
United Arab Emirates	32,923	37,881	38,823
USA	124,675	187,522	208,338
Total (incl. others)	941,785	1,367,620	1,456,386

* Provisional figures.

Transport

RAILWAYS
(traffic)

	2008	2009	2010
Passenger journeys ('000)	1,106	1,124	1,231
Passenger-km (million)	338	338	375
Freight carried ('000 metric tons)	3,395	3,516	3,826
Net freight ton-km (million)	1,691	1,718	1,786

ROAD TRAFFIC
(motor vehicles in use at 31 December)

	1989	1990	1991
Passenger cars	2,550,465	2,664,028	2,762,132
Buses and coaches	50,856	52,136	54,089
Goods vehicles	2,153,297	2,220,658	2,286,541
Total	4,754,618	4,936,822	5,103,205

2005 (motor vehicles in use at 31 December): Passenger cars 3,206,000; Buses and coaches 113,073; Vans and lorries 1,127,900; Motorcycles and mopeds 16,250; Total (incl. others) 4,446,973 (Source: IRF, *World Road Statistics*).

SHIPPING

Flag Registered Fleet
(at 31 December)

	2010	2011	2012
Number of vessels	376	384	403
Total displacement ('000 grt)	1,742.6	1,860.2	2,306.9

Source: Lloyd's List Intelligence (www.lloydslistintelligence.com).

International Sea-borne Freight Traffic
('000 metric tons, excluding crude oil)

	2008	2009	2010
Goods loaded	70,740	81,476	75,636
Goods unloaded	65,233	56,499	64,523

CIVIL AVIATION
(traffic on scheduled services)

	2007	2008	2009
Kilometres flown (million)	179	191	196
Passengers carried ('000)	17,141	16,708	17,508
Passenger-km (million)	26,904	27,736	28,891
Total ton-km (million)	3,659	3,888	3,746

Source: UN, *Statistical Yearbook*.

2010 (Saudi Arabian airlines): Passengers carried ('000) 18,890; Number of flights 155,895; Cargo carried ('000 metric tons) 382.

2011 (Saudi Arabian airlines): Passengers carried ('000) 21,472; Number of flights 162,460; Cargo carried ('000 metric tons) 445.

2012 (Saudi Arabian airlines): Passengers carried ('000) 23,904; Number of flights 168,745; Cargo carried ('000 metric tons) 517.

Tourism

Country of nationality	2008	2009	2010
Algeria	393,609	64,015	96,097
Bahrain	594,188	624,793	820,132
Bangladesh	34,187	23,698	188,584
Egypt	1,853,663	538,287	763,901
India	601,922	247,075	389,116
Indonesia	501,758	205,378	235,636
Iran	349,848	413,656	220,051
Iraq	24,282	64,138	171,913
Jordan	501,269	517,318	451,099
Kuwait	2,589,988	2,475,318	2,507,813
Lebanon	307,492	58,337	116,129
Malaysia	141,778	62,749	152,396
Oman	125,552	165,875	176,687
Pakistan	817,550	336,255	465,571
Qatar	808,072	1,470,382	843,762
Sudan	398,607	88,269	65,352
Syria	708,034	730,306	254,140
Turkey	248,500	154,011	128,927
United Arab Emirates	1,613,574	1,889,187	1,957,613
United Kingdom	284,685	170,467	98,114
Yemen	197,652	101,576	112,472
Total (incl. others)	14,757,444	10,896,712	10,850,187

Total tourist arrivals ('000): 17,336 in 2011 (provisional).

Tourism receipts (US $ million, excl. passenger transport): 5,995 in 2009; 6,712 in 2010; 8,459 in 2011 (provisional).

Source: World Tourism Organization.

PILGRIMS TO MECCA FROM ABROAD

	2010*	2011†	2012‡
Total	1,799,601	1,828,195	1,752,932

* Figures for Islamic year 1431 (18 December 2009 to 06 December 2010).
† Figures for Islamic year 1432 (07 December 2010 to 26 November 2011).
‡ Figures for Islamic year 1433 (27 November 2011 to 14 November 2012).

Communications Media

	2010	2011	2012
Telephones ('000 main lines in use)	4,166	4,633	4,802
Mobile cellular telephones ('000 subscribers)	51,564	53,706	53,012
Internet subscribers ('000)	1,898.0	1,871.4	n.a.
Broadband subscribers ('000)	1,496.6	1,577.0	1,965.8

Personal computers: 17,200,000 (697.9 per 1,000 persons) in 2008.

Source: International Telecommunication Union.

Education

(2011/12)

	Institutions	Teachers	Students
Pre-primary	2,323	12,705	141,422
Primary	13,845	232,453	2,530,744
Intermediate	8,241	125,355	1,212,029
Secondary (general)	5,658	114,625	1,226,205
Special	1,703	8,074	27,439
Adult education	2979	7,899	49,659
Technical and vocational	119	7,858	115,948
Higher	n.a.	59,442	1,206,007

Source: Ministry of Education, Riyadh.

Pupil-teacher ratio (primary education, UNESCO estimate): 11.0 in 2010/11 (Source: UNESCO Institute for Statistics).

Adult literacy rate (UNESCO estimates): 86.6% (males 90.4%; females 81.3%) in 2010 (Source: UNESCO Institute for Statistics).

Directory

The Constitution

The Basic Law of Government was introduced by royal decree in 1992.

Chapter 1 defines Saudi Arabia as a sovereign Arab, Islamic state. Article 1 defines God's Book and the Sunnah of his prophet as the constitution of Saudi Arabia. The official language is Arabic. The official holidays are Id al-Fitr and Id al-Adha. The calendar is the Hegira calendar.

Chapter 2 concerns the system of government, which is defined as a monarchy, hereditary in the male descendants of Abd al-Aziz ibn Abd al-Rahman al-Faisal Al Sa'ud. It outlines the duties of the Heir Apparent. The principles of government are justice, consultation and equality in accordance with Islamic law (*Shari'a*).

Chapter 3 concerns the family. The State is to aspire to strengthen family ties and to maintain its Arab and Islamic values. Article 11 states that 'Saudi society will be based on the principle of adherence to God's command, on mutual co-operation in good deeds and piety and mutual support and inseparability'. Education aims to instil the Islamic faith.

Chapter 4 defines the economic principles of the State. All natural resources are the property of the State. The State protects public money and freedom of property. Taxation is only to be imposed on a just basis.

Chapter 5 concerns rights and duties. The State is to protect Islam and to implement the *Shari'a* law. The State protects human rights in accordance with the *Shari'a*. The State is to provide public services and security for all citizens. Punishment is to be in accordance with the *Shari'a*. The Royal Courts are open to all citizens.

Chapter 6 defines the authorities of the State as the judiciary, the executive and the regulatory authority. The judiciary is independent, and acts in accordance with *Shari'a* law. The King is head of the Council of Ministers and Commander-in-Chief of the Armed Forces. The Prime Minister and other ministers are appointed by the King. It provides for the establishment of a Consultative Council (Majlis al-Shoura).

Chapter 7 concerns financial affairs. It provides for the annual presentation of a state budget. Corporate budgets are subject to the same provisions.

Chapter 8 concerns control bodies. Control bodies will be established to ensure good financial and administrative management of state assets.

Chapter 9 defines the general provisions pertaining to the application of the Basic Law of Government.

The Government

HEAD OF STATE

King: HM King ABDULLAH IBN ABD AL-AZIZ AL SA'UD (acceded to the throne 1 August 2005).

COUNCIL OF MINISTERS
(September 2013)

Prime Minister: King ABDULLAH IBN ABD AL-AZIZ AL SA'UD.

First Deputy Prime Minister and Minister of Defence: Crown Prince SALMAN IBN ABD AL-AZIZ AL SA'UD.

Second Deputy Prime Minister: Prince MUQRIN IBN ABD AL-AZIZ AL SA'UD.

Minister of the Interior: Prince MUHAMMAD IBN NAYEF IBN ABD AL-AZIZ AL SA'UD.

Minister of Municipal and Rural Affairs: Prince MANSOUR IBN MUTAIB IBN ABD AL-AZIZ AL SA'UD.

Minister of Foreign Affairs: Prince SA'UD AL-FAISAL AL SA'UD.

Minister of Petroleum and Mineral Resources: Eng. ALI IBN IBRAHIM AL-NUAIMI.

Minister of Labour: Eng. ADEL BIN MUHAMMAD ABD AL-KADER FAKIEH.

Minister of Social Affairs: Dr YOUSUF ABDULLAH AL-OTHMAN.

Minister of Agriculture: Dr FAHD IBN ABD AL-RAHMAN IBN SULAIMAN BALGHUNAIM.

Minister of Water and Electricity: ABDULLAH IBN ABD AL-RAHMAN AL-HUSSEIN.

Minister of Education: Prince FAISAL IBN ABDULLAH IBN MUHAMMAD AL SA'UD.

Minister of Higher Education: Dr KHALID IBN MUHAMMAD AL-ANGARI.

Minister of Communications and Information Technology: MUHAMMAD IBN JABIL IBN AHMAD MULLA.

Minister of Finance: Dr IBRAHIM IBN ABD AL-AZIZ AL-ASSAF.

Minister of Economy and Planning: MUHAMMAD IBN SULAYMAN AL-JASSER.

Minister of Culture and Information: Dr ABD AL-AZIZ IBN MOHI EL-DIN KHOJA.

Minister of Commerce and Industry: TAWFIQ AL-RABEEAH.

Minister of Justice: Dr MUHAMMAD IBN ABD AL-KARIM IBN ABD AL-AZIZ AL-EISSA.

Minister of Pilgrimage (Hajj) Affairs: BANDAR AL-HAJJAR.

Minister of Awqaf (Religious Endowments), Dawa, Mosques and Guidance Affairs: SALEH IBN ABD AL-AZIZ MUHAMMAD IBN IBRAHIM AL-SHEIKH.

Minister of Health: Dr ABDULLAH IBN ABD AL-AZIZ AL-RABEA.

Minister of the Civil Service: Dr ABDULLAH AL-BARRAK.

Minister of Transport: Dr JUBARAH IBN EID AL-SURAISERI.

Minister of Housing: SHUWAISH AL-DUWAIHI.

Minister of the National Guard: Prince MITAB IBN ABDULLAH AL SA'UD.

Minister of State for Foreign Affairs: NIZAR IBN UBAYD MADANI.

Minister of State for Consultative Council Affairs: Dr SAUD IBN SAEED IBN ABD AL-AZIZ AL-MATHAMI.

Ministers of State: Prince ABD AL-AZIZ IBN ABDULLAH IBN ABD AL-AZIZ AL SA'UD, Dr ABD AL-AZIZ IBN ABDULLAH AL-KHUWEITER, Dr MUTLIB IBN ABDULLAH AL-NAFISA, Dr MUSAID IBN MUHAMMAD AL-AYBAN, Prince ABD AL-AZIZ IBN FAHD AL SA'UD.

MINISTRIES

Most ministries have regional offices in Jeddah.

Council of Ministers: Murabba, Riyadh 11121; tel. (1) 488-2444.

Ministry of Agriculture: Airport Rd, Riyadh 11195; tel. (1) 401-6666; fax (1) 403-1415; e-mail pubrel@moa.gov.sa; internet www.moa.gov.sa.

Ministry of Awqaf (Religious Endowments), Dawa, Mosques and Guidance Affairs: Riyadh 11232; tel. (1) 473-0401; fax 477-2938; internet www.al-islam.com.

Ministry of the Civil Service: POB 18367, Riyadh 11114; tel. (1) 402-6900; fax (1) 405-6258; e-mail mcswebmaster@mcs.gov.sa; internet www.mcs.gov.sa.

Ministry of Commerce and Industry: POB 1774, Airport Rd, Riyadh 11162; tel. (1) 405-6292; fax (1) 403-5567; e-mail public-relation@commerce.gov.sa; internet www.commerce.gov.sa.

Ministry of Communications and Information Technology: Intercontinental Rd, Riyadh 11112; tel. (1) 452-2222; fax (1) 452-2220; e-mail info@mcit.gov.sa; internet www.mcit.gov.sa.

Ministry of Culture and Information: Intercontinental Rd, Riyadh 11112; tel. (1) 401-4440; fax (1) 402-3570; internet www.moci.gov.sa.

Ministry of Defence: POB 26731, Airport Rd, Riyadh 11165; tel. (1) 478-9000; fax (1) 401-1336; internet www.moda.gov.sa.

Ministry of Economy and Planning: POB 358, 44 University St, Riyadh 11182; tel. (1) 401-1444; fax (1) 405-2051; e-mail ministry@planning.gov.sa; internet www.mep.gov.sa.

Ministry of Education: POB 3734, Airport Rd, Riyadh 11148; tel. (1) 404-2888; fax (1) 401-2365; internet www.moe.gov.sa.

Ministry of Finance: Airport Rd, Riyadh 11177; tel. (1) 405-0000; fax (1) 403-3130; e-mail info@mof.gov.sa; internet www.mof.gov.sa.

Ministry of Foreign Affairs: POB 55937, Riyadh 11544; tel. (1) 405-5000; fax (1) 403-0645; e-mail info@mofa.gov.sa; internet www.mofa.gov.sa.

Ministry of Health: Airport Rd, Riyadh 11176; tel. (1) 212-5555; fax (1) 402-9876; e-mail f_otaibi@moh.gov.sa; internet www.moh.gov.sa.

Ministry of Higher Education: POB 225085, Riyadh 11324; tel. (1) 441-5555; fax (1) 441-9004; e-mail contact@mohe.gov.sa; internet www.mohe.gov.sa.

Ministry of Housing: Riyadh.

Ministry of the Interior: POB 2933, Airport Rd, Riyadh 11134; tel. (1) 401-1111; fax (1) 403-3125; internet www.moi.gov.sa.

Ministry of Justice: POB 7775, University St, Riyadh 11137; tel. (1) 405-7777; fax (1) 405-5399; internet www.moj.gov.sa.

Ministry of Labour: POB 21110, King Abd al-Aziz Rd, Riyadh 11475; tel. (1) 200-6666; fax (1) 478-9175; e-mail info@mol.gov.sa; internet www.mol.gov.sa.

Ministry of Municipal and Rural Affairs: POB 955, Nasseriya St, Riyadh 11136; tel. (1) 456-9999; fax (1) 456-3196; e-mail info@momra.gov.sa; internet www.momra.gov.sa.

Ministry of the National Guard: POB 6818, Riyadh 11452; tel. (1) 491-1390; fax (1) 491-6928; internet www.sang.gov.sa.

Ministry of Petroleum and Mineral Resources: POB 247, Al Ma'ather St, Riyadh 11191; tel. (1) 478-1661; fax (1) 479-3596; e-mail info@mopm.gov.sa; internet www.mopm.gov.sa.

Ministry of Pilgrimage (Hajj) Affairs: al-Maazar St, Riyadh 11183; tel. (1) 404-3003; fax (1) 402-2555; internet www.hajinformation.com.

Ministry of Social Affairs: Riyadh 11157; tel. (1) 477-8888; fax (1) 477-7336; e-mail info@mosa.gov.sa; internet www.mosa.gov.sa.

Ministry of Transport: Airport Rd, Riyadh 11178; tel. (1) 874-4444; fax (1) 874-4588; e-mail info@mot.gov.sa; internet www.mot.gov.sa.

Ministry of Water and Electricity: King Fahd Rd, Riyadh 11233; tel. (1) 205-6666; fax (1) 205-2749; e-mail info@mowe.gov.sa; internet www.mowe.gov.sa.

Majlis al-Shura
(Consultative Council)

Al-Yamamh Palace, Riyadh 11212; tel. (1) 4821666; fax (1) 4816985; e-mail webmaster@shura.gov.sa; internet www.shura.gov.sa.

In March 1992 King Fahd issued a decree to establish a Consultative Council of 60 members, whose powers include the right to summon and question ministers. The composition of the Council was announced by King Fahd in August 1993, and it was officially inaugurated in December. Each member serves a term of four years. The Council's membership was increased to 90 when its second term began in July 1997; it was expanded further, to 120, in May 2001, and to 150 in April 2005. King Fahd issued a decree extending the legislative powers of the Council in November 2003, including the right to propose new legislation.

Chairman: Dr Abdullah ibn Muhammad ibn Ibrahim al-Sheikh.

Vice-Chairman: Dr Muhammad Amin Ahmad Jefri.

Secretary-General: Dr Muhammad Abdullah al-Amer.

Political Organizations

There are no political organizations in Saudi Arabia.

Diplomatic Representation

EMBASSIES IN SAUDI ARABIA

Afghanistan: POB 93337, Riyadh 11673; tel. (1) 480-3459; fax (1) 480-3451; e-mail afgembriyad@hotmail.com; Ambassador Sayed Ahmad Umerkhil.

Albania: POB 94004, Riyadh 11693; tel. (1) 281-6534; fax (1) 281-6535; e-mail embassy.riyadh@mfa.gov.al; Ambassador Admirim Banaj.

Algeria: POB 94388, Riyadh 11693; tel. (1) 488-7171; fax (1) 482-1703; e-mail Mail@algerianembassy-saudi.com; internet algerianembassy-saudi.com; Ambassador Abd al-Wahab Derbal.

Argentina: POB 94369, Riyadh 11693; tel. (1) 465-2600; fax (1) 465-3075; e-mail earab@mrecic.gov.ar; internet earab.mrecic.gov.ar; Ambassador Jaime Sergio Cerda.

Australia: POB 94400, Riyadh 11693; tel. (1) 488-7788; fax (1) 488-7973; internet www.saudiarabia.embassy.gov.au; Ambassador Neil Hawkins.

Austria: POB 94373, Riyadh 11693; tel. (1) 480-1217; fax (1) 480-1526; e-mail riyadh-ob@bmeia.gv.at; internet www.bmeia.gv.at/riyadh; Ambassador Gregor W. Koessler.

Azerbaijan: 59 al-Worood Quarter St, off Amir Failsal bin Sa'ud Abd al-Rahman, Aloroba Rd, Riyadh; tel. (1) 419-2382; fax (1) 419-2260; e-mail riyadh@mission.mfa.gov.az; internet www.azembassy.org.sa; Ambassador Rasim Shamsaddin Oglu Rzayev.

Bahrain: POB 94371, Riyadh 11693; tel. (1) 488-0044; fax (1) 488-0208; e-mail riyadh.mission@mofa.gov.bh; Ambassador Sheikh Hamoud bin Abdullah Al Khalifa.

Bangladesh: POB 94395, Riyadh 11693; tel. (1) 419-5300; fax (1) 419-3555; e-mail info@bangladeshembassy.org.sa; internet www.bangladeshembassy.org.sa; Ambassador Muhammad Shahidul Islam.

Belgium: POB 94396, Riyadh 11693; tel. (1) 488-2888; fax (1) 488-2033; e-mail riyadh@diplobel.fed.be; internet www.diplomatie.be/riyadh; Ambassador Marc Vinck.

Bosnia and Herzegovina: POB 94301, Riyadh 11693; tel. (1) 456-7914; fax (1) 454-4360; e-mail baembsaruh@awalnet.net.sa; Ambassador (vacant).

Brazil: POB 94348, Riyadh 11693; tel. (1) 488-0018; fax (1) 488-1073; e-mail embaixada@brazemb-ksa.org; internet www.brazemb-ksa.org; Ambassador Sergio Luiz Canaes.

Brunei: POB 94314, al-Warood, Area 29, al-Fujairah St, Riyadh 11693; tel. (1) 456-0814; fax (1) 456-1594; e-mail riyadh.arabsaudi@mfa.gov.bn; Ambassador Dato Haji Abdul Mokti Daud.

Burkina Faso: POB 94330, Riyadh 11693; tel. (1) 465-2244; fax (1) 465-3397; e-mail burkinafaso.ksa@arab.net.sa; Ambassador Ountana Mansa.

Cameroon: POB 94336, Riyadh 11693; tel. (1) 488-0022; fax (1) 488-1463; e-mail ambacamriyad@ifrance.com; internet www.ambacamriyad.org.sa; Ambassador Iya Tidjani.

Canada: POB 94321, Riyadh 11693; tel. (1) 488-2288; fax (1) 488-1997; e-mail ryadh@international.gc.ca; internet www.canadainternational.gc.ca/saudi_arabia-arabie_saoudite; Ambassador Tom MacDonald.

Chad: POB 94374, Riyadh 11693; tel. and fax (1) 465-7702; Ambassador Saqr Yousuf Anto.

China, People's Republic: POB 75231, Riyadh 11578; tel. (1) 483-2126; fax (1) 281-2070; e-mail chinaemb_sa@mfa.gov.cn; internet www.chinaembassy.org.sa; Ambassador Li Chengwen.

Comoros: Riyadh; tel. (1) 293-4697; fax (1) 293-4797; Ambassador Assiandi Abdou Rahmane Amir.

Côte d'Ivoire: POB 94303, Riyadh 11693; tel. (1) 482-5582; fax (1) 482-9626; e-mail acisa@ambaci-riyadh.org; Ambassador Vazoumana Torre.

Denmark: POB 94398, Riyadh 11693; tel. (1) 488-0101; fax (1) 488-1366; e-mail ruhamb@um.dk; internet saudiarabien.um.dk; Ambassador Christian Kønigsfeldt.

Djibouti: POB 94340, Riyadh 11693; tel. (1) 454-3182; fax (1) 456-9168; e-mail dya_bamakhrama@hotmail.com; Ambassador Dya-Eddine Said Bamakhrama.

Egypt: POB 94333, Riyadh 11693; tel. (1) 481-0464; fax (1) 481-0463; Ambassador Afif Abd al-Wahab.

Eritrea: POB 94002, Riyadh; tel. (1) 480-1726; fax (1) 482-7537; Ambassador Mohammed Omar Mahmoud.

Ethiopia: POB 94341, Riyadh 11693; tel. (1) 482-3919; fax (1) 483-3281; e-mail ethiopian@awalnet.net.sa; Ambassador Dr Muhammad Hasen.

Finland: POB 94363, Riyadh 11693; tel. (1) 488-1515; fax (1) 488-2520; e-mail sanomat.ria@formin.fi; internet www.finland.org.sa; Ambassador Jarno Syrjälä.

France: POB 94367, Riyadh 11693; tel. (1) 488-1255; fax (1) 488-2882; e-mail diplomatie@ambafrance.org.sa; internet www.ambafrance-sa.org; Ambassador Bertrand Besancenot.

Gabon: POB 94325, Riyadh 11693; tel. (1) 456-7171; fax (1) 453-6121; e-mail ambagabonriyad@yahoo.com; Ambassador Ismail Ghalama Lingongo.

The Gambia: POB 94322, Riyadh 11693; tel. (1) 205-2158; fax (1) 456-2024; e-mail gamextriyadh@yahoo.com; Ambassador Omar Gibril Sallah.

Germany: POB 94001, Riyadh 11693; tel. (1) 488-0700; fax (1) 488-0660; e-mail info@riad.diplo.de; internet www.riad.diplo.de; Ambassador Dieter W. Haller.

Ghana: POB 94339, Riyadh 11693; tel. (1) 454-5126; fax (1) 225-2771; e-mail ghanaembrym@yahoo.com; internet www.ghanaembassyksa.com; Ambassador Alhaji Abdulai Salifu.

Greece: POB 94375, Riyadh 11693; tel. (1) 480-1975; fax (1) 480-1969; e-mail gremb.ria@mfa.gr; internet www.mfa.gr/saudi-arabia; Ambassador Ioannis Christofilis.

Guinea: POB 94326, Riyadh 11693; tel. (1) 488-1101; fax (1) 482-6757; e-mail riydambagunee@yahoo.fr; Ambassador el-Hadj Candido Rivas.

Hungary: POB 94014, al-Waha District, Ahmad Tonsy St 23, Riyadh 11693; tel. (1) 454-6707; fax (1) 456-0834; e-mail mission.ryd@mfa.gov.hu; internet www.mfa.gov.hu/emb/riyadh; Ambassador Miklós Kállay.

India: POB 94387, Riyadh 11693; tel. (1) 488-4144; fax (1) 488-4189; e-mail info@indianembassy.org.sa; internet www.indianembassy.org.sa; Ambassador Hamid Ali Rao.

Indonesia: POB 94343, Riyadh 11693; tel. (1) 488-2800; fax (1) 488-2966; e-mail kbri.riyadh@gmail.com; internet riyadh.kemlu.go.id; Ambassador Gatot Abdullah Mansyur.

Iran: POB 94394, Riyadh 11693; tel. (1) 488-1916; fax (1) 488-1890; Ambassador Javad Rasouli Mahallati.

Iraq: Riyadh; tel. (1) 480-6514; e-mail rydemt@iraqmfamail.com; Ambassador Dr Ghanim Alwan Jawad al-Jumaili.

Ireland: POB 94349, Riyadh 11693; tel. (1) 488-2300; fax (1) 488-0927; e-mail riyadhembassy@dfa.ie; internet www.embassyofireland.org.sa; Ambassador Dr Niall Holohan.

Italy: POB 94389, Riyadh 11693; tel. (1) 488-1212; fax (1) 480-6964; e-mail segreteria1.riad@esteri.it; internet www.ambriad.esteri.it; Ambassador Mario Buffo.

Japan: POB 4095, Riyadh 11491; tel. (1) 488-1100; fax (1) 488-0189; e-mail info@jpn-emb-sa.com; internet www.ksa.emb-japan.go.jp; Ambassador Jiro Kodera.

Jordan: POB 94316, Riyadh 11693; tel. (1) 488-0051; fax (1) 488-0072; e-mail jordan.embassy@nesma.net.sa; Ambassador Jamal Hamid al-Shamayleh.

Kazakhstan: POB 94012, Riyadh 11693; tel. (1) 480-6406; fax (1) 480-9106; e-mail office@kazembgulf.net; internet www.kazembsaudi.com; Ambassador Bakhtiyar Tassymov.

Kenya: POB 94358, Riyadh 11693; tel. (1) 488-1238; fax (1) 488-2629; e-mail riyadh@mfa.go.ke; internet www.kenyaembassyriyadh.com; Ambassador Mahmoud Ali Saleh.

Korea, Republic: POB 94399, Riyadh 11693; tel. (1) 488-2211; fax (1) 488-1317; e-mail emsau@mofat.go.kr; internet sau.mofat.go.kr; Ambassador Kim Jong-Yong.

Kuwait: POB 94304, Riyadh 11693; tel. (1) 488-3201; fax (1) 488-3682; Ambassador Sheikh Thamer Jaber al-Ahmed al-Jaber al-Sabah.

Kyrgyzstan: POB 94383, Riyadh 11693; tel. (1) 229-3272; fax (1) 229-3274; e-mail info@kyrgyzembarabia.kg; internet www.kyrgyzembarabia.kg; Ambassador Jusupbek Sharipov.

Lebanon: POB 94350, Riyadh 11693; tel. (1) 480-4060; fax (1) 480-4703; e-mail embassy@lebanon.org.sa; internet www.lebanon.org.sa; Ambassador Abd al-Sattar Muhammad Isa.

Libya: POB 94365, Riyadh 11693; tel. (1) 488-9757; fax (1) 488-3252; e-mail libianembassy@yahoo.com; Ambassador MUHAMMAD ABDULLAH AL-SHAKAL.

Malaysia: POB 94335, Riyadh 11693; tel. (1) 488-7100; fax (1) 482-4177; e-mail malriyadh@kln.gov.my; internet www.kln.gov.my/perwakilan/riyadh; Ambassador Datuk Syed OMAR MUHAMMAD AL-SAGGAF.

Maldives: POB 2228, Riyadh 11451; tel. (1) 462-6787; fax (1) 464-3725; e-mail admin@maldivesembassy.org.sa; Ambassador ADAM HASSAN.

Mali: POB 94331, Riyadh 11693; tel. (1) 464-5640; fax (1) 419-5016; e-mail consulat@sbm.net.sa; Ambassador MUHAMMAD MAHMOUD BEN LABAT.

Malta: POB 94361, Riyadh 11693; tel. (1) 463-2345; fax (1) 463-3993; e-mail maltaembassy.riyadh@gov.mt; internet www.foreign.gov.mt/saudi_arabia; Ambassador STEPHEN BORG.

Mauritania: POB 94354, Riyadh 11693; tel. (1) 464-6749; fax (1) 465-8355; Ambassador MUHAMMAD MAHMOUD OULD ABDULLAH.

Mexico: POB 94391, Riyadh 11693; tel. (1) 480-8822; fax (1) 480-8833; e-mail embassyofmexico@embamex.org.sa; internet embamex.sre.gob.mx/arabiasaudita; Ambassador ARTURO TREJO.

Morocco: POB 94392, Riyadh 11693; tel. (1) 481-1858; fax (1) 482-7016; e-mail consular@moroccanembassy.sa; internet www.moroccanembassy.sa; Ambassador ABDESLAM BARAKA.

Myanmar: Villa No. 5, al-Kadi St, King Fahd Area, Riyadh; tel. (1) 229-3306; e-mail meriyadh@gmail.com; Ambassador KHIN ZAW WIN.

Nepal: POB 94384, Riyadh 11693; tel. (1) 461-1108; fax (1) 464-0690; e-mail info@neksa.org; internet www.neksa.org; Ambassador UDAYA RAJ PANDEY.

Netherlands: POB 94307, Riyadh 11693; tel. (1) 488-0011; fax (1) 488-0544; e-mail riy@minbuza.nl; internet saudiarabia.nlembassy.org; Ambassador J. L. WESTHOFF.

New Zealand: POB 94397, Riyadh 11693; tel. (1) 488-7988; fax (1) 488-7911; e-mail info@nzembassy.org.sa; internet www.nzembassy.com/saudiarabia; Ambassador ROD HARRIS.

Niger: POB 94334, Riyadh 11693; tel. and fax (1) 470-8698; fax (1) 205-4323; e-mail ambassadeduniger_riyadh@yahoo.com; Ambassador IBRAHIM KATCHALLOU MUHAMMAD.

Nigeria: POB 94386, Riyadh 11693; tel. (1) 482-3024; fax (1) 482-4134; e-mail nigeria@nigeria.org.sa; internet www.nigeria.org.sa; Ambassador ABUBAKAR SHEHU BUNU.

Norway: POB 94380, Riyadh 11693; tel. (1) 488-1904; fax (1) 488-0854; e-mail emb.riyadh@mfa.no; internet www.al-norwige.org.sa; Ambassador CARL SCHIÖTZ WIBYE.

Oman: POB 94381, Riyadh 11693; tel. (1) 482-3120; fax (1) 482-3738; e-mail riyadh@mofa.gov.om; Ambassador Dr SAEED AHMAD BIN HILAL BIN SAUD AL-BUSAIDI.

Pakistan: POB 94007, Riyadh 11693; tel. (1) 488-4111; fax (1) 488-7953; e-mail parep_riyadh@yahoo.com; internet www.mofa.gov.pk/saudiarabia; Ambassador MUHAMMAD NAEEM KHAN.

Peru: POB 94433, Riyadh 11693; tel. (1) 482-2474; fax (1) 483-0474; e-mail lepru.riyadh@gmail.com; Ambassador JULIO EDUARDO MARTINETTI MACEDO.

Philippines: POB 94366, Riyadh 11693; tel. (1) 482-0507; fax (1) 488-3945; e-mail filembry@sbm.net.sa; internet www.philembassy-riyadh.org; Ambassador EZZEDIN H. TAGO.

Poland: POB 94016, Riyadh 11693; tel. (1) 454-9274; fax (1) 454-9210; e-mail riyadh@msz.gov.pl; internet www.rijad.polemb.net; Ambassador WITOLD SMIDOWSKI.

Portugal: POB 94328, Riyadh 11693; tel. (1) 482-9042; fax (1) 482-6981; e-mail portriade@nesma.net.sa; Ambassador Dr ANTONIO MARIA DE SOUSA.

Qatar: POB 94353, Riyadh 11461; tel. (1) 482-5544; fax (1) 482-5394; e-mail riyadh@mofa.gov.qa; Ambassador ALI ABDULLAH AL-MAHMOUD.

Romania: POB 94319, Riyadh 11693; tel. (1) 263-0456; fax (1) 456-9985; e-mail office@embrom.org.sa; Chargé d'affaires a.i. MIHAIL-CONSTANTIN COMAN.

Russia: POB 94308, Riyadh 11693; tel. (1) 481-1875; fax (1) 481-1890; e-mail rusembass@mail.ru; internet www.rfemb-ksa.mid.ru; Ambassador OLEG OZEROV.

Rwanda: POB 94383, Riyadh 11693; tel. (1) 454-0808; fax (1) 456-1769; Ambassador SIMON INSONERE.

Senegal: POB 94352, Riyadh 11693; tel. (1) 488-0146; fax (1) 488-3804; Ambassador MOUHAMADOU DOUDOU LO.

Sierra Leone: POB 94329, Riyadh 11693; tel. (1) 465-6204; fax (1) 464-3662; e-mail slembrdh@zajil.net; Ambassador Alhaji WUSU MUNU.

Singapore: POB 94378, Riyadh 11693; tel. (1) 480-3855; fax (1) 483-0632; e-mail singemb_ruh@sgmfa.gov.sg; internet www.mfa.gov.sg/riyadh; Ambassador LAWRENCE ANDERSON.

Somalia: POB 94372, Riyadh 11693; tel. (1) 464-3456; fax (1) 464-9705; Ambassador AHMED ABDULLAH MOHAMED.

South Africa: POB 94006, Riyadh 11693; tel. (1) 442-9716; fax (1) 442-9708; e-mail riyadh.info@foreign.gov.za; Ambassador MUHAMMAD SADIQ JAAFAR.

Spain: POB 94347, Riyadh 11693; tel. (1) 488-0606; fax (1) 488-0420; e-mail emb.riad.info@maec.es; Ambassador JOAQUIN PERTH.

Sri Lanka: POB 94360, Riyadh 11693; tel. (1) 460-8232; fax (1) 460-8846; e-mail mail@srilankaembassyriyadh.com; internet www.lankaemb-riyadh.org; Ambassador AHMED A. JAWAD.

Sudan: POB 94337, Riyadh 11693; tel. (1) 488-7979; fax (1) 488-7729; Ambassador ABD AL-HAFEZ IBRAHIM MUHAMMAD.

Sweden: POB 94382, Riyadh 11693; tel. (1) 482-7796; fax (1) 488-0604; e-mail ambassaden.riyadh@gov.se; internet www.swedenabroad.com/riyadh; Ambassador DAG JUHLIN-DANNFELT.

Switzerland: POB 94311, Riyadh 11693; tel. (11) 488-1291; fax (11) 488-0632; e-mail rya.vertretung@eda.admin.ch; internet www.eda.admin.ch/riad; Ambassador PETER REINHARDT.

Syria: POB 94323, Riyadh 11693; tel. (1) 482-6191; fax (1) 482-6196; Ambassador MAHDI DAKHLALLAH.

Tajikistan: Riyadh; Ambassador Dr ABDULLAH YULDASHEV.

Tanzania: POB 94320, Riyadh 11693; tel. (1) 454-2839; fax (1) 454-9660; e-mail tzriyad@deltasa.com; Ambassador Prof ABDULLAH H. OMARI.

Thailand: POB 94359, Riyadh 11693; tel. (1) 488-1174; fax (1) 488-1179; e-mail thaiemryadsl@awalnet.net.sa; internet www.thaiembassy.org/riyadh; Chargé d'affaires a.i. WIJAK CHITTARAT.

Tunisia: POB 94368, Riyadh 11693; tel. (1) 488-7900; fax (1) 488-7641; e-mail amb.tunisie.riyadh@saudi.net.sa; Ambassador NAJIB AL-MUNIF.

Turkey: POB 94390, Riyadh 11693; tel. (1) 482-0101; fax (1) 488-7823; e-mail embassy.riyadh@mfa.gov.tr; internet riyadh.emb.mfa.gov.tr; Ambassador AHMET MUHTAR GÜN.

Turkmenistan: POB 94019, Riyadh 11693; tel. (1) 205-4898; fax (1) 205-2990; e-mail info@turkmenemb-sa.org; internet www.turkmenemb-sa.org; Ambassador NAZARGULY SHAGULYEV.

Uganda: POB 94344, Riyadh 11693; tel. (1) 454-4910; fax (1) 454-9264; e-mail ugariyadh@hotmail.com; Ambassador Dr RASHID YAHYA SSEMUDDU.

Ukraine: POB 94010, Riyadh 11693; tel. (1) 450-8536; fax (1) 450-8534; e-mail emb_sa@mfa.gov.ua; internet saudiarabia.mfa.gov.ua; Ambassador PETRO KOLOS.

United Arab Emirates: POB 94385, Riyadh 11693; tel. (1) 488-1227; fax (1) 482-7504; e-mail riyadh@mofa.gov.ae; internet uae-embassy.ae/embassies/sa; Ambassador MUHAMMAD SAEED MUHAMMAD AL-DHAHIRI.

United Kingdom: POB 94351, Riyadh 11693; tel. (1) 481-9100; fax (1) 481-9350; e-mail pressoffice.riyadh@fco.gov.uk; internet ukinsaudiarabia.fco.gov.uk; Ambassador JOHN JENKINS.

USA: POB 94309, Riyadh 11693; tel. (1) 488-3800; fax (1) 488-7360; e-mail usembriyadhwebsite@state.gov; internet riyadh.usembassy.gov; Ambassador JAMES B. SMITH.

Uruguay: POB 94346, Riyadh 11693; tel. (1) 462-0739; fax (1) 462-0638; e-mail uruarabia@mrree.gub.uy; Ambassador CARLOS ANTONIO MORA MEDERO.

Uzbekistan: POB 94008, Riyadh 11693; tel. (1) 263-5223; fax (1) 263-5105; Ambassador ALISHER QADIROV.

Venezuela: POB 94364, Riyadh 11693; tel. (1) 480-7141; fax (1) 480-0901; e-mail embvenar@embvenar.org.sa; Ambassador JOSEBA ACHUTEGUI.

Yemen: POB 94356, Riyadh 11693; tel. (1) 488-1769; fax (1) 488-1562; Ambassador MUHAMMAD ALI MOHSEN AL-AHWAL.

Judicial System

Judges are independent and governed by the rules of Islamic *Shari'a*. A new Judicial Law approved in May 2007 provided for a number of significant changes to the courts system. The new legislation called for the establishment of appeal courts, criminal courts and specialized courts. A Supreme Court was to be established in Riyadh, and new appeals courts were planned for each of the kingdom's 13 regions. There were to be general courts to deal with all conflicts except labour, commercial and family disputes, and criminal courts to address crimes. Family and personal conflicts were to be handled by civil courts. However, by 2013 few of these proposed amendments had yet to be implemented and the following courts were in operation:

Supreme Judicial Council: comprises 11 mems; supervises work of the courts; reviews legal questions referred to it by the Minister of Justice and expresses opinions on judicial questions; reviews sentences of death, cutting and stoning; Chair. Dr MUHAMMAD IBN ABD AL-KARIM IBN ABD AL-AZIZ AL-EISSA.

Court of Cassation: consists of Chief Justice and an adequate number of judges; includes department for penal suits, department for personal status and department for other suits.

General (Public) Courts: consist of one or more judges; sentences are issued by a single judge, with the exception of death, stoning and cutting, which require the decision of three judges.

Summary Courts: consist of one or more judges; sentences are issued by a single judge.

Specialized Courts: the setting up of specialized courts is permissible by Royal Decree on a proposal from the Supreme Council of Justice.

Religion

ISLAM

Arabia is the centre of the Islamic faith, and Saudi Arabia includes the holy cities of Mecca and Medina. Except in the Eastern region, where a large number of people follow Shi'a rites, the majority of the population are Sunni Muslims, and most of the indigenous inhabitants belong to the strictly orthodox Wahhabi sect. The Wahhabis originated in the 18th century, but first became unified and influential under Abd al-Aziz (Ibn Sa'ud), who became the first King of Saudi Arabia. They are now the keepers of the holy places and control the pilgrimage to Mecca. In 1986 King Fahd adopted the title of Custodian of the Two Holy Mosques; the title passed to King Abdullah upon his accession to the throne in August 2005. The country's most senior Islamic authority is the Council of Senior Ulama.

Mecca: Birthplace of the Prophet Muhammad, seat of the Grand Mosque and Shrine of Ka'ba, visited by 1,828,195 Muslims from abroad in the Islamic year 1432 (2010/11).

Medina: Burial place of Muhammad, second sacred city of Islam.

Grand Mufti and Chairman of Council of Senior Ulama: Sheikh ABD AL-AZIZ IBN ABDULLAH AL-SHEIKH.

CHRISTIANITY

The Roman Catholic Church

A small number of adherents, mainly expatriates, form part of the Apostolic Vicariate of Northern Arabia. The Vicar Apostolic is resident in Bahrain.

The Anglican Communion

Within the Episcopal Church in Jerusalem and the Middle East, Saudi Arabia forms part of the diocese of Cyprus and the Gulf. The Anglican congregations in the country are entirely expatriate. The Bishop in Cyprus and the Gulf is resident in Cyprus, while the Archdeacon in the Gulf is resident in Bahrain.

Other Denominations

The Greek Orthodox Church is also represented.

The Press

Since 1964 most newspapers and periodicals have been published by press organizations, administered by boards of directors with full autonomous powers, in accordance with the provisions of the Press Law. These organizations, which took over from small private firms, are privately owned by groups of individuals experienced in newspaper publishing and administration (see Publishers).

There are also a number of popular periodicals published by the Government and by the Saudi Arabian Oil Co, and distributed free of charge. The press is subject to no legal restriction affecting freedom of expression or the coverage of news.

DAILIES

Arab News: POB 10452, SRP Bldg, Madinah Rd, Jeddah 21433; tel. (2) 639-1888; fax (2) 639-3223; e-mail arabnews@arabnews.com; internet www.arabnews.com; f. 1975; English; publ. by Saudi Research and Publishing Co; Editor-in-Chief KHALED AL-MAEENA; circ. 110,000.

Al-Bilad (The Country): POB 6340, Jeddah 21442; tel. (2) 672-3000; fax (2) 671-2545; internet www.albilad-daily.com; f. 1934; Arabic; publ. by Al-Bilad Publishing Org; Editor-in-Chief QUINAN AL-GHOMDI; circ. 66,210.

Al-Eqtisadiah: POB 10452, Jeddah 21433; tel. (2) 651-1333; fax (2) 667-6212; internet www.aleqt.com; f. 1992; business and finance; publ. by Saudi Research and Publishing Co; Editor-in-Chief SALMAN IBN YUSUF DOSARI; circ. 81,000.

Al-Jazirah (The Peninsula): POB 354, Riyadh 11411; tel. (1) 487-0911; fax (1) 487-1063; e-mail ccs@al-jazirah.com.sa; internet www.al-jazirah.com; f. 1972; Arabic; publ. by Al-Jazirah Corpn for Press, Printing and Publishing; Dir-Gen. ABD AL-LATIF BIN SAAD; Editor-in-Chief KHALID BIN HAMAD AL-MALIK; circ. 110,000.

Al-Madina al-Munawara (Medina—The Enlightened City): POB 807, Makkah Rd, Jeddah 21421; tel. (2) 671-2100; fax (2) 671-1877; e-mail webmaster@al-madina.com; internet al-madina.com; f. 1937; Arabic; publ. by Al-Madina Press Establishment; Chief Editor FAHD HASSAN AL-AQRAN; circ. 46,370.

Al-Nadwah (The Council): POB 5803, Jarwal Sheikh Sayed Halabi Bldg, Mecca; tel. (2) 520-0111; fax (2) 520-3055; e-mail info@al-nadwah.com; internet www.alnadwah.com.sa; f. 1958; Arabic; publ. by Makkah Printing and Information Establishment; Editor AHMAD BIN SALEH BAYUSUF; circ. 35,000.

Okaz: POB 1508, Seaport Rd, Jeddah 21441; tel. (2) 672-7621; fax (2) 672-4297; e-mail 104127.266@compuserve.com; internet www.okaz.com.sa; f. 1948; Arabic; publ. by Okaz Org. for Press and Publication; Editor-in-Chief MUHAMMAD AL-TUNISI; circ. 110,000.

Al-Riyadh: POB 2943, Riyadh 11476; tel. (1) 487-1000; fax (1) 441-7417; internet www.alriyadh.com; f. 1965; Arabic; publ. by Al-Yamama Press Establishment; Editor TURKI A. AL-SUDARI; circ. 150,000 (Sat.–Thur.), 90,000 (Fri.).

Saudi Gazette: POB 5576, Jeddah 21432; tel. (2) 676-0000; fax (2) 672-7621; e-mail news@saudigazette.com.sa; internet www.saudigazette.com.sa; f. 1976; English; publ. by Okaz Org. for Press and Publication; Editor-in-Chief MUHAMMAD NASIR SHOUKANI; circ. 15,000.

Al-Watan: POB 15156, Airport Road, Abha; tel. (7) 227-3333; fax (7) 227-3756; e-mail editor@alwatan.com.sa; internet www.alwatan.com.sa; f. 1998; publ. by Assir Establishment for Press and Publishing; Dir-Gen. HATEM HAMID; circ. 150,000.

Al-Yaum (Today): POB 565, Dammam 31421; tel. (3) 858-0800; fax (3) 858-8777; e-mail mail@alyaum.com; internet www.alyaum.com; f. 1965; publ. by Dar al-Yaum Press, Printing and Publishing Ltd; Dir-Gen. SALEH ALI HAMID; Editor-in-Chief MUHAMMAD ABDULLAH AL-WAEEL; circ. 40,000.

WEEKLIES

Al-Muslimoon (The Muslims): POB 13195, Jeddah 21493; tel. (2) 669-1888; fax (2) 669-5549; f. 1985; Arabic; cultural and religious affairs; publ. by Saudi Research and Publishing Co; Editor-in-Chief Dr ABDULLAH AL-RIFA'E; circ. 68,665.

Saudi Economic Survey: POB 1989, Jeddah 21441; tel. (2) 657-8551; fax (2) 657-8553; e-mail info@saudieconomicsurvey.com; internet www.saudieconomicsurvey.com; f. 1967; English; review of Saudi Arabian economic and business activity; Publr SAIFUDDIN A. ASHOOR; Gen. Man. WALID S. ASHOOR.

Sayidaty (My Lady): POB 4556, Madina Rd, Jeddah 21412; tel. (2) 639-1888; fax (2) 669-5549; internet www.sayidaty.net; f. 1981; publ. in Arabic and English edns; women's magazine; publ. by Saudi Research and Publishing Co; Editor-in-Chief MUHAMMAD FAHAD AL-HARTHI.

Al-Shams (The Sun): Riyadh; internet shms.pressera.com; f. 2005; tabloid format; sports, culture, entertainment; publishing licence revoked by the Govt in Feb. 2006, but restored after some 6 weeks; Editor-in-Chief KHALAF AL-HARBI.

Al-Yamama: POB 851, Riyadh 11421; tel. (1) 442-0000; fax (1) 441-7114; f. 1952; literary magazine; Editor-in-Chief ABDULLAH AL-JAHLAN; circ. 35,000.

OTHER PERIODICALS

Ahlan Wasahlan (Welcome): POB 8013, Jeddah 21482; tel. (2) 686-2349; fax (2) 686-2006; internet pr.sv.net/aw; monthly; flight journal of Saudi Arabian Airlines; Gen. Man. and Editor-in-Chief YARUB A. BALKHAIR; circ. 150,000.

Al-Daragh: POB 2945, Riyadh 11461; tel. (1) 401-1999; fax (1) 401-3597; e-mail info@aldarahmagazine.com; internet aldarahmagazine.com; history journal; publ. by King Abd al-Aziz Foundation for Research and Archives.

Al-Faysal: POB 3, Riyadh 11411; tel. (1) 465-3027; fax (1) 464-7851; monthly; f. 1976; Arabic; culture, education, health, interviews; Man. Editor ABDULLAH Y. AL-KOWAILEET.

Majallat al-Iqtisad wal-Idara (Journal of Economics and Administration): King Abd al-Aziz University, POB 9031, Jeddah 21413; 2 a year; Chief Editor Prof. ABD AL-AZIZ A. DIYAB.

Al-Manhal (The Spring): POB 2925, Jeddah; tel. (2) 643-2124; fax (2) 642-8853; e-mail info@manhalmagazine.com; f. 1937; monthly; Arabic; cultural, literary, political and scientific; Editor ZUHAIR N. AL-ANSARI.

The MWL Journal: Press and Publications Department, Rabitat al-Alam al-Islami, POB 537, Mecca; fax (2) 544-1622; e-mail info@themwl.org; internet www.themwl.org; monthly; English; Dir MURAD SULAIMAN IRQISOUS.

Al-Rabita: POB 537, Mecca; tel. (2) 560-0919; fax (2) 543-1488; e-mail info@themwl.org; internet www.themwl.org; Arabic; Chief Editor Dr OSMAN ABUZAID.

Saudi Review: POB 4288, Jeddah 21491; tel. (2) 651-7442; fax (2) 653-0693; f. 1966; English; monthly; newsletter from Saudi newspapers and broadcasting service; publ. by Int. Communications Co; Chief Editor SAAD AL-MABROUK; circ. 5,000.

Al-Sharkiah-Elle (Oriental Elle): POB 6, Riyadh; monthly; Arabic; women's magazine; Editor SAMIRA M. KHASHAGGI.

Al-Soqoor (Falcons): POB 2973, Riyadh 11461; tel. (1) 476-6566; f. 1978; 2 a year; air force journal; cultural activities; Editor HAMAD A. AL-SALEH.

Al-Tadhamon al-Islami (Islamic Solidarity): Ministry of Pilgrimage (Hajj) Affairs, Omar bin al-Khatab St, Riyadh 11183; monthly; Editor Dr MUSTAFA ABD AL-WAHID.

Al-Tijarah (Commerce): POB 1264, Jeddah 21431; tel. (2) 651-5111; fax (2) 651-7373; e-mail jcci@mail.gcc.com.bh; f. 1960; monthly; publ. by Jeddah Chamber of Commerce and Industry; Chair. Sheikh ISMAIL ABU DAUD; circ. 8,000.

NEWS AGENCIES

International Islamic News Agency (IINA): POB 5054, Jeddah 21422; tel. (2) 665-2056; fax (2) 665-9358; e-mail iina@islamicnews.org.sa; internet www.islamicnews.org.sa; f. 1972; operates under the auspices of the Org. of the Islamic Conference; Dir-Gen. ABD AL-WAHAB KASHIF.

Saudi Press Agency (SPA): POB 7186, King Fahd Rd, Riyadh 11171; tel. (1) 419-5485; fax (1) 419-5685; e-mail wass@spa.gov.sa; internet www.spa.gov.sa; f. 1970; Dir-Gen. ABDULLAH BIN FAHD AL-HUSSAIN.

Publishers

Assir Establishment for Press and Publishing: POB 15156, Abha; tel. (7) 227-3333; fax (7) 227-3590; f. 1998; publishes *Al-Watan*; Gen. Man. HATEM HAMED MOUMINAH.

Al-Bilad Publishing Organization: POB 6340, al-Sahafa St, Jeddah 21442; tel. (2) 672-3000; fax (2) 671-2545; publishes *Al-Bilad* and *Iqra'a*; Dir-Gen. AMIN ABDULLAH AL-QARQOURI.

Dar al-Maiman Publishers and Distributors: POB 90020, Riyadh 11613; tel. and fax (1) 4627336; fax (1) 2800587.

Dar al-Shareff for Publishing and Distribution: POB 58287, Riyadh 11594; tel. (1) 403-4931; fax (1) 405-2234; f. 1992; fiction, religion, science and social sciences; Pres. IBRAHIM AL-HAZEMI.

Dar al-Yaum Press, Printing and Publishing Ltd: POB 565, Dammam 31421; tel. (3) 858-0800; fax (3) 858-8777; e-mail mail@alyaum.com; internet www.alyaum.com; f. 1964; publishes *Al-Yaum*; Chair. ABD AL-AZIZ MUHAMMAD AL-HUGAIL; Gen. Man. SALIH ALI AL-HUMAIDAN.

International Publications Agency (IPA): POB 70, Dhahran 31942; tel. and fax (3) 895-4925; publishes material of local interest; Man. SAID SALAH.

Al-Jazirah Corpn for Press, Printing and Publishing: POB 354, Riyadh 11411; tel. (1) 487-0911; fax (1) 487-1175; e-mail ccs@al-jazirah.com.sa; internet www.al-jazirah.com.sa; f. 1964; 42 mems; publishes *Al-Jazirah* daily newspaper; Chair. ABD AL-LATIF BIN SAAD AL-ATEEQ; Editor-in-Chief KHALID EL-MALEK.

Al-Madina Press Establishment: POB 807, Jeddah 21421; tel. (2) 671-2100; fax (2) 671-1877; f. 1937; publishes *Al-Madina al-Munawara*; Gen. Man. AHMAD SALAH JAMJOUM.

Makkah Printing and Information Establishment: POB 5803, Jarwal Sheikh Sayed Halabi Bldg, Mecca; tel. (2) 542-7868; publishes *Al-Nadwah* daily newspaper; Chair. MUHAMMAD ABDOU YAMANI.

Okaz Organization for Press and Publication: POB 1508, Jeddah 21441; tel. (2) 672-2630; fax (2) 672-8150; publishes *Okaz* and *Saudi Gazette*; Chair. SAEED AL-HARTHI.

Al-Rushd Publishers: POB 17522, Riyadh 11494; tel. (1) 459-3451; fax (1) 457-3381; e-mail alrushd@alrushdryh.com; internet www.rushd.com.sa; scientific and academic publs.

Saudi Publishing and Distributing House: Umm Aslam District, nr Muslaq, POB 2043, Jeddah 21451; tel. (2) 629-4278; fax (2) 629-4290; e-mail info@spdh-sa.com; internet www.spdh-sa.com; f. 1966; publishers, importers and distributors of English and Arabic books; Chair. MUHAMMAD SALAHUDDIN.

Saudi Research and Publishing Co: POB 478, Riyadh 11411; tel. (1) 441-9933; fax (1) 442-9555; internet www.srpc.com; publs include *Arab News*, *Asharq al-Awsat*, *Al-Majalla*, *Al-Muslimoon* and *Sayidati*; Dep. Gen. Man. SALEH AL-DOWAIS.

Al-Yamama Press Establishment: POB 851, Al Sahafa Qtr, Riyadh 11421; tel. (1) 441-6611; fax (1) 441-7580; publishes *Al-Riyadh* and *Al-Yamama*; Dir-Gen. SAKHAL MAIDAN.

Broadcasting and Communications

TELECOMMUNICATIONS

Ettihad Etisalat: POB 9979, Riyadh 11423; tel. (1) 211-8015; fax (1) 211-8029; e-mail info@mobily.com.sa; internet www.mobily.com.sa; f. 2004; owned by consortium led by Emirates Telecommunications Corpn (United Arab Emirates); awarded the second licence to provide mobile telephone services in 2004; operates under the brand name *Mobily* (launched 2005); 14.8m. subscribers (Dec. 2008); Chair. ABD AL-AZIZ BIN SALEH AL-SUGHAYIR; CEO KHALID AL-KAF.

Saudi Telecommunications Co—Saudi Telecom (STC): POB 87912, Riyadh 11652; tel. (1) 215-3030; fax (1) 215-2734; e-mail contactus@stc.com.sa; internet www.stc.com.sa; f. 1998; partially privatized in 2002; provides telecommunications services in Saudi Arabia; Chair. Eng. ABD AL-AZIZ A. AL-SUGAIR; CEO Dr KHALED BIN ABD AL-AZIZ AL-GHONEIM.

Zain Saudi Arabia: POB 295814, Riyadh 11351; tel. (1) 216-1800; e-mail corporate.communications@sa.zain.com; internet www.sa.zain.com; f. 2007; wholly owned by Mobile Telecommunications Co KSC (Zain Kuwait); awarded the third licence to provide mobile telephone services in 2007; Chair. Prince HUSSAM IBN SA'UD IBN ABD AL-AZIZ AL SA'UD; CEO SAAD AL-BARRAK.

Regulatory Authority

Communications and Information Technology Commission (CITC): POB 75606, Riyadh; tel. (1) 461-8000; fax (1) 461-8002; internet www.citc.gov.sa; f. 2001 under the name Saudi Communications Comm.; present name adopted 2003; independent regulatory authority; Gov. ABDULLAH ABD AL-AZIZ AL-DARRAB.

BROADCASTING

Radio

Saudi Arabian Broadcasting Service: c/o Ministry of Information and Culture, POB 60059, Riyadh 11545; tel. (1) 401-4440; fax (1) 403-8177; e-mail saudi-radio@saudiradio.net.sa; internet www.saudiradio.net; 24 medium- and short-wave stations, incl. Jeddah, Riyadh, Dammam and Abha, broadcast programmes in Arabic and English; 23 FM stations; overseas service in Bengali, English, Farsi, French, Hausa, Indonesian, Somali, Swahili, Turkestani, Turkish and Urdu; Dir-Gen. MUHAMMAD AL-MANSOOR.

Saudi Aramco FM Radio: Bldg 3030 LIP, Dhahran 31311; tel. (3) 876-1845; fax (3) 876-1608; f. 1948; English; private; for employees of Saudi Aramco; Man. ESSAM Z. TAWFIQ.

Television

Saudi Arabian Government Television Service: POB 7971, Riyadh 11472; tel. (1) 401-4440; fax (1) 404-4192; e-mail satepjeng@moci.gov.sa; began transmission 1965; 112 stations, incl. 6 main stations at Riyadh, Jeddah, Medina, Dammam, Qassim and Abha, transmit programmes in Arabic and English; operates 4 channels: Channel 1 (Arabic); Channel 2 (English and French); Channel 3 (sport); Al-Ekhbariya (news); Dir-Gen. ABD AL-AZIZ AL-HASSAN (Channel 1).

Finance

(cap. = capital; res = reserves; dep. = deposits; m. = million; br(s) = branch(es); amounts in Saudi riyals, unless otherwise stated)

BANKING

Central Bank

Saudi Arabian Monetary Agency (SAMA): POB 2992, Riyadh 11169; tel. (1) 463-3000; fax (1) 466-2966; e-mail info@sama.gov.sa; internet www.sama.gov.sa; f. 1952; functions include stabilization of currency, administration of monetary reserves, regulation of banking and insurance sectors, and issue of notes and coins; dep. 962,808m., total assets 1,393,080m. (June 2009); Gov. Dr FAHD IBN ABDULLAH AL-MUBARAK; 10 brs.

National Banks

Alinma Bank: POB 66674, al-Anoud Tower, King Fahad Rd, Riyadh 11586; e-mail info@alinma.com; internet www.alinma.com; f. 2006; cap. 15,000m., res 105m., dep. 17,984m. (Dec. 2011); Chair. ABD AL-AZIZ ABDULLAH AL-ZAMIL; 15 brs.

National Commercial Bank (NCB): POB 3555, King Abd al-Aziz St, Jeddah 21481; tel. (2) 649-3333; fax (2) 644-6468; e-mail contact@alahli.com; internet www.alahli.com; f. 1950; 69.3% govt-owned; cap. 15,000m., res 13,938m., dep. 241,668m. (Dec. 2011); Chair. MANSOUR S. AL-MAIMAN; 258 domestic brs, 2 abroad.

Al-Rajhi Banking and Investment Corpn (Al-Rajhi Bank): POB 28, al-Akariya Bldg, Oleya St, Riyadh 11411; tel. (1) 211-6000; fax (1) 460-0922; e-mail contactus@alrajhibank.com.sa; internet www.alrajhibank.com.sa; f. 1988; operates according to Islamic financial principles; cap. 15,000m., res 17,706m., dep. 180,450m. (Dec. 2011); Chair. Sheikh SULAIMAN BIN ABD AL-AZIZ AL-RAJHI; 700 brs.

Riyad Bank Ltd: POB 22601, King Abd al-Aziz St, Riyadh 11416; tel. (1) 401-3030; fax (1) 404-1255; internet www.riyadbank.com.sa; f. 1957; cap. 15,000m., res 14,285m., dep. 146,064m. (Dec. 2011); Chair. RASHED A. AL-RASHED; Pres. and CEO TALAL I. AL-QUDAIBI; 201 domestic brs, 1 abroad.

Specialist Bank

Arab Investment Co SAA (TAIC): POB 4009, King Abd al-Aziz St, Riyadh 11491; tel. (1) 476-0601; fax (1) 476-0514; e-mail taic@taic.com; internet www.taic.com; f. 1974 by 17 Arab countries for investment and banking; cap. US $700m., res $141m., dep. $1,184m. (Dec. 2011); Chair. YOUSUF IBN IBRAHIM AL-BASSAM; CEO IBRAHIM H. AL-MAZYAD; 1 br.

Banks with Foreign Interests

Arab National Bank (ANB): POB 56921, King Faisal St, North Murabba, Riyadh 11564; tel. (1) 402-9000; fax (1) 402-7747; e-mail info@anb.com.sa; internet www.anb.com.sa; f. 1980; Arab Bank PLC, Jordan, 40%, Saudi shareholders 60%; cap. 8,500m., res 7,057m., dep. 96,683m. (Dec. 2011); Chair. ABD AL-LATIF HAMAD AL-JABR; Man. Dir Dr ROBERT EID; 117 domestic brs, 1 abroad.

Bank al-Jazira: POB 6277, Khalid bin al-Waleed St, Jeddah 21442; tel. (2) 651-8070; fax (2) 653-2478; e-mail info@baj.com.sa; internet www.baj.com.sa; 94.17% Saudi-owned; cap. 3,000m., res 1,726m., dep. 32,464m. (Dec. 2011); Chair. TAHA ABDULLAH AL-KUWAIZ; CEO NABIL AL-HOSHAN; 23 brs.

Banque Saudi Fransi (Saudi French Bank): POB 56006, Ma'ather Rd, Riyadh 11554; tel. (1) 404-2222; fax (1) 289-9999; e-mail communications@alfransi.com.sa; internet www.alfransi.com.sa; f. 1977; present name adopted 2002; Saudi shareholders 68.9%, Calyon, Paris La Défense 31.1%; cap. 7,232m., res 8,601m., dep. 95,842m. (Dec. 2010); Chair. Dr SALEH A. AL-OMAIR; Man. Dir PATRICE COUVEGNES; 79 brs.

SAMBA Financial Group: POB 833, Riyadh 11421; tel. and fax (1) 477-4770; e-mail sambacare@samba.com; internet www.samba.com.sa; f. 1980; merged with United Saudi Bank in 1999; 96.4% owned by Saudi nationals; cap. 9,000m., res 8,078m., dep. 157,885m. (Dec. 2011); Chair. EISA AL-EISA; 66 domestic brs, 2 abroad.

Saudi British Bank (SABB): POB 9084, Prince Abd al-Aziz bin Mossaid bin Jalawi St, Riyadh 11413; tel. (1) 405-0677; fax (1) 405-0660; e-mail sabb@sabb.com; internet www.sabb.com.sa; f. 1978; 60% owned by Saudi nationals, 40% by HSBC Holdings BV; cap. 7,500m., res 6,517m., dep. 111,470m. (Dec. 2011); Chair. KHALED SULIMAN OLAYAN; Man. Dir DAVID DEW; 78 domestic brs, 1 abroad.

Saudi Hollandi Bank (Saudi Dutch Bank): POB 1467, Head Office Bldg, al-Dhabab St, Riyadh 11431; tel. (1) 406-7888; fax (1) 403-1104; e-mail csc@shb.com.sa; internet www.shb.com.sa; f. 1977 to assume activities of Algemene Bank Nederland NV in Saudi Arabia; jt-stock co; ABN AMRO Bank (Netherlands) 40%, Olayan Saudi Investament Co 21.8%; cap. 3,307m., res 3,544m., dep. 44,572m. (Dec. 2011); Chair. Sheikh MUBARAK ABDULLAH AL-KHAFRAH; Man. Dir BERND VAN LINDER; 40 brs.

Saudi Investment Bank (SAIB): POB 3533, Riyadh 11481; tel. (1) 478-6000; fax (1) 477-6781; e-mail info@saib.com.sa; internet www.saib.com.sa; f. 1976; provides a comprehensive range of traditional and specialized banking services; cap. 5,500m., res 2,726m., dep. 37,957m. (Dec. 2011); Chair. Dr ABD AL-AZIZ O'HALI; Gen. Man. MUSAED AL-MINEEFI; 30 brs.

Government Specialized Credit Institutions

Real Estate Development Fund (REDF): POB 5591, Riyadh 11139; tel. (1) 479-2222; fax (1) 479-0148; f. 1974; provides interest-free loans to Saudi individuals and cos for private or commercial housing projects; loans granted amounted to 5,264m. in 2002; Chair. Dr IBRAHIM IBN ABD AL-AZIZ AL-ASSAF (Minister of Finance); Dir-Gen. MUHAMMAD AL-ABDANI; 24 brs.

Saudi Arabian Agricultural Bank (SAAB): POB 1811, Riyadh 11126; tel. (1) 402-3911; fax (1) 402-2359; f. 1963; provides loans to farmers for industry-specific use; loans disbursed amounted to 1,320.0m. in 2002; Controller-Gen. ABDULLAH SAAD AL-MENGASH; Gen. Man. ABD AL-AZIZ MUHAMMAD AL-MANQUR; 70 brs.

Saudi Credit Bank: POB 3401, Riyadh 11471; tel. (1) 402-9128; f. 1973; provides interest-free loans for specific purposes to Saudi citizens of moderate means; loans disbursed amounted to 348.0m. in 2002; Man. IBRAHIM AL-HINAISHIL; 25 brs.

STOCK EXCHANGE

The Electronic Securities Information System (ESIS) was formed in 1990 and operated by the Saudi Arabian Monetary Agency (see Central Bank). The ESIS was superseded by a new market system, Tadawul, in 2001. Since 2003 Tadawul has been supervised by the Capital Market Authority. A total of 57,269m. shares were traded in 2009, amounting to SR 1,262,148.8m.

Saudi Stock Exchange (Tadawul): NCCI Bldg, North Tower, King Fahd Rd, POB 60612, Riyadh 11555; tel. (1) 218-9999; e-mail webinfo@tadawul.com.sa; internet www.tadawul.com.sa; f. 2001; restructured as a jt-stock co in 2007; 157 listed cos in mid-2013; Chair. TAHA A. AL-KUWAIZ; CEO ADEL SALEH AL-GHAMDI.

Regulatory Authority

Capital Market Authority: Faisaliah Tower, King Fahd Rd, POB 220022, Riyadh 11311; fax (1) 279-7770; e-mail info@cma.org.sa; internet www.cma.org.sa; f. 2003 to regulate and develop the Saudi Arabian capital market; Chair. MUHAMMAD IBN ABD AL-MALIK AL-SHEIKH.

INSURANCE

A new Co-operative Insurance Law, promulgated in 2004, required all companies operating in the kingdom to be locally registered and brought the sector under the supervision of the Saudi Arabian Monetary Agency (see Central Bank). In March 2009 some 29 insurance companies were operating in Saudi Arabia.

Ace Arabia Insurance Co Ltd (E.C.): 7th and 8th Floors, Southern Tower, Khobar Business Gate, King Faisal Bin Abd al-Aziz St (Coastal Rd), al-Khobar; tel. (3) 849-3633; fax (3) 849-3660; e-mail ace@ace-arabia.com; internet www.ace-arabia.com; f. 1974; cap. US $1m.; Chair. Sheikh ABD AL-KARIM EL-KHEREIJI; CEO BRUCE C. AITKEN.

Allied Cooperative Insurance Group: POB 7076, Jeddah 21462; tel. (2) 663-3222; fax (2) 661-7421; e-mail csc@acig.com.sa; internet www.acig.com.sa; Chair. KHALID AL-BASSAM; CEO HESHAM AL-SHAREEF.

Bank Al-Jazira Takaful Ta'awuni: POB 6277, Jeddah 21442; tel. and fax (2) 683-6364; e-mail infotakaful@baj.com.sa; internet www.takaful.com.sa; Islamic life insurance; Gen. Man. DAWOOD Y. TAYLOR.

Mediterranean and Gulf Cooperative Insurance and Reinsurance Co (MEDGULF): POB 2302, Riyadh 11451; tel. (1) 405-5550; fax (1) 478-9219; e-mail riyadh@medgulf.com; internet www.medgulf.com.sa; Chair. SALEH A. S. AL-SAGRI; Exec. Pres. and Man. Dir LUTFI F. EL-ZEIN.

Al-Rajhi Co for Co-operative Insurance: Platinum Centre, 3rd Floor, Setteen St, POB 67791, Riyadh 11517; tel. (1) 475-2211; fax (1) 475-5017; e-mail info@alrajhitakaful.com; internet www.alrajhiinsurance.com.sa; f. 1990 as Al-Rajhi Insurance Co; renamed as above 2006; cap. 200m.; Chair. ABDULLAH SULAIMAN AL-RAJHI; CEO ABD AL-AZIZ M. AL-SEDEAS.

Red Sea Insurance Group of Cos: POB 5627, Jeddah 21432; tel. (2) 660-3538; fax (2) 665-5418; e-mail redsea@anet.net.sa; f. 1974; insurance, devt and reinsurance; Chair. KHALDOUN B. BARAKAT.

RSA Saudi Arabia—Al-Alamiya: 1st Floor, Obekan Bldg, Prince Sultan St, POB 2374, Jeddah 21451; tel. (2) 692-7085; fax (2) 692-7125; e-mail alamiya.insurance@sa.rsagroup.com; internet www.alamiyainsurance.com.sa; part of the Royal & Sun Alliance (RSA) Group; total assets US $73.0m. (2002); CEO STUART PURDY.

SABB Takaful Co: POB 9086, Riyadh 11413; tel. (1) 403-0087; fax (1) 402-5832; internet www.sabbtakaful.com; f. 2007; 32.5% owned by Saudi British Bank (SABB), 32.5% by HSBC, 35% by private investors; cap. 100m.; Chair. FOUAD ABD AL-WAHAB BAHRAWI; Man. Dir DAVID ROBERT HUNT.

Sanad Cooperative Insurance and Reinsurance JSC: 3rd Floor, Dareen Centre, Alahsa St, POB 27477, Riyadh 11417; tel. (1) 292-7111; fax 292-7888; e-mail info@sanad.com.sa; internet www.sanad.com.sa; f. 2007; Chair. AHMAD AL-ABDULLAH AL-AKEIL; CEO PHILIP WILLIAM.

Saudi IAIC Cooperative Insurance Co (SALAMA): POB 122392, Jeddah 21332; tel. (2) 664-7877; fax (2) 664-7387; e-mail customers.relation@salama.com.sa; internet www.salama.com.sa; Chair. Dr SALEH J. MALAIKAH.

Saudi National Insurance Co (E.C.): POB 5832, Jeddah 21432; tel. (2) 660-6200; fax (2) 667-4530; e-mail snic@eajb.com.sa; internet www.snic.com.sa; f. 1974; Chair. Sheikh HATEM ALI JUFFALI; Gen. Man. OMAR S. BILANI.

Tawuniya (NCCI): POB 86959, Riyadh 11632; tel. and fax (1) 218-0100; e-mail info@tawuniya.com.sa; internet tawuniya.com.sa; f. 1985 by royal decree as Nat. Co for Co-operative Insurance; name changed as above 2007; owned by 3 govt agencies; proposed privatization approved by the Supreme Economic Council in May 2004; initial public offering of shares in Dec. 2004; auth. cap. 500m.; Chair. SULAYMAN AL-HUMMAYYD; Man. Dir and Gen. Man. ALI A. AL-SUBAIHIN; 13 brs.

United Cooperative Assurance Co (UCA): POB 5019, Medina Rd, Jeddah 21422; tel. (2) 653-0068; fax (2) 651-1936; e-mail jeddah@uca.com.sa; internet www.uca.com.sa; f. 1974 as United Commercial Agencies Ltd; name changed as above 2007; all classes of insurance; cap. 200m.; Chair. HASSAN M. MAHASSINI; CEO MACHAAL A. KARAM.

Wala'a Insurance: POB 31616, al-Khobar 31952; tel. (3) 865-1866; fax (3) 865-1944; e-mail khobar@walaa.com; internet www.walaa.com; f. 1976; fmrly Saudi United Insurance; operated by Saudi United Cooperative Insurance Co; provides all classes of insurance for businesses and govt agencies; majority shareholding held by Ahmad Hamad al-Gosaibi & Bros; cap. US $5m.; Chair. SULAYMAN AL-KADI; CEO JOHNSON VARUGHESE; 6 brs.

Trade and Industry

(Figures for weight are in metric tons)

DEVELOPMENT ORGANIZATIONS

Arab Petroleum Investments Corpn: POB 9599, Dammam 31423; tel. (3) 847-0444; fax (3) 847-0011; e-mail apicorp@apicorp-arabia.com; internet www.apicorp-arabia.com; f. 1975; affiliated to the Org. of Arab Petroleum Exporting Countries; specializes in financing petroleum and petrochemical projects and related industries in the Arab world and in other developing countries; shareholders: Kuwait, Saudi Arabia and the United Arab Emirates (17% each), Libya (15%), Iraq and Qatar (10% each), Algeria (5%), Bahrain, Egypt and Syria (3% each); auth. cap. US $1,200m.; cap. $550m. (Dec. 2006); Chair. ABDULLAH A. AL-ZAID; Gen. Man. and CEO AHMAD BIN HAMAD AL-NUAIMI.

National Agricultural Development Co (NADEC): POB 2557, Riyadh 11461; tel. (1) 404-0000; fax (1) 405-5522; e-mail info@nadec.com.sa; internet www.nadec.com.sa; f. 1981; interests include 6 dairy farms, 2 dairy processing plants and 40,000 ha of land for cultivation of wheat, barley, forage and vegetables, and processing of dates; the Govt has a 20% share; chief agency for agricultural devt; cap. SR 400m.; Chair. SULAYMAN ABD AL-AZIZ AL-RAJHI; Man. Dir ABD AL-AZIZ AL-BABTAIN.

Public Investment Fund: POB 6847, Riyadh 11452; tel. (1) 477-4488; fax (1) 474-2693; e-mail info@mof.gov.sa; internet www.mof.gov.sa/en/docs/ests/sub_invbox.htm; f. 1971 to facilitate devt of the nat. economy; 100% state-owned; under the control of the Ministry of Finance; provides the Govt's share of capital to mixed capital cos; has managed Sanabil al-Saudia, a sovereign wealth fund with cap. of US $5,300m., since 2008; Chair. Dr IBRAHIM IBN ABD AL-AZIZ AL-ASSAF (Minister of Finance); Sec.-Gen. MANSOUR AL-MAIMAN.

Saudi Arabian General Investment Authority (SAGIA): POB 5927, Riyadh 11432; tel. (1) 203-5555; fax (1) 263-2894; e-mail marketing_dept@sagia.gov.sa; internet www.sagia.gov.sa; f. 2000 to promote foreign investment; Gov. ABD AL-LATIF IBN AHMAD AL-UTHMAN.

Saudi Fund for Development (SFD): POB 50483, Riyadh 11523; tel. (1) 279-4000; fax (1) 464-7450; e-mail info@sfd.gov.sa; internet www.sfd.gov.sa; f. 1974 to help finance projects in developing countries; state-owned; had financed 511 projects by 2011; total commitments amounted to SR 35,651.49m; Chair. Dr IBRAHIM IBN ABD AL-AZIZ AL-ASSAF (Minister of Finance); Vice-Chair. and Man. Dir E. YOUSUF I. AL-BASSAM.

Saudi Industrial Development Fund (SIDF): POB 4143, Riyadh 11149; tel. (1) 477-4002; fax (1) 479-0165; e-mail sidf@sidf.gov.sa; internet www.sidf.gov.sa; f. 1974; supports and promotes local industrial devt, providing medium-term interest-free loans; also offers marketing, technical, financial and administrative advice; loans disbursed amounted to SR 8,544m. in 2007; cap. SR 20,000m. (2007); Chair. YOUSUF BIN IBRAHIM AL-BASSAM; Dir-Gen. ABDULLAH MUHAMMAD AL-OBOUDI.

TASNEE: POB 26707, Riyadh 11496; tel. (1) 476-7166; fax (1) 477-0898; e-mail general@tasnee.com; internet www.tasnee.com; f. 1985 as Nat. Industrialization Co to promote and establish industrial projects in Saudi Arabia; cap. SR 785m.; 100% owned by Saudi nationals; Chair. MUBARAK BIN ABDULLAH AL-KHAFRAH; CEO MOAYYED BIN ISSA AL-QURTAS.

CHAMBERS OF COMMERCE

Council of Saudi Chambers of Commerce and Industry: POB 16683, Riyadh 11474; tel. (1) 218-2222; fax (1) 218-2111; e-mail council@saudichambers.org.sa; internet www.saudichambers.org.sa; comprises one delegate from each of the chambers of commerce in the kingdom; Chair. MUHAMMAD ABD AL-QADER AL-FADEL; Sec.-Gen. Dr FAHD AL-SULTAN.

Abha Chamber of Commerce and Industry: POB 722, Abha; tel. (7) 227-1818; fax (7) 227-1919; e-mail info@abhacci.org.sa; internet www.abhacci.org.sa; Pres. ABDULLAH SAID AL-MOBTY; Sec.-Gen. Dr HAMDI ALI AL-MALIKI.

Al-Ahsa Chamber of Commerce and Industry: POB 1519, al-Ahsa 31982; tel. (3) 582-0458; fax (3) 587-5274; internet www.hcci.org.sa; Pres. SULAYMAN A. AL-HAMAAD.

Ar'ar Chamber of Commerce and Industry: POB 440, Ar'ar; tel. (4) 662-6544; fax (4) 662-4581; Sec.-Gen. THANI B. AL-ANEZI.

Al-Baha Chamber of Commerce and Industry: POB 311, al-Baha; tel. (7) 727-0291; fax (7) 828-0146; Pres. ABDULLAH M. AL-MOAGEB; Sec.-Gen. YAHYA AL-ZAHRANI.

Eastern Province Chamber of Commerce and Industry (Asharqia Chamber): POB 719, Dammam 31421; tel. (3) 857-1111; fax (3) 857-0607; e-mail info@chamber.org.sa; internet www.chamber.org.sa; f. 1952; Pres. ABD AL-RAHMAN RASHID AL-RASHID; Sec.-Gen. IBRAHIM ABDULLAH AL-OLAYAN.

Federation of Gulf Co-operation Council Chambers (FGCCC): POB 2198, Dammam 31451; tel. (3) 826-5943; fax (3) 826-6794; e-mail fgccc@zajil.net; internet www.fgccc.org; Pres. SALIM H. ALKHALILI; Sec.-Gen. MUHAMMAD A. AL-MULLA.

Ha'il Chamber of Commerce and Industry: POB 1291, Ha'il; tel. (6) 532-1060; fax (6) 533-1366; e-mail hussa_mk@yahoo.com; internet www.hcc.org.sa; Pres. KHALID A. AL-SAIF.

Jeddah Chamber of Commerce and Industry: POB 1264, Jeddah 21431; tel. (2) 651-5111; fax (2) 651-7373; e-mail customerservice@jcci.org.sa; internet www.jcci.org.sa; f. 1946; 26,000 mems; Chair. Sheikh SALEH KAMEL; Sec.-Gen. Dr HANI M. ABURAS.

Jizan Chamber of Commerce and Industry: POB 201, Jizan; tel. (7) 322-5155; fax (7) 322-3635; Pres. Eng. FAHD A. QALM.

Al-Jouf Chamber of Commerce and Industry: POB 585, al-Jouf; tel. (4) 624-9060; fax (4) 624-0108; Pres. MARZOUK S. AL-RASHID; Sec.-Gen. AHMAD KHALIFA AL-MUSALLAM.

Al-Majma Chamber of Commerce and Industry: POB 165, al-Majma 11952; tel. (6) 432-0268; fax (6) 432-2655; Pres. FAHD MUHAMMAD AL-RABIAH; Sec.-Gen. ABDULLAH IBRAHIM AL-JAAWAN.

Mecca Chamber of Commerce and Industry: POB 1086, Mecca; tel. (2) 534-3838; fax (2) 534-2904; f. 1947; Pres. ADEL ABDULLAH KA'AKI; Sec.-Gen. YASSER ABDULLAH AWAN.

Medina Chamber of Commerce and Industry: POB 443, King Abd al-Aziz Rd, Medina; tel. (4) 838-8909; fax (4) 838-8905; e-mail info@mcci.org.sa; internet www.mcci.org.sa; Pres. MUHAMMAD AL-GHAMDI; Sec.-Gen. Dr AMIR ABDULLAH SLEHM.

Najran Chamber of Commerce and Industry: POB 1138, Najran; tel. (7) 522-2216; fax (7) 522-3926; e-mail ywadidi@najcci.org.sa; internet www.najcci.org.sa; Pres. ALI BIN HAMAD HAMROUR AL-ABAAS; Sec.-Gen. ALI BIN SALEH AL-QUMAISH.

Al-Qassim Chamber of Commerce and Industry: POB 444, Buraydah, al-Qassim 51411; tel. (6) 381-4000; fax (6) 381-2231; e-mail info@qcc.org.sa; internet www.qcc.org.sa; Sec.-Gen. Dr FAISAL AL-KHAMIS.

Al-Qurayat Chamber of Commerce and Industry: POB 416, al-Qurayat; tel. (4) 642-6200; fax (4) 642-3172; Pres. OTHMAN ABDULLAH AL-YOUSUF; Sec.-Gen. JAMAL ALI AL-GHAMDI.

Riyadh Chamber of Commerce and Industry: POB 596, Riyadh 11421; tel. (1) 404-0044; fax (1) 402-1103; e-mail info@rdcci.org.sa; internet www.riyadhchamber.org.sa; f. 1961; acts as arbitrator in business disputes, information centre; Pres. ABD AL-RAHMAN ALI AL-JERAISY; Sec.-Gen. HUSSEIN ABD AL-RAHMAN AL-AZAL; 70,000 mems.

Tabouk Chamber of Commerce and Industry: POB 567, Tabouk; tel. (4) 422-2736; fax (4) 422-7387; internet www.tcci.org.sa; Pres. MUHAMMAD H. AL-WABSI; Sec.-Gen. AWADH AL-BALAWI.

Ta'if Chamber of Commerce and Industry: POB 1005, Ta'if; tel. (2) 736-6800; fax (2) 738-0040; e-mail info@taifchamber.org.sa; internet www.taifcci.com; Pres. NAIF A. AL-ADWANI; Sec.-Gen. Eng. YOUSUF MUHAMMAD AL-SHAFI.

Yanbu Chamber of Commerce and Industry: POB 58, Yanbu; tel. (4) 322-7878; fax (4) 322-6800; f. 1979; publishes quarterly magazine; 5,000 members; Pres. Dr MANSOUR M. AL-ANSARI; Sec.-Gen. KHALED SALMAN AL-SAHALI.

STATE HYDROCARBONS COMPANIES

Saudi Arabian Oil Co (Saudi Aramco): POB 5000, Dhahran 31311; tel. (3) 872-0115; fax (3) 873-8190; e-mail webmaster@aramco.com.sa; internet www.saudiaramco.com; f. 1933; previously known as Arabian-American Oil Co (Aramco); in 1993 incorporated the Saudi Arabian Marketing and Refining Co (SAMAREC, f. 1988) by merger of operations; holds the principal working concessions in Saudi Arabia; operates 5 wholly owned refineries (at Jeddah, Rabigh, Ras Tanura, Riyadh and Yanbu); Pres. and CEO KHALID A. AL-FALIH.

Aramco Gulf Operations Co (AGOC): POB 688, Khafji City 31971; tel. (3) 766-4024; fax (3) 767-5514; e-mail alsultanbf@kjo.com.sa; internet www.agoc.com.sa; f. 2000; wholly owned by Saudi Aramco; holds concession for offshore exploitation of Saudi Arabia's half-interest in the Saudi Arabia-Kuwait Neutral Zone; Pres. and CEO MUHAMMAD A. AL-SHAMMARY.

Petromin Corporation (Petromin Oils): POB 1432, Jeddah 21431; tel. (2) 215-7000; fax (2) 215-7111; e-mail info@petromin.com; internet www.petromin.com; f. 1968; 71% owned by Saudi Aramco, 29% by Mobil; manufacture and marketing of lubricating oils and other related products; production 140m. litres (2002); cap. 110m. riyals; Exec. Dir WAHEED A. SHAIKH; Pres. and CEO SAMIR M. NAWAR.

Rabigh Refining and Petrochemical Co (Petro Rabigh): POB 666, Rabigh 21911; tel. (2) 425-1855; fax (2) 425-2732; internet www.petrorabigh.com; f. 2005; jt venture between Saudi Aramco and Sumitomo Chemical (Japan); operation of integrated oil-refining and petrochemical production facilities at Rabigh; initial public offering of 20% of shares announced in Jan. 2008; Chair. ABD AL-AZIZ F. AL-KHAYYAL; Pres. and CEO SAAD FAHAD AL-DOSARI.

Saudi Aramco Lubricating Oil Refining Co (LUBEREF): POB 5518, Jeddah 21432; tel. (2) 427-5497; fax (2) 636-6933; e-mail webmaster@luberef.com; internet www.luberef.com; f. 1975; owned 70% by Saudi Aramco and 30% by Jadwa Industrial Investment Co; Pres. and CEO ABDULLAH O. AL-BAIZ.

Saudi Aramco Mobil Refinery Co Ltd (SAMREF): POB 30078, Yanbu; tel. (4) 396-4443; fax (4) 396-0942; e-mail amrihh@samref.com.sa; internet www.samref.com.sa; f. 1981; operation of oil-refining facilities at Yanbu; operated by Saudi Aramco and Mobil, capacity 360,000 b/d; Pres. and CEO FAWWAZ I. NAWWAB.

Saudi Aramco Shell Refinery Co (SASREF): POB 10088, Madinat al-Jubail, al-Sinaiyah 31961; tel. (3) 357-2000; fax (3) 357-2525; e-mail info@sasref.com.sa; internet www.sasref.com.sa; operation of oil-refining facilities at Jubail; operated by Saudi Aramco and Shell; capacity 300,000 b/d; exports began in 1985; Chair. HAMID T. AL-SAUDOON.

Saudi Basic Industries Corpn (SABIC): POB 5101, Riyadh 11422; tel. (1) 225-8000; fax (1) 225-9000; e-mail info@sabic.com; internet www.sabic.com; f. 1976 to foster the petrochemical industry and other hydrocarbon-based industries through jt ventures with foreign partners, and to market their products; 70% state-owned; production 55m. tons (2007); Chair. Prince SA'UD BIN THUNAYAN AL SA'UD; Vice-Chair. and CEO MUHAMMAD AL-MADY.

Projects include:

Arabian Petrochemical Co (Petrokemya): POB 10002, Jubail 31961; tel. (3) 358-7000; fax (3) 358-4480; e-mail petrokemya@petrokemya.sabic.com; f. 1981; wholly owned subsidiary of SABIC; produced 2.4m. tons of ethylene, 135,000 tons of polystyrene, 100,000 tons of butene-1, 570,000 tons of propylene, 100,000 tons of butadiene and 150,000 tons of benzene in 2001; owns 50% interest in ethylene glycol plant producing 610,000 tons per year of monoethylene glycol, 65,000 tons per year of diethylene glycol and 3,900 tons per year of triethylene glycol; Pres. SAMI A. AL-SUWAIGH.

Eastern Petrochemical Co (Sharq): POB 10035, Jubail 31961; tel. (3) 357-5000; fax (3) 358-0383; e-mail sharq@sharq.sabic.com; f. 1981 to produce linear low-density polyethylene, ethylene glycol; a SABIC jt venture with Japanese cos led by Mitsubishi Corpn; total capacity 660,000 tons of ethylene glycol and 280,000 tons of polyethylene per year; Chair. ABD AL-AZIZ AL-JARBOOA.

Al-Jubail Petrochemical Co (Kemya): POB 10084, Jubail 31961; tel. (3) 357-6000; fax (3) 358-7858; e-mail kemya@kemya.sabic.com; f. 1980; began production of linear low-density polyethylene in 1984, of high-density polyethylene in 1985, and of high alfa olefins in 1986, capacity of 330,000 tons per year of polyethylene; jt venture with Exxon Corpn (USA) and SABIC; Chair. HOMOOD AL-TUWAIJRI; Pres. ABD AL-AZIZ SULAYMAN AL-HAMAAD.

National Industrial Gases Co (Gas): POB 10110, Jubail 31961; tel. (3) 357-5738; fax (3) 358-8880; e-mail hussainaa@gas.sabic.com; 70% SABIC-owned jt venture with Saudi private sector; total capacity of 876,000 tons of oxygen and 492,750 tons of nitrogen per year; Pres. ALI AL-GHAMDI.

National Plastic Co (Ibn Hayyan): POB 10002, Jubail 31961; tel. (3) 358-7000; fax (3) 358-4736; f. 1984; 86.5% owned by SABIC; produces 390,000 tons per year of vinylchloride monomer and 324,000 tons per year of polyvinylchloride; Pres. KHALED AL-RAWAF.

Saudi-European Petrochemical Co (Ibn Zahr): POB 10330, Jubail 31961; tel. (3) 341-5060; fax (3) 341-2966; e-mail info@ibnzahr.sabic.com; f. 1985; annual capacity 1.4m. tons of methyl-tertiary-butyl ether (MTBE), 0.3m. tons of propylene; SABIC has an 80% share, Ecofuel and APICORP each have 10%; Chair. Dr ABD AL-RAHMAN S. AL-UBAID.

Saudi Kayan Petrochemical Co: POB 10302, Jubail Industrial City 31961; tel. (3) 359-3000; fax (3) 359-3111; e-mail shares@saudikayan.sabic.com; internet www.saudikayan.com; f. 2006; jt venture between SABIC and Al-Kayan Petrochemical Co; initial public offering of 45% of shares in 2008; production of ethylene, propylene, polypropylene, ethylene glycol, butene-1 and specialized products incl. aminomethyls, dimethylformamide and choline chloride; Chair. MUTLAQ HAMAD AL-MORISHED.

Saudi Methanol Co (ar-Razi): POB 10065, Jubail Industrial City 31961; tel. (3) 357-7800; fax (3) 358-5552; e-mail arrazi@arrazi.sabic.com; f. 1979; jt venture with a consortium of Japanese cos; capacity of 3.2m. tons per year of chemical-grade methanol; total methanol exports in 2001 were 3.2m. tons; Pres. NABIL A. MANSOURI; Exec. Vice-Pres. H. MIZUNO.

Saudi Petrochemical Co (Sadaf): POB 10025, Jubail 31961; tel. (3) 357-3000; fax (3) 357-3343; e-mail info@sadaf.sabic.com; f. 1980 to produce ethylene, ethylene dichloride, styrene, crude industrial ethanol, caustic soda and methyl-tertiary-butyl-ether (MTBE); total capacity of 4.3m. tons per year; Shell Chemicals Arabia has a 50% share; Pres. MOSAED S. AL-OHALI.

Saudi Yanbu Petrochemical Co (Yanpet): POB 30333, Yanbu 21441; tel. (4) 396-5000; fax (4) 396-5006; e-mail info@yanpet.sabic.com; f. 1980 to produce 820,000 tons per year of ethylene, 600,000 tons per year of high-density polyethylene and 340,000 tons per year of ethylene glycol; total capacity 1.7m. tons per year by 1990; ExxonMobil and SABIC each have a 50% share; Pres. SULAYMAN AL-HUSSAIN.

Yanbu National Petrochemical Co (Yansab): POB 31396, Yanbu Industrial City 21477; tel. (4) 325-9000; fax (4) 325-6666; e-mail shares@yansab.sabic.com; internet www.yansab.com.sa; f. 2006; 55% owned by SABIC; projected total capacity of over 4.0m. tons per year, incl. 1.3m. tons of ethylene; Chair. MUTLAQ HAMAD AL-MORISHED.

Foreign Concessionaire

Saudi Arabian Chevron: POB 363, Riyadh; tel. (1) 462-7274; fax (1) 464-1992; internet www.sachevron.com; also office in Kuwait; f. 1928; fmrly Getty Oil Co; renamed Saudi Arabian Texaco Inc. 1993, renamed as above 2007; holds concession (5,200 sq km at Dec. 1987) for exploitation of Saudi Arabia's half-interest in the Saudi Arabia-Kuwait Neutral (Partitioned) Zone; Pres. AHMAD AL-OMAR.

UTILITIES

Power and Water Utility Company for Jubail and Yanbu (MARAFIQ): POB 11133, Jubail 31961; tel. (3) 340-1111; fax (3) 340-1168; e-mail marafiqworld@marafiq.com.sa; internet www.marafiq.com.sa; f. 2003; equal ownership held by the Royal Comm. for Jubail and Yanbu, Saudi Aramco, Saudi Basic Industries Corpn and the Public Investment Fund; operation and devt of utility services; Chair. Prince SA'UD IBN ABDULLAH IBN THUNAYAN AL SA'UD; CEO THAMIR S. AL-SHARHAN.

Water and Electricity Co: POB 300091, Riyadh 11372; tel. (1) 211-3362; fax (1) 211-3313; e-mail info@wec.com.sa; internet www.wec.com.sa; f. 2003; jointly owned by Saline Water Conversion Corpn and Saudi Electricity Co; responsible for managing supply and demand of electricity and water; Chair. FAHID AL-SHARIF; CEO OMAR AL-GHAMDI.

Electricity

Electricity and Co-generation Regulatory Authority (ECRA): PO Box 4540, Riyadh 11412; tel. (1) 201-9045; e-mail public@ecra.gov.sa; internet www.ecra.gov.sa; f. 2001 to regulate the power industry and to recommend tariffs for the sector; Gov. Dr FAREED M. ZEDAN.

ACWA Power International: POB 22616, Riyadh 11416; tel. (1) 473-4400; fax (1) 474-9215; e-mail info@acwapower.com; internet www.acwapowerprojects.com; f. 2008; develops privately financed power and water projects; Exec. Chair. MUHAMMAD ABUNAYYAN.

Saudi Electricity Co (SEC): POB 57, Riyadh 11411; tel. (1) 403-2222; fax (1) 405-1191; internet www.se.com.sa; f. 1999 following merger of 10 regional cos, to organize the generation, transmission and distribution of electricity into separate operating cos; jt-stock co;

cap. SR 33,758m.; CEO Ali ibn Salih al-Barrak (until 1 Jan. 2014), Ziad ibn Muhammad al-Shiha (from 1 Jan. 2014).

Water

National Water Co: POB 676, Riyadh 11421; tel. (1) 211-3014; fax (1) 211-3016; e-mail info@nwc.com.sa; internet www.nwc.com.sa; f. 2008 to consolidate all govt-run water and wastewater management services and to facilitate the gradual privatization of the sector; Chair. Abdullah ibn Abd al-Rahman al-Hussein (Minister of Water and Electricity); CEO Loay A. al-Musallam.

Saline Water Conversion Corpn (SWCC): POB 4931, 21412 Jeddah; tel. (2) 682-1240; fax (2) 682-0415; e-mail computerdirector@swcc.gov.sa; internet www.swcc.gov.sa; f. 1974; provides desalinated water; 24 plants; Gov. Fahid al-Sharif; Dir-Gen. Abd al-Aziz Omar Nassief.

MAJOR COMPANIES

(Figures for sales and capital, etc., are in Saudi riyals.)

Saleh & Abd al-Aziz Abahsain Co Ltd: POB 209, al-Khobar 31952; tel. (3) 898-4045; fax (3) 899-1557; e-mail info@abahsain.net; internet www.abahsain.net; f. 1947; trade in general heavy machinery and machinery for construction and engineering; Pres. and CEO Abd al-Aziz Ibrahim Abahsain; Gen. Man. Shaukat Riaz Sheikh; 2,080 employees.

Alhamrani Group: POB 1229, Jeddah 21431; tel. (2) 606-5555; fax (2) 606-0265; e-mail info@alhamrani.net; internet www.alhamrani.net; f. 1953; retail and aftersales services for automotive industry; automated banking and security equipment; construction materials and airport and aviation services; Chair. and CEO Sheikh Abdullah A. al-Hamrani; CEO Saleh Kaki; 2,800 employees.

Haji Hussein Alireza & Co Ltd: POB 8, Jeddah 21411; tel. (2) 647-2233; fax (2) 648-3010; e-mail info@alireza.com; internet www.alireza.com; f. 1845; engineering, supply, installation, maintenance and training for computer and telecommunications networks; security systems; precision engineering; Pres. Ahmad Y. Z. Alireza; Gen. Man. Yahia Tewfiq Hassan; 1,400 employees.

Alpha Trading and Shipping Ltd: POB 205, Jeddah 21411; tel. (2) 644-0808; fax (2) 642-1188; e-mail central@alpha-trading.com; internet www.alpha-trading.com; f. 1946; trade in foodstuffs, raw materials and commodities; Chair. Abd al-Qadir Muhammad al-Fadl; Man. Dir Marios Costanides.

Arab Supply and Trading Corpn (ASTRA Group): POB 245, Tabouk; tel. (4) 422-0400; fax (4) 423-7649; e-mail astra@astra.com.sa; internet www.astra-group.net; f. 1976; farming; manufacturing; tourism; telecommunications; banking and investment; wholesale and retail trade; medical and pharmaceutical products and services; Chair. Sabih al-Taher al-Masri; Man. Dir Kamil A. Sadedin; 1,804 employees.

Arabian Cement Co Ltd: POB 275, Jeddah 21411; tel. (2) 694-9700; fax (2) 423-2033; e-mail info@arabiacement.com; internet www.arabiacement.com; f. 1954; produces ordinary Portland cement and sulphate-resistant cement; owns subsidiary Cement Product Industry Co Ltd; Chair. Abdullah Muhammad Issa; CEO Muhammad Tahir Othman; 870 employees.

Consolidated Contractors Co WLL: POB 234, Riyadh 11411; tel. (1) 465-0311; fax (1) 464-5963; internet www.ccc.gr; general construction and engineering projects, incl. infrastructure and heavy industry; major shareholders are members of Saudi royal family; subsidiary of Consolidated Contractors Co, Athens (Greece); Group Chair. Hassib Sabbagh; Group Pres. Said Khoury; more than 140,000 employees (group total).

Dallah al-Baraka Group: POB 430, Jeddah 21411; tel. (2) 671-0000; fax (2) 671-3603; e-mail prd@dallah.com; internet www.dallah.com; f. 1969; divided into business, finance and media divisions; industrial investment; agriculture; trading; real estate; transport; tourism; construction; financial services; communications; satellite broadcasting; Chair. Sheikh Saleh Kamel; 37,000 employees.

Dar al-Arkan Real Estate Development Co: POB 105633, Riyadh 11656; tel. (1) 206-9888; fax (1) 206-1100; e-mail dcc@alarkan.com; internet www.alarkan.com; f. 1994; real estate devt; Chair. Yousuf bin Abdullah al-Shelash.

Eastern Province Cement Co: POB 4536, Dammam 31412; tel. (3) 827-3330; fax (3) 827-1923; internet www.epcco.com.sa; f. 1982 as Saudi-Kuwaiti Cement Co; present name adopted 1994; Gen. Man. Dr Zamil al-Mokrin; 725 employees.

Al-Faisalia Group (AFG): POB 16460, Riyadh 11464; tel. (1) 440-7799; fax (1) 450-8652; e-mail info@alfaisaliah.com; internet www.alfaisaliah.com; f. 1970; sale, installation and management of electrical, electronic and telecommunications equipment; computers; petrochemicals; dairy and agricultural products; Chair. Muhammad Abdullah al-Faisal; Man. Muhammad Abd al-Rahman al-Ariefy; 5,000 employees.

Grain Silos and Flour Mills Organization: POB 3402, Riyadh 11471; tel. (1) 210-3333; fax (1) 210-4444; internet www.gsfmo.gov.sa; f. 1972; autonomous body formally responsible to the Ministry of Agriculture; production of flour and animal feeds for domestic consumption; Dir-Gen. Walid ibn Abd al-Karim al-Khariji; 1,830 employees.

Hoshan Co Ltd (Hoshanco): POB 509, Riyadh 11421; tel. (1) 217-0000; fax (1) 465-6248; e-mail info@hoshangroup.com; internet www.hoshangroup.com; f. 1964; office furniture and equipment, telecommunications, engineering, information technology and microfilm products; Chair. Sulayman A. K. al-Muhaideb; Pres. Rakan el-Hoshan; 600 employees.

Jabal Omar Development Co: POB 56968, Mecca; tel. (2) 553-3898; fax (2) 527-2935; f. 2006; construction and real estate devt; Chair. Abd al-Rahman Faqeeh.

Jadawel International Co Ltd: POB 61539, Riyadh 11575; tel. (3) 463-1760; fax (3) 465-1013; e-mail info@jadawelinternational.com; internet www.jadawelinternational.com; f. 1984; real estate devt and sale of building supplies; Chair. and CEO Muhammad ibn Isa al-Jaber; 1,230 employees.

Jamjoom Corpn for Commerce and Industry: POB 59, Jeddah 21411; tel. (2) 671-5995; fax (2) 671-5210; e-mail jamjoomco@ogertel.com; internet www.jamjoom.com; f. 1971; general construction, operation and maintenance services; import and distribution of air-conditioning, heating, refrigeration, power-generating, water treatment and desalination equipment; shipping and navigation; environmental pollution control; Chair. and CEO Sheikh Abd al-Qafar Muhammad Jamjoon; 1,700 employees.

Al-Jubail Fertilizer Co (Samad): POB 10046, Jubail 31961; tel. (3) 341-6488; fax (3) 341-7122; f. 1979; jt venture between SABIC and Taiwan Fertilizer Co; capacity of 620,000 tons per year of urea, 40,000 tons per year of ammonia, 150,000 tons per year of 2-ethyl hexanol, 50,000 tons per year of di-octyl phtalate and 180,000 tons per year of ISO-butaraldehyde; Chair. Fahad al-Sheaibi; Pres. Abdullah al-Baker; 430 employees.

Isam Khairy Kabbani Group: POB 5338, Jeddah 21422; tel. (2) 627-8888; fax (2) 627-8000; internet www.ikkgroup.com; f. 1968; oil and gas pipelines; wholesale and retail trade in construction materials, electrical goods, tools, hardware and food products; Chair. Sheikh Isam Kabbani; Pres. Hassan Isam Kabbani; 1,650 employees.

Kingdom Holding Co: POB 1, Riyadh 11321; tel. (1) 211-1111; fax (1) 211-1112; e-mail info@kingdom.com.sa; internet www.kingdom.com.sa; f. 1980; project financing, contracting and trading; Exec. Dir Shadi Sadiq Sanbar.

Manufacturing and Building Co Ltd (MABCO): POB 52743, Riyadh 11573; tel. (1) 498-1222; fax (1) 498-4807; f. 1977; manufacture of pre-cast components for construction of buildings; cap. p.u. 100m.; Pres. Omar Abd al-Fattah Aggad; Gen. Man. Wajih al-Baz; 500 employees.

Al-Marai Co Ltd: POB 8524, Riyadh 11492; tel. (1) 470-0005; fax (1) 470-1555; internet www.almarai.com; f. 1976; jt venture with Masstock International (United Kingdom); agricultural management and dairy farming; Chair. Prince Muhammad bin Saud al-Kabir; CEO Abd al-Rahman al-Fadhli; 2,900 employees.

Marei bin Mahfouz Group & Co Ltd: POB 734, Mecca; tel. (2) 550-0088; fax (2) 550-0099; e-mail info@binmahfouz.net; internet www.binmahfouz.net; f. 1970; manufacturer; investor in real estate; import and export; wholesale and retail; medical services; Chair. Marei Mubarak bin Mahfouz; Man. Dir Abdullah Marei bin Mahfouz; 1,150 employees.

Muhammad Abd al-Aziz Al-Rajhi and Sons Holding Co (MARS): POB 59861, Riyadh 11535; tel. (1) 460-1555; fax (1) 419-1430; e-mail info@al-rajhi.com; internet www.al-rajhi.com; f. 1968; industrial group; five subsidiary cos in the fields of steel, water, home appliances, plastics, and heavy industries; Chair. Khalid Muhammad al-Rajhi; CEO Khalid bin Abd al-Hamid al-Sulaimani; 2,000 employees.

Napco Group: POB 538, Dammam 31421; tel. (3) 847-2288; fax (3) 847-1504; e-mail info@napcogroup.com; internet www.napcogroup.com; f. 1956; manufacture and wholesale trade in plastics; Man. Dir Jamal Abd al-Rahman al-Moaibed; 3,000 employees.

National Gas and Industrialisation Co (GASCO): POB 564, Riyadh 11421; tel. (1) 466-4999; fax (1) 466-4888; e-mail info@gasco.com.sa; internet www.gasco.com.sa; f. 1963; supply and transportation of LPG, LPG tanks and accessories; sales 1,200m. (2007), cap. 750m. (2009); Chair. and Man. Dir Abdullah al-Nuaim; Gen. Man. Muhammad Ibrahim al-Shabnan; 2,044 employees.

National Glass Industries Co (Zoujaj): POB 88646, Riyadh 11531; tel. (1) 206-5115; fax (1) 206-5113; e-mail yas@zoujaj-glass.com; internet zoujaj-glass.com; f. 1990; manufacture of glass products; Chair. Riyadh Muhammad al-Humaidan; Gen. Man. Yousuf al-Salman; 290 employees.

National Gypsum Co: POB 187, Riyadh 11411; tel. (1) 464-1963; fax (1) 463-0612; tel. ngc@gypsco.com.sa; internet www.gypsco.com.sa; f. 1958; Chair. ABDULLAH F. AL-THUNAYAN; Gen. Man. THUNAYAN F. AL-THUNAYAN; 450 employees.

National Industrialization Co (TASNEE): POB 26707, Riyadh 11496; tel. (1) 476-7166; fax (1) 477-0898; e-mail admin@tasnee.com; internet www.tasnee.com; f. 1985; petrochemicals, chemicals, plastics and metal; industrial services; Chair. Eng. MUBARAK IBN ABDALLAH AL-KHAFRA; CEO SALEH BIN FAHAD AL-NAZHA.

National Methanol Co (Ibn Sina): POB 10003, Jubail 31961; tel. (3) 340-5500; fax (3) 340-5604; f. 1981; began commercial production of chemical-grade methanol in Nov. 1984; capacity 1m. tons per year; began commercial production of methyl-tertiary-butyl ether (MTBE) in May 1994; capacity 900,000 tons per year; jt venture of SABIC, Hoechst-Celanese Corpn (USA) and PanEnergy Corpn (USA); Chair. ABDULLAH AL-ASSAF; Pres. NABIL MASOURI; 280 employees.

National Pipe Co Ltd: POB 1099, al-Khobar 31952; tel. (3) 857-8205; fax (3) 477-4969; e-mail qc.dept@npc.com.sa; internet www.npc.com.sa; f. 1978; manufacture and marketing of spiral-welded steel pipes for oil and gas transmission; cap. 50m.; Chair. TEYMOUR ALIREZA; Gen. Man. EIJI MIKAMI; 345 employees.

Olayan Financing Co: POB 8772, Riyadh 11492; tel. (1) 474-9000; fax (1) 474-9108; internet www.olayangroup.com; f. 1947; investment in industrial devt and technology projects; Pres. and CEO PETER DADZIS; 8,600 employees.

Qassim Cement Co (QCC): POB 345, Buraidah, Qassim; tel. (6) 381-8888; fax (6) 381-6041; e-mail qcc@qcc.com.sa; internet www.qcc.com.sa; f. 1976; production of 2,000 metric tons per day; Chair. ABDULLAH ABD AL-ATIF AL-SAIF; Gen. Dir OMER IBN ABDULLAH AL-OMER; 650 employees.

Riyadh Cables: POB 26862, Riyadh 11496; tel. (1) 265-0850; fax (1) 265-0942; e-mail rcgc@riyadh-cables.com; internet www.riyadh-cables.com; f. 1984; mfr of electrical cables; Chair. HIKMAT SA'AD AL-DIN AL-ZAIM; 1,561 employees.

Saad Trading and Contracting Co: POB 3250, al-Khobar 31952; tel. (3) 882-2220; fax (3) 882-8699; f. 1986; design; building and construction contracting; engineering; building maintenance; CEO MA'AN ABD AL-WAHID AL-SANEE; Gen. Man. STUART F. SMITH; 5,350 employees.

Mahmood Saeed Collective Co: POB 17013, Jeddah 21484; tel. (2) 636-0020; fax (2) 637-9093; e-mail info@msgroup.com; internet www.msgroup.com; f. 1957; manufacture of soft drinks and packaging, bedding, perfume and cosmetic products; import of textiles; Chair. MAHMOOD MUHAMMAD SAEED QASSIM; Man. Dir TAISIR TOMALIEH; 2,250 employees.

Al-Safi Danone Ltd: POB 10525, Riyadh 11443; tel. (1) 874-6748; fax (1) 270-3371; internet www.alsafidanone.com; f. 1979; began jt venture in 2001; dairy products; Pres. and CEO Prince MUHAMMAD BIN KHALED AL-ABDULLA AL-FAISAL; Gen. Man. MUHAMMAD AL-SHONAIFY; 1,400 employees.

Saudi Arabian Amiantit Co (Amiantit): POB 589, Dammam 31421; tel. (3) 847-1500; fax (3) 847-1398; e-mail info@amiantit.com; internet www.amiantit.com; f. 1968; production and marketing of pipes, fibreglass and rubber products; sales 3,101m., total income 864.2m. (2009); Chair. Prince KHALED BIN ABDULLAH BIN ABD AL-RAHMAN AL SA'UD; Pres. SULAYMAN AL-TWAIJRI; 1,150 employees.

Saudi Arabian Fertilizer Co (SAFCO): POB 11044, Jubail 31961; tel. (3) 341-1100; fax (3) 341-1257; internet www.safco.com.sa; f. 1965; owned 41% by SABIC, 10% by its staff and 49% by private Saudi investors; Chair. MUHAMMAD H. AL-MADY; Man. Dir ABDULLAH AL-BAKR; 700 employees.

Saudi Arabian Mining Co (Ma'aden): POB 68861, Riyadh 11537; tel. (1) 874-8000; fax (1) 874-8300; e-mail info@maaden.com.sa; internet www.maaden.com.sa; f. 1997; privatization approved by the Supreme Economic Council in May 2004; Chair. ABDULLAH S. A. AL-SAIF; Pres. and CEO KHALID BIN SALEH AL-MUDAIFER.

Saudi Binladin Group: POB 9887, Jeddah 21423; tel. (2) 640-0004; fax (2) 640-4368; e-mail sbg_pbad@pbad.sbg.com.sa; internet www.sbg.com.sa; f. 1931; reorg. and present name adopted 1989; construction and investment holding co; Pres. BAKR M. BIN LADEN.

Saudi Cable Group: POB 4403, Jeddah 21491; tel. (2) 638-0080; fax (2) 635-5916; e-mail aruthman@saudicable.com; internet www.saudicable.com; f. 1975; manufacture of building wires, power and telecommunication cables (including fibre optic cables), copper and aluminium rod, PVC compounds, information technology products, power transmission and distribution products, turnkey services; Chair. KHALID ALIREZA; Pres. WAHIB A. LINJAWI; 2,600 employees.

Saudi Cement Co: POB 306, Dammam 31411; tel. (3) 834-8000; fax (3) 834-3091; e-mail contactus@saudicement.com.sa; internet www.saudicement.com.sa; f. 1955; sales 1,346m. (2010); Chair. OMAR BIN SULAYMAN AL-RAJHI; 1,750 employees.

Saudi Ceramic Co: POB 3893, Riyadh 11481; tel. (1) 464-4244; fax (1) 465-2124; e-mail info@saudiceramics.com; internet www.saudiceramics.com; f. 1977; manufacture and marketing of ceramics; sales 280m., cap. 250m. (2003); Chair. SAAD AL-MOJEL; Gen. Man. ABD AL-KARIM AL-NAFIE; 1,700 employees.

Saudi Fisheries Co (SFC): POB 6535, Dammam 31452; tel. (3) 859-1919; fax (3) 859-3090; e-mail info@saudi-fisheries.com; internet www.saudi-fisheries.com; f. 1981; CEO MUHAMMAD JAPER AL-SAHLI; 1,500 employees.

Saudi International Petrochemical Co (Sipchem): POB 12021, Jubail Industrial City 31961; tel. (3) 359-9999; fax (3) 358-8182; e-mail marketing@sipchem.com; internet www.sipchem.com; f. 1999 to develop and invest in the petrochemical and chemical industries; produces a range of petrochemical and chemical products through its affiliates: Int. Methanol Co, Int. Diol Co, Int. Acetyl Co, Int. Vinyl Acetate Co, Int. Gases Co, Sipchem Marketing and Services Co; sales 830m., total income 236m. (2009); CEO AHMAD A. AL-OHALI; Chair. Eng. ABD AL-AZIZ A. AL-ZAMIL; 696 employees.

Saudi Iron and Steel Co (Hadeed): POB 10053, Jubail 31961; tel. (3) 357-1222; fax (3) 358-2222; e-mail commercial@hadeed.com.sa; internet www.hadeed.com.sa; f. 1979; produced more than 3.4m. tons of steel reinforcing bars, coils of wire rod and light sections in 2002; Pres. MUHAMMAD SALEH AL-JABR; 2,900 employees.

Saudi Oger Ltd: POB 1449, Riyadh 11431; tel. (1) 477-3115; fax (1) 477-0079; e-mail ccd@saudioger.com; internet www.saudioger.com; f. 1978; construction, telecommunications, information technology, real estate devt, water and power supply; Gen. Man. SAAD R. HARIRI.

Saudi Pharmaceutical Industries and Medical Appliances Corpn (Spimaco): POB 20001, Riyadh 11455; tel. (1) 477-4481; fax (1) 477-3961; e-mail general@spimaco.com.sa; internet www.spimaco.com.sa; f. 1986; mfr of pharmaceutical products; Chair. Dr SALEH M. S. AL-KHALIWI; Pres. Dr FAHAD BIN IBRAHIM AL-KHALAF; 505 employees.

Saudi Plastic Products Co Ltd (SAPPCO): POB 4916, Dammam 31412; tel. (1) 847-1703; fax (1) 847-1969; e-mail sapdam@sappco.com.sa; internet www.sappco-dammam.com; f. 1969; mfr and supplier of UPVC pipes and fittings; cap. 75m.; total assets 194m.; Man. Dir FAISAL AL-FALEH; 150 employees.

Saudi United Fertilizers Co (Al-Asmida): POB 4811, Riyadh 11412; tel. (1) 478-1304; fax (1) 478-9581; e-mail alasmida@suf-ksa.com; internet www.suf-ksa.com; f. 1975; import and export of agricultural fertilizers, pesticides, forage seeds, field sprayers and agricultural machinery; Man. Dir SAMIR ALI KABBANI.

Saudia Dairy and Foodstuff Co Ltd (SADAFCO): POB 5043, Jeddah 21422; tel. and fax (2) 629-3366; fax 629-3380; e-mail sadafco@sadafco com; internet www.sadafco.com; f. 1976; mfr and distributor of food products and beverages; sales 920.7m. (2003/04); CEO WALTHERUS MATTHIJS; 2,000 employees.

Savola Group: POB 14455, Jeddah 21424; tel. (2) 657-3333; fax (2) 648-4119; e-mail webmaster@savola.com; internet www.savola.com; production of food and beverages; Chair. SULAYMAN A. K. AL-MUHAIDIB; Man. Dir Dr ABD AL-RAOUF M. MANNAA; 4,000 employees.

Southern Province Cement Co: (Head Office) POB 548, Abha; tel. (7) 227-1500; fax (7) 227-1003; internet www.spcc.com.sa; f. 1974; produced 5.7m. tons of cement (2008); Chair. Prince KHALID IBN TURKI AL-TURKI; CEO SAFAR DHUFAYER; 1,555 employees.

Al-Subeaei United Co: POB 749, Jeddah 21421; tel. (2) 672-2288; fax (2) 672-5924; e-mail info@alsubeaei.com; internet www.alsubeaei.com; f. 1934; import and distribution of foodstuffs, textiles, furniture, hardware and gold; money exchange; Chair. MUHAMMAD IBRAHIM AL-SUBEAEI; Sec. C. H. ABD AL-JALEEL; 150 employees.

Al-Suwaiket Trading and Contracting Co: POB 691, Dhahran Airport 31932; tel. (3) 857-9780; fax (3) 857-2904; e-mail ho@alsuwaiket.com; internet www.alsuwaiket.com; f. 1947; general contracting; electro-mechanical engineering; telecoms and electronics; drilling, wells and pipeline services; Pres. MUBARAK ABDULLAH AL-SUWAIKET; 1,200 employees.

Tamimi Co: POB 172, Dammam 31411; tel. (3) 807-5700; fax (3) 847-1592; e-mail tamimi-ho@al-tamimi.com; internet www.al-tamimi.com; f. 1964; pipeline construction, mechanical and civil construction, industrial catering, real estate; cap. 20m.; Chair. TARIQ A. TAMIMI; 16,000 employees.

Al-Tayyar Travel Group Co Ltd: POB 52660, Riyadh 11573; tel. (1) 463-3133; fax (1) 465-6049; e-mail altayyar@altayyargroup.com; internet www.altayyargroup.com; f. 1983; travel and tourism; customs clearance services; shipping; car hire; advertising; Chair. and CEO FAHAD BIN IBRAHIM AL-JARBOA; 1,156 employees.

Xenel Industries Ltd: POB 2824, Jeddah 21461; tel. (2) 604-8000; fax (2) 643-6344; e-mail communications@xenel.com; internet www.xenel.com; f. 1973; energy, petrochemicals, construction, infrastructure devt, health care, logistics and real estate; Vice-Chair. KHALED ALIREZA.

Yamama Saudi Cement Co: POB 293, Riyadh 11411; tel. (1) 405-8288; fax (1) 403-3292; e-mail admindep@yamamacement.com; internet www.yamamacement.com; f. 1961; production and marketing of cement and paper products; Gen. Man. JEHAD BIN ABD AL-AZIZ AL-RASHED; 1,180 employees.

Yanbu Cement Co: POB 5330, Jeddah 21422; tel. (2) 653-1555; fax (2) 653-1420; e-mail info@yanbucement.com; internet www.yanbucement.com; f. 1977; Chair. Prince MESHAL IBN ABD AL-AZIZ; Dir-Gen. Dr SAUD SALEH ISLAM.

Al-Zamil Group: POB 9, al-Khobar 31952; tel. (3) 882-4888; fax (3) 882-2509; e-mail info@zamil.com; internet www.zamil.com; f. 1930; involved in real estate and land devt as well as the marketing of products from numerous subsidiaries, incl. Al-Zamil Aluminium Factory Ltd, Zamil Soule Steel Building Co Ltd, Yamama Factories, Arabian Gulf Construction Co Ltd, Bahrain Marble Factory, Al-Zamil Nails and Screws Factory, Saudi Plastics Factory; Chair. Dr ABD AL-RAHMAN AL-ZAMIL; Pres. ABD AL-AZIZ A. AL-ZAMIL; 7,500 employees.

TRADE UNIONS

Trade unions are illegal in Saudi Arabia.

Transport

RAILWAYS

Saudi Arabia has the only rail system in the Arabian peninsula. The Saudi Government Railroad comprises 719 km of single and 157 km of double track. The main line is 570 km in length and connects Dammam port, on the Gulf coast, with Riyadh, via Dhahran, Abqaiq, Hufuf, Harad and al-Kharj. New 950-km and 115-km lines, connecting Riyadh with Jeddah and Dammam with Jubail, respectively, known as the Saudi Landbridge Project, were planned. The revamped network was to connect the Red Sea with the Persian (Arabian) Gulf and was to be closely linked with Jeddah Islamic Port and King Abd al-Aziz Port (at Dammam). Bidding for the build-operate-transfer contract was opened in February 2008, but was subsequently delayed owing to developments in the global economic climate. In October 2011 the Government announced that it would carry out the project. In March 2009 a SR 6,900m. contract was awarded for the part one of the first phase of the Haramain High-Speed Rail Project, a proposed 450-km line that would connect the west-coast centres of Mecca, Medina and Jeddah, and provide a passenger service for millions of *Umrah* and *Hajj* pilgrims every year. Contracts for part two were awarded to eight companies, including Saudi Binladin Group and Saudi Oger, in February 2011. Completion of the entire project was anticipated by 2014. The concession for a 2,400-km North–South line, connecting Riyadh, Qassim, Ha'il, al-Zubayrah and al-Jalamid, to be mainly utilized for transporting minerals, was tendered, in several stages, from September 2007 to September 2009.

An 18-km elevated metro system linking the holy sites in Mecca was opened in November 2010. Plans for the construction of a metro system in Jeddah, with 200 stations, at a cost of some US $5,600m., were announced in April 2009, while contracts for construction work on a six-line, 176-km metro system in Riyadh were awarded in July 2013. A total of 1.1m. passengers travelled by rail in the kingdom in 2009. In 2010 the total length of Saudi Arabia's railways was 1,020 route-km.

Saudi Railway Co (SAR): Diplomatic Quarter Bldg S-24, POB 64447, Riyadh 11452; tel. (1) 250-1111; fax (1) 480-7517; e-mail info@sar.com.sa; internet www.sar.com.sa; f. 2006; manages North–South Railway project; CEO RUMAIH AL-RUMAIH; Chair. MANSOUR IBN SALEH AL-MAYMAN.

Saudi Railways Organization (SRO): POB 36, Dammam 31241; tel. (3) 871-3000; fax (3) 827-1130; e-mail sro@sro.org.sa; internet www.saudirailways.org; Pres. ABD AL-AZIZ IBN MUHAMMAD AL-HOQAIL.

ROADS

Asphalted roads link Jeddah to Mecca, Jeddah to Medina, Medina to Yanbu, al-Ta'if to Mecca, Riyadh to al-Kharj, and Dammam to Hufuf, as well as the principal communities and certain outlying points in Saudi Aramco's area of operations. The trans-Arabian highway links Dammam, Riyadh, al-Ta'if, Mecca and Jeddah. In 2007 there were 221,372 km of roads, of which 13,596 km were main roads (including motorways) and 33,924 km were secondary roads. Metalled roads link all the main population centres.

Saudi Public Transport Co (SAPTCO): POB 10667, Riyadh 11443; tel. (1) 2884400; fax (1) 2884411; e-mail info@saptco.com.sa; internet www.saptco.com.sa; f. 1979; operates a public bus service throughout Saudi Arabia and to neighbouring countries; the Govt holds a 30% share; Chair. ABDULLAH AL-MUGHBIL; CEO Eng. KHALID AL-HOGAIL.

SHIPPING

On average over 95% of Saudi Arabia's imports and exports pass through the country's sea ports. Responsibility for the management, operation and maintenance of a number of ports began to be transferred to the private sector from 1997, but all ports remain subject to regulation and scrutiny by the Ports Authority. In January 2008 the Ports Authority announced the signing of a US $586m. contract with the China Harbour Engineering Co Ltd to build a new port at Ras Azzawr.

Jeddah is the principal commercial port and the main point of entry for pilgrims bound for Mecca. It has 58 berths for general cargo, container traffic, roll-on roll-off (ro-ro) traffic, livestock and bulk grain shipments, with draughts ranging from 8 m to 16 m. The port also has a 200-metric ton floating crane, cold storage facilities and a fully equipped ship-repair yard. Dammam is the second largest commercial port and has general cargo, container, ro-ro, dangerous cargo and bulk grain berths. Draughts range from 8 m to 13.5 m. It has a 200-metric ton floating crane and a fully equipped ship-repair yard.

The other three important ports are Jubail, Yanbu and Jazan. Jubail has one commercial and one industrial port. Yanbu, which comprises one commercial and one industrial port, is Saudi Arabia's nearest major port to Europe and North America, and is the focal point of the most rapidly growing area, in the west of Saudi Arabia. Jazan is the main port for the southern part of the country.

At 31 December 2012 Saudi Arabia's flag registered fleet totalled 403 vessels, with an aggregate displacement of 2,306,943 grt, of which 11 were fish carriers, two were gas tankers and six were general cargo ships.

Port Authorities

Saudi Ports Authority: POB 5162, Riyadh 11422; tel. (1) 405-0005; fax (1) 405-3508; e-mail info@ports.gov.sa; internet www.ports.gov.sa; f. 1976; regulatory authority; Pres. Dr ABD AL-AZIZ BIN MUHAMMAD AL-TUWAIJRI; Chair. Dr JUBARAH IBN EID AL-SURAISERI (Minister of Transport).

Dammam: POB 28062, Dammam 31188; tel. (3) 858-3199; fax (3) 857-1727; Dir-Gen. NAEEM IBRAHIM AL-NAEEM.

Dhiba: POB 190, Dhiba; tel. (4) 432-1060; fax (4) 432-2679; Dir-Gen. MAHMOUD AL-HARBI.

Jazan: POB 16, Jazan; tel. (7) 317-1000; fax (7) 317-0777; Dir-Gen. ABD AL-HAMEED SOURI.

Jeddah: POB 9285, Jeddah 21188; tel. (2) 647-1200; fax (2) 647-7411; Dir-Gen. SAHIR M. TAHLAWI.

Jubail Commercial Port: POB 276, Jubail 31951; tel. (3) 362-0600; fax (3) 362-3340; e-mail Jubail@ports.gov.sa; Dir-Gen. Capt. FAHD A. AL-AMER.

Jubail Industrial Port: POB 547, Jubail 31951; tel. (3) 357-8000; fax (3) 357-8011; Dir-Gen. ABDULLAH NASIR AL-TWAIJRI.

Yanbu Commercial Port: POB 1019, Yanbu al-Bahar; tel. (4) 322-2100; fax (4) 322-7643; Dir-Gen. ABDULLAH BIN AWAD AL-ZAIMI.

Yanbu Industrial Port: POB 30325, Yanbu; tel. (4) 396-7048; fax (4) 396-7037; Dir-Gen. ABDULLAH BIN AWAD AL-ZAIMI.

Principal Shipping Companies

Arabian Establishment for Trade and Shipping (AET): POB 832, 2nd Floor, Al-Matbouli Plaza, al-Ruwaiz District, Jeddah 21421; tel. (2) 652-5500; fax (2) 657-1148; e-mail aetjed@aetshipping.com; internet www.aetshipping.com; f. 1963; shipping agency; Gen. Man. ANTHONY ROBINSON.

Arabian Petroleum Supply Co Ltd (APSCO): POB 1408, Al-Qurayat St, Jeddah 21431; tel. (2) 608-1171; fax (2) 637-0966; e-mail marine@apsco-ksa.com; internet www.apsco.com.sa; f. 1961; Chair. Sheikh MUHAMMAD YOUSSUF ALI AL-REZA; Man. Dir MUHAMMAD ALI IBRAHIM ALIREZA.

Baaboud Trading and Shipping Agencies: POB 7262, Jeddah 21462; tel. (2) 627-0000; fax (2) 627-1111; e-mail info@baaboud.net; internet www.baaboud.net; Man. Dir AHMAD M. BAABOUD.

Bakri Navigation Co Ltd: POB 3757, Jeddah 21481; tel. (2) 652-4298; fax (2) 652-4297; e-mail info@bakrinavigation.com; internet www.bakrinavigation.com; f. 1973; owns and operates a fleet of oil tankers, tug boats and utility vessels; Chair. Sheikh A. K. AL-BAKRY; Man. Dir G. A. K. AL-BAKRY.

National Shipping Co of Saudi Arabia (Bahri): POB 8931, NSCSA Bldg No. 569, Sitteen St, Malaz Area, Riyadh 11492; tel. (1) 478-5454; fax (1) 477-8036; e-mail info@bahri.sa; internet www.bahri.sa; f. 1979; transportation of crude petroleum and petrochemical products; routes through Red Sea and Mediterranean to USA and Canada; operates a fleet of 42 ships; due to merge with Vela International Marine Ltd in 2013; Chair. ABDULLAH SULAIMAN AL-RUBAIAN; CEO SALEH AL-JASSER.

Saudi Shipping and Maritime Services Co Ltd (TRANSHIP): POB 7522, Jeddah 21472; tel. (2) 642-4255; fax (2) 643-2821; e-mail bunker@tranship.com; internet www.ssmsc.com; Chair. Prince SA'UD IBN NAYEF IBN ABD AL-AZIZ; Dir Eng. SULAIMAN AL-HUDAIRI.

Shipping Corpn of Saudi Arabia Ltd: POB 1691, Arab Maritime Center, Malik Khalid St, Jeddah 21441; tel. (2) 647-1137; fax (2) 647-8222; e-mail arablines@arabjeddah.com; Pres. and Man. Dir ABD AL-AZIZ AHMAD ARAB.

CIVIL AVIATION

There are 27 commercial airports, which handled some 42m. passengers in 2008. Plans to privatize the kingdom's airports were first announced in 2003. In 2008 concessions were awarded to two foreign companies for the management of the three main airports—King Abd al-Aziz International Airport (KAIA, in Jeddah), King Khalid International Airport (KKIA, in Riyadh) and King Fahd International Airport (KFIA, in the Eastern region, near Dammam). Construction of a new passenger terminal at KAIA, with an annual passenger capacity of 30m., commenced in February 2011 and was expected to be completed by 2014. A further two expansion phases, which would increase annual passenger capacity to about 80m. by 2035, were also planned. Prince Muhammad Bin Abd al-Aziz Airport in Medina, which opened in 1972, began handling international flights in 2006. Plans to build two new terminals, thus increasing capacity to around 12m. passengers per year by 2019, were at an advanced planning stage in 2013.

General Authority of Civil Aviation (GACA): POB 887, Jeddah 21165; tel. (2) 640-5000; fax (2) 640-1477; e-mail gaca-info@gaca.gov.sa; internet www.gaca.gov.sa; f. 1934; as the Presidency of Civil Aviation; name changed as above 1977; regulatory authority; Pres. FAISAL IBN HAMAD AL-SUGAIR.

National Air Services (NAS): POB 18118, 2nd Floor, Al-Jirasi Bldg, Madinah Rd, Jeddah 21415; tel. (2) 6910122; fax (2) 6520394; e-mail info@nasaviation.com; internet www.nasaviation.com; f. 1999; privately owned; also operates low-cost air carrier, Nas Air; CEO SULAIMAN AL-HAMDAN.

Saudi Arabian Airlines (SAUDIA): POB 620, Jeddah 21231; tel. (2) 686-4588; fax (2) 686-4587; e-mail webmaster@saudiairlines.com.sa; internet www.saudiairlines.com; f. 1945; began operations in 1947; carried 18.9m. passengers in 2010; regular services to 25 domestic and 52 international destinations; catering and cargo divisions part-privatized in 2008; further divestment of shares in technical services and training divisions finalized in March 2010; Chair. Prince SULTAN IBN ABD AL-AZIZ; Dir-Gen. KHALID ABDULLAH AL-MULHIM.

Tourism

The vast majority of devout Muslims try to make at least one visit to the holy cities of Medina, the burial place of Muhammad, and Mecca, his birthplace. In 2000 the Government decided to issue tourist visas for the first time. A Supreme Commission for Tourism (now Saudi Commission for Tourism and Antiquities—SCTA) was subsequently established to develop the tourism industry in Saudi Arabia. According to the SCTA, at the end of 2008 there were 1,006 hotels operating in the kingdom, providing more than 270,000 hotel rooms. It was reported in 2008 that the SCTA planned to invest almost US $40,000m. to develop 19 tourism resorts on the Red Sea coast. According to provisional data, tourist arrivals were recorded at some 17.3m. in 2011, while receipts from tourism totalled $8,459m. An estimated 1.8m. foreign pilgrims visited Mecca in 2012.

Saudi Commission for Tourism and Antiquities (SCTA): POB 66680, Riyadh 11586; tel. (1) 880-8855; fax (1) 880-8844; internet www.scta.gov.sa; f. 2001 as Supreme Comm. for Tourism, renamed as above 2008; Pres. Prince SULTAN IBN SALMAN IBN ABD AL-AZIZ AL SA'UD.

Saudi Hotels and Resort Areas Co (SHARACO): POB 5500, Riyadh 11422; tel. (1) 481-6666; fax (1) 480-1666; e-mail info@saudi-hotels.com.sa; internet www.saudi-hotels.com.sa; f. 1975; construction and management of hotels, resorts and other tourism facilities; Saudi Govt has a 40% interest; Chair. MUSAAD AL-SENANY; Dir-Gen. ABD AL-AZIZ AL-AMBAR.

Defence

Chief of the General Staff: Gen. HUSSAIN IBN ABDULLAH IBN HUSSAIN AL-GABEEL.

Director-General of Public Security Forces: Gen. SAEED IBN ABDULLAH AL-QAHTANI.

Commander of Land Forces: Lt-Gen. EID IBN AWADH AL-SHALAWI.

Commander of Air Force: Gen. FAYYAD IBN HAMID IBN RAGAD AL-RUWAILI.

Commander of the Navy: Lt-Gen. DHAKHAIL ALLAH IBN AHMAD IBN MUHAMMAD AL-WAQDANI.

Defence Budget (2011): SR 182,000m.

Total Armed Forces (as assessed at November 2012): 233,500 (army 75,000; navy 13,500; air force 20,000; air defence forces 16,000; national guard 100,000—75,000 active personnel and 25,000 tribal levies); industrial security force 9,000).

Paramilitary Forces (as assessed at November 2012): 15,500: 10,500 frontier force; 4,500 coastguard; and 500 special security force.

Education

The educational system in Saudi Arabia resembles that of other Arab countries. Educational institutions are administered mainly by the Government. The private sector plays a significant role at the first and second levels, but its total contribution is relatively small compared with that of the public sector.

Pre-elementary education is provided on a small scale, mainly in urban areas. Elementary or primary education is of six years' duration and the normal entrance age is six. The total number of pupils at this stage in 2011/12 was estimated at 2,530,744, with 232,453 teachers. Intermediate education begins at 12 and lasts for three years. The total number of pupils at this stage in 2011/12 was estimated at 1,212,029, with teachers numbering 125,355. Secondary education begins at 15 and extends for three years. After the first year, successful pupils branch into science or arts groups. The total number of pupils at this stage in 2011/12 was estimated at 1,226,205, with 114,625 teachers. According to UNESCO estimates, enrolment of children in the primary age-group increased from 32% in 1970 to 90% in 2008/09. Between 1970 and 2009/10 enrolment at the secondary level rose from 9% to 81%. The proportion of females enrolled in Saudi Arabian schools increased from 25% of the total number of pupils in 1970 to 47.7% in 2007. Vocational and technical education programmes can be entered after completion of the intermediate stage. In 2010/11 a total of 81,283 students attended 112 technical and vocational institutes.

In 2010/11 an estimated 925,027 students were enrolled in higher education. In 2008/09 the number of new students admitted to universities increased to 242,835, compared with 68,000 in 2003. In 2006 tertiary institutions included 110 university colleges and 87 colleges exclusively for women. In early 2012 there were 24 Government and nine private universities in the country. Princess Nora bint Abdulrahman University, established as Riyadh University for Women in 1970, moved to a new campus within the capital in May 2011. A planned increase in capacity from 26,000 to 50,000 students would make it the largest women's university in the world. The Imam Muhammad bin Sa'ud Islamic University comprises 11 colleges. It also includes six institutes abroad for teaching Islamic and Arab knowledge in the United Arab Emirates, Mauritania, Djibouti, Indonesia, the USA and Japan. Early in 2006 the Ministry of Higher Education announced that foreign universities would be permitted to establish campuses in the kingdom for the first time. The Government's budget for 2012 envisaged expenditure on education and training of SR 165,000m., equivalent to 24% of total spending.

Bibliography

Aarts, Paul, and Nonneman, Gerd (Eds). *Saudi Arabia in the Balance: Political Economy, Society, Foreign Affairs*. London, C. Hurst & Co, 2005/New York, New York University Press, 2006.

Abir, Mordechai. *Saudi Arabia: Society, Government and the Gulf Crisis*. London, Routledge, 1993.

Alshamsi, Mansoor Jassem. *Islam and Political Reform in Saudi Arabia*. Abingdon, Routledge, 2008.

Anderson, Irvine H. *Aramco, the United States, and Saudi Arabia: A study in the Dynamics of Foreign Oil Policy, 1935–50*. Princeton, NJ, Princeton University Press, 1982.

Benoit-Méchin, S. *Ibn Séoud ou la naissance d'un royaume*. Paris, Albin Michel, 1955.

Bianchi, Robert R. *Guests of God: Pilgrimage and Politics in the Islamic World*. Oxford, Oxford University Press, 2004.

Champion, Daryl. *The Paradoxical Kingdom: Saudi Arabia and the Momentum of Reform*. London, C. Hurst & Co, 2003.

Commins, David. *The Wahhabi Mission and Saudi Arabia*. London, I. B. Tauris, 2009.

Cordesman, Anthony H. *Saudi Arabia Enters the 21st Century: The Military and International Security Dimensions*. Westport, CT, Greenwood Press, 2003.

Saudi Arabia: Guarding the Desert Kingdom. Boulder, CO, Westview Press, 2004.

Cordesman, Anthony H., and Obaid, Nawaf. *National Security in Saudi Arabia*. Westport, CT, Praeger Publishers, 2005.

Crawford, Michael, 'The Da'wa of Muhammad Ibn Abd al-Wahhab before the Al Saud' in *Journal of Arabian Studies*. Vol. 1, No. 2, pp. 147–161, June 2011.

Craze, Joshua (Ed.). *The Kingdom: Saudi Arabia and the Challenge of the 21st Century*. London, C. Hurst & Co, 2009.

Elhadj, Elie. 'Saudi Arabia's Agricultural Project: From Dust to Dust', *Middle East Review of International Affairs* 12 (2), June 2008.

Al-Enazy, Askar H. *The Creation of Saudi Arabia: Ibn Saud and British Imperial Policy, 1914–1927*. Abingdon, Routledge, 2009.

Al-Fahad, Abdulaziz. 'From Exclusivism to Accommodation: Doctrinal and Legal Evolution of Wahhabism', *New York University Law Review* 79 (2), 2004.

Fandy, Mamoun. *Saudi Arabia and the Politics of Dissent*. Basingstoke, Palgrave, 1999.

Field, Michael. *The Merchants: The Big Business Families of Arabia*. London, John Murray, 1984.

Furtig, Henner. *Iran's Rivalry with Saudi Arabia between the Gulf Wars*. Reading, Ithaca Press, 2000.

Hegghammer, Thomas. *Jihad in Saudi Arabia: Violence and Pan-Islamism since 1979*. Cambridge, Cambridge University Press, 2010.

Helms, Christine Moss. *The Cohesion of Saudi Arabia*. London, Croom Helm, 1981.

Hertog, Steffen. *Princes, Brokers, and Bureaucrats: Oil and the State in Saudi Arabia*. Ithaca, NY, Cornell University Press, 2010.

Hill, Ginny, and Nonneman, Gerd. *Yemen, Saudi Arabia and the Gulf States: Elite Politics, Street Protests and Regional Diplomacy*. London, Chatham House, 2011.

Holden, David, Johns, Richard, and Buchan, James. *The House of Saud*. London, Sidgwick & Jackson, 1981.

House, Karen Elliott. *On Saudi Arabia: Its People, Past, Religion, Fault Lines—And Future*. New York, Knopf, 2012.

Howarth, David. *The Desert King: Ibn Sa'ud*. New York, McGraw Hill, 1964.

Ibrahim, Fouad N. *The Shi'is of Saudi Arabia*. London, Saqi Books, 2006.

International Crisis Group. 'Can Saudi Arabia Reform Itself?', *ICG Middle East Report* 28, 14 July 2004.

'Saudi Arabia Backgrounder: Who are the Islamists?', *ICG Middle East Report* 31, 21 September 2004.

'The Shiite Question in Saudi Arabia', *ICG Middle East Report* 45, 19 September 2005.

Lacey, Robert. *Inside the Kingdom*. New York, Hutchison, 2009.

Lacroix, Stéphane. *Les islamistes saoudiens: une insurrection manqué*. Paris, Presses Universitaires de France, 2010.

(trans. Holoch, Georges.) *Awakening Islam: Religious Dissent in Contemporary Saudi Arabia*. Cambridge, MA, Harvard University Press, 2011.

Lees, Brian. *Handbook of the Sa'ud family of Saudi Arabia*. London, Royal Genealogies, 1980.

Lippman, Thomas W. *Inside the Mirage: America's Fragile Relationship with Saudi Arabia*. New York, Perseus Books, 2003.

Saudi Arabia on the Edge. Dulles, VA, Potomac Books, 2012.

Long, David E. *The Kingdom of Saudi Arabia*. Gainesville, FL, University Press of Florida, 1998.

Mackey, Sandra. *The Saudis: Inside the Desert Kingdom*. London, W. W. Norton, revised edn, 2002.

Manea, Elham. *Regional Politics in the Gulf: Saudi Arabia, Oman and Yemen*. London, Saqi Books, 2005.

van der Meulen, D. *The Wells of Ibn Sa'ud*. London, John Murray, 1957.

McLoughlin, Leslie. *Ibn Saud, Founder of a Kingdom*. London, Macmillan, 1993.

Niblock, Tim (Ed.). *State, Society and Economy in Saudi Arabia*. London, Croom Helm, 1981.

Saudi Arabia: Power, Legitimacy and Survival. Abingdon, Routledge, 2006.

The Political Economy of Saudi Arabia (with Monica Malik). Abingdon, Routledge, 2007.

Nonneman, Gerd. 'Saudi-European Relations, 1902–2001: A Pragmatic Quest for Relative Autonomy', *International Affairs* 77 (3), July 2001.

Obaid, Nawaf E. *The Oil Kingdom at 100: Petroleum Policy-Making in Saudi Arabia*. Washington, DC, Washington Institute for Near East Policy, 2001.

Ottaway, David B. *The King's Messenger: Prince Bandar bin Sultan and America's Tangled Relationship with Saudi Arabia*. New York, NY, Walker & Co, 2008.

Peterson, J. E. *Saudi Arabia and the Illusion of Security* (Adelphi Papers). Oxford, Oxford University Press, 2002.

Philby, H. St. J. B. *Arabia and the Wahhabis*. London, 1928.

Arabia. London, Benn, 1930.

The Empty Quarter. London, 1933.

A Pilgrim in Arabia. London, 1946.

Arabian Jubilee. London, 1951.

Saudi Arabia. London, 1955.

The Land of Midian. London, 1957.

Quandt, Willam B. *Saudi Arabia in the 1980s: Foreign Policy, Security and Oil*. Oxford, Basil Blackwell, 1982.

Al-Rasheed, Madawi. *Contesting the Saudi State: Islamic Voices from a New Generation*. Cambridge, Cambridge University Press, 2007.

(Ed.). *Kingdom Without Borders: Saudi Arabia's Political, Religious and Media Frontiers*. London, C. Hurst & Co, 2008.

A History of Saudi Arabia, 2nd edn. Cambridge, Cambridge University Press, 2010.

Al-Rasheed, Madawi, and Vitalis, Robert (Eds). *Counter Narratives: History, Contemporary Society and Politics in Saudi Arabia*. New York, Palgrave, 2004.

Robinson, Jeffrey. *Yamani: The Inside Story*. London, Simon & Schuster, 1988.

Sarhan, Samir (Ed.). *Who's Who in Saudi Arabia*. Jeddah, Tihama, and London, Europa Publications, 3rd edn, 1984.

Al Sa'ud, Faisal bin Salman. *Iran, Saudi Arabia and the Gulf*. London, I. B. Tauris, 2004.

Stenslie, Stig. *Regime Stability in Saudi Arabia: The Challenge of Succession*. Abingdon, Routledge, 2011.

'Power Behind the Veil: Princesses of the House of Saud' in *Journal of Arabian Studies*. Vol. 1, No. 1, pp. 69-79, June 2011.

Thompson, Mark. 'Assessing the Impact of Saudi Arabia's National Dialogue' in *Journal of Arabian Studies*. Vol. 1, No. 2, pp. 63-181, June 2012.

Troeller, Gary. *The Birth of Saudi Arabia*. London, Frank Cass, 1976.

Trofimov, Yaroslav. *The Siege of Mecca: The Forgotten Uprising in Islam's Holiest Shrine and the Rise of Al Qaeda*. New York, NY, Doubleday, 2007.

Vassiliev, Alexei. *The History of Saudi Arabia*. London, Saqi Books, 1998.

Vitalis, Robert. *America's Kingdom: Mythmaking on the Saudi Oil Frontier*. Stanford, CA, Stanford University Press, 2006.

Williams, K. *Ibn Sa'ud: The Puritan King of Arabia*. London, Cape, 1933.

Wilson, Peter W., and Graham, Douglas F. *Saudi Arabia: The Coming Storm*. New York, M. E. Sharpe, 1994.

Wilson, Rodney, al-Salamah, Abdullah, Malik, Monica, and al-Rajhi, Ahmed. *Economic Development in Saudi Arabia*. London, RoutledgeCurzon, 2003.

Yamani, Hani A. Z. *To be a Saudi*. London, Janus, 1998.

Yamani, Mai. *Changed Identities: The Challenge of the New Generation in Saudi Arabia*. London, Royal Institute of International Affairs, 1999.

Cradle of Islam: The Hijaz and the Quest for an Arabian Identity. London, I. B. Tauris, 2004.

SPANISH NORTH AFRICA

The territories of Spanish North Africa comprise mainly Ceuta and Melilla, two enclaves within Moroccan territory on the north African coast. Attached to Melilla, for administrative purposes, are Peñón de Vélez de la Gomera, a small fort on the Mediterranean coast, and two groups of islands, Peñón de Alhucemas and the Chafarinas. Ceuta and Melilla are seen as integral parts of Spain by the Spanish Government and have the status of autonomous cities, although Morocco has put forward a claim to both. Sovereignty over the uninhabited island of Perejil (known as Laila to the Moroccans) is disputed between Spain and Morocco.

CEUTA

Geography

The ancient port and walled city of Ceuta is situated on a rocky promontory on the North African coast overlooking the Strait of Gibraltar, the Strait here being about 25 km wide. Ceuta was retained by Spain as a *plaza de soberanía* (a presidio, or fortified enclave, over which Spain has full sovereign rights) when Morocco became independent from France in 1956, and was administered as part of Cádiz Province until 1995. Ceuta now functions as a bunkering and fishing port, occupying an area of 19.7 sq km. At the census of November 2011, the population was recorded at 83,517, with a density of 4,239 people per sq km.

History

Ceuta was conquered by Juan I of Portugal in 1415. Following the union of the crowns of Spain and Portugal in 1580, Ceuta passed under Spanish rule and in 1694, when Portugal was formally separated from Spain, the territory requested to remain under Spanish control. During the 16th, 17th and 18th centuries, Ceuta endured a number of sieges by the Muslims. Ahmad Gailan, a chieftain in northern Morocco, blockaded the town in 1648–55. The Sultan of Morocco, Mulai Ismail (1672–1727), attacked Ceuta in 1674, 1680 and 1694, after which he maintained a blockade against the town until 1720. Ahmad Ali al-Rifi, a chieftain from northern Morocco, made yet another unsuccessful assault in 1732. A pact of friendship and commerce was negotiated between Spain and Morocco at Aranjuez, Spain, in 1780, a peaceful agreement following in the next year over the boundaries of the enclave. In 1844–45 there was another dispute about the precise limits of Ceuta. Further disagreement led to the war of 1859–60. Spanish forces, after an engagement at Los Castillejos, seized Tetuán from Morocco. Following another battle at Wadi Ras in March 1860, the conflict came to an end. A settlement was then made, which enlarged the enclave of Ceuta and obliged Morocco to forfeit to Spain 100m. pesetas as war indemnities. In 1974 the town became the seat of the Capitanía General de Africa.

Since 1939 both Ceuta and Melilla, the other Spanish enclave in North Africa, have been ruled as integral parts of Spain, though this arrangement is disputed in the territories. All those born in Ceuta, Melilla and the island dependencies are Spanish citizens and subjects. Both Ceuta and Melilla have municipal councils (*ayuntamientos*), and are administered as an integral part of Spain by the Delegado del Gobierno (Government Delegate), who is directly responsible to the Ministry of Home Affairs in Madrid. The Government Delegate is usually assisted by a Sub-Delegate. There is also one delegate from each of the ministries in Madrid. Each enclave elects one deputy and two senators to the Cortes Generales (parliament) in Madrid.

In November 1978 King Hassan of Morocco stated his country's claim to Ceuta and Melilla. In October 1981 Spain declared before the UN that the enclaves were integral parts of Spanish territory. In April 1982, however, Istiqlal, a Moroccan political party, demanded action to recover the territories from Spain, and in March 1983 the Moroccan Government blocked the passage of goods across the frontiers of Ceuta and Melilla. In August the movement of Moroccan workers to Ceuta, Melilla and also Gibraltar was restricted. From 1984 there was increasing unease over Spanish North Africa's future, although Spain continued to reject any comparison between the two enclaves and Gibraltar.

Details of the enclaves' new draft statutes, envisaging the establishment of two local assemblies, with jurisdiction over such matters as public works, agriculture, tourism, culture and internal trade, were announced in August 1985 and approved by the central Government in December. Unlike the assemblies of Spain's Comunidades Autónomas (Autonomous Communities, or regions), those of Ceuta and Melilla were not to be vested with legislative powers, and this denial of full autonomy was much criticized in the enclaves. In March 1986 up to 20,000 people took to the streets of Ceuta in a demonstration to demand autonomy. Tensions also rose over the status of Muslim residents in the enclaves.

At the general election of June 1986 the ruling Partido Socialista Obrero Español (PSOE) was successful in Ceuta. In January 1987, on an official visit to Morocco by the Spanish Minister of the Interior, King Hassan proposed the establishment of a joint commission to seek a solution to the problem of the Spanish enclaves, but the proposal was rejected by Spain. In October 1988 the Moroccan Minister of Foreign Affairs formally presented his country's claim to Ceuta and Melilla to the UN General Assembly. In February of that year it was announced that, in accordance with European Community (EC, now European Union) regulations, Moroccan citizens would in due course require visas to enter Spain. Entry to Spanish North Africa, however, was to be exempt from the new ruling.

In March 1988 it was announced that the central Government and the main opposition parties in Madrid had reached a broad consensus on the draft autonomy statutes for the enclaves. Although it was envisaged that Spain would retain the territories, the possibility of a negotiated settlement with Morocco was not discounted. In July, seven years after the enclaves' first official request for autonomy, the central Government announced that the implementation of the autonomy statutes was to be accelerated. Revised draft statutes were submitted by the PSOE to the main opposition parties for consideration. The statutes declared Ceuta and Melilla to be integral parts of Spain, and, for the first time, the Spanish Government undertook to guarantee financial support for the territories. A further innovation contained in the revised draft provided for the establishment of mixed commissions to oversee the movement of goods and services through the territories. As previously indicated by the Spanish Government, the two Spanish North African assemblies were to be granted 'normative' rather than legislative powers. Each new assembly would elect from among its members a city president. It was later also revealed that the revised statutes encompassed only the enclaves of Ceuta and Melilla, thus excluding the associated Spanish North African islands; the islands had been erroneously incorporated in the preliminary statutes, approved in December 1985. Although remaining the responsibility of the Spanish Ministry of Defence, these islands were not, therefore, to become part of any Spanish Comunidad Autónoma.

At the general election held in October 1989 the ruling PSOE retained its Ceuta seats, despite allegations by the opposition Partido Popular (PP) that many names on the electoral register were duplicated. In April 1990 the Spanish Government decided to open negotiations with the political groupings of Ceuta and Melilla, the autonomy statutes having been presented for discussion in the territories. It was confirmed that the enclaves were to remain an integral part of Spain, and that they were to be granted self-government at municipal, rather than regional, level.

Elections for the 25-member municipal councils of Ceuta and Melilla were held in May 1991, and in each territory the PSOE Mayor was replaced. In Ceuta Francisco Fraiz Armada of the Progreso y Futuro de Ceuta (PFC) became Mayor. In October the draft autonomy statutes of Ceuta and Melilla were submitted to the Congreso de los Diputados (Congress of Deputies—the lower house of the Spanish Cortes) in Madrid for discussion. During the debate the PP accused the PSOE of supporting Moroccan interests. In November thousands of demonstrators, many of whom had travelled from the enclaves, attended a protest march in Madrid organized by the Governments of Ceuta and Melilla, in support of demands for autonomy. In early 1992, however, the central Government confirmed that the Assemblies of Ceuta and Melilla were not to be granted full legislative powers. In May a general strike in Ceuta, to protest against this denial of full autonomy, was widely supported.

At the general election held in June 1993 the PSOE of Ceuta lost its seats in the Cortes to the PP. In March 1994 King Hassan declared his opposition to the forthcoming adoption of the autonomy statutes, repeating Morocco's claim to the territories. Representatives of Ceuta were particularly critical of delays in the presentation of the final statutes to the Cortes in Madrid, and urged the central Government and the opposition PP to bring the matter to a speedy conclusion. In September the final statutes of autonomy were approved by the Spanish Government in preparation for their presentation to the Cortes. The statutes provided for 25-member local assemblies, with powers similar to those of the municipal councils of mainland Spain. Morocco, however, announced that it was initiating a new diplomatic campaign to reassert its claim over the territories. The proposals for limited self-government were generally accepted in Melilla but not in Ceuta, where, in October, a general strike received widespread support. An estimated 20,000 residents participated in a demonstration to demand equality with other Spanish regions and full autonomy for the enclave. Earlier in the month, following expressions of concern regarding the territories' protection in the event of Moroccan aggression, the Minister of Defence confirmed that Spain would continue to maintain an appropriate military presence in Ceuta and Melilla. In December more than 2,000 citizens of Ceuta attended a demonstration in Madrid to demand full autonomy.

Following their approval by the Congreso de los Diputados in December 1994, the autonomy statutes were ratified by the Senado (Senate) in February 1995. This approval of the statutes by the Cortes was denounced by the Moroccan Government, which, upon taking office in March, declared the recovery of Ceuta and Melilla to be one of its major objectives. In April responsibility for two explosions in Ceuta was claimed by the Organización 21 de Agosto para la Liberación de los Territorios Marroquíes Usurpados, a Muslim group that demanded the return of the territories to Morocco, and which the Spanish Government suspected was now receiving covert assistance from the Moroccan authorities.

Elections for the new Assemblies were held in May 1995. In Ceuta the PP won nine of the 25 seats, the PFC six, the nationalist Ceuta Unida four and the PSOE three. Basilio Fernández López of the PFC was re-elected Mayor/President, heading a coalition with Ceuta Unida and the PSOE. Mustafa Mizziam Ammar, leader of the Partido Democrático y Social de Ceuta (PDSC), became the first Muslim candidate ever to be elected in the territory. Fewer than 57% of those eligible voted. A general election was held in March 1996 and in Ceuta the three PP delegates to the Cortes were re-elected. In July Fernández López resigned as Mayor/President after seven months at the head of a minority administration, and was replaced by Jesús Fortes Ramos of the PP, who urged that the enclave be considered a full Comunidad Autónoma.

In the 1990s illegal immigration became a serious issue in the enclaves, and in early 1999 it was conceded that the security barrier on Ceuta's border with Morocco was proving inadequate. Improvements to the barrier, and other security measures, were completed by February 2000. Between January and July 1999 alone a total of 21,411 illegal immigrants were apprehended on Ceuta's frontier and returned to Morocco. Meanwhile, work progressed on a new reception centre in Ceuta to replace the inadequate facilities of the Calamocarro camp, where in mid-1999 more than 1,000 illegal immigrants, mainly from sub-Saharan Africa, were being held. The centre was completed in May 2000 at a cost of 2,800m. pesetas; it had accommodation for 130 immigrants. In February 2000 the Spanish Government liberalized Spain's immigration laws, thereby provoking a dramatic rise in clandestine immigration.

At the elections of June 1999 the most successful party in both Ceuta and Melilla was the Grupo Independiente Liberal (GIL), recently founded by Jesús Gil, the controversial Mayor of Marbella. The GIL secured 12 of the 25 seats in the Assembly of Ceuta. Antonio Sampietro Casarramona of the GIL replaced Jesús Fortes Ramos of the PP as Mayor/President of Ceuta. In January 2000 José María Aznar visited Spanish North Africa, the first visit by a Spanish Prime Minister for 19 years. His decision to visit in his capacity as leader of the PP, however, rather than as head of government, was criticized in Ceuta and Melilla, while the Moroccan Government cancelled the planned visit to Rabat, the Moroccan capital, of the Spanish Minister of Foreign Affairs. At the general election held on 12 March 2000 Ceuta's three PP representatives in Madrid all secured re-election.

In September 2000, following a ruling in the Spanish courts that Ceuta and Melilla could not be considered to be Comunidades Autónomas, the ruling GIL proposed in the Ceuta Assembly that the Spanish Government grant Ceuta greater autonomy. Discussions on the proposal, which proved highly emotive, led to disturbances within the Assembly. The motion was subsequently carried by a majority vote, despite the opposition of the PP and the PSOE, and the abstention of the PDSC.

Five Ceuta councillors resigned their posts and announced their departure from the GIL in January 2001, thus depriving the party of its majority in the Assembly. A motion of censure was subsequently brought against Sampietro by the PP, the PSOE, the PDSC and one of the former GIL councillors. The motion was carried on 10 February with the support of 17 of the 25 deputies, and Juan Jesús Vivas Lara of the PP was appointed Mayor/President of Ceuta.

Morocco's withdrawal of its ambassador from Madrid in October 2001 led to a deterioration in the already strained relations between that country and Spain. In February 2002 the Spanish Ministry of Foreign Affairs again rejected the Moroccan Government's comparison of the status of Ceuta and Melilla with that of Gibraltar, as talks between the Spanish and British Governments regarding the British territory progressed. The situation worsened in mid-July, when a small detachment of Moroccan troops occupied the uninhabited rocky islet of Perejil (known as Laila to the Moroccans). Morocco claimed that it was establishing a surveillance post on the island as part of its campaign against illegal immigration and drugs-trafficking. Madrid responded by demanding the immediate evacuation of Moroccan troops from Perejil, receiving the support of the EU and NATO. Although not making a formal claim of sovereignty over the island, Spain proceeded to increase its military forces in Ceuta and Melilla. On 17 July the Spanish ambassador to Rabat was recalled for an unlimited period, and Spanish special forces removed Moroccan troops from Perejil without casualties on either side. Spanish troops subsequently withdrew from the island and the Spanish Minister of Foreign Affairs, Ana Palacio, and her Moroccan counterpart, Muhammad Benaïssa, concluded an accord on Perejil under which both states agreed to return to the *status quo ante*. In subsequent months the Moroccan authorities frequently closed border crossings to Ceuta and Melilla, while Spanish border patrols tightened security. In October Spain ordered the permanent closure of Ceuta's border with Morocco at Benzu, after a number of border incidents and amid concerns about rising illegal immigration. Early 2003 saw an increase in measures to strengthen border security and in Spain's naval presence, in large part reflecting the growing likelihood of US-led armed intervention to oust the regime of Saddam Hussain in Iraq. In March some 700–1,000 Muslim residents of Ceuta protested against the US-led military campaign in Iraq (q.v.).

At the elections of May 2003 the PP won an absolute majority in Ceuta for the first time, with 19 out of 25 seats, while the Unión Demócrata Ceutí (UDCE), representing the Muslim population, secured three seats. Vivas remained as Mayor/President. After a series of suicide bomb attacks were launched against Western targets in Casablanca, Morocco, in mid-May, border security in the enclaves was increased dramatically.

In 2003 it was estimated that around 3,000 immigrants passed through Ceuta, and the enclave received more than 1,400 asylum requests, compared with 372 in 2002 and 82 in 2001. Official figures stated that 18% of the requests processed in 2003 were successful.

At the March 2004 general election the PP retained the deputy and senators elected by Ceuta. In September Vivas met with the newly elected Spanish Prime Minister, José Luis Rodríguez Zapatero, to discuss the possible change in status of Ceuta from Ciudad Autónoma (Autonomous City) to Comunidad Autónoma (Autonomous Community), in line with other areas of Spain. Following a series of bomb attacks on commuter trains in Madrid in March (in which 191 people died), there were fears that residents of Ceuta might have connections with the terrorists, who were suspected of belonging to a Moroccan Islamist group. In November the central Government unveiled plans to build reception centres for immigrants on the mainland, to which illegal immigrants arrested in Ceuta and Melilla would be transported.

In 2005 potential immigrants continued to attempt to gain access to Europe through Ceuta and Melilla, with a succession of groups of would-be immigrants attempting to scale the walls separating the enclaves from Morocco. In September five potential immigrants were killed by security forces during an attempt by some 600 people to climb the wall into Ceuta. It was announced at a Spanish-Moroccan summit held in late September in Seville, Spain, that security on both sides of the border would be increased following the attempts; however, the waves of immigration continued in early October, and more deaths resulted. In that month the Spanish Government authorized €3m. to improve facilities for immigrants in the enclaves. Heightened security reduced the number of attempts being made to climb the walls, but immigrants began looking for new, and more dangerous, routes to Europe via the Canary Islands.

In early 2006 Zapatero made the first official visit by a Spanish Prime Minister to the enclaves in over 25 years. His visit was condemned by the Moroccan authorities as a provocation, despite the fact that relations between Spain and Morocco had been favourable during the first two years of Zapatero's administration, with increasing co-operation on immigration issues.

In February 2007 the Spanish Government reached an agreement with the Governments of Ceuta and Melilla to abandon plans to change the cities' status to that of Comunidades Autónomas. In return, more powers would be devolved to the cities in the areas of employment and social services, and their budgets would be increased. At elections held in May the PP retained its absolute majority in the Assembly, again winning 19 of the 25 seats; the UDCE, in alliance with the left-wing Izquierda Unida, secured four seats, while the PSOE won two. Vivas resumed office as Mayor/President. The entire regional executive of the PSOE, headed by Secretary-General Antonia Palomo, resigned as a result of the party's poor performance in the elections. In October ongoing divisions within the local branch of the PSOE led to its dissolution. The national leadership of the party delegated a commission to assume temporary responsibility for PSOE activities in Ceuta. (The local branch of the PSOE resumed activities under a newly elected Secretary-General, José Antonio Carracao Meléndez, in December 2008.)

In early November 2007 a two-day visit to Ceuta and Melilla by King Juan Carlos, his first since acceding to the throne in 1975, was warmly welcomed by residents, but provoked considerable anger in Morocco. The Moroccan Government recalled its ambassador from Madrid for consultations ahead of the visit, which it deemed regrettable and provocative. The Spanish Prime Minister sought to defuse tensions, insisting that relations with Morocco, which had improved in recent years, remained strong. However, Morocco's King Muhammad VI noted that Spain risked jeopardizing bilateral relations, and urged Spain to engage in dialogue with Morocco over the disputed enclaves. Later in November the Moroccan Government postponed a planned visit to Rabat by the Spanish Minister of Development. The Moroccan ambassador to Spain returned to Madrid in January 2008, following a visit to Rabat by the Spanish Minister of Foreign Affairs and Co-operation, Miguel Angel Moratinos, who delivered a conciliatory letter from Prime Minister Zapatero to King Muhammad.

At the general election held on 9 March 2008 the PP retained Ceuta's seat in the Congreso de los Diputados and its two seats in the Senado. In April the Government of Ceuta opposed plans to reorganize the Spanish armed forces, amid fears that they would result in a substantial reduction in the number of troops stationed in the city. However, the central Government rejected this suggestion, insisting that the composition of the forces deployed in its North African territories would change, but that it did not intend to reduce overall numbers. The following month José Fernández Chacón was appointed to replace José Jenaro García-Arreciado Batanero as Government Delegate in Ceuta.

In October 2009 the Vice-President and Councillor of the Presidency, Pedro Gordillo Durán, was forced to resign from office, following allegations that he had demanded favours of a sexual nature from a female job-seeker in return for granting her employment in the civil service.

At elections to the Assembly held on 22 May 2011 the PP retained the largest representation, with 18 seats. The 'Caballas' coalition—which comprised the UDCE and the Parti Socialista del Pueblo del Ceuta (PSPC)—won four seats, while the PSOE took the remaining three. A new Council of Government, under the continued leadership of Vivas, took office in mid-June.

At the general election held on 20 November 2011, the PP retained Ceuta's seat in the Congreso de los Diputados and both seats in the Senado. In January 2012 Francisco Antonio González Pérez, a former representative of the enclave at the Congreso, assumed the role of Government Delegate in Ceuta. In March the development and environment portfolio was divided, with responsibility for environmental affairs passing to the Councillor for Public Services and Communities. In late April Vivas announced a further reorganization, citing the need to adapt his administration to the changing economic circumstances in Spain. Most notably, Francisco Márquez de la Rubia assumed responsibility for a new Council of Planning and Relations with Governmental Organizations, and Guillermo Martínez Arcas became Councillor of Finance, the Economy and Human Resources. In June 2013 Emilio Carreira Ruiz joined the Government in place of Martinez, following the latter's resignation.

Economy

Ceuta, like the other Spanish enclave in North Africa—Melilla—is a free port. Both enclaves are in fact of little economic importance, while the other Spanish North African possessions are of negligible significance. The chief reason for Spanish retention of these areas is their predominantly Spanish population, though they also serve a strategic military function. The registered population of Ceuta increased fivefold in the last century, and continued to grow in 2002–09, albeit at an average annual rate of only 0.2%. However, by the census of 2011 the population was recorded at 83,517. There are large numbers of immigrants from Morocco in both enclaves.

In 1991 Ceuta's gross domestic product (GDP) was 33.6% below the average for the whole of Spain. In that year the average disposable family income of Ceuta was only 76.9% of that of Spain. Social security benefits accounted for 22.8% of the average family income. By 1996, although family income per capita was 0.8% below the Spanish average, purchasing power was 3.0% higher. GDP at current prices totalled €1,495.2m. in 2012. Real GDP growth was estimated at 2.5% in 2006, 3.7% in 2007 and 1.8% in 2008. In 2012, according to official estimates, the GDP of Ceuta was equivalent to €19,335 per head, ranking 14th (in terms of GDP per head) in a list of 19 Spanish autonomous regions (the 17 Autonomous Communities, together with Ceuta and Melilla).

The hinterland of both cities is small. Development is restricted by the lack of suitable building land. Ceuta, in particular, suffers from intermittent water shortages.

Agriculture, Industry and Tourism

In 2012 agriculture and fishing provided an estimated 0.2% of GDP, while energy provided 2.7%, construction 8.2% and manufacturing 2.2%. Far more important was the services sector, which accounted for an estimated 86.7% of GDP. Most of the population's food has to be imported, with the exception of fish, which is obtained locally. Sardines and anchovies are the most important items. In 2004 236.8 metric tons of fish were landed in Ceuta. A large proportion of the tinned fish is sold outside Spain. More important to the economies of the cities is the port activity; most of their exports take the form of fuel supplied—at very competitive rates—to ships. Most of the fuel comes from the Spanish refinery in Tenerife. Ceuta's port is busier than Melilla's, receiving a total of 12,943 ships in 2012; 2.1m. metric tons of freight were handled in that year. In 2012 Ceuta's trade deficit increased to around €439m. Mineral fuels and oils accounted for €297.4m. (67.7%) of imports, and textile materials and clothing €20.4m. (4.6%). The leading sources of imports in that year were the People's Republic of China (9.0%), the Netherlands (6.0%) and Turkey (5.7%). Commercial agricultural activity in the territories is negligible, and industry is limited to meeting some of the everyday needs of the cities.

Tourism previously made a significant contribution to the territories' economies. Almost 1m. tourists visited Ceuta in 1986, attracted by duty-free goods. High ferry-boat fares and the opening of the Spanish border with Gibraltar in 1985, however, had an adverse effect on the enclaves' duty-free trade, and tourist numbers declined to 68,205 in 2004, of whom 50,962 were Spanish. In 2012 77,295 visitors arrived in Ceuta, of whom 54,131 were Spanish.

In the second quarter of 2013 the total labour force was estimated at 34,700, of whom 12,100 (34.9%) were unemployed.

Finance and Inward Investment

In 1989 a campaign to attract more investment to Ceuta was launched. Tax concessions and other incentives were offered. In the three years to 1990 the Spanish Government's investment in Ceuta totalled 9,000m. pesetas for the purposes of public works, and its health service was allocated 347m. pesetas. Upon the accession of Spain to the European Community (now European Union—EU) in January 1986, Ceuta and Melilla were considered as Spanish cities and European territory, and joined the Community as part of Spain. They retained their status as free ports. The statutes of autonomy, adopted in early 1995, envisaged the continuation of the territories' fiscal benefits. On 28 February 2002 euro notes and coins entered circulation as sole legal tender in the enclaves. Following the enlargement of the EU in 2004 and corresponding plans to downgrade aid to Spain, in 2005 the Government of Ceuta, together with Melilla and two other Spanish regions, Murcia and Asturias, began a campaign to maintain EU aid at existing levels. However, following a further enlargement of the EU in 2007, Ceuta was no longer eligible for support in the long term; subsidies were to be progressively reduced during 2007–13, with a view to their eventual withdrawal.

Ceuta's budget for 2012 was €242.2m. The city's consolidated budget for 2012 included current and capital transfers from the Spanish state of €69.4m. and €6.3m., respectively. The annual rate of inflation averaged 2.0% in 2006–11; consumer prices increased by 2.1% in 2012, compared with 1.5% in 2010 and 2.4% in 2011.

Statistical Survey

Sources (unless otherwise stated): Administración General del Estado, Beatriz de Silva 4, 51001 Ceuta; tel. (956) 512616; fax (956) 511893; Instituto Nacional de Estadística, Paseo de la Castellana 183, 28071 Madrid; tel. (91) 5839100; fax (91) 5839158; internet www.ine.es; *Memoria Socioeconómico y Laboral de 2004:* Consejo Económico y Social, Edif. La Tahoma, Esquina Salud Tejero y Dueñas, Ceuta; tel. (956) 519131; fax (956) 519146; e-mail ces-ceuta@ceuta.es.

AREA AND POPULATION

Area: 19.7 sq km (7.6 sq miles).

Population (census results): 71,505 at 1 November 2001; 83,517 at 1 November 2011 (males 42,765, females 40,752).

Density (at 2011 census): 4,239 per sq km.

Population by Age and Sex (official estimates at 1 January 2013): *0–14:* 17,626 (males 8,968 females 8,658); *15–64:* 57,684 (males 30,356, females 27,328); *65 and over:* 9,194 (males 4,018, females 5,176); *Total* 84,504 (males 43,342, females 41,162).

Births, Marriages and Deaths (2012): Live births 1,127 (birth rate 14.6 per 1,000); Marriages 356 (marriage rate 4.6 per 1,000); Deaths 486 (death rate 6.3 per 1,000).

Life Expectancy (years at birth, 2011): 79.9 (males 77.2; females 82.8).

Immigration and Emigration (excl. Spanish territory, 2012): Immigrants 399; Emigrants 276.

Economically Active Population ('000 persons aged 16 years and over, 2012): Mining and utilities 0.4; Manufacturing 0.2; Construction 1.1; Trade, transport and accommodation 6.5; Finance, insurance, real estate and business services 1.9; Public administration, defence, education, health and social services 9.7; Other services 1.4; *Total employed* 21.2; Unemployed 13.3; *Total labour force* 34.5 (males 20.0, females 14.5). *April–June 2013:* Total employed 22.6; Unemployed 12.1; Total labour force 34.7.

AGRICULTURE, ETC.

Livestock (animals slaughtered, 2004): Sheep 1,025; Goats 108.

Fishing (metric tons, live weight of catch): 304.1 in 2002; 310.8 in 2003; 236.8 in 2004.

FINANCE

Currency and Exchange Rates: 100 cent = 1 euro (€). *Sterling and Dollar Equivalents* (31 May 2013): £1 sterling = 1.170 euros; US $1 = 0.769 euros; 10 euros = £8.55 = $13.01. *Average Exchange Rate* (euros per US $): 0.7550 in 2010; 0.7194 in 2011; 0.7779 in 2012. Note: The local currency was formerly the Spanish peseta. From the introduction of the euro, with Spanish participation, on 1 January 1999, a fixed exchange rate of €1 = 166.386 pesetas was in effect. Euro notes and coins were introduced on 1 January 2002. The euro and local currency circulated alongside each other until 28 February, after which the euro became the sole legal tender.

Budget (€ '000, 2012): *Revenue:* Current operations 215,157.1 (Direct taxation 9,308.2, Indirect taxation 125,013.1, Rates and other revenue 10,905.4 Current transfers 69,360.2, Property income 570.2); Capital operations 27,037.0 (Capital transfers 6,300.0, Transfers of real investments 5,500.0, Assets 1,667.0, Liabilities 13,570.0); Total 242,194.1. *Expenditure:* Current operations 201,266.4 (Wages and salaries 83,046.3, Goods and services 77,536.2, Financial 5,910.6, Current transfers 34,773.2); Capital operations 40,927.8 (Real investments 17,238.4, Capital transfers 8,278.3, Assets 1,667.0, Liabilities 13,744.1); Total 242,194.1.

Cost of Living (Consumer Price Index; base: 2006 = 100): All items 106.4 in 2009; 108.0 in 2010; 110.6 in 2011. *2012* (base: 2011 = 100): All items 102.1.

Gross Domestic Product (€ million at current prices, estimates): 1,526.2 in 2010; 1,529.1 in 2011; 1,495.2 in 2012.

Gross Domestic Product by Economic Activity (€ million at current prices, 2012, estimates): Agriculture and fishing 2.2; Manufacturing 30.5; Mining and energy 37.4; Construction 112.2; Services 1,189.4; *Sub-total* 1,371.7; Net taxes on products 123.5; *GDP at market prices* 1,495.2.

EXTERNAL TRADE

Principal Commodities (€ million, 2012): *Imports:* Milk and dairy products, eggs, honey, etc. 19.3; Mineral fuels and oils, and products thereof 297.4; Textile materials and clothing 20.4; Footwear 10.1; Machinery and equipment (incl. electrical), and parts thereof 6.6;

Vehicles (excl. rail or tram), and parts thereof 4.3; Total (incl. others) 439.4. *Exports:* Total 0.3.

Principal Trading Partners (€ million, 2012): *Imports:* China, People's Republic 39.5; France 4.9; Germany 6.3; India 4.8; Indonesia 4.2; Netherlands 26.4; Switzerland 4.2; Turkey 25.4; USA 9.9; Viet Nam 6.6; Total (incl. others) 439.4. *Exports:* Switzerland 0.1; Total (incl. others) 0.3.

Source: Foreign Trade Database, Agencia Tributaria (Madrid).

TRANSPORT

Road Traffic (Ceuta and Melilla, 2011): Vehicles registered 3,848 (Passenger cars 2,610, Lorries and vans 423, Motorcycles 802, Trucks 5, Other 8).

Shipping (domestic and international, 2012): Vessels entered 12,943; Goods handled ('000 metric tons) 2,066; Passenger movements ('000) 1,875.

Civil Aviation (2012, provisional): Flights 2,308; Passengers carried ('000) 18; Goods transported 1 metric ton.

TOURISM

Visitor Arrivals (by country of residence, 2002): France 2,653; Germany 700; Italy 1,076; Portugal 1,062; Spain 41,593; United Kingdom 1,430; USA 2,939; Total (incl. others) 61,356. *2012:* Total 77,295 (Spain 54,131).

COMMUNICATIONS MEDIA

Telephones (main lines in use, 2004): 24,849.

EDUCATION

Pre-primary (2005/06): 24 schools; 149 teachers; 2,961 students. *2012/13:* 3,929 students.

Primary (2005/06): 22 schools; 411 teachers (excl. 42 engaged in both pre-primary and primary teaching); 5,948 students. *2012/13:* 6,836 students.

Secondary: First Cycle (2005/06): 16 schools (of which 6 schools also provided second-cycle education and 5 provided vocational education, see below); 209 teachers (excl. 34 engaged in both secondary and primary teaching and 234 engaged in more than one cycle of secondary); 3,874 students. *2012/13:* 4,055 students.

Secondary: Second Cycle (2005/06): 34 teachers; 1,298 students. *2012/13:* 1,576 students.

Secondary: Vocational (2005/06): 83 teachers; 970 students. *2012/13:* 1,764 students.

Source: Ministry of Education, Madrid.

Directory

Government

HEAD OF STATE

King of Spain: HM King JUAN CARLOS I (succeeded to the throne 22 November 1975).

Government Delegate in Ceuta: FRANCISCO ANTONIO GONZÁLEZ PÉREZ.

MEMBERS OF THE SPANISH PARLIAMENT

Deputy elected to the Congress in Madrid: FRANCISCO MÁRQUEZ DE LA RUBIA (PP).

Representatives to the Senate in Madrid: LUZ ELENA SANÍN NARANJO (PP), JOSÉ LUIS SASTRE ÁLVARO (PP).

COUNCIL OF GOVERNMENT
(September 2013)

The executive is formed by members of the Partido Popular (PP).

Mayor/President: JUAN JESÚS VIVAS LARA.

Councillor of the Presidency and Government and of Employment: YOLANDA BEL BLANCA.

Councillor of Planning and Relations with Governmental Organizations: FRANCISCO MÁRQUEZ DE LA RUBIA.

Councillor of Education, Culture and Women: MARÍA ISABEL DEU DEL OLMO.

Councillor of Social Affairs: RABEA MOHAMED TONSI.

Councillor of Finance, the Economy and Human Resources: EMILIO CARREIRA RUIZ.

Councillor of Youth, Sport, Tourism and Festivals: PREMI MIRCHANDANI TAHILRAM.

Councillor of Health and Consumer Affairs: ABDELHAKIM ABDESELAM AL-LAL.

Councillor of Development: SUSANA ROMÁN BERNET.

Councillor of Environment, Public Services and Communities: GREGORIO GARCÍA CASTAÑEDA.

GOVERNMENT OFFICES

Delegación del Gobierno: Beatriz de Silva 4, 51001 Ceuta; tel. (956) 984400; fax (956) 513671; e-mail roberto@ceuta.map.es.

Office of the Mayor/President: Plaza de Africa s/n, Asamblea, 1°, 51001 Ceuta; tel. and fax (956) 528200; e-mail presidencia@ceuta.es; internet www.ceuta.es.

Council of Development: Plaza de Africa s/n, Asamblea, 3°, 51001 Ceuta; tel. and fax (956) 528240; e-mail fomento@ceuta.es.

Council of Education, Culture and Women: Plaza de Africa s/n, Asamblea, 2°, 51001 Ceuta; tel. and fax (956) 528153; e-mail educacion@ceuta.es.

Council of Employment: Edif. Ceuta Center, 1°, 51001 Ceuta; tel. and fax (956) 528386; e-mail economia@ceuta.es.

Council of Environment, Public Services and Communities: Plaza de Africa s/n, Asamblea, 3°, 51001 Ceuta; tel. and fax (956) 528164.

Council of Finance, the Economy and Human Resources: Edif. Ceuta Center, 51001 Ceuta; e-mail hacienda@ceuta.es.

Council of Health and Consumer Affairs: Carretera San Amaro 12, Ceuta; tel. (856) 200680; fax (856) 200723; e-mail sanidad@ceuta.es; internet www.ceuta.es/sanidad.

Council of Planning and Relations with Governmental Organizations: Plaza de Africa s/n, Asamblea, 3°, 51001 Ceuta.

Council of Social Affairs: Carretera San Amaro 12, Ceuta; tel. and fax (856) 200684; e-mail bsocial@ceuta.es.

Council of Youth, Sport, Tourism and Festivals: Avda de Africa s/n, Ceuta; tel. (956) 518844; fax (956) 510295.

Assembly

Election, 22 May 2011

	Seats
Partido Popular (PP)	18
Caballas*	4
Partido Socialista Obrero Español (PSOE)	3
Total	25

* Coalition of Unión Demócrata Ceutí (UDCE) and Parti Socialista del Pueblo de Ceuta (PSPC).

Election Commission

Junta Electoral de Zona de Ceuta (JEZ): Ceuta; Sec. FRANCISCO JAVIER IZQUIERDO CARBONERO.

Political Organizations

Izquierda Unida (IU): General Yagüe 4, 1°, 51001 Ceuta; tel. (956) 811941; e-mail izquierdaunidaceuta@hotmail.com; internet www.izquierda-unida.es; alliance of left-wing parties; Federal Coordinator CAYO LARA MOYA.

Partido Democrático y Social de Ceuta (PDSC): Bolivia 35, 51001 Ceuta; Muslim party; Leader MUSTAFA MIZZIAM AMMAR.

Partido Popular (PP): Teniente Arrabal 4, Edif. Ainara, Bajo, 51001 Ceuta; tel. (956) 518191; fax (956) 513218; e-mail ceuta@pp.es; internet popularesceuta.es; fmrly Alianza Popular; national-level, centre-right party; Pres. JUAN JESUS VIVAS LARA; Sec.-Gen. YOLANDA BEL BLANCA.

Partido Socialista Obrero Español (PSOE): Daóiz 1, 51001 Ceuta; tel. (956) 515553; e-mail psoeceuta@telefonica.net; internet www.ceuta.psoe.es; national-level, centre-left party; Pres. JUAN DIAZ TRIANO; Sec.-Gen. JOSÉ ANTONIO CARRACAO MELÉNDEZ.

Partido Socialista del Pueblo de Ceuta (PSPC): Echegarray 1, Local 1D, 51001 Ceuta; tel. and fax (956) 518869; e-mail pspc@pspc.info; internet www.pspc.es; f. 1986 by dissident members of PSOE and others; contested May 2011 elections as part of 'Caballas' coalition with Unión Demócrata Ceutí; Sec.-Gen. IVÁN CHAVES.

Unión Demócrata Ceutí (UDCE): Avda Teniente-Coronel Gautier 22, 2° dcha, Ceuta; Muslim party; contested May 2011 elections as part of 'Caballas' coalition with Partido Socialista del Pueblo de Ceuta; Leader MUHAMMAD ALÍ.

There are also various civic associations.

Judicial System

Tribunal Superior de Justicia de Andalucía, Ceuta y Melilla: Plaza Nueva, 10, Palacio de la Real Chancillería, 18071 Granada, Spain; tel. (958) 002600; fax (958) 002720; e-mail webmaster.ius@juntadeandalucia.es; internet www.juntadeandalucia.es; Pres. SUSANA DÍAZ PACHECO.

Religion

CHRISTIANITY

The Roman Catholic Church

Bishop of Cádiz and Ceuta: ANTONIO CEBALLOS ATIENZA (resident in Cádiz), Vicar-Gen. FRANCISCO CORRERO TOCÓN, Obispado de Ceuta, Plaza de Nuestra Señora de Africa, 51001 Ceuta; tel. (956) 517732; fax (956) 513208; e-mail obispadoceuta@planalfa.es; internet www.obispadodecadizyceuta.org.

OTHER RELIGIONS

Ceuta has a large Muslim population (estimated at around 30,000), as well as Jewish and Hindu communities.

The Press

El Faro de Ceuta: Sargento Mena 8, 51001 Ceuta; tel. (956) 524035; fax (956) 524147; e-mail ceuta@grupofaro.es; internet www.elfaroceutamelilla.es; f. 1934; morning; Pres. RAFAEL MONTERO PALACIOS; Editors-in-Chief JOSÉ M. GALLARDO, TAMARA CRESPO; circ. 5,000.

El Pueblo de Ceuta: Independencia 11, 1°, 51001 Ceuta; tel. (956) 514367; fax (956) 517650; e-mail elpuebloredaccion@telefonica.net; internet www.elpueblodeceuta.es; f. 1995; daily; Dir and Editor-in-Chief SALVADOR VIVANCOS CANALES.

NEWS AGENCY

Agencia EFE: Milán Astray 1, 1°, Of. 8, 51001 Ceuta; tel. (956) 517550; fax (956) 516639; e-mail ceuta@agenciaefe.net; Correspondent RAFAEL PEÑA SOLER.

PRESS ASSOCIATION

Asociación de la Prensa: Beatriz de Silva 14, 1° E, 51001 Ceuta; tel. (956) 403713; fax (956) 528205; Pres. RAFAEL PEÑA SOLER.

Broadcasting

RADIO

Onda Cero Radio Ceuta: Delgado Serrano 1, 1° dcha, 51001 Ceuta; tel. (956) 200068; fax (956) 200179; internet www.ondacero.es; Dir RAFAEL ROMAGUERA MENA.

Radio Nacional de España: Real 90, 51001 Ceuta; tel. (956) 524688; fax (956) 519067; e-mail prensa@rtve.es; internet www.rtve.es; Dir EDUARDO SÁNCHEZ DORADO.

Radio Popular de Ceuta/COPE: Sargento Mena 8, 1°, 11701 Ceuta; tel. (956) 524200; fax (956) 524202; internet www.cope.es; Dir DANIEL OLIVA.

Radio Televisión Ceuta: Avda Alcalde Sánchez, Prado 3–5, Ceuta; tel. and fax (956) 524420; e-mail televidente@rtvce.es; internet www.rtvce.es; f. 2000; owned by Sociedad Española de Radiodifusión; commercial; Dir DANIEL OLIVA MARTÍN.

TELEVISION

Radio Televisión Ceuta: Real 90, Portón 4, 1° dcha, 51001 Ceuta; tel. (956) 511820; fax (956) 516820; internet www.rtvce.es; Dir MANUEL GONZÁLEZ BOLORINO.

Finance

BANKING

In 2007 there were nine banks operating in Ceuta, all of which were based in mainland Spain.

Banco Bilbao Vizcaya Argentaria (BBVA): Gonzalez de la Vega 8, 51001 Ceuta; tel. (956) 201238; fax (956) 510585; internet www.bbva.es; 4 brs.

Banco de España: Plaza de España 2, 51001 Ceuta; tel. (956) 513253; fax (956) 513108; internet www.bde.es.

Banco Español de Crédito (Banesto): Camoens 5, 51001 Ceuta; tel. (956) 524028; internet www.banesto.es.

Banco Popular Español: Paseo del Revellín 1, 51001 Ceuta; tel. (956) 515340; fax (956) 512970; internet www.bancopopular.es.

Banco Santander Central Hispano (BSCH): Paseo del Revellín 17–19, 51001 Ceuta; tel. (956) 511371; internet www.gruposantander.es; 2 brs.

Caja de Ahorros y Pensiones de Barcelona (La Caixa): Gran Vía s/n, 51001 Ceuta; tel. (956) 515886; fax (956) 513972; internet www.lacaixa.es; 4 brs.

Caja Duero: Sargento Coriat 5, 51001 Ceuta; tel. (956) 518040; fax (956) 517019; tel. www.cajaduero.es; 1 br.

Caja Madrid: Plaza de los Reyes s/n, 51001 Ceuta; tel. (956) 524016; fax (956) 524017; internet www.cajamadrid.es; 6 brs.

Montes de Piedad y Caja de Ahorros de Ronda, Cádiz, Almería, Málaga y Antequera (Unicaja): Paseo Revellín 21, 51001 Ceuta; tel. (956) 518340; fax (956) 519561; internet www.unicaja.es; 2 brs.

INSURANCE

MAPFRE: Paseo Marina Española 92, Edif. Patio Paramo, 51001 Ceuta; tel. (956) 519638; fax (956) 513916; e-mail balfaro@mapfre.com; internet www.mapfre.com; Commercial Man. BORJA ALFARO INFANTE; 3 offices.

Trade and Industry

Cámara Oficial de Comercio, Industria y Navegación: Dueñas 2, 51001 Ceuta; tel. (956) 509590; fax (956) 509589; e-mail camerceuta@camaras.org; internet www.camaraceuta.org; chamber of commerce; Pres. LUIS MORENO NARANJO; Sec.-Gen. MARÍA DEL ROSARIO ESPINOSA SUÁREZ.

Confederación de Empresarios de Ceuta: Paseo de las Palmeras, Edif. Corona 26–28, 51001 Ceuta; tel. (956) 200038; fax (956) 512010; e-mail info@confeceuta.es; internet www.confeceuta.es; employers' confed; Pres. RAFAEL MONTERO AVALOS; Sec.-Gen. ALEJANDRO RAMÍREZ HURTADO.

UTILITIES

Aguas de Ceuta Empresa Municipal, SA (ACEMSA): Solis 1, Edif. San Luis, Ceuta; tel. (956) 524619; e-mail aguasdeceuta@acemsa.es; internet www.acemsa.es; Pres. SUSANA ROMÁN BERNET.

Empresa de Alumbrado Eléctrico de Ceuta SA: Beatriz de Silva 2, Ceuta; tel. (956) 511901; e-mail info@electricadeceuta.com; internet www.electricadeceuta.com; generates and transmits electricity; Rep. ALBERTO RAMÓN GAITÁN RODRÍGUEZ.

TRADE UNION

Comisiones Obreras de Ceuta: Alcalde Fructuoso Miaja 1, 51001 Ceuta; tel. (956) 516243; fax (956) 517991; e-mail ccoo.ce@ceuta.ccoo.es; internet www ceuta.ccoo.es; 3,500 mems (2012); Sec.-Gen. JUAN LUIS ARÓSTEGUI RUIZ.

Transport

Much of the traffic between Spain and Morocco passes through Ceuta; there are ferry services to Algeciras, Melilla, Málaga and Almería. Plans for an airport are under consideration. Helicopter services to Málaga are provided by Helisureste. There were 37 km of paved roads in Ceuta in 2010. The Port of Ceuta is one of the most important in the Mediterranean. In 2012 2.1m. metric tons of goods, 1.9m. passengers and 12,943 ships passed through the port.

Port of Ceuta: Autoridad Portuaria de Ceuta, Muelle de España s/n, 51001 Ceuta; tel. (956) 527000; fax (956) 527001; e-mail apceuta@puertodeceuta.com; internet www.puertodeceuta.com; Pres. JOSÉ FRANCISCO TORRADO LÓPEZ.

Acciona Trasmediterránea: Muelle Cañorero Dato 6, 51001 Ceuta; tel. (956) 505390; fax (956) 504714; e-mail info@trasmediterranea.es; internet www.trasmediterranea.es; f. 1917; services between Algeciras and Ceuta.

Tourism

Visitors are attracted by the historical monuments, the Parque Marítimo and the museums, as well as by the Shrine of Our Lady of Africa. There were 77,295 visitors to Ceuta in 2012, of whom 54,131 were from mainland Spain.

Servicios Turísticos de Ceuta: Baluarte de los Mallorquines, Edrissis s/n, 51001 Ceuta; tel. (856) 200560; fax (856) 200565; e-mail turismo@ceuta.es; internet www.ceuta.es/turismo.

Defence

Military authority is vested in a commandant-general. The enclaves are attached to the military region of Sevilla. In August 2003 Spain had 8,100 troops deployed in Spanish North Africa, compared with 21,000 in mid-1987. Two-thirds of Ceuta's land area are used exclusively for military purposes.

Commandant-General: Gen. José Manuel Sanz Román.

Education

The conventional Spanish facilities are available; however, there are also teachers of the Islamic religion in the city. Enrolment at primary schools in Ceuta totalled 6,836 in 2012/13, while the first cycle (from the ages of 12 to 16) of secondary education had an enrolment of 4,055 students; secondary schools enrolled some 1,576 students for the *bachillerato*, and 1,764 students were enrolled on vocational courses. In higher education, links with the University of Granada are maintained and there is a branch of the Spanish open university (Universidad Nacional de Educación a Distancia—UNED).

MELILLA

Geography

Melilla is situated north of the Moroccan town of Nador, on the eastern side of a small peninsula jutting out into the Mediterranean Sea. It was retained by Spain as a *plaza de soberanía* (a presidio, or fortified enclave, over which Spain has full sovereign rights) when Morocco became independent in 1956, and was administered as part of Málaga Province until 1995. Melilla is an active port. The territory's area totals 12.5 sq km. At the census of November 2011, the population (including the islets governed with Melilla) was recorded at 81,323, giving a density of 6,506 people per sq km.

The Peñón de Vélez de la Gomera, Peñón de Alhucemas and Chafarinas Islands

These rocky islets are administered with Melilla. The Peñón de Vélez de la Gomera is situated 117 km south-east of Ceuta, lying less than 85 m from the Moroccan coast, to which it is connected by a narrow strip of sand. This rocky promontory, of 1 ha in area, rises to an altitude of 77 m above sea level, an ancient fortress being situated at its summit. The Peñón de Alhucemas lies 155 km south-east of Ceuta and 100 km west of Melilla, being 300 m from the Moroccan coast and the town of al-Hocima. It occupies an area of 1.5 ha. The uninhabited rocks of Mar and Tierra lie immediately to the east of the Peñón de Alhucemas. The three Chafarinas Islands (from west to east: Isla del Congreso, Isla de Isabel II and Isla del Rey) are situated 48 km east of Melilla and about 3.5 km from the Moroccan fishing port of Ras el-Ma (Cabo de Agua). The islands are of volcanic origin, their combined area being 61 ha. Spain maintains small military bases on some of the islets.

History

Spain secured control of Melilla in 1556, the town having been conquered in 1497 by the ducal house of Medina Sidonia, which had been empowered to appoint the governor and seneschal with the approval of the Spanish Crown. Rif tribesmen attacked Melilla in 1562–64. Later still, the Sultan of Morocco, Mulai Ismail (1672–1727), assaulted the town in 1687, 1696 and 1697. Sultan Muhammad b. Abdallah (1757–90) besieged Melilla in 1771 and 1774. An agreement concluded between Spain and Morocco in 1780 at Aranjuez, Spain, led, however, in the following year, to a peaceful delimitation of the Melilla enclave. There was a brief period of tension in 1844 and, subsequently, in 1861, under the terms of an agreement signed after Spain's Moroccan campaign of 1860, Melilla's boundaries were extended. Conflict with the Rif tribesmen gave rise in 1893–94 to the so-called 'War of Melilla', which ended with a settlement negotiated at Marrakesh, Morocco. It was not until 1909 that Spanish forces, after a hard campaign, occupied the mountainous hinterland of Melilla between the Wadi Kert and the Wadi Muluya—a region in which, some 15 km behind Melilla, were situated the rich iron mines of Beni Bu Ifrur. In July 1921 the Rif tribes, under the command of Abd al-Krim, defeated a Spanish force near Annual and threatened Melilla itself. Only in 1926, with the final defeat of the Rif rebellion, was Spanish control restored over the Melilla region. Melilla was the first Spanish town to rise against the Government of the Popular Front on 17 July 1936, at the beginning of the Spanish Civil War. (See the section on Ceuta for further details of the status of the two enclaves within Spain, and of Spanish relations with Morocco.)

The Chafarinas Islands came under Spanish control in 1847. The Peñón de Alhucemas was occupied in 1673. The Peñón de Vélez de la Gomera, about 80 km further west, came under Spanish rule in 1508, but was then lost not long afterwards and reoccupied in 1564. All three possessions are, like Melilla, incorporated into the province of Málaga. Spanish sovereignty over the uninhabited island of Perejil (Laila), which lies north-west of Ceuta, is uncertain.

The introduction by the central Government of a new aliens law in July 1985 required all foreigners resident in Spain to register with the authorities or risk expulsion. In Ceuta most Muslims possessed the necessary documentation; however, in Melilla (where the Muslim community was estimated to number 27,000, of whom only 7,000 held Spanish nationality) thousands of Muslims staged a protest against the new legislation in November, as a result of which the central Government gave an assurance that it would assist the full integration into Spanish society of Muslims in the enclaves, and promised to improve conditions. In December an inter-ministerial commission, headed by the Minister of the Interior, was created to formulate plans for investment in the enclaves' social services and other public facilities. Tension in Melilla was renewed in that month, when 40,000 members of the Spanish community attended a demonstration in support of the new aliens law. In January 1986 the brutality with which the police dispersed a peaceful rally by Muslim women provoked widespread outrage. In addition to the hunger strike already being undertaken by a number of Muslims, a two-day general strike was called. In February, however, the Ministry of the Interior in Madrid and the leaders of the Muslim communities of Ceuta and Melilla reached agreement on the application of the aliens law. A joint commission to study the Muslims' problems was to be established, and a census to determine those eligible for Spanish citizenship was to be carried out. The agreement was denounced as unconstitutional by the Spanish populations of the enclaves. The Minister of the Interior visited the territories in April and reiterated that the implementation of the aliens law (the deadline for registration having been extended to 31 March 1986, following three postponements) would not entail mass expulsions of Muslim immigrants.

After negotiations with representatives of the Muslim community, in May 1986 the Government agreed to grant Spanish nationality to more than 2,400 Muslims resident in the enclaves. By mid-1986, however, the number of Muslims applying for Spanish nationality had reached several thousand. As a result of delays in the processing of the applications by the authorities, Aomar Muhammadi Dudú, the leader of the newly founded Muslim party, Partido de los Demócratas de Melilla (PDM), accused the Government of failing to fulfil its pledge to the Muslim residents. At the general election of June 1986 the ruling Partido Socialista Obrero Español (PSOE) was defeated by the centre-right Coalición Popular in Melilla, the result indicating the strong opposition of local Spaniards to the Government's plan to integrate the Muslim population. Tight security surrounded the elections in Melilla, where 'parallel elections', resulting in a vote of confidence in the PDM leader, were held by the Muslim community. The elections were accompanied by several days of unrest, involving right-wing Christians and local Muslims, and there were further violent clashes between the police and Christian demonstrators demanding the resignation of the Government Delegate in Melilla, Andrés Moreno.

Following talks in 1986 in Madrid between representatives of the main political parties in Melilla and the Ministry of the Interior, concessions to the enclave included the replacement of Andrés Moreno as Government Delegate by Manuel Céspedes. The Madrid negotiations were denounced by Dudú, who nevertheless in September agreed to accept a senior post in the Ministry of the Interior in Madrid, with responsibility for relations with the Muslim communities of Spain. It was reported in October that Dudú had travelled to Rabat for secret discussions with the Moroccan Minister of the Interior. In November Muslim leaders announced that they wished to establish their own administration in the enclave, in view of the Madrid Government's failure to fulfil its promise of Spanish citizenship for Muslim residents. The Spanish Minister of the Interior, however, reiterated an assurance of the Government's intention to carry out the process of integration of the Muslim community. Later in the month Muslim traders staged a four-day closure of their businesses to draw attention to their plight, and thousands of Muslims took part in a peaceful demonstration reaffirming support for Dudú, who had resigned from his Madrid post after only two months in office. (Dudú subsequently went into exile in Morocco and lost the support of Melilla's Muslim community.) There was a serious escalation of tension in February 1987, when a member of the Muslim community died from gunshot wounds, following renewed racial clashes.

In February 1988 it was announced that, in accordance with European Community (now European Union—EU) regulations, Moroccan citizens would in due course require visas to enter Spain. Entry to Spanish North Africa, however, was to be exempt from the new ruling. In August 1990 Spain granted its Government Delegate in Melilla direct powers to expel illegal residents from the territory.

At the general election held in October 1989 the results in Melilla were declared invalid, following the discovery of serious irregularities. At the repeated ballot held in March 1990, at which some 52% of the electorate voted, both Senado (Senate) seats and the one seat in the Congreso de los Diputados (Congress of Deputies—the lower house in the Spanish Parliament) were won by the Partido Popular (PP), the latter result stripping the PSOE of its overall majority in the Congreso. The Government Delegate in Melilla claimed that voting irregularities had again occurred.

Following the submission of draft autonomy statutes for Ceuta and Melilla to the Congreso de los Diputados in Madrid for discussion in October 1991, in March 1993 the PP submitted its own draft statute for Melilla to the central Government, which immediately condemned the document as unconstitutional. All political parties in Melilla, except the PSOE, demanded that a local referendum be held on the issue of autonomy. At the subsequent general election held in June, the PSOE candidate defeated the incumbent PP deputy; the PP also lost one of its two seats in the Senado.

Following their approval by the Congreso de los Diputados in December 1994, the autonomy statutes were ratified by the Senado in February 1995. (See chapter on Ceuta for further details.) Elections for the new local assemblies were held in May. In Melilla, where the level of participation was less than 62%, the PP won 14 of the 25 seats, the PSOE five seats, Coalición por Melilla (CpM—a new Muslim grouping), four seats and the right-wing Unión del Pueblo Melillense (UPM) two seats. Ignacio Velázquez (PP/Partido Nacionalista de Melilla) was returned to the position of Mayor/President.

A general election was held in March 1996, when the PSOE lost its seat in the lower house to the PP, which also took Melilla's seats in the Senado. At the end of the month thousands of Muslims took part in a demonstration, organized by CpM, to protest against their marginal position in society.

In March 1997 a motion of censure against Ignacio Velázquez resulted in the Mayor/President's defeat, owing to the defection to the opposition of two PP councillors, Enrique Palacios and Abdelmalik Tahar. The latter subsequently absconded to the Canary Islands. The opposition then declared Enrique Palacios to be Mayor/President, although the central Government continued to recognize Velázquez as the rightful incumbent. In May, for the first time, the Mayor/Presidents of Ceuta and Melilla attended a conference of the autonomous regions' presidents, held in Madrid. Despite the attempted 'coup' in Melilla, the territory was represented by Velázquez. In November, from Tenerife, Abdelmalik Tahar accused Velázquez and five associates of having subjected him to blackmail and threats, as a result of which he had relinquished his seat on the Assembly, thereby permitting the PP to replace him and to regain its majority. In December Tahar, who was now under police protection, declared to the investigating judge that he had been offered a substantial bribe. Following an appeal by Palacios and a judicial ruling that permitted the successful revival of the motion of censure against Ignacio Velázquez in February 1998, Palacios took office as Mayor/President of Melilla, accusing his predecessor, furthermore, of serious financial mismanagement. A new motion of censure, presented by the PP and urging that (despite the bribery charges against him) Ignacio Velázquez be restored to office, was deemed to be illegal and therefore rejected in a decree issued by Palacios. In July Palacios accused the PP of having employed public funds to secure the votes of some 2,500 Muslims at the 1995 local elections, the bribes reportedly having taken the form of building materials for the purposes of residential repairs. The allegations were denied by the PP.

Meanwhile, in June 1997 police reinforcements were drafted into Melilla following renewed disturbances in which one immigrant died. More than 100 illegal immigrants were immediately returned to Morocco as part of a special security operation, and on the same day of action a total of 873 Moroccans were denied entry to Melilla. (More than 10,000 Moroccans daily continued to cross the border legally, in order to work in the enclave.) In July a young Moroccan was shot and wounded, and two civil guards were injured, during a confrontation on the Melilla border. In August various non-governmental organizations condemned the rudimentary conditions in which some 800 illegal immigrants were being held in Melilla. It was further announced that a reception centre housing about 100 Algerians was to close, owing to unsatisfactory conditions. In the same month hundreds of Moroccan children, who had been begging on the streets, were returned to their homeland. The increasing involvement of organized criminal gangs in such activities continued to cause disquiet. In August the Spanish General Prosecutor demanded emergency measures to address the immigrant crisis, having already urged the Ministry of the Interior in June to find an immediate solution.

In January 1999, after 12 years' exile in Morocco, Aomar Muhammadi Dudú returned to Melilla, in preparation for the local elections scheduled to be held in June. At the elections the most successful party in Melilla was the Grupo Independiente Liberal (GIL), recently founded by Jesús Gil, the controversial Mayor of Marbella. The GIL secured seven of the 25 seats in the Melilla Assembly. The two newly elected PSOE councillors defied a central directive to vote with the five PP delegates (in order to obstruct the accession of the GIL to the city presidency), and instead gave their support to Mustafa Hamed Aberchán of CpM, which had won five seats. Aberchán was thus elected to replace Palacios as Mayor/President of Melilla. In July Aberchán and the GIL agreed to form a minority Government.

Following a rift between CpM and the GIL, in September 1999 the Mayor/President of Melilla attempted to form a minority government with representatives of the Partido Independiente de Melilla (PIM), recently established by Palacios. In October, however, Aberchán reached a broad accommodation with members of the PP and the UPM that enabled him to remain in office. In November the Melilla branch of the GIL announced that it was to operate independently of the mainland party. In the same month, following a new agreement between Aberchán and the GIL, the latter announced its intention to renew its participation in the Government of Melilla. As a result, the socialist councillors withdrew from the administration. In December Aberchán announced the composition of a new coalition Government. Crispin Lozano, the local leader of the GIL, was appointed First Vice-President, while Palacios became Second Vice-President. Also in that month Ignacio Velázquez, the former PP Mayor/President of Melilla, was barred from public office for six years, having been found guilty of neglecting his duty during his period in office. He was, however, cleared of charges relating to the misappropriation of public funds. In January 2002 Velázquez resigned as Councillor of the Presidency, after the Supreme Court upheld his conviction.

In May 2000 two GIL deputies and one UPM representative defected to the opposition. Aberchán declared that, despite his Government losing its majority, he would not resign. The opposition announced subsequently that they would request a vote of no confidence in Aberchán's Government at the earliest opportunity. In early July the remaining five GIL members left the Government and joined the opposition. The opposition subsequently introduced a motion of censure against Aberchán, whom they accused of nepotism, a lack of transparency and of harassment of the opposition. Aberchán, who described the accusations as being racially motivated, announced that CpM was to withdraw from the legislature. In mid-July some 2,000 Muslim citizens of Melilla demonstrated in support of Aberchán. At the same time, the Second Vice-President of Melilla, Enrique Palacios, suspended the motion of censure by decree, reportedly without having consulted Aberchán. (Palacios was subsequently barred from public office for seven years, having been found guilty of perverting the course of justice.) The opposition, who had criticized the decree as 'illegal and possibly criminal', later overturned it in the courts, and the vote on the motion of censure against Aberchán was therefore able to proceed. The motion was adopted in September, with the support of 16 of the 25 deputies, and the UPM leader, Juan José Imbroda Ortiz, was elected as Mayor/President.

At the elections of May 2003 a coalition of the PP and the UPM won 15 seats, with CpM taking seven. As a result, Imbroda was able to remain in office. The success of the PP represented, in part, a concerted effort to prevent a perpetuation of the unstable governance that had characterized the previous four years under the GIL. The move to the right was also seen as a response by voters of Spanish origin to increasing fears about immigration.

At the general election held in March 2004 the PP retained its support from Melilla. In May the Government of Melilla announced plans to improve security along the border with Morocco; however, in August, in the first mass entry for three years, approximately 450 people attempted to enter Melilla illegally by climbing the security fence. It was believed that up to 40 people succeeded in entering the territory.

During August–October 2005 increasing numbers of would-be immigrants attempted to scale the security barriers separating Melilla from Morocco, leading to the deaths of a number of people. In October six potential immigrants were reportedly shot in clashes with Moroccan security forces. It was announced that one barrier would be doubled in height, and that border security would be increased; plans to build a third barrier were also unveiled. In the same month the Spanish Government announced funding of €17m. for security in Melilla.

At the local elections held in May 2007 the PP obtained 15 seats in the Assembly, the same number as previously, thereby retaining its overall majority; CpM and the PSOE each won five seats. The constitution of the Assembly was delayed until early July owing to an appeal against the election result levied by CpM, which alleged that the PP had engaged in acts of electoral fraud, including the falsification of postal ballots. The appeal was rejected by the Supreme Court of Justice of Andalusia, which ruled that the evidence presented by CpM was not sufficient to indicate irregularity. Imbroda was subsequently re-elected as Mayor/President.

A two-day visit to Melilla and Ceuta by King Juan Carlos and Queen Sofía in November 2007 was strongly condemned by the Moroccan authorities (see the chapter on Ceuta). Several thousand Moroccans, including politicians and trade union representatives, took part in a demonstration at the border with Melilla to protest against the presence of the Spanish King. The Government of Melilla issued a statement accusing the Moroccan Government of interfering in Spanish domestic affairs by criticizing the visit.

At the March 2008 general election the PP retained Melilla's one seat in the Congreso de los Diputados, although only by a narrow margin, as well as its two seats in the Senado. Later that month Esther Donoso García-Sacristán was appointed as Councillor of Contracting and Heritage to replace María del Carmen Dueñas Martínez, who had been elected to the Senado.

Two suspected Islamist militants were detained in Melilla in April 2008, in accordance with international arrest warrants issued by the Moroccan Government over their alleged involvement in terrorist activities. These included a series of suicide bombings launched against Western targets in Casablanca in May 2003, in which 45 people died.

Attempts by illegal migrants to cross into Melilla from Morocco increased in October 2008 after heavy flooding damaged the recently fortified border fence. Although additional security forces were deployed to patrol the areas affected, it was reported that in one incident almost one-half of a group of some 60 sub-Saharan African migrants succeeded in entering Melilla; 17 others were reportedly arrested. In the weeks that followed further attempts were made to breach the security fence: more than 150 people were reported to have tried to enter Melilla during November and a number of people were injured in clashes with Moroccan and Spanish security forces.

In April 2011 Antonio María Claret García was sworn in as Government Delegate in Melilla. At the local elections, which took place on 22 May, the PP won 15 seats, the same number as it had held in the previous two Assemblies. CpM took six seats, while the PSOE's representation declined to just two. The Partido Populares en Libertad, which had been established in March by former PP Mayor/President Ignacio Velázquez, also won two seats. A new Council of Government, under Imbroda, took office in mid-July. At the general election held on 20 November, the PP retained both Melilla's seat in the Congreso de los Diputados and its two seats in the Senado. In January 2012 Abdelmalik el-Barkani Abdelkader was sworn in as Government Delegate to Melilla, becoming the first Muslim to hold that post. In January 2013 the district court began an investigation into accusations that funds totalling €70,000 from the Council of Culture and Festivals intended for the production of a book discussing the history of Judaism in Melilla had been diverted. The opposition PSOE demanded the resignation of the Councillor, Simi Chocrón Chocrón. However, Chocrón denied any wrongdoing. The case remained under investigation in late 2013.

Economy

Melilla, a free port, is of little economic importance to Spain, while the other possessions governed with Melilla are of negligible significance. The chief reason for Spanish retention of the areas is their predominantly Spanish population, though they also serve a strategic military function. The population of Melilla increased at an annual average rate of 0.8% in 2002–09. However, the census of November 2011 recorded the population at 81,323. There are large numbers of immigrants from Morocco in Melilla.

In 1991 Melilla's gross domestic product (GDP) was 30.5% below the average for the whole of Spain. In that year the average disposable family income was 84.8% that of Spain. Social security benefits accounted for 24.3% of the average family income. By 1996, although family income per capita was 6.0% below the Spanish average, purchasing power was 6.6% higher. However, an unofficial report issued in October 1996 classified Melilla as by far the poorest city in Spain. GDP at current prices was estimated at €1,321.8m. in 2012. In 2012, according to official estimates, the GDP of Melilla was equivalent to €16,981 per head, ranking 17th (in terms of GDP per head) in a list of 19 Spanish autonomous regions (the 17 Autonomous Communities, together with Ceuta and Melilla).

Agriculture, Industry and Tourism

In 2012 agriculture and fishing contributed an estimated 0.1% to GDP, while energy contributed 4.0%, construction 8.7% and manufacturing 1.5%. The services sector was by far the largest, contributing 85.7% in that year. Melilla's hinterland is small, and development is restricted by the lack of suitable building land. Most of the population's food has to be imported, with the exception of fish, which is obtained locally. Sardines and anchovies are the most important items. More important to the economy is the port activity (although Melilla's port is less busy than Ceuta's), most exports taking the form of fuel supplied—at very competitive rates—to ships. Most of the fuel comes from the Spanish refinery in Tenerife. Melilla's port received a total of 1,551 vessels in 2012; in that year 955,000 metric tons of freight were handled by the port. In 2012 Melilla's trade deficit was €191.7m.; imports totalled €193.3m., while exports totalled just €1.6m. Foodstuffs accounted for €86.4m. (44.7%) of imports and textile materials and clothing €21.1m. (10.9%). The leading sources of imports in 2012 were the People's Republic of China (27.4%), the USA (17.3%), Viet Nam (8.8%), Canada (8.2%), Thailand (7.1%) and India (6.4%). Commercial agricultural activity in the enclave is negligible, and industry is limited to meeting some of the everyday needs of the city.

Tourism is a significant contributor to the territory's economy. In 2002 a total of 31,812 tourists entered Melilla, of whom 23,648 were Spanish. In 2012 49,778 visitors arrived in Melilla, of whom 36,697 were Spanish. Successive defence cuts led not only to fears for Spanish North Africa's security, but also to losses in income from military personnel stationed in the territories.

In the second quarter of 2013 the total labour force was estimated at 33,000, of whom 9,500 (28.8%) were unemployed.

Finance and Inward Investment

Upon the accession of Spain to the European Community (now European Union—EU) in January 1986, Ceuta and Melilla were considered as Spanish cities and European territory, and joined the Community as part of Spain. They retained their status as free ports. The statutes of autonomy, adopted in early 1995, envisaged the continuation of the territories' fiscal benefits. On 28 February 2002 euro notes and coins entered circulation as sole legal tender in the enclaves. In June 1994 the EU announced substantial regional aid. With assistance from the European Social Fund, a programme of employment and vocational training for Melilla was announced in 1996. Projected Spanish investment was €16.9m. in 2002 and €45.4m. in 2003, the latter including some €16.7m. for the expansion of the airport. However, the successive enlargements of the EU that took place in 2004 and 2007 limited Spain's access to EU aid, with the result that subsidies for Melilla were to be progressively reduced during the period 2007–13, with a view to their eventual withdrawal. In 2006 it was announced that the central Government would invest some €83m. in 2007–13, 47% less than had been invested in 2000–06.

Melilla's budget for 2012 was €237.9m. The city's consolidated budget for 2012 included current and capital transfers from the Spanish state of €109.2m. and €11.6m., respectively. The annual rate of inflation averaged 2.2% in 2006–11; consumer prices increased by 1.7% in 2012, compared with 2.2% in 2010 and 2.3% in 2011.

Statistical Survey

Source (unless otherwise stated): Instituto Nacional de Estadística, Paseo de la Castellana 183, 28071 Madrid; tel. (91) 5839100; fax (91) 5839158; internet www.ine.es.

AREA AND POPULATION

Area: 12.5 sq km (4.8 sq miles).

Population (census results): 66,411 at 1 November 2001; 81,323 at 1 November 2011 (males 42,067, females 39,256).

Density (at 2011 census): 6,506 per sq km.

Population by Age and Sex (official estimates at 1 January 2013): *0–14:* 19,412 (males 10,030, females 9,382); *15–64:* 56,201 (males 29,663, females 26,538); *65 and over:* 8,150 (males 3,475, females 4,675); *Total* 83,763 (males 43,168, females 40,595).

Births, Marriages and Deaths (2012): Live births 1,513 (birth rate 19.4 per 1,000); Marriages 377 (marriage rate 4.8 per 1,000); Deaths 471 (death rate 6.1 per 1,000).

Life Expectancy (years at birth, 2011): 80.4 (males 77.4; females 83.6).

Immigration and Emigration (excl. Spanish territory, 2012): Immigrants 983; Emigrants 1,709.

Economically Active Population ('000 persons aged 16 years and over, 2012): Mining and utilities 0.3; Manufacturing 0.2; Construction 1.9; Trade, transport and accommodation 5.6; Information and communication 0.1; Finance, insurance, real estate and business services 2.7; Public administration, defence, education, health and social services 10.2; Other services 2.0; *Total employed* 23.0; Unemployed 9.2; *Total labour force* 32.2 (males 19.3, females 12.9). *April–June 2013:* Total employed 23.5; Unemployed 9.5; Total labour force 33.0.

FINANCE

Currency and Exchange Rates: 100 cent = 1 euro (€). *Sterling and Dollar Equivalents* (31 May 2013): £1 sterling = 1.170 euros; US $1 = 0.769 euros; 10 euros = £8.55 = $13.01. *Average Exchange Rate* (euros per US $): 0.7550 in 2010; 0.7194 in 2011; 0.7779 in 2012. Note: The local currency was formerly the Spanish peseta. From the introduction of the euro, with Spanish participation, on 1 January 1999, a fixed exchange rate of €1 = 166.386 pesetas was in effect. Euro notes and coins were introduced on 1 January 2002. The euro and local currency circulated alongside each other until 28 February, after which the euro became the sole legal tender.

Budget (€ '000, 2012): *Revenue:* Current operations 208.515.4 (Direct taxation 13,399.4, Indirect taxation 68,900.0, Rates and other revenue 16,775.4, Current transfers 109,160.6, Property income 280.0); Capital operations 29,405.6 (Capital transfers 11,600.8, Transfers of real investments 3,345.1, Assets 459.7, Liabilities 14,000.0); Total 237,921.0. *Expenditure:* Current operations 199,327.9 (Wages and salaries 68,342.1, Goods and services 92,164.9, Financial 3,808.4, Current transfers 35,012.4); Capital operations 38,593.2 (Real investments 21,870.3, Capital transfers 1,619.0, Assets 459.7, Liabilities 14,644.2); Total 237,921.0.

Cost of Living (Consumer Price Index, annual averages; base: 2006 = 100): All items 106.8 in 2009; 109.1 in 2010; 111.6 in 2011. *2012* (base: 2011 = 100): All items 101.7.

Gross Domestic Product (€ million at current prices, estimates): 1,360.0 in 2010; 1,356.4 in 2011; 1,321.8 in 2012.

Gross Domestic Product by Economic Activity (€ million at current prices, 2012, estimates): Agriculture and fishing 1.4; Manufacturing 18.2; Mining and energy 48.0; Construction 105.6; Services 1,039.5; *Sub-total* 1,212.7; Net taxes on products 109.1; *GDP at market prices* 1,321.8.

EXTERNAL TRADE

Principal Commodities (€ million, 2012): *Imports:* Fruits and vegetables 44.2; Coffee, tea, maté and spices 27.2; Cereals 15.0; Textile materials and clothing 21.1; Footwear 3.7; Vehicles (excl. rail or tram), and parts thereof 3.9; Total (incl. others) 193.3. *Exports:* Man-made filaments 0.4; Plastic, rubber and their articles 0.4; Total (incl. others) 1.6.

Principal Trading Partners (€ million, 2012): *Imports:* Brazil 6.3; Canada 15.8; China, People's Republic 52.9; France 2.2; Germany 8.7; India 12.4; Indonesia 2.2; Iran 2.6; Morocco 2.0; Netherlands 8.7; Thailand 13.8; USA 33.4; Viet Nam 17.0; Total (incl. others) 193.3. *Exports:* Morocco 1.1; Total (incl. others) 1.6.

Source: Foreign Trade Database, Agencia Tributaria (Madrid).

TRANSPORT

Road Traffic (Ceuta and Melilla, 2011): Vehicles registered 3,848 (Passenger cars 2,610, Lorries and vans 423, Motorcycles 802, Trucks 5, Other 8).

Shipping (domestic and international, 2012): Vessels entered 1,551; Goods handled ('000 metric tons) 955; Passenger movements ('000) 811.

Civil Aviation (2012, provisional): Flights 9,433; Passengers transported ('000) 308; Goods transported 236 metric tons.

TOURISM

Visitor Arrivals (by country of residence, 2002): France 476; Germany 432; Italy 331; Netherlands 425; Spain 23,648; Total (incl. others) 31,812. *2012:* Total 49,778 (Spain 36,697).

EDUCATION

Pre-primary (2005/06): 20 schools; 159 teachers, 3,237 students. *2012/13:* 4,442 students.

Primary (2005/06): 15 schools; 422 teachers (excl. 20 engaged in both pre-primary and primary teaching); 5,996 students. *2012/13:* 6,917 students.

Secondary: First Cycle (2005/06): 9 schools (of which 4 schools also provided second-cycle education and 5 provided vocational education); 255 teachers (excl. 10 engaged in both primary and secondary teaching, and 198 engaged in more than one secondary cycle, and excl. 33 specialists); 3,923 students. *2012/13:* 4,372 students.

Secondary: Second Cycle (2005/06): 53 teachers; 1,339 students. *2012/13:* 1,711 students.

Secondary: Vocational (2005/06): 65 teachers; 703 students. *2012/13:* 1,287 students.

Source: Ministry of Education, Madrid.

Directory

Government

HEAD OF STATE

King of Spain: HM King Juan Carlos I (succeeded to the throne 22 November 1975).

Government Delegate in Melilla: Abdelmalik el-Barkani Abdelkader.

MEMBERS OF THE SPANISH PARLIAMENT

Deputy elected to the Congress in Madrid: Antonio Gutiérrez Molina (PP).

Representatives to the Senate in Madrid: María del Carmen Dueñas Martínez (PP), Juan José Imbroda Ortiz (PP).

COUNCIL OF GOVERNMENT

(September 2013)

The executive is formed by members of the Partido Popular (PP).

Mayor/President of Melilla: Juan José Imbroda Ortiz.

First Vice-President and Councillor of Development, Youth and Sports: Miguel Marín Cobos.

Second Vice-President and Councillor of Economy and Finance: Daniel Conesa Mínguez.

Councillor of Public Administration: Catalina Muriel García.

Councillor of Social Welfare and Health: María Antonia Garbín Espigares.

Councillor of Culture and Festivals: Simi Chocrón Chocrón.

Councillor of Education and Social Groups: Antonio Miranda Montilla.

Councillor of the Environment: José Ángel Pérez Calabuig.

Councillor of Presidency and Citizenship: Esther Donoso García-Sacristán.

Councillor of Civic Security: Francisco Javier Calderón Carrillo.

Deputy Councillor to the President: Francisco Javier González García.

GOVERNMENT OFFICES

Delegación del Gobierno: Avda de la Marina Española 3, 52001 Melilla; tel. (95) 2675840; fax (95) 2672657; e-mail puri@melilla.map.es.

Office of the Mayor/President: Palacio de la Asamblea, Plaza de España, 52001 Melilla; tel. (95) 2699100; fax (95) 2679230; e-mail presidencia@melilla.es; internet www.melilla.es.

Council of Civic Security: Jefatura Policía Local, General Astilleros 25, Melilla; tel. (95) 2698111; fax (95) 2698121; e-mail policialocal@melilla.es.

Council of Culture and Festivals: Palacio de la Asamblea, Plaza de España, 52001 Melilla; tel. (95) 2699193; fax (95) 2699158; e-mail consejeriacultura@melilla.es.

Council of Development, Youth and Sports: Antiguo Edif. Mantelete, Duque de Ahumada s/n, 52071 Melilla; tel. (95) 2699223; fax (95) 2699224; e-mail consejeriafomento@melilla.es.

Council of the Economy and Finance: Justo Sancho Miñano 2, 52801 Melilla; tel. (95) 2676241; fax (95) 2676242; e-mail consejeriaeconomia@melilla.es.

Council of Education and Social Groups: Querol 7, 52001 Melilla; tel. (95) 2699214; fax (95) 2699279; e-mail educacion@melilla.es.

Council of the Environment: Palacio de la Asamblea, Plaza de España, 52001 Melilla; tel. (95) 2699134; fax (95) 2699161; e-mail consejeriamedioambiente@melilla.es.

Council of the Presidency and Citizenship: Palacio de la Asamblea, Plaza de España, 52001 Melilla; tel. (95) 2699207; fax (95) 2699137; e-mail consejeriapresidencia@melilla.es.

Council of Public Administration: Palacio de la Asamblea, Plaza de España, 52001 Melilla; tel. (95) 2699102; fax (95) 2699103; e-mail cap@melilla.es.

Council of Social Welfare and Health: Carlos Ramírez de Arellano 10, Melilla; tel. (95) 2699301; fax (95) 2699302; e-mail consejeriabienstarsocial@melilla.es.

Assembly

Election, 22 May 2011

	Seats
Partido Popular (PP)	15
Coalición por Melilla (CpM)	6
Partido Socialista Obrero Español (PSOE)	2
Partido Populares en Libertad (PPL)	2
Total	25

Election Commission

Junta Electoral de Zona y Provincial de Melilla: Melilla; Sec. María José Antolin Pérez.

Political Organizations

Coalición por Melilla (CpM): Ejército Español 21, 1° dcha, 52001 Melilla; tel. (95) 2969188; fax (95) 2699247; internet www.coalicionpormelilla.com; f. 1995 by merger of Partido del Trabajo y Progreso de Melilla and Partido Hispano Bereber; majority of members are from the Muslim community; mem. of left-wing Izquierda Unida coalition; Pres. Mustafa Hamed Mo Aberchán; Sec.-Gen. Hassan Mohatar.

Partido Popular (PP): Roberto Cano 2, 1° izqda, POB 384, 52001 Melilla; tel. (95) 2681095; fax (95) 2684477; e-mail melilla@pp.es; internet www.ppmelilla.es; national-level, centre-right party; absorbed the Unión del Pueblo Melillense in 2007; Pres. Juan José Imbroda Ortiz; Sec.-Gen. María del Carmen Dueñas Martínez.

Partido Populares en Libertad (PPL): Calle Carlos V, 21, Local 1, 52006 Melilla; tel. (95) 2694007; fax (95) 2694627; e-mail popularesenlibertad@gmail.com; internet www.popularesenlibertad.es; f. 2011; centrist, liberal party formed to contest elections of May 2011; Pres. Ignacio Velázquez Rivera; Sec.-Gen. Alberto Weil González.

Partido Socialista de Melilla-Partido Socialista Obrero Español (PSME-PSOE): Edif. Argo, Doctor García Martínez 3, 52006 Melilla; tel. (95) 2677807; fax (95) 2679857; e-mail psoe@psoemelilla.es; internet www.psoe.es/ambito/melilla/index.do; national-level, centre-left party; Pres. Tomás Muñoz Gallardo; Sec.-Gen. Gregorio Escobar Marcos.

There are also various civic associations in Melilla.

Religion

As in Ceuta, most Europeans are Roman Catholics. The registered Muslim community numbered 20,800 in 1990. The Jewish community numbered 1,300. There is also a Hindu community.

ISLAM

Comisión Islámica de Melilla (CIM): García Cabrelles 13, Melilla; Sec.-Gen. Dris Muhammad.

CHRISTIANITY

The Roman Catholic Church

Melilla is part of the Spanish diocese of Málaga.

The Press

El Faro de Melilla: Castelar 5, 1°, Melilla; tel. (95) 2690029; fax (95) 2683992; e-mail melilla@grupofaro.es; internet www.elfaroceutamelilla.es; Pres. RAFAEL MONTERO PALACIOS; Editor-in-Chief ANGELA M. PERAZZI.

Melilla Hoy: Polígono Industrial SEPES, La Espiga, Naves A-1/A-2, 52006 Melilla; tel. (95) 2690000; fax (95) 2675725; e-mail redaccion@melillahoy.es; internet www.melillahoy.es; f. 1985; Pres. ENRIQUE BOHÓRQUEZ LÓPEZ-DÓRIGA; Editor-in-Chief MUSTAFA HAMED; circ. 2,000.

Sur: Músico Granados 2, 52001 Melilla; tel. (95) 2691283; fax (95) 2673674; e-mail surmelilla@rusadirmedia.com; internet www.diariosur.es; local edn of Málaga daily; Perm. Rep. AVELINO GUTIÉRREZ PÉREZ.

El Telegrama de Melilla: Polígono La Espiga, Nave A-8, 52006 Melilla; tel. (95) 2691443; fax (95) 2691469; e-mail telegramademelilla@yahoo.es; internet www.eltelegrama.com; Dir JUAN CARLOS HEREDIA.

NEWS AGENCY

Agencia EFE: Teniente Aguilar de Mera 1, Edificio Monumental, 1°, Local 9, 52001 Melilla; tel. (95) 2685235; fax (95) 2680043; e-mail melilla@efe.es; Correspondent NOELIA RAMOS.

PRESS ASSOCIATION

Asociación de la Prensa: Apdo de Correos 574, 29880 Melilla; e-mail correo@apmelilla.com; Pres. FRANCISCO JAVIER CALDERÓN GALLARDO.

Broadcasting

RADIO

Cadena Dial Melilla: Muelle Ribera 18B, 52005 Melilla; tel. (95) 2682328; fax (95) 2681573; e-mail radiomelilla@unionradio.es; internet www.cadenadial.com; Rep. ROCÍO GONZÁLEZ JUSTO.

Onda Cero Radio Melilla: Músico Granados 2, 52004 Melilla; tel. (95) 2691283; e-mail ondaceromelilla@ondaceromelilla.net; internet www.ondaceromelilla.net; Dir JOSÉ JESÚS NAVAJAS TROBAT.

Radio Melilla: Muelle Ribera s/n, 52005 Melilla; tel. (95) 2681708; fax (95) 2681573; e-mail radiomelilla@unionradio.es; internet www.cadenaser.com; owned by Sociedad Española de Radiodifusión; commercial; Dir ANTONIA RAMOS PELÁEZ.

Radio Nacional de España (RNE): Duque de Ahumada 5, 52001 Melilla; tel. (95) 2681907; fax (95) 2683108; internet www.rtve.es; state-controlled; Rep. MONTSERRAT COBOS RUANO.

TELEVISION

A fibre optic cable linking Melilla with Almería was laid in 1990. From March 1991 Melilla residents were able to receive three private TV channels from mainland Spain: Antena 3, Canal+ and Tele 5.

Antena 3: Edif. Melilla, Urbanización Rusadir, 29805 Melilla; tel. (95) 2688840; internet www.antena3.com.

Finance

BANKING

There were seven banks operating in Melilla in 2007, all of which were based in mainland Spain.

Banco Bilbao Vizcaya Argentaria (BBVA): Teniente Aguilar De Mera 3 52001 Melilla; tel. (952) 686076; fax (952) 685249; internet www.bbva.es; 5 brs.

Banco de España: Plaza de España 3, 52001 Melilla; tel. (95) 2683940; fax (95) 2683942; internet www.bde.es.

Banco Español de Crédito (Banesto): Avda Juan Carlos I 12, 52001 Melilla; tel. (95) 2684348; fax (95) 2683645; internet www.banesto.es; 2 brs.

Banco Popular Español: Avda Juan Carlos I 14, 52001 Melilla; tel. (95) 2684847; fax (95) 2676844; internet www.bancopopular.es.

Banco Santander Central Hispano (BSCH): Ejército Español 1, 52001 Melilla; tel. (95) 2681422; internet www.gruposantander.es; 3 brs.

Caja de Ahorros y Pensiones de Barcelona (La Caixa): Avda Juan Carlos I 28, 52001 Melilla; tel. (95) 2685760; fax (95) 2960276; internet www.lacaixa.es; 2 brs.

Montes de Piedad y Caja de Ahorros de Ronda, Cádiz, Almería, Málaga y Antequera (Unicaja): Ejército Español 9, 52001 Melilla; tel. (952) 682595; fax (952) 683684; internet www.unicaja.es; 4 brs.

INSURANCE

MAPFRE: Avda Democracia 9, 52004 Melilla; tel. (95) 2673189; fax (95) 2674977; e-mail maberna@mapfre.com; internet www.mapfre.com; Commercial Man. BERNABE ESCOZ; 2 offices.

Trade and Industry

Cámara Oficial de Comercio, Industria y Navegación: Cervantes 7, 52001 Melilla; tel. (95) 2684840; fax (95) 2683119; e-mail info@camaramelilla.es; internet www.camaramelilla.es; f. 1906; chamber of commerce; Pres. MARGARITA LÓPEZ ALMENDÁRIZ; Vice-Pres. HAMED MAANAN BENAISA BOUJI.

Confederación de Empresarios de Melilla (CEME-CEOE): Plaza 1 de Mayo, bajo dcha, 52003 Melilla; tel. (95) 2673696; fax (95) 2676175; e-mail ceme@cemelilla.org; internet www.cemelilla.org; f. 1979; employers' confed; Pres. MARGARITA LÓPEZ ALMENDÁRIZ; Sec.-Gen. JERÓNIMO PÉREZ HERNÁNDEZ.

UTILITIES

The Spanish electricity company Endesa operates an oil-fired power station in Melilla. In 2007 a new 12.6-MW generator was installed, increasing capacity by 22%.

TRADE UNION

Confederación Sindical de Comisiones Obreras (CCOO): Calle Primero de Mayo, 1°, 52001 Melilla; tel. (95) 2676535; fax (95) 2672571; e-mail orga.melilla@melilla.ccoo.es; internet www.melilla.ccoo.es; Sec.-Gen. CARIDAD NAVARRO RINCÓN.

Transport

There is a daily ferry service to Málaga and a service to Almería. Melilla airport, situated 4 km from the town, is served by daily flights to various destinations on the Spanish mainland, operated by Iberia Regional/Air Nostrum. There were 26 km of paved roads in Melilla in 2010. The Port of Melilla handled 955,000 metric tons of goods and 811,000 passengers in 2012; 1,551 ships passed through the port in that year.

Port of Melilla: Autoridad Portuaria de Melilla, Avda de la Marina Española 4, 52001 Melilla; tel. (95) 2673600; fax (95) 2674838; e-mail informatica@puertodemelilla.es; internet www.puertomelilla.es; Pres. ARTURO ESTEBAN; Dir JOSÉ LUIS ALMAZÁN.

Acciona Trasmediterránea: Avda General Marina 1, 52001 Melilla; tel. (95) 2681635; fax (95) 2682685; e-mail correom@trasmediterranea.es; internet www.trasmediterranea.es; operates ferry service between Melilla and Almería and Málaga, in mainland Spain.

Tourism

There is much of historic interest to the visitor, while Melilla is also celebrated for its modernist architecture. Several new hotels, including a luxury development, were constructed in the 1990s. In 2012 tourist arrivals numbered 49,778 (including 36,697 visitors from mainland Spain).

Oficina Provincial de Turismo: Pintor Fortuny 21, 52004 Melilla; tel. (95) 2976151; fax (95) 2976153; e-mail info@melillaturismo.com; internet www.melillaturismo.com.

Defence

(See Ceuta.) More than one-half of Melilla's land area is used solely for military purposes.

Commandant-General: Gen. ÁLVARO DE LA PEÑA CUESTA.

Education

In addition to the conventional Spanish facilities, the Moroccan Government finances a school for Muslim children in Melilla, the languages of instruction being Arabic and Spanish. Total enrolment at the primary level in Melilla was recorded at 6,917 in 2012/13, while secondary schools had an enrolment of 4,372 for the first cycle of secondary education (between the ages of 12 and 16); 1,711 students were enrolled for the *bachillerato* and 1,287 students enrolled on vocational courses. The Spanish open university (Universidad Nacional de Educación a Distancia—UNED) maintains a branch in Melilla.

Bibliography

Baeza Herrazti, A. (Ed.). *Ceuta hispano-portuguesa*. Ceuta, Instituto de Estudios Ceutíes, 1993.

Ceuta y Melilla en las relaciones de España y Marruecos. Madrid, Instituto Español de Estudios Estratégicos, Centro Superior de Estudios de la Defensa, 1997.

Domínguez Sánchez, C. *Melilla*. Madrid, Editorial Everest, 1978.

Europa Ethnica (Vols 1–2). *Ceuta and Melilla—Spain's Presence on African Soil*. Vienna, Braumüller, 1999.

Gold, P. *Europe or Africa?: A Contemporary Study of the Spanish North African Enclaves of Ceuta and Melilla*. Liverpool, Liverpool University Press, 2000.

Lafond, P. *Melilla*. Barcelona, Lunwerg Editores, 1997.

Mir Berlanga, F. *Melilla en los Siglos Pasados y Otras Historias*. Madrid, Editora Nacional, 1977.

Resumen de la Historia de Melilla. Melilla, 1978.

Zurlo, Y. *Ceuta et Melilla: Histoire, représentations et devenir de deux enclaves espagnoles*. Paris, L'Harmattan, 2005.

SYRIA

Physical and Social Geography

W. B. FISHER

Before 1918 the term 'Syria' was rather loosely applied to the whole of the territory now forming the modern states of Syria, Lebanon, Israel and Jordan. To the Ottomans, as to the Romans, Syria stretched from the Euphrates to the Mediterranean, and from the Sinai to the hills of southern Turkey, with Palestine as a smaller province of this wider unit. The present Syrian Arab Republic has a much more limited extent, covering 185,180 sq km (71,498 sq miles—including the occupied Golan Heights, see Occupied Territories, see p. 554).

The frontiers of the present-day state are largely artificial, and reflect to a considerable extent the interests and prestige of outside powers—Britain, France and the USA—as these existed in 1918–20. The northern frontier with Turkey is defined by a single-track railway line running along the southern edge of the foothills—probably the only case of its kind in the world—while eastwards and southwards boundaries are highly arbitrary, being straight lines drawn for convenience between salient points. Westwards, the frontiers are again artificial, although less crudely drawn, leaving the headwaters of the Jordan river outside Syria and following the crest of the Anti-Lebanon hills, to reach the sea north of Tripoli.

PHYSICAL FEATURES

Geographically, Syria consists of two main zones: a fairly narrow western part, made up of a complex of mountain ranges and intervening valleys; and a much larger eastern zone that is essentially a broad and open platform dropping gently towards the east and crossed diagonally by the wide valley of the Euphrates river.

The western zone, which contains over 80% of the population of Syria, can be further subdivided as follows. In the extreme west, fronting the Mediterranean Sea, there lies an imposing ridge rising to 1,500 m above sea level, and known as the Jebel Ansariyeh. Its western flank drops fairly gradually to the sea, giving a narrow coastal plain, but on the east it falls very sharply, almost as a wall, to a flat-bottomed valley occupied by the Orontes river, which meanders sluggishly over the flat floor, often flooding in winter, and leaving a formerly malarial marsh in summer. Further east lie more hill ranges, opening out like a fan from the south-west, where the Anti-Lebanon range, with Mount Hermon (2,814 m), is the highest in Syria. Along the eastern flanks of the various ridges lie a number of shallow basins occupied by small streams that eventually dry up or form closed salt lakes. In one basin lies the city of Aleppo, once the second town of the Ottoman Empire and still the largest city of Syria. In another is situated Damascus, irrigated from five streams and famous for its clear fountains and gardens—now the capital of the country. One remaining sub-region of western Syria is the Jebel Druse, which lies in the extreme south-west, and consists of a vast outpouring of lava, in the form of sheets and cones. Towards the west this region is fertile, and produces good cereal crops, but eastwards the soil cover disappears, leaving a barren countryside of twisted lava and caverns. Owing to its difficulty and isolation, the Jebel Druse has tended socially and politically to act independently, remaining aloof from the rest of the country.

The entire eastern zone is mainly steppe or open desert, except close to the banks of the Euphrates, the Tigris and their larger tributaries, where irrigation projects allow considerable cultivation on an increasing scale. The triangularly shaped region between the Euphrates and Tigris rivers is spoken of as the Jezireh (*jazira*, island), but is in no way different from the remaining parts of the east.

The presence of ranks of relatively high hills aligned parallel to the coast has important climatic effects. Tempering and humid effects from the Mediterranean are restricted to a narrow western belt, and central and eastern Syria show marked continental tendencies: that is, a very hot summer with temperatures often above 38°C (100°F) or even 43°C, and a moderately cold winter, with frost on many nights. Very close to the Mediterranean, frost is unknown at any season, but on the hills altitude greatly reduces the average temperature, so that snow may lie on the heights from late December to April, or even May. Rainfall is fairly abundant in the west, where the height of the land tends to determine the amount received, but east of the Anti-Lebanon mountains the amount decreases considerably, producing a steppe region that quickly passes into true desert. On the extreme east, as the Zagros ranges of Persia are approached, there is once again a slight increase, but most of Syria has an annual rainfall of less than 250 mm.

ECONOMIC LIFE

There is a close relationship between climate and economic activities. In the west, where up to 750 mm or even 1,000 mm of rainfall occur, settled farming is possible, and the main limitation is difficult terrain. From the Orontes valley eastwards, however, natural rainfall is increasingly inadequate, and irrigation becomes necessary. The narrow band of territory where annual rainfall lies between 200 mm and 380 mm is sometimes spoken of as the 'Fertile Crescent', since it runs in an arc along the inner side of the hills from Jordan through western and northern Syria as far east as Iraq. In its normal state a steppeland covered with seasonal grass, the Fertile Crescent can often be converted by irrigation and efficient organization into a rich and productive territory. Such it was in the golden days of the Arab caliphate; now, after centuries of decline, it has been revived. From the 1950s onwards, a marked change was seen and, initially because of small-scale irrigation schemes and the installation of motor pumps to raise water from underground artesian sources, large areas of the former steppe began to produce cotton, cereals and fruit.

As a result of its relative openness and accessibility and its geographical situation as a 'waist' between the Mediterranean and the Persian (Arabian) Gulf, Syria has been a land of passage, and for centuries its role was that of an intermediary, both commercial and cultural, between the Mediterranean world and the Far East. From early times until the end of the Middle Ages there was a flow of traffic east and west that raised a number of Syrian cities and ports to the rank of international markets. Since the 1930s, following a long period of decline and eclipse resulting from the diversion of this trade to the sea, there has been a revival of activity, owing to the new elements of air transport and the construction of oil pipelines from Iraq.

PEOPLE AND LANGUAGE

At 1 January 2011 the total Syrian population was officially estimated at 24,504,000. According to the United Nations Relief and Works Agency for Palestine Refugees in the Near East (UNRWA), there were 499,189 Palestinian refugees in Syria at 31 December 2012. Following the outbreak of civil conflict between Government forces and opposition groups opposed to the rule of President Bashar al-Assad in 2011, a significant number of Syrian nationals were displaced by the escalating violence. By late September 2013 some 1.9m. Syrian refugees had been registered with the Office of the UN High Commissioner for Refugees (UNHCR) in countries across the Middle East and North Africa, while 156,579 were awaiting registration. The largest concentrations of Syrian refugees were found in Lebanon (which hosted 654,115 registered refugees in late September), Jordan (523,607) and Turkey (484,320). Some 162,317 refugees were registered in Iraq, predominantly in the north of that country and 111,175 in Egypt.

As a result of Syria's ethnic diversity, there is a surprising variety of language and religion. Arabic is spoken over most of the country, but Kurdish is widely used along the northern frontier and Armenian in the cities. Aramaic, the language of Christ, survives in a small number of villages.

History

Revised by AURORA SOTTIMANO

ANCIENT HISTORY

From the earliest times, Syria has experienced successive waves of Semitic immigration—Canaanites and Phoenicians in the third millenium BC , the Hebrews and Arameans in the second, and, unceasingly, the nomadic tribes of the Arabian peninsula. This process has enabled Syria to assimilate, or reject, the invaders who have established their domination over the land without losing its essentially Semitic character. Before Rome assumed control of Syria in the first century BC, the Egyptians, the Assyrians and the Hittites, and, later, the Persians and the Macedonians had all left their mark. During this time the area was divided into many kingdoms usually centred on its main cities: Damascus is claimed to be the oldest capital city in the world, having been continuously inhabited since about 2000 BC, and Aleppo may be even older.

ARAB AND TURKISH RULE

When, after the death of the Prophet Muhammad in AD 632, the newly created power of Islam began a career of conquest, the populations of Syria, Semitic in their language and culture, viewed the Muslim conquests as an opportunity to gain freedom from the Greek-speaking Orthodox Byzantines, to whom they were ill-disposed. By their decisive victory on the Yarmouk river (636), having seized Damascus in 635, the Muslims virtually secured possession of all Syria. From 661–750 the Umayyad dynasty ruled in Syria, which, after the conquest, had been divided into four military districts or *junds* (Damascus, Homs, Urdun, i.e. Jordan, and Palestine). To these, the Caliph Yazid I (680–83) added a fifth, Kinnasrin, for the defence of northern Syria. Under Abd al-Malik (685–705), Arabic became the official language of the state, in whose administration, hitherto largely carried out by the old Byzantine bureaucracy, Syrians, Muslim as well as Christian, now had an increasing share. Syria had become the heart of a great Empire, and the Arab army of Syria, well trained in the ceaseless frontier warfare with Byzantium, bore the main burden of imperial rule, taking a major part in the two great Arab assaults on Byzantium in 674–78 and in 717–18. In 750, with the accession of the Abbasid dynasty, the centre of the Empire was transferred to Baghdad. Syria once more became a mere province and was the object of dispute by outside powers. Local dynasties, however, achieved from time to time a transitory importance, as did the Hamdanids (a Bedouin family from northern Iraq), who ruled Aleppo in 946–67. By the treaty of 997, northern Syria became Byzantine, while the rest of the country remained in the hands of the Fatimid dynasty, which ruled Egypt from 969. After a short period of rule by the Arab Mirdasid house from about 1027, the Seljuq Turks overran Syria, but failed to establish a united state there.

The interlude of the European Crusader states, who maintained a precarious hold on the coastal area of Syria for some 200 years during the 12th and 13th centuries, left little impact historically. A Muslim counter-offensive initiated by the Turkish general Zangi Atabeg of Mosul was continued by his son Nur al-Din, who captured Damascus in 1154, and by the Kurd Saladin, whose victory over the Crusaders at Hattin (1187) destroyed the kingdom of Jerusalem. Finally, a series of campaigns led by the Mamluk Sultan Baibars (1260–77) and his immediate successors brought about the fall of Antioch (1268), Tripoli (1289) and, with the fall of Acre (1291), the disappearance of the crusading states in Syria.

Mamluk rule in Syria, which endured until 1517, was marked by warfare, periodic famine and plague. A growing tension between the Mamluks and the Ottoman Turks broke out into inconclusive warfare in the years 1485–91. When to this tension was added the possibility of an alliance between the Mamluks and the rising power of the Safavids in Persia, the Ottoman Sultan Selim I (1512–20) was compelled to seek a decisive solution to the problem. In August 1516 the battle of Marj Dabik, north of Aleppo, gave Syria to the Ottomans, thus ushering in 400 years of Ottoman rule. The Ottomans brought only a temporary improvement in the unhappy condition of Syria, now divided into the three provinces of Damascus, Tripoli and Aleppo. As the control of the Sultan at Constantinople (now İstanbul, Turkey) became weaker, the Turkish pashas who administered the important towns in Syria obtained greater freedom of action, until Ahmad Jazzar, Pasha of Acre, virtually ruled Syria as an independent prince (1785–1804).

The 19th century saw important changes. The Ottoman Sultan Mahmoud II (1808–39) had promised Syria to the Pasha of Egypt, Muhammad Ali, in return for the latter's services during the Greek War of Independence. When the Sultan declined to fulfil his promise, Egyptian troops overran Syria (1831–33). Ibrahim Pasha, son of Muhammad Ali, now gave to Syria, for the first time in centuries, a centralized government strong enough to hold separatist tendencies in check and to impose a system of taxation, which, if burdensome, was at least regular in its functioning. However, Ibrahim's rule was not popular, for the landowners resented his efforts to limit their social and political dominance, while the peasantry disliked the conscription, the forced labour and the heavy taxation that he found indispensable for the maintenance of his regime. In 1840 a revolt broke out in Syria, and when the Great Powers intervened on behalf of the Sultan (at war with Egypt since 1839), Muhammad Ali was compelled to renounce his claim to rule there.

Western influence, working through trade, through the protection of religious minorities, and through the cultural and educational efforts of missions and schools, had received encouragement from Ibrahim Pasha. The French Jesuits, returning to Syria in 1831, opened schools, and in 1875 founded their University at Beirut. The American Presbyterian Mission (established at Beirut in 1820) introduced a printing press in 1834, and in 1866 founded the Syrian Protestant College, later renamed the American University of Beirut. Syria also received some benefit from the reform movement within the Ottoman Empire, which, begun by Mahmoud II and continued under his successors, took the form of a determined attempt to modernize the structure of the Empire. The semi-independent pashas of old disappeared, the administration being now entrusted to salaried officials of the central Government; some effort was made to create schools and colleges on Western lines, and much was done to deprive the landowning classes of their feudal privileges, although their social and economic predominance was left unchallenged. As a result of these improvements, there was, in the late 19th century, a revival of Arabic literature, which did much to prepare the way for the growth of Arab nationalism in the 20th century.

MODERN HISTORY

By 1914 Arab nationalist sentiment had made some headway among the educated and professional classes, and especially among army officers. The McMahon Correspondence of July 1915–March 1916 (Documents on Palestine, see p. 56) encouraged the Arab nationalists to hope that the end of the First World War (1914–18) would mean the creation of a greater Arab kingdom. However, as a result of the Sykes-Picot Agreement, negotiated in secret between Britain, France and Russia in 1916 (Documents on Palestine, see p. 56), Syria was to become a French sphere of influence. Meanwhile, the maladministration of the Ottoman Governor Jemal Pasha, which brought famine and hardship to ordinary Syrians, dissolved any residual loyalty to the Ottoman Empire. At the end of the war, and in accordance with this agreement, a provisional French administration was established in the coastal districts of Syria, while in the interior an Arab Government came into being. In March 1920 the Syrian nationalists proclaimed an independent kingdom of Greater Syria (including Lebanon and Palestine); however, in April of the same year the San Remo Conference gave France a mandate for the whole of Syria, and in July French troops occupied Damascus.

By 1925 the French, aware that the majority of the Muslim population resented their rule, and that only among the Christian Maronites of the Lebanon could they hope to find support, had carried into effect a policy based upon the religious divisions so strong in Syria. The area under mandate had been divided into four distinct units: a much enlarged Lebanon (including Beirut and Tripoli), a Syrian Republic, and the two districts of Latakia and Jebel Druse. Despite the fact that French rule gave Syria a degree of law and order that might have rendered possible the transition from a medieval to a more modern form of society, nationalist sentiment opposed the mandate on principle, and deplored the failure to introduce full representative institutions and the tendency to encourage separatism among the religious minorities. This discontent, especially strong in the Syrian Republic, became open revolt in 1925–26.

The next 10 years were marked by a hesitant progress towards self-government and attempts to negotiate a Franco-Syrian treaty. A treaty recognizing the principle of Syrian independence was finally signed in September 1936, under the terms of which the districts of Jebel Druse and Latakia would be annexed to Syria, while France would receive certain economic and military rights in Syria. However, France failed to ratify the treaty, and in 1939 it surrendered the Sanjak of Alexandretta—which formed part of the French mandated territories—to Turkey. The onset of the Second World War precipitated the declaration of Syrian independence. In June 1941, after the Anglo-French invasion to oust the Axis-supporting Vichy French regime, the Free French Government promised independence for Syria. Despite the formation in 1943 of a nationalist Government, with Shukri al-Kuwatli as President of the Syrian Republic, it was not until 17 April 1946 that Syria achieved full independence.

UNSTABLE INDEPENDENCE

The newly independent Syria experienced a long period of turbulence. Its institutions were weak, and continued reliance on political and financial support from foreign powers, notably France, Egypt and Saudi Arabia, was the source of profound disappointment among the people. A disastrous intervention in the 1948–49 war against Israel served merely to highlight the prevalence of corruption and disorder in the country. This was the prelude to several interventions by the army in Syrian politics between 1949 and 1954. The army saw itself as 'a part of the people', and, following a coup in 1951, Syria came under the control of a military autocracy, with Col Adib Shishakli as head of state. The Chamber of Deputies was dissolved in December 1951, while a decree of April 1952 abolished all political parties. After the approval of a new Constitution in July 1953, Shishakli became President of Syria in the following month. However, Shishakli had limited experience in political bargaining and had no programme for social or economic change, beyond the tentative introduction of a limited land reform as a necessary step to modernize the economy. In November of that year politicians hostile to the regime of President Shishakli established a Front of National Opposition, refusing to accept as legal the results of the October elections and declaring as their aim the end of military autocracy and the restoration of democratic rule. Shishakli's flight to France led to the collapse of his regime in early 1954 and the restoration of the 1950 Constitution.

Syrian progressive forces clustered around two poles: Akram al-Hourani and his Arab Socialist Party, and the Baath Party of Michel Aflaq and Salah al-Din Bitar. Their programme of social revolution and Arab unity reflected the ideology of the socialist camp, under the influence of the USSR, and the aspirations of Arab nationalists and anti-imperialists, who looked to the Egyptian President, Gamal Abd al-Nasser, for inspiration. The fusion of these ideas culminated in one of the defining episodes of Syrian history, when, on 1 February 1958, the Government of the two states proclaimed the constitution of a union between Egypt and Syria as the United Arab Republic (UAR).

UNION WITH EGYPT

On 21 February 1958 President Nasser of Egypt became the first head of the combined state. A central Cabinet for the UAR was established in October, and also two regional executive councils, one each for Egypt and Syria. A further move towards integration came in March 1960, when a single National Assembly for the whole of the UAR, consisting of 400 deputies from Egypt and 200 from Syria, was instituted. The realities of the UAR soon disappointed its Syrian supporters. Syrian dissatisfaction with the 'Egyptianization' of the Syrian province of the Union grew as policies were increasingly imposed by Egypt without consultation and with little attention to the specificity of the Syrian Region. The UAR was dissolved following a military coup in September 1961; none the less, the policies implemented in Syria after dissolution—land reform, hostility to foreign capital, nationalization of industry, mobilization of peasants and workers in corporatist unions under the control of the state, and a state role in industrial development—were continued and expanded by successive regimes. Even the secessionist Government—self-proclaimed 'liberals' and supporters of private economic initiative—retained many of the statist innovations of the UAR period. The fact that they themselves stemmed from the discredited political class of the post-independence era, and that their 'liberal' political programme largely ignored popular demands for social and democratic change, sullied them in the eyes of the advocates of radical change. Inspired by a coup in neighbouring Iraq, in early 1963 Baathists within the Syrian military made their move.

THE 1963 BAATHIST REVOLUTION

A military junta, styled the National Council of the Revolutionary Command, seized control in Damascus on 8 March 1963. In May the Baathists took measures to purge the armed forces and the administration of personnel known to favour a close alignment with Egypt. A new Government, formed on 13 May and strongly Baathist in character, carried out a further purge in June and at the same time created a National Guard recruited from members of the Baathist movement. These measures led the pro-Egyptian elements to attempt a *coup d'état* at Damascus on 18 July. The attempt failed, however, resulting in considerable loss of life. In the name of 'unity, socialism and freedom', the Baathist regime nationalized all Arab-owned banks and various industrial enterprises, while also implementing a far-reaching land reform, which included the redistribution of land and the reorganization of agricultural relations. On 25 April 1964 a provisional Constitution was promulgated, describing Syria as a democratic socialist republic forming an integral part of the Arab nation. A Presidential Council was established on 14 May, with Gen. Amin al-Hafiz as de facto head of state.

The Baathist regime depended for its main support on the armed forces, which had been recruited in no small degree from the countryside and from religious minorities in Syria, including adherents of the Alawi faith (a schism of the Shi'a branch of Islam). In general, the mass of the peasant population was thought to have pro-Nasser sympathies; the small working class was divided between pro-Nasser and Baathist elements. The middle and upper classes, as well as conservative Muslims, generally opposed the domination of the Baathists. Tensions were growing as well within the Baathist movement between older politicians, more inclined to the pursuit of a Pan-Arab union, and left-wing elements, for whom the immediate objective of Baathism was a radical transformation of Syria along socialist lines. In terms of implementing a thorough social and economic revolution, the Government took a decisive step with the so-called 'Ramadan Decrees'—issued in January 1965 during the Islamic month of Ramadan—which gave the state ownership of three-quarters of the Syrian economy, including full control over most large and mid-size industrial activity in the country.

On 23 February 1966 a military junta representing the radical elements in the Baath Party seized power in Damascus and placed under arrest a number of personalities belonging to the international leadership controlling the organization throughout the Arab world—among them Michel Aflaq, Gen.

Hafiz, Chairman of the recently established Presidential Council, and Salah al-Din Bitar, Prime Minister of the displaced administration. Yet the overall political orientation of the regime did not change. The new leader, Salah Jadid, prioritized economic development and class struggle within Syria over the search for Arab unity. His refusal to collaborate with regimes he perceived not to possess socialist credentials confined Syria to a self-imposed isolation in the Arab world.

THE ARAB–ISRAELI WAR OF 1967

The friction ever present along the frontier between Syria and Israel had provoked outbreaks of violent conflict during preceding years, particularly in the region of Lake Tiberias (the Sea of Galilee). Now, in the winter of 1966–67, the tension along the border assumed more serious proportions, resulting in fighting between the two countries' forces south-east of Lake Tiberias. The tension became a major influence leading to the war that broke out on 5 June 1967 between Israel and its Arab neighbours Egypt, Syria and Jordan. During the course of hostilities, which lasted six days, Israel defeated Egypt and Jordan and then, after some stubborn fighting, outflanked and overran the Syrian positions on the hills above Lake Tiberias. With the breakthrough accomplished, Israeli forces made a rapid advance and occupied the town of Quneitra, about 65 km from Damascus. On 10 June Israel and Syria announced their formal acceptance of the UN proposal for a cease-fire; however, in September the Baath Party of Syria rejected all idea of a compromise with Israel. A resolution adopted by the UN Security Council in November, urging the withdrawal of the Israelis from the lands occupied by them during the June war and the ending of the belligerency that the Arab Governments had until then maintained against Israel, was rejected by Syria, which alone maintained its commitment to a reunified Palestine.

STRUGGLE FOR POWER, 1968–71

The ruling Baath Party had for some years been divided into two main factions: the 'progressive' group, which held that the socialist transformation of the country was of paramount importance and a precondition for Arab unity; and the opposing 'nationalist' faction, which favoured a pragmatic approach to the economy and improved relations with Syria's Arab neighbours. A new Government was formed in October 1968, incorporating members of the nationalist faction, including its leader, Lt-Gen. Hafiz al-Assad, who assumed control of the all-important Ministry of Defence.

In September 1970 the tension between the two factions of the Baath Party had become acute as a result of differences over support for the Palestinian guerrillas during the fighting with the Jordanian army. Jadid and Yousuf Zeayen, a former Prime Minister, sent 200 tanks into Jordan to support the guerrillas' efforts against the 'reactionary' Jordanian monarchy. This measure was opposed by Hafiz al-Assad and the military faction, who wanted to avoid giving any provocation to Israel and launching the weak Syrian army in a risky adventure. In November the army supported Gen. Assad's seizure of power. Assad drew lessons from the experiences of previous Syrian strongmen, including Shishakli and Jadid: he realized that army support was necessary to seize power, but that in order to maintain that support and to recover the territory lost in the 1967 war, he had to take control of al-Baath and repair relations with other Arab regimes.

ASSAD IN POWER

There was no obvious opposition to the military *coup d'état*. Gen. Assad became Prime Minister and Secretary-General of the Baath Party, while Ahmad al-Khatib took office as acting President. A new Regional Command of the party was also formed. Following amendments to the 1969 provisional Constitution in February 1971, Gen. Assad was elected President for a seven-year term in March. In the following month Maj.-Gen. Abd al-Rahman Khlefawi became Premier, and Mahmoud al-Ayoubi was appointed Vice-President. In February the first legislative body in Syria since 1966, the People's Assembly, was formed. Of its 173 members, 87 represented the Baath Party.

Domestically, the Assad regime slowed the socialist transformation of the country, relaxed trade regulations, and opened up the economy to Syrian entrepreneurs by supporting private and mixed-ownership. In December 1972 a new Government was formed by al-Ayoubi, who allotted 16 of 31 government portfolios to members of the Baath Party. A new Constitution, proclaiming socialist principles, was approved by the People's Assembly in January 1973 and confirmed by a referendum in March. The Sunni Muslims were dissatisfied that the Constitution did not recognize Islam as the state religion, and, as a result of their pressure, an amendment was made declaring that the President must be a Muslim. Under the Constitution, freedom of belief was guaranteed, with the state respecting all religions, although the Constitution recognized that Islamic jurisprudence was 'a principal source of legislation'. In 1972 a National Charter created a National Progressive Front (NPF), a grouping of the Baath Party and its allies. Elections were held in March 1973 for the new People's Assembly, and 140 of the 186 seats were won by the NPF, while 42 seats were won by independents and four by the opposition.

Meanwhile, the regime's foreign policy aimed to reduce Syria's isolation in the Arab world and to prepare the country, militarily and diplomatically, for a new confrontation with Israel. Although Syria continued to reject the November 1967 UN Security Council Resolution (No. 242), relations with the UAR and Jordan improved, and in April 1971 Syria agreed to join a union with the UAR, Sudan and Libya. However, the Federation had little effect. The Assad regime increased the Syrian army's control over the Palestinian guerrilla group al-Saiqa (Thunderbolt, or Vanguard of the Popular Liberation War), and banned guerrilla operations against Israeli positions from the Syrian front. Yet, after the Jordanian Government's final onslaught on the Palestinian guerrillas in northern Jordan in July, Syria closed its border and, in August, severed diplomatic relations. Egyptian mediation reduced the chances of a more serious conflict developing, but diplomatic links remained severed with Jordan until October 1973. Relations with the USSR improved during the last half of 1971 and in 1972. However, Syria was not at this time prepared to sign a friendship treaty with the USSR, as had Egypt and Iraq.

THE FOURTH ARAB–ISRAELI WAR AND ITS AFTERMATH

On 6 October 1973 Egyptian and Syrian forces launched a war against Israel in an effort to regain territories lost in 1967. On both the Egyptian and Syrian fronts complete surprise was achieved, giving the Arabs a strong initial advantage, much of which they subsequently lost (see the essay on Arab–Israeli Relations 1967–2013). Although Egypt signed a disengagement agreement with Israel on 18 January 1974, fighting continued on the Syrian front, in the Golan Heights area, until a disengagement agreement was signed on 31 May, after much diplomacy by the US Secretary of State, Dr Henry Kissinger (Documents on Palestine, see p. 68).

Syria continued to maintain an uncompromising policy regarding the Golan Heights and the Palestinian question, and after the 1973 war it received vast amounts of Soviet military aid in order fully to re-equip its forces. Syria's strong support for the Palestine Liberation Organization (PLO) was vindicated in October 1974 at the Arab summit meeting in Rabat, Morocco, where the PLO's claim to the West Bank was formally recognized. By June 1976, however, Syria was in the position of invading Lebanon to crush the Palestinians, and finding most of the remainder of the Arab world agreeing to send a peace-keeping force to Lebanon to quell the conflict. This reversal for Syria arose out of a lengthy chain of events. An improvement in relations with Jordan took place in 1975, with King Hussein visiting Damascus in April and President Assad visiting Amman in June. Relations deteriorated, however, after Jordan appeared to give guarded support to Egyptian President Anwar Sadat's peace initiative in November 1977. The second Egyptian-Israeli disengagement agreement in Sinai, signed in September 1975, met with Syria's strong condemnation. Syria accused Egypt of weakening the general Arab position and betraying the Palestinians.

Syria had shown considerable interest in the Lebanese civil war since its outbreak in April 1975. Initially, Syria sought to protect the position of the Palestinians in Lebanon, sending in about 2,000 al-Saiqa troops in January 1976. After having secured a cease-fire, Assad pledged that he would control the Palestinians in Lebanon, and the core of the PLO, under Yasser Arafat, began to be apprehensive of Syrian dominance. Syria's long-term aims had been to ensure that Lebanon did not disintegrate into confessional statelets, prone to Israeli influence, but also to avoid a leftist victory, which would give the PLO an independent bargaining position and lead to the installation of a radical government in Lebanon that might challenge Syrian hegemony in the area. By June the fighting in Lebanon was so fierce that Syria felt obliged to intervene overtly. This time Syria's intervention was welcomed by the Christian right-wing parties and condemned by the Palestinians and the Muslim left (and also Egypt). A peace-keeping force, consisting of Syrian and Libyan troops in equal proportions, was sent to Lebanon to effect a cease-fire, but the fighting continued unabated until October, when Arab summit meetings, in Riyadh, Saudi Arabia, and Cairo, Egypt, secured a more lasting cease-fire. A 30,000-strong Arab Deterrent Force, consisting largely of Syrian troops, was given authority at the Arab summit meetings to maintain the peace. President Assad's prestige, in Syria and the Arab world, was considerably strengthened by this success. In August 1976 Syria's Prime Minister, Mahmoud al-Ayoubi, was replaced by his predecessor, Gen. Khlefawi. He held office until March 1978, when he was succeeded by Muhammad Ali al-Halabi, previously Speaker of the People's Assembly.

Relations with the USSR improved, and were consolidated when President Assad visited Moscow, the Soviet capital, in April 1977. With Iraq, however, relations remained poor. Iraq shut off the flow of petroleum from its Kirkuk oilfield to the Syrian port of Banias in protest against Syria's intervention in Lebanon. Another Iraqi grievance was Syria's use of water from the Euphrates river for irrigation projects. Relations between Syria and Egypt deteriorated again as a result of President Sadat's peace initiative in November 1977. Assad strongly criticized the move, and diplomatic relations between the two countries were severed in December. Syria's rift with Egypt widened further after Sadat and Prime Minister Menachem Begin of Israel signed the Camp David agreements (Documents on Palestine, see p. 69) in the USA in September 1978. Syria became the core of the 'Steadfastness and Confrontation Front', comprising Arab countries strongly opposed to Egypt's attempt to make a separate peace with Israel. When the Peace Treaty between Egypt and Israel was finally signed in March 1979 (Documents on Palestine, see p. 71), Syria joined most of the other countries in the League of Arab States (Arab League) at a meeting in Baghdad, Iraq, that endorsed political and economic sanctions against Egypt. A brief improvement in Syria's relations with Iraq followed. The oil pipeline from Iraq to Banias was reopened in 1978, but a new scheme for union between the two countries collapsed when an internal conspiracy in Iraq in July 1979 was attributed to Syrian intrigue.

DIFFICULTIES OF THE EARLY 1980s

Although President Assad was easily returned for a second seven-year term of office in February 1978, there was growing evidence of internal dissatisfaction in Syria with the ascendance of the Alawites, the minority Muslim sect to which Assad belonged. That opposition turned violent after 1977, and in June 1979 more than 60 army cadets, most of them thought to be Alawites, were massacred. The slaughter was officially attributed to the Muslim Brotherhood, which was also held responsible for subsequent killings. President Assad's attempts to end this violence met with little lasting success. In January 1980 he appointed a new Council of Ministers with Dr Abd al-Rauf al-Kassem as Prime Minister. Militias of workers, peasants and students were set up, but were ineffective in helping the regular authorities to curb violence.

During early 1980 the number of Soviet advisers in the country increased to more than 4,000, and in October Syria signed a 20-year treaty of friendship and co-operation with the USSR. Meanwhile, at the outbreak of war between Iraq and Iran in September 1980, Syria supported Iran, on account of its own long-standing distrust of the rival Baath Party in Iraq. A crisis with Jordan soon developed, partly because of Syrian allegations that Muslim Brotherhood treachery was being planned from within Jordan, and partly because of Jordan's support for Iraq in the Iran–Iraq War. Towards the end of 1980 Syrian and Jordanian troops faced each other across the frontier; conflict was only averted by Saudi mediation.

Syria's biggest distraction, however, was its involvement in Lebanon. The 30,000 Syrian troops of the Arab Deterrent Force, in Lebanon since 1976, had been a severe drain on Syrian resources. In mid-1980 clashes developed between Syrian troops and the Phalangist militia occupying the town of Zahle, in the Beqa'a valley. Syria maintained that the area was vital to its security against Israel. Israeli aircraft made repeated sorties into Lebanon, and in April Syria moved surface-to-air missiles into the Beqa'a valley after two Syrian helicopters had been shot down by Israeli planes. A prolonged international crisis developed, with a serious threat of war between Israel and Syria. After Saudi and Kuwaiti mediation, however, the siege of Zahle was lifted in June, and the Phalangist militia withdrew. The missiles remained in the Beqa'a valley, as the Syrians maintained that this was a separate issue.

The following year saw a number of reversals for President Assad. In December 1981 Israel formally annexed the Golan Heights, a development that prompted Syria to seek to obtain more arms from the USSR. A huge car bomb explosion in Damascus in November, attributed to the Muslim Brotherhood, was followed by further unrest, culminating in February 1982 in an uprising in Hama, which lasted for nearly three weeks. This was eventually suppressed by Assad's forces with brutal ferocity, and, although it was again attributed to the Muslim Brotherhood, other opposition elements were also involved.

Domestic problems were completely overshadowed, however, by the Israeli invasion of Lebanon in June 1982. Israeli forces quickly reached Beirut, trapping the PLO guerrillas there; the Syrian missiles in the Beqa'a valley were destroyed, and the Syrian presence in northern Lebanon, in the form of the Arab Deterrent Force, was rendered impotent. In August agreement was reached on the evacuation of PLO and Syrian forces from Beirut, which took place between 21 August and 1 September. None the less, no change occurred in the relative positions of Syrian and Israeli forces in Lebanon as a whole.

In January 1983, shortly after the start of negotiations between Lebanon and Israel for an agreement covering the withdrawal of foreign forces from Lebanon, Syria took delivery of Soviet anti-aircraft missiles, with a range of 240 km, which posed a potential threat to aircraft over Lebanon, parts of Jordan and over Israel almost as far as Jerusalem.

Finally, on 17 May 1983 an agreement was reached between Lebanon and Israel announcing the end of hostilities and imposing a time limit on the withdrawal of foreign troops from Lebanon. President Assad's outright rejection of the agreement created a stalemate with Israel, which refused to leave Lebanon unless Syria and the PLO did so first. President Assad insisted on Israel's unconditional withdrawal, declaring that the status of Syrian troops, invited into Lebanon by the Lebanese Government in 1976, could not be compared with that of the invading Israeli forces.

THE STRUGGLE FOR CONTROL OF THE PLO

By July 1983 about 40,000 Syrian troops camped in the Beqa'a valley, and around 8,000–10,000 PLO guerrillas, entrenched in the eastern Beqa'a and northern Lebanon, faced some 25,000 Israelis in the south of the country. Neither side seemed eager for war, but, equally, neither was prepared to withdraw. Syria continued to supply the militias of the Lebanese Druze and Shi'ite factions in their struggle with the Lebanese Government and the Christian Phalangists in and around Beirut, and continued to try to unite Lebanese opposition groups in a pro-Syrian 'national front'. Syria was also supporting Palestinian rebels involved in the struggle for power within the PLO that erupted in the Beqa'a valley in May. Syrian forces now faced armed opposition in Lebanon, not only from the Israeli army, but also from Sunni Muslims in Tripoli, Maronite Christians in the centre of the country, and guerrillas loyal to Arafat in the Beqa'a valley. Syria lent military support to the rebel PLO forces, led by 'Abu Musa' and 'Abu Saleh', which finally attacked Arafat's last stronghold in Tripoli in November, leading to Arafat's flight from Lebanon in December, under UN protection. Syria had failed to gain control of the Palestine Liberation Movement, though it had been instrumental in effecting a dilution of Arafat's authority within the PLO.

Syria's progress towards a position of pre-eminence in the Arab world was eroded during 1984 as the rehabilitation of Egypt continued. Syria opposed Jordan's restoration of diplomatic relations with Egypt in September, and remained opposed to regional peace moves that excluded it.

SYRIAN INFLUENCE IN LEBANON

Although Israel withdrew its forces from Beirut, redeploying them along the Awali river, south of the capital, in September 1983, Syria's army remained entrenched in northern Lebanon. The state of civil war in and around Beirut eventually compelled the evacuation of the multinational peace-keeping force in early 1984. The withdrawal of the US marines from Beirut in February, and the abrogation by Lebanon of the 17 May agreement days later, represented a considerable political success for Syria. Having undermined the US position with the help of its Lebanese allies, Syria was ready to support a package of reforms that could bring long-term stability.

In March 1984 President Amin Gemayel of Lebanon was forced to accept the controlling influence of Syria in Lebanese affairs. A National Reconciliation Conference was held in Lausanne, Switzerland, with President Gemayel under pressure from Syria to agree constitutional reforms that would give the majority Muslim community of Lebanon greater representation in government, in return for guarantees of internal security from Syria. However, the talks failed to produce the results hoped for by Syria, and marked the beginning of the rapid disintegration of the Lebanese National Salvation Front, comprising leading Lebanese opponents of President Gemayel, which had been created, with Syrian backing, in mid-1983. In April 1984, however, President Gemayel gained approval from President Assad for plans for a government of national unity in Lebanon that gave equal representation in the Cabinet to Muslims and Christians, under the premiership of Rashid Karami; Gemayel was to remain as President. Nevertheless, inter-factional fighting continued and intensified in Beirut, threatening the existence of the new Lebanese Government.

INTERNAL TENSION

In November 1983 President Assad suffered what was thought to be a heart attack, which triggered a struggle for power among high-ranking figures in the military and intelligence services, including the President's brother, Rifaat Assad (who was commander of the defence brigades). Following his recovery, in March 1984 President Assad appointed a new Council of Ministers—the first ministerial reorganization for four years. He also appointed an unprecedented three Vice-Presidents: Rifaat Assad was made Vice-President for Military and National Security Affairs; Abd al-Halim Khaddam, the former Minister of Foreign Affairs, was made Vice-President for Political Affairs; and Zuheir Masharkah was promoted from his post as a regional secretary of the Baath Party to become Vice-President for Internal and Party Affairs.

In what was seen as a disciplinary measure against those principally responsible for the confrontations between military units that took place in and around Damascus after President Assad's illness, in June 1984 Rifaat Assad was sent to Geneva, Switzerland, while Gen. Ali Haydar (commander of the Special Forces élite army unit) and Gen. Shafiq Fayyadh (commander of the Third Armoured Division) were sent to Sofia, Bulgaria, apparently into temporary exile. Meanwhile, the defence brigades were absorbed into the army, with the exception of a few units that were put under the command of Rifaat Assad's son-in-law. Rifaat Assad was permitted to return to Syria in November in his capacity as Vice-President. President Assad was re-elected for a third seven-year term of office in February 1985, and appeared to have regained much of his former authority.

ISRAEL'S WITHDRAWAL FROM LEBANON

By means of Syrian mediation, a security plan for Beirut was agreed and put into operation in July 1984. The plan met with only limited success. In September Syria arranged a truce to end fighting in Tripoli between the pro-Syrian Arab Democratic Party and the Sunni Muslim Tawheed Islami (Islamic Unification Movement). This prepared the way for the Lebanese army to enter the city in November, under the terms of an extended security plan—backed by Syria—to assert the authority of the Lebanese Government in Beirut and Tripoli, and south of the capital.

Syria approved Lebanese participation in talks with the Israelis to co-ordinate the departure of the Israeli Defence Force (IDF) from southern Lebanon with other security forces. Talks repeatedly foundered on the question of which forces should take the place of the IDF. Under Syrian influence, the Lebanese wanted the UN Interim Force in Lebanon (UNIFIL) to police the Israel–Lebanon border (as it had been mandated to do in 1978), and the Lebanese army to deploy north of the Litani river, between UNIFIL and the Syrians in the Beqa'a valley. Israel wanted UNIFIL to be deployed north of the Litani, while the Israeli-backed 'South Lebanon Army' (SLA) patrolled the southern Lebanese border. In the absence of an agreement, on 14 January 1985 the Israeli Cabinet voted to take steps towards a three-phase unilateral withdrawal to the international border.

On 10 June 1985 Israel announced the accomplishment of the final phase of the withdrawal, taking its forces behind the southern Lebanese border and leaving a protective 'buffer zone' inside Lebanon, policed by the SLA with IDF support. The Israeli withdrawal increased Syria's influence, and offered Syria the opportunity of reducing its costly military presence in the north and east of the country. In late June and early July Syria withdrew an estimated 10,000 troops from the Beqa'a valley, leaving some 25,000 in position.

SYRIA'S GRIP ON LEBANON

In spite of the election, in March 1985, of a new Chairman of the Lebanese Forces (LF), Elie Hobeika, who announced his readiness to negotiate with Syria and its Druze allies, Syria was unable to prevent renewed inter-factional fighting in Beirut. Assad's strategy in Lebanon was to allow no group to become powerful enough to challenge his authority. In May and June Syria backed the Amal Movement, a Shi'ite militia, in attempting to suppress a resurgence of the PLO (in particular the pro-Arafat wing of the movement) in the Palestinian refugee camps of Sabra, Chatila and Bourj el-Barajneh in Beirut. In the bloody battle for the camps more than 600 people were killed, but Amal failed to take control. An unforeseen development was the extent to which pro- and anti-Arafat PLO factions united to resist the attack on the Palestinian community. On 17 June a fragile, Syrian-sponsored cease-fire agreement was reached in Damascus between Amal and the Palestinian National Salvation Front (PNSF), representing the pro-Syrian, anti-Arafat elements in the camps.

In June 1985 President Assad was able to demonstrate that he retained some command over events in Lebanon when his intercession was instrumental in securing the release of 39 American hostages from a hijacked TWA airliner, which had been detained by members of the radical Shi'ite group Hezbollah. Four weeks of intensive fighting between rival militias (the pro-Arafat Tawheed Islami and the pro-Syrian Arab Democratic Party) in the Lebanese port town of Tripoli, in September and October, were interpreted as part of Syria's campaign to prevent the re-emergence of the pro-Arafat wing of the PLO in Lebanon. Tripoli's port was allegedly being used to distribute weapons and supplies to Arafat loyalists in other parts of the country. A cease-fire was agreed in Damascus in November, and troops of the Syrian army moved into the town.

After a month of negotiations, under Syrian auspices, between the three main Lebanese militias—the Druze forces,

Amal and the LF—a politico-military settlement of the civil war was finally signed by the three militia leaders (Walid Joumblatt, Nabih Berri and Elie Hobeika, respectively) on 28 December 1985, in Damascus. The agreement provided for an immediate cease-fire and for an end to the state of civil war within one year; the militias would be disbanded, and responsibility for security would pass to a reconstituted and religiously integrated army, supported by Syrian forces. It also recognized Lebanon's community of interest with Syria, and envisaged a 'strategic integration' of the two countries in the fields of military relations, foreign policy and security. Before long, however, fierce dissension over the concessions made by Hobeika led to clashes in east Beirut between elements of the LF who supported the agreement and those who were opposed to its terms. In mid-January 1986 Hobeika was forced into exile, and Samir Geagea resumed command of the LF, urging the renegotiation of the Damascus agreement. The long round of inter-sectarian clashes in Beirut resumed in earnest on 22 January.

Sporadic fighting between Palestinian guerrillas and Shi'ite Amal militiamen for control of the refugee camps in the south of Beirut escalated into major exchanges in May 1986. The Palestinian refugee camps of Sabra, Chatila and Bourj el-Barajneh were increasingly under the control of guerrillas loyal to Yasser Arafat, who were continuing to return to Lebanon. Syria appeared to be powerless to prevent the resurgence of the PLO in Lebanon. Leaders of the Muslim communities in Lebanon met Syrian government officials in Damascus, and agreed to impose a cease-fire around the Palestinian refugee camps in Beirut on 14 June. The cease-fire proved to be the first element in a Syrian-sponsored peace plan for Muslim west Beirut. The Amal, Druze and Murabitoun militias were ordered to leave the streets, and in February 1987 Syrian troops moved into Beirut, supported by members of the Syrian security service, *Mukhabarat* ('information'), under the command of Brig.-Gen. Ghazi Kenaan.

The security plan was successful in curbing the activities of militias in west Beirut, and allowed Syria to avert the danger of an anti-Syrian alliance being formed in west Beirut. However, the plan (and Syria's visible involvement in it) was strongly opposed in Christian east Beirut, and the Syrians hesitated over extending it to the southern suburbs, which contained the majority of the city's Palestinian refugees and was controlled by the Shi'ite Hezbollah, backed by Iran, whose influence was growing at the expense of Amal.

BOMB ATTACKS IN SYRIA

On 13 March 1986 a bomb exploded in Damascus, causing an estimated 60 deaths. Syria blamed Iraqi agents for the attack. Then, on 15 April bombs exploded, almost simultaneously, in five Syrian towns. There were further bomb attacks on public transport targets in several towns, including Damascus, before the end of the month. In May the Government admitted that 144 people had been killed during the April bombing campaign. According to the Voice of Lebanon radio station, a hitherto unknown Syrian group (the 17 October Movement for the Liberation of the Syrian People) claimed responsibility for the campaign, and its message suggested that it was a pro-Iraqi, militant Islamist organization.

SYRIA AND INTERNATIONAL TERRORISM

Although it failed to provide conclusive proof of Syrian involvement, the USA claimed that there was evidence of a link between Syria and the Palestinian terrorists who carried out attacks on airports in Rome, Italy, and Vienna, Austria, in December 1985. President Assad denied that Syria was sponsoring terrorism, and refused to restrict the activities of Palestinian groups (including the Abu Nidal faction, the Fatah Revolutionary Council) on Syrian territory, which, he claimed, were 'cultural and political'.

In October 1986 the British Government severed diplomatic relations with Syria after claiming to have proof of the complicity of Syrian diplomats in an attempt to plant a bomb on an Israeli airliner at London's Heathrow airport in the previous April. In November three Syrian diplomats were expelled from West Germany, after a court in West Berlin ruled that the Syrian embassy in East Berlin was implicated in the bombing of a discothèque in the West of the city in April. Later that month the member states of the European Community (EC, now European Union—EU), with the exception of Greece, imposed limited diplomatic and economic sanctions against Syria, as did the USA and Canada (both of which recalled their ambassadors to Syria).

Syria persistently denied any involvement in international terrorism, and by April 1987 several EC countries—with the exception of the United Kingdom—had made tentative advances to Syria, seeking to upgrade diplomatic relations. France in particular had been an unenthusiastic supporter of the sanctions demanded by the British Government, mindful of the crucial role that Syria had to play in the Middle East peace process, and of the need for its co-operation in securing the release of Western hostages being held by militant Islamist groups in Beirut. For its part, Syria appeared to be anxious to be seen to dissociate itself from terrorist groups and to use its influence in Lebanon to free Western hostages. In June of that year it was reported that the offices of Abu Nidal's Fatah Revolutionary Council, near Damascus, had been closed, and many of its members expelled, by the Syrian authorities, and that Abu Nidal himself had moved to Libya. The EC, with the exception of the United Kingdom, ended its ban on ministerial contacts with Syria in July, and financial aid was resumed in September, although a ban on the sale of arms to Syria remained in force.

PAX SYRIANA IN LEBANON

In February 1987 fierce fighting occurred in west Beirut between Amal forces and an alliance of Druze, Murabitoun and Communist Party militias. Muslim leaders appealed for Syria to intervene to restore order, and about 4,000 Syrian troops were deployed in west Beirut on 22 February. The Syrian force (which was soon increased to some 7,500 troops) succeeded in enforcing a cease-fire in the central and northern districts of west Beirut, and moved into areas occupied by Hezbollah, killing 23 Hezbollah members and forcing others to return to their stronghold in the southern suburbs, into which the Syrians still declined to venture.

A Syrian-supervised cease-fire at the embattled Palestinian refugee camps in Beirut took effect on 6 April 1987. The cease-fire agreement was negotiated by representatives of Syria, Amal and the pro-Syrian PNSF, and brought an end to the worst fighting. Members of the PNSF and Arafat loyalists had made common cause in defence of the camps, and their alliance was a contributory factor in the reunification of the PLO under Arafat's leadership, which took place at the 18th session of the Palestine National Council (PNC) in the Algerian capital, Algiers, in April. The PNC adopted a resolution committing itself to improving PLO relations with Syria.

In January 1988 the leader of Amal, Nabih Berri, announced an end to the siege of the Palestinian refugee camps in Beirut and southern Lebanon. On 21 January Syrian troops replaced Amal militiamen and soldiers of the Lebanese army in positions around the Beirut camps, and the 14-month siege of Rashidiyah camp, near Tyre, was ended. However, PLO guerrillas loyal to Arafat refused to withdraw from their positions overlooking Ain al-Hilweh, interrupting the withdrawal of Amal from around Rashidiyah.

A new political crisis overtook Lebanon in mid-1987. On 1 June the Lebanese Prime Minister, Rashid Karami, a Sunni Muslim who was seen as Syria's most influential ally in Lebanon, was assassinated. Although it was not clear who was responsible for Karami's death, the Muslim community strongly suspected the Christian LF militia of involvement. In July Syria sponsored the formation of the Front for Unification and Liberalization, which included among its members Joumblatt and Berri; however, no representatives of Hezbollah or other pro-Iranian factions participated.

REGIONAL RELATIONS

Relations between Jordan and Syria had been poor since 1979, when Syria had accused Jordan of harbouring anti-Syrian groups. Syria opposed the Jordanian-Palestinian agreement, signed by King Hussein and Yasser Arafat in Amman in

February 1985. In August Syria boycotted the extraordinary meeting of the Arab League in Casablanca, Morocco, which was convened partly to consider the Amman accord. The PLO's persistent refusal to acknowledge the UN Security Council Resolutions (Nos 242 and 338) on the Palestinian issue, and a series of terrorist incidents in the second half of 1985 in which the PLO was implicated, reducing its credibility as a potential partner in peace negotiations, led King Hussein to seek a reconciliation with Syria. Following talks held in Riyadh in October, Jordan and Syria rejected 'partial and unilateral' solutions (ruling out separate negotiations with Israel) and affirmed their adherence to the 1982 Fez plan, omitting all reference to the Jordanian-Palestinian peace initiative. In February 1986 King Hussein withdrew from his political alliance with Arafat, and in April Jordan appointed its first ambassador to Syria since 1980.

Syria severed diplomatic relations with Morocco in July 1986, after King Hassan II held talks with Prime Minister Shimon Peres of Israel. A realignment of Syrian policy towards Iran, which became more apparent during 1987, also led to an increasingly uneasy relationship between Syria and its neighbours. As international opinion turned against Iran in the Iran–Iraq War, Syria's support for Iran became more of a liability. The USSR was critical of Syria's stance (reportedly withholding sales of arms to Syria in July). Following Libya's decision to switch its allegiance to Iraq in September, Syria remained the only Arab country to support Iran. However, Syria's concern to regain the favour of Western nations by distancing itself from Islamist fundamentalist and anti-Arafat terrorist groups, and by seeking the release of Western hostages in Lebanon, eventually brought it into dispute with Iran. To Iran's obvious annoyance, Syrian troops limited Hezbollah's movements and activities in the parts of Lebanon under de facto Hezbollah control. In June 1987 Syria sent tanks and members of the Special Forces to surround the camps of Hezbollah militiamen and several hundred Iranian Revolutionary Guards, who were stationed at Ba'albek in the Beqa'a valley. Syria's relations with Iran were further strained by the kidnapping in that month of an American journalist, allegedly by Hezbollah. When, four weeks later, the hostage escaped, his freedom was attributed to Syrian mediation with Hezbollah. Syrian influence was also instrumental in securing the release in September of a West German hostage, one of 23 Western captives being held in south Beirut. At the beginning of September the US ambassador to Syria, who had been recalled to Washington, DC, in November 1986, returned to Syria, and the US Government withdrew its opposition to operations by US oil companies in Syria.

Assad and President Saddam Hussain of Iraq were reported to have met secretly in Jordan in April 1987. In November the two leaders met again at an extraordinary summit meeting of the Arab League in Amman, Jordan. The summit, which had been convened by King Hussein of Jordan to discuss the Iran–Iraq War, produced a unanimous statement expressing solidarity with Iraq, condemning Iran for its occupation of Arab (i.e. Iraqi) territory, and urging it to observe the cease-fire proposals contained in UN Security Council Resolution 598. It was widely reported that Syria had been offered financial inducements by Saudi Arabia (Syria's principal source of aid), Kuwait and other states of the Persian (Arabian) Gulf to realign its stance on the Iran–Iraq War with majority Arab opinion. However, after the summit meeting Syria announced that it had succeeded in obstructing an Iraqi proposal that Arab states should sever diplomatic relations with Iran; that a reconciliation with Iraq had not taken place; and that Syrian relations with Iran remained unchanged. Syria had used its veto to prevent the adoption of an Iraqi proposal to readmit Egypt to membership of the Arab League, but it could not prevent the inclusion in the final communiqué of a clause permitting individual member nations to re-establish diplomatic relations with Egypt. By February 1988 a total of 11 Arab countries, including Iraq, had resumed diplomatic links with Egypt.

GOVERNMENT CHANGES

A major government reorganization was implemented in November 1987, following the resignation of the Prime Minister, Abd al-Rauf al-Kassem. His Government had been accused of corruption and inefficiency, and of failure to solve the country's severe economic problems. Mahmoud al-Zoubi, the Speaker of the Assembly, was appointed Prime Minister, and 15 new members were appointed to the Council of Ministers.

SYRIAN AND IRANIAN SURROGATES CLASH IN LEBANON

The Syrian-brokered lifting of the siege of the Palestinian refugee camps in January 1988, at a time when the Palestinian *intifada* (uprising) in the Israeli-occupied territories was attracting widespread sympathy for the plight of the Palestinians and increasing support for Arafat, allowed Syria to deploy Amal forces against the Iranian-backed Hezbollah, whose strength was viewed by Syria as a threat to its own ambitions to control Lebanon. The first military confrontation between the two groups occurred in March 1988 in the Nabatiyah area of southern Lebanon, and by May had spread to the southern suburbs of Beirut. Syrian troops became involved in the fighting on 13 May when Hezbollah guerrillas, who had wrested control of about 90% of the 36-sq-km southern suburbs from Amal, briefly advanced into a Syrian-controlled area of west Beirut. On 27 May Syrian troops moved into the southern suburbs of Beirut to enforce a cease-fire agreement reached by Syria, Iran and their militia proxies on the previous day. When the Syrian deployment was complete, Amal and Hezbollah were to close down their military operations in all parts of the southern suburbs, except in areas adjoining the 'Green Line' (which separated west Beirut from the Christian-controlled east of the city). In June, in accordance with the agreement, Nabih Berri announced the disbandment of the Amal militia in Beirut and the Beqa'a valley (areas under Syrian control) and all other areas of the country except the south (which was not controlled by Syrian troops).

ARAFAT LOYALISTS DRIVEN OUT OF BEIRUT

In April 1988 a reconciliation was reported to have taken place between President Assad and Yasser Arafat. The two leaders held discussions when Arafat attended the funeral in Damascus of Khalil al-Wazir ('Abu Jihad'), the military commader of the Palestine Liberation Army. At the end of April Arafat loyalists in the Palestinian refugee camps of Chatila and Bourj el-Barajneh in Beirut, possibly interpreting Syria's support for the Palestinian *intifada* and the rapprochement between their leader and Assad as evidence of the Syrian President's waning commitment to the revolt within the PLO, attempted to drive out the fighters belonging to the Syrian-backed group, al-Fatah Intifada (Fatah Uprising), led by 'Abu Musa'. The Syrian troops who had surrounded the camps in April 1987 did not attempt to intervene in the fighting. On 27 June 1988 the Arafat loyalists in Chatila camp surrendered, and in July Bourj el-Barajneh, Arafat's last stronghold in Beirut, fell to 'Abu Musa'. Following the surrender, Syria granted 220 PLO guerrillas safe passage to the Palestinian camp at Ain al-Hilweh, near Sidon.

Amin Gemayel's term of office as President of Lebanon was due to expire on 22 September 1988, and the National Assembly was required to elect a new President prior to that date. Three main contenders for the presidency (traditionally a post occupied by a Maronite Christian) emerged: Gen. Michel Aoun, the Commander-in-Chief of the armed forces; Raymond Eddé, the exiled leader of the Maronite Bloc National; and Suleiman Franjiya, President of Lebanon between 1970 and 1976. The latter did not announce his candidacy until 16 August 1988, two days before the election was scheduled to take place, and the news immediately united President Gemayel and Samir Geagea, the commander of the Christian LF militia, in opposition to Franjiya's candidature, on the grounds that he represented Syrian interests. It was Franjiya who, as President, had invited Syria to intervene militarily in Lebanon to end the civil war in 1976. On 18 August 1988 only 38 of the 76 surviving members of the National Assembly attended the session at which the new President was to be elected. The President of the Assembly declared the session inquorate, and the election was postponed.

Consultations between Syria and the USA resumed during September 1988 to find a compromise candidate for the presidency. It was reported that they had agreed to support the candidacy of Mikhail al-Daher, a deputy in the National Assembly, but Christian leaders in Lebanon repeated their rejection of any candidate imposed upon them by foreign powers. Instead, a Christian military Government was formed by Gen. Aoun to rival the existing Muslim caretaker Government of Selim al-Hoss, which had the full support of Syria. A second attempt to conduct the presidential election was made on 22 September, but the session of the National Assembly again failed to achieve a quorum. Only minutes before his term of office was due to expire, President Gemayel appointed a six-member interim military administration, composed of three Christian and three Muslim officers, led by Gen. Aoun, to govern until a new President was elected. However, the three Muslim officers refused to take up their posts, while the two Christian members of the existing civilian Government surrendered their posts in recognition of the authority of the interim military administration. Lebanon was plunged into a constitutional crisis, with two governments—one Christian, in east Beirut, and one predominantly Muslim, in west Beirut—claiming legitimacy. Syria refused to recognize the interim military Government, and there were fears that, unless a new President could be elected, the fact of dual authority would formalize what was already an effective partition of the country into Christian and Muslim cantons.

GENERAL AOUN'S 'WAR OF LIBERATION'

In March 1989 the most violent clashes for two years erupted in Beirut between Christian and Muslim brigades of the Lebanese army, loyal to Gen. Aoun, and Syrian-backed Muslim and Druze militias, positioned on either side of the 'Green Line'. The hostilities erupted over the blockade of illegal ports in west and south Beirut by Christian forces. During the ensuing six months, Gen. Aoun's self-declared 'war of liberation' developed into one of the most violent confrontations of the Lebanese conflict. Successive plans for peace foundered on the question of the withdrawal of Syria's estimated 35,000–40,000 troops in Lebanon, on which Gen. Aoun insisted as an essential condition of any cease-fire agreement. A fragile cease-fire was arranged at an emergency summit meeting of Arab leaders in Casablanca in May, but the proposal (supported by Egypt, Iraq, Jordan and the PLO) that Syria should immediately withdraw its troops from Lebanon was abandoned in response to Syrian opposition.

By August 1989 it had become clear that Syria was prepared to disregard international censure of its role in Lebanon and to wage a war of attrition against the Lebanese army. However, Syria was restrained from using its overwhelming military superiority by several factors, including the risk of an Israeli intervention, and the necessity to avoid any further deterioration of its relations both with Western countries and the USSR, which such an assault might have provoked.

In September 1989 the Tripartite Arab Committee on Lebanon announced a seven-point plan for peace in Lebanon, which, unlike its previous diplomatic initiatives, did not demand the withdrawal of Syrian forces from Lebanon. The proposals envisaged a cease-fire; the ending of the Syrian naval blockade of the Christian enclave; and the convening of the Lebanese National Assembly to discuss a 'charter of national conciliation' drafted by the Tripartite Committee. Although Gen. Aoun agreed to the Committee's peace plan for Lebanon, he subsequently vowed to continue the war by political means until the liberation was complete.

In October 1989 the Lebanese National Assembly convened in Saudi Arabia and endorsed a charter of national reconciliation (the Ta'if agreement—for full details, see the chapter on Lebanon), which set out the revised constitutional framework for a united and sovereign Lebanon, and envisaged a role for the Syrian armed forces in the implementation of a security plan incorporated in the agreement. Gen. Aoun rejected the Saudi-brokered accord as a betrayal of Lebanese sovereignty, because it did not provide a timetable for a full withdrawal of Syrian forces, although the conditions for a pull-out were, in fact, defined in the accord. Later in the year Gen. Aoun was dismissed as Commander-in-Chief of the Lebanese army and Gen. Emile Lahoud appointed in his place.

In January 1990 intense fighting erupted between Aoun's forces and the LF, led by Samir Geagea, for control of the Christian enclave in Beirut, but Syria remained reluctant to intervene militarily. Fighting continued in Beirut until Syria intervened decisively in October, when thousands of its troops were deployed to evict Gen. Aoun from the presidential palace at Baabda, after President Elias Hrawi of Lebanon had requested the troops' assistance. Christian resistance to the legitimization of Syrian influence in Lebanon had finally been broken, paving the way for the full implementation of the Ta'if agreement.

FOREIGN RELATIONS, 1987–90

In December 1987 a violent Palestinian uprising erupted in the Occupied Territories against Israeli occupation of the West Bank and Gaza Strip. In February 1988, with the *intifada* showing no sign of moderating in intensity, the US Secretary of State, George Shultz, embarked on a tour of Middle East capitals, including Damascus, in an attempt to solicit support for a new peace initiative. The Shultz Plan proposed an international peace conference and direct talks between Israel and each of its adversaries (excluding the PLO), and an interim period of limited autonomy for Palestinians in the West Bank and the Gaza Strip, pending a permanent negotiated settlement (Documents on Palestine, see p. 73). President Assad stopped short of rejecting the plan outright, but, in certain fundamental respects, it was impossible for any Arab leader to accept: it failed to recognize the right of the PLO to participate in peace negotiations or the right of the Palestinians to self-determination. Unsurprisingly, further talks between Shultz and Assad in April failed to reconcile the two sides.

The extraordinary summit meeting of the Arab League held in Algiers in June 1988 rendered the Shultz Plan effectively moribund by demanding the participation of the PLO in any future peace conference, endorsing the Palestinians' right to self-determination and urging the establishment of an independent Palestinian state in the West Bank. Syria, alone of all the Arab states, refused to recognize the independent Palestinian state proclaimed at the 19th session of the PNC in Algiers in November. The cease-fire in the Iran–Iraq War, which came into force on 20 August, presented Iraq with an opportunity to settle old scores with its Baathist rival, initially by attempting to thwart Syrian plans for domination over Lebanon. In September Iraq was reportedly supplying arms and money to the Christian LF in Lebanon, and, following Lebanon's abortive presidential election, Iraq proclaimed its support for the interim military administration appointed by President Gemayel, which was opposed by Syria. During the 'war of liberation' waged by Gen. Aoun against Syrian forces in Lebanon, Iraq became the principal supplier of arms to the Lebanese army.

Syria found itself on the same side as Iraq in a dispute with Turkey over the diversion of water from the Euphrates river in order to fill the reservoir supplying Turkey's newly constructed Atatürk dam. In January 1990 Syria lodged a formal complaint against Turkey regarding the effects of the diversion on Syria's water and electricity supplies. However, the Turkish Government rejected the complaint, claiming that it had increased the supply of water to Iraq and Syria by 50% between November 1989 and January 1990 in order to make good the loss of water caused by the diversion.

SYRIA AND THE 1990–91 GULF CRISIS

By the end of the 1980s President Assad had responded to the emerging new international order with a significant reorientation of Syrian foreign policy, including the resumption of diplomatic relations with Egypt after a rupture lasting almost 12 years; a tentative rapprochement with the PLO; and a shift of emphasis in Soviet-Syrian relations. Moreover, Syria exploited the diplomatic opportunities arising from Iraq's invasion of Kuwait in August 1990 to improve its relations with the USA.

In May 1990 President Hosni Mubarak of Egypt visited Syria, the first such visit by an Egyptian leader since 1977. Syria supported Egypt's efforts to co-ordinate Arab responses to Iraq's invasion of Kuwait, and agreed, at an emergency summit meeting of the Arab League held in Cairo on 10 August 1990, to send troops to Saudi Arabia as part of a pan-Arab deterrent force supporting the US effort to deter an Iraqi invasion of Saudi Arabia. Despite widespread domestic discontent, Syria committed itself to the demand for an unconditional Iraqi withdrawal from Kuwait, and later in August the first contingent of Syrian troops was deployed in Saudi Arabia, joining a US-led multinational force. To placate domestic and wider Arab criticism, Syria asserted that its troops were in Saudi Arabia purely for defensive purposes. Soon it became apparent that Syria's participation in the US-led multinational force was transforming its relations with the West. In November diplomatic ties were restored between Syria and the United Kingdom. By December an estimated 20,000 Syrian troops had been deployed in Saudi Arabia.

In January 1991 President Saddam Hussain of Iraq rejected a message from President Assad, who sought to persuade him that Iraq's occupation of Kuwait benefited Israel alone. However, following attacks by Iraqi Scud missiles on Israel, Syria warned Israel against military involvement in the Gulf crisis, implying that it might be obliged to withdraw from the multinational force in the event of an Israeli attack on an Arab state. Subsequent statements, however, indicated that Syria would tolerate limited Israeli retaliation against Iraq for the missile attacks.

In early 1991 the overwhelming military defeat of Iraq by the US-led multinational force placed Syria in a stronger position with regard to virtually all of its major regional concerns. Syria consolidated its relations with Egypt, and in March the foreign ministers of the Cooperation Council for the Arab States of the Gulf (Gulf Cooperation Council—GCC) member states met their Egyptian and Syrian counterparts in Damascus to discuss increased co-operation in matters of regional security. The formation of an Arab peace-keeping force, comprising mainly Egyptian and Syrian troops, was subsequently announced.

Syria's decision to ally itself, in opposition to Iraq, with the Western powers and the so-called 'moderate' Arab states led the USA to accept that it could no longer seek to exclude it from any role in the resolution of the Arab–Israeli conflict. After the conclusion of hostilities with Iraq, US diplomacy focused on seeking to initiate negotiations between Israel, the Arab states—including Syria—and Palestinian representatives. Nevertheless, despite attempts in May 1991 by both the USA and the USSR to establish sufficient common ground between Israel and Syria for peace negotiations to begin, significant differences remained regarding the holding of a Middle East peace conference. Syria remained adamant that talks with Israel should take place within the framework of an international conference, with the full participation of the UN, and that afterwards such a conference should reconvene at regular intervals. Israel remained opposed both to UN participation and to the reconvening of the conference after an initial session had been held. The USA, for its part, excluded the possibility of holding a peace conference without Syrian participation.

In July 1991 President Assad agreed for the first time to participate in direct negotiations with Israel at a regional peace conference, for which the terms of reference would be a comprehensive peace settlement based on UN Security Council Resolutions 242 and 338. By agreeing to participate on the terms proposed by the USA, Syria decisively increased the diplomatic pressure on Israel to do likewise. On 4 August the Israeli Cabinet formally agreed to attend a peace conference on the terms put forward by the USA and the USSR.

Following the final dissolution of the USSR in December 1991, and the consequent erosion of its position as a potential counterfoil to the USA's Middle East policies, Syria remained obliged actively to support and participate in the US peace initiative. With regard to other regional issues, however, the Syrian Government appeared determined not to acquiesce in the interests of the USA. In mid-April 1992 Syria announced that it would continue to maintain air links with Libya, in defiance of the sanctions that the UN had imposed on that country (see the chapter on Libya). In late April, in an effort to allay suspicions of its Middle East policies, the US Administration formally assured the Syrian Government that it had no hostile intentions towards it.

NEGOTIATIONS WITH ISRAEL, 1993–2000

By October 1993—following an initial, 'symbolic' session of the conference held in Madrid, Spain, in October 1991, and attended by Israeli, Syrian, Egyptian, Lebanese and Palestinian-Jordanian delegations—11 sessions of bilateral negotiations had been held between Israeli and Syrian delegations. In April 1992 they had proceeded to debate the precise meaning of UN Security Council Resolution 242, but the Israeli Government continued firmly to reject any exchange of occupied land—including the Golan Heights—in return for a peace settlement. In May Syria and Lebanon refused to attend multilateral discussions, convened in Belgium, Austria, Canada and Japan, to discuss, among other issues, water resources and the question of Palestinian refugees. During the sixth round of bilateral negotiations, which commenced on 24 September in Washington, DC, and lasted for a month, the new Labour-dominated coalition Government in Israel (elected in July) reportedly indicated its willingness to consider some form of compromise, although it gave no sign that it was prepared to meet Syria's minimum demand: Israel's full and unconditional compliance with UN Security Council Resolution 242, which required, *inter alia*, the withdrawal of Israeli armed forces from territories occupied in 1967.

The original framework for negotiation—simultaneous bilateral negotiation between Israel and its counterparts Syria, Lebanon and the Palestinians—broke down in September 1993, when the PLO and Israel signed the Declaration of Principles on Palestinian Self-Rule (Documents on Palestine, see p. 76), providing for Palestinian self-rule in the Gaza Strip and Jericho. President Assad regarded the agreement as having weakened the united Arab position in the ongoing peace process with Israel, and indicated that Syria would continue to support those Palestinian factions, such as the Damascus-based Popular Front for the Liberation of Palestine—General Command (PFLP—GC), which opposed the agreement.

On 16 January 1994 President Assad met US President Bill Clinton for talks in Geneva aimed at giving fresh momentum to the negotiations. Bilateral discussions continued with US mediation, despite a temporary suspension following the murder of some 30 worshippers at a mosque in Hebron on the West Bank by a right-wing Jewish extremist in February. Assad continued to reject proposals to hold 'secret' talks with Israel, and ignored Israeli demands to prevent attacks by Lebanese militia groups on the Israeli forces in southern Lebanon.

Syria expressed dissatisfaction at the agreement reached between Israel and Jordan in June 1994, accusing the two sides of placing obstacles in the way of reaching a comprehensive regional peace settlement. President Clinton attended the signing of the peace treaty between Israel and Jordan on 26 October, and he visited Syria the following day—the first visit to the country by a US President for 20 years.

In March 1995—more than a year after their suspension—discussions between Syria and Israel finally resumed, and in May the two countries concluded a 'framework understanding on security arrangements' in order to facilitate the participation in the negotiations of the respective Chiefs of Staff. President Assad spoke publicly about the peace process for the first time in June, taking the unprecedented step of referring to Israel by name. Despite Syria's willingness to compromise on the extension of the demilitarized area on its side of the border, talks between the Israeli and Syrian Chiefs of Staff in Washington, DC, reportedly stalled over Israel's insistence on retaining its early-warning system on Mount Hermon. There were also differences over the delineation of the final border between the two countries, with Syria insisting on a return to the border that existed before the 1967 war, and Israel demanding a return to the pre-1948 border. Many observers concluded that Israeli Prime Minister Itzhak Rabin had decided not to try to reach a full settlement with Syria until after the Israeli elections due to take place in 1996. In November 1995, on becoming Israeli Prime Minister after the assassination of Rabin, Shimon Peres declared that seeking peace with Syria would be his top priority, and appealed for the talks to be expanded to cover a range of political issues in addition to military questions. Syria welcomed Peres's initiative, and the two countries concluded a 10-point agreement to act as a framework for new negotiations. A new round of US-sponsored talks began in December in Maryland, USA, and continued during January–February 1996.

Following a series of suicide bomb attacks in Israel in February and March 1996, in which more than 50 Israelis were killed, Prime Minister Peres broke off negotiations with Syria. Despite pressure from the USA and Egypt, President Assad refused to attend the 'summit of peacemakers' at Sharm el-Sheikh, Egypt, which he considered an attempt to support the embattled Israeli Prime Minister and argued that the only effective means of saving the peace process was to reconvene the Madrid conference. After the summit Israel demanded that Syria should explicitly condemn terrorism before it would resume peace talks. Syria responded that it did condemn terrorism, but stated that violent resistance to Israeli occupation was a legitimate right of the Palestinians. Syria also rejected demands by Israel and the USA that it should close down the offices in Damascus of radical Palestinian groups opposed to the peace process.

Negotiations suffered a further reverse in April 1996, when Israel launched 'Operation Grapes of Wrath', a massive bombardment of Lebanon in response to Hezbollah rocket attacks on Kiryat Shmona and other northern settlements. When both Syria and Lebanon refused to yield to Israeli and US demands, Shimon Peres gave priority once again to negotiations with the Palestinians. Nevertheless, in advance of the Israeli elections in May, Peres made clear his willingness to make territorial compromises over the Golan.

The unexpected victory of Likud and the subsequent formation of a right-wing Government in Israel, under Binyamin Netanyahu, was greeted with alarm in Syria. In a speech to the Knesset (parliament) following his appointment, Prime Minister Netanyahu appealed for the reopening of unconditional peace talks with Arab states, but rejected the 'land-for-peace' policies of his Labour predecessor and told deputies that his emphasis would be on security. He insisted that retaining sovereignty over the Golan Heights must be the basis of any peace settlement with Syria. An emergency Arab League summit meeting, held in Cairo in June 1996, urged the new Israeli Government not to abandon the 'land-for-peace' principle, and appealed for the removal of all Israeli settlements on the Golan Heights and its return to Syria. In response, however, Netanyahu stated that Israel should wait at least two generations before even discussing the possibility of giving up the Golan, even if Syria agreed to normalize relations with Israel.

In August 1996 Netanyahu warned that further attacks by Hezbollah guerrillas might provoke Israeli reprisals against Syria. Tensions mounted as the Syrian Chief of Staff claimed that the military option was still open to Syria in its dispute with Israel, and intelligence sources reported the redeployment of Syrian troops from Lebanon to new positions in Syria, possibly to reinforce the western defences of the capital. An offer by Netanyahu to withdraw Israeli troops from southern Lebanon, on condition that Hezbollah forces be disarmed and that both Lebanon and Syria agree to prevent them launching any new attacks on northern Israel, was rejected by President Assad. Such a move would have denied Syria the option of using Hezbollah to exert pressure on Israel while leaving Israel firmly in control of the Golan. The Syrian President insisted that peace negotiations could only resume if Netanyahu's Government honoured earlier agreements and understandings reached with Itzhak Rabin and Shimon Peres, including the commitment given to the USA by Rabin, prior to his assassination, that Israel would withdraw from the whole of the Golan Heights. However, Netanyahu declared that he was under no obligation to abide by what he referred to as 'theoretical statements' made by his predecessor during the course of negotiations.

During the early part of 1997 the Israeli Government's determination to proceed with the controversial Jewish settlement at Har Homa in Arab East Jerusalem, and the collapse in negotiations between Israel and the Palestinian (National) Authority (PA), further obstructed the Israeli-Syrian peace initiative. In February Israel announced that new Jewish settlements were to be constructed on the Golan Heights, and in July withdrawal from the Golan was made conditional on approval by two-thirds of the Knesset. In April the Israeli press accused Syria of developing weapons of mass destruction, including missiles armed with lethal nerve gas capable of hitting targets inside Israel. Syria denied the allegations.

Syria was sceptical that the US-brokered Wye River Memorandum (Documents on Palestine, see p. 92), signed in October 1998 by Israel and the PA, would increase the likelihood of a lasting peace in the Middle East. President Assad reiterated demands for a resumption of 'land-for-peace' negotiations. Following the defeat of the Likud party at the Israeli general election in May 1999, Israel's new Prime Minister, Ehud Barak (of the Labour-led One Israel coalition), reportedly proposed a five-phase plan to conclude a peace with Syria and to effect an Israeli withdrawal from southern Lebanon. Syria responded by demanding that Barak should uphold his pre-election pledge to withdraw from Lebanon within one year of his election and to resume peace negotiations from their point of deadlock in 1996. In July 1999, at the inauguration of the new Israeli Cabinet, Barak promised to negotiate a bilateral peace with Syria, based on UN Security Council Resolutions 242 and 338, apparently signalling to Syria his intention to return most of the occupied Golan Heights in exchange for peace and normalized relations.

The US Secretary of State, Madeleine Albright, held talks with President Assad in Damascus on 4 September 1999, and with Syria's Minister of Foreign Affairs, Farouk al-Shara', in New York later the same month. For the first time, she openly declared US support for Syrian demands for a complete Israeli withdrawal from the Golan Heights. However, nothing tangible was agreed regarding the resumption of peace talks with Israel, which remained tempered by continuing public disagreement over whether, as Syria claimed, Itzhak Rabin had agreed, during the previous round of negotiations in 1994–96, to a full Israeli withdrawal to its pre-1967 border. Israel asserted that it had only agreed to withdraw to the pre-1948 border between Palestine and Syria.

As a result of diplomatic efforts by US President Clinton, in December 1999 Israel and Syria agreed to resume direct negotiations at ministerial level. The first round of discussions between Farouk al-Shara' and the Israeli premier, Ehud Barak, opened on 15 December in Washington, DC, against a background of increased tension in southern Lebanon, and made little progress beyond an informal cease-fire agreement in order to limit the conflict in Lebanon.

The second round of senior-level talks, held on 3–10 January 2000 in Shepherdstown, West Virginia, USA, with the participation of President Clinton, proved inconclusive. Both Syria and Israel endorsed a 'draft working document' prepared by the US Administration as a basis for a framework agreement, but in mid-January bilateral relations again deteriorated. Syria repeated its assertion that Israel was reneging on promises made during the 1994–96 round of talks, and demanded a written commitment from Israel to withdraw from the Golan Heights prior to a resumption of talks, while Israel demanded the personal involvement of President Assad in the peace process, and that Syria take action to restrain Hezbollah in southern Lebanon. On 17 January 2000, amid an intensification of violence in southern Lebanon, the talks scheduled to begin two days later were postponed indefinitely. The informal truce ended in late January, following the killing by Hezbollah of a senior SLA commander.

In late February 2000 Barak was reported to have admitted that Israel had indeed agreed to withdraw from all of the Golan Heights ahead of the 1994–96 talks. However, he also indicated the intention of a unilateral Israeli withdrawal from southern Lebanon. This was confirmed in early March 2000 when the Israeli Cabinet voted unanimously to withdraw its forces from Lebanon by 7 July, even in the absence of an Israeli-Syrian peace settlement. Israel also sought to increase the pressure on

Syria by increasing the proportion of voters on the Golan Heights that would be required to approve, in a referendum, any deal on a handover to Syria.

On 26 March 2000 President Assad held discussions with US President Clinton in Geneva, amid expectations of a renewed breakthrough in Syrian-Israeli relations. The meeting failed to reach an agreement on the issues of sovereignty over a narrow strip of land along the north-eastern shore of Lake Tiberias, which under the pre-1967 border had been part of Israel, and control of a military early-warning station on Mount Hermon. Syria was willing to grant Israel access to the water of Lake Tiberias but not sovereignty over land; moreover, Syria would allow a third party, but not Israel itself, to run the Mount Hermon station.

As violence escalated in southern Lebanon, hardening Israeli attitudes were further demonstrated by the decision of the Government, on 13 April 2000, to end its suspension of the building of Jewish settlements on the Golan Heights. In early May the foreign ministers of Syria, Egypt and Saudi Arabia held talks regarding the peace process in the Syrian city of Palmyra. It was later reported that Egypt and Saudi Arabia had pledged military support to Syria in the event of an Israeli attack. The death on 10 June of President Hafiz al-Assad, and domestic preoccupations with the issue of his succession, inevitably stalled the Israeli-Syrian process even further.

SYRIAN DOMINANCE IN LEBANON DURING THE 1990S

By aligning itself with the Western powers and the moderate Arab states against Iraq in August 1990, Syria had obtained a free rein to consolidate its interests in Lebanon. In October, as the first step towards the implementation of the Ta'if agreement, it had acted to suppress the revolt led by Gen. Aoun. The Ta'if agreement stipulated a formal role for Syrian forces in Lebanon, assigning to them the responsibility for maintaining security there until the various Lebanese militias had been disbanded and the Lebanese army could itself assume that role. The implementation of the Ta'if agreement accelerated in the aftermath of Iraq's military defeat by the US-led multinational force in February 1991, and it culminated in the signing, in May, of a treaty of 'fraternity, co-operation and co-ordination' between Syria and Lebanon.

In May 1992 there was international concern at the escalating tension between Israel and Syria, as Syria allowed Hezbollah fighters to mount attacks on northern Israeli settlements, in the belief that only by continued coercion would Israel withdraw from occupied Arab territories. The Israeli Government, for its part, cited attacks by Hezbollah fighters in justification of its refusal to comply with UN Security Council Resolution 425 and withdraw its armed forces from the southern Lebanese 'buffer zone'. In July 1993 Israeli armed forces launched an intense offensive ('Operation Accountability') against the positions of Hezbollah in southern Lebanon, and were also reported to have attacked Syrian army positions in the Beqa'a valley. Many civilians were killed, and more than 250,000 Lebanese were forced to flee their homes. Mediation by the USA and Syria produced an informal 'understanding' between Israel and Hezbollah whereby fighting was to be confined to the southern 'security zone'. However, in April 1996 there was a new escalation in the conflict after Hezbollah fighters fired rockets into northern Israel, wounding 36 people, and killed an Israeli soldier in the security zone. Prime Minister Peres launched 'Operation Grapes of Wrath': for almost two weeks Israel attacked targets in the southern part of the zone, the Beqa'a valley and (for the first time in 14 years) the southern suburbs of Beirut. After a week of shuttle diplomacy by the US Secretary of State, Warren Christopher, a cease-fire 'understanding' was reached, under which, as in 1993, it was agreed effectively to confine the conflict to the security zone.

In March 1992 some Syrian troops began to withdraw from Beirut, in preparation for the withdrawal of all Syrian armed forces to eastern Lebanon by September (in accordance with the Ta'if agreement). However, Syrian influence on Lebanese internal affairs remained pervasive, and was regarded by some as having contributed to the resignation of the Lebanese Government in May. The decision of the new Lebanese administration to hold elections to the National Assembly in August and September, before the redeployment of Syrian armed forces to eastern Lebanon had taken place, attracted strong criticism by Maronites and other Christian groups, which argued that the continued presence of the Syrian forces would prejudice the outcome of the elections. However, the Lebanese Government insisted that its own army was still unable to guarantee the country's security, and that the timetable for elections, as stipulated by the Ta'if agreement, should be observed. Syria claimed that the Ta'if agreement allowed for them to remain to assist the Lebanese Government until constitutional reforms had been fully implemented. In October 1995 President Assad gave his support to the Lebanese Prime Minister's proposal to extend Lebanese President Elias Hrawi's term of office by another three years, a measure subsequently approved by the Lebanese National Assembly. Parliamentary elections held in mid-1996 produced an Assembly dominated by pro-Syrian supporters of Prime Minister Rafiq Hariri. (Lebanon's Constitutional Court overturned the results of voting for four seats, accusing Syria of intimidating voters.) During the elections Syria redeployed an estimated 10,000–12,000 of its troops from Lebanon to more secure positions in Syria, amid speculation that Damascus feared Israeli attacks.

In 1997 the US-based Human Rights Watch accused Syrian forces of seizing more than 100 Lebanese and Palestinians in Lebanon and detaining them in Syria, and appealed for Syrian forces to be held accountable for crimes they committed in Lebanon. In August of that year fighting again escalated in southern Lebanon between Syrian-backed Hezbollah guerrillas and Israeli troops supporting the SLA. The rising death toll among Israeli soldiers in Israel's self-declared security zone led to renewed demands within Israel for a unilateral withdrawal of its forces from Lebanon.

In April 1998 the Lebanese and Syrian Governments rejected an offer by Israel to withdraw from its security zone in southern Lebanon, providing that there were adequate security guarantees for its northern border. Syria dismissed the proposal as propaganda to improve Israel's image in the West, and saw Israel's request for direct negotiations with Lebanon as an attempt to undermine Syrian influence in Lebanon. In October this influence was evident in the selection of Gen. Emile Lahoud as the new Lebanese President, and the subsequent appointment of a Lebanese Government of national unity (see the chapter on Lebanon). In December Lebanon and Syria signed a bilateral trade agreement, in preparation for the customs union between the two countries, which entered into effect on 1 January 1999. In October both Governments reaffirmed their commitment to support one another, and further agreements were signed in the spheres of foreign relations, business and the environment.

Following the breakdown in direct talks between the Syrian and Israeli Governments at Shepherdstown in January 2000, there was a marked increase in attacks by Hezbollah fighters against Israeli forces in southern Lebanon. This, in turn, sparked retaliatory raids by Israel against Lebanese targets. However, on 5 March Israel announced that it would unilaterally withdraw from southern Lebanon by 7 July, regardless of whether peace agreements had been secured with Lebanon or Syria. Syrian Minister of Foreign Affairs al-Shara' warned that this would be a 'suicidal' course of action in the absence of such peace settlements. Israel's phased withdrawal ultimately disintegrated to become a rapid retreat, as the Israeli-backed SLA fled and Hezbollah intensified its military actions. Israel's occupation of southern Lebanon finally came to an end on 24 May, several weeks ahead of schedule. Hezbollah declared the withdrawal to be a vindication of its strategy of armed resistance. However, Syria was careful to ensure that its soldiers were not seen to be trying to fill the vacuum created by the Israeli withdrawal. (For further details regarding the Israeli withdrawal, see the chapters on Israel and Lebanon.)

OTHER DIPLOMATIC DEVELOPMENTS, 1995–2000

Throughout 1995–96 Syria's relations with the USA were largely dominated by the US-sponsored peace negotiations with Israel. In early 1996 the USA blamed the collapse of

Israeli-Syrian peace negotiations on President Assad's intransigence, becoming increasingly exasperated with the Syrian regime as it attempted to broker a cease-fire in southern Lebanon. After the right-wing victory in the Israeli elections in May, Syria appealed to the USA to abandon its perceived pro-Israeli bias in favour of a more balanced approach towards the peace process. In November 1997 efforts by Syria to combat drugs production and trafficking in Lebanon's Beqa'a valley (largely controlled by the Syrian army) were rewarded when President Clinton removed both Lebanon and Syria from the list of states allegedly producing or trafficking in illegal drugs. However, as long as Syria continued to support Hezbollah in southern Lebanon, and to host Palestinian 'rejectionist' groups in its territory, it was likely to remain on the US list of countries sponsoring terrorism.

Efforts by the Syrian Government to involve the EU in the peace negotiations with Israel, in order to counterbalance the USA's role, met with some success. In November 1997 the head of an EU mission to the Middle East met President Assad in Damascus and indicated that the EU supported Syria's demand that Israel withdraw completely from the Golan Heights. In July 1998 President Assad made an historic visit to France—the Syrian leader's first state visit outside the Middle East (with the exception of US-Syrian meetings in Switzerland) since 1976. The French President expressed support for the rejection by Syria of Israel's recent proposal for withdrawal from southern Lebanon.

In November 1998 Syria and Russia signed a military agreement whereby Russia would assist in the modernization of Syria's defence systems and provide training to military personnel. However, in January 1999 Syria denied Western reports that it was receiving military assistance from Russia in the development of chemical weapons. On 5–6 July President Assad paid his first visit to the Russian capital, Moscow, since the disintegration of the USSR. Assad held talks with the Russian President, Boris Yeltsin, on the Middle East peace process, military and technical co-operation between the two countries, and the issue of Syria's debt to Russia (estimated to be more than US $10,000m.). Russia reiterated its support for Syria's demand for a complete Israeli withdrawal from the Golan Heights and southern Lebanon, and for the resumption of peace negotiations from the point at which they stalled in 1996. In May 2000 it was reported that a major arms deal had been concluded whereby Russia had agreed to supply Syria with defence equipment, worth $2,000m., to upgrade its air force and air-defence system.

Following a meeting in the Iranian capital, Tehran, in September 1995, the Syrian, Iranian and Turkish Ministers of Foreign Affairs reaffirmed their commitment to the territorial integrity of Iraq. Although Syria had become a centre for elements of the Iraqi opposition, the Syrian regime was concerned that the disintegration of Iraq could set a dangerous precedent for its own minorities. In June 1997, following a round of talks of Syrian and Iraqi economic delegations, border crossings between the two countries were reopened for the first time in 17 years, allowing Iraq to import Syrian food and medical supplies under the UN 'oil-for-food' agreement. At the end of 1997 the Iraqi Deputy Prime Minister, Tareq Aziz, was received in Damascus by al-Shara', the first public meeting between senior ministers of the two countries for 17 years. In February 1998 Syria strongly opposed renewed air-strikes against Iraq. To emphasize this point, President Assad received the Iraqi Minister of Foreign Affairs in Damascus in that month, the first time that he had met publicly with a senior Iraqi official since the early 1980s.

Following Iraq's invasion of Kuwait in 1990, Syria continued to strengthen its links with Saudi Arabia and the Gulf states, while maintaining its 'strategic' relationship with Iran. Relations with Iran deteriorated in late 1995, however, after the Syrian regime voiced support for the United Arab Emirates (UAE) in its dispute with Iran over Abu Musa and the Greater and Lesser Tunb islands. None the less, in September 1998 Iran, Iraq and Syria agreed to the formation of a joint forum to co-ordinate their foreign policy. Iran was swift to explore the possibilities for further improving its relations with Syria following the death of President Hafiz al-Assad in June 2000. Within a week of Bashar al-Assad's assumption of the presidency, Ali Akbar Velayati, Iran's former Minister of Foreign Affairs, visited Damascus.

Syria's relations with Turkey remained strained, owing to continuing disagreements over cross-border water supplies, and regarding the Kurds. Both Syria and Iraq voiced concerns over the pollution level of the water they received, and about new dam projects in Turkey that would reduce the volume of Euphrates water downstream. Syria had traditionally used its support for the separatist Kurdistan Workers' Party (Partiya Karkeren Kurdistan—PKK) to put pressure on its powerful neighbour. The PKK was known to have bases in the Syrian-controlled Beqa'a valley in Lebanon, and at the end of 1995 Kurdish fighters crossed the Turkish border from Syria and launched attacks on Turkish military targets. In February 1996 Turkey accused the Syrian Government of giving refuge to the PKK leader, Abdullah Öcalan, and demanded his extradition to Turkey. Bilateral relations deteriorated sharply in April after it was revealed that Turkey and Israel had signed a military accord earlier in the year allowing the Israeli air force to use Turkish military airfields for training purposes. The crisis was aggravated when Turkey temporarily closed the flood gates of the Euphrates dams for 'technical reasons', resulting in water-rationing in Damascus. There was speculation in May that the Turkish Government might be responsible for a series of small explosions in Syrian cities. In October 1998 Turkey threatened to invade Syria if its demands for an end to Syrian support for the PKK and for the extradition of Abdullah Öcalan (who, they claimed, was directing PKK operations from Damascus) were not met. Turkey's stance was viewed by Syria as evidence of a Turkish-Israeli military and political alliance, and as a result both Syria and Turkey ordered troops to be deployed along their joint border. In late October, following Syrian assurances that Öcalan was not residing in Syria, Turkey and Syria signed an agreement whereby the PKK was to be banned from entering Syrian territory, and its active bases in Syria and Lebanon's Beqa'a valley were to be closed. Turkey and Syria also agreed mutual security guarantees, although Syrian concerns persisted regarding the close nature of Turkish-Israeli relations.

The election of the right-wing Likud Government in Israel in May 1996 resulted in closer contacts between Syria, Egypt, Jordan and the PA. At an Arab League summit in Cairo in June of that year, the Egyptian President, Hosni Mubarak, pledged support for President Assad and urged Turkey to reconsider its military agreement with Israel.

Syria's relations with Jordan improved after direct talks between King Hussein and President Assad at the Cairo summit, and in August 1996 the King met President Assad in Damascus—his first visit to Syria since 1994. Following this visit, the Syrian authorities arrested a number of individuals deemed to have been implicated in organizing attacks in Jordan, and the two countries agreed to reopen talks over the use of water from the Yarmouk river. In February 1999 President Assad unexpectedly attended the funeral of King Hussein of Jordan. The accession of King Abdullah ended five years of Syrian hostility towards Jordan caused by Jordan's signing of a bilateral peace agreement with Israel in 1994. Following an official visit by King Abdullah to Syria in April 1999, several Jordanian prisoners were released by the Syrian authorities, and Syria began to supply Jordan with water. A bilateral trade accord was signed in August after a meeting of the joint Jordanian-Syrian higher committee in Amman. Later that month Syria agreed to allow the free circulation of Jordanian newspapers and publications after a 10-year ban. Following the death of President Hafiz al-Assad in June 2000, King Abdullah was among the most prominent mourners. He visited the new President, Bashar al-Assad, in Damascus in July for talks regarding bilateral issues; Syria again agreed to supply Jordan with drinking water over the summer months of 2000.

A meeting between President Hafiz al-Assad and the PA President, Yasser Arafat, at the Cairo summit in June 1996 marked a temporary improvement in relations between the two men. In the following month Arafat visited Damascus, and his foreign affairs adviser, Farouk Kaddumi, held talks in the Syrian capital with leaders of Palestinian groups opposed to the Oslo Accords. Early in 1997, and again in July 1999, there were reports that the Syrian authorities had warned the Popular Front for the Liberation of Palestine (PFLP) and other Palestinian groups based in Damascus that their offices would be closed down if they continued to organize military operations against Israel from Syria. In August 1999 a diplomatic crisis developed between Syria and the PA after the Syrian Deputy Prime Minister and Minister of Defence, Maj.-Gen. Mustafa Tlass, made a series of personal insults against Arafat. Later that year there were reports of a heavy, Syrian-instigated crackdown on members of Arafat's Fatah movement in Palestinian refugee camps in southern Lebanon.

INTERNAL AFFAIRS, 1990–2000

In May 1990 elections were held to the People's Assembly, in which the number of seats was increased from 195 to 250. Candidates representing the Baath Party were elected to 134 seats, 54% of the total, compared with 66% of the total in elections held in 1986. Other parties that had joined the Baath Party-dominated NPF were elected to 32 seats, while independent candidates were elected to 84 seats. Some 60% of the electorate were reported to have participated in the elections, which were contested by 9,765 candidates.

There was speculation during 1991 that President Assad was preparing to introduce a degree of liberalization into Syria's autocratic political system. However, despite the release of 2,864 political prisoners in December and the announcement, in March 1992, that new political parties might in future be established in Syria, Assad rejected the adoption by Syria of foreign democratic frameworks as unsuited to the country's level of economic development.

In January 1994 the future stability of the regime became uncertain when Assad's eldest son, Basel, who had been expected to succeed his father as President, died in a motor accident. The President's second son, Bashar, was recalled from the United Kingdom, where he was studying, to assume the role of heir apparent. In August 16 senior officials, including the Special Forces commander, Ali Haidar, were removed from office, in an apparent attempt by Assad to consolidate his position, weaken the influence of the old guard and improve the country's international standing. At elections to the People's Assembly, held in that month, more than 7,000 candidates were presented, but turn-out at the polls was recorded at just over 50% of the electorate. The coalition parties in the NPF, dominated by the Baath Party, won 167 seats; the remaining seats were won by pro-regime independents. At the inaugural session of the new Assembly, on 14 November, the Prime Minister, Mahmoud al-Zoubi, announced a programme of major economic reforms.

In November 1995 rallies were held across the country to mark President Assad's 25 years in power, and some 1,200 political prisoners, including members of the banned Muslim Brotherhood, were released. In May 1996 Syrian officials denied reports of a series of bomb explosions in Damascus, Aleppo and Latakia, amid speculation that the attacks had been carried out with Turkish involvement. However, a Jordanian source subsequently claimed that they were intended to trigger an army coup involving Sunni Muslim officers supported by the US and Israeli intelligence services. Later that month two new ministers were appointed, including a new Minister of State for Cabinet Affairs, but rumours of a major cabinet reshuffle proved unfounded.

An anti-corruption campaign resulted in the dismissal, in June 1996, of Nadir al-Nabulsi, then Minister of Petroleum and Mineral Wealth, owing to allegations against him relating to the period when he headed the Al-Furat Petroleum Company. When a bomb exploded on a bus in Damascus in December, killing 11 people, there was speculation that it may have been related to the Government's anti-corruption drive and investigations into the business affairs of the President's family, despite an official statement that accused Israel of responsibility for the attack. In early 1997 President Assad's brothers, Jamil and Rifaat, both came under investigation for their business dealings, and, as a result, Jamil was sent into exile in Paris, France. Later that year there were reports that Bashar al-Assad had been given new responsibilities in economic policy-making, notably in the promotion of privatization and foreign investment, in addition to leading the Government's campaign against corruption and overseeing Syrian interests in Lebanon (especially contacts with the Maronite Christian community), although he still had no specific political post. In February 1998 President Assad dismissed his brother Rifaat from his position as one of Syria's three Vice-Presidents, a post that he had held since 1984. (For much of this period Rifaat had been out of favour and living in exile, but he had been allowed to return to Syria in 1992.) It was reported in June 1998 that some 225 political prisoners had been released, including leading members of the Muslim Brotherhood, communists and associates of Salah Jadid, the leader of the civilian branch of the Baath Party ousted from power by Assad in 1970.

Elections to the 250-seat People's Assembly were held on 30 November and 1 December 1998. The ruling Baath Party won 135 of the 167 seats allocated to the NPF, while the remaining 83 seats were taken up by pro-regime independents. In January 1999 the incoming People's Assembly voted unanimously to nominate President Assad for a fifth term in office. Assad's re-election was confirmed in a national referendum held on 11 February. Meanwhile, Bashar al-Assad had been promoted to the rank of army colonel in January, and it was reported that he had also been granted new powers over the management of state finances.

In June 1999 a campaign, led by Bashar al-Assad, to counter corruption in public office resulted in the arrest of several officials and businessmen. In October a former director of Syria's intelligence service received a lengthy prison sentence, having been found guilty of corruption and embezzlement of public funds. In July President Assad issued a general amnesty for prisoners convicted of certain 'economic' crimes, and for those who had deserted the army or evaded military service. The amnesty was to affect hundreds (some reports claimed thousands) of prisoners, including a number of Muslim Brotherhood activists. In September a huge wave of arrests was carried out by security forces in Damascus and Latakia against supporters of President Assad's brother Rifaat; according to some reports, about 1,000 people were detained by the authorities. Moreover, in October hundreds of people were allegedly killed or injured during several days of violent clashes between Rifaat's supporters and the security forces near Latakia. The Government dismissed such reports, and denied claims that the security forces had acted for political reasons. In November the Government warned Rifaat, who was once again in exile, that he would be prosecuted should he return to Syria. It was also reported that in February 2000 Syria's military intelligence chief, Gen. Ali Duba, had been removed from his post, owing to alleged 'administrative offences'; he was replaced by his deputy, Maj.-Gen. Hassan Khalil.

Bashar al-Assad's status as heir apparent was confirmed when, in November 1999, he held discussions with French President Jacques Chirac in Paris. Bashar's influence was also apparent in the government reorganization announced in March 2000, when President Assad selected the former governor of Aleppo, Muhammad Mustafa Mero, as the new Prime Minister. Mahmoud al-Zoubi, who had occupied the post since 1987, was later accused of 'irregularities and abuses' during his period in office, and was reported to have committed suicide before he could be tried on charges of corruption. The new Council of Ministers included 22 new ministers (among whom were a number of younger reformists and supporters of Bashar al-Assad). Although President Assad's trusted stalwarts retained the crucial defence, interior and foreign affairs portfolios, a new Minister of Information, Adnan Omran, was appointed, raising hopes that Syria's media might be allowed greater freedom in the future, while reformists were appointed to the industry and planning portfolios.

DEATH OF PRESIDENT HAFIZ AL-ASSAD

On 10 June 2000, as preparations were under way for the first general congress of the Baath Party to be held since 1985, President Hafiz al-Assad died following a heart attack. Although his health had long been poor, the reaction both in Syria and abroad was initially one of shock. Assessments of Assad's legacy tended to focus more on his international impact—his commitment to pan-Arabism, his implacable opposition to Israel and his role in later years as a stabilizing influence in the Middle East—and much less on his domestic record, where, according to many observers, he had displayed an indifference to human rights and democratic values, had until his later years been tolerant of official corruption, and had presided over a long period of economic stagnation.

While the First Vice-President, Abd al-Halim Khaddam, assumed the role of acting President, the Syrian establishment moved swiftly to secure Bashar al-Assad's accession to power. By the time of his father's burial, in the family's home village of Qardaha, on 13 June 2000, the People's Assembly had voted unanimously to amend the Constitution to lower the minimum age of eligibility for presidential office from 40 to 34 years, Bashar's exact age. The Regional Command of the Baath Party then hastened to nominate Bashar as head of state. On 11 June a decree was adopted promoting him from his then rank of Staff Colonel to Lieutenant-General, and making him Commander-in-Chief of the Armed Forces.

BASHAR ACCEDES TO THE PRESIDENCY

The general congress of the Baath Party, which began, as scheduled, on 17 June 2000, thus became principally a forum to legitimize Bashar's accession to power. On the final day of the congress Bashar was elected Secretary-General of the party. On 27 June the People's Assembly met to set a date for a referendum on Bashar's presidential candidacy, thereby approving his nomination. The referendum, held on 10 July, produced a 97.29% vote in favour of the succession of the sole candidate. The new President took the oath of office on 17 July, three days before the expiry of the 40 days of official mourning proclaimed following the death of his father. Bashar al-Assad emphasized his commitment to reviving the Syrian economy, and promised greater freedom of expression in the country, provided any criticism of his administration was constructive. The new President also undertook to uphold his father's legacy in foreign policy—above all, his firm stance regarding the Golan Heights.

Bashar's early actions, including the release of a significant number of political prisoners, suggested a leader who sought to modernize Syria in both the economic and political spheres. Nevertheless, he gave no indications that he was willing to allow the dominance of the Baath Party to be challenged, nor that the gradualist strategy towards reform would be abandoned. The pursuit of rapid and large-scale change was thought likely to lead the new President into direct conflict with the 'old guard' in the party and state bureaucracy, which remained very powerful. Furthermore, the need to assuage traditionalists at home appeared to limit Bashar's scope to innovate in the field of foreign policy, where his father's legacy retained overwhelming popular support.

In September 2000 a group of prominent business figures announced that they were interested in forming a new political party: the Syrian Social Nationalist Party, banned since the early 1970s, appeared to be being revived. In the following month a group of 99 writers and intellectuals issued a declaration appealing for an end to martial law, in force since 1963. When a People's Assembly deputy, Mamoun al-Homsi, criticized the excessive powers of the various security agencies and appealed for their merger into one organization, it was reported that Bashar had rejected appeals for him to face official sanctions. Amnesty International welcomed the release of 600 political prisoners in November 2000, although it claimed that more than 900 political prisoners remained in Syrian detention. In December Mezzeh prison in Damascus, which had long been a notorious location for the imprisonment of political opponents, was closed.

Meanwhile, hopes rose that Bashar's commitment to greater freedom in Syria was genuine. Civil society organizations became increasingly confident about operating openly and publicly. Emboldened by the positive signals coming from the Syrian authorities, in January 2001 Riad Seif, an outspoken parliamentarian who, along with former political prisoner Michel Kilo, had formed a group called the Committee of Friends of Civil Society, applied for official permission to form a new 'liberal' and 'nationalist' political party, the Movement for Social Peace. In the same month a 'manifesto' containing over 1,000 signatures was handed to the authorities, appealing for martial law to be lifted. The Government responded by stating that the country's emergency laws had been frozen. In February a prominent cartoonist, Ali Farzat, announced that he had been given permission to publish a weekly private newspaper, *al-Doumari*: this was the first private newspaper to be published in Syria for 38 years.

However, there were already indications that some members of the Government were worried that changes were occurring too fast and too radically. In March 2001 Vice-President Abd al-Halim Khaddam warned civil society groups not to threaten 'national unity'; he announced that henceforth such groups should apply to the authorities 15 days in advance for permission to hold meetings. The freedom to travel abroad, which political critics had enjoyed over the previous few months, began to be restricted again. These developments appeared to confirm fears that any increased political freedom in Syria would be at the discretion of the authorities, rather than by right. A report published in April by the UN Human Rights Committee raised concerns regarding the number of criminal offences punishable by death, the continuing use of administrative detention, a long legacy of extra-judicial executions and 'disappearances' of persons, systematic torture in prisons, violations of the right to fair trial, and the fact that martial law remained in force. The Committee also appealed for the establishment of an independent commission of inquiry to investigate past extra-judicial executions and 'disappearances' of persons.

In May 2001 President Bashar al-Assad sought to capitalize on the visit of Pope John Paul II to Syria in order to increase his prestige at home. He emphasized Syria's religious tolerance, released a number of prisoners, and strongly reaffirmed the country's unconditional insistence on the return in full of the Golan Heights The contradictory signals concerning human rights issues continued in late 2001. During August and September there was a major crackdown on activists and political critics. Among those arrested were Riad Seif, Mamoun al-Homsi and the veteran communist leader and long-term political detainee Riad al-Turk. Increasing co-operation between sections of the Muslim Brotherhood and the Communist Action Party was reportedly one reason behind the authorities' growing reluctance to tolerate dissent. However, in October it was announced that another notorious detention centre, Tadmur prison, was to be closed. In November there was another wave of prisoner releases, this time focused on members of banned communist groups and the Muslim Brotherhood. In February 2002 the Government agreed to allow private broadcasters to operate for the first time in 50 years, although they would only be permitted to broadcast music and advertisements. In March Seif and al-Homsi were each sentenced to five years in prison.

In December 2001 President Bashar al-Assad carried out a long-anticipated reorganization of the Syrian Council of Ministers. The number of independent-minded technocrats in the Government increased, among them Ghassan al-Rifai, who became the Minister of Economy and Foreign Trade, and Dr Issam al-Zaim, the new Minister of Industry. However, the new technocrats in the economic ministries were to report to the new Deputy Prime Minister for Economic Affairs, Muhammad al-Hussain, a known conservative. Maj.-Gen. Ali Hammoud, head of the Department of General Security, was appointed as Minister of the Interior, while the crucial defence and foreign affairs portfolios remained unchanged. Overall, the Baath Party's representation was reduced from 26 to 19 posts, while the number of independents was increased from five to seven. The cabinet reshuffle was accompanied by a reorganization of the army's leadership that affected some 800 middle-ranking officers. Also in December two former ministers in the discredited administration of Mahmoud al-Zoubi were gaoled for 10 years, having been convicted on charges related to the misuse of funds of the state-owned Syrian Arab Airlines. In March 2002 Assad dismissed 23 officials at the Ministry of the Interior for 'misconduct'. Fifteen officials at the Ministry of Transport were arrested on corruption charges in the same month, and the Director-General of the Commercial Bank of Syria was also detained.

Riad al-Turk was sentenced to two-and-a-half years' imprisonment in June 2002, on charges of seeking to change the Constitution by illegal means, although he was unexpectedly released on 'humanitarian grounds' in November. By September of that year a series of trials of pro-democracy activists had resulted in prison sentences for 10 people, including two parliamentarians, of between three and 10 years. Less publicized trials of Islamist activists from Hizb al-Tahrir al-Islami (Islamic Freedom Party) and the Muslim Brotherhood, which had been taking place during the first half of 2002, reportedly resulted in six-year custodial sentences for many of the defendants.

President Bashar al-Assad initiated further changes within the security apparatus during 2002. Legislation approved in February required all military and security officials to retire at 60 years of age. In October, after 20 years as head of intelligence in Lebanon, Lt-Gen. Ghazi Kenaan (reportedly a key member of Bashar's inner circle) was moved to the post of head of political security within Syria.

DIPLOMATIC DEVELOPMENTS UNDER BASHAR AL-ASSAD

On taking power, Bashar al-Assad emphasized the continuity of Syrian policy concerning the Middle East peace process. However, the rapidly deepening crisis on the Israeli-Palestinian track meant that no practical steps towards the resumption of talks with Israel took place. Relations between Israel and Syria became further strained from late September 2000, when intense fighting broke out between Palestinians and Israeli forces in the West Bank and Gaza Strip. Syria declared its solidarity with what quickly became known as the al-Aqsa *intifada*. During an emergency summit meeting of the Arab League, held in Cairo on 21–22 October, Syrian Minister of Foreign Affairs al-Shara' urged all Arab countries to sever diplomatic ties with Israel and supported appeals for the establishment of a war crimes tribunal to try Israeli 'war criminals'. In November Syria boycotted a Euro-Mediterranean summit on the grounds that the EU had failed to condemn Israel's alleged excessive use of force against Palestinian protesters in the Occupied Territories.

The death of President Hafiz al-Assad in June 2000 and the outbreak of the al-Aqsa *intifada* in September had at last created the conditions for decades of mistrust between Fatah and Syria to be overcome. At an Arab League summit in Amman, Jordan, on 27–28 March 2001, Bashar al-Assad and Yasser Arafat declared that their reconciliation was complete. As the Palestinian uprising continued, Syria was forthright in its condemnation of Israel's actions in the West Bank and Gaza, and displayed considerable caution towards all efforts to restart the Oslo peace process that appeared to fall short of a comprehensive solution. The Syrian regime was heavily critical of what it perceived as US bias towards Israel, and it continued to host radical Palestinian factions that rejected peace negotiations with Israel. However, Syria had no appetite for a resumption of military conflict with Israel. This was reflected in its policy in Lebanon, which remained the most likely immediate cause of renewed conflict between the two countries.

Israel's withdrawal from southern Lebanon in May 2000 had not extended to the long-disputed Shebaa Farms area, which Israel claimed was part of Syria and was therefore subject to settlement only as part of a peace deal with Syria itself. Syria, for its part, asserted that Shebaa Farms was Lebanese territory, and criticized the UN's support for the Israeli position. In March 2001 the UN came under further Syrian criticism, following its announcement that UNIFIL's strength was to be scaled down. Syria viewed this as a means of compelling Lebanese forces to move into the border area. Syria did not wish to see Hezbollah's freedom of action curtailed, and joined with the Lebanese Government in affirming that security for Israel would only come with the signing of a comprehensive Middle East peace settlement. In April, accusing Syria of supporting the continuing attacks by Hezbollah, Israel responded by bombing a Syrian radar station 35 km east of Beirut. In June Syria welcomed reports that the UN Secretary-General, Kofi Annan, had stated that the UN now acknowledged that Shebaa Farms should be considered part of Lebanon. The Shebaa Farms stand-off provided Syria with a further pretext for continuing its presence in Lebanon. However, responding to growing demands from within Lebanese political circles, Bashar al-Assad began a careful and cautious process of reducing the scale of the Syrian presence during his early years in office.

Public mourning in Lebanon at the death President Hafiz al-Assad in June 2000 had been at a level comparable to that in Syria itself. The Lebanese President, Emile Lahoud, the Prime Minister, Selim al-Hoss, and the National Assembly President, Nabih Berri, all attended Assad's funeral, and Hezbollah platoons marched through the late President's home village to salute their patron for a final time. However, at the Lebanese parliamentary elections in August–September, the Syrian-sponsored Government of Selim al-Hoss was resoundingly defeated by former premier Rafiq Hariri (see the chapter on Lebanon). Syrian officials none the less played a significant role in consultations leading to the formation of a new Lebanese Government under Hariri, in October. In addition, Syria's allies in the south, Amal and Hezbollah, had won a comprehensive electoral victory. In November al-Shara' stated that the issue of Syrian 'redeployment' would be addressed in accordance with the 1989 Ta'if agreement. In December 2000, addressing a long-standing Maronite Christian grievance, Syria released 46 Lebanese prisoners and allowed them to return to Lebanon.

During the first half of 2001 traditional allies in Lebanon such as the Druze leader, Walid Joumblatt, joined with Maronite Christian groups in demanding Syrian troop withdrawals. Finally, between 14 and 19 June the Syrian army completed the pull-out of its estimated 6,000 troops stationed in Beirut and Mount Lebanon governorates. Most of the troops were reported to have returned to Syria (although some were said to have redeployed in the Beqa'a valley). However, hundreds of intelligence officers were left in place in the capital.

Relations between Syria and Iraq improved steadily during Bashar al-Assad's early years in the presidency. Syria strongly opposed the continuation of UN sanctions against Iraq. Despite international criticism, in particular from the USA, increasing quantities of Iraqi oil were exported to Syria outside the framework of UN sanctions. Rail links were resumed in August 2000, after an interruption of some 20 years, and in November the Iraqi Minister of Foreign Affairs, Tareq Aziz, flew to Damascus on the first direct flight abroad by a senior Iraqi official since 1991. In January 2001 the two countries announced that they had worked out a detailed plan to share water resources. Syria condemned US-British air-strikes on Baghdad in February.

Relations between Syria and Turkey remained uncertain. In January 2001 a high-level military delegation visited Turkey to discuss the normalization of diplomatic ties, but little progress was made on the key issue of water resources. A positive sign for the longer term lay in increased co-operation over border security, and the signing, in June 2002, of a military training agreement.

The Syrian Government condemned the suicide attacks carried out against the USA on 11 September 2001. However, the extent to which the Syrian Government would be prepared actively to support the US Administration of George W. Bush in its demands for a 'world-wide coalition' against terrorism remained unclear in the immediate aftermath of the attacks. In October Syria was elected as a non-permanent member of the UN Security Council for the years 2002–03. While Syrian support for Hezbollah in Lebanon and the Islamic Resistance Movement (Hamas) in the Palestinian territories kept Syria on the US list of 'state sponsors of terrorism', in May 2002 the US Department of State disclosed details of Syrian co-operation and intelligence-sharing with the USA to combat the radical Islamist al-Qa'ida network. Syria later confirmed that there had been extensive intelligence-sharing. Nevertheless, the divergent positions of Syria and the USA on the Middle East peace process prevented genuine rapprochement. Amid continued violence between Israel and the Palestinians, and renewed Hezbollah attacks on Israeli outposts in the Shebaa Farms area in October and November, the USA warned Syria that it would not be able to restrain Israel should such attacks continue. It was unclear whether Syria had even been consulted by Hezbollah prior to its military action. Syria condemned the de facto Israeli reoccupation of the West Bank in March 2002. In May, however, Bashar al-Assad joined with President Mubarak of Egypt and Crown Prince Abdullah of Saudi Arabia in rejecting 'all forms of violence'. This appeared to bring Syria into line with other Arab states in condemning the Palestinian suicide attacks against Israeli civilians.

As Hezbollah attacks in Shebaa Farms intensified in April 2002, Syria announced that it was withdrawing its forces from central and southern Lebanon in accordance with the 1989 Ta'if agreement. The redeployment of most of the estimated 25,000 Syrian troops in Lebanon along the Lebanon–Syria border was widely interpreted as a move to ensure that Syria could not be held responsible for Hezbollah's military actions against Israel. US Secretary of State Colin Powell met President Assad in Damascus in April 2002 to warn Syria once again that Israel held it responsible for the Hezbollah assaults. In May Hezbollah guerrillas unexpectedly withdrew from the border area with Israel. Periodic clashes between Israeli forces and Hezbollah continued in Shebaa Farms in the second half of that year. Syria appeared to be cultivating a lower profile in Lebanon, and the replacement, in October, of the head of Syrian intelligence, Lt-Gen. Ghazi Kenaan, by Col Rustom Ghazaleh after 20 years in the post was viewed as a significant step in that direction. In February 2003 Syria announced the redeployment of a further 4,000 troops from northern Lebanon to Syria. This left an estimated 20,000 Syrian troops in Lebanon—a reduction of some 15,000 troops over a two-year period.

On his visit to Damascus in April 2002, Colin Powell sought Syrian support for a US-sponsored Middle East peace conference. Bashar al-Assad rejected the US and Israeli emphasis on the prior reform of Palestinian institutions before peace negotiations could resume in earnest, and accused the USA of ignoring existing Arab proposals and following an agenda that was considered by the Arab world to have been chosen by Israel. The Syrian position remained unchanged following the emergence in late 2002 of details of the 'roadmap' for peace in the Middle East (Documents on Palestine, see p. 104), a document sponsored by the Quartet group (comprising the USA, the EU, the UN and Russia). Syria criticized the roadmap's focus on the reform of Palestinian institutions, and its failure to address the Israeli-Syrian track of the peace process. In May 2003 Israeli Prime Minister Ariel Sharon offered Syria an unconditional resumption of peace talks. Syria issued a cool response, questioning Sharon's motives for such an offer. In common with other countries in the region, however, Syria's attention was focused upon the unfolding crisis in Iraq.

CONSEQUENCES OF THE US-LED PURSUIT OF 'REGIME CHANGE' IN IRAQ

As the prospect of a US-led military campaign to oust the regime in Iraq increased, relations between the USA and Syria deteriorated seriously. Syria reiterated its opposition to Iraq's becoming the next military target in the 'war on terror', and rejected President Bush's exhortation, during a speech in June 2002, to 'choose the right side in the war on terror', repeating its previous claim that the radical Palestinian and Islamist organizations based in Damascus were 'freedom fighters' rather than terrorists, and that their activities within Syria were restricted to the political level. Syrian support for UN Security Council Resolution 1409, which revised the sanctions regime against Iraq by removing restrictions on 'civilian goods', did not prevent a Syria Accountability Bill from being tabled before the US Congress in August. Although the bill was not sponsored by the US Administration, it was believed that figures close to Bush had given it their tacit support. The bill threatened sanctions against Syria on the grounds that it harboured terrorists, continued to occupy parts of Lebanon, was illegally importing Iraqi oil, and was developing weapons of mass destruction.

While appealing to Iraq to allow the UN weapons inspectors to resume their work, Syria urged Arab states not to co-operate with the USA if it were to launch military action against Iraq. As a non-permanent member of the UN Security Council, Syria voted in favour of Resolution 1441 in November 2002 (see the chapter on Iraq). Syria had come under enormous pressure from the USA and its allies to do so, but had only acquiesced on the understanding that the resolution was geared towards achieving a diplomatic solution to the crisis. In February 2003, however, Syria made it clear that it could not support a further resolution that would legitimize military action. Syria worked hard to achieve a united Arab position on Iraq: it supported a resolution tabled by Arab leaders at a summit meeting held in March in Doha, Qatar, that appealed to Arab states not to participate in a war against the Iraqi regime; it opposed last-minute suggestions from the UAE that Saddam Hussain should go into exile to prevent war (no doubt mindful of the dangerous precedent that this might set); and in late March Syria condemned the commencement of US-led military operations against the Iraqi regime.

In the build-up to the now unavoidable conflict, President Bashar al-Assad made efforts to prevent an outbreak of unrest within the Syrian Kurdish community. In late 2002 he became the first head of state to visit Kurdish areas. However, a demonstration by hundreds of members of one of Syria's banned Kurdish parties in February 2003 was followed by the arrest of two of its leaders. Following the start of the US-led intervention in Iraq, the authorities allowed massive anti-war demonstrations to go ahead in Damascus and other cities.

Meanwhile, the US Administration accused Syria of permitting military supplies and Arab volunteers who wanted to fight for the Iraqi regime of Saddam Hussain to cross its border into Iraq. In March 2003 Secretary of State Powell warned Syria that it would face serious consequences for these acts. In part to seek to deflect the growing US pressure, in late March Syria supported UN Security Council Resolution 1472, which allowed UN officials to act on behalf of the Iraqi Government in conducting the 'oil-for-food' programme for 45 days.

President Bush asserted in April 2003 that Syria possessed chemical weapons, and demanded immediate Syrian co-operation with the USA on all issues of concern. None the less, UN Secretary-General Kofi Annan, the EU and the United Kingdom all intervened against the idea of forced 'regime change' in Damascus. Syria's investment in developing improved diplomatic relations with the United Kingdom during the previous two years had yielded results (in December 2002 President Assad had made an official visit to London), and it quickly became clear that the US Administration had decided to give Syria the opportunity to show its 'good faith'. Following a visit to Damascus by Colin Powell in early May, he declared that there was evidence of Syrian co-operation. Nevertheless, in December President Bush signed the Syria Accountability and Restoration of Lebanese Sovereignty Act, which allowed the USA to impose a range of sanctions on Syria unless the country met a series of conditions (including ending its support for terrorist groups). The sanctions were eventually put in place on 11 May 2004; they included a ban on all US exports to Syria other than food or medicine, and a halt to flights between the two countries.

INTERNAL DISSENT AND EXTERNAL PRESSURES GROW

On 2–3 March 2003 elections were held to the People's Assembly. As expected, the NPF, led by the ruling Baath Party, won 167 of the 250 seats, with the remaining 83 going to independents. Electoral turn-out was estimated to be 63.5%. Opposition parties, grouped in the National Democratic Rally, boycotted the election on the grounds that it was undemocratic. On 9 March the newly reconvened legislature elected the Deputy Prime Minister in charge of Public Services, Muhammad Naji al-Otari, as the new Speaker of the People's Assembly. Al-Otari was replaced as Deputy Prime Minister by Muhammad Safi Abu Wdan in late March.

It was reported in July 2003 that President Bashar al-Assad had adopted a decree ending the Baath Party's monopoly on government, military and public sector positions. The resignation, in early September, of Muhammad Mustafa Mero as Prime Minister was widely ascribed to his failure to accelerate the process of reform. Parliamentary Speaker al-Otari was appointed as the new Prime Minister, and his first Council of

Ministers was announced at the end of the month. Ministers who retained their portfolios from the previous administration included Maj.-Gen. Mustafa Tlass as Minister of Defence and Farouk al-Shara' as Minister of Foreign Affairs; notable new appointments included Dr Muhammad al-Hussein, a former Deputy Prime Minister, as Minister of Finance, and Ahmad al-Hassan as Minister of Information. Soon after the appointment of the new Government, at least 16 government officials were dismissed as part of a new anti-corruption campaign. In September assets belonging to the former Minister of Industry, Dr Issam al-Zaim, were seized in connection with alleged corruption at a state-owned textile plant in Latakia. In May 2004 Tlass retired from the positions of Minister of Defence and Deputy Commander-in-Chief of the Armed Forces; he was succeeded in both posts by armed forces Chief of Staff Hassan al-Turkmani, who was in turn replaced by Gen. Ali Habib. In October of that year Lt-Gen. Ghazi Kenaan, formerly head of Syrian intelligence in Lebanon, was appointed Minister of the Interior.

Issues of civil rights had come to the fore in early 2004. In February the Lebanese newspaper *An-Nahar* published a petition, signed by 1,500 Syrian intellectuals and democratic activists, urging the Government to instigate radical reforms, including the lifting of the state of emergency, in force since 1963, and the release of political prisoners. At the end of the month foreigners were banned from studying at the 20 Islamic schools licensed by the Ministry of Labour and Social Affairs. The decision was widely regarded as a crackdown on foreign Islamists believed to be using their studies as a cover for militant, fund-raising or recruitment activities. During July and August 251 political prisoners were released as part of an amnesty announced by President Assad; they included members of the Muslim Brotherhood and, most notably, Syria's longest-serving political prisoner, Imad Shiash, who was imprisoned in 1975 for his membership of the banned Arab Communist Organization.

There was a widespread outbreak of violent, predominantly Kurdish protest in March 2004. The unrest started on 14 March in the north-eastern town of Al-Qamishli, close to the border with Turkey, when fighting at a football match escalated into large-scale anti-Government protests and fighting between the Arab majority and Kurdish minority; a number of deaths were reported. There were also outbreaks of violence at commemorations for the anniversary of a chemical attack by the former Iraqi regime of Saddam Hussain on the Kurdish town of Halabja, in northern Iraq, in 1988; at least seven Kurds were reported to have been killed in Aleppo and Afrin. In June 2004 the leaders of three major Kurdish parties were reportedly summoned to Damascus and 'advised' that the activities of their organizations would no longer be tolerated. None the less, periodic releases of political prisoners continued: more than 100 were released in December and a further 55 were freed in February 2005.

Meanwhile, in April 2003 US President Bush handed to the Israeli and Palestinian leaderships the so-called 'roadmap' peace plan. In May President Assad reportedly assured Javier Solana, the EU's High Representative for the Common Foreign and Security Policy, that Syria would accept the roadmap unconditionally, although he emphasized that it must run in tandem with the Syrian track of negotiations on the Golan Heights. An offer from Syria to resume peace talks with Israel in July was rejected by Israeli Prime Minister Ariel Sharon as 'insincere'. In October Israel launched an air-strike against an alleged Palestinian militant training camp at Ain Saheb, near Damascus, claiming that it was being used by Hamas and Islamic Jihad, which the latter group denied. Israel insisted that the attack was not directed against Syria, but that it was in retaliation for a suicide bomb attack in Haifa, Israel, in which 19 Israelis had been killed. In January 2004 President Assad rejected Israeli offers to resume peace negotiations, describing them as a 'media manoeuvre'. The assassination of a senior Hamas official in Damascus in September, reportedly on the order of Israeli security forces, provoked an angry response from Syrian officials. On 28 January 2005 the UN Security Council adopted a resolution (No. 1583), in which it clearly stated for the first time that Shebaa Farms was part of Syria rather than Lebanon, thereby effectively delegitimizing the activities of Hezbollah in the area.

Syria joined with other members of the Organization of the Islamic Conference (now the Organization of Islamic Cooperation) in June 2004 in announcing its support for the interim Iraqi Government established in the aftermath of the overthrow of Saddam Hussain. Following a visit to Damascus by the interim Iraqi Prime Minister, Dr Ayad Allawi, the two countries agreed to re-establish diplomatic relations and to co-operate in order to prevent foreign militants from crossing into Iraq across its border with Syria. However, Syria continued to come under international scrutiny for its alleged role in supporting Iraqi and foreign insurgents who were fighting against the US-led occupation in Iraq. In December the USA threatened action against Syria unless it ceased its 'interference' in Iraqi internal affairs.

Syria's relations with Lebanon came under close scrutiny from mid-2003, after unidentified assailants fired rockets at the studios of Prime Minister Rafiq Hariri's Future Television in central Beirut. Syria was blamed for having organized the attack, chiefly as a warning to the Lebanese Prime Minister following remarks he had made on a state visit to Brazil in which he appeared to appeal for an improvement in Arab-Israeli relations. As the attack coincided with a further redeployment of Syrian troops from Lebanon, many believed that Syria was still keen to maintain its influence in Lebanese political affairs. Indeed, this concern was addressed in a UN Security Council resolution (No. 1559), approved on 2 September 2004, reiterating the importance of Lebanese sovereignty, and calling on all foreign forces to withdraw from Lebanon and for all militias to disband. The following day the Lebanese National Assembly voted to grant President Emile Lahoud, a long-standing ally of Syria, a three-year extension to his term in office, which was due to end in October (see the chapter on Lebanon). This triggered a renewed political storm regarding Syria's role in Lebanon. Four Lebanese cabinet ministers resigned immediately afterwards, and on 20 September Prime Minister Hariri also submitted his resignation. He was replaced by a former Prime Minister, Omar Karami, who was viewed as being close to Lahoud.

By contrast with the growing crisis over its role in Lebanon, Syria began to enjoy warmer relations with two of its neighbours. In December 2003 ties with Turkey were strengthened by Syria's decision to hand over 22 suspects sought by the Turkish authorities in connection with four suicide bomb attacks in İstanbul in November. In January 2004 President Assad made the first ever visit by a Syrian head of state to Turkey. Turkey's membership of the North Atlantic Treaty Organization (NATO), and hence its relatively close relationship with the USA, as well as shared concerns about a possible 'ripple effect' of increased Kurdish autonomy in northern Iraq following the removal of the regime of Saddam Hussain, were believed to be among the principal reasons for Syria's initiative to improve its relations with Turkey. Similarly, closer co-operation was sought with Jordan over the issue of shared water resources. In February the launch of the Wahdah dam project on Jordan's Yarmouk river, which aimed to provide Jordan with water and Syria with electricity, effectively ended the diplomatic impasse caused by Jordanian accusations that Syria was easing the passage of Islamist militants into Iraq to join the insurgency against the US-led coalition.

SYRIA WITHDRAWS FROM LEBANON

On 14 February 2005 former Lebanese Prime Minister Rafiq Hariri was assassinated by a car bomb in Beirut (see the chapter on Lebanon). Although a hitherto unknown Islamist organization, al-Nusra wa al-Jihad fi Bilad al-Sham (Aid and Jihad in Greater Syria), quickly claimed responsibility, the Lebanese opposition and the international community immediately assumed Syrian involvement. Amid a wave of anti-Syrian sentiment in Lebanon, the USA and France jointly demanded an immediate withdrawal of Syrian troops from the country and a thorough investigation into the circumstances surrounding Hariri's murder, although they were careful not to accuse Syria directly of involvement in the incident. The Arab League and other Arab states urged Syria to implement a withdrawal under the 1989 Ta'if agreement. Syria's only supporter appeared to be Iran: on 16 February 2005 the two countries agreed to form a united front against 'foreign threats'. In response to the unprecedented international pressure, on 5 March President Assad announced the immediate withdrawal of Syrian troops from Lebanon; the withdrawal was completed on 26 April. Many Syrian guest-workers also left Lebanon, amid reports of harassment and violence against them.

Syria vigorously denied responsibility for Hariri's assassination, and condemned the series of bomb attacks that followed in mainly Christian areas of Beirut. Following allegations that President Assad had threatened Hariri with 'physical harm', the UN Security Council adopted Resolution 1595 on 7 April 2005, establishing an International Independent Investigation Commission (UNIIIC), to be headed by a German prosecutor, Detlev Mehlis. In Lebanon, the overwhelming victory of the Future Movement, led by Rafiq Hariri's son, Saad, in the May–June parliamentary elections produced a new Government committed to bringing Hariri's assassins to justice. The assassination in Beirut in June of prominent anti-Syrian figures (journalist Samir Qasir and the former leader of the Lebanese Communist Party, George Hawi), and reports that Syria had a 'hit list' of anti-Syrian Lebanese personalities, sparked further fears in Lebanon.

In October 2005 Mehlis submitted an interim report asserting that there was evidence that high-ranking members of the Syrian and Lebanese security and intelligence services were involved in Hariri's assassination, while pointing to Syria's lack of 'substantial' co-operation with the commission. A preliminary version of the report, leaked to journalists, implicated the Syrian President's brother, Maher al-Assad, and his brother-in-law, Assef Shawkat—head of Syrian military intelligence since February. Days before the report was released, the reported suicide of Syria's Minister of the Interior, Ghazi Kenaan, who had served as head of military intelligence in Lebanon during 1982–2002, added to the impression that Syria had been involved. On 31 October 2005 the UN Security Council unanimously approved Resolution 1636, requiring Syria to make available for questioning any suspected Syrian national or face unspecified 'further action'. President Assad offered to co-operate 'within the limits of national sovereignty': five unnamed Syrian officials—though including neither Shawkat nor Maher al-Assad—were interviewed before Mehlis released his second report in December. No specified charge was levelled against named Syrian officials, but Mehlis's public statements pointed strongly towards Syrian involvement in the deaths of Rafiq Hariri and other Lebanese anti-Syrian figures (including Gibran Tueni, editor of *An-Nahar*, who had recently been murdered). In January 2006 the UN investigation was placed under the direction of a Belgian prosecutor, Serge Brammertz. Meanwhile, in the previous month former Syrian Vice-President Abd al-Halim Khaddam alleged that Bashar al-Assad had personally threatened Rafiq Hariri in 2004.

The murder of Rafiq Hariri had repercussions for Syria beyond its role in Lebanon. Syria was forced to make concessions on a number of fronts in order to relieve the international pressure it now encountered. In March 2005 the Syrian authorities closed the Damascus press office of Islamic Jihad following its involvement in a suicide bombing in Tel-Aviv, Israel. Syria also handed over to the Iraqi authorities a number of opponents based on Syrian soil, including a half-brother of Saddam Hussain. Although the Syrian leadership sought to cultivate relations with Russia, Israeli and US pressure persuaded Russia to restrict its arm sales to short-range *SA-18* missiles, which would be unable to reach Israeli territory. The EU announced that a proposed Association Agreement with Syria would not be signed until Syria had definitively withdrawn from Lebanon and ceased interference in its internal affairs. Israel stated that it would not resume peace talks over the Golan Heights until Syria had withdrawn from Lebanon. The USA openly endorsed the Israeli line, and maintained its pressure on Syria. The signing with Jordan, in early March, of an agreement ending their long-running border dispute was likely, therefore, to have been of scant comfort to the Syrian regime.

THE INTERNATIONAL SCENE, 2006–07

The beginning of 2006 was marked by a change in tone in relations between Syria and the UN. The first Brammertz report, submitted in March, noted that co-operation with Syria had improved, while the Syrian Government signalled its readiness to comply with UNIIIC's requests. President Assad and Vice-President al-Shara' met UN investigators in Damascus in April. Assad continued to deny Syrian involvement in the murder of Rafiq Hariri, pointing instead to a conspiracy against Syria and the Lebanese resistance. Meanwhile, the UN Security Council approved the formation of an international tribunal to take charge of any future trial, and the US Administration announced in late April that it would freeze the assets of any Syrian suspected of involvement in Hariri's assassination. On 17 May the Security Council adopted Resolution 1680, calling on Syria to delimit the common boundary and establish full diplomatic relations with Lebanon. A few days earlier nearly 300 Lebanese and Syrian intellectuals and political activists had signed the 'Beirut-Damascus Declaration', which appealed for the normalization of relations between the two neighbours.

The Syrian Government questioned the legitimacy of the international tribunal; denounced Resolution 1680 as an intolerable interference in its internal affairs, as well as in its relations with Lebanon; and arrested several of the Syrian signatories of the declaration. In early June 2006 Brammertz released his second report, which stated that Syrian co-operation with the UN inquiry had been 'satisfactory', and stressed that further investigation was required to establish 'evidentiary links'. Despite the statement of solidarity issued by Arab League members during their summit of March 2006, and the rapprochement of Egypt and Saudi Arabia with Syria since its withdrawal from Lebanon, Syria remained politically isolated, except for its alliance with Iran. A state visit to Damascus by the Iranian President, Mahmoud Ahmadinejad, in January of that year, and a visit in April by Ali Akbar Hashemi Rafsanjani, Chairman of Iran's Council to Determine the Expediency of the Islamic Order, highlighted the importance of the bilateral relationship. President Assad gave firm support to Iran over its nuclear programme. In mid-June Syria and Iran were reported to have signed a memorandum of understanding on defence co-operation during a four-day official visit to Tehran by Syria's Minister of Defence, Hassan al-Turkmani.

The military campaign launched by Israel against Hezbollah in Lebanon in mid-July 2006 gave Syria the chance to reassert its influence over that country and to reaffirm its long-standing claim to be an indispensable party to any effort to achieve lasting political stability in the region. (For further details of Israel's war with Hezbollah, see the chapters on Israel and Lebanon.) During the month-long conflict, the Syrian Government repeatedly warned that Syria would respond to Israeli attacks. On 15 August, the day after the UN-brokered ceasefire had taken effect, President Assad gave his first major public address since the onset of the crisis. He criticized European policy in the Middle East; attacked Arab leaders for their failure to exert coercive pressure on Israel; stated that the US plan for a 'new Middle East' had collapsed after Hezbollah's successes in fighting against Israel; and claimed that the international effort to rid Lebanon of Syrian influence, and to bring about the disarmament of Hezbollah, was motivated primarily by the desire to allow Israel to dictate the terms of a regional political settlement. Assad vehemently accused the Government of Lebanese Prime Minister Fouad Siniora of collusion with Israel in its plan to disarm Hezbollah. He added that peace in the Middle East was not possible while the Bush Administration remained in place. Leaders across the region strongly refuted Assad's claims, and Syria remained diplomatically isolated. Thus, Syria's interference in Lebanese affairs, the issue of possible arms transfers to Hezbollah through Syrian territory, in violation of UN Security Council Resolution 1701, its alliance with Iran, and the ongoing UN investigation into the assassination of Hariri all contributed to Syria's inclusion in the 'axis of evil' as defined by US President Bush.

After the end of the conflict, President Assad strongly opposed any deployment of foreign troops along the Syrian border with Lebanon. Moreover, Syria continued its support of Iran, and strengthened relations with Hezbollah and Hamas, while it increased its efforts to reassert influence in Lebanon—policies strongly opposed by the USA and Europe. Syrian policy towards Israel remained consistent with its declared perspective that any settlement falling short of a complete withdrawal from the territories occupied in 1967 did not serve Syria's interests, namely the return of the occupied Golan Heights. Therefore, without confronting Israel directly—which it lacked the power to do—Syria ignored US and Israeli demands to end its support for Hezbollah and Hamas and other opponents of Israel. However, President Assad carefully differentiated his position regarding Israel from that of Iran, and repeatedly signalled Syria's readiness to make significant security guarantees to Israel in order to achieve peace. In a number of interviews with Western media, Assad rejected the accusation that Syria was providing military support to Hezbollah and plotting to bring down the Siniora Government in Lebanon. He denied any collusion between Syria and insurgents in Iraq, but maintained that Syria fully supported the 'concept' of resistance to foreign occupation. He also reiterated Syria's opposition to an ethnically based federal system in Iraq. Although sharply critical of the USA's Middle East policy, Assad emphasized that US involvement as chief broker was essential for any Middle East peace settlement. The publication, in September 2006, of Brammertz's third report, which stated that Syria's co-operation with UNIIIC was timely and efficient, did little to dispel international mistrust of Syria. In November the resignation of six pro-Syrian Lebanese cabinet ministers did not prevent the Lebanese National Assembly from endorsing the creation of a UN tribunal on the Hariri assassination a few days later. US pressure on Syria eased somewhat as the Syrian Government assumed a more co-operative stance towards Iraq. These moves included efforts to prevent militants crossing from Syria into Iraq to join the insurgency there, as well as the restoration, in November, of formal diplomatic ties with Iraq, after a hiatus of more than two decades.

From the beginning of 2007 efforts by European states to engage the Syrian regime more constructively continued. In March the visit to Damascus by the EU High Representative for the Common Foreign and Security Policy, Javier Solana, ended a two-year EU ban on senior-level contacts with the Syrian regime. In April the new Speaker of the US House of Representatives, Nancy Pelosi, became the highest-ranking US politician to meet President Assad in Damascus in recent years. Less than a month later US Secretary of State Condoleezza Rice met the Syrian Minister of Foreign Affairs, Walid Mouallem (appointed following the designation of Farouk al-Shara' as Vice-President in February 2006), in Sharm el-Sheikh, Egypt, on the sidelines of an international conference on the situation in Iraq. Yet, despite these contacts, relations between Syria and the USA remained strained. The main issues of contention continued to be Syria's stance on the Lebanese political crisis, and its support for Iran's nuclear programme.

On 31 May 2007 the UN Security Council approved Resolution 1757, establishing the Special Tribunal for Lebanon (STL)—a joint UN-Lebanese body established in Leidschendam, Netherlands—to try those suspected of Hariri's killing. In response, Syria reiterated its position that the special court violated Lebanese sovereignty, and that any Syrian suspects would be tried in Syria. In July the Syrian Government strongly denied claims that it was supporting Fatah al-Islam, a militant Islamist Palestinian group engaged in conflict with the Lebanese army in Tripoli (see the chapter on Lebanon), amid allegations that the Government was fomenting violent unrest in Lebanon in order to obstruct efforts to set up the tribunal.

SYRIA EMERGES FROM INTERNATIONAL ISOLATION

From mid-2007 Syria gradually emerged from its international isolation. Improved relations with its neighbours led to a gradual rehabilitation within Europe, although Syria's dealings with the USA continued to be problematic.

Both Israel and Syria sent out mixed signals in mid-2007 about their readiness to resume bilateral peace talks. The Israeli Prime Minister, Ehud Olmert, responding to repeated offers of peace negotiations from President Assad, stated that he was prepared for talks if Syria cut its ties with Iran and Hezbollah. Syrian officials rejected all preconditions. Tension between the two countries increased in September following an Israeli air attack on the desert site of al-Kibar in northern Syria, which, according to US intelligence, was a covert nuclear facility. The Syrian authorities denied all such allegations and later agreed to admit International Atomic Energy Agency (IAEA) inspectors, in keeping with Syria's obligations as a signatory of the Nuclear Non-Proliferation Treaty. None the less, in May 2008 bilateral negotiations between Syria and Israel resumed, with Turkish mediation, after an eight-year hiatus. A state visit made by President Assad to Turkey in mid-October highlighted the good relations between Syria and the Government of Recep Tayyip Erdoğan.

More noteworthy than the lack of Syrian military response after the Israeli air-strike was the conspicuous absence of Arab solidarity for Syria, reflecting the country's isolation within the Arab world. In a sign of displeasure with Syrian regional policy, the leaders of three key Arab states—Saudi Arabia, Egypt and Jordan—joined Lebanon in boycotting the Arab League summit held in Damascus in March 2008.

During 2007–08 relations between Lebanon and Syria began to show a gradual improvement. In November 2007 Serge Brammertz released the ninth and final report on the assassination of Rafiq Hariri. His conclusions, contrary to expectations, seemed to be leading away from Syrian culpability. In May 2008 an agreement was reached, at a conference in Doha, to end 18 months of institutional paralysis in Lebanon, during which the conflict between the pro-Western Government of Prime Minister Fouad Siniora and Syria's allies in Lebanon, led by Hezbollah, obstructed the impending presidential election. The Doha Agreement—following Syrian suggestions—led to the election of President Michel Suleiman and granted Syria's allies veto power in the new Government. Following the deal, Syria agreed to establish diplomatic relations with Lebanon for the first time ever, in recognition of Lebanese independence. In August President Suleiman made an official visit to Damascus, and on 14 October President Assad signed a decree approving full diplomatic relations with Lebanon. The Syrian embassy in Beirut was opened in December, and on 24 March 2009 Syria appointed Ali Abd al-Karim (previously the country's ambassador to Kuwait) as ambassador to Lebanon. Syria's positive role in facilitating the Doha Agreement also brought dividends with the visit of the Amir of Qatar to Damascus, as well as offers of substantial economic assistance from the UAE and Kuwait.

Despite widespread regional and international disapproval, Syria strengthened its relations with Iran as the region became increasingly polarized between supporters and opponents of the USA. Iranian involvement in the Syrian economy grew with the inauguration, in December 2007, of two new industrial projects facilitated by Iranian capital investment. Military ties were strengthened with the signature of a bilateral defence agreement in May 2008. Moreover, President Assad supported Iran in its stand-off with major powers over its nuclear ambitions, while denouncing as 'unacceptable' Israel's believed possession of nuclear warheads estimated to number more than 200.

Following the election of President Nicolas Sarkozy in May 2007, France displayed a greater willingness to engage actively with Syria at a diplomatic level as part of a solution to the constitutional crisis in Lebanon. President Sarkozy was eager to bring Syria into his proposed Union for the Mediterranean, and expended much diplomatic capital in courting Damascus. He invited President Assad to the EU-Mediterranean summit in Paris in July 2008, and in September Sarkozy made the first official visit to Syria by a French head of state for more than four years; as part of this visit, a four-way summit was held between Assad, Sarkozy, Sheikh Hamad bin Khalifa Al Thani, the Qatari Amir, and Turkish Prime Minister Erdoğan. The ongoing Syrian-Israeli negotiations in Turkey were believed to be a central theme of the summit.

The resolution of the Lebanese crisis marked an improvement in relations between Syria and the EU. An updated EU-Syria Association Agreement was agreed on 14 December 2008, and the EU declared itself ready to proceed with signature in October 2009; Syria's agreement to sign the accord was pending. Once formalized, the agreement would allow Syria tariff- and quota-free access to the EU, as well as increased EU aid. Yet its main significance was political, in that it represented a milestone in Syria's campaign to improve its relations with the West.

A meeting between President Assad and the newly elected Russian President, Dmitrii Medvedev, in August 2008 prompted speculation regarding greater military co-operation between the two countries, although no announcements were made. However, Russia subsequently cancelled plans to supply *MiG* fighter aircraft to Syria.

Despite Syria's participation in a peace conference convened at Annapolis, Maryland, in November 2007, the Bush Administration continued its policy of isolating Syria. In February 2008 the USA announced the imposition of economic sanctions on Syrian individuals accused of either helping Iraqi insurgents or of corruption. In July the US Department of the Treasury banned US citizens from dealing with two companies controlled by Rami Makhlouf, a cousin of President Assad and one of the most influential businessmen in Syria. This move targeted the leading power circles in Damascus, since Makhlouf's control over key business monopolies had entrenched the influence of the Assad family.

The future of negotiations with Israel, on hold since September 2008, was believed to be dependent on the results of the elections in Israel and the USA. Although President Assad stated his interest in moving from indirect talks to direct peace negotiations, the three-week-long Israeli military assault on the Gaza Strip from mid-December (see the chapters on Israel and the Palestinian Territories) made even indirect talks impossible, and resulted in increased tension between Western-backed Arab states and Syria. Addressing an emergency meeting of the Arab League—held in Doha in January 2009, with the conspicuous absence of Egypt and Saudi Arabia—Assad accused Israel of having destroyed the Saudi peace initiative, and appealed for a reactivation of the Arab boycott of Israel. Nevertheless, the Syrian President avoided rhetorical attacks that would jeopardize the recent improvements in relations with the EU, as well as a possible détente with the incoming US Administration of Barack Obama.

With the inauguration of Obama as US President in January 2009, it was hoped that a new phase in relations between the USA and Syria would ensue. The renewal by the US Congress in May of the Syria Accountability Act—extending restrictions on US exports to Syria and Syrian access to the US financial system for another year—on the grounds that Syria continued to pose a threat to US national security, and economic and foreign policy, appeared to confirm the political distance between the two countries. In June, however, following a series of visits to Damascus by senior US officials, including President Obama's personal envoy to the Middle East, George Mitchell, the US Administration announced its decision to appoint an ambassador to Syria for the first time since the assassination of Rafiq Hariri in 2005. Despite the renewal of the Syria Accountability Act, the USA showed flexibility over the application of sanctions, and withdrew its objections to Syria's bid for accession to the World Trade Organization (WTO). As a result, the WTO gave Syria observer status in May, and in June the US Department of State supported a visit to Syria by a high-level delegation of US technology firms.

A report issued by the IAEA in February 2009 cited the finding of significant traces of uranium at the al-Kibar site, but offered no definitive conclusion on the exact nature of nuclear-related activity there. Meanwhile, despite opposition from the USA, France and the United Kingdom, in November 2008 the IAEA agreed to assist Syria in completing a technical and economic feasibility study regarding the construction and location of a potential nuclear power plant. In June 2009 the IAEA reported traces of undeclared uranium at a second site, a small nuclear research reactor in Damascus. In April 2010 IAEA inspectors visited the research reactor in Damascus, but were denied access to contentious military sites.

Following the Israeli general election of February 2009, the formation in March of a coalition Government dominated by right-wing parties did not bode well for a resumption of peace talks with either Syria or the PA: the new Israeli Prime Minister, Binyamin Netanyahu, took an uncompromising stance on the issues of the construction of settlements in the West Bank and Israeli withdrawal from the Occupied Territories, despite pressure from the US Administration to make positive gestures towards the Palestinians and other Arab parties involved in negotiations.

The Gaza crisis in December 2008–January 2009 acted as a catalyst for a rapprochement between Syria and Saudi Arabia. Bilateral relations had soured with the assassination of Lebanese Prime Minister Rafiq Hariri, and they deteriorated further when Saudi Arabia criticized Hezbollah during its conflict with Israel in mid-2006. The first sign of the shift in Saudi policy was a discussion between King Abdullah ibn Abd al-Aziz Al Sa'ud and President Assad at a summit meeting of Arab heads of state held in Kuwait on 19–20 January 2009. In March of that year President Assad visited Riyadh for the first time in two years to attend a mini-summit with King Abdullah, President Mubarak of Egypt and the Amir of Kuwait, Sheikh Sabah al-Ahmad al-Jaber al-Sabah, in preparation for the annual Arab League summit. In July Saudi Arabia appointed an ambassador to Syria (the post having been vacant since 2008), and the Syrian authorities reopened the offices of the popular Saudi daily *Al-Hayat*. The thaw in relations was confirmed by the historic visit of King Abdullah to Syria in October 2009. On this occasion, the leaders of the two most influential countries in Lebanese affairs reached an understanding to co-operate in policy towards Lebanon. Moreover, Saudi Arabia supported Syria in its feud with the Iraqi Prime Minister, Nuri al-Maliki.

A further indication of improved relations with pro-Western Arab states was Assad's visit to Jordan, in March 2009, for the first time in five years. Moreover, the Syrian Prime Minister, Muhammad Naji al-Otari, made an historic visit to Iraq in April—the first by a senior Syrian official in 30 years—and signed agreements on security and economic co-operation with his Iraqi counterpart. Nevertheless, Syria's relations with Iraq remained tense during 2009, as the Iraqi Government repeatedly accused Syria of facilitating the activities of Baathist insurgents within Iraq. Relations deteriorated sharply in August, shortly after the visit of Prime Minister Nuri al-Maliki to Damascus, after Iraq demanded the handover of two senior Baathists allegedly implicated in bomb attacks in Baghdad in which nearly 100 people were killed. The two countries recalled their respective ambassadors, exchanged only months before after three decades of diplomatic freeze. Bilateral tensions subsequently eased, but, unsurprisingly, Syrian leaders welcomed the success in elections to Iraq's Council of Representatives, in March 2010, of the cross-sectarian Iraqi National Movement bloc of Dr Ayad Allawi, who maintained good relations with Syria. Some 23 polling stations were set up across Syria for Iraqi refugees to cast their votes. The rapprochement initiated in early 2009 was as much an effort to forge a united Arab front regarding Israel as it was an attempt to counter Iranian influence—a move that Syria was not prepared to support. President Assad was among the first leaders to congratulate Mahmoud Ahmadinejad on his controversial re-election following the disputed Iranian presidential election of June, and showed no inclination to downgrade the Syrian strategic relationship with Iran, despite the protests that followed the poll.

Syria did not interfere in the Lebanese legislative elections of June 2009, which resulted in victory for Syria's long-time opponent, the March 14 Alliance, led by Saad Hariri. This paved the way for a further strengthening of ties between Syria, the Western powers and their regional allies. Hariri's visit to Damascus on 20 December appeared to have ushered in a new phase in Lebanese-Syrian relations. Nevertheless, both the USA and Saudi Arabia indicated that any additional improvement in relations would depend on Syria making tangible concessions on a number of issues, including helping to curb Iranian influence in the region, and exerting pressure on Hamas and Islamic Jihad—whose leaders were based in Damascus. Thus, by the end of 2009 Syria had begun to move from international isolation towards relative respectability. Nevertheless, Syria's relationship with Egypt remained severely strained. Moreover, deep-rooted problems such as the ongoing Shebaa Farms dispute, alleged Syrian involvement in arms deliveries to Hezbollah, and the pending verdict of the STL's investigation into Rafiq Hariri's assassination seemed likely to hinder Syria's international relations for the foreseeable future.

THE DOMESTIC SCENE, 2005–06

Within Syria, the level of opposition mobilization remained low. Despite the release of more than 300 political prisoners in March 2005, including many Kurds, Kurdish unrest flared up again in May after a Kurdish religious leader was murdered in unclear circumstances. A wave of arrests followed. Also in that month there were a further nine arrests of members of the political opposition accused of connections with the exiled leader of the Muslim Brotherhood, Ali Sadr al-Din al-Bayanouni.

Hopes for political reform centred on the Syrian Baath Party congress held in June 2005, which resulted in the final removal of the 'old guard' associated with the regime of Hafiz al-Assad. Most notably, Abd al-Halim Khaddam, the Vice-President who had served as second-in-command to the late President for three decades, resigned and subsequently went into self-imposed exile in France. The congress recommended that the state of emergency should apply only to 'crimes that threaten state security', and authorized the creation of new, independent political parties, provided they were neither religiously nor ethnically based. However, Article 8 of the Constitution, which assigned to the Baath Party the 'leading role in state and society', remained unaltered. Steps were announced to recognize the rights of the Kurdish minority. Several resolutions were approved on economic policy, including the replacement of socialism by 'social market economy' as official strategy. Moreover, prominent advocates of economic reform gained promotion around the time of the congress, among them Abdullah al-Dardari, who was appointed as Deputy Prime Minister, responsible for Economic Affairs.

In October 2005 a limited cabinet reshuffle brought Mahdi Dakhlallah, editor of the ruling party's daily newspaper, *Al-Baath*, to the post of Minister of Information, while Ghazi Kenaan was appointed to head the Ministry of the Interior. (The latter committed suicide in December). Also in October there were signs that the divided Syrian opposition groups were beginning to work together. The 'Damascus Declaration', a statement demanding the introduction of a democratic system, the lifting of emergency laws and the release of prisoners of conscience, brought Syria's secular Arab nationalist opposition together with the two forces—Kurds and Islamists—considered to be the main opponents of the ruling Baath Party.

Opposition morale was boosted at the beginning of 2006 by the release of dissidents (including Riad Seif and Mamoun al-Homsi), which appeared to indicate the President's commitment to a gradual introduction of political reforms. In May a new 'Beirut-Damascus Declaration' was released by Syrian and Lebanese dissidents, criticizing Syrian tutelage of Lebanon and demanding democracy in both countries. This brought a wave of arrests, and led to the detention of prominent dissidents (including activists Michel Kilo and Mahmoud Issa, as well as human rights lawyer Anwar al-Bunni). Meanwhile, secular and religious opposition members in exile joined forces around former Vice-President Abd al-Halim Khaddam and Muslim Brotherhood leader Ali Sadr al-Din al-Bayanouni. In June they held the founding conference of the National Salvation Front in Syria, a transitional 'government-in-exile' established as part of a broader programme for regime change in Syria. This drew sharp criticism from opposition leaders within Syria, who dismissed regime change as an invitation to foreign military intervention and ruled out association with Khaddam and other figures involved in 'previous corruption in Syria'.

Tension within Syria between radical Islamists and the state increased in 2006 as official sources reported clashes in Aleppo, Zabadani and Damascus. President Assad sought to enhance his control by appointing his own allies to key government posts left vacant by Kenaan's suicide and Khaddam's defection: in February Brig.-Gen. Bassam Abd al-Majid, chief of the military police, became the new Minister of the Interior, while the long-serving Minister of Foreign Affairs, Farouk al-Shara', was appointed Vice-President, responsible for Foreign Affairs and Information: al-Shara' was the sole member of the inner circle of Hafiz al-Assad who continued to play a prominent role in the country. Shortly afterwards, Dr Najah al-Attar became the first woman to be appointed Vice-President—and the first Vice-President not to be a member of the ruling party. Her brother, a former leader of the Muslim Brotherhood, was living in exile in Europe.

BASHAR AL-ASSAD'S DOMESTIC REFORMS

In line with President Assad's gradual reformist programme, Abdullah al-Dardari pushed ahead with a programme of reforms intended to revive the Syrian economy. With limited prospects for growth, the rapid depletion of oil reserves, a steadily expanding population, mounting unemployment and pressing capital spending needs, the Syrian Government chose to accelerate Syria's evolution towards a 'social market economy', the goal of which was to combine market mechanisms with social justice, while rejecting any reforms imposed from abroad. The Government presented the 10th Development Plan (for the five-year period 2006–10) as a comprehensive programme for reform centred on the liberalization of trade and investment, and combined with a policy of fiscal consolidation. Critical elements of this strategy were the scheduled introduction of a value-added tax (VAT) in 2008 (later postponed) and the phasing out of petroleum price subsidies by 2010. Nevertheless, the possibility of sanctions being imposed on Syria as a result of its alleged involvement in the assassination of Rafiq Hariri, the US decision in March 2006 to ban financial transactions between US banks and the Commercial Bank of Syria, and the delay in bringing the EU-Syria Association Agreement into effect all placed further obstacles in the path of Syria's reformers, while removing potentially useful frameworks for economic renewal.

BASHAR AL-ASSAD'S SECOND TERM

Elections to the 250-member People's Assembly were held on 22 April 2007, with predictable success for the ruling party and its allied formations, which were guaranteed two-thirds of the seats. The remaining seats were reserved for independents, almost all of whom were loyal to the regime. The NPF ended up with 172 seats (of which 135 went to the Baath Party), five more than its two-thirds' quota, while the number of independents fell to 78. According to official figures, the turn-out was 56.1% of registered voters, although exiled opposition groups estimated a participation rate of less than 20%. On 27 May Bashar al-Assad, the sole candidate, secured a second seven-year term in office, with the overwhelming approval of the 11.7m. Syrians who were eligible to vote in a presidential referendum to endorse his unanimous nomination by the People's Assembly. Mass participation in the referendum (reported at more than 95.8%), and the percentage of 'yes' votes (97.6%), were hailed by government officials as an indication of both the President's popularity and a consolidation of democratic principles.

The need to reform the economy while controlling domestic opponents continued to dominate the domestic agenda during Bashar al-Assad's second term. In his inaugural address to the People's Assembly, in mid-July 2007, the President confirmed his intention to press ahead with the transition from a centrally planned system to a social market economy. While substantial political reform was never on the agenda, Assad promised to overhaul the proposed law on political parties and to introduce a second chamber of parliament (Majlis al-Shura) to increase democratic participation in the political process. Assad also pledged to resolve the long-standing issue of Kurdish citizenship—a problem originating from a special survey of 1962, which classified some 120,000 Kurds as foreigners. Subsequently, however, the authorities did little to implement the projected reforms, which, in themselves, fell far short of opposition demands. As a result, the image of President Assad as a liberal reformist was at odds with the reality of a Syrian political arena in which the regime intensified repressive measures against its opponents. Thus, in May 2007 Kamal Labwani, arrested in 2005 after a trip to the USA to rally support for political reform in Syria, was given a 12-year prison sentence, the harshest sentence against a dissident since the accession of Bashar al-Assad in 2000. Several other government critics also fell victim to Syrian justice, including those arrested in connection with the Beirut-Damascus Declaration: Anwar al-Bunni, Michel Kilo and Mahmoud Issa were each sentenced to prison terms of between three and five years for 'weakening national sentiment, spreading false news, and inciting sectarian strife'.

In the second half of 2007 the massive inflow of Iraqi refugees into Syria, which is the most accessible route for those fleeing Iraq, became an increasingly controversial issue. Syria displayed a remarkable ability in absorbing up to 1.5m. Iraqis, but unsustainable pressure on Syrian infrastructure, and rampant inflation as a result of very much greater demand for goods and services forced the Syrian Government to intervene. Visa requirements were imposed on Iraqis from October, and in early 2008 the Syrian authorities for the first time allowed non-governmental organizations (NGOs) to operate in the country in order to assist the refugees.

Mounting unemployment and a widening gap between rich and poor in the country made the issue of economic reform ever more politically sensitive. Aware of the potential for popular unrest during the transitional phase of reform, the Government committed itself to a strategy of gradual liberalization that aimed to combine market mechanisms with social justice. In Bashar al-Assad's first term the reform process had been limited to less controversial moves—such as opening up to private sector activities and foreign investment—but the next steps inevitably touched critical areas such as the Baathist policy of subsidizing basic commodities, including electricity and fuel. In early 2008 the sharp rise in global oil prices and the decline in Syrian oil production made the cost of subsidies for gasoil (which accounted for around 50% of all domestic consumption of petroleum products) unsustainable. Nevertheless, confronting strong opposition from sections of the Baath Party, monopolistic business interests and recipients of lucrative profits from smuggling, the Government chose to defer the issue of subsidy cuts, and to delay the introduction of VAT until 2009. The cut in subsidies on diesel and liquefied petroleum gas, eventually implemented in May 2008, resulted in an increased retail price for diesel, a sharp fall in consumption and an increase in smuggling. To compensate for rising prices for food and heating oil, President Assad announced a 25% increase in salaries and pensions for public sector employees, and Prime Minister al-Otari announced plans to set up social security funds.

INTERNAL TENSION IN 2008

A number of violent events in 2008 belied Syria's reputation as a tightly controlled country. In February Imad Mughniyeh, described by Hezbollah as its 'chief of external operations', was killed in a bomb blast in Damascus. Observers speculated that Israeli agents were involved in the bombing, although Israel denied responsibility. Mughniyeh had been implicated in attacks on the US, French and Israeli embassies, and in the abduction of Westerners in Lebanon during the 1980s. The assassination raised uncomfortable questions about the Syrian intelligence services, including the possible complicity of Syrian internal security at a senior level. It also prompted speculation regarding Syria's readiness to reconsider its relationship with Hezbollah and Iran, in the context of reconciliation with the West.

There was a further political assassination that left many questions unanswered in August 2008, when Brig.-Gen. Muhammad Suleiman was apparently shot dead, in unclear circumstances, at a beach resort near Tartous. Suleiman was reportedly one of the most senior Alawi military officers, close to the Assad family and an adviser to the President. The presence at Suleiman's funeral of Maher al-Assad, the President's brother and head of the Republican Guard, confirmed his prominent place in the Syrian hierarchy.

While seeking international legitimacy, foreign investment and development aid, the Syrian regime continued to crack down on dissidents. In December 2007 human rights organizations reported the arrest of some 30 opposition activists associated with the 2005 Damascus Declaration, among them Fida' al-Hourani, daughter of Akram al-Hourani. In July 2008 a riot involving political prisoners at the military prison of Saydnaya, north-west of Damascus, was violently suppressed by Syrian security forces, who allegedly killed dozens of prisoners. At the end of that month 12 opposition activists linked to the Damascus Declaration, including former People's Assembly member Riad Seif, who had been re-arrested in January, were put on trial on charges that included spreading false information and weakening national sentiment. This was the biggest collective prosecution of Syrian dissidents under Bashar al-Assad's presidency. Some days later the Syrian authorities freed Aref Dalila, who was serving a 10-year prison sentence for weakening national sentiment and seeking to change the Constitution, having been gaoled in 2002 after appealing for civil liberties.

Tensions mounted on 27 September 2008 after a car bomb in Damascus killed 17 people. Later that month Syrian security forces killed three alleged Islamist militants from the Yarmouk camp on the outskirts of Damascus, and arrested 11 members of the Islamist group Fatah al-Islam. Their confessions were broadcast on national television in order to corroborate the Government's claim that Lebanese-based Islamists were targeting Syria. Syrian allegations that the Lebanese Future Movement was involved in financing these terrorist groups were denied by its leader, Saad Hariri, who in turn accused Syria of waging a propaganda campaign in an attempt to influence the result of the forthcoming Lebanese elections.

Bashar al-Assad's successes in improving relations with the West, combined with developments within the region, apparently weakened the domestic opposition at this time. At the beginning of April 2009 the Muslim Brotherhood announced its withdrawal from the National Salvation Front, formed in 2006, and suspension of its opposition activities to concentrate on forming a unified Arab stance in support of Palestinians in Gaza. Nevertheless, the Syrian Government denied rumours that it had engaged in dialogue with Islamist militant groups, and Law 49, mandating the death penalty for those found guilty of membership of the Muslim Brotherhood, remained in place.

SYRIA AND THE 'AXIS OF RESISTANCE'

From 2006 President Assad delineated the prospect of a new Middle East 'whose essence is resistance' as a reaction to the seemingly futile negotiations of the Bush years. The failure of the USA and Europe in solving regional problems; the Lebanon and Gaza wars; Israeli attacks targeting Syrian territory; and the fragmentation of Iraq seemed to confirm this view. Syrian leaders hailed the victories of Hezbollah and of the Palestinian resistance as a vindication of Syria's regional policy, and as key elements in a changed regional equation. In a number of interviews and speeches during 2009 and 2010, Assad spelled out the configuration of the new order that Syria sought to pursue in the region, encompassing Hezbollah and Hamas, and involving economic, political and military co-operation between Syria, Iran and Turkey.

Syria and its allies increasingly presented themselves as a front seeking to move towards a collective logic of deterrence. On 25 February 2010 President Assad hosted the Iranian President, Mahmoud Ahmadinejad, and the leader of Hezbollah, Sheikh Hasan Nasrallah, in Damascus, in an ostensible display of solidarity at a time of mounting regional tensions. The high-profile meeting, which was preceded by the signing of a joint defence agreement in December 2009 and followed by the removal of visa restrictions for nationals travelling between Iran and Syria, sent a strong message to those keen to see Syria removed from Iran's strategic orbit.

Turkey played a pivotal role in helping Syria to break out of isolation and expand its economy, while increasing its leverage within the region and the international community. In September 2009 the two countries mutually revoked visa requirements and established a High-Level Strategic Co-operation Council. Joint military exercises were conducted in April 2010.

The visit of Russian President Dmitrii Medvedev to Damascus in May 2010—the first visit to Syria by a Russian head of state—highlighted the growing importance of Syria's regional role. Following the visit, Russia announced that the sale to Syria of *MiG-29* fighter aircraft and defence missiles was ongoing, and also indicated Russian support for the construction of a Syrian civil nuclear power plant.

In the initial phase of the investigation into the assassination of Rafiq Hariri in 2005, Syria was portrayed as the prime suspect. During 2009–10, however, the focus appeared to have shifted to Hezbollah. As domestic tension escalated in Lebanon, President Assad and Saudi Arabia's King Abdullah held talks in Damascus on 29 July 2010 before travelling to Beirut the following day in an attempt to ease growing tensions there. Earlier that month Syria and Lebanon had signed economic agreements for the first time since Hariri's assassination, after Assad and his Lebanese counterpart, Michel Suleiman, agreed to start demarcating shared land and maritime borders. Moreover, evidence of Syria's reassertion of its political influence in Lebanon appeared once again with visits to Damascus by Lebanese Prime Minister Saad Hariri both before and after his trip to Washington, DC, in May. In September, in an interview with the London-based newspaper *Asharq al-Awsat*, Hariri retracted earlier accusations that Syria had been involved in the death of his father.

Despite expressing his willingness to resume Turkish-mediated peace talks, suspended since 2008, and rejecting allegations—raised in mid-April 2010 by Israel and the USA—that Syria had transferred *Scud* missiles to Hezbollah, President Assad declared in a number of interviews that 'there is no partner for peace in Israel', and confirmed that Syria would continue to back the resistance while it sought to redraw the regional geopolitical map.

President Assad warned in July 2010 that the prospect of war was increasing in the region. Yet, despite the perception that no serious peace talks were possible in the context of a deteriorating regional climate, he told the US Special Envoy, George Mitchell, and Secretary of State Hillary Clinton that he was ready to resume peace talks with Israel on the basis of its complete withdrawal from the Golan Heights. Despite Mitchell's reaffirmation, in September, of a US commitment to a Syria-Israel peace settlement, it seemed unlikely that Israel would comply with this Syrian demand unless Damascus took steps to end its support for Hezbollah and Hamas, and to downgrade its own strategic alliance with Iran. Any prospect of Israeli-Syrian talks apparently vanished, and relations with the USA soured, after Israel, in October, revealed satellite images of Syrian *Scud* missiles and a Hezbollah training base near Damascus. Assad accused Israel of hindering the peace process, while the US Permanent Representative to the UN, Susan Rice, blamed Syria for destabilizing Lebanon by arming Hezbollah.

In December 2010 there were reports that Syria had refused to give IAEA inspectors access to the ruins of the alleged nuclear weapons site of al-Kibar, which had been destroyed in an Israeli attack in September 2007, as well as to other sites where the agency suspected Syria was engaged in undisclosed nuclear activity. The Syrian Government had always denied these allegations, but refused unrestricted access, which, it claimed, would amount to a violation of Syrian sovereignty.

Following the announcement, in September 2010, that Syria and Iraq had restored diplomatic ties, Assad received a visit by Iraqi Prime Minister al-Maliki in October, signalling Syria's acceptance of al-Maliki's unity Government, despite his earlier accusations of Syrian complicity in the August 2009 bomb attacks in Baghdad.

While promoting stability in Iraq, Syria was again accused of interfering in Palestinian and Lebanese affairs. In October 2010 leaders of Fatah accused Assad of subverting their efforts at reconciliation with Hamas, whose political leadership was based in Damascus. In December 2010–January 2011 Syrian and Saudi diplomatic efforts to defuse tension in Lebanon intensified ahead of the announcement of indictments by the STL that would implicate members of Hezbollah in the 2005 assassination of Rafiq Hariri. Hezbollah's leader, Sheikh Hasan Nasrallah, denounced the UN-mandated tribunal as an arm of Israeli policy, and put pressure on the Lebanese Government to dissociate itself from the STL. Mediation efforts broke down in January 2011, after Nasrallah announced the withdrawal of the March 8 Alliance from the Lebanese Government. The ensuing collapse of the Lebanese coalition strained relations between Syria and Saudi Arabia. In an interview with the satellite television broadcaster Al Arabiya, the Saudi Minister of Foreign Affairs, Prince Sa'ud al-Faisal Al Sa'ud, expressed disappointment that Syria was unable to make its Lebanese allies reach a compromise solution. The new Lebanese Prime Minister, Najib Miqati, was reported to have close ties with Bashar al-Assad.

In December 2010 President Obama appointed Robert Ford as US ambassador to Syria, despite US congressional opposition on the grounds of Syrian ties with Iran, Hezbollah and Hamas, its failure to co-operate with the IAEA, and its arms-smuggling to Hezbollah—including long-range *Scud* missiles that would enable it to strike Dimona, the site of Israel's own nuclear reactor. Ford's arrival in Damascus marked a return to high-level diplomatic representation after a hiatus of almost six years, his predecessor having been withdrawn following the assassination of Rafiq Hariri in February 2005. The Obama Administration's policy of engagement with Syria continued in early 2011 with the visit to Damascus of US Under Secretary for Political Affairs William Burns. None the less, President Assad made it clear that he considered 'resistance'—by which he meant maintaining a credible military threat towards Israel through support for Hezbollah, Hamas and Islamic Jihad, as well as the strategic alliance with Iran—to be an integral part of Syrian regional strategy.

Speaking to the US daily *Wall Street Journal* in January 2011, as popular unrest was spreading across the Middle East and North Africa region, President Assad asserted that Syria's policy of resistance to Israeli and Western imperialism reflected the will of its people, unlike the pro-US stance of the Tunisian and Egyptian Governments. He expressed sympathy for Egyptian protesters, and, in mid-February, the Syrian press celebrated the fall of President Mubarak of Egypt as the end of the 'Camp David era'.

DOMESTIC DEVELOPMENTS, 2009–10

President Assad effected a cabinet reorganization in April 2009. He replaced the ministers responsible for the interior, justice, health and local government portfolios and created a new post of Minister of State for Environmental Affairs. The new Minister of the Interior, Gen. Saeed Muhammad Sammour, was reported to be a senior officer in the intelligence services. In June Lt-Gen. Ali Muhammad Habib Mahmoud, a member of the Alawi tribe, replaced Lt-Gen. Hassan al-Turkmani as Minister of Defence. In July the removal of Assef Shawkat, Assad's brother-in-law and one of the most influential figures in the country, from the position of chief of military intelligence prompted speculation that he had been placed under investigation following the assassination of Imad Mughniyeh in February 2008.

In mid-2009 President Assad took cautious steps to limit the role of the Baath Party in Syrian politics, although the significance of such moves remained unclear. Assad reportedly hinted at reforms designed to end the party's automatic majority of seats in parliament, and issued a decree abolishing the Office of National Security, the party organ responsible for vetting appointments to public service positions.

The deepening global financial crisis, at a time when Syria was already struggling to respond to the decline in oil production—despite fresh oil discoveries in the Euphrates basin—as well as to several consecutive years of drought, did not deter the Government from its phased economic reform programme. In February 2009 the Government announced plans to close down state-owned companies that were unable to ensure their financial independence from public subsidy. Moreover, the long-awaited Damascus Securities Exchange was launched in March, marking an important milestone in Syria's transition to a social market economy.

Syria pressed on with gradual economic liberalization during 2010. The Central Bank continued to reduce restrictions on foreign currency transactions, as a result of which a greater number of exports moved out of the 'black' economy, and for the first time bids were invited for the financing of aircraft purchases. In May the People's Assembly approved a new law regulating the telecommunications sector (see Economy), which, *inter alia*, ruled out privatization of the state-owned Syrian Telecommunications Establishment. Meanwhile, the long-deferred introduction of VAT was by this time expected no earlier than 2011.

None the less, the removal of Tayseer Reddawi from his position as head of the State Planning Commission (SPC) in January 2010, following his sharp criticism of the consumption patterns of the small minority of Syrian citizens benefiting from economic growth, indicated that the domestic debate on economic reform remained highly charged. Amer Lotfi was subsequently appointed as the new head of the SPC, while his post as Minister of Economy and Trade was assumed by Lamia Aasi, latterly Syria's ambassador to Malaysia and a former Deputy Minister of Finance.

During 2010 the Syrian Government continued to work to complete the legal framework of the country's social market economy. In April the Government introduced a new labour law allowing employers to dismiss staff, despite strong opposition by labour unions. The law was aimed at making Syria a low-wage platform attractive to investors, while undermining the informal economy. In order to evade the extensive entitlements given to workers under previous legislation dating back to the socialist era, employers commonly refused to give their staff formal contracts and did not pay social insurance contributions on behalf of their employees. Nevertheless, the lack of an effective enforcement mechanism suggested that the impact of the legislation would be limited.

As part of a broader government policy to address social issues, in July 2009 President Assad issued a decree that ended the exemption from custodial sentence for men convicted of so-called 'honour crimes'. However, the Syrian authorities set the minimum prison sentence for such crimes at only two years, and judges retained the power to reduce these sentences. During 2010 the Government took steps to counter the spread of conservative Islamic social practices by banning the wearing of the *niqab* (full-face veil). Local newspapers reported that the authorities had reassigned about 1,000 female schoolteachers to other posts owing to their refusal to uncover their faces.

The gradual process of economic liberalization was not replicated in the political sphere. Notably, the state of emergency, in force since 1963, remained in force. Thus, in May 2009 Kurdish dissident Mishaal al-Tammo was sentenced to three-and-a-half years in prison; in July the human rights lawyer and activist Muhannad al-Hasani was arrested; and in October the prominent human rights lawyer Haitham Maleh—an elderly dissident who spent six years in prison in the 1980s—was sentenced to three months' imprisonment after having been convicted of weakening national sentiment. A new law to provide a system of accreditation and governance for civil society organizations, plans for which were announced in January 2010 by the President's wife, Asmaa al-Assad, did not materialize.

Moreover, the Government continued to refuse to rectify the 1962 survey that had stripped some 120,000 Kurds—whose number had since grown to 300,000—of citizenship, despite explicit promises by President Assad in his inauguration speeches of 2000 and 2007. In November 2009 three leaders of the Kurdish Azadi Party were sentenced to three years in prison for weakening national sentiment, while members of the Kurdish Democratic Party and of the Yekiti Party were sentenced in August 2010 for adhering to illegal political organizations.

The human rights lawyer Muhannad al-Hasani, President of the unlicensed Syrian Human Rights Organization, was sentenced to three years' imprisonment in June 2010 for monitoring the Supreme State Security Court, a special court—with almost no procedural guarantees—used by the Government to prosecute critics of the regime. Haitham Maleh was sentenced in July to three years' imprisonment by a military tribunal on charges of weakening national sentiment, the charge usually used against government critics. Security services also referred a 19-year-old internet blogger, Tal al-Mallohi, to trial by the Supreme State Security Court, on suspicion that she provided information to foreign governments; she was convicted and sentenced to five years' imprisonment in February 2011.

President Assad carried out a limited cabinet reorganization in October 2010, appointing Muhammad Riyad Hussein Ismat, a former ambassador to Qatar, as Minister of Culture, and George Malki Soumi, an agricultural specialist and a member of the Syrian Communist Party, as Minister of Irrigation. Also in October Abdullah al-Dardari launched the 2011–15 Development Plan, which focused on improving Syria's infrastructure, especially transport, in accordance with the strategy to transform the country into a regional trading hub. Among the proposed projects were the construction of new airports and the expansion of existing ones; the construction of two trans-Syria highways totalling 800 km in length (the first to link the port of Tartous with the Iraqi border, the second to cross Syria from the Turkish border to the Jordanian border); the expansion of the ports of Latakia and Tartous; and the construction of an underground railway system in Damascus. According to al-Dardari, Syria was in the early phase of a radical economic transformation, although he acknowledged that there was widespread dissatisfaction and lack of understanding of government economic strategy. Some of the difficulties, such as rising youth unemployment, were related to the transition to a social market economy. Moreover, four years of severe drought had brought increased hardship to farmers and generated a massive population displacement of some 600,000 people to the cities of western Syria.

THE SYRIAN UPRISING

The outbreak of popular anti-Government revolts in many Arab states, following the collapse of the Tunisian regime in January 2011, sparked expectations that authoritarian regimes throughout the region might fall. Unrest soon followed in Syria, and over the next six months it escalated significantly. Speaking to the *Wall Street Journal* on 31 January, President Assad stated that reforms were needed, but that his own Government was secure. Moreover, he was of the opinion that he would be able to implement reforms in a considered way because his anti-US sentiment and his stance against Israel gave him credibility with the Syrian people. Appeals on social networking websites for a 'day of rage' on 4–5 February received only a lukewarm response in Syria and abroad, despite apparent popular dislike of the regime, its business cohorts and the security services. In the following weeks small protests in Damascus were quickly dispersed by the security forces, while the regime sought to project an image of widespread support with crude propaganda celebrating the personality of the President.

It was only in March 2011, a month after the fall of Hosni Mubarak in Egypt, that the Syrian public in cities across Syria finally challenged state authority with another 'day of rage' on 15 March and the biggest demonstration in many years on 18 March. Protests in Dar'a were a critical turning point, when local people, outraged by the detention and torture of schoolboys for anti-Government graffiti, took to the streets. Police and army units reacted with lethal force, which merely emboldened the crowd to make further demands—the release of all political prisoners, trials for those who shot and killed protesters, the repeal of the 48-year state of emergency and an end to corruption—as they set fire to the local Baath Party headquarters and the offices of Syriatel, the telephone company owned by Rami Makhlouf, a cousin of the President. In a week of demonstrations in Dar'a alone, about 100 people were reportedly killed. Soon the conflict between Dar'a and Damascus came to symbolize the grievances of all disaffected Syrians against the regime, and demonstrations spread to the port city of Latakia, a stronghold of Assad, and to the Alawi minority, as well as the town of Baniyas and the village of Bayda on Syria's coastal region.

The absence of civil society forums effectively gave the protests an Islamist aspect, because large demonstrations often took place on Friday after communal prayers in what became a weekly cycle. The Friday protests would result in killings, and the Saturday funerals of 'martyrs' would provoke more protests and more killings. The clashes produced two opposing narratives, with government officials claiming that armed gangs and foreign forces, driven by sectarian and extremist motives, were leading the demonstrations, while dissidents claimed that it was the security forces abetted by paramilitary gangs—the so-called *shabbiha*—who attacked peaceful activists and acted as *agents provocateurs*.

During the first two weeks of mass protests President Assad kept a low profile. While heavy security in the two principal Syrian cities, Damascus and Aleppo, kept protests to a minimum, the regime mounted large-scale rallies to assert that it still had popular support. A presidential adviser, Buthaina Shaaban, announced an imminent set of measures, including salary increases for state employees and the release of political prisoners, while the cabinet led by Prime Minister Muhammad Naji al-Otari, who had been in office since 2003, resigned. Assad finally addressed the People's Assembly on 30 March 2011, his speech proving to be a mix of apology and accusation. Although he acknowledged that he had been slow to address popular demands, he stated that he would not be rushed into hurried reform. Moreover, he accused a conspiracy of 'near and far' enemies of seeking to destabilize Syria in conjunction with extremist Islamist groups and social networking sites. Even though he offered the prospect of future reforms such as the repeal of the state of emergency and the extending of Syrian citizenship to Kurds, he refused any relaxation of authoritarian control. His speech effectively halted any expectations that major reforms would be forthcoming, while the spectacle of a crowd of government supporters surrounding the parliament left many Syrians deeply disappointed.

With the explosion of the Syrian uprising, from the second half of March 2011, there was a recurring sequence. First came popular demonstrations—usually timed for Friday after communal prayers—followed by a brutal security crackdown. Next followed administrative palliatives, policy adjustments and finally a presidential address. The governors of Dar'a, Homs, Hama and Deir el-Zor were replaced between late March and late July after massive protests in those areas. The resignation of the Otari Government was followed by the appointment, on 14 April, of a new administration led by Adel Safar, who had been the Minister of Agriculture and Agrarian Reform in the previous Government. All of the new appointees were loyalists, such as the new Minister of the Interior, Maj.-Gen. Muhammad Ibrahim al-Shaar, former chief of the military police who had also previously served as governor of Saydnaya prison. The most important change was the removal of Abdullah al-Dardari, architect of the programme of economic reform, and the abolition of his post. Thus, the Government signalled that it would abandon the policy of economic liberalization in favour of short-term policies—the revival of heating fuel subsidies, the recruitment of more civil servants and the further postponement of VAT—in order to pacify poor Syrians and ensure the survival of the regime. Moreover, in an effort to appease conservative Islamist opponents, the regime decided on 6 April to allow the wearing of the *niqab* in schools, which had been banned in July 2010, and to close a casino, and announced the creation of an Islamic satellite television channel.

The four speeches given by President Assad between late March and August 2011 had various common themes. He admitted the need for reform, and proposed certain legal and constitutional measures, such as ending the state of emergency, revising the Syrian Constitution and organizing new elections for the People's Assembly, to be realized in the near future. On 19 April the state of emergency, in force since 1963, was indeed revoked, a law was adopted giving citizens the right to hold 'peaceful' protests, and the Supreme State Security Court was abolished. Yet, concurrently, the new Government approved measures requiring citizens to seek the permission of the Ministry of the Interior to hold demonstrations, a few hours before an outright ban was placed on 'political' protests. Assad refused to be coerced into what he saw as hurried and ill-considered change, and accused Islamist and foreign 'colonialist' forces of trying to destabilize the country and introduce sectarian chaos. Thus, security forces were still needed with untrammelled authority to defend national sovereignty and stability. This dual approach of forceful suppression mixed with political and economic concessions—usually announced on the eve of the Islamic weekend—thus continued in a familiar pattern.

During April and May 2011 more than 1,100 people were killed, and an estimated 8,000 detained, in a mass campaign of arrests as thousands of protesters took to the streets in most provincial towns, including the Druze area of Suweida, Homs (the third largest Syrian city, near the Lebanese border), the coastal towns of Jabla and Baniyas, Dar'a, and in some suburbs of Damascus (although not the city centre). Foreign media were kept out of the region as the Syrian army moved in, but images uploaded onto social networking websites apparently showed soldiers directing heavy fire at unarmed civilians. The deployment in Dar'a of units of the Fourth Armoured Division, commanded by the President's brother Maher al-Assad, was a signal of the regime's determination to crush the opposition, despite promises of reform. The unrest increasingly moved from rural areas into the cities, thus becoming a nation-wide popular revolt demanding the fall of the regime.

Some of the largest anti-Government protests took place in June 2011 in Hama, a Muslim Brotherhood stronghold, where a popular uprising in early 1982 had been brutally suppressed by the authorities, with great loss of life. Moreover, there were reports of heavy casualties among security forces in Jisr al-Shughour, in the north-western governorate of Idleb, where some 120 soldiers were killed in unclear circumstances. Meanwhile, a major displacement of people was under way, as more than 11,000 civilians crossed the border into Turkey, seeking refuge from the Syrian army.

Appeals for 'national dialogue' in a speech by President Assad on 20 June 2011 were greeted with widespread derision, and in late June rebels rejected an authorized meeting of 150 dissidents, denouncing it as a 'fig leaf'. A National Dialogue Commission on political reform, opened by Vice-President Farouk al-Shara' on 10 July to much official fanfare, received a similar response from the rebels.

ESCALATING REPRESSION AND SHIFTING SOCIAL DYNAMICS

During the second half of 2011, and while international attitudes to the Syrian crisis remained uncertain, there was a change in both the Assad regime's modus operandi and opposition practices. In July the main focus of the uprising shifted from the north-western areas of the country to the central cities of Hama, Homs and Deir el-Zor (the largest urban centre in the Euphrates valley), parts of which appeared to have fallen outside the control of the regime. Syrian forces further escalated the violence and tempo of the conflict: the initial cycle of concessions and repression gave way to the so-called 'security solution', in which security services were given a freer hand to intimidate the population into obedience and divide Syrian communities with the aim of rolling back the opposition movement. In late July government forces with tanks and armoured vehicles launched a heavy military assault on the rebel cities, in what appeared to be a pre-emptive move on the eve of the Islamic holy month of Ramadan, when daily public gatherings in mosques were expected to add momentum to the protests. During August, with Ramadan under way, the regime continued to use lethal force against protesters in many locations nation-wide. By the end of the month the security forces, led by the Republican Guard and supplemented by the *shabbiha,* appeared to have subdued protests in Homs, Hama, Dar'a and Deir el-Zor, with heavy civilian casualties. According to the UN High Commissioner for Human Rights, Navanethem Pillay, more than 2,200 people had been killed since the protests began in mid-March. Official sources stated that several soldiers had been killed or injured during these operations, as they came under heavy fire from armed insurgents.

Despite their overwhelming superiority in strength of personnel and weapons, loyalist forces failed wholly to suppress the revolt, and security services' tactics backfired. The collapse of what Syrians called 'the wall of fear', and the lack of discernible policy guidance, prompted popular reaction and eventually armed resistance, as army defectors joined anti-regime vigilantes. Elements of the opposition—including the Syrian National Council—sought to maintain the essentially peaceful nature of the protests, but significant numbers of Syrian activists reached the conclusion that they had to seek their own solutions and started to challenge regime forces in increasingly violent clashes. Guerrilla resistance emerged in a number of areas close to Syria's international borders—including Homs, 20 km east of the border with Lebanon; Idleb, bordering Turkey; and Dar'a, on the border with Jordan.

The suspension of Syria from the Arab League on 7 November 2011 galvanized the Free Syrian Army (FSA), a loose rebel grouping of volunteers and army defectors, into increasingly bold action. Later in the month the FSA launched grenade attacks for the first time in Damascus, on an air force Intelligence base at Harasta and on a Baath Party building in Mazraa. The Assad regime's claims that it had been confronted by an armed insurgency thus became a self-fulfilling prophecy.

As the conflict became more violent, social dynamics evolved. Peaceful protest and civil society initiative continued, but the mass protests of the initial months of the uprising gave way to smaller demonstrations of popular defiance, quick to disperse as soon as regime forces intervened. Contrary to government claims, religious fundamentalism was not at this stage a prevalent feature of the opposition. Yet the mostly Alawite composition of both the security forces and the *shabbiha* militia, allegedly responsible for ferocious attack on civilians, gave rise to sectarianism and confessionalism, thus validating the regime's narrative depicting the popular uprising as an anti-Alawite fundamentalist revolt.

Nevertheless, Syria's two largest cities—the capital, Damascus, and the country's main commercial centre, Aleppo—experienced little unrest at this time, indicating that part of the population did support the Assad regime. Furthermore, there had been no sign of major divisions within the Government, despite reports that some 200 Baath Party members had resigned in late April 2011, in protest against the violent suppression of demonstrations, and the replacement of the Minister of Defence, Lt-Gen. Ali Muhammad Habib Mahmoud, in early August, officially attributed to ill health; Gen. Dawoud bin Abdullah Rajiha succeeded Habib in the post.

THE SYRIAN NATIONAL COUNCIL

The protest movement grew, but remained unable to coalesce around a unified leadership or political project. By mid-2011 there had been little co-operation between the spontaneous revolts within Syria, organized by Local Co-ordination Committees (LCCs), and groups of dissidents outside the country. A three-day conference held in Antalya, Turkey, between 31 May and 2 June laid the groundwork for an agreement, the key points of which were the establishment of a secular government with separation between religion and state—finally accepted by the Muslim Brotherhood and other Islamist groups after intense pressure—and the creation of an elected executive board.

Efforts to co-ordinate the uprising and gain international support led to the formation, on 15 September 2011, of a Syrian National Council (SNC), which included online activists, Islamist figures, liberal signatories of the Damascus Declaration, Kurds and Christians. About one-half of the SNC members were Syrians in exile. Nevertheless, the movement projected itself as inclusive of all the various strands in Syrian society, and the SNC's head—the Paris-based academic Burhan Ghalioun—stated that it represented Syrian opposition inside and outside the country, with the aim of establishing a civil state without discrimination on grounds of ethnicity, gender, religion or political affiliation. The role of Islamists within the SNC was a sensitive matter, as the Assad regime claimed to stand as a safeguard against Sunni fundamentalists who aim to repress non-Sunni minorities, in particular the Assad family's Alawi sect and Christians.

Despite presenting itself as the most representative force among the opposition, the SNC was just one of several opposition groupings, including the National Co-ordinating Committee for Democratic Change—among whose members were veteran campaigners for democracy such as Michel Kilo and Aref Dalila. Most opposition groups were in agreement regarding the fundamental aims of overthrowing the Assad regime and replacing it with a democratic system, but there remained sharp differences on key issues, including the use of violence and military intervention by outside forces. While the SNC became the main opposition force active in the international diplomatic arena, much of the information about events within Syria filtered out through the LCC, which had at this time become the main organizing body and the principal voice of the domestic Syrian opposition since the uprising started in March 2011. Eventually, the LCC took the responsibility for managing local resources and local governance.

Meeting in İstanbul on 10 June 2012, the SNC elected Abd al-Baset Sida, another Paris-based academic and a member of the Kurdish minority, as its new leader, following the resignation of Burhan Ghalioun. In his first public statement, Sida urged the international community to act to protect the Syrian civilian population under the terms of Chapter VII of the UN Charter, which sets out conditions for the use of military force. However, the SNC's internal divisions kept Western and Arab states from recognizing it as an opposition government-in-exile. In the eyes of the international community, the opposition remained a fractious collection of political groups, long-term exiles, grassroots organizers and armed militants, divided along ideological, ethnic or sectarian lines, and thus not representing a cogent alternative government.

THE MILITARY SOLUTION

The arrival of the first Arab League monitors, in December 2011, changed the dynamic of the uprising. The opposition stepped up their demonstrations, while the regime temporarily withdrew armoured vehicles from inspected areas and announced the release of hundreds of detainees. None the less, the LCC reported that some 1,000 civilians were killed during the first month of the Arab League mission. In one incident, on the day of the mission's arrival, a car bombing near state security buildings in the Kfar Soussa area of Damascus left 44 people dead. As violence escalated and more bomb attacks followed, a propaganda war broke out, with the opposition accusing the Assad regime of carrying out the bombings, while the authorities claimed that the bombs were the work of al-Qa'ida.

Armed opposition increased markedly as the rate of defections to the FSA accelerated, and several districts of Homs, as well as Zabadani, a hilltop town 30 km from Damascus, fell out of government control and were defended by lightly armed militias under the umbrella of the FSA, thus bringing the country to what the UN High Commissioner for Human Rights, in early December 2011, called the verge of civil war.

The operations mounted by the armed forces in Zabadani and Douma—about 10 km north-east of the capital—in January 2012 signalled the abandonment of counter-insurgency tactics and the beginning of a new phase in the Government's strategy. For the first time in the crisis, the Syrian army subjected residential areas to sustained bombardments in advance of ground operations, which were followed by violence and looting on the part of the militias. Deadly assaults were reported on several towns and villages in Idleb governorate, an FSA stronghold in the north-west, close to the Turkish border. In early February the 'military solution' focused on Homs, the self-proclaimed capital of the revolution. Intensive bombardments were reported in the districts of Khalidiyeh, Bab Amr and Inshaat. The destruction of the impoverished district of Bab Amr attracted global media attention as a result of the presence there of a small group of Western reporters—including a journalist of the British *Sunday Times* newspaper and a French photojournalist who were killed during the offensive. Some 40% of the civilian population fled the devastation, according to the UN Under-Secretary-General for Humanitarian Affairs and Emergency Relief Co-ordinator, Valerie Amos, who was permitted to visit Bab Amr in early March, and armed rebel groups eventually retreated after a month of siege and shelling. Syrian state television celebrated the 'liberation' of the city from 'terrorist groups', and President Assad himself made a visit to Bab Amr in late March to launch a reconstruction effort. Bulletins from the LCC indicated that, at the height of the bombardments in early February, the daily death toll was averaging between 50 and 100.

The retaking of Bab Amr demonstrated the superiority of government forces over the FSA, and the regime's willingness to use this strength. By mid-March 2012 the Syrian army regained control of Idleb, and the authorities subsequently announced a series of victories in opposition enclaves in other parts of the country. The regime showed notable restraint in the Kurdish north-east and the predominantly Druze south. In the main cities of Damascus and Aleppo, government efforts focused on preventing dissent spreading from the generally restive periphery to central districts. However, armed resistance continued in and around Homs and in the mountainous Idleb governorate, and towards the end of March several other fronts sprang up, notably around Damascus and Aleppo, as well as in Hama, Deir el-Zor and Rakka.

The non-engagement of the international community in the face of the destruction of Bab Amr convinced the rebels that the uprising would have to succeed without external assistance. The FSA, equipped with only light weapons, sought better arms and tactics, eventually going on the offensive. During April and May 2012 Damascus, hitherto calm, became the next battleground. The influx of people displaced by the conflict elsewhere in the country energized the popular movement there. Demonstrations multiplied, while armed rebels confronted government forces around the capital, reaching its immediate periphery by July.

Although both the Assad regime and the FSA pledged that they would respect the UN-backed cease-fire agreement, the presence of tanks increased in Syrian towns just days prior to the deadline of 12 April 2012 (see the UN-Arab League Peace Plan), violent clashes continued, and a number of bomb explosions targeting government infrastructure in Damascus and Aleppo killed dozens of civilians. On 10 May suicide bombings of a military intelligence building in Damascus resulted in 55 dead and 372 injured, and marked the end of efforts to forge a truce. Such incidents fuelled the ongoing propaganda war: the regime accused al-Qa'ida and the rebels of carrying out indiscriminate bomb attacks, while opposition groups countered that the regime had itself staged the explosions precisely in order to justify its 'war on terror'. As the number of fatalities escalated, the gulf between government and opposition constituencies grew exponentially. The two sides increasingly saw the conflict as a zero-sum game, in which no party appeared willing to take any meaningful political initiative. The Assad regime still felt very strong, as it was regaining ground militarily, while the international community remained divided, and the President continued to enjoy the support of a share of society apparently torn between distrust of a divided opposition and fear of the unknown. Ultimately, the 'military solution' proved unable to restore security and authority in the supposedly 'liberated' areas. The brutal repression resulted in a growing armed opposition comprising militant activists and army deserters. The use of excessive force on the part of the regime, and the absence of any genuine outreach, ensured that rebel groups retained popular support. Meanwhile, an unrelenting campaign of arrests and detention of moderate dissidents and humanitarian activists in the early months of 2012 demonstrated that the Syrian leadership was not considering any real political solution to the crisis.

REGIME REFORMS

In an effort to portray a sense of normality and to signal the commitment of the Assad regime to implementing reforms, in July 2011 the Syrian Government approved a new election law and adopted legislation to legalize the founding of new political parties. Elections for 17,588 seats on municipal and provincial councils, conducted on 12 December, were presented by the regime as the first step in a process of self-styled democratic reform in response to the uprising. During 2012 the Assad regime maintained that the constitutional route out of the political crisis would not be diverted by foreign-backed terrorists, and it pursued its reform programme—which included a revised Constitution, the election of a new parliament, and the formation of a new Government. A referendum on the new Constitution was held on 26 February, as the assault on Bab Amr endured; and on 7 May the election of the new People's Assembly proceeded while violence raged in many parts of the country. Although opposition groups boycotted the referendum and the parliamentary elections, official media claimed that the turn-out was high in both instances, and that 89.4% of voters had endorsed the amended Constitution. No credible opposition force was prepared to collaborate in Assad's version of reform as long as the regime continued its violent crackdown on dissent. Even the officially tolerated opposition groups within Syria—such as the Movement for Building the State (Tayar), led by Louay Hussein, and the National Co-ordination Body for Democratic Change, led by Hassan Abd al-Azim, which supported negotiations with the regime—refused to take part in the elections to the People's Assembly.

Those who expected a change of course were disappointed by the reforms and the government reorganization that followed. Amendments to the 1973 Constitution included the removal of Article 8, which stated that the Baath Party was the leading force in state and society. Yet the Baath Party itself had long become irrelevant in a political system in which unlimited powers were given to the President and to ruling family networks. The amended Constitution still vests substantial powers in the office of the President, including the right to name the Prime Minister and to dismiss the Government. Moreover, as the newly introduced limit on the presidential mandate, of two seven-year terms, was not retroactive, and with the next presidential election not due until 2014, Bashar al-Assad could remain in office until 2028. Finally, the new parliament was virtually identical to its predecessor, with the National Unity Front (the Baath Party and nine parties of the NPF) holding 184 of the 250 seats. None of the six newly established parties that contested the elections included recognized members of the opposition, and none secured any seats. In late June 2012 President Assad appointed a new Council of Ministers that included two 'loyal' opposition figures: the former communist Qadri Jamil as Deputy Prime Minister for Economic Affairs and Minister of Internal Trade and Consumer Protection; and Ali Haidar, of the Syrian Social Nationalist Party, as Minister of State for National Reconciliation Affairs. The appointment of Riyad Farid Hijab, a Baathist who had held the agriculture portfolio in the previous administration, as the new Prime Minister put an end to the prospect of a 'national unity' government—as advanced by President Assad himself in January. Addressing the People's Assembly on 3 June, Assad proclaimed the reform programme complete, rebuffing any further demands and equating all forms of dissent with terrorism and a global conspiracy.

SYRIA'S DESCENT INTO CIVIL WAR

The installation of the new Government in late June 2012 had no effect on the deepening crisis, as Syria headed rapidly into civil war. A gruesome turning-point in the conflict was the massacre of entire families in predominantly Sunni villages within Alawi heartlands. The massacre, on 25 May, of 108 civilians in Houla, a cluster of villages to the north-west of Homs, gave fresh impetus to the FSA campaign against the regime, and marked the effective abandonment of any prospect of a peaceful resolution of the conflict. There were further massacres of villagers during June and July in Sunni enclaves, including Mazraat al-Qubair and Tremseh, near Hama—suggesting a deliberate strategy, on the part of the Assad regime, of carving out an Alawi zone in the event of a collapse of the Syrian state. Surviving villagers reported to UN observers that the killings had been perpetrated by members of the *shabbiha* militia following an army artillery barrage. Domestic protests progressively took up an anti-Alawi rhetoric, and an increasingly fundamentalist discourse, amid unconfirmed reports that jihadi and Salafi elements were playing a role in the uprising. Nevertheless, a resilient popular movement renewed forms of dissent focusing on national solidarity.

In mid-June 2012 Hervé Ladsous, Under-Secretary-General of the UN Department of Peace-keeping Operations, acknowledged that Syria was, in effect, in a state of civil war. This term was echoed in mid-July by the International Committee of the Red Cross. The British-based Syrian Observatory for Human Rights estimated at this time that the conflict in Syria had resulted in more than 21,000 deaths since March 2011.

During July 2012 the conflict appeared to have entered a new phase, with heavy fighting reaching central Damascus. There was also a surge in high-level defections—including those of Brig.-Gen. Munaf Tlass, son of the long-serving former defence minister Mustafa Tlass and a member of a prominent Sunni family, and Nawef al-Fares, the Syrian ambassador to Iraq. On 18 July a bomb explosion inside the headquarters of the National Security Council in Damascus resulted in the death of four key security figures, among them Assef Shawkat, nominally deputy Minister of Defence but in fact a principal security chief and brother-in-law of the President. The other officials killed were the Minister of Defence, Gen. Rajiha; Gen. Hassan Bakhtiar, head of the National Security Council; and Lt-Gen. Hassan al-Turkmani, former Minister of Defence and national security adviser. Following the attack, heavy bombardments and fierce fighting spread to Aleppo and Damascus, amid indications of increased supplies of weapons to the FSA from neighbouring countries. On 6 August the recently appointed Prime Minister, Riyad Hijab, issued a statement confirming his own defection to the opposition, prompting a further reorganization of the Government. Wael Nader al-Halqi, hitherto Minister of Health, was appointed as Prime Minister on 11 August, and on 16 August the Ministers of Justice and of Industry were replaced, and the health portfolio was reallocated. Hijab's defection seemingly exposed the erosion of the authority of the Assad regime. Unable to negotiate with or to suppress the armed opposition, the regime increasingly appeared as a network of militias seeking to maintain power at all costs.

For a time at this point, the fall of the Assad regime seemed imminent. Along the border with Turkey, large areas seized by rebel units created a de facto liberated zone, and news came that weapons were being smuggled into Syria via Turkey. Signalling a new confidence in its ability to retain territory, on 22 September 2012 the FSA moved its headquarters to an undisclosed location in northern Syria. Crucially, the conflict reached central Damascus and Aleppo, where there was a heavy army presence. On 26 September rebels hit the military headquarters in the heart of the capital, causing extensive damage. On 3 October four bombs were detonated in co-ordinated succession in a district of Aleppo, killing 48 people, many of them soldiers.

The regime responded by concentrating forces in the main urban centres and escalating operations, routinely using strikes from helicopters and fighter aircraft on areas controlled by insurgents. Meanwhile, the Government also tried to win over public and international opinion by fostering a dialogue process with the participation of some 20 political parties. This was co-ordinated by Deputy Prime Minister Qadri Jamil, the leader of the 'loyal' National Opposition Bloc. However, any interest on the part of the regime in any political settlement of the crisis was belied by the brutality of its forces—including the recently formed Army of National Defence, which from mid-2012 institutionalized the *shabbiha*. Scores of civilians were killed during August in clashes between rebels and pro-regime forces in Aleppo. Later in the month more than 500 people were massacred in Daraya, which had been one of the first districts of Damascus to rise up in early 2011. This followed days of heavy bombardments and *shabbiha* incursions, in a pattern reminiscent of the earlier massacres in Houla, Mazraat al-Qubair and Tremseh. On 17 September a report by the Independent International Commission of Inquiry to the UN Human Rights Council stated that the scale and frequency of gross human rights violations in Syria—including indiscriminate, daily attacks against civilians—had increased significantly in recent weeks. (The Commission had been established in August 2011, with a mandate to investigate all alleged violations in Syria of international human rights law since March of that year.)

Despite losing control of parts of northern Syria and border posts with Turkey and Iraq, loyalist forces held the rebels at bay in the main urban centres and maintained control of Syria's principal transport axes. On 9 October 2012 rebel forces who had been fighting to establish a safe zone in the north recaptured Maarrat al-Nu'man. Nevertheless, rebels found it increasingly hard to retain control of 'liberated' areas in the face of the regime's military strength and its increased use of air attacks. In an important change of strategy, rebel groups now turned to guerrilla tactics by targeting military installations such as the notorious air force intelligence and detention centre at Harasta in north-east Damascus, which was bombed in that month. In November rebel groups seized the Marj al-Sultan military air facility outside Damascus, and advanced in the eastern province of Deir el-Zor, bordering Iraq, where they captured the military base of Mayadeen and its artillery stockpile.

THE SYRIAN NATIONAL COALITION

While making significant strategic gains, insurgent forces continued their efforts to achieve better co-ordination among fighting groups, and to secure financial, political and military assistance from abroad. Following talks held in early November 2012 in Doha, the largest ever gathering of opponents of the Assad regime formed the National Coalition for Syrian Revolutionary and Opposition Forces, or Syrian National Coalition, a more inclusive coalition led by a prominent Sunni figure, Ahmad Moaz al-Khatib, former imam at the Umayyad Mosque in Damascus. The Doha agreement provided for the creation of a Supreme Military Command (SMC) to serve as a quasi-defence ministry in an eventual transitional government, and to provide a unified command structure to integrate disparate insurgent groups from all Syrian provinces—with the notable exception of forces, such as jihadist groups, that sought the destruction of the Syrian state. This SMC was launched following a conference of senior military opposition commanders in Antalya, Turkey, in early December. In order to adhere to democratic principles, the meeting elected a command of 30 members—11 former officers and 19 civilians.

The Syrian authorities denounced the Doha gathering as blatant foreign interference in Syrian affairs. Losing ground on the battlefield, and amid reports of clashes between rival Alawite clans in the Assad family's home village of Qardaha, the regime once more appeared to be on the brink of collapse. Intense fighting continued during December in Aleppo; and violence reached new levels in the southern suburbs of Damascus, where air-strikes and clashes caused a mass exodus from the Yarmouk camp. Air-strikes by regime forces reportedly resulted in the death of 90 civilians in Halfaya, in Hama governorate. Moreover, opposition groups stated that more than 200 people had been executed in Deri Baalba, near Homs, on 29 December.

By the end of 2012 violence had spread throughout Syria. Widespread destruction and tens of thousands of civilian casualties, as well as hundreds of thousands of refugees and displaced persons stood as evidence of the regime's brutality and its determination to go to any lengths to stay in power. Air-strikes had reduced to rubble Sunni neighbourhoods in Homs and Christian areas in central Aleppo. Areas 'liberated' by rebels, such as the district of Khalidiyeh in Homs and the suburbs of Daraya and Qudsayya near Damascus, became the target of regime retaliation with mortars and artillery attacks, in order to prevent a return to normality and to raise the stakes of being associated with the opposition. Fearing the same all-out destruction, some isolated rebel strongholds, such as Tell Kalakh, opted to negotiate a truce between regime forces and insurgents.

THE COMPLEXITY OF THE SYRIAN CONFLICT

A dangerous development in the Syrian conflict was the escalation of infighting among insurgent groups, and an increased use of car bombs targeting minority-populated areas. At least 34 people were killed on 28 November 2012 in two car bomb explosions in Jaramana, a predominantly Druze and Christian suburb of Damascus that was reportedly loyal to Assad. The Syrian state news agency, SANA, accused the opposition of carrying out indiscriminate 'terrorist bombings, while the opposition accused the regime of having planted the bombs in order to discredit the rebel forces. In December, in its periodic update for September–December, the Commission of Inquiry for Syria of the UN Human Rights Council warned that the conflict had become overtly sectarian.

The risk that the Syrian conflict would descend into inter-militia warfare was highlighted by clashes reported on 24 October 2012 in the largely Kurdish area of Ashrafiya, Aleppo, between elements of the FSA and the Kurdish Democratic Union—an armed group affiliated with the PKK, which formally opposed the Syrian regime but controlled areas in the far north-east with the apparent consent of President Assad. In early July 2013 the killing in Latakia of a senior FSA commander and member of the SMC by the Salafi group the Islamic State of Iraq and the Levant as they met to co-ordinate battle plans certainly exacerbated such tensions.

The rise of Islamists and jihadists among the forces opposed to the Assad regime illustrates the complexity of the Syrian crisis. In the context of ambivalent support on the part of Western countries, and their reluctance to supply the rebels with a steady flow of sophisticated weaponry, Gulf monarchies and Islamist groups had stepped in with money, arms and fighters. Thus, coupled with the brutality of the Assad regime's war against its own people, it was not surprising that the conflict had become radicalized and had attracted extremists.

By the end of 2012 jihadist elements within the rebel forces had achieved considerable military success in strategic regions, particularly in the Euphrates valley. The Islamist group Jabhat al-Nusra li-Ahl al-Sham (the Front for the Support of the People of Syria) has shown itself to be one of the most efficient groups fighting against Assad's army and the *shabbiha*. In January 2013 the al-Nusra Front seized control of the Taftanaz helicopter base in Idleb governorate; and a month later al-Nusra and allied battalions took control of the Tabqa dam—Syria's largest hydroelectric facility—on the Euphrates in Rakka, as well as the neighbouring town of Tabqa.

The al-Nusra Front comprises some 5,000 men, mostly experienced fighters from different Arab countries. These are well equipped and well organized, all united by the idea that the Syrian revolution is an Islamic issue, and all fighting to 'bring the law of Allah back to its land'. In December 2012 the US Department of State officially designated the al-Nusra Front as being an alias of al-Qa'ida in Iraq—an association that al-Nusra rejected. The al-Nusra Front joined neither the Syrian National Coalition nor the jihadist Liberation Front, which grouped Ansar al-Islam, Ahrar al-Sham and the Deir el-Zor Revolutionary Council, but in April 2013 al-Nusra's leader, Abu Muhammad al-Julani, pledged allegiance to the head of al-Qa'ida, Ayman al-Zawahiri.

Although the Syrian National Coalition leader, Moaz al-Khatib, had previously praised the leading role of the al-Nusra Front in fighting government forces, he denounced the group when it declared its affiliation with al-Qa'ida. The USA's designation of al-Nusra as a terrorist organization, however, reportedly increased the Front's popularity among Islamists within Syria, for whom this served to confirm their perception of US interference as part of a conspiracy to keep them out of power. Nevertheless, reports emerged in August 2013 of people in Rakka, the only provincial capital held by the rebels at this time, demonstrating against the perceived 'Islamization' of those parts of Syria under the control of Islamist rebels through the imposition of strict social behaviour and *Shari'a* courts.

A TIPPING MILITARY BALANCE

Until the beginning of 2013 the conflict followed established patterns, with rebels gaining territories in the north and east, and fighting in the Hawran—the southern plain stretching from Damascus to Jordan—and heavy bombardment by regime forces of these rebel-controlled areas. At the end of January, as the rebels made advances in several areas of the country, the leader of the exiled Syrian National Coalition, Moaz al-Khatib, created a stir among the opposition by urging talks with regime figures considered to be detached from the violence, such as Vice-President Farouk al-Shara'. The unprecedented offer of conditional talks won the support of the UN-Arab League Joint Special Representative for Syria, Lakhdar Brahimi, but was rejected by Syria's Minister of State for National Reconciliation Affairs, Ali Haidar, in an interview with SANA, on the grounds that al-Khatib had failed to denounce the activities of Islamist groups. Furthermore, the Assad regime was unwilling to meet al-Khatib's terms for dialogue, which included the release of 160,000 prisoners.

The regime's terms for talks with the opposition were laid down in a speech made by President Assad on 6 January 2013 to supporters who gathered at the Damascus opera house. His vision of reconciliation and transition included a national dialogue and an elaborate political process—involving a unity government, a revised constitution, referendums and elections—controlled by the regime. This process avoided any real negotiation with rebel forces, let alone any compromise over the core of the regime, where real power is vested in the Assad family and its close circle and security élite. Meanwhile, the army would continue to 'fight terrorism'. Dar'a and Homs, which suffered extensive physical damage, killing and population displacement before being brought back under government control, were presented by Assad as 'models' for a broader settlement of the conflict. Thus, the regime refused talks, international mediation and any moves that might jeopardize the hold of the ruling clique. Cabinet changes in early February, when Assad removed six ministers and appointed seven new ones (splitting the labour and social affairs portfolio), appeared little more than cosmetic: Syrian political institutions had long since lost the ability to implement policy, and the presidential palace remained the locus of real decision-making.

Assad's speech appeared to indicate a resurgence of confidence within the regime, despite continuous fighting. An Israeli air-strike on Syrian territory on the night of 29–30 January 2013, understood to have targeted a weapons convoy bound for Lebanon, did not directly challenge Assad's power. Furthermore, the advances of rebel forces during January and February, including the capture of the Taftanaz helicopter base in Idleb, the seizure of the Tabqa dam on the Euphrates and the capture of oilfields in eastern Syria, did not significantly alter the military balance.

Regime advances came at a high human and material cost. On 15 January 2013 some 80 people were killed in two explosions near the University of Aleppo. Following the usual pattern, the Syrian regime blamed terrorists, while the opposition stated that the attacks were result of air-strikes by regime forces. *Shabbiha* and regime troops were believed to have been responsible for the massacre of more than 100 civilians in Basatin al-Hasiya, outside Homs, two days later. In late February the UN High Commissioner for Refugees, António Guterres, described the humanitarian situation in Syria as 'dramatic beyond description'.

It was all too clear that the new-found opposition coalition was still beset with internal rivalries that delayed the formation of an interim government at talks in İstanbul in mid-March 2013. The newly elected coalition Prime Minister, the little-known Ghassan Hitto, who had effectively been imposed on the Syrian National Coalition by Qatar and the Muslim Brotherhood, joined Moaz al-Khatib and other National Coalition leaders when the opposition formally took Syria's seat at the Arab League summit in Doha on 26 March; and the following day, to great fanfare al-Khatib opened a new Syrian diplomatic mission to represent the opposition in the Qatari capital. Shortly beforehand, however, al-Khatib had announced his intention to resign the National Coalition leadership, and he confirmed this a month later, seemingly frustrated both with the Muslim Brotherhood wing of the coalition and with the refusal of Western countries within the international Friends of Syria grouping to offer the rebels anything other than token aid. On 6 July the National Coalition elected Ahmad Asi al-Jarba, a leader of the Shammar tribe from Qamishli, as its head. A Sunni, al-Jarba was reported to have close ties to Saudi Arabia. His election, and the resignation only two days later of coalition Prime Minister Hitto, suggested that Saudi Arabia would now have a dominant voice in rebel affairs.

In the mean time, the military situation began to tilt in favour of the regime. At the beginning of February 2013 Syrian armed forces launched a fierce assault on the rebel-controlled eastern and southern suburbs of Damascus. Heavy fighting was limited to the outskirts of the capital, which in February and March appeared besieged, while opposition groups increasingly used guerrilla attacks, including suicide and car bombs, against security forces inside the city. In one suicide attack, on a mosque in Damascus on 21 March, 49 people—including a key pro-regime cleric—were killed. Also in March regime forces launched a major offensive with the aim of retaking the strategic city of Homs, on the main road to the Hezbollah strongholds in Lebanon and to the regime bases on the Syrian coast (the main point of entry for Russian support).

The dynamics seemed to change again in early March 2013, when rebel groups captured the northern city of Rakka—the first provincial capital and large urban centre to fall under opposition control. In early April rebel forces operating in the south of the country, with Saudi and Jordanian support, seized a military base near Dar'a. Retaliatory attacks by regime forces on villages accused of harbouring deserters resulted in the death of dozens of civilians in Sanamein and Ghabagheb in Dar'a province. Moreover, the first apparently credible reports of the use of chemical weapons emerged in the second half of March: the Government and rebels accused each other of firing a chemical-loaded rocket near Aleppo on 19 March; and later in the month the opposition denounced what they alleged was a chemical missile attack on Adra, near Damascus.

From April 2013 a string of military successes for the regime once again shifted the media narrative from imminent collapse to long-term endurance. On 14 April loyalist forces broke a six-month siege of the Wadi al-Deif and Hamidiya military compounds outside the north-western city of Maarrat al-Nu'man. In May the regime regained its footing in Damascus, tightened its security control in central Syria, and stabilized the southern front. Apparent massacres of Sunnis in Baniyas and Bayda, where entire families were allegedly slaughtered by loyalist militias in early May, suggested a deliberate strategy of sectarian cleansing in an effort to secure a Shi'a 'buffer zone' along the border with Lebanon. Also in May, after three months' bombardment, loyalist forces retook the strategic town of Khirbet Ghazaleh, near the highway linking Damascus with Jordan, thus re-establishing control of the supply route to Dar'a.

The capture of the town of Qusayr, on 5 June 2013, by regime forces, with the help of local militias and Hezbollah fighters from Lebanon, epitomized the reversal of insurgent fortunes. Located on the route linking Homs with the coast, and adjacent to the Lebanese border and the Beqa'a valley, Qusayr was the last rebel stronghold in central Syria. This strategic area was an important corridor through which rebel arms and fighters moved into Syria from Lebanon, and Iranian weapons flowed to Hezbollah. By securing the contested area around the Lebanese border, the regime cut off insurgent supply lines and isolated the rebel towns in the Qalamoun mountains from the Lebanese hinterland. Building on the capture of Qusayr, loyalist forces then pushed to regain control of central Syria. After weeks of siege and heavy bombardments, pro-Government forces finally progressed in central Homs and captured the district of Khalidiyeh in late July. This returned the strategic city linking Damascus to the Syrian coastal area—the heartland of President Assad's Alawite sect—largely under regime control.

By the end of July 2013 neither the regime nor the opposition had registered conclusive victories in the Syrian conflict. The coastal governorates of Latakia and Tartous remained under the control of loyalist forces, while large swathes of territory in the north and east, including the city of Rakka, had been 'liberated'. Rebel-held regions, including Rakka, were under steady bombardment from the Syrian air force, which still controlled the skies. Although loyalist forces were claiming 'victory' in Qusayr and Homs in July, the insurgency had, for its part, taken key points in Aleppo governorate, including Khan al-Assal, thus reinforcing its siege of Syria's largest city, while maintaining control over most of the territory around the city of Idleb. In Damascus, the regime occupied the high ground at Mount Qasioun, overlooking the city, with military bases and the densely populated Alawite neighbourhoods, but intense fighting persisted in the suburbs, and reports continued of numerous incidents of car bomb explosions. Opposition forces in the south controlled major cities within Dar'a governorate, and were fighting for control of the international highway to Jordan.

Almost two-and-a-half years after the start of the uprising, and contrary to rebel expectations, the Assad regime had proved unexpectedly solid, extreme in its methods and immune to international pressure. In its struggle for survival at all costs, the regime appeared to be increasingly dependent on militia-like forces, and on allies who were pursuing their own strategies. Assad's forces were gaining ground largely because rebel groups were fighting each other; weapons supplies were following the strategic calculations of donors rather than the needs of fighting forces; and Western supporters were unable to decide on international strategic priorities—and feared Islamist radicalization most of all. Furthermore, infighting between competing armed groups had reached unprecedented levels. Exploiting an unfavourable political environment for jihadists, including the growing hostility of the FSA and major powers, Kurdish fighters expelled the Salafists from the town of Ras al-Ayn on 17 July 2013, and soon after took control of the border crossing with Turkey. The Kurdish project—the establishment of a proto-state entity in north-eastern Syria—was stymied by the jihadists' successful extension of their control in this region. Amid growing violence, the marginalization of the civilian opposition revealed the extent to which all players were failing to grapple with the important question of democratic change.

HUMANITARIAN DISASTER AND REFUGEE CRISIS

All regions in Syria have experienced violence. By mid-2013 many of the country's largest cities, including Aleppo, had suffered extensive damage from bombings and air-strikes, while a devastating humanitarian crisis continued to ravage the country. The UN Economic and Social Commission for Western Asia (ESCWA) estimated in April that some 1.2m. houses had been damaged or destroyed. Areas under the control of rebel armed groups suffered the highest levels of destruction, as a result of heavy shelling and aerial bombardments. At the end of June the Syrian Observatory for Human Rights reported that more than 100,000 people had been killed in the Syrian conflict since March 2011, with civilians accounting for one-third of the total deaths.

In the assessment of the Office of the UN High Commissioner for Refugees (UNHCR), the conflict in Syria has created the world's worst refugee crisis since the Rwandan genocide in 1994. The High Commissioner, Guterres, noted on 19 March 2013 that daily arrival figures for refugees registered by UNHCR averaged 3,000 in December 2012, 5,000 in January 2013 and 8,000 in February. By early September some 1.84 million Syrians were registered with UNHCR in Lebanon, Jordan, Turkey, Iraq and Egypt, with a further 184,000 awaiting registration. More than 1m. of the refugees were under 18 years of age, and 740,000 under 11 years. Moreover, increasing numbers of refugees were fleeing to North Africa and Europe, according to UNHCR. Since many Syrians declined to register for various reasons, it was likely that hundreds of thousands more could be added to this total. UNHCR forecast that if there was no political solution to the conflict, the number of refugees could double by the end of 2013. The large number of refugees has exerted significant pressure on the economies of neighbouring countries, stretching their already limited resources and services. In response to these pressures, Iraq, Turkey and Jordan had at this time either closed their borders or limited daily refugee inflows. The number of entrants to Jordan had slowed, although the Government insisted that it had kept its borders open. Iraq had for months restricted admissions because of growing security concerns while new camps were under construction. Meanwhile, Turkey, which was hosting more than 450,000 registered refugees in southern Turkey, maintained a policy of allowing entry only to those with valid documents or after camp space was assured for those without documentation. The border closures and restrictions meant that thousands of displaced Syrians remained trapped on the Syrian side, unable to flee or access humanitarian aid. UN estimates in early August put the total number of people internally displaced by the Syrian conflict at some 4m.

Another host country imposed restrictions on the arrival of Syrian refugees in July 2013, as Egypt revised its refugee policy in the wake of its own political upheaval with the overthrow of President Muhammad Mursi. Moreover, a wave of anti-Syrian sentiment had begun sweeping though parts of the country. The Islamist-dominated Mursi administration had kept in place a long-standing 'open-door' policy that had allowed Syrian nationals to come and go without prior need for a visa. Syrians were eligible to receive medical care at state hospitals, while their children could enrol in state schools.

Meanwhile, more than 730,000 refugees had crossed the border into Lebanon, and it was estimated that by the end of 2013 one in four people in Lebanon would be a Syrian refugee. However, Lebanon remained the only country with an open border policy. Because it was still not opting to accommodate Syrian refugees in designated camps, living conditions for the displaced were becoming ever more difficult. With Lebanon also suffering growing domestic tensions, it was thought that the country might soon revise its policy.

INTERNATIONAL REACTIONS TO THE SYRIAN UPRISING

The violent repression of the Syrian popular uprising initially attracted little international pressure, but eventually brought to an end Syria's recent détente with the USA and other Western states. Syria stands at the heart of several critical regional issues: the Arab–Israeli conflict, and inter-Arab rivalries; the struggle over Iran's regional influence; and Turkey's emerging role. Moreover, Syria shares religious and ethnic minorities with its neighbours; remains in a fragile truce with Israel; and has constructed a web of alliances, including with Lebanon's Hezbollah and Iran's Shi'a theocracy. Therefore, all sides have feared that a destabilized Syria would open other fronts of conflict in the region, while sectarian chaos might replace its hitherto stable Baath regime—and spread beyond its borders. Western states were thus initially cautious in condemning the Assad Government, and showed no inclination for another military intervention as in Libya. None the less, the military operation in Dar'a during March 2011 attracted increased international criticism. France, which had been a leader in engagement with Syria, was the first state to push for EU sanctions. On 10 May the EU announced an arms embargo on Syria, and imposed sanctions against 13 prominent Syrian officials, including the President's younger brother, Maher al-Assad—commander of the Fourth Armoured Division and of the Republican Guard—and four other members of the Assad family (the influential business figure Rami Makhlouf, Col Hafiz Makhlouf, chief of the Damascus branch of General Intelligence, and Mundhir and Fawaz Assad, alleged leaders of the *shabbiha* militia). The list also included Muhammad Ibrahim al-Shaar, the newly appointed Minister of the Interior. On 23 May the EU postponed indefinitely its long-delayed Association Agreement with Syria, and added 10 leading government figures to the sanctions list, among them Vice-President Farouk al-Shara' and President Assad himself.

On 29 April 2011 the USA expanded existing economic sanctions, retained from the presidency of George W. Bush despite the improvement in relations. President Barack Obama blocked the property interests of Maher al-Assad and two other officials, as well as of the Syrian intelligence services and their alleged accomplice in repression, the Iranian Islamic Revolutionary Guards Corps—Qods Force. On 18 May a further US executive order expanded these sanctions to include President Assad, Farouk al-Shara' and five other senior members of the regime. Despite the increased sanctions and the clear message, given by Obama in a key speech on the Middle East situation delivered on 19 May, that Assad had a choice between leading the transition or stepping aside, the USA fell short of asking outright for his resignation, and kept its ambassador in Damascus.

Their hardened tone notwithstanding, the EU and the USA did not demand the removal of the Government, leaving open the possibility that President Assad might enact political reforms. One reason for Western caution was the belief that an openly hostile attitude could play into the hands of the Syrian regime, allowing it to invoke a foreign conspiracy and thus mobilize domestic support. Another was the failure of the UN Security Council to agree on any measures of condemnation, because of opposition from the People's Republic of China and Russia to a resolution concerning Syria that might result in an escalation of the situation, as was occurring in Libya.

On 9 June 2011, in response to the bloody repression of the uprising in Jisr al-Shughour, near the border with Turkey, the French Minister of State and Minister of Foreign Affairs, Alain Juppé, became the first Western leader openly to state that President Assad had lost his legitimacy to govern. On the same day, the IAEA referred Syria to the UN Security Council for its covert nuclear activities at the al-Kibar site, which had been destroyed by Israel in September 2007. On 24 June 2011 the EU imposed a third round of sanctions focused on individuals and entities that supported the repressive measures and were connected with Bashar al-Assad. Included were three senior commanders of the Iranian Revolutionary Guards.

Syria suffered growing isolation in mid-2011, but the willingness on the part of Western countries to support President Assad if he embraced reform—a position reiterated by US Secretary of State Hillary Clinton—remained his crucial asset. Moreover, Assad still retained the backing of most Arab states, as well as that of non-Western allies internationally—including both Russia and China, which were likely to veto any Western-sponsored UN Security Council resolution condemning Syria's actions.

At the regional level, most Arab countries proved more or less supportive of Assad during the first months of the Syrian crisis. The subdued reaction of Syria's neighbours, notably Jordan, Iraq and Lebanon, was due to their fears that any post-Baathist sectarian disorder could spread beyond Syria. Nevertheless, Qatar cancelled major investments in Syria, and later closed its embassy in Damascus after it had been attacked in an expression of Syrian government anger at perceived hostile coverage by the Qatar-based television channel Al Jazeera.

Among Syria's regional allies, Iran and Hezbollah were vocal in condemning the rebellion, which they depicted as a plot to undermine the Syrian leadership and to harm the resistance to Israeli regional hegemony. Syria's repressive response to the demonstrations deeply embarrassed Hamas, which offered only lukewarm statements of support to the Syrian regime, and allegedly refused to hold pro-Assad demonstrations.

The reaction of Israel to the Syrian uprising appeared surprisingly cautious, given the potential payoff from a collapse of this key 'confrontation state'. Remarking that the Syrian border had been the quietest of all its Arab neighbours since the 1973 war, Israeli officials indicated that the Assad regime was preferable to an unpredictable alternative. Unexpectedly, this assessment received the explicit support of Rami Makhlouf, who bluntly declared in an interview with the *New York Times* on 10 May 2011 that Israel's stability was linked to the survival of the Assad regime, and that the Assad family would fight to the end in a struggle that would bring turmoil and even war to the entire Middle East. Many saw the incursion, on 15 May, into the Israeli-occupied Golan Heights by some 100 Palestinians living in Syria—four of whom were killed by Israeli troops after they breached the border fence—as a cynical display of the ability of the Syrian regime to provoke conflict in order to stay in power.

Turkey, which had forged a close relationship with Syria in recent years, adopted an incremental approach to the Syrian crisis. From the beginning of the uprising in mid-March 2011, the Turkish Prime Minister, Erdoğan, maintained regular contacts with President Assad, urging him to implement radical political reforms and expressing deep concern about the mounting violence. Meanwhile, Turkey also engaged with the Syrian opposition: representatives of opposition groups met in Antalya in May–June, and in İstanbul in July, for co-ordination meetings sponsored by Turkey's governing Adalet ve Kalkınma Partisi (Justice and Development Party). In June the flight into Turkey of some 11,000 refugees from the border areas of Jisr al-Shughour and Khirbet al-Juz, under attack from the Syrian armed forces, turned the Syrian crisis into a matter affecting Turkish national security.

SYRIA'S DEEPENING DIPLOMATIC ISOLATION

The international approach to the Syrian uprising changed dramatically in response to the attack by regime supporters against the US and French embassies in Damascus on 11 July 2011. The incident followed a visit to Hama by the two countries' ambassadors, amid mounting fears of a repeat of the 1982 massacre of anti-regime rebels there. After weeks of urging Syria to carry out reforms and stop the brutal crackdown, the US Administration of Barack Obama turned decisively against the Syrian regime, stating that Assad had lost his legitimacy to govern. However, despite the increasing tension, the two ambassadors remained in post, and the UN Security Council issued a relatively weak statement on Syria when it finally met to discuss the situation on 3 August; Lebanon, the Arab representative on the Council, refused to associate itself with this mild censure, in the hope that the reforms announced by the Syrian authorities would lead to progress.

Syria's diplomatic isolation deepened in August 2011, in the aftermath of the military assaults on the cities of Hama and Deir el-Zor. Russia, an important ally of Syria with a military base in Tartous, joined in international condemnation. In early August the President of the UN Security Council issued a statement condemning the violence in Syria, and both the GCC and the Arab League later published similar statements criticizing the Syrian Government's actions. Syrian pro-democracy activists received a warm welcome in Washington, DC; and Italy withdrew its ambassador. Both the EU and the USA expanded their sanctions, and two of the region's most powerful states, Saudi Arabia and Turkey, hardened their position against Assad.

Given its close relationship with Syria, its military capability and its geographical location, Turkey was the only country that could put pressure on, and potentially intervene in, Syria. The Turkish Minister of Foreign Affairs, Ahmet Davutoğlu, travelled to Damascus on 9 August 2011 for talks with President Assad. Turkey's Prime Minister, Recep Tayyip Erdoğan, urged President Assad to embark on radical reforms, and referred pointedly to the vital interest that Turkey had in securing the 850-km border between the two states.

The toughening of the Turkish position was less of a surprise than the sharp intervention of King Abdullah of Saudi Arabia, who became the first Arab leader to take a firm stand against the Syrian regime. After declaring in a speech on 7 August 2011 that the 'continuous bloodshed' in Syria was unacceptable, and that the Syrian leadership must stop the violence and enact meaningful reforms or the country would slide into chaos, King Abdullah recalled the Saudi ambassador 'for consultations'. Kuwait and Bahrain withdrew their ambassadors the next day.

The international reaction to the Syrian regime's crackdown on protests grew steadily in intensity. On 18 August 2011—the eve of the 24th successive Friday of protests—President Obama, the EU High Representative for Foreign Affairs and Security Policy, Catherine Ashton, President Nicolas Sarkozy of France, German Federal Chancellor Angela Merkel and the British Prime Minister, David Cameron, made a co-ordinated appeal to President Assad to step down. In an interview given to Syrian state television on 21 August, while the EU was discussing the extension of sanctions against his regime, Assad described Syria's relationship with the West as a dispute over sovereignty and a struggle against a new imperialism. By late August, and the end of Ramadan, the Syrian crisis was continuing to exacerbate regional polarization. There was a rise in tensions between the two major non-Arab powers, Turkey and Iran, which had hitherto co-existed peacefully. None the less, there were indications that even Iran was rethinking its position, as President Mahmoud Ahmadinejad appealed for 'dialogue' between the Syrian Government and its opponents. In late September Erdoğan told international media that Turkey had ended its ties with the Assad Government and was considering implementing its own sanctions against Syria. Attending the annual meeting of the UN General Assembly, the Turkish premier revealed that, earlier in the month, Turkey had seized a ship destined for Syria, which it claimed was transporting weapons for use by pro-Government forces. On 24 September the EU implemented further sanctions against Syria and individuals linked to the Assad Government; the sanctions included a ban on new investment in Syria's petroleum industry, an embargo on imports on Syrian oil and petroleum products, and a prohibition on the export of Syrian banknotes by EU countries.

In early October 2011 both Russia and China voted against a draft UN Security Council resolution, presented by France, Germany, Portugal and the United Kingdom, that sought to condemn 'the continued grave and systematic human rights violations and the use of force against civilians by the Syrian authorities'. Lebanon, Brazil, India and South Africa abstained. Russia and China emphasized that they would not endorse international action that could result in foreign military intervention in Syria. In backing its long-term allies in Damascus at the expense of the aspirations of the Syrian people, Russia was acting to protect its strategic naval base at Tartus. Thus, Russia continued to support the Syrian regime's plans for political reforms, as well as appeal for the opposition to cease its campaign of violence.

Meanwhile, Western and Arab governments welcomed the formation of the SNC, the umbrella opposition group that was established in September 2011 and formally launched in İstanbul on 2 October, but the Council's internal divisions kept them from recognizing it as a government-in-exile.

Meeting in Cairo on 12 November 2011, the overwhelming majority of Arab League foreign ministers voted to suspend Syria's membership of the League for failing to implement a deal to withdraw troops from urban areas and end the so-called 'security-based' response to the crisis. The suspension was rejected by Lebanon (a position clearly reflecting Syria's continued political hold over the Lebanese Government) and Yemen, and by Syria itself; Iraq abstained. An Arab League monitoring mission, operating from 26 December, was terminated on 28 January 2012 because of lack of progress.

In the absence of a consensus on a co-ordinated international response to the Syrian crisis, Western involvement during 2011 remained a series of small, incremental steps and moral condemnation. The meetings of the Friends of Syria—a group comprising more than 50 countries—in Tunisia and Turkey in early 2012 made clear the persistent divide within the international community over the issue of arming the Syrian opposition. At a press conference on 6 March, US President Obama pointed to the risks associated with a military intervention and arming of the opposition.

THE UN-ARAB LEAGUE PEACE PLAN

On 4 February 2012 a UN Security Council resolution concerning the situation in Syria was again vetoed by Russia and China. A similarly worded, Arab-sponsored resolution, which condemned continued widespread and systematic human rights violations on the part of the Syrian authorities, and called on the Syrian Government and allied forces and armed groups to cease 'all violence or reprisals' with immediate effect, was adopted by the UN General Assembly on 16 February by 137 votes to 12 (with 17 abstentions), but it carried little legal force. On 23 February former UN Secretary-General Kofi Annan was appointed Joint Special Envoy of the UN and the Arab League on the Syrian crisis. On 21 April UN Security Council Resolution 2043, submitted by Russia and adopted unanimously, established the UN Supervision Mission in Syria (UNSMIS) for an initial period of 90 days. The support of Russia and China had been secured at the cost of omitting any reference to President Assad's ceding authority. Annan drew up a six-point plan providing for a UN-supervised cessation of armed violence. President Assad formally agreed to abide by the cease-fire agreement, which came into force on 12 April, but he reserved the right to respond to 'terrorist attacks'. With this conditional acceptance of the cease-fire, Assad continued to conduct a skilled diplomatic game, aimed at buying time with international players and turning the focus from 'regime change' to 'regime concessions'. Indeed, the deployment of UN observers did not prevent Syria's descent into what was increasingly characterized as a civil war. Amid a significant escalation in violence, on 16 June the UN suspended the only initiative that had involved all the players in the crisis—the international community, the Syrian opposition and the Assad regime. The mission's dependence on government co-operation and the absence of enforcement mechanisms contributed to its failure. Crucially, the Annan plan did not bring about any change in the underlying positions of the main participants: the Assad regime remained determined to suppress the opposition movement by force; and the bulk of the opposition remained resolved to overthrow the regime, relying increasingly on the FSA. In the context of Russian and Chinese vetoes at the UN, and with continued Iranian and Russian material support, the regime continued to assess that it was in a position to impose its own conditions.

The escalation in the Syrian conflict dynamics during 2012 did not elicit a decisive reaction from key international interests. An international summit meeting, convened by Kofi Annan in Geneva on 30 June in an effort to get the six-point plan back on track, failed to prompt a change of behaviour from either the Syrian regime or the armed opposition—each locked in the belief that they could win the battle and dictate their own conditions rather than find a negotiated solution.

With no apparent resolution to the crisis in sight, in early August 2012 Annan announced his resignation as Joint Special Envoy, and on 19 August the UNSMIS mandate was terminated. After a series of meetings with President Assad during September, Lakhdar Brahimi, the veteran Algerian diplomat who had, on 17 August, been appointed as new UN-Arab League Joint Special Representative for Syria, described his mission as 'nearly impossible'. Little of substance came from Brahimi's subsequent further meetings with Assad, nor from his visit to Moscow in December, but such engagement did show that Assad was considered an integral part of the ongoing diplomatic process aimed at achieving a political settlement of the crisis.

SYRIA'S ALLIES

Increasingly isolated, the regime of Bashar al-Assad was by the second half of 2012 backed solely by its traditional allies: Iran and the Lebanese Hezbollah, which firmly supported the incumbent administration plus Russia and China. Iran's steadfast support was exemplified by the signing of a new free trade agreement in December 2011, which entered into effect at the end of April 2012, and by the visit to Damascus of the head of the Iranian Supreme National Security Council, Saeed Jalili, in early August. This policy of providing support to its strategic ally did not change in spite of Iran's cautious criticism of the Assad regime's violent response to the uprising, and rumours of communications between Iran and members of the Syrian opposition.

The Lebanese Hezbollah movement, which depends on its alliance with Syria (and Iran) for the supply of arms and funds, continued to offer political support to the Assad regime as a critical element in the 'axis of resistance'. However, Hezbollah remained officially on the periphery of the Syrian conflict for most of 2012, blaming the crisis on US and Israeli interference, and watching closely the influx of predominantly Sunni refugees into the Hezbollah stronghold of the Beqa'a valley. Reports of Hezbollah militiamen fighting for the Syrian regime—amid funerals of fighters killed as 'martyrs'—were denied by Hezbollah until October 2012, when the movement's leader, Sheikh Hasan Nasrallah, stated that individual members were indeed fighting in Syria.

The fourth member of the 'axis of resistance', Hamas, for its part refused to support the Syrian Government, and abandoned Damascus—where its political bureau had been based for more than a decade—after the failure of its attempts to mediate in the crisis. Speaking at the Al-Azhar mosque in Cairo in February 2012, the Hamas leader in Gaza, Ismail Haniya, praised 'the heroic Syrian people who are striving for freedom, democracy and reform'.

The consistent support of Russia and China has been a crucial element in enabling the Assad regime to continue its violent campaign for survival. During visits to Damascus in February 2012 Russia's Minister of Foreign Affairs, Sergei Lavrov, and China's Deputy Minister of Foreign Affairs, Zhai Jun, each expressed their backing for the regime's programme of political reforms, and maintained that the opposition's resort to violence should also be condemned. Both countries repeatedly vetoed UN Security Council resolutions on the situation in Syria, emphasizing that they did not want to see military intervention such as the NATO-led operation that brought about regime change in Libya. There was an apparent shift in Russia's approach to the Syrian crisis when, in early July, at the international summit in Geneva, it joined Western countries in questioning the legitimacy of the Assad regime and urging reform of the Syrian state. On 19 July, however, both Russia and China vetoed a Western-sponsored UN Security Council resolution that sought tougher sanctions against Syria. The blocked resolution prompted the US Permanent Representative to the UN, Susan Rice, to state that the Security Council had 'utterly failed' Syria, and to pledge that the USA would work with 'diverse' partners outside the Security Council to exert pressure on the Assad Government.

The newly appointed Syrian Deputy Prime Minister for Economic Affairs, Qadri Jamil, visited Moscow twice during July and August 2012, and again in December, where he held talks about a fuel supply arrangement and a loan. Amid allegations that Russia had shifted its position concerning the departure of President Assad, Jamil indicated during his August visit that the issue could be discussed during negotiations but was not a precondition for such talks—as the Syrian opposition had demanded. At the end of December the Syrian National Coalition leader, Moaz al-Khatib, rejected Russia's invitation for peace talks, demanding instead that Russia apologize for its continued support for Assad.

REGIONAL IMPLICATIONS

As 2012 progressed, the Syrian people's aspirations for democracy were increasingly being politicized, as governments in the region responded to the deepening crisis according to their diverse strategic interests and their degree of fear of likely post-Baathist instability. In the volatile regional environment, the problem of containing the Syrian conflict—i.e. preventing it from sparking violence in neighbouring countries—seemed more urgent than did stemming the bloodshed within Syria itself. Indeed, by early 2012 the Syrian crisis was already having a major impact on Lebanon's sectarian divisions. Violent clashes between Alawis and Sunnis flared up in the northern city of Tripoli, Lebanon's second largest city, forcing the Lebanese army to intervene on several occasions, while the two main political coalitions aligned themselves for and against the Syrian regime. In early June 15 people were killed in clashes in Tripoli, and heavy fighting resumed there on 20 August in the Sunni district of Bab al-Tabbana and the Alawite district of Jabal Muhsin, leaving at least 16 people dead.

A series of events in mid-2012 demonstrated Lebanon's shifting relations with Syria. These included the arrest in Beirut, in August, of Michel Samaha, a former Lebanese information minister and erstwhile adviser to the Syrian President; and the issuing by the Lebanese authorities of an arrest warrant, *in absentia*, for Assad's special security adviser, Gen. Ali Mamlouk. Both were charged with plotting terrorist attacks against Lebanese political and religious figures in collaboration with the Syrian regime. The assassination in Beirut, on 19 October, of Brig.-Gen. Wissam al-Hassan, the head of intelligence in the Lebanese Internal Security Forces, who had been conducting high-profile investigations into bomb plots in Lebanon, was widely thought to have been orchestrated by the Syrian regime and its Lebanese allies.

Iraqi Shi'ite politicians and religious leaders adopted a pragmatic approach to the Syrian crisis, in order both to protect bilateral trade and to avoid antagonizing Iran. The increase in violence, with growing evidence that local and foreign jihadis had joined the rebels, added to the caution of Prime Minister Nuri al-Maliki and the Iraqi Shi'ite-led Government, which was wary of the Sunni-dominated Syrian opposition. Iraq's vigilance only increased following the al-Nusra Front's pledge of allegiance to al-Qa'ida leader Ayman al-Zawahiri in April 2013, and the near-simultaneous announcement by al-Qa'ida in Iraq that the two groups were merging. By contrast, Masoud Barzani, President of the Kurdish Autonomous Region, admitted in July 2012 that Syrian Kurds who had fled to areas controlled by his administration were being given military training. The vast majority of refugees from Syrian Kurdish areas reportedly fled to Iraqi Kurdistan, which was sheltering more than 180,000 Syrians by September 2013.

Turkey forged close ties with the SNC and the FSA, both of which established bases in southern Turkey. Turkish forces were deployed to the border after Syrian air defences shot down a fighter jet of the Turkish air force off the Syrian coast near Latakia in June 2012, and tensions between Turkey and Syria further escalated when five civilians were killed as a result of Syrian shelling of the border town of Akçakale in early October.

Nevertheless, both countries appeared keen to avert a full-scale military confrontation. Turkey avoided major unilateral actions, instead increasing pressure on NATO and the UN to act. Following a formal request by the Turkish Government, NATO ministers of foreign affairs agreed on 4 December to deploy *Patriot* missiles on the Turkish–Syrian border, with a view to reinforcing Turkey's air defence capabilities following 'repeated violations of Turkey's territory'. A substantial concern for Turkey remains the prospect of an autonomous Kurdish region in northern Syria. In August of that year the Turkish Prime Minister, Recep Tayyip Erdoğan, asserted that he was ready to send troops into Syria should it become a base for Kurdish guerrillas launching incursions into Turkey.

In the absence of an explicit international agreement on a resolution to the Syrian crisis, the Western and Arab approach gradually evolved towards a strategy of proclaiming support for diplomatic solutions while aiding a greater militarization of the opposition. Turkey, Saudi Arabia and Qatar were allegedly providing substantial logistical support to the FSA from bases in refugee camps on the Turkish side of the border with Syria, as well as via sympathetic elements in Lebanon. Indicative of Saudi Arabia's increasingly assertive foreign policy was the invitation to Brig.-Gen. Munaf Tlass, who defected from the Assad regime in July 2012, to appear later that month via the Saudi-owned television news channel Al Arabiya, where he presented himself as the next leader of Syria. Also in July US officials stated that the USA would provide more training and equipment to help improve the combat effectiveness of Syrian opposition forces in their campaign against state armed forces.

Concern increased in neighbouring countries with emerging evidence that jihadist groups suspected of links to al-Qa'ida were behind the rise in the number of suicide bombings in Syria during 2012, and with the alarming flows of Syrian refugees into Turkey, Lebanon and, more recently, Jordan. By mid-2012 the influx of large numbers of Syrian refugees into Lebanon, especially in the northern region of Tripoli and in the Beqa'a valley on the Lebanese–Syrian border, was already causing serious concerns for the stability and the economy of Lebanon. Discussion with regard to the establishment of 'buffer zones' to protect civilians at the Syrian–Turkish border also intensified in mid-2012. A 'safe haven' in the north of Syria, with NATO support, would respond to both humanitarian purposes and to Turkey's concern to bring the Kurdish centres in northern Syria under control. From late July the Jordanian Government opted for building refugee camps for security as well as humanitarian reasons, while there were reports that the Jordanian army was opening fire on Syrian troops seeking to prevent refugees from crossing the border.

Israel's announcement—via its Deputy Prime Minister and Minister of Defence, Ehud Barak, on 22 July 2012—that it was ready to intervene in Syria should chemical weapons fall into the hands of Hezbollah or other militant groups increased the sense of imminent regional conflict that was taking hold in the Middle East in mid-2012. Syria admitted in July that it has chemical weapons, and that it could use them in the event of any 'external aggression'. The Israeli stance was supported by US President Barack Obama, who asserted in late August that evidence of the movement or use of chemical or biological weapons by any actor in the Syrian conflict would constitute a 'red line' that would alter his position on intervention in the crisis. However, the ongoing deadlock within the UN Security Council, and the conflicting agendas of regional powers—seemingly ill-prepared to deal with a post-Assad configuration—apparently condemned Syria to further disorder.

PROXY WARS IN SYRIA

Syria found itself centre stage in the deepening struggle for regional influence between Saudi Arabia and Iran by 2012, with Iran maintaining its steadfast support for the Assad regime while Saudi Arabia reportedly channelled arms and financial support to the rebel FSA. What was originally a Syrian conflict with a regional spillover had gradually become a regional war with a Syrian focus. The opposition to Assad increasingly resembled a Sunni coalition including the Gulf states and Turkey, while the pro-regime camp, which included Iran, Hezbollah and Iraq, appeared to be a Shi'ite alliance. The war reignited sectarian tensions in fragile Iraq and Lebanon, as fighters from both countries battled inside Syria.

By 2013 the conflict had descended into multiple wars by proxy, with the foreign policy objectives of various regional and international countries being fought out on Syrian territory. A number of separate rebel groups, backed by different sponsors, had emerged, and these competed for dominance and international support. The motivations of regional patrons—apparently attempting to fan the flames of sectarianism and engaging in a media war of duelling narratives, while supplying materiel and financial support to their chosen side—seemed more in line with those of rivals in a new Arab 'cold war' than with the democratic aspirations of the Syrian people. Israeli incursions on Syrian territory, aimed at preserving the regional balance of military power, added to the complexity of the regional picture. International actors gradually stepped up their involvement in the Syrian conflict, with Iran and Russia providing backing for the Assad regime and Western powers engaging in 'back-door' as well as UN diplomacy. As the USA, the United Kingdom and France urged action through the UN Security Council, blocked by rival powers Russia and China, the Syrian crisis assumed international dimensions as well.

A NEW ARAB 'COLD WAR'?

On the night of 29–30 January 2013, just days after the Israeli Government warned that it might launch a pre-emptive strike to prevent the transfer of chemical weapons to Hezbollah, an air raid destroyed a Syrian target that was reported by US sources to be a convoy of *SA-17* missiles bound for Syria's ally Hezbollah in Lebanon, and by Syria to be a military research centre at Jamraya, north-west of Damascus, about 10 km from the Lebanese border. Despite widespread concerns that the conflict could escalate, neither Syria nor regional powers appeared ready to retaliate. Fears of wider regional conflict grew after Israeli jets, on 5 May, targeted several military installations in the hills on the north-western outskirts of Damascus, a day after hitting a military convoy close to the Lebanese border that reportedly was transporting either anti-aircraft or ground-to-ground missile batteries. The Israeli Government did not take responsibility for the attacks, but its officials signalled that Israel would take strong action to deal with threats to its security. Such threats included in particular the medium-range ballistic missiles allegedly supplied by Iran to Syria, and by Syria to Hezbollah, since the 2006 war between Hezbollah and Israel in southern Lebanon. A much greater potential threat came in the form of the *S-300* high-altitude anti-aircraft missiles that Syria contracted with Russia to supply in mid-May 2013. President Vladimir Putin stated in June that Russia had not yet supplied the missiles, in the interests of not upsetting the regional balance of power; and on 9 August the Russian producer said that no delivery would be made until 2014.

Israel reportedly reassured Damascus that it did not intend to take sides in Syria's civil war, but only to prevent Hezbollah enhancing its military capabilities vis-à-vis Israel. The Israeli strikes were not met with any Syrian military response, but, in an effort to discourage Israel from undertaking any more such attacks, President Assad stated, in a television interview broadcast by the Hezbollah-affiliated channel Al-Manar on 30 May 2013, that Syria was receiving deliveries of Russian arms, and threatened to open a new 'front of resistance' in the Golan Heights. A number of recent incidents reported in the area, including two rockets fired the day after the second Israeli raid, were believed to have involved errant missiles from the civil conflict, rather than having specifically targeted Israel, and did not elicit a further response from Israel. Israel's diplomatic caution apparently reflected its main security concerns—chemical weapons falling into the wrong hands, and the growth of radical Islamist groups, which a weakened Syrian state will not be able to prevent. A new Israeli airstrike, on 5 July, on a munitions warehouse in the Syrian coastal town of Latakia was reported by US officials, who confirmed that the attack did not succeed in destroying all of the Russian-made *Yakhont* anti-ship missiles that it had targeted.

The approach of the Arab states to the Syrian crisis remained divided, with Qatar and, increasingly, Saudi Arabia acting as the most important patrons of the Syrian opposition—and competing for influence by supporting different rebel groups. The Saudis were backing the FSA, and the Qataris the SNC, the latter of which had been recognized by the Arab League as the legitimate representative of Syria. Qatar first supplied weapons to the Syrian rebels through the intermediary of Turkish intelligence, but began to work with Lebanese agents when Saudi Arabia joined the covert military effort. A crucial disagreement between Doha and Riyadh on the role to be played by the Muslim Brotherhood led to their adoption of divergent agendas with regard to Syrian opposition fighters. Saudi Arabia was supporting both secular rebel factions and Salafi groups that espouse the stricter Wahhabi Islam dominant in Saudi Arabia, while Qatar forged close ties with the Muslim Brotherhood in Syria and regionally. By late 2012 the rivalry had intensified to the point at which the Qataris and Saudis were creating separate military alliances. In November, as the Doha meeting leading to the formation of the Syrian National Coalition was taking place, Al Arabiya and other Saudi Arabian media announced the formation of the Five Fronts Command, which many rebels considered to be a Saudi attempt to create a loyal proxy force. That the Qatari-based Al Jazeera never reported this apparently highlighted the rivalry between the two countries. The Five Fronts Command had little success, but the geographical division into fronts endured as a hallmark of continued Saudi influence. As complaints poured in from Syrian opposition leaders and Western officials, Saudi Arabia and Qatar agreed to bring the structures together under the supreme military command of the Western-backed Gen. Selim Idriss, although Doha and Riyadh also continued to act independently with regard to the Syrian conflict.

Qatar's involvement with Syria's political opposition generated even greater controversy than did its support of rebel groups. In August 2011 Qatar contributed to the funding of the SNC. As the Muslim Brotherhood—the only organized bloc within the SNC—gained the greatest influence within the movement, Western nations pressed Qatar to help form a broader opposition, resulting in the establishment of the Syrian National Coalition in Doha in November 2012. Also from late 2012 the increasing prominence of the al-Nusra Front, the highly effective Islamist fighting group allegedly funded by Qatar and other private Gulf donors, brought Western pressure to marginalize such perceived extremist groups. The leading role played by al-Nusra in dislodging the Syrian regime from military facilities in north-east Syria alarmed the USA, which in December formally designated the al-Nusra Front as being an alias of al-Qa'ida in Iraq. Following the transfer of power in Qatar from Sheikh Hamad bin Khalifa Al Thani to his son Sheikh Tamim in late June 2013, foreign policy under the new Amir seemingly shifted towards adopting a much lower profile in shaping the regional balance of power. In early July, meanwhile, the leadership of the Syrian National Coalition was taken by the Saudi-backed candidate, Ahmad al-Jarba, despite strenuous efforts on the part of the Qataris to retain control. His appointment was swiftly followed by the resignation of the Qatari-sponsored interim Prime Minister within the National Coalition, Ghassan Hitto, and such shifts served to confirm the renewed strength of Saudi Arabia's regional position.

Meanwhile, both Saudi Arabia and Qatar found it difficult to endorse the implicit legitimacy conferred on the Assad regime by the various missions of UN and Arab League envoys, whose programme included mediating a deal with President Assad—to which agenda the Syrian opposition remained opposed.

Iran continued to give logistical, diplomatic and financial support to the Syrian regime, and also to sell Syrian crude oil, in defiance of US and EU sanctions, thus providing valuable income for the Syrian Government. In February 2013 the killing of Gen. Hassan Shateri, of the Iranian Revolutionary Guards Corps, marked the first death of a senior Iranian commander in the Syrian conflict, and confirmed the Western official reports that Iranian advisers and troops were embedded in the military apparatus of the Assad regime. While supporting President Assad, the Iranian authorities also continued to signal their desire to have a role in any political resolution to the Syria crisis. After meeting with the leader of the Syrian National Coalition, Moaz al-Khatib, in the same month, the Iranian Minister of Foreign Affairs, Ali Akbar Salehi, supported al-Khatib's offer of conditional talks with the regime—a stance rejected by other members of the Syrian opposition, who appeared set on a fight to the finish. Both Iran and Russia had rejected the precondition for negotiations set by the Sunni regional powers, namely that Assad should relinquish power early in order to facilitate political change. In mid-2013, despite Iran's insistence that its policy with regard to Syria had not changed, the newly elected President, Hassan Rouhani, raised hopes of diplomatic progress as he apparently sought better relations with Saudi Arabia.

SYRIA'S NEIGHBOURS

Since the start of the uprising in 2011, Syria's immediate neighbours have been watching developments over their borders most keenly. They are well aware that Syria's sectarian and ethnic fault lines—around 75% of the population are Sunni, 12% Alawi, 10% Christian and 3% Druze; and some 90% Arab, 9% Kurdish and 1% others (Turkoman, Circassian, etc.) reflect their own to a greater or lesser degree.

Hezbollah's support for the Assad regime notably increased after October 2012, when the organization's leader, Hasan Nasrallah, confirmed that its members were indeed fighting in Syria. In a defiant speech on 30 April 2013, Nasrallah emphasized that the defeat of the Syrian regime was unacceptable while Hezbollah militiamen were fighting on its behalf in border towns contested between rebels and Syrian government forces. According to Syrian opposition sources, the role of Hezbollah fighters had been essential to the regime's victories in Qusayr and Homs. A recent shift in the Syrian army's tactics to a more flexible posture was apparently influenced by the experience of Iran and Hezbollah in small-unit manoeuvres.

Meanwhile, Hezbollah's greater involvement in the Syrian conflict was accompanied by worsening violence in mixed sectarian areas within Lebanon—particularly in the north of the country—and increased political instability, as Lebanese opposition parties abandoned any pretence of co-operation with Hezbollah on domestic issues. While the Lebanese Prime Minister, Najib Miqati, formally abstained from taking a clear position on the Syrian crisis, the existing divisions between the two Lebanese political camps were sharpened by their support for, or opposition to, the Syrian regime; and the increase or decrease of Syrian influence has become a central political debate in Lebanon.

With the militarization of the Syrian uprising, Lebanese anti-regime forces also engaged in paramilitary activity, smuggling weapons into Syria, and, from late 2012, joining the fight across the border. Despite calls for *jihad* made by leading Salafi clerics in the southern city of Sidon and Tripoli in the north in April 2013, the involvement of Lebanese Sunni fighters remained limited. Nevertheless, the domestic situation deteriorated with the increase in violence arising from the growing involvement of Hezbollah, especially in the border area near Qusayr. This is a strategic junction because of its proximity to both Lebanon's Beqa'a valley and the Damascus–Homs highway in Syria.

Violence in Lebanon thus increased as a result of this split between supporters and opponents of the Syrian regime. The supposedly neutral Lebanese army was deployed in Tripoli and the Beqa'a valley ostensibly to stop violence and cross-border arms-smuggling, but they rarely intervened in an effort to avoid alienating either the Sunni or Shi'a communities. Yet the prolonged and increasingly ferocious Syrian conflict was pushing this precarious equilibrium to the limit, with members of each community accusing the army of siding with the other. The battle for Qusayr brought a flare-up in violence, with increased gun battles in Tripoli in mid- to late May 2013 and intermittent violence across the rest of the country. Areas affected included the capital, Beirut, and Sidon, where some Salafi clerics were blamed for seeking to escalate confrontation with other communities.

The withdrawal of the Syrian army from the Kurdish areas in the far north-east in mid-2012 in effect abandoned these peripheral territories on the border with Turkey to Kurdish fighters. The Turkish Government regarded this as a deliberate strategy that would allow Kurds to cross the border freely and make trouble. The official Turkish position towards the Syrian crisis remained unchanged, however. Turkish mediation efforts continued in late 2012, with the aim of securing Russian and Iranian engagement in a vision for a post-Assad Syria. The battle between jihadist and Kurdish forces for Ras al-Ayn, which extended in three phases from November 2012 until the Kurds captured the town on 17 July 2013, led to speculation that Turkey was sponsoring some jihadist groups against the Kurds. Ankara accused Syrian intelligence agencies of being involved in two car bomb attacks on 11 May that caused the deaths of at least 47 people in the southern Turkish border town of Reyhanlı. Although the Syrian regime denied any involvement, the attacks further impaired bilateral relations. Nevertheless, the Turkish Government repeatedly cautioned against direct military intervention in the Syrian conflict.

The revolt in Syria forced a gradual rapprochement between Syria and Iraq. The Government in Baghdad feared that a victory for the rebels in Syria would have two calamitous consequences for Iraq. The first would be a Sunni-dominated post-Assad neighbour that would be under the influence of hostile Gulf forces. The second would be the resurgence of al-Qa'ida and a revitalized Sunni militant organization in Iraq's Anbar governorate, which borders Syria. The al-Nusra Front had admitted to having Iraqis among its ranks; and in March 2013 the Iraqi Government's fears with regard to the second scenario were apparently realized when Iraqi militants associated with al-Qa'ida ambushed and killed 48 Syrian soldiers who had taken refuge in Iraq, together with nine Iraqi guards. There was a dramatic upsurge in violent attacks in Iraq in May, mostly blamed on Sunni militants, with more than 1,000 people killed in that month—the highest number since the height of the Iraqi civil war in 2006–07. By mid-2013, with the eastern third of Syria and the western third of Iraq having become virtually a single entity in which the only functioning power was al-Qa'ida, Iraqi politicians envisaged the entire western region of Iraq (already the site of anti-Government protests) being lost to tribal elements and al-Qa'ida fighters should Assad fall. As a result, the Iraqi leadership maintained a dual-track policy—publicly calling for dialogue between Assad and the Syrian opposition, while increasingly acting in ways that indicated that it wished to see Assad prevail.

Iraq voted in favour of an Arab-sponsored resolution that was adopted by the UN General Assembly on 3 August 2012, condemning the increasing use of heavy weapons by the Syrian authorities and urging all sides in the conflict to cease armed violence immediately. (The resolution was approved by 133 votes to 12, with 31 abstentions.) Reports emerged in October that Syria had signed an agreement to import 60,000 metric tons per month of fuel oil from Iraq, thus allowing the Assad regime to circumvent sanctions and ameliorate its economic situation. Moreover, Iraq permitted Iranian overflights whereby weapons and supplies were allegedly delivered to the Syrian military, while it did little to stem an increasing flow of Iraqi Shi'ite fighters travelling to Syria to fight on behalf of the Assad regime. On a visit to Baghdad in March 2013, the new US Secretary of State, John Kerry, warned Prime Minister Nuri al-Maliki that Washington was 'watching what Iraq is doing': this was the highest-level criticism thus far of Baghdad's perceived failure to inspect flights that Tehran insisted were carrying humanitarian supplies. By contrast, Iraqi Kurds apparently saw the Syrian conflict as an opportunity to increase the autonomy of the Kurdish people in Syria and to widen their own regional influence—a position that in effect pitted them against both the Assad regime and the Syrian opposition. However, clashes between Kurdish and Islamist militias only weakened the Syrian opposition, while alarming Syrian minorities and alienating potential Western supporters.

Jordan, meanwhile, maintained a neutral official position with regard to the Syrian uprising from 2011, allowing Syrian refugees and defectors to cross the border on to its territory, but carefully refusing to take sides. In June 2013 the Jordanian Prime Minister, Abdullah Ensour, denied media reports that foreign forces had been training rebel units in Jordan since November 2012, but not that some military equipment was being sent to Syrian opposition forces via Jordan. From early April 2013 Jordan reportedly allowed Saudi Arabia to channel arms to Syrian rebels through its territory, in exchange for economic assistance and with the prospect of acquiring a weighty strategic partner.

Egypt withdrew its ambassador from Damascus in February 2012, in protest against the Syrian regime's violent crackdown on the uprising. On 15 June 2013, shortly after leading Sunni clerics assembled in Cairo had made a joint call for *jihad* in support of Syrian rebels, President Muhammad Mursi announced the severing of official ties with Syria, and advocated the establishment of a 'no-fly' zone. The sectarian overtones of these announcements and the encouragement to jihadists to join the conflict, as well as the allusion to a possible Egyptian military role, alarmed the Arab and Western supporters of the Syrian uprising, and apparently caused some consternation within the Egyptian military. The ousting of Mursi's Muslim Brotherhood-led Government in early July was hailed by President Assad as the fall of 'political Islam' and as a vindication of his own administration's fight against the Syrian uprising. It also brought about a swift reversal of official Egyptian policy with regard to the Syrian uprising.

THE INTERNATIONAL STRATEGIC CONTEXT

International efforts to reach a political resolution to the Syrian crisis stalled during 2012, while key external actors were apparently either waiting for or promoting a shift in the military balance on the ground. The lack of assistance from the international community as regional parties strived to promote their respective clients within the Syrian opposition above the others exacerbated its fissiparous tendency and contributed to the rise of Islamist groups. The growing strength of al-Qa'ida affiliates such as the al-Nusra Front made Western governments wary of supplying Syrian rebels with weapons that could fall into the hands of seemingly uncontrollable Islamist groups and help them seize control of areas adjacent to Israel.

The formation, in November 2012, of the opposition Syrian National Coalition (which represented Syria at the Arab League summit in March 2013), and the subsequent establishment of the SMC aimed to facilitate both international diplomatic efforts and the supply of military equipment from supporting states. The new US policy, announced by Secretary of State John Kerry in February 2013, that the USA would provide non-lethal aid to the Syrian rebels, was a response to concerns regarding the emergence of powerful Islamist brigades as much as signalling US endorsement of the SMC's legitimacy. By the beginning of 2013 the Western strategy of urging diplomacy while resorting to halfway measures such as arming the opposition to the point of maintaining a low-level insurgency became increasingly unsustainable in view of the worsening humanitarian situation in Syria and the alarming number of refugees fleeing to neighbouring countries. The deployment of NATO *Patriot* missiles on the Turkish border with Syria from early January 2013 involved Western powers more closely in the conflict and brought revived talk of establishing a 'no-fly' zone. Nevertheless, with Russia and China remaining determined to veto any UN Security Council resolution authorizing the use of force against Syria, and with the USA apparently unwilling to make the necessary concessions for Russia to change its stance, all players seemed to be preparing for a long-term conflict. Adding to the caution of Western powers was the perceived risk that a military engagement in Syria would provoke a further escalation of the conflict, given the scale of regional and international polarization.

The potential for direct military action increased after Israel—and later the USA and France—alleged that the Syrian regime had used chemical weapons. US President Barack Obama had stated, on 20 August 2012, that evidence of the movement or use of chemical or biological weapons by the Assad regime or other players in the Syrian conflict would signify the crossing of a 'red line'. However, with inconclusive evidence, and reports that rebels may well have used nerve gas, the USA was still not ready to take direct action against the Assad regime. In late April 2013 the US Secretary of Defense,

Chuck Hagel, reiterated that the USA's goals focused on the desire to strengthen the Syrian opposition while seeking to minimize the influence of al-Qa'ida-affiliated groups and ensure that chemical weapons and other advanced military equipment (such as Russian-made missiles) did not change hands and alter the regional balance of power. Arresting Iranian influence in the region and preserving Israeli military dominance remained the broader strategic goals of US Middle East policy. Hence, the USA would continue at this time to press for a negotiated political transition in Syria and to provided non-lethal aid to the rebels.

The recapture by Syrian regime forces of the town of Qusayr in early June 2013 marked a turning point in the Syrian conflict, prompting Obama's decision, on 13 June, to arm the Syrian opposition. The US authorities indicated that the weapons would be used to strengthen moderate elements, in the hope that this would help to sideline Islamist groups openly aligned with al-Qa'ida. The fall of Qusayr cast a long shadow over plans for a new peace conference that Russian President Vladimir Putin and US Secretary of State John Kerry had agreed in early May to convene in Geneva in the summer. With the tide of war turning in the regime's favour, the planned summit, termed Geneva 2, was eventually postponed until after September. The ouster of the Muslim Brotherhood regime in Egypt in early July prompted a defiant Assad to proclaim the defeat of political Islam and to reconsider Syria's participation in the talks, in which Iran was to be allowed to take part as an observer. Meanwhile, European diplomatic sources had apparently begun to tone down their anti-Assad rhetoric and to promote a political solution in which the Syrian President would be a partner—and his withdrawal from the Syrian political scene would be a matter for negotiation, rather than a precondition for such talks.

The EU embargo imposed on imports of oil from Syria from September 2011 continued to have a detrimental impact on the Syrian economy. On 22 April 2013 the EU Council decided to amend the sanctions to allow member states to authorize purchases of crude oil and petroleum products, exports of equipment and technology to the Syrian oil and gas industry, and investments in the Syrian oil industry, on condition that this was done in consultation with the opposition Syrian National Coalition and that such transactions did not circumvent EU sanctions particularly with regard to the freeze on assets of those associated with violent repression. This easing of certain sanctions was aimed at helping the Syrian civilian population by enabling a resumption of economic activity in areas that were no longer under regime control. However, such transactions appeared unlikely in the near term, as there was no sanctions-exempt Syrian company from which to purchase oil, and some oilfields were reportedly under the control of Islamist fighters.

Meanwhile, the EU remained divided over the embargo on the supply of weapons to Syria. A ban, in force since May 2011, on the supply of arms and equipment that might be used for internal repression expired at the end of May 2013, following the failure of EU member states to agree the terms of an extension, or alternative measures. This opened the way for the United Kingdom and France—the only EU members that had expressed interest in arming what they regarded as moderate Syrian anti-regime forces—to begin supplying arms to the rebels. However, both governments stated that they had no immediate plans to take direct action to affect the war on the ground by providing air support to the rebels. Moreover, the ending of the arms embargo was not expected to have any major near-term impact on the military balance. The EU itself stated that no deliveries were imminent, and the plethora of safeguards and regulations would prove to be a stumbling block unless the opposition could present a more united front. This delay would provide breathing space for the ongoing US-Russian diplomatic efforts, to which France and the United Kingdom remained committed.

The alleged use of chemical weapons by government forces in air-strikes on the Ghouta area, east of Damascus, on 21 August 2013, in which up to 1,429 people were reported to have been killed, marked an abrupt change in US and European policy. The Obama Administration, along with the British and French Governments, began to advocate retaliatory military action against the Assad Government, in spite of vehement opposition from Russia and China, as well as scepticism within their own countries. Four days after the incident, a UN inspection team commenced an investigation to determine whether chemical weapons had indeed been deployed. The Syrian Government denied claims that it had been responsible for the attack, instead blaming opposition groups. At the end of August the British Government failed to gain the approval of the House of Commons for its participation in any military intervention, despite Prime Minister Cameron taking a prominent role in promoting such a course of action among international leaders. The USA, for its part, claimed that the Assad regime had been responsible for the attack and published details of intelligence reports, which claimed that government chemical weapons units had been operating in the area in the preceding days and that samples taken from the area confirmed the use of chemical agents, most likely sarin gas. France also published intelligence reports, the conclusions of which supported those issued by the US Administration. Russia, however, claimed that the responsibility for the attack was uncertain and that military intervention targeting the Assad Government would therefore be illegitimate and, moreover, risked further destabilizing the region. On 9 September Putin proposed an agreement for Syria to disclose details of its chemical weapons arsenal and to allow for its destruction, under international supervision. The following day Syrian Minister of Foreign Affairs, Mouallem, admitted that Syria did indeed possess such weapons and expressed support for the Russian proposal. President Obama subsequently announced that a scheduled vote in the House of Representatives on US military action was to be postponed in order that the Russian plan might be considered. However, Obama reiterated his Administration's opposition to the use of chemical weapons by the Syrian Government and refused to rule out military intervention at a later date. Following three days of discussions between Russia and the USA in Geneva, Switzerland, on 14 September Kerry and Lavrov agreed a deal whereby Syria would be bound to submit a comprehensive list of all chemical weapons in its possession within one week, and those weapons would be destroyed by mid-2014. The UN inspectors' report to the Secretary-General was published on 16 September. It stated that the inspectors had found 'clear and convincing evidence that surface-to-surface rockets containing the nerve agent sarin' had been used on 21 August, although it did not attribute blame to either government or opposition forces.

Economy

RICHARD GERMAN and ELIZABETH TAYLOR

INTRODUCTION

Syria covers an area of 185,180 sq km (71,498 sq miles), of which about 45% is considered to be arable land. The remainder consists of bare mountain, desert and pastures capable of sustaining only nomadic populations. Population census totals in 1970, 1981 and 1994 were 6,304,685, 9,052,628 and 13,782,315, respectively. According to the census of 2004, the figure had risen to 17,920,844, and by 1 January 2011 it had increased to 24,504,000, according to official estimates. However, the descent into civil war from March 2011 onwards (see History) had, by September 2013, resulted in more than 100,000 deaths and prompted the exodus of some 2.0m. refugees to neighbouring countries, according to UN figures.

The vulnerability of the Syrian economy—traditionally based on exports of petroleum, cotton and phosphates, and a service sector reliant on tourism and transit trade—must be viewed against the background of regional instability and the internal political developments that have taken place since the Baath Arab Socialist Party came to power in 1963. As a 'confrontation state', with a portion of its land under Israeli occupation since the Arab–Israeli war of 1967, Syria has incurred significant levels of defence expenditure, amounting to more than one-half of the country's recurrent budget in some financial years. At the same time, its involvement in Lebanon (see History), combined with the threat of conflict with Israel and the history of poor relations with neighbouring Iraq—which have, in turn, influenced relations with Iran and the moderate Arab states of the Persian (Arabian) Gulf—have all affected the Syrian economy.

Between the Baath-dominated coup in March 1963 and Lt-Gen. Hafiz al-Assad's seizure of power in November 1970 there was a radical transformation of the country's economic structure, as a rigorous programme of nationalization made the public sector dominant. However, Assad relaxed state control soon after coming to power, partly in an attempt to widen his power base, introducing some liberalization of foreign trade and promulgating a foreign investment law. The reconstruction effort necessary to restore the Syrian economy after the Arab–Israeli war of October 1973 was immense, but the Government acted swiftly, introducing further liberalization measures to encourage investment. Business confidence gradually began to return, to the extent that the 1971–75 Development Plan (following two earlier plans, starting from 1961) ended with a flourish of unprecedented growth. This, in turn, prompted the Government to reinforce investment incentives in certain sectors and to initiate an ambitious plan for the period 1976–80, but only to find itself confronted again with the economic repercussions of regional political problems.

The 1981–85 and 1986–90 Development Plans concentrated on trying to finish projects already under way rather than launching ambitious new schemes. The growth targets were noticeably more modest, but even these were not achieved. By the late 1980s the scarcity of foreign exchange had caused a shortage of spare parts and raw materials for industry, and production was substantially below capacity. Corruption and mismanagement in the state industrial and agricultural sectors also affected output. The collapse of the USSR in 1991 presaged further problems for Syria, as large sectors of its economy had been orientated towards exporting low-quality goods to the USSR.

Despite these impediments, the rate of real economic growth averaged an estimated 6% annually during 1991–95, supported by project aid from the national development funds of Kuwait, Saudi Arabia and Abu Dhabi (the United Arab Emirates—UAE) and various Gulf-based multilateral agencies, notably the Arab Petroleum Investments Corpn and the Arab Fund for Economic and Social Development (AFESD). However, despite Syria's participation in the US-led multinational force against Iraq in 1990–91, direct US aid (halted for political reasons in 1983) remained suspended, while Syria's access to European Union (EU) aid funds was largely blocked because of disputes over its debt arrears to certain EU member states.

In September 1997 Syria made its largest ever single repayment of foreign debt, having reached an agreement with the World Bank to settle arrears accumulated since the 1980s. Another important agreement for the settlement of bilateral debt had earlier been negotiated with France, bringing Syria closer to an unblocking of multilateral EU funds (eventually achieved in late 2000 when Syria reached a debt settlement agreement with Germany). Nevertheless, the pace of economic reform and government decision-making within Syria remained chronically slow. Western analysts highlighted many institutional obstacles to the development process, including the banking, tax and legal systems, and were particularly critical of the way in which Investment Law 10 of 1991 (see Other Industries) had provided a major stimulus to private sector imports, but failed to attract large-scale private investment in new industrial projects. Advocates of economic reform welcomed the appointment in March 2000 of a new Government, which was committed to addressing these problems and to introducing wide-ranging anti-corruption measures. The subsequent accession to the presidency in that year of Bashar al-Assad, identified as a supporter of the new Government's economic programme, reinforced Syrian expectations that significant liberalization of the economy might be in prospect.

According to government statistics, Syria's real gross domestic product (GDP) had increased at an average annual rate of 5.7% during the period 1990–99, with an average annual rate of inflation of 8.7%. There had remained, however, an underlying unemployment problem since the rate of job creation rarely kept pace with the increase in the working-age population. Subsequent economic growth was an estimated 3% in 2000, 5.0% in 2001 and 4.2% in 2002, before declining to 2.6% in 2003 in the wake of Syria's declining oil production and the impact of further military conflict in Iraq. Government growth statistics for later years—6.7% in 2004, 4.5% in 2005 and 5.1% for 2006—were significantly higher than the IMF's estimates of 2.8%, 3.3% and 4.4%, respectively (the Fund having cautioned that monitoring and analysis of economic developments in Syria were constrained by the country's weak statistical data and methodological framework).

Reflecting Syria's overall macroeconomic stability, the IMF estimated real GDP growth at 4.2% in 2007 and projected a higher rate of about 5% for 2008 (although the Central Bank's later assessment was 4.3%). According to the Fund, inflation accelerated to 17%–20% by mid-2008, but declined sharply from the fourth quarter (to an average rate of 2.8% in 2009) as commodity prices decreased in response to the global financial crisis and ensuing economic downturn. The impact of the recessionary environment on Syria was nevertheless relatively modest, and was mainly felt in terms of its trading links with the countries of the Cooperation Council for the Arab States of the Gulf (Gulf Cooperation Council) and Europe. Official data put Syria's rate of GDP growth for 2009 at 6.0%, in part reflecting a good harvest and recovery in the agricultural sector.

According to provisional official figures, GDP growth in 2010 slowed to 3.4%. Although there was an increase in oil production and an expansion in the services sector, agricultural performance was weak, prompting a rise in food imports. At the end of 2010 the Government approved the Development Plan for 2011–15. Real GDP was projected to grow by at least 5.5% per year for the duration of the Plan, with an overall investment target of US $87,000m. (50% of which was to be provided by the private sector). Much of this investment was to be directed towards infrastructure improvement, particularly transportation. However, sustained political and social unrest in the country from March 2011 onwards had a negative impact on the economic and planning outlook, as the instability deterred crucial tourism development and foreign direct investment (FDI). The Government initially sought to mollify the protests by reintroducing costly subsidies on fuel and food, increasing salaries for public sector workers and delaying the introduction of a value-added tax (VAT). However, these measures failed to stem public opposition, provoking an increasingly repressive and violent response from the Assad regime, and by mid-2012 the unrest had degenerated into outright civil war. With the significant exceptions of Russia, the People's Republic of China and Iran, international opinion was broadly hostile to the Syrian Government's stance. In particular, the EU suspended aid programmes to Syria in May 2011, depriving the country of a major source of development finance, and in September imposed a ban on imports of Syrian oil (representing 95% of the country's oil export trade). The USA similarly extended its sanctions regime. As the political and security outlook continued to deteriorate during 2012–13, the Syrian Government struggled to counter the evident slowdown in economic activity, reflected in the contraction in GDP (variously estimated at around 6.0% in 2011 and up to 20% in 2012), dwindling foreign reserves, rising budget and trade deficits, and depreciation of the Syrian currency.

AGRICULTURE

Agriculture has been a mainstay of the Syrian economy, contributing around one-fifth of GDP. The main areas of cultivation form a narrow strip of land along the coast, from the Lebanese to the Turkish frontiers, which enjoys a Mediterranean climate, is very fertile, and produces fruit, olives, tobacco and cotton. East of this strip lies the northward continuation of the Lebanon range of mountains, which falls sharply on the east to the Orontes river valley, where the marshes have been reclaimed to form another fertile area. In central Syria this valley joins the steppe-plain, about 150 km wide, which runs from the Jordanian border north-eastward towards the Euphrates valley. The plain is traditionally Syria's major agricultural area, with cereals as the principal crops. Also in this region are the country's main cities, Damascus, Homs, Hama and Aleppo. A fourth area, the Jezireh, lies between the Euphrates in Syria and the Tigris in Iraq. Although fertile lands along the banks of the Euphrates and its tributaries had previously been cultivated, the Jezireh's value was recognized only in the early 1950s, when large-scale cotton cultivation was introduced in former pasture lands. It has since greatly increased its output with the development of the Euphrates dam (see Power and Water). One of the chief characteristics of Syria's agricultural performance has been an extreme fluctuation in annual output, owing to wide variations in rainfall.

Under the 1971–75 Development Plan, the Government devoted the largest share to the Euphrates dam project. The main task for the 1976–80 Plan was to put the dam's stored waters to work and to irrigate an additional 240,000 ha of land in the Euphrates basin by the end of the decade. However, later statistics showed that only some 60,000 ha had actually been irrigated, which meant that it would be a very long time before the final Euphrates irrigation target of 640,000 ha (which, it was originally intended, would be achieved by the end of the century) could be reached. In the mean time, emphasis was also placed on other irrigation schemes, including those on the Yarmouk river and in the Ghab, in order to increase the area available for the cultivation of cereals, sugar beet and cotton. In 1987 Jordan and Syria signed an agreement on the use of the waters of the Yarmouk, whereby the countries undertook to share irrigation systems and the power from a hydroelectricity plant associated with the al-Wahdah dam, which was to be built on the Yarmouk in Jordan. After prolonged and repeated delays due to lack of funds, the al-Wahdah project finally came nearer to fruition in April 2003 when the two countries signed an agreement under which Turkish contractor Ozaltin Construction Co would build the dam, at a total cost of US $86.9m. In January 1993 the European Investment Bank (EIB) had agreed to finance the construction of the 65m.-cu m al-Thawra earthfill dam on the Snobar river, designed to irrigate 10,500 ha of land in the Latakia area. By 2005 figures from the National Agricultural Policy Centre showed that of the 1,425,800 ha of total irrigated land in Syria, a little under 20% was cultivated using modern irrigation techniques. Accordingly, the Ministry of Agriculture and Agrarian Reform launched a $420m. scheme within the 2006–10 Development Plan to extend their adoption, and also signed a $58m. agreement with the International Fund for Agricultural Development aimed at boosting water efficiency in the three north-eastern provinces of Deir el-Zor, Al-Hasakah and Rakka.

Although medium-staple cotton had been grown in Syria for many years, it was the high prices prevalent after the Second World War (1939–45) and during the Korean War (1950–53) that provided the greatest impetus to cotton production. In the early 1950s the previously neglected Jezireh area was opened up for large-scale production on a new capital-intensive basis, relatively free from traditional semi-feudal agricultural practices. The local textile industry (historically one of the Syrian economy's leading sectors) uses an appreciable proportion of the cotton crop. A 21% tax on cotton and cotton textile production was abolished in June 1999, in order to stimulate production and exports. Cotton seed production had declined in recent years, to only 307,100 metric tons in 2010, but increased to 436,600 tons in 2011 (according to FAO).

Another major crop is sugar beet. The annual harvest has fluctuated considerably since the area under cultivation increased from the early 1980s. Production totalled 1.3m. metric tons in 1984, before declining to just 222,000 tons in 1988; however, it had increased to 1.5m. tons by 2002, and rose further, to 1.8m. tons, in 2011.

Syria's cereals crop is also of prime importance. Output has fluctuated considerably from year to year, depending on the rainfall. In 1999 Syria's worst drought for decades reduced that year's wheat production to 2.7m. metric tons and barley output to 426,000 tons (about 32% and 73% below the previous five-year averages, respectively). According to FAO, wheat production was 4.9m. tons in 2006, 4.0m. tons in 2007, 2.1m. tons in 2008 (the poorest harvest in eight years, prompting Syria to issue its first tender to import wheat since 1994), 3.7m. tons in 2009, 3.1m. tons in 2010 and 3.9m. tons in 2011. Barley production rose dramatically, to 2.0m. tons, in 2001, subsequently declining to only 0.5m. tons in 2004 and almost 0.8m. tons in 2005. In 2006 output reached 1.2m. tons, before decreasing again to 784,480 tons in 2007 and 261,100 tons in 2008. Production recovered to 845,700 tons in 2009, but declined to 679,800 tons in 2010 and 666,760 tons in 2011. Maize output has fluctuated from 177,036 tons in 2007 to 281,300 tons in 2008, 183,300 tons in 2009, 133,100 tons in 2010 and 298,400 tons in 2011.There has also been considerable expansion in the production of fruit and vegetables, which in 2011 included 670,560 metric tons of watermelons, 337,960 tons of grapes, 307,760 tons of apples, 1.2m. tons of tomatoes and 715,276 tons of potatoes. Demand for fruit and vegetables has at times necessitated imports from other sources, including Lebanon. Syria's annual production of olives has fluctuated sharply, increasing from 501,000 tons in 2005 to some 1.2m. tons in 2006. Production was recorded at 885,900 tons in 2009, 960,400 tons in 2010 and 1.1m. tons in 2011.

Livestock-raising is another important branch of agriculture. In 2011 there were an estimated 1.2m. cattle, 2.3m. goats, 26.2m. chickens and 18.1m. sheep.

PETROLEUM AND NATURAL GAS

At the end of 2012 Syria had proven petroleum reserves of 2,500m. barrels. The Iraq Petroleum Co (IPC) group had rights throughout Syria, but abandoned them in 1951 after failing to find petroleum in commercial quantities. Concessions were granted to an independent US operator in 1955 and to a West German-led consortium in 1956. These led to the discoveries of the Karatchouk field, in the north-eastern corner of the country, the Al-Suweida field, and the field at nearby Rumelan. However, in addition to the cost of extraction being high, the petroleum from all three oilfields was of low quality. In 1964, several years before any of the three fields had begun production on a commercial basis, Syria became one of the first Arab states to discard the notion of petroleum concessions and to nationalize its operations. For the next 10 years all exploration and exploitation was conducted solely by the state-owned General Petroleum Authority and its offshoot, the Syrian Petroleum Co (SPC), with Soviet assistance.

Output from Al-Suweida and Karatchouk started in 1968 and 1969, respectively. The October War in 1973 reduced production from a level of 6.3m. metric tons in the previous year to just 5.4m. tons, recovering in 1974 to 6.2m. tons. Production remained at about that level in the late 1970s; by the early 1980s, with oil prices declining and its known petroleum reserves being exhausted, Syria was actually a net importer. From the mid-1980s, however, the petroleum industry was transformed by the discovery of large reserves of high-quality crude near Deir el-Zor by a consortium of foreign oil companies.

The new discoveries were the result of the reversal of the Government's 'no-concessions' policy in the mid-1970s. In May 1975 the first Syrian concession to be won by any Western company for over 15 years was awarded to a US group, on production-sharing terms heavily tilted in the Government's favour and stipulating that US $20m. be invested in exploration off shore. In June the Government took its new policy one stage further by offering a dozen onshore oil concessions for international bidding. Altogether, 50,000 sq km were to be made available. The oil companies' response to the invitation was initially slow, and when the first US group, Tripco, relinquished its concession in March 1976 no other company had come forward to join the search. In July 1977, however, a US-Syrian consortium called Samoco took up a concession in the Deir el-Zor area, and in December another concession, in Rakka province, was taken by Shell subsidiaries, Syria Shell Petroleum Development and Pecten Syria Co. Both Shell and Samoco insisted on a larger share of eventual petroleum production than was agreed between the Government and Tripco. This softening of terms reawakened the interest of other firms, including Chevron of the USA.

By 1983, however, Samoco, Chevron and Rompetrol of Romania (which was exploring west of Al-Hasakah) had all relinquished their concessions, leaving Pecten and Marathon Oil of the USA as the only foreign operators in the country. In early 1983 Pecten, together with Royal Dutch Shell and Deminex of the Federal Republic of Germany, assumed control of Samoco's concession area. At the end of 1984 it was revealed that the consortium had discovered reserves of high-quality crude petroleum at al-Thayyem, near Deir el-Zor. In 1985 the three foreign partners and the SPC formed the Al-Furat Petroleum Co (AFPC) to develop the concession. Full commercial production began in September 1986, and, because the oil from the field was light crude with a very low sulphur content, it considerably reduced the need to import light crudes for blending. Previously Syria had imported between 5.0m. and 6.6m. metric tons of oil every year. Related to the main al-Thayyem field were the later discoveries of the al-Ward, al-Asharah, al-Shula and al-Kharata fields. In May 1989 it was reported that al-Thayyem was producing 65,000 barrels per day (b/d), with output from the related fields bringing the total output of this system to 100,000 b/d out of total Syrian production in 1989 of 310,000 b/d.

While AFPC continued to widen the scope of its own development programme (which included increasing use of water-injection techniques to maintain production from mature oilfields), Elf Aquitaine of France was preparing to increase or commence production from new wells in the Atallah North and Jafra areas of the Deir el-Zor field in 1993, while the Shell, Tullow Oil, Unocal and Occidental companies were engaged in active oil exploration programmes in other parts of the country. In late 1994 Shell signed a new exploration agreement covering areas previously relinquished by BP and Total. Unocal ceased exploration in Syria by the end of 1994. Syrian petroleum output averaged 570,000 b/d in both 1993 and 1994, rising to 600,000 b/d in 1995.

In 1997 the Hungarian Oil and Gas Co (MOL) was awarded an exploration block of 5,000 sq km east of Palmyra and an agreement covering a five-block exploration area totalling 4,201 sq km was concluded with a consortium made up of subsidiaries of Elf Aquitaine (40%), Japan's Sumitomo Development Co (30%) and Malaysia's Petronas (30%). In the same year Syria Shell Petroleum Development was granted a new exploration block in the Euphrates basin and the Government concluded two new agreements with international companies, Croatia's INA—Naftaplin and Sweden's Svenska Petroleum Exploration, to explore in the Palmyra and Deir el-Zor areas. In November 1998 Tullow Oil, which had experienced a major decline in output from its Syrian oilfield during the course of the year, announced that it was abandoning its Syrian operations because they were no longer commercially viable.

In February 2000 Syria Shell announced new oil discoveries in its Zenobia exploration contract area in the north-east. In May Tanganyika Oil Co (a Canadian affiliate of Sweden's Lundin Oil) was granted exclusive rights to the Oude development block, comprising 403 sq km close to Syria's north-eastern border with Turkey. Output of heavy crude from the block's one producing field (operated by the SPC since the late 1970s) had declined steadily for some time, and the new arrangement signalled the Syrian Government's acceptance of a need for foreign capital and technology to maximize the potential of the SPC's older fields. In July 2001 the Government invited bids for oil and gas exploration rights in five blocks with a total area of 26,000 sq km. A further 11 blocks totalling 63,000 sq km were opened for a second round of bidding in June 2002, and bids for a third round of 11 blocks were solicited in December. Awards for the first round of five blocks were made in January 2003 to Royal Dutch/Shell, US-based Ocean Energy, Canada's Stratic Energy, and a US-Indian consortium including India's state-run Oil and Natural Gas Corpn. In March the SPC announced a 25-year production agreement with the China National Petroleum Corpn to develop the Kebibe field in north-eastern Syria, and in May signed a joint-venture agreement with two US companies, Devon Energy and Gulfsands Petroleum, relating to an area of 11,000 sq km near the Iraqi border. However, in March 2005 Devon Energy announced its intention to withdraw from Syria and sold its interest to Gulfsands, which then signed a new partnership agreement with Russia's Soyuzneftegaz in May (although Soyuzneftegaz then sold its stake in January 2006 to the United Kingdom's Emerald Energy).

In January 2004 the SPC launched a fourth round of production-sharing exploration licences. A total of 14 blocks were offered, but the response was lukewarm, with six blocks eliciting no interest at all. In February the US company ConocoPhillips announced that it was ending its operations in Syria. For the fifth licensing round, launched in April 2005, the Government offered more flexible and generous investment and production-sharing terms. Nine blocks were offered on the basis of 25-year agreements with a 12.5% royalty from the total amount produced. More than 20 bids had been received by early 2006. In May Soyuzneftegaz signed a 25-year exploration and production-sharing agreement for a block measuring 5,000 sq km in the south-east of the country, while Marathon Oil signed a contract to develop two fields in the northern Homs region. Two more blocks were subsequently awarded to Shell and two others to smaller Ukrainian and French companies. In the sixth licensing round, the Ministry of Petroleum and Mineral Resources asked companies in March 2007 to submit offers for seven onshore blocks. In May the Ministry also invited exploration tenders for four offshore blocks for the first time, although this ultimately elicited no successful bids. In December Canada's Loon Energy, Inc received government approval of an exploration and production agreement for a block covering 10,000 sq km in the north-west of Syria. During 2008 output from a few smaller oilfields increased and new investment was expected, following the takeover in September of Tanganyika Oil Co, which had been developing concessions in the north-east of Syria for several years, by the China Petroleum and Chemical Corpn. Also in 2008 the Ministry of Petroleum and Mineral Resources entered contract negotiations for the award of five new exploration permits and extended existing production-sharing arrangements with Royal Dutch Shell and Total for 10 years.

After peaking in the mid-1990s, the production of Syrian crude petroleum slowed steadily with the decline of some more mature fields, highlighting the pressing need for further exploration and enhanced recovery work to stabilize output. In early 2010 three new discoveries were made in the Euphrates basin by ONGC Videsh Ltd of India and the United Kingdom-based IPR Mediterranean Exploration Ltd, with a combined flow of about 10,000 b/d. At the same time the Ministry of Petroleum and Mineral Resources invited tenders to bid for contracts in order to raise production at seven existing fields. It also launched a new exploration bid round (the first since 2007) for eight onshore blocks in the north and east of the country. A total of 15 bids from 13 companies was received, and Total and Petro-Canada were among the first to be awarded licences during 2011. In mid-2011 the Government invited further bids for licences to explore for both petroleum and gas in three blocks off the Mediterranean coast, and also launched a bidding round for the exploitation of shale oil deposits in the north-west of the country near Aleppo. However, the tender process subsequently stalled in the wake of civil conflict, which also had a significant impact on Syria's production of crude petroleum and the commodity's export potential. Output declined from 385,000 b/d in 2010 to about 330,000 b/d in 2011, as most international oil companies operating in the country suspended production following the imposition of EU import sanctions against Syria, which took effect in November, in response to the Government's brutal crackdown on opposition protests. In 2012–13 the regime's oil output and export capacity was further diminished by the ongoing conflict, as some oilfields came under the control of opposition forces, and by the EU embargo. At the end of May 2013 the Minister of Petroleum and Mineral Resources, Suleiman al-Abbas, told a session of the People's Assembly that crude oil production had fallen to just 20,000 b/d.

Syria has two old petroleum refineries at Homs and Banias, with capacities of about 107,000 b/d and 133,000 b/d, respectively. Plans have long been under consideration for their modernization and redevelopment, and the country's growing thirst for energy has highlighted the need for additional refining facilities. However, foreign companies have proved reluctant to commit investment in view of the civil conflict, and prospective construction projects involving Chinese, Malaysian and Venezuelan interests remained on hold in mid-2013.

Royalties for the transit of foreign crude petroleum through Syrian territory were for many years more valuable than indigenous production. Two pipelines carry petroleum from the Kirkuk oilfield, in Iraq, through Syria. One, built in 1934, leads on to a terminal at Tripoli in Lebanon. The second IPC pipeline, completed in 1952, branches off at Homs to the Syrian terminal at Banias. A third pipeline, belonging to the Trans-Arabian Pipeline Co (Tapline), which used to carry Saudi crude to a terminal near Sidon in Lebanon, crosses about 150 km of Syrian territory, much of which was occupied by Israel in 1967. After nationalizing the IPC in June 1972, the Iraqi Government took over payment of royalties to Syria, and in 1973 both countries signed an agreement on transit dues and the supply of petroleum for Syria's own domestic use. However, the flow of petroleum through the Kirkuk–Banias pipeline has been interrupted periodically since then. In July 1998 Iraq and Syria agreed to reopen the Kirkuk–Banias IPC pipeline, which was subsequently restored to good working order on both sides of the border (and was reportedly available for use from March 2000). From late 2000 it was widely reported that Iraq was pumping oil to Syria without seeking formal clearance from UN sanctions administrators. The reported rate of supply of Iraqi crude to Syrian refineries was 140,000 b/d–150,000 b/d, this being the amount by which Syria was able to increase exports of its own crude petroleum in December 2000. In February 2001 the US Secretary of State stated that he had received assurances from President Assad that Syria accepted that Iraqi oil imported through the Kirkuk–Banias pipeline should be 'under the same kind of [UN] control as other elements of the sanctions regime'. In February 2002, however, the British Government informed the UN Security Council that Syria was continuing to violate UN sanctions by importing up to 200,000 b/d of Iraqi oil. In April 2003 Syria informed crude petroleum customers that it would reduce export volumes by up to 40% for the rest of the year. This was widely seen as confirmation that Syria had been importing oil by pipeline from Iraq in contravention of UN sanctions before the flow stopped in the early days of the US-led military campaign against the Iraqi regime.

Syria's proven reserves of natural gas were estimated at 300,000m. cu m in 2012, mostly owned by the SPC and located mainly in the Palmyra and other north-eastern regions. Major gas development projects were initiated in the 1990s to bring the gas to population centres in the west and south, and to fuel electricity generation at power stations supplying Damascus, Homs and other cities. Production of gas rose five-fold during the 1990s, and by 2011 annual output had risen sharply to 8,748m. cu m as new projects came on stream. However, production declined to 7,593m. cu m in 2012, and exploration came to a virtual standstill as the country's civil conflict intensified and international sanctions began to take effect. The Government has aimed to substitute natural gas for oil in power generation, in order to free up as much oil as possible for export and to make Syria a net exporter of liquefied gas, as well as to use gas feedstock to increase the country's production of fertilizers.

In November 1998 Conoco and what became TotalFinaElf, bidding in partnership, were awarded a contract to develop gas resources in the Deir el-Zor area. Costing an estimated US $430m., this Desgas project entailed the gathering and processing of associated gas currently being flared off in existing oilfields, and the bringing into production of the hitherto undeveloped Tabiyeh gas condensate field. The engineering, procurement and construction (EPC) contract for this project, awarded to Kvaerner ENC in March 2000, required the construction of two processing trains, six compressor stations, a 180-km gathering system and a 270-km pipeline link to the national gas grid serving the main population centres in western Syria. Completion of the system was achieved in September 2001. In early 2004 Petro-Canada and its partners Occidental Petroleum Corpn and Petrofac were selected to enter into negotiations with the Ministry of Petroleum and Mineral Resources to conclude a production-sharing contract for the North and South Middle Area Gas project in the Palmyra region. This project would involve appraising and developing up to 15 gas discoveries in fields located in two clusters, one to the east of the city of Homs and the other south-east of Aleppo. However, negotiations with the consortium broke down in January 2005 and the Ministry announced that the state-owned Syrian Gas Co and the SPC would develop the gas reserves. In November Russia's Stroytransgaz was awarded the contract to build a gas treatment plant near Homs as part of the South Middle Area Gas project, and in mid-2006 the company negotiated to build another treatment plant as part of the North Middle Area project. The plant near Homs was inaugurated in November 2009. In May 2006 US-based Marathon Petroleum, which had discovered gas deposits in the Palmyra area in the early 1980s but had not developed them because of a failure to agree commercial terms with the Government, signed a revised production-sharing contract for these fields. The agreement included a provision entitling Marathon to sell the assets to a third party, and in June 2006 Petro-Canada bought the Marathon acreage. Following the discovery of large gas deposits off the coast of Israel, in 2011 Syria launched a bidding round for three offshore exploration blocks; however, in the wake of ongoing civil conflict, no outcome had been announced by mid-2013.

Syria is a partner in a scheme finalized in 2001 for the construction of an overland pipeline (the Arab Gas Pipeline—AGP) to supply Egyptian gas initially to Jordan (beginning in 2003) and later to Syria, Lebanon and Turkey. By February 2008 the section running from Jordan into Syria (to the Deir Ali power station) was completed, and a further stage extending the pipeline to Aleppo was planned. In January 2008 Syria signed an agreement with Turkey to construct a 63-km pipeline between Aleppo and Kilis in order to connect the AGP with the Turkish grid. However, since the outbreak of conflict in Syria during 2011, progress has been uncertain. Syria supplies small quantities of gas to power plants in northern Lebanon through a short pipeline running from the port of Banias. In January 2008 Syria signed a 25-year agreement for the import of Iranian gas starting in late 2009.

In February 2009 the Government issued decrees creating two new bodies to regulate the upstream and downstream elements of the hydrocarbons sector. The General Organization for Petroleum would oversee exploration and production of oil and gas, pipeline transmission, and crude petroleum exports. The General Organization for Oil Refining and Petroleum Products Distribution would supervise the two existing refineries and any new refinery plans, and also products distribution.

OTHER INDUSTRIES

Syria's manufacturing industry is relatively diversified. Substantial phosphate rock reserves (generating production of 3.76m. metric tons in 2010) have enabled the establishment of a fertilizer industry. Cement output has generally averaged between 5m. and 6m. tons annually in recent years. There are cement factories at Tartous, Adra, Hama, Musulmiya, Aleppo and Abu Shamat. In early 2006 rising demand prompted the Government to announce plans for the privatization of the cement sector in order to increase production through more FDI. In late 2008 a consortium of local and foreign banks agreed to provide US $380m. in financing to the Syrian Cement Co (a joint venture between Lafarge of France, with a 75% stake, and the local MAS Economic Group, with a 25% equity) for the construction of a 3m.-tons-per-year cement plant in Aleppo. The facility, built by FLSmidth of Denmark, commenced production in late 2010. A new private sector cement plant at Abu Shamat, in the south-west, with an annual production capacity of 1.6m. tons, became operational in early 2011.

In addition to existing state-owned sugar plants managed by the General Organization for Sugar, the Government announced plans in 2002 to build one of the largest sugar refineries in the world, which would be jointly contracted by Syrian and Brazilian investors. Construction work on the 1m.-metric-tons-per-year facility south of Homs began in April 2006 and was completed in May 2008.

Syria's automotive industry was traditionally restricted to the manufacture of tractors at a plant in Aleppo. However, in March 2007 the first domestically produced motor car, in a joint venture between local state and private partners and an Iranian company, Iran Khodro, rolled off the assembly line at a factory outside Damascus (cars having previously been imported largely from Japan). Iran Khodro holds a 40% stake in the venture (called the Syrian Iranian Automotive Manufacturing Co), Syria's state-owned General Organization for Engineering Industries owns 35%, and the remaining 25% is held by Sultan Trading (the local agent of Iran Khodro since 2001). A second car plant near Homs was inaugurated in December 2007 in another joint venture between the Syrian company Hmisho Trading (owning 20%) and Iran's Saipa Corpn (with 80%).

Despite the dominance of large-scale state industries, the private sector has played an important role in industrial manufacture. Under Investment Law 10, adopted in May 1991, encouragement was given to Syrian and foreign investment in industrial ventures, particularly in the light industry sector. To qualify for Law 10 status, a project had to involve: investment of more than £S10m. and the approval of the Higher Council for Investment, the project evaluation criteria of which took particular account of the amount of foreign capital to be invested; compatibility with national Development Plans; utilization of advanced or innovatory technology; employment creation; and the utilization of locally available resources. Approved projects were entitled to five or more years' exemption from profit, dividend and real estate taxes, and were subject to a liberalized regime of import regulations and exchange controls (including unrestricted repatriation of profits for foreign investors).

In 1998 a number of amendments were made to Law 10 in order to improve the incentives to investment. These included: the removal of a 75% limit on the proportion of output that could be exported; an increase in the permissible level of foreign representation on company boards; additional tax incentives for projects outside Damascus and Aleppo; and the extension of Law 10 benefits to holding companies. In May 2000 legislation was enacted to permit foreign investors to own or lease land needed for Law 10 projects; to extend by two years the tax exemption period for Law 10 projects sited in remote areas; and to reduce to 25% the rate of corporate taxation levied after the expiry of Law 10 tax exemption periods.

POWER AND WATER

The centrepiece of Syria's 1971–75 Development Plan was the Euphrates dam project, on which construction work began in 1968. The project involved the construction of a dam 4.6 km long and 60 m high, with a width of 500 m at the bottom. The reservoir thus created, Lake Assad, was designed to hold 12,000m. cu m of water, operating eight turbines and enabling the long-term irrigation of 640,000 ha of land. The scheme was undertaken with Soviet technical and financial assistance, under an agreement reached with the USSR in 1966, and the entire project was formally opened in 1978. Despite its advantages, the dam exacerbated friction with Iraq, itself reliant on water from the Euphrates river. Disputes over water rights reached a crisis point in 1974–75, when Turkey started to fill the reservoir behind its Keban dam, also on the Euphrates, at the same time as Syria started to fill Lake Assad, leaving Iraq with much less water than usual. Tension over this issue subsided in 1977–78, but resurfaced in 1984 between Syria and Turkey after the latter had started work on its new Atatürk dam. It was thought that the Atatürk dam and the associated South East Anatolian project (GAP) could remove at least 5,000m. cu m of water per year from the Euphrates, once completed in around 2015. In a serious reverse to Syria's water supply infrastructure, the Zeyzoun dam north of Hama collapsed in June 2002, when almost full to its 70m. cu m capacity; over 20 people were killed in the resultant flood.

Syria has suffered frequent interruptions in the supply of electric power. Electricity demand has soared since the 1970s with industrialization, and the Euphrates dam did not, as was hoped, meet Syria's growing needs, as shortfalls in its water supply due to erratic rainfall and Turkish offtake upstream were compounded by a lack of maintenance of the dam and its generating plant. By 1993 Syria was estimated to have a total of 1,900 MW of operational generating capacity out of a theoretical installed capacity of 3,002 MW, while the minimum operational capacity needed to meet demand was estimated to be 2,500 MW. In a bid to rectify the situation, the authorities approved heavy, aid-financed investment in electricity generation in the early 1990s, with work subsequently completed on the 600-MW Jandar plant, financed by Japan, and on the Saudi-financed 1,000-MW plant in Aleppo. Another important generating project was the installation of eight 128-MW turbines in various locations by an Italian company, with finance from Kuwait. In 1997 Mitsubishi Heavy Industries of Japan was awarded the contract to construct a 600-MW plant at Al-Zara, which was completed in late 2000. A major refit of the 680-MW Banias power station was completed by Japanese contractors in April 2001. Nearly US $1,000m. in Japanese funds were provided for Syrian power projects between 1989 and 2001. In March 2001 a project to link the Syrian, Egyptian and Jordanian electricity networks was inaugurated.

In 2004 a German joint venture between Siemens and Koch was awarded the contract to expand power plants at Nasiriyeh and Zeyzoun. That year the Public Establishment for Electricity Generation and Transmission (PEEGT) also sought bids from international contractors for two EPC contracts to build 750-MW combined-cycle power plants at Deir el-Zor and at Deir Ali, south of Damascus, and announced plans to build a new 750-MW combined-cycle plant at Qattineh, involving the demolition of an existing oil-fired facility. In May 2006 the Islamic Development Bank granted Syria a US $230m. loan to finance partly the construction of the Deir el-Zor and Deir Ali plants (to be built respectively by Spain's Iberdrola and Germany's Siemens and Koch), with additional funding from the EIB and AFESD.

By the end of 2009 installed generating capacity stood at 7,518 MW. However, rising electricity demand continued to outstrip supply, prompting frequent shortages. In mid-2009 the Government initiated an emergency plan to install 20 18-MW generators (burning fuel oil or diesel) in the major cities. Tariffs for heavy energy users were increased at the same time in an effort to curb electricity consumption. Later in the year the PEEGT engaged the International Finance Corpn as an adviser for a proposed independent power project near the existing Nasiriyeh power station. The plant was projected to have a capacity of 250 MW–350 MW, using natural gas or fuel oil, and in early August 2010 the Ministry of Electricity issued a request for qualification to developers. Also in late 2009 the PEEGT finalized a contract with India's Bharat Heavy Electricals Ltd to expand the Tishrin power plant by 400 MW. In early 2010 the Ministry of Electricity awarded new power projects to Iran's Power Plant Projects Management Co (MAPNA), for a 450-MW extension of the Jandar plant, and to the China National Electric Equipment Corpn, to expand the Al-Zara plant near Homs. It was reported in mid-2010 that a Qatari-Syrian joint venture had agreed to invest in the building and operation of two 450-MW combined-cycle power plants at Al-Suweida, in the north of the country, and Adra, near Damascus.

In November 2010 legislation was approved to restructure the power sector. It provided for the establishment of separate entities to oversee generation, transmission and distribution, and for private sector investment in power projects. Syria's domestic electricity grid and distribution network has since suffered considerable damage as a consequence of the civil conflict from March 2011, and power transmission from neighbouring Turkey (estimated at up to 20% of Syria's supply) was suspended in 2012 as bilateral relations deteriorated.

TRANSPORT AND COMMUNICATIONS

Syria's three main state-run ports are Latakia, Tartous and Banias (which is dedicated to the petrol industry). In 1996 the Government announced plans for a major expansion of port capacity (9.5m. metric tons per year at that time), as recommended in studies submitted by the Japan International Cooperation Agency (JICA). Total capacity was targeted to reach 19.3m. tons per year by 2003, rising to 29.1m. tons per year by 2010. The reopening of Syria's land border with Iraq in June 1997 was followed by a Syrian request to the UN that Syrian seaports be added to the list of approved transit points for Iraq's humanitarian imports under the UN-administered 'oil-for-food' scheme. Shipments bound for Iraq subsequently contributed to a rise in Syrian transit trade. In May 2003 it was announced that the EU would lend Syria €50m. to assist in the modernization of Tartous. In November 2006 the Ministry of Transport signed a build-operate-transfer concession with International Container Services of the Philippines to develop the container terminal at Tartous. A project to modernize Latakia and improve the harbour's infrastructure was launched jointly by the Government and JICA in February 2008. The Development Plan for 2011–15 projected further expansion and development of the port facilities at Latakia and Tartous.

The national airline is Syrian Arab Airlines (Syrianair). In November 2005 the Ministry of Transport announced major infrastructure improvements in the aviation sector, including the long-term, phased expansion and modernization of Damascus International Airport (to handle 10m. passengers per year by 2020), and the development of Aleppo airport to accommodate 1.5m. passengers per year. In 2007 Syrianair signed a memorandum of understanding with partner companies to set up a new airline, Syrian Pearl, to serve domestic and international markets. The airline, in which Syrianair held a 25% stake, began operations in May 2009. In August 2010 the Government approved plans for the construction of several new airports and an additional terminal at Damascus International Airport.

In 2010 Syria had a total road network of 69,873 km, of which 45,345 km were asphalted. Plans were prepared in 2009 for the construction of two new highways—one linking Tartous on the coast to the Iraqi border in the east, and the other running from the Turkish border in the north to the Jordanian frontier in the south—with proposed investment of US $2,000m.

In July 2011 the General Establishment of Syrian Railways announced a plan to develop and expand the existing rail network by 2025, including the laying of a second track on the Damascus–Aleppo route and 934 km of new line. The Government also declared its intention to start building a metro system in Damascus.

A contract to install 600,000 new telephone lines (double the number existing at that time) was awarded to Siemens of Germany in 1991. International telecommunications services were upgraded in December 1994 with the inauguration of a new submarine cable linking Syria and Lebanon with Cyprus. By 1996 Syria had an efficient modern telephone system with a total of more than 2m. lines installed. In mid-1998, as part of a new expansion programme, Ericsson of Sweden signed a contract valued at US $120m. for the supply and installation of digital switching systems for 1m. new lines. Samsung Electronics of South Korea was reported to have secured the contract for rural fibre-optic links. The expansion programme was being financed by loans from the AFESD, Kuwait Fund for Arab Economic Development (KFAED) and the Abu Dhabi Development Fund. Two separate Global System for Mobile Communications (GSM) pilot schemes were launched in February 2000 with a combined capacity to serve 60,000 subscribers. In April 2001 they were superseded by two permanent GSM networks, one operated by Spacetel Syria (part of Investcom Holding SA, equipped by Ericsson) and the other by Syriatel (a subsidiary of the Egyptian company Orascom Telecom, equipped by Siemens). Both networks were to be operated under 15-year build-own-operate contracts awarded by the state-run Syrian Telecommunications Establishment (STE—Syrian Telecom). STE was to receive royalties of 30% of the operators' revenue for the first three years, 40% for the next three years and 50% thereafter.

It was announced by Investcom in October 2004 that Spacetel Syria would be rebranded under the name of Areeba Syria, and in mid-2007 the company was renamed MTN Syria, following the acquisition of a 75% stake by the South African telecommunications giant MTN Group. Meanwhile, Syriatel had attracted some 2.4m. subscribers by 2006, representing a 55% share of the Syrian market, and had completed its first international investment with the purchase of a 10% stake in Yemen's third GSM operator, Unitel. By 2009 the number of subscribers to Syriatel and MTN Syria was 7.3m. The number of subscribers to the landline network reached 3.7m. in that year. New legislation restructuring Syria's telecommunications sector and establishing an independent regulatory body, the Telecoms Supervisory Authority (to act as regulator from 1 January 2011), was approved by the People's Assembly in May 2010; however, the Government ruled out any privatization of the STE (which was to be replaced by a new organization, the Syrian Telecommunications Co). Due to the political and social unrest that affected the country from March 2011, the proposed auction for a licence to operate a third mobile telephone network was postponed indefinitely in April. The progress of the tender had earlier been undermined when three of the five prequalified companies withdrew from the process due to reservations over the licence terms.

TOURISM

Syria's many tourist attractions include its Mediterranean coastline, Roman and Byzantine ruins, ancient cities, Islamic shrines, and crusader castles. Most visitors predominantly come from Iran or other Arab states, since Western tourists have for many years been deterred by instability in the region and by fear of terrorist attacks. In 2000 the number of tourist arrivals in Syria numbered more than 3.0m. (mainly from Arab states), contributing about 4% of Syria's GDP. In that year a new sectoral development programme was introduced, which aimed to double the sector's share of GDP by 2020. The main planning targets were a total provision of around 175,000 hotel beds (compared with 35,000 in 2000) and annual visitor numbers of more than 7m. Incentives to foreign investors in tourism projects included concessionary arrangements in respect of land purchase, taxation, import duty and repatriation of profits.

Despite a downturn in tourism in the wake of the September 2001 terrorist attacks on the USA, the number of visitor arrivals recovered in 2002, to reach 4.3m. Visitor numbers totalled 6.2m. in 2004, declined to 5.8m. in 2005 and again to 5.7m. in 2006 (these figures included many arrivals from Iraq—effectively refugees from the violence in the wake of the 2003 US-led invasion). In June 2006 the Minister stated that the 2006–10 Development Plan aimed to increase tourist numbers to 7.5m. and revenues to US $5,000m. by 2010. Syria's largest tourism project to date—a $800m. hotel and leisure complex in Tartous called Antaradus—was initiated in a ceremony in April 2006. In May 2008 the Ministry of Tourism launched the first Internal Tourism Exhibition in Damascus, highlighting the fact that domestic tourism accounted for about 25% of overall annual tourism revenues (£S1,100m. in 2007). Tourist arrivals numbered 7.0m. in 2008, 7.7m. in 2009 and 11.0m. in 2010 (representing an increase of some 42%). In the Development Plan for 2010–15, the Government set a goal of attracting 5.1m. additional tourists annually by 2015. However, the civil conflict that has affected Syria since March 2011 has prompted a serious decline in tourist numbers and the loss of vital foreign exchange. The number of visitor arrivals declined to 5.1m. in 2011, according to provisional figures by the World Tourism Organization and, as the civil war intensified, by mid-2012 Syria's tourism industry had essentially collapsed. Many of the country's historical sites have been damaged or looted during the fighting.

BUDGET, BANKING AND FINANCE

From September 1985 resident Syrians were permitted to open accounts in foreign currency at the Commercial Bank of Syria, to be used for imports. This concession had been granted to foreigners and non-resident Syrians in the previous year. In early 1986 there was a major currency crisis, with the value of the Syrian pound on the 'black' market declining sharply. There were widespread arrests of currency dealers, and large quantities of gold and foreign currency were seized. The effect of these measures was to bring about a short-term appreciation in the value of the currency, but it soon began to depreciate once more, weakened by Syria's shortage of reserves of foreign exchange. Between October 1985 and October 1986 the Syrian pound lost 50% of its value against the US dollar. In August 1986 one of Syria's five exchange rates was devalued from US $1 = £S11.75 to $1 = £S22, a level more comparable with the black market rate. The fixed official rate for government accounts and strategic imports remained at $1 = £S3.925, as it had been since April 1976. 'Decree 24' of September 1986 rendered currency smugglers liable to prison terms of 15–25 years, and smugglers of precious metals to terms of three to 10 years. Possession of hard currency was classed as a criminal offence punishable by imprisonment. Although it was rarely enforced, the latter provision was seen by Syrian businesses as a disincentive to legitimate trading activity, and demands for its repeal were repeatedly made in the 1990s by advocates of economic liberalization. In September 1987 the Syrian pound, according to the official exchange rate, was devalued from $1 = £S3.925 to $1 = £S11.20–£S11.25, a move that many observers considered to be long overdue.

Subsidies have been paid to Syria by other Arab countries since the League of Arab States (Arab League) summit meeting in Khartoum, Sudan, in 1967. They were reinforced at the 1974 summit in Rabat, Morocco, which resulted in the promise of an annual sum of US $1,000m. to Syria in its capacity as a confrontation state. The Arab League summit of 1978, held in Baghdad, Iraq, pledged to increase these subsidies to $1,800m. per year for a period of 10 years, but donations were adversely affected by the Iran–Iraq War (in which Syria's former backers provided financial support to Iraq, while Syria sided with Iran) and by the erosion of the financial surpluses accumulated by members of the Organization of the Petroleum Exporting Countries before the decline in oil prices. Aid to Syria from the Gulf states was estimated to have dropped to $600m.–$700m. by 1986. Political actions by the Syrian leadership that met with the approval of moderate Arab states were often accompanied by reports of large sums being channelled from Saudi Arabia. Thus, it was widely believed that Syria received a substantial reward for attending the Arab summit held in Amman, Jordan, in November 1987, which was critical of Iran's actions in the Iran–Iraq War. Moreover, Syria's participation in the US-led multinational force against Iraq in the Gulf War of 1991 led to further rewards in the form of special aid totalling more than $1,000m.

In May 1994 the currency exchange rate used to levy customs duties on items other than basic commodities and most industrial raw materials was changed from US $1 = £S11.20 to $1 = £S23. There was a further selective modification of exchange rate policy at the start of 1995, when the rate applicable to most sales or purchases of foreign currency through the Syrian banking system was changed from £S23 to £S42 per dollar. It was estimated that 80% of all officially sanctioned foreign exchange transactions in Syria were based on this rate of exchange at the end of that year. The oil industry (hitherto required to use a rate of $1 = £S11.20) was permitted to switch to a rate of $1 = £S22.95 from January 1996 and to the main rate of $1 = £S42 from August.

In October 1996 the exchange rate applicable to most foreign exchange transactions was devalued from US $1 = £S42 to $1 = £S43.50, and the rate decreased further, to $1 = £S45, in July 1997. From October 1996 Syrians were permitted to open hard-currency deposit accounts in Syria without declaring the origin of their funds, but there was no formal repeal of the 1986 law forbidding possession of hard currency. In these circumstances, Syrians continued to rely on the Lebanese banking system for most foreign exchange transactions. In August 1998 the principal exchange rate used by Syrian banks was slightly devalued to $1 = £S46. The free market value of the currency at this time was about $1 = £S52.

The 1999 budget, which provided for total expenditure of £S255,300m. and total revenue of £S244,300m., was not formally submitted to the legislature until the end of that year, government departments having meanwhile operated on the basis of their 1998 spending allocations, restricting any capital investment to projects approved in 1998. The budget for 2000 provided for total expenditure of £S275,400m. (including investment expenditure of £S132,000m.) and total revenues of £S263,141m., although it was subsequently reported that the budget out-turn was in surplus as a result of above-forecast revenue and below-forecast expenditure. In November 2000 the Government abolished price subsidies for white sugar and rice. The 2001 budget provided for total revenue of £S312,798m. and total expenditure of £S322,000m., of which £S161,000m. was investment expenditure, £S123,680m. was current expenditure, and £S37,320m. was an allocation for debt repayments and price subsidies. Although there was a significantly increased provision for capital expenditure, project implementation remained generally slow, highlighting the persistence of established attitudes in the public sector. The budget for 2002 provided for expenditure of £S356,400m.; although no details of anticipated revenues were published, the budget (including an unspecified amount of foreign borrowing) was expected to be balanced. Budget allocations in 2002 included £S184,000m. for infrastructural investment, £S131,900m. for public sector spending and £S40,500m. for debt-servicing (mostly on debts still owed to the former Soviet-bloc countries).

The budget for 2003 provided for a 17.5% increase in expenditure to £S420,000m., comprising investment spending of £S211,000m. and current spending of £S209,000m. Anticipated revenues were £S294,000m., of which £S152,000m. was expected at that time to be generated from oil revenues (although the subsequent war in Iraq had a significant impact on this outcome—see Petroleum and Natural Gas). In December the Government approved the budget for 2004, envisaging expenditure of £S449,500m. and a projected deficit of £S226,500m. due mainly to increased allocations to meet development and investment needs. The 2005 budget provided for an expenditure decrease to £S431,400m., with current spending set at £S277,000m. and £S154,400m. devoted to investment, and for total revenues of S£356,300m. The budget for 2006 projected total expenditure of £S495,000m., divided between capital spending of £S195,000m. and current spending of £S300,000m. The budget for 2008 provided for expenditure of £S600,000m. (compared with £S588,000m. in the 2007 budget), comprising current spending of £S370,000m. and investment spending of £S230,000m. The deficit was forecast at £S192,000m. Current spending, however, was likely to be higher due to public sector wage increases that the Government approved in May 2008. Also in May the Minister of Finance confirmed that a 10% VAT would be introduced in Syria from 2009 (although this was later deferred) in order to boost revenues. The draft budget for 2009 projected a fiscal deficit of £S226,000m., or 9.5% of GDP, with expenditure of £S685,000m. (£S410,000m. in current spending) and revenue of £S459,000m. This was based on an oil price assumption of US $42 per barrel for heavy crude (which constituted about two-thirds of Syrian production) and $51 for light crude. However, in January 2009, against the background of decreasing global oil prices and the slowdown in economic activity, the Minister of Finance warned that the fiscal deficit would exceed the budget projection and also that remittances from Syrians working abroad and FDI would decline.

The draft budget for 2010, according to the IMF, envisaged higher total expenditure of £S749,900m. and revenue of £S577,900m., leaving a projected deficit of £S172,000m. While capital spending was budgeted to rise by about 19%, to reach £S327,000m., current spending was only projected to increase by 4%, to total £S422,900m., reflecting expected savings from the replacement of the fuel subsidy system with more targeted social welfare payments. In October 2010 the Government approved the draft budget for 2011, envisaging total expenditure of £S835,000m. and revenue of £S668,000m. (with an assumed oil price of US $48 per barrel for heavy crude and $55 for light crude). However, these projections were undermined as the Government sought to deflect the political and social unrest that began in March 2011 by restoring expensive price subsidies and suspending the introduction of a VAT (considered an important source of future government income). The 2012 budget, approved by the Government in late 2011, envisaged a sharp increase in expenditure to £S1,326,000m. based on a higher assumed oil price of $75 per barrel for heavy crude and $85 for light crude. Current spending was projected at £S951,000m., including £S386,000m. on subsidies (principally on fuel). An estimate for revenue was not given by the Ministry of Finance. Under the 2013 budget, expenditure was forecast to rise by 4% to £S1,383,000m., including increases in subsidies (to £S512,000m.) and salary spending (to £S236,000m.). However, it was unclear how the Government would raise the additional revenues needed, particularly given the ongoing civil war and the punitive sanctions in place against the country.

A decree was adopted in April 2000 to allow foreign banks to set up branches within Syria's free zone areas (then sited at Dar'a, Damascus, Latakia, Aleppo and Tartous). Early interest in the new scheme was confined to Lebanese bankers. By March 2001 six Lebanese banks had obtained licences to set up branches in Syrian free zones, and two of them had opened their first such branches. The capital requirement for such ventures was US $10m.

In April 2001 the Syrian legislature approved bills to safeguard banking secrecy and to allow the establishment of mainstream private banks throughout the country (ending a public sector monopoly dating from the bank nationalizations of 1963). The key provisions of the legislation were that each private bank should have a minimum capital of US $30m., should have majority Syrian ownership and should not be more than 5% owned by any single individual. The Central Bank of Syria was to supervise the new private banks while continuing to oversee the existing state-owned banks (which the Government intended to leave in place to counteract competition from the private sector). Provision was made for the state to set up new banking ventures as a minority (25% or less) partner of private interests. Further legislation (Law 23) enacted in March 2002 consolidated the legal framework for the establishment and operation of private banks in Syria as private or joint venture companies with shareholdings. It also created a regulator for the sector, the Credit and Monetary Council, chaired by the Governor of the Central Bank. The Council would have as an eventual objective the introduction of a floating exchange rate for the Syrian pound to replace the existing complex system of official, customs and commercial rates and the consequential widespread use of the black market for currency transactions. The approval of Law 23 quickly resulted in several applications being received by the Central Bank from investor groups in other Arab countries wishing to set up private banks in Syria. In April 2003 the Government gave final approval for the granting of licences to three private banks: the International Bank for Trade and Finance, the leading shareholder of which was Jordan's Housing Bank for Trade and Finance; the Bank of Syria and Overseas, a joint venture between the Banque du Liban et d'Outre Mer, in partnership with the International Finance Corpn (the private arm of the World Bank) and private Syrian investors; and Lebanon's Banque Européenne pour le Moyen-Orient in a joint venture with Saudi Arabia's Banque Saudi Fransi and Syrian investors.

In June 2003 the Credit and Monetary Council reduced the interest rates that state banks paid on deposits by 1.0% and on loans by 1.5%, the first such change for 22 years. The following month, in a move to encourage foreign and local investment, the Government lifted restrictions on foreign currency dealings by abrogating Decree 24, in force for 17 years, and subsequent legislation introduced in 2000 that had eased some of the harsher provisions of that Decree. The move was seen as consistent with measures taken over the previous year to modernize Syria's banking and financial system. In January 2004 the first two private banks—Banque BEMO Saudi Fransi SA and the Bank of Syria and Overseas—opened for business, marking an end of the state monopoly of the banking sector. The International Bank for Trade and Finance began operating in July of that year. Also in July Bank Audi Syria SA received approval from the Syrian authorities for its application to set up a Syrian joint banking venture. By early 2005 another two private banks—the Arab Bank Syria SA and Byblos Bank Syria—had also been granted licences. In January 2006 Arab Jordanian Bank opened a branch in Syria, and in April banking licences were issued to three Gulf Islamic banks: the Commercial Bank of Kuwait, Qatar National Bank and Dallah Albaraka of Saudi Arabia. In September licences were issued to the first Syrian Islamic banks—CHAM Bank and Syria International Islamic Bank. These were followed in early 2007 by the United Islamic Bank of Syria, backed by Gulf investors. In mid-2009 the Central Bank granted permission to foreign banks to establish representative offices in Syria in an effort to attract major Western institutions, and in January 2010 new legislation raised the equity stake limit for foreign partners in joint banking ventures from 49% to 60%. In October 2009 the Government had announced that conventional and Islamic banks would have to adhere to higher minimum capital requirements being introduced over a five-year period. In March 2010 EFG-Hermes, an Egyptian-based bank, established an office in Syria with plans to launch a private equity investment fund. EU financial sanctions, which were imposed in response to the repression of political opposition by the Syrian authorities, included banning European firms and banks from transacting with the state-owned Commercial Bank of Syria from October 2011. Moreover, in May 2012 the US Department of the Treasury took punitive action against Syria International Islamic Bank, freezing its US assets and banning US financial institutions from further dealings with the bank.

In 2002 the Government legalized the opening of foreign currency accounts and foreign currency transfers, although this was initially restricted to the Commercial Bank of Syria, which was authorized to sell limited amounts of foreign currency for specific non-commercial purposes. Meanwhile, the Government announced the unification, at the 'neighbouring countries rate' of US $1 = £S46–£S46.5, of the different exchange rates for customs valuation (used for calculating customs tariffs and customs fees). For current account transactions, however, the Syrian pound was still traded by the government-controlled Commercial Bank of Syria at several rates, including the official rate of $1 = £S46 prevailing on public sector imports and exports, and the floating rate of $1 = £S51–£S52 applying to most private sector imports. Despite this step towards exchange rate liberalization, the complex system remained a constraint on business sector activity, preventing progress on the full convertibility of the Syrian pound and the freeing up of capital movements. Then, in May 2005 it was announced that the Central Bank would allow private banks to set the daily exchange rates on foreign currencies (a decision deemed to be the first step towards the opening of a free currency market). In February 2006 the Government announced its decision to switch all of the state's foreign currency transactions from US dollars to euros. This reflected Syria's poor political relationship with the USA, and aimed to make foreign assets more secure. In April a new law to regulate officially dealings in the foreign exchange market was issued. This authorized the Credit and Monetary Council to issue licences to joint-stock companies and money-exchange bureaux to undertake foreign exchange activities. Joint-stock companies had to have a required minimum capital of £S250m., and foreigners and banks operating in Syria could acquire a 25% stake in them. Money exchange bureaux could be established with a minimum capital of £S50m. In May 2006 the Central Bank of Syria announced that plans to issue treasury bills for the first time and to introduce a floating exchange rate were progressing. In July 2007 the Syrian pound's peg to the US dollar was removed in an effort to curb rising import costs and inflation, and a new exchange rate regime linked to a broader range of currencies based on the IMF's special drawing rights was in operation from October. In July 2008 the Central Bank issued treasury bills on a trial basis, and in December 2010 the Ministry of Finance launched a long-awaited £S5,000m. programme of treasury bill offerings.

With the security situation deteriorating and international sanctions mounting, market intervention by the Central Bank during 2011–12 sought to stem the depreciation of the Syrian pound and the drain of liquidity from the banking system (due to withdrawals by depositors). The Bank also imposed restrictions on access to scarce foreign exchange.

In June 2005 the Government issued a decree to establish the Syrian Commission on Financial Markets and Securities, paving the way for the creation of the country's first stock exchange, plans for which had first been announced in November 2003. The seven-member commission was appointed in early 2006. After several postponements, the Damascus Securities Exchange (DSE) was officially launched in March 2009, which marked a significant, but cautious, step in Syria's transition to market economics from state central planning. There were only six listed companies initially. By December 2010 the DSE remained small, with just 18 listed securities, but there had been considerable growth in terms of index value and market capitalization. However, in the wake of the political and social unrest that commenced in March 2011, stocks on the DSE registered substantial declines.

FOREIGN TRADE

Syria's exports increased dramatically during the 1970s, mainly owing to increases in the value of petroleum sales, although oil export earnings declined during the 1980s. Meanwhile, in view of the country's shortage of foreign exchange, there were strict curbs on imports.

IMF statistics gave Syria's 1993 visible trade deficit as US $273m. (exports $3,203m., imports $3,476m.), the 1994 deficit as $1,275m. (exports $3,329m., imports $4,604m.), the 1995 deficit as $146m. (exports $3,858m., imports $4,004m.) and the 1996 deficit as $338m. (exports $4,178m., imports $4,516m.). In 1997 Syria recorded a trade surplus of $454m. (exports $4,057m., imports $3,603m.). IMF figures for 1998 showed that the value of exports had contracted by nearly 23%, to $3,142m. (the main factor being a 32% decline, to $1,700m., in oil export earnings during a year of depressed world prices). Spending on imports (which in 1997 had been sharply reduced in response to restrictive government policies) decreased further, to $3,320m., resulting in a visible trade deficit of $178m. Syria's trade statistics for 1999 showed total export earnings of $3,806m. (reflecting an upturn in oil export prices) and import spending of $3,590m., producing a visible trade surplus of $216m. and a current account surplus of $201m. In 2000 a decline in the volume of Syria's oil production was more than offset by further strong growth in oil prices, which resulted in exports increasing by 35% in value to $5,146m. With imports increasing marginally, to $3,723m., the trade surplus therefore rose sharply, to $1,423m., while the current account showed a surplus of $1,061m. Exports were reportedly valued at $5,706m. in 2001 and $6,668m. in 2002, while imports reached $4,282m. and $4,458m., respectively. By 2010 the principal market for Syrian exports was Italy, followed by Germany, Turkey and Saudi Arabia. Turkey was Syria's main supplier in that year, followed by China, Italy and Russia. According to official figures, the value of exports in 2008, 2009 and 2010 totalled £S707,798m., £S488,330m. and £S569,064m., respectively, and that of imports £S839,419m., £S714,216m. and £S812,209m. Trading volumes then contracted sharply in the wake of the civil conflict that began in March 2011. According to press reports, the value of exports in 2011 totalled £S505,000m. but then plummeted to £S168,000m. in 2012 due to international sanctions on Syrian petroleum sales. Imports similarly declined, from £S965,000m. in 2011 to £S649,000m. in 2012. The further deterioration in the trade deficit, from £S460,000m. in 2011 to £S481,000m. in 2012, added to the downward pressure on the Syrian currency, which continued to weaken in the early months of 2013.

After seven years of negotiations, an association agreement between Syria and the EU was initialled in late 2004, providing for trade liberalization and economic co-operation. This agreement then stalled, partly owing to pressure from the US Government on political grounds, but more particularly because of French suspicions of Syrian involvement in the 2005 assassination of former Lebanese Prime Minister Rafiq Hariri. In December 2008 an updated agreement was signed, reflecting an improvement in EU-Syrian relations, but further progress was again delayed by concerns among some EU states about Syria's human rights record and its alleged nuclear development programme. In March 2010 the Syrian Government announced that it would hold fresh talks with the EU about resolving the outstanding issues between them. However, further contacts were suspended by the EU in May 2011, following the Syrian Government's repressive response to the political and social upheaval that had erupted two months earlier. Turkey adopted a similarly punitive stance, announcing the suspension in December of its free trade agreement with Syria (which had come into force in 2007). Meanwhile, in December 2011 Syria signed a new trade deal with Iran, its main regional ally. The agreement entered into effect in April 2012.

FOREIGN DEBT

Syria's debt arrears to funding institutions have created problems in the past (arrears to the World Bank having led to disbursements of new loans being frozen in 1986), while political events have at times cast a shadow over Western official aid. In 1983 the US Congress voted for US economic aid to Syria to be terminated. Syria's total external debt (including military debt to the former Soviet bloc countries of about US $10,000m.) was estimated by the World Bank to have been $16,815m. at the end of 1991, compared with $3,549m. in the early 1980s. By the end of 1993 it was $19,975m. (over 70% of which was classified as 'bilateral concessional'), while total debt service paid during that year was estimated at $283m. Nearly $4,000m. of the 1993 debt consisted of arrears to official creditors, about 10% of these arrears being owed to the World Bank, about 30% to creditors of the Organisation for Economic Co-operation and Development (OECD), and the balance to the former USSR and other Eastern European countries.

The Minister of Economy and Foreign Trade stated in May 1994 that Syria was at that time making interest payments of US $6m. per month on its World Bank debt of about $500m., and was seeking to negotiate arrangements whereby the Government would pay off one-third of the debt while a 'friends of Syria' donor group would pay off the remainder. However, he ruled out the option of a formal IMF/'Paris Club' arrangement as 'unacceptable in our political climate'. Sweden and Belgium were among the OECD countries with export credit agencies that reached agreements with Syria in 1994 in respect of relatively minor debts. However, Syria's main OECD bilateral creditors (among which France, Japan and Germany were each owed arrears of more than $100m.) were still seeking settlements in mid-1995. Negotiations with Germany were complicated by the inclusion of an estimated $500m. of Syrian debt to former East Germany within Syria's total debt of around $640m. to the unified state. The World Bank estimated Syria's 1994 external debt as $20,557m., including arrears of principal totalling $4,563m. and arrears of interest totalling $1,400m. The Bank estimated that Syria paid $398m. in debt service in 1994 (out of a total of $1,530m. due for payment in that year).

In October 1996 France announced a debt settlement agreement involving the forgiving of a reported 900m. French francs (US $175m.) of arrears of interest and the rolling-over of a further 1,000m. French francs ($195m.) of debt. In July 1997 the Syrian Government signed an agreement to settle its debt to the World Bank. Arrears of principal totalling $269.5m. were repaid in full on 1 September, while arrears of interest totalling $256.9m. were to be repaid in instalments over five years from 1 October. It was reported in September 1997 that Syria was negotiating with the Islamic Development Bank to settle around $300m. of payments' arrears. By mid-1998 Syria's only remaining unresolved debt problems of significance were with Germany and Russia. In November 1998 Italy (then Syria's largest export market and second largest import supplier) agreed an aid programme for 1999–2001, under which loans and grants totalling as much as $65m. were to be made available for agricultural, energy, health, agro-industrial, environmental and scientific projects.

In August 1999 Syria agreed a formula for settling US $502m. of debt owed to Iran. Discussions on the continuing debt dispute with Germany resumed in February 2000, leading to the signature in November of an agreement to reschedule the repayment of $572m. over 20 years from 2001. In April 2000 the Romanian Government announced a debt recovery scheme covering the greater part of Syria's outstanding communist-era debt to Romania. In December the EIB, which had made no new development loans to Syria for the previous decade, announced a $75m. loan for improvements to the electricity supply network. The World Bank estimated that Syria's total external debt at the end of 2000 was $21,655m., compared with a figure of $22,340m. in 1999. In January 2005 a debt settlement agreement was signed between Syria and Russia. Russia agreed to cancel $9,800m., representing 73% of Syria's $13,400m. debt dating back to the Soviet era. In May 2008 Syria settled its debt to the Czech Republic and Slovakia after making the final payments outstanding from an agreement concluded in 2004.

Statistical Survey

Sources (unless otherwise stated): Central Bureau of Statistics, rue Abd al-Malek bin Marwah, Malki Quarter, Damascus; tel. (11) 3335830; fax (11) 3322292; e-mail infocbs@cbssyr.org; internet www.cbssyr.org; Central Bank of Syria, place du 17 avril, Damascus; tel. (11) 2216802; fax (11) 2248329; e-mail info@bcs.gov.sy; internet www.banquecentrale.gov.sy.

Area and Population

AREA, POPULATION AND DENSITY

Area (sq km)	
Land	184,050
Inland water	1,130
Total	185,180*
Population (census results)	
3 September 1994	13,782,315
22 September 2004	
Males	9,196,878
Females	8,723,966
Total	17,920,844
Population (official estimate at 1 January)	
2009	23,027,000
2010	23,695,000
2011	24,504,000
Density (per sq km) at 1 January 2011	132.3

* 71,498 sq miles; including the Israeli-occupied Golan region (1,154 sq km).

Note: According to the United Nations Relief and Works Agency for Palestine Refugees in the Near East (UNRWA), there were 499,189 registered Palestinian refugees in Syria at 31 December 2012 (with an estimated 160,000 resident in refugee camps). Following the outbreak of civil conflict during 2011, large numbers of Syrian nationals fled fierce fighting in the country. By September 2013, according to UNRWA registers, there were some 520,000 Syrian refugees in Jordan, around 650,000 in Lebanon and a further 480,000 in Turkey.

POPULATION BY AGE AND SEX

('000 persons at 2004 census)

	Males	Females	Total
0–14	3,637	3,434	7,071
15–64	5,213	5,046	10,259
65 and over	311	280	591
Total	9,161	8,760	17,921

GOVERNORATES

(official estimates at 1 January 2011)

	Area (sq km)	Population ('000)	Density (per sq km)
Dar'a	3,730	1,126	301.9
Deir el-Zor	33,060	1,692	51.2
Dimashq (Damascus, capital)	—	1,780	—
Halab (Aleppo)	18,500	5,927	320.4
Hamah (Hama)	10,160	2,113	208.0
Al-Hasakah	23,330	1,604	68.8
Hims (Homs)	40,940	2,147	52.4
Idleb	6,100	2,072	34.0
Al-Ladhiqiyah (Latakia)	2,300	1,229	534.3
Quneitra	1,860	489	262.9
Al-Raqqah (Rakka)	19,620	1,008	51.3
Rif Dimashq (Rural Damascus)	18,140*	1,877	103.5
Al-Suweida	5,550	486	87.6
Tartous	1,890	954	504.8
Total	185,180	24,504	132.3

* Includes area for Dimashq (Damascus, capital).

BIRTHS, MARRIAGES AND DEATHS

(excl. nomad population and Palestinian refugees, estimates)

	Registered live births		Registered marriages	Registered deaths
	Number	Rate (per 1,000)		
1997	496,140	32.9	128,146	53,366
1998	505,008	32.4	130,835	57,893
1999	503,473	31.3	136,157	56,564
2000	505,484	31.0	139,843	57,759
2001	524,212	31.4	153,842	60,814
2002	471,970	27.6	174,449	53,252
2003	492,639	28.1	n.a.	53,778
2004	491,476	n.a.	178,166	57,855

2009: Live births 721,587; Marriages 241,422; Deaths 86,642.

2010: Live births 870,100; Marriages 227,808; Deaths 91,981.

Source: UN, *Demographic Yearbook*.

Life expectancy (years at birth): 75.8 (males 74.3; females 77.5) in 2011 (Source: World Bank, World Development Indicators database).

ECONOMICALLY ACTIVE POPULATION
(labour force sample survey, persons aged 15 years and over, 2011)*

	Males	Females	Total
Agriculture, hunting, forestry and fishing	579,191	75,696	654,887
Mining and quarrying	39,933	3,851	43,784
Manufacturing	657,319	45,017	702,336
Electricity, gas and water	42,268	5,002	47,270
Construction	757,739	4,594	762,333
Wholesale and retail trade	795,327	27,673	823,000
Restaurants and hotels	60,979	2,340	63,319
Transport, storage and communications	310,625	13,241	323,866
Financing, insurance, real estate	124,794	18,886	143,680
Public administration and defence	560,426	83,167	643,593
Community, social and personal services	405,133	336,039	741,172
Total employed	4,333,734	615,506	4,949,240
Unemployed	503,622	362,663	866,285
Total labour force	4,837,356	978,169	5,815,525

* Figures refer to Syrians only, excluding armed forces.

Health and Welfare

KEY INDICATORS

Total fertility rate (children per woman, 2011)	2.9
Under-5 mortality rate (per 1,000 live births, 2011)	15
HIV/AIDS (% of persons aged 15–49, 2003)	<0.1
Physicians (per 1,000 head, 2008)	1.5
Hospital beds (per 1,000 head, 2010)	1.5
Health expenditure (2010): US $ per head (PPP)	175
Health expenditure (2010): % of GDP	3.4
Health expenditure (2010): public (% of total)	46.0
Access to water (% of persons, 2011)	90
Access to sanitation (% of persons, 2011)	95
Total carbon dioxide emissions ('000 metric tons, 2009)	65,312.9
Carbon dioxide emissions per head (metric tons, 2009)	3.3
Human Development Index (2012): ranking	116
Human Development Index (2012): value	0.648

For sources and definitions, see explanatory note on p. vi.

Agriculture

PRINCIPAL CROPS
('000 metric tons)

	2009	2010	2011
Wheat	3,701.8	3,083.1	3,858.3
Barley	845.7	679.8	666.8
Maize	183.3	133.1	298.4
Potatoes	705.6	673.2	715.3
Sugar beet	732.7	1,493.0	1,805.2
Chick-peas	57.4	42.9	50.1
Lentils	102.5	77.3	112.5
Almonds	97.0	73.1	130.3
Olives	885.9	960.4	1,095.0
Cabbages and other brassicas	44.4	44.7	42.3
Lettuce and chicory	52.2	62.4	61.8
Tomatoes	1,165.6	1,156.4	1,155.0
Cauliflowers	35.9	36.8	36.9
Pumpkins, squash and gourds	121.8	120.9	122.3
Cucumbers and gherkins	132.9	155.0	154.4
Aubergines (Eggplants)	147.0	149.1	141.7
Chillies and peppers, green	48.4	76.9	59.0
Onions and shallots, green	74.9	51.8	69.4
Onions, dry	81.7	109.6	84.9
Oranges	689.8	668.9	734.0
Lemons and limes	140.6	142.2	161.6
—continued	2009	2010	2011
Apples	361.0	393.1	308.8
Apricots	98.9	62.0	75.9
Sweet cherries	56.9	58.1	62.2
Peaches and nectarines	62.6	48.8	54.4
Grapes	358.0	325.7	338.0
Watermelons	749.7	538.7	670.6
Cantaloupes and other melons	106.5	75.9	99.3
Figs	53.7	41.0	42.9
Cotton lint	224.3	165.4	151.3
Cotton seed	423.8	307.1	436.6

Aggregate production ('000 metric tons, may include official, semi-official or estimated data): Total cereals 4,739 in 2009, 3,901 in 2010, 4,829 in 2011; Total roots and tubers 706 in 2009, 673 in 2010, 715 in 2011; Total oilcrops 276 in 2009, 273 in 2010, 319 in 2011; Total vegetables (incl. melons) 3,089 in 2009, 2,983 in 2010, 3,207 in 2011; Total fruits (excl. melons) 2,253 in 2009, 2,152 in 2010, 2,217 in 2011.

Source: FAO.

LIVESTOCK
('000 head, year ending September)

	2009	2010	2011
Horses	14.7	14.0	15.0
Asses	92.7	109.0	97.0
Cattle	1,084.5	1,010.0	1,158.0
Camels	32.5	50.0	55.0
Sheep	18,336.0	15,511.0	18,071.0
Goats	1,508.0	2,057.0	2,294.0
Chickens	24,490	25,401	26,203

Source: FAO.

LIVESTOCK PRODUCTS
('000 metric tons)

	2009	2010	2011
Cattle meat	63.0	61.6	70.9
Sheep meat	189.5	153.2	172.4
Chicken meat	182.2	189.7	179.0
Cows' milk	1,600.3	1,453.0	1,701.8
Sheep's milk	706.0	644.3	705.6
Goats' milk	97.0	139.0	145.0
Hen eggs	162.4	163.3	171.9
Wool, greasy	21.9	18.7	21.1

Source: FAO.

Forestry

ROUNDWOOD REMOVALS
('000 cubic metres, excl. bark, FAO estimates)

	2008	2009	2010
Sawlogs, veneer logs and logs for sleepers	16	16	16
Other industrial wood	24	24	24
Fuel wood	26	27	28
Total	66	67	68

2011: Production assumed to be unchanged from 2010 (FAO estimates).

Sawnwood production ('000 cubic metres): *1980*: Coniferous (softwood) 6.6; Broadleaved (hardwood) 2.4; Total 9.0. *1981–2011:* Production as in 1980 (FAO estimates).

Source: FAO.

Fishing

(metric tons, live weight)

	2009	2010	2011*
Capture	6,607	6,635	4,900
Freshwater fishes	3,500	3,679	2,700
Aquaculture	8,697	8,610	8,000
Common carp	3,739	3,862	3,700
Tilapias	3,914	3,163	2,940
Total catch	15,304	15,245	12,900

* FAO estimates.

Source: FAO.

Mining

('000 metric tons unless otherwise indicated)

	2009	2010	2011
Phosphate rock	2,466	3,765	3,100
Salt (unrefined)	78	81	80
Gypsum	403	540	500
Natural gas (million cu m)	5,572	8,048	8,748
Crude petroleum	19,967	19,171	16,293

2012: Crude petroleum ('000 metric tons) 8,186; Natural gas (million cu m) 7,593.

Sources: US Geological Survey; BP, *Statistical Review of World Energy*.

Industry

SELECTED PRODUCTS

('000 metric tons unless otherwise indicated)

	2009	2010	2011
Plywood (cu m)*	7.8	7.8	7.8
Paper and paperboard*	75	75	75
Cement (hydraulic)	5,176	6,000	9,000†
Olive oil (virgin)	168.2	195.0	208.3
Soybean oil‡	91.3	91.4	55.9
Cottonseed oil‡	46.7	43.8	41.6
Motor spirit (petrol, '000 barrels)	11,589	12,958	13,000†
Distillate fuel oils ('000 barrels)	29,689	29,346	30,000†
Residual fuel oils ('000 barrels)	27,415	33,653	33,000†

* FAO estimates.

† Estimate.

‡ Unofficial figures.

Sources: FAO; US Geological Survey.

Electric energy (million kWh): 41,170 in 2008; 43,406 in 2009; 46,590 in 2010.

Finance

CURRENCY AND EXCHANGE RATES

Monetary Units

100 piastres = 1 Syrian pound (£S).

Sterling, Dollar and Euro Equivalents (30 April 2013)

£1 sterling = £S148.747;
US $1 = £S95.830;
€1 = £S125.269;
£S1,000 = £6.723 sterling = $10.435 = €7.983.

Exchange Rate Between April 1976 and December 1987 the official mid-point rate was fixed at US $1 = £S3.925. On 1 January 1988 a new rate of $1 = £S11.225 was introduced. In addition to the official exchange rate, there is a promotion rate (applicable to most travel and tourism transactions) and a flexible rate.

BUDGET

(£S '000 million)

Revenue	2008	2009	2010
Oil-related proceeds	131.4	128.2	196.1
Non-oil tax revenue	258.0	290.2	261.6
Income and profits	88.6	126.1	81.4
International trade	33.1	37.1	40.9
Excises	16.6	8.6	10.1
Other	119.7	118.3	129.2
Non-oil non-tax revenue	101.5	182.4	176.7
Total	490.9	600.8	634.4

Expenditure	2008	2009	2010
Current expenditure	375.3	442.2	452.3
Wages and salaries	234.7	275.2	298.4
Goods and services	27.5	30.8	34.9
Interest payments	25.5	28.0	21.6
Subsidies and transfers	77.5	83.1	72.8
Development expenditure	173.1	212.4	243.1
Social	65.9	77.8	91.1
Agriculture	16.1	19.9	27.5
Extractive industries	15.5	17.4	13.8
Manufacturing industries	5.9	7.7	7.0
Utilities	36.3	44.4	59.1
Construction	0.8	0.9	1.4
Trade	2.5	3.5	2.3
Transport and communications	25.2	35.6	36.0
Finance	3.8	4.1	3.9
Other	1.0	1.0	1.0
Total	548.4	654.6	695.4

2011 (£S '000 million, estimates): Total revenue 835.0; Total expenditure 835.0.

Source: Ministry of Finance, Damascus.

INTERNATIONAL RESERVES

(excluding foreign exchange, US $ million at 31 December)

	2008	2009	2010
Gold (national valuation)	38	38	54
IMF special drawing rights	56	438	430
Total	94	476	484

2011: IMF special drawing rights 429.

2012: IMF special drawing rights 430.

Source: IMF, *International Financial Statistics*.

MONEY SUPPLY

(£S million at 31 December)

	2008	2009	2010
Currency outside depository corporations	468,820	480,952	540,246
Transferable deposits	469,456	507,088	610,145
Other deposits	717,811	810,695	890,649
Broad money	1,656,087	1,798,734	2,041,040

Source: IMF, *International Financial Statistics*.

COST OF LIVING

(Consumer Price Index; base: 2000 = 100)

	2008	2009	2010
Food and beverages	181.8	182.2	190.8
Electricity, gas and other fuels (incl. water)	173.4	228.6	249.4
Clothing and footwear	139.0	134.9	141.9
Rent	182.7	177.2	176.8
All items (incl. others)	161.4	165.9	173.2

Source: ILO.

All items (Consumer Price Index; base: 2005 = 100): 18.9 in 2011; 203.6 in 2012 (Source: IMF, *International Financial Statistics*).

NATIONAL ACCOUNTS

(£S million at current prices)

Expenditure on the Gross Domestic Product

	2008	2009	2010*
Government final consumption expenditure	274,879	301,815	346,055
Private final consumption expenditure	1,390,933	1,508,579	1,691,479
Gross fixed capital formation	408,725	451,605	579,911
Changes in stocks	351,583	304,709	165,163
Total domestic expenditure	2,426,120	2,566,708	2,782,608
Exports of goods and services	919,542	732,502	911,773
Less Imports of goods and services	897,602	778,505	902,606
GDP in market prices	2,448,060	2,520,705	2,791,775
GDP at constant 2000 prices	1,341,516	1,420,832	1,469,703

* Provisional.

Gross Domestic Product by Economic Activity

	2008	2009	2010*
Agriculture, hunting, forestry and fishing	456,746	570,177	547,475
Mining and quarrying Manufacturing Electricity, gas and water	787,430	635,310	778,312
Construction	78,174	78,590	106,003
Wholesale and retail trade	513,092	582,617	620,710
Transport and communications	225,157	237,677	265,548
Finance and insurance	128,380	123,513	142,979
Government services	224,304	244,004	278,517
Other community, social and personal services	53,621	61,664	68,615
Non-profit private services	1,002	1,152	1,268
Sub-total	2,467,906	2,534,704	2,809,427
Import duties	33,112	37,118	41,448
Less Imputed bank service charges	52,958	51,117	59,100
GDP in market prices	2,448,060	2,520,705	2,791,775

* Provisional.

BALANCE OF PAYMENTS

(US $ million)

	2008	2009	2010
Exports of goods	15,334	10,883	12,273
Imports of goods	–16,107	–13,933	–15,876
Balance on goods	–773	–3,049	–3,603
Exports of services	4,415	4,798	7,333
Imports of services	–3,171	–2,734	–3,533
Balance on goods and services	471	–985	197
Primary income received	540	344	313
Primary income paid	–1,689	–1,451	–1,827
Balance on goods, services and primary income	–678	–2,092	–1,317
Secondary income received	1,335	1,247	1,450
Secondary income paid	–185	–185	–500
Current balance	472	–1,030	–367
Capital account (net)	73	210	287
Direct investment from abroad	1,466	2,570	1,469
Portfolio investment assets	–55	–241	–193
Other investment assets	–631	–626	61
Other investment liabilities	–42	212	–85
Net errors and omissions	–1,232	–747	905
Reserves and related items	50	348	2,076

Source: IMF, *International Financial Statistics*.

External Trade

PRINCIPAL COMMODITIES

(distribution by SITC major group, £S million)

Imports	2008	2009	2010
Food and live animals	96,531	122,366	130,513
Beverages and tobacco	3,829	10,697	17,754
Crude materials, inedible, except fuels	36,603	44,173	37,633
Mineral fuels and lubricants	265,332	91,544	159,610
Animal and vegetable oils and fats	7,034	10,097	8,356
Chemicals and related products	102,839	98,915	105,918
Basic manufactures	217,264	204,515	138,633
Machinery and transport equipment	98,469	119,882	167,211
Total (incl. others)	839,419	714,216	812,209

Exports	2008	2009	2010
Food and live animals	87,576	107,950	99,526
Beverages and tobacco	53,583	9,996	5,301
Crude materials, inedible, except fuels	26,462	13,500	20,089
Mineral fuels and lubricants	261,275	169,577	261,933
Animal and vegetable oils and fats	7,629	4,465	4,317
Chemicals and related products	35,198	31,796	32,518
Basic manufactures	118,927	54,888	64,851
Machinery and transport equipment	31,575	18,216	11,288
Total (incl. others)	707,798	488,330	569,064

PRINCIPAL TRADING PARTNERS

(£S million)

Imports c.i.f.	2008	2009	2010
China, People's Republic	91,500	60,621	71,497
Egypt	28,701	40,522	34,245
France	9,351	10,475	16,169
Germany	17,414	21,055	34,161
India	17,223	15,317	19,483
Italy	39,164	25,786	59,786
Japan	9,545	8,815	10,656
Lebanon	7,885	7,221	8,456
Netherlands	11,253	6,356	11,809
Romania	5,641	9,537	8,018
Russia	108,790	42,879	51,283
Saudi Arabia	31,030	28,908	37,357
Spain	11,724	8,724	8,446
Turkey	23,064	54,269	77,332
United Arab Emirates	15,043	9,559	10,477
USA	16,390	21,740	26,442
Total (incl. others)	839,419	714,216	812,209

Exports f.o.b.	2008	2009	2010
Egypt	34,011	16,927	17,972
France	47,434	31,474	22,426
Germany	75,984	44,409	68,315
Italy	55,147	27,537	70,308
Jordan	21,006	16,182	18,774
Lebanon	62,179	16,292	20,176
Netherlands	9,593	11,205	18,369
Russia	667	586	15,411
Saudi Arabia	48,019	27,418	25,095
Spain	19,860	15,907	10,848
Turkey	29,593	14,707	29,100
United Arab Emirates	8,799	8,101	4,174
USA	16,373	10,459	18,479
Total (incl. others)	707,798	488,330	569,064

Transport

RAILWAYS
(traffic)

	2008	2009	2010
Passengers carried ('000)	3,369	3,676	3,587
Passenger-km ('000)	1,120,146	1,224,098	1,195,100
Freight ('000 metric tons)	9,307	8,842	8,578
Freight ton-km (million)	2,370	2,263	2,196

ROAD TRAFFIC
(motor vehicles in use)

	2008	2009	2010
Passenger cars	551,858	637,604	741,260
Buses	6,201	6,611	7,486
Lorries, trucks, etc.	552,841	623,359	683,906
Motorcycles	205,518	242,090	380,852

SHIPPING

Flag Registered Fleet
(at 31 December)

	2010	2011	2012
Number of vessels	100	76	70
Total displacement ('000 grt)	255.6	144.7	99.1

Source: Lloyd's List Intelligence (www.lloydslistintelligence.com).

International Sea-borne Traffic

	1996	1997	1998
Vessels entered ('000 net regd tons)	2,901*	2,640	2,622
Cargo unloaded ('000 metric tons)	4,560	4,788	5,112
Cargo loaded ('000 metric tons)	1,788	2,412	2,136

* Excluding Banias.

Vessels entered ('000 net registered tons): 2,928 in 1999; 2,798 in 2000; 2,827 in 2001.

Source: mainly UN, *Monthly Bulletin of Statistics* and *Statistical Yearbook*.

CIVIL AVIATION
(traffic on scheduled services)

	2007	2008	2009
Kilometres flown (million)	23	26	26
Passengers carried ('000)	1,272	1,359	1,343
Passenger-km (million)	2,333	2,519	2,507
Total ton-km (million)	221	250	246

Source: UN, *Statistical Yearbook*.

2011 ('000): Passengers carried 1,437 (Source: World Bank, World Development Indicators database).

Tourism

FOREIGN VISITOR ARRIVALS
(incl. excursionists)*

Country of nationality	2008	2009	2010
Iran	361,605	455,012	891,807
Iraq	889,463	894,477	1,006,434
Jordan	1,044,564	1,062,990	1,949,551
Kuwait	126,977	146,724	134,255
Lebanon	1,587,115	1,815,003	2,291,802
Saudi Arabia	403,140	476,346	484,087
Turkey	562,832	733,132	1,459,580
Total (incl. others)	6,950,852	7,720,795	10,969,682

* Figures exclude Syrian nationals resident abroad.

Total tourist arrivals ('000): 5,070 in 2011 (provisional).

Tourism receipts (US $ million, excl. passenger transport): 3,757 in 2009; 6,190 in 2010.

Source: World Tourism Organization.

Communications Media

	2010	2011	2012
Telephones ('000 main lines in use)	4,069	4,345	4,423
Mobile cellular telephones ('000 in use)	11,799	13,117	12,928
Internet subscribers ('000)	986	n.a.	n.a.
Broadband subscribers ('000)	69.8	121.3	378.0

Source: International Telecommunication Union.

Education

(2010/11 unless otherwise indicated)

			Pupils/Students		
	Institutions*	Teachers	Males	Females	Total
Pre-primary	1,431	9,189	90,196	81,310	171,506
Primary	n.a.	132,099†	1,303,300	1,204,101	2,507,400
Secondary: general	1,140	162,758†	1,376,696	1,320,882	2,697,578
Secondary: vocational	595	18,607	73,602	49,731	123,333
Higher*	5	8,084	141,310	138,304	279,614

* Excluding private universities; data for 2006/07.

† 2007/08.

Source: mainly UNESCO Institute for Statistics.

Pupil-teacher ratio (primary education, UNESCO estimate): 17.8 in 2007/08 (Source: UNESCO Institute for Statistics).

Adult literacy rate (UNESCO estimates): 83.4% (males 89.9%; females 76.9%) in 2010 (Source: UNESCO Institute for Statistics).

Directory

The Constitution

A new and permanent Constitution was endorsed by 97.6% of voters in a national referendum held on 12 March 1973. The 157-article Constitution defines Syria as a 'Socialist popular democracy' with a 'pre-planned Socialist economy'. Under the new Constitution, Lt-Gen. Hafiz al-Assad remained President, with the power to appoint and dismiss his Vice-President, Premier and government ministers, and also became Commander-in-Chief of the Armed Forces, Secretary-General of the Baath Socialist Party and President of the National Progressive Front. According to the Constitution, the President is elected by direct popular vote for a seven-year term. Legislative power is vested in the People's Assembly, with 250 members elected for a four-year term by universal adult suffrage.

Following the death of President Hafiz al-Assad on 10 June 2000, the Constitution was amended to allow his son, Lt-Gen. Bashar al-Assad, to accede to the presidency. Bashar al-Assad also became Commander-in-Chief of the armed forces, Secretary-General of the Baath Socialist Party and President of the National Progressive Front.

At a national referendum, held on 26 February 2012, a new Constitution was approved by 89.4% of participating voters.

Turn-out was officially reported at 57.4%, although this figure was disputed by the opponents of President Assad. Among the most significant of its new provisions, the document imposed upon the President a limit of two seven-year terms (although this was not retroactive) and removed reference to the 'leading role' of the ruling Baath Arab Socialist Party. The Constitution entered into effect on 27 February.

The Government

HEAD OF STATE

President: Lt-Gen. BASHAR AL-ASSAD (assumed office 17 July 2000).

Vice-President, responsible for Foreign Affairs and Information: FAROUK AL-SHARA'.

Vice-President: Dr NAJAH AL-ATTAR.

COUNCIL OF MINISTERS
(September 2013)

Prime Minister: Dr WAEL NADER AL-HALQI.

Deputy Prime Minister and Minister of Foreign Affairs and Expatriates: WALID MOUALLEM.

Deputy Prime Minister for Economic Affairs: Dr QADRI JAMIL.

Deputy Prime Minister for Services Affairs and Minister of Local Administration: OMAR IBRAHIM GHALAWANJI.

Minister of Defence: Lt-Gen. FAHD JASSEM AL-FREIJ.

Minister of Communications and Technology: Dr IMAD ABD AL-GHANI SABOUNI.

Minister of Awqaf (Religious Endowments): Dr MUHAMMAD ABD AL-SATTAR AL-SAYYID.

Minister of Presidential Affairs: MANSOUR AZZAM.

Minister of Justice: NAJIM HAMID AL-AHMAD.

Minister of the Interior: Lt-Gen. MUHAMMAD IBRAHIM AL-SHAAR.

Minister of Finance: Dr ISMAEL ISMAEL.

Minister of Health: SAAD ABD AL-SALAM AL-NAYEF.

Minister of Tourism: BISHR RIYAD YAZIGI.

Minister of Electricity: IMAD MUHAMMAD DEEB KHAMIS.

Minister of Water Resources: BASSAM HANNA.

Minister of Agriculture and Agrarian Reform: AHMAD AL-QADRI.

Minister of Higher Education: Dr MALIK ALI.

Minister of Education: Dr HAZWAN AL-WAZZ.

Minister of Economy and Foreign Trade: Dr KHODR ORFALI.

Minister of Industry: KAMAL EDDIN TU'MA.

Minister of Internal Trade and Consumer Protection: SAMIR IZZAT QADI AMIN.

Minister of Transport: Dr MAHMOUD IBRAHIM SAID.

Minister of Housing and Urban Development: HUSSEIN FARZAT.

Minister of Public Works: HUSSEIN ARNOUS.

Minister of Petroleum and Mineral Resources: SULEIMAN AL-ABBAS.

Minister of Culture: Dr LUBANAH MSHAWEH.

Minister of Labour: Dr HASSAN HIJAZI.

Minister of Social Affairs: Dr KINDA AL-SHAMMAT.

Minister of Information: OMRAN AHED AL-ZOUBI.

Minister of State for National Reconciliation Affairs: Dr ALI HAIDAR.

Minister of State for Environmental Affairs: Dr NAZIRA FARAH SARKIS.

Ministers of State: HUSSEIN MAHMOUD FARZAT, JOSEPH JURJI SUWAID, MUHAMMAD TURKI AL-SAYYED, HASSIB ELIAS SHAMMAS, ABDULLAH KHALIL HUSSEIN, JAMAL SHAABAN SHAHIN.

MINISTRIES

Office of the President: Damascus.

Office of the Prime Minister: rue Chahbandar, Damascus; tel. (11) 2226000; fax (11) 2237842.

Ministry of Agriculture and Agrarian Reform: rue Jabri, place Hedjaz, Baramkeh, Damascus; tel. (11) 2213613; fax (11) 2244078; e-mail info@moaar.gov.sy; internet www.syrian-agriculture.org.

Ministry of Awqaf (Religious Endowments): place al-Misat, Damascus; tel. (11) 4470005; fax (11) 4470006; e-mail admin@syrianawkkaf.org; internet www.syrianawkkaf.org.

Ministry of Communications and Technology: rue Abed, Damascus; tel. (11) 2221133; fax (11) 2323273; e-mail info@moct.gov.sy; internet www.moct.gov.sy.

Ministry of Culture: rue George Haddad, Rawda, Damascus; tel. (11) 3331556; fax (11) 3342606; e-mail info@moc.gov.sy; internet www.moc.gov.sy.

Ministry of Defence: place Omayad, Damascus; tel. (11) 7770700; fax (11) 2237842.

Ministry of Economy and Foreign Trade: rue Maysaloun, Damascus; tel. (11) 2324680; fax (11) 2225695; e-mail econ-min@net.sy; internet www.syrecon.org.

Ministry of Education: rue Shahbander, al-Masraa, Damascus; tel. (11) 3313206; fax (11) 4420435; e-mail info@syrianeducation.org.sy; internet www.syrianeducation.org.sy.

Ministry of Electricity: BP 4900, rue al-Kouatly, Damascus; tel. (11) 5810730; fax (11) 5811689; e-mail pmoe@net.sy; internet moe.gov.sy.

Ministry of Finance: BP 13136, rue Jule Jammal, Damascus; tel. (11) 2211300; fax (11) 2224701; e-mail mof@net.sy; internet www.syrianfinance.org.

Ministry of Foreign Affairs and Expatriates: Kafarsouseh, Damascus; tel. (11) 2181000; fax (11) 2146252; e-mail info@mofaex.gov.sy; internet www.mofaex.gov.sy.

Ministry of Health: rue Majlis al-Sha'ab, Damascus; tel. (11) 3311020; fax (11) 3311114; e-mail info@moh.gov.sy; internet www.moh.gov.sy.

Ministry of Higher Education: BP 9251, place Mezzeh Gamarik, Damascus; tel. (11) 2119865; fax (11) 2128919; e-mail mhe@mhe.gov.sy; internet www.mhe.gov.sy.

Ministry of Housing and Urban Development: place Yousuf al-Azmeh, al-Salheyeh, Damascus; tel. (11) 2211494; fax (11) 2259400; e-mail diwan@mohc.gov.sy; internet www.mhc.gov.sy.

Ministry of Industry: BP 12835, rue Maysaloun, Damascus; tel. (11) 3720959; fax (11) 2231096; e-mail industry-min@mail.sy; internet www.moid.gov.sy.

Ministry of Information: Immeuble Dar al-Baath, Autostrade Mezzeh, Damascus; tel. and fax (11) 6664681; e-mail info@moi.gov.sy; internet www.moi.gov.sy.

Ministry of the Interior: rue al-Bahsah, al-Marjeh, Damascus; tel. (11) 2219400; fax (11) 2324835; e-mail admin@civilaffair-moi.gov.sy; internet www.syriamoi.gov.sy.

Ministry of Internal Trade and Consumer Protection: Damascus.

Ministry of Justice: rue al-Nasr, Damascus; tel. (11) 2214105; fax (11) 2246250.

Ministry of Labour: place Yousuf al-Azmeh, al-Salheyeh, Damascus; tel. (11) 2325387; fax (11) 2255143.

Ministry of Local Administration: rue 17 Nissan, Damascus; tel. (11) 2145700; fax (11) 2145731; e-mail info@mla-sy.org; internet mla-sy.org.

Ministry of Petroleum and Mineral Resources: BP 40, al-Adawi, Insha'at, Damascus; tel. (11) 4451624; fax (11) 4463942; e-mail mopmr-central@mail.sy.

Ministry of Public Works: Damascus.

Ministry of Social Affairs: Damascus.

Ministry of State for Environmental Affairs: BP 3773, Damascus; tel. (11) 2138682; fax (11) 2320885; e-mail env-min@net.sy; internet www.gcea.gov.sy.

Ministry of State for National Reconciliation Affairs: Damascus.

Ministry of Tourism: BP 6642, rue Barada, Damascus; tel. (11) 2210122; fax (11) 2242636; e-mail info@syriatourism.org; internet www.syriatourism.org.

Ministry of Transport: BP 33999, rue al-Jala'a, Damascus; tel. (11) 3316840; fax (11) 3323317; e-mail min-trans@net.sy; internet www.mot.gov.sy.

Ministry of Water Resources: Damascus.

Legislature

Majlis al-Sha'ab
(People's Assembly)

People's Council, Damascus; tel. (11) 2226127; fax (11) 3712532; e-mail info@parliament.sy; internet www.parliament.gov.sy.

Speaker: MUHAMMAD JIHAD AL-LAHAM.

Election, 7 May 2012

Party	Seats
National Progressive Front*	184
Others	7
Independents	59
Total	250

* The National Progressive Front (NPF) reportedly comprised 10 political parties, headed by the Baath Arab Socialist Party, which accounted for 162 of the 184 seats won by the NPF.

Political Organizations

National Progressive Front (NPF—Al-Jabha al-Wataniyah al-Taqadumiyah), headed by the late President Hafiz al-Assad, was formed in March 1972 as a coalition of five political parties. At the time of the legislative elections in May 2012, the NPF consisted of 10 parties:

Arab Democratic Unionist Party (Hizb al-Ittihad al-'Arabi al-Dimuqrati): f. 1981, following split from the Arab Socialist Union; considers the concerns of the Arab world in general as secondary to those of Syria itself in the pursuit of pan-Arab goals; Chair. GHASSAN AHMAD OSMAN.

Arab Socialist Movement (Harakat al-Ishtiraki al-'Arabi): Damascus; f. 1963, following split from Arab Socialist Union; contested the 2007 election to the People's Assembly as two factions (see also National Vow Movement); Leader AHMAD AL-AHMAD.

Arab Socialist Union (al-Ittihad al-Ishtiraki al-'Arabi): Damascus; f. 1973, following the separation of the Syrian branch from the international Arab Socialist Union; Nasserite; supportive of the policies of the Baath Arab Socialist Party; Leader SAFWAN AL-QUDSI.

Baath Arab Socialist Party (al-Hizb al-Ba'th al-'Arabi al-Ishtiraki): National Command, BP 9389, Autostrade Mezzeh, Damascus; tel. (11) 6622142; fax (11) 6622099; e-mail baath@baath-party.org; internet www.baath-party.org; Arab nationalist socialist party; f. 1947, as a result of merger between the Arab Revival (Baath) Movement (f. 1940) and the Arab Socialist Party (f. 1940); in power since 1963; supports creation of a unified Arab socialist society; approx. 1m. mems in Syria; brs in most Arab countries; Pres. Lt-Gen. BASHAR AL-ASSAD.

Democratic Socialist Unionist Party (al-Hizb al-Wahdawi al-Ishtiraki al-Dimuqrati): f. 1974, following split from the Arab Socialist Union; Chair. FADLALLAH NASR AL-DIN.

National Vow Movement (Harakat al-'ahd al-Watani): a breakaway party from the Arab Socialist Union; a faction of the Arab Socialist Movement; awarded three seats in 2007 election to the People's Assembly; Leader GHASSAN ABD AL-AZIZ OSMAN.

Socialist Unionists (Al-Wahdawiyyun al-Ishtirakiyyun): e-mail alwahdawinet@hotmail.com; internet www.alwahdawi.net; f. 1961, through split from the Baath Arab Socialist Party following that organization's acceptance of Syria's decision to secede from the United Arab Republic; Nasserite; aims for Arab unity, particularly a new union with Egypt; produces weekly periodical *Al-Wehdawi*; Chair. FAYEZ ISMAIL.

Syrian Arab Socialist Union Party: Damascus; tel. (11) 239305; Nasserite; Sec.-Gen. SAFWAN KOUDSI.

Syrian Communist Party (Bakdash) (al-Hizb al-Shuyu'i al-Suri): BP 7837, Damascus; tel. (11) 4455048; fax (11) 4446390; e-mail info@syriancp.org; internet www.syriancp.org; f. 1924 by Fouad Shamal in Lebanon and Khalid Bakdash (died 1995); until 1943 part of joint Communist Party of Syria and Lebanon; party split into two factions under separate leaders, Bakdash and Faisal (q.v.), in 1986; Marxist-Leninist; publishes fortnightly periodical *Sawt al-Shaab*; Sec.-Gen. AMMAR BAKDASH.

Syrian Communist Party (Faisal) (al-Hizb al-Shuyu'i al-Suri): Damascus; f. 1986, following split of Syrian Communist Party into two factions under separate leaders, Faisal and Bakdash (q.v.); aims to end domination of Baath Arab Socialist Party and the advantages given to mems of that party at all levels; advocates the lifting of the state of emergency and the release of all political prisoners; publishes weekly periodical *An-Nour*; Sec.-Gen. YOUSUF RASHID FAISAL.

Syrian Social Nationalist Party (Centralist Wing) (al-Hizb al-Suri al-Qawmi al-Ijtima'i): e-mail administrator@ssnp.com; internet www.ssnp.com; f. 1932 in Beirut, Lebanon; fmrly mem. of NPF, but withdrew prior to 2012 legislative elections; also known as Parti populaire syrien; seeks creation of a 'Greater Syrian' state, incl. Syria, Lebanon, Jordan, the Palestinian territories, Iraq, Kuwait, Cyprus and parts of Egypt, Iran and Turkey; advocates separation of church and state, the redistribution of wealth, and a strong military; supports Syrian involvement in Lebanese affairs; has brs worldwide, and approx. 90,000 mems in Syria; Pres. ALI HAIDAR.

There are numerous opposition parties, within Syria or in exile, which are forced to operate on a clandestine basis. Formed in 1980, the **National Democratic Rally** (NDR—Tajammu' al-Watani al-Dimuqrati) is an alliance of banned, secularist opposition parties, several of which are opposition wings of parties that joined the ruling NPF.

A current member of the NDR, the **Syrian Democratic People's Party** (al-Hizb al-Sha'ab al-Suri al-Dimuqrati—leader ABULLAH HOSHA) was founded in 1973 as the Syrian Communist Party (Political Bureau), following the decision by founder Riad at-Turk to split from that party after its leader, Khalid Bakdash, decided to allow the organization to join the NPF. The party adopted its current name in 2005. The party publishes an online newsletter (www.arraee.com).

There is also a **Marxist-Leninist Communist Action Party**, which regards itself as independent of all Arab regimes.

An illegal Syrian-based organization, the **Islamic Movement for Change (IMC)**, claimed responsibility for a bomb attack in Damascus in December 1996.

Diplomatic Representation

EMBASSIES IN SYRIA

In February 2012 both Switzerland and the USA closed their embassies in Damascus, citing concerns regarding the safety of diplomatic staff, amid ongoing use of violence by the Syrian armed forces to quell protests against the rule of President Bashar al-Assad. Meanwhile, Libya and Tunisia were ordered to close their embassies in Damascus by the Syrian Government, following the expulsion of Syria's representatives to those countries. By mid-2012 several other countries, including Belgium, Canada, Finland, France, Germany, Greece, Italy, Japan, the Netherlands, Norway, Spain, Turkey and the United Kingdom, as well as the member states of the Cooperation Council for the Arab States of the Gulf (Gulf Cooperation Council), had also closed their respective embassies, and by early 2013 the operations of most diplomatic missions in Syria had been significantly reduced owing to the escalating civil conflict.

Algeria: Immeuble Noss, Raouda, Damascus; tel. (11) 3331446; fax (11) 3334698; Ambassador SALEH BOUSHEH.

Argentina: BP 116, Damascus; tel. (11) 3334167; fax (11) 3327326; e-mail easir@net.sy; Ambassador ROBERTO AHUAD.

Armenia: 2 Saad Ben Abi Uakksi, Bldg 2, West Mezze, Damascus; tel. (11) 6133617; fax (11) 6133618; e-mail armsyriaembassy@mfa.am; Ambassador ARSHAK POLADIAN.

Austria: BP 5634, Immeuble Mohamed Naim al-Deker, 1 rue Farabi, Mezzeh Est, Damascus; tel. (11) 61380100; fax (11) 6116734; e-mail damaskus-ob@bmeia.gv.at; Ambassador ISABEL RAUSCHER.

Belarus: BP 16239, 27 rue Qurtaja, Mezzeh Est, Damascus; tel. (11) 6118097; fax (11) 6631143; e-mail syria@mfa.gov.by; internet syria.mfa.gov.by; Ambassador ALEG YERMALOVICH.

Brazil: BP 2219, 39 rue al-Farabi, Mezzeh Est, Damascus; tel. (11) 6124551; fax (11) 6124553; e-mail braemsyr@net.sy; Ambassador EDGAR ANTONIO CASIANO.

Bulgaria: BP 2732, 8 rue Pakistan, place Arnous, Damascus; tel. (11) 3318445; fax (11) 4419854; e-mail bul_emb@abv.bg; internet www.mfa.bg/bg/62/; Ambassador DIMITAR MIHAILOV.

Chile: BP 3561, 6 rue Ziad bin Abi Soufian, Rawda, Damascus; tel. (11) 3338443; fax (11) 3331563; e-mail embachile.siria@gmail.com; internet chileabroad.gov.cl/siria; Chargé d'affaires a.i. ROBERTO ABU-EID AYUB.

China, People's Republic: BP 2455, 83 rue Ata Ayoubi, Damascus; tel. (11) 3339594; fax (11) 3338067; e-mail chinaemb_sy@mfa.gov.cn; internet sy.chineseembassy.org; Ambassador ZHANG XUN.

Cuba: Immeuble Istouani and Charbati, 40 rue al-Rachid, Damascus; tel. (11) 3339624; fax (11) 3333802; e-mail embajador@sy.embacuba.cu; internet www.cubadiplomatica.cu/siria; Ambassador LUIS ERINEL MARISY FIGUEREDO.

Cyprus: BP 9269, 278G rue Malek bin Rabia, Mezzeh Ouest, Damascus; tel. (11) 6130812; fax (11) 6130814; e-mail cyembdam@scs-net.org; Ambassador ANTONIS GRIVAS.

Czech Republic: BP 2249, place Abou al-Ala'a al-Maari, Damascus; tel. (11) 3331383; fax (11) 3338268; e-mail damascus@embassy.mzv.cz; internet www.mzv.cz/damascus; Ambassador EVA FILIPI.

Denmark: BP 2244, Fatmeh Idriss 6, rue al-Ghazzawi, Mezzeh Ouest, Damascus; tel. (11) 61909000; fax (11) 61909033; e-mail damamb@um.dk; internet www.ambdamaskus.um.dk; Ambassador CHRISTINA MARKUS LASSEN.

Egypt: BP 12443, rue al-Gala'a, Abou Roumaneh, Damascus; tel. (11) 3330756; fax (11) 33500911; e-mail egypt@tvcabo.co.mz; Ambassador SHAWKI ISMAIL ALI SOLIMAN.

Eritrea: BP 12846, Autostrade al-Mazen West, 82 rue Akram Mosque, Damascus; tel. (11) 6112357; fax (11) 6112358; Chargé d'affaires a.i. HUMMED MOHAMED SAEED KULU.

Holy See: BP 2271, 14 rue Masr, Damascus (Apostolic Nunciature); tel. (11) 3332601; fax (11) 3327550; e-mail noncesy@mail.sy; Apostolic Nuncio Most Rev. MARIO ZENARI (Titular Archbishop of Iulium Carnicum).

Hungary: BP 2607, 12 rue al-Salam, Mezzeh Est, Damascus; tel. (11) 6110787; fax (11) 6117917; e-mail mission.dam@mfa.gov.hu; internet www.mfa.gov.hu/kulkepviselet/sy; Ambassador JÁNOS BUDAI.

India: BP 685, 3455 rue ibn al-Haitham, Abou Roumaneh, Damascus; tel. (11) 3347351; fax (11) 3347912; e-mail amb.damascus@mea.gov.in; internet www.indianembassysyria.com; Chargé d'affaires a.i. S. D. SHARMA.

Indonesia: BP 3530, Immeuble 26, Bloc 270A, 132 rue al-Madina al-Munawar, Mezzeh Est, Damascus; tel. (11) 6119630; fax (11) 6119632; e-mail kbridams@net.sy; Ambassador WAHIB ABDUL JAWAD.

Iran: BP 2691, Autostrade Mezzeh, nr al-Razi Hospital, Damascus; tel. (11) 6117675; fax (11) 6110997; e-mail iran-dam@net.sy; Ambassador MUHAMMAD REZA RAOUF SHEIBANI.

Iraq: Damascus; tel. (11) 3341290; fax (11) 3341291; e-mail dmkemb@iraqmofamail.net; Ambassador Dr ALA'A HUSSAIN AL-JAWADI.

Jordan: rue Abou Roumaneh, Damascus; tel. (11) 3334642; fax (11) 3336741; internet www.jordanembassydemascus.gov.jo; Ambassador OMAR AL-AMED.

Korea, Democratic People's Republic: rue Fares al-Khouri-Jisr Tora, Damascus; Ambassador CHOE SU HON.

Lebanon: Abou Roumaneh, Damascus; Ambassador MICHEL EL-KHOURY.

Malaysia: Immeuble 117, Mezzeh Est Villas, Damascus; tel. (11) 6122811; fax (11) 6122814; e-mail malsyria@kln.gov.my; Ambassador MAT DRIS BIN Haji YAACOB.

Mauritania: ave al-Jala'a, rue Karameh, Damascus; tel. (11) 3339317; fax (11) 3330552; Ambassador AAL OULD AHMADO.

Morocco: 35 rue Abu Bakr al-Karkhi Villas, Mezzeh Est, Damascus; tel. (11) 6110451; fax (11) 6117885; e-mail sifmar@scs-net.org; Ambassador MUHAMMAD LAKHSASSI.

Pakistan: BP 9284, rue al-Farabi, Mezzeh Est, Damascus; tel. (11) 6132694; fax (11) 6132662; e-mail parepdam@scs-net.org; Ambassador WAHEED AHMAD.

Panama: Bldg 10, Office 4, rue al-Bizm, Malki St, Damascus; tel. (11) 3739001; fax (11) 3738801; e-mail consulado depanamadamasco@gmail.com; Chargé d'affaires HAISAM CHEHABI.

Philippines: BP 36849, 56 rue Hamzeh bin al-Mutaleb, Mezzeh, Damascus; tel. (11) 6132626; fax (11) 6110152; e-mail info@ambaphilsyria.com; Chargé d'affaires a.i. NESTOR N. PADALHIN.

Poland: BP 501, rue Baha Eddin Aita, Abou Roumaneh, Damascus; tel. (11) 3333010; fax (11) 3315318; e-mail damaszek.amb.sekretariat@msz.gov.pl; internet www.damaszek.msz.gov.pl; Ambassador MICHAŁ MURKOCIŃSKI.

Romania: BP 4454, 8 rue Ibrahim Hanano, Damascus; tel. (11) 3327572; fax (11) 3327571; e-mail damascamb@gmail.com; internet damasc.mae.ro; Ambassador DANUT FLORIN SANDOVICI.

Russia: BP 3153, rue Umar bin al-Khattab, al-Dawi, Damascus; tel. (11) 4423155; fax (11) 4423182; e-mail ruembsyria@mail.ru; internet www.syria.mid.ru; Ambassador AZAMAT KULMUKHAMETOV.

Serbia: BP 739, 18 rue al-Jala'a, Abou Roumaneh, Damascus; tel. (11) 3336222; fax (11) 3333690; e-mail ambasada@srbija-damask.org; internet www.srbija-damask.org; Ambassador JOVAN VUJASINOVIĆ.

Slovakia: BP 33115, 158 rue al-Shafi, Mezzeh Est, Damascus; tel. (11) 6132114; fax (11) 6132598; e-mail emb.damascus@mzv.sk; internet www.damascus.mfa.sk; Ambassador IVAN SURKOS.

Somalia: 7 rue Abu Bakr al-Karkhi Villas, Mezzeh Est, Damascus; tel. and fax (11) 6111220; e-mail webmaster@somaligov.net; internet www.syria.somaligov.net; Ambassador ABD AL-RAHMAN NUR MUHAMMAD DINAARI.

South Africa: BP 9141, rue al-Ghazaoui, 7 Jadet Kouraish, Mezzeh Ouest, Damascus; tel. (11) 61351520; fax (11) 6111714; e-mail admin.damascus@foreign.gov.za; Ambassador SHAUN EDWARD BYNEVELDT.

Sudan: BP 3940, Immeuble al-Kassar Assadi, Damascus; tel. (11) 6112901; fax (11) 6112904; e-mail sud-emb@net.sy; Ambassador ABD AL-RAHMAN DIRAR.

Sweden: BP 4266, Immeuble du Patriarcat Catholique, rue Chakib Arslan, Abou Roumaneh, Damascus; tel. (11) 33400700; fax (11) 3327749; e-mail ambassaden.damaskus@foreign.ministry.se; internet www.swedenabroad.com/damascus; Ambassador NIKLAS KEBBON.

Turkmenistan: Miset. 4097 Ruki el-Din, 2e étage, Damascus; tel. (11) 2241334; fax (11) 3320905.

Ukraine: BP 33944, 14 rue al-Salam, Mezzeh Est, Damascus; tel. (11) 6113016; fax (11) 6121355; e-mail emb_sy@mfa.gov.ua; internet www.mfa.gov.ua/syria; Chargé d'affaires a.i. YEVHEN ZHUPEYEV.

Venezuela: BP 2403, Immeuble al-Tabbah, 5 rue Lisaneddin bin al-Khateb, place Rauda, Damascus; tel. (11) 6124835; fax (11) 6124833; e-mail embavenez@tarassul.sy; internet www.embavensiria.com; Ambassador IMAD SAAB.

Yemen: Abou Roumaneh, Charkassieh, Damascus; Ambassador (vacant).

Judicial System

The Courts of Law in Syria are principally divided into two juridical court systems: Courts of General Jurisdiction and Administrative Courts. Since 1973 the Supreme Constitutional Court has been established as the paramount body of the Syrian judicial structure.

The Supreme Constitutional Court: Damascus; tel. (11) 3331902; This is the highest court in Syria. It has specific jurisdiction over: (i) judicial review of the constitutionality of laws and legislative decrees; (ii) investigation of charges relating to the legality of the election of members of the Majlis al-Sha'ab (People's Assembly); (iii) trial of infractions committed by the President of the Republic in the exercise of his functions; (iv) resolution of positive and negative jurisdictional conflicts and determination of the competent court between the different juridical court systems, as well as other bodies exercising judicial competence. The Supreme Constitutional Court is composed of a Chief Justice and six Justices. They are appointed by decree of the President of the Republic for a renewable period of four years; Chief Justice ADNAN ZUREIQ.

Courts of General Jurisdiction: The Courts of General Jurisdiction in Syria are divided into six categories: (i) The Court of Cassation; (ii) The Courts of Appeal; (iii) The Tribunals of First Instance; (iv) The Tribunals of Peace; (v) The Personal Status Courts; (vi) The Courts for Minors. Each of the above categories (except the Personal Status Courts) is divided into Civil, Penal and Criminal Chambers; (i) The Court of Cassation: This is the highest court of general jurisdiction. Final judgments rendered by Courts of Appeal in penal and civil litigations may be petitioned to the Court of Cassation by the Defendant or the Public Prosecutor in penal and criminal litigations, and by any of the parties in interest in civil litigations, on grounds of defective application or interpretation of the law as stated in the challenged judgment, on grounds of irregularity of form or procedure, or violation of due process, and on grounds of defective reasoning of judgment rendered. The Court of Cassation is composed of a President, seven Vice-Presidents and 31 other Justices (Councillors); (ii) The Courts of Appeal: Each court has geographical jurisdiction over one governorate (*mohafazat*). Each court is divided into Penal and Civil Chambers. There are Criminal Chambers, which try felonies only. The Civil Chambers hear appeals filed against judgments rendered by the Tribunals of First Instance and the Tribunals of Peace. Each Court of Appeal is composed of a President and sufficient numbers of Vice-Presidents (Presidents of Chambers) and Superior Judges (Councillors). There are 54 Courts of Appeal; (iii) The Tribunals of First Instance: In each governorate there are one or more Tribunals of First Instance, each of which is divided into several Chambers for penal and civil litigations. Each Chamber is composed of one judge. There are 72 Tribunals of First Instance; (iv) The Tribunals of Peace: In the administrative centre of each governorate, and in each district, there are one or more Tribunals of Peace, which have jurisdiction over minor civil and penal litigations. There are 227 Tribunals of Peace; (v) Personal Status Courts: These courts deal with marriage, divorce, etc. For Muslims, each court consists of one judge, the 'Qadi Shari'i'. For Druzes, there is one court consisting of one judge, the 'Qadi Mazhabi'. For non-Muslim communities, there are courts for Roman Catholics, Orthodox believers, Protestants and Jews; (vi) Courts for Minors: The constitution, officers, sessions, jurisdiction and competence of these courts are determined by a special law.

Public Prosecution: Public prosecution is headed by the Attorney-General, assisted by a number of Senior Deputy and Deputy Attorneys-General, and a sufficient number of chief prosecutors, prosecutors and assistant prosecutors. Public prosecution is represented at all levels of the Courts of General Jurisdiction in all criminal and penal litigations and also in certain civil litigations as required by the law. Public prosecution controls and supervises enforcement of penal judgments.

Administrative Courts System: The Administrative Courts have jurisdiction over litigations involving the state or any of its governmental agencies. The Administrative Courts system is divided into two courts: the Administrative Courts and the Judicial Administrative Courts, of which the paramount body is the High Administrative Court.

Military Courts: The Military Courts deal with criminal litigations against military personnel of all ranks and penal litigations against officers only. There are two military courts: one in Damascus, the other in Aleppo. Each court is composed of three military judges. There are other military courts, consisting of one judge, in every governorate, which deal with penal litigations against military personnel below the rank of officer. The different military judgments can be petitioned to the Court of Cassation.

Religion

The majority of Syrians follow a form of Islamic Sunni orthodoxy. There are also a considerable number of religious minorities: Shi'a Muslims; Isma'ili Muslims; the Isma'ili of the Salamiya district, whose spiritual head is the Aga Khan; a large number of Druzes, the Nusairis or Alawites of the Jebel Ansariyeh (a schism of the Shi'a branch of Islam, to which about 11% of the population, including President Assad, belong) and the Yezidis of the Jebel Sinjar; and a minority of Christians.

The Constitution states only that 'Islam shall be the religion of the head of the state'. The original draft of the 1973 Constitution made no reference to Islam at all, and this clause was inserted only as a compromise after public protest. The Syrian Constitution is thus unique among the constitutions of Arab states (excluding Lebanon) with a clear Muslim majority in not enshrining Islam as the religion of the state itself.

ISLAM

Grand Mufti: Sheikh AHMAD BADER EL-DIN HASSOUN, BP 7410, Damascus; tel. (11) 2688601; fax (11) 2637650; e-mail info@drhassoun.com; internet www.drhassoun.com.

CHRISTIANITY

Orthodox Churches

Greek Orthodox Patriarchate of Antioch and all the East: BP 9, Damascus; tel. (11) 5424400; fax (11) 5424404; e-mail info@antiochpat.org; internet www.antiochpat.org; Patriarch of Antioch and all the East His Beatitude JOHN X; has jurisdiction over Syria, Lebanon, Iran and Iraq.

Syrian Orthodox Patriarchate of Antioch and all the East: BP 22260, Bab Touma, Damascus; tel. (11) 54498989; e-mail patriarch-z-iwas@scs-net.org; Patriarch of Antioch and all the East His Holiness IGNATIUS ZAKKA I IWAS; the Syrian Orthodox Church includes one Catholicose (of India), 37 Metropolitans and one Bishop, and has an estimated 4m. adherents throughout the world.

The Armenian Apostolic Church is also represented in Syria.

The Roman Catholic Church

Armenian Rite

Patriarchal Exarchate of Syria: Exarchat Patriarcal Arménien Catholique, BP 22281, Bab Touma, Damascus; tel. (11) 5413820; fax (11) 5419431; e-mail damazmcath@hotmail.com; f. 1985; represents the Patriarch of Cilicia (resident in Beirut, Lebanon); 4,500 adherents (31 Dec. 2011); Exarch Patriarchal Bishop JOSEPH ARNAOUTIAN.

Archdiocese of Aleppo: Archevêché Arménien Catholique, BP 97, 33 al-Tilal, Aleppo; tel. (21) 2123946; fax (21) 2116637; e-mail armen.cath@mail.sy; 17,500 adherents (31 Dec. 2007); Archbishop BOUTROS MARAYATI.

Diocese of Kamichlié: Evêché Arménien Catholique, BP 17, al-Qamishli; tel. (53) 424211; fax (53) 422711; e-mail armen.cath@mail.sy; 5,400 adherents (2012); Archbishop BOUTROS MARAYATI.

Chaldean Rite

Diocese of Aleppo: Evêché Chaldéen Catholique, BP 4643, 1 rue Patriarche Elias IV Mouawwad, Soulémaniyé, Aleppo; tel. (21) 4441660; fax (21) 4600800; e-mail audoa@scs-net.org; 15,000 adherents (31 Dec. 2007); Bishop ANTOINE AUDO.

Latin Rite

Apostolic Vicariate of Aleppo: BP 327, 19 rue al-Fourat, Aleppo; tel. (21) 2682399; fax (21) 2689413; e-mail vicariatlatin@mail.sy; f. 1762; 12,000 adherents (31 Dec. 2008); Vicar Apostolic GIUSEPPE NAZZARO (Titular Bishop of Forma).

Maronite Rite

Archdiocese of Aleppo: Archevêché Maronite, BP 203, 57 rue Fares el-Khoury, Aleppo; tel. and fax (21) 2118048; e-mail maronite@scs-net.org; 4,000 adherents (31 Dec. 2007); Archbishop YOUSUF ANIS ABI-AAD.

Archdiocese of Damascus: Archevêché Maronite, BP 2179, 6 rue al-Deir, Bab Touma, Damascus; tel. (11) 5412888; fax (11) 5436002; e-mail mgrsamirnassar@gmail.com; f. 1527; 14,000 adherents (31 Dec. 2007); Archbishop SAMIR NASSAR.

Diocese of Latakia: Evêché Maronite, BP 161, rue Hamrat, Tartous; tel. (43) 223433; fax (43) 322939; 33,000 adherents (31 Dec. 2007); Bishop YOUSUF MASSOUD MASSOUD.

Melkite Rite

Melkite Greek Catholic Patriarchate of Antioch: Patriarcat Grec-Melkite Catholique, BP 22249, 12 ave al-Zeitoun, Bab Charki, Damascus; tel. (11) 5441030; fax (11) 5417900; e-mail pat.melk@scs-net.org; internet www.pgc-lb.org; or BP 70071, Antélias, Lebanon; tel. (4) 413111; fax (4) 418113; f. 1724; jurisdiction over 1.5m. Melkites throughout the world (incl. 234,000 in Syria); Patriarch of Antioch and all the East, of Alexandria and of Jerusalem His Beatitude GREGORIOS III LAHAM; the Melkite Church includes the patriarchal sees of Damascus, Cairo and Jerusalem and four other archdioceses in Syria; seven archdioceses in Lebanon; one in Jordan; one in Israel; and seven eparchies (in the USA, Brazil, Canada, Australia, Venezuela, Argentina and Mexico).

Archdiocese of Aleppo: Archevêché Grec-Catholique, BP 146, 9 place Farhat, Aleppo; tel. (21) 2119307; fax (21) 2119308; e-mail gr.melkcath@mail.sy; 17,000 adherents (31 Dec. 2007); Archbishop JEAN-CLÉMENT JEANBART.

Archdiocese of Busra and Hauran: Archevêché Grec-Catholique, Khabab, Hauran; tel. (15) 855012; e-mail derbosra@hotmail.com; 27,000 adherents (31 Dec. 2007); Archbishop BOULOS NASSIF BORKHOCHE.

Archdiocese of Homs: Archevêché Grec-Catholique, BP 1525, rue el-Mo'tazila, Boustan al-Diwan, Homs; tel. (31) 2482587; fax (31) 2464587; e-mail isidore_battikha@yahoo.fr; 30,000 adherents (31 Dec. 2007); Archbishop (vacant).

Archdiocese of Latakia: Archevêché Grec-Catholique, BP 151, rue al-Moutannabi, Latakia; tel. (41) 460777; fax (41) 476002; e-mail saouafnicolas@yahoo.fr; 10,000 adherents (31 Dec. 2007); Archbishop NICOLAS SAWAF.

Syrian Rite

Archdiocese of Aleppo: Archevêché Syrien Catholique, place Mère Teresa de Calcutta, Azizié, Aleppo; tel. (21) 2126750; fax (21) 2126752; e-mail a_chahda@hotmail.com; 8,000 adherents (31 Dec. 2007); Archbishop DENYS ANTOINE CHAHDA.

Archdiocese of Damascus: Archevêché Syrien Catholique, BP 2129, 157 rue Al-Mustaqeem, Bab Charki, Damascus; tel. and fax (11) 5445343; e-mail psamirm@cyberia.met.lb; 14,000 adherents (31 Dec. 2007); Archbishop GRÉGOIRE ELIAS TABÉ.

Archdiocese of Hassaké-Nisibi: Archevêché Syrien Catholique, BP 6, Hassaké; tel. (52) 320812; e-mail b.hindo@hotmail.com; 35,000 adherents (31 Dec. 2007); Archbishop JACQUES BEHNAN HINDO.

Archdiocese of Homs: Archevêché Syrien Catholique, BP 303, rue Hamidieh, Homs; tel. (31) 221575; fax (21) 224350; 10,000 adherents (31 Dec. 2007); Archbishop THÉOPHILE GEORGES KASSAB.

The Anglican Communion

Within the Episcopal Church in Jerusalem and the Middle East, Syria forms part of the diocese of Jerusalem (see the chapter on Israel).

Other Christian Groups

Protestants in Syria are largely adherents of either the National Evangelical Synod of Syria and Lebanon or the Union of Armenian Evangelical Churches in the Near East (for details of both organizations, see the chapter on Lebanon).

The Press

Since the Baath Arab Socialist Party came to power, the structure of the press has been modified according to socialist patterns. Most publications are issued by political, religious or professional associations (such as trade unions), and several are published by government ministries. However, two privately owned daily newspapers have been launched in recent years. Anyone wishing to establish a new paper or periodical must apply for a licence.

The major dailies are *Al-Baath* (the organ of the party), *Tishreen*, *Al-Thawra* and the *Syria Times*, all published in Damascus.

PRINCIPAL DAILIES

Al-Baath (Renaissance): BP 9389, Autostrade Mezzeh, Damascus; tel. (11) 6622142; fax (11) 6622099; e-mail baath@baath-party.org; internet www.albaath.news.sy; f. 1946; morning; Arabic; organ of the Baath Arab Socialist Party; Editor ILYAS MURAD; circ. 45,000.

Baladna: BP 2000, al-Huda Bldg, al-Eskandaria St, Damascus; tel. (11) 6122515; fax (11) 6122514; e-mail info@ug.com.sy; internet www.baladnaonline.net; Arabic; privately owned; publ. by United Group for Publishing, Advertising and Marketing; Chief Editor SAMIR AL-SHIBANI.

Champress: Immeuble Arnos, place Arnos, Damascus; tel. (11) 44681199; fax (11) 44681190; e-mail mail@champress.com; internet www.champress.com; privately owned; political; online only; Arabic; Dir ALI JAMALO.

Al-Fida' (Redemption): Hama; Al-Wahda Foundation for Press, Printing and Publishing, BP 2448, Dawar Kafr Soussat, Damascus; tel. (11) 225219; fax (11) 2216851; e-mail fedaa@thawra.com; internet fedaa.alwehda.gov.sy; morning; Arabic; political; Editor A. AULWANI; circ. 4,000.

Al-Furat: Al-Wahda Foundation for Press, Printing and Publishing, BP 2448, Dawar Kafr Soussat, Damascus; tel. (51) 224494; fax (51) 218418; e-mail furat@thawra.com; internet furat.alwehda.gov.sy; Editor ADNAN OWAID.

Al-Horubat: Homs; Al-Wahda Foundation for Press, Printing and Publishing, BP 2448, Dawar Kafr Soussat, Damascus; tel. (11) 225219; fax (11) 2216851; e-mail ouroba@thawra.com; internet ouruba.alwehda.gov.sy; morning; Arabic; political; circ. 5,000.

Al-Jamahir (The People): Aleppo; Al-Wahda Foundation for Press, Printing and Publishing, BP 2448, Dawar Kafr Soussat, Damascus; tel. (21) 214309; fax (21) 214308; e-mail jamahir@thawra.com; internet jamahir.alwehda.gov.sy; Arabic; political; Chief Editor MORTADA BAKACH; circ. 10,000.

Syria Times: BP 5452, Medan, Damascus; tel. (11) 2247359; fax (11) 2231374; e-mail syriatimes@teshreen.com; internet syriatimes.tishreen.info; English; publ. by Tishreen Foundation for Press and Publishing; Editor FOUAD MARDOUD; circ. 15,000.

Al-Thawra (Revolution): Al-Wahda Foundation for Press, Printing and Publishing, BP 2448, Dawar Kafr Soussat, Damascus; tel. (11) 2210850; fax (11) 2216851; e-mail admin@thawra.com; internet thawra.alwehda.gov.sy; f. 1963; morning; Arabic; political; Editor ASAAD ABBOUD; circ. 40,000.

Tishreen (October): BP 5452, Medan, Damascus; tel. (11) 2131100; fax (11) 2246860; e-mail tnp@mail.sy; internet www.tishreen.info; Arabic; publ. by Tishreen Foundation for Press and Publishing; Chief Editor KHALAF AL-JARAAD; circ. 50,000.

Al-Wahda (Unity): Latakia; Al-Wahda Foundation for Press, Printing and Publishing, BP 2448, Dawar Kafr Soussat, Damascus; tel. (11) 225219; fax (11) 2216851; e-mail wehda@thawra.com; internet wehda.alwehda.gov.sy; Arabic; political.

Al-Watan: Duty Free Zone, Damascus; tel. (11) 2137400; fax (11) 2139928; internet www.alwatan.sy; f. 2006; Arabic; political; privately owned; Chief Editor WADDAH ABED RABBO.

WEEKLIES AND FORTNIGHTLIES

Abyad wa Aswad (White and Black): 8 rue Hekmat Alasale, Almastaba 4, Muhajirin; tel. (11) 3739968; fax (11) 3739949; e-mail a-and-a@scs-net.org; internet www.awaonline.net; f. 2002; weekly; Arabic; political; privately owned; Editor AYMAN AL-DAQUQ.

Al-Iqtisadiya: rue Abd al-Munim Riyad 13, Damascus; tel. (11) 3737344; fax (11) 3737348; e-mail info@iqtissadiya.com; internet www.iqtissadiya.com; f. 2001; weekly; Arabic; economic; privately owned; Editor WADDAH ABD AL-RABBO.

Kantsasar: BP 133, Aleppo; tel. and fax (21) 2246753; e-mail kantsasar@excite.com; internet www.periotem.com; weekly; publ. by Armenian Prelacy of Aleppo; Editor MARY MERDKHANIAN.

Kassioun: BP 35033, Damascus; tel. (11) 3346681; fax (11) 3346681; e-mail general@kassioun.org; internet www.kassioun.org; weekly; publ. by the Syrian Communist Party (Bakdash).

Kifah al-Oummal al-Ishtiraki (The Socialist Workers' Struggle): Fédération Générale des Syndicats des Ouvriers, rue Qanawat, Damascus; weekly; Arabic; labour; publ. by Gen. Fed. of Labour Unions; Editor SAEED AL-HAMAMI.

Al-Maukef al-Riadi (Sport Stance): Al-Wahda Foundation for Press, Printing and Publishing, BP 2448, Dawar Kafr Soussat, Damascus; tel. (11) 225219; e-mail riadi@thawra.com; internet riadi.alwehda.gov.sy; weekly; Arabic; sports; circ. 50,000.

An-Nour (Light): BP 7394 Damascus; tel. (11) 3324914; fax (11) 3342571; e-mail annour@mail.sy; internet www.an-nour.com; f. 2001; weekly; Arabic; political and cultural; organ of the Syrian Communist Party (Faisal); Editor-in-Chief YAQUB GARRO.

Sawt al-Shaab (Voice of the People): Damascus; f. 1937, but publ. suspended in 1939, 1941, 1947 and 1958; relaunched in 2001; fortnightly; Arabic; organ of the Syrian Communist Party (Bakdash).

OTHER PERIODICALS

Al-Arabieh (The Arab Lady): Syrian Women's Asscn, BP 3207, Damascus; tel. (11) 3313275; fax (11) 3311078; monthly; Editor MAJEDA KUTEIT.

Al-Fikr al-Askari (The Military Idea): BP 4259, blvd Palestine, Damascus; fax (11) 2125280; f. 1950; 6 a year; Arabic; official military review publ. by the Political Administration Press.

Al-Ghad (Tomorrow): Association of Red Cross and Crescent, BP 6095, rue Maysat, Damascus; tel. (11) 2242552; fax (11) 7777040; monthly; environmental health; Editor K. ABED-RABOU.

Al-Irshad al-Zirai (Agricultural Information): Ministry of Agriculture and Agrarian Reform, rue Jabri, Damascus; tel. (11) 2213613; fax (11) 2216627; 6 a year; Arabic; agriculture.

Jaysh al-Sha'ab (The People's Army): Ministry of Defence, BP 3320, blvd Palestine, Damascus; fax (11) 2125280; f. 1946; monthly; Arabic; army magazine; publ. by the Political Dept of the Syrian Army.

Al-Kalima (The Word): Al-Kalima Association, Aleppo; monthly; Arabic; religious; Publr and Editor FATHALLA SAKAL.

Al-Kanoun (The Law): Ministry of Justice, rue al-Nasr, Damascus; tel. (11) 2214105; fax (11) 2246250; monthly; Arabic; juridical.

Layalina: Damascus; tel. (11) 6122515; fax (11) 6122514; e-mail info@layalinamag.com; internet layalina.sy.pressera.com; monthly; Arabic; social and lifestyle; publ. by United Group for Publishing, Advertising and Marketing; Chair. MAJD SULEIMAN.

Al-Maaloumatieh (Information): National Information Centre, BP 11323, Damascus; tel. (11) 2127551; fax (11) 2127648; e-mail nice@net.sy; f. 1994; quarterly; computer magazine; Editor ABD AL-MAJID AL-RIFAI; circ. 10,000.

Al-Ma'arifa (Knowledge): Ministry of Culture, rue al-Rouda, Damascus; tel. (11) 3336963; f. 1962; monthly; Arabic; literary; Editor ABD AL-KARIM NASIF; circ. 7,500.

Al-Majalla al-Batriarquia (The Magazine of the Patriarchate): Syrian Orthodox Patriarchate, BP 914, Damascus; tel. (11) 4447036; f. 1962; monthly; Arabic; religious; Editor SAMIR ABDOH; circ. 15,000.

Al-Majalla al-Tibbiya al-Arabiyya (Arab Medical Magazine): rue al-Jala'a, Damascus; tel. (11) 3331890; e-mail kfkallas@net.sy; internet www.arabmedmag.com; monthly; Arabic and English; publ. by Arab Medical Comm; Dir KHALID KALLAS; Editor Dr AL-LOUJAMI MAZEN.

Majallat Majma' al-Lughat al-Arabiyya bi-Dimashq (Magazine of the Arab Language Academy of Damascus): Arab Academy of Damascus, BP 327, Damascus; tel. (11) 3713145; fax (11) 3733363; e-mail mla@net.sy; f. 1921; quarterly; Arabic; Islamic culture and Arabic literature, Arabic scientific and cultural terminology; Chief Editor Dr SHAKER FAHAM; circ. 1,600.

Al-Mouallem al-Arabi (The Arab Teacher): National Union of Teachers, BP 2342-3034, Damascus; tel. (11) 225219; f. 1948; monthly; Arabic; educational and cultural.

Al-Mouhandis al-Arabi (The Arab Engineer): Order of Syrian Engineers and Architects, BP 2336, Immeuble Dar al-Mouhandisen, place Azme, Damascus; tel. (11) 2214916; fax (11) 2216948; e-mail lbosea@net.sy; f. 1961; 4 a year; Arabic; scientific and cultural; Dir Eng. M. FAYEZ MAHFOUZ; Chief Editor Dr Eng. AHMAD AL-GHAFARI; circ. 50,000.

Al-Munadel (The Militant): c/o BP 11512, Damascus; fax (11) 2126935; f. 1965; monthly; Arabic; magazine of Baath Arab Socialist Party; Dir Dr FAWWAZ SAYYAGH; circ. 100,000.

Al-Nashra al-Iktissad (Economic Bulletin): Damascus Chamber of Commerce; tel. (11) 2218339; fax (11) 2225874; e-mail dcc@dcc-sy.com; f. 1922; quarterly; finance and investment; Editor GHASSAN KALLA; circ. 3,000.

Al-Sinaa (Industry): Damascus Chamber of Commerce, BP 1305, rue Mou'awiah, Harika, Damacus; tel. (11) 2222205; fax (11) 2245981; e-mail dcc@dcc-sy.com; monthly; commerce, industry and management; Editor Y. HINDI.

Souriya al-Arabiyya (Arab Syria): Ministry of Information, Immeuble Dar al-Baath, Autostrade Mezzeh, Damascus; tel. (11) 6622141; fax (11) 6617665; monthly; publicity; in four languages.

Syria Today: Baramkeh, Free Zone, Damascus; tel. (11) 88270310; fax (11) 2137343; e-mail mail@syria-today.com; internet www.syria-today.com; monthly; English; economic and social development; Chair. LOUMA TARABINE; Man. Editor FRANCESCA DE CHÂTEL.

Al-Tamaddon al-Islami (Islamic Civilization Society): Darwichiyah, Damascus; tel. (11) 2240562; fax (11) 3733563; e-mail isltmddn@hotmail.com; f. 1932; monthly; Arabic; religious; published by Al-Tamaddon al-Islami Asscn; Pres. of Asscn AHMAD MOUAZ AL-KHATIB.

Al-Yakza (The Awakening): Al-Yakza Association, BP 6677, rue Sisi, Aleppo; f. 1935; monthly; Arabic; literary social review of charitable institution; Dir HUSNI ABD AL-MASSIH; circ. 12,000.

Al-Zira'a (Agriculture): Ministry of Agriculture and Agrarian Reform, rue Jabri, Damascus; tel. (11) 2213613; fax (11) 2244023; f. 1985; monthly; Arabic; agriculture; circ. 12,000.

NEWS AGENCY

Syrian Arab News Agency (SANA): BP 2661, Baramka, Damascus; tel. (11) 2129702; fax (11) 2228265; e-mail public-relation@sana.sy; internet www.sana.sy; f. 1966; supplies bulletins on Syrian news to foreign news agencies; 16 offices abroad; 16 foreign correspondents; Dir-Gen. AHMAD DAWA.

Publishers

Arab Advertising Organization: BP 2842-3034, 28 rue Moutanabbi, Damascus; tel. (11) 2225219; fax (11) 2220754; e-mail sy-adv@net.sy; internet www.elan-sy.com; f. 1963; exclusive govt establishment responsible for advertising; publishes *Directory of Commerce and Industry*, *Damascus International Fair Guide*, *Daily Bulletin of Official Tenders*; Dir-Gen. MONA F. FABAH.

Damascus University Press: Baramkeh, Damascus; tel. (11) 2119890; fax (11) 2235779; e-mail noubough@gmail.com; internet www.damascusuniversity.edu.sy; f. 1923; medicine, engineering, social sciences, law, agriculture, arts, etc.; Dir NOUBOUGH YASSIN.

Dar al-Awael: BP 10181, Damascus; tel. (11) 44676270; fax (11) 44676273; e-mail alawael@scs-net.org; internet www.daralawael.com; f. 1999; academic publr; Dir-Gen. ISMAIL ABDULLAH.

Dar al-Fikr: BP 962, Damascus; tel. (11) 2211166; fax (11) 2239716; e-mail fikr@fikr.net; internet www.fikr.com; f. 1957; Islamic studies, academic and gen. non-fiction; Dir-Gen. MUHAMMAD ADNAN SALIM.

Institut Français du Proche-Orient: BP 344, Damascus; tel. (11) 3330214; fax (11) 3327887; e-mail secretariat@ifporient.org; internet www.ifporient.org; f. 1922; sociology, anthropology, Islamic studies, archaeology, history, language and literature, arts, philosophy, geography, religion; publs include *Syria* (bi-annual journal), *Bulletin d'Etudes Orientales* (annual journal), *Bibliotheque Archeologique et Historique* (series), *Publications de l'Instituit Français de Damas* (series); Dir FRANÇOIS BURGAT.

OFA-Business Consulting Center—Documents Service: BP 3550, 3 place Chahbandar, Damascus; tel. (11) 3318237; fax (11) 4426021; e-mail ofa1@net.sy; internet www.ofa-bcc.com; f. 1964; numerous periodicals, monographs and surveys on political and economic affairs; Dir-Gen. SAMIR A. DARWICH; has one affiliated br., OFA-Business Consulting Centre (foreign co representation and services).

The Political Administration Press: BP 3320, blvd Palestine, Damascus; fax (11) 2125280; publishes *Al-Fikr al-Askari* (six a year) and *Jaysh al-Sha'ab* (monthly).

Syrian Documentation Papers: BP 2712, Damascus; f. 1968; publishers of *Bibliography of the Middle East* (annual), *General Directory of the Press and Periodicals in the Arab World* (annual), and numerous publications on political, economic, literary and social affairs, as well as legislative texts concerning Syria and the Arab world; Dir-Gen. LOUIS FARÈS.

Tishreen Foundation for Press and Publishing: BP 5452, Medan, Damascus; tel. (11) 2131100; fax (11) 2246860; publishes *Syria Times* and *Tishreen* (dailies).

United Group for Publishing, Advertising and Marketing: Immeuble al-Huda, rue al-Eskandaria, Mazzeh, Damascus; tel. (11) 6122515; fax (11) 6122514; e-mail info@ug.com.sy; internet www.ug.com.sy; publs *Baladna* newspaper, *Layalina* magazine, *What's On* magazine; Chair. MAJD SULEIMAN.

Al-Wahda Foundation for Press, Printing and Publishing (Institut al-Ouedha pour l'impression, édition et distribution): BP 2448, Dawar Kafr Soussat, Damascus; tel. (11) 225219; internet www.alwehda.gov.sy; publs *Al-Fida'*, *Al-Horubat*, *Al-Jamahir*, *Al-Thawra* and *Al-Wahda* (dailies), *Al-Maukef al-Riadi* (weekly) and other commercial publs; Dir-Gen. FAHD DIYAB.

Broadcasting and Communications

TELECOMMUNICATIONS

Syrian Telecommunications Establishment (STE—Syrian Telecom): BP 11774, Autostrade Mezzeh, Damascus; tel. (11) 2240000; fax (11) 6110000; e-mail ste-gm@net.sy; internet www.ste.gov.sy; f. 1975; Gen. Dir Dr NAZEM BAHSAS.

MTN Syria: BP 34474, Immeuble al-Mohandis al-Arabi, Autostrade Mezzeh, Damascus; fax (11) 6666094; e-mail customercare@mtn.com.sy; internet www.mtn.com.sy; f. 2001 as Spacetel Syria; name changed to Areeba Syria in 2004; present name adopted in 2007 following the acquisition of a 75% stake by MTN Group (South Africa); provider of mobile telephone services; Chair. JAMAL RAMADAN; CEO ISMAIL JAROUDI.

Syriatel: Immeuble STE, 6e étage, rue Thawra, Damascus; tel. (11) 932190000 (mobile); fax (11) 3341917; e-mail info@syriatel.com.sy; internet syriatel.sy; f. 2000; provider of mobile telephone services; Chair. RAMI MAKHLOUF; CEO NADER KALAI; 3.5m. subscribers (2007).

BROADCASTING

Radio

General Organization of Radio and Television (ORTAS—Organisme de la Radio-Télévision Arabe Syrienne): place Omayyad, Damascus; tel. (11) 720700; fax (11) 2234930; e-mail contact@rtv.gov.sy; internet www.rtv.gov.sy; radio broadcasts started in 1945, television broadcasts in 1960; radio directorate consists of four departments: Radi, Shaab, Shabab FM, and a multilingual news service; television directorate operates one satellite and two terrestrial channels, broadcasting in Arabic, English and French; Dir-Gen. FAYEZ AL-SAYEGH; Dirs NAIF HAMMOUD (Radio), Dr FOUAD SHERBAJI (Television).

Syriana FM Radio: Damascus; f. 2012.

Television

General Organization of Radio and Television: see Radio.

Addounia TV: Damascus; tel. (11) 4472630; fax (11) 4472632; e-mail info@addounia.tv; internet www.addounia.tv; privately owned news channel; awarded broadcasting licence mid-2007; began broadcasting Oct. 2008; Gen. Man. FOUAD AL-SHARBAJI.

Talaqi TV: Damascus; f. 2012; Head MAHER AL-KHOULI.

Finance

(cap. = capital; res = reserves; dep. = deposits; m.= million; brs = branches; amounts in £S unless otherwise indicated)

BANKING

Central Bank

Central Bank of Syria (Banque Centrale de Syrie): place du 17 avril, Damascus; tel. (11) 2212642; fax (11) 2248329; e-mail info@bcs.gov.sy; internet www.banquecentrale.gov.sy; f. 1956; cap. and res 5,027m., dep. 620,946m. (Dec. 2008); Gov. Dr ADIB MAYALEH; 12 brs.

Other Banks

Agricultural Co-operative Bank: BP 4325, rue al-Tajehiz, Damascus; tel. and fax (11) 2213462; e-mail syrianagrobank@gmail.com; internet www.agrobank.org; f. 1888; cap. 10,000m., res 671m., dep. 12,000m. (Dec. 2001); Chair. Dr ABD AL-RAZZAQ KASSEM; 106 brs.

Arab Bank Syria SA (ABS): BP 38, rue al-Mahdi bin Barakeh, Abou Roumaneh, Damascus; tel. (11) 3348125; fax (11) 3349844; e-mail ali.zatar@arabbank-syria.com; internet www.arabbank-syria.com; f. 2005; jt venture between Syrian investors (51%) and Arab Bank (Jordan—49%); private commercial bank; cap. 3,180m., res 303m., dep. 36,905m. (Dec. 2010); Chair. Dr KHALID WASSIF AL-WAZANI; Gen. Man. MUHAMMAD AL-HASSAN; 9 brs.

Bank Audi Syria SA: BP 6228, Damascus; e-mail contactus.syria@banqueaudi.com; internet www.banqueaudi.com/basy/syria.html; f. 2005; 47% owned by Audi Saradar Group (Lebanon), 26% by Syrian investors, 2% by a Saudi investor; remaining 25% oversubscribed in an initial public offering in Aug. 2005; private commercial bank; cap. 5,000m., res 171m., dep. 68,114m. (Dec. 2009); Chair. GEORGES ACHI; CEO BASSEL S. HAMWI; 19 brs.

Bank of Syria and Overseas: BP 3103, Harika-Bab Barid, Lawyers' Syndicate Bldg, nr Chamber of Commerce, Damascus; tel. (11) 2460560; fax (11) 2460555; e-mail bsomail@bso.com.sy; internet www.bso.com.sy; f. 2004; jt venture between Banque du Liban et d'Outre Mer (BLOM, Lebanon—39%), the World Bank's Int. Finance Corpn (10%) and Syrian investors (51%); private commercial bank; cap. 4,000m., res 1,087m., dep. 62,132m. (Dec. 2011); Chair. Dr RATEB AL-SHALLAH; CEO AMR AZHARI; 11 brs.

Banque BEMO Saudi Fransi SA (BBSF): 39 rue Ayyar, Salhiah, Damascus; tel. (11) 2317778; fax (11) 2318778; e-mail bbsf@mail.sy; internet www.bbsfbank.com; f. 2004; jt venture between Syrian investors (51%), Banque Saudi Fransi (Saudi Arabia—27%) and Banque Européenne pour le Moyen-Orient (Lebanon—22%); private commercial bank; cap. 3,705m., res 789m., dep. 107,435m. (Dec. 2010); Chair. RIAD OBEGI; CEO NABIL HCHAIME; 22 brs.

Byblos Bank Syria: BP 5424, al-Chaalan, rue Amine Loutfi Hafez, Damascus; tel. (11) 3348240; fax (11) 3348205; e-mail byblosbanksyria@byblosbank.com; internet www.byblosbank.com.lb/aboutbbkgroup/byblosbank/bbk_sa/board/index.shtml; f. 2005; 41.5% owned by Byblos Bank SAL (Lebanon), 51% by Syrian investors and 7.5% by the Org. of Petroleum Exporting Countries' Fund for Int. Devt; private commercial bank; cap. 4,000m., res 224m., dep. 37,432m. (Dec. 2010); Chair. and Gen. Man. Dr FRANÇOIS S. BASSIL; 9 brs.

CHAM Bank: BP 33979, place al-Najmeh, Damascus; tel. (11) 3348720; fax (11) 3348731; e-mail info@chambank.com; internet www.chambank.com; f. 2006; jt venture between Dar Investment Co (Kuwait—12.5%), Commercial Bank of Kuwait (10%), Islamic Devt Bank (Kuwait—9%) and several Syrian and other Gulf investors; cap. 4,981m., res −87m., dep. 11,895m., (Dec. 2010); private commercial bank run on Islamic principles; Chair. ALI YOUSEF AL-AWADHI.

Commercial Bank of Syria (Banque Commerciale de Syrie): BP 933, place Yousuf al-Azmeh, Damascus; tel. (11) 2218890; fax (11) 2216975; e-mail cbos@mail.sy; internet www.cbs-bank.com; f. 1967; govt-owned bank; cap. US $1,616m., res $699m., dep. $13,237m. (Dec. 2009); Chair. Dr ISAM RUDWAN KHOORI; Gen. Man. AHMAD MUHAMMAD DIAB; 84 brs.

Industrial Bank: BP 7578, Immeuble Dar al-Mohandessin, rue Maysaloon, Damascus; tel. and fax (11) 2222222; e-mail info@industrialbank.gov.sy; internet www.industrialbank.gov.sy; f. 1959; nationalized bank providing finance for industry; cap. 257m., total assets 8,131m. (Dec. 2001); Gen. Man. ANIS AL-MARAWI; 17 brs.

International Bank for Trade and Finance: place Hejazz, Damascus; tel. (11) 2460500; fax (11) 2460505; e-mail info@ibtf.com; internet www.ibtf.com.sy; f. 2004; 49% owned by Housing Bank for Trade and Finance (Jordan), 51% by Syrian investors; cap. 5,000m., res 849m., dep. 68,844m. (Dec. 2010); private commercial bank; Chair. Dr MICHAEL MARTO; CEO SULTAN AL-ZU'BI; 30 brs.

Popular Credit Bank: BP 2841, 6e étage, Immeuble Dar al-Mohandessin, rue Maysaloon, Damascus; tel. (11) 2227604; fax (11) 2211291; f. 1967; govt-owned bank; provides loans to the services sector and is sole authorized issuer of savings certificates; Pres. and Gen. Man. MUHAMMAD HASSAN AL-HOUJJEIRI; 50 brs.

Real Estate Bank: BP 2337, place Yousuf al-Azmeh, Damascus; tel. (11) 2218602; fax (11) 2233107; e-mail realestate@realestate-sy.com; internet www.reb.sy; f. 1966; govt-owned bank; provides loans and grants for housing, schools, hospitals and hotel construction; cap. 10,000m., res 7,650m., dep. 197,487m. (Dec. 2010); Chair. MUHAMMAD SALEH KENG; Gen. Man. Dr MULHAM DIBO; 21 brs.

Syria International Islamic Bank: BP 35494, Damascus; tel. (11) 2241135; fax (11) 2241132; e-mail info@siib.sy; internet www.siib.sy; f. 2006; 49% Qatari-owned (incl. Qatar Int. Islamic Bank—30%); private commercial bank run on Islamic principles; cap. 5,461m., res 242m., dep. 70,427m. (Dec. 2010); Chair. YOUSUF AHMAD AL-NAAMA; CEO ABD AL-QADER AL-DUWAIK; 14 brs.

Syrian Lebanese Commercial Bank SAL (SLCB): c/o Commercial Bank of Syria, BP 933, Immeuble G.M., 6e étage, place Yousuf Azmeh, Damascus; tel. (11) 2225206; fax (11) 2243224; e-mail hamra@slcbk.com; internet www.slcb.com.lb; f. 1974; 84.2% owned by Commercial Bank of Syria, 10% by Banque du Crédit Populaire SAL, 5% by Syrian Insurance Co; head office in Beirut, Lebanon; brs in Damascus and Aleppo; cap. 125,000m., res 26,331m., dep. 516,142m. (Dec. 2009); Chair. ANTOINE FRANJIEH; 2 brs.

STOCK EXCHANGE

Six companies were listed on the Damascus Securities Exchange when it opened for trading in March 2009.

Damascus Securities Exchange: BP 6564, Damascus; tel. (11) 5190000; fax (11) 5190099; e-mail info@dse.sy; internet www.dse.sy; f. 2009; 18 listed cos (Sept. 2010); Chair. Dr RATEB AL-SHALLAH.

Supervisory Body

Syrian Commission on Financial Markets and Securities: BP 31845, Damascus; tel. (11) 3310487; fax (11) 3310722; e-mail info@scfms.sy; internet www.scfms.sy; f. 2005; Chair. MUHAMMAD AL-IMADY.

INSURANCE

A legislative decree, issued in 2005, allowed for the establishment of privately owned insurance companies.

Arabia Insurance Co—Syria (AICS): rue al-Alam, Damascus; tel. (11) 6627745; fax (11) 6627750; e-mail arabia-insurance@arabiasyria.com; f. 2006; Asst Gen. Man. ROGER COTON.

General Social Security Organization: BP 2684, rue Port Said, Damascus; tel. (11) 2316932; fax (11) 2323115; e-mail taminat@gov.sy; internet www.taminat.gov.sy; Dir-Gen. KHALAF AL-ABDULLAH.

Syria International Insurance (Arobe Syria): BP 33015, Hosari Bldg, 1st Floor, al-Brazil St, Tajheez, Damascus; tel. (11) 3348350; fax (11) 3348144; e-mail info@aropesyria.com; internet www.aropesyria.com; f. 2006; owned by Arope Insurance (Lebanon); all classes of insurance; Chair. AMR AZHARI.

Syrian General Organization for Insurance (Syrian Insurance Co): BP 2279, 29 rue Ayyar, Damascus; tel. (11) 2218430; fax (11) 2220494; e-mail syrinsur@syrian-insurance.com; internet www.syrian-insurance.com; f. 1953; auth. cap. 1,000m.; nationalized co; operates throughout Syria; Chair. ADEL AL-KADAMANI; Dir-Gen. SULAYMAN AL-HASSAN.

Syrian Kuwaiti Insurance Co: BP 5778, Immeuble 4, King Abd al-Aziz Al Sa'ud St, Abou Roumaneh, Damascus; tel. (11) 3328060; fax (11) 3328061; e-mail info@skicins.com; internet www.skicins.com; f. 2006; owned by Gulf Insurance Co of Kuwait; cap. 850m.; all classes of insurance; Chair. KHALID SAUD AL-HASSAN.

Trust Syria Insurance Co: BP 30578, Immeuble Trust, rue Murshid Khatir, Damascus; tel. (11) 4472650; fax (11) 4472652; e-mail mail@trustsyria.com; internet www.trustsyria.com; f. 2006; all classes of insurance; CEO TAHER BIN TALEB KAMAL AL-HERAKI.

United Insurance Co: BP 4419, Damascus; tel. (11) 3341933; fax (11) 3341934; e-mail info@uic.com.sy; internet www.uic.com.sy; awarded Syria's first-ever private insurance co licence in 2006; Gen. Man. MUHAMMAD AL-SABI.

Supervisory Body

Syrian Insurance Supervisory Commission (SISC): BP 5648, 5e étage, Immeuble Insurance, rue 29 mai, Damascus; fax (11) 2226224; e-mail sisc.sy@mail.sy; internet www.sisc.sy; f. 2004; Gen. Man. EYAD ZAHRA.

Trade and Industry

STATE ENTERPRISES

Syrian industry is almost entirely under state control. There are national organizations responsible to the appropriate ministry for the operation of all sectors of industry, of which the following are examples:

Cotton Marketing Organization: BP 729, rue Bab al-Faraj, Aleppo; tel. (21) 2238486; fax (21) 2218617; e-mail cmo-aleppo@mail.sy; internet www.cmo.gov.sy; f. 1965; governmental authority for purchase of seed cotton, ginning and sales of cotton lint; Pres. and Dir-Gen. Dr AHMAD SOUHAD GEBBARA.

General Company for Phosphate and Mines (GECOPHAM): BP 288, Homs; tel. (31) 2751122; fax (31) 2751123; e-mail gecopham@net.sy; internet www.gecopham.com; f. 1970; production and export of phosphate rock; Gen. Dir Eng. FARHAN AL-MOHSEN.

General Organization for Engineering Industries: BP 3120, Damascus; tel. (11) 2121834; fax (11) 2116201; e-mail g.o.eng.ind@net.sy; internet www.handasieh.org; 13 subsidiary cos.

General Organization for the Exploitation and Development of the Euphrates Basin (GOEDEB): Rakka; Dir-Gen. Dr Eng. AHMAD SOUHAD GEBBARA.

General Organization for Food Industry (GOFI): BP 105, rue al-Fardous, Damascus; tel. (11) 2457008; fax (11) 2457021; e-mail foodindustry@mail.sy; internet www.syriafoods.net; f. 1975; food-processing and marketing; Chair. and Gen. Dir KHALIL JAWAD.

General Organization for the Textile Industries: BP 620, rue al-Fardoss, Bawabet al-Salhieh, Damascus; tel. (11) 2216200; fax (11) 2216201; e-mail syr-textile@mail.syr; internet textile.org.sy; f. 1975; control and planning of the textile industry and supervision of textile manufacture; 27 subsidiary cos; Dir-Gen. Dr JAMAL AL-OMAR.

Syrian Petroleum Company (SPC): BP 2849, Damascus; tel. (11) 3137935; fax (11) 3137979; e-mail spccom1@scs-net.org; internet www.spc-sy.com; f. 1958; state agency; holds the oil and gas concession for all Syria; exploits the Al-Suweida, Karatchouk, Rumelan and Jbessseh oilfields; also organizes exploration, production and marketing of oil and gas nationally; Chair. and Man. Dir Dr Eng. OMAR AL-HAMAD.

Al-Furat Petroleum Company: BP 7660, Damascus; tel. (11) 6183333; fax (11) 6184444; e-mail afpc@afpc.net.sy; internet www.afpc-sy.com; f. 1985; 50% owned by SPC and 50% by a foreign consortium of Syria Shell Petroleum Devt B.V. and Deminex Syria GmbH; exploits oilfields in the Euphrates river area; Chair. SAID HUNEDI; Gen. Man. OLE MYKLESTAD.

DEVELOPMENT ORGANIZATIONS

State Planning Commission: Rukeneddin, Damascus; tel. (11) 5161015; fax (11) 5161010; e-mail info@planning.gov.sy; internet www.planning.gov.sy; Head AMER HOSNI LUTFI.

Syrian Consulting Bureau for Development and Investment: BP 12574, Bldg 1, 2nd Floor, cnr Zuheir Ben Abi Sulma St and ibn al-Khateeb St, Rawda, Damascus; tel. (11) 3345757; fax (11) 3340711; e-mail scb@scbdi.com; internet www.scbdi.com; f. 1991; independent; Man. Dir NABIL SUKKAR.

CHAMBERS OF COMMERCE AND INDUSTRY

Federation of Syrian Chambers of Commerce: BP 5909, rue Mousa Ben Nousair, Damascus; tel. (11) 3337344; fax (11) 3331127; e-mail syr-trade@mail.sy; internet www.fedcommsyr.org; f. 1975; Pres. GHASSAN AL-QALLA'A; Sec.-Gen. BASSAM GHRAWI.

Aleppo Chamber of Commerce: BP 1261, Aleppo; tel. (21) 2238236; fax (21) 2213493; e-mail alepchmb@mail.sy; internet www.aleppochamber.org; f. 1885; Pres. Dr HASSAN ZEIDO; Gen. Sec. MUHAMMAD MANSOUR.

Aleppo Chamber of Industry: BP 1859, rue al-Moutanabbi, Aleppo; tel. (21) 3620601; fax (21) 3620040; e-mail info@aleppo-coi.org; internet www.aleppo-coi.org; f. 1935; Pres. SALEH AL-MALLAH; Gen. Man. MUHAMMAD GHREWATI; 7,705 mems.

Damascus Chamber of Commerce: BP 1040, rue Mou'awiah, Damascus; tel. (11) 2245475; fax (11) 2225874; e-mail dcc@net.sy; internet www.dcc-sy.com; f. 1890; Pres. MUHAMMAD GHASSAN AL-QALLAA; Gen. Sec. BASSAM GHRAOUI; 11,500 mems.

Damascus Chamber of Industry: BP 1305, rue Harika Mou'awiah, Damascus; tel. (11) 2215042; fax (11) 2245981; e-mail dci@mail.sy; internet www.dci-syria.org; Pres. Eng. IMAD GHRIWATI; Sec. Eng. AYIMEN MAOULAWI.

Hama Chamber of Commerce: BP 147, rue al-Kouatly, Hama; tel. (33) 2525203; fax (33) 2517701; e-mail hamacham@scs-net.org; internet hama-chamber.org; f. 1934; Pres. HAMZEH KASSAB BASHI; Man. Dir ABD AL-RAZZAK AL-HAIT.

Homs Chamber of Commerce: BP 440, rue Abou al-Of, Homs; tel. (31) 2471000; fax (31) 2464247; e-mail hcc@homschamber.org.sy; internet www.homschamber.org.sy; f. 1928; Pres. Eng. M. ADEL TAYYARA; Gen. Man. M. FARES AL-HUSSAMY.

Latakia Chamber of Commerce and Industry: 8 rue Attar, Latakia; tel. (41) 479531; fax (41) 478526; e-mail lattakia@chamberlattakia.com; internet www.chamberlattakia.com; Pres. KAMAL ISMAIL AL-ASSAD.

Tartous Chamber of Commerce and Industry: POB 403, Tartous; tel. (43) 329852; fax (43) 329728; e-mail info@tcci-sy.com; internet tcci-sy.net; Pres. WAHIB KAMEL MERI; Gen. Man. MANAH ASSAF.

EMPLOYERS' ORGANIZATIONS

Fédération de Damas: Damascus; f. 1949.

Fédération Générale à Damas: Damascus; f. 1951; Dir TALAT TAGLUBI.

Fédération des Patrons et Industriels à Lattaquié: Latakia; f. 1953.

UTILITIES

Electricity

Public Establishment for Electricity Generation and Transmission (PEEGT): BP 3386, 17 rue Nessan, Damascus; tel. (11) 2229654; fax (11) 2229062; e-mail peegt@net.sy; f. 1965; present name adopted 1994; state-owned; operates 11 power stations through subsidiary cos; Dir-Gen. Dr AHMAD AL-ALI; Gen. Man. HISHAM MASIAJ.

Gas

Syrian Gas Company: BP 4499, Homs; tel. (31) 2451925; fax (31) 2451933; e-mail info@sgc.gov.sy; internet www.sgc.gov.sy; f. 2003; state-owned; responsible for production, processing and distribution of gas supplies; Dir-Gen. ALI ABBAS.

Water

The Ministry of Housing and Urban Development is responsible for planning and regulation in the Syrian water sector; it oversees the operations of 14 regional water establishments that manage the provision of drinking water and sewerage facilities. The Ministry of Water Resources is responsible for the management of water resources and the provision of irrigation water. An Integrated Water Resource Management Project, co-ordinated by the State Planning Commission, was initiated in 2006 with the aim of modernizing and integrating the various authorities responsible for the sector (see www.water.co.sy).

MAJOR INVESTMENT HOLDING COMPANIES

CHAM Holding: Sahnaya–Dar'a Highway, Damascus; tel. (11) 9962; fax (11) 6731274; e-mail info@chamholding.sy; internet www.chamholding.sy; f. 2007; investment holding; real estate, utilities, transport, tourism, financial services; Chair. NABIL KUZBARI.

Nahas Enterprises Group: BP 3050, Damascus; tel. (11) 2234000; fax (11) 2235004; e-mail nahasent@scs-net.org; internet www.nahas.me; f. 1900; transport, tourism, hospitality, chemicals and infrastructure; Chair. SAEB NAHAS.

Souria Holding: BP 3852, Immeuble 3, rue Misr, Abou Roumaneh, Damascus; tel. (11) 3329100; fax (11) 3316065; e-mail info@souriaholding.com; internet www.souriaholding.com; f. 2007; real estate, hospitality, retail, health care and infrastructure; Chair. HAYTHAM SOUBHI JOUD.

MAJOR COMPANIES

Fouad Takla Co: BP 2785, Immeuble Takla 15, place Arnos, Damascus; tel. (11) 4416761; fax (11) 4421910; e-mail contact@fouadtakla.com; internet www.fouadtakla.com; f. 1964; construction and devt; Man. Partner TALAL TAKLA.

Al-Matin Group: BP 1191, Homs; tel. (31) 2133092; fax (31) 2133091; e-mail marketing@almatin.com; internet almatin.com; f. 1976; mfrs of polypropylene bags, packaging materials and plastic pipes.

NASCO Group: BP 3993, Damascus; tel. (11) 3319200; fax (11) 3319220; e-mail nasco@net.sy; internet www.thenascogroup.com; f. 1988; oilfield contracting and services; five affiliate cos; Chair. NAWAR SUKKAR.

National Co for Pharmaceutical Industry (NCPI): BP 13020, Aleppo; tel. (21) 2630051; fax (21) 2630053; e-mail info@ncpipharma.com; internet www.ncpipharma.com; f. 1989; drugs mfrs; Chair. HAYSSAM AL-KAMAL.

National Sugar Co: 3e étage, Villa Garbeih, rue al-Ghazzawi, Mezzeh Ouest, Damascus; tel. (11) 6132873; fax (11) 6132860; e-mail info@nsc-sy.com; internet www.nsc-sy.com; f. 2008; sugar mfrs; CEO ANLO DU PISANI.

TRADE UNION

General Federation of Labour Unions (Ittihad Naqabat al-'Ummal al-'Am fi Suriya): BP 2351, rue Qanawat, Damascus; f. 1948; Chair. MUHAMMAD SHAABAN AZZOUZ; Sec. MAHMOUD FAHURI.

Order of Syrian Engineers and Architects: BP 2336, Immeuble al-Mohandessin, place Azmeh, Damascus; tel. (11) 2214916; fax (11) 2216948; e-mail osea@net.sy; internet www.syrianengineers.com; Pres. M. FAYEZ MAHFOUZ.

Transport

RAILWAYS

In 2010 the total length of Syrian railways was 2,139 route-km. A new railway line linking Aleppo with Mersin in southern Turkey began operating in March 2009. Another new line connecting Aleppo with Gaziantep, also in southern Turkey, was inaugurated in December; services commenced in late 2010. Meanwhile, by 2011 plans were under way for a mixed underground/elevated metro system in Damascus. Construction work on the Green Line, consisting of a 16.5-km line and 17 stations, was initially scheduled to commence in 2012, with completion anticipated by 2016. However, the project was thought to have been halted by the country's descent into civil conflict.

General Establishment of Syrian Railways: Ministry of Transport, BP 182, Aleppo; tel. (21) 2294690; fax (21) 2225697; e-mail cfs-syria@net.sy; internet www.cfssyria.org; f. 1897; Dir-Gen. GEORGE MAKABARI.

General Organization of the Hedjaz-Syrian Railway: BP 2978, rue Hedjaz, Damascus; tel. (11) 3331625; e-mail generaldirector@hijazerail.com; internet hijazerail.com; f. 1908; the Hedjaz Railway has 347 km of track (gauge 1,050 mm) in Syria; services operate between Damascus and Amman, Jordan, on a branch line of about 24 km from Damascus to Katana, and there is a further line of 64 km from Damascus to Serghaya; Dir-Gen. MAHMOUD SAQBANI.

ROADS

Arterial roads run across the country linking the north to the south and the Mediterranean to the eastern frontier. In 2010 Syria's total road network was 69,873 km, of which 45,345 km were asphalted. In mid-2009 the Government announced plans for the construction of two major new motorways: a north–south highway linking Bab al-Hawha, near the Turkish border, with Nasib, on the border with Jordan; and an east–west highway linking the Mediterranean port of Tartous with the Iraqi border.

Public Establishment for Road Communications: BP 34203, Damascus; tel. (11) 2458411; fax (11) 2452682; e-mail director-g@

perc.gov.sy; internet www.perc.gov.sy; f. 2003; Dir-Gen. Dr YOUSEF AL-HAMOUD.

SHIPPING

Latakia is Syria's principal port; it has a 972-m quay with draughts ranging from 11.8 m–13.3 m. A concession to manage and operate the container terminal at Latakia was awarded to a consortium led by the French CMA CGM Group in March 2009. Latakia handled 8.9m. tons of cargo in 2010. The other major ports are at Banias and Tartous. Tartous handled 15.4m. tons of cargo in 2010.

At 31 December 2013 Syria's flag registered fleet totalled 70 vessels, with an aggregate displacement of 99,074 grt, of which one was a bulk carrier and 45 were general cargo ships.

Regulatory and Port Authorities

General Directorate of Syrian Ports: BP 505, Algazaer St, Latakia; tel. (41) 479041; fax (41) 475805; e-mail gdp-itm@syrianport.com; internet www.syrianports.com; Dir-Gen. Rear-Adm. GHAZI HAMDAN.

Latakia Port Authority: BP 220, rue Baghdad, Latakia; tel. (41) 476452; fax (41) 475760; e-mail info@lattakiaport.gov.sy; internet www.lattakiaport.gov.sy; Gen. Man. SULEIMAN A. BALOUCH.

Syrian General Authorities for Maritime Transport (SYRIAMAR): BP 314, place Zat al-Sawary, Latakia; tel. (41) 370681; fax (41) 371013; internet syriamar.net.

Tartous Port Authority: BP 86, Tartous; tel. (43) 225150; fax (43) 315602; e-mail ta-pco@mail.sy; internet www.tartousport.com; Gen. Man. ZAKI E. NAJIB.

Principal Shipping Companies

Ismail, A. M., Shipping Agency Ltd: BP 74, rue al-Mina, Tartous; tel. (43) 221987; fax (43) 318949; operates 8 general cargo vessels; Man. Dir MAHMOUD ISMAIL.

Muhieddine Shipping Co: BP 1099, rue al-Chourinish, Tartous; tel. (43) 323090; fax (43) 317139; e-mail info@muhieddineshipping.net; internet www.muhieddineshipping.net; operates 7 general cargo ships.

Riamar Shipping Co Ltd: BP 284, Immeuble Tarwin, rue du Port, Tartous; tel. (43) 314999; fax (43) 212616; e-mail aksabra@riamar.org; operates 6 general cargo vessels; Chair. and Man. Dir ABD AL-KADER SABRA.

Al-Sham Shipping Co: BP 33436, Damascus; tel. (11) 3311960; fax (11) 3311961; e-mail al-sham@al-sham.com; internet www.al-sham.com; f. 1994; operates 2 general cargo vessels; Chair. MUHAMMAD A. HAYKAL.

Syro-Jordanian Shipping Co: BP 148, rue Port Said, Latakia; tel. (41) 471635; fax (41) 470250; e-mail syjomar@net.sy; f. 1976; operates 2 general cargo ships; Chair. OSMAN LEBBADY; Tech. Man. M. CHOUMAN.

Tartous International Container Terminal JSC: BP 870, Tartous; tel. (43) 328882; fax (43) 328831; e-mail info@ictsi.sy; internet www.ictsi-sy.com; f. 2006; owned by Int. Container Terminal Services, Inc; awarded 10-year concession to operate a container terminal at Tartous; CEO and Gen. Man. ROMEO A. SALVADOR.

CIVIL AVIATION

There are international airports at Damascus and Aleppo. Syrianair also operates domestic flights from airports in al-Qamishli and Deir el-Zor. Extensive renovation work at Deir el-Zor was completed in 2008. Damascus International Airport handled 4.2m. passengers in 2010, while Aleppo handled 0.6m. passengers in the same year.

Syrian Civil Aviation Authority (SCAA): BP 6257, place Nejmeh, Damascus; tel. (11) 3331306; fax (11) 2232201; internet www.scaasy.com; Dir-Gen. Dr WAFIK HASAN.

Cham Wings Airlines: rue al-Fardous, Damascus; tel. (11) 2244086; fax (11) 2454506; e-mail info@chamwings.com; internet www.chamwings.com; f. 2007; first private int. airline in Syria; flights from Damascus serving seven destinations in the Middle East and Europe; Chair. ISSAM SHAMMOUT.

Syrian Arab Airlines (Syrianair): BP 417, Social Insurance Bldg, 5th Floor, Youssef al-Azmeh Sq., Damascus; tel. (11) 2220700; fax (11) 224923; e-mail syr-air@syriatel.net; internet www.syriaair.com; f. 1946; refounded 1961 to succeed Syrian Airways, after revocation of merger with Misrair (Egypt); domestic passenger and cargo services (from Damascus, Aleppo, Latakia and Deir el-Zor) and routes to Europe, the Middle East, North Africa and the Far East; Chair. and Man. Dir NACHAAT NUMIR; Dir-Gen. GHAYDA ABD AL-LATIF.

Syrian Pearl Airlines: BP 31219, Damascus; tel. (11) 5010; fax (11) 3349557; e-mail info@flysyrianpearl.com; internet www.flysyrianpearl.com; f. 2008; commenced operations May 2009; 69% owned by CHAM Holding, 25% by Syrian Arab Airlines and 6% by Kuwaiti investors; domestic flights, and services to Sharm el-Sheikh (Egypt), Jeddah (Saudi Arabia) and İstanbul (Turkey); flights suspended in June 2009; Chair. Dr ABD AL-RAHMAN AL-ATTAR; CEO FINN THAULOW.

Tourism

Syria's tourist attractions include a pleasant Mediterranean coastline, the mountains, town bazaars, and the antiquities of Damascus, Aleppo and Palmyra, as well as hundreds of deserted ancient villages in the north-west of the country. According to provisional figures, an estimated 5.1m. tourists visited Syria in 2011; tourism receipts totalled US $6,190m. in 2010.

Ministry of Tourism: BP 6642, rue Barada, Damascus; tel. (11) 2210122; fax (11) 2242636; e-mail min-tourism@mail.sy; internet www.syriatourism.org; f. 1972; Counsellor to the Minister SAWSAN JOUZY; Dir of Tourism Promotion and Marketing NIDAL MACHFEJ.

Middle East Tourism: BP 201, Malki St, Shawki ave, Damascus; tel. (11) 3325655; fax (11) 3326266; e-mail daadouche@net.sy; internet www.daadouche.com; f. 1952; Pres. MAHER DAADOUCHE; 7 brs.

Syrian Arab Co for Hotels and Tourism (SACHA): BP 5549, Mezzeh, Damascus; tel. (11) 2223286; fax (11) 2219415; f. 1977; Chair. DIRAR JUMA'A; Gen. Man. ELIAS ABOUTARA.

Defence

Commander-in-Chief of the Armed Forces: Lt-Gen. BASHAR AL-ASSAD.

Minister of Defence and Deputy Commander-in-Chief of the Armed Forces: Lt-Gen. FAHD JASSEM AL-FREIJ.

Chief of Staff of the Armed Forces: Lt-Gen. ALI ABDULLAH AYYUB.

Air Force Commander: Maj.-Gen. JAMIL HASSAN.

Republican Guard Commander: Gen. MAHER AL-ASSAD.

Defence Budget (2012): est. £S243,000m.

Military Service: 30 months.

Total Armed Forces (as assessed at November 2012): 178,000 (army 110,000—including conscripts; air defence command—an army command—36,000; navy 5,000; air force 27,000); reserves 314,000 (army 280,000; air force 10,000; air defence 20,000; navy 4,000).

Education

Primary education, which begins at six years of age and lasts for six years, is officially compulsory. In 2008/09 primary enrolment included 93% of children in the relevant age-group. In 2009/10 an estimated 2,429 450 pupils were enrolled in primary education (males 1,265,470; females 1,163,980). Secondary education, beginning at 12 years of age, lasts for a further six years, comprising two cycles of three years each. In 2009/10 enrolment at secondary schools included 67% of children in the appropriate age-group. An estimated 2,625,382 pupils (males 1,338,083; females 1,287,299) were enrolled in secondary education (excluding vocational courses) in 2009/10.

There are agricultural and technical schools for vocational training, and by 2006/07 there were eight private universities and numerous private schools. In that year there were 250,000 students at state universities, 6,000 at private institutions and a further 2,500 at the Syrian Virtual University (which offers degree courses via the internet). In 2012 there were six government universities and eight private universities. The main language of instruction in schools is Arabic, but English and French are widely taught as second languages. The combined budgetary expenditure of the Ministries of Education and of Higher Education in 2008 was an estimated S£63,286m. (equivalent to some 10.5% of total government spending).

The UN Relief and Works Agency for Palestine Refugees in the Near East (UNRWA) provides education for Palestinian refugees in Syria. During the academic year 2010/11 UNRWA operated 118 schools in Syria, with a total enrolment of 66,014 pupils.

Bibliography

Abboud, Samer, and Arslanian, Ferdinand. *Syria's Economy and the Transition Paradigm*. St Andrews Papers on Contemporary Syria, Boulder, CO, Lynne Rienner Publishers, 2008.

Abboud, Samer, and Said, Salam. *Syrian Foreign Trade and Economic Reform*. Boulder, CO, Lynne Rienner Publishers, 2009.

Abd-Allah, Dr Umar. *The Islamic Struggle in Syria*. Berkeley, Mizan Press, 1984.

Abu Jaber, Kamal S. *The Arab Baath Socialist Party*. New York, Syracuse University Press, 1966.

Beshara, Adel (Ed.). *The Origins of Syrian Nationhood: Histories, Pioneers and Identity*. Abingdon, Routledge, 2011.

Chaitani, Youssef. *Post-colonial Syria and Lebanon: The Decline of Arab Nationalism and the Triumph of the State*. London, I. B. Tauris, 2007.

Commins, David. *Historical Dictionary of Syria*. Lanham, MD, Scarecrow Press, 2004.

Cordesman, Anthony H. *Israel and Syria: The Military Balance and Prospects of War*. Westport, CT, Praeger Security International, 2008.

Degeorge, Gérard. *Syrie*. Paris, Editions Hermann, 1983.

Devlin, John F. *Syria: A Profile*. London, Croom Helm, 1982.

Donati, Caroline. *L'exception syrienne: entre modernisation et résistance*. Paris, Editions La Découverte, 2009.

Dostal, Jörg Michael, and Zorob, Anja. *Syria and the Euro-Mediterranean Relationship*. St Andrews Papers on Contemporary Syria, Boulder, CO, Lynne Rienner Publishers, 2008.

Drysdale, Alastair, and Hinnebusch, Raymond A. *Syria and the Middle East Peace Process*. New York, Council on Foreign Relations, 1992.

Ehteshami, Anoush, and Hinnebusch, Raymond. *Syria and Iran: Middle Powers in a Penetrated Regional System*. London, Routledge, 1997.

Fedden, Robin. *Syria: an Historical Appreciation*. London, 1946.

Syria and Lebanon. London, John Murray, 1966.

Firro, Kais M. *Metamorphosis of the Nation (al-Umma): The Rise of Arabism and Minorities in Syria and Lebanon, 1850–1940*. Eastbourne, Sussex Academic Press, 2009.

Florence, Ronald. *Blood Libel: The Damascus Affair of 1840*. Wisconsin, University of Wisconsin Press, 2004.

George, Alan. *Syria: Neither Bread nor Freedom*. London, Zed Books, 2003.

Goodarzi, Jubin. *Syria and Iran: Diplomatic Alliance and Power Politics in the Middle East*. London, I. B. Tauris, 2009.

Haddad, Bassam. *Business Networks in Syria: The Political Economy of Authoritarian Resilience*. Palo Alto, CA, Stanford University Press, 2011.

Haddad, J. *Fifty Years of Modern Syria and Lebanon*. Beirut, 1950.

Helbaoui, Youssef. *La Syrie*. Paris, 1956.

Heydemann, Steven. *Authoritarianism in Syria: Institutions and Social Conflict, 1946–1970*. Ithaca, NY, Cornell University Press, 1998.

Heydemann, Steven, and Leenders, Reinoud (Eds). *Middle East Authoritarianisms: Governance, Contestation, and Regime Resilience in Syria and Iran*. Redwood City, CA, Stanford University Press, 2013.

Hinnebusch, Raymond E. *Authoritarian Power and State Formation in Ba'thist Syria: army, party and peasant*. Oxford, Westview Press, 1990.

Syria: Revolution From Above. Abingdon, Routledge, 2002.

Hinnebusch, Raymond E. *et al. Syrian Foreign Policy and the United States: From Bush to Obama*. St Andrews Papers on Contemporary Syria, Boulder, CO, Lynne Rienner Publishers, 2009.

Hinnebusch, Raymond E., and Schmidt, Søren. *The State and the Political Economy of Reform in Syria*. St Andrews Papers on Contemporary Syria, Boulder, CO, Lynne Rienner Publishers, 2008.

Hitti, Philip K. *History of Syria; including Lebanon and Palestine*. New York, 1951.

Hokayem, Emile. *Syria's Uprising and the Fracturing of the Levant*. London, International Institute for Strategic Studies, 2013.

Homet, M. *L'Histoire secrète du traité franco-syrien*. New edn, Paris, 1951.

Hureau, Jean. *La Syrie aujourd'hui*. Paris, Editions Afrique, 1977.

Kedar, Mordechai. *Asad in Search of Legitimacy: Messages and Rhetoric in the Syrian Press, 1970–2000*. Brighton, Sussex Academic Press, 2004.

Khatib, Line. *Islamic Revivalism in Syria: The Rise and Fall of Ba'thist Secularism*. Abingdon, Routledge, 2011.

Kienle, Eberhard (Ed.). *Contemporary Syria: Liberalization between Cold War and Cold Peace*. London, I. B. Tauris, 1994.

Lawson, Fred H. *Why Syria Goes to War: Thirty Years of Confrontation*. Cornell University Press, 1996.

(Ed.). *Demystifying Syria*. London, Saqi Books, 2009.

Lesch, David W. *The New Lion of Damascus: Bashar al-Asad and Modern Syria*. Yale University Press, 2005.

Leverett, Flynt L. *Inheriting Syria: Bashar's Trial by Fire*. Washington, DC, Brookings Institution Press, 2005.

Lloyd-George, D. *The Truth about the Peace Treaties, Vol. II*. London, 1938.

Lobmeyer, Hans Gunther. *Opposition and Resistance in Syria*. London, I. B. Tauris, 2004.

Longrigg, S. H. *Syria and Lebanon Under French Mandate*. Oxford University Press, 1958.

Ma'oz, Moshe. *Syria and Israel: From War to Peace-making*. Oxford University Press, 1995.

McGilvary, Margaret. *The Dawn of a New Era in Syria*. Reading, Garnet Publishing, 2002.

Mundy, Martha, and Saumarez Smith, Richard. *Governing Property, Making the Modern State: Law, Administration and Production in Modern Syria*. London, I. B. Tauris, 2007.

Perthes, Volker. *The Political Economy of Syria Under Asad*. London, I. B. Tauris, 1995.

Syria under Bashar al-Asad: Modernisation and the Limits of Change. Abingdon, Routledge, 2005.

Petran, Tabitha. *Syria*. London, Benn, 1972.

Pipes, Daniel. *Greater Syria: the History of an Ambition*. New York, Oxford University Press, 1990.

Provence, Michael. *The Great Syrian Revolt and the Rise of Arab Nationalism*. Austin, TX, University of Texas Press, 2005.

Rabil, Robert G. *Syria, the United States, and the War on Terror in the Middle East*. Westport, CT, and London, Praeger Security International, 2006.

Rabinovich, Itamar. *The Brink of Peace. The Israeli-Syrian Negotiations*. Princeton, NJ, Princeton University Press, 1999.

The View from Damascus: State, Political Community and Foreign Relations in Twentieth-Century Syria. London, Vallentine Mitchell & Co Ltd, 2008.

Rathmell, Andrew. *Secret War in the Middle East: The Covert Struggle for Syria, 1949-1961*. London, I. B. Tauris, 1995.

Reed, Fred A. *Shattered Images: The Rise of Militant Iconoclasm in Syria*. Vancouver, Talon Books, 2003.

Rubin, Barry. *The Truth About Syria*. London, Palgrave Macmillan, 2007.

Seale, Patrick, and Hourani, Albert. *The Struggle for Syria*. London, I. B. Tauris, 1986.

Sottimano, Aurora, and Selvik, Kjetil. *Changing Regime Discourse and Reform in Syria*. St Andrews, University of St Andrews Centre for Syrian Studies, 2008.

Springett, B. H. *Secret Sects of Syria and the Lebanon*. London, 1922.

Sunayama, Sonoko. *Syria and Saudi Arabia: Collaboration and Conflicts in the Oil Era*. London, I. B. Tauris, 2007.

Tejel, Jordi. *Syria's Kurds: History, Politics and Society*. Abingdon, Routledge, 2008.

Thubron, C. A. *Mirror to Damascus*. London, Heinemann, 1967.

Tibawi, A. L. *Syria*. London, 1962.

American Interests in Syria 1800–1901. New York, Oxford University Press, 1966.

Torrey, Gordon H. *Syrian Politics and the Military*. Ohio State University, 1964.

Van Dam, Nikolaos. *The Struggle for Power in Syria*. London, Croom Helm, 1979.

Yamak, L. Z. *The Syrian Social Nationalist Party*. Cambridge, MA, Harvard University Press, 1966.

Yildiz, Kerim. *The Kurds in Syria: The Forgotten People*. London, Pluto Press, 2005.

Zachs, Fruma. *Making of a Syrian Identity: Intellectuals and Merchants in Nineteenth-Century Beirut*. Leiden, Brill, 2005.

Zisser, Eyal. *Asad's Legacy: Syria in Transition*. London, C. Hurst & Co, 2000.

Commanding Syria; Bashar al-Asad and the First Years in Power. London, I. B. Tauris, 2006.

TUNISIA

Physical and Social Geography

D. R. HARRIS

Tunisia is the smallest of the countries that comprise the 'Maghreb' of North Africa, but it is more cosmopolitan than Algeria or Morocco. It forms a wedge of territory, 163,610 sq km (63,170 sq miles) in extent, between Algeria and Libya. It includes the easternmost ridges of the Atlas Mountains, but most of the country is low-lying and bordered by a long and sinuous Mediterranean coastline that faces both north and east. Ease of access by sea and by land from the east has favoured the penetration of foreign influences, and Tunisia owes its distinct national identity and its varied cultural traditions to a succession of invading peoples: Phoenicians, Romans, Arabs, Turks and French. It was more effectively Arabized than either Algeria or Morocco and remnants of the original Berber population are confined to a few isolated localities in the south.

At the April 1994 census the population was 8,785,364 and the overall density was 57.9 per sq km. Most of the people live in the more humid, northern part of the country, and at the 1994 census about 7.7% (674,100) lived in Tunis. At the April 2004 census the population had reached 9,910,872 and the overall density was 64.1 per sq km. The population of Tunis had increased to 728,453 (about 7.4% of the population) in 2004. Situated where the Sicilian Channel links the western with the central Mediterranean and close to the site of ancient Carthage, Tunis combines the functions of capital and chief port. No other town approaches Tunis in importance, but on the east coast both Sfax (population 294,875 in mid-2012) and Sousse (population 217,734) provide modern port facilities, as does Bizerta (population 124,957) on the north coast, while some distance inland the old Arab capital and holy city of Qairawan, now known as Kairouan (population 134,304), serves as a regional centre. Other sizeable towns include Ettadhamen (143,826) and Gabès (130,830). At mid-2012 the population had increased to an estimated 10,777,500 and the overall density was 69.7 per sq km, while the population of Tunis was estimated at 651,710. (The apparent decline in the population of Tunis is attributable to the creation of Sidi Hassine—population 79,381 at the 2004 census—as a separate municipality in August 2004.) The capital's population can sometimes be cited as much higher, owing to the designation of other large settlements, including Ariana and Ettadhamen, as suburbs.

The principal contrasts in the physical geography of Tunisia are between a humid and relatively mountainous northern region, a semi-arid central expanse of low plateaux and plains, and a dry Saharan region in the south. The northern region is dominated by the easternmost folds of the Atlas mountain system that form two separate chains, the Northern and High Tell, separated by the valley of the River Medjerda, the only perennially flowing river in the country. The Northern Tell, which is a continuation of the Algerian Tell Atlas, extends along the north coast at heights of between 300 m and 600 m. South of the Medjerda valley lies the broader Tell Atlas, which is a continuation of the Saharan Atlas of Algeria, and comprises a succession of rugged sandstone and limestone ridges. Near the Algerian frontier these reach a maximum height of 1,544 m at Djebel Chambi, the highest point in Tunisia, but die away eastward towards the Cap Bon peninsula, which extends north-east to within 145 km of Sicily.

South of the High Tell or Dorsale ('backbone') central Tunisia consists of an extensive platform sloping gently towards the east coast. Its western half, known as the High Steppe, comprises alluvial basins rimmed by low, barren mountains, but eastward the mountains give way first to the Low Steppe, a gravel-covered plateau, and ultimately to the flat coastal plain of the Sahel. Occasional watercourses cross the Steppes, but they flow only after heavy rain and usually fan out and evaporate in salt flats, or sebkhas, before reaching the sea.

The central Steppes give way southward to a broad depression occupied by two great seasonal salt lakes or shotts. The larger of these, the Shott Djerid, lies at 16 m below sea level and is normally covered by a salt crust. It extends from close to the Mediterranean coast near Gabès almost to the Algerian frontier and is adjoined on the north-west by the Shott al-Rharsa, which lies at 21 m below sea level. South of the shotts Tunisia extends for over 320 km into the Sahara. Rocky, flat-topped mountains, the Monts des Ksour, separate a flat plain known as the Djeffara, which borders the coast south of Gabès, from a sandy lowland partly covered by the dunes of the Great Eastern Erg.

The climate of northern Tunisia is Mediterranean in type, with hot, dry summers followed by warm, wet winters. Average rainfall reaches 1,500 mm in the Kroumirie Mountains, the wettest area in north Africa, but over most of the northern region it varies from 400 mm to 1,000 mm. The wetter and least accessible mountains are covered with forests in which cork oak and evergreen oak predominate, but elsewhere lower rainfall and over-grazing combine to replace forest with meagre scrub growth. South of the High Tell rainfall is reduced to between 200 mm and 400 mm annually, which is insufficient for the regular cultivation of cereal crops without irrigation, and there is no continuous cover of vegetation. Large areas of the Steppes support only clumps of wiry esparto grass, which is collected and exported for paper manufacture. Southern Tunisia experiences full desert conditions. Rainfall is reduced to below 200 mm annually and occurs only at rare intervals. Extremes of temperature and wind are characteristic, and vegetation is completely absent over extensive tracts. The country supports only a sparse nomadic population except where supplies of underground water make cultivation possible.

History

Revised by NEIL PARTRICK

PRE-COLONIAL AND COLONIAL PERIODS

In antiquity Tunisia enjoyed great prosperity under the Carthaginians and then the Romans. In the seventh century AD Arab invasions from the east destroyed Byzantine rule, and for a short time the newly established Arab city of Kairouan in central Tunisia became the centre of Arab rule in the Maghreb. Over the following centuries, despite numerous revolts by the local Berber inhabitants against successive Arab dynasties, the region was progressively Islamized and Arabized. By the end of the 15th century Tunisia became involved in the struggle between the rival Spanish and Ottoman Empires for control of the Mediterranean, and in the late 16th century Ottoman forces captured Tunis.

The Ottomans established the 'regency' of Tunis, but direct Ottoman rule was brief, with authority passing to a military caste who administered the country enjoying a large measure of autonomy from İstanbul. At the beginning of the 18th century one of these Turkish officers of Cretan origin established the Husainid dynasty, which reigned until 1957. Husainid rule brought some semblance of order, but was threatened by the growing strength of the European powers. In the early 19th century the European powers forced the *Bey* (ruler) to suppress the activities of the corsairs (pirates operating along the Barbary Coast), which had provided a considerable part of state revenues.

As France, Britain and Italy competed for influence, Tunisia tried to modernize its society and institutions, but quickly fell into debt, and in 1869 the *Bey* was obliged to accept financial control by the European powers. In order to secure its own position, particularly in the face of Italian imperial expansion, France decided on military intervention in April 1881. The French encountered no serious resistance and the Marsa Convention of 1883 formally established a French protectorate over Tunisia. The *Bey* remained the nominal ruler but, although Tunisian traditional institutions were retained, effective power passed to the French resident-general and the French administration. There was an influx of European settlers—French, Italian and Maltese—but it was not until 1931 that the French outnumbered the Italians. Nevertheless, by the last decade of French rule Europeans represented only 7% of the total population and much of Tunisian society remained intact.

INDEPENDENCE

Inspired by the nationalist movement in Egypt, the Destour (Constitution) movement was founded in 1920, calling for a self-governing constitutional regime with a Legislative Assembly. French attempts to conciliate opinion by administrative reforms failed to satisfy the more radical elements, and in 1925 the movement was dissolved. The movement was revived in the 1930s, but split when younger members formed the Néo-Destour in 1934. Under the leadership of Habib Bourguiba, a French-trained lawyer, the Néo-Destour became an effective mass party and later established an important alliance with the labour movement, the Union Générale des Travailleurs Tunisiens (UGTT, now the Union Générale Tunisienne du Travail), led by Farhat Hached. After the Second World War peaceful progress towards autonomy came to a halt owing to growing settler opposition, procrastination on the part of the French Government, and the consequent alienation of the nationalists. Tunisian resentment erupted in strikes and demonstrations in early 1952, and a wave of violence spread throughout the country. Lengthy negotiations eventually led to an accord in June 1955 granting internal autonomy to Tunisia, which was accepted by Bourguiba and a majority of the Néo-Destour, although the party reaffirmed that it would be satisfied only with complete independence. Negotiations led by Bourguiba resulted in an agreement in March 1956 under which France formally recognized the independence of Tunisia. In July 1957 the Constituent Assembly, elected immediately after the declaration of independence, voted to abolish the monarchy, proclaimed Tunisia a republic and designated Bourguiba President. Tunisian demands for the evacuation of French forces from the French base at Bizerta were rejected by the French Government, preoccupied as it was with the deteriorating situation in neighbouring Algeria. Periodic clashes, anti-French rioting and diplomatic skirmishes occurred sporadically for a number of years over the presence of French troops in Tunisia. However, following clashes between Tunisian and French forces in June 1961 around the French base at Bizerta, during which over 1,000 Tunisians were killed, new negotiations resulted in the evacuation of the base in October 1963.

BOURGUIBA ESTABLISHES HIS SUPREMACY

After independence Bourguiba set about constructing a political system that devolved from and depended on him. The authority that he was able to command derived from his successful leadership of the independence movement, and his ability to manipulate and control the political system that he created, thereby preventing the emergence of anyone who could pose a challenge to him. He quickly strengthened his control over the Néo-Destour party (renamed the Parti Socialiste Destourien—PSD—in 1964) and, by exploiting rivalries within the UGTT, brought the powerful trade union movement within the Bourguiba system. A new Constitution promulgated in June 1959 confirmed the authority of the President, who was empowered to formulate general policy, choose the members of the Government, hold supreme command of the armed forces and make all appointments to civil and military posts. In contrast, the National Assembly, elected for five years, met for only six months of the year and its role was largely limited to the ratification of policy decisions taken by the President. There was no effective cabinet and no parliamentary control. The system was in many respects a presidential monarchy, and indeed Bourguiba saw himself as assuming the position of the former *Bey*, even continuing some of the ceremonial practices of the monarchy. In presidential elections in November 1959 Bourguiba was elected unopposed, and in elections to the National Assembly all 90 seats were won by the Néo-Destour party. The Communists were unable to compete with the nationalism of the Néo-Destour and from 1963 were suppressed. Later, a new left wing emerged composed mainly of intellectuals and lacking support among the working class. Bourguiba's attempt to give a liberal interpretation to Islam led to some resistance from conservative religious forces, but Bourguiba could count on the influential writings of Islamic reformer Tahar al-Haddad, who, prior to independence, had advocated the emancipation of women. While not implementing a wholly secular political system, in 1956 Bourguiba instituted a secular-style personal status law (in contrast to the presumed civil status of Muslims under Shariah law), and abolished Shariah courts.

In 1961 Bourguiba appointed Ahmed Ben Salah as Secretary of State for Planning and Finance, and quickly added agriculture and education to his minister's responsibilities. Ben Salah embarked on an ambitious programme of reform centred on the introduction of the co-operative system in former French agricultural estates. However, the co-operatives operated at a loss, largely due to poor management, and were opposed by the peasantry and the bourgeoisie. By 1968 resistance to the new system began to increase. Ben Salah's response was to extend the agricultural co-operative system across the whole country, even though there were no funds or trained personnel to support this. By the middle of 1969, after the army fired on peasants demonstrating against the co-operatives, Bourguiba withdrew his support from Ben Salah, who was removed from office, arrested, tried and sentenced to 10 years' imprisonment.

After a brief period when the political system was opened to free discussion, Bourguiba quickly reasserted his authority within the PSD and the state. In November 1974 Bourguiba was re-elected President of the Republic and elections to the

National Assembly were uncontested, with the electorate being offered only a single party list. The new Assembly voted amendments to the Constitution allowing Bourguiba to be appointed President-for-life. As Bourguiba reasserted his authority, the coercive force of the state was increasingly deployed, targeting students and members of left-wing groups. Meanwhile, the UGTT was becoming an increasingly vocal critic of government policy and an outlet for political dissenters. It appealed for urgent changes in the method of government and an end to the use of 'intimidation' in suppressing strikes and demonstrations. In January 1978 the union organized a general strike as a warning to the Government and in retaliation for attacks on union offices. Rioting ensued in Tunis and several other cities, the army intervened and over 50 people were killed, while hundreds more were injured. Hundreds of demonstrators were arrested, tried and imprisoned and the union's Secretary-General, Habib Achour, and other members of the executive were also taken into custody and charged with subversion. The modernization project was stalling and disaffection with the system increased dramatically. In January 1980 there was an attack on the town of Gafsa in central Tunisia by guerrillas, originally estimated to number 300, although only 60 were later brought to trial. The Tunisian army quickly regained control of the town, but 41 deaths were reported. Responsibility for the attack was claimed by a hitherto unknown group, the Tunisian Armed Resistance, which declared that it aimed to free Tunisia from the 'dictatorship' of the PSD. The Tunisian Government claimed that the attackers were Tunisian migrant workers who had been trained in Libya and encouraged to make the attack in order to destabilize the Bourguiba regime. Libya denied the allegations and referred to the incident as a 'popular uprising'. The attack caused international concern, particularly in France, which sent military aircraft to Gafsa and naval vessels to the Tunisian coast. The Gafsa attack was condemned by the more established opposition groups within Tunisia, although the same groups condemned the execution of 13 of the guerrillas.

LIMITED POLITICAL LIBERALIZATION; MOUNTING UNREST

The sudden illness of Premier Hedi Nouira, Bourguiba's designated successor, in February 1980 renewed political uncertainty. In April Muhammad Mzali was appointed Prime Minister and his new Government included a member of the opposition Mouvement des Démocrates Socialistes (MDS) and three ministers who had resigned in 1977 in protest at the harsh measures taken against strikers. Most political prisoners were released during 1980, and in January 1981 a pardon was granted to nearly 1,000 members of the UGTT who had been convicted of involvement in the 1978 riots. At the same time greater tolerance was shown towards opposition groups: in mid-1980 permission was granted for the MDS to publish two weekly periodicals, and in the following February an amnesty was granted to all members of the radical Mouvement de l'Unité Populaire (MUP) except its leader-in-exile, Ben Salah. In April 1981 Bourguiba declared that he saw no objection to the emergence of political parties provided that they rejected violence and religious fanaticism and were not dependent 'ideologically or materially' on any foreign group. He promised that any group participating in legislative elections scheduled for November that gained a minimum of 5% of the votes cast would be officially recognized as a political party. In July the one-party system ended with the official recognition of the Parti Communiste Tunisien (PCT), which had been banned since 1963. In contrast, some 50 members of the Mouvement de la Tendance Islamique (MTI), established in 1981, were arrested and given prison sentences in September. Bourguiba began to perceive the rise of political Islam as the most important threat to his rule and decided that co-opting his former enemies on the left would strengthen his position and increase the stability of the regime. At parliamentary elections in November the Front national, a joint electoral pact formed by the PSD and the UGTT, won all seats in the National Assembly and gained 94.6% of votes cast; the MUP and the MDS failed to win 5% of the vote, but were finally accorded official status in November 1983.

These limited moves towards political liberalization did nothing to stop mounting domestic unrest. In January 1984 widespread rioting and looting broke out in the south of the country and quickly spread to the north, including the capital, Tunis. The Government declared a state of emergency, and troops were brought in to control street demonstrations. The resulting clashes between troops and demonstrators left 89 people dead and 938 injured, according to official figures, and more than 1,000 people were arrested. After a week of disturbances Bourguiba intervened to reverse the increases in the price of bread and other staple foods that had prompted the disturbances, and order was re-established.

Throughout 1984 and 1985 a series of strikes by public sector workers took place and the confrontation between the Government and the UGTT intensified. In October 1985 the union's Secretary-General, Achour, who had been released in December 1981, was again arrested and imprisoned. The appointment in April 1986 of a senior military officer and former head of military security, Gen. Zine al-Abidine Ben Ali, as Minister of the Interior, was considered a significant change in domestic policy. Bourguiba had always been suspicious of the armed forces and ensured that they were kept out of politics. In July Mzali was replaced as premier by Rachid Sfar (previously Minister of Finance) and dismissed as PSD Secretary-General. Mzali subsequently fled the country, but was sentenced *in absentia* to four years' imprisonment and 15 years' hard labour. New parliamentary elections in November were boycotted by all the opposition parties and once again the PSD won all the seats in the Assembly.

SUPPRESSION OF ISLAMIST ACTIVISTS

By 1987 the Government had consolidated its control over the UGTT, and left-wing militancy was no longer perceived as a threat. 'Islamic fundamentalism', meanwhile, was regarded as the greatest threat to the regime. Certainly, the failure of Bourguiba's economic policies, the fast pace of modernization and international events all contributed to the rise of political Islam. The movement was dominated by the MTI, but also included other smaller but more radical groups whose precise relationship to the MTI was unclear. The early months of 1987 saw a crackdown on Islamists, scores of whom were arrested for a number of offences, including terrorism. In March the Secretary-General of the MTI, Sheikh Rachid Ghannouchi, was arrested on charges of violence and collusion with foreign powers to overthrow the Government. Relations with Iran soured and Iranian diplomats in Tunis were accused of inciting terrorism and helping to plan the overthrow of Bourguiba. On this pretext, another series of arrests of Islamists ensued. According to the authorities, 1,500 people were detained, although opposition parties estimated that the total reached more than 3,000. In May the Government approved the creation of the Association for the Defence of Human Rights and Public Liberty, as a rival to the independent Ligue Tunisienne des Droits de l'Homme (LTDH), which the Government accused of favouring the MTI. In June 37 Islamists, mostly students, were sentenced to terms of imprisonment of between two and six years for taking part in illegal demonstrations in April and for defaming Bourguiba. After 13 foreign tourists were injured by bomb explosions in Sousse and Monastir in August, the Government promptly insisted that the MTI was responsible, even though a radical group, Islamic Jihad, had claimed responsibility. Six young Tunisians later confessed to planting the bombs, and stated that they were members of the MTI. They alleged that the bombings were part of an operation to damage the tourist industry on which Tunisia depended. In September the trial opened of 90 Islamists accused of threatening state security and plotting against the Government. Despite the prosecution's demand that all 90 defendants should receive the death penalty, only seven were sentenced to death, five of them *in absentia*. Fourteen defendants were acquitted and 69 (including Ghannouchi) received prison sentences.

FOREIGN RELATIONS UNDER BOURGUIBA

Although relations with France were strained during the first decade of independence, by the early 1970s France had become a major source of financial assistance to Tunisia, and on his first official visit to Paris in July 1972 Bourguiba paid eloquent tribute to the former colonial power. Links with the USA, established before independence when the Tunisian nationalists enjoyed the support of the American labour movement, were strengthened, and the USA became another major source of financial aid. Bourguiba refused to subscribe to the conventional view that the USA was an 'imperialist' power in the Middle East, and this reinforced the USA's view of Tunisia as a friendly, moderate regime. In the Arab world Bourguiba was critical of the leadership of President Nasser of Egypt and Nasserist policies were described by his Minister of Foreign Affairs as 'micro-imperialism'. After a visit to Palestinian refugee camps in Jordan in 1965, Bourguiba expressed strong support for the Palestinian cause but controversially also called for direct negotiations with Israel on the basis of the UN partition plan for Palestine of 1947. Tunisia refused to participate in meetings of the League of Arab States (the Arab League) and severed diplomatic relations with Egypt.

However, the war between Israel and the Arab states in June 1967 led to immediate reconciliation with the Arab world. The Arab states' humiliating defeat led to a wave of demonstrations in Tunisia in support of Nasser and pan-Arabism, and there were a number of hostile actions against Tunisia's small Jewish community, which had traditionally enjoyed good relations with its Muslim neighbours. A number of Jews had held cabinet posts in the early years after independence. Diplomatic relations with the United Arab Republic (as Egypt continued to be known despite the earlier collapse of its union with Syria and Iraq) were restored, and although Bourguiba warned of the dangers of renewed warfare in the Middle East, he accepted that armed struggle was the only option open to the Palestinians and reaffirmed Tunisia's support for the Palestine Liberation Organization (PLO). Tunisia sent a small military force to Egypt during the October War of 1973 and gave active diplomatic support for the Arab cause. However, after Egypt signed a peace treaty with Israel in 1979, Tunisia severed diplomatic relations with Cairo. The Arab League imposed a political and economic boycott on Egypt and transferred its headquarters from Cairo to Tunis. When Israel invaded Lebanon in 1982 and destroyed the PLO's political and military base in Beirut, Tunisia allowed the organization to establish new headquarters in Tunis, drawing Tunisia more deeply into the Arab–Israeli conflict. In 1985 the Israeli air force attacked the PLO headquarters in Tunis, killing some 60 people and injuring many more, some of them Tunisian civilians. The raid was in retaliation for the murder of a number of Israelis in Cyprus by Palestinian guerrillas a month earlier.

Relations between Tunisia and its wealthy eastern neighbour, Libya, remained close but uneasy and often tense, so there was widespread surprise when in January 1974, at a meeting in Djerba, Bourguiba and Libyan leader Muammar al-Qaddafi signed an agreement to establish a union between their two countries. The agreement was signed when Prime Minister Nouira was out of the country and on his return Bourguiba made a tactical retreat and his Minister of Foreign Affairs, Muhammad Masmoudi, who had played a key role in the agreement, was dismissed and went into exile. After the abortive union, relations between the two countries became strained. One source of contention was the delimitation of their respective sectors of the continental shelf in the Gulf of Gabès, in which important deposits of petroleum were to be found. In June 1977 both sides agreed to submit to arbitration by the International Court of Justice (ICJ), and agreement was finally reached in February 1982. Relations declined further in August 1985, following Qaddafi's decision to expel some 30,000 Tunisian migrants working in Libya and in September Tunisia severed diplomatic relations with Libya, following the expulsion of four Libyan diplomats who had been accused of sending letter-bombs to Tunisian journalists. It was not until late 1987 that Tunisia announced that the dispute with Libya was over. Consular links were resumed the following month when the border between the two countries was reopened.

Earlier, in 1983 the demarcation of the frontier with Algeria was one of the issues discussed at a meeting between Bourguiba and President Chadli of Algeria. The two leaders agreed on closer co-operation and, together with Mauritania, subsequently signed the Maghreb Fraternity and Co-operation Treaty.

BEN ALI TAKES OVER FROM BOURGUIBA

During the second half of 1987 Bourguiba's behaviour became increasingly erratic. Reports emerged that he was demanding the retrial of the Islamists who had been sentenced in September, with the aim of having the death sentence imposed on all 90 defendants. A disagreement about the fate of the Islamists allegedly ensued between Bourguiba and Ben Ali, who had been appointed Prime Minister in October. In early November seven doctors declared that Bourguiba was unfit to govern, owing to senility and ill health, and in accordance with the Constitution, Ben Ali was sworn in as President. There was no apparent opposition to Ben Ali's takeover, which had been approved in advance by the majority of ministers and senior military officers.

On assuming power President Ben Ali immediately began a policy of national reconciliation, ordering the release of a large number of political and non-political prisoners, including Ghannouchi and other leading members of the MTI, and the MDS leader, Ahmad Mestiri, while Ben Salah was pardoned and returned to Tunisia from exile. Ben Ali also promised to increase political freedom and introduce a more democratic system of government, which would see the emergence of a truly competitive multi-party system. Under amendments to the Constitution, the post of President-for-life was abolished; the President was to be elected every five years and limited to two consecutive terms in office. In April 1988 the National Assembly passed legislation instituting a multi-party-system, although in order to gain legal recognition, political parties had to uphold the aims of, and work within, the Constitution, and were not permitted to pursue purely religious, racial, regional or linguistic policies. In July the National Assembly modified the Press Code, relaxing some of its repressive clauses. In the same month Tunisia became the first Arab country to ratify the UN convention against torture and other inhuman or degrading treatment. Ben Ali restated his desire to 'open a new page of pluralism and democracy' and began consultations with opposition parties, the UGTT, employers' organizations and youth and women's groups, which led to the announcement of a National Pact in September. Basic freedoms were guaranteed, although political parties could be formed only with the approval of the Minister of Interior. The leftist Rassemblement Socialiste Progressiste (RSP) and the liberal Parti Social pour le Progrès, together with the newly formed Union Démocratique Unioniste (UDU), were all granted legal recognition. Relations with the Islamists improved. The authorities emphasized Tunisia's Arab and Islamic identity. Nevertheless, the MTI, now transformed into a political party and with a new name, Hizb al-Nahdah—or Parti de la Renaissance—was denied official status.

Meanwhile, the ruling party changed its name to the Rassemblement Constitutionnel Démocratique (RCD), and at its first congress Ben Ali was re-elected party Chairman, despite speculation that he would relinquish his party post, and Prime Minister Hedi Baccouche was appointed Vice-Chairman. In parliamentary elections in April 1989, the first multi-party elections for almost a decade, the RCD won all 141 seats, with 80% of the votes cast. Hizb al-Nahdah, forbidden from campaigning as a party, presented 'independent' candidates in 19 of the 25 constituencies, taking 13% of total votes and 25% of votes in many constituencies (30% in Tunis) and replacing the MDS as the main opposition force. Ben Ali was confirmed as President by a reassuring 99% of voters. After the elections Ghannouchi went into voluntary exile in Paris and Abd-al-Fattah Mourou, a lawyer, assumed the leadership of al-Nahdah within Tunisia. In December a second application by the party for official recognition was refused, although the party was permitted to publish limited numbers of a weekly journal, *Al-Fajr*. Critics of Ben Ali argued that the National Pact and the relaxation of the restrictive measures in place were simply a device for him to bide his time and strengthen his authoritarian grip on power.

SUPPRESSION OF THE ISLAMIST MOVEMENT

Following their failure to secure legal recognition, the Islamists increased their political agitation, particularly in universities. In December 1989 96 students began a hunger strike after the Government tried to divide its opponents by dissolving the Theological Faculty of Zitouna University. A campus police station in Kairouan was ransacked, and casualties were reported on the campus in Sfax. In February 1990 the protests culminated in clashes between police and students belonging to the Union Générale des Étudiants de Tunisie (UGET), an organization considered close to al-Nahdah. About 600 student activists were detained. The Government accused al-Nahdah of exploiting the students and of inciting unrest among the work-force, including a strike by 10,000 municipal workers. Political tension increased following severe floods in January 1990, which killed 30 people and caused widespread damage to property. Some 800 demonstrators, incited by Islamist leaders who condemned the Government's dilatory relief efforts, attacked government offices in Sidi Bouzid, and 26 were arrested. Al-Nahdah, together with the six legal opposition groups, boycotted municipal elections in June on the grounds that they were neither free nor fair. Despite a change in the electoral law under which the winning party gained only 50% of the seats, while the remaining seats were divided between all the parties according to the number of votes received, the RCD won control of all but one of the 245 municipal councils. In November several members of al-Nahdah were arrested, following the discovery of explosives that were allegedly to have been used for terrorist activities. Al-Nahdah's senior officials denied that the movement was involved in terrorism, although some independent reports claimed that the party had a military wing. In December senior officials of al-Nahdah were arrested, together with more than 100 other people, and accused of attempting to establish an Islamic state. In February 1991 there was an armed attack on RCD offices in Tunis, in which a caretaker was burned to death. The authorities stated that al-Nahdah had planned the attack, and Ghannouchi appeared to condone it by stating that the violence was in response to state violence. Five Islamists were later sentenced to death for their part in the attacks and three were subsequently executed.

The crackdown on the Islamist movement intensified. The UGET was disbanded by the authorities after the police claimed to have found weapons and subversive material linked to al-Nahdah. In May 1991 some 300 people, including about 100 members of the security forces, were arrested in connection with an alleged Islamist plot. The success of the Front Islamique du Salut in the first round of parliamentary elections in Algeria in December encouraged the Tunisian authorities to redouble their efforts against the Islamists. Suppression of al-Nahdah continued with widespread arrests and a large security presence on the streets. In July 1992 almost 200 alleged al-Nahdah members were put on trial for plotting to take power by force. In August the courts announced long prison sentences for the defendants. Among those receiving life sentences were three exiled al-Nahdah leaders, Ghannouchi, Salah Karkar and Habib Mokni. It was claimed that Ghannouchi had received funds from the Governments of Iran, Sudan and Saudi Arabia to overthrow the Tunisian regime and was organizing a violent Islamist revolution. These mass trials were seen as the culmination of the Tunisian Government's long campaign against al-Nahdah, whose organizational structures within the country were largely destroyed and its leaders imprisoned or forced into exile, mainly in Europe. The Minister of the Interior claimed that 'a Tunisian terrorist network' had been completely dismantled.

THE 1994 ELECTIONS: BEN ALI RE-ELECTED FOR A SECOND TERM

In preparation for presidential and parliamentary elections in March 1994, changes were made to the electoral system. The number of seats in the National Assembly was increased from 141 to 163, of which 144 were to be contested according to the existing majority list or 'first past the post' system, with the remaining 19 seats distributed among the parties that did not secure a majority in the constituencies according to their proportion of the vote at the national level. All six legal opposition parties accepted the new system and indicated that they would participate in the elections. Their acceptance of the extremely modest and largely cosmetic electoral reform measures were an indication of the weakness of the legal and secular opposition parties, reduced to an obedient official opposition to the ruling RCD.

The elections themselves brought few surprises. President Ben Ali was elected for a second term, winning 99.9% of the vote, according to official sources, which also reported that 94.9% of eligible voters had participated in the election. Abderrahmane el-Hani, a lawyer and leader of a political party not recognized by the Government, and Moncef Marzouki, the former President of the LTDH and a persistent critic of the regime's human rights record, had both been arrested after announcing their intention to stand for the presidency. In parliamentary elections the RCD swept to victory, winning 97.7% of the vote and taking all 144 seats allocated under the majority list system. The legal opposition secured only 2.3% of the vote, but, under the new electoral formula, was allocated 19 'guaranteed' seats.

In early October 1995, the day after the MDS made public a letter sent to Ben Ali by its leader, Muhammad Mouada, in which he complained that measures to control society were worse under Ben Ali than during Bourguiba's presidency, Mouada was arrested and charged with maintaining secret contacts with foreign agents, endangering the country's security and accepting money from a foreign country. The security forces claimed to have found documents at his home that indicated he had received substantial sums of money from Libya. A Libyan informer alleged that the payments were for secret political and military information about Tunisia. In November Khemais Chamari, the deputy leader of the MDS, was stripped of his parliamentary immunity in order to allow charges (relating to Mouada's trial) to be brought against him. In February 1996 Mouada was sentenced to 11 years in prison. Chamari was detained in May, and in July was sentenced to five years' imprisonment for breaching security proceedings relating to Mouada's trial. Both men denied the charges. Mouada's arrest and detention provoked a bitter struggle for leadership in the MDS, further weakening the party. In December, however, Mouada and Chamari were granted a conditional release, but remained under police surveillance. A year later Mouada was rearrested and subsequently charged with attempting to destabilize the regime in alliance with a 'terrorist network'.

CONSTITUTIONAL CHANGES

Towards the end of 1997 a number of political reforms aimed at 'strengthening democracy' that had first been announced by Ben Ali in 1996 were approved by the National Assembly and incorporated into the Constitution. They included a guarantee that: opposition parties would be given at least 20% of the seats in the National Assembly; no party was to be allowed to hold more than 80% of seats on municipal councils; the minimum age of parliamentary candidates was to be reduced from 25 to 23 years; citizens with Tunisian mothers (in addition to those with Tunisian fathers) were to be allowed to stand for parliament; all political parties would have to respect republican values, human rights and the rights of women and not be based on religion, language, race or region or have links with foreign countries; and the President was to be allowed to hold a referendum on issues of national importance.

Early in 1999 parliament approved a further amendment to the Constitution, whereby the number of candidates eligible to stand for president was increased. Under the terms of the amendment leaders of opposition parties could stand for the presidency provided they had led their party for five consecutive years, and that their party had at least one seat in the Chamber of Deputies. Previously, candidates for the presidency had to obtain the support of 30 members of parliament or mayors, which effectively disqualified all those who were not nominees of the ruling RCD.

BEN ALI'S THIRD PRESIDENTIAL TERM

In Tunisia's first contested presidential election since independence, held on 24 October 1999, two candidates opposed Ben Ali: Abderrahmane Tlili, Secretary-General of the UDU, and Muhammad Belhadj Amor, Secretary-General of the PUP. They obtained less than 1% of the total vote between them. Ben Ali's victory was never in doubt—he won 99.4% of the vote—and the other two candidates gave the illusion of political pluralism. In parliamentary elections held at the same time, the ruling RCD swept to victory, securing 91.6% of votes cast and winning all 148 of the contested seats in the National Assembly. Of the 34 seats reserved for the opposition parties and distributed according to the number of votes gained, the MDS received 13, the UDU seven, the PUP seven, the Mouvement Ettajdid five and the Parti Social Libéral (PSL), represented for the first time, two. Thus, despite the President's declaration that the elections heralded a new order of multi-party politics, the ruling RCD retained a massive majority in the new Assembly, although Tunisian and international observers declared the elections to have been free and fair.

Ben Ali was sworn in as President on 15 November 1999, and declared that the task of reducing unemployment would be his 'priority of priorities', promised new legislation to ensure greater transparency in the electoral process and to guarantee freedom of the press, and pledged to strengthen the judicial system to improve the protection of human rights, and to reform the education system and the administration.

Shortly after the elections Ben Ali appointed Muhammad Ghannouchi as Prime Minister in place of Hamed Karoui, who had held the premiership for a decade. Ghannouchi, who had been the Minister of International Co-operation and Foreign Investment since 1992, was an economist with wide experience in economic planning, finance and investment and in negotiations with the major international financial agencies.

In November 1999 Ben Ali released 600 political prisoners as part of an amnesty under which some 1,800 prisoners were freed and another 1,200 had their sentences reduced. Most of the freed political prisoners were members of al-Nahdah, but they also included some members of the banned Parti Communiste des Ouvriers Tunisiens (PCOT). Meanwhile, Abderraouf Chamari, formerly deputy leader of the MDS and a leading human rights activist, who had been sentenced to one year in prison for allegedly slandering the authorities, was released after only two months of his sentence, and shortly afterwards Khemais Ksila, Vice-President of the LTDH, sentenced to three years' imprisonment in early 1998, was also released. Early in 2000 the former MDS leader, Mouada, was released from house arrest.

In April 2000 Taoufik Ben Brik, a Tunisian national and Tunis correspondent for the Swiss daily *La Croix* and several other European newspapers, began a 42-day hunger strike in protest at police harassment. The repercussions of the Ben Brik affair were felt in government circles. Ben Ali quickly replaced Dali Jazi, Minister-delegate to the Prime Minister in charge of Human Rights, Communications and Relations with the National Assembly, with Afif Hendaoui and also made changes among senior staff at the ministry of information, in the state-controlled media and at the official press agency. At the same time the President replaced some senior military officers including Gen. Salah Laouani, head of the Brigades d'Ordre Publique, and Gen. Gmati, Commander of the National Guard, who had both been closely involved in Ben Ali's takeover in 1987.

During a visit to London, United Kingdom, in June 2000 Marzouki announced that a national democratic conference was planned for early December to lay the foundations for a democratic state in Tunisia within a decade. Marzouki, now the spokesman for the Conseil National des Libertés en Tunisie (CNLT), a grouping of some 35 Tunisian dissidents, founded in late 1998 but officially banned, expressed the hope that members of al-Nahdah would participate in the proposed conference, thus bringing together the hitherto divided secular and Islamist opponents of the Ben Ali regime. In July Marzouki was dismissed from his university post after publicly criticizing the Tunisian authorities during a visit to Europe. Marzouki received a one-year prison sentence in December, having been convicted of belonging to an illegal organization and disseminating false information.

In November 2000 President Ben Ali announced a series of initiatives aimed at furthering the democratization process and promoting human rights in Tunisia. The measures included: state compensation to anyone taken into custody or imprisoned unlawfully and later found to be innocent; improved access to legal aid; legislation to improve conditions in the country's prisons and to guarantee prisoners' rights; the transfer of responsibility for the prison system to the Ministry of Justice from the Ministry of the Interior; a revised press code reducing censorship and prosecution of journalists without good reason, removing imprisonment for infringements of the code, and removing the charge of 'defamation of public order'. In return for these changes the President called on journalists and publishers to prepare a code of ethics in order to protect journalism from excesses.

In a reshuffle of the Council of Ministers in January 2001 President Ben Ali replaced the Minister of the Interior, Abdallah Kallel, with the Government Secretary-General, Abdallah Kaâbi. Dali Jazi succeeded Muhammad Jegham as the Minister of National Defence. In February Slaheddine Maâoui, the former Minister of Tourism, Leisure and Handicrafts, was appointed to the sensitive post of Minister-delegate to the Prime Minister in charge of Human Rights, Communications and Relations with the National Assembly, where he replaced Afif Hendaoui, who had only held the post from mid-2000. Although there were few changes to senior ministerial posts, the number of under-secretaries was increased from 12 to 24. Most of those appointed to these posts were less than 40 years old and were university graduates brought in to improve the Government's management of the economy and to accelerate the pace of economic reform. At the same time a number of changes were made to the RCD's political bureau: the Prime Minister, Muhammad Ghannouchi, became a member, Ali Chaouch returned to the post of Secretary-General and Muhammad Jegham was replaced by Dali Jazi.

In mid-January 2001 a Tunisian living in exile in Switzerland began legal proceedings against Kallel, the former Minister of the Interior, who was receiving medical treatment in Geneva, Switzerland, at that time, on the grounds that he had been tortured in the Ministry of the Interior in 1992. However, by the time the Swiss police began to investigate the allegations, Kallel had left the country. Shortly afterwards Ben Ali appointed Kallel to the post of presidential councillor.

In March 2001 almost 100 moderate political figures signed a petition denouncing President Ben Ali's plans to amend the Constitution to allow him a fourth term in office, accusing him of corruption and nepotism. Meanwhile, al-Nahdah released a joint communiqué with a dissident faction of the MDS, led by Mouada, in which they proposed a National Democratic Front of opposition groups, uniting Islamists and liberals against the Ben Ali regime. On 19 June Mouada was arrested and imprisoned for allegedly breaking the terms of his conditional release, imposed in December 1996.

In late April 2001 President Ben Ali instructed the Ministry of the Interior to investigate all alleged abuses by the security forces against Tunisian citizens and to ensure that those found guilty were punished. The following month the President gave an increasingly rare interview to a Tunisian newspaper, in which he expressed his commitment to accelerating the pace of democratic change and reaffirmed that those responsible for human rights abuses would be brought to justice. To reinforce his message, the President made various conciliatory gestures, ordering the release of a number of political prisoners. At the same time a court ruled that the LTDH could resume its activities. Under revisions to the press code announced in May, the offence of 'defamation of public order' was abolished, together with prison sentences for some violations of the code. However, the changes did little encourage freedom of expression, with the regime maintaining tight surveillance over the local press and foreign publications.

In June 2001 Trifi, President of the LTDH, launched a campaign calling for a general amnesty law, an initiative that was supported by Marzouki and a former Minister of Education, Muhammad Charfi, and later by the Secretary-General of the UGTT, Abdessalem Jerad. In early July Judge

Mokhtar Yahyaoui addressed an open letter to President Ben Ali condemning the pressure exerted by the regime on judges, forcing them to give judgments 'dictated in advance, to which there was no appeal and which were not in accordance with the law'. This was the first time that a senior member of the judiciary had spoken out publicly in this way, and his remarks commanded particular attention as Yahyaoui was unaffiliated to any political party or group and had a reputation for integrity and professionalism. Yahyaoui was suspended from duty and deprived of his salary, and in December was dismissed from his post. The Association des Magistrats Tunisiens, which in May had passed a resolution calling for the independence of the judiciary, issued a communiqué expressing support for Judge Yahyaoui. At the end of July, in a speech marking the 44th anniversary of the Republic, Ben Ali stressed the importance of applying the law and of punishing those who disregarded it in the name of democracy and civil liberties, and rejected demands for the release of opponents of the regime and an end to the prosecution of others. At the end of September the RCD's central committee nominated Ben Ali as the party's official candidate for the 2004 presidential election.

In October 2001, in an interview with *Le Monde*, Kamel el-Taief, a former political adviser to Ben Ali and until the early 1990s a close ally, spoke out against the Ben Ali regime, stating that the country was ruled by a 'mafia' linked to the President's family and that Tunisians were scandalized by the widespread corruption and angered by the lack of civil liberties. He claimed that opposition existed within the regime, and that even some ministers were opposed to the Ben Ali 'clique' and the ruling party. El-Taief was arrested in November and sentenced to one year's imprisonment in February 2002. Shortly before President Jacques Chirac of France visited Tunis in December 2001, the Tunisian authorities decided to lift the travel restrictions imposed on Marzouki to enable him to leave Tunisia to take up a university post in France.

In February 2002, after spending some four years in hiding from the police, Hamma Hammami, leader of the PCOT, and two other party members were brought before a Tunis court. The three men had come out of hiding to protest against the nine-year prison sentences imposed on them *in absentia* in 1999 for belonging to a banned political party. Nevertheless, the court confirmed the original sentences and sentenced one of the men, Samir Taamallah, to an additional two years' imprisonment for contempt of court. In March 2002 the Court of Appeal reduced the sentences to 38 months for Hammami and 21 months for his two associates. Hammami was not included in the group of prisoners granted a presidential pardon on the 25 July, the anniversary of independence.

In January 2002, following the arrest in Belgium of Tarak Maaroufi, a Tunisian with Belgian citizenship, on suspicion of being a key member of Osama bin Laden's al-Qa'ida terrorist network in Europe, Walid Bennani, President of al-Nahdah's Consulative Committee, wrote to the Belgian Minister of Justice stating that Maaroufi had never been a member of the banned Tunisian Islamist party and strongly denying claims by the Tunisian regime of links between al-Nahdah and al-Qa'ida. In February three men were brought before a military tribunal in Tunis accused of having links with al-Qa'ida. Some 31 other suspects were being tried *in absentia*, including Sami Essed Ben Khemaies, a Tunisian awaiting trial in Italy on charges of being the leader of the Milan cell of the Groupe Salafiste pour la Prédication et le Combat (GSPC—renamed 'the al-Qa'ida Organization in the Land of the Islamic Maghreb', or AQIM, in early 2007—see the chapter on Algeria), which provided logistical support for, and was preparing terrorist attacks in Europe on behalf of, al-Qa'ida.

On 11 April 2002 a tanker lorry exploded outside the Ghriba synagogue on the island of Djerba in south-eastern Tunisia, killing 21 people, most of them German tourists, and wounding 20 others. The synagogue was one of the main tourist sites on the island, a popular destination for European holidaymakers. At first the Tunisian Government insisted that the explosion was an accident, but the German authorities, who sent police investigators to the scene, were convinced that it was a suicide bomb attack linked to events in the Middle East. Several days later the Tunisian authorities admitted that it had been a 'premeditated criminal act'. Shortly afterwards two Arabic newspapers based in London claimed that al-Qa'ida was responsible for the suicide bomb attack, its first operation since the 11 September 2001 suicide attacks on the USA. German police were investigating contacts between a suicide bomber, Nizar Ben Muhammad Nasr Nawar, alias Saif al-Din al-Tunissi, a young Tunisian employed by a foreign tourist agency in Djerba, and a German national arrested near Duisburg. In June 2002 the Qatar-based television station Al Jazeera broadcast a statement by Sulayman Abu Ghaith, spokesman for al-Qa'ida, confirming that the attack was carried out by a young member of al-Qa'ida 'who could not see his Palestinian brothers killed while Jews walked freely in Djerba to enjoy themselves and practise their religion'. At the same time as the attack in Djerba, the synagogue at La Marsa in the capital was vandalized and another synagogue in the southern city of Sfax was desecrated by a gang of youths who had joined a demonstration in the city in support of the Palestinians. Arrests of alleged accomplices of the Tunisian suicide bomber continued in Europe in the early months of 2003.

In late April 2002, two weeks after the tanker bomb attack on the Djerba synagogue, President Ben Ali replaced the Minister of the Interior and the Director of National Security, the two most senior officials responsible for internal security. Hedi M'henni, hitherto Minister of Social Affairs, replaced Kaâbi at the Ministry of the Interior, and Muhammad Hedi Ben Hassine, a retired general and former director of military security, replaced Ali Ganzaoui as head of national security. At its congress held in Djerba in the previous month the UGTT had pledged to re-establish its independence from the Ben Ali regime, to encourage links with other civil society groups, and to promote greater democracy within the organization itself. Delegates expressed solidarity with the strike by the lawyers' association, called for respect for civil liberties, expressed support for the embattled LTDH, and demanded an end to legal proceedings against PCOT leader Hamma Hammami. However, the Secretary-General, Abdessalem Djerad, later declared that Ben Ali could count on the support of workers and trade unionists in his efforts 'to consolidate the foundations of the Republican regime'.

FURTHER CONSTITUTIONAL CHANGES

In November 2001, in a speech marking the 14th anniversary of his accession to power, Ben Ali announced what he termed a 'fundamental reform' of the Constitution, although he gave few details of the proposed changes. Most commentators concluded that Ben Ali was determined to secure a fourth mandate and that the proposed changes would probably include increasing the number of presidential candidates, so as to lend greater credibility to the 2004 elections, and the addition of a clause devoted to upholding human rights and liberties. The Parti Démocrate Progressiste (PDP), the dissident faction of the MDS not represented in parliament, together with the unrecognized Forum Démocratique pour le Travail et les Libertés (FDTL), led by Dr Mustapha Ben Jafaâr, and the Congrès pour la République, founded by Marzouki, set up a 'democratic co-ordination committee' to campaign against a fourth mandate for Ben Ali and to press for an amnesty for political prisoners, freedom of expression and the independence of the judiciary. In December the PUP became the first legal opposition party to express support for Ben Ali's candidature. In February 2002 the Chamber of Deputies met in special session to examine proposals for revisions to the Constitution prepared by a team of experts headed by Abdelaziz Ben Dhia, special adviser to the President. The proposed revisions included: the creation of a second chamber, the Chamber of Advisers, to ensure better representation of the regions and professional bodies; and the removal of restrictions on the number of times the presidential mandate could be renewed. Presidential elections would involve more than one candidate. After discussions in the Chamber of Deputies the revisions would be put to a referendum, which Ben Ali announced would be held in conditions of transparency with observers and journalists from neighbouring and friendly countries allowed to monitor the proceedings. Legal political parties taking part in the referendum campaign would benefit from financial assistance and access to radio and television. The opposition Mouvement Ettajdid's political bureau deplored the fact that the proposals had been presented to parliament without prior consultation with opposition parties or civil society, and later was the only party represented in parliament to condemn the referendum. There was particular concern that under the proposed changes the head of state would enjoy legal immunity during his term of office, and also after the end of his mandate for actions carried out during his term of office.

In April 2002 the Chamber of Deputies adopted the proposals, which were put to a referendum held on 26 May. In the final draft the maximum age for presidential candidates had notably been increased from 70 to 75 years, giving Ben Ali (who would be 68 years of age at the 2004 election) the opportunity to seek two additional mandates and fuelling speculation that he intended to make himself 'President for life'. While the PDP demanded a boycott of the referendum, the first official results indicated that 99.52% of voters had approved the changes, with voter participation put at 95%.

In September 2002 Ben Ali implemented a major cabinet reorganization, replacing a number of ministers and reducing the number of posts from 54 to 40. Although there were no changes at key ministries such as interior, foreign affairs and defence, the Ministry of Human Rights was abolished and its functions transferred to the Ministry of Justice. No explanation was given for this decision, which aroused disquiet among human rights groups. In October the President finally legalized the FDTL. The party had tried to obtain legal status for eight years. The LTDH President, Trifi, declared that these presidential gestures were totally insufficient and that what was needed was the liberalization of political life, a general amnesty and an independent judiciary.

In January 2003 parliament adopted a new law under which all opposition parties with at least one seat in the Chamber of Deputies would be allowed to nominate a member of their executive as a candidate in presidential elections. Despite persistent speculation regarding his health, at the opening of the RCD's party conference in Tunis in July, Ben Ali announced that he would seek a fourth term as President.

President Ben Ali made a number of changes to the composition of the Council of Ministers in late August 2003. At the end of August the UDU stated that the party's leader, Abderrahmane Tlili, had been attacked in the street and seriously injured, and that documents had been stolen from his car. The party appealed to what it termed all democratic, progressive forces to condemn such acts and to make every effort to stop the use of force in political life. In September Tlili was arrested in connection with alleged financial irregularities arising from his tenure as head of the country's Office de l'Aviation Civile et des Aéroports. In June 2004 he was sentenced to nine years' imprisonment and fined heavily, having been found guilty of corruption in awarding contracts. Many suspected a political motive behind the charges.

In January 2004 Bouchiha, Secretary-General of the PUP, announced that he would contest the forthcoming presidential election on a platform of democratic pluralism and political reform. Mounir Béji, leader of the PSL, also indicated that he would be a candidate and would aim to 'consolidate democracy'. In the same month Muhammad Daouas was replaced as Governor of the Banque Centrale de Tunisie by the former Minister of Finance, Taoufik Baccar, and assigned to 'other functions'. Daouas, a vociferous supporter of economic reform, had urged greater transparency in private sector companies, and there was speculation that this had alarmed many wealthy business executives, some of whom had close links with Ben Ali and his entourage, and may have precipitated his replacement.

Shortly before President Chirac of France made an official visit to Tunisia and Tunisia hosted the '5+5 Dialogue Summit' in December 2003, Zouhair Yahyaoui of TUNeZINE, who had been arrested in June 2002, was released. In February 2004 former deputy Khemais Chamari, a human rights activist and one of the leading opponents of Ben Ali, announced that he was returning to Tunisia after seven years of exile in France to continue the struggle against what he called repression and human rights abuses.

THE PRESIDENTIAL AND LEGISLATIVE ELECTIONS OF OCTOBER 2004

In April 2004, at a meeting of the national council of the PSL, the organization's President, Mounir Béji, stated that the party would participate in the next presidential, legislative and municipal elections. In mid-June the successor to the PCT, Mouvement Ettajdid, announced that the President of its national council, Muhammad Ali Halouani, a university professor active in the trade union movement, would be the party's candidate in the forthcoming presidential election. In late June a rally organized by a grouping of opposition parties (the FDTL, the PDP and the PCOT) under the slogan 'No to a life presidency' urged voters to boycott the presidential election in October, rejected changes made to the Constitution in 2002 permitting Ben Ali to stand for a fourth term, and declared that the result was a foregone conclusion. Addressing regional governors at the end of June 2004, Ben Ali called for the neutrality of the administration and full respect for the electoral code during the October presidential and legislative elections, in the interests of bringing about 'further achievements on the path of democracy and the consecration of pluralism'.

In the presidential election held on 24 October 2004 Ben Ali was re-elected for a fourth mandate with 94.49% of the vote, according to official sources; this percentage was slightly lower than in the three previous elections, when he received over 99% of the vote. Bouchiha, leader of the PUP, gained 3.78% of the vote, Muhammad Ali Halouani, the candidate of Initiative Démocratique, a coalition of Mouvement Ettajdid and independent candidates, 0.95%, and Mounir Béji, leader of the PSL, 0.79%. The MDS and the UDU had decided not to field candidates of their own but to support Ben Ali's re-election. Bouchiha and Béji, moreover, had both declared that they were not running against Ben Ali but with him 'to advance the democratic process', leaving Halouani as the only candidate to oppose Ben Ali and publicly denounce his absolute personal power.

In legislative elections held on the same day, the RCD, with its powerful party machine, again won a landslide victory, winning all 152 contested seats in the National Assembly out of a total of 189. The MDS received 14 of the 37 seats reserved for the weak and divided opposition parties. Turn-out in the elections was officially put at 91%, but independent sources claimed that the real figure was much lower, especially in Tunis.

BEN ALI'S FOURTH TERM

Addressing the nation in November 2004 after being sworn in for a fourth term, President Ben Ali pledged to adopt an approach that would balance the need for stability, continued progress and comprehensive and sustained development with 'the irreversible process of democratic pluralism'. He emphasized that freedom of the press and of expression was a 'deeply rooted value' and promised greater opportunity for discussion in the media and the strengthening of the role of the various components of civil society—political parties, organizations and associations—to allow them to express their respective views. Elections to a new upper house, the Chamber of Advisers, would be held in 2005 'to enrich our democratic process and strengthen the participation of regions, social parties and cadres in the management of public affairs'. The creation of an upper house had been a key demand of the European Union (EU). The President reiterated his commitment to promoting the role of women in all fields of activity. A major reorganization of the Council of Ministers brought some younger ministers into the Government, but major policy changes were considered unlikely. The personnel changes included the appointment of Abdelbaki Hermassi as Minister of Foreign Affairs, replacing Ben Yahia, who left the cabinet, M'henni as Minister of National Defence in place of Dali Jazi, who retired, and Rafik Belhaj Kacem, former presidential adviser, as Minister of the Interior and Local Development.

In elections by indirect suffrage to the newly created Chamber of Advisers held at the beginning of July 2005, the ruling RCD secured 71 of the 85 elected seats. All 43 seats reserved for representatives of the regions (one or two seats per governorate on the basis of population size) were taken by the RCD, with no opposition candidates. All the seats allocated to farmers (14) and employers (14) also went to RCD loyalists, but the 14 seats reserved for the trade unions remained vacant as the UGTT decided not to participate, stating that it wanted to choose its own representatives rather than having candidates chosen by an electoral college composed of deputies, mayors and municipal councillors and thus dominated by the RCD. The remaining 41 seats in the Chamber of Advisers were filled by presidential appointees in August.

In a speech at the end of July 2005 on the anniversary of the Republic, Ben Ali emphasized the crucial importance of upholding the rule of law. He reaffirmed his strong commitment to promoting democratic dialogue in public life, but insisted that dialogue could only be held with parties and organizations that were officially recognized and respected the Constitution. There would be no dialogue with any political group acting under the cover of religion, a clear reference to al-Nahdah. Some opposition parties had called for a general amnesty for imprisoned members of al-Nahdah, and there had been speculation that the authorities might be prepared to hold talks with the banned party.

President Ben Ali further reorganized the Council of Ministers in August 2005. Among notable changes were the appointment of Abdelwahab Abdallah, a long-serving principal adviser to the President, as Minister of Foreign Affairs, in place of Abdelbaki Hermassi, and of Kamel Morjane, previously Assistant UN High Commissioner for Refugees, as Minister of National Defence; M'henni, who had latterly held the defence portfolio, was subsequently appointed Secretary-General of the governing RCD.

Tunisia hosted the second World Summit on the Information Society (WSIS) on 16–18 November 2005. Attended by delegates from 176 countries, the WSIS was the largest meeting ever organized under UN auspices. For the Ben Ali regime, the summit was intended to showcase Tunisia as a modern country that had mastered information technologies thanks to its investments. However, critics claimed that it merely highlighted the reality of a police state that did not tolerate criticism, curtailed press freedom and routinely blocked access to internet sites used by dissidents. In October eight leading political opponents, including both socialists and Islamists, began a hunger strike to call for greater freedom and the release of some 500 political prisoners from Tunisian gaols; the protest continued throughout the summit.

In January 2006 opponents of the Government announced the creation of a new 'democratic coalition', which included the Mouvement Ettajdid, two small left-wing parties and independent figures. However, joint action with al-Nahdah was ruled out as the group declared that 'no political parties can speak in the name of Allah'. In contrast, Marzouki, a supporter of co-operation with al-Nahdah, called for the foundation of a 'democratic front' that would exclude only those Islamists who advocated violence and the introduction of *Shari'a* law and opposed equality between men and women.

In February 2006 Ben Ali pardoned 1,298 prisoners and granted conditional release to a further 359 detainees, including more than 70 members of al-Nahdah and the eight men sentenced in 2004 for engaging in subversive activities on the internet. Hamadi Jebali, a former member of al-Nahdah's political bureau who had spent more than 15 years in gaol, later stated that his release was 'a positive step on the right path' and supported demands by the secular opposition for a general amnesty and for freedom of expression and association. Jebali called for talks between all parties, including the Government, and stated that the (modest) electoral success recently achieved by Islamist parties in Egypt, Morocco, (and more significantly in) the Palestinian territories and in Turkey disproved claims that Islamists were opposed to democracy. However, the regime continued to argue that al-Nahdah was a fundamentalist movement and therefore no contact seemed likely between the two.

In late June 2006 the Tunisian press reported that 10 university students had been arrested in Gafsa on suspicion of links with al-Qa'ida; the police later detained another group of 10 youths, whom, it was claimed, had planned to join the Base of Holy War in the Land of the Two Rivers (Tanzim Qa'idat al-Jihad fi Bilad al-Rifidain) organization, also known as al-Qa'ida in Iraq. The Government's concerns over the operations of terrorist groups linked to al-Qa'ida appeared to be validated in January 2007, when the Minister of the Interior and Local Development, Belhaj Kacem, stated that police had shot dead 14 members of a suspected militant Islamist organization and arrested a number of others in Soliman, near Tunis. Two members of the security forces were killed during the operation. Belhaj Kacem reported that the group—which had been assembled by six militants who had entered the country from Algeria, and which was suspected of having links to AQIM—had been in possession of explosives and details of foreign embassies and diplomatic staff in Tunis. It appeared that the crackdown on al-Nahdah, which had always advocated peaceful means to conduct politics, was driving some militants into the arms of more extremist groups linked to international terrorist networks. In January 2008 a court in Tunisia issued its judgment on the suspected militants: two of the defendants received death penalties, eight were sentenced to life imprisonment, and a further 20 received prison terms ranging from five to 30 years.

In July 2007, in a speech to commemorate the 50th anniversary of the proclamation of the Republic, Ben Ali focused his attention on the improving socio-economic indicators, which made Tunisia one of the leading countries in the developing world in terms of modernization. Ben Ali stressed the country's achievements in improving access to education, social security, health care and access to better services, such as safe drinking water. He also announced plans for the development of new infrastructure and the upgrading of tourist facilities, and spoke of the necessity to attract more foreign investment. While in many respects a cause for optimism, such socio-economic successes also masked some of the harsher realities and tensions within the country.

In November 2007, in a speech in Radès to mark the 20th anniversary of his accession to power, Ben Ali proposed a reduction in the voting age, from 20 to 18 years, and an amendment of the electoral law to preclude any single party from holding more than 75% of seats in municipal councils. Nine imprisoned members of the banned al-Nahdah party were also reportedly pardoned to mark the anniversary. During the speech Ben Ali announced a range of measures designed to promote democracy and human rights in the country; these included increasing the level of funding allocated to opposition parties and their press. Nevertheless, in May 2008 the recently founded Syndicat National des Journalistes Tunisiens (SNJT—which replaced the pro-Government Association des Journalistes Tunisiens) made renewed calls for a review of media regulations in line with international standards of press freedom.

During early 2008 riots erupted in the mining town of Redeyef, near Gafsa, situated in one of the country's most under-developed regions. The local population had been particularly severely affected by rising prices and growing unemployment, and peaceful demonstrations escalated into violence as protesters clashed with police. Local people were reportedly angered by the recruitment policies implemented by the state-owned Compagnie des Phosphates de Gafsa (CPG—a phosphate mining operation), one of the few sources of employment in the area. It was apparently felt that the introduction of these policies exacerbated a sense of socio-political neglect in the region. In June one man was killed and some 22 others injured after security forces opened fire on protesters in the town.

President Ben Ali was unanimously re-elected Chairman of the RCD at the party congress in late July 2008, effectively nominating him as the RCD candidate for the 2009 presidential election. Concerns were raised by opposition parties and human rights organizations alike about the implications of a continuation of the Ben Ali regime into 2014. At the congress Ben Ali also announced a series of amendments to the RCD party structure, including the addition of new, younger members and a reduction in the number of vice-presidents from two to one. Following this announcement, Karoui was removed from his post as first vice-president of the party, with Prime Minister Muhammad Ghannouchi becoming sole vice-president. M'henni, who had served as the organization's Secretary-General, was replaced by Muhammad Ghariani.

On 29 August 2008 the President appointed six new ministers—four of whom entered the Government for the first time.

Meanwhile, the Government intensified its campaign against radical Islamists, but scaled back its restrictions upon and condemnation of al-Nahdah. Following the imprisonment in August 2008 of 13 Islamists convicted of instituting a terrorist cell, 14 other militants were arrested in October on suspicion of planning terrorist attacks. The arrests raised the number of detentions on terrorism charges in the country to over 160 within a year. In November, however, President Ben Ali authorized the release of 21 prisoners, most of whom were al-Nahdah members. This official pardon marked the 21st anniversary of Ben Ali's presidency and seemed to indicate that he no longer regarded al-Nahdah as a threat to his rule.

President Ben Ali promised once again that Tunisia would move towards greater democracy, giving assurances that the presidential election scheduled for October 2009 would be 'transparent' and would be held under 'conditions of integrity'. He also pledged that opposition candidates would be permitted wider representation in the media, in order to 'reinforce democracy and consolidate pluralism'. His words were received with considerable scepticism, however, as just a week earlier an opposition newspaper, *Mouwatinoun* (an organ of the FDTL), had been banned from publication for printing 'unlawful allegations' in an opinion piece.

During December 2008 three opposition leaders announced their candidacy for the 2009 presidential election, taking advantage of a temporary amendment to the electoral law adopted in July 2008, which permitted the leader of any party to contest the election if he had held that position for at least two years. Bouchiha, Secretary-General of the PUP, Ahmed Innoubli, Secretary-General of the UDU, and Ahmed Brahim, Secretary-General of the Mouvement Ettajdid, all put their names forward. (The former Secretary-General of the PDP, Chebbi, had announced his intention to contest the election in February.)

In March 2009 the Chamber of Deputies approved changes to the electoral code first proposed by Ben Ali in November 2007. Among these new measures, which were promulgated by the President in April 2009, were an increase in the proportion of seats allocated to the opposition in the Chamber of Deputies, from 20% to 25%, and the imposition of a 75% upper limit on the share of seats that could be obtained by any one list in the municipal councils (regardless of the number of votes obtained). Furthermore, the voting age was to be reduced from 20 to 18 years.

In April 2009 the Government announced that international observers would not be permitted to monitor the forthcoming election because Tunisia was not 'an emerging democracy'. Although the Government subsequently reneged on this statement after criticism by opposition activists, residual concerns about its commitment to transparency were expressed by one of the opposition presidential candidates in May.

Also in June 2009, the Minister of Trade and Handicrafts, Ridha Touiti, was replaced by Ridha Ben Mosbah, formerly a secretary of state within the Ministry of Higher Education, Scientific Research and Technology. Touiti's position had come under increasing pressure since the significant deterioration in Tunisia's trade position resulting from the impact of the global economic downturn upon the country's main export markets in Europe (see Economy). Nevertheless, Touiti remained in the Government as Minister-delegate to the Prime Minister.

Preparations for the presidential election continued in mid-2009. On 25 August President Ben Ali officially announced his candidacy and subsequently received the endorsement of several political and social organizations, including the UGTT. However, the previous day Chebbi withdrew from the election, citing the 'lack of freedom and transparency' in the electoral process.

The run-up to the October 2009 elections was marked, as previously, by an all-pervasive media and publicity campaign in support of Ben Ali and the RCD, together with repressive measures against any attempts by the opposition parties to broadcast their messages or even organize meetings.

BEN ALI'S FIFTH TERM

With five of the eight officially sanctioned opposition parties publicly declaring their support for President Ben Ali, the result of the presidential election, on 25 October 2009, was widely predicted. According to official figures, Ben Ali won 89.6% of the 4.7m. votes cast, with the three other candidates, Muhammad Bouchiha, head of the PUP, Ahmed Innoubli, leader of the UDU, and Ahmed Brahim, leader of the Mouvement Ettajdid, winning just 5.0%, 3.8% and 1.6% of the votes, respectively.

At concurrent legislative elections, the RCD took all the 161 seats contested under the first-past-the-post system. Under constitutional amendments adopted in 2002, the remaining 53 seats (25% of the total) were divided among the opposition parties in proportion to their share of the vote.

The main dissident opposition parties complained that the elections had been neither free nor fair, although 31 international election observers, allowed to monitor the polling day itself, expressed satisfaction at the conduct of the poll. However, officials from the US Department of State questioned the credibility of those observers.

In April 2010 the Government suspended the licence of Tunisia's oldest private university, the Université Libre de Tunis (ULT), for alleged administrative and educational irregularities. It was claimed that the Government's actions were in response to a book written by the ULT's founder, Muhammad Bouebdelli, and published online, in which Bouebdelli catalogued his long-standing dispute with the Government.

Meanwhile, in late November 2009 Ben Ali was reported to be suffering from ill health. Widespread rumours that his illness was serious raised much speculation over his succession, particularly since he would be over 75 years of age at the presidential election scheduled for 2014, and, under the terms of the Constitution, ineligible to stand. The rumours were further fuelled by a cabinet reshuffle in January 2010, when the Minister of National Defence, Kamel Morjane, was reassigned to the foreign affairs portfolio, thus assuming responsibility for the third of the three major portfolios in the Government (having previously served as Minister of the Interior). Morjane's position was further consolidated the following month, when he was appointed to the Political Bureau, the highest committee of the ruling RCD party. In the reorganization seven ministers were removed, while six new ministers joined the Government, the most notable of whom was Muhammad Ridha Chalghoum, a former director of the state-owned Banque Nationale Agricole, who became Minister of Finance. Ridha Grira assumed the national defence portfolio, in place of Morjane.

REVOLUTION AND THE DEPARTURE OF BEN ALI

Universal and long-latent public disaffection with the repressive nature of the Ben Ali regime finally culminated into mass mobilization against it in December 2010, following the widely reported self-immolation of a fruit seller in the small town of Sidi Bouzid. The incident came shortly after the publication of classified US diplomatic cables by the WikiLeaks organization, which highlighted US embassy officials' belief that corruption was endemic in the ruling élite.

Muhammad Bouazizi, who has since become a symbol of the unrest that spread throughout the Middle East and North Africa region in 2011 and became known as the 'Arab spring', set himself alight in the main square of Sidi Bouzid on 17 December 2010, after police arrested him for selling fruit and vegetables without a permit. His apparent plight—lack of economic opportunity, compounded by official interference and corruption—reflected that of many other young Tunisians, who quickly took up his cause. Riots ensued in Sidi Bouzid and rapidly spread to neighbouring towns; as reports of fatalities, allegedly perpetrated by the security services, began to emerge, the protests spread throughout the country, overwhelming the Government's capacity to contain them. At the end of December demonstrations erupted in Tunis, by which time the concessions offered by the Government and Ben Ali himself to appease the protesters merely galvanized them further. Ben Ali adopted increasingly drastic measures, such as the removal of principal key ministers, but serious protests in early January 2011 signalled that the regime's ability to retain control was rapidly disintegrating. Clearly sensing the political mood, on 14 January Ben Ali fled the country and sought refuge in Saudi Arabia, bringing his 23-year rule to an abrupt end.

Violence and protests continued after Ben Ali's departure, as the remnants of the ruling RCD attempted to restore political control in the face of widespread opposition. Prime Minister Muhammad Ghannouchi assumed the presidency when Ben Ali left the country, but was forced to resign after a Constitutional Court ruling, which stated that, under the Constitution, the parliamentary speaker, Fouad Mebazaa, was the legitimate interim President. Mebazaa formed a new coalition Government, comprising some former RCD figures, as well as opposition politicians, on 17 January 2011, and was duly sworn in on 15 February. However, the involvement of former government officials angered the public and further protests ensued; as a result, just 10 days later, Mebazaa announced the establishment of a new and enlarged administration, which excluded RCD members. Soon afterwards, the National Assembly conferred on Mebazaa the power to rule by decree, in order to seek to contain the persistent protests, which continued to focus on the presence of former regime officials within the state apparatus. However, it became apparent that the public would settle for nothing less than wholesale change and finally, on 7 March, a third interim Government was installed, under a new Prime Minister, Béji Caïd Essebsi, who had served as a Minister of Foreign Affairs during the presidency of Bourguiba. The new Government appeared to meet with public approval and the unrest began to subside. Its first act was to dissolve the hated state security administration and it confirmed its commitment to democratic elections and the suspension of the 1959 Constitution.

A High Authority for the Achievement of the Objectives of the Revolution, Political Reform and Democratic Transition was established to implement a 'road-map to democracy', and plans were initiated for the organization of elections to a national constituent assembly on 24 July 2011. However, these plans advanced haltingly; the Commission's initial meetings were often acrimonious and failed to make any progress, while the interim Government inexplicably disbanded a second commission set up to investigate official corruption and embezzlement. However, efforts to remove all remaining vestiges of the Ben Ali regime continued apace; officials were barred from office and on 9 March the RCD itself was dissolved. Officials who had served in the Ben Ali Government in the previous 10 years, including those who had held senior posts within the regime, were banned from contesting the forthcoming elections. Meanwhile, a wide range of charges against Ben Ali and his family were gradually drawn up and by June, when he was tried for the first time, *in absentia*, he faced at least 18 civil lawsuits and some 182 military charges. By August he and his wife had both been convicted of embezzling state funds and convicted to 35 years' imprisonment, with an additional 15 years each for the illegal possession of weapons and illicit drugs.

The High Authority continued to experience difficulty in gaining consensus over the elections and transition to democracy, suffering a major reverse when al-Nahdah withdrew its participation on two occasions, owing to disagreements. Eventually, the authority admitted that the organization of elections in July 2011 was too great a political and logistical challenge, and the poll was postponed until 23 October.

Public wariness over the intentions of the interim Government persisted throughout much of the transitional period, and various opposition groups continued to stage demonstrations and strikes in 2011. In addition, the weakness of the central authorities resulted in the deterioration of public services and, in particular, of the maintenance of law and order. By late August, with elections still three months away, the sense of political drift was increasing public uncertainty; however, it appeared that Tunisia had consigned its successive dictatorships to the past and was firmly committed to a new democratic future.

The elections to the National Constituent Assembly (NCA) took place on 23 October 2011. It had been agreed that a majority in the new Assembly should determine who held power in the new government, but that the body should also draft a new constitution determining the details of the new political system. At an election featuring some 81 parties and associations, Hizb al-Nahdah emerged with the largest representation in the NCA, winning some 89 of the 217 seats contested, but needed to form a coalition with two secular parties, the liberal Congrès pour la République (CPR), led by Moncef Marzouki, and the left-leaning Forum Démocratique pour le Travail et les Libertés (Ettakatol), in order to govern. The three parties together commanded 138 seats in the Assembly, the CPR having secured 29 seats and Ettakatol 20. It is arguable that participation in a coalition has helped to strengthen the dominant moderate Islamist trend in Hizb al-Nahdah that is represented by its leader, Rachid Ghannouchi. In June 2012 the al-Qa'ida leader, Ayman al-Zawahiri, condemned al-Nahdah for not imposing *Shari'a* law in Tunisia and termed their Islamism 'US-approved'. Demonstrating the dramatic shift in Tunisian politics, Marzouki was approved by the NCA as an interim (and symbolic) President. He, in turn, appointed Hamadi Jebali, an al-Nahdah senior figure and a long-standing opponent of the former regime, as Prime Minister.

It is expected that, when it eventually finishes it work, the NCA will confirm that a parliamentary system of democracy will continue to operate. Among the other challenges for the Assembly to resolve is the role of religion in public life. In order to counter the possible exploitation by political Salafists of the greater political space afforded by regime change, the Assembly's members are considering measures to prevent any of the country's approximately 4,000 mosques from being used for partisan political activities. At the same time, the Constitution is likely to seek to uphold the legal independence of mosques. The new Government is aware of the ideological challenge of Tunisia's Salafists and the willingness of some of them to either support or be involved in some of the new external struggles, as in the previously conducted *jihad* (holy war) in the Sahel or the Middle East.

A seemingly genuine move toward a pluralist political system resulted from the upheaval in Tunisia (unlike the more limited, leadership-orientated, changes in Egypt and Yemen, for instance). However, aspects of the old state apparatus remained in, for example, the powers of the largely unreconstructed Ministry of the Interior. This was the focus of political complaints in April 2012, after the heavy-handed policing of an opposition protest in Tunis.

In July 2012 Hizb al-Nahdah leader Ghannouchi, who earlier that month had been re-elected by over 70% of party members, defeating those committed to the imposition of Shari'a law, commented that the Government, led by his Islamist party, was interested in broadening its base, a statement that was received with somewhat guarded enthusiasm by some secular parties. Amid reported tensions within the coalition over the Government's direction, the announcement was regarded by some observers as an indication that al-Nahdah was seeking to restructure the Government. On 30 June the CPR's Secretary-General, Muhammad Abbou, resigned as Minister-delegate to the Prime Minister, in charge of Administrative Reform, citing frustration over the limited scope of his post, although speculation continued that his resignation was linked to ongoing disagreement within the governing coalition. On 27 July the Minister of Finance, Houcine Dimassi, submitted his resignation. This followed the approval by the NCA earlier that month of a presidential decree removing Mustapha Kamel Nabli from the post of Governor of the central bank. (The economist Chédli Ayari became the new Governor and subsequently maintained better relations with the Government.) Slim Besbes, hitherto Dimassi's deputy, assumed the finance portfolio on an interim basis until December, when Elyès Fakhfekh was appointed to the post (whilst retaining his tourism portfolio).

The assassination of Chokri Belaid, a leading secular opposition politician, in early February 2013 fuelled a political crisis. The NCA had failed to agree on a new constitution, amid arguments that largely divided on Islamist–secular lines. Salafists associated with the banned Ansar al-Sharia group, which had refused to recognize the legitimacy of the new political process, were accused of responsibility for the murder, although Hizb al-Nahdah was also criticized for being inhibited within the Government it led from taking action against Salafists, who were involved in illegal activity. On 19 February the premier, leading Hizb al-Nahdah figure Jebali, resigned and President Marzouki appointed the Minister of the Interior, Ali Laârayedh, to replace him. In March a new Council of Ministers, which included Lotfi Ben Jiddou as the new Minister of the Interior, was established. The overthrow of the elected Muslim Brotherhood presidency and Government of Muhammad Mursi in neighbouring Egypt in June increased tensions in Tunisia still further, especially when young secular activists formed a group modelled on one in Egypt, known as Tamarrud ('resistance'), in opposition to the Tunisian Islamist-led Government. The murder of another secular leftist figure, Muhammad Brahimi, outside his home near Tunis on 25 July caused further dissent, which prompted what were variously reported as between 60 and 70 defections from the NCA, and confrontations in Bardo Square in Tunis and in Sidi Bouzid, Brahimi's home town where the December 2010 revolt had first erupted. Ben Jiddou accused Boubaker Hakim, a militant already in hiding, of carrying out the murders of Belaid and Brahimi. Hakim was associated with Ansar al-Sharia, which denied involvement in either attack. Speculation by some that the actual cause of the murders was an intent to provoke clashes in order to justify a state clampdown appeared incompatible with the Tunisian military's limited tradition of political intervention. For this reason, it seemed unlikely at mid-2013 that an Egyptian-style military intervention would take place in Tunisia.

In late July 2013 Ettakatol announced that it would withdraw from the ruling coalition unless a new government of national unity was formed. The independent Minister of Education, Salem Labyadh, also tendered his resignation. A grouping of opposition parties, the Front de Salut National, was formed to co-ordinate pressure for the governing institutions to be dissolved. The largest and most powerful union, the UGTT, began to organize strike action in support of demands that the Government resign.

The Front Populaire opposition grouping, of which Belaid and Brahimi were leading figures, demanded the dissolution of the Government and the organization of fresh elections. There were widespread calls for urgent political agreement on the constitution prior to elections in an effort to overcome the increasing crisis. However, the 'legitimate' Salafists, those committed to peaceful political activity, continued to argue that even majority backing for a secular constitution in a plebiscite would be illegitimate. Hizb al-Nahdah leader Ghannouchi stressed that the NCA was legitimately elected and should not have to suspend itself. On 30 July 2013 Prime Minister Laârayedh announced that elections would take place on 17 December. However, it was unclear if the promised elections depended on agreement on the constitution, and, if the latter was not resolved, then the prospect of elections might not be enough to prevent the political situation from deteriorating further. Mass anti-Government demonstrations continued in August and September. Nevertheless, al-Nahdah declared that it was open to the formation of a new governing coalition, following further negotiations. As long as al-Nahdah enjoyed the support of its coalition partners, or possibly of some new parties added to the coalition, then major confrontation could be averted.

FOREIGN RELATIONS

Relations with the West

President Ben Ali continued to pursue a moderate, pro-Western foreign policy. Relations with the USA remained cordial, and in March 1988 US Secretary of State George Shultz announced US support for Ben Ali's political reforms. Co-operation between France and Tunisia was strengthened following a state visit by Ben Ali to Paris in September and a state visit to Tunis by President Mitterrand in June 1989. However, relations with the USA and its European allies became strained after Iraq invaded Kuwait in August 1990. Ben Ali condemned the deployment of a US-led multinational force in the Gulf region, clearly in order to appeal to his domestic audience, arguing that it was not in the interests of either the Arabs or world peace. A National Committee for Support to Iraq was created, including the secular opposition parties and professional associations, and there were widespread popular demonstrations to express solidarity with Iraq. The Islamists, who had links in the Gulf Arab states, were caught in a dilemma. They opposed foreign forces in the region and condemned Iraq's invasion of Kuwait. They declared that pro-Iraqi feeling in Tunisia was a rejection of 'US imperialism'. France was also the target of public anger. For a brief period in the aftermath of the Gulf War, Tunisia's stance damaged relations with those countries that had participated in military operations to liberate Kuwait.

In February 1991 the USA reduced economic aid, and ended military assistance, although subsequent investment agreements with the USA indicated a rapid improvement in relations. Robert Pelletreau, the US Assistant Secretary of State, visited Tunis in December 1995 for talks with President Ben Ali and leading ministers. He praised the country's economic reforms, stated that military co-operation between the two countries would continue and announced that any threat to Tunisia would be viewed 'with concern'. In May 1997 a delegation led by Tunisia's Minister of National Defence visited Washington, DC, for a meeting of the joint committee for military co-operation. During a visit to Tunis in June 1998, US Under-Secretary of State Stuart Eizenstat praised Tunisia as a 'model for the developing world' and stated that the USA was keen to promote greater economic co-operation with Tunisia and its other Maghreb neighbours. In a report to the US Senate Committee on Foreign Relations in February 2001 the US State Department reiterated its strong criticism of Tunisia's human rights record, but the new US Administration of George W. Bush continued to regard Tunisia as an important strategic ally, and as in the case of previous presidencies, conveniently disregarded these criticisms.

Relations with Tunisia's key European allies also quickly recovered after the Gulf War but, although relations remained close, especially with France, they were strained by Tunisian disquiet at the activities of its Islamist opponents who had been granted asylum in Europe, and continuing concern in Europe over human rights abuses in Tunisia. On a visit to Paris in February 1993, Tunisia's Minister of the Interior criticized the French authorities for granting asylum to Tunisian Islamist militants, and in October Charles Pasqua, Minister of the Interior in the new French administration, pledged that France would not become a base for Islamist activists. In January 1995 the French and Tunisian interior ministers met in Tunis with their counterparts from Italy, Spain, Portugal, Algeria and Morocco to discuss security matters arising from Islamist militancy. They condemned 'terrorism, fundamentalism and every form of extremism and fanaticism' and agreed to exchange information on a regular basis. Jacques Chirac's election to the French presidency was welcomed by the Tunisian authorities, and it was hoped that the new French administration would support Tunisia in its negotiations with the EU over the association agreement and maintain an unyielding policy towards Islamist militants in France. In June French police arrested a number of Tunisians and Algerians living in France who were alleged to be part of a network providing arms to Islamist groups in Algeria and to the Front Islamiste Tunisien (which appeared to have close links with the radical Algerian Groupe Islamique Armée—GIA—although Rachid Ghannouchi, the leader of al-Nahdah, denied any contacts between his party and this group). In October President Chirac made a state visit to Tunis, where he praised Ben Ali for promoting modernization, democracy and social harmony, and promised an increase in aid to Tunisia.

Ben Ali's state visit to France, which should have taken place in September 1996, was cancelled amid speculation that the President feared public criticism of Tunisia's human rights record. However, in February 1997 an agreement was reached on further military co-operation. Ben Ali's state visit to Paris finally took place in October. French leaders acknowledged Tunisia's difficult regional position and pledged continued support for economic reforms, but appealed for further progress in democracy and human rights. During the visit two economic agreements were signed, providing additional

French financial support for Tunisia. The long-standing dispute over French-owned property in Tunisia was also resolved. Nevertheless, while economic co-operation continued to develop, relations at the political level were soured by highly critical reports about the Ben Ali regime in the French media during the Tunisian presidential and parliamentary elections in October 1999. There was renewed tension in early 2001 when the French Government criticized the growing use of violence against human rights activists.

Italy was Tunisia's second largest trading partner after France and the third biggest source of foreign investment, but relations between the two countries were strained during the 1990s owing to the problem of illegal immigration from Tunisia into Italy and disputes over fishing rights. Italy insisted that Tunisia do more to curb illegal immigrants, mainly Moroccans and Tunisians, entering Italy from Tunisia. The arrival in Tunisia in 1994 of former Italian Prime Minister, Bettino Craxi, sentenced *in absentia* by the Italian courts to 18 years in prison for corruption, proved embarrassing for the Tunisian authorities. In June 1995 Italy requested that Tunisia extradite Craxi; however, the matter proved complicated because the extradition agreement between the two countries excluded political offences. Craxi, who maintained close links with the Tunisian leadership, was reported to be too ill to leave his villa in Hammamet and died in Tunisia in 2000. After meeting Ben Ali in Tunis in June 1998, the Italian Prime Minister, Romano Prodi, insisted that problems over fishing zones and illegal immigration could easily be resolved. In July, however, a sharp increase in the number of illegal immigrants arriving from Tunisia provoked an angry rebuke from the Italian Minister of Foreign Affairs, who accused the Tunisian authorities of not doing enough to stem the flow. The conflict quickly subsided, and in August the two countries signed an accord under which Tunisia agreed to do more to prevent Tunisians from entering Italy illegally and to take back illegal immigrants apprehended by the Italian authorities in exchange for a substantial aid agreement. Later in the year the two countries agreed to promote greater maritime co-operation in order to improve the detection of illegal immigrants entering Italy from Tunisia, and to reduce illegal fishing by Italian vessels in Tunisian waters. Nevertheless, disputes over fishing rights continued to cause friction between the two countries, although co-operation on illegal immigration into Italy made some progress. During the second half of 2000 new agreements were signed with Italy on defence co-operation and the employment of Tunisian workers.

Relations with Spain were strengthened in October 1995 when a treaty of friendship and co-operation was signed during a visit to Tunisia by the Spanish Prime Minister, Felipe González. The first annual meeting between leaders of the two countries, as agreed under the 1995 treaty of friendship and co-operation, was held in Madrid in January 1997. Although the meeting dealt primarily with economic co-operation, the Spanish Prime Minister, José María Aznar, appealed for further improvement in Tunisia's record on human rights. The issue of human rights and political freedoms had also been raised when the Tunisian Minister of Foreign Affairs held talks with his Spanish counterpart in Madrid in July 1996. Prime Minister Aznar again visited Tunis in May 1998 for the annual meeting between senior officials, and urged Spanish firms to take greater advantage of investment opportunities in Tunisia.

In December 1993 the EU's Council of Ministers mandated the European Commission to begin talks with Tunisia on a new partnership agreement to replace the co-operation agreement signed in 1976. The Tunisian Ministry of Foreign Affairs welcomed the talks, which it described as 'a political signal' marking European approval of Tunisia's progress towards political pluralism and its respect for human rights. Talks with the EU began in Brussels in March 1994, and negotiations were completed in July 1995 when Tunisia became the first southern Mediterranean country to sign a new economic association agreement as part of the EU's plan for a Euro-Mediterranean Partnership. The agreement involved the gradual removal of tariffs on industrial imports from the EU, a high-risk strategy for the country's vulnerable manufacturing sector. The European Commission insisted that such partnership agreements with the Maghreb states were essential and, by strengthening the economies of those countries, would lessen Islamist violence and stem the flow of emigrants to Europe.

In May 1996 the European Parliament for the first time passed a resolution condemning Tunisia's treatment of opposition politicians and strongly criticizing its human rights record. The resolution reiterated that the 1995 association agreement required Tunisia to respect democratic principles and human rights, and urged the European Commission to persuade the Tunisian Government to meet these obligations. The resolution was greeted with an indignant response from the Tunisian Government and from several opposition parties. The association agreement was formally implemented in March 1998 after it had been ratified by all EU member states. Despite receiving highly critical reports from international human rights organizations about the situation in Tunisia, and expressions of concern by some member states over civil liberties in the country, the EU chose not to condemn the Ben Ali regime's human rights record, preferring instead to focus on the country's stability while insisting that some progress was being made towards greater democracy. Early in 2000 Tunisia, keen to increase its agricultural exports to Europe, opened preliminary talks with the EU about the liberalization of trade in agricultural goods. The Ben Brik affair provoked renewed criticism of Tunisia's human rights record in the European Parliament, and in June some of its deputies demanded that the association agreement should be suspended.

The President of the European Commission, Romano Prodi, visited Tunis in January 2001 as part of a tour of the Maghreb aimed at reviving the Euro-Mediterranean Partnership. During his visit he met with a delegation from the LTDH. It was reported that Tunisia had become increasingly disillusioned with the EU accord, arguing that European financial support had not been sufficient to offset the losses resulting from the progressive reduction of tariffs on European imports and the costs of preparing the economy for free trade. Tension also resulted from what the Tunisian Government perceived as EU interference in the country's internal affairs, notably criticism of its human rights record.

Relations with the West after 11 September 2001

Following the September 2001 suicide attacks on New York and Washington, DC, President Ben Ali vehemently denounced those who had carried out the attacks and reiterated Tunisia's 'principled and deeply anchored stand against terrorism in all its forms and manifestations'. In contrast to the 1991 Gulf War, there were no popular demonstrations against the US offensive in Afghanistan, but some observers believed that Tunisian popular opinion was in favour of Osama bin Laden. In December William Burns, the US Assistant-Secretary of State with responsibility for the Middle East, visited Tunis as part of a tour of Maghreb capitals. During talks with Ben Ali he reaffirmed Washington's interest in promoting US co-operation with the Maghreb states, and thanked the Tunisian leadership and people for their expressions of solidarity following the attacks. Tunisian security services were co-operating with the US Federal Bureau of Intelligence to track down suspects of Tunisian origin based in Europe. In April 2001 Italian police had arrested a number of Tunisians who were accused of belonging to the Milan cell of the Algerian-based GSPC, which was providing logistical support for, and planning terrorist attacks in Europe on behalf of, al-Qa'ida. The Italian police believed that more Tunisians were members of the GSPC network, which had cells in several European countries. Following the attacks the Tunisian press accused the banned Islamist party, al-Nahdah, whose leadership was based in Europe, of having links with al-Qa'ida, allegations that were strongly denied by al-Nahdah representatives. In December 2002 Burns again visited Tunis, where discussions focused on economic and political issues, the Middle East crisis and the US-led 'war on terror'.

Anti-war demonstrations were held in Tunisia after the US-led military intervention in Iraq that commenced in March 2003. On a visit to Austria, the Tunisian Minister of Foreign Affairs stated that the military campaign in Iraq represented a failure for all those who had been working for a peaceful solution to the crisis. In December US Secretary of State Colin Powell began a brief tour of the Maghreb states in Tunisia, regarded by the USA as a staunch ally in the 'war on terror'. He chose to ignore long-standing criticism by his own State Department of the human rights situation in Tunisia, praised the Tunisian Government's efforts in education, health and women's rights, and invited Ben Ali to visit President Bush at the White House in February 2004. He told reporters that more political reform in Tunisia was expected, and that he had discussed the need for an open press with the Tunisian leadership. In January 2004, during a visit by the Tunisian Minister of Foreign Affairs to Washington, DC, Powell highlighted the strong relationship between Tunisia and the USA, and referred to Tunisia as a voice of moderation and regional harmony. He also noted that Ben Ali had played an important role in encouraging Qaddafi to change his policy towards the West. When Ben Ali visited Washington, DC, in February, President Bush thanked him for working with the USA in the 'war on terror', and praised Tunisia's modern education system and the equal rights granted to women. A spokesman for the US President stated that Bush had encouraged Ben Ali to make progress in areas such as press freedom, the right of Tunisians to organize and work peacefully for reform, and the need for free and competitive elections and equal justice under the law. Such advances, the USA considered, could give Tunisia a leading role in bringing reform and freedom to the wider Middle East region. Ben Ali was the first Arab leader to visit Washington, DC, after Bush presented his initiative on democracy in the Middle East, and at the end of 2003 William Burns announced that the USA had chosen Tunisia as the regional centre for its Middle East Partnership Initiative to promote democracy and political reform. Ben Ali responded to criticism of this by reiterating that he was introducing democratic reforms in a measured way so that extremists could not take advantage of freedoms intended for law-abiding citizens. In May 2004 Ben Ali received Burns, who emphasized the importance that Washington attached to efforts from within the region to carry out reforms, while declaring that the USA had no intention of imposing such reforms. Ben Ali was one of a small group of Arab leaders invited by President Bush to attend the summit meeting of the Group of Eight (G8) leading industrialized nations held in Georgia, USA, in June; however, although the White House announced that the Tunisian President would be participating in the meeting, he did not attend.

In September 2004 the Tunisian Minister of Foreign Affairs, Habib Ben Yahia, visited Washington, DC, for talks with Secretary of State Colin Powell about prospects for the US initiative for political reforms in the Middle East and North African region. Yahia emphasized his country's commitment 'to continued movement in that direction'. Following presidential and legislative elections in October, the US Department of State expressed concern that opportunities for political participation 'were not everything we had hoped for'.

In March 2006 US Secretary of Defense Donald Rumsfeld visited Tunis for talks with President Ben Ali and Minister of National Defence Kamel Morjane, as part of a tour of Maghreb countries; the discussions covered issues including military co-operation and counter-terrorism. In May US Under-Secretary of State Robert Zoellick visited the Tunisian capital for talks with Ben Ali. He acknowledged the positive role that Tunisia had played in the normalization of relations between the USA and Libya (see the chapter on Libya). In June 2007 the Minister of Foreign Affairs, Abdelwahab Abdallah, met both Vice-President Cheney and Secretary of State Condoleezza Rice during an official visit to Washington, DC. The meetings were described as friendly and positive. The two parties discussed the deterioration of the situation in the Palestinian territories and other recent developments in the Middle East. The US Administration reiterated its support for Tunisia and praised its leaders for their stance in the 'war on terror' and their efforts in furthering democratic reforms. Bilateral relations were further strengthened in early September 2008, when Rice visited Tunisia during a brief tour of Maghreb states. She met with President Ben Ali and held talks with several Tunisian officials on issues including counter-terrorism and domestic reform. In a statement to the press, Rice praised the progress that Tunisia had made in promoting women's rights and urged the country to make every effort to ensure that the 2009 presidential elections would be 'free and fair'.

Following the September 2001 attacks in the USA the French authorities quickly reassessed their attitude to the Ben Ali regime. After Tunisia had been diplomatically ostracized by senior French politicians, the French Minister of Foreign Affairs, Hubert Védrine, visited Tunis in October, followed by President Chirac, who held talks with Ben Ali in December as part of a tour of Maghreb capitals and declared that both Governments were in complete agreement on the need to eradicate international terrorism. Chirac shocked and angered the Tunisian opposition by praising Ben Ali for his 'exemplary policy of combating terrorism'. Just before President Chirac's visit, the Tunisian authorities had allowed Moncef Marzouki to leave the country and take up a university post in France. At a meeting of the Commission Mixte Franco-Tunisienne in Paris at the end of January 2002, chaired by Hubert Védrine, his Tunisian counterpart, Ben Yahia, stressed that democracy must be developed in security and stability, and accused the Islamists of using human rights as part of their campaign to take power. Following the suicide bomb attack in Djerba in April, French police arrested several alleged accomplices of the Tunisian suicide bomber. The marked improvement in relations between France and the Ben Ali regime continued. In October France's new Minister of the Interior visited Tunis to discuss anti-terrorism issues, and in November the Minister of Foreign Affairs, Dominique de Villepin, visiting Tunis as part of a tour of Maghreb capitals, stated that 'an open and dynamic Tunisia under the leadership of President Ben Ali deserved the full support of France'. In December French police arrested Khemais Toumi, a prosperous businessman living in Marseilles, who provided financial backing for the secular opposition in Tunisia, after the Tunisian authorities requested his extradition. In 1997 Toumi had been sentenced *in absentia* by a Tunis court to five years' imprisonment on fraud charges, but no request had been made at that time for his extradition. Lawyers for Toumi expressed concern that, with the marked improvement in relations between Paris and Tunis, their client would be handed over to the Tunisian authorities and fears were expressed for his physical safety.

President Chirac made a three-day state visit to Tunis in December 2003, and angered dissidents and human rights activists by declaring that Tunisia had made great advances in 'the first human right which is the right to eat, receive health care and an education and have a place to live'. Members of his entourage had no illusions about the absence of democracy under the Ben Ali regime, but insisted that discreet diplomacy was more effective than grand declarations. In July 2004 the French Minister of Foreign Affairs, Michel Barnier delivered to President Ben Ali a personal message of friendship from President Chirac and an invitation to join him in Toulon in August for the celebrations to mark the liberation of southern France during the Second World War. Barnier emphasized the Euro-Mediterranean dimension of Franco-Tunisian relations, and expressed hope that the two countries could work together to bring about a new momentum in relations between the EU and the Maghreb through the so-called Barcelona Process (the co-operation and dialogue instituted by the Euro-Mediterranean Partnership). In addition to talks on Franco-Tunisian co-operation, which focused on security questions, counter-terrorism and clandestine immigration, Barnier also discussed the Middle East with Tunisian government ministers, and stated that both France and Tunisia were in agreement on the main issues involved, notably on the situation in Iraq and the Israeli–Palestinian conflict. President Chirac sent a message of congratulations to Ben Ali on his re-election in October and the French Ministry of Foreign Affairs stated that France would always 'stand by Tunisia for the continuation of its social and economic development'.

Shortly after being elected, French President Nicolas Sarkozy made an official visit to Tunisia in July 2007, during which he expressed praise for Tunisia and its project of modernization and democratization. While Sarkozy raised the issue of human rights with regard to some individual cases, he declared that he was not in Tunisia to lecture the regime but to praise its efforts in moving towards democracy. The main items discussed with Ben Ali were security issues, with Sarkozy calling for closer co-operation between Tunisian and French counter-terrorism security services. He also launched the idea of a Mediterranean Union that he hoped would build upon the Barcelona Process to foster closer economic, political and cultural ties between all countries bordering the Mediterranean Sea. In April 2008 President Sarkozy met again with Ben Ali during a state visit to Tunisia, where the two leaders supervised the signing of several agreements designed to increase nuclear and aviation co-operation. Ben Ali also expressed his support for Sarkozy's recently renamed Union for the Mediterranean, which had been modified in early 2008 to encompass not just those nations bordering the Mediterranean Sea, but all EU member states. When the Union for the Mediterranean was officially inaugurated at a summit meeting in Paris on 13 July, President Ben Ali was among the many leaders of the 43 member nations to be in attendance. In a speech during the summit, Ben Ali emphasized the importance of closer collaboration with EU states on matters of environmental policy in order to 'promote the abilities of the more fragile Mediterranean countries to deal with climate change'.

Relations with France became strained for a brief period in March 2009, when the French Minister of Foreign and European Affairs, Bernard Kouchner, accused the Tunisian Government of 'attacks on human rights [and] the harassment and sometimes jailing of journalists'. However, in April French Prime Minister, François Fillon, praised the democratization process under Ben Ali, following a two-day visit to Tunisia. The fickleness of bilateral relations was exposed once again in the aftermath of Ben Brik's arrest and imprisonment following the elections. French ministers publicly expressed their disapproval, raising the ire of Ben Ali. In consequence, Tunisian ministers refused invitations to a banquet at the French embassy in Tunis in early December. However, relations thawed in time for French national day on 14 July 2010, when Ben Ali sent Sarkozy a message of support. It was against this background that France initially misjudged the determination of sections of the Tunisian public to overthrow the regime evidenced in the wave of protests that began in late 2010. Three days before Ben Ali fled Tunisia in January 2011, France's Minister of Foreign and European Affairs, Michèle Alliot-Marie, offered to send French security forces to help his regime tackle the burgeoning protests.

Following the change of regime, efforts were made by the Governments of Tunisia and France to improve bilateral relations. France issued positive statements about Tunisia's application for 'EU advanced partner' status. In July 2012 Tunisia's interim President, Moncef Marzouki, met the new French President, François Hollande, in Paris, where discussions were conducted on enhancement of the two countries' relationship. In July 2013 Hollande conducted an official visit to Tunis, accompanied by, *inter alia*, a human rights activist and a liberal film director of Tunisian origin. The political message, following his Government's strong condemnation of the murder of Belaid that February, seemed clear. However, Hollande announced his support for the transitional process in Tunisia and signed a series of bilateral economic agreements.

The issue of terrorism was discussed during visits to Tunis by Italian President Carlo Azeglio Ciampi and Minister of Foreign Affairs Renato Ruggiero in October 2001 and by Italian Prime Minister Silvio Berlusconi in November. A number of Tunisians had been arrested in Italy on terrorism charges both before and after the September 2001 attacks in the USA. Some progress in handling questions of illegal immigration and fishing rights resulted in an improvement in bilateral relations. In July 2003, after a sharp increase in the number of illegal immigrants trying to reach Italy by sea from Tunisia, the Tunisian Minister of the Interior promised new legislation aimed at both migrants seeking illegally to enter Italy and traffickers. Ben Ali made an official visit to Italy in May 2004 at the invitation of the Italian President. The Government of Romano Prodi, in power from May 2006, made the Mediterranean and the wider Middle East a foreign policy priority. The Minister of Foreign Affairs, Massimo D'Alema, visited Tunisia in April 2007 and stated that both countries were committed to achieving peace and security in the area. Human rights issues were not mentioned, as the meeting between D'Alema and Ben Ali focused almost exclusively on the Arab–Israeli conflict. Following the change of regime in Tunisia in January 2012, Italy sought to improve bilateral relations, and in May, during a two-day official visit to Tunis by Italian President Giorgio Napolitano, Tunisian Minister of Foreign Affairs Rafik Ben Abdessalem and his Italian counterpart, Giulio Terzi di Santagata, signed a strategic agreement that included Italy's commitment to Tunisia obtaining EU advanced partner status.

A visit by the Spanish premier, Aznar, in September 2001 was mainly devoted to discussions about the international coalition against terrorism. In June 2004 Spain's Minister of Foreign Affairs and Co-operation, Miguel Ángel Moratinos, held talks in Tunis with Ben Ali; this was the first visit to Tunisia by a member of the new socialist Government of José Luis Rodríguez Zapatero. (Moratinos had praised the Tunisian Government repeatedly in 2006 and 2007 for its efforts in curbing illegal immigration into Spain and for its stance in the 'war on terror'.) In April 2003, meanwhile, during a visit to Tunis by the German Minister of the Interior, Otto Schily, Germany and Tunisia signed an agreement to fight terrorism and organized crime. Most of the foreign tourists killed in the suicide bomb attack on a synagogue in Djerba in April 2002 had been German nationals, and the German authorities had sent a team of police officers to Tunisia to assist in the investigations. Spanish Minister of Foreign Affairs José Manuel García-Margallo visited Tunis in March 2012, when he committed Spain to deeper relations with Tunisia, following the success of what he called the 'democratic transition' in the country.

Romano Prodi, then the President of the European Commission, visited Tunis in April 2003 to discuss bilateral relations between Tunisia and the EU. Prodi called for the strengthening of economic and political relations between the EU and all the southern Mediterranean countries. In December Tunis hosted the first '5+5 Dialogue Summit' of the heads of state and government of the Union of the Arab Maghreb (UMA) and of France, Italy, Malta, Portugal and Spain. The meeting, organized on the initiative of President Ben Ali, was intended in part to act as a forum to express concerns about the impending enlargement of the EU amid fears that this would be at the expense of the Maghreb countries, and also as a further attempt to revive the UMA. Prodi stated that the enlarged EU must give priority to strengthening co-operation with Algeria, Morocco and Tunisia, but pointed out that this would prove less difficult if the Maghreb countries resolved their own internal disputes and accelerated 'the continuous progress towards democracy'. However, the meeting appeared to have done little to alleviate issues of contention between the Maghreb states, notably the Western Sahara issue. In November 2005 Gijs de Vries, the EU Co-ordinator for Counter-Terrorism, called for even closer ties between European intelligence services and their North African counterparts. Meanwhile, in February 2004 Reporters sans Frontières, an international organization concerned with press freedom, urged the EU to end its support programme for the Tunisian news media and instead to assist the few newspapers and television stations based outside Tunisia in their efforts to convey alternative news to Tunisians. The EU did not follow these recommendations, instead contributing €2.15m. in 2004/05 to a project for the training of journalists in Tunisia. While the European Parliament has often been critical of the Tunisian regime and its human rights record, the EC has been on friendlier terms with Tunisia and has financed a number of projects aimed at strengthening the Tunisian economy.

Following the commencement of negotiations in June 2009 between Tunisia and the EU over Tunisia's application for advanced partner status in its partnership with the EU, the mixed opinions among EU members were revealed in a debate on the issue in the European Parliament in January 2010. Some EU members expressed concerns over Tunisia's democratic and human rights failings, concerns which were reiterated by an European Commission report, published in May, on Tunisia's progress in implementing a five-year Action Plan it had agreed with the EU in 2005. The report praised Tunisia's progress in economic reform, but highlighted 'persistent shortcomings' in democratic advancement, the rule of law and human rights.

Tunisia remains keen to gain advanced partner status, since it confers additional benefits such as preferential trade terms, membership of various European agencies and observer status at the Council of Europe. In June 2010, demonstrating Tunisian sensitivity on the subject, the National Assembly approved amendments to the penal code outlawing any action that 'incites foreigners to take action that harms the country's economic interests'. The amendments were reportedly aimed at Tunisian opposition figures who had been lobbying against the granting by the EU of advanced partner status until Tunisia improved its record on human rights. Since the change of regime in Tunisia in 2011, the prospects for it securing EU advanced partner status in the short to medium term have greatly improved, with a number of countries either backing it outright or sounding very positive about the prospect. However, there is evidence of some residual caution within the EU to ensure that human rights advances in Tunisia are irreversible. Indicative of the improved relationship, in 2012 the EU committed itself to more than doubling its planned aid disbursements to the Tunisian Government.

The EU and leading EU states welcomed the transition to a relatively democratic and representative government and NCA. Following the political upheaval in 2013, however, there has been a cautious response, with European attention concentrated on the much greater clashes in neighbouring Egypt. The EU has not condemned the forced removal from office of an Islamist President, though it seeks to encourage a peaceful outcome to the crisis in Egypt. Consequently, it is not expected that the EU would take a decisive role in the current crisis in Tunisia, unless events were to escalate out of control.

Following the popular protests of early 2011, US President Barack Obama indicated his Administration's support for the aims of the protesters, while calling for all parties to avoid violence. Obama also urged the Tunisian Government to demonstrate respect for human rights and to commit to holding elections. In February US Secretary of State Hillary Clinton made an official visit to Tunisia, during which she met with interim President Mebazaa and Prime Minister Essebsi, pledging US assistance in Tunisia's efforts to institute political and social reforms. In February 2012 Clinton pledged that the USA would aid Tunisia's economic development, and three months later the US Under Secretary of State for Economic, Business and Agricultural Affairs, Robert Hormats, stated that Tunisia was 'on the right track' in the pursuit of democratic reform.

In April 2012 the USA committed to a sovereign loan guarantee of nearly US $500m. for a Tunisian bond issue, and to the payment of Tunisia's relatively modest debts to the World Bank and African Development Bank. Bilateral 'anti-terrorism training' was resumed after a seven-year hiatus, reflecting both the US Administration's desire to ensure that the Government in Tunisia supported US interests, and that a worsening security situation in Libya threatening to weaken border security in Tunisia and Algeria, and already impacting on some neighbouring Sahel states, did not aid al-Qa'ida or related groups in North and West Africa. On 20 June the Tunisian Minister of National Defence, Abdelkarim Zebidi, signalled the Government's desire to enhance its defence relations with the USA when he stressed to the US ambassador to Tunisia the need, as he perceived it, for the logistical capabilities of the country's armed forces to be improved. Relations were adversely affected in September, however, when the angry reaction in much of the Muslim world to a US-made film denigrating the Prophet Muhammad prompted—or provided an excuse for—an attack on the US embassy, in which several Tunisians were killed. Tunisian Salafists, possibly connected to the banned Ansar al-Sharia group, were suspected of involvement. In the context of a larger-scale attack on a US consulate in neighbouring Libya earlier in September that was linked to al-Qa'ida, the US Administration was all the more perturbed by the incident in Tunisia and by what it perceived as the al-Nahdah-led Government's ongoing leniency towards the country's Salafists, who, even if some of them accepted the need to work politically, were regarded as complicit in the instability at the very least. After efforts were made to improve Tunisian-US relations, they became strained again in May 2013, when 20 Tunisians were found guilty of involvement in the attack but only received suspended sentences. The USA strongly condemned the murders of two leading secular opposition politicians in February and July, which precipitated a political crisis in the country, which was compounded by subsequent events in Egypt.

Relations with other Maghreb States

After Ben Ali came to power, relations with Libya improved substantially. Qaddafi visited Tunis in February 1988, when it was agreed to abolish entry visas for Tunisians and Libyans crossing the Tunisian–Libyan border, and that both countries would abide by the judgment of the ICJ concerning the delineation of their respective sectors of the continental shelf in the Gulf of Gabès. In May Ben Ali and Qaddafi held an unscheduled summit on the island of Djerba. The two leaders signed an agreement providing for a social and economic union of the two countries, the free movement of people and goods across their common frontier, the establishment of a common identity card system and the freedom to live, work and own property. A number of joint industrial, economic and cultural projects were initiated immediately after the summit. In August Ben Ali visited Libya, where he and Qaddafi signed a series of co-operation agreements and an agreement concerning the settlement of the dispute over the continental shelf in the Gulf of Gabès. During the visit a technical commission was established to examine means of accelerating co-operation and some degree of unification between Tunisia and Libya. In September an agreement was signed establishing a joint Tunisian-Libyan company, which would exploit the offshore '7 November' oilfield in the Gulf of Gabès. An agreement to link the two countries' electricity grids was signed. During a visit to Tunis in December Qaddafi addressed the National Assembly, stating that he favoured 'constitutional unity' between the two countries but would not try to impose it. However, despite a great deal of rhetoric, Qaddafi appeared reluctant actually to implement co-operation agreements such as the joint exploration of the Gulf of Gabès and the financing of infrastructure projects in Tunisia. Tunisia and Libya, with Algeria, Mauritania and Morocco, were founder members of the UMA in February 1989. However, the UMA never developed into a coherent and functioning union.

The decision by the UN Security Council in April 1992 to impose sanctions against Libya over the Lockerbie affair (see the chapter on Libya) was reluctantly accepted by Tunisia. Although flights to and from Libya were suspended, Tunisia insisted that land and sea links would remain open. Tunisia was Libya's principal trading partner in the Arab world. Sanctions against Libya created a mini-boom in southern Tunisia, amid a sharp increase in cross-border trade and in transit traffic, but relations deteriorated sharply in September, when the Libyan leader remarked that Tunisia had no future and was doomed to unite with either Libya or Algeria. Despite these differences, the Tunisian Government made efforts to negotiate a solution to the Lockerbie affair. In April 1993 Ben Ali visited Libya and consulted with President Muhammad Hosni Mubarak of Egypt in a further attempt to resolve the deadlock between Libya and the West in the approach to the UN Security Council's sanctions review. Failure to resolve the Lockerbie affair also frustrated Ben Ali's efforts to forge closer relations between the UMA and the EU. On a visit to Tunis in December, the French Minister of Defence left the President in no doubt that Libya's membership of the UMA was a serious impediment to closer relations between the UMA and EU. As a result of UN sanctions, Tunisia became the main point of entry for international companies working in Libya. In September 1995 Tunisia appealed for the lifting of UN sanctions against Libya and also supported Libya's request to participate in the Euro-Mediterranean summit held in Barcelona, Spain, in November. A series of economic agreements were signed in October, when the Tunisian Prime Minister met the Secretary-General of the Libyan People's Committee, and Ben Ali held talks with Qaddafi in January 1996. A Tunisian delegation led by the Prime Minister attended a meeting in Tripoli in July, and bilateral relations improved after a visit to Tunis by Qaddafi in October when he addressed the National Assembly. Several agreements on investment, trade and co-operation were signed subsequently and progress was made on a number of joint economic projects during 1997–98.

The Libyan Secretary for Foreign Liaison and International Co-operation, Omar al-Muntasir, visited Tunis in February 1999 at the same time as the US Secretary of Defense, William Cohen, who asked Ben Ali to show more support for UN sanctions against Libya and to use his influence with Qaddafi to persuade Libya to surrender the two suspects in the Lockerbie affair. In January, however, Ben Ali had repeated an appeal for the lifting of sanctions against Libya 'to end the suffering of the Libyan people', arguing that sanctions had also aggravated regional tensions and undermined Tunisia's own economic development plans. Nevertheless, Tunisia did not follow some sub-Saharan African states in openly flouting the air embargo. President Ben Ali held talks with Qaddafi at the summit meeting of the Organization of African Unity (OAU, now the African Union—AU) in Algiers in July, and the Libyan leader visited Tunis on his return from the meeting. Ben Ali attended the special OAU summit meeting in Libya in September, which coincided with extensive celebrations to mark the 30th anniversary of Qaddafi's regime. The Libyan leader visited Tunisia in May 2003, at the invitation of President Ben Ali, to review bilateral relations and progress in various joint projects. Tunisia declared that it would continue its efforts to achieve the final lifting of UN sanctions against Libya, and the two countries reiterated their solidarity with the Iraqi people and their commitment to Iraq's independence and territorial integrity.

In February 2004 Ben Ali held talks with the Libyan Secretary for Foreign Liaison and International Co-operation. Their discussions were reported to have covered reinforcing bilateral relations, reviving the UMA (which was at that time under Libyan presidency), and the Arab League summit that was to be held in Tunis in March. Ben Ali was invited to the extraordinary summit meeting of the AU, to be held in Libya later in February. In June Ben Ali held talks with the Secretary of the Libyan General People's Committee, Shukri Muhammad Ghanem, in the course of which they reviewed progress in bilateral relations and discussed reviving the UMA. In July 2006 the new Secretary of the Libyan General People's Committee, Al-Baghdadi Ali al-Mahmoudi, visited Tunis for the 19th session of the Joint Tunisian-Libyan Commission, at which discussions focused on strengthening economic co-operation. The lifting of sanctions on Libya and the re-admission of the Libyan leadership to the international system meant closer co-operation with Tunisia. Trade between the two countries increased as Libya began to catch up after years of isolation. In April 2007 it was announced by the two Governments that Tunisian building firms would help Libya to build over 40,000 homes by 2010. Libya's Secretary for the Economy, Trade and Investment spoke of the necessity to increase exchanges, which stood at US $2,000m. per year.

Regime change in Libya was welcomed by 'post-revolution' Tunisia. Indicative of their improved relations, in April 2012 Libya's transitional Government and Tunisia signed a land border agreement to combat organized crime, terrorism and trafficking. In July they signed an agreement to increase co-operation in the sector of information technology. Their greatly improved relationship also gave impetus to renewed talk in the Maghreb of reviving the almost defunct UMA. Any significant progress will, however, require improved Moroccan-Algerian relations, and a more stable Libya, from the point of view of neighbouring Tunisia and Algeria in particular. Following the near collapse of the Libyan state and the rise of armed militias, a west Libyan Berber tribe reportedly engaged in confrontation with local Arabs. From early 2013 there were widespread reports that AQIM forces were seeking to enter Algeria via Tunisia. Jebel Chaambi, a mountainous area west of Kasserine and close to the Algerian border, was the scene of repeated fighting involving jihadi militia and both Tunisian and Algerian security forces from April, when mines killed security personnel. On 29 July eight Tunisian security personnel were killed in an apparent ambush by jihadi militia.

Tunisia's relations with Algeria continued to be dominated by the Islamist threat. In December 1991 Rachid Ghannouchi and other senior al-Nahdah members were reportedly expelled from Algeria to Sudan. Relations with Algeria improved appreciably after the second round of Algeria's legislative elections were cancelled in January 1992 following the military takeover depriving the Front Islamique du Salut (FIS) of victory in the polls. The situation in Algeria was a constant factor in Tunisian decision-making with respect to domestic opposition and the choices made to counter political Islamism. Tunisia welcomed the appointment of Muhammad Boudiaf as Chairman of the High Council of State, and the military junta's campaign to suppress the FIS. In February 1993 Boudiaf's successor, Ali Kafi, visited Tunis, and during his stay letters were exchanged with President Ben Ali to ratify the official demarcation of the 1,000-km border between the two countries. Ben Ali and Kafi also expressed their determination to work together to counter the threat of terrorism (assumed by many commentators more accurately to mean the threat of militant Islamism) in the region. In December the Algerian and Tunisian ministers responsible for foreign affairs met at Tabarka, Tunisia, to celebrate the final demarcation of the frontier between the two countries, the precise line of which had been disputed for some years after independence. The new Algerian head of state, Liamine Zéroual, visited Tunis for the UMA summit meeting in April 1994 and held further talks with Ben Ali after the meeting ended. The two leaders issued a statement expressing their commitment to democracy, pluralism and the promotion of human rights, and condemning fanaticism and extremism. Zéroual's appeals for dialogue with Algeria's banned Islamist party seemed certain to have alarmed Ben Ali, who had rejected any negotiations with the Tunisian Islamist opposition. After an attack by Algerian Islamist militants against a Tunisian frontier post near Tozeur in February 1995, in which six Tunisian soldiers were reported to have been killed, security along the border was strengthened. It was well known that Tunisia had been co-operating with Algeria on security matters for some years and the co-operation may have extended beyond sharing intelligence to joint operations against armed Islamist groups (involving Tunisians as well as Algerians) operating in border areas. Some difficulties that had arisen over the employment of Algerians in Tunisia and over trade relations between the two countries appeared to have been resolved when Prime Minister Karoui visited Algiers in June 1996. The Algerian Prime Minister, Ahmed Ouyahia, made a reciprocal visit to Tunis in December and indicated his support for Tunisia's efforts to revive the UMA. Ben Ali held talks with Algeria's new President, Abdelaziz Bouteflika, at the OAU summit meeting in Algiers in July 1999 and again during the special OAU summit meeting in Libya in September, during which they discussed improving bilateral co-operation and the revival of the UMA. In May 2000 the Tunisian authorities announced that their security forces had repulsed a cross-border attack by a group of Algerian Islamist guerrillas linked to Hassan Hattab's Da'wa wal Djihad, during which three militants were killed and two Tunisian soldiers injured. The incident, the most serious since 1995, occurred shortly after Tunisia signed a customs agreement with Algeria aimed at combating smuggling which, Algeria insisted, helped to finance its radical Islamist opponents. Nevertheless, in June 2000 President Bouteflika visited Tunis, where he addressed the Tunisian parliament.

President Ben Ali made an official visit to Algiers in February 2002 to discuss bilateral relations and reviving the UMA. Earlier, in April and November 2001, the Algerian army Chief of Staff, Gen. Muhammad Lamari, had visited Tunis for talks with Ben Ali and his military and security officials about intensifying the battle against Islamist militants, better surveillance of their borders to prevent Tunisian and Algerian members of al-Qa'ida from returning to their country of origin from Afghanistan, and dismantling North African Islamist networks in Europe. It was reported that numerous Islamist activists from Tunisia, who had taken refuge in Algeria and joined local GIA groups, had been arrested and handed over to the Tunisian authorities. In December 2002 the Prime Ministers of Algeria and Tunisia opened the 13th Joint Algerian-Tunisian Committee in Tunis. In June 2006 the Tunisian press reported that a group of 10 Tunisians, who had participated in training at a GSPC camp in eastern Algeria, had been arrested by the Tunisian security forces as they crossed the border between the two countries. It was believed that the Tunisians had planned to travel to Iraq in order to join the insurgency against US and allied forces. Local sources suggested that young Tunisian Islamists who wanted to join al-Qa'ida in Iraq now transited via the GSPC network in Algeria rather than through networks in Libya. In December 2008 Prime Minister Ghannouchi and his Algerian counterpart, Ahmed Ouyahia, signed a preferential trade agreement, following a meeting of the Algerian-Tunisian High Joint Committee in Tunis. The need for mutual co-operation was emphasized by the collapse of the Qaddafi regime in Libya. This resulted in instability at their borders with Libya and an exodus of regime figures, as well as migrants from sub-Saharan Africa. In August 2011 Tunisia and Algeria were reported to be conducting talks to discuss enhanced security co-operation.

Tunisia's normally good relations with Morocco were strained in May 1994 after Tunisia expelled some 600 Moroccans who the authorities claimed were living there without permission or had broken Tunisian laws. Towards the end of the year the Tunisian authorities expelled several hundred Moroccans on the grounds that they were trying to enter Italy as illegal immigrants. The route through Tunisia was used by many of the Moroccans who enter Italy illegally every year. In early 1996 Tunisia condemned Morocco for trying to block UMA activities in retaliation for alleged Algerian interference in the Western Sahara dispute. However, after a visit to Rabat by Karoui in September, a commitment was made to improve economic and political co-operation. In November both countries appealed for the revival of the UMA. This message was repeated in March 1999, when President Ben Ali made a state visit to Rabat. During the visit a free trade agreement was signed between the two countries as part of a plan to increase bilateral trade. Morocco's new ruler, King Muhammad VI, visited Tunis in May. President Ben Ali made an official visit to Morocco in July 2001 at the invitation of King Muhammad, when discussions were held about increasing bilateral trade.

Ben Ali was closely involved in the movement towards Maghreb unity, and in February 1989 Tunisia signed the treaty creating the UMA with Algeria, Morocco, Libya and Mauritania. Tunisia was chosen as the site of the new Maghreb Investment and Foreign Trade Bank, and a Tunisian diplomat, Muhammad Amamou, was appointed UMA Secretary-General. In January 1993 Tunisia assumed the annual presidency of the organization. Tunisian officials stressed that Ben Ali's presidency had been a success and that 11 co-operation agreements had been signed during his one-year term of office, including plans for a Maghreb free trade zone. Yet, in reality, he failed to give new impetus to the organization, largely because two of its members, Algeria and Libya, remained preoccupied with their own problems: Algeria plunged into civil war by escalating Islamist violence and Libya subjected to even tighter UN sanctions. Algeria and Morocco's rivalry over the issue of Western Sahara also undermined the workings of the UMA. The summit meeting that should have marked the end of Tunisia's presidency was delayed three times and did not take place until April 1994 when Ben Ali handed over the presidency to the new Algerian head of state, Liamine Zéroual. Neither King Hassan of Morocco nor Qaddafi was present. Although at least 40 accords had been adopted by the UMA, only five had been ratified by all five member states, indicating that little progress had been made in translating rhetoric into reality and developing a unified Maghreb. Ben Ali, in line with the long-standing policy of Tunisia to maintain good relations with all of its Maghreb neighbours, continued to urge the other four member states to try to overcome the obstacles facing the organization by joint action, but little progress was made. Following the suspension of UN sanctions against Libya in April 1999, some tentative moves were made to revive the organization; however, plans for a heads of state summit meeting in Algiers in November—the first for five years—were cancelled owing to renewed tensions between Algeria and Morocco. At a meeting of UMA ministers responsible for foreign affairs in Algiers in January 2002 former Tunisian Minister of Foreign Affairs, Habib Boularès, was appointed UMA Secretary-General to replace Muhammad Amamou, who had stepped down because of ill health. However, the long-delayed summit meeting of UMA heads of state that was to have been held in Algiers in June 2002 was cancelled. Renewed attempts to convene the summit in Algiers in December 2003 failed after King Muhammad of Morocco stated that he would not be attending.

Ben Ali attended the Arab League summit in Algiers in March 2005. At the end of the summit, the Tunisian Minister of Foreign Affairs participated in a meeting of UMA foreign ministers, but the long-awaited UMA heads of state summit due to be held in Tripoli in late May was postponed indefinitely at the last minute after King Muhammad of Morocco announced that he would not be attending. During the WSIS held in Tunis in November, Ben Ali held discussions with Bouteflika and Qaddafi on ways of strengthening co-operation and solidarity between Maghreb countries; King Muhammad of Morocco did not attend the summit. In February 2006 former Tunisian Minister of Foreign Affairs, Habib Ben Yahia, replaced Boularès as Secretary-General of the UMA. In April 2008 celebrations were held in Tangier, Morocco, to mark the 50th anniversary of the summit at which the idea of a union of Arab Maghreb states was first proposed. In spite of some residual tension between Moroccan and Algerian officials, the event ended peacefully with renewed calls for greater regional collaboration and a galvanized UMA. The prospects of this have been enhanced by the series of regime or governmental changes in the Maghreb; however, instability is also a deterrent against a deepening of the union even though it has enhanced security co-operation.

Relations with the Middle East

After Ben Ali came to power in 1987 his Prime Minister, Hedi Baccouche, toured the Arab Gulf states, which ranked among Tunisia's major sources of economic aid, to explain to Arab leaders the new administration's domestic and foreign policies. In January 1988 the Tunisian Government announced that it would be resuming diplomatic relations with Egypt, severed in 1979 after Egypt signed a peace agreement with Israel. In January 1989 Dr Boutros Boutros-Ghali, then Minister of State for Foreign Affairs, became the first Egyptian minister to visit Tunisia for a decade. In March 1990 Ben Ali made the first visit to Cairo by a Tunisian President since 1965, and signed several agreements on bilateral co-operation with Egypt. In September a majority of Arab League members decided to move the organization's headquarters from Tunis (where it had been 'temporarily' established in 1979) back to Cairo. The Tunisian Government protested at the decision, and the League's Tunisian Secretary-General, Chedli Klibi, resigned. Relations with Saudi Arabia also remained cordial, but, despite a high level of co-operation between the two countries, the Tunisian Government was concerned about the extent of Saudi support for Tunisian Islamists.

Meanwhile, Tunisia was the scene of another Israeli operation against the PLO. In April 1988 Khalil al-Wazir ('Abu Jihad'), the deputy of PLO Chairman Yasser Arafat, was killed by an Israeli assassination squad at his home in Tunis. The Israeli operation was a source of embarrassment for the Tunisian authorities, as it was revealed that Mossad (Israeli secret service) operatives had been based in Tunisia for some time before the assassination was carried out.

President Ben Ali's decision to condemn the deployment of a UN-authorized, US-led multi-national force in the Gulf region following Iraq's invasion of Kuwait in August 1990, and the expression of strong pro-Iraqi sentiments among Tunisians during the crisis, seriously strained Tunisia's previously close relations with Saudi Arabia and the Gulf Arab states, notably Kuwait, which withdrew its ambassador from Tunis. Ben Ali had not explicitly condemned Iraq's invasion of Kuwait, and the Tunisian National Committee of Support to Iraq had expressed support for the annexation. After the cease-fire in the Gulf War in February 1991, Tunisia quickly sought to restore links that had been cut by its support for Iraq. Ben Ali sent a cordial message to the Amir of Kuwait, congratulating him upon regaining his sovereignty. However, it was not until April 1994—when Sheikh Sabah al-Ahmad al-Jaber, the Kuwaiti Minister of Foreign Affairs and First Deputy Prime

Minister, visited Tunis—that it was reported that normal diplomatic relations would be restored. Bilateral co-operation finally resumed in April 1996. A state visit to Tunis by the Amir of Qatar, Sheikh Hamad bin Khalifa Al Thani, in June 1997 provided further evidence of the improvement in Tunisia's relations with the Gulf Arab States. However, in February 2001, after the Qatar-based satellite television channel Al Jazeera broadcast live interviews with several leading human rights activists, and with exiled al-Nahdah leader Ghannouchi, Tunisia responded by recalling its ambassador from Qatar. Since 2011 Qatar has tried to position itself at the forefront of regime change (in some countries at least) in the Arab world. As a result, the Qatari heir apparent, Sheikh Tamim bin Hamad bin Khalifa Al Thani, visited Tunisia in July 2012 and signed a number of economic agreements intended to facilitate increased Qatari investment in the energy and power sectors. Tunisia's relations with Saudi Arabia were complicated by Ben Ali obtaining refuge in that country, and allegedly also appropriating a large amount of Tunisia's state funds. However, there are periodic negotiations on the matter. Saudi Arabia has conducted high-level meetings with senior Tunisian officials since the change of regime. In July it also confirmed development loans of nearly US $200m. at low interest for Tunisia's energy and power sector, and for vocational training. While Saudi Arabia appeared to have encouraged the Egyptian military's overthrow of President Mursi, it has less obvious interests in trying to influence events in Tunisia, despite alleged connections with some local Salafists.

Efforts were also made to re-establish cordial relations with Egypt, and both Governments found common cause in the fight against Islamist militancy. In early 1997 the Egyptian Prime Minister, Kamal al-Ganzouri, visited Tunis where he signed several economic and cultural co-operation agreements. Both countries pledged to work together to increase bilateral trade, and agreement was reached in principle on the creation of a free trade zone. In early 1998 the two countries signed an agreement in Cairo at a meeting of the Tunisian-Egyptian Joint Higher Committee to dismantle customs duties over the next 10 years. Ben Ali held talks in Egypt with President Mubarak in November 1999, and in February 2001 Mubarak made an official visit to Tunis to discuss the escalation in violence between Israel and the Palestinians. Following the change of leadership in both countries, Tunisia sought to improve its most important African and Arab relationship, that with Egypt. On 16 July 2012 President Marzouki visited the new Egyptian President, Muhammad Mursi, in Cairo, where the latter strongly praised the role of Tunisia in beginning the 'Arab spring' of revolutionary protests in the Middle East and North Africa. The forced removal of Mursi from office in July 2013 was strongly condemned by Tunisia, and resulted in a deterioration in relations, exacerbated by Tunisia's own political crisis.

At the same time Tunisia continued to maintain good relations with Iraq, and the Tunisian Government regularly urged the UN to lift sanctions against that country. US and British air-strikes against Iraq in December 1999 were strongly criticized by the Government and condemned by the Chamber of Deputies and by several opposition parties. However, there were no street demonstrations in support of Iraq, although security around the US embassy in Tunis was increased. In May 1999 Tunisia signed a trade agreement with Iraq, and Tunisia's Minister of Trade and Handicrafts, Mondher Zenaïdi, made a number of visits to Baghdad to discuss bilateral trade under the UN's 'oil-for-food' programme for Iraq. By the end of the year Tunisia was reported to have won contracts worth US $200m. to supply goods to Iraq since the 'oil-for-food' programme began. Responding to pressure from public opinion, in October 2000 Tunisia defied the air embargo against Iraq and sent two aircraft to Baghdad carrying humanitarian and medical aid. A trade delegation led by the Minister of Trade travelled on one of the flights. Tunisia expressed deep regret at the US and British air-strikes against targets near Baghdad in mid-February 2001. During a visit to Tunis by the Iraqi Vice-President, Taha Yassin Ramadan, in late February the two countries signed a free trade agreement. At the beginning of March 2003, as the Iraq crisis deepened, Tunisia was appointed to a special committee of the Arab League to try to find a peaceful solution, and in mid-March the Tunisian Minister of Foreign Affairs, in a last-minute peace effort, visited Baghdad for talks with Iraqi leader, Saddam Hussain. Towards the end of the month Ben Ali expressed 'deep regret' at the US-led military intervention in Iraq. He called on the international community to end the war and resolve the crisis by peaceful means within the framework of the UN.

Tunisia claimed to have played a leading role, together with Norway, in the secret talks between the PLO and Israel that led to the signing of the Declaration of Principles on Palestinian Self-Rule (Documents on Palestine, see p. 76) in September 1993. Tunisia welcomed the breakthrough in PLO-Israeli relations, and shortly afterwards an Israeli delegation arrived in Tunis for talks with Tunisian and PLO officials. Salah Masawi, the PLO director-general of foreign relations, declared that there was no obstacle to Tunisia establishing diplomatic relations with Israel. The Tunisian Ministry of Foreign Affairs welcomed the PLO-Israel Cairo Agreement of May 1994 on implementing Palestinian self-rule in Gaza and Jericho. The PLO offices in Tunis were closed in June as Arafat and the Palestinian leadership prepared to move to Gaza, where the Palestinian (National) Authority (PA) was to be established.

As the PLO departed, Tunisia made new moves towards the normalization of relations with Israel. The first party of Israeli tourists to visit Tunisia since independence arrived in June 1994, following an agreement made in October 1993 with Israeli Deputy Minister of Foreign Affairs Yossi Beilin, the first senior Israeli minister to visit Tunisia, and direct telephone links were established with Israel in July. In October the Tunisian and Israeli ministers responsible for foreign affairs met at the UN General Assembly in New York and agreed in principle to open interests sections (which Tunisia referred to as 'economic channels') in the Belgian embassies in Tunis and Tel-Aviv. At a meeting at the US State Department in Washington, DC, with Warren Christopher and the Israeli Minister of Foreign Affairs, Shimon Peres, the Tunisian Minister of Foreign Affairs, Ben Yahia, stated that this was the first step towards full diplomatic relations. In February 1995 Tunisia, together with Israel, Morocco, Mauritania and Egypt, took part in talks with NATO in Brussels, Belgium, on security co-operation. Before the talks the Secretary-General of NATO, Willy Claes, had made the controversial statement that he saw Islamist extremism as the biggest single threat to the West since the collapse of communism. In March Tunisia participated in naval exercises off the Tunisian coast with Israel, Canada, Morocco, Algeria, Egypt and four of the Gulf Arab states.

In October 1995 Arafat met Ben Ali in Tunis to review progress made on the implementation of Palestinian self-rule. After the Palestinian elections in January 1996, an agreement was reached between Tunisia and Israel to proceed with low-level diplomatic relations from April. Tunisia thus became the fourth Arab state to establish diplomatic relations with Israel, after Egypt, Jordan and Morocco. At the same time Tunisia agreed to recognize passports issued by the PA. In April 1996 Israel opened an interests office in the Belgian embassy in Tunis; however, Tunisia delayed sending its own representative to Tel-Aviv in response to Israeli attacks on southern Lebanon. Nevertheless, some contacts between the two countries were made, but the victory of Binyamin Netanyahu in the Israeli elections in May and the formation of a right-wing Government quickly brought the process of normalization to a halt. President Ben Ali attended the emergency Arab summit meeting in Cairo in June and, as current Chairman of the Arab League, made one of the two keynote speeches. After the conference he defended the actions of those countries that had taken steps to normalize relations with Israel, stating that they were intended 'to push the peace process forward'. However, in November the Tunisian leadership condemned Israeli intransigence towards the peace process and criticized the building of Jewish settlements in the Occupied Territories. The normalization of relations was suspended, the head of the Tunisian interests office in Tel-Aviv departed in August 1997 and the only remaining Tunisian diplomat returned to Tunis early in 1998. After the appointment of a new Government in Israel headed by the Labour leader, Ehud Barak, and a revival of the Middle East peace process, relations with Israel improved, and the Israeli interests office in Tunis reopened in October 1999. In October 2000, in response to violent clashes between Israel and the Palestinians, Tunisia again closed its interests office in Tel-Aviv and imposed a freeze on normalization of relations with the Jewish state. Many Tunisians remained deeply hostile towards Israel, and several large pro-Palestinian demonstrations were held, including one led by Ben Ali and the Palestinian leader, Arafat. These protests were carefully controlled by the authorities, and university students were forbidden to hold their own demonstrations in support of the Palestinians.

In late March 2004 President Ben Ali caused a diplomatic storm when, at just two days' notice, he postponed indefinitely the annual summit-level meeting of the Arab League Council, due to be held in Tunis on 29–30 March. Despite the numerous divisions and differences between the Arab states, this was the first time in the history of the League that a summit had been cancelled after the preliminary meetings at ministerial level had already begun. Plans to relaunch the Saudi-sponsored Arab peace plan (originally endorsed by the League's summit held in Beirut, Lebanon, two years earlier) had been dealt a serious blow by Israel's 'targeted killing' of Sheikh Ahmad Yassin, the founder and spiritual leader of the militant Islamic Resistance Movement (Hamas), and Saudi Arabia, Bahrain, Oman and the United Arab Emirates had already declared that they would not attend the summit. According to Tunisia's Ministry of Foreign Affairs, the decision had been taken to postpone the summit because agreement had not been reached on issues including certain amendments and proposals regarded by Tunisia as essential to a political reform programme formulated in response to the Bush Administration's Greater Middle East Initiative. However, representatives of several other Arab League states asserted that there had been no serious differences on the reform programme, and that the Tunisian amendments had been incorporated. The League's Secretary-General, Amr Moussa, stated that Tunisia's decision would have dangerous consequences for joint Arab action, and accepted an offer by Egypt to host the summit as soon as possible. In response, Tunisia insisted that, as it held the rotating chairmanship of the League, it retained the right to host the meeting at a date to be arranged. The summit, which was also to have discussed the situation in Iraq, was to have been the League's first meeting at this level since the commencement of the US-led military campaign to overthrow the regime of Saddam Hussain, and its postponement was regarded by many as reinforcing the image of a divided and ineffective Arab world.

At the beginning of April 2004 Moussa announced that a consensus had been reached on rescheduling the summit, and it was later announced that it would be held in Tunis on 22–23 May. Ben Ali stated in his opening address that there should be more international efforts to reactivate the 'roadmap' for a permanent solution to the Israeli–Palestinian conflict (sponsored by the USA, the UN, the EU and Russia) and for the protection of the Palestinian people, and emphasized the need for Iraq to regain its sovereignty. The meeting produced vague pledges on political reforms, called for a revival of the Middle East peace process, condemned spiralling violence in the Israeli–Palestinian conflict and appealed for the UN to assume a stronger role in Iraq. The Libyan leader, Qaddafi, walked out of the opening session; four other Arab leaders departed before the closing session, and eight did not attend the meeting at all.

In July 2004 Ben Yahia chaired the first meeting of the so-called Arab 'troika' on Iraq, comprising Tunisia, Algeria and Bahrain, established in May during the Tunis Arab League summit. The Secretary-General of the Arab League and Iraq's Minister of Foreign Affairs, Hoshiyar Mahmud Muhammad al-Zibari, also attended the session, at which Iraq's request for Arab troops to be sent to Baghdad to protect the UN mission and for Arab participation in the reconstruction of Iraq were discussed. At the May summit Arab states had refused to send troops to Iraq under the supervision of the US-led force. Before the troika meeting al-Zibari briefed his Tunisian counterpart on the political and security situation in Iraq following the previous month's transfer of power to the Interim Government.

In February 2005, after Israeli premier Ariel Sharon accepted an invitation from Ben Ali to attend the Second WSIS to be hosted by Tunisia in November, Tunisian opposition parties and human rights groups condemned the proposed visit, which would be the first by an Israeli Prime Minister, stating that it would bring 'lasting shame' on the country, and vowed to stop it. Tunisian officials played down the invitation, stating that the summit was an international event, to which every country in the world was invited. The PA called on Ben Ali to cancel the invitation to Sharon. In the event, Israel was represented by the Deputy Prime Minister and Minister of Foreign Affairs, Silvan Shalom. Protesters chanting anti-Israeli slogans denounced the visit as an attempt to normalize relations between the two countries. In June 2007 Tunisia called for an ending of the confrontation between Fatah and Hamas in the Palestinian territories, with the Minister of Foreign Affairs calling for 'logic and reason to prevail' in order to preserve the unity of the Palestinian people. Tunisia remained suspicious of Islamist movements, Hamas included, and supported the peace efforts of President Abbas.

In early 2001 Prime Minister Muhammad Ghannouchi became the first Tunisian premier to visit Iran since the 1979 Revolution. Tunisia had severed diplomatic relations with Iran in 1987 after accusing Tehran of supporting Islamist militancy in Tunisia, but relations had been restored in September 1990. In January 2006 the Iranian Vice-President in charge of Legal and Parliamentary Affairs, Sayed Ahmad Mousavi, visited Tunis for talks with Ben Ali. In February Tunisian Minister of Foreign Affairs Abdelwahab Abdallah held talks in Tehran with the Iranian President, Mahmoud Ahmadinejad, and his Iranian counterpart, at which eight co-operation agreements were signed. During the visit Ahmadinejad expressed his gratitude for Tunisia's support for Iran's right to access nuclear technology for peaceful purposes. In the wake of the political upheaval in Tunisia in 2010–11, Iran was keen to present itself as the ally of revolt in the Arab world against countries it viewed as being in the sway of the USA. However, following the change of regime, Tunisia was keen to indicate that its moderate Islamist direction did not make it an automatic ally of Shi'a Islamist-led Iran. Relations have become more cordial, but not substantive.

Economy

Revised for this edition by NEIL PARTRICK

In the 1980s Tunisia's economy entered a period of turbulence, following an impressive record in the previous decade. A decline in petroleum production from 1980 and a series of droughts, together with the sudden fall in the international oil price in 1986, resulted in a balance of payments crisis, forcing the Government to seek assistance from the IMF (see Planning).

Austerity measures were adopted in 1991 in order to counter the effects of the Gulf War on exports, tourism revenues and external funding sources. In protest at Tunisia's ambivalence at the time of the 1990–91 crisis, Kuwait and Saudi Arabia curtailed planned investment and aid, and the USA also reduced its support. Nevertheless, gross domestic product (GDP) growth in 1991 was around 3.5%, reflecting a record harvest, a recovery in tourism and an upturn in the industrial sector. In July 1992 a new five-year Development Plan (1992–96—see Planning) was inaugurated, amid optimism that Tunisia was set to become North Africa's leading centre for venture capital and technology. Having risen sharply by 7.8% in 1992, GDP growth then declined again, to only 2% in 1993, 3.3% in 1994 and 2.4% in 1995 (largely reflecting the effects of drought on agricultural production) before recovering to 6.9% in 1996 and an estimated 5.6% in 1997. Unemployment, particularly acute in the poorer south, centre and north-west, remained a problem, affecting between 15% and 20% of the economically active population by 1997. GDP rose by 5% in 1998 and by 6.2% in 1999 (by which time GDP per head in Tunisia was the highest in the Maghreb). Despite further contractions in agriculture as a result of poor rainfall, GDP grew by an estimated 5% in 2000 and 5.1% in 2001—evidence of the positive effects of gradual liberalization and diversification on the economy. Meanwhile, average inflation remained subdued at 3.1% in 1998, 2.7% in 1999, 2.9% in 2000 and 1.9% in 2001 (its lowest rate for over a quarter of a century).

According to the IMF, GDP growth in 2002 decelerated sharply, to an estimated 1.7%. Fiscal policy was tightened in response to excessive demand, while the economy was affected by a series of shocks, including a terrorist attack, a slowdown in export markets and another year of drought. This led to a correction in the external balance of payments, despite a decline in tourism. Growth of non-agricultural GDP was maintained at an estimated 3.5% in 2002, mainly supported by non-manufacturing industries and services (despite the weakness of tourism-related sectors). The economy returned to a higher growth rate of 5.6% in 2003, driven by the recovery in agricultural output after successive years of drought, and inflation was stable at 2.7%. The Government, meanwhile, continued its prudent budget policy. As a result of more favourable weather and a recovery in tourism, GDP growth was 6.0% in 2004, although inflation rose to 3.6%. In 2005, while the tourism and energy sectors performed well and the textile industry survived the challenge from Asian competition, there was again a slowdown in agriculture, and growth slipped to an estimated 4.2%. As international petroleum prices continued to rise sharply, the cost of fuel subsidies increased, leading the Government to raise retail oil prices and launch an energy-saving strategy. The inflation rate was estimated at 2.1% in 2005. GDP growth accelerated to 5.6% in 2006, owing to an agricultural recovery, the expansion of non-textile manufacturing and the strength of the services sector. However, inflation increased to 4.5%, leading to a tightening of monetary policy in the second half of the year. The IMF praised the authorities' good economic management for yielding strong macroeconomic results in Tunisia in 2007: growth accelerated to 6.3% and inflation averaged 3.1%. The current account deficit widened (largely because of worsening terms of trade) and the dinar recorded a slight depreciation of about 3%, but both were nevertheless comfortably financed by higher foreign direct investment (FDI), as reflected by an increase in international reserves. However, there were concerns over the impact that the high global commodity prices would have on inflation and fiscal performance and over the need to reform the subsidy system. In early 2008 there was unrest, particularly in south-western Tunisia, as people protested against the rising cost of living and unemployment (see History). Inflation rose to 4.9% in 2008, fuelled by rapidly increasing import costs, which in turn precipitated a widening of the trade deficit. Real GDP growth slowed slightly, but remained robust at 4.6%. The global economic downturn, which particularly affected European Union (EU) countries (Tunisia's main export destination), had taken full effect by early 2009. As a result, exports declined in that year by 18%, although the trade deficit narrowed slightly, as imports also fell markedly. Owing to falling demand for Tunisia's manufactured goods, industrial production declined by 7%. Overall growth was supported by growth in both agriculture and services; however, the pace of real GDP growth slowed to 3.1%, thus easing price pressures and reducing inflation, to 3.5%. Although domestic demand remained at a low level, and the real value of agriculture and fisheries output contracted in 2010, exports rebounded strongly, by 21%, as the eurozone started to recover. As a result, overall growth additionally showed a slight rise in 2010, to 3.7%. Expanding economic activity also had an impact on domestic consumer prices, however, with inflation rising to 4.1%, according to the ILO. In 2011, according to the Institut National de la Statistique (INS), a contraction of 2.2% in real GDP occurred, compared with 2010. This largely reflected political upheaval that contributed to a reduction in manufacturing and other (non-agricultural) business activities, softened domestic consumption, reduced FDI, and shrunken foreign remittances when Tunisia's large work-force in Libya were obliged by the conflict there to return home. Inflation fell to 3.5%, although at August 2013 the INS was stating that average inflation in 2011 was 4.3%, following a 5.2% rise in 2010.

A real GDP rise of 4.8% occurred in the first quarter of 2012, compared with the corresponding period of 2011. This was not surprising, given that a 3.7% contraction was recorded in the first quarter of 2011, compared with the corresponding period of the previous year. By the end of 2012 the INS reported that the annual real GDP rise was 4.1%, a reflection of heightened economic activity due to relative political stabilization. However foreign remittances have not recovered to the position seen in 2010, chiefly due to ongoing upheaval in some neighbouring Arab states, while demand growth from Europe, the largest market for Tunisian goods, was modest. The IMF put real GDP growth in 2012 at 3.6%, somewhat less than the INS figure and markedly below the average of 4.9% over 2006–11.

Concerns over the Government's commitment to an anti-inflationary monetary policy were expressed in July 2012, when the Governor of the Banque Centrale de Tunisie (BCT), Mustapha Kamel Nabli, was dismissed. He had raised concerns about the inflationary consequences of both promoting bank lending and expanding government spending. It was feared by some observers that his replacement, Chédli Ayari, formerly of the World Bank, would simply follow the Government's prioritization of growth. This concern appeared to be vindicated as average monthly inflation rose by 7% in 2012 compared with 2011. The six-month inflation average to the end of June 2013 was 8.25%, compared with the same period in the previous year. Imported inflation in turn followed government-encouraged growth.

In July 1995 Tunisia had signed an association agreement with the EU (see Trade) under which Tunisian manufacturers would progressively be exposed to increasingly strong competitive pressures. The agreement formally came into force in March 1998, although Tunisia began dismantling trade barriers to EU industrial goods from January 1996.

Despite pressure from the World Bank, the IMF and Tunisia's own central bank, until the late 1990s the Government had moved relatively slowly to privatize public companies, fearing that this would lead to reductions in the work-force and aggravate unemployment. By 1998 there was some evidence that political resistance to privatization had weakened and that the Government had accepted that an acceleration in the sale of public companies was essential to strengthen the economy. In 2006, recognizing Tunisia's relatively high level of external debt compared with other emerging market economies with similar ratings, the Government, consistent with IMF advice, allocated two-thirds of the proceeds from the partial privatization of Tunisie Télécom (see Transport and Communications) to reduce external debt. Although Tunisia's external debt stock had risen slightly to TD 21,301m. by 2008, it had fallen considerably in relative terms, to 38.6% of GDP, compared with 54% in 2005. A fall in asset prices, brought on by the global economic downturn in 2009, temporarily slowed the Government's divestment programme, and over the course of the year only one state-owned enterprise, the Société Tunisienne d'Industrie Automobile, was sold off, for an insubstantial TD 2m. for its outstanding stake. However, the Government earned considerably more from the sale of a fixed-line and mobile-phone concession, for TD 257m. The Government aimed to sell off up to 12 state-owned enterprises during 2010. The Government released 22.2% of its shareholding of Tunis Re, an insurance company, to private investors in April, while in May it sought expressions of interest for its 51.6% stake in a tyre manufacturer, Société Tunisienne des Industries de Pneumatiques. However, efforts to revive the sale of Banque Franco-Tunisienne failed to make progress. In 2010 external public debt rose significantly, after remaining level in 2009, to TD 23,582m. (equivalent to 37.2% of real GDP). After elections in October 2011, the Islamist-led Government committed itself to the sale of state-funded media company, Al-Wataniya, while indicating that a number of companies recently taken over by the state, having formerly been privately owned by the Ben Ali family, would be divested. It is estimated that Tunisian banks leveraged around US $2,000m. for these assets. In May 2012 TD 205m. was raised from the sale of two telecom licences to operator Tunisiana (in which Qatar Telecom has a 75% stake). The Islamist-led Government is committed to ongoing privatization, and projected that this and the granting of licences would generate TD 1,000m in 2012, a target that seemed to require them to finally act on selling off Tunisie Télécom. However this did not occur. At the end of 2012 the Government stated that the total of 'privatization and grants' had risen by more than TD 1,000m. compared with 2011. However, the Government expects that this revenue will fall by a similar amount in 2013.

The incoming Islamist-led Government began a review of the operation of the existing investment law. This could, in theory, bring foreign onshore ownership (presently limited to 49%, excluding the agricultural sector) in line with the 60% of equity that it is possible for foreign investors to hold in offshore Tunisian companies.

In 1999 former President Zine al-Abidine Ben Ali had declared that reducing unemployment was his 'priority of priorities', and a national fund was set up to finance training and work programmes and to help those wishing to establish their own businesses. The President also highlighted the importance of increasing domestic and foreign investment, improving the competitiveness of the economy and strengthening exports. Despite marked improvements in the standard of living in the country, both the IMF and the World Bank identified unemployment as Tunisia's greatest problem and stated that annual growth rates of 6%–7% would have to be achieved through increased levels of domestic and foreign investment, faster export growth and further structural reforms. However, some analysts argued that many foreign investors were deterred by the repressive policies of the Ben Ali regime and evidence of widespread corruption and nepotism. In 2002 unemployment remained high, at 15.3%; it only declined marginally, to 14.2%, in 2004. Having remained at around this level since then, signs emerged in early 2009 of a deterioration in the job market, owing to the global economic downturn. Unemployment increased to 14.7% in 2009, as industrial output contracted. In March 2010 the Government announced that it was to allocate TD 187m. to support job creation, with a focus on helping graduates into work, following the publication of a World Bank study that indicated that some 38% of graduates had never been in employment and that 66% remained unemployed 18 months after graduation. Following Ben Ali's downfall amid popular, youth-orientated, revolt, the subsequent interim Government announced an emergency economic stimulus plan of US $1,500m. aimed at tackling unemployment and regional disparities (unemployment and related underdevelopment are far worse in the central-western part of the country). In mid-2012 the World Bank estimated that 44% of university graduates were unemployed. Overall unemployment was 18.9% at the end of 2011, and only fell slightly, to 18.1%, by the end of the first quarter of 2012. By the end of 2011 upheaval in Libya had encouraged many Tunisian migrants to return home where the domestic economy was floundering. By the end of 2012, however, unemployment had fallen slightly, to 16.7%. In contrast, at that time youth unemployment was, at 33%, very high, despite an increase in public spending and improved political conditions.

The Tunisian Government's projection of 4% real GDP growth in 2013 is based on the assumption that non-agricultural growth will run at 4.5% (the same increase seen in 2012). Notably, however, the growth projection was adjusted downwards in April 2013, following a political crisis in February after a senior opposition figure was assassinated (see History), and reflecting the impact of ongoing modest European demand. The IMF agreed a two year stand-by agreement with the Tunisian Government in June, making US $1,750m. available upon request in support of the economy should it face financing problems.

In its attempts to realize its target of a US $2,000m. in additional FDI, the Tunisian Government has continued to court Gulf state governments and businesses. Some Gulf governments have been responsive. The state-run Kuwait Investment Authority, a majority investor in the mutual investment fund for Tunisia, Consortium Tuniso-Koweitien de Développement, announced in June 2013 that it was increasing the fund's capital from €48m. to €221m.

AGRICULTURE

From the point of view of agriculture, Tunisia may be regarded as made up of five different areas: the mountainous north, with its large fertile valleys; the north-east, including the Cap Bon, where the soil suits the cultivation of oranges and other citrus fruit; the Sahel, where olives grow; the centre, with its high tablelands and pastures; and the south, with oases and gardens, where dates are prolific. Harvests vary considerably in size, determined by the uncertain rainfall. The main cereal crops are wheat, barley, maize, oats and sorghum. Fruit is also important, with grapes, olives, dates, oranges and figs grown for export as well as for the local market.

Agriculture's contribution to GDP has declined steadily from 22% in 1965 to 9.5% in 2011, to 8.6% as of the end of 2012, according to the INS. The sector's share of national employment has also fallen significantly, from 46% in 1960 to 16.4% (including fishing) in the first quarter of 2013, according to the INS. The 2002–06 Development Plan endorsed food self-sufficiency as a national objective, but Tunisia has generally had a negative food trade balance since the 1980s: the deficit stood at TD 511.7m. in 2003, TD 162.4m. in 2004 and TD 174.1m. in 2005. By 2011 it had reached TD 1,300m., and only fell slightly, to TD 1,200m., in 2012. In the first half of 2013 the deficit was narrowing again, at TD 349m, as exports rose substantially in the early months of the year compared with recent trends.

Agricultural output has been steadily increasing since the drought of 2010. The INS's latest figures indicate that, measured from a base of 100 in 2000, total agricultural production reached a monthly average of 127.7 in 2011 (after falling to 121.9 in 2010 from 125.1 the year before). It rose to 132.7 in 2012, and averaged 136 per month in the first half of 2013.

The fragmentation of landholdings and the need to consolidate them into larger, more efficient units has remained not only an obstacle to increasing the profitability of the agricultural sector but also a highly sensitive issue for the Government. In 1998 the Ministry of Agriculture reported that, while the area devoted to agriculture was declining as farmland was taken over for urban and industrial uses, the number of landholders had increased from 326,000 in 1962 to 471,000 in 1995, with the average size of landholdings declining from

16 ha to 11 ha. Many farms were too small to be profitable, and this discouraged investment and the use of modern farming methods. Also in 1998, the Ministry announced that state-owned farms would be leased to foreign investors with expertise in livestock and vineyard management.

Grown in a belt across the northern part of the country, wheat is the main cereal crop. The Government guarantees the price to the grower. Cereal production has continued to fluctuate markedly from year to year. There was a dramatic decline in 1987–88 as a result of drought and the worst plague of locusts for 30 years, while particularly good harvests were recorded in 1992 (2.6m. metric tons) and 1996 (2.8m. tons). Then, in 2001–02 Tunisia experienced one of the worst droughts in more than 50 years. The Government estimated output at only 0.6m. tons for 2002, with demand projected at 2.5m. tons. In 2003 production recovered to reach 2.9m. tons, and the 2004 crop, following plentiful rainfall, was estimated at 2.5m. tons. In 2005 production declined to 2.1m. tons, despite favourable weather conditions; the wheat crop was down by 5%, and the barley crop fell by 24% because of a decrease in the areas under cultivation. In 2006 the wheat and barley crops were estimated at 1.2m. tons and 395,000 tons, respectively, and imports of cereals increased by 8.2%. The 2007 harvest was the worst in almost a decade, falling to 1.19m. tons in total, on account of poor rains. Wheat production fell by 37% to 918,999 tons, while barley output dropped by over 50% to 269,100 tons. In response to this decline in production, the Government intervened in support of cereal farmers, offering them fixed prices for their produce, freezing the price of seeds and improving the availability of credit and grants. A 2007 World Bank study of Tunisia's agricultural sector stated that cereal production was inefficient, uncompetitive and used up precious water resources. However, the Tunisian Government prefers to reduce reliance on food imports. Cereal output showed no improvement in 2008, reaching just 1.1m. tons, although after a significantly improved harvest it reached 2.5m. tons in 2009. However, an extremely poor harvest in 2010 reduced yields significantly and, according to the INS, cereal production fell to just 1.1m. tons. In 2011 an improved harvest helped push up total cereal production to 2.3m. tons.

Grapes are grown around Tunis and Bizerte. Wine production reached a peak of almost 2.0m. hl in 1963. However, annual output had declined to around 340,000 hl by the early 1990s. Following new investment in vineyards, production then increased to 469,000 hl in 1999, but declined to 325,000 hl in 2002 as a result of the drought. Output recovered to 402,000 hl in 2006, but contracted again in 2008, to 300,000 hl. Stimulated by rising domestic demand and favourable prices, production of table grapes has increased significantly in recent years; by 2002 production had reached 75,000 metric tons, and by 2008 had risen to 122,000 tons. Production continued to increase thereafter, reaching 133,000 tons in 2009 and 141,000 tons in 2010.

Tunisia is the world's fourth largest producer of olive oil. Reform of the export marketing system for olive oil included the ending in 1994 of a requirement to negotiate all export contracts through the industry's national marketing board. In 1998 the Government abolished export taxes on olive oil and introduced a number of other measures to increase exports and improve the quality of the oil produced. In the 2000/01 agricultural year a national programme was initiated to safeguard olive groves from the adverse effects of drought, but there was still a fall in production to 30,000 metric tons, the lowest for 10 years. Olive oil production in the 2002/03 season increased to 72,000 tons, with 39,000 tons destined for export, and to 280,000 tons in 2003/04, with exports of 209,000 tons. Production in the 2004/05 season fell to 130,000 tons, with 98,000 tons destined for export (lower output typically following an exceptionally good year). In 2005/06 production increased to 220,000 tons, with exports of 160,000 tons, and then fell in 2006/07 to 170,000 tons, with exports (mainly to Italy and Spain) set at 120,000 tons. A return to growth was experienced once again in 2007/08, when production reached 200,000 tons, with exports of 169,000 tons. This level of production was maintained over 2009 and 2010. The US Department of Agriculture states that it was maintained at 180,000 tons over 2011–12 and, so far, in 2013. However it believes that in 2010 output declined to 135,000 tons, from 150,000 tons in 2009. Production of oil olives (for olive oil) has been falling steadily since 2008, when 1m. tons were produced. Just 600,000 tons were produced in 2011.

Citrus fruits are grown mainly in the Cap Bon peninsula. In 2000/01 production totalled 271,000 metric tons, but decreased to 236,000 tons in 2001/02 and fell again in 2002/03 to about 225,000 tons, which was attributable to the effects of drought. Production in 2003/04 continued to decline, to about 209,000 tons, owing to damage caused by heavy rainfall; it increased to 243,000 tons in 2004/05 and 262,000 tons in 2005/06, before declining to 247,000 tons in 2006/07. In the 2007/08 season output increased significantly, to 300,000 tons, with 27,400 tons designated for export. By the 2010/11 season, the most recent period for which data is available, output had been raised further, to 352,000 tons.

Dates are mainly exported to the EU, principally France, although new markets include Asia and North America. Date production in 2006/07 was 131,000 metric tons and exports reached 60,000 tons, but declined in 2007/08, to 124,000 tons, although total exports in this latter period rose slightly to 62,000 tons. In subsequent seasons, date production rose significantly. By 2010 Tunisia produced 174,000 tons, and in 2011 production rose to 189,500 tons. Government efforts to increase sugar beet output, by persuading farmers to grow the crop in rotation with cereals, were not successful and, after several years of steady decline, production was discontinued in 2001. Other crops include tomatoes, chillies and peppers, melons, watermelons and almonds. In 2010, according to FAO estimates, Tunisia's livestock included 1.3m. goats, 7.2m. sheep and some 671,000 cattle. A modest but expanding part of Tunisia's crop production is organic produce: in 2011 the land designated for its cultivation tripled, and some 6,000 tons of organic olives were produced, of which two-thirds were exported.

Sfax is the main centre of the fishing industry. The industry has received substantial state investment for fleet modernization, the upgrading of fishing ports and for research. The majority of fishing vessels are concentrated in the south, along the Gulf of Gabès (although pollution and overfishing have reduced this region's contribution to the country's total annual catch) and the ports of Sousse, Mahdia and Monastir in the central region. The Government has sought to offset overfishing in the Gulf of Gabès by offering incentives for the development of fishing grounds along the northern coastline. The total catch has been relatively steady in recent years. According to FAO figures, in 2008 the total catch was recorded at 101,500 metric tons. In 2009 it increased to 102,800 tons, before increasing again in 2010 to 103,100 tons. A larger increase, to 110,900 tons, was recorded in 2011.

MINERALS

Oil was first discovered in 1964 at al-Borma, in the south of the country near the Algerian border, and important finds were subsequently made offshore at Ashtart, east of Sfax in the Gulf of Gabès (these deposits accounting for a substantial proportion of Tunisia's total output by the mid-1980s). At January 2013 the USA's Energy Information Administration estimated Tunisia's total reserves of petroleum at 430m. barrels.

Production has come principally from al-Borma, Ashtart and four other concessions—Adam, Didon, Miskar and Oued Zar. In 2005 the Adam field, located in the Borj el-Khadra concession, became Tunisia's largest producing oilfield at 18,000 barrels per day (b/d), with the al-Borma and Ashtart fields producing around 12,000 b/d and 11,500 b/d, respectively. Although annual oil production declined progressively from the 1980s, falling to 3.3m. tons by 2006, it was estimated to have increased to 4.6m. tons in 2007, following new discoveries and the development of the Oudna field. However, production declined slightly, to 4.2m. tons, in 2008, and then further still, to 4.0m., tons in 2009 and to 3.8m. tons in 2010. Oil production fell further in 2011, when it reportedly declined to 3.3m. tons (of which 2.7m. was exported). However, according to reports from the Ministry of Trade and Industry, in the first two months of 2012 oil output recovered, albeit amidst increased domestic usage. Oil production was 73,000 b/d in February, up on 65,000 b/d in January.

In the late 1990s, despite the absence of a major petroleum strike for many years, several companies were engaged in exploration work in Tunisia, including Pluspetrol of Argentina, Anadarko Petroleum Corpn and ExxonMobil of the USA, and Agip of Italy. During 1998 the discovery of petroleum in the Guebiba field was announced, while production began at the offshore al-Biban field and at the Didon offshore field in the Gulf of Gabès. In 1999 production began at the Sabria field in the southern Kebili area, and in 2002 discoveries were reported in the Baraka offshore block, in the Ghadamès basin and in the Hasdrubal well. In 2003 discoveries and successful testing were reported in the southern Borj el-Khadra concession and in the Douleb field wells in north-western Tunisia. In 2004 further discoveries of both oil and gas were made in the Ksar Hadada block in the south of the country.

In 2006 a 35-year-old oil exploration dispute between Tunisia and Malta was resolved as the two countries signed an agreement providing for joint development of the continental shelf area. Also in that year Lundin Petroleum of Sweden and Sinochem Corpn of the People's Republic of China announced the start of production from the Oudna offshore field in the Gulf of Hammamet; new discoveries were reported by Eni in the Adam concession and Borj el-Khadra; and exploration permits were granted to Anadarko, Shell, Petro-Canada and Rigo Oil Co. According to ETAP, 44 international and domestic oil companies were involved in exploration activities in 29 onshore and 17 offshore blocks by early 2007. Later that year further discoveries were reported by Pioneer Natural Resources in Jenein-Nord and by OMV in Jenein-Sud. In early 2008 OMV also acquired an interest in Sidi Mansou offshore, while exploration licences were awarded to Cygam Energy Inc of Canada in the Sud Tozeur concession, to Canada's Madalena Ventures Inc and partners in Remada Sud, to Petrovietnam for acreage near Gabès, and to French-Australian group Primoil in the Le Kef and Jendouba provinces. Meanwhile, Eni announced that it would invest US $409.8m. in new projects in Tunisia over the following four years, including the development of two oil and gas fields in the Gulf of Hammamet. Some of this work progressed; however, plans were delayed by the political upheaval throughout much of 2011. The Italian company remains committed to investing $500m.–$600m. a year, an undertaking it first made in early 2011, and which it reiterated a year later

Tunisia's petroleum refinery, at Bizerte, has a capacity of about 34,000 b/d. Plans to increase it have long been abandoned, and in December 2005 the Government announced that it would build a new refinery at La Skhirra. In 2007 it was announced that Qatar Petroleum International was to invest US $2,500m. in the new facility. In July 2012 a visit by the Qatari Heir Apparent (now Amir), Sheikh Tamim, revived the state's former commitment and a new 'build, own, operate' arrangement by Qatar Petroleum was announced. It was envisaged that this would eventually enable total refined oil production to reach 154,000 b/d, providing for a theoretical surplus of 60,000 b/d for export above projected domestic demand.

There are five oil export terminals on the Mediterranean coast, the largest of which is at La Skhirra, which also handles about 22% of Algeria's oil exports. The others are at Gabès, Zarzis, Bizerte and the Ashtart offshore terminal. In 2001 a 126-km pipeline with a capacity of 22,000 b/d was completed to link the Sidi al-Kilani oilfield to the petroleum storage facilities at La Skhirra. Tunisia became a member of the Organization of Arab Petroleum Exporting Countries (OPEC) in 1982, but withdrew from the organization in 1986 owing to the decline in its oil output.

Tunisian reserves of natural gas were estimated at about 65,000m. cu m as of January 2011. Total gas production in 2006 was 2,149m. cu m; this rose to 2,288m. cu m in 2008. Output declined again slightly in 2009, to 2,762m. cu m, before rising once again, to 3,293m. cu m, in 2010. Almost all of the country's gas production came from the al-Borma field until 1995, when the offshore Miskar field was brought on stream by BGIT, which invested US $600m. to develop the field, the biggest foreign investment ever made in the country. The Miskar project, completed in 1997, has since supplied around 90% of total national production. BGIT has a long-term contract to deliver gas to the Société Tunisienne d'Electricité et du Gaz (STEG). In 2007 BGIT said it would invest a further $500m. to extend the life of the Miskar field and would cover $800m. of the $1,200m. cost of developing the offshore Hasdrubal gasfield, located just south of Miskar. ETAP would contribute the remainder. In November 2006 Petrofac LTD was awarded a $400m. contract to build new Hasdrubal onshore gas storage and liquefied petroleum gas (LPG) production facilities. In addition to al-Borma, Miskar and Hasdrubal, there are gasfields at El Franig, Baguel and Zinnia. The El Franig and Baguel gasfields in the south-west of the country, jointly owned and developed since 1997 by CMS Nomeco International of the USA and ETAP, are linked to the national pipeline system. The Government approved a liquid petroleum gas project in Tataouine, the poor southern Governorate, in April 2012. This followed disturbances in the area fomented by demands for employment and, specifically, calls for the much discussed 'LPG of the South' project to get under way.

The Transmed gas pipeline constructed to supply Algerian natural gas to Italy crosses Tunisia and became operational in 1983. Liftings from the pipeline became a new source of natural gas for STEG. Work to expand its annual capacity from 16,000m. cu m to 24,000m. cu m was completed during 1997. In 2003 Tunisia and Libya established a joint venture gas company, Jointgas, to manage the construction of a gas pipeline from Libya in order to provide a new source of supply in addition to the gas that Tunisia receives from the Transmed pipeline in the form of dues.

In 2008 Tunisia was the world's fifth largest producer of phosphate rock, accounting for about 5% of world supply, which is chiefly mined in the central area of the country. The Compagnie des Phosphates de Gafsa (CPG) is responsible for production, about 80% of which is processed locally into fertilizers and phosphoric acid in plants belonging to Groupe Chimique, the state processing company. Since the early 1990s annual production of raw phosphates has ranged from about 6m. to 8m. metric tons. In 2006 output was 7.8m. tons (compared with 8.2m. tons in the previous year), with exports of 731,000 tons worth TD 37m. Output rose to 8m. tons in 2007, with exports increasing to 1.2m. tons, valued at TD 71m., while production diminished slightly, to 7.5m. tons, in 2008 and again, to 7.2m. tons, in 2009. According to INS figures published in March 2012, this trend was reversed in 2010 and output rose to 8.2m. tons. However, the annual data for 2008 belied a sharp downturn in production in the second half of the year as Groupe Chimique halted production at three of its five plants. This drastic action represented an attempt to arrest the steep decline in global prices for phosphoric acid, which had plummeted by 50% in just three months, severely eroding profits. The fall in prices also raised concerns over government plans to expand the phosphate sector, for which it had pledged investment of over US $2,000m. The political upheaval delayed production for much of 2011, as strikes and protests interrupted the flow of materials to and from mines. Export revenues for mining products and phosphates fell by more than 40% from 2010 to 2011. In November 2011 Groupe Chimique suspended production when a protest was staged in its Gabès plant in the south-west of the country by unemployed workers; industrial action halted production again in February 2012. In May the Government announced an investment by the Chinese company Wengfu in the phosphate mine in the interior province of El-Kef, an area of significant economic deprivation.

Production of iron ore declined after independence in 1956, when it was more than 1m. metric tons per year. By 1995 output was down to 225,000 tons. The Jerissa mine has been responsible for about 70% of total production, while the remainder has been extracted from the Tamera-Douaria mine. According to the latest, slightly revised INS figures, total production was 214,300 tons in 2006, declining to 180,400 tons in 2007, but recovering to 206,500 tons in 2008. After a pronounced decline in 2009, to 151,300 tons, when demand slumped, output rebounded in 2010, reaching 180,500 tons.

Lead output fell steadily until the early 1990s, but then recovered to post production figures of 5,000 metric tons in 2003, 5,470 tons in 2004 and 8,708 in 2005. Annual zinc production was about 36,000 tons in the period 2001–03, but fell to 29,011 tons in 2004 and to 15,889 tons in 2005. This decline reflected the closure between May 2004 and September 2005 of three lead-zinc mines (Fej Lahdoum, Boujabeur and Bougrine) owing to the depletion of reserves.

INDUSTRY

Tunisia's industrial sector ranges from traditional activities, such as textiles and leather, to 'downstream' industries based on the country's phosphate reserves. The greater part of Tunisia's industry is located in Tunis. Other industrial centres are Sousse, Sfax, Gabès, Bizerte, Gafsa, Béja and Kasserine. There are two free trade zones at Bizerte and Zarzis, which opened in the 1990s. Although located on state-owned land, each is privately managed. Companies established in the zones, officially known as 'Parcs d'Activités Economiques', receive tax concessions and are exempt from most customs duties.

From the late 1980s private sector small and medium-sized businesses became increasingly prominent. The 1987–91 Development Plan allocated more investment to small-scale development and placed a greater emphasis on attracting private investment into industry. Exports of industrial goods (particularly textiles) rose steadily during the period. Under the 1992–96 Plan, the 6% annual GDP growth target was to be achieved mainly by means of expansion in the manufacturing and services sector. Manufacturing exports rose from 63% of total exports in 1992 to about 70% in 1996. Under the 1997–2001 Plan, overall industrial production was projected to grow by 6.9% a year, by 2001 industry was reported to be generating 18.5% of GDP and more than 80% of exports, despite growing competition from the EU. After three years of sustained growth, manufacturing slowed in 2002, with a growth rate down to 1.9% in real terms. This was due in particular to reduced activity in the textile and mechanical/electrical industries, affected by weak demand from abroad. Consequently, the sector's contribution to GDP remained about the same, at 18.6%. In 2003 investment in manufacturing increased to TD 1,020m., with higher levels invested in building materials, food, and mechanical and electrical industries. In 2004 manufacturing's share of GDP was 19.6%. All component sectors performed well that year, although textiles suffered from overseas competition. The following year manufacturing contributed 18.7% of GDP, the fall reflecting a decline in the production of olive oil and continuing competition in textiles. Investment in manufacturing reached TD 1,030m. The sector accounted for 18.6% of GDP in 2006 and 18.4% in 2007. The decline in export demand, and consequently in output, had a marked effect on the manufacturing sector in 2009, with its share of GDP falling to 16.8%, a level at which it remained in 2010, rising slightly, to 17.1%, in 2011, before falling to 16.3% in 2012.

The textiles sector remains an important contributor in manufacturing and exports. Virtually all textile exports go to the EU, especially to France, Germany, Italy and Belgium. In the shoe and leather goods sector about one-third of firms produce exclusively for export, principally shoes. Following the expiry of the World Trade Organization Agreement on Textiles and Clothing in January 2005 and the abolition of trade quotas, Tunisian producers were exposed to increased competition from Asian companies and the sector contracted in that year (to total some 2,000 companies and 250,000 jobs). Textiles made up 37.7% of overall exports in 2005 and 33.6% in 2006, when their respective values were TD 5,133.1m. and TD 5,150.6m., but Tunisia maintained its position as the fourth largest supplier to the EU, after China, India and Turkey. In 2007 several EU companies, including Benetton and Martinelli Ginetto, relocated their textile operations to Tunisia to capitalize on the experienced work-force, while some local companies started production of higher-value goods. These developments further augmented the value of textiles exports, which amounted to TD 5,189.7m. in 2007. This level was maintained in 2008, before declining in 2009 to TD 4,728.5m., as demand in Europe slumped. However, exports recovered again in 2010, to TD 5,048.5m. Textiles, clothing and leather goods represented 3.3% of GDP in 2012, down from 3.6% in 2010.

Steel production has declined because of technical difficulties at the al-Fouladh complex at Menzel Bourguiba, at which production was suspended indefinitely in 2007 as the result of a fire. Another steel mill, with a capacity of 100,000 tons per year, is sited at Bizerte. According to the IMF, manufacturing of mechanical and electrical products was the fastest growing sector in 2007, accounting for some 27% of exported goods. By 2009 the value of exports by the sector had reached over TD 6,000m. Overseas motor companies operating in Tunisia include Isuzu, Pirelli, Fiat, GM and Ford. In 2007 the Government sold the Société Tunisienne des Industries Automobiles (involved in vehicle assembly and coach-building) to the local Groupe Mabrouk. After the disruption of 2011, foreign automotive companies based in Tunisia expressed optimism again in mid-2012 about the expansion of production.

Cement production during the late 1990s averaged around 4.7m. metric tons. Privatization of the cement companies began in 1998, when two state-owned cement plants were sold: the Société des Ciments de Jebel Oust to Cimpor of Portugal for TD 241m., and the Société des Ciments d'Enfidha to Uniland of Spain for TD 168m. The sale of the two plants provided the bulk of revenue obtained from privatization during that year. The Société des Ciments de Gabès was sold in early 2000 to another Portuguese firm for TD 311m. and in May an Italian firm purchased the Société des Ciments Artificiels de Tunis (CAT) for TD 50.5m. In 2004 Feriana Tuniso-Algérienne de Ciment Blanc (SOTACIB) was sold to the Spanish Grupo Prasa for TD 14.5m. Overall cement production rose to 6.4m. tons in both 2004 and 2005, and increased gradually in the intervening years to yield 7.2m. tons by 2008, according to the latest figures, and 8.1m. tons by 2010. Meanwhile, a group of investors from Europe and Saudi Arabia announced plans to build a TD 175m. cement plant, with a capacity of 1.5m. tons per year, at Al-Akarit. In 2007 Spain's Aricam began construction of a new plant in Gafsa to serve the domestic market.

The chemical sector, comprising the state-owned Industries chimiques maghrébines at Gabès and 'mixed' (partly state-owned) companies at Sfax, processes phosphate rock into phosphatic fertilizers and phosphoric acid. Since 1995 production of the latter has vacillated between 1.0m. and 1.2m. metric tons. In 2000 the state-owned Chemical Products and Detergents Co and the Cosmetics, Detergents and Perfumes Co were sold to a Dutch multinational company. In 2005 CPG and Groupe Chimique signed a memorandum of understanding with two Indian companies, Coromandel Fertiliser and Gujarat State Fertiliser Corpn, to build a US $180m. plant at Skhirra to manufacture phosphoric acid for export to India.

Under the terms of the association agreement with the EU in the mid-1990s, Tunisia has been dismantling trade barriers to EU industrial goods in stages over a 12-year period. The Ministry of Industry and Technology estimated at that time that as many as 2,000 companies could collapse as a result of increased competition unless efforts were made to improve productivity and the quality of their goods. Therefore, in advance of the implementation of the agreement, the Government started an industrial modernization programme to improve the competitiveness of Tunisian industry, with financial support from the EU, the World Bank and two Tunisian state funds (the Fonds de promotion et de maîtrise de technologie and the Fonds pour le développement de la compétitivité industrielle). By the end of 2006 the programme covered 3,671 companies, of which 2,434 had received approval for their restructuring plans involving a total investment of TD 3,795m. As the global economic downturn began to impact upon the Tunisian economy, more companies sought support under the programme: the Government reported that 90 companies had applied during the first quarter of 2009, representing an increase of 70%, compared with the same period of the previous year. In 2012 the prospect of receiving 'advanced status' under an extant EU association agreement country raised worries among some Tunisians. There may be further vulnerabilities to EU imports and competition, as trade relations are increased.

STEG is responsible for the transmission and distribution of electricity, but lost its monopoly on generation in 1996 as the Government sought to open up the construction, operation and ownership of power facilities to private investors. Nevertheless, STEG still handles about 80% of production. Tunisia is linked to Algeria and Morocco through a 220-kV grid.

In 2009 the Government published plans for the development of renewable energy sources, the aim of which was to take more than 4% of the country's energy from renewables by 2014. Research suggests that Tunisia is capable of producing up to 1,000 MW of wind power; however, by 2009 the country's installed capacity was only 55 MW. The Tunisian Government signed a nuclear co-operation agreement with France in 2008. A planned nuclear power station, which could produce up to 1,000 MW of energy, was not expected to be operational until 2023.

By the end of 2007 total electricity production in Tunisia had reached 13,960m. kWh, with total national consumption standing at 12,085m. kWh, but consumption was forecast to rise to 17,800m. kWh by 2010, requiring a doubling of installed capacity to 4,000 MW by that year. However, the economic downturn brought about a decline in demand towards the end of 2008, resulting in a fall in output to 11,078m. kWh in that year. According to the INS, consumption fell slightly to 12,962m. kWh in 2011, from 13,015m. kWh in 2010. Output rose subsequently, to reach 14,795m. kWh by 2010. An additional 500 MW of extra capacity is required every two years in order to reach the Government's total installed capacity target of 5,600 MW by 2016.

TRANSPORT AND COMMUNICATIONS

Tunisia inherited a relatively modern system of road and rail communications from the period of colonial rule, and substantial work has since been carried out to modernize and extend the highway and railway networks. Tunisia has some 20,000 km of primary and secondary roads, most of which are surfaced and relatively well-maintained. Since 1995 the Government's policy on motorway building has been to seek private sector financing for the construction of toll roads, with public sector investment channelled into the maintenance and improvement of existing roads. In 1998 the Government announced plans for two new sections of motorway, one from Tunis to Bizerte and another from Bizerte to Menzel Bourguiba. Construction began in 2000 on the Tunis–Bizerte motorway, a US $120m. project funded in part by a loan from the AFESD. In 2005 work was under way on the construction of a 98-km motorway from M'Saken to Sfax and the 100-km Tunis–Béja motorway, while in 2007 Tunisia and Libya announced plans to build a toll highway between Sfax and Tripoli, the Libyan capital.

Tunisia's rail network is operated by the state-owned Société Nationale des Chemins de Fer Tunisiens and consists of a north–south coastal line and four east–west branch lines to Jendouba, Le Kef, Kasserine and Tozeur. In 2008 passenger numbers totalled 39.2m., but this total fell to 38.6m. in 2009. Urban railway transport is handled by the Société des Transports de Tunis.

There are international airports at Tunis-Carthage, Djerba-Zarzis, Monastir-Skanès, Sfax-Thyna, Tabarka-7 Novembre, Tozeur-Nefta and Gafsa-Ksar. The second phase of the Tunis-Carthage airport expansion project, to increase passenger capacity from 3.5m. to 4.5m. per year, was completed in 1998. Construction of a new international airport at Enfidha, some 60 km south of Tunis, was completed in late 2009. Initial passenger-handling capacity at Zine al-Abidine Ben Ali (now Enfidha-Hammamet) International Airport, totalled 7m. passengers; after further expansion schemes, it is scheduled to become Tunisia's largest airport, with a capacity of 30m. passengers. In 1995 the state's 85% shareholding in TunisAir, the national airline, was reduced to 45.2% as part of the Government's privatization programme, and the company announced that it would offer 20% of its capital to public subscription. Tunisian charter airlines include Carthage Airlines and Nouvel Air. In 2011, when the tourism industry was in decline due to the political upheaval, incoming air passenger numbers were significantly reduced, falling from 5.6m. in 2010 to 3.8m. in 2011.

There are ports at Tunis-La Goulette, Sousse, Sfax, Gabès, Skhirra, Bizerte, Radès and Zarzis. The state-owned shipping company, the Compagnie Tunisienne de Navigation, is the main shipping company in Tunisia. The Office de la Marine Marchande et des Ports is responsible for the management of ports. The number of ships entering Tunisia's main ports increased from 5,938 in 1995 to 7,864 in 2008, much of this traffic being handled by Tunis-La Goulette-Radès. In 2005 a feasibility study was launched into the possibility of building a deep water port at Enfidha capable of accommodating large ships up to a capacity of 80,000 metric tons; bids were invited for the construction of the port from early 2009. In 2007 the Government announced that it would privatize port management and cargo handling. In April 2008 a new direct sea link between Tunisia and Morocco was inaugurated to accelerate shipments between the two countries and reduce the costs of using indirect routes via Europe.

Investment of some TD 1,500m. (US $1,300m.) was allocated to the telecommunications sector under the 1997–2001 Development Plan, with the aim of increasing the number of telephone lines to 1m. In 1998 the country's first GSM cellular phone system began operations for 30,000 subscribers in the Tunis-Nabeul-Hammamet region. Orascom Telecom of Egypt was awarded the country's second GSM licence in 2002. In October Orascom signed an agreement with Kuwait's Wataniya Telecom to jointly operate the licence under the name Tunisiana. In 2004 China's ZTE was awarded the contract to supply and install a third generation (3G) mobile telecommunications network in Tunisia. The United Arab Emirates-based TECOM Investments and Dubai Investment Group purchased a 35% stake in Tunisie Télécom (TT) in 2006.

In 2009 a combined fixed-line and mobile telephone licence was eventually awarded to a consortium of France Télécom and a Tunisian company, Divona Télécom. The licence was to encapsulate a whole range of services, from fixed-line to 2G and 3G mobile telecommunications services, as well as high-speed broadband internet access. The licence represented part of the Government's plan to develop the most advanced telecommunications network in the region, although it stated that it would not issue any further licences until at least 2013, to allow time for the new provider to establish itself. Tunisiana purchased licences from the Government in 2012 for mobile and fixed line services. In late July the Government announced that it would be selling its 25% stake in Tunisiana by auction. However the Tunisian Government has not privatized its stake in TT. According to a Dubai press report in June 2013, the Dubai authorities have offered to put up for sale their 35% share.

According to the International Telecommunications Union (ITU), in 2012 there were 1.1m. fixed-line subscribers (which has been on a slightly downward trend since 2010), representing 10% of the population, and approximately 12.8m. mobile subscribers in total, a significant increase from the 8.6m. mobile subscribers recorded in 2008. In 2012 the ITU listed 41.4% of the population as having 'access to the internet', compared with 27.5% in 2008, while the number having fixed broadband subscriptions nearly doubled from the end of 2008 to the end of 2012, from 227,303 to 512,254.

FINANCE AND BUDGET

The BCT is the sole bank of issue of Tunisia's national currency, the dinar. It performs all the normal central banking functions, although in 1994 a new foreign exchange market opened in Tunis, ending the BCT monopoly on quoting prices for the dinar against hard currencies. By 2005 there were 20 commercial banks and two development banks in the country. In 1994 the Government introduced legislation to tighten banking regulation, and ordered Tunisian banks to set aside 50% of their profits to cover bad debts, meet a capital adequacy requirement of 5%, cease making unsecured loans and reduce their exposure to any single sector to no more than 25%. By the late 1990s a restructuring of the banking system was under way, with financial assistance from the World Bank, the African Development Bank (AfDB) and the EU. Then, in 2001, a new banking law tightened the rules on investments and bank licensing, and increased the minimum capital requirement limits. The legislation required banks to obtain external auditor reports and certified financial statements on each borrower above a certain loan threshold, and to tighten their exposure limits. Also, the bank restructuring process was to be accelerated with the privatization of state banks.

In 2005 the Government adopted a number of further measures to promote good governance and strengthen the legal framework for banks, including a new law on financial security that aimed to guarantee the transparency and reliability of accounting. A revision to the banking law, adopted in 2006, simplified the operating conditions for banks and prohibited the distribution of dividends that were inadequately provisioned.

In 2007 the Government's holdings in three small banks—Banque Tuniso-Koweitienne, Banque Franco-Tunisienne and Banque de Tunisie et des Emirats d'Investissement—were put up for sale and in early 2008 France's Caisse d'Epargne bought the stake in Banque Tuniso-Koweitienne. The Société Tunisienne de Banque also divested two of its subsidiaries to local companies. In June 2008 the BCT announced that it was planning to increase bank reserve requirements for the second time that year in order to reduce excess liquidity and control inflationary pressures. The BCT also announced that the dinar was expected to become fully convertible by the end of 2009. In December 2007 banks were authorized to manage, within a 20% limit, their assets in foreign currency on international markets. The global financial crisis forced the Government to delay its plans, but the Prime Minister stated in September 2009 that it was still committed to the scheme. Various capital reforms, such as a floating exchange rate, needed to put in place before full convertibility can be achieved, and in November President Ben Ali announced that he was abolishing the requirement that foreign companies receive official consent to repatriate investment allowances. It appeared unlikely that the dinar would be made fully convertible much before 2014, a date that was confirmed by Ben Ali in November 2010. The new interim Government, which was installed following Ben Ali's departure from office in January 2011, was expected to adhere to this deadline, by which time Tunisia hoped to have finalized preparations to turn Tunis into a regional financial centre.

In mid-2010 the BCT took steps in support of these plans. It announced the creation of two public banking holding companies, designed to bolster the local financial sector in advance of its liberalization and the arrival of foreign competitors into the market. Tunisia's first locally owned Islamic bank, Banque Zitouna, which was capitalized at TD 35m, was also established in that year. It opened with nine branches, but planned rapid domestic expansion as well as further growth throughout the Maghreb region.

The 'offshore' banking sector was first regulated by legislation in 1976, which placed strict limits on the banks' activities. In 1985 a new law gave them greater freedom to do business in the local currency and to participate in dinar treasury operations. By 2005 there were eight offshore banks, including Tunis International Bank, Alubaf International Bank and North Africa International Bank. In 1995 Tunisia's first merchant bank, International Maghreb Merchant Bank, began operating. A second merchant bank, the Banque d'Affaires de Tunisie, opened in 1997, with the STB as the major shareholder. In 1998 the Banque Internationale Arabe de Tunisie raised US $40m. through the issue of global depository receipts. This was Tunisia's first international equity offering.

The Tunis stock exchange, the Bourse des Valeurs Mobilières de Tunis (Bourse de Tunis), was established as a state-run institution in 1969 and then converted in 1994 into a private company, regulated by an independent monitoring body. Regulations were introduced in 1995 to make it easier for foreign investors to do business on the exchange, with the proviso that no quoted company's share capital could be more than 10% foreign-owned without the permission of the Tunisian authorities. (The investment regulations allowed foreign ownership of non-quoted companies' shares to reach 30% before permission was required.) In 1997 the limit on foreign ownership of companies was raised to 49.9%. Yet, despite government efforts to stimulate the stock market, by the end of 1998 fewer then 40 firms were listed, many of them banks, and few foreign investors had shown interest. Despite increased activity and interest in blue-chip stocks, such as TunisAir, by 2001 the number of firms listed had only increased to 45. In 2002 the Government introduced additional investment incentives, including further tax concessions, for foreign investors. In 2008 an alternative stock market, the Marché Alternatif, was launched. According to the BCT, the stock market index closed at 2,614 points in 2007, rising to 4,292 by the end of 2009. Over the course of the year the market capitalization of the bourse had risen by 47% to TD 12,200m. In March 2010 the Government announced plans to develop the bourse by offering a reduction in corporation tax to 20% for five years to companies that offered at least 30% of their capital to the public before the end of 2014. This was countered with separate plans to introduce a 10% capital gains tax on profits above TD 10,000 and on shares bought on or after 1 January 2011 and held for less than one year. However, the plans adversely affected investor confidence and the bourse fell, prompting the Government to reconsider its proposal. The measure was not introduced at the beginning of the year, by which time political turmoil had erupted throughout the country.

In 1994 the Government launched its first placement on the Japanese bond market (to help cover Tunisia's balance of payments deficit), and in 1996 finalized a US $200m. syndicated sovereign loan on the international market. A further syndicated loan of $150m. was signed later that year. In 1999 Tunisia entered the Eurobond market for the first time, raising $242m. in 10-year bonds. In 2000 the Government launched a 50,000m. yen global Samurai bond. This was followed in 2001 by a sovereign bond for 55,000m. yen ($450m.) and a 30-year global bond for an additional 20,000m. yen ($167m.). In 2002 the Government launched a 10-year global dollar bond for $650m. and in 2003 issued a 10-year euro-denominated sovereign bond worth €300m. ($323.8m.). Despite the uncertain international environment at that time, this issue was well received on the international market, prompting international credit agencies to raise their long-term and short-term credit ratings for Tunisia. In 2004 the Government issued a seven-year €450m. sovereign bond and a 15-year €400m. debenture bond, and in August 2007 issued a 30,000m. yen bond.

The 2000 budget was based on real GDP growth of 6%, with the deficit projected at 2.7% of GDP. Almost two-thirds of revenue (projected at TD 10,510m.) was to come from tax and non-fiscal revenue, with the rest from borrowing. A sharp rise in tax revenues was forecast (with tax increases on tobacco, alcohol and cars) in order to compensate in part for a fall in customs revenue as tariffs were removed under the terms of the EU accord. The IMF estimated that, excluding grants and privatization receipts, the actual budget deficit for 2000 was TD 786m. (2.9% of GDP) compared with a projected TD 947m. The 2001 budget was set at TD 10,800m., based on real GDP growth of 6.2% and inflation at 3%, with the deficit projected to fall to 2.4% of GDP. Current spending was forecast to increase by 7.2%, taking into account wage increases and the recruitment of additional public sector workers in the health and education sectors. Total investment was forecast to increase by 10% to TD 7,800m. (equivalent to 26.4% of GDP), 55% of which was derived from the private sector. The IMF estimated that, excluding grant and privatization receipts, the actual budget deficit was 3.5% of GDP in 2001. The 2002 budget was set at TD 11,533m. with the deficit projected to fall to 2.2% of GDP. Expenditure was projected to rise by 6.6% and inflation to 3%. However, as a result of difficult economic circumstances, the Government revised the original budget estimates to keep the deficit under control. Once austerity measures had been introduced, including a TD 347m. reduction in expenditure, official figures put the deficit at 2.6% of GDP.

The 2003 budget was set at TD 11,410m., with overall expenditure set to increase by 2%. It forecast GDP growth of 5.5% based on the assumption of a strong economic recovery. The deficit was projected to fall to TD 734m., equivalent to 2.2% of GDP, while revenues were expected to increase by 2.5%, to TD 10,670m. The 2004 budget was set at TD 12,730m., with a deficit projected at 2.1% of GDP. It also provided for the reduction in the number of customs tariffs and the narrowing of the differential between most-favoured-nation tariffs and those applicable under the association agreement with the EU. The 2005 budget was set at TD 12,990m., with the deficit forecast at 2.3% of GDP. The 2006 budget, based on an oil price assumption of US $60 per barrel, was set at TD 13,652m. The 2007 budget was based on projected GDP growth of 6%, with the deficit set at 3.1% of GDP. Expenditure was forecast at TD 14,460m., while overall investment was set to fall by about 10% as the Government looked to the private sector to fund infrastructure projects. Actual out-turn data indicated that the budget deficit at the end of 2007 was not as high as the Government had projected, although it did reach TD 1.3m., equivalent to 2.9% of GDP. The 2008 budget was set at TD 15,342m., assuming real GDP growth of 6.1% and a projected deficit of 3% of GDP, based on an average oil price of $75 per barrel. Current spending was forecast to rise to over TD 8,000m. The Government announced significant increases in public sector pay, while maintaining subsidies on fuel and food to offset the continuing rise in oil and food prices on world markets. Taxation revenue (accounting for 85% of government income) was forecast to reach TD 10,000m., and total investment was expected to rise by 15%, with 60% coming from the private sector. The 2009 budget, drafted just as the global financial system was heading toward recession, attempted to stabilize the Tunisian economy. It was predicated on a slight decline in growth, to 5%, owing to an expected weakening of the export market and a decline in tourism receipts. Prime Minister Muhammad Ghannouchi declared the Government's intention to raise expenditure in order to stimulate consumption, increasing spending by 12.5% to TD 17.200m., and observed that reduced revenues were likely to result in a deficit of 3% of GDP. However, in July 2009 the Government was forced to issue a supplementary budget, as slower than expected growth resulted in much poorer tax receipts than had been anticipated. In order to compensate for reduced revenues, the supplementary budget announced higher spending, which the Government predicted would push the deficit up to 3.8% of GDP. The 2010 budget set an increase in expenditure of 5.4%, to TD 18,300m., with capital spending rising by 18% to TD 4,600m. and wages rising by 8%, to TD 6,800m. Owing to the uncertain economic conditions at the time of the budget, the Government did not release full data, leaving revenue projections open to speculation. However, the fiscal stimulus, put in place by the mid-2009 supplementary budget, was extended in order to provide ongoing support to ailing businesses and to stimulate job creation. The 2011 budget projected real GDP growth of 5.4% in that year, on the basis of a 6.1% rise in revenues to TD 15,400m. and a 4.9% rise in spending to TD 19,200m. However, the political turmoil and widespread unrest forced the interim Government, which assumed power after the overthrow of Ben Ali, to introduce a supplementary budget. It raised spending by 11%, to TD 21,300m., in order to boost subsidies and salaries to meet the immediate demands of the protesters, while growth was reduced significantly, to just 1%. The incoming Government in November 2011 introduced an ambitious and optimistic budget for 2012 that raised spending by 7.5% over 2011, and committed 37% of total expenditure to wages and 40% to the impoverished interior regions. Earlier projected cost savings by cutting fuel subsidies were abandoned and food subsidies were increased. The budget deficit was projected at 6% of GDP by the end of 2012. In presenting its budget, the Government assumed that it could contain the deficit on the basis of real economic growth of 4.5% and a strong rise in foreign investment, after the contraction experienced in 2011. The actual out-turn in 2012, according to the BCT, was a budget deficit that was a little under the projection, at 5.1% of GDP, or TD 3,600m. (excluding, according to BCT calculations, privatization receipts or grants). BCT public finance data state that this was partly offset by a total of TD 1,700m. in 'privatization and grants' in 2012.

In June 2012 the USA committed itself to a US $30m. sovereign loan guarantee (see History) for a planned Tunisian government bond issue worth at least $450m., which, assuming it is successful, will ease the growing public debt burden. There have also been discussions with Islamic financial institutions in the Gulf about issuing a *sukuk* (Islamic bond) to assist in easing the debt burden. In June 2013 the parliament approved the issuance of a $700m *sukuk*, which has been scheduled for November or December. A Turkish loan of $200m. was ratified by that country's parliament in June. It will be used over a six-year period for Tunisian public infrastructure projects. An additional $200m is to be lent by Turkey's Exim Bank to assist Tunisia's ability to import goods from Turkey, including for public projects.

PLANNING

The Government started comprehensive planning in the 1960s, beginning with a three-year Development Plan for 1962–64 and then four-year Plans for 1965–68, 1969–72 and 1973–76. These were followed by successive five-year Plans covering 1977–81, 1982–86, 1987–91, 1992–96, 1997–2001, 2002–06, 2007–11 and, most recently, 2010–14.

Although Tunisia relied initially on petroleum to underpin economic growth, it had to plan for a future in which it would become a net importer of fuel. The need for adjustments became more pressing in 1986 with the collapse of international petroleum prices. With help from the IMF, the Government adopted a radical four-year programme designed to provide a secure basis for the economy for the next decade. The strategy depended on an increase in exports of agricultural and manufactured goods, a rise in revenues from tourism, and severe reductions in the Government's investment budget. Meanwhile, trade was to be liberalized and the Tunisian dinar was to be devalued, in an attempt to maintain export competitiveness. The economy broadly recovered over the period of the programme, but fluctuations in performance continued to reflect movements in the international price of oil and the susceptibility of the harvest to recurring droughts. The 1992–96 Plan envisaged total investment of TD 17,400m., of which 52.3% would be generated by the private sector, and the creation of 320,000 jobs. Also planned were further reductions in subsidies on consumer and other products, the disposal of state assets except in strategic sectors, the elimination of price controls on manufactured goods, and the introduction of selective charges for health, education and other services. Although projected to increase at an average rate of 6% per year, GDP grew at only about 4.5% over the plan period. Meanwhile, in 1995 the Government announced that major infrastructural projects would in future be open to private sector investment.

The 1997–2001 Plan envisaged total spending of TD 42,000m. over the five-year period, of which the government budget would provide TD 33,775m. with the remainder funded by external financing. The Plan targeted an average rate of real GDP growth of 6% per year, while the unemployment rate was to fall from 15.5% to 13% by 2001. Meanwhile, the Government had announced new measures in 1996 to encourage foreign investment during the 1997–2001 period, including allowing investors to buy up to 49% of any local company without prior authorization. (The limit on foreign ownership of companies listed on the stock exchange was raised to 49.9% in 1997.)

The 2002–06 Plan set a per caput growth rate target of 4.8% and a 5.4% annual economic growth rate by 2006, with increasing emphasis on private sector involvement in the transport, telecommunications and banking sectors. The Plan for 2007–11 sought to accelerate economic growth to around 6.1% per year and to reduce unemployment. The Government intended to continue the gradual liberalization of the economy, increasing the role of private sector activity to 75.4% and the proportion of private investment to 63.5%, and cutting external financing. The budget and current account deficits were forecast to converge at 2.1% and 2.0% of GDP, respectively, with inflation remaining low, at 2.5%. The principal sectors for development were information technology, the engineering and electrical industries, and chemicals.

In early July 2010 the National Assembly approved the Government's 12th economic development plan, covering the years 2010–14. The plan incorporated necessary revisions forced by the economic downturn. The Government sought to attain an average annual growth rate of 5.5% (compared with the target of 6.1% in the 11th Plan) and to lift income per caput to more than TD 8,300 by 2014. The Plan aimed to create 415,000 jobs and to reduce the unemployment rate to 11.6%, while increasing the level of investment to the equivalent of 26% of GDP. In addition, the plan was intended to attract an average of TD 3,250m. of FDI per year. A budget deficit target of below 2.7% of GDP was set, as well as a reduction in the level of public debt to 40.4% of GDP.

TRADE

Tunisia's trade growth in recent years has centred principally on the expansion of its links with the EU since the signing of the association agreement in 1995. The country's major exports include textiles, agricultural products, leather goods and phosphates. The main imports are consumer goods, machinery, raw and processed materials, and agricultural and industrial equipment. Tunisia's balance of trade deficit has been traditionally offset by earnings from tourism and remittances from Tunisians working abroad.

According to the IMF, total exports as a share of GDP rose from 28.5% in 1990 to 33% in 2001, in which year the value of exports increased by 18.7% to TD 9,503.7m. and the value of imports by 16.4% to TD 13,658.3m., resulting in a trade deficit of TD 4,154.6m. (equivalent to 11.8% of GDP). Exports from the textile sector and the mechanical engineering and electrical industries recorded significant growth. The import value increase was the result of a 25% rise in consumer goods, a 19.5% rise in raw materials and semi-finished products, and a 7.2% increase in capital goods. The current account deficit increased to TD 1,241m. in 2001, equivalent to 4.3% of GDP. It then narrowed to TD 1,138m. in 2002, equivalent to 3.8% of GDP, following higher inflows of foreign investment from privatization during that year. The trade deficit narrowed by 7.8% to TD 3,866.1m. in 2002. Exports totalled TD 9,646.2m. and imports totalled TD 13,512.3m. Although the overall balance of services declined by 18%, attributable to a 14% fall in tourism earnings, factor income recorded a surplus with a 12% increase in workers' remittances. In 2003 exports increased to TD 10,343m. and imports to TD 14,039m., resulting in a 1.8% reduction in the overall trade deficit to TD 3,696m. The higher export growth came from increased sales of textiles and mechanical and electrical goods, accounting for 47.2% and 20.8% of exports, respectively. Imports from the EU totalled TD 10,011m. (an increase of 5.5% over 2002) while exports totalled TD 8,343.4m. (an 8.9% increase). The current account deficit narrowed again in 2003, to TD 941m., equivalent to 2.9% of GDP, and the trade deficit amounted to TD 3,696m. Final trade figures for 2004 indicated exports valued at TD 12,055m. and imports at TD 15,960m., resulting in a 5.8% widening of the trade deficit to TD 3,905m. In 2004 the favourable balance of services (with higher receipts from tourism) resulted in a further fall in the current account deficit to TD 691m., equivalent to 2% of GDP. In 2005 the value of exports increased by 12.9%, to TD 13,608m., and that of imports rose by 7.2%, to TD 17,102m., reducing the trade deficit by about 10%; the current account deficit narrowed to 1.1% of GDP. Remittances from abroad in 2005 increased to TD 1,807m. from TD 1,783m. in 2004, while tourism receipts rose to TD 2,587m. from TD 2,290m. in the previous year. In 2006 the value of exports and imports reached TD 15,316m. and TD 19,768m., respectively, resulting in a deficit of 7.4% of GDP. The current account deficit increased (as a result of higher oil prices) to 2.3% of GDP. Tunisia's largest trading partners that year were France (taking 32.0% of exports), Italy (22.0%) and Germany (7.9%). In 2007 the value of exports increased to TD 19,409.6m., but imports increased to TD 24,438.7m. (reflecting strong local demand and the impact of continued trade liberalization), thus widening the trade deficit to more than TD 5,000m. The current account deficit increased to an estimated 2.6% of GDP. In 2008, as global commodity prices rose significantly, the value of imports increased considerably, to TD 30,241.2m. The growth in exports was less marked, rising to TD 23,637m., causing a widening of the trade deficit to TD 6,604.2m. Although the non-merchandise surplus increased, it was not sufficient to prevent a widening of the overall current account deficit, which expanded to 4.2% of GDP.

The trade deficit narrowed in 2009, as the decline in the value of imports exceeded that in the value of exports. Imports decreased to TD 25,692m., while exports fell to TD 19,469m., resulting in a slightly reduced deficit of TD 6,223m. Mining products and phosphates exports fell in value to TD 1,300m. (from TD 2,200m. in 2010). The non-merchandise surplus widened, primarily on account of a rise in tourism receipts. As a result, the overall current account deficit narrowed to TD 1,513m. In 2010 the trade deficit widened considerably to TD 8,293m., following a sharp rise in imports. However, the non-merchandise surplus grew, supported in the main by greatly increased remittances from Tunisians working in Europe, and as a result the overall current account deficit narrowed to TD 1,345m. In 2011 the trade deficit widened once again, to TD 8,610m., as import costs continued to rise and exports increased only modestly. Generally, the size of the non-merchandise surplus offsets a large portion of the deficit, but the decline in tourism revenues and in foreign remittances, due principally to instability in Libya, minimized this and resulted in a current account deficit of TD 4,500m. With the decline in net FDI, the Government drew down some of its foreign exchange reserves to finance partially the shortfall on the current account. Foreign exchange fell by TD 2,400m. from the end of 2010 to the end of 2011. In 2011 declining tourism revenue and falling foreign remittances helped the current account deficit to rise to TD 4,766m., or 9% of real GDP.

An only modest economic recovery for much of 2012 helped to widen the trade deficit further, to TD 11,635m., with a higher volume, and rising international prices, of imports, and a relatively modest increase in exports. However, according to the latest BCT data, a marked recovery in tourism receipts and a more modest, but still strong, rise in foreign remittances helped ease the services deficit. However, the rising trade imbalance caused the overall current account deficit to rise still further, to TD 5,765m., or 10.9% of real GDP. In the first half of 2013 a slight rise in the trade deficit compared with the corresponding period of 2012 occurred, from TD 5,469m. to TD 5,553m.

In July 1995 Tunisia signed an association agreement with the EU, which took effect from 1998. Its main provisions were as follows. EU capital goods and semi-finished goods that were not also manufactured in Tunisia (accounting for 12% of Tunisia's imports from the EU at that time) would be exempt from import duty from the date the agreement entered into force. EU exports of specified goods that were also manufactured in Tunisia (28% of Tunisian imports from the EU) would be subject to the progressive elimination of import duties over a period of five years after entry into force. Duties on EU exports of goods that were deemed to be 'more sensitive' in the Tunisian economic context (30% of Tunisian imports from the EU) would be phased out over a period of 12 years. Duties on EU exports of goods that were deemed to be 'most sensitive' (29.5% of Tunisian imports from the EU at that time) would be maintained for the first five years of the agreement before being phased out over a seven-year period. Duties on traditional handicraft and textile products (0.5% of Tunisian imports from the EU) would not be phased out under the agreement. During the 12-year transition period following the agreement's entry into force, Tunisia would have the option of reimposing import duties of up to 25% on EU exports that were considered to threaten emerging industries in Tunisia, provided that such duties did not affect more than 15% of all imports from the EU and were not maintained for more than five years. Tunisia (which already had duty-free access to the EU market for industrial goods) would benefit from a limited relaxation of EU quota and tariff restrictions on some agricultural exports, although olive oil exports to the EU remained subject to existing restrictions. In January 2000 negotiations began with the EU on the extension of free trade to agricultural products, and an agreement came into effect from January 2001. This raised the annual quota of olive oil exports entering the EU duty-free from 46,000 metric tons to 50,000 tons, with further annual increases to a maximum of 56,000 tons by 2005. It also fixed the quantities of other agricultural exports permitted to enter the EU duty-free. The EU's quota for soft wheat exports to Tunisia was raised to 460,000 tons, and a quota for 100,000 tons of vegetable oil exports was also introduced.

The Tunisian Government expected that investment of around TD 2,200m. (60% for the modernization of businesses and 40% for infrastructural development and other initiatives to improve the business environment) would be required during the first five years of exposure to increased EU competition.

Preparatory studies had indicated that about one-third of Tunisian industrial companies were likely to be put out of business by the new trade measures, while a further third would find the transition difficult. Under the association agreement, the EU pledged to provide financial assistance to help the Tunisian economy adjust, including support for industrial restructuring, training and promotion of the private sector. Although the agreement did not come into force formally until March 1998, Tunisia began implementing its provisions from January 1996, when import duties on EU capital goods were abolished.

Tunisia signed free trade agreements with Jordan and Egypt in 1998 and with Morocco in 1999, and trade co-operation agreements in 2002 with Iran, Egypt, Portugal and Morocco. In February 2004 Morocco, Jordan, Egypt and Tunisia signed an agreement towards the creation of a Euro-Mediterranean free trade area by 2010. However, this was subsequently superseded by those countries' adhesion to the Greater Arab Free Trade Area. A number of trade agreements, including a preferential trade exchange agreement exempting a broad tranche of goods from customs duties, were signed between Tunisia and Algeria at a meeting of the Algerian-Tunisian High Joint Committee in December 2008.

TOURISM

Tourism is a major source of foreign currency earnings for Tunisia, accounting for about 6% of GDP in 2010. The main centres for tourists are Hammamet, Sousse, Djerba, Monastir and Tunis. Since the 1960s the country has been a popular destination for Western European visitors. However, it has had to compete with many other Mediterranean holiday destinations, and foreign tourists have sometimes been deterred by fear of terrorist incidents. More recently, Tunisia has been looking to attract new visitors from Eastern Europe, China, Japan and Australia, and to diversify its range of tourist attractions.

The number of foreign tourist arrivals grew to 5.2m. in 2000, representing a rise of about 7% on the previous year, while tourism revenues increased to TD 2,100m. Despite a sharp decline in the fourth quarter, receipts increased to TD 2,400m. in 2001, with 5.4m. tourist arrivals. In 2002, however, tourist arrivals decreased to 5.1m., reflecting a 19% drop in European visitors, in part due to a terrorist incident. Tourism earnings declined to TD 2,024m., but still contributed over 6% of GDP and 17% of external receipts, and employed 13.5% of the labour force. Tourism receipts were down by 4.6%, to TD 1,929m., in 2003, although the number of tourist arrivals increased marginally, to 5.1m., reflecting an increase in the number of visitors from Arab countries. The number of European tourists decreased by 2.7%. In 2004 arrivals totalled some 6.0m. and receipts rose to TD 2,290m. The number of tourists from other Maghreb countries reached 2.3m. In the same year the Government established the National Tourism Commission, chaired by the Minister of Tourism and Handicrafts. There were 6.4m. tourist arrivals in 2005 and receipts reached TD 2,587m. Arrivals from European countries increased by 11.1%. In 2006 arrivals reached 6.5m. while receipts totalled TD 2,751m., and in 2007 a further rise in the sector, to 6.8m. arrivals with receipts of TD 3,045m., was recorded. Despite the rise in arrivals, the tourism sector's dependence on the mass low-cost market has been highlighted in a report by the European Investment Bank (EIB). It noted that numbers of tourists from Europe (with the exception of France) had fallen and that the sector had failed to respond to the needs of independent and other higher-spending visitors. In April 2009 the Government launched a new strategy for tourism, which was designed specifically to attract higher-spending visitors, and increase the number of visitors from the Gulf states and China. After an increase in arrivals to 7.1m. in 2008, tourism showed signs of being affected by the economic downturn in Europe. However, arrivals for 2009 totalled 6.9m. In 2011 the political upheaval resulted in a decline in tourist arrivals, to 4.8m., while revenues fell by about one-third, to TD 2,400m. In January 2012 the Government launched a new tourism promotion initiative. However, the combination of social unrest in Tunisia and the ongoing debt crisis in the eurozone has not helped to ease the decline in Tunisian tourism. The sector has not yet recovered from the political upheaval that took place over much of 2011. Data published by the INS in July 2013 revised the tourist arrivals figure for 2011 downward to 3.1m. According to the BCT, 'tourist earnings' declined from TD 3,500m. in 2010 to TD 2,400m. in 2011. It can be concluded from data that the BCT has made available for 2012 that the recovery that year was modest, even though incoming tourist numbers improved from 2011. The World Travel and Tourism Council (WTTC) estimated that the revenue from incoming tourism travel and spending (i.e. excluding expenditure by Tunisian tourists) had risen from TD 1,190m. in 2011 to TD 1,320m. in 2012. The WTTC expected the latter figure to remain fairly constant in 2013.

However, ICT first quarter data for 2013 shows tourist arrivals of around 923,400, a rise of 50% compared with the corresponding period in 2011. In June 2013 the Government claimed that 2.5m. tourists had visited Tunisia in the first six months of that year alone, generating TD 1,500m. in revenue (a figure at variance with WTTC data above, but compatible with the official, seemingly all inclusive, 'tourism earnings' data). However, political upheaval is liable to constrain earnings in the second half of 2013. According to the IMF's Country Report, issued in June, tourism had fallen by 35% from 2010. The report also cited structural problems in the tourism sector: an over-reliance on debt and, relatedly, on sometimes inefficient state-owned banks, weak corporate governance and what it calls a non specialized 'cover all' business model.

FOREIGN AID

The principal sources of economic aid for Tunisia continue to be Western countries and international institutions. The World Bank group has been the most important multilateral donor, providing loans and credits for investment in a variety of projects. The AfDB is another large multilateral donor. Important bilateral donors have included France, the USA and Gulf Arab states (although in 1991 the US Government reduced its aid because of Tunisia's muted support for Iraq during the Gulf crisis). Japan has also extended substantial credit to Tunisia for the purchase of Japanese goods and services. Tunisia's receipts of official development aid had risen from US $178m. in 1984 to $393m. by 1990, and during the 1990s it continued to obtain substantial external funds, principally from the World Bank, the EU and Organisation for Economic Co-operation and Development countries. By March 2003 the World Bank portfolio in Tunisia comprised 21 active projects, amounting to a total net commitment of $1,200m. In June 2004 the World Bank approved a new country assistance strategy to be implemented over a four-year period starting in 2005, including a lending programme in the range of $200m.–$300m. a year to achieve key development objectives: the first and most urgent objective was to reduce unemployment, which remained high at 15%; the second was to improve the education system; and the third was to boost the performance of social programmes while maintaining budget balances. In July 2004 the World Bank approved a $130m. loan for the second phase of an education programme and a $13m. loan to develop the information and communication technologies sector. The Bank additionally approved a $36m. loan for export development projects. Also in 2004 the OPEC Fund for International Development signed a $12m. loan agreement to help finance the construction of a Higher Institute of Technology in Béja. In 2005–06 the World Bank approved further loans to support water supply and sewerage projects, while the OPEC Fund agreed to finance an energy project in the south-east of the country. In May 2009 the AfDB signed a $250m. loan agreement to support Tunisia's efforts towards integration into the global economy. The agreement was approved by the Chamber of Deputies in July, along with further loans from the International Bank for Reconstruction and Development and the EIB. Following the outbreak of political unrest in December 2010 and the overthrow of Ben Ali's regime a month later, Tunisia's need for financial support rose dramatically, not least to support the additional promises made by the interim Government to address the protesters' grievances over salaries and prices. The AfDB and the World Bank provided $1,500m. in emergency funding almost immediately, and subsequently the Group of Eight (G8) leading industrialized nations pledged an additional $25,000m. in loans over the next five years.

Tunisia's total foreign debt had increased from US $3,526m. in 1980 to $8,475m. by 1992 and to $11,379m. by 1996. After a decline in 1998, to $10,850m., debt rose to $11,872m. in 1999, of which $9,487m. was long-term public debt. The debt-servicing ratio was 15.9% in 1999, up from 15.4% in 1998. Under the terms of the 2000 budget, external borrowing was set at TD 1,500m., compared with TD 1,117m. in 1999 and TD 977m. in 1998. In 2000 total foreign debt was $11,500m. and the debt servicing ratio was 22.6%. According to the IMF, total external debt that year rose to 60.2% of GDP from 59.6% of GDP in 1999. Foreign exchange reserves stood at TD 2,810m. at the end of 2001. In 2002 external debt was 61% of GDP and the debt-servicing ratio was 17.2%. Foreign exchange reserves totalled $2,437m. at June 2003.

The outstanding balance of medium- and long-term external debt, measured in TD, amounted to 17,357m. at the end of 2003, compared with TD 16,115m. at the end of 2002. The debt service ratio was down to 13.1% and reserves increased to TD 3,645m. At the end of 2004 external debt had increased to TD 19,238m., while reserves rose to TD 4,733m., and by the end of 2005 the debt balance amounted to TD 20,435m., with reserves standing at TD 5,872m. In 2006, according to the latest and revised figures from the BCT, external debt eased to TD 19,728m. as a result of some early repayments, with the ratio to GDP standing at 43%. However, it rose again slightly, in absolute terms, in 2008 to TD 21,301m., but fell as a proportion of GDP, to 38.6%. However, by the end of 2010 external debt was a slightly lower proportion of strongly rising GDP, at 37.2%, and totalled TD 23,582m. According to the BCT, the debt-service ratio was a manageable 9.3%. At the end of 2011 the BCT stated external debt had risen to TD 25,391m., which, in a poor economic year, represented around 39% of GDP.

Foreign currency reserves totalled TD 8,756m. at the end of 2006, increasing to TD 9,638m. at the end of 2007; by the end of 2008 they had risen further, to TD 11,742m. The level of reserves rose to TD 14,932m. in 2009, and then again, to TD 17,978m., in 2010. In 2011 reserves were estimated by the Economist Intelligence Unit (EIU) to have dropped by as much as TD 1,500m., as export earnings declined and the economy contracted amid the political upheaval; however, in the first half of 2012 reserves were anticipated to have recovered fairly strongly. In June 2013 an EIU report estimated that foreign reserves had fallen to under US $7,000m. (about TD 11,475m.), less than 100 days of import cover, and argued that the promised *sukuk* should ensure sufficient cover.

Statistical Survey

Source (unless otherwise stated): Institut National de la Statistique, 70 rue el-Cham, BP 265, 1002 Tunis; tel. (71) 891-002; fax (71) 792-559; e-mail ins@ins.tn; internet www.ins.nat.tn.

Area and Population

AREA, POPULATION AND DENSITY

Area (sq km)	
Land	154,530
Inland waters	9,080
Total	163,610*
Population (census results)	
20 April 1994	8,785,364
28 April 2004	
Males	4,965,435
Females	4,945,437
Total	9,910,872
Population (official estimates at 1 July)†	
2010	10,549,100
2011	10,673,800
2012	10,777,500
Density (per sq km) at 1 July 2012	69.7‡

* 63,170 sq miles.
† Estimates are rounded to the nearest 100 persons.
‡ Land area only.

POPULATION BY AGE AND SEX
(UN estimates at mid-2013)

	Males	Females	Total
0–14	1,305,175	1,244,938	2,550,113
15–64	3,786,721	3,870,169	7,656,890
65 and over	359,149	430,364	789,513
Total	5,451,045	5,545,471	10,996,516

Source: UN, *World Population Prospects: The 2012 Revision*.

GOVERNORATES
(population estimates at 1 July 2012)

	Area (sq km)*	Population†	Density (per sq km)
Tunis	346	1,003,700	2,900.9
Ariana	498	528,500	1,061.2
Ben Arous	761	600,900	789.6
Manouba	1,060	375,700	354.4
Nabeul	2,788	773,100	277.3
Zaghouan	2,768	174,000	62.9
Bizerte	3,685	556,000	150.9
Béja	3,558	305,400	85.8
Jendouba	3,102	424,200	136.8
Le Kef	4,965	255,100	51.4
Siliana	4,631	234,000	50.5
Kairouan	6,712	566,700	84.4
Kasserine	8,066	438,400	54.4
Sidi Bouzid	6,994	417,900	59.8
Sousse	2,621	641,700	244.8
Monastir	1,019	539,400	529.3
Mahdia	2,966	400,500	135.0
Sfax	7,545	955,500	126.6
Gafsa	8,990	344,500	38.3
Tozeur	4,719	105,900	22.4
Kébili	22,084	154,300	7.0
Gabès	7,175	367,500	51.2
Médenine	8,588	466,700	54.3
Tataouine	38,889	147,900	3.8
Total	154,530	10,777,500	69.7

* Land area only.
† Estimates are rounded to the nearest 100 persons, therefore total may not be equal to the sum of components.

PRINCIPAL TOWNS
(official population estimates at 1 July 2012)

Tunis (capital)	651,710	El Mourouj	128,203
Sfax (Safaqis)	294,875	Bizerta (Bizerte)	124,957
Sousse	217,734	Soukra	117,698
Ettadhamen	143,826	Ariana	115,601
Kairouan (Qairawan)	134,304	Gafsa	103,079
Gabès	130,830		

BIRTHS, MARRIAGES AND DEATHS

	Registered live births		Registered marriages		Registered deaths	
	Number	Rate (per 1,000)	Number	Rate (per 1,000)	Number	Rate (per 1,000)
2004	166,551	16.8	68,976	6.9	48,651	4.9
2005	170,999	17.1	73,971	7.4	49,768	5.0
2006	173,390	17.1	81,340	8.0	48,529	4.8
2007	177,503	17.4	76,809	7.5	48,308	4.7
2008	182,990	17.7	78,748	7.6	51,258	5.0
2009	184,282	17.7	81,605	7.8	51,082	4.9
2010	196,039	18.6	87,081	8.3	51,728	4.9
2011	201,120	18.8	91,590	8.6	56,469	5.3

Life expectancy (years at birth): 74.9 (males 72.9; females 76.9) in 2011.

ECONOMICALLY ACTIVE POPULATION
(labour force survey, '000 persons aged 15 years and over, April–June)

	2011	2012
Agriculture, forestry and fishing	510.0	550.0
Manufacturing	578.0	597.9
Electricity, gas and water*	31.6	37.2
Construction	441.7	432.4
Trade	388.1	386.3
Hotels and restaurants	106.1	111.4
Transport and communications	175.3	193.6
Financial intermediation	25.7	31.3
Real estate, renting and business activities	133.6	140.6
Public administration, education and health	588.1	611.5
Other community, social and personal services	138.9	129.2
Sub-total	3,117.1	3,221.4
Activities not adequately defined	22.7	10.2
Total employed	3,139.8	3,231.6
Unemployed	704.9	691.6
Total labour force	3,844.6	3,923.2
Males	2,817.9	2,852.3
Females	1,026.7	1,070.9

* Including mining and quarrying.

Mid-2013 (estimates in '000): Agriculture, etc. 810; Total labour force 4,134 (Source: FAO).

Health and Welfare

KEY INDICATORS

Total fertility rate (children per woman, 2011)	2.1
Under-5 mortality rate (per 1,000 live births, 2011)	16
HIV/AIDS (% of persons aged 15–49, 2011)	<0.1
Physicians (per 1,000 head, 2009)	1.2
Hospital beds (per 1,000 head, 2010)	2.1
Health expenditure (2010): US $ per head (PPP)	544
Health expenditure (2010): % of GDP	5.7
Health expenditure (2010): public (% of total)	54.3
Access to water (% of persons, 2011)	96
Access to sanitation (% of persons, 2011)	90
Total carbon dioxide emissions ('000 metric tons, 2009)	25,155.6
Carbon dioxide emissions per head (metric tons, 2009)	2.4
Human Development Index (2012): ranking	94
Human Development Index (2012): value	0.712

For sources and definitions, see explanatory note on p. vi.

Agriculture

PRINCIPAL CROPS
('000 metric tons)

	2009	2010	2011
Wheat	1,654	822	1,606
Barley	850	237	681
Potatoes	324	370	367
Broad beans, horse beans, dry	70	48	73
Almonds, with shell	60	52	61
Olives	800	750	863
Artichokes	16	14	18
Tomatoes	1,135	1,296	1,284
Pumpkins, squash and gourds	51	49	48*
Cucumbers and gherkins	38	42	41*
Chillies and peppers, green	281	304	268
Onions and shallots, green†	210	217	210
Onions, dry†	140	145	140
Peas, green	14	11	11*
Carrots and turnips	62	57	55*
Watermelons	570	498	470*
Oranges	116	137	139*
Tangerines, mandarins, clementines and satsumas	44	37	48
Lemons and limes	42	37	48
Grapefruit and pomelos*	84	87	93
Apples	110	126	128
Pears	60	66	61
Apricots	30	24	30
Peaches and nectarines	118	117	123*
Grapes	97	97	114
Figs	28	26	26
Dates	162	174	180

* FAO estimate(s).

† Unofficial figures.

Aggregate production ('000 metric tons, may include official, semi-official or estimated data): Total cereals 2,564 in 2009, 1,109 in 2010, 2,342 in 2011; Total roots and tubers 324 in 2009, 370 in 2010, 367 in 2011; Total pulses 116 in 2009, 93 in 2010, 127 in 2011; Total vegetables (incl. melons) 2,825 in 2009, 2,961 in 2010, 2,860 in 2011; Total fruits (excl. melons) 1,180 in 2009, 1,221 in 2010, 1,314 in 2011.

Source: FAO.

LIVESTOCK
('000 head, year ending September)

	2009	2010	2011
Horses*	57	57	57
Asses*	240	240	240
Cattle	679	671	656
Camels*	235	235	237
Sheep	7,362	7,234	6,999
Goats	1,455	1,296	1,282
Chickens*	70,000	80,000	82,000
Turkeys*	5,800	5,800	6,100

* FAO estimates.

Source: FAO.

LIVESTOCK PRODUCTS
('000 metric tons)

	2009	2010	2011
Cattle meat	51.6	55.8	54.6
Sheep meat	49.1	50.0	51.5
Chicken meat	103.0	113.2	120.0
Cows' milk	1,048	1,059	1,054
Sheep's milk*	19.0	19.5	19.5
Goats' milk*	13.2	13.4	13.4
Hen eggs*	88	91	91
Wool, greasy*	10.3	10.4	10.4

* FAO estimates.

Source: FAO.

Forestry

ROUNDWOOD REMOVALS
('000 cu m, excl. bark, FAO estimates)

	2009	2010	2011
Sawlogs, veneer logs and logs for sleepers	25	25	25
Pulpwood	75	75	75
Other industrial wood	118	118	118
Fuel wood	2,177	2,185	2,188
Total	2,395	2,403	2,406

Source: FAO.

SAWNWOOD PRODUCTION
('000 cu m, incl. sleepers)

	1992	1993	1994
Coniferous (softwood)	2.2	5.8	6.8
Broadleaved (hardwood)	4.0	13.6	13.6
Total	6.2	19.4	20.4

1995–2011: Production as in 1994 (FAO estimates).

Source: FAO.

Fishing

('000 metric tons, live weight)

	2009	2010	2011
Capture	97.9	97.7	102.8
Mullets	7.1	7.3	7.3
Common pandora	3.3	3.9	2.8
Sargo breams	0.4	0.4	0.4
Bogue	2.9	2.8	2.9
Jack and horse mackerels	8.2	9.4	6.3
Sardinellas	14.2	15.1	14.0
European pilchard	19.0	14.4	21.5
Chub mackerel	3.1	3.4	4.7
Common cuttlefish	3.9	4.7	3.0
Aquaculture	4.9	5.4	8.1*
Total catch (incl. others)	102.8	103.1	110.9*

* FAO estimate.

Source: FAO.

Mining

('000 metric tons unless otherwise indicated)

	2009	2010	2011
Crude petroleum	3,950	3,770	3,235
Natural gas (million cu m)†	3,200	3,400	3,500
Iron ore: gross weight	151	180	171
Iron ore: metal content†	79	94	90
Phosphate rock‡	7,409	8,149	2,480
Salt (marine)	1,280	1,804	1,181
Gypsum (crude)	360	435	535

* Source: BP, *Statistical Review of World Energy*.
† Estimated production.
‡ Figures refer to gross weight. The estimated phosphoric acid content (in '000 metric tons) was: 1,115 in 2009; 1,214 in 2010; 518 in 2011.

2012: Crude petroleum 3,090 (Source: BP, *Statistical Review of World Energy*).

Lead concentrates (metric tons): 8,708 in 2005 (figure refers to metal content of concentrates).

Zinc concentrates (metric tons): 15,889 in 2005 (figure refers to metal content of concentrates).

Source (unless otherwise indicated): US Geological Survey.

Industry

SELECTED PRODUCTS
('000 metric tons unless otherwise indicated)

	2009	2010	2011
Superphosphates	747	740	350
Cement	7,186	7,561	7,200
Crude steel	155	115	119
Quicklime	366	343	283
Motor gasoline ('000 barrels)	2,372	2,372	2,226
Kerosene and jet fuel oil ('000 barrels)	7,702	11,169	9,636
Distillate fuel oil ('000 barrels)	4,387	4,387	3,796
Residual fuel oil ('000 barrels)	4,330	4,307	1,533
Electric energy (million kWh)	15,693	n.a.	n.a.

Sources: partly UN Industrial Commodity Statistics Database; US Geological Survey.

Finance

CURRENCY AND EXCHANGE RATES

Monetary Units
1,000 millimes = 1 Tunisian dinar (TD).

Sterling, Dollar and Euro Equivalents (31 May 2013)
£1 sterling = 2.493 dinars;
US $1 = 1.639 dinars;
€1 = 2.131 dinars;
100 Tunisian dinars = £40.12 = $61.03 = €46.93.

Average Exchange Rate (dinars per US $)
2010 1.4314
2011 1.4078
2012 1.5619

BUDGET
(million dinars)*

Revenue†	2010	2011‡	2012§
Tax revenue	12,699	13,668	14,653
Direct taxes	5,033	5,936	6,238
Trade taxes	564	564	589
Value-added tax	3,750	3,818	4,177
Excise	1,563	1,512	1,559
Other taxes	1,789	1,839	2,091
Non-tax revenue	2,070	2,362	2,080
Capital revenue	—	—	8
Total	14,769	16,030	16,741

Expenditure‖	2010	2011‡	2012§
Current expenditure	11,153	13,660	16,175
Wages and salaries	6,785	7,679	8,614
Goods and services	841	860	1,151
Interest payments	1,152	1,190	1,286
Domestic	557	592	646
External	595	598	640
Transfers and subsidies	2,375	3,931	4,524
Non-allocated	–	–	600
Capital expenditure	4,326	4,727	5,446
Direct investment	1,450	1,459	2,806
Capital transfers and equity	2,876	3,269	2,640
Total	15,479	18,387	21,621

* Figures refer to the consolidated accounts of the central Government, including administrative agencies and social security funds. The data exclude the operations of economic and social agencies with their own budgets.
† Excluding grants from abroad and receipts from privatization (million dinars): 84 in 2010; 591 in 2011 (estimate); 1,739 in 2012 (projected).
‡ Estimates.
§ Projected figures.
‖ Excluding net lending (million dinars): –35 in 2010; –88 in 2011 (estimate); 46 in 2012 (projected).

Source: IMF, *Tunisia: 2012 Article IV Consultation—Staff Report; Public Information Notice on the Executive Board Discussion; and Statement by the Executive Director for Tunisia* (September 2012).

CENTRAL BANK RESERVES
(US $ million at 31 December)

	2008	2009	2010
Gold (national valuation)	3.4	3.3	3.0
IMF special drawing rights	5.2	379.1	372.3
Reserve position in IMF	31.2	31.7	86.6
Foreign exchange	8,812.9	10,646.5	9,000.3
Total	8,852.7	11,060.6	9,462.2

2011: Gold (national valuation) 2.9; IMF special drawing rights 371.3; Reserve position in IMF 86.4.

2012: Gold (national valuation) 2.8; IMF special drawing rights 371.7; Reserve position in IMF 86.4; Foreign exchange 7,899.1; *Total* 8,360.0.

Source: IMF, *International Financial Statistics.*

MONEY SUPPLY
(million dinars at 31 December)

	2010	2011	2012
Currency outside banks	5,518	6,816	6,550
Demand deposits at commercial banks	10,012	11,300	13,062
Total money (incl. others)	16,454	19,733	20,843

Source: IMF, *International Financial Statistics.*

COST OF LIVING
(Consumer Price Index; base: 2000 = 100)

	2008	2009	2010
Food	132.6	138.3	147.2
Electricity, gas and other fuels	146.7	150.0	167.8
Clothing	118.4	121.0	125.3
Rent	131.3	136.1	141.3
All items (incl. others)	128.8	133.6	139.1

2011: Food 152.6; All items (incl. others) 143.9.

2012: Food 164.1; All items (incl. others) 152.0.

Source: ILO.

NATIONAL ACCOUNTS
(million dinars at current prices)

Expenditure on the Gross Domestic Product

	2009	2010	2011
Government final consumption expenditure	9,758.7	10,479.2	11,618.0
Private final consumption expenditure	36,390.1	39,683.7	42,784.2
Gross fixed capital formation	14,278.2	15,497.3	14,015.6
Change in inventories	−26.3	1,030.7	1,127.4
Total domestic expenditure	60,400.7	66,690.9	69,545.2
Exports of goods and services	26,428.1	31,210.3	31,299.2
Less Imports of goods and services	28,151.6	34,460.4	36,113.9
GDP in purchasers' values	58,677.2	63,440.9	64,730.5
GDP at constant 2005 prices	50,994.0	52,833.9	52,710.1

2012 (million dinars): GDP in purchasers' values 70,490.7; GDP at constant 2005 prices 54,890.0.

Gross Domestic Product by Economic Activity

	2010	2011	2012
Agriculture and fishing	4,741.3	5,459.4	5,979.0
Mining (excluding hydrocarbons)	486.8	271.5	338.0
Manufacturing (excluding hydrocarbons)	10,680.1	10,766.2	11,278.0
Hydrocarbons, electricity and water	4,808.0	5,196.8	5,649.6
Construction and public works	2,639.1	2,687.4	2,814.9
Maintenance and repair	226.3	232.5	247.3
Transport and telecommunications	8,294.6	7,989.6	8,832.8
Hotels and restaurants	3,163.0	2,626.3	3,211.8
Trade, finance, etc.	14,411.5	15,421.4	16,541.9
Non-market services	9,815.5	10,982.7	12,295.3
Sub-total	59,266.3	61,633.7	67,188.7
Less Imputed bank service charges	822.2	874.6	941.8
Gross value added at factor cost	58,444.1	60,759.2	66,246.9
Indirect taxes, *less* subsidies	4,996.7	3,971.4	4,243.8
GDP in purchasers' values	63,440.9	64,730.6	70,490.7

BALANCE OF PAYMENTS
(US $ million)

	2009	2010	2011
Exports of goods	14,481	16,493	17,876
Imports of goods	−18,117	−21,005	−22,623
Balance on goods	−3,636	−4,512	−4,747
Exports of services	5,334	5,632	4,618
Imports of services	−2,872	−3,234	3,178
Balance on goods and services	−1,174	−2,115	−3,306
Primary income received	318	431	455
Primary income paid	−2,328	−2,355	−2,434
Balance on goods, services and primary income	−3,185	−4,039	−5,285
Secondary income received	1,979	1,972	1,946
Secondary income paid	−28	−37	−47
Current balance	−1,234	−2,104	−3,386
Capital account (net)	164	82	184
Direct investment liabilities	1,525	1,335	433
Portfolio investment liabilities	−89	−26	−44
Other investment assets	−13	−240	−33
Other investment liabilities	1,217	700	1,063
Net errors and omissions	67	33	74
Reserves and related items	1,639	−222	−1,709

Source: IMF, *International Financial Statistics.*

External Trade

PRINCIPAL COMMODITIES
(US $ million)

Imports c.i.f.	2008	2009	2010
Food and live animals	1,912.7	1,128.4	1,452.4
Cereal and cereal preparations	1,229.0	484.0	777.2
Mineral fuels, lubricants, etc.	4,151.0	2,178.2	2,793.7
Petroleum and related products	3,299.3	1,686.9	2,160.5
Gas, natural and manufactured	844.7	487.0	623.3
Chemicals and related products	2,345.6	2,065.3	2,301.6
Plastics in primary forms	531.0	416.7	507.7
Basic manufactures	5,598.2	4,334.1	4,797.3
Textile yarn, fabrics and related products	2,087.6	1,749.0	1,844.7
Cotton fabrics, woven	987.0	829.3	844.7
Machinery and transport equipment	6,725.9	6,604.1	7,751.4
General industrial machinery and equipment	1,048.0	983.0	1,099.3
Electrical machinery, apparatus and appliances	1,920.0	1,756.6	2,239.3
Road vehicles	1,454.4	1,408.4	1,604.3
Miscellaneous manufactured articles	1,778.6	1,684.7	1,764.4
Total	24,638.4	19,096.2	22,215.4

Exports f.o.b.	2008	2009	2010
Food and live animals	856.6	758.6	769.1
Mineral fuels, lubricants, etc.	3,345.2	1,969.2	2,328.0
Petroleum and related products	3,345.0	1,969.0	2,320.3
Petroleum oils and oils obtained from bituminous materials, crude	2,630.8	1,553.1	2,080.8
Animal and vegetable oils	771.2	497.6	428.0
Chemicals and related products	2,942.8	1,521.1	1,790.4
Fertilizers	1,525.4	661.2	812.8
Basic manufactures	1,786.1	1,474.0	1,630.6
Machinery and transport equipment	4,044.1	3,624.9	4,678.2
Electrical machinery, apparatus and appliances	2,538.8	2,214.7	2,651.1
Miscellaneous manufactured articles	5,111.4	4,319.1	4,461.1
Articles of clothing and clothing accessories	3,765.6	3,120.3	3,089.2
Men's or boy's outerwear	1,020.7	760.5	722.5
Footwear	608.0	512.3	566.4
Total	19,320.0	14,445.1	16,426.6

Source: UN, *International Trade Statistics Yearbook*.

2011 (distribution by HS, million dinars): *Imports c.i.f.:* Vegetables and vegetable products 1,953.6 (Cereals 1,267.1); Mineral products 5,315.3; Chemicals and related products 2,371.8; Rubber and plastic, and articles thereof 1,913.3 (Plastic articles 1,687.1); Textiles and textile articles 3,827.2; Iron and steel; other base metals and articles of base metal 3,153.1; Machinery and mechanical appliances; electrical equipment; parts thereof 8,137.1 (Boilers, etc. 3,665.3, Electrical equipment 4,471.8); Vehicles 2,377.7; Total imports (incl. others) 33,695.4; *Exports f.o.b.:* Vegetables and vegetable products 1,599.2; Mineral products 1,330.0; Chemicals and related products 1,453.3; Textiles and textile articles 5,305.8; Footwear, headgear, etc. 834.3; Iron and steel; other base metals and articles of base metals 989.4; Machinery and mechanical appliances; electrical equipment; parts thereof 7,012.5 (Electrical equipment 6,300.4); Vehicles 830.3; Total exports (incl. others) 25,091.9.

2012 (million dinars): *Imports c.i.f.:* Agricultural products 4,213.9; Energy, fuels and lubricants 6,404.3; Textiles 4,273.2; Mechanical and electrical machinery and equipment 15,952.9; Miscellaneous manufacturing products 6,374.2; Total imports (incl. others) 38,182.7; *Exports f.o.b.:* Agricultural products 2,577.1; Energy, fuels and lubricants 4,450.3; Textiles 5,927.8; Mechanical and electrical machinery and equipment 9,714.8; Miscellaneous manufacturing products 2,228.0; Total exports (incl. others) 26,547.6.

PRINCIPAL TRADING PARTNERS
(US $ million)*

Imports c.i.f.	2008	2009	2010
Algeria	724.3	501.2	621.5
Argentina	404.5	161.7	149.9
Belgium	444.2	383.1	466.0
Brazil	303.3	197.7	259.0
China, People's Republic	919.6	956.6	1,344.1
Egypt	249.6	167.8	172.8
France (incl. Monaco)	4,546.3	3,832.1	4,203.2
Germany	1,717.0	1,672.5	1,696.6
India	218.4	223.9	279.7
Italy	4,245.4	3,108.9	3,907.3
Japan	325.9	237.9	312.6
Korea, Republic	173.1	159.7	346.4
Libya	1,073.7	560.6	283.7
Malta	126.8	267.2	197.2
Netherlands	345.0	285.3	441.6
Russia	1,855.7	688.1	1,034.4
Spain	951.2	867.0	1,025.3
Turkey	732.3	576.6	631.7
Ukraine	516.4	327.4	303.0
United Kingdom	456.0	341.3	377.3
USA	748.8	764.8	905.2
Total (incl. others)	24,638.4	19,096.2	22,215.4

Exports f.o.b.	2008	2009	2010
Algeria	408.1	451.2	474.7
Belgium	430.0	319.6	320.3
France (incl. Monaco)	5,507.5	4,283.3	4,717.3
Germany	1,338.0	1,270.1	1,388.1
India	595.2	238.3	307.2
Iran	234.7	127.8	53.2
Italy	3,991.7	3,038.4	3,264.9
Libya	871.2	831.8	732.3
Morocco	234.2	209.4	232.0
Netherlands	422.3	232.7	360.1
Spain	946.1	486.9	637.1
Switzerland (incl. Liechtenstein)	456.0	133.3	263.7
Turkey	309.4	170.8	214.2
United Kingdom	898.6	686.7	824.8
USA	323.1	196.8	388.5
Total (incl. others)	19,320.0	14,445.1	16,426.6

* Imports by country of production; exports by country of last destination.

Source: UN, *International Trade Statistics Yearbook*.

2011 (million dinars): *Imports c.i.f.:* Algeria 896.4; Argentina 433.7; Belgium 599.0; Brazil 642.7; China, People's Republic 2,048.3; France 6,164.7; Germany 2,487.7; India 493.6; Italy 5,331.8; Japan 412.9; Russia 1,936.9; Spain 1,593.1; Turkey 1,195.9; Ukraine 468.8; USA 1,232.6; Total imports (incl. others) 33,695.4; *Exports f.o.b.:* Algeria 656.0; Belgium 473.4; France 7,395.4; Germany 2,271.4; Italy 5,432.3; Libya 1,103.3; Netherlands 587.2; Spain 1,079.4; USA 388.9; Total exports (incl. others) 25,091.9.

2012 (million dinars): Total imports 38,182.7; Total exports 26,547.6.

Transport

RAILWAYS
(traffic)

	2008	2009	2010
Passengers carried ('000)	39,226	38,576	40,153
Passenger-km (million)	1,494	1,486	1,534
Freight carried ('000 metric tons)	10,528	9,318	10,446
Freight net ton-km (million)	2,073	1,821	2,024

ROAD TRAFFIC
(estimates, motor vehicles in use at 31 December)

	2000	2001	2002
Passenger cars	516,525	552,897	585,194
Buses and coaches	11,143	11,973	12,181
Lorries and vans	240,421	253,760	266,499
Road tractors	8,307	9,165	9,605

2010: Passenger cars 915,926; Buses and coaches 16,818; Lorries and vans 381,154; Motorcycles 6,724.

Source: IRF, *World Road Statistics*.

SHIPPING

Flag Registered Fleet
(at 31 December)

	2010	2011	2012
Number of vessels	61	62	62
Total displacement ('000 grt)	266.6	311.8	358.5

Source: Lloyd's List Intelligence (www.lloydslistintelligence.com).

International Sea-borne Freight Traffic
('000 metric tons)

	2008	2009	2010
Goods loaded*	7,939	7,817	8,145
Goods unloaded	16,520	14,553	16,326

* Excluding Algerian crude petroleum loaded at La Skhirra.

CIVIL AVIATION
(traffic on scheduled services)

	2007	2008	2009
Kilometres flown (million)	34	37	35
Passengers carried ('000)	2,055	2,275	2,279
Passenger-km (million)	2,960	3,357	3,220
Total ton-km (million)	303	343	326

Source: UN, *Statistical Yearbook*.

Passengers carried ('000): 2,740 in 2010; 2,747 in 2011 (Source: World Bank, World Development Indicators database).

Tourism

FOREIGN TOURIST ARRIVALS BY NATIONALITY
('000)

	2008	2009	2010
Algeria	968.5	961.3	1,060.0
Belgium	169.1	168.1	163.1
France	1,395.3	1,344.7	1,385.3
Germany	521.5	484.2	458.6
Italy	444.5	383.9	354.1
Libya	1,766.9	1,995.2	1,825.5
Poland	207.5	175.3	151.4
United Kingdom	254.9	275.7	353.3
Total (incl. others)	7,050.4	6,901.4	6,902.7

Total tourist arrivals ('000): 4,782 in 2011 (provisional).

Receipts from tourism (US $ million, excl. passenger transport): 2,773 in 2009; 2,645 in 2010; 1,805 in 2011 (provisional).

Source: World Tourism Organization.

Communications Media

	2010	2011	2012
Telephones ('000 main lines in use)	1,289.6	1,217.8	1,105.6
Mobile cellular telephones ('000 subscribers)	11,114.2	12,387.7	12,841.3
Internet subscribers ('000)	543.3	604.1	n.a.
Broadband subscribers ('000)	481.8	544.4	512.3

Personal computers: 997,150 (96.6 per 1,000 persons) in 2008.

Source: International Telecommunication Union.

Education

(2011/12 unless otherwise indicated)

	Institutions	Teachers	Students
Primary (public)			
1st cycle	4,523	58,833	1,014,836
2nd cycle	2,116	37,900*	469,368
Secondary (public)	521	37,416*	453,090
Higher	195	22,411†	330,541†

* 2010/11 figure.
† Full-time equivalent.

Pupil-teacher ratio (primary education, UNESCO estimate): 17.4 in 2010/11 (Source: UNESCO Institute for Statistics).

Adult literacy rate (UNESCO estimates): 77.6% (males 86.4%; females 71.0%) in 2008 (Source: UNESCO Institute for Statistics).

Directory

The Constitution

A new Constitution for the Republic of Tunisia was promulgated on 1 June 1959 and amended on 12 July 1988; further amendments were approved by national referendum on 26 May 2002. However, the Constitution was abrogated following the removal from office of President Zine al-Abidine Ben Ali in January 2011. On 16 December a Constitutional Law on the Provisional Organization of Public Institutions entered into effect, replacing the 1959 Constitution until a new permanent constitution could be approved. The main provisions of the 1959 Constitution are summarized below:

NATIONAL ASSEMBLY

Legislative power is exercised by a bicameral parliament: the Chamber of Deputies and the Chamber of Advisers, which was established by the constitutional amendments approved in May 2002. Every citizen who has had Tunisian nationality for at least five years and who has attained 20 years of age has the right to vote. The Chamber of Deputies, which is elected (at the same time as the President) every five years, shall hold two sessions every year, each session lasting not more than three months. Additional meetings may be held at the demand of the President or of a majority of the deputies. The Chamber of Advisers currently consists of 126 members; while this number is revised every six years, it must never exceed two-thirds of the number of members of the Chamber of Deputies. One-third of the members of the Chamber of Advisers is composed of representatives of the main professional unions and federations, one-third by representatives of the 24 governorates (one or two from each governorate, depending on the size of its population), and the remainder are appointed by the President. The members of the

Chamber of Advisers serve a six-year term; one-half of its members are replaced every three years.

HEAD OF STATE

The President of the Republic is both head of state and head of the executive. He must be not less than 40 years of age and not more than 75 (not more than 70, prior to the May 2002 amendments). The President is elected by universal suffrage for a five-year term. The amendments approved in May 2002 removed restrictions on the renewal of the presidential mandate (previously, this was renewable twice consecutively). The President is also the Commander-in-Chief of the army and makes both civil and military appointments. The Government may be censured by the National Assembly, in which case the President may dismiss the Assembly and hold fresh elections. If censured by the new Assembly thus elected, the Government must resign. Should the presidency fall vacant for any reason before the end of a President's term of office, the President of the National Assembly shall take charge of affairs of the state for a period of 45 to 60 days. At the end of this period a presidential election shall be organized. The President of the National Assembly shall not be eligible as a presidential candidate.

COUNCIL OF STATE

Comprises two judicial bodies: an administrative body dealing with legal disputes between individuals and state or public bodies, and an audit office to verify the accounts of the state and submit reports.

ECONOMIC AND SOCIAL COUNCIL

Deals with economic and social planning and studies projects submitted by the National Assembly. Members are grouped in seven categories representing various sections of the community.

The Government

HEAD OF STATE

President: MONCEF MARZOUKI (ad interim; sworn in on 13 December 2011).

COUNCIL OF MINISTERS
(September 2013)

A coalition of the Parti de la Renaissance/Hizb al-Nahdah, Congrès pour la République (CPR), Forum Démocratique pour le Travail et les Libertés (Ettakatol) and independents (Ind.).

Prime Minister: ALI LAÂRAYEDH (Hizb al-Nahdah).

Minister of Justice: NADHIR BEN AMMOU (Ind.).

Minister of National Defence: RACHID SABBAGH (Ind.).

Minister of the Interior: LOTFI BEN JEDDOU (Ind.).

Minister of Foreign Affairs: OTHMAN JARANDI (Ind.).

Minister of Human Rights and Transitional Justice: SAMIR DILOU (Hizb al-Nahdah).

Minister of Social Affairs: KHALIL ZAOUIA (Ettakatol).

Minister of Finance: ELYÈS FAKHFEKH (Ettakatol).

Minister of Religious Affairs: NOUREDDINE KHADEMI (Ind.).

Minister of Education: SALEM LABYADH (Ind.).

Minister of Culture: MEHDI MABROUK (Ind.).

Minister of Higher Education and Scientific Research: MONCEF BEN SALEM (Hizb al-Nahdah).

Minister of Industry: MEHDI JOMAÂ (Ind.).

Minister of Trade and Handicrafts: ABDELWAHEB MAÂTAR (CPR).

Minister of Tourism: JAMEL GHAMRA (Ind.).

Minister of Agriculture: MUHAMMAD BEN SALEM (Hizb al-Nahdah).

Minister of Family and Women's Affairs: SIHEM BADI (CPR).

Minister of State Properties and Real Estate Affairs: SLIM BEN HMIDANE (CPR).

Minister of Professional Training and Employment: NAOUFEL JAMMELI (Ind.).

Minister of Development and International Co-operation: LAMINE DOGHRI (Ind.).

Minister of Youth and Sports: TAREK DHIAB (Ind.).

Minister of Public Works and the Environment: MUHAMMAD SALMANE (Ind.).

Minister of Transport: ABDELKARIM HAROUNI (Hizb al-Nahdah).

Minister of Public Health: ABDELLATIF MEKKI (Hizb al-Nahdah).

Minister of Information and Communication Technologies: MONGI MARZOUK (Hizb al-Nahdah).

Minister-delegate to the Prime Minister: NOUREDDINE BHIRI (Hizb al-Nahdah).

Minister-delegate to the Prime Minister, in charge of Economic Affairs: RIDHA SAIDI (Hizb al-Nahdah).

Minister-delegate to the Prime Minister, in charge of Governance and Anti-Corruption: ABDERRAHMANE LADGHAM (Ettakatol).

There are, in addition, 10 Secretaries of State. The Governor of the Central Bank also has full ministerial status.

MINISTRIES

Office of the President: Palais de Carthage, 2016 Carthage; tel. (71) 242-038; e-mail contact@carthage.tn; internet www.carthage.tn.

Office of the Prime Minister: pl. du Gouvernement, La Kasbah, 1030 Tunis; tel. (71) 565-400; e-mail boc@pm.gov.tn; internet www.pm.gov.tn.

Ministry of Agriculture: 30 rue Alain Savary, 1002 Tunis; tel. (71) 786-833; fax (71) 780-391; e-mail mag@ministeres.tn.

Ministry of Culture: 8 rue 2 mars 1934, la Kasbah, 1006 Tunis; tel. (71) 563-006; fax (71) 563-816; e-mail minculture@email.ati.tn; internet www.culture.tn.

Ministry of Development and International Co-operation: Tunis.

Ministry of Education: blvd Bab Benat, 1030 Tunis; tel. (71) 568-768; e-mail ministere@minedu.edunet.tn; internet www.education.gov.tn.

Ministry of Family and Women's Affairs: 2 rue d'Alger, 1001 Tunis; tel. (71) 252-514; fax (71) 349-900; e-mail maffepa@email.ati.tn; internet www.femmes.tn.

Ministry of Finance: pl. du Gouvernement, La Kasbah, 1008 Tunis; tel. (71) 571-888; fax (71) 572-390; e-mail pcontenu@finances.gov.tn; internet www.portail.finances.gov.tn.

Ministry of Foreign Affairs: ave de la Ligue des états arabes, 1030 Tunis; tel. (71) 847-500; fax (71) 785-025; e-mail mae@diplomatie.gov.tn; internet www.diplomatie.gov.tn.

Ministry of Higher Education and Scientific Research: ave Ouled Haffouz, 1030 Tunis; tel. (71) 786-300; fax (71) 786-701; e-mail mes@mes.rnu.tn; internet www.mes.tn.

Ministry of Human Rights and Transitional Justice: ave 2 Mars 1934, 2000 Bardo, Tunis; tel. (71) 702-288; fax (71) 702-822.

Ministry of Industry: Immeuble Beya, 40 rue 8011, Montplaisir, 1002 Tunis; tel. (71) 905-132; fax (71) 902-742; e-mail contact@mit.gov.tn; internet www.industrie.gov.tn.

Ministry of Information and Communication Technologies: 3 bis rue d'Angleterre, 1000 Tunis; tel. (71) 359-000; fax (71) 352-353; e-mail info@infocom.tn; internet www.infocom.tn.

Ministry of the Interior: ave Habib Bourguiba, 1000 Tunis; tel. (71) 333-000; fax (71) 340-888; e-mail mint@ministeres.tn.

Ministry of Justice: 31 ave Bab Benat, 1019 Tunis; tel. (71) 561-440; fax (71) 586-106; e-mail info@e-justice.tn; internet www.e-justice.tn.

Ministry of National Defence: blvd Bab Menara, 1008 Tunis; tel. (71) 560-240; fax (71) 561-804; e-mail defnat@defense.tn; internet www.defense.tn.

Ministry of Professional Training and Employment: 10 blvd Ouled Haffouz, 1002 Tunis; tel. (71) 798-196; fax (71) 794-615; e-mail webmaster@mfpe.gov.tn; internet www.emploi.gov.tn.

Ministry of Public Health: Bab Saâdoun, 1006 Tunis; tel. (71) 577-000; fax (71) 567-100; e-mail msp@ministeres.tn; internet www.santetunisie.rns.tn.

Ministry of Public Works and the Environment: blvd de la terre, Centre Urbain Nord, 1080 Tunis; tel. (71) 728-644; fax (71) 728–655; e-mail webmaster@environnement.nat.tn; internet www.environnement.gov.tn.

Ministry of Religious Affairs: 76 ave Bab Benat, 1019 Tunis; tel. (71) 570-147; fax (71) 572-296; e-mail mar@ministeres.tn; internet www.affaires-religieuses.tn.

Ministry of Social Affairs: 27 blvd Bab Benat, 1006 Tunis; tel. (71) 567-502; fax (71) 150-000; e-mail masste@rnas.gov.tn; internet www.social.tn.

Ministry of State Properties and Real Estate Affairs: 19 ave de Paris, 1000 Tunis; tel. (71) 340-265; fax (71) 342-552; e-mail brc@mdeaf.gov.tn; internet www.mdeaf.gov.tn.

Ministry of Tourism: 1 ave Muhammad V, 1001 Tunis; tel. (71) 341-077; fax (71) 354-223; e-mail boc@tourisme.gov.tn; internet www.tourisme.gov.tn.

Ministry of Trade and Handicrafts: Tunis.

Ministry of Transport: ave Muhammad Bouazizi, 2035 Tunis; tel. (71) 772-110; fax (71) 807-203; e-mail mtr@ministeres.tn; internet www.transport.tn.

Ministry of Youth and Sports: ave Med Ali Akid, Cité El Khadhra, 1003 Tunis; tel. (71) 841-433; fax (71) 800-267; e-mail mjsep@sport .tn; internet www.sport.tn.

President and Legislature

PRESIDENT

On 12 December 2011 the National Constituent Assembly elected Moncef Marzouki to serve as interim President of the Republic. Marzouki—a long-standing opponent of former President Zine al-Abidine Ben Ali and leader of the Congrès pour la République party—was sworn into office the following day.

Presidential Election, 25 October 2009

Candidate	Votes	% of votes
Zine al-Abidine Ben Ali	4,238,711	89.62
Muhammad Bouchiha	236,955	5.01
Ahmed Inoubli	176,726	3.80
Ahmed Brahim	74,257	1.57
Total*	4,729,649	100.00

* Excluding 7,718 invalid votes.

LEGISLATURE

Majlis al-Watani al-Taasisi (National Constituent Assembly)

Palais du Bardo, 2000 Tunis; tel. (71) 510-200; fax (71) 514-608; e-mail anc@anc.tn; internet www.anc.tn.

President: MUSTAPHA BEN JAÂFAR.

General Election, 23 October 2011

	Seats
Parti de la renaissance/Hizb al-Nahdah	89
Congrès pour la République (CPR)	29
Pétition populaire pour la liberté, la justice et le développement (al-Aridha)	26
Forum démocratique pour le travail et les libertés (Ettakatol)	20
Parti démocrate progressiste (PDP)	16
L'Initiative (al-Moubadara)	5
Pôle démocratique moderniste (al-Qotb)*	5
Afek Tounes	4
Parti communiste des ouvriers tunisiens (PCOT)	3
Movement du peuple (Echaâb)	2
Mouvement des démocrates socialistes (MDS)	2
Others	16
Total	217

* Coalition of five civil associations and four parties, led by Mouvement ettajdid.

Political Organizations

Following the removal from office of former President Zine al-Abidine Ben Ali in January 2011, a number of previously outlawed political organizations—including the Islamist Parti de la renaissance/Hizb al-Nahdah—were granted legal status, while several new parties also participated in elections to the National Constituent Assembly held on 23 October.

Congrès pour la République (CPR): 45 rue Ali Dargouth, 1001 Tunis; tel. (71) 346-001; fax (71) 346-002; e-mail cprtunisie@yahoo.fr; internet www.cprtunisie.net; f. 2001; Sec.-Gen. IMAD ALDAIMI.

Forum démocratique pour le travail et les libertés (Ettakatol—FDTL): 4 rue d'Angleterre, 1001 Tunis; tel. and fax (71) 320-258; e-mail contact@fdtl.org; internet www.ettakatol.org; f. 1994; Sec.-Gen. Dr MUSTAPHA BEN JAÂFAR.

L'Initiative (al-Moubadara): Tunis; internet www.almoubadara.tn; f. 2011; Leader KAMEL MORJANE.

Mouvement des démocrates socialistes (MDS): Tunis; in favour of a pluralist political system; participated in 1981 election and was officially recognized in Nov. 1983; 11-mem Political Bureau and 60-mem Nat. Council, normally elected by the party Congress; Sec.-Gen. AHMED KHASKHOUSSI.

Mouvement ettajdid: 7 ave de la liberté, Tunis; tel. (71) 349-307; fax (71) 350-748; internet ettajdid.org; f. 1993 as Mouvement du renouveau, successor to Parti communiste tunisien; leading party in the Pôle démocratique moderniste coalition; Sec.-Gen. AHMAD BRAHIM; Pres. of Nat. Council MUHAMMAD ALI HALOUANI.

Parti de la renaissance/Hizb al-Nahdah: Montplaisir, Tunis; tel. (71) 900-907; fax (71) 901-679; e-mail webmaster@nahdha.tn; internet www.ennahdha.tn; fmrly Mouvement de la tendance islamique (banned in 1981); awarded legal status in March 2011; Islamist-orientated; Leader RACHID GHANNOUCHI; Sec.-Gen. HAMADI JEBALI.

Parti républicain: Tunis; f. 2012 by merger of fmr Parti démocrate progressiste, Afek Tounes and 7 others; centrist; promotes freedom of expression and seeks to uphold democratic process; Sec.-Gen. MAYA JRIBI; Exec. Sec. YASSINE BRAHIM.

Parti social libéral (PSL): 42 ave Hédi Chaker, 1002 Tunis; tel. (71) 789-089; fax (71) 789-060; e-mail p.s.l@gnet.tn; f. 1988; officially recognized in Sept. 1988 as the Parti social pour le progrès; adopted present name in 1993; liberal; Pres. Dr MONDHER THABET.

Parti des travailleurs tunisiens (POT): Tunis; e-mail pcot@ albadil.org; internet www.albadil.org; f. 1986 as Parti communiste des ouvriers tunisiens; name changed as above 2012; legalized 2011; Sec.-Gen. HAMMA HAMMAMI.

Parti de l'unité populaire (PUP): 7 rue d'Autriche, 1002 Tunis; tel. (71) 791-436; fax (71) 835-152; internet www.elwahda.org.tn; breakaway faction from Mouvement de l'unité populaire; officially recognized in Nov. 1983; Sec.-Gen. HASSINE HAMMAMI.

Parti des verts pour le progrès (PVP): 2 ave de France, bureau 335, 3ème étage, 1000 Tunis; tel. (71) 328-439; fax (71) 328-438; e-mail contact@partivert-tunisie.com; internet www .partivert-tunisie.com; f. 2006; seeks to promote awareness of the environment; Sec.-Gen. MONGI KHAMASSI.

Pétition populaire pour la liberté, la justice et le développement (al-Aridha): Tunis; f. 2011; key demands include formation of a democratic constitution, adoption of a system of free health care and dispensation of grants to the unemployed; Leader MUHAMMAD HECHMI HAMDI.

Pôle démocratique moderniste (PDM) (al-Qotb): Tunis; internet www.pole.tn; f. 2011; coalition of 5 civil associations and 4 parties, led by Mouvement ettajdid; Leaders RIADH BEN FADL, MUSTAPHA BEN AHMED.

Union démocratique unioniste (UDU): Tunis; officially recognized in Nov. 1988; supports Arab unity; Sec.-Gen. AHMED INOUBLI.

Diplomatic Representation

EMBASSIES IN TUNISIA

Algeria: 18 rue de Niger, 1002 Tunis; tel. (71) 783-166; fax (71) 788-804; e-mail ambalg@gnet.tn; Ambassador ABD EL-KADER HADJAR.

Argentina: rue du Lac Victoria, BP 12, 1053 Tunis; tel. (71) 964-871; fax (71) 963-006; e-mail etune@mrecic.gov.ar; Ambassador SERGIO ALBERTO BAUR.

Austria: 16 rue ibn Hamdiss, BP 23, al-Menzah, 1004 Tunis; tel. (71) 239-038; fax (71) 755-427; e-mail tunis-ob@bmeia.gv.at; Ambassador Dr GERHARD WEINBERGER.

Bahrain: 72 Mouaouia ibn Soufiane Ave, Almanzah Althamen, 2037 Tunis; tel. (71) 750-865; fax (71) 766-549; e-mail tunis.mission@mofa .gov.bh; Ambassador Sheikh MUHAMMAD BIN ALI BIN HAMAD AL KHALIFA.

Belgium: 47 rue du 1er juin, BP 24, 1002 Tunis; tel. (71) 781-655; fax (71) 792-797; e-mail tunis@diplobel.fed.be; internet www.diplomatie .be/tunis; Ambassador PATRICK DE BEYTER.

Brazil: rue du Lac Léman, Les Berges du Lac, BP 93, 1053 Tunis; tel. (71) 965-455; fax (71) 846-995; e-mail brasemb.tunis@gnet.tn; internet tunis.itamaraty.gov.br/fr; Ambassador JULIO GLINTERNICK BITELLI.

Bulgaria: 5 rue Ryhane, BP 6, Cité Mahragène, 1082 Tunis; tel. (71) 798-962; fax (71) 791-667; e-mail embassy.tunis@mfa.bg; internet www.mfa.bg/embassies/tunisia; Ambassador MIHAIL NIKOLOVSKI.

Canada: rue de la Feuille d'Erable, Les Berges du Lac II, BP 48, 1053 Tunis; tel. (71) 010-200; fax (71) 010-393; e-mail tunis@international .gc.ca; internet www.canadainternational.gc.ca/tunisia-tunisie; Ambassador SÉBASTIEN BEAULIEU.

China, People's Republic: 22 rue Dr Burnet, 1002 Tunis; tel. (71) 780-064; fax (71) 792-631; e-mail chinaemb_tn@mfa.gov.cn; internet tn.china-embassy.org; Ambassador HUO ZHENGDE.

Congo, Democratic Republic: 11 rue Tertullien, Notre Dame, Tunis; tel. (71) 281-833; Ambassador MBOLADINGA KATAKO.

Côte d'Ivoire: 17 rue el-Mansoura, BP 21, Belvédère, 1002 Tunis; tel. (71) 755-911; fax (71) 755-901; e-mail acitn@ambaci-tunis.org; Ambassador IDRISSA BAYO.

Cuba: 1 rue Amilcar, al-Menzah VIII, 1004 Tunis; tel. (71) 767-235; fax (71) 755-922; e-mail embajador-tunez@topnet.tn; internet emba .cubaminrex.cu/tunezar; Ambassador SERAFÍN GIL RODRÍGUEZ VALDÉS.

Czech Republic: 98 rue de Palestine, BP 53, Belvédère, 1002 Tunis; tel. (71) 781-916; fax (71) 793-228; e-mail tunis@embassy.mzv.cz; internet www.mzv.cz/tunis; Ambassador ALEXANDR SLABÝ.

Egypt: ave Muhammad V, Quartier Montplaisir, rue 8007, Tunis; tel. (71) 792-233; fax (71) 794-389; e-mail egyembassy.tunis@planet .tn; Ambassador AYMEN JAMELEDDINE ABD EL-FATTEH MACHRAFA.

Finland: Dar Nordique, rue du Lac Neuchâtel, Les Berges du Lac, 1053 Tunis; tel. (71) 861-777; fax (71) 961-080; e-mail sanomat.tun@ formin.fi; internet www.finlandtunis.org; Ambassador TANJA JÄÄSKELÄINEN.

France: 2 pl. de l'Indépendence, 1000 Tunis; tel. (71) 105-111; fax (71) 105-100; e-mail courier@ambassadefrance-tn.org; internet www .ambassadefrance-tn.org; Ambassador FRANÇOIS GOUYETTE.

Germany: 1 rue al-Hamra, BP 35, Mutuelleville, 1002 Tunis; tel. (71) 143-200; fax (71) 788-242; e-mail reg1@tunis.diplo.de; internet www.tunis.diplo.de; Ambassador JENS UWE PLÖTNER.

Greece: 6 rue Saint Fulgence, Notre Dame, 1082 Tunis; tel. (71) 288-411; fax (71) 285-849; e-mail gremb.tun@mfa.gr; internet www.mfa .gr/tunis; Ambassador ANNA KORKA.

Hungary: 12 rue Achtart, BP 572, Nord Hilton, 1082 Tunis; tel. (71) 780-544; fax (71) 781-264; e-mail mission.tun@kum.hu; internet www.mfa.gov.hu/emb/tunis; Ambassador GYÖRGY PÁNTOS.

India: 4 pl. Didon, Notre Dame, 1002 Tunis; tel. (71) 787-819; fax (71) 783-394; e-mail amb.tunis@mea.gov.in; internet www .indianembassytunis.com; Ambassador NAGMA MUHAMMAD MALLICK.

Indonesia: 15 rue du Lac Malaren, BP 58, 1053 Tunis; tel. (71) 860-377; fax (71) 861-758; e-mail kbritun@gnet.tn; Ambassador MOHAMMAD IBNU SAID.

Iran: 10 rue de Docteur Burnet, Belvédère, 1002 Tunis; tel. (71) 790-084; fax (71) 793-177; Ambassador Dr PEIMAN DJEBELLI.

Iraq: ave Tahar B. Achour, route X2 m 10, Mutuelleville, Tunis; tel. (71) 965-824; fax (71) 964-750; e-mail tunemb@iraqmofamail.net; Ambassador JABER HABIB JABER.

Italy: 37 rue Gamal Abd al-Nasser, 1000 Tunis; tel. (71) 321-811; fax (71) 324-155; e-mail ambitalia.tunisi@esteri.it; internet www .ambtunisi.esteri.it; Ambassador RAIMONDO DE CARDONA.

Japan: 9 rue Apollo XI, BP 163, Cité Mahrajène, 1082 Tunis; tel. (71) 791-251; fax (71) 786-625; e-mail eoj.tunis@tn.mofa.go.jp; internet www.tn.emb-japan.go.jp; Ambassador JUICHI TAKAHARA.

Jordan: 10 Nahj al-Shankiti, 1002 Tunis; tel. (71) 785-829; fax (71) 786-461; e-mail emb.jordan@planet.tn; Ambassador ZUHEIR DMOUR.

Korea, Republic: 3 rue de l'Alhambra, BP 297, Mutuelleville, 1002 Tunis; tel. (71) 799-905; fax (71) 791-923; e-mail tunisie@mofat.go.kr; internet tun.mofat.go.kr; Ambassador JOO BOK-RYONG.

Kuwait: 40 route Ariane, al-Menzah, Tunis; tel. (71) 754-811; fax (71) 767-659; e-mail tunis@mofa.gov.kw; Ambassador FAHAD AL-AWADHI.

Lebanon: rue d'Ormia, 1053 Les Berges du Lac, Tunis; tel. and fax (71) 960-001; e-mail ambassadeliban@planet.tn; Ambassador BASSAM NOOMANI.

Libya: 48 bis rue du 1er juin, Mutuelleville, 1002 Tunis; tel. (71) 780-866; fax (71) 795-338; Ambassador JEMAL JARNAZ.

Mali: 3 impasse Aboul Atahya, rue Dr Burnet, Mutueville, 1002 Tunis; BP 109, Cité Mahrajène, 1082 Tunis; tel. (71) 792-589; fax (71) 791-453; e-mail ambamali@planet.tn; Ambassador SIRAGATA TRAORÉ.

Malta: Immeuble Carthage Centre, rue du Lac de Constance, BP 71, Les Berges du Lac, Tunis; tel. (71) 965-811; fax (71) 965-977; e-mail maltaembassy.tunis@gov.mt; Ambassador CARMEL INGUANEZ.

Mauritania: 17 rue Fatma Ennechi, BP 62, al-Menzah, Tunis; tel. (71) 234-935; Ambassador MAHFOUDH OULD MUHAMMAD AHMED.

Morocco: 39 rue du 1er juin, Mutuelle Ville, 1002 Tunis; tel. (71) 782-775; fax (71) 787-103; e-mail ambamaroc@sifamatunis.net; Ambassador MUHAMMAD FARAJ DOUKKALI.

Netherlands: 6–8 rue Meycen, Cité Mahrajène, 1082 Tunis; tel. (71) 155-300; fax (71) 155-330; e-mail tun@minbuza.nl; internet tunesie .nlambassade.org; Ambassador HANS VAN VLOTEN DISSEVELT.

Pakistan: 35 rue Ali Ayari, al-Menzah 9A, Tunis; tel. (71) 871-330; fax (71) 871-410; e-mail pareptunis@yahoo.com; Ambassador MUSHTAQ ALI SHAH.

Poland: Le Grand Blvd de la Corniche, 2045 Les Berges du Lac II, Tunis; tel. (71) 196-193; fax (71) 196-203; e-mail tunis.amb .sekretariat@msz.gov.pl; internet www.tunis.polemb.net; Ambassador IWO BYCZEWSKI.

Portugal: 2 rue Sufétula, Belvédère, 1002 Tunis; tel. (71) 893-981; fax (71) 791-008; e-mail ambport@hexabyte.tn; Ambassador LUIS FARO RAMOS.

Qatar: rue Alhadi Krai, Northern al-Omran Quarter, 1082 Tunis; tel. (71) 849-600; fax (71) 749-073; e-mail tunis.amb@mofa.gov.qa; internet www.qatarembassy.tn; Ambassador SAAD BIN NASSER AL-HUMAIDI.

Romania: 18 ave d'Afrique, BP 57, al-Menzah V, 1004 Tunis; tel. (71) 766-926; fax (71) 767-695; e-mail ambroum@planet.tn; internet tunis .mae.ro; Ambassador NICOLAE NĂSTASE.

Russia: 4 rue Bergamotes, BP 48, el-Manar I, 2092 Tunis; tel. (71) 882-446; fax (71) 882-478; e-mail ambrustn@mail.ru; internet www .tunisie.mid.ru; Ambassador ALEKSANDR P. SHENI.

Saudi Arabia: ave Muhammad Bouazizi, Centre Urbain Nord C, Mahrajène, 1080 Tunis; tel. (71) 233-466; fax (71) 751-441; Ambassador Dr KHALED BIN MUSAID AL-ANQARI.

Senegal: BP 22, Belvédère, 1002 Tunis; tel. (71) 802-397; fax (71) 780-770; e-mail ambassene@planet.tn; internet www.ambasenegal .intl.tn; Ambassador KHADIJATOU TALL DIANÉ.

Serbia: 4 rue de Libéria, Belvédère, 1002 Tunis; tel. (71) 783-057; fax (71) 796-482; e-mail amb.serbia@gnet.tn; Ambassador MILICA CUBRILO FILIPOVIĆ.

Somalia: 6 rue Hadramout, Mutuelleville, Tunis; tel. (71) 289-505; Ambassador AHMAD ABDALLAH MUHAMMAD.

South Africa: 7 rue Achtart, Nord Hilton, BP 251, 1082 Tunis; tel. (71) 800-311; fax (71) 796-742; e-mail sa@emb-safrica.intl.tn; internet www.southafrica.intl.tn; Ambassador NONCEBA NANCY LOSI-TUTU.

Spain: 24 ave Dr Ernest Conseil, Cité Jardin, 1002 Tunis; tel. (71) 782-217; fax (71) 786-267; e-mail emb.tunez@maec.es; Ambassador ANTONIO COSANO PÉREZ.

Sudan: 37 rue d'Afrique, al-Menzah V, 1008 Tunis; tel. (71) 231-322; fax (71) 751-756; e-mail contact@soudanembassy-tn.com; Ambassador FADHEL ABDALLAH FADL IDRISS.

Switzerland: BP 56, Les Berges du Lac, 1053 Tunis; tel. (71) 962-997; fax (71) 965-796; e-mail tun.vertretung@eda.admin.ch; internet www.eda.admin.ch/tunis; Ambassador PIERRE COMBERNOUS.

Syria: 119 Azzouz Ribai-Almanar 3, Tunis; tel. (71) 888-188; Ambassador (vacant).

Turkey: 4 ave Hédi Karay, Centre Urbain Nord, BP 134, 1082 Tunis; tel. (71) 132-300; fax (71) 767-045; e-mail ambassade.tunis@mfa.gov .tr; internet tunis.emb.mfa.gov.tr; Ambassador ÖMER GÜCÜK.

Ukraine: 7 rue Saint Fulgence, Notre Dame, 1002 Tunis; tel. (71) 845-861; fax (71) 840-866; e-mail emb_tn@mfa.gov.ua; internet www .mfa.gov.ua/tunis; Ambassador (vacant).

United Arab Emirates: 9 rue Achtart, Nord Hilton, Belvédère, 1002 Tunis; tel. (71) 788-888; fax (71) 788-777; e-mail media.tunis@ mofa.gov.ae; Ambassador SALEM ISSA ALI AL-KUTAM ZOUGHABI.

United Kingdom: rue du Lac Windermere, Les Berges du Lac, 1053 Tunis; tel. (71) 108-700; fax (71) 108-749; e-mail british.embassy@ planet.tn; internet www.gov.uk/government/world/tunisia; Ambassador HAMISH COWELL.

USA: Les Berges du Lac, 1053 Tunis; tel. (71) 107-000; fax (71) 963-263; e-mail tuniswebsitecontact@state.gov; internet tunisia .usembassy.gov; Ambassador JACOB WALLES.

Yemen: rue Mouaouia ibn Soufiane, al-Menzah VI, Tunis; tel. (71) 237-933; Ambassador HUSSEIN DHAIFULLAH AL-AWADHI.

Judicial System

The **Cour de Cassation** in Tunis has three civil and one criminal sections. There are three **Cours d'Appel** at Tunis, Sousse and Sfax, and 13 **Cours de Première Instance**, each having three chambers, except the **Cour de Première Instance** at Tunis, which has eight chambers. **Justices Cantonales** exist in 51 areas.

Religion

The Constitution of 1959 recognizes Islam as the state religion, with the introduction of certain reforms, such as the abolition of polygamy. An estimated 99% of the population are Muslims. Minority religions include Judaism (an estimated 1,500 adherents in 2008) and Christianity. The Christian population comprises Roman Catholics, Greek Orthodox, and French and English Protestants.

ISLAM

Grand Mufti of Tunisia: Sheikh KAMAL AL-DIN JA'EIT.

CHRISTIANITY

The Roman Catholic Church

There were an estimated 20,500 adherents in Tunisia in December 2007.

Archbishop of Tunis: Most Rev. MAROUN ELIAS LAHHAM, Evêché, 4 rue d'Alger, 1000 Tunis; tel. (71) 335-831; fax (71) 335-832; e-mail eveche.tunisie@evechetunisie.org; internet www.diocesetunisie.org.

The Protestant Church

Reformed Church of Tunisia: 36 rue Charles de Gaulle, 1000 Tunis; tel. (71) 327-886; e-mail eglisereformee@yahoo.fr; f. 1880; c. 220 mems; Pastor WILLIAM BROWN.

The Press

DAILIES

Al-Chourouk (Sunrise): 25 rue Jean Jaurès, BP 36619, Tunis; tel. (71) 331-000; fax (71) 253-024; e-mail directiongenerale@alchourouk.com; internet www.alchourouk.com; Arabic; Dir SLAHEDDINE AL-AMRI; Editor-in-Chief ABD AL-HAMID RIAHI; circ. 70,000.

Essahafa: 6 rue Ali Bach-Hamba, 1000 Tunis; tel. (71) 341-066; fax (71) 349-720; e-mail contact@essahafa.info.tn; internet www.essahafa.info.tn; f. 1936; Arabic; Editor-in-Chief NEJI ABBASSI.

La Presse de Tunisie: 6 rue Ali Bach-Hamba, 1000 Tunis; tel. (71) 341-066; fax (71) 349-720; e-mail contact@lapresse.tn; internet www.lapresse.tn; f. 1936; French; Editors-in-Chief MONGI GHARBI, FAOUZIA MEZZI; circ. 40,000.

Le Quotidien: 25 rue Jean Jaurès, 1000 Tunis; tel. (71) 331-000; fax (71) 253-02; e-mail directiongenerale@lequotidien-tn.com; internet www.lequotidien-tn.com; f. 2001; French; Dir SLAHEDDINE AL-AMRI; Editor-in-Chief CHOUKRY BAKOUCHE; circ. 20,000.

As-Sabah (The Morning): ave Muhammad Bouazizi, BP 441, al-Menzah, 1004 Tunis; tel. (71) 238-222; fax (71) 232-761; e-mail redaction@assabah.com.tn; internet www.assabah.com.tn; f. 1951; Arabic; Dir MUSTAPHA AL-JABER; Editor-in-Chief NOUREDDINE ACHOUR; circ. 30,000.

Le Temps: ave Muhammad Bouazizi, al-Menzah, 1004 Tunis; tel. (71) 238-222; fax (71) 232-761; e-mail redaction@letemps.com.tn; internet www.letemps.com.tn; f. 1975; French; Dir MUSTAPHA AL-JABER; Editor-in-Chief RAOUF KHALSI; circ. 42,000.

Tunisia Live: 17 rue Charles de Gaulle, Tunis; tel. (71) 324-703; e-mail contact@tunisialive.net; internet www.tunisia-live.net; f. 2011; English; online only; Founders RAMLA JABER, YOUSSEF GAIGI, ZIED MHIRSI.

PERIODICALS

Afrique Economie: 16 rue de Rome, BP 61, 1015 Tunis; tel. (71) 347-441; fax (71) 353-172; e-mail iea@planet.tn; f. 1970; monthly; Dir MUHAMMAD ZERZERI.

Al-Akhbar (The News): 1 passage d'al-Houdaybiyah, 1000 Tunis; tel. (71) 344-100; fax (71) 355-079; internet www.akhbar.tn; f. 1984; weekly; Arabic; general; Dir MUHAMMAD BEN YOUSUF; circ. 75,000.

Al-Anouar al-Tounissia (Tunisian Lights): 25 rue al-Cham, 5000 Tunis; tel. (71) 331-000; fax (71) 253-024; internet www.alanouar.com; Arabic; Dir SLAHEDDINE AL-AMRI; circ. 165,000.

Attariq al-Jadid (New Road): 6 rue Metouia, 1069 Tunis; tel. (71) 256-400; fax (71) 240-981; internet www.attariq.org; f. 1981; weekly; Arabic; organ of the Mouvement ettajdid; Editor-in-Chief HATEM CHAÂBOUNI.

Al-Bayan (The Manifesto): 61 rue Abderrazek, Chraîbi, 1001 Tunis; tel. (71) 339-633; fax (71) 338-533; e-mail darelbayane@gnet.tn; f. 1976; weekly; general; organ of the Union tunisienne de l'industrie, du commerce et de l'artisanat; Dir HÉDI DJILANI; circ. 100,000.

Al-Biladi (My Country): 15 rue 2 mars 1934, Tunis; f. 1974; Arabic; political and general weekly for Tunisian workers abroad; Dir HÉDI AL-GHALI; circ. 90,000.

Bulletin Mensuel de Statistiques: Institut National de la Statistique, 70 rue al-Cham, BP 265, 1080 Tunis; tel. (71) 891-002; fax (71) 792-559; e-mail ins@mdci.gov.tn; internet www.ins.nat.tn; monthly.

Conjoncture: 37 ave Kheireddine Pacha, 1002 Tunis; tel. (71) 891-826; fax (71) 200-706; e-mail conjoncture2003@yahoo.fr; f. 1974; monthly; economic and financial surveys; Dir HABIB BEDHIAFI; circ. 5,000.

Démocratie: Tunis; f. 1978; monthly; French; organ of the MDS; Dir HASSIB BEN AMMAR; circ. 5,000.

Echaâb: 41 ave Ali Dargouth, 1001 Tunis; tel. (71) 255-020; fax (71) 355-139; e-mail journal.echaab@planet.tn; internet www.echaab.info.tn; weekly; Dirs HUSSAIN ABBASI, SAMI TAHIRI.

L'Economiste Maghrébin: 3 rue el-Kewekibi, 1002 Tunis; tel. (71) 790-773; fax (71) 793-707; e-mail info@leconomistemaghrebin.com; internet www.leconomiste.com.tn; f. 1990; bi-weekly; French; Dir HÉDI MÉCHRI; circ. 30,000.

L'Expert: 69 rue Echam, 1002 Tunis; tel. (71) 784-970; fax (71) 794-130; internet www.lexpertjournal.com.tn.

El-Fallah: 8451 rue Alain Savary, al-Khadra, 1003 Tunis; tel. (71) 806-800; fax (71) 809-181; e-mail utap.tunis@email.ati.tn; internet www.utap.org.tn; weekly; organ of the Union Tunisienne de l'Agriculture et de la Pêche (UTAP); Dir MABROUK BAHRI; Editor GHARBI HAMOUDA; circ. 7,000.

L'Hebdo Touristique: rue 8601, 40, Zone Industrielle, La Charguia 2, 2035 Tunis; tel. (71) 786-866; fax (71) 794-891; e-mail haddad.tijani@planet.tn; f. 1971; weekly; French; tourism; Dir TIJANI HADDAD; circ. 5,000.

IBLA: Institut des Belles Lettres Arabes, 12 rue Jemaâ el-Haoua, 1008 Tunis; tel. (71) 560-133; fax (71) 572-683; e-mail ibla@gnet.tn; internet www.iblatunis.org; f. 1937; 2 a year; French, Arabic and English; social and cultural review on Maghreb and Muslim-Arab affairs; Dir JEAN FONTAINE; circ. 600.

Irfane (Children): 6 rue Muhammad Ali, 1000 Tunis; tel. (71) 256-877; fax (71) 351-521; f. 1965; monthly; Arabic; Dir-Gen. RIDHA EL-OUADI; circ. 100,000.

Jeunesse Magazine: 6 rue Muhammad Ali, 1000 Tunis; tel. (71) 256-877; fax (71) 351-521; f. 1980; monthly; Arabic; Dir-Gen. RIDHA EL-OUADI; circ. 30,000.

Journal Les Annonces: 6 rue de Sparte, BP 1343, Tunis; tel. (71) 350-177; fax (71) 347-184; e-mail nejib.azouz@planet.tn; internet www.elilane.com; f. 1978; 2 a week; French and Arabic; Dir MUHAMMAD NEJIB AZOUZ; circ. 170,000.

Journal Officiel de la République Tunisienne: ave Farhat Hached, 2040 Radès; tel. (71) 299-914; fax (71) 297-234; f. 1860; official gazette; Arabic and French; 2 a week; publ. by Imprimerie Officielle (State Press); Pres. and Dir-Gen. ROMDHANE BEN MIMOUN; circ. 20,000.

Al-Mawkif: 10 rue Eve Nohelle, 1001 Tunis; tel. (71) 332-271; fax (71) 332-194; e-mail mawkef_21@yahoo.fr; f. 1984; weekly; organ of the Parti démocrate progressiste (which merged into Parti républicain in 2012); Man. Dir AHMED NÉJIB CHEBBI; Editor-in-Chief RACHID KHECHANA.

Al-Moussawar: 10 rue al-Cham, Tunis; tel. (71) 289-000; fax (71) 289-357; internet www.almoussawar.com; weekly; circ. 75,000.

Mouwatinoun (Citizens): Tunis; internet www.fdtl.org; f. 2007; weekly; Arabic; organ of the Forum démocratique pour le travail et les libertés (FDTL).

Réalités: 6–7 rue de Cameroun, 1002 Tunis; tel. (71) 893-489; fax (71) 787-160; e-mail redaction@realites.com.tn; internet www.realites.com.tn; f. 1979; weekly; Arabic and French; Dir TAÏEB ZAHAR; Editor-in-Chief ZYED KRICHEN; circ. 25,000.

Tounes el Khadra: 8451 rue Alain Savary, al-Khadra, 1003 Tunis; tel. (71) 806-800; fax (71) 809-181; e-mail utap.tunis@email.ati.tn; internet www.utap.org.tn; f. 1976; bi-monthly; agricultural, scientific and technical; organ of the UTAP; Dir MABROUK BAHRI; Editor GHARBI HAMOUDA; circ. 5,000.

Tunis Hebdo: 1 passage d'al-Houdaybiyah, 1000 Tunis; tel. (71) 344-100; fax (71) 355-079; e-mail tunishebdo@tunishebdo.com.tn; internet www.tunishebdo.com.tn; f. 1973; weekly; French; general and sport; Dir and Editor-in-Chief MUHAMMAD BEN YOUSUF; circ. 35,000.

NEWS AGENCY

Tunis Afrique Presse (TAP): 7 ave Slimane Ben Slimane, al-Manar, 2092 Tunis; tel. (71) 889-000; fax (71) 883-500; e-mail dg.tap@tap.info.tn; internet www.tap.info.tn; f. 1961; Arabic, French and English; offices in Algiers (Algeria), Rabat (Morocco), Paris (France) and New York (USA); daily news services; Pres. and Man. Dir MUHAMMAD TAIEB YOUSEFFI.

Publishers

Al-Dar al-Arabia Lil Kitab: 4 ave Mohieddine el-Klibi, BP 32, al-Manar 2, 2092 Tunis; tel. (71) 888-255; fax (71) 888-365; e-mail mal@gnet.tn; f. 1975; general literature, children's books, non-fiction; Chief Officer LOTFI BEN MBAREK.

Centre de Publications Universitaires: Campus Universitaire, BP 255, 1080 Tunis; tel. (71) 874-000; fax (71) 871-677; e-mail cpu@cpu.rnu.tn; internet www.mes.tn/cpu; educational books, journals.

Cérès Editions: 6 rue Alain Savary, Belvédère, 1002 Tunis; tel. (71) 280-505; fax (71) 287-216; e-mail info@ceres-editions.com; internet www.ceres-editions.com; f. 1964; social sciences, art books, literature, novels; Man. Editor KARIM BEN SMAÏL.

Dar Cheraït: Centre Culturel et Touristique Dar Cheraït, Route Touristique, 2200 Tozeur; tel. (76) 452-100; fax (76) 452-329; e-mail darcherait@planet.tn; internet www.darcherait.com.tn.

Dar al-Kitab: 5 ave Bourguiba, 4000 Sousse; tel. (73) 25097; f. 1950; literature, children's books, legal studies, foreign books; Pres. TAÏEB KACEM; Dir FAYÇAL KACEM.

Dar as-Sabah: ave Muhammad Bouazizi, BP 441, al-Menzah, 1004 Tunis; tel. (71) 717-222; fax (71) 232-761; e-mail redaction@assabah.com.tn; internet www.assabah.com.tn; f. 1951; 200 mems; publishes daily and weekly papers, including the dailies *As-Sabah* and *Le Temps*, which circulate throughout Tunisia, North Africa, France, Belgium, Luxembourg and Germany; Chair. MUHAMMAD SAKHER EL MATERI; Dir-Gen. MUSTAPHA AL-JABER.

Editions Apollonia: 4 rue Claude Bernard, 1002 Tunis; tel. (71) 786-381; fax (71) 799-190; e-mail apolloniaeditions@gmail.com; internet www.apollonia.com.tn; art, literature, essays, poetry.

Editions Bouslama: 15 ave de France, 1000 Tunis; tel. (71) 240-056; fax (71) 381-100; f. 1960; history, children's books; Man. Dir ALI BOUSLAMA.

Institut National de la Statistique: 70 rue al-Cham, BP 265, 1080 Tunis; tel. (71) 891-002; fax (71) 792-559; e-mail ins@mdci.gov.tn; internet www.ins.nat.tn; publishes a variety of annuals, periodicals and papers concerned with the economic policy and devt of Tunisia.

Librairie al-Manar: 60 ave Bab Djedid, BP 179, 1008 Tunis; tel. (71) 253-224; fax (71) 336-565; e-mail librairie.almanar@planet.tn; f. 1938; general, educational, Islam; Man. Dir HABIB M'HAMDI.

Société d'Arts Graphiques, d'Edition et de Presse (SAGEP): 15 rue 2 mars 1934, La Kasbah, 1000 Tunis; tel. (71) 564-988; fax (71) 569-736; f. 1974; prints and publishes daily papers, magazines, books, etc.; Dir-Gen. MAHMOUD MEFTAH.

Sud Editions: 79 rue de Palestine, 1002 Tunis; tel. (71) 785-179; fax (71) 848-664; e-mail sud.editions@planet.tn; f. 1976; Arab literature, art and art history, history, sociology, religion; Man. Dir MUHAMMAD MASMOUDI.

GOVERNMENT PUBLISHING HOUSE

Imprimerie Officielle de la République Tunisienne: 40 ave Farhat Hached, 2098 Radès; tel. (71) 434-211; fax (71) 434-234; e-mail iort@iort.gov.tn; internet www.iort.gov.tn; f. 1860; Pres. and Dir-Gen. AHMED ZARROUK.

Broadcasting and Communications

TELECOMMUNICATIONS

Orange Tunisie: rue du Lac de Côme, Les Berges du Lac, 1053 Tunis; tel. (71) 167-900; fax (71) 961-808; internet www.orange.tn; f. 2010; launched mobile telephone network in May 2010; 49% stake owned by France Télécom; Chair. MARWAN MABROUK.

Orascom Telecom Tunisia (Tunisiana): Immeuble Zénith, Les Jardins du Lac, 1053 Tunis; tel. (22) 120-000; e-mail servicerp@tunisiana.com; internet www.tunisiana.com; f. 2002; Chair. TAWFIQ JELASSI; CEO KENNETH CAMPBELL.

Société Tunisienne d'Entreprises de Télécommunications (SOTETEL): rue des Entrepreneurs, Zone Industrielle, BP 640, La Charguia 2, 1080 Tunis; tel. (71) 941-100; fax (71) 940-584; e-mail contact@sotetel.tn; internet www.sotetel.net; f. 1981; privatized in 1998; Pres. ALI GHODBANI; Dir-Gen. JAMEL MHEDHBI.

Tunisie Télécom: Jardins du Lac II, 1053 Tunis; tel. (71) 901-717; fax (71) 900-777; e-mail actel.virtuelle@ttnet.tn; internet www.tunisietelecom.tn; 65% state-owned, 35% owned by Tecom-Dig (Dubai, United Arab Emirates); CEO RAOUF CHKIR.

Regulatory Authority

Instance Nationale des Télécommunications (INT): rue Echabia, Montplaisir, 1073 Tunis; tel. (71) 900-868; fax (71) 909-435; e-mail contact@intt.tn; internet www.intt.tn; f. 2001; Pres. KAMEL SAADAOUI.

BROADCASTING

Office National de la Télédiffusion (ONT) (National Broadcasting Corporation of Tunisia): Cité Ennassim 1, Montplaisir, BP 399, 1080 Tunis; tel. (71) 908-177; fax (71) 904-923; e-mail ont@telediffusion.net.tn; internet www.telediffusion.net.tn; f. 1993 supervision and management of the radio and television broadcasting networks.

Radio

Etablissement de la Radiodiffusion Tunisienne: 71 ave de la Liberté, 1002 Tunis; tel. (71) 847-300; fax (71) 780-993; e-mail portail@radiotunisienne.tn; internet www.radiotunisienne.tn; govt service; originally merged with Télévision Tunisienne; became independent 2006; broadcasts in Arabic, French, German, Italian, Spanish and English; radio stations at Gafsa, El-Kef, Monastir, Sfax, Tataouine and Tunis (3); television stations Tunis 7 and Canal 21; Pres. and Man. Dir MUHAMMAD MEDDEB.

Express FM: 1 rue Monastir 2045, l'Aouina Tunis; tel. (71) 760-769; e-mail contact@expressfm.tn; internet www.radioexpressfm.com; f. 2010; Gen. Man. NAJOUA RAHOUI.

Jawhara FM: rue des Orangers, Khzema Est, BP 120, 4051 Sousse; tel. (73) 275-800; fax (73) 275-810; e-mail direction@jawharafm.net; internet www.jawharafm.net; Dir Gen. ALI BELHAJ YOUSSEF.

Mosaïque FM: Tunis; tel. (71) 287-246; e-mail dg@mosaiquefm.net; internet www.mosaiquefm.net; f. 2003; first privately owned radio station when launched in 2003; broadcasts in Arabic and French to Tunis and the north-east of the country; Dir-Gen. NOUREDDINE BOUTAR.

Shems FM: 5 rue du Lac d'Annecy, Les Berges du Lac, Tunis; tel. (71) 167-070; e-mail contact@shemsfm.net; internet www.shemsfm.net; f. 2010; Dir-Gen. FATHI BHOURY.

Zitouna FM: 61 ave Habib Bourguiba, 2016 Carthage Hannibal; internet www.zitounafm.net; f. 2007.

Television

Etablissement de la Télévision Tunisienne: ave de la Ligue des Etats Arabes, Notre Dame, 1030 Tunis; e-mail info@tunisiatv.com; internet www.tunisie7.tn; formerly merged with Radiodiffusion Tunisienne; became independent 2006; Pres. and Man. Dir ADNENE KHEDR.

Hannibal TV: 85 ave du 13 Août, Choutrana II, Soukra, 2036 Tunis; e-mail contact@hannibaltv.com; internet www.hannibaltv.com.tn; f. 2005; privately owned channel; CEO LARBI NASRA.

Nessma TV: 14, rue 8006, Montplaisir, 1073 Tunis; tel. (71) 909-222; fax (71) 893-503; e-mail communication@nessmatv.tv; internet www.nessma.tv; f. 2009; covers Maghreb region; 50% owned by Karoui Group and rest by Quinta Communication and Mediaset Group; Pres. and CEO NABIL KAROUI.

Finance

(cap. = capital; dep. = deposits; res = reserves; m. = million; br(s) = branch(es); amounts in dinars, unless otherwise stated)

BANKING

Central Bank

Banque Centrale de Tunisie (BCT): 25 rue Hédi Nouira, BP 777, 1080 Tunis; tel. (71) 340-588; fax (71) 354-214; e-mail boc@bct.gov.tn; internet www.bct.gov.tn; f. 1958; cap. 6m., res 90m., dep. 5,752m. (Dec. 2009); Gov. CHÉDLI AYARI; 12 brs.

Commercial Banks

Amen Bank: ave Muhammad V, 1002 Tunis; tel. (71) 835-500; fax (71) 833-517; e-mail amenbank@amenbank.com.tn; internet www.amenbank.com.tn; f. 1967 as Crédit Foncier et Commercial de Tunisie; name changed as above in 1995; cap. 100m., res 241m., dep. 3,783m. (Dec. 2010); Chair. RACHID BEN YEDDER; Gen. Man. AHMAD EL-KARM; 81 brs.

Arab Banking Corpn Tunisie (ABC Tunisie): Immeuble ABC, rue du Lac d'Annecy, Les Berges du Lac, 1053 Tunis; tel. (71) 861-861; fax (71) 860-921; e-mail abc.tunis@arabbanking.com; internet www.arabbanking.com; f. 2000; cap. 50m., res –22m., dep. 189m. (Dec. 2009); Chair. MUHAMMAD HUSSAIN LAYAS; Pres. and Chief Exec. HASSAN ALI JUMA; 4 brs.

Arab Tunisian Bank: 9 rue Hédi Nouira, BP 520, 1001 Tunis; tel. (71) 351-155; fax (71) 342-852; e-mail atbbank@atb.com.tn; internet www.atb.com.tn; f. 1982; 64.2% owned by Arab Bank PLC (Jordan); cap. 100m., res 260m., dep. 2,926m. (Dec. 2010); Pres. Dr SAMAR EL-MOLLA; Dir-Gen. MUHAMMAD FERID BEN TANFOUS; 107 brs.

Attijari Bank: 14 ave de la Liberté, Tunis; tel. (71) 141-400; fax (71) 782-663; e-mail courrier@attijaribank.com.tn; internet www.attijaribank.com.tn; f. 1968 as Banque du Sud; present name adopted 2006; 37.11% owned by Attijariwafa Bank (Morocco), 17.46% by Banco Santander (Spain); cap. 168m., res 102m., dep. 3,465m. (Dec. 2010); Pres. MONCEF CHAFFAR; CEO MUHAMMAD EL-KETTANI; Dir-Gen. HICHAM SEFFA; 93 brs.

Banque de l'Habitat: 21 ave Kheireddine Pacha, BP 242, 1002 Tunis; tel. (71) 001-800; fax (71) 951-048; e-mail banquehabitat@bh

.fin.tn; internet www.bh.com.tn; f. 1984; 32.62% govt-owned; cap. 89m., res 312m., dep. 3,436m. (Dec. 2010); CEO BRAHIM HAJJI; 79 brs.

Banque Internationale Arabe de Tunisie (BIAT): 70–72 ave Habib Bourguiba, BP 520, 1080 Tunis; tel. (71) 340-733; fax (71) 346-454; e-mail correspondent.banking@biat.com.tn; internet www.biat .com.tn; f. 1976; cap. 170m., res 287m., dep. 5,509m. (Dec. 2010); Chair. ISMAIL MABROUK; Gen. Man. SLAHEDDINE LADJIMI; 138 brs.

Banque Nationale Agricole (BNA): rue Hédi Nouira, 1001 Tunis; tel. (71) 831-000; fax (71) 832-807; e-mail bna@bna.com.tn; internet www.bna.com.tn; f. 1989 by merger of Banque Nationale du Développement Agricole and Banque Nationale de Tunisie; cap. 160m., res 175m., dep. 4,887m. (Dec. 2010); Chair. and CEO JAAFAR KHATTECHE; 157 brs.

Banque de Tunisie SA: 2 rue de Turquie, BP 289, 1001 Tunis; tel. (71) 125-510; fax (71) 125-410; e-mail finance@bt.com.tn; internet www.bt.com.tn; f. 1884; cap. 112m., res –3m., dep. 2,219m. (Dec. 2010); CEO HABIB BEN SAAD; 103 agencies.

Société Tunisienne de Banque (STB): rue Hédi Nouira, BP 638, 1001 Tunis; tel. (71) 340-477; fax (71) 348-400; e-mail stb@stb.com.tn; internet www.stb.com.tn; f. 1957; 24.81% govt-owned; merged with Banque Nationale de Développement Touristique and Banque de Développement Economique de Tunisie in 2000; cap. 124m., res 378m., dep. 5,200m. (Dec. 2010); Chair. and Gen. Man. SAMIRA GHRIBI; 119 brs.

Union Bancaire pour le Commerce et l'Industrie (UBCI): 139 ave de la Liberté, Belvédère, 1002 Tunis; tel. (71) 842-000; fax (71) 849-338; e-mail saber.mensi@bnpparibas.com; internet www .ubcinet.net; f. 1961; affiliated with, and 50% owned by, BNP Paribas (France); cap. 50m., res 114m., dep. 1,525m. (Dec. 2009); Pres. and Gen. Man. PATRICK POUPON; 110 brs.

Union Internationale de Banques SA: 65 ave Habib Bourguiba, BP 109, 1000 Tunis; tel. (71) 347-000; fax (71) 353-090; e-mail lilia .meddeb@uib.fin.tn; internet www.uib.com.tn; f. 1963 as a merging of Tunisian interests by the Société Franco-Tunisienne de Banque et de Crédit with Crédit Lyonnais (France) and other foreign banks, incl. Banca Commerciale Italiana; 52.3% owned by Société Générale (France); cap. 196m., res –123m., dep. 2,009m. (Dec. 2009); Chair. DAVID BERNARD; Dir-Gen. KAMEL NEJI; 94 brs.

Merchant Banks

Banque d'Affaires de Tunisie (BAT): 10 bis rue Mahmoud El Matri, Mutuelleville, 1002 Tunis; tel. (71) 143-800; fax (71) 891-678; e-mail bat@bat.com.tn; internet www.bat-tunisie.com; f. 1997; cap. 4.5m.; Pres. and CEO MUHAMMAD HABIB KARAOULI.

International Maghreb Merchant Bank (IM Bank): Immeuble Maghrebia, Bloc B, 3ème étage, Les Berges du Lac, 2045 Tunis; tel. (71) 860-816; fax (71) 860-057; e-mail imbank@imbank.com.tn; internet www.imbank.com.tn; f. 1995; Pres. OLIVIER PASTRÉ; Exec. Dirs NASREDINE DEKLI, AHMED BESBES.

Development Banks

Banque de Tunisie et des Emirats (BTE): 5 bis blvd Muhammad Badra, 1002 Tunis; tel. (71) 112-000; fax (71) 286-409; e-mail dg@bte .com.tn; internet www.bte.com.tn; f. 1982 as Banque de Tunisie et des Emirats d'Investissement; name changed as above in 2005; owned by the Govt of Tunisia and Abu Dhabi Investment Authority; cap. 90m., res 41m., dep. 258m. (Dec. 2010); Chair. SALAM RACHID AL-MOHANNADI; Gen. Man. GOLSOM JAZIRI; 12 brs.

Banque Tunisienne de Solidarité (BTS): 56 ave Muhammad V, 1002 Tunis; tel. (71) 844-040; fax (71) 845-537; e-mail bts@email.ati .tn; internet www.bts.com.tn; f. 1997; provides short- and medium-term finance for small-scale projects; cap. 40m.; Man. Dir LAMINE HAFSAOUI; 25 brs.

Banque Tuniso-Libyenne: 25 ave Kheireddine Pacha, BP 150, Montplaisir, 1007 Tunis; tel. (71) 901-350; fax (71) 902-818; e-mail btl@gnet.tn; internet www.btl.com.tn; f. 1983 as Banque Arabe Tuniso-Libyenne de Développement et de Commerce; present name adopted 2005; promotes trade and devt projects between Tunisia and Libya, and provides funds for investment in poorer areas; cap. 70.0m., res 2.2m., dep. 309.1m. (Dec. 2008); Chair. and Gen. Man. BADREDDINE BARKIA.

Société Tuniso-Séoudienne d'Investissement et de Développement (STUSID): 32 rue Hédi Karray, BP 20, 1082 Tunis; tel. (71) 718-233; fax (71) 719-233; e-mail commercial@stusid.com.tn; internet www.stusid.com.tn; f. 1981; provides long-term finance for devt projects; cap. 100.0m., res 84.4m., dep. 10.5m. (Dec. 2002); Chair. Dr ABD AL-AZIZ A. AL-NASRALLAH; Pres. and Dir-Gen. ABD AL-WAHEB NACHI.

'Offshore' Banks

Albaraka Bank Tunisia: 88 ave Hédi Chaker, 1002 Tunis; tel. (71) 790-000; fax (71) 780-235; e-mail bestbank@planet.tn; f. 1983; as Beit Ettamouil Saoudi Tounsi; name changed to above in 2009; Islamic bank; Chair. ABDELILAH SOUBAHI; Vice-Chair. and Man. Dir AISSA HIDOUSSI.

Alubaf International Bank: 8007 rue Montplaisir, BP 51, Belvédère, 1002 Tunis; tel. (71) 783-500; fax (71) 793-905; e-mail alub@ alubaf.com.tn; internet www.alubaf.com.tn; f. 1985; 100% owned by Libyan Arab Foreign Bank; cap. US $25m., res $5m., dep. $333m. (Dec. 2010); Chair. Dr AHMAD MNEISSI ABD EL-HAMID; Gen. Man. ALTAHER M. AL-SHAMES.

North Africa International Bank (NAIB): ave Kheireddine Pacha, BP 485, 1002 Tunis; tel. (71) 950-800; fax (71) 950-840; e-mail naib@naibank.com; internet www.naibbank.com; f. 1984; cap. US $30m., res $17m., dep. $365m. (Dec. 2010); Chair. and Gen. Man. GIUMA M. WAHEBA; 1 br.

Tunis International Bank: 18 ave des Etats-Unis d'Amérique, BP 81, 1002 Tunis; tel. (71) 782-411; fax (71) 782-479; e-mail tib1.tib@ planet.tn; internet www.tib.com.tn; f. 1982; 86.6% owned by United Gulf Bank (Bahrain); cap. US $50m., res $22m., dep. $433m. (Dec. 2010); Chair. MASOUD J. HAYAT; Dep. Chair. and Man. Dir MUHAMMAD FEKIH; 3 brs.

STOCK EXCHANGE

Bourse des Valeurs Mobilières de Tunis (Bourse de Tunis): 34 ave de la Bourse, Les Berges du Lac II, 1053 Tunis; tel. (71) 197-910; fax (71) 197-903; e-mail info@bvmt.com.tn; internet www.bvmt.com .tn; f. 1969; Chair. MUHAMMAD FADHEL ABD EL-KEFI; Dir-Gen. MUHAMMAD BICHIOU.

INSURANCE

BEST Reinsurance (BEST Re): Rue du Lac de Côme, Les Berges du lac, BP 484, 1080 Tunis; tel. (71) 860-355; fax (71) 861-011; e-mail general@best-re.com; internet www.best-re.com; f. 1985; operates according to Islamic principles; cap. US $100m.; Chair. Dr SALEH J. MALAIKAH.

Caisse Tunisienne d'Assurances Mutuelles Agricoles—Mutuelle Générale d'Assurances (CTAMA—MGA): 6 ave Habib Thameur, 1069 Tunis; tel. (71) 340-933; fax (71) 332-276; e-mail ctama@planet.tn; internet www.ctamamga.com; f. 1912; Pres. NEJI HANNACHI; Dir-Gen. MANSOUR NASRI.

Cie d'Assurances Tous Risques et de Réassurance (ASTREE): 45 ave Kheireddine Pacha, BP 780, 1002 Tunis; tel. (71) 792-211; fax (71) 794-723; e-mail courrier@astree.com.tn; internet www.astree .com.tn; f. 1949; cap. 4m.; Pres. and Dir-Gen. MUHAMMAD HABIB BEN SAAD.

Cie Tunisienne pour l'Assurance du Commerce Extérieur (COTUNACE): ave Muhammad V, Montplaisir I, rue 8006, 1002 Tunis; tel. (71) 783-000; fax (71) 782-539; e-mail cotunace.ddc@ planet.tn; internet www.cotunace.com.tn; f. 1984; cap. 5m.; 65 mem. cos; Pres. and Dir-Gen. MONCEF ZOUARI.

Société Tunisienne d'Assurance et de Réassurance (STAR): ave de Paris, 1000 Tunis; tel. (71) 340-866; fax (71) 340-835; e-mail star@star.com.tn; internet www.star.com.tn; f. 1958; Pres. and Dir-Gen. LASSAAD ZARROUK.

Tunis Re (Société Tunisienne de Réassurance): 12 ave du Japon, Montplaisir 1, BP 29, 1073 Tunis; tel. (71) 904-911; fax (71) 904-930; e-mail tunisre@tunisre.com.tn; internet www.tunisre.com.tn; f. 1981; various kinds of reinsurance; cap. 45m. (2011); Chair. and Gen. Man. LAMIA BEN MAHMOUD.

Trade and Industry

GOVERNMENT AGENCIES

Centre de Promotion des Exportations (CEPEX): Centre Urbain, BP 225, 1080 Tunis; tel. (71) 234-200; fax (71) 237-325; e-mail info@cepex.nat.tn; internet www.cepex.nat.tn; f. 1973; state export promotion org.; Pres. and Dir-Gen. ABDELLATIF HAMMEM.

Foreign Investment Promotion Agency (FIPA): rue Slaheddine al-Ammami, Centre Urbain Nord, 1004 Tunis; tel. (71) 752-540; fax (71) 231-400; e-mail fipa.tunisia@fipa.tn; internet www .investintunisia.tn; f. 1995; Dir-Gen. NOUREDDINE ZEKRI.

Office du Commerce de la Tunisie (OCT): 65 rue de Syrie, 1002 Tunis; tel. (71) 785-619; fax (71) 784-491; e-mail OCT@Email.ati.tn; internet www.infocommerce.gov.tn; f. 1962; Pres. and Dir-Gen. SLAHEDDINE MAKHLOUF; Sec.-Gen. MUSTAPHA DEBBABI.

CHAMBERS OF COMMERCE AND INDUSTRY

Chambre de Commerce et d'Industrie du Centre: rue Chadli Khaznadar, 4000 Sousse; tel. (73) 225-044; fax (73) 224-227; e-mail ccis.sousse@planet.tn; internet www.ccicentre.org.tn; f. 1895; 30 mems; Pres. NÉJIB MELLOULI; Dir FATEN BASLY.

Chambre de Commerce et d'Industrie du Nord-Est: Tom Bereaux Bizerte Center, angle rues 1er mai, Med Ali, 7000 Bizerte; tel. (72) 431-044; fax (72) 431-922; e-mail ccine.biz@gnet.tn; internet www.ccibizerte.org.tn; f. 1902; 30 mems; Pres. FAOUZI BEN AISSA; Dir MOUFIDA CHAKROUN.

Chambre de Commerce et d'Industrie de Sfax: rue du Lieutenant Hammadi Tej, BP 794, 3000 Sfax; tel. (74) 296-120; fax (74) 296-121; e-mail ccis@ccis.org.tn; internet www.ccis.org.tn; f. 1895; 35,000 mems; Pres. ABDESSALEM BEN AYED; Dir SOFIENE SALLEMI.

Chambre de Commerce et d'Industrie de Tunis: 31 ave de Paris, 1000 Tunis; tel. (71) 247-322; fax (71) 354-744; e-mail ccitunis@planet.tn; internet www.ccitunis.org.tn; f. 1885; 30 mems; Pres. MOUNIR MOUAKHAR.

INDUSTRIAL AND TRADE ASSOCIATIONS

Agence des Ports et des Installations de Pêches (APIP): Port de Pêche de La Goulette, BP 64, 2060 Tunis; tel. (71) 736-012; fax (71) 735-396; e-mail apip@apip.com.tn; internet www.apip.nat.tn; fishing ports authority; Pres. and Dir-Gen. SGHAÏER HOUCINE.

Agence de Promotion de l'Industrie (API): 63 rue de Syrie, 1002 Tunis; tel. (71) 792-144; fax (71) 782-482; e-mail api@api.com.tn; internet www.tunisieindustrie.nat.tn; f. 1987 by merger; co-ordinates industrial policy, undertakes feasibility studies, organizes industrial training and establishes industrial zones; overseas offices in Belgium, France, Germany, Italy, Sweden, the United Kingdom and the USA; 24 regional offices; Gen. Man. MUHAMMAD BEN ABDALLAH.

Centre Technique du Textile (CETTEX): ave des Industries, Zone Industrielle, Bir el-Kassaâ, BP 279, Ben Arous, 2013 Tunis; tel. (71) 381-133; fax (71) 382-558; e-mail cettex@cettex.com.tn; internet www.cettex.com.tn; f. 1992; responsible for the textile industry; Dir-Gen. SAMIR HAOUET.

Cie des Phosphates de Gafsa (CPG): Cité Bayech, 2100 Gafsa; tel. (76) 226-022; fax (76) 224-132; e-mail cpg.gafsa@cpg.com.tn; internet www.gct.com.tn; f. 1897; production and marketing of phosphates; Pres. and Dir-Gen. MUHAMMAD FADHEL ZRELLI.

Entreprise Tunisienne d'Activités Pétrolières (ETAP): 27 ave Kheireddine Pacha, BP 83, 1073 Tunis; tel. (71) 902-688; fax (71) 906-141; e-mail dexprom@etap.com.tn; internet www.etap.com.tn; f. 1974; state-owned; responsible for exploration, production, trade and investment in hydrocarbons; Pres. and CEO KHALED BECHEIKH.

Office des Céréales: Ministry of Agriculture and Environment, 30 rue Alain Savary, 1002 Tunis; tel. (71) 780-550; fax (71) 794-152; e-mail office.cereales@email.ati.tn; f. 1962; responsible for the cereals industry; Chair. and Dir-Gen. YOUSUF NEJI.

Office National des Mines: 24 rue 8601, BP 215, 1080 Tunis; tel. (71) 788-242; fax (71) 794-016; e-mail contact@onm.nat.tn; internet www.onm.nat.tn; f. 1963; mining of iron ores; research and study of mineral wealth; Dir-Gen. ABDELBAKI MANSOURI.

Office des Terres Domaniales (OTD): 60 rue Alain Savary, 1002 Tunis; tel. (71) 771-086; fax (71) 795-026; e-mail boc@otd.nat.tn; internet www.otd.nat.tn; f. 1961; responsible for agricultural production and the management of state-owned lands; Pres. and Dir-Gen. ABDELHAKIM KHALDI.

UTILITIES

Electricity and Gas

Société Tunisienne de l'Electricité et du Gaz (STEG): 38 rue Kemal Atatürk, BP 190, 1080 Tunis; tel. (71) 341-311; fax (71) 349-981; e-mail dpsc@steg.com.tn; internet www.steg.com.tn; f. 1962; responsible for generation and distribution of electricity and for production of natural gas; Pres. and Dir-Gen. TAHAR LAÂRIBI; 35 brs.

Water

Société Nationale d'Exploitation et de Distribution des Eaux (SONEDE): ave Slimane Ben Slimane, el-Manar 2, 2092 Tunis; tel. (71) 887-000; fax (71) 871-000; e-mail sonede@sonede.com.tn; internet www.sonede.com.tn; f. 1968; production and supply of drinking water; Pres. and Dir-Gen. HÉDI BELHAJ.

MAJOR COMPANIES

Compagnie Générale des Salines de Tunisie (COTUSAL): 19 rue de Turquie, 1001 Tunis; tel. (71) 347-666; fax (71) 336-163; e-mail direction@cotusal.com.tn; internet www.cotusal.tn; f. 1949; production of edible and industrial sea salt; Man. Dir NORBERT DE GUILLEBON; 450 employees.

Entreprise Ali Mheni (EAM): 12 bis rue de Russie, BP 609, 1000 Tunis; tel. (71) 332-433; fax (71) 323-001; f. 1969; construction and civil engineering, public works, building; Pres. and Dir-Gen. RAOUF MHENI; 1,000 employees.

Les Grands Ateliers du Nord SA: GP 1 Km 12, el-Zahra 2034, Tunis; tel. (71) 216-803; fax (71) 216-675; e-mail info.gam@poulina.com.tn; internet www.montblanc-electromenager.com; f. 1975; manufacture of agricultural equipment, electrical home appliances and office furniture; Pres. ABDELAZIZ GUIDARA; 1,000 employees.

Groupe Chimique Tunisien: 7 rue du Royaume d'Arabie Saoudite, 1002 Tunis; tel. (71) 784-488; fax (71) 783-495; e-mail gct@gct.com.tn; internet www.gct.com.tn; f. 1947; production of phosphoric acid and fertilizers; Pres. and Dir-Gen. MUHAMMAD NÉJIB MRABET; 4,300 employees.

Industries Maghrébines de l'Aluminium (IMAL): 14 rue 8612, Zone Industrielle, La Charguia 1, 2035 Tunis; tel. (71) 206-750; fax (71) 206-752; f. 1964; manufacture and distribution of aluminium products; cap. p.u. TD 450,000; Chair. MONCEF EL-HORRY; 50 employees.

Industries Mécaniques Maghrébines (IMM): route de Tunis, Zone Industrielle, 3100 Kairouan; tel. (77) 271-800; fax (77) 272-685; e-mail latrous.tahas@gnet.tn; f. 1982; production suspended 1988, recommenced 1991; 4.8% owned by Gen. Motors (USA), 2.4% by Isuzu Motors (Japan) and 92.8% by local investors; production of light commercial vehicles; Man. Dir TAHAR LATROUS; 348 employees.

Skanes Meubles SA: route de Sousse, BP 27, 5000 Monastir; tel. (73) 501-337; fax (73) 501-339; f. 1962; manufacture of furniture and hotel equipment, toys; Pres. RIDHA BCHIR.

Société Industrielle de Pêches et de Conserves Alimentaires SA: 66 ave Habib Bourguiba, 2014 Megrine-Riadh; tel. (71) 308-010; fax (71) 308-060; fish, fruit and vegetable processing and canning; Dir-Gen. ALI MABROUK; 150 employees.

Société Tunisienne Automobile, Financière, Immobilière et Maritime (STAFIM): rue du Lac Léman, Les Berges du Lac, 1053 Tunis; tel. (71) 860-444; fax (71) 862-622; e-mail stafim@peugeot.com.tn; f. 1930; distribution and sales of cars, spare parts, engines and mechanical machinery; Dir-Gen. PASCAL MOREL; 267 employees.

Tunisienne de Conserves Alimentaires (TUCAL): route de Mateur, Km 8.5, 2010 La Manouba; tel. (71) 601-833; fax (71) 601-251; e-mail contact@tucal.tn; internet www.tucal.com.tn; manufacture and distribution of canned food products; Pres. and Gen. Man. AMOR BEN SÉDRINE.

TRADE UNION

Union Générale des Etudiants de Tunisie (UGET): 11 rue d'Espagne, Tunis; f. 1953; 600 mems; Pres. MEKKI FITOURI.

Union Générale Tunisienne du Travail (UGTT): 29 pl. Muhammad Ali, 1000 Tunis; tel. (71) 332-400; fax (71) 354-114; e-mail ugtt.tunis@email.ati.tn; internet www.ugtt.org.tn; f. 1946 by Farhat Hached; affiliated to ITUC; 360,000 mems in 24 affiliated unions; 18-mem. exec. bureau; Gen. Sec. ABDESSALEM JERAD.

Union Nationale de la Femme Tunisienne (UNFT): 56 blvd Bab Benat, 1006 Tunis; tel. (71) 560-181; fax (71) 567-131; e-mail unft@email.ati.tn; internet www.unft.org.tn; f. 1956; promotes the rights of women; 150,000 mems; 28 regional delegations, 199 professional training centres, 13 professional alliances; Pres. KHIRA LAGHA; Vice-Pres. FAÏZA AZOUZ; 23 brs abroad.

Union Tunisienne de l'Agriculture et de la Pêche (UTAP): rue 8451, ave Alain Savary, 1003 Tunis; tel. (71) 806-800; fax (71) 809-181; e-mail utap.tunis@email.ati.tn; internet www.utap.org.tn; f. 1955 as Union Nationale des Agriculteurs Tunisiens (which supplanted the Union Générale des Agriculteurs Tunisiens, f. 1950); name changed as above in 1995; Pres. AHMED HAIDAR JARALLAH.

Union Tunisienne de l'Industrie, du Commerce et de l'Artisanat (UTICA): rue Ferjani Bel Haj Ammar, Cité el-Khadhra, 1003 Tunis; tel. (71) 142-000; fax (71) 142-100; internet www.utica.org.tn; f. 1946; mems: 15 national federations and 170 syndical chambers at national levels; Pres. WIDAD BOUCHAMAOUI.

Transport

RAILWAYS

In 2010 the total length of Tunisian railways was 1,119 route-km; 38.6m. passengers travelled by rail in Tunisia in 2009.

Société Nationale des Chemins de Fer Tunisiens (SNCFT): Gare de Tunis ville, pl. Barcelone, 1001 Tunis; tel. (71) 334-444; fax (71) 254-320; e-mail sncft@sncft.com.tn; internet www.sncft.com.tn; f. 1956; state org. controlling all Tunisian railways; Pres. and Dir-Gen. MUHAMMAD NAJIB FITOURI.

Société des Transports de Tunis (TRANSTU): 1 ave Habib Bourgiba, BP 660, 1025 Tunis; tel. (71) 259-422; fax (71) 342-727; e-mail contact@snt.com.tn; internet www.snt.com.tn; f. 2003 following merger of the Société Nationale des Transports and the Société du Métro Léger de Tunis; operates 5 light train routes with 136 trains, and 206 local bus routes with 1,050 buses; also operates in the suburbs of Tunis-Goulette-Marsa, with 18 trains; plans approved in 2006 for expansion of the light rail system, with 5 new express lines; Pres. and Dir-Gen. CHEDLY HAJRI.

ROADS

In 2010 there were 356 km of motorways, 4,746 km of highways, main or national roads, 6,496 km of secondary or regional roads and 7,820 km of other roads. The total length of the road network was 19,418 km.

Société Nationale de Transport Interurbain (SNTRI): ave Muhammad V, BP 40, Belvédère, 1002 Tunis; tel. (71) 784-433; fax (71) 791-621; e-mail marketing@sntri.com.tn; internet www.sntri.com.tn; f. 1981; Dir-Gen. SASSI YAHIA.

Société des Transports de Tunis: see Railways.

There are 12 **Sociétés Régionales des Transports**, responsible for road transport, operating in different regions in Tunisia.

SHIPPING

Tunisia has seven major ports: Tunis-La Goulette, Radès, Bizerta, Sousse, Sfax, Gabès and Zarzis. There is a special petroleum port at La Skhirra. In April 2009 the Government invited bids for the construction of a new deep-water port at Enfidha.

At 31 December 2012 Tunisia's flag registered fleet totalled 62 vessels, with an aggregate displacement of 358,504 grt, of which one was a bulk carrier, five were fish carriers and two were general cargo ships.

Port Authority

Office de la Marine Marchande et des Ports (OMMP): Bâtiment Administratif, Port de la Goulette, 2060 La Goulette; tel. (71) 735-300; fax (71) 735-812; e-mail ommp@ommp.nat.tn; internet www.ommp.nat.tn; maritime port administration; Pres. and Dir-Gen. OMAR MAJDOUB.

Principal Shipping Companies

Cie Générale Maritime: Bloc D7, Apt 74, 1003 Tunis; tel. and fax (71) 860-430; e-mail logwan.girgen@gnet.tn; Chair. ELIAS MAHERZI.

Cie Tunisienne de Navigation SA (CTN): 5 ave Dag Hammarskjöld, BP 40, 1001 Tunis; tel. (71) 341-777; fax (71) 345-736; e-mail cotunav@ctn.com.tn; internet www.ctn.com.tn; f. 1959; state-owned; brs at Bizerta, La Goulette, Sfax and Sousse; Pres. and Dir-Gen. ALI KHALIFA.

Gabès Marine Tankers (GMT): Immeuble SETCAR, route de Sousse, Km 13, 2034 Tunis; tel. (71) 454-644; fax (71) 450-350; e-mail gabesmarine@gmt.com.tn; internet www.setcar-group.com; f. 1994; part of the Setcar Group; Chair. FÉRID ABBÈS.

Gas Marine: Immeuble SETCAR, route de Sousse, Km 13, 2034 el-Zahra; tel. (71) 454-644; fax (71) 454-650; Chair. HAMMADI ABBÈS.

Hannibal Marine Tankers: 2ème Etage, Residence Lakeo, rue du Lac Michigan, Les Berges du Lac, 1053 Tunis; tel. (71) 960-037; fax (71) 960-243; e-mail hannibal.tankers@gnet.tn; Gen. Man. AMEUR MAHJOUB.

Société Nouvelle de Transport Kerkennah (SONOTRAK): 179 ave Muhammad Hédi Khefacha, Gare Maritime de Kerkenna, 3000 Sfax; tel. (74) 498-216; fax (74) 497-496; e-mail jabeur.m@planet.tn; internet kerkennah.free.fr/sonotrak/indexsonotrak.htm; Chair. TAOUFI JRAD.

Tunisian Shipping Agency: Zone Industrielle, Radès 2040, BP 166, Tunis; tel. (71) 448-379; fax (71) 448-410; e-mail tsa.rades@planet.tn; Chair. MUHAMMAD BEN SEDRINE.

CIVIL AVIATION

There are international airports at Tunis-Carthage, Sfax, Djerba, Monastir, Tabarka, Gafsa and Tozeur. Zine al-Abidine Ben Ali airport, located at Enfidha, 100 km south of Tunis, began operations in December 2009. The airport, with an initial annual capacity of 7m. passengers, was officially inaugurated by Zine al-Abidine Ben Ali in early 2010. However, following Ben Ali's ouster in January 2011, the airport was renamed Enfidha-Hammamet International Airport.

Office de l'Aviation Civile et des Aéroports: BP 137 and 147, Aéroport International de Tunis-Carthage, 1080 Tunis; tel. (71) 755-000; fax (71) 755-133; e-mail relations.exterieures@oaca.nat.tn; internet www.oaca.nat.tn; f. 1970; civil aviation and airport authority; Pres. and Gen. Dir SALAH GHARSALLAH.

Nouvelair Tunisie: Zone Touristique Dkhila, 5065 Monastir; tel. (73) 520-600; fax (73) 520-650; e-mail info@nouvelair.com.tn; internet www.nouvelair.com; f. 1989 as Air Liberté Tunisie; name changed as above in 1996; Tunisian charter co; flights from Tunis, Djerba and Monastir airports to Scandinavia and other European countries; Chair. AZIZ MILAD.

Sevenair: 10 rue de l'Artisanat, La Charguia 11, Tunis; tel. (71) 942-323; fax (71) 942-272; e-mail info@sevenair.com.tn; internet www.sevenair.com.tn; f. 1992 as Tuninter; Tunisian charter co; Gen. Man. MONCEF ZOUARI.

TunisAir (Société Tunisienne de l'Air): ave Muhammad Bouazizi, 2035 Tunis; tel. (71) 700-100; fax (71) 700-897; e-mail Resaonline@tunisair.com.tn; internet www.tunisair.com; f. 1948; 45.2% govt-owned; 20% of assets privatized in 1995; flights to Africa, Europe and the Middle East; Pres. and Dir-Gen. NABIL CHETTAOUI.

Tunisavia (Société de Transports, Services et Travaux Aériens): blvd du leader Yasser Arafat, Tunis-Carthage International Airport, 2035 Tunis; tel. (71) 280-555; fax (71) 281-333; e-mail siege@tunisavia.com.tn; internet www.tunisavia.com.tn; f. 1974; helicopter and charter operator; CEO MUHAMMAD AZIZ MILAD; Gen. Man. MOHSEN NASRA.

Tourism

The main tourist attractions are the magnificent sandy beaches, Moorish architecture and remains of the Roman Empire. Tunisia contains the site of the ancient Phoenician city of Carthage. Tourism, a principal source of foreign exchange, has expanded rapidly, following extensive government investment in hotels, improved roads and other facilities. The number of hotel beds increased from 71,529 in 1980 to 188,600 in 1999. The political instability following the ouster of former President Zine al-Abidine Ben Ali in February 2011 had a significant effect on the tourism industry. According to provisional figures, there were 4.8m. foreign tourist arrivals in 2011, compared with 6.9m. in the previous year. Receipts from tourism were estimated at US $1,805m. in 2011, compared with $2,645m. in 2010.

Office National du Tourisme Tunisien: 1 ave Muhammad V, 1001 Tunis; tel. (71) 341-077; fax (71) 350-997; e-mail ontt@email.ati.tn; internet www.bonjour-tunisie.com; f. 1958; Dir-Gen. KHALED CHEIKH.

Defence

Chief of Staff of the Army: Gen. MUHAMMAD SALAH HAMDI.

Chief of Staff of the Navy: Vice-Adm. MUHAMMAD KHAMMASSI.

Chief of Staff of the Air Force: Gen. BÉCHIR BÉDOUI.

Estimated Defence Budget (2012): TD 1,900m.

Military Service: 1 year (selective).

Total Armed Forces (as assessed at November 2012): 35,800: army 27,000 (22,000 conscripts); navy est. 4,800; air force 4,000.

Paramilitary Forces (as assessed at November 2012): 12,000 National Guard.

Education

Education is compulsory in Tunisia for a period of nine years between the ages of six and 16. Primary education begins at six years of age and normally lasts for six years. Secondary education begins at 12 years of age and lasts for seven years, comprising a first cycle of three years and a second cycle of four years. In 2008/09, according to UNESCO estimates, the total enrolment at primary schools included 98% of children in the relevant age-group. In that year the total enrolment at secondary schools was equivalent to 90% of children in the relevant age-group. In 2011 some TD 3,000.2m. was allocated to education and professional training (equivalent to 14.9% of budgeted government expenditure).

In early 2012 there were 13 universities, including a virtual university, and a General Directorate of Technological Studies. Arabic is the first language of instruction in primary and secondary schools, but French is also used. French is used almost exclusively in higher education. The University of Tunis was opened in 1959/60. In 1988 the university was divided into two separate institutions: one for science, the other for arts. It has 54 faculties and institutes. In 1986 two new universities were opened, at Monastir and Sfax. In 2010/11 the number of full-time students enrolled at higher educational establishments in Tunisia was 336,017.

Bibliography

Alexander, Christopher. *Tunisia: Stability and Reform in the Modern Maghreb*. Abingdon, Routledge, 2010.

Anthony, John. *About Tunisia*. London, 1961.

Azaiez, Tahar Letaief. *Tunisie, changements politiques et emploi (1956–1996)*. Paris, L'Harmattan, 2000.

Basset, André. *Initiation à la Tunisie*. Paris, 1950.

Belkhodja, Tahar. *Les trois décennies de Bourguiba*. Paris, Arcanteres-Publisud, 1998.

Ben Brik, Taoufik. *Une si douce dictature: chroniques tunisiennes 1990–2000*. Paris, La Découverte: Reporters sans frontières, 2000.

Ben Romdhane, Mahmoud. *Tunisie: État, économie et société*. Paris, Éditions Publisud, 2011.

Bessis, Sophie, and Belhassen, Souhayr. *Bourguiba Tome 1: A la conquête d'un destin (1901–1957)*. Paris, Jeune Afrique Livres, 1988.

Bourguiba, Habib. *La Tunisie et la France*. Paris, 1954.

Hadith al-Jamaa. (Collected Broadcasts) Tunis, 1957.

Brunschvig, Robert. *La Tunisie au haut Moyen Age*. Cairo, 1948.

Camau, Michel. *Tunisie au présent. Une modernité au-dessus de tout soupçon?* Paris, Centre National de la Recherche, 1987.

Camau, Michel, and Geisser, Vincent. *Le syndrome autoritaire. Politique en Tunisie de Bourguiba à Ben Ali*. Paris, Presses de Sciences Po, 2003.

Cambon, Henri. *Histoire de la régence de Tunisie*. Paris, 1948.

Duvignaud, Jean. *Tunisie*. Lausanne, Editions Rencontre, 1965.

Duwaji, Ghazi. *Economic Development in Tunisia*. New York, Praeger, 1967.

Erdle, Steffen. *Ben Ali's 'New Tunisia' (1987–2009): A Case Study of Authoritarian Modernization in the Arab World*. Berlin, Klaus Schwarz Verlag, 2010.

Garas, Félix. *Bourguiba et la naissance d'une nation*. Paris, 1956.

Geyer, Georgie A. *Tunisia: The Story of a Country that Works*. London, Stacey International, 2003.

Goussaud-Falgas, Geneviève. *Français de Tunisie: Les dernières années du Protectorat*. Saint-Cyr-sur-Loire, Editions Alan Sutton, 2004.

Guen, Moncef. *La Tunisie indépendante face à son économie*. Paris, 1961.

Guitouni, M., Dupont, L., and Brissette, Y. *La Tunisie de Ben Ali : Les défis de l'émergence*. Paris, Eska, 2005.

Hamdi, Mohamed, E. *The Politicisation of Islam: A Case Study of Tunisia*. Boulder, CO, Westview Press Inc, 2001.

King, Stephen J. *Liberalization Against Democracy: The Local Politics of Economic Reform in Tunisia*. Bloomington, IN, Indiana University Press, 2003.

Knapp, W. *Tunisia*. London, Thames and Hudson, 1972.

Ling, Dwight D. *Tunisia, from Protectorate to Republic*. Indiana University Press, 1967.

Memmi, Albert. *Le Pharaon*. Paris, Julliard, 1988.

Micaud, C. A. *Tunisia, the Politics of Moderation*. New York, 1964.

Moore, C. H. *Tunisia since Independence*. Berkeley, University of California Press, 1965.

Murphy, Emma C. *Economic and Political Change in Tunisia: from Bourguiba to Ben Ali*. London, St Martin's Press, 2000.

Nerfin, M. *Entretiens avec Ahmed Ben Salah*. Paris, F. Maspero, 1974.

Perkins, Kenneth J. *Historical Dictionary of Tunisia* (African Historical Dictionaries, No. 45). Metuchen, NJ, and London, The Scarecrow Press, 1989.

A History of Modern Tunisia. Cambridge, Cambridge University Press, 2004.

Powel, Brieg, and Sadiki, Larbi. *Europe and Tunisia: Democratization via Association*. Abingdon, Routledge, 2010.

Raymond, André. *La Tunisie*. Series *Que sais-je*. No. 318, Paris, 1961.

Rudebeck, Lars. *Party and People: A Study of Political Change in Tunisia*. London, C. Hurst, 1969.

Salem, Norma. *Habib Bourguiba, Islam and the Creation of Tunisia*. London, Croom Helm, 1984.

Sylvester, Anthony. *Tunisia*. London, Bodley Head, 1969.

White, Gregory. *A Comparative Political Economy of Tunisia and Morocco: On the Outside of Europe Looking In*. Albany, NY, State University of New York Press, 2001.

World Bank. *Tunisia's Global Integration and Sustainable Development: Strategic Choices for the 21st Century*. World Bank, 1997.

Ziadeh, Nicola, A. *The Origins of Tunisian Nationalism*. Beirut, 1962.

TURKEY

Physical and Social Geography

W. B. FISHER

Turkey consists essentially of the large peninsula of Asia Minor, which has strongly defined natural limits: sea on three sides (the Black Sea to the north, the Aegean to the west and the Mediterranean to the south) and high mountain ranges on the fourth (eastern) side. The small region of European Turkey, containing the cities of İstanbul (Constantinople) and Edirne (Adrianople), is, by contrast, defined by a purely artificial frontier, the exact position of which has varied considerably since the 19th century, according to the fluctuating fortunes and prestige of Turkey itself. Another small territory, the Hatay, in southern Turkey and centred on İskenderun (Alexandretta), is bordered to the west by the Mediterranean sea and to the east by Syria, from which it was acquired as part of a diplomatic bargain in 1939. The total area of Turkey is estimated at 783,562 sq km (302,535 sq miles), of which 769,604 sq km is land and 13,958 sq km is inland waterways. According to the results of the census conducted in October 2000, the country's population numbered 67,803,927. By December 2012, according to official figures, the population had increased to 75,627,384, giving an average population density per sq km of 98.3 inhabitants (land area only).

PHYSICAL FEATURES

The geological structure of Turkey is extremely complicated, and rocks of almost all ages occur, from the most ancient to most recent. Broadly speaking, Turkey consists of a number of old plateau blocks, against which masses of younger rock series have been squeezed to form fold mountain ranges of varying size. As there were several of these plateau blocks, rather than just one, the fold mountains run in many different directions, with considerable irregularity, and hence no simple pattern can be discerned—instead, one mountain range gives place to another abruptly, and can pass suddenly from highland to plain or plateau.

In general outline, Turkey consists of a ring of mountains enclosing a series of inland plateaux, with the highest mountains to the east, close to Armenia and Iran. Mount Ararat is the highest peak in Turkey, reaching 5,165 m, and there are neighbouring peaks almost as high. In the west the average altitude of the hills is distinctly lower, though the highest peak (Mount Erciyas, or Argaeus) is over 3,900 m. The irregular topography of Turkey has given rise to many lakes, some salt and some fresh, and generally more numerous than elsewhere in the Middle East. The largest, Lake Van, covers nearly 4,000 sq km.

Two other features may be mentioned. Large areas of the east and some parts of the centre of Asia Minor have been covered in sheets of lava, which are often of such recent occurrence that soil has not yet been formed—consequently, wide expanses are sterile and uninhabited. Second, in the north and west, cracking and disturbance of the rocks has taken place on an enormous scale. The long, indented coast of the Aegean Sea, with its numerous oddly shaped islands and estuaries, is due to cracking in two directions, which has split the land into detached blocks of roughly rectangular shape. Often the lower parts have sunk and been drowned by the sea. The Bosphorus and Dardanelles owe their origin to this faulting action, and the whole of the Black Sea coast is due to subsidence along a great series of fissures. Movement and adjustment along these cracks has by no means ceased, so that at the present day earthquakes are frequent in the north and west of Turkey.

Owing to the presence of mountain ranges close to the coast, and the great height of the interior plateaux (varying from 800 m to 2,000 m), Turkey has special climatic conditions, characterized by great extremes of temperature and rainfall, with wide variation from one district to another. In winter, conditions are severe in most areas, except for those lying close to sea level. Temperatures of −30°C to −40°C can occur in the east, and snow lies there for as many as 120 days each year. The west has frost on most nights of December and January, and (again apart from the coastal zone) has an average winter temperature below 1°C. In summer, however, temperatures over most of Turkey exceed 30°C, with 43°C in the south-east. There can hence be enormous seasonal variations of temperature—sometimes over 50°C, among the widest in the world.

Rainfall, too, is remarkably variable. Along the eastern Black Sea coast, towards the Georgian frontier, over 2,500 mm fall annually; elsewhere, amounts are very much smaller. Parts of the central plateau, being shut off by mountains from the influence of sea winds, are arid, with annual totals of under 250 mm, and expanses of salt steppe and desert are frequent. The main towns of Anatolia, including Ankara, the capital, are placed away from the centre and close to the hills, where rainfall tends to be greater and water supplies better.

It is necessary to emphasize the contrast that exists between the Aegean coastlands, which, climatically, are by far the most favoured regions of Turkey, and the rest of the country. Round the Aegean, winters are mild and fairly rainy, and the summers hot, but tempered by a persistent northerly wind, the Meltemi, or Etesian wind, which is of great value in ripening fruit, especially figs and sultana grapes.

LANGUAGE

The Turkish language, which is of central Asiatic origin, is spoken over most, but by no means all, of the country. This was introduced into Turkey in Seljuq times, and was written in Arabic characters, but, as these are not really well adapted to the sound of Turkish, Roman (i.e. European) script has been compulsory since 1928. In addition, there are a number of non-Turkish languages. Kurdish is widely spoken in the south-east, along the Syrian and Iraqi frontiers; and Caucasian dialects, quite different from either Turkish or Kurdish, occur in the north-east. Greek and Armenian were once widespread but, following the deportations which began in the 1920s, both forms of speech are now current only in the city of İstanbul, where considerable numbers of Greeks and Armenians still live.

History

Revised for this edition by GARETH JENKINS.

ANCIENT HISTORY

Turkey's history stretches back to the very beginnings of human civilization. Excavations at Çatal Hüyük, in central Turkey south of Konya, show that agriculture, urban settlement and trade were flourishing more than 6,000 years ago in Turkey. Written history begins much later, with colonies of merchants from Assyria at Kültepe, near present-day Kayseri, just after 2000 BC. Around 1700 BC the Hittites established an empire which lasted until around 1200 BC, and was one of the dominant states of the eastern Mediterranean, having diplomatic and military relations with Egypt. The Hittite Empire collapsed soon after 1200 BC, as a result of a wave of immigrants—the Phrygians, Cimmerians, Lydians and others whose archaeological remains are often impressive but who left virtually no written records. Among these invaders were Greek-speakers who established towns along Turkey's western coast on the Aegean, in the region known as Ionia, and later expanded along the Mediterranean and Black Sea coasts.

In 546 BC Persia conquered the whole of Anatolia. However, this and the subsequent conquest by Alexander the Great in 334 BC and the establishment of the Roman province of Asia in 133 BC did not impede the steady spread of Greek language and culture in the cities.

In AD 330 the Emperor Constantine founded a new capital at Byzantium, until then a trade settlement and relatively minor city, and renamed it Constantinople. The city quickly became one of the world's major urban centres. It was the Roman/Byzantine capital until 1453 and remained the Turkish capital up to the proclamation of the Republic in 1923.

SELJUQS AND OTTOMANS

The disappearance of the Byzantine Empire was the outcome of a process which began at the Battle of Manzikert in August 1071 when Byzantine armies were defeated by the Seljuq Turks and central and eastern Anatolia passed permanently under Turkish and Islamic rule. The following 400 years saw the loss of the remaining Byzantine possessions and the expansion of Ottoman power northwards into the Balkans. Though the Byzantines had been fighting their Muslim Arab neighbours for several hundred years, the Turks were newcomers. Their conquests were made easier by the Fourth Crusade, which conquered Constantinople from the Byzantines in 1204 and effectively fragmented Byzantine territory. The Seljuqs swiftly established a new Islamic empire in Anatolia after 1071, based at Konya, and the Turkish language quickly began to supplant Greek for official purposes, while a Persian court culture and Arabic religious culture replaced Roman and Greek traditions. Turkmen and other nomads moved into Anatolia, changing both its demographics and the pattern of agriculture. Substantial numbers of Greeks and other non-Muslims remained part of Anatolian society until the early 20th century. Within a few centuries of Manzikert, and even before the fall of Constantinople, Anatolia was widely known as 'Turkey' in many European countries.

Seljuq ascendancy was short-lived as a result of the Mongol invasions of the 13th century that broke the Empire's power. Authority passed to local emirates across Anatolia. The emirate closest to the Byzantine heartlands was established at Söğüt by Osman Gazi, founder of the Ottoman dynasty, in north-western Anatolia around 1290. His armies conquered the important city of Bursa in 1324 and the second Ottoman ruler proclaimed himself 'Sultan', although several decades would pass before this title was widely recognized. Ottoman armies first crossed the Dardanelles in 1348, immediately after the Black Death. Adrianople, the capital of Thrace, was taken in 1365 and became a new capital. The invasion of Timur resulted in a major military reverse at the Battle of Ankara in 1402, but the Ottoman conquests were resumed less than a generation later. The conquest of Constantinople completed the transformation of a frontier-warrior emirate into a new world empire. (The city was officially renamed İstanbul in 1935.)

The conquest of Constantinople was followed by further expansion into the Balkans and also into the Middle East. By 1530 the Ottoman territory extended from Hungary to Egypt.

After Süleyman I ('the Magnificent'), the Ottoman Empire began losing ground to the West. The Battle of Lepanto (in Turkish İnebaht) in 1579 meant the end of Ottoman sea domination and the abandonment of hopes of expansion into Italy. A generation ago scholars spoke confidently of an 'Ottoman' decline, but this word is out of vogue with many early 21st century historians. None the less, it is clear first that, with some exceptions (military technology being the main one), the Ottomans did not experience the set of dynamic changes and innovations that were taking place in Europe. Most importantly, the printing press was not allowed to operate until the early 18th century. This used to be attributed to the obscurantism of the *ulama* (or Islamic learned class) and its opposition to *bidat* (innovations). Nevertheless, Turkish military power was still capable of staging major incursions into Central Europe: for instance, the famous but unsuccessful siege of Vienna in 1689.

Ottoman attempts at reform were made in the 1730s, with the recruiting of officers from France, but the Janissary armies, hereditary warrior guilds, were strongly resistant to change. The rise of Russian power was witnessed under Peter the Great (1675–1725) and Catherine I (1684–1727). Military reverses culminated in the loss of the Crimea, and the important commercial routes it controlled, to the Russians at the Treaty of Küçük Kaynarca in 1774. The Empire was now so weak that its survival was in doubt. It was not until the reign of Selim III during 1787–1807 that the Ottoman Government began to respond to the challenge to its survival by promoting not only military reforms but a wide range of other changes, and systematically exploiting international alliances and diplomacy. Napoleon's invasion of Egypt in 1798 was the final wake-up call for the Empire.

The immediate and most serious danger to the Ottomans was from Russia, which fought a total of eight wars with the Empire between 1774 and 1918. The threat of Russian expansion enabled the Turks to obtain diplomatic and practical support from the British and the French, but in the Balkans the Christian nationalities of the Empire began to struggle for independence, beginning with the Serbs in 1804 and the Greek War of Independence (1821–30). At the outset of this period the Ottomans had no army in the modern sense and no civil service—only 2,000 scribes. By the end of the 19th century Turkey had a modern army, which might have been capable of defeating the Balkan Christians if allowed to do so by the European powers, and an imperial civil service of about 100,000 officials. A second major thread in 19th century Ottoman history is the arrival of several million Muslim migrants from Circassia, the Caucasus and the Balkans as a result of Christian conquests in those areas. These migrations tipped the balance in Anatolia in favour of Muslims even before the First World War, and without them much of present-day Turkey might not have remained either Turkish or Muslim. At least one-half of the Turkish population today is descended from these immigrants.

In 1839 the Ottoman Government embarked on a period of education, legal and administrative reform known as the *Tanzimat* (reordering). This process accelerated in the wake of the Crimean War (1853–56) after the United Kingdom and France rejected Russian proposals for a joint partition of the Ottoman Empire and instead fought a war to protect it. However, in the 1870s, after the deaths of the *Tanzimat* reformers, the Empire slid rapidly into financial bankruptcy. Christian uprisings began in Bulgaria and the western Balkans, and harsh reprisals (known as the Bulgarian Atrocities) ended the friendship between the United Kingdom and Turkey for the next half a century and created a permanent image problem for Turkey that has persisted to this day.

Efforts to built a modern, liberal empire under Mithat Pasha foundered in the ensuing war. Mithat Pasha was dismissed and eventually murdered, and a new pro-Islamic and anti-British Sultan, Abdülhamit II, closed Turkey's first ever parliament and ruled as an autocrat until 1908. During this period Turkey was effectively a collective protectorate of the European 'Great Powers' with only limited freedom of action, and its final disappearance was widely supposed to be only a matter of time. None the less, technological and economic modernization continued, and the late 19th century was a period of prosperity for Turkey.

Abdülhamit was replaced by the Committee of Union and Progress (CUP), an underground political party formed of army officers and officials, bent on modernization and 'Turkification'. It took the CUP several years to consolidate its hold on power. During this period attacks first by Italy (1911) and then by an alliance of Greece, Bulgaria and Serbia (1912–13) succeeded in taking all Turkey's Balkan and Aegean territories other than those that the country continues to retain.

By early 1914 the Government was in the hands of a triumvirate of the original revolutionaries of 1908, consisting of Enver Pasha, Ahmed Cemal Pasha and Talat Bey (the only civilian member of the junta). Although civilian public opinion seems to have expected Turkey to stay neutral in the First World War, Enver Pasha was staunchly pro-German and struck at Russian targets in the Black Sea to make war inevitable. His actions were followed by Russian invasion and occupation of eastern Turkey for several years. The Russian incursion raised the question of the loyalty of the Christian Armenian population, some of whom had previously staged armed revolts against Ottoman rule. In what appeared to have been a combination of prejudice and a pre-emptive move to guard against further Armenian rebellions, in 1915, with the exception of the Armenians in İstanbul, which was also home to the foreign diplomatic community, virtually the entire Armenian population of Anatolia was dispatched on forced marches to what is now Syria. The vast majority of those deported were believed either to have been killed or to have died of hunger and disease during the journey.

The acrimonious historical debate that followed now revolves less around whether such things happened than whether or not the deaths constituted a 'genocide' (requiring that Turkey should pay reparations) and what the exact numbers were. In what are purported to be his personal notes, Minister of the Interior Mehmet Talat, who oversaw the deportations, put the number of Armenians who were forcibly displaced at 924,158. Demographers of the Ottoman Empire estimate that in all about 3.3m. Ottomans of all faiths died as a result of the wars between 1911 and 1923, out of a population of about 17m. The largest number of dead, upwards of 2.3m., were, perhaps surprisingly to Western opinion, Muslims, though disease and famine were often responsible. Demographic estimates place Greek deaths at around 350,000 and those of Armenians at around 600,000–700,000. These academic estimates are challenged by Armenians in particular, who claim around 1.5m. deaths; however, Western demographers of the Ottoman Empire compute on the basis of censuses and other evidence that such a number is greater than the total Armenian population of the Ottoman Empire. Whatever the exact truth of the matter, the legacy of 'the Armenian massacres' remains a very strong influence on Western perceptions of the Turks, while Turkish families with their own direct memories of suffering in the First World War are often equally uncompromising. Some European politicians would like to see acknowledgement of guilt for the events of 1915 made a condition for Turkish admission to the European Union (EU), although this is not part of the Union's formal position.

Despite Turkey's defeats by Russia, the Ottoman armies scored some important successes. An invading British army suffered a humiliating defeat at Kut al-Amara, on the Euphrates river, and a bold but mismanaged Allied landing on the Dardanelles Straits intended to force open the routes to Russia via İstanbul led to an equally great military disaster at Gallipoli in 1915 and 500,000 deaths. Two years later, however, the Ottoman Arab lands fell quickly to a British army entering from Egypt, and soon afterwards Bulgaria surrendered, severing Turkish links with Germany. On 30 October 1918 an armistice was signed at Mudros, and French, Italian and British occupation forces moved into Turkey.

Preliminary discussions about the post-war partitioning of the Ottoman lands had been taking place between the British and French since 1915; areas of influence in the Arab world were defined in the 1916 Sykes-Picot Agreement. It was taken for granted that the Arab territories would be permanently removed from Ottoman control. Yet Greece, the Armenians and some of the Western powers also eyed the Empire's Turkish heartlands. A partition treaty signed at Sèvres in August 1920 reduced Turkey to a small rump state, and gave areas of Anatolia to Greece, France, Italy and new Kurdish and Armenian states, while the United Kingdom would effectively have İstanbul and its free zone. The treaty was signed by four representatives of the Sultan but never ratified by Turkey. It was the lowest point in Turkey's fortune as a nation and has remained something of an obsession with Turkish public opinion ever since.

The agreement signed at Sèvres was the logical outcome of numerous discussions of partition over the previous century. The difficulty had always been to implement them. By the time the Treaty of Sèvres was signed, Greek armies had been in possession of İzmir for over a year and were advancing eastwards along the Menderes valley. The Greeks had hoped to use *force majeure* to seize most of western Turkey and make it part of a Greater Greece. However, a nationalist resistance movement had been established in Ankara with its own National Assembly.

THE RISE OF ATATÜRK

The Young Turk Government had collapsed with the armistice of 1918; its leaders fled abroad and the CUP dispersed. Though there continued to be an Ottoman legislative assembly in İstanbul, power had effectively returned to the Sultan, who was now propped up by the forces of the occupying powers.

Meanwhile, the Allied powers were at last completing arrangements for the partition of the Ottoman Empire. After a series of conferences, a treaty was drawn up and signed by the Allied representatives and those of the Sultan's Government at Sèvres on 10 August 1920. The Treaty of Sèvres was very harsh—far more so than that imposed on Germany. The Turks would effectively have been pushed into central Anatolia. The possibility of national extinction that Sèvres implied remains a strong factor in Turkish politics. the Treaty of Sèvres was, however, never implemented. While the Allies were imposing their terms on the Sultan and his Government in İstanbul, a nationalist movement arose in the interior of Anatolia, based on the rejection of the treaty and the principles on which it was founded.

The leader of the movement was a general, Mustafa Kemal, who was born in 1880 in Salonika, then an Ottoman city. A career army officer by education, Kemal was sidelined during the 'Young Turk' revolution, but made his name within the Ottoman military when he served with distinction as commander of a division during the Allied invasion at Gallipoli in 1915.

Yet, he remained unknown to the public at large and was not regarded as a potential threat by the Allies that occupied İstanbul. Kemal also appeared to enjoy the confidence of the Sultan and was given the task of disbanding the Ottoman army in Anatolia. On 19 May 1919—four days after the Greek landing in İzmir—he arrived at Samsun, on the Black Sea coast. After meeting with British officials, he continued his journey into Anatolia, where, instead of disbanding the Ottoman army, he set about organizing a resistance movement against foreign occupation.

Leading figures moved to Ankara, the base of the resistance, from İstanbul to take part in the struggle. On 23 July 1919 Mustafa Kemal and his associates convened the first National congress in Erzurum and drew up a national programme. Delegates from all over the country attended a second congress, held in September. An Executive Committee, presided over by Kemal, was formed, and chose Ankara, then a minor provincial town, as its headquarters. Ankara soon became the effective capital of the Resistance movement and forces. On 28 January 1920 the last Ottoman parliament, which was dominated by the Resistance, approved the National Pact, which decisively rejected the occupation of territories inhabited by a Muslim—i.e. Turkish or Kurdish—majority. At the end of April a new Grand National Assembly of 350 deputies met in Ankara, proclaiming sovereignty in the name of the nation and adopting the National Pact.

There remained the military task of expelling the invaders. The Greco–Turkish war fell into three stages, covering roughly the campaigns of 1920, 1921 and 1922. In the first campaign, the Resistance, hopelessly outmatched in numbers and material, was badly defeated and the Greeks advanced far into Anatolia. Greek gunfire was even heard in Ankara. The second campaign began with Greek successes, but the Turks rallied and defeated the invaders first at İnönü—from which İsmet Pasha, who commanded the Turkish forces there, later took his surname—and then, on 24 August 1921, in a major battle on the Sakarya river, where the Turkish forces were under the personal command of Mustafa Kemal. This victory considerably strengthened the Resistance, which was henceforth generally perceived as the effective Government of Turkey. The French and Italians withdrew from the areas of Anatolia assigned to them under the Treaty of Sèvres and negotiated separate terms with the new Government. The Soviets, now established on Turkey's eastern frontier, had already done so at the beginning of the year.

In August 1922 the third and final phase of the war of independence began. The Turkish army drove the Greeks back to the Aegean and reoccupied İzmir on 9 September. Mustafa Kemal now prepared to cross to Thrace. To do so he had to cross the Straits, still under Allied occupation. The French and Italian contingents withdrew, and the British followed. On 11 October an armistice was signed at Mudanya, whereby the Allied Governments agreed to the restoration of Turkish sovereignty in Eastern Thrace. In November the last Sultan, Vahdettin (Mehmet VI), was deposed and went into exile. A peace conference opened at Lausanne, Switzerland, in November. The Treaty of Lausanne, a landmark in the history of the region, was eventually signed on 24 July 1923. It recognized Turkish sovereignty over virtually all of Turkey's present territories, defining relations between Greece and Turkey, and abolishing privileges for foreigners in the country. The only reservations related to the status of Mosul, in northern Iraq, which was not settled until 1926, and the demilitarization of the Straits, which were not to be fortified without the consent of the powers. This consent, given at the Montreux Conference in 1936, continues to define international rights over the Turkish waterways of the Dardanelles and the Bosphorus.

THE TURKISH REPUBLIC

Once peace was established, Mustafa Kemal (who was to assume the name of Atatürk—'Father of the Turks'—in 1934) saw the solution of Turkey's problems in a process of Westernization and the integration of Turkey, on a basis of equality, into the modern Western world. Between 1922 and 1938, the year of his death, Kemal carried through a series of far-reaching reforms intended to establish a strong nation-state.

The first changes were constitutional. On 29 October 1923 Turkey was declared a Republic, with Kemal as President. After the deposition of Sultan Vahdettin in November 1922, a brief experiment was made with a purely religious sovereignty and Abdülmecit II was proclaimed as Caliph but not Sultan. The experiment was not successful. Abdülmecit II followed his predecessor into exile in 1924. The Kemalist regime was effectively a single party dictatorship, with the Cumhuriyet Halk Partisi (CHP—Republican People's Party) forming the main instrument for the enforcement of government policy. The Constitution of 20 April 1924 made the elected parliament the sole repository of sovereign power. Executive power was to be exercised by the President and a cabinet chosen by him.

The next object of attack was the religious system, already weakened by the removal of the Sultan-Caliph, which Kemal saw as the source of Turkey's backwardness and thus the near-extinction of the country. In 1924 the office of the Sheikh ul-Islam (Şeyhülislam—the head of the Sunni Muslim religious establishment in the Ottoman Empire) was replaced by a state-controlled Directorate of Religious Affairs. The separate Islamic schools (*medreses*) were simultaneously closed down. Symbolically, the most striking reform was the abolition of the fez in 1925. However, this was probably less important in the long run than the abrogation of the old legal system in 1926 and the introduction of new civil, criminal and commercial codes of law adapted from Europe. These meant that Turkey had finally broken completely with *Shari'a* (Islamic) law. The replacement of the Arabic script with a version of the Latin alphabet in 1928 was probably equally important, since it cut off Turks from their Islamic past and also (since it was better adapted to the needs of the Turkish language) helped boost literacy levels, then only around 6%.

Turkey's national policy-making in 1923, as was the case later, had as its principal goal the defence of national sovereignty, but the pursuit of economic development and prosperity came a close second. During the mid-1920s economic policy was generally conceived of along free market lines, though it was assumed that there should be 'national' ownership of business and that foreign nationals were unwelcome. As a result, from 1928 the 'colonies' of foreign business people in İstanbul were encouraged to leave. Many Turkish indigenous businesses set up in the early Republic proved unviable. By 1932 restrictions were in place on the currency that remained in force until the late 1980s. Industry was to be set up by the state along lines loosely copied from the USSR. Factories for staple commodities, including textiles, paper, chemicals, glass, and iron and steel, were established. By the beginning of the Second World War the Turkish economy was still overwhelmingly agricultural and traditional, but at least the foundations of a new order had been laid.

The foreign policy of the Republic was, for a long time, one of strict non-involvement in foreign disputes, and the maintenance of friendly relations with as many powers as possible. By the late 1930s, however, the growing threat of German, and more especially Italian, aggression prompted Turkey to strengthen its economic links with the United Kingdom, culminating in a mutual defence pact in May 1939 between Turkey, France and the United Kingdom.

In 1925 there was a major Kurdish revolt in the south-eastern provinces. It was defeated and its leader, Şeyh Sait, was hanged. Kurdish leaders were exiled, but further revolts followed. One of the most serious was the Dersim Uprising of 1937, which briefly challenged the central Government, before being defeated. Public use of Kurdish was discouraged (though it only became illegal in 1982) and manifestations of Kurdish ethnic identity were prohibited. However, ethnic Kurds were to be found at all levels in the civilian Government and the army.

The death of Mustafa Kemal Atatürk in November 1938 was a great shock to Turkey. He was succeeded as President by İsmet İnönü (then known as İsmet Pasha). İnönü, a less charismatic but more socially orthodox figure than Atatürk, ruled Turkey until May 1950. His initial aim was to hold elections and proceed to multi-party democracy, but the advent of the Second World War made this impossible.

TURKEY DURING THE SECOND WORLD WAR

Despite the May 1939 Pact with the French and the British, the Turkish Government decided to remain neutral at the outbreak of the Second World War. In June 1941, when German expansion in the Balkans had brought the German armies within 100 miles of İstanbul, the Turkish Government further protected itself by signing a friendship and trade agreement with Germany.

One main consideration holding Turkey back from active participation in the war was mistrust of the USSR, and the widespread feeling that Nazi conquest and Soviet 'liberation' were equally to be feared. Hence, it was not until August 1944 that the Turks broke off diplomatic relations with Germany. On 23 February 1945 they declared war on Germany in order to comply with the formalities of entry to the UN Conference.

The war years subjected Turkey to severe economic strains, which made İnönü's Government deeply unpopular. Between

1945 and 1950 Turkish opposition politicians, backed by the USA, began to press for the right to set up their own parties and to contest free elections. When the Charter of the UN was introduced for ratification in the Turkish parliament in 1945, a group of members, led by Celâl Bayar, Adnan Menderes, Fuad Köprülü and Refik Koraltan, used the occasion to press for democratic freedoms in Turkey and were expelled from the ruling party. In November President İnönü announced the end of the single-party system. In January 1946 the opposition leaders registered the new Demokrat Parti (DP—Democrat Party).

TURKEY UNDER THE DP

In the general election of July 1946 the DP opposition won 70 out of 416 parliamentary seats, but there can be little doubt that completely free elections would have given them many more. During the years that followed a series of changes in both law and practice ensured the growth of democratic liberties. Freedom of the press and of association were extended, martial law was ended and on 15 February 1950 a new electoral law was approved, guaranteeing free and fair elections. On 28 May a new general election was held, in which the DP won an overwhelming victory. İnönü resigned voluntarily and Celâl Bayar became President. A new cabinet was formed, with Adnan Menderes as Prime Minister. The new regime adopted an economic policy friendlier to private enterprise, both Turkish and foreign, but its policies were erratic and its control over the economy weakened as time passed. Its ability to satisfy rural voter aspirations was the primary determinant of its political success for the DP. During the first half of the 1950s the Turkish economy grew rapidly, with the result that the DP won a resounding victory in the general election of May 1954.

By the second half of the 1950s the economy was in serious trouble, with lower growth, a spiralling trade deficit and a sharp increase in inflation. Hence, in the 1957 general election the DP's share of the vote fell to less than 50%, although it retained power.

FOREIGN AFFAIRS, 1945–60

In foreign affairs, both the CHP and the DP Governments followed a firm policy of unreserved identification with the West in the Cold War. From May 1947 the USA extended economic and military aid to Turkey on an increasing scale, and in 1950 a first indication of both the seriousness and the effectiveness of Turkish policy was given with the dispatch of Turkish troops to Korea. In August 1949 Turkey became a member of the Council of Europe, and early in 1952 acceded to full membership of the North Atlantic Treaty Organization (NATO).

In January 1957 the USA announced a new programme of economic and military assistance for those countries of the area that were willing to accept it. At a further meeting held in Ankara the Muslim states belonging to the Baghdad Pact expressed their approval of this 'Eisenhower Doctrine'. From the mid-1950s relations with Greece steadily deteriorated, bringing the two countries, both NATO allies, close to outright war on several occasions. A compromise over Cyprus's independence from Britain was reached between Greek and Turkish Cypriots. Cyprus, with Turkey, Greece and the United Kingdom as guarantor powers, eventually agreed on a constitution for an independent, bi-communal Cyprus, and gained independence in August 1960.

Adherence to NATO and the Central Treaty Organization remained the basis of Turkey's foreign policy during the late 1950s. By the beginning of 1960, however, the Menderes Government was beginning to explore the possibilities of an improved bilateral relationship with the USSR. This was the start of a general multilateralization of Turkish foreign policy in the years ahead that would expose conflicts between Turkey's regional interests and its commitment to an alliance with the USA.

THE 1960 COUP

Heavy trade deficits, followed by inflation, continued to generate severe political difficulties for the DP Turkish Government. Hostility between the DP and the opposition CHP grew steadily more marked, and was sharpened towards the end of 1959 by suspicions that the DP was planning to hold elections in the near future, ahead of schedule.

In May 1959 political tension between the two main parties had already broken into violence during a political tour of Anatolia conducted by the opposition leader, İsmet İnönü. The Government banned all political meetings, tightened censorship and increasingly suppressed opposition activities. At the end of April 1960 student unrest led to the imposition of martial law. As martial law administrator, the Turkish army found itself, for the first time in half a century, sucked into politics. In the early hours of 27 May, with civilian politics on the point of collapse, the military seized power. President Bayar, Prime Minister Menderes, most DP deputies and a number of officials and senior officers were arrested. The Government was replaced by a junta of military officers, 'the Committee of National Unity', headed by Gen. Cemal Gürsel.

The coup was immediately successful and initially almost bloodless. The Menderes regime was accused of violating the Constitution and moving towards dictatorship. However, the officers insisted that they were temporary custodians of authority and would hand over to the duly constituted civilian authorities.

THE RETURN TO CIVILIAN GOVERNMENT

The Committee of National Unity, which originally comprised 37 members, was reduced to 23 on 13 November 1960. This purge completed, preparations for a return to political democracy continued. A new Constituent Assembly, to act as a temporary parliament, was convened at the beginning of January 1961. It comprised the 23 members of the Committee of National Unity, acting jointly with a House of Representatives of 271 members, both elected and nominated. In this the CHP predominated. At the same time party politics were again legalized and a number of new parties emerged. Some of them proved short-lived, but one, the Adalet Partisi (AP—Justice Party), founded by Gen. Ragip Gümüşpala, who had been Commander of the Third Army at the time of the coup, attracted the support of many former adherents of the DP, which was now illegal.

A special committee of the Assembly framed a new Constitution, which included significant departures from the 1924 version. It provided for a court to determine the constitutionality of laws and for a bicameral legislature (comprising a National Assembly and a Senate), and it included a reference to 'social justice' as one of the aims of the state. Meanwhile, in September 1961 the former Prime Minister, Adnan Menderes, and two of his former ministers were hanged, following an 11-month trial. In September 1990, following a prolonged campaign by right-wing factions (including the ruling Anavatan Partisi—ANAVATAN—Motherland Party), their bodies were exhumed and reburied in İstanbul with state honours.

On 15 October 1961 the CHP won 173 seats and the AP 158 seats in the general election to the National Assembly, and 36 and 70 seats, respectively, in the Senate. Since support for the DP was still strong and the CHP had failed to achieve an overall working majority, a coalition became necessary. On 10 November İnönü, the leader of the CHP, was asked to form a government and, after much hesitation and strong pressure from the army, the AP agreed to join forces with its rival. A new administration was formed, with İnönü as Prime Minister, Akıf İyidoğan of the AP as Deputy Prime Minister and 10 further ministers from each of the two coalition parties.

DEMIREL GOVERNMENT

For all this, the question of Cyprus continued to give the opposition ammunition with which to harass the İnönü Government. At the Senate elections in June 1964 the AP won 31 out of the 51 seats contested, thus increasing its already large majority in this house. Its success was clouded by the death of the party's leader, Gen. Gümüşpala. In November Süleyman Demirel was elected leader in his place, although he was without a seat in parliament. İnönü survived more than one narrow vote of confidence, but was finally defeated on

13 February 1965 during voting in the National Assembly on the budget.

At the general election of 11 October 1965, the AP under Demirel won an overall majority. In spite of its working majority, the Demirel Government proved only marginally more successful than its predecessors in achieving its objectives. However, elections in June 1966 for one-third of the seats in the Senate showed that the AP was not losing popularity. Meanwhile, in March President Gürsel had been succeeded by Senator Cevdet Sunay, also a former army Chief of Staff.

Bülent Ecevit, Minister of Labour in 1961–65, was elected Secretary-General of the CHP, with the declared intention of turning it into a party of democratic socialism. However, six months later 48 senators and members of the National Assembly resigned from the party on the grounds that it was becoming overly radical.

MILITARY INTERVENTION

Demirel's AP Government was faced by growing political violence from early 1968 onwards. Disorder in the universities, emanating from non-political educational grievances and from clashes between political extremists of the right and the left, took an increasingly violent form. Parliamentary politics also became deeply confused, with divisions on all sides. Elections in October 1969 produced an enlarged majority for the AP, but the party soon split, a number of Demirel's right-wing opponents forming a new DP. A new party, the Milli Nizam Partisi (MNP—National Order Party), with right-wing policies and theocratic tendencies, was formed in January 1970 by Prof. Necmettin Erbakan. It was the first sign of the Islamist revival in Turkey.

Disorder increased, but it was still a considerable surprise when, on 12 March 1971, the Chief of the General Staff and the army, navy and air force commanders delivered a memorandum to the President, demanding the cabinet's resignation. Later that day Demirel resigned. It later emerged that the commanders had intervened ahead of a more radical coup by less senior officers.

MILITARY DOMINATION OF POLITICS

A new army-backed Government was formed by a former Prime Minister, Dr Nihat Erim, with the support of both the AP and the CHP. Bülent Ecevit, the CHP Secretary-General, resigned from office and refused to collaborate. Erim's programme promised sweeping reforms in taxation, land ownership, education, power and industry, but the Government's attention was first directed to the suppression of political violence. The military ultimatum was followed by further bombings, kidnappings and clashes between right- and left-wing students and between students and police. On 28 April 1971 martial law was proclaimed, initially for one month, in 11 provinces, including Ankara and İstanbul. Newspapers were suppressed, strikes were banned and large numbers of left-wing supporters were arrested.

In May 1972 a Council of Ministers drawn from the AP, the National Reliance Party and the CHP, headed by Ferit Melen, was approved. There was a shift to the left within the CHP in May; Inönü resigned after 34 years as Chairman, and was replaced by Bülent Ecevit. Meanwhile, martial law was prolonged at two-month intervals. Military rule ended abruptly after a crisis over the election of a new president. President Sunay's term of office expired in March 1973. Gen. Faruk Gürler, who had been army commander during the 1971 coup, resigned his post as Chief of Staff in order to stand for the presidency, his candidature receiving the strong support of the armed forces. Despite obvious military support for Gen. Gürler, 14 ballots failed to produce a result, and eventually the AP, CHP and Cumhuriyetci Güven Partisi (CGP—Republican Reliance Party) agreed on a compromise candidate, Senator Fahri Korutürk, a former head of the navy, with no party political affiliation. He was elected President on 6 April 1973. The following day Melen resigned, and was succeeded as Prime Minister by Naim Talu, an independent senator, who formed a Government with AP and CGP participation. Gradually, the armed forces withdrew from political affairs and martial law was lifted, coming to an end in September.

FOREIGN POLICY DEVELOPMENTS

Relations between Turkey and Cyprus had been difficult in the 1960s. The 1960 Settlement broke down in December 1962 and Turkish military intervention on the island was avoided only by international pressure, mainly from the USA, after attacks had been made on Turkish enclaves by Greek Cypriots in November 1967. In February 1974 Greece announced that petroleum had been found in Greek territorial waters in the Aegean. This led to a dispute over the extent of national jurisdiction over the continental shelf and territorial waters, with both sides making aggressive moves in Thrace and the Aegean. The already tense situation in the Aegean was followed by a coup in Cyprus in July.

This coup was carried out by the Cypriot National Guard, led by officers from Greece, apparently with the support of the Greek military regime. Declaring its intention of protecting the Turkish community in Cyprus and preventing the union of Cyprus with mainland Greece, Turkey proclaimed its right to intervene as a guarantor state under the Zürich agreement of 1959. On 20 July 1974 Turkish troops landed in Cyprus, and took control of the northern areas of the island. Negotiations were under way in August when Turkey launched a second offensive that gave it about one-third of the total area of Cyprus but at a very high cost in terms of its standing in the world.

The flight of Greek Cypriot refugees from the north early in 1975 effectively left the Turks free to take over the administration and economy, and to establish a de facto partition of the island. The Turkish Cypriots unilaterally declared a 'Turkish Federated State' in northern Cyprus on 13 February, and continued pressing for the establishment of a bi-regional federal state system in Cyprus. Subsequent rounds of negotiations between Greece and Turkey failed to achieve results. The US Congress imposed an embargo on military aid and the supply of arms to Turkey in February, on the grounds that US military equipment had been used in the Turkish invasion of Cyprus in July 1974 and that Turkey had failed to make substantial progress towards resolving the Cyprus crisis. After lengthy negotiations, a new bilateral defence agreement was reached between the two countries in March 1976, but the agreement was not immediately ratified, owing to the strength of the Greek lobby in the US Congress.

In January 1978, at the beginning of his term of office, Ecevit stated that his foreign policy would be aimed at the exploration at the highest level of possible compromises between Greece and Turkey. A summit meeting took place at Montreux, Switzerland, on 9 March, at which the progress made in personal relations between Ecevit and the Greek Prime Minister, Konstantinos Karamanlis, contributed to a general lessening of tension in the Aegean.

Finally, after lengthy negotiations, a five-year defence and economic co-operation agreement between Turkey and the USA was signed on 29 March 1980. In return for economic aid to help Turkey modernize its army and fulfil its NATO obligations, the USA was to obtain access to more than 25 military establishments, allowing expanded surveillance of the USSR. The USA's readiness to come to an agreement increased after the Soviet invasion of Afghanistan in December 1979, which heightened Turkey's strategic importance.

ECEVIT GOVERNMENT

Elections to the National Assembly and for 52 Senate seats were held on 14 October 1973. In the National Assembly, the CHP, with 185 seats, replaced the AP as the largest party but failed to win an overall majority. The CHP was believed to have won many votes from former supporters of the banned Türkiye İşçi Partisi (Workers' Party of Turkey), while the AP lost support to the DP and a new organization, the Milli Selamet Partisi (MSP—National Salvation Party). The latter, led by Erbakan, had been founded in 1972 to replace his banned MNP, sharing its fundamentalist Islamist policies, and became the third largest party in the new National Assembly. Prime Minister Talu resigned, but then remained in office for a further three months while negotiations on the formation of a coalition government continued. On 25 January 1974 a Government was formed by the CHP and the MSP, with Bülent Ecevit as Prime Minister and Erbakan as his deputy. The

Council of Ministers was composed of 18 CHP members and seven from the MSP.

The new Government, an apparently unlikely coalition of the left-of-centre CHP and the reactionary MSP, proclaimed its reforming intentions, but made significant concessions to the demands of its Muslim supporters. In February 1974 Turkey was for the first time represented at a summit meeting of the Organization of the Islamic Conference (OIC, now Organization of Islamic Cooperation).

The differences between the MSP and the CHP had been submerged during the Cyprus crisis, but once more became apparent in September 1974 as the MSP wanted a hard line taken on Cyprus, while Ecevit favoured early elections, which he seemed likely to win. On 16 September Ecevit resigned. He had miscalculated about being able to force early elections. Turkey remained without a government with a parliamentary majority for more than six months. In November Prof. Sadi Irmak attempted unsuccessfully to form a coalition to prepare for new elections in 1975, but remained in office in an interim capacity.

DEMIREL RETURNS TO POWER

In March 1975 Süleyman Demirel returned to power, leading a hardline right-wing coalition, the Nationalist Front, consisting of four parties: Demirel's AP, the MSP, the CGP and the neo-fascist Milliyetçi Hareket Partisi (MHP—Nationalist Action Party) founded by Col Alparslan Türkeş, who became Deputy Prime Minister. The precarious nature of this coalition meant that the Government had to avoid taking radical measures that would upset the co-operation between the four parties. This prevented Demirel's Government from addressing the pressing problems of a deteriorating economy and increasing political violence, for Erbakan refused to countenance the austerity measures demanded by the IMF, while Türkeş stood in the way of a crackdown on political violence, some of which the 'Grey Wolves' of the MHP were thought to have instigated.

In spite of its weakness, the Demirel Government continued in power by suspending all action over controversial issues, such as the economy, Cyprus and Greece and relations with the European Community (EC, now EU) and NATO, pending the general election scheduled for October 1977. Increasing political violence throughout Turkey and especially in the universities, between left- and right-wing groups, persuaded the authorities to bring forward the general election to June. The political inactivity was matched by economic paralysis as it became clear that the economy was overloaded with short-term debt and banks struggled to meet foreign-currency bills of payment.

However, the election of June 1977 failed to produce a decisive majority. While the CHP increased its share of seats in the National Assembly to 213 of 450, the AP also increased its representation from 149 to 189 seats. Ecevit, the leader of the CHP, formed a Council of Ministers, but failed to agree a coalition with the smaller parties, and a week later was defeated in a vote of confidence in the legislature. Demirel, the leader of the AP, was subsequently invited to form a new administration and on 1 August members of the MSP and the MHP were awarded key portfolios in a coalition Government. There was a flare-up of violence on campuses. By mid-December one-third of the universities were shut and 250 people had died in political violence.

After losing a no confidence vote in the legislature, the Demirel Government resigned on 31 December 1977. On 2 January 1978 Ecevit returned to power with a new coalition.

ECEVIT RETURNS TO POWER

After the chaos of Demirel's administration, the appointment of Ecevit as Prime Minister was widely welcomed; however, his popular support was not reflected in the National Assembly. His majority was dependent upon the support of a small group of defectors from the AP, 10 of whom became ministers, while the number of deputies who had changed allegiance had resulted in a 'pool' of about 20 independents. Radical reforms were urged on Ecevit, but the insecure parliamentary majority, the country's economic weakness and the unwanted reputation of the CHP in the conservative rural areas as a radical party made him cautious. The Government adopted an economic stabilization programme, signed a stand-by arrangement with the IMF and began work on restructuring the severe short-term debt burden. However, it was unable to secure the huge amounts of international financial assistance necessary to make the stabilization programme work and few of the economic targets were reached. Ecevit was unwilling to take further austerity measures demanded by the IMF as a condition for further aid. Moreover, political violence continued to escalate. Although calm returned to the universities, elsewhere more and more people were killed in acts of terrorism.

By December 1978 more than 800 people had been killed, particularly in the eastern provinces. These new areas of violence reflected a change of tactics by the MHP, which during 1978 campaigned in central and eastern Anatolia where the traditional elements of society had been least affected by modernization. Türkeş's appeal to nationalism gained him supporters, particularly in areas where Turks lived with other ethnic groups, notably the Kurds. The violence culminated in December at the south-eastern town of Kahramanmaraş in the most serious outbreak of ethnic fighting since the 1920s. There the historic enmity between the orthodox Sunni majority and the heterodox Alevi minority had been exacerbated by the activities of right- and left-wing agitators. On 21 December 1978 the Alevis turned the funeral of two members of the left-wing teachers' association, murdered the day before, into a large-scale demonstration. The mourners were fired on by Sunni supporters of Türkeş and indiscriminate rioting erupted. After three days, more than 100 people had been killed, at least 1,000 had been injured and large parts of the Alevi quarters had been reduced to ruins. Order was not restored until the army intervened on 24 December.

MARTIAL LAW

The violence led to the imposition of martial law on 26 December 1978. Martial law was imposed for two months (renewed subsequently at two-monthly intervals) in 13 provinces, all, except İstanbul and Ankara, in the east, although the mainly Kurdish areas of the south-east were excluded to prevent friction. Ecevit announced that it was to be 'martial law with a human face', and instituted a co-ordination committee for its implementation, comprising himself, Gen. Kenan Evren, the Chief of the General Staff, and Lt-Gen. Sahap Yardimoğlu, the Chief Martial Law Administrator.

In April 1979 six ministers, defectors from the AP, issued a public memorandum criticizing Ecevit for taking insufficient account of their views and demanding tougher measures to combat political violence, particularly by left-wing groups, and Kurdish separatism. They also demanded a redirection of economic policies to allow more Western investment and greater freedom for private enterprise. The gulf between their views and those of Ecevit's left-wing supporters in the CHP became more and more pronounced, and the impossibility of reconciling the left- and right-wing elements in the coalition became clear. In response to the growth of Kurdish separatism, and alarmed by Kurdish violence in Iran, Ecevit agreed to extend martial law into six more provinces, all in the Kurdish south-east. Three CHP deputies promptly resigned, reducing the party's minority representation in the National Assembly to 211 of 450.

During the next few months Ecevit's parliamentary majority gradually dwindled, after a series of resignations by CHP deputies, and in October 1979 by-elections the AP achieved substantial gains. Ecevit promptly resigned on 16 October. Eight days later Demirel formed a new Government with the backing of the right-wing MHP and the MSP, affording the Government a majority of four.

Disorder grew steadily, as did the warning signs of military involvement in politics. On 2 January 1980 the Turkish generals issued a public warning to all political parties, criticizing them for arguing and urging them to reach a consensus of opinion on anti-terrorist measures. The weakness of the Government was illustrated by parliament's inability to choose a new head of state when President Korutürk's term expired in April. Since neither the right nor the left was prepared to compromise on the choice of candidate, the President of the

National Assembly, Ihsan Sabri Çağlayangil, took office as acting President. By August political violence had almost reached the proportions of a civil war. Although martial law continued to be extended every two months in 20 of the 67 provinces, clashes between right and left had caused some 2,000 deaths since the beginning of the year, and there was a growing trend towards the assassination of national figures.

THE 1980 COUP AND ITS AFTERMATH

On 11 September 1980 the armed forces, led by Gen. Evren, seized power in a bloodless coup, the third in 20 years. The main reasons for their intervention were the failure of the Government to deal with the country's political and economic chaos or to combat left- and right-wing terrorism. The leaders of the coup formed a five-member National Security Council (NSC), sworn in on 18 September. The Chairman of the NSC, Gen. Evren, became Head of State. Martial law was extended to the whole country and the legislature was dissolved. On 21 September the NSC appointed a mainly civilian Council of Ministers, with a retired naval commander, Bülent Ulusu, as Prime Minister and Turgut Özal as Deputy Prime Minister and Minister for Economic Affairs. Former political leaders, suspected terrorists and political extremists were detained, while all political activity was banned and trade union activities were restricted.

Though its rule was harsh, the military Government was committed to the eventual return of civilian rule within a framework that would prevent disorder. In October 1981 a Consultative Assembly was formed to draft a new constitution and to prepare the way for a return to parliamentary rule.

The new Constitution, extremely restrictive and authoritarian, was approved by referendum on 7 November 1982, with a 91% majority, largely because to refuse it would have meant continued military rule. An appended 'temporary article' automatically installed Gen. Evren as President for a seven-year term. The opposition was not allowed to canvass openly against the new Constitution.

During its period in power the military regime purged several hundred left-wing university professors, closed newspapers, tightened press censorship and held mass trials of labour leaders and others. Torture and ill-treatment appeared to be routine during interrogation and just under 50 convicted terrorists were executed. In May 1983 the President revoked the 30-month ban on political activity and allowed political parties to be formed under strict rules. All the former political parties, which had been dissolved in October 1981, were to remain proscribed, along with 723 former members of the legislature and leading party officials who were banned from active politics for 10 years. Despite its excessive harshness, the military achieved their twin aims of restoring political stability and ushering in economic growth. Turkey after 1982 was a very different country from what it had been in the 1970s.

CIVILIAN RULE RETURNS UNDER ÖZAL

A general election was held on 6 November 1983, and parliamentary rule was restored, with a 400-seat unicameral Grand National Assembly (Büyük Millet Meclisi). Election was on the basis of proportional representation (with a minimum requirement of 10% of the total votes, to discourage small parties), voting was compulsory and every candidate had to be approved by the NSC.

The President banned a total of 11 parties from participating in the general election. The conservative ANAVATAN, led by Turgut Özal, won 211 of the 400 seats in the Grand National Assembly and the armed forces' preferred party, the centre-right Milliyetçi Demokratik Partisi (MDP—Nationalist Democracy Party), was beaten into third place, with the centre-left Halkçı Parti (Populist Party) coming second. The result reflected the great popularity of Özal as the architect of economic recovery after 1980. He was appointed Prime Minister and named his Council of Ministers in December 1983. The MDP voted to disband itself in May 1986. Many of its members joined the new right-wing Hür Demokrat Partisi (HDP—Free Democratic Party), which was formed by Mehmet Yazar. By the end of 1986, therefore, there were four recognized parliamentary groups in the Grand National Assembly—ANAVATAN, the Sosyal Demokrat Halkçı Parti (SHP—Social Democratic Populist Party), the Demokratik Sol Parti (DSP—Democratic Left Party) and the Doğru Yol Partisi (DYP—True Path Party).

Concern continued throughout the 1980s and the early 1990s regarding the persistent and widespread use of torture against political prisoners. In December 1985 a case brought before the Human Rights Commission of the Council of Europe by five European countries, alleging that Turkey had violated the European Convention for the Protection of Human Rights and Fundamental Freedoms, was settled out of court. Turkey agreed to rescind all martial law decrees within 18 months, to introduce an amnesty for political prisoners and to allow independent observers from the Council of Europe to monitor progress. In July 1987 all martial law decrees in Turkey were repealed; by that time an official state of emergency had been declared in a total of nine provinces. In November the eight-year state of emergency in İstanbul was revoked.

FURTHER STEPS TOWARDS DEMOCRACY

In a national referendum, held in September 1987, a narrow majority approved the repeal of the restrictions imposed on over 200 politicians in 1981, banning them from taking an active part in public life for a period of 10 years. This result enabled Bülent Ecevit to take over the leadership of the DSP (he never returned to the CHP), while Süleyman Demirel was elected as leader of the DYP.

As the polls for the referendum closed, the Prime Minister, who had campaigned against the repeal of the ban, immediately announced that a general election would be held on 1 November 1987 (a year earlier than required). Seven parties contested the general election, which was the first free election in Turkey since the 1980 military coup. ANAVATAN obtained 36.3% of the votes cast (which, because of the 'weighted' electoral system, meant that it was allotted 292 of the seats in the Grand National Assembly, now enlarged from 400 to 450 seats), while the SHP (24.7% of the votes) won 99 seats and the DYP (19.1% of the votes) won 59 seats. Özal formed a new, expanded Council of Ministers in December.

ÖZAL BECOMES PRESIDENT

In mid-October 1989 Özal declared his candidacy for the presidential election to be conducted in the Grand National Assembly on 31 October. On 9 November Özal succeeded Gen. Evren as President, and unexpectedly appointed Yıldırım Akbulut, the Speaker of the Grand National Assembly and a former Minister of the Interior, to succeed him as Prime Minister. Akbulut was subsequently elected as party leader.

At an ANAVATAN party congress, convened on 15 June 1991, former Minister of Foreign Affairs Mesut Yılmaz defeated Akbulut in a contest for the party leadership. The following day Akbulut resigned as Prime Minister and, on 17 June, in accordance with the Constitution, President Özal invited Yılmaz to head a new administration.

THE 1991 GENERAL ELECTION

At the general election on 20 October 1991, the DYP, under the leadership of Demirel, received an estimated 27.3% of the votes cast, narrowly defeating ANAVATAN (with 23.9%) and the SHP (with 20.6%). Demirel assumed the premiership at the head of a coalition, comprising members of the DYP and the SHP: one effect of military rule had been to end the feud between politicians of the centre-left and centre-right. On 25 November the coalition partners announced a programme for political and economic reform that included the drafting of a new constitution, improvements in anti-terrorist legislation and matters of human rights, and increased levels of cultural recognition and of autonomy in local government for Kurds in Turkey.

FOREIGN AFFAIRS, 1980–93

Turkey–EC relations were poor in the 1970s, with the country lacking the significance of Greece's 1975 application to enter the EC. In January 1982, as a result of the human rights situation in Turkey and particularly the imprisonment of Bülent Ecevit by the military, the European Parliament voted to suspend relations with Turkey, and in March aid to Turkey was frozen.

In 1981 Greece joined the EC, adding a new dimension to Turkish–EC difficulties and the normalization of relations. In September 1986 the Turkish–EC Association Council (which was established in 1963, but had been suspended since the army coup in 1980) met for talks in Brussels, Belgium. Turkey, however, failed to gain access to the suspended EC aid because of Greek vetoes. In April 1987 Turgut Özal, ignoring the advice of EC ambassadors in Ankara, made a formal application to become a full member of the EC. Overruling Greek objections, the EC Council of Ministers agreed to submit the application to the Commission of the European Communities to formulate its opinion on the merits of the case. Yet in December 1989 the EC rejected Turkey's application to start negotiations, at least until 1993.

Meanwhile, Turgut Özal moved to boost Turkish–US relations. Following the forcible annexation of Kuwait by Iraq in August 1990, he broke with Turkish diplomatic tradition and allowed US troops logistical support in the coming Gulf War. In mid-January 1991 a resolution to extend the war powers of the Government and effectively endorse the unrestricted use of Turkish airbases by coalition forces was agreed by the Grand National Assembly. On the following day US aircraft began bombing missions into north-east Iraq from NATO bases inside south-east Turkey. In February and March the USA announced substantial increases in military and economic aid to Turkey for 1991 and 1992.

Although Greece and Turkey had agreed to ease tensions in April 1982, relations were further strained when the Turkish-backed 'Turkish Federated State of Cyprus' unilaterally declared independence, as the 'Turkish Republic of Northern Cyprus' ('TRNC'), in November 1983. Turkey remains the only country to have recognized this state and to have exchanged ambassadors with it (in May 1984). In July 1986 Turgut Özal became the first Turkish Prime Minister to make an official visit to the 'TRNC'. Tension between Greece and Turkey came to a head in March 1987, when a disagreement between the two countries over petroleum-prospecting rights in disputed areas of the Aegean Sea almost resulted in the outbreak of military conflict. However, relations between Turkey and Greece improved considerably in 1988: in February the Turkish Government officially annulled a decree, issued in 1964, that curbed the property rights of Turkey's ethnic Greek population. In return, the Greek Prime Minister, Andreas Papandreou, officially accepted Turkey's status as an associate member of the EC by signing the Protocol of Adaptation (consequent on Greece's accession to the EC) to the EC-Turkey Association Agreement in April 1988, which the Greek Government had hitherto refused to do. However, the situation deteriorated somewhat later in the same month, when Greece insisted on linking the possibility of Turkey's entry into the EC with the ending of the Turkish presence in Cyprus.

Following the formal dissolution of the USSR in December 1991, the Turkish Government sought to further its political, economic and cultural influence in the Central Asian region, and in particular to forge strong links with the six Muslim states of the former USSR. In June 1992 leaders of 11 countries, including both Turkey and Greece and six former Soviet republics, established a Black Sea economic alliance (now the Organization of the Black Sea Economic Cooperation, based in İstanbul), and expressed their commitment to promoting greater co-operation with regard to transport, energy, information, communications and ecology.

TURKEY AND THE IRAQI KURDS

In August 1988 the Iraqi armed forces launched a major offensive against Kurdish separatists in northern Iraq. Thousands of Kurdish refugees (an estimated 100,000–150,000 by early September) fled to the Turkish border, where, after initial hesitation, the Turkish Government admitted them on 'humanitarian grounds' and provided asylum in makeshift camps. In addition, the Turkish Government refused a request by Iraq to allow Iraqi forces to pursue Kurdish guerrillas in Turkish territory.

POLICY TOWARDS THE TURKISH KURDS, 1980–93

During the 1980s Kurdish-nationalist terrorism became a serious problem for Turkey in its south-eastern provinces. In 1984 the outlawed Marxist Partiya Karkeren Kurdistan (PKK—Kurdistan Workers' Party), led by Abdullah Öcalan, which demanded the creation of revolutionary Kurdish and Turkish national homelands in Turkey and its neighbours, launched a violent guerrilla campaign against the Turkish authorities in these provinces. The PKK concentrated its attacks on the local militia and civilians. However, by July 1987, as a result of international pressure to return to democracy, martial law was replaced by a state of emergency under a district governor in all of these provinces. In spite of this concession, the violence in the south-east grew and attracted steadily more international attention. It also meant that the military once more began to play a central part in Turkish national politics on the grounds of national security.

In late 1992 Turkish air and ground forces (in excess of 20,000 troops) struck at PKK bases inside northern Iraq, hoping to take advantage of losses inflicted upon the Kurdish rebels by a simultaneous offensive, initiated by Iraqi Kurdish *peshmerga* forces in October, with the aim of forcing the PKK out of Iraq. By mid-December most Turkish ground forces had been withdrawn from Iraqi territory.

ÇILLER BECOMES PRIME MINISTER

In April 1993 President Özal died. On 16 May he was succeeded by Süleyman Demirel. This meant that a new leader had to be chosen for the DYP; in early June Minister of State Tansu Çiller was elected, thus becoming Turkey's first female Prime Minister. Çiller announced the composition of her Council of Ministers in late June.

On taking office as Prime Minister, Çiller was immediately confronted with a dramatic increase in separatist violence. The PKK ended its unilateral cease-fire, which had been announced in March 1993, by declaring 'war' on all Turkish targets. There followed a wave of bomb explosions in Turkish tourist resorts and abductions of foreign nationals by the PKK, as well as a series of attacks upon Turkish diplomatic missions and business interests in Europe. This triggered increased military action and a political crackdown on Kurdish activities.

The pro-Kurdish Halkın Emek Partisi (HEP—People's Labour Party) was outlawed in July 1993. In March 1994 'mainstream' parliamentarians voted to strip seven members of the Demokrasi Partisi (DEP—Democracy Party, the successor to HEP) and one independent Kurdish deputy of their parliamentary immunity from prosecution, and six deputies were subsequently detained. On 16 June Turkey's Constitutional Court banned the DEP and ruled that its 13 deputies should be expelled from the Grand National Assembly, owing to associations with the PKK. In August the six deputies detained since March, along with two DEP deputies arrested in July, went on trial on charges of supporting separatist movements. In December they were found guilty and received prison sentences of between three-and-a-half and 15 years, despite international protests. In October 1995 the Supreme Court released two of the deputies but upheld the sentences on the four deputies remaining in prison.

By early 1994 the Government not only had problems in the south-east of the country but the Turkish economy had suffered its biggest collapse since that of 1979. The beneficiary was the Islamist movement. Taking advantage of a fragmented political scene, it moved into a dominating position in Turkish national politics that it maintained thereafter. In the March 1994 local elections the Islamist Refah Partisi (RP—Welfare Party) won 19% of the votes cast and took control of both Ankara and İstanbul. These elections marked a permanent shift in the country's political life.

Despite continuing dissension within the Government, and the resignation of several cabinet ministers, Çiller's coalition held together throughout the remainder of 1994, sustained, not least, by mutual fear of the RP. The Government's main priorities now related to passing basic democratic reforms so as to enable the customs union with the EU, planned since the 1960s and prepared for in a series of reductions in tariffs over 25 years, to go ahead. Turkey and the EU agreed on the customs union arrangements in March 1995. Turkey agreed not to block the accession of the Republic of Cyprus to the EU. For the customs union to come into force on 1 January 1996, the European Parliament had to ratify the change, and there was no prospect of this without significant progress on human rights in Turkey. In July Çiller secured approval from the Grand National Assembly for several democratization measures, including the lowering of the minimum voting age and the removal of certain restrictions on trade unions and political participation. In addition, the number of parliamentary seats was to be increased by 100, to 550.

Another factor was Turkey's relations with Greece. These were still strained and deteriorated in 1994, after Greece signed the UN Convention on the Law of the Sea, permitting the extension of its territorial waters in the Aegean Sea from six to 12 nautical miles. The Turkish Government, fearing the loss of shipping access to international seas, insisted that any expansion of territorial waters would be considered an act of aggression on the part of Greece, to which Turkey would respond. As the Convention entered into force in mid-November, both sides conducted military exercises in the Aegean. Tensions between the two countries were manifest in early 1995 during negotiations to conclude the customs union between the EU and Turkey. Greece finally withdrew its opposition to the agreement in March, following the adoption of a formal timetable for accession negotiations to commence with Cyprus. In Cyprus President Glavkos Klerides, elected in 1993, had created a bilateral defence agreement with Greece that, in Turkish eyes, upset the strategic balance between the two countries. In June 1994 the Grand National Assembly granted the Government military powers to defend the country's interests in the Aegean, following ratification of the Law of the Sea Convention by the Greek Parliament.

In early September 1995 Deniz Baykal was elected as the new leader of the CHP. Negotiations subsequently failed to agree on the continuation of the ruling coalition. In early October Çiller was again able to form a coalition, having secured the backing of the MHP and the DSP parliamentary groups.

THE ISLAMISTS ENTER GOVERNMENT

The overriding objective of Tansu Çiller's caretaker administration prior to the general election, scheduled for 24 December 1995, was to secure endorsement by the EU of the long-proposed customs union. In October the Supreme Court had cancelled the charges against four Kurdish former deputies, while the Grand National Assembly voted to amend the 'anti-terror' laws, one of the outstanding concerns of the European Parliament, in order to permit greater freedom of expression. The customs union was finally approved by the European Parliament on 13 December, and entered into force on 1 January 1996.

During the election campaign domestic issues, such as the high rate of inflation, were the dominant concerns. The outcome of the election failed to resolve the country's political uncertainties: the RP won 158 of the 550 seats in the enlarged Grand National Assembly, having obtained 21.4% of the votes cast, while the DYP secured 135 seats (19.2%), ANAVATAN 132 seats (19.7%), the DSP 76 seats (14.6%) and the CHP 49 seats (10.7%). The remaining votes were shared among smaller parties, which gained no representation.

President Demirel gave the RP, as the largest party in the new Grand National Assembly, the first opportunity to form a government. Protracted negotiations between the parties ensued over the next two months. Despite the apparently conciliatory approach of the RP leader, Erbakan, the party failed to secure the secular coalition partner that it needed to form the first predominantly Islamist government in the history of modern Turkey. The question increasingly became whether the two secular right-wing parties, the DYP and ANAVATAN, could agree terms for a coalition that would prevent the formation of an RP administration. Finally, on 28 February 1996 ANAVATAN and the DYP concluded an agreement. A rotating premiership arrangement was to be undertaken, according to which the ANAVATAN leader, Mesut Yılmaz, was to occupy the office in the first year. The DYP was given most of the economic ministries, while ANAVATAN took control of the defence and security portfolios. The new coalition still needed the support of the DSP if it was to control an absolute majority in the Grand National Assembly, but a formal arrangement proved impossible to secure.

Within weeks it was evident that the DYP-ANAVATAN coalition would not last long, not least because of the intense personal animosity between Yılmaz and Çiller. By the end of May 1996 Çiller was publicly urging Yılmaz to resign. The atmosphere of crisis within the country was deepened by an unsuccessful attempt to assassinate President Demirel on 19 May. In early June the Grand National Assembly, with the support of DYP deputies, voted to debate a censure motion against the Government; however, on 6 June Yılmaz resigned.

On 7 June 1996 Erbakan was invited to form a government, and negotiations to establish a new coalition began. The nomination of the veteran Islamist as Prime Minister indicated how deeply Turkey was changing—but it was profoundly disagreeable to many of his opponents. On 28 June the RP and DYP reached agreement, and their coalition won a confidence vote in the Grand National Assembly on 8 July. Erbakan, as leader of the RP, became Prime Minister, while Çiller assumed the deputy premiership and foreign affairs portfolio. The new Government announced that its objective was to secure political and economic stability; it promised to pursue further European integration and undertook to honour existing international and strategic agreements, providing they did not threaten national interest. Almost immediately Erbakan embarked on a tour of Middle East and Asian Islamic countries.

YILMAZ REPLACES ERBAKAN

In the context of persistent rumours of an imminent military coup and a new censure motion against the Government, tabled in protest at proposals to introduce Islamic reforms, a meeting of the military-dominated NSC on 28 February 1997 led to the publication of an 18-point memorandum setting out recommendations to ensure the protection of secularism in Turkey. On 5 March, under intense pressure, Erbakan reluctantly signed the memorandum, whereby the Government was committed to: increasing the length of compulsory state education from five to eight years; closing unauthorized Islamist schools and acting against Muslim brotherhoods (*tarikatlar*); halting the employment of soldiers expelled from the army for fundamentalist activities; and reducing co-operation with Iran.

Although the immediate political crisis had apparently been resolved, DYP dissidents began to call for the dissolution of the Government and the organization of early elections. In June 1997, following the loss of his parliamentary majority, Erbakan resigned. He expected to become the junior partner in a new coalition with Çiller. However, President Demirel selected not Çiller but ANAVATAN leader Mesut Yılmaz to form a new coalition. On 30 June 1997 Yılmaz was appointed Prime Minister, having successfully gained the support of the DSP and the newly founded Demokrat Türkiye Partisi (Democratic Turkey Party), along with that of several DYP defectors, to form a coalition with a nominal 12-seat majority. The new Government's programme, announced on 7 July, stressed its commitment to secularism and echoed many of the recommendations of the 18-point memorandum drawn up by the NSC (including the controversial education reforms). The Government received a vote of confidence from the Grand National Assembly on 12 July. Legislation promulgating the education reforms secured parliamentary approval in mid-August, as did a press amnesty law that suspended the sentences of imprisoned editors (believed to number at least six) who had been convicted of publishing articles posing a threat to national security. Later that month the trial began of a total of 48 members of the security forces, including 11 officers, for the murder of the journalist Metin Göktepe in 1996. Doubts were raised about the effectiveness of the trial when the defendants failed to attend the court; delays to the case resulted in demonstrations in İstanbul in January 1998. In March, however, five of the officers were sentenced to more than seven years' imprisonment, while the remaining six were acquitted.

On 16 October 1997 Turkey agreed an out-of-court settlement in a case of alleged torture that had been taken to the ECHR. Later that month a human rights activist, Esber Yağmurdereli, was sentenced to 23 years' imprisonment for supporting terrorist activity and disseminating separatist propaganda. Following both foreign and domestic condemnation of his detention, he was released in November, ostensibly on the grounds of ill health.

Meanwhile, in May 1997 the armed forces launched their most ambitious military incursion into northern Iraq to date, in pursuit of PKK activists, in an operation entailing the mobilization of some 50,000 troops. The most severe critics of the exercise were Iran and Syria, which accused Turkey of seeking to establish a permanent military presence in northern Iraq. A further offensive against PKK positions in northern Iraq in October was accompanied by the lifting of the 10-year-old state of emergency in three of the nine south-eastern provinces (Bitlis, Batman and Bingöl).

FOREIGN RELATIONS, 1997–99

In April 1997 the Greek and Turkish ministers responsible for foreign affairs held bilateral talks in Malta under EU auspices, during which it was agreed that each country would establish a committee of experts to help resolve bilateral disputes. The two committees were to be separate and independent and were to communicate through the EU. In July, at a NATO summit in Madrid, Spain, direct talks took place between Demirel and the Greek Prime Minister, Konstantinos Simitis (the first such meeting for three years). An agreement was signed on 8 July whereby both sides pledged to respect the other's sovereign rights and to renounce violence, and the threat of violence, in their dealings with each other. Turkey announced the formation of a joint committee to implement partial integration between Turkey and the 'TRNC', in response to the EU's agreement to commence accession talks with Cyprus. Turkey also declared in September that should the EU continue to conduct membership talks with the Greek Cypriot Government, it would seek further integration with the 'TRNC'.

In January 1999 Turkey accused Greece of escalating tension in the Aegean and urged reconciliation through negotiations. Relations with Greece deteriorated in early 1999, following repeated Turkish accusations of Greek support for the PKK; Greece denied the accusations, and Öcalan was later captured at the Greek embassy in Kenya.

DOMESTIC DIFFICULTIES PERSIST

On 16 January 1998 the Constitutional Court issued a judgment banning the RP on the grounds that it had a 'hidden' fundamentalist agenda and had conspired against the secular order. In addition, former Prime Minister Erbakan and six other RP officials were banned from holding political office for five years. A month later some 100 former RP deputies joined the new Fazilet Partisi (FP—Virtue Party), which had been founded in December 1997 under the leadership of İsmail Alptekin, and by early March the FP had become the largest party in the Grand National Assembly.

At the end of the month, the NSC criticized the Government for advocating a relaxation of the enforcement of anti-Islamic legislation; the Government subsequently proposed further measures to curb Islamist radicalism, and the universities announced their decision to enforce the dress code.

Also in March 1998 the Court of Appeals ruled that former Prime Minister Çiller could not be prosecuted over allegations that she had misused government funds during her premiership. While admitting that she had withdrawn substantial sums from a secret government 'slush fund', Çiller had claimed that she could not disclose the destination of the money for reasons of national security. In May the Grand National Assembly confirmed that an inquiry would be conducted into corruption allegations against Prime Minister Yılmaz connected with tendering for government contracts. In early June Yılmaz announced that he would resign at the end of the year to make way for a broadly based interim government that would oversee the holding of early legislative elections in April 1999. In August 1998 12 former RP politicians, including Erbakan and the FP leader, Recai Kutan, were charged with illegally diverting funds from the party prior to its dissolution.

Following corruption allegations against Prime Minister Yılmaz connected with the privatization of the Türk Ticaret Bankası, on 25 November 1998 the Grand National Assembly approved a motion of no confidence in the Government, which subsequently resigned. Protracted political manoeuvring resulted in the formation, in January 1999, of an interim administration headed by Ecevit, comprising members of the DSP and independents.

ÖCALAN CAPTURED

Ecevit thus happened to be in power when the Turkish Government scored one of its most striking successes. Relations with Syria, which had already deteriorated in July 1998 (owing to Syria's repeated claim to the Hatay region of Turkey), worsened in early October after Turkey threatened the use of force if Syria did not expel PKK leader Abdullah Öcalan (known to be residing in that country) and close down terrorist training camps both in Syria and the Beqa'a valley in Lebanon. Following a meeting of Turkish and Syrian officials in late October, an agreement was signed under which Syria would not allow the PKK to operate on its territory. Öcalan was also forced to leave the country.

Turkey recalled temporarily its ambassador to Italy in October 1998, after that country hosted a meeting of the Kurdish parliament-in-exile. Relations deteriorated further, following the arrest of Öcalan upon his arrival in Italy in November, as a result of Italy's refusal to extradite him to Turkey and of his application for asylum. Öcalan's request for asylum was denied, and in January 1999 he was reported to have left Italy. On 15 February Öcalan, who had apparently been using a Greek Cypriot passport, was captured at the Greek embassy in Kenya, and returned to Turkey. Widespread protests were held throughout Europe.

Öcalan was charged with treason on 23 February 1999, and held personally responsible for the deaths of some 30,000 people during the 15-year Kurdish struggle for autonomy. PKK violence in protest at the trial continued in that month. In April a further operation was launched against the PKK, involving the deployment of some 15,000 Turkish troops in northern Iraq. On 29 June, however, the PKK leader was found guilty and sentenced to death. On 2 August Öcalan issued a statement from his prison cell announcing that the PKK would cease all offensive operations and pursue its goals by peaceful means.

1999 GENERAL ELECTION

On 18 April 1999 elections took place to the 550-seat Grand National Assembly. Some 87% of the electorate voted, and Ecevit's DSP became the largest party in the Grand National Assembly with 136 seats, closely followed by the MHP (129 seats) and the FP (111). ANAVATAN and the DYP obtained 86 seats and 85 seats, respectively; three seats were won by independents. The Halkin Demokrasi Partisi (HADEP—People's Democracy Party) performed strongly in the south-east, but failed to secure the 10% of the national vote necessary for a seat in the Grand National Assembly. The CHP leader, Deniz Baykal, resigned, following the poor performance of his party. President Demirel on 3 May invited Bülent Ecevit to form a new administration, and on 28 May a three-party coalition Government, composed of the DSP, the MHP and ANAVATAN, was announced. The new Government commanded 351 seats in the Grand National Assembly, and was thus the first since 1995 to command an overall parliamentary majority. In the same month the Chief Prosecutor instituted a court case against the FP, with the aim of dissolving the party.

SERIOUS PRISON UNREST—EXTERNAL AND DOMESTIC DEVELOPMENTS

In September 1999 unrest broke out in prisons across the country led by the Devrimci Halk Kurtuluş Partisi-Cephesi (DHKP-C—Revolutionary People's Liberation Party-Front); 10 prisoners were killed and a number of guards were held hostage. The Minister of Justice asserted that he would not resign over the unrest; he later announced that a special force was to be established to ensure prison security. Some 100 people were arrested in İstanbul while trying to issue a press release on the prison incidents. Unrest continued in prisons in late 1999 and early 2000. In February 2000 a protocol was signed providing for the education of prison inmates.

There was a marked improvement in Turkish–Greek relations, which in turn contributed to Greek acceptance of the decision of the EU summit meeting in Helsinki, Finland, in December 1999 to grant Turkey the status of a candidate for EU membership. Ankara responded by encouraging the Turkish Cypriots to participate in long-sought UN-sponsored negotiations on the Cyprus problem, although there seemed little prospect of a solution in the near future. An exchange of visits by the Greek and Turkish Ministers of Foreign Affairs in January and February 2000, the first for nearly 40 years, confirmed the improvement in relations; during these visits several bilateral agreements were signed and a joint working group on the reduction of military tensions in the Aegean region was established.

Although the Court of Appeals and the Chief Prosecutor rejected Abdullah Öcalan's appeal against his death sentence, the Government on 12 January 2000 granted a stay of execution until such time as the ECHR had considered the PKK leader's case.

SEZER ELECTED PRESIDENT

On 29 March 2000 the Grand National Assembly rejected constitutional amendments proposed by the Government, including measures that sought to reduce the presidential term of office from seven to five years, to introduce a system of direct presidential elections and to allow an incumbent Head of State to seek re-election—the specific aim of this last provision being to enable President Demirel to serve a second term. Following a second rejection of the amendments on 5 April, on 5 May the Assembly elected Ahmet Necdet Sezer, hitherto President of the Constitutional Court and the Government's nominee, as Turkey's 10th President, with 330 votes out of 533 in a third round of voting.

FEBRUARY 2001 FINANCIAL CRISIS AND AFTERMATH

Turkey experienced its worst financial crisis for many years in late February 2001, when the Government was forced to float the lira. The crisis followed months of increasing pressure on the currency and was finally prompted by a public clash between President Sezer and Prime Minister Ecevit at a meeting of the NSC on 19 February. Ecevit walked out when the President accused him of protecting ministers suspected of corruption. The immediate reaction of the markets was a massive flight of capital and a collapse in share prices. After three days of abortive resistance, the Government released the lira from its 'peg' with the US dollar on 22 February, thereby effectively devaluing the currency by about one-third. Ecevit resisted opposition calls for his resignation, instead appointing Kemal Derviş, a senior World Bank official, as Minister of State responsible for economic policy with extensive new powers.

Derviş quickly drew up a recovery plan, envisaging the implementation of long-delayed privatization and liberalization measures, and applied to the IMF for emergency support. Protracted negotiations ensued, during which the IMF insisted on key steps being taken before it would agree to new loans, including the closure of loss-making, state-owned banks and privatization of the telecommunications industry. After the Government had secured parliamentary approval for these and other measures in early May 2001, the IMF on 15 May approved additional stand-by credit of US $8,000m., bringing total IMF resources available to Turkey to a record $19,000m.

BANNING OF THE FP—OTHER PARTY DEVELOPMENTS, 2001–02

In common with its three Islamist predecessors, the FP was banned by the Constitutional Court on 22 June 2001, with immediate effect, and ordered to surrender its assets to the state, on the grounds that the party had become the focus of anti-secular activities in breach of the Constitution. The Court also ordered the expulsion from the Grand National Assembly of two FP deputies for particular anti-secular offences, the remaining FP deputies being required to become independents. Kutan described the ruling as 'a blow to Turkey's search for democracy and law'.

In July 2001, with the support of about one-half of the former FP deputies, Kutan announced the formation of a new Islamist party, to be called Saadet Partisi (Felicity Party), stating that it would seek to protect religious rights but would not challenge the secular basis of the Turkish state. Most of the remaining FP deputies declared their support for a more reformist Islamist party, the Adalet ve Kalkınma Partisi (AKP—Justice and Development Party), founded in August by the former mayor of İstanbul, Recep Tayyip Erdoğan. At the end of July the ECHR ruled by four votes to three that the Turkish Constitutional Court had not violated the European Convention on Human Rights in January 1998 in proscribing the RP (the predecessor of the FP). The AKP quickly emerged not only as the stronger of the two successor Islamist parties but also the best-supported party in the country in opinion polls. In what appeared to be a concerted establishment campaign against Erdoğan, the Constitutional Court ruled in January 2002 that the AKP leader's conviction on a sedition charge in 1999 had disqualified him from politics, and banned him from standing in the next general election. The electoral commission confirmed the decision in June 2002.

EXTERNAL RELATIONS, 2001–02

The Grand National Assembly in October 2001 gave the Government authority to send Turkish troops abroad to participate in the US-led military operation against the militant Islamist al-Qa'ida network and Taliban forces in Afghanistan (mounted in the wake of the September suicide attacks in the USA) and also to allow more foreign troops to be stationed in Turkey. In December the US Secretary of State, Colin Powell, visited Ankara in the course of a 10-nation tour to rally support for military action in Afghanistan. In the following month, as Ecevit had talks with President George W. Bush in Washington, DC, Turkey supplied a contingent to the multinational International Security Assistance Force being deployed in Afghanistan. A Turkish-supported decision by the Turkish Cypriots to resume the UN-sponsored negotiations in Cyprus in January 2002 helped to reactivate the process of rapprochement between Turkey and Greece, as required by the EU as a precondition for the opening of formal accession negotiations with Turkey. Senior Turkish and Greek officials met in Ankara in March to discuss the Aegean Sea delimitation and related issues, and were reported to have agreed to submit intractable differences to the International Court of Justice, based in The Hague, Netherlands. The two sides also signed an agreement for the construction of a pipeline through which Turkey would supply gas to Greece.

2002 GOVERNMENT CRISIS

Early in October 2001 the Government secured the Grand National Assembly's approval of several amendments to the Constitution intended to facilitate Turkey's accession to the EU, including an easing of the ban on the Kurdish language. In the following month the legislature approved revisions to the Civil Code under which women obtained equal status with men in the sphere of the family. However, there remained strong parliamentary opposition, particularly from the MHP, to abolishing the death penalty—a key EU requirement—and to giving legislative force to other human rights reforms.

The political deadlock deepened in May 2002, when Ecevit became seriously incapacitated by illness but refused to resign. He also resisted demands for an early general election, not only from the opposition, but also from within the ruling coalition. The crisis appeared to have been defused in June, when the MHP agreed to remain in the Government, while allowing the human rights legislation and the abolition of capital punishment to be approved in the Grand National Assembly by an alliance of the other two coalition parties and opposition members.

Derviş also announced his resignation from the Government in July 2002, but was persuaded by the President to remain in office to reassure the financial markets and the IMF; he therefore delayed his resignation until 10 August. He was, nevertheless, present when Deputy Prime Minister Hüsamettin Özkan and Minister of Foreign Affairs İsmail Cem launched a new pro-EU organization, the Yeni Türkiye Partisi (YTP—New Turkey Party), as opinion polls indicated that none of the three existing coalition parties would secure the minimum percentage of 10% of votes in an election required for legislative representation. The new party joined the widespread demands for an early poll, to which the increasingly isolated Ecevit was forced to submit after the MHP officially voiced its support for an election. As confirmed by the Grand National Assembly at the end of July, a general election was set for 3 November, nearly 18 months ahead of schedule. This decision cleared the way for the Grand National Assembly's formal approval in early August of the delayed human rights and other reforms, including: the abolition of the death penalty except in time of war; the ending of the ban on broadcasting in languages other than Turkish; authorization of Kurdish teaching in regulated private schools; the lifting of penalties for criticism of the armed forces and other state institutions; the easing of restrictions on public demonstrations and association; greater freedom for non-Muslim religions; the redefinition of police duties and powers; and the revision of press laws and regulations.

2002 PARLIAMENTARY ELECTIONS—ERDOĞAN BECOMES PRIME MINISTER

On 20 September 2002 Turkey's High Electoral Board concurred in the Constitutional Court's decision to prohibit Erdoğan and Erbakan, from participating in the forthcoming elections. Nevertheless, in the polling on 3 November the AKP achieved a decisive victory, securing 363 of the 550 Grand National Assembly seats, with 34.3% of the votes. The parties of the incumbent Ecevit coalition all failed to win any parliamentary seats, and their leaders, Ecevit, Yılmaz and Devlet Bahçeli, resigned as heads of their parties. The CHP was the only other party to achieve representation in the Assembly, winning 178 seats with 19.4% of the vote (far exceeding the 10% minimum), while nine seats were secured by independent candidates (to whom the minimum percentage requirement did not apply). In view of Erdoğan's exclusion, the AKP deputy leader, Abdullah Gül, became Prime Minister and Minister of Foreign Affairs, heading a Council of Ministers, which was reduced from 38 to 25 members. However, Erdoğan was recognized as the real leader of the new Government and immediately undertook a tour of EU capitals. Following the rapid adoption of appropriate constitutional amendments and their reluctant approval by President Sezer, Erdoğan was elected to the Grand National Assembly in a by-election on 9 March 2003 and was installed as Prime Minister two days later. He subsequently formed a new 23-member Council of Ministers, which included Gül as Minister of Foreign Affairs.

The commutation of Öcalan's death sentence to life imprisonment in October 2002 was followed in January 2003 by Turkey's signature of the protocol of the European Convention of Human Rights proscribing the death penalty in peacetime. In June the Grand National Assembly adopted a further series of human rights reforms, including further legislation to permit education and broadcasting in Kurdish and other minority languages and to amend the existing legal definition of terrorism. Further measures approved by the Assembly in July included the downgrading of the predominantly military NSC to make it an entirely advisory body (in accordance with EU requirements).

NOVEMBER 2003 BOMBINGS IN İSTANBUL

Turkey experienced its worst peacetime violence in November 2003, when four massive suicide bombings were mounted in İstanbul within five days. The first two truck bombs exploded outside two synagogues on the Jewish Sabbath on 15 November. Five days later two truck bombs exploded outside the Turkish headquarters of the Hong Kong and Shanghai Banking Corporation and the British consulate. In total, the attacks killed 63 people, including the drivers of the vehicles, and injured over 700 more. The dead included three Britons, among them the Consul-General, Roger Short, and six members of Turkey's Jewish community. Intensive investigations by the security authorities found evidence that the bombings had been carried out by members of a group of Kurdish militants connected to the al-Qa'ida network, all of whom had been trained outside Turkey.

VOTE AGAINST US TROOP DEPLOYMENT—DEVELOPMENTS FOLLOWING THE US-LED CAMPAIGN IN IRAQ

The major foreign policy dilemma facing the new AKP Government in early 2003 was whether to accede to a US request for permission to deploy US troops in the south-east of Turkey, in the event of an invasion of Iraq. After protracted disagreement over financial terms, concluding in an offer by the USA of US $30,000m. in aid and loans, the Government agreed in late February to submit a resolution on US troop deployment to a parliamentary vote. However, amid overwhelming popular opposition to a US-led campaign in Iraq, the Grand National Assembly on 1 March failed to provide the required two-thirds' majority for a government motion authorizing the deployment of US troops. Nevertheless, later in March, after the invasion of Iraq had begun, the Assembly approved the opening of Turkish airspace to US military aircraft for a six-month period, in return for US aid and loans of up to $9,400m. Controversially, the approved motion also authorized the deployment of Turkish troops in northern Iraq, where Kurdish aspirations and PKK (at that time known as the Congress for Freedom and Democracy in Kurdistan—KADEK) bases were viewed as posing a threat to Turkish national security and where there had been a small, unofficial Turkish military presence since 1997. During a visit to Ankara in early April 2003, US Secretary of State Colin Powell pledged that northern Iraq would not come under the control of Kurdish separatists and that Turkey would have a role in the post-war reconstruction of Iraq. Massed Turkish troops therefore did not cross the border during the war, despite outrage in Ankara over the fall of the petroleum-rich northern Iraqi city of Kirkuk to Iraqi Kurds in mid-April. A declaration by the Turkish Ministry of Foreign Affairs that a permanent Kurdish military presence in Kirkuk was 'unacceptable' elicited a promise by Powell that Kurdish forces in that city would be replaced by US troops and that Iraq would remain a single sovereign state. In early July, while Turkish–US relations were still at a low ebb, 11 Turkish soldiers were among 24 Turks arrested by US forces in Sulaimaniya over an alleged plot against local Kurdish leaders. The soldiers were taken as captives to Baghdad—an incident that was seen as a national slight by the Turkish public.

DOMESTIC POLITICS AND THE KURDISH QUESTION, 2004–06

The local government elections, which took place on 28 March 2004, indicated a strong increase in support for the AKP, which secured 41.6% of votes cast; the CHP, regarded as being out of touch with its followers and intent on pursuing a nationalist line rather than a centre-left one, won only 18.2% of the votes. Almost certainly, the Government's successful economic performance, in restraining the rate of inflation and restoring the annual gross domestic product growth rate, was the main reason for its continued public support. In May, in the latest of the series of reforms intended to make Turkey compliant with EU human rights and democratic standards, the Grand National Assembly adopted draft constitutional amendments to confirm the abolition of the death penalty and dissolve anti-terrorist state security courts, to guarantee full equality for women and to establish full parliamentary control over the budget of the armed forces.

The contest between the AKP Government on the one side, and the staunchly secularist state establishment, notably the army and the judiciary on the other, continued to act as the major divide in Turkish politics. A particular issue of contention was the demand by the AKP (supported by some 70% of the population) that female students should be allowed to wear Muslim-style headscarves in university premises. This was firmly rejected by the university authorities, as well as the courts, as an unacceptable symbolic infringement of Kemalist secularism. The AKP leaders supported proposals for ending the ban, but wisely decided not to press for a constitutional amendment to make this possible, since it would have resulted in direct conflict with the secularist authorities.

PKK VIOLENCE AND OFFICIAL RETALIATION

Exploiting the instability in northern Iraq, in June 2004 the PKK abandoned the cease-fire it had declared in 1999, following Öcalan's capture. Although its attacks were on a far lower scale than in the 1990s, the end of the cease-fire opened up a serious breach between the Turkish and US administrations, since about 5,000 PKK militants continued to enjoy a safe haven in northern Iraq, in territory ostensibly controlled by the Iraqi Kurdish leaders. Although the US Government officially classified the PKK as a terrorist organization, the US authorities in Iraq refused to take military action against them, leading to Turkish accusations that they were applying double standards. In November 2005 a bomb exploded outside a bookshop in the town of Semdinli, in the remote south-eastern province of Hakkari, killing two people and injuring another 12. It quickly emerged that the bomb had been planted by local non-commissioned officers (NCOs) of the gendarmerie, the semi-military force that is responsible for law and order outside the main cities. In June 2006 two NCOs and a former PKK informant were convicted of causing the explosion and sentenced to long prison terms, but the affair prompted violent protests in the south-east, causing several deaths. Earlier, Erdoğan had tried to appease Kurdish opinion in August 2005, when he visited Diyarbakır and promised that 'we will resolve all problems with more democracy, more civil rights and more prosperity'. On the Kurdish side, in the following month the successor of HADEP (DEHAP—Demokratik Halk Partisi or the Democratic People's Party) was formally dissolved, having been merged with the Demokratik Toplum Partisi (DTP—Democratic Society Party). The DTP called on the PKK to restore its cease-fire, but its appeal went unheeded.

The most immediate problem for Turkey, however, during 2005–07 remained the revival and escalation of PKK terrorist attacks in the south-east of the country, dispelling hopes that the movement had been defeated militarily at the end of the 1990s.

IRAQ-BASED PKK VIOLENCE STRAINS TURKISH–US RELATIONS

The attacks reflected the ability of PKK operatives to strike at targets within Turkey from bases in the Qandil Mountains on the eastern borders of northern Iraq and Iran. Turkey blamed responsibility for the renewed PKK activity on the USA (the occupying force in Iraq) and the Iraqi Kurdish authorities. During early to mid-2006 there were signs that PKK activities in northern Iraq might stimulate Turkey and Iran to forge closer military links. Iranian forces, taking advantage of the proximity of the Qandil bases to the Iranian–Iraqi frontier bombarded the Qandil bases in May and June 2006. A subsequent clash between the Iranian forces and the PKK killed 17 militants on 24 February 2007. The USA responded belatedly in September 2006 to growing Turkish complaints about PKK terrorism by appointing a senior retired general, Joseph Ralston, to co-operate in joint action with Turkey over northern Iraq, but, as the months passed, it became increasingly evident that no practical action was contemplated.

Gen. Ralston visited Turkey several times after his appointment, but his Turkish counterpart, Gen. (retd) Edip Başar, was dismissed on 20 May 2007 for warning that defeating the PKK would not be easy. In the absence of action against the PKK bases, the military raised the possibility of an incursion deep into Iraqi territory. The contrast between the US-led invasion of 2003, carried out against a perceived terrorist threat which proved not to exist in reality, and the situation in Turkey—where soldiers were actually being killed by cross-border incursions but retaliation was not permitted—became a major source of tension between Turkey and the USA and its Iraqi allies.

TOWARDS DEADLOCK? THE TURKEY–EU RELATIONSHIP, 2004–07

Turkey's hopes of joining the EU increased in 2004 and 2005, but during 2006 and 2007 negotiations became steadily more deadlocked, while opinion in some EU countries hardened against Turkey and Turkish popular support for membership of the Union waned dramatically. The shift began in February 2004, when the AKP Government dramatically reversed previous Turkish policies on Cyprus by supporting a settlement of the Cyprus issue based on proposals by UN Secretary-General Kofi Annan, which provided for a bi-communal federal state, thereby shifting from its previous stance of support for a sovereign Turkish Cypriot state. The Turkish authorities gained some credit in the EU for the Turkish Cypriots' vote in favour of the plan, but the Greek Cypriots rejected the deal by a ratio of three to one and went on to join the Union. Though the Greek Cypriot Government officially declared that it would not veto Turkey's membership application, Turkey did not recognize the Republic of Cyprus, creating a serious new obstacle for its membership prospects. An official visit to Greece by Erdoğan in early May (the first by a Turkish premier in 16 years) reflected the improvement in relations between the two countries; bilateral discussions particularly concerned Turkey's application for EU membership.

An EU summit meeting held in Brussels in December 2004 announced the decision to set 3 October 2005 as the date for the opening of formal accession negotiations with Turkey, subject to strict conditions being met. Requirements included the Turkish signature of an additional protocol extending its customs union with the EU to the 10 new member states, including the Republic of Cyprus, this stipulation being a last-minute compromise after Erdoğan had ruled out recognition of the Greek Cypriot Government of a divided Cyprus. With regard to the negotiations, Turkey was given no guarantee that they would lead to full EU membership and was warned that they could be suspended at any stage if Turkey was found to be in breach of EU civil rights and rule of law standards. In addition, Turkey was informed that any accession treaty would include 'permanent safeguards', allowing other member states to impose restrictions on migration from Turkey.

New complications for Turkey's EU aspirations arose from the decisive rejection of the proposed EU constitutional treaty by the electorates of France and the Netherlands on 29 May and 1 June 2005, respectively. A major factor in both votes was popular opposition to the admission of Turkey to the EU, for which the proposed constitution made provision at a future date. Opposition by the French public to eventual Turkish accession was reflected in a statement by the French Prime Minister, Dominique de Villepin, on 2 August implying that accession negotiations with Turkey could not start until the Turkish Government recognized the Republic of Cyprus. The French President, Jacques Chirac, later dropped this condition, but attention then shifted to Germany, where the centre-right Christian Democrats insisted that Turkey could only be offered an (ill-defined) 'privileged partnership' rather than full membership of the EU. Fortunately for Turkey, however, the centre-right failed to win an overall majority in the German general election held on 18 September, so that the Christian Democrat leader, Angela Merkel, was forced into a coalition with the Social Democrats, who had long supported the principle of Turkish accession. Hence, the new German Government continued to support Turkey's eventual accession in principle. Meanwhile, in late July Turkey finally signed the additional protocol extending its EU customs union to Cyprus and the other nine new EU member states. However, it appended a declaration emphasizing that the signing did not amount to any form of recognition of the Republic of Cyprus and that Turkey continued to regard the Greek Cypriot Government as only having authority south of the UN buffer zone. Moreover, the protocol could not come into effect until it was ratified by the Turkish parliament. Since implementation of the protocol would require Turkey to open its harbours and airports to Greek Cypriot ships and aircraft, the AKP Government refused to submit it for parliamentary ratification until the EU also, in exchange, lifted its embargo on direct trade and flights to the 'TRNC'.

All these issues came to a head in the run-up to an emergency meeting of EU foreign ministers called by the British EU presidency on 2 October 2005, to agree on a Negotiating Framework Document for Turkey. On the question of recognition of the Republic of Cyprus by Turkey, it was agreed that Turkey would have to take this step as part of the eventual accession process, but it would not be demanded as a condition for the start of negotiations. Similarly, Turkey was not required to implement the additional protocol immediately. However, the EU strongly urged it to do so, and stated that it would re-examine the question by the end of 2006, implying that there could be an impediment to the negotiations on this issue by the end of the following year. Even after these obstacles had been overcome, however, the Austrian Government made a belated demand for a reference to 'privileged partnership' as an alternative to full membership in the Negotiating Framework Document, and abandoned this condition only after the EU agreed to open negotiations with Croatia at the same time as those with Turkey. Hence, the negotiating process officially began on 3 October 2005. Before substantive negotiations could begin, there was first a screening process, in which European Commission officials briefed the Turkish and Croatian Governments on the *acquis communautaire*, the EU's body of law. Officials of the two Governments then explained the progress made so far in applying these, and how they intended to proceed. By 12 June 2006 sufficient progress had been made to allow a meeting of EU foreign ministers, with the Turkish Deputy Prime Minister and Minister of Foreign Affairs, Abdullah Gül, to open and close the substantive negotiations on Chapter 24, dealing with science and research, in a single day.

THE EU AND FREEDOM OF EXPRESSION ISSUES

The EU continued to press Turkey for further human rights improvements, notably: the reduction of the political role of the military; the removal of some legal restrictions affecting Turkey's small non-Muslim communities; and wider freedom of expression.

On the last issue, a critical case arose in December 2005, when Orhan Pamuk, Turkey's best known modern novelist, was charged under Article 301 of the Penal Code for having 'denigrated Turkey and the Turkish people' for comments to a Swiss radio station about the Armenian massacres of 1915. The decision to prosecute him under Article 301 aroused a furore. Faced by an international outcry, the courts retreated and in January 2006 the charges against Pamuk were dropped.

By contrast, the Turkish Armenian newspaper editor Hrant Dink was convicted under Article 301. The novelist Elif Şafak was indicted under Article 301 for remarks made by a character in one of her novels, but acquitted in August 2006. A professor of Sumerian studies, Muazzez İlmiye Çığ, was tried in November for an article on ancient temple prostitutes, which allegedly insulted religion, while Perihan Mağden, a novelist and journalist, was prosecuted twice during the year, once for allegedly inciting disrespect towards the armed forces and later for alleged insult towards the teenage murderer of Father Andrea Santoro, the Trabzon priest killed in February (see below). The leftist magazine *Özgür Gündem* was barred for two weeks from printing and distributing operations.

On 19 January 2007 the situation took a much more serious turn when Hrant Dink was shot dead outside his office in İstanbul. His assailant, detected by a closed-circuit television camera, was a 17-year-old boy from Trabzon with apparent links to nationalist-religious movements of the far right. The killing was strikingly similar to the apparently ideologically motivated murder of a Roman Catholic priest, Andrea Santoro, by a youth in Trabzon in February 2006. The murder of Dink, a popular and respected figure among intellectual circles in İstanbul, caused a world-wide outcry and allegations of failure by the security forces to perform their duties effectively. The murder exposed the sharp divisions in Turkish society. After the killing, several thousand Turkish demonstrators marched under the slogan 'We are all Armenians', but the detained murderer was treated as a hero by some of the police officers holding him.

On 18 April 2007 there was further violence when three Protestant Christian missionaries, two foreign nationals and one Turkish Christian convert, had their throats cut and were repeatedly stabbed at a missionary publishing house in the central Anatolian town of Malatya by a group of youths. The killings brought a warning to Turkey from German Chancellor Angela Merkel on 23 April to do more to combat intolerance; 10 people were arrested in connection with the killings.

Turkish–French relations were already strained, creating an additional obstacle to Turkey's chances of EU accession. During mid-2006 the Government of President Jacques Chirac took several steps that seemed to point to growing alignment with Turkey's regional opponents. One was a military pact with the Greek Cypriots, allowing French forces to use the Andreas Papandreou Base in southern Cyprus. A second was a visit by President Chirac to Armenia on 29 September, in which he came close to saying that recognition of the 1915 events as a 'genocide' would be a pre-condition for Turkey's accession to the EU.

With the question of access by Greek Cypriot vessels to Turkish airports and harbours unresolved, EU leaders met in December 2006 to consider retaliatory measures. On 15 December it was agreed at the European Council that eight of the 35 chapters of the *acquis communautaire* would be blocked, and negotiations could not be closed on any chapter, until Turkey opened its ports.

THE 2007 PRESIDENTIAL AND PARLIAMENTARY ELECTIONS

In May 2007 the seven-year term of office of President Ahmet Necdet Sezer was due to end. Sezer had been a major stumbling block for the AKP Government during its time in office, making frequent use of his veto, not only for legislation but also for civil service appointments. He was also widely regarded, along with the military, as the main barrier preventing the AKP Government from introducing Islamist legislation, frequently warning the public that Turkey and its secular traditions were in danger.

Initially, Prime Minister Erdoğan planned to stand for the presidency himself. However, after repeated warnings from the military that it would not tolerate a First Lady who, like Erdoğan's wife, wore the Islamic headscarf, he decided to nominate the Minister of National Defence, Mehmet Vecdi Gönül, whose wife did not cover her head. However, the Speaker of the Grand National Assembly, Bülent Arınç, the leader of the more strongly Islamist faction in the AKP, insisted that the party's candidate should be the Deputy Prime Minister and Minister of Foreign Affairs, Abdullah Gül, whose wife wore the headscarf.

The first round of the presidential election was held on 27 April 2007, but the opposition CHP boycotted the polls. The AKP failed to get the requisite 367 votes, but could have expected to win the necessary straight majority in the later rounds. However, later that day the military posted a statement on its website implicitly threatening to stage a coup if the AKP persevered with Gül's candidacy. On 1 May the Constitutional Court upheld an application by the CHP to annul the vote on the grounds that the Grand National Assembly had been inquorate. The AKP responded by announcing that early parliamentary elections would be held on 22 July.

The AKP secured a resounding victory in the general election, with 46.7% of the popular vote, securing 341 seats in the Grand National Assembly. The CHP received 20.9% and 112 seats, an increase of 1.5% since 2002, but 66 fewer seats. This was because a third party had entered parliament. The MHP won 14.3% of the votes, enabling it to clear the 10% national barrier and re-enter the National Assembly with 71 members. Pro-Kurdish deputies contested the elections as independents, winning 23 seats and promptly forming a group for the DTP. It was the first time for 13 years that openly pro-Kurdish representatives had held seats in the Grand National Assembly.

Despite the AKP's landslide election victory, Erdoğan remained mindful of the military's threat and offered Gül the chance to withdraw his candidacy for the presidency. However, Gül remained undeterred and was duly elected President on 28 August 2007, securing the support of 339 deputies at the fourth round of voting.

Gül's first action as Head of State was to confirm the new Government under Erdoğan's premiership. The new Council of Ministers approved on 29 August 2007 included Ali Babacan as Minister of Foreign Affairs and Chief Negotiator of Turkey for European Union Affairs, and Beşir Atalay as Minister of Internal Affairs; however, it generally contained no surprises and very few changes. The new Government's programme contained a pledge to produce a new constitution, work on which was being carried out by a commission. On economic matters, the Government indicated that it intended to continue with free market policies aimed at boosting national prosperity. The new programme was put to a vote of confidence on 5 September, which was won easily, with 337 deputies voting in favour of the Government and 197 votes against; there was one abstention.

POST-ELECTION POLITICS—BID TO CLOSE THE AKP

Hopes that a new and more liberal era was about to open in Turkish politics proved misplaced. Although proposals for a new constitution were debated throughout the second half of 2007, as the year ended the AKP quietly shelved the issue. In the early months of 2008 the Government focused instead on a single and more contentious issue, the ending of the ban on Islamic female headdress in universities. The necessary two-thirds' majority in the National Assembly was secured after the MHP decided to support the change. However, the amendments were annulled by the Constitutional Court on 5 June, although by then the Government was facing a much more serious challenge. On 16 March the chief public prosecutor had applied to the Constitutional Court for the AKP to be outlawed on the grounds that it was attempting to eradicate secularism. He also appealed for 70 of its leading figures, including Prime Minister Erdoğan, to be expelled from the National Assembly and banned from holding political office for five years. The Constitutional Court announced its verdict on 30 July, finding the AKP guilty of attempting to undermine secularism, but narrowly voting to impose a US $20m. fine rather than closing the party down.

Emboldened by the Court's decision, the AKP began to shift from secularist practices to ones more in line with Muslim traditions, with education a key area of contention. Changes in the previously secularist-dominated higher education system began on 7 December 2007, with the replacement of the retiring head of the Higher Education Council, Erdoğan Teziç, with an AKP supporter, Yusuf Ziya Özcan. The first signs of a shift in university administration away from secularists and towards academics closer to the AKP came on 5 August 2008, when President Gül announced the appointments of 21 new university rectors, provoking the resignations in protest of several senior figures in the İstanbul Technical University and other universities.

ERGENEKON TRIAL AND ARRESTS OF AKP OPPONENTS

On 20 October 2008 the trial began of 86 people charged with belonging to an organization known as 'Ergenekon', a reference to a mythical valley in Central Asia where the early Turks were said to have taken refuge from their enemies. Prosecutors alleged that the suspects—many of whom were rivals or bitter enemies—were all members of a vast clandestine network that was attempting to stage a campaign of violence to undermine the AKP and precipitate a military coup. The case polarized opinion in Turkey. Newspapers supporting the Government presented allegations against those accused as if they were fact, and there were attempts to widen the accusations to include serving army officers and even some opposition leaders. Sceptics pointed to legal flaws in the process and to the unlikelihood of such a wide and disparate band of people, ranging from the disreputable to the highly respectable, being linked in a single conspiracy. The main common characteristic among the early waves of Ergenekon detainees was that they were all outspoken critics of the Government. However, the vociferous campaign in support of the prosecution, coming from leftist intellectuals (many of them former detainees under military rule) and Islamists, initially drowned out the protests of doubters, although the handling of the arrests and trials would have been regarded elsewhere as highly prejudicial.

THE PKK AND IRAQ: SUPPORT FROM THE USA

PKK violence remained a serious problem during the second half of 2007 and into 2008, with attacks continuing in south-eastern Turkey and occasional attacks on targets in metropolitan Turkey, such as the bomb attacks in Güngören, İstanbul, on 27 July 2008. Seventeen people were killed in what was believed to be the work of a PKK offshoot. A series of high-profile killings of Turkish troops serving in the east during the latter months of 2007 led Turkey to threaten a major incursion into Iraq. On 17 October the Grand National Assembly voted by 507 to 19, in a session held in camera, to authorize an incursion into Iraq to target PKK bases there.

The PKK continued to step up its attacks in south-eastern Turkey in late 2007, and on 22 October, less than a week after the Turkish parliamentary vote, 17 Turkish soldiers were killed near the Iraqi border. However, with Turkey clearly prepared to fight a regional war to stop PKK terrorist incursions into its territory, US policy changed. When Erdoğan visited the USA, he emerged from a meeting with President Bush on 5 November with the news that he had obtained US approval for air-strikes on PKK positions in northern Iraq. The USA also agreed to extensive intelligence-sharing, including the provision of satellite imagery of PKK assets.

On 16 December 2007 Turkish warplanes attacked PKK camps in northern Iraq, particularly the PKK headquarters on Mount Qandil, close to the Iranian border. However, despite these strikes and ongoing US support, PKK attacks continued to claim the lives of Turkish soldiers in south-eastern Anatolia into 2008.

Meanwhile, the civilian wing of the Kurdish nationalist movement in Turkey, the DTP, emerged from the July 2007 elections with 21 seats (originally elected as independents). However, the party was undermined by the removal of its chairman, Nurettin Demirtaş, to do military service, and by the threat of closure from the Constitutional Court.

EFFORTS TO IMPROVE RELATIONS WITH ARMENIA

Signs of a possible *détente* between Turkey and Armenia had been increasing in the previous few months. In August 2008 Armenia's President Serge Sarkissian issued an invitation to President Gül to attend a football match between the two countries. Gül accepted and travelled to the Armenian capital, Yerevan, on 6 September. It appeared for a while as if there might be a breakthrough in Turkish–Armenian relations. However, this failed to transpire as it became clear that Armenia's neighbour and Turkey's close partner, Azerbaijan, would not agree to Turkey lifting its sanctions against Armenia. These were introduced in the early 1990s after Armenia seized about 17% of Azerbaijan's territories, including Muslim majority districts around the disputed enclave of Nagornyi Karabakh, driving about a million people to seek refuge in Azerbaijan. Although the Turkish and Armenian Foreign Ministers met in Washington, DC, on 7 April 2009, and President Sarkissian indicated that recognition of the genocide would not be a precondition for the normalization of relations, there was no further discernible progress. On 31 August, however, the Turkish and Armenian Ministries of Foreign Affairs issued a joint statement, in which they announced an agreement to establish full diplomatic relations. On 10 October Turkey and Armenia signed a protocol in Geneva, Switzerland, which outlined the steps that they would take to restore full diplomatic and political ties. News of the agreement prompted a furious reaction from Azerbaijan. Fearful of losing one of its closest allies in the region, and the key to the AKP's goal of establishing Turkey as a hub for the transportation of hydrocarbons to Europe, the Turkish Government rapidly backed down, assuring Azerbaijan that any normalization of ties with Armenia would be dependent on the latter relinquishing its control over Nagornyi Karabakh. The parliaments in both Turkey and Armenia refused to ratify the protocol, and hopes of a rapprochement evaporated.

DOMESTIC POLITICS—PARTIAL SETBACK FOR THE AKP IN LOCAL ELECTIONS

The timing of the 29 March 2009 local elections was problematic for the AKP, as they coincided with the unemployment rate rising to around 15%. Nevertheless, the AKP comfortably won more votes than any other party, taking 39% of the ballot, compared with 23% for the main opposition CHP and 16.4% for the MHP. Although the AKP remained far ahead of its rivals, its total share of the vote had fallen far short of its expectations. Significantly, it lost ground to the pro-Kurdish DTP in the south-east of the country, with the AKP and the DTP each receiving around 50% of the votes in 15 provinces.

Erdoğan indicated that he had heard the warning messages from the voters, and on 1 May 2009 he responded with a major reorganization of his cabinet. In total, eight members of the previous cabinet were dropped and nine new ones appointed. The best known of the discarded ministers was the Minister of Finance, Kemal Unakıtan, who had held the role since 2002. He was replaced by Mehmet Şimşek, previously the Minister of State for the Economy and a former investment banker. The changes amounted to a slight strengthening of the pro-Islamist wing of the Government. Bülent Arınç, former President of the National Assembly and a leading member of the more conservative wing of the party, joined the Government as a Deputy Prime Minister. Prof. Dr Ahmet Davutoğlu, hitherto the main foreign policy adviser of the Prime Minister, replaced Ali Babacan as Minister of Foreign Affairs. Egemen Bağış, who was appointed Chief Negotiator of Turkey for European Union Affairs on 10 January, became a Minister of State for the first time. An important reform in education occurred in July 2009, when the Government removed restrictions that had prevented graduates of vocational high schools from entering university, and which effectively gave those schools—including those for training Islamist clergy—parity with the secular system. The change, which was likely to result in secondary education in Turkey gaining an increasingly religious hue, passed with little or no opposition from the once vociferous secular middle classes, a sign of their growing marginalization.

PROGRESS ON THE KURDISH ISSUE STALLED

In July 2009 the Government launched a series of meetings and consultations in order to identify Kurdish grievances and formulate ways to address them, but the process soon lost momentum. In an attempt to revitalize it, in October the Government announced that a group of PKK militants would soon arrive at Turkey's Habur border crossing with Iraq to commence what it described as a process by which the entire organization would eventually lay down its arms. However, the Government had neither sufficiently prepared the Turkish public nor established a legal framework to deal with the repatriation of the returning militants. When eight militants duly crossed the border on 19 October, they were greeted as conquering heroes by thousands of PKK supporters. The scale of the reception provoked strong criticism from nationalist opposition parties, which accused the Government of granting an amnesty to terrorists, and prompted a nationalist backlash, including violent public protests and attacks on ethnic Kurds living in western Turkey. Alarmed by the public outcry, the Government cancelled plans for the return of another group of PKK militants and instead launched a crackdown on the Kurdish nationalist movement. On 11 December the Constitutional Court formally outlawed the DTP, dissolving the party and confiscating its assets. Over the months that followed hundreds of Kurdish nationalists were imprisoned on charges of belonging to a PKK 'umbrella' organization, the Koma Civakên Kurdistan (KCK—Union of Communities of Kurdistan).

Although most of the DTP's parliamentary deputies transferred to another pro-Kurdish party, the Bariş ve Demokrasi Partisi (BDP—Peace and Democracy Party), the dissolution of the DTP and the KCK arrests appeared to strengthen those who argued that the only way to extract concessions from the Turkish state was through violence. In June 2010 the PKK announced that it was intensifying its campaign of violent action.

TENSION OVER CONSTITUTIONAL REFORM

In March 2010 the Government announced a package of proposed constitutional reforms, which it claimed would expedite Turkey's accession to the EU and resolve persistent constitutional disputes between the executive, legislative, judicial and military branches of the Turkish state. The chief amendments proposed by the Government included: a restructuring of the Supreme Council of Judges and Public Prosecutors, the Constitutional Court, and the Council of State, which would result in greater government control over their composition and activities; revised criteria for the dissolution of political parties and the establishment of a parliamentary commission to oversee closure cases; measures to allow the trial of military personnel in civilian courts and to limit the jurisdiction of military courts over civilians; the removal of immunity from prosecution for the instigators of the 1980 military coup; allowing collective bargaining for civil servants; the establishment of the office of Ombudsman; and the removal of barriers to the introduction of positive gender discrimination. The Government embarked on a series of consultations with opposition parties in an effort to secure the required two-thirds' parliamentary majority for the legislation, but refused to allow separate votes on the individual measures, insisting that they be voted on as a single bill. The CHP rejected the proposals, accusing the ruling party of seeking to increase its control over the apparatus of the judiciary. None the less, the AKP possessed sufficient support within the Grand National Assembly to trigger a public referendum on the package. Following the approval of President Gül, it was announced by the High Electoral Board that a public referendum on the reforms was to be held on 12 September 2010. As with the parliamentary vote, the measures were put to a referendum as a single package, denying voters the ability to approve or reject specific changes. The Government's refusal to include any measures to address the grievances of Turkey's Kurdish minority resulted in the pro-Kurdish BDP organizing a largely successful boycott of the referendum in predominantly Kurdish areas of the country. Nevertheless, in Turkey as a whole, 57.9% of voters approved the reforms. Over the following months the Government implemented the changes that increased its control over the judiciary, including restructuring all of the higher courts and reducing the jurisdiction of military tribunals, although by mid-2012 the other measures had yet to be introduced.

A NEW ERA IN THE CHP

In mid-May 2010 Deniz Baykal was forced to resign as leader of the CHP, following allegations published in the media regarding his private life. At a party conference held in Ankara later that month, Kemal Kılıçdaroğlu was elected unopposed as leader. Although it was ostensibly a social-democratic party, under Baykal the CHP had become characterized by strident Turkish nationalist rhetoric and its relentless criticism of the AKP's policies rather than an ability to offer solutions. Despite his failure to inspire the Turkish electorate, Baykal had proved highly adept at consolidating his power base within the party. As a result, before he could return it to its social-democratic roots, Kılıçdaroğlu had first to purge the CHP of Baykal loyalists. After an initial surge following Kılıçdaroğlu's appointment, popular support for the CHP began to wane during mid-2010, amid very public party infighting. Kılıçdaroğlu's first test came during the campaign for the September referendum on the Government's proposed changes to the Constitution, which the CHP opposed. A normally reserved politician, in the referendum campaign Kılıçdaroğlu made the mistake of trying to match Prime Minister Erdoğan's abrasive, hectoring rhetorical style, an approach that was as unconvincing as it was ultimately unsuccessful. Nevertheless, during late 2010 and early 2011 Kılıçdaroğlu gradually succeeded in removing nationalist Baykal loyalists from positions of power in the CHP, replacing them with liberals and social democrats and moving the party's policy platform towards the centre-left. However, in a country with a traditionally strong electoral bias towards parties of the centre-right, this appeared likely to reduce rather than enhance the CHP's prospects of eventually assuming power. A further disadvantage was that Kılıçdaroğlu was a member of the Alevi religious community, at a time when there had been a marked increase in the Sunni majority's sense of Islamic identity.

DETERIORATION IN RELATIONS WITH ISRAEL

Since early 2009, following a public disagreement in January between Prime Minister Erdoğan and Israeli President Shimon Peres regarding the conflict in the Gaza Strip, the previously cordial relations between Turkey and Israel deteriorated significantly. In October Turkey announced the cancellation of Israel's involvement in a major military exercise.

In May 2010, nine Turks were killed during a raid by Israeli marine commandos on a ship, the MV *Mavi Marmara*, bound for the Gaza Strip. The ship had been chartered by a Turkish charitable organization, İnsan Hak ve Hürriyetleri ve İnsani Yardım Vakfi (IHH—the Foundation for Human Rights and Freedoms and Humanitarian Relief), as part of a flotilla of vessels attempting to break the Israeli blockade of Gaza. Erdoğan responded by recalling the Turkish ambassador to Israel, while also accusing Israel of carrying out an act of 'state terror'. Israeli Prime Minister Netanyahu insisted that Israeli troops had acted in self-defence after being attacked by pro-Palestinian activists on board the ship. Erdoğan responded by declaring that the re-establishment of normal ties between the two countries was impossible unless Israel issued a formal apology, paid compensation to the families of those killed and lifted its blockade of Gaza. Israel offered to express its regret over the incident but refused to apologize or meet any of Erdoğan's other demands. In early September 2011, following the publication of the findings of a UN inquiry into the incident, Davutoğlu announced that Turkey would, with immediate effect, downgrade its relations with Israel to second secretary level and suspend military co-operation between the two countries, citing the Israeli Government's refusal to apologize for the deaths.

RENEWED CONCERNS OVER FREEDOM OF EXPRESSION

The Ergenekon investigation was expanded from late 2008, and many more government opponents were arrested and imprisoned on charges of belonging to an alleged clandestine organization dedicated to conspiring to overthrow the AKP administration. The accused comprised journalists, academics, doctors, lawyers, public prosecutors, members of organized crime groups, serving and retired military personnel, former covert operatives, opposition politicians, and members of secular non-governmental organizations (NGOs).

Many other cases followed, most notably the 'Sledgehammer' investigation into an alleged coup plot. A detailed plan of the alleged coup was given anonymously to a pro-AKP journalist in January 2010. During the months that followed over 200 serving and retired members of the Turkish military, including more than 10% of the country's serving generals and admirals, were arrested and imprisoned on charges of complicity in the alleged coup plot. Initially, many people had been prepared to accept the main allegations in the cases. However, as the absurdities and contradictions of the cases began to emerge, those who questioned the conduct of the investigations became targets themselves. In August Hanefi Avci, a respected police chief, wrote a book detailing how he believed the police force had been infiltrated by AKP supporters who falsified evidence and fabricated charges against the Government's opponents. On 28 September, two days before he was due to hold a press conference at which he had promised to provide documentary proof to back up his allegations, Avci was arrested and imprisoned. He was subsequently charged with membership of Ergenekon.

In early February 2011 an internet television channel, OdaTV, announced that it had acquired video footage of the police involved in the Ergenekon investigation planting evidence, including arms caches, in premises associated with some of the accused. On 14 February the police raided OdaTV's office, arrested the journalists who had uncovered the video footage and charged them with membership of Ergenekon. On 3 March nine left-wing journalists, who had initially welcomed the Ergenekon investigation but had recently begun to express concerns that the police were fabricating evidence, were arrested and imprisoned on charges of being members of Ergenekon. Fearful of meeting a similar fate, most independent journalists began to exercise self-censorship. In July, when a court was forced to release a young army officer, Emrah Küçükakça, after he provided irrefutable proof that the police had planted evidence in his apartment, the news received almost no coverage in the Turkish media, nor was any attempt made to launch an investigation into the police officers involved.

THE 2011 GENERAL ELECTION

Increasing concerns about freedom of expression and the politicization of the police and justice system intensified in the run-up to the general election of 12 June 2011. In late 2010 the AKP had announced that, if re-elected, it would introduce a new constitution to replace the one promulgated in 1982 during a period of military rule. During early 2011 opinion polls consistently suggested that the AKP would win the election by a comfortable margin. The only question was whether it would win the 367 seats required to approve a new constitution through parliament or the 330 seats necessary to put the draft of a new charter to a referendum.

Opinion polls indicated that popular support for the CHP was running at 26%–28% and 11%–12% for the ultra-nationalist MHP. As a result, the AKP sought to attract Turkish ultra-nationalist voters to push the MHP under the 10% threshold for representation in the Grand National Assembly and to increase the number of AKP seats. During the election campaign AKP officials adopted fierce Turkish nationalist, and often anti-Kurdish, rhetoric in an attempt to undermine the MHP. More disturbing was the broadcasting on the internet of a series of covertly recorded videos of leading members of the MHP apparently engaged in sexual relations. A total of 10 leading members of the MHP, including nine of the 17 members of the party's National Executive, subsequently stood down as parliamentary candidates in the election. The number of the videos, and the professional manner in which they had been recorded, led to accusations that they were the work of government sympathizers in the police. No evidence was ever produced to incriminate AKP sympathizers. However, the perception that the MHP was the victim of a government-backed defamation campaign resulted in a net increase, rather than a decline, in its popular support, and the party won 13.0% of the votes in the general election and 53 seats in the Grand National Assembly. Candidates backed by the BDP, who were running as independents in order to circumvent the 10% threshold for political parties, won another 36 seats, more than expected, mainly as a result of traditionally pro-AKP Kurds being alienated by the Turkish ultra-nationalist rhetoric adopted by the ruling party during the election campaign. Nevertheless, the AKP still won 49.8% of the vote and 326 seats, well ahead of the CHP with 26.0% and 135 seats.

Further controversy followed when the Yüksek Seçim Kurulu (YSK—High Electoral Board) declared one of the successful BDP-supported candidates to be ineligible for election, citing a previous criminal conviction. The YSK instead awarded the seat to a member of the AKP, thus reducing the number of pro-BDP parliamentary deputies to 35 and increasing the AKP's representation to 327 seats. In an equally controversial move, the courts refused to release from gaol two successful CHP candidates, who were being held on remand under the Ergenekon investigation, and five successful pro-BDP candidates, who were being held on remand as part of the KCK trial.

KURDISH DECLARATION OF DEMOCRATIC AUTONOMY

Since it launched its second insurgency in 2004, the PKK has primarily used violence in order to pressure the Turkish authorities into making political concessions rather than to seek a military victory. Short, intense bursts of violence were followed by longer periods of lower levels of activity, in an attempt to give the Government an opportunity to make concessions or engage in dialogue.

On 31 May 2010 the PKK launched another period of sustained activity when it killed six members of the military in an attack on a naval base near İskenderun, on Turkey's eastern Mediterranean coast. Over the next weeks, PKK militants staged a series of attacks on military targets in south-east Turkey, as well as carrying out a number of bombings in cities in the west of the country. On 13 August the PKK announced that it would once again scale back its campaign during the run-up to the constitutional referendum of 12 September, in the hope that the AKP would use the subsequent consolidation of its grip on power to initiate peace negotiations. Hopes of dialogue were raised still further by the gradual acknowledgment in a series of public statements by Prime Minister Erdoğan that the Turkish state had long been engaged in intermittent negotiations with imprisoned PKK founder Öcalan.

However, not only was no dialogue forthcoming, but the Turkish authorities continued to arrest and imprison Kurdish nationalists on charges of membership of, or support for, the PKK. On 28 February 2011, shortly before the spring thaw began to open the mountain passes in the PKK's main battlegrounds in south-east Turkey, the organization announced another period of intensified violence. Previously, the PKK leadership in the Qandil mountains of northern Iraq had consulted with Öcalan before making any important strategic decisions, communicating with him by means of his weekly meetings with his lawyers. However, when the Turkish authorities repeatedly prevented Öcalan's lawyers from meeting with him, the PKK leadership announced the intensification in violence, leaving Öcalan with little option than to endorse a *fait accompli*.

Another shift in the focus of Kurdish nationalism occurred during early 2011, when a coalition of groups and organizations led by the BDP and known collectively as the Demokratik Toplum Kongresi (DTK—Democratic Society Congress) launched a campaign of civil disobedience in protest against the continuing arrests of Kurdish nationalists, particularly in relation to the KCK trial. The campaign was largely symbolic, including mass public protests and appeals for the boycotting of state-controlled mosques. However, the DTK warned that, unless the AKP started to address Kurdish grievances, it would begin to push for what it termed 'democratic autonomy' and the devolution of some of the powers of the central Government to the regions.

Both the PKK and the DTK scaled back their campaigns in the run-up to the 12 June 2011 general election in the hope that, emboldened by a renewed mandate, the AKP would finally focus on Kurdish concerns. However, such hopes rapidly faded when, after its landslide victory, the Government continued with the Turkish nationalist rhetoric that had characterized the AKP's election campaign. In frustration at the Government's refusal to address Kurdish grievances and the ongoing arrests and detentions of Kurdish nationalists, on 14 July the DTK issued a proclamation of democratic autonomy. In the short term, the announcement appeared unlikely to have a practical impact on the administration of the Kurdish regions in the south-east of the country. However, in terms of long-term Kurdish demands, it effectively set a new minimum level for the concessions that the Kurdish nationalists would accept.

The DTK's proclamation of democratic autonomy was warmly endorsed by the PKK, amid further signs that the organization's leadership in the Qandil mountains was now making all major strategic decisions independent of Öcalan. On 29 July 2011, in apparent response to what he feared was his growing marginalization within the Kurdish nationalist movement, Öcalan issued a statement announcing his withdrawal from any attempt to solve the Kurdish issue and fiercely criticizing both the BDP and the PKK.

ADJUSTING TO THE ARAB REVOLUTIONS

The appointment of Ahmet Davutoğlu as Minister of Foreign Affairs in May 2009 was followed by an intensification of Turkey's efforts to form closer political and economic ties with the other Muslim countries of the Middle East. Bilateral trade boomed, and Turkey established what it termed 'High-Level Strategic Co-operation Councils', in which ministers from Iraq, Syria, Jordan and Lebanon held regular joint meetings with their Turkish counterparts. In addition, the AKP Government abolished visa requirements for almost all of the Muslim countries in the Middle East.

To the concern of its Western allies, particularly the USA, the Turkish Government also cultivated closer ties with Iran. In September 2009 Erdoğan defended Iran's lack of transparency over its uranium enrichment programme and dismissed evidence that the country was accelerating its pursuit of weapons-grade material as 'gossip'. During early 2010 Davutoğlu travelled several times to Tehran, the Iranian capital, to try to broker an agreement that would prevent additional international sanctions. In May, acting together with Brazil, Turkey persuaded Iran to accept an agreement that included an exchange of 1,200 kg of its own low-enriched uranium for foreign nuclear fuel for a research reactor. However, the deal was rejected by the international community, which moved forward with plans for additional sanctions. In June Turkey, then a non-permanent member of the UN Security Council, voted against the imposition of further UN sanctions on Iran, although its opposition was not enough to prevent the approval of the measures.

Although it was sometimes portrayed as a strategic shift from West to East, Turkey's eagerness to foster closer ties with other Muslim countries was based more on a desire to establish itself as a regional power. The Turkish Government's attempt to create its own zone of influence was built primarily on forming close links with the ruling élites in the region. The main exception was Egypt, where the ruling AKP had always aligned itself more closely with the opposition Muslim Brotherhood than the regime of President Muhammad Hosni Mubarak. As a result, after cautiously endorsing the popular protest movement in Tunisia, the AKP administration vigorously welcomed the uprising in Egypt. On 1 February 2011 Erdoğan became the first world leader to urge Mubarak to step down.

However, the situation changed when the unrest in the Arab world during early 2011 spread to Libya. The Turkish Government had enjoyed a warm relationship with Libyan leader Muammar al-Qaddafi, and in November 2010 Erdoğan had even flown to Libya to receive the Qaddafi International Prize for Human Rights. Initially, the Government was outspoken in its support for the Qaddafi regime, and on 1 March 2011 Erdoğan publicly warned that Turkey would veto any attempt by NATO to intervene on the side of the rebels in the civil war in Libya. However, amid growing concerns within the Government that Turkey risked not only international isolation but also supporting the losing side, its position began to shift. On 27 May Turkey joined other NATO members in approving a plan under which the Alliance would assume command of all air operations in Libya.

The Turkish Government had formed even closer political and personal ties with the regime of Syrian President Bashar al-Assad than it had with Libya. Similarly, the AKP administration initially refused to condemn Syria's brutal suppression of pro-reform protests. However, as the death toll began to mount and thousands of Syrian refugees fled into Turkey, the Government's policy started to change. Gradually, it began to distance itself from the Syrian regime, appealing to the Syrian security forces to exercise restraint and urging Assad to implement comprehensive reforms. At the same time, the Turkish authorities began to allow Syrian opposition groups, including the Free Syrian Army (FSA), to operate freely in the country, particularly in the growing refugee camps along the Turkish–Syrian border. With Assad still showing no sign of willingness to implement reforms, on 22 November 2011

Erdoğan again publicly urged him to resign. Over the following months Turkey became one of the most outspoken supporters of the Syrian rebel groups fighting to overthrow Assad, allowing elements of the Free Syrian Army (FSA) to operate in Turkey and helping to facilitate its purchases of arms and equipment with funds supplied by Qatar and Saudi Arabia.

The Arab uprisings also had a negative effect on Turkey's relations with Iran. The Turkish Government suspected that Iran had been instrumental in fomenting Bahrain's Shi'a Muslim majority against the ruling Sunni élite in February 2011, while the deployment in eastern Anatolia of an early warning radar as part of NATO's proposed missile shield was heavily criticized by Iran. Turkish officials vigorously denied that the radar was aimed at Iran in particular. However, the Iranian Government was unconvinced and accused Turkey of acting as a proxy for the USA, even threatening to target Turkey if Iran ever came under attack by the USA or Israel.

A NEW DOMESTIC POWER STRUGGLE

In the run-up to the June 2011 election, Erdoğan had announced that it would be the last time that he would stand for parliament. Although he had refrained from saying so publicly, it was an open secret that, once the AKP had been returned to power, Erdoğan planned to push through a new constitution replacing Turkey's parliamentary system with a presidential one and then to have himself elected President for two successive five-year terms.

Initially, the scale of the AKP's electoral victory boosted his presidential ambitions by demonstrating that none of the opposition parties was in a position to challenge him. However, this also galvanized dissident elements within the Turkish Islamist movement, particularly followers of the Islamic preacher Fethullah Gülen, who had gone into exile in the USA in 1999. Since the 1980s, Gülen's followers had gradually built up a vast network of schools, NGOs, businesses and media organizations. Although relations between Erdoğan and Gülen's supporters had always been strained, they had allied themselves with the AKP against the secularist regime which had ruled Turkey since the foundation of the Republic in 1923.

Gülen's supporters had become particularly influential in the police and judicial systems and—allied with the organization's media outlets—had been the main driving force behind controversial investigations such as Ergenekon and 'Sledgehammer'. However, they were now moved to action by Erdoğan's steps toward the establishment of a presidential system. On 8 February 2012, while Erdoğan was recovering from surgery, public prosecutors affiliated with the Gülen Movement issued a summons to Fidan regarding allegations that he had collaborated with the PKK in holding secret negotiations in Oslo in 2010. Before being appointed to head MİT, Fidan had served as Erdoğan's security advisor and was considered to be an ally of Erdoğan. As a result, Erdoğan interpreted the summons as a direct challenge to his authority.

The public prosecutors who had issued the summons were promptly reassigned to other duties. During the months that followed, hundreds of suspected Gülen sympathizers in the police and judicial system were marginalized or reassigned to lowly positions in the provinces. Although Erdoğan appeared to have won the first round of the power struggle, the Gülen Movement still exercised considerable influence through its network of NGOs and media outlets and more tensions appeared likely as Erdoğan pushed ahead with his plans to introduce a presidential system.

DIALOGUE WITH ÖCALAN

In July 2012 the PKK launched a new phase in its long-term insurgency, increasing its attacks against the Turkish security forces and—for the first time since the early 1990s—attempting to control territory in south-eastern Turkey. Initially, the strategy was successful. By late August 2012 large areas of the mountainous district of Şemdinli on the Turkish–Iraqi border had become virtually impassable to the Turkish security forces. During September, however, the Turkish military gradually regained the initiative. By late October, when winter conditions put an end to the campaigning season, it had reduced the area under PKK control and used its superior strength to inflict heavy casualties. However, the PKK's initial successes had given it confidence and it began to prepare to return to the offensive in the spring of 2013.

Even though his isolation on the prison island of İmralı meant that he could no longer influence the organization's tactics and strategies, Öcalan remained a revered figure, both to the PKK and to the broader Kurdish nationalist movement. From December 2012 Turkish officials held discussions with Öcalan about a possible negotiated end to the PKK insurgency. They also began to ease the terms of his confinement, allowing him to receive occasional visits from representatives of the BDP, who were then able to relay messages from Öcalan to the rest of the Kurdish nationalist movement.

Many in the PKK regarded the dialogue with Öcalan as a Turkish Government ruse to weaken the organization and prevent it from returning to the offensive in the spring of 2013. Öcalan was more optimistic, appearing confident that he could persuade the Turkish state to introduce reforms to address Kurdish demands, including for greater cultural rights and a large measure of autonomy for south-eastern Turkey. When, on 22 March, Öcalan called for a suspension of violence, owing to his iconic status the PKK had little option but to comply. On the following day the organization announced an indefinite unilateral cease-fire. On 8 May it began to withdraw its fighting units from Turkey, pending a successful conclusion of Öcalan's negotiations with the Turkish state.

Öcalan had expected the Turkish state to begin substantive peace negotiations as soon as the PKK militants began to withdraw. However, Turkish officials refused even to start talks until the withdrawal was complete, a process that was expected to continue until October 2013. Meanwhile, in his public speeches Erdoğan explicitly excluded the possibility of ever allowing the Kurds full language rights or autonomy.

In mid-July 2013 both Öcalan and the PKK leadership in northern Iraq issued statements setting the Turkish Government a deadline of October for the implementation of substantial concessions to their demands or risk a return to violence. Turkish officials continued to insist that they would not even begin negotiations until all of the PKK's fighting units had withdrawn from Turkish territory.

REGIONAL ISOLATION

When Erdoğan publicly called on President Assad to resign in November 2011, the AKP had calculated that the civil conflict in Syria would be short and that Assad's Alawite regime would be replaced by a predominantly Sunni government, which would look to Turkey for leadership. However, the conflict increasingly exposed the limitations of Turkey's external ambitions. On 22 June 2012 Syria's air defences shot down a Turkish F-4E *Phantom* reconnaissance aircraft, after it crossed into Syrian air space. The AKP threatened retribution and increased its military presence along the Turkish–Syrian border. With Turkish public opinion overwhelmingly opposed to any military intervention in Syria, however, the AKP's response was confined to rhetoric.

As the Syrian civil war intensified, the number of Syrians seeking refuge in Turkey steadily rose. In mid-2012 there were an estimated 20,000 Syrian refugees in Turkey. By September 2013 the number of Syrian refugees registered with the Office of the UN Commissioner for Refugees (UNHCR) in Turkey had increased to more than 484,000, either housed in one of the 17 organized camps or scattered through towns and cities close to the border, resulting in considerable friction with the local population.

From early 2013 Turkey had begun to come under increasing pressure from its Western allies, particularly the USA, to suppress the movements of members of extremist organizations such as the al-Nusra Front. The AKP started to restrict movements across the Turkish–Syrian border, which caused tensions—and occasional clashes—between the Turkish security forces and the rebel groups. On 11 February a car bomb at the Cilvegözü border-crossing killed 17 people. On 11 May two car bombings in the Turkish border town of Reyhanlı killed 52 people. Although no conclusive evidence has emerged to identify the perpetrators, in the weeks following the attack the local people in Reyhanlı staged a series of public demonstrations, accusing the AKP of pursuing policies that had involved their community in the violence of the Syrian civil war.

The AKP's hopes of regional pre-eminence suffered another blow when the Egyptian army ousted President Muhammad Mursi on 3 July 2013. Although the Muslim Brotherhood had regional aspirations of its own, the AKP had regarded Mursi's retention of power as key to its goal of an alliance of conservative Sunni regimes, which—it was hoped—Turkey would eventually dominate. The AKP vigorously denounced the military intervention in Egyptian politics and its subsequent crackdown on the Brotherhood. However, this brought Turkey into conflict with its former allies in the bid to overthrow Assad, Saudi Arabia and Qatar, both of which had welcomed Mursi's overthrow.

CONSERVATIVE AUTHORITARIANISM AND THE GEZI PROTESTS

During late 2012 and early 2013 Erdoğan sought to concentrate ever more de facto political power in his own hands and become more assertive in seeking to implement measures which reflected his personal views and values. In November 2012 the producers of a television series set in the Ottoman imperial court were forced to change both its script and its costumes, after Erdoğan complained that it failed to reflect the Ottomans' adherence to conservative Muslim values. In April 2013 he declared that he had decided that the non-alcoholic yoghurt beverage *ayran* would now be known as the Turkish national drink. In early May he announced that legislation would be introduced to restrict the sale of alcohol. The legislation was hurriedly adopted in the Grand National Assembly in the early hours of 24 May, with Erdoğan adding a number of last-minute changes. These included a requirement that any depiction of alcoholic beverages on television or in the cinema was to be blurred, on the grounds that it would otherwise encourage alcohol consumption. On 29 May the AKP held an inaugural ceremony for the construction of a third bridge across the Bosphorus. It was announced that the bridge would be named after Sultan Selim I, who is reviled by members of the country's Alevi minority for massacring many thousands of the Alevi community in the 16th century.

Erdoğan had long sought to make his mark on İstanbul by redeveloping the Taksim Square area, the symbolic heart of the modern city. His plans included the construction of a shopping mall and mosque complex at Gezi Park adjacent to the square. Despite the lack of necessary permits, preliminary work on the project had started in late 2012. On 28 May 2013 a small number of environmentalists began a peaceful protest in the park in an attempt to prevent workers uprooting its trees. Whenever they were driven out by riot police, they waited and then returned to resume their peaceful protests. On 31 May, as a video of a particularly brutal assault by the police was widely viewed on the internet, the number of protesters suddenly began to rise. By the end of that day many thousands—most of them young members of Turkey's previously largely apolitical educated middle class—had joined the protests. Finally, on 1 June the police were forced to withdraw from Taksim Square and Gezi Park.

The Gezi Park protests precipitated weeks of similar demonstrations across the country. Five protesters were killed, thousands injured and over 700 arrested. Erdoğan furiously condemned the protests as a plot by foreign 'dark forces' who were jealous of Turkey's return to greatness under his rule. The police eventually regained control of Taksim Square and Gezi Park. By mid-July 2013 the Taksim Square redevelopment project had been suspended pending a court ruling on its legality, and the number of protests and their intensity had both declined. The protests had, nevertheless, transformed the domestic political environment, further polarizing an already deeply divided society.

Economy

Revised for this edition by MEHMET UĞUR

INTRODUCTION

Turkey is about 1,450 km (900 miles) long and some 500 km (300 miles) wide, covering an area of 783,562 sq km (302,535 sq miles). The census of October 2000 recorded the population at 67,803,927. At December 2012, and on the basis of the new address-based population registration methodology, the population was reported at 75,627,384. These totals excluded Turks working abroad, the majority of whom are in Germany. Turkey's population density increased from 72.4 per sq km in October 1990 to 98.3 per sq km at the end of 2012. İstanbul, the country's largest city, had an estimated population of 13.7m. at December 2012 (compared with 8.8m. in 2000). It is followed by Ankara (the capital) and İzmir, with estimated populations of 4.8m. and 3.7m., respectively. Projections indicate that Turkey's population will exceed that of Germany by 2025.

The country possesses significant natural advantages: fertile land yielding a wide variety of grains, fruit and vegetables, and other products; an extensive range of minerals; and a number of natural ports. The climate is varied and, on the whole, favourable. Turkey's gross domestic product (GDP) per head on a purchasing-power parity (PPP) basis was US $15,320 in 2010, well below the average of $34,025 for Organisation for Economic Co-operation and Development (OECD) member states. Since the late 1960s millions of Turks have gone abroad to seek employment, mainly in Western Europe, but also in some Middle Eastern countries such as Libya, Saudi Arabia and the other states of the Persian (Arabian) Gulf. However, out-migration has recently fallen due to stricter visa regimes in Europe and falling demand for Turkish labour in the Middle East.

Severe economic, political and social volatility in the late 1970s led to a recession in 1980, when gross national income (GNI) contracted by 1.1%. In 1980–90 GNI, at constant 1987 prices, increased at an average annual rate of 5.5%, with a growth rate of 9.2% in 1990. In 1991 the adverse effects of the Gulf War led to growth of just 0.9%. GNI growth improved in 1992 and 1993, but, after a severe financial crisis early in 1994 and an austerity programme in April, GNI contracted by 6.1% in that year. Nevertheless, GNI growth resumed quickly, increasing by 8% in 1995 and 7.9% in 1996. The strongest sectoral growth in both years was recorded in trade and industry.

Figures published by OECD revealed that, although income per head rose by 6.1% in 1995, to US $2,928, the wealthiest 20% of the population had an income of $8,037 per head, while the poorest had only $717, giving Turkey the worst income distribution of all OECD countries, except Mexico. According to World Bank estimates, GNI rose by 8.6% in 1997, yielding a GNI per head of $3,130 on a conventional exchange-rate basis and $6,470 on a PPP basis. In 1998, as a result of adverse external factors such as the financial crisis in Russia (Turkey's second most important trading partner), GNI growth decelerated to 3.9%, yielding GNI of $3,160 per head on a conventional exchange-rate basis and $6,594 on a PPP basis.

A sharp decline in economic growth had already been predicted for 1999 before two major earthquakes in north-western Turkey in August and November inflicted huge damage on industry and infrastructure. Consequently, GNI contracted by 6.4%, resulting in per-head income decreasing to US $2,878 and GDP declining by 5%. By mid-2000 a recovery appeared to be under way, as reflected in the 5.6% GDP growth in the first quarter. In November, however, the fragility of the recovery was exposed by a major banking and stock market crisis, in which the Central Bank of the Republic of Turkey expended some US $7,000m. to support the lira, before the Government secured an additional stand-by facility of $7,000m. from the IMF in December. In 2000 overall GDP growth stood at 3.5%; total GDP amounted to $198,800m. (or $455,500m. on a PPP basis), producing GDP per head of $3,000 ($6,800 at PPP).

The respite proved to be only temporary. First, a Central Bank plan to restore credibility to the currency after a decade of high inflation, by introducing a new lira equivalent to TL 1m. on 1 January 2001, was abandoned. Then, following a public clash between the President and the Prime Minister in February over the latter's alleged failure to combat corruption, the financial system neared collapse in Turkey's worst economic crisis in recent years. A massive flight of capital forced the Government to float the lira and to accept an immediate devaluation of over one-third (see Budget, Investment and Finance). The devaluation-induced consumer price increases prompted widespread protests, amid rumours that another military takeover was imminent. Difficult negotiations with the IMF resulted in the approval in May of a further stand-by credit equivalent to US $8,000m. (bringing the total granted to Turkey since December 1999 to a record $19,000m.), but only on even stricter conditions that long-promised economic restructuring and counter-inflationary measures would at last be implemented, including reductions in subsidies, reform of the banking sector and privatization of state-owned enterprises. Following the crisis, which was aggravated by the economic effects of the September 2001 suicide attacks on the USA, expected GDP growth of 4.5% in 2001 turned into a contraction of 7.4%. GNI decreased by 9.4% and inflation rose to 68.5%. Total GDP in that year declined to $148,166m. (or $427,000m. at PPP), giving a per caput GDP figure of $2,226 (or $6,419 at PPP).

The economic crisis necessitated the conclusion in February 2002 of a new agreement with the IMF for a stand-by credit of SDR 12,800m., with renewed pledges of structural reform. Although the political crisis that developed in mid-2002 and the calling of a general election for early November created new uncertainties for the economy, a growth rate of 7.8% was recorded in 2002, with total GDP rising to US $182,848m. (or $453,300m. at PPP). According to the World Bank, total GNI was $173,300m. ($438,000m. at PPP) in 2002 and GNI per head was $2,500 ($6,300 at PPP). The official rate of unemployment rose to 10.3% in 2002 (from 8.4% in 2001), while the inflation rate was restrained to 29.7%.

The US-led military campaign in Iraq during March–April 2003 posed further difficulties for the Turkish economy, not least because Turkey opted to forgo around US $30,000m. in aid and loans from the USA by refusing to allow US troops to pass through Turkey to invade Iraq. The US Government eventually granted a loan of $8,500m. in return for access to Turkish airspace, but Turkey encountered new difficulties with the IMF, which in May withheld a $476m. tranche of the latest stand-by credit, owing to slow progress in the Turkish economic reform programme. However, an extended review of Turkey's compliance resulted in the IMF Executive Board deciding in August to release the stand-by tranche and to extend the repayment period into 2006. Further releases of $502m. in December 2003, $495m. in April 2004 and $661m. in July of that year brought total disbursements under the 2002 stand-by arrangement to about $17,000m. of the $19,000m. available.

Strong economic growth of 5.9% in 2003 produced a GDP of US $492,900m. and per caput income of $7,216 (both on a PPP basis). The official rate of unemployment increased slightly, to 10.5% of a total labour force of 23.6m., while the inflation rate was restrained to 18.4%. Vigorous growth continued in 2004, at a rate of 9.9%, and inflation was halved to 9.5%, while official unemployment declined to 9.3%, its lowest level for 30 years. On a PPP basis, total GDP in 2004 was $551,900m. while GDP per head stood at $8,015. In May 2005 the IMF approved a further stand-by arrangement of SDR 6,660m. (about $10,000m.) to support Turkey's economic and financial programme until May 2008 (see Budget, Investment and Finance).

Economic recovery and more solid financial foundations were symbolized by the long-delayed introduction on 1 January 2005 of the new Turkish lira (YTL), equivalent to 1m. old lira and subdivided into 100 kuruş. (The name of the currency reverted to Turkish lira on 1 January 2009, although YTL banknotes and coins remained in circulation for a further year.) The GDP growth rate remained high in 2005, at 7.7%, but it subsequently began to slow down towards the 5% long-run growth rate projected by OECD. Even before the global financial crisis affected the country, GDP growth rates were in decline, decreasing to 5.0% in 2007 and 1.1% in 2008. In 2009 GDP contracted by some 4.8% as the effects of the financial crisis took hold. Growth resumed in 2010, with GDP expanding by 8.2% and continued in 2011, when growth was recorded at 8.5%. However, lower GDP growth rates have been recorded in recent years due to implementation of tighter monetary policy to deal with inflationary pressures, and reduce the current account deficit, which was equivalent to about 10% of GDP in 2011. GDP growth was 2.2% in 2012. OECD estimated growth rates of 3.1% for 2013 and 4.6% for 2014.

AGRICULTURE AND FISHING

Turkey relies substantially on agriculture. It is the largest producer and exporter of agricultural products in the Middle East and North Africa, although the sector's overall role has shrunk considerably over recent decades and Turkey has not been self-sufficient in food production in recent years. In 2011 the agricultural sector accounted for 25.5% of total employment. The sector has been constrained by high rates of interest and inflation, structural deficiencies such as fragmented and small land holdings, a lack of grassroots farmers' organizations and poor marketing facilities. Efforts to remedy such deficiencies formed part of the Government's structural reform programme that followed the financial crises of November 2000 and February 2001 and was shaped by Turkey's aspiration to join the European Union (EU) and its commitments under the IMF conditionality. Although the slow pace of eliminating subsidies came under repeated IMF and World Bank criticism in 2002–03, the producer support estimate (PSE) of 26.5% in 2004 (as a percentage of the value of gross farm receipts) was lower than the OECD average of 29.9%. However, by 2005 the PSE in Turkey had increased to 32.1%, overtaking the OECD average, which declined to 27.8% in that year. By 2009 Turkey's PSE had increased further, to 36.9%, while the OECD average had declined to just 22.4%.

Nearly 25m. ha, or about one-third of the total land area, are in some sort of agricultural use. However, the area devoted to permanent crops decreased from 4.1% in 1980 to 3.2% in 1996, while irrigated land rose from 9.6% to 15.4% of cropland over the same period. The irrigated area rose from 4.3m. ha in 1996 to 4.9m. ha in 2003. Of Turkey's 4m. agricultural units, about 60% are small, the average size of a family farm being only 6 ha. The principal agricultural exports by value are hazelnuts, cotton, tobacco, grapes and citrus fruits. Other important crops are barley, sunflower and other oilseeds, maize, sugar beet, potatoes, tea, and olives.

Following the introduction of land reforms and the improved utilization of land, machinery and farmer education resources, agricultural output increased by some 30% in 1971, but in subsequent years the expansion targets set in successive five-year plans were not met. In 1980–90 the rate of increase continued to fluctuate, leading to an average annual growth rate of 1.3%. In 1990–96 an average annual increase of 1.2% was recorded. By 2000–04 the average annual growth rate had declined to 0.8%. Agriculture provided 59.4% of total export revenue in 1979, but the proportion declined to about 20% in the late 1980s and to 13.6% in 1994, increasing to 15.8% in 1999. The sector's share of export revenue then contracted to 13.9% in 2000 and 9.4% in 2004. In 2007 agriculture's share of export revenue was less than 7%. The agricultural sector, including forestry and fishing, contributed 14.9% of GDP in 1999. Thereafter, agriculture's share of GDP declined, from around 12% in 2000–04 to 7.7% in 2008. However, the sector's share increased to 9.1% during the recession in 2009 and remained higher than the levels observed after the mid-2000s. Agriculture's share of GDP was 9.5% in 2010 and 9.2% in 2011.

Government policy aims to increase agricultural productivity and improve animal husbandry, but budget constraints mean that funding comes mainly from international sources, notably the World Bank. However, there is increasing foreign commercial interest in developing Turkish agro-industry, particularly for Middle East export markets. In an attempt to alleviate the poverty of the south-eastern provinces of Turkey, the Government drew up the South-East Anatolia Project (Güneydogu Anadolu Projesi—GAP) in the early 1980s, covering a total area of 74,000 sq km. Some 495 projects were integrated into GAP, which envisaged the construction of 22 dams on the Tigris and Euphrates rivers and their tributaries, 19 power plants, and an irrigation network with the potential to cover 8.5m. ha. GAP has been affected by delays resulting from attacks by Kurdish separatists and disputes over financing. In 1994 two water pipelines were opened. At the end of 2010 TL 30,600m. of a total projected TL 42,100m. had been invested in GAP.

About one-half of the cultivated area is devoted to cereals, of which the most important is wheat. The principal wheat-growing area is the central Anatolian plateau, but the uncertain climate causes wide fluctuations in production. Barley, rye and oats are other important crops grown on the central plateau. Maize is grown along the Black Sea coastal regions, and leguminous crops in the İzmir hinterland. Rice, normally sufficient for domestic needs, is grown in various parts of the country. In the 1990s the annual wheat harvest usually stayed above 18m. metric tons per year, owing to good weather, improved cultivation methods and increased levels of irrigation. Between 2005 and 2009 annual wheat production stood at approximately 21m. tons, declining to 17.7m. tons in 2008, before recovering to 20.6m. tons in 2009. Wheat production was 19.7m. tons in 2010 and 21.8m. ton in 2011.

Production of tuber crops (mainly potatoes and onions) was 7.8m. metric tons in 1995, and fluctuated at around 7.0m. tons per year in 2002–05 and 6.0m. tons in 2006–10. In 2010 and 2011, tuber crop production remained stable, at 6.5m. tons. Output of pulses declined from 1.8m. tons in 1995 to just under 1.2m. tons on average in 2010 and 2011. Total vegetable production increased from 18.3m. tons in 1995 to 25.8m. tons on average in 2010 and 2011.

Cotton has traditionally been Turkey's main export earner, grown mainly in the İzmir and Adana regions. In recent years it has lost some of its traditional importance, although the irrigation of agricultural land in the eastern Haran region has revived its fortunes. Production of cotton lint decreased from 851,487 metric tons in 1995 to 791,000 tons in 2000, before increasing to 900,000 tons in 2003. From 2004 to 2006 average production of cotton lint was approximately 900,000 tons, and stood at 960,000 tons in 2007. Turkey remained the world's seventh largest producer of cotton lint, with production recorded at 816,705 and 954,600ton in 2010 and 2011. Cotton seed output amounted to 1.3m. tons in 1995 and, according to FAO figures, remained at about that level in 2003–07. Turkey was the seventh largest producer of cotton seed, with output recorded at 1.3m. and 1.5m. tons in 2010 and 2011. Sugar beet production increased from 11.2m. tons in 1995 to an estimated 18.8m. tons in 2000, as a result of a 25% increase in the land area devoted to the crop (440,000 ha). As a result of reduced subsidies, sugar beet production decreased after 2002 and remained at around 14.5m. tons during 2004–06. In 2007 sugar beet production declined to 12.4m. tons, before increasing to 15.5m. tons in 2008, 17.9m. tons in 2010 and 16.1m. tons in 2011.

Turkey produces what is regarded as a particularly fine type of tobacco for consumers. The three principal producing regions are the Aegean district, the Black Sea coast and the Marmara-Thrace region. The bulk of the crop is produced in the Aegean region, where the tobacco is notable for its light golden colour and mild taste. The finest tobacco is grown on the Black Sea coast, around Samsun. Although a traditional Turkish export, its relative position as an export staple has been declining in recent years. Most of Turkey's tobacco exports go to buyers in the USA and Eastern European countries. Until the end of the 1990s, production fluctuated considerably—from a record level of 324,000 metric tons in 1976 and 1993 to a low level of 204,000 tons in 1995. Production rose to 286,000 tons in 1997, but decreased to 200,000 tons in 2000. In 2000–03 tobacco production averaged about 150,000 tons, and this declined to an average level of 136,000 tons during 2004–06. In 2007 tobacco production declined significantly, to 74,584 tons, but it rose to 93,400 tons in 2008, before decreasing again, to 85,000 tons in 2009, 55,000 tons in 2010 and 45,000 tons in 2011. In 1999 260,000 ha were devoted to the crop, compared with 210,000 ha in 1995, but by 2003 the area had declined to 183,000 ha, before increasing slightly, to 190,000 ha, in 2004 and 2005. The area devoted to tobacco cultivation stood at 147,000 ha in 2008, 139,000 ha in 2009, 81,000 ha in 2010 and 80,000 ha in 2011.

In 1984 the Government permitted the first legal imports of foreign cigarettes in more than 40 years, breaking the monopoly over sales and distribution held by the state-owned tobacco and beverages agency, TEKEL. A new cigarette factory in İzmir, as part of a joint venture between the US tobacco company Philip Morris and the local Hacı Ömer Sabancı Holding AŞ, produces popular US brands for the domestic market. However, TEKEL (the privatization of which was completed in 2005) has responded by raising capacity and output and improving the quality of its brands, notably by producing cigarettes with Virginia tobacco.

The coastal area of the Aegean, with mild winters and hot, dry summers, produces grapes, citrus fruits, figs and olives. Exports of dried figs were valued at US $53m. in 1993, France being the main customer. Production of figs declined from 240,000 metric tons in 2000 to 235,000 tons in 2001, before rising to 280,000 tons in 2003. In 2004–06 average annual fig production was around 285,000 tons, but production decreased to 205,000 tons in 2008. Production of figs subsequently increased once again, to 244,000 tons in 2009, 255,000 tons in 2010 and 260,508 tons in 2011. The outstanding product, however, is the sultana type of raisin. Turkey normally ranks second in the world as a sultana producer, but in years of good yields becomes the largest producer in the world. Average sultana production was around 245,000 tons per year during 2000–04, increasing to an average of 260,000 tons in 2005–07. Production of all varieties of grapes fluctuated between 3.5m. tons and 4.0m. tons during 2000–08, with a trough of 3.3m. tons in 2001 and a peak of 4.0m. tons in 2006. Grape output averaged 4.3m. tons per year in 2009–11.

The citrus fruit sector expanded steadily from 1995 to 2001. Over this period annual production of oranges increased from 842,000 metric tons to 1.25m. tons; mandarins from 453,000 tons to 580,000 tons; and grapefruit from 65,000 tons to 135,000 tons. In 2003 citrus fruit production included 1.25m. tons of oranges, 550,000 tons of mandarins and 135,000 tons of grapefruit. Between 2005–11 these figures averaged 1.6m. tons for oranges, 845,000 tons for mandarins and tangerines, 190,000 tons for grapefruit and pomelos and 760,000 tons for lemons. Other significant fruit production in 2011 included 2.7m. tons of apples, 676,000 tons of apricots, 439,000 tons of sweet cherries, 546,000 tons of peaches and nectarines, 386,000 tons of pears, and 269,000 tons of plums and sloes.

The Black Sea area, notably around Giresun and Trabzon, produces the greatest quantity of hazelnuts (filberts) of any region in the world, having been grown there since 300 BC. A harvest of 625,000 metric tons was recorded in 2001. Subsequently, production declined to 350,000 tons in 2004, owing to reduced support prices, before increasing to 661,000 tons in 2006. Hazelnut production rose to 800,791 tons in 2008, but decreased to 500,000 tons in 2009 before increasing once again, to 600,000 tons in 2010. In 2011, hazelnut production followed the bi-annual cycle and fell to 430,000 tons, Turkey is the world's leading producer and exporter of hazelnuts, accounting for more than 50% of global output and trade in hazelnuts. Significant quantities of walnuts, almonds and pistachios are also grown, with an output of 183,000 tons of walnuts, 69,838 tons of almonds and 112,000 tons of pistachios in 2011.

Tea is grown at the eastern end of the Black Sea, around Rize, and in other areas. Production increased from the early 1980s to reach 199,000 metric tons in 1999, but declined to 139,000 tons in 2000; output had recovered to 154,000 tons by 2003, increasing further, to 218,000 tons, in 2005, before declining to 206,160 tons in 2007. Average tea production was around 220,000 tons during 2008–11.

Turkey is also an important producer of oilseeds, principally sunflower, groundnut, soybean and sesame. Total oilseed production was 1.2m. metric tons in 2000, but decreased to an annual average of 980,000 tons in 2004–07. Moreover, the country is a major producer of olives, the output of which is subject to fluctuations owing to the two-year flowering cycle. Olive production was 850,000 tons in 2003, before surging to 1.6m. tons in 2004. During 2004–11 average olive production was 1.5m. tons per year.

Until 1972, Turkey was one of the seven countries with the right to export opium under the UN Commission on Narcotic Drugs. Much opium, however, was exported illegally, particularly to the USA and Iran. Partly as a result of pressure from the US Government, the Turkish Government made the cultivation of opium poppies illegal in 1972, but the ban was lifted in July 1974 and the flowers are grown in certain provinces under strict controls. Opium gum is no longer tapped from the living plant. The poppy pods (opium straw) are sold to the Government, which processes them into concentrate for export as the basis for morphine and other drugs.

Sheep and cattle are raised on the grazing lands of the Anatolian plateau. Stock-raising forms an important branch of the agricultural sector. The sheep population is mainly of the Karaman type and is used primarily as a source of meat and milk. The bulk of the clip comprises coarse wool suitable only for carpets, blankets and poorer grades of clothing fabric. However, efforts have been made in recent years to encourage breeding for wool, and there are some 200,000 Merino sheep in the Bursa region. The Angora (Ankara) goat produces the fine, soft wool known as mohair. Turkey is one of the world's largest producers of mohair, with an average output of about 9,000 metric tons per year. Poultry meat has displaced traditional meats such as lamb, mutton and goat in domestic consumption patterns. In 2011 the number of heads of cattle, sheep and goats was 11.3m., 23.1m. and 6.3m., respectively. Although several government projects have been introduced to increase productivity, the ratio of meat output to heads of livestock animals has remained largely stable.

Turkey has 8,333 km of coastline and some 1,200 inland water resources, but fishing potential has been curtailed by over-fishing, pollution and ecological changes. Although the fisheries sector grew by 8% in 1997 and by 6% in 1998, it accounted for only 2% of overall agricultural production in 1998. The development of aquaculture in inland waters has been one of the aims of the GAP, while the Black Sea Fishery Improvement Project aims to increase catches within a sustainable framework. In 1998 a five-year project for increasing turbot production was launched at the Black Sea port of Trabzon, with Japanese technical and financial assistance. In 1999 there were 17,475 Turkish fishing vessels and 55,000 fishermen were licensed, while 200,000 people were directly employed in the fishing industry and 2m. indirectly. In 2003 the fisheries sector contributed TL 1,307,900,000m. to GNI; its share rose to TL 1,786,500,000m. in 2004, representing 0.4% of GNI. The total catch fell from 587,700 metric tons in 2003 to 546,100 tons in 2005, but amounted to 623,900 tons by 2009, rising further to 655,000 tons in 2010 and 703,700 in 2011. The total included a significant increase in aquaculture fishing, which climbed up from 119,200 tons in 2005 to 188,900 metric tons in 2011.

MINERALS AND MINING

Turkey has a diversity of rich mineral resources, including significant quantities of bauxite, borax, coal and lignite, chromium, copper, iron ore, manganese and sulphur. The mining and quarrying sector employed some 134,000 workers in 1999. The size of the work-force employed in the sector declined to 83,000 in 2003, before increasing again, to 119,000 in 2005 and 128,000 in 2006 and 2007. In 2010 the size of the sectoral work-force decreased to 115,000, but it increased slightly, to 125,000, in 2011. In that year the sector's share of GDP, at 1.7%, was negligible, and it engaged only 0.5% of the employed population. Similarly, the share of mining and quarrying exports including oil and gas in total export earnings also remained low, at approximately 0.3% in 2011 and 2012. In contrast, the share of mining and quarrying products in the total cost of imports was 22.5% and 25.5%, respectively, in those years. Imports of oil and raw materials are major contributors to Turkey's persistently high current account deficit.

The most important state-owned enterprise in the mining sector was Etibank, established in 1935, which worked through its subsidiaries, Ereğli Coal Mines, East Chromium Mines, Turkish Copper, Keban Lead Mines and Keçiborlu Sulphur Mines. During the early 1960s state-owned enterprises increased their predominance over the private sector, with an investment programme that was supported by the Mining Investment Bank, established in 1962. The policy of encouraging the private sector to play a greater part in the mining industry, through the establishment of the Turkish Mining Bank Corpn in 1968, has failed to overcome the general reluctance of private investors to view mining as a worthwhile area for long-term investment, with the result that the private sector is under-capitalized. An additional factor militating against the development of mining has been the long-held suspicion of foreign investment in mining. A law enacted in 1973 restricted foreign participation in mining development projects. However, this restriction was relaxed in January 1980, allowing up to 49% foreign participation in mining ventures. In response, the publicly owned Etibank entered into a joint-venture agreement with a US company (Phelps Dodge) in 1983 for copper-mining. Etibank was privatized in 2001, followed by the mining department (Eti Holding AŞ). Eti Holding AŞ disposed of most of its mining subsidiaries and in 2004 was renamed as Eti Mine Works. Eti Mine Works is still publicly owned, but its mining operations are limited mainly to boron production.

Bituminous and anthracite coal is found at and around Zonguldak, on the Black Sea coast. Most of the seams are of good coking quality, the coke being used in the steel mills nearby Karabük. In 2004 total coke production amounted to 2.8m. metric tons, compared with 3.3m. tons in 2002 and 3.1m. tons in 2003. Coke production increased slightly, to approximately 3.1m. tons in 2005 and 2006 and to 3.2m. tons in 2007. As of 2011, coke production was 5.6m. tons. Lignite is found in many parts of central and western Anatolia, and possible total reserves are estimated at up to 8,000m. tons. Production of lignite amounted to 49.6m. tons in 2002, declining to 43.7m. tons in 2003 and 2004. However, production increased during 2005–09, reaching 82.3m. tons in the latter year. In 2010 and 2011, lignite production was 74.4 m. and 89.8m. tons, respectively. Lignite is used to generate almost 50% of Turkey's electricity output. Seams located in western Turkey are operated by the West Lignite Mines. The other main mines are at Soma, Degirmisaz and Tunçbilek. Lignite deposits at Afsin Elbistan are being developed, with extensive German and international financial assistance, as part of an ambitious integrated energy project designed to increase capacity generating by 1,360 MW.

Practically all of Turkey's iron ore comes from the Divrigi mine, situated between Sivas and Erzurum, in the north-east of the country, and operated by the Turkish Iron and Steel Corpn (Ereğli Demir ve Çelik Fabrikalari TAŞ—Erdemir). The average grade of ore is from 60% to 66%, and reserves were estimated at 149.9m. metric tons in 2005. Output of gross iron ore increased from 1.7m. tons in 1979 to a peak of 5.5m. tons in 1992, but had declined to 3.4m. tons in 2002. Then output increased to 4.6m. tons in 2005. Between 2006-2011, the average level of production remaind close to 5m. tons per year.

Turkey is one of the world's largest producers of chromite (chromium ore). The richest deposits are in Güleman, south-eastern Turkey, in the vicinity of İskenderun; in the area around Eskişehir, north-western Anatolia; and between Fethiye and Antalya on the Mediterranean coast. The Güleman mines, producing 25% of the country's total, are operated by East Chromium Mines. Other mines are owned and worked by private enterprise. Little chromium is used domestically, but the mineral is a major earner of foreign exchange. Output of chromite declined from a peak of 0.8m. metric tons of ore, mined in 1977, to less than 0.5m. tons per year in the early 1980s, but recovered to reach 1.5m. tons in 1989. In the 1990s chromium production fluctuated between 0.5m. tons and 1.5m. tons, most of this in the private sector. Chromium output decreased sharply in the early 2000s, before recovering to 0.5m. tons in 2004 and 0.7m. tons in 2005. After a decline in

2006, chromium production increased to 1.7m. tons in 2007, 1.9m. tons in 2008 and 1.6m. tons in 2009. In 2010 and 2011 production was around 1.9m. tons. Turkey accounts for less than 1% of world chromium ore reserves but produces more than 8% of the world output.

Copper has been mined in Turkey since ancient times. Current production comes from the Ergani Mines, at Maden in Elazığ, and the Morgul Copper Mine, at Borçka, in Çorum province. Production of blister copper has tended to fluctuate, decreasing from 36,000 metric tons in 1986 to 27,500 tons in 1994. Since 1996 annual production of blister copper has consistently been about 33,000 tons, but increased to 58,000 tons in 2003. By 2007, however, production had increased to 81,000 tons. Further increases were recorded in 2008 and 2009, with outputs of 100,000 and 105,000 tons, respectively, In 2010 and 2011 copper production fell significantly to 97,000 and 80,000 tons, respectively. Crude aluminium (aluminia) output was around 162,000 tons in 2003; and has remained at that level since then. Most of the output is exported to Germany, the United Kingdom and the USA. Known reserves of copper ore are estimated at 90m. tons.

Eskişehir, in north-western Anatolia, is the world's leading centre for meerschaum-mining. Meerschaum, a soft white mineral that hardens on exposure to the sun and looks like ivory, has long been used by Turkish craftsmen for pipes and cigarette holders.

Manganese, magnesite, lead, sulphur, salt, asbestos, antimony, zinc and mercury are important mineral resources. Of these, manganese ranks first in importance. Deposits, worked by private enterprise, are found in many parts of the country, but principally near Eskişehir and in the Ereğli district. In 2005 manganese production stood at 52,273 metric tons and accounted for 0.5% of world production. Lead is mined at Keban, west of Elazığ, with an average annual production of 25,000 tons per year from 2009-2011. Production of sulphur (public sector only), mainly from the Keciborlu mine, in Isparta province, totalled 39,000 tons in 1987. Antimony is mined near Balıkesir and Niğde. Antimony production in 2005 stood at 28,377 tons, accounting for 20.7% of world output. Antimony reserves in Turkey represented 2.7% of world reserves in 2005. An important source of mercury deposits, which may amount to 440,000 tons, has been found at Sizma, in Konya province. Large uranium deposits have been discovered in the Black Sea, between 1 km and 2 km below sea level. Turkey's first commercially viable silver mine was opened in January 1988. In April 1996 a project to develop Turkey's first gold mine (reserves were discovered in 1990) near Bergama, in İzmir province, was finally approved. In 2002 potential gold reserves were officially estimated at 440 tons. Despite public opposition, successive governments have encouraged gold-mining in western Turkey. Consequently, gold production increased to 9,920 kg in 2007 and 14,469 kg in 2009. As of 2011, gold production stood at 23,248 kg.

The Uludağ (Bursa) tungsten deposits are among the richest in the world. However, Turkey is not a major producer of tungsten. Other minerals are barytes, perlite, phosphate rock, boron minerals, cinnabar and emery. Turkey supplies more than 80% of the world market for emery.

PETROLEUM AND NATURAL GAS

Petroleum was first discovered in Turkey in 1950, and all subsequent discoveries have been in the Hakkari basin, in the south-east of the country. It is mostly heavy-grade petroleum with a fairly high sulphur content. Production of crude petroleum has fluctuated since it reached 3.5m. metric tons in 1973. Owing to the small size of Turkey's main oilfields in the fractured terrain of the south-eastern Hakkari basin, petroleum production declined steadily from 1980 to 1985. Production increased in the early 1990s and reached 3.9m. tons in 1993; then it declined gradually to 3.4m. tons in 1997, 2.9m. tons in 1999 and 2.6m. tons in 2001. In 2003 petroleum production rose to 2.8m. tons, at an average of 59,000 barrels per day (b/d), but output decreased to an 2.1m. tons (43,000 b/d) in 2004. Recently, production was around 2.5m. tons over the period 2008-2011. Petroleum production in Turkey covers only about 8% of total consumption.

Turkey also produces natural gas, its largest non-associated field being the offshore Marmara Kuzey field in the Thrace-Gallipoli basin of the Sea of Marmara. In July 2001 it was announced that gas had been discovered in Mersin and İskenderun bays in south-western Turkey, while in March 2002 the new Gocerler gas field in the Thrace basin began production 16 months after its discovery. Annual gas production stood at about 800m. cu m during 2005–07 but fell to 650m. cu m during 2008–11. Gas production was 669.8m. cu m in 2011. However, domestic production never exceeded 5% of domestic consumption, which was 21,180m. cu m in 2004 and 35,100m. cu m in 2009. In the latter year 53% of the gas consumed was utilized for electricity generation, 25% was used by industry and 22% by households; almost 98% of the gas consumed in 2009 was imported. Domestic gas consumption of 41,200m. cu m was recorded in 2011.

Imports of mineral fuels and oils rose from US $5,375.3m. in 1999 to $9,529.3m. in 2000, when they accounted for 17.5% of the value of total imports. In 2001 imports declined to $8,288.6m., but accounted for a larger share (20.3%) of total imports as the latter fell dramatically due to the deep recession in that year. In 2002 their value was $9,021.6m., accounting for 17.6% of total imports. The corresponding figures in 2003 and 2004 were $11,574.9m. (16.7%) and $14,407.1m. (14.8%). Between 2009 and 2012 mineral fuel and oil imports continued to increase, accounting for 25.5% of total imports by 2012. Turkey's dependence on imported petroleum and gas has increased as domestic growth rates and international prices increased. Petroleum and gas imports accounted for 6.3% of the total value of imports in 2011 and 8% in 2012. Saudi Arabia is Turkey's main supplier of petroleum, with substantial volumes also imported from Iran, Libya and Iraq. Russia supplies 70% of Turkey's gas imports, with most of the remaining balance coming from Algeria and Nigeria.

Three main companies produce petroleum: the Turkish Petroleum Corpn (TPAO), a 99% state-owned Turkish company, which accounts for about 80% of total oil output; subsidiaries of the Royal Dutch Shell Group; and of the US ExxonMobil group. In 1983 the Government introduced a new law intended to liberalize conditions for foreign companies, enabling them to export as much as 35% of any onshore petroleum that they discovered, and up to 45% of any offshore output, prompting several joint venture exploration agreements between major foreign oil companies and TPAO.

Refining and other downstream operations are dominated by the state-owned Turkish Petroleum Refineries Corpn (TÜPRAŞ), which has four refining complexes: Batman in the south-east, Aliaga near İzmir, İzmit near İstanbul and the Central Anatolian Refinery at Kırıkkale near Ankara. Of the country's total refining capacity of 720,000 b/d, TÜPRAŞ has a market share of about 80% and has instituted a modernization programme to switch to lighter refined products. The country's largest refinery, at İzmit, with a capacity of 226,000 b/d, suffered extensive fire damage following an earthquake in August 1999. Turkey's sole private refinery is ATAŞ, near Mersin on the Mediterranean coast, a joint venture of Mobil, Shell, BP and a local company.

Having privatized a 31.5% stake in TÜPRAŞ (for US $2,300m.) in 2000, the Government confirmed in July 2001 that its holding would be reduced to under 50% by a further offering. In 2000 the Government had also privatized a majority stake in Petrol Ofisi AŞ (POAŞ), the dominant petroleum distributor, while plans were drawn up for partially privatizing the state oil and gas pipeline authority, BOTAŞ. In May 2001 new legislation liberalized the country's gas market, ended BOTAŞ's monopoly in gas importation, and separated the company into units for gas importation, transport, storage and distribution by 2009, in preparation for their privatization (except for the transport unit). The Government sold its remaining shares in POAŞ through a public tender in 2002 and a deal with the controlling group in August. Responding to IMF pressure, the Government confirmed in the same month that it intended to privatize most of the rest of the country's energy sector. A major petroleum market reform bill, proposed in March 2003, provided for the liberalization of the pricing of oil and oil products, as well as the integration of pipeline, refining and distribution functions. Further legislation approved in December aimed to remove remaining state controls in the sector, to liberalize pricing of petroleum and petroleum products, to end restrictions on merging procedures, and to integrate pipeline, refining and distribution functions. In early 2005 14.8% of government-owned shares in TÜPRAŞ were sold to institutional investors based abroad. In a privatization tender process in September, a consortium comprising Koç Holding AŞ and Royal Dutch Shell acquired a 51% share in TÜPRAŞ for $4,140m.

TPAO operates a 500-km pipeline running from the oilfields around Batman to Dörtyol on the Gulf of İskenderun. A 986-km pipeline from Kirkuk, in northern Iraq, to Turkey has a capacity of 1.5m. b/d. Completion and full commissioning of a second pipeline, alongside the first, took place in July 1987. Following the imposition of economic sanctions on Iraq by the UN in August 1990, the twin pipeline from Kirkuk to Turkey's Mediterranean terminal at Ceyhan remained closed until December 1996, costing BOTAŞ an estimated US $400m. per year in lost revenues. However, the reopening of the pipeline did little to curb the large-scale smuggling of Iraqi oil into Turkey, estimated at up to 100,000 b/d and costing the Turkish treasury large sums in lost tax revenue. Turkey's National Security Council launched a new operation in March 2000 to suppress oil-smuggling, not only from Iraq but also from Iran, Georgia, Azerbaijan, Syria and Bulgaria, and by July claimed to have reduced such activity by 50%.

Turkey is looking to the Caspian Sea and Central Asia to provide most of its future oil and gas needs, and is involved in several projects to develop supplies there. In 1994 TPAO became part of the Azerbaijan International Operating Company, a consortium of foreign petroleum companies in a production-sharing agreement with Azeri state oil company SOCAR, to develop offshore oilfields in the Caspian Sea. TPAO also became a partner in the Azeri Shah Deniz field in 1996 and has established a petroleum exploration company with the Government of Kazakhstan.

Oil and gas transportation is a controversial issue in the Caspian Sea and Central Asia regions. Turkey, Russia and Iran are competing to route the rich energy resources of Azerbaijan, Kazakhstan, Turkmenistan and Uzbekistan through their territories en route to Western markets. Turkey's main priority has been a 1,760-km oil pipeline to transport 1m. b/d of Azeri and Kazakh Caspian Sea petroleum from Baku in Azerbaijan through Georgia and then across Turkey to the Mediterranean port of Ceyhan, at an estimated construction cost of US $4,000m. The Governments of Turkey, the USA and Azerbaijan all declared their support for the Baku–Ceyhan route, which would reduce dependence of Caspian Sea energy exports on Russia and bypass Iran. In November 1999 Turkey, Azerbaijan, Georgia and Kazakhstan signed a legal framework agreement to enable what was renamed the Baku–Tbilisi–Ceyhan (BTC) pipeline to proceed. In February 2001 Chevron Texaco of the USA, which had previously opposed the pipeline, announced its willingness to join the Main Export Pipeline Company (MEPCO), while the following month a memorandum of understanding on the pipeline was signed in Astana, the Kazakh capital, by the Governments of Turkey, Azerbaijan, Georgia and Kazakhstan. Construction of the Turkish section of the pipeline began in September 2002, and the pipeline was finally opened in May 2005, at a ceremony in Baku. The BTC pipeline has a projected lifespan of 40 years. In 2009 it transported 1m. b/d (160,000 cu m) of oil. The volume of oil transported through BTC increased to 1.2m. b/d in 2010 and 1.4m. b/d in 2011.

Turkey's enthusiasm for the BTC pipeline has been due to its concerns about the use of the crowded Bosphorus to export petroleum. In July 1994 Turkey imposed stricter controls for ships transporting hazardous goods through the Bosphorus, following a collision in March. Russia, which exports some 70% of its petroleum by way of the Bosphorus, protested against the measure. As a longer-term solution to potentially dangerous congestion in the Bosphorus and resultant expensive delays to supertankers, a number of 'Bosphorus bypass' pipelines are under consideration, including one linking the Black Sea coast, north of İstanbul, to the Aegean Sea near the border with Greece. In 2011 the Government announced a plan to build a 50-km-long canal linking the Black Sea to the Sea of Marmara through the European part of İstanbul, in an attempt to alleviate congestion in the Bosphorus. Feasability studies for the project commenced in early 2012.

Demand for natural gas is projected to rise steadily in Turkey over the next two decades, although not as dramatically as was being forecast before the economic crisis in 2001 and resultant price deregulation. The main consumers are still expected to be industry and power plants, in view of the Government's identification of gas as the preferred fuel for future power generation for economic, environmental and regional political reasons. However, as a result of the downward revision of demand forecasts, in 2001–02 Turkey found itself committed to 'take or pay' contracts for far more natural gas than it was expected to need, the excess being projected at more than 25% by 2010. Nevertheless, the risks caused by this 'excess commitment' are now less significant because of the intensified search among Western European countries to diversify their sources of supply in the face of dependence on Russia.

In December 1997 Turkey and Russia signed a 25-year contract (the so-called 'Blue Stream' agreement) for a large increase in Russian natural gas supplies, mostly to be delivered via a 1,210-km dual pipeline, linking Isobilnoye in southern Russia to Dzhugba on the Black Sea coast, under the sea to the Turkish port of Samsun and on to Ankara, and possibly eventually to Lebanon, Syria, Israel and Greece. The agreement envisaged the import of an additional 3,000m. cu m of gas per year through the pipeline, with an increase to 16,000m. cu m by 2010. Russian supplies received through the Black Sea pipeline would supplement those received by Turkey through the existing pipeline route (crossing Ukraine, Moldova, Romania and Bulgaria), so that Russia would continue to provide at least one-half of Turkey's total annual demand for imported gas well into the 21st century. Work on what would be the world's deepest underwater gas pipeline was finally completed, one year behind schedule, in October 2002, at a cost of US $3,200m., with gas flows commencing in March 2003. In the following month, however, Turkey announced a six-month halt to imports through the pipeline because of over-supply of gas, thus raising doubt over whether the agreement with Russia would be fully discharged. In November Gazprom announced that it had resolved the dispute, reportedly agreeing a significantly lower price for the gas being supplied.

Another source of natural gas supply to Turkey is via a pipeline from Iran, for which a US $20,000m. agreement was concluded in August 1996, for the construction of a 1,400-km pipeline from Tabriz, in Iran, to Ankara. Despite US disapproval, Turkey proceeded with the project and awarded the contract for the construction of the first section of the pipeline, from the Iranian border to Erzurum, in early 1997; the second section, from Erzurum to Ankara, was to be built at a later date. Each country was to be responsible for financing the section of the pipeline in its own territory. Following delays in completion, for which each side blamed the other, an agreement was reached in January 2000 that deliveries would commence in mid-2001. However, in July inauguration of the pipeline was postponed, owing to what Turkey described as technical difficulties on the Iranian side, although Iran denied that it was to blame for the further delay. The pipeline was eventually inaugurated in January 2002, with Iranian supplies of gas to Turkey expected to rise from 3,000m. cu m in 2002 to 10,000m. cu m by 2007. By early 2011 Iran was reported to be the largest supplier of crude petroleum to Turkey, accounting for 30% of the total.

A separate scheme for the shipment of gas from Turkmenistan to Turkey is the Trans-Caspian Gas Pipeline (TCGP), on which BOTAŞ signed an agreement with Turkmenistan in May 1999, envisaging the construction of a 1,690-km pipeline running under the Caspian and via Azerbaijan and Georgia to Turkey. The pipeline would transport up to 30,000m. cu m of gas per year to Turkey, with additional gas possibly being sent onwards to Europe. However, although Turkish officials argued that Turkey's anticipated future gas needs would support more than one new pipeline, some observers regarded the TCGP proposal as a direct competitor to the 'Blue Stream' and other pipeline projects and pointed out that major gas reserves recently discovered in Azerbaijan's Shah Deniz field are much closer to Turkey. Pending further progress on the TCGP project, in March 2001 Turkey signed a bilateral agreement with Azerbaijan providing for the supply of gas, mainly from the Shah Deniz field over 15 years, starting in 2005 with imports of 2,000m. cu m, which were expected to rise to 6,500m. cu m by 2008. In late 2001 the Azeri and Georgian parliaments ratified the necessary transit agreements for a 1,000-km pipeline linking Baku to Erzurum via Georgia, which would have an initial capacity of 22,000m. cu m a year, rising to 30,000m. cu m, and so would be able to pipe gas from Turkmenistan, when, and if, the TCGP was constructed, to Baku. The South Caucasus pipeline came on stream in December 2006, and supplies to Turkey began early the following year.

In December 2003 Turkey signed an agreement with Greece, providing for the construction of a 300-km pipeline through which, commencing in 2006, up to 11,000m. cu m per year of gas would be pumped from Bursa in Turkey to Komotini in northern Greece, for onward diversion to Western European markets. Work on the pipeline officially began in July 2005 with a ceremony, attended by the Turkish and Greek Prime Ministers, on the River Meric/Evros border between the two countries. It was stated that the longer-term aim was to extend the pipeline to Italy as part of the Southern Europe Gas Ring Project.

Nabucco is a further pipeline project, involving the construction of a pipeline extending 3,300 km. The Nabucco Pipeline will be connected near Erzurum with the Tabriz–Erzurum pipeline, and with the South Caucasus Pipeline. As a result, Nabucco will also be connected with the planned Trans-Caspian Gas Pipeline. When complete, it will allow transportation of natural gas from the Middle East and the Caspian region countries such as Iran, Azerbaijan and Turkmenistan to Western Europe and to the countries along its path. The western end of the pipeline will be Baumgarten an der March, a major natural gas hub in Austria. The construction work is estimated to cost €9,000m. (US $12,600m.), and the transport capacity of the pipeline is estimated to reach up to 31,000m. cu m per year by around 2020. The Nabucco project is included in the EU Trans-European Energy Network programme. In July 2009 the EU and Turkey settled their dispute over the terms and conditions of the Nabucco project, and an intergovernmental agreement was signed by the Turkish Prime Minister, Recep Tayyip Erdoğan, and the heads of government of the four other transit countries (Austria, Hungary, Romania and Bulgaria) on 13 July, following a summit meeting in Ankara. In May 2012 Nabucco submitted a proposal to the Shah Deniz consortium, but the bid was rejected in favour of Turkey's Trans-Anatolia Gas Pipeline (TANAP), a project based on an agreement between Turkey and Azerbaijan, which will link the Southern Caucasus pipeline corridor through Georgia to a number of proposed links in EU countries. The launch of TANAP was co-ordinated with the start of the Shah Deniz II gas drilling project in the Caspian Sea. Commercial production at Shah Deniz II is expected to begin in 2017. The announcement in May 2013 that Nabucco had failed to secure the bid for gas from Shah Deniz II raised new doubts about the viability of the Southern Gas Corridor, which the EU considered necessary for energy diversification and supply security.

The energy market is regulated by the Energy Market Regulatory Authority (EMRA), which was established in 2001 with an initial remit to regulate the electricity market. In 2002–05 EMRA's remit was broadened to include the natural gas, petroleum and liquefied petroleum gas (LPG) markets. Its role is to ensure a 'financially viable, stable and transparent energy market', which will function within a 'competitive environment' in order to provide 'sufficient electricity, natural gas, petroleum and LPG of good quality to consumers, at low cost, in a reliable and environment friendly manner'. EMRA is a public corporation linked to the Ministry of Energy and Natural Resources, with some administrative and financial autonomy, and focuses particularly upon privatization and market liberalization.

MANUFACTURING AND INDUSTRY

State Economic Enterprises (SEEs) played a leading role in Turkey's industrialization process from the 1930s. However, from the 1960s the private sector generated nearly one-half of industrial output and invested at rates similar to the public sector. The symbiotic relationship between the private and public sectors began to break down in the second half of the 1970s. After a long period of economic and political uncertainty, the Government announced its long-awaited plans for privatization of the SEEs in May 1987. Initially, the Government's share in 22 private companies would be sold, followed by the denationalization of the more efficient and profitable SEEs.

As a first measure, one-half of the Government's shareholding of 40% in Teletas, a telecommunications company, was sold to the private sector in early 1988. A sharp reduction in share prices on the İstanbul Stock Exchange (ISE) then slowed the privatization programme. Five state-owned cement works were sold directly to a French company (although the completion of this sale was suspended in 1991). Similarly, USAS, an aircraft services firm, was sold directly to a Scandinavian airline in early 1989. The fact that these were sold directly to foreign companies, rather than to the public on the ISE, attracted widespread criticism. As the ISE recovered at the end of 1989, the Government proceeded with the sale of its minority shareholdings in private sector companies. Such holdings in six companies were sold in early 1990. Subsequent privatizations enjoyed varying degrees of success. Small portions of state-owned shareholdings were sold in a number of major companies, such as Petkim Petrokimya Holding AŞ, the petrochemicals giant, and Erdemir, the iron and steel complex. In the first half of 1992 the Government of Süleyman Demirel undertook five such sales, with estimated total revenue of TL 552,000m. In July the Government announced the sale of 11 state cement companies, which together accounted for 18% of total cement production in Turkey. In late 1992 and 1993 the privatization programme continued at a steady rate, but, under the Government of Tansu Çiller, few sales were completed. In July 1994 legislation to accelerate privatization was declared to be unconstitutional by the Constitutional Court, although new legislation was approved in November. None the less, the programme generated only US $354m. in 1994 and $576m. in 1995; the target revenue was $5,000m.

Although every Government from the mid-1980s claimed that privatization was a key part of economic policy, only US $3,500m. had been raised from the sale of state enterprises by 1997. In May 1998 the Privatization Administration (OIB) sold a 12.2% stake in Türkiye İş Bankası (one of the country's leading commercial banks) for $651m., while in July it accepted a bid of $1,160m. for a 51% holding in the petrol distributor POAŞ. However, this bid effectively lapsed some weeks later, when the prospective buyer (a consortium of four local firms) failed to secure the necessary finance. In April 1999 the OIB suspended the privatization of POAŞ, having previously been obliged to defer the sale of several other organizations in the second half of 1998, in view of adverse market trends and pre-election political uncertainties. In July, however, following a change of government, the OIB relaunched the privatization programme—a key element of the economic restructuring programme agreed with the IMF in December 1998 (see Budget, Investment and Finance). The sale of a 51% share in POAŞ was finally completed in March 2000 (for $1,260m.), while a 31.5% holding in TÜPRAŞ was sold in April (for $2,300m.). Other enterprises designated for early complete or partial privatization included Türk Telekomünikayson, Erdemir, the İskenderun Iron and Steel Works (İSDEMIR), and Petkim, as well as the national carrier Turkish Airlines (Türk Hava Yolları) and parts of the power generation industry. Privatizing a strategic share in Türk Telekomünikayson proved to be especially controversial. A first offer of a 33.5% stake was abandoned after no bids had been received by the 15 September 2000 deadline, whereupon the proposal was restructured so that the purchaser would obtain majority management rights. Following the massive financial crisis of February 2001, privatization of a 51% stake in Türk Telekomünikayson (currently valued at $10,000m.) was a condition of further IMF assistance. The disposal of a 45% share received reluctant parliamentary approval in May, on the basis that the

Government would retain a 'golden share', giving it the power to block any onward disposal thought to be undesirable.

The privatization programme was further delayed by the impact of the crisis in 2001, in which industrial output declined by 9% and the contribution of the industrial sector to GNI contracted by 7%. In a letter of intent to the IMF in July 2002, the Government stated that the OIB had adopted a new strategy for reducing the state's holding in TÜPRAŞ to under 50%, through a tender for a strategic partner and/or the placement of exchangeable bonds, since a public offering was not feasible in current market conditions. The Government continued by stating that it had reduced its stake in Erdemir to below 50% by means of a sale to an investment fund, that its remaining 25.8% stake in POAŞ would shortly be sold to the existing strategic investor, and that at least 51% of the shares in Petkim would be offered by October. The letter expressed confidence that these and other sales would meet the indicative target of US $700m. in privatization proceeds in 2002. As regards other plans, the letter recorded that 'roadmaps' had been drawn up for the privatization of Türk Telekomünikayson, the TEKEL tobacco and alcohol monopoly, and the Türkiye Şeker Fabrikaları sugar company, that all state-owned thermal generation and electricity distribution assets would be offered in February 2003 (with the exception of projects eligible for Treasury guarantee), and that two distribution subsidiaries of the BOTAŞ pipeline authority would be privatized by the end of that year. Few of these targets were achieved, however, and the Government was obliged in April 2004 to submit a new timetable to the IMF, under which the sale of the remaining 55% state-owned share of Türk Telekomünikayson (now Telekomünikayson Kurumu) to the Saudi-led Oger Telecoms Joint Venture Group for $6,550m. was approved in mid-2005, while a tender was launched for a block sale of 49.5% of Erdemir.

Overall, the value of privatized assets remained low, at an annual average of US $546m. from 1989 to 2003. This was mainly due to uncertainty about successive governments' privatization policies and the recurrent economic crises of the 1990s. However, the value of privatized assets increased significantly, to $1,266m. in 2004 and $8,209m. in 2005. Following the re-election of the Adalet ve Kalkınma Partisi (AKP—Justice and Development Party) in 2007, privatization proceeds increased from $4,259m. in that year to $6,300m. in 2008, with the sale of Petkim generating $2,000m. Privatization revenues decreased significantly, to $2,300m., in 2009 due to the global financial crisis, but increased again, to $3,100m., in 2010.

Turkey's growth rates were industry-led until the mid-1990s. As a result, the share of industry (including manufacturing industry, mining and utilities) in the economy increased from 12% of GDP in 1952 to 26% in 1995. However, the sector's share remained stagnant at around 28%–29% during 2000–05. In 2007 industry accounted for 21% of GDP. In 2008–12 industry's share in GDP remained at about 20%, as the share of services continued to increase and share of agriculture remained stagnant, at around 8%.

A 5% reduction in industrial output in 1999 was followed by a 5.6% expansion in 2000, during which lower interest rates helped to boost consumer demand, especially for motorcars and household appliances. A sharp contraction of industrial output in 2001 was followed by renewed growth of 9.2% in 2002 and 9.1% in 2003. Overall, the average annual growth rate of industrial GDP was 7.8% in 1980–90, slowing to 2.8% in 1990–2002. The growth rate picked up again after the 2001 crisis and remained at 6%–10%. Between 1980 and 1998 the share of industrial products in total exports increased from 36% to 77.4%, with the share increasing further, to 93.2%, in 2003. The share was about 85% in 2004–08 and 83% in 2009–12.

The textiles and clothing sector employs around one-fifth of Turkey's industrial labour, accounting for 21.5% of total industrial output in 2002 (at a value of US $27,700m.) and 33.8% of export revenue (at a value of $12,200m.). From 2003 onwards the share of textiles and clothing in export revenue began to decline as exports of other industrial products such as motor vehicles began to increase. In 2007 the share of textiles and clothing in export revenue was 20.9%, whereas motor vehicles accounted for 15.8% (compared with 10% in 2002). In 2009 the share of textiles and clothing in export revenue was 20.5%. Since then, the share of textiles and clothing in export revenue has begun to decline, averaging around 17% per year in 2010–12.

Inaugurated in the late 1930s, the iron and steel industry in Turkey has been one of the fastest-growing in the world, and prospects continue to be relatively good, following difficulties in the early 1980s. Total output of crude steel reached 14.3m. tons in 2000, increasing to 18.3m. tons in 2003. In July 1996 an agreement was signed with the European Coal and Steel Community (part of the EU) for the elimination of duties by both sides, with effect from 1 August 1996. The value of iron and steel exports declined to US $1,600m. in 1998, from $2,000m. in 1997. Iron and steel exports increased from $1,737m in 1999 to $3,842.4m. in 2003. The increase in the value of iron and steel exports was sustained in the next five years, rising to $16,841m. in 2008. In 2009–12 iron and steel products accounted for about 10% of export earnings, with an average value of $11,000m. Although iron and steel products make a significant contribution to expert earnings, Turkey remains a net importer of these products.

Cement production, on the strength of the expansion in the construction industry (owing largely to the Government's mass housing programme), rose to a record 20m. metric tons in 1986. The industry is now almost entirely privately owned as a result of the privatization programme of the 1990s. Following privatization, production has continued to increase, with occasional declines in years when the economy as a whole has done badly. Output stood at 30.0m. tons in 2001, rising to 35m. tons in 2003. Figures for the period 2004–07 showed a further expansion in cement output, which reached 49.6m. tons in 2007. During 2008–10 average production of cement was approximately 57m. tons per year.

Among food industries, the state-controlled sugar industry was the most important. In 1994 total production of raw sugar was 1.7m. metric tons, with the private sector accounting for only slightly over 25% of this total. Total production declined slightly, to 1.3m. tons, in 1995, but had doubled to 2.6m. tons by 1998. Sugar production then decreased to an estimated 1.8m. tons in 2003–07 before increasing to approximately 2.4m. tons per year during 2008–10. There have been plans to privatize the sugar industry since 2001. By 2004–05 three state-owned refineries had been privatized. Since then, only one of six refineries scheduled for privatization was sold in 2011.

While a majority of motor vehicles sold in Turkey were imported, production of its automotive industry rose from 261,400 units in 2001 to 516,600 in 2003 (including passenger vehicles, tractors, lorries and buses). In 2006 the Turkish motor vehicle industry produced 756,381 passenger cars, 136,594 pick-up trucks, 46,510 trucks and 42,496 tractors. In 2007 the production figures were as follows: 855,460 passenger cars, 154,979 pick-up trucks and 38,264 buses/minibuses. After a significant reduction in output in 2009 due to the effects of the global financial crisis, 885,135 passenger cars and 28,463 buses and minibuses were produced in 2010.

Since 2005 the value of exported motor vehicles (including passenger cars, tractors, trucks and buses) has exceeded the value of imports, leading to an increase in the trade surplus from US $1,200m. in 2005 to $7,900m. in 2008. The trade balance was still positive in 2009, but declined to $4,600m. owing to lower export demand during the global economic downturn. In 2010–12 imports of motor vehicles and trailers began to exceed exports, leading to an annual average trade deficit of approximately $2,000m. Durable consumer goods is another manufacturing industry in which Turkey's output and export performance have demonstrated significant progress. As of 2010, according to provisional figures, production of some durable goods was as follows: 7.2m. refrigerators and freezers, 5.2m. washing machines, 8.3m. ovens, 2.2m. vacuum cleaners and 9.2m. television sets. Durable consumer goods also constituted a significant source of export revenue, accounting for 9.5% of total export value in 2004, 7.9% in 2007 and 6.5% in 2010.

In 1970 Turkey's first petrochemicals complex, situated at İzmit, began production of ethylene, polythene, polyvinyl chloride, chlorine and caustic soda. Two other petrochemicals plants were established at Aliaga, near İzmir, and at

Yumurtalık, near Adana. They had been operated by the state-owned firm Petkim, which was largely privatized in 2005 and 2008. The state-owned Turkish Nitrates Corpn has a nitrate plant at Kütahya, a triple superphosphate plant at Samsun and a superphosphate plant at Elazığ. There are several privately owned fertilizer plants, including triple superphosphate plants at İskenderun and Yarimca. Turkey produces 75% of its requirements of fertilizers and, when new plants are completed, it will be self-sufficient. Production of fertilizer was an estimated 3.6m. tons in 2010. Other manufacturing industries include tobacco, chemicals, pharmaceuticals, metal-working, engineering, leather goods, glassware and ferro-chrome.

The power sector, along with the transport, communications and tourism sector, has continued to hold priority in the Government's development programmes for every year since 1989. Official sources indicated that domestic power production rose by 10.5% in 1996 but still failed to keep pace with increase in demand, which grew by 12%. Despite the progress made in power plant construction in recent years, many more units will have to be built to meet increased domestic and industrial demand, although official projections in the late 1980s that demand would increase five-fold to 100,000 MW by 2020 were revised downwards in 2003 (see Minerals and Mining). Gas-fuelled plants will generate most new capacity, with the private sector playing an increasingly important role.

Output from stations operated by the Turkish Electricity Board currently accounts for about 60% of all electricity generated, while chartered companies and private generators provide the remainder. The number of villages with electricity rose from 2,371 in 1970 to 18,345 in 1980, increasing further to 35,191 in 1990 and 37,411, in 2003. Total electricity generation increased from 124,922m. kWh in 2000 to 176,299m. kWh in 2006 and 198,418m. kWh in 2008. In both 2010 and 2011 electricity generation in Turkey stood at about 198,500m. kWh.

In mid-1995 construction of a gas-fuelled generating station in Marmara was initiated by a consortium of one Turkish and three foreign companies. The power plant, which was estimated to cost US $540m., had a potential capacity of 3,600m. kWh. In November an agreement was signed with foreign creditors and contractors for the construction of the 672-MW Birecik hydroelectric plant on the Euphrates river. The agreement was the first of many planned build-operate-transfer (BOT) schemes, under which the ownership of the plant was to be transferred to the Turkish Government once it became fully operational and profitable, or after a period of 15 years.

More controversial among new hydroelectric power projects is the proposed 1,200-MW Ilisu dam on the Tigris river in south-eastern Turkey, which has been strongly opposed on environmental and social grounds as its reservoir will displace up to 30,000 people and submerge the ancient Kurdish town of Hasankeyf. The dam is also opposed by Syria and Iraq, on the grounds that the Tigris water flow would be reduced, although Turkey denies that this would be the case. Another similarly controversial dam is proposed for the Coruh river at Yusefeli in north-eastern Turkey. Up to 15,000 people, mostly from Turkey's Georgian minority, are expected to lose their homes if the project proceeds as planned. In March the British-based AMEC construction company announced its withdrawal from the Yusefeli dam project, citing purely commercial reasons. Turkish officials responded by insisting that construction of the Ilisu and Yusefeli dams would go ahead as planned. In addition, the AKP Government has accelerated the pace of constructing dams and increasing the hydroelectric power output, leading to local and nation-wide protests since 2010.

From mid-1996 preparations were undertaken for the construction of the country's first nuclear generator, at Akkuyu on the southern Mediterranean coast. The US $4,000m. plant was put out to tender in December and construction was to have been completed in 2005. The 1,300-MW plant would have supplied some 2% of Turkey's energy needs. In July 2000, however, the Government announced that the project, which had attracted much environmentalist and regional opposition, had been suspended indefinitely on cost grounds, although it might be reconsidered in the future, should nuclear technology improve. In 2010 the Government announced that the project was finally to proceed with Russian assistance.

Turkey has imported electricity from Bulgaria for some time, and in March 1997 Ankara signed a new five-year energy agreement with that country. Turkey also imports power from Georgia and Iran, and has signed a memorandum of understanding with other Black Sea Economic Co-operation members to examine the creation of a regional power grid. Other recent initiatives to diversify supply sources include the signature in May 1999 of an agreement for Turkmen electricity to be supplied to Turkey.

Joint-venture defence manufacturing with foreign partners is a major element of foreign investment in Turkish industry (a development that began with the US $4,000m. agreement concluded in 1983 with the US Government and a US company, General Dynamics, to assemble and later manufacture F-16 fighter aircraft at Murted outside Ankara). The Defence Industry and Support Administration (DIDA), established in 1985, was to co-ordinate Turkey's 10-year programme, costing $15,000m., to modernize the armed forces. The modernization was to involve, to a large extent, locally manufactured equipment and weapons.

TOURISM

Tourism is one of Turkey's fastest growing industries and is an important source of foreign currency. In the 1990s Kurdish nationalist activity and associated violence affecting tourist centres posed less of a threat to the prospects of the tourism industry, which were more governed by international factors such as the economic fortunes of the European countries from where most tourists to Turkey originate. Following a 20.6% year-on-year decline in tourist arrivals in 1999, and a concomitant decline in tourist revenue to US $5,203m. (from $7,177m. in 1998), owing to political unrest and earthquake-related disruption, arrivals recovered to 10.4m. in 2000, while revenue increased to $7,636m. The tourism sector performed well in 2001, despite the country's economic and financial crisis, the number of arrivals totalling 10.8m. and revenue increasing to $10,067m. In 2002 tourist arrivals increased to 12.8m., and tourism revenue rose to $11,901m. In the first half of 2003 the US-led military action in neighbouring Iraq resulted in tourist arrivals decreasing by about 11%, compared with the same period in 2002, but a strong recovery in the second half of the year produced a total of 13.3m. in 2003, generating increased tourism revenue of $13,203m. Despite concern that the bomb attacks in İstanbul in late 2003 and in 2004 (see History) would have a negative impact, tourist arrivals rose by some 26% in 2004, to 16.8m., and tourism revenue increased to $15,888m. The increase in tourist arrivals and revenue continued in 2005 and 2006, with an average number of arrivals of 20m. and average revenue of $17,500m. per year. In 2007 and 2008 the number of tourist arrivals stood at 23.3m. and 26.3m., respectively, while revenue was reported at $18,487m. and $21,951m., respectively. Between 2000 and 2008 tourism revenue had experienced an average annual growth rate of 11.7%. Between 2009 and 2012 the average number of foreign visitors was approximately 30m., and average tourism revenue was $22,000m.

In October 1999 the OIB invited bids for various state-owned tourist assets, including hotels and land, as part of the Government's strategy of promoting private sector development of the tourism sector. Plans were also drafted in 2000–01 for the diversification of tourism away from coastal resorts, to inland attractions such as hot springs and to winter sports, with the aim of bringing tourists to Turkey throughout the year rather than mainly in the summer season. The Government's longer-term objective is to achieve a total of 60m. tourist arrivals per year by 2020, generating annual revenue of US $50,000m. Currently, this target seems to be over-ambitious, given the slow economic growth in Europe and some evidence of saturation in the arrival of tourists from Russia and Middle Eastern countries. In 2012 the total number of tourist arrivals was 31.8m. and receipts amounted to $23,440m. In that year the major countries of origin were Germany (15.8% of total tourist arrivals), Russia (11.3%), the United Kingdom (7.8%) and the Netherlands (4.2%).

BUDGET, INVESTMENT AND FINANCE

In the 1960s and 1970s Five-Year Economic Development Plans aimed to achieve self-sustained economic growth through import-substituting industrialization. In the 1980s import substitution was replaced with emphasis on export-led growth and liberalization, even though the Government continued to play a significant role as producer and employer. In May 1989 the Government published the sixth Five-Year Plan (1990–94), which envisaged an average annual growth rate of 7%, reaching 8.3% in 1994. However, actual growth in this period remained low, at an average of 2.2% per year. Owing to an economic crisis in 1994, the preparation for the seventh Plan was postponed by one year in September and an intermediary plan had to be implemented in 1995. In May 1995 the Government published the seventh Plan, for the period 1996–2000, which envisaged economic growth increasing to an annual 7.1%, but actual growth remained at 3.2%. The eighth Five-Year Plan, for 2001–05, was approved by the Grand National Assembly in June 2000. This was followed by a new planning framework that was linked to Turkey's third Pre-Accession Economic Programme, agreed with the EU in August 2003. The first National Development Plan under the new framework covered the 2004–06 period and set the following objectives: achieving high and sustainable growth; creating a high-technology-oriented economy that could compete in international markets; developing human resources and increasing employment; improving infrastructure services and environmental protection; and reducing the developmental differences among the regions, ensuring rural development and reducing social imbalances. Growth rates after the 2001 crises remained high, ranging between 7.6% and 9.9% during 2002–05, before slowing down to 5.9% in 2006 and 5.0% in 2007. As a result of the global financial crisis, the GDP growth rate declined to 1.1% in 2008, and recorded a contraction of 4.8% in 2009. Growth resumed in 2010 and 2011, with impressive rates of over 8% in each year. However, the growth rate fell to 2.2% in 2012, with OECD forecasts indicating an annual growth rate of 4%–5% in the medium term.

The Central Bank (Merkez Bankası) started operations on 3 October 1931. Historically, the Central Bank controlled exchange operations and extended credits to state-owned enterprises by discounting the treasury-backed bonds issued by these institutions. Legislation adopted in 1987 granted the Government wide-ranging powers over the Central Bank. Following the stand-by agreement with the IMF in April 1994, however, the ability of the Government to draw on central bank credits was curtailed. Although the Government reneged on its commitment during the elections of 1995, the IMF was instrumental in the signing of a protocol between the Central Bank and the Treasury, leading to significant limitations to central bank credits to the Government. In addition, the protocol, for the first time in the history of the country, transferred the power of setting short-term interest rates to the Central Bank. The independence of the Central Bank acquired a new impetus after the 2001 financial crisis and the stand-by agreement with the IMF. Until 1997 its monetary policy was geared towards controlling public and private expenditures through money supply as an intermediate target. From 1997 onwards, however, there was a gradual shift towards inflation targeting, which was implicit until 2005 and became explicit in 2006. The Central Bank was relatively more successful in achieving the implicit target during 2003–05, but it failed to hit the explicit target during 2006–08. For 2009 the Central Bank upwardly revised the target to 7.5%, which helped it to meet its goal for the first time since the transition to explicit inflation targeting, with inflation standing at 6.3% in that year. However, inflation increased to 8.6% in 2010. Although the inflation rate fell to 6.5% in 2011, it increased again to 8.9% in 2012.

In June 1999 a law was approved providing for the reform of the financial sector. The legislation, which came into effect in early 2000, incorporated core principles of the Basel Committee on Banking Supervision relating to risk-based capital requirements, loan administration procedures, auditing practices and credit risk issues, and envisaged the establishment of an independent Regulatory and Supervisory Board for Banking, the members of which (appointed for six-year terms) were to be nominated by the treasury, the Ministry of Finance, the Central Bank, the state planning organization, the Capital Markets Board and the Banks' Association of Turkey. This new body would monitor the observance of financial regulations (which had hitherto been regularly breached by some smaller institutions) and would have powers to order the merger or acquisition of institutions experiencing financial difficulty. In 1999 Turkey had 81 banks; at least 14 of these concerns were in difficulties because of over-lending to affiliated companies, eight being taken over by the Savings Deposit Insurance Fund, with bad debts of some US $5,000m. In June 2000 the Central Bank initiated preparations for the restructuring and sale of the eight banks, possibly as a merged group or groups, as part of a longer-term programme of privatization of the state-owned banking sector.

The principal sources of budgetary revenue are income tax, import taxes and duties, taxes and fees on services, and revenues from state monopolies. In late 1984 the Government introduced value-added tax to replace the previous unwieldy system of production taxes.

From 1989 onwards political instability affected the Government's ability to implement its economic plans. The appointment of Tansu Çiller as Prime Minister in 1993 was a popular choice with the business community, but while she quickly identified economic priorities, internal problems hampered attempts to implement reform. In 1993 the budget deficit was three times that of the previous year and reached 9.2% of GNI. In early 1994 two US credit rating agencies downgraded Turkey's credit rating, which resulted in a 'run' on foreign currencies. The value of the lira was officially devalued by 12% against the US dollar. However, the currency continued to decline. Interest rates rose to 150%–200% as the Government and the Central Bank desperately tried to bring the financial markets under control. In April the Government announced a programme of austerity measures to reduce the budget deficit, lower inflation, and restore domestic and international confidence in the economy. The programme included a freezing of wages, price increases of up to 100% on state monopoly goods, as well as longer-term restructuring measures such as the closure of loss-making state enterprises and an accelerated privatization process. By May the lira stabilized at around TL 30,000 to the dollar, having stood at some TL 16,000 at the beginning of the year. In August the value of the lira declined once more but was steadied at a rate of TL 34,000 per dollar, following an increase in interest rates from 70% to 240%. The austerity measures then began to have a measure of success, the markets stabilized and the lira stayed below 40,000 to the dollar until the end of the year. The measures also helped to restore a degree of international confidence in the Turkish economy and to secure an IMF stand-by loan, approved in July, of SDR 610m. (approximately US $873m.). The budget deficit for 1994 was substantially reduced in real terms, accounting for 3.7% of GNI. None the less, the budget deficit continued to exert serious inflationary pressure on the economy and to attract much domestic and international criticism. The Government continued to borrow heavily on the domestic market, although foreign borrowing became prohibitively expensive because of the crisis and was thus reduced. Inflation increased dramatically to 106.3% in 1994, from 66.1% in 1993.

Inflation remained high at 93.6% in 1995 and the actual budget deficit increased to TL 320,000,000m. Çiller abandoned the 14-month IMF stand-by agreement in September, after the collapse of her Government. The resultant political uncertainty and negotiations were accompanied by the largest series of strikes since the 1970s, which caused the closure of ports and a halt in production at state-owned industrial and transport companies. By October the strike action was costing the country an estimated US $500m. in lost export revenue and production, and threatened to undermine attempts to control inflation and restore economic stability. Prior to the general election in December, Çiller was able to settle the public sector wage dispute and, more importantly, to secure ratification of the EU customs union, which entered into force on 1 January 1996 (see Foreign Trade and Balance of Payments).

The general election of December 1995 failed to produce a clear victory for any one party, and the period of uncertainty that followed precluded the adoption of any stabilizing measures to improve the economic situation. In June 1996 a new Government was established, led by the Islamist fundamentalist Welfare Party, with the True Path Party as a coalition partner. In July the new administration approved an increase in the minimum wage and salary increases of 50% for state workers and pensioners. During his first five months in office Prime Minister Necmettin Erbakan announced three economic packages, which, he claimed, would raise a total of US $30,000m. in revenue, to meet the pay awards and limit the budget deficit. Nevertheless, the budget deficit remained high, at 8.2% of GNI, and the annual rate of inflation fell only slightly, to 82.4%.

In November 1996 the Grand National Assembly approved the Government's ambitious and controversial budget for 1997, in which Erbakan vowed to increase expenditure, end domestic borrowing and yet produce a 'zero-deficit' through a massive increase in government income from privatization. Although it was presented as the 'dream' budget, it encountered strong criticism from political opponents and from the country's business community. The Government's privatization plans received a welcome boost in January 1997, when the Constitutional Court gave its approval to the sale of a major stake in the state company Türk Telekomünikasyon. However, objections to a number of Erbakan's revenue-raising packages remained, notably against his attempt to sell large public real estate holdings and lease state-owned power projects. Early in 1997 Erbakan made new promises of additional pay increases to state workers and pensioners, over and above those included in that year's budget, which did little to inspire confidence in the Government's economic competence.

The coalition Government of Prime Minister Mesut Yılmaz, which took office in mid-1997, made a determined effort in its first year to stem the rise in inflation and improve economic management, notably by accelerating privatization. Revised economic targets for 1997 were announced, including: growth in GNI of 5.5%–6%, compared with the previous target of 4%; a reduction in the trade deficit, from US $20,500m. to $20,000m.; and a budget deficit at the end of the year of TL 2,400,000m., including a supplementary budget of TL 2,000,000m. In fact, GNI expanded by an impressive 8.6% in 1997, whereas inflation worsened to 99%. By July 1998 year-on-year inflation had declined to 72% from 101% in January. The reduction was achieved largely through a freeze in public sector prices. In June the Government signed an accord with the IMF under which the Fund would monitor the Turkish economy for 18 months. The agreement, which committed the Government to keeping a tight rein on public expenditure and boosting privatization and tax receipts, set targets for wholesale inflation of 50% by the end of 1998 and 20% by the end of 1999. Tax reform legislation, adopted in July, reduced the tax burden for most people and aimed to encourage full declaration of earnings. However, in the same month the Government was forced to compromise on its pledge to keep down public sector pay increases when it agreed to an immediate 20% rise, with a further 10% for the three months from October. In 1998 the Government recorded an actual budget deficit of TL 3,697,824,000m., equivalent to 6.7% of GNI. This was in spite of a primary surplus (excluding expenditure on debt-servicing) of TL 2,479,000,000m., equivalent to 4.3% of GNI. The inflation reduction target was not met, with the consumer price index rising by 70% in 1998.

Following the elections held in April 1999, the new Government declared its intention to implement a programme of structural reforms. It was announced in early July that the IMF monitoring programme introduced in 1998 would remain in place, with a view to applying for an IMF stand-by arrangement. The increasing need for social security reform, and the importance attached to it by the IMF, led the Government to publish a draft bill proposing an increase in the pensionable retirement age, from 38 to 58 for women and from 43 to 60 for men, over a 10-year period. Legislation to reform the financial sector was enacted in June, and in the same month the Government imposed a 20% ceiling on public sector pay increases, despite trade union demands that increases be linked to the prevailing inflation rate of more than 60%. On 13 August constitutional amendments were approved, permitting international arbitration in disputes between state bodies and foreign investors and allowing the privatization of state-owned utilities. The lack of international arbitration clauses in contracts for BOT projects had previously deterred many potential foreign partners from investing in infrastructure development, including high-priority work in the energy sector.

The 1999 budget envisaged a deficit of TL 9,236,000,000m. (including debt-servicing requirements), equivalent to 11.6% of GNI. Budgeted expenditure for 1999 was TL 27,266,000,000m., including TL 10,300,000,000m. for debt-servicing, while revenue totalled TL 18,030,000,000m. The anticipated surplus on the 1999 primary budget (excluding interest payments) was TL 1,064,000,000m. The increase in the 1999 debt-servicing requirement (which was 67% higher than in 1998) was the result of a larger than expected rise in the interest payable on the Government's domestic borrowing. In fact, the disruption of state finances caused by the earthquakes of August and November contributed to a primary budget deficit equivalent to 2.7% of GNI, while consumer price inflation during the year was recorded at 68.8%.

The 2000 budget, approved in December 1999, provided for a deficit after debt-servicing of TL 14,383,000,000m., equivalent to 11.5% of GNI, although a projected 70% increase in tax receipts, to TL 24,000,000,000m., was expected to contribute to a primary budget surplus of 2.2% of GNI (3.7% excluding earthquake-related expenditure). In the previous month the Grand National Assembly had approved a new 'national solidarity' tax law, intended to raise in excess of TL 700,000,000m. (about US $1,360m.,) to finance post-earthquake reconstruction. The specific measures included: an additional 5% tax on 1998 corporate earnings and on personal earnings exceeding TL 12,000m.; a tax of between 4% and 19% (depending on maturity date) on proceeds from government bonds issued before 1 December 1999; a doubling of motor vehicle and real estate tax in 2000; a 25% surcharge on mobile telephone fees; a charge of TL 600,000 on every bank cheque written; special transaction taxes on lotteries, domestic airline fares and gun licences; and authorization to increase petroleum products consumption tax from 300% to 500%. The new tax on government bonds resulted in a 6% decline in share values on the ISE, with particularly heavy losses being sustained by banks as major holders of such bonds.

The 2000 budget was a key component of the Government's economic restructuring programme for the period 2000–02; the first tranche of a SDR 2,892m. (about US $3,800m.) IMF stand-by credit was released, following the Fund's approval of the programme in December 1999. With the ambitious goal of increasing the rate of GNI growth to 5.8% in 2002, its key elements were: 'up-front' fiscal adjustment to achieve a stable primary budget surplus of around 4% of GNI; a more diversified debt management policy and increased privatization to contain the burden of interest payments; reduction of consumer and wholesale price inflation to 25% and 20%, respectively, in 2000, and to 7% and 5%, respectively, in 2002; a firm exchange-rate commitment supported by consistent incomes policies; and structural reform to strengthen public finances, reduce inequalities in the tax burden and curb waste in public expenditure. As part of the anti-inflation programme, a new 'exchange rate substitution' policy took effect on 1 January 2000, under which the managed peg used since 1994 was abandoned in favour of a peg set according to a predetermined devaluation rate (20% in 2000), itself set against a 'basket' of the US dollar and the euro. The IMF arrangement was supplemented in May 2000 by a World Bank 'economic reform loan' of $750m., with a maturity of 15 years, including a five-year grace period.

The Government's sale of a 51% stake in POAŞ in March 2000 (for US $1,260m.) and of a 31.5% stake in TÜPRAŞ in April (for $2,300m.) were the main components of first-half proceeds from privatization of some $5,000m., so that the full-year target of $7,600m. was likely to be exceeded in the second half, during which the sale of a 20% stake in Türk Telekomünikayson was scheduled. The Government also raised $2,500m. from the sale to a Turkish-Italian consortium of a third global system for mobiles (GSM) licence. GDP growth in the first half of 2000 of more than 5%, compared with the same period in 1999, suggested that the economy was recovering from the 1999 reverse, although consumer price inflation remained well above the Government's 25% target for 2000. However, the Government's intentions were again frustrated by a major banking liquidity crisis and flight of capital in November, during which the Central Bank expended $7,000m. of its reserves in supporting the lira before the IMF eased the situation in December by granting a supplemental reserve facility of SDR 5,800m. (about $7,000m.). Another package of reforms agreed with the IMF included the familiar objectives of curbing inflation, reducing the budget deficit and expediting privatization. The resultant 2001 budget provided for expenditure of TL 48,400,000,000m. and revenue of TL 43,100,000,000m., with the target deficit of TL 5,300,000,000m. representing 3.5% of projected GNI. It also targeted economic growth of 4.5% in 2001 (compared with 3.5% in 2000) and a reduction in consumer price inflation to 12% (from 39% in 2000).

No sooner had the new programme been introduced than Turkey's gravest economic crisis in three decades struck in February 2001, as a result of a public clash between President Ahmet Necdet Sezer and Prime Minister Bülent Ecevit over the latter's alleged inaction against ministers and officials suspected of corruption. The immediate reaction of the markets was a decline in the share price index to over 60% below its 2000 high, capital flight involving the movement of some US $5,000m. out of Turkey on 19 February 2001 alone and a rise in overnight interest rates to the equivalent of 4,000% annually, as the Central Bank mounted an abortive effort to defend the lira. Ceding to market forces, the Government ended the 'crawling peg' with the US dollar on 22 February and allowed the lira to float freely, with the result that its value decreased by 36% over two days. Ecevit responded by appointing a new Central Bank governor and installing Kemal Derviş, hitherto a senior World Bank official, as Minister of State responsible for economic policy, charged in particular with securing yet another IMF disbursement of funds. To that end, Derviş quickly drew up a 'recovery' plan for a radical restructuring of the banking sector, including the placing of the three main state-owned banks under a joint administration headed by technocrats, the liquidation of other insolvent banks and full independence for the Central Bank. Also envisaged was swift action to privatize debt-laden, state-owned enterprises long allocated for divestment, beginning with a 51% share in Türk Telekomünikayson and including major stakes in Turkish Airlines and the state sugar, alcohol and tobacco monopolies.

Protracted negotiations with the IMF resulted in approval being given on 15 May 2001 to an additional stand-by facility of SDR 6,000m. (about US $8,000m.), bringing the total made available to Turkey since December 1999 to SDR 15,100m. Of this amount, Turkey had drawn SDR 8,100m. (about $10,000m.) by mid-May. In addition, the World Bank undertook to provide further loans of up to $2,500m. The IMF approved the latest facility only after the Turkish Government had secured parliamentary approval of its 'recovery' plan, in the face of strong opposition on the grounds that Turkey was surrendering its national economic sovereignty. However, the strength of such opposition, not least within the ruling coalition, raised immediate doubts about the Government's commitment to reform, with the result that the IMF suspended disbursements in late June, thus provoking further sharp depreciation of the lira (to just over 50% of its pre-February value) and a further slump in share prices. The disbursements were resumed on 12 July, after the Government had given new assurances, in particular on its commitment to reform of the banking sector and to privatization of Türk Telekomünikayson. In early August the IMF Executive Board 'commended the Turkish authorities on the strong implementation of their ambitious economic reform programme'. However, the Government's hopes that GDP contraction could be contained to 3% in 2001 were shattered by the negative effects on the already beleaguered Turkish economy of the global economic slowdown, aggravated by the effects of the September suicide attacks on the USA. The outcome was that Turkey's GDP declined by 7.4% (and GNI by 9.4%) in that year, while year-on-year inflation almost doubled to 68.5% and the budget deficit reached the equivalent of 17.2% of GNI.

As approved in December 2001, the 2002 budget once again aimed to correct persistent fiscal imbalances, providing for expenditure of TL 97,831,000,000m. and revenue of TL 70,918,000,000m., with a projected deficit of just under TL 27,000,000,000m., equivalent to about 10% of anticipated GNI. At the same time the budget provided for a public sector primary surplus of 6.5% of GNI. A resumption of economic growth at 3%–4% was forecast for 2002, while the Government aimed to reduce the annual inflation rate to 35%. An accompanying restatement of economic reform objectives included the completion of the restructuring of the banking sector by the end of 2002, improved transparency in the use of public funds, the enhancement of the private sector through a revitalized privatization programme, and the removal of obstacles to foreign and domestic investment.

The 2002 budget package and associated measures secured the endorsement of the IMF, which, on 4 February, approved a new three-year stand-by credit of SDR 12,800m. (about US $17,500m.) for Turkey, enabling the Government to draw SDR 7,300m. immediately. The new arrangement replaced the December 1999 stand-by credit as expanded in May 2001, the remaining undisbursed element of which (SDR 3,300m.) was included in the new credit. By August 2002 Turkey had drawn SDR 9,000m., although in approving the release of a third tranche on 7 August the IMF warned that the country's latest political crisis had unsettled domestic financial markets and revealed 'vulnerabilities', demonstrating that strict adherence to the reform programme was essential. In 2002 a budget deficit of TL 39,085,000,000m. (14% of GDP) was recorded, and the Government failed to achieve the IMF-supported target of a public sector primary surplus of 6.5% of GNI. However, the net public debt to GNI ratio declined to less than 80% at the end of 2002, compared with more than 90% at the end of 2001.

Finalization of the budget for 2003 by the new AKP Government was delayed until March, owing to uncertainties about the economic impact on Turkey of hostilities in neighbouring Iraq. Turkey suffered a loss of some US $30,000m. in US grants and loans, following the Grand National Assembly's rejection of US troop deployment through Turkey. Although the USA subsequently pledged $9,400m. in return for full access to Turkish airspace, the $20,000m. shortfall necessitated the presentation of an austerity budget in 2003, which provided for higher tobacco and excise duties, new vehicle and property taxes, and reductions in spending totalling more than TL 3,000,000,000m. The IMF welcomed the austerity budget and also the Government's renewed commitment to the structural reform programme and the achievement of a public sector primary surplus of 6.5% of GNI in 2003. By May, however, familiar slippages were already apparent in meeting reform objectives, with the result that the IMF suspended the transfer of the latest stand-by tranche of $476m., citing in particular the Government's failure to address obstacles to foreign investment, to simplify the social security system and to expedite the privatization of Türk Telekomünikasyon. The Fund eventually agreed in August to release the withheld tranche. The outcome for 2003 was economic growth of 5.9% and an inflation rate reduced to 18.4%, although the public sector primary surplus was just below target, at 6.2% of GNI.

The Government's budget for 2004, adopted by the Grand National Assembly in December 2003, provided for expenditure of TL 150,000,000,000m. and revenue of TL 103,000,000,000m., the stated aim being to maintain economic growth at above 5% and reduce inflation to 12%. However, a sizeable fiscal differential of about 1.8% of GNI rapidly emerged, mainly owing to above-inflation increases in minimum wages and 20% rises in pensions, with the result that in March 2004 the Government obtained parliamentary approval for a supplementary budget reducing discretionary spending for all ministries by 13%, and increasing excise duties on petroleum, alcohol, tobacco and gas. This corrective action, together with continuing economic growth of more than 5% and a further reduction of inflation to under 10% year-on-year by mid-2004, enabled the IMF in July to release the latest US $661m. tranche of the 2002 stand-by arrangement. Meanwhile, an Investment Advisory Council, established in March, was charged in particular with improving Turkey's low level of foreign direct investment (FDI), which had averaged only about $800m. per year in the previous decade, well below FDI received by comparable emerging economies.

The Government's budget for 2005 was based on an expectation of GDP growth of 5%, providing for a shift in expenditure towards public investment and scientific research, and reductions in corporation tax and the top rate of personal income tax. In approving a further three-year US $10,000m. stand-by arrangement for Turkey in May 2005, the IMF commended the authorities' recent economic achievements, adding that they would 'reduce Turkey's remaining vulnerabilities'. Capital outflows and pressure on the currency in 2006 demonstrated that Turkey remained vulnerable to global liquidity conditions, but the fiscal consolidation process continued. For example, in 2005 the primary balance recorded a surplus of 6.2% of gross national product (GNP) (quite close to the IMF requirement of 6.5% of GNP), whereas the overall budget deficit remained relatively low, at 1.4% of GNP. This trend continued in 2006, when the primary surplus and the overall budget deficit were estimated at 6.7% and 0.7% of GNP, respectively.

Until early 2005 the AKP Government remained essentially tied to the pre-existing IMF-sponsored stabilization programme. For example, in a Letter of Intent dated 5 April 2003, the Prime Minister's Office stated that the new Government was committed to implementing the existing programme with strengthened resolve. It also stated that the programme targets specified under the stand-by agreement were appropriate and achievable. Finally, it requested the IMF to complete the fourth review and renew the existing stand-by agreement with Turkey. Similar statements were made in the Letter of Intent dated 2 April 2004.

Encouraged by the growth performance in 2003 and 2004, however, the AKP Government began to signal that it had eventually come of age and could begin to cash in the rewards for compliance with the IMF conditionality. The Letter of Intent dated 26 April 2005 reflected this change of mood by requesting a new stand-by agreement. The Government acknowledged that it was still in need of the IMF anchor, but by proposing a three-year economic policy programme of its own it also wanted to signal that its economic policy would be informed by the Government's own assessment of the economic conditions—not only by the IMF's diagnosis.

The programme for 2005–08 stated that the economic policies of the preceding two years had led to sustainable improvement in economic performance, that the Government wanted to consolidate this achievement and that strengthening the convergence towards EU norms was an essential target for the next three years. Given these aims, the Government introduced explicit inflation targeting in 2006 and indicated that reliance on ad hoc revenue measures would be reduced, that the tax base would be widened and that the social security system would be reformed.

Thus far, evidence concerning progress and/or success on these fronts is mixed. For example, the IMF was impressed by Turkey's continued success in meeting the primary surplus target of 6.5% of GDP, but its concerns about the heavy reliance on ad hoc revenue measures for achieving the target became more visible. In a recent proposal for discussion, the IMF recommended a move away from the primary surplus rule towards an expenditure ceiling rule, with a view to encouraging fiscal reform aimed at widening the tax base and reducing excessive reliance on employment-and income-related tax rates. Similarly, there were some attempts to reform the social security system (for example, extension of the retirement age, amalgamation of public insurance schemes, and some reforms aimed at rationalizing health care expenditures), but evidence does not show a significant impact on the level of expenditures.

These mixed results, combined with an unplanned fiscal stimulus in 2007, have led to friction in the hitherto cosy relationship between the IMF and the Turkish Government. The IMF review published in August 2008 on the current stand-by agreement suggested that economic developments had become less favourable since their last review in May 2007. The IMF drew attention to both supply-side shocks that slowed growth and led to increased inflationary pressure, and to policy changes and wider political developments that distracted attention away from the economic policy reform agenda. Around the time of the IMF review, Turkey first began to feel the impact of the global financial crisis. Although the financial sector was not exposed to pre-crisis vulnerabilities as experienced in Europe and the USA, Turkey entered into recession in the final quarter of 2008. GDP contracted by 4.8% in 2009, and the primary balance target of 6.5% of GDP was abandoned in favour of a counter-cyclical deficit target for 2010–12. This counter-cyclical policy amendment contributed to the resumption of growth in 2010, but ambiguity surrounded the Government's exit strategy and concerns remained regarding the expenditure-dependent nature of Turkey's growth performance.

Such concerns were underpinned by two perennial issues: high real interest rates and persistent current account deficits. Turkey has the second highest level of real interest rates globally after Brazil, with an average of 15% over the last decade. This has been the case despite disinflation and fiscal consolidation. An IMF working paper published in 2008 reported that doubts about the sustainability of disinflation, high risk premiums and fiscal policy variables were significant determinants of high real interest rates in Turkey. The current account deficit peaked at 6.1% of GDP in 2006 and remained well above the critical 5% level in subsequent years. Due to economic contraction in 2009, the current account deficit narrowed to 1.9% of GDP. However, it subsequently started to deteriorate again, reaching 6.1% of GDP in 2010, 9.6% in 2011 and about 6% in 2012.

A heavy burden of foreign debt, contracted in the late 1970s and extended through subsequent rescheduling, has severely hampered the Government's structural adjustment efforts, which have also been complicated by rising domestic debt. At the end of 1998 foreign debt stock totalled US $101,000m., while domestic debt totalled $44,500m. During 1998 the Government borrowed a total of $2,400m. on international capital markets (later raised to $2,600m. through the issue of additional bonds). In 1999 its international borrowing target (as formulated prior to the August earthquake) was about $3,000m., with an additional estimated $1,000m. for project financing. At the end of 1999 the outstanding external debt stock totalled $111,215m., while domestic debt totalled TL 26,679,144,000m. in March 2000, the corresponding figures rising to $119,600m. at the end of 2000, and TL 90,332,000,000m. by June 2001, respectively. By the end of 2001 domestic debt had risen to TL 122,157,260,000m., while external debt had fallen to $113,901m. By the end of 2002 domestic debt had risen further to TL 149,869,691,000m., while total external debt had increased to $131,058m. The corresponding figures at the end of 2003 were TL 194,386,700,000m. and $147,035m., after which external debt increased to $160,000m. by January 2005 and domestic debt to YTL 234,800m. by June. The ratio of net public debt (the combined total of foreign and domestic currency-denominated debt) to GNP declined from 90.5% in the crisis year of 2001 to 44.8% in 2006.

During 2007–11 Turkey's debt-to-GDP ratio fluctuated between 39% and 46% and remained far below the 60% level prescribed in the convergence criteria for EU membership. In addition, the Turkish Government repaid all outstanding IMF loans in 2013. Nevertheless, the reduction in public debt has been accompanied by increased private-sector borrowing. In 2013 external borrowing by the private sector was equivalent to 51% of GDP, making Turkey one of the most-leveraged emerging market economy in the world. The surge in private sector borrowing is a major contributor to Turkey's high current account deficit.

FOREIGN TRADE AND BALANCE OF PAYMENTS

Turkey has had a persistent foreign trade deficit since 1947. Following the economic reforms of 1980 and the introduction of export-led policies, however, the deficit decreased in the early 1980s. In the early 1990s Turkey's trade deficit began to increase again and has become a constraint on Turkey's economic performance. Annual trade deficits in the 1990s and 2000s have been closely associated with the growth rate in each year and with the manufacturing industry's dependence on imported investment and intermediate goods, which constituted around 90% of total imports throughout the period. In 1990 exports and imports stood at US $13,000m. and $22,300m., generating an export/import ratio of 58%. In 1995 the corresponding figures were: $21,600m. of exports, $35,700m. of imports and an export/import ratio of 60%. The value of both exports and imports continued to record high growth rates each year, but the trade balance continued to be negative. For example, in 2000 the value of exports and imports increased to $27,700m. and $54,500m., respectively, generating an export/import ratio of 51%. Between 2005 and 2008 export and import growth continued and the export/import ratio improved. In 2008 there were $132,027m. of exports and $201,964m. of imports, with an export/import ratio of 65.4%. During the recession of 2009 imports declined more rapidly than exports, leading to an improved export/import ratio of 72.5%. However, as growth resumed, the export/import ratio deteriorated to 61.4% in 2010 and 56% in 2011. The export/import ratio was 64.4% in 2012.

Turkey's trade deficit has been partly offset, for some time, by a net surplus on invisible earnings (services and transfers), particularly helped by expatriate workers' remittances. A major contributor to the invisibles balance since the early 1980s has been the contribution from Turkish contractors working in the Middle East and, increasingly, in Russia, Azerbaijan and the Turkic republics of Central Asia. In March 1997 a Russian official stated that 150 Turkish contractors were working on 200 construction projects in Russia, worth some US $5,000m., making Turks the leading foreign contractors in that country. Workers' remittances were for a long time an important source of foreign exchange, although their contribution has declined in recent years. They totalled $5,356m. in 1998, but decreased to $4,572m. in 1999, before declining slightly, to $4,560m., in 2000. In 2001 they decreased sharply, to $2,786m., declining further, to $1,936m. in 2002 and $729m. in 2003, before rising to $804m. in 2004. In 2008 total workers' remittances amounted to $1,324m. Receipts from tourism represent another important source of foreign exchange.

A current account deficit of US $2,437m. was recorded in 1996, increasing to an unprecedented level of $9,821m. in 2000, as a result of an overvalued lira, rising oil prices and strong domestic demand. Owing to a major financial and economic crisis, the current account showed a surplus of $3,392m. in 2001, but reverted to rising deficit positions of $1,523m. in 2002, $8,036m. in 2003 and $15,604m. in 2004. In 2005 and 2006 the current account deficit stood at $22,603m. and $31,764m., amounting to 6.4% and 6.5% of GDP, respectively. The current account deficit remained high, at around 10% of GDP in 2011, leading to renewed concerns about its sustainability and its implications for the Turkish economy's external vulnerabilities. The main determinant of the current account deficit in Turkey has been the high level of dependence on the import of energy and intermediate goods, which accounted for more than two-thirds of total imports from 2005 onwards. Raw materials and intermediate goods accounted for 70% of Turkey's imports in 2010 and 2011, and 74% in 2012. Recently, it has been reported that domestic credit expansion and external borrowing by the private sector are additional determinants of the current account deficit in Turkey.

The overall balance of payments recorded a small surplus of US $441m. in 1998 that increased significantly, to $5,354m., in 1999. In 2000 Treasury borrowing on the international capital markets and a doubling of net capital inflow to $9,400m. financed most of the record current account deficit, but an overall balance of payments deficit of $3,934m. was recorded. In the crisis year of 2001 the deficit rose sharply, to $12,888m., but in 2002 the overall deficit was reduced to $214m., while in 2003 an overall surplus of $4,087m. was recorded, rising slightly, to $4,307m., in 2004. In 2005 the overall surplus on the balance of payments increased substantially, to $23,176m., but it declined to $10,621m. in 2006—mainly owing to capital outflows that tested the credibility of the new Central Bank Governor during the global liquidity squeeze. In 2008 the balance of payments recorded a deficit of $2,800m., primarily owing to a large current account deficit and substantial capital outflows. However, as growth resumed, Turkey became a preferred destination for international investors again, and increased portfolio investment inflows led to a balance of payments surplus of $14,971m. in 2010. A modest surplus of $1,008m. was recorded in 2011. The Central Bank's foreign exchange reserves (excluding gold) rose from $17,755m. at the end of 2001 to $25,527m. at the end of 2002, $32,058m. at the end of 2003 and $34,374m. at the end of 2004. Extensive capital inflows (until the recent global financial crisis) led to a significant increase in foreign currency reserves, which reached $70,000m. in 2008 and 2009, before rising to $81,000m. in 2010 and $93,036m. in 2011. Despite the increase in foreign currency reserves, the reserves-to-external debt coverage ratio in Turkey has remained lower than other emerging markets such as Chile, South Africa, Brazil and India.

Turkey's principal imports in 2004 by value were machinery and appliances (23%), mineral fuels (17%), iron and steel products (8%), road vehicles and parts (8%), and plastics (5%). The principal exports were clothing and textiles (23%), electrical machinery and appliances (18%), road vehicles and parts (11%), iron and steel (9%), and agricultural products and foodstuffs (8%). The picture remained largely similar in 2007, with machinery and transport equipment accounting for 29.2%, mineral fuels for 19.4%, road vehicles for 7.0%, and iron and steel for 6.4% of total imports. The principal export categories were machinery and transport equipment (31.9%), textiles and clothing (21.0%), and iron and steel (8.8%). In 2010 the country's main imports were raw materials and intermediate goods (71%), investment goods (16%) and consumption goods (13%). On the other hand, the main export categories consisted of machinery and transport equipment (27.9%), textiles and clothing (19%), and iron and steel products (9.6%). The three principal import and export categories remained the same in 2011 and 2012.

The EU is Turkey's principal trading partner, taking about 55% of its exports and supplying 44% of its imports until 2007. From 2008 onwards the EU's share in Turkey's foreign trade declined gradually to 39% of exports and 37% of imports in 2012. In terms of individual countries, Germany was Turkey's main trading partner until 2005. In that year Germany received 12.8% of Turkish exports and supplied 11.6% of its imports. During 2006–12 Germany continued to be the largest market for Turkish exports, but its share has declined slightly, amounting to 8.6% in 2012. Although the United Kingdom, France and Italy remain important destinations, the second largest market for Turkish exports in 2012 was Iraq (7.1%), and the third largest was Iran (6.5%). Historically, European countries, particularly Germany, constituted the main sources of Turkish imports. Russia's share in Turkish imports has increased from 11% in 2005 to 15.5% in 2008. In 2012 Russia became the largest supplier of imports, accounting for 11.3% of the total, followed by Germany and the People's Republic of China, which both contributed 9.0%. The rise in Russia's share in Turkish imports has been the result of increased imports of energy. Foreign trade figures consequently indicate that Turkey has diversified the sources of its imports and destinations for its exports, with the decline in the share of the EU and principal EU countries, and the emergence of new partners in Africa, Asia and Latin America.

In 1963 the Government signed an association agreement with the European Community (EC, now the EU), under which Turkey was granted financial aid and preferential tariff quotas. A package of minor improvements was introduced at the end of 1976 and the association agreement was revised in July 1980, offering Turkey a five-year financial aid package. Since the military coup of September 1980, aid from EC countries became increasingly dependent upon the restoration of democracy and human rights in Turkey. NATO members have been divided over support for the Turkish regime: in December 1981 the USA promised to accelerate aid to Turkey, but in March 1982 EC aid worth US $586m. was frozen. This aid remained blocked, despite the reconvening of the Turkey-EC Association Council in September 1986. In 1987 Turkey submitted an application for full EC membership, followed by a concerted diplomatic effort to win support for its application in Europe. The frozen aid was partly released in early 1988. At the end of 1989 the European Commission published its report in response to Turkey's application for full membership. The report drew attention to both economic and political problems in Turkey, as well as the country's unsatisfactory human rights record, and proposed that negotiations should not start until after 1992. Although an agreement to construct a customs union as of 1 January 1995 was secured in 1993, its establishment was postponed in late 1994, owing to persisting concerns regarding the Turkish Government's record on human rights, democracy and the rule of law. Negotiations in early 1995 finally led to an agreement providing for the removal of barriers to non-agricultural trade, which was signed at a meeting of the EU-Turkey Association Council in March. The accord was formally ratified by the European Parliament in December, and came into effect on 1 January 1996. The EU was to provide ECU 1,800m. over a five-year period, in order to assist the implementation of the new trade regime and to alleviate any initial hardships resulting from the agreement. However, some $470m. in EU adjustment funds to support the customs union was blocked in September 1996 by Greece, and by the European Parliament as a result of concern over Turkey's human rights record.

Turkey's relations with the EU remained strained throughout 1996, and they suffered a further set-back in December 1997, when the EU decided to exclude Turkey from the list of countries eligible to join the organization in the near future. Although the European Commission subsequently published a strategy in March 1998 for enhancing co-operation by building on the customs union that came into force in 1996, EU financial assistance to Turkey remained blocked at the insistence of Greece. However, the improvement in Greek-Turkish relations in the wake of the August 1999 earthquake resulted in Greece ending its veto on EU aid to Turkey and also backing the decision of the EU summit in Helsinki, Finland, in December, to grant Turkey candidate status. In December 2000 the EU and Turkey concluded an accession partnership agreement, which provided a framework for EU support in return for legal and administrative reforms aimed at satisfying the EU's Copenhagen criteria for accession. Nevertheless, Turkish membership was not taken into account in the arrangements for European Parliament seats and qualified majority voting rights in the future. This was a signal indicating that EU-Turkey accession negotiations would be long winded. In March 2001 the Government published a detailed programme for meeting the requirements of EU membership, setting out plans for the harmonization of economic, social and administrative structures with the EU's *acquis communautaire*. However, the Government acknowledged that implementation of the programme would not be possible unless Turkey found solutions to its deep-seated economic weaknesses. The post-February 2001 economic crisis created further difficulties for Turkey's EU application, although the Government remained firmly committed to the goal of membership. In December 2002 an EU summit in Copenhagen, Denmark, decided that Turkey's progress towards compliance with EU democratic and human rights criteria would be reviewed in December 2004 and that accession negotiations would begin 'without delay' if the review were positive. The Government thereafter pursued a programme of enacting the constitutional, legal and human rights reforms required by the EU. However, further difficulties with the EU arose over Turkey's signature in August 2003 of a customs union with the 'Turkish Republic of Northern Cyprus' without consulting the European Commission.

In December 2004 an EU summit meeting finally set 3 October 2005 as the date for the opening of accession negotiations with Turkey, subject to strict conditions being met. These included the Turkish signature of an additional protocol extending its customs union with the EU to the 10 new member states, including the Republic of Cyprus. After some hesitation, Turkey signed the additional protocol in late July, but issued a declaration emphasizing that this does not imply recognition of the Greek Cypriot Government. Accession negotiations began, as scheduled, in October, and the science and technology chapter of the *acquis communautaire* was completed in 2006. However, the extension of the additional protocol to Cyprus remained an unresolved issue that could derail Turkey's accession negotiations. A much talked about 'train crash' was avoided only marginally towards the end of that year, but further obstacles were subsequently raised by the then French President, Nicolas Sarkozy (in office during 2007–12), who questioned Turkey's European credentials.

Derailment of EU-Turkey accession negotiations was avoided at the margins, but the EU Council suspended the opening of eight chapters of the *acquis communautaire* in December 2006. This was in response to Turkey's failure to extend the additional protocol to Cyprus, allowing free access of Cypriot vessels to Turkish ports and airports. The suspended chapters included free movement of goods, right of establishment and freedom to provide services, financial services, agriculture and rural development, fisheries, transport policy, customs union and external relations. In addition, the Council decided that Turkey can open accession talks in policy areas other than those eight chapters, but the other chapters cannot be closed unless the Commission has confirmed that Turkey has implemented its commitments with respect to the additional protocol.

Developments between 2007 and 2011 were characterized by a further decline in Turkey's reform implementation and in the EU's commitment to Turkish membership. During this period nine chapters that were not subject to suspension under the Council Decision of 2006 were opened for negotiations. However, progress was slow and these chapters cannot be closed even if negotiations are completed. In addition, France blocked the opening of five more chapters in 2008, as these were considered to be directly linked to accession—a prospect that France and Germany would prefer to substitute with a special partnership that falls short of membership. Although the European Commission announced in May 2012 that the EU would seek to revive the accession negotiations with the Turkish Government, the process remained stalled. In June 2013 the EU eventually agreed to resume the accession negotiations with Turkey by opening the regional policy chapter. However, excessive use of police force against demonstrators protesting against increasing authoritarianism, insensitivity towards environmental issues and religiously motivated interventions into lifestyles resulted in a further postponement of negotiations, pending the publication of a progress report on Turkey in October.

Under a Free Zones Law of 1985, Turkey has established a number of special sites within the country deemed to be outside the customs border. Consequently, they are exempt from foreign trade and other regulations, providing Turkish and foreign companies operating within them with special incentives. The free zones established by 2002 were Mersin (1987), Antalya (1987), Aegean (1990), İstanbul Atatürk Airport (1990), Trabzon (1992), İstanbul-Leather (1995), Eastern Anatolia (1995), Mardin (1995), İstanbul International Stock Exchange (1997), İzmir Menemen-Leather (1998), Rize (1998), Samsun (1998), İstanbul Thrace (1998), Kayseri (1998), Europa (1999), Gaziantep (1999), Adana Yumurtalık (1999), Bursa (2001), Denizli (2001), Kocaeli (2001) and Tubitak-Marmara Research Technology Centre (2002).

ECONOMIC PROSPECTS

Turkey appeared in mid-2005 to have recovered fully from the major financial crises of November 2000 and February 2001, which had again exposed chronic underlying economic weaknesses and the failure of successive governments to correct them. In approving the new three-year stand-by arrangement for Turkey in May 2005, the IMF commented: 'Turkey's economic performance is at its strongest for a generation. Growth was 8% on average over the last three years, while inflation has fallen to single digits, its lowest level in more than 30 years. Through their strong policies, the Turkish authorities have transformed Turkey's economic performance, while reforms associated with EU accession negotiations hold out the promise for further economic advance. Turkey deserves the support of the international community on the strength of its impressive track record under the last Fund-supported programme and the policies proposed under the new arrangement. The challenge now for the authorities is to implement the new programme in full in order to sustain and build on this recent success.' The IMF assessment concluded that 'the overriding goals of the new programme are to create conditions for sustained growth that will raise living standards and reduce unemployment, facilitate convergence towards EU economies and bring about an orderly exit from Fund support'. To achieve these objectives, continued the IMF, the Turkish authorities needed to 'deal effectively with short-term macroeconomic challenges and, in particular, reduce the current account deficit to more sustainable levels; secure permanently lower inflation, by retaining the floating exchange rate, preserving Central Bank independence and adopting formal inflation targeting; make the government debt position more sustainable through continued sizable primary surpluses, shifting towards longer debt maturities and underpinning the fiscal adjustment with structural fiscal reforms; restore Turkey's net foreign exchange reserve position and strengthen its resilience to unexpected external developments; maintain financial sector stability by further improving the supervisory and regulatory framework, accelerating asset recovery and restructuring state banks; and implement a structural reform agenda that enhances Turkey's growth prospects, lowers unemployment and improves the investment climate'.

The Government's resolve was strengthened by its awareness that continued reform was essential for achieving the objective of admission to the EU. The EU's decision in December 2004 to set 3 October 2005 as the date for the opening of formal accession negotiations with Turkey was a major achievement for the Turkish Government, although the attached conditions were the strictest ever imposed on a candidate country. Although negotiations commenced as planned, Turkey is expected to face a long process of negotiations on the terms of eventual EU accession. Turkey's EU membership prospects was tested in May–June 2006, when the new Turkish lira depreciated by about 15% and interest rates had to be increased by four percentage points. Although a financial crisis appears to have been avoided, owing to the existence of a flexible exchange rate and sound fiscal policy, large current account deficits continue to make Turkey highly vulnerable to external shocks, such as global liquidity contractions or adverse developments in the accession negotiations.

Developments in 2007 and 2008 indicated that the success of the post-economic crisis period would be difficult to replicate in the near future. The Central Bank failed to meet its inflation target in three successive years since the introduction of explicit inflation targeting in 2006, and the gap is widening. One reason was the adverse capital movements and the depreciation of the Turkish currency that occurred in mid-2006. The second was the damage to the credibility of the Central Bank caused by the Government's opaque approach to the appointment of the current Central Bank Governor in that year. These factors, together with high current account deficits, have led to a widening of the gap between actual and expected inflation and, in turn, to higher real interest rates. The current account deficit was expected to increase to about 6%, after declining to about 4.75% owing to recession in 2009, while real interest rates were expected to remain above 10% in the medium term.

Current forecasts by OECD and the IMF indicate two principal sources of vulnerability in Turkey: high inflation rates and large current account deficits as a percentage of GDP. Slower growth rates from 2010 onwards were expected to help reduce both inflation and the current account deficit. However, these predictions have proved optimistic. The current account deficit was 9.8% of GDP in 2011 and was projected to improve only slightly, to 8.9%, in 2012. Similarly, inflation remained high in 2011 and 2012, exceeding the ceiling of the Central Bank's inflation target. Despite tight monetary policy, the rate of inflation remained high, at 8.5%, between June 2012 and June 2013. Nevertheless, the IMF and OECD are optimistic about Turkey's economic outlook, although both organizations predict lower growth rates, of around 4%–5%, in the medium term.

The period after 2005 proved to be disappointing with regard to the pace of reform under EU conditionality. The commitment of the AKP Government to reform and EU membership began to falter under pressure from its religious core supporters to prioritize issues closer to their preferences. Concerns have been raised by pro-business organizations regarding an apparent realignment in Turkish foreign policy in favour of countries in the wider Middle East region. Although mixed signals from some EU member states (especially Germany, France and Austria) proved to be a convenient excuse for weakening the Government's reform commitment, informed observers tend to assign a significant weight to the change in government preferences following the AKP's victory in the local elections of 2004. So far, a weaker commitment to reform and EU membership has not been associated with excessive volatility, as was the case in the 1990s and early 2000s. However, the evidence over the last five years (2009–13) indicates that certain vulnerabilities still exist, mainly due to persistent inflation, large current account deficits, and the high indebtedness of the private sector in foreign currency.

Statistical Survey

Source (unless otherwise stated): T. C. Başbakanlık Türkiye İstatistik Kurumu (Turkish Statistical Institute), Necatibey Cad. 114, 06580-Yücetepe/Ankara; tel. (312) 400410; internet www.turkstat.gov.tr.

Area and Population

AREA, POPULATION AND DENSITY

Area (sq km)	
Land	769,604
Inland water	13,958
Total	783,562*
Population (periodic census results)	
21 October 1990	56,473,035
22 October 2000	
Males	34,346,735
Females	33,457,192
Total	67,803,927
Population (annual census results at 31 December)†	
2010	73,722,988
2011	74,724,269
2012	75,627,384
Density (per sq km) at 31 December 2012	98.3‡

* 302,535 sq miles.

† In accordance with new methodology employing Address Based Population Registration System introduced in 2007.

‡ Land area only.

POPULATION BY AGE AND SEX
(annual population census at 31 December 2012)

	Males	Females	Total
0–14	9,678,382	9,178,797	18,857,179
15–64	25,803,873	25,284,329	51,088,202
65 and over	2,473,913	3,208,090	5,682,003
Total	37,956,168	37,671,216	75,627,384

PROVINCES
(annual population census at 31 December 2012)

	Area (sq km)	Population	Density (per sq km)
Adana	14,046	2,125,635	151.3
Adıyaman	7,606	595,261	78.3
Afyon	14,719	703,948	47.8
Ağri	11,499	552,404	48.0
Aksaray	7,966	379,915	47.7
Amasya	5,704	322,283	56.5
Ankara	25,402	4,965,542	195.5
Antalya	20,791	2,092,537	100.6
Ardahan	4,968	106,643	21.5
Artvin	7,367	167,082	22.7
Aydın	7,904	1,006,541	127.3
Balıkesir	14,473	1,160,731	80.2
Bartın	2,080	188,436	90.6
Batman	4,659	534,205	114.7
Bayburt	3,739	75,797	20.3
Bilecik	4,307	204,116	47.4
Bingöl	8,254	262,507	31.8
Bitlis	7,095	337,253	47.5
Bolu	8,323	281,080	33.8
Burdur	7,135	254,341	35.6
Bursa	10,886	2,688,171	246.9
Çanakkale	9,950	493,691	49.6
Çankırı	7,492	184,406	24.6
Çorum	12,796	529,975	41.4
Denizli	11,804	950,557	80.5
Diyarbakır	15,204	1,592,167	104.7
Düzce	2,593	346,493	133.6
Edirne	6,098	399,708	65.5
Elazığ	9,281	562,703	60.6
Erzincan	11,728	217,886	18.6
Erzurum	25,331	778,195	30.7
Eskişehir	13,902	789,750	56.8
Gaziantep	6,845	1,799,558	262.9
Giresun	6,832	419,555	61.4
Gümüşhane	6,437	135,216	21.0
Hakkari	7,179	279,982	39.0
Hatay	5,831	1,483,674	254.4
Iğdir	3,588	190,409	53.1
Isparta	8,871	416,663	47.0
İstanbul	5,315	13,854,740	2,606.7
İzmir	12,016	4,005,459	333.3
Kahramanmaraş	14,457	1,063,174	73.5
Karabük	4,109	225,145	54.8
Karaman	8,869	235,424	26.5
Kars	10,139	304,821	30.1
Kastamonu	13,158	359,808	27.3
Kayseri	17,109	1,274,968	74.5
Kırıkkale	4,570	274,727	60.1
Kırklareli	6,300	341,218	54.2
Kırşehir	6,530	221,209	33.9
Kilis	1,428	124,320	87.1
Kocaeli	3,625	1,634,691	450.9
Konya	40,814	2,052,281	50.3
Kütahya	12,014	573,421	47.7
Malatya	12,103	762,366	63.0
Manisa	13,229	1,346,162	101.8
Mardin	8,806	773,026	87.8
Mersin	15,512	1,682,848	108.5
Muğla	12,949	851,145	65.7
Muş	8,067	413,260	51.2
Nevşehir	5,392	285,190	52.9
Niğde	7,365	340,270	46.2
Ordu	5,952	741,371	124.6
Osmaniye	3,196	492,135	154.0
Rize	3,922	324,152	82.6
Sakarya	4,880	902,267	184.9
Samsun	9,364	1,251,722	133.7
Siirt	5,473	310,879	56.8
Sinop	5,817	201,311	34.6
Sivas	28,567	623,535	21.8
Şanlıurfa	19,336	1,762,075	91.1
Şırnak	7,152	466,982	65.3

—*continued*	Area (sq km)	Population	Density (per sq km)
Tekirdağ	6,342	852,321	134.4
Tokat	10,073	613,990	61.0
Trabzon	4,664	757,898	162.5
Tunceli	7,686	86,276	11.2
Uşak	5,363	342,269	63.8
Van	22,983	1,051,975	45.8
Yalova	850	211,799	249.2
Yozgat	14,074	453,211	32.2
Zonguldak	3,310	606,527	183.2
Total	783,562	75,627,384	96.5

PRINCIPAL TOWNS
(population at annual census of 31 December 2012)

İstanbul	13,710,512	Hatay	742,590
Ankara (capital)	4,842,136	Balıkesir	711,743
İzmir (Smyrna)	3,661,930	Eskişehir	710,830
Bursa	2,402,012	Sakarya	680,637
Adana	1,886,624	Kahramanmaraş	675,589
Gaziantep	1,604,933	Denizli	670,812
Konya	1,563,863	Aydın	611,846
Kocaeli	1,527,407	Tekirdağ	589,049
Antalya	1,492,674	Van	548,717
Mersin	1,327,870	Erzurum	509,474
Diyarbakır	1,155,258	Malatya	504,793
Kayseri	1,116,393	Mardin	458,112
Şanlıurfa	975,455	Sivas	428,426
Manisa	904,513	Trabzon	426,882
Samsun	840,399	Ordu	423,295

BIRTHS, MARRIAGES AND DEATHS

	Live births		Marriages		Deaths	
	Number	Rate (per 1,000)	Number	Rate (per 1,000)	Number*	Rate (per 1,000)
2004	1,213,545	17.9	615,357	8.6	433,000	6.1
2005	1,231,678	18.0	641,241	8.9	436,000	6.1
2006	1,238,725	17.8	636,121	8.7	440,000	6.0
2007	1,266,503	18.0	638,311	8.6	447,000	6.1
2008	1,262,333	17.8	641,973	9.0	454,000	6.4
2009	1,270,000	17.7	591,742	8.2	461,000	6.4
2010	1,279,000	17.6	582,715	8.0	459,000	6.3
2011	1,278,000	17.2	592,775	8.0	465,000	6.3

* Figures are estimates derived from address-based population registration.

Marriages: 603,751 in 2012 (marriage rate 8.0 per 1,000).

Sources: partly UN, *Demographic Yearbook* and *Population and Vital Statistics Report*.

Recorded births (province and district centres only): 1,255,937 in 2010; 1,241,412 in 2011; 1,279,864 in 2012.

Recorded deaths (province and district centres only): 365,707 in 2010; 375,367 in 2011; 374,855 in 2012.

Life expectancy (years at birth): 73.9 (males 71.7; females 76.3) in 2011 (Source: World Bank, World Development Indicators database).

ECONOMICALLY ACTIVE POPULATION
(sample surveys, '000 persons aged 15 years and over)

	2010	2011	2012
Agriculture, hunting, forestry and fishing	5,683	6,143	6,097
Mining and quarrying	115	125	113
Manufacturing	4,216	4,367	4,420
Electricity, gas and water	165	212	218
Construction	1,431	1,676	1,709
Wholesale and retail trade; repair of motor vehicles, motorcycles and personal and household goods	3,326	3,476	3,502
Hotels and restaurants	1,084	1,141	1,206
Transport, storage and communications	1,213	1,255	1,333
Financial intermediation	273	280	264
Real estate, renting and business activities	490	581	691
Public administration and defence; compulsory social security	1,292	1,337	1,458
Education	1,019	1,106	1,224
Health and social work	590	693	808
Other community, social and personal service activities	1,699	1,717	1,780
Total employed	22,594	24,110	24,821
Unemployed	3,046	2,615	2,518
Total labour force	25,641	26,725	27,339
Males	18,257	18,867	19,147
Females	7,383	7,859	8,192

Note: Totals may not be equal to the sum of components, owing to rounding.

Health and Welfare

KEY INDICATORS

Total fertility rate (children per woman, 2011)	2.1
Under-5 mortality rate (per 1,000 live births, 2011)	15
HIV/AIDS (% of persons aged 15–49, 2011)	<0.1
Physicians (per 1,000 head, 2009)	1.5
Hospital beds (per 1,000 head, 2009)	2.5
Health expenditure (2010): US $ per head (PPP)	1,039
Health expenditure (2010): % of GDP	6.7
Health expenditure (2010): public (% of total)	74.8
Access to water (% of persons, 2011)	100
Access to sanitation (% of persons, 2011)	91
Total carbon dioxide emissions ('000 metric tons, 2009)	277,844.9
Carbon dioxide emissions per head (metric tons, 2009)	3.9
Human Development Index (2012): ranking	90
Human Development Index (2012): value	0.722

For sources and definitions, see explanatory note on p. vi.

Agriculture

PRINCIPAL CROPS
('000 metric tons)

	2009	2010	2011
Wheat	20,600	19,674	21,800
Rice, paddy	750	860	900
Barley	7,300	7,250	7,600
Maize	4,250	4,310	4,200
Rye	343	367	366
Oats	218	204	218
Potatoes	4,398	4,548	4,613
Sugar beet	17,275	17,942	16,127
Beans, dry	181	213	201
Chick peas	563	531	487
Lentils	302	447	406
Walnuts	177	178	183
Hazelnuts, with shell	500	600	430
Olives	1,291	1,415	1,750
Sunflower seed	1,057	1,320	1,335
Cabbages and other brassicas	707	693	710
Lettuce and chicory	438	419	424
Spinach	225	218	222
—continued	2009	2010	2011
Tomatoes	10,746	10,052	11,003
Cauliflowers and broccoli	157	159	162
Pumpkins, squash and gourds	412	430	411
Cucumbers and gherkins	1,735	1,739	1,749
Aubergines (Eggplants)	816	847	822
Chillies and peppers, green	1,837	1,987	1,975
Onions and shallots, green	169	165	154
Onions, dry	1,850	1,900	2,141
Garlic	105	77	79
Beans, green	604	588	615
Carrots and turnips	594	533	602
Watermelons	3,810	3,683	3,864
Cantaloupes and other melons	1,679	1,612	1,648
Bananas	205	210	207
Oranges	1,690	1,711	1,730
Tangerines, mandarins, etc.	846	859	872
Lemons and limes	784	787	790
Grapefruit and pomelos	191	214	219
Apples	2,782	2,600	2,680
Pears	384	380	386
Quinces	96	121	128
Apricots	695	476	676
Sweet cherries	418	418	439
Sour cherries	193	195	182
Peaches and nectarines	547	535	546
Plums and sloes	246	241	269
Strawberries	292	300	302
Grapes	4,265	4,255	4,296
Figs	244	255	261
Tea	199	235	222
Anise, badian, fennel and coriander	9	14	15
Tobacco, unmanufactured	85	55	45

Aggregate production ('000 metric tons, may include official, semi-official or estimated data): Total cereals 33,570 in 2009, 32,765 in 2010, 35,195 in 2011; Total roots and tubers 4,399 in 2009, 4,549 in 2010, 4,614 in 2011; Total pulses 1,237 in 2009, 1,345 in 2010, 1,234 in 2011; Total vegetables (incl. melons) 26,702 in 2009, 25,901 in 2010, 27,407 in 2011; Total fruits (excl. melons) 14,223 in 2009, 13,946 in 2010, 14,388 in 2011.

Source: FAO.

LIVESTOCK
('000 head, year ending September)

	2009	2010	2011
Horses	180	167	155
Asses	274	234	212
Cattle	10,860	10,724	11,370
Buffaloes	86	87	85
Camels	1	1	1
Pigs	2	2	2
Sheep	23,975	21,795	23,090
Goats	5,594	5,128	6,293
Chickens	244,280	229,969	234,918
Ducks	470	413	397
Geese and guinea fowls	1,063	945	716
Turkeys	3,230	2,755	2,942

Source: FAO.

LIVESTOCK PRODUCTS
('000 metric tons)

	2009	2010	2011
Cattle meat	325.3	618.6	644.9
Buffalo meat	1.0	3.4	1.6
Sheep meat*	262	240	253
Goat meat*	37.0	33.9	41.6
Horse meat*	1.8	1.8	1.8
Chicken meat	1,293.3	1,444.1	1,613.3
Cows' milk	11,583.3	12,480.5	13,802.4
Buffalo milk	32.4	35.5	40.4
Sheep milk	734.2	816.8	892.8
Goats' milk	192.2	272.8	320.6
Hen eggs	864.5	740.0	810.0†
Honey	82.0	81.1	94.2

* FAO estimates.
† Unofficial figure.

Source: FAO.

Forestry

ROUNDWOOD REMOVALS
('000 cubic metres, excl. bark)

	2009	2010	2011
Sawlogs, veneer logs and logs for sleepers	7,805	8,321	8,719
Pulpwood	6,200	7,027	7,288
Other industrial wood	247	347	416
Fuel wood	5,048	4,902	4,616
Total	19,300	20,597	21,039

Source: FAO.

SAWNWOOD PRODUCTION
('000 cubic metres, incl. railway sleepers)

	2009	2010	2011
Coniferous (softwood)	3,777	3,984	4,192
Broadleaved (hardwood)	2,076	2,259	2,269
Total	5,853	6,243	6,461

Source: FAO.

Fishing

('000 metric tons, live weight)

	2009	2010	2011
Capture	464.2	487.3	514.8
Common carp	11.0	12.1	10.0
Tarek	10.7	11.4	9.2
Whiting (incl. Poutassou)	12.7	14.8	10.4
Mullets	9.6	11.9	10.0
European pilchard	30.1	27.6	34.7
European sprat	53.4	57.0	87,141
European anchovy	204.7	229.0	228.5
Atlantic bonito	7.0	9.4	10.0
Bluefish	6.0	4.7	3.1
Atlantic horse mackerel	8.0	6.1	6.9
Mediterranean horse mackerel	20.4	14.4	18.1
Sand smelts (Silversides)	7.9	5.9	8.2
Striped venus	24.6	26.9	30.2
Marine molluscs	39.6	41.2	42.7
Aquaculture	159.6	167.7	188.9*
Trout	80.9	85.2	107.9
Gilthead seabream	28.4	28.2	32.2
Seabasses	46.6	50.8	47.0
Total catch	623.9	655.0	703.7*

* FAO estimate.

Source: FAO.

Mining

('000 metric tons unless otherwise indicated)

	2009	2010	2011
Hard coal	3,774	3,667	5,619
Lignite	82,263	74,437	89,806
Iron ore: gross weight	4,170	5,188	5,754
Iron ore: metal content[1]	2,200	2,700	3,000
Copper[1,2]	105	97	80
Bauxite	1,473.2	1,311.1	1,500.0[1]
Lead: mine output[1,2]	26	23	26
Lead: concentrates[1,2]	23	21	23
Chromium[3]	1,574.0	1,904.5	1,900.0[1]
Silver (kilograms)	351,600	363,520	450,000[1]
Gold (kilograms)[2,4]	14,469	16,890	25,000[1]
Marble ('000 cu m)	2,715.6	3,352.1	3,500.0[1]
Limestone[5]	243,184	270,441	270,000[1]
Quartzite	1,943.9	2,500.0	2,500.0[1]
—continued			
Dolomite	11,152.1	15,224.5	15,000.0[1]
Bentonite	932.4	798.4	379.9
Kaolin	727.6	711.5	1,002.4
Silica sand[6]	4,499.2	4,022.4	3,250.0[1]
Gypsum	4,369.6	6,321.9	6,400.0[1]
Magnesite: mine output	861.2	2,316.8	2,300.0[1]
Feldspar: mine output	4,212.5	6,281.6	4,478.0
Borate minerals: mine output	3,923.5	4,442.9	6,306.6
Borate minerals: concentrates	1,800.0[1]	2,200.0[1]	2,273.1
Nitrogen[1,7]	100.0	200.0	200.0
Perlite: mine output	522.8	545.6	429.8
Pumice	4,322.5	4,000.0[1]	4,000.0[1]
Pyrites[6]	124.1	131.3	130.0[1]
Sodium sulphate: concentrates	4,592.0	1,600.6	1,500.0[1]

[1] Estimated production.
[2] Figures refer to metal content of ores and concentrates.
[3] Figures refer to gross weight of ores.
[4] Figures include estimated output from the by-products of refining other base metals.
[5] Excluding production used for making cement.
[6] Figures refer to gross weight of minerals.
[7] Nitrogen content of ammonia.

Source: US Geological Survey.

Crude petroleum ('000 metric tons): 2,602 in 2010; 2,427 in 2011; 2,399 in 2012.

Natural gas (million cu metres): 660.4 in 2009; 625.7 in 2010; 669.8 in 2011.

Industry

SELECTED PRODUCTS
('000 metric tons, unless otherwise indicated)

	2010	2011	2012*
Flour	7,106.0	7,815.4	4,532.8
Sugar	2,436.7	2,358.9	2,304.4
Cotton yarn	1,077.6	1,068.9	933.9
Wool yarn	75,776.3	70,945.7	37,001.7
Crude steel	30,677.9	38,072.8	38,957.8
Cement	70,800.7	68,208.0	63,134.8
Fertilizers (incl. mineral or chemical)	3,479.1	3,969.2	3,713.7
Domestic refrigerators and freezers ('000)	7,164.7	7,965.8	8,661.6
Domestic washing machines ('000)	5,560.2	6,072.0	6,104.0
Ovens ('000)	6,778.4	7,823.1	7,119.5
Vacuum cleaners ('000)	3,289.3	3,335.6	3,215.7
Television receivers ('000, colour)	9,266.7	10,765.3	n.a.
Tyres for automobiles ('000 units)	18,390.8	20,119.0	17,985.8
Tractors (number)	45,200	72,565	60,261
Passenger motor cars (number)	886,201	935,988	857,369
Buses and minibuses (number)	28,909	37,803	53,257
Electric energy (gross production, million kWh)	211,207.7	229,395.1	n.a.

* Provisional figures.

2010 ('000 metric tons unless otherwise indicated, provisional): Margarine 599.7; Beer (million litres) 1,024.0; Alcoholic spirits (million litres) 72.2; Cigarettes (with filter) 115.2; Products of the paper industry 5,001.9; Wood block flooring ('000 sq m) 64,801.8; Motor oil 4,976.2; Motor gasoline 3,882.8; Liquefied petroleum gas 683.3; Asphalt 2,789.0.

Finance

CURRENCY AND EXCHANGE RATES

Monetary Units

100 kuruş = 1 Turkish lira.

Sterling, Dollar and Euro Equivalents (31 May 2013)

£1 sterling = 2.842 liras;
US $1 = 1.868 liras;
€1 = 2.429 liras;
100 Turkish liras = £35.19 = US $53.54 = €41.16.

Average Exchange Rate (Turkish liras per US $)

2010 1.5029
2011 1.6749
2012 1.7960

Note: A new currency, the new Turkish lira, equivalent to 1,000,000 of the former units, was introduced on 1 January 2005. Figures in this survey have been converted retrospectively to reflect this development. (The name of the currency reverted to Turkish lira on 1 January 2009, although new Turkish lira banknotes and coins remained in circulation for a further year.).

CONSOLIDATED BUDGET

(million Turkish liras)

Revenue	2010	2011	2012*
Tax revenue	216,109	260,262	286,117
Direct taxes	61,295	76,012	85,530
Indirect taxes	147,422	175,155	190,891
Taxes on wealth	7,392	9,095	9,696
Non-tax revenue	19,447	23,836	27,449
Special revenues and funds	150,263	184,254	215,762
Total	385,819	468,352	529,328

Expenditure	2010	2011	2012*
Current expenditure	187,871	215,946	251,041
Investment expenditure	37,545	43,322	49,848
Fixed capital	37,712	43,136	49,672
Inventory variation	–166	187	176
Transfers	197,317	217,801	252,627
Current transfers	184,540	205,841	241,403
Capital transfers	12,777	11,960	11,224
Total	422,734	477,070	553,516

* Provisional figures.

Source: Ministry of Development, Ankara.

INTERNATIONAL RESERVES

(US $ million at 31 December)

	2010	2011	2012
Gold (national valuation)	5,258	9,888	19,235
IMF special drawing rights	1,494	1,490	1,489
Reserve position in IMF	174	173	173
Foreign exchange	79,046	76,659	98,280
Total	85,972	88,210	119,177

Source: IMF, *International Financial Statistics*.

MONEY SUPPLY

(million Turkish liras at 31 December)

	2010	2011	2012
Currency outside depository corporations	43,623	48,592	52,020
Transferable deposits	114,031	132,168	144,019
Other deposits	457,908	519,298	569,861
Securities other than shares	1,113	10,338	18,492
Broad money	616,674	710,395	784,392

Source: IMF, *International Financial Statistics*.

COST OF LIVING

(Consumer Price Index; base: 2003 = 100)

	2010	2011	2012
Food and non-alcoholic beverages	186.2	197.8	214.5
Alcoholic beverages and tobacco	292.4	302.8	345.2
Clothing and footwear	124.6	132.8	143.6
Housing, water, electricity, gas and other fuels	208.0	220.1	245.3
Household goods	142.3	153.4	167.4
Health	127.6	128.3	130.1
Transport	171.0	188.0	202.4
Communications	112.1	112.6	116.2
Recreation and culture	146.0	148.2	156.4
Education	185.9	196.0	207.8
Restaurants and hotels	229.1	247.5	270.2
Miscellaneous goods and services	191.7	216.2	244.2
All items	178.4	190.0	206.8

NATIONAL ACCOUNTS

(million Turkish liras at current prices)

Expenditure on the Gross Domestic Product

	2010	2011	2012
Government final consumption expenditure	157,513.6	180,707.8	209,198.6
Private final consumption expenditure	787,752.8	923,836.2	992,745.2
Increase in stocks	6,707.7	22,528.4	–357.4
Gross fixed capital formation	207,815.6	283,163.2	287,681.7
Total domestic expenditure	1,159,789.7	1,410,235.6	1,489,268.1
Exports of goods and services	233,045.9	311,148.0	374,615.8
Less Imports of goods and services	294,036.3	423,670.4	447,067.1
GDP in purchasers' values	1,098,799.3	1,297,713.2	1,416,816.8
GDP at constant 1998 prices	105,885.6	115,174.7	117,753.7

Gross Domestic Product by Economic Activity

	2010	2011	2012
Agriculture, forestry and fishing	92,739.0	103,635.3	112,635.0
Mining and quarrying	15,785.4	19,132.9	21,103.5
Manufacturing	172,112.1	210,674.2	220,338.7
Electricity, gas and water	25,455.0	28,768.0	32,347.0
Construction	45,669.5	57,751.3	61,806.9
Wholesale and retail trade	120,869.4	155,908.3	172,624.2
Hotels and restaurants	25,589.6	30,027.8	33,314.2
Transport, storage and communications	144,427.5	175,665.2	197,988.7
Financial institutions	40,501.6	40,575.8	46,987.2
Ownership of dwellings	123,028.9	129,265.0	137,712.8
Real estate, renting and business activities	52,742.8	60,939.4	70,472.4
Public administration and defence; compulsory social security	46,090.3	52,248.9	60,359.3
Education	36,802.7	42,717.2	49,197.8
Health and social work	17,939.5	19,384.5	21,784.0
Other community, social and personal services	18,696.6	21,379.9	22,074.4
Private households with employed persons	2,097.0	2,379.6	2,709.7
Sub-total	980,547.0	1,150,453.1	1,263,456.0
Taxes, *less* subsidies	137,671.7	164,583.7	175,750.8
Less Financial intermediation services indirectly measured	19,419.3	17,323.6	22,390.0
GDP in purchasers' values	1,098,799.3	1,297,713.2	1,416,816.8

BALANCE OF PAYMENTS
(US $ million)

	2010	2011	2012
Exports of goods	120,991	143,497	163,329
Imports of goods	–177,315	–232,535	–228,957
Balance on goods	–56,324	–89,038	–65,628
Exports of services	36,451	40,974	44,198
Imports of services	–19,882	–20,945	–20,783
Balance on goods and services	–39,755	–69,009	–42,213
Primary income received	4,477	3,952	5,034
Primary income paid	–11,692	–11,793	–11,709
Balance on goods, services and primary income	–46,970	–76,850	–48,888
Secondary income received	2,107	2,503	2,297
Secondary income paid	–584	–745	–930
Current balance	–45,447	–75,092	–47,521
Capital account (net)	–51	–25	–44
Direct investment assets	–1,464	–2,349	–4,074
Direct investment liabilities	9,036	16,047	12,555
Portfolio investment assets	–3,524	2,688	2,648
Portfolio investment liabilities	19,617	19,298	38,132
Other investment assets	7,012	11,136	–449
Other investment liabilities	28,384	19,878	20,416
Net errors and omissions	1,408	9,427	1,157
Reserves and related items	14,971	1,008	22,820

Source: IMF, *International Financial Statistics*.

External Trade

PRINCIPAL COMMODITIES
(distribution by SITC, US $ million, excl. military goods)

Imports c.i.f.	2010	2011	2012
Crude materials (inedible) except fuels	15,394.6	20,051.9	18,630.1
Metalliferous ores and metal scrap	8,201.8	11,141.6	10,754.1
Mineral fuels, lubricants, etc.	38,497.0	54,116.8	60,115.8
Petroleum, petroleum products, etc.	11,390.6	15,245.9	16,179.2
Chemicals and related products	25,446.3	31,191.1	29,685.7
Organic chemicals	4,172.2	5,282.9	4,882.8
Medicinal and pharmaceutical products	4,777.7	5,083.1	4,343.1
Plastics in primary forms	7,650.0	9,932.2	9,929.0
Basic manufactures	31,802.2	38,429.5	36,040.2
Textile yarn, fabrics, etc.	6,701.8	7,719.4	6,593.6
Iron and steel	9,720.8	11,544.6	11,095.9
Machinery and transport equipment	53,875.8	67,076.8	61,605.7
Power-generating machinery and equipment	6,716.8	6,894.6	6,806.2
Machinery specialized for particular industries	5,138.9	7,789.9	7,522.9
General industrial machinery, equipment and parts	6,873.2	8,985.5	8,710.3
Road vehicles	13,174.4	16,782.2	14,184.6
Miscellaneous manufactured articles	11,638.1	14,137.6	13,153.3
Non-monetary gold, unwrought or semi-manufactured	2,523.5	6,726.3	8,392.1
Total (incl. others)	185,544.3	240,841.7	236,545.0

Exports f.o.b.	2010	2011	2012
Food and live animals	10,498.6	12,285.6	12,686.0
Vegetables and fruit	6,152.5	6,695.7	6,552.3
Mineral fuels, lubricants, etc.	4,469.4	6,538.9	7,707.8
Petroleum, petroleum products, etc.	4,026.3	6,027.7	6,964.7
Chemicals and related products	6,805.8	8,047.2	8,913.7
Basic manufactures	33,181.5	40,327.7	41,262.6
Textile yarn, fabrics, etc.	8,969.6	10,783.2	11,083.7
Non-metallic mineral manufactures	3,708.4	3,729.3	3,758.4
Iron and steel	10,199.5	12,836.9	13,093.0
Machinery and transport equipment	31,811.2	37,441.6	37,432.1
Road vehicles	13,522.2	15,444.5	14,664.3
Miscellaneous manufactured articles	19,763.1	22,463.9	24,318.9
Clothing and accessories (excl. footwear)	12,745.6	13,945.0	14,277.9
Total (incl. others)	113,883.2	134,906.9	152,464.4

PRINCIPAL TRADING PARTNERS
(US $ million, excl. military goods*)

Imports c.i.f. (excl. grants)	2010	2011	2012
Algeria	2,276.0	1,150.3	924.9
Belgium	3,213.6	3,959.3	3,690.3
Bulgaria	1,702.5	2,474.6	2,753.6
China, People's Republic	17,180.8	21,693.3	21,295.2
France	8,176.6	9,229.6	8,589.9
Germany	17,549.1	22,985.6	21,400.6
Greece	1,541.6	2,568.8	3,539.9
India	3,409.9	6,498.7	5,843.6
Iran	7,645.0	12,461.5	11,964.8
Italy	10,203.7	13,449.9	13,344.5
Japan	3,297.8	4,263.7	3,601.4
Korea, Republic	4,764.1	6,298.5	5,660.1
Netherlands	3,156.0	4,005.0	3,660.6
Poland	2,621.0	3,496.2	3,058.1
Romania	3,449.2	3,801.3	3,236.4
Russia	21,600.6	23,952.9	26,625.3
Saudi Arabia	2,437.2	2,001.5	2,171.0
Spain	4,840.1	6,196.5	6,023.6
Sweden	1,922.8	2,284.4	2,135.4
Switzerland	3,153.7	5,019.0	4,304.9
Ukraine	3,832.7	4,812.1	4,394.2
United Arab Emirates	698.4	1,649.5	3,596.5
United Kingdom	4,680.6	5,840.4	5,629.5
USA	12,318.7	16,034.1	14,130.5
Total (incl. others)	185,544.3	240,841.7	236,545.0

Exports f.o.b.	2010	2011	2012
Algeria	1,504.6	1,470.5	1,813.0
Azerbaijan	1,550.5	2,064.0	2,584.7
Belgium	1,960.4	2,451.0	2,359.6
Bulgaria	1,497.4	1,622.8	1,685.0
China, People's Republic	2,269.2	2,466.3	2,833.3
Egypt	2,250.6	2,759.3	3,679.2
France	6,054.5	6,805.8	6,198.6
Germany	11,479.1	13,950.8	13,124.6
Greece	1,455.7	1,553.3	1,401.5
Iran	3,044.2	3,589.6	9,921.6
Iraq	6,036.4	8,310.1	10,822.1
Israel	2,080.1	2,391.1	2,329.7
Italy	6,505.3	7,851.5	6,373.2
Libya	1,932.4	747.6	2,139.4
Netherlands	2,461.4	3,243.1	3,244.6
Poland	1,504.3	1,758.3	1,853.7
Romania	2,599.4	2,878.8	2,495.6
Russia	4,628.2	5,992.6	6,680.8
Saudi Arabia	2,217.7	2,763.5	3,676.6

Exports f.o.b.—*continued*	2010	2011	2012
Spain	3,536.2	3,917.6	3,717.5
Switzerland	2,056.9	1,484.3	2,124.5
Ukraine	1,260.4	1,729.8	1,829.3
United Arab Emirates	3,332.9	3,706.7	8,174.6
United Kingdom	7,235.9	8,151.4	8,693.9
USA	3,762.9	4,584.0	5,604.4
Total (incl. others)	113,883.2	134,906.9	152,464.4

* Imports by country of origin, exports by country of last consignment.

Transport

RAILWAYS
(traffic)

	2010	2011	2012
Passengers carried ('000)	84,173	85,752	70,284
Passenger-km (million)	5,491	5,882	4,598
Freight carried ('000 metric tons)*	24,355	25,421	25,666
Freight ton-km (million)	11,462	11,677	11,670

* Excluding parcels and departmental traffic.

ROAD TRAFFIC
(motor vehicles by use)

	2010	2011	2012
Passenger cars	7,544,871	8,113,111	8,648,875
Minibuses	386,973	389,435	396,119
Buses and coaches	208,510	219,906	235,949
Small trucks	2,399,038	2,611,104	2,794,606
Trucks	726,359	728,458	751,650
Motorcycles and mopeds	2,389,488	2,527,190	2,657,722
Special purpose vehicles	35,492	34,116	33,071

SHIPPING

Flag Registered Fleet
(at 31 December)

	2010	2011	2012
Number of vessels	1,291	1,297	1,325
Total displacement ('000 grt)	6,070.6	6,457.3	6,680.1

Source: Lloyd's List Intelligence (www.lloydslistintelligence.com).

International Sea-borne Traffic

	2005	2006	2007
Vessels entered (number)	33,181	32,810	33,477
Passengers disembarked (number)	698,915	613,533	588,108
Goods unloaded ('000 metric tons)*	107,526	n.a.	n.a.
Vessels cleared (number)	23,245	23,564	24,941
Passengers embarked (number)	705,937	608,654	594,385
Goods loaded ('000 metric tons)*	36,601	n.a.	n.a.

* Including timber.

CIVIL AVIATION
(scheduled services)

	2003	2004	2005
Domestic services:			
Kilometres flown ('000)	28,180	28,489	35,886
Number of passengers	4,991,517	5,805,291	7,151,491
Passenger-km ('000)	2,751,910	3,223,299	3,991,885
Freight handled (metric tons)	29,146	30,710	31,504
Total ton-km ('000)	275,681	321,118	392,055
International services:			
Kilometres flown ('000)	101,738	109,038	122,899
Number of passengers	4,802,897	5,617,506	6,486,320
Passenger-km ('000)	12,223,997	14,227,375	16,359,597
Freight handled (metric tons)	88,993	93,736	87,851
Total ton-km ('000)	1,617,729	1,849,177	2,104,407

Passengers carried (million): 102.8 in 2010; 117.6 in 2011; 130.4 in 2012.

Freight handled ('000 metric tons): 2,021.1 in 2010; 2,249.5 in 2011; 2,249.1 in 2012.

Tourism

VISITOR ARRIVALS BY NATIONALITY

Country	2010	2011	2012
Austria	500,321	528,966	505,560
Azerbaijan	486,381	578,685	593,238
Belgium	543,003	585,860	608,071
Bulgaria	1,433,970	1,491,561	1,492,073
France	928,376	1,140,459	1,032,565
Georgia	1,112,193	1,152,661	1,404,882
Germany	4,385,263	4,826,315	5,028,745
Greece	670,297	702,017	669,823
Iran	1,885,097	1,879,304	1,186,343
Israel	109,559	79,140	83,740
Italy	671,060	752,238	714,041
Netherlands	1,073,064	1,222,823	1,273,593
Russia	3,107,043	3,468,214	3,599,925
Sweden	447,270	571,917	617,811
Ukraine	568,227	602,404	634,663
United Kingdom	2,673,605	2,582,054	2,456,519
USA	642,768	757,143	771,837
Total (incl. others)	28,632,204	31,456,076	31,782,832

Tourism receipts (million US $, excl. passenger transport, incl. expenditure of Turkish nationals residing abroad): 20,806.7 in 2010; 23,020.4 in 2011; 23,440.4 in 2012.

Communications Media

	2010	2011	2012
Telephones ('000 main lines in use)	16,201.5	15,210.8	13,859.7
Mobile cellular telephones ('000 subscribers)	61,769.6	65,321.7	67,680.5
Internet subscribers ('000)	7,224.4	7,652.2	n.a.
Broadband subscribers ('000)	7,087.7	7,554.7	7,858.2

Personal computers: 4,400,000 (61.0 per 1,000 persons) in 2006.

Source: International Telecommunication Union.

Education

(2012/13, unless otherwise indicated, provisional figures)

	Institutions	Teachers	Students
Pre-primary	27,197	62,933	1,077,933
Primary	46,156	551,802	11,160,896
Secondary:			
general	4,214	119,393	2,725,972
vocational and teacher training	6,204	135,502	2,269,651
Higher*	1,914	118,839	4,112,687

* Figures for 2011/12.

Adult literacy rate (UNESCO estimates): 90.8% (males 96.4%, females 85.3%) in 2009 (Source: UNESCO Institute for Statistics).

Directory

The Constitution

In October 1981 the National Security Council (NSC), which took power in September 1980, announced the formation of a Consultative Assembly to draft a new constitution, replacing that of 1961. The Assembly consisted of 40 members appointed directly by the NSC and 120 members chosen by the NSC from candidates put forward by the governors of the 67 provinces; all former politicians were excluded. The draft Constitution was approved by the Assembly in September 1982 and by a national referendum in November. Its main provisions (including subsequent amendments) are summarized below:

Legislative power is vested in the unicameral Turkish Grand National Assembly (TGNA), which comprises 550 deputies. The election of deputies is by universal adult suffrage for a four-year term (reduced from five years, following an amendment in May 2007). Executive power is vested in the President of the Republic, who is elected by universal suffrage for a five-year term. The President may not serve for more than two terms of office. The President is empowered to: appoint a Prime Minister and senior members of the judiciary, the Central Bank and broadcasting organizations; dissolve the Assembly; and declare a state of emergency entailing rule by decree.

In July 2003 the TGNA approved an amendment reducing the number of NSC members from 13 to six. The NSC was henceforth to be a predominantly civilian advisory body, comprising the President, Prime Minister, Chief of General Staff, and Ministers of Foreign Affairs, National Defence and Internal Affairs. Amendments approved by the Assembly in May 2004 included guarantees of equal rights between men and women, the removal of references to capital punishment and the abolition of State Security Courts. At a national referendum held in September 2010, a package of amendments to the Constitution, including a restructuring of the Supreme Council of Judges and Public Prosecutors, limitations on the judicial powers of the Constitutional Court and the Council of State, and restrictions on the jurisdiction of military tribunals, were approved by 57.9% of participating voters. (For details regarding further constitutional amendments, see History.)

The Government

HEAD OF STATE

President: ABDULLAH GÜL (took office 28 August 2007).

COUNCIL OF MINISTERS
(September 2013)

The executive is formed by the Adalet ve Kalkınma Partisi (AKP).

Prime Minister: RECEP TAYYIP ERDOĞAN.

Deputy Prime Ministers: BÜLENT ARINÇ, ALI BABACAN, BEŞIR ATALAY, BEKIR BOZDAĞ.

Minister of Justice: SADULLAH ERGIN.

Minister of Family and Social Policy: FATMA ŞAHIN.

Minister of European Union Affairs: EGEMEN BAĞIŞ.

Minister of Science, Industry and Technology: NIHAT ERGÜN.

Minister of Labour and Social Security: FARUK ÇELIK.

Minister of the Environment and Urban Planning: ERDOĞAN BAYRAKTAR.

Minister of Foreign Affairs: Prof. Dr AHMET DAVUTOĞLU.

Minister of the Economy: MEHMET ZAFER ÇAĞLAYAN.

Minister of Energy and Natural Resources: Dr TANER YILDIZ.

Minister of Youth and Sports: SUAT KILIÇ.

Minister of Food, Agriculture and Livestock: Dr MEHMET MEHDI EKER.

Minister of Customs and Trade: HAYATI YAZICI.

Minister of Internal Affairs: MUAMMER GÜLER.

Minister of Development: CEVDET YILMAZ.

Minister of Culture and Tourism: ÖMER ÇELIK.

Minister of Finance: MEHMET ŞIMŞEK.

Minister of National Education: NABI AVCI.

Minister of National Defence: İSMET YILMAZ.

Minister of Forestry and Water Works: VEYSEL EROĞLU.

Minister of Health: Dr MEHMET MÜEZZINOĞLU.

Minister of Transport, Maritime Affairs and Communications: BINALI YILDIRIM.

MINISTRIES

President's Office: Cumhurbaşkanlığı Genel Sekreterliği, 06689 Çankaya, Ankara; tel. (312) 4702308; fax (312) 4701316; e-mail cumhurbaskanligi@tccb.gov.tr; internet www.cankaya.gov.tr.

Prime Minister's Office: Vekaletler Cad., Başbakanlık Merkez Bina, 06573 Kızılay, Ankara; tel. (312) 4221000; fax (312) 4180476; e-mail bimer@basbakanlik.gov.tr; internet www.basbakanlik.gov.tr.

Deputy Prime Ministers' Office: Başbakan yard. ve Devlet Bakanı, Bakanlıklar, Ankara; tel. (312) 4191621; fax (312) 4191547.

Ministry of Culture and Tourism: Kültür ve Turizm Bakanlığı, Atatürk Bul. 29, 06050 Opera, Ankara; tel. (312) 3090850; fax (312) 3124359; e-mail info@kulturturizm.gov.tr; internet www.kultur.gov.tr.

Ministry of Customs and Trade: Ankara.

Ministry of Development: Ankara.

Ministry of the Economy: Ankara.

Ministry of Energy and Natural Resources: Enerji ve Tabii Kaynaklar Bakanlığı, Türk Ocağı Cad. 2, 06100 Ankara; tel. (312) 2126420; fax (312) 2225760; e-mail bilgi@enerji.gov.tr; internet www.enerji.gov.tr.

Ministry of the Environment and Urban Planning: Ankara.

Ministry of European Union Affairs: Mustafa Kemal Mah. 2082 Cad. 4, 06510 Bilkent, Ankara; tel. (312) 2181300; fax (312) 2181464; e-mail bilgiedinme@ab.gov.tr; internet www.abgs.gov.tr.

Ministry of Family and Social Policy: Ankara.

Ministry of Finance: Maliye Bakanlığı, Dikmen Cad. 06450, Ankara; tel. (312) 4152900; fax (312) 4257816; e-mail bilgi@sgb.gov.tr; internet www.maliye.gov.tr.

Ministry of Food, Agriculture and Livestock: Tarım ve Hayvancılık Bakanlığı, Kampüsü Eskişehir Yolu 9 km Lodumlu, Ankara; tel. (312) 2873360; fax (312) 2863964; e-mail admin@tarim.gov.tr; internet www.tarim.gov.tr.

Ministry of Foreign Affairs: Dr Sadık Ahmet Cad. 8, 06100 Balgat, Ankara; tel. (312) 2921000; fax (312) 2873869; e-mail info@mfa.gov.tr; internet www.mfa.gov.tr.

Ministry of Forestry and Water Works: Çevre ve Orman Bakanliği, Söğütözü Cad. 14E, Ankara; tel. (312) 2075000; fax (312) 2076299; e-mail webmaster@cevreorman.gov.tr; internet www.cevreorman.gov.tr.

Ministry of Health: Sağlık Bakanlığı, Mithatpasa Cad. 3 Sihhiye, 06434 Ankara; tel. (312) 5852250; fax (312) 4339885; e-mail info@saglik.gov.tr; internet www.saglik.gov.tr.

Ministry of Internal Affairs: Içişleri Bakanlığı, Bakanlıklar, Ankara; tel. (312) 4224000; fax (312) 4181795; e-mail basin@icisleri.gov.tr; internet www.icisleri.gov.tr.

Ministry of Justice: Adalet Bakanlığı, 06659 Kizilay, Ankara; tel. (312) 4177770; fax (312) 4193370; e-mail akilic1@adalet.gov.tr; internet www.adalet.gov.tr.

Ministry of Labour and Social Security: Çalışma ve Sosyal Güvenlik Bakanlığı, İnönü Bul. 42, 06520 Emek, Ankara; tel. (312) 2966000; fax (312) 4179765; e-mail iletisim@csgb.gov.tr; internet www.csgb.gov.tr.

Ministry of National Defence: Milli Savunma Bakanlığı, 06100 Ankara; tel. (312) 4026100; fax (312) 4184737; internet www.msb.gov.tr.

Ministry of National Education: Milli Eğitim Bakanlığı, Atatürk Bul., Bakanlıklar, Ankara; tel. (312) 4191410; fax (312) 4177027; e-mail meb@meb.gov.tr; internet www.meb.gov.tr.

Ministry of Science, Industry and Technology: Sanayi ve Ticaret Bakanlığı, Eskişehir Yolu üzeri 7 km 2151 Cad. 154, 06510 Ankara; tel. (312) 2015000; fax (312) 2196738; e-mail webmaster@sanayi.gov.tr; internet www.sanayi.gov.tr.

Ministry of Transport, Maritime Affairs and Communications: T.C. Ulaştırma Denizcilik ve Haberleşme Bakanlığı, Hakkı Turayliç Cad. 5, 06338 Emek, Ankara; tel. (312) 2031116; fax (212) 2124930; e-mail okm@ubak.gov.tr; internet www.ubak.gov.tr.

Ministry of Youth and Sports: Ankara.

Legislature

Grand National Assembly (Büyük Millet Meclisi)

TBMM 06543, Bakanlıklar, Ankara; tel. (312) 4205151; fax (312) 4206756; e-mail assembly@tbmm.gov.tr; internet www.tbmm.gov.tr.

Speaker: CEMIL ÇIÇEK.

General Election, 12 June 2011

Party	Valid votes cast	% of valid votes	Seats
Adalet ve Kalkınma Partisi (AKP)	21,399,082	49.83	327
Cumhuriyet Halk Partisi (CHP)	11,155,972	25.98	135
Milliyetçi Hareket Partisi (MHP)	5,585,513	13.01	53
Independents*	2,819,917	6.57	35
Saadet Partisi (SP)	543,454	1.27	0
Total (incl. others)	42,941,763†	100.00	550

* Affiliated to the Bariş ve Demokrasi Partisi (BDP).
† Excluding 973,185 invalid votes.

Election Commission

Yüksek Seçim Kurulu (YSK) (High Electoral Board): Kızılırmak Cad. 9, 06640 Küçükesat, Ankara; tel. (312) 4191040; fax (312) 4195308; e-mail bilgiedinme@ysk.gov.tr; internet www.ysk.gov.tr; independent; Chair. SADI GÜVEN.

Political Organizations

Political parties were banned from 1980–83. Legislation enacted in March 1986 stipulated that a party must have organizations in at least 45 provinces, and in two-thirds of the districts in each of these provinces, in order to take part in an election. A political party is recognized by the Government as a legitimate parliamentary group only if it has at least 20 deputies in the Grand National Assembly.

In mid-1992, following the adoption of less restrictive legislation concerning the formation of political parties, several new parties were established, and the left-wing CHP, dissolved in 1981, was reactivated.

Adalet ve Kalkınma Partisi (AKP) (Justice and Development Party): Söğütözü Cad. 6, Çankaya, Ankara; tel. (312) 2045000; fax (312) 2045000; e-mail rte@akparti.org.tr; internet www.akparti.org.tr; f. 2001; Islamist-orientated; Chair. RECEP TAYYIP ERDOĞAN.

Bağımsız Türkiye Partisi (BTP) (Independent Turkey Party): Cankiri Cad. 24, Kat 5 Ulus, Ankara; tel. (312) 3092001; fax (312) 3092003; e-mail btp@btp.org.tr; internet www.btp.org.tr; f. 2001; Chair. Prof. Dr HAYDAR BAŞ.

Bariş ve Demokrasi Partisi (BDP) (Peace and Democracy Party): Oguz Mah., Baris Manco Cad. 1388, Sok 37, Balgat, Ankara; tel. (312) 2201950; fax (312) 2201977; e-mail bdpbasin@gmail.com; internet www.bdp.org.tr; f. 2008; Kurdish nationalist, social democratic; following the dissolution of the pro-Kurdish Demokratik Toplum Partisi in 2009, that party's representatives in the Grand National Assembly and some elected officials at the provincial and local levels joined the BDP; Chair. SELAHATTIN DEMIRTAŞ, GÜLTEN KIŞANAK.

Büyük Birlik Partisi (BBP) (Great Unity Party): Gazi Mah., Silahtar Cad. 90, BBP Genel Merkezi Yenimahalle, Ankara; tel. (312) 4340923; fax (312) 4355818; e-mail bbp.duyuru@gmail.com; internet www.bbp.org.tr; f. 1993; Pres. MUSTAFA DESTICI; Sec.-Gen. ÜZEYIR TUNÇ.

Cumhuriyet Halk Partisi (CHP) (Republican People's Party): Anadolu Bul. 12, Söğütözü, Ankara; tel. (312) 2074000; fax (312) 2074039; e-mail chp@chp.org.tr; internet www.chp.org.tr; f. 1923 by Mustafa Kemal (Atatürk); dissolved in 1981 and reactivated in 1992; merged with Sosyal Demokrat Halkçı Parti (Social Democratic Populist Party) in Feb. 1995 and with the Yeni Türkiye Partisi in Oct. 2004; left-wing; Chair. KEMAL KILIÇDAROĞLU; Sec.-Gen. BIHLUN TAMAYLIGIL.

Demokrat Parti (DP) (Democratic Party): Akay Cad. 16, Kızılay, Ankara; tel. (312) 4441946; fax (312) 4168683; e-mail dp@dp.org.tr; internet www.dp.org.tr; f. 1983 as Doğru Yol Partisi (True Path Party); renamed as above in May 2007; merged with Anavatan Partisi (Motherland Party) in Nov. 2009; centre-right; Chair. GÜLTEKIN UYSAL.

Demokratik Sol Parti (DSP) (Democratic Left Party): Mareşal Fevzi Çakmak Cad. 17, Ankara; tel. (312) 2124950; fax (312) 2124188; e-mail dsp@dsp.org.tr; internet www.dsp.org.tr; f. 1985, drawing support from mems of the fmr Republican People's Party; centre-left; Chair. MASUM TÜRKER; Gen.-Sec. HASAN ERÇELEBI.

Emek Partisi (EMEP) (Labour Party of Turkey): Fevzi Çakmak 1 Sok. 15/5, Kızılay, Ankara; tel. (312) 2324198; fax (312) 2324197; e-mail emekpartisi@emep.org; internet www.emep.org; f. 1996; advocates scientific socialism; Chair. SELMA GURKAN.

Genç Parti (GP) (Youth Party): İller Sok. 7, Mebusevleri, 06580 Tandoğan, Ankara; fax (312) 2969757; f. 2002; populist, nationalist; Chair. CEM UZAN.

Halkın Sesi Partisi (HAS Parti) (People's Voice Party): Oğuzlar Mah. 1397, Sok. 14, 06520 Balgat, Ankara; tel. (312) 2852484; fax (312) 2852480; e-mail iletisim@hasparti.org.tr; f. 2010 by fmr Chair. of Saadet Partisi; Chair. Prof. Dr NUMAN KURTULMUŞ.

Halkın Yükselişi Partisi (HYP) (People's Ascent Party): Filistin Sok. 30, Gaziosmanpaşa, Ankara; tel. (312) 4480621; fax (312) 4476968; e-mail hypgenelmerkez@hyp.org.tr; internet www.hyp.org.tr; f. 2005; advocates social democratic principles; Pres. RAGIP ÖNDER GÜNAY.

İşçi Partisi (IP) (Workers' Party): Toros Sok. 9, Sıhhıye, Ankara; tel. (312) 2318111; fax (312) 2292994; e-mail int@ip.org.tr; internet www.ip.org.tr; f. 1992; Chair. DOĞU PERINÇEK.

Liberal Demokrat Parti (LDP) (Liberal Democrat Party): İstanbul; tel. (533) 3323165; fax (212) 2550291; e-mail ldp@ldp.org; internet www.ldp.org.tr; f. 1994; Chair. CEM TOKER.

Millet Partisi (MP) (Nation Party): Atatürk Bul. 72/37, Kızılay, Ankara; tel. (312) 4194060; fax (312) 3127651; e-mail milletpartisi@hotmail.com; internet www.milletpartisi.org; f. 1992; Chair. AYKUT EDIBALI.

Milliyetçi Hareket Partisi (MHP) (Nationalist Action Party): Ceyhun Atif Kansu Cad. 128, Balgat, Ankara; tel. (312) 4725555; fax (312) 4731544; e-mail bilgi@mhp.org.tr; internet www.mhp.org.tr; f. 1983; fmrly the Democratic and Conservative Party; Chair. DEVLET BAHÇELI; Sec.-Gen. İSMET BÜYÜKATAMAN.

Özgürlük ve Dayanisma Partisi (ODP) (Freedom and Solidarity Party): GMK Bul. 87/13, Maltepe, Ankara; tel. (312) 2317232; fax 2320347; e-mail odp@odp.org.tr; internet www.odp.org.tr; f. 1996; Chairs ALPER TAŞ, BILGE SEÇKIN ÇETINKAYA.

Özgür Toplum Parti (OTP) (Free Society Party): f. 2003; associated with Halkın Demokrasi Partisi; Leader AHMET TURAN DEMIR.

Saadet Partisi (SP) (Felicity Party): Ziyabey Cad. 2, Sok. 15, 06520 Balgat, Ankara; tel. (312) 2848800; fax (312) 2856246; e-mail bilgi@saadet.org.tr; internet www.saadet.org.tr; f. 2001; replaced conservative wing of Islamist fundamentalist and free-market advocating Fazilet Partisi (Virtue Party), which was banned in that year; Chair. Prof. Dr MUSTAFA KAMALAK.

Türkiye Komünist Partisi (TKP) (Communist Party of Turkey): Osmanağa Mah. Serasker Cad. Kazasker Sok. 10, Kadıköy, İstanbul; tel. (216) 4146504; fax (216) 3461137; e-mail tkp@tkp.org.tr; internet www.tkp.org.tr; f. 1981 as the Party of Socialist Power; name changed as above in 2001; Chair. ERKAN BAŞ.

Yurt Partisi (Homeland Party): Meşrutiyet Cad. Bayındır 2, Sok. 59/5, Kızılay, Ankara; tel. (312) 4189034; fax (312) 4189364; e-mail iletisim@yurtpartisi.org.tr; internet www.yurtpartisi.org.tr; f. 2002; nationalist and conservative party; Leader SAADETTIN TANTAN.

The following proscribed organizations were engaged in an armed struggle against the Government:

Devrimci Halk Kurtuluş Partisi—Cephesi (DHKP—C) (Revolutionary People's Liberation Party—Front): e-mail dhkc@ozgurluk.org; faction of Dev-Sol; subsumed parent org. in 1996.

Partiya Karkeren Kurdistan (PKK) (Kurdistan Workers' Party): internet www.pkkonline.net; f. 1978; 57-mem. directorate; launched struggle for an independent Kurdistan in 1984; declared cease-fire 2000; renamed Congress for Freedom and Democracy in Kurdistan (KADEK) April 2002 and KONGRA-GEL Nov. 2003; return to fmr name, PKK, announced April 2005, following resumption of armed struggle; name KONGRA-GEL continued to be used by some elements; military wing, Hezên Parastina Gel (HPG—People's Defence Forces), re-emerged 2004; Chair. MURAT KARAYILAN; Leader ABDULLAH ÖCALAN.

Diplomatic Representation

EMBASSIES IN TURKEY

Afghanistan: Cinnah Cad. 88, 06550 Çankaya, Ankara; tel. (312) 4422325; fax (312) 4426256; e-mail info@afghanembassy.org.tr; internet afghanembassy.org.tr; Ambassador Dr AMANULLAH JAYHOON.

Albania: Ebu Ziya Tevfik Sok. 17, Çankaya, Ankara; tel. (312) 4416103; fax (312) 4416109; e-mail embassy.ankara@mfa.gov.al; Ambassador GENCI MUÇAJ.

Algeria: Şehit Ersan Cad. 42, 06680 Çankaya, Ankara; tel. (312) 4687719; fax (312) 4687593; e-mail cezayirbe@yahoo.fr; Ambassador MOULOUD HAMAI.

Angola: Kennedy Cad. 155, 1-2-3 Gaziosmanpaşa, Ankara; tel. (312) 4282770; fax (312) 4282772; e-mail embaixada.turquia@mirex.gov.ao; Ambassador JOSÉ GUERREIRO ALVES PRIMO.

Argentina: Uğur Mumcu Cad. 60/1, 06700 Gaziosmanpaşa, Ankara; tel. (312) 4462062; fax (312) 4462063; e-mail embargturquia@yahoo.com.ar; Chargé d'affaires a.i. RAIMUNDO MARCELO APPELHANS.

Australia: Uğur Mumcu Cad. 88, 7th Floor, 06700 Gaziosmanpaşa, Ankara; tel. (312) 4599500; fax (312) 4464827; e-mail info-ankara@dfat.gov.au; internet www.turkey.embassy.gov.au; Ambassador IAN DAVID GRAINGE BIGGS.

Austria: Atatürk Bul. 189, 06680 Kavaklıdere, Ankara; tel. (312) 4055190; fax (312) 4189454; e-mail ankara-ob@bmeia.gv.at; internet www.aussenministerium.at/botschaft/ankara.html; Ambassador KLAUS WÖLFER.

Azerbaijan: Diplomatik Site, Bakü Sok. 1, 06450 Oran, Ankara; tel. (312) 4911681; fax (312) 4920430; e-mail ankara@mission.mfa.gov.az; Ambassador FAIG BAGIROV.

Bahrain: İlkbahar Mah. 606, Sok. 19, Oran-Çankaya, Ankara; tel. (312) 4912656; fax (312) 4912676; e-mail ankara.mission@mofa.gov.bh; Ambassador IBRAHIM YOUSUF AL-ABDULLAH.

Bangladesh: Birlik Mah. 391, Cad. 16, 06610 Çankaya, Ankara; tel. (312) 4952719; fax (312) 4952744; e-mail bdootankara@ttmail.com; Ambassador ZULFIQUR RAHMAN.

Belarus: Abidin Daver Sok. 17, 06550 Çankaya, Ankara; tel. (312) 4416769; fax (312) 4416674; e-mail turkey@mfa.gov.by; internet www.turkey.mfa.gov.by; Ambassador VALERY KOLESNIK.

Belgium: Mahatma Gandhi Cad. 55, 06700 Gaziosmanpaşa, Ankara; tel. (312) 4056166; fax (312) 4468251; e-mail ankara@diplobel.fed.be; internet www.diplomatie.be/ankara; Ambassador POL DE WITTE.

Bosnia and Herzegovina: Turan Emeksiz Sok., Park Bloklan, B Blok 3/9–10, Gaziosmanpaşa, Ankara; tel. (312) 4273602; fax (312) 4273604; e-mail bh_emba@ttmail.com; Ambassador DAMIR DZANKO.

Brazil: Reşit Galip Cad., İlkadım Sok. 1, 06700 Gaziosmanpaşa, Ankara; tel. (312) 4481840; fax (312) 4481838; e-mail brasemb@brasembancara.org; internet www.brasembancara.org; Ambassador ANTONIO LUIS ESPINOLA SALGADO.

Bulgaria: Atatürk Bul. 124, 06680 Kavaklıdere, Ankara; tel. (312) 4672071; fax (312) 4686956; e-mail Embassy.Ankara@mfa.bg; internet www.mfa.bg/embassies/turkey; Ambassador KRASIMIR TULECHKI.

Canada: Cinnah Cad. 58, 06690 Çankaya, Ankara; tel. (312) 4092700; fax (312) 4092712; e-mail ankra@international.gc.ca; internet www.turkey.gc.ca; Ambassador JOHN HOLMES.

Chile: Reşit Galip Cad., İrfanli Sok. 14/1–3, 06700 Gaziosmanpaşa, Ankara; tel. (312) 4473418; fax (312) 4474725; e-mail embassy@chile.org.tr; internet www.chile.org.tr; Ambassador JORGE PATRICIO ARANCIBIA REYES.

China, People's Republic: Gölgeli Sok. 34, 06700 Gaziosmanpaşa, Ankara; tel. (312) 4360628; fax (312) 4464248; e-mail chinaemb_tr@mfa.gov.cn; internet www.chinaembassy.org.tr; Ambassador GONG XIAOSHENG.

Colombia: Koza Sok. 91/5, 06570 Gaziosmanpaşa, Ankara; tel. (312) 4464388; fax (312) 4464399; e-mail eankara@cancilleria.gov.co; Ambassador FERNANDO PANESSO.

Congo, Democratic Republic: Turan Emeksiz Sok. 16/1, Gaziosmanpaşa, Ankara; tel. (312) 4660916; fax (312) 4660918; e-mail missionrdcankara@gmail.com; Ambassador MARCEL MULUMBA TSHIDIMBA.

Croatia: Kelebek Sok. 15/A, 06700 Gaziosmanpaşa, Ankara; tel. (312) 4469460; fax (312) 4464700; e-mail ankara@mvep.hr; internet tr.mvp.hr; Ambassador DRAŽEN HRASTIĆ.

Cuba: Şölen Sok. 8, 06550 Çankaya, Ankara; tel. (312) 4428970; fax (312) 4426115; e-mail embacubatur@tr.net; Ambassador JORGE QUESADA CONCEPCIÓN.

Czech Republic: Kaptanpaşa Sok. 15, Gaziosmanpaşa, Ankara; tel. (312) 4056139; fax (312) 4463084; e-mail ankara@embassy.mzv.cz; internet www.mzv.cz/ankara; Ambassador VÁCLAV HUBINGER.

Denmark: Mahatma Gandhi Cad. 74, 06700 Gaziosmanpaşa, Ankara; tel. (312) 4466141; fax (312) 4472498; e-mail ankamb@um.dk; internet www.ambankara.um.dk; Ambassador RUBEN MADSEN.

Djibouti: İlkbahar Mah. Galip Erdem Cad. 613, Sok. 6, Yıldız-Çankaya, Ankara; tel. (312) 4919513; fax (312) 4919510; e-mail djib.embassytr@gmail.com; Ambassador ADEN HOUSSEIN ABDILLAHI.

Ecuador: Kelebek Sok. 21/1, Gaziosmanpaşa, Ankara; tel. (312) 4460160; fax (312) 4460173; e-mail eecuturquia@mmrree.gov.ec; Ambassador AUGUSTO ALEJANDRO SAA CORRIERE.

Egypt: Atatürk Bul. 126, 06680 Kavaklıdere, Ankara; tel. (312) 4261026; fax (312) 4270099; e-mail embassy_egypt@yahoo.com; internet www.egyptturkey.com; Ambassador ABD AL-RAHMAN SALAH EL-DIN.

Estonia: Gölgeli Sok. 16, 06700 Gaziosmanpaşa, Ankara; tel. (312) 4056970; fax (312) 4056976; e-mail embassy.ankara@mfa.ee; internet www.estemb.org.tr/embassy; Ambassador MIKO HALJAS.

Ethiopia: Uğur Mumcu Sok. 74/1–2, 06700 Gaziosmanpaşa, Ankara; tel. (312) 4360400; fax (312) 4481938; e-mail ethembank@ttnet.net.tr; Ambassador MULATU TESHOME WIRTU.

Finland: Kader Sok. 44, 06700 Gaziosmanpaşa, Ankara; tel. (312) 4574400; fax (312) 4680072; e-mail sanomat.ank@formin.fi; internet www.finland.org.tr; Ambassador NINA VASKUNLAHTI.

France: Paris Cad. 70, 06540 Kavaklıdere, Ankara; tel. (312) 4554545; fax (312) 4554527; e-mail ambaank@yahoo.fr; internet www.ambafrance-tr.org; Ambassador LAURENT BILI.

The Gambia: Hilal Mah., Hollanda Cad., 31 Yıldız, Ankara; tel. (312) 4425771; fax (312) 4425707; Ambassador GIBRIL JOOF.

Georgia: Kılıç Ali Sok. 12, Oran, Ankara; tel. (312) 4918030; fax (312) 4918032; e-mail ankara.emb@mfa.gov.ge; internet www.turkey.mfa.gov.ge; Ambassador IRAKLI KOPLATADZE.

Germany: Atatürk Bul. 114, 06690 Kavaklıdere, Ankara; tel. (312) 4555100; fax (312) 4555337; e-mail info@ankara.diplo.de; internet www.ankara.diplo.de; Ambassador EBHARD POHL.

Ghana: Gölgeli Sok. 9, Gaziosmanpaşa, Çankaya, Ankara; tel. (312) 4425479; fax (312) 4418569; e-mail ghanaembassyturkey@yahoo.com; Ambassador İBRAHIM ABASS.

Greece: Zia ür-Rahman Cad. 9–11, 06670 Gaziosmanpaşa, Ankara; tel. (312) 4480873; fax (312) 4463191; e-mail gremb.ank@mfa.gr; Ambassador KYRIAKOS LOUKAKIS.

Holy See: Apostolic Nunciature, Birlik Mah. 3, Cad. 37, PK 33, 06552 Çankaya, Ankara; tel. (312) 4953514; fax (312) 4953540; e-mail vatican@tr.net; Apostolic Nuncio Most Rev. ANTONIO LUCIBELLO (Titular Archbishop of Thurio).

Hungary: Sancak Mah. Layoş, Koşut Cad. 2, 06550 Yıldız, Çankaya, Ankara; tel. (312) 4422273; fax (312) 4415049; e-mail mission.ank@mfa.gov.hu; internet www.mfa.gov.hu/kulkepviselet/tr/hu; Ambassador Dr JÁNOS HÓVÁRI.

India: Cinnah Cad. 77A, 06680 Çankaya, Ankara; tel. (312) 4382195; fax (312) 4403429; e-mail chancery@indembassy.org.tr; internet www.indembassy.org.tr; Ambassador SUSMITA GONGULEE THOMAS.

Indonesia: Abdullah Cevdet Sok. 10, 06680 Çankaya, Ankara; tel. (312) 4382190; fax (312) 4382193; e-mail kbriank@ttmail.com; Ambassador NAHARI AGUSTINI.

Iran: Tahran Cad. 10, 06700 Kavaklıdere, Ankara; tel. (312) 4682821; fax (312) 4682823; e-mail iranemb.ank@mfa.gov.ir; Ambassador ALIREZA BIGDELI.

Iraq: Turan Emeksiz Sok. 11, 06700 Gaziosmanpaşa, Ankara; tel. (312) 4687421; fax (312) 4684832; e-mail ankemb@iraqmofamail.com; Ambassador ABD AL-AMIR KAMAL ABU TABIKH.

Ireland: Uğur Mumcu Cad. 88, MNG Binası B Blok Kat 3, 06700 Gaziosmanpaşa, Ankara; tel. (312) 4591000; fax (312) 4468061; e-mail ankaraembassy@dfa.ie; internet www.embassyofireland.org.tr; Ambassador KENNETH THOMPSON.

Israel: Mahatma Gandhi Cad. 85, 06700 Gaziosmanpaşa, Ankara; tel. (312) 4597500; fax (312) 4597555; e-mail info@ankara.mfa.gov.il; internet ankara.mfa.gov.il; Chargé d'affaires a.i. YOSEF LEVY SFARI.

Italy: Atatürk Bul. 118, 06680 Kavaklıdere, Ankara; tel. (312) 4574200; fax (312) 4574280; e-mail ambasciata.ankara@esteri.it; internet www.ambankara.esteri.it; Ambassador GIANPAOLO SCARANTE.

Japan: Reşit Galip Cad. 81, 06692 Gaziosmanpaşa, Ankara; tel. (312) 4460500; fax (312) 4371812; e-mail culture@jpn-emb.org.tr; internet www.tr.emb-japan.go.jp; Ambassador KIYOSHI ARAKI.

Jordan: Dede Korkut Sok. 18 Mesnevi, 06690 Çankaya, Ankara; tel. (312) 4402054; fax (312) 4404327; e-mail ankara@fm.gov.jo; Ambassador AMJAD AL-ADAILEH.

Kazakhstan: Kiliç Ali Sok. 6, Diplomatik Site, 06450 Oran, Ankara; tel. (312) 4919100; fax (312) 4904455; e-mail ankara@mfa.kz; Ambassador ZHANSEIT TUIMEBAYEV.

Kenya: İlkbahar Mah., Turan Güneş Bul. 571, Cad. 612, Sok. 10, 06550 Yıldız, Çankaya; tel. (312) 4914508; fax (312) 4914516; Chargé d'affaires a.i. LINDSAY KIPTINESS.

Korea, Republic: Cinnah Cad., Alaçam Sok. 5, 06690 Çankaya, Ankara; tel. (312) 4684822; fax (312) 4267872; e-mail turkey@mofat.go.kr; internet tur-ankara.mofat.go.kr; Ambassador LEE SANG-KYU.

Kosovo: Hirfanli Sok. 14/2, Gaziosmanpaşa, Ankara; tel. (312) 4467054; fax (312) 4467055; e-mail embassy.turkey@ks-gov.net; internet www.ambasada-ks.net/tr; Ambassador AVNI SPAHIU.

Kuwait: Reşit Galip Cad., Kelebek Sok. 110, Gaziosmanpaşa, Ankara; tel. (312) 4450576; fax (312) 4462826; e-mail kuwait@ada .net.tr; Ambassador ABDULLAH ABD AL-AZIZ AL-DUWAIKH.

Kyrgyzstan: İlkbahar Mah., Galip Erdem Cad. 25, Çankaya, Ankara; tel. (312) 4913506; fax (312) 4913513; e-mail info@ kgembassy.org.tr; Ambassador ERMEK IBRAIMOV.

Latvia: Reşit Galip Cad. 95, Çankaya, Ankara; tel. (312) 4056136; fax (312) 4056137; e-mail embassy.turkey@mfa.gov.lv; Ambassador ATIS SJANITS.

Lebanon: Kızkulesi Sok. 44, Gaziosmanpaşa, 06700 Ankara; tel. (312) 4467485; fax (312) 4461023; e-mail lebembas@ttnet.net.tr; Ambassador MANSOUR ABDALLAH.

Libya: Cinnah Cad. 60, 06690 Çankaya, Ankara; tel. (312) 4381110; fax (312) 4403862; e-mail infolibya@yahoo.com; Ambassador ABD UL-RAZAQ MUKHTAR AHMED ABD AL-GADER.

Lithuania: Mahatma Gandhi Cad. 17/8–9, 06700 Gaziosmanpaşa, Ankara; tel. (312) 4470766; fax (312) 4470663; e-mail amb.tr@urm.lt; internet tr.mfa.lt; Ambassador KESTUTIS KUDZMANAS.

Luxembourg: Reşit Galip Cad. 70/2, 2 Gaziosmanpaşa, Ankara; tel. (312) 4591400; fax (312) 4365055; e-mail ankara.amb@mae.etat.lu; Ambassador ARLETTE CONZEMIUS.

Macedonia, former Yugoslav republic: Karaca Sok. 24/5–6, 06700 Gaziosmanpaşa, Ankara; tel. (312) 4399204; fax (312) 4399206; e-mail ankara@mfa.gov.mk; Ambassador GORAN TASKOVSKI.

Malaysia: Mahatma Gandhi Cad. 58, 06700 Gaziosmanpaşa, Ankara; tel. (312) 4463547; fax (312) 4464130; e-mail malankara@ kln.gov.my; internet www.kln.gov.my/perwakilan/ankara; Ambassador Dato' SAIPUL ANUAR ABD AL-MUIN.

Mauritania: Oran Mah. Şemsettin Bayramoğlu Sok. 7, Çankaya, Ankara; tel. (312) 4917063; fax (312) 4917064; e-mail moritanya .buyukelciligi@gmail.com; Ambassador MUHAMMAD AHMED LEHWEIRTHI.

Mexico: Kırkpınar Sok. 18/6, 06540 Çankaya, Ankara; tel. (312) 4423033; fax (312) 4420221; e-mail mexico@embamextur.com; internet www.mexico.org.tr; Ambassador MARTHA BÁRCENA COQUI.

Moldova: Kaptanpaşa Sok. 49, 06700 Gaziosmanpaşa, Ankara; tel. (312) 4465527; fax (312) 4465816; e-mail ankara@mfa.md; internet www.turcia.mfa.md; Ambassador IGOR BOLBOCEANU.

Mongolia: A. Fethi Okyar Sok. 4, Oran Diplomatik Sitesi, 06700 Oran, Ankara; tel. (312) 4921027; fax (312) 4921064; e-mail ankara@ mfat.gov.mn; Ambassador BATKHISHIG BADAMDORJ.

Montenegro: Büyükesat, Gökçek Sok. 11, 06700 Ankara; tel. (312) 4364698; fax (312) 4361546; e-mail turkey@mfa.gov.me; Ambassador RAMO BRALIĆ.

Morocco: Reşit Galip Cad., Rabat Sok. 11, 06700 Gaziosmanpaşa, Ankara; tel. (312) 4376020; fax (312) 4468430; e-mail sifamatr@tr .net; Ambassador MUHAMMAD LOTFI AOUAD.

Netherlands: Hollanda Cad. 5, 06550 Yıldız, Ankara; tel. (312) 4091800; fax (312) 4091898; e-mail ank@minbuza.nl; internet turkey .nlembassy.org; Ambassador JAN PAUL DIRKSE.

New Zealand: Kizkulesi Sok. 11, Gaziosmanpaşa, Ankara; tel. (312) 4463333; fax (312) 4463317; e-mail nzembassyankara@ttmail.com; internet www.nzembassy.com/turkey; Ambassador TAHAMOANA (TAHA) AISEA MACPHERSON.

Niger: Mahatma Gandhi Cad. 40, Gaziosmanpaşa, Ankara; tel. (312) 4361013; fax (312) 4361017; e-mail niger@ambassadeturquie .org; Ambassador ADAM ABDOULAYE DAN-MARADI.

Nigeria: Uğur Mumcu Sok. 56, 06700 Gaziosmanpaşa, Ankara; tel. (312) 4481077; fax (312) 4481082; e-mail embassynigeriaturkey@ yahoo.co.uk; Ambassador AHMED ABDULHAMID.

Norway: Kirkpinar Sok. 18/3–4, 06540 Çankaya, Ankara; tel. (312) 4084800; fax (312) 4084899; e-mail emb.ankara@mfa.no; internet www.norway.org.tr; Ambassador JANIS BJØRN KANAVIN.

Oman: Diplomatik Alan, Besim Atalay Sok. 7, Oran, Ankara; tel. (312) 4910940; fax (312) 4900682; e-mail omanembassy@yahoo.com; Ambassador Sayyid QAIS BIN SALIM BIN ALI AL-SAID.

Pakistan: İran Cad. 37, Çankaya, Ankara; tel. (312) 4271410; fax (312) 4671023; e-mail perepankhara@yahoo.com; internet www .pakembassyankara.com; Ambassador MUHAMMAD HAROON SHAUKAT.

Peru: Reşit Galip Cad. 70/1, 06700 Ankara; tel. (312) 4469039; fax (312) 4474026; e-mail peruankara@gmail.com; Ambassador JORGE ABARCA DEL CARPIO.

Philippines: Mahatma Gandhi Cad. 56, 06700 Gaziosmanpaşa, Ankara; tel. (312) 4465831; fax (312) 4465733; e-mail ankara_pe@ yahoo.com; Ambassador SENEN T. MANGALILE.

Poland: Atatürk Bul. 241, 06650 Kavaklıdere, Ankara; tel. (312) 4572000; fax (312) 4678963; e-mail ankara.amb.sekretariat@msz .gov.pl; internet ankara.msz.gov.pl; Chargé d'affaires PIOTR KRAWCZYK.

Portugal: Kuleli Sok. 39, Gaziosmanpaşa, Ankara; tel. (312) 4056028; fax (312) 4463670; e-mail embaixada@portugal.org.tr; internet www.portugalembassy.org.tr; Ambassador JORGE TITO DE VASCONCELES NOGUEIRA DIAS CABRAL.

Qatar: Bakü Sok. 6, Diplomatik Site, Oran, Ankara; tel. (312) 4907274; fax (312) 4906757; e-mail qeank@yahoo.com; Ambassador SALEM MUBAREK AL-SHAFI.

Romania: Bükreş Sok. 4, 06680 Çankaya, Ankara; tel. (312) 4663706; fax (312) 4271530; e-mail romanyabyk@dsl.ttmail.com; internet ankara.mae.ro; Ambassador RADU ONOFREI.

Russia: Karyağdı Sok. 5, 06692 Çankaya, Ankara; tel. (312) 4392122; fax (312) 4383952; e-mail rus-ankara@yandex.ru; internet www.turkey.mid.ru; Chargé d'affaires a.i. ANDREI V. BURABOV.

Saudi Arabia: Turan Emeksiz Sok. 6, 06700 Gaziosmanpaşa, Ankara; tel. (312) 4685540; fax (312) 4274886; e-mail tremb@mofa .gov.sa; Ambassador ADIL BIN SERAJ MIRDAD.

Senegal: Hilal Mah., Alexander Dubcek Cad. 8, Yıldız, Ankara; tel. (312) 4420046; fax (312) 4420056; e-mail senegalbuyukelciligi@ gmail.com; Ambassador ISSAKHA MBACKE.

Serbia: Paris Cad. 47, 06691 Kavaklıdere, Ankara; tel. (312) 4260236; fax (312) 4278345; e-mail embserank@gmail.com; Chargé d'affaires a.i. LJILJANA BELOJEVIĆ.

Singapore: Yıldızevler Mah., 4. Cad., 718 Sok. 13/14, 06550 Çankaya, Ankara; tel. (312) 4424330; fax (312) 4426144; e-mail singemb_ank@sgmfa.gov.sg; internet www.mfa.gov.sg/ankara; Chargé d'affaires LORLING LEE.

Slovakia: Atatürk Bul. 245, 06692 Kavaklıdere, Ankara; tel. (312) 4675075; fax (312) 4682689; e-mail emb.ankara@mzv.sk; Ambassador MILAN ZACHAR.

Slovenia: Kırlangıç Sok. 36, 06700 Gaziosmanpaşa, Ankara; tel. (312) 4054980; fax (312) 4260216; e-mail van@gov.si; Ambassador MILAN JAZBEC.

Somalia: Rabat Sok. 24/2, 06700 Gaziosmanpaşa, Ankara; tel. (312) 4364028; fax (312) 4364029; e-mail somemb.ankara@gmail.com; internet www.somaliembassytr.org; Ambassador MOHAMMED MURSAL SHEIKH ABDIRAHMAN.

South Africa: Filistin Sok. 27, 06700 Gaziosmanpaşa, Ankara; tel. (312) 4056861; fax (312) 4466434; e-mail general.ankara@foreign .gov.za; internet www.southafrica.org.tr; Ambassador VIKA M. KHUMALO.

South Sudan: Kız Kulesi Sok. 1, Gaziosmanpaşa, Ankara; tel. (312) 4360285; fax (312) 4360284; e-mail info@southsudanankara.org; internet www.southsudanankara.org; Ambassador JOHN GAI YOH.

Spain: Abdullah Cevdet Sok. 8, 06550 Çankaya, Ankara; tel. (312) 4401796; fax (312) 4395170; e-mail emb.ankara@maec.es; internet www.maec.es/embajadas/ankara; Ambassador CRISTOBAL GONZÁLEZ-ALLER JURADO.

Sri Lanka: Kırlangıç Sok. 41, 06700 Gaziosmanpaşa, Ankara; tel. (312) 4271021; fax (312) 4271026; Ambassador BHARATHI DAVINA WIJERATNE.

Sudan: Mahatma Gandhi Cad. 48, 06700 Gaziosmanpaşa, Ankara; tel. (312) 4466327; fax (312) 4468506; e-mail ankara@mfa.gov.sd; Ambassador OMER HAIDAR ABU ZAID.

Sweden: Katip Çelebi Sok. 7, 06692 Kavaklıdere, Ankara; tel. (312) 4554100; fax (312) 4554120; e-mail ambassaden.ankara@gov.se; internet www.swedenabroad.com/ankara; Ambassador HÅKAN AKESSON.

Switzerland: Atatürk Bul. 247, 06692 Kavaklıdere, Ankara; tel. (312) 4573100; fax (312) 4671199; e-mail ank.vertretung@eda.admin .ch; internet www.eda.admin.ch/ankara; Ambassador WALTER HAFFNER.

Syria: Sedat Simavi Sok. 40, 06550 Çankaya, Ankara; tel. (312) 4409657; fax (312) 4385609; Chargé d'affaires a.i. MOUNZER MOUNZER.

Tajikistan: Ferit Recai Ertuğrul Cad. 20, 25009 Oran, Ankara; tel. (312) 4911607; fax (312) 4911603; e-mail tajemb_turkey@yahoo.com; Ambassador FARRUH SHARIPOV.

Thailand: Koza Sok. 87, 06700 Gaziosmanpaşa, Ankara; tel. (312) 4374318; fax (312) 4378495; e-mail thaiank@ttmail.com; Ambassador RATHAKIT MANATHAT.

Tunisia: Ferit Recai Ertuğrul Cad. 19, Oran Diplomatic Site, Ankara; tel. (312) 4919635; fax (312) 4919634; e-mail at.ankara@ superonline.com; Chargé d'affaires a.i. NEYLA CHALA EP CHEBAANE.

'Turkish Republic of Northern Cyprus': Rabat Sok. 20, 06700 Gaziosmanpaşa, Ankara; tel. (312) 4461036; fax (312) 4465238; e-mail info@kktcbe.org.tr; internet www.kktcbe.org; Ambassador MUSTAFA LAKADAMYALI.

Turkmenistan: Koza Sok. 28, 06700 Çankaya, Ankara; tel. (312) 4416122; fax (312) 4417125; e-mail tmankara@ttnet.net.tr; Ambassador ATA SERDAROV.

Uganda: Uğur Mumcu Sok. 59, Gaziosmanpaşa, Ankara; tel. (312) 4370194; fax (312) 4370178; e-mail ugandaembassyturkey@gmail.com; Chargé d'affaires a.i. MOSES KASUJJA KALULE.

Ukraine: Sancak Mah. 512 Sok. 17, 06550 Çankaya, Ankara; tel. (312) 4415499; fax (312) 4406815; e-mail emb_tr@mfa.gov.ua; internet www.mfa.gov.ua/turkey; Ambassador SERGEI KORSUNSKII.

United Arab Emirates: Turan Güneş Bul. 13, Galip ERdem Cad. 613, Ylkbahar Mah., Çankaya, Ankara; tel. (312) 4901414; fax (312) 4912333; e-mail uaeemb@uaeemb.net; internet www.uaeemb.net; Ambassador KHALID KHALIFA A. RASHED AL-MU'ALLA.

United Kingdom: Şehit Ersan Cad. 46/A, 06680 Çankaya, Ankara; tel. (312) 4553344; fax (312) 4553352; e-mail info.officer@fco.gov.uk; internet ukinturkey.fco.gov.uk; Ambassador DAVID REDDAWAY.

USA: Atatürk Bul. 110, 06100 Kavaklıdere, Ankara; tel. (312) 4555555; fax (312) 4670019; e-mail webmaster_ankara@state.gov; internet turkey.usembassy.gov; Ambassador FRANCIS J. RICCIARDONE, Jr.

Uzbekistan: Sancak Mah. 549 Sok. 3, Yıldız, 06550 Çankaya, Ankara; tel. (312) 4413871; fax (312) 4427058; e-mail uzemb_ankara@yahoo.com; Ambassador ULFAT S. KADYROV.

Venezuela: Hilal Mah., Hollanda Cad., 696. Sok. 20A, Yıldız, 06550 Çankaya, Ankara; tel. (312) 4412145; fax (312) 4406755; e-mail mision-ankara@embavenez-turquia.com; Ambassador JOSÉ GREGORIO BRACHO REYES.

Viet Nam: Koza Sok. 109, Gaziosmanpaşa, Çankaya, Ankara; tel. (312) 4468049; fax (312) 4465623; e-mail dsqvnturkey@yahoo.com; internet www.vietnamembassy-turkey.org; Ambassador NGUYEN THE CUONG.

Yemen: Fethiye Sok. 2, 06700 Gaziosmanpaşa, Ankara; tel. (312) 4462637; fax (312) 4461778; e-mail yemenemb@superonline.com; Chargé d'affaires a.i. TARIQ ABD AL-LATIF MUHAMMAD DHAIFALLAH.

Judicial System

Until the foundation of the Turkish Republic, a large part of the Turkish civil law—the laws affecting the family, inheritance, property, obligations, etc.—was based on the Koran, and this holy law was administered by special religious (*Shari'a*) courts. The legal reform of 1926 was not only a process of secularization, but also a radical change of the legal system. The Swiss Civil Code and the Code of Obligation, the Italian Penal Code and the Neuchâtel (Cantonal) Code of Civil Procedure were adopted and modified to fit Turkish customs and traditions.

According to current Turkish law, the power of the judiciary is exercised by judicial (criminal), military and administrative courts. These courts render their verdicts in the first instance, while superior courts examine the verdict for subsequent rulings.

Constitutional Court: Consists of 17 members, appointed by the President. Reviews the constitutionality of laws, at the request of the President of the Republic, parliamentary groups of the governing party or of the main opposition party, or of one-fifth of the members of the National Assembly, and sits as a high council empowered to try senior members of state. The rulings of the Constitutional Court are final. Decisions of the Court are published immediately in the Official Gazette, and shall be binding on the legislative, executive and judicial organs of the state; Chief Justice HAŞIM KILIÇ.

Court of Appeals: Atatürk Bul. 100, 06658 Bakanlıklar, Ankara; tel. (312) 4161000; e-mail iletisim@yargitay.gov.tr; internet www.yargitay.gov.tr; the court of the last instance for reviewing the decisions and verdicts rendered by judicial courts. It has original and final jurisdiction in specific cases defined by law. Members are elected by the Supreme Council of Judges and Public Prosecutors; Chief Justice ALI ALKAN.

Council of State: An administrative court of the first and last instance in matters not referred by law to other administrative courts, and an administrative court of the last instance in general. Hears and settles administrative disputes and expresses opinions on draft laws submitted by the Council of Ministers. Three-quarters of the members are appointed by the Supreme Council of Judges and Public Prosecutors; the remaining quarter is selected by the President of the Republic.

Military Court of Appeals: A court of the last instance to review decisions and verdicts rendered by military courts, and a court of first and last instance with jurisdiction over certain military persons, stipulated by law, with responsibility for the specific trials of these persons. Members are selected by the President of the Republic from nominations made by the Military Court of Appeals.

Supreme Military Administrative Court: A military court for the judicial control of administrative acts concerning military personnel. Members are selected by the President of the Republic from nominations made by the Court.

Court of Jurisdictional Disputes: Settles disputes among judicial, administrative and military courts arising from disagreements on jurisdictional matters and verdicts.

Court of Accounts: A court charged with the auditing of all accounts of revenue, expenditure and government property, which renders rulings related to transactions and accounts of authorized bodies on behalf of the National Assembly.

Supreme Council of Judges and Public Prosecutors: The Minister of Justice serves as the President of the Supreme Council, while the Under-Secretary to the Minister of Justice is an ex officio member. The remaining 20 members of the Council comprise four appointed directly by the President of the Republic, three nominated by the Court of Appeals, two by the Council of State, one by the Justice Academy and 10 elected by judges and prosecutors; each of these members is appointed for a four-year term. Decides all personnel matters relating to judges and public prosecutors.

Public Prosecutor: The law shall make provision for the tenure of public prosecutors and attorneys of the Council of State and their functions. The Chief Prosecutor of the Republic, the Chief Attorney of the Council of State and the Chief Prosecutor of the Military Court of Appeals are subject to the provisions applicable to judges of higher courts.

Military Trial: Military trials are conducted by military and disciplinary courts. These courts are entitled to try the military offences of military personnel and those offences committed against military personnel or in military areas, or offences connected with military service and duties. Military courts may try non-military persons only for military offences prescribed by special laws.

Religion

ISLAM

More than 99% of the Turkish people are Muslims. However, Turkey is a secular state. Although Islam was stated to be the official religion in the Constitution of 1924, an amendment in 1928 removed this privilege. Since 1950 subsequent Governments have tried to re-establish links between religion and state affairs, but secularity was protected by the revolution of 1960, the 1980 military takeover and the 1982 Constitution.

Diyanet İşleri Başkanlığı (Presidency of Religious Affairs): Eskişehir Yolu 9 km Çankaya, Ankara; tel. (312) 2957000; e-mail protokol@diyanet.gov.tr; internet www.diyanet.gov.tr; Pres. Prof. Dr ALI BARDAKOĞLU.

CHRISTIANITY

The town of Antioch (now Antakya) was one of the earliest strongholds of Christianity, and by the 4th century had become a patriarchal see. Formerly in Syria, the town was incorporated into Turkey in 1939. Constantinople (now İstanbul) was also a patriarchal see, and by the 6th century the Patriarch of Constantinople was recognized as the Ecumenical Patriarch in the East. Gradual estrangement from Rome developed, leading to the final breach between the Catholic West and the Orthodox East, usually assigned to the year 1054.

There are estimated to be about 100,000 Christians in Turkey.

The Orthodox Churches

Armenian Patriarchate: Ermeni Patrikliği, Sevgi Sok. 6, 34130 Kumkapı, İstanbul; tel. (212) 5170970; fax (212) 5164833; e-mail haybadtivan@gmail.com; internet www.lraper.org; f. 1461; 100,000 adherents (incl. workers from Armenia—2007); Patriarch MUTAFYAN II; Deputy Patriarch ARAM ATESHIAN.

Bulgarian Orthodox Church: Bulgar Ortodoks Kilisesi, Halâskâr Gazi Cad. 319, Şişli, İstanbul; Rev. Archimandrite GANCO ÇOBANOF.

Greek Orthodox Church: The Ecumenical Patriarchate (Rum Ortodoks Patrikhanesi), Sadrazam Ali Paşa Cad. 35, 34220 Fener-Haliç, İstanbul; tel. (212) 5255416; fax (212) 5316533; e-mail patriarchate@ec-patr.org; internet www.ec-patr.org; Archbishop of Constantinople (New Rome) and Ecumenical Patriarch BARTHOLOMEW I.

The Roman Catholic Church

Turkey Catholic Bishops' Conference: Conferenza Episcopale di Turchia, Satırcı Sok. 2, Harbiye, 34373 İstanbul; tel. (212) 2307312; fax (212) 2303195; e-mail v.cancellarius@yahoo.com; internet www.katolikkilisesi.org; f. 1987; Pres. Most Rev. RUGGERO FRANCESCHINI (Archbishop of İzmir).

Armenian Rite

Patriarchate of Cilicia: f. 1742; Patriarch NERSES BEDROS TARMOUNI XIX (resident in Beirut, Lebanon).

Archdiocese of İstanbul: Sakızağacı Cad. 31, PK 183, 80072 Beyoğlu, İstanbul; tel. (212) 2441258; fax (212) 2432364; f. 1928; Archbishop HOVHANNES TCHOLAKIAN.

Byzantine Rite

Apostolic Exarchate of İstanbul: Hamalbaşı Cad. 44, PK 259, 80070 Beyoğlu, İstanbul; tel. (212) 2440351; fax (212) 2411543; f. 1911; Apostolic Admin. LOUIS PELÂTRE (Titular Bishop of Sasima).

Bulgarian Catholic Church: Bulgar Katolik Kilisesi, Eski Parmakkapı Sok. 15, Galata, İstanbul.

Latin Rite

Metropolitan Archdiocese of İzmir: Church of St Polycarp, Necatibey Bul. 2, PK 267, 35210 İzmir; tel. (232) 4840531; fax (232) 4845358; e-mail curiaves@yahoo.it; f. 1818; Archbishop of İzmir Most Rev. RUGGERO FRANCESCHINI.

Apostolic Vicariate of Anatolia: Mithat Paša Cad. 5, PK 75, 31200 Iskenderum; tel. (326) 6175916; fax (326) 6139291; e-mail curiaves@yahoo.it; f. 1990; Vicar Apostolic (vacant).

Apostolic Vicariate of İstanbul: Papa Roncalli Sok. 65/A, 34373 Inönü Mah., Şişli, İstanbul; tel. (212) 2480775; fax (212) 2411543; e-mail vapostolique@yahoo.fr; f. 1742; Vicar Apostolic LOUIS PELÂTRE (Titular Bishop of Sasima).

Maronite Rite

The Maronite Patriarch of Antioch, Cardinal Nasrallah Pierre Sfeir, is resident in Bkerké, Lebanon.

Melkite Rite

The Greek Melkite Patriarch of Antioch, Grégoire III Laham, is resident in Damascus, Syria.

Syrian Rite

The Syrian Catholic Patriarch of Antioch, Ignace Pierre VIII Abdel Ahad, is resident in Beirut, Lebanon.

Patriarchal Exarchate of Turkey: Sarayarkası Sok. 15, PK 84, 34437 Ayazpaşa, İstanbul; tel. (212) 2432521; fax (212) 2490261; e-mail info@suryanikatolikkilisesi.com; f. 1908; Patriarchal Exarch Fr YUSUF SAĞ.

The Anglican Communion

Within the Church of England, Turkey forms part of the diocese of Gibraltar in Europe. The Bishop is resident in the United Kingdom.

Anglican Chaplaincy in İstanbul: Christ Church, Serdar Ekram Sok. 82, Karaköy, İstanbul; tel. (212) 2515616; fax (212) 2435702; e-mail parson@tnn.net; internet www.anglicanistanbul.com; Chaplain Rev. Canon IAN SHERWOOD.

JUDAISM

There are estimated to be about 23,000 Jews in Turkey.

Jewish Community of Turkey: Türkiye Hahambaşılığı, Yemenici Sok. 21, Beyoğlu, 34430 Tünel, İstanbul; tel. (212) 2938794; fax (212) 2441980; e-mail info@musevicemaati.com; internet www.musevicemaati.com; Chief Rabbi ISAK HALEVA.

The Press

Almost all İstanbul papers are also printed in Ankara and İzmir on the same day, and some in Adana. The most popular national dailies are *Zaman*, *Posta*, *Hürriyet* and *Sabah*; *Yeni Asır*, published in İzmir, is the best-selling quality daily of the Aegean region. There are numerous provincial newspapers with a limited circulation.

PRINCIPAL DAILIES

Akşam (Evening): Davutpaşa Cad. 34, 34020 Zeytinburnu, İstanbul; tel. (212) 4493000; fax (212) 4819561; e-mail editor@aksam.com.tr; internet www.aksam.com.tr; publ. by Türkmedya AŞ; Man. Dir MUSTAFA DOLU; circ. 150,053 (April 2009).

Bugün (Today): Meliha Avni Sozen Cad. 17, Block B, Mecidiyeköy, Sisli, İstanbul; tel. (212) 3558580; fax (212) 2730954; e-mail bugun@bugun.com.tr; internet www.bugun.com.tr; f. 2003; publ. by Koza Davetiye; Editor-in-Chief SELAHATTIN SADIKOĞLU; circ. 60,770 (April 2009).

Cumhuriyet (Republic): Prof. Nurettin Mazhar Öktel Sok. 2, 34381 Şişli, İstanbul; tel. (212) 3437274; fax (212) 2914976; e-mail portal@cumhuriyet.com.tr; internet www.cumhuriyet.com.tr; f. 1924; morning; left-wing, nationalist; Editor-in-Chief IBRAHIM YILDIZ; circ. 65,132 (April 2009).

Fotomaç: Barbaros Bul. 153, Cam Han, Beşiktaş, İstanbul; tel. (212) 3543368; fax (212) 3543557; e-mail spor@fotomac.com.tr; internet www.fotomac.com.tr; f. 1991; sport; publ. by Turkuvaz Radyo Televizyon Gazetecilik ve Yayıncılık AŞ (a subsidiary of Çalık Holding); Editor-in-Chief ZEKI UZUNDURUKAN; circ. 214,441 (April 2009).

Gazete Haberturk: Abdülhakhamit Cad. 25, Beyoğlu, İstanbul; tel. (212) 3136000; fax (212) 3136590; internet www.htgazete.com; f. March 2009; publ. by Ciner Yayın Holding; Editor-in-Chief FATIH ALTAYLI; weekly circ. 297,709 (April 2009).

Günes (Sun): Merkezefendi Mah. Davutpaşa Cad. 34, 34020 Zeytinburnu, İstanbul; tel. (212) 4493010; fax (212) 4819571; internet www.gunes.com; f. 1997; publ. by Türkmedya AŞ; Editor-in-Chief MURAT BÜYÜKÇELEBI; circ. 128,619 (April 2009).

Hürriyet (Freedom): Hürriyet Medya Towers, 34212 Güneşli, İstanbul; tel. (212) 6770000; fax (212) 6770846; e-mail interneteditor@hurriyet.com.tr; internet www.hurriyet.com.tr; f. 1948; morning; political; independent; publ. by Doğan Yayın Holding (Doğan Media Group); Chief Editor ENIS BERBEROĞLU; circ. 495,567 (April 2009).

Hürriyet Daily News and Economic Review: Sogutozu Mah., Dumlupinar Bul. 102, 06510 Çankaya, Ankara; tel. (312) 2070090; fax (312) 2070094; e-mail hdn@hurriyet.com.tr; internet www.turkishdailynews.com; f. 1961 as Daily News; later renamed Turkish Daily News; renamed as above 2008; English language; publ. by Doğan Yayın Holding (Doğan Media Group); CEO RAGIP NEBIL ILSEVEN; Editor-in-Chief DAVID JUDSON; circ. 6,106 (April 2009).

Milliyet: Doğan Medya Center, Bağcilar, 34204 İstanbul; tel. (212) 5056111; fax (212) 5056233; e-mail webadmin@milliyet.com.tr; internet www.milliyet.com.tr; f. 1950; morning; political; publ. by Doğan Yayın Holding (Doğan Media Group); Editor-in-Chief DERYA SAZAK; circ. 200,532 (April 2009).

Posta (Post): Yüzyıl Mah., Doğan Medya Center, 34204 Bağcılar, İstanbul; tel. (212) 5056111; fax (212) 5056520; e-mail internet@posta.com.tr; internet www.posta.com.tr; f. 1995; publ. by Doğan Yayın Holding (Doğan Media Group); Editor-in-Chief RIFAT ABABAY; circ. 516,136 (April 2009).

Radikal: Hürriyet Medya Towers, 34212 Güneşli, İstanbul; tel. (212) 6770000; fax (212) 4496047; e-mail iletisim@radikal.com.tr; internet www.radikal.com.tr; f. 1996; liberal; merged with economics and business daily *Referans* in 2010; publ. by Doğan Yayın Holding (Doğan Media Group); Man. Editor EYÜP CAN SAĞLIK.

Sabah (Morning): Barbaros Bul. 153, Cam Han, Beşiktaş, İstanbul; tel. (212) 3543000; e-mail editor@sabah.com.tr; internet www.sabah.com.tr; publ. by Turkuvaz Radyo Televizyon ve Gazetecilik AŞ (a subsidiary of Çalık Holding); Exec. Editor ERDAL ŞAFAK; circ. 380,851 (April 2009).

Star: Yeni Bosna Merkez Mah., Kavak Sok. 3/2, Ser Plaza, İstanbul; tel. (212) 4962020; fax (212) 4962179; e-mail editor@stargazete.com; internet www.stargazete.com; f. 1999; Man. Editor MUSTAFA KARAALIOĞLU; circ. 102,706 (April 2009).

Takvim (Calendar): Barbaros Bul. 153, Cam Han 5, Beşiktaş, İstanbul; tel. (212) 3543000; fax (212) 3470677; e-mail takvim@takvim.com.tr; internet www.takvim.com.tr; lifestyle, entertainment and sport; publ. by Turkuvaz Radyo Televizyon ve Gazetecilik AŞ (a subsidiary of Çalık Holding); Man. Editor ERGÜN DILER; circ. 150,053 (April 2009).

Today's Zaman: Ahmet Taner Kışlalı Cad. 6, 34194 Yenibosna, İstanbul; tel. (212) 4541454; fax (212) 4541497; e-mail editor@todayszaman.com; internet www.todayszaman.com; f. 2007; English language; publ. by Zaman Media Group; Editor-in-Chief BÜLENT KENEŞ; circ. 4,677 (April 2009).

Türkiye (Turkey): Ekim Cad. 29, 34197 Yenibosna, İstanbul; tel. (212) 4543000; fax (212) 4543100; e-mail info@tg.com.tr; internet www.turkiyegazetesi.com.tr; f. 1970; nationalist, pro-Islamic; Editor-in-Chief NUH ALBAYRAK; circ. 141,313 (April 2009).

Vakit (Time): Ada 55, İstoç Bağcılar, İstanbul; tel. (212) 6592056; fax (212) 4474209; e-mail haber@vakit.com.tr; internet www.vakit.com.tr; f. 1978; Editor-in-Chief AHMET KARAHASANOĞLU; circ. 52,204 (April 2009).

Vatan (Homeland): Büyükdere Cad. 123, 34349 Gayrettepe, İstanbul; tel. (212) 3545454; internet www.gazetevatan.com; f. 2002; publ. by Doğan Yayın Holding (Doğan Media Group); Man. Editor ISMAIL YUVACAN; circ. 204,819 (April 2009).

Yeni Asır (New Century): Gaziosmanpaşa Bul. 5, 35260 Çankaya, İzmir; tel. (232) 4415000; fax (232) 4464222; e-mail yasir@yeniasir.com.tr; internet www.yeniasir.com.tr; f. 1895; political; publ. by Turkuvaz İzmir Gazete Dergi Basın Yayın AŞ (subsidiary of Çalik Holding); Chair. AHMET ÇALIK; Man. Editor ŞEBNEM BURSALI; circ. 38,760 (April 2009).

Yeni Çağ (New Age): Çobançeşme Mah., Kalender Sok. 12, 34550 Yenibosna, İstanbul; tel. (212) 4524040; fax (212) 4524055; e-mail yenicag@yenicaggazetesi.com.tr; internet www.yg.yenicaggazetesi

.com.tr; f. 2002; nationalist; Man. Editor HAYRI KÖKLÜ; circ. 51,190 (April 2009).

Yeni Şafak (New Dawn): Yenidoğan Mah., Kızılay Sok. 39, Bayrampaşa, İstanbul; tel. (212) 6122930; fax (212) 6121903; e-mail halklailiskiler@yenisafak.com.tr; internet yenisafak.com.tr; f. 1995; Editor-in-Chief YUSUF ZIYA CÖMERT; circ. 103,598 (April 2009).

Zaman (Era): Ahmet Taner Kislali Cad. 6, 34194 Yenibosna, İstanbul; tel. (212) 4541454; fax (212) 4541467; e-mail h.dikmen@zaman.com.tr; internet www.zaman.com.tr; f. 1962; morning; Man. Editor EKREM DUMANLI; circ. 773,228 (April 2009).

WEEKLIES

Aksiyon: Fevzi Çakmak Mah., A. Taner Kışlalı Cad. 6, 34194 Yenibosna, İstanbul; tel. (212) 4541400; fax (212) 4548625; e-mail okur@aksiyon.com.tr; internet www.aksiyon.com.tr/aksiyon; f. 1994; news, politics, economics; Man. Editor BÜLENT KORUCU; circ. 38,184 (Nov. 2009).

BusinessWeek Türkiye: Ebulula Mardin Cad. 4, Gazeteciler Sitesi A8-1, 34330 Akatlar, İstanbul; tel. (212) 3245515; fax (212) 3245505; internet www.businessweek.com.tr; business and economics; publ. by Infomag Publishing Ltd and Bloomberg LP (USA); Man. Editor SERDAR TURAN.

Ekonomist: Hürriyet Medya Towers, 34212 Güneşli, İstanbul; tel. (212) 4103256; fax (212) 4103255; e-mail ekonomist@doganburda.com; internet www.ekonomist.com.tr; f. 1991; business and economics; publ. by Doğan Burda Dergi Yayıncılık ve Pazarlama AŞ; Man. Editor TALAT YEŞILOĞLU; circ. 9,505 (Nov. 2009).

Newsweek Türkiye: Abdülhakhamit Cad. 25, Beyoğlu, İstanbul; tel. (212) 3136000; fax (212) 3137455; internet www.newsweek.com.tr; news, business, economics; publ. by Ciner Gazete Dergi Basım Yayıncılık Sanayi ve Ticaret AŞ; Man. Editor SELÇUK TEPELI; circ. 4,500 (Nov. 2009).

Para: Toprak Center, Ihlamur Yıldız Cad. 10, 34353 Beşiktaş, İstanbul; tel. (212) 3263333; fax (212) 3543792; e-mail para@paradergi.com.tr; internet www.paradergi.com.tr; business and economics; publ. by Turkuvaz Gazete Dergi Basım AŞ; Man. Editor OĞUZ DEMIR; circ. 8,380 (Nov. 2009).

Tempo: Hürriyet Medya Towers, 34212 Güneşli, İstanbul; tel. (212) 4103282; fax (212) 4103311; internet www.tempoonline.com.tr; f. 1987; celebrity gossip, lifestyle; publ. by Doğan Burda Dergi Yayıncılık ve Pazarlama AŞ; Editor-in-Chief AYŞEGÜL SAVUR.

Yeni Aktüel: Toprak Center, Ihlamur Yıldız Cad. 10, 34353 Beşiktaş, İstanbul; tel. (212) 3263334; fax (212) 3543792; internet www.yeniaktuel.com.tr; culture; publ. by Turkuvaz Gazete Dergi Basım AŞ; Man. Editor DEFNE ASAL ER; circ. 6,381 (Nov. 2009).

PERIODICALS

Atlas: Hürriyet Medya Towers, 34212 Güneşli, İstanbul; tel. (212) 4103566; fax (212) 4103564; e-mail atlas@doganburda.com; internet www.kesfetmekicinbak.com; f. 1993; monthly; archaeology, geography; publ. by Doğan Burda Dergi Yayıncılık ve Pazarlama AŞ; Man. Editor ÖZCAN YÜKSEK.

Capital: Hürriyet Medya Towers, 34212 Güneşli, İstanbul; tel. (212) 4103228; fax (212) 4103227; e-mail capital@doganburda.com; internet www.capital.com.tr; f. 1993; monthly; business, economics; publ. by Doğan Burda Dergi Yayıncılık ve Pazarlama AŞ; Man. Editor SEDEF SEÇKIN BÜYÜK.

Chip: Hürriyet Medya Towers, 34212 Güneşli, İstanbul; tel. (212) 4103200; fax (212) 4103357; internet www.chip.com.tr; f. 1996; monthly; computing; publ. by Doğan Burda Dergi Yayıncılık ve Pazarlama AŞ; Man. Editor MAHMUT KARSLIOĞLU.

Global: Büyükdere Cad. 65, Saadet Apt 8/15, Mecidiyeköy, İstanbul; tel. (212) 2133881; fax (212) 2133884; e-mail info@globaldergisi.com; internet www.globaldergisi.com; business, economics; Man. Editor MÜGE MEŞE.

Güncel Hukuk: Hürriyet Medya Towers, 34212 Güneşli, İstanbul; tel. (212) 4103534; fax (212) 4103531; e-mail guncelhukuk@doganburda.com; internet www.guncelhukuk.com.tr; monthly; law; publ. by Doğan Burda Dergi Yayıncılık ve Pazarlama AŞ; Man. Editor Prof. Dr KÖKSAL BAYRAKTAR.

Infomag: Ebulula Mardin Cad. 4, Gazeteciler Sitesi A-8/1, Akatlar 1, Levent, İstanbul; tel. (212) 3245515; fax (212) 3245505; e-mail info@infomag.com.tr; internet www.infomag.com.tr; monthly; business; Man. Editor SERDAR TURAN.

Platin: Davutpaşa Cad. 34, 34020 Topkapı, İstanbul; tel. (212) 4493400; fax (212) 4819581; e-mail info@platinonline.com; internet www.platinonline.com; monthly; business, economics; publ. by Türkmedya AŞ; Editor LEVENT ERTEM.

NEWS AGENCIES

Anadolu Ajansı: Mustafa Kemal Bul. 128/C, Tandoğan, Ankara; tel. (312) 2317000; fax (312) 2312174; e-mail ozelbulten@aa.com.tr; internet www.aa.com.tr; f. 1920; Chair. and Dir-Gen. S. HILMI BENGI.

ANKA Ajansı: Cinnah Cad. 11/5 Kavaklıdere, Ankara; tel. (312) 4682500; fax (312) 4268471; e-mail anka@ankaajansi.com.tr; internet www.ankaajansi.com.tr; Dir-Gen. VELI ÖZDEMIR.

Bagımsiz Basın Ajansı (BBA): Saglam Fikir Sok. 9, Esentepe, 34394 İstanbul; tel. (212) 2122936; fax (212) 2122940; e-mail bba@bba.tv; internet www.bba.tv; f. 1971; provides camera crewing, editing and satellite services in Turkey, the Balkans, the Middle East and the former Soviet republics to broadcasters world-wide; Pres. BEDRI KAYABAL.

Cihan News Agency: Çobançeşme Mah. Kalender Sok. 16, 34530 Yenibosna, Bahçelievler, İstanbul; tel. (212) 5524057; fax (212) 4541456; e-mail newssales@cihan.com.tr; internet www.cihanmedia.com; f. 1992; part of Feza Media Corpn; Production Man. HAKAN ÇIDAL.

Doğan Haber Ajansı (Doğan News Agency): Doğan TV Center, 34204 Bağcılar, İstanbul; tel. (212) 4135555; fax (212) 4135598; internet www.dha.com.tr; f. 1999 by merger of Hürriyet Haber Ajansı and Milliyet Haber Ajansı; subsidiary of Doğan Yayın Holding (Doğan Media Group); 34 bureaux world-wide; Dir-Gen. UĞUR ÇEBECI.

İKA Haber Ajansı (Economic and Commercial News Agency): Atatürk Bul. 199/A-45, Kavaklıdere, Ankara; f. 1954; Dir ZIYA TANSU.

TEBA—Türk Ekonomik Basın Ajansı (Turkish Economic Press Agency): Süleyman Hacı Abdullahoğlu Cad. 5, D3 Balgat, Ankara; tel. (312) 2842006; fax (312) 2840638; e-mail teba@tebahaber.com.tr; internet www.tebahaber.com.tr; f. 1981; private economic news service; Propr YELDA CALTAS; Editor AKIN TOKATLI.

Ulusal Basın Ajansı (UBA): Meşrutiyet Cad. 5/10, Ankara; Man. Editor OĞUZ SEREN.

JOURNALISTS' ASSOCIATION

Türkiye Gazeteciler Cemiyeti: Türkocağı Cad. 1, Cağaloğlu, İstanbul; tel. (212) 5138300; fax (212) 5268046; e-mail tgc@tgc.org.tr; internet www.tgc.org.tr; f. 1946; Pres. ORHAN ERINÇ; Sec.-Gen. CELAL TOPRAK.

Publishers

Altın Kitaplar Yayınevi Anonim ŞTİ: Göztepe Mah. Kazım Karabekir Cad., İstanbul; tel. (212) 4463888; e-mail iletisim@altinkitaplar.tr; internet www.altinkitaplar.com.tr; f. 1959; fiction, non-fiction, biography, children's books, encyclopedias, dictionaries; Publrs FETHI UL, TURHAN BOZKURT; Chief Editor MÜRSIT UL.

Arkadas Co Ltd: Yuva Mah. 3702, Sok. 4, 06105 Yenimahalle, Ankara; tel. (312) 3960111; fax (312) 3960141; e-mail info@arkadas.com.tr; internet www.arkadas.com.tr; f. 1980; fiction, educational and reference books; Gen. Man. CUMHUR OZDEMIR.

Arkeoloji ve Sanat Yayınları (Archaeology and Art Publications): Hayriye Cad. 5/2 Mateo Mratoviç Apt., 34425 Beyoğlu, İstanbul; tel. (212) 2930378; fax (212) 2456877; e-mail info@arkeolojisanat.com; internet www.arkeolojisanat.com; f. 1978; classical, Byzantine and Turkish studies, art and archaeology, numismatics and ethnography books; Publr NEZIH BASGELEN; Senior Editor BRIAN JOHNSON.

Bilgi Yayınevi: Meşrutiyet Cad. 46/A, Yenişehir, 06420 Ankara; tel. (312) 4318122; fax (312) 4317758; e-mail info@bilgiyayinevi.com.tr; internet www.bilgiyayinevi.com.tr.

Doğan Burda Dergi Yayıncılık ve Pazarlama AŞ: Hürriyet Medya Towers, 34212 Güneşli, İstanbul; tel. (212) 4780300; fax (212) 4103581; e-mail dalan@doganburda.com; internet www.doganburda.com; jt venture between Doğan Yayın Holding (Doğan Media Group) and Hubert Burda Media Holding GmbH & Co KG (Germany); publishes 27 magazines and periodicals; Chair. PAUL-BERNHARD KALLEN; CEO MEHMET Y. YILMAZ.

Iletisim Yayınları: Binbirdirek Meydanı Sok., Iletisim Han 7/2, 34122 Cağaloğlu, İstanbul; tel. (212) 5162260; fax (212) 5161258; e-mail iletisim@iletisim.com.tr; internet www.iletisim.com.tr; f. 1984; fiction, non-fiction, encyclopedias, reference; Gen. Man. NIHAT TUNA.

Inkilap Kitabevi: Çobançeşme Mah. Altay Sok. 8 Yenibosna, İstanbul; tel. (212) 4961111; fax (212) 4961112; e-mail info@inkilap.com; internet www.inkilap.com; f. 1935; general reference and fiction; Man. Dir A. FIKRI; Dir of Foreign Rights S. DIKER.

Kabalci Yayınevi: Ankara Cad. 47, Cağaloğlu, İstanbul; tel. (212) 5226305; fax (212) 5268495; e-mail info@kabalci.com.tr; internet www.kabalci.com.tr; art, history, literature, social sciences; Pres. SABRI KABALCI.

Metis Yayınları: Ipek Sok. 5, 34433 Beyoğlu, İstanbul; tel. (212) 2454696; fax (212) 2454519; e-mail rights@metisbooks.com; internet www.metisbooks.com; f. 1982; fiction, literature, non-fiction, social sciences; Dir SEMIH SÖKMEN.

Nobel Medical Publishing: Millet Cad. 111 Çapa, İstanbul; tel. (212) 6328333; fax (212) 5870217; e-mail info@nobeltip.com; internet www.nobeltip.com; f. 1974; medical books and journals; CEO ERSAL BINGÖL.

Nurdan Yayınları Sanayi ve Ticaret Ltd Sti: Prof. Kâzim Ismail Gürkan Cad. 13, Kat 1, 34410 Cağaloğlu, İstanbul; tel. (212) 5225504; fax (212) 5125186; e-mail nurdan@nurdan.com.tr; internet www.nurdan.com.tr; f. 1980; children's and educational; Dir NURDAN TÜZÜNER; Editor ÇIĞDEM TÜZÜNER.

Parantez Yayınları AŞ: Asmalı Mescid Mah. Tünel Meydanı, Tünel Geçidi İşhanı C Blok, D 424 Beyoğlu, İstanbul; tel. and fax (212) 2526516; e-mail parantez@yahoo.com; internet www.parantez.net; f. 1991; Publr METIN ZEYNIOĞLU.

Payel Yayınevi: Cağaloğlu Yokusu Evren han Kat 3/51, 34400 Cağaloğlu, İstanbul; tel. (212) 5284409; fax (212) 5124353; f. 1966; science, history, literature; Editor AHMET ÖZTÜRK.

Remzi Kitabevi AŞ: Akmerkez E3 Blok Kat. 14, Etiler, İstanbul; tel. (212) 2822080; fax (212) 2822090; e-mail post@remzi.com.tr; internet www.remzi.com.tr; f. 1927; general and educational; Dirs EROL ERDURAN, ÖMER ERDURAN, AHMET ERDURAN.

Seckin Yayınevi, Inc.: Saglik Sok. 21, 06410 Sihhiye, Ankara; tel. (312) 4353030; fax (312) 4352472; e-mail satis@seckin.com.tr; internet www.seckin.com.tr; f. 1959; accounting, computer science, economics, law, engineering; CEO KORAY SEÇKIN.

Türk Dil Kurumu (Turkish Language Institute): Atatürk Bul. 217, 06680 Kavaklıdere, Ankara; tel. (312) 4575200; fax (312) 4680783; e-mail bilgi@tdk.org.tr; internet tdk.gov.tr; f. 1932; non-fiction, research, language; Pres. Prof. Dr MUSTAFA S. KAÇALIN.

Varlık Yayınları AŞ: Ayberk Ap. Piyerloti Cad. 7–9, Çemberlitaş, 34400 İstanbul; tel. (212) 5162004; fax (212) 5162005; e-mail varlik@varlik.com.tr; internet www.varlik.com.tr; f. 1933; fiction and non-fiction books, and cultural monthly review; Dirs FILIZ NAYIR DENIZTEKIN, OSMAN DENIZTEKIN.

GOVERNMENT PUBLISHING HOUSE

Ministry of Culture and Tourism: Directorate of Publications, Necatibey Cad. 55, 06440 Kızılay, Ankara; tel. (312) 2315450; fax (312) 2315036; e-mail yayimlar@kutuphanelergm.gov.tr; internet www.kultur.gov.tr; f. 1973; Dir ALI OSMAN GÜZEL.

PUBLISHERS' ASSOCIATION

Türkiye Yayıncılar Birliği Derneği (Publishers' Association of Turkey): Kazım Ismail Gürkan Cad. 12/3, Ortaklar Han, 34440 Cağaloğlu, İstanbul; tel. (212) 5125602; fax (212) 5117794; e-mail info@turkyaybir.org.tr; internet www.turkyaybir.org.tr; f. 1985; Pres. METIN CELÂL ZEYNIOĞLU, NIYAZI ŞIMŞEK; Sec. KENAN KOCATÜRK; 300 mems.

Broadcasting and Communications

TELECOMMUNICATIONS

Avea İletşim Hizmetleri AŞ: Abdi İpekçi Cad. 75, 34367 Maçka, İstanbul; tel. (212) 4601500; internet www.avea.com.tr; f. Feb. 2004 as TT&TIM İletişim Hizmetleri AŞ; present name adopted Oct. 2004; 81.13% stake owned by Türk Telekom, 18.87% owned by İş Bankası; provides mobile cellular telecommunications services; 11.4m. subscribers (2010); Chair. MUHAMMAD HARIRI; CEO ERKAN AKDEMIR.

Turkcell İletişim Hizmetleri AŞ: Turkcell Plaza, Mesrutiyet Cad. 71, 34430 Tepebaşi, İstanbul; tel. (212) 3131000; fax (212) 2925393; e-mail musteri.hizmetleri@turkcell.com.tr; internet www.turkcell.com.tr; f. 1994; provides mobile cellular telecommunications services; 13.07% by TeliaSonera AB (Sweden); 33.9m. subscribers at Sept. 2010; Chair. COLIN J. WILLIAMS; CEO SÜREYYA CILIV.

Türksat AŞ: Konya Yolu 40 km, Gölbaşı, Ankara; tel. (312) 6153000; fax (312) 4995115; e-mail info@turksat.com.tr; internet www.turksat.com.tr; satellite and cable telecommunications services; CEO ÖZKAN DALBAY.

Türk Telekomünikasyon AŞ (Türk Telekom): Turgut Özal Bul., 06103 Aydınlıkevler, Ankara; tel. (312) 3060733; fax (312) 3245311; e-mail iletisim@turktelekom.com.tr; internet www.turktelekom.com.tr; 55% owned by Oger Telecoms Joint Venture Group, 30% by Turkish Govt and 15% by private investors; fixed-line telecommunications services; Chair. MUHAMMAD HARIRI; CEO Dr K. GÖRKHAN BOZKURT.

Vodafone Telekomünikasyon AŞ (Vodafone Türkiye): Vodafone Plaza, Büyükdere Cad. 67, 34398 Maslak, İstanbul; tel. (212) 3670000; fax (212) 3670010; internet www.vodafone.com.tr; f. 1994 as Telsim; name changed 2006, following acquisition by Vodafone Group PLC (United Kingdom); offers mobile cellular telecommunications services; CEO SERPIL TIMURAY.

Regulatory Authorities

Bilgi Teknolojileri ve İletişim Kurumu (Information and Communication Technologies Authority): Yeşilırmak Sok., 16 Demirtepe, 06430 Ankara; tel. (312) 2947200; fax (312) 2947145; e-mail info@tk.gov.tr; internet www.tk.gov.tr; f. 2000; Chair. Dr TAYFUN ACARER.

General Directorate of Communications: Hakkı Turayliç Cad. 5 Kat 7–8, Emek, Ankara; tel. (312) 2031000; fax (312) 2121775; e-mail soytas@ubak.opr.tr; internet hgm.ubak.gov.tr; Dir-Gen. ATILLA ÇELIK.

BROADCASTING

Regulatory Authority

Radyo ve Televizyon Üst Kurulu (RTÜK) (Radio and Television Supreme Council): Bilkent Plaza B2 Blok, Bilkent, 06530 Ankara; tel. (312) 2975000; fax (312) 2661985; e-mail rtuk@rtuk.org.tr; internet www.rtuk.org.tr; f. 1994; responsible for assignment of channels, frequencies and bands, controls transmitting facilities of radio stations and TV networks, draws up regulations on related matters, monitors broadcasting and issues warnings in case of violation of the Broadcasting law; Pres. DAVUT DURSUN.

Radio

Türkiye Radyo ve Televizyon Kurumu (TRT) (Turkish Radio and Television Corpn): Turan Güneş Bul., 06450 Oran, Ankara; tel. (312) 4632330; fax (312) 4632335; e-mail aktifhat@trt.net.tr; internet www.trt.net.tr; f. 1964; controls Turkish radio and television services, incl. four national radio channels; Dir-Gen. İBRAHIM ŞAHIN; Head of Radio ÇETIN TEZCAN.

Voice of Turkey: PK 333, 06443 Yenişehir, Ankara; tel. (312) 4633270; fax (312) 4633277; e-mail tsr@trt.net.tr; internet www.trt.net.tr; f. 1937; external service of the TRT; Head of Dept SULEYMAN KOKSOY.

There are also more than 50 local radio stations, an educational radio service for schools and a station run by the Turkish State Meteorological Service. The US forces have their own radio and television service.

Television

Digitürk: tel. (212) 4737373; fax (212) 3260099; e-mail destek@digiturk.com.tr; internet www.digiturk.gen.tr; f. 1999; subsidiary of Çukurova Holding; subscription-based satellite television service offering 170 channels; also internet service provider; CEO ERTAN ÖZERDEM.

Türkiye Radyo ve Televizyon Kurumu (TRT) (Turkish Radio and Television Corpn): Oran Sitesi Turan Günes Bul. A Blok Kat 6, 06450 Oran, Ankara; tel. (212) 2597275; e-mail aktifhat@trt.net.tr; internet www.trt.net.tr; four national, one regional and two international channels in 2008; Kurdish-language channel (TRT 6) launched January 2009; Arabic-language service (TRT 7) launched April 2010; Dir-Gen. İBRAHIM ŞAHIN; Head of Television NILGÜN ARTUN; Dir Ankara TV GÜRKAN ELÇI.

As of 2008 there were 23 national, 16 regional and 212 local terrestrial television broadcasters. There are also cable and satellite channels.

Finance

(cap. = capital; res = reserves; dep. = deposits; m. = million; br(s) = branch(es); amounts in Turkish liras; note: figures have been converted retrospectively to reflect the introduction on 1 January 2005 of the new unit of currency, equivalent to 1,000,000 of the old Turkish lira)

The Central Bank of the Republic of Turkey (Türkiye Cumhuriyet Merkez Bankası AŞ) was founded in 1931, and constituted in its present form in 1970. The Central Bank is the bank of issue and is also responsible for the execution of monetary and credit policies, the regulation of the foreign and domestic value of the Turkish lira jointly with the Government, and the supervision of the credit system. In 1987 a decree was issued to bring the governorship of the Central Bank under direct government control. In 2001 the Central Bank was granted policy independence.

In June 1999 an independent supervisory body, the Regulatory and Supervisory Board for Banking, was established by law to monitor the financial sector. The treasury, the Ministry of Finance, the Central Bank, the state planning organization, the Capital Markets Board and the Banks' Association of Turkey were each to nominate one member to the Board for a six-year term. The Board was operational from mid-2000. Other legislation passed in June 1999 incorporated core principles of the Basle Committee on Banking Supervision relating to risk-based capital requirements, loan administration procedures, auditing practices and credit risk issues.

The largest of the private-sector Turkish banks is the Türkiye İş Bankası AŞ, which operates 1,088 branches in the country.

There are several credit institutions in Turkey, including the Türkiye Sınai Kalkınma Bankası AŞ (Industrial Development Bank of Turkey), which was founded in 1950, with the assistance of the World Bank, to encourage private investment in industry by acting as underwriter in the issue of share capital.

There are numerous co-operative organizations, including agricultural co-operatives in rural areas. There are also a number of savings institutions.

In 1990 the Turkish Government announced plans to establish a structure for offshore banking. A decree issued in October of that year exempted foreign banks, operating in six designated free zones, from local banking obligations.

At the end of 1999 the number of banks operating in Turkey (excluding the Central Bank) totalled 81, of which seven were state-owned. Following a number of liquidations, mergers and acquisitions in the banking system after 2000, the number of banks had been reduced to 43 by the end of 2008. Of this total, 13 were development and investment banks; the number of state-owned banks had been reduced to three, with the control of Birleşik Fon Bankasi AŞ (formerly Bayindirbank) passing to the Savings Deposit Insurance Fund. There were 11 private commercial banks and 16 foreign-owned banks.

BANKING

Regulatory Authority

Bancacılık Düzenleme ve Denetleme Kurumu (BDDK) (Banking Regulation and Supervisory Agency): Atatürk Bul. 191, 06680 Kavaklidere, Ankara; tel. (312) 4556500; fax (312) 4240879; e-mail bilgi@bddk.org.tr; internet www.bddk.org.tr; Chair. MUKIM ÖZTEKIN.

Central Bank

Türkiye Cumhuriyet Merkez Bankası AŞ (Central Bank of the Republic of Turkey): Head Office, İstiklal Cad. 10 Ulus, 06100 Ankara; tel. (312) 5075000; fax (312) 5075640; e-mail iletisimbilgi@tcmb.gov.tr; internet www.tcmb.gov.tr; f. 1931; bank of issue; cap. 46.2m., res 3,691.2m., dep. 89,359.6m. (Dec. 2009); Gov. Dr ERDEM BAŞÇI; 21 brs.

State Banks

Türkiye Cumhuriyeti Ziraat Bankası (Agricultural Bank of the Turkish Republic): Doğanbey Mah., Atatürk Bul. 8, 06107 Ulus, Ankara; tel. (312) 5842000; fax (312) 5844053; e-mail zbmail@ziraatbank.com.tr; internet www.ziraat.com.tr; f. 1863; absorbed Türkiye Emlâk Bankası AŞ (Real Estate Bank of Turkey) in July 2001; cap. 2,500m., res 8,457m., dep. 113,771m. (Dec. 2011); Chair. MUHARREM KARSLI; Gen. Man. CAN AKIN ÇAĞLAR; 1,225 brs in Turkey, 11 brs abroad.

Türkiye Halk Bankası AŞ: Esikişehir Yolu, 2 Cad. 63, Söğütözü, 06520 Ankara; tel. (312) 2892000; fax (312) 2893575; e-mail info@halkbank.com.tr; internet www.halkbank.com.tr; f. 1938; absorbed Türkiye Öğretmenler Bankası TAŞ in 1992; acquired 96 brs of Türkiye Emlak Bankası in 2001; merged with Pamukbank TAŞ in 2004; cap. 2,578m., res 506m., dep. 66,724m. (Dec. 2011); Chair. HASAN CEBECI; Gen. Man. SÜLEYMAN ASLAN; 705 brs in Turkey, 4 brs abroad.

Türkiye Vakıflar Bankası TAO (Vakifbank) (Foundation Bank of Turkey): Camlik Cad. Cayir Cimen Sok. 2, 34330 1 Levent, İstanbul; tel. (212) 3167116; fax (212) 3167126; e-mail international@vakifbank.com.tr; internet www.vakifbank.com.tr; f. 1954; cap. 3,300m., res 1,411m., dep. 62,260m. (Dec. 2011); Chair. HALIL AYDOĞAN; Gen. Man. SÜLEYMAN KALKAN; 603 brs in Turkey, 2 brs abroad.

Principal Commercial Banks

Akbank TAŞ: Sabancı Center, 34330 4 Levent, 80745 İstanbul; tel. (212) 3855555; fax (212) 2697787; e-mail investor.relations@akbank.com; internet www.akbank.com; f. 1948; absorbed Ak Uluslararası Bankası AŞ in Sept. 2005; 20% owned by Citigroup; cap. 4,000m., res 3,003m., dep. 81,411m. (Dec. 2011); Chair. SUZAN SABANCI DINÇER; CEO HAKAN BINBAŞGIL; 926 brs in Turkey, 1 br. abroad.

Alternatifbank AŞ: Cumhuriyet Cad. 22–24, Elmadağ, 34367 İstanbul; tel. (212) 3156500; fax (212) 2331500; e-mail kalite@abank.com.tr; internet www.abank.com.tr; f. 1991; 95.6% owned by Anadolu Group; cap. 300m., res 3m., dep. 3,642m. (Dec. 2011); Chair. TUNCAY ÖZILHAN; CEO HAMIT AYDOĞAN; 56 brs.

ING Bank AS: Eski Büyükdere Cad., Ayazaga Köyyolu 6, Maslak, 34398 İstanbul; tel. and fax (212) 4440600; internet www.ingbank.com.tr; f. 1990; fmrly Oyak Bank; owned by ING Groep NV (Netherlands); name changed as above in 2008; cap. 2,159m., res 117m., dep. 11,385m. (Dec. 2011); Chair. JOHN T. MCCARTHY; CEO PINAR ABAY; 365 brs in Turkey, 1 br. in Bahrain.

Şekerbank TAŞ: Büyükdere Cad. 171, Metrocity İş Merkezi, A Blok 34330 1 Levent, İstanbul; tel. (212) 3440737; fax (212) 3197162; e-mail intdiv@sekerbank.com.tr; internet www.sekerbank.com.tr; f. 1953; 33.98% owned by TuranAlem Securities (Kazakhstan); cap. 1,000m., res 24m., dep. 9,192m. (Dec. 2011); Chair. HASAN BASRI GÖKTAN; Gen. Man. MERIÇ ULUŞAHIN; 250 brs.

Tekstil Bankasi AŞ (Tekstilbank): Büyükdere Cad. 63, 34398 Maslak, İstanbul; tel. (212) 3355335; fax (212) 3281328; e-mail ir@tekstilbank.com.tr; internet www.tekstilbank.com.tr; f. 1986; cap. 420m., res 29m. dep. 2,687m. (Dec. 2011); 75.4% owned by GSD Holdings; Chair. AKGÜN TÜRER; Gen. Man. ÇIM GÜZELAYDINLI; 44 brs.

Türk Ekonomi Bankası AŞ (TEB): Meclisı Mebusan Cad. 57, 34427 Fındıklı, İstanbul; tel. (212) 2512121; fax (212) 2525058; internet www.teb.com.tr; f. 1927; fmrly Kocaeli Bankası TAŞ; jt venture between Colakoğlu Group and BNP Paribas SA (France); Fortis Bank AS merged into TEB in 2011; cap. 2,204m., res 102m., dep. 30,710m. (Dec. 2011); Chair. YAVUZ CANEVI; Exec. Dir and Gen. Man. VAROL CIVIL; 275 brs in Turkey, 1 br. in Bahrain.

Türkiye Garanti Bankası AŞ (Garantibank): Nispetiye Mah, Aytar Cad. 2, 34340 Levent Beşiktaş, İstanbul; tel. (212) 3181818; fax (212) 3181888; e-mail mutlus@garanti.com.tr; internet www.garantibank.com; f. 1946; owned by Doğuş Group; cap. 5,145m., res 845m., dep. 93,235m. (Dec. 2011); Chair. FERIT FAIK ŞAHENK; Pres. and CEO ERGUN ÖZEN; 808 brs in Turkey, 2 brs abroad.

Türkiye İş Bankası AŞ (İşbank): İş Kuleleri, 34330 Levent, İstanbul; tel. (212) 3160000; fax (212) 3160900; e-mail halkla.iliskiler@isbank.com.tr; internet www.isbank.com.tr; f. 1924; cap. 6,115m., res 2,156m., dep. 100,090m. (Dec. 2011); Chair. ERSIN ÖZINCE; CEO and Dir ADNAN BALI; 1,088 brs in Turkey, 15 abroad.

Yapı ve Kredi Bankası AŞ: Yapı Kredi Plaza, Blok D, 80620 İstanbul; tel. (212) 3397000; fax (212) 3396000; internet www.ykb.com.tr; f. 1944; cap. 4,286m., res 536m., dep. 78,264m. (Dec. 2011); merged with Koçbank AŞ in 2006; Exec. Dir and Dep. CEO CARLO VIVALDI; CEO FAIK AÇIKALIN; 838 brs.

Development and Investment Banks

İller Bankasi Genel Müdürülügü: Atatürk Bul. 21, 06053 Opera, Ankara; tel. (312) 5087000; fax (312) 5087399; e-mail ilbank@ilbank.gov.tr; internet www.ilbank.gov.tr; Chair. and Gen. Man. HIDAYET ATASOY; 19 brs.

Türkiye Kalkınma Bankası (Development Bank of Turkey): İzmir Cad. 35, 06440 Kızılay Ankara; tel. (312) 4179200; fax (312) 4183967; e-mail rkalkinmahaberlesme@kalkinma.com.tr; internet www.kalkinma.com.tr; cap. 160m., res 346m. (Dec. 2011); Chair. AHMET YAMAN (acting); Gen. Man. METIN PEHLIVAN (acting).

Türkiye Sınai Kalkınma Bankası AŞ (Industrial Development Bank of Turkey): Meclisi Mebusan Cad. 81, Findikli, 34427 İstanbul; tel. (212) 3345050; fax (212) 3345234; e-mail info@tskb.com.tr; internet www.tskb.com; f. 1950; cap. 613.5m., res 58.0m., dep. 1,395.6m. (Dec. 2009); Chair. ADNAN BALI; CEO H. FEVZI ONAT; 2 brs.

Savings Deposit Insurance Fund Bank

Birleşik Fon Bankası AŞ: Büyükdere Cad. 143, 34394 Esentepe, İstanbul; tel. (212) 3401000; fax (212) 3473217; e-mail callcenter@fonbank.com.tr; internet www.fonbank.com.tr; fmrly Bayindirbank; name changed as above 2005; control passed to Savings Deposit Insurance Fund in 2001; Chair. SALIM ALKAN; Gen. Man. RECEP SÜLEYMAN ÖZDIL.

Banking Organization

Banks' Association of Turkey: Nıspetıye Cad. Akmerkez B3 Blok. Kat 13–14, 34340 Etiler, İstanbul; tel. (212) 2820973; fax (212) 2820946; e-mail gensek@tbb.org.tr; internet www.tbb.org.tr; f. 1958; Chair. HUSEYIN AYDIN.

STOCK EXCHANGE

İstanbul Menkul Kıymetler Borsası (İMKB): Resitpaşa Mah., Tuncay Artun Cad., 34467 Emirgan, İstanbul; tel. (212) 2982100; fax (212) 2982500; e-mail international@imkb.gov.tr; internet www.ise.org; f. 1866; revived in 1986 after being dormant for about 60 years; 104 mems of stock market, 132 mems of bond and bills market (April 2008); Chair. and CEO HÜSEYIN ERKAN; Senior Vice-Chair. ARIL SEREN.

INSURANCE

Principal Companies

AKSigorta AŞ: Meclis-i Mebusan Cad. 67, 34427 Fındıklı, İstanbul; tel. (212) 3934300; fax (212) 3343900; e-mail info@aksigorta.com.tr; internet www.aksigorta.com.tr; f. 1960; life and non-life; Chair. AHMET CEMAL DÖRDÜNCÜ; Gen. Man. UĞUR GÜLEN.

Allianz Sigorta AŞ: Bağlarbaşı, Kısıklı Cad. 13, 34662 Altunizade, İstanbul; tel. (216) 5566666; fax (216) 5566777; e-mail info@allianz.com.tr; internet www.allianz.com.tr; f. 1923; general, non-life; also offers life insurance through its subsidiary, Allianz Hayat ve Emeklilik AŞ; fmrly Koç Allianz Sigorta AŞ; 84% owned by Allianz AG (Germany); Chair. Dr RÜŞDÜ SARAÇOĞLU; CEO GEORGE D. SARTOREL.

Anadolu Sigorta TAŞ (Anadolu Insurance Co): Büyükdere Cad. İş Kuleleri Kule 2 Kat. 23–26 34330 4 Levent, İstanbul; tel. (212) 3500350; fax (212) 3500355; e-mail bilgi@anadolusigorta.com.tr; internet www.anadolusigorta.com.tr; f. 1925; life and non-life; 35.53% owned by Türkiye İş Bankası AŞ; Chair. BURHAN KARAGÖZ; CEO MUSTAFA ALI SU.

AvivaSA Emeklilik ve Hayat AŞ (AvivaSA): İnkılap Mah., Küçüksu Cad., Akçakoca Sk. 8, 34768 Ümraniye, İstanbul; tel. (216) 6333333; fax (216) 6343888; e-mail musteri@avivasa.com.tr; internet www.aviva.com.tr; f. 2007 by merger of Aviva Hayat ve Emeklilik and AK Emeklilik; life; 49.7% stakes owned by AK Sigorta AŞ and Aviva PLC (United Kingdom); Chair. HAKAN AKBAŞ; Gen. Man. MERAL EGEMEN.

AXA Sigorta AŞ: Meclis-i Mebusan Cad. Oyak İş Hanı 15, 34427 Salıpazarı, İstanbul; tel. (212) 3342424; fax (212) 2521515; e-mail iletisim@axasigorta.com.tr; internet www.axasigorta.com.tr; life and non-life; Chair. and CEO HAKKI CEMAL ERERDI; 10 brs.

ERGO Sigorta AŞ: Saray Mah., Dr Adnan Büyükdeniz Cad. 4, Akkom Ofis Park, Blok Kat. 10–14, Ümraniye, İstanbul; tel. (216) 5548100; fax (216) 6667777; e-mail ergoisvicre@ergoisvicre.com.tr; internet www.ergoturkiye.com; f. 1926 as La Suisse Umum Sigorta, acquired by İsviçre in 1981; acquired by ERGO Versicherungsgrüppe AG (Germany) in 2008; name changed as above 2010; fire, accident, marine, engineering, agricultural; Chair. AKIN KOZANOĞLU; Gen. Man. Dr THOMAS BARON; 11 regional brs.

Eureko Sigorta: Büyükdere Cad., Nurol Plaza 257, 34398 Maslak, İstanbul; tel. (212) 3041000; fax (212) 2854424; e-mail esmusterihizmetleri@eurekosigorta.com.tr; internet www.eurekosigorta.com.tr; f. 1989 as Garanti Sigorta; renamed as above in Oct. 2007; 80% owned by Eureko BV (Netherlands) and 20% by Türkiye Garanti Bankası AŞ; non-life; Chair. ERGUN ÖZEN; CEO OKAN UTKUERI.

Groupama Sigorta AŞ: Groupama Plaza, Eski Büyükdere Cad. 2, 34398 Maslak, İstanbul; tel. (212) 3676767; fax (212) 3676868; e-mail sigorta@groupama.com.tr; internet www.groupama.com.tr; f. 1959 as Başak Sigorta; 56.67% stake acquired by Groupama SA (France) in 2006; adopted present name 2009, following merger with Güven Sigorta TAŞ; life and non-life; Chair. PIERRE LEFEVRE; Gen. Man. ALAIN BAUDRY.

Güneş Sigorta: Günes Plaza, Büyükdere Cad. 110, 34394 Esentepe-Şişli, İstanbul; tel. (212) 4441957; fax (212) 3556464; e-mail gunes@gunessigorta.com.tr; internet www.gunessigorta.com.tr; f. 1957; non-life; 51.3% stake owned by Türkiye Vakıflar Bankası TAO, 45% owned by Groupama (France); Chair. BILAL KARAMAN; Gen. Man. MEHMET İLKER AVCI.

Yapı Kredi Sigorta AŞ: Yapı Kredi Plaza, A Blok, Büyükdere Cad., 34330 Levent, İstanbul; tel. (212) 3360606; fax (212) 3360808; e-mail yksigorta@yksigorta.com.tr; internet www.yksigorta.com.tr; f. 1943 as Halk Sigorta; present name adopted 2000; life and non-life; 53.1% stake owned by Yapı ve Kredi Bankası AŞ; Chair. TAYFUN BAYAZIT; Gen. Man. Dr S. GIRAY VELIOĞLU.

Insurance Organization

Türkiye Sigorta ve Reasürans Şirketleri Birliği (Asscn of the Insurance and Reinsurance Companies of Turkey): Büyükdere Cad., Büyükdere Plaza 195, 1-2, 34394 Levent, İstanbul; tel. (212) 3241950; fax (212) 3256108; e-mail genel@tsrsb.org.tr; internet www.tsrsb.org.tr; f. 1954 by merger of the Association of the Insurance Companies of Turkey and the Central Office of Insurers; present name adopted 1975; 57 mems (2009); Pres. HULUSI TAŞKIRAN; Sec.-Gen. ERHAN TUNÇAY.

Trade and Industry

GOVERNMENT AGENCIES

Özelleştirme İdaresi Başkanlığı (ÖİB) (Privatization Administration): Ziya Gökalp Cad. 80, Kurtuluş, 06600 Ankara; tel. (312) 4304560; fax (312) 4359342; e-mail info@oib.gov.tr; internet www.oib.gov.tr; co-ordinates privatization programme; Pres. METIN KILCI.

Rekabet Kurumu (Turkish Competition Authority): Bilkent Plaza B3 Blok, 06800 Bilkent, Ankara; tel. (312) 2914444; fax (312) 2667920; e-mail rek@rekabet.gov.tr; internet www.rekabet.gov.tr; f. 1997; prevents restriction of competition, oversees mergers and monitors state aid; Pres. and Chair. Prof. Dr NURETTIN KALDIRIMCI.

Türkiye Atom Enerjisi Kurumu (Turkish Atomic Energy Authority): Eskişehir Yolu 9km, 06530 Lodumlu, Ankara; tel. (312) 2958700; fax (312) 2878761; e-mail bilgi_taek@taek.gov.tr; internet www.taek.gov.tr; f. 1956; controls the development of peaceful uses of atomic energy; 7 mems; Pres. Prof. Dr ÜNER ÇOLAK.

CHAMBERS OF COMMERCE AND INDUSTRY

Türkiye Odalar ve Borsalar Birliği (TOBB) (Union of Chambers and Commodity Exchanges of Turkey): Dumlupınar Bul. 252, Eskişehir Yolu 9 Km, 06530 Ankara; tel. (312) 2182000; fax (312) 2194090; e-mail info@tobb.org.tr; internet www.tobb.org.tr; f. 1950; represents 365 chambers and commodity exchanges; Pres. RIFAT HISARCIKLIOĞLU.

Ankara Sanayi Odası (ASO) (Ankara Chamber of Industry): Atatürk Bul. 193, Kavaklıdere, Ankara; tel. (312) 4171200; fax (312) 4175205; e-mail aso@aso.org.tr; internet www.aso.org.tr; f. 1963; Pres. M. NURETTIN ÖZDEBIR.

Ankara Tabip Odası (ATO) (Ankara Chamber of Commerce): Mithatpaşa Cad. 62/18 Kızılay, 06420 Ankara; tel. (312) 4188700; fax (312) 4187794; e-mail ato@ato.org.tr; internet www.ato.org.tr; Pres. Prof. Dr GÜLRIZ ERSÖZ.

İstanbul Sanayi Odası (İSO) (İstanbul Chamber of Industry): Meşrutiyet Cad. 62, 34430 Tepebaşi, İstanbul; tel. (212) 2522900; fax (212) 2495084; e-mail info@iso.org.tr; internet www.iso.org.tr; f. 1952; more than 12,500 mems (2006); Chair. C. TANIL KÜÇÜK; Gen. Sec. METE MELEKSOY.

İstanbul Ticaret Odası (İstanbul Chamber of Commerce): Reşadiye Cad. 34112 Eminönü, İstanbul; tel. (212) 4556000; fax (212) 5131565; e-mail info@us-istanbul.com; internet www.ito.org.tr; f. 1952; more than 300,000 mems; Pres. MURAT YALÇINTAŞ.

EMPLOYERS' ASSOCIATIONS

Türk Sanayicileri ve İşadamları Derneği (TÜSİAD) (Turkish Industrialists' and Businessmen's Association): Meşrutiyet Cad. 74, 34420 Tepebaşı, İstanbul; tel. (212) 2491929; fax (212) 2491350; e-mail tusiad@tusiad.org; internet www.tusiad.org; f. 1971; c. 600 mems; Chair. ÜMIT BOYNER; Sec.-Gen. ZAFER ALI YAVAN.

Türkiye İşveren Sendikaları Konfederasyonu (TİSK) (Turkish Confederation of Employer Associations): Hoşdere Cad. Reşat Nuri Sok. 108, 06540 Çankaya, Ankara; tel. (312) 4397717; fax (312) 4397592; e-mail tisk@tisk.org.tr; internet www.tisk.org.tr; f. 1962; represents (on national level) 23 employers' asscns; official representative in labour relations; Pres. TUĞRUL KUDATGOBILIK; Sec.-Gen. BÜLENT PIRLER.

UTILITIES

Plans for the privatization of the electricity distribution grid were announced in 2004. Following numerous delays, the privatization process resumed in 2008, under the supervision of the Privatization Administration.

Electricity

Elektrik Üretim Anonim Şirketi (EÜAŞ) (Electricity Generation Co Inc): İnönü Bul. 27, Bahçelievler, 06490 Ankara; tel. (312) 2126900; fax (312) 2130103; e-mail basinhalk@euas.gov.tr; internet www.euas.gov.tr; f. 2001, following devolution of responsibilities of fmr Elektrik Üretim-İletim AŞ into separate entities for generation, transmission and wholesale activities; responsible for electricity generation; Chair. SEFER BÜTÜN.

Türkiye Elektrik Dağıtım AŞ (TEDAŞ): İnönü Bulv. 27, Bahçelievler, 06490 Ankara; tel. (312) 2126915; fax (312) 2138873; e-mail bilgi@tedas.gov.tr; internet www.tedas.gov.tr; responsible for distribution and sale of electricity; owns 20 regional distribution cos; Pres. and Man. Dir HAŞIM KEKLIK.

Türkiye Elektrik Iletim Anonim Şirketi (TEIAŞ) (Turkish Electricity Transmission Company): İnönü Bul. 27, Bahçelievler, 06490 Ankara; tel. (312) 2038061; fax (312) 2228160; e-mail basinmail@teias.gov.tr; internet www.teias.gov.tr; f. 2001 (see EÜAŞ); responsible for electricity transmission; Chair. and Gen. Man. KEMAL YILDIR.

Water

Devlet Su İşleri Genel Müdürlüğü (DSİ) (General Directorate of State Hydraulic Works): İnönü Bul., Yücetepe, 06100 Ankara; tel. (312) 4178300; fax (312) 4182498; e-mail idarim@dsi.gov.tr; internet www.dsi.gov.tr; f. 1954; controlled by the Ministry of Energy and Natural Resources; responsible for the planning and devt of water resources; Dir-Gen. HAYDAR KOÇAKER.

MAJOR INVESTMENT HOLDING COMPANIES

Alarko Şirketler Topluluğu: Muallim Naci Cad. 69, Ortaköy, İstanbul; tel. (212) 2275200; e-mail info@alarko.com.tr; internet www.alarko.com.tr; f. 1954; interests in industry, tourism, real estate, energy and food processing sectors; Chair. İSHAK ALATON; CEO AYHAN YAVRUCU; c. 6,000 employees.

Anadolu Endüstri Holding AŞ: Umut Sok. 12, 34752 İçerenköy, İstanbul; tel. (216) 5788500; internet www.anadolugroup.com; 65 subsidiary cos in automotive, financial services, food and beverages, health and manufacturing sectors; Chair. and CEO TUNCAY ÖZILHAN; c. 13,000 employees.

Çalık Holding AŞ: Büyükdere Cad. 163, 34394 Zincirlikuyu, İstanbul; tel. (212) 3065000; fax (212) 3065600; internet www.calik.com; f. 1997; subsidiary cos active in energy, construction, textiles, finance, media and telecommunications sectors; Chair. AHMET ÇALIK; CEO BERAT ALBAYRAK; 19,855 employees.

Çukurova Holding: Büyükdere Cad. Yapı Kredi Plaza A Blok, Kat. 16 1, Levent, 34330 İstanbul; tel. (212) 3701200; fax (212) 3701235; e-mail cukurovaholding@cukurovaholding.com.tr; internet www.cukurova.com.tr; f. 1978; industrial and commercial conglomerate; stakes in 140 companies in industry, manufacturing, construction, telecommunications, media, transport, energy and financial services; Chair. MEHMET EMIN KARAMEHMET; Exec. Dir F. ŞADI GÜCÜM; 36,150 employees world-wide.

Doğan Şirketler Grubu Holding AŞ: Oymacı Sok. 15/1, Altunizade, 34662 Üsküdar, İstanbul; tel. (216) 5569000; fax (216) 5569284; e-mail press@doganholding.com.tr; internet www.doganholding.com.tr; f. 1980; investment holding; interests in energy, media, industrial, trade, financial services and tourism sectors; owns and operates several of Turkey's largest-selling national newspapers (incl. *Hürriyet*, *Milliyet* and *Vatan*, as well as holding interests in radio and television broadcasting, and publishing; Chair. ARZUHAN DOĞAN YALÇINDAĞ; CEO Dr RAGIP NEBIL İLSEVEN.

Doğuş Grubu Binaları (Doğuş Group): Eski Büyükdere Cad., Ayazağa Mah., Oycan Plaza 15, Kat. 4, Maslak, İstanbul; tel. (212) 3353232; fax (212) 3353090; e-mail dmail@dogusholding.com.tr; internet www.dogusgrubu.com.tr; f. 1951; interests in financial services, automotive and construction industries, tourism, energy, real estate and media; subsidiary cos incl. Doğuş İnşaat, Doğuş Otomotiv and Garanti Bank; Chair. FERIT F. ŞAHENK; CEO HÜSNÜ AKHAN; 20,000 employees.

Eczacıbaşı Holding AŞ: Kanyon Ofis, Büyükdere Cad. 185, 34394 Levent, İstanbul; tel. (212) 3717000; fax (212) 3717110; internet www.eczacibasi.com.tr; f. 1912; production of pharmaceuticals, health and beauty products, and building products; Chair. BÜLENT ECZACIBAŞI; Pres. and CEO Dr ERDAL KARAMERCAN; 9,500 employees.

Hacı Ömer Sabancı Holding AŞ: Sabancı Centre, 80745 4 Levent, İstanbul; tel. (212) 3858080; fax (212) 3858888; internet www.sabanci.com.tr; f. 1967; 69 subsidiaries and jt-venture cos in financial services, automotive, tire manufacturing and repair, retail, cement and energy sectors; Chair. and Man. Dir GÜLER SABANCI; CEO ZAFER KURTUL; 51,120 employees (2008).

İhlas Holding AŞ: 29 Ekim Cad. 23, 34197 Yenibosna, İstanbul; tel. (212) 4542000; fax (212) 4542136; e-mail ihlas@ihlas.com.tr; internet www.ihlas.com.tr; f. 1993; media and publishing, broadcasting, manufacturing, construction, mining and energy; Pres. Dr ENVER ÖREN; CEO AHMET MÜCAHID ÖREN; 2,722 employees.

Koç Holding AŞ: Nakkaştepe Azizbey Sok. 1, 34674 Kuzguncuk, İstanbul; tel. (216) 5310000; fax (216) 5310099; e-mail iletsim@koc.com.tr; internet www.koc.com.tr; f. 1926; subsidiary cos incl. Arçelik, Ford Otomotiv and Tüpraş; Chair. MUSTAFA V. KOÇ; CEO BÜLENT BULGURLU; 73,677 employees world-wide (Dec. 2008).

Ordu Yardımlaşma Kurumu (OYAK) (Armed Forces' Pension Fund): Ziya Gökalp Cad. 64, 06600 Kurtuluş, Ankara; tel. (312) 4156000; fax (312) 4322705; internet www.oyak.com.tr; f. 1961; holds investments in 26 cos in manufacturing, finance and services sectors, incl. ERDEMİR and Oyak-Renault; CEO ŞERIF COŞKUN ULUSOY; 29,871 employees.

Tekfen Holding Co Inc: Kültür Mah., Tekfen Sitesi, Aydinlik Sok., A Blok 7, 34340 Beşiktaş, İstanbul; tel. (212) 3593300; fax (212) 3593305; e-mail tefken@tekfen.com.tr; internet www.tekfen.com.tr; comprises 49 cos dealing in construction, engineering and manufacturing, agriculture and industry, banking, real estate and investment; Pres. and CEO ERHAN ÖNER; 16,868 employees (Dec. 2008).

Zorlu Holding AŞ: Zorlu Plaza, 34310 Avcılar, İstanbul; tel. (212) 4562000; internet www.zorlu.com; f. 1968; manufacture of textiles and consumer goods, energy generation, tourism, property management; subsidiary cos incl. Vestel; Chair. AHMET ZORLU.

MAJOR COMPANIES

Akçansa Çimento Sanayi ve Ticaret AS: Hüseyin Bağdatlıoğlu İş Merkezi, Kaya Sultan Sok. 97 Kat. 5, Kozyatağı, 34742 İstanbul; tel. (216) 5713000; fax (216) 5713091; internet www.akcansa.com.tr; f. 1996; jt venture between Hacı Ömer Sabancı Holding AŞ and HeidelbergCement Group (Germany); production of cement; Chair. MEHMET GÖÇMEN; Gen. Man. HAKAN GÜRDAL; 1,032 employees.

Aksa (Akrilik Kimya San. AŞ): Miralay Şekipbey Sok. Ak Han 15–17, Kat. 5/6, 34437 Gumuşsuyu, İstanbul; tel. (212) 2514500; fax (212) 2514507; e-mail aksa@aksa.com; internet www.aksa.com; f. 1968; produces acrylic fibres and general chemical products; Chair. MEHMET ALI BERKMAN; Gen. Man. CENGIZ TAŞ; 750 employees.

Anadolu Efes Biracılık ve Malt Sanayii AŞ (Anadolu Efes): Fatih Sultan Mehmet Mah., Balkan Cad. 58, 34771 İstanbul; tel. (216) 5868000; fax (216) 4887863; e-mail efes@efespilsen.com; internet www.anadoluefes.com; f. 1969; subsidiary of Anadolu Endüstri Holding AŞ; production of beverages; Chair. TUNCAY ÖZILHAN; Gen. Man. ALEJANDRO JIMENEZ; 18,054 employees.

Arçelik AŞ: Karaağaç Cad. 2–6, Sütlüce, 34445 İstanbul; tel. (212) 3143434; fax (212) 3143482; e-mail corporateinfo@arcelik.com; internet www.arcelikas.com.tr; f. 1955; 57% owned by Koç Holding; produces domestic appliances; subsidiary: Grundig Elektronik AŞ; Chair. RAHMI M. KOÇ; CEO LEVENT ÇAKIROĞLU; 17,000 employees world-wide.

Aygaz AŞ: Büyükdere Cad. Aygaz Han 145/1, 34394 Zincirikuyu, İstanbul; tel. (212) 3541515; fax (212) 2883963; e-mail aygazhizmethatti@aygaz.com.tr; internet www.aygaz.com.tr; f. 1961; 40.68% stake owned by Koç Holding; supply and distribution of liquefied petroleum gas; Chair. RAHMI M. KOÇ; Gen. Man. YAĞIZ EYÜBOĞLU; 1,431 employees (Dec. 2008).

BİM Birleşik Mağazalar AŞ: Ebubekir Cad. 73, 34887 Samandıra, İstanbul; tel. (216) 5640303; fax (216) 3117978; e-mail iletisim@bim.com.tr; internet www.bim.com.tr; f. 1995; retailer of food and basic consumer goods; Chair. MUSTAFA LATIF TOPBAŞ; 13,681 employees (Dec. 2008).

Çolakoğlu Metalurji AŞ: Rüzgarlıbahçe Mah., Kavak Sok., Kat. 16, Kavacık, İstanbul 34805; tel. (216) 4442627; fax (216) 5371401; e-mail colakoglu@colakoglu.com.tr; internet www.colakoglu.com.tr; f. 1968; manufactures steel wire rod in coils, reinforcing bars, billets and slabs; Gen. Man. UĞUR DALBELER.

Ereğli Demir ve Çelik Fabrikalari TAŞ (Erdemir): Merdivenköy Yolu Cad. 7, Küçükbakkalköy Ataşehir, 34750 İstanbul; tel. (372) 3294639; fax (372) 3294138; e-mail erdemir_ir@erdemir.com.tr; internet www.erdemir.com.tr; f. 1960; fmr state-owned enterprise; majority owned by Oyak Group since 2006; 9 subsidiary cos; manufactures steel and iron products; Chair. and Man. Dir DINÇ KIZILDEMIR; CEO SEDAT ORHAN.

Ford Otomotiv San AŞ: Fatih Mah. Hasan Basri Cad., Köymenkent, 34885 Samandıra, İstanbul; tel. (216) 5647236; fax (216) 5647278; e-mail ykokten@ford.com.tr; internet www.ford.com.tr; f. 1959; jt venture between Koç Holding and Ford Motor Co (USA); manufactures passenger cars, trucks and engines; Gen. Man. MICHAEL FLEWITT; 8,000 employees.

Habaş (Habaş Sınai ve Tibbi Gazlar İstihsal Endüstrisi AŞ): Fuat Paşa Sok. 26, 34880 Soğanlık, İstanbul; tel. (216) 4536400; fax (216) 4522570; internet www.habas.com.tr; production of medical and industrial gases, electricity, steel, machinery; distribution of natural gas; also owns Anadolubank; Chair. MEHMET RÜŞTÜ BAŞARAN.

Hedef Alliance Holding AŞ: Basın Ekspres Yolu, Kavak Sok., Ser Plaza 3, A Blok Kat. 3, 34530 Yenibosna, İstanbul; tel. (212) 4527200; fax (212) 4527228; internet www.hedefalliance.com.tr; f. 1987; present name adopted 2001; distribution of pharmaceutical and cosmetic products; Chair. ETHEM SANCAK.

İÇDAŞ: 34212 Güneşli, İstanbul; tel. (212) 6040404; fax (212) 5502024; e-mail icdas@icdas.com.tr; internet www.icdas.com.tr; f. 1970; produces steel bars and high alloy steels; Gen. Man. BÜLEND ENGIN.

Kordsa Global AŞ: Sabancı Centre Kule 2, Kat. 17, 4 Levent, 34330 İstanbul; tel. (212) 3858657; fax (212) 2820012; internet www.kordsaglobal.com; f. 1973; manufactures nylon and polyester yarn, industrial and cord fabrics; subsidiary of Hacı Ömer Sabancı Holding AŞ; Chair. MEHMET NURETTIN PEKARUN; Pres. and CEO CENK ALPER; 4,500 employees world-wide.

Mercedes-Benz Türk AŞ: Tem Otoyolu Hadımköy Çıkışı, Mercedes Cad., 34500 Bahçeşehir, İstanbul; tel. (212) 8673000; fax (212) 8674400; internet www.mercedes.com.tr; manufactures civil and military vehicles; CEO WOLF-DIETER KURZ.

Migros Ticaret AŞ: Turgut Özal Cad. 6, 34758 Ataşehir, İstanbul; tel. (216) 5793000; fax (216) 4565909; e-mail iletisim@migros.com.tr; internet www.migroskurumsal.com; f. 1954; retail, marketing and distribution; in 2005 took over Tansaş retail chain; Chair. FEVZI BÜLEND ÖZAYDINLI; Gen. Man. ÖMER ÖZGÜR TORT.

Oyak-Renault Otomobil Fabrikaları AŞ: Fatih Sultan Mah., Balkan Cad. 47, 34770 Ümraniye, İstanbul; tel. (216) 6456666; fax (216) 6456688; internet www.renault.com.tr; f. 1969; 51% owned by Renault (France), 49% owned by Oyak Group; manufactures automobiles; CEO TARIK TUNALIOĞLU.

Petkim Petrokimya Holding AŞ: PK 12, 35801 Aliağa, İzmir; tel. (232) 6163240; fax (232) 6161248; internet www.petkim.com.tr; f. 1965; 51% owned by a consortium of Socar (Azerbaijan) and Turcas Petrol AŞ (Turkey); 39% owned by private investors; 10% state-owned; produces petrochemicals; Chair. VAGIF ALIYEV; Gen. Man. SADETTIN KORKUT; 2,612 employees.

Petrol Ofisi AŞ (POAŞ): Ayazağa Büyükdere Cad. 33, 34398 Maslak, İstanbul; tel. (212) 3291500; fax (212) 3291888; e-mail info@poas.com.tr; internet www.poas.com.tr; f. 1941; fmr State Economic Enterprise, privatized in 2000; 54.17% owned by Doğan Şirketler Grubu Holding AŞ, 41.58% owned by ÖMV AG (Austria); distribution of petroleum and petroleum products; Chair. GERHARD ROISS; CEO MELIH TÜRKER; 1,061 employees (Dec. 2008).

Philsa: 7 Eylül Mah., Philsa Cad. 32, 35860 Torbalı, İzmir; tel. (232) 8501111; fax (232) 8501122; f. 1991; 75% owned by Philip Morris Int. (USA) and 25% by Hacı Ömer Sabancı Holding AŞ; manufactures cigarettes; Gen. Man. SEDAT MÜDERRISOĞLU.

Sanko Textile and Trading Co: Sani Konukoglu Bul., PK 83, Gaziantep; tel. (342) 2116000; fax (342) 2116429; e-mail info@sankotextile.com; internet www.sankotextile.com; f. 1943; manufacturers and exporters of yarns and knitted fabrics; 12,000 employees.

Sarkusyan Elektrolitik Bakır Sanayii ve Ticaret AŞ: Emek Mah., Asiroglu, St 147, 41700 Darcia-Kocaeli; tel. (262) 6766600; fax (262) 6766680; e-mail info@sarkuysan.com; internet www.sarkusyan.com; f. 1972; produces copper products, cast iron parts for the manufacture of automobiles and machinery; Chair. and Pres. HAYRETTIN ÇAYCI.

Tofaş (Türk Otomobil Fabrikası AŞ): Büyükdere Cad. 145/5, 34400 Zincirlikuyu, İstanbul; tel. (212) 2753390; fax (212) 2753988; internet www.tofas.com.tr; f. 1968; jt venture between Koç Holding AŞ and Fiat Auto SpA (Italy); manufactures automobiles and automobile parts; Pres. ALI AYDIN PANDIR.

Toyota Otomotiv Sanayi Türkiye AŞ: Arifiye, 54580 Sakarya; tel. (264) 2950295; fax (264) 2951295; e-mail iletisim@toyotatr.com; internet www.toyotatr.com; f. 1990; 90% owned by Toyota Motor Europe NV/SA, 10% by Mitsui & Co Ltd; CEO ORHAN ÖZER; 2,875 employees.

Türkiye Kömür İşletmeleri Kurumu (TKI) (General Directorate of Turkish Coal Enterprises): Hipodrom Cad. 12, 06330 Yenimahalle, Ankara; tel. (312) 5401000; fax (312) 3841635; e-mail tkiadmin@tki.gov.tr; internet www.tki.gov.tr; f. 1957; coal mining; Pres. and Gen. Man. MUSTAFA AKTAS; 9,068 employees.

Türkiye Petrol Rafinerileri AŞ (TÜPRAŞ): 41790 Körfez, Kocaeli; tel. (262) 3163000; fax (262) 3163010; e-mail info@tupras.com.tr; internet www.tupras.com.tr; f. 1983; privatization completed 2005; 75% owned by Koç Holding AŞ, 20% by Aygaz AŞ, 3% by OPET Petrolcülük AŞ, 1.9% by Shell Overseas Investment BV and 0.1% by Shell Co of Turkey Ltd; refining of crude oil; Chair. ÖMER M. KOÇ; CEO YAVUZ ERKUT.

Türkiye Petrolleri Anonim Ortaklığı (TPAO) (Turkish Petroleum Corpn): Sögütözü Mah. 2, Cad. 86 06100 Çankaya, Ankara; tel. (312) 2072000; fax (312) 2869000; e-mail tpaocc@petrol.tpao.gov.tr; internet www.tpao.gov.tr; f. 1954; State Economic Enterprise; explores for, drills and produces crude petroleum and natural gas; Chair. and Gen. Man. BESIM ŞIŞMAN; 3,730 employees.

Türkiye Şeker Fabrikaları AŞ: Mithatpaşa Cad. 14, 06100 Yenişehir, Ankara; tel. (312) 4585500; fax (312) 4585800; e-mail yonet@turkseker.gov.tr; internet www.turkseker.gov.tr; produces sugar and manufactures machinery used in sugar production; Chair. and Gen. Dir Dr BÜLENT ÜZÜMCÜ; 2,865 employees.

Tütün, Tütün Mamülleri, Tuz ve Alkol İşletmeleri AŞ (TTA): Orhantepe Mah, Tekel Cad., 34865 Cevizli, İstanbul; tel. (212) 5331900; fax (212) 5320527; e-mail iletisim@tekel.gov.tr; internet www.tekel.gov.tr; f. 1862; production and distribution of tobacco products, alcohol and salt; Pres. and Gen. Man. KASIM DEMIREL.

Ülker: PK 366, Topkapı, İstanbul; tel. (212) 5671567; fax (212) 3102838; internet www.ulker.com.tr; f. 1944; manufacture and distribution of food products and beverages; Chair. MURAT ÜLKER.

Vestel AŞ: Ambarli, Petrol Ofisi Dolum Tesisleri Yolu, 34840 Avcilar, İstanbul; tel. (212) 4562200; fax (212) 4220335; internet www.vestel.com.tr; subsidiary of Zorlu Holding; manufacture and distribution of domestic appliances and other electronic goods; group comprises 24 cos world-wide; Group Chair. AHMET NAZIF ZORLU.

TRADE UNIONS

(Note: Statistics correct to July 2009)

Confederations

DİSK (Türkiye Devrimci İşçi Sendikaları Konfederasyonu) (Confederation of Progressive Trade Unions of Turkey): Cad. Abide-I Hürriyet 117, Nakiye Elgün Sok. 91, Şişli, İstanbul; tel. (212) 2910005; fax (212) 2342075; e-mail disk@disk.org.tr; internet www.disk.org.tr; f. 1967; member of ITUC and European Trade Union Confed; Pres. EROL EKICI; Sec.-Gen. ADNAN SERDAROĞLU; 17 affiliated unions with 400,000 mems.

Hak-İş (Hak İşçi Sendikaları Konfederasyonu) (Confederation of Turkish Real Trade Unions): Tunus Cad. 37, 06680 Kavaklıdere, Ankara; tel. (312) 4178002; fax (312) 4250552; e-mail hakis@hakis.org.tr; internet www.hakis.org.tr; f. 1976; mem. of ITUC and European Trade Union Confed; Pres. MAHMUT ARSLAN; Gen. Sec. Dr OSMAN YILDIZ; 13 affiliated unions with 550,000 mems.

KESK (Kamu Emekçileri Sendikaları Konfederasyonu) (Confederation of Public Employees' Trade Unions): Çehre Sok. 6/1, Gaziosmanpaşa, Ankara; tel. (312) 4367111; fax (312) 4367470; e-mail kesk@kesk.org.tr; internet www.kesk.org.tr; f. 1995; mem. of ITUC and European Trade Union Confed; Pres. LAMI ÖZGEN; Gen. Sec. ISMAIL HAKKI TOMBUL; 11 affiliated unions with 224,413 mems.

Memur-Sen (Memur Sendikaları Konfederasyonu) (Confederation of Public Servants' Trade Unions): Özveren Sok. 9, 4 Demirtepe, Ankara; tel. (312) 2304898; fax (312) 2303989; e-mail info@memursen.org.tr; internet www.memursen.org.tr; f. 1995; Pres. AHMET GÜNDOĞDU; Gen. Sec. MAHMUT KAÇAR; 12 affiliated unions with 376,355 mems.

Türk-İş (Türkiye İşçi Sendikaları Konfederasyonu) (Confederation of Turkish Trade Unions): Bayındır Sok. 10, 06410 Kizilay, Ankara; tel. (312) 4333125; fax (312) 4336809; e-mail turkis@turkis.org.tr; internet www.turkis.org.tr; f. 1952; mem. of ITUC, European Trade Union Confed. and OECD/Trade Union Advisory Cttee; Pres. MUSTAFA KUMLU; Gen. Sec. PEVRUL KAVLAK; 33 affiliated unions and federations with 2.2m. mems.

Türkiye Kamu-Sen (Türkiye Kamu Çalışanları Sendikaları Konfederasyonu) (Confederation of Turkish Public Employees' Unions): Dr Mediha Eldem Sok. 85, Kocatepe, Çankaya, Ankara; tel. (312) 4242200; fax (312) 4242208; e-mail kamusen@kamusen.org.tr; internet www.kamusen.org.tr; f. 1992; Pres. ISMAIL KONCUK; Gen. Sec ÖNDER KAHVECI; 13 affiliated unions with 400,000 mems.

Principal Affiliated Trade Unions

Belediye-İş (Türkiye Belediyeler ve Genel Hizmetler İşçiler Sendikası) (Municipal and Public Services Workers): Necatibey Cad. 59, Kızılay, Ankara; tel. (312) 2318343; fax (312) 2320874; e-mail belediyeis@belediyeis.org.tr; internet www.belediyeis.org.tr; f. 1983; affiliated to Türk-İş; Pres. NIHAT YURDAKUL; Gen. Sec. NIHAT AYÇIÇEK; 205,666 mems.

Genel-İş (Türkiye Genel Hizmetler İşçileri Sendikası) (Municipal Workers): Çankırı Cad. 28, Kat. 8, 06030 Ulus, Ankara; tel. (312) 3091547; fax (312) 3091046; e-mail bilgi@genel-is.org.tr; internet www.genel-is.org.tr; f. 1983; affiliated to DİSK; Pres. EROL EKICI; Gen. Sec. KANI BEKO; 83,976 mems.

Hizmet-İş Sendikası (Municipal and Public Service Workers): Gazi Mustafa Kemal Bul. 86, Maltepe, 06570 Çankaya, Ankara; tel. (312) 2318710; fax (312) 2319889; e-mail hizmet-is@hizmet-is.org.tr; internet www.hizmet-is.org.tr; f. 1979; affiliated to Hak-İş; Pres. MAHMUT ARSLAN; Gen. Sec. DEVLET SERT; 130,942 mems.

Petrol-İş (Türkiye Petrol, Kimya ve Lastik İşçileri Sendikası) (Petroleum, Chemicals and Rubber Industry): Altunizade Mah., Kuşbakışı Cad. 23, Üsküdar, İstanbul; tel. (212) 4749870; fax (212) 4749867; e-mail merkez@petrol-is.org.tr; internet www.petrol-is.org.tr; f. 1950; affiliated to Türk-İş; Pres. MUSTAFA ÖZTAŞKIN; Gen. Sec. ALI UFUK YAŞAR; 89,442 mems.

Sağlık-Sen (Sağlık ve Sosyal Hizmet Çalışanları Sendikası) (Health and Social Workers): GMK Bul., Özveren Sok. 9/2, Demirtepe, Ankara; tel. (312) 4441995; fax (312) 2308365; internet www.sagliksen.org.tr; f. 1995; affiliated to Memur-Sen; Pres. METIN MEMIŞ; Gen. Sec. SEMIH DURMUŞ; 169,000 mems.

Tarım-İş (Türkiye Orman, Topraksu, Tarım ve Tarım Sanayii İşçileri Sendikası) (Forestry, Agriculture and Agricultural Industry Workers) Bankacı Sok. 10, 06700 Kocatepe, Ankara; tel. (312) 4190456; fax (312) 4193113; e-mail info@tarimis.org.tr; internet www.tarimis.org.tr; f. 1961; affiliated to Türk-İş; Pres. BEDRETTIN KAYKAÇ; Gen. Sec. MUSTAFA ÇARDAKÇI; 43,337 mems.

Tekgıda-İş (Türkiye Tütün, Müskirat Gıda ve Yardımcı İşçileri Sendikası) (Tobacco, Drink, Food and Allied Workers): 4 Levent Konaklar Sok. 1, İstanbul; tel. (212) 2644996; fax (212) 2789534; e-mail bilgi@tekgida.org.tr; internet www.tekgida.org.tr; f. 1952; affiliated to Türk-İş; Pres. MUSTAFA TÜRKEL; Gen. Sec. MECIT AMAÇ; 191,641 mems.

Teksif (Türkiye Tekstil, Örme ve Giyim Sanayii İşçileri Sendikası) (Textile, Knitting and Clothing Workers): Ziya Gökalp Cad. Aydoğmuş Sok. 1, Kurtuluş, 06600 Ankara; tel. (312) 4312170; fax (312) 4357826; e-mail teksif@oda.net.tr; internet www.teksif.org.tr; f. 1951; affiliated to Türk-İş; Pres. NAZMI IRGAT; Gen. Sec. MUSTAFA BURGAZ; 338,835 mems.

Tes-İş (Türkiye Enerji, Su ve Gaz İşçileri Sendikası) (Electricity, Water and Gas Workers): Meriç Sok. 23, 06510 Beştepeler, Ankara; tel. (312) 2126510; fax (312) 2126552; e-mail info@tes-is.org.tr; internet www.tes-is.org.tr; f. 1963; affiliated to Türk-İş; Pres. MUSTAFA KUMLU; Gen. Sec. MUSTAFA ŞAHIN; 122,350 mems.

Türk Eğitim-Sen (Türkiye Eğitim ve Öğretim Bilim Hizmetleri Kolu Kamu Çalışanları Sendikası) (Teachers and University Lecturers): Bayındır 2., Sok. 46, Kızılay, Ankara; tel. (312) 4240960; fax (312) 4240968; e-mail gds@turkegitimsen.org.tr; internet www.turkegitimsen.org.tr; affiliated to Türkiye Kamu-Sen; Pres. İSMAIL KONCUK; Gen. Sec. MUSA AKKAŞ; 155,021 mems.

Türk Maden-İş (Türkiye Maden İşçileri Sendikası) (Mining): Strazburg Cad. 7, Sıhhiye, Ankara; tel. (312) 2317355; fax (312) 2298931; e-mail genelmerkez@madenis.org.tr; internet www.madenis.org.tr; affiliated to Türk-İş; Pres. NURETTIN AKÇUL; Gen. Sec. VEDAT ÜNAL; 58,591 mems.

Türk-Metal (Türkiye Metal, Çelik, Mühimmat, Makina ve Metalden Mamul, Eşya ve Oto, Montaj ve Yardımcı İşçileri Sendikası) (Auto, Metal and Allied Workers): Beştepe Mah., Yaşam Cad. 1. Sok. 7/A, Söğütözü, Yenimahalle, Ankara; tel. (312) 2926400; fax (312) 2844018; e-mail bilgiislem@turkmetal.org.tr; internet www.turkmetal.org.tr; f. 1963; affiliated to Türk-İş; Pres. PEVRUL KAVLAK; Gen. Sec. YÜCEL YÜCEL; 343,263 mems.

Türkiye Çimse-İş (Türkiye Çimento, Seramik, Toprak ve Cam Sanayii İşçileri Sendikası) (Cement, Ceramics, Clay and Glass Industries): Esat Cad. 43, Küçükesat, Çankaya, Ankara; tel. (312) 4195830; fax (312) 4251335; internet www.cimse-is.org.tr; f. 1963; affiliated to Türk-İş; Pres. ZEKERIYE NAZLIM; Gen. Sec. KAZIM BELEK; 71,510 mems.

Yol-İş (Türkiye Yol, Yapı ve İnşaat İşçileri Sendikası) (Road, Construction and Building Workers): Sümer 1 Sok. 18, Kızılay, Ankara; tel. (312) 2324687; fax (312) 2324810; e-mail yildirimkoc@yol-is.org.tr; internet www.yol-is.org.tr; f. 1963; affiliated to Türk-İş; Pres. RAMAZAN ADAR; Gen. Sec. TEVFIK ÖZÇELIK; 165,505 mems.

Transport

RAILWAYS

The total length of the railways in operation within the national frontiers was 12,008 km in 2012, of which 9,642 km were main lines. There are direct rail links with Bulgaria, Iran and Syria. Construction work on a new line connecting Turkey with Georgia and Azerbaijan commenced in late 2007. However, construction was temporarily suspended in August 2008, owing to military conflict between Georgia and Russia in the Georgian secessionist region of South Ossetia. Environmental concerns further delayed the project, which consequently was not expected to be completed until 2014. Construction work on a 533-km high-speed rail link between Ankara and İstanbul commenced in 2003. A 245-km section of the line between Ankara and Eskişehir became operational in March 2009; the line was scheduled to be fully operational by the end of 2013. Construction work on the Marmaray Project, a 76-km suburban line between the European and Asian sections of İstanbul, incorporating a 13.6-km tunnel under the Bosphorus strait, commenced in 2004. Following several delays, the project was expected to be completed in 2015. İstanbul operates a two-line, 34.7-km light railway system and two metro lines totalling 42 km in length. The second of those lines, servicing 16 stations between Kadıköy and Kartal in the Asian part of the city, was inaugurated in 2012. Ankara, Adana, Bursa and İzmir also operate metro and light railway systems.

Türkiye Cumhuriyeti Devlet Demiryolları (TCDD) (Turkish State Railways): Talatpaşa Bul., 06330 Gar, Ankara; tel. (312) 3090515; fax (312) 3126247; e-mail byhim@tcdd.gov.tr; internet www.tcdd.gov.tr; f. 1924; operates all railways and connecting ports of the State Railway Admin., which acquired the status of a state economic enterprise in 1953, and a state economic establishment in 1984; Chair. of Bd and Dir-Gen. SÜLEYMAN KARAMAN.

ROADS

In January 2012 the total road network was estimated at 65,049 km of classified roads, of which 2,119 km were motorways, 31,372 km were highways and 31,558 km were secondary roads.

Karayolları Genel Müdürlüğü (KGM) (General Directorate of Highways): İnönü Bul., Yücetepe, 06100 Ankara; tel. (312) 4157000; fax (312) 4172851; e-mail info@kgm.gov.tr; internet www.kgm.gov.tr; f. 1950; Dir-Gen. MEHMET CAHIT TURHAN.

SHIPPING

At 31 December 2012 Turkey's merchant fleet comprised 1,325 vessels and had an aggregate displacement of 6,680,140 grt, of which 111 were bulk carriers, 27 were fish carriers, seven were gas tankers and 437 were general cargo ships.

The ports of Bandırma, Derince, Haydarpaşa (İstanbul), İskenderun and İzmir, all of which are connected to the railway network, are operated by Turkish State Railways (TCDD), while the port of İstanbul and five smaller ports are operated by the Turkish Maritime Organization. Responsibility for some 13 ports, including those of Antalya and Trabzon, was transferred from the Turkish Maritime Organization to private companies under separate 30-year agreements in 1997–2003. In 2007 control of the port of Mersin was transferred from TCDD to the private sector under a 36-year concession agreement. A similar arrangement involving the port of Samsun commenced in April 2010. In 2011 Prime Minister Recep Tayyip Erdoğan announced plans to construct a 50-km canal through the European portion of the country, connecting the Black and Mediterranean Seas. The 'Canal İstanbul' project was intended to relieve congestion on the Bosphorus Strait.

Regulatory and Port Authorities

Turkish Maritime Organization (TDI): Genel Müdürlüğü, Rıhtım Cad. Merkez Han 32, 34425 Karaköy, İstanbul; tel. (212) 2515000; fax (212) 2495391; e-mail tdibasin@tdi.gov.tr; internet www.tdi.com.tr; Gen. Man. BURHAN KÜLÜNK.

Port of Bandırma: TCDD Liman İşletme Müdürlüğü, Bandırma; tel. (266) 7187530; fax (266) 7136011; e-mail bandirmaliman@tcdd.gov.tr; Port Man. OKKES DEMIREL; Harbour Master RUSEN OKAN.

Port of Derince: TCDD Liman İşletme Müdürlüğü, Derince; tel. (262) 2399021; e-mail derinceliman@tcdd.gov.tr; Port Man. ALI ARIF AYTAÇ; Harbour Master HAYDAR DOĞAN.

Port of Haydarpaşa (İstanbul): TCDD Liman İşletme Müdürlüğü Haydarpaşa, İstanbul; tel. (216) 3488020; fax (216) 3451705; e-mail haydarpasaliman@tcdd.gov.tr; Port Man. NEDIM OZCAN; Harbour Master İSMAIL SAFAER.

Port of İskenderun: TCDD Liman İşletme Müdürlüğü, İskenderun; tel. (326) 6140044; fax (326) 6132424; e-mail iskenderunliman@tcdd.gov.tr; Port Man. HILMI SÖNMEZ; Harbour Master İSHAK ÖZDEMIR.

Port of İzmir: TCDD Liman İşletme Müdürlüğü, İzmir; tel. (232) 4631600; fax (232) 4632248; e-mail izmirliman@tcdd.gov.tr; Port Man. TURAN YALÇIN.

Port of Mersin: Yeni Mah. 101, Cad. 5307, Sok. 5, 33100 Mersin; tel. (324) 2412920; fax (324) 2290849; e-mail marketing@mersinport.com.tr; internet www.mersinport.com.tr; f. 2007; managed by a consortium of PSA Int. (Singapore) and Akfen (Turkey) under a 36-yr concession; Gen. Man. JOHN PHILLIPS; Harbour Master RACI TARHUSOĞLU.

Port of Samsun: TCDD Liman İşletme Müdürlüğü, Samsun; tel. (362) 2332293; fax (362) 4451626; e-mail samsunliman@tcdd.gov.tr; managed since April 2010 by Cey Group (Turkey) under a 36-year concession; Port Man. SAFFET YAMAK; Harbour Master Capt. ARIF H. UZUNOĞLU.

Principal Shipping Companies

Akmar Shipping Group: Küçükbakkalköy Mah. Cicek Sok. 4, Aksoy Plaza, 34750 Kadıköy, İstanbul; tel. (216) 5762666; fax (216) 5727195; e-mail info@akmar.com.tr; internet www.akmar.com.tr; f. 2004; Chair. NECDET AKSOY.

Deniz Nakliyatı TAŞ (Turkish Cargo Lines): Fahrettin Kerim Gökay Cad. Denizciler İş Merkezi No. 18, 1A Blok Kat. 1, Altunizade/Üsküdar, İstanbul; tel. (216) 4747400; fax (216) 4747430; e-mail tcl@tcl.com.tr; internet www.tcl.com.tr; f. 1955; bulk carriers; Chair. M. GÜNDÜZ KAPTANOĞLU; Gen. Man. CEMIL GÜCÜYENER; 2 large and 2 small handy bulk/ore carriers.

İstanbul Deniz Otobusleri Sanayi ve Ticaret AŞ: Kennedy Cad., Hizli Feribot Iskelesi Yenikapi, İstanbul; tel. (212) 4556900; fax (212) 5173958; e-mail info@ido.com.tr; internet www.ido.com.tr; f. 1987; state-owned; ferry co; scheduled for privatization; Gen. Man. Dr AHMET PAKSOY; 90 vessels.

Kiran Group of Shipping Companies: Fahrettin Kerim Gorkay Cad. 18, Denizciler İş Merkezi, B Blok Kat. 2, 34662 Altunizade, İstanbul; tel. (216) 5541400; fax (216) 5541414; e-mail kiran@kiran.com.tr; internet www.kiran.com.tr; f. 1959; Chair. TURGUT KIRAN; Man. Dir TAMER KIRAN; 19 vessels.

Ozsay Deniz Elektroniği AŞ: Güzelyalı, E-5 Üzeri 18, 34903 Pendik, İstanbul; tel. (216) 4933610; fax (216) 4930306; e-mail ozsay@tnn.net; internet www.ozsay.com; f. 1976; Pres. RECEP KALKAVAN; Man. Dir OMER KALKAVAN; 10 vessels.

Türkiye Denizcilik İşletmeleri Denizyolları İşletmesi Müdürlüğü (TDI): Meclisı Mebusan Cad. 18, 80040 Salıpazarı, İstanbul;

tel. (212) 2521700; fax (212) 2515767; e-mail bilgiedinme@tdi.gov.tr; internet www.tdi.com.tr; ferry co; Chair. ERKAN ARIKAN; Man. Dir KADIR KURTOĞLU; 5 vessels.

Yardimci Shipping Group of Companies: Aydintepe Mah. Tersaneler Cad. 50 Sok. 7, 34947 Tuzla, İstanbul; tel. (216) 4938000; fax (216) 4928080; e-mail info@yardimci.gen.tr; internet www.yardimci.gen.tr; f. 1976; Chair. KEMAL YARDIMCI; Man. Dir HUSEYIN YARDIMCI; 9 vessels.

CIVIL AVIATION

There are 40 airports for international and domestic flights in Turkey. The largest of these are Atatürk and Sabiha Gökçen (both serving İstanbul), Esenboğa (Ankara), Adnan Menderes (İzmir), Antalya, Dalaman, Milas–Bodrum, Adana, Trabzon, Isparta Süleyman Demirel and Nevşehir–Kapadokya. A second terminal building at Sabiha Gökçen International Airport was inaugurated in October 2009. Earlier that year plans were announced to increase total passenger capacity at the airport to 20m. by 2018. In August 2012 the Government confirmed that it would seek to build a third international airport to serve İstanbul, located in the European part of the city. The first phase of the project, which was intended to accommodate up to 90m. passengers per year, was scheduled for completion by 2015.

Devlet Hava Meydanları İşletmesi Genel Müdürlüğü (General Directorate of State Airports Authority): Konya Yolu Üzeri No. 66, 06330 Etiler, Ankara; tel. (312) 2042000; fax (312) 2123917; e-mail dhmi@dhmi.gov.tr; internet www.dhmi.gov.tr; f. 1984; manages 36 airports nation-wide; responsible for air traffic control in Turkish airspace; Chair. of Bd and Dir-Gen. ORHAN BIRDAL.

Sivil Havacılık Genel Müdürlüğü (Directorate General of Civil Aviation): Bosna Hersek Cad. 5, 06510 Emek, Ankara; tel. (312) 2036000; fax (312) 2124684; e-mail ozelkalem@shgm.gov.tr; internet web.shgm.gov.tr; Dir-Gen. BILAL EKŞI.

Atlasjet Havacilik AŞ: Yeşilyurt Mah. Eski Halkali Yolu Alacati Evleri Yani 5B, 34153 Florya, İstanbul; tel. (212) 6632000; fax (212) 6632751; e-mail info@atlasjet.com; internet www.atlasjet.com; f. 2001; passenger and cargo; 17 aircraft; CEO ORHAN COŞKUN.

Onur Air Taşımacılık AŞ: Atatürk Havalimanı B Kapısı, Teknik Hangar Yanı 34149, Yeşilköy, İstanbul; tel. (212) 4686687; fax (212) 4686696; e-mail info@onurair.com.tr; internet www.onurair.com.tr; f. 1992; international and domestic passenger and cargo charter services; 22 aircraft; Gen. Man. ŞAHABETTIN BOLUKÇU.

Pegasus Hava Taşımacılığı AŞ (Pegasus Airlines): Basın Ekspres Yolu 2, Halkalı, İstanbul; tel. (212) 6977777; fax (212) 6939777; internet www.flypgs.com; f. 1990; domestic and international scheduled and charter services; 23 aircraft; Chair. ALI SABANCI; Gen. Man. SERTAÇ HAYBAT.

SunExpress (Güneş Ekspres Havacilik AŞ): Mehmetçik Mah. Aspendos Bul. Aspendos İş Merkezi 63/1–2, 07300 Antalya; tel. (242) 3102626; fax (242) 3102650; e-mail travelcenter@sunexpress.com; internet www.sunexpress.com; f. 1989; 50% owned by Deutsche Lufthansa AG (Germany) and 50% by Turkish Airlines; charter and scheduled passenger and freight; serves European destinations; 26 aircraft; Man. Dir PAUL SCHWAIGER.

TAV Havalimanları Holding AŞ: İstanbul Atatürk Havalimanı, Dış Hatlar Terminali, 34149 Yeşilköy, İstanbul; tel. (212) 4633000; fax (212) 4655050; e-mail info@tav.aero; internet www.tavairports.com; f. 1997; construction and management of airport facilities; manages Atatürk (İstanbul), Esenboğa (Ankara), Adnan Menderes (İzmir) and Gazipaşa (Antalya) airports, as well as airports in Georgia and Tunisia; Chair. HAMDI AKIN; Pres. and CEO Dr MUSTAFA SANI ŞENER.

Türk Hava Yolları AO (THY) (Turkish Airlines Inc): Genel Müdürlük Binas, Atatürk Hava Limanı, 34830 Yeşilköy, İstanbul; tel. (212) 4636363; fax (212) 4652388; e-mail customer@thy.com; internet www.thy.com.tr; f. 1933; 49.12% state-owned; extensive internal network and scheduled and charter flights to destinations in the Middle East, Africa, the Far East, Cen. Asia, the USA and Europe; 133 aircraft; Chair. HAMDI TOPÇU; Gen. Man. TEMEL KOTIL.

Tourism

Visitors to Turkey are attracted by the climate, fine beaches and ancient monuments. With government investment, the country has rapidly become a leading holiday destination for European tourists (particularly from the United Kingdom and Germany). In 2012 the number of tourists increased to 31.8m. (compared with 7.5m. in 1999); receipts from tourism reached US $23,440m. in 2012.

Ministry of Culture and Tourism: See The Government—Ministries; Dir-Gen. of Information MUSTAFA SYAHHAN; Dir-Gen. of Investments and Establishments KUDRET ASLAN.

Defence

Chief of the General Staff: Gen. NECDET ÖZEL.

Ground Forces Commander: Gen. HULUSI AKAR.

Navy Commander: Adm. BÜLENT BOSTANOĞLU.

Air Force Commander: Gen. AKIN ÖZTÜRK.

Gendarmerie Commander: Gen. SERVET YÖRÜK.

Defence Budget (2012): TL 30,700m.

Military Service: 15 months.

Total Armed Forces (as assessed at November 2012): 510,600: army 402,000 (est. 325,000 conscripts); navy 48,600 (34,500 conscripts); air force 60,000. Reserves 378,700.

Paramilitary Forces (as assessed at November 2012): 150,000 gendarmerie; 3,250 coast guard.

Education

When the Turkish Republic was formed, the Ministry of Education became the sole authority in educational matters, replacing the dual system of religious schools and other schools. One of the main obstacles to literacy was the Arabic script, which required years of study before proficiency could be attained. In 1928, therefore, a Turkish alphabet was introduced, using Latin characters. At the same time the literary language was simplified, and purged of some of its foreign elements. In 2012 government expenditure on education was budgeted at about TL 39,100m.

PRIMARY EDUCATION

Primary education may be preceded by an optional pre-school establishment for children between three and six years of age. In the 2011/12 academic year, according to provisional figures, there were 28,625 such schools, with 55,883 teachers. In the same year 1,169,556 children were enrolled at pre-schools.

An education reform bill approved in March 2012 extended the duration of compulsory education from eight to 12 years. It includes four years of elementary school, four years of middle school and four years of high school. Elementary school starts from the age of six.

Primary education is now entirely free, and co-education is the accepted basis for universal education. According to provisional figures, the number of primary schools has risen from 12,511 in 1950 to 32,108 in 2011/12, and the number of teachers from 27,144 to 515,852. In the same year 10,979,301 children were enrolled at primary schools. In 2008/09, according to UNESCO estimates, 97% of children in the relevant age-group were enrolled in primary education.

SECONDARY EDUCATION

Secondary education lasts for a minimum of four years after primary education, and provides for students intending to proceed to higher educational institutions. The secondary education system encompasses general high schools, and vocational and technical high schools. In addition, since 1992/93 'open' high schools have provided secondary education opportunities to young working people through the media and other new technologies.

Those students who wish to proceed to an institute of higher education must pass the state matriculation examination. The study of a modern language (English, French or German) is compulsory. In 2011/12, according to provisional figures, there were 4,171 general high schools, with 122,716 teachers. In that year 2,666,066 children were enrolled in general secondary education. In 2008/09, according to UNESCO estimates, 74% of children in the relevant age-group were enrolled in secondary education.

VOCATIONAL EDUCATION

In 2011/12, according to provisional figures, a total of 2,090,220 students attended 5,501 vocational and teacher-training high schools, with 113,098 teachers. In addition, there are colleges for commerce, tourism, communication, local administration and secretarial skills.

HIGHER EDUCATION

Higher educational institutions in Turkey were established, and are administered, by the state. In early 2012 there were 139 universities, 45 of which were private. The main university at İstanbul, originally established in 1453, was attended by 73,061 students in 2003. A total of 2,181,217 students were enrolled at institutes of higher education in the 2005/06 academic year.

Bibliography

General and Historical Context

Adly, Amr. *State Reform and Development in the Middle East: Turkey and Egypt in the Post-Liberalization Era*. Abingdon, Routledge, 2013.

Ahmad, Feroz. *The Young Turks*. Oxford, Oxford University Press, 1969.

The Turkish Experiment in Democracy 1950–1975. London, Hurst, for Royal Institute of International Affairs, 1977.

Akçam, Taner. *From Empire to Republic: Turkish Nationalism and the Armenian Genocide*. London, Zed Books, 2004.

Aksin, Sina. *Turkey from Empire to Revolutionary Republic: The Emergence of the Turkish Nation from 1789 to the Present*. New York, New York University Press, 2006.

Turkey from Empire to Revolutionary Republic: The Emergence of the Turkish Nation from 1789 to the Present. London, C. Hurst & Co, 2007.

Alderson, A. D. *The Structure of the Ottoman Dynasty*. Oxford, 1956.

Allen, W. E. D., and Muratoff, P. *Caucasian Battlefields: A History of the Wars on the Turco-Caucasian Border, 1828–1921*. Cambridge, 1953.

Barchard, David. *Turkey and the West*. London, Routledge and Kegan Paul, 1985.

Bean, G. E. *Aegean Turkey*. London, Benn, 1966.

Turkey's Southern Shore. London, Benn, 1968.

Bisbee, Eleanor. *The New Turks*. London, Greenwood Press.

The People of Turkey. New York, 1946.

Boghossian, Roupen. *Le conflit turco-arménien*. Beirut, Altapress, 1987.

Cahen, Claude. *Pre-Ottoman Turkey*. London, Sidgwick and Jackson, 1968.

Cassels, Lavender. *The Struggle for the Ottoman Empire, 1717–1740*. London, John Murray, 1967.

Coles, Paul. *The Ottoman Impact on Europe*. London, Thames and Hudson, 1968; New York, Brace and World, 1968.

Davison, Roderic H. (updated by Dodd, Clement H.). *Turkey. A Short History*. Huntingdon, Eothen Press, 3rd edn, 1998.

De Bellaigue, Christopher. *Rebel Land: Among Turkey's Forgotten People*. London, Bloomsbury, 2009.

Goodwin, Jason. *Lords of the Horizons: A History of the Ottoman Empire*. New York, Henry Holt, 1999.

Gül, Murat. *The Emergence of Modern Istanbul: Transformation and Modernisation of a City*. London, I. B. Tauris, 2009.

Hale, William. *The Political and Economic Development of Modern Turkey*. London, Croom Helm, 1981.

Turkish Foreign Policy, 1774–2000. London, Frank Cass, 2002.

Hanioğlu, Şükrü. *A Brief History of the Late Ottoman Empire*. Princeton, NJ, Princeton University Press, 2008.

Atatürk: An Intellectual Biography. Princeton, NJ, Princeton University Press, 2011.

Heyd, Uriel. *Foundations of Turkish Nationalism: The Life and Teachings of Ziya Gökalp*. London, Luzac and Harvill Press, 1950.

Language Reform in Modern Turkey. Jerusalem, 1954.

Hotham, David. *The Turks*. London, John Murray, 1972.

Jacoby, Tim, and Mann, Michael. *Social Power and the Turkish State*. London, Taylor and Francis, 2004.

Kasaba, Resat. *The Ottoman Empire and the World Economy: The Nineteenth Century*. Albany, NY, State University of New York Press, 1989.

Kazamias, A. M. *Education and the Quest for Modernity in Turkey*. London, Allen and Unwin, 1967.

Kazancigil, Ali, and Ozbudun, Ergun (Eds). *Atatürk: Founder of a Modern State*. London, Hurst, 1981.

Kedourie, Elie. *England and the Middle East: The Destruction of the Ottoman Empire, 1914–1921*. Cambridge, 1956.

Ker-Lindsay, James. *Crisis and Conciliation: A Year of Rapprochement Between Greece and Turkey*. London, I. B. Tauris, 2007.

Kerslake, Celia, Öktem, Keren, and Robins, Philip (Eds). *Turkey's Engagement with Modernity: Conflict and Change in the Twentieth Century*. Basingtoke, Palgrave Macmillan, 2010.

Kinnane, Dirk. *The Kurds and Kurdistan*. Oxford, 1965.

Kinross, Lord. *Within the Taurus*. London, 1954.

Europa Minor: Journeys in Coastal Turkey. London, 1956.

Turkey. London, 1960.

Kinross, Patrick. *Atatürk: The Rebirth of a Nation* (New edn). London, Phoenix, 2001.

Kinzer, Stephen. *Crescent and Star: Turkey between Two Worlds*. New York, Farar, Straus and Giroux, 2001.

Koray, Enver. *Türkiye Tarih Yayınları Bibliografyası 1729–1950; A Bibliography of Historical Works on Turkey*. Ankara, 1952.

Kushner, David. *The Rise of Turkish Nationalism*. London, Frank Cass, 1980.

Lamb, Harold. *Suleiman the Magnificent: Sultan of the East*. New York, 1951.

Landau, Jacob M. *Pan-Turkism: A Study in Irredentism*. London, Hurst, 1981.

Lewis, Bernard. *Istanbul and the Civilization of the Ottoman Empire*. Norman, OK, University of Oklahoma Press, 1963.

The Emergence of Modern Turkey (3rd edn). New York, NY, Oxford University Press, 2001.

Lewis, Geoffrey. *La Turquie, le déclin de l'empire, les réformes d'Ataturk, la république moderne*. Belgium, Verviers, 1968.

Lewis, G. L. *Turkey* ('Nations of the Modern World' series). London, 1955; 3rd edn, New York, Praeger, 1965.

Lewy, Günter. *The Armenian Massacres in Ottoman Turkey: A Disputed Genocide*. Salt Lake City, UT, University of Utah Press, 2005.

Liddell, Robert. *Byzantium and Istanbul*. London, 1956.

Linke, L. *Allah Dethroned*. London, 1937.

Çatal Hüyük. London, Thames and Hudson, 1967.

Lloyd, Seton. *Early Anatolia*. London, 1956.

Mango, Andrew. *Atatürk*. London, John Murray, 1999.

Turkey and the War on Terror: For Thirty Years We Fought Alone. Abingdon, Routledge, 2005.

Mellaart, James. *Earliest Civilizations of the Near East*. London, Thames and Hudson, 1965.

Mantran, Robert. *Histoire de la Turquie*. Paris, 1952.

McDowall, David. *A Modern History of the Kurds*. London, I. B. Tauris, 1996.

Miller, William. *The Ottoman Empire and its Successors, 1801–1927*. Cambridge, 1934.

Moorehead, A. *Gallipoli*. London, Wordsworth Editions, 1997.

Newman, Bernard. *Turkish Crossroads*. London, 1951.

Turkey and the Turks. London, Herbert Jenkins, 1968.

Nezir-Akmese, H. *The Birth of Modern Turkey: The Ottoman Military and the March to WWI (International Library of Twentieth Century History)*. London, I. B. Tauris, 2005.

Olsson, Tord, Ozdalga, Elisabeth, and Raudvere, Catharina (Eds). *Alevi Identity*. London, RoutledgeCurzon, 1998.

Orga, İrfan, and Orga, Margarete. *Atatürk*. London, 1962.

Ostrogorsky, G. *History of the Byzantine State*. Oxford, 1956.

Plate, Herbert. *Das Land der Türken*. Graz, Vienna (Wien), and Cologne (Köln), Verlag Styria, 1957.

Pope, Hugh. *Sons of the Conquerors: The Rise of the Turkic World*. New York, Overlook Press, 2005.

Price, M. Philips. *A History of Turkey: From Empire to Republic*. London, 1956.

Quataert, Donald. *The Ottoman Empire, 1700–1922*. Cambridge, Cambridge University Press, 2000.

Ramsaur, E. E. *The Young Turks and the Revolution of 1908*. Princeton, NJ, Princeton University Press, 1957.

Reisman, Arnold. *Turkey's Modernization: Refugees from Nazism and Atatürk's Vision*. Washington, DC, New Academia Publishing, 2006.

Rice, Tamara Talbot. *The Seljuks*. London, 1962.

Robinson, Richard D. *The First Turkish Republic*. Cambridge, MA, Harvard University Press, 1963.

Rugman, Jonathan, and Hutchings, Roger. *Atatürk's Children: Turkey and the Kurds*. London, Cassell, 1996.

Runciman, Sir Steven. *The Fall of Constantinople, 1453*. Cambridge, Cambridge University Press, 1965.

Salter, Cedric. *Introducing Turkey*. London, Methuen, 1961.

Shankland, David. *Islam and Society in Turkey*. Huntingdon, Eothen Press, 1999.

The Alevis in Turkey: The Emergence of a Secular Islamic Tradition. London, RoutledgeCurzon, 2003.

Shaw, Stanford. *History of the Ottoman Empire*. Cambridge, Cambridge University Press, 1976.

Stark, Freya. *Ionia*. London, 1954.

Lycian Shore. London, 1951.

Riding to the Tigris. London, 1956.

Steinhaus, Kurt. *Soziologie der turkischen Revolution*. Frankfurt, 1969.

Stone, Norman. *Turkey: A Short History*. London, Thames and Hudson, 2011.

Sumner, B. H. *Peter the Great and the Ottoman Empire*. Oxford, 1949.

Toynbee, A. J., and Kirkwood, D. P. *Turkey*. London, 1926.

Tunaya, T. Z. *Atatürk, the Revolutionary Movement and Atatürkism*. İstanbul, Baha, 1964.

Üngör, Uğur Ümit. *The Making of Modern Turkey: Nation and State in Eastern Anatolia, 1913-1950*. Oxford, Oxford University Press, 2012.

Vaughan, Dorothy. *Europe and the Turk: A Pattern of Alliances, 1350–1700*. Liverpool, 1954.

Vere-Hodge, Edward Reginald. *Turkish Foreign Policy, 1918–1948*. London, 2nd revised edn, 1950.

Vertigans, S. *Islamic Roots and Resurgence in Turkey: Understanding and Explaining the Muslim Resurgence*. New York, Praeger, 2003.

Volkan, Vamik D., and Itzkowitz, Norman. *Turks and Greeks, Neighbours in Conflict*. Huntingdon, Eothen Press, 1994.

Webster, D. E. *The Turkey of Atatürk: Social Progress in the Turkish Reformation*. Philadelphia, PA, 1939.

Wittek, P., and Heywood, C. (Ed.). *The Rise of the Ottoman Empire: Studies on the History of Turkey, 13th–15th Centuries*. London, Curzon Press, 2002.

Yılmaz, Bahri. *Challenges to Turkey: The New Role of Turkey in International Politics since the Dissolution of the Soviet Union*. New York, St Martin's Press, 2004 and 2005.

Contemporary Political History

Abramowitz, Morton (Ed.). *Turkey's Transformation and the American Policy*. Washington, DC, Century Foundation Press, 2001.

Akçapar, Burak. *Turkey's New European Era: Foreign Policy on the Road to EU Membership*. Lanham, MD, Rowman & Littlefield Publishers, 2006.

Aktar, Ayhan, Kızılyürek, Niyazi, and Özkırımlı, Umut (Eds). *Nationalism in the Troubled Triangle: Cyprus, Greece and Turkey*. Basingstoke, Palgrave Macmillan, 2010.

Alexander, Yonah, Brenner, Edgar H., and Krause, Serhat Tutuncuoglu (Eds). *Turkey: Terrorism, Civil Rights, and the European Union*. Abingdon, Routledge, 2008.

Alisa, Marcus. *Blood and Belief: The PKK and the Kurdish Fight for Independence*. New York, New York University Press, 2007.

Allen, H. E. *The Turkish Transformation*. Chicago, IL, University of Chicago Press, 1935.

Altunisik, Meliha Benli, and Kavli, Özlem Tur. *Turkey: Challenges of Continuity and Change (The Contemporary Middle East)*. London, Routledge, 2004.

Armstrong, H. C. *Grey Wolf: Mustafa Kemal, an Intimate Study of a Dictator*. London, 1937.

Atasoy, Yildiz. *Turkey, Islamists and Democracy: Transition and Globalization in a Muslim State*. London, I. B. Tauris, 2005.

Aydn, M. and Erhan, C. (Eds). *Turkish-American Relations: Past, Present and Future*. London, Frank Cass, 2003.

Azak, Umut. *Islam and Secularism in Turkey: Kemalism, Religion and the Nation State*. London, I. B. Tauris, 2010.

Bahrampour, Firouz. *Turkey, Political and Social Transformation*. New York, Gaus, 1967.

Barkley, Henri J. (Ed.). *Reluctant Neighbour: Turkey's Role in the Middle East*. Washington, DC, US Institute of Peace Press, 1997.

Bengio, Ofra. *The Turkish-Israeli Relationship: Changing Ties of Middle Eastern Outsiders*. Basingstoke, Palgrave Macmillan, 2010.

Berkes, Niyazi. *The Development of Secularism in Turkey*. London, C. Hurst and Co, 1999 (2nd edn; first published 1964).

Birand, Mehmet Ali. *The Generals' Coup in Turkey: An Inside Story of September 12, 1980*. Oxford, Brassey's, 1987.

Bozdaglioglu, Y. *Turkish Foreign Policy and Turkish Identity: A Constructivist Approach (International Relations Series)*. London, Routledge, 2003.

Bürger, Christian. *Türkei ante portas—Der Beitritt der Türkei zur Europäischen Union*. Frankfürt am Main, Peter Lang, 2009.

Çarkoğlu, A., and Kalaycıoğlu, M. E. *The Rising Tide of Conservatism in Turkey*. Basingstoke, Palgrave Macmillan, 2009.

Çarkoğlu, A., and Rubin, B. M. (Eds). *Turkey and the European Union: Domestic Politics, European Integration, and International Dynamics*. London, Frank Cass, 2003.

Greek-Turkish Relations in an Era of Detente. London, Frank Cass, 2004.

Religion and Politics in Turkey. Abingdon, Routledge, 2005.

Casier, Marlies, and Jongerden, Joost (Eds). *Nationalisms and Politics in Turkey: Political Islam, Kemalism and the Kurdish Issue*. Abingdon, Routledge, 2010.

Ciddi, Sinan. *Kemalism in Turkish Politics: The Republican People's Party, Secularism and Nationalism*. Abingdon, Routledge, 2010.

Cizre, Ümit. *Secular and Islamic Politics in Turkey: The Making of the Justice and Development Party*. Abingdon, Routledge, 2007.

Cohn, Edwin J. *Turkish Economic, Social and Political Change*. New York, Praeger, 1970.

Cooke, Hedley V. *Challenge and Response in the Middle East: The Quest for Prosperity, 1919–1951*. New York, 1952.

Cornell, Erik. *Turkey in the 21st Century: Opportunities, Challenges, Threats*. London, RoutledgeCurzon, 2000.

Davutoğlu, Ahmet. *Stratejik derinlik: Türkiye'nin uluslararası konumu (Strategic Depth: Turkey's International Position)*. İstanbul, Küre Yayınları, 2001.

Dismorr, Ann. *Turkey Decoded*. London, Saqi Books, 2008.

Dodd, Clement H. *Politics and Government in Turkey*. Manchester, Manchester University Press, 1969.

Edgecumbe, Sir C. N. E. *Turkey in Europe*. New York, Barnes and Noble, 1965.

Eligür, Banu. *The Mobilization of Political Islam in Turkey*. Cambridge, Cambridge University Press, 2010.

Frey, F. W. *The Turkish Political Elite*. Cambridge, MA, MIT Press, 1965.

Fuller, Graham. *The New Turkish Republic: Turkey as a Pivotal State in the Muslim World*. Washington, DC, US Institute of Peace Press, 2007.

Geyikdagi, Mehmet Yaşar. *Political Parties in Turkey: The Role of Islam*. New York, Praeger, 1986.

Gökalp, Ziya. *Turkish Nationalism and Western Civilisation*. London, 1960.

Gokay, Bulent. *Soviet Eastern Policy and Turkey, 1920–1991 (Routledge Studies in the History of Russia and Eastern Europe)*. Abingdon, Routledge, 2006.

Gordon, Philip H., and Taspinar, Omer. *Winning Turkey: How America, Europe and Turkey Can Revive a Fading Partnership*. Washington, DC, Brookings Institution Press, 2008.

Güneş, Cengiz. *The Kurdish National Movement in Turkey: From Protest to Resistance*. Abingdon, Routledge, 2011.

Hale, William. *Aspects of Modern Turkey*. Epping, Bowker Publishing, 1977.

Turkey, the US and Iraq. London, Saqi Books, 2007.

Politics of Modern Turkey. Abingdon, Routledge, 2008.

Hale, William, and Özbudun, Ergun. *Islamism, Democracy and Liberalism in Turkey*. Abingdon, Routledge, 2009.

Harris, George S. *The Origins of Communism in Turkey*. Stanford, CA, Hoover Institution, 1967.

Houston, Christopher. *Islam, Kurds and the Turkish Nation State*. Oxford, Berg, 2001.

Howe, Marvine. *Turkey Today: A Nation Divided over Islam's Revival*. Boulder, CO, Westview Press, 2000.

Ibrahim, Ferhad, and Gurbey, Gulistan (Eds). *The Kurdish Conflict in Turkey: Obstacles and Chances for Peace and Democracy*. New York, Palgrave Macmillan, 2001.

Ifantis, Kostas, and Verney, Susannah. *Turkey's Road to European Union Membership: National Identity and Political Change*. Abingdon, Routledge, 2008.

Jabar, Faleh A. (Ed.). *The Kurds: Nationalism and Politics*. London, Saqi Books, 2006.

Jenkins, Gareth. *Context and Circumstance: The Turkish Military and Politics*. Oxford, Oxford University Press, 2001.

Political Islam in Turkey. New York, Palgrave Macmillan, 2006.

Joseph, Joseph S. *Turkey and the European Union*. New York, Palgrave Macmillan, 2006.

Kamer, Heinz. *A Changing Turkey: Challenges to Europe and the US*. Washington, DC, Brookings Institution Press, 2000.

Karasipahi, Sena. *Muslims in Modern Turkey: Kemalism, Modernism and the Revolt of the Islamic Intellectuals*. London, I. B. Tauris, 2008.

Karpat, Kemal. *Turkey's Politics, The Transition to a Multi-Party System*. Princeton, NJ, 1959.

Kaylan, M. *The Kemalists: Islamic Revival And The Fate Of Secular Turkey*. New York, Prometheus Books, 2005.

Kumbaracıbaşı, Arda Can. *Turkish Politics and the Rise of the AKP: Dilemmas of Institutionalization and Leadership Strategy*. Abingdon, Routledge, 2009.

Lewis, Bernard. *The Emergence of Modern Turkey*. London and New York, Oxford University Press, revised edn, 1970.

Liel, Alon. *Turkey in the Middle East: Oil, Islam and Politics*. Boulder, CO, Lynne Reiner, 2001.

Moustakis, F. *The Greek-Turkish Relationship and NATO*. London, Frank Cass, 2003.

Muller, Mark, and Yildiz, Kerim. *The European Union and Turkish Accession: Human Rights and the Kurds*. London, Pluto Press, 2008.

Nachmani, A. *Turkey: Facing a New Millennium: Coping with Intertwined Conflicts*. Manchester, Manchester University Press, 2003.

Öcalan, Abdullah (trans. Klaus Happel). *Prison Writings: The Roots of Civilisation*. London, Pluto Press, 2007.

Öktem, Kerem. *Angry Nation: Turkey Since 1989*. London, Zed Books, 2010.

Özcan, Ali Kemal. *A Theoretical Analysis of the PKK and Abdullah Öcalan*. Abingdon, Routledge, 2005.

Park, Bill. *Modern Turkey: People, State and Foreign Policy in a Globalised World*. Abingdon, Routledge, 2011.

Pettifer, James. *The Turkish Labyrinth: Atatürk and the New Islam*. London, Viking, 1997.

Pope, Nicole and Pope, Hugh. *Turkey Unveiled: Atatürk and After*. London, John Murray, 1997.

Poulton, Hugh. *Top Hat, Grey Wolf and Crescent: Turkish Nationalism and the Turkish Republic*. London, Hurst and Co, 1997.

Rabasa, Angel. *The Rise of Political Islam in Turkey*. Santa Monica, CA, RAND Corporation, 2008.

Ringman, Jonathan, Hutchings, Roger, and Simpson, John. *Atatürk's Children: Turkey and the Kurds*. Herndon, VA, Cassell Academic, 2001.

Robins, Philip. *Turkish Foreign Policy since the Cold War*. London, C. Hurst, 2002.

Roy, O. *Turkey Today: A European Nation?* London, Anthem Press, 2005.

Rubin, Barry, and Çarkoğlu, Ali. (Eds). *Religion and Politics in Turkey*. Abingdon, Routledge, 2009.

Shankland, David (Ed.). *The Turkish Republic at Seventy-Five Years*. Huntingdon, Eothen Press, 1999.

Szyliowicz, Joseph S. *Political Change in Rural Turkey: Erdemli*. The Hague, Mouton, 1966.

Taspinar, Omar. *Kurdish Nationalism and Political Islam in Turkey: Kemalist Identity in Transition*. London, Routledge, 2011.

Thomas, L. V., and Frye, R. N. *The United States and Turkey and Iran*. Cambridge, MA, 1951.

Toynbee, A. J. *The Western Question in Greece and Turkey*. London, Constable, 1923.

Uğur, Mehmet, and Canefe, Nergis. *Turkey and European Integration: Accession Prospects and Issues (Europe and the Nation State)*. London, Routledge, 2004.

Ünal, Mustafa. *Counterterrorism in Turkey: Policy Choices and Policy Effects Toward the Kurdistan Workers' Party (PKK)*. Abingdon, Routledge, 2011.

Uslu, Nasuh. *Turkish Foreign Policy in the Post-Cold War Period*. Hauppauge, NY, Nova Publishers, 2007.

Vali, Ferenc A. *Bridge across the Bosphorus: The Foreign Policy of Turkey*. Baltimore, MD, Johns Hopkins University Press, 1970.

Ward, Barbara. *Turkey*. Oxford, 1942.

Winrow, Gareth. *Turkey and the Caucasus: Domestic Interests and Security Concerns*. London, Royal Institute of International Affairs, 2001.

Yavuz, M. H. *Islamic Political Identity in Turkey (Religion and Global Politics)*. Oxford, Oxford University Press, 2003.

Secularism and Muslim Democracy in Turkey. Cambridge, Cambridge University Press, 2009.

Yıldız, K. *The Kurds in Turkey: EU Accession and Human Rights*. London, Pluto Press, 2005.

Yıldız, Kerim, and Breau, Susan. *The Kurdish Conflict: International Humanitarian Law and Post-Conflict Mechanisms*. Abingdon, Routledge, 2010.

Yılmaz, Bahri. *Challenges to Turkey: The New Role of Turkey in International Politics Since the Dissolution of the Soviet Union*. New York, St Martin's Press, 2006.

Economy

Aydin, Z. *The Political Economy of Turkey*. London, Pluto Press, 2005.

Insel, Ahmet. *La Turquie entre l'ordre et le développement*. Paris, L'Harmattan, 1984.

Issawi, Charles. *The Economic History of Turkey*. Chicago, IL, University of Chicago Press, 1980.

Kara, Alper, and Altunbas, Yener. *Banking under Political Instability and Chronic High Inflation: The Case of Turkey*. New York, Palgrave Macmillan, 2007.

Nas, Tevfik. *Tracing the Economic Transformation of Turkey from the 1920s to EU Accession*. Leiden, Martinus Nijhoff Publishers, 2008.

Odekon, M. *The Costs of Economic Liberalization in Turkey*. Bethlehem, PA, Lehigh University Press, 2005.

Onis, Z., and Rubin, B. M. (Eds). *The Turkish Economy in Crisis*. London, Frank Cass, 2003.

Rittenberg, Libby (Ed.). *The Political Economy of Turkey in the Post-Soviet Era*. Westport, CT, Praeger Publishing, 1998.

Shorter, Frederic C. (Ed.). *Four Studies on the Economic Development of Turkey*. London, Cass, 1967; New York, Kelley, 1968.

Togan, Sübidey. *Economic Liberalization and Turkey*. Abingdon, Routledge, 2010.

THE UNITED ARAB EMIRATES

ABU DHABI AJMAN DUBAI FUJAIRAH RAS AL-KHAIMAH SHARJAH UMM AL-QAIWAIN

Geography

The coastline of the seven United Arab Emirates (UAE) extends for nearly 650 km (400 miles) from the frontier of the Sultanate of Oman to Khor al-Udaid, on the Qatari peninsula, in the Persian (Arabian) Gulf, interrupted only by an isolated outcrop of the Sultanate of Oman, which lies on the coast of the Persian Gulf to the west and the Gulf of Oman to the east at the Strait of Hormuz. Six of the emirates lie on the coast of the Persian Gulf, while the seventh, Fujairah, is situated on the eastern coast of the peninsula, and has direct access to the Gulf of Oman. The area is one of extremely shallow seas, with offshore islands and coral reefs, and often an intricate pattern of sand-banks and small gulfs as a coastline. There is a considerable tide. The waters of the Gulf contain abundant quantities of fish, hence the important role of fishing in local life.

The climate is arid, with very high summer temperatures; except for a few weeks in winter, air humidity is also very high. The total area of the UAE has been estimated at 77,700 sq km (30,000 sq miles), relatively small compared with neighbouring Oman and Saudi Arabia, and it has a rapidly growing population, totalling 5,066,000 at mid-2009, according to official estimates. The population is concentrated in the emirates of Abu Dhabi and Dubai, the principal commercial regions of the country. Abu Dhabi is the largest emirate, with an area of about 67,350 sq km and a population of an estimated 2,120,700 in mid-2011, according to the Statistics Centre of Abu Dhabi. The town of Abu Dhabi is also the capital of the UAE. The most important port is Dubai, the capital of the UAE's second largest emirate (which had an estimated population of 2,105,875 at the end of 2012, according to the Dubai Statistics Centre. Its significance derives from its position on one of the rare deep creeks of the area, and it now has a very large transit trade.

Many inhabitants are still nomadic Arabs, and the official language is Arabic, which is spoken by most of the native inhabitants. Arabs are outnumbered, however, by non-Arab immigrant workers. In the coastal towns there are many Iranians, Indians, Pakistanis and Africans. Most of the native inhabitants are Muslims, mainly of the Sunni sect.

History

Revised for this edition by KHALID ALMEZAINI; Based on an original essay by GERD NONNEMAN

Settlement of the area of the United Arab Emirates (UAE) appears to have begun in the Bronze Age; the so-called Umm al-Nar culture thrived near today's Abu Dhabi in the third millennium BC. In the Classical Age ancient Persia and Greece were the dominant external influences. The supremacy of the Sasanid Empire of Persia was swept away by the spread of Islam to the Gulf coast of Arabia in the seventh century AD, and by the 14th century much of today's UAE was part of the Kingdom of Hormuz. The Portuguese first arrived in the Gulf in 1498 as part of their effort to take control of the Arab role in trading between Europe and the Far East. In the process they defeated the Arab rulers of Hormuz, destroying the port of Khor Fakkan (on the Gulf of Oman) in 1506 and conquering the port of Julfar (near today's Ras al-Khaimah) by 1515, where they constructed a fort in 1631. By the early 17th century the Portuguese commercial monopoly of the Gulf area was already being challenged by other European traders, and in 1650 they were expelled from Oman and the Gulf by the new Omani Yaariba dynasty. A period of commercial and political rivalry between the Dutch and the British followed, punctuated by Persian and occasionally Ottoman attempts to establish a claim—although the area of the UAE (contrary to Bahrain and Qatar) never experienced an Ottoman presence. The initial Dutch predominance weakened and in 1766 came practically to an end, while the British were consolidating their position in India.

The greatest challenge to British influence came from the Qawasim (singular: Qasimi), who were the strongest coastal power on the Arab side of the Gulf (indeed extending to the Persian coast at Lingeh), with their main centres at Sharjah and Ras al-Khaimah. In 1818 Britain launched an attack against Ras al-Khaimah and other harbours along the coast, destroying many of the forts and ships, and largely defeating the Qawasim. In 1820 a general peace treaty to suppress piracy and slave traffic was concluded between Great Britain, the principal sheikhs of the 'Pirate Coast' and Bahrain (the latter were also believed to retain some power in Qatar). A strong British squadron was stationed at Ras al-Khaimah to enforce the treaty.

Maritime attacks persisted, but in 1835 the sheikhs agreed, in a 'maritime truce', not to engage—under any circumstances—in hostilities by sea during the pearl-diving season. The advantages of this were sufficiently noticeable—and British pressure sufficiently persuasive—for the sheikhs to prove willing to renew the truce for increasing periods until, in May 1853, a 'treaty of maritime peace in perpetuity' was concluded, establishing a 'perpetual maritime truce' on the newly named 'Trucial Coast' (also called Trucial Oman). It was supervised by the British Government, to whom the signatories would refer any breach. The British did not interfere in conflicts between the sheikhs on land.

South of the area controlled principally by the Qawasim, two other sheikhdoms had emerged, ruled by different sections of the Bani Yas tribe—traditionally the dominant tribal grouping in the area now comprising the emirates of Abu Dhabi and Dubai, and the main rival to the Qawasim. Originally based mainly in the Liwa oasis, some settled on the coast, on the island of Abu Dhabi. The tribe's leading family, the Al Bu Falah, also known as the Al Nahyan, supplied the Bani Yas's paramount sheikh. In 1833 a different clan of the Bani Yas, the Al Bu Falasah (or Al Maktoum) migrated further north along the coast and established themselves by the creek of Dubai, effectively escaping the dominance of the Al Bu Falah. Dubai was very quickly recognized as a separate sheikhdom but one that, in contrast to Abu Dhabi, would prove more urban-based and centred around trade.

Towards the end of the 19th century France, Germany and Russia showed increasing interest in the Gulf area; and in 1892 Britain entered into separate but identical 'exclusive' treaties with the Trucial rulers, whereby the sheikhs undertook not to cede, mortgage or otherwise dispose of parts of their territories to anyone except the British Government, nor to enter into any relationship with another government without British consent. Britain had already undertaken to protect the states from external attack in the perpetual maritime treaty of 1853.

In 1820, when the general treaty was signed, there had been only four recognized sheikhdoms (including the Khalifa family's rule over Bahrain and Qatar). Dubai had emerged as a separate sheikhdom by the time of the 1853 treaty. In 1866, on the death of the paramount Sheikh of the Qawasim, who had ruled from Sharjah, his domains were divided among his four sons, the separate branches of the family being established at Sharjah, Ras al-Khaimah, and at Dibba and Kalba on the Gulf of Oman. Effective control of the Qawasim domains (comprising all territories north of a line from Sharjah town to Kalba, with the exceptions of Ajman, Umm al-Qaiwain and Musandam) was rarely completely centralized, but the main seats of power remained Sharjah and Ras al-Khaimah. The latter was recognized by Britain as a separate sheikhdom in 1921, following several periods of virtual independence under rival members of the ruling family.

The pre-eminent position of Sharjah and the Qawasim on the lower Gulf coast, based on their maritime power and trade, was lost to the Bani Yas of Abu Dhabi and Dubai as British naval control increased the importance of the latter's land-based power. A revival came with the establishment of a British airfield in Sharjah in 1932. Even so, Kalba was recognized as a separate sheikhdom four years later, a development coinciding with the establishment of an emergency airstrip there at a time when the local Qasimi sheikh was proving to be independently powerful. However, Kalba was again incorporated into Sharjah in 1952. By contrast, when it became clear that the ruler of Sharjah no longer commanded effective authority over Fujairah, the latter was recognized as a separate sheikhdom in that same year, and its ruler, the Sheikh of the Sharqi tribe dominant in Fujairah, acceded to the treaties. These involved recognition of the British Government's right to define state boundaries, to settle disputes between the Trucial sheikhdoms and to render assistance to the Trucial Oman Scouts, a recently founded force of some 1,600 men, officered and paid for by the United Kingdom. Henceforth, therefore, there were seven recognized sheikhdoms (excluding Bahrain and Qatar), respectively ruled by the Al Nahyan—also 'Al Nuhayyan'—(Abu Dhabi), the Al Maktoum (Dubai), two branches of the Qawasim (Sharjah and Ras al-Khaimah), the Al Mu'alla—or Al Ali—(Umm al-Qaiwain), the Nu'ayyim (Ajman) and the al-Sharqi family (Fujairah).

In 1952, on British advice, a trucial council was established, at which all seven Rulers met at least twice a year, under the chairmanship of the British political agent in Dubai. Its object was to encourage the pursuit of a common policy in administrative matters, possibly leading to a federation of the states.

The advent of the commercial production of petroleum in mid-1962 gave Abu Dhabi an excellent opportunity for development. Sheikh Shakhbut bin Sultan Al Nahyan, the Ruler of Abu Dhabi since 1928, was regarded by both the majority of the ruling family and the British as insufficiently competent or willing to translate this growing wealth into development of the emirate. In August 1966 he was replaced by his younger brother, Sheikh Zayed bin Sultan, until that time the able and popular Governor of Al Ain. Subsequently, Abu Dhabi's society was transformed rapidly by the acquisition of immense wealth. In 1966 petroleum was discovered in neighbouring Dubai, which also benefited from the petroleum boom while simultaneously developing its trading and transshipment economy.

By contrast, Sharjah saw its relative position diminish further as it failed to halt the silting up of its creek, and in the mid-1960s Britain selected Dubai as the headquarters for the Trucial States Council and the Trucial States Development Office. In June 1965 Sheikh Saqr bin Sultan of Sharjah was deposed. In spite of an appeal to the UN, supported by Iraq and the United Arab Republic (Egypt), the accession of his cousin, Sheikh Khalid bin Muhammad, proceeded without incident.

Intending to relocate its major military base in the Middle East, the United Kingdom started work in 1966 on a base in Sharjah, which by 1968 had become the principal base in the Gulf. However, the British Labour Government stated in that year that it would withdraw forces from all areas 'east of Suez' by the end of 1971, precipitating serious concerns among local rulers—as well as in Britain itself—about the security vacuum that this might create. The Trucial Oman Scouts, based in Sharjah, were proposed as the nucleus of a federal security force after the British withdrawal, but some states, notably Abu Dhabi, were already creating their own defence forces. Under pressure from the British and with the central support of Sheikh Zayed, the concept of a federation of nine sheikhdoms was proposed. This federation was to include Qatar and Bahrain, but in the end they opted for separate independence.

Meanwhile, definition of the borders between the various rulers' domains had been ongoing since the 1950s, arbitrated and documented by British diplomats on the basis of surveys of local realities and tribal allegiances: this became necessary as oil-prospecting meant that territory assumed unprecedented importance, while those prospecting needed to know to which ruler they should apply for effective protection. The resulting patchwork of territories includes several where sovereignty is shared between two or more emirates, and in some instances also with Oman. It also resulted in the exclave of Musandam (to Oman), and a small Omani enclave near the UAE's Gulf of Oman coast.

On 1 December 1971 the United Kingdom terminated all existing treaties with the Trucial States. On the following day Abu Dhabi, Dubai, Sharjah, Umm al-Qaiwain, Ajman and Fujairah formed the UAE, and a treaty of friendship was made with the United Kingdom. Ras al-Khaimah, proud of its former status and seeking equality with Abu Dhabi and Dubai, initially stayed out of the treaty. It also apparently hoped that support would be forthcoming in Sharjah for reviving a joint independent Qawasim emirate. In January 1972 the Ruler of Sharjah, Sheikh Khalid, was killed by rebels under the leadership of his cousin, Sheikh Saqr, who had been deposed in 1965, and on whose support the Ruler of Ras al-Khaimah appears to have counted. Yet the rebels were captured, and Sheikh Sultan bin Muhammad succeeded his brother as Ruler, confirming a continuation of the late Khalid's relatively liberal principles of government, and Sharjah's membership of the UAE. Ras al-Khaimah's leadership, taking into account the difficulties of creating a militarily and economically secure separate state, reconsidered its position and joined the UAE on 10 February 1972.

Much of the 'glue' for the creation—and, indeed, survival—of this federation was afforded by the financial generosity of Abu Dhabi and by Sheikh Zayed's personal charisma and commitment to the initiative. The federation approved a provisional Constitution, which was to expire after five years, when a formal constitution would be drafted. However, the provisional Constitution was repeatedly renewed until 1996 (when it was made permanent), and this lent a flexibility to the developing emirates, allowing the process of centralization to follow a gradual course and averting any serious dispute that could arise from an emirate's contravention of formal constitutional decrees. At independence, Sheikh Zayed, the Ruler of Abu Dhabi, took office as the first President of the UAE. Sheikh Rashid bin Said Al Maktoum, the Ruler of Dubai since 1958, became Vice-President, while his eldest son, Sheikh Maktoum bin Rashid (Crown Prince of Dubai), became Prime Minister. In December 1971 the UAE became a member of both the League of Arab States (Arab League) and the UN.

The borders between Qatar, Abu Dhabi and Dubai were settled early in 1970—although not without objection from Saudi Arabia, the territorial claims of which considerably overlapped with those of Abu Dhabi. In late 1974 a border agreement was signed with Saudi Arabia on the Liwa oases, whereupon Saudi Arabia recognized the UAE and ambassadors were exchanged.

Although the UAE remained one of the most conservative Arab states, it gave considerable support to the Arab cause in the October War of 1973 and participated in the associated petroleum-supply reductions and boycotts. It was the first state to impose a total ban on exports of petroleum to the USA, and subsequently supported the Arab ostracism of Egypt that followed the negotiation of the Camp David agreements between Egypt and Israel in 1978 and the 1979 peace treaty between those two countries. In this period, the UAE's financial support to Arab states contributed significantly to its recognition as an independent state.

TOWARDS GREATER CENTRALIZATION

Together with the presidency, judiciary, Supreme Council of Rulers and Council of Ministers, the UAE also instituted a consultative and 'supervisory' legislature called the Federal National Council (FNC). This body consists of 40 members, with eight each from Abu Dhabi and Dubai, six each from Sharjah and Ras al-Khaimah, and four each from Ajman, Umm al-Qaiwain and Fujairah; until the introduction of elections for one-half of their number in 2006, all were appointed by the respective Rulers. The FNC first met in February 1972. However, real power still resides with the emirs and senior members of the ruling families. In December 1973 the separate Abu Dhabi Government was disbanded and, in a ministerial reorganization, some of its members became federal ministers. Most notably, the Abu Dhabi minister responsible for petroleum, Dr Mana bin Said al-Oteiba, became the first federal Minister of Petroleum and Mineral Resources. In May 1975, at a session of the Supreme Council, the seven emirs gave their consent, in principle, to additional moves towards centralization. In November Sharjah merged the Sharjah National Guard with the Union Defence Force, and granted control of its broadcasting station to the federal Ministry of Communications, its police to the Ministry of the Interior and its courts to the Ministry of Justice. The Sharjah, Fujairah and Abu Dhabi flags were abolished in favour of the federal tricolour.

The merger of the main defence forces (the Union Defence Force, the Abu Dhabi Defence Force and the Dubai Defence Force) was finally agreed in May 1976, when Sheikh Khalifa bin Zayed Al Nahyan, the Crown Prince of Abu Dhabi, was made Deputy Supreme Commander (Sheikh Zayed became Supreme Commander). In November the provisional Constitution was amended so that the right to levy armed forces and acquire weapons was placed exclusively in the hands of federal government—although practice, in many ways, remained different, not least on the part of Dubai.

In 1976 Sheikh Zayed, impatient with the slow rate of federal evolution, threatened not to stand for a second term as President of the UAE. In the event, he was re-elected unanimously in November, after the Supreme Council had granted the federal Government greater control over defence, intelligence services, immigration, public security and border control. A reorganization of the Council of Ministers followed in January 1977, with ministers chosen on the principle of merit rather than equitable representation of the seven emirates. The new 40-member FNC, inaugurated on 1 March, included only seven members from the first five-year session (1971–76).

A joint Cabinet-FNC committee was established in 1978 to discuss methods of enhancing UAE integration. The Iranian Revolution of 1979 and the resultant security threat prompted a full meeting of the Council of Ministers and the FNC in February. This produced a 10-point memorandum, which was submitted to the Supreme Council, advocating the abolition of all internal borders, the unification of defence forces and the merging of revenues in a federal budget. Despite widespread support in most of the emirates, these proposals aggravated the long-standing rivalry between Abu Dhabi, the financial mainstay of the federation, and Dubai, which had become increasingly critical of the centralized federal Government. Dubai rejected the memorandum completely and, together with Ras al-Khaimah, boycotted a Supreme Council meeting in March.

The deadlock was broken when Sheikh Rashid, Ruler of Dubai, replaced his son as Prime Minister of the federal Government (while retaining the vice-presidency) in July 1979. A new Council of Ministers was formed, preserving a similar balance of power between the emirates as before. Ras al-Khaimah integrated its defence force with the federal force, and both Abu Dhabi and Dubai pledged to contribute 50% of their revenues from petroleum to the federal budget. In practice, however, Dubai's forces remained a separate entity. Further attempts at integration included the construction of national roads, the installation of telecommunications, and the central planning and financing of health, education and agriculture. In November 1981 Sheikh Rashid was re-elected Prime Minister by the Supreme Council, and Sheikh Zayed was re-elected President.

FOREIGN POLICY FOLLOWING THE IRAN–IRAQ WAR, 1980–88

One component of the response to the new regional climate created by the Iran–Iraq War was the establishment in May 1981 of the Cooperation Council for the Arab States of the Gulf (Gulf Cooperation Council—GCC). Its ostensible aim was to work towards economic, political and social integration in the Gulf, and security aims were rhetorically minimized to avoid riling either Iraq or Iran (both of whom had opposed such a grouping before). However, as the regional threat became more acute, and especially after the discovery of a plot to effect a coup in Bahrain, with suspected Iranian involvement, the issue of security rose up the GCC's agenda. The organization also became a useful means for the UAE and other member states to send messages, which might diverge from their individual positions, to different audiences.

Enhanced reliance on Western defence co-operation and substantially increased defence expenditure, however, became a major strand of policy for the UAE, in common with the other GCC states. The UAE also signed a defence agreement with Saudi Arabia in 1982, despite border conflict between the two countries. Furthermore, the UAE increased its annual military expenditure by 30%–40% between the end of the 1980s and the early 1990s.

When the UN Security Council adopted Resolution 598 on 20 July 1987, which urged an immediate cease-fire, Iran refused to accede. In November, at an extraordinary meeting of the Arab League in Amman, Jordan, the UAE joined the other member states in condemning Iran for prolonging the war against Iraq, deploring its occupation of Arab territory, and urging it to accept Resolution 598 without preconditions. Yet by the end of the war, the UAE quickly drifted back to a more nuanced and, indeed, diverse policy towards Iran, not least given Dubai's very extensive trade and commercial links with the country and the large presence within the emirate of Iranians and others of Iranian extraction.

DOMESTIC DEVELOPMENTS, 1987–2001

An attempted coup took place in Sharjah in June 1987, when Sheikh Abd al-Aziz, a brother of the Ruler, Sheikh Sultan bin Muhammad al-Qasimi, issued a statement in his brother's absence announcing the latter's abdication on the grounds that he had mismanaged the economy. (Sharjah had incurred debts, estimated at US $920m. in mid-1987, as the result of a major programme of construction ordered by the Ruler.) However, Dubai intervened and convened a meeting of the Supreme Council of Rulers that endorsed Sheikh Sultan's claim to be the legitimate ruler of Sharjah, and restored him to power. In a compromise arrangement, Sheikh Abd al-Aziz was given the title of Crown Prince; however, in February 1990 Sheikh Sultan revoked this decision. In July Sheikh Sultan appointed Sheikh Ahmad bin Muhammad al-Qasimi, the head of Sharjah's Petroleum and Mineral Affairs Department, as Deputy Ruler of Sharjah (but not Crown Prince).

On 7 October 1990 the long-serving Ruler of Dubai, Prime Minister and Vice-President of the UAE, Sheikh Rashid bin Said Al Maktoum, died. He was succeeded in all of his offices by his eldest son, Sheikh Maktoum bin Rashid Al Maktoum, although it was clear that it was Sheikh Muhammad—his energetic younger brother and the Minister of Defence for the UAE—who was going to be the power behind the throne and the driving force behind Dubai's economic and infrastructural boom. In October 1991 the Supreme Council confirmed Sheikh Zayed and Sheikh Maktoum as President and Vice-President, respectively, for a further five-year term. The provisional federal Constitution was also renewed for another period of five years, as it had been ever since the first extension in 1976.

The UAE became involved in a major international financial scandal in July 1991, when the regulatory authorities in seven countries closed down the operations of the Bank of Credit and Commerce International (BCCI), in which the Abu Dhabi ruling family and its agencies had held a controlling interest (77%) since April 1990. This followed the disclosure by an auditor's report, commissioned by the Bank of England, of large-scale fraud by BCCI authorities (perpetrated before April 1990). By the end of July 1991 BCCI's activities had been suspended in all 69 countries in which it had operated.

In January 1995 the Ruler of Dubai, Sheikh Maktoum bin Rashid Al Maktoum, named Sheikh Muhammad bin Rashid Al Maktoum as Crown Prince. In June 1996 legislation designed to make the provisional Constitution permanent was endorsed by the FNC, following its approval by the Supreme Council of Rulers. At the same time Abu Dhabi was formally designated capital of the UAE. Sheikh Zayed was subsequently re-elected to the presidency.

In April 2001 Dubai's Director-General of Ports and Customs, Dr Obeid Saqer bin Busit, was sentenced to 27 years' imprisonment on charges of corruption; he was the highest-ranking civil servant ever to have been tried for corruption in the UAE. Six other defendants (three UAE nationals and three Pakistani expatriates) were also convicted—among them the head of Dubai's Hamriya port. The arrests had been ordered by Dubai's Crown Prince following a two-year investigation. The federal Minister of Justice and Islamic Affairs proposed the establishment of an anti-corruption commission and the institution of more stringent legislation to counter corruption. Those convicted were later reportedly pardoned, but the episode highlighted a new determination to tackle the issue.

DOMESTIC DEVELOPMENTS, 11 SEPTEMBER 2001–04

Following the terrorist attacks on New York and Washington, DC, USA, on 11 September 2001, the UAE's banking sector was subject to considerable international scrutiny, after US investigators claimed to have discovered evidence of financial transactions between banks in the UAE and US bank accounts used by those involved in the attacks (one of whom was a UAE national). The Central Bank ordered the freezing of assets in the UAE belonging to 27 individuals and organizations accused by the USA of being actively involved in the promotion of terrorism. In October a decree was adopted that sought to prohibit the 'laundering' of funds through the UAE's banking sector; henceforth all banks would be required to inform the Central Bank of the receipt or transfer of amounts in excess of US $10,900. Those convicted on charges connected to money-laundering activities would, furthermore, receive increased fines and prison sentences of up to seven years. The decree also formally established a national commission to combat such practices. However, the *hawala* finance system—a traditional alternative remittance system operating outside the control of the conventional banking sector—was unaffected by the changes; much of the funding destined for militant groups and activities is believed to be channelled in this way. In June 2002 the police in Dubai made their first ever arrests on charges of money-laundering; the detainees were believed to include both Arabs and Europeans.

The UAE celebrated the 30th anniversary of its creation in December 2001, when the seven Rulers re-elected Sheikh Zayed as President for a further five-year term. In mid-June 2003 the frail Sheikh Saqr bin Muhammad al-Qasimi, the Ruler of Ras al-Khaimah, deposed his eldest son, Khalid, as Crown Prince and installed a younger son, Sa'ud, in his place. Sheikh Khalid was said to be deeply unhappy with the decision, which he claimed had been influenced by his father's ill health. Tanks from the federal UAE armed forces arrived in the emirate on 15 June to 'maintain stability and public order', in an apparent attempt to prevent tribesmen loyal to Khalid from convening in Ras al-Khaimah city. However, tension eased on 16 June, after Sheikh Khalid departed for Oman. In January 2004 Sheikh Sa'ud continued his brother's reform programme by ordering the release of 124 prisoners, including several of those who had demonstrated against his appointment; however, Sa'ud, a businessman, was clearly less intent on controlling development on environmental and other grounds than his brother had been.

DOMESTIC DEVELOPMENTS FOLLOWING THE DEATH OF SHEIKH ZAYED, 2004–10

The death of Sheikh Zayed was announced on 2 November 2004, after a prolonged period of ill health. His eldest son, Crown Prince Khalifa, immediately succeeded to the throne in Abu Dhabi and the next day was elected by the Supreme Council as the new President of the UAE. Sheikh Khalifa's half-brother, Sheikh Muhammad bin Zayed Al Nahyan, became the new Crown Prince. The new President moved quickly to reorganize the federal Council of Ministers, bringing in a number of younger technocrats and the first female minister, Sheikha Lubna bint Khalid al-Qasimi, who was given control of the economy and planning portfolio. A new Ministry of Energy replaced the Ministries of Petroleum and Mineral Resources and of Electricity and Water. In December Sheikh Khalifa announced the largest restructuring of the Abu Dhabi Executive Council for decades, reducing the number of the emirate's ministries from 12 to seven and bringing in some younger ministers to run them.

In January 2005 it was announced that the federal Government was to spend US $408m. on providing assistance to the less developed northern emirates. In June the latent issue between Abu Dhabi and Dubai over the latter's property laws also moved towards a resolution, when it was announced that a new federal law was being prepared allowing foreigners to own property. The announcement was made by a member of Abu Dhabi's ruling family, and the sale of the Al Raha Beach development commencing in the emirate the same month was the first evidence that Abu Dhabi itself would henceforth allow such foreign ownership. Subsequently, a new property law was enacted in Dubai in March 2006, formally giving limited freehold ownership rights to foreigners in designated areas—thereby finally implementing an intention first announced in 2002.

On 1 December 2005 Sheikh Khalifa announced that elections would be introduced to choose one-half of the members of the FNC, which would also eventually be expanded from the current 40 members and see its powers enhanced. Thus far, the UAE had been the only GCC state without elections of any kind. These elections would be undertaken by the individual emirate councils which, although also to be expanded, were for the present to continue to be appointed by the emirs.

On 4 January 2006 the Ruler of Dubai, Sheikh Maktoum bin Rashid Al Maktoum, died while on a visit to Australia. His brother, Sheikh Muhammad, succeeded him, also becoming Vice-President and Prime Minister of the UAE. Given the new Ruler's long-established role in managing the emirate's affairs, in many respects business proceeded as usual; something of a cultural change permeated government affairs at a federal level, however, as the new Prime Minister applied his business-like management style to the Council of Ministers and the administration.

The evolving national and foreign policy challenges to the UAE were recognized by the establishment in June 2006 of a Supreme National Security Council (SNSC) in order to address UAE security issues more effectively. Although it was described as being concerned with economic, social, cultural and environmental security, as well as more traditional security matters, the SNSC's composition perhaps reflects the latter's preponderance: it includes the President, Prime Minister, Minister of Foreign Affairs, Deputy Supreme Commander of the Armed Forces, Minister of Defence, Chief of Staff of the Armed Forces, Chief of National Security and the National Security Adviser.

A National Electoral Committee was established in August 2006 to preside over the partial elections to the FNC, which took place in December, following a major awareness campaign. Considerable competition among the 450 candidates (including 65 women) was not, however, reflected in country-wide enthusiasm for the vote, with some intellectuals expressing their disappointment at the limited nature of the exercise—in particular the fact that from the whole citizenry, only the electoral colleges of 6,689 pre-selected individuals (including 1,189 women) had the right to vote. Official turn-out figures of these pre-approved voters ranged from 60% in Abu Dhabi and 71% in Dubai, to 80%–90% in the smaller emirates (based on smaller numbers to start with). In Abu Dhabi one woman was elected, although the 20 appointed members of the new Council, which was inaugurated in February 2007, included nine women. In December 2008 the Supreme Council of Rulers endorsed a draft constitutional amendment extending the FNC's term from two to four years; the amendment was approved by the FNC in January 2009. Despite the widespread political apathy, concerns over governance, transparency and rights were being debated among some of the non-political élite and intelligentsia. Indeed, some from within the FNC itself suggested that the body's electorate and powers should be expanded.

THE UAE AND THE GLOBAL FINANCIAL CRISIS

The ramifications of the financial and economic crisis that engulfed the world in 2008–09 also came to be felt in the UAE, where the impact went beyond the purely economic (see Economy). Indeed, with property prices, especially in Dubai, crashing to one-half of their pre-crisis value, and the Dubai Financial Market losing 75% of its value in late 2008, the whole 'Dubai model' appeared to have suffered a major reverse. This raised inevitable questions over the management of the emirate, not only among international creditors but also within Dubai and in Abu Dhabi. Initially, the UAE authorities, including those in Dubai, appeared to talk down the impact, but by early 2009 the sheer scale of the crisis was becoming apparent. By 2009 developers had to be bailed out, major projects were suspended (including work on Palm Deira, the third phase of the artificial Palm Islands project), and Dubai itself issued a US $20,000m. bond, one-half of which was taken up in February by the federal Central Bank—in effect by Abu Dhabi. There were also strong rumours that Dubai had to give Abu Dhabi a share in a number of its projects and enterprises, in case the emirate would prove unable to start repaying some of its loans. In addition, after the bailout Dubai had to concede more political weight to Abu Dhabi in the areas of domestic and foreign policies. Dubai, to a great extent, lost the little political power that it had held before 2008. This was reflected in 2010 when Dubai for the first time agreed to implement UN economic sanctions against Iran despite the strong relationship between Tehran and Dubai.

Dubai's reputation and solvency were brought into question after state holding company Dubai World unexpectedly announced a moratorium on the repayment of its £26,000m. debt. The emirate's total debt was recorded at some £80,000m., but by other measures was estimated to be much higher. Senior personnel at some of the emirate's financial and commercial institutions were replaced, and in March 2010 Dubai World announced a debt-restructuring proposal, which it hoped would result in a return to stability. In a telling move in August 2011, Sheikh Muhammad declared himself President of the Higher Board of the Dubai International Financial Centre—one instance of the senior Al Maktoum enhancing their direct control over key institutions.

While Sheikh Muhammad of Dubai remained Prime Minister of the UAE, and maintained good relations with key members of the Al Nahyan, and while Abu Dhabi certainly did not want to see Dubai's economy crash nor lose international credibility, the general perception was that Dubai would henceforth lose some of its ability to function as a virtually independent entity within the UAE, going its own way in development, legal innovation or foreign policy. The good relationship between Abu Dhabi's Sheikh Muhammad bin Zayed Al Nahyan and Sheikh Muhammad bin Rashid Al Maktoum further contributed to the support of Dubai's economy.

Yet, by the same token, the leadership in Abu Dhabi continued to see Dubai not only as a rival but also as a key element of the UAE's economy and international standing. Indeed, while the financial crisis undoubtedly provoked some readjustment of Dubai's vision of the future, including some of the grander schemes and the previously assumed rates of growth, the emirate's economy, being well-ensconced next to Abu Dhabi and endowed with excellent service facilities and tourism infrastructure, in addition to its pre-eminent transshipment function and aluminium-smelting capacity, was widely expected to be able to rebound. The UAE as a whole also suffered from the downturn, but, owing to the huge financial cushion provided by Abu Dhabi, its damaging effects were significantly curtailed—the crisis even brought increased international involvement and raised the profile of the larger emirate. Indeed, both the crisis and Abu Dhabi's ongoing development strategy seemed likely to result in a UAE that was viewed as both more coherent and with a pre-eminent role for Abu Dhabi. Nevertheless, it became clear in 2010 and 2011 that even Abu Dhabi was reassessing some of its spending patterns, with budget reductions in several departments. By 2011, however, it was also evident that the UAE was benefiting from a widespread perception that it was a haven of relative stability in a turbulent region.

ADDRESSING THE QUESTION OF LABOUR AND HUMAN RIGHTS

The question of labour and foreign workers—so crucial to the UAE's economy and ambitious development plans, and to its overall 'social contract' with its citizens—emerged as one of the country's most problematic issues from 2005. On 1 July a new law came into effect banning labourers from working in the open sun between 12.30 p.m. and 4.30 p.m. during the months of July and August, although it remains unclear how effectively this has been enforced.

A series of unprecedentedly high-profile workers' demonstrations and strikes took place from September 2005, bringing the labour issue to a head. Hundreds of workers from India, Pakistan and Bangladesh demonstrated on Palm Island over unpaid wages, and groups of disgruntled workers staged several other demonstrations at the Dubai and Abu Dhabi Ministries of Labour. The Government's response was as swift as it was extraordinary: after meeting representatives of the Palm Island demonstrators, the Minister of Labour, Dr Ali bin Abdullah al-Kaabi, ruled that the contractor—Al Hamad Development and Construction, led by a prominent local individual—must pay its employees total back pay of US $7m. within 24 hours and, in addition to a penalty fee, prohibited it from further hiring for six months. Officials indicated that these measures were intended to show that prominent employers would no longer be protected for employment regulations breaches. However, further damaging international publicity was attracted in March 2006, when a violent strike erupted at the iconic Burj Dubai building project, as 2,500 workers staged a protest for better treatment and higher wages (labourers having been paid as little as $4 per day). Direct confrontation took place between the workers and police; the protesters burned cars, threw bricks and other building materials, blocked streets and fought a running battle with the riot police. Attention was consequently focused on such reports as that by the US-based organization Human Rights Watch, which had criticized the treatment of workers in the UAE and had asserted that the country's construction sites had claimed 850 deaths in a single year. Local embassies, meanwhile, reported that 84 South Asian workers had committed suicide in 2005.

Again, the Government responded to both its domestic and foreign critics. The Ministry of Labour interceded to help settle the Burj Dubai dispute (as it would once again in May, when 400 workers went on strike in Jebel Ali regarding unpaid wages), announcing in late March 2006 that a law was being drafted that would, for the first time, allow labourers to form trade unions and pursue collective wage bargaining—both, thus far, illegal—and that measures were being introduced to improve conditions for migrant workers, including checks on timely payment of wages, and the introduction of compulsory health insurance from the end of 2006. Yet this proved insufficient to assuage the concerns of Human Rights Watch, which issued another critical report in November 2006, accusing the Government of having 'failed to stop employers from seriously abusing the rights of the country's half million migrant construction workers' and claiming that one key problem was that the Government did not enforce its own laws, in part because of insufficient numbers of inspectors. Days before the report's publication, and presumably aware of its contents, the Prime Minister, Sheikh Muhammad, issued an order to the Minister of Labour, Dr al-Kaabi, to 'take all necessary steps to organize the affairs of foreign workers ... and to assure them of all the conditions of health, security and a dignified life, both in their places of residence and at work'. Planned measures included the introduction of a system of health insurance for all categories of workers, the creation of a special court to address workers' complaints and of an inspectorate to monitor, in the Prime Minister's words, the 'application of humanitarian laws and regulations in force in the emirates, as well as the protection and defence of the rights and dignity of foreign workers'. He also appealed for the development of an 'efficient and binding mechanism' to ensure that wages would be paid within two months and to give workers the right to change jobs. In late November, in recognition of the problem of implementation, a major inspection campaign was launched to assess companies' adherence to the labour law, and reporting requirements were put in place that would be sanctionable by fines and prison sentences. By the end of the month more than 100 labour camps had been closed down over failures to observe basic conditions for workers.

From April 2007 new contract standards became effective for the employment of construction workers, and it was announced that a centralized agency would be established to supervise the supply of labour to companies. Most importantly, a new labour law was being prepared, and, in a striking departure from regional custom, a draft of the proposed law was made available to the public on a dedicated website, with an invitation to comment. In addition to numerous responses from nationals and expatriate workers, and discussion in the print media, one response came again from Human Rights Watch, which welcomed many of the suggested improvements and the Government's openness, while criticizing aspects of the draft. Key criticisms regarded strong limitations on the right to strike (ruled out while mediation or arbitration is in progress), the exclusion of domestic, agricultural and public workers from the rights and protection set out in the draft law, and the absence of provisions on the right to organize and join trade unions (a law on trade union activity mooted in late 2006 had failed to materialize). Al-Kaabi welcomed the comments from Human Rights Watch, and held out the possibility of further adjustments, although the interim law on strikes issued in November 2006, which resulted in numerous deportations in subsequent months, seemed to indicate that by no means all the organization's concerns would be addressed in the final version of the labour law.

The removal of al-Kaabi from his post in the government reorganization of February 2008 was seen by some as a sign that his proactive attempts to deal with labour rights issues (simultaneous with a tough meritocratic approach to his own civil servants) had been judged to have gone far enough and was adding to project cost inflation. Even so, al-Kaabi's replacement as Minister of Labour, former ambassador to the USA Saqr Ghobash Said Ghobash, was clearly aware of the significance of these issues in terms of the UAE's international reputation.

The question of labour rights and the UAE's international standing gained prominence again in 2009, following the publication of a report by Human Rights Watch in May that highlighted what it said were the abuses still being inflicted on thousands of South Asian workers engaged in the Saadiyat Island project (the island in Abu Dhabi is under development as the emirate's international culture and leisure hub). The report pressed representatives of the Guggenheim Museum, New York University (NYU) and the French Museum Agency (responsible for the Louvre Abu Dhabi project), which were all creating outposts on Saadiyat, to obtain contractual guarantees that construction companies engaged on their projects would protect the fundamental rights of workers. The Government rejected the tenor of the report, stressing the measures it had taken to improve the situation and pointing to Human Rights Watch's own recognition that the UAE Government had moved to improve housing conditions and ensure the timely payment of wages in recent years. In 2010 NYU Abu Dhabi adopted an explicit policy insisting on workers' rights being observed. Furthermore, most of the larger construction companies involved in the project began building labour compounds equipped with very high quality services (including health, sport and social facilities). These compounds are monitored on a regular basis by government bodies.

Addressing another long-standing human rights issue, the Minister of the Interior, Sheikh Saif bin Zayed Al Nahyan, announced in October 2006 that a preliminary list was being finalized of *bidoun* (stateless people) who would have a right to citizenship. His ministry estimated the number of *bidoun* in the country at about 10,000 (however, outside estimates have ranged as high as 100,000). Sheikh Khalifa had instructed a commission, set up earlier that year to deal with the issue, to 'find a comprehensive solution to the question of stateless people in order to resolve the matter permanently'. By the end of 2006 nearly 1,300 were in the process of being granted citizenship, and inconclusive evidence suggests that a few hundred at most were added to this list in 2007 and the first part of 2008. Yet, from September 2008, when registration centres were opened, several thousand applications were thought to have been made. Nevertheless, the issue remained unresolved in mid-2013.

In July 2009 at least 120 Shi'a Lebanese families and a number of Palestinians from the Gaza Strip were expelled from the UAE at short notice. Some of those affected had lived in the country for decades, and lost extensive assets in the process. The Lebanese Government, the international media and Human Rights Watch expressed concern at this development. Explanations offered by the UAE authorities indicated that the reason for the expulsions was the violation of residency law. However, some reports (based on interviews with those expelled) suggested that the individuals had been forced to leave the UAE owing to security issues related to Hezbollah and the Islamic Resistance Movement (Hamas—a Palestinian militant Islamist organization). The Government reportedly believed that the former residents had been providing financial support to these Islamist organizations.

Meanwhile, in April 2009 a US television channel broadcast a video purporting to show the torture of a grain merchant by Sheikh Issa bin Zayed Al Nahyan, a brother of Sheikh Khalifa, with the apparent assistance of police officers. The video had formed part of evidence presented to a court in Houston, USA, by a former business associate of Sheikh Issa. Following the widespread reporting of the allegations by the international media, the UAE authorities announced that Sheikh Issa had been placed under house arrest and that an investigation was under way. This was a striking development as the senior members of the royal families had long been perceived as immune from criminal procedures. However, Sheikh Issa was acquitted in January 2010, while his accusers were convicted *in absentia* of 'drugging, recording and publishing a video, and blackmail', verdicts that attracted criticism from the US Government and Human Rights Watch.

In light of this and of the official attitude towards media coverage of the financial crisis of 2008–09, Human Rights Watch and others expressed their concerns over the new pending Media Law that was announced in April 2009. It was claimed that some of the provisions in the new legislation—in particular the ban on insulting members of the Government and royal family—could imperil journalists' ability to report on such cases, and contained too many vague stipulations open to exploitation by the authorities should they wish to suppress the media. However, the head of the National Media Council responded robustly, pointing out that the law reconciled local cultural practice with the requirements of a free press, and only personal attacks on members of the royal family and Government, not criticism of their professional performance, were out of bounds. In response to concerns over Article 33, which states that fines may be imposed as penalties for press coverage that is deemed to harm the country's reputation, foreign relations or obligations, or that damages its national identity, or 'harms the country's national economy', it was stressed that only where journalists had printed information that they knew to be false, and where this was proven in court, would penalties apply. Information that turned out to be false, but had been printed in good faith, would not be so liable. Moreover, it was pointed out, the law did not apply to Dubai Media City, where most of the foreign press, and some local media, were based. Reporting on the sensitive issue of financial and economic trouble in Dubai after the crisis of 2008–09, therefore, would not be out of bounds under the law. Even so, it remained clear that local media outlets in particular continued to err on the side of caution by, in effect, self-censoring. Since presidential ratification of the law remained pending in mid-2013, the country continues to operate under the 1980 Press and Publications Law. Interestingly, however, the Emirates News Agency (WAM) noted in early 2012 that Sheikh Muhammad's statement that journalists should not go to gaol for doing their job should be considered law. This bears placing in the context, though, of the overall security-conscious retrenchment that became reinforced as the 'Arab spring' unfolded.

DOMESTIC POLITICS FOLLOWING THE 'ARAB SPRING', 2011–12

The so-called 'Arab spring' of popular uprisings in the Middle East and North Africa, which began in Tunisia and Egypt in early 2011, also had secondary effects in the UAE, albeit more by way of moving government attitudes further in a security-centred direction than any significant overt political activism. This was really a continuation of a trend that had become visible earlier, as Abu Dhabi's weight was increasingly being felt in policy matters. This was exemplified in April and May by the dissolution, and replacement by government appointees, of the boards of long-established non-governmental organizations, such as the Jurists' Association and the Teachers' Association, who had signed an online petition advocating further political reform in the UAE. After the drawing-up of this petition, the UAE Government ordered the arrest of some 94 activists over the following year, including academics, lawyers, doctors, high-ranking government officials, etc., who were among the more vociferous advocates of democracy in the country, for 'opposing the Government' and 'insulting the President, the Vice-President and the Crown Prince of Abu Dhabi'. Most of the detainees were members of the Islamist group al-Islah (Reform), which has suspected links to the Muslim Brotherhood.

Yet another instance was the unexplained decision in mid-2011 not to renew the operating licence of the independent Gulf Research Center, just after an international survey had ranked it as the Arab world's second most important 'think tank'. This enhanced security stance in part reflects the background and persuasions of Crown Prince Sheikh Muhammad bin Zayed, but also, in particular, his and others' concerns over possible Iranian influence, not least given the developments in Bahrain, along with lingering concern over the possibility of radical Islamist elements gaining support in the country.

It was against the background of the 'Arab spring' that the UAE's second elections to the FNC were held in September 2011. A total of 468 candidates stood for the 20 elected seats (still out of 40), and this time the electorate was expanded to 129,274. However, the 28% turn-out was low by any standards, and tribal voting was prominent. It also did not seem coincidental that, amid the regional turmoil, the Government also promised a major investment programme for the five northern emirates to help to address the poverty and development gap. It was reported that Abu Dhabi had pledged to invest up to US $10,000m. in the infrastuctures of the northern emirates.

The overall atmosphere in the country nevertheless remained one of security-focused retrenchment and control, explained in part by fears at senior level, especially in Abu Dhabi, about the possible effects at home of the 'Arab spring', in part by similarly Abu Dhabi-centered suspicion of Iran's influence, and in part by the already mentioned relative ascendancy of the Al Nahyan post-Sheikh Zayed. The trial of the 'UAE Five' (five signatories to the online petition) arrested in April 2011 began two days after the elections. Observers and human rights organizations claimed that flagrant flaws in due process meant that the right to a free and fair trial had been compromised. The trial of the other detained activists commenced in March 2013; in early July 69 of the defendants were convicted of planning an Islamist coup against the Government and were sentenced to up to 15 years in prison (the other 25 activists were acquitted).

The UAE leadership's worries about Muslim Brotherhood-linked activity in the country were also heightened by the 'Arab spring', and in December 2011 the citizenship was revoked of seven men accused of foreign loyalties; all were understood to have close links with the Muslim Brotherhood. Once again this led to condemnation by international human rights organizations, especially as it was revealed in 2012 that at least one of the men had been pressed to accept a Comoros passport and then had to accept deportation to Thailand after the Comoros had ultimately refused to accept him. In a further sign of nervousness regarding any independent activism, in February 2012 30 Syrians who had demonstrated against the regime of President Bashar al-Assad in front of the Syrian consulate in Dubai had their residency permits cancelled and were thus effectively expelled from the country. A UAE national who criticized the Government's action on the social networking site Twitter was arrested by Dubai police in Ras al-Khaimah. The episode had diplomatic reverberations when the Qatar-based Egyptian cleric Yusuf al-Qaradawi lambasted the UAE leadership on the Al Jazeera television network for the decision, in turn provoking a furious response from Abu Dhabi and, indeed, from Dubai's increasingly vocal and high-profile chief of police, Gen. Dahi Khalfan Tamim. (The diplomatic spat was quelled after the Heir Apparent of Qatar, Sheikh Tamim bin Hamad Al Thani, intervened and repeat broadcasts dropped Qaradawi's comments.) Relations between the UAE and Qatar became more tense in February 2013 following the arrest of a Qatari citizen at Dubai airport on charges of attempting to provide financial support for members of the Muslim Brotherhood in the UAE (at August the Qatari detainee remained in jail and his family had not been informed of the precise reasons for his incarceration). However, relations between the two countries appeared to be improving following the inauguration of Sheikh Tamim as Qatar's new Amir in June.

The security-focused trend continued in the glare of international criticism when both the US State Department-funded National Democratic Institute and Germany's Konrad Adenauer Stiftung were informed in March 2012 that they had three months to leave the country. The decision was criticized by both the US and German Governments, with German Federal Chancellor Angela Merkel commenting that this was part of a more general crackdown on foundations in the UAE. Some thought that the foundations' work on other countries in the region (probably including Bahrain) may have brought pressure from those Governments, as neither organization did much work specifically on the UAE. In another incident, in February 2013 the UAE Government barred a British academic from the London School of Economics and Political Science from entering the country owing to criticisms of the UAE authorities' attitude towards civil liberties and political freedom in his recent published works.

Striking confirmation of the authorities' concern about Muslim Brotherhood activity came when a member of Ras al-Khaimah's ruling family, Sheikh Sultan bin Kayed Al Qasimi, the Chairman of al-Islah and a first cousin of the Ruler, was arrested on 20 April 2012, since then being kept under house arrest at the Ruler's palace. It appears that this may have been a move by the family itself, but it clearly did not occur in a vacuum. Sheikh Sultan was among those who had criticized the revocation of citizenship of seven members of al-Islah. The emirate's Ruler, Sheikh Saud, has taken a strong line against criticism of the UAE's leadership, similar to that adopted by the Abu Dhabi ruling family—in part, no doubt, because of the latter's financial support for the poorer emirate, especially since 2011.

In July 2012 a further eight members of al-Islah were arrested, including the high-profile, internationally respected human rights lawyer Dr Muhammad al-Roken, who had represented the previous seven activists, and also the 'UAE Five' in 2011.

REGIONAL RELATIONS SINCE 1990

Iraq's occupation of Kuwait, in August 1990, caused a political and economic crisis throughout the Gulf region. The UAE responded by supporting resistance to Iraqi aggression, and on 20 August the UAE ordered all nationals to join the armed forces for six weeks' military training. Armed forces opposing Iraq's invasion, including units from the British and French air forces, were granted facilities in the country. In February 1991, after the outbreak of hostilities between Iraq and a US-led multinational force, the UAE air force conducted four raids against Iraqi targets.

In October 1995 Sheikh Zayed appealed for reconciliation with Iraq and the easing of UN sanctions. The UAE sent several shipments of aid containing food and medicine to Iraq. In late 1997, as the crisis developed between Iraq and weapons inspectors of the UN Special Commission (UNSCOM, see the chapter on Iraq), the UAE refused US requests to allow the deployment of US fighter aircraft in the UAE, and strongly advocated a diplomatic solution. In August 1998 it was announced that the UAE was to restore diplomatic ties with Iraq. Thereafter, the amount of aid from the UAE to Iraq increased significantly.

The UAE reopened its embassy in the Iraqi capital, Baghdad, in April 2000. However, it lent its support to a declaration of the GCC annual summit meeting in December that urged Iraq to conform with UN Security Council Resolutions. It was generally considered that the UAE had been compelled to endorse the declaration in return for emphasis of GCC support for the UAE in its territorial dispute with Iran.

Following the kidnap of one of its diplomats in Iraq in May 2006, the UAE withdrew its most senior diplomat, the chargé d'affaires, from Baghdad. However, in June 2008, Sheikh Abdullah bin Zayed Al Nahyan, the UAE's Minister of Foreign Affairs, became the first senior government official from a GCC country to visit Baghdad since the US-led invasion to overthrow Saddam Hussain in 2003. In July 2008 Iraqi Prime Minister Nuri al-Maliki made an official visit to Abu Dhabi, during which Sheikh Khalifa announced plans to reinstate full diplomatic relations and approved the cancellation of some US $7,000m. of Iraqi debt. The first UAE ambassador to Iraq since 1990 took up his post in Baghdad in September 2008.

The focus on Iraq did not dispel the long-standing territorial tensions with Iran. Rival claims to the island of Abu Musa had been made by Sharjah and Iran in 1970, when petroleum exploration began. In 1971 agreement was reached to divide any oil revenues. However, in August 1992 it was reported that Iran had annexed Abu Musa after 20 years of joint control. It was claimed that Iranian authorities had denied landing permission to more than 100 residents of the island who were returning from Sharjah, and that Iran was refusing a compromise agreement. Iran subsequently claimed sovereignty over Abu Musa, together with the Greater Tunb and Lesser Tunb islands. Discussions between the two sides in Abu Dhabi at the end of September collapsed almost immediately, with Iran refusing to discuss ownership of two of the three islands. A GCC summit meeting held in Abu Dhabi in December demanded that Iran reverse the 'virtual annexation' of the islands. In April 1993 a GCC statement expressed support for bilateral negotiations. In the same month it was reported that all persons who had been expelled from (or refused entry to) Abu Musa in 1992 had been permitted to return. Both the UAE and Iran periodically proclaimed their commitment to direct talks; however, by late 1994 no significant progress had been made towards resolving the conflict, and in December the UAE announced its intention to refer the dispute to the International Court of Justice (ICJ). In February 1995 it was alleged that Iran had deployed air defence systems on the islands. Relations between the two countries deteriorated further when Iran opened an airport on Abu Musa in March 1996, and a power station on the island of Greater Tunb in the following month. No solution was reached at talks in March 1997, and in June the UAE protested to the UN about a pier that Iran had allegedly constructed on Greater Tunb. In March 1999 the GCC issued a statement criticizing Iranian naval exercises near the disputed islands.

Given this context, the UAE was also highly critical of a developing rapprochement between Iran and Saudi Arabia, the latter having offered to mediate in the dispute over the islands. Relations with Saudi Arabia deteriorated further following a visit to that country by President Muhammad Khatami of Iran, although the Saudi authorities insisted that a rapprochement with Iran would not be at the expense of its relations with any other country. In November 1999 a tripartite committee, established by the GCC and comprising representatives of Oman, Qatar and Saudi Arabia, announced that it would continue in its efforts to facilitate a settlement over ownership of the disputed islands. At the end of the month Sheikh Zayed decided not to attend a meeting of GCC leaders in Saudi Arabia, in protest against the lack of attention given to the dispute by the other members of the GCC at a time when they were improving relations with Iran. In December the UAE renewed its request for Iran either to enter into direct negotiations or to agree to international arbitration over the islands. When Iran announced in March 2000 that it would be prepared to negotiate, the UAE welcomed the statement, but referred it to the tripartite GCC committee. In September 2006 Iran rejected the UAE's proposal to refer the dispute to the ICJ.

An Iranian official suggested in early May 2007 that Iran would be willing to resolve the matter through dialogue and with reference to the 1971 memorandum of understanding on joint control of Abu Musa, and a state visit to the UAE by the Iranian President, Mahmoud Ahmadinejad, appeared to ease relations. However, these conciliatory moves were undermined by the UAE's capture in May 2007 of several Iranian divers (later released), and Iran's capture in June of the crew of three UAE vessels. In July an opinion piece in the Iranian newspaper *Kayhan* by its editor, Hossein Shariatmadari, claimed Bahrain as a province of Iran and demanded the full return of the islands. Although the author was known for adopting fairly outlandish positions, the fact that he also served as adviser to the country's Supreme Religious Leader, Ayatollah Khamenei, gave the article added impact. The GCC reacted by asserting the independence of Bahrain and the UAE's sovereignty over the three islands, and the Iranian Government made it clear that, indeed, the article did not reflect its policy.

Tempers flared again in May 2008, when an announcement by the Speaker of the FNC that a delegation had requested Russian mediation was rejected by Iran, which insisted on any 'misunderstanding' being dealt with bilaterally. This in turn brought a furious statement from a UAE Ministry of Foreign Affairs official that there was no misunderstanding about the islands being occupied, adding: 'Occupation is occupation, whether it is by Israel, Iran or any other country.' The revelation in August that Iran had set up two administrative maritime offices on Abu Musa was met with strong protests from the UAE. This was backed up with an unequivocal statement from the GCC describing Iran's activity as 'illegitimate action on an indivisible part of the UAE'. The Iranian response was predictably resolute: Iran's Permanent Representative to the UN, in a letter to the UN in September, emphasized his country's desire for 'brotherly relations' with the UAE, but maintained that Abu Musa was 'Iranian' and that Iran was simply operating within its 'sovereign rights'. In April 2010 Sheikh Abdullah Al Nahyan described the Iranian presence on the islands as 'a shameful occupation'. Predictably, this prompted dismissive comments from Iran, but in June the FNC hardened its position by formally insisting that any official reference to the islands dispute should henceforth use the term 'occupation'.

Meanwhile, following the disputed Iranian presidential election in June 2009 (see the chapter on Iran), the UAE authorities had to walk a fine line. A majority of the Iranian and Iranian-origin population, especially in Dubai, wanted to express its fury at what it saw as President Ahmadinejad's theft of victory. For several days in mid-June hundreds of anti-Ahmadinejad demonstrators staged protests in front of the Iranian consulate in Dubai, despite the Iranian ambassador requesting that they be halted by the authorities. However, Dubai's police subsequently stopped the protests, arguing that this was necessary to avoid clashes with Ahmadinejad supporters. As Dubai's influence diminished due to its debt crisis in 2009–10, and as the policy preferences of Abu Dhabi and the federation took increasing precedence, it seemed likely that UAE policy towards Iran would harden, particularly in light of US demands for sanctions on Iran. Indeed, revelations that emerged through the WikiLeaks organization in 2010 and 2011 showed that Crown Prince Muhammad bin Zayed, in particular, had for some time been taking a hardline position on the question of Iran in confidential meetings with US officials.

Relations deteriorated again in mid-April 2012, following a visit by President Ahmadinejad to the disputed island of Abu Musa. The UAE recalled its ambassador to Iran, while later that month the GCC issued a statement in which it referred to the visit as a 'provocation' on the part of Iran. In February 2013 the UAE reacted angrily to an announcement by Iran that it was to carry out an inspection tour of the islands before drawing up a national security and foreign affairs policy for the disputed territory.

The occasional friction with Saudi Arabia caused by the question of the islands accompanied other fluctuating bilateral disputes. The UAE boycotted a meeting of GCC oil ministers in March 1999, in protest against a Saudi decision to begin petroleum production on disputed territory. Tension escalated very publicly again after an announcement in May that the GCC Monetary Council would be located in Riyadh, capital of Saudi Arabia, the largest GCC economy. It is unclear how this statement came to be issued without UAE approval, or whether UAE representatives had mishandled the issue, but later that month the UAE Government announced that it would no longer take part in the monetary union project.

The recurrent tension between the two countries was also manifested in Saudi objections over the planned Dolphin gas pipeline and mooted causeway between Qatar and the UAE—both of obvious importance to the UAE (not least given its need for supplies of non-associated gas for its rapidly increasing consumption of energy)—with Saudi Arabia holding up both projects for some time by raising territorial and maritime claims. Rival claims have been made over the territory adjoining the Khor al-Udaid, which is prominently displayed as part of the UAE on a map printed on the country's identification cards. This map was a factor underlying the tightened Saudi border controls in mid-2009, which led to lengthy queues of trucks at the border, particularly at the Al-Ghuwaifat crossing. Meanwhile, the UAE protested against the Saudi-Qatari boundary agreement, which was submitted to the Arab League in June; the UAE claimed that this was incompatible with its own 1969 agreement with Qatar, although Saudi Arabia argued that it had never recognized that agreement.

In November 2009 the UAE submitted documents to the UN which claimed that, while Saudi Arabia had indicated its readiness to enter into negotiations, there had not been 'any change in Saudi position in such a way that would lead to a settlement of all boundary matters'. The UAE also criticized the encroachment of Saudi patrol boats into its territorial waters in September. A new Border Council headed by Sheikh Muhammad bin Zayed was established in December. In March 2010 there were unconfirmed reports of a minor maritime clash in the area; two Saudi border guards were reported to have been arrested and interrogated, before being taken to the Saudi embassy in Abu Dhabi.

Relations between the UAE and Oman (which had long observed a *modus vivendi* with Iran) improved with a 1999 agreement demarcating their joint border, which was fully formalized in June 2002, and a statement by the two countries' leaders in May 2007 that they would forge a 'strategic partnership'. However, by 2010 tensions had increased, with the border being tightly monitored, including at the previously easily crossed borders of Musandam and Buraimi. In 2011 the Government of Oman brought accusations against the UAE of espionage activities, although mediation by the Kuwaiti Amir appeared to calm tensions over this issue somewhat.

In January 2010 Mahmoud al-Mabhouh, a senior member of Hamas, was assassinated in a Dubai hotel. Following an investigation, the Dubai police accused the Israeli external intelligence service, Mossad, of having carried out the assassination, alleging that Israeli agents had entered Dubai using false European and Australian passports. Condemnation of Israel by the British Government and other authorities followed, although mainly for the theft and abuse of nationals' passports (see the chapter on Israel).

From early 2011 the UAE also became more actively engaged in the crisis ensuing from anti-Government protests in Yemen (see the chapter on Yemen). This was recognized as one of the most pressing security issues for the country, and the Government took a close interest in the situation, both in development assistance and through involvement with the Friends of Yemen group of countries. It also supported a GCC plan for a transfer of power by the regime in Yemen, which was proposed in early 2011.

The most notable development in 2011 was the UAE's involvement in the civil conflict in Libya (see the chapter on Libya), in which it took a strong stance in favour of the insurgents (as did Qatar): it was among the first states to recognize the National Transitional Council established by rebel forces, supported the GCC's and the Arab League's efforts to follow suit, offered financial assistance and training to the rebels, and dispatched a number of aircraft and personnel to participate in a NATO operation against the forces of Libyan leader Muammar al-Qaddafi. Following the establishment of the new regime in Libya, the UAE also began to build on this record to enhance bilateral relations.

The UAE's policy towards President Assad's Syria also shifted in the second half of 2011, although more slowly than that of Qatar, Saudi Arabia and Bahrain. However, the UAE withdrew its ambassador from the Syrian capital, Damascus, and asked the Syrian ambassador to leave, following the GCC's decision in February 2012 to do so collectively. It closed ranks with its fellow GCC members in demanding an end to the Syrian regime's use of violence against those deemed to be opposed to it, and a political transition. The UAE's relatively early ambivalence must be understood in light of the leadership's conflicting concerns for: setting precedents of revolutionary activity in long-established regimes with which the country had good (including commercial) relations, not least given its aversion to domestic political activism combined with the fear of a breakthrough of the Muslim Brotherhood in another key Arab country; and the perception that the Syrian conflict was turning into a proxy fight between Sunnis and Iranian-supported Shi'a. The UAE has become one of the leading aid donors to the Syrian refugees who have fled in their thousands to Jordan, Turkey and Lebanon. The UAE Red Crescent, in co-operation with the UAE Government, opened a refugee camp in Jordan which can currently host some 5,000 refugees and has the potential to be expanded to accommodate about 25,000 individuals.

One peculiar aspect and illustration of the increasingly authoritarian atmosphere in the UAE has been the recurring comments on social media and elsewhere by Dubai's outspoken police chief, Gen. Dahi Khalfan Tamim. In June 2012, in an anti-Muslim Brotherhood tirade against Muhammad Mursi, Egypt's newly elected President, Gen. Dahi generated a diplomatic incident, causing the UAE ambassador to Cairo to be summoned to Egypt's Ministry of Foreign Affairs, and the UAE's deputy foreign minister being sent to the Egyptian capital to explain that these were merely 'personal' remarks. However, many believed that the UAE Government had given Gen. Dahi the 'green light' freely to speak and criticize the Egyptian leader.

OTHER EXTERNAL RELATIONS SINCE 1990

Beyond the region itself, in July 1994 the UAE signed a defence agreement with the USA, which extended the agreement signed in 1991 in the aftermath of the Gulf conflict. This coincided with the announcement of plans to reduce the size of the UAE armed forces by 10,000, to 50,000. In January 1995 a defence agreement with France followed, providing for 'consultations' in the event of aggression against or threats to UAE territory. Negotiations over a similar agreement with the United Kingdom stalled for a period over British reluctance to accept UAE jurisdiction over British troops deployed there. An agreement was finally signed in November 1996 whereby the United Kingdom undertook to defend the UAE in the event of an external attack. As part of a US $15,000m. weapons procurement programme, the Government signed a contract in December 1997 for the modernization of its 33 *Mirage* 2000 jets, and for the purchase of 30 new *Mirage* 2000-9 fighter aircraft. In May 1998 an order for 80 US F-16 fighter aircraft (worth at least $6,000m.) was announced, representing the largest defence purchase in the country's history. While Abu Dhabi provides 80% of the UAE's total military manpower and defence budget, arms procurement remains only partly centralized, so equipment is inadequately standardized; nor does the country have the local trained manpower to operate all the equipment fully. A great proportion of the UAE's defence purchases may be regarded, in part, as diplomatic and as an insurance policy to secure foreign protectors, rather than as effective defence infrastructure acquisitions in their own right.

In response to the 11 September 2001 attacks against the USA, and ensuing pressure from Washington, the UAE severed diplomatic relations with the Taliban regime in Afghanistan in late September. Hitherto, the UAE had been one of only three states to maintain official ties with the Taliban. After diplomatic relations had been ended, the UAE's Minister of Foreign Affairs stated that the emirates had made 'intense efforts' to persuade the Taliban authorities to hand over the leader of al-Qa'ida, Osama bin Laden, so that he might stand trial in an international court. The UAE pledged support to the USA in its efforts to bring to justice the perpetrators of acts of terrorism, and in October a suspected militant Islamist was extradited from the UAE to France, where he was wanted for questioning. At a December GCC summit in Muscat, Oman, the UAE joined its fellow members in agreeing to establish a Supreme Joint Defence Council and to formulate a joint strategy on terrorism.

At the same time the country maintained its delicate diplomatic balance by emphasizing that the success of the USA's 'global coalition' against terrorism must be linked to a resumption of the Arab-Israeli peace process. At an Arab League summit in Beirut, Lebanon, in March 2002, the UAE stated its opposition to any US-led attack on Iraq.

As the diplomatic crisis over Iraq deepened during the second half of 2002, the UAE continued to try to remain diplomatically even-handed, calling for Iraqi co-operation with the UN while emphasizing the need for a peaceful solution. At an Arab League summit in Doha, Qatar, in March 2003, the UAE supported a resolution in which Arab states agreed not to participate in military action in Iraq—even if the UAE, in common with the other Gulf monarchies, would permit US aircraft to use its airspace in the event of such action. Sheikh Zayed's proposal that Saddam Hussain and other senior officials in the Iraqi Government should go into exile in order to avoid war, to be replaced by an interim UN administration, was not tabled for formal debate at the summit. Following the overthrow of Saddam Hussain's regime by the US-led coalition in April and the announcement later in that month that US military forces were to be withdrawn from Saudi Arabia, the US Secretary of Defense, Donald Rumsfeld, announced that the USA would spend US $25m. on upgrading the al-Dhafra airbase in Abu Dhabi for use by its aircraft in the region. During and in the immediate aftermath of the conflict in Iraq, the UAE provided the country with humanitarian aid, and also planned to secure a significant role in Iraqi reconstruction. In 2004 the UAE agreed to write off most of Iraq's $7,000m. debt.

In July 2004 the UAE signed a Trade and Investment Framework Agreement with the USA, and negotiations towards a Free Trade Agreement (FTA) began in March 2005. This irked the Saudi Government, which had previously argued that the GCC should negotiate a trade deal as a single body, and complained that Bahrain's signing of a bilateral FTA with the USA earlier that year contravened the GCC's common external tariff agreement. In late 2007, however, the Office of the US Trade Representative announced that the UAE and the USA had agreed that they would be unable to conclude an FTA during the tenure of the incumbent US Administration. Despite the inauguration of Barack Obama as the new US President in January 2009 (and his re-election in November 2012), substantive negotiations on an FTA had not recommenced by September 2013.

In addition to seeking closer economic ties with the USA, the UAE signalled its determination to strengthen relations with two key emerging trade and investment partners, the People's Republic of China and India, with several official statements to this effect in 2007 in particular, and a state visit to India by Prime Minister Sheikh Muhammad in March of that year. The move that drew the most international comment was the agreement for France to establish a permanent naval base in the UAE—albeit capable of accommodating only 500 personnel. The new base, which also included an air base and a training facility, was inaugurated by President Nicolas Sarkozy in May 2009. France was hoping to persuade the UAE to replace its fleet of French *Mirage* 2000 combat planes with 60 new multi-role *Rafale* jets, and to obtain the contract for the construction of the UAE's planned nuclear power stations. However, in an unexpected development and to the chagrin of the French authorities, in December 2009 a US $40,000m. contract for the construction of four civil nuclear reactors was signed with a consortium led by the Korea Electric Power Corpn of the Republic of Korea (South Korea), rather than, as had been expected, the French company Areva. The first of the plants was expected to start operations in 2017, with the other three scheduled for completion by 2020. Apparently in response to the ongoing financial crisis in the eurozone and other Western countries, the UAE appeared to be shifting its attention eastward, particularly towards fostering closer economic relations with India, China, South Korea and Japan.

For the UAE, this represented a continuation of its explicit security and diplomatic diversification strategy. This did not, however, threaten its close security and defence ties with the USA. One illustration of this came in the form of some US $4,000m. in arms supply deals with US companies announced in February 2009 (mainly with Boeing, Lockheed and Raytheon), to 'modernize the country's air transport fleet'.

Economy

Revised for this edition by RICHARD GERMAN and ELIZABETH TAYLOR

INTRODUCTION

Prior to the discovery of petroleum, the economy of the seven sheikhdoms, or emirates, that comprised the Trucial States was based on pearling, fishing, trade and a limited amount of agriculture. In the 19th century piracy, as defined by the Western powers that became dominant in the area, also formed an important source of income for the coastal tribes. Since 1958, when petroleum was first discovered off the coast of Abu Dhabi, and in particular from June 1962 when it was first exported, the economy of the area has undergone dramatic change. The pace of this change increased appreciably following independence in 1971, leading to the creation of the federal state of the United Arab Emirates (UAE), and the increases in the price of oil dictated by the Organization of the Petroleum Exporting Countries (OPEC), of which the UAE is a member.

The pace of the UAE's rapid economic change can be seen in the dramatic increase in its population during the last fifty years. At the March 1968 census the population was recorded at 179,126. By the December 1980 census, it had reached 1,042,099, and results from the December 1985 census indicated that the figure grew by some 55.7% in the intervening five years, to 1,622,464, of whom about 670,000 were inhabitants of Abu Dhabi. The December 1995 census recorded a population of 2,411,041. During 1995–2005 it increased by an annual average of 6.5%. The most recent census took place in December 2005, the results of which recorded a population of 4,106,427, comprising 3,280,932 non-UAE nationals and 825,495 UAE citizens (of whom 50.6% were males, and 49.4% females). The largest relative increases in population were in the smallest emirates, reflecting their policy of economic expansion. The unequal distribution of the sexes is indicative of the large amount of immigration that has been necessary to sustain the country's economic growth. In 2004 it was estimated that the total number of people in employment was 2,459,145, and this figure had increased to around 3,397,000 in 2008, with over 20% working in construction. However, the onset of a global financial crisis and economic downturn in the latter part of 2008 led to substantial redundancies in the construction, property, tourism and financial services sectors (particularly in Dubai), forcing many expatriate workers to leave the emirates. The results of the 2009 labour force survey conducted by the National Bureau of Statistics showed that almost 25% of the population was below the age of 15 and that workers constituted 53% of the total population. The UAE's sixth census, which had been scheduled to take place in April 2010, was postponed indefinitely, apparently because of financial issues. According to official figures (which were based on administrative records of births and deaths and net migration), the population in mid-2010 reached 8,264,070, 11.4% of whom were UAE nationals. According to UN estimates, this figure had risen to 9,346,127 by mid-2013.

Despite progress towards political integration, there has been little co-ordination in the economic affairs of the emirates. Abu Dhabi's wealth, based on its petroleum resources, has dominated the UAE economy. In contrast, Dubai has pursued an independent strategy of diversification away from reliance on the oil industry and become an entrepôt for regional trade. The northern emirates remain comparatively undeveloped. There is, nevertheless, a federal budget, which is essentially concerned with the implementation of federal infrastructure policy. Individual emirates also draw up separate budgets for municipal expenditure and local projects. The Constitution provides for social services, such as health and education, to come under federal control. Abu Dhabi contributes around 70%–80% of the federal budget revenue.

Iraq's invasion of Kuwait in August 1990 initially had a destabilizing effect upon the UAE economy, but by the end of that year confidence had revived. Relatively steady revenue from petroleum exports and rapidly growing non-oil trade provided a strong financial base to support the Government's ambitious plans for industrial expansion and diversification through most of the 1990s.

The sharp fall in international petroleum prices in 1998 caused gross domestic product (GDP) to decline in that year. A recovery from late 1999 was then undermined by the general downturn in the global economy in the aftermath of the suicide attacks on the USA in September 2001. According to the Central Bank, real GDP growth slipped to 1.9% in 2002 before increasing significantly in 2003 to reach 11.9%, owing to rising international petroleum prices. As prices remained buoyant, there was continued high growth of 9.7% in 2004. IMF figures indicated that real non-hydrocarbon GDP grew by 11% in 2005, while the hydrocarbons sector registered a growth rate of 2.1%. However, rising inflation, which reached 6.2% in 2005, caused concern, with official figures for 2006 recording a rate of 9.3%. This rise was driven by strong domestic demand and also by sharp increases in the prices of services and in rents, particularly in Dubai, where the Government imposed a 15% cap on rent rises for all leased properties in the emirate until the end of 2006. Non-hydrocarbon GDP, driven particularly by Dubai's diversification, rose by 11.1% (comprising 62.5% of federal GDP in that year), while the oil sector recorded growth of 6.0%. Rising rents continued to affect inflation, and in November 2006 Abu Dhabi introduced a 7% rent cap. In January 2007 Dubai lowered its 15% ceiling on rent increases to match that of Abu Dhabi. GDP growth was estimated by the IMF at 9.4% in 2006, and, although remaining buoyant, it slowed to 7.4% in 2007, according to the UAE Ministry of Economy. However, housing shortages and high demand continued to prompt rent rises, which, together with the weakness of the US dollar, interest rate cuts and increases in commodity prices, added to inflationary pressures. As a result, consumer price inflation reached 11.1% in 2007.

The Central Bank reportedly estimated real GDP growth at 7.4% in 2008. However, the economy slowed markedly in the latter part of the year in the wake of the global financial crisis and a fall in oil prices on international markets in response to weakening demand. The UAE, and particularly Dubai, also saw a dramatic reversal in the property market, which had previously experienced rapid expansion. Dubai had borrowed heavily to fund growth in property and infrastructure, leaving the emirate exposed to debt and prompting negative credit assessments from major international rating agencies. To mitigate the impact of the international downturn on the domestic economy, the Government intervened to support the banking sector, including by means of a precautionary guarantee on deposits, and to maintain major infrastructure projects that were struggling to secure financing or risked postponement or cancellation.

According to the IMF, GDP contracted by 0.7% in 2009, reflecting a decline in petroleum output in line with OPEC-agreed production cuts and lower non-oil growth associated with a property market correction in Dubai and tight credit conditions. The hydrocarbons sector declined by 6.3%, and non-hydrocarbon growth slowed from an annual average of 8% in 2006–08 to 1% in 2009. Inflation fell substantially from a peak of 12% in 2008, to 1% in 2009, reflecting in large part a reduction in rents and consumer spending. Prospects for economic recovery were threatened when, in November 2009, the Dubai Government announced that the flagship state-owned investment corporation, Dubai World, would seek a six-month postponement of repayments on debts totalling an estimated US $59,000m. The announcement provoked fears of a major default on the emirate's sovereign debt, leading to a sharp decline in international share prices. The following month Abu Dhabi provided funding of $10,000m. for a restructuring process to prevent Dubai from defaulting on a $4,100m. bond repayment owed by the government-owned property developer Nakheel, while the Dubai authorities implemented measures to maintain confidence in the banking system and mitigate the impact on economic activity of further financial turmoil. In May 2010 Dubai World reached an agreement with creditors on restructuring some $23,500m of debt; by that time, however, some other government-related entities (GREs) were also in difficulties and having to pursue debt-restructuring arrangements (see Budget, Banking and Finance).

The IMF considered that the economic recovery gained strength during 2010, supported by a more favourable international environment and higher hydrocarbon prices, although some sectors, particularly property, still laboured under the effects of the global financial crisis. Real GDP grew by an estimated 3.2% in that year, while average inflation fell to 0.9%. Social and political unrest then erupted across much of the Arab world from early 2011. Although the impact of the popular uprisings was not significant in the UAE, it prompted the federal Government to increase spending on infrastructure in the less affluent northern emirates and to subsidize the price of basic foods. The Government also introduced reforms to the employment sponsorship system from January 2011, in an effort to improve the operation of the labour market and to deter abuses. The economic recovery continued in 2011, despite the continuing uncertain global environment and regional political turmoil. Real GDP grew by 4.9%, according to the IMF, supported by high oil prices and additional oil production by the UAE to offset the disruption to output from Libya. Non-hydrocarbon growth also increased, by 2.7%, mainly on account of the trade and tourism sectors. The Dubai World debt-restructuring was completed, but the IMF emphasized the continuing fiscal risks posed by other GREs still in need of debt-refinancing and reliant on external funding. Inflation averaged 0.9% in 2011, with the low rate mainly reflecting a continuing decline in rents.

According to the IMF, the economic recovery was maintained in 2012, with GDP growth of 4.3%, following higher oil prices and capital inflows. Hydrocarbon production increased by around 5.2%, and non-oil growth, driven by the service sectors, accelerated to 3.8%, while average inflation remained subdued, at 0.7%. The property sector stabilized in Abu Dhabi and started to recover in Dubai. The UAE, meanwhile, benefited from its perceived tranquillity amidst turmoil in much of the broader Middle East region. Preliminary estimates indicated that Dubai's real GDP rose by 4.3% in 2012, following slower growth of 3.4% and 2.8% in 2011 and 2010, respectively, and the recession of 2009, when output declined by 2.4%.

Until 1981 development expenditure in the UAE came from the annual federal budget, and there was no attempt at detailed long-term integrated economic planning, although Abu Dhabi did have a loose development plan for 1977–79. The first five-year plan, intended to run from 1981–85, was hampered by the fall in petroleum revenues over that period. This experience meant that there was little enthusiasm for further federal plans, and the emirates returned to a more flexible approach to defining and planning development priorities. However, in April 2007 the Prime Minister (and Ruler of Dubai) announced the UAE's first ever national strategy, covering economic, infrastructure, social, government, justice and rural development. It focused particularly on greater federal co-operation in policy-making and administration, and set targets for all the federation's ministries to achieve over three years. Later in 2007 Abu Dhabi introduced its own plan for strategic growth for 2008–12, aiming to diversify the economy away from the oil sector, expand infrastructure and increase tourism. In 2010 the federal Government released its strategy for 2011–13, the key priorities of which included upgrading the education and health care systems, social development and the improvement of government services. Following a review of its development strategy, in January 2012 the Abu Dhabi Government approved a series of new projects across a range of sectors, such as infrastructure, social services, housing, health and education. At the beginning of 2013 the Abu Dhabi authorities announced a US $90,000m. package of spending on capital projects for 2013–17, including infrastructure development and diversification ventures particularly focused outside the centre of the capital. In late 2012 the Dubai authorities approved the resumption of a number of postponed development projects and also announced plans for a new major scheme, Muhammad bin Rashid City. However, the IMF warned that new investments should be structured in a way that strictly limited risk-taking by the still highly-indebted GRE sector.

PETROLEUM AND GAS

The economy of the UAE is dominated by petroleum. At the end of 2012 proven oil reserves totalled 97,800m. barrels (5.9% of world reserves), more than 90% of which are in Abu Dhabi. Between 1971 and 1980 the UAE's revenue from petroleum increased about 25-fold. In this period public sector spending increased at an average annual rate of 72%. However, there was a major recession in the mid-1980s, and, owing to the surplus of global petroleum supplies, government revenue from oil exports was greatly reduced. By 1997 the petroleum sector's contribution to GDP had declined to 29%, from 63% in 1980. Nevertheless, crude petroleum exports still constituted about 40% of total commodity exports in that year. Lower international oil prices in 1998 again led to a decline in the UAE's real GDP, and, as a result, the oil sector's contribution fell to just 20.3%. However, the sector recovered to contribute 36.8% of GDP by 2008. It then declined to 28.9% in 2009, before rising again to 31.5% in 2010, 39.3% in 2011 and 40% in 2012.

During 1985–88 the UAE regularly exceeded its OPEC production quota. Widely acknowledged to be the most flagrant overproducer in OPEC, it repeatedly rejected the quotas that it had been allocated, claiming that they were inconsistent with its large reserves and disproportionate to the quotas allotted to other OPEC member states. Iraq's invasion of Kuwait in August 1990 led to the suspension of OPEC quotas as member states agreed to compensate for the loss of Iraqi and Kuwaiti production of petroleum due to the UN's mandatory trade embargo. In March 1991 OPEC agreed to reduce production levels by 5% in the second quarter of the year. The UAE agreed to reduce its level of production to 2.320m. barrels per day (b/d). From March 1992 the UAE's OPEC quota was set at 2.244m. b/d, which the UAE appeared to be observing, notwithstanding Abu Dhabi's decision to proceed with a $5,000m. development programme designed to add an extra 600,000 b/d of oil production capacity by 1996. In 1992 crude petroleum production averaged 2.283m. b/d. UAE petroleum production fluctuated little during 1993–96, remaining at around its OPEC quota (set in April 1993) of 2.161m. b/d.

In November 1997 OPEC production quotas were increased to reflect actual production (many OPEC members, including the UAE, having exceeded their quotas during that year) and the expected increase in demand in 1998; the UAE's new quota was 2.366m. b/d. However, declining petroleum prices in 1998 led to production cuts. In addition to the fall in prices, the UAE was also more directly affected by the economic crisis in Asia, as more than 50% of its exports in 1996 went to Japan, the Republic of Korea (South Korea) and Singapore. Petroleum prices continued to decline, and in March 1999 the UAE agreed to reduce production further, to 2.000m. b/d (effective from 1 April), in conjunction with both OPEC and non-OPEC countries in an effort to stabilize the market. By mid-1999 a notable recovery in world petroleum prices had been achieved as a result. Following a continued rise in petroleum prices in 2000, the UAE agreed to raise its level of production to 2.219m. b/d, effective from 1 July. The recovery continued for much of 2000, and further increases in output were agreed in October.

Production quotas were reduced by OPEC in early 2001, in an effort to counter a downward trend in world prices as demand fell. Thus, from 1 February the UAE agreed a reduction in output to 2.201m. b/d, and a further decrease, to 2.113m. b/d, was effected from 1 April. However, these decreases failed sufficiently to offset the impact on prices of the slowing of international demand, necessitating a further round of production cuts from 1 September whereby the UAE's production quota was reduced to 2.025m. b/d (of an OPEC total of 23.201m. b/d). Following the suicide attacks on the USA later that month, international demand slumped even further. The UAE's production quota was reduced to 1.894m. b/d, from 1 January 2002. International petroleum prices recovered significantly from March, but they were increasingly volatile during the second half of 2002 as the impending crisis over Iraq deepened (see History). This volatility was exacerbated by problems of overproduction by OPEC countries, although the UAE adhered relatively tightly to its quota. In January 2003 the UAE's quota was increased to 2.008m. b/d, and one month later it was raised further to 2.138m. b/d. Quotas were suspended by OPEC during the US-led military campaign to oust the regime of Saddam Hussain in Iraq during March–April 2003. From 1 April 2004 the UAE's quota was 2.051m. b/d, and, following four further rises between mid-2004 and early 2005, it was increased to 2.444m. b/d from 1 July, as OPEC sought to offset increases in international oil prices. The quota was then reduced between October 2006 and April 2007, to 2.300m. b/d. According to industry sources, overall production in the UAE totalled 2.900m. b/d in 2007. In November of that year the quota was increased by 42,000 b/d, and production in 2008 reached 2.936m. b/d. Output then declined to 2.599m. b/d in 2009, in response to further quota revisions by OPEC. Production increased to 2.849m. b/d in 2010, and to 3.322m. b/d in 2011, as efforts continued to maintain price stability in the oil market, and reached 3.389m. in 2012. The likelihood of further major petroleum discoveries in the UAE is low, but enhanced recovery techniques are being used to increase the extraction rates of mature oilfields.

The UAE's proven reserves of natural gas totalled 6,100,000m. cu m (3.3% of world reserves) in 2012. Whereas in the past much gas was simply burnt off, increasingly the UAE has exploited this resource both for internal energy usage and as a lucrative source of export earnings. A US $1,000m. onshore gas development programme (OGD-2) at the Habshan natural gas complex near the Bab oil- and gasfield, was inaugurated in 1998 and completed in 2001. The associated $700m. Asab gas project, supporting industries in Ruwais, was completed in 1999. During 2006 work progressed on the third phase of the onshore gas development programme (OGD-3) and the second phase of the Asab gas development project.

Demand in the UAE for natural gas is growing at 7% annually, and that figure is expected to double by 2020. Despite the level of reserves and the inauguration in 2007 of the Dolphin pipeline linking Qatar to Abu Dhabi, Dubai and Oman, there remains a shortfall in gas supply, and the country is exploring other options in order to meet its power generation needs (see Electricity).

Abu Dhabi

The first company to obtain a concession to explore for petroleum in Abu Dhabi was the Trucial Coast Development Oil Co, which was granted a concession over the entire territory in 1939. In 1962 the consortium was renamed the Abu Dhabi Petroleum Co (ADPC), and during the 1960s it gradually relinquished much of its concession. The second largest oil company in Abu Dhabi was founded in 1954 as Abu Dhabi Marine Areas Ltd (ADMA), which in 1971 was a consortium of British Petroleum (BP) and Compagnie Française des Pétroles (CFP). In 1972 BP sold 45% of its shares to the Japan Oil Development Co, and by 1974 the Abu Dhabi Government, in the form of Abu Dhabi National Oil Co (ADNOC), had acquired a 60% share. In 1977 ADNOC and ADMA agreed to establish a new company, ADMA-OPCO (with the same shareholders as ADMA), for offshore work, and in 1978 the Abu Dhabi Co for Onshore Oil Operations (ADCO) was formed from ADPC for onshore work. The main onshore oilfields at that time were the Murban, Bu Hasa and Asab fields, while the main offshore ones were Umm Shaif and Lower Zakum. By 1986 Abu Dhabi was producing approximately 1.3m. b/d.

In March 1991 Abu Dhabi announced that, as part of a US $7,000m. development plan for 1991–95, $2,800m. was to be spent on doubling exports of liquefied natural gas (LNG), increasing long-term oil production capacity from 2m. b/d to 2.6m. b/d and doubling refining capacity to more than 250,000 b/d. Formal approval had been obtained for the release of the estimated $500m. required to expand capacity at the onshore Bab field and the offshore Upper Zakum field. At the Bab field ADCO aimed to increase capacity from 60,000 b/d to 350,000 b/d. The capacity at the Upper Zakum field was to be increased by 200,000 b/d. Small discoveries that had been ignored over the past decade were also to be reappraised. In late 1994 the broad division of crude petroleum production within Abu Dhabi was 425,000 b/d from ADMA-OPCO offshore fields, 470,000 b/d from the Upper Zakum offshore field and 920,000 b/d from ADCO's onshore fields. In November 2005 the Government announced that oil production capacity would rise further, to 3.5m. b/d (from 2.5m. b/d), by 2009–10, through the development of new fields and the expansion of existing ones. In March 2006 ADNOC finalized a contract with ExxonMobil of the USA to increase the capacity of the offshore Upper Zakum field from 550,000 b/d to 750,000 b/d, and to introduce enhanced recovery technologies to prolong the field's productive life. By mid-2007 other upgrading or development projects to raise sustainable production capacity were planned or under way in the Bu Hasa, Bab, Sahil-Asab-Shah, Umm al-Lulu, Nasr, Qusahwira and Bida al-Qemzan oilfields. In 2008 Occidental was awarded a concession to develop two fields near the city of Abu Dhabi, which were expected to add an initial 20,000 b/d to production capacity. ADCO awarded onshore expansion contracts to United Kingdom-based Petrofac International (for the Asab field, worth $2,500m.) and Spain's Tecnicas Reunidas (for the Sahil and Shah fields, worth $1,200m.) in 2009. ADCO also awarded an $800m. contract to South Korea's SK Engineering to improve capacity at the Bab field, and ADMA-OPCO awarded a contract to France-based Technip to begin development of the offshore Nasr field.

In February 2011 the Government awarded the Abu Dhabi Oil Co a 30-year extension on its interest in the Mubarraz, Umm al-Anbar and Neewat al-Ghalan fields, and a new offshore concession in the Hail field. The agreement formed part of a series of pending negotiations with ADNOC's main partners (including ExxonMobil, Shell, BP and Total) to renew concessions that would start to expire in 2014 (although it was subsequently reported in mid-2012 that BP was not involved in these negotiations). In March 2011 ADNOC and the Korea National Oil Corpn (KNOC) signed a preliminary agreement concerning the development of Abu Dhabi's oilfields, which would guarantee South Korea stakes in reserves of at least 1,000m. barrels. The agreement also allowed for the storage of 6m. barrels of Abu Dhabi crude petroleum in South Korean facilities free of charge. In a separate agreement, KNOC was granted exploration rights to three undeveloped oil concessions, with reserves estimated at nearly 600m. barrels. In January 2012 ADNOC and the China National Petroleum Corpn signed a strategic agreement to collaborate in upstream projects in undeveloped areas, and in July Technip and Abu Dhabi's National Petroleum Construction Co were awarded a contract, worth between US $820m. and $1,000m., for an expansion project in the offshore Upper Zakum field. In April 2013 ADMA-OPCO signed engineering, procurement and construction contracts worth $2,400m. for the development of the offshore Satah Al Razboot oilfield with South Korea's Hyundai Engineering and with Petrofac International.

Abu Dhabi's exports of petroleum are transported through two main terminals—the Jebel Dhanna terminal and Das terminal—and smaller terminals at Abu al-Bukhoosh and Mubarraz.

In the 1970s the Government sought to develop its downstream production, and its first refinery, at Umm al-Nar, started up in 1976 with a capacity of 15,000 b/d. A second refinery, at Ruwais, went into operation in June 1981. By 1999 the Ruwais refinery was producing 132,050 b/d, and a subsequent expansion of the complex to a capacity of 420,000 b/d was completed in January 2006 by Technip, at a cost of US $480m. In June 2012 the Abu Dhabi Oil Refining Co (Takreer) awarded South Korea's Samsung Engineering a $2,470m. contract to build a carbon black and delayed coker plant in Ruwais.

During the early 1970s much of the gas produced in association with petroleum was flared off, but in 1977 an LNG plant at Das Island started recovering offshore associated gas, and in 1981 the GASCO (Abu Dhabi Gas Industries) plant began onshore gas collection. In 1981 a new gasfield was found underlying the offshore Zakum oilfield, and in 1984 exploration began in Abu Dhabi's share of the Khuff formation, thought to be one of the largest offshore gasfields in the world. In 1983 the Abu Dhabi Gas Liquefaction Co (ADGAS) borrowed US $500m. to upgrade its Das island complex by building three new storage tanks for LNG and four for liquefied petroleum gas (LPG), together with vapour recovery units. The Thamama C Gas project came on stream in 1984, processing gas from the Thamama C foundation of the Bab field. In 1988 Das Island produced 2.48m. metric tons of LNG for export to ADGAS's sole long-term contract customer, Japan's Tokyo Electric Power Co. A third LNG production train and 34m. cu m per day of additional gas-gathering facilities were completed in 1994, raising the plant's capacity to 5m. tons per year. In early 1995 ADGAS made several LNG shipments to Belgian, Spanish and French importers under single-cargo sales agreements. It subsequently secured short-term contracts to supply a total of nearly 1m. tons of LNG to the same customers between July 1995 and April 1996.

ADNOC's ambitious plans for the further expansion of its upstream gas industry have included the Asab field gas development scheme and the onshore gas development programme (OGD). During 2002 it began implementing the biggest investment programme in Abu Dhabi's oil and gas sector for a decade. An estimated US $5,000m. of new engineering, procurement and construction work was to be tendered, with the objective of increasing sustainable oil capacity by 300,000 b/d to within 500,000 b/d of Abu Dhabi's medium-term target at that time of 3m. b/d. In relation to the gas sector, the programme was geared towards meeting an anticipated doubling of demand from 2007 to 3,000m. cu ft/d. The Dolphin project would be crucial in meeting this demand. In March 2009 ADNOC renewed its GASCO concession with Total, Shell, and Partex Oil and Gas for 20 years, and in July signed an agreement with ConocoPhillips to develop natural gas and condensate reservoirs in the Shah gasfield (one of the largest in the Middle East). However, ConocoPhillips withdrew from the project in April 2010, and in January 2011 ADNOC selected Occidental Petroleum as a new partner. Under the new agreement, signed in March, Occidental Petroleum was to hold a 40% participating interest in the 30-year contract.

In 2009 GASCO awarded contracts worth more than US $10,000m. for its Integrated Gas Development facility to process associated gas from the Umm Shaif field and sour gas from Habshan and Ruwais. The facility, with five gas-processing trains, was due to become operational in late 2013. GASCO also awarded a contract to Petrofac to add a fourth natural gas liquid train at the Ruwais plant. Two new gas-processing plants on Das Island and an undersea pipeline are to provide additional volumes to Habshan, as is the Bab Gas

Compression project, which was inaugurated in February. In April ADNOC selected Shell to participate in a 30-year joint venture to develop the major Bab sour gas reservoirs.

Dubai

Dubai is the second largest producer of petroleum in the UAE. In 1963 Conoco acquired the petroleum concession that had been held from 1937 to 1961 by the Iraq Petroleum Co, and formed the Dubai Petroleum Co (DPC), concentrating on offshore production. In 1954 CFP and Hispanoil had obtained an onshore concession, and formed Dubai Marine Areas Ltd (DUMA). DPC acquired a 50% share in DUMA's concession in 1963, and then released some of its shares to other companies, so that by the late 1960s CFP, Hispanoil, Continental Oil, Texaco, Sun Oil and Wintershall all had shares in DUMA-DPC's concession. By 1974 the Government of Dubai had acquired a 60% share in participation in DUMA-DPC. Nevertheless, the former concessionaire companies continued to operate under the same conditions until 1979, when the Government decided to buy back 50% of the production to market it direct.

Although petroleum was first discovered in Dubai in 1966, production did not commence until 1969. Output averaged 34,236 b/d in 1970, rising to 362,346 b/d in 1978. Production was mainly from the two offshore oilfields of Fateh and South West Fateh, but some petroleum was also lifted from the Rashid and Falah offshore fields. In May 1982 a major new onshore discovery was made in the Margham field. A 59-km pipeline, linking the Margham field with the gas-processing plant at Jebel Ali, was brought into operation in April 1989. In August 2006, in a development that signalled the end of the DPC, the Government announced that it would assume direct control of its offshore oil resources, from April 2007, through a new state-owned entity, the Dubai Petroleum Establishment (DPE). The DPE would be responsible for operating the oilfields and for all future business related to hydrocarbons production. In February 2010 the Government reported the discovery of another offshore oilfield, named Al Jalila, to the east of the Rashid field.

During the 1970s Dubai's natural gas was flared off, but in 1980 a gas treatment plant, owned by the Dubai Natural Gas Co (DUGAS), began operations. Dubai's gas reserves were estimated at 125,000m. cu m at that time, and the DUGAS plant, at Jebel Ali, began operations with a treatment capacity of 3m. cu m per day. In 1985 the plant had a production capacity of between 825 and 850 metric tons per day (t/d) of propane, 600 t/d of butane and 850 t/d–900 t/d of condensate. In 1988 DUGAS and two foreign companies, ASCO (of the USA) and BP, signed an agreement to process associated gas from the Margham field at Jebel Ali. Previously this gas had been flared. Construction of a new DUGAS plant to produce methyl-tertiary-butyl ether (MTBE), a lead substitute in petrol, was completed in February 1995. In July 1997 the Dubai-based Emirates National Oil Corpn awarded a contract for the construction of a condensate-processing plant to Technipetrol of Italy. The installation of an unleaded petrol plant was also planned at Jebel Ali. In February 1998 Abu Dhabi agreed to supply Dubai with gas (which was previously supplied mainly by Sharjah). To meet rising demand, the gas and condensate-bearing capacity at the Margham field at Jebel Ali was to be expanded. From 2007 Dubai was to draw on supplies from the regional Dolphin project. In mid-2006 the emirate embarked on the construction of a new LNG facility near Jebel Ali port, with a capacity of up to 3m. metric tons, for storing, blending and trading LNG; the aim was to draw maximum benefits from seasonal gas price differentials. In April 2008 Dubai agreed a contract with Qatargas and Shell to import up to 3m. tons of LNG per year at the Jebel Ali port; the first delivery was made in December 2010.

Sharjah

According to industry sources, Sharjah has the third largest share of the UAE's proven oil reserves, with an estimated 1,500m. barrels. Production of petroleum began in Sharjah in 1974, with the Mubarak field producing at a rate of 60,000 b/d. The field lies in a 'protocol area', which is occupied by Iran, and in the north it lies in Iranian territorial concessions for hydrocarbons exploration. Sharjah has production and drilling rights, but shares production and revenue with Iran. This situation caused considerable difficulties following the onset of hostilities between Iran and Iraq, and in 1984 oil exploration was interrupted when Iranian patrol boats arrived near Abu Musa island. The security problems facing Sharjah became more apparent when Iranian naval forces attacked the Mubarak oilfield in April 1988, thereby causing its closure for a period of two months. At the end of 1980 Amoco announced a major new onshore discovery of petroleum and natural gas. Exports of crude petroleum from this Sajaa field started in mid-1982 at a rate of 25,000 b/d. Sharjah maintained production levels at an average of 65,000 b/d during 1987–90, although in 1991 output was about 25% lower, owing to problems at the Mubarak field. By 1992 output from the Mubarak field had fallen to 8,000 b/d.

Average production from Sharjah's two gasfields, Sajaa 1 and Sajaa 2, reached 16.98m. cu m per day in 1986. A pipeline costing US $190m. was completed in 1984 to carry gas from the Sajaa fields to power stations in Ras al-Khaimah, Fujairah, Ajman and Umm al-Qaiwain, and in 1985 this pipeline had a capacity of 60,000 b/d of condensate and 1.1m. cu m per day of gas. Following the settlement of the border dispute between Sharjah and Dubai in 1985, a pipeline was built to supply gas from the Sajaa field to Dubai's power and desalination plant at Jebel Ali. An agreement was also reached in 1983 for Amoco to drill six wells over the ensuing 15 months, to bring the capacity of the Sajaa field to 14.2m. cu m per day. An LPG plant began production in July 1986, with a capacity of 13,000 b/d of mixed LPGs, 7,500 b/d of propane, 6,000 b/d of butane and 6,000 b/d of condensate.

Many projects were postponed during the recession of the mid-1980s, but the economic revival following the 1990–91 Gulf crisis enabled the Government to revive development plans. In July 1992 the Amoco Sharjah Oil Co (owned 60% by the Sharjah Government and 40% by Amoco Corpn) announced significant new gas discoveries. A new contract to supply gas to power stations in the northern emirates was awarded by the UAE federal authorities in June 1994. It was estimated that 50%–60% of Sharjah's dry gas production was piped to Dubai in 1995, with the remainder going to Sharjah and the northern emirates' power stations. Production of condensates and natural gas liquids was 40,000 b/d–45,000 b/d in that year. In December 1995 Amoco Corpn signed a memorandum of understanding with the Government of Oman, whereby the US company was granted exclusive representation to market Omani gas in the UAE. Amoco's proposal was to build a pipeline from Oman's gasfields to Amoco Sharjah's gas-treatment plant, which would be expanded to deal with a significantly increased throughput.

In July 2002 Sharjah and Ajman announced a joint production-sharing agreement for the development of the offshore Zora gasfield. The announcement was seen as an example of the sort of co-operation between northern emirates that would be necessary for the region to develop its natural resources most efficiently. Negotiations began during 2003 between Emarat (the Emirates General Petroleum Corpn) and Dolphin Energy Ltd to off-take gas from the Dolphin network, via a branch line, to its distribution facility in Sharjah. The gas would be supplied to all the northern emirates. In 2010 the Sharjah National Oil Corpn was established by royal decree, and the local company Crescent Petroleum formed a joint venture with Russia's Rosneft to drill for gas in the emirate.

Ajman, Fujairah, Ras al-Khaimah and Umm al-Qaiwain

Of the remaining emirates, Ras al-Khaimah appears to have the largest reserves of petroleum and natural gas. Offshore discoveries, made in 1976 and 1977, proved not to be commercially exploitable, but Gulf Oil made new discoveries off the west coast in 1981. In the same year an onshore concession was granted to a consortium of Amoco and Gulf Oil, and, following seismic tests, Gulf Oil announced significant discoveries of petroleum and gas in the second offshore test well, Saleh One X, in February 1983. The well started production in February 1984, at 5,000 b/d, followed in April by Saleh Two X, at 3,500 b/d, and production there has since increased. At the beginning of 1985, however, Ras al-Khaimah was producing oil at a rate of only between 8,000 b/d and 10,000 b/d. A new well, Saleh Four X, began operating in February, with a production rate of between 7,000 b/d and 8,000 b/d of oil, and a further well, Saleh Five X, was drilled in April. In 1987 production was only 11,000 b/d, most of the revenue from which was used to finance exploration and development. By the end of 1987 a seventh well had been drilled in the Saleh field, and production was reported to be about 12,000 b/d. By mid-1986 the four-stage programme to establish a downstream oil industry in Ras al-Khaimah, at a cost of US $45m.–$50m., had been completed. This consisted of pipelines from the Saleh field to the mainland, separation and stabilization facilities, onshore storage facilities for 500,000 barrels, and an LPG plant. In 1991 the Omani Government agreed to allow gas from its Bukha offshore field to be processed at Ras al-Khaimah. Output was expected to be limited to around 5,000 b/d of condensate, 800 b/d of LPG and 40 cu ft of dry gas per day. The emirate has been processing gas at Khor Khuwair since 1985, but utilization has been minimal. In January 1996 a new company, Ras al-Khaimah Oil and Gas, whose principal shareholder was a US investor, signed an agreement to undertake onshore and offshore exploration work in the emirate.

Umm al-Qaiwain's first well was drilled in 1981, and a Canadian concession in the emirate was due to start production in 1985. Exploration continued in Umm al-Qaiwain, as it did in Ajman, where drilling for petroleum finally began in 1982. In July 1983 Ajman formed the Ajman National Oil Co, with a capital of US $37m. In February 1984 it was announced that two Canadian oil companies had been granted offshore concessions in Fujairah, and in 1988 Broken Hill Petroleum of Australia conducted a seismic survey offshore from the emirate. In late 1995 a 30,000-b/d refinery, purchased second-hand from a major multinational by the Greek company Metro Oil, went into production in Fujairah. The refinery's product mix was configured to supply the needs of shipping using Fujairah's bunkering facilities. In 1995 Fujairah's deep-water port was one of the world's largest bunkering stations. It had about 500,000 cu m of product storage capacity and was well placed to act as a bulk oil trade centre for the Gulf and the Indian subcontinent. A major new tank-terminal venture, with a projected initial capacity of 465,000 cu m and a projected final capacity of 700,000 cu m, was under development in Fujairah in 1996 by a consortium led by Royal Van Ommeren (a Dutch company with world-wide oil storage interests). A pipeline to deliver crude petroleum from Abu Dhabi's Habshan fields to a new export terminal in Fujairah (providing an alternative export route for Abu Dhabi to avoid the Gulf's congested and strategically vulnerable Strait of Hormuz) became operational in June 2012. In early 2013 it was reported that the Abu Dhabi-owned International Petroleum Investment Co (IPIC) would invest $3,000m. in a new Fujairah refining complex, with a targeted capacity of 250,000 b/d.

ELECTRICITY

The federal Ministry of Energy (formerly the Ministry of Electricity and Water) is responsible for power stations at Umm al-Qaiwain, Falaj al-Mualla, Dhaid, Masfut, Manama, Uzun, Masafi, Fujairah, Qidfa and Dibba. Dubai, Ras al-Khaimah, Sharjah and Abu Dhabi are responsible for their own power. In addition to the old diesel, gas and steam stations, Abu Dhabi's power is provided by the Umm al-Nar East and West stations, Units 9 and 10, a 600-MW station at Bani Yas, and stations at Saadiyat and al-Ain. Until the late 1990s the Government of Abu Dhabi operated power and electricity services direct through the Abu Dhabi Water and Electricity Department (ADWED). However, in early 1998 a government committee recommended that ADWED be transformed into a semi-autonomous regulatory body, the Abu Dhabi Water and Electricity Authority (ADWEA), and that Abu Dhabi's power stations should be partially or totally privatized. In April 1989 it was announced that the Taweelah A power station, under construction since 1984, would begin operation in August 1989, supplying Abu Dhabi with 250 MW of power and 20m. gallons per day (g/d) of water. The second phase, originally approved in January 1987, entailed the construction of a power station (Taweelah B) with a capacity of 732 MW, and a desalination unit with a capacity of 76m. g/d. Work on the Taweelah project was interrupted by the Gulf crisis of 1990–91. The 'turnkey' contract was awarded for the Taweelah B project in July 1992 to a Swiss consortium. The Al-Taweelah Power Co was to manage the Taweelah B facility; with the addition of two new gas-turbine units its capacity would rise to 1,220 MW.

With ever-rising demand for power, the Government has pressed ahead rapidly with expansion projects. By 1994 the total installed capacity of the UAE's power stations was 5,000 MW, while the anticipated demand in 2000 was 7,500 MW. In April 1997 the Abu Dhabi Government approved the US $700m. expansion of the Taweelah A power and desalination plant, to be implemented as an independent water and power project (IWPP). Under its new owners, the Emirates CMS Power joint venture, it assumed full-scale production of electricity and desalinated water in 2001. Plans were also announced for the expansion of the Jebel Ali E station by 232 MW to 472 MW, and for the construction of a new power station, Jebel Ali G, with a capacity of 440 MW. A major generation station built at Mirfa, near Ruwais, already supplied many villages and islands in Abu Dhabi with 246 MW and 16.2m. g/d of water. It was to expand its capacity via an $80m. investment by the new Al Mirfa Power Co. Similar upgrading was planned for the Umm al-Nar plant, run by a private company of the same name. In April 2002 ADWEA invited bids from foreign companies for a 40% stake in the new project company that was to be established to upgrade Umm al-Nar. Later in the same year it was announced that Al Mirfa's capacity was to be increased to 1,500 MW and 100m. g/d once plans to upgrade Umm al-Nar were further advanced. In April 2002 a consortium led by the British company International Power was awarded the contract to build Umm al-Nar. A project company, the Arabian Power Co, was established. ADWEA, with 60%, and International Power, with 20%, were the main shareholders in the new company. In December 1999 bids were received for a 1,500-MW and 100m.-g/d IWPP at Shuweihat, west of Abu Dhabi, and in August 2001 the US/British joint venture CMS Energy and International Power signed a 20-year power and water purchase agreement for the first phase of the project; CMS took a 40% stake in a new utility company, the Shuweihat CMS International Power Co, while ADWEA secured a 60% stake. In December loan-financing agreements were signed for the first phase, and Siemens were awarded the 'turnkey' contract to build the plant. Fisia Italimpianti was awarded the contract to build the associated desalination plant. The cost of construction was estimated at $1,600m., and the plant began commercial operations in 2004.

In July 2002 the Union Water and Electric Co announced its intention to build a 650-MW and 100m.-g/d water and power plant at Qidfa in Fujairah. The plant commenced operations in 2004. In July 2006 ADWEA and Singapore's Sembcorp signed a privatization agreement to expand the Fujairah facility, with Sembcorp acquiring a 40% stake in the project. The project was to involve the addition of a further 225 MW in capacity. The Dubai Electricity and Water Authority (DEWA), which owns and operates its own generating plants, started the third phase of expansion of Al Aweer Power Station H, designed to add 830 MW of new generation capacity and scheduled for completion in 2008. By mid-2006 the total capacity for electricity production in the UAE as a whole had risen to about 16,000 MW, with ADWEA accounting for 53%, DEWA 29%, Sharjah Electricity and Water Authority 11% and the federal Government 7%. In 2007 DEWA invited tenders for the construction of the Hassyan power and desalination plant, which should provide 9,000 MW of electricity and 600m. g/d of water on completion in 2020; and ADWEA started the second phase of the Shuweihat project, with planned capacity of 1,600 MW and 100m. g/d. Also in 2007 Abu Dhabi launched the Masdar renewable energy initiative, including plans to create the first zero-carbon, zero-waste city—with a university (the Masdar Institute of Science and Technology), a special economic zone offering business incentives, and a solar power plant. In January 2008 the Crown Prince of Abu Dhabi announced a US $15,000m. investment in the initiative. In July critical power shortages prompted the Ajman Government to agree a $2,000m. contract with Malaysia's MMC Utilities to develop a 1,000-MW coal-fired power plant.

The federal Government announced in 2009 that it would seek to generate 7% of electricity from renewable energy sources by 2020, and that the newly established International Renewable Energy Agency was to be located in Abu Dhabi. It was also planning the Taweelah C IWPP, with projected capacity of at least 1,500 MW and 100m. g/d of water. In early 2010 the Dubai Government was, for the first time, preparing to invite private investment in the electricity and water sector. DEWA issued a tender for a consultancy contract to manage the launch of its first IWPP at Hassyan and to create an independent regulator. DEWA also increased its generating capacity with the inauguration of a new 600-MW plant at Jebel Ali. At the end of 2010 the Fujairah Asia Power Co, owned by the United Kingdom's International Power and Japan's Marubeni Corpn, was completing a 2,000-MW power and desalination plant project using gas supplied by Dolphin Energy.

In March 2011 the federal Government announced plans to spend US $1,600m. on upgrading the water and electricity infrastructure in the northern emirates, where unemployment among nationals is among the highest, and which suffer most from disruption to power and water supplies. In contrast with Abu Dhabi and Dubai, the northern emirates lack their own water and electricity authorities, and thus depend on federal supplies for the provision of essential utilities.

As a result of the shortage of gas supplies to meet power generation and desalination requirements, the federal Government appointed Thorium Power of the USA to study the feasibility of a nuclear energy programme to meet growing demand, and in 2008 set up the Emirates Nuclear Energy Corpn. The UAE also signed nuclear co-operation agreements with France, the United Kingdom and the USA in that year, and with Japan in January 2009. These developments were followed in December by the award of a US $20,000m. contract to a South Korean-US consortium, led by Korea Electric Power Corpn, to build and operate four nuclear power plants, each with the capacity to generate 1,400 MW. The plants were expected to provide 25% of the UAE's electricity demand by 2020. In January 2012 DEWA announced plans to build a 1,000-MW solar park in Dubai, and in March 2013 the world's largest concentrated solar power plant, Shams 1, began operations in Abu Dhabi's western region.

The federal Government has been engaged in a major project to create an integral power grid in the region of the Cooperation Council of the Arab States of the Gulf (Gulf Cooperation Council—GCC). In mid-2011 the UAE was connected to the grid, which began operating in 2009 and was completed in 2012. The country has also sought to unify its own power grid by connecting stations along its western coast with those in the central region.

INDUSTRY

Since the UAE was formed in 1971, the diversification of the economy away from petroleum has been a clearly stated government policy. Industrial development has been manned largely by immigrant labour.

Abu Dhabi

Most of Abu Dhabi's heavy industry is centred on the Jebel Dhanna-Ruwais industrial zone, 250 km west of Abu Dhabi city, which was officially opened in March 1982. In 1979 the General Industries Corpn (GIC) was set up to co-ordinate non-petroleum development, and an industrial bank, the Emirates Industrial Bank, was founded in 1983 to fund new industrial projects. The government-owned Abu Dhabi Investment Co launched an industrial investment programme in 1993.

A joint-stock company called Abu Dhabi Ship Building (ADSB) was established in 1995 with the US company Newport News (40%) and the Abu Dhabi Government (18.5%) as founding shareholders. The remaining 41.5% of the share capital was raised through a heavily over-subscribed public offering. ADSB's repair and construction facilities for naval and merchant vessels were to be located initially at an established dry dock at Mussafah, pending construction of a purpose-built yard.

A decree was issued in July 1996 to establish Abu Dhabi's first free zone on Saadiyat island, east of Abu Dhabi city, with the aim of investing US $3,300m. to develop storage, transportation and trading facilities for various commodities, from ores, grain and foodstuffs to precious metals and gems. The island is linked to Abu Dhabi city by a 6-km bridge. In August 1997 it was announced that both local and international investors would be offered a $1,700m. equity stake in the initial public offering in the Saadiyat Free Zone Authority (which would regulate the free zone). A project development company would build and operate the facilities on the island under a 25-year renewable concession agreement.

In its drive to develop and diversify the emirate's economy, the Abu Dhabi Government established the Higher Corpn for Specialized Economic Zones in June 2004 to develop strategic industry clusters and promote investment through the creation of dedicated zones with integrated modern infrastructure and services. The first of many planned specialized zones, the Industrial City of Abu Dhabi (ICAD), was subsequently established in Mussafah. By late 2005 some 45 factories were operational in the zone. In December ICAD 2 was launched, and the Government also passed a law to attract foreign investment into the emirate by allowing 100% ownership by foreign investors in the specialized zones. In late 2010 the first phase of the Khalifa Industrial Zone Abu Dhabi (KIZAD) project was launched by the Abu Dhabi Ports Co. The venture would be one of the largest integrated industrial zones in the world, and would offer full foreign ownership for investors. New industrial development projects approved by the Government in January 2012 included the construction of two new industrial zones in Ruwais and Medinat Zayed, and major investment in automobile manufacturing.

In 2007 Emirates Aluminium, a joint venture between Abu Dhabi's Mubadala Development Co. and Dubai Aluminium (DUBAL), began the US $5,700m. first-phase development of greenfield aluminium smelter plant at Taweelah. The smelter became operational in December 2009, and full first-phase capacity of 750,000 metric tons per year was reached at the start of 2011. In mid-2011 a further investment of $4,500m., to increase capacity in the second phase to 1.3m. tons per year by 2014, was announced. The Mubadala Development Co and the Investment Corpn of Dubai announced in June 2013 the creation of Emirates Global Aluminium—a jointly-held, equal-ownership company to integrate the businesses of DUBAL and Emirates Aluminium.

Petrochemical industry developments in the emirate have included the establishment of the FERTIL fertilizer complex and an ethane cracker at the Abu Dhabi Polymers Co complex, both at Ruwais. The Abu Dhabi National Chemical Co, established in 2008 and part-owned by ADNOC, announced plans to build two integrated chemical plants, and in 2009 Borouge, a plastics company jointly owned by ADNOC and Austria's Borealis, signed a US $2,600m. contract to expand polyethylene and polypropylene production facilities at Ruwais.

Large-scale construction projects proliferated in Abu Dhabi in 2005–06, creating opportunities for local and international investors. Major schemes included the 20-sq km Mohammed bin Zayed City, the Abu Dhabi central market development, the Al-Gurm resort scheme and the Raha Beach complex. However, many projects stalled in 2008 with the onset of the international financial crisis and economic downturn. In April 2011 Abu Dhabi's Urban Planning Council awarded contracts worth a total of US $5,700m. for new residential and commercial property development in order to meet supply shortages. In May 2012 the government-owned Aabar Investments signed an agreement with China State Construction Engineering Corpn to undertake property development projects worth $2,000m. in Abu Dhabi, with funding from the Industrial and Commercial Bank of China.

Dubai

Dubai has taken the lead in developing non-petroleum industry and attracting foreign investors as an offshore financial, business and tourism centre. This has been centred on the Jebel Ali port and industrial area, 30 km west of Dubai city.

The first major plant to begin production in Dubai was an aluminium smelter, which commenced operations at the end of 1979. It was built at a cost of US $800m., and initially had an installed capacity of 135,000 metric tons of aluminium ingots per year. Following a series of expansions, production capacity had increased to 960,000 tons per year by 2009. An industrial plant operated by cable manufacturer DUCAB also began production in 1979. By 1994 DUCAB produced nearly 20,000 tons of copper and aluminium cable. In 1995 it expanded its product range to include specialist lead-sheathed cables for the oil, gas and petrochemical industries. Initially, DUCAB was jointly owned by BICC of the United Kingdom and the Dubai Government, but in June 1997 the Abu Dhabi Government bought a 35% share in the company.

In 1980, in an effort to promote Dubai's industrial development, Sheikh Rashid decreed that Jebel Ali should be a free trade zone. The Jebel Ali Free Zone Authority, offering the advantages of duty-free trade, was finally inaugurated, under full foreign ownership, in 1985. By mid-1994 around 630 companies had set up businesses in the Jebel Ali Free Zone, and new companies were arriving there at an average rate of 15 per month. Major foreign companies locating there included Xerox, Union Carbide, 3M, Black & Decker, Mitsubishi, York International, BP Amoco Arabian Agencies and Shell Markets. Local firms at Jebel Ali include Dubai's National Cement Co and the National Flour Mills. A second area for light industry was also developed around the extended port area of Mina Rashid in Dubai itself.

The authorities introduced a new law in 1993 that explicitly excluded licensed national firms from the 'offshore' provisions of the original free trade zone legislation; confirmed their liability to the provisions of Dubai's standard company laws; and made the granting of a licence subject to proof of at least 51% UAE or GCC ownership of the company concerned and at least 40% locally added value in its products. It was hoped that the removal of former ambiguities would encourage more local companies to take advantage of the infrastructure benefits of manufacturing within the zone.

In 1994 the Jebel Ali Free Zone Authority adopted a policy of not granting new licences to garment manufacturers, on the grounds that it did not wish to encourage labour-intensive industries. By mid-2006 more than 1,000 companies were operating in the zone, drawn from all parts of the world. Distribution and sales operations (often serving markets far beyond the Gulf region) outnumbered manufacturing and assembly operations by about two to one, although manufacturing and assembly accounted for some four-fifths of total investment in the zone. At this time India's Southern Petroleum Industries Corpn announced plans to locate a fertilizer plant at Jebel Ali to serve the Indian market.

Dubai's investment in high-technology ventures has included its US $200m. Internet City (DIC), a 25-sq km collection of offices to attract international names in e-commerce. By September 2000 a total of 180 companies had apparently rented all available space in the DIC, which included an internet university.

The Burj Dubai skyscraper became the world's tallest building in July 2007 as it reached 512 m during construction, to surpass the Taipei 101 office block in the Republic of China (Taiwan). By January 2010, when the building (renamed Burj Khalifa) was officially opened, it had reached a height of some 828 m. However, by late 2008, as market conditions deteriorated in the context of the global financial crisis, other prestigious projects, including Jumeirah Gardens (planned by real estate company Meraas Development as an integrated city in central Dubai) and proposals by the financially exposed property developer Nakheel (see Budget, Banking and Finance) to build a 1 km-high tower, were postponed.

In October 2012 Link Global Group proposed a US $1,000m. project to construct a replica of India's Taj Mahal in Dubai, which would include hotel, retail and commercial premises. In November the Dubai Government announced plans for a major development by Dubai Holding and Emaar Properties, Muhammad bin Rashid City, which was to incorporate the largest shopping mall in the world, as well as leisure and entertainment facilities.

The Northern Emirates

Industrial development in the remaining emirates has been based largely on the construction industry and port expansion. Two container ports have been developed in Sharjah, where there is also a lubricating oil plant, a rope factory, the Sharjah Oxygen Co, a factory making plastic pipes and a cement plant. The Gulf Industries Complex in Sharjah's industrial zone opened in 1981, producing furniture and household utensils. In the following year a fodder factory opened at Mina Khaled, operated by the Gulf Co for Agricultural Development. An LPG plant came into operation on the site in 1986. Sharjah had built 15 industrial parks on the border with Dubai by 1996. The main industries are food, furniture, gold and jewellery, plastics and building materials. By 2001 Sharjah's share of the UAE's light and medium-sized industries had risen to 43%; a total of 1,052 manufacturing units had been set up in the emirate. In 2002 manufacturing contributed 19% to Sharjah's GDP. Heavy industry is concentrated in Hamriyah Free Zone. The continued growth in the industrial sector in Sharjah has put heavy pressure on gas capacity, and high prices are the main deterrent to potential investors. The emirate's Economic Development Department registered 5,351 new companies in 2005 (up from 4,145 in 2004), while licence renewals increased to 31,142 in 2005 (from 22,725 in 2004). By early 2006 Sharjah accounted for about 45% of the UAE's industrial output, with 19 industrial areas and two free zones. In 2006 the Essar Group was planning a 1m.-metric tons-per-year steel rolling mill in Hamriyah Free Zone, and Saudi Arabia's Al-Ruya Industries was pursuing the construction of a 3.6m.-tons-per-year cement plant, also in the Hamriyah zone.

Ras al-Khaimah has developed a valuable export business in aggregate (stones used in making concrete) from the Hajar Mountains. The first explosives factory in the Gulf was opened there in 1980, and a pharmaceutical factory was opened in 1981. The emirate also established an asphalt company and a lime kiln, and in 1981 the Ras al-Khaimah Co for White Cement was created to build the Gulf's first white cement factory at Khor Khuwair. This joint Kuwaiti-UAE venture commenced operations in 1986, producing 300,000 metric tons of white cement per year. More recently, prestigious real estate projects under way in the emirate in early 2007 included: Airport City, a mixed-use development surrounding the emirate's international airport; Al-Marjan Island, a 3.8-sq km hotel, residential and marina complex; Gateway City, a business and exhibition centre; and Mina al-Arab, a US $5,430m. tourism and leisure coastal development. In an effort to develop a downstream petrochemicals industry, initiated in 2005, Ras al-Khaimah planned a joint venture with Iran's National Petrochemical Co to build a 320,000-tons-per-year monoethylene glycol complex in the emirate.

At the end of 1980 the Government of Fujairah established a Department of Industry and Economy to organize industrial development. The emirate has since set up factories producing marble, tiles, rockwool insulation, concrete blocks, tyres and shoes. Many of these industries use materials from the Hajar Mountains, where surveys have indicated significant quantities of copper, chromite, talc and magnesium. Commercial production of 1,600 metric tons per day began at a new cement plant in Dibba in 1982, when Fujairah's US $4.9m. rockwool factory also started operations, with an annual capacity of 5,000 tons. Cement production capacity was due to rise to 2,500 tons per day during 1996. A new, 11-berth port was opened in Fujairah in 1982. A crushing plant, designed to produce 3m. tons per year of aggregate for cement production, went into production in 1985. A free zone facility in Fujairah was the base for 55 enterprises in mid-1995. Its total trade volume in the first half of that year was 6,152m. tons (principally foodstuffs, textiles, electronic goods, medical equipment, packaging and steel commodities), with a value of AED 260m. In 2005 a joint venture of the Fujairah Government, Dubai Investment Group and Egypt's Orascom Construction Industries established Emirates Cement Co to build a $360m., 3,000-tons-per-day cement facility in the Hast al-Bana area.

Umm al-Qaiwain has concentrated on construction, with cement production and related activities as the dominant sector. A free zone was established by royal decree in 1987. Large-scale real estate projects in progress in 2010 included Al Salam City, a US $8,300m. commercial, residential and retail complex (which had been on hold since 2008 as a result of difficulties regarding electricity and water supplies) and White Bay, a $4,000m. residential and commercial community scheme.

Ajman, the smallest emirate, has a cement factory, a dry dock and a ship repair yard. There is a pressing need for improved infrastructure there. In December 2001 an international consortium was awarded a wastewater concession by the Ajman Government, construction of which began in February 2003. In 1991 the federal Government announced plans for a 240-MW increase in the electricity production capacity of the northern emirates. Contracts to install an extra 210 MW of capacity were awarded in late 1994. Plans were being drawn up in 1995 for new west-coast electricity distribution links between Ras al-Khaimah, Ajman and Umm al-Qaiwain, while a proposal to connect the northern emirates to the Abu Dhabi grid was under consideration as a future development option. In 1997 the federal Ministry of Electricity and Water signed contracts for the interconnection of the west-coast power distribution network in the northern emirates.

AGRICULTURE

Since the establishment by FAO of an agricultural experimental station at Digdagga (Ras al-Khaimah) in 1955, agriculture in the UAE has undergone a transformation. Traditionally, agriculture was based on nomadic pastoralism, in association with some oasis cultivation on the east coast and at Liwa, Dhaid, al-Ain and Falaj al-Mualla. This cultivation was totally dominated by dates. Although dates are still the major crop in terms of area cultivated (producing an estimated return of 775,000 metric tons in 2010), production of vegetables has increased dramatically—particularly tomatoes, output of which was 165,000 tons in 2010. This increase in vegetable cultivation and an extensive forestry programme have nevertheless led to problems with the water tables, which the Government has attempted to alleviate through the construction of desalination plants.

The UAE's livestock in 2011 numbered 20m. chickens, 2m. goats, 1.4m. sheep, 390,000 camels and 64,000 cattle, according to FAO estimates. In the same year the UAE's total annual fishing catch was 75,319 metric tons.

TRADE, TRANSPORT, TOURISM AND COMMUNICATIONS

During the 1970s the UAE's earnings from exports of petroleum enabled the country to retain a healthy overall balance of trade. Decreases in output of petroleum in the early 1980s resulted in a relative decline in the country's trade surplus. The Iran–Iraq War of 1980–88 brought considerable problems for the economies of other countries in the region, but Dubai continued to benefit from its trade links with Iran. Trade surpluses were markedly lower in 1992–94, but from 1995 they began steadily to widen. Both exports and imports rose, but the rate of growth of the former outstripped the latter. By 2007 the balance of trade had achieved a surplus in 2007 amounting to AED 170,850m. The value of exports in that year increased to AED 664,345m., while imports reached AED 428,194m. According to the Central Bank, the surplus narrowed from AED 231,092m. in 2008 to AED 154,760m. in 2009, largely reflecting a decline in the value of exports by the hydrocarbons sector. Export revenue fell from AED 878,508m. in 2008 to AED 705,828m. in 2009, while the cost of imports also declined, from AED 647,417m. to AED 551,068m. There was an increase in the trade surplus in 2010, mainly because of higher petroleum prices. The surplus widened to AED 186,849m., with exports valued at AED 779,639m. and imports at AED 592,790m. Estimates for both 2011 and 2012 indicated further rises in the surplus, to AED 291,951m. and AED 470,900m., respectively, as exports reached AED 1,034,323m. in 2011 and AED 1,285,828m. in 2012, compared with imports of AED 742,372m. and AED 814,889m., respectively.

The UAE was admitted to the General Agreement on Tariffs and Trade (GATT) in 1994, and to its successor, the World Trade Organization (WTO), in 1996. Negotiations with the USA over a free trade agreement commenced in March 2005, but have since stalled.

One way in which trade has been allocated is through the designation of free trade zones, such as Jebel Ali and Port Zayed. From April 1982 customs duties in Dubai and Sharjah were lowered from 3% to 1%, to bring them in line with Abu Dhabi. In 1983 all the emirates introduced a 4% unified import tariff, following a GCC unified economic agreement in 1981, although this tariff was not uniformly applied throughout the federation until August 1994 (when individual emirates formally abandoned inconsistent customs practices). Imports from within the GCC area were exempt from the 4% tariff, as were many industrial raw materials, agricultural inputs, medicines and certain food items. The GCC unified tariff has not been properly observed by other member states within the region. The UAE supported a relaunch of the initiative at the December 2001 GCC summit meeting in Muscat, Oman, at which it was agreed that a 5% unified tariff would come into effect in January 2003. The Jebel Ali Free Zone has offered various incentives to investors, including: the right to 100% foreign ownership; the absence of taxes, import or export duties; and the right to full repatriation of profits and capital. There has also been an ample supply of cheap labour. In December 2007 the GCC summit held in Qatar agreed to launch the Gulf common market, which—in addition to allowing the free flow of capital—would give GCC nationals freedom of movement, residency and employment in any of the six countries. The common market duly entered effect in January 2008.

One of the main characteristics of the country's economy over recent years has been the expansion in the number of major airports. Dubai International Airport is the busiest of the UAE's airports, handling 41m. passengers in 2009, 47.2m. in 2010, 51.0m. in 2011 and a record 57.7m. in 2012. In July 2011 the Dubai Government approved expenditure of AED 28,800m. to expand the capacity of Dubai International from 60m. to 90m. passengers per year by 2018. A second airport in Dubai—Al Maktoum International Airport—was opened at Jebel Ali in June 2010; it was initially to be used exclusively by cargo carriers, with passenger services to be launched at a later date. The new airport was expected to have a total annual passenger-handling capacity of 160m. upon completion. Traffic through Abu Dhabi International Airport increased by some 20% per year from 2001, taking the total number of passengers to 5m. by 2005. A US $6,800m. expansion of the airport began in 2011, to allow further growth and to increase annual passenger capacity to 20m. In March 2006 the Government formed the Abu Dhabi Airports Co to operate all airports within the emirate. The international airport in Sharjah handles the bulk of the UAE's air cargo, as well as providing up-to-date facilities for passengers. Although Sharjah airport is also in the process of being upgraded, its proximity to Dubai International Airport has led to a downturn in its fortunes. The other UAE airports are in al-Ain, Fujairah and Ras al-Khaimah. It was announced in mid-2006 that Ras al-Khaimah's international airport would spend AED 1,000m. up to the end of 2008 on an expansion project set to continue until 2020. In December 2007 Ajman awarded a contract to build and operate an international airport to a Spanish consortium.

Dubai founded its own operator, Emirates Airline, in 1985, and Abu Dhabi's national carrier, Etihad Airways, was established in 2003. Ras al-Khaimah's RAK Airways, which was established in 2006, briefly ceased operations in 2009–10 because of financial strains. Dubai's new budget airline, flydubai (Dubai Aviation Corpn), meanwhile, started its first flights in 2009. Having issued a US $1,000m. bond in June 2011, in November Emirates placed a record $18,000m. order for 50 Boeing 777 aircraft. It had earlier placed a major order for additional Airbus A380 aircraft. Etihad Airways, which in 2011 handled 8.29m. passengers and reported its first annual profit, has sought investment opportunities overseas, taking stakes in Air Berlin (Germany), Air Seychelles, Aer Lingus (Ireland) and Virgin Australia. In September 2012 Emirates Airline announced a 10-year alliance with Qantas Airways to compete for a share of the Australian market.

Port facilities in the UAE have been greatly expanded, particularly at the Dubai ports of Mina Jebel Ali and Mina Rashid. In 2002 the shipbuilding facility at a new port at Taweelah in Abu Dhabi was opened, and in 2003 work to deepen Mina Jebel Ali's main basin was completed, opening up the port to a new generation of container vessels. A project was announced in January 2003 to increase the capacity of Mina Jebel Ali to 21.8m. 20-foot equivalent units (TEUs) by 2020. Throughput at Sharjah's port, Khor Fakkan, in that year was 1.44m. TEUs. In February 2006 Dubai Ports World (DP World—created in September 2005 by the merger of the Dubai Ports Authority and Dubai Ports International) completed an arrangement to take control of the British ports and shipping firm P&O. In March, however, faced with US congressional hostility to the takeover, it agreed to sell off P&O's US port interests. In mid-2008 DP World, in partnership with ZIM Ports of Israel, agreed to purchase the Spanish port operator Contarsa, owner of the concession for the Tarragona Container Port Terminal. In May 2006 it was reported that Sharjah was developing a maritime city in Hamriyah Free Zone as an exclusive zone for shipbuilding and servicing, and for marine infrastructure related to the oil and gas sector. Sharjah's port facilities have been expanded with the completion of a project to increase handling capacity at Khor Fakkan Container Terminal and further development of Hamriyah port. Abu Dhabi, meanwhile, has been in the process of transferring its container traffic from the older Mina Zayed terminal to the new Khalifa port at Taweelah (which inaugurated commercial operations in September 2012). Khalifa will also accommodate new cargo generated by the surrounding industrial zone (KIZAD), and is expected to become one of the largest ports in the world when all phases are completed. DP World listed on the London Stock Exchange in June 2011, with the aim of attracting a broader range of investors.

Following Dubai Municipality's decision in 2002 to develop an urban rail transit system, the authority awarded the AED 14,300m. contract to Dubai Rapid Link (DURL—a consortium headed by Mitsubishi Corpn of Japan) in mid-2005, soon after which construction work began. The first phase of the advanced driverless Dubai Light Rail (or Metro) project, with 10 of the 29 planned stations in operation on the Red Line, opened in September 2009. By late 2011 a total of 27 stations were in operation. The Green Line was inaugurated in September 2011, with 18 of its planned 20 stations in operation. In May 2006 it was announced that Abu Dhabi would build a metro system, to be linked to the Dubai Light Rail, as part of a public transport master plan for the period up to 2030. In March 2009 the federal Government formally approved the construction of the first phase of a 1,500-km rail network linking all the emirates, to be overseen by Etihad Rail (formerly the Union Railway Co). The construction contract, worth AED 3,300m., was awarded in October 2011 to a consortium led by Italy's Saipem.

Plans for the construction of a causeway between the UAE and Qatar were announced in December 2004, but further progress was delayed because of Saudi Arabia's objections to the proposed route. A new 75-km motorway linking Fujairah and Dubai opened in 2011. In March 2006 Sharjah launched a major road construction and upgrading programme, costing an estimated AED 2,000m., while in June and July of that year contracts were tendered for a bridge and highway linking the Abu Dhabi port area and international airport with Saadiyat island. In mid-2007 Dubai launched a US $12,000m. road construction plan for the period to 2020, envisaging 500 km of new roadways, 95 new interchanges and nine new ring roads. In January 2012 Abu Dhabi approved the construction of the Mafraq–Ghoueifat highway, which will link the emirate with neighbouring countries, and also the expansion of the existing Emirates Road between Abu Dhabi and Dubai.

The UAE's tourism industry has undergone rapid expansion. In Dubai, the principal centre for UAE tourism, the main emphasis has been on diversification into luxury beach and resort developments catering predominantly for holiday-makers—rather than the business travellers who constituted the core clientele of many of Dubai's older-established hotels. Promotion of the UAE as a year-round destination for 'sunshine tourism' has been aimed principally at the upper end of the European, Japanese and US markets. An ambitious project was announced in May 2001 to develop 120 km of coastline in Dubai: the Palm Islands Project involved the construction of 2,000 residential villas, as many as 40 hotels and extensive other tourist facilities. In April 2003 plans were made public for another major offshore tourism project in Dubai, the Globe Archipelago, at an estimated cost of US $409m., and in August of the same year plans for the construction of Hydropolis, a $550m., 220-suite underwater hotel, were announced. Construction of the Dubai Sports City complex was also under way by 2005. Ski Dubai, an indoor mountain-themed ski resort and retail complex, opened in Dubai in November of that year. Annual tourist arrivals in Dubai reached 10.6m. by 2012, and in May 2013 the Government announced that it aimed to attract 20m. visitors each year by 2020.

Abu Dhabi is seeking to increase the number of visitors to 3m. per year by 2015, from fewer than 1m. in 2004. During 2005 the Abu Dhabi Tourism Authority (ADTA, formed in 2004) approved private hotel projects adding 4,000 extra hotel rooms and apartments over three years. In April 2006 ADTA set up a subsidiary, the Tourism Development and Investment Co, to develop the emirate's flagship Saadiyat Island project. Costing $27,000m., the project would transform the 27-sq km natural island, 500 m off shore from Abu Dhabi City, into an international tourism destination in three phases between 2006 and 2018. The Yas Marina Circuit opened in November 2009 in Abu Dhabi, and hosted the UAE's inaugural Formula One motor-racing Grand Prix. Sharjah received 1.3m. tourists in 2005, compared with just 650,000 five years earlier. Total tourist arrivals to the UAE increased from 6.8m. in 2009 to 7.4m. in 2010, and to a provisional 8.1m. in 2011. In 2012 the Abu Dhabi Authority for Tourism and Culture replaced the emirate's two main tourism agencies, the ADTA and the Abu Dhabi Authority for Culture and Heritage. In May 2013 the UAE rejoined the World Tourism Organization.

According to the Telecommunications Regulatory Authority (TRA), there were an estimated 11.2m. mobile phone subscribers, 1.7m. landline subscriptions and 1.4m. internet subscribers at the beginning of 2011. The GCC region (including the UAE) has a much higher internet penetration than the Arab world as a whole. In February 2000 the UAE created an Electronic Commerce and Media Zone to encourage international and regional Arab media firms to relocate. However, a law of 1988 still applies that encourages self-censorship in the established newspapers, and this may have dissuaded media concerns from moving to the UAE. In August 2003 the state-run Emirates Telecommunications Corpn (Etisalat) invited international equipment suppliers to submit bids for a third-generation (3G) mobile network, the second such network in the Middle East. In December 2005 Emirates Integrated Telecommunications Co (du) was established as the UAE's second national licensed (and first integrated) telecommunications operator, providing mobile, fixed-line and broadband internet services. In May 2006 the TRA signed a new, 20-year full-service licence agreement with Etisalat; and in August of that year it was announced that Etisalat and du had agreed to connect their networks, having resolved all commercial, technical and legal issues. Following severe disruption to communication networks in the Gulf region in January and February 2008, Etisalat, together with Saudi Telecom, Telecom Egypt and Ogero of Lebanon, agreed to invest US $400m. in a new undersea cable between India and Europe. In March 2010 the TRA awarded Al-Yah Satellite Communications Co a 10-year contract to establish satellite telecommunications services. In December 2012 the Government outlined a new tax structure to be applied to the telecommunication operators' revenues and profits until 2016.

BUDGET, BANKING AND FINANCE

The unit of currency in the UAE is the dirham, which was created in 1973 to replace the Bahraini dinar and the Qatar/Dubai riyal, formerly used in the emirates. With effect from March 1996 'AED' superseded 'Dh' as the Central Bank's official abbreviation for the currency unit. The dirham is linked officially to the IMF's Special Drawing Right (SDR), but in practice to the US dollar. In December 2001 the GCC summit in Muscat agreed to establish a single currency for the region, to be called the dinar, by January 2010. However, following the decision in May 2009 to locate the headquarters of the GCC Monetary Council in Riyadh, Saudi Arabia, the UAE federal Government announced that it would not join the currency arrangement.

In many economic matters, the individual emirates have pursued their own separate policies, although they rarely publish detailed budgets. Abu Dhabi (as the largest emirate and principal oil producer) and, to a lesser extent, Dubai are by far the biggest contributors to the federal budget (which only forms part of the UAE's consolidated fiscal account).

The 1995 federal budget provided for total spending of AED 17,949m. and total revenue of AED 16,903m., leaving a deficit of AED 1,046m. The deficit rose gradually during 1996–98. In 1999, however, there was a small surplus (of AED 63m. from revenue of AED 20,268m. and expenditure of AED 20,205m.), but the budget returned to deficit in 2000 and 2001. The draft budget for 2002 projected a deficit of AED 2,169m. from revenue of AED 20,987m. and expenditure of AED 23,156m.

The 2003 budget anticipated an increased deficit of AED 2,207m., which, as in previous years, was likely to be offset by petroleum prices reaching a higher level than projected. None the less, the IMF advised that further privatizations were needed in order to close the gap between revenue and expenditure. The Council of Ministers approved a slightly smaller draft deficit for 2004 of AED 2,160m; 42.2% of the increased total expenditure (of AED 23,880m.) was earmarked for the justice and security sector. The 2005 budget anticipated a fiscal balance that was again likely to result in an actual surplus due to higher than forecast petroleum prices. According to an official economic report issued in June 2006, the UAE recorded a surplus in the consolidated government financial accounts in 2005, after two decades of fiscal deficit. The Council of Ministers approved its second balanced federal budget in March 2006, forecasting revenue and expenditure for the year of AED 27,880m., although a surplus was again likely to be recorded because of surging petroleum prices. The budgets for 2007, 2008 and 2009 similarly maintained a fiscal balance, with revenue and expenditure forecast at AED 28,425m., AED 34,900m. and AED 42,200m., respectively.

The federal budget for 2010 projected an increase of 3.4% in expenditure, to AED 43,600m. Social sectors, including education and health, were to receive 41% of total expenditure, with a further 17.5% for infrastructure development (although a considerable proportion of spending on infrastructure projects is borne by individual emirates rather than the federal authorities). Meanwhile, Dubai's 2010 budget projected a decline in expenditure of about 6%, and a fall in revenue of some 12%, in the wake of the collapse of the property sector. A deficit equivalent to 2% of GDP was forecast for the year. The budget for 2011 projected a 6% decrease in expenditure, to AED 41,000m. The spending plan was part of a three-year budget for 2011–13 (the first multi-year budget to be introduced in the UAE). Revenue was forecast at AED 38,000m., leaving a deficit of AED 3,000m. Abu Dhabi was expected to contribute about 19% less to federal revenue in 2011 than in 2010; the emirate projected its own 2011 budget to be balanced, after having run deficits in both 2009 and 2010. Dubai, in its budget, projected revenue of AED 29,900m. and expenditure of AED 33,700m. for 2011 (a decline of 6.4% compared with spending in 2010). A marginal increase in expenditure, to AED 41,800m., with revenue of AED 41,400m., was forecast in the 2012 federal budget, resulting in a small deficit. Dubai's 2012 budget projected a 4.4% decrease in expenditure, to AED 32,200m., and a deficit of AED 1,800m. According to the IMF, Abu Dhabi was to start implementing a fiscal consolidation plan in 2012, having completed a review of its development strategy. In November the Government approved a balanced federal budget for 2013, which envisaged a 6.7% increase in expenditure to AED 44.600m., with revenue projected to rise by 7.7%. The federal budget only accounts for around 11% of total expenditure, while the individual emirates account for the remainder. The Dubai budget increased public spending for 2013 by 6%.

In 1991 the Bank of Commerce and Credit International (BCCI), operating in many countries around the world and in which the Abu Dhabi Government was a major shareholder and depositor, collapsed after a damaging scandal involving widespread fraud and money-laundering. Following years of international litigation and creditor compensation claims, in mid-2013 the UAE central bank formally announced the liquidation of BCCI branches in the emirates. With effect from July 1993, the central bank had introduced new banking regulations whereby the minimum ratio for capital adequacy was raised to 10% (2% higher than the internationally recommended minimum). Moreover, the legal definition of a bank's 'core' capital and its 'supplementary' capital was re-specified in accordance with current international standards. All on- and off-balance-sheet items were required to be ranked according to a schedule of risk. Banks were required to maintain a minimum level of 10% of total risk-weighted assets relative to their capital base, in which core capital must reach a minimum of 6% of total risk-weighted assets, while supplementary capital would be considered only up to a maximum of 67% of core capital. Banks would henceforth be required to report to the central bank every three months.

In October 1993 the central bank issued a circular tightening the banking regulations still further with effect from the beginning of 1994 (with provision for deferral on a case-by-case basis until the end of 1995). This circular limited any bank's exposure to the following proportion of its capital base: 25% if the exposure was to a government-owned commercial entity; 5% to a director or board member, and no more than 25% in aggregate to the bank's entire board; 6% in aggregate to bank employees; 7% to one of its shareholders, to a single borrower, or to a group of related borrowers; 20% to a subsidiary or affiliate. There were also ceilings on funded inter-bank exposures, letters of credit and guarantee, and other contingent liabilities. Banks were required to report large exposures (including those of subsidiaries) to the central bank on a quarterly basis, a large exposure being defined in the circular as all exposures to a single borrower or a group of related borrowers that total 7% or more of a bank's capital base. The central bank later agreed to exclude contingent liabilities from its definition of a large exposure, which was to be calculated after deductions for provisions, cash collateral and deposits under lien. It also agreed to draw up a list of acceptable securities against which banks would be permitted to lend without reference to the 'large exposure' limits. During 1994 UAE banks increased their capital by more than US $200m. in order to comply with international adequacy standards and UAE banking regulations.

The reputation of the UAE's banking system was the subject of renewed scrutiny following the suicide attacks on the mainland USA in September 2001, when it emerged that financial transactions between branches of Citibank in the UAE and the USA had provided the means to finance the attacks. In late September the UAE central bank froze the assets of some 27 individuals and organizations accused of sponsoring terrorist activities; at least 62 private bank accounts were suspended. In October a decree was issued that sought to prohibit the laundering of funds through the UAE's banking sector; henceforth all banks were required to inform the Central Bank of the receipt or transfer of amounts in excess of US $10,900. Those convicted on charges connected to money-laundering activities, furthermore, would receive increased fines and prison sentences of up to seven years. The decree also formally established a national commission to seek to combat such practices. However, the *hawala* finance system—a traditional alternative remittance system operating outside the control of the conventional banking sector—was unaffected by the changes.

In July 2007 Abu Dhabi issued its US $1,000m. inaugural sovereign bond. Also in that month the National Bank of Dubai and Emirates Bank International agreed the terms of a merger, creating Emirates NBD—the largest bank in the UAE and one of the largest in the GCC.

The UAE, and particularly Dubai, were affected adversely by the turmoil in global financial markets in the latter half of 2008. Despite their strong profit growth in preceding years, banks were overexposed to property market financing. The central bank created an AED 50,000m. emergency lending facility to maintain liquidity in September; and, while asserting that the financial system remained strong, it announced in October a three-year guarantee on the deposits of local banks, and of foreign banks with core operations in the UAE. In February 2009 Abu Dhabi announced that it would inject a further US $4,300m. into five of its own banks, and Dubai announced a $20,000m. bond issue, one-half of which was purchased by the central bank (demonstrating the federal Government's commitment to supporting Dubai and reassuring the financial markets). Meanwhile, the central bank took measures to strengthen banking supervision, including the establishment of a new Financial Stability Unit.

In July 2009 the Dubai Financial Support Fund (DFSF) was established to support state-backed entities and projects deemed to be of strategic importance within the emirate. Concerns remained, however, about Dubai's ability to meet its financial commitments, particularly the repayment by Dubai World's property development subsidiary, Nakheel, of a US $3,500m. Islamic bond due to mature in December. In September 2009 Dubai World began debt-rescheduling talks with banks, seeking a 'standstill' on property-related debt until May 2010 to allow time for an orderly restructuring. The standstill and restructuring would apply to bilateral bank loans, syndicated loans and bonds. The announcement led credit ratings agencies to downgrade most of Dubai's government-owned companies. In December 2009 it was announced that Abu Dhabi had extended a bail-out credit to address Dubai World's obligations and to protect the UAE economy and banking system. The DFSF authorized the repayment of the Islamic bond, while a new insolvency regime was to be implemented to facilitate the restructuring of other debt. In mid-2010 Dubai World announced that it had agreed with creditors the terms of a restructuring arrangement covering $23,500m. of debt. The Dubai Government would also convert $8,900m. of its loans to Dubai World into equity. Meanwhile, the state-backed investment conglomerate Dubai Holding also entered into talks with advisers over the restructuring of its debt. To limit future excessive borrowing, in December of that year the federal Government approved new legislation to place a ceiling on public debt (set at 25% of GDP) and to regulate the issuing and trading of government securities.

The IMF estimated that Dubai held US $31,000m. of debt due in 2011–12, and that the emirate's total debt stood at $113,000m.—68% of which was owed by GREs. Abu Dhabi's total debt amounted to $104,000m., also with the greater proportion (88%) stemming from GRE borrowings. In late 2010 and early 2011 Dubai Holding companies Dubai International Capital and Dubai Holding Commercial Operations Group agreed restructuring and refinancing deals, while several other GREs similarly entered into debt-restructuring negotiations with banks. In June 2011 Nakheel reached an agreement whereby it would be separated from its parent company and brought under the direct management of the Dubai Government. The Investment Corpn of Dubai, with stakes in prominent Dubai entities including Emirates Airline and DP World, was also enabled to raise a refinancing loan. Earlier in the year Abu Dhabi had provided a $5,200m. package to support Aldar Properties, one of the emirate's largest property developers. The Dubai Government had, meanwhile, set up the Tayseer programme in 2010 to arrange funding for various stalled construction and development projects, and in 2011 it began to provide financial services to property developers. After the Dubai World restructuring agreement had been finalized, in September 2010 the Dubai Government had returned to the market with a $1,250m. bond issue, which was four times oversubscribed. The Government also successfully issued a $500m. 10-year bond in June of that year, and announced its intention to raise up to a further $5,000m. under a new bond programme. In Abu Dhabi, meanwhile, issues included a $2,500m. bond from IPIC and a $1,500m. bond raised by the Mubadala Development Co in April 2011. Also in 2011 Abu Dhabi Commercial Bank and Abu Dhabi Islamic Bank turned to the Islamic bond market to raise $500m. each. In February 2012 Emirates NBD Bank similarly issued a $500m. bond, and in May the Dubai Government launched two $1,250m. Islamic bonds. The first quarter of 2012 also saw two major conventional bond issues: by Dolphin Energy for $1,000m. and by the National Bank of Abu Dhabi for $750m. In April Dubai International Capital announced a $2,500m. debt-restructuring arrangement. Earlier, in December 2011, Aldar Properties received a second bail-out from Abu Dhabi. During 2012 DP World and IPIC made early debt repayments and the Dubai International Finance Centre (DIFC) and the Dubai Islamic Bank paid in full on maturity. In early 2013 Nakheel and Aabar Investments were engaged in talks with lenders to extend repayments on loans, while Sorouh Real Estate and Aldar Properties, both bail-out recipients, agreed to merge to form a new entity, to be called Aldar Sorouh Properties. In August 2012 international credit rating agency Moody's reaffirmed the UAE's long-term creditworthiness to be stable, although in December it downgraded three Dubai banks—Emirates NBD, the Commercial Bank of Dubai and Mashreqbank—for poor asset quality, and also placed Dubai Islamic Bank on credit watch. Market confidence in the UAE was, nevertheless, reflected in the oversubscription for the Dubai Government's issuance of Islamic bonds in January 2013.

During 2012 the Central Bank imposed a limit on bank lending to GREs, capped lending to single borrowers and announced that all banks were required to hold high-quality liquid assets equal to 10% of their liabilities from January 2013 to help them cover bad loans and to comply with recognized global standards (although implementation of this measure was postponed in December for further consideration). The Central Bank also introduced a new regulation in December 2012 to cap mortgage lending to avoid another property 'bubble'. However, the measure prompted complaints by lenders and in May 2013 the Bank agreed to raise the level of the cap. Meanwhile, the Bank announced plans to launch a pilot programme for a credit bureau, prior to an official start-up in 2014.

In 2002 plans had been announced for the creation of the DIFC, a financial free zone. Concerns were expressed that there might not be sufficient demand in the Gulf region for two such centres, given Bahrain's established record in this area. Nevertheless, a law formally setting down the powers and status of the DIFC was finally approved by the Government in 2003, and the DIFC was launched in September 2004. In April 2013 Abu Dhabi also issued a decree establishing a financial free zone, to be called Global Marketplace Abu Dhabi. The zone would permit international financial companies to operate without restrictions on foreign ownership, and was intended to rival the DIFC for the attention of firms attracted by the UAE's stability and connections with other Gulf markets. The decree also established a new regulator, the Financial Services Regulations Bureau, as well as the Global Marketplace Registration Bureau and Global Marketplace courts, including a court of first instance and an appellate court. The UAE's restrictions on foreign ownership of companies operating outside free zones would remain largely unchanged. According to the UN Conference on Trade and Development (UNCTAD), foreign direct investment in the UAE reached US $9,602m. in 2012, having fallen to $4,003m. in 2009, which reflected improving confidence in the economy but also concerns over the political instability elsewhere in the Middle East region. UNCTAD also disclosed that the UAE was the largest purchaser engaged in cross-border acquisitions in 2011, amounting to $5,944m.

The UAE had been considering the establishment of a stock exchange since 1985, and the Dubai Financial Market (DFM) finally opened in March 2000, although it was initially affected by the adverse economic impact of the suicide attacks on the USA in September 2001. In September 2005 the Dubai International Financial Exchange (DIFX), located within the DIFC, began operations as an international stock exchange. By December 2006 there were 21 securities listed on the DIFX, of which 16 were traded. Meanwhile, in 2002 the Dubai Metals and Commodities Centre was created as a free trade zone offering a 50-year tax moratorium and 100% foreign ownership potential to resident companies trading in diamonds and gold and other valuable metals. The Dubai Gold and Commodities Exchange subsequently began operations in November 2005 as the first international commodities derivatives market in the Middle East region. During 2007 the Dubai Mercantile Exchange, the first international energy futures and commodities exchange in the Middle East, began trading. New regulations were approved in that year permitting local companies to list on the DIFX. The Dubai Government, meanwhile, consolidated its holdings in the DFM and the DIFX into a new holding company, Borse Dubai. In late 2008 the DFM suffered a dramatic fall in share values in reaction to concerns about Dubai's debt levels and the drop in property prices in the context of the global financial crisis. In February 2009 Borse Dubai received more than US $1,000m. from the federal Government to prevent the company defaulting on a $2,500m. loan that it was attempting to refinance. The DFM acquired Nasdaq Dubai (as the DIFX had been renamed in 2008) in 2009. In April 2011 the Dubai Government amended the laws regulating the operation of the DIFC to improve transparency and co-ordination. The DFM index was the worst performing Gulf exchange in 2011, posting losses of 17%, amid concerns over the impact of the regional political turmoil and the debt crisis in the eurozone. However, it rose by nearly 20% in 2012, as Dubai started to show signs of recovery. In June 2013 it was announced that the UAE would be upgraded to emerging market status by Morgan Stanley Capital International, opening the country's exchanges to increased global investment flows.

The UAE has several sovereign wealth funds that have invested in Western companies, including the Abu Dhabi Investment Authority, IPIC, Mubadala Development Co, Dubai Investment Capital, Dubai Investment Group, Istithmar World and RAK Investment Authority. Emirates Investment Authority, established in 2007, is the first federal sovereign wealth fund for all seven emirates. The Abu Dhabi Investment Authority, considered to be one of the world's largest funds, published its first ever annual review in early 2010, representing a break with its customary policy of privacy. Holdings were targeted toward conventional investments, such as stocks and bonds, primarily in North America and Europe.

Statistical Survey

Source (unless otherwise stated): Central Bank of the UAE, POB 854, Abu Dhabi; tel. (2) 6652220; fax (2) 6652504; e-mail admin@cbuae.gov.ae; internet www.centralbank.ae; National Bureau of Statistics, POB 93000, Abu Dhabi; tel. (2) 6271100; fax (2) 6261344; e-mail contactus@nbs.gov.ae; internet www.uaestatistics.gov.ae.

Area and Population

AREA, POPULATION AND DENSITY

Area (sq km)	77,700*
Population (census results)	
17 December 1995	2,411,041
5 December 2005	
UAE nationals	825,495
Males	417,917
Females	407,578
Non-UAE nationals	3,280,932
Total	4,106,427
Population (official estimate at mid-year)	
2010	8,264,070†
Density (per sq km) at mid-2010	106.4

* 30,000 sq miles.

† Comprising 947,997 UAE nationals and 7,316,073 non-UAE nationals.

Mid-2013 (UN estimate): Total population 9,346,127 (Source: UN, *World Population Prospects: The 2012 Revision*).

POPULATION BY AGE AND SEX
(UN estimates at mid-2013)

	Males	Females	Total
0–14	711,928	691,104	1,403,032
15–64	5,812,073	2,093,872	7,905,945
65 and over	25,200	11,950	37,150
Total	6,549,201	2,796,926	9,346,127

Source: UN, *World Population Prospects: The 2012 Revision*.

Population by Sex (official estimates at mid-2010): Total 8,264,070 (males 6,161,820, females 2,102,250).

POPULATION BY EMIRATE
(official estimates at mid-2010, UAE nationals only)

	Area (sq km)	Population	Density (per sq km)
Abu Dhabi	67,340	404,546	6.0
Dubai	3,885	168,029	43.3
Sharjah	2,590	153,365	59.2
Ajman	259	42,186	162.9
Ras al-Khaimah	1,684	97,529	57.9
Fujairah	1,166	64,860	55.6
Umm al-Qaiwain	777	17,482	22.5
Total	77,700	947,997	12.2

Note: Figures for non-nationals, totalling 7,316,073, were not available.

PRINCIPAL TOWNS
(estimated population at mid-2003)

Dubai	1,171,000	Ras al-Khaimah	102,000
Abu Dhabi (capital)	552,000	Fujairah	54,000
Sharjah	519,000	Umm al-Qaiwain	38,000
Al-Ain	348,000	Khor Fakkan	32,000
Ajman	225,000		

2012 (official estimate at 31 December): Dubai 2,105,875 (Source: Statistics Centre, Municipality of Dubai, *Dubai in Figures*).

BIRTHS, MARRIAGES AND DEATHS

	Live births		Marriages*		Deaths	
	Number	Rate (per 1,000)	Number	Rate (per 1,000)	Number	Rate (per 1,000)
2003	61,165	15.1	12,277	3.0	6,002	1.5
2004	63,113	14.6	12,794	2.9	6,123	1.4
2005	64,623	15.7	12,984	3.2	6,361	1.5
2006	62,969	14.9	13,190	3.1	6,483	1.5
2007	67,689	15.1	12,987	2.9	7,414	1.7
2008	68,779	14.4	15,041	3.2	7,755	1.6
2009	76,366	15.1	15,155	3.0	7,788	1.5
2010	79,625	n.a.	15,104	n.a.	7,414	n.a.
2011	83,950	n.a.	15,105	n.a.	7,350	n.a.

* Muslim marriages only.

Life expectancy (years at birth): 76.7 (males 75.8; females 77.7) in 2011 (Source: World Bank, World Development Indicators database).

EMPLOYMENT
(persons aged 15 years and over)

	2005	2006*	2007†
Agriculture, hunting, forestry and fishing	193,044	209,066	225,499
Mining and quarrying	38,694	41,906	45,199
Oil and gas	33,200	35,956	38,783
Manufacturing	336,585	364,521	393,173
Electricity, gas and water supply	34,207	37,046	39,958
Construction	534,398	578,753	624,242
Wholesale and retail trade; repair of motor vehicles, motorcycles and personal and household goods	502,427	544,129	586,897
Hotels and restaurants	116,615	126,294	136,220
Transport, storage and communications	162,768	176,278	190,133
Financial intermediation	31,015	33,589	36,229
Real estate, renting and business activities	77,858	84,320	90,947
Public administration and defence; compulsory social security	286,105	309,851	334,207
Community, social and personal service activities	114,736	124,259	134,026
Private households with employed persons	222,506	240,975	259,916
Total employed	2,650,958	2,870,987	3,096,646

* Preliminary figures.
† Estimates.

2008 ('000 persons aged 15 years and over): Agriculture, hunting, forestry and fishing 233; Mining and quarrying 47 (Oil and gas 40); Manufacturing 431; Electricity, gas and water 39; Construction 757; Wholesale and retail trade; repair of motor vehicles, motorcycles and personal and household goods 643; Hotels and restaurants 146; Transport, storage and communications 204; Financial intermediation 42; Real estate, renting and business activities 97; Public administration and defence; compulsory social security 353; Community, social and personal service activities 142; Private households with employed persons 264; *Total employed* 3,397.

Health and Welfare

KEY INDICATORS

Total fertility rate (children per woman, 2011)	1.7
Under-5 mortality rate (per 1,000 live births, 2011)	7.0
HIV/AIDS (% of persons aged 15–49, 1994)	0.18
Physicians (per 1,000 head, 2007)	1.9
Hospital beds (per 1,000 head, 2008)	1.9
Health expenditure (2010): US $ per head (PPP)	1,562
Health expenditure (2010): % of GDP	3.7
Health expenditure (2010): public (% of total)	73.0
Access to sanitation (% of persons, 2011)	98
Total carbon dioxide emissions ('000 metric tons, 2009)	156,822.9
Carbon dioxide emissions per head (metric tons, 2009)	22.6
Human Development Index (2012): ranking	41
Human Development Index (2012): value	0.818

For sources and definitions, see explanatory note on p. vi.

Agriculture

PRINCIPAL CROPS
('000 metric tons, FAO estimates)

	2009	2010	2011
Potatoes	7.1	7.8	9.5
Cabbages	9.5	9.3	8.4
Lettuce	1.1	1.2	1.1
Spinach	1.1	1.1	0.9
Tomatoes	150.0	165.0	159.6
Cauliflowers and broccoli	8.5	9.0	11.9
Pumpkins, squash and gourds	30.5	32.0	32.6
Cucumbers and gherkins	23.0	24.0	26.2
Aubergines (Eggplants)	13.5	14.0	14.0
Chillies and peppers, green	7.5	8.2	8.2
Onions and shallots, green	15.1	14.1	15.2
Beans, green	1.0	1.4	1.6
Carrots and turnips	8.6	8.3	9.5
Watermelons	1.0	1.2	1.2
Cantaloupes and other melons	2.5	2.8	2.8
Lemons and limes	5.0	4.6	4.6
Mangoes, mangosteens and guavas	11.0	10.6	13.0
Dates	759.0	825.3	900.0

Aggregate production ('000 metric tons, may include official, semi-official or estimated data): Total fruits (excl. melons) 795.7 in 2009, 861.1 in 2010, 940.3 in 2011.

Source: FAO.

LIVESTOCK
('000 head, year ending September)

	2009	2010	2011*
Cattle	62†	62†	64
Camels	380†	380†	390
Sheep	1,475	1,450*	1,400
Goats	1,941	1,988†	2,000
Chickens*	18,000	20,000	21,000

* FAO estimate(s).
† Unofficial figure.

Source: FAO.

LIVESTOCK PRODUCTS
('000 metric tons, FAO estimates)

	2009	2010	2011
Cattle meat	14.8	15.0	15.4
Camel meat	29.7	30.1	30.2
Sheep meat	12.1	7.0	6.9
Goat meat	37.6	38.1	38.4
Chicken meat	39.6	40.8	41.4
Cows' milk	22.0	23.5	23.5
Camels' milk	40.4	42.4	42.4
Sheep's milk	15.8	17.5	17.5
Goats' milk	40.0	42.0	42.0
Hen eggs	30.0	26.1	26.1

Source: FAO.

Fishing

('000 metric tons, live weight)

	2009	2010	2011
Capture	77.7	79.6	75.1*
Groupers and seabasses	3.4	4.1*	3.9*
Grunts and sweetlips	2.0	2.1	1.9
Emperors (Scavengers)	3.3	6.8*	6.4*
King soldier bream	3.1	3.1	2.9
Sardinellas	0.8	0.8	0.8
Narrow-barred Spanish mackerel	8.3	8.7	8.3
Jacks and crevalles	1.5	1.0	n.a.
Carangids	8.1	8.7	8.2
Indian mackerel	0.6	1.5	1.4
Pink ear emperor	10.7	10.0*	9.5*
Aquaculture	—	—	0.2
Total catch (incl. others)	77.7	79.6*	75.3*

* FAO estimate.

Source: FAO.

Mining

	2010	2011	2012
Crude petroleum (million metric tons)	133.3	151.3	154.1
Natural gas (million cu metres)*	51,280	52,308	51,661

* Excluding gas flared or recycled.

Source: BP, *Statistical Review of World Energy*.

Industry

SELECTED PRODUCTS
('000 barrels, unless otherwise indicated)

	2009	2010	2011
Cement ('000 metric tons)	18,997	18,000*	18,000*
Aluminium ('000 metric tons)	955	1,400	1,750
Motor spirit (petrol)	12,994	15,732	20,914
Kerosene and jet fuel	35,405	39,092	49,202
Gas-diesel (distillate fuel) oil	26,682	29,018	36,427
Residual fuel oils	5,584	5,804	6,680
Liquefied petroleum gas	5,840	6,570	8,103

* Estimate.

Source: US Geological Survey.

Electric energy (million kWh): 86,260 in 2008; 90,573 in 2009; 97,728 in 2010 (Source: UN Industrial Commodity Statistics Database).

Finance

CURRENCY AND EXCHANGE RATES

Monetary Units
100 fils = 1 UAE dirham (AED).

Sterling, Dollar and Euro Equivalents (31 May 2013)
£1 sterling = 5.587 dirhams;
US $1 = 3.673 dirhams;
€1 = 4.776 dirhams;
100 UAE dirhams = £17.90 = $27.23 = €20.94.

Exchange Rate: The Central Bank's official rate was set at US $1 = 3.671 dirhams in November 1980. This remained in force until December 1997, when the rate was adjusted to $1 = 3.6725 dirhams.

BUDGET OF THE CONSOLIDATED GOVERNMENTS
(million UAE dirhams)

Revenue	2009	2010	2011*
Hydrocarbon	174,129	233,986	362,576
Non-hydrocarbon	81,135	79,205	77,498
Customs	8,546	8,062	9,701
Profit transfers	4,033	5,089	6,564
Income tax	1,340	1,113	1,093
Fees and charges	24,803	26,157	23,293
Investment income	19,701	15,748	12,196
Other	22,712	23,037	24,651
Total	255,264	313,191	440,074

Expenditure	2009	2010	2011*
Current expenditure	210,920	229,917	257,091
Salaries and wages	33,248	31,136	32,059
Goods and services	68,216	36,614	40,013
Subsidies and transfers	46,034	41,004	53,899
Development expenditure	45,548	35,446	37,253
Loans and equity	117,948	68,193	101,563
Foreign grants	3,287	2,613	5,585
Total	377,702	336,170	401,492

* Estimates.

Source: IMF, *United Arab Emirates: Selected Issues and Statistical Appendix* (June 2012).

2012 (consolidated accounts of the federal governments of Abu Dhabi, Dubai and Sharjah, '000 million UAE dirhams, projections): *Revenue* (including IMF estimates of revenues from other government entities operating in the oil and gas sector): Total 490.4 (Hydrocarbons 404.3, Non-hydrocarbon 86.1). *Expenditure and grants:* Total 231.2 (Foreign grants 5.9) (Source (2011–12): IMF, *United Arab Emirates: Staff Report for the 2012 Article IV Consultation*—May 2012).

INTERNATIONAL RESERVES
(excluding gold, US $ million at 31 December)

	2010	2011	2012
IMF special drawing rights	833.5	831.8	833.1
Reserve position in IMF	200.8	347.0	376.0
Foreign exchange*	31,750.9	36,090.5	45,826.1
Total	32,785.3	37,269.3	47,035.2

* Figures exclude the Central Bank's foreign assets and accrued interest attributable to the governments of individual emirates.

Source: IMF, *International Financial Statistics*.

MONEY SUPPLY
(million UAE dirhams at 31 December)

	2010	2011	2012
Currency outside banks	38,560	41,591	45,615
Demand deposits at commercial banks	194,401	222,505	253,558
Total money	232,961	264,096	299,173

Source: IMF, *International Financial Statistics*.

COST OF LIVING
(Consumer Price Index; base: 2007 = 100)

	2010	2011	2012
Food, beverages and tobacco	122.4	129.6	136.4
Clothing and footwear	108.4	106.4	108.9
Housing (incl. rent)	113.6	110.8	108.0
Furniture, etc.	118.9	123.1	125.7
Medical care and health services	105.3	105.7	106.9
Transport	114.5	118.8	119.0
Communication	98.1	98.2	98.2
Recreation and culture	109.3	114.3	114.6
Education	128.9	133.6	139.6
All items (incl. others)	115.0	116.0	116.8

NATIONAL ACCOUNTS
(million UAE dirhams at current prices)

Gross Domestic Product by Emirate

	2007	2008	2009*
Abu Dhabi	545,368	705,159	596,434
Dubai	310,056	342,900	294,158
Sharjah	54,002	65,026	60,946
Ajman	12,633	14,441	13,885
Ras al-Khaimah	14,580	16,413	15,738
Fujairah	9,172	9,904	9,330
Umm al-Qaiwain	2,246	2,424	2,314
Total	948,056	1,156,267	992,805

* Preliminary figures.

Expenditure on the Gross Domestic Product

	2010	2011	2012*
Government final consumption expenditure	90,141	93,657	97,310
Private final consumption expenditure	622,358	661,763	701,264
Increase in stocks	12,123	12,201	10,231
Gross fixed capital formation	262,575	281,690	309,173
Total domestic expenditure	987,197	1,049,311	1,117,978
Exports of goods and services	827,322	1,156,229	1,341,168
Less Imports of goods and services	758,962	925,325	1,049,644
GDP in purchasers' values	1,055,557	1,280,215	1,409,502
GDP at constant 2007 prices	937,007	973,602	1,016,102

* Preliminary figures.

Gross Domestic Product by Economic Activity

	2010	2011	2012*
Agriculture, livestock and fishing	8,992	9,354	10,363
Mining and quarrying	334,047	505,767	568,788
Oil and gas	331,584	503,225	566,128
Manufacturing	94,546	112,982	126,201
Electricity and water	25,706	29,734	32,053
Construction	122,352	120,130	125,536
Wholesale and retail trade, and repairs	136,995	140,907	148,939
Restaurants and hotels	21,566	24,777	28,122
Transport, storage and communications	89,517	100,460	113,018
Financial institutions and insurance	74,017	80,060	86,065
Real estate and business services	112,621	120,491	127,600
Government services	57,151	60,204	65,984
Community, social and personal services	23,586	27,158	31,367
Private households with employed persons	4,651	5,104	5,283
Sub-total	1,105,746	1,337,129	1,469,319
Less Imputed bank service charge	50,189	56,914	59,817
GDP in purchasers' values	1,055,557	1,280,215	1,409,502

* Preliminary figures.

BALANCE OF PAYMENTS
('000 million UAE dirhams)

	2010	2011	2012*
Exports of goods f.o.b.	784.22	1,109.23	1,285.83
Imports of goods f.o.b.	–604.35	–717.76	–814.89
Trade balance	179.87	391.47	470.94
Services (net)	–111.51	–160.56	–179.42
Income (net)	–0.37	0.40	1.09
Balance on goods, services and income	67.99	231.31	292.61
Current transfers (net)	–41.40	–44.20	–48.20
Current balance	26.59	187.11	244.42
Capital and financial accounts (net)	18.46	–109.15	–145.75
Net errors and omissions	–18.12	–61.34	–62.30
Overall balance	26.93	16.62	36.37

* Preliminary estimates.

External Trade

PRINCIPAL COMMODITIES
(distribution by HS, million UAE dirhams)

Imports c.i.f.	2009	2010	2011
Vegetable products	18,683.9	20,187.3	24,299.6
Prepared foodstuffs, beverages, spirits and tobacco	8,868.2	10,423.5	12,283.7
Chemical products, etc.	24,063.4	27,122.0	33,044.7
Plastics, rubber and articles thereof	13,720.2	15,368.2	17,730.1
Textiles and textile articles	17,494.7	17,826.8	20,683.6
Pearls, precious or semi-precious stones, precious metals, etc.	101,497.7	139,191.3	188,431.7
Base metals and articles of base metal	41,206.3	41,755.7	55,814.9
Machinery and electrical equipment	108,134.3	94,294.2	106,099.7
Vehicles and other transport equipment	57,205.1	60,346.2	72,184.4
Total (incl. others)	447,393.8	485,413.9	602,757.3

Exports f.o.b.*	2009	2010	2011
Animals and animal products	773.4	923.4	1,180.9
Prepared foodstuffs, beverages, spirits and tobacco	4,265.1	5,825.8	6,281.2
Mineral products	3,713.3	3,330.4	6,299.4
Chemical products, etc.	1,692.9	2,198.7	2,979.8
Plastics, rubber and articles thereof	5,211.4	5,909.7	6,828.1
Textiles and textile articles	1,005.0	1,177.2	1,057.0
Stone, plaster, cement, ceramic and glassware	1,903.6	2,329.8	2,440.0
Base metals and articles of base metal	8,019.5	7,633.4	11,155.1
Machinery and electrical equipment	1,386.9	1,504.4	1,439.6
Vehicles and other transport equipment	1,718.4	6,190.6	5,094.8
Total (incl. others)†	65,278.9	83,077.7	114,038.3

* Excluding petroleum exports and excluding re-exports; re-exports amounted to 147,693.4m. dirhams in 2009; 185,863.3m. dirhams in 2010; 210,842.8m. dirhams in 2011.

† Excluding free zone exports.

SELECTED MAJOR TRADING PARTNERS
(million UAE dirhams)

Imports	2009	2010	2011
Australia	6,365.4	7,500.0	8,956.8
Belgium	6,496.8	6,718.8	10,819.2
Brazil	3,750.2	4,471.3	5,773.2
Canada	4,323.7	3,525.1	5,435.0
China, People's Republic	47,825.6	49,905.3	54,960.0
France (incl. Monaco)	14,027.1	12,779.3	15,982.9
GCC countries	21,537.6	22,336.3	27,821.8
Germany	29,998.0	29,679.5	30,656.1
Hong Kong	4,054.6	3,853.0	6,305.5
India	61,564.8	83,187.4	105,132.2
Italy (incl. San Marino)	17,417.6	15,150.9	19,966.9
Japan	26,903.7	28,501.6	30,010.1
Korea, Republic	16,899.2	12,140.3	22,919.2
Netherlands	4,800.7	4,925.2	5,064.8
Pakistan	5,764.9	6,547.5	7,201.8
Saudi Arabia	12,179.3	11,969.9	15,048.3
Sudan	2,334.3	4,962.0	7,442.3
Switzerland	9,819.9	11,488.4	15,289.6
Thailand	7,518.4	7,785.4	8,975.4
Turkey	9,362.3	9,108.9	8,962.5
United Kingdom	18,762.4	17,238.8	21,477.5
USA	41,524.9	41,303.6	53,274.9
Total (incl. others)	447,393.8	485,413.9	602,757.3

Exports*	2009	2010	2011
Bahrain	669.5	905.0	1,239.6
Belgium	3,451.2	4,014.5	556.3
Brazil	256.7	3,079.3	1,903.9
Canada	316.1	197.1	2,935.9
Egypt	801.8	1,243.7	1,403.3
GCC countries	33,311.3	32,365.1	13,217.8
Hong Kong	188.0	611.5	1,751.3
India	46,497.0	80,218.0	36,234.9
Kuwait	1,161.7	1,667.5	3,252.9
Oman	1,858.9	1,818.3	1,194.3
Pakistan	1,806.5	2,100.7	1,316.3
Qatar	4,897.4	1,817.9	1,870.6
Saudi Arabia	3,007.0	3,743.5	5,660.4
Singapore	475.2	612.1	3,284.4
Switzerland	8,727.0	13,418.5	14,457.6
Thailand	260.7	380.2	2,130.0
Turkey	681.8	586.1	3,241.8
United Kingdom	1,551.2	2,618.3	594.9
USA	3,323.1	3,331.4	1,177.8
Total (incl. others)	212,972.3	268,940.9	114,038.3

* Data for non-petroleum exports and all re-exports.

Transport

ROAD TRAFFIC
('000 registered motor vehicles in use)

	2000	2001	2002
Passenger cars (incl. taxis)	561.9	654.2	606.1
Trucks (incl. public)	83.3	66.2	66.2
Buses (incl. public)	14.7	13.3	16.0
Other	13.2	11.2	13.1

Total vehicles in use ('000): 767 in 2002; 792 in 2003.

2007 (motor vehicles registered at 31 December): Passenger cars 1,279,098; Buses and coaches 48,205; Vans and lorries 39,424; Motorcycles and mopeds 13,639 (Source: IRF, *World Road Statistics*).

SHIPPING

Flag Registered Fleet
(at 31 December)

	2010	2011	2012
Number of vessels	716	730	738
Total displacement ('000 grt)	1,572.8	1,515.3	1,348.8

Source: Lloyd's List Intelligence (www.lloydslistintelligence.com).

International Sea-borne Shipping
(estimated freight traffic, '000 metric tons)

	1988	1989	1990
Goods loaded	63,380	72,896	88,153
Crude petroleum	54,159	63,387	78,927
Other cargo	9,221	9,509	9,226
Goods unloaded	8,973	8,960	9,595

Source: UN, *Monthly Bulletin of Statistics*.

CIVIL AVIATION
(traffic on scheduled services)*

	2007	2008	2009
Kilometres flown (million)	483	573	655
Passengers carried ('000)	25,088	28,432	31,762
Passenger-km (million)	108,262	124,831	143,849
Total ton-km (million)	16,971	19,337	21,823

* Figures include an apportionment (one-quarter) of the traffic of Gulf Air, a multinational airline with its headquarters in Bahrain.

Source: UN, *Statistical Yearbook*.

Passengers carried ('000): 44,775 in 2010; 49,481 in 2011 (Source: World Bank, World Development Indicators database).

Tourism

FOREIGN TOURIST ARRIVALS*

Country	2002	2003	2004
Canada	95,878	55,297	57,718
Egypt	111,822	121,221	131,635
France	90,735	98,624	112,429
Germany	236,660	235,147	337,594
India	336,046	357,941	356,446
Iran	270,350	334,453	336,734
Jordan	73,140	76,553	76,308
Lebanon	74,225	83,137	90,409
Pakistan	154,711	183,724	173,152
Russia	267,655	324,484	340,716
United Kingdom	491,604	496,147	644,688
USA	123,112	175,116	192,948
Total (incl. others)†	5,445,367	5,871,023	6,195,006

* Figures refer to international arrivals at hotels and similar establishments.

† Total includes domestic tourists.

Total tourist arrivals ('000): 6,812 in 2009; 7,432 in 2010; 8,129 in 2011 (provisional).

Receipts from tourism (US $ million, excl. passenger transport): 7,352 in 2009; 8,577 in 2010; 9,204 in 2011 (provisional).

Source: World Tourism Organization.

Communications Media

	2010	2011	2012
Telephones ('000 main lines in use)	1,479.5	1,825.5	1,967.5
Mobile cellular telephones ('000 subscribers)	10,926.0	11,727.4	13,775.3
Internet subscribers ('000)	1,374.9	1,324.1	n.a.
Broadband subscribers ('000)	786.8	867.0	951.8

Source: International Telecommunication Union.

Education

(Government schools only)

	2008/09	2009/10	2010/11
Institutions	721	725	725
Teachers*	27,469	28,856	29,348
Students			
Pre-primary	23,910	24,821	26,171
Primary	175,761	175,968	177,516
Secondary	60,903	63,032	61,540
Other schools	1,799	1,610	3,948

* Includes administrative and technical staff.

Source: Ministry of Education, United Arab Emirates.

Pupil-teacher ratio (primary education, UNESCO estimate): 17.0 in 2010/11 (Source: UNESCO Institute for Statistics).

Adult literacy rate (UNESCO estimates): 90.4% (males 90.9%; females 89.2%) in 2007 (Source: UNESCO Institute for Statistics).

Directory

The Constitution

A provisional Constitution for the UAE took effect in December 1971. This laid the foundation for the federal structure of the Union of the seven emirates, previously known as the Trucial States.

The highest federal authority is the Supreme Council of Rulers, which comprises the Rulers of the seven emirates. It elects the President and Vice-President from among its members. The President appoints a Prime Minister and a Council of Ministers. Proposals submitted to the Council require the approval of at least five of the Rulers, including those of Abu Dhabi and Dubai. The legislature is the Federal National Council (FNC), a consultative assembly comprising 40 members, of whom one-half are appointed by the emirates and the remainder are chosen by electoral colleges for a two-year term. A constitutional amendment extending the FNC's term to four years was endorsed by the Supreme Council of Rulers in December 2008 and approved by the FNC in January 2009.

In July 1975 a committee was appointed to draft a permanent federal constitution, but the FNC decided in 1976 to extend the provisional document for five years. The provisional Constitution was extended for another five years in December 1981, and for further periods of five years in 1986 and 1991. In November 1976, however, the Supreme Council amended Article 142 of the provisional Constitution so that the authority to levy armed forces was placed exclusively under the control of the federal Government. Legislation designed to make the provisional Constitution permanent was endorsed by the FNC in June 1996, after it had been approved by the Supreme Council of Rulers.

The Government

HEAD OF STATE

President: Sheikh KHALIFA BIN ZAYED AL NAHYAN (Ruler of Abu Dhabi, elected by the Supreme Council of Rulers as President of the UAE on 3 November 2004; re-elected 3 November 2009).

Vice-President: Sheikh MUHAMMAD BIN RASHID AL MAKTOUM (Ruler of Dubai).

SUPREME COUNCIL OF RULERS
(with each Ruler's date of accession)

Ruler of Abu Dhabi: Sheikh KHALIFA BIN ZAYED AL NAHYAN (2004).

Ruler of Dubai: Sheikh MUHAMMAD BIN RASHID AL MAKTOUM (2006).

Ruler of Sharjah: Sheikh SULTAN BIN MUHAMMAD AL-QASIMI (1972).

Ruler of Ras al-Khaimah: Sheikh SAUD BIN SAQR AL-QASIMI (2010).

Ruler of Umm al-Qaiwain: Sheikh SAUD BIN RASHID AL-MU'ALLA (2009).

Ruler of Ajman: Sheikh HUMAID BIN RASHID AL-NUAIMI (1981).

Ruler of Fujairah: Sheikh HAMAD BIN MUHAMMAD AL-SHARQI (1974).

COUNCIL OF MINISTERS
(September 2013)

Prime Minister and Minister of Defence: Sheikh MUHAMMAD BIN RASHID AL MAKTOUM.

Deputy Prime Minister and Minister of the Interior: Lt-Gen. Sheikh SAIF BIN ZAYED AL NAHYAN.

Deputy Prime Minister and Minister of Presidential Affairs: Sheikh MANSOUR BIN ZAYED AL NAHYAN.

Minister of Finance: Sheikh HAMDAN BIN RASHID AL MAKTOUM.

Minister of Foreign Affairs: Sheikh ABDULLAH BIN ZAYED AL NAHYAN.

Minister of Higher Education and Scientific Research: Sheikh HAMDAN BIN MUBARAK AL NAHYAN.

Minister of Public Works: ABDULLAH BIN MUHAMMAD AL-NUAIMI.

Minister of Economy: SULTAN BIN SAID AL-MANSOURI.

Minister of Development and International Co-operation: Sheikha LUBNA BINT KHALID AL-QASIMI.

Minister of Justice: Dr HADIF JOWAN AL-DHAHIRI.

Minister of Energy: SUHAIL BIN MUHAMMAD AL-MAZROUI.

Minister of Labour: SAQR GHOBASH SAID GHOBASH.

Minister of Social Affairs: Dr MARIAM MUHAMMAD KHALFAN AL-ROUMI.

Minister of Education: HUMAID MUHAMMAD OBAID AL-QATTAMI.

Minister of the Environment and Water: Dr RASHID AHMAD AL-FAHD.

Minister of Culture, Youth and Community Development: Sheikh NAHYAN BIN MUBARAK AL NAHYAN.

Minister of Health: ABD AL-RAHMAN BIN MUHAMMAD AL-OWAIS.

Minister of Cabinet Affairs: MUHAMMAD BIN ABDULLAH AL-GARGAWI.

Minister of State for Financial Affairs: OBAID HUMAID AL-TAYER.

Minister of State for Foreign Affairs and for Federal National Council Affairs: Dr ANWAR MUHAMMAD GARGASH.

Ministers of State: REEM IBRAHIM AL-HASHEMI, Dr MAITHA SALIM AL-SHAMSI, SULTAN AHMAD AL-JABER, ABDULLAH BIN MUHAMMAD GOBASH.

FEDERAL MINISTRIES

Office of the Prime Minister: POB 12848, Dubai; tel. (4) 3534550; fax (4) 3530111; e-mail info@primeminister.ae; internet www.uaepm.ae.

Office of the Deputy Prime Minister: POB 831, Abu Dhabi; tel. (2) 4451000; fax (2) 4450066.

Ministry of Cabinet Affairs: POB 899, Abu Dhabi; tel. (2) 4450777; fax (2) 4453418; e-mail contactus@moca.gov.ae; internet www.moca.gov.ae.

Ministry of Culture, Youth and Community Development: POB 17, Abu Dhabi; tel. (2) 4466145; fax (2) 4452504; e-mail info@mcycd.gov.ae; internet www.mcycd.ae.

Ministry of Defence: POB 46616, Abu Dhabi; tel. (2) 4461300; fax (4) 3531974; e-mail mod@mod.gov.ae; internet www.mod.gov.ae.

Ministry of Development and International Co-operation: POB 110555, Abu Dhabi; tel. (2) 4956000; fax (2) 4499164.

Ministry of Economy: POB 901, Abu Dhabi; tel. (2) 3161111; fax (2) 6260000; e-mail economy@economy.ae; internet www.economy.ae.

Ministry of Education: POB 3962, Abu Dhabi; tel. (2) 4089999; fax (4) 2176006; e-mail ccc.moe@moe.gov.ae; internet www.moe.gov.ae.

Ministry of Energy: POB 59, Abu Dhabi; tel. (2) 6126500; fax (2) 6272291; e-mail moenr@moenr.ae; internet www.moenr.gov.ae.

Ministry of the Environment and Water: POB 213, Old Airport Rd, Abu Dhabi; tel. (2) 4444740; fax (2) 4490444; e-mail adarchieve@moew.gov.ae; internet www.moew.gov.ae.

Ministry of Finance: POB 433, Abu Dhabi; tel. (2) 6726000; fax (2) 6768414; e-mail estifsarat@mof.gov.ae; internet www.mof.gov.ae.

Ministry of Foreign Affairs: POB 1, Abu Dhabi; tel. and fax (2) 2222000; fax (2) 2222000; e-mail info@mofa.gov.ae; internet www.mofa.gov.ae.

Ministry of Health: POB 848, Abu Dhabi; tel. (2) 6330000; fax (2) 6726000; e-mail info@moh.gov.ae; internet www.moh.gov.ae.

Ministry of Higher Education and Scientific Research: POB 45253, Abu Dhabi; tel. (2) 6428000; fax (2) 6428778; e-mail mohe@uae.gov.ae; internet www.mohesr.ae.

Ministry of the Interior: POB 398, Abu Dhabi; tel. (2) 4414666; fax (2) 4022762; e-mail moi@moi.gov.ae; internet www.moi.gov.ae.

Ministry of Justice: POB 260, Abu Dhabi; tel. (2) 6921000; fax (2) 6810680; e-mail moj@uae.gov.ae; internet ejustice.gov.ae.

Ministry of Labour: POB 809, Abu Dhabi; tel. (2) 6671700; fax (2) 4494293; e-mail minister@mol.gov.ae; internet www.mol.gov.ae.

Ministry of Presidential Affairs: POB 280, Abu Dhabi; tel. (2) 6222221; fax (2) 6222228; e-mail ihtimam@mopa.ae; internet www.mopa.ae.

Ministry of Public Works: POB 878, Abu Dhabi; tel. (4) 2610001; fax (4) 2125544; e-mail info@mopw.gov.ae; internet www.mopw.gov.ae.

Ministry of Social Affairs: POB 809, Abu Dhabi; tel. (4) 2637777; fax (4) 2633525; e-mail info@msa.gov.ae; internet www.msa.gov.ae.

Ministry of State for Federal National Council Affairs: POB 130000, Abu Dhabi; tel. (2) 4041000; fax (2) 4041155; e-mail mfnca@mfnca.gov.ae; internet www.mfnca.gov.ae.

Ministry of State for Financial Affairs: POB 433, Abu Dhabi; tel. (2) 771133; fax (2) 793255.

Ministry of State for Foreign Affairs: POB 1, Abu Dhabi; tel. (2) 6660888; fax (2) 6652883.

Legislature

Federal National Council (FNC)

POB 836, Abu Dhabi; tel. (2) 6199500; fax (2) 6812846; e-mail info@almajles.gov.ae; internet www.almajles.gov.ae.

Formed under the provisional Constitution, the Council is composed of 40 members from the various emirates (eight each from Abu Dhabi and Dubai, six each from Sharjah and Ras al-Khaimah, and four each from Ajman, Fujairah and Umm al-Qaiwain). Each emirate appoints its own representatives separately. The Council studies laws proposed by the Council of Ministers and can reject them or suggest amendments. In December 2005 Sheikh Khalifa announced that elections would be introduced to choose one-half of the members of the FNC, which would also be expanded and granted enhanced powers. In August 2006 a National Electoral Committee was established to preside over the elections, which were held during 16–20 December. A constitutional amendment extending the Council's term from two to four years was endorsed by the Supreme Council of Rulers in December 2008 and approved by the FNC in January 2009. A further round of elections took place on 24 September 2011.

Speaker: MUHAMMAD AHMAD AL-MURR.

Political Organizations

There are no political organizations in the UAE.

Diplomatic Representation

EMBASSIES IN THE UNITED ARAB EMIRATES

Afghanistan: POB 5687, Abu Dhabi; tel. (2) 4472666; fax (2) 4472660; e-mail afgem555@emirates.net.ae; internet www.afghanembassy-uae.com; Ambassador Dr NAJIBULLAH MOJADIDI.

Algeria: POB 3070, Abu Dhabi; tel. (2) 448949; fax (2) 4447068; e-mail emalgadhabi@hotmail.com; Ambassador HAMID CHEBIRA.

Angola: POB 36532, Abu Dhabi; tel. (2) 4477042; fax (2) 4477043; e-mail info@adangola.ae; internet www.adangola.ae; Ambassador FLÁVIO SARAIVA DE CARVALHO FONSECA.

Argentina: POB 3325, Abu Dhabi; tel. (2) 4436838; fax (2) 4431392; e-mail eearb@cancilleria.gob.ar; Ambassador RUBÉN EDUARDO CARO.

Armenia: POB 6358, Abu Dhabi; tel. (2) 4444196; fax (2) 4444197; e-mail armemiratesembassy@mfa.am; internet uae.mfa.am; Ambassador GEGHAM GHARIBJANYAN.

Australia: POB 32711, al-Muhairy Centre, 8th Floor, Sheikh Zayed I St, Abu Dhabi; tel. (2) 4017500; fax (2) 4017501; e-mail abudhabi.embassy@dfat.gov.au; internet www.uae.embassy.gov.au; Ambassador PABLO KANG.

Austria: POB 35539, Abu Dhabi; tel. (2) 6944999; fax (2) 6944988; e-mail abu-dhabi-ob@bmeia.gv.at; internet www.bmeia.gv.at/en/embassy/abu-dhabi; Ambassador PETER ELSNER-MACKAY.

Azerbaijan: POB 45766, Plot N-297, W-16, al-Bateen Area, Abu Dhabi; tel. (2) 6662848; fax (2) 6663150; e-mail azembasy@eim.ae; internet www.azembassy.ae; Ambassador ELKHAN GAHRAMANOV.

Bahrain: POB 3367, Abu Dhabi; tel. (2) 6657500; fax (2) 6674141; e-mail abudhabi.mission@mofa.gov.bh; Ambassador MUHAMMAD SAQR AL-MAAWDA.

Bangladesh: POB 2504, Villa 21, Delma St, al-Rowdha, Abu Dhabi; tel. (2) 4462853; fax (2) 4464733; e-mail mission.abudhabi@mofa.gov.bd; internet www.bdembassyuae.org; Ambassador MUHAMMAD IMRAN QAWNAIN.

Belarus: POB 30337, Plot 111, Villa 2, East 19, Sharq Area, Abu Dhabi; tel. (2) 4453399; fax (2) 4451131; e-mail uae@mfa.gov.by; internet uae.mfa.gov.by; Ambassador ROMAN GOLOVCHENKO.

Belgium: POB 3686, al-Masood Tower, 6th Floor, Hamdan St, Abu Dhabi; tel. (2) 6319449; fax (2) 6319353; e-mail abudhabi@diplobel.fed.be; internet www.diplomatie.be/abudhabi; Ambassador CHRISTIAAN TANGHE.

Bosnia and Herzegovina: POB 43362, Abu Dhabi; tel. (2) 6444164; fax (2) 6443619; e-mail ambassador.rk@bhmc.ae; internet www.bhmc.ae; Ambassador MILUTIN VASILJEVIĆ.

Brazil: POB 3027, Villa 3, St 5, Madinat Zayed, Abu Dhabi; tel. (2) 6320606; fax (2) 6327727; e-mail brasemb.abudhabi@itamaraty.gov.br; internet abudhabi.itamaraty.gov.br; Ambassador JOSÉ DE MENDONÇA E LIMA.

Brunei: POB 5836, Abu Dhabi; tel. (2) 4486999; fax (2) 4486333; e-mail kbdauh98@amirates.net.ae; Ambassador MUHAMMAD YUSRA SALIH.

Canada: POB 6970, Abu Dhabi Trade Towers, West Tower, 9th and 10th Floors, Abu Dhabi; tel. (2) 6940300; fax (2) 6940399; e-mail abdbi@international.gc.ca; internet www.dfait-maeci.gc.ca/abudhabi; Ambassador ARIF LALANI.

Chile: St 4, nr St 23, al-Mushrif, Abu Dhabi; tel. (2) 4472022; fax (2) 4472023; e-mail info@chile-uae.com; internet chile-uae.com; Ambassador JEAN-PAUL TARUD.

China, People's Republic: POB 2741, Plot 26, W-22, Abu Dhabi; tel. (2) 4434276; fax (2) 4436835; e-mail chinaemb_ae@mfa.gov.cn; internet ae.chineseembassy.org; Ambassador HUANG JIEMIN.

Cyprus: POB 63013, 426 al-Khaleej al-Arabi St, Abu Dhabi; tel. (2) 6654480; fax (2) 6657870; e-mail cyembadb@eim.ae; Ambassador ELPIDOFOROS ECONOMOU.

Czech Republic: POB 27009, City Bank Bldg, Corniche Plaza, Abu Dhabi; tel. (2) 6782800; fax (2) 6795716; e-mail abudhabi@embassy.mzv.cz; internet www.mzv.cz/abudhabi; Ambassador JAROSLAV LUDVA.

Denmark: POB 105415, Abu Dhabi; tel. (2)4410104; fax (2) 4410021; e-mail auhamb@um.dk; internet fae.um.dk; Ambassador POUL O. G. HOINESS.

Egypt: POB 4026, Abu Dhabi; tel. (2) 8137000; fax (2) 4449878; e-mail egemb_abudhabi@mfa.gov.eg; Ambassador TAMER MANSOUR.

Eritrea: POB 2597, Abu Dhabi; tel. (2) 6331838; fax (2) 6790060; e-mail erimb75@emirates.net.ae; Chargé d'affaires a.i. ALAMIN NAFIE YOUSEF.

Fiji: Abu Dhabi; Ambassador ROBIN NAIR.

Finland: POB 3634, al-Masood Tower, Hamdan St, Abu Dhabi; tel. (2) 6328927; fax (2) 6325063; e-mail sanomat.abo@formin.fi; internet www.finland.ae; Ambassador ILKKA-PEKKA SIMILÄ.

France: POB 4014, Abu Dhabi; tel. (2) 4435100; fax (2) 4434158; e-mail contact@ambafrance.ae; internet www.ambafrance-eau.org; Ambassador ALAIN AZOUAOU.

The Gambia: POB 3675, Abu Dhabi; tel. (2) 6678033; fax (2) 6678030; e-mail gamsyuae@emirates.net.ae; Ambassador (vacant).

Germany: POB 2591, Abu Dhabi Mall, West Tower, 14th Floor, Abu Dhabi; tel. (2) 6446693; fax (2) 6446942; e-mail info@abu-dhabi.diplo.de; internet www.abu-dhabi.diplo.de; Ambassador NIKOLAI VON SCHOEPFF.

Greece: POB 5483, Abu Dhabi; tel. (2) 4492550; fax (2) 4492455; e-mail gremb.abd@mfa.gr; internet www.mfa.gr/abu; Ambassador DIONISIOS ZOIS.

Hungary: POB 44450, Abu Dhabi; tel. (2) 6766190; fax (2) 6766215; e-mail mission.abu@mfa.gov.hu; internet www.mfa.gov.hu/emb/abudhabi; Ambassador JANCSI ZOLTÁNRENDKÍVÜLI.

India: POB 4090, Abu Dhabi; tel. (2) 4492700; fax (2) 4444685; e-mail ambassador@indembassyuae.org; internet www.indembassyuae.org; Ambassador M. K. LOKESH.

Indonesia: POB 7256, Abu Dhabi; tel. (2) 4454448; fax (2) 4455453; e-mail indoemb@emirates.net.ae; internet www.kemlu.go.id/abudhabi; Ambassador SALMAN AL-FARISI.

Iran: POB 4080, Abu Dhabi; tel. (2) 4447618; fax (2) 4448714; e-mail iranemb@emirates.net.ae; internet www.iranembassy.org.ae; Ambassador MUHAMMAD REZA FAYYAZ.

Iraq: POB 6389, Embassies Area, 41 West 59/2, Abu Dhabi; tel. (2) 4418022; fax (2) 4418155; e-mail adbemb@mofaml.gov.iq; internet www.mofamission.gov.iq/abudhabi; Ambassador ARSHAD TAWFIQ.

Ireland: POB 61581, 1–2 Khalifa al-Suwaidi Development, 19th St (off 32nd St), al-Bateen Area, Abu Dhabi; tel. (2) 4958200; fax (2) 6819233; e-mail irishvisaofficedubai@gmail.com; internet www.embassyofireland.ae; Ambassador PAT HENNESSY.

Italy: POB 46752, Villa 438–439, St 26, al-Manaseer Area, Abu Dhabi; tel. (2) 4435622; fax (2) 4434337; e-mail italianembassy.abudhabi@esteri.it; internet www.ambabudhabi.esteri.it; Ambassador GIORGIO STARACE.

Japan: POB 2430, Abu Dhabi; tel. (2) 4435696; fax (2) 4434219; e-mail embjpn@ab.mofa.go.jp; internet www.uae.emb-japan.go.jp; Ambassador YOSHIHIKO KAMO.

Jordan: POB 4024, Abu Dhabi; tel. (2) 4447100; fax (2) 4449157; e-mail abudhabi@fm.gov.jo; internet www.jordanembassy.ae; Ambassador NAYEF ZEIDAN.

Kazakhstan: 593 Rashid bin Said Al Maktoum St, al-Safarat District, Abu Dhabi; tel. (2) 4498778; fax (2) 4498775; e-mail abudhabi@mfa.kz; internet www.kazembemirates.net; Ambassador ASKAR A. MUSSINOV.

Kenya: POB 3854, Abu Dhabi; tel. (2) 6666300; fax (2) 6652827; e-mail kenyarep@emirates.net.ae; internet www.kenyaembassy.ae; Ambassador MUHAMMED ABDI GELLO.

Korea, Republic: POB 3270, Abu Dhabi; tel. (2) 6439122; fax (2) 6439130; e-mail uae@mofat.go.kr; internet are.mofat.go.kr; Ambassador KWON HAE-RYONG.

Kuwait: POB 926, Abu Dhabi; tel. (2) 4477146; fax (2) 4477675; e-mail q8embassy@gmail.com; Ambassador SALEH MUHAMMAD AL-BUAIJAN.

Lebanon: POB 4023, Abu Dhabi; tel. (2) 4492100; fax (2) 4493500; e-mail lebanon3@eim.ae; Ambassador HASSAN YUSUF SAAD.

Libya: POB 5739, Abu Dhabi; tel. (2) 4450030; fax (2) 4450033; e-mail libya_emb_ae@foreign.gov.ly; Ambassador Dr ARIF ALI AL-NAYEDH.

Malaysia: POB 3887, Abu Dhabi; tel. (2) 4482775; fax (2) 4482779; e-mail admin@malaysianembassy.ae; internet www.kln.gov.my/perwakilan/abudhabi; Ambassador AHMAD ANWAR BIN ADNAN.

Mauritania: POB 2714, Abu Dhabi; tel. (2) 4462724; fax (2) 4465772; e-mail mminejih@hotmail.com; Ambassador HAMID OULD AHMAD TALEB.

Mexico: POB 108543, Villa 1, Sector 23, Plot 7A, Bain al-Jessrain, Abu Dhabi; tel. (2) 5580088; fax (2) 5580077; e-mail embamex@eim.ae; internet embamex.sre.gob.mx/emiratosarabesunidos; Ambassador FRANCISCO JAVIER ALONSO ESCOBAR.

Morocco: POB 4066, Abu Dhabi; tel. (2) 4433973; fax (2) 4433917; e-mail sifmabo@yahoo.com; internet www.moroccan-emb.ae; Ambassador MUHAMMAD AIT OUALI.

Nepal: POB 38282, Abu Dhabi; tel. (2) 6344767; fax (2) 6344469; e-mail info@nepalembassyuae.org; internet www.nepalembassyuae.org; Ambassador DHANANJAYA JHA.

Netherlands: POB 46560, al-Masood Tower, 6th Floor, Sheikh Hamdan St, Abu Dhabi; tel. (2) 6958000; fax (2) 6313158; e-mail abu@minbuza.nl; internet www.netherlands.ae; Ambassador Dr GERALD MICHELS.

New Zealand: Villa 226/2, al-Karamah St (24th St, between 11th & 13th), al-Karamah Area, Abu Dhabi; tel. (2) 4411222; fax (2) 4411555; e-mail nzembassy.abu.dhabi@mfat.govt.nz; internet www.nzembassy.com/united-arab-emirates; Ambassador MALCOLM MILLAR.

Nigeria: POB 110171, Abu Dhabi; tel. (2) 4431503; fax (2) 4431792; e-mail nigerabudhabi@yahoo.co.uk; Ambassador OMOLADE OLUWATERU.

Norway: POB 47270, Abu Dhabi; tel. (2) 6211221; fax (2) 6213313; e-mail emb.abudhabi@mfa.no; internet www.norway.ae; Ambassador STEN ANDERS BERGE.

Oman: POB 2517, Said bin Tahnon Sq., al-Mushraf Area, Abu Dhabi; tel. (2) 4463333; fax (2) 4464633; e-mail abudhabi@mofa.gov.om; Ambassador Sheikh MUHAMMAD BIN ABDULLAH ALI AL-QATABI.

Pakistan: Plot 2, Sector W59, Embassies Area, Abu Dhabi; tel. (2) 4447800; fax (2) 4447172; e-mail parepabudhabi@pakistanembassyuae.org; internet www.pakistanembassyuae.org; Ambassador JAMIL AHMAD KHAN.

Philippines: POB 3215, Villa 8, St 8, Sector 94, Zone 2, Abu Dhabi; tel. (2) 6390006; fax (2) 6390002; e-mail auhpe@philembassy.ae; internet philembassy.ae; Ambassador GRACE RELUCIO PRINCESA.

Poland: POB 2334, Abu Dhabi; tel. (2) 4465200; fax (2) 4462967; e-mail abudhabi.amb.sekretariat@msz.gov.pl; internet www.abuzabi.polemb.net; Ambassador ADAM KRZYMOWSKI.

Qatar: POB 3503, 26th St, al-Minaseer, Abu Dhabi; tel. (2) 4493300; fax (2) 4493311; e-mail qatar-embassy2009@hotmail.com; Ambassador ABDULLAH M. AL-UTHMAN.

Romania: POB 70416, Abu Dhabi; tel. (2) 4459919; fax (2) 4461143; e-mail romaniae@emirates.net.ae; internet abudhabi.mae.ro; Ambassador ADRIAN MĂCELARU.

Russia: POB 8211, Abu Dhabi; tel. (2) 6721797; fax (2) 6788731; e-mail rusembuae@gmail.com; internet www.uae.mid.ru; Ambassador ALEKSANDR EFIMOV.

Saudi Arabia: POB 4057, Abu Dhabi; tel. (2) 4445700; fax (2) 4448491; e-mail aeemb@mofa.gov.sa; Ambassador IBRAHIM AL-SAAD AL-IBRAHIM.

Somalia: POB 4155, Abu Dhabi; tel. and fax (2) 6651580; fax (2) 6651580; e-mail webmaster@somaligov.net; internet www.uae.somaligov.net; Ambassador AHMED MUHAMMAD IGAL.

South Africa: POB 29446, Abu Dhabi; tel. (2) 4473446; fax (2) 4473031; e-mail info@southafrica.ae; internet www.southafrica.ae; Ambassador MPETJANE KGAOGELO LEKGORO.

Spain: POB 46474, al-Saman Tower, Hamdan St, Abu Dhabi; tel. (2) 6269544; fax (2) 6274978; e-mail emb.abudhabi@maec.es; Ambassador JOSÉ EUGENIO SALARICH.

Sri Lanka: POB 46534, Abu Dhabi; tel. (2) 6316444; fax (2) 6331661; e-mail lankemba@emirates.net.ae; internet www.srilankaembassyuae.com; Ambassador MAHINDA BALASURIYA.

Sudan: POB 4027, Abu Dhabi; tel. (2) 4446699; fax (2) 4490540; e-mail sudembll@emirates.net.ae; Ambassador AHMAD YUSUF MUHAMMAD.

Sweden: POB 31867, Abu Dhabi; tel. (2) 4178800; fax (2) 4178850; e-mail ambassaden.abu-dhabi@gov.se; internet www.swedenabroad.com/abudhabi; Ambassador MAX BJUHR.

Switzerland: POB 46116, Abu Dhabi; tel. (2) 6274636; fax (2) 6269627; e-mail adh.vertretung@eda.admin.ch; internet www.eda.admin.ch/uae; Ambassador ANDREA REICHLIN.

Syria: POB 4011, Abu Dhabi; tel. (2) 4448768; fax (2) 4449387; e-mail info@syrianembassy.ae; internet www.syrianembassy.ae; Ambassador Dr ABD AL-LATIF AL-DABBAGH.

Thailand: POB 47466, Abu Dhabi; tel. (2) 5576551; fax (2) 5576552; e-mail thaiauh@emirates.net.ae; internet www.thaiembassy.org/abudhabi; Ambassador WARAWUDH CHUWIRACH.

Tunisia: POB 4166, Abu Dhabi; tel. (2) 6811331; fax (2) 6812707; e-mail pol_ambtunad@eim.ae; Ambassador TAREK BETTAIEB.

Turkey: POB 3204, Abu Dhabi; tel. (2) 4109999; fax (2) 4109905; e-mail embassy.abudhabi@mfa.gov.tr; internet abudhabi.emb.mfa.gov.tr; Ambassador Ş. VURAL ALTAY.

Uganda: Villa 28, West 17/02, al-Falah St 9, al-Bateen, Abu Dhabi; tel. (2) 6659931; fax (2) 6659934; e-mail info@ugandaembassyuae.com; internet www.ugandaembassyuae.com; Ambassador Prof. IRENE FLORENCE PERSIS WEKIYA.

Ukraine: POB 35572, Abu Dhabi; tel. (2) 6327586; fax (2) 6327506; e-mail embua@embukr.ae; internet www.oae.mfa.gov.ua/oae; Ambassador YURIY V. POLUREZ.

United Kingdom: POB 248, Abu Dhabi; tel. (2) 6101100; fax (2) 6101586; e-mail consular.uae@fco.gov.uk; internet ukinuae.fco.gov.uk; Ambassador DOMINIC JERMEY.

USA: POB 4009, Abu Dhabi; tel. (2) 4142200; fax (2) 4142469; e-mail webmasterabudhabi@state.gov; internet abudhabi.usembassy.gov; Ambassador MICHAEL H. CORBIN.

Yemen: POB 2095, Abu Dhabi; tel. (2) 4448457; fax (2) 4443691; e-mail yemenemb@emirates.net.ae; Ambassador AHMAD ABDULLAH SALEH.

Judicial System

The 95th article of the Constitution of 1971 provided for the establishment of the Union Supreme Court and Union Primary Tribunals as the judicial organs of State.

The Union has exclusive legislative and executive jurisdiction over all matters that are concerned with the strengthening of the federation, such as foreign affairs, defence and Union armed forces, security, finance, communications, traffic control, education, currency, measures, standards and weights, matters relating to nationality and emigration, Union information, etc.

The late President Sheikh Zayed signed the law establishing the new federal courts on 9 June 1978. The new law effectively transferred local judicial authorities into the jurisdiction of the federal system.

Primary tribunals in Abu Dhabi, Sharjah, Ajman and Fujairah are now primary federal tribunals, and primary tribunals in other towns in those emirates have become circuits of the primary federal tribunals.

The primary federal tribunals may sit in any of the capitals of the four emirates and have jurisdiction on all administrative disputes between the Union and individuals, whether the Union is plaintiff or defendant. Civil disputes between Union and individuals will be heard by primary federal tribunals in the defendant's place of normal residence.

The law requires that all judges take a constitutional oath before the Minister of Justice and that the courts apply the rules of *Shari'a* (Islamic religious law) and that no judgment contradicts the *Shari'a*. All employees of the old judiciaries will be transferred to the federal authority without loss of salary or seniority.

Shari'a Court: In February 1994 President Sheikh Zayed ordered that an extensive range of crimes, including murder, theft and adultery, be tried in *Shari'a* courts rather than in civil courts; Chief Shari'a Justice AHMAD ABD AL-AZIZ AL-MUBARAK.

Federal Supreme Court: Pres. and Chief Justice ABD AL-WAHAB ABDUL.

Religion

ISLAM

Most of the inhabitants are Sunni Muslims, while about 16% of Muslims are Shi'ites.

CHRISTIANITY

Roman Catholic Church

Apostolic Vicariate of Southern Arabia: POB 54, Abu Dhabi; tel. (2) 4461895; fax (2) 4465177; e-mail info@ccsarabia.org; internet www.ccsarabia.org; f. 1889; fmrly Apostolic Vicariate of Arabia; renamed as above, following reorganization in 2011; responsible for most of the Arabian peninsula (incl. the UAE, Oman and Yemen), containing an estimated 850,000 Catholics (31 December 2011);

Vicar Apostolic Bishop PAUL HINDER (Titular Bishop of Macon, Georgia).

The Anglican Communion

Within the Episcopal Church in Jerusalem and the Middle East, the UAE forms part of the diocese of Cyprus and the Gulf. The Anglican congregations in the UAE are entirely expatriate. The Bishop in Cyprus and the Gulf resides in Cyprus, while the Archdeacon in the Gulf is resident in Bahrain.

The Press

The state regulator for the sector is the National Media Council, under the Chairmanship of SAQR GHOBASH SAID GHOBASH (Minister of Labour).

ABU DHABI

Abu Dhabi Magazine: POB 662, Abu Dhabi; tel. (2) 6214000; fax (2) 6348954; f. 1969; Arabic, some articles in English; monthly; Editor ZUHAIR AL-QADI; circ. 18,000.

Abu Dhabi Official Gazette: POB 19, Abu Dhabi; tel. (2) 6688413; fax (2) 6669981; e-mail gazette@ecouncil.ae; f. 1965; Arabic; daily; official reports and papers.

Abu Dhabi Tempo: POB 33760, Abu Dhabi; tel. (2) 6673349; fax (2) 6673389; e-mail info@abudhabitempo.com; internet www.abudhabitempo.com; f. 2009; monthly; local community news; distributed free of charge; publ. by BrandMoxie; Editor SANA BAGERSH; circ. 30,000.

Al-Ain Times: POB 15229, al-Ain; tel. (3) 7671995; fax (3) 7671997; e-mail alaintimes@gmail.com; internet www.alaintimesuae.com; f. 2006; English and Arabic; weekly; publ. by Alpha Beta Publrs and Media Consultants; Chief Editor FADWA M. B. AL-MUGHARIBI.

Akhbar al-Arab: POB 54040, Abu Dhabi; tel. (2) 4486000; e-mail info@akhbaralarab.ae; internet www.akhbaralarab.co.ae; f. 1999; daily; political; circ. 50,000.

Alrroya Aleqtisadiya (Economic Vision): POB 112494, Abu Dhabi; tel. (2) 6517777; fax (2) 6517772; internet www.alrroya.com; f. 2009; Arabic; business daily; publ. by Imedia LLC; Man. Editor REFAAT JAAFAR.

Hiya (She): POB 2488, Abu Dhabi; tel. (2) 4474121; Arabic; weekly for women; publ. by Dar al-Wahdah.

Al-Ittihad (Unity): POB 791, Abu Dhabi; tel. (2) 4455555; fax (2) 4455126; e-mail editor@alittihad.co.ae; internet www.alittihad.ae; f. 1972; Arabic; daily and weekly; publ. by Abu Dhabi Media Co; Man. Editor ALI ABU AL-RISH; circ. 58,000 daily, 60,000 weekly.

Majid: POB 791, Abu Dhabi; tel. (2) 4451804; fax (2) 4451455; e-mail majid-magazine@emi.co.ae; internet www.majid.ae; f. 1979; Arabic; weekly; children's magazine; publ. by Abu Dhabi Media Co; Man. Editor AHMAD OMAR; circ. 164,000.

The National: Abu Dhabi Media Co, 4th St, Sector 18, Zone 1, Abu Dhabi; tel. (2) 4144000; fax (2) 4144001; internet www.thenational.ae; f. 2008; English; daily; publ. by Abu Dhabi Media Co; Editorial Dir MARTIN NEWLAND; Editor-in-Chief HASSAN FATTAH.

Zahrat al-Khaleej (Splendour of the Gulf): POB 791, Abu Dhabi; tel. (2) 4461600; fax (2) 4451653; e-mail abedrabbo@admedia.ae; f. 1979; Arabic; weekly; women's magazine; publ. by Abu Dhabi Media Co; Editor-in-Chief TALAL TOHME; circ. 10,000.

DUBAI

Al-Bayan (The Official Report): POB 2710, Dubai; tel. (4) 3444400; fax (4) 3447846; e-mail readers@albayan.ae; internet www.albayan.ae; f. 1980; Arabic; daily; publ. by Awraq Publishing, a subsidiary of Arab Media Group; CEO SAMI AL-QAMZI; Editor-in-Chief DA'EN SHAHIN; circ. 82,575.

Emarat Al-Youm: POB 502012, Dubai; e-mail 1971ey@gmail.com; internet www.emaratalyoum.com; Arabic; business daily; publ. by Awraq Publishing, a subsidiary of Arab Media Group; Editor SAMI AL-RIYAMI.

Emirates 24/7: POB 191919, Dubai; tel. (4) 3062222; fax (4) 3407698; e-mail news@emirates247.com; internet www.emirates247.com; f. 2005; English; online; Editor-in-Chief RIYAD MICKDADY.

Emirates Woman: POB 2331, Dubai; tel. (4) 2824060; fax (4) 2827593; e-mail faye@motivate.co.ae; f. 1981; English; monthly; fashion, health and beauty; publ. by Motivate Publishing; Editor FAYE JAMES; circ. 20,324.

Gulf News: Sheikh Zayed Rd, POB 6519, Dubai; tel. (4) 3447100; fax (4) 3441627; e-mail editor@gulfnews.com; internet www.gulfnews.com; f. 1978; English; daily; two weekly supplements, *Junior News* (Wed.), *Gulf Weekly* (Thur.); publ. by Al-Nisr Publishing; Editor-in-Chief ABD-AL HAMID AHMAD; circ. 103,000.

Al-Jundi (The Soldier): POB 2838, Dubai; tel. (4) 3532222; fax (4) 3744272; e-mail mod5@eim.ae; f. 1973; Arabic; monthly; military and cultural; Editor-in-Chief Brig. MUHAMMAD ALI ABDULLAH AL-EASSA; circ. 10,000.

Khaleej Times: POB 11243, Dubai; tel. (4) 3383535; fax (4) 3383345; e-mail ktimes@emirates.net.ae; internet www.khaleejtimes.com; f. 1978; a Galadari enterprise; English; daily; distributed throughout the region and in India, Pakistan and the United Kingdom; free weekly supplement, *Weekend* (Fri.); Publr and Editor-in-Chief MUHAMMAD A. R. GALADARI; Man. Dir QASSIM MUHAMMAD YOUSUF; circ. 70,000.

Al-Manara: Office 129, Bldg 10, Dubai Media City; tel. (4) 3901777; fax (4) 3904554; e-mail dar@almanaramagazine.ae; internet www.almanaramagazine.ae; Arabic; lifestyle; Editor WALID AL-SAADI.

Trade and Industry: POB 1457, Dubai; tel. (4) 2280000; fax (4) 2211646; e-mail dcciinfo@dcci.org; internet www.dubaichamber.ae; f. 1975; Arabic and English; monthly; publ. by Dubai Chamber of Commerce and Industry; circ. 26,000.

UAE Digest: POB 500595, Dubai; tel. (4) 3672245; fax (4) 3678613; e-mail info@sterlingp.ae; internet www.sterlingp.ae; English; monthly; publ. by Sterling Publications; current affairs; Man. Editor K. RAVEENDRAN.

Viva: POB 500024, Dubai; tel. (4) 2108000; fax (4) 2108080; e-mail vivaletters@itp.com; internet www.vivamagazine.ae; f. 2004; publ. by ITP; Editor MANDIE GOWER; circ. 23,000.

What's On: POB 2331, Dubai; tel. (4) 2824060; fax (4) 2827593; e-mail editor-wo@motivate.co.ae; internet www.whatsonlive.com; f. 1979; English; monthly; publ. by Motivate Publishing; Group Editor and Man. Partner IAN FAIRSERVICE; circ. 31,055.

Xpress: POB 6519, Dubai; tel. (4) 3447100; fax (4) 3420433; e-mail editor@alnisrmedia.com; internet www.xpress4me.com; f. 2007; English; weekly; publ. by Al-Nisr Publishing; Editor NIRMALA JANSSEN.

RAS AL-KHAIMAH

Akhbar Ras al-Khaimah (Ras al-Khaimah News): POB 87, Ras al-Khaimah; Arabic; monthly; local news.

Al-Ghorfa: POB 87, Ras al-Khaimah; tel. (7) 2333511; fax (7) 2330233; f. 1970; Arabic and English; free monthly; publ. by Ras al-Khaimah Chamber of Commerce and Industry; Editor ZAKI H. SAQR.

Ras al-Khaimah Magazine: POB 200, Ras al-Khaimah; Arabic; monthly; commerce and trade; Chief Editor AHMAD AL-TADMORI.

SHARJAH

Al-Azman al-Arabia (Times of Arabia): POB 5823, Sharjah; tel. (6) 5356034.

The Gulf Today: POB 30, Sharjah; tel. (6) 5777999; fax (6) 5777737; e-mail tgt@gulftoday.ae; internet gulftoday.ae; f. 1996; English; daily; Editor-in-Chief AYSHA TARYAM; circ. 38,000.

Al-Khaleej (The Gulf): POB 30, Sharjah; tel. (6) 5625304; fax (6) 5598547; e-mail kh_readers@alkhaleej.ae; internet www.alkhaleej.co.ae; f. 1970; Arabic; daily; political; independent; Editor GHASSAN TAHBOUB; circ. 82,750.

Al-Sharooq (Sunrise): POB 30, Sharjah; tel. (6) 5598777; fax (6) 5599336; f. 1970; Arabic; weekly; general interest; Editor YOUSUF AL-HASSAN.

Al-Tijarah (Commerce): Sharjah Chamber of Commerce and Industry, POB 580, Sharjah; tel. (6) 5116600; fax (6) 5681119; e-mail scci@sharjah.gov.ae; internet www.sharjah.gov.ae; f. 1970; Arabic/English; monthly magazine; circ. 50,000; annual trade directory; circ. 100,000.

NEWS AGENCY

Emirates News Agency (WAM): POB 3790, Abu Dhabi; tel. (2) 4454545; fax (2) 4044200; e-mail wamnews@eim.ae; internet www.wam.org.ae; f. 1977; operated by the Govt; Dir-Gen. IBRAHIM AL-ABED; Chief Editor JAMAL NASSER.

Publishers

All Prints: POB 857, Abu Dhabi; tel. (2) 6336999; fax (2) 6320844; e-mail allprints@allprints.co.ae; internet www.all-prints.com; f. 1968; publishing and distribution; Partners BUSHRA KHAYAT, TAHSEEN S. KHAYAT.

ITP: POB 500024, Dubai; tel. (4) 4443000; fax (4) 4443030; e-mail info@itp.com; internet www.itp.com; f. 1987; publishes more than 60 magazines, incl. *Ahlan!*, *Arabian Business*, *Time Out Dubai*, *Viva*; CEO WALID AKAWI.

Kalimat Publishing and Distribution: POB 21969, Sharjah; tel. (6) 5566696; fax (6) 5566691; e-mail info@kalimat.ae; internet www.kalimat.ae; f. 2007; children's books; CEO Sheikha BODOUR AL-QASIMI.

Motivate Publishing: POB 2331, Dubai; tel. (4) 2824060; fax (4) 2820428; e-mail motivate@motivate.ae; internet www.motivatepublishing.com; f. 1979; books and magazines; Man. Partner and Group Editor IAN FAIRSERVICE.

Sterling Publications: POB 500595, Dubai; tel. (4) 3672245; fax (4) 3678613; e-mail info@sterlingp.ae; publs include *UAE Digest*, *Banking*, *Business Review* and *Ajman Today*; Man. Dir SANKARA NARAYANAN; Man. Editor K. RAVEENDRAN.

Broadcasting and Communications

TELECOMMUNICATIONS

Emirates Integrated Telecommunications Co (du): POB 502666, Dubai; tel. (4) 3600000; fax (4) 3604440; e-mail talk-to-us@du.ae; internet www.du.ae; f. 2006; commenced operations under the brand name *du* in Feb. 2007; 40% owned by the federal Govt, 20% by TECOM Investment, 20% by Mubadala Devt Co and 20% by public shareholders; provides telecommunications services throughout the UAE; Chair. AHMAD BIN BYAT; CEO OSMAN SULTAN.

Emirates Telecommunications Corpn (Etisalat): POB 3838, Abu Dhabi; tel. (2) 6182091; fax (2) 6334448; e-mail prd@etisalat.co.ae; internet www.etisalat.co.ae; f. 1976; provides telecommunications services throughout the UAE; Chair. MUHAMMAD HASSAN OMRAN; CEO MUHAMMAD AL-QAMZI.

Regulatory Authority

Telecommunications Regulatory Authority (TRA): POB 26662, Abu Dhabi; tel. (2) 6269999; fax (2) 6118209; e-mail info@tra.ae; internet www.tra.ae; f. 2004; Chair. MUHAMMAD BIN AHMAD AL-QAMZI; Dir-Gen. MUHAMMAD AL-GHANEM.

BROADCASTING

Radio

Abu Dhabi Radio: Abu Dhabi Media Co, 4th St, Sector 18, Zone 1, Abu Dhabi; tel. (2) 4144000; fax (2) 4144001; internet www.admedia.ae; f. 1969; broadcasts in Arabic over a wide area; also broadcasts in French, Bengali, Filipino and Urdu; affiliated channels include Emarat FM, Quran Kareem Radio, Sawt Al Musiqa; owned and operated by Abu Dhabi Media Co; Dir-Gen. ABD AL-WAHAB AL-RADWAN.

Arabian Radio Network: POB 502012, Dubai; tel. (4) 3912000; fax (4) 3912007; e-mail info@arn.ae; internet www.arn.ae; f. 2001; owned by Arab Media Group; operates 8 stations; CEO MUHAMMAD AL-MULLA.

Capital Radio: POB 63, Abu Dhabi; tel. (2) 4451000; fax (2) 4451155; govt-operated; English-language FM music and news station; Station Man. AIDA HAMZA.

Channel 4 Radio Network: POB 442, Ajman; tel. (6) 7461444; e-mail chris@channel4fm.com; internet www.channel4fm.com; operates 89.1 Radio 4, 104.8 Channel 4, 103.2 Coast, 101.3 Gold and 107.8 Radio Al Rabia stations; owned by Ajman Independent Studios LLC; Head CHRIS ROSE.

Ras al-Khaimah Broadcasting Station: POB 141, Ras al-Khaimah; tel. (7) 2851151; fax (7) 2352300; five transmitters broadcast in Arabic, Urdu, Malayalam, Telugu, Tamil and Bangla; Chair. ABD AL-MALIK BIN KAYED AL-QASSIMI.

Sharjah Radio and Television: POB 111, Sharjah; tel. (6) 5661111; fax (6) 5669999; e-mail info@sharjahtv.ae; internet www.sharjahtv.ae; Dir AMNA KHAMIS GHARIB AL-NAKHI.

Umm al-Qaiwain Broadcasting Station: POB 444, Umm al-Qaiwain; tel. (6) 7666044; fax (6) 7666055; e-mail uaqfm@emirates.net.ae; f. 1978; broadcasts music and news in Arabic, Malayalam, Sinhala and Urdu; Gen. Man. ALI JASSEM.

Television

Abu Dhabi Television: Abu Dhabi Media Co, 4th St, Sector 18, Zone 1, Abu Dhabi; tel. (2) 4144000; fax (2) 4144001; internet www.adtv.ae; f. 1969; reorg. 2008; broadcasts entertainment and news programmes; affiliated channels include Emirates Channel, Abu Dhabi Sports; owned by Abu Dhabi Media Co; Exec. Dir KARIM SARKIS.

Ajman Television Network: POB 442, Ajman; tel. (6) 7465000; fax (6) 7465135; e-mail progajtv@ajmantv.com; internet www.ajmantv.com; f. 1996; broadcasts in Arabic and English; Chair. ABDULLAH MUHAMMAD.

Arabian Television Network: Arab Media Group, POB 500666, Dubai; tel. (4) 3062222; fax (4) 3479965; e-mail info@arabmediagrouponline.com; internet www.arnonline.com; f. 2007; broadcasts own entertainment channels, incl. SHOOFtv and Noor Dubai TV; also adapts international brands for Arab market, such as MTV Arabia; owned by Arab Media Group; Gen. Man. MARYAM AL-FALASI.

City 7 TV: POB 502209, Bldg 4, Dubai Media City, Dubai; tel. (4) 3678142; fax (4) 3678060; e-mail info@city7tv.com; internet www.city7tv.com; Pres. MOHI EL-DIN BIN HENDI.

Dubai Media Inc: POB 835, Dubai; tel. (4) 3369999; fax (4) 3360060; e-mail info@dmi.ae; internet www.dmi.gov.ae; f. 2004; channels include Dubai Television, Dubai One, Sama Dubai, Dubai Sports; state-owned; Chair. Sheikh MAKTOUM BIN MUHAMMAD BIN RASHID AL MAKTOUM; Man. Dir AHMAD ABDULLAH AL-SHEIKH.

Middle East Broadcasting Center (MBC): POB 76267, Dubai; tel. (4) 3919999; fax (4) 3919900; e-mail infotv@mbc.ae; internet www.mbc.net; f. 1991; broadcasts throughout region via satellite; channels include Al-Arabiya News Channel, MBC Persia (Farsi service), MBC 1, 2, 3 and 4 (entertainment); Chair. Sheikh WALID AL-IBRAHIM.

Sharjah Radio and Television: see Radio.

Finance

(cap. = capital; res = reserves; dep. = deposits; m. = million; brs = branches; amounts in dirhams, unless otherwise indicated)

BANKING

Central Bank

Central Bank of the United Arab Emirates: POB 854, Abu Dhabi; tel. (2) 6652220; fax (2) 6652504; e-mail admin@cbuae.gov.ae; internet www.centralbank.ae; f. 1973; acts as issuing authority for local currency; superseded UAE Currency Bd in Dec. 1980; cap. 300m., res 1,200m., dep. 156,274m. (Dec. 2009); Chair. KHALIFA MUHAMMAD AL-KINDI; Gov. SULTAN BIN NASSER AL-SUWAIDI; 5 brs.

Principal Banks

Abu Dhabi Commercial Bank (ADCB): POB 939, Abu Dhabi; tel. (2) 6962222; fax (2) 6450384; e-mail info@adcb.com; internet www.adcb.com; f. 1985 by merger; 65% govt-owned, 35% owned by private investors; cap. 5,595m., res 12,768m., dep. 113,748m. (Dec. 2011); Chair. MUHAMMAD GHANIM AL-SUWAIDI; Exec. Dir ALA'A MUHAMMAD KHALIL ERAIQAT; 40 brs in the UAE, 2 brs in India.

Abu Dhabi Islamic Bank: POB 313, Abu Dhabi; tel. (2) 6100600; fax (2) 6656028; e-mail adib@adib.co.ae; internet www.adib.ae; f. 1997; cap. 4,364m., res 2,892m., dep. 57,103m. (Dec. 2011); Chair. JAWAN AWAIDHA SUHAIL AL-KHAILI; CEO TIRAD MAHMOUD; 60 brs.

Ajman Bank PJSC: POB 7770, Block C, 13th Floor, al-Mina Rd, Ajman Free Zone, Ajman; tel. (6) 7479999; fax (6) 7479990; e-mail info@ajmanbank.ae; internet www.ajmanbank.ae; f. 2008; 25% owned by Govt of Ajman; *Shari'a*-compliant services; cap. 1,000m., res −12m., dep. 2,897m. (Dec. 2011); Chair. Sheikh AMMAR BIN HUMAID AL-NUAIMI; CEO MUHAMMAD AMIRI (acting); 2 brs.

Bank of Sharjah: POB 1394, Sharjah; tel. (6) 5694411; fax (6) 5694422; e-mail enquire@bankofsharjah.com; internet www.bankofsharjah.com; f. 1973; cap. 2,100m., res 1,430m., dep. 14,801m. (Dec. 2010); Chair. AHMAD AL-NOMAN; Exec. Dir and Gen. Man. VAROUJAN NERGUIZIAN; 2 brs.

Commercial Bank of Dubai PSC: POB 2668, Mankhool St, Dubai; tel. (4) 2121000; fax (4) 2121911; e-mail cbd-ho@cbd.ae; internet www.cbd.ae; f. 1969; 20% owned by Govt of Dubai; cap. 1,941m., res 2,948m., dep. 30,380m. (Dec. 2011); Chair. SAEED AHMED GHOBASH; CEO PETER BALTUSSEN; 24 brs.

Commercial Bank International PSC: POB 4449, al-Riqah St, Dubai; tel. (4) 2275265; fax (4) 2279038; e-mail cbiho@emirates.net.ae; internet www.cbiuae.com; f. 1991; cap. 1,407m., res 210m., dep. 9,139m. (Dec. 2011); Chair. MUHAMMAD SULTAN AL-QADI; CEO KRIS BABICCI; 9 brs.

Dubai Bank PJSC: POB 65555, Sheikh Zayed Rd, Dubai; e-mail info@dubaibank.ae; internet www.dubaibank.ae; tel. (4) 3328989; fax (4) 3290071; f. 2002 by Emaar Properties, a real estate developer; cap. 1,500m., res 113m., dep. 15,306m. (Dec. 2009); Chair. MUHAMMAD HADI AHMED AL-HUSSAINI.

Dubai Islamic Bank PJSC: POB 1080, Airport Rd, Deira, Dubai; tel. (4) 2953000; fax (4) 2954111; e-mail contactus@dib.ae; internet www.alislami.ae; f. 1975; cap. 3,797m., res 4,394m., dep. 68,823m. (Dec. 2011); Chair. Dr MUHAMMAD EBRAHIM AL-SHAIBANI; CEO ABDULLAH AL-HAMLI; 44 brs.

Emirates Investment Bank PJSC: POB 5503, Office 904, Twin Towers, Baniyas St, Deira, Dubai; tel. (4) 2328080; fax (4) 2328134; e-mail aeibank@emirates.net.ae; internet www.aeibank.com; f. 1976 as Arab Emirate Investment Bank Ltd; name changed as above in 2010; cap. 49m., res 54m., dep. 1,130m. (Dec. 2011); Chair. OMAR ABDULLAH AL-FUTTAIM.

Emirates Islamic Bank PJSC: POB 5547, Baniyas Rd, Deira, Dubai; tel. (4) 2287474; fax (4) 2272172; e-mail info@emiratesislamicbank.ae; internet www.emiratesislamicbank.ae; f. 1976 as Middle East Bank; became a Public Joint Stock Co (PJSC) in 1995; present name adopted 2004; subsidiary (99.8% owned) of Emirates Bank Int; cap. 2,430m., res 319m., dep. 27,934m. (Dec. 2010); Chair. HESHAM ABDULLA AL-QASSIM; CEO JAMAL SAEED BIN GHALAITA; 32 brs.

Emirates NBD PJSC: POB 2923, Baniyas Rd, Deira, Dubai; tel. (4) 2256256; fax (4) 2227662; e-mail ibrahims@emiratesbank.com; internet www.emiratesnbd.com; f. 2007 by merger of Emirates Bank Int. PJSC with Nat. Bank of Dubai PJSC; 56% owned by Govt of Dubai; cap. 9,557m., res 17,789m., dep. 219,419m. (Dec. 2011); Chair. Sheikh AHMAD BIN SAID AL MAKTOUM; CEO RICK PUDNER; 132 brs.

First Gulf Bank: POB 6316, Sheikh Zayed St, Abu Dhabi; tel. (2) 6816666; fax (2) 6814282; e-mail info@fgb.ae; internet www.fgb.ae; f. 1979; cap. 1,500m., res 16,894m., dep. 111,721m. (Dec. 2011); Chair. Sheikh MANSOUR BIN ZAYED AL NAHYAN; Man. Dir ABD AL-HAMID SAID; CEO ANDRÉ SAYEGH; 19 brs.

Investbank PSC: POB 1885, Sharjah; tel. (6) 5694440; fax (6) 5694442; e-mail custserv@invest-bank.ae; internet www.investbank.ae; f. 1975; cap. 1,155m., res 502m., dep. 7,657m. (Dec. 2011); Chair. Dr ABDULLAH OMRAN TARYAM; Gen. Man. SAMI R. FARHAT; 12 brs.

Mashreqbank PSC: POB 1250, Omer bin al-Khattab St, Deira, Dubai; tel. (4) 2223333; fax (4) 2226061; internet www.mashreqbank.com; f. 1967 as Bank of Oman; present name adopted 1993; cap. 1,690m., res 779m., dep. 52,640m. (Dec. 2011); Chair. and Pres. ABDULLAH BIN AHMAD AL-GHURAIR; CEO ABD AL-AZIZ ABDULLAH AL-GHURAIR; 57 brs in the UAE, 22 brs abroad.

Al-Masraf: POB 46733, ARBIFT Bldg, Hamdan St, Tourist Club Area, Abu Dhabi; tel. (2) 6721900; fax (2) 6777550; e-mail arbiftho@emirates.net.ae; internet www.arbift.com; f. 1976 as Arab Bank for Investment and Foreign Trade; renamed as above in 2007; jointly owned by the UAE Federal Govt, the Libyan Arab Foreign Bank and the Banque Extérieure d'Algérie; cap. 1,500m., res 1,201m., dep. 9,333m. (Dec. 2011); Chair. MUHAMMAD SAIF AL-SUWAIDI; Gen. Man. A. S. PILLAI (acting); 7 brs in the UAE.

National Bank of Abu Dhabi (NBAD): POB 4, Tariq ibn Ziad St, Abu Dhabi; tel. (2) 6111111; fax (2) 6275738; e-mail CustomerSupport@nbad.com; internet www.nbad.com; f. 1968; 73% owned by Abu Dhabi Investment Council, 3% by foreign institutions and the remainder by UAE citizens; issued Islamic bonds for the first time in June 2010; cap. 2,870m., res 15,106m., dep. 191,612m. (Dec. 2011); Chair. NASSER AHMAD KHALIFA AL-SUWAIDI; Group Chief Exec. MICHAEL H. TOMALIN; 73 brs in the UAE, 31 brs abroad.

National Bank of Fujairah PSC: POB 2979, Dubai; tel. (4) 3971700; fax (4) 3973922; e-mail nbfho@nbf.ae; internet www.nbf.ae; f. 1982; owned jointly by Govt of Fujairah (36.78%), Govt of Dubai (9.78%), and UAE citizens and cos (51.25%); cap. 1,100m., res 563m., dep. 10,338m. (Dec. 2011); Chair. Sheikh SALEH BIN MUHAMMAD AL-SHARQI; CEO VINCE COOK; 11 brs.

National Bank of Ras al-Khaimah PSC (RAKBANK): POB 5300, Rakbank Bldg, Oman St, al-Nakheel, Ras al-Khaimah; tel. (7) 2281127; fax (7) 2283238; e-mail nbrakho@emirates.net.ae; internet www.rakbank.ae; f. 1976; 52.75% owned by Govt of Ras al-Khaimah; cap. 1,385m., res 2,154m., dep. 18,624m. (Dec. 2011); Chair. Sheikh OMAR BIN SAQR AL-QASIMI; CEO GRAHAM HONEYBILL; 16 brs.

National Bank of Umm al-Qaiwain PSC: POB 800, Umm al-Qaiwain Private Properties Dept Bldg, King Faisal St, Umm al-Qaiwain; tel. (6) 7655225; fax (6) 7655440; e-mail nbuq@nbq.ae; internet www.nbq.ae; f. 1982; cap. 1,600m., res 1,018m., dep. 7,090m. (Dec. 2011); Chair. Sheikh SAUD BIN RASHID AL-MU'ALLA; Man. Dir and CEO Sheikh NASSER BIN RASHID AL-MU'ALLA; 16 brs.

Noor Islamic Bank PJSC: POB 8822, Dubai; tel. (4) 4268888; fax (4) 3456789; internet www.noorbank.com; f. 2008; *Shari'a*-compliant services; 25% owned by Investment Corpn of Dubai, 25% by Dubai Group, 5% by UAE Federal Govt, 45% by private investors; total assets 22,000m.; Chair. Sheikh AHMAD BIN SAEED AL MAKTOUM; CEO HUSSAIN AL-QEMZI; 10 brs.

Sharjah Islamic Bank: POB 4, Al-Borj Ave, Sharjah; tel. (6) 5115123; fax (6) 5681699; e-mail contact.center@sib.ae; internet www.sib.ae; f. 1976 as Nat. Bank of Sharjah; present name adopted 2005, reflecting the bank's conversion to *Shari'a*-compliant operations; commercial bank; cap. 2,425m., res 1,396m., dep. 11,299m. (Dec. 2011); Chair. Sheikh SULTAN BIN MUHAMMAD BIN SULTAN AL-QASSIMI; CEO MUHAMMAD AHMAD ABDULLAH; 13 brs.

Union National Bank (UNB): POB 3865, Salam St, Abu Dhabi; tel. (2) 6741600; fax (2) 6786080; e-mail feedback@unb.co.ae; internet www.unb.co.ae; f. 1983; fmrly Bank of Credit and Commerce (Emirates); cap. 4,495m., res 2,333m., dep. 60,884m. (Dec. 2011); Chair. Sheikh NAHYAN BIN MUBARAK AL NAHYAN; CEO MUHAMMAD NASR ABDEEN; 26 brs in the UAE.

United Arab Bank: POB 25022, HE Sheikh Abdullah bin Salem al-Qassimi Bldg, 6th Floor, al-Qassimi St, Sharjah; tel. (6) 5733900; fax (6) 5733907; e-mail uarbae@emirates.net.ae; internet www.uab.ae; f. 1975; affiliated to Société Générale, France; 35% owned by Commercial Bank of Qatar; cap. 996m., res 610m., dep. 8,693m. (Dec. 2011); Chair. Sheikh FAISAL BIN SULTAN BIN SALEM AL-QASSIMI; CEO PAUL TROWBRIDGE; 9 brs.

Development Bank

Emirates Industrial Bank: POB 2722, Arab Monetary Fund Bldg, 6th Floor, Corniche Rd, Abu Dhabi; tel. (2) 6339700; fax (2) 6319191; e-mail projects_auh@emiratesindustrialbank.net; internet www.eib.ae; f. 1982; offers low-cost loans to enterprises with at least 51% local ownership; 100% state-owned; cap. 200m.; Chair. OBAID HUMAID AL-TAYER; Gen. Man. MUHAMMAD ABD AL-BAKI MUHAMMAD.

Bankers' Association

United Arab Emirates Bankers' Association: POB 44307, Abu Dhabi; tel. (2) 4467706; fax (2) 4463718; e-mail ebauae@emirates.net.ae; internet www.eba-ae.com; f. 1983; Chair. AHMAD HUMAID AL-TAYER (Chair., Commercial Bank of Dubai); Gen. Man. FATHI M. SKAIK.

SOVEREIGN WEALTH FUNDS

Abu Dhabi Investment Authority (ADIA): POB 3600, 211 Corniche, Abu Dhabi; tel. (2) 4150000; fax (2) 4151000; internet www.adia.ae; f. 1976; manages Govt of Abu Dhabi's investment portfolio; Chair. Sheikh KHALIFA BIN ZAYED AL NAHYAN (President of the UAE and Ruler of Abu Dhabi); Man. Dir Sheikh HAMAD BIN ZAYED AL NAHYAN.

Abu Dhabi Investment Company (Invest AD): POB 46309, Abu Dhabi; tel. (2) 6658100; fax (2) 6650575; e-mail info@investad.ae; internet www.investad.ae; f. 1977; investment of govt funds, and advisory activities in the UAE and the Middle East; 98% owned by Abu Dhabi Investment Council and 2% by Nat. Bank of Abu Dhabi; Chair. KHALIFA M. AL-KINDI; CEO NAZEM FAWWAZ AL-KUDSI.

Emirates Investment Authority: POB 3235, Abu Dhabi; e-mail careers@eia.gov.ae; internet www.eia.gov.ae; f. 2007; federal sovereign wealth fund; Chair. Sheikh MANSOUR BIN ZAYED AL NAHYAN (Deputy Prime Minister and Minister of Presidential Affairs); CEO MUBARAK RASHID AL-MANSOURI.

Investment Corporation of Dubai: POB 333888, Dubai International Financial Center, 6th Floor, DIFC Gate Village, Dubai; tel. (4) 7071333; fax (4) 7071444; e-mail info@icd.gov.ae; internet www.icd.gov.ae; f. 2006; manages Govt of Dubai's investment portfolio; Chair. Sheikh MUHAMMAD BIN RASHID AL MAKTOUM (Ruler of Dubai); Exec. Dir and CEO MUHAMMAD I. AL-SHAIBANI.

RAK Investment Authority: POB 31291, Ras al-Khaimah; tel. (7) 2446533; fax (7) 2447202; e-mail gm@rakinvestmentauthority.com; internet www.rak-ia.com; f. 2005; sovereign wealth fund of Ras al-Khaimah Govt; cap. US $1,200m. (2009); CEO Dr KHATER MASAAD.

STOCK EXCHANGES

Abu Dhabi Securities Exchange (ADX): POB 54500, Abu Dhabi; tel. (2) 6277777; fax (2) 6128728; e-mail info@adx.ae; internet www.adx.ae; f. 2000 as Abu Dhabi Securities Market, renamed as above 2008; 67 listed cos (Jan. 2010); Chair. NASSER AHMAD AL-SUWAIDI; Dir-Gen. TOM HEALY.

Dubai Financial Market (DFM): POB 9700, Dubai; tel. (4) 3055555; fax (4) 3314924; e-mail helpdesk@dfm.co.ae; internet www.dfm.co.ae; f. 2000; restructured to comply with *Shari'a* principles in 2006; 63 listed cos, 7 bonds, 15 mutual funds (Sept. 2008); market capitalization AED 61,370m. (Feb. 2004); Chair. ABD AL-JALIL YOUSUF; CEO and Man. Dir ESSA ABD AL-FATTAH KAZIM.

NASDAQ Dubai: POB 53536, The Exchange Bldg, Level 7, Gate District, Dubai International Financial Centre, Dubai; tel. (4) 3055455; fax (4) 4534068; e-mail corpcomm@nasdaqdubai.com; internet www.nasdaqdubai.com; f. 2005 as Dubai Int. Financial Exchange; renamed as above 2008; Chair. ABD AL-WAHED AL-FAHIM; CEO HAMED ALI.

Regulatory Authority

Securities and Commodities Authority: POB 33733, Abu Dhabi; tel. (2) 6277888; fax (2) 6274600; e-mail contactus@sca.ae; internet sca-mo1.sca.ae; f. 2000; Chair. SULTAN BIN SAID AL-MANSOURI (Minister of Economy); CEO ABDULLAH SALEM AL-TURIFI.

INSURANCE

Abu Dhabi National Insurance Co (ADNIC): POB 839, Abu Dhabi; tel. (2) 8040100; fax (2) 6268600; e-mail adnic@adnic.ae; internet www.adnic.ae; f. 1972; subscribed 25% by the Govt of Abu Dhabi and 75% by UAE nationals; all classes of insurance; Chair. KHALIFA MUHAMMAD AL-KINDI.

Al-Ahlia Insurance Co: POB 128, Ras al-Khaimah; tel. (7) 2221479; e-mail contactus@alahli.com; internet www.alahli.com; f. 1977; Chair. ABDULLAH S. BAHAMDAN; Gen. Man. YAHYA NOUR EL-DIN; 3 brs.

Al-Ain Ahlia Insurance Co: POB 3077, Abu Dhabi; tel. (2) 4459900; fax (2) 4456685; e-mail alainins@emirates.net.ae; internet www.alaininsurance.com; f. 1975; Chair. MUHAMMAD BIN J. R. AL-BADIE AL-DHAHIRI; Gen. Man. MUHAMMAD MAZHAR HAMADEH; brs in Dubai, Sharjah, Tarif, Ghouifat and al-Ain.

Dubai Insurance Co PSC: POB 3027, Dubai; tel. (4) 2693030; fax (4) 2693727; e-mail info@dubins.ae; internet www.dubins.ae; f. 1970; Chair. BUTI OBAID AL-MULLA.

Al-Fujairah National Insurance Co PSC: POB 277, Fujairah; tel. (9) 2233355; fax (9) 2224344; e-mail ho@fujinsco.ae; internet www.afnic.ae; f. 1976; 84.75% owned by Govt of Fujairah; cap. 75m.; Chair. ABD AL-GHAFOUR BAHROUZIAN; Gen. Man. ANTOINE MAALOULI.

Sharjah Insurance Co: POB 792, Sharjah; tel. (6) 5686690; fax (6) 5686545; e-mail sico@emirates.net.ae; internet www.shjins.com; f. 1970; Chair. Sheikh MUHAMMAD BIN SAOUD AL-QASSIMI; Gen. Man. AHMED KHATER.

Union Insurance Co PSC: POB 1225, Ajman; tel. (6) 7466996; fax (6) 7466997; e-mail unins@emirates.net.ae; internet www.unioninsuranceuae.com; national insurance co of Ajman emirate; Chair. ABDULLAH HUMAID AL-MAZROUI; Gen. Man. SAMER S. BUSHNAQ.

Trade and Industry

DEVELOPMENT ORGANIZATIONS

Abu Dhabi Fund for Development (ADFD): POB 814, al-Salam St, Abu Dhabi; tel. (2) 6441000; fax (2) 6440800; e-mail ifo@adfd.ae; internet www.adfd.ae; f. 1971; offers economic aid to other Arab states and developing countries in support of their development; cap. AED 4,000m.; Dir-Gen. SAID KHALFAN MATAR AL-ROMAITHI.

Abu Dhabi Investment Council (ADIC): POB 3600, Abu Dhabi; tel. (2) 4150000; fax (2) 4151000; f. 2007; responsible for co-ordinating Abu Dhabi's investment policy; Chair. Sheikh KHALIFA BIN ZAYED AL NAHYAN; 1 br. overseas.

Department of Economic Development Abu Dhabi: POB 12, Abu Dhabi; tel. (2) 6727200; fax (2) 6727749; e-mail ier@adeconomy.ae; internet www.adeconomy.ae; f. 1974; supervises Abu Dhabi's Economic Vision 2030 programme; Chair. NASSER AL-SOWAIDI; Under-Sec. MUHAMMAD OMAR ABDULLAH.

General Holding Corpn (GHC): POB 4499, Abu Dhabi; tel. (2) 6144444; fax (2) 6312857; e-mail info@ghc.ae; internet www.ghc.ae; f. 1979 as Gen. Industry Corpn; name changed as above 2004; responsible for the promotion of non-petroleum-related industry; Chair. Sheikh HAMAD BIN ZAYED AL NAHYAN; Vice-Chair. NASSER AHMAD AL-SOWAIDI.

CHAMBERS OF COMMERCE

Federation of UAE Chambers of Commerce and Industry: POB 3014, Abu Dhabi; tel. (2) 6214144; fax (2) 6339210; POB 8886, Dubai; tel. (4) 2955500; fax (4) 2941212; e-mail info@fcciuae.ae; internet www.fcciuae.ae; f. 1976; seven mem. chambers; Chair. SALAH SALEM BIN OMAIR AL-SHAMSI; Sec.-Gen. ABDULLAH SULTAN ABDULLAH.

Abu Dhabi Chamber of Commerce and Industry: POB 662, Abu Dhabi; tel. (2) 6214000; fax (2) 6215867; e-mail services@adcci.gov.ae; internet www.abudhabichamber.ae; f. 1969; 45,000 mems; Pres. SALAH SALEM BIN OMAIR AL-SHAMSI; Dir-Gen. MUHAMMAD RASHID AL-HAMELI.

Ajman Chamber of Commerce and Industry: POB 662, Ajman; tel. (6) 7422177; fax (6) 7471666; e-mail info@ajcci.gov.ae; internet www.ajcci.gov.ae; f. 1977; Chair. OBEID BIN ALI AL-MUHAIRI; Dir-Gen. MUHAMMAD AL-HAMRANI.

Dubai Chamber of Commerce and Industry: POB 1457, Dubai; tel. (4) 2280000; fax (4) 2211646; e-mail customercare@dubaichamber.ae; internet www.dubaichamber.ae; f. 1965; 108,000 mems (2007); Chair. ABD AL-RAHMAN SAIF AL-GHURAIR; Dir-Gen. HAMAD BUAMIM.

Fujairah Chamber of Commerce, Industry and Agriculture: POB 738, Fujairah; tel. (9) 2222400; fax (9) 2221464; internet www.fujcci.ae; Pres. SAID ALI KHAMAS; Dir-Gen. MUHAMMAD KHALID AL-JASSEM.

Ras al-Khaimah Chamber of Commerce and Industry: POB 87, Ras al-Khaimah; tel. (7) 2260000; fax (7) 2260112; e-mail rcci@rakchamber.ae; internet www.rakchamber.ae; f. 1967; 17,840 mems (Dec. 2007); Chair. YOUSUF AL-NEAIMI; Dir-Gen. Dr NASER AHMED SALMEEN.

Sharjah Chamber of Commerce and Industry: POB 580, Sharjah; tel. (6) 5116600; fax (6) 5681119; e-mail scci@sharjah.gov.ae; internet www.sharjah.gov.ae; f. 1970; 33,500 mems; Chair. AHMAD MUHAMMAD AL-MIDFA'A; Dir-Gen. SAID OBAID AL-JARWAN.

Umm al-Qaiwain Chamber of Commerce and Industry: POB 436, Umm al-Qaiwain; tel. (6) 7651111; fax (6) 7657056; e-mail uaqcci@emirates.net.ae; Pres. ABDULLAH RASHID AL-KHARJI; Man. Dir SHAKIR AL-ZAYANI.

STATE HYDROCARBONS COMPANIES

Abu Dhabi

Supreme Petroleum Council: POB 898, Abu Dhabi; tel. (2) 602000; fax (2) 6023389; f. 1988; assumed authority and responsibility for the administration and supervision of all petroleum affairs in Abu Dhabi; Chair. Sheikh KHALIFA BIN ZAYED AL NAHYAN; Sec.-Gen. YOUSUF BIN OMEIR BIN YOUSUF.

Abu Dhabi National Oil Co (ADNOC): POB 898, Abu Dhabi; tel. (2) 6020000; fax (2) 6023389; e-mail adnoc@adnoc.com; internet www.adnoc.ae; f. 1971; cap. AED 7,500m.; state co; deals in all phases of oil industry; owns two refineries: one on Umm al-Nar island and one at Ruwais; Habshan Gas Treatment Plant (scheduled for partial privatization); gas pipeline distribution network; a salt and chlorine plant; holds 60% participation in operations of ADMA-OPCO and ADCO, and 88% of ZADCO; has 100% control of Abu Dhabi Nat. Oil Co for Oil Distribution (ADNOC-FOD), Abu Dhabi Nat. Tanker Co (ADNATCO), Nat. Drilling Co (NDC) and interests in numerous other cos, both in the UAE and overseas; ADNOC is operated by Supreme Petroleum Council; Chair. Sheikh KHALIFA BIN ZAYED AL NAHYAN (Pres. of the UAE and Ruler of Abu Dhabi); CEO ABDULLAH NASSER AL-SUWAIDI.

Subsidiaries include:

Abu Dhabi Co for Onshore Oil Operations (ADCO): POB 270, Abu Dhabi; tel. (2) 6040000; fax (2) 6665523; e-mail webmaster@adco.ae; internet www.adco.ae; f. 1978; shareholders are ADNOC (60%), BP, Shell and Total (9.5% each), ExxonMobil (9.5%) and Partex (2%); oil exploration, production and export operations from onshore oilfields; average production (1990): 1.2m. b/d; Chair. YOUSUF BIN OMEIR BIN YOUSUF; Gen. Man. ABD AL-MUNIM SAIF AL-KINDI.

Abu Dhabi Drilling Chemicals and Products Ltd (ADDCAP): POB 46121, Abu Dhabi; tel. (2) 6029000; fax (2) 6029010; e-mail addcap@emirates.net.ae; f. 1975; production of drilling chemicals and provision of marine services; wholly owned subsidiary of ADNOC; Chair. YOUSUF BIN OMEIR BIN YOUSUF; Gen. Man. MAHFOUD A. DARBOUL AL-SHEHHI.

Abu Dhabi Gas Industries Co (GASCO): POB 665, Abu Dhabi; tel. (2) 6030000; fax (2) 6037414; e-mail info@gasco.ae; internet www.gasco.ae; f. 1978; started production in 1981; recovers condensate and LPG from Asab, Bab and Bu Hasa fields for delivery to Ruwais natural gas liquids fractionation plant; capacity of 22,000 metric tons per day; 68% owned by ADNOC; Total, Shell Gas and Partex have a minority interest; Chair. YOUSUF OMEIR BIN YOUSUF; Gen. Man. MUHAMMAD SAHOO AL-SUWAIDI.

Abu Dhabi Gas Liquefaction Co (ADGAS): POB 3500, Abu Dhabi; tel. (2) 6061111; fax (2) 6065500; e-mail info@adgas.com; internet www.adgas.com; f. 1973; 70% owned by ADNOC, 15% by Mitsui and Co, 10% by BP, 5% by Total; operates LGSC and the LNG plant on Das Island, which uses natural gas produced in association with oil from offshore fields and has a design capacity of approx. 2.3m. metric tons of LNG per year and 1.29m. tons of LPG per year; the liquefied gas is sold to the Tokyo Electric Power Co, Japan; Chair. ABDULLAH NASSER AL-SUWAIDI; Gen. Man. SAIF AHMAD AL-GHAFLI.

Abu Dhabi Marine Operating Co (ADMA-OPCO): POB 303, Abu Dhabi; tel. (2) 6060000; fax (2) 6064888; e-mail webmaster@adma.ae; internet www.adma-opco.com; operates a concession 60% owned by ADNOC, 40% by Abu Dhabi Marine Areas Ltd (BP, Total and Japan Oil Devt Co); f. 1977 as an operator for the concession; production (1984): 67.89m. barrels (8.96m. metric tons); Chair. YOUSUF BIN OMEIR BIN YOUSUF; Gen. Man. ALI R. AL-JARWAN.

Abu Dhabi Oil Refining Co (TAKREER): POB 3593, Abu Dhabi; tel. (2) 6027000; fax (2) 6027001; e-mail publicrelation@takreer.com; internet www.takreer.com; refining of crude petroleum; production of chlorine and related chemicals; Chair. YOUSUF BIN OMEIR BIN YOUSUF; Gen. Man. JASIM ALI AL-SAYEGH.

ADNOC Distribution: POB 4188, Abu Dhabi; tel. (2) 6771300; fax (2) 6722322; e-mail Information@adnoc-dist.ae; internet www.adnoc-dist.co.ae; 100% owned by ADNOC; distributes petroleum products in UAE and world-wide; Chair. YOUSUF BIN OMEIR BIN YOUSUF; Gen. Man. JAMAL JABER AL-DHAREEF.

National Drilling Co (NDC): POB 4017, Abu Dhabi; tel. (2) 6776100; fax (2) 6779937; e-mail webmaster@ndc.ae; internet www.ndc.ae; drilling operations; Chair. ABDULLAH NASSER AL-SUWAIDI; Gen. Man. ABDALLAH SAEED AL-SUWAIDI.

National Petroleum Construction Co (NPCC): POB 2058, Abu Dhabi; tel. (2) 5549000; fax (2) 5549111; e-mail npccnet@eim.ae; internet www.npcc.ae; f. 1973; 'turnkey' construction and maintenance of offshore facilities for the petroleum and gas industries; cap. AED 100m.; Chair. HUSSAIN JASEM AL-NOWAIS; CEO AQEEL A. MADHI.

Ajman

Ajman National Oil Co (AJNOC): POB 410, Ajman; tel. (6) 7421218; f. 1983; 50% govt-owned, 50% held by Canadian and private Arab interests.

Dubai

Dubai Petroleum Establishment: POB 2222, Dubai; tel. (4) 3432222; fax (4) 3012200; internet www.dubaipetroleum.ae; f. 1963 as Dubai Petroleum Co; reorg. and renamed as above 2007; wholly owned by Dubai authorities; responsible for managing Dubai's offshore petroleum assets; Gen. Man. JEFF SEVERIN.

DUGAS (Dubai Natural Gas Co Ltd): POB 4311, Dubai (Location: Jebel Ali); tel. (4) 8846000; fax (4) 8846118; wholly owned by Dubai authorities; Dep. Chair. and Dir SULTAN AHMAD BIN SULAYEM.

Emarat: POB 9400, Dubai; tel. (4) 3434444; fax (4) 3433393; e-mail info@emarat.ae; internet www.emarat.ae; f. 1981 as Emirates General Petroleum Corpn, renamed as above 1996; wholly owned by Ministry of Finance; marketing and distribution of petroleum; Chair. OBAID HUMAID AL-TAYER (Minister of State for Financial Affairs); Gen. Man. JAMAL AL-MIDFA.

Emirates National Oil Co (ENOC): POB 6442, ENOC Complex, Sheikh Rashid Rd, Dubai; tel. (4) 3374400; fax (4) 3134702; e-mail webmaster@enoc.com; internet www.enoc.com; f. 1993; responsible for management of Dubai-owned cos in petroleum-marketing sector; Chief Exec. SAEED KHOORY.

Emirates Petroleum Products Co Pvt. Ltd (EPPCO): POB 5589, Dubai; tel. (4) 372131; fax (4) 3031605; e-mail f&e@eppcouae.com; internet www.eppcouae.com; f. 1980; jt venture between Govt of Dubai and Caltex Alkhaleej Marketing; sales of petroleum products, bunkering fuel and bitumen; Chair. Sheikh HAMDAN BIN RASHID AL MAKTOUM.

Sedco-Houston Oil Group: POB 702, Dubai; tel. (4) 3224141; holds onshore concession of over 400,000 ha as well as the offshore concession fmrly held by Texas Pacific Oil; Pres. CARL F. THORNE.

Sharjah

Sharjah Petroleum Council: POB 188, Sharjah; f. 1999; Chair. Sheikh AHMAD BIN SULTAN AL-QASIMI (Deputy Ruler of Sharjah); Sec.-Gen. Eng. WALEED RASHID DEMAS.

Sharjah Liquefied Petroleum Gas Co (SHALCO): POB 787, Sharjah; tel. (6) 5286333; fax (6) 5286111; e-mail shalco@shalco.ae; f. 1984; 100% owned by Sharjah authorities; gas-processing; producer of liquified commercial propane and commercial butane; Dir-Gen. SALEH AL-ALI.

Umm al-Qaiwain

Petroleum and Mineral Affairs Department: POB 9, Umm al-Qaiwain; tel. (6) 7666034; Chair. Sheikh SULTAN BIN AHMAD AL-MU'ALLA.

UTILITIES

Abu Dhabi

Regulation and Supervision Bureau: POB 32800, Abu Dhabi; tel. (2) 4439333; fax (2) 4439334; e-mail bureau@rsb.gov.ae; internet www.rsb.gov.ae; f. 1998; regulatory authority; Chair. MUHAMMAD AHMAD AL-BOWARDI; Dir-Gen. NICK CARTER.

Abu Dhabi Water and Electricity Authority (ADWEA): POB 6120, Abu Dhabi; tel. (2) 6943333; fax (2) 6943192; e-mail pr@adwea.gov.ae; internet www.adwea.gov.ae; f. 1998 to manage the water and electricity sectors and oversee the privatization process; Chair. Dr AHMAD BIN MUBARAK AL-MAZROUI; Dir-Gen. ABDULLAH SAIF AL-NUAIMI.

Abu Dhabi Distribution Co: POB 219, Abu Dhabi; tel. (2) 6423000; fax (2) 6426033; e-mail contactcentre@addc.ae; internet www.addc.ae; f. 1998; distribution of water and electricity; Chair. Sheikh DIAB BIN ZAYED AL NAHYAN.

Abu Dhabi National Energy Co (TAQA): POB 55224, Abu Dhabi; tel. (2) 6943662; fax (2) 6422555; e-mail info@taqa.ae; internet www.taqa.ae; f. 2005; 51% owned by ADWEA; owns assets in power, water, petroleum and mineral sectors in the UAE and abroad; provides more than 85% of the water and electricity produced in Abu Dhabi; Chair. HAMAD AL-HURR AL-SUWAIDI; CEO CARL SHELDON.

Abu Dhabi Transmission and Dispatch Co: POB 173, Abu Dhabi; tel. (2) 6414000; fax (2) 6426333; internet www.transco.ae; f. 1999; operation and devt of the transmission network for water and electricity; Chair. Dr ABDULLAH AL-SUWAIDI; Man. Dir DAVID COPESTAKE.

Abu Dhabi Water and Electricity Co (ADWEC): POB 51111, Abu Dhabi; tel. (2) 6943333; fax (2) 6425773; e-mail webmaster@adwec.ae; internet www.adwec.ae; f. 1999; responsible for forecasting and managing the supply and demand of electricity and water; Chair. AHMAD SAIF AL-DARMAKI; Man. Dir GERHARDT GLEISSNER.

Al-Ain Distribution Co: POB 1065, al-Ain; tel. (3) 7636000; fax (3) 7629949; e-mail customercare@aadc.ae; internet www.aadc.ae; f. 1999; distribution of water and electricity; Chair. Sheikh DIAB BIN ZAYED AL NAHYAN.

Bayounah Power Co: POB 33477, Abu Dhabi; tel. (2) 6731100; fax (2) 6730403; e-mail webmaster@adwea.gov.ae; internet www.bpc.ae; f. 1999; operates two power stations at Abu Dhabi (also water desalination) and al-Ain; Chair. AHMAD HILAL AL-KUWAITI; Man. Dir ABD AL-JALEEL AL-KHOURY.

Al-Mirfa Power Co: POB 32277, Abu Dhabi; tel. (2) 8833044; fax (2) 8833011; e-mail info@ampc.ae; internet www.ampc.ae; f. 1999 to control Mirfa and Madinat Zayed plants; capacity 300 MW electricity per day, 37m. gallons water per day; Chair. MUHAMMAD FOULAD; Gen. Man. PHILIP GRAHAM TILSON.

As part of the privatization programme, several independent power and water projects (IWPPs) have been established, including Arabian Power Co, Emirates CMS Power Co, Gulf Total Tractebel Power Co, Shuweihat CMS International Power Co, and Taweelah Asia Power Co (TAPCO). In each IWPP, ADWEA retains a 60% shareholding while the remaining 40% is owned by private investors.

Dubai

Dubai Electricity and Water Authority (DEWA): POB 564, Dubai; tel. (4) 3244444; fax (4) 3248111; e-mail customercare@dewa.gov.ae; internet www.dewa.gov.ae; f. 1992 following merger of Dubai Electricity Co and Dubai Water Dept; management and devt of the water and electricity sectors; CEO and Man. Dir SAID MUHAMMAD AHMAD AL-TAYER.

Northern Emirates (Ajman, Fujairah, Ras al-Khaimah and Umm al-Qaiwain)

Federal Water and Electricity Authority: POB 1672, Dubai; tel. (4) 2315555; fax (4) 2809977; e-mail cs@fewa.gov.ae; internet www.fewa.gov.ae; generation and distribution of electricity and water in the northern emirates; operates six power-generating plants and three water desalination plants; scheduled for part-privatization; Gen. Man. MUHAMMAD MUHAMMAD SALEH.

Sharjah

Sharjah Electricity and Water Authority (SEWA): Sharjah; tel. (2) 5288888; fax (2) 5288000; e-mail contactus@sewa.gov.ae; internet www.sewa.gov.ae; Chair. Sheikh SULTAN BIN MUHAMMAD AL-QASSIMI.

MAJOR COMPANIES

Abu Dhabi

Abu Dhabi Media Co (ADMC): POB 63, 4th St, Sector 18, Zone 1, Abu Dhabi; e-mail communications@admedia.ae; internet www.admedia.ae; f. 2007; fmrly Emirates Media, Inc; owns Abu Dhabi Television, 5 radio stations (Abu Dhabi FM, Abu Dhabi Classic FM, Emarat FM, Quran Kareem FM and Star FM) and 4 newspapers (*Al-Ittihad*, *Majid*, *The National*, and *Zahrat al-Khaleej*); Chair, MUHAMMAD MUBARAK AL-MAZROUE; CEO AYMAN SAFADI.

Abu Dhabi National Chemicals Co (Chemaweyaat): POB 43237, Abu Dhabi; tel. (2) 4110000; fax (2) 6359259; e-mail info@chemaweyaat.com; internet www.chemaweyaat.com; f. 2008; jt venture between Abu Dhabi Investment Council (40%), Int. Petroleum Investment Co (40%), Abu Dhabi Nat. Oil Co (ADNOC) (20%); devt of major petrochemicals complex at Chemaweyaat Industrial City, Taweelah; production of aromatics, olefins and fertilizers expected to commence in late 2013; Chair. Sheikh MANSOUR BIN ZAYED AL NAHYAN.

Abu Dhabi Polymers (Borouge): POB 6925, Abu Dhabi; tel. (2) 6070300; fax (2) 6070999; e-mail info@borouge.com; internet www.borouge.com; f. 1998; 60% owned by Abu Dhabi Nat. Oil Co (ADNOC), 40% by Borealis (Austria); production and marketing of polyethylene and polypropylene products; 0.6m. metric tons per year production capacity (2009); a major expansion of production facilities, which commenced in 2007, was expected to increase capacity to

2m. tons per year by 2010 and 4.5m. tons per year by 2013; CEO ABD AL-AZIZ ABDULLAH AL-HAJRI; over 1,600 employees.

Admak General Contracting Co: POB 650, Abu Dhabi; tel. (2) 6264626; fax (2) 6264636; e-mail admak@emirates.net.ae; f. 1968 as M. A. Kharafi; present name adopted 1981; general civil engineering and road contractors; part of the M. A. Kharafi Group of Kuwait; Man. Dir MOHSEN KAMEL MOSTAFA; Exec. Dir SAID A. FOTOUH; 2,600 employees.

ALDAR Properties PJSC: POB 51133, Abu Dhabi; tel. (2) 8105555; fax (2) 8105550; e-mail info@aldar.com; internet www.aldar.com; f. 2005; real estate development, management and investment; Chair. ABUBAKER SADDIQ AL-KHOORI; CEO SAMI ASAD.

Emirates Aluminium (Emal): POB 11023, Abu Dhabi; tel. (2) 5092222; fax (2) 5093333; e-mail info@emal.ae; internet www.emal.ae; f. 2007; jt venture between Dubai Aluminium (Dubal) and Mubadala Devt Co; construction of an aluminium smelting complex ongoing late 2013; projected capacity of 1.3m. metric tons on completion of second phase, due 2014; CEO SAID FADHIL AL-MAZROUI.

Emirates Steel Industries: POB 9022, Abu Dhabi Industrial City; tel. (2) 5511187; fax (2) 5510911; e-mail inquiry@esi-steel.com; internet www.esi-steel.com; f. 2001 as Emirates Iron and Steel Factory; 100% govt-owned; subsidiary of Abu Dhabi Basic Industries Corpn; production capacity 2m. metric tons per year; Chair. SAID GHUMRAN AL-RUMAITHI; 1,200 employees.

Hafilat Industries LLC: POB 91207, Abu Dhabi; tel. (2) 6733336; fax (2) 6733776; e-mail info@hafilatme.com; internet www.hafilatme.com; jt venture between Specialised Investment Group, Emirates Link Group and Volgren (Australia); bus and coach manufacturing; Chair. KHALAF SAGHIR AL-QUBAISI.

Mechanical and Civil Engineering Contractors (MACE) Ltd: POB 2307, Abu Dhabi; tel. (2) 6666462; fax (2) 6662616; e-mail mace@emirates.net.ae; internet www.macecontractors.com; f. 1968; Chair. and Man. Dir WILLIAM A. T. HADDAD; 1,200 employees.

National Central Cooling Co PJSC (Tabreed): POB 29478, Abu Dhabi; tel. (2) 6455007; fax (2) 6455008; e-mail info@tabreed.ae; internet www.tabreed.com; f. 1998; manufacture of air conditioning and district cooling systems; CEO JASIM HUSEIN THABET; Chair. WALID AL-MOKARRAB AL-MUHAIRI.

Pilco (Pipeline Construction Co): POB 2021, Abu Dhabi; tel. (2) 5554500; fax (2) 5559053; e-mail pilco@emirates.net.ae; f. 1968; fabrication of steel, piping, tanks, pressure vessels and machine components; general services to the oil industry; Gen. Man. E. N. HAWA; 200 employees.

Dubai

Al-Ahmadiah Contracting and Trading: POB 2596, Dubai; tel. (4) 3981999; fax (4) 3983327; e-mail admin@alahmadiah.ae; internet www.alahmadiah.com; f. 1970; building and civil engineering contractors; part of the Al-Fajer Group; Pres. and Propr Sheikh HASHER MAKTOUM JUMA AL MAKTOUM; Dir S. K. JOSHI; 1,500 employees.

Arabtec Construction LLC: POB 3399, St No. 4, Al Quoz, Sheikh Zayed Rd, Dubai; tel. (4) 3400700; fax (4) 3404004; e-mail arabtec@arabtecuae.com; internet www.arabtecuae.com; f. 1970; specializes in large real estate and infrastructure projects; Chair. HASAN ABDULLAH ISMAIK.

Dubai Aluminium Corpn (DUBAL): POB 3627, Dubai; tel. (4) 8846666; fax (4) 8846919; e-mail info@dubal.ae; internet www.dubal.ae; f. 1979; production of primary aluminium; capacity of 30m. gallons of potable water per day; produced 1.0m. metric tons of cast metal products in 2009; Chair. Sheikh HAMDAN BIN RASHID AL MAKTOUM; CEO ABDULLAH KALBAN.

Al-Futtaim Engineering: POB 159, Dubai; tel. (4) 2119111; fax (4) 2119299; e-mail alfengg@alfuttaim.ae; internet www.engineeringuae.com; f. 1974; CEO OMAR AL-FUTTAIM; 150 employees.

Galadari Brothers Group: POB 138, Dubai; tel. (4) 3388800; fax (4) 3381918; e-mail contact@gabros.ae; internet www.galadarigroup.com; automobiles, engineering, industrial equipment, information technology, media, real estate, retail; Chair. MUHAMMAD IBRAHIM AL-SHAIBANI.

Al-Ghurair Group: POB 1, Dubai; tel. (4) 2623377; fax (4) 2623388; e-mail info@alghurairgroup.ae; internet www.alghurair.com; f. 1960/61; general contracting, banking, import and export, aluminium extrusion and manufacture of aluminium doors, windows, etc., PVC pipes, tiles and marbles, cement and mineral waters; gold and exchange dealers, owners of grain silos and flour mills, printing press, packaging factory, real estate dealers; cap. AED 1,000m.; Chair. ABD AL-RAHMAN SAIF AL-GHURAIR; CEO MAJID SAIF AL-GHURAIR; 5,000 employees.

Gulf Eternit Industries Co Ltd: POB 1371, Dubai; tel. (4) 2857256; fax (4) 2852498; e-mail info@gulf-eternit.com; internet www.gei.ae; f. 1971; design, manufacture and installation of piping systems for industrial, petrochemical, municipal, civil and irrigation applications; part of the Future Pipe Group; sales AED 245.5m., cap. AED 50m. (1998); Pres. FOUAD MAKHZOUMI; Exec. Vice-Pres. Dr OMAR ASHER.

Gulf Extrusions Co LLC: POB 5598, Jebel Ali Industrial Area, Dubai; tel. (4) 8846146; fax (4) 8846830; e-mail sales@gulfex.com; internet www.gulfex.com; f. 1975; member of the Al-Ghurair Group; over 9,000 aluminium product profiles for domestic construction projects and export to other Gulf, European, South East Asian and Canadian markets; Gen. Man. MODAR AL-MEKDAD.

Al-Habtoor Group LLC: POB 25444, Dubai; tel. (4) 3941444; fax (4) 3949990; internet www.habtoor.com; f. 1970; civil and building contracting; engineering; hotels and catering; insurance; leasing; transport services; Chair. KHALAF A. AL-HABTOOR; about 6,000 employees.

Bin Ladin Contracting Group UAE: POB 1555, Dubai; tel. (4) 2991500; fax (4) 691350; e-mail binladin@emirates.net.ae; f. 1967; civil engineering, roadworks, piling, ground services and building, electrical contracting; Man. Dir ABU BAKR SALIM AL-HAMID; 4,000 employees.

National Cement Co PSC: POB 4041, Dubai; tel. (4) 3388885; fax (4) 3388886; e-mail cement@nationalcement.ae; internet www.nationalcement.ae; production and sale of cement; Chair. MUHAMMAD A. AL-GHURAIR.

Al-Shirawi Group of Companies: POB 93, Dubai; tel. (4) 2821000; fax (4) 2821534; e-mail shirawi@eim.ae; internet www.alshirawi.com; f. 1971; over 30 subsidiary cos active in construction, manufacturing, industrial equipment, logistics, electronics and printing; Chair. ABDULLAH AL-SHIRAWI.

United Foods Co PSC: POB 5836, Dubai; tel. (4) 3382688; fax (4) 3381987; e-mail aseel@emirates.net.ae; internet www.aseelandsafi.com; f. 1976; manufacture and trading of hydrogenated vegetable oil and edible oils; Chair. ALI BIN HUMAID AL-OWAIS; CEO FETHI MUHAMMAD KHIARI; 400 employees.

Fujairah

Fujairah Building Industries PSC: POB 383, Fujairah; tel. (9) 2222051; fax (9) 2227314; e-mail fbi_fuj@emirates.net.ae; internet www.fujfbi.ae; govt-owned; subsidiaries include Emirates Ceramic Factory, Fujairah Concrete Products, Fujairah Marble and Tiles Factory; Chair. MUHAMMAD OBEID BIN MAJED AL-ALEELI.

Fujairah Cement Industries (FCI): POB 600, Fujairah; tel. (9) 2223111; fax (9) 2227718; e-mail fujcem82@emirates.net.ae; internet www.fujairahcement.com; f. 1979; cement manufacture and supply; Chair. Sheikh HAMAD BIN SAIF AL-SHARQI; Gen. Man. NASSER ALI KHAMAS; 225 employees.

Ras al-Khaimah

Alltek Emirates Ltd: POB 1569, Ras al-Khaimah; tel. (7) 2668864; fax (7) 2668977; e-mail alltekem@emirates.net.ae; f. 1985; manufacture and marketing of spray plasters, decorative paints and limestone powder.

RAK Ceramics: POB 4714, Ras al-Khaimah; tel. (7) 2445046; fax (7) 2445270; e-mail mktgservices@rakceram.com; internet www.rakceramics.com; f. 1989; manufacture of ceramic tiles and sanitary ware; CEO ABDULLAH MASSAAD.

Raknor (PVT) Ltd: POB 883, Ras al-Khaimah; tel. (7) 2668351; fax (7) 2668910; e-mail raknor@emirates.net.ae; internet www.raknor.com; f. 1976; manufacture of concrete blocks; Chair. Sheikh SA'UD BIN SAQR AL-QASSIMI; Gen. Man SAMI RIDA SAMI.

Sharjah

CME Contracting Marine Engineering: POB 1859, Sharjah; tel. (6) 354511; f. 1975; turnkey industrial projects, water and electricity plants, construction, building, marine works; joint venture between Chair. and German cos Klaus Stuff, Helma Greuel-Mainz; Chair. Dr F. AL-GAWLY; 323 employees.

Conforce Gulf Ltd Co: POB 289, Sharjah; tel. (6) 591433; f. 1979; building contractor, exporter of building and electrical materials; Man. ABDULLAH MUHAMMAD BUKHATIR.

Dafco Trading and Industrial Co WLL: POB 515, Sharjah; tel. (6) 5621333; fax (6) 5620999; internet www.dafcogroup.com; f. 1969; general contracting trading co; operates factories producing bricks and concrete; Man. M. AL-FARHAN.

General Enterprises Co: POB 28, Sharjah; tel. (6) 5684558; fax (6) 5684558; internet www.gecouae.com; general trading and contracting; Gen. Man. Sheikh AHMAD BIN MUHAMMAD SULTAN AL-QASIMI.

Gulf Building Materials Co Ltd (GBM): POB 1612, Sharjah; tel. (6) 354683; production and supply of building materials: cement, marble and aluminium.

Hempel Paints (Emirates) LLC: POB 2000, Sharjah; tel. (6) 5310140; fax (6) 5310141; e-mail hempelae@eim.ae; f. 1976;

manufacture and sale of paints for offshore marine, domestic and industrial use; Chair. SA'UD ABD AL-AZIZ AL-RASHID; CEO and Gen. Man. JOHN R. SPENDLOVE.

Sharjah Electrodes: POB 2019, Sharjah; tel. (6) 5331000; fax (6) 5337244; f. 1976; manufacture and distribution of arc-welding electrodes and wire nails; Man. Dir MUHAMMAD ABDULLAH AL-KHAYYAL.

Umm al-Qaiwain

Umm al-Qaiwain Aluminium Co (UMALCO): POB 225, Umm al-Qaiwain.

Umm al-Qaiwain Industries Corpn: POB 547, Umm al-Qaiwain; tel. (6) 7671772; fax (6) 7671011; e-mail uaqind@emirates.net.ae; Chair. Sheikh ALI BIN RASHID AL-MU'ALLA; Gen. Man. SALIM SAIF AL-GHOBBI.

Transport

RAILWAYS

The first phase of an urban light-railway system, Dubai Metro—with 10 of the 29 planned stations in operation on the Red Line—opened in September 2009. By early 2012 all 29 stations had been opened. The 23-km Green Line was inaugurated in September 2011, with 18 of its planned 20 stations in operation. In September 2013 plans were announced for further extensions to both the Red and Green lines, to be operational by 2020. In 2006 the Abu Dhabi authorities announced plans for the construction of a 130-km metro system, projected for completion by 2015. Plans for the construction of a federal railway network for passengers and freight, linking the seven emirates, gained final government approval in March 2009. The 1,000-km network was to be constructed in two phases, with the first phase expected to take five years to complete.

Etihad Rail: f. 2009 as Union Railway Co; current name adopted 2011; charged with construction of, and eventual operations of, a federal railway network for both passengers and freight, to extend throughout the UAE; first phase of construction—comprising a 264-km freight line between Ruwais and Habshan and Shah in Abu Dhabi—expected to commence in 2013; wholly state-owned; Chair. NASIR AL-SUWAIDI; CEO NASIR AL-MANSOURI.

ROADS

The road network in the UAE is undergoing rapid development. Abu Dhabi and Dubai are linked by a good road that is dual carriageway for most of its length. This road forms part of a west coast route from Shaam, at the UAE border with the northern enclave of Oman, through Dubai and Abu Dhabi to Tarif. An east coast route links Dibba with Muscat, Oman. Other roads include the Abu Dhabi–al-Ain highway and roads linking Sharjah and Ras al-Khaimah, and Sharjah and Dhaid. An underwater tunnel links Dubai Town and Deira by dual carriageway and pedestrian subway. An extensive development plan announced in July 2006—the Dubai Strategic Plan—was to allocate AED 44,000m. to road infrastructure up to 2020 and to include the construction of 500 km of new roads, and upgrades of the emirate's existing road network. In 2008 there was a total paved road network of 4,080 km.

SHIPPING

Dubai has been the main commercial centre in the Gulf for many years. Abu Dhabi has also become an important port since the opening of the first section of its artificial harbour, Port Zayed. The Khalifa Port and Industrial Zone in Abu Dhabi, with a capacity of 2.5m. 20-ft equivalent units (TEU) per year, was inaugurated in September 2012. There are smaller ports in Sharjah, Fujairah, Ras al-Khaimah and Umm al-Qaiwain. Dubai possesses two docks capable of handling 500,000-metric-ton tankers, seven repair berths and a third dock able to accommodate 1,000,000-ton tankers. The Dubai port of Mina Jebel Ali, which was to be expanded at a cost of some US $1,362m., has the largest man-made harbour in the world. Plans were under way to expand Ras al-Khaimah's Mina Saqr Port. The first phase of the Mina Saqr project was completed in 2007, increasing the port's annual capacity to 350,000 TEUs; upon completion of the second phase, capacity would increase to 1.7m. TEUs per year.

At 31 December 2012 the United Arab Emirates' flag registered fleet totalled 738 vessels, with an aggregate displacement of 1,348,804 grt, of which four were bulk carriers, two were fish carriers and 28 were general cargo ships.

Abu Dhabi

Abu Dhabi Ports Co (ADPC): POB 54477, Mina Zayed, Abu Dhabi; tel. (2) 6952000; fax (2) 6952177; e-mail info@adpc.ae; internet www.adpc.ae; responsible for the devt and regulation of Abu Dhabi's ports and related industrial zones; Chair. Dr SULTAN AHMAD AL-JABER; CEO (vacant).

Abu Dhabi Terminals (ADT): POB 422, Port Zayed, Abu Dhabi; tel. (2) 6730600; fax (2) 6731023; e-mail info@adterminals.ae; internet www.adterminals.ae; f. 2006; replaced Abu Dhabi Seaports Authority (f. 1972); administers Port Zayed, Musaffah port and Freeport; facilities at Port Zayed include 21 deep-water berths and 5 container gantry cranes of 40 metric tons capacity; cold storage 20,500 tons; handled a total of 390,087 TEUs in 2008; jt venture between ADPC and Mubadala; Chair. TAWFIQ YOUSUF AL-MUBARAK; CEO MUHAMMAD AL-MANNAEI.

Abu Dhabi National Tanker Co (ADNATCO): POB 2977, Sheikh Khalifa Energy Complex, Takreer Tower, Abu Dhabi; tel. (2) 6028400; fax (2) 6723999; e-mail info@adnatcongsco.com; internet www.adnatco.com; f. 1975; subsidiary co of ADNOC, operating owned and chartered tankships, and transporting crude petroleum, refined products and sulphur; Gen. Man. ALI OBAID AL-YABHOUNI.

Abu Dhabi Petroleum Ports Operating Co (IRSHAD): POB 61, Abu Dhabi; tel. (2) 6028000; fax (2) 6742094; e-mail info@irshad.ae; internet www.irshad.ae; f. 1979; 60% owned by ADNOC, 40% by LAMNALCO Kuwait; manages Jebel Dhanna, Ruwais, Das Island, Umm al-Nar and Zirku Island SPM terminal, Mubarraz; operates fleet of 36 vessels; cap. AED 50m.; Chair. YOUSUF BIN OMEIR BIN YOUSUF; Gen. Man. KHALIFA M. AL-GOBAISI.

Dubai

Dubai Ports World (DP World): POB 17000, JAFZA 17, 5th Floor, Dubai; tel. (4) 8811110; fax (4) 48811331; e-mail info@dpworld.com; internet www.dpworld.ae; f. 2005 by merger of Dubai Ports Authority (f. 1991 by merger of Mina Jebel Ali and Mina Rashid) and Dubai Ports Int. (f. 1999); subsidiary of state-controlled Dubai World; 23% sold via initial public offering Nov. 2007; storage areas and facilities for loading and discharge of vessels; operates ports of Mina Jebel Ali and Mina Rashid in Dubai, Port Zayed in Abu Dhabi, Fujairah Port and numerous other international facilities; handled 42m. TEUs world-wide in 2006; CEO MUHAMMAD SHARAF; Sr Vice-Pres. and Man. Dir, UAE Region MUHAMMAD AL-MUALLEM.

Drydocks World—Dubai: POB 8988, Dubai; tel. (4) 3450626; fax (4) 3450116; e-mail drydocks@drydocks.gov.ae; internet www.drydocks.gov.ae; f. 1983; state-owned; dry-docking and repairs, tank-cleaning, construction of vessels and floating docks, conversions, galvanizing, dredging, etc.; Chair. KHAMIS JUMA BUAMIM.

Fujairah

Port of Fujairah: POB 787, Fujairah; tel. (9) 2228800; fax (9) 2228811; e-mail info@fujairahport.ae; internet www.fujairahport.ae; f. 1983; operated by Dubai Ports World; offers facilities for handling container, general cargo and roll on, roll off (ro-ro) traffic; handled 565,723 TEUs in 1999; Chair. Sheikh SALEH BIN MUHAMMAD AL-SHARQI; Gen. Man. Capt. MOUSA MURAD.

Ras al-Khaimah

Saqr Port Authority: POB 5130, Ras al-Khaimah; tel. (7) 2668444; fax (7) 2668533; e-mail info@saqrport.ae; internet www.saqrport.ae; govt-owned; port operators handling bulk cargoes, containers, general cargo and ro-ro traffic; Gen. Man. Capt. COLIN CROOKSHANK.

Sharjah

Department of Seaports and Customs: POB 510, Sharjah; tel. (6) 5281666; fax (6) 5281425; e-mail shjports@eim.ae; internet www.sharjahports.ae; the authority administers Port Khalid, Hamriyah Port and Port Khor Fakkan and offers specialized facilities for container and ro-ro traffic, reefer cargo and project and general cargo; in 2003 Port Khalid handled 145,482 TEUs of containerized shipping, and Port Khor Fakkan 1,444,451 TEUs; Port Khalid and Hamriyah Port together handled over 4m. metric tons of non-containerized cargo; Chair. (Ports and Customs) Sheikh KHALID BIN ABDULLAH AL-QASIMI; Dir-Gen. ISSA JUMA AL-MUTAWA.

Umm al-Qaiwain

Ahmed bin Rashid Port and Free Zone Authority: POB 279, Umm al-Qaiwain; tel. (6) 7655882; fax (6) 7651552; e-mail abrpaftz@emirates.net.ae; Pres. KHALID BIN RASHID AL-MU'ALLA; Gen. Man. MURTAZA K. MOOSAJEE.

CIVIL AVIATION

There are seven international airports, two in Dubai, and one in each of Abu Dhabi, al-Ain, Fujairah and Ras al-Khaimah, as well as a smaller one at Sharjah, which forms part of Sharjah port, linking air, sea and overland transportation services. The second airport in Dubai, Al Maktoum International Airport, was officially inaugurated in June 2010. Initially, the airport was open exclusively to cargo carriers. Part of the Dubai World Central commercial and residential infrastructure development, the new airport was expected, upon completion of a secondary phase of construction, to have five runways, four terminal buildings and an annual capacity of 160m. passengers and 12m. metric tons of freight, rendering it the largest airport in the world. It was reported that passenger carriers would begin to serve the airport from October 2013. Meanwhile, an expansion project at the Dubai International Airport, to increase annual capacity from 60m. to 90m. passengers, was scheduled for completion in 2018. Plans for the construction of a new terminal at Abu Dhabi International Airport, with a projected annual passenger capacity of 30m., were under way in 2013; the terminal was expected to be completed by 2017. Plans to construct a new terminal at Sharjah International Airport, at a cost of US $354m., were announced in late 2008.

General Civil Aviation Authority: POB 6558, Abu Dhabi; tel. (2) 4447666; fax (2) 4054535; e-mail info@gcaa.ae; internet www.gcaa.ae; f. 1996; responsible for all aspects of civil aviation; Chair. SULTAN BIN SAID AL-MANSOURI (Minister of Economy); Dir-Gen. SAIF MUHAMMAD AL-SUWAIDI.

Abu Dhabi Aviation: POB 2723, Abu Dhabi; tel. (2) 5758000; fax (2) 5757775; e-mail adava@abudhabiaviation.com; internet www.abudhabiaviation.com; f. 1976; domestic charter flights; Chair. NADER AHMAD MUHAMMAD AL-HAMADI; Gen. Man. MUHAMMAD IBRAHIM AL-MAZROUI.

Air Arabia: POB 132, Sharjah; tel. (6) 5088888; fax (6) 5580244; e-mail hraydan@airarabia.com; internet www.airarabia.com; f. 2003; 55% owned by private investors, 45% by the Sharjah Govt; low-fare airline; serves 46 destinations across the Middle East, N. Africa, S. and Cen. Asia, and Europe; handled 3.6m. passengers in 2008; Chair. Sheikh ABDULLAH BIN MUHAMMAD AL THANI; CEO ADEL ALI.

Emirates Airline: POB 686, Dubai; tel. (4) 2951111; fax (4) 2955817; e-mail corpcom@emiratesairline.com; internet www.emirates.com; f. 1985; owned by the Dubai Govt; operates services to over 130 destinations in over 70 countries; carried 34.0m. passengers and 1.8m. metric tons of freight in 2011/12; Chair. and Chief Exec. Sheikh AHMAD BIN SAID AL MAKTOUM; Exec. Vice-Chair. Sir MAURICE FLANAGAN; Pres. TIM CLARK.

Etihad Airways: POB 35566, Khalifa City A, Abu Dhabi; tel. (2) 5110000; fax (2) 5111200; internet www.etihadairways.com; f. 2003; owned by the Abu Dhabi Govt; operates 56 aircraft serving more than 66 destinations in 43 countries; carried 4.6m. passengers in 2007; Chair. Sheikh HAMAD BIN ZAYED AL NAHYAN; CEO JAMES HOGAN.

Falcon Express Cargo Airlines (FECA): Dubai International Airport, POB 93722, Dubai; tel. (4) 2826886; fax (4) 2823125; e-mail admin@feca.bz; internet www.falcongroup.bz; f. 1995; dedicated courier freight.

RAK Airways: POB 31457, Ras al-Khaimah; tel. (7) 2075000; fax (7) 2447387; e-mail info@rakairways.com; internet www.rakairways.com; f. 2006; flights commenced 2007; owned by Govt of Ras al-Khaimah; operates from Ras al-Khaimah Int. Airport; serves destinations in Bangladesh, Egypt, India and Saudi Arabia; Chair. Sheikh OMAR BIN SAQR AL-QASIMI; CEO OMAR JAHAMEH.

Tourism

Each emirate develops and promotes its tourist attractions separately, although a federal tourism authority, the National Council of Tourism and Antiquities, commenced operations in late 2009. Dubai is the UAE's most popular tourist destination; its wide range of luxury hotels and resorts, and entertainment and shopping facilities attracted around 7m. visitors in 2008. Abu Dhabi is developing its tourism industry, with an emphasis on leisure, heritage and cultural facilities, as well as luxury hotels and resorts. An extensive commercial, residential and leisure project is being developed at Saadiyat Island, which will incorporate beaches, hotels, golf courses and a cultural district that will accommodate branches of the Louvre and Guggenheim museums, as well as the Sheikh Zayed National Museum. There are established tourism sectors in Sharjah and Ras al-Khaimah, and plans are being implemented to foster tourism in Ajman and Fujairah. According to provisional figures, in 2011 there were 8.1m. foreign visitors to the UAE, compared with 616,000 in 1990. Receipts from tourism totalled US $9,204m. in 2011, according to provisional figures.

National Council of Tourism and Antiquities (NCTA): Abu Dhabi; f. 2008; commenced operations 2009; Dir-Gen. MUHAMMAD KHAMIS BIN HARIB AL-MUHAIRI.

Abu Dhabi Tourism Authority (ADTA): POB 94000, Abu Dhabi; tel. (2) 4440444; fax (2) 4440400; e-mail contact@abudhabi.ae; internet www.abudhabitourism.ae; f. 2004; Chair. Sheikh SULTAN BIN TAHNUN AL NAHYAN; Dir-Gen. MUBARAK HAMAD AL-MUHEIRI.

Tourism Development and Investment Authority (TDIC): POB 126888, Abu Dhabi; tel. (2) 4061400; e-mail info@tdic.ae; internet www.tdic.ae; 100% owned by ADTA; responsible for the devt of a range of major projects incl. Saadiyat Island; CEO LEE TABLER.

Dubai Department of Tourism and Commerce Marketing: POB 594, Dubai; tel. (4) 2230000; fax (4) 2230022; e-mail info@dubaitourism.co.ae; internet www.dubaitourism.co.ae; f. 1997; 18 offices abroad; Chair. Sheikh MUHAMMAD BIN RASHID AL MAKTOUM (Ruler of Dubai); Dir-Gen. HILAL AL-MARRI.

Fujairah Tourism and Antiquities Authority: POB 829, Fujairah; tel. (9) 2231554; fax (9) 2231006; e-mail fujtourb@emirates.net.ae; internet fujairah-tourism.gov.ae; f. 1995; Chair. Sheikh SAEED BIN SAEED AL-SHARQI; Gen. Man. SAEED AL-SAMAHI.

National Corporation for Tourism and Hotels (NCTH): POB 6942, Abu Dhabi; tel. (2) 4099999; fax (2) 4099990; e-mail ncth@emirates.net.ae; internet www.ncth.com; 20% owned by Govt of Abu Dhabi; Chair. HAMDAN BIN MUBARAK AL-NAYHAN.

Ras al-Khaimah Tourism Promotion Board: POB 31219, Ras al-Khaimah; tel. (7) 2445125; fax (7) 2447463; internet www.raktourism.com; f. 2006; Chair. Sheikh ABD AL-AZIZ BIN HUMAID AL-QASIMI; CEO Dr KHATER MASSAAD.

Sharjah Commerce and Tourism Development Authority: POB 26661, Crescent Tower, 9th Floor, Buheirah Corniche, Sharjah; tel. (6) 5566777; fax (6) 5563000; e-mail sctda@sharjah.org; internet www.sharjahtourism.ae; f. 1996; Dir-Gen. MUHAMMAD ALI AL-NOMAN.

Defence

The Union Defence Force and the armed forces of the various emirates were formally merged in May 1976. Abu Dhabi and Dubai retain a degree of independence. Military service is voluntary.

Chief of Staff of the Federal Armed Forces: Lt-Gen. HAMAD MUHAMMAD THANI AL-RUMAITHI.

Defence Budget (2011): AED 34,200m.; federal expenditure on defence has been substantially reduced since the early 1980s, but procurement and project costs are not affected, as individual emirates finance these separately.

Total armed forces (as assessed at November 2012): 51,000 (army 44,000; navy est. 2,500; air force 4,500).In May 2009 a French military base, comprising naval, air force and army facilities, was inaugurated in Abu Dhabi; at November 2011, a force numbering 800 was deployed at the base.

Education

Primary education is compulsory, beginning at six years of age and lasting for six years. Secondary education, starting at the age of 12, lasts for three years. After one year, students can choose between science- or arts-based streams. According to UNESCO estimates, enrolment at primary schools included 90% of children in the relevant age-group in 2008/09, while the comparable ratio for secondary enrolment was 83%. In 2010/11 a total of 26,733 children attended government pre-primary schools, and 177,911 attended primary schools in the UAE. In the same year secondary enrolment in government schools totalled 61,061. There are primary and secondary schools in all the emirates, and further education in technical fields is available in the more advanced areas. Many students receive higher education abroad. The UAE has 14 universities. A branch of the Université Paris-Sorbonne opened in Abu Dhabi in October 2006, while a branch of New York University opened in 2009. Two American universities are in operation, in Sharjah and Dubai. A British university and a Canadian university operate in Dubai, which also hosts branches of universities from Australia, others from the United Kingdom, and the USA. Four higher colleges of technology (two for male and two for female students) in Abu Dhabi opened in 1988. According to UNESCO, in 2008/09 a total of 87,006 students were enrolled in university and other higher education; some 60% of students in tertiary education in that year were females. Budgeted federal government expenditure by the Ministries of Education and of Higher Education and Scientific Research in 2012 totalled an estimated AED 8,200m. (equivalent to 20% of total expenditure by the central Government).

Bibliography

Abdullah, M. Morsy. *The Modern History of the United Arab Emirates*. London, Croom Helm, 1978.

al-Abed, Ibrahim, and Hellyer, Peter (Eds). *The United Arab Emirates*. London, Trident Press, 2001.

Albaharna, H. M. *The Legal Status of the Arabian Gulf States*. Manchester, Manchester University Press, 1969.

Ali, Syed. *Dubai: Gilded Cage*. New Haven, CT, Yale University Press, 2010.

al-Alkim, Hassan Hamdan. *The Foreign Policy of the United Arab Emirates*. London, Saqi Books, 1989.

Almezaini, Khaled. *The UAE and Foreign Policy: Foreign Aid, Identities and Interests*. Abingdon, Routledge, 2011.

Anthony, John Duke. *Arab States of the Lower Gulf: People, Power, Politics*. Washington, DC, Middle East Institute, 1975.

The United Arab Emirates: Dynamics of State Formation. Abu Dhabi, Emirates Center for Strategic Research, 2002.

Busch, B. C. *Britain and the Persian Gulf 1894–1914*. Berkeley, CA, University of California Press, 1967.

Cordesman, Anthony. *Bahrain, Oman, Qatar, and the UAE*. Boulder, CO, Westview Press, 1997.

Daniels, John. *Abu Dhabi: A Portrait*. London, Longman, 1974.

Davidson, Christopher. *The United Arab Emirates: A Study in Survival*. Boulder, CO, Lynne Rienner Publishers, 2005.

Dubai: The Vulnerability of Success. London, Hurst & Co, 2008.

Abu Dhabi: Oil and Beyond. London, Hurst & Co, 2009.

Davies, Charles. *The Blood Red Arab Flag: An Investigation into Qasimi Piracy*. Exeter, University of Exeter Press, 1997.

Elsheshtawy, Yasser. *Dubai: Behind an Urban Spectacle*. Abingdon, Routledge, 2009.

Fenelon, K. G. *The United Arab Emirates: An Economic and Social Survey*. London, Longman, 1973.

Gabriel, Erhard F. (Ed.). *The Dubai Handbook*. Ahrensburg, Germany, Institute for Applied Economic Geography, 1989.

Ghareeb, Edmund, and al-Abed, Ibrahim (Eds). *Perspectives on the United Arab Emirates*. London, Trident Press, 1997.

Hawley, Donald Frederick. *The Trucial States*. London, George Allen and Unwin, 1971.

Heard-Bey, Frauke. *From Trucial States to United Arab Emirates* (3rd edn). Dubai, Motivate Publishing, 2004.

Khalifa, Ali Mohammad. *The United Arab Emirates: Unity in Fragmentation*. London, Croom Helm, 1980.

Krane, Jim. *City of Gold: Dubai and the Dream of Capitalism*. New York, NY, St. Martin's Press, 2009.

Lienhardt, Peter, and Shahi, al-Ahmed (Ed.). *Shaikhdoms of Eastern Arabia*. New York, St Martin's Press, 2001.

Mann, Clarence. *Abu Dhabi: Birth of an Oil Sheikhdom*. Beirut, Khayats, 1964.

Mahdavi, Parvis. *Gridlock: Labor, Migration, and Human Trafficking in Dubai*. Palo Alto, CA, Stanford University Press, 2011.

Mattair, Thomas. *The Three Occupied UAE Islands: The Tunbs and Abu Musa*. Abu Dhabi, Emirates Center for Strategic Studies and Research, 2005.

Ministry of Information and Culture. *United Arab Emirates: A Record of Achievement, 1971–1996; 25 Years of Development*. Abu Dhabi, 1996.

Oteiba, Mani al-Said. *Petroleum and the Economy of the United Arab Emirates*. London, Croom Helm, 1977.

Peck, M. C. *The UAE—A Venture in Unity*. Boulder, CO, Westview Press, 1986.

al-Qasimi, Sultan bin Muhammad. *The Myth of Arab Piracy in the Gulf*. London, Croom Helm, 1986.

Rugh, Andrea B. *The Political Culture of Leadership in the United Arab Emirates*. New York, Palgrave Macmillan, 2007.

Schofield, Richard. *Unfinished Business: Iran, the UAE, Abu Musa and the Tunbs*. London, Royal Institute of International Affairs, 2003.

Suleiman, Atef. *The Petroleum Experience of Abu Dhabi*. Abu Dhabi, Emirates Center for Strategic Studies and Research, 2008.

Taryam, Abdullah Omran. *The Establishment of the UAE, 1950–85*. London, Croom Helm, 1987.

Wilkinson, John. *Arabia's Frontiers: The Story of Britain's Boundary Drawing in the Desert*. London, I. B. Tauris, 1987.

Zahlan, Rosemarie Said. *The Origins of the United Arab Emirates*. London, Macmillan, 1978.

YEMEN

Geography

On 22 May 1990 the Yemen Arab Republic (YAR) and the People's Democratic Republic of Yemen (PDRY) merged to form the Republic of Yemen. Yemen consists of the south-west corner of the Arabian peninsula—the highlands inland and the coastal strip along the Red Sea; and the former British colony of Aden (195 sq km or 75.3 sq miles) and the Protectorate of South Arabia (about 333,000 sq km), together with the islands of Perim (13 sq km) and Kamaran (57 sq km). The Republic of Yemen lies at the southern end of the Arabian peninsula, approximately between longitude 43°E and 56°E, with Perim Island a few kilometres due west, in the strait marking the southern extremity of the Red Sea, and Socotra in the extreme east. Yemen has frontiers with Saudi Arabia and Oman, although atlases have shown considerable variation in the precise boundaries of the three countries, or sometimes have not indicated them at all. (A final agreement on delineation of the border with Saudi Arabia, with the exception of some eastern sections, was signed in 2000, while the border with Oman was officially demarcated in 1995.) The capital of the Republic of Yemen is San'a, which lies on the al-Jehal plateau (2,175 m above sea level).

Physically, Yemen comprises the dislocated southern edge of the great plateau of Arabia. This is an immense mass of ancient granites, once forming part of Africa, and covered in many places by shallow, mainly horizontal, layers of younger sedimentary rocks. The whole plateau has undergone down-warping in the east and elevation in the west, so that the highest land (over 3,000 m) occurs in the extreme west, near the Red Sea, with a gradual decline to the lowest parts (under 300 m) in the extreme east. The whole of the southern and western coasts of Yemen were formed by a series of enormous fractures, which produced a flat but very narrow coastal plain, rising steeply to the hill country a short distance inland. Percolation of molten magma along the fracture-lines gave rise to a number of volcanic craters, now extinct, and one of these, partly eroded and occupied by the sea, forms the site of Aden port.

An important topographical feature is the Wadi Hadramout, an imposing valley running parallel to the coast at 160 km–240 km distance inland. In its upper and middle parts this valley is broad, and occupied by a seasonal torrent; in its lower (eastern) part it narrows considerably, making a sudden turn south-eastwards and reaching the sea. This lower part is largely uninhabited, but the upper parts, where alluvial soil and intermittent flood water are available, support a farming population.

Rainfall is generally scarce, but relatively more abundant on the highlands and in the west. The climate of the highlands is considered to be the best in all Arabia since it experiences a regime rather like that of East Africa: a warm, temperate and rainy summer, and a cool, moderately dry winter with occasional frost and some snow. Aden receives 125 mm of rain annually, all of it during winter (December–March), while in the lowlands of the extreme east, it may rain only once in five or 10 years. In the highlands a few miles north of Aden, falls of up to 760 mm occur, for the most part during summer, and this rainfall also gradually declines eastwards, giving 380 mm–500 mm in the highlands of Dhofar. As much as 890 mm of rain may fall annually on the higher parts of the interior, off the Red Sea coast, with 400 mm–500 mm over much of the plateau, but the coast receives less than 130 mm generally, often in the form of irregular downpours. There is, therefore, the phenomenon of streams and even rivers flowing perennially in the western highlands but failing to reach the coast.

Ultimately, to the north and east, rainfall becomes almost negligible, as the edges of the Arabian Desert are reached. This unusual situation of a reversal in climatic conditions over a few miles is thought to be the result of two streams of air: an upper one, damp and unstable in summer, and originating in the equatorial regions of East Africa; and a lower current, generally drier and related to conditions prevailing over the rest of the Middle East. In this way the low-lying coastal areas have a maximum of rainfall in winter, and the hills of Yemen a maximum in summer. Temperatures are high everywhere, particularly on the coastal plain, which has a southern aspect: mean figures of 25°C (January) to 32°C (June) occur at Aden town, although temperatures of more than 38°C are common. Owing to this climate gradation from desert to temperate conditions, Yemen has a similar gradation of crops and vegetation. In the interior, off the Red Sea coast, the highest parts appear as 'African', with scattered trees and grassland. Crops of coffee, qat, cereals and vegetables are grown, while, lower down, 'Mediterranean' fruits appear, with millet and, where irrigation water is available, bananas. The date palm is the only tree to grow successfully in the coastal region.

To the east, except on the higher parts, which have a light covering of thorn scrub (including dwarf trees that exude a sap from which incense and myrrh are derived), and the restricted patches of cultivated land, the territory is devoid of vegetation. Cultivation is limited to small level patches of good soil on flat terraces alongside the river beds, on the floor and sides of the Wadi Hadramout, or where irrigation from wells and occasionally from cisterns can be practised. The most productive areas are: Lahej, close to Aden town; two districts near Mukalla (about 480 km east of Aden); and parts of the middle Hadramout. Irrigation from cisterns hollowed out of the rock has long been practised, and Aden town has a famous system of this kind, dating back many centuries. Today, however, the main system of irrigation is provided by floodwater.

The area of Yemen is approximately 536,869 sq km (207,286 sq miles). Its population was 14,587,807 at the census of 16 December 1994. The population was recorded as 19,685,161 at the census of 16 December 2004, giving a population density of 36.7 persons per sq km. According to UN estimates, the population had reached 24,407,381 by mid-2013, resulting in a population density of 45.5 persons per sq km.

History

Revised for this edition by RICHARD SPENCER

EARLY HISTORY

With a flourishing agriculture, based on a sophisticated system of irrigated terraces, the incense trade and the use of its ports as a link between India, China, Africa and the Mediterranean region, Yemen was one of the richest regions in the ancient world. The South Arabian states constituted an advanced civilization by the second millennium. The ancient Kingdom of Yemen gave way to a group of smaller states, of which Saba was the most prominent between the years 750 BC and 115 BC. From about 400 BC, Saba's neighbouring kingdoms of Main, Qataban and Hadramout shared in its prosperity, plying the 'incense road' and the west coast of the Arabian Peninsula. Their goods reached as far as Rome and its tributaries. The Semitic 'South Arabian' script, sometimes incorrectly referred to as 'Himyaritic', examples of which have been found among the Mesopotamian tablets and as far afield as Palestine, developed among these prosperous trading communities. With the rise of Islam in the seventh century AD, a large number of Yemenis served in the Islamic armies that conquered territories from the Atlantic to the borders of China. Although part of a succession of Islamic empires, Yemen often reasserted its individuality, and local rulers gained a measure of independence. In the early 16th century the fear that the Portuguese might establish a presence in southern Arabia led to the first Ottoman occupation of Yemen, although in the early 17th century local rulers, the Zaidi Imams, launched a guerrilla war against the Turks, which led to their withdrawal.

In 1839 Britain occupied the port of Aden, a valuable fuelling station on the route to India. Aden became a free port in 1850 and an important military base, and from 1869 benefited from the substantial increase in shipping that resulted from the opening of the Suez Canal. During the second half of the 19th century, as the Turks attempted to reassert their control over Yemen, the British established a protectorate over tribes in the Aden hinterland, consolidating their position with a series of treaties with the tribes, which, in return for protection from outside attack and regular subsidies, undertook to refrain from correspondence with foreign powers, to whom they were not to cede any territory without approval. These events were significant in Yemeni history because, for the first time, southern Arabia was formally divided into two distinct territories separated by a boundary recognized by international treaty. At the inception of the 20th century events in Yemen, as in almost all of the Arabian Peninsula, were affected by the recapture of Riyadh by Abd al-Aziz ibn Abd al-Rahman of the Al Sa'ud family, and the ensuing decline of the Al Rashid dynasty that had ruled much of the region since 1874. The Wahhabi influence of the House of Sa'ud, dating from the proselytizing of Muhammad ibn Abd al-Wahhab in the early 18th century, was strongest in the Najd (Nejd) region of central Arabia, but it pervaded most of the tribes, with its injunction to return to the true teaching of the Prophet. In the 1930s Abd al-Aziz (commonly referred to as Ibn Sa'ud) invaded Yemen to settle a border dispute. The Ta'if agreement allocated Tihama and Hajran to the Saudi king. The legacy of the Wahhabi version of Islam remains strong in Yemen and is relevant to the 21st-century manifestation of jihadism.

BRITAIN, ADEN AND THE IMAMS

Following the withdrawal of Turkish forces from Yemen at the end of the First World War (1914–18), the Zaidi Imam, Yahya, reasserted his control over Yemen and challenged the right of the British authorities in Aden to have relations with the tribes in the Protectorate, which he insisted were his subjects. However, in 1934 Imam Yahya tacitly accepted the boundaries agreed between Britain and the Turks, although he considered this as merely permitting Aden to administer part of his territory. Relations with Britain subsequently improved, although the Imam resented the toleration of his political opponents in Aden and, while the British were concerned about his apparent friendship with Fascist Italy, during the Second World War (1939–45) he remained strictly neutral. Under Yahya's rule Yemen remained backward and isolated, and in 1948 he was assassinated in the first post-war coup in the Arab world. His successor, Ahmad, ruled as autocratically as his father had done, but ended the country's isolation and accepted Soviet and Chinese assistance to develop the country's weak infrastructure. Ahmad remained intensely suspicious of Britain and encouraged subversion among tribes in the Aden Protectorate. Nevertheless, his eventual hostility to President Gamal Abd al-Nasir (Nasser) of Egypt, the champion of radical Arab nationalism, eventually led to a certain rapprochement with the British. Ahmad died in September 1962 and shortly afterwards his successor, Badr, was overthrown by Yemeni officers with the help of Egypt, which quickly deployed troops in Yemen. A republic was proclaimed, with a senior officer, Col Abd Allah Sallal, as President.

By the late 1950s Aden Colony was a prosperous port city with the largest British military base outside Europe, among the best social services, the most free press in the Arab world, and a vigorous trade union movement. In the Protectorate rulers were encouraged to accept a resident political adviser in an effort to improve security and local administration, and encourage economic and social development. Egyptian propaganda against 'the occupied South' was one of the factors that persuaded the British to create the Federation of South Arabia in 1959. Two years later Aden was merged into the new federation in an attempt to weaken the nationalists in the Colony. The federation, essentially a government of Sultans dependent on British officials and finances, was never recognized by Arab Governments and was beset by mutual jealousies among the rulers. At a conference held in London, United Kingdom, in December 1963, it was announced that independence would come in 1968, but planned reforms were not implemented for there was no agreement as to who should occupy the principal offices, and outside Aden there was still no real administrative structure and no political organization to mobilize the people in support of the federation.

Meanwhile, young men from the Protectorate, inspired by the ideals of Arab nationalism, formed the National Liberation Front (NLF), declaring that they intended not merely to expel British troops but to bring about a socialist revolution. Their first triumph was to provoke a tribal revolt in Radfan, which was suppressed by the use of British troops, helicopters and even heavy bombers, a campaign that led to widespread criticism within the Arab world and among left-wingers in Britain. A campaign of urban terror was launched in Aden in which 60 people were killed and 350 injured between December 1963 and May 1966.

In February 1966 the Labour Government in the United Kingdom announced that there was no further need for the Aden base, the defence of which had been the paramount reason for creating the federation, and that there would be no further British military presence in South Arabia after independence in 1968. From then on, the British Government was preoccupied with withdrawing from South Arabia with the minimum cost in terms of British lives. The federal leaders, realizing that they had isolated themselves from much of the Arab world by supporting the British, felt betrayed and defenceless. In December 1966 the NLF declared itself the sole representative of the people of South Arabia. It wrested control of the Aden streets from its former ally, the Front for the Liberation of Occupied South Yemen (FLOSY) and began to take control of state after state in the hinterland. Although the NLF was known to have extreme left-wing views, the British preferred it to the pro-Nasser FLOSY and assisted its assumption of power. The handover to the NLF, formalized by a meeting in Geneva, Switzerland, took place on 30 November 1967.

YEMEN ARAB REPUBLIC

After the military coup that overthrew Imam Badr in September 1962 the royalists rallied and, with assistance from Saudi Arabia, attempted to regain control of the country from the new republican regime of Col Sallal, who was supported by a large force of Egyptian troops. A stalemate developed, but the situation was transformed by Egypt's defeat by Israel in the June War of 1967. Nasser, now dependent on Saudi Arabian financial assistance, agreed to withdraw his troops from Yemen and this was completed by the end of November 1967. Sallal was deposed and succeeded by a three-man Council, headed by Qadi Abd al-Rahman al-Iryani. The royalists launched a major offensive in December, but the republicans, despite the withdrawal of Egyptian troops, succeeded in reconquering much of the country, helped by intensified royalist feuding. By February 1970 King Faisal ibn Abd al-Aziz Al Sa'ud had decided that he could tolerate the moderate republic of al-Iryani, and indeed use it as an ally against the communist south. He therefore terminated all aid to the royalists and ordered them to cease fighting. Nearly all the royalists were integrated into the new regime, which was then recognized by Saudi Arabia and the United Kingdom. An estimated 200,000 people had been killed during the eight years of civil war.

Abd al-Rahman al-Iryani played an indispensable role in national reconciliation after the civil war but had to contend with a central Government weakened by the war, conservative tribal sheikhs and the *ulama* (religious scholars), and young modernizers and townsfolk anxious for reform against a background of financial crisis, with an army demanding expensive new equipment. His Government was also dependent for financial assistance on Saudi Arabia, which also extended its largesse to the tribal chiefs. In June 1974, after a plot backed by Iraq to overthrow the regime was discovered, al-Iryani opposed any strong action. When the army and tribal leaders threatened a coup, he resigned and went to live in exile. His successor, Lt-Col Ibrahim al-Hamadi, suspended the Constitution and the Consultative Council, made a determined effort to eradicate corruption, and succeeded in reducing dependence on Saudi Arabia and improving relations with the People's Democratic Republic of Yemen (PDRY). He aimed at a strong centralized state with wide political participation, and encouraged the emergence of the leftist National Democratic Front (NDF). These moves offended the practically independent northern tribal leaders, some of whom rebelled and were consequently bombed by the air force. In October 1977 al-Hamadi was murdered, but his assassins were never caught. He was succeeded by the Chief of Staff, Ahmad al-Ghashmi, a tribesman of the powerful Hashid confederation, but he too was murdered in June 1978.

Al-Ghashmi was succeeded as President by Lt-Col Ali Abdullah Saleh, who was, like his predecessor, a tribesman of the Hashid. At first his position was extremely precarious: he narrowly escaped an assassination attempt in September 1978 and also survived what appeared to be an attempted military coup with the backing of the PDRY in October. With the Shafai South stirred up by the NDF based in Aden and reports of fighting in other regions, the Yemen Arab Republic (YAR) appeared to be on the point of collapse. Saleh was forced to revert to the old Imamic policy of relying on the Hashid and Bakil tribal confederations to deal with internal threats. Only the intervention of other Arab states saved the country from complete disaster during the war with the PDRY in September 1979. During 1981 the NDF overran considerable areas, but then Aden decreased its support and the Zaidi tribes, worried about the advance of the 'godless', rallied to the support of Saleh. Early in 1982 Saleh ordered a full-scale offensive, defeated the NDF and allowed the survivors to be reintegrated in the North.

In 1983 Saleh, who had quickly acquired many of the skills used by the old Imams required to rule an unusually difficult country, was unanimously re-elected for a further five years. In 1985 the YAR held its first free elections to local councils, and in 1988 the long-postponed general election took place for 128 seats in the new 159-member Consultative Council, which was empowered to legislate, ratify treaties and supervise the work of the Government. The remaining 31 members were appointed by the President. Approximately one-sixth of the elective seats, including all six constituencies in the capital, San'a, were won by candidates sympathetic to the Muslim Brotherhood and many others by tribesmen of conservative background. The Council's first action was to re-elect Saleh for a further five years.

In foreign policy Saleh avoided total commitment to either the East or the West. Saudi Arabia continued to provide financial support, but Saleh also sought aid and investment from the West and maintained good relations with the USSR, the YAR's principal supplier of arms.

PEOPLE'S DEMOCRATIC REPUBLIC OF YEMEN

After the British withdrawal from Aden, NLF leader Qahtan al-Shaabi declared South Yemen a unitary state, abolished the old sheikhdoms and proclaimed himself President, Prime Minister and Commander-in-Chief. Other parties were banned, the press was controlled, and a State Security Supreme Court was created and rapidly established firm control throughout the country by means of a police force trained by East Germans. Relations with the United Kingdom deteriorated rapidly as advisers who had remained to assist in the build-up of the new armed forces were expelled and replaced by advisers from the USSR, which also provided arms. As a result of the ending of British subsidies and the closure of the Suez Canal, which badly affected the port of Aden, the country was in a desperate plight.

Al-Shaabi was opposed by an extreme left-wing group within the NLF under the leadership of Abd al-Fattah Ismail and Ali Salim al-Baid, who demanded the nationalization of banks and foreign trade, the collectivization of land, and the export of revolution throughout the Arabian Peninsula. Although al-Shaabi subsequently moved to the left, speaking of the socialist path and the redistribution of land, he was deposed in a bloodless coup in June 1969 and replaced by a five-man Presidential Council, chaired by Salim Rubai Ali and including Abd al-Fattah Ismail. The shift to the left was signalled immediately by the recognition of the German Democratic Republic (East Germany), the severing of diplomatic relations with the USA and calls for revolution in the 'Occupied Gulf'. There followed a period of harsh repression, with constant speeches about conspiracies, and mass arrests, with special courts untrammelled by ordinary law created 'to review anti-state activity'. A large number of citizens, estimated by some at up to one-quarter of the population, fled abroad. The army and the police were subjugated through purges and indoctrination. A new Constitution, with its adoption of the new name the PDRY, was announced, with a commitment to socialism, tolerance of Islam and women's rights, and vesting all power in the single party. Salim Rubai Ali returned from a visit to the People's Republic of China inspired by Maoist ideas of spreading the revolution to the countryside by encouraging the seizure of land by the peasants and concentrating most economic activities in the hands of the state. The country was in perpetual crisis and only aid from the USSR kept it afloat.

Despite numerous declarations expressing a desire to unite with the North, relations with the YAR rapidly deteriorated owing to the presence there of thousands of exiles armed and funded by Saudi Arabia. Border incidents escalated into widespread fighting in September 1972 and a cease-fire was only agreed after mediation by the League of Arab States (the Arab League). To general surprise, the two countries reached an agreement on unification, but little progress was made and relations again deteriorated. In the following years Salim Rubai Ali and Abd al-Fattah Ismail struggled for control of the PDRY's foreign policy and in July 1978 Ali was overthrown, having been found guilty of numerous crimes, and executed. Several days of fighting ensued, causing a new flood of refugees to the North. In December Ismail became Head of State and succeeded in his ambition of changing the NLF into a 'Vanguard Party'—the Yemen Socialist Party (YSP). In February 1979 the PDRY launched a well-planned attack against the North in an effort to bring about unity by force. As the YAR army appeared to be on the verge of disintegration, other Arab states intervened to end the fighting. The two states again signed an agreement to unite, but few practical steps were taken towards its implementation.

In January 1986 Ali Nasser Muhammad, who had assumed the presidency in 1980 after Ismail resigned on grounds of ill heath, attempted to arrest or kill his opponents at a meeting of the politburo, leading to a brief but intense civil war in which at least 2,000 people, including 55 senior party figures, were killed. Some 6,000 foreigners were evacuated to Djibouti. Muhammad fled into exile and his Prime Minister, Haidar Abu Bakr al-Attas, assumed his posts of President and Secretary-General of the YSP. Muhammad was sentenced to death *in absentia* along with 35 of his supporters, although only five were actually executed and a series of amnesties persuaded most of his supporters who had fled to return. There appeared to be little change in internal affairs under the new regime, and close co-operation with the USSR continued. Nevertheless, relations with Saudi Arabia and the Gulf States improved significantly, as did those with the United Kingdom and the USA.

In 1989 the USSR announced that there was no need for the Aden base after the end of the Cold War, and Soviet aid declined dramatically. With the economy on the verge of collapse after two decades of ideologically led mismanagement, and the people on the verge of starvation, important changes were set in motion by the Government. Private and foreign investment was encouraged, the ponderous bureaucracy was dismantled and government monopolies were ended. The YSP ended its monopoly of political life, and several political parties were recognized. The ban on foreign publications was lifted and, later, permits were issued for a range of independent newspapers and journals.

THE ROAD TO UNITY

After the withdrawal of the British from Aden in 1967 the new independent South Yemen had declared that the aim of its Revolution was to unite both parts of Yemen. A number of agreements to unite were signed but never implemented. There were no common ideological grounds between the North and the South, and the financial dependence of one on Saudi Arabia and the other on the USSR prevented any effective move towards unity. In 1988 President Saleh declared that the long-standing dispute over the border between North and South could only be resolved through unification, and YSP Secretary-General Ali Salim al-Baid travelled to San‘a and negotiated a series of agreements. There was a declaration that there should be no recognition of frontiers drawn up during foreign occupation or during the Imamate, existing border posts would be replaced by new ones jointly manned, movement between the two states should be unrestricted, troops should be withdrawn from frontier areas and there should be joint exploration of the Marib/Shabwah area, which would be demilitarized. A number of practical results followed, and al-Baid spoke of ‘creating unified economic interests that would be the material basis for the political success of unity’. It was clear that neither state could finance its own development unilaterally, or attract enough outside assistance, but through unification this might be possible. It appeared that the two Yemens were now set upon economic integration at least.

However, shortly afterwards, amid the general ferment that accompanied the financial crisis leading to *perestroika* (restructuring) in the PDRY, the stability of the YAR became more attractive. In November 1989 senior officials from both countries discussed a 136-article constitution, based on agreements reached by the Constitutional Committee established following the war in 1979. President Saleh proposed that it should be referred to both legislatures and then be put to a referendum; this set a target date for unification of November 1990. It was agreed that the YSP and the General People’s Congress (GPC), which was regarded as its northern equivalent, should preserve their independence, but that there should be room for other political parties. Saleh welcomed ‘a multi-party system provided that it is of Yemeni origin’. In February 1990, at a joint cabinet meeting, 46 laws were approved on such matters as customs procedures, taxation, trade unions and education. Plans were drawn up for a single currency to be issued from a unified central bank. Delegations were sent to the Arab countries to inform them of the intention to form a single state, and after a visit to Riyadh, Saudi Arabia, Saleh announced that King Fahd fully supported unity, although many doubted that he would really welcome a united democratic Yemen on his southern flank.

However, there still appeared to be opposition among hard-line communists in Aden, while in the North dissatisfaction among religious and tribal leaders was more public. To pre-empt the opposition, it was decided to bring forward the date of unification to 22 May 1990. On 21 May the agreement to unite was approved unanimously in Aden, but in San‘a a number of Islamist members walked out or abstained amid demonstrations by their supporters. The following day a joint session of the two Assemblies elected a five-man Presidential Council, headed by Saleh and with al-Baid as Vice-President. At a referendum held in May 1991, the new Constitution for the unified state was approved by a large majority, although fewer than 50% of the electorate registered to vote. Members of the newly formed Yemeni Congregation for Reform (al-Islah) and other Islamists had urged a boycott, insisting that the new Constitution was un-Islamic and, together with other opposition groups, claimed that irregularities in the voting procedure had rendered the result null and void.

The two government parties, the northern GPC and the southern YSP, had agreed to share power equally until elections were held in November 1992, but within months of the referendum there were reports that extremists within each were increasing their stocks of weapons for use against the other. Owing to the disparity in the population—10m. in the North and 2m. in the South—posts had to be found in the North for southerners, who were regarded as secularists, indeed as former communists, and whose presence was resented. Northerners were shocked by the un-Islamic lifestyle of many in Aden and by the enhanced role of women. Towards the end of 1991 and during 1992 there were several attacks on YSP leaders and a number of the party’s officials were killed. There were also reports of bomb attacks on the homes of GPC members. Meanwhile, the economic situation had deteriorated sharply as a result of the Gulf crisis and the social unrest proved fertile soil for the Islamists, who provided education and a range of other social services that the state could not.

YEMEN AND THE GULF CRISIS

Iraq’s invasion and annexation of Kuwait in August 1990 placed the Government of the newly unified Yemen in an extremely difficult situation. Iraq was an important trade partner and a source of aid, but Yemen was heavily dependent on financial support from Saudi Arabia, which also hosted large numbers of Yemeni expatriate workers. Moreover, there was evidence of widespread popular support in Yemen for Iraq’s President Saddam Hussain. These factors explain the Government’s equivocal response to the Iraqi invasion of Kuwait and to subsequent developments in the Gulf region. In the immediate aftermath of the invasion, the Government condemned Iraq, but also criticized the arrival of US and other Western military forces to defend Saudi Arabia. At the summit meeting of leaders of Arab League member states, held in Cairo, Egypt, on 10 August, Yemen voted against the proposal to send Arab forces to Saudi Arabia as part of a US-led multinational force to deter aggression by Iraq. Yemen also abstained in the UN Security Council vote to impose economic sanctions against Iraq, although by late August it appeared to be reluctantly implementing UN sanctions. In October Yemen’s Minister of Foreign Affairs, Abd al-Karim al-Iryani, announced that Yemen would support any measures taken to achieve a peaceful withdrawal of Iraqi troops from Kuwait, but that this should be followed by withdrawal of all foreign forces from the area.

In November 1990 Yemen voted against the UN Security Council resolution to authorize the multinational contingent in the Gulf to use ‘all necessary means’ against Iraq if it had not withdrawn its forces from Kuwait by 15 January 1991. This prompted a visit to Yemen by US Secretary of State James Baker, in an attempt to persuade Yemen to modify its position. In December 1990 Yemen assumed the chair of the UN Security Council and increased its efforts to mediate in the Gulf crisis; the Vice-President, Ali Salim al-Baid, met King Hussein of Jordan in Amman, and the Iraqi President in Baghdad, for talks concerning the crisis. In January 1991 Yemen presented a peace plan in an attempt to prevent war in the Gulf; the proposals included an Iraqi withdrawal from Kuwait, the withdrawal of the multinational military force, and the holding of an international conference on the Arab–Israeli conflict. Despite numerous diplomatic initiatives undertaken by Yemen prior to the UN deadline of 15 January, the peace plan failed to prevent the outbreak of war in the Gulf on the following day. Following the US-led military offensive against Iraq, Yemen issued a statement in which it condemned the action, and hundreds of thousands of Yemenis demonstrated in support of Iraq.

The Government estimated that the Gulf crisis had cost the Yemeni economy US $3,000m. Yemen's relations with Saudi Arabia and the Gulf states deteriorated as a result of Yemen's stance during the crisis, which was not quickly forgotten. Saudi Arabia ceased its financial support of some $600m. a year and expelled some 500,000 to 800,000 Yemeni workers, whose return caused widespread economic and social disruption. In April 1992 Saudi Arabia warned the four oil companies prospecting in the eastern desert, in an area where the frontier had not been precisely delimited, that they were trespassing on Saudi territory, and, to the great indignation of the Yemenis, the companies ceased work. The Saudis also disapproved of Yemen's increasing friendship with Iran. The Cooperation Council for the Arab States of the Gulf (Gulf Cooperation Council—GCC) stopped funding the expansion of Aden port, and Kuwait instructed its airline not to sell tickets to Yemenis. Yemen's one ally in the Arabian peninsula was its neighbour Oman, with frequent high-level visitors exchanging messages between Sultan Qaboos and President Saleh. In late 1992 Yemen and Oman signed and ratified an agreement to establish the demarcation of the border, and in April 1993 the two countries agreed on measures to open border points and increase bilateral trade. Relations with Bahrain, the United Arab Emirates (UAE) and Qatar also showed signs of gradual improvement and those with Egypt were quickly repaired. Yemen continued to oppose sanctions against Iraq, but in March 1993 Saddam Hussain sent his half-brother to San‘a to protest against Yemeni attempts to improve its relations with the Gulf states.

Reconciliation with the Western powers was smoother. Relations with the USA, which had severely reduced its aid to Yemen in January 1991, quickly improved and relations were soon fully restored with the United Kingdom. Meanwhile, Yemen had increasingly been drawn into the affairs of its neighbours across the Red Sea, helping to settle disputes in Djibouti and receiving more than 60,000 Somali refugees from the civil war in Somalia during 1992 and 1993.

THE 1993 ELECTIONS AND THE ENSUING POLITICAL CRISIS

In spite of the climate of unrest, legislative elections were held in April 1993, the first nation-wide, multi-party elections based on universal suffrage in the Arabian peninsula. After lively campaigning in the months preceding the elections, turn-out was very high, and international observers expressed broad satisfaction with the conduct of the elections. Inevitably, there were reports of disturbances in several towns and accusations of fraudulent practices by both leading parties. When the results were announced, the GPC, led by President Saleh, had won the majority of the vote and secured 123 of the 301 seats in the House of Representatives, most of them in the former YAR. Al-Islah, widely reported to have received substantial assistance from Saudi Arabia, took second place with 62 seats, again mainly in the YAR, relegating the YSP, led by Vice-President al-Baid, to third place with 56 seats, most of them in the former PDRY. The Baath party took seven seats, minor parties five seats and independents 48 seats. Of the 50 women candidates who stood for election, only two won seats.

After the election the three main parties eventually agreed to form a coalition, with the GPC and YSP each taking two seats on the Presidential Council and al-Islah the one remaining seat. Al-Islah was also allocated six posts in the Council of Ministers, but these did not include the portfolios of education and finance, which the party had demanded. However, the al-Islah leader, Sheikh Abdullah bin Hussain al-Ahmar, became Speaker of the House of Representatives. The YSP, disappointed by the election results, became increasingly apprehensive and resentful about the emerging alliance between the GPC and al-Islah. The GPC found it easier to co-operate with al-Islah than with the YSP on a number of important political issues, especially proposed constitutional changes; this co-operation was assisted by the fact that President Saleh's tribe, the Sanhan, belonged to the Hashid tribal federation, of which the al-Islah leader was the paramount Sheikh.

In August 1993 the Vice-President refused to take part in the Government and decided to return to Aden. His departure from San‘a marked the official beginning of a political crisis that was to lead to civil war. This crisis intensified following a series of assassinations of YSP officials, including the Vice-President's nephew. It was widely rumoured in San‘a that these assassinations were ordered by the President's 'entourage', notably his brother and three half-brothers, who commanded key military units and the security services.

In November 1993 al-Baid declared that the North was attempting to annex the South rather than unifying with it. Chronic economic problems that had already been exacerbated by the isolation of the country in the 1990–91 Gulf conflict led to riots in San‘a and Taiz in January 1994. More political killings followed—al-Baid claimed that more than 150 YSP members had been killed since May 1990—as well as kidnappings of foreign nationals.

On 20 February 1994 the President and Vice-President signed a document of reconciliation at a public ceremony in Amman, Jordan, but there was no rapprochement between the two leaders, and al-Baid demanded that Saleh order the immediate arrest of his brothers. Al-Baid and his principal lieutenants walked out of follow-up talks and further strained relations with the President by visiting Saudi Arabia and the Gulf states to seek support for their cause. The day after the ceremony there were clashes between rival military units in the southern province of Abyan and in other parts of the country. After unification, the armed forces of the former YAR and PDRY had not been integrated; the GPC continued to control the northern forces and the YSP those of the South. The fighting that continued sporadically for some months involved not only forces under the command of the GPC and YSP, but also YSP forces loyal to the former South Yemen President, Ali Nasser Muhammad, as well as tribal militias, which used the opportunity to promote their own interests.

THE CIVIL WAR

On 27 April 1994, the first anniversary of the general election, a major tank battle took place between rival army units at Amran, some 60 km to the north of San‘a. It was the biggest clash between the opposing forces since the crisis began. Some 200 tanks were involved in the fighting; 85 tanks were reported to have been destroyed and more than 400 soldiers killed or wounded. Both sides claimed that the other attacked first. The YSP claimed that the attack was tantamount to a declaration of war, while the President accused al-Baid of secessionism and pledged to fight to defend the unity of the country. During the night of 4 May fighter aircraft under the command of the YSP attacked northern airports at San‘a, Taiz and Hodeida, the presidential palace in San‘a, the country's two main power stations, Hodeida port, and petroleum storage and pipeline facilities at Marib. Northern aircraft retaliated on 5 May, badly damaging the airport at Aden. The civil war had begun in earnest. The President declared a 30-day state of emergency and dismissed the Vice-President. France announced that it was evacuating its nationals and the USA advised its citizens to leave. On 10 May Prime Minister al-Attas, a southerner, was dismissed after he appealed for outside forces to help end the civil war. The Minister of Petroleum and Minerals was among other YSP members dismissed from their posts in the Council of Ministers. On 21 May al-Baid proclaimed the breakaway 'Democratic Republic of Yemen' (DRY) and began diplomatic efforts to secure recognition of the old frontier. Al-Attas, the former Prime Minister of Yemen, who had joined the secessionist government in Aden, travelled to Egypt to seek the backing of Arab moderates and appealed to the West for support and recognition for the southern government. Al-Baid was named 'President' of the new state, with a five-man 'Presidential Council' drawn from a range of political and tribal affiliations.

On 1 June 1994 the UN Security Council unanimously adopted Resolution 924, appealing for an immediate cease-fire and requesting the dispatch of a UN commission of inquiry to assess prospects for a renewed dialogue between the belligerents. However, before the commission of inquiry, led by former Algerian Minister of Foreign Affairs Lakhdar Brahimi, began its work, the Ministers of Foreign Affairs of the GCC, meeting on 4–5 June, issued a statement effectively blaming the North for the conflict and implicitly recognizing the DRY. The ministers warned that continued hostilities would have repercussions for the GCC states, forcing them to adopt appropriate measures against 'the party that does not abide by the cease-fire'; only Qatar dissented. Dr Abd al-Karim al-Iryani, the Minister of Planning and Development and principal political counsellor to President Saleh, maintained that arms purchased with Saudi funds were being supplied to the South. The North accused Saudi Arabia of encouraging the secessionists in order to create a new petroleum emirate in the Hadramout under Saudi influence and providing it with an outlet to the Indian Ocean.

A cease-fire and talks arranged in Cairo by Brahimi both collapsed. It was reported that the South had acquired military equipment, including tanks and missiles, and new *MiG*-29 fighter planes from Eastern Europe, with Gulf funding, and was using its air power to bomb the Marib oilfields.

At the end of June 1994 the UN Secretary-General reported that UN efforts to mediate between the two rival factions had made no progress. The Security Council, meeting on 29 June, adopted Resolution 931, which requested that the Secretary-General continue to mediate between the two factions in order to secure a durable cease-fire and appealed for a monitoring force to supervise the truce. Several observers pointed to the critical role of the USA, which finally decided to support a unified Yemen and warned Saudi Arabia against interfering. Despite talks in Moscow, Russia, on 30 June and again in New York, USA, on 2 July on implementing and supervising a cease-fire, northern forces continued their advance and by 4 July had entered northern districts of Aden, which was without water or electricity. On 7 July Aden surrendered to northern forces and the self-proclaimed DRY collapsed. Al-Baid fled to Oman, and his 'Vice-President', Abd al-Rahman al-Jifri, to Saudi Arabia. President Saleh reported that 931 civilians and soldiers had been killed in the civil war and 5,000 had been wounded, although others claimed that the death toll was much higher. It was estimated that the war against the southern secessionists had cost the central Government US $8,000m. Saleh estimated that it would cost $7,500m. in post-war reconstruction. Following the announcement of a general amnesty and the termination of the state of emergency, southern Yemeni soldiers began returning to the country.

After the fall of Aden to northern forces, the victorious North pledged to work for national reconciliation. On 7 July 1994 a document was submitted to the UN Secretary-General stating that military operations would cease immediately, a general amnesty would be declared, democracy and political pluralism, together with human rights, freedom of speech and of the press would be respected, and national dialogue within the framework of constitutional legitimacy would be resumed.

On 28 September 1994 the House of Representatives in San'a adopted a series of constitutional reforms, which greatly strengthened the position of the President, including the abolition of the Presidential Council. Following the defeat of the secular YSP and the dispersal of its military and political power base, al-Islah began asserting its authority. As part of the constitutional reforms, *Shari'a* (Islamic law) became the only, rather than the principal, source of legislation, and the last references to the specific rights of women were removed from the Constitution. On 1 October Saleh was re-elected President of the Republic and, despite much rhetoric about reconciliation, the YSP was excluded from the new Government. The GPC retained the majority of posts within the new Council of Ministers, but al-Islah increased its membership from six to nine, including the influential portfolios of education and justice. The South was represented in the new cabinet by four ministers, together with Vice-President Maj.-Gen. Abd al-Rabbuh Mansur Hadi.

Despite its minority representation in government, al-Islah was the most influential party in the country, with the best and most dynamic organization. Its officials were active in the towns and even in remote parts of the countryside, and its broad-based constituency included the tribes, the commercial bourgeoisie and the influential Muslim Brotherhood. In September 1994 the al-Islah congress elected members of the Muslim Brotherhood to most of its key posts. Yet, despite the ascendancy of its ideologues, al-Islah moved cautiously and was careful in its public statements to stress its commitment to political pluralism and to a market economy, while condemning violence and terrorism in all its forms. Al-Islah ministers acted with discretion but determination. The Minister of Education, Abdo Ali al-Qubati, for example, did not overturn existing teaching programmes, but he did increase the hours devoted to Koranic studies at the expense of science teaching, and suspended teachers suspected of socialist and secular sympathies. He also gradually phased out co-educational classes in schools and in the university in the southern provinces, and 'recommended' that female teachers and students observe the 'proper dress code'. The Minister of Justice, Dr Abd al-Wahab Lufti al-Daylami, dismissed women judges whose appointment had survived from the former PDRY, stating that they were totally incompetent in Islamic law. Al-Islah and the GPC, meanwhile, co-operated to destroy the YSP and appeared determined to 'Islamize' the southern provinces. The Government seized all properties belonging to the YSP, and thousands of civil servants suspected of socialist sympathies were dismissed.

In June 1995 President Saleh was re-elected head of the GPC at the party's first general assembly to be held since 1988, and was given the new title of party Chairman. The Deputy Prime Minister and Minister of Foreign Affairs, Abd al-Karim al-Iryani, assumed Saleh's previous position of Secretary-General, and the post of party Vice-Chairman was taken by the country's Vice-President, Abd al-Rabbuh Mansur Hadi. In accordance with a decision to rationalize and restructure the party, the permanent committee, elected to represent the constituencies, was reduced to 300 members, and the size of the politburo, elected by the permanent committee, was reduced from 23 to seven members.

Tensions that had emerged between the GPC and al-Islah in early 1995 continued as the year progressed, with differences over many aspects of policy becoming more pronounced. While some elements in al-Islah were keen to further Islamist influence over the country's banking system, the GPC was in favour of its privatization. Al-Islah, which had established its own system of educational establishments, quite separate from the state-run education system, was also opposed to the GPC's aim of educational integration and unification. Al-Islah expressed its opposition to economic reforms recommended by the World Bank, and criticized the GPC for attending an economic summit meeting in Jordan, in October, at which representatives of Israel were present. Moreover, in December the party's Minister of Trade and Supply, Muhammad Ahmad Afandi, resigned from his post, citing political and economic differences with the GPC. With the collapse of the YSP, the southern governorates felt increasingly marginalized and neglected, and reconstruction work in the South was mainly financed by foreign governments and organizations. Violent outbreaks continued in 1996 with explosions in Aden and other southern towns. In June 19 people died in riots in Mukalla and a bomb attack on the Egyptian embassy in July was blamed on 'separatist elements'.

The leaders of the GPC and al-Islah met in January 1997 and renewed their coalition agreement. Earlier, opposition parties had accused both the GPC and al-Islah of monopolizing access to the state-controlled media and using public funds for their election campaigns.

In the elections to the House of Representatives, held on 27 April 1997, the GPC secured a clear majority, winning 187 of the 301 seats, 64 more than in 1993. Al-Islah, its only serious rival, won just 53 seats, compared with 62 in 1993. Independent candidates increased their representation from 48 to 54 seats. Of these, 39 declared their support for the GPC and six for al-Islah. International observers were critical of some aspects of the elections, but pronounced them reasonably free and fair, despite violence in which at least 20 people were reported to have been killed. A new Council of Ministers was named in May 1997; 25 of the 29 members were GPC members, three were independents and there was one member of al-Haq, a conservative Islamist party that won no seats in the election. The GPC emphasized that they were 'participants' and not partners in government. An independent, Faraj Said bin Ghanim, was appointed Prime Minister, while Alawi Saleh al-Salami regained the post of Minister of Finance, which he had held during 1986–94.

As a result of its move to opposition, al-Islah forfeited all its ministerial portfolios and consequently its control over the Ministry of Education, and immediately after the election the President confirmed that al-Islah's religious institutes would be incorporated into the state education system and their finances and curriculum brought into line with those of state schools. In a move seen by many as the first step towards the creation of an upper house of parliament, President Saleh appointed 59 members to a new Consultative Council, designed to broaden the base of participation. Although lacking executive or legislative authority, the Council's committee structure paralleled that of the Council of Ministers and was given a mandate to draft laws on local administration, including the politically sensitive issue of the reorganization of provincial boundaries. In December 1997 the House of Representatives approved the promotion of President Saleh from lieutenant-general to the rank of field marshal.

THREATS TO THE STATE EMERGE

Yemeni affairs following the civil war are inextricably connected to those of Pakistan, Afghanistan and the Arabian peninsula. Yemen's relations with other countries in the region and its internal stability cannot be considered without reference to the international phenomenon of jihadism. Its manifestation in Yemeni society, where it is supported by many thousands of Afghan war veterans, has become a potent factor in the complex ideological, tribal and territorial mix.

Since 2004 another major threat to President Saleh's rule has developed in the northern province of Saada, near the Saudi Arabian border, following a wave of rebellions originally led by the al-Houthi family. The origins of the dispute are unclear, but it is estimated that some 150,000 people have been displaced by the intense military activity in the region.

After two bombs exploded in Aden in July 1997, 120 people were arrested throughout the southern governorates, mainly members of those opposition parties that had boycotted the recent elections. The authorities claimed that the opposition parties were responsible for the bombings, but Abd al-Rahman al-Jifri, leader of the League of the Sons of Yemen (RAY), insisted that the bombs had been planted by the Yemeni Government in an attempt to discredit the opposition. Later in the year the authorities stated that most of those detained had been released, but the opposition claimed that the majority of them were still in prison and that two had died after being tortured. The arrests provoked demonstrations during August and September in Mukalla, the capital of the Hadramout, where support for the exiled separatist leader al-Baid was strong. The demonstrators were also reacting to a decision by the newly formed Consultative Council to divide the province of Hadramout into two parts, a move that was interpreted as an attempt to isolate the coastal areas, including the towns of Mukalla and Shihr (where the YSP retained a strong presence), from the interior of the province. There were further bombings in Aden in October.

Elsewhere in the country, the Government's economic reforms were provoking widespread and often violent protests. In October 1997, after fuel prices were increased, local people in Dhammar, Marib and al-Jawf protested by blocking roads to the capital. Tribal leaders supported the protesters' actions and the authorities responded by dispatching troops to reopen the roads. At Dhammar three people died in clashes between armed tribesmen and the security forces. Foreigners were no longer considered immune from violent attacks, and there was a sharp increase in the number of kidnappings of foreign residents and tourists, mainly by tribes seeking to extract material benefits from the state or to demonstrate their dissatisfaction with certain government actions. In November Brig. Hussain Muhammad Arab, the Minister of the Interior, linked the increase in the number of kidnappings with the Aden bombings, describing them as part of a campaign to 'tarnish Yemen's image and shake its stability'. In the same month 31 people alleged to be 'foreign agents' were put on trial in San'a, charged with attacking and robbing military posts.

In a report published in March 1997, Amnesty International described Yemen as a 'major violator of human rights', despite having ratified or acceded to most human rights treaties and incorporated many of their safeguards into its domestic legislation. The report criticized the activities of the political branch of the security forces and the dramatic increase in the use of the death penalty since 1990, and alleged the systematic use of torture in prisons and the arbitrary arrest and detention of political opponents. It also listed abuses against women. The Deputy Prime Minister expressed surprise at the criticism, but the Government promised to investigate the alleged abuses and gave assurances that the political security branch would be brought under judicial control. At the beginning of April 1997 the European Parliament urged the European Commission to put pressure on the Yemeni authorities to improve the country's human rights record, and a new co-operation agreement signed with the European Union (EU) at the end of the month (replacing the 1984 agreement) was made conditional on progress in both human rights and democracy in Yemen. Later in 1997 Amnesty International deplored the increase in extra-judicial punishments and instances where international standards to ensure fair trials were disregarded. In a number of cases, following lenient sentencing, crowds of armed civilians took the law into their own hands and the authorities made little effort to curb the increase in vigilante activity. In October a formal Yemeni application for membership of the Commonwealth (which comprises former British dependencies) was rejected on the grounds that Yemen did not meet the required standards in terms of democracy, the rule of law and respect for human rights. In February 1998 Mansur Rajih, who had been adopted as a prisoner of conscience by several human rights organizations, was released after 15 years in prison under threat of execution.

At the end of March 1998 the year-long trial of 15 members of the separatist southern Yemeni leadership during the 1994 civil war finally came to an end. Five of the men, including al-Baid and former Prime Minister Haidar al-Attas, were condemned to death; three, including Abd al-Rahman al-Jifri, were sentenced to 10 years in prison; five received suspended sentences; and two were acquitted. All the accused had fled abroad after the southern secessionists were defeated by northern forces, and were tried *in absentia*. Demonstrations and bomb explosions ensued. Kidnapping of foreigners by tribesmen continued; there were 21 kidnappings in 1997, and six attempted and 16 actual kidnappings in the early part of 1998, and little prospect of those involved being arrested. In June three British journalists were arrested for filming illegally in Yemen and were only released following diplomatic exchanges. The Government claimed that the murder of a group of nuns in July was the work of 'deranged extremists'. In August a decree was issued whereby the maximum legal penalty upon conviction of kidnapping was increased to death.

Meanwhile, in March 1998 the Prime Minister, Faraj Said bin Ghanim, left for Switzerland, ostensibly for medical treatment, but on his return to Yemen in April he resigned from the premiership, after only 11 months in office, citing corruption and incompetence among his ministers as the reason behind his decision. Bin Ghanim subsequently became head of the Consultative Council. The President appointed al-Iryani to head a provisional administration, and in May al-Iryani was confirmed in the post when a new, enlarged Council of Ministers was announced. Presenting the new Government's programme to the House of Representatives in June, al-Iryani pledged to continue wider-ranging measures to tackle the country's economic problems and to begin implementing comprehensive administrative, employment and legal reforms. The Government also indicated that it would proceed with efforts to settle the long-standing border dispute with Saudi Arabia.

The Government's decision, in June 1998, to increase prices of fuel and some basic foodstuffs by up to 40%, with immediate effect, led to a week of riots and demonstrations in the capital and several other towns, including Taiz, Dhammar, Ibb and Marib. Some 100 people were thought to have died, including 21 soldiers. Tribesmen also seriously damaged the Hunt Oil pipeline from Marib to the Red Sea, although both the Government and Hunt Oil played down the seriousness of the incident. At the same time at least two explosions were reported in Aden. By the end of the year there had been 17 separate attacks on the Marib oil pipeline since June. Party tensions were elevated throughout these events and there was an attempt on President Saleh's life.

As an early indication of the increasing jihadist presence in the country, in December 1998 the 'Islamic Aden-Abyan Army', a small faction of the Yemeni Islamist group Islamic Jihad, under the leadership of Zein al-Abidine al-Mihdar (also known as 'Abu Hassan'), kidnapped 16 tourists in Yemen, of whom four were killed during a rescue attempt (including three Britons). This was followed in October 2000 by the deaths of 17 US servicemen, in an attack by Islamist militants on a US Navy warship, the USS *Cole*, off the coast of Aden. By 2001, following the declaration by the USA of a 'war on terror', it was clear that the Yemeni connection was significant.

Islamic Jihad's international connections date back to the war in Afghanistan, and include links with Osama bin Laden (see the chapter on Saudi Arabia), who had proposed that the Afghan war veterans should overthrow the Marxist PDRY. Islamic Jihad was operating a military training camp in the mountains of southern Yemen, which the Yemeni authorities had been trying to close for some time. The actions of the Yemeni security forces were heavily criticized in the British media. The deaths of the four hostages in 1998 sparked a diplomatic row between the United Kingdom and Yemen. It was suggested that the incident may have been a reprisal for the US-British air-strikes against Iraq earlier in December. After the incident, the Islamic Army of Aden-Abyan, which was thought to have influence with members of the ruling élite, demanded the overthrow of the Government and its replacement by a broad-based administration including *ulama*, tribal chiefs and notables. A court in Zinjibar sentenced the three kidnappers to death in May 1999.

The kidnappings in Abyan were linked to the arrest a few days previously of five young British Muslims and an Algerian (who had been living in the United Kingdom), who were believed to have been planning to bomb the British consulate and a British-built church in Aden. The authorities claimed that the men were members of a London-based extremist Islamist group, 'Supporters of the *Shari'a*', and had been sent to Yemen by the group's leader, Abu Hamza al-Masri. In October 1998 Abu Hamza's group had issued a communiqué in Arabic on behalf of the Islamic Aden-Abyan Army, warning 'unbelievers' to leave the Arabian Peninsula. It later emerged that one of the British Muslims arrested was the stepson of Abu Hamza. At a press conference in London in January 1999 Abu Hamza demanded the overthrow of the Yemeni Government and warned non-Muslims against visiting Yemen on pain of death.

The six suspects went on trial at the end of January 1999, accused of membership of an armed group and of planning to commit acts of sabotage against Yemeni and foreign interests in Aden. The men all denied the charges and claimed to have been tortured. A further four men, including a son of Abu Hamza (Mustafa Kamil), were put on trial in connection with the Abyan kidnappings. In March British police arrested Abu Hamza in London for questioning, but released him three days later. Abu Hamza had earlier issued a new threat on behalf of the Islamic Aden-Abyan Army, warning the British and US ambassadors to leave Yemen. After court challenges citing torture, in August the court in Aden found the 10 defendants guilty as charged; seven were sentenced to terms of imprisonment of three to seven years, while the other three were given shorter sentences which they were regarded as having already served while awaiting trial. Subsequently three of the men returned to the United Kingdom. In April 2000 Yemen's Supreme Court upheld the prison sentences imposed on the remaining five Britons in 1999. The Yemeni authorities continued to accuse Abu Hamza of being the main instigator of recent terrorist operations in Yemen, and to condemn the United Kingdom for refusing to extradite him to Yemen. However, the United Kingdom insisted that after investigating Abu Hamza's activities it had no grounds for deporting him. Meanwhile, in October 1999, after two unsuccessful appeals against his death sentence, the leader of the Islamic Aden-Abyan Army, Abu Hassan, was executed, although his two accomplices later had their sentences commuted to life imprisonment. There were reports that the Government had come under strong pressure, notably from the al-Islah leader, Sheikh Abdullah bin Hussain al-Ahmar, to take decisive action against the kidnappers. After the arrest at the end of October of two men alleged to be the new leaders of the Islamic Aden-Abyan Army, the authorities claimed that the group now consisted of only small, low-level units, which were under close surveillance by the security forces. In response to Abu Hassan's execution, the Islamic Army had threatened to strike against Western interests in Yemen. Meanwhile, the Government announced the creation of a separate court to try kidnappers and those involved in acts of sabotage against oil pipelines.

Despite increasing violence, rising numbers of kidnappings and assassinations, and a growing sense that the country was sliding into chaos, Yemen's political institutions continued to function. Saleh won Yemen's first direct presidential election on 23 September 1999 (with 96.3% of the vote), in which some two-thirds of the eligible voters participated according to official figures. Also in 1999 Ahmad, Saleh's son, was appointed as head of the Republican Guard. In January 2000 the House of Representatives finally approved a bill setting out the structure and powers of local and regional government. The new law established district and governorate councils: governors and district managers were to be appointed by the President while their deputies would be elected, though their powers were unclear. The Constitution was amended in November, giving more authority to the executive and weakening the legislature. The amendments were approved by referendum in February 2001. Also in that month disputed local elections were held, and five months later the Government partially abolished the councils. Nationally, Abd al-Karim al-Iryani was replaced as Prime Minister by Abd al-Qadir Bajammal in April and Yemen's first female minister, Prof. Wahiba Fare'e, was appointed to the newly created post of Minister of State for Human Rights. Legislative elections, postponed in 2001, were held on 27 April 2003: the GPC won 228 seats, al-Islah 47 seats and the YSP seven seats. Two minor opposition parties, the Nasserite Unionist Popular Organization and the Arab Socialist Baath Party, secured three seats and two seats, respectively, while independents took the remaining 14. The new Government's programme included a controversial measure to incorporate religious institutes (estimated to number some 400, with 250,000 students) into the state education system. These institutes, basically Koranic schools, were developed in North Yemen in the 1970s primarily to counteract the spread of Marxist ideas from the PDRY, but by the 1990s had come to be widely regarded as a vehicle for al-Islah propaganda and recruitment. In January 2002 the private al-Iman University run by Sheikh Abd al-Majid al-Zindani, the Chairman of al-Islah's Shura Council, was also briefly closed down. Sheikh al-Zindani, notorious for his fierce anti-Western and anti-Jewish rhetoric, was reported to have assumed a low public profile in late 2001, as his university was regarded by many as an academic centre of Islamist extremism where a culture of intolerance was promoted. In the aftermath of the 11 September 2001 terrorist attacks on the US mainland, the Government maintained that the closures were part of the ongoing 'war on terror'. By February 2002 it was reported that some 600 foreign students enrolled in religious institutes had been deported.

THE USS *COLE* ATTACK AND THE 'WAR ON TERROR'

On a visit to San'a in October 1997, the US Assistant Secretary of State for Middle East and Near East Affairs, Martin Indyk, expressed continued US support for all measures to strengthen security and stability in the region and stated that the US Government was keen to promote and expand co-operation with Yemen. He praised the Yemeni Government for its 'rational approach' to the border dispute with Saudi Arabia. In May and December 1998 the Commander-in-Chief of the US Central Command, Anthony Zinni, visited Yemen for talks with President Saleh on military co-operation, and in November US and Yemeni forces carried out one of a series of joint military exercises. Zinni made a third visit to Yemen in April 1999 when he inspected the work of US military staff assisting Yemen's mine-clearance programme. The visit fuelled rumours that the Government was planning to offer the USA military facilities on the Yemeni island of Socotra, at the entrance to the Gulf of Aden, despite strenuous denials by President Saleh. In March the editor of an opposition newspaper, *Al-Haqq*, was arrested after the paper published a report accusing the Government of allowing the USA to use Socotra as a military base. The US military had a commercial agreement under which its ships could refuel at Aden, but there was no evidence that plans were underway to station US military personnel in Yemen on a permanent basis. In May Yemen's Minister of Foreign Affairs indicated that the USA would be permitted to use the country's military bases on a temporary basis but only if this was part of an operation that was in Yemen's interests. Despite increased military co-operation and a general improvement in bilateral relations, the two countries remained divided on policy towards Iraq and Iran. Yemen, for example, had condemned as 'flagrant aggression' the US and British air-strikes against Iraq in December 1998 known as Operation Desert Fox. Meanwhile, the USA expressed concern when part of a consignment of *T-55* tanks purchased by Yemen from Poland found their way to Sudan; there were similar anxieties after the Czech Republic agreed in September 1999 to sell Yemen 100 *T-54* and *T-55* tanks because of fears that some of this weaponry might also be destined for Sudan or even Iraq. In July 2000 the Czech Republic confirmed that it had dispatched 30 tanks to Yemen and planned to deliver another 76 by the end of the year. In May Russia had also sent a consignment of tanks to Yemen. As President Saleh had stated that Yemen was committed to reducing military expenditure following the border accord with Saudi Arabia, these shipments inevitably aroused suspicions that, despite the criticisms voiced by the USA, Yemen was continuing to purchase arms destined for sale to 'pariah' states such as Sudan.

In March 2000 President Saleh made an official visit to Washington, DC, where he held talks with President Bill Clinton and senior members of his Administration, which were reported to have covered aid, plans for increased military co-operation, and regional issues, notably the Middle East peace process. In April the US Department of State reported that Yemen was a 'safe haven' for terrorist groups, in part because the Government had only limited control over much of the interior of the country and its borders. It noted that the Palestinian Islamic Resistance Movement (Hamas) was allowed to maintain an official representative in Yemen, and that members of the extremist Algerian Groupe Islamique Armé (GIA) and Egyptian Islamic Jihad, or those sympathetic to these groups, were living openly in Yemen. Concern was also expressed by the US Department of State about human rights and the significant limitations placed on democratic institutions such as elections.

On 12 October 2000 a total of 17 US naval personnel were killed and 38 wounded in a bomb attack against the destroyer USS *Cole* while it was refuelling at Aden. At first, President Saleh stated that there had been an explosion on board the US vessel, but he later conceded that there had been a terrorist attack and offered full co-operation in investigating the incident. US sources immediately pointed to a link between the suicide bombers and the militant Islamist Osama bin Laden, and suggested that even if bin Laden were not directly involved in the attack on the USS *Cole* he may well have inspired those responsible, whose aim was to deter the USA from its political engagement and military involvement in the Middle East. According to the Yemeni Government, some of those detained after the attack were members of Islamic Jihad with links to Osama bin Laden. However, three Yemeni Islamist groups claimed responsibility for the attack, the Islamic Aden-Abyan Army and two previously unknown groups—Muhammad's Army and the Islamic Deterrence Force. The US Administration defended its policy of refuelling ships at Aden, stating that 25 ships had been safely refuelled there in the previous 18 months. Addressing the US Senate's Armed Services Committee, Gen. Anthony Zinni, recently retired as Commander of US forces in the Middle East, insisted that the decision to allow US ships to refuel at Aden had not been made for political reasons and argued that the Yemeni port had appeared a safer location to refuel than many others in a volatile region. He rejected any suggestion that the navy might have compromised security to support the political goal of improving US-Yemeni relations.

Yemeni officials announced in December 2000 that six people accused of being involved in the attack on the USS *Cole* would go on trial in January 2001. The accused included some civil servants who were alleged to have provided forged papers. Early in 2001, however, the Yemeni authorities announced that the trial would be delayed, and it was reported that US officials had requested more time to gather additional evidence. Co-operation between the Yemeni and US teams investigating the attack had proved difficult, but in November 2000 the two sides had come to an agreement that defined their respective roles in the investigation. Nevertheless, in an interview with *The Washington Post* in December, President Saleh stated that US officials would not be allowed to question Yemeni suspects unless Yemeni investigators were present, and insisted that Yemen would not consider any requests for the extradition of Yemeni suspects. In April 2001 it was reported that another three suspects had been arrested. In July William Burns, the new US Assistant Secretary of State for Near Eastern Affairs, visited San'a for discussions about security issues. The Yemeni authorities continued to complain of intrusive behaviour by US officials of the Federal Bureau of Investigation (FBI) investigating the USS *Cole* incident, but towards the end of 2001 Yemen was reported to have provided the USA with important information regarding the case. In November the official newspaper *26 September* published claims that the individual suspected of planning the attack had subsequently sought refuge in Afghanistan. The man was named as Muhammad Omar al-Harazi, and was also believed to have been one of the principal organizers of the 1998 attacks on the US embassies in Kenya and Tanzania. In February 2002 it was reported that the trial of eight of the suspects in the bombing of the USS *Cole* had been postponed at the request of the US authorities because of the possibility that new information about the case would be obtained during interrogation of al-Qa'ida and Taliban (an Islamist organization that ruled Afghanistan during 1996–late 2001) prisoners captured by US military forces in Afghanistan in late 2001 and held in detention at the US military base at Guantánamo Bay, Cuba. In April 2003 a total of 10 of the Yemenis accused of involvement in the USS *Cole* attack escaped from a political security prison; seven others remained in detention. The following month two of the fugitives were captured and charged with the murder of US military personnel. In September 2004 a Yemeni court imposed the death sentence on two of six men convicted of involvement in the attack on the USS *Cole* and prison sentences of between five and 10 years on the remaining four. In February 2005 an appeal court ruling upheld one of the death sentences, but commuted the other to 15 years in prison and reduced the sentence of one of the other men from eight to five years.

In September 1999 President Saleh had accused the United Kingdom of harbouring Abu Hamza al-Masri. In October 2000, shortly after the USS *Cole* bombing, there was a large explosion at the British embassy in San'a. British officials stated that an explosive device thrown over the perimeter wall had struck the embassy's generator. There were no injuries to embassy staff, and a man was later arrested by the Yemeni authorities and charged with the attack. Some analysts suggested that they were probably precipitated, as violence escalated in the West Bank and Gaza Strip, by mounting Arab dissatisfaction with the USA and its Western allies for their support for Israel. In July 2001 four Yemenis were found guilty of planning and carrying out the attack on the embassy and were sentenced to between four and 15 years' imprisonment. Two of those convicted had pleaded guilty, stating that the attack was in retaliation for Israeli violence against the Palestinians.

After the terrorist attacks on New York and Washington, DC, on 11 September 2001, US commentators frequently identified Yemen as one of those states believed to be harbouring militant Islamists and described it as a possible target for future US-led military intervention as part of the US Government's declared 'war on terror'. President Saleh, who was no doubt determined to avoid the diplomatic isolation and economic sanctions that followed Yemen's support for Iraq during the 1990–91 Gulf crisis, immediately pledged full support for the USA's global campaign against terrorism.

Security co-operation with the US Administration brought diplomatic and financial benefits to Yemen, but also served to intensify popular animosity towards the USA for its uncompromising support for Israel and its continuing bombing campaign against Iraq. Responding to expressions of popular resentment towards the USA, President Saleh emphasized that any US-led military action should be undertaken only in accordance with guidelines established by the UN and should seek to minimize casualties among Muslim civilians. On several occasions the President also described Yemen as a victim of the rise of global terrorism, pointing to kidnappings and violent anti-Government activities.

In early February 2002 a team of Yemeni investigators visited the Guantánamo Bay base in Cuba (where the USA was holding Taliban and al-Qa'ida prisoners) in order to assist in questioning some 20–30 Yemeni nationals held there; Yemenis formed the second largest national group in detention (after suspects from Saudi Arabia).

The Yemeni authorities stated that they had increased security measures to protect US interests in the country and had arrested five Yemeni nationals suspected of belonging to an al-Qa'ida terrorist cell. President Saleh stated during an interview that 84 terrorist suspects had been arrested during the current anti-terrorism campaign, and, although he denied the existence of al-Qa'ida bases in Yemen, he admitted that some suspected terrorists had been employed in government departments or agencies but not in the military and security forces. US Vice-President Dick Cheney made a brief visit to Yemen in March 2002—the first visit by a senior US official since 1986—as part of a diplomatic tour of the Middle East region. For security reasons, Cheney did not leave the airport. His talks with President Saleh were reported to have focused on the Israeli–Palestinian crisis, Yemen's role in the 'war on terror' and Iraq. Official sources reported that three teams of US military advisers and trainers, each with 20–30 members, were being sent to Yemen. Eight political parties in Yemen issued a statement condemning Cheney's visit and accusing the USA of seeking military domination of the region. The day after the visit two grenades were thrown at the US embassy in San'a, but no one was injured in the explosions.

The Israeli military intervention in Palestinian-controlled areas of the West Bank at the end of March 2002 provoked popular demands for Yemen to end security co-operation with the USA, and on several occasions large crowds tried to protest outside the heavily protected US embassy in the capital. In April a large explosion and gun-fire were heard near the embassy. In the same month there were several bomb attacks against offices of Yemen's secret police, the Political Security Organization (PSO), and the homes of its officials. A new radical Islamist group calling itself the Sympathizers of al-Qa'ida claimed responsibility for the attacks, and also issued threats of 'suicide' attacks against the intelligence services and senior political figures unless al-Qa'ida suspects held at PSO headquarters were released. Meanwhile, opposition parties appealed for action against US economic and oil interests in the Arab region because of the US Government's apparent unconditional support for what they termed 'Israeli terrorist attacks in Palestine', and demanded an end to all forms of co-operation between Yemen and the USA. At the same time the Yemeni House of Representatives, where the GPC enjoyed a strong majority, appealed to Arab and Muslim countries to suspend all forms of co-operation with both the USA and the United Kingdom until they renounced their 'one-sided policies towards Israel'. Nevertheless, security co-operation with the US Government continued. President Saleh announced that a team of 40 US military experts had arrived in Yemen to provide counter-terrorism training for the security forces. The USA was also helping to install computers and surveillance equipment at airports and border crossings to monitor those entering and leaving the country more closely. It was also reported that new terms had been agreed for refuelling US ships at the port of Aden, including a provision that would allow US marines to assist with security at the port. US officials, however, stated that there were no immediate plans to resume refuelling at Aden. In May a spokesman for President Saleh declared that Yemen would not grant military facilities to the USA or any other country at any of its ports. Later that month Prime Minister Bajammal defended the continuing co-operation with the USA in the 'war on terror' and insisted that Yemen could only benefit from US military training expertise. In June, at a seminar organized by the Yemen Centre for Future Studies, attended by journalists, lawyers, and some parliamentary deputies, speakers appeared to confirm that some al-Qa'ida terrorist cells were indeed operating in Yemen and would become stronger in the future unless the authorities took decisive action to dismantle them. However, in July Sheikh Abdullah al-Ahmar, the al-Islah leader, rejected official claims that the 84 people being held in custody in Yemen were linked to al-Qa'ida and insisted that the accusations against them had been made merely to appease the US Administration. Moreover, al-Ahmar claimed that hundreds of Yemenis had been detained by the authorities since 11 September 2001 and Yemen's decision to co-operate with the USA in the 'war on terror'.

In October 2002 there was an explosion on a French supertanker, the *Limburg*, as it arrived at the al-Dabba oil-export terminal near the Yemeni port of al-Shahr, killing a Bulgarian crew member and releasing some 90,000 barrels of oil into the Gulf of Aden. A week later the Yemeni authorities agreed with French and US investigators that it was a terrorist attack and that, as in the case of the attack on the USS *Cole* in 2000, a small boat filled with explosives had been piloted into the tanker. It was not clear whether it was a suicide bomb attack or whether the explosives were detonated by remote control. US investigators insisted that the attack was linked to al-Qa'ida. Yemen subsequently increased sea and air patrols of its coastline. In August 2004 a total of 15 men were convicted of participating in the *Limburg* bombing, one *in absentia*; one man received the death penalty and the others prison sentences ranging from five to 10 years. In February 2005 an appeal court upheld the death sentence, imposed the death penalty on a second man and increased the prison sentences of two others.

Five suspected al-Qa'ida members, including Qaed Salim Sinan al-Harethi, described as al-Qa'ida's chief operative in Yemen and who was believed to have co-ordinated the attack on the USS *Cole*, were assassinated in Marib province in November 2002, by a missile fired from a US Central Intelligence Agency (CIA) *Predator* drone aircraft. According to US and Yemeni officials, a US citizen of Yemeni origin, Ahmad Hijazi, alleged to have links with an al-Qa'ida cell in Buffalo, New York, USA, was among those killed. Amnesty International condemned the attack, stating that it violated international treaties banning extra judicial executions. A Spanish warship taking part in the US-led 'war on terror' discovered 15 Scud missiles and other military equipment from the People's Democratic Republic of Korea (North Korea) hidden under a cargo of cement on a ship bound for Yemen in December. After having taken charge of the vessel, US naval forces allowed it to proceed under escort to Yemen. The missiles were then unloaded after the USA had received assurances from the Yemeni authorities that they would remain in Yemen. For some years there had been suspicions that Yemen was continuing to purchase arms destined for sale to certain 'pariah' states. The incident caused some friction between Yemen and the USA as the Yemeni authorities initially denied that the missiles belonged to them. They later insisted that the shipment was legal and that the missiles were for defensive use only.

Yemen initially endorsed US President George W. Bush's initiative on promoting democratic change in the Middle East, and hosted a regional conference on democracy and human rights of 600 delegates from 40 countries. President Saleh called democracy the 'choice of the modern age for all peoples' and the 'rescue ship' for political regimes. The meeting, however, strongly rejected the idea that democracy could be imposed from outside and insisted that the impetus for change must come from within their own society.

In February 2004 the USA accused Sheikh Abd al-Majid al-Zindani of being a terror suspect because of his long history of working with Osama bin Laden. Al-Zindani denied the accusation, and, under pressure from al-Islah, the Yemeni Government asked the Bush Administration to provide the evidence on which the accusation was made. President Saleh was one of the Arab leaders invited by President Bush to attend the 'Group of Eight' (G8) industrialized nations summit in Georgia, USA, in June. In August, after opposition parties accused the Yemeni authorities of permitting the US ambassador to monitor the anti-terrorism campaign, President Saleh charged them with attempting to discredit the Government. He insisted that Yemen was co-operating with, not taking orders from, the USA in the 'war on terror', and described US assistance to Yemen in the fight against terrorism as 'limited'.

During 2005 President Saleh continued to struggle to balance internal and external political interests. US Under Secretary for Global Affairs, Paula Dobriansky, acknowledged Yemen's contribution to the 'war on terror' and described Yemen as 'an effective partner with the international community'. In March, however, after the US Department of State released its annual report on human rights, which stated that Yemeni police and security forces arbitrarily continued to arrest, detain and torture people, President Saleh accused the USA of double standards and argued that it should change its own conduct and improve conditions of detainees in Iraq and Afghanistan and at Guantánamo Bay. A report by Amnesty International published at the beginning of August quoted testimonies from two Yemenis who stated that, after their arrests, they had been held for more than 18 months in two secret US detention centres in Indonesia and Jordan before being transferred to prison in Yemen.

In September 2005 Yemen officially requested that the USA remove Sheikh Abd al-Majid al-Zindani from its list of people suspected of supporting terrorist activities, claiming that the accusations were based on inaccurate information from biased sources, and in February 2006 continued to reject US requests for his arrest. President Saleh visited Washington, DC, in November 2005 for talks with President Bush, declaring Yemen's firm resolve to continue to work with the USA and the international community to combat terrorism. In a speech in December President Saleh declared that only his personal intervention and resolve had prevented the USA from occupying Aden after the bombing of the USS *Cole*. Meanwhile, officials denied that the USA had requested permission to open detention centres in Yemen for terrorist suspects. In March 2006 the Government criticized comments relating to Yemen in a human rights report published by the US State Department, insisting that the information was inaccurate and did not reflect the reality of the situation in Yemen. After three detainees at Guantánamo Bay committed suicide in June, one of them Yemeni, a human rights organization in Yemen accused the USA of killing the three men and appealed to the Yemeni authorities to take an active stand against 'this crime committed by the US Government'. However, the increase in foreign military financial aid allocated to Yemen by the Bush Administration, from US $1.9m. in 2003 to $8.4m. in 2006, reflected the improvement, on balance, in bilateral co-operation on security issues.

THE 'AL-HOUTHIS' AND OTHER INTERNAL THREATS TO STABILITY, 2002–08

As the Yemeni authorities struggled to respond to the phenomenon of jihadism and the 'war on terror', tensions, both traditional and modern, were never far below the surface of Yemeni society and contributed to the threatened disintegration of the country. In June 2002 the YSP appealed for the sentences against those secessionists condemned *in absentia* in 1998 to be revoked, for a general amnesty to be granted to all persons punished for political reasons related to past conflicts, and for the return of all those forced into exile for political reasons.

It was reported in February 2002 that the Ministry of the Interior had closed down *Al-Shoma'a*, an independent weekly, following a dispute with the editor-in-chief, who had written articles accusing senior government officials of corruption. Some time previously six journalists working on the weekly had been arrested, but they were later released on instructions from President Saleh. In May three Yemeni journalists working for *Al-Thawry*, the YSP's weekly publication, were arrested after writing a series of articles criticizing government policies and demanding equality for all citizens. They were accused of 'encouraging confessional, regional and secessionist sentiments, criticizing the President and inciting the public against the ruling regime'; they were sentenced to five months' imprisonment in June, but in the following month a court of appeal ordered their release subject to guarantees that they would appear at future hearings.

In March 2002 four people were killed in clashes between rival tribal clans in Ibb governorate, provoked by disputes over water rights. Soon afterwards, further clan fighting left 11 people dead. In an interview with *The Yemen Times* in June, Sheikh Yahya al-Ukaymi, a prominent native of the al-Jawf region, rejected allegations that the tribal areas were a 'breeding ground' for terrorism, although he acknowledged that elements of terrorist groups such as al-Qa'ida might take advantage of the poverty and chaos that characterized these areas. Al-Ukaymi denied that his tribe was sheltering al-Qa'ida suspects, claiming that it was attempting to locate al-Qa'ida supporters and bring them to justice. In July London-based Arabic press sources reported that a military helicopter had come under fire from tribesmen in the al-Jawf region, slightly injuring a senior military officer, Brig. Ali Muhammad Saleh, Deputy Chief-of-Staff and head of the Security Committee of the Supreme Elections Committee. The officers on board had been visiting military units stationed in the al-Jawf governorate and border areas. According to local sources, the tribesmen had acted because they feared that the helicopter was about to open fire on their villages. Some weeks prior to the incident President Saleh had named al-Jawf as one of three governorates where the authorities had declared a state of high alert to prevent possible terrorist attacks, and the security forces had targeted a number of local tribes believed to be sheltering suspected al-Qa'ida members. In April 2002 a recently formed organization calling itself the Sympathizers of al-Qa'ida claimed responsibility for a series of explosions that targeted the offices of the PSO and the homes of some of its senior officials, although no one was injured. The Sympathizers of al-Qa'ida later issued an ultimatum through the Yemeni media, threatening further bomb attacks unless the authorities released 173 of their comrades, who they claimed were being detained by the PSO. In May the group claimed responsibility for an explosion close to the homes of the Prime Minister and of the deputy director of the PSO. President Saleh largely dismissed the threat posed by the organization and insisted that the small number of al-Qa'ida activists in Yemen were being carefully monitored by the security services. However, some local commentators argued that the authorities, in their zeal to co-operate with the US authorities in the search for suspected supporters of al-Qa'ida, had ignored domestic political considerations and should reappraise their policies, especially the detention of suspects for long periods without trial. In July a car bomb exploded outside the home in San'a of Brig. Fadhi al-Kawsee, the senior security official for Amran governorate.

Following the legislative elections of April 2003, President Saleh asked Prime Minister Bajammal to form a new administration. In the new, 35-member Council of Ministers there were 17 new ministers, but the key portfolios of defence, the interior, petroleum and mineral resources, and foreign affairs remained unchanged. The only woman in the new Government was Amat al-Alim al-Susua, who was appointed Minister of Human Rights. All members of the Council of Ministers were GPC members. During his first meeting with the Council of Ministers, the President was reported to have urged the Minister of Religious Endowments and Guidance to take special care in training moderate and enlightened imams. President Saleh also appointed a prominent southerner, Salem Saleh Muhammed, who had returned from exile in early 2002, as his senior adviser on counter-terrorism. Al-Islah leader Sheikh Abdullah bin Hussain al-Ahmar was re-elected Speaker of the House of Representatives.

In May 2003, in a televised address to mark the 13th anniversary of independence, President Saleh announced an amnesty for the five southern secessionist leaders living in exile: former Vice-President Ali Salim al-Baid, former Prime Minister Haidar al-Attas, former Minister of Defence Haitham Qassem, former Deputy Prime Minister Saleh Obeid Ahmed, and the erstwhile Governor of Aden, Saleh Munassar al-Siyali. The YSP leadership welcomed the President's announcement and expressed the hope that it heralded a change in the country's political landscape, which was currently dominated by the GPC. Later in the month, during a visit to the UAE, the President was reported to have met Qassem and pledged that he and the other four secessionists could return to Yemen, where they would be allowed full political and civil rights. In September Siad Nooman, a former Speaker of the House of Representatives and a leading member of the YSP, returned to Yemen after having spent nine years in self-imposed exile in the UAE.

In July 2003 the security forces killed six Islamist militants and injured five others during a military operation in Abyan province, where suspected members of the Islamic Aden-Abyan Army had taken refuge after attacking a military medical team some days before. They also discovered a large quantity of weapons and explosives.

It was reported in August 2003 that the Government was determined to remove imams suspected of affiliation to al-Islah. A senior GPC official accused al-Islah of seeking to dominate the mosques and appealed to all political forces to fight against religious fanaticism, insisting that it was one of the reasons behind the emergence of a culture of violence, extremism and terrorism that threatened Yemen's security and stability. Later, the Minister of Religious Endowments and Guidance stated that the message from the mosques should advocate moderation and tolerance. He announced that the Government had formulated a programme to train imams to promote these values and was determined to prevent the preaching of *jihad* against the West or Israel or support for suicide bomb attacks. Nevertheless, in early 2004 the Friday sermons from the Great Mosque in San'a regularly appealed for support for the destruction of the 'Zionist and American enemies of Islam'. In June the Director of the Ministry of Religious Endowments and Guidance stated that firm measures would be taken against imams who preached opposition to the Government and incited worshippers to violence. The Ministry was in the process of organizing training and guidance programmes for some 2,500 imams with the aim of correcting their religious pronouncements and persuading them to preach Islamic tolerance. In late June the Council of Ministers gave orders to close down all unlicensed religious schools (estimated to number more than 4,000) in an effort to combat extremism, and stated that an extensive review of religious education in public schools was urgently needed to ensure that teaching about Islam advocated moderation. Some commentators argued that the Government was merely responding to pressure from the US Administration.

In 2003, meanwhile, President Saleh formed a committee of religious scholars, chaired by Judge Hammud al-Hitar, to engage in dialogue with those detained on suspicion of being al-Qa'ida members or sympathizers. By using religious arguments, the committee hoped to persuade them that *jihad* need not necessarily involve violence. Judge Hitar insisted that dialogue was one of the basic pillars of Yemen's anti-terrorism policy, and was aimed at eradicating the ideological roots of extremism. When the committee was satisfied that a detainee had made satisfactory progress, he was required to sign a pledge renouncing violence and extremism and undertaking to respect the country's Constitution and legislation, before being released on probation. In October it was reported that three leaders of the Islamic Aden-Abyan Army, including Khalid Abd al-Nabi, considered to be the successor to Abu Hassan (who was executed in 1999), had pledged to disband the organization and to renounce all political and military activities following dialogue with the committee. They had also signed pledges on behalf of all their followers. In November some 93 prisoners were reportedly released under the new programme and a further 54 pardoned with the expectation that they would be released at a later date. However, the work of the committee was criticized by the USA and senior members of Yemen's own security forces, who claimed to have apprehended released militants engaged in subversive activities. The Minister of the Interior also voiced concerns about the programme. Some independent observers argued that dialogue was merely a piece of presidential 'window dressing' for the benefit of the West and was intended to encourage Western donors to increase economic aid to Yemen. Judge Hitar was keen to stress the importance of solving the country's economic problems, which he claimed were being exploited by extremist elements, and to persuade international partners in the fight against terrorism to increase their financial assistance to Yemen.

As part of efforts to combat violence and extremism, the Government stated that it had spent over US $32m. since 2002 purchasing weaponry on the open market and seeking to persuade ordinary citizens to sell their weapons to the authorities. Purchases of arms from tribes in the Marib area revealed a frightening array of weaponry, including rocket and grenade launchers and land-mines. However, officials indicated that they were unable to continue the scheme due to a lack of resources and had approached the USA for financial assistance. The authorities confronted the formidable task of trying to control the long-established and lucrative trafficking of weapons both into and out of Yemen.

Meanwhile, the struggle to track down members of al-Qa'ida operating in Yemen continued. In November 2003 the security forces arrested Muhammad Hamdi al-Ahdal, who was believed to have taken over as chief operative of al-Qa'ida in Yemen after the assassination of Qaed Salim Sinan al-Harethi in December 2002. According to the local press, al-Ahdal admitted under questioning that al-Qa'ida was attempting to infiltrate the security services and claimed that the group had received funds from Saudi Arabia and Kuwait as well as from supporters in Yemen. In March 2004 the security forces captured Abd al-Rauf Nassib, a senior aide to al-Harethi, and the sole survivor of the missile attack that killed al-Harethi and five other suspected al-Qa'ida members. He was one of 12 militants captured during the siege of an Islamist stronghold in the mountains of Abyan province.

Violent clashes occurred in June 2004 in the mountainous region near Saada in northern Yemen between the security forces and militant supporters of Hussain al-Houthi, the leader of al-Shabab al-Mo'men (Faithful Youth), a movement commonly known as the 'al-Houthis'. The authorities claimed that the group had established its own militia near the border with Saudi Arabia and was responsible for attacks on government buildings and mosques in Saada. The movement appeared to be motivated by bitter opposition to the USA and Israel but was not linked to al-Qa'ida. Several attempts at mediation by tribal and political figures failed to persuade al-Houthi to end his rebellion and to surrender voluntarily. It was reported that some 300 al-Houthi militants had been killed since the conflict began, with hundreds of rebels wounded or arrested.

In September 2004 al-Houthi was killed by members of the security forces, but at the end of the month there were reports that violent clashes continued between al-Houthi's supporters, led by the group's new military chief, Sheikh Abdullah al-Ruzami, and government troops; many soldiers were reported to have been killed in a series of suicide bomb attacks in Saada.

Clashes between al-Houthi's supporters and government forces erupted again in late March–April 2005 in Saada following attacks on military patrols and checkpoints, and an estimated 280 people were killed in the fighting. Government forces appeared to have prevailed, but independent sources argued that hundreds of armed rebels remained unaccounted for and predicted that it might prove difficult to stamp out the rebellion completely.

President Saleh and the GPC accused the opposition parties, excluding al-Islah, of supporting al-Houthi's rebellion and also referred to help from 'parties outside Yemen', believed to refer to some wealthy Saudi Arabian Shi'a. The President declared that the Joint Forum, an alliance of opposition parties, had abused their freedom of expression and committed treason by supporting the rebel leader; he warned that he would have to take 'constitutional measures' against them. Several members of an opposition party, al-Haq, were subsequently arrested and in October 2004 the party reported that its politburo chief, Hassan Muhammad Zeid, had been physically assaulted in San'a. Abd al-Karim al-Khaiwani, Editor-in-Chief of the United Popular Forces' weekly newspaper, *Al-Shoura*, was arrested in September, accused of supporting al-Houthi and sentenced to a year in prison for incitement, insulting the President, publishing false news and causing tribal and sectarian discrimination; the paper was closed down for six months. *Al-Shoura* insisted that it had reported events in Saada with 'extreme neutrality', and al-Khaiwani's arrest provoked widespread protests. In February 2005 Amnesty International appealed for al-Khaiwani's release and expressed concern about his harsh treatment in prison. The International Federation of Journalists (based in Brussels, Belgium) and the US-based Committee to Protect Journalists also condemned al-Khaiwani's detention. In a speech in May President Saleh stated that Abdul Malik al-Houthi (Hussain al-Houthi's son) and his followers constituted the military wing of al-Haq and the United Popular Forces parties.

At the end of October 2004 the GPC accused the opposition of a scheme to 'spread corruption' in government departments and of 'harming the country's image'. In January 2005 al-Imam University, run by Sheikh al-Zindani, Chairman of al-Islah's Shura Council, strongly denied a report published on the GPC's website that it had a military wing preparing to carry out operations aimed at creating anarchy in Yemen. The following month, the GPC's weekly paper, *al-Mithaq*, carried an unprecedented attack on al-Islah leader and Speaker of the House of Representatives Sheikh Abdullah bin Hussain al-Ahmar. President Saleh immediately ordered an investigation and insisted that there was no disagreement whatsoever between him and al-Ahmar.

In March 2005 the authorities accused opposition parties of provoking violent anti-Government demonstrations held across the country to protest against a new sales tax and to demand the Government's resignation. Dozens of protesters were arrested by the police, who were fired on when they tried to contain the demonstrations. At the end of the month President Saleh ordered the establishment of a committee, headed by his political adviser and former premier, Abd al-Karim al-Iryani, to reopen talks with opposition parties, and the GPC appealed to all political parties to take part in the national dialogue.

At a ceremony celebrating the 27th anniversary of his rise to power, in July 2005 President Saleh announced that he would not seek re-election to the presidency in September 2006 even though, under the terms of the Constitution, he was permitted to serve a further term of office. It was suggested that a reference to 'young qualified leaders' indicated that he was grooming his son, Ahmad, head of the Republican Guard, to succeed him, a rumour that was denied by the President.

In July 2005 a total of 39 people were killed (including four members of the security forces), at least 50 protesters were injured, and dozens were arrested in San'a, Aden and a number of other towns in two days of rioting against the Government's decision to remove subsidies on fuel, thus nearly doubling the price of petroleum products. The riots were the worst the country had experienced since June 1998.

In September 2005 President Saleh announced a general amnesty for several hundred supporters of al-Houthi, saying 'We pardon them despite the bloodshed they caused'—more than 700 people had been killed in the uprising. Some 36 rebels, accused of plotting to kill the President and senior army officers, were excluded from the amnesty. Saleh also announced that Yemen's exiled royal family (the last Zaidi Imam—Badr—died in 2002) would be compensated 'in a just manner'. However, at the end of November 2005 there was renewed fighting between al-Houthi's supporters and the security forces in Saada province. Soldiers and police, supported by tanks and armoured vehicles, attempted to seal off part of the province where the rebels were concentrated. At least 16 rebels were killed in two days of fighting with the security forces. President Saleh accused the rebels of failing to respect the amnesty, while one of the rebel leaders blamed the Government for the renewed hostilities, insisting that the President's amnesty was not being implemented on the ground. Some tribal leaders reported that many of the 400 rebels released under the amnesty had taken up arms again and rejoined the uprising. At the beginning of December one imam was sentenced to death and another to 10 years' imprisonment for supporting the al-Houthi rebels and spying for Iran. Both were accused of having contacts with the Iranian ambassador in San'a, of travelling to Iran to seek support for the al-Houthi rebels and of conspiring to overthrow the Republican regime.

Meanwhile, in November 2005 the New York-based Committee to Protect Journalists expressed its concern over attacks on journalists in Yemen—a number of journalists working for opposition newspapers had been assaulted by the security services in recent months—and the unwillingness or inability of the authorities to arrest and punish those responsible. The organization asserted that this called into question the Government's commitment to a free press and the safety of journalists. In January 2006 a delegation from the committee visiting Yemen expressed alarm at the deterioration in press freedom. They urged the President to ensure that the perpetrators of physical attacks on journalists were brought to justice. They also condemned the authorities for closing down outspoken newspapers and for using extra-legal methods to harass the press. In February the chief editors of three independent newspapers were arrested and publication of their newspapers was suspended after they printed copies of caricatures of the Prophet Muhammad that had originally been published in a Danish newspaper. The caricatures caused a storm of protest throughout the Middle East. The prosecution demanded the death penalty and compensation for readers who had been subjected to 'mental suffering'. These demands were supported by a faction within al-Islah led by the popular and influential Sheikh al-Zindani. The Paris-based organization Reporters sans frontières launched an appeal for the release of the journalists. Meanwhile, large demonstrations protesting against the cartoons had taken place in a number of the main cities.

In December 2005 and January 2006 there were several incidents in which European tourists were kidnapped. In December 2005 two Austrian tourists were abducted in Marib by tribesmen demanding the release of relatives imprisoned in San'a. They were quickly released, unharmed, following mediation by tribal leaders. Shortly afterwards a former German diplomat and his family were kidnapped during a group tourist visit to Shabwah province in the South by tribesmen similarly demanding the release of imprisoned relatives. They were also released unharmed within a few days. President Saleh pledged that kidnappers would be pursued and punished, condemning their activities as irresponsible and inhumane. Nevertheless, at the beginning of January 2006 five Italians were abducted in Marib province, although they appeared to have been kidnapped by members of an armed gang rather than tribesmen. Following failed negotiations, the hostages were released after a few days when security forces surrounded the area where they were being held and intervened.

In December 2005 three Somalis died, many others were injured and numerous arrests were made during violent clashes with the security forces who used tear gas and clubs to disperse a sit-in by hundreds of Somali refugees outside the offices of the UN High Commissioner for Refugees (UNHCR) in San'a. The refugees, including women and children, had begun their sit-in a month earlier to protest against poor living conditions and plans for their repatriation. (Thousands of Somalis arrived by boat in Yemen each year fleeing the violence in their homeland and bound for the Gulf states or Europe.) According to the Yemeni authorities, UNHCR was preparing to send some 5,000 Somali refugees back to Somalia as part of a repatriation plan.

In February 2006 a total of 23 prisoners serving sentences for terrorist acts escaped from a prison in San'a run by the PSO. They included militants linked to al-Qa'ida who carried out the attacks on the USS *Cole* in 2000 and on the *Limburg* in 2002. The escape prompted an international alert and was received with 'extreme disquiet' in the USA. Investigations later revealed that a number of security officials working for the PSO were involved in the escape and serious questions were raised as to why so many al-Qa'ida militants had been detained in the same prison. In May 2006 it was reported that nine of the prisoners had either been rearrested or had surrendered voluntarily to the authorities. Meanwhile, Sheikh Abdullah bin Hussain al-Ahmar, the Speaker of the House of Representatives and Chairman of al-Islah, dismissed the threat posed by the escaped prisoners and referred to al-Qa'ida as a 'weapon the USA used to threaten people'. In July a San'a court acquitted 19 people, including five Saudi nationals, who had been arrested at the beginning of the year on charges of planning attacks against US and other Western interests in Yemen.

Escalating political violence and killings accompanied the run-up to the presidential and local elections of 20 September 2006, although an EU Election Observation Mission concluded that the polls 'succeeded in providing for an open and competitive political contest in which all major parties were fully engaged and where voters were offered a genuine choice between candidates'. Saleh received 77.17% of the votes (4,149,673), while Faysal bin Shamlan, a former businessman and minister in the former PDRY Government, of the Joint Meeting Parties (JMP—a loose alliance of Islamist, socialist and Nasserite opposition parties) garnered 21.82% (1,173,075). Independent candidate Fathi Muhammad al-Azab received 24,524 votes, Yassin Abdo Saeed Nu'man of the National Council of Opposition 21,642 votes and Ahmad Abdallah al-Majidi, another independent candidate, 8,324 votes. A total of 1,612 candidates stood for the 431 governorate seats, and 18,901 for the 6,896 district council seats; of these, 35 women were elected to the local authorities. The ruling GPC won 85% of the governorate seats, the JMP 10% and independents the remainder. Of the district council seats, the GPC won 76%, the JMP 15% and independents 8%.

During the latter half of 2006 and in 2007 President Saleh's Government was beset by further internal threats arising from renewed activity from al-Houthi's supporters and domestic jihadist militants. The resurgence of the al-Houthi rebels in January 2007 was met with intense military retaliation in which the whole Saada region was put under military control; help was provided by Saudi Arabia. Between 700 and 1,000 soldiers died. The response also took a political turn as the administration emphasized the al-Houthi supporters' adherence to the Zaidi Imams, members of a Shi'a sect, thereby introducing a divisive Sunni–Shi'a element to the dispute.

This drew criticism of the Saleh Government from Shi'a religious leaders including Grand Ayatollah Ali al-Sistani, the pre-eminient Shi'a cleric in Iraq. A temporary unity between the USA, Saudi Arabia and Sunni radicals, including some from al-Islah, was established to confront a common foe. After the violence, a cease-fire and withdrawal of troops was requested by al-Houthi's supporters, together with the release of prisoners and recognition of an al-Houthi political party. A cease-fire was agreed in June 2007.

The al-Houthi politico-religious dispute had an impact on the second domestic threat challenging the Government in 2006–07, namely the influence of individuals and groups purportedly involved in advocating terrorism. As described above, al-Zindani was designated as a global terrorist by the USA, but he and other Sunni radicals had hitherto been protected in Yemen and were useful allies against the al-Houthi threat. The co-operation between Yemen and the USA in the aftermath of the 11 September 2001 attacks with regard to terrorism and the incorporation of Yemen into the Greater Middle East Initiative had dissipated in recent years, and the most recent dispute with the al-Houthi rebels may have distracted Western attention away from the ongoing internal jihadist activity, which continued, inspired by bin Laden's Hadramouti inheritance, and fuelled by the legal and illegal transfer of arms and materials across the Saudi border. As the arms trade declined, there was a gradual increase in the deployment of car bombs using fertilizers and explosive ingredients. Between September 2006 and July 2007 there was a stream of incidents and arrests, beginning with two failed suicide attacks on oil facilities in Marib and Hadramout. In October and December 2006 a number of suspects were killed while attempting attacks in San'a. In October a large group of men of Yemeni and foreign origin were arrested for attempting to supply Somali Islamists with weapons, the East Africa-Yemeni connections being highly developed. However, in November 19 alleged militants were acquitted of the more serious charges against them of terrorist activity.

There was an escalation of violence in early July 2007 when four buses carrying Spanish tourists were blown up by a suicide bomber in Marib. Eight tourists and two local drivers were killed in the attack. Arrests were made in San'a and a week later three cars believed to have been intended as car bombs were discovered in Aden. In August four al-Qa'ida militants were killed by Yemeni security forces, including, it was believed, Kassim al-Raimi, who had been accused of planning the bus bombing. Al-Raimi had escaped from San'a prison in February 2006, along with other prisoners connected with al-Qa'ida. In late 2007 al-Raimi was convicted *in absentia* and sentenced to 12 years' imprisonment.

The unexpected use of soft targets and the employment of suicide attacks indicated an intensification of tactics by Sunni jihadists. Meanwhile, in June 2007 seven oil workers were shot, one fatally, at an airfield in Marib; to what extent this was an isolated opportunist event or part of the wider terrorist threat was unclear. Two messages were apparently issued later that month by al-Qa'ida in Yemen, one of which claimed that al-Wahisi (another escaped prisoner from San'a) was its leader and attacked the 'ideological programming' of jihadists—a reference to the experimental attempts of Judge Hitar to detach jihadists from violent methods.

DETERIORATING DOMESTIC SITUATION, 2008–09

The year 2008 saw President Saleh assailed by further domestic pressures: from the al-Houthi rebels and the al-Qa'ida-associated jihadists; from a dissident group in central Yemen that had been active in mosques, condemning the Government's 'pro-Western' stance and criticizing the World Bank; and in Aden, where there had been pressure to dissociate the wealthier south from the troublesome north. The hopes for Yemen as an ally in the US-led 'war on terror' post-11 September 2001 had now largely evaporated, and the perception was growing in the West that the country was close to becoming a 'failed state'.

The al-Houthi rebels in the northern area around Saada were increasingly depicted as players in a religious sectarian conflict in Yemen: they are drawn from a Shi'a tradition that, according to the President, has a reactionary agenda, supported by Iran. Religious clerics in Saudi Arabia, which views the events so close to its border with concern, condemned the movement, likening it to Hezbollah in Lebanon. In May 2008 the JMP demanded an end to 'this absurd war' and to the restrictions on reporting it, but with little hope of success. Five cease-fires had broken down since the conflict began in 2004. A plan to end the fighting, mediated by Qatar, also failed.

In an attempt to control the internal situation, the Ministry of the Interior introduced a number of restrictions including: the division of the country into 12 security regions; special security checkpoints on highways, manned by military and special security forces; development of the Yemeni Coast Guard Authority (supported by the USA since the USS *Cole* attack); development of the Counter-Terrorism Unit; and a plan for disarming citizens and monitoring arms sales. The Government also disrupted mobile telephone networks in the Saada region, in which it was thought 100,000 people had been displaced by the fighting since 2004. Reporting on the conflict was censored; in 2004 journalist Abd al-Karim al-Khaiwani was imprisoned for publicizing the devastation caused by the fighting, when he was editor-in-chief of *Al-Shoura*. In August 2007 he was abducted and beaten for a critical article published in another newspaper. According to Amnesty International, al-Khaiwani was sentenced to six years' imprisonment on conspiracy charges in June 2008; several human rights publications had reported the alleged mistreatment of the journalist in custody.

The recent jihadist activity was carried out principally by an organization called Jund al-Yemen, based in the Hadramout. Jund al-Yemen was linked to al-Qa'ida and was believed to be led or inspired by Nasir al-Wuhayshi and Kassim al-Raimi, who was reported to have been killed in 2007 by security forces. The *Gulf States Newsletter* of 2 May 2008 suggested that Jund al-Yemen was responsible for the 15 September 2006 oil attacks as well as violence on 7 July 2007. In 2008 its tally included three deaths on 18 January (when tourists were targeted); an attack on the US embassy on 18 March; a further attack on a pipeline in March and on the Canadian oil company Nexen in San'a on 10 April; and an explosion at a post office in Saada, in which five people died. The organization's publicity included references to 'al-Qa'ida in Yemen' and the 'al-Qa'ida Organization for Jihad in the Southern Arabian Peninsula'. In addition, on 9 April an explosion at a security checkpoint in Marib killed seven people.

In southern Yemen, which includes the strategically vital Bab-al-Mandab entrance to the Red Sea, there were several civilian protests in mid-2008 in which up to 20 people died. Earlier protests, starting in mid-2007, against the perceived favouritism shown to the North in appointments and economic development were exploited and expanded to include demands for greater accountability and transparency in Yemen's institutions and government and even for the 'liberation' of southern Yemen: influential Yemenis argued that autonomy for the South, with its oil reserves, or at least distance from San'a might be one route out of the country's troubles.

The first ever elections to the governorships of Yemen's 21 provinces were held on 18 May 2008. The electorate comprised 7,500 elected members of local councils; 36 candidates competed, but the country's opposition parties boycotted the elections. As a result, the GPC took most of the posts, although three independent candidates won in Al-Baida, Marib and Al-Jawf provinces.

Yemen's slide towards the status of 'failed state' accelerated in 2008–09. In July 2008, the 30th anniversary of President Saleh's rule, another cease-fire with the al-Houthi militants had been announced, partly in response to international concern at the humanitarian situation in the Saada region, where 130,000 people had been displaced by mid-2008, and homes and infrastructure had been destroyed by shelling and air attacks. Despite the establishment of a reconstruction fund and the Government's announcement of a four-year strategy to rehabilitate the war-ravaged province, the widespread destruction and loss of life resulted in increased support for the al-Houthi movement. The cease-fire was broken with sporadic violent incidents throughout late 2008 and early 2009, and both government and al-Houthi representatives accused the opposing side of breaching the fragile truce. When a group of nine foreign nationals, who were connected to an aid agency, were kidnapped in the north of the country in mid-June, the Government initially blamed the al-Houthi movement. However, this was strongly denied by the rebels and it became clear that the newly formed al-Qa'ida in the Arabian Peninsula (AQAP), which had promised such incidents earlier in the year, were more likely the responsible party. In July 16 al-Qa'ida-affiliated militants were convicted of involvement in a series of violent attacks over a two-year period, which included attacks on foreign tourists and oil facilities; six of those convicted were sentenced to death. Of the kidnapped foreigners, three female nurses—two Germans and a South Korean—were found dead a few days after their abduction. In January 2010, in advance of a visit to Yemen by the German Minister of Foreign Affairs, Guido Westerwelle, the authorities announced that they had evidence that the remaining six hostages, including a German couple and their three children, were still alive. In mid-May the Saudi authorities announced that two of the remaining German hostages had been found alive near the border between Saudi Arabia and Yemen. The kidnap of the nine foreigners had been preceded by the deaths in September 2008 of 19 people, including seven assailants, in a double car bomb attack at the US embassy in San'a, and the deaths of four South Korean tourists and their Yemeni guide in a suicide bomb attack in the Hadramout province in March 2009.

The International Crisis Group (ICG) reported in May 2009 that, in Yemen's predominantly tribal society, the violence was spreading far beyond its original reach. According to the ICG, the conflicts that had beset Yemen in the North and the South, not initially connected with jihadism, were proliferating and becoming more complicated as a result of the numerous tribal conflicts, government support for certain groups over others, and the growing influence of the jihadist groups. In March some 500,000 people in the south of Yemen had demonstrated against the Government, while in July as many as 37 civilians and soldiers died in a series of violent incidents in the country.

The jihadists—and the other dissident groups—thrived in Yemen in part because of the state's weakness and lack of authority. The deputy leader of AQAP, Said Ali al-Shihri, and several other jihadist fighters escaped from Saudi Arabia into Yemen; others were believed to have moved there from other 'terror hotspots', such as Somalia, Iraq and Pakistan. The growth of jihadism was also encouraged by financial support from Saudi sources for Wahhabi/Salafi *madrassas* (Islamic schools) in Yemen, despite the relatively successful Saudi campaign against jihadism within its own borders.

In an interview published by the *International Herald Tribune* on 23 June 2008 President Saleh's frustration at trying to placate the USA, deal with internal dissent and retain a balance of political power at home was apparent. He referred to the US Administration as 'cowboys', criticizing their interference and, by implication, their hypocrisy over the Yemeni Guantánamo Bay prisoners. In August the Yemeni citizen Salem Ahmad Hamdan was convicted of supporting terrorism at the first of the military trials to be conducted at Guantánamo Bay. Hamdan was a driver and occasional bodyguard for Osama bin Laden, and was seized in Afghanistan shortly after the September 2001 attacks. He was acquitted of a more serious charge of conspiracy and received a five-and-a-half year sentence, of which over five years had already been served at Guantánamo Bay. He was returned to Yemen and released in January 2009. Jamal al-Badawi, wanted by the USA in connection with the bombing of the USS *Cole*, surrendered in 2007 to the Yemeni authorities and was believed to be helping with Yemen's anti-terrorist strategy; the Government refused to extradite him to the USA.

The failure of the Government and the opposition to reach agreement on a programme of electoral reform led to an escalating political crisis during 2008–09. Following the appointment of a new Supreme Commission for Elections and Referendums (SCER) by the Government in August 2008, without opposition agreement, the JMP appealed for a boycott of the registration process for the legislative elections, which were scheduled for April 2009. Violent clashes between police and protesters ensued, and in November 2008 the House of Representatives voted to delay the forthcoming municipal elections, also due to be held in April 2009. The JMP and other opposition groups stated their intention not to participate in the legislative elections, and, in late February, after negotiations between the Government and the opposition, the House of Representatives voted to postpone the elections for two years, during which time, it was hoped, agreement could be reached on the reform of the electoral system. In August the leader of the JMP, Hamid al-Ahmar, an influential businessman and the son of the late Sheikh Abdullah bin Hussain al-Ahmar, publicly accused President Saleh of corruption and demanded that he resign.

AL-QA'IDA IN THE ARABIAN PENINSULA

In January 2009 the formation of AQAP, by a merger of the Yemeni and Saudi Arabian al-Qa'ida organizations, was officially announced. Its leader was Nasir al-Wuhayshi, a former personal secretary to Osama bin Laden, and its deputy leader was Said Ali al-Shihri, also known as Abu Sufyan al-Azdi al-Shihri, a former Guantánamo detainee, released in November 2007, who was accused of involvement in the US embassy attack of September 2008. AQAP declared its intention of attacking infrastructure, tourists and military targets via several audio and video messages. The organization was linked to the kidnapping and killing of foreigners in June, possibly in revenge for the arrest by the Yemeni authorities of an AQAP financier. Al-Wuhayshi also offered support to secessionists in the South and denounced President Saleh, in an audio message broadcast on the internet in May. In an earlier message, he accused the Western 'crusaders' combating piracy in the Gulf of Aden of 'surrounding the island of Islam'. It was feared that the consolidation of AQAP might signal a new phase of disorder in which the jihadists would exploit the existing conflicts and use Yemen as a base from which to threaten the security of other states in the region.

In November 2009 three senior Yemenis, including the head of the PSO in Hadramout, Col Ahmed Ba-Wazir, were killed in an ambush by AQAP militants. In December three attacks were mounted by Yemeni armed forces, with US support, against AQAP. Among the more than 30 militants killed were fighters from Saudi Arabia, Pakistan and Egypt, according to the Deputy Prime Minister. It was reported in early 2010 that 42 civilians, including women and children, had been killed in the three raids. The Government subsequently offered an apology for the civilian deaths and announced that it would pay compensation to relatives of the victims. In January the Somali Islamist organization al-Shabaab (The Youth) had offered to send fighters to Yemen to assist AQAP, and the two groups claimed to be co-operating closely.

The provision of US intelligence led in June 2010 to the arrests of 30 foreigners living in Yemen, some of whom had links to the San'a Institute for the Arabic Language, where Nigerian student Omar Farouk Abdulmutallab had received instruction. Abdulmutallab had been arrested in the USA for allegedly attempting to detonate an explosive device during a flight between Amsterdam, the Netherlands, and Detroit, Michigan, USA, on 25 December 2009. AQAP claimed three days later that it had orchestrated the attempted attack in response to a 'bombardment of cluster bombs and cruise missiles launched from US ships occupying the Gulf of Aden against the courageous Yemeni tribes'. Meanwhile, 14 people were killed in June 2010 when four armed men, suspected of being members of AQAP, attacked a high-security gaol in Aden and released some of the prisoners. In July a further 11 people were killed during an attack on a government building in Zinjibar in Abyan province, which the Yemeni authorities blamed on AQAP.

EXTERNAL RELATIONS AFTER THE CIVIL WAR

In the aftermath of the civil war of 1994, President Saleh quickly embarked on a diplomatic offensive to isolate the secessionists and ensure that they could not regroup in neighbouring countries, most of which had supported the South during the two-month conflict. Oman and Djibouti promised the prompt return of military equipment brought there by the fleeing southern forces, and most states, including Egypt, expressed their support for a unified Yemen. Relations with Oman were strengthened further in June 1995 when the demarcation of the Yemeni–Omani border (initiated in 1992) was officially completed. Relations with Sudan also improved and Iran showed growing interest in Yemen and began providing some medical assistance. However, the arrival of militants from Algeria's banned Front Islamique du Salut (FIS), and later from the extremist GIA, provoked a strong protest from the Algerian Government and in January 1995 Algeria recalled its ambassador from San'a. Al-Islah was known to have provided military training and political indoctrination for Islamist militants from Algeria and also from Egypt, while declaring publicly that the party supported an end to violence in Algeria and dialogue leading to free, multi-party elections. The Yemeni Government strongly denied the existence of training camps for militant Islamists until 1995 when President Saleh, on a visit to Cairo, declared that his security forces had discovered a cell of the militant Egyptian group Islamic Jihad and offered to exchange members of the group for Yemeni separatists based in Cairo. Towards the end of 1997 the Yemeni authorities were reported to have arrested a number of Yemeni and foreign Islamist militants, including the so-called 'Arab Afghans', possibly in a move to curb the activities of the more extremist elements within al-Islah.

Long-standing difficulties with Yemen's powerful neighbour, Saudi Arabia, continued to dominate foreign relations. After the civil war ended, Saudi Arabia provided assistance for the reconstruction of Aden hospital, and promises of further assistance for health projects were made during a visit by Saudi Arabia's Deputy Minister of Health in December 1994, the first sign since the end of the Gulf War that Saudi Arabia might begin to resume financial aid to Yemen. Yemen promised to begin a new chapter in its relations with Saudi Arabia based on 'co-operation, security and stability'. However, in late December tensions between the two countries increased over the disputed border, and there were reports of armed clashes between Saudi and Yemeni forces in disputed territory. The Saudi Minister of Defence, Prince Sultan ibn Abd al-Aziz Abd Al Sa'ud, was reported to have told Yemen's Prime Minister, Abd al-Aziz Abd al-Ghani, that the Saudi air force would bomb Yemen unless it withdrew military units stationed in certain frontier areas. A large Saudi force of 20,000 men, together with 400 tanks, armoured vehicles and pieces of heavy artillery, penetrated some 70 km inside Yemeni territory. The intervention of the Syrian Vice-President, Abd al-Halim Khaddam, defused the situation and produced a compromise in January 1995. After a month of difficult negotiations the two countries signed a memorandum of understanding in Mecca, Saudi Arabia, on 26 February, establishing the basis for future discussions. Under the memorandum, Yemen accepted the terms of the 1934 Ta'if agreement, which had lapsed in 1994, thereby effectively conceding sovereignty over the provinces of Najran, Gizan and Asir, which were annexed by Saudi Arabia in 1934. Although the Ta'if agreement dealt principally with the border area in the north-west of the country, Yemen's Minister of Foreign Affairs succeeded in ensuring that future talks would deal with the entire length of the border between the two countries. The memorandum signed in Mecca provided for the establishment of six joint committees to delineate the land and sea borders and develop economic and commercial ties; both sides also agreed that they would not permit their country to become 'a base and centre for aggression' against the other. If the negotiations did not lead to agreement, the memorandum provided for international arbitration, a point initially rejected by Prince Sultan. On 8 March 1995 the memorandum was approved by the Yemeni Council of Ministers. In a joint statement, issued at the end of President Saleh's official visit to Saudi Arabia in June, the two Governments expressed their satisfaction with the memorandum of understanding and, in addition, pledged their commitment to strengthening economic, commercial and cultural co-operation. Yemen clearly hoped that the memorandum would lead to the normalization of relations with Saudi Arabia, and that negotiations could lead to the return of at least some of the 800,000 Yemeni workers expelled from Saudi Arabia during the Gulf crisis, as well as the resumption of significant Saudi aid.

By the end of 1995 some progress had been made in implementing the February memorandum of understanding. It was assumed that many Yemenis expelled in 1990 would return to their former employers and businesses in the kingdom, although it was thought unlikely that the level of emigration would be as great as before the expulsion. In December 1995 reports of armed clashes along the disputed border were denied by Saudi Arabia and early in 1996 the two countries reached a preliminary agreement on their land frontier. Talks also began on the delimitation of the maritime boundary between the two countries. In July the two countries signed a bilateral security agreement aimed mainly at combating cross-border drugs-trafficking, but also at preventing Yemen from becoming a refuge for radical Saudi dissidents. In the past Yemen had been accused of providing refuge for foreign dissidents, particularly members of Islamist groups, but since mid-1995 the Government had moved to arrest and extradite many such dissidents, including the Arab *mujahidin* who fought in Afghanistan against the Soviet occupation. The two countries concluded a new trade agreement in September 1996. During August and September a number of high-level meetings were held between Saudi and Yemeni officials.

However, tensions between the two countries quickly re-emerged. After a visit to Jeddah, the new Minister of Foreign Affairs, Abd al-Karim al-Iryani, a noted critic of Saudi Arabia, complained that he had not been treated with the correct diplomatic protocol. Tensions arose again after a Saudi-owned television station in London, the Middle East Broadcasting Corporation, transmitted an interview with the southern Yemeni leader, al-Baid, who was on trial *in absentia* in Yemen. Later in 1997, after further high-level meetings between the two sides, including a meeting between President Saleh and Prince Sultan, the Yemeni press suggested that a settlement of the border dispute was imminent. However, in October al-Iryani accused Saudi Arabia of supporting the tribal unrest in Yemen, and the Yemeni authorities also claimed to have evidence that Saudi Arabia was involved in a series of bombings in Aden. Further border clashes occurred in November in which several soldiers were reported to have been killed. Despite the renewal of immigration visas for Yemenis in May 1998, for the first time since the end of the 1991 Gulf crisis the border dispute flared up at the end of the month, when it was reported that Saudi forces had occupied several islands in the Red Sea, which were also claimed by Yemen, and expelled the resident population. While this was regarded as an attempt by Saudi Arabia to establish its own claim to the area, some also interpreted it as signalling Saudi disapproval of the new Yemeni Government headed by al-Iryani. The occupation may also have been motivated, in part, by Saudi Arabia's desire to prevent Yemen from supporting Ethiopia in its dispute with Eritrea. In July 1998 Saudi Arabian forces shelled the disputed islands, killing three Yemenis, only one week after they had crossed the land border to take part in pacification operations against local tribes supported by Saudi Arabia in their struggle against the Yemeni Government. There were protests from President Saleh, but the two countries later agreed to work towards a peaceful solution to their differences. A joint military committee meeting attended by the respective Chiefs of Staff was held in August, but only agreements governing 'guarantees and rules' between the two countries were concluded.

According to some observers, Saudi Arabia's reluctance to finalize a border agreement was due to rivalries within the royal family over the succession. Whereas Crown Prince Abdullah was believed to favour an early settlement, his brother and main rival, Prince Sultan, took a hard-line stance towards Yemen and was opposed to it. Amid growing frustration in Yemen, President Saleh was reported to have urged Saudi Arabia to honour the accord he had signed in Italy in 1997 with Prince Sultan, in which most of the disputed border from Jebel Thaniyah to the border with Oman had evidently been settled, at least in basic outline. The President also stated that Saudi Arabia was now insisting on a revision of the 1934 Ta'if agreement. At the same time, President Saleh again suggested that international arbitration might be the only way of achieving a settlement to the long-running dispute, a proposal to which Saudi Arabia remained strongly opposed. To demonstrate its displeasure, Saudi Arabia expelled 3,000 Yemeni workers from the kingdom in December 1999, amid renewed tensions between the two countries. In January 2000 serious border clashes broke out between Yemeni and Saudi forces in which some 10 Yemeni soldiers were reported to have been killed. In February the USA offered to mediate between the two parties, but the offer was politely rejected by Saudi Arabia. Some commentators were predicting that it might take years before a settlement was finally reached. However, in May Crown Prince Abdullah attended celebrations in San'a to mark the 10th anniversary of Yemeni unification, and in June the two countries signed an agreement described as 'a final and permanent' treaty for maritime and land borders. The new treaty incorporated both the 1934 Ta'if agreement and the 1995 memorandum of understanding, but did not define the entire frontier. The maritime border was clearly defined, along with the north-western section of the land frontier, which, with some minor amendments, confirmed the line set out in the Ta'if agreement. However, the long eastern section of the border, running from Jabel Thar to the intersection of the Saudi, Oman and Yemen borders, remained undefined, and the treaty merely stated that the two sides had agreed to demarcate this sector 'in an amicable way', without making any specific arrangement for settling disputes. The two Governments agreed to appoint an international company to demarcate the border and produce maps, which, following approval by both sides, would form part of the agreement. The new treaty also incorporated a number of clauses from the 1995 memorandum of understanding not directly related to the border. The two sides agreed to promote economic, commercial and cultural relations and not to allow their territories to be used as bases for aggression or for political, military or propaganda purposes against the other.

It was reported that the new agreement was being hailed in political circles in San'a as an event as memorable as the unification of North and South Yemen a decade before. There were high hopes that improved relations with their powerful neighbour would bring economic rewards, improving prospects for Yemeni workers in the kingdom and encouraging Saudi investment in Yemen. Both countries denied rumours that Saudi Arabia had agreed to support Yemen's application for membership of the GCC, and that the privileges enjoyed by Yemeni workers in the kingdom before the 1990–91 Gulf crisis would be restored, although Saudi Arabia was expected to allow more Yemeni workers to enter the country. The border agreement was ratified by Yemen's House of Representatives and appeared to have popular support, even though some opposition groups insisted that efforts should have been made to recover territories lost under the 1934 Ta'if accord. In July 2000 the interior ministers of the two countries agreed a timetable for implementing the new accord and, after further discussions by a joint Saudi-Yemeni technical committee in October, a German firm, Hansa Luftbild, was awarded the contract to delineate the border. The company had been involved in demarcating the border between Oman and Saudi Arabia and between Oman and Yemen. After a visit to Yemen by Saudi Arabia's Minister of the Interior, Prince Nayef ibn Abd al-Aziz Al Sa'ud, in January 2001 a joint statement was issued indicating that progress was being made on implementing the border agreement and that the next step would be to consider ways of organizing border authorities and crossings.

The first significant sign of improved relations with Saudi Arabia came in December 2000, when the two countries held the first meeting of their joint co-operation council for more than 10 years. Saudi Arabia pledged US $300m. in loans for development projects and agreed to reschedule $330m. of Yemeni debt. Pledges were also made on co-operation in education, health, trade, investment, transport and civil aviation. The issue of Yemeni workers in the kingdom would be addressed at a later meeting. With the border accord in place, President Saleh declared that Yemen would reduce the size of its armed forces in order to decrease military expenditure. In April 2001 there were reports that Yemen and Saudi Arabia had signed a contract worth $1,000m. with Hansa Luftbild, authorizing the company to demarcate the border, and had reached an agreement on the location of four border crossing-points, which would be open throughout the year.

However, despite improved relations with Saudi Arabia, some difficulties remained, notably Saudi concerns over the smuggling trade across the Yemeni border. Saudi officials maintained that most weapons used by militants in the kingdom were smuggled in from Yemen. The Yemeni authorities responded by expressing their concern about alleged Saudi funding of militant groups in Yemen. In January 2004 Yemen protested when Saudi Arabia began building a barrier along the border, stating that it violated the 2000 border agreement. However, during an official visit to Saudi Arabia in February 2004, President Saleh stated that the two countries had agreed measures to control the border more effectively. In March 2005 the Saudi Minister of the Interior visited Yemen for talks with President Saleh and senior ministers on co-operation in the field of maintaining security and fighting terrorism. President Saleh attended the funeral of King Fahd at the beginning of August. In June 2006 the Saudi Crown Prince, Sultan ibn Abd al-Aziz, visited Yemen for talks with President Saleh on strengthening bilateral co-operation and to take part in the 17th session of the Saudi-Yemeni Co-ordination Council. In July President Saleh made a state visit to Saudi Arabia, and his talks with King Abdullah and Crown Prince Sultan focused on bilateral relations and regional issues.

The complicated ties of history, geography, religion and tribe made permanent resolution of the two neighbouring countries' differences extremely difficult. Technology may provide a long-term partial solution to the border problem: Saudi Arabia contracted the European Aeronautic Defence and Space Company to build a sophisticated security and surveillance system along its 1,000-km border with Yemen. For some Yemenis, the cross-border traffic of drugs, arms and people was highly lucrative, and the trade in weapons enriched tribal leaders in Saada, who thus had a vested interest in the continuance of violence and armed conflict in the region. Border violations—and resulting military action by Saudi Arabia—were once again a major issue as the al-Houthi rebellion, the influence of jihadism and other threats to Yemen's stability as a state had grown in recent years.

GCC MEMBERSHIP AND REGIONAL RELATIONS

Close co-operation with the USA has brought some diplomatic rewards at the regional level. In December 2001 the GCC granted Yemen membership of four of its non-political committees and there was unanimous support for Yemen eventually being admitted to full membership of the organization, although the Omani foreign minister stated some time later that this process would take at least 10 years. In October 2002 Yemen and the GCC signed a protocol setting out their mutual relations, and in February 2003 Yemen hosted a meeting of the executive panel of the GCC health ministers' board in San'a, the first GCC meeting to be held in Yemen.

In February 2004, despite government opposition, Kuwait's National Assembly voted in favour of an investigation into allegations made by one of its deputies that in January 2003 President Saleh had advised former President Saddam Hussain of Iraq to invade Kuwait and to safeguard Baghdad by making Kuwait the battleground with US-led forces. Yemen vehemently denied the allegations, and the Speaker of the National Assembly wrote to his Kuwaiti counterpart urging him to put an end to verbal attacks against Saleh by Kuwaiti deputies. In December 2003 the Kuwaiti legislature had refused to ratify two technical co-operation agreements with Yemen in the light of this issue. While the Kuwaiti Government was anxious to safeguard improved relations with Yemen, the issue suggested continuing resentment in political circles over Yemen's stance during the 1990–91 Gulf crisis. In September 2005 a delegation of Kuwaiti deputies visited Yemen in an effort to improve bilateral relations and held talks with government officials and members of parliament. In January 2006 Yemen announced three days of mourning following the death of the Amir of Kuwait, and President Saleh, accompanied by a high level delegation, travelled to Kuwait to present his condolences to the Kuwaiti Government and people. President Saleh later sent his congratulations to Sheikh Sabah al-Ahmad al-Jaber al-Sabah on his accession as the new Emir of Kuwait. In July President Saleh visited Qatar for talks with the Amir, Sheikh Hamad, on bilateral relations and the conflict between Israel, Lebanon and the Palestinians. On a visit to San'a in March 2005 the GCC's Secretary-General, Abd al-Rahman al-Attiya, announced that Yemen would also be allowed to take part in the GCC's free trade, patenting and standardization co-operation. However, Yemen's Minister of Foreign Affairs, Abu Bakr al-Kurbi, admitted that there were currently no negotiations on Yemen's full admission to membership of the GCC. In February 2006 Yemen's Minister of Public Health and Population attended a meeting of the GCC's ministers responsible for health in Bahrain, and in March GCC ministers responsible for foreign affairs urged that co-operation with Yemen—then covering education, health, labour, social affairs, sports and youth—should be expanded to include standardization and industrial consultations. In an interview in June the Prime Minister stated that Yemen's membership of the GCC had become a reality, especially after recent comments by King Abdullah of Saudi Arabia that he had 'closed the door to the possibility of backing down on Yemen's joining the GCC'. In July Yemen began negotiations to join the World Trade Organization, which were still ongoing in mid-2013.

In March 2002 Egypt's Minister of the Interior visited San'a for talks on co-operation against terrorism. Relations with Egypt had been strained during the 1990s owing to Yemen's refusal to extradite Egyptian nationals accused of belonging to the banned Islamic Jihad. In February, however, the Yemeni authorities had arrested a number of Egyptian nationals during their campaign to shut down certain religious institutes. This campaign created tension with Indonesia and Malaysia in February, after 44 Indonesian students studying in Yemen were arrested. The Indonesian ambassador subsequently protested to the Yemeni authorities and demanded their immediate release, warning that their continued detention could undermine the good relations between the two countries. The Yemeni authorities resolved that those students who had been studying at the Dar al-Hadith schools in Marib and Saada would be deported and in future all Indonesian students wishing to study in Yemen would be obliged to obtain permission from the Indonesian Government and pursue their studies at an establishment recognized and approved by the Yemeni authorities. During February and March a number of Malaysian students were detained on suspicion of being involved in political and terrorist activities, while others fled and sought refuge in the Malaysian embassy. Reports suggested that some 300 Malaysians were studying in Yemen, many of them at al-Iman University.

In an interview with *Al-Hayat* in February 2002, President Saleh was reported to have warned the US Government that a US-led attack on Iraq, as part of its 'war on terror', would jeopardize the continued support of its traditional allies in the Arab region. However, Saleh was careful to emphasize his own ongoing efforts to persuade the Iraqi authorities to accept the return of UN weapons inspectors. At the end of March, as Israel undertook an uncompromising military intervention in Palestinian-controlled areas of the West Bank, thousands of Yemenis demonstrated across the country in support of the Palestinian cause. They also demanded an end to UN sanctions against Iraq and expressed their opposition to any US military action in that country. In a message to the Secretary-General of the Arab League at the beginning of April, President Saleh urged Arab states to break contacts with Israel and to end all moves towards normalization of relations with the Jewish state. Shortly afterwards the House of Representatives appealed to Arab and Muslim states to donate money to the Palestinian *intifada* (uprising), urging those states that had established relations with Israel to end all co-operation and invoking the use of oil embargoes to force concessions from the West on this issue. There were demands that Israel withdraw immediately from Palestinian lands and comply with all UN resolutions pertinent to the Arab–Israeli conflict. In April more than 100,000 demonstrators took part in a protest march through San'a organized by al-Islah to protest against the action of the Israeli armed forces in the Palestinian-controlled areas. In a televised address, President Saleh urged Yemenis to support the Palestinians by donating blood and money.

US threats of military action against Iraq provoked widespread demonstrations of protest in Yemen, in which leading politicians from across the political spectrum took part. Demonstrators also denounced Israeli policies towards the Palestinians in the West Bank and Gaza, and US and Israeli flags were burnt in the streets. Some commentators argued that these demonstrations were encouraged by the authorities in order to divert public opinion away from the regime's close but unpopular co-operation with the USA in the run-up to parliamentary elections. In February 2003 President Saleh declared that a US-led military campaign to oust the regime of Saddam Hussain in Iraq would be a threat to stability and peace in the region, and denounced the proposed 'regime change' in Iraq as 'a dangerous precedent'. Later in the month he stated that UN weapons inspectors should be given enough time to complete their mission and reiterated his desire to see the Iraq crisis resolved through dialogue. Amid mounting popular opposition to war, the President asked why US and British troops were not being deployed to protect the Palestinians from Israeli violence. At the end of February the United Kingdom, citing possible terrorist attacks, announced that it was closing its embassy in San'a and the consulate-general in Aden to the public, and withdrawing all non-essential staff. The British foreign office advised Britons not to travel to Yemen and those living and working there to consider leaving. The Dutch embassy also reduced its staff, and Dutch nationals were likewise advised to leave. In late March, after the commencement of hostilities in Iraq, anti-war demonstrations were held almost every day across the country, some of which became violent. There were reports that two people had been killed when police opened fire on an unauthorized demonstration in San'a in order to stop protesters reaching the US embassy. Several leading officials from Islamist and pan-Arab political parties were arrested. Also in March a US national was among three people killed at an oil facility in Marib province belonging to the US company Hunt Oil, although this may have been the result of a local dispute and not directly connected to mounting anti-US feeling in the country. In May President Saleh stated that Yemen was following the 'regrettable developments' in Iraq with concern and insisted that Iraqis should be allowed to administer their own affairs.

In an interview with *Al-Arabiya* in January 2004, President Saleh stated that the campaigns against the US-led occupation of Iraq, like those against the Israeli occupation of the Palestinian territories, were 'legitimate resistance'. In February a Yemeni national was arrested in Kirkuk, Iraq, on suspicion of involvement in devastating suicide bomb attacks against two Kurdish political parties in Arbil. In March Yemen welcomed the signing of the interim constitution in Iraq, describing it as a step towards Iraq recovering its sovereignty, but continued to press for the USA and its allies to withdraw their forces from the country. At the end of June the Yemeni Ministry of Foreign Affairs welcomed the formal transfer of power to an Iraqi Interim Government as an important step towards the complete handover of authority to the Iraqi people. In August the Minister of Foreign Affairs confirmed that Yemen was prepared to send a peace-keeping force to Iraq under mandates from the Arab League and the UN, but only following the withdrawal of the US-led coalition forces.

In March 2004 the Council of Ministers strongly condemned Israel's assassination of Sheikh Ahmad Yassin, the spiritual leader of Hamas, and urged the international community to impose sanctions against Israel and bring its Prime Minister, Ariel Sharon, before an international court to answer charges of 'war crimes'. In November President Saleh attended the military funeral of Yasser Arafat in Cairo. In January 2006 President Saleh congratulated Hamas on its victory in Palestinian legislative elections and in March Khalid Meshaal, the head of Hamas's political bureau, visited Yemen as part of a tour of Arab countries to inform the Yemeni authorities about the latest developments in the Palestinian territories. President Saleh reiterated Yemen's continuing support for the Palestinian cause and their right to an independent state and ordered the Council of Ministers to collect contributions from institutions and the public to assist the Palestinian people. In May President Saleh received the Palestinian Minister of Foreign Affairs, Mahmud al-Zahhar, who briefed him on the hardships currently experienced by the inhabitants of the West Bank and Gaza. In July thousands of people, including politicians and trade unionists, demonstrated in San'a to condemn Israeli actions against unarmed Palestinians and to demand the release of members of the Cabinet and legislature arrested by the Israeli authorities. Later, President Saleh condemned Israel's military offensive in Lebanon as 'state terrorism', praised the resistance of both the Lebanese and Palestinian people and appealed for an emergency meeting of the Arab League to discuss the crisis. When the proposed summit was cancelled because of a poor response to Saleh's initiative, the President blamed what was happening in Lebanon and the Palestinian areas on 'an absence of Arab solidarity'. In August the Palestinian President, Mahmud Abbas, visited San'a for talks with President Saleh on the crisis.

In his address to the Arab League summit held in Khartoum in March 2006, President Saleh praised the peace efforts of the Sudanese Government, appealed to the Arab states to support reconciliation between Somalia's warring clans and urged the leaders of Ethiopia and Eritrea to enter into dialogue and avoid military confrontation. He stated that the Arab nation wanted peace with Israel but insisted that there must be full withdrawal from Arab territories. In July the Ministry of Foreign Affairs denied media reports that former Iraqi Vice-President Izzat Ibrahim al-Duri was receiving medical treatment in a San'a hospital.

President Muhammad Khatami of Iran visited Yemen in May 2003, as part of a tour of Arab states—the first visit of an Iranian president since the 1979 Islamic Revolution. Khatami and President Saleh discussed developments in the region, particularly in the Palestinian territories and Iraq. A number of co-operation agreements, dealing with security, trade, culture and financial aid, were signed. In October 2005, after meeting Iranian envoys, President Saleh stated that both countries wanted to strengthen co-operation and declared that Iran had the right to develop nuclear energy for peaceful purposes. In December one person was sentenced to death and another to 10 years' imprisonment for spying on behalf of Iran and seeking Iranian support for the al-Houthi rebels. The Turkish Prime Minister visited Yemen in October 2005, when he signed a number of economic co-operation agreements and discussed political developments in the region. The President of Pakistan visited Yemen in December for talks with President Saleh on co-operation in combating terrorism and expanding political and economic links. President Saleh, at the head of a high-level delegation, made a state visit to Pakistan in April 2006, when five co-operation agreements were signed and the two countries reiterated their resolve to fight against terrorism and extremism.

In November 1995 there were reports that Eritrean troops had attempted to land on the Red Sea island of Greater Hanish, one of three islands (the others being Lesser Hanish and Zuqar) claimed by both Yemen and Eritrea. The attempted invasion had apparently been prompted by Yemen's announced intention to develop Greater Hanish as a tourist resort, and its subsequent refusal to comply with an Eritrean demand that the island be evacuated. Negotiations in Yemen and Eritrea in late November and early December failed to defuse the crisis, and on 15 December fighting broke out between the two sides, resulting in the deaths of six Eritrean and three Yemeni soliders. On 17 December Yemen and Eritrea agreed to a cease-fire, to be monitored by a commission comprising a senior official from each country and two US diplomats. None the less, fighting was renewed the following day and Eritrean forces succeeded in occupying Greater Hanish. The cease-fire was subsequently adhered to, and some 180 Yemeni soliders (captured during the fighting) were released at the end of the month. Attempts by the Ethiopian and Egyptian Governments to broker an agreement between the two sides proved unsuccessful. In January 1996 France assumed the role of mediator. On 21 May representatives of Eritrea and Yemen signed an arbitration accord in Paris, France, whereby the two sides agreed that they were prepared to submit the dispute to an international tribunal. France and the USA subsequently undertook to observe and supervise military movements in the area around the disputed islands. In August, however, Eritrean troops occupied Lesser Hanish and Yemen threatened to send troops to force them to withdraw. After intervention by the UN and France, Eritrea withdrew its forces and in October the two countries reaffirmed their agreement to allow an international arbitration panel to settle the dispute. The five-member panel began work in January 1997 and in October 1998 awarded the main Hanish islands to Yemen while Eritrea was given two groups of tiny islets and fishing rights in Yemen waters. Eritrea accepted the ruling and withdrew its forces from the islands soon after the arbitration panel's decision was announced. Yemen assumed control of the majority of the Hanish islands on 1 November. In December 1999 the panel concluded its work, declaring that the maritime boundary between Yemen and Eritrea should be the median line between the coastlines of the two countries and rejected Eritrean claims to mineral rights on certain Yemeni islands. However, the panel was careful to define the maritime boundary between the two countries only as far as 15° 42′10″ N (a point just north of Jebel al-Thayr islands) so as to avoid areas that might be claimed by Saudi Arabia. Yemen had requested that the boundary be defined as far north as latitude 16° N, a move strongly opposed by Saudi Arabia. Despite some misgivings, both Yemen and Eritrea indicated that they would accept the decision, but relations between the two countries remained strained. In October Yemen had signed a joint security agreement with Eritrea's neighbour, Ethiopia, at a time when the two states were engaged in a long and bitter war. In June 2003 Eritrean navy patrols intercepted a number of Yemeni fishing boats and detained 133 Yemeni crew members in fishing areas around the Hanish Islands; the men were released one month later. There were reports that since early 2001 tensions had arisen between the two countries over the interpretation of the international tribunal's decision of 1999 with regard to fishing rights. Relations between the two countries had been further strained when, in May 2003, the Secretary-General of the Eritrean National Alliance, a coalition of armed opposition groups, allegedly stated that the alliance was receiving funds from Yemen.

In December 2003 Yemen joined Sudan and Ethiopia in establishing the Tripartite San'a Co-operation Forum, with the declared aim of promoting stability, security and peace in the region. Eritrean officials claimed that the new grouping was an alliance against their country, but in January 2004, at a meeting with the Eritrean Minister of Foreign Affairs, President Saleh invited Eritrea to join the new grouping and appealed for all conflicts in the region to be resolved through dialogue and peaceful means so that the member states could focus on reconstruction and development. In December 2005 a summit of leaders of the Co-operation Forum, now expanded to include the Transitional Government of Somalia, was held in Aden, constituting their fourth round of talks. Four co-operation agreements were signed, and President Saleh offered to mediate in the dispute between Ethiopia and Eritrea. In January 2006 Somali leaders signed a peace agreement in Aden to attempt to resolve their factional differences and thanked President Saleh for his efforts in uniting the Somali people. In that year, according to UNHCR, Yemen was home to 84,000 registered refugees from the violence in Somalia, although many more were thought to be there illegally. Thousands continued to arrive in Yemen during 2007–08.

The situation in Somalia deteriorated again during 2007–08 and the opposition Alliance for the Reliberation of Somalia (ARS) split into two factions, one based in Djibouti and the other in Eritrea. In August 2008 successful private talks were held in Yemen to mend the differences between the head of the ARS (Sharif Ahmed) and the Islamist members over the signing by Sheikh Ahmed of a pact with the Somali Prime Minister.

In April 2006 President Saleh, heading a powerful contingent, visited China, where topics of discussion included economic co-operation and recent developments in the Middle East. China agreed to fund development projects in Yemen worth US $1,500m. President Saleh made a point of stating that, in offering assistance to Yemen, China did not impose any conditions, whereas the EU insisted that its development aid must be associated with democratic reforms and progress on human rights. Yemen, he affirmed, wished to carry out its own reforms rather than have them imposed by others. China, with Russia, has been the main supplier of arms to Yemen since 2001.

A FAILING STATE?

In 2010, a decade after the attack on the USS *Cole*, the indications were that Yemen was in danger of collapse. During those 10 years the country had suffered almost constant instability, resulting from a series of formidable domestic problems: the ruling northern élite, led by President Saleh since 1978, was accused of maintaining power for itself through control of the GPC, the institutions of government and the country's dwindling oil revenues; the impoverished population of 24m. could not be supported by the country's main cash crop, the narcotic qat; fuel was subsidized, encouraging smuggling, corruption and inefficiency, but attempts to raise taxation were met with violence; and the country proved to be fertile ground for jihadist militants and al-Houthi insurgents, owing to weak central authority and a dissatisfied population.

US special forces were now active in the country, operating against AQAP and gathering intelligence for counter-terrorism. In April 2009 the Commander of the US Central Command, Gen. David Petraeus, told the US Senate Armed Services Committee that 'the inability of the Yemeni Government to secure and exercise control over all of its territory offers terrorist and insurgent groups in the region, especially al-Qa'ida, a safe haven in which to plan, organize and support terrorist operations'. A large number of Yemenis remained in detention at Guantánamo Bay; repatriation to Yemen was viewed as a hazardous option owing to recent incidents in which prisoners had escaped from the country's gaols, possibly in collaboration with members of the security authorities.

The al-Houthi rebellion in the north of Yemen, which had turned into a more general insurgency movement, continued unabated, spreading across the border into Saudi Arabia. A major military offensive in August 2009, and a cease-fire, failed to end the conflict, which drew Saudi air power into Yemeni territory.

A conference on Yemen was held in London in January 2010, at which commitments were made to help Yemen combat AQAP and maintain security, and it was agreed that an intergovernmental Friends of Yemen grouping would be formed (the first meeting of which was held in Abu Dhabi, UAE, in late March). Throughout much of 2010 all indicators continued to show an economic and political system in terminal, if gradual, decline.

Domestic politics continued to reflect the determination by the ruling clique to hold onto power, and by President Saleh to hand over power to the next generation (which official cables published by the WikiLeaks organization revealed to have involved assassination attempts against senior army commander and President Saleh's chief military adviser Gen. Ali Mohsen al-Ahmar). Protests against perceived corruption among the northern-based élite and discrimination became increasingly strident in the southern provinces; after harsh suppression of the protests, elements of the Southern Movement (also known as Hirak—a separatist group led by former military officers) adopted violent tactics, attacking security force bases; southern political leaders were arrested and held for lengthy periods without trial. Following concurrent clashes in the North, a truce was concluded on 11 February 2010 with the Zaidi revivalist al-Houthi movement, although sporadic skirmishes and manoeuvres continued, often through proxy tribal forces. The opposition JMP continued to negotiate with the ruling GPC over the delayed elections, and what they perceived as attempts by the GPC to rig the electoral process, such as by appointing a disproportionate number of loyalists to the SCER.

Three major terrorist events attracted international attention: AQAP launched a suicide bomb attack against the British ambassador in west San'a on 26 April 2010; fired a grenade at a British embassy vehicle on 6 October; and sent two bombs via courier services to two synagogues in the USA on 30 October (following intelligence received from Saudi Arabia, these were intercepted at airports in the United Kingdom and Dubai, UAE). The Yemeni-US cleric Anwar al-Awlaki was believed to have been involved in the attacks. Less noted but more consequential was the killing of Jabir al-Shabwani, (the Deputy Governor of Marib Province and an important Abida tribal sheikh) in a US air-strike, while he was en route to negotiate the surrender of an AQAP member. The air attack was variously reported as having been accidental, or the result of poor information provided by the Yemeni Intelligence Service. As a result, tribal forces in the Abida region attacked the Safar pipeline to Ras Isa, road checkpoints and power lines to San'a.

Economically, both crude petroleum and fresh water outputs continued to fall, while the Yemeni riyal depreciated by 16% in the first seven months of 2010, before intervention by the Central Bank. Unemployment remained high, at 35%–40%, particularly among those under 25 years of age.

In November 2010 the WikiLeaks organization published leaked classified US Department of State cables, including some originating from the US embassy in San'a. It was revealed, *inter alia*, that not only had the Government of Yemen promised to take responsibility for US military activity (which had long been suspected), but that Deputy Prime

Minister for Defence and Security Affairs Rashad Muhammad al-Alimi had joked to US officials that he had deceived the House of Representatives about this. Al-Alimi was subsequently summoned by the House of Representatives to explain his remarks.

ANTI-GOVERNMENT PROTESTS AND ATTACK AGAINST PRESIDENT SALEH

In early 2011, as during the previous year, President Saleh continued to reject attempts by the opposition (both political and popular) to reform his regime. Even in mid-January, he was widely believed to be trying to manipulate the electoral system until such time as his eldest son, Ahmad, reached the age of 40—the minimum age to hold the presidential office—when the President could resign in Ahmad's favour. All this changed, however, with the revolutionary events in the Middle East and North Africa known as the 'Arab spring', when Yemenis (like many across the Middle East) saw that modern communications could enable and protect peaceful rebellion against Arab 'strongmen', such as Tunisian President Zine al-Abidine Ben Ali or Egypt's President Hosni Mubarak.

Initially, the GPC called for dialogue with the JMP, which was perceived as an effort to curtail anti-Government protests. Neither the JMP nor the people regarded this as anything other than the President's delaying tactics. Small marches and demonstrations began in San'a, with protesters chanting the slogan 'the people want the regime to fall'. These increased steadily in size, and spread to other cities of north Yemen, such as Taiz, Hodeida, Dhamar and Ibb. Often these demonstrations were attacked by so-called *baltajiyun* (thugs), who were rumoured to have been paid by the Government to terrorize the population into acquiescence. The tactic failed, and the demonstrations gathered momentum. Denied entry to Tahrir Square in central San'a, the protestors took up permanent positions in several towns; in San'a, the area in front of the University was dubbed Taghayr ('Change') Square.

Cracks started appearing in the façade of the ruling GPC: on 23 February 2011 seven parliamentary deputies resigned to form an independent political bloc. Resignations and demonstrations continued steadily. On 10 March Saleh countered a transition plan presented by prominent Yemenis a week earlier with a proposal to draft a new constitution providing for a parliamentary system; however, this was rejected by the JMP.

On 18 March 2011 unidentified gunmen on rooftops around 'Change Square' in San'a killed 52 protesters during morning prayers. The President declared a 30-day state of emergency, and two days later dismissed his Government. On 21 March Saleh's long-time follower Gen. al-Ahmar declared his support for the opposition, bringing with him several other senior military officials; many other politicians and diplomats resigned from their posts.

During the following eight weeks unproductive negotiations were conducted, first at a national level, then mediated by the GCC Secretary-General, Abd al-Latif al-Zayani, seeking a peaceful transitional process, with President Saleh and some of his entourage being offered amnesty. While he often agreed, in principle, to a transition to the opposition, the President would rapidly revoke this in rallies with his supporters. Violence in the countryside, particularly the South, increased in frequency and severity. The death toll mounted steadily. This phase reached a climax on 22 May 2011—the day after the 21st anniversary of Yemeni unification—when al-Zayani and many foreign ambassadors were besieged for 10 hours inside the UAE embassy by armed supporters of Saleh. After a helicopter and ground evacuation to the presidential palace, Saleh refused to sign the GCC transition plan, despite all the opposition and GPC representatives having done so. Armed clashes ensued in San'a between tribal forces loyal to Sheikh Abdullah bin Hussain al-Ahmar and government forces, continuing for about one week. About 50 were killed, including senior figures in a mediation party, and several hundred were injured. Thousands of civilians fled San'a.

On 29 May 2011 government forces stormed the main square in Taiz, which had been occupied by opposition activists. At least 50 protesters were killed, and an unknown number injured. As a result, local tribes engaged in militant activity, and violent clashes with members of the Republican Guard erupted.

On 3 June 2011 President Saleh and many senior government officials (including the Prime Minister, two Deputy Prime Ministers, the Speakers of the House of Representatives and al-Islah's Shura Council) were severely wounded in an explosion while praying in a mosque; it was subsequently confirmed to have been caused by a bomb placed inside the building. Most of those injured in the incident, including President Saleh, were evacuated to Saudi Arabia for medical treatment, and the Saudis brokered a truce between the Government and the al-Ahmar tribal forces. Following Saleh's departure, the Vice-President, Maj.-Gen. (later Field Marshal) Abd al-Rabbuh Mansur al-Hadi, nominally became acting President, although President Saleh's sons and nephews (who commanded various security units) retained tight control of San'a. The opposition, prominent Yemenis and the people, as well as foreign diplomats and emissaries, tried without success to convince al-Hadi to begin the transitional process. On 7 July Saleh appeared on state television, calling for dialogue, and again three days later in a meeting with a US emissary. After no further progress, on 16 July one of the main groupings within the Youth Revolutionary coalition movement formed by protesters proclaimed a 17-member Transitional Presidential Council, mostly comprising experienced opposition politicians. On 21 July there was an unsuccessful attempt to assassinate Muhammad al-Yadumi, Secretary-General of al-Islah, by attacking his car in San'a.

From March 2011 onwards, many of the security forces were withdrawn from outlying areas, a decision variously assessed as being to reinforce presidential protection, or to allow the strength of AQAP to grow across the land (and thus revive US support for the regime). On 27 March an Islamist group seized the town of Jaar in Abyan, and the following day about 150 civilians were killed and 100 injured when a munitions factory being looted exploded. In the absence of government forces, Islamist militants slowly continued their advance (although tribes formed militias to provide security in their districts), eventually occupying Zinjibar, besieging army troops in their barracks, before being halted and then rapidly expelled by an alliance between government and tribal forces in mid-July. In the north, the al-Houthi rebels consolidated their positions and acclaimed a self-appointed Governor of Saada. In early July they advanced southwards in al-Jawf, coming into conflict with more centrist tribal militias.

In early September 2011 it was reported that the GPC had approved a new transition plan, under the terms of which President Saleh would formally transfer his powers to Vice-President al-Hadi over a three-month period. It was reported that Saleh had given his personal approval to the plan and had asked al-Hadi to conduct talks with the opposition with a view to signing the agreement. However, the plan and the call for talks were rejected by the opposition. Later that month violence began once again to escalate, as government forces and troops who had defected to the opposition clashed in San'a: on 18 September at least 21 people were killed after government forces opened fire on demonstrators in 'Change Square'. On 23 September it was announced that Saleh had returned to Yemen from Saudi Arabia and resumed his duties as President. Meanwhile, clashes in San'a had continued and, following another attack on protesters in 'Change Square' on 24 September, it was reported that at least 100 people had been killed since fighting resumed on 18 September. In his first televised address since returning to the country, on 25 September Saleh insisted that he was committed to holding talks with the opposition and called for a 'peaceful exchange of power through early elections'. However, the opposition remained sceptical of his intent to implement those measures. Two days later seven soldiers were killed in a bomb attack on a convoy carrying the Minister of Defence, Brig.-Gen. Muhammad Nasser Ahmad Ali, in Aden. Despite its calls for Saleh to leave office, the US Administration's co-operation with the Yemeni Government in its efforts to combat AQAP continued: on 30 September both countries confirmed that Yemeni-US cleric (and alleged Islamist ideologue and recruiter) Anwar al-Awlaki had been killed in an air-strike on a vehicle convoy in al-Jawf province.

INTERIM GOVERNMENT

Tensions continued to rise in Yemen throughout late 2011. Loyalist forces attacked protesters and intense skirmishes occurred between factions of the army loyal to President Saleh, the dissident First Armoured Division commanded by Maj.-Gen. Ali Mohsen al-Ahmar, and the Hashid tribal federation of Sheikh Sadeq al-Ahmar. Many inside and outside Yemen feared an imminent civil war. Diplomatic efforts by Western and regional countries continued to urge President Saleh to resign; however, he and his allies resisted the pressures, in particular presenting the death of al-Awlaki as proof of the regime's importance in the counter-terrorist campaign.

Foreign pressure continued to increase: on 21 October 2011 the UN Security Council unanimously adopted Resolution 2014, which called for acceptance of the GCC plan; at the end of that month the prospect of President Saleh's assets being frozen, and a travel ban imposed on him was also raised. Saleh then began to negotiate in earnest, securing key concessions for his faction, and on 23 November he finally signed the GCC-mediated agreement in Riyadh. This provided for a phased transition of power, ending in his formal replacement by al-Hadi on 21 February 2012. In exchange, he and his associates would receive immunity from prosecution. In addition, a National Dialogue Conference (NDC) would be conducted to reunite all sectors of Yemeni society, the Constitution would be revised, and a further presidential election would be held in 2014.

The Office of the UN High Commissioner for Human Rights and international non-governmental human rights organizations both condemned the immunity clauses as being against international law, while the people, who had borne the brunt of the regime's attempted suppression, also objected vehemently. Public displeasure was demonstrated on 25 November 2011, termed the 'Friday of Ongoing Revolution', when thousands of protesters rallied in San'a and Yemen's other major cities in opposition to the proposed immunity for Saleh and his associates.

After lengthy negotiations, a 34-member Government of national unity was sworn in on 10 December 2011, replacing the interim administration that had been officially dismissed by President Saleh in March. Seventeen members of the new Government were representatives of Saleh's GPC and 17 of the opposition JMP grouping. The following week civil servants and service personnel staged mass demonstrations to demand the resignation of the President's appointees; some less important to the GPC left, but others—particularly in key military and security positions—remained in office. Another part of the GCC deal was the demobilization of armed groups in San'a and the cities: on 18 December the similarly cross-party Demilitarization Committee began to remove checkpoints and outposts of all three factions in San'a and elsewhere, in accordance with the agreement. This reduced tensions, and the likelihood of the outbreak of further conflict.

The public, which had succeeded in ousting President Saleh where the JMP had failed, was deeply dissatisfied at what was perceived to be an arrangement between the élite which ignored their concerns for a reform of the entire political system, and failed to bring Saleh and his clique to justice. Protesters mounted a 'March of Life' rally from Taiz to San'a, arriving on 23 December, where 14 were killed in the ensuing clashes with police. Two days later, there were huge demonstrations in Aden by Southern Movement supporters against al-Hadi's forthcoming, unopposed election. Saleh's loyalists countered these protests with a rally in their usual Saba'een Square to remind the public that the terms of the GCC agreement included immunity from prosecution.

2012 PRESIDENTIAL ELECTION

Having agreed to relinquish power, President Saleh and GPC members loyal to his regime waged a campaign to disrupt the transitional arrangements and undermine the designated President's authority. On 6 January 2012 senior members of the GPC even denounced al-Hadi as a traitor for defying President Saleh's authority; the Vice-President responded by threatening to leave Yemen if this did not cease. On 31 January the new Minister of Information, who had adopted a less compliant attitude towards Saleh, survived an assassination attempt, while on 2 February armed regime loyalists seized the offices of the state-owned *Al-Thawry* newspaper to protest at the new editor's removal of Saleh's picture from the title page the previous day.

The draft legislation providing immunity for Saleh and his associates was proposed in the Council of Ministers on 8 January 2012, and referred to the House of Representatives on 10 January, where it was met with opposition from some deputies; anti-immunity 'Marchers for Dignity' from Saada staged further protests.

The demobilization of armed groups in San'a continued: the Demilitarization Committee ordered Sheikh Sadeq al-Ahmar's Hashid tribal forces to leave San'a on 11 January 2012, giving them two days to comply. Three days later, al-Hadi announced that he would not submit his nomination for election to the legislature unless Ali Mohsen al-Ahmar's First Armoured Division units withdrew from their positions in the north-west of the San'a region.

In an unexpected attack, a local tribal leader with links to Ansar al-Shari'a (the Islamist insurgents occupying several cities in the southern province of Abyan) seized Rada district in Al-Baida province on 16 January 2012. While the majority of the security forces fled, his followers killed several policemen and freed several hundred prisoners from the gaol, many of whom were Islamist militants. Four days later, the leader was killed at his home in the town by his pro-Government half-brother, who was himself killed by another half-brother; several other tribesmen were also killed in the fighting.

On 21 January 2012 the House of Representatives adopted the legislation providing immunity, and accepted Vice-President al-Hadi's candidacy for the presidency, prompting further large public protests, which continued intermittently over the next month. The following day, under intense US pressure (to reduce further interference), President Saleh left for medical treatment in the USA, travelling via Oman to prevent any possibility of claiming asylum in the USA. He was met with demonstrations by Yemenis in the diaspora. The day after Saleh had left for the USA, thousands of air force officers and men in both San'a and Taiz began to protest against the continued tenure of his half-brother, Gen. Muhammad Saleh al-Ahmar, as commander of the air force.

Having consolidated to the north and west of Saada, the Shi'a revivalist al-Houthis continued to battle both the Salafis of the Dammaj Institute near Saada city, and followers of al-Islah and tribesmen in Amran and Hajjah provinces. Some 200 fighters (on all sides) were killed and many more wounded in half a dozen clashes from mid-January to late March 2012. On 15 February the al-Houthi forces also stormed al-Islah's office in Saada, removed the posters of Vice-President al-Hadi, and prevented any electoral posters from being displayed.

Al-Hadi's electoral campaign, which was officially launched on 7 February 2012, was met with some resistance, with the organization of a day of 'Completing all Goals of Revolution' protests in San'a and 14 main cities on 10 February. This was countered by a comparable turn-out of demonstrators in similar locations the following week, who observed a 'Your Vote is a Gain for the Revolution' protest in support of al-Hadi. For many people in the North, however, the formality of the election was a matter of indifference.

This was not the case in the former PDRY, where there were regular clashes between supporters of the Southern Movement and security forces. The former also targeted locations and personnel of the SCER in particular, attempting to disrupt the conduct of the election: the Al-Dhaleh region was attacked twice in early February 2012; the head of the SCER in Al-Baida together with the commander of the local Republican Guard unit was ambushed on 16 February; and on 14 February a bomb was detonated outside the SCER office in Aden, killing the perpetrator and causing al-Hadi to cancel his campaign rallies in the South.

Despite all the disruption, the presidential election took place on 21 February 2012, under the supervision of some 103,000 security forces personnel. Al-Hadi, as the sole candidate, was confirmed as President with 99.8% of the votes cast; a participation rate of 65% of the electorate was recorded.

PRESIDENT AL-HADI

On 25 February 2012, as President al-Hadi took office, a suicide attack against the Presidential Palace in Mukalla, in Hadramout province, killed 26 Republican Guard soldiers and wounded many more. Two days later former President Saleh took part in the inauguration ceremony in San‘a, at which al-Hadi stated that he also intended to hand over to a successor in two years. However, the inauguration was boycotted by many JMP personnel, owing to Saleh's attendance, an issue that GPC deputies subsequently raised in the House of Representatives.

On 2 March 2012, when thousands of people staged a nationwide protest termed the 'Friday of Restructuring the Army', demanding that members of the former President's family be removed from their military and security appointments, the new President replaced the Governor and security chief of Aden, and the commander of the Southern Military Region. The outgoing regional commander, Brig. Mahdi Maquala, was a regime insider, and this high-profile dismissal was regarded as the first step in security sector reform, for which there was domestic and international demand. Three days later, Islamists attacked an army operating base in Abyan, killing 185 soldiers and seizing armoured vehicles and heavy weapons. Many alleged complicity in the offensive by the outgoing commander.

REFORM PROCESS

Protests demanding more security sector reform continued, as did demonstrations demanding that former President Saleh should face justice, and Southern Movement protests. Clashes between Islamists (who had been reinforced by 300 al-Shabaab members from Somalia in mid-February 2012) and the security forces continued. The Islamists continued to expand their control, making inroads into government territory surrounding their main base in Abyan. They advanced into Al-Baida province (where a suicide bomb attack killed eight people on 13 March), Lahj province (killing 28 soldiers, and injuring or capturing many more on 31 March), Hadramout province (where they ambushed and killed seven soldiers on 1 April) and Shabwah province (where they killed seven more soldiers on 10 April). This period included sporadic heavy fighting in Abyan itself, centred around Zinjibar and Jaar. As a result of these clashes, the number of internally displaced persons increased, those from Abyan alone reaching 100,000. The growing food insecurity was exacerbated by the general increase in the cost of staples, leading to widespread famine throughout much of coastal Yemen. In addition to their insurgency, Islamists were also involved in attacks on foreigners: in mid-March a US teacher was killed in Taiz and a Swiss teacher was kidnapped in Hodeida.

On 7 April 2012 a presidential decree announced a major reorganization of senior military commanders, removing many of Saleh's associates and relatives and replacing them with professional officers. This did not include Ali Mohsen al-Ahmar (commander of the dissident First Armoured Division), Gen. Ahmad Ali Abdullah (commander of the Republican Guard), Gen. Yahya Muhammad Abdullah (the Central Security Forces Chief of Staff), or Ammar Muhammad Abdullah (deputy head of the National Security Bureau). It did, however, include both Gen. Muhammad Saleh al-Ahmar (commander of the air force) and Col Tariq Muhammad Abdullah (commander of the presidential guard). While some accepted their dismissals, al-Ahmar refused to leave his base at San‘a Airport, and Tariq Muhammad Abdullah, though surrendering command of the presidential guard, refused his appointment in Hadramout, instead taking command of the powerful Third Brigade of the Republican Guard in a key location just north of San‘a. With the support of foreign diplomats, on 15 April al-Hadi gave al-Ahmar a deadline of 48 hours to leave the air force headquarters and relinquish the post to his successor, Gen. Rashed Nasir Ali al-Janad.

After thousands of people protested in Yemen on 13 April 2012 to demand further security sector reform, former President Saleh's supporters staged a counter-demonstration on 16 April, urging his return to power. He addressed the gathering, stating that 'no one may surrender himself to death or liquidation', which was interpreted as a veiled warning not to remove his relatives from their senior army and security posts. The following day al-Ahmar defied the Demilitarization Committee and prevented its representatives from entering the air force headquarters. A military confrontation ensued over several days, during which time al-Ahmar threatened to fire on civilian aircraft using San‘a Airport. Meanwhile, thousands of protesters across Yemen demanded the prosecution of military commanders who had disobeyed the President's orders regarding their positions. Al-Ahmar was eventually persuaded to leave on 24 April by the UN Special Envoy to Yemen.

The mutiny in the Third Republican Guard Brigade was more protracted. While Tariq Muhammad Abdullah was eventually convinced to cede his post by the UN Special Envoy on 4 May 2012, the new commander was prevented from taking up command by the Brigade Chief of Staff, a former regime loyalist who resisted all pressure. The mutiny was eventually resolved on 7 June by junior officers and soldiers, who seized the tanks and heavy weapons at the brigade headquarters from the mutineers and forced their surrender.

On 6 May 2012 it was reported that Fahd al-Qusu al-Aulaqi—an al-Qa‘ida member who had been involved in many terrorist plots since the time of the attack on the USS *Cole*—had been killed by a US drone attack in Rafd, in Shabwah province. Two days later, it was leaked that the information to target him had been provided by a Western double agent who had infiltrated al-Qa‘ida, and been trained to use a disguised bomb device. The agent had successfully left Yemen, before surrendering the device to his US controllers.

Despite intelligence of an imminent attack, al-Qa‘ida managed to infiltrate a suicide bomber into San‘a. On 21 May 2012, while wearing a Central Security Force uniform, the attacker detonated a bomb amid soldiers at the dress rehearsal for the Unification Day parade at Saba‘een Square. Some 96 people were killed and several hundred wounded by the blast, which al-Qa‘ida claimed was targeted at the Chief of the General Staff. The deputy head of the National Security Bureau, Ammar Muhammad Saleh, was removed, while his brother Yahya, the Central Security Forces Chief of Staff, was replaced with a more effective commander.

The day after Unification Day, an international contact group chaired jointly by the United Kingdom and Saudi Arabia—the Friends of Yemen—held a donors' conference in Riyadh, at which various pledges of financial assistance totalling US $4,000m. were made; most of this amount comprised a pledge of $3,500m. from Saudi Arabia to support infrastructure and security.

With US intelligence, logistical and close air support, the Yemeni army fought its way back into Abyan during late May and June 2012, regaining control of Zinjibar, Jaar and al-Shaqra and finally seizing Ansar al-Shari‘a's last stronghold on 23 June. While many foreign combatants had been killed or captured in the fighting, it was suspected that many Yemeni insurgents had merely blended into the population once more. The liberation of Abyan was accompanied by prominent casualties. On 18 June Maj.-Gen. Salim Qatan, the commander of the South Military Region, who had led the operation, was killed by a suicide bomb attack against his convoy as it was driving through Aden.

During July 2012 there was a series of small bomb attacks and shootings, mainly targeting security force personnel; most of these were attributed to al-Qa‘ida. A suicide bomb attack was also staged against cadets leaving the police academy in San‘a on 11 July, in which nine were killed and about 15 injured. Despite having been driven from Abyan, and apparently having adopted a terrorist (rather than insurgent) campaign, on 25 July Islamists attacked Jaar in Abyan once again. In early September the Government claimed that Said Ali al-Shihri had been killed in Hadramout province.

The toll on the Yemeni civilian population of the combined political instability was immense. By mid-2012 fuel prices were estimated to have risen by as much as 500%, while sugar and flour prices had increased by more than 50%. In a report published in April, the UN World Food Programme estimated that more than 10m. Yemenis had insufficient food, and that more than 267,000 children were living under life-threatening levels of malnutrition at the end of 2011.

THE ROAD TO TRANSITION

The combination of simmering internecine strife and explosive terrorist activity continued throughout 2012, with a powerful Saleh loyalist being kidnapped by tribesmen just north of San'a in early July, and only released after high-level intervention. The Yemeni police academy in San'a was attacked by a suicide bomber on 11 July; at least 10 people were killed. However, despite the violence, the political process continued, with the newly formed, Salafi al-Rashad Party announcing on 16 July that it wished to participate in the forthcoming NDC. Against this backdrop, UN Special Adviser on Yemen Jamal Benomar briefed the UN Security Council on 17 July on the political, humanitarian and security challenges to transition, and in particular on the major interference caused by former President Saleh. Indeed, only a fortnight later, irregular policemen loyal to Saleh stormed the Ministry of the Interior, killing 15 people and wounding 43 more (as well as destroying much of the contents of the Ministry). Three days later, on 1 August, an Italian security guard was kidnapped by tribesmen outside the Italian embassy and released a few days later. Also on 1 August Benomar was officially confirmed in the role of Special Adviser to UN Secretary-General Ban Ki-Moon.

A major step towards security sector reform (and evicting members of the Saleh family and loyalists from the establishment) occurred when President al-Hadi issued a decree on 6 August 2012 dissolving the Republican Guard (formerly commanded by Saleh's eldest son). Some units were transferred into a newly formed Presidential Protective Force, while others were dispersed among regional commands. Units from Maj.-Gen. Ali Mohsen al-Ahmar's First Armoured Division were also moved into the presidential force or under regional command. While Benomar lauded this as an important step towards creating democratic armed forces, on 10 August hundreds of loyalist Republican Guards surrounded the Ministry of Defence for several hours in protest. Reform was also taking place in the judicial sector: on 29 August al-Hadi dismissed the unpopular Chairman of the Supreme Judicial Council and appointed a new one, despite a campaign by Yemeni judges to win the right to elect the Chairman and members of the Council.

Despite these reforms to the military, other policies of the Saleh regime continued: Ahmed Abdullah al-Hassani, a former Yemeni ambassador and southern leader, was arrested at Aden airport on 15 August 2012 as he returned after seven years of exile in the United Kingdom. He was released four days later. Another attack on a leading southerner came on 30 August, when Yassin Sa'id Nu'man, Secretary-General of the YSP and a presidential adviser, was the target of a failed assassination attempt, which resulted in widespread youth protest.

Meanwhile, the terrorist attacks and reprisals continued: a suicide bomber detonated his explosive belt at a funeral of a Popular Revolutionary Committee militia member in Jaar on 30 August 2012, killing 45 mourners and wounding many more. Three days later a US drone targeting Abd al-Ra'uf al-Dhahab, a relative of the local tribal leader who seized Rada district in January, fired a missile that hit a minibus, killing 14 civilians in al-Baida province. Abd al-Ra'uf escaped unharmed. On 11 September the Minister of Defence, Brig.-Gen Muhammad Nasser Ahmad Ali, survived a car bomb attack in San'a that killed 12 people and injured many others. In response, the following day President al-Hadi replaced several senior pro-Saleh security and intelligence officials and simultaneously carried out a minor cabinet reshuffle.

On 12 September 2012, after the existence of an anti-Islamic film produced privately in the USA was widely publicized, mobs attacked the US embassy in San'a. The embassy was breached, with suggestions of a politically motivated complacency by remaining Saleh loyalists within the security forces. President al-Hadi issued an apology for the breach of security to the US President. One month later the Yemeni security chief for the US embassy was murdered in unexplained circumstances.

REFORMS CONTINUE

Reform of the political establishment gathered pace in Yemen in the latter half of 2012, with a GPC former minister admitting that the southerners had legitimate grievances, and suggesting a six-region federal system, with each region enjoying autonomy, including over natural resources. Soon afterwards, on 27 September, at a high-level Friends of Yemen meeting on the margins of the UN General Assembly, the UN Security Council urged all Yemeni parties to continue to act in the spirit of reconciliation. As preparations for the NDC got under way, hardline elements of the Southern Movement declared their intention to boycott the event. Nevertheless, the formation of a steering committee was announced on 6 October, as well as the principle of equal representation from the South and the North, and that a minimum of 30% of members would be women. A further major step forward came at the end of the following month, when the SCER was appointed, based on the recommendations of the newly purged Supreme Judicial Council, and according to the provisions of the GCC Initiative. Meanwhile, in late November a Saudi diplomat and his bodyguard were shot dead in their vehicle in San'a by attackers wearing police uniforms.

Military reform took another few steps forward with the announcement in mid-December 2012 that a court martial had sentenced 93 Republican Guard officers and men to between three and seven years' imprisonment on charges of insubordination and mutiny for their assault on the Ministry of Defence in August. A major advance occurred four days later, on 18 December, with the announcement by President al-Hadi that the armed forces were to be restructured to become five branches: Land, Air, Naval and Coastguard, Border Guards, and Strategic Reserve, the latter comprising the Presidential Protection Force, Missile Defence Command, and Special Operations Command.

In early 2013, in a move thought by many to have been made under foreign pressure to improve the chances of reconciliation, former President Saleh departed abroad, ostensibly for medical treatment. Indeed, the following day it was reported that, in addition to purging Saleh loyalists from the security forces, President al-Hadi was to address the forcible discharge of tens of thousands of former southern soldiers after the 1994 civil war—a major issue for many southerners. Nevertheless, on 13 January hundreds of thousands of supporters of the Southern Movement rallied in Aden in favour of secession.

On 23 January 2013 the Yemeni coastguard and the USS *Farragut* intercepted a ship carrying military equipment (including surface-to-air missiles and electronic circuits) from Iran. Yemen accused Iran of supplying weapons to the al-Houthis and referred the matter to the UN Security Council. Following an investigation by a UN panel of experts tasked with monitoring compliance with UN sanctions against Iran, it was noted that some of the cargo may have been bound for Somalia. In the same month AQAP's senior cleric, Zubayr Adil bin Abdullah al-Abab, was killed in a US drone strike in Shabwah province.

On 27 January 2013 all 15 members of the UN Security Council, led by the United Kingdom and Morocco, visited Yemen for the first time to evaluate the implementation of UN Security Council Resolution No. 2051, which was adopted in June 2012, and to assess the progress of political transition. They met President al-Hadi and representatives of parliament, civil societies and the GCC. Two weeks later the Security Council reiterated a threat of sanctions against anyone found to be interfering in the transition, naming former President Saleh and former Vice-President al-Baid explicitly. (A few days later Saleh opened a museum in San'a dedicated to himself, documenting his 33-year rule.) In late February Qussim Askar Jubran, a prominent leader of the secessionist wing of the Southern Movement, was arrested at his home in Aden.

THE NDC BEGINS

The Friends of Yemen held their fifth meeting in London on 7 March 2013. The meeting was held to show continued support for Yemen's political transition, in particular its development and reform plans in the political, economic, security and humanitarian sectors. The Friends stressed their support for the unity, sovereignty, independence and territorial integrity of Yemen and focused discussion on five key subjects: the NDC and constitutional reform; preparations for the February 2014 elections; delivery of the US $7,900m. of aid committed to Yemen in 2012; the severe humanitarian situation (with an estimated 13m. people in need of assistance); and security and justice sector reform. The Friends urged the Yemeni authorities to ensure that the security forces exercised restraint in response to peaceful protests.

On 18 March 2013, two years after a murderous attack on youth demonstrators in San'a, the NDC—established as a socially and geographically representative consultative and debating process—began. Despite some initial political, and even cultural, clashes between the 565 participants, they soon embarked on constructive, if not amicable, dialogue and the formation of nine working groups on contentious issues such as development, the Southern question, the al-Houthi issue and the Constitution. The intention was for delegates to identify a list of grievances and redresses, and to make recommendations for a new constitution and system of government, all in the next six months. Outside the venue, however, the violence continued: on 23 March a group of armed men attempted to murder an al-Houthi delegate from al-Jawf province just after he had left an NDC session.

At the end of March 2013 a Swiss woman, who had been held hostage for almost a year, was freed, possibly through Qatari mediation. International affairs occupied much of April, with a major issue being Saudi Arabia's decision to enforce a law requiring foreigners to work only for those Saudis who had sponsored their entry into the kingdom. This resulted in the deportation of around 20,000 Yemenis within a few weeks, with the prospect of many more remittance-earners likewise being sent home. While the Saudis claimed that the issue was solely legal, there was much suspicion in Yemen that the cause was Saudi desire for preferential treatment over the recent discovery of petroleum reserves in al-Jawf province on the border between the two states.

On 10 April 2013 President al-Hadi executed the final major piece in his military reform programme, with the reorganization of Yemeni ground forces from five military regions into seven smaller ones. Simultaneously, the appointment of members of the Saleh family (including Gen. Ahmad Ali Abdullah) and Gen. Ali Mohsen al-Ahmar to non-military posts (mostly abroad) removed their physical presence from Yemen. On 27 April a court ordered a new inquiry into the involvement of former President Saleh and 12 of his loyalists in the killing of 45 protesters on 18 March 2011 in 'Change Square'—the so-called 'Friday of Dignity' massacre. The following day the General District Attorney ordered an inquiry into Saleh's role in the shelling of Hashid tribal federation leader Sheikh Sadeq al-Ahmar's home in May 2011.

On 28 April 2013 supporters of the Southern Movement gathered across southern Yemen to commemorate the 19th anniversary of the 1994 civil war. (A further rally was held in Mukalla on 8 July, the day the war ended in defeat for the DRY.) On 29 April four imprisoned secessionist leaders were released from gaols in San'a and Aden under presidential directives and were greeted by Yemeni officials.

Nearly one year after a bill was adopted on freedom of information, President al-Hadi appointed Yemen's first Information Commissioner, although his lack of political standing and limited budget were quickly seized upon as weaknesses in the concept. Three days later, on 9 May 2013, al-Hadi, in his role as President of the NDC, launched the field visits by NDC teams to study developments at the local level, and discuss popular needs and opinions.

The contentious issue of Guantánamo detainees returned to the political spotlight when, on 24 May 2013, US President Barack Obama lifted the moratorium on repatriation of low-level detainees to Yemen and announced the appointment of a delegate charged with ensuring that this was carried out. Five days later Yemen's Minister of Human Rights appealed for funds to build a rehabilitation centre to receive the detainees. Angered at the apparent lack of progress in this matter, Yemeni and US human rights protesters demonstrated outside the US embassy in San'a on 17 June, demanding their immediate release.

June 2013 began with an increase in violence in the South: two US drone strikes killed seven suspected AQAP members in Abyan; Yemeni security guards foiled a suicide car bomb attack on a gas pumping station in Shabwah province, and then on 5 June the Yemeni army launched a assault on Ghayl Ba-Wazir in Hadramout to remove AQAP fighters from the town. On 2 June Kassim al-Raimi, AQAP's military commander, had released a video stating that US citizens would not be safe unless their leaders respected the security of other nations and did not attack or oppress them.

As a token of good will, the Yemeni Government returned the body of Hussain al-Houthi (the founder of the eponymous movement) to his family for burial, nine years after his death in combat. His funeral in Saada was attended by tens of thousands of Zaidi Muslims. Three days later President al-Hadi initiated the second round of the NDC in San'a, hailing the progress that had been achieved since March 2013: the nine working groups had met nearly 11,000 officials and civil society members from all 17 provinces. Yet, as before, there was violence surrounding the conference. Al-Houthis demonstrated in front of the headquarters of the National Security Bureau to demand the release of detained adherents of the movement; 10 al-Houthis were killed during the protest and 38 wounded. The following day thousands demonstrated to protest against the killings.

Economy

Revised for this edition by PHILIP McCRUM

INTRODUCTION

Despite possessing substantial oil and gas resources and a significant tract of agriculturally productive land, Yemen has been consistently ranked among the world's lowest-income countries. According to the World Bank, Yemen's gross national income (GNI) was US $25,959m. ($1,110 per head) in 2011 on a conventional exchange rate basis, compared with $4,949m. ($321 per head) in 1995. Measured on the basis of purchasing-power parity (PPP), GNI amounted to $2,310 per head in 2011. In 1989, the last year before Yemeni unification, the World Bank had estimated Yemen's GNI per head as $650 (conventionally measured), based on aggregated data for the then Yemen Arab Republic (YAR, or North Yemen) and the People's Democratic Republic of Yemen (PDRY, or South Yemen). Data from a year earlier showed that the YAR had fared better economically, achieving a GNI per head of $640 by 1988 (according to the World Bank), whereas the PDRY's equivalent statistic was $430. These estimated statistics, suggesting a significant decline in GNI per head in the years following unification in May 1990, appear to be broadly consistent with the turbulent course of events in the new Republic of Yemen. Early plans for economic development and integration were quickly disrupted by the Gulf crisis of 1990–91, while subsequent plans were undermined by the outbreak of civil war in 1994 and the eruption of nation-wide anti-Government protests in 2011, which seriously destabilized the country.

Unification in 1990 created a country of 536,869 sq km with a population estimated at 11,282,000, excluding up to 2.5m. Yemenis working abroad, mainly in Saudi Arabia. Of the two components, the YAR had a population of 9,274,173 (including nationals abroad) in 1986, while the PDRY had a population of 2,345,266 in 1988. The results of Yemen's first post-unification census, carried out on 16 December 1994, indicated a total population of 14,587,807 (23% of whom lived in urban areas). A household budget survey conducted in 1998 indicated that the proportion of Yemen's population living in poverty (as defined by current UN measures of living standards) rose from 19% in 1992 to 33% in 1998, with the main concentrations of poverty in rural areas. By 2005 this figure had risen to over 50%. During 1996–2006 it was estimated by the World Bank that the population increased at an average annual rate of 3.2%; this rate declined slightly to 2.9% during 2006–10. The resident population at the 16 December 2004 census was recorded as 19,685,161. The UN estimated the population at 24,407,381 in mid-2013.

In the mid-1980s the economic prospects of both the YAR and the PDRY were significantly improved by the discovery of hydrocarbons in commercial quantities, and the perceived need for rapid joint development of their oil and gas sectors was a major factor in the two countries' decision to unite.

Prior to the invasion in 1990 of Kuwait by Iraq, Yemen had been greatly dependent on trade with both countries. It had also relied heavily, for balance of payments purposes, on hard currency remittances from Yemeni workers in Saudi Arabia and the Gulf States. However, many of these workers returned home in large numbers, when, in September, Saudi Arabia terminated Yemeni workers' privileges in retaliation for Yemen's opposition to the US-led military build-up in the Persian (Arabian) Gulf region. In October the Government, in support of a request for special aid from the international community, calculated its actual and prospective losses in 1990–91 at US $1,686m. Later Yemeni estimates of the overall cost of the crisis included one by President Ali Abdullah Saleh in May 1991, putting Yemen's total prospective losses, including 1992, at over $3,000m. Moreover, in April 1991 the Government valued property and assets lost by Yemeni nationals forced to leave Saudi Arabia at $7,900m. By then the total number of returnees from Saudi Arabia was estimated by Yemeni officials at up to 1m., representing a 10% increase in the country's population and giving rise to serious social problems and pressure on scarce resources.

In November 1991 President Saleh conceded that Yemen was experiencing an economic crisis, with unemployment between 25% and 30%, and lost aid and other negative effects producing a 50% shortfall in government receipts compared with the original 1991 budget. In response, the Government implemented austerity measures, including reductions in food subsidies and defence expenditure, and co-operated informally with the IMF and other international agencies in adjusting short-term economic policy. On the positive side, activity in the oil and gas sectors accelerated sharply in 1991–92, on the strength of discoveries of significant new reserves, although output from existing oilfields declined in 1992, when government oil revenue remained modest in relation to the country's current financial needs. By mid-1993 there were signs that relations with Saudi Arabia and other states of the Cooperation Council for the Arab States of the Gulf (Gulf Cooperation Council—GCC) were beginning to improve, and in August oil production started to rise when the first shipments were made from a newly developed field.

In 1994 political events led once more to deep economic crisis as the armed conflict of May–July further destabilized the deficit-ridden public finances and burdened the country with a costly agenda of post-war repair work to be undertaken before the normal development programme could resume. The Yemeni Government estimated the overall cost of the war at US $4,000m., and anticipated a $3,500m. spending requirement for reconstruction work. Widespread shortages of food, water and electricity continued to be reported in many parts of the country in September, causing a five-fold rise in the prices of some basic foodstuffs and, inevitably, popular discontent. It was subsequently estimated by the IMF that Yemen's real gross domestic product (GDP), measured at constant 1990 prices, had declined at an average annual rate of 0.2% in the period 1991–94, and consumption per head had declined by an average 26.5% per year, while the inflation rate had averaged 57.3% per year.

A delegation of World Bank and IMF officials visited San'a in January 1995 to assess the situation and draw up proposals for immediate remedial action. It was estimated at this point that prices were rising at an annual rate of 60%, despite direct and indirect government subsidies totalling more than US $400m. per year, while the unemployment rate was around 30%, despite widespread over-manning throughout the public sector. By March the inflation rate was reported to have risen to 100%, and the unemployment rate to 50%, as the country awaited a major economic policy initiative by the Government.

The main components of this initiative were: curbing the budget deficit; the adoption of a more liberal exchange rate policy; and a commitment to implement wide-ranging structural reforms (to be finalized in consultation with the IMF and World Bank) from 1996 onwards. Implementation of an IMF-approved reform programme began on schedule in January 1996, and in July the Government published a detailed development plan for the remainder of the decade. At the end of 1996 the World Bank congratulated the Yemeni Government on its 'remarkable success' in stabilizing the currency and reducing the rate of price inflation (which by November 1996 was less than 10% on an annualized basis).

According to the IMF, Yemen's real GDP at constant prices increased at an average annual rate of 5.6% in the period 1995–99 (9.8% for the oil and gas sector and 4.7% for the non-oil economy), while real consumption per head grew at an average rate of 2.9% per year and inflation averaged 25.3% per year. The IMF estimated the year-on-year growth rates in real GDP as 7.9% in 1995, 2.9% in 1996, 8.1% in 1997, 4.9% in 1998 and 3.7% in 1999.

The recovery in international oil prices in 1999 and 2000 heralded a more favourable economic environment, and the IMF estimated the rate of real GDP growth at 4.4% in 2000 and 4.6% in 2001. Also in 2001 the Yemeni Government finalized its five-year development plan for the period 2001–05, having previously adopted a far-reaching structural reform programme (including privatization and public sector rationalization) drawn up in consultation with advisers from the IMF and World Bank. The plan incorporated a detailed poverty reduction strategy designed to reduce the estimated 40% of the population living below internationally recognized levels of poverty and to address associated social problems. Yemen's border treaty with Saudi Arabia, concluded in June 2000, was widely portrayed in Yemen as an event of major economic significance, opening the way to substantial increases in trade, investment and economic co-operation. In December of that year Saudi Arabia agreed to resume economic aid to Yemen, confirming the full normalization of relations after a decade of estrangement.

The international economic downturn in the aftermath of the 11 September 2001 suicide attacks on the US mainland posed some difficulties for Yemen, notably in terms of increased transport costs and dwindling tourism receipts, but revenue from petroleum remained healthy, underpinning growth in real GDP of 3.9% in 2002. Real GDP growth remained at a similar level in 2003 (3.8%) and in 2004 (3.9%), despite a slowdown in oil production of 5.9% in 2004, reflecting diminishing recovery from existing ageing fields and the absence of significant new discoveries. Despite a persistent decline in oil production each consecutive year, Yemen has managed to maintain positive growth thanks to buoyant non-oil expansion. In 2005 real GDP growth increased to 5.9%, before slowing to 3.2% in 2006, its lowest rate for a decade. In 2007 real growth rose marginally, to 3.5%, before declining to 3.2% again in 2008. In 2009 real GDP growth recovered slightly, reaching 3.8%, before increasing strongly in 2010, to an estimated 6.2%. However, owing to the political turmoil that affected the country from early 2011, real GDP contracted considerably during that year, narrowing by 12.8%. Actual data for real GDP growth in 2012 was not publicly available by mid-2013, but official estimates indicated that the economy expanded by 2.0%.

Annual average inflation rose from 10.8% in 2003 to 12.5% in 2004, owing largely to expansionary fiscal and monetary policies and to higher food prices caused by adverse weather conditions. Inflation slowed slightly in 2005, to 11.8%, before increasing at the rapid rate of 20.8% in 2006, according to the Central Bank of Yemen. In 2007 price growth decelerated, although it remained strong, at 10%. In 2008 inflation rose to 19%, as food and housing-related costs (such as cooking gas) surged on the back of high global commodity prices and record-high oil prices. However, the global economic downturn resulted in a marked decline in the price of commodities, and consumer price growth slowed dramatically in 2009, to 5.4%. A strong economic recovery in 2010 pushed prices up by 11.2%, while in 2011 protracted political unrest caused widespread shortages of basic goods and consumer prices spiked dramatically. Over the course of the year the cost of living increased sharply, with annual average inflation reaching 19.3%, although, given the shortage of data published during the year, the true figure is likely to have been much higher. Indeed, transport costs alone rose by more than one-half, owing to sustained interruptions to domestic oil supply. As the disorder eased slightly during the early part of 2012, price pressures moderated somewhat, but overall consumer price inflation remained elevated for the year as a whole, at 10.1%.

In 2005 the World Bank had stated that additional financial support to Yemen would be conditional on the implementation of policy reforms. In July 2006, having recognized that the economic situation had begun to improve slowly, the Bank approved a new financial support strategy for Yemen covering the period 2006–09, aimed at increasing non-oil GDP growth, raising human development indicators, and improving fiscal and resource sustainability. Meanwhile, the International Finance Corpn was to continue supporting the development of the private sector through investments and technical assistance activities.

High oil prices helped buoy Yemen's economy in 2008, but the global economic downturn resulted in a sharp decrease in oil prices, which coincided with an ongoing decline in Yemen's oil output. In the first half of 2009 government oil revenues were just one-quarter of the amount accrued in the same period during the previous year; as a consequence, Yemen was forced to appeal to Saudi Arabia for emergency budgetary support. Yemen's deteriorating internal security situation prompted an international conference in London, United Kingdom, in January 2010, which acknowledged that the country's ailing economy was the underlying cause of its wider problems. At the summit, in return for concerted support for Yemen, the Government agreed to commit itself to an economic reform programme arranged in tandem with the IMF, which focused on fiscal stability, eliminating subsidies and building non-oil revenue streams. During the first four months of 2010 the price of diesel oil was raised twice. The move prompted strikes, but the Government appeared committed to its programme; in July it reduced the electricity subsidy and also implemented more fully a general sales tax (GST), which it had only partially imposed in 2005. In return for persisting with these measures, it also became clear that international donors were honouring their pledges and significant sums of aid were starting to flow into the country.

However, the reform programme was effectively abandoned in early 2011 after the onset of widespread anti-Government demonstrations. President Saleh, in an attempt to appease the protesters, widened subsidies once again and increased public sector salaries. Donor aid virtually stopped as Yemen's international stakeholders lost confidence in the Saleh regime, and by mid-2011 the economy was deteriorating rapidly. The country received some financial support over the course of the year, mainly from its neighbours, notably Saudi Arabia, but the amounts involved were limited, with most of the aid supplied in the form of oil. By the end of the year the Yemeni Government had appealed once more to the international community for further aid donations; the Minister of Planning and International Co-operation announced that the unrest had cost the country over US $15,000m. and that it would need support of at least $8,700m. to stimulate the country's economic recovery. In April 2012 the IMF resumed financial support for Yemen, immediately disbursing almost $100m. in emergency aid, while in May the Friends of Yemen (a group of international stakeholders, including key bilateral and multilateral donors) committed themselves to providing further financial support for the Yemeni Government. However, a full donor conference scheduled for June, at which the funding was to be negotiated, was postponed until September. Following that meeting, held in New York, USA, the Yemeni Government managed to secure pledges for further funds, taking the total pledged to Yemen over the course of the year to over $8,000m. However, this total remained short of the $12,000m. it was hoping to secure. In order to accelerate the disbursal of the funds, the Government subsequently established the Executive Bureau for the Acceleration of Aid Absorption. However, by mid-2013 it had failed to find a candidate to lead the body.

The significant economic contraction experienced by the Yemeni economy over the course of the period of political unrest resulted in deepening hardship for all the population, but particularly those living close to the poverty line. In a report published in early 2012, the World Food Programme stated that some 5.3m. Yemenis were suffering from severe food insecurity in 2011, representing a sharp increase from 2.8m. in 2009. Acute malnutrition was recorded at 13% in that year, just below the World Health Organization (WHO) emergency threshold of 15%.

AGRICULTURE AND FISHING

The contribution of the agriculture, hunting, forestry and fisheries sector to GDP declined from 24.2% in 1990 to 13.2% in 2007, decreasing further to 13.1% in 2009 and 13.0% in 2010. However, this contribution picked up in 2011, to 15.7%, before declining again to 14.6% in 2012. Agriculture remains a disproportionately large source of employment in Yemen. The sector provided 58% of male employment and 95% of female employment among the 77% of Yemen's population who lived in rural areas at the time of the December 1994 census. The 1999 labour market survey showed that the sector employed some 1.3m. persons (1.2m. men and 0.1m. women), representing about 43% of those in employment. According to official data, in 2006 the sector's share of employment declined noticeably, to 33.1% of the total labour force; by 2010 it had fallen further to 24%, primarily owing to a much smaller proportion of women working in the sector.

According to the Central Bank, the rate of real annual growth in agricultural production averaged 5.1% between 2002 and 2008, rising only slightly in 2009 to 5.2%. Growth slowed in 2010 to 4.1%, slowing further to 2.9% in 2011. Only 6% of Yemen's land area is categorized by the World Bank as arable (and only one-half of this as 'crop land'), while 7% is classed as forest and woodland and 30% as permanent pasture. The remaining 57% is largely desert and scrub. Of a total cultivable area of 1.6m. ha, 1.4m. ha were under cultivation in 2012, with 57% devoted to cereals, 11% to fodder, and 6% each to cash crops (such as cotton), fruit, and vegetables.

The greater part of the arable land is in the western part of the country, which is the most fertile area of the Arabian peninsula, with a long tradition of intensive cultivation by smallholders. The wide range of climatic conditions across the hillsides, mountains, valleys, coastal plains and highland plateaux of western Yemen make it possible to cultivate a diversity of crop types, including dates, tobacco and cotton, on the drought-prone Tihama plain and in coastal areas further to the south; coffee (at altitudes above 1,300 m); the qat bush (mainly at altitudes between 1,500 m and 2,500 m); sorghum or durra (at altitudes up to 3,000 m); and other cereals including wheat, barley and maize. Traditional fruit and vegetable crops in the highland areas include citrus fruits, apricots, peaches, grapes, tomatoes and potatoes, while newer crops encouraged since the 1970s under agricultural development programmes (often backed by bans on fruit and vegetable imports) include watermelons, cucumbers, peas, cauliflowers and lettuces. Mangoes, bananas and papayas are grown at lower altitudes where sub-tropical conditions prevail. The less favourable climate and terrain of Yemen's desert interior restrict agricultural production mainly to the wadi areas with sufficient water resources to support farming. The fertile Wadi Hadramout, extending across 160 km of eastern Yemen, is the largest wadi system in the Arabian peninsula. Livestock-farming and animal-herding are important activities in most parts of Yemen, supplying much of the local demand for meat and dairy products and providing a small exportable surplus of hides and skins.

Agricultural development projects, mainly financed by foreign aid, featured prominently in the development plans of the former YAR and the PDRY and have remained a priority since unification. Established in 1993, the Fish and Agriculture Promotion Fund had by 2001 financed some 3,340 programmes and projects, including more than 700 in the field of irrigation and water construction. The building of a major new Marib dam at Wadi Abida was completed in 1986 with financing from the Abu Dhabi Fund for Development. The dam has a storage capacity of 390m. cu m and was designed to provide perennial irrigation for 6,000 ha of cereal crops, with 5,000 ha of intermittent irrigation. Plans for a second development phase of the Marib dam scheme were finalized in 2000. Small-scale dam-building projects have been undertaken in many other wadi areas throughout Yemen.

Fish catches were around 50,000 metric tons in the former PDRY and 21,000 tons in the former YAR in the mid-1980s. It had long been recognized that the Arabian Sea fishing grounds off southern Yemen and, to a lesser extent, the Red Sea grounds off western Yemen had considerable untapped development potential. Ongoing fisheries expansion schemes at the time of unification in May 1990 included a long-term programme in the south, which was then midway through its third phase. Fourth-phase funding was subsequently secured in 1991–92 from the International Development Association (IDA), the International Fund for Agricultural Development, and the European Community (EC, now European Union—EU). According to official figures, fish production reached 228,100 tons in 2003. The Government subsequently set a target of a 10% annual increase in fishery production, to reach 560,000 tons by 2010. By 2007 total production had reached 494,600 tons, although this decreased dramatically in 2008 to 214,400 tons, recovering only marginally in 2009, to 255,000 tons. In 2010, however, the total catch rose further to 280,000 tons, falling once again to 230,516 tons by 2012.

The Government is trying to build capacity in the sector, with a particular focus on upgrading and expanding cold storage and processing facilities. The labour-intensive nature of the fisheries sector means that it is highly strategic. According to the Ministry of Fisheries, the sector employed 315,000 people in 2004, equal to 3.5% of Yemen's economically active population. More importantly, though, the Ministry estimated that these workers supported a further 1.7m. people—about 9% of the total population.

Yemen's trade in agricultural produce has been heavily in deficit, annual production of exportable cash crops (such as coffee, cotton, sesame, tobacco and qat—a mildly narcotic plant) having remained at fairly modest levels while local production of staple food crops has supplied a diminishing proportion of local demand. Efforts to increase cereals output have been hampered by uncertain rainfall, so that Yemen has continued to rely on imports, particularly of wheat, at an annual level of 2m.–3m. metric tons in recent years. According to official figures, production in 2005 included 495,591 tons of cereals, 694,797 tons of vegetables, 768,350 tons of fruit and 190,360 tons of cash crops. In 2006 cereal production increased significantly, to 726,297 tons; vegetable production rose to 711,652 tons and fruit production totalled 865,543 tons. In 2007 cereal production picked up significantly once more, reaching 1,028,875 tons, vegetable production remained static at 712,360 tons, while fruit production declined slightly, to 854,520 tons. In 2008 the total output of cereals reached 713,739 tons; vegetable production totalled 1,037,246 tons and fruit production 958,977 tons. In 2009 cereals output declined to 674,500 tons; vegetable production rose slightly to 1,100,300 tons and fruit production picked up to 988,700 tons. A good harvest in 2010 gave a significant boost to production levels: output of cereals rose to 1,012,900 tons, vegetable production increased to 1,165,000 tons and fruit production reached 1,036,900 tons. By 2012, following the widespread political turbulence, overall production had fallen, with cereals output at 909,741 tons, vegetables at 1,132,852 tons, and fruit production falling to 1,001,411 tons. Yemen had 1.68m. cattle, 9.42m. sheep, 9.16m. goats and 0.44m. camels in 2012.

The true balance between food crops and cash crops in the agriculture of Yemen is difficult to assess accurately because qat is not reliably recorded in official statistics. There is no doubt that the qat bush is by far the most profitable cash crop, although its growers are not eligible for such benefits as concessionary agricultural loans and do not have access to export markets (qat use being banned in neighbouring Arab countries and elsewhere in the world). However, inside Yemen, the chewing of qat leaves is a regular social ritual for the majority of the adult population. Qat-growing occupies a significant proportion of Yemen's best agricultural land and entails weekly irrigation. By 2012, some 167,682 ha were allocated to qat production, representing 11% of all available cultivable land in the country. Correspondingly, its share of total water use had risen to 23%.

Qat grows year-round, permanently occupying land that might have been used for crop rotation, and has no nutritional value. The World Bank has estimated that Yemen's internal trade in qat generates at least 25% of GDP and 16% of employment. A 20% tax on retail sales of qat yielded YR 1,600m. in 1999 despite serious enforcement problems.

A World Bank study of regional water resources, published in 1997, said that the Government had, in effect, contributed to Yemen's water crisis by banning the importation of qat (which is also cultivated in Ethiopia, Somalia and Kenya), banning the importation of fruit and vegetables, and failing to abolish all subsidies on the price of diesel (the main fuel for water pumps). Yemen's Prime Minister acknowledged in mid-1998 that the water crisis was his country's 'greatest problem'. There was, he said, a case for differential pricing in the agricultural sector to curb wasteful usage by qat growers. In May 1999 it was announced that President Saleh had ceased to use qat and had launched a campaign to encourage other prominent Yemenis to follow his example. Qat-chewing in public buildings and during working hours was banned in late 1999. Nevertheless, qat production was officially recorded as having risen to 108,043 metric tons in 2000, from cultivated land totalling 102,934 ha, yielding revenue of YR 64,178m. By 2007 qat production had risen to 147,444 tons, increasing to 165,668 tons in 2008, 173,900 tons in 2009 and 176,400 tons in 2010. By 2012 it had risen further to 190,896 tons.

Critics of qat cultivation in Yemen include experts on water resource depletion. The quantity of rainwater per year in Yemen is estimated at 68,000m.–73,000m. cu m; since very little of it is captured, more than 40% evaporates. The 1997 World Bank study described Yemen as the most 'water-stressed' country in the Middle East and North Africa, with only 176 cu m of water available per head of population per year from renewable underground reserves, compared with a regional average of 1,250 cu m and a world average of 7,500 cu m. ('Availability' in this context is the maximum rate of extraction from aquifers without causing irreversible depletion of reserves.) In 1994 the report said Yemen pumped an estimated 2,800m. cu m of water from aquifers whose sustainable withdrawal rate was 2,100m. cu m per year. With all available surface water resources in full use, more than 60% of Yemen's total 1994 water supply was from aquifers, and 93% of the withdrawals from aquifers were for agricultural use. There were at least 45,000 groundwater wells in Yemen in 1994.

Despite efforts to boost the harvesting of rainwater (see Power and Water), a report in 2010 by the Deutsche Gesellschaft für Technische Zusammenarbeit, a German development organization, recommended that Yemen curtail agricultural output because of its excessive water consumption. The report suggested that Yemen should conserve its water for residential and industrial use, given that the country would never be self-sufficient in food. Another study, by an international non-governmental organization, the Small Arms Survey, claimed that violent conflict over scarce land and water resources was on the rise in Yemen and that 4,000 Yemenis die every year as a direct result of disputes over water and land.

MINING AND ENERGY

Although it does not qualify for membership of the Organization of the Petroleum Exporting Countries (OPEC), Yemen is a producer of crude petroleum and natural gas, revenue from which provides crucial support for the state budget and investment programme. The sector's contribution to GDP rose from 6% in 1994 to 33.7% in 2000, in which year petroleum accounted for 75.8% of the Government's revenue, compared with 64.1% in 1999. However, as Yemen's oil output declined, the sector's contribution to GDP waned, and was just 14.7% in 2008, decreasing further to 13.1% in 2009, according to the Central Bank. By 2011 oil revenues still made up around 70% of total government income. At the end of 2012 Yemen's proven reserves of petroleum (virtually all situated in fields discovered between 1984 and 1993) totalled 3,000m. barrels, according to the *BP Statistical Review of World Energy*.

The discovery in July 1984 of significant petroleum deposits in the Marib/al-Jawf region, in the north-east of the YAR, was followed by discoveries across the border in the neighbouring Shabwa region of the PDRY. Small-scale production of crude petroleum began in the YAR at the end of 1985, and in the PDRY in mid-1987. Talks between the YAR and PDRY Governments on closer economic co-operation led to the establishment in January 1989 of a joint company to administer oil exploration and development rights in a cross-border area totalling 2,200 sq km. At the time of Yemeni unification in May 1990 aggregate oil output averaged 180,000 barrels per day (b/d), of which fewer than 10,000 b/d were produced in the former PDRY's Shabwa region.

After Yemeni unification, more than 10 significant oilfields were discovered in the 1,260 sq km Masila exploration block in the eastern Hadramout region. Yemen's annual average oil output rose from 210,000 b/d in 1993 to 345,000 b/d in 1994 (about 45% of the 1994 total coming from Masila). In the East Shabwa concession area, immediately west of the Masila fields, Total-CFP (the operator for a consortium of French, Kuwaiti, US and Australian oil companies) brought the Kharir oilfield into production at the end of 1997 at an initial rate of 20,000 b/d. However, expectations of production growth in the main Shabwa exploration areas (situated 200 km west of the East Shabwa block) were not fulfilled in the 1990s despite extensive exploration work.

Competition between foreign oil companies for new oil concessions had been strongest in Yemen's 1991–92 licensing round, which notably included Shabwa blocks, regarded at that time as prime development sites. There was a general improvement in 1995–96 in the terms offered to new concession-holders, including an increase of 5% in average cost recovery allowances, and the Government made particular efforts during 1997 to attract new investment in smaller blocks and blocks that had been assessed as marginal on the basis of previous exploration work. In 1997 the state-owned Yemen General Oil and Gas Corpn was authorized to acquire minority equity stakes (of 15% to 25%) in newly awarded exploration blocks. In late 1999 the Government announced that Yemen's next oil-licensing round would incorporate improved incentives for investment, including reductions in concession-holders' initial 'signature' payments, reductions in minimum royalty rates, and increases in cost-recovery allowances. Five onshore and two offshore blocks were opened to bidding on the improved terms in 2000.

Four new blocks in territory bordering Saudi Arabia (and unavailable for exploration until the conclusion of the June 2000 border treaty) were awarded in 2000–01. Seven blocks in other areas of Yemen were included in a licensing round in 2001, and it was announced that up to 40 more blocks were to be made available in 2002. In January 2005 the Minister of Oil and Minerals stated that licensing and exploration would be increased during the coming year to arrest a decline in crude petroleum production in 2004 and subsequently invited bids for seven oil concessions (one offshore and six onshore blocks) across the country. Also in 2005 the Norwegian company DNO announced that its Nabrajah field had begun production, while Austria's OMV reported a significant oil discovery in Shabwa province, which was confirmed as Yemen's largest discovery in recent years. The Ministry signed agreements with a number of international oil companies in 2005–06. Parliament, meanwhile, decided to terminate a Hunt Oil concession in al-Jawf when it expired in November 2005, despite an earlier agreement to extend it by five years, and the Government then approved the transfer of the block to a state-owned firm, Safir. Hunt Oil and ExxonMobil (also of the USA) reacted by filing arbitration proceedings against the Government. Safir eventually won the international arbitration hearing. In a similar move at the end of 2011, a separate, newly formed Yemeni oil company, the Masila Company for Petroleum Exploration and Production (MCPEP), took over Nexen's concession at the Masila field, when its licence expired in December. It was anticipated that Safir would collaborate with the MCPEP on production at the Masila field.

In September 2006 the Ministry of Oil and Minerals launched a new international licensing round. Fourteen blocks were made available and concessions were awarded for eight of them. The remainder failed to attract interest mainly because of their location in the Empty Quarter and the lack of seismic data. In January 2008 the Ministry launched its fourth licensing round, focusing on offshore fields. It accepted 25 bids out of 30 received for exploration rights in 11 offshore oil blocks. Major international oil companies (IOCs), including ExxonMobil, Total, Norway's StatoilHydro and Spain's Repsol, all tendered bids, highlighting the increased viability of offshore exploration and production on account of the sustained high global oil prices. In late 2010 the Government awarded three onshore licences to OMV, DNO and Total. However, owing to the subsequent unrest over the following two years, little activity took place on these concessions. In May 2013 the Government opened another licensing round, for five blocks. The high level of interest from IOCs—some 23 companies registered for pre-qualification—prompted the Government to announce that it would offer a further 15 blocks in due course.

Yemen's total oil output averaged 350,000 b/d in 1995, 355,000 b/d in 1996 and 370,000 b/d in 1997. The Government's reported oil export revenue rose to a record US $1,012m. in 1997, reflecting an increase in production during a period of relatively strong export prices. In the first half of 1998, however, a slump in the world oil market reduced the average price of Yemen's main export grade by 32% (from $17.27 per barrel in January–June 1997 to $11.80 per barrel in January–June 1998). Yemen was one of several non-members of OPEC to make a public pledge of support for OPEC production decreases designed to counteract the 1998 price slump. A March 1998 statement from Yemen's Ministry of Oil and Minerals said that a Yemeni oil production cut-back of 2%–3% was to be introduced (although the state oil corporation continued to forecast an 11% production increase by the end of 1998). In the event, average 1998 oil output was 380,000 b/d (2.7% higher than the 1997 average). In 1999 production increases were reported from several areas (including Masila, where output averaged 210,000 b/d in the second quarter of the year, and Jannah, where output reached 65,000 b/d in the third quarter of the year), while export prices recovered from the depressed levels of 1998. Overall, Yemen's average oil output rose by 4.6% to 395,000 b/d in 1999. In 2000 Yemen's oil output was 160.6m. barrels, from an average of 440,000 b/d. Production in 2001 rose to an average of 458,000 b/d, although this was well below government plans for output levels approaching 500,000 b/d. In 2002 output decreased to an average of 443,300 b/d, but rose again in 2003 to an average of 465,000 b/d. Production then declined to about 400,000 b/d in 2004, but recovered slightly, to 426,000 b/d, in 2005 as output from new fields helped to offset declining returns from older ones. However, in 2006 production declined again, to 390,000 b/d, and it decreased further, to 340,000 b/d, in 2007. The decline continued into 2008, with total daily output averaging just 310,000 b/d, and by the end of 2009 this figure had decreased to 287,000 b/d. Production lowered slightly in 2010, to around 270,000 b/d, before declining dramatically in the first half of 2011, when anti-Government tribesmen destroyed the oil pipeline connecting the Marib field to the export terminal at Ras Isa. By the end of 2011 output was recorded at just 228,000 b/d. Repeated attacks on the pipeline and other oil infrastructure, not just by discontented tribesmen, but also by Islamist militants, had caused considerable disruption to domestic oil supplies throughout that year. This was compounded by the evacuation of foreign employees of oil companies as the unrest deepened, and subsequently by a strike at the Masila field by workers dissatisfied with their severance payments when the MCPEP took over the concession from Nexen. As a result, oil output failed to recover, and, with supply disruptions continuing into 2012, production declined still further, to just 180,000 b/d. Indeed, repeated sabotage on oil infrastructure continued throughout 2012 and into 2013. As a result, Yemen has become increasingly reliant on expensive oil imports.

Yemen has two ageing oil refineries in Aden (which opened in 1954) and in Marib, the former operated by the state-owned Aden Refinery Co and the latter by Yemen Hunt Oil. The Aden Refinery Co, set up by the former PDRY Government when the predominantly export-orientated Aden refinery was nationalized in 1977, obtained crude petroleum-processing contracts from various countries during the 1980s, including Algeria, India, Iran, Iraq, Kuwait, Libya, Saudi Arabia and the USSR. At the time of the Iraqi invasion of Kuwait in August 1990, Iraq (30,000 b/d) and Kuwait (20,000 b/d) were the Aden refinery's principal suppliers of preferentially priced crude petroleum. Part of unified Yemen's own recently developed crude petroleum production (which in mid-1990 came wholly from oilfields in the former YAR) was subsequently diverted from its intended export markets in order to cover the refinery's loss of imports resulting from the UN embargo on trade with Iraq and Iraqi-occupied Kuwait. Only about one-third of the refinery's nominal processing capacity of 170,000 b/d was in use in the early 1990s, when the Government of unified Yemen was seeking financing for a two-phase modernization programme to raise that capacity by 80,000 b/d (the first 30,000 b/d at an estimated cost of US $150m., and the final 50,000 b/d at an estimated cost of $200m.). The Aden refinery was closed for some weeks during and immediately following the 1994 civil war after several of its storage tanks were destroyed in the fighting. There was no major damage to the distillation facilities, and the plant was operating at its normal pre-war production volume by early August 1994. At the end of 1995 the Aden refinery was processing an average 60,000 b/d of domestic crude petroleum and 40,000 b/d of imported crude petroleum. In 1996 plans were drawn up for an upgrade to the refinery. However, after the upgrading project had been subjected to three successive rounds of tendering, the Government decided in late 1997 to seek private investment in the Aden Refinery Co. In December 2000 the Prime Minister said that preparations were being made to seek a private buyer for an initial 51% stake in the project, and the Government reaffirmed its commitment to the project in November 2001. However, by 2007 there had been no progress towards privatization, and in August of that year the Ministry of Oil and Minerals announced that the plans had been abandoned by the Government, with the Aden Refinery Co to remain under public ownership for the foreseeable future.

In December 2002 the Government signed an agreement with the Hadramout Refinery Co, backed by Saudi investors, for a US $300m. facility with a capacity of 40,000 b/d, to be built at Mukalla. In May 2004 a Korean consortium of Samsung Corpn and SK Engineering & Construction was awarded the engineering, procurement and construction (EPC) contract for the refinery. However, in July 2006 it was reported that the Government had decided to terminate the agreement with the investors. In 2007 discussions were initiated with an Indian company, the Oil and Natural Gas Corporation, to construct the plant, but to no effect. In early 2008 plans to build a second, 45,000-b/d refinery at Ras Isa faltered, when Hood Oil, the US company administering the project, put the scheme on hold because of declining crude feedstock coming from the Marib field.

In early 2005 four international companies submitted bids for the EPC contract to build a US $100m. liquefied petroleum gas (LPG) plant at Marib. The same four bidders, and two further contractors, were also invited to tender for the construction of an LPG export terminal at the Red Sea port of Salif. In the same year Denmark's Ramboll was awarded the consultancy contract on a project to build a 565-km natural gas pipeline linking Safir to Marib before splitting into two branches running on to Aden and Hodeida. The pipeline, costing between $450m.–$500m., was to supply gas feedstock to a planned power plant at Marib (see Power and Water) and fuel industrial development in Aden and Hodeida.

At the end of 2007 Yemen had proven reserves of natural gas totalling 490,000m. cu m, discovered both separately and in association with oil by companies drilling in oil concession areas (the main discoveries of non-associated gas having been made in the Marib/al-Jawf and Jannah blocks).

Throughout the first half of the 1990s various proposals were put forward for a major gas development project centred on the export of liquefied natural gas (LNG). In March 1997 the Yemeni legislature approved the establishment of a consortium to organize the planned project. As constituted in October 1997, the consortium comprised Total-CFP (the project leader, with a 36% interest), the state-owned General Gas Corpn (21%), Hunt Oil (15.1%), Exxon (14.5%), and the South Korean companies Yukong (8.4%) and Hyundai (5%). It was envisaged that gas would be piped from Marib to a liquefaction plant on the Gulf of Aden with a production capacity of 6.7m. metric tons per year. However, the consortium's sole memorandum of understanding, with the Turkish company BOTAŞ, was not renewed on its expiry at the end of 1997, by which time many target markets in Asia were experiencing severe economic downturns. In May 2000 the consortium (by then operating under the name Yemen LNG) announced its decision to invite bids for the project's EPC contracts. The published specifications included a liquefaction plant with two LNG trains (each capable of producing 3.1m. tons per year), a 300-km gas supply pipeline and two smaller pipelines. By the end of 2000 the consortium had received several bids for each of the project's construction contracts. However, it had not secured any customers for the LNG that it proposed to produce. Its marketing efforts were similarly unproductive in 2001 and in the first half of 2002, and in June of that year Exxon and Hunt Oil left the consortium (although Hunt Oil later retracted its withdrawal). The project then remained dormant until 2004, when it was reported that the consortium—by then comprising France's Total (with 43%), Yemen Gas (23%), Hunt Oil (18%) and the Korean companies SK Engineering & Construction (10%) and Hyundai (6%)—was bidding to sell gas to South Korea under a long-term supply contract. Offtake agreements were subsequently signed in the first half of 2005 with Korea Gas Corpn (KOGAS), Belgium's Tractebel and Total, prompting the issue of new EPC tenders for the proposed US $2,000m. LNG plant (to be sited at the port of Bal Haf) and its associated gas pipelines. In August 2006 KOGAS purchased 2.88% of shares from Hyundai, increasing its stake in the project to 8.88%, and Punj Lloyd (India) was awarded a sub-contract worth $69m. for the civil and mechanical, electrical and instrumentation works to serve the 6.8m. tons-a-year facility. In September 2005 a team led by Technip (Italy) and JGC Corpn (Japan) was awarded the EPC contract, while the pipeline contract was awarded to A Hak Pijpleidingen of the Netherlands and AMEC Spie Capag of France. Slight delays affected the project in mid-2007, owing both to the Government's arbitration case with Hunt Oil (Hunt Oil owned the Marib field from where the gas feedstock was to be sourced) and to the increased global demand for related construction materials and equipment. However, in November 2008 the liquefaction and export facility at Balhaf was officially inaugurated by President Saleh, and in August 2009 Yemen's first shipment of LNG, totalling some 120,000 cu m, was finally despatched. It is estimated that Yemen's LNG project will provide the country with up to $50,000m. of revenue over its 25-year life-cycle. In April 2010 the facility inaugurated its second production train, raising output to full capacity, and increasing revenues to $370m. per year. In addition, the project employed some 700 Yemeni workers and supported a further 10,000 jobs through its demand for local services and supplies.

Yemen's principal non-hydrocarbon mine and quarry products include rock salt, limestone, marble, gypsum, granite, basalt and clay. This sector contributed only 0.1% of GDP in 2000, when Yemen produced 2.5m. metric tons of quarried stone, 819,000 tons of sand and gravel aggregate, 150,000 tons of salt, and 100,000 tons of crude gypsum. Deposits of copper, nickel, zinc, lead, coal, iron, sulphur, silver, gold and uranium are known to exist. Improved mapping and evaluation of hard mineral resources have been prioritized by the post-unification Government, which has obtained financial assistance from the World Bank, the United Nations Development Programme (UNDP) and IDA for surveying work. The Government is particularly interested in the possibility of Yemen becoming a significant producer of gold, which Soviet surveyors first discovered at Medden (50 km west of Mukalla) in the early 1980s. Gold-prospecting licences were held by Irish, Dutch and

British companies in 1992, and in 1993 prospecting rights in a further 30,000 sq km were granted to a Yemeni company. In 1997 a Canadian company, Menora Resources, carried out a pre-feasibility drilling programme at Medden, where the measured resource of gold was recorded at 280,000 oz. In early 1998 the Government announced that five companies were currently engaged in mineral-prospecting, including exploration for zinc and lead, and that new gold discoveries had been made by Canadian, US and Indonesian prospecting companies. In July 2000 a Canadian company signed an agreement to develop nickel, copper and cobalt deposits in the Haja region. The Yemeni Government signed three memorandums of understanding with Bateman of South Africa in November 2003 to explore for copper, nickel, gold and other minerals in three concession areas. In May 2004 British company Scott Wilson was awarded a contract to conduct a financial feasibility study on a gold-mining project about 110 km north east of San'a. In December 2005 Yemen signed an exploration agreement with the British company ZincOx to mine for zinc at the estimated 12.6m.-ton Jabali deposit; final designs for a zinc oxide facility at the site were completed in early 2007. In early 2008 ZincOx secured the necessary funding, in the form of a US $120m. high-yield bond, in order to initiate the project. Investment in the project was believed to total $75m., with ZincOx holding a 60% interest in the joint venture, while Anglo American PLC (United Kingdom) and Yemeni company Ansan Wikfs (Hadramout) Ltd each retained a 20% stake. ZincOx planned to extract ore at a rate of 800,000 metric tons per year (t/y), to produce up to 70,000 t/y of high-quality zinc oxide. The mine has a life of 12 years and is expected to contribute up to $600m. to the economy. The project was inaugurated in February 2009 and mining operations began in the following month.

Giving a further boost to the mining sector, in January 2008 the Government finally completed its mineral survey. This had revealed significant quantities of gold deposits in the country, particularly in the Harraz mountain massif. The region is estimated to contain about 678 tons of minerals, of which 15% are gold and 11% silver. The survey indicated more than 40 potential gold-mining sites.

MANUFACTURING AND INDUSTRY

The industrial sector, broadly defined to include manufacturing, construction, and the supply of electricity, gas and water, contributed some 13.3% of GDP in 2012. Manufacturing accounted for the largest proportion of this, at 8.9%, followed by construction, with 3.6%.

The state-owned Yemen Corpn for Cement Production and Marketing (also known as Yemen Cement Co) had an installed production capacity of about 1.3m. metric tons per year in mid-2005 at its plants at Bajil (established in 1973), Amran (established in 1982) and Mafraq (established in 1993). Production from these plants was sufficient to supply an estimated 40%–50% of Yemen's annual demand for cement, the balance being supplied by imports from neighbouring countries. Bids were submitted in January 2002 for a contract to add up to 1.2m. tons of new capacity to the Amran plant, the contract being subsequently awarded to Ishikawajima-Harima Heavy Industries of Japan. In June 2004 the Yemen Corpn for Cement Production and Marketing invited bids for a US $100m. contract to expand the Bajil plant to a capacity of 800,000 tons per year (later awarded to China National Machinery and Equipment Import and Export Corpn). In 2005 two private sector projects by Yemen-Saudi joint ventures to build cement plants at Batis and Mukalla began In 2006 the International Finance Corpn extended a $35m. loan to the National Cement Co to support the construction of a greenfield cement plant at al-Anad (about 70 km north of Aden).

The centrepiece of unified Yemen's industrial development strategy is a commercial and industrial free zone development at Aden (the port city having been designated the country's economic capital), modelled on similar initiatives in other developing countries. Inaugurated in May 1991 (at which time 50 industrial projects had already received outline approval), the zone was to be developed in stages over a period of years. A proposal submitted by US consultants in 1993 recommended total investment of US $5,600m. in four phases over a period of 25 years, centred on the development of port infrastructure to take full advantage of Aden's potential as a transshipment centre for the container traffic of regional ports situated further away from the main international shipping lanes. The plan included proposals for new harbour facilities, an airport extension, a new 300-MW gas-turbine power station and new manufacturing infrastructure, and recommended that development should operate on a fully privatized basis. The Yemen Free Zones Public Authority (YFZPA) subsequently announced its intention to seek full privatization of all administrative operations at the port and airport, to countenance full private ownership of the proposed extensions, and to open up Aden's existing port and airport facilities to some form of joint venture participation by private interests.

In March 1996 the YFZPA finalized an agreement whereby a company called Yemen Investment and Development International (Yeminvest—a joint venture between Yemen Holdings, owned by Saudi Arabian private interests, and PSA Corpn, formerly known as the Port of Singapore Authority) became the concession holder and project co-ordinator for the Aden development programme. PSA was to manage and operate a new Aden container terminal (ACT) for 20 years following completion of the first phase of construction, scheduled for March 1999. Costing up to US $280m., the first-phase works included dredging harbour channels, building six quays and a new transshipment terminal, installing a small power plant, equipping the terminal with cranes and other facilities, and providing access roads and other ancillary features. The handling capacity of the terminal would be 500,000 20-ft-equivalent units (TEUs) per year. The ACT opened on schedule in March 1999, on completion of the bulk of the first-phase development work. The ACT's average monthly throughput exceeded 15,000 TEUs in the last quarter of 1999. Annual throughput rose from 247,913 TEUs in 2000 to 377,367 TEUs in 2001, despite a 15% decline in traffic following the events of 11 September 2001. However, the bombing by the militant Islamist organization al-Qa'ida of an oil tanker, the French-flagged *Limburg*, off Mukalla in October 2002, severely dented container traffic into Aden. Throughput at the ACT slumped by some 70% to 115,921 TEUs in 2003. The ACT only managed to regain its former level of activity by 2006, when throughput rose to 397,080 TEUs. This improved further in 2007, when throughput reached 503,325 TEUs. However, by the end of 2008, piracy in the Gulf of Aden was taking its toll on shipping and activity showed signs of slowing. Throughput declined by 2% to 429,197 TEUs, but by early 2009, when piracy was reaching its peak, throughput was starting to slow dramatically, decreasing by almost one-quarter year on year by the end of March. By the end of 2009 total throughput at the port had decreased to 381,834 TEUs, declining further to 370,382 TEUs in 2010. The increasing unrest in 2011 had a negative impact on port activity, and by the end of the year throughput had fallen to just 180,000 TEUs. The easing of political tensions supported the port's recovery in 2012 and container throughput rose significantly over the year, to reach 262,624 TEUs.

Yeminvest withdrew from its long-term agreement to run the ACT in October 2003. In June 2004 the Yemen Ports Authority (in co-operation with the World Bank, which advises the Government on the overall development of the country's ports) awarded a contract to a Dutch firm to manage the process of selecting a new operator for the terminal. Dubai Ports World (DP World) was subsequently awarded the 35-year concession to operate and manage the Aden and neighbouring Ma'alla terminals at the end of 2007, with the details of the agreement finalized in July 2008. In return for a management lease, DP World is required to invest some US $220m. in the development of port facilities in the five years following the start of the lease in November 2008, focusing on the construction of an additional 400-m berth at the ACT. However, debt problems encountered by Dubai World, owner of DP World, put the expansion programme in Aden in doubt, despite Dubai World insisting that it would go ahead. By the end of 2010, with throughput volumes continuing to decline, wider concerns were being raised over the management of the ACT, with speculation arising that DP World was deliberately undermining the competitiveness of the terminal, by increasing fees in order to boost the performance of the other four ports that it owned in the region. DP World countered these allegations, insisting that it had invested considerably in the terminal's expansion. The new Yemeni Government, which was finally established in early 2012 (see History), announced shortly afterwards that it would investigate many of the large contracts signed by the regime of President Saleh. Foremost among these was the DP World contract, which the new Government intimated was mired in corruption. Perhaps sensing an imminent legal tussle, in September DP World announced that it was withdrawing from Aden, and by mid-2013 the port was left without an operator and activity there remained listless.

It was intended that completion of the port facilities should be followed by the development of a 1,350-ha site for export-orientated industries; modernization and improvement of infrastructure and facilities and expansion of cargo-handling capacity at Khormaksar international airport; construction of a new power station; and (as the final phase of the development programme) construction of a World Trade Centre complex including 100,000 sq m of office space and 9,300 sq m of exhibition space. According to Yeminvest's initial revenue projections, the free zone development would be self-financing by its seventh year, with the container port playing an important income-generating role. The Yemeni Government's entitlement to revenue from free zone operations was to increase gradually from 25% to 100% over the 25-year duration of the concession. Construction work on the initial phase of the Aden free zone's industrial and commercial estate (known as Aden Distripark) was completed in 2001. In March Yeminvest signed a memorandum of understanding for a sugar refinery with a capacity of 200,000 metric tons per year of refined sugar and 13,000 tons of molasses (the largest project so far planned for the estate). The scheme collapsed shortly after that following accusations of widespread corruption, but plans for the free zone were resurrected in early 2007, following the award of a large economic support package by international donors at a conference in London the previous November. The Government announced that some of the funds would be allocated to ensuring that the scheme finally got under way.

Yemen's General Investment Authority (GIA) was established in 1991 to encourage and supervise new investment in Yemen (including investment by Yemenis resident abroad), offering an extensive range of tax and other incentives. GIA promotional campaigns have placed particular emphasis on investment in labour-intensive export industries, including the manufacture of textiles, for which Yemen offered the advantage of quota-free access to the EU, the USA and other principal markets.

POWER AND WATER

A main planning priority in the power sector after unification in 1990 was to link the electricity grids of the former YAR and the PDRY. This was finally achieved in July 1997 at a total cost of US $64m. (of which $54m. was provided by the Arab Fund for Economic and Social Development—AFESD). The World Bank estimated that the Public Electricity Corpn's total 1997 installed capacity was a nominal 596 MW, of which only 408 MW was effectively available because of the technical limitations of Yemen's power plants and distribution lines. High growth of energy demand—stimulated partly by subsidized tariffs—had placed Yemen's electricity supply system under severe pressure for some years. San'a had experienced particularly bad power shortages since 1993, and some generating and transmission facilities had suffered damage in the 1994 civil war. In 1997 the Government drew up a $51m. emergency power project to cover Yemen's electricity needs until the year 2001. As submitted to IDA (from which funding was sought), the project envisaged the rapid installation of 30 MW of additional generating capacity at the Dhahban power plant serving San'a; the rehabilitation of 20 MW of existing diesel generating capacity at the same plant; and the improvement of transmission lines to ensure that the plant's increased output was fully available to the grid.

By 2002 Yemen had a total installed generating capacity of about 810 MW. Pending the creation of new capacity, industry sources maintained that power shortages could be partly remedied by recovering the 30% of current electricity output lost as a result of the inefficiency of the national grid. In May 2002 the Yemeni Government signed an agreement for the operation of a proposed independent power project put forward by Marib Power Co Yemen, a joint venture between Delma Power Co (based in the USA) and Consolidated Contractors International Co (based in Greece). Under these proposals, a gas-fired plant with an initial generating capacity of 300 MW would be constructed near Marib and would supply electricity at significantly lower cost than existing oil-fired plants. In March 2003 the Public Electricity Corpn (PEC) invited bids for two associated contracts on the project, the first covering the supply and installation of a 200-km overhead transmission line from Marib to San'a, with the inclusion of two substations, and the second covering the supply and installation of gas turbines for the Marib plant. Germany's Lahmeyer International was chosen in May 2004 by PEC to provide consultancy services on the $230m. plant. In September the contract for the transmission line and substations was awarded to South Korea's Hyundai and to an Iranian contractor. In the same month a consortium of Germany's Siemens and Saudi Arabia's Arabian Bemco Contracting was selected for the $159m. EPC contract for infrastructure work on the first phase of the plant, which was being financed by the AFESD and the Saudi Fund for Development. In May 2006 Aggreko International of the United Kingdom signed a two-year contract with the Government to supply 50 MW of extra generating capacity to power the infrastructure development. The project received a further boost in November 2007, when Saudi Arabia announced the offer of a grant worth $101m. to assist with the plant's funding. In the same month the French development agency Agence Française de Développement (AFD) provided Yemen with a $37m. concessional loan to help build capacity in Yemen's electricity sector. Separately, the AFD, in collaboration with the World Bank and the Islamic Development Bank, agreed to provide $49.5m. to fund a rural electrification project. In March 2007 Aggreko secured the contract to provide 50 MW of generating capacity for two years to power stations in Amran, Aden, Taiz and Lahij. In September 2009 construction of the Marib power station was completed and the project was inaugurated in April 2010. However, acts of sabotage on transmission lines surrounding the plant prompted temporary closures from May. At the end of 2012 Yemen was producing a total of 1,532 MW.

Major water supply initiatives in post-unification Yemen included a project to bring drinking water to 45,000 people in over 100 villages to the north of Aden. The first phase of this project, involving the drilling of wells in the coastal Wadi Bani and the construction of the means of raising the water 1,500 m to the Laboos plateau, began in late 1991, as did the Radaa water supply and sanitation project, involving the supply of drinking water to some 30,000 people. Aden's water supply system and sewerage facilities were severely disrupted during the civil war in 1994, and serious water shortages continued to be reported three months after the end of the fighting in the city. UN agencies identified an emergency requirement for essential repairs costing up to US $5m. to water and sewerage infrastructure. New water and sewerage schemes under consideration in 1996 included the construction of a wastewater treatment plant in San'a (to be financed by the World Bank, the AFESD and the OPEC Fund for International Development). Two loan agreements ($25m. from the World Bank and KD 18m. from the AFESD) were subsequently approved by the Yemeni legislature in May 1999, and the first phase of the wastewater project was put out to tender in 2001.

According to a World Bank study, about 88% of Yemen's urban households had access to piped water supplies in 1997, although such supplies were often erratic and interruptions of up to eight weeks could be experienced in certain areas. In some large cities, including Taiz and San'a, more than one-fifth of the population depended on private sector water suppliers. It was estimated that two-thirds of all water consumed in San'a in 1997 was provided by these largely unregulated private suppliers. About 90% of Yemen's urban households were estimated to have access to adequate wastewater facilities, although in the majority of cases these took the form of closed pit systems rather than public sewer networks. The disposal of solid waste was a particular problem in urban Yemen in the mid-1990s, as municipal collections tended to be limited to market areas and main streets, leading to accumulations of rubbish in side streets and to uncontrolled dumping of waste outside towns. Laws on environmental protection and waste management were introduced in 1995 to provide a basis for improving this situation. A local consortium was awarded a US $22m. contract in May 2005 to supply and install a water supply and sewerage disposal system to serve about 300,000 residents in Taiz. The project was financed by the World Bank.

In March 2004 the World Bank approved a US $40m. credit to Yemen for a groundwater and soil conservation project to improve water use efficiency and increase surface water and groundwater availability. An additional $15m. to support this project was received in July 2008, at around the same time that the Government produced its rainwater-harvesting plan. The Bank approved a further $50m. credit in 2006 to support power projects, while the Saudi Fund for Development announced the establishment of a financing mechanism for electricity generation projects in Yemen, starting with two facilities in San'a and Aden.

A plan entitled A Road Map to Harvesting Rainwater in Yemen, drafted in mid-2008 by the Ministry of Water and the Environment, highlighted San'a as a priority target. The plan aimed to collect and reuse 70% of rainwater in San'a by 2012 and to use it to feed the severely depleted San'a basin and provide drinking and irrigation water to the city. These water capture techniques would be rolled out to the rest of the country, with a target of collecting 40% of the rainwater by 2020, while by that time it was hoped that 100% of the rainwater in the main conurbations, such as San'a and Taiz, would be gathered and harvested. The plan is based on updated data collected by the Ministry in 2005, published in the National Strategy for Reforming the Water Sector. The data showed that the amount of water used in the country in 2000 was 3,400m. cu m—about 25% more than renewed water resources. Current estimates suggest that Yemen today has an annual 'water deficit' of 900m. cu m. However, the city of Mukalla in the Hadramout received a boost in mid-2009, when a huge underground aquifer was discovered near the city. It will provide the city with 50 years-worth of potable water and its nine wells can produce up to 30 litres of water per second.

TRANSPORT AND COMMUNICATIONS

Transportation, storage and communications contributed some 18.1% of GDP in 2011, according to official figures. In 2012 the total length of Yemen's asphalted roads was 16,811 km, around 14% of the total road network. In 2010 some 872,702 road vehicles were in use. Road-building and maintenance are important development priorities and have been funded to a large extent by foreign aid donors in recent years. After Yemeni unification in 1990 there was an increased emphasis on the improvement of road links across the former YAR–PDRY border. In 1993 the Government of Oman agreed to finance a highway across Oman's newly opened border with Yemen. Road-building schemes scheduled to go to tender in 1998 included 180 km in the south (between Aden and Mukalla) and 65 km in the west (between Salif and Hodeida), both of which were to be financed by the World Bank. More than 800 km of existing roads were included in upgrading plans under consideration in 1998. In July 2003 an Australian firm, Snowy Mountains Engineering Corpn, was awarded a 16-month consultancy contract for a major rural roads development project to be funded by the World Bank. The AFESD signed a US $52m. loan agreement with the Yemeni Government in December that year to finance the Dhamar road project, a 250-km construction scheme. The design tender for a fly-over link between the ACT and Ma'alla port was under preparation in June 2006; estimated at $55m., the project constitutes part of Yemen's National Highways and Rural Access masterplan, designed by Halcrow (United Kingdom) for the Ministry of Public Works and Urban Development. Proposals to build a highway between Aden and the border with Saudi Arabia advanced in June 2003 as the Ministry awarded a contract to draw up feasibility and design studies. In 2013 it was reported that the Government had secured some $550m. of grant finance from the Saudi Fund for Development and the World Bank towards the first of three phases of construction work on the 710-km highway. The first phase was to link Aden with Taiz, the second Taiz with San'a and the third San'a with the border region.

The port of Aden, developed around a natural deep harbour, was ideally placed to benefit from the growth of international Suez Canal traffic during the period of British colonial rule. Its trade was hit especially hard by the closure of the Canal from 1967 to 1975 and the subsequent failure of the PDRY Government to respond adequately to changing shipping patterns (including the rapid growth of containerization). The first phase of a major modernization and expansion of Aden's port facilities was completed in 1999 (see Manufacturing and Industry). The port's existing freight and distribution services were transferred to seven private contractors in mid-1998 as part of the Government's privatization programme. The volume of imports passing through Aden's established port facilities (i.e. excluding traffic through the newly opened container terminal) exceeded 1.7m. metric tons in 1999, having doubled since 1997. The main port serving the easternmost region of Yemen is Mukalla, an important fishing centre with deep-water harbour facilities developed during the 1980s. The region's main oil export terminal is situated about 35 km east of Mukalla. The main port on Yemen's Red Sea coast is Hodeida, which was greatly expanded in the 1970s and 1980s in line with the growth in the import trade of the former YAR. The selection of Aden as unified Yemen's commercial capital in 1990 implied some slowdown in the future expansion of port facilities at Hodeida. The port of Mocha, situated south of Hodeida (and therefore closer to Aden), cancelled many of its own expansion plans after unification. In contrast, the port of Salif, north of Hodeida, benefited in the 1990s from its proximity to Yemen's Red Sea oil export terminal at Ras Isa. In January 2003 the World Bank approved a US $23m. loan for the first phase of a 12-year, three-part Port Cities Development Programme to invest a total of $96m. in infrastructure and facilities in Aden, Hodeida and Mukalla.

Aden's international airport at Khormaksar was extensively upgraded in the late 1980s with Soviet financial assistance. However, its terminal building, capable of handling 250,000 passengers annually, was damaged during the 1994 civil war. Repairs to the terminal, as well as the construction of a new control tower and related technical facilities, were included in a World Bank-supported airport rehabilitation project, which was put out to tender at the beginning of 1998. In June 1999 a US $24m. contract was awarded for the project, which was scheduled for completion over a period of 30 months. Yemen's other international airports are at San'a, Hodeida, Taiz and Mukalla. Plans for upgrading San'a airport were approved in 2002. By July 2005 several companies had submitted bids to build a third terminal, and in March 2006 China's Beijing Urban Construction Investment Development Co was awarded the $114.7m. EPC contract.

Yemen's national carrier, Yemen Airways or Yemenia, was established in May 1996 through the merger of the former YAR airline (also called Yemenia) and the former PDRY airline (Al-Yemen, previously known as Alyemda). The Government holds a 51% shareholding in the merged airline, while the remaining 49% is held by Saudi Arabia.

Yemen has modern international telecommunications links via satellite stations and microwave relays, as well as relatively good links between major centres within the country. However, many smaller towns and rural areas still had fairly limited telephone networks in the mid-1990s, while there was a generally inadequate provision of lines within urban centres. Overall, Yemen had only 1.29 fixed telephone lines per 100 inhabitants in 1996. There were 8,800 cellular telephone subscribers in the same year (although mobile telecommunications services, suspended during the 1994 civil war, were not restored until September 1996). Contracts worth US $3m. were awarded in November 1996 for an expansion of the telephone network within San'a and the upgrading of links between San'a and other population centres. In late 1997 the French company Alcatel was awarded a $14m. contract to install 82,000 new lines throughout the country. Alcatel subsequently won a contract to install a modern telecommunications system on Socotra island. The provision of fixed telephone lines by the state-owned Public Telecommunications Corpn totalled 417,100 (2.38 per 100 inhabitants) in 2000. According to a report published by the Communications and Information Technology Commission in March 2006, compound annual growth in the country's telecommunications sector had achieved 15% over the previous five years, while mobile telephone and fixed-line penetration rates were 57% and 16%, respectively. By the end of 2010 figures from the International Telecommunication Union showed that there were 46 mobile telephone subscribers for every 100 inhabitants, compared with just 14 in 2006. By 2012 there were 13.9m. mobile subscribers, more than one-half of the population. Internet usage also increased significantly, from just 1.3 users per 100 people in 2006, to 11 users per hundred people in 2010 and more than 17 in 2012. Conversely, the number of fixed-line subscribers per 100 inhabitants had declined slightly, from 4.6 in 2006 to 4.4 in 2010. By 2012 there were 1.1m. fixed line subscribers.

International telephone services are provided by TeleYemen, of which 51% was owned by the United Kingdom's Cable & Wireless and 49% by the Public Telecommunications Corpn until the end of 2003, when Cable & Wireless withdrew from the venture. France Télécom was awarded a five-year contract to manage TeleYemen, beginning in January 2004, and Cable & Wireless's stake was bought back by the Yemeni Government. In 1999 Yemen's analogue mobile telephone network (set up in 1992) had 18,000 subscribers, more than 60% of them based in San'a. A new mobile satellite communications service, serving the hydrocarbons, agricultural and tourism sectors, was licensed in June 1999. In the same month the Government announced its intention to seek two service providers to set up competing Global Systems for Mobile Communications (GSM) networks in Yemen. The two GSM contracts were awarded in July 2000. The two GSM operators, SabaFon and Spacetel Yemen (now MTN Yemen), launched their services in February 2001. In late 2002 SabaFon, with more than 100,000 subscribers, awarded a contract to Siemens of Germany to expand its mobile network. By early 2003 Spacetel Yemen provided coverage to about 60% of the population, and in March the company selected Alcatel to expand its network to provide capacity for over 300,000 GSM subscribers across the entire country. It was reported in mid-2004 that the Ministry of Communications and Information Technology would launch a public tender for a third mobile licence, rather than invite local operators to bid, in a move prompted by the imminent expiry of the four-year exclusive rights agreement with the two incumbent operators, SabaFon and Spacetel Yemen. In May 2005 the Ministry invited international operators to tender for the third licence by early August. The winner of the tender was to have a majority interest in the new operator, with the remaining stake likely to be offered for public subscription. In October a consortium comprising China Mobile and local Yemeni investors (Unitel) was awarded the licence with a bid of US $150m. It was then reported that Unitel was unable to pay the costs. The Government cancelled the award of the concession, and in early 2006 invited Omantel (the second highest bidder) to negotiate terms for the operating licence. However, in July Kuwait Finance and Investment Co and Saudi Arabia's House for Integrated Technology and Systems (HITS) acquired a stake in Unitel, and subsequently reached an agreement with the Government restoring the mobile concession to Unitel. Alcatel was meanwhile awarded a contract by the Public Telecommunications Corpn to supply and integrate a network operation centre for its fixed and mobile networks. By 2012 there were four mobile operators in the country: Yemen Mobile, Sabafon, MTN, and Y.

TOURISM

In 1995 there were 61,400 tourist arrivals in unified Yemen, more than one-half of them from European countries, generating an estimated revenue of US $50m. Yemen's largest tourism company, Universal Travel and Tourism, had links with some 300 overseas tour operators in Europe, the USA and Japan in 1995, when several major hotel developments were in progress to cater for a projected rise in visitor numbers. The main developer was the Tourism Investment Co (50% owned by Universal Travel and Tourism). Yemen earned around $55m. from tourism in 1996, when there were 229 registered hotels in the country. An Egyptian-led consortium submitted proposals in mid-1998 for a tourism resort development on the thinly populated Yemeni island of Socotra (where conservation of the natural environment was an issue of major concern to international environmental experts).

Tourist numbers decreased by one-third, to 58,370, in 1999 as a result of adverse publicity about Yemen's internal security situation, remaining relatively depressed in 2000 as kidnappings and terrorist attacks continued to be reported. Financial aid was secured from the EU in August 2000 for the development of a detailed action plan to revive Yemen's tourism industry. The decline in tourist numbers coincided with a growth in the provision of hotel accommodation. The number of hotels in Yemen doubled between 1996 and 2000, with the result that occupancy rates of 30% or less were reported in 2000. However, the September 2001 attacks on the US mainland and the subsequent US-led 'war on terror' did not have the expected adverse effect on tourism and by 2003 the industry appeared to have partly recovered; arrivals in that year increased to 154,667 and estimated revenue from tourism was US $139m. Some two-thirds of tourist arrivals in 2003 came from other countries in the Middle East region; the number of arrivals from Europe and North America remained considerably lower than in the late 1990s. There were 273,732 arrivals in 2004 and, according to official figures, 284,221 tourists visited the country in 2005 (raising $262m. in receipts); the World Tourism Organization reported the much higher figures of 336,030 arrivals in 2005 and 382,332 arrivals in 2006. Most visitors came from Saudi Arabia (accounting for 46.7% of the total in 2006). Total visitor arrivals had risen to 433,921 by 2009, according to the Ministry of Tourism, bringing in revenue of $903m. Despite persistent political insecurity throughout 2010, tourist arrivals increased further to 536,020, according to government figures, generating revenue of $1,161m. in that year. However, widespread unrest and conflict in 2011 deterred visitors and tourist numbers fell to just 387,498 in 2011, before recovering to 459,329 in 2012.

BUDGET, INVESTMENT AND FINANCE

After unification, the respective currencies of the two former Yemeni states were legal tender in the Republic of Yemen and could be used at a rate of 1 (South) Yemeni dinar = 26 (North) Yemeni riyals until 20 June 1996, when the old dinar was formally abolished and the riyal became the sole currency unit for the unified Yemen. In mid-1993, when the standard official exchange rate was US $1 = YR 12.01 (as it had been since February 1990), the black market value of the Yemeni currency was approximately $1 = YR 46 (reflecting, in part, the country's annual inflation rate of about 200% at that time). In 1992 the Government had introduced a 'customs rate' of $1 = YR 18 for all non-essential imports, and in May 1993 it had introduced an 'incentive rate' of YR 25 to the dollar for oil companies and tourists.

In the unified state's first budget, for 1991, expenditure was projected at YR 50,980m. (compared with an aggregate figure of YR 46,256m. in 1990) and revenue at YR 35,218m. (YR 24,704m. in 1990). The resultant forecast deficit of YR 15,762m. represented a 27% reduction against the 1990 combined deficit of YR 21,552m. The biggest allocation in the 1991 budget was for defence (YR 12,700m.), followed by investment and development (YR 11,000m.) and education (YR 8,300m.). The investment and development allocation did not include loans and grants from external sources, which were seen as crucial for offsetting losses attributable to the Gulf crisis.

The 1992 budget provided for estimated revenue of YR 45,778m. and expenditure of YR 58,114m., and thus for a deficit of YR 12,336m. The Government's financial projections for the year envisaged: that its foreign exchange resources would total US $2,185m. to meet anticipated commitments of $2,349m. (as against resources of $1,836m. and outgoings of $2,212m. in 1991); that imports of wheat, flour, rice and essential drugs would cost $368m.; that all foreign debt obligations would be met in 1992; and that defence spending would be reduced by 12% compared with 1991. The Government did not publish budget proposals for 1993, and was assumed to be organizing its finances on a month-to-month basis, using its 1992 spending as a guideline for the current year. According to press reports (said to be based on internal Ministry of Finance records), actual spending in 1992 had totalled YR 58,060m. (of which YR 53,637m. was current spending), while actual revenue had amounted to only YR 32,008m. (about one-third of estimated GNI). The largest single component of expenditure in 1992 was the public sector salary bill, reported to total YR 32,735m. In 1994 the Government again failed to reach any agreement on a national budget, and was assumed to be maintaining a form of month-to-month accounting system until May, when established procedures were disrupted by the onset of civil war.

According to estimates published by independent Yemeni economists in January 1994, the Government spent YR 74,000m. in 1993 and collected revenue of YR 32,000m., leaving a deficit of YR 42,000m., equivalent to more than one-third of GDP (which was estimated at between YR 110,000m. and YR 120,000m.). It was not known how the budget deficit had been financed. Following the end of the civil war in July 1994, the Government stated that it planned to issue bonds to raise funds for post-war reconstruction work. The Yemeni currency's unofficial exchange rate against the US dollar, which had declined to YR 80 before the outbreak of hostilities, decreased below YR 100 for the first time during June 1994. Retrospective budget statistics for 1994, published long after the end of that year, showed total revenue of YR 41,384m. and total expenditure of YR 85,875m. The overall deficit was YR 44,491m.

In 1995 the Government prepared a formal budget (approved by the legislature on 30 April) providing for total expenditure of YR 111,128m. and total revenue of YR 89,646m., leaving a deficit of YR 21,482m. It had previously been announced in December 1994 that capital spending in 1994 would total around YR 35,000m., of which YR 20,000m. would be spent on post-war reconstruction and infrastructural development. The 1995 budget was preceded by a package of economic measures designed to limit the size of the budget deficit (which would otherwise have reached an estimated YR 60,000m.). On 30 March a unified official exchange rate of YR 50 per US dollar was introduced, and on 7 May local banks were authorized to carry out currency trading at prevailing free-market exchange rates (which remained far weaker than the new official rate).

Following talks with delegations from the World Bank and the IMF, the Government announced in late May 1995 that it was drawing up a five-year plan to restructure the economy over the period 1996–2000. The draft plan envisaged the flotation of the riyal within three years; progressive withdrawal of price subsidies on basic goods, including grain, rice and flour; liberalization of the food distribution system; far-reaching administrative reforms, including some decentralization measures; full harmonization of the northern and southern legal systems; and the introduction of a privatization programme (to be followed by the establishment of a stock market). Joint public-private sector ventures would be encouraged in infrastructural and other projects, and particular efforts would be made to secure high levels of private investment in labour-intensive projects. Seven publicly owned companies in Aden (five of which were food-processing concerns) were earmarked for early privatization, as were a number of small-scale power generation facilities. The Government was expected to finalize the content of the five-year plan after further consultations with representatives of the Bretton Woods institutions, which were understood to favour a 50% reduction in public sector employment and a two-year phasing-out period for all government price subsidies. The Yemeni Government, for its part, was hoping that IMF/World Bank financial assistance for structural reforms would be complemented by measures to secure a reduction in Yemen's external indebtedness.

In July 1995 the Central Bank of Yemen raised its maximum deposit rate from 9% to 22% to stimulate savings in local currency, and used an estimated US $27m. of its foreign assets to support the free-market exchange rate of the riyal, which had declined in late June to its lowest ever level of YR 165 to the dollar (a level previously reached on the unofficial currency market in April, prior to the authorization of free-market currency dealing through the banking system). In mid-July Yemen's Prime Minister said that the public finances were currently showing a slightly smaller deficit than had been forecast in the 1995 budget, while a senior World Bank official expressed strong confidence in government economic policy and foresaw a tripling of World Bank assistance to Yemen if the Government moved quickly to implement key structural reforms. The free-market exchange rate per dollar strengthened to YR 55 during August, before declining to YR 114 in November and YR 130 in December. At the beginning of December the Central Bank held its first ever auction of treasury bills, having announced that it would be issuing short-dated bills with a total face value of YR 12,000m. over the next six months, with the aim of reducing excess liquidity in the country's economy.

In January 1996 the Government announced the immediate abolition of the official exchange rate of YR 50 per dollar, while asserting its readiness to intervene in the currency market if the riyal's free-market value weakened beyond 'the real and practical rate'. (At the same time the so-called customs exchange rate—now the main indicator of current government estimates of the 'real and practical' value of the currency—was devalued to YR 100 per dollar.) The Central Bank was authorized to use up to US $480m. of foreign reserves to support the riyal during the first 15 months of the floating exchange rate regime. Intervention by the Central Bank caused the exchange rate to strengthen to YR 100 per dollar at some points during the first quarter of 1996. In April, when the Central Bank did not intervene in the local currency market, the rate declined to YR 134 per dollar.

As well as abolishing the official exchange rate at the beginning of 1996, the Government reduced official price subsidies for many basic foodstuffs. Market prices rose sharply, and some commodities were in short supply for a time as a result of hoarding prompted by expectations of future price increases. In January the Government announced that electricity prices were to rise by 50%–100% and water charges by 40%–60%, depending on consumption. Prices of oil products and domestic gas were also increased, although the price increase for diesel (originally 100%) was reduced to 33% after protest action by farmers.

The 1996 budget provided for expenditure of YR 181,416m. (a 63.2% increase over the previous budget) and revenue of YR 155,886m. (an increase of 73.9%), resulting in a deficit of YR 25,530m. (19% less than the 1995 budget deficit). The spending allocations included YR 1,000m. to alleviate the severity of economic reforms for the most vulnerable sections of the population. A January 1996 meeting of multilateral, regional and bilateral donors commended Yemen's current economic policies and pledged a total of US $500m. of new funding in 1996 ($350m. in support of structural reforms and $150m. to finance development projects). The Arab Monetary Fund was to provide $68m. under a loan agreement signed in November 1995. A 15-month stand-by credit of SDR 132m. (about $194m.) was formally approved by the IMF in March 1996, and the World Bank approved an $80m. structural-reform programme in April, to be supplemented by further credits for a number of civil works projects designed to provide short-term employment for labourers. It was announced in June that the Government was to set up a $20m. Social Development and Employment Fund, through which investment in job creation and related programmes would be channelled.

In July 1996 the Government finalized its development plan for the period 1996–2000, which included a GDP growth target of 7.2% per annum. Oil and gas production was targeted to grow by 55% during the period of the plan. It was envisaged that total investment would amount to YR 818,000m. (more than US $5,800m. at the prevailing exchange rate). Of this, nearly YR 390,000m. represented foreign investment in the oil and gas sector (three-quarters of which was for the planned LNG export scheme). There was YR 207,000m. of foreign aid,

YR 121,600m. of public investment and the balance (nearly YR 100,000m.) came from private sector investment.

As originally adopted, Yemen's 1997 budget provided for total expenditure of YR 313,985m. and total revenue of YR 301,222m., leaving a deficit of YR 12,763m. However, additional expenditure of YR 12,610m. was approved by the legislature in September, increasing the final 1997 budget deficit to YR 25,373m. When capital items were excluded, the revised 1997 budget was in surplus by YR 2,690m. on the current account. The Central Bank's foreign exchange reserves increased from US $564m. at the end of 1995 to $969m. at the end of 1996 and stood at $1,072m. in mid-1997. The currency exchange rate averaged around YR 130 to the dollar in the year to mid-1997. The Central Bank's minimum interest rate on riyal bank deposits (which had been 20% in April 1997) was reduced to 12% in August and 11% in December.

In pursuance of its structural reform programme, the Government introduced substantial price increases for fuel, wheat and flour at the start of July 1997, while at the same time increasing public sector wages by 10%. In September the Government announced its intention to establish an official stock exchange in early 1998 and to begin preparations to privatize the National Bank of Yemen (established in 1970 through the nationalization of foreign commercial banks' operations in the PDRY).

At the end of October 1997 the IMF approved a US $512m. loan and credit package in support of the Government's economic programme for the period 1997–2000. The package comprised SDR 264.8m. ($366m.) in loans under the IMF's Enhanced Structural Adjustment Facility, plus a credit of SDR 105.9m. ($146m.) under the Extended Fund Facility. The objectives of the medium-term strategy for 1997–2000 were to achieve average non-oil GDP growth of 6% per annum in real terms; to keep the core inflation rate at or below 5% per annum; to restrict the external current account deficit to 2% of GDP; and to maintain sufficient foreign exchange reserves to cover 4.5 months of imports. The budget deficit was to be limited to an average 2% of GDP. The structural adjustment process was to involve reorienting spending towards social sectors and infrastructure; reforming direct and indirect taxation; eliminating price subsidies; introducing administrative, civil service and financial sector reforms; implementing a 'rapidly moving and broad privatization programme'; and taking steps to 'enhance the competitive environment'. The World Bank approved two new loans in November 1997: SDR 58.9m. ($80m.) to assist the structural reform process in the financial and banking sector and SDR 17.7m. ($24.7m.) to support rural development in southern Yemen.

Yemen's 1998 budget provided for an 11.7% increase in total revenue, to YR 336,583m., while expenditure was set at YR 350,054m. (7% higher than the revised 1997 total). The resultant deficit of YR 13,471m. was wholly attributable to capital spending, as the current account was expected to show a surplus of YR 31,028m. The central assumption in the 1998 revenue estimates was that crude petroleum prices would average US $18 per barrel in that year. In practice, oil prices decreased by around one-third in the opening months of 1998 (see Mining and Energy), with the result that Yemen's budget deficit stood at YR 36,200m., instead of an expected YR 4,400m., at the end of April.

In April 1998 the Government announced forthcoming 40% increases in wheat and flour prices, and stated that it intended to phase out all subsidies on these items by the end of the century. Further price rises in June, affecting various subsidized commodities including gasoline, kerosene, bottled gas and basic foodstuffs, sparked protest demonstrations in San'a and several other urban centres. The Government raised public sector wages by 15% from the start of July, having secured IMF approval for a higher 1998 budget deficit (5% of GDP) than had originally been targeted. There was an increase in 1998 in kidnappings of foreigners and government officials by armed tribesmen in rural areas, reportedly aimed at publicizing grievances over low levels of development spending. There was also a reported increase in petty damage to oil pipelines by disaffected tribesmen.

Yemen made it known in 1998 that Saudi Arabia had begun to issue entry visas to Yemeni workers for the first time since the Gulf War, although Yemenis were now required to have Saudi sponsors and to obtain work and residence permits (requirements that had previously been waived for Yemenis). An estimated 400,000 Yemenis were already working in Saudi Arabia in early 1998. There was no expectation of a large-scale influx of Yemenis into Saudi Arabia at this time, not least because the Saudi economy was itself adversely affected by the sharp downturn in world oil prices.

The 1999 budget provided for expenditure of YR 335,500m. (4.1% less than in 1998) and revenue of YR 294,400m., leaving a deficit of YR 41,100m. In contrast to the situation in 1998, when revenue decreased far below budgeted levels because of depressed oil export prices, the outlook in mid-1999 was for above-budget revenue in the current year, reflecting the unexpectedly strong recovery of the oil market since the end of 1998. An IMF report issued in March 1999 noted the severe impact of reduced oil income on all sectors of Yemen's economy in 1998, the final fiscal deficit in 1998 being equivalent to about 6% of GDP, while the estimated 1998 inflation rate was around 11% and GDP growth was below 3%, in real terms. In July 1999 the IMF was forecasting a fiscal deficit equivalent to around 3% of GDP in 1999, coupled with inflation of less than 10% and real growth of 4% in non-oil GDP. By that month a total of SDR 153m. (US $206m.) had been approved for disbursement under the October 1997 IMF support programme for Yemen.

In April 1999 the Government raised public sector salaries while reducing some price subsidies. In the following month the prices of kerosene, fuel oil and bottled gas were increased. The currency exchange rate declined to YR 170 per US dollar in June, necessitating an increase in the minimum interest rate for riyal bank deposits (which had been moving upwards since October 1998) to 20%—a level last seen in 1997. At the same time the minimum proportion of deposits that banks were required to hold in riyals was raised from 10% to 15%. In mid-August 1999 the currency exchange rate was YR 148 per dollar. Against a background of strong improvement in the national finances, the benchmark interest rate was reduced in stages, standing at 13% in July 2000. In early August 2000 the exchange rate was YR 156 per dollar. Yemen's budget for 2000 provided for expenditure of YR 422,250m. and revenue of YR 388,950m., leaving a deficit of YR 33,300m. Oil revenue was expected to total around YR 246,520m. in that year.

In March 2001 the IMF estimated that the actual 2000 budget out-turn was likely to show a surplus equivalent to 9% of GDP, compared with a deficit equivalent to 0.4% of GDP in 1999. While acknowledging that strong growth in oil export earnings was the main factor in the transformation of the public finances in 2000, the IMF welcomed the Yemeni authorities' efforts 'to restrain public expenditures in the face of rising pressures for a relaxation of the adjustment effort'. Yemen's budget for 2001 provided for expenditure of YR 501,882m. and revenue of YR 487,843m., leaving a deficit of YR 14,039m. The budget's oil revenue projections reportedly assumed an average export price of US $22 per barrel in 2001. The Government rejected demands put forward in the legislature and the press for an additional YR 20,000m. of expenditure (based on a higher oil price projection). In July 2001 the Government took the unpopular step of raising the price of diesel fuel from YR 10 to YR 17 per litre as part of its subsidy reduction programme.

The approved budget for 2002 provided for expenditure of YR 531,829m. (a 6% increase over 2001) and revenue of YR 482,021m. (1% less than in 2001), the resulting projected deficit of YR 49,808m. being equivalent to 2.4% of anticipated GDP (compared with an out-turn surplus of 2.8% in 2001). Priority was given to augmenting allocations for defence (to YR 104,844m.) and internal security (to YR 26,300m.) to finance Yemen's anti-terrorism endeavours, although the budget also provided for the implementation of outstanding economic reforms. Approval of the budget in January 2002 was accompanied by the enactment of a law on the introduction of a GST, although implementation was deferred pending a review of the indirect taxation system. It was subsequently announced that the GST, which attracted widespread public antipathy, was to come into effect on 1 July 2005. The exchange rate in August 2002 was YR 176 per dollar. The Central Bank's foreign exchange reserves stood at US $3,659m. at the end of April 2002, compared with $2,953m. at the end of January 2001.

The budget for 2003, approved in January, projected a deficit of YR 64,000m., which represented 3% of anticipated nominal GDP. It provided for total revenue of YR 604,300m. (with petroleum exports accounting for some 34% of this figure) and for expenditure of YR 668,400m. At the end of 2002 foreign exchange reserves had reached US $4,365.6m.

In 2003 the Central Bank issued a circular raising the reserve requirement on foreign currency deposits with the banks operating in the country from 10% to 20%. In October of that year the Government approved the draft budget for 2004. It forecast a deficit of YR 63,500m. (or 3% of nominal GDP), based on expenditure of YR 744,600m. and revenue of YR 681,100m. Foreign exchange reserves increased to US $4,982.0m. by the end of 2003.

The draft budget for 2005 was approved by the Government in October 2004, and reportedly forecast a 12% increase in expenditure, to YR 836,400m. Revenue was expected to rise by 16%, to YR 791,000m., leaving a budget deficit of 3% of GDP. Foreign exchange reserves had risen to US $5,613.5m. by the end of 2004. In its March 2005 appraisal of the Yemeni economy (see Introduction), the IMF was critical of the Government's management of public expenditure, stating that very little had been done to improve internal control mechanisms, budget execution or fiscal reporting. In December 2005 parliament finally approved the 2006 budget after protracted debate. Revenue was expected to increase by 38%, to YR 1,052,000m., and expenditure by 40%, to YR 1,180,000m., resulting in a budget deficit equivalent to more than 3.5% of GDP. The higher deficit forecast reflected the adoption of a national wage strategy (see Introduction). Also in December Al Watani Bank for Trade and Investment was declared bankrupt in the wake of allegations of irregularities, raising concerns about the precarious nature of Yemen's banking system.

In July 2006 the Government approved the draft of a national planning and development strategy for the period 2006–10, focusing on increasing the rate of economic growth to over 7% per year, raising Yemen's human development profile from the low- to middle-group of countries, and halving the level of poverty by 2015. A proportion of the increased revenues from oil and LNG was meanwhile being channelled into improving social infrastructure, such as a scheme to develop a new medical centre near San'a, as part of the Government's second five-year development plan. Meanwhile, in a bid to attract higher levels of foreign investment into Yemen, the Government amended legislation governing commercial transactions so as to allow foreign interests to trade with one another within Yemen; prior to this reform, the law had required at least one trading partner to be local.

The fiscal out-turn in 2006 showed a very small surplus—the first since 2001. Revenues totalled YR 1,500m., while expenditure reached YR 1,400m. However, owing to a sustained decline in oil revenues, the 2007 budget projected a deficit of some 5.3% of GDP. This projection was in fact surpassed, with the actual end-of-year data showing a budget deficit of YR 251m., equivalent to 5.8% of GDP. The 2008 budget envisaged a worsening of this position, with the budget widening further to 7.6% of GDP, as Yemen's oil production continued its decline. However, in the event, the oil price surged during the first three-quarters of 2008, reaching record highs, and consequently the Government's fiscal position improved slightly, with the deficit narrowing to YR 232m., equating to 6.1% of GDP. Nevertheless, with the subsequent decrease in the oil price and the continued decline in oil production, the 2009 budget foresaw the widening of the deficit once again, to 7.4% of GDP. In an attempt to reduce expenditure, the Government announced plans to curtail spending on development projects, but as the oil price continued its precipitous decline, the Government was forced to reduce its budget significantly, with some expenditure items being lowered by as much as 50%. In an effort to boost revenue, it announced the elimination of customs tariff exemptions and stated that it would push through plans to amend the legislation on income tax. By the end of 2009 the Government's worst fears were realized: oil revenues had declined by more than 50% to just US $1,960m., the lowest level for six years, compared with record receipts of $4,400m. in 2008. This slump in income was compounded by the costly oil subsidy bill, and the Government was forced to appeal to Saudi Arabia for financial support. The budget deficit widened significantly in 2009 to a sum equivalent to 10.2% of GDP.

The Government's dwindling finances resulted in the delivery of a prudent budget for 2010. Revenues were projected at YR 1,520.4m., with the contribution from oil declining to around 60% of the total. The budget also anticipated a rise in tax income, presumably taking into account the implementation of the GST, although the announcement in November 2009 that the Government was reducing corporation tax from 35% to 15% raised doubts over these figures. Projected expenditure still forecast a large subsidy bill, but the Government remained committed to reducing this gradually. In expectation that Yemen's donors would honour their outstanding aid commitments, the capital expenditure budget was greatly reduced. Overall expenditure was therefore forecast at YR 2,012.1m., leaving a reduced deficit of YR 491.7m., equating to around 7% of GDP.

The outbreak of serious political violence in early 2011, which precipitated the effective collapse of the Government and the temporary departure of President Saleh to Saudi Arabia, prevented the publication of budget out-turn figures, but it was estimated that the Government's fiscal position improved in 2010 owing to the high price of petroleum. The 2011 budget projected a 9.5% decline in expenditure, bringing the fiscal deficit back down to just 3.6% of GDP. However, the budget was abandoned amid the subsequent political turmoil. Although no official figures are available, the consensus among international financial institutions is that the Government spent heavily in 2011, increasing subsidies, wages and social welfare expenditure in an unsuccessful attempt to ease socio-economic tensions. With oil production declining considerably, the fiscal deficit is believed to have widened dramatically to over 8% of GDP.

One of the first tasks of the new Government was to produce the budget for the 2012 fiscal year in May; perhaps understandably, it placed emphasis on supporting the immediate needs of the population. However, as a result, it committed itself to further spending rises, for which it hoped a recovery in oil production, combined with the sustained high international price of oil, would compensate. The budget set the deficit at YR 561,600m. The subsequent budget of 2013 anticipated a further deepening of the deficit, to YR 682,000m., a rise of 21%. The Government projected revenues of YR 2,080,000m., against expenditure of YR 2,770,000m.

The Government's rapidly deteriorating fiscal position, coupled with a worrying decline in the domestic security situation, placed an ever-increasing strain on the riyal, as importers struggled to obtain sufficient hard currency to pay for their imports and as savers sought to buy US dollars in anticipation of a slump in the value of the riyal. The riyal had begun to weaken against the dollar in the latter half of 2009, and the Central Bank was forced to use large sums of hard currency to reinforce it. During 2009 the Central Bank intervened at least six times, spending over US $1,000m. in support of the riyal. Pressure on the local currency continued into 2010, and the Bank spent some $850m. to buttress the riyal in the first quarter of 2010 alone. Further efforts by the Central Bank to stem the decline had little effect: in March it was announced that commercial banks were no longer permitted to transfer their customers' riyal deposits into dollars, and the minimum deposit rate was increased twice in three days, rising from 12% to 20%. In an attempt to restore confidence in the system, in early April the Governor of the Central Bank, Ahmed Abdel-Rahman al-Samaawi, was replaced by Muhammad Awad bin Humam. The decline in the riyal eventually eased, but a secondary mini-slump in May demonstrated that the currency remained under considerable strain. As a result of the Central Bank's efforts to support the riyal, its foreign reserves decreased from $8,100m. at the end of 2008, to less than $6,000m. by the end of the first quarter of 2010. The onset of political violence in early 2011 only increased demand for dollars, and between February and the beginning of June the riyal lost 20% of its value. Ongoing attempts by the Central Bank to shore up the currency reduced its stock of reserves even further, to around $5,000m., according to official data; however, independent observers believed that reserves were much lower. By the end of the year reserves had indeed fallen further to critical levels, but, following the replacement of the Saleh regime, currency pressures started to ease slightly, and over the first half of 2012 reserves increased for the first time in almost three years, reaching $4,700m. by June and recovering even more rapidly over the latter part of the year to finish 2012 at $6,158m.

FOREIGN TRADE AND BALANCE OF PAYMENTS

There is a deficiency of accurate and detailed trade and payments statistics for Yemen, particularly relating to labour migration and workers' remittances, while some official trade figures give unrealistically low import totals (smuggling having been particularly widespread in the former YAR in the late 1970s and early 1980s). The blurring of such statistics reflects the very high levels of economic interdependence that developed within the Arabian Peninsula in the 1970s and 1980s, as Saudi Arabia and other oil-rich Gulf states provided mass employment opportunities for Yemeni workers. In so far as they were used to offset the large deficits in the Yemeni states' basic commodity trade, the inflows of remittance income from the oil states strengthened the overall balance of payments positions of the YAR and the PDRY. (In practice, significant amounts of remittance income were spent on imported consumer goods, particularly in the YAR.) However, remittance income did not eliminate either state's heavy dependence on foreign aid to finance development projects and budget deficits, nor did it represent a stable and predictable income source, being highly dependent on fluctuations in the host countries' economic cycles, which were closely linked to swings in world oil prices. In the 1990s unified Yemen benefited from a stronger export base as it developed its own oilfields. At the same time import demand was boosted, and remittance income reduced, as the country absorbed the impact of the large repatriations of Yemeni workers arising from the 1990–91 Gulf crisis. Having become accustomed to modest rises in export earnings as oil production developed, Yemen was in 1998 adjusting to a major slump in world oil prices. In late 1997 Yemen secured substantial relief in respect of its major arrears of foreign debt (including debt stemming from the former PDRY's heavy reliance on Soviet aid).

Until the late 1980s the former YAR's merchandise exports covered less than 3% of the value of imports. World Bank statistics showed that in the period 1965–80 exports grew at an average annual rate of only 2.8%, whereas imports grew by 23.3% per year. In the period 1980–88, however, the average annual growth in exports was 35.6%, while imports declined by 10% per year. The improvement in export performance was attributable to the start of crude petroleum exports at the end of 1987. In 1987 YAR exports were worth only US $19m., against imports of $1,311m.; in 1988 exports rose sharply, to $485m., against imports of $1,310m. In the early 1980s the YAR's official annual trade deficit ran at about $1,500m., decreasing to around $1,200m. per year in 1986 and 1987 and to $835m. in 1988. The estimated value of goods smuggled into the former YAR to avoid high import duties was $1,000m. in 1983. According to the World Bank, oil and other minerals accounted for 88% of YAR exports by value in 1988 (compared with 9% in 1965), manufactured goods for 11% (0% in 1965) and other primary commodities for 1% (91% in 1965). In the same year food accounted for 28% of total imports by value (compared with 41% in 1965), manufactured goods for 55% (47% in 1965), fuels for 8% (6% in 1965) and other primary commodities for 6% (6% in 1965).

According to the World Bank, the former PDRY's exports declined in value in the period 1965–80 at an average annual rate of 13.7%, while imports decreased by 7.5% per year. In the period 1980–88, however, exports increased by an average of 1.9% per year and imports by 4.4% per year. In 1988 exports were worth US $80m., while imports reached $598m. The former PDRY's main export commodities (excluding refined petroleum products) were cotton, hides and skins, fish, rice, and coffee. The chief imports (excluding crude petroleum) were manufactured goods for development projects, clothing, foodstuffs and livestock. Fuels and minerals accounted for 90% of total PDRY exports by value in 1988 (against 80% in 1965), other primary commodities for 9% (14% in 1965), and manufactured goods for 1% (8% in 1965).

Following unification, Yemen's external trade was temporarily disrupted by the UN embargo on trade with Iraq and Kuwait, which necessitated a diversion to the Aden refinery of Yemeni crude petroleum that would otherwise have gone for export (see Manufacturing and Industry). The value of Yemen's merchandise exports in 1990 totalled YR 7,066m. (including YR 6,188m. from oil), whereas merchandise imports totalled YR 20,863m., producing a visible trade deficit of YR 13,795m., compared with a combined deficit for the YAR and the PDRY in 1989 of YR 11,533m. (exports YR 6,765m., imports YR 18,298m.). There was a visible trade deficit of YR 18,238.4m. in 1992 (exports YR 6,075.9m., imports YR 24,314.3m.). The provisional trade figures for 1993 showed a deficit of YR 25,382.3m. (exports YR 5,693.3m., imports YR 31,075.6m.). In 1994 Yemen's merchandise trade was in surplus by US $302.1m. (exports $1,824m., imports $1,521.9m.). There were visible trade deficits of $11m. in 1995 and $30.8m. in 1996. In 1997 merchandise trade was in deficit by $132.5m. (exports $2,274m., imports $2,406.5m.), while in 1998 there was a sharply increased deficit of $726.8m., export earnings having declined by 34%, to $1,500.1m., as a result of that year's downturn in world oil prices, whereas import spending was reduced by 7.4%, to $2,227.8m. Official trade figures for 1999 showed a surplus of $357.8m. (exports $2,478.3m., imports $2,120.4m.), there having been a rise of more than 73% (from $1,228.7m. to $2,131.2m.) in the value of Yemen's oil exports.

A further substantial rise in oil prices in 2000, combined with a 10.8% rise in the volume of Yemen's oil exports, boosted the provisional calculation of the visible trade surplus to US $1,312.8m. (exports $3,797.2m., imports $2,484.4m.). Central Bank figures indicated a reduced trade surplus of $766.4m. (exports $3,366.9m., imports $2,600.4m.) in 2001 and $779m. (exports $3,584m., imports $2,805m.) in 2002. Crude petroleum exports in 2002 increased to $3,122m., from $2,905m. in 2001, representing 87% of the total value of exports. In 2003 the trade balance, according to the Central Bank, recorded a surplus of $376.9m., reflecting exports valued at $3,934.4m. and imports at $3,557.4m. The total value of crude petroleum exports in 2003 amounted to $3,459.1m., forming 87.9% of the total value of exports. According to Central Bank preliminary data, the visible trade balance recorded a surplus of $1,700.3m. in 2005 (compared with a surplus of $817.1m. in 2004), with exports increasing to $6,413.2m. in value and imports to $4,712.9m. Reflecting the surge in international oil prices, crude petroleum exports reached $5,952m. in value, forming 93% of the total value of exports. Sustained high oil prices in 2006 boosted the trade balance further, with exports rising to $7,316.4m. A significant rise in the cost of imports, totalling $5,926m., on account of rising global commodity prices, only offset these gains to a degree, leaving a slightly reduced trade balance of $1,390.3m. In 2007 the rising cost of global commodities pushed up the import bill considerably, to $5,926.1m., while declining oil output and static oil prices resulted in a slight reduction in oil export earnings. As a result, Yemen's trade account moved into deficit for the first time in over a decade. Despite record oil export earnings of $7,700m. in 2008, the trade account remained in deficit. In 2009 the situation deteriorated markedly, as oil export revenues contracted by over 42%. Although there was a concomitant reduction in the import bill, owing to a decline in global commodity prices, a trade deficit of over $2,000m. was recorded. The trade account recovered considerably in 2010, with a strong rise in revenues due to the higher oil price; by the end of the year the deficit had been reduced to $1,050.7m. Remarkably, the trade position improved further in 2011, owing to a record oil price and a marked decline in imports on account of the deteriorating domestic economy and the significant contraction in commercial and manufacturing activity. As a result, the trade deficit narrowed considerably to YR 514,608m. in 2011, before deteriorating again in 2012 as export earnings declined slightly, but import values recovered considerably following the improvement in the domestic situation. The trade deficit widened to YR 906,873m.

Yemen had a current account deficit of YR 1,711m. in 1990, compared with a combined YAR and PDRY deficit of YR 9,853m. in 1989. The services account showed receipts of YR 17,518m. in 1990 (YR 5,519m. in 1989), exceeding payments of YR 5,432m. (YR 3,839m. in 1989). The strong upturn in private remittances in 1990 was attributable to Yemeni nationals returning from Saudi Arabia because of the Gulf crisis. The World Bank assessed Yemen's net remittance income at US $800m. in 1991, and suggested that the current account was $20m. in surplus in that year. Prior to the 1990 Gulf crisis, remittance income had averaged around $2,000m. per year. According to World Bank estimates, a decline in Yemen's net remittance income to $340m. in 1992 was a contributory factor in an overall current account deficit of $1,582m. in that year. In mid-1994 the Arab Monetary Fund extended a $47m. loan to Yemen to support the financing of the country's 1993 balance of payments deficit. Yemen had a current account deficit of $1,248m. and an overall balance of payments deficit of $1,113m. in 1993. In 1994 there was a current account surplus of $366m. and an estimated overall deficit of $653m. In 1995 Yemen received estimated remittance income of $1,120m. and recorded a surplus of $183m. on the current account. In 1996 Yemen received remittance income of $1,182m. and recorded a current account deficit of $70m. In 1997 net current transfers totalling $1,255.3m. were received, producing a current account surplus of $51.6m. when set against the merchandise trade deficit of $142.5m., a services deficit of $426.3m. (credits $207.6m., debits $633.9m.) and an invisible income deficit of $634.9m. (credits $69.6m., debits $704.5m.). In 1998 net remittance income was estimated to be virtually unchanged, at $1,256.3m., leaving the current account in deficit by $228.1m. when set against the merchandise trade deficit of $700.5m., a services deficit of $362m. (credits $207.5m., debits $569.5m.) and an invisible income deficit of $421.9m. (credits $65.5m., debits $487.4m.). The 30.8% reduction in outgoings on the invisibles account in 1998 was attributable, in part, to debt-rescheduling agreements with overseas creditors. In 1999 the balance of payments showed a current account surplus of $549.6m. and an overall surplus of $268.9m. Net remittance income in 1999 was $1,314m.

Provisional figures for 2000 showed a current account surplus of US $1,336.6m. and an overall balance of payments surplus of $1,388.5m. In 2001 the current account surplus decreased to $670.9m., declining further, to $519.5m., in 2002, according to preliminary Central Bank figures. The overall balance of payments surplus in 2002 was $758m., compared with $653.2m. in the previous year. Preliminary data from the Central Bank for 2003 indicated that the overall balance of payments realized a surplus of $335.6m. The surplus on the current account declined to $148.7m. According to the IMF, in 2005 the overall balance of payments recorded a surplus of $433.8m., up from $372.5m. in 2004. The current account registered a surplus of $624.1m. in 2005, compared with $224.6m. in 2004. In 2006 this surplus was reduced to $205.7m., although the overall balance of payments widened significantly to $1,111.7m., as Yemen attracted significant capital inflows. In 2007 Yemen's current account slipped into deficit for the first time in a decade, as oil production contracted by 12%. The deficit was $1,508m., equal to 7.1% of GDP. Although a spike in the oil price pushed up export earnings in 2008, a rising import bill, as well as increased non-merchandise payments—piracy in the Gulf of Aden had pushed up import-related services costs considerably—ensured that the current account remained in deficit, albeit slightly narrowed at $1,251m., or 4.9% of GDP. The overall balance of payments had returned to surplus, at $354m. The non-merchandise deficit narrowed slightly in 2009, as global interest rates declined and as Yemen paid reduced services costs on its fewer imports. However, with the country recording its largest trade deficit for many years, the current account deficit widened worryingly, to $2,560m., equivalent to around 8.5% of GDP. Owing to much stronger trade figures, Yemen's current account deficit narrowed in 2010, to around $1,381.2m. The non-merchandise deficit remained largely unchanged, however, as increased remittance inflows were offset by larger services and income debits. Despite the improvement in Yemen's merchandise trade position in 2011, the overall current account failed to reflect that level, as oil companies repatriated their higher earnings, while expatriate Yemeni remittances declined owing to the deteriorating global economy. The current account deficit improved, to $527.4m. The position of the non-merchandise account improved considerably in 2012, owing mainly to a sharp rise in remittance inflows, as more Yemenis were able to work in the neighbouring Gulf states and the economies there began to improve. However, the marked widening of the trade deficit ensured that the overall current account deficit also widened, to $985.6m.

In June 1990 the World Bank confirmed that Yemen would be entitled to concessionary finance and that loan programmes and development projects under way in the YAR and the PDRY would continue in the unified country. Unified Yemen's receipts of official development aid amounted to US $405m. in 1990 and $313m. in 1991 (in which year it represented 3.9% of GNI).

Figures disclosed in July 1990 showed unified Yemen's total foreign debt as US $7,256m., of which $4,366m. was debt attributable to the former PDRY (owed mainly to the USSR, China and Eastern European countries) and $2,890m. to the former YAR. In September 1990 France agreed to cancel all of Yemen's outstanding debt to it—some $55m.—and Japan also granted debt relief aid. According to the World Bank, Yemen's external debt totalled $6,598m. at the end of 1992. In mid-1995 Japan's cumulative debt-relief grants to Yemen totalled $68.4m. In September 1996 the 'Paris Club' of official creditors agreed to recommend the rescheduling of about $100m. of Yemen's debt, and in April 1997 the USA announced a rescheduling of Yemeni debt over a period of 40 years, including a 20-year exemption period.

Russia, which became a member of the 'Paris Club' in 1997, disclosed that it was owed US $400m. of commercial debt by Yemen, three-quarters of which was overdue for repayment. However, the bulk of the former USSR's lending had been on non-commercial terms within the framework of bilateral co-operation agreements with the former PDRY and YAR. The total lending under these agreements was almost $6,700m., of which $6,500m. (including nearly $2,700m. of arrears) was still outstanding. Loan agreements had been denominated in roubles, with typical repayment periods of between five and 15 years and typical interest rates of 2% to 5%, and had usually specified repayment in hard currency by the YAR or 'in the national currency for subsequent purchase of goods' by the PDRY. The former USSR had by 1988 acceded to 19 requests for postponements of debt repayments, the total value of all repayments received being less than 170m. roubles.

At a 'Paris Club' meeting in November 1997 Russia agreed to waive about US $5,360m. of Yemeni debt (80% of $6,700m.) and to apply so-called 'Naples conditions' (67% of debt written off and 33% rescheduled over a greatly extended period at very low interest rates) to the remainder. Yemen's debts to the other 'Paris Club' countries were to be reviewed by each country with a view to rescheduling on 'Naples' terms. Total Yemeni indebtedness to foreign creditors other than Russia was estimated to be about $1,500m. in 1997. Yemen's Prime Minister stated after the November 1997 'Paris Club' meeting that creditor countries in two regions—the Arab world and Eastern Europe—had not as yet discussed debt rescheduling with Yemen. In the case of Eastern Europe, the amounts involved were relatively modest and were not considered a problem by Yemen. In the case of major Arab creditor countries, including Saudi Arabia, Kuwait and Iraq, the Yemeni Government had requested rescheduling negotiations with a view to obtaining terms similar to those applied by 'Paris Club' countries. However, there had been no response from any of the countries concerned, with the result that all debts to other Arab governments remained 'in place and frozen' at the end of 1997. In June 1999 it was reported that Yemen's current net outstanding debt to Russia totalled $426m. and was to be repaid over 33 years at an interest rate of 1.19%. A formal analysis of Yemen's end-1999 external debt position, carried out by the Government in collaboration with the IMF and the World Bank, concluded that the present debt was 'sustainable over the medium term'.

Agreements were reported in December 2000 on the rescheduling of some of Yemen's debts to Saudi Arabia and Kuwait. The Saudi-Yemeni Co-operation Council (which had last met prior to the outbreak of the Gulf crisis of 1990–91) agreed that a resumption of Saudi funding for Yemeni development projects was to be based partly on the provision of new loans of up to US $300m. and partly on a restructuring of earlier debt totalling more than $330m. Yemen's external debt stood at $4,945m. at the end of 2002, increasing marginally by 1.5% from the level recorded at the corresponding time a year earlier. The ratio of foreign debt to GDP decreased from 52% in 2001 to 49.7% in 2002. According to the Central Bank, the outstanding balance of external public debt at the end of 2003 amounted to $5,376.8m., the ratio to GDP declining to 48% (representing one of the lowest ratios in the Middle East). Of this figure, $2,473.2m. (or 46% of the total) was owed to international institutions (mainly the IDA, the IMF and the AFESD), $1,811m. (33.7%) to 'Paris Club' member countries (particularly to Russia), and $1,092.6m. (20.3%) to other donors (notably the Saudi Fund for Development, Kuwait Development Fund, and China). External debt declined to $5,167.9m. at the end of 2005 (from $5,335.8m. at the end of 2004), and the ratio to GDP declined further to 33% (from 39% in 2004).

During 2003–06 the Japanese Government was reported to have waived about US $31.5m. of Yemen's debt. In August 2006 Japan agreed to cancel a further debt of $7.8m., and in 2007 the Japanese embassy in San'a indicated that Japan would cancel $6m. of the debt accrued by Yemen in that year, demonstrating confidence in a bilateral relationship that has afforded significant cumulative debt relief to the Gulf state in recent years. This relationship was further reinforced in July 2008, when Japan cancelled a further $17m. of outstanding debt.

By 2007 Yemen's debt had increased slightly, owing to the award of a massive economic support package at a donors' conference held in London in November 2006. At the conference, which was attended by a large number of international donors, including multilateral institutions, as well as 'Paris Club' and non-'Paris Club' members, Yemen received pledges worth some US $5,300m. in a mixture of grants and concessional loans. Some of these were disbursed throughout 2007 and early 2008, pushing up Yemen's external debt by 6% in 2007 to $5,800m., equal to around 25% of GDP. By the end of 2009 Yemen's debt had risen to just over $6,000m., although by mid-2010 this had declined again to around $5,800m. However, debt levels increased in the latter half of the year, and by early 2011 total external debt had risen to over $6,200m. With very few disbursements during 2011, Yemen's overall external debt remained at about that level by the end of the year, but significant pledges made throughout 2012 and into 2013, totalling over $8,000m., sent debt levels higher once more. By the end of 2012 only a proportion of the funds pledged had been actually disbursed, and so official data did not reflect the full amount Yemen was to receive. None the less, total external debt was recorded at $7,200m. at the end of that year.

Statistical Survey

Sources (unless otherwise indicated): Republic of Yemen Central Statistical Organization, POB 13434, San'a; tel. (1) 250619; fax (1) 250664; e-mail csoi@y.net.ye; internet www.cso-yemen.org; Central Bank of Yemen, POB 59, Ali Abd al-Mughni St, San'a; tel. (1) 274314; fax (1) 274360; e-mail cbyh@y.net.ye; internet www.centralbank.gov.ye.

Area and Population

AREA, POPULATION AND DENSITY

Area (sq km)	536,869*
Population (census results)	
16 December 1994†	14,587,807
16 December 2004‡	
Males	10,036,953
Females	9,648,208
Total	19,685,161
Population (UN estimates at mid-year)§	
2011	23,304,210
2012	23,852,408
2013	24,407,381
Density (per sq km) at mid-2013	45.5

* 207,286 sq miles.
† Excluding adjustment for underenumeration.
‡ Population is *de jure*.
§ Source: UN, *World Population Prospects: The 2012 Revision*.

POPULATION BY AGE AND SEX
(UN estimates at mid-2013)

	Males	Females	Total
0–14	5,000,874	4,801,738	9,802,612
15–64	6,966,634	6,938,836	13,905,470
65 and over	336,681	362,618	699,299
Total	12,304,189	12,103,192	24,407,381

Source: UN, *World Population Prospects: The 2012 Revision*.

PRINCIPAL TOWNS
(population at 1994 census)

San'a (capital)	954,448	Hodeida	298,452
Aden	398,294	Mukalla	122,359
Taiz	317,571	Ibb	103,312

Source: UN, *Demographic Yearbook*.

Mid-2011 ('000, incl. suburbs, UN estimate): San'a 2,419 (Source: UN, *World Urbanization Prospects: The 2011 Revision*).

BIRTHS, MARRIAGES AND DEATHS
(annual averages, UN estimates)

	1995–2000	2000–05	2005–10
Birth rate (per 1,000)	41.9	37.5	33.5
Death rate (per 1,000)	9.9	8.7	7.8

Source: UN, *World Population Prospects: The 2012 Revision*.

Registered births: 318,936 in 2010; 239,980 in 2011, 279,719 in 2012.

Registered deaths: 28,494 in 2010; 23,662 in 2011; 28,596 in 2012.

Marriages (2002, estimate): 10,934 (Source: UN, *Demographic Yearbook*).

Life expectancy (years at birth): 65.5 (males 64.0, females 67.0) in 2011 (Source: World Bank, World Development Indicators database).

EMPLOYMENT
(persons aged 15 years and over, 2005/06)

	Males	Females	Total
Agriculture, hunting and forestry	1,260,796	113,797	1,374,593
Fishing	31,506	—	31,506
Mining and quarrying	14,225	735	14,959
Manufacturing	200,339	21,799	222,138
Electricity, gas and water	18,466	308	18,773
Construction	485,048	816	485,864
Trade, restaurants and hotels	641,117	9,697	650,814
Transport, storage and communications	235,681	3,796	239,477
Hotels and restaurants	72,992	1,063	74,054
Finance, insurance and real estate	37,368	2,539	39,907
Education	196,594	49,535	246,129
Health and social welfare	38,146	16,763	54,909
Personal and social services	72,163	5,282	77,445
Public administration and defence	436,802	16,730	453,532
Private households with employed persons	15,196	8,106	23,302
Sub-total	3,756,438	250,967	4,007,404
Unspecified	73,363	68,679	142,043
Total	3,829,801	319,646	4,149,447

Mid-2013 (estimates in '000): Agriculture, etc. 2,390; Total labour force 6,684 (Source: FAO).

Health and Welfare

KEY INDICATORS

Total fertility rate (children per woman, 2011)	5.1
Under-5 mortality rate (per 1,000 live births, 2011)	77
HIV/AIDS (% of persons aged 15–49, 2011)	0.2
Physicians (per 1,000 head, 2009)	0.3
Hospital beds (per 1,000 head, 2010)	0.7
Health expenditure (2010): US $ per head (PPP)	155
Health expenditure (2010): % of GDP	5.6
Health expenditure (2010): public (% of total)	21.0
Access to water (% of persons, 2011)	55
Access to sanitation (% of persons, 2011)	53
Total carbon dioxide emissions ('000 metric tons, 2009)	23,996.8
Carbon dioxide emissions per head (metric tons, 2009)	1.0
Human Development Index (2012): ranking	160
Human Development Index (2012): value	0.458

For sources and definitions, see explanatory note on p. vi.

Agriculture

PRINCIPAL CROPS
('000 metric tons)

	2009	2010	2011*
Wheat	222	265	278
Barley	23	40	38
Maize	56	89	89
Millet	62	111	131
Sorghum	312	507	603
Potatoes	278	303	368
Chick-peas	51	51*	57
Sesame seed	24	25	28
Seed cotton	25	25	29
Tomatoes	251	262	253
Cucumbers and gherkins	16	17*	18
Chillies and peppers, green	21	22*	22
Onions, dry	216	224	237
Garlic	4	4*	5
Beans, green	4	4	5
Carrots and turnips	15	16*	19
Okra	23	24*	24
Watermelons	172	189	187
—continued			
Cantaloupes and other melons	32	35	34
Bananas	132	133	136
Oranges	113	122†	127
Tangerines, mandarins, etc.	22	22†	23
Grapes	129	166	167
Mangoes, mangosteens and guavas	405	401	472
Dates	57	58	60
Papayas	25	26	21
Coffee, green	19	19	20
Tobacco, unmanufactured	23	23	20

* FAO estimate(s).
† Unofficial figure.

Aggregate production ('000 metric tons, may include official, semi-official or estimated data): Total cereals 674 in 2009, 1,013 in 2010, 1,139 in 2011; Total roots and tubers 278 in 2009, 304 in 2010, 369 in 2011; Total vegetables (incl. melons) 820 in 2009, 868 in 2010, 887 in 2011; Total fruits (excl. melons) 981 in 2009, 1,031 in 2010, 1,112 in 2011.

Source: FAO.

LIVESTOCK
('000 head, year ending September)

	2009	2010	2011*
Horses	2†	2†	2
Asses*	500	500	500
Cattle	1,567	1,605	1,610
Camels	384	403†	405
Sheep	9,087	9,206	9,250
Goats	8,883	9,016	9,050
Chickens*	58,000	60,000	60,000

* FAO estimates.
† Unofficial figure.

Source: FAO.

LIVESTOCK PRODUCTS
('000 metric tons)

	2009	2010	2011*
Cattle meat	96.7	107.5	109.9
Sheep meat	30.7	34.3	36.0
Goat meat	31.6	35.0	37.0
Chicken meat	139.7	144.1	149.7
Camels' milk*	19.0	19.4	19.4
Cows' milk	291.1	301.3*	301.3
Sheep's milk	42.1	43.0*	43.0
Goats' milk	52.3	53.5*	53.5
Hen eggs	58.6†	60.6†	60.6
Wool, greasy	7.6†	7.7†	7.7

* FAO estimate(s).
† Unofficial figure.

Source: FAO.

Forestry

ROUNDWOOD REMOVALS
('000 cubic metres, excl. bark, estimates)

	2009	2010	2011
Total (all fuel wood)	425	441	441

Source: FAO.

Fishing

('000 metric tons, live weight of capture)

	2009	2010	2011
Demersal percomorphs*	5.0	4.5	4.0
Indian oil sardine	43.5	36.5	39.0
Yellowfin tuna	27.8	23.3	24.9
Pelagic percomorphs*	30.0	33.0	22.0
Sharks, rays and skates, etc.	10.3	8.9	9.5
Cuttlefish and bobtail squids	10.8	8.8	9.2
Total catch (incl. others)*	179.6	163.9	157.3

* FAO estimates.

Source: FAO.

Mining

('000 metric tons unless otherwise indicated)

	2009	2010	2011
Crude petroleum	14,426	14,173	10,567
Natural gas (million cu m)*	29,632	29,200	29,600
Salt	65	75†	75†
Gypsum (crude)	100	100†	100†

* Gross production.

† Estimate.

2012: Crude petroleum ('000 metric tons) 8,332.

Sources: BP, *Statistical Review of World Energy*; US Geological Survey.

Industry

SELECTED PRODUCTS

('000 barrels unless otherwise indicated)

	2009	2010	2011
Liquefied petroleum gas ('000 metric tons)	735	736	585
Motor spirit	5,110	5,110	5,110
Kerosene	4,052	4,050	4,050
Distillate fuel oils	7,775	7,780*	7,780
Residual fuel oils	14,750	14,800	14,800
Cement ('000 metric tons)	2,118	3,500*	3,500*
Electric energy (million kWh)	6,749	7,755	6,206

* Estimated figure.

2008 (estimates): Mineral water (million litres) 401; Soft drinks (million litres) 270; Cigarettes (million packets) 215; Paints ('000 litres) 47,551; Plastic bags (metric tons) 39,768.

2012: Electric energy (million kWh) 6,580; Liquefied petroleum gas ('000 metric tons) 670.

Source: partly US Geological Survey.

Finance

CURRENCY AND EXCHANGE RATES

Monetary Units

100 fils = 1 Yemeni riyal (YR).

Sterling, Dollar and Euro Equivalents (31 May 2013)

£1 sterling = YR 326.93;
US $1 = YR 214.89;
€1 = YR 279.49;
YR 1,000 = £3.059 = $4.65 = €3.58.

Average Exchange Rate (YR per US $)

2010 219.590
2011 213.800
2012 214.351

Note: The exchange rate of US $1 = YR 9.76, established in the YAR in 1988, remained in force until February 1990, when a new rate of $1 = YR 12.01 was introduced. Following the merger of the two Yemens in May 1990, the YAR's currency was adopted as the currency of the unified country. In March 1995 the official exchange rate was amended from YR 12.01 to YR 50.04 per US dollar. The rate has since been adjusted. From mid-1996 data refer to a market-determined exchange rate, applicable to most private transactions

CENTRAL GOVERNMENT BUDGET

(YR '000 million)

Revenue*	2009	2010	2011†
Oil and gas	715.8	1,090.1	1,226.8
Exports	349.4	569.6	787.9
Domestic revenues	366.4	520.5	438.9
Non-oil revenues	562.7	684.8	462.2
Tax revenues	409.5	454.6	376.1
Non-tax revenues	153.2	230.2	86.1
Total	1,278.5	1,774.9	1,689.0

Expenditure	2009	2010	2011†
Current expenditure	1,478.2	1,750.1	1,875.6
Civil wages and salaries	569.4	569.0	662.6
Materials and services	199.2	222.0	193.5
Interest	124.6	159.9	233.2
Domestic	113.9	148.2	218.1
Foreign	10.7	11.8	15.1
Transfers and subsidies	555.5	734.5	712.4
Current transfers	158.4	170.5	177.3
Subsidies	397.1	564.0	535.1
Other current expenditure	29.5	32.7	35.7
Capital development expenditure	269.8	275.1	127.0
Net lending	75.9	61.0	18.9
Total	1,823.9	2,086.3	2,021.5

* Excluding grants received (YR '000 million): 27.6 in 2009; 34.2 in 2010; 17.3 in 2011 (preliminary).

† Preliminary figures.

INTERNATIONAL RESERVES

(US $ million at 31 December)

	2010	2011	2012
Gold (national valuation)	74.4	82.4	90.0
IMF special drawing rights	280.5	253.9	253.8
Foreign exchange	5,587.8	4,195.0	5,813.8
Total	5,942.7	4,531.3	6,157.6

Source: IMF, *International Financial Statistics*.

MONEY SUPPLY

(YR million at 31 December)

	2010	2011	2012
Currency outside banks	547,284	777,407	803,407
Demand deposits at commercial banks	175,592	162,300	231,544
Total money (incl. others)	786,560	993,031	1,104,891

Source: IMF, *International Financial Statistics*.

COST OF LIVING

(Consumer Price Index; base: 2008 = 100)

	2010	2011	2012
Food and non-alcoholic beverages	116.2	133.5	147.4
Clothing and footwear	107.5	121.8	133.3
Housing and related items	119.7	142.4	157.4
Health	126.8	145.8	161.8
Transport	111.2	131.8	173.2
Communications	115.0	129.2	131.1
Education	103.5	112.0	125.5
All items (incl. others)	116.4	138.9	152.9

NATIONAL ACCOUNTS

(YR million at current prices)

National Income and Product

	2009	2010*	2011*
Domestic factor incomes	5,693,224	6,867,744	6,864,482
Consumption of fixed capital	357,608	395,928	261,001
Gross domestic product (GDP) at factor cost	6,050,831	7,263,672	7,125,483
Indirect taxes, *less* subsidies	–277,916	–419,769	–410,590
GDP in purchasers' values	5,772,915	6,843,903	6,714,893
Factor income from abroad (net)	–219,392	–376,175	–476,931
Gross national product (GNP)	5,553,524	6,467,728	6,237,962
Less Consumption of fixed capital	357,608	395,928	261,001
National income in purchasers' values	5,195,916	6,071,800	5,976,961
Other transfers from abroad (net)	287,927	442,396	433,400
National disposable income	5,483,843	6,514,196	6,410,361

Expenditure on the Gross Domestic Product

	2009	2010*	2011*
Government final consumption expenditure	826,645	886,613	945,539
Private final consumption expenditure	4,281,535	4,899,780	4,573,171
Changes in stocks	96,937	12,255	378,959
Gross fixed capital formation	1,142,324	1,344,701	886,444
Total domestic expenditure	6,347,441	7,143,349	6,784,113
Exports of goods and services	1,424,381	2,034,046	2,220,108
Less Imports of goods and services	1,998,906	2,333,491	2,289,329
GDP in purchasers' values	5,772,915	6,843,903	6,714,893
GDP at constant 2000 prices	2,667,820	2,819,774	2,459,809

2012 (estimates): Government final consumption expenditure 1,135,636; Private final consumption expenditure 5,272,866; Changes in stocks 312,977; Gross fixed capital formation 1,385,477; *Total domestic expenditure* 8,106,957; Exports of goods and services 1,874,924; *Less* Imports of goods and services 2,944,618; *GDP in purchasers' values* 7,037,263; *GDP at constant 2000 prices* 2,509,477.

Gross Domestic Product by Economic Activity

	2009	2010*	2011*
Agriculture, hunting, forestry and fishing†	727,505	815,855	926,363
Mining and quarrying	1,142,151	1,605,419	1,808,230
Manufacturing	472,512	573,265	514,685
Electricity, gas and water	44,114	53,226	54,114
Construction	331,738	365,055	222,606
Trade, restaurants and hotels	1,175,749	1,361,514	1,087,091
Transport, storage and communications	693,628	757,663	695,506
Finance, insurance, real estate and business services	474,741	551,829	581,269
Government services	595,015	629,938	709,072
Other community, social and personal services	52,530	57,201	54,729
Private non-profit services and services to households	5,305	5,939	4,910
Sub-total	5,714,988	6,776,904	6,658,575
Import duties (net)	57,927	66,999	56,318
GDP in purchasers' values	5,772,915	6,843,903	6,714,893

* Provisional.

† Including production of qat.

2012 (estimates): Agriculture, hunting, forestry and fishing (incl. production of qat) 1,014,620; Mining and quarrying 1,581,889; Manufacturing 619,728; Electricity, gas and water 52,590; Construction 252,181; Trade, restaurants and hotels 1,132,862; Transport, storage and communications 753,097; Finance, insurance, real estate and business services 648,604; Government services 833,247; Other community, social and personal services 58,356; Private non-profit services and services to households 5,252; *Sub-total* 6,952,426; Import duties (net) 84,837; *GDP in purchasers' values* 7,037,263.

BALANCE OF PAYMENTS

(US $ million)

	2009	2010	2011
Exports of goods	5,855.0	7,649.8	8,662.2
Imports of goods	–7,867.8	–8,700.5	–8,248.4
Balance on goods	–2,012.8	–1,050.7	413.7
Exports of services	1,237.2	1,611.7	1,247.9
Imports of services	–2,132.8	–2,348.5	–2,273.1
Balance on goods and services	–2,908.5	–1,787.5	–611.5
Primary income received	115.0	54.5	53.3
Primary income paid	–1,286.3	–1,771.6	–2,604.9
Balance on goods, services and primary income	–4,079.8	–3,504.6	–3,163.1
Secondary income received	1,628.3	1,837.5	1,549.6
Secondary income paid	–113.4	–57.7	–49.6
Current balance	–2,564.9	–1,724.8	–1,663.1
Capital account (net)	—	88.4	—
Direct investment liabilities	129.2	–93.3	–712.8
Portfolio investment assets	–13.5	–358.1	114.5
Other investment assets	–574.9	61.3	38.4
Other investment liabilities	142.1	–209.1	–252.6
Net errors and omissions	1,589.6	674.7	354.7
Reserves and related items	–1,292.4	–1,561.0	–2,121.0

Source: IMF, *International Financial Statistics*.

External Trade

PRINCIPAL COMMODITIES
(distribution by SITC, YR '000 million)

Imports c.i.f.	2010	2011	2012
Food and live animals	521.6	597.7	764.0
Cereal and cereal preparations	252.0	308.8	419.7
Wheat and meslin	154.9	205.7	283.7
Rice	54.1	50.5	74.2
Sugars, sugar preparations and honey	78.6	111.5	107.7
Mineral fuels and lubricants	496.2	633.3	655.2
Petroleum and petroleum products	489.9	627.2	648.6
Animal and vegetable oils and fats	69.6	41.8	54.4
Chemicals and related products	154.5	140.1	184.5
Drugs and pharmaceutical items	58.3	54.0	75.0
Basic manufactures	284.7	201.0	266.9
Iron and steel	112.9	61.5	89.4
Machinery and transport equipment	438.1	312.3	350.3
Machinery specialized for particular industries	64.1	45.2	36.3
General industrial machinery, equipment and parts	54.5	42.9	35.9
Road vehicles	195.6	124.7	184.5
Passenger motor vehicles (excl. buses)	138.3	88.6	110.8
Miscellaneous manufactured articles	77.3	65.8	90.5
Total (incl. others)	2,095.1	2,037.4	2,421.4

Exports f.o.b.*	2010	2011	2012
Food and live animals	93.4	101.3	90.7
Fish and fish preparations	47.1	51.9	45.5
Mineral fuels and lubricants	1,274.2	1,314.4	1,316.5
Petroleum and petroleum products	992.4	984.6	1,143.7
Petroleum oils and oils obtained from bituminous minerals, crude	120.9	61.7	53.7
Chemicals and related products	22.9	49.2	49.3
Machinery and transport equipment	32.0	26.8	31.3
Road vehicles	8.3	9.5	12.4
Total (incl. others)	1,457.8	1,523.8	1,514.5

* Including re-exports.

PRINCIPAL TRADING PARTNERS
(distribution by SITC, YR '000 million)

Imports c.i.f.	2010	2011	2012
Argentina	29.3	33.8	
Australia	38.9	38.4	98.1
Brazil	83.4	72.7	81.3
Canada	11.8	1.8	2.4
China, People's Republic	144.1	121.4	171.5
Egypt	42.9	40.0	45.0
France (incl. Monaco)	56.4	46.9	45.0
Germany	34.4	25.7	32.4
India	61.6	93.1	124.1
Italy	29.2	14.1	11.3
Japan	39.2	17.7	29.1
Korea, Republic	24.0	16.0	25.3
Kuwait	82.3	85.7	74.6
Malaysia	74.6	46.8	57.6
Netherlands	132.1	157.9	218.5
Oman	45.3	37.2	47.5
Pakistan	19.2	27.8	19.0
Russia	16.1	15.7	39.8
Saudi Arabia	173.8	212.6	185.9
Singapore	21.1	30.8	27.4
Switzerland-Liechtenstein	24.0	174.5	218.1
Thailand	41.5	31.1	40.5
Turkey	63.5	49.3	81.8
United Arab Emirates	399.8	323.7	342.0
United Kingdom	27.5	23.9	13.3
USA	106.0	102.3	113.6
Total (incl. others)	2,095.1	2,037.4	2,421.4

Exports f.o.b.*	2010	2011	2012
Belgium	1.2	20.5	1.7
China, People's Republic	312.7	491.5	619.3
Egypt	9.4	15.0	10.4
France (incl. Monaco)	5.6	6.7	1.1
Greece	27.4	14.0	0.1
India	475.3	202.3	171.7
Japan	9.5	20.4	20.8
Korea, Republic	60.3	119.3	66.5
Kuwait	16.0	4.5	0.9
Malaysia	35.2	0.8	27.1
Netherlands	5.3	7.9	7.9
New Zealand	—	—	33.6
Saudi Arabia	58.7	86.2	62.6
Singapore	142.3	20.8	39.6
Somalia	20.4	15.0	13.6
South Africa	0.1	0.4	23.9
Switzerland-Liechtenstein	0.1	5.7	20.6
Thailand	50.8	271.5	290.9
United Arab Emirates	126.1	62.1	25.4
United Kingdom	10.8	27.9	0.2
USA	27.6	59.2	3.5
Viet Nam	6.1	12.1	8.5
Total (incl. others)	1,457.8	1,523.8	1,514.5

* Including re-exports.

Transport

ROAD TRAFFIC
(vehicles in use at 31 December)

	1994	1995	1996
Passenger cars	227,854	229,084	240,567
Buses and coaches	2,712	2,835	3,437
Goods vehicles	279,154	279,780	291,149

2004: Private cars 285,335; Taxi cars 36,371; Buses 22,214; Lorries 127,213; Motorcycles 64,845.

2007: Total vehicles 777,734.

Source: IRF, *World Road Statistics*.

SHIPPING

Flag Registered Fleet
(at 31 December)

	2010	2011	2012
Number of vessels	41	41	40
Total displacement ('000 grt)	221.9	221.9	221.0

Source: Lloyd's List Intelligence (www.lloydslistintelligence.com).

International Sea-borne Freight Traffic
('000 metric tons, unless otherwise indicated, excluding dhows)

	2010	2011	2012
Vessels called (number)	2,813	2,152	2,061
Dry cargo:*			
goods loaded	487	377	312
goods unloaded	8,298	6,341	8,279
Oil products:			
goods loaded	5,026	3,832	4,329
goods unloaded	10,933	9,029	9,970

* Excluding livestock and vehicles.

CIVIL AVIATION
(traffic on scheduled services)

	2007	2008	2009
Kilometres flown (million)	22	24	24
Passengers carried ('000)	1,039	1,065	1,051
Passenger-km (million)	3,041	3,029	3,015
Total ton-km (million)	344	315	307

Source: UN, *Statistical Yearbook*.

2011: Passengers carried ('000) 1,129 (Source: World Bank, World Development Indicators database).

Tourism

TOURIST ARRIVALS

	2010	2011	2012
Africa	20,257	15,719	19,210
Djibouti	8,636	3,852	4,547
Ethiopia	9,359	8,134	12,557
Sudan	4,494	2,852	3,294
Americas	28,006	18,275	27,894
Asia	64,292	38,068	46,365
India	26,112	13,251	16,407
Indonesia	6,832	5,389	5,150
Pakistan	7,681	5,350	8,953
Turkey	5,673	5,127	5,759
Europe	32,057	13,380	16,354
France	5,567	2,724	2,101
Germany	4,559	1,235	1,504
Italy	2,003	791	562
United Kingdom	10,949	4,704	7,331
Middle East	390,112	301,631	348,939
Bahrain	4,568	2,255	5,861
Egypt	18,204	8,855	10,029
Iraq	3,271	2,669	2,322
Jordan	9,069	7,600	4,972
Oman	49,659	38,497	49,597
Saudi Arabia	235,412	198,823	217,287
Syria	14,668	12,876	17,657
United Arab Emirates	21,681	10,904	17,994
Total (incl. others)	536,020	387,498	459,329

Tourism receipts (US $ million): 1,161 in 2010; 780 in 2011; 849 in 2012.

Communications Media

	2010	2011	2012
Telephones ('000 main lines in use)	1,046	1,075	1,104
Mobile cellular telephones ('000 subscribers)	11,085	11,668	13,900
Internet subscribers ('000)	582	n.a.	n.a.
Broadband subscribers ('000)	84	109	167

Source: International Telecommunication Union.

Education

(2010/11)

			Students		
	Schools	Teachers	Males	Females	Total
Pre-primary	485	1,999	16,143	13,713	29,856
Primary	12,376	120,339	2,667,272	1,989,118	4,656,390
Secondary	331	6,891	382,708	232,883	615,591
Higher	34	10,649	188,097	80,958	296,055

Pupil-teacher ratio (primary education, UNESCO estimates): 30.3 in 2010/11 (Source: UNESCO Institute for Statistics).

Adult literacy rate (UNESCO estimates): 63.9% (males 81.2%; females 46.8%) in 2010 (Source: UNESCO Institute for Statistics).

Directory

The Constitution

A draft Constitution for the united Republic of Yemen, based on that endorsed by the Yemen Arab Republic (YAR) and the People's Democratic Republic of Yemen (PDRY) in December 1981, was published in December 1989; it was approved by a popular referendum on 15–16 May 1991.

On 29 September 1994 a total of 52 articles were amended, 29 added and one cancelled, leaving a total of 159 articles in the Constitution. Further amendments to the Constitution were adopted by the House of Representatives in late November 2000 and approved in a national referendum on 20 February 2001.

The Constitution defines the Yemeni Republic as an independent and sovereign Arab and Islamic country. The document states that the Republic 'is an indivisible whole, and it is impermissible to concede any part of it. The Yemeni people are part of the Arab and Islamic nation'. The Islamic *Shari'a* is identified as the basis of all laws.

The revised Constitution provides for the election, by direct universal suffrage, of the President of the Republic; the President is elected for a seven-year term (increased from five years by the amendments approved in 2001). The President is empowered to appoint a Vice-President. The President of the Republic is, ex officio, Supreme Commander of the Armed Forces. The Constitution as amended in 2001 requires presidential candidates to obtain the endorsement of 5% of a combined vote of the appointed Consultative Council and the elected House of Representatives (in place of 10% of the latter chamber alone).

Legislative authority is vested in the 301-member House of Representatives, which is elected, by universal suffrage, for a six-year term (increased from four years by amendment in 2001). The role of the House of Representatives is defined as to 'monitor' the executive. The President is empowered to dissolve the legislature and call new elections within a period of 60 days.

The upper house of the legislature, the Consultative Council, has 111 members (increased from 59 by amendment in 2001), nominated by the President.

The President of the Republic appoints the Prime Minister and other members of the Government on the advice of the Prime Minister.

The Constitution delineates the separation of the powers of the organs of State, and guarantees the independence of the judiciary. The existence of a multi-party political system is confirmed. Serving members of the police and armed forces are banned from political activity.

The Government

HEAD OF STATE

President: Field Marshal ABD AL-RABBUH MANSUR AL-HADI (took office 25 February 2012).

COUNCIL OF MINISTERS
(September 2013)

Prime Minister: MUHAMMAD SALEM BASINDWA.

Minister of Local Administration: ALI MUHAMMAD AL-YAZIDI.

Minister of Planning and International Co-operation: MUHAMMAD AL-SA'ADI.

Minister of the Interior: ABD AL-QADER QAHTAN.

Minister of Finance: SAKHR AHMED AL-WAJIH.

Minister of Oil and Minerals: HISHAM SHARAF.

Minister of Social Affairs and Labour: AMAT AL-RAZZAK ALI HAMAD.

Minister of Human Rights: HOURIAH AHMED MASHHOUR.

Minister of Transport: WA'ED ABDULLAH BATHIB.

Minister of Information: AHMED ALI AL-AMRANI.

Minister of Foreign Affairs: ABU BAKR AL-KURBI.

Minister of Expatriate Affairs: MUJAHID AL-QUHALI.

Minister of Electricity: SALEH HASAN SUMAI.

Minister of Legal Affairs: MUHAMMAD AHMED AL-MIKHLAFI.

Minister of Religious Endowments and Guidance: HAMOUD MUHAMMAD ABAD.

Minister of Culture: ABDULLAH AUBAL MANDHOUQ.

Minister of Agriculture and Irrigation: FARID AHMED MUJAWAR.

Minister of Industry and Trade: SAAD AL-DIN ALI BIN TALIB.

Minister of Public Health and Population: AHMED QASSIM AL-ANSI.

Minister of Education: ABD AL-RAZZAQ YAHYA AL-ASHWAL.

Minister of Fisheries: AWADH SAAD AL-SOCATRI.

Minister of Justice: MURSHED ALI AL-ARASHANI.

Minister of Higher Education and Scientific Research: YAHYA AL-SHU'AIBI.

Minister of Technical Education and Vocational Training: ABD AL-HAFEZ NOMU'AN.

Minister of Tourism: QASIM SALLAM.

Minister of the Civil Service and Social Security: NABIL SHAMSAN.

Minister of Telecommunications and Information Technology: AHMED OBAID BIN DAGHR.

Minister of Defence: Brig.-Gen. MUHAMMAD NASSER AHMAD ALI.

Minister of Public Works and Highways: OMAR ABDULLAH AL-KURSHUMI.

Minister of Water and the Environment: ABDO RAZZAZ SALEH KHALED.

Minister of Youth and Sports: MUAMMAR AL-ERYANI.

Minister of State for Parliament and Shura Council Affairs: RASHAD AHMAD AL-RASSAS.

Minister of State for Cabinet Affairs: JAWHARAH HAMOUD THABET.

Minister of State: SHAIF EZI SAGHIR.

Minister of State: HASAN AHMED SHARAF AL-DIN.

MINISTRIES

Ministry of Agriculture and Irrigation: POB 2805, San'a; tel. (1) 296456; fax (1) 277177; e-mail alahmadi@hotmail.com; internet www.agricultureyemen.com.

Ministry of Civil Service and Social Security: POB 1992, San'a; tel. (1) 282404; fax (1) 283592; e-mail mocsi@mocsi.gov.ye; internet www.mocsi.gov.ye.

Ministry of Culture: San'a; tel. (1) 235461; fax (1) 251557; e-mail moc@y.net.ye; internet www.mocyemen.com.

Ministry of Defence: POB 1399, San'a; tel. (1) 252374; fax (1) 252378.

Ministry of Education: San'a; tel. (1) 252726; fax (1) 274555; e-mail moe@yemen.net.ye; internet www.yemenmoe.net.

Ministry of Electricity: POB 11422, San'a; tel. (1) 326191; fax (1) 326214; e-mail yempec@y.net.ye.

Ministry of Expatriate Affairs: San'a; tel. (1) 402643; fax (1) 400710; e-mail info@iayemen.org; internet www.iayemen.org.

Ministry of Finance: POB 190, San'a; tel. (1) 260365; fax (1) 263040; e-mail support@mofyemen.net; internet www.mof.gov.ye.

Ministry of Fisheries: San'a; tel. (1) 268583; fax (1) 263182.

Ministry of Foreign Affairs: POB 1994, San'a; tel. (1) 276612; fax (1) 286618; e-mail mofa1@mofa.gov.ye; internet www.mofa.gov.ye.

Ministry of Higher Education and Scientific Research: San'a.

Ministry of Human Rights: San'a; internet www.mhryemen.org.

Ministry of Industry and Trade: POB 22210, San'a; tel. (1) 252345; fax (1) 252337; e-mail info@moitye.net; internet www.moit.gov.ye.

Ministry of Information: POB 3040, San'a; tel. (1) 274011; fax (1) 282004; e-mail yemen-info@y.net.ye.

Ministry of the Interior: POB 4991, San'a; tel. (1) 274147; fax (1) 332511; e-mail moi@yemen.net.ye; internet www.moi.gov.ye.

Ministry of Justice: San'a.

Ministry of Legal Affairs: POB 1192, San'a; tel. (1) 402213; fax (1) 402162; e-mail legal@y.net.ye; internet www.legalaffairs.gov.ye.

Ministry of Local Administration: POB 2198, San'a; tel. (1) 252532; fax (1) 251513; internet www.molayemen.gov.ye.

Ministry of Oil and Minerals: POB 81, San'a; tel. (1) 202306; fax (1) 202314; e-mail mom@y.net.ye; internet www.mom.gov.ye.

Ministry of Planning and International Co-operation: POB 175, San'a; tel. (1) 250713; fax (1) 250662; e-mail kamalmasoud@hotmail.com; internet www.mpic-yemen.org.

Ministry of Public Health and Population: POB 274160, San'a; tel. (1) 252193; fax (1) 252247; e-mail his@moh.gov.ye; internet www.mophp-ye.org.

Ministry of Public Works and Highways: San'a; tel. (1) 262602; fax (1) 262609; e-mail info@mpwh-ye.net; internet www.mpwh-ye.net.

Ministry of Religious Endowments and Guidance: San'a.

Ministry of Social Affairs and Labour: San'a; tel. (1) 274921; fax (1) 262806.

Ministry of State for Cabinet Affairs: San'a.

Ministry of State for Parliament and Shura Council Affairs: San'a.

Ministry of Technical Education and Vocational Training: POB 25235, San'a; tel. (1) 469279; fax (1) 202362; e-mail mtevt@yemen.net.ye; internet www.mtevt.info.

Ministry of Telecommunications and Information Technology: San'a.

Ministry of Tourism: POB 5607, San'a; tel. (1) 251033; fax (1) 251034; e-mail tourism@yementourism.com; internet www.yementourism.com/gov.

Ministry of Transport: POB 2781, San'a; tel. (1) 260903; fax (1) 260901; e-mail info@mot.gov.ye; internet www.mot.gov.ye.

Ministry of Water and the Environment: San'a; tel. (1) 418290; fax (1) 418282; internet www.mweye.org.

Ministry of Youth and Sports: POB 2414, San'a; tel. (1) 472901; fax (1) 472900; e-mail hamod.obad@yahoo.com.

President and Legislature

PRESIDENT

In accordance with an agreement between President Field Marshal Ali Abdullah Saleh and representatives of the opposition signed in Riyadh, Saudi Arabia, in late November 2011, Saleh transferred his constitutional powers to his Vice-President, Maj.-Gen. (latterly Field Marshal) Abd al-Rabbuh Mansur al-Hadi, on 23 December 2011, while retaining the title of President for a further three months. On 21 February 2012 an early presidential election took place, at which al-Hadi was the sole candidate. At the election, al-Hadi's candidacy was approved by 99.8% of participating voters. He was officially sworn into office on 25 February.

LEGISLATURE

House of Representatives

POB 623, San'a; tel. (1) 272761; fax (1) 276099; e-mail parliament.SG@y.net.ye.

Speaker: YAHYA ALI AL-RA'EI.

General Election, 27 April 2003

Party	Seats*
General People's Congress (GPC)	228
Yemeni Congregation for Reform (al-Islah)	47
Independents	14
Yemen Socialist Party (YSP)	7
Nasserite Unionist Popular Organization	3
Arab Socialist Baath Party	2
Total	301

* Includes the results of three by-elections held in July 2003.

Election Commission

Supreme Commission for Elections and Referendums (SCER): POB 15491, San'a; tel. (1) 202345; fax (1) 402685; e-mail scer@y.net.ye; internet www.scer.gov.ye; f. 1992; Chair. MUHAMMAD HUSSEIN HAIDAR AL-HAKIMI.

Political Organizations

In the former PDRY the Yemen Socialist Party (YSP) was the only legal political party until December 1989, when the formation of opposition parties was legalized. There were no political parties in the former YAR. The two leading parties that emerged in the unified Yemen were the General People's Congress and the YSP. During 1990 an estimated 30–40 further political parties were reported to have been formed, and in 1991 a law regulating the formation of political parties was approved. Following the civil war from May to July 1994, President Saleh excluded the YSP from the new Government formed in October. There were 22 registered political parties in April 2003.

General People's Congress (GPC): San'a; e-mail gpc@y.net.ye; internet www.almotamar.net; f. 1982; a broad grouping of supporters of President Saleh; Chair. Field Marshal ALI ABDULLAH SALEH; Sec.-Gen. YAHYA ALI AL-RA'EI.

Al-Haq: San'a; f. 1995; conservative Islamic party; operates within the JMP opposition coalition; Sec.-Gen. HASSAN MUHAMMAD ZAID.

Joint Meeting Parties (JMP): San'a; f. 2006 as a coalition of five parties incl. al-Haq, al-Islah and the YSP; a sixth party, the Arab Socialist Baath Party, joined in 2008; Chair. SULTAN AL-SAMI.

League of the Sons of Yemen (Rabitat Abna' al-Yemen—RAY): Aden; e-mail services@ray-party.org; internet www.ray-party.org; f. 1951; represents interests of southern tribes; Leader ABD AL-RAHMAN AL-JIFRI; Sec.-Gen. MOHSIN MUHAMMAD BIN FAREED.

Nasserite Unionist Popular Organization: Aden; tel. (1) 536497; e-mail alwahdawinet@hotmail.com; internet www.alwahdawi.net; f. 1989 as a legal party; operates within the JMP opposition coalition; Sec.-Gen. SULTAN AL-ATWANI.

National Opposition Council: San'a; a coalition of eight small opposition parties.

Yemen Socialist Party (YSP): San'a; f. 1978 to succeed the United Political Organization—National Front (UPO—NF); fmrly Marxist-Leninist 'vanguard' party based on 'scientific socialism'; has Political Bureau and Cen. Cttee; mem. of the JMP opposition coalition; Sec.-Gen YASIN SAID NO'MAN.

Yemeni Congregation for Reform (al-Islah): POB 23090, San'a; tel. (3) 131001; fax (1) 383879; e-mail islah@al-islah.net; internet www.al-islah.net; f. 1990 by mems of the legislature, other political figures and tribal leaders; seeks constitutional reform based on Islamic law; a leading mem. of the JMP opposition coalition; Chair. Sheikh MUHAMMAD BIN ABDULLAH AL-YADOUMI; Sec.-Gen. ABD AL-WAHAB AL-ANISI.

Other parties in Yemen include the **Arab Socialist Baath Party**; the **Federation of Popular Forces**; the **Liberation Front Party**; the **Nasserite Democratic Party**; the **National Democratic Front**; the **National Social Party**; the **Popular Nasserite Reformation Party**; the **Social Green Party**; the **Yemen League**; the **Yemeni Unionist Congregation Party**; and the **Yemeni Unionist Rally Party**

Diplomatic Representation

EMBASSIES IN YEMEN

Algeria: POB 509, 67 Amman St, San'a; tel. (1) 206350; fax (1) 209688; e-mail ambalg-sa-ye@y.net.ye; Ambassador ABDELWAHAB BOZAHER.

Bulgaria: POB 1518, Asr, St 4, Residence 5, San'a; tel. (1) 208469; fax (1) 207924; e-mail embassy.sanaa@mfa.bg; internet www.mfa.bg/embassies/yemen; Ambassador BORIS BORISOV.

China, People's Republic: POB 482, az-Zubairy St, San'a; tel. (1) 275337; fax (1) 275341; e-mail chinaem@y.net.ye; internet ye.china-embassy.org; Ambassador CHANG HUA.

Cuba: POB 15256, St 6B, Blk 9, House 3, Safia Zone, nr Amman St, San'a; tel. (1) 442321; fax (1) 442322; e-mail embacubayemen@y.net.ye; Ambassador (vacant).

Djibouti: POB 3322, 6 Amman St, San'a; tel. (1) 445236; fax (1) 445237; e-mail youssouf@y.net.ye; Ambassador MOHAMMED HERSI.

Egypt: POB 1134, Gamal Abd al-Nasser St, San'a; tel. (1) 275948; fax (1) 274196; Ambassador ABU BAKR AL-QIRBI.

Eritrea: POB 11040, Western Safia Bldg, San'a; tel. (1) 209422; fax (1) 214088; Ambassador MOUSA YASSIN SHEIKH ALDDIN.

Ethiopia: POB 234, Al-Hamadani St, San'a; tel. (1) 208833; fax (1) 213780; e-mail ethoembs@y.net.ye; Ambassador ATO HASSEN ABDELLA.

France: POB 1286, cnr Sts 2 and 21, San'a; tel. (1) 268888; fax (1) 269160; e-mail sanaa@ambafrance-ye.org; internet www.ambafrance-ye.org; Ambassador FRANCK GELLET.

Germany: POB 2562, Hadda, San'a; tel. (1) 413174; fax (1) 413179; e-mail info@sanaa.diplo.de; internet www.sanaa.diplo.de; Ambassador CAROLA MÜLLER-HOLTKEMPER.

India: POB 1154, Bldg 12, Djibouti St, San'a; tel. (1) 441251; fax (1) 441257; e-mail indiaemb@y.net.ye; internet www.eoisanaa.com.ye; Ambassador AUSAF SAYEED.

Indonesia: POB 19873, Bldg 16, Beirut St, Haddah, San'a; tel. (1) 427210; fax (1) 427212; e-mail indosan@y.net.ye; Ambassador WAJID FAUZ.

Iran: POB 1437, Haddah St, San'a; tel. (1) 413552; fax (1) 414139; e-mail iriranemb@y.net.ye; Ambassador MAHMOUD ALI ZADA.

Iraq: POB 498, South Airport Rd, San'a; tel. (1) 440184; fax (1) 440187; e-mail snaemb@iraqmofamail.net; internet www.mofamission.gov.iq/yem; Ambassador ASAAD ALI YASEEN.

Italy: POB 1152, Haddah St No. 131, San'a; tel. (1) 432587; fax (1) 432590; e-mail ambasciata.sanaa@esteri.it; internet www.ambsanaa.esteri.it; Ambassador LUCIANO GALLI.

Japan: POB 817, Haddah Area, San'a; tel. (1) 423700; fax (1) 417850; e-mail info@ye.emb-japan.go.jp; internet www.ye.emb-japan.go.jp; Ambassador MASAKAZU TOSHIKAGE.

Jordan: POB 2152, Hadat Damascus St, San'a; tel. (1) 413276; fax (1) 414516; e-mail sanaa@fm.gov.jo; Ambassador SULEIMAN GHWEIRI.

Korea, Democratic People's Republic: POB 1209, al-Hasaba, Mazda Rd, San'a tel. (1) 232340; Ambassador CHANG MYONG SON.

Korea, Republic: POB 5005, San'a; tel. (1) 431801; fax (1) 431806; e-mail yemen@mofat.go.kr; internet yem.mofat.go.kr/eng/af/yem/main; Ambassador LEE YOUNG-HO.

Kuwait: POB 3746, South Ring Rd, San'a; tel. (1) 268876; fax (1) 268875; Ambassador FAHD SAAD SAEED AL-MAI'A.

Lebanon: POB 38, St 12, San'a; tel. (1) 203959; fax (1) 201120; e-mail lebem@y.net.ye; Ambassador (vacant).

Libya: POB 1506, Ring Rd, St 8, House 145, San'a; Secretary of Libyan Brotherhood Office RAMADAN PAZAMA.

Malaysia: POB 16157, San'a; tel. (1) 429781; fax (1) 429783; e-mail malsanaa@kln.gov.my; internet www.kln.gov.my/perwakilan/yemen; Ambassador ABDULLAH FAIZ ZAIN.

Mauritania: POB 19383, No. 6, Algeria St, San'a; tel. (1) 264188; fax (1) 215926; Ambassador MUHAMMAD MAHFOUZ OULD AL-QADI.

Morocco: POB 3181, Faj Attan, Hay Assormi, ave Beyrouth, San'a; tel. (1) 426628; fax (1) 426627; e-mail sifama_sanaa@hotmail.com; Ambassador MUHAMMAD HAMMA.

Netherlands: POB 463, off 14th October St, San'a; tel. (1) 421800; fax 417280; e-mail saa@minbuza.nl; internet yemen.nlembassy.org; Ambassador J. VERHEUL.

Oman: POB 6133, 14th October St, al-Gala Quarter, Bldg 2, Khormaskar, San'a; tel (1) 208874; fax (1) 204586; e-mail sanaa@mofa.gov.om; Ambassador (vacant).

Pakistan: POB 2848, Ring Rd, off Haddah St, San'a; tel. (1) 248814; fax (1) 248866; e-mail pakembassy@yemen.net.ye; internet www.pakistanembassyyemen.com; Ambassador AHMED AL-DILAI.

Qatar: POB 19717, San'a; tel. (1) 304640; fax (1) 304645; e-mail sanaa@mofa.gov.qa; Ambassador MUHAMMAD BIN HAMAD AL-FAHAID.

Russia: POB 1087, 26 September St, San'a; tel. (1) 278719; fax (1) 283142; e-mail remb@y.net.ye; internet www.rusemb-ye.org; Ambassador VLADIMIR P. DEDUSHKIN.

Saudi Arabia: POB 1184, Zuhara House, Hadda Rd, San'a; tel. (1) 240429; Ambassador ALI BIN MUHAMMAD AL-HAMDAN.

Somalia: POB 101, San'a; tel. (1) 208864; e-mail webmaster@somaligov.net; internet www.yemen.somaligov.net; Ambassador AHMED OMAR HAMIIDI.

Spain: POB 7108, San'a; tel. (1) 429899; fax (1) 429893; e-mail emb.sanaa@maec.es; Ambassador FRANCISCO JAVIER HERGUETA GARNICA.

Sudan: POB 2561, 82 Abou al-Hassan al-Hamadani St, San'a; tel. (1) 265231; fax (1) 265234; Ambassador AWAD HUSSEIN RIZIQ.

Syria: POB 494, Hadda Rd, Damascus St 1, San'a; tel. (1) 414891; Ambassador (vacant).

Tunisia: POB 2561, Diplomatic Area, St 22, San'a; tel. (1) 471845; fax (1) 471840; Ambassador JAMAL AL-JUWEILI.

Turkey: POB 18371, San'a; tel. (1) 432890; fax (1) 434828; e-mail embassy.sanaa@mfa.gov.tr; internet sanaa.emb.mfa.gov.tr; Ambassador FAZLI ÇORMAN.

United Arab Emirates: POB 2250, Ring Rd, San'a; tel. (1) 248777; fax (1) 248779; e-mail sanaa@mofa.gov.ae; internet uae-embassy.ae/embassies/ye; Ambassador ABDULLAH MATAR AL-MAZROUEI.

United Kingdom: POB 1287, 938 Thaher Himiyar St, East Ring Rd, San'a; tel. (1) 308114; fax (1) 302454; e-mail britishembassysanaa@fco.gov.uk; internet www.gov.uk/government/world/organisations/british-embassy-sana-a; Ambassador JANE MARRIOTT.

USA: POB 22347, Sa'awan St, Sheraton Hotel District, San'a; tel. (1) 7552000; fax (1) 303182; e-mail passanaa@state.gov; internet yemen.usembassy.gov; Ambassador GERALD M. FEIERSTEIN.

Judicial System

Yemen's Constitution guarantees the independence of the judiciary and identifies Islamic law (*Shari'a*) as the basis of all laws.

Yemen is divided into 20 governorates in addition to the Capital Secretariat of San'a (a municipality), each of which is further divided into districts. Each district has a Court of First Instance in which all cases are heard by a single magistrate. Appeals against decisions of the Courts of First Instance are referred to a Court of Appeal. Each governorate has a Court of Appeal with four divisions: Civil, Criminal, Matrimonial and Commercial, each of which consists of three judges.

The Supreme Court of the Republic, which sits in San'a, rules on matters concerning the Constitution, appeals against decisions of the Courts of Appeal and cases brought against members of the legislature. The Supreme Court has eight divisions, each of which consists of five judges.

Supreme Judicial Council: The Supreme Judicial Council supervises the proper function of the courts, and its Chairman is the President of the Republic; Chief of Supreme Judicial Council Dr ALI NASSER SALEM.

Religion

ISLAM

The majority of the population are Muslims. Most are Sunni Muslims of the Shafi'a sect, except in the north-west of the country, where Zaidism (a moderate sect of the Shi'a order) is the dominant persuasion.

CHRISTIANITY

The Roman Catholic Church

Apostolic Vicariate of Southern Arabia: POB 54, Abu Dhabi, United Arab Emirates; tel. (2) 4461895; fax (2) 4465177; e-mail info@ccsarabia.org; internet www.ccsarabia.org; f. 1889 as Apostolic Vicariate of Arabia; renamed as above, following reorganization in 2011; responsible for a territory comprising the UAE, Oman and Yemen, with an estimated 650,000 Roman Catholics (31 December 2010); Vicar Apostolic PAUL HINDER (Titular Bishop of Macon, Georgia, resident in the UAE); Vicar-Gen. Most Rev. LENNIE CONNULLY.

The Anglican Communion

Within the Episcopal Church in Jerusalem and the Middle East, Yemen forms part of the diocese of Cyprus and the Gulf. The Anglican congregations in San'a and Aden are entirely expatriate; the Bishop in Cyprus and the Gulf is resident in Cyprus, while the Archdeacon in the Gulf is resident in Bahrain.

HINDUISM

There is a small Hindu community.

The Press

Legislation embodying the freedom of the press in the unified Republic of Yemen was enacted in May 1990. The lists below include publications that appeared in the YAR and the PDRY prior to their unification in May 1990.

DAILIES

Al-Ayyam: POB 648, al-Khalij al-Imami, Crater, Aden; tel. (2) 255170; fax (2) 255692; e-mail editor@al-ayyam-yemen.com; internet www.al-ayyam.info; f. 1958; Editor HISHAM BASHRAHEEL.

Al-Jumhuriya: Taiz Information Office, Taiz; tel. (4) 216748; Arabic; Deputy Editor ZAID MUHAMMAD AL-GHABIRI; circ. 100,000.

Al-Rabi' 'Ashar Min Uktubar (14 October): POB 4227, Crater, Aden; f. 1968; not publ. on Sat; Arabic; Editorial Dir FAROUQ MUSTAFA RIFAT; Chief Editor MUHAMMAD HUSSAIN MUHAMMAD; circ. 20,000.

Al-Sharara (The Spark): POB 4227, Crater, Aden; Arabic; circ. 6,000.

Al-Thawra (The Revolution): POB 2195, San'a; tel. (1) 262626; fax (1) 274139; e-mail contact@althawranews.net; internet www.althawranews.net; Arabic; govt-owned; Editor MUHAMMAD AL-ZORKAH; circ. 110,000.

PERIODICALS

Almotamar Net: San'a; tel. (1) 208934; fax (1) 402983; e-mail editing@almotamar.net; internet www.almotamar.net; online news organ of the General People's Congress; Editor-in-Chief ABD AL-MALIK AL-FUAIDI.

Attijarah (Trade): POB 3370, Hodeida; tel. (3) 213784; fax (3) 211528; e-mail hodcci@y.net.ye; monthly; Arabic; publ. by Hodeida Chamber of Commerce.

Al-Balagh: San'a; tel. (1) 280581; fax (1) 280584; internet www.al-balagh.net; Arabic; weekly; Editor ABDULLAH IBRAHIM.

Al-Bilad (The Country): POB 1438, San'a; weekly; Arabic; centre-right; Editor-in-Chief ABD AL-MALIK AL-FAISHANI.

Dar al-Salam (Peace): POB 1790, San'a; tel. (1) 272946; f. 1948; weekly; Arabic; political, economic and general essays; Editor ABDULLAH MUKBOOL AL-SICGUL.

Al-Hares: Aden; fortnightly; Arabic; publ. by Ministry of the Interior; circ. 8,000.

Al-Hikma (Wisdom): POB 4227, Crater, Aden; monthly; Arabic; publ. by the Writers' Union; circ. 5,000.

Al-Mithaq (The Charter): San'a; weekly; organ of the Gen. People's Congress.

Al-Ra'i al-'Am (Public Opinion): POB 293, San'a; tel. (1) 253785; fax (1) 223378; e-mail alraialaam2002@yahoo.com; internet www.alraialaam.com.ye; weekly; independent; Editor KAMAL ALUFI.

Ray: Aden; tel. (1) 400532; internet www.ray-yem.com; Arabic; organ of League of the Sons of Yemen.

Al-Risalah: POB 55777, 26 September St, Taiz; tel. (4) 214215; fax (4) 221164; e-mail alaws@y.net.ye; f. 1968; weekly; Arabic; publ. by Assalam Trading Houses.

Al-Sahwa (Awakening): POB 11126, Hadda Rd, San'a; tel. (1) 247892; fax (1) 269218; e-mail aa230317@yahoo.com; internet www.alsahwa-yemen.net; weekly; publ. by Yemeni Congregation for Reform (al-Islah); Editor-in-Chief MUHAMMAD YOUSUFI.

Sawt al-Yemen (Voice of Yemen): POB 302, San'a; weekly; Arabic.

Al-Shoura: POB 15114, San'a; tel. (1) 251106; fax (1) 251104; e-mail shoura@y.net.ye; internet www.y.net.ye/shoura; circ. 15,000.

Al-Thawry (The Revolutionary): POB 4227, Crater, Aden; internet www.althawry.org; weekly, on Sat.; Arabic; organ of Cen. Cttee of Yemen Socialist Party.

26 September: POB 17, San'a; tel. (1) 262626; fax (1) 274139; e-mail 26sept@yemen.net.ye; internet www.26september.info; armed forces weekly; Editor-in-Chief ALI AL-SHATIR; circ. 25,000.

Al-Wahda al-Watani (National Unity): Al-Baath Printing House, POB 193, San'a; tel. (1) 77511; f. 1982; fmrly Al-Omal; monthly; Editor MUHAMMAD SALEM ALI; circ. 40,000.

Al-Wahdawi: POB 13010, San'a; tel. (1) 536497; e-mail alwahdawinet@hotmail.com; internet www.alwahdawi.net; weekly; organ of Nasserite Unionist Popular Org.

Yemen Observer: POB 19183, San'a; tel. (1) 505466; fax (1) 260504; e-mail contact@yobserver.com; internet www.yobserver.com; f. 1996; twice-weekly; English; publ. by Yemen Observer Publishing House; Editor-in-Chief ZAID AL-ALAYA'A.

Yemen Post: POB 15531, San'a; tel. (1) 000202; fax (1) 539268; e-mail editor@yemenpost.net; internet www.yemenpost.net; f. 2007; English; weekly; Editor-in-Chief HAKIM AL-MASMARI.

The Yemen Times: POB 2579, Hadda St, San'a; tel. (1) 268661; fax (1) 268276; e-mail yementimes@yementimes.com; internet www.yementimes.com; f. 1990; Mon. and Thur.; English; privately owned; Editor-in-Chief NADIA AL-SAQQAF; circ. 30,000.

Yemen Today: POB 19183, San'a; tel. (1) 248444; fax (1) 260504; e-mail info@yemen-today.com; internet www.yemen-today.com; f. 2007; monthly; English; politics and current affairs; publ. by Yemen Observer Publishing House; Man. Editor DAVID MACDONALD.

Yemeni Women: POB 4227, Crater, Aden; monthly; circ. 5,000.

PRESS ASSOCIATION

Yemeni Journalists Syndicate: San'a; internet yemenjournalist.org; Chair. YASSIN AL-MASOUDI; Sec.-Gen. MARWAN AL-DAMMAJ.

NEWS AGENCY

Yemen News Agency (SABA): Five Story Office Bldg and Printing Plant, al-Jama'ah al-Arabia St, al-Hasaba, San'a; tel. (1) 252944; fax (1) 251586; e-mail info@sabanews.net; internet www.sabanews.net; f. 1990 by merger of Saba News Agency and Aden News Agency following reunification of Yemen; mem. of the Fed. of Arab News Agencies and of the Non-Aligned News Agencies; Editor-in-Chief NASR TAHA MUSTAFA.

Publishers

Armed Forces Printing Press: POB 17, San'a; tel. (1) 274240; publishes *26 September*.

14 October Corpn for Printing, Publishing, Distribution and Advertising: POB 4227, Crater, Aden; under control of the Ministry of Information; publs include *Al-Rabi' 'Ashar Min Uktubar*; Chair. AHMAD AL-HUBAISHI.

Al-Thawrah Corpn: POB 2195, San'a; fax (1) 251505; Chair. M. R. AL-ZURKAH.

Yemen Observer Publishing House: POB 19183, San'a; tel. (1) 248444; fax (1) 260504; e-mail contact@yobserver.com; internet www.yobserver.com; f. 1996; publs include *Yemen Observer* and *Yemen Today*; Publr FARIS ABDULLAH SANABANI.

PUBLISHERS' ASSOCIATION

Yemeni Publishers' Association: f. 2008; Man. Dr NABIL ABADI.

Broadcasting and Communications

TELECOMMUNICATIONS

HiTs-Unitel (Y): San'a; tel. (700) 700111; internet www.y-gsm.com; f. 2007; provides mobile telephone services; Chair. NADER KALAI; CEO IMAD HAMAD.

MTN Yemen: POB 4562, San'a; e-mail ashahidi@mtn.com.ye; internet www.mtn.com.ye; f. 2000 as Spacetel Yemen; renamed as above in 2006, following merger of MTN Group Ltd with Investcom LLC; provides mobile services; CEO RAED AHMAD.

Public Telecommunications Corpn: POB 17045, Airport Rd, al-Jiraf, San'a; tel. and fax (1) 331109; e-mail ptc@yemen.net.ye; internet www.ptc.gov.ye; state-owned; Dir-Gen. MUHAMMAD AL-KASSOUS.

Yemen International Telecommunications Co (TeleYemen): POB 168, al-Tahreer Area, San'a; tel. (1) 7522000; fax (1) 270848; e-mail teleyemen@y.net.ye; internet www.teleyemen.com.ye; f. 1990 as a jt venture with Cable and Wireless PLC (United Kingdom); wholly owned by Public Telecommunications Corpn since 2003; provides fixed-line, mobile and internet services; CEO HESHAM AL-ALAILI.

Yemen Mobile Co: San'a; internet www.yemenmobile.com.ye; f. 2004 as a subsidiary of Yemen Int. Telecommunications Co (TeleYemen); initial public offering of 45% of shares in 2006; provides mobile services; Chair. ALI NAJI NASRI; CEO SADEK MUHAMMAD MOUSLEH; 1.9m. subscribers (2009).

Yemen Co for Mobile Telephony (SabaFon): POB 18550, San'a; e-mail website@sabafon.com; internet www.sabafon.com; f. 2001; shareholders include Al-Ahmar Group For Trade, the Iran Foreign Investment Co and Batelco (Bahrain); provides mobile services; Chair. Sheikh HAMID AL-AHMAR; CEO TARIK AL-HAIDARY.

BROADCASTING

Yemen Radio and Television Corpn: POB 2182, San'a; tel. (1) 230654; fax (1) 230761; e-mail info@yemenradio.net; internet www.yemenradio.net; state-controlled; operates two television channels and eight regional radio stations for San'a, Taiz, Mukalla, Aden, Lahij, Sayoun, Hodeida and Abyan; Chair. ABDULLAH AL-ZALAB; Gen. Man. AHMAD T. SHAYANY.

Finance

(cap. = capital; res = reserves; dep. = deposits; m. = million; brs = branches; amounts in Yemeni riyals unless otherwise indicated)

BANKING

Central Bank

Central Bank of Yemen: POB 59, Ali Abd al-Mughni St, San'a; tel. (1) 274314; fax (1) 274360; e-mail cbyh@y.net.ye; internet www.centralbank.gov.ye; f. 1971; merged with Bank of Yemen in 1990; cap. 6,000m., res 275,871m., dep. 773,681m. (Dec. 2009); Gov. MUHAMMAD AWAD BIN HUMAM; Dep. Gov. MUHAMMAD AL-RUBIDI; 20 brs.

Principal Banks

Co-operative and Agricultural Credit Bank (CACBANK): POB 2015, Banks Complex, al-Zubairy St, San'a; tel. and fax (1) 250009; e-mail info@cacbank.com.ye; internet www.cacbank.com.ye; f. 1976; cap. 11,000m., res 310m., dep. 212,861m. (Dec. 2011); Chair. MEHDAR ABDULLAH AL-SAGGAF; 54 brs.

International Bank of Yemen YSC: POB 4444, 106 al-Zubairy St, San'a; tel. (1) 407000; fax (1) 407020; e-mail info@ibyemen.com; internet www.ibyemen.com; f. 1980; commercial bank; 75% private Yemeni interests; 25% foreign shareholders; cap. 8,000m., res 1,950m., dep. 168,712m. (Dec. 2010); Chair. HAYEL A. HAQ BESHER (acting); Gen. Man. AHMAD T. N. AL-ABSI; 19 brs.

Islamic Bank of Yemen for Finance and Investment: POB 18452, Mareb Yemen Insurance Co Bldg, al-Zubairy St, San'a; tel. (1) 206117; fax (1) 206116; internet www.islbank.com; f. 1996; savings, commercial, investment and retail banking; cap. 3,568m., res 1,449m., dep. 12,616m. (Dec. 2009); Chair. ABD AL-KAREM AL-ASWADI; Man. Dir KHALED AL-DUSARI; 5 brs.

National Bank of Yemen: POB 5, Arwa Rd, Crater, Aden; tel. (2) 253753; fax (2) 252325; e-mail nby.ho@y.net.ye; internet www.nbyemen.com; f. 1970 as Nat. Bank of South Yemen; reorg. 1971; 100% state-owned; cap 10,000m., res 3,554m., dep. 92,125m. (Dec. 2010); Chair. AHMED OBAID AL-FADHLI; Gen. Man. ESAM ALAWI AL-SAKKAF; 28 brs.

Shamil Bank of Yemen and Bahrain: POB 19382, Haddah St, San'a; tel. (1) 411847; fax (1) 411848; e-mail shamilbank@y.net.ye; internet www.sbyb.net; f. 2002; cap. 6,000m., res 136m., dep. 22,586m. (Dec. 2010); Chair. AHMAD ABUBAKER OMER BAZARA; Gen. Man. SAEED MUHAMMAD BAZARA.

Tadhamon International Islamic Bank: POB 2411, al-Saeed Commercial Bldg, al-Zubairy St, San'a; e-mail tib@y.net.ye; internet www.tiib.com; f. 1995 as Yemen Bank for Investment and Devt; became Tadhamon Islamic Bank in 1996; name changed as above in 2002; cap. 20,000m., res 29,113m., dep. 323,016m. (Dec. 2010); Chair. ABD AL-GABBAR HAYEL SAID; Man. Dir SHAWKI AHMED HAYEL; 21 brs.

Yemen Bank for Reconstruction and Development (YBRD): POB 541, 26 September St, San'a; tel. (1) 270483; fax (1) 271684; e-mail ybrdho@y.net.ye; internet www.ybrd.com.ye; f. 1962; 51% state-owned; 49% owned by public shareholders; cap. 10,000m., res 4,225m., dep. 111,158m. (Dec. 2010); Chair. HUSSAIN FADHL MUHAMMAD HARHARA; Gen. Man. ABD AL-NASER NOMAN AL-HAJ; 43 brs.

Yemen Commercial Bank (YCB): POB 19845, al-Rowaishan Bldg, al-Zubairy St, San'a; tel. (1) 277224; fax (1) 277291; e-mail info@ycb.com.ye; internet www.ycb.com.ye; f. 1993; cap. 6,926m., res 619m., dep. 83,351m. (Dec. 2010); Board Dir Sheikh MUHAMMAD BIN YAHYA AL-ROWAISHAN; Exec. Pres. and Gen. Man. AYED AL-MASHNI; 13 brs.

INSURANCE

Aman Insurance Co (YSC): POB 1133, al-Zubairy St, San'a; tel. (1) 202106; fax (1) 209452; e-mail akil@amaninsurance-ye.com; internet www.y.net.ye/amaninsurance; all classes of insurance; Chair. MUHAMMAD ABDULLAH AL-SUNIDAR; Man. Dir AKIL AL-SAKKAF.

Mareb Yemen Insurance Co: POB 2284, al-Zubairy St, San'a; tel. (1) 206111; fax (1) 206118; e-mail maryinsco74@y.net.ye; internet www.marebinsurance.com.ye; f. 1974; all classes of insurance; cap. 150m.; Chair. and CEO ALI MUHAMMAD HASHIM; Gen. Man. ALI ABD AL-RASHID.

Saba Yemen Insurance Co: POB 19214, Ishaq Bldg, al-Zubairy St, San'a; tel. (1) 240908; fax (1) 240943; e-mail saba-ins@y.net.ye; internet www.saba-insurance.com; f. 1990; all classes of insurance; cap. 400m. (Jan. 2006); Chair. Sheikh MUHAMMAD BIN YAHIAH AL-ROWAISHAN; Man. Dir MUHAMMAD HUSSEIN ZAWIYAH.

Trust Yemen Insurance and Reinsurance Co: POB 18392, San'a; tel. (1) 425007; fax (1) 412570; e-mail trust-yemen@y.net.ye; internet www.trustgroup.net/Main; f. 1995; all classes of insurance; Chair. ALI DHIB; Gen. Man. HUSSAIN AYYOUB.

United Insurance Co: POB 1883, al-Saeed Commercial Bldg, 2nd Floor, al-Zubairy St, San'a; tel. (1) 555555; fax (1) 214012; e-mail uicyemen@uicyemen.com; internet www.uicyemen.com; f. 1981; general and life insurance; cap. 400m. (2005); Chair. AHMAD SAID; Gen. Man. TAREK A. HAYEL SAID.

Al-Watania Insurance Co (YSC): POB 15497, al-Kasr St, San'a; tel. (1) 272874; fax (1) 272924; e-mail gm@alwataniains.com; internet www.alwataniains.com; f. 1993; all classes of insurance; cap. 100m. (2005); Exec. Chair. YOUSUF ABD AL-WADUD SAID.

Yemen General Insurance Co (SYC): POB 2709, YGI Bldg, 25 Algiers St, San'a; tel. (1) 442489; fax (1) 442492; e-mail ygi-san@y.net

.ye; internet www.yginsurance.com; f. 1977; all classes of insurance; cap. 500m. (2005); Chair. ABD AL-GABBAR THABET; Gen. Man. BAKIR AL-MUNSHI.

Yemen Insurance Co: POB 8437, San'a; tel. (1) 272806; fax (1) 274177; e-mail sanaa@yemenins.com; internet yemenins.com; f. 1990; all classes of insurance; cap. 100m.; Chair. MUHAMMAD MUBARAK ADHBAN; Gen. Man. KHALID BASHIR TAHIR.

Yemen Insurance and Reinsurance Co: POB 456, Aden; tel. (2) 54286; fax (2) 57336; e-mail yireico@y.net.ye; f. 1969; Lloyd's Agents; cap. 5m.; Gen. Man. HUSSAIN AL-HADDAD.

Trade and Industry

GOVERNMENT AGENCIES

General Investment Authority (GIAY): POB 19022, Hadda St, San'a; tel. (1) 434312; fax (1) 434314; e-mail info@investinyemen.gov.ye; internet www.investinyemen.gov.ye; f. 1992; promotes and facilitates strategic investment in Yemen; Chair. SALEH MUHAMMAD SAID AL-ATTAR.

Yemen Economic Corpn: POB 1207, San'a; tel. (1) 262501; fax (1) 262508; e-mail yeco@yeco.biz; internet www.yeco.biz; f. 1973; promotes and facilitates investment and development across various sectors of the economy; Gen. Man. ALI MUHAMMAD AL-KUHLANI.

DEVELOPMENT ORGANIZATIONS

Agricultural Research and Extension Authority: POB 87148, Dhamar; tel. (6) 423913; fax (6) 423914; e-mail area@yemen.net.ye; internet www.area.gov.ye; Chair. Dr ISMAIL A. MUHARRAM.

Social Fund for Development (SFD): POB 15485, Fij Attan, San'a; tel. (1) 449669; fax (1) 449670; e-mail sfd@sfd-yemen.org; internet www.sfd-yemen.org; f. 1997; autonomous devt agency, governed by a bd of dirs representing the Govt, non-governmental orgs and the private sector, chaired by the Prime Minister.

Tihama Development Authority: POB 3792, Doreihemy Rd, Hodeida; e-mail arcechodeida@y.net.ye; agricultural devt agency under the supervision of the Ministry of Agriculture and Irrigation; Chair. MUHAMMAD YAHIA AL-GASHAM.

Yemen Free Zone Public Authority: POB 5842, Aden; tel. (2) 241210; fax (2) 221237; e-mail yfzpa@y.net.ye; internet www.yemenfreezone.com; f. 1991; supervises creation of a free zone for industrial investment; Vice-Chair. ABD AL-GALIL SHAIF AL-SHAIBI.

CHAMBERS OF COMMERCE

Chamber of Commerce and Industry—Aden: POB 473, Crater 101, Aden; tel. (2) 251104; fax (2) 255446; e-mail cciaden@yemen.net.ye; internet www.adenchamber.org; f. 1886; 9,000 mems; Chair. MUHAMMAD OMER BAMASHMUS; Dir-Gen. KHALIL TAHA KHALIL.

Federation of Chambers of Commerce: POB 16992, San'a; tel. (1) 232445; fax (1) 221765; e-mail moh-saeed@fycci.org; internet www.fycci.org; Chair. MUHAMMAD ABDO SAID AN'AM; Dir-Gen. MUHAMMAD AL-MAITAMI.

Hadramout Chamber of Commerce and Industry: POB 8302, Main St, Mukalla City, Hadramout; tel. (5) 353258; fax (5) 303437; e-mail hdramoutchamber@y.net.ye; Chair. OMER A. R. BAJARASH.

Hodeida Chamber of Commerce: POB 3370, 20 al-Zubairy St, Hodeida; tel. (3) 217401; fax (3) 211528; e-mail hodcci@y.net.ye; f. 1960; 6,500 mems; cap. YR 10m.; Dir NABIL AL-WAGEEH.

Ibb Chamber of Commerce and Industry: POB 70004, Ibb; tel. (4) 404868; fax (4) 403893.

Saadah Chamber of Commerce and Industry: POB 3754-2566, Saadah; tel. (7) 521524; fax (7) 513671; Chair. MUHAMMAD R. JARMAN.

San'a Chamber of Commerce and Industry: Airport Rd, al-Hasabah St, POB 195, San'a; tel. (1) 232361; fax (1) 232412; e-mail sanaacomyemen@y.net.ye; f. 1959; over 35,000 mems; Chair. HASSAN AL-KABOUS; Gen. Man. MUHAMMAD AL-MAHALLA.

Taiz Chamber of Commerce and Industry: POB 5029, Chamber St, Taiz; tel. (4) 210580; fax (4) 212335; e-mail taizchamber@y.net.ye; internet www.taizchamber.com; f. 1962; 5,600 mems; Chair. AHMED HAYEL SAID; Dir MOFID A. SAIF.

Thamar Chamber of Commerce and Industry: POB 87010, Thamar; tel. (5) 502200; fax (6) 501191.

STATE ENTERPRISES

While the Government is committed to privatization in all areas of trade and industry, there are still numerous state-owned enterprises:

General Corpn for Foreign Trade and Grains: POB 710, San'a; tel. (1) 202361; fax (1) 209511; f. 1976; Dir-Gen. ABD AL-RAHMAN AL-MADWAHI.

General Corpn for Manufacturing and Marketing of Cement: POB 1920, San'a; tel. (1) 215691; fax (1) 263168; Chair. AMIN ABD AL-WAHID AHMAD.

National Co for Foreign Trade: POB 90, Crater, Aden; tel. (2) 42793; fax (2) 42631; f. 1969; incorporates main foreign trading businesses (nationalized in 1970) and arranges their supply to the National Co for Home Trade; Gen. Man. AHMAD MUHAMMAD SALEH (acting).

National Co for Home Trade: POB 90, Crater, Aden; tel. (2) 41483; fax (2) 41226; f. 1969; marketing of general consumer goods, building materials, electrical goods, motor cars and spare parts, agricultural machinery, etc.; Man. Dir ABD AL-RAHMAN AL-SAILANI.

National Dockyards Co: POB 1244, Hedjuff, Aden; tel. (2) 244503; fax (2) 241681; f. 1969; maintenance and repair of ships and vessels; marine engineering; Man. Dir ABDULLAH ALI MUHAMMAD.

Yemen Drug Co for Industry and Commerce (YEDCO): POB 40, San'a; tel. (1) 370210; fax (1) 370209; e-mail yedco@y.net.ye; import, maufacture and distribution of pharmaceutical products, chemicals, medical supplies, baby foods and scientific instruments; Chair. MUHAMMAD AL-KOHLANI; Gen. Man. MUHAMMAD ALI AL-KADIR.

Yemen Trading and Construction Co: POB 1092, San'a; tel. (1) 264005; fax (1) 240624; e-mail ytcc@y.net.ye; f. 1979; initial cap. YR 100m.; Gen. Man. GHASSAN AMIN KASSIM.

STATE HYDROCARBONS COMPANIES

General Corpn for Oil and Mineral Resources: San'a; f. 1990; state petroleum co; Pres. AHMAD BARAKAT.

Ministry of Oil and Minerals: POB 81, San'a; tel. (1) 202306; fax (1) 202314; e-mail mom@y.net.ye; internet www.mom.gov.ye; responsible for the refining and marketing of petroleum products, and for prospecting and exploitation of indigenous hydrocarbons and other minerals; subsidiaries include:

Aden Refinery Co: POB 3003, Aden 110; tel. (2) 376214; fax (2) 376600; e-mail info@arc-ye.com; internet www.arc-ye.com; f. 1952; operates petroleum refinery; capacity 8.6m. metric tons per year; operates two general tankers and one chemical tanker; Exec. Dir FATHI SALEM ALI; Refinery Man. MUHAMMAD YESLAM.

Petroleum Exploration and Production Authority (PEPA): POB 7196, Haddah St, San'a; tel. (1) 442630; fax (1) 442632; e-mail pepa-expo.com@y.net.ye; internet www.pepa.com.ye; f. 1990; manages petroleum concessions; Chair. NASSER ALI AL-HOMADY.

Safer Exploration and Production Operations Co: POB 481, San'a; tel. (1) 416080; e-mail webmaster@sepocye.com; internet www.sepocye.com; f. 1997; operation of Marib/Al-Jawf Blk 18 since 2005; Exec. Man. MUHAMMAD HUSSAIN AL-HAJ.

Yemen Co for Investment in Oil and Minerals: POB 11993, San'a; tel. (1) 203925; fax (1) 203923; e-mail yicom@y.net.ye; internet www.yicom.net; promotes investment in new exploration areas; supervises operators in several exploration blocks; Exec. Gen. Man. Eng. ALI AL-KADI.

Yemen Gas Co: al-Raqas St, San'a; internet www.yemengasco.com; f. 1993 as Gen. Gas Corpn; renamed as above 1996; 100% govt-owned; production and distribution of LPG; Deputy Dir NAJEEB AL-OUD.

Yemen General Oil and Gas Corporation: POB 19137, San'a; tel. (1) 446857; fax (1) 446417; e-mail info@yogc.com.ye; internet www.yogc.com.ye; f. 1996; Exec. Dir ABD AL-KADER SHAEA.

Yemen National Oil Co: POB 5050, Ma'alla, Aden; importer and distributor of petroleum products; Gen. Man. MUHAMMAD ABD HUSSEIN.

Yemen Oil Refinery Co: POB 15203, San'a; tel. and fax (1) 218962; e-mail info@yorco.net; internet www.yorco.net; f. 1996; operates petroleum refinery at Marib; Gen. Man. Eng. MUSAD AHMAD AL-SUBARI.

Yemen Petroleum Co: tel. (1) 444046; fax (1) 447691; internet www.ypcye.com; f. 1961; responsible for marketing of oil in domestic market; Exec. Dir OMAR MUHAMMAD ISMAIL AL-ARHABI.

Yemen LNG Co Ltd: POB 15347, San'a; tel. (1) 438000; fax (1) 428042; e-mail pr@yemenlng.com; internet www.yemenlng.com; f. 2005; shareholders include Total SA (France—39.62%), Hunt Oil (USA—17.22%), Yemen Gas Co (16.73%), SK Corpn (Repub. of Korea—9.55%); operates a two-train LNG plant in Marib region; Chair. HISHAM SHARAF (Minister of Oil and Minerals); Gen. Man. JACQUES AZIBERT.

UTILITIES

Electricity

Public Electricity Corpn: POB 178, Airport Rd, San'a; tel. (1) 328141; fax (1) 328150; e-mail ypecnt@y.net.ye; Man. Dir ABD AL-MONIM MUTAHAR.

Water

General Authority for Rural Water Supply Projects (GARWSP): San'a; govt agency responsible for water supply in rural areas.

National Water Resources Authority (NWRA): POB 8944, Amran St, al-Hassaba, San'a; tel. (1) 231733; e-mail info@nwra-yemen.org; internet www.nwra-yemen.org; govt agency responsible for management of water resources; Chair. SALEM HASSAN BASHUEB.

National Water and Sewerage Authority (NWSA): POB 104, San'a; tel. (1) 250158; fax (1) 251536; e-mail nwsa@y.net.ye; govt agency responsible for water supply in urban areas.

MAJOR COMPANIES

Al-Ahwal Holding Group: Djibouti St, San'a; tel. (1) 447573; fax (1) 442058; e-mail nabil.yassin@alahwal.com.ye; internet www.alahwal.com.ye; f. 1961; import and distribution of products in sectors incl. agricultural and industrial machinery, automotive and foodstuffs; subsidiaries include Al-Ahwal Gen. Trading Co, ATMA Trading Co and Four Stars Co.

Al-Gharasi International Trading Co: POB 1270, San'a; tel. (1) 683179; fax (1) 683173; e-mail info@algharasi.com; internet www.algharasi.com; f. 1972; 8 cos; general trading, distribution of medical supplies and mfrs of food products, plastics and tissue papers.

Al-Hadha Group: al-Hadha Bldg, al-Zubeiry St, San'a; tel. (1) 211161; fax (1) 211164; e-mail alhadha@al-hadha.com; internet www.al-hadha.com; 12 cos in Yemen, four abroad; general trading, distribution of LPG, currency exchange, construction, shipping; Chair. ABDULLAH H. AL-HADHA.

Hayel Saeed Anam Group: POB 5302, Taiz; tel. (4) 215171; fax (4) 212334; e-mail info@hsagroup.com; internet www.hsagroup.com; 14 cos in Yemen incl. Yemen Co for Industry and Commerce, Yemen Co for Ghee and Soap Industry, National Dairy and Food Co, National Co for Cement; trading, manufacturing, services and agricultural and marine resources sectors; Chair. ABD AL-RAHMAN HAYEL SAEED.

Thabet Brothers Group of Cos: Thabet Group Bldg, POB 5106, Madram Rd, Aden; tel. (2) 246000; fax (2) 246013; e-mail info@tehama.com.ye; 12 cos incl. Hodeida Shipping and Transport Co, Red Sea Contracting and Construction, Tehama, Yemen Gen. Insurance Co; general trading, shipping, construction, insurance, foodstuffs; Chair. MUHAMMAD ABDO THABET.

Tihama Tractors and Engineering Co Ltd: POB 49, 17 Algeria St, San'a; tel. (1) 471809; fax (1) 472007; e-mail titra@y.net.ye; internet www.tihama-group.com; f. 1963 as Yemen Trading and Shipping Co; present name adopted 1967; originally established for sale and distribution of agricultural machinery and industrial products; has diversified into management of major telecommunications and infrastructure projects; Chair. AMIN DIRHEM; Gen. Man. AHMAD ALI AL-ARASHI.

TRADE UNIONS

Agricultural Co-operatives Union: POB 649, San'a; tel. (1) 270685; fax (1) 274125.

General Confederation of Workers: POB 1162, Ma'alla, Aden; f. 1956; affiliated to WFTU; 35,000 mems; Pres. RAJEH SALEH NAJI; Gen. Sec. ABD AL-RAZAK SHAIF.

Trade Union Federation: San'a; Pres. ALI SAIF MUQBIL.

Transport

RAILWAYS

There are no railways in Yemen.

ROADS

In 1996 Yemen had a total road network of 64,725 km, including 5,234 km of main roads and 2,474 km of secondary roads. In 2006 there were an estimated 73,200 km of roads; some 13.7% of the road network was paved.

General Corpn for Roads and Bridges: POB 1185, al-Zubairy St, Asir Rd, San'a; tel. (1) 202278; fax (1) 209571; e-mail gcrb@y.net.ye; responsible for maintenance and construction.

Yemen Land Transport Co: POB 279, Taiz St, San'a; tel. (1) 262108; fax (1) 263117; f. 1961; incorporates fmr Yemen Bus Co and all other public transport of the fmr PDRY; oversees provision of public transport; scheduled for privatization; Chair. YAHYA AHMED AL-KOHLANI; Gen. Man. SALEH ABDULLAH ABD AL-WALI.

SHIPPING

Aden is the main port. Aden Main Harbour has 28 first-class berths. In addition, there is ample room to accommodate vessels of light draught at anchor in the 18-ft dredged area. There is also 800 ft of cargo wharf accommodating vessels of 300 ft length and 18 ft draught. Aden Oil Harbour accommodates four tankers of 57,000 metric tons and up to 40 ft draught. A long-term concession to operate Aden Container Terminal and nearby Ma'alla Container Terminal, in partnership with the Gulf of Aden Port Corporation, was signed by Dubai Ports World (DP World), of the United Arab Emirates, in late 2005 and came into effect in November 2008, incorporating an estimated US $220m. upgrade programme; this was expected to increase the annual capacity from 700,000 containers in 2007 to 1.5m. containers by 2012. However, DP World withdrew from the contract in September 2012. Total container throughput at Aden was 265,459 20-ft equivalent units in 2009. Hodeida port, on the Red Sea, also handles a considerable amount of traffic. The port of Bal Haf has been developed to accommodate natural gas liquefaction and export facilities; shipments commenced in late 2009. Al-Mukalla port, in Hadramout province, is an important regional centre for trade, fishing and shipbuilding. Plans to develop a new industrial port at Dhabah, also in Hadramout, were announced in 2009.

At 31 December 2012 Yemen's flag registered fleet comprised 40 vessels, with a combined displacement of some 220,977 grt, of which one was a fish carrier and six were general cargo ships.

Regulatory and Port Authorities

Maritime Affairs Authority: POB 1443, San'a; tel. (2) 221581; fax (2) 221448; e-mail maa-headoffice@y.net.ye; internet www.maa-yemen.net; f. 1990 as Public Corpn for Maritime Affairs; renamed as above 2001; protection of the marine environment; registration of ships; implementation of international maritime conventions; Capt. ABDULLAH IBRAHIM ABKAR AL-NEGRI.

Yemen Arabian Sea Ports Corpn: POB 50793, al-Mukalla, Hadramout; tel. (5) 305560; fax (5) 303508; e-mail info@portofmukalla.com; internet www.portofmukalla.com; management and supervision of ports at al-Mukalla and Socotra; Chair. ABD AL-HAFEDH AL-QUAITI.

Yemen Gulf of Aden Ports Corpn: POB 1316, Tawahi, Aden; tel. (2) 202666; fax (2) 203521; e-mail info@portofaden.net; internet www.portofaden.net; f. 1888; management and supervision of Port of Aden and other ports in the western Gulf of Aden; Chair. Capt. MUHAMMAD ISHAQ; Port Officer Capt. SHAKEEB M. ABD AL-WAHED.

Yemen Red Sea Ports Corpn: Hodeida; tel. (3) 211603; fax (3) 211561; e-mail chairman@portofhodeidah.com; internet www.portofhodeidah.com; management and supervision of the Port of Hodeida as the main port and ports of Mocha and Salif as secondary ports.

Principal Shipping Companies

Atlas Shipping and Transport Co Ltd: POB 3182, Hodeida; tel. (3) 202053; fax (3) 202057; e-mail atlas@atlasye.com; internet www.atlasye.com; f. 1998; subsidiary of Al-Hadha Group; shipping agents, cargo, bunkering.

Al-Bukari Shipping Co Ltd: POB 3358, Hodeida; tel. (3) 222888; fax (3) 211741; e-mail bukari@y.net.ye; internet www.bukarishipping.com; f. 1978; shipping agents, stevedoring, cargo, bunkering; Man. Dir SULEIMAN H. AL-BUKARI.

Elkirshi Shipping and Stevedoring Co: POB 3813, al-Hamdi St, Hodeida; tel. (3) 204448; fax (3) 241199; operates at ports of Hodeida, Mocha and Salif; Contact FATHI ALI MUHAMMAD.

Gulf of Aden Shipping Co: POB 1439, Tawahi, Aden; tel. (2) 271080; fax (2) 237912; e-mail almansoob@y.net.ye; internet www.almansoob.com.ye; f. 1990; cargo operations, arranges crew changes, bunkers and repairs; Operations Man. MUHAMMAD ADAM.

Hodeida Shipping and Transport Co Ltd: POB 3337, Hodeida; tel. (3) 228543; fax (3) 228533; e-mail hodship_1969@y.net.ye; internet www.hodship.aden.com.ye; f. 1969; shipping agents, stevedoring, Lloyd's agents; clearance, haulage, land transportation, cargo and vessel surveys; Gen. Man. HASSAN A. KASSIM.

Middle East Shipping Co Ltd (Mideast): POB 3700, Hayel Saeed Bldg, al-Tahreer St, Hodeida; tel. (3) 203977; fax (3) 203910; e-mail mideast@mideastshipping.com; internet www.mideastshipping.com; f. 1962; Chair. ABD AL-WASA HAYEL SAID; Gen. Man. AHMAD GAZEM SAID; brs in Mocha, Aden, Taiz, Mukalla, San'a, Salif, Ras Isa, al-Shihr.

National Shipping Co: POB 1228, Steamer Point, Aden; tel. 733553888 (mobile); fax (2) 202344; e-mail natship@y.net.ye; shipping, bunkering, clearing and forwarding, and travel agents; Dir-Gen. MOHSEN SALEM BIN BREIK.

Saba Shipping and Stevedoring Co Ltd: POB 3378/3173, Meena St, Hodeida; tel. (3) 226628; fax (3) 211588; e-mail sabaship@y.net.ye; internet www.sabashipping.com; f. 1983; shipping agents, stevedoring, cargo, bunkering.

CIVIL AVIATION

There are six international airports—San'a International (13 km from the city), Aden Civil Airport (at Khormaksar, 11 km from the port of Aden), al-Ganad (at Taiz), Mukalla (Riyan), Seyoun and Hodeida. Work on the second phase of an expansion of San'a international airport was initially expected to be completed in 2009, but was subsequently delayed. In late 2013 it was reported that the Government was preparing to request bids for the second phase of construction.

Civil Aviation and Meteorology Authority: POB 1042, San'a; tel. (1) 274717; fax (1) 274718; e-mail hasconst@cama.gov.ye; internet www.cama.gov.ye; supervisory body for civil aviation and meteorology affairs; Chair. HAMED AHMAD FARAG.

Felix Airways: Al-Hasaba St, Airport Rd, San'a; tel. (1) 252992; fax (1) 252989; e-mail hassan.thabet@felixairways.com; internet www.felixairways.com; f. 2008; 75% owned by Islamic Corpn for the Devt of the Private Sector, 25% by Yemen Airways; low-cost carrier providing domestic services from San'a and Aden and regional services to the United Arab Emirates, Oman, Saudi Arabia and Djibouti; CEO Eng. MUHAMMAD ABDULLAH AL-ARASHA; Chair. Sheikh SALEH AL-AWAJI.

Yemen Airways (Yemenia): POB 1183, Airport Rd, San'a; tel. (1) 232400; fax (1) 252991; e-mail info@yemenia.com; internet www.yemenia.com; f. 1961 as Yemen Airlines; nationalized as Yemen Airways Corpn 1972; present name adopted 1978; merged with airlines of fmr PDRY in 1996; owned 51% by Yemeni Govt and 49% by Govt of Saudi Arabia; scheduled for privatization; supervised by a ministerial cttee under the Ministry of Transport; internal services and external services to more than 30 destinations in the Middle East, Asia, Africa, Europe and the USA; Chair. and CEO ABD AL-KALEK S. AL-KADI; Man. Dir ABD AL-AZIZ AL-HAZMI.

Tourism

Yemen boasts areas of beautiful scenery, a favourable climate, and towns of historic and architectural importance. UNESCO has named San'a, Shibam and Zabid as World Heritage sites because of their cultural significance; in 2008 the Socotra Archipelago was added to the list of World Heritage sites as a natural landmark. However, the growth of tourism has, in recent years, been hampered by political instability, with a number of foreign tourists being victims of fatal attacks and kidnappings. In 2012 some 459,329 tourists visited Yemen, compared with just 387,498 in 2011; tourism receipts totalled US $849m. in 2012.

Association of Yemen Tourism and Travel Agencies: San'a; e-mail ysaleh@y.net.ye; internet www.aytta.org.ye; f. 1996; Chair. YAHYA M. A. SALEH.

General Authority of Tourism: POB 129, San'a; tel. (1) 252319; fax (1) 252317; e-mail gtda@gtda.gov.ye; internet www.gtda.gov.ye; Chair. MUTAHAR TAQI.

Yemen Tourism Promotion Board: POB 5607, 48 Amman St, San'a; tel. (1) 251033; fax (1) 251034; e-mail ytpb@yementourism.com; internet www.yementourism.com; f. 1999; Exec. Dir AHMAD AL-BIEL.

Defence

The armed forces of the former YAR and the PDRY were officially merged in May 1990, but by early 1994 the process had not been completed and in May civil war broke out between the forces of the two former states, culminating in victory for the North. In October former President Saleh announced plans for the modernization of the armed forces, which would include the banning of party affiliation in the security services and armed forces, and in March 1995 the full merger of the armed forces was announced.

Supreme Commander of the Armed Forces: President Field Marshal ABD AL-RABBUH MANSUR AL-HADI.

Chief of the General Staff: Brig.-Gen. AHMAD ALI AL-ASHWAL.

Chief of the Air Force: Gen. RASHED NASIR ALI AL-JANAD.

Defence Budget (2013): YR 357,000m.

Military Service: Two years.

Total Armed Forces (as assessed at November 2012): 66,700: army 60,000; navy 1,700; air force 3,000; air defence 2,000.

Paramilitary Forces (as assessed at November 2012): an estimated 50,000-strong Ministry of the Interior Force, at least 20,000 tribal levies, and a coast guard of about 1,200.

Education

Primary education in Yemen is compulsory from the age of six and lasts for six years. Secondary education, beginning at 13, lasts for a further six years. In the 2009/10 academic year enrolment at primary schools included 78% of children in the relevant age-group (boys 85%; girls 70%). In the same year enrolment at secondary schools included 40% of students in the appropriate age-group (males 49%; females 31%). In 2009/10 a total of 26,044 pupils were in pre-primary education, and 4,402,679 pupils attended primary institutions. There were 574,899 pupils in secondary education in that year, while 266,096 students were enrolled at public and private universities. In 2010 public expenditure on education amounted to an estimated YR 279,000m., equivalent to 19% of total government spending. A Basic Education Development project, for which the World Bank provided a loan of US $65m., aims to increase enrolment in primary schools to 85% over 40 years.

Bibliography

al-Attar, Mohamed Said. *Le sous-développement économique et social du Yémen*. Algiers, Editions Tiers-Monde, 1966.

Badeeb, Said M. *The Saudi–Egyptian Conflict over North Yemen 1962–70*. Colorado, Westview Press, 1986.

Balsan, François. *Inquiétant Yémen*. Paris, 1961.

Bidwell, Robin. *The Two Yemens*. London, Longman, 1983.

Blumi, Isa. *Chaos in Yemen: Societal Collapse and the New Authoritarianism*. Abingdon, Routledge, 2010.

Brehony, Noel. *Yemen Divided: The Story of a Failed State in South Arabia*. London, I. B. Tauris, 2011.

Burrowes, Robert D. *The Yemen Arab Republic: The Politics of Development 1962–1986*. London, Croom Helm, 1987.

Historical Dictionary of Yemen (2nd edn). Lanham, MD, Scarecrow Press, 2010.

Carapico, Sheila. *Civil Society in Yemen: The Political Economy of Activism in Modern Arabia*. Cambridge University Press, 1998.

Caton, Steven C. *An Anthropology of War and Mediation*. New York, Hill and Wang, 2006.

Central Office of Information. *Aden and South Arabia*. London, HMSO, 1965.

Clark, Victoria. *Yemen: Dancing on the Heads of Snakes*. New Haven, CT, Yale University Press, 2010.

Colburn, Marta. *The Republic of Yemen: Development Challenges in the 21st Century*. London, Catholic Institute for International Relations, 2004.

Colonial Office. *Accession of Aden to the Federation of South Arabia*. London, HMSO, 1962.

Aden and the Yemen. London, HMSO, 1960.

Treaty of Friendship and Protection between the United Kingdom and the Federation of South Arabia. London, HMSO, 1964.

Detalle, Renaud. *Tensions in Arabia: The Saudi–Yemeni Fault Line*. Baden-Baden, Nomos Verlagsgesellschaft, 2000.

Doe, Brian. *Southern Arabia*. London, Thames and Hudson, 1972.

Dresch, Paul. *Tribes, Government and History in Yemen*. New York, NY, Oxford University Press, 1994.

A History of Modern Yemen. Cambridge, Cambridge University Press, 2001.

Enders, Klaus, Williams, Sherwyn E., Choueiri, Nada G., Sobolev, Yuri V., and Walliser, Jan. *Yemen in the 1990s: From Unification to Economic Reform* (IMF Occasional Paper). Washington, DC, IMF Publication Services, 2002.

Federation of South Arabia. *Conference on Constitutional Problems of South Arabia*. HMSO, 1964.

Gavin, R. J. *Aden 1839–1967*. London, Hurst, 1973.

Halliday, Fred. *Revolution and Foreign Policy: The Case of South Yemen, 1967–1987*. Cambridge, Cambridge University Press, 2002.

Helfritz, H. *The Yemen: A Secret Journey*. London, Allen and Unwin, 1958.

Heyworth-Dunne, G. E. *Al-Yemen: Social, Political and Economic Survey*. Cairo, 1952.

Hickinbotham, Sir Tom. *Aden*. London, Constable, 1959.

Hull, Edmund J. *High Value Target: Countering Al-Qaeda in Yemen*. Dulles, VA, Potomac Books, 2011.

Ingrams, Doreen. *A Survey of the Social and Economic Conditions of the Aden Protectorate*. London, 1949.

Ingrams, Doreen, and Ingrams, Leila (Eds). *The Records of Yemen 1798–1960*. London, Archive Editions, 1995.

Ingrams, Harold. *The Yemen: Imams, Rulers and Revolutions*. London, 1963.

Ingrams, W. H. *A Report on the Social, Economic and Political Conditions of the Hadhramaut, Aden Protectorate*. London, 1936.

Ismail, Tareq Y., and Jacqueline S. *The People's Democratic Republic of Yemen. Politics, Economics and Society*. London, Pinter, 1986.

Jenner, Michael. *Yemen Rediscovered*. London, Longman, 1983.

King, Gillian. *Imperial Outpost—Aden*. New York, Oxford University Press, 1964.

Kostiner, Joseph. *Yemen: The Tortuous Quest for Unity 1990–94*. London, Royal Institute of International Affairs, 1996.

Kour, Z. H. *The History of Aden, 1839–1972*. London, Frank Cass, 1980.

Kuehn, Thomas. *Empire, Islam, and Politics of Difference: Ottoman Rule in Yemen, 1849–1919*. Leiden, Brill, 2011.

Lackner, Helen. *The People's Democratic Republic of Yemen: Outpost of Socialist Development in Arabia*. London, Ithaca Press, 1985.

Ledger, David. *Shifting Sands: The British in South Arabia*. London, Peninsula Publishing, 1983.

Leveau, R., Mermier, F., and Steinbach, U. (Eds). *Le Yémen contemporain*. Paris, Editions Karthala, 1999.

Lichtenthäler, Gerhard. *Political Ecology and the Role of Water: Environment, Society and Economy in Northern Yemen*. Aldershot, Ashgate, 2003.

Macro, Eric. *Bibliography of the Yemen, with Notes on Mocha*. University of Miami Press, 1959.

Yemen and the Western World since 1571. London, C. Hurst, and New York, Praeger, 1968.

Mahdi, K. A., Würth, A., and Lackner, H. *Yemen into the Twenty-First Century: Continuity and Change*. Reading, Ithaca Press, 2007.

Manea, Elham. *Regional Politics in the Gulf: Saudi Arabia, Oman and Yemen*. London, Saqi Books, 2005.

Mercier, Eric. *Aden: un parcours interrompu*. Tours, Centre Français d'Etudes Yéménites-URBAMA, 1997.

Naumkin, Vitaly. *Red Wolves of Yemen: The Struggle for Independence*. Cambridge, Oleander Press, 2004.

O'Ballance, Edgar. *The War in the Yemen*. London, Faber, 1971.

Page, Stephen. *The Soviet Union and the Yemens: Influence in Asymmetrical Relationships*. New York, Praeger, 1985.

Paget, Julian. *Last Post: Aden 1964–67*. London, Faber and Faber, 1969.

Peterson, J. E. *Yemen, the Search for a Modern State*. London, Croom Helm, 1981.

Phillips, Sarah. *Yemen's Democracy Experiment in Regional Perspective: Patronage and Pluralized Authoritarianism*. London, Palgrave Macmillan, 2008.

Yemen and the Politics of Permanent Crisis. Abingdon, Routledge, 2011.

Pieragostini, Karl. *Britain, Aden and South Arabia*. London, Macmillan, 1992.

Pridham, B. R. (Ed.). *Contemporary Yemen: Politics and Historical Background*. London, Croom Helm, 1984.

Economy and Society and Culture in Contemporary Yemen. London, Croom Helm, 1985.

Qat Commission of Inquiry. *Report*. Aden, 1958.

al-Rasheed, Madawai, and, Vitalis, Robert (Eds). *Counter-Narratives: History, Contemporary Society and Politics in Saudi Arabia and Yemen*. London, Palgrave Macmillan, 2004.

Saif, Ahmad A. *A Legislature in Transition: The Yemeni Parliament*. Aldershot, Ashgate Publishing, 2001.

Schmidt, Dana Adams. *Yemen, the Unknown War*. London, Bodley Head, 1968.

Schwedler, Jillian. *Faith in Moderation: Islamist Parties in Jordan and Yemen*. Cambridge, Cambridge University Press, 2007.

Scott, H. *In the High Yemen*. London, Murray, 1942.

Searight, Sarah. *Yemen: Land and People*. Pallas Athene, 2002.

Serjeant, R. B. *The Portuguese off the South Arabian Coast*. Oxford, Clarendon, 1963; reprinted Beirut, 1974.

Smith, G. Rex. *The Yemens*. Oxford, World Bibliographical Series, Clio Press, 1984.

Stookey, Robert W. *Yemen: The Politics of the Yemen Arab Republic*. Westview Press, 1978.

al-Suwaidi, Jamal S. (Ed.). *The Yemeni War of 1994: Causes and Consequences*. London, Saqi Books, 1995.

Trevaskis, Sir Kennedy. *Shades of Amber: A South Arabian Episode*. London, Hutchinson, 1967.

vom Bruck, Gabriele. *Islam, Memory and Morality in Yemen: Ruling Families in Transition*. London, Palgrave Macmillan, 2005.

Walker, Jonathan. *Aden Insurgency: The Savage War in South Arabia, 1962–67*. Staplehurst, Spellmount Publrs, 2004.

Waterfield, Gordon. *Sultans of Aden*. London, Murray, 1968.

Wedeen, Lisa. *Peripheral Visions: Publics, Power, and Performance in Yemen*. Chicago, University of Chicago Press, 2008.

Weir, Shelagh. *A Tribal Order: Politics and Law in the Mountains of Yemen*. London, British Museum Press, 2007.

World Bank. *Economic Growth in the Republic of Yemen: Sources, Constraints and Potentials*. Washington, DC, World Bank Publications, 2002.

PART THREE

Regional Information

REGIONAL ORGANIZATIONS

United Nations

Address: United Nations, New York, NY 10017, USA.

Telephone: (212) 963-1234; **fax:** (212) 963-4879; **internet:** www.un.org.

The United Nations (UN) was founded on 24 October 1945. The organization, which has 193 member states, aims to maintain international peace and security and to develop international co-operation in addressing economic, social, cultural and humanitarian problems. The principal organs of the UN are the General Assembly, the Security Council, the Economic and Social Council, the International Court of Justice and the Secretariat. The General Assembly, which meets for three months each year, comprises representatives of all UN member states. The Security Council investigates disputes between member countries, and may recommend ways and means of peaceful settlement: it comprises five permanent members (the People's Republic of China, France, Russia, the United Kingdom and the USA) and 10 other members elected by the General Assembly for a two-year period. The Economic and Social Council comprises representatives of 54 member states, elected by the General Assembly for a three-year period: it promotes co-operation on economic, social, cultural and humanitarian matters, acting as a central policy-making body and co-ordinating the activities of the UN's specialized agencies. The International Court of Justice comprises 15 judges of different nationalities, elected for nine-year terms by the General Assembly and the Security Council: it adjudicates in legal disputes between UN member states.

Secretary-General: BAN KI-MOON (Republic of Korea) (2007–15).

MEMBER STATES IN THE MIDDLE EAST AND NORTH AFRICA

(with assessments for percentage contributions to UN budget during 2013–15, and year of admission)

Algeria	0.137	1962
Bahrain	0.039	1971
Cyprus	0.047	1960
Egypt	0.134	1945
Iran	0.356	1945
Iraq	0.068	1945
Israel	0.396	1949
Jordan	0.022	1955
Kuwait	0.273	1963
Lebanon	0.042	1945
Libya	0.142	1955
Morocco	0.062	1956
Oman	0.102	1971
Qatar	0.209	1971
Saudi Arabia	0.864	1945
Syria	0.036	1945
Tunisia	0.036	1956
Turkey	1.328	1945
United Arab Emirates	0.595	1971
Yemen	0.010	1947/67*

* The Yemen Arab Republic became a member of the UN in 1947, and the People's Democratic Republic of Yemen was admitted in 1967. The two countries formed the Republic of Yemen in 1990.

SOVEREIGN STATE NOT IN THE UNITED NATIONS

Palestine

Note: Palestine was granted non-member observer state status at the UN in November 2012.

Diplomatic Representation

PERMANENT MISSIONS TO THE UNITED NATIONS

(September 2013)

Algeria: 326 East 48th St, New York, NY 10017; tel. (212) 750-1960; fax (212) 759-5274; e-mail mission@algeria-un.org; internet www.algeria-un.org; Permanent Representative MOURAD BENMEHIDI.

Bahrain: 866 Second Ave, 14th/15th Floor, New York, NY 10017; tel. (212) 223-6200; fax (212) 319-0687; e-mail bahrain1@un.int; Permanent Representative JAMAL FARES ALROWAIEI.

Cyprus: 13 East 40th St, New York, NY 10016; tel. (212) 481-6023; fax (212) 685-7316; e-mail mission@cyprusun.org; internet www.un.int/cyprus; Permanent Representative NICHOLAS EMILIOU.

Egypt: 304 East 44th St, New York, NY 10017; tel. (212) 503-0300; fax (212) 725-3467; e-mail egypt@un.int; Permanent Representative MOOTAZ AHMADEIN KHALIL.

Iran: 622 Third Ave, 34th Floor, New York, NY 10017; tel. (212) 687-2020; fax (212) 867-7086; e-mail iran@un.int; internet www.un.int/iran; Permanent Representative MOHAMMAD KHAZAEE.

Iraq: 14 East 79th St, New York, NY 10075; tel. (212) 737-4433; fax (212) 772-1794; e-mail iraqny@un.int; Permanent Representative MOHAMED ALI ALHAKIM.

Israel: 800 Second Ave, New York, NY 10017; tel. (212) 499-5520; fax (212) 499-5515; e-mail info-un@newyork.mfa.gov.il; internet www.israel-un.org; Permanent Representative RON PROSOR.

Jordan: 866 Second Ave, 4th Floor, New York, NY 10017; tel. (212) 832-9553; fax (212) 832-5346; e-mail missionun@jordanmissionun.com; Permanent Representative Prince ZEID RA'AD ZEID AL-HUSSEIN.

Kuwait: 321 East 44th St, New York, NY 10017; tel. (212) 973-4300; fax (212) 370-1733; e-mail kuwaitmission@msn.com; internet www.kuwaitmission.com; Permanent Representative MANSOUR AYYAD AL-OTAIBI.

Lebanon: 866 United Nations Plaza, Rm 531–533, New York, NY 10017; tel. (212) 355-5460; fax (212) 838-2819; e-mail contact@lebanonun.org; internet www.un.int/lebanon; Permanent Representative NAWAF A. SALAM.

Libya: 309–315 East 48th St, New York, NY 10017; tel. (212) 752-5775; fax (212) 593-4787; e-mail libyanmis2011@yahoo.com; internet www.libyanmission-un.org; Permanent Representative IBRAHMIN O. A. DABBASHI.

Morocco: 866 Second Ave, 6th and 7th Floors, New York, NY 10017; tel. (212) 421-1580; fax (212) 980-1512; e-mail info@morocco-un.org; Permanent Representative MOHAMMED LOULICHKI.

Oman: 3 Dag Hammarskjöld Plaza, 305 East 47th St, 12th Floor, New York, NY 10017; tel. (212) 355-3505; fax (212) 644-0070; e-mail oman@un.int; Permanent Representative LYUTHA S. AL-MUGHAIRY.

Qatar: 809 United Nations Plaza, 4th Floor, New York, NY 10017; tel. (212) 486-9335; fax (212) 758-4952; e-mail pmun@mofa.gov.qa; Permanent Representative MESHAL HAMAD MOHAMED JABR AL-THANI.

Saudi Arabia: 809 United Nations Plaza, 10th and 11th Floors, New York, NY 10017; tel. (212) 557-1525; fax (212) 983-4895; e-mail saudi-mission@un.int; Permanent Representative ABDULLAH YAHYA AL-MOUALLIMI.

Syria: 820 Second Ave, 15th Floor, New York, NY 10017; tel. (212) 661-1313; fax (212) 983-4439; e-mail exesec.syria@gmail.com; internet www.syria-un.org; Permanent Representative BASHAR JA'AFARI.

Tunisia: 31 Beekman Pl., New York, NY 10022; tel. (212) 751-7503; fax (212) 751-0569; e-mail tunisnyc@nyc.rr.com; Permanent Representative MOHAMED KHALED KHIARI.

Turkey: 821 United Nations Plaza, 10th Floor, New York, NY 10017; tel. (212) 949-0150; fax (212) 949-0086; e-mail tr-delegation.newyork@mfa.gov.tr; internet www.turkuno.dt.mfa.gov.tr; Permanent Representative YAŞAR HALIT ÇEVIK.

United Arab Emirates: 3 Dag Hammarskjöld Plaza, 305 East 47th St, 7th Floor, New York, NY 10017; tel. (212) 371-0480; fax (212) 371-4923; e-mail uae@uaemission.com; Permanent Representative LANA ZAKI NUSSEIBEH.

Yemen: 413 East 51st St, New York, NY 10022; tel. (212) 355-1730; fax (212) 750-9613; e-mail ymiss-newyork@mofa.gov.ye; Permanent Representative JAMAL ABDULLAH AL-SALLAL.

OBSERVERS

Intergovernmental organizations, etc., active in the region that participate in the sessions and the work of the UN General Assembly as Observers, maintaining permanent offices at the UN.

African Union: 305 East 47th St, 5th Floor, 3 Dag Hammarskjöld Plaza, New York, NY 10017; tel. (212) 319-5490; fax (212) 319-7135; e-mail aumission_ny@yahoo.com; internet www.africa-union.org; Permanent Observer TÉTÉ ANTÓNIO.

Asian-African Legal Consultative Organization: 188 East 76th St, Apt 26B, New York, NY 10021; tel. (917) 623-2861; fax (206) 426-5442; e-mail aalco@un.int; Permanent Observer ROY LEE.

Cooperation Council for the Arab States of the Gulf: One Dag Hammarskjöld Plaza, 885 Second Ave, 40th Floor, New York, NY 10017; tel. (212) 319-3088; fax (212) 319-3434; Permanent Observer ADNAN AHMED ABDULLAH AL-ANSARI.

International Committee of the Red Cross: 801 Second Ave, 18th Floor, New York, NY 10017; tel. (212) 599-6021; fax (212) 599-6009; e-mail newyork@icrc.org; Head of Delegation WALTER A. FÜLLEMANN.

International Criminal Police Organization (INTERPOL): One United Nations Plaza, Suite 2610, New York, NY 10017; tel. (917) 367-3463; fax (917) 367-3476; e-mail nyoffice@interpol.int; internet www.interpol.int; Special Representative WILLIAM J. S. ELLIOTT (Canada).

International Development Law Organization: 336 East 45th St, 11th Floor, New York, NY 10017; tel. (212) 867-9707; fax (212) 867-9717; e-mail pcivili@idlo.int; Permanent Observer PATRIZIO M. CIVILI.

International Institute for Democracy and Electoral Assistance: 336 East 45th St, 14th Floor, New York, NY 10017; tel. (212) 286-1084; fax (212) 286-0260; e-mail unobserver@idea.int; Permanent Observer MASSIMO TOMMASOLI.

International Olympic Committee: 708 Third Ave, 6th Floor, New York, NY 10017; tel. (212) 209-3952; fax (212) 209-7100; e-mail IOC-UNObserver@olympic.org; Permanent Observer MARIO PESCANTE.

Inter-Parliamentary Union: 336 East 45th St, 10th Floor, New York, NY 10017; tel. (212) 557-5880; fax (212) 557-3954; e-mail ny-office@mail.ipu.org; internet www.ipu.org/Un-e/un-opo.htm; Permanent Observer (vacant).

International Union for Conservation of Nature (IUCN): 551 Fifth Ave, Suites 800 A-B, New York, NY 10176; tel. (212) 346-1163; fax (212) 346-1046; e-mail iucn@un.int; internet www.iucn.org; Permanent Observer NARINDER KAKAR (India).

League of Arab States: 866 United Nations Plaza, Suite 494, New York, NY 10017; tel. (212) 838-8700; fax (212) 355-3909; e-mail arableague@un.int; Permanent Observer AHMED FATHALLA.

Organization of Islamic Cooperation: 320 East 51st St, New York, NY 10022; tel. (212) 883-0140; fax (212) 883-0143; e-mail oicny@un.int; internet www.oicun.org; Permanent Observer UFUK GOKCEN.

Palestine: 115 East 65th St, New York, NY 10021; tel. (212) 288-8500; fax (212) 517-2377; e-mail palestine@un.int; internet www.un.int/palestine; Permanent Observer RIYAD H. MANSOUR.

Partners in Population and Development: 336 East 45th St, 14th Floor, New York, NY 10017; tel. (212) 286-1082; fax (212) 286-0260; e-mail srao@ppdsec.org; internet www.partners-popdev.org; Permanent Observer MOHAMMAD NURUL ALAM.

University for Peace: 551 Fifth Ave, Suites 800 A-B, New York, NY 10176; tel. (212) 346-1163; fax (212) 346-1046; e-mail nyinfo@upeace.org; internet www.upeace.org; Permanent Observer NARINDER KAKAR (India).

The African Development Bank, the Economic Cooperation Organization, the Islamic Development Bank, the OPEC Fund for International Development, the Organization of the Black Sea Economic Cooperation, and the Parliamentary Assembly of the Mediterranean are among a number of intergovernmental organizations that have a standing invitation to participate as Observers, but do not maintain permanent offices at the UN.

United Nations Information Centres/Services

Algeria: POB 444, Hydre, Algiers; tel. and fax (21) 92 54 42; e-mail unic.dz@undp.org; internet algiers.unic.org.

Bahrain: POB 26814, UN House, Bldg 69, Rd 1901, Manama 319; tel. 17311676; fax 17311600; e-mail unic.manama@unic.org; internet www.manama.unic.org; also covers Qatar and the United Arab Emirates.

Egypt: 1 Osiris St, Garden City, Cairo; tel. (2) 7900022; fax (2) 7953705; e-mail info@unic-eg.org; internet www.unic-eg.org; also covers Saudi Arabia.

Iran: POB 15875-4557; 8 Shahrzad Blvd, Darrous, Tehran; tel. (21) 2287-3837; fax (21) 2287-3395; e-mail unic.tehran@unic.org; internet www.unic-ir.org.

Lebanon: UN House, Riad es-Solh Sq., POB 11-8575, Beirut; tel. (1) 981301; fax (1) 970424; e-mail unic-beirut@un.org; internet www.unicbeirut.org; also covers Jordan, Kuwait and Syria.

Libya: POB 286, Khair Aldeen Baybers St, Hay al-Andalous, Tripoli; tel. (21) 4770251; fax (21) 4777343; e-mail tripoli@un.org; internet tripoli.unic.org.

Morocco: BP 601; rue Tarik ibn Zyad 6, Rabat; tel. (3) 7768633; fax (3) 7768377; e-mail unicmor@unicmor.ma; internet www.unicmor.ma.

Tunisia: BP 863, 41 ave Louis Braille, Tunis; tel. (71) 902-203; fax (71) 906-811; e-mail unic.tunis@unic.org; internet www.unictunis.org.tn.

Turkey: PK 407, Birlik Mahallesi, 2 Cad. No. 11, 06610 Cankaya, Ankara; tel. (312) 4541052; fax (312) 4961499; e-mail unic.ankara@unic.org; internet www.unicankara.org.tr.

Yemen: POB 237; St 5, off Al-Boniya St, Handhal Zone, San'a; tel. (1) 274000; fax (1) 274043; e-mail unicyem@y.net.ye; internet www.unic-yem.org.

ECONOMIC COMMISSION FOR AFRICA—ECA

Address: Menelik II Ave, POB 3001, Addis Ababa, Ethiopia.

Telephone: (11) 5517200; **fax:** (11) 5514416; **e-mail:** ecainfo@uneca.org; **internet:** www.uneca.org.

The UN Economic Commission for Africa (ECA) was founded in 1958 by a resolution of the UN Economic and Social Council (ECOSOC). The Commission promotes sustainable socio-economic development in Africa and aims to advance economic integration among African countries, and economic co-operation between Africa and other parts of the world.

MEMBERS

Algeria	Eritrea	Niger	Congo, Democratic Republic	Malawi	Swaziland
Angola	Ethiopia	Nigeria	Congo, Republic	Mali	Tanzania
Benin	Gabon	Rwanda	Côte d'Ivoire	Mauritania	Togo
Botswana	The Gambia	São Tomé and Príncipe	Djibouti	Mauritius	Tunisia
Burkina Faso	Ghana	Senegal	Egypt	Morocco	Uganda
Burundi	Guinea	Seychelles	Equatorial Guinea	Mozambique	Zambia
Cameroon	Guinea-Bissau	Sierra Leone		Namibia	Zimbabwe
Cape Verde	Kenya	Somalia			
Central African Republic	Lesotho	South Africa			
Chad	Liberia	South Sudan			
Comoros	Libya	Sudan			
	Madagascar				

Organization

(September 2013)

COMMISSION

The Commission may only act with the agreement of the government of the country concerned. It is also empowered to make recommendations on any matter within its competence directly to the government of the member or associate member concerned, to governments admitted in a consultative capacity, and to the UN Specialized Agencies. The Commission is required to submit for prior consideration by ECOSOC any of its proposals for actions that would be likely to have important effects on the international economy.

CONFERENCE OF AFRICAN MINISTERS

The Conference, which meets every year, is attended by ministers responsible for finance, planning and economic development, representing the governments of member states, and is the main deliberative body of the Commission. The Commission's responsibility to promote concerted action for the economic and social development of Africa is vested primarily in the Conference, which considers matters of general policy and the priorities to be assigned to the Commission's programmes, considers inter-African and international economic policy, and makes recommendations to member states in connection with such matters.

SECRETARIAT

The Secretariat provides the services necessary for the meeting of the Conference of Ministers and the meetings of the Commission's subsidiary bodies, carries out the resolutions and implements the programmes adopted there. It comprises the Office of the Executive Secretary and (following a radical restructuring, which took effect in March 2013) the following divisions: Gender; Governance; Innovation and Technology; Macroeconomic Policy; Natural Resource Management; Regional Integration and Trade; Social Development; and Capacity Development and Special Initiatives. An Office of Partnerships, also established in 2013, includes teams from the AU and NEPAD.

Executive Secretary: Dr CARLOS LOPES (Guinea-Bissau).

AFRICAN POLICY CENTRES

The following are focal points for continental policy making and programming:

African Centre for Statistics;

African Climate Policy Centre;

African Institute for Economic Development and Planning;

African Minerals Development Centre;

African Trade Policy Centre;

Land Policy Initiative.

SUB-REGIONAL OFFICE

North Africa: BP 2062 Rabat Ryad, Morocco; tel. (3) 771-78-29; fax (3) 771-27-02; e-mail srdc-na@uneca.org; internet www.uneca.org/sro-na.

Activities

The Commission's activities are focused on two pillars: promoting regional integration in support of the visions and priorities of the African Union (AU, formerly the Organization of African Unity—OAU), through research and policy analysis on regional integration issues, capacity building, and the provision of technical assistance to the institutions (including the regional economic communities, see below) underpinning the regional integration agenda; and on meeting emerging global challenges and the special needs of Africa, with particular emphasis on achieving the Millennium Development Goals (MDGs). The Secretariat is guided in its efforts by major regional strategies, including the Abuja Treaty on the establishment of an African Economic Community, signed under the aegis of the OAU in 1991, the UN System-wide Support to the AU and the New Partnership for Africa's Development (NEPAD—approved in 2006, see below), and the Framework, Roadmap and Architecture for Fast Tracking the Establishment of a Continental Free Trade Area, and an Action Plan for Boosting Intra-African Trade, adopted in January 2012 by AU leaders. The following regional economic communities are regarded as pillars of continental economic integration: the Common Market for Eastern and Southern Africa (COMESA), the East African Community (EAC) and the Southern African Development Community (SADC) (which together form the EAC-COMESA-SADC Tripartite FTA initiative); the Communauté Économique des États de l'Afrique Centrale (CEEAC), the Economic Community of West African States (ECOWAS), the Intergovernmental Authority on Development (IGAD), and the Union of the Arab Maghreb.

GENDER

ECA aims to improve the socio-economic prospects of women through the promotion of equal access to resources and opportunities, and equal participation in decision-making. An African Centre for Gender and Development (renamed as above in 2006) was established in 1975 to service all national, sub-regional and regional bodies involved in development issues relating to gender and the advancement of women. The Centre manages the African Women's Development Fund, which was established in June 2000. An African Women's Rights Observatory (AWRO), launched in 1995, monitors gender equality and the advancement of women. An African Gender and Development Index, measuring how far member states had met their commitments towards international agreements on gender equality and women's advancement, was inaugurated in January 2005; the most recent Index, reflecting the state of progress in 2011, was issued in January 2012. The African Women's Decade, covering 2010–20, was launched in October 2010 under the theme 'Grassroots approach to gender equality and women's empowerment'.

GOVERNANCE

ECA aims to improve member states' capacity for good governance and development management. The Commission provides support for the African Peer Review Mechanism, a NEPAD initiative whereby participating member governments mutually assess compliance with a number of codes, standards and commitments that uphold good governance and sustainable development. ECA assists civil society organizations to participate in governance; supports the development of private sector enterprises; and helps to improve public administration in member states. To achieve these aims the Commission provides technical assistance and advisory services, conducts studies, and organizes training workshops, seminars and conferences at national, sub-regional and regional levels for ministers, public administrators and senior policy-makers, as well as for private and non-governmental organizations (NGOs). The Commission and the AU jointly provide support to the African Governance Forum (AGF) process, which is implemented through UNDP's Regional Bureau for Africa; such fora have been convened periodically since 1997. AGF VIII, addressing the theme 'Democracy, Elections, and the Management of Diversity in Africa', was held in Gaborone, Botswana, in 2012. In 2005 the first *African Governance Report (AGR-1)* was published by ECA, monitoring progress towards good governance in 27 countries. *AGR-2*, issued in August 2009, found improvements over the past few years in the observance of human rights and the rule of law, as well as in competitive electoral politics and the scope of political representation, although party and electoral systems were deemed to be weak and poorly structured. Advances were judged to have been made in economic governance, public sector management, private sector development and corporate governance, while weaknesses were highlighted in the management of the tax system and in service delivery, and corruption was cited as a major challenge to achieving sustainable economic progress and development in Africa. *AGR-3*, addressing elections and diversity management in Africa, was released in August 2013. A *Mutual Review of Development Effectiveness in Africa Report (MRDE)* is jointly compiled by ECA's Governance Division and the Organisation for Economic Co-operation and Development (OECD); the Review considers progress achieved hitherto in delivering commitments made by African countries and their development partners, and outlines future key priorities. The sixth edition was issued in July 2013.

INNOVATION AND TECHNOLOGY

The ICT (Information and Communications Technology), Science and Technology Division has responsibility for co-ordinating the implementation of the Harnessing Information Technology for Africa project, and for implementing the African Information Society Initiative (AISI), which was founded in 1996 and supports the development of the pan-continental information and communications infrastructure. ECA was given responsibility for the Task Force on e-Government, mandated by the second session of the World Summit on Information Society (WSIS), convened in Tunis, Tunisia, in November 2005. The Commission maintains the Africa Knowledge for Development Networks (accessible at knowledge.africa-devnet.-org), an internet-based platform for promoting knowledge sharing on regional economic and social development. In July 2009 the first International Conference on African Digital Libraries and Archives, held under ECA auspices, urged the establishment of an ECA African Digital Library and Archives Programme. In February of that year representatives of UN agencies, NEPAD, the AU, and media executives, convened the first Regional Media Dialogue, in The Vaal, South Africa, at the end of which they adopted a Consensus Declaration and series of recommendations relating to the increasing role of the media in Africa's development. A second Regional Media Dialogue, held in June 2011, in Maseru, Lesotho, adopted the Maseru Declaration, recommending the development of a continent-wide framework for structured engagement with the media. In September 2012 the Division launched a new African Forum for Geospatial Information Systems (GIS), aimed at enhancing the capacity of African media professionals to promote GIS. A World Geospatial Data Infrastructure Conference and Africa-GIS Conference were to be held concurrently in November 2013, in Addis Ababa, on the theme 'Spatial Enablement in Support of Economic Development and Poverty Reduction'. In October 2011 ECA, with the AU, launched a new Africa Internet Governance Forum (AfIGF), in accordance with the recommendations of the WSIS. ECA hosts the AfIGF's secretariat.

The 2012 session of the AfIGF, held in October, in Cairo, Egypt, urged regional collaboration to combat cybercrime. The 2013 session was to be held in late September, in Nairobi, Kenya. In June of that year a meeting of experts on cyber legislation from member states in eastern, southern and northern Africa, held under the auspices of the ECA, AU, and relevant regional economic communities, adopted the Addis Ababa Declaration on the harmonization of cyber legislation in Africa. ECA has provided technical support to the AU in developing a new AU Convention on Cybersecurity, which is expected to be finalized in 2013.

In August 2012 ECA and the UN Institute for Training and Research launched a series of free internet-based e-Learning courses aimed at supporting the objective of establishing a Continental Free Trade Area by 2017. The Commission supports the Electronic Rural School in Local Languages (ERELA) programme, administered by the Government of Finland with the aim of promoting learning and use of communications technologies in local African mother tongues.

In March 2008 ECA organized a conference entitled Science with Africa to link African science-based organizations and businesses with their global counterparts; the second Science with Africa conference, held in June 2010, adopted a set of recommendations on how African countries might leverage science and technology to carry forwards their development agenda. In September 2012 ECA launched a new Access to Scientific Knowledge in Africa (ASKIA) online portal (accessible at askia.uneca.org/askia), providing scientific and socio-economic information of relevance to scientists, policy-makers, and other researchers in the region.

Since 2007 ECA has organized biennial Technology in Government in Africa (TIGA) awards, with the objective of recognizing the effective use by regional governments and institutions of ICTs for public service delivery. In 2011 ECA, jointly with the Switzerland-based African Innovation Foundation, launched an annual Innovation Prize for Africa (IPA), which aims to reward regional innovation in the areas of science, technology and engineering.

MACROECONOMIC POLICY

ECA advocates for a sound regional macroeconomic policy framework, with the aim of supporting and enabling inclusive growth, private sector development, value addition, employment, sustainable development, and the transformation of the region's economies from low-income to middle-income status. The Commission supports the economic development of member states through the collection and analysis of data; the preparation of annual economic surveys; the compilation of reports on regional economic conditions, governance and development management; the production of regional and national policy studies covering economic reforms, international and illicit financial flows, domestic resource mobilization, external debt, and exchange rate management; and the dissemination of best practices relating to specific aspects of economic management.

In June 2009 ECA and the AU hosted, in Cairo, a joint meeting of African ministers of finance and economic affairs, which considered the impact on the region of the global crisis. During that month a joint report of all five UN Regional Commissions, entitled *The Global Economic and Financial Crisis: Regional Impacts, Responses and Solutions*, was launched. In October 2010 ECA, the AU and the AfDB established a Joint Secretariat (based at ECA headquarters) to enhance coherence and collaboration in support of Africa's development agenda. In May 2011 ECA launched the *ECA LDC Monitor*, an internet-based tool aimed at assessing economic progress in member Least-Developed Countries. The theme of the 2013 *Economic Report on Africa*, released by ECA and the AU Commission in June of that year, was 'Making the Most of Africa's Commodities: Industrializing for Growth, Jobs, and Economic Transformation'. ECA, the AfDB, OECD and UNDP jointly prepare an annual *African Economic Outlook*: the focus of the 2013 edition, issued in May, was 'Structural Transformation and Natural Resources'. Since 2006 ECA and AfDB have organized an annual African Economic Conference (AEC), aimed at enabling an exchange of ideas among economists and policy-makers on development policy. The eighth AEC was to be held in Johannesburg, South Africa, in October 2013, on the theme 'Regional Integration in Africa'.

ECA's African Institute for Economic Development and Planning (IDEP), founded in 1962, undertakes pan-African capacity development and training programmes, and also conducts policy research, and dialogue initiatives. The African Centre for Statistics was established in 2006 to encourage the use of statistics in national planning, to provide training and technical assistance for the compilation, analysis and dissemination of statistics, and to assist member states with the compilation of population censuses. An Advisory Board on Statistics in Africa, comprising 15 experts from national statistical offices, sub-regional bodies and training institutes, meets annually to advise ECA on statistical developments in Africa and guide its activities. The Statistical Commission for Africa (StatCom-Africa), comprising representatives of national statistical offices, regional and international institutions and development partners, meets every two years as the principal body overseeing statistical development in Africa, with annual working groups monitoring progress and deciding on activities. In January 2012 StatCom-Africa, meeting in Cape Town, South Africa, adopted the Robben Island Declaration on Statistical Development, which aimed to strengthen methods of data collection and analysis, of harmonizing statistics in Africa and upgrading the system of national accounts. ECA assists its member states in population data collection and data processing; analysis of demographic data obtained from censuses or surveys; training demographers; formulation of population policies and integrating population variables in development planning, through advisory missions and through the organization of national seminars on population and development; and in dissemination of demographic information. The first conference of African ministers responsible for civil registration was convened in August 2010, in Addis Ababa, and the second was held in September 2012, in Durban, South Africa. ECA commemorates African Statistics Day annually on 18 November.

SOCIAL DEVELOPMENT

ECA undertakes research and develops tools and guidelines in support of the formulation, implementation and evaluation of regional and national policies aimed at achieving inclusive, equitable and sustainable development. The Commission provides information on global processes on social policy, including on the International Conference on Population and Development and the development of the UN's post-2015 development agenda. A Regional Conference on Population and Development Beyond 2014 was to be convened in Addis Ababa, under ECA auspices, during late September–early October 2013.

A Commission on HIV/AIDS and Governance in Africa, with its secretariat based at ECA headquarters, was launched in September 2003. The Commission, an initiative of the UN Secretary-General, was mandated to assess the impact of the HIV/AIDS pandemic on national structures and African economic development and to incorporate its findings in a Final Report; this was issued in October 2005.

NATURAL RESOURCE MANAGEMENT

ECA undertakes research in support of policy, legal and regulatory frameworks underpinning the proper management of natural resources in Africa. ECA works to strengthen regional and national human and institutional capacities and to widen stakeholder participation in the protection of Africa's environment and in the management of the continent's mineral resources. The Commission promotes the use of science and technology in achieving sustainable development.

From 2005 ECA increased its work devoted to the changes in climate caused by global warming, and the resulting threat posed by drought, floods and other extreme events. In 2006, with the AU and the AfDB, the Commission established a 10-year Climate for Development in Africa Programme (Clim-Dev Africa) to improve the collection of climate-related data and assist in forecasting and risk management. ECA provides the technical secretariat for Clim-Dev Africa. In December 2007 ECA announced the establishment of an African Climate Policy Centre (ACPC), to help member states to incorporate climate-related concerns in their development policies so as to counter the impact of climate change. The first Climate Change and Development in Africa Conference (CCDA-I) was held in Addis Ababa, Ethiopia, in October 2011. Members were encouraged, inter alia, to incorporate climate change data and analysis in their policy-making decisions, to identify means of increasing agricultural productivity, including water management and soil enrichment, and to develop strategies for low carbon development. CCDA-II was held in October 2012, again in Addis Ababa, on the theme 'Leveraging State-Society Dialogue for Improving Natural Resource Governance in Africa'. In September 2012 a series of ACPC workshops on upgrading hydro-meteorological networks and recovering hydro-meteorological data was launched in Ethiopia; workshops were subsequently to be held in Gambia, Mali, Mozambique and Rwanda.

ECA assists member states in the assessment and use of water resources and the development of river and lake basins common to more than one country. ECA encourages co-operation between countries with regard to water issues and collaborates with other UN agencies and regional organizations to promote technical and economic co-operation in this area. In 1992, on the initiative of ECA, the Interagency Group for Water in Africa (now UN-Water/Africa) was established to co-ordinate and harmonize the water-related activities of the UN and other organizations on the continent. ECA has been particularly active in efforts to promote the integrated development of the water resources of the Zambezi river basin and of Lake Victoria. In December 2003 ECA hosted the Pan-African Implementation and Partnership Conference on Water (PANAFCON).

In July 2011 the 17th regular summit of AU heads of state and government invited African states to work on a common continental position for the UN Conference on Sustainable Development—UNCSD (convened in Rio de Janeiro, Brazil, in June 2012). Consequently, in October 2011 ECA organized a UNCSD Africa Regional

Preparatory Conference which noted emerging challenges to sustainable development in Africa, including low adaptive capacity to the effects of climate change; increasing severe biodiversity loss, desertification and land degradation, aggravated by the effects of climate change; and rapid urbanization. The conference urged the international community to meet its commitments to the continent in terms of transfer of financial and technological resources, and committed African states to enhancing efforts to improve national governance and development effectiveness, and to formulating national strategies for sustainable development. ECA, in collaboration with other agencies, compiles a Sustainable Development Report on Africa (SDRA); the fifth issue, on the theme 'Achieving sustainable development in Africa through inclusive green growth', was being prepared in 2013.

ECA promotes food security in African countries through raising awareness of the relationship between population, food security, the environment and sustainable development; encouraging the advancement of science and technology in member states; and providing policy analysis support and technical advisory services aimed at strengthening national population policies. In March 2010 ECA issued a report urging member countries to build upon the outcomes of the Abuja Food Security Summit, organized by the AU in December 2006, by establishing a common market of strategic food and agricultural commodities.

In 2006 ECA, the AU and the AfDB established the Land Policy Initiative (LPI), a joint programme that promotes equitable access to, and the efficient and sustainable utilization of land. The LPI's Secretariat is based at ECA headquarters, and is assisted by an African Task Force on Land. An LPI Framework and Guidelines on Land Policy in Africa was finalized in 2009. The LPI aims to advance women's secure access to land, and the recognition of African customary land rights.

REGIONAL INTEGRATION AND TRADE

ECA supports the implementation of the AU's regional integration agenda, through research; policy analysis; strengthening capacity and the provision of technical assistance to the regional economic communities; and working on transboundary initiatives and activities across a variety of sectors. In October 2008 ECA launched an Observatory on Regional Integration in Africa, an internet-based repository of knowledge and information aimed at supporting the activities of policy-makers, member states, regional economic communities, and other stakeholders. The Commission conducts research and outreach activities aimed at ensuring best practice in trade policy development and undertakes research and dissemination activities on bilateral and international trade negotiations (such as the ongoing multilateral trade negotiations under the World Trade Organization) with a view to helping African countries to benefit from globalization through trade. In July 2012 ECA, the AU and the AfDB issued their fifth joint *Assessing Regional Integration in Africa* report (ARIA V), which addressed the ongoing process towards establishing, by 2017, an operational Continental Free Trade Area. The African Trade Policy Centre (ATPC), established in 2003, aims to strengthen the human, institutional and policy capacities of African governments to formulate and implement sound trade policies and participate more effectively in international trade negotiations. The Centre takes both a national and regional perspective, and provides a rapid response to technical needs arising from ongoing trade negotiations. In November 2011 the ATPC organized the first Africa Trade Forum (ATF). During ATF II, held in September 2012 on the theme 'Boosting Intra-Africa Trade and Establishing the Continental Free Trade Area', the ATPC launched a new Africa Corridor Management Alliance (ACMA), with the aim of making more efficient the cost of moving goods through Africa's trade and transit corridors, and across international borders. Issues to be addressed by the ACMA included unofficial fees, roadblocks, and corruption; as well as variance in national laws relating to vehicle standards and inspection requirements; inefficient administrative procedures; and delays in the clearance of goods at ports.

ECA and the World Bank jointly co-ordinate the sub-Saharan Africa Transport Programme (SSATP), established in 1987, which aims to facilitate policy development and related capacity building in the continent's transport sector. In April 2012 ECA formally invited the AU Commission to join the SSATP Board. A meeting of all participants in the programme is held annually. The regional Road Management Initiative (RMI) under the SSATP seeks to encourage a partnership between the public and private sectors to manage and maintain road infrastructure more efficiently and thus to improve country-wide communications and transportation activities. An Urban Mobility component of the SSATP aims to improve sub-Saharan African urban transport services, while a Trade and Transport component aims to enhance the international competitiveness of regional economies through the establishment of more cost-effective services for shippers. The Railway Restructuring element focuses on the provision of financially sustainable railway enterprises. The first session of a forum on Central African regional integration, organized by the ECA SRO for Central Africa, took place in November 2009, in Douala, Cameroon. The second session was held in May–June 2012, also in Douala, on the theme 'Sub-regional Trade and Transport Infrastructure Development in Central Africa'. In November 2005 a meeting of sub-Saharan African ministers of transport, convened in Bamako, Mali, on the fringes of the SSATP Annual General Meeting, adopted a resolution aimed at developing Africa's transport infrastructure, focusing on the importance of incorporating transport issues into poverty reduction strategies, ensuring sustainable financing for Africa's road programmes, and prioritizing road safety issues. The first African Road Safety Conference, held in Accra, Ghana, in February 2007, by African ministers responsible for transport and health, reaffirmed road safety as a key development priority and pledged to set and achieve measurable national targets for road safety and the prevention of traffic injuries in all member states. In November 2011 the second African Road Safety Conference, convened by ECA within the framework of the SSATP, approved an Action Plan, which aimed to halve the number of road crash fatalities by 2020. A meeting of experts convened in September 2011 to review the development of interconnected Trans-African Highways (TAH) reported that by that time the TAH comprised some nine principal axes of roads across the continent, but that about one-quarter of an envisaged final network was yet to be constructed. The meeting recommended the adoption of an intergovernmental agreement on the TAH, and adopted a series of 10 recommendations aimed at accelerating the development of the highways interconnection initiative.

The Division supports efforts to advance the development of Africa's extensive mineral and energy resources, focusing on promoting co-operation, integration and public-private sector partnerships; facilitating policy decisions and dissemination of best practices; and supporting capacity building. An African Minerals Development Centre was being established during 2012–13 by ECA, the AU and the AfDB, with a mandate to implement the African Mining Vision, endorsed in February 2009 by AU heads of state. ECA's Energy Programme provides assistance to member states in the development of indigenous energy resources and the formulation of energy policies to extricate member states from continued energy crises. In May 2004 ECA was appointed as the secretariat of a UN-Energy/Africa initiative which aimed to facilitate the exchange of information, good practices and knowledge-sharing among UN organizations and with private sector companies, NGOs, power utilities and other research and academic institutions. In December 2011 ECA and the AU organized a second conference of African ministers responsible for mineral resources development.

SPECIAL INITIATIVES AND CAPACITY DEVELOPMENT

ECA provides guidance to the policy-making organs of the UN and the AU on the formulation of policies supporting the achievement of Africa's development objectives. It contributes to the work of the General Assembly and of specialized agencies by providing an African perspective in the preparation of development strategies. The former UN System-wide Special Initiative on Africa, covering the decade 1995–2006, aimed to mobilize resources and to implement a series of political and economic development objectives; the Initiative was followed by the UN System-wide Support to the AU and NEPAD, launched in 2006. NEPAD was established by the AU in 2001, and ECA was assigned the task of co-ordinating UN support for NEPAD at the regional level. In February 2010 a new NEPAD Planning and Co-ordination Committee (NPCC) was established as a technical body of the AU, to replace the former NEPAD Secretariat, with the aim of improving the implementation of NEPAD projects at country level. In April 2010 ECA and the NPCC concluded a Memorandum of Understanding strengthening collaboration between the two bodies.

Joint meetings of ECA ministers of economy, planning and economic development and AU ministers of economy and finance are convened annually (most recently in March 2013).

In October 1999 the first African Development Forum (ADF)—initiated by ECA as a process to formulate an agenda for effective sustainable development in African countries—was organized in Addis Ababa. Regular ADF meetings are held, each addressing a specific development issue. ADF VIII was convened in October 2012, on the theme 'Governing and Harnessing Natural Resources for Africa's Development'. In March 2011 ECA launched the Africa Platform for Development Effectiveness (APDEv, accessible at www.africa-platform.org), a multi-stakeholder platform and organizing mechanism for policy-makers in the continent.

In March 2009 the Coalition for Dialogue on Africa (CoDA) was launched by ECA, the AU and the AfDB, as an independent African forum to serve as an umbrella for all existing fora on Africa. ECA hosts its secretariat. CoDA meetings, including a multi-stakeholder dialogue forum, were convened in Tunis, in November, to consider Africa's recovery from the global economic and financial crisis, and regional integration. In February 2010 CoDA met, again in Tunis, to discuss transforming the Coalition into a fully independent, non-governmental African initiative, with a chief executive; and to develop a work programme. A CoDA policy forum was held in Abidjan, Côte d'Ivoire, in May, on 'Financing Regional Integration in Africa'. Meeting in October 2010, on the sidelines of ADF VII, CoDA urged African leaders to continue to pursue participation multinational negotiations on climate change. A CoDA policy forum on foreign direct investments in land in Africa was convened in Lisbon, Portugal, in June 2011.

Finance

ECA's proposed regular budget for the two-year period 2012–13, an appropriation from the UN budget, was US $138.3m.

Publications

Africa Climate Policy Bulletin.
African Gender and Development Index.
African Governance Report.
African Review Report on Chemicals.
African Statistical Yearbook.
African Women's Report.
Africa Youth Report.
Assessing Regional Integration in Africa.
ECA Policy Brief.
Eastern Africa News (issued by the SRO for East Africa).
Echos d'Afrique Centrale (issued by the SRO for Central Africa).
Economic Report on Africa.
Insight ECA-SA (issued by the SRO for Southern Africa).
MDG Report: Assessing Progress in Africa.
Mutual Review of Development Effectiveness in Africa (jointly with OECD).
Sustainable Development Report on Africa (every 2 years).
Country reports, policy and discussion papers, reports of conferences and meetings, training series, working paper series.

Economic and Social Commission for Western Asia—ESCWA

Address: Riad el-Solh Sq., POB 11-8575, Beirut, Lebanon.
Telephone: (1) 981301; **fax:** (1) 981510; **e-mail:** webmaster-escwa@un.org; **internet:** www.escwa.un.org.

The UN Economic Commission for Western Asia was established in 1974 by a resolution of the UN Economic and Social Council (ECOSOC), to provide facilities of a wider scope for those countries previously served by the UN Economic and Social Office in Beirut (UNESOB). The name Economic and Social Commission for Western Asia (ESCWA) was adopted in 1985.

MEMBERS

Bahrain	Palestine
Egypt	Qatar
Iraq	Saudi Arabia
Jordan	Sudan
Kuwait	Syria
Lebanon	Tunisia
Libya	United Arab Emirates
Morocco	Yemen
Oman	

Organization

(September 2013)

COMMISSION

The Commission meets every two years in ministerial session to determine policy and establish work directives. Representatives of UN bodies and specialized agencies, regional organizations, other UN member states, and non-governmental organizations having consultative status with ECOSOC may attend as observers. The 27th ministerial session of the Commission was convened in May 2012.

PREPARATORY COMMITTEE

The Committee has the task of reviewing programming issues and presenting recommendations in that regard to the sessions of the Commission. It is the principal subsidiary body of the Commission and functions as its policy-making structure. Seven specialized intergovernmental committees have been established (see below) to consider specific areas of activity, to report on these to the Preparatory Committee and to assist the Committee in formulating ESCWA's medium-term work programmes: they meet every two years, except for the Committee on Transport, which meets annually.

SUBSIDIARY COMMITTEES

Statistical Committee: established in 1992;
Committee on Social Development: established in 1994;
Committee on Energy: established in 1995;
Committee on Water Resources: established in 1995;
Committee on Transport: established in 1997;
Committee on Liberalization of Foreign Trade and Economic Globalization: established in 1997;
Committee on Women: established in 2003.

In addition, an Advisory Committee meets every four months at ESCWA headquarters: it comprises the heads of diplomatic missions in the host country, and a senior representative of the host country, and fulfils a consultative role, while providing a means of communication between member governments and the ESCWA Secretariat. A further Technical Committee, made up of senior officials from member countries, was established pursuant to a decision of the 24th ministerial session of the Commission held in May 2006. The Committee held its inaugural meeting in January 2008 and was to convene every six months, with a mandate to advise and assist the Secretariat in formulating strategy and future priorities and implementing programmes of work. The Consultative Committee on Scientific Technological Development and Technological Innovation was established in 2001 and meets every two years. It comprises experts from public institutions, the private sector, civil society and research centres.

SECRETARIAT

The Secretariat comprises an Executive Secretary, a Deputy Executive Secretary, and the following administrative and programme divisions: Administrative Services; Economic Development and Globalization; Information and Communications Technology; Programme Planning and Technical Co-operation; Social Development; Statistics; and Sustainable Development and Productivity. Each division is headed by a Chief, who is accountable to the Executive Secretary. In addition, there is an ESCWA Centre for Women (established in 2003, formerly part of the Social Development Division), and a Unit for Emerging and Conflict Related Issues, established in 2006.

Executive Secretary: RIMA KHALAF (Jordan).

Activities

ESCWA aims to support development and to further economic co-operation and integration in western Asia. ESCWA undertakes or sponsors studies of economic, social and development issues of the region, collects and disseminates information, and provides advisory services to member states in various fields of economic and social development. It also organizes conferences and intergovernmental and expert group meetings and sponsors training workshops and seminars. ESCWA adopts biennial strategic frameworks as the basis for its programme planning.

Much of ESCWA's work is carried out in co-operation with other UN bodies, as well as with other international and regional organizations, for example the League of Arab States (Arab League), the Cooperation Council for the Arab States of the Gulf (GCC) and the Organization of Islamic Cooperation (OIC). In May 2009 ESCWA co-hosted, with the International Labour Organization and the Syrian Government, a Regional High-Level Consultative Forum on the Impacts of the International Financial Crisis on the ESCWA Member Countries. The meeting adopted the Damascus Declaration, comprising a set of proposals for member countries to respond more effectively to the crisis, including support for greater investment in the region by ESCWA's sovereign wealth funds, adopting fiscal stimulus policies, and strengthening the efficiency of their regulatory frameworks. The Forum identified ESCWA as being key to enhancing the participation of Arab and Islamic financial institutions in member countries' efforts to counter the effects of the crisis. In June 2013 ESCWA and the Arab League concluded a Memorandum of Understanding, reflecting new modalities of co-operation in respect to emerging regional challenges. Henceforth ESCWA was to participate in ministerial sessions and meetings of the Economic and Social Council of the League.

In May 2010 ESCWA's 26th ministerial session was convened, on the theme 'The Role of Youth and their Empowerment'. In June 2011 ESCWA hosted the 15th meeting of a Regional Co-ordination Mechanism for Arab States, at which regional directors and officials from more than 20 UN agencies and other international and regional organizations considered the recent political and social reforms in several Arab countries. The grouping reaffirmed its commitment to strengthening co-operation in order to support more inclusive and sustainable development in the region. It also resolved to establish a new thematic working group to achieve greater regional integration. In mid-2011 ESCWA undertook an internal review of its work programmes in order to enhance its capacity to address the emerging needs of societies in transition. In January 2012 the UN Secretary-General addressed a High-level Meeting on Reform and Transition to Democracy, organized by ESCWA. The meeting emphasized the need to incorporate human rights and principles of social justice as essential elements of future economic strategies in countries in the region in order to secure democracy, as well as to protect and promote the empowerment of women and to stimulate youth employment opportunities. The 27th ministerial session was convened in May, on the theme 'The role of participation and social justice in achieving sustainable and balanced development'. In February 2013 a High-Level Meeting on Beyond Populism: Economic Challenges and Opportunities in Democratic Transitions was convened, under ESCWA auspices, in Rabat, Morocco.

ECONOMIC DEVELOPMENT AND GLOBALIZATION

Through its Economic Development and Globalization Division ESCWA aims to assist member states to achieve sustainable economic development in the region and to integrate more fully into the world economy. A Financing for Development Team aims to assist member countries to implement the recommendations of the Monterrey Consensus, adopted at the International Conference on Financing for Development, held in Monterrey, Mexico, in March 2002. Other concerns are to encourage domestic, intra-regional and foreign investment, to facilitate transboundary flows of goods, services, people and capital, by integrating regional markets (for example through the Greater Arab Free Trade Area) and to support member countries with debt management. The Division's Trade Team works to advance regional trading integration, as well as greater participation of the region in the multilateral trading system. It acts as a forum for member countries in preparation for multilateral trade negotiations, such as those within the Doha Round of negotiations under the World Trade Organization. An Economic Analysis Team aims to increase the capacity of member countries to co-ordinate economic policies. It makes continuous assessments of the region's macroeconomic performances; conducts economic research, modelling and forecasting; monitors the region's progress towards the UN Millennium Development Goals (MDGs); and disseminates its findings to support dialogue at various regional meetings. The Division aims to help member countries to increase their exports and to encourage domestic and foreign investment. The work of the Division's Transport Team includes the development of an integrated transport system in the Arab Mashreq region; development of a regional transport information system; formation of national and regional transport and trade committees, representing both the private and public sectors; simplification of cross-border trading procedures; and the use of electronic data exchange for more efficient transport and trade. In May 2008 the 25th ministerial session of the Commission adopted a Convention on International Multi-modal Transport of Goods in the Arab Mashreq.

The first Arab Economics Forum was convened by ESCWA in November 2012, in Beirut, Lebanon, with participation by academics, experts and policy-makers from the ESCWA region, as well as from neighbouring countries in Europe and Asia. The Forum was funded by the European Union. In April 2013 ESCWA launched a new regional Infrastructure Investments and PPPs Initiative, in co-operation with the Geneva-based ECE International Centre of Excellence on PPPs. Under the Initiative a regional PPP network and PPP specialist centres (including on Islamic finance, renewable energy and infrastructure) were to be established.

EMERGING AND CONFLICT-RELATED ISSUES

In January 2006 a Unit for Emerging and Conflict-related Issues (ECRI) was established to consolidate and develop ESCWA's activities in conflict and post-conflict countries and areas, including Iraq, the Palestinian territories and, initially, southern Lebanon. Following the Israeli military strikes that targeted the Lebanese bases of the militant Shi'a organization Hezbollah in July–August of that year, the mandate of ECRI was expanded to cover all of Lebanon. ECRI's priority areas include analysis and policy formulation for reducing the causes of conflict; capacity building to improve the effectiveness of public administration and the rule of law; forging partnerships among civic entities at local and regional level; and working with other ESCWA divisions to meet the special needs of countries affected by conflicts. ESCWA administers an E-Caravan mobile computer school programme, to provide information and communications technology (ICT) training to communities in southern Lebanon. Other projects include the provision of regional and local 'networking academies' in Iraq, to give training in information technology; the Smart Communities Project, providing modern technology for villages in Iraq; the improvement of statistics related to gender in Iraq; and the support of the Coalition of Arab-Palestinian Civil Society Organizations. Regional expert group meetings organized by ECRI have included 'Strengthening Good Governance Practices in Conflict Affected Countries: Current Priorities and Future Interventions', and 'Policies for Peace-building and Conflict Prevention in Western Asia'. In September 2011 ESCWA hosted an expert group meeting, in part chaired by ECRI, to consider the impact of conflict on progress towards achieving the MDGs in countries in the region. In the following month ECRI contributed to a seminar on participatory governance in crisis-affected Arab countries. In July 2012 ESCWA hosted a round-table discussion on 'Reconciliation, Reform and Resilience' in post-conflict Lebanon.

ESCWA CENTRE FOR WOMEN

The ESCWA Centre for Women was established in October 2003. Its main focus of activities is the empowerment and advancement of women. It also aims to incorporate issues relating to gender in regional projects and programmes. The Centre monitors developments, compiles country profiles on the status of women, provides support for formulating relevant legislation, raises awareness by publishing reports and studies, and organizes conferences. In December 2003 ESCWA issued its first *Status of Arab Women* report; this was to assess the situation of Arab women at two-yearly intervals. The 2011 edition focused on equal participation in decision-making. In September 2008 the ESCWA Secretary-General launched a guide entitled *Gender in the Millennium Development Goals*, which summarized the key regional gender issues in the context of each MDG and provided a statistical framework for evaluating and following up adherence to international agreements relating to gender equality, in the context of reporting progress in achieving (by 2015) the Arab MDGs. In 2012 the Centre's activities included organizing a seminar on 'Women in the Arab Uprisings' (in January), participating in a regional collaborative workshop on 'Women in Computing in the Arab World' (in March), convening a sub-regional workshop on strengthening legislative frameworks to address violence against women (in April), organizing a workshop on 'Women in Arab Parliaments' (in July), and (in December) organizing a training workshop on developing national action plans for the implementation of UN Security Council Resolution 1325 (2000), relating to the role of women in conflict management, conflict resolution, and sustainable peace.

INFORMATION AND COMMUNICATIONS TECHNOLOGY

The Information and Communications Technology Division works to increase the capabilities of ESCWA member countries in harnessing ICT in support of sustainable development and regional integration. It aims to narrow the so-called digital gap between Arab countries and other regions, and, consequently, to improve the competitiveness of local industries and the effectiveness of local services. It supports the formation of ICT policies and infrastructure, by providing technical assistance, pilot projects, studies and meetings of experts. ESCWA was responsible for advising member countries on the implementation of recommendations issued by the first phase of the World Summit on the Information Society (WSIS), held in December 2003, and on preparations for the second phase of the Summit, which was convened in Tunis, Tunisia, in November 2005. As a follow-up to the Summit, ESCWA undertook to collate a profile of the region's information society based on national profile reports. A Regional Follow-up to the Outcome of the WSIS was held in Damascus, Syria, in June 2009. In November ESCWA organized a regional workshop on Arabic domain names and internet governance, held in Sharm el-Sheikh, Egypt. In July 2011 ESCWA co-organized, with the Arab League and International Telecommunication Union, a Partnership Building Forum for the Implementation of the Arab Top Level Domains. The inaugural meeting of a new Arab Internet Governance Forum (AIGF)—established under the auspices of ESCWA and the Arab League—was convened in October 2012, in Kuwait. The 26th session of the Commission, held in May 2010, resolved to establish an ESCWA Technology Centre, in order to strengthen member states' ICT capabilities. The Centre was inaugurated, in El Hassan Science City, Jordan, in November 2011. In May 2012 the 27th Commission session launched a set of directives on Cyber Legislation. In 2012 ESCWA undertook a Digital Arabic Content Survey, which analysed the use of Arabic language content by ICT sector companies.

SOCIAL DEVELOPMENT

ESCWA's Social Development Division encourages regional co-operation in promoting comprehensive and integrated social policies, so as to achieve greater social equality and well-being, and to alleviate poverty, social exclusion, gender imbalances and social tension. It advises governments on the importance of integrating social analysis into policy-making, identifies methods for the effective formulation, implementation and monitoring of social policy, and assists national and regional research on social development. ESCWA's objectives with regard to population are to increase awareness and understanding of links between population factors and poverty, human rights and the environment, and to strengthen the capacities of member states to analyse and assess demographic trends and migration. In the area of social participatory development ESCWA aims to further the alleviation of poverty and to generate a sustainable approach to development through greater involvement of community groups, institutions and users of public services in decision-making. The Division's work on social policy in the city analyses urban problems, such as poverty, unemployment, violence, and failure to integrate vulnerable and marginal groups, and aims to assist policy-makers in ensuring that all city-dwellers have equal access to public services. ESCWA provides a forum for preparatory and follow-up meetings to global conferences. In December 2011 ESCWA organized a second regional review meeting of the International Plan of Action on Ageing, which resulted from the World Assembly, held in Madrid, Spain in 2002. In May 2010 ESCWA's 26th ministerial session emphasized the need to secure employment opportunities for young people. Efforts to increase the involvement of young people, and of women, in development programmes were also promoted, in particular at a time when the region was attempting to recover from the effects of the global financial and economic crisis. In 2010 an estimated 60% of the region's population were under 25 years of age. In November 2011 ESCWA organized an inter-regional seminar on 'Participatory Development and Conflict Resolution: Path of Democratic Transition and Social Justice', to address aspects of the political and social changes taking place in several countries in the region.

STATISTICS

ESCWA helps to develop the statistical systems of member states in accordance with the UN Fundamental Principles of Official Statistics, in order to improve the accuracy and comparability of economic and social data, and to make the information more accessible to planners and researchers. It aims to improve human and institutional capacities, in particular in the use of statistical tools for data analysis, to expand the adoption and implementation of international statistical methods, and to promote co-operation to further the regional harmonization of statistics. ESCWA assists members in preparing for population and housing censuses, in accordance with the UN 2010 World Population and Housing Census Programme. In December 2011 ESCWA hosted a workshop on Population Census Preparedness. A Trade and Transport Statistics Team compiles, processes and disseminates statistics on international trade and transport within the region, and assists member countries to develop their statistical capacity in this sector.

SUSTAINABLE DEVELOPMENT AND PRODUCTIVITY

The work of ESCWA's Sustainable Development and Productivity Division is undertaken by four teams, covering: energy for sustainable development; water and environment; technology and enterprise development; and sustainable agriculture and rural development. ESCWA aims to counter the problem of an increasing shortage of freshwater resources and deterioration in water quality resulting from population growth, agricultural land use and socio-economic development, by supporting measures for more rational use and conservation of water resources, and by promoting public awareness of and community participation in water and environmental protection projects. The Division assists governments in the formulation and implementation of capacity-building programmes and the development of surface and groundwater resources. ESCWA promotes greater co-operation among member and non-member countries in the management and use of shared water resources, and supports the Arab Integrated Water Resources Management Network (AWARENET, comprising some 120 research and training institutes). in September 2013 ESCWA and the German Federal Institute for Geosciences and Natural Resources launched an Inventory of Shared Water Resources in Western Asia, which aimed to identify and review the state of transboundary surface and groundwater resources in the Middle East. ESCWA supports co-operation in the establishment of electricity distribution and supply networks throughout the region and promotes the use of alternative sources of energy and the development of new and renewable energy technologies. It places a special emphasis on increasing the access of poor people to cheap energy and water, and on the creation of new jobs. The Division promotes the application of environmentally sound technologies in order to achieve sustainable development, as well as measures to recycle resources, minimize waste and reduce the environmental impact of transport operations and energy use. ESCWA collaborates with national, regional and international organizations in monitoring and reporting on emerging environmental issues and to pursue implementation of Agenda 21, which was adopted at the June 1992 UN Conference on Environment and Development, with particular regard to land and water resource management and conservation. In July 2011 ESCWA hosted a regional meeting concerned with 'Economic Policies Supporting the Transition to a Green Economy in the Arab Region'. In September ESCWA hosted a conference on 'The Role of Green Industries in Promoting Socio-Economic Development in the Arab Countries'. In February 2012 ESCWA organized, jointly with the International Food Policy Research Institute, an international conference on food security in the Arab region.

ESCWA, in co-operation with the Arab League and UNEP's Office for West Asia, organized a series of preparatory meetings to formulate a regional strategy for the UN Conference on Sustainable Development (Rio+20), which was held in Rio de Janeiro, Brazil, in June 2012. In May the 27th ministerial session requested the Commission's Secretariat to report back to the membership on the outcomes of Rio+20, and to support member states in building capacity to address these. In May 2013, jointly with the Arab League, UNEP's Office for West Asia, and other partners, ESCWA organized a Regional Arab Implementation Meeting, in Dubai, which issued the Dubai Document addressing the regional implementation of the 2012 Conference outcomes.

Finance

ESCWA's proposed regular budget allocation from the UN budget for the two years 2012–13 was US $62.6m.

Publications

ESCWA Annual Report.

UN-ESCWA Weekly News.

Analysis of Performance and Assessment of Growth and Productivity in the ESCWA Region.

Annual Review of Developments in Globalization and Regional Integration.

Compendium of Environment Statistics.

Compendium of Social Statistics and Indicators.

Country and Regional Profiles for Sustainable Development Indicators.

ESCWA Centre for Women Newsletter (monthly).

Estimates and Forecasts for GDP Growth in the ESCWA Region.

External Trade Bulletin of the ESCWA Region (annually).

International Comparison Program Newsletter.

Review of Industry in ESCWA Member Countries.

Review of Information and Communications Technology and Development.

Status of Arab Women Report (every 2 years).

Survey of Economic and Social Developments in the ESCWA Region.

Transport Bulletin.

Weekly News.

ESCWA publishes reports, case studies, assessments, guides and manuals on the subjects covered by its various Divisions.

United Nations Children's Fund—UNICEF

Address: 3 United Nations Plaza, New York, NY 10017, USA.

Telephone: (212) 326-7000; **fax:** (212) 887-7465; **e-mail:** info@unicef.org; **internet:** www.unicef.org.

UNICEF was established in 1946 by the UN General Assembly as the UN International Children's Emergency Fund, to meet the emergency needs of children in post-war Europe. In 1950 its mandate was expanded to respond to the needs of children in developing countries. In 1953 the General Assembly decided that UNICEF should become a permanent branch of the UN system, with an emphasis on programmes giving long-term benefits to children everywhere, particularly those in developing countries. In 1965 UNICEF was awarded the Nobel Peace Prize.

Organization

(September 2013)

EXECUTIVE BOARD

The Executive Board, as the governing body of UNICEF, comprises 36 member governments from all regions, elected in rotation for a three-year term by ECOSOC. The Board establishes policy, reviews programmes and approves expenditure. It reports to the General Assembly through ECOSOC.

SECRETARIAT

The Executive Director of UNICEF is appointed by the UN Secretary-General in consultation with the Executive Board. The administration of UNICEF and the appointment and direction of staff are the responsibility of the Executive Director, under policy directives laid down by the Executive Board, and under a broad authority delegated to the Executive Director by the Secretary-General. Around 85% of UNICEF staff positions are based in field offices.

Executive Director: Anthony Lake (USA).

Deputy Executive Director: Johanna (Yoka) Brandt (Netherlands).

UNICEF OFFICES

Regional Office for the Middle East and North Africa: POB 1551, 11821 Amman, Jordan; tel. (6) 5502400; fax (6) 5531112; e-mail amman@unicef.org.jo; internet www.unicef.org/jordan.

UNICEF Innocenti Research Centre: Piazza SS. Annunziata 12, 50122 Florence, Italy; tel. (055) 20330; fax (055) 2033220; e-mail florence@unicef.org; internet www.unicef-irc.org; f. 1988; undertakes research in two thematic areas: Social and economic policies and children; and Child protection and implementation of international standards for children; Dir Gordon Alexander.

UNICEF Supply Division: Oceanvej 10–12, 2100 Copenhagen, Denmark; tel. 35-27-35-27; fax 35-26-94-21; e-mail supply@unicef.org; internet www.unicef.org/supply; responsible for overseeing UNICEF's global procurement and logistics operations.

Further strategic supply hubs are located in Dubai, United Arab Emirates; Douala, Cameroon; Colón, Panama; and Shanghai, People's Republic of China.

Activities

UNICEF is dedicated to the well-being of children, adolescents and women and works for the realization and protection of their rights within the frameworks of the Convention on the Rights of the Child, which was adopted by the UN General Assembly in 1989, and by 2013 was almost universally ratified, and of the Convention on the Elimination of All Forms of Discrimination Against Women, adopted by the UN General Assembly in 1979. Promoting the full implementation of the Conventions, UNICEF aims to ensure that children worldwide are given the best possible start in life and attain a good level of basic education, and that adolescents are given every opportunity to develop their capabilities and participate successfully in society. The Fund also continues to provide relief and rehabilitation assistance in emergencies. Through its extensive field network in more than 150 developing countries and territories, UNICEF undertakes, in co-ordination with governments, local communities and other aid organizations, programmes in health, nutrition, education, water and sanitation, the environment, gender issues and development, and other fields of importance to children. Emphasis is placed on low-cost, community-based programmes. UNICEF programmes are increasingly focused on supporting children and women during critical periods of their life, when intervention can make a lasting difference. Since the 1950s UNICEF has engaged the services of prominent individuals as Goodwill Ambassadors and Advocates, who can use their status to attract attention to particular causes and support UNICEF's objectives. UNICEF advocates for increased focus on children in national budgets and development plans.

The principal themes of UNICEF's medium-term strategic plan for the period 2006–13 are young child survival and development; basic education and gender equality (including the Fund's continued leadership of the UN Girls' Education Initiative, see below); HIV/AIDS and children (including participation in the Joint UN Programme on HIV/AIDS—UNAIDS—see below); child protection from violence, exploitation and abuse; and policy advocacy and partnerships for children's rights. These priority areas are guided by the relevant UN Millennium Development Goals (MDGs) adopted by world leaders in 2000, and by the 'A World Fit for Children' declaration and plan of action endorsed by the UN General Assembly Special Session on Children in 2002. The 'A World Fit for Children' declaration reaffirmed commitment to the agenda of the 1990 World Summit for Children. The plan of action resolved to work towards the attainment by 2015 of 21 new goals and targets supporting the MDGs in the areas of education, health and the protection of children; these included: a reduction in mortality rates for infants and children under five by two-thirds; a reduction in maternal mortality rates by three-quarters; a reduction by one-third in the rate of severe malnutrition among children under the age of five; and enrolment in primary education by 90% of children. UNICEF issues regular reports that monitor progress in achieving the MDGs. UNICEF supports the Global Strategy for Women's and Children's Health, launched by heads of state and government participating in the September 2010 UN Summit on the MDGs; some US $40,000m. has been pledged towards women's and child's health and achieving goals (iv) Reducing Child Mortality and (v) Improving Maternal Health. A draft roadmap towards the Fund's next medium-term strategic plan, to cover the period 2014–17, was to be passed to the Executive Board for approval in late 2013. In 2013 UNICEF was a co-leader of the following five of the 11 global thematic consultations on the post-2015 development agenda: addressing inequalities; conflict, disaster and violence; education; health; and water. In September 2012 UNICEF organized the inaugural forum of a new Global Partnership on Children with Disabilities, which aimed to include issues pertaining to disabled children in the post-2015 development agenda.

UNICEF estimates that more than 500,000 women die every year during pregnancy or childbirth, largely because of inadequate maternal health care, and nearly 4m. newborns die within 28 days of birth. For every maternal death, approximately 30 further women suffer permanent injuries or chronic disabilities as a result of complications during pregnancy or childbirth. Under the Global Partnership for Maternal, Newborn and Child Health, UNICEF works with the World Health Organization (WHO), the UN Population Fund (UNFPA) and other partners in countries with high maternal mortality to improve maternal health and prevent maternal and newborn death through the integration of a continuum of home, community, outreach and facility-based care, embracing every stage of maternal, newborn and child health. UNICEF and partners work with governments and policy-makers to ensure that antenatal and obstetric care is a priority in national health plans. UNICEF's recent activities in this area have included support for obstetric facilities and training in, and advocacy of, women's health issues, such as ending child marriage, eliminating female genital mutilation/cutting (FGM/C), preventing malaria and promoting the uptake of tetanus toxcid vaccinations and iron and folic acid supplements among pregnant women.

YOUNG CHILD SURVIVAL AND DEVELOPMENT

In 2012 UNICEF allocated some 53% of total programme assistance to young child survival and development. In 2012 UNICEF estimated that around 6.6m. children under five years of age died (compared with some 20m. child mortalities in 1960 and some 13m. in 1990)—mainly in developing countries (four-fifths of such premature deaths occurring in sub-Saharan African and South Asia), and the majority from largely preventable causes, such as birth asphyxia, diarrhoea, malaria, pneumonia and prematurity. More than one-third of all deaths of children under five in that year occurred in India (22% of all deaths) and Nigeria (13%). UNICEF has worked with WHO and other partners to increase global immunization coverage against the following six diseases: measles, poliomyelitis, tuberculosis, diphtheria, whooping cough and tetanus. In 2003 UNICEF, WHO, the World Bank and other partners established a new Child Survival Partnership, which acts as a forum for the promotion of co-ordinated action in support of efforts to save children's lives in 68 targeted developing countries. UNICEF, WHO, the World Bank and the UN Population Division established an Inter-agency Group for Child Mortality Estimation (IGME) in 2004, to advance work on monitoring progress towards meeting the MDG on reducing child mortality. In September 2012 IGME reported that in 2011 an estimated 6.9m. children died under the age of five years old, compared with around

12m. such deaths in 1990. In September 2005 UNICEF, WHO and other partners launched the Partnership for Maternal, Newborn and Child Health, which aimed to accelerate progress towards the attainment of the MDGs to reduce child and maternal mortality. In 2000 UNICEF, WHO, the World Bank and a number of public and private sector partners launched the Global Alliance for Vaccines and Immunization (GAVI), subsequently renamed the GAVI Alliance, which aims to protect children of all nationalities and socio-economic groups against vaccine-preventable diseases. GAVI's strategy includes improving access to sustainable immunization services, expanding the use of existing vaccines, accelerating the development and introduction of new vaccines and technologies and promoting immunization coverage as a focus of international development efforts. From 2006 a Global Immunization Meeting was convened annually by UNICEF, WHO and GAVI Alliance partners. In 2006 UNICEF, WHO and other partners launched the Global Immunization Vision and Strategy (GIVS), a global 10-year framework, covering 2006–15, aimed at reducing deaths due to vaccine-preventable diseases by at least two-thirds compared to 2000 levels, by 2015; and increasing national vaccination coverage levels to at least 90%. (In 2011 the global child vaccination coverage rate was estimated at 83%.) In May 2012 the 65th World Health Assembly endorsed a Global Vaccine Action Plan (GVAP), building on the GIVS, which aimed to facilitate more equitable access to vaccines by 2020. In June 2012 UNICEF, and the Ethiopian, Indian and US Governments launched Committing to Child Survival: A Promise Renewed; the initiative, which was to be administered from a small secretariat hosted by UNICEF, aimed to terminate preventable child mortality through the pursuit of the following goals: mobilizing political leadership; achieving consensus on a global roadmap of proven strategies; and driving sustained collective action and mutual accountability.

UNICEF works to improve safe water supply, sanitation and hygiene, and thereby reduce the risk of diarrhoea and other water-borne diseases. In partnership with other organizations the Fund supports initiatives to make schools in more than 90 developing countries safer through school-based water, sanitation and hygiene programmes. UNICEF places great emphasis on increasing the testing and protection of drinking water at its source as well as in the home. UNICEF, the World Bank and other partners participate in the Global Public-Private Partnership for Handwashing with Soap, which was established in 2001 with the aim of empowering communities in developing countries to prevent diarrhoea and respiratory infections through the promotion of the practice of thorough hand-washing with soap. In 2006 UNICEF and partners established the Global Task Force on Water and Sanitation with the aim of providing all children with access to safe water, and accelerating progress towards MDG targets on safe drinking water and basic sanitation.

UNICEF-assisted programmes for the control of diarrhoeal diseases promote the low-cost manufacture and distribution of pre-packaged salts or home-made solutions. The use of 'oral rehydration therapy' has risen significantly in recent years, and is believed to prevent more than 1m. child deaths annually. During 1990–2000 diarrhoea-related deaths were reduced by one-half. UNICEF also promotes the need to improve sanitation and access to safe water supplies in developing nations in order to reduce the risk of diarrhoea and other water-borne diseases (see 20/20 initiative, below). To control acute respiratory infections, another leading cause of death in children under five in developing countries, UNICEF works with WHO in training health workers to diagnose and treat the associated diseases. A report released by UNICEF in July 2012 entitled *Pneumonia and diarrhoea: tackling the deadliest diseases for the world's poorest children*, stated that pneumonia and diarrhoea account for nearly one-third of deaths among children under five globally. In 2011 UNICEF supported the introduction of a new pneumococcal vaccine into routine immunization programmes in Kenya; this reportedly reached in that year some 90% of Kenyan children below the age of one. At the UN General Assembly Special Session on Children, in 2002, goals were set to reduce measles deaths by 50%. Expanded efforts by UNICEF, WHO and other partners led to a reduction in world-wide measles deaths by 78% between 2000 and 2008. Around 1m. children die from malaria every year, mainly in sub-Saharan Africa. In October 1998 UNICEF, together with WHO, the UN Development Programme (UNDP) and the World Bank, inaugurated a new global campaign, Roll Back Malaria, to fight the disease. UNICEF is actively engaged in developing innovative and effective ways to distribute highly subsidized insecticide-treated mosquito nets at the local level, thereby increasing the proportion of children and pregnant women who use them.

According to UNICEF estimates, around 25% of children under five years of age are underweight, while each year malnutrition contributes to more than one-third of the child deaths in that age group and leaves millions of others with physical and mental disabilities. UNICEF supports national efforts to reduce malnutrition, for example, fortifying staple foods with micronutrients, widening women's access to education, improving the nutritional status of pregnant women, strengthening household food security and basic health services, providing food supplies in emergencies, and promoting sound childcare and feeding practices. Since 1991 more than 19,000 hospitals in about 130 countries have been designated 'baby-friendly', having implemented a set of UNICEF and WHO recommendations entitled '10 steps to successful breast-feeding'. The Executive Director of UNICEF chairs the Lead Group of the Scaling Up Nutrition (SUN) initiative, which convened its first meeting in April 2012, and comprises 27 national leaders and agencies jointly providing strategic guidance with a view to improving child and maternal nutrition. SUN, initiated in 2009, and co-ordinated by the UN Secretary-General's Special Representative for Food Security and Nutrition, aims to increase the coverage of interventions that improve nutrition during the first 1,000 days of a child's life (such as exclusive breastfeeding, optimal complementary feeding practices, and provision of essential vitamins and minerals); and to ensure that national nutrition plans are implemented and that government programmes take nutrition into account. The activities of SUN are guided by the Framework for Scaling up Nutrition, which was published in April 2010 and subsequently endorsed by more than 100 partners, including UN agencies, governments, research institutions, and representatives of civil society and of the private sector; and by the SUN Roadmap, finalized in September 2010.

BASIC EDUCATION AND GENDER EQUALITY

In 2012 UNICEF allocated some 20% of total programme assistance to basic education and gender equality. UNICEF considers education to be a fundamental human right, and works to ensure all children receive equal access to quality education. UNICEF participated in and fully supports the objectives and framework for action adopted by the World Education Forum in Dakar, Senegal, in April 2000, including the Education for All initiative. UNICEF was assigned formal responsibility within the initiative for education in emergencies, early childhood care and technical and policy support. UNICEF leads and acts as the secretariat of the United Nations Girls' Education Initiative (UNGEI), which aims to increase the enrolment of girls in primary schools in more than 100 countries. It is estimated that more than 100m. school-age children world-wide, of whom more than one-half are girls, remain deprived of basic education. In May 2010 UNGEI convened the first international conference on 'Engendering Empowerment: Education and Equality' ('E4'), in Dakar, Senegal. The E4 conference unanimously adopted the Dakar Declaration on Accelerating Girls' Education and Gender Equality, in which it urged that increased focus should be placed on accelerating access to education for the most socially deprived girls, deemed to be the most disadvantaged group in education. UNICEF supports inclusive fee-free education. On 11 October 2012 the first International Day of the Girl Child (approved by the UN General Assembly in December 2011) was commemorated, on the theme 'Ending Child Marriage'.

UNICEF advocates the implementation of the Child Friendly School model, designed to facilitate the delivery of safe, quality education. UNICEF, in partnership with UNESCO, has developed an Essential Learning Package to support countries to reduce disparities in the provision of basic education. The initiative was implemented for the first time by Burkina Faso in 2003, and has since been adopted by a further 11 countries in West and Central Africa.

HIV/AIDS AND CHILDREN

In 2012 UNICEF allocated some 3% of total programme assistance to combating HIV/AIDS. UNICEF is concerned at the danger posed by HIV/AIDS to the realization of children's rights and aims to provide expertise, support, logistical co-ordination and innovation towards ending the epidemic and limiting its impact on children and their mothers. In 2012 it was estimated that 3.4m. children under the age of 15 were living with HIV/AIDS world-wide. During 2011 some 330,000 children under the age of 15 were estimated to have been newly infected with HIV, while 230,000 died as a result of AIDS and AIDS-related illnesses. Around 17m. children world-wide have lost one or both parents to AIDS since the start of the pandemic, and as a result of HIV/AIDS many children have suffered poverty, homelessness, discrimination, and loss of education and other life opportunities. UNICEF's priorities in this area include prevention of infection among young people (through, for example, support for education programmes and dissemination of information through the media), reduction in mother-to-child transmission, care and protection of orphans and other vulnerable children, and care and support for children, young people and parents living with HIV/AIDS. UNICEF works closely in this field with governments and co-operates with other UN agencies in the Joint UN Programme on HIV/AIDS (UNAIDS), which became operational on 1 January 1996. Young people aged 15–24 are reported to account for around 45% of new HIV infections world-wide. UNICEF advocates Life Skills-Based Education as a means of empowering young people to cope with challenging situations and of encouraging them to adopt healthy patterns of behaviour. In July 2004 UNICEF and other partners produced a

Framework for the Protection, Care and Support of Orphans and Vulnerable Children Living in a World with HIV and AIDS. In October 2005 UNICEF launched Unite for Children, Unite against AIDS, a campaign that was to provide a platform for child-focused advocacy aimed at reversing the spread of HIV/AIDS amongst children, adolescents and young people; and to provide a child-focused framework for national programmes based on the following four 'pillars' (known as the 'Four Ps'): the prevention of mother-to-child HIV transmission; improved provision of paediatric treatment; prevention of infection among adolescents and young people; and protection and support of children affected by HIV/AIDS. In November 2010 UNICEF issued its fifth *Children and AIDS: A Stocktaking Report*, detailing ongoing progress and challenges. In October 2010 UNICEF issued its first Mother-Baby Pack, containing drugs to prevent mother-to-child transmission of HIV in the poorest households. UNICEF supports the Global Plan towards the Elimination of New HIV Infections among Children by 2015 and Keeping Their Mothers Alive, which was endorsed in June 2011 by a UN High Level Meeting on HIV/AIDS, and aims to reduce by 90% of new HIV infections among children, and halve the number of deaths among their mothers.

At December 2011 it was estimated that some 15,000 children aged between 0–14 in the Middle East and North Africa were living with HIV/AIDS.

CHILD PROTECTION FROM VIOLENCE, EXPLOITATION AND ABUSE

In 2012 some 11% of total programme resources were allocated to child protection. UNICEF is actively involved in global-level partnerships for child protection, including the Inter-Agency Coordination Panel on Juvenile Justice; the Inter-Agency Working Group on Unaccompanied and Separated Children; the Donors' Working Group on Female FGM/C (see above); the Better Care Network; the Study on Violence Against Children; the Inter-Agency Standing Committee (IASC) Task Force on Protection from Sexual Exploitation and Abuse in Humanitarian Crises; and the IASC Task Force on Mental Health and Psychological Support in Emergency Settings.

UNICEF estimates that the births of around 48m. children annually (about 36% of all births) are not registered, and that some 63% of births occuring in South Asia, and 55% of births in sub-Saharan Africa, are unregistered. UNICEF promotes universal registration in order to prevent the abuse of children without proof of age and nationality, for example through trafficking, forced labour, early marriage and military recruitment. In 2012 the Fund supported the registration at birth of around 29.5m. children in some 80 countries. The Fund has promoted the organization of birth registration data in rural areas of developing countries through RapidSMS text messaging.

UNICEF estimates that some 158m. children aged from five–14 are engaged in child labour, while around 1.2m. children world-wide are trafficked each year. The Fund, which vigorously opposes the exploitation of children as a violation of their basic human rights, works with the International Labour Organization and other partners to promote an end to exploitative and hazardous child labour, and supports special projects to provide education, counselling and care in developing countries. UNICEF promotes ratification of the Optional Protocol to the Convention on the Rights of the Child on the sale of children, child prostitution and child pornography. The Fund co-sponsored and actively participated in the Third Congress Against Commercial Sexual Exploitation of Children, held in Rio de Janeiro, Brazil, in November 2008.

More than 250,000 children are involved in armed conflicts as soldiers, porters and forced labourers. UNICEF encourages ratification of the Optional Protocol to the Convention on the Rights of the Child on the involvement of children in armed conflict, which was adopted by the General Assembly in May 2000 and entered into force in February 2002, and bans the compulsory recruitment of combatants below the age of 18. The Fund also urges states to make unequivocal statements endorsing 18 as the minimum age of voluntary recruitment to the armed forces. UNICEF, with Save the Children, co-chairs the Steering Group of the Paris Principles, which aims to support the implementation of a series of 'Commitments and Guidelines'—first endorsed by an international conference convened by UNICEF and the French Government in Paris, France, in February 2007—to end the recruitment of children, support the release of children from the armed forces and facilitate their reintegration into civilian life. By the end of 2012 105 countries had voluntarily signed up to the Paris Commitments. It is estimated that landmines kill and maim between 8,000 and 10,000 children every year. UNICEF supports mine awareness campaigns, and promotes the full ratification of the Convention on the Prohibition of the Use, Stockpiling, Production and Transfer of Anti-Personnel Mines and on their Destruction, which was adopted in December 1997 and entered into force in March 1999. By October 2012 the Convention had been ratified by 160 countries.

POLICY AND ADVOCACY AND PARTNERSHIPS FOR CHILDREN'S RIGHTS

In 2012 UNICEF allocated some 9% of total programme assistance to policy and advocacy and partnerships for children's rights.

The Fund promotes the collection and analysis of statistical data relating to the well being of children. UNICEF's annual publication *The State of the World's Children* presents such data annually; the theme of the 2013 report, issued in May, was 'Children with Disabilities'. UNICEF's Multiple Indicator Cluster Survey (MICS) method of data collection, initiated in 1995, analyses data on child protection, education, health (including HIV and AIDS), nutrition, and water and sanitation, and is a main tool used in measuring progress towards the achievement of the UN MDGs. The fifth MICS round was being undertaken during 2012–14. During 2012 UNICEF developed a new Multiple Overlapping Deprivation Analysis (MODA) tool to assess poverty and inequalities within countries. In recent years the Fund has become increasingly concerned about the numbers of children who are not included in statistical information on development markers, and who have become isolated from vital services owing to factors such as urbanization, political volatility, natural disasters, and environmental challenges.

Since 2005 young people from the Group of Eight (G8) nations (Canada, France, Germany, Italy, Japan, Russia, the United Kingdom and the USA) and selected emerging countries (including Brazil, China, Egypt, India, Mexico and South Africa) have participated in a Junior 8 (J8) summit, which is organized with support from UNICEF on the fringes of the annual G8 summit. The J8 summits address issues including education, energy, climate change, HIV/AIDS, the global financial crisis, and tolerance. Since 2010 G(irls)20 summits have been convened alongside summits of G20 leaders; the participants represent the G20 countries, and include, also, young female representatives of the African Union and European Union.

UNICEF aims to break the cycle of poverty by advocating for the provision of increased development aid to developing countries, and aims to help poor countries obtain debt relief and to ensure access to basic social services. UNICEF was the leading agency in promoting the 20/20 initiative, which was endorsed at the World Summit for Social Development, held in Copenhagen, Denmark, in March 1995. The initiative encouraged the governments of developing and donor countries to allocate at least 20% of their domestic budgets and official development aid to health care, primary education, and low-cost safe water and sanitation. In May 2012 UNICEF initiated its first Social Protection Strategic Framework, promoting child-sensitive inclusive social protection systems.

Through this focus area, UNICEF seeks to work with partners to strengthen capacities to design and implement cross-sectoral social and economic policies, child-focused legislative measures and budgetary allocations that enable countries to meet their obligations under the Convention on the Rights of the Child and the Convention on the Elimination of All Forms of Discrimination against Women. UNICEF has identified the following priority areas of support to 'upstream' policy work: child poverty and disparities; social budgeting; decentralization; social security and social protection; holistic legislative reform for the two Conventions; and the impact of migration on children.

HUMANITARIAN RESPONSE

UNICEF provides emergency relief assistance to children and young people affected by conflict, natural disasters and food crises. In situations of violence and social disintegration the Fund provides support in the areas of education, health, mine-awareness and psychosocial assistance, and helps to demobilize and rehabilitate child soldiers. In 2012 UNICEF responded to 286 humanitarian challenges in 79 countries. In January 2013 UNICEF launched an appeal for nearly US $1,400m. to support the urgent requirements of children in 45 territories affected by conflict, natural disasters, and other complex emergencies that year.

UNICEF's emergency education assistance includes the provision of 'Edukits' in refugee camps and the reconstruction of school buildings. In the area of health the Fund co-operates with WHO to arrange 'days of tranquillity' in order to facilitate the immunization of children in conflict zones. Psychosocial assistance activities include special programmes to support traumatized children and help unaccompanied children to be reunited with parents or extended families.

In 2013 UNICEF was supporting children and families affected by the civil war in Syria, including Syrian refugees sheltering in neighbouring countries (Lebanon, Jordan, Turkey, Iraq and Egypt), through the delivery of an uninterrupted education to around 118,000 children; the supply of anti-measles vaccines to 1.3m. children; the provision of psychosocial support to 167,000 children; and through the delivery of water supplies to 222,000 people. In August of that year it was reported that the number of UNICEF-registered children who had fled the Syrian conflict had exceeded 1m.; of these more than 768,000 were believed to be aged under 11. The Fund issued a statement condemning the chemical attack on 21 August on several thousand civilians, including children, in Ghouta, Damascus.

In 2013 UNICEF was providing assistance to Palestinian children and women in the Palestinian territories, Jordan and Lebanon. In March of that year UNICEF issued a briefing paper entitled *Children in Israeli Military Detention: Observations and Recommendations*, with a focus on the rights of Palestinian child detainees.

Since 1998 UNICEF's humanitarian response has been structured within a framework of identified Core Commitments for Children in Humanitarian Action (CCCs). Revised CCCs were issued in April 2010 to reflect new humanitarian structures and best practices. The revised CCCs incorporated UNICEF's commitment to working in partnership with international organizations, national authorities and civil society in order to strengthen risk reduction, disaster preparedness and response, and early recovery. During 2005 the UN's Inter-Agency Standing Committee (IASC), concerned with co-ordinating the international response to humanitarian disasters, developed a concept of organizing agency assistance to IDPs through the institutionalization of a 'Cluster Approach', comprising 11 core areas of activity. UNICEF is the lead agency for the clusters on Education (jointly with Save The Children); Nutrition; and Water, Sanitation and Hygiene. In addition, it leads the Gender-based Violence Area of Responsibility sub-cluster (jointly with UNFPA) and the Child Protection Area of Responsibility sub-cluster within the Protection Cluster.

Finance

UNICEF, UNDP and UNFPA are committed to integrating their budgets from 2014.

United Nations Development Programme—UNDP

Address: One United Nations Plaza, New York, NY 10017, USA.

Telephone: (212) 906-5300; **fax:** (212) 906-5364; **e-mail:** hq@undp.org; **internet:** www.undp.org.

The Programme was established in 1965 by the UN General Assembly. Its central mission is to help countries to eradicate poverty and achieve a sustainable level of human development, an approach to economic growth that encompasses individual well-being and choice, equitable distribution of the benefits of development, and conservation of the environment. UNDP advocates for a more inclusive global economy. UNDP co-ordinates global and national efforts to achieve the UN Millennium Development Goals, and is contributing to the formulation of a post-2015 UN system-wide development framework.

Organization

(September 2013)

UNDP is responsible to the UN General Assembly, to which it reports through ECOSOC.

EXECUTIVE BOARD

The Executive Board is responsible for providing intergovernmental support to, and supervision of, the activities of UNDP and the UN Population Fund (UNFPA). It comprises 36 members: eight from Africa, seven from Asia and the Pacific, four from Eastern Europe, five from Latin America and the Caribbean and 12 from Western Europe and other countries. Members serve a three-year term.

SECRETARIAT

Offices and divisions at the Secretariat include an Operations Support Group; Offices of the United Nations Development Group, the Human Development Report, Development Studies, Audit and Performance Review, Evaluation, and Communications; and Bureaux for Crisis Prevention and Recovery; Partnerships; Development Policy; and Management. Five regional bureaux, all headed by an assistant administrator, cover Africa; Asia and the Pacific; the Arab states; Latin America and the Caribbean; and Europe and the Commonwealth of Independent States. UNDP's Administrator (the third most senior UN official, after the Secretary-General and the Deputy Secretary-General) is in charge of strategic policy and overall co-ordination of UN development activities (including the chairing of the UN Development Group), while the Associate Administrator supervises the operations and management of UNDP programmes.

Administrator: HELEN CLARK (New Zealand).

Associate Administrator: REBECA GRYNSPAN (Costa Rica).

Assistant Administrator and Director of the Regional Bureau for Arab States: SIMA SAMI BAHOUS (Jordan).

COUNTRY OFFICES

In almost every country receiving UNDP assistance there is an office, headed by the UNDP Resident Representative, who usually also serves as the UN Resident Co-ordinator, responsible for the co-ordination of all UN technical assistance and development activities in that country, so as to ensure the most effective use of UN and international aid resources.

OFFICES OF UN RESIDENT CO-ORDINATORS IN THE MIDDLE EAST AND NORTH AFRICA

Algeria: 9A rue Emile Payen Hydra, BP 823, Algiers 16000; tel. and fax (2) 21-92-54-42; e-mail registry.dz@undp.org; internet www.dz.undp.org; Resident Co-ordinator CRISTINA AMARAL.

Bahrain: 69 UN House, Rd 1901, Hoora 319, POB 26814, Manama; tel. 311600; fax 311500; e-mail registry.bh@undp.org; internet www.undp.org.bh; Resident Co-ordinator PETER GROHMANN.

Egypt: CEDARE Bldg, 2 el Hegaz St, Roxy, Heliopolis, Cairo; tel. (2) 2566209; fax (2) 2561647; e-mail registry.eg@undp.org; internet www.undp.org.eg; Resident Co-ordinator ANITA NIRODY.

Iran: 8 Shahrzad Blvd, POB 15875-4557, Darrous 1948773911, Tehran; tel. (21) 22860691; fax (21) 22869547; e-mail registry.ir@undp.org; internet www.undp.org.ir; Resident Co-ordinator GARY LEWIS.

Iraq: Bldg No. 153, 102 Abi Nawas St, POB 2048 (Alwiyah), Baghdad; tel. (1) 907-6358; fax (1) 886-2523; e-mail press.iraq@undp.org; internet www.iq.undp.org; Regional Co-ordinator JACQUELINE BADCOCK.

Jordan: Bldg 16, Ishaq Al Edwan St, Amman; tel. (6) 533-8167; fax (6) 534-0782; e-mail registry.jo@undp.org; internet www.undp-jordan.org; Resident Co-ordinator COSTANZA FARINA.

Kuwait: POB 2993, 13030 Safat; tel. 5308000; fax 5399358; e-mail registry.kw@undp.org; internet www.undp-kuwait.org; Resident Co-ordinator MUBASHAR RIAZ SHEIKH.

Lebanon: Arab African International Bank Bldg, Riad El Solh St, Nejmeh, Beirut; tel. (1) 962500; fax (1) 962491; e-mail registry@undp.org.lb; internet www.undp.org.lb; Resident Co-ordinator ROBERT WATKINS.

Libya: 69–71 Turkiya St, POB 358, Tripoli; tel. (21) 333-0852; fax (21) 333-7349; e-mail registry.ly@undp.org; internet www.undp.org.ly; Resident Co-ordinator GEORG CHARPENTIER.

Morocco: 13 ave Ahmed Balafrej Souissi, 10000 Rabat; tel. 37633090; fax 37633089; e-mail registry.ma@undp.org; internet www.pnud.org.ma; Resident Co-ordinator BRUNO POUEZAT.

Palestinian Territories: POB 51359, Jerusalem; tel. 2-6268200; fax 2-6268222; e-mail registry.papp@undp.org; internet www.undp.ps; Resident Co-ordinator JAMES W. RAWLEY.

Saudi Arabia: United Nations Building, Ibn El-Nafis St, Diplomatic Quarter, POB 94623, Riyadh 11641; tel. (1) 488-5301; fax (1) 488-5309; e-mail registry.sa@undp.org; internet www.undp.org.sa; Resident Co-ordinator REYAD M. AL-AHMAD.

Syria: Mezzeh, West Villas, Gazawi St, No. 8, Damascus; tel. (11) 6129811; fax (11) 6114541; e-mail registry.sy@undp.org; internet www.undp.org.sy; Resident Co-ordinator YACOUB EL HILLO.

Tunisia: 41 bis, ave Louis Braille, Cité El Khadhra, Tunis 1003; tel. (71) 904-011; fax (71) 900-668; e-mail registry.tn@undp.org; internet www.tn.undp.org; Resident Co-ordinator MOUNIR TABET.

Turkey: 11 2. Cad., 06610 Birlik Mahallesi, Ankara; tel. (312) 4541100; fax (312) 4961463; e-mail registry.tr@undp.org; internet www.undp.org.tr; Resident Co-ordinator KAMAL MALHOTRA.

United Arab Emirates: UN House, Plot 26-E 19/2, al-Nahya Camp, Abu Dhabi; tel. (2) 4467600; fax (2) 4467050; e-mail registry.ae@undp.org; internet www.undp.org.ae; Resident Co-ordinator SAYED AQA.

Yemen: POB 551, Sana'a; tel. (1) 448605; fax (1) 448841; e-mail registry@undp.org.ye; internet www.undp.org.ye; Resident Co-ordinator ISMAIL OULD-CHEIKH AHMED.

Activities

UNDP describes itself as the UN's global development network, advocating for change and connecting countries to knowledge, experience and resources to help people to build a better life. In

2013 UNDP was active in 177 countries. It provides advisory and support services to governments and UN teams with the aim of advancing sustainable human development and building national development capabilities. Assistance is mostly non-monetary, comprising the provision of experts' services, consultancies, equipment and training for local workers. Developing countries themselves contribute significantly to the total project costs in terms of personnel, facilities, equipment and supplies. UNDP also supports programme countries in attracting aid and utilizing it efficiently.

From the mid-1990s UNDP assumed a more active co-ordinating role within the UN system. In 1997 the UNDP Administrator was appointed to chair the UN Development Group (UNDG), which promotes coherent policy at country level through the system of UN Resident Co-ordinators (see above), the Common Country Assessment mechanism (CCA, a process for evaluating national development needs), and the UN Development Assistance Framework (UNDAF, for planning and co-ordination development operations at country level, based on the CCA). UNDP maintains a series of Thematic Trust Funds to channel support to priority programme activities.

The 2008–13 Strategic Plan emphasized UNDP's 'overarching' contribution to achieving sustainable human development through capacity development strategies, to be integrated into all areas of activity. Other objectives identified by the Plan included strengthening national ownership of development projects and promoting and facilitating South-South co-operation. A successor Plan was being developed for 2014–17, which aimed to strengthen UNDP's capacity to deliver results.

In 2013 UNDP was working to advance the UN's development agenda through engagement with the MDGs Acceleration Framework and by contributing to the formulation of a post-2015 system-wide development framework.

A framework to promote a development partnership between African countries and the international community was initiated in 1993 at the Tokyo International Conference on African Development (TICAD). A second conference was convened in 1998, a third in September 2003, and a fourth in May 2008. TICAD V, held in June 2013, in Yokohama, Japan, adopted the Yokohama Declaration and Action Plan for 2013–17, focusing on the role played by national health systems and maintaining a healthy workforce in underpinning social and economic growth. In the interim periods the process is pursued through follow-up meetings, regional forums, trade conferences and seminars. UNDP and the Government of Japan sponsor the Africa-Asia Business Forum (AABF); the fifth AABF took place in June 2009, in Kampala, Uganda. In October 2002 the UN General Assembly recognized the New Partnership for Africa's Development (NEPAD) as the framework for the international community's support of development in Africa. UNDP supported the establishment and operation of a voluntary NEPAD initiative providing for countries to evaluate standards of governance in other participating states, the so-called African Peer Review Mechanism, and manages a trust to support the mechanism. In October 2011 the UNDP Regional Bureau for Africa and NEPAD signed a Memorandum of Understanding on pursuing the following main areas of co-operation: development policy and strategy; governance; capacity development; South-South co-operation and aid effectiveness; knowledge management; environment and climate change; and gender equity and women's empowerment.

UNDP, jointly with the World Bank, leads an initiative on 'additional financing for the most vulnerable', the first of nine activities that were launched in April 2009 by the UN System Chief Executives Board for Co-ordination (CEB), with the aim of alleviating the impact on poor and vulnerable populations of the developing global economic crisis.

MILLENNIUM DEVELOPMENT GOALS

UNDP, through its leadership of the UNDG and management of the Resident Co-ordinator system, has a co-ordinating function as the focus of UN system-wide efforts to achieve the so-called Millennium Development Goals (MDGs), pledged by UN member governments attending a summit meeting of the UN General Assembly in September 2000. The objectives were to establish a defined agenda to reduce poverty and improve the quality of lives of millions of people and to serve as a framework for measuring development. There are eight MDGs, as follows, for which one or more specific targets have been identified:

i) to eradicate extreme poverty and hunger, with the aim of reducing by 50% (compared with the 1990 figure) the number of people with an income of less than US $1 a day and those suffering from hunger by 2015, and to achieve full and productive employment and decent work for all, including women and young people;

ii) to achieve universal primary education by 2015;

iii) to promote gender equality and empower women, in particular to eliminate gender disparities in primary and secondary education by 2005 and at all levels by 2015;

iv) to reduce child mortality, with a target reduction of two-thirds in the mortality rate among children under five by 2015 (compared with the 1990 level);

v) to improve maternal health, specifically to reduce by 75% the numbers of women dying in childbirth and to achieve universal access to reproductive health by 2015 (compared with the 1990 level);

vi) to combat HIV/AIDS, malaria and other diseases, with targets to have halted and begun to reverse the incidence of HIV/AIDS, malaria and other major diseases by 2015 and to achieve universal access to treatment for HIV/AIDS for all those who need it by 2010;

vii) to ensure environmental sustainability, including targets to integrate the principles of sustainable development into country policies and programmes, to reduce by 50% (compared with the 1990 level) the number of people without access to safe drinking water by 2015, and to achieve significant improvement in the lives of at least 100m. slum dwellers by 2020;

viii) to develop a global partnership for development, including an open, rule-based, non-discriminatory trading and financial system, and efforts to deal with international debt, to address the needs of least developed countries (LDCs) and landlocked and small island developing states, to provide access to affordable, essential drugs in developing countries, and to make available the benefits of new technologies.

UNDP plays a leading role in efforts to integrate the MDGs into all aspects of UN activities at country level and to ensure that the MDGs are incorporated into national development strategies. The Programme supports efforts by countries, as well as regions and sub-regions, to report on progress towards achievement of the goals, and on specific social, economic and environmental indicators, through the formulation of MDG reports. These form the basis of a global report, issued annually by the UN Secretary-General since mid-2002. UNDP also works to raise awareness of the MDGs and to support advocacy efforts at all levels, for example through regional publicity campaigns, target-specific publications and the Millennium Campaign to generate support for the goals in developing and developed countries. UNDP provides administrative and technical support to the Millennium Project, an independent advisory body established by the UN Secretary-General in 2002 to develop a practical action plan to achieve the MDGs. Financial support of the Project is channelled through a Millennium Trust Fund, administered by UNDP. In January 2005 the Millennium Project presented its report, based on extensive research conducted by teams of experts, which included recommendations for the international system to support country level development efforts and identified a series of 'Quick Wins' to bring conclusive benefit to millions of people in the short-term. International commitment to achieve the MDGs by 2015 was reiterated at a World Summit, convened in September 2005. In December 2006 UNDP and the Spanish Government concluded an agreement on the establishment of the MDG Achievement Fund (MDG-F), which aims to support the acceleration of progress towards the achievement of the MDGs and to enhance co-operation at country level between UN development partners. UNDP and the UN Department of Economic and Social Affairs (UNDESA) are lead agencies in co-ordinating the work of the MDG Gap Task Force, which was established by the UN Secretary-General in May 2007 to track, systematically and at both international and country level, existing international commitments in the areas of official development assistance, market access, debt relief, access to essential medicines and technology. In November the UN, in partnership with two major US companies, launched an online MDG Monitor (www.mdgmonitor.org) to track progress and to support organizations working to achieve the goals. In September 2010 UNDP launched the MDGs Acceleration Framework, which aimed to support countries in identifying and overcoming barriers to eradicating extreme poverty and achieving sustainable development. The 2012 edition of the *Millennium Development Goals Report*, issued in July of that year, indicated that targets in the areas of poverty, slum dwelling and water had been met three years in advance of 2015.

POST-2015 DEVELOPMENT FRAMEWORK

In January 2012 the UN Secretary-General established a UN System Task Team—led jointly by the UNDP Administrator-General and the UN Under-Secretary-General for Economic and Social Affairs—which supports system-wide consultations in 11 thematic areas, each led by specified UN agencies, on the advancement of the post-2015 global development agenda. In May and July, respectively, the Co-Chairs and membership were announced of a new High-level Panel to Advise on the Global Development Agenda Beyond 2015, and in September 2012 the Panel's Executive Secretary was appointed and the Panel's inaugural meeting was held, on the sidelines of the UN General Assembly. In May 2013 the Panel presented to the UN Secretary-General a draft document entitled *A New Global Partnership: Eradicate Poverty and Transform Economies through Sustain-*

able Development, which set out a universal agenda to eradicate extreme poverty globally by 2030, and to pursue and deliver sustainable development. The Panel consulted closely with a working group of experts tasked by the UN Conference on Sustainable Development (convened in June 2012) to formulate a series of Sustainable Development Goals.

The thematic areas in which consultations were under way in 2013 are as follows:

i) Conflict and fragility: led by UNDP, UNICEF, the UN Peacebuilding Support Office and the Inter-Agency Secretariat of the International Strategy for Disaster Reduction;

ii) Education, led by UNESCO and UNICEF;

iii) Energy, led by UN-Energy, the Sustainable Energy for All initiative of the UN Secretary-General, UNDP, UNIDO, UNDESA, and the World Bank;

iv) Environmental sustainability, led by UNDP and UNEP;

v) Food security and Nutrition, led by WFP and FAO;

vi) Governance, led by UNDP and OHCHR;

vii) Growth and employment, led by UNDP, the ILO and UNDESA;

viii) Health, led by WHO and UNICEF;

ix) Inequalities, led by UNDP, the ILO and UNDESA;

x) Population dynamics, led by UNFPA, UN-Habitat, the International Organization for Migration and UNDESA;

xi) Water, facilitated by UN-Water, and co-led by UNICEF and UNDESA.

DEMOCRATIC GOVERNANCE

UNDP supports national efforts to ensure efficient and accountable governance, to improve the quality of democratic processes, and to build effective relations between the state, the private sector and civil society, which are essential to achieving sustainable development. As in other practice areas, UNDP assistance includes policy advice and technical support, the capacity building of institutions and individuals, advocacy and public information and communication, the promotion and brokering of dialogue, and knowledge networking and sharing of good practices.

UNDP works to strengthen parliaments and other legislative bodies as institutions of democratic participation. It assists with constitutional reviews and reform, training of parliamentary staff, and capacity building of political parties and civil organizations as part of this objective. In April 2012, jointly with the Inter-Parliamentary Union, UNDP released the *Global Parliamentary Report*, which addressed means of improving strategies to meet public expectations of parliaments. UNDP undertakes missions to help prepare for and ensure the conduct of free and fair elections. It helps to build the long-term capacity of electoral institutions and practices within a country, for example by assisting with voter registration, the establishment of electoral commissions, providing observers to verify that elections are free and fair, projects to educate voters, and training journalists to provide impartial election coverage.

Within its justice sector programme UNDP undertakes a variety of projects to improve access to justice, in particular for the poor and disadvantaged, and to promote judicial independence, legal reform and understanding of the legal system. UNDP also works to promote access to information, the integration of human rights issues into activities concerned with sustainable human development, and support for the international human rights system.

UNDP is mandated to assist developing countries to fight corruption and improve accountability, transparency and integrity (ATI). It has worked to establish national and international partnerships in support of its anti-corruption efforts and used its role as a broker of knowledge and experience to uphold ATI principles at all levels of public financial management and governance. UNDP publishes case studies of its anti-corruption efforts and assists governments to conduct self-assessments of their public financial management systems. UNDP leads the new secretariat of the International Aid Transparency Initiative, which was inaugurated, in collaboration with other members of the multi-stakeholder steering committee, in September 2013.

In March 2002 a UNDP Governance Centre was inaugurated in Oslo, Norway, to enhance the role of UNDP in support of democratic governance and to assist countries to implement democratic reforms in order to achieve the MDGs. In 2012 the Centre's areas of focus were access to information and e-governance; access to justice and rule of law; anti-corruption; civic engagement; electoral systems and processes; human rights; local governance; parliamentary development; public administration; and women's empowerment. The Democratic Governance Network (DGP-Net) allows discussion and the sharing of information. An iKnow Politics Network, supported by UNDP, aims to help women become involved in politics.

During 2011 UNDP worked to support the transition to democracy in Egypt, Tunisia and Yemen through the provision of technical expertise and election training. In 2012 UNDP helped to promote an initiative in Libya which encouraged 1.3 m. women to register to vote in legislative elections held in July; it also provided training and other technical support to female candidates.

In March 2012 UNDP published the second *Arab Knowledge Report*, an assessment of the current state of knowledge in the Arab region, with a particular focus on preparing future generations for the 'knowledge society'. (The first report had been issued in October 2009.) In May 2013 UNDP and the Iraqi authorities initiated new curricula for primary and secondary schools in Iraq that aimed to raise awareness of the concepts of integrity, transparency and human rights.

POVERTY REDUCTION

UNDP aims to promote sustainable human development by ensuring that national development policies emphasize the needs of the poor and marginalized, and by supporting developing countries in integrating human rights principles and standards into the design and implementation of development policies (on the basis that equal opportunities and freedoms are conducive to the promotion of economic growth with an inclusive impact). Activities aimed at facilitating poverty eradication include support for capacity-building programmes and initiatives to generate sustainable livelihoods, for example by improving access to credit, land and technologies, and the promotion of strategies to improve education and health provision for the poorest elements of populations (especially women and girls). UNDP aims to help governments to reassess their development priorities and to design initiatives for sustainable human development. The World Summit for Social Development, convened in March 1995, in Copenhagen, Denmark, adopted the Copenhagen Declaration and related Programme of Action, placing people as the focus of development activities. Following the introduction, in 1999, by the World Bank and IMF of Poverty Reduction Strategy Papers (PRSPs), UNDP has helped governments to draft these documents, and, since 2001, has linked the papers to efforts to achieve and monitor progress towards the MDGs. In 2004 UNDP inaugurated the International Poverty Centre for Inclusive Growth (IPC-IG), in Brasília, Brazil, which fosters the capacity of countries to formulate and implement poverty reduction strategies and encourages South-South co-operation in all relevant areas of research and decision-making. In particular, the Centre aims to assist countries to meet MDGs through research into and implementation of pro-poor policies that encourage social protection and human development, and through the monitoring of poverty and inequality. UNDP's Secretariat hosts the UN Office for South-South Cooperation, which was established, as the Special Unit for South-South Cooperation, by the United Nations General Assembly in 1978.

UNDP country offices support the formulation of national human development reports (NHDRs), which aim to facilitate activities such as policy-making, the allocation of resources, and monitoring progress towards poverty eradication and sustainable development. In addition, the preparation of Advisory Notes and Country Co-operation Frameworks by UNDP officials helps to highlight country-specific aspects of poverty eradication and national strategic priorities. In January 1998 the Executive Board adopted eight guiding principles relating to sustainable human development that were to be implemented by all country offices, in order to ensure a focus to UNDP activities. Since 1990 UNDP has published an annual *Human Development Report*, incorporating a Human Development Index, which ranks countries in terms of human development, using three key indicators: life expectancy, adult literacy and basic income required for a decent standard of living. The Report also includes a Human Poverty Index and a Gender-related Development Index, which assesses gender equality on the basis of life expectancy, education and income. The 2013 edition of the Report, *The Rise of the South: Human Progress in a Diverse World*, was released in April. UNDP proposed to the June 2012 UNCSD a future 'Sustainable Human Development Index', which would recognize the impact on future generations of contemporary development, and place a high value on factors such as dignity and sustainability, alongside economic development. Jointly with the International Labour Organization (ILO), UNDP operates a Programme on Employment for Poverty Reduction, which undertakes analysis and studies, and supports countries in improving their employment strategies. In March 2012 the first Global Human Development Forum was convened, under UNDP auspices, in Istanbul, Turkey; delegates (comprising experts on development, and representatives of the UN, governments, the private sector and civil society) adopted the Istanbul Declaration, urging that the global development agenda should be redrafted, and calling for concerted global action against social inequities and environmental degradation.

UNDP is committed to ensuring that the process of economic and financial globalization, including national and global trade, debt and capital flow policies, incorporates human development concerns. It aimed to ensure that the Doha Development Round of World Trade Organization (WTO) negotiations should achieve an expansion of trade opportunities and economic growth to less developed countries. UNDP is a partner—with the IMF, the International Trade Centre, the UN Conference on Trade and Development (UNCTAD), the World Bank and the WTO—in the Enhanced Integrated Framework (EIF) for trade-related assistance to LDCs, a multi-donor programme which aims to support greater participation by LDCs in the global trading system; EIF funds are channelled through a dedicated EIF Trust Fund. The EIF replaced in 2007, and builds upon, a previous Integrated Framework, which was established in 1997.

UNDP issues an annual *Arab Human Development Report*. UNDP's Arab Regional Trade, Economic Governance and Human Development Project aims to help Arab states (through policy studies, training, advisory services and knowledge-sharing) to take advantage of globalization and regional integration for the benefit of sustainable human development. A national report for Qatar: *Expanding the Capacities of Qatari Youth: Mainstreaming Young People in Development* was issued in 2012.

In 1996 UNDP initiated a process of collaboration between city authorities world-wide to promote implementation of the commitments made at the 1995 Copenhagen summit for social development and to help to combat aspects of poverty and other urban problems, such as poor housing, transport, the management of waste disposal, water supply and sanitation. The World Alliance of Cities Against Poverty was formally launched in 1997, in the context of the International Decade for the Eradication of Poverty. The eighth global Forum of the Alliance convened in Dublin, Ireland, in February 2013.

UNDP sponsors the International Day for the Eradication of Poverty, held annually on 17 October.

ENVIRONMENT AND ENERGY

UNDP plays a role in developing the agenda for international co-operation on environmental and energy issues, focusing on the relationship between energy policies, environmental protection, poverty and development. UNDP promotes development practices that are environmentally sustainable, for example through the formulation and implementation of Poverty Reduction Strategies and National Strategies for Sustainable Development. Together with the UN Environment Programme (UNEP) and the World Bank, UNDP is an implementing agency of the Global Environment Facility (GEF), which was established in 1991 to finance international co-operation in projects to benefit the environment.

UNDP recognizes that desertification, land degradation and drought (DLDD) are major causes of rural poverty and promotes sustainable land management, drought preparedness and reform of land tenure as means of addressing the problem. It also aims to reduce poverty caused by land degradation through implementation of environmental conventions at a national and international level. During 2002–09 UNDP implemented the first phase (IDDP I) of an Integrated Drylands Development Programme, which aims to ensure that the needs of people living in arid regions are met and considered at a local and national level. IDDP II was launched in 2010, with a focus on mainstreaming drylands issues and climate change adaptation and mitigation into national policy and development frameworks; building the capacity of drylands communities to address environmental, economic and socio-cultural challenges; and supporting drylands communities through improved local governance, management and utilization of natural resources. The Drylands Development Centre delivers IDDP II via UNDP country offices in 17 African and West Asian states. In June 2009 UNDP and the Secretariat of the UN Convention to Combat Desertification in Those Countries Experiencing Serious Drought and/or Desertification, Particularly in Africa (UNCCD) agreed a pilot strategic working partnership, based on the UNCCD's strategic priorities in combating DLDD and on UNDP's implementation support capabilities at the national level. A formal UNDP/UNCCD programme of co-operation was concluded in March 2012. UNDP is also concerned with sustainable management of forestries, fisheries and agriculture. Since 1992 UNDP has administered a Small Grants Programme, funded by the GEF, to support community-based initiatives concerned with biodiversity conservation, prevention of land degradation and the elimination of persistent organic pollutants. The Equator Initiative, inaugurated in 2002, as a partnership between UNDP and representatives of governments, civil society and businesses, aims to reduce poverty in communities along the equatorial belt by fostering local partnerships, harnessing local knowledge and promoting conservation and sustainable practices. UNDP is a partner agency of the Climate and Clean Air Coalition to Reduce Short Lived Climate Pollutants (SLCPs), which was launched in February 2012 with the aim of combating SLCPs, including methane, black carbon and certain hydrofluorocarbons. UNDP also implements projects funded by the International Climate Initiative (launched in 2008 by the German Government).

In December 2005 UNDP (in collaboration with Fortis, a private sector provider of financial services) launched the MDG Carbon Facility, whereby developing countries that undertake projects to reduce emissions of carbon dioxide, methane and other gases responsible for global warming may sell their 'carbon credits' to finance further MDG projects.

UNDP supports efforts to promote international co-operation in the management of chemicals. It was actively involved in the development of a Strategic Approach to International Chemicals Management which was adopted by representatives of 100 governments at an international conference convened in Dubai, United Arab Emirates, in February 2006.

UNDP works to ensure the effective governance of freshwater and aquatic resources, and promotes co-operation in transboundary water management. It works with other agencies to promote safe sanitation, ocean and coastal management, and community water supplies. In 1996 UNDP, with the World Bank and the Swedish International Development Agency, established a Global Water Partnership to promote and implement water resources management. UNDP, with the GEF, supports a range of projects which incorporate development and ecological requirements in the sustainable management of international waters. including the Global Mercury Project, a project for improved municipal waste-water management in coastal cities of the African, Caribbean and Pacific states, a Global Ballast Water Management Programme and an International Waters Learning Exchange and Resources Network.

In the Middle East and North Africa UNDP projects concerned with protecting international waters have included the UNDP/GEF Nubian Aquifer Project (in partnership with IAEA and UNESCO) and protection of the Red Sea and the Gulf of Aden.

CRISIS PREVENTION AND RECOVERY

UNDP is not primarily a relief organization, but collaborates with other UN agencies in countries in crisis and with special circumstances to promote relief and development efforts, in order to secure the foundations for sustainable human development and thereby increase national capabilities to prevent or mitigate future crises. In particular, UNDP is concerned to achieve reconciliation, reintegration and reconstruction in affected countries, as well as to support emergency interventions and management and delivery of programme aid. It aims to facilitate the transition from relief to longer-term recovery and rehabilitation. Special development initiatives in post-conflict countries include the demobilization of former combatants and destruction of illicit small armaments, rehabilitation of communities for the sustainable reintegration of returning populations and the restoration and strengthening of democratic institutions. UNDP is seeking to incorporate conflict prevention into its development strategies. It has established a mine action unit within its Bureau for Crisis Prevention and Recovery in order to strengthen national and local de-mining capabilities including surveying, mapping and clearance of anti-personnel landmines. It also works to increase awareness of the harm done to civilians by cluster munitions, and participated in the negotiations that culminated in May 2008 with the adoption of an international Convention on Cluster Munitions, which in February 2010 received its 30th ratification, enabling its entry into force on 1 August. UNDP also works closely with UNICEF to raise awareness and implement risk reduction education programmes, and manages global partnership projects concerned with training, legislation and the socio-economic impact of anti-personnel devices. In 2005 UNDP adopted an '8-Point Agenda' aimed at improving the security of women and girls in conflict situations and promoting their participation in post-crisis recovery processes. In late 2006 UNDP began to administer the newly established UN Peacebuilding Fund, the purpose of which is to strengthen essential services to maintain peace in countries that have undergone conflict. During 2008 UNDP developed a new global programme aimed at strengthening the rule of law in conflict and post-conflict countries; the programme placed particular focus on women's access to justice, institution building and transitional justice.

In 2006 UNDP launched an Immediate Crisis Response programme (known as 'SURGE') aimed at strengthening its capacity to respond quickly and effectively in the recovery phase following a conflict or natural disaster. Under the programme Immediate Crisis Response Advisors—UNDP staff with special expertise in at least one of 12 identified areas, including early recovery, operational support and resource mobilization—are swiftly deployed, in a 'SURGETeam', to UNDP country offices dealing with crises.

UNDP is the focal point within the UN system for strengthening national capacities for natural disaster reduction (prevention, preparedness and mitigation relating to natural, environmental and technological hazards). UNDP's Bureau of Crisis Prevention and Recovery, in conjunction with the Office for the Co-ordination of Humanitarian Affairs and the secretariat of the International Strategy for Disaster Reduction, oversees the system-wide Capacity for Disaster Reduction Initiative (CADRI), which was inaugurated in 2007, superseding the former United Nations Disaster Management Training Programme. In February 2004 UNDP introduced a

Disaster Risk Index that enabled vulnerability and risk to be measured and compared between countries and demonstrated the correspondence between human development and death rates following natural disasters. UNDP was actively involved in preparations for the second World Conference on Disaster Reduction, which was held in Kobe, Japan, in January 2005. Following the Kobe Conference UNDP initiated a new Global Risk Identification Programme. During 2005 the Inter-Agency Standing Committee, concerned with co-ordinating the international response to humanitarian disasters, developed a concept of providing assistance through a 'cluster' approach, comprising core areas of activity (see OCHA). UNDP was designated the lead agency for the Early Recovery cluster, linking the immediate needs following a disaster with medium- and long-term recovery efforts. UNDP has participated in a series of consultations on a successor arrangement for the Hyogo Framework for Action that were launched in 2012 by the UN International Strategy for Disaster Reduction (UN/ISDR—the focal point of UN disaster planning); it was envisaged that the planned post-Hyogo arrangement (to be adopted by the third World Conference on Disaster Reduction, to be held in 2014 in Japan) would specify measurable outcomes of disaster risk reduction planning, in addition to detailing processes, and that, in view of rapidly increasing urbanization globally, it would have a focus on building safer cities. UNDP hosts the Global Risk Identification Programme (GRIP), initiated in 2007 to support activities world-wide aimed at identifying and monitoring disaster risks. In August 2012 the UNDP Administrator, stating that disaster risk management should become central to development planning, announced that UNDP disaster reduction assistance would be doubled over the next five years.

In March 2013 UNDP, UN/ISDR, the League of Arab States and other partners organized the First Arab Conference on Disaster Risk Reduction, with participation by senior government officials, civil mayors and civil society representatives from Arab states. The Conference launched the Arab Regional Platform on Disaster Risk Reduction.

In December 2010 UNDP and the EU agreed to support the establishment of an Arab League Crisis Response Centre and Warning System, based in Cairo, Egypt, during 2011–12.

HIV/AIDS

UNDP regards the HIV/AIDS pandemic as a major challenge to development, and advocates making HIV/AIDS a focus of national planning and national poverty reduction strategies; supports decentralized action against HIV/AIDS at the community level; helps to strengthen national capacities at all levels to combat the disease; and aims to link support for prevention activities, education and treatment with broader development planning and responses. UNDP places a particular focus on combating the spread of HIV/AIDS through the promotion of women's rights. UNDP is a co-sponsor, jointly with the World Health Organization (WHO) and other UN bodies, of the Joint UN Programme on HIV/AIDS (UNAIDS), which became operational on 1 January 1996. UNAIDS co-ordinates UNDP's HIV and Development Programme. UNDP works in partnership with the Global Fund to Fight HIV/AIDS, Tuberculosis and Malaria, in particular to support the local principal recipient of grant financing and to help to manage fund projects.

UNDP administers a global programme concerned with intellectual property and access to HIV/AIDS drugs, to promote wider and cheaper access to antiretroviral drugs, in accordance with the agreement on Trade-Related Aspects of Intellectual Property Rights (TRIPS), amended by the WTO in 2005 to allow countries without a pharmaceutical manufacturing capability to import generic copies of patented medicines.

Finance

UNDP and its various funds and programmes are financed by the voluntary contributions of members of the UN and the Programme's participating agencies, cost-sharing by recipient governments and third-party donors. Of UNDP's total provisional programme expenditure of US $4,608m. in 2011, some 28% was allocated to achieving the MDGs and reducing poverty; 26% was allocated to fostering democratic governance; 24% to supporting crisis prevention and recovery; and 12% to managing energy and the environment for sustainable development. Some $503m. (11% of total provisional expenditure) was allocated to the Arab states. For the period 2008–11 total voluntary contributions to UNDP were projected at $20,600m., of which $5,300m. constituted regular (core) resources, $5,000m. bilateral donor contributions, $5,500m. contributions from multilateral partners, and $4,800m. cost-sharing by recipient governments.

UNDP, UNFPA and UNICEF are committed to integrating their budgets from 2014.

Publications

Annual Report of the Administrator.

Choices (quarterly).

Human Development Report (annually).

Poverty Report (annually).

Results-Oriented Annual Report.

Associated Funds and Programmes

UNDP is the central funding, planning and co-ordinating body for technical co-operation within the UN system. A number of associated funds and programmes, financed separately by means of voluntary contributions, provide specific services through the UNDP network. UNDP manages a trust fund to promote economic and technical co-operation among developing countries.

GLOBAL ENVIRONMENT FACILITY (GEF)

The GEF, which is managed jointly by UNDP, the World Bank (which hosts its secretariat) and UNEP, began operations in 1991 and was restructured in 1994. Its aim is to support projects in the six thematic areas of climate change; the conservation of biological diversity; the protection of international waters; reducing the depletion of the ozone layer in the atmosphere; arresting land degradation; and addressing the issue of persistent organic pollutants. Capacity building to allow countries to meet their obligations under international environmental agreements, and adaptation to climate change, are priority cross-cutting components of these projects. The GEF acts as the financial mechanism for the Convention on Biological Diversity and the UN Framework Convention on Climate Change. UNDP is responsible for capacity building, targeted research, pre-investment activities and technical assistance. UNDP also administers the Small Grants Programme of the GEF, which supports community-based activities by local NGOs, and the Country Dialogue Workshop Programme, which promotes dialogue on national priorities with regard to the GEF; by September 2013 the Small Grants Programme had co-financed 16,866 community projects in more than 120 countries. In October 2010 donor countries pledged US $4,350m. for the fifth periodic replenishment of GEF funds (GEF-5), covering the period 2011–14; negotiations on GEF-6 were initiated in April 2013.

In 2012 21 countries in the Middle East and North Africa implemented 24 GEF-financed projects with UNDP support, receiving some US $59m. in grant funding from the Facility.

Chair. and CEO: Dr Naoko Ishii (Japan).

Executive Co-ordinator of UNDP-GEF Unit: Yannick Glemarec; 304 East 45th St, 9th Floor, New York, NY 10017, USA; fax (212) 906-6998; e-mail gefinfo@undp.org; internet www.undp.org/gef/.

MDG ACHIEVEMENT FUND (MDG-F)

The Fund, established in accordance with an agreement concluded in December 2006 between UNDP and the Spanish Government, aims to support the acceleration of progress towards the achievement of the MDGs and to advance country-level co-operation between UN development partners. The Fund operates through the UN development system and focuses mainly on financing collaborative UN activities addressing multi-dimensional development challenges. The Spanish Government provided initial financing to the Fund of nearly €528m., adding some €90m. in September 2008. By 2013 some 130 programmes were under way in 50 countries, in the thematic areas of children and nutrition; climate change; conflict prevention; culture and development; economic governance; gender equality and women's empowerment; and youth employment.

Senior Adviser, MDG-F Secretariat: Paloma Durán; MDG-F Secretariat, c/o UNDP, One United Nations Plaza, New York, NY 10017, USA; tel. (212) 906-6180; fax (212) 906-5364; e-mail pb.mdgf.secretariat@undp.org; internet www.mdgfund.org.

MONTREAL PROTOCOL

Through its Montreal Protocol/Chemicals Unit UNDP collaborates with public and private partners in developing countries to assist them in eliminating the use of ozone-depleting substances (ODS), in accordance with the Montreal Protocol to the Vienna Convention for the Protection of the Ozone Layer, through the design, monitoring and evaluation of ODS phase-out projects and programmes. In particular, UNDP provides technical assistance and training, national capacity building and demonstration projects and technology transfer investment projects.

PROGRAMME OF ASSISTANCE TO THE PALESTINIAN PEOPLE (PAPP)

PAPP, established in 1978, is committed to strengthening institutions in the Israeli-occupied Territories and emerging Palestinian autonomous areas, to creating employment opportunities and to stimulating private and public investment in the area to enhance trade and export potential. Examples of PAPP activities include the following: construction of sewage collection networks and systems in the northern Gaza Strip; provision of water to 500,000 people in rural and urban areas of the West Bank and Gaza; construction of schools, youth and health centres; support to vegetable and fish traders through the construction of cold storage and packing facilities; and provision of loans to strengthen industry and commerce. In January 2009, in response to the intensive bombardment of the Gaza Strip by Israeli forces during December 2008–January 2009, with the stated aim of ending rocket attacks launched by Hamas and other militant groups on Israeli targets ('Operation Cast Lead'), PAPP distributed food packages to more than 30,000 Palestinians in the territory who were not served by UNRWA. In September 2011 PAPP launched a Consolidated Plan of Assistance, covering the period 2012–14, which aimed to support the Palestinian people in the following areas: energy resources; transport and management systems; affordable and adequate housing; education; public health services and systems; and heritage conservation.

UNDP Special Representative in the Occupied Palestinian Territories: FRODE MAURING (Norway); POB 51359, Jerusalem; tel. (2) 6268200; fax (2) 6268222; e-mail registry.papp@undp.org; internet www.undp.ps.

UNDP DRYLANDS DEVELOPMENT CENTRE (DDC)

The Centre, based in Nairobi, Kenya, was established in February 2002, superseding the former UN Office to Combat Desertification and Drought (UNSO). (UNSO had been established following the conclusion, in October 1994, of the UN Convention to Combat Desertification in Those Countries Experiencing Serious Drought and/or Desertification, Particularly in Africa; in turn, UNSO had replaced the former UN Sudano-Sahelian Office.) The DDC was to focus on the following areas: ensuring that national development planning takes account of the needs of communities based in drylands (arid, semi-arid and dry sub-humid areas, with vulnerable ecoystems), particularly in poverty reduction strategies; helping countries to cope with the effects of climate variability, especially drought, and to prepare for future climate change; and addressing local issues affecting the utilization of resources. The DDC delivers UNDP's Integrated Drylands Development Programme (currently in its second phase).

UN Gigiri Compound, United Nations Ave, POB 30552, 00100 Nairobi, Kenya; tel. (20) 7624640; fax (20) 7624648; e-mail ddc@undp.org; internet www.undp.org/drylands.

UNITED NATIONS CAPITAL DEVELOPMENT FUND (UNCDF)

The Fund was established in 1966 and became fully operational in 1974. It invests in poor communities in LDCs through local governance projects and microfinance operations, with the aim of increasing such communities' access to essential local infrastructure and services and thereby improving their productive capacities and self-reliance. UNCDF encourages participation by local people and local governments in the planning, implementation and monitoring of projects. The Fund aims to promote the interests of women in community projects and to enhance their earning capacities. UNCDF helps to develop financial services for poor communities and supports UNDP's MicroStart initiative, which assists private sector and community-based initiatives aimed at generating employment opportunities. In November 2008 UNCDF launched MicroLead, a fund (initially amounting to US $26m.) that provides loans to leading microfinance institutions and other financial service providers (MFIs/FSPs) in developing countries; MicroLead was also to focus on the provision of early support to countries in post-conflict situations. In September 2011 UNCDF and The MasterCard Foundation agreed a $23m. six-year expansion of MicroLead with a focus on sub-Saharan Africa. In October 2012 MicroLead was extended into Myanmar, with a $7m. grant from LIFT Myanmar (a multi-donor trust fund). In 2013 UNCDF had country offices in 37 LDCs.

Executive Secretary: MARC BICHLER (Luxembourg); Two United Nations Plaza, 26th Floor, New York, NY 10017, USA; fax (212) 906-6479; e-mail info@uncdf.org; internet www.uncdf.org.

UNITED NATIONS VOLUNTEERS (UNV)

The United Nations Volunteers is an important source of middle-level skills for the UN development system supplied at modest cost, particularly in the LDCs. Volunteers expand the scope of UNDP project activities by supplementing the work of international and host country experts and by extending the influence of projects to local community levels. UNV also supports technical co-operation within and among the developing countries by encouraging volunteers from the countries themselves and by forming regional exchange teams comprising such volunteers. UNV is involved in areas such as peace-building, elections, human rights, humanitarian relief and community-based environmental programmes, in addition to development activities.

The UN International Short-term Advisory Resources (UNISTAR) Programme, which is the private sector development arm of UNV, has increasingly focused its attention on countries in the process of economic transition. Since 1994 UNV has administered UNDP's Transfer of Knowledge Through Expatriate Nationals (TOKTEN) programme, which was initiated in 1977 to enable specialists and professionals from developing countries to contribute to development efforts in their countries of origin through short-term technical assignments. In March 2000 UNV established an Online Volunteering Service to connect development organizations and volunteers using the internet; in 2012 11,037 online volunteers, working on 16,196 assignments, made their skills available through the Online Volunteering Service.

In December 2011 UNV issued the first *State of the World's Volunteerism Report*, on the theme 'Universal Values for Global Well-being'.

During 2012 some 6,807 national and international UNVs were deployed in 127 countries, on 6,912 assignments; some 13% of UNV assignments were undertaken in the Arab states in that year.

Executive Co-ordinator: RICHARD DICTUS (Netherlands); POB 260111, 53153 Bonn, Germany; tel. (228) 8152000; fax (228) 8152001; e-mail information@unvolunteers.org; internet www.unv.org.

United Nations Environment Programme—UNEP

Address: POB 30552, Nairobi 00100, Kenya.

Telephone: (20) 621234; **fax:** (20) 623927; **e-mail:** unepinfo@unep.org; **internet:** www.unep.org.

The United Nations Environment Programme was established in 1972 by the UN General Assembly, following recommendations of the 1972 UN Conference on the Human Environment, in Stockholm, Sweden, to encourage international co-operation in matters relating to the human environment.

Organization

(September 2013)

GOVERNING COUNCIL

The main functions of the Governing Council (which meets every two years in ordinary sessions, with special sessions taking place in the alternate years) are to promote international co-operation in the field of the environment and to provide general policy guidance for the direction and co-ordination of environmental programmes within the UN system. In December 2012 the UN General Assembly resolved to expand UNEP's Governing Council from 58 members to universal representation of all UN member states. The first meeting of the enlarged Council was held in February 2013 on the theme 'Rio+20: From Outcome to Implementation'. A Global Ministerial Environment Forum (first convened in 2000) meets annually as part of the Governing Council's regular and special sessions. The Governing Council is assisted in its work by a Committee of Permanent Representatives.

SECRETARIAT

Offices and divisions at UNEP headquarters in Nairobi, Kenya, include the Offices of the Executive Director and Deputy Executive Director; the Secretariat for Governing Bodies; Offices for Evaluation and Oversight, Programme Co-ordination and Management, Resource Mobilization, and Global Environment Facility Co-ordination; and Divisions of Communications and Public Information, Early Warning and Assessment, Environmental Policy Implementation, Technology, Industry and Economics, Regional Co-operation, and Environmental Law and Conventions.

Executive Director: ACHIM STEINER (Germany).

Deputy Executive Director: IBRAHIM THIAW (Mauritania).

REGIONAL OFFICES

UNEP maintains six regional offices. These work to initiate and promote UNEP objectives and to ensure that all programme formulation and delivery meets the specific needs of countries and regions. They also provide a focal point for building national, sub-regional and regional partnerships and enhancing local participation in UNEP initiatives. A co-ordination office has been established at headquarters to promote regional policy integration, to co-ordinate programme planning, and to provide necessary services to the regional offices.

Africa: POB 30552, Nairobi, Kenya; tel. (20) 7621234; fax (20) 7624489; e-mail roainfo@unep.org; internet www.unep.org/roa.

West Asia: POB 10880, Manama, Bahrain; tel. 17812777; fax 17825110; e-mail uneprowa@unep.org.bh; internet www.unep.org/rowa.

OTHER OFFICES

Basel, Rotterdam and Stockholm Conventions, Secretariat: 11–13 chemin des Anémones, 1219 Châtelaine, Geneva, Switzerland; tel. 229178729; fax 229178098; e-mail brs@brsmeas.org; internet www.basel.int; www.pic.int; www.pops.int; Exec. Sec. JIM WILLIS (USA).

Convention on International Trade in Endangered Species of Wild Fauna and Flora (CITES): 15 chemin des Anémones, 1219 Châtelaine, Geneva, Switzerland; tel. 229178139; fax 227973417; e-mail info@cites.org; internet www.cites.org; Sec.-Gen. JOHN SCANLON (Australia).

Global Programme of Action for the Protection of the Marine Environment from Land-based Activities: GPA Co-ordination Unit, UNEP, POB 30552, 00100 Nairobi, Kenya; tel. (20) 7621206; fax (20) 7624249; internet www.gpa.unep.org.

Mediterranean Action Plan on the Implementation of the Barcelona Convention, Secretariat: Leoforos Vassileos Konstantinou 48, POB 18019, 11610 Athens, Greece; tel. (210) 7273100; fax (210) 7253196; e-mail unepmedu@unepmap.gr; internet www.unepmap.org.

Multilateral Fund for the Implementation of the Montreal Protocol, Secretariat: Suite 4100, 1000 De La Gauchetière St, Montreal, QC H3B 4W5, Canada; tel. (514) 282-1122; fax (514) 282-0068; e-mail secretariat@unmfs.org; internet www.multilateralfund.org; Chief Officer MARIA NOLAN (United Kingdom).

UNEP/CMS (Convention on the Conservation of Migratory Species of Wild Animals), Secretariat: Platz der Vereinten Nationen 1, 53113 Bonn, Germany; tel. (228) 8152402; fax (228) 8152449; e-mail secretariat@cms.int; internet www.cms.int; Exec. Sec. BRADNEE CHAMBERS.

UNEP Division of Technology, Industry and Economics: 15 rue de Milan, 75441 Paris, Cedex 09, France; tel. 1-44-37-14-50; fax 1-44-37-14-74; e-mail unep.tie@unep.fr; internet www.unep.org/dtie; Dir SYLVIE LEMMET (France).

UNEP International Environmental Technology Centre (IETC): 2–110 Ryokuchi koen, Tsurumi-ku, Osaka 538-0036, Japan; tel. (6) 6915-4581; fax (6) 6915-0304; e-mail ietc@unep.org; internet www.unep.org/ietc; Dir MATTHEW GUBB.

UNEP Ozone Secretariat: POB 30552, Nairobi, Kenya; tel. (20) 762-3851; fax (20) 762-4691; e-mail ozoneinfo@unep.org; internet ozone.unep.org; Exec. Sec. MARCO GONZÁLEZ (Costa Rica).

UNEP Post-Conflict and Disaster Management Branch: 11–15 chemin des Anémones, 1219 Châtelaine, Geneva, Switzerland; tel. 229178530; fax 229178064; e-mail postconflict@unep.org; internet www.unep.org/disastersandconflicts; Chief Officer HENRIK ALEXANDER SLOTTE.

UNEP Risoe Centre on Energy, Environment and Sustainable Development: Risoe Campus, Technical University of Denmark, Frederiksborgvej 399, Bldg 142, POB 49, 4000 Roskilde, Denmark; tel. 46-77-51-29; fax 46-32-19-99; e-mail unep@risoe.dtu.dk; internet uneprisoe.org; f. 1990 as the UNEP Collaborating Centre on Energy and Environment; supports UNEP in the planning and implementation of its energy-related policy and activities; provides technical support to governments towards the preparation of national Technology Needs Assessments on climate change adaptation; Head JOHN CHRISTENSEN.

UNEP-SCBD (Convention on Biological Diversity, Secretariat): 413 St Jacques St, Suite 800, Montréal, QC, H2Y 1N9, Canada; tel. (514) 288-2220; fax (514) 288-6588; e-mail secretariat@cbd.int; internet www.cbd.int; Exec. Sec. BRAULIO FERREIRA DE SOUZA DIAS (Brazil).

UNEP Secretariat for the UN Scientific Committee on the Effects of Atomic Radiation: Vienna International Centre, Wagramerstr. 5, POB 500, 1400 Vienna, Austria; tel. (1) 26060-4330; fax (1) 26060-5902; e-mail malcolm.crick@unscear.org; internet www.unscear.org; Sec. Dr MALCOLM CRICK.

Activities

UNEP represents a voice for the environment within the UN system. It is an advocate, educator, catalyst and facilitator, promoting the wise use of the planet's natural assets for sustainable development. It aims to maintain a constant watch on the changing state of the environment; to analyse the trends; to assess the problems using a wide range of data and techniques; and to undertake or support projects leading to environmentally sound development. It plays a catalytic and co-ordinating role within and beyond the UN system. Many UNEP projects are implemented in co-operation with other UN agencies, particularly the UN Development Programme (UNDP), the World Bank Group, FAO, UNESCO and WHO. About 45 intergovernmental organizations outside the UN system and 60 international non-governmental organizations (NGOs) have official observer status on UNEP's Governing Council, and, through the Environment Liaison Centre in Nairobi, Kenya, UNEP is linked to more than 6,000 non-governmental bodies concerned with the environment. UNEP also sponsors international conferences, programmes, plans and agreements regarding all aspects of the environment.

In February 1997 the Governing Council, at its 19th session, adopted a ministerial declaration (the Nairobi Declaration) on UNEP's future role and mandate, which recognized the organization as the principal UN body working in the field of the environment and as the leading global environmental authority, setting and overseeing the international environmental agenda. In June a special session of the UN General Assembly, referred to as Rio+5, was convened to review the state of the environment and progress achieved in implementing the objectives of the UN Conference on Environment and Development (UNCED—known as the Earth Summit), that had been held in Rio de Janeiro, Brazil, in June 1992. UNCED had adopted Agenda 21 (a programme of activities to promote sustainable development in the 21st century) and the Rio+5 meeting adopted a Programme for Further Implementation of Agenda 21 in order to intensify efforts in areas such as energy, freshwater resources and technology transfer. The meeting confirmed UNEP's essential role in advancing the Programme and as a global authority promoting a coherent legal and political approach to the environmental challenges of sustainable development. An extensive process of restructuring and realignment of functions was subsequently initiated by UNEP, and a new organizational structure reflecting the decisions of the Nairobi Declaration was implemented during 1999. UNEP played a leading role in preparing for the World Summit on Sustainable Development (WSSD), held in August–September 2002 in Johannesburg, South Africa, to assess strategies for strengthening the implementation of Agenda 21. Governments participating in the conference adopted the Johannesburg Declaration and WSSD Plan of Implementation, in which they strongly reaffirmed commitment to the principles underlying Agenda 21 and also pledged support to all internationally agreed development goals, including the UN Millennium Development Goals (MDGs) adopted by governments attending a summit meeting of the UN General Assembly in September 2000. Participating governments made concrete commitments to attaining several specific objectives in the areas of water, energy, health, agriculture and fisheries, and biodiversity. The UN Conference on Sustainable Development (UNCSD) (also known as Earth Summit 2012 and as Rio+20), convened in June 2012, again in Rio de Janeiro, with participation by more than 100 heads of state and government, and by an estimated 50,000 representatives of international and non-governmental organizations, civil society groups, and the private sector, determined to strengthen the institutional framework and intergovernmental arrangements for sustainable development; and to establish a high-level intergovernmental forum to promote system-wide co-ordination and coherence of sustainable development policies and to follow up the implementation of sustainable development objectives. The forum—which was to build on the work of, and eventually replace, the UN Commission on Sustainable Development —was established in July 2013, and met for the first time in September, at the start of the 68th UN General Assembly. The Conference determined that UNEP's role should be strengthened as the lead agency in setting the global environmental agenda and co-ordinating UN system-wide implementation of the environmental dimension of sustainable development. The Conference decided to ask the UN General Assembly, during its 67th session (commencing in September 2012), to adopt a resolution that would upgrade UNEP by establishing universal membership of the Governing Council; ensuring increased financial resources to enable the Programme to fulfil its mandate; strengthening UNEP's participation in the main UN co-ordinating bodies; and empowering UNEP to lead efforts to develop UN system-wide strategies on the environment. The resolution was approved by the General Assembly in December. The participants in Rio+20 endorsed an outcome document, entitled *The Future We Want*, which, *inter alia*, reaffirmed commitment to working towards an economically, socially and environmentally sustainable future, and to the eradication of poverty as an indispensable requirement for sustainable development; and deemed the implementation of green economy policy options, in the context of sustainable development and poverty eradication, to be an important tool for achieving sustainable development. UNCSD approved a set of Sustainable Development Goals (SDGs), setting global targets in sustainable development challenges; it was envisaged that, post-2015, the SDGs would complement the MDGS. A 10-year framework on sustainable consumption and production was also announced, and the Conference decided to develop a new global wealth indicator that was to incorporate more dimensions than gross national product (the traditional indicator). The Conference invited all UN agencies and entities to mainstream sustainable development in their mandates, programmes, and strategies. The importance of enhancing the participation of developing countries in international economic decision-making was emphasized. UNEP was to provide the Secretariat with a 10-Year Framework of Programmes (YFP) on Sustainable Consumption and Production that was adopted by the UNCSD participating states. A World Congress on Justice, Governance and Law for Environmental Sustainability, which convened during UNCSD, with participation by leading judges, prosecutors and auditor generals, adopted a landmark series of principles to guide the Advancement of Justice, Governance and Law for Environmental Sustainability. In 2012 UNEP established a nine-member International Advisory Council, comprising senior judges, auditors and academics, with a mandate to provide strategic guidance to the international community in improving the legal foundations for achieving international environmental goals.

In May 2000 UNEP's first annual Global Ministerial Environment Forum (GMEF), was held in Malmö, Sweden, attended by environment ministers and other government delegates from more than 130 countries. Participants reviewed policy issues in the field of the environment and addressed issues such as the impact on the environment of population growth, the depletion of earth's natural resources, climate change and the need for fresh water supplies. The Forum issued the Malmö Declaration, which identified the effective implementation of international agreements on environmental matters at national level as the most pressing challenge for policy-makers. The Declaration emphasized the importance of mobilizing domestic and international resources and urged increased co-operation from civil society and the private sector in achieving sustainable development. The GMEF has subsequently convened annually, most recently in February 2013.

CLIMATE CHANGE

UNEP worked in collaboration with the World Meteorological Organization (WMO) to formulate the 1992 UN Framework Convention on Climate Change (UNFCCC), with the aim of reducing the emission of gases that have a warming effect on the atmosphere (known as greenhouse gases). (See Secretariat of the UN Framework Convention on Climate Change, below.) In 1998 UNEP and WMO established the Intergovernmental Panel on Climate Change (IPCC, see below), as an objective source of scientific information about the warming of the earth's atmosphere.

UNEP's climate change-related activities have a particular focus on strengthening the capabilities of countries (in particular developing countries) to integrate climate change responses into their national development processes, including improving preparedness for participating in UN Reduced Emissions from Deforestation and Forest Degradation (UN-REDD) initiatives; Ecosystem Based Adaptation; and Clean Tech Readiness.

UN-REDD, launched in September 2008 as a collaboration between UNEP, UNDP and FAO, aims to enable donors to pool resources (through a trust fund established for that purpose) to promote a transformation of forest resource use patterns. In August 2011 UN-REDD endorsed a Global Programme Framework covering 2011–15. Leaders from countries in the Amazon, Congo and Borneo-Mekong forest basins participated, in June 2011, in the Summit of Heads of State and Government on Tropical Forest Ecosystems, held in Brazzaville, Republic of the Congo; the meeting issued a declaration recognising the need to protect forests in order to combat climate change, and to conduct future mutual dialogue. In that month UNEP issued a report focusing on the economic benefits of expanding funding for forests.

UNEP is a founding member of the Climate and Clean Air Coalition to Reduce Short Lived Climate Pollutants (SLCPs), which was launched in February 2012 as a partnership of international agencies, governments, environmentalists, and representatives of the private sector and civil society, with the aim of combating SLCPs, including methane, black carbon and certain hydrofluorocarbons.

UNEP's Technology Needs Assessment and Technology Action Plan aims to support some 35–45 countries with the implementation of improved national Technology Needs Assessments within the framework of the UNFCCC, involving, *inter alia*, detailed analysis of mitigation and adaptation technologies, and prioritization of these technologies. The UNEP Risoe Centre of Denmark supports governments in the preparation of these Assessments. It was announced in February 2013 that UNEP would lead a consortium, including the UN Industrial Development Organization (UNIDO) and other agencies, as the hosts of a new Climate Technology Centre and Network (CTCN), which was to accelerate the transfer of climate-related technology and expertise to developing nations.

UNEP encourages the development of alternative and renewable sources of energy, as part of its efforts to mitigate climate change. To achieve this, UNEP has created the Global Network on Energy for Sustainable Development, linking 21 centres of excellence in industrialized and developing countries to conduct research and exchange information on environmentally sound energy technology resources. UNEP's Rural Energy Enterprise Development (REED) initiative (operating within Africa as AREED) helps the private sector to develop affordable 'clean' energy technologies, such as solar crop-drying and water-heating, wind-powered water pumps and efficient cooking stoves. UNEP is a member of the Global Bioenergy Partnership initiated by the G8 group of industrialized countries to support the sustainable use of biofuels. Through its Transport Programme UNEP promotes the use of renewable fuels and the integration of environmental factors into transport planning, leading a world-wide Partnership for Clean Fuels and Vehicles, a Global Fuel Economy Initiative, and a Non Motorised Transport 'Share the Road' scheme. Meanwhile, UNDP's Sustainable Buildings and Construction Initiative promotes energy efficiency in the construction industry. In conjunction with UN-Habitat, UNDP, the World Bank and other organizations and institutions, UNEP promotes environmental concerns in urban planning and management through the Sustainable Cities Programme, and projects concerned with waste management, urban pollution and the impact of transportation systems. In June 2012 UNEP and other partners inaugurated a new Global Initiative for Resource-Efficient Cities, which aimed to lower pollution levels, advance efficiency in the utilization of resources (including through the promotion of energy-efficient buildings), and reduce infrastructure costs in urban areas world-wide with populations in excess of 500,000.

During 2007 UNEP (with WMO and the WTO) convened a second International Conference on Climate Change and Tourism, together with two meetings on sustainable tourism development and a conference on global eco-tourism. In June 2009 UNEP and WTO jointly issued a report entitled *Trade and Climate Change*, reviewing the intersections between trade and climate change from the perspectives of the science of climate change; economics; multilateral efforts to combat climate change; and the effects on trade of national climate change policies.

GREEN ECONOMY

In October 2008, in response to the global economic, fuel and food crises that escalated during that year, UNEP launched the *Green Economy Initiative (GEI)*, also known as the 'Global Green New Deal', which aimed to mobilize and refocus the global economy towards investments in clean technologies and the natural infrastructure (for example the infrastructures of forests and soils), with a view to, simultaneously, combating climate change and promoting employment. The UNEP Executive Director stated that the global crises were in part related to a broad market failure that promoted speculation while precipitating escalating losses of natural capital and nature-based assets, compounded by an over-reliance on finite, often subsidized fossil fuels. The three principal dimensions of the GEI were: the compilation of the *Green Economy Report*, to provide an analysis of how public policy might support markets in accelerating the transition towards a low-carbon green economy; the Green Jobs Initiative, a partnership launched by UNEP, the ILO and the International Trade Union Confederation in 2007 (and joined in 2008 by the International Organisation of Employers); and the Economics of Ecosystems and Biodiversity (TEEB) partnership project, focusing on valuation issues. In April 2009 the UN System Chief Executives Board for Co-ordination (CEB) endorsed the GEI as the fourth of nine UN initiatives aimed at alleviating the impact of the global economic crisis on poor and vulnerable populations. UNEP participates in the SEED Initiative, a global partnership for action on sustainable development and the green economy that was launched collaboratively with UNDP and the International Union for the Conservation of Nature at the 2002 WSSD. SEED supports innovative locally driven small-scale businesses that actively work towards providing social and environmental benefits. A Green Economy Coalition was established in 2008 as a loose grouping of UNEP and other UN agencies, research institutes, business interests, trade unions, and

NGOs, with the aim of promoting environmental sustainability and social equity.

In February 2013 UNEP, the ILO, UNIDO and the United Nations Institute for Training and Research launched the Partnership for Action on Green Economy (PAGE), which aimed, over the period 2013–20, to support 30 countries in developing national green economy strategies aimed at generating employment and skills, promoting clean technologies, and reducing environmental risks and poverty.

In June 2009 UNEP welcomed OECD's 'Green Growth' declaration, which urged the adoption of targeted policy instruments to promote green investment, and emphasized commitment to the realization of an ambitious and comprehensive post-2012 global climate agreement. In January 2012 UNEP, OECD, the World Bank, and the Global Green Growth Institute (established in June 2010 in Seoul, Republic of Korea—South Korea) launched the Green Growth Knowledge Platform. The Platform, accessible at www.greengrowthknowledge.org, aims to advance efforts to identify and address major knowledge gaps in green growth theory and practice, and to support countries in formulating and implementing policies aimed at developing a green economy.

In January 2011 UNEP and the World Tourism Organization launched the Global Partnership for Sustainable Tourism, also comprising other UN agencies, OECD, 18 governments, and other partners, with the aim of guiding policy and developing projects in the area of sustainable tourism, providing a global platform for discussion, and facilitating progress towards a green economy.

UNEP Finance Initiatives (FI) is a programme encouraging banks, insurance companies and other financial institutions to invest in an environmentally responsible way: an annual FI Global Roundtable meeting is held, together with regional meetings. In April 2007 UNEP hosted the first annual Business for Environment (B4E) meeting, on corporate environmental responsibility, in Singapore; the 2013 meeting was held in April, in New Delhi, India. During 2007 UNEP's Programme on Sustainable Consumption and Production established an International Panel for Sustainable Resource Management (comprising experts whose initial subjects of study were to be the environmental risks of biofuels and of metal recycling), and initiated forums for businesses and NGOs in this field. In May 2011 the International Panel issued a *Decoupling Report* that urged the separation of the global economic growth rate from the rate of natural resource consumption. The report warned that, by 2050, without a change of direction, humanity's consumption of minerals, ores, fossil fuels and biomass were on course to increase threefold. Later in May 2011 the Panel released a report focusing on the need to increase the recycling of metals world-wide.

In 1994 UNEP inaugurated the International Environmental Technology Centre (IETC), based in Osaka, Japan. The Centre promotes and implements environmentally sound technologies for disaster prevention and post-disaster reconstruction; sustainable production and consumption; and water and sanitation (in particular waste-water management and more efficient use of rainwater).

EARLY WARNING AND ASSESSMENT

The Nairobi Declaration resolved that the strengthening of UNEP's information, monitoring and assessment capabilities was a crucial element of the organization's restructuring, in order to help establish priorities for international, national and regional action, and to ensure the efficient and accurate dissemination of information on emerging environmental trends and emergencies.

UNEP's Division of Early Warning and Assessment analyses the world environment, provides early warning information and assesses global and regional trends. It provides governments with data and helps them to use environmental information for decision-making and planning.

UNEP's Global Environment Outlook (GEO) process of environmental analysis and assessment, launched in 1995, is supported by an extensive network of collaborating centres. The fifth 'umbrella' report on the GEO process (*GEO-5*) was issued in June 2012, just in advance of the UN Conference on Sustainable Development. The fifth report assessed progress achieved towards the attainment of some 90 environmental challenges, and identified four objectives—the elimination of the production and use of ozone layer-depleting substances; the removal of lead from fuel; access to improved water supplies; and promoting research into reducing pollution of the marine environment—as the areas in which most progress had been made. Little or no progress, however, was found to have been attained in the pursuit of 24 objectives, including managing climate change, desertification and drought; and deterioration was found to have occurred in the state of the world's coral reefs. In recent years regional and national GEO reports have been issued focusing on Africa, the Andean region, the Atlantic and Indian oceans, Brazil, the Caucasus, Latin America and the Caribbean, North America, and the Pacific; and the following thematic GEO reports have been produced: *The Global Deserts Outlook* (2006) and *The Global Outlook for Ice and Snow* (2007).

UNEP's Global International Waters Assessment (GIWA) considers all aspects of the world's water-related issues, in particular problems of shared transboundary waters, and of future sustainable management of water resources. UNEP is also a sponsoring agency of the Joint Group of Experts on the Scientific Aspects of Marine Environmental Pollution and contributes to the preparation of reports on the state of the marine environment and on the impact of land-based activities on that environment. In November 1995 UNEP published a Global Biodiversity Assessment, which was the first comprehensive study of biological resources throughout the world. The UNEP-World Conservation Monitoring Centre (UNEP-WCMC), established in June 2000 in Cambridge, United Kingdom, manages and interprets data concerning biodiversity and ecosystems, and makes the results available to governments and businesses. In October 2008 UNEP-WCMC, in partnership with the IUCN, launched the World Database on Protected Areas (WDPA), an online resource detailing the world's national parks and protected areas; by 2013 images of more than 200,000 sites could be viewed on the site. In 2007 the Centre undertook the 2010 Biodiversity Indicators Programme, with the aim of supporting decision-making by governments so as to reduce the threat of extinction facing vulnerable species. UNEP is a partner in the International Coral Reef Action Network—ICRAN, which was established in 2000 to monitor, manage and protect coral reefs world-wide. In June 2001 UNEP launched the Millennium Ecosystem Assessment, which was completed in March 2005. Other major assessments undertaken include the International Assessment of Agricultural Science and Technology for Development; the Solar and Wind Energy Resource Assessment; the Regionally Based Assessment of Persistent Toxic Substances; the Land Degradation Assessment in Drylands; and the Global Methodology for Mapping Human Impacts on the Biosphere (GLOBIO) project.

In June 2010 delegates from 85 countries, meeting in Busan, South Korea, at the third conference addressing the creation of a new Intergovernmental Science-Policy Platform on Biodiversity and Ecosystem Services (IPBES), adopted the Busan Outcome Document finalizing details of the establishment of the IPBES; the Outcome Document was subsequently approved by the UN General Assembly. The Platform, inaugurated in April 2012, was to undertake, periodically, assessments, based on current scientific literature, of biodiversity and ecosystem outputs beneficial to humans, including timber, fresh water, fish and climatic stability.

The 2001 UNEP publication *The Mesopotamian Marshlands: Demise of an Ecosystem* charted the erosion of some 90% of Mesopotamian wetlands (located mainly in southern Iraq, at the confluence of the Tigris and Euphrates rivers) as a result of draining and damming activities. UNEP continued to monitor the area and, in 2003, estimated that an additional 3% (some 325 sq km) had disappeared. Following the fall of the Saddam Hussein regime local residents began reflooding the area. In 2004 UNEP launched a Marshland Management Project. Funded by the UN Iraq Trust Fund and the Italian and Japanese Governments, the Project (ongoing) aims to support sustainable development for the returning Marsh Arabs and restoration of the wetlands. By end-2006 nearly one-half of the 1970s extent of the Marshlands had been reclaimed. In June 2009 UNEP and UNESCO jointly launched an initiative entitled 'Natural Cultural Management of the Iraqi Marshlands as World Heritage', with the objective of listing the area as a World Heritage Site; in 2013 *Marshlands of Mesopotamia* was under consideration on the list of tentative World Heritage Sites.

DISASTERS AND CONFLICTS

UNEP aims to minimise environmental causes and consequences of disasters and conflicts, and supports member states in combating environmental degradation and natural resources mismanagement, deeming these to be underlying risk factors for conflicts and natural hazards. UNEP promotes the integration of environmental concerns into risk reduction policy and practices. In 2011 UNEP targeted activities aimed at reducing conflict and disaster risk at 16 countries, 12 of which had adopted national policies aimed at mitigating post-conflict and post-disaster environmental risks. During 2011 training on environment and disaster risk reduction was conducted in India, Sri Lanka and Thailand.

UNEP undertakes assessments to establish the risks posed by environmental impacts on human health, security and livelihoods, and provides field-based capacity building and technical support, in countries affected by natural disaster and conflict. Since 1999 UNEP has conducted post-crisis environmental assessments in Afghanistan, the Balkans, the Democratic Republic of the Congo, Lebanon, Nigeria (Ogoniland), the Palestinian territories, Rwanda, Sudan, and Ukraine, and in the countries affected by the 2004 Indian Ocean tsunami.

An independent report of the Senior Advisory Group to the UN Secretary-General on Civilian Capacity in the Aftermath of Conflict, issued in February 2011, identified natural resources as a key area of focus. The report designated UNEP as the lead agency for identifying best practices in managing natural resources in support of peace-building.

ENVIRONMENTAL GOVERNANCE

UNEP promotes international environmental legislation and the development of policy tools and guidelines in order to achieve the sustainable management of the world environment. It helps governments to implement multilateral environmental agreements, and to report on their results. At a national level it assists governments to develop and implement appropriate environmental instruments and aims to co-ordinate policy initiatives. Training in various aspects of environmental law and its applications is provided. The ninth Global Training Programme on Environmental Law and Policy was conducted by UNEP in November 2009; regional training programmes are also offered. UNEP supports the development of new legal, economic and other policy instruments to improve the effectiveness of existing environmental agreements. It updates a register of international environmental treaties, and publishes handbooks on negotiating and enforcing environmental law. It acts as the secretariat for a number of regional and global environmental conventions (see list above). In June 2011 UNEP launched the Multilateral Environmental Agreements Information and Knowledge Management Initiative, which aimed to expand the sharing of information on more than 12 international agreements relating to the protection of the environment.

In June 2009 the first meeting was convened, in Belgrade, Serbia, of a new Consultative Group of Ministers and High-level Representatives on International Environment Governance; the meeting reviewed UNEP's role and stressed the linkages between sustainable environmental policies and development. From end-June–early July five successive UNEP Executive Directors and other prominent environmentalists met, in Glion, Switzerland, to discuss means of bringing about change in the functioning of the world economy to prioritize a sustainable approach to using and preserving the environment for the benefit of long-term human welfare.

UNEP is the principal UN agency for promoting environmentally sustainable water management. It regards the unsustainable use of water as one of the most urgent environmental issues, and estimates that two-thirds of the world's population will suffer chronic water shortages by 2025, owing to rising demand for drinking water as a result of growing populations, decreasing quality of water because of pollution, and increasing requirements of industries and agriculture. In 2000 UNEP adopted a new water policy and strategy, comprising assessment, management and co-ordination components. The Global International Waters Assessment (see above) is the primary framework for the assessment component. The management component includes the Global Programme of Action (GPA) for the Protection of the Marine Environment from Land-based Activities (adopted in November 1995), which focuses on the effects of pollution on freshwater resources, marine biodiversity and the coastal ecosystems of small island developing states. UNEP promotes international co-operation in the management of river basins and coastal areas and for the development of tools and guidelines to achieve the sustainable management of freshwater and coastal resources. In 2007 UNEP initiated a South-South Co-operation programme on technology and capacity building for the management of water resources. UNEP provides scientific, technical and administrative support to facilitate the implementation and co-ordination of 13 regional seas conventions and associated regional plans of action. UNEP's Regional Seas Programme aims to protect marine and coastal ecosystems, particularly by helping governments to put relevant legislation into practice.

UNEP was instrumental in the drafting of a Convention on Biological Diversity (CBD) to preserve the immense variety of plant and animal species, in particular those threatened with extinction. The Convention entered into force at the end of 1993; by September 2013 192 states and the European Union (EU) were parties to the CBD. The CBD's Cartagena Protocol on Biosafety (so called as it had been addressed at an extraordinary session of parties to the CBD convened in Cartagena, Colombia, in February 1999) was adopted at a meeting of parties to the CBD in January 2000, and entered into force in September 2003; by September 2013 the Protocol had been ratified by 166 states parties. The Protocol regulates the transboundary movement and use of living modified organisms resulting from biotechnology, in order to reduce any potential adverse effects on biodiversity and human health. It establishes an Advanced Informed Agreement procedure to govern the import of such organisms. In January 2002 UNEP launched a major project aimed at supporting developing countries with assessing the potential health and environmental risks and benefits of genetically modified (GM) crops, in preparation for the Protocol's entry into force. In February the parties to the CBD and other partners convened a conference on ways in which the traditional knowledge and practices of local communities could be preserved and used to conserve highly threatened species and ecosystems. The sixth conference of parties to the CBD, held in April 2002, adopted detailed voluntary guidelines concerning access to genetic resources and sharing the benefits attained from such resources with the countries and local communities where they originate; a global work programme on forests; and a set of guiding principles for combating alien invasive species. In October 2010 the 10th conference of the parties to the CBD, meeting in Nagoya, Japan, approved the Nagoya-Kuala Lumpur Supplementary Protocol to the CBD, with a view to establishing an international regime on access and benefit sharing (ABS) of genetic resources, alongside a strategic 10-year Strategic Plan for Biodiversity, comprising targets and timetables to combat loss of the planet's nature-based resources. The Supplementary Protocol was opened for signature in March 2011, and by September 2013 had been signed by 92 states and ratified by 19. The 12th conference of the parties to the CBD, convened in October 2012, in Hyderabad, India, agreed that developed countries should double by 2015 resources dedicated towards biodiversity protection. The conference pledged to focus particular attention towards the sustainable management of marine areas, such as the Sargasso Sea and Tonga archipelago, and determined formally to classify marine areas of ecological or biological significance. The UN Decade on Biodiversity was being celebrated during 2011–20. UNEP supports co-operation for biodiversity assessment and management in selected developing regions and for the development of strategies for the conservation and sustainable exploitation of individual threatened species (e.g. the Global Tiger Action Plan). It also provides assistance for the preparation of individual country studies and strategies to strengthen national biodiversity management and research. UNEP administers the Convention on International Trade in Endangered Species of Wild Flora and Fauna (CITES), which entered into force in 1975 and comprised 178 states parties at September 2013 (Lebanon having most recently ratified the Convention, in March). CITES, whose states parties meet in conference every three years, regulates international trade in nearly 35,000 species of plants and animals, as well as products and derivatives therefrom. The Convention has special programmes on the protection of elephants (including an African Elephant Action Plan, finalized in 2010), falcons, great apes, hawksbill turtles, sturgeons, tropical timber (jointly with the International Tropical Timber Organization), and big leaf mahogany. Meeting in St Petersburg, Russia, in November 2010, at the International Tiger Forum, the heads of UNODC, the Convention on International Trade in Endangered Species of Wild Fauna and Flora (CITES), the World Customs Organization, INTERPOL and the World Bank jointly approved the establishment of a new International Consortium on Combating Wildlife Crime (ICCWC), with the aim of combating the poaching of wild animals and illegal trade in wild animals and wild animal products. The 2013 CITES conference, which was held in March, in Bangkok, Thailand, strengthened the international regime covering trade in precious tropical hardwoods (including rosewoods and ebonies; with special procedures to be implemented for musicians travelling with instruments made therefrom); tortoises and turtles; five species of shark that are harvested for their fins or meat; manta rays (whose gill plates are traded); elephants (including stronger controls on e-commerce, and stricter monitoring of ivory stockpiles); rhinoceros; and big cats (with a focus on trophy leopard hunting). The conference agenda focused on means of combating the over-exploitation of marine and forest reserves, and escalating wildlife crime, determined to consider the use of the GEF as a financial instrument for the Convention, and declared 3 March as annual World Wildlife Day. ICCWC organized the first global meeting of wildlife enforcement networks on the sidelines of the Conference.

The Convention on the Conservation of Migratory Species of Wild Animals (CMS, also referred to as the Bonn Convention), concluded under UNEP auspices in 1979, aims to conserve migratory avian, marine and terrestrial species throughout the range of their migration. The secretariat of the CMS is hosted by UNEP. At September 2013 there were 119 states parties to the Convention. A number of agreements and Memoranda of Understanding (MOU) concerning conservation have been concluded under the CMS. The CMS Agreement on Cetaceans of the Black Seas, Mediterranean, and Contiguous Atlantic Area (ACCOBAMS) entered into force in 2001. An agreement and action plan to protect migratory birds of prey in Africa and Eurasia, supported by UNEP and the CMS, was concluded in October 2008 by 28 countries meeting in Abu Dhabi, United Arab Emirates. Signatory governments committed to protecting the birds from illegal killing (such as poisoning and shooting) and from unsustainable exploitation. In August 2012 the conference of parties to the CMS determined to develop a new strategic plan to guide the Convention over the period 2015–23.

In October 1994 87 countries, meeting under UN auspices, signed a Convention to Combat Desertification (see UNDP Drylands Development Centre), which aimed to provide a legal framework to counter the degradation of arid regions. An estimated 75% of all drylands have suffered some land degradation, affecting approximately 1,000m. people in 110 countries. UNEP continues to support the implementation of the Convention, as part of its efforts to protect land resources. UNEP also aims to improve the assessment of dryland degradation and desertification in co-operation with governments and other international bodies, as well as identifying the causes of degradation and measures to overcome these.

ECOSYSTEM MANAGEMENT

The Millennium Ecosystem Assessment, a scientific study of the state of 24 ecosystems, that was commissioned by the UN Secretary-General and published in 2001, found that 15 of the ecosystems under assessment were being used unsustainably, thereby inhibiting, particularly in developing countries, the achievement of the UN MDGs of reducing poverty and hunger. UNEP's Ecosystem Management Programme aims to develop an adaptive approach that integrates the management of forests, land, freshwater and coastal systems, focusing on sustaining ecosystems to meet future ecological needs, and to enhance human well-being. UNEP places particular emphasis on six ecosystem services deemed to be especially in decline: climate regulation; water regulation; natural hazard regulation; energy; freshwater; nutrient cycling; and recreation and ecotourism. Secondary importance is given to water purification and waste treatment; disease regulation; fisheries; and primary production. UNEP supports national and regional governments to build capacity in order to promote the role of sustainably managed ecosystems in support of social and economic development; to determine which ecosystem services to prioritize; and to incorporate an ecosystem management approach into their national and developmental planning and investment strategies.

In February 2012 UNEP and the Chinese Academy of Sciences (CAS) signed an agreement to establish the International Ecosystem Management Partnership of the United Nations Environment Programme (UNEP-IEMP), a new global centre on ecosystem management to be based in Beijing, with a mandate to promote ecosystem management in developing nations.

UNEP's Billion Tree Campaign, initiated in February 2007, initially encouraged governments, community organizations and individuals to plant 1,000m. trees before the end of the year, and exceeded that target; by September 2013 some 12,611m. trees had been planted under the continuing campaign.

HARMFUL SUBSTANCES AND HAZARDOUS WASTE

UNEP administers the Basel Convention on the Control of Transboundary Movements of Hazardous Wastes and their Disposal, which entered into force in 1992 with the aim of preventing the uncontrolled movement and disposal of toxic and other hazardous wastes, particularly the illegal dumping of waste in developing countries by companies from industrialized countries. At September 2013 179 countries and the EU were parties to the Convention.

In 1996 UNEP, in collaboration with FAO, began to work towards promoting and formulating a legally binding international convention on prior informed consent (PIC) for hazardous chemicals and pesticides in international trade, extending a voluntary PIC procedure of information exchange undertaken by more than 100 governments since 1991. The Convention was adopted at a conference held in Rotterdam, Netherlands, in September 1998, and entered into force in February 2004. It aims to reduce risks to human health and the environment by restricting the production, export and use of hazardous substances and enhancing information exchange procedures. UNEP played a leading role in formulating a multilateral agreement to reduce and ultimately eliminate the manufacture and use of Persistent Organic Pollutants (POPs), which are considered to be a major global environmental hazard. The Stockholm Convention on POPs, targeting 12 particularly hazardous pollutants, was adopted by 127 countries in May 2001 and entered into force in May 2004. In May 2009 the fourth conference of parties to the Stockholm Convention agreed on a list of nine further POPs; these were incorporated into the Convention in an amendment that entered into force in August 2010.

In January 2013, meeting in Geneva, Switzerland, more than 140 governments adopted the Minamata Convention on Mercury, which provides for controls relating to the usage, release, mining, import and export, and safe storage of mercury, and for the phasing-out by 2020 of the production of several mercury-containing products. The Convention—which had been under negotiation since February 2009—was to be opened for signature at a meeting to be convened in Japan, in October 2013. Pending the entry into force of the Convention a voluntary Global Mercury Partnership addresses activities related to combating mercury pollution. A Global Alliance to Eliminate Lead Paint was endorsed in May 2009 by the second International Conference on Chemicals Management (q.v.), with the aim of minimizing occupational exposure to, and preventing children's exposure to paints containing lead. The first and second meetings of the Global Alliance were convened, respectively, in May 2010 (in Geneva) and in July 2012 (in Bangkok, Thailand).

UNEP was the principal agency in formulating the 1987 Montreal Protocol to the Vienna Convention for the Protection of the Ozone Layer (1985), which provided for a 50% reduction in the production of chlorofluorocarbons (CFCs) by 2000. An amendment to the Protocol was adopted in 1990, which required complete cessation of the production of CFCs by 2000 in industrialized countries and by 2010 in developing countries. The Copenhagen Amendment, adopted in 1992, stipulated the phasing out of production of hydrochlorofluorocarbons (HCFCs) by 2030 in developed countries and by 2040 in developing nations. Subsequent amendments aimed to introduce a licensing system for all controlled substances, and imposed stricter controls on the import and export of HCFCs, and on the production and consumption of bromochloromethane (Halon-1011, an industrial solvent and fire extinguisher). In September 2007 the states parties to the Vienna Convention agreed to advance the deadline for the elimination of HCFCs to 2020 in developed countries and to 2030 in developing countries. A Multilateral Fund for the Implementation of the Montreal Protocol was established in June 1990 to promote the use of suitable technologies and the transfer of technologies to developing countries, and support compliance by developing countries with relevant control measures. UNEP, UNDP, the World Bank and UNIDO are the sponsors of the Fund, which by February 2012 had approved financing for more than 6,875 projects and activities in 145 developing countries at a cost of more than US $2,800m. The eighth replenishment of the Fund, covering the period 2012–14, raised $400m. in new contributions from donors. In September 2009, following ratification by Timor-Leste, the Montreal Protocol, with 196 states parties, became the first agreement on the global environment to attain universal ratification. UNEP's OzonAction branch promotes information exchange, training and technological awareness, helping governments and industry in developing countries to undertake measures towards the cost-effective phasing-out of ozone-depleting substances.

UNEP encourages governments and the private sector to develop and adopt policies and practices that are cleaner and safer, make efficient use of natural resources, incorporate environmental costs, ensure the environmentally sound management of chemicals, and reduce pollution and risks to human health and the environment. In collaboration with other organizations UNEP works to formulate international guidelines and agreements to address these issues. UNEP also promotes the transfer of appropriate technologies and organizes conferences and training workshops to provide sustainable production practices. Relevant information is disseminated through the International Cleaner Production Information Clearing House. By 2013 more than 40 National Cleaner Production Centres (NCPCs), and, in Latin America, a regional network of cleaner production centres, had been established, under a joint UNEP/UNIDO programme that was launched in 1994 to promote the use and development of environmentally sustainable technologies and to build national capacities in cleaner production. In October 2009 UNIDO and UNEP endorsed the creation of the global network for Resource Efficient and Cleaner Production (RECPnet), with the aim of utilizing the capabilities of NCPCs in developing and transition countries. RECPnet was launched in November 2011. In October 1998 UNEP adopted an International Declaration on Cleaner Production, with a commitment to implement cleaner and more sustainable production methods and to monitor results. In 1997 UNEP and the Coalition for Environmentally Responsible Economies initiated the Global Reporting Initiative, which, with participation by corporations, business associations and other organizations, develops guidelines for voluntary reporting by companies on their economic, environmental and social performance. In April 2002 UNEP launched the 'Life Cycle Initiative', which evaluates the impact of products over their entire life cycle (from manufacture to disposal) and aims to assist governments, businesses and other consumers with adopting environmentally sound policies and practice, in view of the upward trend in global consumption patterns.

In accordance with a decision made by UNEP's Governing Council in February 2002, a Preparatory Committee for the Development of a Strategic Approach to International Chemicals Management was established; the work of the Committee culminated in the first session, held in February 2006, in Dubai, United Arab Emirates, of the International Conference on Chemicals Management (ICCM-1), comprising governments and intergovernmental and non-governmental organizations. ICCM-1 adopted the Strategic Approach to International Chemicals Management (SAICM), a policy framework to promote the sound management of chemicals in support of the objective (determined by the 2002 WSSD) of ensuring that, by 2020, chemicals are produced and used in ways that minimize significant adverse impacts on the environment and human health. ICCM-2, convened in May 2009, in Geneva, reviewed the implementation of the SAICM and adopted 20 indicators to measure its future progress. ICCM-3, held in September 2012, in Nairobi, evaluated data on the 20 indicators. UNEP provides technical support for implementing the Convention on Persistent Organic Pollutants (see above), encouraging the use of alternative pesticides, and monitoring the emission of pollutants through the burning of waste. With UNDP, UNEP helps governments to integrate sound management of chemicals into their development planning. In September 2012 UNEP published the *Global Chemical Outlook*, highlighting the effect of chemicals on human health and the environment, and assessing the negative impact on emerging and developing economies.

In March 2013 UNEP and WHO issued a joint report entitled *State of the Science of Endocrine Disrupting Chemicals*, which assessed the potential disrupting effects on the human hormone system and the environment of synthetic chemicals found in many household products.

Pollutant Release and Transfer Registers (PRTRs), for collecting and disseminating data on toxic emissions, are under development in Cyprus, Egypt and Turkey.

GLOBAL ENVIRONMENT FACILITY

UNEP, together with UNDP and the World Bank, is an implementing agency of the Global Environment Facility (GEF), established in 1991 to help developing countries, and those undergoing economic transition, to meet the costs of projects that benefit the environment in six specific areas: biological diversity; climate change; international waters; depletion of the ozone layer; land degradation; and persistent organic pollutants. Important cross-cutting components of these projects include capacity building to allow countries to meet their obligations under international environmental agreements (described above), and adaptation to climate change. During 1991–2011 some 522 projects were approved by the GEF to be implemented by UNEP, with a total value amounting to US $1,646m. UNEP services the Scientific and Technical Advisory Panel, which provides expert advice on GEF programmes and operational strategies.

COMMUNICATIONS AND PUBLIC INFORMATION

UNEP's public education campaigns and outreach programmes promote community involvement in environmental issues. Further communication of environmental concerns is undertaken through coverage in the press, broadcasting and electronic media, publications (see below), an information centre service and special promotional events, including World Environment Day (celebrated on 5 June; slogan in 2013: 'Think.Eat.Save. Reduce Your Footprint'—relating to an anti-food wastage theme), the Focus on Your World photography competition, and the awarding of the annual Sasakawa Prize (to recognize distinguished service to the environment by individuals and groups) and of the Champions of the Earth awards (for outstanding environmental leaders from each of UNEP's six regions). An annual Global Civil Society Forum (preceded by regional consultative meetings) is held in association with UNEP's Governing Council meetings. From April 2007 UNEP undertook a two-year programme on strengthening trade unions' participation in environmental processes. UNEP's Tunza programme for children and young people includes conferences, online discussions and publications. UNEP co-operates with the International Olympic Committee, the Commonwealth Games organizing body and international federations for football, athletics and other sports to encourage 'carbon neutral' sporting events and to use sport as a means of outreach.

Finance

Project budgetary resources approved by the Governing Council for UNEP's activities during 2012–13 totalled US $474m. UNEP is allocated a contribution from the regular budget of the United Nations, and derives most of its finances from voluntary contributions to the Environment Fund and to trust funds.

Publications

Annual Report.

CBTF (Capacity Building Task Force on Trade, Environment and Development) Newsletter.

DEWA / GRID Europe Quarterly Bulletin. E+ (Energy, Climate and Sustainable Development).

Emissions Gap Report.

The Environment and Poverty Times.

Global Chemicals Outlook.

Great Apes Survival Project Newsletter.

Green Economy Report.

IETC (International Environmental Technology Centre) Insight.

Life Cycle Initiatives Newsletter.

Our Planet (quarterly).

Planet in Peril: Atlas of Current Threats to People and the Environment.

ROA (Regional Office for Africa) News (2 a year).

Tourism Focus (2 a year).

RRC.AP (Regional Resource Centre for Asia and the Pacific) Newsletter.

Sustainable Consumption Newsletter.

Tunza (quarterly magazine for children and young people).

UNEP Chemicals Newsletter.

UNEP Year Book (annually).

World Atlas of Biodiversity.

World Atlas of Coral Reefs.

World Atlas of Desertification.

Studies, reports (including the *Global Environment Outlook* series), legal texts, technical guidelines, etc.

Associated Bodies

Intergovernmental Panel on Climate Change (IPCC): c/o WMO, 7 bis, ave de la Paix, 1211 Geneva 2, Switzerland; tel. 227308208; fax 227308025; e-mail ipcc-sec@wmo.int; internet www.ipcc.ch; established in 1988 by the World Meteorological Organization (WMO) and UNEP; comprises some 3,000 scientists as well as other experts and representatives of all UN member governments. Approximately every five years the IPCC assesses all available scientific, technical and socio-economic information on anthropogenic climate change. The IPCC provides, on request, scientific, technical and socio-economic advice to the Conference of the Parties to the UN Framework Convention on Climate Change (UNFCCC) and to its subsidiary bodies, and compiles reports on specialized topics, such as *Aviation and the Global Atmosphere*, *Regional Impacts of Climate Change*, and (issued in March 2012) *Managing the Risks of Extreme Events and Disasters to Advance Climate Change Adaptation*. The IPCC informs and guides, but does not prescribe, policy. In December 1995 the IPCC presented evidence to 120 governments, demonstrating 'a discernible human influence on global climate'. In 2001 the Panel issued its *Third Assessment Report*, in which it confirmed this finding and presented new and strengthened evidence attributing most global climate warming over the past 50 years to human activities. The IPCC's *Fourth Assessment Report*, the final instalment of which was issued in November 2007, concluded that increases in global average air and ocean temperatures, widespread melting of snow and ice, and the rising global average sea level, demonstrate that the warming of the climate system is unequivocal; that observational evidence from all continents and most oceans indicates that many natural systems are being affected by regional climate changes; that a global assessment of data since 1970 has shown that it is likely that anthropogenic warming has had a discernable influence on many physical and biological systems; and that other effects of regional climate changes are emerging. The *Fourth Assessment Report* was awarded a share of the Nobel Peace Prize for 2007. In January 2010 the IPCC accepted criticism that an assertion in the 2007 *Report*, concerning the rate at which Himalayan glaciers were melting, was exaggerated, and in February 2010 the Panel agreed that the *Report* had overstated the proportion of the Netherlands below sea level. In late February it was announced that an independent board of scientists would be appointed to review the work of the IPCC. The *Fifth Assessment Report* of the IPCC was to be published in 2014. In May 2011 a meeting of delegates from IPCC member states determined that a 13-member executive committee, under the leadership of the IPCC Chairman, should be established to supervise the day-to-day operations of the Panel and to consider matters requiring urgent action.

Chair.: RAJENDRA K. PACHAURI (India).

UN Convention to Combat Desertification in Those Countries Experiencing Serious Drought and/or Desertification, Particularly in Africa, Secretariat (UNCCD): Hermann-Ehlers-Str. 10, 53113 Bonn, Germany; tel. (228) 815-2800; fax (228) 815-2898; e-mail secretariat@unccd.int; internet www.unccd.int; the UN Conference on Environment and Development, convened in June 1992, in Rio de Janeiro, Brazil, endorsed an integrated approach to addressing the issue of accelerating desertification, with an emphasis on promoting sustainable development at the community level, and requested the UN General Assembly to establish a negotiating committee to draft the UNCCD; consequently, the Convention was adopted in June 1994, and came into force in December 1996. In October 1998 a Global Mechanism was established under UNCCD, to provide strategic advisory services to developing countries on means of attracting and increasing investments in sustainable land management, for example by channelling investments from innovative financial sources such as micro-finance and climate change funds. The eighth session of the UNCCD Conference of the Parties (COP), held in September 2007, in Madrid,

Spain, adopted The Strategy, a 10-year strategic plan and framework, which covered the period 2008–18, and aimed to enhance the implementation of the Convention, with a focus on forging global partnerships towards the reversal and prevention of desertification and land degradation, and on establishing a global framework to support the development and implementation of national and regional poverty reduction policies. COP 10, convened in October 2011, in Changwon, Republic of Korea, adopted the Changwon Initiative, which was to complement activities being undertaken in accordance with The Strategy, including enhancing UNCCD scientific processes; mobilizing additional resources and facilitating partnership arrangements; and supporting a global framework for the promotion of best practice. COP 11, the most recent Conference, was held in Windhoek, Namibia, in September 2013. By that time the UNCCD had been ratified by 194 states and the EU.

Executive Secretary: MONIQUE BARBUT (France).

UN Framework Convention on Climate Change, Secretariat (UNFCCC): Haus Carstanjen, Martin-Luther-King-Str. 8, 53175 Bonn, Germany; tel. (228) 815-1000; fax (228) 815-1999; e-mail secretariat@unfccc.int; internet unfccc.int; the World Meteorological Organization (WMO) and UNEP worked together to formulate the Convention, in response to the first report of the IPCC, issued in August 1990, which predicted an increase in the concentration of 'greenhouse' gases (i.e. carbon dioxide and other gases that have a warming effect on the atmosphere) owing to human activity. The UNFCCC was signed in May 1992 and formally adopted at the UN Conference on Environment and Development, held in June. It entered into force in March 1994. It committed countries to submitting reports on measures being taken to reduce the emission of greenhouse gases and recommended stabilizing these emissions at 1990 levels by 2000; however, this was not legally binding. Following the second session of the Conference of the Parties (COP) of the Convention, held in July 1996, multilateral negotiations ensued to formulate legally binding objectives for emission limitations. At the third COP, held in Kyoto, Japan, in December 1997, 38 industrial nations endorsed mandatory reductions of combined emissions of the six major gases by an average of 5.2% during the five-year period 2008–12, to pre-1990 levels. The so-called Kyoto Protocol was to enter into force on being ratified by at least 55 countries party to the UNFCCC, including industrialized countries with combined emissions of carbon dioxide in 1990 accounting for at least 55% of the total global greenhouse gas emissions by developed nations. The fourth COP, convened in Buenos Aires, Argentina, in November 1998, adopted a plan of action to promote implementation of the UNFCCC and to finalize the operational details of the Kyoto Protocol. These included the Clean Development Mechanism, by which industrialized countries may obtain credits towards achieving their reduction targets by assisting developing countries to implement emission-reducing measures, and a system of trading emission quotas. The fifth COP, held in Bonn, Germany, in October–November 1999, and the first session of the sixth COP, convened in The Hague, Netherlands, in November 2000, failed to reach agreement on the implementation of the Buenos Aires plan of action, owing to a lack of consensus on several technical matters, including the formulation of an effective mechanism for ascertaining compliance under the Kyoto Protocol, and adequately defining a provision of the Protocol under which industrialized countries may obtain credits towards achieving their reduction targets in respect of the absorption of emissions resulting from activities in the so-called land-use, land-use change and forestry (LULUCF) sector. Further, informal, talks were held in Ottawa, Canada, in early December. Agreement on implementing the Buenos Aires action plan was finally achieved at the second session of the sixth COP, held in Bonn in July 2001. The seventh COP, convened in Marrakesh, Morocco, in October–November, formally adopted the decisions reached in July, and elected 15 members to the Executive Board of the Clean Development Mechanism. In March 2002 the USA (the most prolific national producer of harmful gas emissions) announced that it would not ratify the Kyoto Protocol. The Kyoto Protocol eventually entered into force on 16 February 2005, 90 days after its ratification by Russia. Negotiations commenced in May 2007 on establishing a new international arrangement eventually to succeed the Kyoto Protocol. Participants in COP 13, convened in Bali, Indonesia, in December 2007, adopted the Bali Roadmap, detailing a two-year process leading to the planned conclusion of the schedule of negotiations in December 2009. Further rounds of talks were held during 2008 in Bangkok, Thailand (March–April); Bonn (June); and Accra, Ghana (August). The UN Climate Change Conference (COP 14), convened in Poznań, Poland, in December 2008, finalized the Kyoto Protocol's Adaptation Fund, which was to finance projects and programmes in developing signatory states that were particularly vulnerable to the adverse effects of climate change. Addressing the Conference, the UN Secretary-General urged the advancement of a 'Green New Deal', to address simultaneously the ongoing global climate and economic crises. COP 15 was held, concurrently with the fifth meeting of parties to the Kyoto Protocol, in Copenhagen, Denmark, in December 2009. Heads of state and government and other delegates attending the Conference approved the Copenhagen Accord, which determined that international co-operative action should be taken, in the context of sustainable development, to reduce global greenhouse gas emissions so as to hold the ongoing increase in global temperature below 2°C. It was agreed that enhanced efforts should be undertaken to reduce vulnerability to climate change in developing countries, with special reference to least developed countries, small island states and Africa. Developed countries agreed to pursue the achievement by 2020 of strengthened carbon emissions targets, while developing nations were to implement actions to slow down growth in emissions. A Green Climate Fund was to be established to support climate change mitigation actions in developing countries, and a Technology Mechanism was also to be established, with the aim of accelerating technology development and transfer in support of climate change adaptation and mitigation activities. COP 16, convened, concurrently with the sixth meeting of parties to the Kyoto Protocol, in Cancún, Mexico, in November–December 2010, adopted several decisions (the 'Cancún Agreements'), which included mandating the establishment of a Cancún Adaptation Framework and associated Adaptation Committee, and approving a work programme which was to consider approaches to environmental damage linked to unavoidable impacts of climate change in vulnerable countries, as well as addressing forms of adaptation action, such as: strengthening the resilience of ecological systems; undertaking impact, vulnerability and adaptation assessments; engaging the participation of vulnerable communities in ongoing processes; and valuing traditional indigenous knowledge alongside the best available science. UN system-wide activities to address climate change are co-ordinated by an action framework established by the UN Chief Executives Board for Co-ordination under the UN *Delivering as One* commitment. COP 17, held in Durban, South Africa, in November–December 2011 concluded with an agreement on a 'Durban Platform for Enhanced Action'. The Platform incorporated agreements to extend the Kyoto provisions regarding emissions reductions by industrialized nations for a second phase, to follow on from the expiry at end-2012 of the first commitment phase, and to initiate negotiations on a new, inclusive global emissions arrangement, to be concluded in 2015, that would come into effect in 2020 with 'legal force'. During the conference sufficient funds were committed to enable the inauguration of the Green Climate Fund, and a commitment was concluded to establish the Adaptation Committee. In December 2012 COP 18, convened in Doha, Qatar, approved an amendment of the Kyoto Protocol to initiate a second commitment period of eight years and endorsed the timetable for negotiating a new climate agreement by May 2015 (with a meeting of world heads of state to be convened in 2014). States parties committed to reducing greenhouse gas emissions by at least 18% below 1990 levels during 2013–20. COP 18 also secured a commitment by developed nations to mobilize US $100,000m. by 2020 to support climate change adaptation and mitigation initiatives in affected developing countries. The meeting confirmed that the Green Climate Fund would become operational in late 2013, based in Songdo, South Korea. As at September 2013 the Kyoto Protocol had 192 states parties (191 countries and the European Community). The USA has not signed the Protocol. Canada withdrew its participation with effect from December 2012.

Executive Secretary: CHRISTIANA FIGUERES (Costa Rica).

United Nations High Commissioner for Refugees—UNHCR

Address: CP 2500, 1211 Geneva 2 dépôt, Switzerland.

Telephone: 227398111; **fax:** 227397312; **e-mail:** unhcr@unhcr.org; **internet:** www.unhcr.org.

The Office of the High Commissioner was established in 1951 to provide international protection for refugees and to seek durable solutions to their problems. In 1981 UNHCR was awarded the Nobel Peace Prize.

Organization

(September 2013)

HIGH COMMISSIONER

The High Commissioner is elected by the United Nations General Assembly on the nomination of the Secretary-General, and is responsible to the General Assembly and to the UN Economic and Social Council (ECOSOC).

High Commissioner: António Manuel de Oliveira Guterres (Portugal).

Deputy High Commissioner: Thomas Alexander Aleinikoff (USA).

EXECUTIVE COMMITTEE

The Executive Committee of the High Commissioner's Programme (ExCom), established by ECOSOC, gives the High Commissioner policy directives in respect of material assistance programmes and advice in the field of international protection. In addition, it oversees UNHCR's general policies and use of funds. ExCom, which comprises representatives of 66 states, both members and non-members of the UN, meets once a year.

ADMINISTRATION

Headquarters, based in Geneva, Switzerland, include the Executive Office, comprising the offices of the High Commissioner, the Deputy High Commissioner and the two Assistant High Commissioners (for Operations and Protection). The Inspector General, the Director of the UNHCR liaison office in New York, and the Director of the Ethics Office (established in 2008) report directly to the High Commissioner. The principal administrative Divisions cover International Protection; Programme and Support Management; Emergency Security and Supply; Financial and Administrative Management; Human Resources Management; External Relations; and Information Systems and Telecommunications. A UNHCR Global Service Centre, based in Budapest, Hungary, was inaugurated in 2008 to provide administrative support to the headquarters. There are five regional bureaux covering Africa, Asia and the Pacific, Europe, the Americas, and North Africa and the Middle East. In 2013 UNHCR employed around 7,200 regular staff, of whom about 85% were working in the field. At that time there were 396 UNHCR offices in 123 countries.

Activities

The competence of the High Commissioner extends to any person who, owing to well-founded fear of being persecuted for reasons of race, religion, nationality or political opinion, is outside the country of his or her nationality and is unable or, owing to such fear or for reasons other than personal convenience, remains unwilling to accept the protection of that country; or who, not having a nationality and being outside the country of his or her former habitual residence, is unable or, owing to such fear or for reasons other than personal convenience, is unwilling to return to it. This competence may be extended, by resolutions of the UN General Assembly and decisions of ExCom, to cover certain other 'persons of concern', in addition to refugees meeting these criteria. Refugees who are assisted by other UN agencies, or who have the same rights or obligations as nationals of their country of residence, are outside the mandate of UNHCR.

In recent years there has been a significant shift in UNHCR's focus of activities. Increasingly UNHCR has been called upon to support people who have been displaced within their own country (i.e. with similar needs to those of refugees but who have not crossed an international border) or those threatened with displacement as a result of armed conflict. In addition, greater support has been given to refugees who have returned to their country of origin, to assist their reintegration, and UNHCR is working to enable local communities to support the returnees, frequently through the implementation of Quick Impact Projects (QIPs). In 2004 UNHCR led the formulation of a UN system-wide Strategic Plan for internally displaced persons (IDPs). During 2005 the UN's Inter-Agency Standing Committee (IASC), concerned with co-ordinating the international response to humanitarian disasters, developed a concept of organizing agency assistance to IDPs through the institutionalization of a 'Cluster Approach', currently comprising 11 core areas of activity (see OCHA). UNHCR is the lead agency for the clusters on Camp Co-ordination and Management (in conflict situations; the International Organization for Migration leads that cluster in natural disaster situations), Emergency Shelter, and (jointly with OHCHR and UNICEF) Protection. The IASC maintains a series of *Guidelines on Mental Health and Psychosocial Support in Emergency Settings*, and, in November 2012 UNHCR, jointly with WHO, issued *Assessing Mental Health and Psychosocial Needs and Resources: Toolkit for Humanitarian Settings*.

From the mid-2000s the scope of UNHCR's mandate was widened from the protection of people fleeing persecution and violence to encompass, also, humanitarian needs arising from natural disasters.

In July 2006 UNHCR issued a '10 Point Plan of Action on Refugee Protection and Mixed Migration' (*10 Point Plan*), a framework document detailing 10 principal areas in which UNHCR might make an impact in supporting member states with the development of comprehensive migration strategies. The 10 areas covered by the Plan were as follows: co-operation among key players; data collection and analysis; protection-sensitive entry systems; reception arrangements; mechanisms for profiling and referral; differentiated processes and procedures; solutions for refugees; addressing secondary movements; return of non-refugees and alternative migration options; and information strategy. A revised version of the *10 Point Plan* was published in January 2007. Addressing the annual meeting of ExCom in October 2007 the High Commissioner, while emphasizing that UNHCR was not mandated to manage migration, urged a concerted international effort to raise awareness and comprehension of the broad patterns of global displacement and migration. In order to fulfil UNHCR's mandate to support refugees and others in need of protection within ongoing mass movements of people, he urged better recognition of the mixed nature of many 21st-century population flows, often comprising both economic migrants and refugees, asylum seekers and victims of trafficking who required detection and support. It was also acknowledged that conflict and persecution—the traditional reasons for flight—were being increasingly compounded by factors such as environmental degradation and the detrimental effects of climate change. A Dialogue on Protection Challenges, convened by the High Commissioner in December 2007, agreed that the *10 Point Plan* should be elaborated further.

In 2009 UNHCR launched the first annual Global Needs Assessment (GNA), with the aim of mapping comprehensively the situation and needs of populations of concern falling under the mandate of the Office. The GNA is intended to represent a blueprint for planning and decision-making for UNHCR, populations of concern, governments and other partners.

All UNHCR personnel are required to sign, and all interns, contracted staff and staff from partner organizations are required to acknowledge, a Code of Conduct, to which is appended the UN Secretary-General's bulletin on special measures for protection from sexual exploitation and sexual abuse. The post of Senior Adviser to the High Commissioner on Gender Issues was established in 2004. In June 2011 UNHCR issued an updated strategy on Action against Sexual and Gender-Based Violence.

UNHCR's global strategic priorities for 2012–13 were to promote a favourable protection environment; to promote fair protection processes and increase levels of documentation; to ensure security from violence and exploitation; to provide basic needs and services; and to pursue durable solutions.

At December 2012 the total global population of concern to UNHCR, based on provisional figures, amounted to 35.8m. At that time the refugee population world-wide totalled 10.5m., of whom 6.7m. were being assisted by UNHCR. UNHCR was also concerned with some 525,941 recently returned refugees, 17.7m. IDPs, 1.5m. returned IDPs, 3.3m. stateless persons, and 936,740 asylum seekers. UNHCR maintains an online statistical population database.

UNHCR is one of the 10 co-sponsors of UNAIDS.

World Refugee Day, sponsored by UNHCR, is held annually on 20 June. The theme in 2013 was 'One family torn apart by war is too many'.

INTERNATIONAL PROTECTION

As laid down in the Statute of the Office, UNHCR's primary function is to extend international protection to refugees and its second function is to seek durable solutions to their problems. In the exercise of its mandate UNHCR seeks to ensure that refugees and asylum seekers are protected against *refoulement* (forcible return), that they receive asylum, and that they are treated according to internationally recognized standards. UNHCR pursues these objectives by a variety of means that include promoting the conclusion and ratification by states of international conventions for the protection of refugees. UNHCR promotes the adoption of liberal practices of asylum by states, so that refugees and asylum seekers are granted admission, at least on a temporary basis.

The most comprehensive instrument concerning refugees that has been elaborated at the international level is the 1951 United Nations Convention relating to the Status of Refugees. This Convention, the scope of which was extended by a Protocol adopted in 1967, defines the rights and duties of refugees and contains provisions dealing with a variety of matters which affect the day-to-day lives of refugees. The application of the Convention and its Protocol is supervised by UNHCR. The Office has actively encouraged states to accede to the Convention (which had 145 parties at September 2013) and the Protocol (146 parties at September 2013). Important provisions for the treatment of refugees are also contained in a number of instruments adopted at the regional level. These include the 1969 Convention Governing the Specific Aspects of Refugee Problems adopted by the Organization of African Unity (now the African Union—AU) member states in 1969, the European Agreement on the Abolition of Visas for Refugees, and the 1969 American Convention on Human Rights. In October 2009 AU member states adopted the AU Convention for the Protection and Assistance of IDPs in Africa, the first legally binding international treaty providing legal protection and support to internally displaced populations. An increasing number of states have also adopted domestic legislation and/or administrative measures to implement the international instruments, particularly in the field of procedures for the determination of refugee status. UNHCR has sought to address the specific needs of refugee women and children, and has also attempted to deal with the problem of military attacks on refugee camps, by adopting and encouraging the acceptance of a set of principles to ensure the safety of refugees. From 2009 UNHCR strengthened its focus on protecting and finding solution refugees residing in urban areas (who by 2013 represented more than one-half of all refugees). In recent years the Office has formulated a strategy designed to address the fundamental causes of refugee flows.

UNHCR has increasingly placed a focus on statelessness (lack of legal nationality), and promotes new accessions to the 1951 Convention Relating to the Status of Stateless Persons and the 1961 Convention on the Reduction of Statelessness. UNHCR maintains that a significant proportion of the global stateless population has not hitherto been systematically identified. A series of *UN Guiding Principles on Internal Displacement* was finalized in 1998. In December 2011 UNHCR organized a ministerial meeting, in Geneva, to commemorate the 60th anniversary of the 1951 Refugee Convention and the 50th anniversary of the 1961 Convention on the Reduction of Statelessness, and to reaffirm commitment to the central role played by these instruments. A number of participants at the meeting made pledges to address statelessness, including improving procedures for identifying stateless people on their territories, enhancing civil registration systems, and raising awareness of the options available to stateless people. During 2013 UNHCR aimed to follow up pledges made at the meeting; some US $79m. was allocated by the Office in that year to 61 projects on addressing statelessness.

ASSISTANCE ACTIVITIES

The first phase of an assistance operation uses UNHCR's capacity of emergency response. This enables UNHCR to address the immediate needs of refugees at short notice, for example, by employing specially trained emergency teams and maintaining stockpiles of basic equipment, medical aid and materials. A significant proportion of UNHCR expenditure is allocated to the next phase of an operation, providing 'care and maintenance' in stable refugee circumstances. This assistance can take various forms, including the provision of food, shelter, medical care and essential supplies. Also covered in many instances are basic services, including education and counselling.

As far as possible, assistance is geared towards the identification and implementation of durable solutions to refugee problems—this being the second statutory responsibility of UNHCR. Such solutions generally take one of three forms: voluntary repatriation, local integration, or resettlement onwards to a third country. UNHCR supports the implementation of the Guidance Note on Durable Solutions for Displaced Persons, adopted in 2004 by the UN Development Group.

Where voluntary repatriation, generally the preferred solution, is feasible, the Office assists refugees to overcome obstacles preventing their return to their country of origin. This may be done through negotiations with governments involved, or by providing funds either for the physical movement of refugees or for the rehabilitation of returnees once back in their own country. Some 526,000 refugees repatriated voluntarily to their home countries in 2012.

When voluntary repatriation is not an option, efforts are made to assist refugees to integrate locally and to become self-supporting in their countries of asylum. This may be done either by granting loans to refugees, or by assisting them, through vocational training or in other ways, to learn a skill and to establish themselves in gainful occupations. One major form of assistance to help refugees re-establish themselves outside camps is the provision of housing.

In cases where resettlement through emigration is the only viable solution to a refugee problem, UNHCR negotiates with governments in an endeavour to obtain suitable resettlement opportunities, to encourage liberalization of admission criteria and to draw up special immigration schemes. During 2012 an estimated 71,000 refugees were resettled under UNHCR auspices.

UNHCR integrates certain priority considerations into its programme planning and implementation, including awareness of specific problems confronting refugee women, the needs of refugee children, the environmental impact of refugee programmes and long-term development objectives. A Policy Development and Evaluation Service (PDES) reviews systematically UNHCR's operational effectiveness. In 2013 the PDES was supporting the formulation and implementation of the Office's policy on refugee protection and solutions in urban areas, by undertaking a global survey on the implementation of urban refugee policy; establishing internet-based compilation of effective operational practices in urban areas; and by implementing a review of an urban refugee programme then ongoing in New Delhi, India.

NORTH AFRICA AND THE MIDDLE EAST

UNHCR co-ordinates humanitarian assistance for the estimated 165,000 Sahrawis registered as refugees in five camps in the Tindouf area of Algeria. The Office also supports an urban refugee population in Algiers. (Activities in Algiers were temporarily suspended from December 2007 following a terrorist attack that devastated UNHCR's offices there.) In September 1997 an agreement was reached on implementing the 1991 Settlement Plan for the Western Sahara. Accordingly, UNHCR was to help organize the registration and safe return of some 120,000 Sahrawi refugees provisionally identified as eligible to vote in the planned referendum on the future of the territory. In addition, UNHCR was to facilitate the reintegration of the returnees and monitor their rehabilitation. By 2013, however, little progress had been achieved towards the implementation of the Settlement Plan and subsequent alternative settlement proposals. UNHCR was continuing to provide basic relief items and to facilitate family visits for the residents of the Tindouf camps; in September 2009 UNHCR resolved to expand its confidence-building programme, which was launched in 2004 mainly to facilitate family visits; by 2013 around 12,000 people had participated in family visits under the programme. In July 2012 and February 2013 UNHCR organized two seminars, in the Azores and in Faro, Portugal, respectively, covering the role of women and the importance of the tent (al-khaima) in Western Saharan culture.

As a result of serious instability in Libya from mid-February 2011, nearly 100,000 people soon became displaced from the eastern coastal city of Benghazi and surrounding areas; furthermore large numbers (estimated at 656,000 by August) of Libyans and former foreign residents in Libya fled to nearby countries, including 57,221 Libyan nationals who were seeking shelter in Tunisia, and 63,747 Libyans in Egypt. UNHCR dispatched teams to Egypt and Libya to provide support. In response to the crisis within Libya, UNHCR—which maintained a small international staff in the Libyan capital, Tripoli, and organized presences in Benghazi and Tobruk in the east of the country—transported supplies into Libya and provided material assistance to refugees and other vulnerable groups there. During the initial months of the crisis UNHCR airlifted tents, and items such as blankets, sleeping mats, jerrycans, and kitchen sets, to several thousand people gathered in border areas. At the request of the Tunisian Government, UNHCR and other agencies established a number of camps at the Libya-Tunisia border. Furthermore, thousands of Libyans (mainly Berbers) fled Libya's Western Mountain region into Tunisia, the majority being accommodated there by local families. By late August UNHCR had registered nearly 60,000 Libyan refugees sheltering in southern Tunisia. UNHCR distributed ration cards to Libyan refugees in urban areas of Tunisia. UNHCR expressed reiterated concern in September 2011 for the safety of foreign nationals (mainly migrant workers) remaining in Libya. Sub-Saharan Africans were reported to be at particular risk of persecution. Meanwhile, in early 2011, UNHCR and IOM jointly conducted the humanitarian evacuation of more than 100,000 third country nationals from Egypt and Tunisia, which had also experienced serious civil unrest. In 2012 UNCHR shifted its focus in Libya from the provision of humanitarian relief to support for the establishment of an effective national mixed migration and asylum framework. UNHCR's work plan in Libya in 2013 included strengthening registration and refugee status determination processes, and ensuring that border officials refer asylum seekers to the correct authorities; ensuring that all individuals of concern have protection documentation; promoting and facilitating durable solutions, and providing vocational training in support of community empowerment and self-reliance; strengthening services for refugees with specific needs, for example for the elderly and the disabled; and building security against sexual and gender-based violence.

Yemen has historically hosted refugees fleeing political instability and intermittent drought in the Horn of Africa. UNHCR operates two reception centres to process incomers, and four other offices, in Yemen. At 31 December 2012 Yemen was hosting an estimated 237,182, mostly Somali refugees (about 95% of the total); the majority of these were residing in urban areas, while some 20,000 were accommodated in the al-Kharaz camp. Some 22,300 new Somali refugees arrived in Yemen in 2012. Ongoing violent conflict in northern Yemen has also generated internal displacement, and at the end of 2012 there were an estimated 385,320 IDPs in Yemen. UNHCR's priorities in Yemen in 2013 included improving registration and profiling processes for people of concern; improving security from sexual abuse or gender-based violence; strengthening the protection of children; providing education and vocational training, especially for refugees in camps; exploring livelihood opportunities for populations of concern; monitoring an ongoing expansion of the al-Kharaz camp; advocating for the finalization of a national refugee legal framework; and exploring resettlement as a durable solution.

In March 2003 UNHCR and the International Federation of Red Cross and Red Crescent Societies signed an agreement to co-operate in providing humanitarian relief in Iraq and neighbouring countries. From mid-2003, following the overthrow of the Saddam Hussain regime by a US-led force, UNHCR developed plans for the eventual phased repatriation of more than 500,000 of the large population of Iraqis exiled world-wide, and for the return to their homes of some 800,000 IDPs. The Office assumed responsibility for assisting about 50,000 refugees from other countries (including some 34,000 Palestinians—of whom an estimated 11,740 remained in 2013) who had been supported by the previous Iraqi administration but were now suffering harassment; many had abandoned their homes in Iraq owing to insufficient security and inadequate supplies. Negotiations with Iran were initiated in mid-2003 to enable Iranian refugees to repatriate across the Iraq–Iran border. From March–May 2003, and following the bomb attack in August on the UN headquarters in Baghdad, all international UN humanitarian personnel were withdrawn from Iraq, leaving national staff to conduct operations on the ground. During 2003–05 some 315,000 spontaneous returns by Iraqi refugees and asylum seekers and 496,000 returns by IDPs were reported. However, owing to the ongoing unstable security situation, UNHCR and the Iraqi Interim Government (inaugurated in June 2004) discouraged Iraqi refugees from returning home, and UNHCR warned governments hosting Iraqi refugees against repatriation, as well as advising continued protection of Iraqi asylum seekers. During 2006–07, owing to escalating violent sectarian unrest, it was reported that more than 1.5m. Iraqis had become newly displaced and that many people—including skilled and professional workers—had left Iraq, further inhibiting the national recovery process. In April 2007 an International Conference on Addressing the Humanitarian Needs of Refugees and Internally Displaced Persons inside Iraq and in Neighbouring Countries was convened in Geneva by the UN High Commissioner for Refugees. UNHCR remains highly concerned for foreign refugees remaining in Iraq (totalling 35,189 at end-2011). UNHCR has a small international presence (re-established in March 2008) in Baghdad, Basrah, Erbil, Kirkuk and Mosul, as well as 18 Protection and Assistance Centres, six Return Integration and Community Centres, and 40 mobile teams. Through its network of offices UNHCR monitors population movements and the well-being of refugees, IDPs and returnees throughout Iraq. At 31 December 2012, the total Iraqi IDP population amounted to 1.1m., around 219,000 IDPs having returned to their homes during that year. The Office provides returnees, in accordance with a case-by-case approach, with counselling, limited transportation and livelihood grants. UNHCR's priorities in Iraq in 2013 included advocating for accession by the Iraq Government to the principal international refugee and statelessness instruments, and for the establishment of an effective national asylum system; capacity-building programmes for governmental and local agencies; legal interventions on behalf of refugees, IDPS, stateless persons, and returnees; efforts to combat sexual and gender-based violence; provision of material assistance; and the implementation of projects providing shelter for and promoting self-reliance among IDPs and returnees. UNHCR was also to maintain an emergency stockpile of basic non-food items to support Syrian refugees in Iraq. A new Comprehensive Plan to End Displacement, developed in 2012 by the Iraqi authorities with UNHCR support, was being implemented in 2013.

At the end of 2012 it was estimated that there were 480,000 Iraqis sheltering in Syria (51,300 UNHCR-assisted) and 450,500 (29,000 UNHCR-protected) in Jordan, as well as smaller groups of Iraqis in other neighbouring countries, placing considerable strain on local infrastructure and services. In 2010 UNHCR and the Syrian Government concluded a Co-operation Agreement providing the legal basis for the Office's activities in that country. UNHCR's activities in support of Iraqi populations of concern has included the provision of remedial classes; outreach to parents by education volunteers; distribution of education grants; and support with access to health care. UNHCR has particularly focused assistance on vulnerable refugees with specific needs, such as female-headed households, children and the elderly. UNHCR has pursued accelerated departures and resettlement opportunities for the most vulnerable Iraqi refugees. The violent unrest that emerged in Syria from 2011, and escalated during 2012–13, disrupted resettlement activities relating to Iraqi refugees there. In 2011 28,230 returns by Iraqis from Syria to Iraq were recorded (only 3,071 of these UNHCR-assisted), and around 50,000 further Iraqis were reported to have repatriated voluntarily from Syria in 2012.

At the end of 2012 Kuwait was hosting 94,503 people of concern to UNHCR, mainly *bidoun* (stateless people, totalling 93,000), Iraqis and Palestinians.

In March 2012, in view of mounting unrest in Syria since March 2011, humanitarian agencies launched an inter-agency Syria Regional Response Plan. The Plan, drafted and led by UNHCR, aims to assist Syrians who have fled to neighbouring countries (which have continued to keep their borders open to the influx). The agencies initially appealed jointly for US $84m. to fund the plan in 2012; in September this was increased to $347m. An appeal for some $2,900m. was made under a new edition of the Plan to cover the protection needs of Syrian refugees throughout 2013, although this was only partially (40%) funded by September. By that month some 1,929,227 Syrian refugees (of a total 2,102,582 persons of concern) had been registered by UNHCR in neighbouring countries. At that time 518,613 Syrian refugees were registered in Jordan, 645,381 in Lebanon, 484,291 in Turkey, 161,500 in Iraq, and 105,153 in Egypt. In 2013 a UNHCR presence in Jordan was managing the overcrowded Za'atri refugee camp, near Mafraq, which opened in July 2012 with capacity for around 60,000 residents, and was by September 2013 accommodating around 120,000 Syrian refugees. A second, smaller camp, Mrajeeb al-Fhood, was opened near Zarqa in April. The Office aimed to establish new registration sites and refugee help desks in Jordan during 2013. UNHCR was advocating with the Lebanese authorities in 2013 for the establishment of an efficient framework for the protection of persons of concern. Meanwhile, the Office was registering and determining the status of incoming refugees from Syria; assisting refugees with the attainment of civil status documentation; supplying food, hygiene kits and other basic essential items; providing health assistance; providing educational grants to children; and offering vocational training. Although there were no formal refugee camps in Lebanon, several informal tented encampments were operating in 2013. More than 90% of the Syrian refugees in Iraq were sheltering in the Kurdistan region, and, of these, around three-fifths were being hosted by local communities. In 2013 UNHCR was maintaining a permanent presence at the al-Qa'im and Dohuk refugee camps in Kurdistan, was assisting the reception and registration of refugees, and was distributing essential basic relief items, such as kitchen sets, mattresses and blankets. Meanwhile, at that time, UNHCR was providing essential services and seeking durable solutions for Syrian refugees accommodated in 17 camps in Turkey. Within Syria—where, by September 2013, the IDP population had reached 4.3m., and a total of 6.8m. people were reported to be in need of immediate support as a consequence of the ongoing conflict—UNHCR has provided food, health, hygiene, and registration and counselling services, and has undertaken community visits to distribute relief items such as kitchen sets, jerrycans, blankets and mattresses. With the Syrian Red Crescent UNHCR was implementing a cash-for-shelter project in al-Nabek, a village near Homs which was hosting several thousand IDPs. At 31 December 2012 Syria was also accommodating a significant population of stateless people, totalling 221,000.

In response to the intensive bombardment of the Gaza Strip by Israeli forces conducted during late-December 2008–January 2009, with the stated aim of ending rocket attacks launched by Hamas and other militant groups on Israeli targets, UNHCR assisted UNRWA (which has responsibility for protecting the Palestinian refugee population in Gaza) through the provision of non-food items and logistical support.

From the late 1970s civil strife in Afghanistan resulted in massive population displacements, including movements of refugees from that country into Pakistan and Iran which created a massive refugee population, reaching a peak of almost 6.3m. people in 1990. In September 2001, prompted by the threat of impending military action directed by a US-led global coalition against targets in the Taliban-administered areas of Afghanistan, UNHCR launched an emergency relief operation to cope with the potentially large further movement of Afghan refugees and IDPs. UNHCR urged the adoption of more liberal border policies by surrounding countries and began substantially to reinforce its presence in Iran and Pakistan. Movements of Afghan refugees into Iran were reported following the initiation of the US-led military action in October. In March 2002 tripartite accords on repatriation were concluded by UNHCR with the Afghan authorities and with Iran and Pakistan. In that month UNHCR signed a new agreement with the Iranian Government to grant access to Afghans in detention centres throughout that country and to undertake a screening programme for asylum seekers, in order to deal with the problem of undocumented refugees. During 2008 the Iranian authorities implemented an online refugee registration process, referred to as Amayesh, under which the details of more than 900,000 people were registered; identity cards were issued to refugees registered under Amayesh, and, subsequently, temporary work-permits began to be issued to Amayesh card holders with a view to finding temporary solutions in Iran for the Afghan refugees. UNHCR envisaged utilizing the data collated under Amayesh in its planning processes. At the end of December 2012 more than 860,000 UNHCR-assisted Afghan refugees remained in Iran (in addition to about 1m. unregistered Afghan migrants). During 2011 a quadripartite consultation process was initiated, involving Afghanistan, Iran, Pakistan and UNHCR, with the aim of developing a strategy for Afghan refugees over the period 2012–14; the resulting 'Solutions Strategy' was endorsed by a stakeholders' conference convened in May 2012.

CO-OPERATION WITH OTHER ORGANIZATIONS

UNHCR works closely with other UN agencies, intergovernmental organizations and non-governmental organizations (NGOs) to increase the scope and effectiveness of its operations. Within the UN system UNHCR co-operates, principally, with WFP in the distribution of food aid, UNICEF and WHO in the provision of family welfare and child immunization programmes, OCHA in the delivery of emergency humanitarian relief, UNDP in development-related activities and the preparation of guidelines for the continuum of emergency assistance to development programmes, and the Office of the UN High Commissioner for Human Rights. UNHCR also has close working relationships with the International Federation of Red Cross and Red Crescent Societies and the International Organization for Migration. UNHCR planned to engage with nearly 700 NGOs in 2012–13. In recent years UNHCR has pursued a strategy to engage private sector businesses in supporting its activities through the provision of donations (cash contributions and 'in kind'), of loaned expertise, and of marketing related to designated causes.

TRAINING

UNHCR organizes training programmes and workshops to enhance the capabilities of field workers and non-UNHCR staff, in the following areas: the identification and registration of refugees; people-orientated planning; resettlement procedures and policies; emergency response and management; security awareness; stress management; and the dissemination of information through the electronic media.

Finance

The United Nations' regular budget finances a proportion of UNHCR's administrative expenditure. The majority of UNHCR's programme expenditure (about 98%) is funded by voluntary contributions, mainly from governments. The Private Sector and Public Affairs Service aims to increase funding from non-governmental donor sources, for example by developing partnerships with foundations and corporations. Following approval of the Unified Annual Programme Budget any subsequently identified requirements are managed in the form of Supplementary Programmes, financed by separate appeals. UNHCR's projected funding requirements for 2013 totalled US $3,920.0m.

Publications

Global Trends (annually).

Refugees (quarterly, in English, French, German, Italian, Japanese and Spanish).

Refugee Resettlement: An International Handbook to Guide Reception and Integration.

Refugee Survey Quarterly.

Refworld (annually).

Sexual and Gender-based Violence Against Refugees, Returnees and Displaced Persons: Guidelines for Prevention and Response.

The State of the World's Refugees (every 2 years).

Statistical Yearbook (annually).

UNHCR Handbook for Emergencies.

Press releases, reports.

Statistics

PERSONS OF CONCERN TO UNHCR IN THE MIDDLE EAST AND NORTH AFRICA*

('000 persons, at 31 December 2012, provisional figures)

Host Country	Refugees	Asylum seekers	Returnees	Others of concern
Algeria	94.1	1.7	0.0	—
Egypt	109.9	17.0	—	0.1
Iran	868.2	0.2	0.0	—
Iraq	98.8	4.9	82.3	1,470.0
Israel	48.5	5.7	—	0.0
Jordan	302.7	2.9	—	—
Kuwait	0.7	0.8	—	93.0
Lebanon	133.9	1.9	—	—
Libya	7.1	6.6	1.1	236.9
Saudi Arabia	0.6	0.1	0.0	70.0
Syria	576.5	2.2	68.6	221.0
Turkey	267.1	14.1	—	10.9
Yemen	237.2	6.5	—	492.2

* The table shows only those countries where the total number of persons of concern to UNHCR amounted to more than 10,000. The figures are provided mostly by governments, based on their own methods of estimation. The data do not include the 4,919,917 Palestinian refugees who come under the care of UNRWA at 31 December 2012.

United Nations Peace-keeping

Address: Department of Peace-keeping Operations, Room S-3727B, United Nations, New York, NY 10017, USA.

Telephone: (212) 963-8077; **fax:** (212) 963-9222; **internet:** www.un.org/Depts/dpko/.

United Nations peace-keeping operations have been conceived as instruments of conflict control. The UN has used these operations in various conflicts, with the consent of the parties involved, to maintain international peace and security, without prejudice to the positions or claims of parties, in order to facilitate the search for political settlements through peaceful means such as mediation and the good offices of the UN Secretary-General. Each operation is established with a specific mandate, which requires periodic review by the UN Security Council. In 1988 the United Nations Peace-keeping Forces were awarded the Nobel Peace Prize.

United Nations peace-keeping operations fall into two categories: peace-keeping forces and observer missions. Peace-keeping forces are composed of contingents of military and civilian personnel, made available by member states. These forces assist in preventing the recurrence of fighting, restoring and maintaining peace, and promoting a return to normal conditions. To this end, peace-keeping forces are authorized as necessary to undertake negotiations, persuasion, observation and fact-finding. They conduct patrols and interpose physically between the opposing parties. Peace-keeping forces are permitted to use their weapons only in self-defence.

Military observer missions are composed of officers (usually unarmed), who are made available, on the Secretary-General's request, by member states. A mission's function is to observe and report to the Secretary-General (who, in turn, informs the Security Council) on the maintenance of a cease-fire, to investigate violations and to do what it can to improve the situation. Peace-keeping forces and observer missions must at all times maintain complete impartiality and avoid any action that might affect the claims or positions of the parties.

The UN's peace-keeping forces and observer missions are financed in most cases by assessed contributions from member states of the organization. (The exceptions are UNFICYP, which is funded partly by voluntary contributions; and UNMOGIP and UNTSO, which are financed from the UN regular budget.) In recent years a significant expansion in the UN's peace-keeping activities has been accompanied by a perpetual financial crisis within the organization, as a result of the increased financial burden and some member states' delaying payment. At 30 June 2013 outstanding assessed contributions to the peace-keeping budget amounted to some US $1,240m.

By September 2013 the UN had deployed a total of 68 peace-keeping operations, of which 13 were authorized in the period 1948–88 and 55 since 1988. At 31 July 2013 115 countries were contributing some 97,369 uniformed personnel to the 15 operations that were ongoing at that time, of whom 82,351 were peace-keeping troops, 13,209 police and 1,809 military observers.

UNITED NATIONS DISENGAGEMENT OBSERVER FORCE—UNDOF

Address: Camp Faouar, Syria.

Force Commander: Maj.-Gen. IQBAL SINGH SINGHA (India).

Establishment and Mandate: UNDOF was established for an initial period of six months by a UN Security Council resolution in May 1974, following the signature in Geneva, Switzerland, of a disengagement agreement between Syrian and Israeli forces. The mandate has since been extended by successive resolutions. The initial task of the mission was to take over territory evacuated in stages by the Israeli troops, in accordance with the disengagement agreement, to hand over territory to Syrian troops, and to establish an area of separation on the Golan Heights.

Activities: UNDOF continues to monitor the area of separation; it carries out inspections of the areas of limited armaments and forces; uses its best efforts to maintain the cease-fire; carries out demining activities; and undertakes activities of a humanitarian nature, such as arranging the transfer of prisoners and war dead between Syria and Israel. The Force operates exclusively on Syrian territory.

From December 2008 indirect negotiations between Israel and Syria on the Golan Heights situation stalled. During 2011 demonstrations by anti-Government protesters in Syria extended to the area of UNDOF's operations. In mid-May and early June groups of Palestinian protesters gathered at a site known as the 'family shouting place', opposite the village of Majdal Chams in the area of limitation on the Israeli-occupied Golan side; on the second occasion the protesters attempted to breach the cease-fire line. UNDOF monitored the proceedings using armoured patrols, engaged with the Syrian and Israeli militaries, and attempted to diffuse tensions. Subsequently, UNDOF strengthened its force protection measures, including the fortification of its positions. During 2012–13 UNDOF's area of operations continued to be affected by escalating instability in Syria. The Syrian armed forces expanded their deployment in the mission's area of operations, in violation of the 1974 agreement on disengagement of forces. Significant population movements were also noted: in July 2012 more than 800 Syrian civilians vacated Jabbata al Khashab, in the area of separation, seeking shelter in villages further south. UNDOF protested against all violations of the 1974 disengagement agreement and continued to monitor the area of separation through the use of fixed positions and patrols, attempting to ensure the exclusion from it of military forces; the mission also undertook fortnightly inspections of equipment and force levels in the areas of limited armaments and forces. On several occasions UNDOF provided direct emergency medical treatment, including to wounded Syrian opposition and national military personnel; the mission also provided assistance to the Syrian Red Crescent.

In March 2013 armed Syrian opposition combatants stopped and detained 21 UNDOF peace-keepers, in the al-Jimla area. The UN Secretary-General and Security Council strongly condemned the action and demanded the immediate and unconditional release of the mission personnel; the detainees were released soon afterwards. In May a further four UNDOF peace-keepers were temporarily detained by Syrian opposition militants in the vicinity of al-Jimla. In June the UN Security Council extended UNDOF's mandate until 31 December. Expressing concern that military activities impinging upon the area of separation had the potential to escalate tensions between Israel and Syria the Council requested the UN Secretary-General to ensure that the mission was sufficiently equipped to fulfil its mandate in a safe and secure way. Reporting on the mission's activities in September the Secretary-General noted several reports of firing across the cease-fire line in recent months, by the Syrian military and opposition forces, and also by the Israeli military claiming retaliation. UNDOF continued to man static positions to ensure the exclusion of all military forces from the area of separation, and from July the Observer Group Golan set up several temporary observation posts along the cease-fire line with a view to enhancing the Force's situational awareness of the area of separation.

Operational Strength: At 31 July 2013 the mission comprised 1,165 troops and 68 police, supported by 144 international and local civilian personnel (as at 30 June). Military observers of UNTSO's Observer Group Golan help UNDOF in the performance of its tasks, as required.

Finance: The General Assembly appropriation for the operation over the period 1 July 2013–30 June 2014 amounted to US $48.0m.

UNITED NATIONS INTERIM FORCE IN LEBANON—UNIFIL

Address: Naqoura, Lebanon.

Force Commander and Chief of Mission: Maj.-Gen. PAOLO SERRA (Italy).

Maritime Task Force Commander: Rear Admiral JOESE DE ANDRADE BANDEIRA LEANDRO (Brazil).

Establishment and Mandate: UNIFIL was established by UN Security Council Resolution 425 in March 1978, following an invasion of Lebanon by Israeli forces. The force was mandated to confirm the withdrawal of Israeli forces, to restore international peace and security, and to assist the Government of Lebanon in ensuring the return of its effective authority in southern Lebanon. UNIFIL also extended humanitarian assistance, including the provision of food, water, and medical and dental services, to the population of the area, particularly following the second Israeli invasion of Lebanon in 1982. In April 1992, in accordance with its mandate, UNIFIL completed the transfer of part of its zone of operations to the control of the Lebanese army. UN Security Council Resolution 1701, approved in August 2006—following an eruption of conflict in July between the Israeli armed forces and Hezbollah militia—expanded the mission's mandate to include monitoring the cease-fire between the two sides, supporting the deployment of Lebanese troops in southern Lebanon, and facilitating humanitarian activities and safe IDP returns. Resolution 1701 also authorized the establishment of a UNIFIL Maritime Task Force.

Activities, 1998–2005: In March 1998 the Israeli Government announced that it recognized Security Council Resolution 425, requiring the unconditional withdrawal of its forces from southern Lebanon. It stipulated, however, that any withdrawal of its troops must be conditional on receiving security guarantees from the Lebanese authorities. In April 2000 the Israeli Government formally notified the UN Secretary-General of its intention to comply with Security Council Resolution 425. The Security Council endorsed an operational plan to enable UNIFIL to verify the withdrawal. In mid-June the UN Secretary-General confirmed that Israeli forces had fully evacuated from southern Lebanon. UNIFIL, reinforced with additional troops, patrolled the area vacated by the Israeli forces, monitored the line of withdrawal (the so-called Blue Line), undertook de-mining activities, and continued to provide humanitarian assistance. From August the Lebanese Government deployed a Joint Security Force to the area and began re-establishing local administrative structures and reintegrating basic services into the rest of the country. However, the authorities declined to deploy military personnel along the border zone, on the grounds that a comprehensive peace agreement with Israel would first need to be achieved. In November, following two serious violations of the Blue Line in the previous month by both Israeli troops and Hezbollah militia, the Security Council urged the Lebanese Government to take effective control of the whole area vacated by Israel and to assume international responsibilities. In January 2001 the UN Secretary-General reported that UNIFIL no longer exercised control over the area of operation, which remained relatively stable. The Security Council endorsed his proposals to reconfigure the Force in order to focus on its remaining mandate of maintaining and observing the cease-fire along the line of withdrawal; this was completed by the end of 2002. Violations of the Blue Line were reported throughout 2002 and 2003 and, despite restrictions on its movements, UNIFIL increased its patrols. UNIFIL also helped to clear areas of land of anti-personnel devices and to assist the integration of the formerly occupied zone into the rest of the country. In July 2004 UNIFIL representatives with other UN officials, worked to defuse tensions following an alleged Hezbollah sniper attack against Israeli forces and subsequent Israeli violations of Lebanese airspace. At the end of that year the UN expressed concern at further repeated violations of the Blue Line from both sides. A serious breach of the cease-fire occurred in May 2005. In June UNIFIL reported attacks on Israeli troop positions by Hezbollah militia and a forceful response by the Israeli Defence Force. In November UNIFIL brokered a cease-fire following further hostilities across the Blue Line, initiated by Hezbollah; however, there were reports of a missile attack on Israeli positions in the following month. The Security Council subsequently urged all parties to end violations of the Blue Line and for the Lebanese Government to maintain order and exert greater authority throughout its territory.

2006–13: In mid-July 2006 a full-scale conflict erupted between the Israeli armed forces and Hezbollah, following the capture by Hezbollah of two Israeli soldiers, and the killing of three others. An estimated 1,000 Lebanese civilians were killed and 900,000 displaced from their homes during the unrest. A cease-fire between Hezbollah and Israel entered into effect in mid-August, following the adoption by the UN Security Council of Resolution 1701. The provisions of the resolution also demanded 'the immediate cessation by Hezbollah of all attacks and the immediate cessation by Israel of all offensive military operations' in Lebanon; welcomed a recent decision of the Lebanese Government to deploy 15,000 armed troops in southern Lebanon; increased the Force's authorized troop strength to a maximum of 15,000; and expanded its mandate to include monitoring the cease-fire, supporting the Lebanese troop deployment in southern Lebanon, facilitating humanitarian access to civilian communities, and assisting voluntary and safe returns of people displaced by the conflict. Resolution 1701 also (at the request of the Lebanese authorities) established a UNIFIL Maritime Task Force (MTF)—the first naval task force to participate in a UN peace-keeping mission—which was deployed from October to support the Lebanese Navy in monitoring and securing Lebanon's territorial waters and coastline, and preventing the unauthorized entry of arms by sea into Lebanon. In September 2006 a new Strategic Military Cell, reporting to the Under-Secretary-General for Peace-keeping Operations, was established to provide military guidance to UNIFIL. A UN Mine Action Co-ordination Centre of South Lebanon was also established to co-ordinate efforts to locate and destroy unexploded munitions.

In June 2007 six soldiers serving under UNIFIL were killed in a car bomb attack in south-eastern Lebanon. In January 2008 the Security Council condemned an attack on a UNIFIL patrol. In August the Security Council, while authorizing a 12-month extension to the mission's mandate, recognized UNIFIL's contribution to achieving a stable security environment since the 2006 conflict and welcomed an increase in co-ordinated activities between UNIFIL and Lebanese forces. In January 2009 UNIFIL initiated an investigation into evidence that rockets had been fired from Lebanon towards Israel, and others had been discovered ready to fire, and strengthened border patrols. A review of UNIFIL's operational effectiveness was conducted in late 2009; in February 2010 recommendations were issued, on the basis of the review, on means of making the Force in future more task-oriented and flexible. The review also emphasized the need to formalize a mechanism for regular strategic dialogue between UNIFIL and the Lebanese armed forces. In August the Force Commander convened an extraordinary tripartite meeting with senior representatives of the Lebanese Armed Forces and the Israeli Defence Forces, following a violent encounter along the Blue Line.

In February 2011 UNIFIL conducted a large-scale disaster preparedness exercise with the Lebanese Armed Forces in the Tyre area. The UN Security Council strongly condemned a terrorist attack perpetrated against a UNIFIL convoy near Saida in late July, injuring six peace-keepers. At the beginning of August Lebanese and Israeli forces briefly exchanged fire across the Blue Line in the Wazzani River area; UNIFIL subsequently investigated the incident, and made a number of recommendations aimed at preventing a recurrence.

Worsening unrest in Syria during 2012–13 generated insecurity at the Lebanon–Syria border, and led to large numbers of Syrians (numbering around 748,600 by September 2013) seeking shelter on the Lebanese side. Illegal transfers of arms reportedly occurred across the Lebanon–Syria boundary in both directions. In April 2012 the UN Secretary-General urged Lebanon and Syria to delineate fully their common border, and thereby to enhance control of the border. Meanwhile in 2012–13 UNIFIL repeatedly reported and protested Israeli violations of Lebanese airspace—mainly by unmanned vehicles, but occasionally by fighter aircraft. In April 2013 the UN Secretary-General called upon the leadership of Hezbollah (which, in early 2012, had made public acknowledgement of support received by the Iranian authorities) to cease making efforts to acquire weapons and build unilateral paramilitary capabilities.

In 2013 UNIFIL was conducting around 300 patrols daily on foot and in vehicles, as well as regular helicopter patrols of its area of operations, and UNIFIL and the Lebanese armed forces were jointly conducting daily co-ordinated activities, in addition to operating seven checkpoints on the Litani River in southern Lebanon. Joint UNIFIL-Lebanese armed forces activities included capability exercises, training exercises on land and at sea, and counter-rocket-launching operations. UNIFIL was also working to mark visibly the Blue Line, involving the clearance of minefields, measuring co-ordinates, and constructing Blue Line markers. The UNIFIL MTF—operating in September 2013 under the command of Brazil—was continuing to work closely with the Lebanese Navy in training and capacity-building activities, and was continuing to conduct maritime surveillance operations. During October 2006–September 2013 the Task Force hailed some 52,773 vessels and referred 3,717 vessels to the Lebanese authorities for further inspections. UNIFIL's mandate was most recently extended by the UN Security Council by one year, to 31 August 2014.

Operational Strength: At 31 July 2013 the Force comprised 10,585 military personnel; it was supported (at 30 June) by 327 international and 650 local civilian staff. UNIFIL is assisted in its tasks by military observers of the United Nations Truce Supervision Organization (q.v.).

Finance: The General Assembly appropriation for the operation for the period 1 July 2013–30 June 2014 amounted to US $492.6m.

UNITED NATIONS MISSION FOR THE REFERENDUM IN WESTERN SAHARA—MINURSO

Address: el-Aaiún, Western Sahara.

Special Representative of the UN Secretary-General and Chief of Mission: WOLFGANG WEISBROD-WEBER (Germany).

Force Commander: Maj.-Gen. IMAM EDY MULYONO (Indonesia).

Establishment and Mandate: In April 1991 the UN Security Council endorsed the establishment of MINURSO to verify a cease-fire in the disputed territory of Western Sahara, which came into effect in September 1991, and to implement a settlement plan, involving the repatriation of Western Saharan refugees (in co-ordination with UNHCR), the release of all Sahrawi political prisoners, and the organization of a referendum on the future of the territory. Western Sahara is claimed by Morocco, the administering power since 1975, and by the Algerian-supported (and based) Frente Popular para la Liberación de Saguia el Hamra y Río de Oro—Frente Polisario. Although originally envisaged for January 1992, the referendum was postponed indefinitely. IAn operation to compile a satisfactory electoral list was formally initiated in August 1994. In December 1995 the UN Secretary-General reported that the identification of voters had stalled, owing to persistent obstruction of the process on the part of the Moroccan and Frente Polisario authorities. In May 1996 the Security Council suspended the identification process until all sides demonstrate their willingness to co-operate with the mission. The Council decided that MINURSO's operational capacity should be reduced by 20%, with sufficient troops retained to monitor and verify the cease-fire.

Activities, 1997–2000: In 1997 the Secretary-General of the UN appointed James Baker, a former US Secretary of State, as his Personal Envoy to the region to revive efforts to negotiate a resolution to the dispute. Baker obtained the support of Morocco and the Frente Polisario to conduct direct talks; these were initiated in June, in Lisbon, Portugal, under the auspices of the UN, and attended by Algeria and Mauritania in an observer capacity. In September the two sides concluded an agreement which aimed to resolve the outstanding issues of contention, including a commitment by both parties to identify eligible Sahrawi voters on an individual basis, in accordance with the results of the last official census in 1974, and a code of conduct to ensure the impartiality of the poll. In October 1997 the Security Council increased the strength of the mission, to enable it to supervise nine identification centres. The process of voter identification resumed in December, and by September 1998 the initial identification process had been completed. However, the controversial issue of the eligibility of 65,000 members of three Saharan tribal groups remained unresolved. In October the Security Council endorsed a series of measures to advance the referendum, including a strengthened Identification Commission to consider requests from any applicant from the three disputed tribal groups on an individual basis. In November, following a visit to the region by the UN Secretary-General, the Frente Polisario accepted the proposals, and in March 1999 the Moroccan Government signed an agreement with the UN to secure the legal basis of the MINURSO operation. In July the UN published the first part of a provisional list of qualified voters. An appeals process then commenced, in accordance with the settlement plan. In November almost 200 Moroccan prisoners of war were released by the Frente Polisario, following a series of UN-led negotiations. The identification of applicants from the three disputed Saharan tribal groups was completed at the end of December. In January 2000 the second, final part of the provisional list of qualified voters was issued, and a six-week appeals process ensued.

2001–06: In June 2001 the Personal Envoy of the UN Secretary-General elaborated a draft Framework Agreement on the Status of Western Sahara as an alternative to the settlement plan. The draft Agreement envisaged the disputed area remaining part of Morocco, but with substantial devolution of authority. Any referendum would be postponed. The Security Council authorized Baker to discuss the proposals with all concerned parties. However, the Frente Polisario and Algeria rejected the draft Agreement. In November the Security Council, at the insistence of the Frente Polisario, requested the opinion of the UN Legal Counsel regarding the legality of two short-term reconnaissance licences granted by Morocco to international petroleum companies for operation in Western Sahara. In January 2002 the Secretary-General's Personal Envoy visited the region and met with leaders of both sides. He welcomed the release by the Frente Polisario of a further 115 Moroccan prisoners, but urged both sides to release all long-term detainees. In July the Frente Polisario released a further 101 Moroccan prisoners, leaving a total of 1,260 long-term detainees, of whom 816 had been held for more than 20 years. During February–November 2003 the Frente Polisario released 643 more prisoners. Morocco continued to detain 150 Sahrawi prisoners. In January the Secretary-General's Personal Envoy presented to both sides and to the Governments of neighbouring states a new arrangement for a political settlement, providing for self-determination, that had been requested by Resolution 1429 of the Security Council. In July the Frente Polisario accepted the so-called Peace Plan for Self-Determination of the People of Western Sahara. This was, however, rejected by the Moroccan Government in April 2004.

In March 2004 MINURSO co-operated with UNHCR to implement a family visits programme, providing for exchange of contacts of relatives divided by the dispute. MINURSO provided transport and other logistical support for the scheme, which was intended to be part of a series of humanitarian confidence-building measures. James Baker resigned as Personal Envoy of the Secretary-General in June. In September the Special Representative of the UN Secretary-General (SRSG), who had assumed responsibility for pursuing a political solution, held his first series of formal meetings with all parties to the dispute. In April 2005 the Secretary-General advised that MINURSO's force strength be maintained given the lack of progress in negotiating a political settlement. In July the Secretary-General appointed a new Personal Envoy for the Western Sahara, Peter van Walsum, who undertook his first visit to heads of state in the region in October in an attempt to review the 2003 Peace Plan. The Frente Polisario released all remaining Moroccan prisoners in August 2005.

2007–13: In early 2006 Morocco established a Royal Advisory Council for Saharan Affairs that comprised Moroccan political parties and Sahrawi leaders, but not the Frente Polisario. In February a ministerial delegation of the Moroccan Government presented the member states of the Group of Friends of Western Sahara (France, Russia, Spain, the United Kingdom and the USA), as well as Germany and the UN Secretary-General, with the basics of a possible future plan for granting extended autonomy to Western Sahara. Direct talks between representatives of the Moroccan Government and the Frente Polisario, attended by representatives of Algeria and Mauritania, were held in June 2007 under the auspices of the Personal Envoy of the UN Secretary-General in Manhasset, NY, USA. Further negotiations were conducted in August. Both sides were reported to have agreed that the process should continue and that the current status quo in Western Sahara was unacceptable. The third and fourth rounds of discussions between the two sides, held in January and March 2008, respectively, secured further commitment by both sides to continue the process of negotiations. In February 2009 the newly appointed Personal Envoy, Christopher Ross, visited the region for the first time to meet with representatives of the Moroccan Government, Frente Polisario authorities and the Group of Friends. Ross visited the region for a second time in June to prepare for an informal meeting of the main parties. The talks, which were held in Dürnstein, Austria, in August, secured a commitment by the Moroccan Government and the Frente Polisario to continue negotiations as soon as possible. At a second informal meeting, held in Westchester County, NY, USA, in February 2010, both parties agreed once again to continue with negotiations; however, an impasse remained, concerning the issue of self-determination, with the Frente Polisario requesting a referendum for Western Sahara that would present multiple options, including independence, and the Moroccan Government favouring a negotiated autonomy for the area. At the third, fourth and fifth rounds of talks, held, respectively, in November and December 2010, and in January 2011, no significant progress was achieved. In early February 2011 the parties met with UNHCR to review the humanitarian confidence-building measures initiated during 2004. A sixth, seventh and eighth round of negotiations were convened in March. June and July 2011, and again ended in impasse, with each party continuing to reject the other's proposal as the sole basis of future negotiations. Negotiations were renewed in March 2012, at the Greentree Estate, in Manhasset, again without progression. From August 2012–early 2013 the UN Secretary-General undertook a series of visits to mediate between the parties to the conflict, and also to the capitals of the Group of Friends and to Germany and Switzerland, with the aim of strengthening international support for the pursuit of a political settlement. In April 2013 the Security Council extended MINURSO's mandate until 30 April 2014. During 2013 both sides to the conflict raised concerns that ongoing violent unrest in nearby Mali might spill over into the region and might contribute to radicalizing Western Saharan refugee camps.

During March 2012–March 2013, MINURSO conducted 9,214 ground patrols and 589 aerial patrols, including air reconnaissance, while maintaining good communications with the Royal Moroccan Army and the Frente Polisario. During 2013 MINURSO continued to monitor a temporary deployment line comprising 326 observation posts of the Royal Moroccan Army, positioned some 15 km to the west of the 'Berm' (the 2,700 km-long Moroccan-built wall separating the Moroccan- and Frente Polisario-controlled areas).

The mission has headquarters in the north and south of the disputed territory. There are liaison office in Tindouf, Algeria—which was established in order to maintain contact with the Frente Polisario and the Algerian Government—and in Dakhla, Western Sahara. The mission's military component is deployed at nine team sites.

Operational Strength: At 31 July 2013 MINURSO comprised 202 military observers, 27 troops and five police officers; it was supported by 12 UN Volunteers, and (at 30 June) by 94 international and 167 local civilian personnel.

Finance: The General Assembly appropriation to cover the cost of the mission for the period 1 July 2013–30 June 2014 amounted to US $60.5m.

UNITED NATIONS PEACE-KEEPING FORCE IN CYPRUS—UNFICYP

Address: Nicosia, Cyprus.

Special Representative of the UN Secretary-General and Chief of Mission: Lisa M. Buttenheim (USA).

Force Commander: Maj.-Gen. Chao Liu (People's Republic of China).

Establishment and Mandate: UNFICYP was established in March 1964 by a UN Security Council resolution (initially for a three-month duration) to prevent a recurrence of fighting between the Greek and Turkish Cypriot communities, and to contribute to the maintenance of law and order and a return to normal conditions. The Force controls a 180-km buffer zone, established (following the Turkish intervention in 1974) between the cease-fire lines of the Turkish forces and the Cyprus National Guard. It is mandated to investigate and act upon all violations of the cease-fire and buffer zone. The Force also performs humanitarian functions, such as facilitating the supply of electricity and water across the cease-fire lines, and offering emergency medical services. Meanwhile, the UN Secretary-General's good offices have supported the conduct of negotiations between the Greek and Turkish Cypriot leaders.

In October 2004 the Security Council endorsed the recommendations of the Secretary-General's review team, which included a reduction in the mission's authorized strength from 1,230 to 860 military personnel, to include 40 military observers and liaison officers, and an increase in the deployment of civilian police officers from 44 to 69.

Activities, 1997–2008: In July 1997 a series of direct negotiations between the leaders of the two communities was initiated, in the presence of the UN Secretary-General's Special Adviser; however, the talks were suspended at the end of that year. In November 1999 the Greek Cypriot and Turkish Cypriot leaders agreed to participate in proximity negotiations, to be mediated by the UN. Consequently, five rounds of these took place during the period December 1999–November 2000. In January 2002 a new series of direct talks between the leaders of the two communities commenced, under the auspices of the Secretary-General's Special Adviser. In May the Secretary-General visited Cyprus and met the two leaders. Further meetings between the Secretary-General and the two leaders took place in September (in Paris, France) and October (New York, USA). In November he submitted to them for consideration a document providing the basis for a comprehensive settlement agreement; a revised version of the document was released in the following month. A further revised version of the draft settlement plan document was presented to the leaders of the two communities during a visit by the Secretary-General to Cyprus in late February 2003. He urged that both sides put this to separate simultaneous referendums at the end of March, in the hope that, were the settlement plan approved, Cyprus would be able to accede to the European Union (EU) in a reunited state on 1 May 2004. Progress stalled, however, at a meeting between the two sides held in early March 2003 in The Hague, Netherlands. In April the Security Council adopted a resolution calling upon both parties to continue to work towards a settlement using the Secretary-General's plan as the unique basis for future negotiations. In reports to the Security Council the UN Secretary-General has consistently recognized UNFICYP as being indispensable to maintaining calm on the island and to creating the best conditions for his good offices. In November he noted that a number of restrictions placed on UNFICYP's activities during 2000 by the Turkish Cypriot authorities and Turkish forces remained in place. In February 2004 the Greek Cypriot and Turkish Cypriot leaders committed themselves to the Secretary-General's settlement plan. Negotiations on settling outstanding differences were chaired by the Secretary-General's Special Adviser for Cyprus throughout March and a finalized text was presented at the end of that month. The proposed Foundation Agreement was subsequently approved by two-thirds of Turkish Cypriot voters in a referendum held in April, but rejected by some 75% of Greek Cypriot voters. In June the Secretary-General determined to undertake a comprehensive review of UNFICYP's mandate and force levels, in view of the political developments on the island. In November 2004 UNFICYP troops initiated an EU-funded project to remove anti-personnel landmines from the buffer zone separating the two communities. A second phase of the project was launched in August 2005 (and completed in November 2006); it terminated in February 2011, by which time an estimated 27,000 landmines had been removed.

In July 2006 the Turkish Cypriot leader and the Greek Cypriot President meeting under the auspices of the UN Secretary-General, agreed on a set of principles and decisions aimed at reinstating the negotiating process. In September 2007 UNFICYP hosted a second meeting of the leaders of the two communities. They agreed on a need to initiate a settlement process and confirmed that they would continue a bi-communal dialogue under UN auspices. In March 2008 the Special Representative of the UN Secretary-General (SRSG) convened a meeting of the two leaders, who agreed to the establishment of technical committees and working groups in preparation for detailed political negotiations. The leaders also agreed to reopen a crossing between the two communities at Ledra Street, Nicosia. A ceremony to mark the event was held in early April. A second round of discussions was held, at the residence of the SRSG, in May. In July the two leaders agreed in principle on the issue of a single sovereignty and citizenship and initiated a review of the technical committees and working groups.

2008–13: Full negotiations on a political settlement for the island were inaugurated in September 2008, supported by the newly appointed Special Adviser of the UN Secretary-General, Alexander Downer. By August 2009 the two leaders had met 40 times in the preceding 12-month period, discussing issues concerning governance and power sharing, the EU, security and guarantees, territory, property, and economic matters. The second round of full negotiations commenced in September, and by September 2010 a further 44 meetings had been conducted. UNFICYP personnel during that year focused efforts on the maintenance of the military status quo, demining, and the facilitation of civilian activities in the buffer zone. In October the Limnitis/Yesilirmak crossing point was reopened. In November the UN Secretary-General met directly with the two leaders in order to reinvigorate the settlement discussions. A further meeting between the Secretary-General and the leaders of the two communities was convened in January 2011, at which both sides agreed to intensify efforts to reach substantive agreement on outstanding core issues of contention. In July a tripartite meeting of the Secretary-General and the Greek Cypriot and Turkish Cypriot leaders agreed on an intensified schedule of regular negotiations, with enhanced engagement by the UN. In October 2011 and January 2012 further tripartite meetings were held, in Greentree, NY, USA, aimed at assessing progress made in the ongoing negotiations, and at addressing unresolved core issues, especially related to power-sharing, contentious property ownership issues, territory and citizenship. Bilateral meetings continued, in Nicosia, in February–March 2012, but were reported at that time by the UN Secretary-General to be almost deadlocked on outstanding core issues. In April the Special Adviser of the Secretary-General indicated that the UN's participation in negotiations would be reduced to the level of technical-level discussions and confidence-building measures, pending the achievement of significant progress in bilateral discussions between the Greek and Turkish Cypriot leaders. In January 2013 the Security Council urged both communities to continue to pursue negotiations on reunification, to increase the participation of civil society representatives in the negotiations process, and to engage with UNFICYP on the demarcation of a buffer zone. The election in February of Nicos Anastasiades as the new Greek Cypriot leader brought hope of renewed momentum to the negotiations process, and in May the Special Adviser of the UN Secretary-General hosted a meeting between Anastasiades and his Turkish counterpart, Derviş Eroğlu. In July the Council extended the mission's mandate until 31 January 2014.

During the first half of 2013 UNFICYP delivered weekly humanitarian assistance to 347 Greek Cypriots and 124 members of the Roman Catholic Maronite community in northern Cyprus; monitored the functioning of Greek Cypriot schools in the north; addressed legal and humanitarian issues relating to the detention of four Turkish Cypriots in the south and to five Greek Cypriots/Maronites in the north; regularly visited, and facilitated family visits to, inmates at detention facilities in both territories; observed court hearings; and facilitated some 86 events in support of bi-communal co-operation.

Operational Strength: At 31 July 2013 UNFICYP had an operational strength of 922 troops and 68 police officers, supported by 154 international and local civilian staff (as at 30 June).

Finance: The General Assembly appropriated US $56.6m. to the Special Account for UNFICYP to supplement voluntary donations in financing the period 1 July 2013–30 June 2014.

UNITED NATIONS TRUCE SUPERVISION ORGANIZATION—UNTSO

Address: Government House, Jerusalem.

Head of Mission and Chief-of-Staff: Maj.-Gen. MICHEL FINN (Ireland).

Establishment and Mandate: UNTSO was established initially to supervise the truce called by the UN Security Council in Palestine in May 1948 and has assisted in the application of the 1949 Armistice Agreements. Its activities have evolved over the years, in response to developments in the Middle East and in accordance with the relevant resolutions of the Security Council. There is no periodic renewal procedure for UNTSO's mandate.

Activities: UNTSO observers assist UN peace-keeping forces in the Middle East, at present UNIFIL and UNDOF. The mission maintains offices in Beirut, Lebanon and Damascus, Syria. In addition, UNTSO operates a number of outposts in the Sinai region of Egypt to maintain a UN presence there. UNTSO observers have been available at short notice to form the nucleus of new peace-keeping operations.

In July 2006 the UN Secretary-General strongly condemned the killing by Israeli fire of four members of UNTSO who had been supporting UNIFIL during the full-scale conflict that erupted in that month between the Israeli armed forces and Hezbollah.

Military Strength: The operational strength of UNTSO at 31 July 2013 was 149 military observers, supported by 92 international and 136 local civilian staff (as at 30 June).

Finance: UNTSO expenditures are covered by the regular budget of the United Nations. The appropriation for the two-year period 2012–13 was US $70.3m.

United Nations Peace-building

Address: Department of Political Affairs, United Nations, New York, NY 10017, USA.

Telephone: (212) 963-1234; **fax:** (212) 963-4879; **internet:** www.un.org/Depts/dpa.

The Department of Political Affairs provides support and guidance to UN peace-building operations and political missions working in the field to prevent and resolve conflicts or to promote enduring peace in post-conflict societies.

The World Summit of UN heads of state held in September 2005 approved recommendations made by the UN Secretary-General in his March 2005 report entitled *In Larger Freedom: Towards Development, Security and Human Rights for All* for the creation of an intergovernmental advisory Peace-building Commission. In December the UN Security Council and General Assembly authorized the establishment of the Commission; it was inaugurated, as a special subsidiary body of both the Council and Assembly, in June 2006. A multi-year standing peace-building fund, financed by voluntary contributions from member states and mandated to support post-conflict peace-building activities, was established in October 2006. A Peace-building Support Office was established within the UN Secretariat to administer the fund, as well as to support the Commission.

OFFICE OF THE UNITED NATIONS SPECIAL CO-ORDINATOR FOR LEBANON—UNSCOL

Address: UN House, Riad el-Solh Sq., POB 11, 8577 Beirut, Lebanon.

Special Co-ordinator for Lebanon: DEREK PLUMBLY (United Kingdom).

Establishment and Mandate: The Office of the United Nations Special Co-ordinator for Lebanon was established in February 2007, replacing the Office of the Personal Representative of the UN Secretary-General for southern Lebanon (established in August 2000). The Office co-ordinates the UN presence in Lebanon and is the focal point for the core group of donor countries supporting Lebanon. The Office works closely with the expanded UN peace-keeping mission in Lebanon, UNIFIL. The Special Co-ordinator is responsible for supervising implementation of Security Council Resolution 1701, which was adopted in August 2006, and called for a cessation of hostilities in Lebanon.

Operational Strength: At 31 July 2013 UNSCOL comprised 20 international civilian and 61 local civilian personnel.

OFFICE OF THE UNITED NATIONS SPECIAL CO-ORDINATOR FOR THE MIDDLE EAST PEACE PROCESS—UNSCO

Address: Gaza; Jerusalem; Ramallah.

Special Co-ordinator for the Middle East Peace Process: ROBERT R. SERRY (Netherlands).

Establishment and Mandate: The Office of the United Nations Special Co-ordinator for the Middle East (UNSCO) was established in June 1994 after the conclusion of the Declaration of Principles on Interim (Palestinian) Self-Government Arrangements—the Oslo Accord. UNSCO was to seek, during the transition process envisaged by the Declaration, to ensure 'an adequate response to the needs of the Palestinian people and to mobilise financial, technical, economic and other assistance'. In 1995 UNSCO's mandate was reconfigured as the Office of the Special Co-ordinator for the Middle East Peace Process and Personal Representative of the Secretary-General to the Palestine Liberation Organization and the Palestine (National) Authority (PA).

Activities: The Office has been mandated to assist in all issues related to the humanitarian situation confronting the Palestinian people, and supports negotiations and the implementation of political agreements. The Regional Affairs Unit (RAU) of the Office assists in the fulfilment of that part of the Office's mandate that requires it to co-ordinate its work and to co-operate closely with all of the parties to the Middle East peace process, including the Governments of Israel, Lebanon, Syria, Jordan and Egypt, the PA, Palestinian civil society, the Arab League, and individual Arab states that have assumed a key role in facilitating the peace process. The Special Co-ordinator also collaborates closely with key international actors, in particular those that, together with the UN, constitute the Middle East Quartet, i.e. the European Union, Russia and the USA, and serves as the Envoy of the UN Secretary-General to the Quartet. In addition to the RAU, UNSCO maintains a Media Office and a Co-ordination Unit.

Operational Strength: At 31 July 2013 UNSCO comprised 28 international civilian and 30 local civilian personnel.

UNITED NATIONS ASSISTANCE MISSION FOR IRAQ—UNAMI

Address: Amman, Jordan.

Telephone: (6) 5504700; **fax:** (6) 5504705; **e-mail:** unami-information@un.org; **internet:** unami.unmissions.org.

Special Representative of the UN Secretary-General for Iraq: NICKOLAY MLADENOV (Bulgaria).

Deputy Special Representative of the UN Secretary-General for Political, Electoral and Constitutional Support: GYÖRGY BUSZTIN (Hungary).

Deputy Special Representative of the UN Secretary-General for Development and Humanitarian Support: JACQUELINE BADCOCK (United Kingdom).

Establishment and Mandate: The United Nations Assistance Mission for Iraq (UNAMI) was initially established by UN Security Council Resolution 1500 (14 August 2003) as a one-year mission to co-ordinate and support humanitarian efforts in post-conflict Iraq. Later in August, however, terrorist attacks on the UNAMI headquarters in Baghdad killed the newly appointed Special Representative of the UN Secretary-General (SRSG) for Iraq (and UN High Commissioner for Human Rights), Sergio Vieira de Mello, and 21 other UN personnel. UN international staff were subsequently withdrawn from Iraq, and, until the formation of the Iraqi Interim Government at the end of June 2004, UNAMI operated primarily from outside Iraq (from Cyprus, Jordan and Kuwait). Meanwhile, political and security concerns were urgently reviewed by the UN Secretary-General. UNAMI consists of two 'pillars'—political and reconstruction and development—and a Human Rights Office (HRO), which maintains links with the Office of the UN High Commissioner for Human Rights (OHCHR). (The HRO and OHCHR jointly publish reports on the human rights situation in Iraq.) Generally, the work of the political pillar is carried out in support of the good offices and facilitation role of the SRSG. The political office also supports, as necessary, the HRO and the reconstruction and development pillar. In April–May 2004 the UN helped to establish an Independent Electoral Commission of Iraq (IECI). In accordance with the mandate afforded it under UN Security Council Resolution 1546 (June 2004), UNAMI assisted in the convening of an Iraqi national conference in August, including in the selection of a Consultative Council. UNAMI is mandated, under Resolution 1546, 'to promote the protection of human rights, national reconciliation, and judicial and legal reform in order to strengthen the rule of law in Iraq'. Through two units, the HRO monitors and reports on the human rights situation and addresses the reconstruction of Iraqi national human rights institutions. HRO activities include providing technical support and training to the ministries of justice, defence and human rights; the establishment of a national centre for missing and disappeared persons in Iraq; and the establishment of a national human rights institution. UNAMI is also mandated to promote dialogue and effective procedures to resolve disputed international boundaries.

In August 2007 the UN Security Council approved Resolution 1770, which expanded UNAMI's mandate to incorporate a responsibility to promote, support and facilitate the implementation of the International Compact (see under Activities), as well as the co-ordination and delivery of humanitarian assistance, and to support and advise on national reconciliation efforts.

Activities: In January 2005 elections were held in Iraq to form a Transitional National Assembly that would be charged with drafting a permanent constitution, as well as to help establish a Transitional Government and presidency. UNAMI's electoral unit assisted and advised the IECI, which was responsible for the organization and conduct of these elections. From May until October 2005, in response to requests for assistance from the Transitional Government, UNAMI provided support and advice to the constitution-making process. In early 2007 UNAMI facilitated and observed the process of reconfiguring the IECI as the Independent High Electoral Commission (IHEC). UNAMI has continued to assist the IHEC in capacity and institution building and provided technical support during provincial and national legislative elections conducted in 2009–10. In December 2011 the Iraqi authorities requested that UNAMI serve in an impartial advisory capacity in the then ongoing process to select IHEC commissioners; the selection process was completed in September 2012. Provincial elections were held in Iraq, under IHEC auspices, in April and June 2013, and legislative elections were scheduled to be held during 2014. UNAMI participated during 2013 in meetings of the IHEC Board of Commissioners.

With regard to reconstruction and development, UNAMI aims are to address the long-term challenge of achieving sustainable food security; to strengthen the overall quality of education and service delivery at all levels; to support policy development, and preserve and conserve the tangible and intangible Iraqi cultural heritage; to improve the human development situation in Iraq and promote good governance by strengthening institutional capacity, contributing to the creation of employment opportunities and providing policy advice; to support the national health strategy of the Iraqi Ministry of Health in meeting basic health needs; to formulate and implement programmes on institutional/policy reform, capacity building, and service provision necessary to rehabilitate and develop the infrastructure of human settlements, and to support the Iraqi authorities in providing adequate assistance and effective protection to uprooted populations in Iraq, and to assist them in preventing new displacement as well as in achieving durable solutions. UNAMI works closely with other UN agencies, funds and programmes to co-ordinate assistance activities through the UN Country Team for Iraq.

In April 2009 the SRSG presented a report on the disputed internal boundaries of northern Iraq, concluding a year-long process of analysis and consultation. In June the Special Representative launched a Task Force on Dialogue, with senior representatives of the Iraqi Prime Minister and Kurdistan Regional Government to consider the UNAMI report and facilitate further political dialogue.

UNAMI endorsed the International Compact for Iraq, a five-year framework for co-operation between Iraq and the international community jointly chaired by the Iraqi Government and the UN Secretariat, that was launched in May 2007. In August 2008 UNAMI and the Iraqi Government signed a UN Assistance Strategy for Iraq 2008–10, which focused on greater collaboration and co-financing of projects. In May 2010 a new UN Development Assistance Framework was signed by the UN and the Iraqi Government, covering the period 2011–14. The Framework identified as priority areas for UN support inclusive economic growth; environmental management; promoting good governance and protection of human rights; ensuring access to improved basic services for all; and investment in the capacities of women, youth and children to enable their full participation in all aspects of life in Iraq. During 2011–13 UNAMI, with UNHCR, monitored the situation at the Iraq–Syria border, as increasing numbers of refugees crossed into Iraq in flight from the ongoing civil war in Syria. In 2013 UNAMI and UNHCR were continuing to pursue durable solutions for individuals within Iraq with identified international protection needs.

In July 2013 the UN Secretary-General reported that heightening inter-sectarian tensions, demonstrations and unrest were posing a significant threat to stability and security in Iraq; UNAMI, meanwhile, was seeking at that time to create space for and mediate political dialogue. In early September the mission strongly condemned an outbreak of violent unrest at Camp Ashraf, in eastern Iraq, which resulted in the deaths of 52 inmates, and urged the Iraqi authorities to establish forthwith a board of inquiry into the incident. The camp was closed down later in that month.

Operational Strength: At 31 July 2013 UNAMI personnel (based in Iraq, Jordan and Kuwait) comprised 268 troops, four military advisers, and four police officers; they were assisted by 346 international civilian staff and 464 local civilian staff (as at 30 June).

UNITED NATIONS SUPPORT MISSION IN LIBYA—UNSMIL

Address: Tripoli, Libya.

Special Representative of the UN Secretary-General: TAREK MITRI (Lebanon).

Establishment and Mandate: Following the outbreak of conflict in Libya in February 2011, UNSMIL was established in September, for an initial period of three months, with a mandate to support Libya's transitional authorities in restoring public security and the rule of law; promoting inclusive political dialogue and national reconciliation; embarking upon the process of drafting a new constitution and preparing for democratic elections. UNSMIL is also mandated to support the Libyan authorities in extending state authority, through the strengthening of emerging accountable institutions; restoring public services; promoting and protecting human rights (particularly for vulnerable groups); supporting transitional justice; taking the immediate steps required to initiate economic recovery; and co-ordinating support that may be requested from other multilateral and bilateral actors. UNSMIL had not been preceded by a UN peacekeeping mission. In December the UN Security Council extended the mission for a further three month period, and the mission's mandate was further extended, for 12 months, in March 2012: at that time the mandate was modified to include assisting the Libyan authorities to define national needs and priorities; managing the process of democratic transition; promoting the rule of law and monitoring and protecting human rights, particularly those of women and vulnerable groups; restoring public security; countering the illicit proliferation of all arms and related materiel of all types, in particular man-portable surface-to-air missiles; co-ordinating international assistance; and building government capacity across all relevant sectors. In December UNSMIL, the Libyan authorities and UNDP organized a conference on 'Truth and Reconciliation in Libya: the Way Forward'.

Operational Strength: At 31 July 2013 the Office was served by nine police officers and three UN Volunteers, as well as (as at 30 June) by 145 international civilian and 68 local civilian staff members.

United Nations Relief and Works Agency for Palestine Refugees in the Near East—UNRWA

Address: Gamal Abd al-Nasser St, Gaza City.

Telephone: (8) 2887701; **fax:** (8) 2887707.

Address: Bayader Wadi Seer, POB 140157, Amman 11814, Jordan.

Telephone: (6) 5808100; **fax:** (6) 5808335; **e-mail:** unrwa-pio@unrwa.org; **internet:** www.unrwa.org.

UNRWA was established by the UN General Assembly to provide relief, health, education and welfare services for Palestine refugees in the Near East, initially on a short-term basis. UNRWA began operations in May 1950 and, in the absence of a solution to the refugee problem, its mandate has subsequently been extended by the General Assembly.

Organization

(September 2013)

UNRWA employs an international staff of about 120 and more than 24,200 local staff, mainly Palestine refugees. The Commissioner-General is the head of all UNRWA operations and reports directly to the UN General Assembly. UNRWA has no governing body, but its activities are reviewed annually by an Advisory Commission. In November 2005 the UN General Assembly approved an expansion of the Commission from 10 members to 21, reflecting the funding commitments in recent years of the governments concerned. It also authorized the Palestinian authorities, the European Community and the League of Arab States to attend as observers.

Commissioner-General: FILIPPO GRANDI (Italy).

Deputy Commissioner-General: MARGOT B. ELLIS (USA).

FIELD OFFICES

Each field office is headed by a director and has departments responsible for education, health and relief and social services programmes, finance, administration, supply and transport, legal affairs and public information. Operational support officers work in Gaza and the West Bank to monitor and report on the humanitarian situation and facilitate UNRWA field activities.

Gaza: POB 61, Gaza City; Al Azhar Rd, Rimal Quarter, Gaza City; tel. (8) 2887457; fax (8) 2887219; Dir ROBERT TURNER.

Jordan: POB 143464, 11814 Amman; tel. (6) 5809100; fax (6) 5809134; Dir MARTA COLBURN.

Lebanon: POB 11-0947, Beirut 1107 2060; Bir Hassan, Ghobeiri, opp. City Sportive, Beirut; tel. (1) 840490; fax (1) 840466; e-mail lebanon@unrwa.org; Dir ANN DISMORR.

Syria: POB 4313, Damascus; UN Compound, Mezzah Highway/Beirut Rd, Damascus; tel. (11) 6133035; fax (11) 6133047; Dir MICHAEL KINGSLEY-NYINAH.

West Bank: POB 19149, Jerusalem; Sheik Jarrah Qtr, East Jerusalem; tel. (2) 5890400; fax (2) 5322714; Dir FELIPE SANCHEZ.

There are UNRWA liaison offices in Brussels, Belgium (for the European Union); Cairo, Egypt; Geneva, Switzerland; and New York and Washington, DC, USA.

Activities

ASSISTANCE ACTIVITIES

Since 1950 UNRWA has been the main provider of relief, health, education and social services for Palestine refugees in Lebanon, Syria, Jordan, the West Bank and the Gaza Strip. For UNRWA's purposes, a Palestine refugee is one whose normal residence was in Palestine for a minimum of two years before the 1948 conflict and who, as a result of the Arab–Israeli hostilities, lost his or her home and means of livelihood. To be eligible for assistance, a refugee must reside in one of the five areas in which UNRWA operates and be in need. A refugee's descendants who fulfil certain criteria are also eligible for UNRWA assistance. After the renewal of Arab–Israeli hostilities in the Middle East in June 1967, hundreds of thousands of people fled from the fighting and from Israeli-occupied areas to east Jordan, Syria and Egypt. UNRWA provided emergency relief for displaced refugees and was additionally empowered by a UN General Assembly resolution to provide 'humanitarian assistance, as far as practicable, on an emergency basis and as a temporary measure' for those persons other than Palestine refugees who were newly displaced and in urgent need. In practice, UNRWA lacked the funds to aid the other displaced persons and the main burden of supporting them devolved on the Arab governments concerned. The Agency, as requested by the Government of Jordan in 1967 and on that Government's behalf, distributes rations to displaced persons in Jordan who are not registered refugees of 1948. UNRWA's emergency humanitarian support activities for Palestinian refugees include the provision of basic food and medical supplies; the implementation of a programme of emergency workdays, which aims to provide employment and income for labourers with dependants, while improving the local infrastructure; the provision of extra schooling days to make up for those missed because of the conflict, trauma counselling for children, and post-injury rehabilitation; and the reconstruction of shelters. UNRWA undertook a US $52m. emergency relief programme to support Palestinian refugees during 1982–85, following the Israeli invasion of southern Lebanon in June 1982. An expanded programme of assistance was implemented in the West Bank and Gaza during 1987–92 in response to the social and economic consequences of the so-called first Palestinian *intifada* (uprising) against Israel, and Israeli countermeasures. In June 2004 UNRWA and the Swiss Government hosted an international conference, convened in Geneva, with participation by representatives of 67 countries and 34 international organizations, aimed at addressing the humanitarian needs of Palestinian refugees; further to a decision of the conference a Department of Infrastructure and Camp Improvement was established at UNRWA headquarters, to address the deteriorating living conditions in many camps. In recent years diminishing funding has necessitated a retrenchment of the Agency's assistance activities, with the average annual spending per refugee falling by about one-half since 1975.

At 31 December 2012 UNRWA was providing essential services to 4.9m. registered refugees. Of these, about one-third were living in 61 camps serviced by the Agency (of which: 19 were in the West Bank; 15 in Lebanon; 10 in Jordan; nine in Syria; and eight in Gaza), while the remaining refugees had settled in local towns and villages of the host countries. UNRWA's three principal areas of activity are 'Acquired knowledge and skills', 'A long and healthy life', and 'A decent standard of living'. Some 86% of the Agency's 2013 regular budget was devoted to these three operational programmes.

'Acquired knowledge and skills' accounted for 54% of UNRWA's 2013 regular budget. In the 2011/12 school year there were 485,754 pupils enrolled in 699 UNRWA schools, and 19,217 educational staff. UNRWA also operated 10 vocational and teacher-training centres, which provided a total of 6,652 training places, and three other educational sciences faculties. Technical co-operation for the Agency's education programme is provided by UNESCO. During the 2010/11 school year UNRWA was prevented from enrolling some 40,000 eligible children in schools in Gaza as building materials required for the construction of necessary new schools had not been supplied to the territory since 2007. In March 2012 UNRWA convened an international conference in Brussels, Belgium, on the theme 'Engaging Youth: Palestine Refugees in a Changing Middle East', and published a list of 10 'Youth Commitments' through which the Agency was to strengthen its support to young Palestinian refugees. These included: expanding a pilot skills programme; providing enhanced vocational training and micro-finance opportunities; promoting fundraising towards scholarships; and increasing co-operation with global youth initiatives.

'Long and healthy lives' accounted for 19% of UNRWA's 2013 regular budget. At 1 January 2012 there were 138 primary health care units providing outpatient medical care, disease prevention and control, maternal and child health care and family planning services, of which 117 also offered dental care and a further 123 had laboratory services. At that time the number of health staff totalled 3,595. UNRWA also operates a hospital in the West Bank and offers assistance towards emergency and other secondary treatment, mainly through contractual agreements with non-governmental and private hospitals. Technical assistance for the health programme is provided by the World Health Organization. UNRWA offers mental health care to refugees, in particular children, experiencing psychological stress. The Agency aims to provide essential environmental health services. Nearly all camp shelters are connected to water networks, and by January 2012 87% were connected to sewerage networks.

'Decent standard of living' accounted for 13.7% of UNRWA's regular budget for 2013. These services comprise the distribution of food rations, the provision of emergency shelter and the organization of welfare programmes for the poorest refugees (at 1 January 2012 293,718 refugees, or nearly 6% of the total registered refugee population, were eligible to receive special hardship assistance). In 2012 UNRWA provided technical and financial support to 49 women's programme centres and 35 community-based rehabilitation centres.

In order to encourage Palestinian self-reliance the Agency issues grants to ailing businesses and loans to families who qualify as special hardship cases. In 1991 UNRWA launched a micro-finance programme which aims to promote income-generating opportunities for Palestinian refugees as well as to low-income communities living near refugee populations. Under the programme credit and complimentary financial services are extended to small- and micro-business owners, and to households, with the objective of creating sustainable employment, and with a particular focus on empowering women and children. The programme was initiated in the Occupied Territories and was extended to Palestinian refugees in Jordan and Syria in 2003. By January 2012 265,571 loans, with a total estimated value of US $302m., had been awarded under the programme. A report issued by UNRWA in December 2011 found that the rate of unemployment among refugees in Gaza exceeded 33% in that year, one of the highest in the world.

UNRWA Microfinance Department Headquarters: POB 19149, Jerusalem; 21 Zalman Sharagi St, Sheikh Jarrah Qtr, East Jerusalem; tel. (2) 5890221; fax (2) 5890230; the micro-finance programme also operates through national field offices and several local branch offices.

RECENT EMERGENCIES

From the commencement, in the second half of 2000, of the so-called second Palestinian al-Aqsa *intifada*, and Israel's restriction from that time on the issuing of permits to enter or leave Gaza to only medical humanitarian cases, UNRWA became the lead agency with responsibility for the co-ordination and delivery of emergency assistance, as well as for monitoring the immediate needs of the local populations, and launched successive emergency appeals for assistance to Palestinian refugees in Gaza and the West Bank. The UNRWA Commissioner-General repeatedly expressed deep concern at the worsening humanitarian situation in the Palestinian territories, at the demolition of homes in Gaza and the West Bank by Israeli military forces, at the entry restrictions imposed by Israel against the Gaza Strip, which were causing extreme food shortages, and at restrictions on the movements of UN international staff within Gaza, which were severely impeding the Agency's activities. UNRWA repeatedly expressed concern at the construction by Israel, from 2002, of the West Bank security fence, or barrier, which was estimated to affect some 200,000 people through loss of land, water, agricultural resources and education, and hindered UNRWA's ability to provide and distribute humanitarian assistance. UNRWA has continued to monitor closely the construction and impact of the barrier.

Following the victory by the militant Islamic Resistance Movement (Hamas, opposed to any accommodation with Israel) at legislative elections held in the Palestinian Autonomous Territories in January 2006 and the installation of a Hamas-led administration there in March, the European Union (EU) and USA announced that they would withhold direct aid to the Palestinian National Authority (PA), but would increase their contributions to humanitarian organizations engaged in the region. During 2006 UNRWA protested repeatedly that its activities in Gaza were being severely disrupted owing to the constant closure of the Karni crossing between Gaza and Israel. In late August the Agency reported that its operations in Gaza were nearly stalled and that the difficulties with access to the area had resulted in acute shortages of food, fuel and construction supplies. In July of that year UNRWA appealed for US $7.2m. to fund emergency humanitarian assistance for Palestinian refugees based in Lebanon and Syria who had been affected as a consequence of the conflict that erupted in that month between the Israeli armed forces and the militant Shi'a organization Hezbollah. By the end of 2006 UNRWA reported its extreme concern at the socio-economic crisis affecting the Palestinian people, caused partly by the withholding of official donor assistance and ongoing restrictions on access and movement of people and goods. It launched an appeal for $246.2m. in emergency funding, mostly to meet basic humanitarian requirements, in 2007. In July 2007 UNRWA announced that it had suspended all public works rehabilitation and construction projects in Gaza owing to a lack of basic supplies resulting from a land, sea and air blockade imposed since June of that year on the Gaza Strip by Israel and Egypt (strengthening the existing border restrictions).

In May 2007 sectarian violence in northern Lebanon disrupted UNRWA's supply of humanitarian assistance and forced an estimated 27,000 people to leave their homes. In June UNRWA issued a flash appeal for US $12.7m. to meet the immediate needs of the displaced refugees and to improve the conditions at Beddawi camp, which was providing temporary shelter to the majority of those fleeing the fighting. In September UNRWA issued an emergency appeal for northern Lebanon, amounting to $54.8m. for the period 1 September 2007–31 August 2008, to meet the needs of the affected population and to support the rehabilitation of the Nahr el-Bared camp, which had been extensively damaged by the fighting. In mid-2012 around 5,900 families remained displaced from Nahr el-Bared.

In December 2008 UNRWA issued an appeal for more than US $275m. in international donations for 2009 under the UN Consolidated Appeals Process (CAP), in view of the deepening vulnerability of Palestinian refugees affected by the continuing blockade imposed by Israel, entrenched poverty and unprecedented high levels of unemployment. The Agency stated that the dependency of Gaza and the West Bank on external aid had deepened during 2008. In late December, in response to the intensive bombardment of the Gaza Strip by Israeli forces that commenced at that time with the stated aim of ending rocket attacks launched by Hamas and other militant groups on Israeli targets, the UNRWA Commissioner-General expressed horror at the extensive destruction and loss of life caused by the Israeli action and, while recognizing Israel's legitimate security concerns, urged the Israeli military to cease the bombardment and to respect all international conventions regarding the protection of non-combatants in times of conflict to which Israel is a signatory. At the end of December UNRWA launched a flash appeal for $34m. to meet Gaza's urgent humanitarian requirements (including the provision of essential health supplies, food, cash assistance, materials for housing repairs, fuel, and shelter requirements for displaced Palestinian civilians) over a period of four months. Israeli air strikes were reported by UNRWA at that time to have inflicted significant damage to Gaza's fragile infrastructure and to have destroyed its public service capacity. The Agency, which had suspended its food assistance during the second half of December owing to insufficient supplies, demanded that border crossings should be reopened permanently. At the beginning of January 2009 Israeli forces initiated a ground invasion of Gaza.

In early January 2009 the UN Secretary-General urged an immediate cease-fire in Gaza and denounced as unacceptable recent Israeli attacks on three UNRWA-run schools that had resulted in a substantial number of civilian fatalities and injuries. At that time around 25 UNRWA schools were serving as temporary shelters to Palestinians who had been displaced by the ongoing violence. Soon afterwards UNRWA suspended its movements through Gaza (including, once again, food distribution) owing to Israeli air strikes on humanitarian convoys that had caused several fatalities. On 8 January the UN Security Council adopted Resolution 1860 demanding an immediate cease-fire in Gaza, culminating in the full withdrawal of Israeli forces; the unimpeded provision throughout Gaza of food, fuel and medical treatment; improved international arrangements to prevent arms and ammunition smuggling; intra-Palestinian reconciliation; and renewed efforts to achieve a comprehensive long-term peace between Israel and Palestine. In mid-January UNRWA's field headquarters in Gaza was struck and set alight by Israeli shells that reportedly contained incendiary white phosphorus; the UN Secretary-General protested strongly against the attack. On 18 January Israel, while maintaining its positions in Gaza, ceased hostilities; Hamas responded by announcing a week-long cessation of hostilities against Israeli targets, in order to permit Israel to withdraw its armed forces fully from the territory. The Israeli withdrawal was completed on 21 January. By the time of the cease-fire the Israeli offensive had reportedly killed 1,340 people in Gaza (including 460 children and 106 women), and had wounded some 5,320 people (including 1,855 children and 795 women). At the height of the crisis UNRWA provided refuge for 50,896 Palestinians in 50 shelters.

In late January 2009 the UN launched a flash appeal for US $615m. (in addition to its CAP appeal for 2009) to cover the emergency requirements of UNRWA and other aid agencies over a period of six–nine months in supporting civilians in Gaza through the provision of food, water, sanitation, health care and shelter, other basic services, education, psychological care, emergency repairs and rehabilitation, and clearing unexploded ordnance. At that time UNRWA was serving some 900,000 refugees in Gaza, while other civilians were being supported by the WFP. For several days in early February UNRWA suspended the importation of humanitarian supplies into Gaza following the confiscation by the Hamas authorities of deliveries of foodstuffs and blankets. At that time UNRWA's activities in Gaza were also being restricted by the refusal of the Israeli authorities to permit entry into the territory of nylon pellets for making plastic food distribution bags, and paper and exercise books for educational use. In early March the UN Secretary-General appealed to international donors participating in the International Conference on the Palestinian Economy and Gaza Reconstruction, convened in Sharm el-Sheikh, Egypt, for contributions to support and rebuild Gaza. The Secretary-General emphasized at that meeting the importance of maintaining a durable cease-fire, open border crossings into Gaza, and Palestinian reconciliation. In August UNRWA issued a Gaza Ramadan Appeal, requesting an additional $181m. in donations to fund food assistance, shelter improvements, job creation and the rehabilitation of education and health facilities for the poorest and most vulnerable groups of refugees living in Gaza.

In January 2010 UNRWA launched its emergency appeal for that year, amounting to US $323.3m. At the end of May the UNRWA Commissioner-General and the UN Special Co-ordinator for the Middle East Peace Process issued a joint statement strongly condemning an attack perpetrated at that time by Israeli security forces against a flotilla of vessels that was travelling through international waters with the aim of carrying humanitarian aid to Gaza; the Israeli action resulted in the deaths of nine civilians and wounded more than 40 further passengers. The joint statement stressed that such fatalities would be avoidable if Israel were to terminate its blockade of Gaza. In December 2011 UNRWA appealed for $318.2m. in support of its activities in 2012. In January 2012 the UN General Assembly adopted a resolution that urged donor nations to increase contributions to the Agency, in order to address its funding shortfall. UNRWA appealed, in February 2013, for some $300m. to fund its emergency activities during 2013, of which $243.4m. was for Gaza and $55.9m. for the West Bank. Some $78m. was required to fund the supply of food assistance to nearly 75,000 food-insecure Palestinians in the Gaza Strip, while around 250,000 refugees deemed to be surviving below the abject poverty line were to be provided during 2013 with small cash grants, refugee families with children were to be supported in the 2013/14 school year with back-to-school cash assistance, and households whose food security and productive assets had been disrupted by Israeli military operations were to receive tailored cash compensation. Furthermore, some 36,600 cash-for-work positions, both skilled and unskilled, were to be created in 2013. UNRWA identified three strategic priorities for its emergency operations during 2013: preventing further deterioration in food security; protecting and upholding the rights of refugees, including access to services; and ensuring that the Agency maintains sufficient capacity to undertake its emergency interventions.

Following the emergence of civil conflict in Syria from March 2011 the Syrian authorities ceased to provide health services to Palestinian refugees in that country (numbering 499,189 at 31 December 2012), leaving UNRWA as the sole health service provider. In 2013 UNRWA was working to provide essential services and supplies to conflict-affected Palestinian refugees in Syria. In September 2013 529,000 Palestinian refugees remained in Syria, of whom 235,000 were displaced within that country (more than 200,000 were in the Damascus area), and 420,000 were deemed by the Agency to require urgent humanitarian assistance. By September 2013 UNRWA had, since the start of the conflict, provided food and cash assistance to more than 278,000 Syria-based Palestinian refugees; distributed non-food items to 77,000 of the refugees; and supplied some 90,000 family food parcels. During September UNRWA was accommodating around 8,650 displaced people—mainly women and children, 85% of whom were Palestinians—in 21 Agency facilities, such as schools, in Syria. A further 4,030 Palestinian refugees were being shelterd in 14 non-UNRWA facilities. At that time a reduced service of 10 UNRWA health centres and six health points remained operational in Syria, and the Agency was able to open only 49 of a total of its 118 schools in that country at the start, in September, of the 2013/14 school year. UNRWA has monitored movements of Palestinian refugees from Syria into neighbouring Jordan (numbering more than 8,880 by September 2013) and Lebanon (around 45,000), and liaised with local authorities there to ensure that the humanitarian needs of the incoming refugees are met. In June 2013 UNRWA appealed, through its 2013 Syria Humanitarian Response Plan, for US $200m. in assistance until the end of December for emergency activities relating to Palestinian refugees within Syria and for those who had fled from Syria to alternative refuge in Jordan and Lebanon. In mid-June the UNRWA Commissioner-General stated that seven of the 12 camps in Syria accommodating Palestinian refugees had become 'theatres of war', and were frequently inaccessible to UNRWA personnel. The Agency has repeatedly urged the Syrian authorities to afford protection to all civilians, including refugees, to ensure the safety of humanitarian personnel, and to comply with its obligations under international law.

Statistics

REFUGEES REGISTERED WITH UNRWA*
(31 December 2012)

Country	Number	% of total
Jordan	2,034,641	41
Gaza Strip	1,203,135	24
West Bank	741,409	15
Syria	499,189	10
Lebanon	441,543	9
Total	4,919,917	100

* Additionally, UNRWA was providing assistance at 31 December 2012 to some 351,976 eligible other registered persons.

Finance

UNRWA is financed almost entirely by voluntary contributions from governments and the European Union, the remainder being provided by UN bodies, non-governmental organizations, business corporations and private sources, which also contribute to extra-budgetary activities. UNRWA's regular budget for 2012–13, covering recurrent expenditure on sectoral activities, totalled US $1,251m.

Publications

Annual Report of the Commissioner-General of UNRWA.
Reports on labour markets, micro-finance, youth outreach, etc.

World Food Programme—WFP

Address: Via Cesare Giulio Viola 68, Parco dei Medici, 00148 Rome, Italy.

Telephone: (06) 65131; **fax:** (06) 6513-2840; **e-mail:** wfpinfo@wfp.org; **internet:** www.wfp.org.

WFP, the principal food assistance organization of the United Nations, became operational in 1963. It aims to alleviate acute hunger by providing emergency relief following natural or man-made humanitarian disasters, and supplies food assistance to people in developing countries to eradicate chronic undernourishment, to support social development and to promote self-reliant communities.

Organization

(September 2013)

EXECUTIVE BOARD

The governing body of WFP is the Executive Board, comprising 36 members, 18 of whom are elected by the UN Economic and Social Council (ECOSOC) and 18 by the Council of the Food and Agriculture Organization (FAO). The Board meets four times each year at WFP headquarters, in Rome, Italy.

SECRETARIAT

WFP's Executive Director is appointed jointly by the UN Secretary-General and the Director-General of FAO and is responsible for the management and administration of the Programme. Around 90% of WFP staff members work in the field. WFP administers some 87 country offices, in order to provide operational, financial and management support at a more local level, and maintains six regional bureaux, located in Bangkok, Thailand (for Asia), Cairo, Egypt (for the Middle East, Central Asia and Eastern Europe), Panama City, Panama (for Latin America and the Caribbean), Johannesburg, South Africa (for Southern Africa), Kampala, Uganda (for Central and Eastern Africa), and Dakar, Senegal (for West Africa). A Vulnerability Analysis and Mapping (VAM) unit is maintained within the Secretariat.

Executive Director: ERTHARIN COUSIN (USA).

Activities

WFP is the only multilateral organization with a mandate to use food assistance as a resource. It is the second largest source of assistance in the UN, after the World Bank Group, in terms of actual transfers of resources, and the largest source of grant aid in the UN system. WFP handles more than one-third of the world's food assistance. WFP is also the largest contributor to South–South trade within the UN system, through the purchase of food and services from developing countries (at least three-quarters of the food purchased by the Programme originates in developing countries). WFP's mission is to provide food assistance to save lives in refugee and other emergency situations, to improve the nutrition and quality of life of vulnerable groups, and to help to develop assets and promote the self-reliance of poor families and communities. WFP aims to focus its efforts on the world's poorest countries and to provide at least 90% of its total assistance to those designated as 'low-income food-deficit'. During 2012 WFP food assistance, distributed through development projects, emergency operations (EMOPs) and protracted relief and recovery operations (PRROs), benefited some 97.2m. people, including 82.1m. women and children, and 6.5m. internally displaced persons (IDPs), in 80 countries. Total food deliveries in 2012 amounted to 3.5m. metric tons.

WFP rations comprise basic food items (staple foods such as wheat flour or rice; pulses such as lentils and chickpeas; vegetable oil fortified with vitamins A and D; sugar; and iodized salt). Where possible basic rations are complemented with special products designed to improve the nutritional intake of beneficiaries. These include fortified blended foods, principally Corn Soya Blend, containing important micronutrients; Super Cereals; ready-to-use foods, principally peanut-based pastes enriched with vitamins and minerals trade-marked as Plumpy'Doz and Plumpy'Sup, which are better suited to meeting the nutritional needs of young and moderately malnourished children; high energy biscuits, distributed in the first phases of emergencies when cooking facilities may be scarce; micronutrient powder ('sprinkles'), which can be used to fortify home cooking; and compressed food bars, given out during disaster relief operations when the distribution and preparation of local food is not possible. Some 9.8m. children were in receipt of special nutrition support in 2012. The Programme's food donations must meet internationally agreed standards applicable to trade in food products. In May 2003 WFP's Executive Board approved a policy on donations of genetically modified (GM) foods and other foods derived from biotechnology, determining that the Programme would continue to accept donations of GM/biotech food and that, when distributing it, relevant national standards would be respected. It is WFP policy to buy food as near to where it is needed as possible, with a view to saving on transport costs and helping to sustain local economies. From 2008 targeted cash and voucher schemes started to be implemented, as an alternative to food rations. It was envisaged that the cash and voucher approach would reduce the cost to WFP of transporting and storing food supplies, and would also benefit local economies (both being long-term WFP policy objectives). Vouchers are considered to be relatively easy to monitor, and also may be flexibly increased or reduced depending upon the severity of an emergency situation. There were some 6.0m. beneficiaries of cash and voucher programmes in 2012. During 2011 WFP and several corporate partners started to implement pilot schemes in targeted areas in Bangladesh and Indonesia under a new Project Laser Beam (PLB) initiative, aimed at addressing child malnutrition. With other UN agencies, governments, research institutions, and representatives of civil society and of the private sector, WFP supports the Scaling up Nutrition (SUN) initiative, which was initiated in 2009, under the co-ordination of the UN Secretary-General's Special Representative for Food Security and Nutrition, with the aim of increasing the coverage of interventions that improve nutrition during the first 1,000 days of a child's life (such as exclusive breastfeeding, optimal complementary feeding practices, and provision of essential vitamins and minerals); and ensuring that nutrition plans are implemented at national level, and that government programmes take nutrition into account. In 2013 WFP, with FAO, was co-leading global consultations on formulating a post-2015 development framework in the thematic area of food and nutrition.

WFP aims to address the causes of chronic malnourishment, which it identifies as poverty and lack of opportunity. It emphasizes the role played by women (who are most likely to sow, reap, harvest and cook household food) in combating hunger, and endeavours to address the specific nutritional needs of women, to increase their access to food and development resources, and to promote girls' education. WFP estimates that females represent four-fifths of people engaged in farming in Africa and three-fifths of people engaged in farming in Asia, and that globally women are the sole breadwinners in one-third of households. Increasingly WFP distributes food assistance through women, believing that vulnerable children are more likely to be reached in this way. WFP also urges the development of new food assistance strategies as a means of redressing global inequalities and thereby combating the threat of conflict and international terrorism.

The Programme also focuses resources on supporting the nutrition and food security of households and communities affected by HIV/AIDS, and on promoting food security as a means of mitigating extreme poverty and vulnerability and thereby combating the spread and impact of HIV/AIDS. In February 2003 WFP and the Joint UN Programme on HIV/AIDS (UNAIDS) concluded an agreement to address jointly the relationship between HIV/AIDS, regional food shortages and chronic hunger, with a particular focus on Africa, South-East Asia and the Caribbean. In October of that year WFP became a co-sponsor of UNAIDS.

WFP is a participant in the High Level Task Force (HLTF) on the Global Food Security Crisis, which was established by the UN Secretary-General in April 2008 with the aim of addressing the global impact of soaring levels of food and commodity prices, and of formulating a comprehensive framework for action. In January 2009 the HLTF determined to establish a Global Partnership for Agriculture, Food Security and Nutrition. During 2009 the long-standing Committee on World Food Security (CFS), open to member states of WFP, FAO and IFAD, underwent reform, becoming a central component of the new Global Partnership; thereafter the CFS was tasked with influencing hunger elimination programmes at global, regional and national level, taking into account that food security relates not just to agriculture but also to economic access to food, adequate nutrition, social safety nets and human rights. WFP participated in a World Summit on Food Security, organized by FAO, in Rome, in November 2009, which aimed to secure greater coherence in the global governance of food security and set a 'new world food order'. WFP, with FAO, IFAD and other agencies, contributes to the Agriculture Market Information System, established in 2011 to improve transparency in agricultural markets and contribute to stabilizing food price volatility.

WFP, with FAO and IFAD, implements a food security initiative to strengthen feeding programmes and expand support to farmers in developing countries, the second of nine activities that were launched in April 2009 by the UN System Chief Executives Board for Co-ordination (CEB), with the aim of alleviating the impact on poor and vulnerable populations of the developing global economic crisis. WFP also solely leads an initiative on emergency activities to meet humanitarian needs and promote security, the seventh of the CEB activities launched in April 2009.

In June 2008 WFP's Executive Board approved a strategic plan, covering the period 2008–13, that shifted the focus of WFP's activities from the supply of food to the supply of food assistance, and provided a new institutional framework to support vulnerable populations affected by the ongoing global food crisis and by possible future effects of global climate change. The five principal objectives of the 2008–13 plan were saving lives and protecting livelihoods in emergencies; preparing for emergencies; restoring and rebuilding lives after emergencies; reducing chronic hunger and undernutrition everywhere; and strengthening the capacity of countries to reduce hunger. The plan emphasized prevention of hunger through early warning systems and analysis; local purchase of food; the maintenance of efficient and effective emergency response systems; and the use of focused cash and voucher programmes (including electronic vouchers) to ensure the accessibility to vulnerable people in urban environments of food that was locally available but, owing to the high level of market prices and increasing unemployment, beyond their financial means. A draft new strategic plan, to cover the period 2014–17, was under consideration in 2013.

WFP has developed a range of mechanisms to enhance its preparedness for emergency situations (such as conflict, drought and other natural disasters) and to improve its capacity for responding effectively to crises as they arise. Through its Vulnerability Analysis and Mapping (VAM) project, WFP aims to identify potentially vulnerable groups by providing information on food security and the capacity of different groups for coping with shortages, and to enhance emergency contingency-planning and long-term assistance objectives. VAM—co-ordinated from a dedicated unit at the WFP Secretariat in Rome, and also comprising, in 2013, VAM Programme Advisers in each regional office, and 14 full-time country officers—produces food security analysis reports, guidelines, reference documents and maps. In 2011 VAM launched an online Food and Commodity Price Data Store relating to data on the most commonly consumed staples in 1,070 markets in 68 countries. The key elements of WFP's emergency response capacity are its strategic stores of food and logistics equipment (drawn from 'stocks afloat': ships loaded with WFP food supplies that can be re-routed to assist in crisis situations; development project stocks redesignated as emergency project contingency reserves; and in-country borrowing from national food reserves enabled by bilateral agreements); stand-by arrangements to enable the rapid deployment of personnel, communications and other essential equipment; and the Augmented Logistics Intervention Team for Emergencies (ALITE), which undertakes capacity assessments and contingency-planning. When engaging in a crisis WFP dispatches an emergency preparedness team to quantify the amount and type of food assistance required, and to identify the beneficiaries of and the timescale and logistics (e.g. means of transportation; location of humanitarian corridors, if necessary; and designated food distribution sites, such as refugee camps, other emergency shelters and therapeutic feeding centres) underpinning the ensuing EMOP. Once the EMOP has been drafted, WFP launches an appeal to the international donor community for funds and assistance to enable its implementation. WFP special operations are short-term logistics and infrastructure projects that are undertaken to facilitate the movement of food aid, regardless of whether the food is provided by the Agency itself. Special operations typically complement EMOPs or longer rehabilitation projects.

During 2000 WFP led efforts, undertaken with other UN humanitarian agencies, for the design and application of local UN Joint Logistics Centre facilities, aimed at co-ordinating resources in an emergency situation. In 2001 a UN Humanitarian Response Depot was opened in Brindisi, Italy, under the direction of WFP experts, for the storage of essential rapid response equipment. In that year the Programme published a set of guidelines on contingency planning. Since 2003 WFP has been mandated to provide aviation transport services to the wider humanitarian community. During 2005 the UN's Inter-Agency Standing Committee (IASC), concerned with co-ordinating the international response to humanitarian disasters, developed a concept of organizing agency assistance to IDPs through the institutionalization of a 'Cluster Approach', currently comprising 11 core areas of activity. WFP was designated the lead agency for the clusters on Emergency Telecommunications (jointly with the Office for the Co-ordination of Humanitarian Affairs and UNICEF) and Logistics. A new cluster on Food Security, established in 2011, is led jointly by WFP and FAO, and aims to combine expertise in food aid and agricultural assistance in order to boost food security and to improve the resilience of food-insecure disaster-affected communities.

WFP aims to link its relief and development activities to provide a continuum between short-term relief and longer-term rehabilitation and development. In order to achieve this objective, WFP aims to promote capacity-building elements within relief operations, e.g. training, income-generating activities and environmental protection measures; and to integrate elements that strengthen disaster mitigation into development projects, including soil conservation, reafforestation, irrigation infrastructure, and transport construction and rehabilitation. In all its projects WFP aims to assist the most vulnerable groups (such as nursing mothers and children) and to ensure that beneficiaries have an adequate and balanced diet. Through its development activities, WFP aims to alleviate poverty in developing countries by promoting self-reliant families and communities. No individual country is permitted to receive more than 10% of the Programme's available development resources. WFP's Food-for-Assets development operations pay workers living in poverty with food in return for participation in self-help schemes and labour-intensive projects, with the aim of enabling vulnerable households and communities to focus time and resources on investing in lasting assets with which to raise themselves out of poverty (rather than on day-to-day survival). Food-for-Assets projects provide training in new techniques for achieving improved food security (such as training in new agricultural skills or in the establishment of home gardening businesses); and include, for example, building new irrigation or terracing infrastructures; soil and water conservation activities; and allocating food rations to villagers to enable them to devote time to building schools and clinics. In areas undermined by conflict WFP offers food assistance as an incentive for former combatants to put down their weapons and learn new skills. In 2012 some 15.1m. people were in receipt of food from WFP as an incentive to build assets, attend training, strengthen resilience to shocks and preserve livelihoods. WFP focuses on providing good nutrition for the first 1,000 days of life, from the womb to two years of age, in order to lay the foundations for a healthy childhood and adulthood. WFP's '1,000 days plus' approach supports children over the age of two through school feeding activities, which aim to expand educational opportunities for poor children (given that it is difficult for children to concentrate on studies without adequate food and nutrition, and that food-insecure households frequently have to choose between educating their children or making them work to help the family to survive), and to improve the quality of the teaching environment. During 2012 school feeding projects benefited 24.7m. children. As an incentive to promote the education of vulnerable children, including orphans and children with HIV/AIDS, and to encourage families to send their daughters to school, WFP also implements 'take-home ration' projects, under which it provides basic food items to certain households, usually including sacks of rice and cans of cooking oil. WFP's Purchase for Progress (P4P) programme, launched in September 2008, expands the Programme's long-term 'local procurement' policy, enabling smallholder and low-income farmers in developing countries to supply food to WFP's global assistance operations. Under P4P farmers are taught techniques and provided with tools to enable them to compete competitively in the market-place. P4P also aims to identify and test specific successful local practices that could be replicated to benefit small-scale farmers on a wider scale. During 2008–13 P4P initiatives were initiated in 21 countries, in Africa, Latin America and Asia. By 2013 WFP had established links under P4P with more than 1,000 farmers' organizations representing more than 1.1m. farmers world-wide. In September 2009 WFP, the Global Alliance for Improved Nutrition and other partners launched Project Laser Beam (PLB), a five-year public-private partnership aimed at eradicating eradicating child malnutrition; PLB initially undertook pilot projects in Bangladesh and India.

Since 1999 WFP has been implementing PRROs, where the emphasis is on fostering stability, rehabilitation and long-term development for victims of natural disasters, displaced persons and refugees. PRROs are introduced no later than 18 months after the initial EMOP and last no more than three years. When undertaken in collaboration with UNHCR and other international agencies, WFP has responsibility for mobilizing basic food commodities and for related transport, handling and storage costs.

In 2013 WFP operational expenditure in the Middle East, North Africa, Eastern Europe and Central Asia was (subject to subsequent re-assessments and excluding costs that might be incurred in respect of emerging crises) forecast at US $1,381.9m. (some 25% of total expenditure in that year); this was to assist some 14.6m beneficiaries.

During July 2012–December 2013 an EMOP, costing US $510m., was being implemented—in conjunction with the UNHCR-led UN inter-agency Syria Regional Response Plan—to provide food assistance to vulnerable Syrians sheltering from protracted conflict in their native country in nearby Egypt, Iraq, Jordan, Lebanon and Turkey. Beneficiaries of the EMOP were given vouchers to purchase food items from local markets, with a view to supporting local economies. In September 2013 WFP distributed food vouchers to Syrian refugees sheltering in the large Za'atri camp in Jordan, enabling them to select food items, including fresh produce, from designated camp shops. A Joint Rapid Food Security Needs Assessment on Syria, conducted in June 2012 by WFP, FAO and the Syrian Government, found that by that time nearly 3m. Syrians were in need of food, crops and livestock assistance. It was reported that significant damage had occurred to crops (including wheat and barley cultivation, cherry and olive trees, and vegetable production), and that working conditions for farmers had deteriorated, compounded by increasing unavailability of labour, rises in fuel costs, and power cuts that were restricting water supply. During October 2011–December 2013 WFP was undertaking a $525.9m. EMOP to assist people affected by the violent unrest within Syria, through the distribution of supplementary food rations covering (from January 2013) 80% of daily energy requirements. In January 2013 the Syrian Arab Red Crescent reported that some 4m. people in Syria were in need of assistance, causing the UN immediately to declare the crisis a system-wide 'Level Three' emergency. Accordingly, during 2013 WFP was progressively increasing the number of target beneficiaries of the EMOP from 2.5m. at the start of the year to 4m. from October. WFP was, however, only able to reach 2.4m. beneficiaries within Syria in August, owing to logistical difficulties and intensifying unrest; the Agency was co-ordinating with other agencies, including UNHCR and the Red Cross, to facilitate rapid relief transport and delivery capabilities in Syria. An immediate response EMOP to provide food assistance to people affected by intensification of civil unrest was initiated in December 2012, following air strikes and shellings against densely populated areas of the Syrian capital, Damascus; the operation was targeted at 25,000 families. An EMOP to assist 150,000 Iraqi refugees in Syria was undertaken during May 2010–March 2012, but, owing to limited resources, WFP terminated the operation, and from April 2012 responsibility for feeding Iraqi refugees in Syria was transferred to UNHCR.

From 1 January 2012–31 December 2013 WFP was implementing a US $95m. EMOP to provide food assistance to the non-refugee population of the Gaza Strip (numbering 542,600 people). A PRRO targeting food assistance in support of destitute and marginalized groups in the West Bank was under way during 1 January 2011–31 December 2013; the $152m. scheme was to help some 454,500 beneficiaries annually, focusing on meeting immediate food needs, enhancing food consumption, and improving dietary diversity, and aimed to promote long-term resilience by supporting the re-establishment of agricultural livelihoods in conflict-affected areas. An electronic food voucher system implemented by WFP in the Palestinian territories during 2010 assisted 32,000 people in the West Bank and more than 15,000 in Gaza; the vouchers could be spent in selected shops, thereby also benefiting local shop-owners and food producers. WFP was implementing an EMOP in Yemen during 2013 to provide emergency food and nutrition support to some 4.9m. food-insecure and conflict-affected people, at a total cost to WFP of $242m. A survey produced in March 2012 by WFP—in conjunction with UNICEF and the Yemen authorities—on the food situation in that country, reported that levels of hunger had doubled since 2009. A PRRO was being undertaken in that country during 1 January 2013–31 December 2014 aimed at providing food assistance to 131,000 refugees sheltering there.

In response to the outbreak of conflict in Libya from mid-February 2011, WFP launched a US $4m. operation to augment and co-ordinate logistics and emergency telecommunications in that country. In mid-April WFP announced that it had opened a humanitarian corridor for the transportation of food and other assistance to communities in western areas of the country, which had hitherto been isolated by heavy fighting. A $121.6m. emergency operation aimed at supplying food aid to vulnerable populations affected by the conflict in Libya, and in Egypt and Tunisia (which had also been affected by violent unrest in early 2011), was implemented during March 2011–February 2012.

Finance

The Programme is funded by voluntary contributions from donor countries, intergovernmental bodies such as the European Commission, and the private sector. Contributions are made in the form of commodities, finance and services (particularly shipping). Commitments to the International Emergency Food Reserve (IEFR), from which WFP provides the majority of its food supplies, and to the Immediate Response Account of the IEFR (IRA), are also made on a voluntary basis by donors. WFP's projected expenditure for 2013 amounted to some US $5,533.3m., which was to assist some 74.6m. beneficiaries.

Publications

Food and Nutrition Handbook.

School Feeding Handbook.

State of Food Insecurity in the World (annually, with FAO and IFAD).

World Hunger Series.

Year in Review.

Food and Agriculture Organization of the United Nations—FAO

Address: Viale delle Terme di Caracalla, 00100 Rome, Italy.

Telephone: (06) 5705-1; **fax:** (06) 5705-3152; **e-mail:** fao-hq@fao.org; **internet:** www.fao.org.

FAO, the first specialized agency of the UN to be founded after the Second World War, aims to achieve food security for all, and serves as a co-ordinating agency for development programmes in the whole range of food and agriculture, including forestry and fisheries. It helps developing countries to promote educational and training facilities and to create appropriate institutions.

Organization

(September 2013)

CONFERENCE

The governing body is the FAO Conference of member nations. It meets every two years, formulates policy, determines the organization's programme and budget on a biennial basis, and elects new members. It also elects the Director-General of the Secretariat and the Independent Chairman of the Council. Regional conferences are also held each year.

COUNCIL

The FAO Council is composed of representatives of 49 member nations, elected by the Conference for rotating three-year terms. It is the interim governing body of FAO between sessions of the Conference, and normally holds at least five sessions in each biennium. There are eight main Governing Committees of the Council: the Finance, Programme, and Constitutional and Legal Matters Committees, and the Committees on Commodity Problems, Fisheries, Agriculture, Forestry, and World Food Security.

HEADQUARTERS

At 1 July 2012 there were 1,847 FAO professional staff and 1,729 support staff, of whom about 55% were based at headquarters in Rome, Italy. FAO maintains five regional offices (see below), 10 sub-regional offices, five liaison offices (in Yokohama, Japan; Washington, DC, USA; Geneva, Switzerland, and New York, USA: liaison with the UN; and Brussels, Belgium: liaison with the European Union), and more than 130 country offices. The Office of the Director-General includes the Office of Evaluation; Office of the Inspector-General; Legal Office; Ethics Office; Office for Communication, Partnerships and Advocacy; and Office of Strategy, Planning and Resources Management. Work is undertaken by the following departments: Agriculture and Consumer Protection; Economic and Social Development; Fisheries and Aquaculture; Forestry; Natural Resources Management and Environment; Corporate Services, Human Resources and Finance; and Technical Co-operation.

Director-General: Dr José Graziano da Silva (Brazil).

REGIONAL OFFICES

Near East: 11 El-Eslah el-Zerai St, Dokki, POB 2223, Cairo, Egypt; tel. (2) 3316000; fax (2) 7495981; e-mail fao-rne@fao.org; internet www.fao.org/world/Regional/RNE/index_en.htm; a biennial Regional Conference for the Near East (NERC) is convened (most recently in May 2012, in Rome, Italy); Regional Rep. Abdessalam Ould Ahmed.

Sub-regional Office for Central Asia: Ivedik Cad. 55, 06170 Yenimahalle, Ankara, Turkey; tel. (312) 307-9500; fax (312) 307-

1705; e-mail FAO-SEC@fao.org; internet www.fao.org/europe/sec/en/; Sub-regional Rep. MUSTAPHA SINACEUR.

Sub-regional Office for North Africa: BP 300, Tunis, Tunisia; tel. (1) 847553; fax (1) 791859; e-mail fao-snea@fao.org; internet www.fao.org/world/subregional/snea; Sub-regional Rep. BENOÎT HOREMANS.

Sub-regional Office for the Gulf Cooperation Council States and Yemen: POB 62072, Abu Dhabi, United Arab Emirates; tel. (2) 6586774; e-mail FAO-SNG@fao.org; Sub-Regional Rep. ABDU GASEM AL-SHAREEF AL-ASSIRI.

Activities

In pursuit of its objectives of raising levels of nutrition, improving the production and distribution of food and other commodities derived from farms, fisheries and forests, ameliorating the lives of rural populations, and achieving global food security, FAO focuses on four priority areas of activity: serving as a knowledge network; sharing policy expertise; providing a neutral forum for nations; and bringing knowledge directly to the field. World Food Day, commemorating the foundation of FAO, is held annually on 16 October.

ECONOMIC AND SOCIAL DEVELOPMENT

The Economic and Social Development Department comprises divisions of Agricultural Development; Economics; Statistics; Trade and Markets; and Gender, Equity and Rural Employment. The Department's priority areas of focus are: the world food situation; investment in agriculture; long-term perspectives in agriculture; gender right to food; and food volatility in agricultural markets.

FAO provides a focal point for economic research and policy analysis relating to food security and sustainable development. Participants in the World Food Summit, convened under FAO auspices in November 1996, approved the Rome Declaration on World Food Security and the World Food Summit Plan of Action, with the aim of halving the number of people then afflicted by undernutrition, no later than 2015; this objective was subsequently incorporated into a long-term Strategic Framework for the period 2000–15 that was approved by the FAO Conference in November 1999, and also into the UN Millennium Development Goals (MDGs, adopted in 2000 by UN heads of state and government). The commitment was further reaffirmed by World Food Summit: Five Years Later, held in June 2002 to review the 1996 conference.

With a view to countering an escalation from 2006 in commodity prices, FAO launched, in October 2007, an online Global Forum on Food Security and Nutrition; and inaugurated, in December of that year, an Initiative on Soaring Food Prices, which sought to boost food production in low-income developing countries by improving smallholders' access to agricultural supplies. In April 2008 the UN Secretary-General appointed FAO's Director-General as Vice-Chairman of a High Level Task Force on the Global Food Security Crisis, which aimed to address the impact of the still soaring levels of food and fuel prices and formulate a comprehensive framework for action. A High Level Conference on World Food Security and the Challenges of Climate Change and Bioenergy that was hosted in June by FAO adopted a Declaration on Food Security, urging the international donor community to increase investment in rural development, agriculture and agribusiness in developing countries and countries with economies in transition. In January 2009 a follow-up high-level meeting, convened in Madrid, Spain, agreed to initiate a consultation process with regard to the establishment of a Global Partnership for Agriculture, Food Security and Nutrition to strengthen international co-ordination and governance for food security. During 2009 the long-standing Committee on World Food Security (CFS), open to member states of FAO, the World Food Programme (WFP) and the International Fund for Agricultural Development (IFAD), underwent reform, becoming a central component of the new Global Partnership; thereafter the CFS was tasked with influencing hunger elimination programmes at global, regional and national level, taking into account that food security relates not just to agriculture but also to economic access to food, adequate nutrition, social safety nets and human rights. The CFS appoints the steering committee of the High Level Panel of Experts on Food Security and Nutrition, established in October 2009. In July of that year the FAO Director-General welcomed the Food Security Initiative—with commitments of US $20,000m.—approved in that month by leaders of the Group of Eight (G8) industrialized nations. In November FAO organized a World Summit on Food Security, in Rome, which adopted the Five Rome Principles for Sustainable Global Food Security: (i) investment in country-owned plans aimed at channelling resources to efficient results-based programmes and partnerships; (ii) fostering strategic co-ordination at the national, regional and global level to improve governance, promote better allocation of resources, avoid duplication of efforts and identify response gaps; (iii) striving for a comprehensive twin-track approach to food security comprising direct action to combat hunger in the most vulnerable, and also medium- and long-term sustainable agricultural, food security, nutrition and rural development programmes to eliminate the root causes of hunger and poverty, including through the progressive realization of the right to adequate food; (iv) ensuring a strong role for the multilateral system by sustained improvements in efficiency, responsiveness, co-ordination and effectiveness of multilateral institutions; and (v) ensuring sustained and substantial commitment by all partners to investment in agriculture and food security and nutrition, with provision of necessary resources in a timely and reliable fashion, aimed at multi-year plans and programmes.

FAO, with WFP and IFAD, leads an initiative to strengthen feeding programmes and expand support to farmers in developing countries, the second of nine activities that were launched in April 2009 by the UN System Chief Executives Board for Co-ordination (CEB), with the aim of alleviating the impact on poor and vulnerable populations of the developing global economic crisis. In May 2010 FAO launched an online petition entitled the *1billionhungry project*, with the aim of raising awareness of the plight of people world-wide suffering from chronic hunger. In May 2012 the CFS endorsed a set of landmark Voluntary Guidelines on the Responsible Governance of Tenure of Land, Fisheries and Forests in the Context of National Food Security, with the aim of supporting governments in safeguarding the rights of citizens to own or have access to natural resources. The FAO Director-General welcomed a new 'Zero Hunger Challenge' initiative announced by the UN Secretary-General in the following month, which aimed to eliminate malnutrition through measures such as boosting the productivity of smallholders, creating sustainable food systems, and reducing food wastage. In January 2013 FAO and the International Finance Corporation signed a Memorandum of Understanding (MOU) jointly to promote responsible private investment in agribusiness, and to promote the development of economic opportunities for rural communities.

In February 2011 FAO's Food Price Index recorded the highest levels of global food prices since 1990 (reaching 238 points). In June agriculture ministers from G20 countries adopted an action plan aimed at stabilizing food price volatility and agriculture, with a focus on improving international policy co-ordination and agricultural production; promoting targeted emergency humanitarian food reserves; and developing, under FAO auspices, an Agricultural Market Information System (AMIS) to improve market transparency and help stabilize food price volatility. FAO maintains, additionally to the Food Price Index—which averaged 201.8 points in August 2013—price indices for cereal, dairy, oils and fats, meat, and sugar.

The 2012 edition of the joint FAO-IFAD-WFP annual *State of Food Insecurity in the World* report, released in October, found that nearly 870m. people globally were suffering from chronic malnutrition, some 852m. of whom resided in developing countries in Asia and Africa. The report maintained that support for economic development, including smallholder agricultural growth, should be promoted alongside safety nets for the very vulnerable; and that a higher priority should be given to quality nutrition, to reduce the occurrence of obesity and non-communicable diseases. In 2013 FAO, with WFP, was co-leading global consultations on formulating a post-2015 development framework in the thematic area of food and nutrition.

FAO produces studies and reports on agricultural development, the impact of development programmes and projects, and the world food situation, as well as on commodity prices, trade and medium-term projections. It supports the development of methodologies and guidelines to improve research into food and agriculture and the integration of wider concepts, such as social welfare, environmental factors and nutrition, into research projects. In November 2004 the FAO Council adopted a set of voluntary Right to Food Guidelines, and established a dedicated administrative unit, that aimed to 'support the progressive realization of the right to adequate food in the context of national food security' by providing practical guidance to countries in support of their efforts to achieve the 1996 World Food Summit commitment and MDG relating to hunger reduction. FAO's Statistical Division assembles, analyses and disseminates statistical data on world food and agriculture and aims to ensure the consistency, broad coverage and quality of available data. The Division advises member countries on enhancing their statistical capabilities. It maintains FAOSTAT (accessible at faostat.fao.org) as a core database of statistical information relating to nutrition, fisheries, forestry, food production, land use, population, etc. In 2004 FAO developed a new statistical framework, CountrySTAT, to provide for the organization and integration of statistical data and metadata from sources within a particular country. By 2013 CountrySTAT systems had been developed in 27 developing countries. FAO's internet-based interactive World Agricultural Information Centre (WAICENT) offers access to agricultural publications, technical documentation, codes of conduct, data, statistics and multimedia resources. FAO compiles and co-ordinates an extensive range of international databases on agriculture, fisheries, forestry, food and statistics, the most important of these being AGRIS (the International Information System for the Agricultural Sciences and

Technology) and CARIS (the Current Agricultural Research Information System). In June 2000 FAO organized a high-level Consultation on Agricultural Information Management (COAIM), which aimed to increase access to and use of agricultural information by policy-makers and others. The second COAIM was held in September 2002 and the third meeting was convened in June 2007.

In 1999 FAO signed an MOU with UNAIDS on strengthening co-operation to combat the threat posed by the HIV/AIDS epidemic to food security, nutrition and rural livelihoods. FAO is committed to incorporating HIV/AIDS into food security and livelihood projects, to strengthening community care and to highlighting the importance of nutrition in the care of those living with HIV/AIDS.

FAO's Special Programme for Food Security (SPFS), initiated in 1994, assists low-income countries with a food deficit to increase food production and productivity as rapidly as possible, primarily through the widespread adoption by farmers of improved production technologies, with emphasis on areas of high potential. Under the Programme, which promotes South-South co-operation, some 40 bilateral co-operation agreements are in effect. In 2013 some 62 countries were categorized formally as 'low-income food-deficit'.

FAO's Global Information and Early Warning System (GIEWS), which become operational in 1975, monitors and maintains a database on the crop and food outlook at the global, regional, national and sub-national level in order to detect emerging food supply difficulties and disasters and to ensure rapid intervention in countries experiencing food supply shortages. It publishes regular reports on the weather conditions and crop prospects in sub-Saharan Africa and in the Sahel region, issues special alerts which describe the situation in countries or sub-regions experiencing food difficulties, and recommends an appropriate international response. The publication *Crop Prospects and Food Situation* reviews the global situation, and provides regional updates and a special focus on countries experiencing food crises and requiring external assistance, on a quarterly basis. *Food Outlook*, issued in June and November, analyses developments in global food and animal feed markets.

In March 2012 GIEWS published a special report on the food production situation in Syria; the report recommended—in view of ongoing violent conflict in that country—that the food security situation should be closely monitored and that a detailed assessment of requirements should be drafted.

AGRICULTURE AND CONSUMER PROTECTION

The Department of Agriculture and Consumer Protection comprises the following divisions: Animal Production and Health; Food Safety and Quality; Plant Production and Protection; Rural Infrastructure and Agro-Industries; and the Joint FAO/IAEA Division of Nuclear Techniques in Food and Agriculture.

FAO is concerned to improve crop and grassland and pasture productivity and to develop sustainable agricultural systems. It provides member countries with technical advice for plant improvement, the application of plant biotechnology, the development of integrated production systems and rational grassland management. There are groups concerned with the main field cereal crops, i.e. rice, maize and wheat, which *inter alia* identify means of enhancing production, collect and analyse relevant data and promote collaboration between research institutions, government bodies and other farm management organizations. In 1985 and 1990 FAO's International Rice Commission endorsed the use of hybrid rice, which had been developed in the People's Republic of China, as a means of meeting growing demand for the crop, in particular in the Far East, and it has subsequently assisted member countries to acquire the necessary technology and training to develop hybrid rice production. In Africa FAO has collaborated with the West African Rice Development Association to promote and facilitate the use of new rice varieties and crop management practices. FAO actively promotes the concept of Conservation Agriculture, which aims to minimize the need for mechanical soil tillage or additional farming resources and to reduce soil degradation and erosion.

FAO is also concerned with the development and diversification of horticultural and industrial crops, for example oil seeds, fibres and medicinal plants. FAO collects and disseminates data regarding crop trials and new technologies. It has developed an information processing site, Ecocrop, to help farmers identify appropriate crops and environmental requirements.

FAO's plant protection service incorporates a range of programmes concerned with the control of pests and the use of pesticides. Negotiations initiated in 1996 under the auspices of FAO and the UN Environment Programme (UNEP) culminated in September 1998 in the adoption of the Rotterdam Convention on the Prior Informed Consent Procedure for Certain Hazardous Chemicals and Pesticides in International Trade, which required that hazardous chemicals and pesticides banned or severely restricted in at least two countries should not be exported unless explicitly agreed by the importing country. The treaty entered into force in February 2004. In November 2002 FAO launched a revised International Code of Conduct on the Distribution and Use of Pesticides (first adopted in 1985) to reduce the inappropriate distribution and use of pesticides and other toxic compounds, particularly in developing countries. FAO co-operates with UNEP to provide secretariat services for the Convention. FAO has promoted the use of Integrated Pest Management (IPM) initiatives to encourage the use, at the local level, of safer and more effective methods of pest control, such as biological control methods and natural predators.

FAO hosts the secretariat of the International Plant Protection Convention (first adopted in 1951, revised in 1997) which aims to prevent the spread of plant pests and to promote effective control measures. The secretariat helps to define phytosanitary standards, promote the exchange of information and extend technical assistance to contracting parties (179 at September 2013).

FAO's Animal Production and Health Division is concerned with the control and management of major animal diseases, and, in recent years, with safeguarding humans from livestock diseases. Other programmes are concerned with the contribution of livestock to poverty alleviation, the efficient use of natural resources in livestock production, the management of animal genetic resources, promoting the exchange of information and mapping the distribution of livestock around the world. During 2001–10 FAO implemented a Pro-Poor Livestock Policy Initiative to support the formulation and implementation of livestock-related policies to improve the livelihood and nutrition of the world's rural poor.

The Emergency Prevention System for Transboundary Animal and Plant Pests and Diseases (EMPRES) was established in 1994 to strengthen FAO's activities in the prevention, early warning, control and, where possible, eradication of pests and highly contagious livestock diseases (which the system categorizes as epidemic diseases of strategic importance, such as rinderpest or foot-and-mouth; diseases requiring tactical attention at international or regional level, e.g. Rift Valley fever; and emerging diseases, e.g. bovine spongiform encephalopathy—BSE). EMPRES has a desert locust component, and has published guidelines on all aspects of desert locust monitoring. A web-based EMPRES Global Animal Disease Information System (EMPRES-i) aims to support veterinary services through the timely release of disease information to enhance early warning and response to transboundary animal diseases, including emergent zoonoses. FAO assumed responsibility for technical leadership and co-ordination of the Global Rinderpest Eradication Programme (GREP), which had the objective of eliminating that disease by 2011; in June 2011 the FAO Conference adopted a resolution declaring global freedom from rinderpest. FAO and the World Organisation for Animal Health (OIE) adopted two resolutions during 2011 relating to the destruction/safe storage of remaining stocks of rinderpest virus and on banning the use of the live virus in research. In June 2012 a conference convened in Bangkok, Thailand, under the auspices of FAO, the OIE and the Thai Government, endorsed a new Global Foot and Mouth Disease Control Strategy. In November 1997 FAO initiated a Programme Against African Trypanosomiasis, which aimed to counter the disease affecting cattle in almost one-third of Africa. In November 2004 FAO established a specialized Emergency Centre for Transboundary Animal Disease Operations (ECTAD) to enhance FAO's role in assisting member states to combat animal disease outbreaks and in co-ordinating international efforts to research, monitor and control transboundary disease crises. In May 2004 FAO and the OIE signed an agreement to clarify their respective areas of competence and improve co-operation, in response to an increase in contagious transboundary animal diseases (such as foot-and-mouth disease and avian influenza, see below). The two bodies agreed to establish a global framework on the control of transboundary animal diseases, entailing improved international collaboration and circulation of information. In 2006 FAO, the OIE and the World Health Organization (WHO) launched a Global Early Warning and Response System for Major Animal Diseases, including Zoonoses (GLEWS), in order to strengthen their joint capacity to detect, monitor and respond to animal disease threats. In October of that year FAO inaugurated a Crisis Management Centre to co-ordinate (in close co-operation with the OIE) the organization's response to major emergencies related to animal or food health.

In September 2004 FAO and WHO declared an ongoing epidemic in certain East Asian countries of the H5N1 strain of highly pathogenic avian influenza (HPAI) to be a 'crisis of global importance': the disease was spreading rapidly through bird populations and was also transmitting to human populations through contact with diseased birds (mainly poultry). In April 2005 FAO and the OIE established an international network of laboratories and scientists (OFFLU) to exchange data and provide expert technical advice on avian, equine and swine influenza. In the following month FAO, with WHO and the OIE, launched a global strategy for the progressive control of avian influenza. In November a conference on Avian Influenza and Human Pandemic Influenza, jointly organized by FAO, WHO and the OIE and the World Bank, issued a plan of action identifying a number of responses, including: expanding national and regional capacity in surveillance, diagnosis and alert and response systems; expanding the network of influenza laboratories; establishing multi-country networks for the control or prevention of animal transboundary diseases; expanding the global antiviral stockpile; strengthening veterinary infrastructures; and mapping a strategy for the co-ordination of antiviral and influenza vaccine research and development. In June 2006 FAO and the OIE convened a scientific conference on the spread and management of H5N1 that advocated early detection of the disease in wild birds, improved biosecurity and hygiene in the poultry trade, rapid response to disease outbreaks, and the establishment of a global tracking and monitoring facility, as well as investment in telemetry/satellite technology to improve tracking capabilities. In October 2008, at the sixth international ministerial conference on avian influenza, convened in Sharm el-Sheikh, Egypt, FAO, with WHO, UNICEF, the OIE, the World Bank and the UN System Influenza Co-ordinator, presented a new strategic framework within the concept of a 'One World, One Health' policy focused on caring for the health of animals, humans, and the ecosystems that support them. The framework aimed to advance co-operation with respect to emerging infectious diseases, to strengthen animal and public health surveillance and to enhance response mechanisms. During 2003–mid-2013 outbreaks of H5N1 were recorded in 63 countries and territories, and more than 400m. domestic and wild birds consequently died or were culled. FAO warned in January 2013—at which time the virus remained endemic in parts of Asia and the Middle East—that the implementation of global health measures aimed at monitoring and controlling H5N1 and other diseases of animal origin (with particular reference to Peste des Petits Ruminants, affecting goats and sheep) was being put at risk by national budgetary restrictions arising from the ongoing global economic downturn.

In December 2011 the conference of parties to the Convention on Migratory Species (CMS) established a Scientific Task Force on Wildlife and Ecosystem Health, with FAO participation, reflecting the ongoing 'One World, One Health' policy; a Task Force on Avian Influenza and Wild Birds, established under the CMS in August 2005, was to continue as a core focus area within the larger Scientific Task Force.

In April 2009, in response to a major outbreak in humans of the swine influenza variant pandemic (H1N1) 2009, the FAO Crisis Management Centre mobilized a team of experts to increase animal disease surveillance and maintain response readiness to protect the global pig farming sector from infection with the emerging virus.

FAO is committed to promoting food quality and safety in all different stages of food production and processing. It supports the development of integrated food control systems by member states, which incorporate aspects of food control management, inspection, risk analysis and quality assurance. The joint FAO/WHO Codex Alimentarius Commission, established in 1962, aims to protect the health of consumers, ensure fair trade practices and promote the co-ordination of food standards activities at an international level. The Commission maintains databases of standards for food additives, and for maximum residue levels of veterinary drugs maximum and pesticides. In July 2001 the Codex Alimentarius Commission agreed the first global principles for assessing the safety of foods derived from biotechnology (i.e. genetically modified—GM—foods), and approved a series of maximum levels of environmental contaminants in food. In January 2003 FAO organized a technical consultation on biological risk management in food and agriculture which recognized the need for a more integrated approach to so-called biosecurity, i.e. the prevention, control and management of risks to animal, human and plant life and health. FAO has subsequently developed a *Toolkit*, published in 2007, to help countries to develop and implement national biosecurity systems and to enhance biosecurity capacity. In June 2004 FAO published guidelines for assessing possible risks posed to plants by living modified organisms.

FAO aims to assist member states to enhance the efficiency, competitiveness and profitability of their agricultural and food enterprises. FAO extends assistance in training, capacity building and the formulation of agribusiness development strategies. It promotes the development of effective 'value chains', connecting primary producers with consumers, and supports other linkages within the agribusiness industry. Similarly, FAO aims to strengthen marketing systems, links between producers and retailers and training in agricultural marketing, and works to improve the regulatory framework for agricultural marketing. FAO promotes the use of new technologies to increase agricultural production and extends a range of services to support mechanization, including training, maintenance, testing and the promotion of labour-saving technologies. Other programmes are focused on farm management, post-harvest management, food and non-food processing, rural finance, and rural infrastructure. FAO helps reduce immediate post-harvest losses, with the introduction of improved processing methods and storage systems.

FAO's Joint Division with the International Atomic Energy Agency (IAEA) is concerned with the use of nuclear techniques in food and agriculture. It co-ordinates research projects, provides scientific and technical support to technical co-operation projects and administers training courses. A joint laboratory in Seibersdorf, Austria, is concerned with testing biotechnologies and in developing non-toxic fertilizers (especially those that are locally available) and improved strains of food crops (especially from indigenous varieties). In the area of animal production and health, the Joint Division has developed progesterone-measuring and disease diagnostic kits. Other sub-programmes of the Joint Division are concerned with soil and water, plant breeding and nutrition, insect pest control and food and environmental protection.

NATURAL RESOURCES MANAGEMENT AND ENVIRONMENT

FAO's Natural Resources Management and Environment Department is mandated to provide leadership, knowledge, and technical and policy advice regarding the sustainable use of the planet's land, water, genetic resources and biodiversity; to improve responses to challenges to the global environment that affect food and agriculture, including climate change and land degradation; to address issues related to bioenergy; and to serve as a neutral forum for dialogue on the sustainable use of natural resources. The Department comprises two divisions: Climate, Energy and Tenure, and Land and Water. FAO hosts the secretariat of the Commission on Genetic Resources for Food and Agriculture, established in 1983, with a mandate to address the impact of biodiversity on food and agriculture.

The Climate, Energy and Tenure Division supports member states to develop adaptive capacities in the agriculture, fisheries and forestry sectors to enhance the resilience of agricultural systems to climate change (which increases the risk of crop and livestock failure in fragile ecosystems, causing changing growing conditions and an increase in extreme weather events); and to promote sustainable agricultural practices aimed at reducing the emission of greenhouse gases. The Division serves as the secretariat for FAO interdepartmental working groups on climate change and on bioenergy. Emissions can also be reduced by sustainable agricultural practices. In 2006 FAO established the International Bioenergy Platform to serve as a focal point for research, data collection, capacity building and strategy formulation by local, regional and international bodies concerned with bioenergy. FAO also serves as the secretariat for the Global Bioenergy Partnership, which was inaugurated in May 2006 to facilitate the collaboration between governments, international agencies and representatives of the private sector and civil society in the sustainable development of bioenergy. In 2012 FAO initiated a new Energy-Smart Food for people and climate (ESF) programme, which aims to support states in promoting energy-smart agrifood systems, through the identification, development and implementation of energy, water, food security and climate-smart strategies that promote agricultural growth and rural development. The organization has also developed a Sustainable Bioenergy Support Package, to promote good practices and monitoring of bioenergy development.

FAO aims to enhance the sustainability of land and water systems, and as a result to secure agricultural productivity, through the improved tenure, management, development and conservation of those natural resources. The organization promotes equitable access to land and water resources and supports integrated land and water management, including river basin management and improved irrigation systems. FAO has developed AQUASTAT as a global information system concerned with water and agricultural issues, comprising databases, country and regional profiles, surveys and maps. AquaCrop, CropWat and ClimWat are further productivity models and databases which have been developed to help to assess crop requirements and potential yields. Since 2003 FAO has participated in UN Water, an inter-agency initiative to co-ordinate existing approaches to water-related issues. In August 2012 FAO launched an initiative entitled 'Coping with water scarcity: An action framework for agriculture and food security', which aimed to support the improved management of water resources in agricultural production, including through the development of irrigation schemes, the recycling and re-using of waste water, and the implementation of measures to reduce water pollution.

In December 2008 FAO organized a Ministerial Conference on Water for Agriculture and Energy in Africa: 'the Challenges of Climate Change', in Sirte, Libya, which was attended by representatives of 48 African member countries and other representatives of international, regional and civil organizations.

FAO is concerned with the conservation and sustainable use of plant and animal genetic resources. It works with regional and international associations to develop seed networks, to encourage the use of improved seed production systems, to elaborate quality control and certification mechanisms and to co-ordinate seed security activities, in particular in areas prone to natural or man-made disasters. FAO has developed a World Information and Early Warning System (WIEWS) to gather and disseminate information concerning plant genetic resources for food and agriculture and to undertake periodic assessments of the state of those resources. FAO is also developing, as part of the WIEWS, a Seed Information Service to extend information to member states on seeds, planting and new technologies. In

November 2001 the FAO Conference adopted the International Treaty on Plant Genetic Resources for Food and Agriculture (also referred to as the Seed Treaty), with the aim of providing a framework to ensure access to plant genetic resources and to related knowledge, technologies, and—through the Treaty's Benefit-sharing Fund (BSF)—funding. The Seed Treaty entered into force in June 2004, and had 128 states parties by September 2013. The BSF assists poor farmers in developing countries with conserving, and also adapting to climate change, their most important food crops. By 2013 around 1,750 gene banks had been established world-wide, storing more than 7m. plant samples.

FAO's Agro-Ecological Zoning (AEZ) methodology, developed jointly with the International Institute for Applied Systems Analysis, is the main tool used for land resources assessment; agro-ecological zones are defined as homogenous and contiguous areas possessing similar soil, land and climate characteristics. A global AEZ database is updated periodically (most recently in May 2012).

FAO is the UN lead agency of an initiative, 'Education for Rural People', which aims to improve the quality of and access to basic education for people living in rural areas and to raise awareness of the issue as an essential element of achieving the MDGs. FAO also hosts the secretariat of the Global Forum on Agricultural Research, which was established in 1996 as a collaboration of research centres, non-governmental and private sector organizations and development agencies. The Forum aims to strengthen research and promote knowledge partnerships concerned with the alleviation of poverty, the increase in food security and the sustainable use of natural resources. Furthermore FAO hosts the secretariat of the Science Council of the Consultative Group on International Agricultural Research (CGIAR), which, specifically, aims to enhance and promote the quality, relevance and impact of science within the network of CGIAR research centres and to mobilize global scientific expertise.

A High-level Meeting on National Drought Policy, organized in March 2013, in Geneva, Switzerland, by FAO, WMO, and the UN Convention to Combat Desertification, issued a declaration that urged governments to develop and implement national drought management policies consistent with their development objectives, and provided supporting scientific and policy guidance.

FISHERIES AND AQUACULTURE

FAO's Fisheries and Aquaculture Department comprises divisions of fisheries and aquaculture policy and economics; and fisheries and aquaculture resources use and conservation. Fish was estimated in 2012 to be the primary source of protein for 17% of the global population, and for about one-quarter of the populations of 'low-income food-deficit' countries. Aquaculture contributes almost one-third of annual global fish landings, and was estimated in 2012 to account for nearly one-half of fish consumed by humans.

FAO undertakes extensive monitoring, publishing every two years *The State of World Fisheries and Aquaculture*, and collates and maintains relevant databases. It formulates country and regional profiles and has developed a specific information network for the fisheries sector, GLOBEFISH, which gathers and disseminates information regarding market trends, tariffs and other industry issues. FAO aims to extend technical support to member states with regard to the management and conservation of aquatic resources, and other measures to improve the utilization and trade of products, including the reduction of post-harvest losses, preservation marketing and quality assurance.

FAO aims to facilitate and secure the long-term sustainable development of fisheries and aquaculture, in both inland and marine waters, and to promote its contribution to world food security. In March 1995 a ministerial meeting of fisheries adopted the Rome Consensus on World Fisheries, which identified a need for immediate action to eliminate overfishing and to rebuild and enhance depleting fish stocks. In November the FAO Conference adopted a Code of Conduct for Responsible Fishing (CCRF), which incorporated many global fisheries and aquaculture issues (including fisheries resource conservation and development, fish catches, seafood and fish processing, commercialization, trade and research) to promote the sustainable development of the sector. In February 1999 the FAO Committee on Fisheries adopted new international measures, within the framework of the Code of Conduct, in order to reduce over-exploitation of the world's fish resources, as well as plans of action for the conservation and management of sharks and the reduction in the incidental catch of seabirds in longline fisheries. The voluntary measures were endorsed at a ministerial meeting, held in March, which issued a declaration to promote the implementation of the Code of Conduct and to achieve sustainable management of fisheries and aquaculture. Several international plans of action (IPOA) have been elaborated within the context of the CCRF: the IPOA for Conservation and Management of Sharks (IPOA-Sharks, 1999); the IPOA for the Management of Fishing Capacity (IPOA-Capacity, 1999); the IPOA for Reducing Incidental Catch of Seabirds in Longline Fisheries (IPOA-Seabirds, 1999); and the IPOA to Prevent, Deter and Eliminate Illegal, Unreported and Unregulated Fishing (IPOA-IUU, 2001). FAO has prepared guidelines to support member countries with implementing IPOAs and has encouraged states to develop national plans of action to complement the international plans. FishCode, an interregional assistance programme, supports developing countries in implementing the CCRF.

In 2001 FAO estimated that about one-half of major marine fish stocks were fully exploited, one-quarter under-exploited, at least 15% over-exploited, and 10% depleted or recovering from depletion. IUU was estimated to account for up to 30% of total catches in certain fisheries. In October FAO and the Icelandic Government jointly organized the Reykjavík Conference on Responsible Fisheries in the Marine Ecosystem, which adopted a declaration on pursuing responsible and sustainable fishing activities in the context of ecosystem-based fisheries management (EBFM). EBFM involves determining the boundaries of individual marine ecosystems, and maintaining or rebuilding the habitats and biodiversity of each of these so that all species will be supported at levels of maximum production. In March 2005 FAO's Committee on Fisheries adopted voluntary guidelines for the so-called eco-labelling and certification of fish and fish products, i.e. based on information regarding capture management and the sustainable use of resources. In November 2009 an Agreement on Port State Measures to Prevent, Deter and Eliminate Illegal, Unreported and Unregulated Fishing, negotiated by the Committee, and denying port access to fishing vessels involved in IUU activities, was endorsed by the FAO Conference. In May 2011 FAO initiated a Technical Consultation on flag state performance, aimed at assessing the performance of flag states, and establishing means of preventing vessels from flying the flags of irresponsible states. Voluntary Guidelines for Flag State Performance were approved by a session of the Technical Consultation that was held in February 2013. FAO was committed to supporting the development of the guidelines and providing assistance to countries to implement them effectively. The guidelines were to be presented to the Committee on Fisheries at its next session in June 2014.

FAO promotes aquaculture as a valuable source of animal protein and income-generating activity for rural communities. It has undertaken to develop an ecosystem approach to aquaculture (EAA) and works to integrate aquaculture with agricultural and irrigation systems. In February 2000 FAO and the Network of Aquaculture Centres in Asia and the Pacific (NACA) jointly convened a Conference on Aquaculture in the Third Millennium, which adopted the Bangkok Declaration and Strategy for Aquaculture Beyond 2000. In September 2010 FAO and NACA convened the Global Conference on Aquaculture, in Phuket, Thailand, on the theme 'Farming the Waters for People and Food'; the Global Conference adopted a set of recommendations on further advancing aquaculture. In October 2012 development agencies, governments and research institutions launched a new three-year project 'Aquaculture for Food Security, Poverty Alleviation and Nutrition' (AFSPAN)—under FAO management and with funding by the European Union—with the aim of advancing understanding of the role of aquaculture in maintaining food security in poorer countries, and using that knowledge to develop sustainable policies for improving livelihoods.

FORESTRY

FAO's Forestry Department comprises divisions of forest economics, policy and products; and forest assessment, management and conservation.

FAO is committed to the sustainable management of trees, forests and forestry resources. It aims to address the critical balance of ensuring the conservation of forests and forestry resources while maximising their potential to contribute to food security and social and economic development. In March 2009 the Committee on Forestry approved a new 10-year FAO Strategic Plan for Forestry, replacing a previous strategic plan initiated in 1999. The new plan, which was 'dynamic' and was to be updated regularly, covered the social, economic and environmental aspects of forestry. The first World Forest Week, sponsored by FAO, was held in March 2009, and the first World Forest Day, sponsored by FAO and the UN Forum on Forests, was observed on 21 March 2013. 2011 was declared the International Year of Forests by the UN General Assembly. In May 2013 FAO hosted an International Conference on Forests for Food Security and Nutrition.

FAO assists member countries to formulate, implement and monitor national forestry programmes, and encourages the participation of all stakeholders in developing plans for the sustainable management of tree and forest resources. FAO also helps to implement national assessments of those programmes and of other forestry activities. At a global level FAO undertakes surveillance of the state of the world's forests and publishes a report every two years. A separate *Forest Resources Assessment* is published every five years; the process to compile the 2015 edition was initiated in June 2011. In 2012 FAO issued a report on *The State of the World's Forest Genetic Resources*. FAO is committed to collecting and disseminating accurate information and data on forests. It maintains the Forestry

Information System (FORIS) to make relevant information and forest-related databases widely accessible.

In September 2008 FAO, with UNEP and UNDP, launched the UN Collaborative Programme on Reducing Emissions from Deforestation and Forest Degradation in Developing Countries (UN-REDD), with the aim of enabling donors to pool resources (through a trust fund established for that purpose) to promote a transformation of forest resource use patterns. In August 2011 UN-REDD endorsed a Global Programme Framework covering 2011–15.

FAO is a member of the Collaborative Partnership on Forests, an informal, voluntary arrangement among 14 agencies with significant forestry programmes, which was established in April 2004 on the recommendation of the UN's Economic and Social Council. FAO organizes a World Forestry Congress, generally held every six years; the 14th Congress was to be held in September 2015, in Durban, South Africa.

TECHNICAL CO-OPERATION

The Technical Co-operation Department has responsibility for FAO's operational activities, including policy and programme development assistance to member countries; the mobilization of resources; investment support; field operations; emergency operations and rehabilitation; and the Technical Co-operation Programme.

FAO provides policy advice to support the formulation, implementation and evaluation of agriculture, rural development and food security strategies in member countries. It administers a project to assist developing countries to strengthen their technical negotiating skills, in respect to agricultural trade issues. FAO also aims to co-ordinate and facilitate the mobilization of extrabudgetary funds from donors and governments for particular projects. It administers a range of trust funds, including a Trust Fund for Food Security and Food Safety, established in 2002 to generate resources for projects to combat hunger, and the Government Co-operative Programme. In February 2013 a new Africa Solidarity Trust Fund was inaugurated, which aimed to mobilize Africa-to-Africa financial resources in support of strengthening regional food security. FAO's Investment Centre, established in 1964, aims to promote greater external investment in agriculture and rural development by assisting member countries to formulate effective and sustainable projects and programmes. The Centre collaborates with international financing institutions and bilateral donors in the preparation of projects, and administers cost-sharing arrangements, with, typically, FAO funding 40% of a project. The Centre is a co-chair (with the German Government) of the Global Donor Platform for Rural Development, which was established in 2004, comprising multilateral, donor and international agencies, development banks and research institutions, to improve the co-ordination and effectiveness of rural development assistance.

FAO's Technical Co-operation Programme, which was inaugurated in 1976, provides technical expertise and funding for small-scale projects to address specific issues within a country's agriculture, fisheries or forestry sectors. An Associate Professional Officers programme co-ordinates the sponsorship and placement of young professionals to gain experience working in an aspect of rural or agricultural development.

FAO organizes an annual series of fund-raising events, 'TeleFood', some of which are broadcast on television and the internet, in order to raise public awareness of the problems of hunger and malnutrition. Since its inception in 1997 public donations to TeleFood have exceeded some US $29m. (2013), financing more than 3,200 'grassroots' projects in 130 countries. The projects have provided tools, seeds and other essential supplies directly to small-scale farmers, and have been especially aimed at helping women.

The Technical Co-operation Division co-ordinates FAO's emergency operations, concerned with all aspects of disaster and risk prevention, mitigation, reduction and emergency relief and rehabilitation, with a particular emphasis on food security and rural populations. FAO works with governments to develop and implement disaster prevention policies and practices. It aims to strengthen the capacity of local institutions to manage and mitigate risk and provides technical assistance to improve access to land for displaced populations in countries following conflict or a natural disaster. Other disaster prevention and reduction efforts include dissemination of information from the various early-warning systems and support for adaptation to climate variability and change, for example by the use of drought-resistant crops or the adoption of conservation agriculture techniques. Following an emergency FAO works with governments and other development and humanitarian partners to assess the immediate and longer-term agriculture and food security needs of the affected population. It has developed an Integrated Food Security and Humanitarian Phase Classification Scheme to determine the appropriate response to a disaster situation. Emergency co-ordination units may be established to manage the local response to an emergency and to facilitate and co-ordinate the delivery of inter-agency assistance. In order to rehabilitate agricultural production following a natural or man-made disaster FAO provides emergency seed, tools, other materials and technical and training assistance. Under the UN's cluster approach to co-ordinating the international response to humanitarian disasters with a focus on core areas of activity, FAO and WFP jointly lead the Food Security cluster, which was established in 2011, and aims to combine expertise in agricultural assistance and food aid to improve the resilience of food-insecure disaster-affected communities. FAO also contributes the agricultural relief and rehabilitation component of the UN's Consolidated Appeals Process (CAP), which aims to co-ordinate and enhance the effectiveness of the international community's response to an emergency; during 2012 FAO received US $222m. in funding in response to its appeals under the 2012 CAP process. In April 2004 FAO established a Special Fund for Emergency and Rehabilitation Activities to enable it to respond promptly to a humanitarian crisis before making an emergency appeal for additional resources.

FAO is undertaking several agricultural sector initiatives in Iraq, including an Agricultural Growth and Employment Support project covering the period 2010–13. A regional bio-ecological pest control project aimed at managing the T. absoluta tomato borer was being undertaken during 2013–14 in Egypt, Iran, Iraq, Jordan, Lebanon, Syria and Yemen; and in 2010–13 a regional project was being implemented throughout the Near East, to manage the deep-rooted invasive plant *Solanum elaegnifolium* (silver-leafed nightshade), which depletes soil of nutrients and water, and is toxic to livestock. It was reported in 2011 that more than 60% of cultivated land in Syria was infested with this weed. FAO appealed for $12m. under the 2013 UN Consolidated Appeals Process (CAP) to fund the following projects in Yemen (where there was significant unrest and internal displacement, particularly in southern areas, and some northern regions): Resilient livelihood improvement based on the rehabilitation and efficient use of water harvesting techniques; Strengthening food security and agriculture co-ordination (jointly with WFP); Integrated Food Security Phase Classification, phase II; Protection and improvement of agricultural livelihood assets of displaced families and their host communities in Hajjah; and Improving vulnerable households' food insecurity status in Hajjah through female-led backyard food production. FAO also appealed under the 2013 CAP for $12m. to support the following projects in Gaza and the West Bank: Emergency support to vulnerable herding communities in Area C of the West Bank; Emergency backyard food production activities in vulnerable and marginalized areas of the West Bank and Gaza Strip; Improving protection for fishers and farmers in access-restricted border areas in the Gaza Strip; Restoring damaged agricultural assets and productive capacities of farmers and herders affected by external shocks and demolitions; Strengthening the food security coordination platform in the occupied Palestinian territory (jointly with WFP and UNWRA); and Quick impact emergency interventions to protect the endangered livelihoods of poor and small-scale farmers in Area C, the Seam Zone and Gaza Strip against external shocks.

Following rains in southwestern Libya and southeastern Algeria (the location of locust breeding grounds) in early October 2011, and a disruption to normal ground survey activities during 2011 in Libya owing to violent insecurity, an outbreak of desert locusts occurred in southwestern areas of Libya from January 2012. Infestations receded in June as vegetation that had been supporting bands and swarms of locusts dried out. The Commission for Controlling the Desert Locust in the Western Region and FAO organized for national locust control units to spray with pesticides some 60,000 ha on either side of the Algeria-Libya border in 2012.

FAO Statutory Bodies and Associated Entities

(based at the Rome headquarters, unless otherwise indicated)

Agricultural Market Information System (AMIS): AMIS Secretariat, FAO, Viale delle Terme di Caracalla, 00153 Rome, Italy; tel. (6) 5705-2057; fax (6) 5705-3152; e-mail amis-secretariat@fao.org; internet www.amis-outlook.org; f. 2011 to improve transparency in agricultural markets and contribute to stabilizing food price volatility; a partnership of FAO, the International Food Policy Research Institute, IFAD, OECD, UNCTAD, the World Bank, WFP, WTO, and the UN High Level Task Force on the Global Food Security Crisis (f. 2008).

Agriculture, Land and Water Use Commission for the Near East (ALAWUC): c/o FAO Regional Office for the Near East, POB 2223, Cairo, Egypt; f. 2000 by merger of the Near East Regional Commission on Agriculture and the Regional Commission on Land and Water Use in the Near East; seventh session of ALAWUC held in May 2012, in Cairo, Egypt; 23 mem. states.

Codex Alimentarius Commission (Joint FAO/WHO Food Standards Programme): e-mail codex@fao.org; internet www.codexalimentarius.org; f. 1962 to make proposals for the co-ordination of all international food standards work and to publish a code of international food standards; Trust Fund to support participation by least-developed countries was inaugurated in 2003; there are numerous specialized Codex committees, e.g. for food labelling, hygiene, additives and contaminants, pesticide and veterinary residues, milk and milk products, and processed fruits and vegetables; and an intergovernmental task force on antimicrobial resistance; 185 mem. states and the EU; 220 observers (at September 2013).

Commission for Controlling the Desert Locust in Southwest Asia: internet www.fao.org/ag/locusts/SWAC; f. 1964 to carry out all possible measures to control plagues of the desert locust in Afghanistan, India, Iran and Pakistan; 28th session: Dec. 2012, New Delhi, India; 4 mem. states.

Commission for Controlling the Desert Locust in the Central Region: c/o FAO Regional Office for the Near East, POB 2223, Cairo, Egypt; e-mail eclo@fao.org; internet www.fao.org/ag/locusts/en/info/info/index.html; covers north-eastern Africa and the Middle East; reported in Sept. 2012 that limited expansion of the locust population might occur in Red Sea coastal areas of Yemen that had received recent rainfall; 28th session: Nov. 2012, Jeddah, Saudi Arabia; 16 mem. states.

Commission for Controlling the Desert Locust in the Western Region: 30 rue Asselah Hocine, BP 270, Algiers, Algeria; e-mail clcpro@fao.org; internet www.clcpro-empres.org; f. 2002; covers north-western Africa; has implemented a preventive control programme to strengthen locust surveillance and control in member countries (first phase: 2006–11; second phase 2011–14); and has advocated to help member countries establish autonomous national locust control units; works closely with EMPRES; sixth session: March 2012, Tunis, Tunisia; 10 mem. states.

Emergency Prevention System for Transboundary Animal and Plant Pests and Diseases (EMPRES): e-mail vincent.martin@fao.org; internet www.fao.org/ag/againfo/programmes/en/empres.html; f. 1994 to strengthen FAO's activities in prevention, early warning, control and eradication of pests and highly contagious livestock diseases; maintains an internet-based EMPRES Global Animal Disease Information System (EMPRES-i).

FAO Desert Locust Control Committee: f. 1955 as a primary forum bringing together locust-affected countries, international donors and other agencies, to advise FAO on the management of desert locusts; 40th session: June 2012, Rome.

Fishery Committee for the Eastern Central Atlantic: f. 1967 to promote improvements in inland fisheries in the Eastern Central Atlantic area between Cape Spartel (Morocco) and the Congo River; 20th session: March 2012, in Rabat, Morocco; 33 mem. states and the EU.

General Fisheries Commission for the Mediterranean: internet www.gfcm.org; f. 1949 (as the General Fisheries Council for the Mediterranean, name changed with adoption of amendments to the GFCM agreement in 1997) to develop aquatic resources, to encourage and co-ordinate research in the fishing and allied industries, to assemble and publish information, and to recommend the standardization of equipment, techniques and nomenclature; covers the Mediterranean, Black Sea and connecting waters; 37th session: May 2013, in Croatia; 23 mem. states and the EU.

Governing Body of the International Treaty on Plant Genetic Resources (Seed Treaty): e-mail pgrfa-treaty@fao.org; internet www.planttreaty.org; f. 2004 to oversee the implementation of the Seed Treaty; fourth session: March 2011, Nusa Dua, Bali; 126 mem. states and the EU (at Sept. 2012).

International Poplar Commission: internet www.fao.org/forestry/ipc/en; f. 1947 to study scientific, technical, social and economic aspects of poplar and willow cultivation; to promote the exchange of ideas and material between research workers, producers and users; to arrange joint research programmes, congresses, study tours; to make recommendations to the FAO Conference and to National Poplar Commissions; 24th session: Oct.–Nov. 2012, in Dehradun, India; 37 mem. states.

International Rice Commission (IRC): internet www.fao.org/ag/irc; f. 1949 to promote national and international action on production, conservation, distribution and consumption of rice, except matters relating to international trade; supports the International Task Force on Hybrid Rice, the Working Group on Advanced Rice Breeding in Latin America and the Caribbean, the Interregional Collaborative Research Network on Rice in the Mediterranean Climate Areas, and the Technical Co-operation Network on Wetland Development and Management/Inland Valley Swamps; in July 2012 27 experts from 22 IRC member countries convened a Global Rice Roundtable, in Le Corum, Montpelier, France, to consider possible future directions of the IRC; 62 mem. states (accounting for around 93% of global rice production).

Near East Forestry and Range Commission: c/o FAO Regional Office for the Near East, 11 El-Eslah el-Zerai St, Dokki, POB 2223, Cairo, Egypt; f. 1953 to advise on formulation of forest policy and review and co-ordinate its implementation throughout the region; to exchange information and advise on technical problems; 21st session: Jan. 2014, Cairo; 27 mem. states.

Silva Mediterranea: e-mail silva.mediterranea@fao.org; internet www.fao.org/forestry/silvamed; f. 1911, became a statutory body of FAO in 1948; FAO committee on Mediterranean forestry issues convened under the auspices of the FAO Forestry Commissions for Africa, Europe, and Near-East; 26 mem. states and the EU.

Finance

FAO's Regular Programme, which is financed by contributions from member governments, covers the cost of FAO's Secretariat, its Technical Co-operation Programme (TCP) and part of the cost of several special action programmes. The regular budget for the two-year period 2012–13 totalled US $1,006m. Much of FAO's technical assistance programme and emergency (including rehabilitation) support activities are funded from extra-budgetary sources, predominantly by trust funds that come mainly from donor countries and international financing institutions; voluntary donor contributions to FAO were projected at around $1,400m. in 2011–13.

Publications

Commodity Review and Outlook (annually).

Crop Prospects and Food Situation (5/6 a year).

Desert Locust Bulletin.

Ethical Issues in Food and Agriculture.

FAO Statistical Yearbook (annually).

FAOSTAT Statistical Database (online).

Food Outlook (2 a year).

Food Safety and Quality Update (monthly; electronic bulletin).

Forest Resources Assessment (every 5 years).

The State of Agricultural Commodity Markets (every 2 years).

The State of Food and Agriculture (annually).

The State of Food Insecurity in the World (annually, with IFAD and WFP).

The State of World Fisheries and Aquaculture (every 2 years).

The State of the World's Forests (every 2 years).

Unasylva (quarterly).

Yearbook of Fishery Statistics.

Yearbook of Forest Products.

Commodity reviews, studies, manuals. A complete catalogue of publications is available at www.fao.org/icatalog/inter-e.htm.

International Atomic Energy Agency—IAEA

Address: POB 100, Wagramerstrasse 5, 1400 Vienna, Austria.
Telephone: (1) 26000; **fax:** (1) 26007; **e-mail:** official.mail@iaea.org; **internet:** www.iaea.org.

The International Atomic Energy Agency (IAEA) is an intergovernmental organization, established in 1957 in accordance with a decision of the General Assembly of the United Nations. Although it is autonomous, the IAEA is administratively a member of the United Nations, and reports on its activities once a year to the UN General Assembly. Its main objectives are to enlarge the contribution of atomic energy to peace, health and prosperity throughout the world and to ensure, so far as it is able, that assistance provided by it or at its request or under its supervision or control is not used in such a way as to further any military purpose. The 2005 Nobel Peace Prize was awarded, in two equal parts, to the IAEA and to the Agency's Director-General.

Organization

(September 2013)

GENERAL CONFERENCE

The Conference, comprising representatives of all member states, convenes each year for general debate on the Agency's policy, budget and programme. It elects members to the Board of Governors, and approves the appointment of the Director-General; it admits new member states.

BOARD OF GOVERNORS

The Board of Governors consists of 35 member states elected by the General Conference. It is the principal policy-making body of the Agency and is responsible to the General Conference. Under its own authority, the Board approves all safeguards agreements, important projects and safety standards.

SECRETARIAT

The Secretariat, comprising some 2,470 staff, is headed by the Director-General, who is assisted by six Deputy Directors-General. The Secretariat is divided into six departments: Technical Co-operation; Nuclear Energy; Nuclear Safety and Security; Nuclear Sciences and Applications; Safeguards; and Management. A Standing Advisory Group on Safeguards Implementation advises the Director-General on technical aspects of safeguards.

Director-General: YUKIYA AMANO (Japan).

Activities

The Agency's activities are supported by three pillars: technology (assisting research on and practical application of atomic energy for peaceful uses), safety, and verification (ensuring that special fissionable and other materials, services, equipment and information made available by the Agency or at its request or under its supervision are not used for any non-peaceful purpose).

TECHNICAL CO-OPERATION AND TRAINING

The IAEA provides assistance in the form of experts, training and equipment to technical co-operation projects and applications worldwide, with an emphasis on radiation protection and safety-related activities. Training is provided to scientists, and experts and lecturers are assigned to provide specialized help on specific nuclear applications. The IAEA supported the foundation in September 2003 of the World Nuclear University, comprising a global network of institutions that aim to strengthen international co-operation in promoting the safe use of nuclear power in energy production, and in the application of nuclear science and technology in areas including sustainable agriculture and nutrition, medicine, fresh water resources management and environmental protection.

FOOD AND AGRICULTURE

In co-operation with FAO, the Agency conducts programmes of applied research on the use of radiation and isotopes in fields including efficiency in the use of water and fertilizers; improvement of food crops by induced mutations; eradication or control of destructive insects by the introduction of sterilized insects (radiation-based Sterile Insect Technique); improvement of livestock nutrition and health; studies on improving efficacy and reducing residues of pesticides, and increasing utilization of agricultural wastes; and food preservation by irradiation. The programmes are implemented by the Joint FAO/IAEA Division of Nuclear Techniques in Food and Agriculture and by the FAO/IAEA Agriculture and Biotechnology Laboratory, based at the IAEA's laboratory complex in Seibersdorf, Austria. A Training and Reference Centre for Food and Pesticide Control, based at Seibersdorf, supports the implementation of national legislation and trade agreements ensuring the quality and safety of food products in international trade. The Agency's Marine Environment Laboratory (IAEA-MEL), in Monaco, studies radionuclides and other ocean pollutants. In June 2012 IAEA announced the establishment of a new Ocean Acidification International Coordination Centre (OA-ICC), under the management of IAEA-MEL, with a mandate to facilitate, promote and communicate global actions on ocean acidification.

LIFE SCIENCES

In co-operation with the World Health Organization (WHO), the IAEA promotes the use of nuclear techniques in medicine, biology and health-related environmental research, provides training, and conducts research on techniques for improving the accuracy of radiation dosimetry.

The IAEA/WHO Network of Secondary Standard Dosimetry Laboratories (SSDLs) comprises 81 laboratories in 62 member states. The Agency's Dosimetry Laboratory in Seibersdorf performs dose inter-comparisons for both SSDLs and radiotherapy centres. The IAEA undertakes maintenance plans for nuclear laboratories; national programmes of quality control for nuclear medicine instruments; quality control of radioimmunoassay techniques; radiation sterilization of medical supplies; and improvement of cancer therapy in low- and middle-income countries through the IAEA Programme of Action for Cancer Therapy (PACT), inaugurated in 2004. By the end of 2012 47 member states had received imPACT (integrated missions of the Programme of Action for Cancer) reviews, which provide comprehensive assessments of national cancer control capabilities and support radiotherapy capacity building. In May 2009 the IAEA and WHO launched a new Joint Programme on Cancer Control, aimed at enhancing efforts to fight cancer in the developing world. In June 2010 the inaugural meeting took place of an IAEA Advisory Group on Increasing Access to Radiotherapy Technology (AGaRT) in low and middle income countries.

PHYSICAL AND CHEMICAL SCIENCES

The Agency's programme on physical sciences includes industrial applications of isotopes and radiation technology; application of nuclear techniques to mineral exploration and exploitation; radiopharmaceuticals; and hydrology, involving the use of isotope techniques for assessment of water resources. Nuclear data services are provided, and training is given for nuclear scientists from developing countries. The Physics, Chemistry and Instrumentation Laboratory in Seibersdorf supports the Agency's research in human health, industry, water resources and environment. The Abdus Salam International Centre for Theoretical Physics, based in Trieste, Italy, operates in accordance with a tripartite agreement in force between the IAEA, UNESCO and the Italian Government.

NUCLEAR POWER

In 2013 there were 437 nuclear power plants in operation and 68 reactors under construction world-wide. Nuclear power accounts for about 13% of total electrical energy generated globally. The IAEA helps developing member states to introduce nuclear-powered electricity-generating plants through assistance with planning, feasibility studies, surveys of manpower and infrastructure, and safety measures. The Agency also assesses life extension and decommissioning strategies for ageing nuclear power plants. It issues publications on numerous aspects of nuclear power, and provides training courses on safety in nuclear power plants and other topics. An energy data bank collects and disseminates information on nuclear technology, and a power-reactor information system monitors the technical performance of nuclear power plants. The use of nuclear technology in seawater desalination and of radiation hydrology techniques to provide potable water are addressed. IAEA has since 1992 been actively engaged in the process to develop an International Thermonuclear Experimental Reactor (ITER), to expand the use of fusion energy. In October 2007 the ITER International Organization—comprising the EU, People's Republic of China, India, Japan, Republic of Korea, Russia and the USA—was inaugurated, with responsibility for constructing, operating and decommissioning the reactor. The construction phase commenced in 2010, in Cadarache, France, and it is envisaged that the reactor will enter fully into operation by 2026. In May 2001 the International Project on Innovative Nuclear Reactors and Fuel Cycles (INPRO) was inaugurated. INPRO, which has 39 members (38 IAEA member states and the European Commission), aims to promote nuclear energy as a means of meeting future sustainable energy requirements and to facilitate the exchange of information by member states to advance innovations in nuclear technology. The IAEA is a permanent observer at the Generation IV International Forum (GIF), which was inaugurated in 2000 to undertake research and development activities aimed at developing the feasibility and performance capabilities of next generation nuclear energy systems. In 2010 the IAEA established an Integrated Nuclear Infrastructure Group (ING), which aimed to integrate information from disparate databases to enable more effective planning; to offer training in the use of planning tools; to provide legislative assistance; and to provide guidance on ensuring self-assessment capabilities among governmental and operating organizations. Integrated Nuclear Infrastructure Review (INIR) missions are conducted in member states, and in 2012 a new INIR methodology was introduced. An advisory Technical Working Group on Nuclear Power Infrastructure was also initiated during 2010. In that year the Executive Board endorsed the establishment of a Low Enriched Uranium (LEU) Bank, to be funded from extra-budgetary sources, with the aim of supplying LEU for the purpose of nuclear power generation.

An IAEA International Ministerial Conference on Nuclear Energy in the 21st Century, with a focus on the role of nuclear energy in climate change mitigation and on meeting increasing global demand for energy, was convened in June 2013 in St Petersburg, Russia, with support from the OECD Nuclear Energy Agency and the Russian Government.

RADIOACTIVE WASTE MANAGEMENT

The Agency provides practical help to member states in the management of radioactive waste. The Waste Management Advisory Programme (WAMAP) was established in 1987, and undertakes advisory missions in member states. A code of practice to prevent the illegal dumping of radioactive waste was drafted in 1989, and another on the international transboundary movement of waste was drafted in 1990. A ban on the dumping of radioactive waste at sea came into effect in 1994, under the Convention on the Prevention of Marine Pollution by Dumping of Wastes and Other Matters; the IAEA was to determine radioactive levels, for purposes of the Convention, and to provide assistance to countries for the safe disposal of radioactive wastes. A new category of radioactive waste—very low level waste (VLLW)—was introduced in the early 2000s. A VLLW repository, at Morvilliers, France, became fully operational in 2004. The Agency has issued modal regulations for the air, sea and land transportation of all radioactive materials.

In September 1997 the IAEA adopted a Joint Convention on the Safety of Spent Fuel Management and on the Safety of Radioactive Waste Management. The first internationally binding legal device to address such issues, the Convention was to ensure the safe storage and disposal of nuclear and radioactive waste, during both the construction and operation of a nuclear power plant, as well as following its closure. The Convention entered into force in June 2001, and had been ratified by 68 parties at September 2013.

NUCLEAR SAFETY

The IAEA's nuclear safety programme encourages international co-operation in the exchange of information, promoting implementation of its safety standards and providing advisory safety services. It includes the IAEA International Nuclear Event Scale (INES), which measures the severity of nuclear events, incidents and accidents; the Incident Reporting System; an emergency preparedness programme (which maintains an Emergency Response Centre, located in Vienna, Austria); operational safety review teams; the International Nuclear Safety Group (INSAG); the Radiation Protection Advisory Team; and a safety research co-ordination programme. The safety review teams provide member states with advice on achieving and maintaining a high level of safety in the operation of nuclear power plants, while research programmes establish risk criteria for the nuclear fuel cycle and identify cost-effective means to reduce risks in energy systems. A new version of the INES, issued in July 2008, incorporated revisions aimed at providing more detailed ratings of activities including human exposure to sources of radiation and the transportation of radioactive materials.

The nuclear safety programme promotes a global safety regime, which aims to ensure the protection of people and the environment from the effects of ionizing radiation and the minimization of the likelihood of potential nuclear accidents, etc. Through the Commission on Safety Standards (which has sub-committees on nuclear safety standards, radiation safety standards, transport safety standards and waste safety standards) the programme establishes IAEA safety standards and provides for their application. In September 2006 the IAEA published a new primary safety standard, the Fundamental Safety Principles, representing a unified philosophy of nuclear safety and protection that was to provide the conceptual basis for the Agency's entire safety standards agenda. The IAEA's *Safety Glossary Terminology Used in Nuclear Safety and Radiation Protection* is updated regularly. In 2010 IAEA established a Global Safety Assessment (G-SAN), facilitating collaboration between experts world-wide with the aim of harmonizing nuclear safety.

The Convention on the Physical Protection of Nuclear Material, signed in 1980commits contracting states to ensuring the protection of nuclear material during transportation within their territory or on board their ships or aircraft; amendments aimed at strengthening the Convention were adopted in July 2005.

Following a serious accident at the Chernobyl nuclear power plant in Ukraine (then part of the USSR) in April 1986, two conventions were formulated by the IAEA and entered into force in October. The first, the Convention on Early Notification of a Nuclear Accident, commits parties to provide information about nuclear accidents with possible transboundary effects at the earliest opportunity (it had 117 parties by September 2013); and the second, the Convention on Assistance in the Case of a Nuclear Accident or Radiological Emergency, commits parties to endeavour to provide assistance in the event of a nuclear accident or radiological emergency (this had 110 parties by September 2013). During 1990 the IAEA organized an assessment of the consequences of the Chernobyl accident, undertaken by an international team of experts, who reported to an international conference on the effects of the accident, convened at the IAEA headquarters in Vienna in May 1991. In February 1993 INSAG published an updated report on the Chernobyl incident, which emphasized the role of design factors in the accident, and the need to implement safety measures in the RBMK-type reactor. In March 1994 an IAEA expert mission visited Chernobyl and reported continuing serious deficiencies in safety at the defunct reactor and the units remaining in operation. An international conference reviewing the radiological consequences of the accident, 10 years after the event, was held in April 1996, co-sponsored by the IAEA, WHO and the EC. The last of the Chernobyl plant's three operating units was officially closed in December 2000. During the 2000s the IAEA offered a wide range of assistance with the decommissioning of Chernobyl. In November 2008 the IAEA and other UN agencies approved a UN Action Plan on Chernobyl to 2016, which had been developed by the UN Development Programme (UNDP), and was envisaged as a framework for the regeneration of affected areas of Ukraine, Belarus and Russia.

An International Convention on Nuclear Safety, which was adopted at an IAEA conference in June 1994, and entered into force in October 1996, applies to land-based civil nuclear power plants: adherents commit themselves to fundamental principles of safety, and maintain legislative frameworks governing nuclear safety.

In October 2003 a protocol entered into force that revised the 1963 Vienna Convention on Civil Liability for Nuclear Damage, fixing the minimum limit of liability for the operator of a nuclear reactor at 300m. Special Drawing Rights (SDRs, the accounting units of the IMF) in the event of an accident. The amended protocol also extended the length of time during which claims may be brought for loss of life or injury. The International Expert Group on Nuclear Liability (INLEX) was also established in 2003. A Convention on Supplementary Compensation for Nuclear Damage established a further compensatory fund to provide for the payment of damages following an accident; contributions to the Fund were to be calculated on the basis of the nuclear capacity of each member state. The Convention had four contracting states by September 2013.

In June 2003 IAEA published the results of an assessment undertaken in 2002 of the possible long-term radiological impact of depleted uranium residues, derived from the 1991 Gulf War, at several locations in Kuwait; it determined that the residues did not pose a health threat to local populations.

In May 2001 the IAEA convened an international conference to address the protection of nuclear material and radioactive sources from illegal trafficking. In September, in view of the perpetration of major terrorist attacks against targets in the USA during that month, the IAEA General Conference adopted a resolution that emphasized the importance of the physical protection of nuclear material in preventing its illicit use or the sabotage of nuclear facilities and nuclear materials. Three main potential threats were identified: the acquisition by a terrorist group of a nuclear weapon; acquisition of nuclear material to construct a nuclear weapon or cause a radiological hazard; and violent acts against nuclear facilities to cause a radiological hazard. In March 2002 the Board of Governors approved in principle an action plan to improve global protection against acts of terrorism involving nuclear and other radioactive materials. The plan addressed the physical protection of nuclear materials and facilities; the detection of malicious activities involving radioactive materials; strengthening national control systems; the security of radioactive sources; evaluation of security and safety at nuclear facilities; emergency response to malicious acts or threats involving radioactive materials; ensuring adherence to international guidelines and agreements; and improvement of programme co-ordination and information management. In March 2003 the IAEA organized an International Conference on Security of Radioactive Sources, held in Vienna. In April 2005 the UN General Assembly adopted the International Convention for the Suppression of Acts of Nuclear Terrorism. The Convention, which opened for signature in September of that year and entered into force in July 2007, established a definition of acts of nuclear terrorism and urged signatory states to co-operate in the prevention of terrorist attacks by sharing information and providing mutual assistance with criminal investigations and extradition proceedings. Under the provisions of the Convention it was required that any seized nuclear or radiological material should be held in accordance with IAEA safeguards. By the end of 2012 a total of 2,331 incidents had been reported to the Illicit Trafficking Database (ITDB) since its creation in 1995; of the 160 incidents that were reported to have occurred during 2012, 17 involved illegal possession of and attempts to sell nuclear material or radioactive sources; 24 involved reported theft or loss; and 119 concerned discoveries of uncontrolled material, unauthorized disposals, and inadvertent unauthorized shipments and storage. The ITDB had 120 participant states in that year. In July 2012 ITDB participant states convened to discuss means of improving the sharing of information on incidents of unauthorized activities involving radioactive materials.

In June 2004 the IAEA Board of Governors approved an international action plan on the decommissioning of nuclear facilities; the plan was revised in 2007. In September 2007 the IAEA launched a Network of Centres of Excellence for Decommissioning. In 2013 the Agency was managing four ongoing international projects related to safe decommissioning.

In October 2008 the IAEA inaugurated the International Seismic Safety Centre (ISSC), within the Agency's Department of Safety and Security. The ISSC was to serve as a focal point for avoiding and mitigating the consequences of extreme seismic events on nuclear installations world-wide, and was to be supported by a committee of high-level experts in the following areas: geology and tectonics; seismology; seismic hazard; geotechnical engineering; structural engineering; equipment; and seismic risk. In March 2011, in the aftermath of the severe earthquake and tsunami flooding that had struck and severely damaged the Fukushima Daiichi nuclear power plant, the Japanese authorities requested IAEA support in monitoring the effects of the ensuing release of radiation on the environment and on human health. Accordingly, the IAEA dispatched radiation monitoring teams to Japan to provide assistance to local experts, with a particular focus on: worker radiation protection; food safety; marine and soil science; and Boiling Water Reactor (BWR) technology. In late March the IAEA, FAO and WHO issued a joint statement on food safety issues following the Fukushima nuclear emergency, emphasizing their commitment to mobilizing knowledge and expertise in support of the Japanese authorities. During late May–early June an IAEA team comprising 20 international experts visited Japan to assess the ongoing state of nuclear safety in that country. The emergency phase of the Fukushima accident ended with the attainment of Cold Shutdown Condition, in mid-December 2011. In 2011–13 the IAEA issued regular status reports on the situation at Fukushima Daiichi, covering environmental radiation monitoring; workers' exposure to radiation; and ongoing conditions at the plant.

In June 2011, in view of the Fukushima Daiichi accident, the IAEA Ministerial Conference on Nuclear Safety adopted a Ministerial Declaration which formed the basis of the first IAEA Action Plan on Nuclear Safety. The Plan, which was unanimously endorsed in September by the 55th General Conference, emphasized greater transparency in nuclear safety matters and the improvement of safety regimes, including the strengthening of peer reviews, emergency and response mechanisms, and national regulatory bodies. Safety standards were to be reviewed and an assessment of the vulnerabilities of nuclear power plants was to be undertaken. In March 2012 the IAEA convened an International Experts' Meeting on Reactor and Spent Fuel Safety, and in June a meeting of experts was held on Enhancing Transparency and Communications Effectiveness in the Event of a Nuclear or Radiological Emergency, resulting in a 12-point Plan of Action. In September the IAEA and the World Association of Nuclear Operators signed a new Memorandum of Understanding (MOU), to reflect enhanced co-operation in the aftermath of the Fukushima Daiichi event. A ministerial conference on nuclear safety convened jointly by the IAEA and the Japanese Government in Fukushima in December 2012, with participation by representatives of 117 states and 13 international organizations, aimed to share lessons learnt and knowledge gained from the Fukushima Daiichi accident. In January–February 2013 the IAEA organized an International Experts' Meeting on Decommissioning and Remediation After a Nuclear Accident, within the context of implementation of the 2011 IAEA Action Plan on Nuclear Safety.

In May 2011 the IAEA convened a technical meeting on the theme 'Newly Arising Threats in the Cybersecurity of Nuclear Facilities'; the meeting proposed revisions to current international guidance relating to computer security at nuclear facilities, and recommended that the Agency undertake further reviews of current security guidance and identify best practices relating to cybersecurity in nuclear installations.

DISSEMINATION OF INFORMATION

The International Nuclear Information System (INIS), which was established in 1970, provides a computerized indexing and abstracting service. Information on the peaceful uses of atomic energy is collected by member states and international organizations and sent to the IAEA for processing and dissemination (see list of publications below). The IAEA also co-operates with FAO in an information system for agriculture (AGRIS) and with the World Federation of Nuclear Medicine and Biology, and the non-profit Cochrane Collaboration, in maintaining an electronic database of best practice in nuclear medicine. The IAEA Nuclear Data Section provides cost-free data centre services and co-operates with other national and regional nuclear and atomic data centres in the systematic world-wide collection, compilation, dissemination and exchange of nuclear reaction data, nuclear structure and decay data, and atomic and molecular data for fusion.

SAFEGUARDS

The Treaty on the Non-Proliferation of Nuclear Weapons (known also as the Non-Proliferation Treaty or NPT), which entered into force in 1970, requires each 'non-nuclear-weapon state' (one which had not manufactured and exploded a nuclear weapon or other nuclear explosive device prior to 1 January 1967) which is a party to the Treaty to conclude a safeguards agreement with the IAEA (an IAEA comprehensive safeguards agreement—CSA). Under such an agreement, the state undertakes to accept IAEA safeguards on all nuclear material in all its peaceful nuclear activities for the purpose of verifying that such material is not diverted to nuclear weapons or other nuclear explosive devices. In May 1995 the Review and Extension Conference of parties to the NPT agreed to extend the NPT indefinitely, and reaffirmed support for the IAEA's role in verification and the transfer of peaceful nuclear technologies. At the next review conference, held in April–May 2000, the five 'nuclear-weapon states'—China, France, Russia, the United Kingdom and the USA—issued a joint statement pledging their commitment to the ultimate goal of complete nuclear disarmament under effective international controls. A further review conference was convened in May 2005. The 2010 review conference, held in May of that year, unanimously adopted an outcome document containing a 22-point action plan aimed at advancing nuclear disarmament, non-proliferation and the peaceful uses of nuclear energy over the following five years. The Conference also proposed that a regional conference should be convened to address means of eliminating nuclear and other weapons of mass destruction in the Middle East; resolved that the nuclear-weapon states should commit to further efforts to reduce and ultimately eliminate all types of nuclear weapons, including through unilateral, bilateral, regional and multilateral measures, with specific emphasis on the full implementation of the Treaty on Measures for the Further Reduction and Limitation of Strategic Offensive Arms (known as the New START Treaty), signed by the Presidents of Russia and the USA in April 2010 (and in effect from February 2011); and determined that the Conference on Disarmament should immediately establish a subsidiary body to address nuclear disarmament within the context of an agreed and comprehensive programme of work. At September 2013 185 non-nuclear-weapon states and the five nuclear-weapon states were parties to the NPT. A number of non-nuclear-weapon states, however, had not complied, within the prescribed time-limit, with their obligations under the Treaty regarding the conclusion of the relevant safeguards agreement with the Agency.

The five nuclear-weapon states have concluded safeguards agreements with the Agency that permit the application of IAEA safeguards to all their nuclear activities, excluding those with 'direct national significance'. A Comprehensive Nuclear Test Ban Treaty (CTBT) was opened for signature in September 1996, having been adopted by the UN General Assembly. The Treaty was to enter into international law upon ratification by all 44 nations with known nuclear capabilities. A verification body, the Comprehensive Nuclear-Test-Ban Treaty Organization (CTBTO), was to be established upon the Treaty's entry into force; meanwhile, an interim Preparatory Commission for the CTBTO, based in Vienna, became operational in 1997. By September 2013 183 countries had signed the CTBT and 159 had ratified it, including 36 of the 44 states with known nuclear capabilities (known as the 'Annex II states', of which the remaining eight were China, Egypt, Iran, Israel, and the USA, which were at that time signatories to the CTBT; and the Democratic People's Republic of Korea—North Korea, India, and Pakistan, which had not signed the Treaty). In October 1999 ratification of the CTBT was rejected by the US Senate. President Obama of the USA indicated in April 2009 that ratification of the Treaty would be pursued by his regime. The May 2010 NPT review conference determined that all nuclear-weapon states should undertake to ratify the CTBT, and emphasized that, pending the entry into force of the CTBT, all states should refrain from conducting test explosions of nuclear weapons.

To enable the Agency to be able to conclude that all nuclear material in a state is channelled towards peaceful activities both a CSA and an Additional Protocol to the CSA must be in effect. Additional Protocols, which were introduced from 1997, bind member states to provide inspection teams with improved access to information concerning existing and planned nuclear activities, and to allow access to locations other than known nuclear sites within the country's territory. By 31 December 2012 119 states and the European Atomic Energy Community (Euratom) had ratified Additional Protocols to their safeguards agreements. At the end of 2012 some 114 states had both a CSA and an Additional Protocol in force. Integrated Safety Assessments of Research Reactors (INSARR) missions are conducted in member states, on the basis of IAEA safety standards, and, during 2012, a programme of complementary Operation and Maintenance Assessment for Research Reactors (OMARR) missions was initiated.

Several regional nuclear weapons treaties require their member states to conclude CSAs with the IAEA, including the Treaty for the Prohibition of Nuclear Weapons in Latin America (Tlatelolco Treaty, with 33 states parties at September 2013); the South Pacific Nuclear-Free Zone Treaty (Rarotonga Treaty, 13 states parties at September 2013); the Treaty in the South-East Asia Nuclear-Weapon Free Zone (Treaty of Bangkok, adopted in 1995, 10 states parties at September 2013); and the African Nuclear-Weapon Free Zone Treaty (Pelindaba Treaty, adopted in 1996, with 36 states parties at September 2013). In September 2006 experts from Kazakhstan, Kyrgyzstan, Tajikistan, Turkmenistan and Uzbekistan adopted a treaty on establishing a Central Asian Nuclear Weapon Free Zone (CANWFZ); all five states subsequently ratified the treaty. At the end of 2012 664 IAEA safeguards agreements were in force with 179 states, covering 692 nuclear facilities. During that year the Agency conducted 1,965 inspections. Expenditure on the Safeguards Regular Budget for 2012 was €121.2m., and extra-budgetary programme expenditure amounted to €25.5m. The IAEA maintains an imagery database of nuclear sites, and has installed digital surveillance systems (including unattended and remote monitoring capabilities) at sites to replace obsolete analogue systems: by the end of 2012 some 1,283 cameras were connected to 591 systems, operating at 252 facilities in 33 countries.

Under a long-term strategic plan for safeguards, covering the period 2012–23, the IAEA aims to develop the concept of a safeguards approach that is driven by outcomes and customized to the circumstances of individual states, and thereby to move away from a prescriptive facility-based approach.

The IAEA's Safeguards Analytical Laboratory (at the Seibersdorf complex) analyses nuclear fuel cycle samples collected by IAEA safeguards inspectors. Construction of a new Nuclear Material Laboratory was under way at Seibersdorf in 2013, and was scheduled for completion in 2014.

In April 1991 the UN Security Council requested the IAEA to conduct investigations into Iraq's capacity to produce nuclear weapons, following the end of the war between Iraq and the UN-authorized, US-led multinational force. The IAEA was to work closely with a UN Special Commission of experts (UNSCOM), established by the Security Council, whose task was to inspect and dismantle Iraq's weapons of mass destruction (including chemical and biological weapons). In July the IAEA declared that Iraq had violated its safeguards agreement with the IAEA by not submitting nuclear material and relevant facilities in its uranium-enrichment programme to the Agency's inspection. This was the first time that a state party to the NPT had been condemned for concealing a programme of this nature. In October the sixth inspection team, composed of UNSCOM and representatives of the IAEA, was reported to have obtained conclusive documentary evidence that Iraq had a programme for developing nuclear weapons. By February 1994 all declared stocks of nuclear-weapons-grade material had been removed from Iraq. Subsequently, the IAEA pursued a programme of long-term surveillance of nuclear activity in Iraq, under a mandate issued by the UN Security Council. In September 1996 Iraq submitted to the IAEA a 'full, final and complete' declaration of its nuclear activities. However, in September–October 1997 the IAEA recommended that Iraq disclose further equipment, materials and information relating to its nuclear programme. In April 1998 IAEA technical experts were part of a special group that entered eight presidential sites in Iraq to collect baseline data, in accordance with an MOU concluded between the UN Secretary-General and the Iraqi authorities in February. The accord aimed to ensure full Iraqi co-operation with UNSCOM and IAEA personnel. In August, however, Iraq suspended co-operation with UN inspectors, which prevented IAEA from implementing its programme of ongoing monitoring and verification (OMV) activities. In October the IAEA reported that while there was no evidence of Iraq having produced nuclear weapons or having retained or obtained a capability for the production of nuclear weapons, the Agency was unable to guarantee that all items had been found. All IAEA inspectors were temporarily relocated from Iraq to Bahrain in November, in accordance with a decision to withdraw UNSCOM personnel owing to Iraq's failure to agree to resume co-operation. In March 2000 UNSCOM was replaced by a new arms inspection body, the UN Monitoring, Verification and Inspection Commission (UNMOVIC). Although the IAEA carried out inventory verifications of nuclear material in Iraq in January 2000, January 2001 and January 2002, pursuant to Iraq's NPT safeguards agreement, full inspection activities in conjunction with UNMOVIC remained suspended. In September 2002 the US President expressed concern that Iraq was challenging international security owing to its non-compliance with successive UN resolutions relating to the elimination of weapons of mass destruction. In November the UN Security Council adopted Resolution 1441 providing for an enhanced inspection mission and a detailed timetable according to which Iraq would have a final opportunity to comply with its disarmament obligations. Following Iraq's acceptance of the resolution, experts from the IAEA's so-called Iraq Nuclear Verification Office and UNMOVIC resumed inspections on 27 November, with Council authorization to have unrestricted access to all areas and the right to interview Iraqi scientists and weapons experts. In early December Iraq submitted a declaration of all aspects of its weapons programmes, as required under Resolution 1441. In mid-March 2003 Dr Mohamed el-Baradei, then the IAEA Director-General, reported that no evidence had been found of nuclear weapons programme activities in Iraq, while also stating that the Agency had not had sufficient time to complete its investigations. Shortly before the initiation of unilateral military action against Iraq by US and allied forces on 19 March IAEA and UNMOVIC personnel were withdrawn from the country. Following the overthrow in April of the Saddam Hussain regime, responsibility for weapons inspections in Iraq were assumed by a US-led Iraq Survey Group. In late April el-Baradei emphasized the necessity of securing the sites of Iraq's declared nuclear materials from looting and damage. In June 2007 the UN Security Council, noting testimonials that all of Iraq's known weapons of mass destruction had deactivated and that the Iraqi Government had declared its support for international non-proliferation regimes, voted to terminate the mandates of the IAEA weapons inspectors in Iraq and of UNMOVIC. Under the provisions of Iraq's safeguards agreement the IAEA continued to manage its existing information on Iraq, including satellite images; to update its knowledge of facilities in Iraq; and to undertake a physical inventory verification of the nuclear material present in that country.

In September 2003 the IAEA adopted a resolution demanding that the Iranian Government sign, ratify and fully implement an Additional Protocol to its CSA promptly and unconditionally. The Agency also urged Iran to suspend its uranium enrichment and reprocessing activities, pending satisfactory application of the provisions of the Additional Protocol. Iran issued a declaration of its nuclear activities in October, and, in December, signed an Additional Protocol and agreed to suspend uranium enrichment processing. The Agency dispatched inspectors to Iran from October to conduct an intensive verification process. In April 2004 the IAEA Director-General visited Iran and concluded an agreement on a joint action plan to address the outstanding issues of the verification process. Iran provided an initial declaration under the (as yet unratified) Additional Protocol in May. In June, however, the Director-General expressed his continued concern at the extent of Iranian co-operation with IAEA inspectors. In September the Board of Governors adopted a resolution in which it strongly regretted continuing enrichment-related and reprocessing activities by Iran and requested their immediate suspension. The Director-General announced in late November that the suspension had been verified. In August 2005 the Agency adopted a resolution condemning Iran for resuming uranium conversion. In the following month a further resolution was adopted by the Board of Governors, in support of a motion by the EU, citing Iran's non-compliance with the NPT and demanding that Iran accelerate its co-operation with the Agency regarding the outstanding issues. In February 2006 the Board of Governors adopted a resolution that recalled repeated failures by Iran to comply with its obligations under its NPT safeguards agreement, expressed serious concern at the nature of Iran's nuclear programme, and urged that, with a view to building confidence in the exclusively peaceful nature of the programme, Iran should suspend fully all activities related to uranium enrichment (reportedly resumed in January) and reprocessing; ratify and fully implement the Additional Protocol agreed in 2003; and implement transparency measures extending beyond its formal arrangements with the Agency. The resolution requested the IAEA Director-General to report the steps required of Iran to the UN Security Council and to inform the Security Council of all related IAEA documents and resolutions. In response, the Iranian authorities declared that they would suspend all legally non-binding measures imposed by the IAEA, including containment and surveillance measures provided for under the Additional Protocol, and that consequently all IAEA seals and cameras should be removed from Iranian sites by mid-February 2006. At the end of July the UN Security Council, having reviewed the relevant information provided by the IAEA Director-General, issued Resolution 1696, in which it demanded that Iran suspend all enrichment-related and reprocessing activities, including research and development, within a period of one month, and stipulated that non-compliance might result in the imposition on Iran of economic and diplomatic sanctions. The resolution requested that the IAEA Director-General submit to the Council at the end of August a report on Iran's response. The report, which was made public in mid-September, found that Iran had not suspended its enrichment-related activities and was still not in compliance with the provisions of the Additional Protocol. In December the Security Council imposed sanctions against Iran, and in March 2007 the Council imposed a ban on the export of arms from that country.

In June 2007 the IAEA Director-General and the Iranian authorities agreed to develop within 60 days a plan on the modalities for resolving outstanding safeguards implementation issues; accordingly, in August, a workplan on this area (also detailing procedures and timelines) was finalized. At that time the IAEA declared that previous Agency concerns about plutonium reprocessing activities in Iran were now resolved, as its findings had verified earlier statements made by the Iranian authorities. In February 2008 the IAEA Board of Governors reported that Iran was still pursuing its uranium enrichment activities, and that the Iranian Government needed to continue to build confidence about the scope and purported peaceful nature of its nuclear programme. Consequently, in the following month, the UN Security Council adopted a new resolution on Iran in which it professed concern for the proliferation risk presented by the Iranian nuclear programme and authorized inspections of any cargo to and from Iran suspected of transporting prohibited equipment; and strengthened sanctions against Iran.

In May 2008 the IAEA Director-General, at the request of the UN Security Council, circulated a report to both the Security Council and the IAEA Board of Governors on the *Implementation of the NPT Safeguards Agreement and Relevant Provisions of Security Council Resolutions 1737 (2006), 1747 (2007), and 1803 (2008) in the Islamic Republic of Iran*, which concluded that there remained several areas of serious concern, including an ongoing 'green salt' project; high explosives testing; a missile re-entry vehicle project; some procurement activities of military-related institutions; outstanding substantive explanations regarding information with a possible military dimension; and Iran's continuing enrichment-related activities. In September the UN Security Council adopted a new resolution that reiterated demands that Iran cease enriching uranium. Reporting on the situation in February 2009, the IAEA Director-General stated that Iran continued to enrich uranium. Iran was urged once again to implement its Additional Protocol and other transparency measures.

In September 2009 the IAEA was informed by Iran that a second uranium enrichment facility was under construction in its territory; the Iranian authorities stated that the facility was to be used for peaceful purposes. The IAEA determined to send safeguards inspectors to examine the plant, located at the Fordo underground site near Qom, south-west of Tehran. In November the IAEA Board of Governors adopted a resolution urging Iran to suspend immediately construction at Fordo; to engage with the IAEA on resolving all outstanding issues concerning its nuclear programme; to comply fully and without qualification with its safeguards obligations, specifically to provide requested clarifications regarding the purpose of the Fordo enrichment plant and the chronology of its design and construction; and to confirm that no other undeclared facilities were planned or under construction. A report by the IAEA Secretary-General issued in February 2010 stated that, while the IAEA continued to verify the non-diversion of declared nuclear material in Iran, the Iranian authorities had not provided the necessary degree of co-operation to enable the Agency to confirm that all nuclear material in Iran was not being diverted for military purposes. In June the UN Security Council adopted Resolution 1929 further strengthening the UN sanction regime against Iran. Resolution 1929 also established a panel of experts to assist with monitoring and enforcing the implementation of the Iran sanctions. In November 2011 the IAEA Board of Governors adopted a resolution expressing 'deep and increasing concern' over the unresolved issues regarding the Iranian nuclear programme and calling upon Iran to engage seriously and without preconditions in discussions aimed at restoring international confidence in the exclusively peaceful nature of its nuclear activities. With a view to intensifying dialogue, senior IAEA experts visited Iran in late January–early February 2012, and again in late February. On both occasions the IAEA team requested, but was denied, access to the military complex at Parchin, south-east of Tehran, which was suspected to be the site of an explosives containment vessel; clarification of unresolved issues relating to possible military dimensions of Iran's nuclear programme was not achieved. An IAEA report on the Iran situation, issued in late February, found that uranium enrichment had increased three-fold since late 2011, in particular at the underground site at Fordo near Qom; it was maintained by the Iranian authorities, however, that this material was required for a medical research reactor. The report also claimed that the installation of centrifuges at the Natanz uranium enrichment plant, in central Iran, had accelerated. Meeting in May 2012 the IAEA Director-General and senior Iranian officials discussed the adoption of a document on a 'Structured Approach' as a framework for future discussions. In late August the IAEA reported that Iran's Fordo nuclear installation had, since May, doubled production capacity. The IAEA Board of Governors adopted a resolution in September that urged Iran fully and promptly to comply with all requirements set by the Board and with all that country's obligations established by relevant resolutions of the UN Security Council. A further 10 rounds of talks between representatives of the IAEA and the Iranian authorities on the adoption of the proposed Structured Approach were convened in December 2012–May 2013, and another round was scheduled to be held at the end of September 2013, in Vienna. In early April of that year the IAEA's International Seismic Safety Centre reported that an earthquake that had just struck southern Iran was some 91 km removed from a nuclear power plant at Bushehr; the Iranian Government informed the Agency that the plant was undamaged. In August the Board of Governors reiterated that Iran was not providing sufficient co-operation with the Agency, including by not implementing its Additional Protocol, and was not providing credible assurances about the absence of undeclared nuclear material and activities.

The IAEA Conference adopted a resolution in September 2009 that expressed concern about Israel's nuclear capabilities and called upon Israel to accede to the NPT and to place all its nuclear facilities under comprehensive IAEA safeguards. In early July 2013 an INSARR mission was sent to Israel to conduct a peer review of the safety of a reactor at the centrally located Soreq Nuclear Research Center.

In June 2011 the IAEA Board of Governors adopted a resolution noting with serious concern the conclusion of the Agency that a building destroyed at Dair Alzour, Syria, in September 2007, was very likely an undeclared nuclear reactor; the resolution requested Syria to remedy urgently non-compliance with its Safeguards Agreement and called upon that country promptly to bring into force and implement an Additional Protocol to its CSA. IAEA officials visited Syria in October 2011 to pursue the matter, but were not granted sufficient access to locations believed to be functionally related to the Dair Alzour site. In November the IAEA Director-General demanded that Syria co-operate fully with the Agency in connection with unresolved issues relating to Dair Alzour and other locations. In August 2012 the Board of Governors reiterated this request. In September 2013, at which time the possibility of initiating punitive military action against targets in the Syrian capital, Damascus, was under consideration by the US leadership, Russia urged a gathering of the Board of Governors to consider the potential impact, were such action accidentally to strike a nuclear reactor located near that city.

Following the announcement by Libya in mid-December 2003 that it would conclude an Additional Protocol to its CSA with the IAEA, the Agency worked closely with that country to verify the extent of its past undeclared and present nuclear materials and activities. The Libyan authorities signed an Additional Protocol in March 2004.

While assessing nuclear activities in Iran and Libya from late 2003 the Agency also undertook investigations into the supply routes and sources of the technology and materials used in their past undeclared nuclear programmes, demonstrating evidence of a complex 'black market'. The Agency demanded full co-operation from the source countries involved.

In November 2011 the IAEA convened, in Vienna, a Forum on the Experience of Possible Relevance to the Creation of a Nuclear-Weapon-Free-Zone in the Middle East.

NUCLEAR FUEL CYCLE

The Agency promotes the exchange of information between member states on technical, safety, environmental, and economic aspects of nuclear fuel cycle technology, including uranium prospecting and the treatment and disposal of radioactive waste; it provides assistance to member states in the planning, implementation and operation of nuclear fuel cycle facilities and assists in the development of advanced nuclear fuel cycle technology. The Agency operates a number of databases and a simulation system related to the nuclear fuel cycle through its Integrated Nuclear Fuel Cycle Information System (iNFCIS). Every two years, in collaboration with OECD, the Agency prepares estimates of world uranium resources, demand and production.

Finance

The Agency is financed by regular and voluntary contributions from member states. Expenditure approved under the regular budget for 2013 amounted to some €341.5m., while the target for voluntary contributions to finance the IAEA technical co-operation programme in that year was €84.4m. In 2010 the IAEA Peaceful Uses Initiative (PUI) was launched, a funding vehicle aimed at raising extra-budgetary contributions for Agency activities in the peaceful uses of nuclear technology.

Publications

Annual Report.

Atoms for Peace.

Fundamental Safety Principles.

IAEA Bulletin (quarterly).

IAEA Safety Glossary Terminology Used in Nuclear Safety and Radiation Protection.
IAEA Yearbook.
INIS Atomindex (bibliography, 2 a month).
INIS Reference Series.
INSAG Series.
Legal Series.
Meetings on Atomic Energy (quarterly).
The Nuclear Fuel Cycle Information System: A Directory of Nuclear Fuel Cycle Facilities.
Nuclear Data Newsletter.
Nuclear Fusion (monthly).
Nuclear Safety Review (annually).
Nuclear Technology Review (annually).
Panel Proceedings Series.
Publications Catalogue (annually).
Safeguards Implementation Report.
Safety Series.
Technical Directories.
Technical Cooperation Report.

International Bank for Reconstruction and Development—IBRD (World Bank)

Address: 1818 H St, NW, Washington, DC 20433, USA.
Telephone: (202) 473-1000; **fax:** (202) 477-6391; **e-mail:** pic@worldbank.org; **internet:** www.worldbank.org.

The IBRD was established in December 1945. Initially it was concerned with post-war reconstruction in Europe; since then its aim has been to assist the economic development of member nations by making loans where private capital is not available on reasonable terms to finance productive investments. Loans are made either directly to governments, or to private enterprises with the guarantee of their governments. The World Bank, as it is commonly known, comprises the IBRD and the International Development Association (IDA). The affiliated group of institutions, comprising the IBRD, IDA, the International Finance Corporation (IFC), the Multilateral Investment Guarantee Agency (MIGA) and the International Centre for Settlement of Investment Disputes (ICSID, see below), is referred to as the World Bank Group.

Organization

(September 2013)

Officers and staff of the IBRD serve concurrently as officers and staff in IDA. The World Bank has offices in New York, Brussels, Paris (for Europe), Frankfurt, London, Geneva and Tokyo, as well as in more than 100 countries of operation. Country Directors are located in some 30 country offices.

BOARD OF GOVERNORS

The Board of Governors consists of one Governor appointed by each member nation. Typically, a Governor is the country's finance minister, central bank governor, or a minister or an official of comparable rank. The Board normally meets once a year.

EXECUTIVE DIRECTORS

The general operations of the Bank are conducted by a Board of 25 Executive Directors. Five Directors are appointed by the five members having the largest number of shares of capital stock, and the rest are elected by the Governors representing the other members. The President of the Bank is Chairman of the Board.

PRINCIPAL OFFICERS

The principal officers of the Bank are the President of the Bank, three Managing Directors, two Senior Vice-Presidents and 25 Vice-Presidents.

President and Chairman of Executive Directors: Dr Jim Yong Kim (USA).

Vice-President, Middle East and North Africa: Inger Andersen (Denmark).

Activities

The World Bank's primary objectives are the achievement of sustainable economic growth and the reduction of poverty in developing countries. In the context of stimulating economic growth the Bank promotes both private sector development and human resource development and has attempted to respond to the growing demands by developing countries for assistance in these areas. In September 2001 the Bank announced that it was to become a full partner in implementing the UN Millennium Development Goals (MDGs), and was to make them central to its development agenda. The objectives, which were approved by governments attending a special session of the UN General Assembly in September 2000, represented a new international consensus to achieve determined poverty reduction targets. The Bank was closely involved in preparations for the International Conference on Financing for Development, which was held in Monterrey, Mexico, in March 2002. The meeting adopted the Monterrey Consensus, which outlined measures to support national development efforts and to achieve the MDGs. During 2002/03 the Bank, with the IMF, undertook to develop a monitoring framework to review progress in the MDG agenda. The first *Global Monitoring Report* was issued by the Bank and the IMF in April 2004 and has since been published annually. In 2013 the Bank, with other agencies including the UNIDO, UNDP and UN-Energy, was co-leading global consultations on formulating a post-2015 development framework in the thematic area of energy.

In October 2007 the Bank's President defined the following six strategic themes as priorities for Bank development activities: the poorest countries; fragile and post-conflict states; middle-income countries; global public goods; the Arab world; and knowledge and learning. In May 2008 the Bank established a Global Food Crisis Response Programme (GFRP, see below) to assist developing countries affected by the escalating cost of food production. In December the Bank resolved to establish a new facility to accelerate the provision of funds, through IDA, for developing countries affected by the global decline in economic and financial market conditions. The Bank participated in the meeting of heads of state and government of the Group of 20 (G20) leading economies, that was held in Washington, DC, USA, in November 2008 to address the global economic situation, and pursued close collaboration with other multinational organizations, in particular the IMF and OECD, to analyse the impact of the ongoing economic instability. During early 2009 the Bank elaborated its operational response to the global economic crisis. Three operational platforms were devised to address the areas identified as priority themes, i.e. protecting the most vulnerable against the effects of the crisis; maintaining long-term infrastructure investment programmes; and sustaining the potential for private sector-led economic growth and employment creation. Consequently, a new Vulnerability Financing Facility was established, incorporating the GFRP and a new Rapid Social Response Programme, to extend immediate assistance to the poorest groups in affected low- and middle-income countries. Infrastructure investment was to be supported through a new Infrastructure Recovery and Assets Platform, which was mandated to release funds to secure existing infrastructure projects and to finance new initiatives in support of longer-term economic development. Private sector support for infrastructure projects, bank recapitalization, microfinance, and trade financing was to be led by IFC.

The Bank's efforts to reduce poverty include the compilation of country-specific assessments and the formulation of country assistance strategies (CASs) to review and guide the Bank's country programmes. In 1998/99 the Bank's Executive Directors endorsed a Comprehensive Development Framework (CDF) to effect a new approach to development assistance based on partnerships and country responsibility, with an emphasis on the interdependence of the social, structural, human, governmental, economic and environmental elements of development. The CDF, which aimed to enhance the overall effectiveness of development assistance, was formulated after a series of consultative meetings organized by the Bank and attended by representatives of governments, donor agencies, financial institutions, non-governmental organizations, the private sector and academics. In December 1999 the Bank introduced a new approach to implement the principles of the CDF, as part of its strategy to enhance the debt relief scheme for heavily indebted poor countries (HIPCs, see below). Applicant countries were requested to formulate, in consultation with external partners and other stakeholders, a results-oriented national strategy to reduce poverty, to be presented in the form of a Poverty Reduction Strategy Paper (PRSP). In cases where there might be some delay in issuing a full PRSP, it was permissible for a country to submit a less detailed 'interim' PRSP (I-PRSP) in order to secure the preliminary qualification for debt relief. The approach also requires the publication of annual progress reports. In 2001 the Bank introduced a new Poverty Reduction Support Credit to help low-income countries to implement the policy and institutional reforms outlined in their PRSP. Increasingly, PRSPs have been considered by the international community to be the appropriate country-level framework to assess progress towards achieving the MDGs.

The Bank's annual publication *World Development Report* addresses specific aspects of development. The 2013 edition focused on jobs, including the impact of productive employment on social and economic development. The 2014 WDR was scheduled to be published in late 2013, on the theme 'Managing Risk for Development'.

In September 2011 the Bank introduced a Corporate Scorecard, which uses a framework of performance indicators to monitor the IBRD and IDA's ongoing progress and achievement of development results. In April 2012 an interactive internet-based version of the Corporate Scorecard was introduced.

FINANCIAL OPERATIONS

IBRD capital is derived from members' subscriptions to capital shares, the calculation of which is based on their quotas in the IMF. At 30 June 2012 the total subscribed capital of the IBRD was US $205,394m., of which the paid-in portion was $12,418m. (6.0%); the remainder is subject to call if required. Most of the IBRD's lendable funds come from its borrowing, on commercial terms, in world capital markets, and also from its retained earnings and the flow of repayments on its loans. IBRD loans carry a variable interest rate, rather than a rate fixed at the time of borrowing.

IBRD loans usually have a 'grace period' of five years and are repayable over 15 years or fewer. Loans are made to governments, or must be guaranteed by the government concerned, and are normally made for projects likely to offer a commercially viable rate of return. In 1980 the World Bank introduced structural adjustment lending, which (instead of financing specific projects) supports programmes and changes necessary to modify the structure of an economy so that it can restore or maintain its growth and viability in its balance of payments over the medium term.

The IBRD and IDA together made 253 new lending and investment commitments totalling US $35,335m. during the year ending 30 June 2012. During 2011/12 the IBRD alone approved commitments totalling $20,582m. (compared with $26,747m. in the previous year), of which $1,433m. (7%) was allocated to projects in the Middle East and North Africa. Total disbursements by the IBRD in the year ending 30 June 2012 amounted to $28,775m. The Bank's operational strategy in the region has focused on the following five key areas: improving governance; private sector development; strengthening water management; education; and inclusion. In April 2011 the Bank's President asserted the need to formulate a new regional strategy based on a 'Social Contract for Development', in order to support political and social movements in the region pressing for greater democracy, citizen participation and accountable governance. The Bank works with the Arab League to support programmes and initiatives to counter the problem of high youth employment.

In September 1996 the World Bank/IMF Development Committee endorsed a joint initiative to assist HIPCs to reduce their debt burden to a sustainable level, in order to make more resources available for poverty reduction and economic growth. A new Trust Fund was established by the World Bank in November to finance the initiative. The Fund, consisting of an initial allocation of US $500m. from the IBRD surplus and other contributions from multilateral creditors, was to be administered by IDA. In early 1999 the World Bank and IMF initiated a comprehensive review of the HIPC initiative. In June the G8 countries, meeting in Cologne, Germany, agreed to increase contributions to the HIPC Trust Fund and to cancel substantial amounts of outstanding debt, and proposed more flexible terms for eligibility. In September the Bank and IMF reached an agreement on an enhanced HIPC scheme, with further revenue to be generated through the revaluation of a percentage of IMF gold reserves. It was agreed that, in order to qualify for debt relief and additional concessional lending, countries were to formulate a PRSP, and should demonstrate prudent financial management in the implementation of the strategy for at least one year. Those countries still deemed to have an unsustainable level of debt at the pivotal 'decision point' of the process were to qualify for assistance. In the majority of cases a sustainable level of debt was targeted at 150% of the net present value (NPV) of the debt in relation to total annual exports (compared with 200%–250% under the original HIPC scheme). Other countries with a lower debt-to-export ratio were to be eligible for assistance under the initiative, providing that their export earnings were at least 30% of GDP (lowered from 40%) and government revenue at least 15% of GDP (reduced from 20%). In September 2005 the Bank and IMF endorsed a proposal of the G8 to cancel all debt owed by countries that had reached their completion point, under a new Multilateral Debt Relief Initiative. By December 2012 35 countries had reached completion point and a further two had reached decision point of the process.

In January 2012 the Bank launched the Program for Results (PforR), a new lending instrument that links the disbursement of funds to the delivery of pre-defined results. By August 2013 eight PforR projects had been approved and a further 10 were under consideration.

During 2000/01 the World Bank strengthened its efforts to counter the problem of HIV and AIDS in developing countries. In November 2001 the Bank appointed its first Global HIV/AIDS Adviser. In September 2000 a new Multi-Country HIV/AIDS Programme for Africa (MAP) was launched, initially with US $500m., in collaboration with UNAIDS and other major donor agencies and non-governmental organizations. In February 2002 the Bank approved an additional $500m. for a second phase of MAP. The Bank has undertaken research into the long-term effects of HIV/AIDS, and hosts the Global HIV/AIDS Monitoring and Evaluation Support Team of UNAIDS. In November 2004 the Bank launched an AIDS Media Center to improve access to information regarding HIV/AIDS, in particular to journalists in developing countries. It has also established a resource library to strengthen HIV/AIDS monitoring and evaluation systems. In July 2009 the Bank published a report, with UNAIDS, concerned with the impact of the global economic crisis on HIV prevention and treatment programmes. A new regional report on HIV/AIDS in the Middle East and North Africa, entitled *Time for Strategic Action*, was published in June 2010.

In March 2007 the Board of Executive Directors approved an action plan to develop further its Clean Energy for Development Investment Framework, which had been formulated in response to a request by the G8 heads of state, meeting in Gleneagles, United Kingdom, in July 2005. The action plan focused on efforts to improve access to clean energy, in particular in sub-Saharan Africa; to accelerate the transition to low carbon emission development; and to support adaptation to climate change. In October 2008 the Bank Group endorsed a new Strategic Framework on Development and Climate Change, which aimed to guide the Bank in supporting the efforts of developing countries to achieving growth and reducing poverty, while recognizing the operational challenges of climate change. In June 2010 the Bank appointed a Special Envoy to lead the Bank's representation in international discussions on climate change. In February 2012 the Bank supported the establishment of a Global Partnership for Oceans.

TECHNICAL ASSISTANCE AND ADVISORY SERVICES

In addition to providing financial services, the Bank also undertakes analytical and advisory services, and supports learning and capacity-building, in particular through the World Bank Institute, the Staff Exchange Programme and knowledge-sharing initiatives. The Bank has supported efforts, such as the Global Development Gateway, to disseminate information on development issues and programmes, and, since 1988, has organized the Annual Bank Conference on Development Economics (ABCDE) to provide a forum for the exchange and discussion of development-related ideas and research. The 2013 gathering was held, in June, on the theme 'Risk and Vulnerability'. In September 1995 the Bank initiated the Information for Development Programme (InfoDev) with the aim of fostering partnerships between governments, multilateral institutions and private sector experts in order to promote reform and investment in developing countries through improved access to information technology.

The provision of technical assistance to member countries has become a major component of World Bank activities. The economic and sector work (ESW) undertaken by the Bank is the vehicle for considerable technical assistance and often forms the basis of CASs and other strategic or advisory reports. In addition, project loans and credits may include funds earmarked specifically for feasibility studies, resource surveys, management or planning advice, and training. The World Bank Institute has become one of the most important of the Bank's activities in technical assistance. It provides training in national economic management and project analysis for government officials at the middle and upper levels of responsibility. It also runs overseas courses aiming to build up local training capability, and administers a graduate scholarship programme. Technical assistance (usually reimbursable) is also extended to countries that do not need Bank financial support, e.g. for training and transfer of technology. The Bank encourages the use of local consultants to assist with projects and to strengthen institutional capability.

The Project Preparation Facility (PPF) was established in 1975 to provide cash advances to prepare projects that may be financed by the Bank. In 1992 the Bank established an Institutional Development Fund (IDF), which became operational on 1 July; the purpose of the Fund was to provide rapid, small-scale financial assistance, to a maximum value of US $750,000, for capacity-building proposals. In 2002 the IDF was reoriented to focus on good governance, in particular financial accountability and system reforms.

ECONOMIC RESEARCH AND STUDIES

In the 1990s the World Bank's research, conducted by its own research staff, was increasingly concerned with providing information to reinforce the Bank's expanding advisory role to developing countries and to improve policy in the Bank's borrowing countries. The principal areas of current research focus on issues such as maintaining sustainable growth while protecting the environment and the poorest sectors of society, encouraging the development of the private sector, and reducing and decentralizing government activities.

The Bank chairs the Consultative Group on International Agricultural Research (CGIAR), which was founded in 1971 to raise financial support for international agricultural research work for improving crops and animal production in developing countries; it supports 15 research centres.

CO-OPERATION WITH OTHER ORGANIZATIONS

The World Bank co-operates with other international partners with the aim of improving the impact of development efforts. It collaborates with the IMF in implementing the HIPC scheme and the two agencies work closely to achieve a common approach to development initiatives. The Bank has established strong working relationships with many other UN bodies, in particular through a mutual commitment to poverty reduction objectives. In May 2000 the Bank signed a joint statement of co-operation with OECD. The Bank holds regular consultations with other multilateral development banks and with the European Union with respect to development issues. The Bank-NGO Committee provides an annual forum for discussion with non-governmental organizations (NGOs). Strengthening co-operation with external partners was a fundamental element of the Comprehensive Development Framework, which was adopted in 1998/99 (see above). In 2001/02 a Partnership Approval and Tracking System was implemented to provide information on the Bank's regional and global partnerships. In June 2007 the World Bank and the UN Office on Drugs and Crime launched a joint Stolen Asset Recovery (StAR) initiative, as part of the Bank's new Governance and Anti-Corruption (GAC) strategy. In April 2009 the G20 recommended that StAR review and propose mechanisms to strengthen international co-operation relating to asset recovery. The first global forum on stolen asset recovery and development was convened by StAR in June 2010.

The Bank is a partner, with the IMF, the UN Conference on Trade and Development (UNCTAD), UNDP, the World Trade Organization (WTO) and the International Trade Commission, in the Enhanced Integrated Framework (EIF) for trade-related assistance to least developed countries (LDCs), which aims to facilitate greater participation by LDCs in the global trading system; EIF activities are supported by a dedicated EIF Trust Fund. The EIF replaced in 2007, and builds upon, a previous Integrated Framework, established in 1997. In 1997 a Partnerships Group was established to strengthen the Bank's work with development institutions, representatives of civil society and the private sector. The Group established a new Development Grant Facility, which became operational in October, to support partnership initiatives and to co-ordinate all of the Bank's grant-making activities. The Bank establishes and administers trust funds, open to contributions from member countries and multilateral organizations, NGOs, and private sector institutions, in order to support development partnerships. By 30 June 2012 the Bank had a portfolio of 1,064 active trust funds, with assets of some US $29,200m.

In June 1995 the World Bank joined other international donors (including regional development banks, other UN bodies, Canada, France, the Netherlands and the USA) in establishing a Consultative Group to Assist the Poorest (CGAP), with the aim of channelling funds to the most needy through grass-roots agencies. An initial credit of approximately US $200m. was committed by the donors. The Bank manages the CGAP Secretariat, which is responsible for the administration of external funding and for the evaluation and approval of project financing. The CGAP provides technical assistance, training and strategic advice to microfinance institutions and other relevant bodies. As an implementing agency of the Global Environment Facility (GEF) the Bank assists countries to prepare and supervise GEF projects relating to biological diversity, climate change and other environmental protection measures. It is an example of a partnership in action which addresses a global agenda, complementing Bank country assistance activities. A new international partnership, the African Stockpiles Programme, was initiated in June 2004 with the aim of disposing of an estimated 50,000 metric tons of obsolete pesticides throughout the region. The Bank was to manage the Programme's Multi-Donor Trust Fund and to host the unit acting as a secretariat for the Programme's Steering Committee. Ethiopia, Mali, Morocco, Niger, South Africa, Tanzania and Tunisia were to be the first participants in the project, which was anticipated to last for 12–15 years at a cost of US $250m. In 2005/06 a multi-donor trust fund was established to finance a study into the feasibility of transferring water from the Red Sea to the Dead Sea. Other funds administered by the Bank include the Global Program to Eradicate Poliomyelitis, launched during the financial year 2002/03, the Least Developed Countries Fund for Climate Change, established in September 2002, an Education for All Fast-Track Initiative Catalytic Trust Fund, established in 2003/04, and a Carbon Finance Assistance Trust Fund, established in 2004/05. In 2006/07 the Bank established a Global Facility for Disaster Reduction and Recovery. In September 2007 the Bank's Executive Directors approved a Carbon Partnership Facility and a Forest Carbon Partnership Facility to support its climate change activities. In March 2008 the Bank established a new trust fund to channel resources in support of a Palestinian Reform and Development Plan (2008–10). In May the Bank inaugurated the Global Food Crisis Response Programme (GFRP) to provide financial support, with resources of some $1,200m., to help meet the immediate needs of countries affected by the escalating cost of food production and by food shortages. Grants and loans were to be allocated on the basis of rapid needs assessments, conducted by the Bank with the FAO, the WFP and IFAD. As part of the facility a Multi-Donor Trust Fund was to be established to facilitate co-ordination among donors and to leverage financial support for the rapid delivery of seeds and fertilizer to small-scale farmers. In April 2009 the Bank increased the resources available under the GFRP to $2,000m. By March 2013 $1,560m. had been approved under the GFRP for initiatives in 49 countries, of which some $1,390m. had been disbursed. In January 2011 the Bank signed a Memorandum of Understanding with the League of Arab States within the framework of the Arab World Initiative, in order to strengthen co-operation in areas of regional economic and social development. In May the Bank inaugurated a new Arab Financing Facility for Infrastructure (AFFI), as a partnership between the Bank, IFC and the Islamic Development Bank, in order to improve access to financing for public and private infrastructure projects in the region.

The Bank is a lead organization in providing reconstruction assistance following natural disasters or conflicts, usually in collaboration with other UN agencies or international organizations, and through special trust funds. In May 2003 a Bank representative participated in an international advisory and monitoring board to assess reconstruction and development needs following international conflict in Iraq and removal of its governing regime. In October the Bank, with the UN Development Group, published a report identifying 14 priority areas for reconstruction, with funding requirements of US $36,000m. over the period 2004–07, which was presented to an international donor conference held later in that month. The conference, in Madrid, Spain, approved the establishment of an International Reconstruction Fund Facility for Iraq to channel international donations and to co-ordinate reconstruction activities. In January 2004 the Bank's Board of Executive Directors authorized the Bank to administer an integral part of the facility, the Iraq Trust Fund, to finance a programme of emergency projects and provide technical assistance. By January 2009 the ITF was financing 18 project grants, amounting to $481.6m. The Bank was a partner, with the Iraqi Government, the UN Secretariat, the IMF and other financial institutions, in the International Compact with Iraq, a five-year framework for co-operation that was launched in May 2007. In September 2006 the Bank established an Emergency Service Support Programme Multi-Donor Trust Fund for the Palestine (National) Authority, to generate funds for essential basic services which may be affected by a decline in external funding assistance following the election, earlier in that year, of a Hamas-led government.

The Bank has worked with FAO, the World Health Organization (WHO) and the World Organisation of Animal Health (OIE) to develop strategies to monitor, contain and eradicate the spread of highly pathogenic avian influenza. In September 2005 the Bank organized a meeting of leading experts on the issue and in November it co-sponsored, with FAO, WHO and the OIE, an international partners' conference, focusing on control of the disease and preparedness planning for any future related influenza pandemic in humans. In January 2006 the Bank's Board of Directors approved the establishment of a funding programme (the Global Program for Avian Influenza Control and Human Pandemic Preparedness and Response—GPAI), with resources of up to US $500m., to assist countries to combat the disease. Later in that month the Bank co-sponsored, with the European Commission and the People's Republic of China, an International Ministerial Pledging Conference on Avian and Human Pandemic Influenza (AHI), convened in Beijing. Participants pledged some $1,900m. to fund disease control and pandemic preparedness activities at global, regional and country levels. Commitments to the AHI facility amounted to $126m. at January

2009. In June the Bank approved an additional $500m. to expand the GPAI in order to fund emergency operations required to prevent and control outbreaks of the new swine influenza variant pandemic (H1N1).

EVALUATION

The Independent Evaluation Group is an independent unit within the World Bank. It conducts Country Assistance Evaluations to assess the development effectiveness of a Bank country programme, and studies and publishes the results of projects after a loan has been fully disbursed, so as to identify problems and possible improvements in future activities. In addition, the department reviews the Bank's global programmes and produces the *Annual Review of Development Effectiveness*. In 1996 a Quality Assurance Group was established to monitor the effectiveness of the Bank's operations and performance. In March 2009 the Bank published an Action Plan on Aid Effectiveness, based on the Accra Agenda for Action that had been adopted in September 2008 during the Third High Level Forum on Aid Effectiveness, held in Ghana.

In September 1993 the Bank established an independent Inspection Panel, consistent with the Bank's objective of improving project implementation and accountability. The Panel, which began operations in September 1994, was to conduct independent investigations and report on complaints from local people concerning the design, appraisal and implementation of development projects supported by the Bank. By August 2013 the Panel had received 88 formal requests for inspection.

IBRD INSTITUTIONS

World Bank Institute (WBI): founded in March 1999 by merger of the Bank's Learning and Leadership Centre, previously responsible for internal staff training, and the Economic Development Institute (EDI), which had been established in 1955 to train government officials concerned with development programmes and policies. The new Institute aimed to emphasize the Bank's priority areas through the provision of training courses and seminars relating to poverty, crisis response, good governance and anti-corruption strategies. The Institute supports a Global Knowledge Partnership, which was established in 1997 to promote alliances between governments, companies, other agencies and organizations committed to applying information and communication technologies for development purposes. Under the EDI a World Links for Development programme was also initiated to connect schools in developing countries with partner establishments in industrialized nations via the internet. In 1999 the WBI expanded its programmes through distance learning, a Global Development Network, and use of new technologies. A new initiative, Global Development Learning Network (GDLN), aimed to expand access to information and learning opportunities through the internet, video conferences and organized exchanges. The WBI had also established 60 formal partnership arrangements with learning centres and public, private and non-governmental organizations to support joint capacity building programmes; many other informal partnerships were also in place. During 2009/10 new South-South Learning Middle-income country (MIC)–OECD Knowledge Exchange facilities were established. By 2013 the WBI was focusing its work on the following areas: climate change; fragile and conflict-affected states; governance; growth and competitiveness; health systems; public-private partnerships in infrastructure; and urban development; Vice-Pres. SANJAY PRADHAN (India); publs *Annual Report*, *Development Outreach* (quarterly), other books, working papers, case studies.

International Centre for Settlement of Investment Disputes (ICSID): founded in 1966 under the Convention of the Settlement of Investment Disputes between States and Nationals of Other States. The Convention was designed to encourage the growth of private foreign investment for economic development, by creating the possibility, always subject to the consent of both parties, for a Contracting State and a foreign investor who is a national of another Contracting State to settle any legal dispute that might arise out of such an investment by conciliation and/or arbitration before an impartial, international forum. The governing body of the Centre is its Administrative Council, composed of one representative of each Contracting State, all of whom have equal voting power. The President of the World Bank is (ex officio) the non-voting Chairman of the Administrative Council. At August 2013 437 cases had been registered with the Centre, of which 268 had been concluded and 169 were pending consideration. At that time 149 countries had signed and ratified the Convention to become ICSID Contracting States; Sec.-Gen. MEG KINNEAR (Canada).

Publications

Abstracts of Current Studies: The World Bank Research Program (annually).
African Development Indicators (annually).
Annual Report on Operations Evaluation.
Annual Report on Portfolio Performance.
Annual Review of Development Effectiveness.
Doing Business (annually).
Global Commodity Markets (quarterly).
Global Development Finance (annually).
Global Economic Prospects (annually).
Global Financial Development Report (annually).
ICSID Annual Report.
ICSID Review—Foreign Investment Law Journal (2 a year).
Joint BIS-IMF-OECD-World Bank Statistics on External Debt (quarterly).
News from ICSID (2 a year).
Poverty Reduction and the World Bank (annually).
Poverty Reduction Strategies Newsletter (quarterly).
Research News (quarterly).
Staff Working Papers.
The World Bank and the Environment (annually).
World Bank Annual Report.
World Bank Atlas (annually).
World Bank Economic Review (3 a year).
World Bank Research Observer.
World Development Indicators (annually).
World Development Report (annually).

Statistics

IBRD LOANS APPROVED IN THE MIDDLE EAST AND NORTH AFRICA, JULY 2011–JUNE 2012
(US $ million)

Country	Purpose	Amount
Egypt	Giza North power project	240.0
	Emergency labor intensive investment	200.0
Jordan	First programmatic development policy loan	250.0
Lebanon	Cultural heritage and urban development	27.0
Morocco	Ouarzazate I concentrated solar power plant	200.0
	First skills and employment development policy loan	100.0
	Judicial performance enhancement for service to citizen	15.8
	National initiative for human development 2—Program for results loan	300.0
	Micro, small and medium enterprise development	50.0
Tunisia	Micro, small and medium enterprise development	50.0
Turkey*	Private sector renewable energy and energy efficiency (additional financing)	500.0
	Third programmatic environmental sustainability and energy sector development policy loan	600.0

* Classified under Europe and Central Asia by the World Bank.

Source: World Bank, *Annual Report 2012*.

International Development Association—IDA

Address: 1818 H Street, NW, Washington, DC 20433, USA.

Telephone: (202) 473-1000; **fax:** (202) 477-6391; **internet:** www.worldbank.org/ida.

The International Development Association began operations in November 1960. Affiliated to the International Band for Reconstruction and Development (IBRD), IDA advances capital to the poorer developing member countries on more flexible terms than those offered by the IBRD.

Organization

(September 2013)

Officers and staff of the IBRD serve concurrently as officers and staff of IDA.

President and Chairman of Executive Directors: Dr Jim Yong Kim (USA).

Activities

IDA assistance is aimed at the poorer developing countries (i.e. those with an annual gross national income (GNI) per capita of less than US $1,195 were to qualify for assistance in 2012/13) in order to support their poverty reduction strategies. Under IDA lending conditions, credits can be extended to countries whose balance of payments could not sustain the burden of repayment required for IBRD loans. Terms are more favourable than those provided by the IBRD; credits are for a period of 35 or 40 years, with a 'grace period' of 10 years, and carry no, or very low, interest and service charges. From 1 July 2011 the maturity of credits was to be 25 or 40 years, with a grace period of five or 10 years. In 2013 82 countries were eligible for IDA assistance, including 13 small-island economies with a GNI per head greater than $1,195, but which would otherwise have little or no access to Bank funds, and 17 so-called blend borrowers which are entitled to borrow from both IDA and the IBRD.

IDA's total development resources, consisting of members' subscriptions and supplementary resources (additional subscriptions and contributions), are replenished periodically by contributions from the more affluent member countries. In March 2010 negotiations on the 16th replenishment of IDA funds (IDA16) commenced, in Paris, France. Participants determined that the overarching theme of IDA16 should be achieving development results, and the following areas of focus be 'special themes': gender; climate change; fragile and conflict affected states; and crisis response. Replenishment meetings were subsequently held in Bamako, Mali, in June, and in Washington, DC, USA, in October. An agreement was concluded in December, at a meeting convened in Brussels, Belgium. The IDA16 replenishment amounted to $49,300m., to cover the period 1 July 2011–30 June 2014, of which $26,400m. was committed by 51 donor countries.

During the year ending 30 June 2012 new IDA commitments amounted to US $14,753 for 160 projects, compared with $16,269m. for 230 projects in the previous year. In that financial year some 32% of lending was for infrastructure projects, 24% for social sector projects, and 23% for projects in the area of public administration and law.

In December 2008 the Bank's Board of Executive Directors approved a new IDA facility, the Financial Crisis Response Fast Track Facility, to accelerate the provision of up to US $2,000m. of IDA15 resources to help the poorest countries to counter the impact of the global economic and financial crisis. The first operations approved under the Facility, in February 2009, were for Armenia (amounting to $35m.) and the Democratic Republic of Congo ($100m.) in support of employment creation and infrastructure development initiatives and meeting the costs of essential services. In December the Board of Executive Directors approved a pilot Crisis Response Window to deploy an additional $1,300m. of IDA funds to support the poorest countries affected by the economic crisis until the end of the IDA15 period (30 June 2011), with the aim of assisting those countries to maintain spending on sectors critical to achieving the Millennium Development Goals. Permanent funding for the Crisis Response Window, which additionally was to assist low-income countries manage the impact of natural disasters, was agreed as part of the IDA16 replenishment accord in December 2010. In mid-2011 $250m. was allocated from the Crisis Response Window to provide relief and longer-term rehabilitation assistance to areas of the Horn of Africa affected by severe drought. In September the World Bank announced that $30m. of those funds were to be disbursed through UNHCR in order to improve basic facilities in settlements occupied by persons displaced as a result of the drought. In December the World Bank's Board of Executive Directors approved the establishment of an Immediate Response Mechanism in order to accelerate the provision of assistance to IDA-eligible countries following a natural disaster or economic crisis.

IDA administers a Trust Fund, which was established in November 1996 as part of a World Bank/IMF initiative to assist heavily indebted poor countries (HIPCs). In September 2005 the World Bank's Development Committee and the International Monetary and Financial Committee of the IMF endorsed a proposal of the Group of Eight (G8) industrialized nations to cancel the remaining multilateral debt owed by HIPCs that had reached their completion point under the scheme (see IBRD). In December IDA convened a meeting of donor countries to discuss funding to uphold its financial capability upon its contribution to the so-called Multilateral Debt Relief Initiative (MDRI). IDA's participation in the scheme was approved by the Board of Executive Directors in March 2006 and entered into effect on 1 July. During IDA15 US $6,300m. was allocated to the provision of debt relief under the MDRI, $1,700m. under the HIPC initiative and a further $1,100m. to finance arrears clearance operations. At July 2011 the estimated cost of the HIPC initiative was $76,000m., of which IDA commitments totalled $14,900m.; IDA's contribution to the MDRI was estimated at $35,300m. in nominal value terms (or some 67% of the total cost of the MDRI). By June 2013 35 countries had reached completion point to receive assistance under the initiative.

Publication

Annual Report.

Statistics

IDA CREDIT APPROVED IN THE MIDDLE EAST AND NORTH AFRICA, JULY 2011–JUNE 2012
(US $ million)

Country	Purpose	Amount
Yemen . .	Labour intensive public works	61.0

Source: World Bank, *Annual Report 2012*.

International Finance Corporation—IFC

Address: 2121 Pennsylvania Ave, NW, Washington, DC 20433, USA.

Telephone: (202) 473-3800; **fax:** (202) 974-4384; **e-mail:** information@ifc.org; **internet:** www.ifc.org.

IFC was founded in 1956 as a member of the World Bank Group to stimulate economic growth in developing countries by financing private sector investments, mobilizing capital in international financial markets, and providing technical assistance and advice to governments and businesses.

Organization

(September 2013)

IFC is a separate legal entity in the World Bank Group. Executive Directors of the World Bank also serve as Directors of IFC. The President of the World Bank is ex officio Chairman of the IFC Board of Directors, which has appointed him President of IFC. Subject to his overall supervision, the day-to-day operations of IFC are conducted by its staff under the direction of the Executive Vice-President. The senior management team includes 10 Vice-Presidents responsible for regional and thematic groupings. At the end of June 2012 IFC had 3,763 staff members, of whom 56% were based in field offices in 92 countries.

PRINCIPAL OFFICERS

President: Dr JIM YONG KIM (USA).

Executive Vice-President: JIN-YONG CAI (People's Republic of China).

Vice-President, Eastern and Southern Europe, Central Asia, Middle East and North Africa: DIMITRIS TSITSIRAGOS (Greece).

OFFICES IN THE MIDDLE EAST AND NORTH AFRICA

IFC Advisory Services: Nile City Towers, 2005 Corniche el-Nil, North Tower, 24th Floor, Boulac, Cairo, Egypt; tel. (2) 2461-9140; fax (2) 2461-9160; Dir MOUAYED MAKHLOUF.

Algeria: 5 bis chemin Mackley, 16306 Ben Aknoun, Algiers; tel. (37) 65-24-79; e-mail jcobein@ifc.org; Principal Country Officer JOUMANA COBEIN.

Egypt: Nile City Towers, 2005 Corniche el-Nil, North Tower, 24th Floor, Boulac, Cairo; tel. (2) 2461-9140; fax (2) 2461-9160; e-mail nshousha@ifc.org; Principal Country Officer NADA SHOUSHA.

Iraq: Baghdad; tel. (1) 120-0000; e-mail zbadr@ifc.org; Country Man. ZIAD BADR.

Jordan: 38 Ahmed Orabi St, Shemeesani, Amman 11195; tel. (6) 567-8050; fax (6) 567-8040; e-mail aattiga@ifc.org; Principal Country Officer AHMED ATTIGA.

Lebanon: World Bank Office, A. Beyhum St, Al Marfaa, Bourie, House, Solidere Beirut, 1107 2270; tel. (1) 987800; fax (1) 987601; e-mail tjacobs@ifc.org; Senior Country Officer THOMAS JACOBS.

Morocco: 7 rue Larbi Ben Abdellah, Rabat-Souissi; tel. (37) 65-24-79; fax (37) 65-28-93; e-mail jcobein@ifc.org; Principal Country Officer JOUMANA COBEIN.

Saudi Arabia: Diplomatic Quarter, UN Bldg, POB 5900, Riyadh 11432; tel. (1) 4834956; fax (1) 4885311; e-mail walmurshed@ifc.org; Senior Country Officer WALID AL MURSHED.

Tunisia: Tunis; tel. (71) 967-197; e-mail acourcelle@ifc.org; Principal Operations Officer ANTOINE COURCELLE-LABROUSSE.

Turkey: Buyukdere Cad. 185, Kanyon ofis Blogu Kat 10, Levent, 34394 Istanbul; tel. (212) 385-3000; fax (212) 385-3001; e-mail slazar@ifc.org; Assoc. Dir SYBILE LAZAR.

UAE: The Gate, West Side, 10th floor, D.I.F.C., POB 118071, Dubai; tel. (4) 3601000; fax (4) 3601010; e-mail dkhanna@ifc.org; Chief Investment Officer DEEPAK C. KHANNA.

West Bank and Gaza: World Bank Bldg, 6th Floor, Dahiet al Barid, POB 54842, Jerusalem, Israel; tel. (2) 236 6538; fax (2) 236-6521; e-mail yhabesch@ifc.org; Country Officer YOUSSEF HABESCH.

Yemen: POB 18152, Hadda, St no. 40, San'a; tel. (1) 413708; fax (1) 431376; e-mail rconway@ifc.org; Country Officer RAYMOND JOSEPH CONWAY.

Activities

IFC aims to promote economic development in developing member countries by assisting the growth of private enterprise and effective capital markets. It finances private sector projects, through loans, the purchase of equity, quasi-equity products, and risk management services, and assists governments to create conditions that stimulate the flow of domestic and foreign private savings and investment. IFC may provide finance for a project that is partly state-owned, provided that there is participation by the private sector and that the project is operated on a commercial basis. IFC also mobilizes additional resources from other financial institutions, in particular through syndicated loans, thus providing access to international capital markets. IFC provides a range of advisory services to help to improve the investment climate in developing countries and offers technical assistance to private enterprises and governments. In 2008 IFC formulated a policy document to help to increase its impact during the three-year period 2009–11. The IFC Road Map identified five strategic 'pillars' as priority areas of activity: strengthening the focus on frontier markets (i.e. the lowest-income countries or regions of middle-income countries, those affected by conflict, or underdeveloped industrial sectors); building long-term partnerships with emerging 'players' in developing countries; addressing climate change and securing environmental and social sustainability; promoting private sector growth in infrastructure, health and education; and developing local financial markets. From late 2008 IFC's overriding concern was to respond effectively to the difficulties facing member countries affected by the global economic and financial crisis and to maintain a sustainable level of development. In particular it aimed to preserve and create employment opportunities, to support supply chains for local businesses, and to provide credit.

To be eligible for financing projects must be profitable for investors, as well as financially and economically viable; must benefit the economy of the country concerned; and must comply with IFC's environmental and social guidelines. IFC aims to promote best corporate governance and management methods and sustainable business practices, and encourages partnerships between governments, non-governmental organizations and community groups. In 2001/02 IFC developed a Sustainability Framework to help to assess the longer-term economic, environmental and social impact of projects. The first Sustainability Review was published in mid-2002. In 2002/03 IFC assisted 10 international banks to draft a voluntary set of guidelines (the Equator Principles), based on IFC's environmental, social and safeguard monitoring policies, to be applied to their global project finance activities. In September 2009 IFC initiated a Performance Standards Review Process to define new standards to be applied within the Equator Principles framework. At mid-2013 78 financial institutions had signed up to the Equator Principles.

In November 2004 IFC announced the establishment of a Global Trade Finance Programme (GTFP), with initial funding of some US $500m., which aimed to support small-scale importers and exporters in emerging markets, and to facilitate South–South trade in goods and services, by providing guarantees for trade transactions, as well as extending technical assistance and training to local financial institutions. Additional funding of $500m. was approved in January 2007, and in October 2008. In December, as part of a set of measures to support the global economy, the Board of Directors approved an expansion of the GTFP, doubling its funding to $3,000m. By July 2013 more than 250 global and regional confirming banks operating in around 100 countries were participating in the Programme. Other initiatives included the establishment of an Infrastructure Crisis Facility to provide investment for existing projects affected by a lack of private funding, and a new Bank Capitalization Fund (to be financed, up to $3,000m., with the Japan Bank for International Co-operation) to provide investment and advisory services to banks in emerging markets. In May 2009 IFC established an Asset Management Company, as a wholly owned subsidiary, to administer the Capitalization Fund. In February of that year IFC inaugurated a Microfinance Enhancement Facility, with a German development bank, to extend credit to microfinancing institutions and to support lending to low-income borrowers, with funds of up to $500m. IFC committed $1,000m. in funds to a new Global Trade Liquidity Program (GTLP), which was inaugurated by the World Bank Group in April, with the aim of mobilizing support of up to $50,000m. in trade transactions through financing extended by governments, other development banks and the private sector. In October IFC established a Debt and Asset Recovery Program to help to restore stability and growth by facilitating loan restructuring for businesses and by investing in funds targeting distressed assets and companies. IFC pledged to contribute $1,550m. to the Program over a three-year period, and aimed to mobilize resources through partnerships with other international financial institutions and private sector companies. IFC's first Green Bond (due in April 2014) was issued in April 2010, and a second was issued in April 2012. Proceeds from IFC Green Bonds are to be invested in energy efficient, renewable energy, and other climate-friendly projects. During 2011/12 IFC launched a Critical Commodities Finance Program, which aimed to expand agricultural-commodity trade finance in developing countries, providing up to $18,000m. in trade over a period of three years.

IFC's authorized capital is US $2,580m. (In July 2010 the Board of Directors recommended a special capital increase of $130m., to raise authorized capital from $2,450 to the current $2,580m; the increase took effect on 27 June 2012, having received the approval of the Board of Governors.) At 30 June 2012 paid-in capital was $2,372m. The World Bank was originally the principal source of borrowed funds, but IFC also borrows from private capital markets. IFC's net income amounted to $1,328m. (after a $330m. grant transfer to IDA) in 2011/12, compared with $1,579m. in 2010/11 (after a $600m. transfer to IDA). In December 2008 the Board of Directors approved a Sovereign Funds Initiative to enable IFC to raise and manage commercial capital from sovereign funds.

In the year ending 30 June 2012 project financing approved by IFC amounted to US $20,358m. for 576 projects in 103 countries (compared with $18,660m. for 518 projects in the previous year). Of the total approved in 2011/12, $15,462m. was for IFC's own account, while $4,896m. was in the form of loan syndications and parallel loans, underwriting of securities issues and investment funds and funds mobilized by the IFC Asset Management Company. Generally, IFC limits its financing to less than 25% of the total cost of a project, but may take up to a 35% stake in a venture (although never as a majority shareholder). Disbursements for IFC's account amounted to $7,981m. in 2011/12.

During the year ending 30 June 2012 IFC approved total financing of US $2,210m. for projects in the Middle East and North Africa (including Afghanistan and Pakistan, but excluding Turkey which it classifies under the Europe and Central Asia region), compared with $1,603m. in the previous year. An additional $668m. was mobilized during 2011/12 in the form of loan participation, parallel loans and structured finance. The main areas of IFC activities in the region are financial institutions, infrastructure, manufacturing and the oil and gas sectors. During 2011/12 IFC launched 25 advisory projects in the Middle East and North Africa. In July 2011 IFC committed $150m. to a new World Bank facility to support micro and small enterprises (MSMEs) in the region.

IFC's Advisory Services are a major part of the organization's involvement with member countries to support the development of private enterprises and efforts to generate funding, as well as to enhance private sector participation in developing infrastructure. Advisory services cover the following five main areas of expertise: the business enabling environment (i.e improving the investment climate in a country); access to financing (including developing financing institutions, improving financial infrastructure and strengthening regulatory frameworks); infrastructure (mainly encouraging private sector participation); environment and social sustainability; and corporate advice (in particular in support of small and medium-sized enterprises—SMEs). In December 2008 the Board of Directors determined to provide additional funding to IFC advisory services in order to strengthen the capacity of financial institutions and governments to respond to the crisis in the global financial markets. At 30 June 2012 there were more than 630 active Advisory Service projects in 105 countries. Total expenditure on Advisory Services during that year amounted to US $197.0m. IFC manages, jointly financed with the World Bank and MIGA, the Foreign Investment Advisory Service (FIAS), which provides technical assistance and advice on promoting foreign investment and strengthening the country's investment framework at the request of governments. Under the Technical Assistance Trust Funds Program (TATF), established in 1988, IFC manages resources contributed by various governments and agencies to provide finance for feasibility studies, project identification studies and other types of technical assistance relating to project preparation. In 2004 a Grassroots Business Initiative was established, with external donor funding, to support businesses that provide economic opportunities for disadvantaged communities in Africa, Latin America, and South and South-East Asia. Since 2002 IFC has administered an online SME Toolkit to enhance the accessibility of business training and advice. By 2013 the service was available in 18 languages.

Since 2004 IFC has presented an annual Client Leadership Award to a chosen corporate client who most represents IFC values in innovation, operational excellence and corporate governance.

Publications

Annual Report.

Doing Business (annually).

Emerging Stock Markets Factbook (annually).

Lessons of Experience (series).

Outcomes (quarterly).

Results on the Ground (series).

Review of Small Businesses (annually).

Sustainability Report (annually).

Other handbooks, discussion papers, technical documents, policy toolkits, public policy journals.

Multilateral Investment Guarantee Agency—MIGA

Address: 1818 H Street, NW, Washington, DC 20433, USA.

Telephone: (202) 473-6163; **fax:** (202) 522-2630; **internet:** www.miga.org.

MIGA was founded in 1988 as an affiliate of the World Bank. Its mandate is to encourage the flow of foreign direct investment to, and among, developing member countries, through the provision of political risk insurance and investment marketing services to foreign investors and host governments, respectively.

Organization

(September 2013)

MIGA is legally and financially separate from the World Bank. It is supervised by a Council of Governors (comprising one Governor and one Alternate of each member country) and an elected Board of Directors (of no less than 12 members).

President: Dr JIM YONG KIM (USA).

Executive Vice-President: KEIKO HONDA (Japan).

Activities

The convention establishing MIGA took effect in April 1988. Authorized capital was US $1,082m., although the convention provided for an increase of capital stock upon the admission of new members. In April 1998 the Board of Directors approved an increase in MIGA's capital base. A grant of $150m. was transferred from the IBRD as part of the package, while the capital increase (totalling $700m. callable capital and $150m. paid-in capital) was approved by MIGA's Council of Governors in April 1999. A three-year subscription period then commenced, covering the period April 1999–March 2002 (later extended to March 2003). At 30 June 2012 110 countries had subscribed $749.8m. of the general capital increase. At that time total subscriptions to the capital stock amounted to $1,915.1m., of which $365.4m. was paid-in.

MIGA guarantees eligible investments against losses resulting from non-commercial risks, under the following main categories:

(i) transfer risk resulting from host government restrictions on currency conversion and transfer;

(ii) risk of loss resulting from legislative or administrative actions of the host government;

(iii) repudiation by the host government of contracts with investors in cases in which the investor has no access to a competent forum;

(iv) the risk of armed conflict and civil unrest;

(v) risk of a sovereign not honouring a financial obligation or guarantee.

Before guaranteeing any investment, MIGA must ensure that it is commercially viable, contributes to the development process and is not harmful to the environment. During the fiscal year 1998/99 MIGA and IFC appointed the first Compliance Advisor and Ombudsman to consider the concerns of local communities directly affected by MIGA- or IFC-sponsored projects. In February 1999 the Board of Directors approved an increase in the amount of political risk insurance available for each project, from US $75m. to $200m. During 2003/04 MIGA established a new fund, the Invest-in-Development Facility, to enhance the role of foreign investment in attaining the Millennium Development Goals. In 2005/06 MIGA supported for the first time a project aimed at selling carbon credits gained by reducing greenhouse gas emissions; it provided $2m. in guarantee coverage to the El Salvador-based initiative. In April 2009 the Board of Directors approved modifications to MIGA's policies and operational regulations in order to enhance operational flexibility and efficiency, in particular in the poorest countries and those affected by conflict. In November 2010 the Council of Governors approved amendments to MIGA's convention (the first since 1988) to broaden the eligibility for investment projects and to enhance the effectiveness of MIGA's development impact. In April 2013 the Board of Directors approved a new Conflict-Affected and Fragile Economies Facility, with the aim of providing political risk insurance to enable projects to be implemented in challenging environments that might assist with reconstruction, bring in capital, and generate employment.

During the year ending 30 June 2012 MIGA issued 66 investment insurance contracts for 50 projects with a value of US $2,657m. (compared with 50 contracts amounting to $2,099m. in 2011/12). Since 1990 the total investment guarantees issued amounted to some $27,200m., through 1,096 contracts in support of 701 projects.

MIGA works with local insurers, export credit agencies, development finance institutions and other organizations to promote insurance in a country, to ensure a level of consistency among insurers and to support capacity building within the insurance industry. MIGA also offers investment marketing services to help to promote foreign direct investment in developing countries and in transitional economies, and to disseminate information on investment opportunities. MIGA's annual flagship report *World Investment and Political Risk*, accessible at www.miga.org/wipr, is the focal point of the Agency's knowledge dissemination of resources on political risk management and insurance. In early 2007 MIGA's technical assistance services were amalgamated into the Foreign Advisory Investment Service (FIAS, see IFC), of which MIGA became a lead partner, along with IFC and the World Bank. During 2000/01 an office was established in Paris, France, to promote and co-ordinate European investment in developing countries, in particular in Africa and Eastern Europe. In March 2002 MIGA opened a regional office, based in Johannesburg, South Africa. In September a new regional office was inaugurated in Singapore, in order to facilitate foreign investment in Asia. A Regional Director for Asia and the Pacific was appointed, for the first time, in August 2010 to head a new Asian Hub, operating from offices in Singapore, Hong Kong SAR and the People's Republic of China.

In November 2008 a West Bank and Gaza Investment Guarantee Trust Fund was inaugurated to encourage greater private sector investment in those territories. The new fund, co-sponsored by the European Investment Bank, the Japanese Government and the Palestinian (National) Authority, was to be administered by MIGA. During 2011/12 some US $8.7m. in guarantees was issued through the Trust Fund in support of two projects.

Publications

Annual Report.

MIGA News (online newsletter; every 2 months).

World Investment and Political Risk (annually).

Other guides, brochures and regional briefs.

International Fund for Agricultural Development—IFAD

Address: Via Paolo di Dono 44, 00142 Rome, Italy.

Telephone: (06) 54591; **fax:** (06) 5043463; **e-mail:** ifad@ifad.org; **internet:** www.ifad.org.

IFAD was established in 1977, following a decision by the 1974 UN World Food Conference, with a mandate to combat hunger and eradicate poverty on a sustainable basis in the low-income, food-deficit regions of the world. Funding operations began in January 1978.

Organization

(September 2013)

GOVERNING COUNCIL

Each member state is represented in the Governing Council (the Fund's highest authority) by a Governor and an Alternate. Sessions are held annually with special sessions as required. The Governing Council elects the President of the Fund (who also chairs the Executive Board) by a two-thirds' majority for a four-year term. The President is eligible for re-election.

EXECUTIVE BOARD

Consists of 18 members and 18 alternates, elected by the Governing Council, who serve for three years. The Executive Board is responsible for the conduct and general operation of IFAD and approves loans and grants for projects; it holds three regular sessions each year. An independent Office of Evaluation reports directly to the Board.

The governance structure of the Fund is based on the classification of members. Membership of the Executive Board is distributed as follows: eight List A countries (i.e. industrialized donor countries), four List B (petroleum-exporting developing donor countries), and six List C (recipient developing countries), divided equally among the three Sub-List C categories (i.e. for Africa, Europe, Asia and the Pacific, and Latin America and the Caribbean).

President and Chairman of Executive Board: KANAYO F. NWANZE (Nigeria).

Activities

IFAD provides financing primarily for projects designed to improve food production systems in developing member states and to strengthen related policies, services and institutions. In allocating resources IFAD is guided by the need to increase food production in the poorest food-deficit countries; the potential for increasing food production in other developing countries; and the importance of improving the nutrition, health and education of the poorest people in developing countries, i.e. small-scale farmers, artisanal fishermen, nomadic pastoralists, indigenous populations, rural women, and the rural landless. All projects emphasize the participation of beneficiaries in development initiatives, both at the local and national level. Issues relating to gender and household food security are incorporated into all aspects of its activities. IFAD is committed to achieving the Millennium Development Goals (MDGs), pledged by governments attending a special session of the UN General Assembly in September 2000, and, in particular, the objective to reduce by 50% the proportion of people living in extreme poverty by 2015. In 2001 the Fund introduced new measures to improve monitoring and impact evaluation, in particular to assess its contribution to achieving the MDGs.

In May 2011 the Executive Board adopted IFAD's Strategic Framework for 2011–15, in which it reiterated its commitment to improving rural food security and nutrition, and enabling the rural poor to overcome their poverty. The 2011–15 Strategic Framework was underpinned by five strategic objectives: developing a natural resource and economic asset base for poor rural communities, with improved resilience to climate change, environmental degradation and market transformation; facilitating access for the rural poor to services aimed at reducing poverty, improving nutrition, raising incomes and building resilience in a changing environment; supporting the rural poor in managing profitable, sustainable and resilient farm and non-farm enterprises and benefiting from decent employment opportunities; enabling the rural poor to influence policies and institutions that affect their livelihoods; and enabling institutional and policy environments that support agricultural production and the related non-farm activities.

From 2009 IFAD implemented a new business model, with the direct supervision of projects, and maintaining a stable presence in countries of operations, as its two main pillars. Consequently, by 2011 the Fund directly supervised some 93% of the projects it was funding, compared with 18% in 2007.

IFAD is a participant in the High Level Task Force (HLTF) on the Global Food Security Crisis, which was established by the UN Secretary-General in April 2008 and aims to address the impact of soaring global levels of food and fuel prices and to formulate a comprehensive framework for action. In June IFAD participated in the High-Level Conference on World Food Security and the Challenges of Climate Change and Bioenergy, convened by FAO in Rome, Italy. The meeting adopted a Declaration on Food Security, which noted an urgent need to develop the agricultural sectors and expand food production in developing countries and countries with economies in transition, and for increased investment in rural development, agriculture and agribusiness. In January 2009 the HLTF participated in a follow-up high-level meeting convened in Madrid, Spain, which agreed to initiate a consultation process with regard to the establishment of a Global Partnership for Agriculture, Food Security and Nutrition. During 2009 the long-standing Committee on World Food Security (CFS), open to member states of IFAD, FAO, and the World Food Programme (WFP), underwent reform, becoming a central component of the new Global Partnership; thereafter the CFS was tasked with influencing hunger elimination programmes at the global, regional and national level, taking into account that food security relates not just to agriculture but also to economic access to food, adequate nutrition, social safety nets and human rights. IFAD contributes, with FAO, WFP and other agencies, to a new Agricultural Market Information System (AMIS), which was agreed by a meeting of agriculture ministers from G20 countries, held in June 2011 to increase market transparency and to address the stabilization of food price volatility. IFAD welcomed a commitment made, in May 2012, by G8 heads of state and government and leaders of African countries, to supporting a New Alliance for Food Security and Nutrition; the Alliance was to promote sustainable and inclusive agricultural growth over a 10-year period. The 2012 edition of the joint IFAD-FAO-WFP annual *State of Food Insecurity in the World* report, released in October, maintained that support for economic development, including smallholder agricultural growth, should be promoted alongside safety nets for the most vulnerable populations.

IFAD, with FAO and WFP, leads an initiative on ensuring food security by strengthening feeding programmes and expanding support to farmers in developing countries, the second of nine activities that were launched in April 2009 by the UN System Chief Executives Board for Co-ordination (CEB), with the aim of alleviating the impact on poor and vulnerable populations of the developing global economic crisis.

In March 2010 the Executive Board endorsed a new IFAD Climate Change Strategy, under which the Fund aimed to create a climate-smart portfolio, and to support smallholder farmers increase their resilience to climate change. In October 2012 a new Adaptation for Smallholder Agriculture Programme (ASAP) became operational; under the ASAP finance for climate adaptation initiatives was to be integrated into IFAD-supported investments.

In 1996 IFAD supported the establishment of the Support Group of the Global Forum on Agricultural Research (GFAR), which facilitates dialogue between research centres and institutions, farmers' organizations, non-governmental bodies, the private sector and donors. IFAD is a leading repository of knowledge, resources and expertise in the field of rural hunger and poverty alleviation. In 2001 it renewed its commitment to becoming a global knowledge institution for rural poverty-related issues. Through its technical assistance grants, IFAD aims to promote research and capacity building in the agricultural sector, as well as the development of technologies to increase production and alleviate rural poverty. In recent years IFAD has been increasingly involved in promoting the use of communication technology to facilitate the exchange of information and experience among rural communities, specialized institutions and organizations, and IFAD-sponsored projects. Within the strategic context of knowledge management, IFAD has supported initiatives to establish regional electronic networks, such as Electronic Networking for Rural Asia/Pacific (ENRAP, conducted over three phases during the period 1998–2010), and FIDAMERICA in Latin America and the Caribbean (conducted over four phases during 1995–2009), as well as to develop other lines of communication between organizations, local agents and the rural poor.

IFAD has funded efforts to improve the production of durum wheat in the dryland areas of West Asia and North Africa and to support the establishment of a regional animal surveillance and control network to identify and prevent outbreaks of livestock diseases in North Africa, the Middle East and the Arab Peninsula.

IFAD is empowered to make both loans and grants. Loans are available on highly concessionary, hardened, intermediate and ordinary terms. Highly concessionary loans carry no interest but have an annual service charge of 0.75% and a repayment period of 40 years; loans approved on hardened terms carry no interest charge, have an annual service charge of 0.75%, and are repaid over 20 years; intermediate loans are subject to a variable interest charge, equivalent to 50% of the interest rate charged on World Bank loans, and are repaid over 20 years; and ordinary loans carry a variable interest charge equal to that levied by the World Bank, and are repaid over 15–18 years. New Debt Sustainability Framework (DSF) grant financing was introduced in 2007 in place of highly concessional loans for heavily indebted poor countries (HIPCs). In 2012 highly concessionary loans represented some 33% of total lending in that year, DSF grants 32%, ordinary loans 30%, and intermediate loans 4%. Research and technical assistance grants are awarded to projects focusing on research and training, and for project preparation and development. In order to increase the impact of its lending resources on food production, the Fund seeks as much as possible to attract other external donors and beneficiary governments as cofinanciers of its projects. In 2012 external co-financing accounted for some 29.1% of all project funding, while domestic contributions, i.e. from recipient governments and other local sources, accounted for 22.4%.

The IFAD Indigenous Peoples Assistance Facility was created in 2007 to fund microprojects that aim to build upon the knowledge and natural resources of indigenous communities and organizations. Under IFAD's Policy on Engagement with Indigenous Peoples, adopted by the Executive Board in September 2009, an Indigenous Peoples' Forum was established in February 2011; this was to be hosted by IFAD and to convene every two years. The inaugural session of the Forum was held in February 2013. In September 2010, the Executive Board approved the establishment of a new Spanish Food Security Cofinancing Facility Trust Fund (the 'Spanish Trust Fund'), which is used to provide loans to IFAD borrower nations. On 31 December 2010 the Spanish Government provided, on a loan basis, €285.5m. to the Spanish Trust Fund.

In November 2006 IFAD was granted access to the core resources of the HIPC Trust Fund, administered by the World Bank, to assist in financing the outstanding debt relief on post-completion point countries participating in the HIPC debt relief initiative (see under IBRD). By October 2012 36 of 39 eligible countries had passed their decision points, thereby qualifying for HIPC debt relief assistance from IFAD, and 34 countries had reached completion point, thereby qualifying for full and irrevocable debt reduction.

IFAD's development projects usually include a number of components, such as infrastructure (e.g. improvement of water supplies, small-scale irrigation and road construction); input supply (e.g. improved seeds, fertilizers and pesticides); institutional support (e.g. research, training and extension services); and producer incentives (e.g. pricing and marketing improvements). IFAD also attempts to enable the landless to acquire income-generating assets: by increasing the provision of credit for the rural poor, it seeks to free them from dependence on the capital market and to generate productive activities

In addition to its regular efforts to identify projects and programmes, IFAD organizes special programming missions to selected countries to undertake a comprehensive review of the constraints affecting the rural poor, and to help countries to design strategies for the removal of these constraints. In general, projects based on the recommendations of these missions tend to focus on institutional improvements at the national and local level to direct inputs and services to small farmers and the landless rural poor. Monitoring and evaluation missions are also sent to check the progress of projects and to assess the impact of poverty reduction efforts.

The Fund supports projects that are concerned with environmental conservation, in an effort to alleviate poverty that results from the deterioration of natural resources. In addition, it extends environmental assessment grants to review the environmental consequences of projects under preparation. IFAD administers the Global Mechanism of the 1996 Convention to Combat Desertification in those Countries Experiencing Drought and Desertification, particularly in Africa The Mechanism mobilizes and channels resources for the implementation of the Convention, and IFAD is its largest financial contributor. IFAD is an executing agency of the Global Environmental Facility, specializing in the area of combating rural poverty and environmental degradation.

During 2012 IFAD approved four projects in the Near East and North Africa region (which, according to IFAD's classification, includes parts of Central and Eastern Europe, Djibouti, Somalia and Sudan), amounting to some US $93.9m. in lending (9.5% of total IFAD lending in that year). In 1998 the IFAD Governing Council approved the establishment of a Fund for Gaza and the West Bank which enabled the Fund to provide financial assistance to those territories. At the end of 2012 46 programmes and projects were ongoing in 18 countries in the region.

In September 2012 IFAD—participating with other agencies and international donors in a consultative group meeting on Yemen, held in Riyadh, Saudi Arabia—pledged US $41m. in funding for new agriculture and rural development projects in that country over 2012–14, with some $10m. to be channelled through the new ASAP.

During 1998 the Executive Board endorsed a policy framework for the Fund's provision of assistance in post-conflict situations, with the aim of achieving a continuum from emergency relief to a secure basis from which to pursue sustainable development. In September 2012 a High Level Expert Forum on Food Insecurity in Protracted Crises, convened by IFAD, FAO and WFP within the framework of the CFS, drafted an Agenda for Action. The document recommended utilizing integrated strategies—with a focus on building resilience—to address food insecurity in protracted crises, i.e. integrating food security into peace-building and governance initiatives at the national and regional level, and integrating food security into regional and global initiatives aimed at improving governance and addressing vulnerability.

IFAD co-operates with other agencies and partners within the context of the Global Partnership for Effective Development Co-operation, established by the Fourth High Level Forum on Aid

Effectiveness, convened in Busan, Republic of Korea, in November–December 2011. Since the late 1990s IFAD has established partnerships within the agribusiness sector, with a view to improving performance at project level, broadening access to capital markets, and encouraging the advancement of new technologies. In October 2001 IFAD became a co-sponsor of the Consultative Group on International Agricultural Research (CGIAR). In 2006 IFAD reviewed the work of the International Alliance against Hunger, which was established in 2004 to enhance co-ordination among international agencies and non-governmental organizations concerned with agriculture and rural development, and national alliances against hunger. In November 2009 IFAD and the Islamic Development Bank concluded a US $1,500m. framework co-financing agreement for jointly financing priority projects during 2010–12 in many of the 52 countries that had membership of both organizations.

Finance

In accordance with the Articles of Agreement establishing IFAD, the Governing Council periodically undertakes a review of the adequacy of resources available to the Fund and may request members to make additional contributions. In February 2012 a target of US $1,500m. was set for the ninth replenishment of IFAD funds (IFAD9), covering the period 2013–15. IFAD9 became effective on 30 November 2012. (A Fund replenishment becomes effective upon receipt of one-half of the funds pledged; by the end of December 2012 member states had pledged 92% of the ninth replenishment target.) The provisional regular budget for administrative expenses for 2013 amounted to $144.1m., while some $3.7m. was budgeted in that year to the Fund's capital budget.

Publications

Annual Report.
IFAD Update (2 a year).
Rural Poverty Report.
Staff Working Papers (series).
State of Food Insecurity in the World (annually, with FAO and WFP).

International Monetary Fund—IMF

Address: 700 19th St, NW, Washington, DC 20431, USA.

Telephone: (202) 623-7000; **fax:** (202) 623-4661; **e-mail:** publicaffairs@imf.org; **internet:** www.imf.org.

The IMF was established at the same time as the World Bank in December 1945, to promote international monetary co-operation, to facilitate the expansion and balanced growth of international trade and to promote stability in foreign exchange.

Organization

(September 2013)

Managing Director: CHRISTINE LAGARDE (France).

First Deputy Managing Director: DAVID LIPTON (USA).

Deputy Managing Directors: NAOYUKI SHINOHARA (Japan), NEMAT SHAFIK (Egypt/United Kingdom/USA), MIN ZHU (People's Republic of China).

Director, African Department: ANTOINETTE MONSIO SAYEH (Liberia).

Director, Middle East and Central Asia Department: MASOOD AHMED (Pakistan).

BOARD OF GOVERNORS

The highest authority of the Fund is exercised by the Board of Governors, on which each member country is represented by a Governor and an Alternate Governor. The Board normally meets annually. The voting power of each country is related to its quota in the Fund. An International Monetary and Financial Committee (IMFC, formerly the Interim Committee) advises and reports to the Board on matters relating to the management and adaptation of the international monetary and financial system, sudden disturbances that might threaten the system and proposals to amend the Articles of Agreement.

BOARD OF EXECUTIVE DIRECTORS

The 24-member Board of Executive Directors is responsible for the day-to-day operations of the Fund. The USA, United Kingdom, Germany, France and Japan each appoint one Executive Director. There is also one Executive Director from the People's Republic of China, Russia and Saudi Arabia, while the remainder are elected by groups of the remaining countries.

REGIONAL REPRESENTATION

There is a network of regional offices and Resident Representatives in more than 90 member countries. In addition, special information and liaison offices are located in Tokyo, Japan (for Asia and the Pacific), in New York, USA (for the United Nations), and in Europe (Paris, France; Geneva, Switzerland; Belgium, Brussels; and Warsaw, Poland, for Central Europe and the Baltic states).

Activities

The purposes of the IMF, as defined in the Articles of Agreement, are:

(i) To promote international monetary co-operation through a permanent institution which provides the machinery for consultation and collaboration on monetary problems;

(ii) To facilitate the expansion and balanced growth of international trade, and to contribute thereby to the promotion and maintenance of high levels of employment and real income and to the development of members' productive resources;

(iii) To promote exchange stability, to maintain orderly exchange arrangements among members, and to avoid competitive exchange depreciation;

(iv) To assist in the establishment of a multilateral system of payments in respect of current transactions between members and in the elimination of foreign exchange restrictions which hamper the growth of trade;

(v) To give confidence to members by making the general resources of the Fund temporarily available to them, under adequate safeguards, thus providing them with the opportunity to correct maladjustments in their balance of payments, without resorting to measures destructive of national or international prosperity;

(vi) In accordance with the above, to shorten the duration of and lessen the degree of disequilibrium in the international balances of payments of members.

In joining the Fund, each country agrees to co-operate with the above objectives. In accordance with its objective of facilitating the expansion of international trade, the IMF encourages its members to accept the obligations of Article VIII, Sections two, three and four, of the Articles of Agreement. Members that accept Article VIII undertake to refrain from imposing restrictions on the making of payments and transfers for current international transactions and from engaging in discriminatory currency arrangements or multiple currency practices without IMF approval. At the end of 2011 some 90% of members had accepted Article VIII status.

In 2000/01 the Fund established an International Capital Markets Department to improve its understanding of financial markets and a separate Consultative Group on capital markets to serve as a forum for regular dialogue between the Fund and representatives of the private sector. In mid-2006 the International Capital Markets Department was merged with the Monetary and Financial Systems Department to create the Monetary and Capital Markets Department, with the intention of strengthening surveillance of global financial transactions and monetary arrangements. In June 2008 the Managing Director presented a new Work Programme, comprising the following four immediate priorities for the Fund: to enable member countries to deal with the current crises of reduced economic growth and escalating food and fuel prices, including efforts by the Fund to strengthen surveillance activities; to review the Fund's lending instruments; to implement new organizational tools and working practices; and to advance further the Fund's governance agenda.

The deceleration of economic growth in the world's major economies in 2007 and 2008 and the sharp decline in global financial market conditions, in particular in the second half of 2008, focused international attention on the adequacy of the governance of the international financial system and of regulatory and supervisory frameworks. The IMF aimed to provide appropriate and rapid financial and technical assistance to low-income and emerging economies most affected by the crisis and to support a co-ordinated, multinational recovery effort. The Fund worked closely with the Group of 20 (G20) leading economies to produce an Action Plan, in November 2008, concerned with strengthening regulation, transparency and integrity in financial markets and reform of the international financial system. In March 2009 the IMF released a study on the 'Impact of the Financial Crisis on Low-income Countries', and in that month convened, with the Government of Tanzania, a high-level conference, held in Dar es Salaam, to consider the effects of the global financial situation on African countries, as well as areas for future partnership and growth. Later in that month the Executive Board approved a series of reforms to enhance the effectiveness of the Fund's lending framework, including new conditionality criteria, a new flexible credit facility and increased access limits (see below).

In April 2009 a meeting of G20 heads of state and government, convened in London, United Kingdom, determined to make available substantial additional resources through the IMF and other multinational development institutions in order to strengthen global financial liquidity and support economic recovery. There was a commitment to extend US $250,000m. to the IMF in immediate bilateral financial contributions (which would be incorporated into an expanded New Arrangements to Borrow facility) and to support a general allocation of special drawing rights (SDRs), amounting to a further $250,000m. It was agreed that additional resources from sales of IMF gold were to be used to provide $6,000m. in concessional financing for the poorest countries over the next two to three years. The G20 meeting also resolved to implement several major reforms to strengthen the regulation and supervision of the international financial system, which envisaged the IMF collaborating closely with a new Financial Stability Board. In September G20 heads of state and government endorsed a Mutual Assessment Programme, which aimed to achieve sustainable and balanced growth, with the IMF providing analysis and technical assistance. In January 2010 the IMF initiated a process to review its mandate and role in the 'post-crisis' global economy. Short-term priorities included advising countries on moving beyond the policies they implemented during the crisis; reviewing the Fund's mandate in surveillance and lending, and investigating ways of improving the stability of the international monetary system; strengthening macro-financial and cross-country analyses, including early warning exercises; and studying ways to make policy frameworks more resilient to crises. In November 2011 G20 heads of state and government, meeting in Cannes, France, agreed to initiate an immediate review of the Fund's resources, with a view to securing global financial stability which had been undermined by high levels of debt in several eurozone countries. In December European Union heads of state and government agreed to allocate to the IMF additional resources of up to $270,000m. in the form of bilateral loans.

A joint meeting of the IMFC, G20 ministers responsible for finance and governors of central banks, convened in April 2012, in Washington, DC, welcomed a decision in March by eurozone member states to strengthen European firewalls through broader reform efforts and the availability of central bank swap lines, and determined to enhance IMF resources for crisis prevention and resolution, announcing commitments from G20 member states to increasing, by more than US $430,000m., resources to be made available to the IMF as part of a protective firewall to serve the entire IMF membership. Additional resources pledged by emerging economies (notably by the People's Republic of China, Brazil, India, Mexico and Russia) at a meeting of G20 heads of state and government held in June, in Los Cabos, Baja California Sur, Mexico, raised the universal firewall to $456,000m. Meeting in October, in Tokyo, Japan, the IMFC urged national policy-makers to implement policies agreed in recent months aimed at restarting economic growth and promoting job creation. The global economy was reported to have decelerated to a greater extent than had been previously anticipated: a contraction in output in the eurozone was noted, and, additionally, a slow-down in economic activity in many other advanced economies and also in emerging markets and developing economies, reflecting weaker external and domestic demand, and also in some cases the impact of policies aimed at addressing inflationary pressures.

In August 2009 the Fund's Board of Governors approved the new general allocation of SDRs, amounting to SDR 161,200m., which became available to all members, in proportion to their existing quotas, from 28 August. A further SDR 21,400m. (equivalent to US $33,000m.) became available on 9 September under a special allocation provided for by the Fourth Amendment to the Articles of Agreement, which entered into force in the previous month having been ratified by members holding 85% of the total voting power.

In September 2011 the IMF joined other international financial institutions active in the Middle East and North Africa region to endorse the so-called Deauville Partnership, established by the Group of Eight (G8) industrialized nations in May to support political and economic reforms being undertaken by several countries, notably Egypt, Jordan, Morocco and Tunisia. The Fund was committed to supporting those countries to maintain economic and financial stability, and to promote inclusive growth.

QUOTAS

MEMBERSHIP AND QUOTAS IN THE MIDDLE EAST AND NORTH AFRICA
(million SDR*)

Country	September 2013
Algeria	1,254.7
Bahrain	135.0
Cyprus	158.2
Egypt	943.7
Iran	1,497.2
Iraq	1,188.4
Israel	1,061.1
Jordan	170.5
Kuwait	1,381.1
Lebanon	266.4
Libya	1,123.7
Morocco	588.2
Oman	237.0
Qatar	302.6
Saudi Arabia	6,985.5
Syria	293.6
Tunisia	286.5
Turkey	1,455.8
United Arab Emirates	752.5
Yemen	243.5

* The Special Drawing Right (SDR) was introduced in 1970 as a substitute for gold in international payments, and was intended eventually to become the principal reserve asset in the international monetary system. Its value (which was US $1.51177 at 3 September 2013 and averaged $1.53169 in 2012) is based on the currencies of the five largest exporting countries. Each member is assigned a quota related to its national income, monetary reserves, trade balance and other economic indicators; the quota approximately determines a member's voting power and the amount of foreign exchange it may purchase from the Fund. A member's subscription is equal to its quota. Quotas are reviewed at intervals of not more than five years, to take into account the state of the world economy and members' different rates of development. In December 2010 the Board of Governors concluded the 14th General Review, with an agreement to increase quotas by 100%, to realign quota shares to ensure greater representation of emerging economies and to preserve the basic votes share of low-income countries. The reforms required approval by member states constituting 85% of total quotas in order to enter into effect. By July 2013 140 members accounting for 75.69% of the Fund's voting power had accepted the amendment. A Quota and Voice Reform agreement, concluded in March 2008 to increase quotas by a total of SDR 20,800m. for 54 member countries, entered into effect in March 2011. As at 3 September 2013 total quotas in the Fund amounted to SDR 238,118.0m.

RESOURCES

Members' subscriptions form the basic resource of the IMF. They are supplemented by borrowing. Under the General Arrangements to Borrow (GAB), established in 1962, the Group of Ten industrialized nations (G10—Belgium, Canada, France, Germany, Italy, Japan, the Netherlands, Sweden, the United Kingdom and the USA) and Switzerland (which became a member of the IMF in May 1992 but which had been a full participant in the GAB from April 1984) undertake to lend the Fund as much as SDR 17,000m. in their own currencies to assist in fulfilling the balance of payments requirements of any member of the group, or in response to requests to the Fund from countries with balance of payments problems that could threaten the stability of the international monetary system. In 1983 the Fund entered into an agreement with Saudi Arabia, in association with the GAB, making available SDR 1,500m., and other borrowing arrangements were completed in 1984 with the Bank for International Settlements, the Saudi Arabian Monetary Agency, Belgium and Japan, making available a further SDR 6,000m. In 1986 another borrowing arrangement with Japan made available SDR 3,000m. In May 1996 GAB participants concluded an agreement in principle to expand the resources available for borrowing to SDR 34,000m., by securing the support of 25 countries with the financial capacity to support the international monetary system. The so-called New Arrangements to Borrow (NAB) was approved by the Executive Board in January 1997. It was to enter into force, for an initial five-year period, as soon as the five largest potential creditors participating in NAB had approved the initiative and the total credit arrangement of participants endorsing the scheme had reached at least SDR 28,900m. While the GAB credit arrangement was to remain in effect, the NAB was expected to be the first facility to be activated in the event of the Fund's requiring supplementary resources. In July 1998 the GAB was activated for the first time in more than 20 years in order to provide funds of up to US $6,300m. in support of an IMF emergency assistance package for Russia (the first time the GAB had been used for a non-participant). The NAB became effective in November, and was used for the first time as part of an extensive programme of support for Brazil, which was adopted by the IMF in early December. (In March 1999, however, the activation was cancelled.) In November 2008 the Executive Board initiated an assessment of IMF resource requirements and options for supplementing resources in view of an exceptional increase in demand for IMF assistance. In February 2009 the Board approved the terms of a borrowing agreement with the Government of Japan to extend some SDR 67,000m. (some $100,000m.) in supplemental funding, for an initial one-year period. In April G20 heads of state and government resolved to expand the NAB facility, to incorporate all G20 economies, in order to increase its resources by up to SDR 367,500m. ($500,000m.). The G20 summit meeting held in September confirmed that it had contributed the additional resources to the NAB. In April 2010 the IMF's Executive Board approved the expansion and enlargement of NAB borrowing arrangements; these came into effect in March 2011, having completed the ratification process. By July 2012 38 members or state institutions were participating in the NAB, and had committed SDR 369,997m. in supplementary resources.

FINANCIAL ASSISTANCE

The Fund makes resources available to eligible members on an essentially short-term and revolving basis to provide members with temporary assistance to contribute to the solution of their payments problems. Before making a purchase, a member must show that its balance of payments or reserve position makes the purchase necessary. Apart from this requirement, reserve tranche purchases (i.e. purchases that do not bring the Fund's holdings of the member's currency to a level above its quota) are permitted unconditionally. Exchange transactions within the Fund take the form of members' purchases (i.e. drawings) from the Fund of the currencies of other members for the equivalent amounts of their own currencies.

With further purchases, however, the Fund's policy of conditionality means that a recipient country must agree to adjust its economic policies, as stipulated by the IMF. All requests other than for use of the reserve tranche are examined by the Executive Board to determine whether the proposed use would be consistent with the Fund's policies, and a member must discuss its proposed adjustment programme (including fiscal, monetary, exchange and trade policies) with IMF staff. New guidelines on conditionality, which, *inter alia*, aimed to promote national ownership of policy reforms and to introduce specific criteria for the implementation of conditions given different states' circumstances, were approved by the Executive Board in September 2002. In March 2009 the Executive Board approved reforms to modernize the Fund's conditionality policy, including greater use of pre-set qualification criteria and monitoring structural policy implementation by programme review (rather than by structural performance criteria).

Purchases outside the reserve tranche are made in four credit tranches, each equivalent to 25% of the member's quota; a member must reverse the transaction by repurchasing its own currency (with SDRs or currencies specified by the Fund) within a specified time. A credit tranche purchase is usually made under a Stand-by Arrangement with the Fund, or under the Extended Fund Facility. A Stand-by Arrangement is normally of one or two years' duration, and the amount is made available in instalments, subject to the member's observance of 'performance criteria'; repurchases must be made within three-and-a-quarter to five years. In March 2012 the Executive Board approved an amendment to the Extended Fund Facility permitting extended arrangements to be approved from the start for up to a maximum of four years (the Facility had hitherto been approved for up to three years, with the possibility of a subsequent one-year extension). The member must submit detailed economic programmes and progress reports for each year; repurchases must be made within four-and-a-half to 10 years. In October 1994 the Executive Board approved an increase in members' access to IMF resources, on the basis of a recommendation by the then Interim Committee. The annual access limit under IMF regular tranche drawings, Stand-by Arrangements and Extended Fund Facility credits was increased from 68% to 100% of a member's quota, with the cumulative access limit set at 300%. In March 2009 the Executive Board agreed to double access limits for non-concessional loans to 200% and 600% of a member's quota for annual and cumulative access respectively. In 2011/12 regular funding arrangements approved (and augmented) amounted to SDR 52,601.2m. (compared with SDR 129,628m. in the previous financial year, SDR 74,175m. in 2009/10 and SDR 66,736m. in 2008/09).

In October 1995 the Interim Committee of the Board of Governors endorsed recent decisions of the Executive Board to strengthen IMF financial support to members requiring exceptional assistance. An Emergency Financing Mechanism was established to enable the IMF to respond swiftly to potential or actual financial crises, while additional funds were made available for short-term currency stabilization. The Mechanism was activated for the first time in July 1997, in response to a request by the Philippines Government to reinforce the country's international reserves, and was subsequently used during that year to assist Thailand, Indonesia and South Korea. It was used in 2001 to accelerate lending to Turkey. In September 2008 the Mechanism was activated to facilitate approval of a Stand-by Arrangement amounting to SDR 477.1m. for Georgia, which urgently needed to contain its fiscal deficit and undertake rehabilitation measures following a conflict with Russia during the previous month. In November the Board approved a Stand-by Arrangement of SDR 5,169m., under the Emergency Financing Mechanism procedures, to support an economic stabilization programme in Pakistan, one for Ukraine, amounting to SDR 11,000m., and another of SDR 10,538m. for Hungary, which constituted 1,015% of its quota, to counter exceptional pressures on that country's banking sector and the Government's economic programme. An arrangement for Latvia, amounting to SDR 1,522m., was approved in the following month. In May 2010 the Board endorsed a three-year Stand-by Arrangement for Greece amounting to SDR 26,400m., accounting for some 2,400% of that country's new quota (under the 2008 quota reform). The Arrangement was approved under the Emergency Financing Mechanism, as part of a joint financial assistance package with the eurozone countries, which aimed to alleviate Greece's sovereign debt crisis and to support an economic recovery and reform programme. In July 2011 the Fund completed a fourth review of the country's economic performance under the Stand-by Arrangement, enabling a further disbursement of SDR 2,900m. In March 2012, following the cancellation of the Stand-by Arrangement, the Executive Board approved an allocation of SDR 23,800m. to be distributed over four years under the Extended Fund Facility—representing access to IMF resources amounting to 2,159% of Greece's quota—in support of the country's ongoing economic adjustment programme; some SDR 1,400m, was to be disbursed immediately. An allocation of SDR 19,465.8m., to be distributed over three years, was approved in December 2010 for Ireland under the Emergency Financing Mechanism, in conjunction with a eurozone assistance programme for that country aimed at supporting the restoration of stability in its financial sector. In May 2011 the Fund allocated SDR 23,742m. to Portugal over three years under the Extended Fund Facility, again under the Emergency Financing Mechanism and in tandem with a wider eurozone package of assistance that was supporting the Portuguese Government's ongoing economic adjustment programme. In March 2013 the IMF Managing Director, the President of the European Central Bank, and eurozone finance ministers agreed, in principle, to develop a joint programme of support to alleviate the sovereign debt crisis in Cyprus. In early April an IMF team and the Cypriot authorities reached a provisional agreement on the terms of a €10,000m. finance package that included a three-year SDR 891m. (equivalent to around €1,000m.) IMF allocation under the Extended Fund Facility; the arrangement was approved by the Board of Executive Directors in May.

In October 2008 the Executive Board approved a new Short-Term Liquidity Facility (SLF) to extend exceptional funds (up to 500% of quotas) to emerging economies affected by the turmoil in international financial markets and economic deceleration in advanced economies. Eligibility for lending under the new Facility was to be based on a country's record of strong macroeconomic policies and having a sustainable level of debt. In March 2009 the Executive Board decided to replace the SLF with a Flexible Credit Line (FCL) facility, which, similarly, was to provide credit to countries with very strong economic foundations, but was also to be primarily considered as precautionary. In addition, it was to have a longer repayment period (of up to five years) and have no access 'cap'. The first arrangement under the FCL was approved in April for Mexico, making available funds of up to SDR 31,528m. for a one-year period. In August 2010 the duration of the FCL, and credit available through it, were increased, and a Precautionary Credit Line (PCL) was established for member states with sound economic policies that had not yet meet the requirements of the FCL. In November 2011 the PCL was replaced by a new, more flexible Precautionary and Liquidity Line (PLL), which was to be made available to countries 'with sound economic fundamentals' and 'sound policies', for use in broader circumstances than the PCL, including as insurance against shocks and as a short-term liquidity window; PLL arrangements may have a duration of either six months or 1–2 years. One FCL arrangement, amounting to SDR 3,870m., was approved in 2011/12, for Colombia;

meanwhile existing FCL arrangements remained in place for Mexico and Poland.

In January 2010 the Fund introduced new concessional facilities for low-income countries as part of broader reforms to enhance flexibility of lending and to focus support closer to specific national requirements. The three new facilities aimed to support country-owned programmes to achieve macroeconomic positions consistent with sustainable poverty reduction and economic growth. They carried zero interest rate, although this was to be reviewed every two years. An Extended Credit Facility (ECF) succeeded the existing PRGF to provide medium-term balance of payments assistance to low-income members. ECF loans were to be repayable over 10 years, with a five-and-a-half-year grace period. A Standby Credit Facility (SCF) replaced the high-access component of a former Exogenous Shocks Facility (operational from January 2006–December 2009) in order to provide short-term balance of payments financial assistance in response to the adverse economic impact of events beyond government control, including on a precautionary basis. SCF loans were to be repayable over eight years, with a grace period of four years. A new Rapid Credit Facility was to provide rapid financial assistance to PRGF-eligible members requiring urgent balance of payments assistance, under a range of circumstances. Loans were repayable over 10 years, with a five-and-a-half-year grace period. A Post-Catastrophe Debt Relief (PCDR) Trust was established in June 2010 to enable the Fund—in the event of a catastrophic disaster—to provide debt relief to any vulnerable low-income eligible member state in order to free up resources to meet exceptional balance of payments needs. In November 2011 a new Rapid Financing Instrument (RFI) was launched, for which all member states were to be eligible, and which was to support urgent balance of payments requirements, including those arising from exogenous shocks such as commodity price changes, natural disasters, and post-conflict and other fragile situations. Low-income member states may also make use of a non-financial Policy Support Instrument (PSI), providing access to IMF monitoring and other support aimed at consolidating economic performance.

During 2011/12 members' purchases from the general resources account amounted to SDR 32,270m., compared with SDR 26,616m. in the previous year. Outstanding IMF credit at 30 April 2012 totalled SDR 94,182m., compared with SDR 65,539m. in 2010/11. The five largest users of IMF credit during the 2011/12 financial year were Greece, Portugal, Ireland, Romania, and Ukraine.

IMF participates in an initiative to provide exceptional assistance to heavily indebted poor countries (HIPCs), in order to help them to achieve a sustainable level of debt management. In all 41 HIPCs were identified, of which 33 were in sub-Saharan Africa. Resources for the HIPC initiative were channelled through the PRGF Trust. In early 1999 the IMF and the World Bank initiated a comprehensive review of the HIPC scheme, in order to consider modifications of the initiative and to strengthen the link between debt relief and poverty reduction. A consensus emerged among the financial institutions and leading industrialized nations to enhance the scheme, in order to make it available to more countries, and to accelerate the process of providing debt relief. In September the IMF Board of Governors expressed its commitment to undertaking an off-market transaction of a percentage of the Fund's gold reserves (i.e. a sale, at market prices, to central banks of member countries with repayment obligations to the Fund, which were then to be made in gold), as part of the funding arrangements of the enhanced HIPC scheme; this was undertaken during the period December 1999–April 2000. Under the enhanced initiative it was agreed that countries seeking debt relief should first formulate, and successfully implement for at least one year, a national poverty reduction strategy (see above). In May 2000 Uganda became the first country to qualify for full debt relief under the enhanced scheme. In September 2005 the IMF and World Bank endorsed a proposal by G8 nations to achieve the cancellation by the IMF, IDA and African Development Bank of 100% of debt claims on countries that had reached completion point under the HIPC initiative, in order to help them to achieve their Millennium Development Goals. The debt cancellation was to be undertaken within the framework of a Multilateral Debt Relief Initiative (MDRI). The IMF's Executive Board determined, additionally, to extend MDRI debt relief to all countries with an annual per capita of GDP US $380, to be financed by IMF's own resources. Other financing was to be made from existing bilateral contributions to the PRGF Trust Subsidy Account. The initiative became effective in January 2006 once the final consent of the 43 contributors to the PRGF Trust Subsidy Account had been received. As at July 2011 the IMF had committed some $6,500m. in debt relief under the HIPC initiative, of a total of $76,000m. pledged for the initiative (in 2010 net present value terms); at that time the cost to the IMF of the MDRI amounted to some $3,900m. (in nominal value terms). In June 2010 the Executive Board approved the establishment of a Post-Catastrophe Debt Relief Trust (PCDR Trust) to provide balance of payments assistance to low-income members following an exceptional natural disaster.

The IMF is a partner in the Enhanced Integrated Framework (EIF) for trade-related assistance to Least Developed Countries (LDCs), a multi-donor programme which aims to support greater participation by LDCs in the global trading system.

SURVEILLANCE

Under its Articles of Agreement, the Fund is mandated to oversee the effective functioning of the international monetary system. Accordingly, the Fund aims to exercise firm surveillance over the exchange rate policies of member states and to assess whether a country's economic situation and policies are consistent with the objectives of sustainable development and domestic and external stability. The Fund's main tools of surveillance are regular, bilateral consultations with member countries conducted in accordance with Article IV of the Articles of Agreement, which cover fiscal and monetary policies, balance of payments and external debt developments, as well as policies that affect the economic performance of a country, such as the labour market, social and environmental issues and good governance, and aspects of the country's capital accounts, and finance and banking sectors. In April 1997 the Executive Board agreed to the voluntary issue of Press Information Notices (PINs) following each member's Article IV consultation, to those member countries wishing to make public the Fund's views. Other background papers providing information on and analysis of economic developments in individual countries continued to be made available. The Executive Board monitors global economic developments and discusses policy implications from a multilateral perspective, based partly on World Economic Outlook reports and Global Financial Stability Reports. In addition, the IMF studies the regional implications of global developments and policies pursued under regional fiscal arrangements. The Fund's medium-term strategy, initiated in 2006, determined to strengthen its surveillance policies to reflect new challenges of globalization for international financial and macroeconomic stability. The IMF, with the UN Department for Economic and Social Affairs, leads an initiative to strengthen monitoring and analysis surveillance, and to implement an effective warning system, one of nine initiatives that were endorsed in April 2009 by the UN System Chief Executives Board for Co-ordination (CEB), with the aim of alleviating the impact of the global crisis on poor and vulnerable populations. In September 2010 the Executive Board decided that regular financial stability assessments, within the Financial Sector Assessment Programme framework (see below), were to be a mandatory exercise for 25 jurisdictions considered to have systemically important financial sectors. In July 2012 the Executive Board adopted a Decision on Bilateral and Multilateral Surveillance (the so-called Integrated Surveillance Decision), which aimed to strengthen the legal framework underpinning surveillance activities. In September the Board endorsed a Financial Surveillance Strategy detailing steps towards further strengthening the financial surveillance framework.

In April 1996 the IMF established the Special Data Dissemination Standard (SDDS), which was intended to improve access to reliable economic statistical information for member countries that have, or are seeking, access to international capital markets. In March 1999 the IMF undertook to strengthen the Standard by the introduction of a new reserves data template. By April 2013 71 countries had subscribed to the Standard. The eurozone also voluntarily issues metadata in SDDS format. The financial crisis in Asia, which became apparent in mid-1997, focused attention on the importance of IMF surveillance of the economies and financial policies of member states and prompted the Fund further to enhance the effectiveness of its surveillance through the development of international standards in order to maintain fiscal transparency. In December 1997 the Executive Board approved a new General Data Dissemination System (GDDS), to encourage all member countries to improve the production and dissemination of core economic data. The operational phase of the GDDS commenced in May 2000. By April 2013 107 countries were actively participating in the GDDS. The Fund maintains a Dissemination Standards Bulletin Board, which aims to ensure that information on SDDS subscribing countries is widely available.

In April 1998 the then Interim Committee adopted a voluntary Code of Good Practices on Fiscal Transparency: Declaration of Principles, which aimed to increase the quality and promptness of official reports on economic indicators, and in September 1999 it adopted a Code of Good Practices on Transparency in Monetary and Financial Policies: Declaration of Principles. The IMF and World Bank jointly established a Financial Sector Assessment Programme (FSAP) in May 1999, initially as a pilot project, which aimed to promote greater global financial security through the preparation of confidential detailed evaluations of the financial sectors of individual countries. In September 2009 the IMF and World Bank determined to enhance the FSAP's surveillance effectiveness with new features, for example introducing a risk assessment matrix, targeting it more closely to country needs, and improving its cross-country analysis and perspective. As part of the FSAP Fund staff may conclude a Financial System Stability Assessment (FSSA), addressing issues relating to macroeconomic stability and the strength of a country's financial system. A separate component of the FSAP are Reports on the Observance of Standards and Codes (ROSCs), which are compiled after an assessment of a country's implementation and observance of internationally recognized financial standards.

TECHNICAL ASSISTANCE

Technical assistance is provided by special missions or resident representatives who advise members on every aspect of economic management, while more specialized assistance is provided by the IMF's various departments. In 2000/01 the IMFC determined that technical assistance should be central to the IMF's work in crisis prevention and management, in capacity building for low-income countries, and in restoring macroeconomic stability in countries following a financial crisis. Technical assistance activities subsequently underwent a process of review and reorganization to align them more closely with IMF policy priorities and other initiatives.

The IMF delivers some technical assistance, aimed at strengthening local capacity in economic and financial management, through regional centres. In October 2004 a new technical assistance centre for the Middle East (METAC) was inaugurated, based in Beirut, Lebanon.

In May 2009 the IMF launched the first of a series of Topical Trust Funds (TTFs—providing support to member states towards addressing economic policy challenges), on Anti-Money Laundering and Combating the Financing of Terrorism. In May 2011 two further TTFs were created, on Tax Policy and Administration, and on Managing Natural Resource Wealth.

In May 2012, following the merger of the former IMF Institute (established in 1964) and Office of Technical Assistance Management, a new Institute for Capacity Development was inaugurated, to provide technical assistance and training to support member countries with developing the capacity of national economic and financial institutions. The IMF is a co-sponsor, with the Austrian authorities, the European Bank for Reconstruction and Development, Organisation for Economic Co-operation and Development and the World Trade Organization, of the Joint Vienna Institute, which was opened in the Austrian capital in October 1992 and which trains officials from former centrally planned economies in various aspects of economic management and public administration. In May 1998 an IMF-Singapore Regional Training Institute was inaugurated, in collaboration with the Singaporean Government, in order to provide training for officials from the Asia-Pacific region. In 1999 a Joint Regional Training Programme, administered with the Arab Monetary Fund, was established in the United Arab Emirates, and during 2000/01 a joint training programme for Chinese government officials was established in Dalian, Liaoning Province. A Joint Regional Training Centre for Latin America became operational in Brasília, Brazil, in 2001. In July 2006 a Joint India-IMF Training Programme was inaugurated in Pune, India. In May 2011 a new IMF-Middle East Center for Economics and Finance was inaugurated in Kuwait.

Publications

Annual Report.
Balance of Payments Statistics Yearbook.
Civil Society Newsletter (quarterly).
Direction of Trade Statistics (quarterly and annually).
Emerging Markets Financing (quarterly).
F & D—Finance and Development (quarterly).
Financial Statements of the IMF (quarterly).
Global Financial Stability Report (2 a year).
Global Monitoring Report (annually, with the World Bank).
Government Finance Statistics Yearbook.
Handbook on Securities Statistics (published jointly by IMF, BIS and the European Central Bank).
IMF Commodity Prices (monthly).
IMF Financial Activities (weekly, online).
IMF in Focus (annually).
IMF Research Bulletin (quarterly).
IMF Survey (monthly, and online).
International Financial Statistics (monthly and annually).
Joint BIS-IMF-OECD-World Bank Statistics on External Debt (quarterly).
Quarterly Report on the Assessments of Standards and Codes.
Staff Papers (quarterly).
World Economic Outlook (2 a year).
Other country reports, regional outlooks, economic and financial surveys, occasional papers, pamphlets, books.

United Nations Educational, Scientific and Cultural Organization—UNESCO

Address: 7 place de Fontenoy, 75352 Paris 07 SP, France.

Telephone: 1-45-68-10-00; **fax:** 1-45-67-16-90; **e-mail:** bpi@unesco.org; **internet:** www.unesco.org.

UNESCO was established in 1946 'for the purpose of advancing, through the educational, scientific and cultural relations of the peoples of the world, the objectives of international peace and the common welfare of mankind'.

Organization

(September 2013)

GENERAL CONFERENCE

The supreme governing body of the Organization, the Conference meets in ordinary session once in two years and is composed of representatives of the member states. It determines policies, approves work programmes and budgets and elects members of the Executive Board.

EXECUTIVE BOARD

The Board, comprising 58 members, prepares the programme to be submitted to the Conference and supervises its execution; it meets twice a year.

SECRETARIAT

UNESCO is headed by a Director-General, appointed for a four-year term. There are Assistant Directors-General for the main thematic sectors, i.e education, natural sciences, social and human sciences, culture, and communication and information, as well as for the support sectors of external relations and co-operation and of administration.

Director-General: IRINA BOKOVA (Bulgaria).

CO-OPERATING BODIES

In accordance with UNESCO's constitution, national Commissions have been set up in most member states, which help to integrate work within the member states and the work of UNESCO. Most members also have their own permanent delegations to UNESCO. UNESCO aims to develop partnerships with cities and local authorities.

FIELD CO-ORDINATION

UNESCO maintains a network of offices to support a more decentralized approach to its activities and enhance their implementation at field level. Cluster offices provide the main structure of the field co-ordination network. These cover a group of countries and help to co-ordinate between member states and with other UN and partner agencies operating in the area. In 2013 there were 27 cluster offices covering 148 states. In addition 21 national offices serve a single country, including those in post-conflict situations or economic transition and the nine most highly populated countries. The regional bureaux (see below) provide specialized support at the national level.

REGIONAL BUREAUX

Regional Bureau for Education in Africa (BREDA): 12 ave L. S. Senghor, BP 3311, Dakar, Senegal; tel. 849-23-23; fax 823-86-23; e-mail dakar@unesco.org; internet www.dakar.unesco.org; Dir ANN THERESE NDONG-JATTA.

Regional Bureau for Sciences in Africa: POB 30592, Nairobi, Kenya; tel. (20) 7621-234; fax (20) 7622-750; e-mail nairobi@unesco.org; internet www.unesco-nairobi.org; f. 1965 to execute UNESCO's regional science programme, and to assist in the planning and execution of national programmes; Dir MOHAMMED DJELID.

Regional Bureau for Education in the Arab States: POB 5244, Cité Sportive, Beirut, Lebanon; tel. (1) 850013; fax (1) 834854; e-mail beirut@unesco.org; internet www.unesco.org/en/beirut; Dir HAMED AL-HAMMAMI.

Regional Bureau for Sciences in the Arab States: 8 Abdel Rahman Fahmy St, Garden City, Cairo 11511, Egypt; tel. (2) 7945599; fax (2) 7945296; e-mail cairo@unesco.org; internet www.unesco.org/new/en/cairo/natural-sciences; also covers informatics; Dir Dr TAREK GALAL SHAWKI.

Activities

In the implementation of all its activities UNESCO aims to contribute to achieving the UN Internationally Agreed Development Goals, and the UN Millennium Development Goal (MDG) of halving levels of extreme poverty by 2015, as well as other MDGs concerned with education and sustainable development. UNESCO was the lead agency for the International Decade for a Culture of Peace and Non-violence for the Children of the World (2001–10). In November 2007 the General Conference approved a medium-term strategy to guide UNESCO during the period 2008–13. UNESCO's central mission as defined under the strategy was to contribute to building peace, the alleviation of poverty, sustainable development and intercultural dialogue through its core programme sectors (Education; Natural Sciences; Social and Human Sciences; Culture; and Communication and Information). The strategy identified five 'overarching objectives' for UNESCO in 2008–13, within this programme framework: Attaining quality education for all; Mobilizing scientific knowledge and science policy for sustainable development; Addressing emerging ethical challenges; Promoting cultural diversity and intercultural dialogue; and Building inclusive knowledge societies through information and communication. In 2013 UNESCO, with UNICEF, was co-leading global consultations on formulating a post-2015 development framework in the thematic area of education.

The 2008–13 medium-term strategy reaffirmed UNESCO's commitment to prioritizing Africa and its development efforts. In particular, it was to extend support to countries in post-conflict and disaster situations and strengthen efforts to achieve international targets and those identified through the New Partnership for Africa's Development (NEPAD, see under African Union). A further priority for UNESCO, to be implemented through all its areas of work, was gender equality. Specific activities were to be pursued in support of the welfare of youth, least developed countries (LDCs) and small island developing states.

EDUCATION

UNESCO recognizes education as an essential human right, and an overarching objective for 2008–13 was to attain quality education for all. Through its work programme UNESCO is committed to achieving the MDGs of eliminating gender disparity at all levels of education and attaining universal primary education in all countries by 2015. The focus of many of UNESCO's education initiatives are the nine most highly populated developing countries (Bangladesh, Brazil, the People's Republic of China, Egypt, India, Indonesia, Mexico, Nigeria and Pakistan), known collectively as the E-9 ('Education-9') countries.

UNESCO leads and co-ordinates global efforts in support of 'Education for All' (EFA), which was adopted as a guiding principle of UNESCO's contribution to development following a world conference, convened in March 1990. In April 2000 several UN agencies, including UNESCO and UNICEF, and other partners sponsored the World Education Forum, held in Dakar, Senegal, to assess international progress in achieving the goal of Education for All and to adopt a strategy for further action (the 'Dakar Framework'), with the aim of ensuring universal basic education by 2015. The Dakar Framework, incorporating six specific goals, emphasized the role of improved access to education in the reduction of poverty and in diminishing inequalities within and between societies. UNESCO was appointed as the lead agency in the implementation of the Framework, focusing on co-ordination, advocacy, mobilization of resources, and information sharing at the international, regional and national level. It was to oversee national policy reforms, with a particular focus on the integration of EFA objectives into national education plans. An EFA Global Action Plan was formulated in 2006 to reinvigorate efforts to achieve EFA objectives and, in particular, to provide a framework for international co-operation and better definition of the roles of international partners and of UNESCO in leading the initiative. UNESCO's medium-term strategy for 2008–13 committed the organization to strengthening its role in co-ordinating EFA efforts at the global and national level, promoting monitoring and capacity-building activities to support implementation of EFA objectives, and facilitating mobilization of increased resources for EFA programmes and strategies (for example through the EFA-Fast Track Initiative, launched in 2002 to accelerate technical and financial support to low-income countries). An EFA Global Monitoring Report is prepared annually; the 2012 edition (released in October), focused on the theme 'Youth and Skills: Putting Education to Work'. In September 2012 the UN Secretary-General launched 'Education First', a new initiative aimed at increasing access to education, and the quality thereof, world-wide.

UNESCO advocates 'Literacy for All' as a key component of Education for All, regarding literacy as essential to basic education and to social and human development. UNESCO was the lead agency of the UN Literacy Decade (2003–12), which aimed to formulate an international plan of action to raise literacy standards throughout the world and to assist policy-makers to integrate literacy standards and goals into national education programmes. The Literacy Initiative for Empowerment (LIFE) was developed as an element of the Literacy Decade to accelerate efforts in some 35 countries where illiteracy is a critical challenge to development. UNESCO is also the co-ordinating agency for the UN Decade of Education for Sustainable Development (2005–14), through which it aims to establish a global framework for action and strengthen the capacity of education systems to incorporate the concepts of sustainable development into education programmes. In 2014 UNESCO was to organize, with the Government of Japan, a UNESCO World Conference on Education for Sustainable Development, to assess the implementation of the UN Decade. The April 2000 World Education Forum recognized the global HIV/AIDS pandemic to be a significant challenge to the attainment of Education for All. UNESCO, as a co-sponsor of UNAIDS, takes an active role in promoting formal and non-formal preventive health education. Through a Global Initiative on HIV/AIDS and Education (EDUCAIDS) UNESCO aims to develop comprehensive responses to HIV/AIDS rooted in the education sector, with a particular focus on vulnerable children and young people. An initiative covering the 10-year period 2006–15, the Teacher Training Initiative in sub-Saharan Africa, aims to address the shortage of teachers in that region (owing to HIV/AIDS, armed conflict and other causes) and to improve the quality of teaching.

A key priority area of UNESCO's education programme is to foster quality education for all, through formal and non-formal educational opportunities. It assists members to improve the quality of education provision through curricula content, school management and teacher training. UNESCO aims to expand access to education at all levels and to work to achieve gender equality. In particular, UNESCO aims to strengthen capacity building and education in natural, social and human sciences and promote the use of new technologies in teaching and learning processes. In May 2010 UNESCO, jointly with ITU, established a Broadband Commission for Digital Development, to comprise high level representatives of governments, industry and international agencies concerned with the effective deployment of broadband networks as an essential element of economic and social development objectives; the Commission's first report, *State of Broadband 2012: Achieving Digital Inclusion for All*, was released in September 2012.

The Associated Schools Project (ASPnet—comprising more than 9,000 institutions in 180 countries in 2013) has, since 1953, promoted the principles of peace, human rights, democracy and international co-operation through education. It provides a forum for dialogue and for promoting best practices. At tertiary level UNESCO chairs a University Twinning and Networking (UNITWIN) initiative, which was established in 1992 to establish links between higher education institutions and to foster research, training and programme development. A complementary initiative, Academics Across Borders, was inaugurated in November 2005 to strengthen communication and the sharing of knowledge and expertise among higher education professionals. In October 2002 UNESCO organized the first Global Forum on International Quality Assurance, Accreditation and the Recognition of Qualifications to establish international standards and promote capacity building for the sustainable development of higher education systems.

Within the UN system UNESCO is responsible for providing technical assistance and educational services in the context of emergency situations. This includes establishing temporary schools, providing education for refugees and displaced persons, as well as assistance for the rehabilitation of national education systems. In Palestine, UNESCO collaborates with the UN Relief and Works Agency for Palestine Refugees in the Near East (UNRWA) to assist with the training of teachers, educational planning and rehabilitation of schools. In February 2010 UNESCO agreed to form an International Co-ordination Committee in support of Haitian culture, in view of the devastation caused by an earthquake that had struck that country in January, causing 230,000 fatalities and the destruction of local infrastructure and architecture.

In February 2010 a high-level meeting on Education for All, comprising ministers of education and international co-operation, and representatives from international and regional organizations, civil society and the private sector, was held to assess the impact on education of the ongoing global economic crisis, and to consider related challenges connected to social marginalization.

NATURAL SCIENCES

The World Summit on Sustainable Development, held in August–September 2002, recognised the essential role of science (including mathematics, engineering and technology) as a foundation for achieving the MDGs of eradicating extreme poverty and ensuring environmental sustainability. UNESCO aims to promote this function within the UN system and to assist member states to utilize and foster the benefits of scientific and technical knowledge. A key objective for the medium-term strategy (2008–13) was to mobilize science knowledge and policy for sustainable development. Throughout the natural science programme priority was to be placed on Africa, LDCs and small island developing states. The Local and Indigenous Knowledge System (LINKS) initiative aims to strengthen dialogue among traditional knowledge holders, natural and social scientists and decision-makers to enhance the conservation of biodiversity, in all disciplines, and to secure an active and equitable role for local communities in the governance of resources. In June 2012, in advance of the UN Conference on Sustainable Development (Rio+20), which was convened later in that month, UNESCO, with the International Council of Scientific Unions and other partners, participated in a Forum on Science, Technology and Innovation for Sustainable Development, addressing the role to be played by science and innovation in promoting sustainable development, poverty eradication, and the transition to a green economy.

In November 1999 the General Conference endorsed a Declaration on Science and the Use of Scientific Knowledge and an agenda for action, which had been adopted at the World Conference on Science, held in June–July 1999, in Budapest, Hungary. By leveraging scientific knowledge, and global, regional and country level science networks, UNESCO aims to support sustainable development and the sound management of natural resources. It also advises governments on approaches to natural resource management, in particular the collection of scientific data, documenting and disseminating good practices and integrating social and cultural aspects into management structures and policies. UNESCO's Man and the Biosphere Programme supports a world-wide network of biosphere reserves (comprising 621 biosphere reserves in 117 countries, including 12 transboundary sites, in September 2013), which aim to promote environmental conservation and research, education and training in biodiversity and problems of land use (including the fertility of tropical soils and the cultivation of sacred sites). The third World Congress of Biosphere Reserves, held in Madrid, Spain, in February 2008, adopted the Madrid Action Plan, which aimed to promote biosphere reserves as the main internationally designated areas dedicated to sustainable development. UNESCO also supports a Global Network of National Geoparks (91 in 27 countries in 2013) which was inaugurated in 2004 to promote collaboration among managed areas of geological significance to exchange knowledge and expertise and raise awareness of the benefits of protecting those environments. Member geoparks must have effective management structures that facilitate sustainable development, with a particular emphasis on sustainable tourism. UNESCO organizes regular International Geoparks Conferences; the fifth was held in May 2012, in Unzen Volcanic Area Global Geopark, Japan, and the sixth was to take place in Stonehammer, Canada, in September 2014.

UNESCO promotes and supports international scientific partnerships to monitor, assess and report on the state of Earth systems. With the World Meteorological Organization and the International Council of Science, UNESCO sponsors the World Climate Research Programme, which was established in 1980 to determine the predictability of climate and the effect of human activity on climate. UNESCO hosts the secretariat of the World Water Assessment Programme (WWAP), which prepares the periodic *World Water Development Report*. UNESCO is actively involved in the 10-year project, agreed by more than 60 governments in February 2005, to develop a Global Earth Observation System of Systems (GEOSS). The project aims to link existing and planned observation systems in order to provide for greater understanding of the earth's processes and dissemination of detailed data, for example predicting health epidemics or weather phenomena or concerning the management of ecosystems and natural resources. UNESCO's Intergovernmental Oceanographic Commission (UNESCO-IOC) serves as the Secretariat of the Global Ocean Observing System. The International Geoscience Programme, undertaken jointly with the International Union of Geological Sciences (IUGS), facilitates the exchange of knowledge and methodology among scientists concerned with geological processes and aims to raise awareness of the links between geoscience and sustainable socio-economic development. The IUGS and UNESCO jointly initiated the International Year of Planet Earth (2008).

From 2005 UNESCO-IOC developed a Tsunami Early Warning and Mitigation System in the North-eastern Atlantic, the Mediterranean and Connected Seas (NEAMTWS), which conducted its first tsunami training exercise (NEAMWave12) in November 2012.

UNESCO is committed to contributing to international efforts to enhance disaster preparedness and mitigation. Through education UNESCO aims to reduce the vulnerability of poorer communities to disasters and improve disaster management at local and national levels. It also co-ordinates efforts at an international level to establish monitoring networks and early warning systems to mitigate natural disasters, in particular in developing tsunami early warning systems in Africa, the Caribbean, the South Pacific, the Mediterranean Sea and the North-East Atlantic similar to those already established for the Indian and Pacific oceans. Other regional partnerships and knowledge networks were to be developed to strengthen capacity building and the dissemination of information and good practices relating to risk awareness and mitigation and disaster management. Disaster education and awareness were to be incorporated as key elements in the UN Decade of Education for Sustainable Development (see above). UNESCO is also the lead agency for the International Flood Initiative, which was inaugurated in January 2005 at the World Conference on Disaster Reduction, held in Kobe, Japan. The Initiative aims to promote an integrated approach to flood management in order to minimize the damage and loss of life caused by floods, mainly with a focus on research, training, promoting good governance and providing technical assistance. The fifth International Conference on Flood Management was convened in Tsukuba, Japan, in September 2011.

A priority of the natural science programme has been to promote policies and strengthen human and institutional capacities in science, technology and innovation. At all levels of education UNESCO aims to enhance teaching quality and content in areas of science and technology and, at regional and sub-regional level, to strengthen co-operation mechanisms and policy networks in training and research. With the International Council of Scientific Unions and the Third World Academy of Sciences, UNESCO operates a short-term fellowship programme in the basic sciences and an exchange programme of visiting lecturers.

UNESCO is the lead agency of the NEPAD Science and Technology Cluster and the NEPAD Action Plan for the Environment.

SOCIAL AND HUMAN SCIENCES

UNESCO is mandated to contribute to the world-wide development of the social and human sciences and philosophy, which it regards as of great importance in policy-making and maintaining ethical vigilance. The structure of UNESCO's Social and Human Sciences programme takes into account both an ethical and standard-setting dimension, and research, policy-making, action in the field and future-oriented activities. One of UNESCO's so-called overarching objectives in the period 2008–13 was to address emerging ethical challenges.

A priority area of UNESCO's work programme on Social and Human Sciences has been to promote principles, practices and ethical norms relevant for scientific and technological development. The programme fosters international co-operation and dialogue on emerging issues, as well as raising awareness and promoting the sharing of knowledge at regional and national levels. UNESCO supports the activities of the International Bioethics Committee (IBC—a group of 36 specialists who meet under UNESCO auspices) and the Intergovernmental Bioethics Committee, and hosts the secretariat of the 18-member World Commission on the Ethics of Scientific Knowledge and Technology (COMEST), established in 1999, which aims to serve as a forum for the exchange of information and ideas and to promote dialogue between scientific communities, decision-makers and the public.

The priority Ethics of science and technology element aims to promote intergovernmental discussion and co-operation; to conduct explorative studies on possible UNESCO action on environmental ethics and developing a code of conduct for scientists; to enhance public awareness; to make available teaching expertise and create regional networks of experts; to promote the development of international and national databases on ethical issues; to identify ethical issues related to emerging technologies; to follow up relevant declarations, including the Universal Declaration on the Human Genome and Human Rights (see below); and to support the Global Ethics Observatory, an online world-wide database of information on applied bioethics and other applied science- and technology-related areas (including environmental ethics) that was launched in December 2005 by the IBC.

UNESCO itself provides an interdisciplinary, multicultural and pluralistic forum for reflection on issues relating to the ethical dimension of scientific advances, and promotes the application of international guidelines. In May 1997 the IBC approved a draft version of a Universal Declaration on the Human Genome and

Human Rights, in an attempt to provide ethical guidelines for developments in human genetics. The Declaration, which identified some 100,000 hereditary genes as 'common heritage', was adopted by the UNESCO General Conference in November and committed states to promoting the dissemination of relevant scientific knowledge and co-operating in genome research. In October 2003 the General Conference adopted an International Declaration on Human Genetic Data, establishing standards for scientists working in that field, and in October 2005 the General Conference adopted the Universal Declaration on Bioethics and Human Rights. At all levels UNESCO aims to raise awareness and foster debate about the ethical implications of scientific and technological developments and promote exchange of experiences and knowledge between governments and research bodies.

UNESCO recognizes that globalization has a broad and significant impact on societies. It is committed to countering negative trends of social transformation by strengthening the links between research and policy formulation by national and local authorities, in particular concerning poverty eradication. In that respect, UNESCO promotes the concept that freedom from poverty is a fundamental human right. In 1994 UNESCO initiated an international social science research programme, the Management of Social Transformations (MOST), to promote capacity building in social planning at all levels of decision-making. In 2003 the Executive Board approved a continuation of the programme but with a revised strategic objective of strengthening links between research, policy and practice. In 2008–13 UNESCO aimed to promote new collaborative social science research programmes and to support capacity building in developing countries.

UNESCO aims to monitor emerging social or ethical issues and, through its associated offices and institutes, formulate preventative action to ensure they have minimal impact on the attainment of UNESCO's objectives. As a specific challenge UNESCO is committed to promoting the International Convention against Doping in Sport, which entered into force in 2007. UNESCO also focuses on the educational and cultural dimensions of physical education and sport and their capacity to preserve and improve health.

Fundamental to UNESCO's mission is the rejection of all forms of discrimination. It disseminates information aimed at combating racial prejudice, works to improve the status of women and their access to education, promotes equality between men and women, and raises awareness of discrimination against people affected by HIV/AIDS, in particular among young people. In 2004 UNESCO inaugurated an initiative to enable city authorities to share experiences and collaborate in efforts to counter racism, discrimination, xenophobia and exclusion. As well as the International Coalition of Cities against Racism, regional coalitions were to be formed with more defined programmes of action. An International Youth Clearing House and Information Service (INFOYOUTH) aims to increase and consolidate the information available on the situation of young people in society, and to heighten awareness of their needs, aspirations and potential among public and private decision-makers. Supporting efforts to facilitate dialogue among different cultures and societies and promoting opportunities for reflection and consideration of philosophy and human rights, for example the celebration of World Philosophy Day, are also among UNESCO's fundamental aims.

CULTURE

In undertaking efforts to preserve the world's cultural and natural heritage UNESCO has attempted to emphasize the link between culture and development. In December 1992 UNESCO established the World Commission on Culture and Development, to strengthen links between culture and development and to prepare a report on the issue. The first World Conference on Culture and Development was held in June 1999, in Havana, Cuba. In November 2001 the General Conference adopted the UNESCO Universal Declaration on Cultural Diversity, which affirmed the importance of intercultural dialogue in establishing a climate of peace. UNESCO's medium-term strategy for 2008–13 recognized the need for a more integrated approach to cultural heritage as an area requiring conservation and development and one offering prospects for dialogue, social cohesion and shared knowledge.

UNESCO aims to promote cultural diversity through the safeguarding of heritage and enhancement of cultural expressions. In January 2002 UNESCO inaugurated the Global Alliance on Cultural Diversity, to promote partnerships between governments, non-governmental bodies and the private sector with a view to supporting cultural diversity through the strengthening of cultural industries and the prevention of cultural piracy. In October 2005 the General Conference approved an International Convention on the Protection of the Diversity of Cultural Expressions. It entered into force in March 2007 and the first session of the intergovernmental committee servicing the Convention was convened in Ottawa, Canada, in December.

UNESCO's World Heritage Programme, inaugurated in 1978, aims to protect historic sites and natural landmarks of outstanding universal significance, in accordance with the 1972 UNESCO Convention Concerning the Protection of the World Cultural and Natural Heritage, by providing financial aid for restoration, technical assistance, training and management planning. The medium-term strategy for 2008–13 acknowledged that new global threats may affect natural and cultural heritage. It also reinforced the concept that conservation of sites contributes to social cohesion. States parties compile 'Tentative Lists', detailing sites under consideration for nomination to the formal 'World Heritage List'; at September 2013 some 172 countries had compiled Tentative Lists, comprising some 1,566 prospective sites. During mid-2013–mid-2014 the World Heritage List comprised 981 sites globally, of which 759 had cultural significance, 193 were natural landmarks, and 29 were of 'mixed' importance. UNESCO is assisting in the exploration of prehistoric sites in Libya, and in the preservation of sites and monuments in other countries, for example Carthage and Al-Qairawan (Tunisia), Fez (Morocco), Tyre (Lebanon) and the Casbah of Algiers (Algeria). The Organization has assisted Iraq in the establishment of a regional training centre for the conservation of cultural property in the Arab countries. UNESCO also maintains a 'List of World Heritage in Danger'. In September 2013 this comprised 44 sites world-wide, including six sites in Syria: the ancient city of Damascus, the site of Palmyra, the ancient city of Bosra, the ancient city of Aleppo, Crac des Chevaliers and Qal'at Salah El-Din, and ancient villages of northern Syria (all inscribed in 2013); the Church of the Nativity (built on the site identified in Christian tradition as the birthplace of Jesus) and the Pilgrimage Route, Bethlehem, Palestine (inscribed in 2012); the old city of Jerusalem and its walls; the Abu Mena archeological site near Alexandria, Egypt; the ancient city of Ashur and Samarra Archaeological City in Iraq; the historic town of Zabid in Yemen; and the Cultural Landscape of Bam, Iran (added to the List in 2004, following an earthquake which had devastated the town in December 2003). In May and June–July 2003, following the overthrow of the Saddam Hussain regime, UNESCO sent two assessment missions to Iraq to compile an inventory of cultural property and record the condition of major institutions and archaeological sites. In July UNESCO and INTERPOL signed an agreement on the compilation of a database of objects of cultural importance that had been looted in Iraq during the period of unrest. The UNESCO Director-General expressed deep concern in August 2012 at the reported ongoing destruction of sites of Sufi religious significance—including shrines and libraries—in Libya; and, in October, at fire damage to the ancient souk (market) in Aleppo, Syria, resulting from the ongoing civil war in that country.

UNESCO supports the safeguarding of humanity's non-material 'intangible' heritage, including oral traditions, music, dance and medicine. An Endangered Languages Programme was initiated in 1993. By 2013 the Programme estimated that, of the more than 6,000 languages spoken world-wide, about one-half were endangered. It works to raise awareness of the issue, for example through publication of the *Atlas of the World's Languages in Danger of Disappearing,* to strengthen local and national capacities to safeguard and document languages, and administers a Register of Good Practices in Language Preservation. In October 2003 the UNESCO General Conference adopted a Convention for the Safeguarding of Intangible Cultural Heritage, which provided for the establishment of an intergovernmental committee and for participating states to formulate national inventories of intangible heritage. The Convention entered into force in April 2006 and the intergovernmental committee convened its inaugural session in November. A Representative List of the Intangible Cultural Heritage of Humanity, inaugurated in November 2008, comprised, at the end of 2012, 259 elements ('masterpieces of the oral and intangible heritage of humanity') deemed to be of outstanding value; these included: Chinese calligraphy; falconry; several dances, such as the tango, which originated in Argentina and Uruguay, and the dances of the Ainu in Japan; the Mesir Macunu festival in Turkey; craftsmanship of Horezu ceramics in Romania; and the Ifa divination system in Nigeria. The related List of Intangible Cultural Heritage in Need of Urgent Safeguarding comprised 31 elements at December 2012, such as the Naqqāli form of story-telling in Iran, the Saman dance in Sumatra, Indonesia, earthenware pottery-making skills in Kgatleng District, Botswana, and the Qiang New Year Festival in Sichuan Province, China. UNESCO's culture programme also aims to safeguard movable cultural heritage and to support and develop museums as a means of preserving heritage and making it accessible to society as a whole.

In November 2001 the General Conference authorized the formulation of a Declaration against the Intentional Destruction of Cultural Heritage. In addition, the Conference adopted the Convention on the Protection of the Underwater Cultural Heritage, covering the protection from commercial exploitation of shipwrecks, submerged historical sites, etc., situated in the territorial waters of signatory states. UNESCO also administers the 1954 Hague Convention on the Protection of Cultural Property in the Event of Armed Conflict and the 1970 Convention on the Means of Prohibiting and Preventing the Illicit Import, Export and Transfer of Ownership of Cultural Property. In 1992 a World Heritage Centre was established to enable rapid mobilization of international technical assistance for the preservation of cultural sites. Through the World Heritage Information Network (WHIN), a world-wide network of more than 800 information providers, UNESCO promotes global awareness and information exchange.

UNESCO aims to support the development of creative industries and or creative expression. Through a variety of projects UNESCO promotes art education, supports the rights of artists, and encourages crafts, design, digital art and performance arts. In October 2004 UNESCO launched a Creative Cities Network to facilitate public and private sector partnerships, international links, and recognition of a city's unique expertise. In 2013 34 cities were participating in the Network, including Aswan, Egypt (City of Craft and Folk Art). UNESCO is active in preparing and encouraging the enforcement of international legislation on copyright, raising awareness on the need for copyright protection to uphold cultural diversity, and is contributing to the international debate on digital copyright issues and piracy.

Within its ambition of ensuring cultural diversity, UNESCO recognizes the role of culture as a means of promoting peace and dialogue. Several projects have been formulated within a broader concept of Roads of Dialogue. In Central Asia a project on intercultural dialogue follows on from an earlier multidisciplinary study of the ancient Silk Roads trading routes linking Asia and Europe, which illustrated many examples of common heritage. Other projects include a study of the movement of peoples and cultures during the slave trade, a Mediterranean Programme, the Caucasus Project and the Arabia Plan, which aims to promote world-wide knowledge and understanding of Arab culture. UNESCO has overseen an extensive programme of work to formulate histories of humanity and regions, focused on ideas, civilizations and the evolution of societies and cultures. These have included the *General History of Africa, History of Civilizations of Central Asia,* and *History of Humanity*. UNESCO endeavoured to consider and implement the findings of the Alliance of Civilizations, a high-level group convened by the UN Secretary-General that published a report in November 2006. UNESCO signed a Memorandum of Understanding with the Alliance during its first forum, convened in Madrid, Spain, in January 2008.

COMMUNICATION AND INFORMATION

UNESCO regards information, communication and knowledge as being at the core of human progress and well-being. It advocates the concept of knowledge societies, based on the principles of freedom of expression, universal access to information and knowledge, promotion of cultural diversity, and equal access to quality education. In 2008–13 UNESCO determined to consolidate and implement this concept, in accordance with the Declaration of Principles and Plan of Action adopted by the second phase of the World Summit on the Information Society (WSIS) in November 2005. UNESCO hosted the WSIS+10 Review meeting, in February 2013 (the first WSIS phase having taken place in December 2003), in Paris, on the theme 'Towards Knowledge Societies for Peace and Sustainable Development'.

A key strategic objective of building inclusive knowledge societies is enhancing universal access to communication and information. At the national and global level UNESCO promotes the rights of freedom of expression and of access to information. It promotes the free flow and broad diffusion of information, knowledge, data and best practices, through the development of communications infrastructures, the elimination of impediments to freedom of expression, and the development of independent and pluralistic media, including through the provision of advisory services on media legislation, particularly in post-conflict countries and in countries in transition. UNESCO recognizes that the so-called global digital divide, in addition to other developmental differences between countries, generates exclusion and marginalization, and that increased participation in the democratic process can be attained through strengthening national communication and information capacities. UNESCO promotes policies and mechanisms that enhance provision for marginalized and disadvantaged groups to benefit from information and community opportunities. Activities at local and national level include developing effective 'infostructures', such as libraries and archives and strengthening low-cost community media and information access points, for example through the establishment of Community Multimedia Centres (CMCs). Many of UNESCO's principles and objectives in this area are pursued through the Information for All Programme, which entered into force in 2001. It is administered by an intergovernmental council, the secretariat of which is provided by UNESCO. UNESCO also established, in 1982, the International Programme for the Development of Communication (IPDC), which aims to promote and develop independent and pluralistic media in developing countries, for example by the establishment or modernization of news agencies and newspapers and training media professionals, the promotion of the right to information, and through efforts to harness informatics for development purposes and strengthen member states' capacities in this field. In March 2013 the IPDC approved funding for 63 new media development projects in developing and emerging countries world-wide. In 2011, on the basis of discussions held at the 2010 session of the Internet Governance Forum (established by the second phase of the WSIS to support the implementation of the Summit's mandate) UNESCO published a report entitled 'Freedom of Connection-Freedom of Expression: the Changing Legal and Regulatory Ecology Shaping the Internet'. UNESCO has engaged with the Freedom Online Coalition, launched in December 2011 by the first Freedom Online Conference, held in The Hague, Netherlands, with the objective of facilitating global dialogue regarding the role of governments in furthering freedom on the internet. The second Freedom Online Conference was convened in Nairobi, Kenya, in September 2012, and the third Conference was held in Tunis, Tunisia, in June 2013, by which time the Freedom Online Coalition had 21 member states.

UNESCO supports cultural and linguistic diversity in information sources to reinforce the principle of universal access. It aims to raise awareness of the issue of equitable access and diversity, encourage good practices and develop policies to strengthen cultural diversity in all media. In 2002 UNESCO established Initiative B@bel as a multidisciplinary programme to promote linguistic diversity, with the aim of enhancing access of under-represented groups to information sources as well as protecting underused minority languages. In December 2009 UNESCO and the Internet Corporation for Assigned Names and Numbers (ICANN) signed a joint agreement which aimed to promote the use of multilingual domain names using non-Latin script, with a view to promoting linguistic diversity. UNESCO's Programme for Creative Content supports the development of and access to diverse content in both the electronic and audio-visual media. The Memory of the World project, established in 1992, aims to preserve in digital form, and thereby to promote wide access to, the world's documentary heritage. Documentary material includes stone tablets, celluloid, parchment and audio recordings. By September 2013 299 inscriptions had been included on the project's register; five inscriptions originated from international organizations, including the Archives of the ICRC's former International Prisoners of War Agency, 1914–23, submitted by the ICRC, and inscribed in 2007; the League of Nations Archives, 1919–46, submitted by the UN Geneva Office, and inscribed in 2009; and documentary heritage of the International Commission for the International Tracing Service (ITS), submitted by the ITS, and inscribed in 2013. In September 2012 UNESCO organized an international conference on the 'Memory of the World in the Digital Age: Digitization and Preservation', in Vancouver, Canada. The conference adopted the Vancouver Declaration, emphasizing that every individual should be guaranteed access to information, including in digital format, and that digital information should be available in the long term. UNESCO also supports other efforts to preserve and disseminate digital archives and, in 2003, adopted a Charter for the Preservation of Digital Heritage. In April 2009 UNESCO launched the internet based World Digital Library, accessible at www.wdl.org, which aims to display primary documents (including texts, charts and illustrations), and authoritative explanations, relating to the accumulated knowledge of a broad spectrum of human cultures.

UNESCO promotes freedom of expression, of the press and independence of the media as fundamental human rights and the basis of democracy. It aims to assist member states to formulate policies and legal frameworks to uphold independent and pluralistic media and infostructures and to enhance the capacities of public service broadcasting institutions. In regions affected by conflict UNESCO supports efforts to establish and maintain an independent media service and to use it as a means of consolidating peace. UNESCO also aims to develop media and information systems to respond to and mitigate the impact of disaster situations, and to integrate these objectives into wider UN peace-building or reconstruction initiatives. UNESCO is the co-ordinating agency for 'World Press Freedom Day', which is held annually on 3 May; it also awards an annual World Press Freedom Prize. A conference convened in Tunis, in celebration of the May 2012 World Press Freedom Day—held on the theme 'New Voices: Media Freedom Helping to Transform Societies', with a focus on the transition towards democracy in several countries of North Africa and the Middle East—adopted the Carthage Declaration, urging the creation of free and safe environments for media workers and the promotion of journalistic ethics. The Declaration also requested UNESCO to pursue implementation of the UN Plan of Action on the Safety of Journalists and the Issue of Impunity, which had been drafted with guidance from UNESCO, and endorsed in April by the UN System Chief Executives Board for Co-ordination. UNESCO maintains an Observatory on the Information Society, which provides up-to-date information on the development of new ICTs, analyses major trends, and aims to raise awareness of related ethical, legal and societal issues. UNESCO promotes the upholding of human rights in the use of cyberspace. In 1997 it organized the first International Congress on Ethical, Legal and Societal Aspects of Digital Information ('INFOethics').

UNESCO promotes the application of information and communication technology for sustainable development. In particular it supports efforts to improve teaching and learning processes through electronic media and to develop innovative literacy and education initiatives, such as the ICT-Enhanced Learning (ICTEL) project. UNESCO also aims to enhance understanding and use of new technologies and support training and ongoing learning opportunities for librarians, archivists and other information providers.

Finance

UNESCO's activities are funded through a regular budget provided by contributions from member states and extrabudgetary funds from other sources, particularly the UN Development Programme, the World Bank, regional banks and other bilateral Funds-in-Trust arrangements. UNESCO co-operates with many other UN agencies and international non-governmental organizations.

UNESCO's Regular Programme budget for the two-year period 2012–13 was US $685.7m.

In response to a decision, in late October 2011, by a majority of member states participating in the UNESCO General Conference to admit Palestine as a new member state, the USA decided to withhold from UNESCO significant annual funding. In the following month UNESCO launched an Emergency Multi-Donor Fund, as a channel for donations made by international donors with the aim of addressing the funding shortfall.

Publications

(mostly in English, French and Spanish editions; Arabic, Chinese and Russian versions are also available in many cases)

Atlas of the World's Languages in Danger of Disappearing (online).
Best Practices of Island and Coastal Biospheres.
Copyright Bulletin (quarterly).
Encyclopedia of Life Support Systems (online).
Education for All Global Monitoring Report.
International Review of Education (quarterly).
International Social Science Journal (quarterly).
Memory of the World, The Treasures that Record our History from 1700 BC to the Present Day.
Museum International (quarterly).
Nature and Resources (quarterly).
The New Courier (quarterly).
Prospects (quarterly review on education).
UNESCO Sources (monthly).
UNESCO Statistical Yearbook.
UNESCO World Atlas of Gender Equality in Education.
World Communication Report.
World Educational Report (every 2 years).
World Heritage Review (quarterly).
World Information Report.
World Science Report (every 2 years).
Books, databases, video and radio documentaries, statistics, scientific maps and atlases.

Specialized Institutes and Centres

Abdus Salam International Centre for Theoretical Physics: Strada Costiera 11, 34151 Trieste, Italy; tel. (040) 2240111; fax (040) 224163; e-mail sci_info@ictp.it; internet www.ictp.it; f. 1964; promotes and enables advanced study and research in physics and mathematical sciences; organizes and sponsors training opportunities, in particular for scientists from developing countries; aims to provide an international forum for the exchange of information and ideas; operates under a tripartite agreement between UNESCO, IAEA and the Italian Government; Dir FERNANDO QUEVEDO (Guatemala).

International Bureau of Education (IBE): POB 199, 1211 Geneva 20, Switzerland; tel. 229177800; fax 229177801; e-mail doc .centre@ibe.unesco.org; internet www.ibe.unesco.org; f. 1925, became an intergovernmental organization in 1929 and was incorporated into UNESCO in 1969; the Council of the IBE is composed of representatives of 28 member states of UNESCO, designated by the General Conference; the Bureau's fundamental mission is to deal with matters concerning educational content, methods, and teaching/learning strategies; an International Conference on Education is held periodically; Dir CLEMENTINA ACEDO (Venezuela); publs *Prospects* (quarterly review), *Educational Innovation* (newsletter), educational practices series, monographs, other reference works.

UNESCO Institute for Information Technologies in Education: 117292 Moscow, ul. Kedrova 8, Russia; tel. (499) 129-29-90; fax (499) 129-12-25; e-mail liste.info.iite@unesco.org; internet iite .unesco.org; f. 1988; the Institute aims to formulate policies regarding the development of, and to support and monitor the use of, information and communication technologies in education; it conducts research and organizes training programmes; Dir a.i. DENDEV BADARCH.

UNESCO Institute for Lifelong Learning: Feldbrunnenstr. 58, 20148 Hamburg, Germany; tel. (40) 448-0410; fax (40) 410-7723; e-mail uil@unesco.org; internet www.unesco.org/uil/index.htm; f. 1951, as the Institute for Education; a research, training, information, documentation and publishing centre, with a particular focus on adult basic and further education and adult literacy; Dir ARNE CARLSEN.

UNESCO Institute for Statistics: CP 6128, Succursale Centre-Ville, Montréal, QC, H3C 3J7, Canada; tel. (514) 343-6880; fax (514) 343-5740; e-mail uis.information@unesco.org; internet www.uis .unesco.org; f. 2001; collects and analyses national statistics on education, science, technology, culture and communications; Dir HENDRIK VAN DER POL (Netherlands).

UNESCO Institute for Water Education: Westvest 7, 2611 AX Delft, Netherlands; tel. (15) 2151715; fax (15) 2122921; e-mail info@ unesco-ihe.org; internet www.unesco-ihe.org; f. 2003; activities include education, training and research; and co-ordination of a global network of water sector organizations; advisory and policy-making functions; setting international standards for postgraduate education programmes; and professional training in the water sector; Rector ANDRÁS SZÖLLÖSI-NAGY (Hungary).

UNESCO-UNEVOC International Centre for Technical and Vocational Education and Training: UN Campus, Hermann-Ehlers-Str. 10, 53113 Bonn, Germany; tel. (228) 8150-100; fax (228) 8150-199; e-mail unevoc@unesco.org; internet www.unevoc.unesco .org; f. 2002; the centre assists member states to strengthen and upgrade their vocational education and training (TVET) systems; promotes high-quality lifelong technical and vocational education, with a particular focus on young people, girls and women, and the disadvantaged; Head SHYAMAL MAJUMDAR (India).

UNESCO International Institute for Capacity Building in Africa (UNESCO–IICBA): ECA Compound, Africa Ave, POB 2305, Addis Ababa, Ethiopia; tel. (11) 5445284; fax (11) 514936; e-mail info@unesco-iicba.org; internet www.unesco-iicba.org; f. 1999 to promote capacity building in the following areas: teacher education; curriculum development; educational policy, planning and management; and distance education; Dir ARNALDO NHAVOTO.

UNESCO International Institute for Educational Planning (IIEP): 7–9 rue Eugène Delacroix, 75116 Paris, France; tel. 1-45-03-77-00; fax 1-40-72-83-66; e-mail info@iiep.unesco.org; internet www .unesco.org/iiep; f. 1963; serves as a world centre for advanced training and research in educational planning; aims to help all member states of UNESCO in their social and economic development efforts, by enlarging the fund of knowledge about educational planning and the supply of competent experts in this field; legally and administratively a part of UNESCO, the Institute is autonomous, and its policies and programme are controlled by its own Governing Board, under special statutes voted by the General Conference of UNESCO; a satellite office of the IIEP is based in Buenos Aires, Argentina; Dir KHALIL MAHSHI (Jordan).

World Health Organization—WHO

Address: 20 ave Appia, 1211 Geneva 27, Switzerland.

Telephone: 227912111; **fax:** 227913111; **e-mail:** info@who.int; **internet:** www.who.int.

WHO, established in 1948, is the lead agency within the UN system concerned with the protection and improvement of public health.

Organization

(September 2013)

WORLD HEALTH ASSEMBLY

The Assembly meets in Geneva, Switzerland, once a year. It is responsible for policy-making and the biennial programme and budget; appoints the Director-General; admits new members; and reviews budget contributions. The 66th Assembly was convened in May 2013.

EXECUTIVE BOARD

The Board is composed of 34 health experts designated by a member state that has been elected by the World Health Assembly to serve on the Board; each expert serves for three years. The Board meets at least twice a year to review the Director-General's programme, which it forwards to the Assembly with any recommendations that seem necessary. It advises on questions referred to it by the Assembly and is responsible for putting into effect the decisions and policies of the Assembly. It is also empowered to take emergency measures in case of epidemics or disasters. Meeting in November 2011 the Board agreed several proposals on reforms to the Organization aimed at improving health outcomes, achieving greater coherence in global health matters, and promoting organizational efficiency and transparency.

Chairman: Prof. JANE HALTON (Australia).

SECRETARIAT

Director-General: Dr MARGARET CHAN (People's Republic of China).

Deputy Director-General: Dr ANARFI ASAMOA-BAAH (Ghana).

Assistant Directors-General: Dr BRUCE AYLWARD (Canada) (Polio, Emergencies and Country Collaboration), FLAVIA BUSTREO (Italy) (Family, Women's and Children's Health), OLEG CHESTNOV (Russia) (Non-communicable Diseases and Mental Health), KEIJI FUKUDA (USA) (Health Security and Environment), MOHAMED ABDI JAMA (Somalia) (General Management), MARIE-PAULE KIENY (France) (Health Systems and Innovation), HIROKI NAKATANI (Japan) (HIV/AIDS, TB, Malaria and Neglected Tropical Diseases).

PRINCIPAL OFFICES

Each of WHO's six geographical regions has its own organization, consisting of a regional committee representing relevant member states and associate members, and a regional office staffed by experts in various fields of health.

Africa Office: Cité du Djoue BP 06, Brazzaville, Republic of the Congo; tel. 83-91-00; fax 83-95-01; e-mail regafro@whoafro.org; internet www.afro.who.int; Dir Dr LUÍS GOMES SAMBO (Angola).

Eastern Mediterranean Office: POB 7608, Abdul Razzak al Sanhouri St, Cairo (Nasr City) 11371, Egypt; tel. (2) 2765000; fax (2) 6702492; e-mail postmaster@emro.who.int; internet www.emro.who.int; Dir Dr ALA ALWAN (Iraq).

International Health Regulations Coordination—WHO Lyon Office: 58 ave Debourg, 69007 Lyon, France; tel. 4-72-71-64-70; fax 4-72-71-64-71; e-mail ihrinfo@who.int; internet www.who.int/ihr/lyon/en/index.html; supports (with regional offices) countries in strengthening their national surveillance and response systems, with the aim of improving the detection, assessment and notification of events, and responding to public health risks and emergencies of international concern under the International Health Regulations.

WHO Centre for Health Development: I. H. D. Centre Bldg, 9th Floor, 5–1, 1-chome, Wakinohama-Kaigandori, Chuo-ku, Kobe, Japan; tel. (78) 230-3100; fax (78) 230-3178; e-mail wkc@wkc.who.int; internet www.who.or.jp; f. 1995 to address health development issues; Dir ALEX ROSS (USA).

Activities

WHO is the UN system's co-ordinating authority for health (defined as 'a state of complete physical, mental and social well-being and not merely the absence of disease and infirmity'). WHO's objective is stated in its constitution as 'the attainment by all peoples of the highest possible level of health'. The Organization's core functions, outlined in its 11th programme of work covering 2006–13, are to provide leadership on global public health matters, in partnership, where necessary, with other agencies; to help shape the global health research agenda; to articulate ethical and evidence-based policy options; to set, and monitor the implementation of, norms and standards; to monitor and assess health trends; and to provide technical and policy support to member countries. Aid is provided in emergencies and natural disasters. In May 2013 the 66th World Health Assembly adopted the Organization's 12th General Programme of Work, to guide its activities during 2014–19.

In its work WHO adheres to a six-point agenda: promoting development; fostering health security; strengthening health systems; harnessing research, information and evidence; enhancing partnerships; and improving performance.

WHO has developed a series of international classifications, including the *International Statistical Classification of Disease and Related Health Problems (ICD)*, providing an etiological framework of health conditions, and currently in its 10th edition; and the complementary *International Classification of Functioning, Disability and Health (ICF)*, which describes how people live with their conditions.

WHO keeps diseases and other health problems under constant surveillance, promotes the exchange of prompt and accurate information and of notification of outbreaks of diseases, and administers the International Health Regulations (the most recently revised version of which entered into force in June 2007). WHO undertakes to: collect and disseminate health data and undertake statistical analyses and comparative studies in such diseases as cancer, heart disease and mental illness; set standards for the quality control of drugs, vaccines and other substances affecting health, and communicate reports or any known adverse reactions to drugs to all member states; formulate health regulations for international travel; and promote improved environmental conditions, including housing, sanitation and working conditions.

A global programme of collaborative research and exchange of scientific information is carried out in co-operation with about 1,200 national institutions. Particular emphasis is given to the widespread communicable diseases of the tropics, and the countries directly concerned are assisted in developing their research capabilities. Co-operation among scientists and professional groups is encouraged. WHO negotiates and sustains national and global partnerships. It may propose international conventions and agreements, or promote the development and testing of new technologies, tools and guidelines. WHO assists in developing an informed public opinion on matters of health.

In the implementation of all its activities WHO aims to contribute to achieving by 2015 the UN Millennium Development Goals (MDGs) that were agreed by the September 2000 UN Millennium Summit. WHO has particular responsibility for the MDGs of reducing child mortality, with a target reduction of two-thirds in the mortality rate among children under five; improving maternal health, with a specific goal of reducing by 75% the numbers of women dying in childbirth; and combating HIV/AIDS, malaria and other diseases. In addition, it directly supports the following millennium 'targets': halving the proportion of people suffering from malnutrition; halving the proportion of people without sustainable access to safe drinking water and basic sanitation; and providing access, in co-operation with pharmaceutical companies, to affordable, essential drugs in developing countries. Furthermore, WHO reports on 17 health-related MDG indicators; co-ordinates, jointly with the World Bank, the High-Level Forum on the Health MDGs, comprising government ministers, senior officials from developing countries, and representatives of bilateral and multilateral agencies, foundations, regional organizations and global partnerships; and undertakes technical and normative work in support of national and regional efforts to reach the MDGs. In 2013 WHO, with UNICEF, was co-leading consultations on formulating a post-2015 development framework in the thematic area of health.

The 2006–13 General Programme of Work defined a policy framework for pursuing the principal objectives of building healthy populations and combating ill health. The Programme took into account increasing understanding of the social, economic, political and cultural factors involved in achieving better health and the role played by better health in poverty reduction; the increasing complexity of health systems; the importance of safeguarding health as a component of humanitarian action; and the need for greater co-ordination among development organizations. It incorporated four interrelated strategic directions: lessening excess mortality, morbidity and disability, especially in poor and marginalized populations; promoting healthy lifestyles and reducing risk factors to human health arising from environmental, economic, social and behavioural causes; developing equitable and financially fair health systems; and establishing an enabling policy and an institutional environment for the health sector and promoting an effective health dimension to social, economic, environmental and development policy. WHO is the sponsoring agency for the Health Workforce Decade (2006–15).

During 2005 the UN's Inter-Agency Standing Committee (IASC), concerned with co-ordinating the international response to humanitarian disasters, developed a concept of organizing agency assistance to IDPs through the institutionalization of a 'Cluster Approach', comprising 11 core areas of activity. WHO was designated the lead agency for the Health Cluster. The 65th World Health Assembly, convened in May 2012, adopted a resolution endorsing WHO's role as Health Cluster lead and urging international donors to allocate sufficient resources towards health sector activities during humanitarian emergencies.

WHO, with the International Labour Organization (ILO), leads the Social Protection Floor initiative, the sixth of nine activities that were launched in April 2009 by the UN System Chief Executives Board for Co-ordination (CEB), with the aim of alleviating the impact on poor and vulnerable populations of the global economic downturn. In October 2011 a Social Protection Floor Advisory Group, launched in August 2010 under the initiative, issued a report entitled *Social Protection Floor for a Fair and Inclusive Globalization*, which urged that basic income and services should be guaranteed for all, stating that this would promote both stability and economic growth globally.

COMMUNICABLE DISEASES

WHO identifies infectious and parasitic communicable diseases as a major obstacle to social and economic progress, particularly in developing countries, where, in addition to disabilities and loss of productivity and household earnings, they cause nearly one-half of all deaths. Emerging and re-emerging diseases, those likely to cause epidemics, increasing incidence of zoonoses (diseases or infections passed from vertebrate animals to humans by means of parasites, viruses, bacteria or unconventional agents), attributable to factors such as environmental changes and changes in farming practices, outbreaks of unknown etiology, and the undermining of some drug therapies by the spread of antimicrobial resistance, are main areas of concern. In recent years WHO has noted the global spread of communicable diseases through international travel, voluntary human migration and involuntary population displacement.

WHO's Communicable Diseases group works to reduce the impact of infectious diseases world-wide through surveillance and response; prevention, control and eradication strategies; and research and product development. The group seeks to identify new technologies and tools, and to foster national development through strengthening health services and the better use of existing tools. It aims to strengthen global monitoring of important communicable disease problems, and to create consensus and consolidate partnerships around targeted diseases and collaborates with other groups at all stages to provide an integrated response. In 2000 WHO and several partner institutions in epidemic surveillance established the Global Outbreak Alert and Response Network (GOARN). Through the Network WHO aims to maintain constant vigilance regarding outbreaks of disease and to link world-wide expertise to provide an immediate response capability.

From March 2003 WHO began to co-ordinate an international investigation into the global spread of Severe Acute Respiratory Syndrome (SARS), a previously unknown atypical pneumonia. In 2013 WHO was monitoring the spread of Middle East respiratory syndrome coronavirus (MERS-CoV), a related acute respiratory condition; by 7 September 114 laboratory-confirmed cases of MERS-CoV had been reported to the Organization since September 2012, and 54 of those affected had died. The reported cases had arisen in Jordan, Qatar, Saudi Arabia and the United Arab Emirates (UAE). Laboratory-confirmed cases had also been reported in France, Germany, Italy, Tunisia and the United Kingdom, relating to patients who had recently been in the source region, or had been transferred to a third country for care. From the end of 2003 WHO was monitoring the spread through several Asian countries of the virus H5N1 (a rapidly mutating strain of zoonotic highly pathogenic avian influenza—HPAI) that was transmitting to human populations through contact with diseased birds, mainly poultry. It was feared that H5N1 would mutate into a form transmissable from human to human. In March 2005 WHO issued a *Global Influenza Preparedness Plan*, and urged all countries to develop national influenza pandemic preparedness plans and to stockpile antiviral drugs. In May, in co-operation with FAO and the World Organisation for Animal Health (OIE), WHO launched a Global Strategy for the Progressive Control of Highly Pathogenic Avian Influenza. A conference on Avian Influenza and Human Pandemic Influenza that was jointly organized by WHO, FAO, the OIE and the World Bank in November 2005 issued a plan of action identifying a number of responses for disease control, preparedness, response and vaccine research. An International Pledging Conference on Avian and Human Influenza, convened in January 2006 in Beijing, People's Republic of China, and co-sponsored by the World Bank, European Commission and Chinese Government, in co-operation with WHO, FAO and the OIE, requested a minimum of US $1,200m. in funding towards combating the spread of the virus. By 27 August 2013 a total of 637 human cases of H5N1 had been laboratory confirmed, in Azerbaijan, Bangladesh, Cambodia, China, Djibouti, Egypt, Indonesia, Iraq, Laos, Myanmar, Nigeria, Pakistan, Thailand, Turkey and Viet Nam, resulting in 378 deaths. Cases in poultry had become endemic in parts of Asia and Africa, and outbreaks in poultry had also occurred in some European and Middle Eastern countries. Two further general subtypes of avian influenza—H7 and H9—have also been reported in humans. In April 2013 WHO and the Chinese authorities deployed a joint mission to investigate and make recommendations concerning the control of an outbreak of H7N9 in humans that had emerged in the previous month in China. By 12 August 135 cases of H7N9 in humans, resulting in 44 deaths, had been reported to WHO.

In April 2009 GOARN sent experts to Mexico to work with health authorities there in response to an outbreak of confirmed human cases of a new variant of swine influenza A(H1N1) that had not previously been detected in animals or humans. In late April, by which time cases of the virus had been reported in the USA and Canada, the Director-General of WHO declared a 'public health emergency of international concern'. All countries were instructed to activate their national influenza pandemic preparedness plans (see above). At the end of April the level of pandemic alert was declared to be at phase five of a six-phase (phase six being the most severe) warning system that had been newly revised earlier in the year. Phase five is characterized by human-to-human transmission of a new virus into at least two countries in one WHO region. On 11 June WHO declared a global pandemic (phase six on the warning scale, characterized by human-to-human transmission in two or more WHO regions). The status and development of pandemic influenza vaccines was the focus of an advisory meeting of immunization experts held at the WHO headquarters in late October. In June 2010 the WHO Director-General refuted allegations, levelled by a British medical journal and by the Parliamentary Assembly of the Council of Europe, regarding the severity of pandemic (H1N1) 2009 and the possibility that the Organization had, in declaring the pandemic, used advisers with a vested commercial interest in promoting pharmaceutical industry profitability. In August 2010 the WHO Director-General declared that transmission of the new H1N1 virus had entered a post-pandemic phase. In May 2011 the 64th World Health Assembly adopted a Pandemic Influenza Preparedness (PIP) Framework, which aimed to broaden access to anti-influenza vaccines.

One of WHO's major achievements was the eradication of smallpox. Following a massive international campaign of vaccination and surveillance (begun in 1958 and intensified in 1967), the last case was detected in 1977 and the eradication of the disease was declared in 1980. In May 1996 the World Health Assembly resolved that, pending a final endorsement, all remaining stocks of the variola virus (which causes smallpox) were to be destroyed on 30 June 1999, although 500,000 doses of smallpox vaccine were to remain, along with a supply of the smallpox vaccine seed virus, in order to ensure that a further supply of the vaccine could be made available if required. In May 1999, however, the Assembly authorized a temporary retention of stocks of the virus until 2002. In late 2001, in response to fears that illegally held virus stocks could be used in acts of biological terrorism (see below), WHO reassembled a team of technical experts on smallpox. In January 2002 the Executive Board determined that stocks of the virus should continue to be retained, to enable research into more effective treatments and vaccines. The state of variola virus research was to be reviewed in 2014, by the 67th World Health Assembly, which was to discuss nominating a deadline for the destruction of the remaining virus stocks.

In 1988 the World Health Assembly launched the Global Polio Eradication Initiative (GPEI), which aimed, initially, to eradicate poliomyelitis by the end of 2000; this target was subsequently extended to the end of 2018 (see below). Co-ordinated periods of Supplementary Immunization Activity (SIA, facilitated in conflict zones by the negotiation of so-called 'days of tranquility'), including National Immunization Days (NIDs), Sub-National Immunization Days (SNIDs), mop-up campaigns, VitA campaigns (Vitamin A is administered in order to reduce nutritional deficiencies in children and thereby boost their immunity), and Follow up/Catch up campaigns, have been employed in combating the disease, alongside the strengthening of routine immunization services. Since the inauguration of the GPEI WHO has declared the following regions 'polio-free': the Americas (1994); Western Pacific (2000); and Europe (2002). Furthermore, type 2 wild poliovirus has been eradicated globally (since 1999), although a type 2 circulating vaccine-derived poliovirus (cVDPV) was reported to be active in northern Nigeria during 2006–early 2010. In January 2004 ministers responsible for health of affected countries, and global partners, meeting under the auspices of WHO and UNICEF, adopted the Geneva Declaration on the Eradication of Poliomyelitis, in which they made a commitment to accelerate the drive towards eradication of the disease, by improving the scope of vaccination programmes. In February 2007 the GPEI launched an intensified eradication effort aimed at identifying and addressing the outstanding operational, technical and financial barriers to eradication. The May 2008 World Health Assembly adopted a resolution urging all remaining polio-affected member states to achieve the vaccination of every child. Some 223 polio cases were confirmed world-wide in 2012, of which 217 were in the then three polio-endemic countries (Nigeria, 122 cases; Pakistan, 58 cases, and Afghanistan, 35 cases), and six cases were recorded in non-endemic countries (five cases in Chad and one case in Niger). (In 1988, by comparison, 35,000 cases had been confirmed in 125 countries, with the actual number of cases estimated at around 350,000.) India was declared to be no longer polio-endemic in February 2012. In April 2013, acting upon a request made in May 2012 by the 65th World Health Assembly, the GPEI issued a new Polio Eradication and Endgame Strategic Plan covering the period 2013–18.

WHO is committed to the elimination of leprosy (the reduction of the prevalence of leprosy to less than one case per 10,000 population). The use of a highly effective combination of three drugs (known as multi-drug therapy—MDT) resulted in a reduction in the number of leprosy cases world-wide from 10m.–12m. in 1988 to 181,941 registered cases in January 2012. The Global Alliance for the Elimination of Leprosy was launched in November 1999 by WHO, in collaboration with governments of affected countries and several private partners, including a major pharmaceutical company, to support the eradication of the disease through the provision of free MDT treatment; WHO has supplied free MDT treatment to leprosy patients in endemic countries since 1995. Most cases occur in Africa, Asia and South America.

The objective of providing immunization for all children by 1990 was adopted by the World Health Assembly in 1977. Six diseases (measles, whooping cough, tetanus, poliomyelitis, tuberculosis and diphtheria) became the target of the Expanded Programme on Immunization (EPI), in which WHO, UNICEF and many other organizations collaborated. As a result of massive international and national efforts, the global immunization coverage increased from 20% in the early 1980s to the targeted rate of 80% by the end of 1990. In 2006 WHO, UNICEF and other partners launched the Global Immunization Vision and Strategy (GIVS), a global 10-year framework, covering 2006–15, aimed at reducing deaths due to vaccine-preventable diseases by at least two-thirds compared to 2000 levels, by 2015; and increasing national vaccination coverage levels to at least 90%. In 2011 the global child vaccination coverage rate was estimated at 83%. In May 2012 the 65th World Health Assembly endorsed a Global Vaccine Action Plan (GVAP), building on the GIVS, which aimed to facilitate more equitable access to vaccines by 2020.

WHO provides policy guidance relating to Antimicrobial Resistance (AMR): the spread of infections caused by micro-organisms (including bacteria, viruses and certain parasites) that are resistant to conventional treatments (antibiotics, antivirals and antimalarials), such as multidrug-resistant TB and methicillin-resistant Staphylococcus Aureus (MRSA). WHO has also issued guidelines which aimed to mitigate the risks associated with the use of antimicrobials in livestock reared for human consumption.

HIV/AIDS, TB, MALARIA AND NEGLECTED TROPICAL DISEASES

Combating the human immunodeficiency virus/acquired immunodeficiency syndrome (HIV/AIDS), tuberculosis (TB) and malaria are organization-wide priorities and, as such, are supported not only by their own areas of work but also by activities undertaken in other areas. TB is the principal cause of death for people infected with the HIV virus and an estimated one-third of people living with HIV/AIDS globally are co-infected with TB. In July 2000 a meeting of the Group of Seven industrialized nations and Russia, convened in Genoa, Italy, announced the formation of a new Global Fund to Fight AIDS, TB and Malaria (as previously proposed by the UN Secretary-General and recommended by the World Health Assembly).

The HIV/AIDS epidemic represents a major threat to human well-being and socio-economic progress. Some 95% of those known to be infected with HIV/AIDS live in developing countries, and AIDS-related illnesses are the leading cause of death in sub-Saharan Africa. It is estimated that around 30m. people world-wide died of AIDS during 1981–2011. WHO supports governments to develop effective health sector responses to the HIV/AIDS epidemic through enhancing their planning and managerial capabilities, implementation capacity, and health systems resources. The Joint UN Programme on HIV/AIDS (UNAIDS) became operational on 1 January 1996, sponsored by WHO and other UN agencies; the UNAIDS secretariat is based at WHO headquarters. People living with HIV/AIDS in developing countries have often failed to receive advanced antiretroviral therapy (ART) that is widely available in industrialized countries, owing to its high cost. In May 2000 the World Health Assembly adopted a resolution urging WHO member states to improve access to the prevention and treatment of HIV-related illnesses and to increase the availability and affordability of drugs. A WHO-UNAIDS HIV Vaccine Initiative was launched in that year. In June 2001 governments participating in a special session of the UN General Assembly on HIV/AIDS adopted a Declaration of Commitment on HIV/AIDS. WHO participates in the 'Accelerating Access' initiative, which aims to expand access to care, support and ART for people with HIV/AIDS. In March 2002, under its 'Access to Quality HIV/AIDS Drugs and Diagnostics' programme, WHO published a comprehensive list of HIV-related medicines deemed to meet recommended standards. The secretariat of the International HIV Treatment Access Coalition, founded in December of that year by governments, non-governmental organizations (NGOs), donors and others to facilitate access to ART for people in low- and middle-income countries, is based at WHO headquarters. In September 2006, Brazil, Chile, France, Norway and the United Kingdom launched UNITAID, an international drug purchase facility aiming to provide sustained, strategic market intervention, with a view to reducing the cost of medicines for priority diseases and increasing the supply of drugs and diagnostics. In July 2008, UNITAID created the Medicines Patent Pool to focus on increasing access to HIV medicines in developing countries. WHO advocates providing—regardless of T-cell count—ART to HIV-positive partners in serodiscordant (mixed HIV-status) couples, to HIV-positive pregnant women, and to populations deemed to be at risk of infection. WHO guidance for serodiscordant couples was published in April 2012. In July WHO published the first report detailing levels of HIV drug resistance in low- and middle-income countries; the overall rate was estimated at that time to be 6.8%. WHO guidelines on the use of ART were first released in 2002, and have subsequently been revised, with the most recent update released in June 2013. In the following month UNAIDS initiated the Treatment 2015 framework, aimed at facilitating the provision by 2015 of ART to some 15m. people infected with HIV. At mid-2013 it was reported that around 10m. requiring ART globally had access to the treatment.

WHO supports the following 'Three Ones' principles, endorsed in April 2004 by a high-level meeting organized by UNAIDS, the United Kingdom and the USA, with the aim of strengthening national responses to the HIV/AIDS pandemic: for every country there should be one agreed national HIV/AIDS action framework; one national AIDS co-ordinating authority; and one agreed monitoring and evaluation system. In May 2011 the 64th World Health Assembly adopted a new Global Health Sector Strategy on HIV/AIDS, covering 2011–15, which aimed to promote greater innovation in HIV prevention, diagnosis, treatment, and the improvement of care services to facilitate universal access to care for HIV patients. In December 2011 the UN General Assembly adopted a Political Declaration on HIV/AIDS, outlining 10 targets to be attained by 2015: reducing by 50% sexual transmission of HIV; reducing by 50% HIV transmission among people who inject drugs; eliminating new HIV infections among children, and reducing AIDS-related maternal deaths; ensuring that at least 15m. people living with HIV are receiving ART; reducing by 50% TB deaths in people living with HIV; reaching annual global investment of at least US $22,000m. in combating AIDS in low- and medium-resource countries; eliminating gender inequalities and increasing the capacity of women and girls to self-protect from HIV; promoting the adoption of legislation and policies aimed at eliminating stigma and discrimination against people living with HIV; eliminating HIV-related restrictions on travel; strengthening the integration of the AIDS response in global health and development efforts.

At December 2011 some 300,000 people in the Middle East and North Africa were reported to have HIV/AIDS.

In 1995 WHO established a Global Tuberculosis Programme to address the challenges of the TB epidemic, which had been declared a global emergency by the organization in 1993. According to WHO estimates, one-third of the world's population carries the TB bacillus. In 2011 this generated 8.7m. new active cases (13% in people co-infected with HIV), and killed 1.4m. people (430,000 of whom were also HIV-positive). Some 22 countries account for four-fifths of global TB cases. The largest concentration of TB cases is in South-East Asia. WHO provides technical support to all member countries, with special attention given to those with high TB prevalence, to establish effective national tuberculosis control programmes. WHO's strategy for TB control includes the use of the expanded DOTS (direct observation treatment, short-course) regime, involving the following five tenets: sustained political commitment to increase human and financial resources and to make TB control in endemic countries a nation-wide activity and an integral part of the national health system; access to quality-assured TB sputum microscopy; standardized short-course chemotherapy for all cases of TB under proper case-management conditions; uninterrupted supply of quality-assured drugs; and maintaining a recording and reporting system to enable outcome assessment. Simultaneously, WHO is encouraging research with the aim of further advancing DOTS, developing new tools for prevention, diagnosis and treatment, and containing new threats (such as the HIV/TB co-epidemic). Inadequate control of DOTS in some areas, leading to partial and inconsistent treatments, has resulted in the development of drug-resistant and, often, incurable strains of TB. The incidence of so-called Multidrug Resistant TB (MDR-TB) strains has risen in recent years; an estimated 3.7% of new TB cases were reported to be MDR in 2011. MDR-TB cases occur most frequently in China, India, Russia and South Africa; it was reported in 2011 that in Russia around 20% of new cases and 46% of cases presenting for retreatment were MDR. WHO has developed DOTS-Plus, a specialized strategy for controlling the spread of MDR-TB in areas of high prevalence. By the end of 2011 some 84 countries had reported at least one case of Extensive Drug Resistant TB (XDR-TB), defined as MDR-TB plus resistance to any fluoroquinolone, and to any of the three second-line anti-TB drugs. XDR-TB is believed to be most prevalent in Eastern Europe and Asia. TB cases resistant to all drugs have been reported in Europe and in Iran. In 2007 WHO launched the Global MDR/XDR Response Plan, which aimed to expand diagnosis and treatment to cover, by 2015, some 85% of TB patients with MDR-TB.

The 'Stop TB' partnership, launched by WHO in 1999, in partnership with the World Bank, the US Government and a coalition of NGOs, co-ordinates the Global Plan to Stop TB, which represents a roadmap for TB control covering the period 2006–15. The Global Plan aims to facilitate the achievement of the MDG of halting and beginning to reverse by 2015 the incidence of TB by means of access to quality diagnosis and treatment for all; to supply ART to 3m. TB patients co-infected with HIV; to treat nearly 1m. people for MDR-TB (this target was subsequently altered by the 2007 Global MDR/XDR Response Plan, see above); to develop a new anti-TB drug and a new vaccine; and to develop rapid and inexpensive diagnostic tests at the point of care. A second phase of the Global Plan, launched in late 2010 and covering 2011–15, updated the Plan to take account of actual progress achieved since its instigation in 2006. The Global TB Drug Facility, launched by 'Stop TB' in 2001, aims to increase access to high-quality anti-TB drugs for sufferers in developing countries. In 2007 'Stop TB' endorsed the establishment of a Global Laboratory Initiative with the aim of expanding laboratory capacity.

In December 2010 WHO endorsed a new rapid nucleic acid amplification test (NAAT) that provided an accurate diagnosis of TB in around 100 minutes; it was envisaged that NAAT, by eliminating the wait of up to three months for a TB diagnosis, would greatly enhance management of the disease and patient care.

In October 1998 WHO, jointly with UNICEF, the World Bank and UNDP, formally launched the Roll Back Malaria (RBM) programme. The disease acutely affects at least 350m.–500m. people, and kills an estimated 1m. people, every year. Some 85% of all malaria cases occur in sub-Saharan Africa. It is estimated that the disease directly causes nearly one-fifth of all child deaths in that region. The Democratic Republic of the Congo and Nigeria have the highest levels of infection in sub-Saharan Africa. The global RBM Partnership, linking governments, development agencies, and other parties, aims to mobilize resources and support for controlling malaria. The RBM Partnership Global Strategic Plan for the period 2005–15, adopted in November 2005, lists steps required to intensify malaria control interventions with a view to attaining targets set by the Partnership for 2010 and 2015 (the former targets include ensuring the protection of 80% of people at risk from malaria and the diagnosis and treatment within one day of 80% of malaria patients, and reducing the global malaria burden by one-half compared with 2000 levels; and the latter: achieving a 75% reduction in malaria morbidity and mortality over levels at 2005). WHO recommends a number of guidelines for malaria control, focusing on the need for prompt, effective antimalarial treatment, and the issue of drug resistance; vector control, including the use of insecticide-treated bednets; malaria in pregnancy; malaria epidemics; and monitoring and evaluation activities. WHO, with several private and public sector partners, supports the development of more effective anti-malaria drugs and vaccines through the 'Medicines for Malaria' venture.

In May 2013 the 66th World Health Assembly adopted a resolution on Neglected Tropical Diseases that urged member states to ensure country ownership of prevention, control, elimination and eradication programmes, urged international partners to supply adequate funding in support of these, and encouraged the development of new technologies aimed at supporting vector control and infection prevention.

Joint UN Programme on HIV/AIDS (UNAIDS): 20 ave Appia, 1211 Geneva 27, Switzerland; tel. 227913666; fax 227914187; e-mail communications@unaids.org; internet www.unaids.org; established in 1996 to lead, strengthen and support an expanded response to the global HIV/AIDS pandemic; activities focus on prevention, care and support, reducing vulnerability to infection, and alleviating the socio-economic and human effects of HIV/AIDS; launched the Global Coalition on Women and AIDS in Feb. 2004; guided by UN Security Council Resolution 1308, focusing on the possible impact of AIDS on social instability and emergency situations, and the potential impact of HIV on the health of international peace-keeping personnel; by the UN Millennium Development Goals adopted in Sept. 2000; by the Declaration of Commitment on HIV/AIDS agreed in June 2001 by the first-ever Special Session of the UN General Assembly on HIV/AIDS, which acknowledged the AIDS epidemic as a 'global emergency'; and the Political Declaration on HIV/AIDS, adopted by the June 2006 UN General Assembly High Level Meeting on AIDS; in Nov. 2012 UNAIDS appointed Aung San Suu Kyi as Global Advocate for Zero Discrimination; co-sponsors: WHO, UN Women, UNICEF, UNDP, UNFPA, UNODC, the ILO, UNESCO, the World Bank, WFP, UNHCR; Exec. Dir MICHEL SIDIBÉ (Mali).

NON-COMMUNICABLE DISEASES AND MENTAL HEALTH

The Non-communicable Diseases (NCDs) and Mental Health group comprises departments for the surveillance, prevention and management of uninfectious diseases, and departments for health promotion, disability, injury prevention and rehabilitation, substance abuse and mental health. The surveillance, prevention and management of NCDs, tobacco, and mental health are organization-wide priorities.

Addressing the social and environmental determinants of health is a main priority of WHO. Tobacco use, unhealthy diet and physical inactivity are regarded as common, preventable risk factors for the four most prominent NCDs, i.e. cardiovascular diseases, cancer, chronic respiratory disease and diabetes. It is estimated that these NCDs are collectively responsible for an estimated 35m. deaths—60% of all deaths—globally each year, and that up to 80% of cases of heart disease, stroke and type 2 diabetes, and more than one-third of cancers, could be prevented by eliminating shared risk factors, the main ones being tobacco use, unhealthy diet, physical inactivity and harmful use of alcohol. WHO aims to monitor the global epidemiological situation of NCDs, to co-ordinate multinational research activities concerned with prevention and care, and to analyse determining factors such as gender and poverty. In May 2013 the 66th World Health Assembly endorsed a Global Action Plan for 2013–20 for the Prevention and Control of NCDs, incorporating nine targets for reducing the impact of NCDs, as well as a monitoring framework; the Action Plan built upon a Global Strategy on NCDs first endorsed in 2000 and a previous Plan covering the period 2008–13.

The sixth Global Conference on Health Promotion, convened jointly by WHO and the Thai Government, in Bangkok, Thailand, in August 2005, adopted the Bangkok Charter for Health Promotion in a Globalized World, which identified ongoing key challenges, actions and commitments. In October 2011 WHO convened a global conference on the social determinants of health, in Rio de Janeiro, Brazil; the conference adopted the Rio Political Declaration on Social Determinants of Health, expressing commitment to reducing inequities in health and healthcare provision.

In May 2004 the World Health Assembly endorsed a Global Strategy on Diet, Physical Activity and Health; it is estimated that more than 1,000m. adults world-wide are overweight, and that, of these, some 300m. are clinically obese. WHO has studied obesity-related issues in co-operation with the International Association for the Study of Obesity (IASO). The International Task Force on Obesity, affiliated to the IASO, aims to encourage the development of new policies for managing obesity. WHO and FAO jointly commissioned an expert report on the relationship of diet, nutrition and physical activity to chronic diseases, which was published in March 2003.

WHO's programmes for diabetes mellitus, chronic rheumatic diseases and asthma assist with the development of national initiatives, based upon goals and targets for the improvement of early detection, care and reduction of long-term complications. WHO's cardiovascular diseases programme aims to prevent and control the major cardiovascular diseases, which are responsible for more than 14m. deaths each year. It is estimated that one-third of these deaths could have been prevented with existing scientific knowledge.

The programme on cancer control is concerned with the prevention of cancer, improving its detection and cure, and ensuring care of all cancer patients in need. In May 2004 the World Health Assembly adopted a resolution on cancer prevention and control, recognizing an increase in global cancer cases, particularly in developing countries, and stressing that many cases and related deaths could be prevented. The resolution included a number of recommendations for the improvement of national cancer control programmes. In May 2009 WHO and the International Atomic Energy Agency (IAEA) launched a Joint Programme on Cancer Control, aimed at enhancing efforts to fight cancer in the developing world. Inter-agency collaboration on combating cancer was intensified following the Political Declaration on the Prevention and Control of Non-communicable Diseases made in September 2011 by a High-level Meeting of the UN

General Assembly. WHO is a co-sponsor of the Global Day Against Pain, which is held annually on 11 October to highlight the need for improved pain management and palliative care for sufferers of diseases such as cancer and AIDS, with a particular focus on patients living in low-income countries with minimal access to opioid analgesics, and to promote recognition of access to pain relief as a basic human right.

The WHO Human Genetics Programme manages genetic approaches for the prevention and control of common hereditary diseases and of those with a genetic predisposition representing a major health factor. The Programme also concentrates on the further development of genetic approaches suitable for incorporation into health care systems, as well as developing a network of international collaborating programmes.

WHO works to assess the impact of injuries, violence and sensory impairments on health, and formulates guidelines and protocols for the prevention and management of mental problems. The health promotion division promotes decentralized and community-based health programmes and is concerned with developing new approaches to population ageing and encouraging healthy lifestyles and self-care. It also seeks to relieve the negative impact of social changes such as urbanization, migration and changes in family structure upon health. WHO advocates a multi-sectoral approach—involving public health, legal and educational systems—to the prevention of injuries, which represent 16% of the global burden of disease. Several health promotion projects have been undertaken, in collaboration between WHO regional and country offices and other relevant organizations, including the Global School Health Initiative, to bridge the sectors of health and education and to promote the health of school-age children; the Global Strategy for Occupational Health, to promote the health of the working population and the control of occupational health risks; Community-based Rehabilitation, aimed at providing a more enabling environment for people with disabilities; and a communication strategy to provide training and support for health communications personnel and initiatives. In 2000 WHO, UNESCO, the World Bank and UNICEF adopted the joint Focusing Resources for Effective School Health (FRESH Start) approach to promoting life skills among adolescents.

WHO supports the UN Convention, and its Optional Protocol, on the Rights of Persons with Disabilities, which came into force in May 2008, and seeks to address challenges that prevent the full participation of people with disabilities in the social, economic and cultural lives of their communities and societies; at that time the WHO Director-General appointed a Taskforce on Disability to ensure that WHO was reflecting the provisions of the Convention overall as an organization and in its programme of work. In December 2011 WHO and the World Bank jointly released the first *World Report on Disability*, focusing on the areas of health care, rehabilitation, education, employment and support services, and detailing a number of recommendations for governments aimed at creating environments that would enable people with disabilities to flourish. In May 2013 the 66th World Health Assembly adopted a resolution urging member states to develop national action plans for the implementation of the Convention on the Rights of Persons with Disabilities.

In February 1999 WHO initiated the ongoing programme, 'Vision 2020: the Right to Sight', which aimed to eliminate avoidable blindness (estimated to be as much as 80% of all cases) by 2020. Blindness was otherwise predicted to increase by as much as two-fold, owing to the increased longevity of the global population. In May 2013 the 66th World Health Assembly endorsed a Global Action Plan, covering 2014–19, that focused on improving eye health, reducing avoidable visual impairment, and securing access to rehabilitation services.

In 2012 WHO estimated that tobacco would lead to more than 8m. deaths annually by 2030 (through lung cancer, heart disease, chronic bronchitis and other effects). The Tobacco or Health Programme aims to reduce the use of tobacco, by educating tobacco-users and preventing young people from adopting the habit. In May 1999 the World Health Assembly endorsed the formulation of a Framework Convention on Tobacco Control (FCTC) to help to combat the increase in tobacco use (although a number of tobacco growers expressed concerns about the effect of the convention on their livelihoods). The FCTC entered into force in February 2005. In 2008 WHO published a comprehensive analysis of global tobacco use and control, the *WHO Report on the Global Tobacco Epidemic*, which designated abuse of tobacco as one of the principal global threats to health, and predicted that during the latter part of the 21st century the vast majority of tobacco-related deaths would occur in developing countries. The report identified and condemned a tobacco industry strategy to target young people and adults in the developing world, and detailed six key proven strategies, collectively known as the 'MPOWER package', aimed at combating global tobacco use: monitoring tobacco use and implementing prevention policies; protecting people from tobacco smoke; offering support to people to enable them to give up tobacco use; warning about the dangers of tobacco; enforcing bans on tobacco advertising, promotion and sponsorship; and raising taxes on tobacco. The MPOWER package provided a roadmap to support countries in building on their obligations under the FCTC. The FCTC obligates its states parties to require 'health warnings describing the harmful effects of tobacco use' to appear on packs of tobacco and their outside packaging, and recommends the use of warnings that contain pictures. WHO provides technical and other assistance to countries to support them in meeting this obligation through the Tobacco Free Initiative. WHO encourages governments to adopt tobacco health warnings meeting the agreed criteria for maximum effectiveness in convincing consumers not to smoke. In November 2012 the fifth Conference of the Parties to the FCTC adopted a Protocol to Eliminate Illicit Trade in Tobacco Products. This was opened for signature in January 2013 and required ratification by 40 member states to enter into force.

WHO's Mental Health and Substance Abuse department was established in 2000 from the merger of formerly separate departments to reflect the many common approaches in managing mental health and substance use disorders. WHO defines mental health as a 'state of well-being in which every individual realizes his or her own potential, can cope with the normal stresses of life, can work productively and fruitfully, and is able to make a contribution to her or his community'. WHO's Mental Health programme is concerned with mental health problems that include unipolar and bipolar affective disorders, psychosis, epilepsy, dementia, Parkinson's disease, multiple sclerosis, drug and alcohol dependency, and neuropsychiatric disorders such as post-traumatic stress disorder, obsessive compulsive disorder and panic disorder. WHO aims to address mental problems by increasing awareness of mental health issues and promoting improved mental health services and primary care. In October 2008 WHO launched the so-called mental health Gap Action Programme (mhGAP), which aimed to improve services addressing mental, neurological and substance use disorders, with a special focus on low and middle income countries. It was envisaged that, with proper care, psychosocial assistance and medication, many millions of patients in developing countries could be treated for depression, schizophrenia, and epilepsy; prevented from attempting suicide; and encouraged to begin to lead normal lives. A main focus of mhGAP concerns forging strategic partnerships to enhance countries' capacity to combat stigma commonly associated with mental illness, reduce the burden of mental disorders, and promote mental health. In August 2013 WHO extended mhGAP to incorporate new clinical protocols and guidelines aimed at supporting healthcare workers in treating post-traumatic stress disorder. In May of that year the 66th World Health Assembly adopted a Mental Health Action Plan covering the period 2013–20, with the objectives of strengthening effective mental health leadership and governance; providing comprehensive, integrated and responsive mental health and social care services in community-based settings; implementing strategies for mental health prevention and promotion; and strengthening information systems, evidence and research. WHO is a joint partner in the Global Campaign against Epilepsy: Out of the Shadows, which aims to advance understanding, treatment, services and prevention of epilepsy world-wide.

The Substance Abuse programme addresses the misuse of all psychoactive substances, irrespective of legal status and including alcohol. WHO provides technical support to assist countries in formulating policies with regard to the prevention and reduction of the health and social effects of psychoactive substance abuse, and undertakes epidemiological surveillance and risk assessment, advocacy and the dissemination of information, strengthening national and regional prevention and health promotion techniques and strategies, the development of cost-effective treatment and rehabilitation approaches, and also encompasses regulatory activities as required under the international drugs-control treaties in force. In May 2010 WHO endorsed a new global strategy to reduce the harmful use of alcohol; this promoted measures including taxation on alcohol, minimizing outlets selling alcohol, raising age limits for those buying alcohol, and the employment of effective measures to deter people from driving while under the influence of alcohol.

WHO forecasts that by 2050 nearly 2,000m. people globally will be aged over 60. In June 2010 WHO launched the Global Network of Age-Friendly Cities, as part of a broader response to the ageing of populations world-wide. The Network aims to support cities in creating urban environments that would enable older people to remain active and healthy. The first International Conference on Age-Friendly Cities was convened in September 2011, in Dublin, Ireland; the second was held in Québec, Canada, in September 2013 on the theme 'Living and Aging Together in our Community'.

FAMILY, WOMEN'S AND CHILDREN'S HEALTH

WHO's Family and Community Health group addresses the following areas of work: child and adolescent health, research and programme development in reproductive health, making pregnancy safer and men's and women's health. Making pregnancy safer is an organization-wide priority. The group's aim is to improve access to sustainable health care for all by strengthening health systems and fostering individual, family and community development. Activities include newborn care; child health, including promoting and protecting the health and development of the child through such approaches as promotion of breastfeeding and use of the mother-baby package, as well as care of the sick child, including diarrhoeal and acute respiratory disease control, and support to women and children in difficult circumstances; the promotion of safe motherhood and maternal health; adolescent health, including the promotion and development of young people and the prevention of specific health problems; women, health and development, including addressing issues of gender, sexual violence, and harmful traditional practices; and human reproduction, including research related to contraceptive technologies and effective methods. In addition, WHO aims to provide technical leadership and co-ordination on reproductive health and to support countries in their efforts to ensure that people: experience healthy sexual development and maturation; have the capacity for healthy, equitable and responsible relationships; can achieve their reproductive intentions safely and healthily; avoid illnesses, diseases and injury related to sexuality and reproduction; and receive appropriate counselling, care and rehabilitation for diseases and conditions related to sexuality and reproduction.

WHO supports the Global Strategy for Women's and Children's Health, launched by heads of state and government participating in the September 2010 UN Summit on the MDGs; some US $40,000m. has been pledged towards women's and child's health and achieving goals (iv) Reducing Child Mortality and (v) Improving Maternal Health. In May 2012 the World Health Assembly adopted a resolution on raising awareness of early marriage (entered into by more than 30% of women in developing countries) and adolescent pregnancy, and the consequences thereof for young women and infants.

In September 1997 WHO, in collaboration with UNICEF, formally launched a programme advocating the Integrated Management of Childhood Illness (IMCI). IMCI recognizes that pneumonia, diarrhoea, measles, malaria and malnutrition cause some 70% of the approximately 11m. childhood deaths each year, and recommends screening sick children for all five conditions, to obtain a more accurate diagnosis than may be achieved from the results of a single assessment. WHO encourages national programmes aimed at reducing childhood deaths as a result of diarrhoea, particularly through the use of oral rehydration therapy and preventive measures. In November 2009 WHO and UNICEF launched a Global Action Plan for the Prevention and Control of Pneumonia (GAPP), which aimed to accelerate pneumonia control through a combination of interventions of proven benefit. In April 2013 WHO and UNICEF launched a new Integrated Global Action Plan for the Prevention and Control of Pneumonia and Diarrhoea, focusing on interventions such as improved nutrition and maintaining a clean environment to protect children from contracting both diseases. Accelerated efforts by WHO to promote vaccination against measles through its Measles Initiative (subsequently renamed the Measles and Rubella Initiative), established in 2001, contributed to a three-quarters' reduction in global mortality from that disease during the period 2000–10. In April 2012 WHO and other partners launched a global strategy that aimed to eliminate measles deaths and congenital rubella syndrome.

HEALTH SECURITY AND ENVIRONMENT

The Sustainable Development and Healthy Environments group focuses on the following areas of work: health in sustainable development; nutrition; health and environment; food safety; and emergency preparedness and response. Food safety is an organization-wide priority.

WHO promotes recognition of good health status as one of the most important assets of the poor. The Sustainable Development and Healthy Environment group seeks to monitor the advantages and disadvantages for health, nutrition, environment and development arising from the process of globalization (i.e. increased global flows of capital, goods and services, people, and knowledge); to integrate the issue of health into poverty reduction programmes; and to promote human rights and equality. WHO collaborates with FAO, WFP, UNICEF and other UN agencies in pursuing its objectives relating to nutrition and food safety. It has been estimated that 780m. people world-wide cannot meet basic needs for energy and protein, more than 2,000m. people lack essential vitamins and minerals, and that 170m. children are malnourished. In December 1992 WHO and FAO hosted an international conference on nutrition, at which a World Declaration and Plan of Action on Nutrition was adopted to make the fight against malnutrition a development priority. Following the conference, WHO promoted the elaboration and implementation of national plans of action on nutrition. WHO aims to support the enhancement of member states' capabilities in dealing with their nutrition situations, and addressing scientific issues related to preventing, managing and monitoring protein-energy malnutrition; micronutrient malnutrition, including iodine deficiency disorders, vitamin A deficiency, and nutritional anaemia; and diet-related conditions and NCDs such as obesity (increasingly affecting children, adolescents and adults, mainly in industrialized countries), cancer and heart disease. In 1990 the World Health Assembly resolved to eliminate iodine deficiency (believed to cause mental retardation); a strategy of universal salt iodization was launched in 1993. In collaboration with other international agencies, WHO is implementing a comprehensive strategy for promoting appropriate infant, young child and maternal nutrition, and for dealing effectively with nutritional emergencies in large populations. Areas of emphasis include promoting health-care practices that enhance successful breast-feeding; appropriate complementary feeding; refining the use and interpretation of body measurements for assessing nutritional status; relevant information, education and training; and action to give effect to the International Code of Marketing of Breast-milk Substitutes. (WHO reported in July 2013 that only 37 countries world-wide had adopted legislation reflecting all the recommendations of the International Code.) The food safety programme aims to protect human health against risks associated with biological and chemical contaminants and additives in food. With FAO, WHO establishes food standards (through the work of the Codex Alimentarius Commission and its subsidiary committees) and evaluates food additives, pesticide residues and other contaminants and their implications for health. The programme provides expert advice on such issues as food-borne pathogens (e.g. listeria), production methods (e.g. aquaculture) and food biotechnology (e.g. genetic modification). In July 2001 the Codex Alimentarius Commission adopted the first global principles for assessing the safety of genetically modified (GM) foods. In March 2002 an intergovernmental task force established by the Commission finalized 'principles for the risk analysis of foods derived from biotechnology', which were to provide a framework for assessing the safety of GM foods and plants. In February 2003 the FAO/WHO Project and Fund for Enhanced Participation in Codex was launched to support the participation of poorer countries in the Commission's activities. WHO supports, with other UN agencies, governments, research institutions, and representatives of civil society and of the private sector, the initiative on Scaling up Nutrition (SUN), which was initiated in 2009, under the co-ordination of the UN Secretary-General's Special Representative for Food Security and Nutrition, with the aim of increasing the coverage of interventions that improve nutrition during the first 1,000 days of a child's life (such as exclusive breastfeeding, optimal complementary feeding practices, and provision of essential vitamins and minerals); and ensuring that nutrition plans are implemented at national level, and that government programmes take nutrition into account. The activities of SUN are guided by the Framework for Scaling up Nutrition, which was published in April 2010, and by the SUN Roadmap, finalized in September 2010.

WHO's programme area on environmental health undertakes a wide range of initiatives to tackle the increasing threats to health and well-being from a changing environment, especially in relation to air pollution, water quality, sanitation, protection against radiation, management of hazardous waste, chemical safety and housing hygiene. In April 2013 WHO reported that household and outdoor air pollution were the cause of, respectively 3.5m. and 3.3m. global deaths annually. In 2012 it was estimated that some 783m. people world-wide had no access to clean drinking water, while a further 2,500m. people are denied suitable sanitation systems. WHO helped to launch the Water Supply and Sanitation Council in 1990 and regularly updates its *Guidelines for Drinking Water Quality*. In rural areas the emphasis continues to be on the provision and maintenance of safe and sufficient water supplies and adequate sanitation, the health aspects of rural housing, vector control in water resource management, and the safe use of agrochemicals. In urban areas assistance is provided to identify local environmental health priorities and to improve municipal governments' ability to deal with environmental conditions and health problems in an integrated manner; promotion of the 'Healthy City' approach is a major component of the programme. Other programme activities include environmental health information development and management, human resources development, environmental health planning methods, research and work on problems relating to global environment change, such as UV-radiation. The WHO Global Strategy for Health and Environment, developed in response to the WHO Commission on Health and Environment which reported to the UN Conference on Environment and Development in June 1992, provides the framework for programme activities. In May 2008 the 61st World Health Assembly adopted a resolution urging member states to take action to address the impact of climate change on human health.

Through its International EMF Project WHO is compiling a comprehensive assessment of the potential adverse effects on human health deriving from exposure to electromagnetic fields (EMF). In May 2011 the International Agency for Research on Cancer, an agency of WHO, classified radiofrequency EMF as possibly carcinogenic to humans, on the basis of an increased risk of glioma (malignant brain cancer) associated with the use of wireless phones.

In March 2013 WHO and the UN Environment Programme (UNEP) issued a joint report entitled *State of the Science of Endocrine Disrupting Chemicals*, which assessed the potential disrupting effects on the human hormone system and the environment of synthetic chemicals found in many household products.

WHO's work in the promotion of chemical safety is undertaken in collaboration with the ILO and UNEP through the International Programme on Chemical Safety (IPCS), the Central Unit for which is located in WHO. The Programme provides internationally evaluated scientific information on chemicals, promotes the use of such information in national programmes, assists member states in establishment of their own chemical safety measures and programmes, and helps them strengthen their capabilities in chemical emergency preparedness and response and in chemical risk reduction. In 1995 an Inter-organization Programme for the Social Management of Chemicals was established by UNEP, the ILO, FAO, WHO, the UN Industrial Development Organization (UNIDO) and OECD, in order to strengthen international co-operation in the field of chemical safety.

Since the major terrorist attacks perpetrated against targets in the USA in September 2001, WHO has focused renewed attention on the potential malevolent use of bacteria (such as bacillus anthracis, which causes anthrax), viruses (for example, the variola virus, causing smallpox) or toxins, or of chemical agents, in acts of biological or chemical terrorism. In September 2001 WHO issued draft guidelines entitled 'Health Aspects of Biological and Chemical Weapons'. In March 2013 the UN Secretary-General announced that a mission comprising UN weapons experts, in co-operation with specialists from WHO and the Organisation for the Prohibition of Chemical Weapons, would initiate an investigation into the alleged misuse of chemical weapons by combatants in the ongoing conflict in Syria. In mid-September the mission issued a report on the alleged use on 21 August of chemical weapons against unarmed civilians in the rebel-held area of Ghouta, Damascus, causing significant injuries and fatalities, in which it found 'clear and convincing evidence' of the use of surface-to-surface rockets containing sarin gas, and that chemical weapons had been used on a relatively large scale generally during the Syrian conflict, including against children.

Within the UN system, WHO's Department of Emergency and Humanitarian Action co-ordinates the international response to emergencies and natural disasters in the health field, in close co-operation with other agencies and within the framework set out by OCHA. In this context, WHO provides expert advice on epidemiological surveillance, control of communicable diseases, public health information and health emergency training. Its emergency preparedness activities include co-ordination, policy-making and planning, awareness-building, technical advice, training, publication of standards and guidelines, and research. Its emergency relief activities include organizational support, the provision of emergency drugs and supplies and conducting technical emergency assessment missions. The Division's objective is to strengthen the national capacity of member states to reduce the adverse health consequences of disasters. In responding to emergency situations, WHO always tries to develop projects and activities that will assist the national authorities concerned in rebuilding or strengthening their own capacity to handle the impact of such situations. WHO appeals through the UN's inter-agency Consolidated Appeals Process (CAP) for funding for its emergency humanitarian operations.

WHO has, since 1950, provided technical supervision of UNRWA's programme to provide healthcare to Palestinians living in the Occupied Territories. A WHO Special Representative is based at UNRWA's headquarters.

In March 1996 a survey of health conditions in Iraq, published by WHO, generated concern at the impact on the population of the ongoing international trade embargo and, in particular, the widespread incidence of nutritional deficiencies and increasing infant mortality rates. Under the terms of Resolution 986 of the UN Security Council, which permitted the limited sale of petroleum by the Iraqi authorities in order to facilitate the purchase of essential humanitarian supplies, WHO was responsible for distributing medicines and medical supplies, for supervising the distribution of medicines by the Iraqi authorities in central and southern Iraq and for implementing an epidemiological surveillance network in the northern Kurdish provinces of Iraq. The distribution of medicines to an anticipated 600 hospitals and health centres was initiated in May 1997. In response to the collapse of much of Iraq's local health infrastructure following the campaign by US and allied troops to overthrow the Saddam Hussain regime in March/April 2003 and subsequent unrest throughout the country, WHO provided technical assistance to local governments with an emphasis on restarting disease surveillance and response capabilities, rebuilding primary health care functions, and enabling the supply of urgent medicines.

HEALTH SYSTEMS AND INNOVATION

The Information, Evidence and Research group addresses the following areas of work: evidence for health policy; health information management and dissemination; and research policy and promotion and organization of health systems. Through the generation and dissemination of evidence the Information, Evidence and Research group aims to assist policy-makers assess health needs, choose intervention strategies, design policy and monitor performance, and thereby improve the performance of national health systems. The group also supports international and national dialogue on health policy.

WHO co-ordinates the Health InterNetwork Access to Research Initiative (HINARI), which was launched in July 2001 to enable relevant authorities in developing countries to access biomedical journals through the internet at no or greatly reduced cost, in order to improve the world-wide circulation of scientific information; by 2013 more than 8,500 journals and 7,000 e-books were being made available to health institutions in more than 100 countries.

In 2004 WHO developed the World Alliance on Patient Safety, further to a World Health Assembly resolution in 2002. Since renamed WHO Patient Safety, the programme was launched to facilitate the development of patient safety policy and practice across all WHO member states.

In 2003 WHO launched a virtual Healthy Academy. In May 2005 the World Health Assembly adopted a resolution asking WHO to extend the accessibility of the Health Academy, and urging WHO to support member states in integrating 'eHealth' into national health systems and services. The Academy provides eLearning courses, on topics such as HIV/AIDS; malaria; oral health; and safer food

WHO's Health Technology and Pharmaceuticals group, made up of the departments of essential drugs and other medicines, vaccines and other biologicals, and blood safety and clinical technology, covers the following areas of work: essential medicines—access, quality and rational use; immunization and vaccine development; and world-wide co-operation on blood safety and clinical technology. Blood safety and clinical technology are an organization-wide priority.

In May 2013 the World Health Assembly determined to establish an open-ended working group to address means of eliminating so-called Substandard/Spurious/Falsely-labelled/Falsified/Counterfeit (SSFFC) medical products.

In January 1999 the Executive Board adopted a resolution on WHO's Revised Drug Strategy which placed emphasis on the inequalities of access to pharmaceuticals, and also covered specific aspects of drugs policy, quality assurance, drug promotion, drug donation, independent drug information and rational drug use. Plans of action involving co-operation with member states and other international organizations were to be developed to monitor and analyse the pharmaceutical and public health implications of international agreements, including trade agreements. In April 2001 experts from WHO and the World Trade Organization participated in a workshop to address ways of lowering the cost of medicines in less developed countries. In the following month the World Health Assembly adopted a resolution urging member states to promote equitable access to essential drugs, noting that this was denied to about one-third of the world's population. WHO participates with other partners in the 'Accelerating Access' initiative, which aims to expand access to antiretroviral drugs for people with HIV/AIDS.

WHO reports that 2m. children die each year of diseases for which common vaccines exist. In September 1991 the Children's Vaccine Initiative (CVI) was launched, jointly sponsored by the Rockefeller Foundation, UNDP, UNICEF, the World Bank and WHO, to facilitate the development and provision of children's vaccines. The CVI has as its ultimate goal the development of a single oral immunization shortly after birth that will protect against all major childhood diseases. An International Vaccine Institute was established in Seoul, South Korea, as part of the CVI, to provide scientific and technical services for the production of vaccines for developing countries. A comprehensive survey, *State of the World's Vaccines and Immunization*, was published by WHO, jointly with UNICEF, in 1996; revised editions of the survey were issued in 2003 and 2010. In 1999 WHO, UNICEF, the World Bank and a number of public and private sector partners formed the Global Alliance for Vaccines and Immunization (GAVI), which aimed to expand the provision of existing vaccines and to accelerate the development and introduction of new vaccines and technologies, with the ultimate goal of protecting children of all nations and from all socio-economic backgrounds against vaccine-preventable diseases.

WHO supports states in ensuring access to safe blood, blood products, transfusions, injections, and health-care technologies.

In May 2011 WHO launched a new internet-based Global Health Observatory, a repository of data on health topics, which also provides online access to WHO's annual *World Health Statistics*. In May 2013 the 66th World Health Assembly adopted a resolution on e-Health standardization and interoperability, noting the importance of health data in underpinning the efficient functioning of health systems and services, as well as the need to protect the security of such information and the privacy of personal clinical data.

Finance

WHO's regular budget is provided by assessment of member states and associate members. An additional fund for specific projects is provided by voluntary contributions from members and other sources, including UNDP and UNFPA.

Publications

Bulletin of WHO (monthly).

Eastern Mediterranean Health Journal (annually).

International Classification of Functioning, Disability and Health—ICF.

International Pharmacopoeia.

International Statistical Classification of Disease and Related Health Problems.

International Travel and Health.

Model List of Essential Medicines (every 2 years).

Pan-American Journal of Public Health (annually).

Toxicological Evaluation of Certain Veterinary Drug Residues in Food (annually).

Weekly Epidemiological Record (in English and French, paper and electronic versions available).

WHO Drug Information (quarterly).

World Health Statistics.

World Malaria Report.

WHO Model Formulary.

WHO Report on the Global Tobacco Epidemic.

World Health Report (annually, in English, French and Spanish).

World Cancer Report.

World Malaria Report (with UNICEF).

Zoonoses and Communicable Diseases Common to Man and Animals.

Technical report series; catalogues of specific scientific, technical and medical fields available.

Other UN Organizations Active in the Region

OFFICE FOR THE CO-ORDINATION OF HUMANITARIAN AFFAIRS—OCHA

Address: United Nations Plaza, New York, NY 10017, USA.

Telephone: (212) 963-1234; **fax:** (212) 963-1312; **e-mail:** ochany@un.org; **internet:** unocha.org.

The Office was established in January 1998 as part of the UN Secretariat, with a mandate to co-ordinate international humanitarian assistance and to provide policy and other advice on humanitarian issues. It administers the Humanitarian Early Warning System, as well as Integrated Regional Information Networks (IRIN), to monitor the situation in some 70 different countries, and a Disaster Response System. A complementary service, Reliefweb monitors crises and publishes information on the internet.

In June 2013 OCHA issued a revision to its 2013 Syria Humanitarian Assistance Response Plan (SHARP, launched in December 2012), in view of the further intensification and expansion during the first half of 2013 of the crisis that emerged in that country in March 2011. The revised SHARP, requiring funding of US $4.4m., was to target some 6.8m. people in Syria requiring humanitarian assistance, including 4.3m. IDPs, with project activities to be based on the findings of several sectoral assessments undertaken during the first half of 2013 by UN agencies, the Syrian Arab Red Crescent, government ministries, and other humanitarian bodies.

In March 2013 UN/ISDR, UNDP, the League of Arab States and other partners organized the First Arab Conference on Disaster Risk Reduction, with participation by senior government officials, civil mayors and civil society representatives from Arab states. The Conference launched the Arab Regional Platform on Disaster Risk Reduction.

Under-Secretary-General for Humanitarian Affairs and Emergency Relief Co-ordinator: VALERIE AMOS (United Kingdom).

Inter-Agency Secretariat of the International Strategy for Disaster Reduction—UN/ISDR: International Environment House II, 7–9 Chemin de Balexert, 1219 Châtelaine, Geneva 10, Switzerland; tel. 229178908; fax 229178964; e-mail isdr@un.org; internet www.unisdr.org; operates as secretariat of the International Strategy for Disaster Reduction (ISDR), adopted by UN member states in 2000 as a strategic framework aimed at guiding and co-ordinating the efforts of humanitarian organizations, states, intergovernmental and non-governmental organizations, financial institutions, technical bodies and civil society representatives towards achieving substantive reduction in disaster losses, and building resilient communities and nations as the foundation for sustainable development activities; UN/ISDR promotes information sharing to reduce disaster risk, and serves as the focal point providing guidance for the implementation of the Hyogo Framework for Action (HFA), adopted in 2005 as a 10-year plan of action for protecting lives and livelihoods against disasters; organizes the biennial sessions of the Global Platform for Disaster Risk Reduction (fourth session: held in May 2013, in Geneva); in early 2012 UN/ISDR initiated consultations on formulating a blueprint on a post-2015 disaster risk reduction framework in advance of the third World Conference on Disaster Reduction that was scheduled to be held in 2014, in Japan; it is also a co-leader of the global consultations on addressing conflict and fragility in the post-2015 development framework; UN/ISDR implements a 'Making Cities Resilient' campaign in view in increasing urbanization world-wide; Head, Special Representative of the UN Secretary-General for Disaster Risk Reduction MARGARETA WAHLSTRÖM.

UN WOMEN—UNITED NATIONS ENTITY FOR GENDER EQUALITY AND THE EMPOWERMENT OF WOMEN

Address: 304 East 45th St, 15th Floor, New York, NY 10017, USA.

Telephone: (212) 906-6400; **fax:** (212) 906-6705; **internet:** www.unwomen.org.

UN Women was established by the UN General Assembly in July 2010 in order to strengthen the UN's capacity to promote gender equality, the empowerment of women, and the elimination of discrimination against women and girls. It commenced operations on 1 January 2011, incorporating the functions of the Office of the Special Adviser on Gender Issues and Advancement of Women, the Division for the Advancement of Women of the Secretariat, the United Nations Development Fund for Women (UNIFEM) and the International Research and Training Institute for the Advancement of Women (INSTRAW).

In 2011 UN Women deployed experts to Tunisia to support that country's newly formed electoral subcommission in its work to ensure gender parity, and also to assist with transitional justice and reconciliation processes. During that year UN Women helped Tunisian women's groups with refreshing advocacy skills. In 2011 UN Women also provided support to a coalition of 500 women's groups in Egypt.

Executive Director: PHUMZILE MLAMBO-NGCUKA (South Africa).

UNITED NATIONS OFFICE FOR DISARMAMENT AFFAIRS—UNODA

Address: UN Plaza, Rm S-3185, New York, NY 10017, USA.

Fax: (212) 963-4066; **e-mail:** UNODA-web@un.org; **internet:** www.un.org/disarmament.

UNODA—established in 1982 as the UN Department for Disarmament Affairs, with its current name adopted in 2007—works to promote nuclear disarmament and non-proliferation; to strengthen disarmament regimes with regard to biological and chemical weapons and other weapons of mass destruction; and to support disarmament activities relating to conventional weapons, with a particular focus on landmines and small arms. UNODA maintains subsidiary offices in Geneva, Switzerland; Kathmandu, Nepal; Lima, Peru; Lomé, Togo; and Vienna, Austria.

In March 2013 the UN Secretary-General announced that a mission comprising UN weapons experts, in co-operation with specialists from the World Health Organization and the Organisation for the Prohibition of Chemical Weapons, would initiate an investigation into the alleged use of chemical weapons in the ongoing Syrian conflict. (Syria was not at that time a signatory to the 1992 Convention on the Prohibition of the Development, Production, Stockpiling and Use of Chemical Weapons and on their Destruction, and the presence in that country of stockpiles of chemical nerve agents had been alleged.) At the end of that month the Secretary-General appointed a Swedish scientist, Dr Åke Sellström, to head the mission. On 18 August the Sellström-led team arrived in Syria to investigate three previously reported chemical attacks. The alleged use on 21 August of chemical weapons against unarmed civilians in the rebel-held area of Ghouta, Damascus, prompted widespread international condemnation. In the immediate aftermath of the incident several thousand patients were treated for apparently neurotoxic symptoms, and up to around 1,400 fatalities were reported. The UN Secretary-General expressed shock at the atrocity and announced his intention immediately to initiate an impartial and thorough investigation into the situation, urging the Syrian Government promptly to confirm its willingness to co-operate with the existing UN chemical weapons inspection mission. On 24–25 August 2013 the High Representative for Disarmament Affairs engaged in this respect with representatives of the Syrian authorities, and from 26–30 August the UN mission visited the site of the attack, to examine the scene and to take relevant soil and biological samples. In early September the Russian foreign minister, US Secretary of State and Joint UN-Arab League Special Representative gave consideration to a proposal by Russia that Syria should surrender its chemical stockpiles to international control. Soon afterwards the Syrian regime notified the UN Secretary-General that it was taking measures to accede to the 1992 Chemical Weapons Convention and would observe the obligations imposed by the Convention prior to its national entry into force. In mid-September the Sellström weapons inspection mission issued its report on the 21 August atrocity, finding 'clear and convincing evidence' of the use of surface-to-surface rockets containing sarin gas in Ghouta, Damascus, and that chemical weapons had been used on a relatively large scale generally during the Syrian conflict, including against children.

Under-Secretary-General and High Representative for Disarmament Affairs: ANGELA KANE (Germany).

UNITED NATIONS OFFICE ON DRUGS AND CRIME—UNODC

Address: Vienna International Centre, POB 500, 1400 Vienna, Austria.

Telephone: (1) 26060-0; **fax:** (1) 26060-5866; **e-mail:** unodc@unodc.org; **internet:** www.unodc.org.

The Office was established in November 1997 (as the UN Office of Drug Control and Crime Prevention) to strengthen the UN's integrated approach to issues relating to drug control, crime prevention and international terrorism.

Executive Director: YURI FEDOTOV (Russia).

OFFICE OF THE UNITED NATIONS HIGH COMMISSIONER FOR HUMAN RIGHTS—OHCHR

Address: Palais Wilson, 52 rue de Paquis, 1201 Geneva, Switzerland.

Telephone: 229179290; **fax:** 229179022; **e-mail:** infodesk@ohchr.org; **internet:** www.ohchr.org.

The Office is a body of the UN Secretariat and is the focal point for UN human-rights activities. Since September 1997 it has incorporated the Centre for Human Rights. The High Commissioner is the UN official with principal responsibility for UN human rights activities.

At September 2013 OHCHR was concerned with 36 thematic mandates and with 13 country mandates, including for Iran (mandate established in 2011; and most recently extended in 2013), the Palestinian Territories (1993, to be maintained pending 'the end of the Israeli occupation'), and Syria (established in 2011).

High Commissioner: NAVANETHEM PILLAY (South Africa).

UNITED NATIONS INDEPENDENT COMMISSION OF INQUIRY (COI) ON SYRIA

The CoI on Syria was established in March 2011 by the UN Human Rights Council, with a mandate to report on the human rights situation in that country. The CoI's first report was published in November of that year, and regular updates have been issued subsequently. An emergency meeting of the Human Rights Council convened at the beginning of June 2012 on the deteriorating situation in Syria—following the shelling, in late May, allegedly by Syrian government forces, of a residential neighbourhood, which resulted in the deaths of an estimated 108 men, women and children—adopted a resolution condemning the use of force against civilians as 'outrageous', condemning the Syrian authorities for failure to protect, and to promote the rights of, all Syrians, and calling for the CoI on Syria to conduct a special investigation into the massacre, with a view to holding to account those responsible for 'violations that may amount to crimes against humanity'. In mid-August the CoI on Syria issued a report which concluded that both Syrian government forces and opposition combatants had committed crimes against humanity (murder and torture), war crimes and gross violations of international human rights and humanitarian law, including unlawful killing, indiscriminate attacks against civilian populations, arbitrary detention, torture, and acts of sexual violence. The CoI subsequently reported that the frequency and the extent of gross human rights violations in Syria were increasing significantly, with indiscriminate attacks against civilians being reported constantly. It was reported in February 2013 that a confidential list of individuals and entities believed to be responsible for perpetrating crimes during the conflict would be passed to the UN Commissioner for Human Rights. In June the CoI reported that the incidence of war crimes and gross human rights violations was continuing to escalate, with government forces and affiliated militias allegedly carrying out systematic and widespread crimes against humanity against civilians, while anti-government armed militia were also accused of committing war crimes, particularly in the Aleppo area, including hostage-taking, torture, extra-judicial executions, and pillage. The CoI also found at that time that there were reasonable grounds to believe that chemical weapons had been used in the conflict, without specifying the side responsible. The Commission reiterated its consistent position that a political settlement was the only means of curtailing the violent conflict. The sixth report of the CoI, released in mid-September, urged the pursuit of a political settlement to the conflict, and maintained that any international military action undertaken in response to the gas attack that occurred on 21 August, against civilians in Ghouta, Damascus, would intensify the crisis within Syria and would adversely affect the achievement of a political settlement.

UNITED NATIONS HUMAN SETTLEMENTS PROGRAMME—UN-HABITAT

Address: POB 30030, Nairobi, Kenya.

Telephone: (20) 621234; **fax:** (20) 624266; **e-mail:** infohabitat@unhabitat.org; **internet:** www.unhabitat.org.

UN-Habitat was established, as the United Nations Centre for Human Settlements, in October 1978 to service the intergovernmental Commission on Human Settlements. It became a full UN programme on 1 January 2002, serving as the focus for human settlements activities in the UN system.

Executive Director: JOAN CLOS (Spain).

Regional Office for Africa and the Arab States: POB 30030, Nairobi, Kenya 00100; tel. (20) 623221; fax (20) 623904; e-mail roaas@unhabitat.org.

UNITED NATIONS CONFERENCE ON TRADE AND DEVELOPMENT—UNCTAD

Address: Palais des Nations, 1211 Geneva 10, Switzerland.

Telephone: 229171234; **fax:** 229070057; **e-mail:** info@unctad.org; **internet:** www.unctad.org.

UNCTAD was established in 1964. It is the principal organ of the UN General Assembly concerned with trade and development, and is the focal point within the UN system for integrated activities relating to trade, finance, technology, investment and sustainable development. It aims to maximize the trade and development opportunities of developing countries, in particular least-developed countries, and to assist them to adapt to the increasing globalization and liberalization of the world economy. UNCTAD undertakes consensus-building activities, research and policy analysis and technical co-operation.

Secretary-General: MUKHISA KITUYI (Kenya).

Deputy Secretary-General: PETKO DRAGANOV (Bulgaria).

UNITED NATIONS POPULATION FUND—UNFPA

Address: 605 Third Ave, New York, NY 10158, USA.

Telephone: (212) 297-5000; **fax:** (212) 370-0201; **e-mail:** hq@unfpa.org; **internet:** www.unfpa.org.

Created in 1967 as the Trust Fund for Population Activities, the UN Fund for Population Activities (UNFPA) was established as a Fund of the UN General Assembly in 1972 and was made a subsidiary organ of the UN General Assembly in 1979, with the UNDP Governing Council (now the Executive Board) designated as its governing body. In 1987 UNFPA's name was changed to the United Nations Population Fund (retaining the same acronym).

In August 2013 the Executive Director of UNFPA stated his concern for the impact of the ongoing conflict in Syria, and in particular its recent escalation in Damascus, on women, young people and families; the increased risk of gender-based violence, and the need to provide unhindered access to women and girls in need of emergency obstetric care, as well as other emergency assistance, were emphasized.

Executive Director: BABATUNDE OSOTIMEHIN (Nigeria).

Regional Office for the Arab States: 31 Palestine St, New Maadi, Cairo, Egypt; tel. (2) 2706-7040; fax (2) 2706-7086; internet arabstates.unfpa.org.

UN Specialized Agencies

INTERNATIONAL CIVIL AVIATION ORGANIZATION—ICAO

Address: 999 University St, Montréal, QC H3C 5H7, Canada.

Telephone: (514) 954-8219; **fax:** (514) 954-6077; **e-mail:** icaohq@icao.org; **internet:** www.icao.int.

ICAO was founded in 1947, on the basis of the Convention on International Civil Aviation, signed in Chicago, in 1944, to develop the techniques of international air navigation and to help in the planning and improvement of international air transport.

Secretary-General: RAYMOND BENJAMIN (France).

Middle East Office: POB 85, Cairo Airport Post Office Terminal One, Cairo 11776, Egypt; tel. (2) 267-4840; fax (2) 267-4843; e-mail icaomid@cairo.icao.int; internet www.icao.int/mid.

INTERNATIONAL LABOUR ORGANIZATION—ILO

Address: 4 route des Morillons, 1211 Geneva 22, Switzerland.

Telephone: 227996111; **fax:** 227988685; **e-mail:** ilo@ilo.org; **internet:** www.ilo.org.

ILO was founded in 1919 to work for social justice as a basis for lasting peace. It carries out this mandate by promoting decent living standards, satisfactory conditions of work and pay and adequate employment opportunities. Methods of action include the creation of international labour standards; the provision of technical co-operation services; and training, education, research and publishing activities to advance ILO objectives.

Director-General: GUY RYDER (United Kingdom).

Regional Office for Africa: BP 2788, Africa Hall, 6th Floor, Menelik II Ave, Addis Ababa, Ethiopia; tel. (11) 544-4480; fax (11) 544-5573; e-mail addisababa@ilo.org; internet www.ilo.org/addisababa.

Regional Office for Arab States: POB 11-4088, Beirut, Lebanon; tel. (1) 752400; fax (1) 752405; e-mail beirut@ilo.org; internet www.ilo.org/beirut.

INTERNATIONAL MARITIME ORGANIZATION—IMO

Address: 4 Albert Embankment, London, SE1 7SR, United Kingdom.

Telephone: (20) 7735-7611; **fax:** (20) 7587-3210; **e-mail:** info@imo.org; **internet:** www.imo.org.

The Inter-Governmental Maritime Consultative Organization (IMCO) began operations in 1959, as a specialized agency of the UN to facilitate co-operation among governments on technical matters affecting international shipping. Its main aims are to improve the safety of international shipping, and to control pollution caused by ships. IMCO became IMO in 1982.

A high-level sub-regional meeting of states from the Western Indian Ocean, the Gulf of Aden and Red Sea areas, held under IMO auspices in Djibouti, in January 2009, adopted the Djibouti Code of Conduct concerning the Repression of Piracy and Armed Robbery. The Code, which by September 2013 had been signed by 20 of the 21 countries eligible as signatories, promotes the implementation of those aspects of relevant UN Security Council resolutions, and of a February 2009 General Assembly resolution on oceans and the law of the sea, which fall within IMO's area of competence.

Secretary-General: KOJI SEKIMIZU (Japan).

INTERNATIONAL TELECOMMUNICATION UNION—ITU

Address: Place des Nations, 1211 Geneva 20, Switzerland.

Telephone: 227305111; **fax:** 227337256; **e-mail:** itumail@itu.int; **internet:** www.itu.int.

Founded in 1865, ITU became a specialized agency of the UN in 1947. It acts to encourage world co-operation for the improvement and use of telecommunications, to promote technical development, to harmonize national policies in the field, and to promote the extension of telecommunications throughout the world. ITU helped to organize the World Summit on the Information Society, held, in two phases, in 2003 and 2005, and supports follow-up initiatives. ITU has assumed responsibility for issues relating to cybersecurity. In December 2012 a World Conference on International Communications endorsed new International Telecommunication Regulations (ITRs), updating those previously set down in 1988. The new ITRs included provisions to secure freedom of expression, to assist developing countries to enhance their telecommunications infrastructure, to promote accessibility to persons with disabilities, to limit unsolicited bulk electronic communications, and to improve the energy efficiency of telecommunications networks.

Secretary-General: HAMADOUN TOURÉ (Mali).

UNITED NATIONS INDUSTRIAL DEVELOPMENT ORGANIZATION—UNIDO

Address: Vienna International Centre, Wagramerstr. 5, POB 300, 1400 Vienna, Austria.

Telephone: (1) 260260; **fax:** (1) 2692669; **e-mail:** unido@unido.org; **internet:** www.unido.org.

UNIDO began operations in 1967 and became a specialized agency in 1985. Its objectives are to promote sustainable and socially equitable industrial development in developing countries and in countries with economies in transition. It aims to assist such countries to integrate fully into global economic system by mobilizing knowledge, skills, information and technology to promote productive employment, competitive economies and sound environment.

Director-General: LI YONG (People's Republic of China).

UNIVERSAL POSTAL UNION—UPU

Address: CP 13, 3000 Bern 15, Switzerland.

Telephone: 313503111; **fax:** 313503110; **e-mail:** info@upu.int; **internet:** www.upu.int.

The General Postal Union was founded by the Treaty of Berne (1874), beginning operations in July 1875. Three years later its name was changed to the Universal Postal Union. In 1948 UPU became a specialized agency of the UN. It aims to develop and unify the international postal service, to study problems and to provide training.

Director-General: BISHAR ABDIRAHMAN HUSSEIN (Kenya).

WORLD INTELLECTUAL PROPERTY ORGANIZATION—WIPO

Address: 34 chemin des Colombettes, 1211 Geneva 20, Switzerland.

Telephone: 223389111; **fax:** 227335428; **e-mail:** wipo.mail@wipo.int; **internet:** www.wipo.int.

WIPO was established in 1970. It became a specialized agency of the UN in 1974 concerned with the protection of intellectual property (e.g. industrial and technical patents and literary copyrights) throughout the world. WIPO formulates and administers treaties embodying international norms and standards of intellectual property, establishes model laws, and facilitates applications for the protection of inventions, trademarks etc. WIPO provides legal and technical assistance to developing countries and countries with economies in transition and advises countries on obligations under the World Trade Organization's agreement on Trade-Related Aspects of Intellectual Property Rights (TRIPS).

Director-General: FRANCIS GURRY (Australia).

WORLD METEOROLOGICAL ORGANIZATION—WMO

Address: 7 bis, ave de la Paix, 1211 Geneva 2, Switzerland.

Telephone: 227308111; **fax:** 227308181; **e-mail:** wmo@wmo.int; **internet:** www.wmo.int.

WMO was established in 1950 and was recognized as a Specialized Agency of the UN in 1951, aiming to improve the exchange of information in the fields of meteorology, climatology, operational hydrology and related fields, as well as their applications. WMO jointly implements, with UNEP, the UN Framework Convention on Climate Change. In June 2011 the 16th World Meteorological Congress endorsed a new Global Framework for Climate Services.

Secretary-General: MICHEL JARRAUD (France).

WORLD TOURISM ORGANIZATION—UNWTO

Address: Capitán Haya 42, 28020 Madrid, Spain.

Telephone: (91) 5678100; **fax:** (91) 5713733; **e-mail:** omt@unwto.org; **internet:** www.world-tourism.org.

The World Tourism Organization was established in 1975 and was recognized as a Specialized Agency of the UN in December 2003. It works to promote and develop sustainable tourism, in particular in support of socio-economic growth in developing countries.

Secretary-General: TALEB RIFAI (Jordan).

Special High Level Appointments of the UN Secretary-General

High-level Co-ordinator for Compliance by Iraq with its Obligations Regarding the Repatriation or Return of all Kuwaiti and Third Country Nationals or their Remains, as well as the Return of all Kuwaiti Property, including Archives seized by Iraq: GENNADY P. TARASOV (Russia).

Humanitarian Envoy for Kuwait: ABDULLAH AL-MATOUQ (Kuwait).

Joint Special Representative of the UN and the League of Arab States for Syria: LAKHDAR BRAHIMI (Algeria).

Personal Envoy for Western Sahara: CHRISTOPHER ROSS (USA).

Special Adviser on Cyprus: ALEXANDER DOWNER (Australia).

Special Co-ordinator for Lebanon: DEREK PLUMBLY (United Kingdom).

Special Co-ordinator for the Middle East Peace Process, Personal Representative to the Palestine Liberation Organization and the Palestinian Authority, and the Secretary-General's Envoy to the Quartet: ROBERT H. SERRY (Netherlands).

Special Envoy for the Implementation of UN Security Council Resolution 1559 (on Lebanon): TERJE ROED-LARSEN (Norway).

Further Special Representatives and other high-level appointees of the UN Secretary-General are listed in entries on UN peace-keeping and peace-building missions.

Affiliated Body

SPECIAL TRIBUNAL FOR LEBANON

Address: POB 115, 2260 AC Leidschendam, Netherlands.

Telephone: (70) 800-3400; **e-mail:** stl-pressoffice@un.org; **internet:** www.stl-tsl.org.

In March 2006 the UN Security Council adopted a resolution requesting the UN Secretary-General to negotiate an agreement with the Lebanese Government on the establishment of an international tribunal to try those suspected of involvement in a terrorist attack that, in February 2005, had killed 23 people, including the former Prime Minister of Lebanon, Rafik Hariri. The resulting agreement on the Special Tribunal for Lebanon was endorsed by the Security Council in May 2007. The Tribunal, which became operational on 1 March 2009, comprises both international and Lebanese judges and applies Lebanese (not international) law. On its establishment the Tribunal took over the mandate of a terminated UN International Independent Investigation Commission (UNIIIC), which had been created by a resolution of the Security Council in April 2005 in order to gather evidence and assist the Lebanese authorities in their investigation into the February 2005 attacks, and whose mandate had later been expanded to investigate other assassinations that had occurred before and after the February 2005 attack. A Defence Office has been established within the Tribunal to protect the rights of the suspects, accused and their counsel, providing legal assistance and support where necessary. In June 2011 the Tribunal passed to the Lebanese authorities arrest warrants for four Lebanese suspects, Salim Jamil Ayyash, Mustafa Amine Badreddine, Hussein Hassan Oneissi and Assad Hassan Sabra, who were indicted on charges of conspiracy to commit a terrorist act; in February 2012 the Tribunal announced that it would try the four suspects *in absentia*, as it appeared that they had absconded. Also in February 2012, the UN Secretary-General extended the mandate of the Special Tribunal for a further three years, with effect from 1 March. In July 2012 it was announced that trial proceedings would provisionally commence in March 2013; however, in February 2013 it was announced that the commencement of proceedings would be postponed. In August a new tentative date of 13 January 2014 was set for the start of trial proceedings. The Tribunal maintains an office in Beirut, Lebanon.

President of the Court: Sir DAVID BARAGWANATH (New Zealand).

Chief Prosecutor: NORMAN FARELL (Canada).

Registrar: DARYL A. MUNDIS (USA).

Head of Defence Office: FRANÇOIS ROUX (France).

AFRICAN DEVELOPMENT BANK—AfDB

Address: Statutory Headquarters: rue Joseph Anoma, 01 BP 1387, Abidjan 01, Côte d'Ivoire.

Telephone: 20-20-44-44; **fax:** 20-20-49-59; **e-mail:** afdb@afdb.org; **internet:** www.afdb.org.

Address: Temporary Relocation Agency: 15 ave du Ghana, angle des rues Pierre de Coubertin et Hedi Nouira, BP 323, 1002 Tunis Belvédère, Tunisia.

Telephone: (71) 103-900; **fax:** (71) 351-933.

Established in 1964, the Bank began operations in July 1966, with the aim of financing economic and social development in African countries. The Bank's headquarters are officially based in Abidjan, Côte d'Ivoire. Since February 2003, however, in view of ongoing insecurity in Côte d'Ivoire, the Bank's operations have been conducted, on a long-term temporary basis, from Tunis, Tunisia. In May 2013 the Bank's Board of Governors approved a roadmap for a structured return to Côte d'Ivoire by the end of 2014.

AFRICAN MEMBERS

Algeria	Eritrea	Namibia
Angola	Ethiopia	Rwanda
Benin	Gabon	São Tomé and Príncipe
Botswana	The Gambia	Senegal
Burkina Faso	Ghana	Seychelles
Burundi	Guinea	Sierra Leone
Cameroon	Guinea-Bissau	Somalia
Cape Verde	Kenya	South Africa
Central African Republic	Lesotho	South Sudan
Chad	Liberia	Sudan
Comoros	Libya	Swaziland
Congo, Democratic Republic	Madagascar	Tanzania
Congo, Republic	Malawi	Togo
Côte d'Ivoire	Mali	Tunisia
Djibouti	Mauritania	Uganda
Egypt	Mauritius	Zambia
Equatorial Guinea	Morocco	Zimbabwe
	Mozambique	
	Namibia	
	Niger	

There are also 24 non-African members.

Organization

(September 2013)

BOARD OF GOVERNORS

The highest policy-making body of the Bank, which also elects the Board of Directors and the President. Each member country nominates one Governor, usually its Minister of Finance and Economic Affairs, and an alternate Governor or the Governor of its Central Bank. The Board meets once a year. The 2013 meeting was held in Marrakesh, Morocco, in May.

BOARD OF DIRECTORS

The Board, elected by the Board of Governors for a term of three years, is responsible for the general operations of the Bank and meets on a weekly basis. The Board has 20 members.

OFFICERS

The President is responsible for the organization and the day-to-day operations of the Bank under guidance of the Board of Directors. The President is elected for a five-year term and serves as the Chairperson of the Board of Directors. The President oversees the following senior management: Chief Economist; Vice-Presidents of Finance, Corporate Services, Country and Regional Programmes and Policy, Sector Operations, and Infrastructure, Private Sector and Regional Integration; Auditor General; General Counsel; Secretary-General; and Ombudsman. Bank field offices are located in around 35 member countries under a strategy of decentralization. In January 2011 a Permanent Committee on the Review and Implementation of the Decentralization was established. In accordance with a Roadmap on Decentralization, adopted by the Board of Directors in April 2011, and covering the period 2011–16, greater responsibility for portfolio management was to be transferred to the Bank's field offices; the Bank's presence in Fragile States was to be enhanced, through the extension of the field office network to Burundi, Central African Republic, Liberia (which was inaugurated in September 2012), South Sudan and Togo; and five regional resource centres were to be established with the aim of consolidating regional capacity. The Bank's first external representation office (for Asia) was inaugurated in Tokyo, Japan, in October 2012, and two further external representation offices were also to be opened: for the Americas, to be based in Washington, DC, USA; and for Europe, to be based in Brussels, Belgium.

Executive President and Chairperson of Board of Directors: DONALD KABERUKA (Rwanda).

FINANCIAL STRUCTURE

The African Development Bank (AfDB) Group of development financing institutions comprises the African Development Fund (ADF) and the Nigeria Trust Fund (NTF), which provide concessionary loans, and the AfDB itself. The Group uses a unit of account (UA), which, at December 2012, was valued at US $1.53692.

The capital stock of the Bank was at first exclusively open for subscription by African countries, with each member's subscription consisting of an equal number of paid-up and callable shares. In 1978, however, the Governors agreed to open the capital stock of the Bank to subscription by non-regional states on the basis of nine principles aimed at maintaining the African character of the institution. The decision was finally ratified in May 1982, and the participation of non-regional countries became effective on 30 December. It was agreed that African members should still hold two-thirds of the share capital, that all loan operations should be restricted to African members, and that the Bank's President should always be a national of an African state. In May 1998 the Board of Governors approved an increase in capital of 35%, and resolved that the non-African members' share of the capital be increased from 33.3% to 40%. In May 2010 the Board of Governors approved a general capital increase of 200%. At 31 December 2012 the Bank's authorized capital was UA 66,980.0m. (compared with UA 66,054.5m. at the end of 2011); subscribed capital at the end of 2012 was UA 65,220.0m. (of which the paid-up portion was UA 4,960.0m.).

Activities

At the end of 2012 the Bank Group had approved total lending of UA 72,202.8m. since the beginning of its operations in 1967. In 2012 the Group approved 199 lending operations amounting to UA 4,253.8m. compared with UA 5,720.3m. in the previous year. Of the total amount approved in 2012 UA 3,602.8m. was for loans and grants, UA 248.0m. for heavily indebted poor countries (HIPC) debt relief, UA 133.9m. for equity participation and UA 269.0m. for special funds. Of the total loans and grants approved in 2012, UA 1,763.5m. (49%) was for infrastructure projects (of which UA 889.7m. was for energy supply initiatives); UA 604.2m. (17%) was for transport projects; UA 505.4m. (14%) for multisector projects; and UA 402.8m. (11%) for projects in the finance sector. Some 31% of Bank Group loan and grant approvals in 2012 were allocated to countries in North Africa, 12.8% to Southern Africa, 12.4% to East Africa, 12.2% to West Africa, and 8.8% to Central Africa.

In 2006 the Bank established a High Level Panel of eminent personalities to advise on the Bank's future strategic vision. The Panel issued its report, *Investing in Africa's future—The AfDB in the 21st Century*, in February 2008. A Roadmap on Development Effectiveness was approved by the Board in March 2011, focusing on areas deemed most likely to bring about transformational change, including strengthening transparency and accountability; and accelerating decentralization. The Bank's Strategy for 2013–22, adopted in April 2013, focused on achieving inclusive growth and promoting the transition to green growth, with infrastructure development, regional integration, private sector development, governance and accountability, and skills and technology designated as core areas of priority. Further areas of special emphasis included fragile states, gender, agriculture, and food security. In mid-2008 the Bank established an African Food Crisis Response initiative to extend accelerated support to members affected by the sharp increase in the cost of food and food production. The initiative aimed to reduce short-term food poverty and malnutrition, with funds of some UA 472.0m., and to support long-term sustainable food security, with funding of UA 1,400m. In February 2009 the Bank hosted a meeting of the heads of multilateral development banks and of the IMF to discuss recent economic developments, the responses of each institution and future courses of action. In March the Bank's Board of Directors endorsed four new initiatives to help to counter the effects of the crisis: the establishment of an Emergency Liquidity Facility, with funds of some US $1,500m., to assist members with short-term financing difficulties; a new Trade Finance Initiative, with funds of up to $1,000m., to provide credit for trade financing operations; a Framework for the Accelerated Resource Transfer of ADF Resources; and enhanced policy advisory support. The Bank also agreed to contribute $500m. to a multinational Global Trade Liquidity Program, which commenced operations in mid-2009. In September the Bank initiated a consultative process for a sixth general capital increase. An increase of 200% was endorsed by a committee of the governing body representing the Bank's shareholders, meeting in April 2010, to enable the Bank to sustain its increased level of lending. The capital increase was formally approved by the Board of Governors in May.

In November 2008 the Bank hosted a special conference of African ministers of finance and central bank governors to consider the impact on the region of the contraction of the world's major economies and the recent volatility of global financial markets. The meeting determined to establish a Committee of African Finance Ministers and Central Bank Governors, comprising 10 representatives from each Bank region, with a mandate to examine further the impact of the global financial crisis on Africa, to review the responses by member governments, and to develop policy options. The so-called Committee of Ten (C10) convened for its inaugural meeting in Cape Town, South Africa, in January 2009. In March the C10 adopted a paper outlining the major concerns of African countries in preparation for the meeting of heads of state of the Group of 20 (G20) major economies, held in London, United Kingdom, in early April. The third meeting of the Committee, held in Abuja, Nigeria, in July, reviewed economic indicators and developments since the G20 meeting and appealed for all commitments to low-income countries pledged at the summit to be met. The Committee also issued a series of messages for the next G20 summit meeting, held in Pittsburgh, PA, USA, in September, including a request for greater African participation in the G20 process and in international economic governance. The fourth meeting of the C10, convened in February 2010, determined that it should meet formally two times a year, with other informal meetings and meetings of deputies to be held in between; the Secretariat of the Committee was to be provided by the AfDB.

In May 2011 the Group of Eight (G8) industrialized nations, in collaboration with regional and international financial institutions and the governments of Egypt and Tunisia, established a Deauville Partnership to support political and economic reforms being undertaken by several countries in North Africa and the Middle East, notably Egypt, Jordan, Morocco and Tunisia. The AfDB supported the establishment of the Partnership and was to chair a Co-ordination Platform. In September Kuwait, Qatar, Saudi Arabia, Turkey and the United Arab Emirates joined the Partnership.

Since 1996 the Bank has collaborated closely with international partners, in particular the World Bank, in efforts to address the problems of HIPCs (see IBRD). Of the 41 countries identified as potentially eligible for assistance under the scheme, 33 were in sub-Saharan Africa. Following the introduction of an enhanced framework for the initiative, the Bank has been actively involved in the preparation of Poverty Reduction Strategy Papers, that provide national frameworks for poverty reduction programmes. In April 2006 the Board of Directors endorsed a Multilateral Debt Relief Initiative (MDRI), which provided for 100% cancellation of eligible debts from the ADF, the IMF and the International Development Association to secure additional resources for countries to help them attain their MDGs. ADF's participation in the MDRI, which became effective in September, was anticipated to provide some UA 5,570m. (US $8,540m.) in debt relief.

The Bank contributed funds for the establishment, in 1986, of the Africa Project Development Facility, which assists the private sector in Africa by providing advisory services and finance for entrepreneurs: it was managed by the International Finance Corporation (IFC), until replaced by the Private Enterprise Partnership for Africa in April 2005. In 1989 the Bank, in co-ordination with IFC and the UN Development Programme (UNDP), created the African Management Services Company (AMSCo), which provides management support and training to private companies in Africa. The Bank is one of three multilateral donors, with the World Bank and UNDP, supporting the African Capacity Building Foundation, which was established in 1991 to strengthen and develop institutional and human capacity in support of sustainable development activities. The Bank hosts the secretariat of an Africa Investment Consortium, which was inaugurated in October 2005 by several major African institutions and donor countries to accelerate efforts to develop the region's infrastructure. An Enhanced Private Sector Assistance Initiative was established, with support from the Japanese Government, in 2005 to support the Bank's strategy for the development of the private sector. The Initiative incorporated an Accelerated Cofinancing Facility for Africa and a Fund for African Private Sector Assistance. In October 2010 the Board of Directors agreed to convert the Fund into a multi-donor trust fund.

In November 2006 the Bank Group, with the UN Economic Commission for Africa (ECA), organized an African Economic Conference (AEC), which has since become an annual event. The seventh AEC was held in Kigali, Rwanda, in October–November 2012 on the theme 'Inclusive and Sustainable Development in an Age of Economic Uncertainty'. In September 2011 the Bank organized a regional meeting on peace-building and state-building in Africa, in preparation for the Fourth High Level Forum on Aid Effectiveness, which was convened in Busan, Republic of Korea, in November–December.

In March 2000 African ministers of water resources endorsed an African Water Vision and a Framework for Action to pursue the equitable and sustainable use and management of water resources in Africa in order to facilitate socio-economic development, poverty alleviation and environmental protection. An African Ministers' Council on Water (AMCOW) was established in April 2002 to provide the political leadership and focus for implementation of the Vision and the Framework for Action. AMCOW requested the Bank to establish and administer an African Water Facility Special Fund, in order to provide the financial requirements for achieving their objectives; this became operational in December. In March the Bank approved a Rural Water Supply and Sanitation Initiative to accelerate access in member countries to sustainable safe water and basic sanitation, in order to meet the requirements of several MDGs. In March 2008 the Bank hosted the first African Water Week, organized jointly with AMCOW, on the theme of 'Accelerating Water Security for the Socio-economic Development of Africa'. The Bank co-ordinated and led Africa's regional participation in the Sixth World Water Forum, which was held in Marseilles, France, in March 2012. The Bank was actively involved in preparing for the fifth Africa Carbon Forum, which was convened in Abidjan, Côte d'Ivoire, in July 2013 (previous fora having been held in September 2008, March 2010, July 2011 and April 2012).

The Bank hosts the secretariat of the Congo Basin Forest Fund, which was established in June 2008, as a multi-donor facility, with initial funding from Norway and the United Kingdom, to protect and manage the forests in that region. The Bank also hosts the secretariat of an African Fertilizer Financing Mechanism (AFFM), established in 2007 to boost agricultural productivity, food security, and the sustainable management of natural resources in Africa. The inaugural meeting of the AFFM Governing Council was convened in Tunis, Tunisia, in November 2009; the second Governing Council meeting was hosted by the Bank in March 2013.

Through the Migration and Development Trust Fund, launched in 2009, the Bank supports the development of financial services for migrant workers, and facilitates channelling remittances towards productive uses in workers' countries of origin.

The Bank provides technical assistance to regional member countries in the form of experts' services, pre-investment feasibility studies, and staff training. Much of this assistance is financed through bilateral trust funds contributed by non-African member states. The Bank's African Development Institute provides training for officials of regional member countries in order to enhance the management of Bank-financed projects and, more broadly, to strengthen national capacities for promoting sustainable development. The Institute also manages an AfDB/Japan Fellowship programme that provides scholarships to African students to pursue further education. In 1990 the Bank established the African Business Round Table (ABR), which is composed of the chief executives of Africa's leading corporations. The ABR aims to strengthen Africa's private sector, promote intra-African trade and investment, and attract foreign investment to Africa. The ABR is chaired by the Bank's Executive President. In 2008 the Bank endorsed a Governance Strategic Directions and Action Plan as a framework for countering corruption and enhancing democratic governance in Africa in the period 2008–12.

A joint secretariat supports co-operation activities between the African Union (AU), the ECA and the AfDB. In March 2009 a new Coalition for Dialogue on Africa was inaugurated by the Bank, the ECA and the AU. In 1999 a Co-operation Agreement was formally concluded between the Bank and the Common Market for Eastern and Southern Africa. In March 2000 the Bank signed a Memorandum of Understanding (MOU) on its strategic partnership with the World Bank. Other MOUs were signed during that year with the United Nations Industrial Development Organization, the World Food Programme, and the Arab Maghreb Union. In September 2008 the Bank supported the establishment of an African Financing Partnership, which aimed to mobilize private sector resources through partnerships with regional development finance institutions. The Bank hosts the secretariat of the Partnership. It also hosts the secretariat of the Making Finance Work for Africa Partnership, which was established, by the G8, in October 2007, in order to support the development of the financial sector in the sub-Saharan region. In December 2010 the Bank signed an MOU with the Islamic Development Bank to promote economic development in common member countries through co-financing and co-ordinating projects in priority areas. It signed an MOU with the European Bank for Reconstruction and Development in September 2011. The Bank is actively involved in the New Partnership for Africa's Development (NEPAD), established in 2001 to promote sustainable development and eradicate poverty throughout the region. Since 2004 it has been a strategic partner in NEPAD's African Peer Review Mechanism. In 2011 the Bank supported the development of a Program for Infrastructure Development in Africa, as a joint initiative with NEPAD and the AU. During 2013 the AfDB, AU and UN Economic Commission for Africa were jointly developing AU Agenda 2063, a vision to guide the economic and social transformation of Africa over the coming 50 years, within the context of which a series of African Development Goals (ADGs) were being formulated. AU Agenda 2063 was to be finalized by June 2014. In May 2013 the Board of Governors endorsed a new Africa50Fund, which was to finance, in partnership with regional institutions, transformational projects with a focus on enhancing the trans-continental infrastructure.

AFRICAN DEVELOPMENT BANK

The Bank makes loans at a variable rate of interest, which is adjusted twice a year, plus a commitment fee of 0.75%. Lending approved amounted to UA 2,080.5m. for 48 operations in 2012, including resources allocated under the HIPC debt relief initiative, the Post-conflict Country Facility (see below), and equity participations, compared with UA 3,689.4m., for 59 operations, in the previous year. Lending for private sector projects amounted to UA 753m. in 2012. Since October 1997 fixed and floating rate loans have been made available.

AFRICAN DEVELOPMENT FUND

The Fund commenced operations in 1974. It grants interest-free loans to low-income African countries for projects with repayment over 50 years (including a 10-year grace period) and with a service charge of 0.75% per annum. Grants for project feasibility studies are made to the poorest countries.

In December 2007 donor countries committed US $8,900m. to replenish the Fund for the period 2008–10 (ADF-11), during which there was to be a focus on infrastructure, governance and regional integration. The funding arrangements for ADF-11 allocated UA 408m. to a new Fragile States Facility to support the poorer regional member countries, in particular those in a post-conflict or transitional state. The Facility was to incorporate the Post-Conflict Country Facility, which was established in 2003 to help certain countries to clear their arrears and accelerate their progress within the HIPC process. An agreement was concluded by donors in October 2010 to increase contributions to the Fund by 10.6%, to some $9,350m., under ADF-12, covering the period 2011–13. ADF-12 was to support ongoing institutional reform and capacity building, as well as efforts to stimulate economic growth in Africa's lowest income countries. Operational priorities included climate change adaptation and mitigation measures, regional economic integration, and private sector development. The first replenishment meeting for ADF-13 was held in Tunis, Tunisia, in February 2013; a second meeting was held in June and the concluding meeting was scheduled to be convened in late September.

In 2012 lending under the ADF amounted to UA 1,890.2m. for 98 projects, compared with UA 1,831.9m. for 87 projects in the previous year.

NIGERIA TRUST FUND

The Agreement establishing the NTF was signed in February 1976 by the Bank and the Government of Nigeria. The Fund is administered by the Bank and its loans are granted for up to 25 years, including grace periods of up to five years, and carry 0.75% commission charges and 4% interest charges. The loans are intended to provide financing for projects in co-operation with other lending institutions. The Fund also aims to promote the private sector and trade between African countries by providing information on African and international financial institutions able to finance African trade.

Operations under the NTF were suspended in 2006, pending a detailed assessment and consideration of the Fund's activities which commenced in November. The evaluation exercise was concluded in July 2007 and an agreement was reached in November to authorize the Fund to continue activities for a further 10-year period. Three operations, amounting to UA 14.1m., were approved in 2012.

Publications

Annual Development Effectiveness Review.

AfDB Business Bulletin (10 a year).

AfDB Statistics Pocketbook.

AfDB Today (every 2 months).

African Competitiveness Report.

African Development Report (annually).

African Development Review (3 a year).

African Economic Outlook (annually, with OECD).

Annual Report.

African Statistical Journal (2 a year).

Annual Procurement Report.

Economic Research Papers.

Gender, Poverty and Environmental Indicators on African Countries (annually).

OPEV Sharing (quarterly newsletter).

Quarterly Operational Summary.

Selected Statistics on African Countries (annually).

Summaries of operations and projects, background documents, Board documents.

Statistics

SUMMARY OF BANK GROUP OPERATIONS
(millions of UA)

	2011	2012	Cumulative total*
AfDB approvals†			
Number	59	48	1,366
Amount	3,689.43	2,080.46	41,777.96
Disbursements	1,868.79	2,208.17	24,618.55
ADF approvals†			
Number	87	98	2,572
Amount	1,831.86	1,890.17	29,430.22
Disbursements	1,296.65	1,169.60	17,268.11
NTF approvals			
Number	3	3	85
Amount	10.88	14.10	396.31
Disbursements	8.67	1.76	237.50
Special Funds‡			
Number	35	50	158
Amount approved	188.12	269.0	598.3
Group total†			
Number	184	199	4,184
Amount approved	5,720.29	4,253.75	72,202.76
Disbursements	3,174.11	3,379.53	42,124.15

* Since the initial operations of the three institutions (1967 for AfDB, 1974 for ADF and 1976 for NTF).

† Approvals include loans and grant operations, private and public equity investments, emergency operations, HIPC debt relief, loan reallocations and guarantees, the Post-Conflict Country Facility and the Fragile States Facility.

‡ Includes the African Water Fund, the Rural Water Supply and Sanitation Initiative, the Global Environment Facility, the Congo Basin Forest Fund, the Fund for African Private Sector Assistance, and the Migration and Development Trust Fund.

BANK GROUP APPROVALS BY SECTOR, 2012

Sector	Number of projects	Amount (millions of UA)
Agriculture and rural development	20	308.1
Social	21	535.3
Education	8	191.6
Health	6	3.7
Other	7	330.1
Infrastructure	46	1,763.5
Water supply and sanitation	13	269.7
Energy supply	14	889.7
Communication	—	—
Transportation	19	604.2
Finance	4	402.8
Multisector	43	505.4
Industry, mining and quarrying	1	97.7
Environment	—	—
Total (loans and grants)	135	3,602.8
HIPC debt relief	5	248.0
Equity participations	9	133.9
Special funds	50	269.0
Other approvals	64	650.9
Total approvals	199	4,253.8

Source: African Development Bank, *Annual Report 2012*.

AFRICAN UNION—AU

Address: Roosevelt St, Old Airport Area, POB 3243, Addis Ababa, Ethiopia.

Telephone: (11) 5517700; **fax:** (11) 5517844; **e-mail:** webmaster@africa-union.org; **internet:** au.int.

In May 2001 the Constitutive Act of the African Union entered into force. In July 2002 the African Union (AU) became fully operational, replacing the Organization of African Unity (OAU), which had been founded in 1963. The AU aims to support unity, solidarity and peace among African states; to promote and defend African common positions on issues of shared interest; to encourage human rights, democratic principles and good governance; to advance the development of member states by encouraging research and by working to eradicate preventable diseases; and to promote sustainable development and political and socio-economic integration, including co-ordinating and harmonizing policy between the continent's various 'regional economic communities' (see below).

MEMBERS*

Algeria	Eritrea	Nigeria
Angola	Ethiopia	Rwanda
Benin	Gabon	São Tomé and Príncipe
Botswana	The Gambia	Senegal
Burkina Faso	Ghana	Seychelles
Burundi	Guinea	Sierra Leone
Cameroon	Guinea-Bissau	Somalia
Cape Verde	Kenya	South Africa
Central African Republic†	Lesotho	South Sudan
Chad	Liberia	Sudan
Comoros	Libya	Swaziland
Congo, Democratic Republic	Madagascar†	Tanazania
Congo, Republic	Malawi	Togo
Côte d'Ivoire	Mali	Tunisia
Dijbouti	Mauritania	Uganda
Egypt†	Mauritius	Zambia
Equatorial Guinea	Mozambique	Zimbabwe
	Namibia	
	Niger	

* The Sahrawi Arab Democratic Republic (SADR–Western Sahara) was admitted to the OAU in February 1982, following recognition by more than one-half of the member states, but its membership was disputed by Morocco and other states which claimed that a two-thirds' majority was needed to admit a state whose existence was in question. Morocco withdrew from the OAU with effect from November 1985, and has not applied to join the AU. The SADR ratified the Constitutive Act in December 2000 and is a full member of the AU.

† In March 2009 Madagascar's participation in the activities of the AU was suspended, following the forced resignation of its elected President and transfer of power to the military. In April 2012 Guinea-Bissau was suspended following a military coup, pending the restoration of constitutional order. In March 2013 the Central African Republic's participation was suspended, also after a military coup. Following the overthrow of the elected Egyptian regime in July of that year, that country was also suspended from participation in meetings of the Union.

Note: The Constitutive Act stipulates that member states in which Governments accede to power by unconstitutional means are liable to suspension from participating in the Union's activities and to the imposition of sanctions by the Union.

Organization

(September 2013)

ASSEMBLY

The Assembly, comprising member countries' heads of state and government, is the supreme organ of the Union and meets at least once a year (with alternate sessions held in Addis Ababa, Ethiopia) to determine and monitor the Union's priorities and common policies and to adopt its annual work programme. Resolutions are passed by a two-thirds' majority, procedural matters by a simple majority. Extraordinary sessions may be convened at the request of a member state and on approval by a two-thirds' majority. A chairperson is elected at each meeting from among the members, to hold office for one year. The Assembly ensures compliance by member states with decisions of the Union, adopts the biennial budget, appoints judges of the African Court of Human and Peoples' Rights, and hears and settles disputes between member states. The first regular Assembly meeting was held in Durban, South Africa, in July 2002, and a first extraordinary summit meeting of the Assembly was convened in Addis Ababa in February 2003. The 21st ordinary session of the Assembly—commemorating 50 years since the 1963 foundation of the former Organization of African Unity—was held in May 2013, in Addis Ababa, on the theme 'Panafricanism and African Renaissance'.

Chairperson: (2013/14) HAILEMARIAM DESALEGN (Pres. of Ethiopia).

EXECUTIVE COUNCIL

Consists of ministers of foreign affairs and others and meets at least twice a year (in February and July), with provision for extraordinary sessions. The Council's Chairperson is the minister of foreign affairs (or another competent authority) of the country that has provided the Chairperson of the Assembly. Prepares meetings of, and is responsible to, the Assembly. Determines the issues to be submitted to the Assembly for decision, co-ordinates and harmonizes the policies, activities and initiatives of the Union in areas of common interest to member states, and monitors the implementation of policies and decisions of the Assembly.

PERMANENT REPRESENTATIVES COMMITTEE

The Committee, which comprises Ambassadors accredited to the AU and meets at least once a month. It is responsible to the Executive Council, which it advises, and whose meetings, including matters for the agenda and draft decisions, it prepares.

COMMISSION

The Commission is the permanent secretariat of the organization. It comprises a Chairperson (elected for a four-year term of office by the Assembly), Deputy Chairperson and eight Commissioners (responsible for peace and security; political affairs; infrastructure and energy; social affairs; human resources, science and technology; trade and industry; rural economy and agriculture; and economic affairs) who are elected on the basis of equal geographical distribution. Members of the Commission serve a term of four years and may stand for re-election for one further term of office. Further support staff assist the smooth functioning of the Commission. The Commission represents the Union under the guidance of, and as mandated by, the Assembly and the Executive Council, and reports to the Executive Council. It deals with administrative issues, implements the decisions of the Union, and acts as the custodian of the Constitutive Act and Protocols, and other agreements. Its work covers the following domains: control of pandemics; disaster management; international crime and terrorism; environmental management; negotiations relating to external trade; negotiations relating to external debt; population, migration, refugees and displaced persons; food security; socio-economic integration; and all other areas where a common position has been established by Union member states. It has responsibility for the co-ordination of AU activities and meetings.

Chairperson: Dr NKOSAZANA DLAMINI-ZUMA (South Africa).

SPECIALIZED TECHNICAL COMMITTEES

There are specialized committees for monetary and financial affairs; rural economy and agricultural matters; trade, customs and immigration matters; industry, science and technology, energy, natural resources and environment; infrastructure; transport, communications and tourism; health, labour and social affairs; and education, culture and human resources. These have responsibility for implementing the Union's programmes and projects.

PAN-AFRICAN PARLIAMENT

The Pan-African Parliament comprises five deputies (including at least one woman) from each AU member state, presided over by an elected President assisted by four Vice-Presidents. The President and Vice-Presidents must equitably represent the central, northern, eastern, southern and western African states. The Parliament convenes at least twice a year; an extraordinary session may be called by a two-thirds' majority of the members. The Parliament currently has only advisory and consultative powers. Its eventual evolution into an institution with full legislative authority is planned. The Parliament is headquartered at Midrand, South Africa.

President: BETHEL NNAEMEKA AMADI (Nigeria).

AFRICAN COURT OF JUSTICE AND HUMAN RIGHTS

An African Court of Human and Peoples' Rights (ACHPR) was created following the entry into force in January 2004 of the Protocol to the African Charter on Human and Peoples' Rights Establishing the ACHPR (adopted in June 1998). In February 2009 a protocol (adopted in July 2003) establishing an African Court of Justice entered into force. The Protocol on the Statute of the African Court of Justice and Human Rights, aimed at merging the ACHPR and the African Court of Justice, was opened for signature in July 2008, and had, by September 2013, been ratified by five states.

PEACE AND SECURITY COUNCIL

The Protocol to the Constitutive Act of the African Union Relating to the Peace and Security Council of the African Union entered into force on 26 December 2003; the 15-member elected Council was formally inaugurated in May 2004. It acts as a decision-making body for the prevention, management and resolution of conflicts.

ECONOMIC, SOCIAL AND CULTURAL COUNCIL

The Economic, Social and Cultural Council (ECOSOCC), inaugurated in March 2005, was to have an advisory function and to comprise representatives of civic, professional and cultural bodies at national, regional and diaspora levels. Its main organs were to be an elected General Assembly; Standing Committee; Credential Committee; and Sectoral Cluster Communities. It is envisaged that the Council will strengthen the partnership between member governments and African civil society. The General Assembly was inaugurated in September 2008. The Sectoral Cluster Communities were to be established to formulate opinions and influence AU decision-making in the following 10 areas: peace and security; political affairs; infrastructure and energy; social affairs and health; human resources, science and technology; trade and industry; rural economy and agriculture; economic affairs; women and gender; and cross-cutting programmes.

NEW PARTNERSHIP FOR AFRICA'S DEVELOPMENT (NEPAD)

NEPAD Planning and Co-ordination Agency (NPCA): POB 1234, Halfway House, Midrand, 1685 South Africa; tel. (11) 256-3600; fax (11) 206-3762; e-mail media@nepad.org; internet www.nepad.org; f. Feb. 2010, as a technical body of the AU, to replace the former NEPAD Secretariat, with the aim of improving the country-level implementation of projects; NEPAD was launched in 2001 as a long-term strategy to promote socio-economic development in Africa; adopted Declaration on Democracy, Political, Economic and Corporate Governance and the African Peer Review Mechanism in June 2002; the July 2003 AU Maputo summit decided that NEPAD should be integrated into AU structures and processes; a special 'Brainstorming on NEPAD' summit, held in Algiers, Algeria in March 2007, issued a 13-point communiqué on the means of reforming the Partnership; a further Review Summit on NEPAD, convened in Dakar, Senegal, in April 2008, reaffirmed the centrality of NEPAD as the overarching developmental programme for Africa; the UN allocated US $12.6m. in support of NEPAD under its 2012–13 budget; CEO Dr IBRAHIM ASSANE MAYAKI.

PROPOSED INSTITUTIONS

In 2013 three financial institutions, for managing the financing of programmes and projects, remained to be established: an African Central Bank; an African Monetary Fund; and an African Investment Bank.

Activities

In May 1963 30 African heads of state adopted the Charter of the Organization of African Unity (OAU). In May 1994 the Abuja Treaty Establishing the African Economic Community (AEC, signed in June 1991) entered into force.

An extraordinary summit meeting, convened in September 1999, in Sirte, Libya, at the request of the then Libyan leader Col Muammar al-Qaddafi, determined to establish an African Union, based on the principles and objectives of the OAU and AEC, but furthering African co-operation, development and integration. Heads of state declared their commitment to accelerating the establishment of regional institutions, including a pan-African parliament, a court of human and peoples' rights and a central bank, as well as the implementation of economic and monetary union, as provided for by the Abuja Treaty Establishing the AEC. In July 2000 at the annual OAU summit meeting, held at Lomé, Togo, 27 heads of state and government signed the draft Constitutive Act of the African Union, which was to enter into force one month after ratification by two-thirds of member states' legislatures; this was achieved on 26 May 2001. The Union was inaugurated, replacing the OAU, on 9 July 2002, at a summit meeting of heads of state and government held in Durban, South Africa, after a transitional period of one year had elapsed since the endorsement of the Act in July 2001. During the transitional year, pending the transfer of all assets and liabilities to the Union, the OAU Charter remained in effect. A review of all OAU treaties was implemented, and those deemed relevant were retained by the AU. The four key organs of the AU were launched in July 2002. Morocco is the only African country that is not a member of the AU. The AU aims to strengthen and advance the process of African political and socio-economic integration initiated by the OAU. The Union operates on the basis of both the Constitutive Act and the Abuja Treaty.

The AU has the following areas of interest: peace and security; political affairs; infrastructure and energy; social affairs; human resources, science and technology; trade and industry; rural economy and agriculture; and economic affairs. In July 2001 the OAU adopted a New African Initiative, which was subsequently renamed the New Partnership for Africa's Development (NEPAD). NEPAD, which was officially launched in October, represents a long-term strategy for socio-economic recovery in Africa and aims to promote the strengthening of democracy and economic management in the region. The heads of state of Algeria, Egypt, Nigeria, Senegal and South Africa played leading roles in its preparation and management. In June 2002 NEPAD heads of state and government adopted a Declaration on Democracy, Political, Economic and Corporate Governance and announced the development of an African Peer Review Mechanism (APRM—whose secretariat was to be hosted by the UN Economic Commission for Africa). Meeting during that month the Group of Seven industrialized nations and Russia (the G8) welcomed the formation of NEPAD and adopted an Africa Action Plan in support of the initiative. The inaugural summit of the AU Assembly, held in Durban, South Africa, in July 2002, issued a Declaration on the Implementation of NEPAD, which urged all member states to adopt the Declaration on Democracy, Political, Economic and Corporate Governance and to participate in the peer review process. By 2013 some 16 nations had joined the APRM process. NEPAD focuses on the following sectoral priorities: infrastructure (covering information and communication technologies, energy, transport, water and sanitation); human resources development; agriculture; culture; science and technology; mobilizing resources; market access; and the environment. It implements action plans concerned with capacity building, the environment and infrastructure. The summit meeting of the AU Assembly convened in Maputo, Mozambique, in July 2003 determined that NEPAD should be integrated into AU structures and processes. In March 2007 a special NEPAD summit held in Algiers, Algeria, issued a 13-point communiqué on the best means of achieving this objective without delay. The centrality of NEPAD as the overarching developmental programme for Africa was reaffirmed by a further summit meeting, convened in Dakar, Senegal, in April 2008, which also published a number of further key decisions aimed at guiding the future orientation of the Partnership. In February 2010 African leaders approved the establishment of the NEPAD

Planning and Co-ordination Agency (NPCA), a technical body of the AU, to replace the former NEPAD Secretariat, with the aim of improving the implementation of projects at country level. The Chairperson of the African Union Commission (AUC) exercises supervisory authority over the NPCA. NEPAD's Programme for Infrastructure Development in Africa (PIDA), of which the African Development Bank (AfDB) is the executing agency, aims to develop the continental energy, ICT, transport and transboundary water resources infrastructures. Some 80 programmes and projects aimed at regional integration, with a particular focus on developing the continental infrastructure, were being undertaken in the context of an AU/NEPAD African Action Plan (AAP) covering the period 2010–15.

The eighth AU Assembly, held in January 2007 in Cairo, Egypt, adopted a decision on the need for a 'Grand Debate on the Union Government', concerned with the possibility of establishing an AU Government as a precursor to the eventual creation of a United States of Africa. The ninth Assembly, convened in July 2007 in Accra, Ghana, adopted the Accra Declaration, in which AU heads of state and government expressed commitment to the formation of a Union Government of Africa and ultimate aim of creating a United States of Africa, and pledged, as a means to this end, to accelerate the economic and political integration of the African continent; to rationalize, strengthen and harmonize the activities of the regional economic communities; to conduct an immediate audit of the organs of the AU ('Audit of the Union'); and to establish a ministerial committee to examine the concept of the Union Government. A panel of eminent persons was subsequently established to conduct the proposed institutional Audit of the Union; the panel became operational at the beginning of September, and presented its review to the 10th Assembly, which was held in January–February 2008 in Addis Ababa, Ethiopia. A committee comprising 10 heads of state was appointed to consider the findings detailed in the review.

In March 2005 the UN Secretary-General issued a report on the functioning of the United Nations which included a clause urging donor nations to focus particularly on the need for a 10-year plan for capacity building within the AU. The UN System-wide Support to the AU and NEPAD was launched in 2006, following on from the UN System-wide Special Initiative on Africa, which had been undertaken over the decade 1996–2005.

In May 2012, with a view to increasing the involvement in the African development agenda of people of African origin living beyond the continent, the AU hosted the first Global African Diaspora Summit, in Midrand, South Africa.

In May 2013 the 21st ordinary session of the Assembly, which commemorated 50 years since the 1963 foundation of the former OAU, adopted a Strategic Plan to guide the activities of the Union during 2014–17. During 2013 the AU, AfDB and UN Economic Commission for Africa (ECA) were jointly developing AU Agenda 2063, a vision to guide the economic and social transformation of the continent over the coming 50 years, within the context of which a series of African Development Goals (ADGs) were being formulated. AU Agenda 2063 was to be finalized by June 2014.

PEACE AND SECURITY

The Protocol to the Constitutive Act of the African Union Relating to the Establishment of the Peace and Security Council, adopted by the inaugural AU summit of heads of state and government in July 2002, entered into force in December 2003, superseding the 1993 Cairo Declaration on the OAU Mechanism for Conflict Prevention, Management and Resolution. The Protocol provides for the development of a collective peace and security framework (known as the African Peace and Security Architecture—APSA). This includes a 15-country Peace and Security Council, operational at the levels of heads of state and government, ministers of foreign affairs, and permanent representatives, to be supported by a five-member advisory Panel of the Wise, a Continental Early Warning System, an African Standby Force (ASF) and a Peace Fund (superseding the OAU Peace Fund, which was established in June 1993). In March 2004 the Executive Council elected 15 member states to serve on the inaugural Peace and Security Council. The activities of the Peace and Security Council include the promotion of peace, security and stability; early warning and preventive diplomacy; peace-making mediation; peace support operations and intervention; peace-building activities and post-conflict reconstruction; and humanitarian action and disaster management. The Council was to implement the common defence policy of the Union, and to ensure the implementation of the 1999 OAU Convention on the Prevention and Combating of Terrorism (which provided for the exchange of information to help to counter terrorism and for signatory states to refrain from granting asylum to terrorists). Member states were to set aside standby troop contingents for the planned ASF, which was to be mandated to undertake observation, monitoring and other peace-support missions; to deploy in member states as required to prevent the resurgence or escalation of violence; to intervene in member states as required to restore stability; to conduct post-conflict disarmament and demobilization and other peace-building activities; and to provide emergency humanitarian assistance. The Council was to harmonize and co-ordinate the activities of other regional security mechanisms. An extraordinary AU summit meeting, convened in Sirte, in February 2004, adopted a declaration approving the establishment of the multinational ASF, comprising five regional brigades—the Central African Multinational Force, the Eastern Africa Standby Force, the Economic Community of West Africa (ECOWAS) Standby Force, the North African Regional Capability, and the Southern African Development Community (SADC) Standby Brigade—to be deployed in African-led peace support operations. A Policy Framework Document on the establishment of the ASF and the Military Staff Committee was approved by the third regular summit of AU heads of state, held in July 2004. It was envisaged that the ASF, which is composed of rapidly deployable multidimensional military, police and civilian capabilities, would become fully operational by 2015. In October 2010 the ASF conducted an exercise known as 'AMANI AFRICA', with pan-continental participation, in Addis Ababa. A roadmap on achieving the full operationalization of the ASF (ASF Roadmap III) was finalized in April 2011.

The extraordinary OAU summit meeting convened in Sirte, in September 1999 determined to hold a regular ministerial Conference on Security, Stability, Development and Co-operation in Africa (CSSDCA): the first CSSDCA took place in Abuja, Nigeria, in May 2000. The CSSDCA process provides a forum for the development of policies aimed at advancing the common values of the AU and AEC in the areas of peace, security and co-operation. In December 2000 OAU heads of state and government adopted the Bamako Declaration, concerned with arresting the circulation of small arms and light weapons (SALW) on the continent. It was envisaged that the Central African Convention for the Control of SALW, their Ammunition, Parts and Components that can be used for their Manufacture, Repair or Assembly (Kinshasa Convention), adopted by Central African states in April 2010, would contribute to the AU's SALW control capacity. In September 2011 AU member states, met in Lomé, to debate a draft strategy on SALW control and to elaborate an African Common Position on global negotiations towards a comprehensive Arms Trade Treaty (ATT, to guide trade in conventional weapons). In May 2012 an African Regional Consultation on the ATT was organized at AU headquarters by the Regional Centre for Peace and Disarmament in Africa (UNREC, a subsidiary of the UN Office for Disarmament Affairs). The ATT was eventually adopted by the UN General Assembly in April 2013.

In January 2005 the AU Non-Aggression and Common Defence Pact was adopted to promote co-operation in developing a common defence policy and to encourage member states to foster an attitude of non-aggression. The Pact, which entered into force in December 2009, establishes measures aimed at preventing inter- and intra-state conflicts and arriving at peaceful resolutions to conflicts. It also sets out a framework defining, *inter alia,* the terms 'aggression' and 'intervention' and determining those situations in which intervention may be considered an acceptable course of action. As such, the Pact stipulates that an act, or threat, of aggression against an individual member state is to be considered an act, or threat, of aggression against all members states.

In recent years the AU has been involved in peace-making and peace-building activities in several African countries and regions. An AU Special Representative on Protection of Civilians in Armed Conflict Situations in Africa was appointed in September 2004.

In March 2011 a High-Level Ad Hoc Committee on Libya, comprising the leaders of Republic of the Congo, Mali, Mauritania, South Africa and Uganda, was formed to facilitate dialogue among the parties to the conflict that had emerged in Libya in early 2011. In mid-March the Committee urged an immediate halt to the military intervention in Libya that followed the adoption by the UN Security Council of Resolution 1973, which, *inter alia*, imposed a no-fly zone in Libya's airspace and authorized UN member states to take 'all necessary measures to protect civilians and civilian populated areas under threat of attack' by forces loyal to Col al-Qaddafi, 'while excluding a foreign occupation force of any form on any part of Libyan territory'. During March the Committee developed a Roadmap for the Peaceful Resolution of the Crisis in Libya, which urged an immediate cessation of hostilities; the facilitation by the Libyan authorities of the delivery of humanitarian assistance to vulnerable populations; the protection of all foreign nationals, including African migrant workers; the adoption and implementation of political reforms to eliminate the causes of the conflict; and better co-ordination of the international community's crisis resolution efforts. In early April it was reported that the Libyan regime had accepted the provisions of the AU Roadmap; the opposition forces active in Libya, however, refused to approve it, demanding that al-Qaddafi relinquish power. The 17th regular summit of AU heads of state and government, convened in late June–early July 2011, endorsed a set of Proposals on a Framework Agreement for a Political Solution to the Crisis in Libya, which had been developed by the High-Level Ad Hoc Committee in the context of the AU Roadmap. The summit also determined to disregard the arrest warrant for al-Qaddafi and members of his regime that had been issued in late June by the International Criminal Court. In early July the High-Level Ad Hoc Committee formally presented the Proposals for a Framework Agreement to the parties to the Libyan conflict; these were rejected by the rebel forces.

In mid-August 2011, following several months of civil conflict in Libya, and of Security Council Resolution 1973-mandated NATO action there, anti-government forces began to make significant advances against the al-Qaddafi regime, and, by 23 August, the rebels had taken control of the Libyan capital, Tripoli, and had conquered al-Qaddafi's fortified compound in the city. Meeting shortly afterwards, at the level of heads of state and government, the AU Peace and Security Council noted with deep appreciation the efforts undertaken by the High-Level Ad Hoc Committee on Libya in pursuit of a political solution to the ongoing conflict, within the context of the AU Roadmap and the Proposals on a Framework Agreement. The Council urged Libyan stakeholders to accelerate the process leading to the formation of an all-inclusive transitional government for that country, and emphasized the commitment of the AU to work with the UN, the League of Arab States, the Organization of Islamic Cooperation, NATO, and the EU, in support of the Libyan people. In late September the AU reiterated its concerns for the security of African migrant workers based in Libya. In September 2011 the AU recognized the National Transitional Council as the de facto government of Libya.

In early July 2013, in response to the overthrow in a coup d'etat of the elected Egyptian president, Mohamed Morsi, the AU Peace and Security Council suspended Egypt from participation in meetings of the Union; and authorized the establishment of an International Consultative Forum on Egypt (ICF-Egypt), also with Arab League and UN participation, to address and facilitate a co-ordinated response to the crisis. Furthermore, the Chairperson of the AU Commission immediately appointed an AU High-Level Panel for Egypt—under the leadership of Alpha Oumar Konaré, the former President of Mali and former Chairperson of the AU Commission—with a mandate to engage with Egyptian stakeholders, with a view to stimulating constructive political dialogue towards national reconciliation and a prompt return to constitutional order. The Panel aimed to consolidate advancements to the democratic process that had been attained since the popular uprising that had occurred in Egypt in January-February 2011 resulting in the overthrow of the authoritarian regime of former President Hosni Mubarak. The July 2013 suspension of Egypt represented the first suspension of one of the Union's principal financially contributing nations.

The EU assists the AU financially in the areas of: peace and security; institutional development; governance; and regional economic integration and trade. In June 2004 the European Commission activated for the first time its newly established Africa Peace Facility (APF), which represents the main source of funding to the African peace and security agenda, and has, since 2007, provided short-term crisis response funding, as well as contributing to longer-term peace and security institutional capacity building in connection with the AU and other African regional economic communities, in the areas of conflict prevention, post-conflict stabilization, and accelerating decision making and co-ordination processes. During 2007–13 APF funds were channelled as follows: €600m. to peace support operations (the Fund's core area of activity); €100m. towards the operationalization of the African Peace and Security Architecture and Africa-EU dialogue; €40m. for unforeseen contingencies; and €15m. towards early response. A €300m. replenishment of the APF, to cover 2011–13, was agreed in August 2011. It was announced in March 2012 that €11.4m. would be allocated through the APF over the period 1 February 2012–31 January 2014 towards the training of the ASF, and towards the establishment of an African e-library comprising documentation of relevance to the Force. APF programming for the period 2014–20 was being prepared in 2013.

INFRASTRUCTURE, ENERGY AND THE ENVIRONMENT

Meeting in Lomé, in July 2001, OAU heads of state and government authorized the establishment of an African Energy Commission (AFREC), with the aim of increasing co-operation in energy matters between Africa and other regions. AFREC was launched in February 2008. It was envisaged at that time that an African Electrotechnical Standardization Commission (AFSEC) would also become operational, as a subsidiary body of AFREC.

In 1964 the OAU adopted a Declaration on the Denuclearization of Africa, and in April 1996 it adopted the African Nuclear Weapons Free Zone Treaty (also known as the 'Pelindaba Treaty'), which identifies Africa as a nuclear weapons-free zone and promotes co-operation in the peaceful uses of nuclear energy; the Pelindaba Treaty entered into force in July 2009.

In 1968 OAU member states adopted the African Convention on the Conservation of Nature and Natural Resources. The Bamako Convention on the Ban of the Import into Africa and the Control of Transboundary Movement and Management of Hazardous Wastes within Africa was adopted by OAU member states in 1991 and entered into force in April 1998.

In June 2010 a consultative meeting was convened between the AU, the Common Market for Eastern and Southern Africa (COMESA), IGAD, and other regional partners, aimed at advancing co-ordination and harmonization of their activities governing the environment. It was envisaged that the AU would facilitate the development of a comprehensive African Environmental Framework, to guide pan-continental and regional economic community environmental activities. At that time the AU was in the process of integrating two regional fora—the African Ministerial Conference on Water (AMCOW) and the African Ministerial Conference on the Environment (AMCEN)—into its structures, as specialized institutes.

The 17th regular summit of AU heads of state and government, held in late June–early July 2011, adopted a decision inviting member states to work on a common African position for the United Nations Conference on Sustainable Development—UNCSD (also referred to as Rio+20), which was held in Rio de Janeiro, Brazil, in June 2012. Consequently an Africa Regional Preparatory Conference for UNCSD was convened, under the auspices of the UN ECA, in October 2011. The Conference noted emerging challenges to continental sustainable development, including low adaptive capacity to the effects of consequences of climate change; increasing severe biodiversity loss, desertification and land degradation, aggravated by the effects of climate change; and rapid urbanization. The conference urged the international community to meet its commitments to the continent in terms of transfer of financial and technological resources, and committed African states to enhancing efforts to improve national governance and development effectiveness, and to developing national strategies for sustainable development.

In February 2007 the first Conference of African Ministers responsible for Maritime Transport was convened to discuss maritime transport policy in the region. A draft declaration was submitted at the Conference, held in Abuja, outlining the AU's vision for a common maritime transport policy aimed at 'linking Africa' and detailing programmes for co-operation on maritime safety and security and the development of an integrated transport infrastructure. The subsequently adopted Abuja Maritime Transport Declaration formally provided for an annual meeting of ministers responsible for maritime transport, to be hosted by each region in turn. In July 2009 the AU Assembly decided to establish an African Agency for the Protection of Territorial and Economic Waters of African Countries. In June 2011 a task force was inaugurated to lead the development and implementation of a new '2050 Africa's Integrated Maritime Strategy' (2050 Aim-Strategy); the Strategy was to address maritime challenges affecting the continent, including the development of aquaculture and offshore renewable energy resources; unlawful activities, such as illegal fishing, acts of maritime piracy (particularly in the Gulfs of Aden and Guinea), and trafficking in arms and drugs; and environmental pressures, such as loss of biodiversity, degradation of the marine environment, and climate change. The first Conference of African Ministers responsible for Maritime-related Affairs was held in April 2012, alongside a workshop on developing the 2050 AIM-Strategy.

In January 2012 the Executive Council endorsed a new African Civil Aviation Policy (AFCAP); and also endorsed the African Action Plan for the UN 2011–20 Decade of Action on Road Safety.

In February 2009 AU heads of state adopted the Africa Mining Vision (AMV), which promotes the contribution of mining to sustainable local development, aiming to ensure that employees and communities benefit from industrial mining enterprises, and that priority is given to the protection of local environments. An African Minerals Development Centre was being established during 2012–13 by the AU, the ECA and the AfDB, with a mandate to implement the AMV.

POLITICAL AND SOCIAL AFFAIRS

The African Charter on Human and People's Rights, which was adopted by the OAU in 1981 and entered into force in October 1986, provided for the establishment of an 11-member African Commission on Human and People's Rights, based in Banjul, The Gambia. A Protocol to the Charter, establishing an African Court of People's and Human Rights, was adopted by the OAU Assembly of Heads of State in June 1998 and entered into force in January 2004. In February 2009 a protocol (adopted in July 2003) establishing an African Court of Justice entered into force. The Protocol on the Statute of the African Court of Justice and Human Rights, aimed at merging the African Court of Human and Peoples' Rights and the African Court of Justice, was opened for signature in July 2008. A further Protocol, relating to the Rights of Women, was adopted by the July 2003 Maputo Assembly. The African Charter on the Rights and Welfare of the Child was opened for signature in July 1990 and entered into force in November 1999. A Protocol to the Abuja Treaty Establishing the AEC relating to the Pan-African Parliament, adopted by the OAU in March 2001, entered into force in December 2003. The Parliament was inaugurated in March 2004 and was, initially, to exercise advisory and consultative powers only, although its eventual evolution into an institution with full legislative powers is envisaged. In March 2005 the advisory Economic, Social and Cultural Council was inaugurated.

In April 2003 AU ministers of labour and social affairs requested the AU Commission to develop, in consultation with other stakeholders, a pan-African Social Policy Framework (SPF). The SPF, finalized in November 2008, identified the following thematic social issues: population and development; social protection; labour and employment; education; health; HIV/AIDS, TB, malaria and other infectious diseases; the family; children, adolescents and youth; migration; agriculture, food and nutrition; ageing; disability; gender equality and women's empowerment; culture; urban development; environmental sustainability; the impact of globalization and trade liberalization; and good governance, anti-corruption and rule of law. The following areas of focus: drug abuse and crime prevention; civil conflict; foreign debt; and sport were given special consideration under the Framework. Recommendations were outlined in the SPF that were aimed at supporting AU member states in formulating and implementing national social policies.

The July 2002 inaugural summit meeting of AU heads of state and government adopted a Declaration Governing Democratic Elections in Africa, providing guidelines for the conduct of national elections in member states and outlining the AU's electoral observation and monitoring role. In April 2003 the AU Commission and the South African Independent Electoral Commission jointly convened an African Conference on Elections, Democracy and Governance. In February 2012 a new African Charter on Democracy, Elections and Governance entered into force, having been ratified at that time by 15 AU member states.

In recent years several large population displacements have occurred in Africa, mainly as a result of violent conflict. In 1969 OAU member states adopted the Convention Governing the Specific Aspects of Refugee Problems in Africa, which entered into force in June 1974 and had been ratified by 45 states at September 2013. The Convention promotes close co-operation with UNHCR. The AU maintains a Special Refugee Contingency Fund to provide relief assistance and to support repatriation activities, education projects, etc., for displaced people in Africa. In October 2009 AU member states participating in a regional Special Summit on Refugees, Returnees and IDPs in Africa, convened in Kampala, Uganda, adopted the AU Convention for the Protection and Assistance of IDPs in Africa, the first legally binding international treaty providing legal protection and support to people displaced within their own countries by violent conflict and natural disasters; the Convention entered into force in December 2012, and by September 2013 had been ratified by 17 countries. The AU aims to address pressing health issues affecting member states, including the eradication of endemic parasitic and infectious diseases and improving access to medicines. An African Summit on HIV/AIDS, TB and other related Infectious Diseases was convened, under OAU auspices, in Abuja in March 2001 and, in May 2006, an AU Special Summit on HIV/AIDS. TB and Malaria was convened, also in Abuja, to review the outcomes of the previous Summit. The 2006 Special Summit adopted the Abuja Call for Accelerated Action on HIV/AIDS, TB and Malaria, and, in September of that year AU ministers of health adopted the Maputo Plan of Action for the Operationalisation of the Continental Policy Framework for Sexual and Reproductive Health, covering 2007–10, aimed at advancing the goal of achieving universal access to comprehensive sexual and reproductive health services in Africa; in July 2010 the Plan was extended over the period 2010–15. In January 2012 the 18th AU Assembly meeting decided to revitalize AIDS Watch Africa (AWA), an advocacy platform established in April 2001, and hitherto comprising several regional heads of states, to be henceforth an AU Heads of State and Government Advocacy and Accountability Platform with continent-wide representation. AWA's mandate was to be extended to cover, also, TB and malaria. In March 2012 NEPAD and UNAIDS signed an agreement on advancing sustainable responses to HIV/AIDS, health and development across Africa. An AU Scientific, Technical and Research Commission is based in Abuja, Nigeria.

In July 2004 the Assembly adopted the Solemn Declaration on Gender Equality in Africa (SDGEA), incorporating a commitment to reporting annually on progress made towards attaining gender equality. The first conference of ministers responsible for women's affairs and gender, convened in Dakar, in October 2005, adopted the Implementation Framework for the SDGEA, and Guidelines for Monitoring and Reporting on the SDGEA, in support of member states' reporting responsibilities.

The seventh AU summit, convened in Banjul, in July 2006, adopted the African Youth Charter, providing for the implementation of youth policies and strategies across Africa, with the aim of encouraging young African people to participate in the development of the region and to take advantage of increasing opportunities in education and employment. The Charter outlined the basic rights and responsibilities of youths, which were divided into four main categories: youth participation; education and skills development; sustainable livelihoods; and health and well-being. The Charter, which entered into force in August 2010, also details the obligations of member states towards young people.

AU efforts to combat human trafficking are guided by the 2006 Ouagadougou Action Plan to Combat Trafficking in Human Beings. In June 2009 the AU launched AU COMMIT, a campaign aimed at raising the profile of human trafficking on the regional development agenda. It was estimated at that time that nearly 130,000 people in sub-Saharan Africa and 230,000 in North Africa and the Middle East had been recruited into forced labour, including sexual exploitation, as a result of trafficking; many had also been transported to Western Europe and other parts of the world.

In December 2012 the AU adopted a Plan of Action on Drug Control and Crime Prevention covering the period 2003–17.

TRADE, INDUSTRY AND ECONOMIC CO-OPERATION

In October 1999 a conference on Industrial Partnerships and Investment in Africa was held in Dakar, jointly organized by the OAU with the UN Industrial Development Organization, the ECA, the AfDB and the Alliance for Africa's Industrialization. In June 1997 the first meeting between ministers of the OAU and the EU was convened in New York, USA. In April 2000 the first EU-Africa summit of heads of state and government was held in Cairo, under the auspices of the EU and OAU, with participation also by Morocco. The summit adopted the Cairo Plan of Action, which addressed areas including economic integration, trade and investment, private-sector development in Africa, human rights and good governance, peace and security, and development issues such as education, health and food security. The second EU-Africa summit meeting was initially to have been held in April 2003 but was postponed, owing to disagreements concerning the participation of President Mugabe of Zimbabwe, against whom the EU had imposed sanctions. Held eventually (with participation by Mugabe) in December 2007, in Lisbon, Portugal, the second EU-Africa Summit adopted a Joint Africa-EU Strategy (JAES), outlining a long-term vision of the future partnership between the two regions. The third EU-Africa Summit, held in November 2010, in Tripoli, Libya, confirmed commitment to the JAES and adopted an action plan on co-operation, covering 2011–13. The fourth Africa-EU Summit—to convene in Brussels, Belgium, in April 2014—was to consider proposed reforms to the JAES, aimed at enhancing the implementation of agreed action programmes, and expanding engagement with civil society stakeholders. A fifth EU-Africa Business Forum was organized in September 2012, also in Brussels. A Joint Africa-EU Task Force meets regularly, most recently in February 2013, to consider areas of co-operation.

Co-operation between African states and the People's Republic of China is undertaken within the framework of the Forum on China-Africa Co-operation (FOCAC). The first FOCAC ministerial conference was held in October 2000; the second in December 2003; the third (organized alongside a China-Africa leaders' summit) in November 2006; the fourth in November 2009; and the fifth in July 2012. During the fifth FOCAC the Chinese President announced strengthened China-Africa co-operation in the following priority areas: support for sustainable development in Africa, including investment in the development of transnational and transregional infrastructure, agricultural technology, manufacturing, and small and medium-sized enterprises; implementation of an 'African Talents Program', which was to provide skills training; capacity building in meteorological infrastructure, in the protection and management of forests, and in water supply projects; and the implementation of a new 'Initiative on China-Africa Cooperative Partnership for Peace and Security'. Africa–USA trade is underpinned by the US African Growth and Opportunity Act (AGOA), adopted in May 2000 to promote the development of free market economies in Africa. Regular Africa-EU and Africa-South America ('ASA') summits are convened. The second ASA summit, convened by the AU and Union of South American Nations—UNASUR in Porlamar, Margarita Island, Venezuela, in September 2009, adopted the Margarita Declaration and Action Plan, covering issues of common concern, including combating climate change, and developing an alternative financial mechanism to address the global economic crisis. The third ASA summit took place in May 2012, in Malabo, Equatorial Guinea.

The AU aims to reduce obstacles to intra-African trade and to reverse the continuing disproportionate level of trade conducted by many African countries with their former colonial powers. In June 2005 an AU conference of Ministers of Trade was convened, in Cairo, to discuss issues relating to the development of Trade in Africa, particularly in the context of the World Trade Organization's Doha Work Programme. The outcome of the meeting was the adoption of the Cairo Road Map on the Doha Work Programme, which addressed several important issues including the import, export and market access of agricultural and non-agricultural commodities, development issues and trade facilitation.

The 1991 Abuja Treaty Establishing the AEC initially envisaged that the Economic Community would be established by 2028, following a gradual six-phase process involving the co-ordination, harmonization and progressive integration of the activities of all existing and future sub-regional economic unions. (The AU recognizes the following eight so-called regional economic communities, or RECs, in Africa: the COMESA, the East African Community—EAC and the SADC, which together comprise the EAC-COMESA-SADC Tripartite FTA initiative; the Communauté Economique des Etats de l'Afrique Centrale—CEEAC, the ECOWAS, the IIGAD, and the Union of the Arab Maghreb. The subsidiary RECs are the Communauté Economique et Monétaire de l'Afrique Centrale—CEMAC, the Community of Sahel-Saharan States—CEN-SAD, the Economic Community of the Great Lakes Countries, the Indian Ocean Commission—IOC, the Mano River Union, the Southern African Customs Union, and the Union Economique et Monétaire Ouest-Africaine—UEMOA.) The inaugural meeting of the AEC took place in June 1997. In July 2007 the ninth AU Assembly adopted a Protocol on Relations between the AU and the RECs, aimed at facilitating the harmonization of policies and ensuring compliance with the schedule of the Abuja Treaty.

In January 2012 the 18th summit of AU leaders endorsed a new Framework, Roadmap and Architecture for Fast Tracking the Establishment of a Continental Free Trade Area (CFTA), and an Action Plan for Boosting Intra-African Trade. The summit determined that the implementation of the CFTA process should follow these milestones: the finalization by 2014 of the EAC-COMESA-SADC Tripartite FTA initiative; the completion during 2012–14 of other REC FTAs; the consolidation of the Tripartite and other regional FTAs into the CFTA initiative during 2015–16; and the establishment of an operational CFTA by 2017. The January 2012 summit invited ECOWAS, CEEAC, CEN-SAD and the Union of the Arab Maghreb to draw inspiration from the EAC-COMESA-SADC Tripartite initiative and to establish promptly a second pole of regional integration, thereby accelerating continental economic integration. In the context of UNCSD, held later in that year, the summit recognized the need to strengthen the AU's institutional framework for sustainable development, deeming that promoting the transition to 'green' and 'blue' economies would accelerate continental progress towards sustainable development.

In February 2008 the AU Assembly endorsed the AU Action Plan for the Accelerated Industrial Development of Africa (AIDA), which had been adopted in September 2007 by the first extraordinary session of the Conference of African Ministers of Industry. The Action Plan details a set of programme and activities aimed at stimulating a competitive and sustainable industrial development process.

A roadmap and plan of action for promoting microfinance in Africa was finalized in 2009, and was under consideration in 2013.

The AU leadership participated in the summit meeting of G8 heads of state and government that was convened in Huntsville, Canada, in June 2010; the summit also included an African Outreach meeting with the leaders of Algeria, Ethiopia, Malawi, Nigeria, Senegal and South Africa.

In October 2010 the AU, ECA and the AfDB established a Joint Secretariat to enhance coherence and collaboration in support of Africa's development agenda.

RURAL ECONOMY AND AGRICULTURE

In July 2003 the second Assembly of heads of state and government adopted the Maputo Declaration on Agriculture and Food Security in Africa, focusing on the need to revitalize the agricultural sector and to combat hunger on the continent by developing food reserves based on African production. The leaders determined to deploy policies and budgetary resources to remove current constraints on agricultural production, trade and rural development; and to implement the Comprehensive Africa Agriculture Programme (CAADP). The CAADP, which is implemented through NEPAD, focuses on the four pillars of sustainable land and water management; market access; food supply and hunger; and agricultural research. CAADP heads of state have agreed the objective of allocating at least 10% of national budgets to investment in agricultural productivity. The CAADP aims by 2015 to achieve dynamic agricultural markets between African countries and regions; good participation in and access to markets by farmers; a more equitable distribution of wealth for rural populations; more equitable access to land, practical and financial resources, knowledge, information, and technology for sustainable development; development of Africa's role as a strategic player in the area of agricultural science and technology; and environmentally sound agricultural production and a culture of sustainable management of natural resources.

In December 2006 AU leaders, convened at a Food Security Summit in Abuja, adopted a declaration of commitment to increasing intra-African trade by promoting and protecting as strategic commodities at the continental level cotton, legumes, maize, oil palm, rice and beef, dairy, fisheries and poultry products; and promoting and protecting as strategic commodities at the sub-regional level cassava, sorghum and millet. The AU leaders also declared a commitment to initiating the implementation of the NEPAD Home-grown School Feeding Project, the African Regional Nutrition Strategy, the NEPAD African Nutrition Initiative, and the NEPAD 10-Year Strategy for Combating Vitamin and Mineral Deficiency.

In December 2006 the AU adopted the Great Green Wall of the Sahara and Sahel Initiative (GGWSSI), comprising a set of cross-sectoral actions and interventions (including tree planting) that were aimed at conserving and protecting natural resources, halting soil degradation, reducing poverty, and increasing land productivity in some 20 countries in the Sahara and Sahel areas.

The AU's Programme for the Control of Epizootics (PACE) has co-operated with FAO to combat the further spread of the Highly Pathogenic Avian Influenza (H5N1) virus, outbreaks of which were reported in poultry in several West African countries in the 2000s; joint activities have included establishing a regional network of laboratories and surveillance teams and organizing regional workshops on H5N1 control.

In April 2009 AU ministers responsible for agriculture met to address the challenges to the continent posed by high food prices, climate change and the ongoing global financial and economic crisis. In July the 13th regular session of the Assembly issued a Declaration on Land Issues and Challenges in Africa, and the Sirte Declaration on Investing in Agriculture for Economic Growth and Food Security. The Sirte Declaration urged member states to review their land sector policies, and determined to undertake studies on the establishment of an appropriate institutional framework, and to launch an African Fund for Land Policy, in support of these efforts. The meeting also urged the establishment of a 'South to South Forum for Agricultural Development in Africa', recommitted to the Maputo Declaration, and urged member states to expand efforts to accelerate the implementation of the CAADP.

In January 2011 the Executive Council endorsed the Accelerated African Agribusiness and Agro-Industries Development Initiative (3ADI), which had been launched at a high-level conference on the development of agribusiness and agro-industries in Africa, convened in Abuja, Nigeria, in March 2010. The framework for the implementation of the 3ADI is the Strategy for the Implementation of the AU Plan of Action for the Accelerated Industrial Development of Africa (AIDA), adopted by African ministers responsible for industry, in October 2008; the Ministerial Action Plan for the Least Developed Countries (LDCs), adopted in December 2009 by LDC ministers responsible for industry and trade; and the Abuja Declaration on Development of Agribusiness and Agro-industries in Africa, adopted by the March 2010 Abuja high-level conference. The initiative aims to mobilize private sector investment, from domestic, regional and international sources, in African agribusiness and agro-industrial development, with the long-term objective of achieving, by 2020, highly productive and profitable agricultural value chains.

The First Conference of African Ministers of Fisheries and Aquaculture (CAMFA) was convened in September 2010, in Banjul. In January 2011 the Executive Council urged member states to adopt and integrate ecosystem approaches in their national and regional fisheries management plans; to strengthen measures to address Illegal, Unreported and Unregulated (IUU) fishing; and to eliminate barriers to intra-regional trade in fish and fishery products.

HUMANITARIAN RESPONSE

In December 2005 a ministerial conference on disaster reduction in Africa, organized by the AU Commission, adopted a programme of action for the implementation of the Africa Regional Strategy for Disaster Risk Reduction (2006–15), formulated in the context of the Hyogo Framework of Action that had been agreed at the World Conference on Disaster Reduction held in Kobe, Japan, in January 2005. A second ministerial conference on disaster reduction, convened in April 2010, urged all member states, and the RECs, to take necessary measures to implement the programme of action. In August 2010 the AU and the UN Office for the Co-ordination of Humanitarian Affairs signed an agreement detailing key areas of future co-operation on humanitarian issues, with the aim of strengthening the AU's capacity in the areas of disaster preparedness and response, early warning, co-ordination, and protection of civilians affected by conflict or natural disaster.

In August 2011 AU leaders, convened at the first AU Pledging Conference, promised to donate some US $350m. towards relief efforts to alleviate the impact of severe drought and famine in the Horn of Africa, which was reported at that time to be affecting up to 12.5m. people.

Finance

The 2013 budget, adopted by the Executive Council in July 2012, totalled US $278 2m., comprising an operational budget of $117.5m. and a programme budget $160.7m. Some 75% of the operational budget is financed by contributions—of 15% of the total each—from Algeria, Egypt, Libya, Nigeria and South Africa. Around 90% of programme budgetary funding derives from the AU's development partners.

Specialized Agencies

African Academy of Languages (ACALAN): BP 10, Koulouba-Bamako, Mali; tel. 2023-84-47; fax 2023-84-47; e-mail acalan@acalan.org; internet www.acalan.org; f. 2006 to foster continental integration and development through the promotion of the use—in all domains—of African languages; aims to restore the role and vitality of indigenous languages (estimated to number more than 2,000), and to reverse the negative impact of colonialism on their perceived value; implements a Training of African Languages Teachers and Media Practitioners Project; a core programme is the promotion of the Pan-African Masters and PhD Program in African Languages and Applied Linguistics (PANMAPAL), inaugurated in 2006 at the University of Yaoundé 1 (Cameroon), Addis Ababa University (Ethiopia), and at the University of Cape Town (South Africa); identified in 2009 some 41 'Vehicular Cross-Border Languages'; Vehicular Cross-Border Language Commissions were to be established for 12 of these: Beti-fang and Lingala (Central Africa); Kiswahili, Somali and Malagasy (East Africa); Standard modern Arab and Berber (North Africa); Chichewa/Chinyanja and Setswana (Southern Africa); and Hausa, Mandenkan and Fulfulde (West Africa); in Dec. 2011 organized a workshop on African languages in cyberspace; ACALAN is developing a linguistic Atlas for Africa; Exec. Dir Dr SOZINHO FRANCISCO MATSINHE.

African Civil Aviation Commission (AFCAC): 1 route de l'Aéroport International LSS, BP 2356, Dakar, Senegal; tel. 859-88-00; fax 820-70-18; e-mail secretariat@afcac.org; internet www.afcac.org; f. 1969 to co-ordinate civil aviation matters in Africa and to co-operate with ICAO and other relevant civil aviation bodies; promotes the development of the civil aviation industry in Africa in accordance with provisions of the 1991 Abuja Treaty; fosters the application of ICAO Standards and Recommended Practices; examines specific problems that might hinder the development and operation of the African civil aviation industry; 53 mem states; promotes co-ordination and better utilization and development of African air transport systems and the standardization of aircraft, flight equipment and training programmes for pilots and mechanics; organizes working groups and seminars, and compiles statistics; Sec.-Gen. IYABO O. SOSINA.

African Telecommunications Union (ATU): ATU Secretariat, POB 35282 Nairobi, 00200 Kenya; tel. (20) 4453308; fax (20) 4453359; e-mail sg@atu-uat.org; internet www.atu-uat.org; f. 1999 as successor to Pan-African Telecommunications Union (f. 1977); promotes the rapid development of information communications in Africa, with the aim of making Africa an equal participant in the global information society; works towards universal service and access and full inter-country connectivity; promotes development and adoption of appropriate policies and regulatory frameworks; promotes financing of development; encourages co-operation between members and the exchange of information; advocates the harmonization of telecommunications policies; 46 national mems, 18 associate mems comprising fixed and mobile telecoms operators; Sec.-Gen. ABDOULKARIM SOUMAILA.

Pan-African Institute of Education for Development (IPED): 49 ave de la Justice, BP 1764, Kinshasa I, Democratic Republic of the Congo; tel. (81) 2686091; fax (81) 2616091; f. 1973, became specialized agency in 1986, present name adopted 2001; undertakes educational research and training, focuses on co-operation and problem-solving, acts as an observatory for education; responsible for Education Management Information Systems (EMIS) under the Second Decade for Education for Africa (2006–15); publs *Bulletin d'Information* (quarterly), *Revue africaine des sciences de l'éducation* (2 a year), *Répertoire africain des institutions de recherche* (annually).

Pan-African News Agency (PANAPRESS): BP 4056, ave Bourguiba, Dakar, Senegal; tel. 869-12-34; fax 824-13-90; e-mail panapress@panapress.com; internet www.panapress.com; f. 1979 as PanAfrican News Agency, restructured under current name in 1997; regional headquarters in Khartoum, Sudan; Lusaka, Zambia; Kinshasa, Democratic Republic of the Congo; Lagos, Nigeria; Tripoli, Libya; began operations in May 1983; receives information from national news agencies and circulates news in Arabic, English, French and Portuguese; publs *Press Review*, *In-Focus*.

Pan-African Postal Union (PAPU): POB 6026, Arusha, Tanzania; tel. (27) 2543263; fax (27) 2543265; e-mail sg@papu.co.tz; internet www.upap-papu.org; f. 1980 to extend members' co-operation in the improvement of postal services; 43 mem. countries; Sec.-Gen. YOUNOUSS DJIBRINE (Cameroon); publ. *PAPU News*.

ARAB FUND FOR ECONOMIC AND SOCIAL DEVELOPMENT—AFESD

Address: POB 21923, Safat, 13080 Kuwait.

Telephone: 24959000; **fax:** 24815760; **e-mail:** hq@arabfund.org; **internet:** www.arabfund.org.

Established in 1968 by the Economic Council of the Arab League, the Fund began its operations in 1974. It participates in the financing of economic and social development projects in the Arab states.

MEMBERS

All member countries of the League of Arab States.

Organization

(September 2013)

BOARD OF GOVERNORS

The Board of Governors consists of a Governor and an Alternate Governor appointed by each member of the Fund. The Board of Governors is considered as the General Assembly of the Fund, and has all powers.

BOARD OF DIRECTORS

The Board of Directors is composed of eight Directors elected by the Board of Governors from among Arab citizens of recognized experience and competence. They are elected for a renewable term of two years.

The Board of Directors is charged with all the activities of the Fund and exercises the powers delegated to it by the Board of Governors.

Director-General and Chairman of the Board of Directors: ABDLATIF YOUSUF AL-HAMAD (Kuwait).

FINANCIAL STRUCTURE

The Fund's authorized capital is 800m. Kuwaiti dinars (KD) divided into 80,000 shares having a value of KD 10,000 each. In April 2008 the Board of Governors approved a transfer of KD 1,337m. from the Fund's additional capital reserves to paid-up capital, increasing subscribed capital from KD 663m. to KD 2,000m. At 31 December 2012 shareholders' equity amounted to KD 2,808.6m. (including KD 808.6m. in reserves).

Activities

Pursuant to the Agreement Establishing the Fund (as amended in 1997 by the Board of Governors), the purpose of the Fund is to contribute to the financing of economic and social development projects in the Arab states and countries by:

1. Financing economic development projects of an investment character by means of loans granted on concessionary terms to governments and public enterprises and corporations, giving preference to projects which are vital to the Arab entity, as well as to joint Arab projects;

2. Financing private sector projects in member states by providing all forms of loans and guarantees to corporations and enterprises (possessing juridical personality), participating in their equity capital, and providing other forms of financing and the requisite financial, technical and advisory services, in accordance with such regulations and subject to such conditions as may be prescribed by the Board of Directors;

3. Forming or participating in the equity capital of corporations possessing juridical personality, for the implementation and financing of private sector projects in member states, including the provision and financing of technical, advisory and financial services;

4. Establishing and administering special funds with aims compatible with those of the Fund and with resources provided by the Fund or other sources;

5. Encouraging, directly or indirectly, the investment of public and private capital in a manner conducive to the development and growth of the Arab economy;

6. Providing expertise and technical assistance in the various fields of economic development.

The Fund co-operates with other Arab organizations such as the Arab Monetary Fund, the League of Arab States and the Organization of Arab Petroleum Exporting Countries in preparing regional studies and conferences, for example in the areas of human resource development, demographic research and private sector financing of infrastructure projects. It also acts as the secretariat of the Co-ordination Group of Arab National and Regional Development Financing Institutions. These organizations work together to produce a *Joint Arab Economic Report*, which considers economic and social developments in the Arab states. The 2012 edition of the Report was themed 'Opportunities and Challenges of Access to Financial and Banking Services and Financing in the Arab World'. The Fund has, since 2011, organized jointly with the World Bank annual Arab Development Symposiums. The inaugural Symposium, held in March 2011, in Kuwait, concerned 'Water and Food Security in the Arab World', and the second, convened in June 2012, also in Kuwait, focused on the developmental role of micro, small and medium-sized enterprises in inclusive economic growth, job creation and poverty reduction. In September 2011 the Fund endorsed the so-called Deauville Partnership, which had been established by the Group of Eight industrialized countries in May in order to assist countries in the Middle East and North Africa undergoing social and economic transformations. The Fund joined some nine other international financial institutions active in the region to establish a Co-ordination Platform to facilitate and promote collaboration among the institutions extending assistance under the Partnership.

During 2012 the Fund approved 13 loans, totalling KD 379m., to help 12 new and one previously financed public sector projects in nine member countries. One private sector project was appraised in 2012: a storage services initiative in Egypt. At the end of that year total lending since 1974 amounted to KD 7,958.1m., which had helped to finance 499 projects in 17 Arab countries. In 2012 33% of financing was for transport and telecommunications projects, while 27% was for projects in the energy and electricity sector. During the period 1974–2012 70% of project financing was for infrastructure sector projects and 20% for projects in the productive sectors.

During 2012 the Fund extended 14 inter-Arab and national grants, totalling KD 2.8m., providing for technical assistance, training, research activities and other emergency assistance programmes. The cumulative total number of grants provided by the end of 2012 was 1,009, with a value of KD 183.4m.

In December 1997 AFESD initiated an Arab Fund Fellowships Programme, which aimed to provide grants to Arab academics to conduct university teaching or advanced research. During 2010 the Fund contributed US $100m. to a new Special Account to finance small and medium-sized private sector projects in Arab countries, which had first been proposed in January 2009. The Fund administers the Account, and hosted its inaugural meeting in October 2010.

Publications

Annual Report.

Joint Arab Economic Report (annually).

Statistics

LOANS BY SECTOR

	2012		1974–2012
Sector	Amount (US $ million)	%	%
Infrastructure sectors	292.0	77.0	69.7
Transport and telecommunications	124.0	32.7	26.3
Energy and electricity	103.0	27.2	33.1
Water and sewerage	65.0	17.1	10.3
Productive sectors	0.0	0.0	20.0
Industry and mining	0.0	0.0	5.8
Agriculture and rural development	0.0	0.0	14.2
Social services	42.0	11.1	7.6
Other	45.0	11.9	2.7
Total	379.0	100.0	100.0

Source: AFESD, *Annual Report 2012*.

ARAB MONETARY FUND

Address: Arab Monetary Fund Bldg, Corniche Rd, POB 2818, Abu Dhabi, United Arab Emirates.

Telephone: (2) 6171400; **fax:** (2) 6326454; **e-mail:** centralmail@amfad.org.ae; **internet:** www.amf.org.ae.

The Agreement establishing the Arab Monetary Fund was approved by the Economic Council of Arab States in Rabat, Morocco, in April 1976 and entered into force on 2 February 1977.

MEMBERS

Algeria	Morocco
Bahrain	Oman
Comoros	Palestine
Djibouti	Qatar
Egypt	Saudi Arabia
Iraq*	Somalia*
Jordan	Sudan*
Kuwait	Syria
Lebanon	Tunisia
Libya	United Arab Emirates
Mauritania	Yemen

* From July 1993 loans to Iraq, Somalia and Sudan were suspended as a result of non-repayment of debts to the Fund. Sudan was readmitted in April 2000, following a settlement of its arrears; a Memorandum of Understanding, to incorporate new loan repayments was concluded in September 2001. An agreement to reschedule Iraq's outstanding arrears was concluded in 2008. In 2011 an agreement was signed with Comoros concerning the settlement of that country's debt to the Fund. Somalia and Syria were in arrears at end-2012.

Organization

(September 2013)

BOARD OF GOVERNORS

The Board of Governors is the highest authority of the Arab Monetary Fund. It formulates policies on Arab economic integration and the liberalization of trade among member states. With certain exceptions, it may delegate to the Board of Executive Directors some of its powers. The Board of Governors is composed of a governor and a deputy governor appointed by each member state for a term of five years. It meets at least once a year; meetings may also be convened at the request of half the members, or of members holding half of the total voting power.

BOARD OF EXECUTIVE DIRECTORS

The Board of Executive Directors exercises all powers vested in it by the Board of Governors and may delegate to the Director-General such powers as it deems fit. It is composed of the Director-General and eight non-resident directors elected by the Board of Governors. Each director holds office for three years and may be re-elected.

DIRECTOR-GENERAL

The Director-General of the Fund is appointed by the Board of Governors for a renewable five-year term, and serves as Chairman of the Board of Executive Directors.

The Director-General supervises Committees on Loans, Investments, and Administration. Other offices include the Economic and Technical Department, the Economic Policy Institute, the Investment Department, the Legal Department, an Internal Audit Office, and the Finance and Computer Department.

Director-General and Chairman of the Board of Executive Directors: Dr Jassim Abdullah al-Mannai.

FINANCE

The Arab Accounting Dinar (AAD) is a unit of account equivalent to three IMF Special Drawing Rights (SDRs). (The average value of the SDR in 2012 was US $$1.53169.)

In April 1983 the authorized capital of the Fund was increased from AAD 288m. to AAD 600m. The new capital stock comprised 12,000 shares, each having the value of AAD 50,000. At the end of 2012 total paid-up capital was AAD 596.04m.

CAPITAL SUBSCRIPTIONS
(million Arab Accounting Dinars, 31 December 2012)

Member	Paid-up capital
Algeria	77.90
Bahrain	9.20
Comoros	0.45
Djibouti	0.45
Egypt	58.80
Iraq	77.90
Jordan	9.90
Kuwait	58.80
Lebanon	9.20
Libya	24.69
Mauritania	9.20
Morocco	27.55
Oman	9.20
Palestine	3.96
Qatar	18.40
Saudi Arabia	88.95
Somalia	7.35
Sudan	18.40
Syria	13.25
Tunisia	12.85
United Arab Emirates	35.30
Yemen	28.30
Total*	596.04

* Excluding Palestine's share (AAD 3.96m.), which was deferred by a Board of Governors' resolution in 1978.

Activities

The creation of the Arab Monetary Fund was seen as a step towards the goal of Arab economic integration. It assists member states in balance of payments difficulties, and also has a broad range of aims.

The Articles of Agreement define the Fund's aims as follows:

(*a*) to correct disequilibria in the balance of payments of member states;

(*b*) to promote the stability of exchange rates among Arab currencies, to render them mutually convertible, and to eliminate restrictions on current payments between member states;

(*c*) to establish policies and modes of monetary co-operation to accelerate Arab economic integration and economic development in the member states;

(*d*) to tender advice on the investment of member states' financial resources in foreign markets, whenever called upon to do so;

(*e*) to promote the development of Arab financial markets;

(*f*) to promote the use of the Arab dinar as a unit of account and to pave the way for the creation of a unified Arab currency;

(*g*) to co-ordinate the positions of member states in dealing with international monetary and economic problems; and

(*h*) to provide a mechanism for the settlement of current payments between member states in order to promote trade among them.

The Arab Monetary Fund functions both as a fund and a bank. It is empowered:

(*a*) to provide short- and medium-term loans to finance balance of payments deficits of member states;

(*b*) to issue guarantees to member states to strengthen their borrowing capabilities;

(*c*) to act as intermediary in the issuance of loans in Arab and international markets for the account of member states and under their guarantees;

(*d*) to co-ordinate the monetary policies of member states;

(*e*) to manage any funds placed under its charge by member states;

(*f*) to hold periodic consultations with member states on their economic conditions; and

(*g*) to provide technical assistance to banking and monetary institutions in member states.

Loans are intended to finance an overall balance of payments deficit and a member may draw up to 75% of its paid-up subscription, in convertible currencies, for this purpose unconditionally (automatic loans). A member may, however, obtain loans in excess of this limit, subject to agreement with the Fund on a programme aimed at reducing its balance of payments deficit (ordinary and extended loans, equivalent to 175% and 250% of its quota, respectively). From 1981 a country receiving no extended loans was entitled to a loan under the Inter-Arab Trade Facility (discontinued in 1989) of up to 100% of its quota. In addition, a member has the right to borrow under a compensatory loan in order to finance an unexpected deficit in its balance of payments resulting from a decrease in its exports of goods and services or a large increase in its imports of agricultural products following a poor harvest. In 2009 the access limit was doubled to 100% of paid-up capital.

Automatic and compensatory loans are repayable within three years, while ordinary and extended loans are repayable within five and seven years, respectively. Loans are granted at concessionary and uniform rates of interest that increase with the length of the period of the loan. In 1996 the Fund established the Structural Adjustment Facility, initially providing up to 75% of a member's paid-up subscription and later increased to 175%. This may include a technical assistance component comprising a grant of up to 2% of the total loan. In 2009, in order to enhance the flexibility and effectiveness of its lending to meet the needs of member countries affected by the global financial crisis, the Fund determined to extend an access limit of 175% for lending for both the public finance sector and for the financial and banking sector under the Structural Adjustment Facility. In 2007 the Fund established an Oil Facility to assist petroleum-importing member countries to counter the effects of the escalation in global fuel prices. Eligible countries were entitled to borrow up to 200% of their paid-up subscription under the new Facility. A new Short Term Liquidity Facility was approved in 2009 to provide resources to countries with previously strong track records undergoing financial shortages owing to the sharp contraction in international trade and credit.

Over the period 1978–2012 the Fund extended 160 loans, amounting to AAD 1,600m., to 14 countries. During 2012 the Fund approved lending of AAD 118m. (compared with AAD 116m. in 2011), including an automatic loan, amounting to AAD 7.4m., for Jordan; a compensatory loan (amounting to AAD 24m.) and ordinary loan AAD (21m.), extended to Yemen; an automatic loan (9.6m.), a compensatory loan (12.8m.) and a loan under the Structural Adjustment Facility (16.0m.) in the public finance sector, for Tunisia; and an AAD 27.4m. compensatory loan for Morocco, which aimed to support financing the purchase of agricultural imports.

The Fund's technical assistance activities are extended through either the provision of experts to the country concerned or in the form of specialized training of officials of member countries. In view of the increased importance of this type of assistance, the Fund established, in 1988, the Economic Policy Institute (EPI), which offers regular training courses and specialized seminars for middle-level and senior staff, respectively, of financial and monetary institutions of the Arab countries. During 2012 the EPI organized 13 training events, attended by 369 people. In April 1999 the Fund signed a Memorandum of Understanding with the International Monetary Fund (IMF) to establish a joint regional training programme. The Fund also co-operates with the IMF in conducting workshops and technical advice missions under the Arab Credit Reporting Initiative and the Arab Debt Markets Development Initiative.

AMF collaborates with Arab Fund for Economic and Social Development (AFESD), the League of Arab States and the Organization of Arab Petroleum Exporting Countries in writing and publishing a *Joint Arab Economic Report*. The Fund also co-operates with AFESD, with the technical assistance of the IMF and the World Bank, in organizing an annual seminar. The Fund provides the secretariat for the Council of Arab Central Banks, comprising the governors of central banks and the heads of the monetary agencies in Arab countries, and also serves as the technical secretariat of the Board of Arab finance ministers. In 1991 the Council established the Arab Committee on Banking Supervision. In 2005 the Council inaugurated a second technical grouping, the Arab Committee on Payments and Settlements Systems. In September 2011 the Fund endorsed the so-called Deauville Partnership, which had been established by the Group of Eight industrialized countries in May in order to assist countries in the Middle East and North Africa undergoing social and economic transformations. The Fund joined some nine other international financial institutions active in the region to establish a Co-ordination Platform to facilitate and promote collaboration among the institutions extending assistance under the Partnership.

TRADE PROMOTION

Arab Trade Financing Program (ATFP): POB 26799, Arab Monetary Fund Bldg, 7th Floor, Corniche Rd, Abu Dhabi, United Arab Emirates; tel. (2) 6316999; fax (2) 6316793; e-mail finadmin@atfp.ae; internet www.atfp.org.ae; f. 1989 to develop and promote trade between Arab countries and to enhance the competitive ability of Arab exporters; operates by extending lines of credit to Arab exporters and importers through national agencies (some 198 agencies designated by the monetary authorities of 19 Arab and five other countries); the Arab Monetary Fund provided 56% of ATFP's authorized capital of US $500m; participation was also invited from private and official Arab financial institutions and joint Arab/foreign institutions; administers the Inter-Arab Trade Information Network (IATIN), and organizes Buyers-Sellers meetings to promote Arab goods; by the end of 2012 the Program had extended lines of credit with a total value of $9,200m; Chair. and Chief Exec. Dr Jassim Abdullah al-Mannai; publ. *Annual Report* (Arabic and English).

Publications

Annual Report.

Arab Capital Markets (quarterly).

Arab Countries: Economic Indicators (annually).

Foreign Trade of the Arab Countries (annually).

Joint Arab Economic Report (annually).

Money and Credit in the Arab Countries.

National Accounts of the Arab Countries (annually).

Statistical Bulletin of Arab Countries.

Reports on commodity structure (by value and quantity) of member countries' imports from and exports to other Arab countries; other studies on economic, social, management and fiscal issues.

Statistics

LOANS APPROVED, 1978–2012

Type of loan	Number of loans	Amount (AAD '000)
Automatic	60	362,126
Ordinary	12	125,751
Compensatory	16	130,785
Extended	24	340,344
Structural Adjustment Facility	27	430,162
Oil Facility	3	32,489
Inter-Arab Trade Facility (cancelled in 1989)	11	64,730
Total	153	1,550,487

LOANS APPROVED, 2012

Borrower	Type of loan	Amount (AAD '000)
Jordan	Automatic loan	7,365
Morocco	Compensatory loan	27,350
Tunisia	Automatic loan	9,562
	Compensatory loan	12,750
	Structural Adjustment Facility	15,935
Yemen	Compensatory loan	24,000
	Ordinary loan	21,000

Source: *Annual Report 2012*.

COOPERATION COUNCIL FOR THE ARAB STATES OF THE GULF

Address: POB 7153, Riyadh 11462, Saudi Arabia.
Telephone: (1) 482-7777; **fax:** (1) 482-9089; **internet:** www.gcc-sg.org.

More generally known as the Gulf Cooperation Council (GCC), the organization was established on 25 May 1981 by six Arab states. Its charter describes the GCC as providing the means for realizing co-ordination, integration and co-operation in all economic, social and cultural affairs.

MEMBERS*

Bahrain	Oman	Saudi Arabia
Kuwait	Qatar	United Arab Emirates

* In December 2001 the Supreme Council admitted Yemen (which applied to join the organization as a full member in 1996) as a member of the GCC's Arab Bureau of Education for the Gulf States, as a participant in meetings of GCC ministers of health and of labour and social affairs, and, alongside the GCC member states, as a participant in the biennial Gulf Cup football tournament. In September 2008 Yemen's inclusion in future GCC development planning was approved and Yemen was admitted to GCC control and auditing apparatuses. Negotiations were ongoing on the full accession of Yemen to the GCC by 2016. In May 2011 the GCC invited Jordan and Morocco to submit membership applications.

Organization

(September 2013)

SUPREME COUNCIL

The Supreme Council is the highest authority of the GCC. It comprises the heads of member states and holds one regular session annually, and in emergency session if demanded by two or more members. The Council also convenes an annual consultative meeting. The Presidency of the Council is undertaken by each state in turn, in alphabetical order. The Supreme Council draws up the overall policy of the organization; it discusses recommendations and laws presented to it by the Ministerial Council and the Secretariat General in preparation for endorsement. The GCC's charter provided for the creation of a commission for the settlement of disputes between member states, to be attached to and appointed by the Supreme Council. The Supreme Council convenes the commission for the settlement of disputes on an ad hoc basis to address altercations between member states as they arise. An extraordinary summit of GCC heads of state was convened in May 2012 to discuss an ongoing initiative to transform the Council into an Arab Gulf Union Council (q.v.). The 33rd annual meeting of the Supreme Council was convened in December 2012 in Manama, Bahrain.

CONSULTATIVE COMMISSION

The Consultative Commission, comprising 30 members (five from each member state) nominated for a three-year period, acts as an advisory body, considering matters referred to it by the Supreme Council. In 2013 the creation of a regulatory authority to oversee food and drugs in the GCC states; the establishment of a joint GCC specialized centre for public and preventative health; the development of a GCC media strategy; the creation of mechanisms aimed at combating corruption and removing obstacles to development; and children's cultural programmes were under consideration by the Commission.

COMMISSION FOR THE SETTLEMENT OF DISPUTES

The Commission for the Settlement of Disputes is formed by the Supreme Council for each case, on an ad hoc basis in accordance with the nature of each specific dispute.

MINISTERIAL COUNCIL

The Ministerial Council consists of the ministers of foreign affairs of member states (or other ministers acting on their behalf), meeting every three months, and in emergency session if demanded by two or more members. It prepares for the meetings of the Supreme Council, and draws up policies, recommendations, studies and projects aimed at developing co-operation and co-ordination among member states in various spheres. GCC ministerial committees have been established in a number of areas of co-operation; sectoral ministerial meetings are held periodically.

SECRETARIAT GENERAL

The Secretariat assists member states in implementing recommendations by the Supreme and Ministerial Councils, and prepares reports and studies, budgets and accounts. The Secretary-General is appointed by the Supreme Council for a three-year term renewable once. The position is rotated among member states in order to ensure equal representation. The Secretariat comprises the following divisions and departments: Political Affairs; Economic Affairs; Human and Environmental Affairs; Military Affairs; Security; Legal Affairs; the Office of the Secretary-General; Finance and Administrative Affairs; a Patent Bureau; an Administrative Development Unit; an Internal Auditing Unit; an Information Centre; and a Telecommunications Bureau (based in Bahrain). Five Assistant Secretaries-General are appointed by the Ministerial Council upon the recommendation of the Secretary-General. All member states contribute in equal proportions towards the budget of the Secretariat. There is a GCC delegation office in Brussels, Belgium.

Secretary-General: ABDUL LATIF BIN RASHID AL-ZAYANI (Bahrain).

Activities

ARAB GULF UNION COUNCIL

In December 2011 the 32nd summit of the Supreme Council welcomed a proposal by King Abdullah of Saudi Arabia specifying that the basis of GCC collaboration should progress from the stage of co-operation to full political, economic and military union (as an 'Arab Gulf Union Council'). The summit directed the Ministerial Council to form a specialized commission, to comprise three members from each member state, to study the proposal. The initiative was regarded as a means of consolidating the organization in view of the Arab uprisings of 2011 and consequent changed regional political landscape. At the inaugural meeting of the commission, held in February 2012, the GCC Secretary-General noted that the full economic integration of member states would precede political union. An extraordinary summit of GCC heads of state was held in May to discuss the initiative, which, at that time, was most strongly supported by the Governments of Saudi Arabia and Bahrain.

COMPREHENSIVE DEVELOPMENT STRATEGY FOR 2010–25

In December 1998 the Supreme Council approved a long-term strategy for regional development, covering the period 2000–25, aimed at achieving integrated, sustainable development in all member states and the co-ordination of national development plans. Meeting in December 2010 the 31st summit of GCC heads of state adopted a revised comprehensive development strategy for member states, covering 2010–25. The updated strategy identified several ongoing challenges including: promoting integration over competition, and collective over national development efforts, within the grouping; scarcity of water resources in the region, the high salinity content in local water, and the high cost of alternative water resources; limitations on cultivating farming lands; the disproportionate engagement of national citizens in state employment and dependence on foreign workers in the non-governmental labour market; incompatibility between educational and training goals and the needs of the labour market (the region has a large non-resident population); investment decline in certain sectors, and migration of national capital abroad owing to limited local investment opportunities; the existence of budgetary deficits; the potential impacts of climate change on the environment; and global development, security and economic challenges. The following strategic goals were outlined: pursuing a framework enabling sustainable development; ensuring adequate water for development needs; achieving self-sufficiency in meeting the security and defence needs of the GCC development process; achieving integrated economic partnership; eliminating sources of vulnerability from the GCC economic environment; deriving maximum benefit from infrastructure facilities; technical and scientific capacity building; enhancing social development in the areas of education and training, health, and intellectual and cultural development; and enhancing the productivity of the GCC labour force.

ECONOMIC CO-OPERATION

In November 1981 GCC ministers drew up a Unified Economic Agreement covering freedom of movement of people and capital, the abolition of customs duties, technical co-operation, harmonization of banking regulations and financial and monetary co-ordination. At the same time GCC heads of state approved the formation of a Gulf Investment Corporation, to be based in Kuwait (see below). In March 1983 customs duties on domestic products of the Gulf states were abolished, and new regulations allowing free movement of workers and vehicles between member states were also introduced. A common minimum customs levy (of between 4% and 20%) on foreign imports was imposed in 1986. In February 1987 the governors of the member states' central banks agreed in principle to co-ordinate their rates of exchange, and this was approved by the Supreme Council in November. It was subsequently agreed to link the Gulf currencies to a 'basket' of other currencies. In April 1993 the Gulf central bank governors decided to allow Kuwait's currency to become part of the GCC monetary system that was established following Iraq's invasion of Kuwait in order to defend the Gulf currencies. Meeting in September 1992 GCC ministers reached agreement on the application of a unified system of tariffs by March 1993. A meeting of the Supreme Council, held in December 1992, however, decided to mandate GCC officials to formulate a plan for the introduction of common external tariffs, to be presented to the Council in December 1993. Only the tax on tobacco products was to be standardized from March 1993, at a rate of 50% (later increased to 70%). In April 1994 ministers of finance agreed to pursue a gradual approach to the unification of tariffs. A technical committee, which had been constituted to consider aspects of establishing a customs union, met for the first time in June 1998. In November 1999 the Supreme Council concluded an agreement to establish the customs union by 1 March 2005. However, in December 2001 the Supreme Council, meeting in Muscat, Oman, adopted a new agreement on regional economic union ('Economic Agreement Between the Arab GCC States'), which superseded the 1981 Unified Economic Agreement. The new accord brought forward the deadline for the establishment of the proposed customs union to 1 January 2003 and provided for a standard tariff level of 5% for foreign imports (with the exception of 53 essential commodities previously exempted by the Supreme Council). The agreement also provided for the introduction, by January 2010, of a GCC single currency, linked to the US dollar (this deadline, however, was not met—see below). The Supreme Council also authorized the creation of a new independent authority for overseeing the unification of specifications and standards throughout member states.

The GCC customs union was launched, as planned, on 1 January 2003. In July the GCC entered into negotiations with Yemen on harmonizing economic legislation. In December 2005 the Supreme Council approved standards for the introduction of the planned single currency. The GCC Common Market was inaugurated on 1 January 2008. Oman and the United Arab Emirates (UAE) withdrew from the process to introduce a single currency in 2007 and 2009, respectively. An accord on Gulf Monetary Union was signed in June 2009 by Bahrain, Kuwait, Qatar and Saudi Arabia, and was approved by the 30th meeting of the Supreme Council, held in Kuwait in December. In May 2010 the GCC Secretary-General stated that the introduction of the single currency was unlikely to occur for at least five years.

In April 1993 GCC central bank governors agreed to establish a joint banking supervisory committee, in order to devise rules for GCC banks to operate in other member states. In December 1997 GCC heads of state authorized guidelines to this effect. These were to apply only to banks established at least 10 years previously with a share capital of more than US $100m.

The 29th summit meeting of heads of state, held in Muscat, in December 2008, discussed the ongoing global financial crisis, and directed relevant ministerial committees to intensify co-ordination among member states to mitigate the negative impact of the global situation on the region's economies.

TRADE AND INDUSTRY

In 1985 the Supreme Council endorsed a common industrial strategy for the Gulf states. It approved regulations stipulating that priority should be given to imports of GCC industrial products, and permitting GCC investors to obtain loans from GCC industrial development banks. In November 1986 resolutions were adopted on the protection of industrial products, and on the co-ordination of industrial projects, in order to avoid duplication. In 1989 the Ministerial Council approved the Unified GCC Foreign Capital Investment Regulations, which aimed to attract foreign investment and to co-ordinate investments among GCC countries. Further guidelines to promote foreign investment in the region were formulated during 1997. In December 1999 the Supreme Council amended the conditions determining rules of origin on industrial products in order to promote direct investment and intra-Community trade. In September 2000 GCC ministers of commerce agreed to establish a technical committee to promote the development of electronic commerce and trade among member states.

In December 1992 the Supreme Council endorsed Patent Regulations for GCC member states to facilitate regional scientific and technological research. A GCC Patent Office for the protection of intellectual property in the region was established in 1998. In December 2006 the Supreme Council endorsed a system to unify trademarks in GCC states.

In December 2001 the Supreme council adopted unified procedures and measures for facilitating the intra-regional movement of people and commercial traffic, as well as unified standards in the areas of education and health care. In August 2003 the GCC adopted new measures permitting nationals of its member states to work in, and to seek loans from financial institutions in, any other member state. In December 2005 the Supreme Council approved a plan to unify member states' trade policies. The Council adopted further measures aimed at facilitating the movement of people, goods and services between member countries, with consideration given to environmental issues and consumer protection, and agreed to permit GCC citizens to undertake commercial activities in all member states.

AGRICULTURE

The GCC states aim to achieve food security through the best utilization of regional natural resources. A unified agricultural policy for GCC countries, initially endorsed in 1985, was revised in December 1996. Unified agricultural quarantine laws were adopted by the Supreme Council in December 2001. In 2006 an agreement was entered into with FAO on the regional implementation of a technical programme on agricultural quarantine development, aimed at protecting the agricultural sector from plant disease epidemics. A permanent committee on fisheries aims to co-ordinate national fisheries policies, to establish designated fishing periods and to undertake surveys of the fishing potential in the Arabian (Persian) Gulf. In December 2010 the summit meeting of GCC leaders called for a comprehensive review of agricultural sector development, with a focus on policies aimed at preserving water resources; the regional scarcity of water, and its high saline content, have been an area of concern.

COMMUNICATIONS, INFORMATION AND TRANSPORT

GCC ministers responsible for telecommunications, posts and information technology, and ministers of information, convene regularly. The 2001 Economic Agreement provided for member states to take all necessary means to ensure the integration of their telecommunication policies, including telephone, post and data network services. A simplified passport system was approved in 1997 to facilitate travel between member countries. In December 2006 the Supreme Council requested that all GCC members conclude studies on the implementation of a GCC rail network, which was to interconnect all member states, with a view to enhancing economic development. It was announced in 2010 that the GCC states would invest nearly US $119,600m. in infrastructure projects during 2010–20, of which 90% was to be allocated to developing the regional rail infrastructure. A report, issued in April 2011, on the status of GCC infrastructure development schemes, stated that some $452m. of infrastructure projects were under way in the region. It was envisaged that increased expenditure on infrastructure projects, representing a diversification from petroleum-based growth, might strengthen the regional economy during the ongoing global economic slowdown.

In December 2012 the 33rd GCC summit meeting, held in Manama, Bahrain, approved the creation of a GCC commission for civil aviation.

ENERGY AND ENVIRONMENT

In 1982 a ministerial committee was established to co-ordinate hydrocarbons policies and prices. Ministers adopted a petroleum security plan to safeguard individual members against a halt in their production, to form a stockpile of petroleum products, and to organize a boycott of any non-member country when appropriate. In December 1987 the Supreme Council adopted a plan whereby a member state whose petroleum production was disrupted could 'borrow' petroleum from other members, in order to fulfil its export obligations. GCC ministers responsible for petroleum hold occasional co-ordination meetings to discuss the agenda and policies of OPEC, to which all six member states belong. In November 2003 ministers of petroleum determined to develop a GCC Common Mining Law.

The Unified Economic Agreement provided for the establishment and co-ordination of an infrastructure of power-generating stations and desalination plans. The 2001 Economic Agreement also stressed that member states should adopt integrated economic policies with regard to developing the basic utilities infrastructure. In December 1997 GCC heads of state declared that work should commence on the first stage of the plan to integrate the electricity networks of the six member countries, under the management of an independent authority. The estimated cost of the project was more than US $6,000m. The Gulf Council Interconnection Authority was established in 1999, with its headquarters in Dammam, Saudi Arabia. In 2001 a GCC Electric Interconnection Commission was established, which was to support the project. The first phase of the project was completed, and in trial operation, by 2009.

In February 2001 GCC ministers responsible for water and electricity determined to formulate a common water policy for the region. Ministers responsibility for electricity and water approved an Electric Interconnection Agreement in November 2009, setting out the relations between the contracting parties. A GCC conference on Power and Water Desalination was convened in Qatar in October 2011. A Common Water Emergency Plan is under development.

In December 2006 the Supreme Council declared its intention to pursue the use of nuclear energy technology in the GCC region. The Council commissioned a study to develop a joint nuclear energy programme, but emphasized that any development of this technology would be for peaceful purposes only and fully disclosed to the international community. In February 2009 representatives of GCC member states attended a workshop organized by the International Atomic Energy Agency (IAEA).

In December 2001 GCC member states adopted the Convention on the Conservation of Wildlife and their Natural Habitats in the Countries of the GCC; the Convention entered into force in April 2003. In December 2007 the Supreme Council adopted a green environment initiative, aimed at improving the efficiency and performance of environmental institutions in member states.

CULTURAL CO-OPERATION

The GCC Folklore Centre, based in Doha, Qatar, was established in 1983 to collect, document and classify the regional cultural heritage, publish research, sponsor and protect regional folklore, provide a database on Gulf folklore, and to promote traditional culture through education. The December 2005 summit of heads of state adopted the Abu Dhabi Declaration, which stressed that member states should place a strong focus on education and on the development of human resources in order better to confront global challenges. Periodically cultural fora are held, including on folklore (most recently in 2001); poetry (2004); drama (2009); and intellectual matters (2006). An occasional Exhibition of Creative Arts and Arabic Calligraphy is convened, most recently in 2006. A Strategy for GCC Youth was approved by the 33rd GCC summit in December 2012.

REGIONAL SECURITY

Although no mention of defence or security was made in the original charter, the summit meeting which ratified the charter also issued a statement rejecting any foreign military presence in the region. The Supreme Council meeting in November 1981 agreed to include defence co-operation in the activities of the organization: as a result, ministers responsible for defence met in January 1982 to discuss a common security policy, including a joint air defence system and standardization of weapons. In November 1984 member states agreed to form the Peninsula ('Al Jazeera') Shield Force for rapid deployment against external aggression, comprising units from the armed forces of each country under a central command to be based in north-eastern Saudi Arabia.

In December 1987 the Supreme Council approved a joint pact on regional co-operation in matters of security. In August 1990 the Ministerial Council condemned Iraq's invasion of Kuwait as a violation of sovereignty, and demanded the withdrawal of all Iraqi troops from Kuwait. The Peninsula Shield Force was not sufficiently developed to be deployed in defence of Kuwait. During the crisis and the ensuing war between Iraq and a multinational force which took place in January and February 1991, the GCC developed closer links with Egypt and Syria, which, together with Saudi Arabia, played the most active role among the Arab countries in the anti-Iraqi alliance. In March the six GCC nations, Egypt and Syria formulated the Declaration of Damascus, which announced plans to establish a regional peace-keeping force. The Declaration also urged the abolition of all weapons of mass destruction in the area, and recommended the resolution of the Palestinian question by an international conference. In June Egypt and Syria, whose troops were to have formed the largest proportion of the proposed peace-keeping force, announced their withdrawal from the project, reportedly as a result of disagreements with the GCC concerning the composition of the force and the remuneration involved. In December 1997 the Supreme Council approved plans for linking the region's military telecommunications networks and establishing a common early warning system.

In December 1997 the Council expressed concern at the escalation of tensions owing to Iraq's failure to co-operate with the UN Special Commission (UNSCOM). In February 1998 the US Secretary of Defense visited each of the GCC countries in order to generate regional support for any punitive military action against Iraq, given that country's obstruction of UN weapons inspectors. Kuwait was the only country to declare its support for the use of force (and to permit the use of its bases in military operations against Iraq), while other member states urged a diplomatic solution to the crisis. The GCC supported an agreement concluded between the UN Secretary-General and the Iraqi authorities at the end of February 1998, and urged Iraq to co-operate with UNSCOM in order to secure an end to the problem and a removal of the international embargo against the country. This position was subsequently reiterated by the Supreme Council. In September 2002 the US Secretary of State met representatives of the GCC to discuss ongoing US pressure on the UN Security Council to draft a new resolution insisting that Iraq comply with previous UN demands, setting a time frame for such compliance and authorizing the use of force against Iraq in response to non-compliance. In March 2003, in response to the initiation of US-led military action against Iraq for perceived non-compliance with the resulting Security Council resolution (1441, adopted in November 2002), the GCC Secretary-General urged the resumption of negotiations in place of military conflict. The GCC summit meeting held in Kuwait, in December 2003, issued a statement accepting the USA's policies towards Iraq at that time, emphasizing the importance of UN participation there, condemning ongoing operations by terrorist forces, and denoting the latter as anti-Islamic.

In December 2000 GCC leaders adopted a joint defence pact aimed at enhancing the grouping's defence capability. The pact formally committed member states to defending any other member state from external attack, envisaging the expansion of the Peninsula Shield Force from 5,000 to 22,000 troops and the creation of a new rapid deployment function within the Force. In March 2001 the GCC member states inaugurated the first phase of the long-envisaged joint air defence system. In December GCC heads of state authorized the establishment of a supreme defence council, comprising member states' ministers of defence, to address security-related matters and supervise the implementation of the joint defence pact. The council was to convene on an annual basis. Meeting in emergency session in early February 2003 GCC ministers of defence and foreign affairs agreed to deploy the Peninsula Field Force in Kuwait, in view of the then impending US military action against neighbouring Iraq. The full deployment of 3,000 Peninsula Shield troops to Kuwait was completed in early March; the force was withdrawn two months later. In December 2005 the Supreme Council, meeting in Abu Dhabi, UAE, agreed that the Peninsula Shield Force should be reconstituted. Proposals to develop the Force were endorsed by the 2006 heads of state summit, held in December, in Riyadh, Saudi Arabia. In December 2009 the 30th Supreme Council meeting ratified a new defence strategy that included upgrading the capabilities of the Peninsula Shield, undertaking joint military projects, and pursuing co-operation in combating the illegal trade of armaments to GCC member states.

In 1992 Iran extended its authority over the island of Abu Musa, which it had administered under a joint arrangement with the UAE since 1971. In September 1992 the GCC Ministerial Council condemned Iran's continued occupation of the island and efforts to consolidate its presence, and reiterated support of UAE sovereignty over Abu Musa, as well as the largely uninhabited Greater and Lesser Tunb islands (also claimed by Iran). All three islands are situated in the approach to the Strait of Hormuz, through which petroleum exports are transported. The GCC has condemned repeated military exercises conducted by Iran in the waters around the disputed islands as a threat to regional security and a violation of the UAE's sovereignty. Successive GCC summit meetings have restated support for the UAE's right to regain sovereignty over the three islands (and over their territorial waters, airspace, continental shelf and economic zone). In December 2010 the 31st summit meeting stated disappointment at the failure of repeated contacts with Iran over the matter. The meeting welcomed international efforts to engage with Iran over its controversial nuclear programme, particularly by the 5+1 Group (comprising the People's Republic of China, France, Germany, Russia and the United Kingdom). In December 2012 the 33rd summit meeting urged Iran to co-operate with the IAEA, deeming that its nuclear programme threatened international as well as regional security.

In March 2011, in response to a request from the Bahrain Government following a series of violent clashes between opposition protesters and security forces in that country, the GCC dispatched a contingent of Peninsula Shield Force troops (numbering some 1,000 from Saudi Arabia and 500 from the UAE, with more than 100 armoured vehicles), to Bahrain to protect strategic facilities and help maintain order.

The December 2005 summit of GCC heads of state issued a statement declaring that the Gulf region should be a zone free of weapons of mass destruction.

In December 2009 the 30th Supreme Council meeting emphasized the GCC's support for Iraq's sovereignty, independence and territorial integrity, on non-interference in Iraq's internal affairs, and on the preservation of its Arab and Islamic identity; and urged inclusive national reconciliation. The meeting also stated concern over acts of marine piracy in the Gulf of Aden, the Red Sea and other regional waterways, and emphasized the need to intensify co-operation in challenging the perpetrators. The December 2010 summit meeting expressed appreciation at efforts made by the GCC naval forces in combating maritime piracy and protecting shipping corridors.

In July 2007 the Ministerial Council determined to establish a GCC Disaster Control Center; a team of experts in disaster management was to be established there. In December 2010 the GCC summit approved a regional plan of action to prepare for and respond to radiation risks.

In December 2012 the 33rd GCC summit welcomed the inauguration of an International Excellence Center for Curbing Violent Extremism (Hidayah), in Abu Dhabi.

EXTERNAL RELATIONS

In June 1988 an agreement was signed by the GCC and European Community (EC) ministers of economic co-operation; this took effect from January 1990. Under the accord a joint ministerial council (meeting on an annual basis) was established, and working groups were subsequently created to promote co-operation in several specific areas, including business, energy, the environment and industry. In October 1990 GCC and EC ministers of foreign affairs commenced negotiations on formulating a free trade agreement. GCC heads of state, meeting in December 1997, condemned statements issued by the European Parliament, as well as by other organizations, regarding human rights issues in member states and insisted they amounted to interference in GCC judicial systems. In January 2003 the GCC established a customs union (see above), which was a precondition of the proposed GCC-European Union (EU, as the restructured EC was now known) free trade agreement. Negotiations on the agreement, initiated in 2003, were suspended by the GCC in May 2010, owing to a dispute over export duties; by 2013 the negotiations had not been formally restarted, although informal contacts were ongoing. In June 2010 the GCC and EU adopted a Joint Action Programme for 2010–13, aimed at strengthening economic, financial and monetary co-operation, as well as co-operation in other key strategic areas of investment, including trade, energy and the environment, transport, industry, telecommunications and information technology, education and scientific research. In June 2012 the GCC and EU determined to develop a joint work programme covering 2013–16 that would deepen bilateral co-operation in areas including peace and security, regional integration, economic growth, and sustainable development. In April 2008 the GCC and the European Free Trade Association (EFTA) finalized negotiations on the conclusion of a bilateral free trade agreement; the agreement was signed in July 2009, in Norway.

In September 1994 GCC ministers of foreign affairs decided to end the secondary and tertiary embargo on trade with Israel. In December 1996 the foreign ministers of the Damascus Declaration states, convened in Cairo, Egypt, requested the USA to exert financial pressure on Israel to halt the construction of settlements on occupied Arab territory. In December 2001 GCC heads of state issued a statement holding Israeli government policy responsible for the escalating crisis in the Palestinian territories. The consultative meeting of heads of state held in May 2002 declared its support for a Saudi-proposed initiative aimed at achieving a peaceful resolution of the crisis. GCC heads of state summits have repeatedly urged the international community to encourage Israel to sign the Nuclear Non-Proliferation Treaty. In December 2012 the 33rd GCC summit welcomed the granting of observer status to Palestine by the UN General Assembly in the previous month.

In June 1997 ministers of foreign affairs of the Damascus Declaration states agreed to pursue efforts to establish a free trade zone throughout the region, which they envisaged as the nucleus of a future Arab common market. Meanwhile, the Greater Arab Free Trade Area, an initiative of the League of Arab States, entered into effect on 1 January 2005.

The GCC-USA Economic Dialogue, which commenced in 1985, convenes periodically as a government forum to promote co-operation between the GCC economies and the USA. Since the late 1990s private sector interests have been increasingly represented at sessions of the Dialogue. It was announced in March 2001 that a business forum was to be established under the auspices of the Dialogue, to act as a permanent means of facilitating trade and investment between the GCC countries and the USA.

In December 2008 an agreement establishing a GCC-Singapore Free Trade Area (GSFTA) was signed, in Doha. An inaugural meeting of ministers of foreign affairs of the GCC and the Association of Southeast Asian Nations (ASEAN) was held in June 2009, in Manama. The meeting adopted a GCC-ASEAN Joint Vision as a framework for future co-operation between the two groupings. A second meeting, held in Singapore, in May–June 2010, approved an ASEAN-GCC Action Plan, which identified specific measures for closer co-operation to be undertaken in the two-year period 2010–12. Meeting in October 2012 ASEAN and GCC ministers responsible for foreign affairs determined to extend the Plan into 2013.

The GCC Secretary-General denounced the major terrorist attacks that were perpetrated in September 2001 against targets in the USA. Meeting in an emergency session in mid-September, in Riyadh, GCC ministers of foreign affairs agreed to support the aims of the developing international coalition against terrorism. Meanwhile, however, member states urged parallel international resolve to halt action by the Israeli security forces against Palestinians. In December the Supreme Council declared the organization's full co-operation with the anti-terrorism coalition. In December 2006 the Supreme Council determined to establish a specialized security committee to counter terrorism.

In March 2011 GCC leaders issued a statement urging the League of Arab States to take measures to protect citizens in Libya from the effects of violent measures against opposition elements being taken at that time by the regime of the then Libyan leader Col Muammar al-Qaddafi. In October the Council met in emergency session to discuss ongoing violent unrest in Syria, where suppression by the regime of anti-government protests during that year had resulted in more than 3,000 civilian fatalities. In early 2012 all GCC member states withdrew their diplomatic presence from Syria in protest at the Syrian regime's violent suppression of mass anti-government protests. In December the 33rd summit formally recognized the National Coalition for Syrian Revolutionary and Opposition Forces, formed in November, as the 'sole lawful representative' of the Syrian people.

In April 2011, in response to mounting political unrest in Yemen, the GCC proposed a mediation plan whereby President Saleh of Yemen would resign and receive immunity from prosecution, anti-Government activists would desist from protesting, and a new government of national unity would be appointed, pending the staging of a presidential election within two months of Saleh's proposed withdrawal. Saleh, however, refused to sign the plan at that time, and, in late May, the GCC mediation attempt was suspended. In September Saleh indicated that he might be willing to approve the plan although opposition elements expressed scepticism that Saleh would fully adhere to the peace initiative. In October the UN Security Council unanimously approved a resolution that expressed serious concern over the worsening security situation in Yemen; demanded that all sides immediately reject the use of violence to achieve their political goals; and called on all parties to sign the GCC peace initiative. In late November President Saleh finally signed the GCC-mediated agreement. Accordingly, Saleh relinquished his constitutional powers and, in February 2012, presidential elections were held.

In November 2012 GCC foreign ministers and their counterparts from Jordan and Morocco, meeting in Manama, Bahrain, endorsed a joint co-operation initiative; a meeting of GCC foreign ministers was convened in July 2013 to develop plans for implementing the initiative.

ASSOCIATED BODIES

Gulf Investment Corporation (GIC): POB 3402, Safat 13035, Kuwait; tel. 2225000; fax 2225010; e-mail gic@gic.com.kw; internet www.gic.com.kw; f. 1983 by the six member states of the GCC, each contributing 16.6% of the total capital; total assets US $6,292m. (Dec. 2012); investment chiefly in the Gulf region, financing industrial projects (including pharmaceuticals, chemicals, steel wire, aircraft engineering, aluminium, dairy produce and chicken-breeding); provides merchant banking and financial advisory services, and in 1992 was appointed to advise the Kuwaiti Government on a programme of privatization; CEO and Chief Investment Officer IBRAHIM A. AL-QADHI; publ. *The GIC Gazetteer* (annually).

Gulf International Bank: POB 1017, ad-Dowali Bldg, 3 Palace Ave, Manama 317, Bahrain; tel. 17534000; fax 17522633; e-mail info@gibbah.com; internet www.gibonline.com; f. 1976 by the six GCC states and Iraq; became a wholly owned subsidiary of the GIC (without Iraqi shareholdings) in 1991; in April 1999 a merger with Saudi Investment Bank was concluded; total assets US $20,134m. (30 June 2013); CEO Dr YAHYA ALYAHYA.

Publications

GCC News (monthly, available online in Arabic).

GCC: A Statistical Glance.

Statistical Bulletin on Water.

At-Ta'awun (periodical).

ECONOMIC COOPERATION ORGANIZATION—ECO

Address: 1 Golbou Alley, Kamranieh St, POB 14155-6176, Tehran, Iran.
Telephone: (21) 22831733; **fax:** (21) 22831732; **e-mail:** registry@ecosecretariat.org; **internet:** www.ecosecretariat.org.

The Economic Cooperation Organization (ECO) was established in 1985 as the successor to the Regional Cooperation for Development, founded in 1964.

MEMBERS

Afghanistan	Kyrgyzstan	Turkey
Azerbaijan	Pakistan	Turkmenistan
Iran	Tajikistan	Uzbekistan
Kazakhstan		

The 'Turkish Republic of Northern Cyprus' has been granted special guest status.

Organization

(September 2013)

SUMMIT MEETING

The first summit meeting of heads of state and of government of member countries was held in Tehran, Iran, in February 1992. Summit meetings are generally held at least once every two years. The 12th summit was held in October 2012, in Baku, Azerbaijan.

COUNCIL OF MINISTERS

The Council of Ministers, comprising ministers of foreign affairs of member states, is the principal policy- and decision-making body of ECO. It meets at least once a year.

REGIONAL PLANNING COUNCIL

The Council, comprising senior planning officials or other representatives of member states, meets at least once a year. It is responsible for reviewing programmes of activity and evaluating results achieved, and for proposing future plans of action to the Council of Ministers.

COUNCIL OF PERMANENT REPRESENTATIVES

Permanent representatives or Ambassadors of member countries accredited to Iran meet regularly to formulate policy for consideration by the Council of Ministers and to promote implementation of decisions reached at ministerial or summit level.

SECRETARIAT

The Secretariat is headed by a Secretary-General, who is supported by two Deputy Secretaries-General. The following Directorates administer and co-ordinate the main areas of ECO activities: Trade and investment; Transport and communications; Energy, minerals and environment; Agriculture, industry and tourism; Project and economic research and statistics; Human resources and sustainable development; and International relations. The Secretariat services regular ministerial meetings held by regional ministers responsible for agriculture; energy and minerals; finance and economy; industry; trade and investment; and transport and communications.

Secretary-General: SHAMIL ALESKEROV (Azerbaijan).

Activities

The Regional Cooperation for Development (RCD) was established in 1964 as a tripartite arrangement between Iran, Pakistan and Turkey, which aimed to promote economic co-operation between member states. ECO replaced the RCD in 1985, and seven additional members were admitted to the organization in November 1992. The main areas of co-operation are transport (including the building of road and rail links, of particular importance as seven member states are landlocked), telecommunications and post, trade and investment, energy (including the interconnection of power grids in the region), minerals, environmental issues, industry, and agriculture. ECO priorities and objectives for each sector are defined in the Quetta Plan of Action and the Istanbul Declaration; an 'Almaty Outline Plan', which was adopted in 1993, is specifically concerned with the development of regional transport and communication infrastructure. Meeting in October 2005, in Astana, Kazakhstan, the ECO Council of Ministers adopted a document entitled *ECO Vision 2015*, detailing basic policy guidelines for the organization's activities during 2006–15, and setting a number of targets to be achieved in the various areas of regional co-operation. The 10th ECO summit meeting, convened in Tehran, Iran, in March 2009, reaffirmed commitment to ongoing co-operation, and observed that the global financial crisis had originated in factors such as world-wide systemic weaknesses, unsound practices, and excessive use of resources, necessitating closer future co-operation among member states. At the 11th summit meeting, held in Istanbul, Turkey, in December 2010, it was reported that Iraq had applied to join ECO.

In 1990 an ECO College of Insurance was inaugurated. A joint Chamber of Commerce and Industry was established in 1993. The third ECO summit meeting, held in Islamabad, Pakistan, in March 1995, concluded formal agreements on the establishment of several other regional institutes and agencies: an ECO Trade and Development Bank, headquartered in Istanbul (with main branches in Tehran and Islamabad) (the Bank's headquarters was inaugurated in late 2006, and commenced operations in 2008); a joint shipping company (now operational), airline (project abandoned, see below), and an ECO Cultural Institute (inaugurated in 2000), all based in Iran; and an ECO Reinsurance Company (draft articles of agreement relating to its creation were finalized in May 2007) and an ECO Science Foundation, with headquarters in Pakistan. In addition, heads of state and of government endorsed the creation of an ECO eminent persons group and signed the following two agreements in order to enhance and facilitate trade throughout the region: the Transit Trade Agreement (which entered into force in December 1997); and the Agreement on the Simplification of Visa Procedures for Businessmen of ECO Countries (which came into effect in March 1998). In May 2001 the Council of Ministers agreed to terminate the ECO airline project, owing to its unsustainable cost, and to replace it with a framework agreement on co-operation in the field of air transport. In October 2012 the Council of Ministers endorsed the Charter of the Parliamentary Assembly of the Economic Cooperation Organization Countries (PAECO). PAECO's inaugural conference was convened in Islamabad, in February 2013; a Women Parliamentarians' Meeting was held within the framework of the conference. The second PAECO conference was to take place in Afghanistan in early 2014. The Assembly was to have a permanent secretariat, which was to be based in Islamabad and was to be financed by the Pakistan Government.

In September 1996, at an extraordinary meeting of the ECO Council of Ministers, held in Izmir, Turkey, member countries signed a revised Treaty of Izmir, the organization's founding charter. An extraordinary summit meeting, held in Aşgabat, Turkmenistan, in May 1997, adopted the Aşgabat Declaration, emphasizing the importance of the development of the transport and communications infrastructure and the network of transnational petroleum and gas pipelines through bilateral and regional arrangements in the ECO area. In May 1998, at the fifth summit meeting, held in Almatı, Kazakhstan, ECO heads of state and of government signed a Transit Transport Framework Agreement (TTFA) and a Memorandum of Understanding (MOU) to help combat the cross-border trafficking of illegal goods. (The TTFA entered into force in May 2006.) The meeting also agreed to establish an ECO Educational Institute in Ankara, Turkey; in April 2012 the Institute was formally inaugurated. In June 2000 the sixth ECO summit encouraged member states to participate in the development of information and communication technologies through the establishment of a database of regional educational and training institutions specializing in that field. The seventh ECO summit, held in Istanbul, in October 2002, adopted the Istanbul Declaration, which outlined a strengthened and more proactive economic orientation for the organization.

Convening in conference for the first time in March 2000, ECO ministers of trade signed a Framework Agreement on ECO Trade Cooperation (ECOFAT), which established a basis for the expansion of intra-regional trade. The Framework Agreement envisaged the eventual adoption of an accord providing for the gradual elimination of regional tariff and non-tariff barriers between member states. The so-called ECO Trade Agreement (ECOTA) was endorsed at the eighth ECO summit meeting, held in Dushanbe, Tajikistan, in September 2004; ECOTA entered into force in April 2008, having been ratified by Afghanistan, Iran, Pakistan, Tajikistan and Turkey. Heads of state and government participating in the 12th ECO summit meeting, held in October 2012, urged that ECOTA should become operational between the contracting parties during 2013. In May 2011 the Permanent Steering Committee on Economic Research, meeting for the first time, adopted the ECO Plan of Action for Economic Research. The first meeting of ECO Heads of Tax Administrations was convened in January 2013, in Tehran.

ECO ministers responsible for agriculture, convened in July 2002, in Islamabad, adopted a declaration on co-operation in the agricultural sector, which specified that member states would contribute to agricultural rehabilitation in Afghanistan, and considered instigating a mechanism for the regional exchange of agricultural and cattle products. In December 2004, meeting in Antalya, Turkey, agriculture ministers approved the Antalya Declaration on ECO Cooperation in Agriculture and adopted an ECO plan of action on drought management and mitigation. In March 2007, meeting in Tehran, ECO ministers approved the concept of an ECO Permanent Commission for Prevention and Control of Animal Diseases and Control of Animal Origin Food-Borne Diseases (ECO-PCPCAD). An ECO Veterinary Commission (ECO-VECO) was established, in Tehran, in October 2012. ECO implements a Regional Programme for Food Security (RPFS), supported by FAO, which comprises nine regional components, as well as a country programme for community-based food production in Afghanistan. In April 2007 an ECO experts' group convened to develop a work plan on biodiversity in the ECO region with the aim of promoting co-operation towards achieving a set of agreed biodiversity targets over the period 2007–15. The ECO member states agreed, in July 2008, to establish the ECO Seed Association (ECOSA); ECOSA hosted its first international seed trade conference in December 2009, and thereafter regular conferences have been held (the fifth was to be convened in September 2013, in Bishkek, Kyrgyzstan). In December 2008 the first ECO expert meeting on tourism adopted a plan of action on ECO co-operation in the field of ecotourism, covering 2009–13. In September 2007 the ECO Regional Center for Risk Management of Natural Disasters was inaugurated in Mashhad, Iran; the Center was to promote co-operation in drought monitoring and early warning. The sixth ECO International Conference on Disaster Risk Management was convened in February 2012, in Kabul, Afghanistan. In February 2006 a high-level group of experts on health was formed; its first meeting, held in the following month, focused on the spread of avian influenza in the region. The first ECO ministerial meeting on health, convened in February 2010, considered means of enhancing co-operation on health issues with regard to attaining the relevant UN Millennium Development Goals, and addressed strengthening co-operation in the areas of blood transfusion and pharmaceuticals. The meeting adopted the Baku Declaration, identifying key priority areas for future ECO area health co-operation. In June 2011 ECO ministers responsible for the environment adopted a Framework Plan of Action on Environmental Cooperation and Global Warming, covering the period 2011–15.

A meeting of ministers of industry, convened in November 2005, approved an ECO plan of action on privatization, envisaging enhanced technical co-operation between member states, and a number of measures for increasing cross-country investments; and adopted a declaration on industrial co-operation. The first meeting of the heads of ECO member states' national statistics offices, convened in January 2008 in Tehran, adopted the ECO Framework of Cooperation in Statistics and a related plan of action. An ECO Trade Fair was staged in Pakistan, in July 2008. The organization maintains ECO TradeNet, an internet-based repository of regional trade information.

ECO has co-operation agreements with several UN agencies and other international organizations in development-related activities. In December 2007 the ECO Secretary-General welcomed, as a means of promoting regional peace and security, the inauguration of the UN Regional Centre for Preventive Diplomacy in Central Asia (UNRCCA), based in Aşgabat. In that month ECO and the Shanghai Cooperation Organization signed an MOU on mutual co-operation in areas including trade and transportation, energy and environment, and tourism. An ECO-International Organization on Migration MOU on co-operation was concluded in January 2009. In March 2011 ECO, the UN Economic Commission for Europe and the Islamic Development Bank signed a trilateral MOU on co-operation. ECO has been granted observer status at the UN, the Organization of Islamic Cooperation and the World Trade Organization.

ECO prioritizes activities aimed at combating the cultivation of and trade in illicit drugs in the region (which is the source of more than one-half of global seizures of opium, with more than 90% of global opium production occurring in Afghanistan, and many ECO member states are used in transit for its distribution). An ECO-UNODC Drug Control and Co-ordination Unit (ECO-DOCCU) was inaugurated, in Tehran, in July 1999. During 2008–13 the ECO Secretariat and European Commission were jointly implementing a project entitled 'Fight against Illicit Drug Trafficking from/to Afghanistan'. The inaugural meeting of heads of INTERPOL of ECO member states was held in June 2010, in Tehran, and, in August, the first conference of ECO police chiefs with responsibility for anti-narcotics was convened, also in Tehran. In February 2013 representatives of ECO-DOCCU and ECO member states participated in an experts' group meeting on the scientific detection of crime, convened by INTERPOL in Tehran. In November 2012 a meeting of heads of anti-corruption organizations and ombudsmen of the ECO member states, held in Dushanbe, Tajikistan, approved the Statute of the ECO Regional Center for Cooperation of Anti-Corruption Agencies and Ombudsmen (RCCACO).

In November 2001 the UN Secretary-General requested ECO to take an active role in efforts to restore stability in Afghanistan and to co-operate closely with his special representative in that country. In June 2002 the ECO Secretary-General participated in a tripartite ministerial conference on co-operation for development in Afghanistan that was convened under the auspices of the UN Development Programme and attended by representatives from Afghanistan, Iran and Pakistan. ECO operates a Special Fund for the Reconstruction of Afghanistan, which was established in April 2004; by 2013 more than US $11m. had been pledged to the Fund. By that time the Fund had approved four ECO projects targeted towards the education and health sectors. ECO envisages connecting Afghanistan to the regional rail road system. In January 2010 the ECO Secretary-General participated in a Regional Summit Meeting of Afghanistan and Neighbours, hosted by the Turkish Government in Istanbul, with participation by representatives of regional governments and organizations; and, in July 2010, he attended the first International Conference on Afghanistan to be convened on that country's territory, in the Afghan capital, Kabul.

Finance

Member states contribute to a centralized administrative budget.

ECO Annual Economic Report.

ECO Bulletin (quarterly).

ECO Economic Journal.

ECO Environment Bulletin.

EUROPEAN UNION—EU

Presidency of the Council of the European Union: Lithuania (July–December 2013); Greece (January–June 2014); Italy (July–December 2014).

President of the European Council: HERMAN VAN ROMPUY (Belgium).

High Representative of the Union for Foreign Affairs and Security Policy: CATHERINE ASHTON (United Kingdom).

ENLARGEMENT

Turkey, which had signed an association agreement with the EC in 1963 (although this was suspended between 1980 and 1986, following a military coup), applied for membership of the EU on 14 April 1987. As a populous, predominantly Muslim nation, with a poor record on human rights and low average income levels, Turkey encountered objections to its prospective membership, which opponents claimed would disturb the balance of power within the EU and place an intolerable strain on the organization's finances. The Helsinki (Finland) European Council of 1999, however, granted Turkey applicant status and encouraged it to undertake the requisite political and economic reforms for eventual membership. By accelerating the pace of reforms, Turkey had made significant progress towards achieving compliance with the so-called Copenhagen criteria by 2004, including far-reaching reforms of the Constitution and the penal code. Turkish ambitions for EU membership were adversely affected in April 2004 by the failure of the UN plan for the reunification of Cyprus, which was rejected in a referendum by the Greek Cypriots in the south of the island (see above). Cyprus has been divided since 1974 when Turkey invaded the northern third of the country in response to a Greek-sponsored coup aiming to unite the island with Greece. Turkey refuses to recognize the Greek Cypriot Government and is the only country to recognize the Government of the northern section of the country, known as the 'Turkish Republic of Northern Cyprus', where it has 30,000 troops deployed. The requirement for the successful resolution of all territorial disputes with members of the EU meant that failure to reach a settlement in Cyprus remained a significant impediment to Turkey's accession to the EU, although the Turkish authorities had expressed strong support for the peace plan. In December 2004, however, the EU agreed to begin accession talks with Turkey in early October 2005, although it specified a number of conditions, including the right to impose 'permanent safeguard' clauses in any accession accord. The safeguard clauses related to the freedom of movement of Turkish citizens within the EU (seeking to allay fears about large numbers of low-paid Turkish workers entering other EU member states) and restrictions on the level of subsidy available to Turkey for its infrastructure development or agriculture. The EU warned that negotiations could last between 10 and 15 years and that eventual membership was not guaranteed. Turkey was also obliged to sign a protocol to update its association agreement with the EU prior to accession negotiations in October, to cover the 10 new members that had joined the organization in May 2004, including Cyprus. The Turkish Government had previously refused to grant effective recognition to the Greek Cypriot Government and, although it signed the protocol at the end of July 2005, it still insisted that the extension of the association agreement did not constitute formal recognition. In a report issued in November 2006, the Commission demanded that Turkey open its ports to Cypriot ships by mid-December, in compliance with its agreement to extend its customs union to the 10 new member states in 2005. Turkey announced that there could be no progress on this issue until the EU implemented a regulation drafted in 2004 to end the economic isolation of the 'Turkish Republic of Northern Cyprus', the adoption of which had been blocked by Cyprus. In December 2006, therefore, the EU Council stipulated that talks would not commence in eight policy areas affected by the restrictions placed on Cypriot traffic by Turkey. In its 2011 annual report on enlargement strategy and progress, the Commission expressed regret that negotiations had not opened in any new policy areas for over a year. By 2013 negotiations had opened in 13 of the total of 33 policy areas, with talks provisionally closed in one area; 18 areas remained blocked, and no new areas of negotiation had opened since mid-2010.

THE MIDDLE EAST AND THE MEDITERRANEAN

A scheme to negotiate a series of parallel trade and co-operation agreements encompassing almost all of the non-member states on the coast of the Mediterranean was formulated by the European Community (EC) in 1972. Association Agreements, intended to lead to customs union or the eventual full accession of the country concerned, had been signed with Greece (which eventually became a member of the Community in 1981) in 1962, Turkey in 1964 and Malta in 1971; a fourth agreement was signed with Cyprus in 1972. (In May 2004 Malta and Cyprus became members of the European Union—EU, as the EC became known in May 2003.) These established free access to the Community market for most industrial products and tariff reductions for most agricultural products. Annexed were financial protocols under which the Community was to provide concessional finance. During the 1970s a series of agreements covering trade and economic co-operation were concluded with the Arab Mediterranean countries and Israel, all establishing free access to EC markets for most industrial products. Access for agricultural products was facilitated, although some tariffs remained. In 1982 the Commission formulated an integrated plan for the development of its own Mediterranean regions and recommended the adoption of a new policy towards the non-Community countries of the Mediterranean. This was to include greater efforts towards diversifying agriculture, in order to avoid surpluses of items such as citrus fruits, olive oil and wine (which the Mediterranean countries all wished to export to the Community) and to reduce these countries' dependence on imported food. From 1 January 1993 the majority of agricultural exports from Mediterranean non-Community countries were granted exemption from customs duties.

In June 1995 the European Council endorsed a proposal by the Commission to reform and strengthen the Mediterranean policy of the EU. In November a conference of ministers of foreign affairs of the EU member states, 11 Mediterranean non-member countries (excluding Libya) and the Palestinian authorities was convened in Barcelona, Spain. The conference issued the Barcelona Declaration, outlining the main objective of the partnership, which was to create a region of peace, security and prosperity. The Declaration set the objective of establishing a Euro-Mediterranean free trade area. The process of co-operation and dialogue under this agreement became known as the Euro-Mediterranean Partnership or Barcelona Process until 2008.

In March 2008 the European Council approved a proposal formally to transform the Barcelona Process into a Union for the Mediterranean. In mid-July heads of state and of government from the 27 EU member states and from the member states and observers of the Barcelona Process attended the Paris Summit for the Mediterranean, at which the new Union for the Mediterranean was officially launched. (Bosnia and Herzegovina, Croatia, Monaco and Montenegro were also admitted to the Union for the Mediterranean.) Six co-operation projects were approved at the summit, which were to focus on: improving pollution levels in the Mediterranean; constructing maritime and land highways; civil protection; the creation of a Mediterranean Solar Plan; the establishment of a Euro-Mediterranean University (which was established in Slovenia in June 2008); and the launch of a Mediterranean Business Development Initiative. A meeting of Euro-Mediterranean ministers of foreign affairs, convened in Marseilles, in November, endorsed the new Union. A Euro-Mediterranean Regional and Local Assembly (ARLEM) held its inaugural meeting in Barcelona in January 2010, and a Secretariat was established in Barcelona in March.

The European Neighbourhood Policy (ENP) was established by the European Commission in 2004, to enhance co-operation with 16 countries that neighboured the EU following its enlargement. Algeria, Egypt, Israel, Jordan, Lebanon, Libya, Morocco, the Palestinian Autonomous Areas, Syria and Tunisia were covered by the ENP (which became known as the Southern Neighbourhood), which was intended to complement the Barcelona Process, in addition to several countries to the east of the Union (the Eastern Neighbourhood). Under the ENP, the EU negotiated bilateral Action Plans with 12 neighbouring countries, establishing targets for further political and economic co-operation over a three- to five-year period. The Action Plans aimed to build on existing contractual relationships between the partner country and the EU (e.g. an Association Agreement or a Partnership and Co-operation Agreement). The eventual conclusion of more ambitious relationships with partner countries achieving significant progress in meeting the priorities set out in the Action Plans was envisaged. On the expiry of the initial Action Plans, new documents were being adopted. In October 2008 Morocco was granted advanced status under the ENP, and in November 2012 negotiations for a new ENP Action Plan for 2013–17 were concluded.

The EU's primary financial instrument for the implementation of the Euro-Mediterranean Partnership was the MEDA programme, providing support for the reform of economic and social structures within partnership countries. It was followed by MEDA II, which was granted a budget of €5,350m. for 2000–06. In 2007 a new European Neighbourhood and Partnership Instrument (ENPI) replaced MEDA and the Technical Assistance to the Commonwealth of Independent States (TACIS) programme (which was concerned with EU co-operation with the countries of the former USSR). The ENPI was conceived as a flexible, policy-orientated instrument to target sustainable development and conformity with EU policies and standards. In 2007–13 some €12,000m. was available, within its framework, to support ENP Action Plans and the Strategic Partnership with Russia. An ENPI cross-border co-operation programme covered activities across the external borders of the EU in the south and the east, supported by funds totalling €1,180m. in 2007–13. From 2014 the ENPI was to be replaced by the European Neighbourhood Instrument (ENI).

Turkey, which had signed an Association Agreement with the EC in 1963 (although this was suspended between 1980 and 1986 following a military coup), applied for membership of the EU in April 1987 (see Enlargement). Accession talks began in October 2005, and effectively stalled in 2010. In May 2012 the EU and Turkey launched a new 'positive agenda', which sought to identify areas for future bilateral co-operation, and focus resources on them. Such areas included: conformity with EU law; political reform; visas, mobility and migration; trade; energy; counter-terrorism; and foreign policy issues.

Co-operation agreements concluded in the 1970s with the Maghreb countries (Algeria, Morocco and Tunisia), the Mashreq countries (Egypt, Jordan, Lebanon and Syria) and Israel covered free access to the Community market for industrial products, customs preferences for certain agricultural products, and financial aid in the form of grants and loans from the EIB. A co-operation agreement negotiated with the Republic of Yemen was non-preferential. In June 1992 the EC approved a proposal to conclude new bilateral agreements with the Maghreb countries, incorporating the following components: political dialogue; financial, economic, technical and cultural co-operation; and the eventual establishment of a free trade area. A Euro-Mediterranean Association Agreement with Tunisia was signed in July 1995 and entered into force in March 1998. A similar agreement with Morocco (concluded in 1996) entered into force in March 2000. (In July 1987 Morocco applied to join the Community, but its application was rejected on the grounds that it is not a European country.) In March 1997 negotiations were initiated between the European Commission and representatives of the Algerian Government on a Euro-Mediterranean Association Agreement that would incorporate political commitments relating to democracy and human rights; this was signed in December 2001 and entered into force in September 2005. An Association Agreement with Jordan was signed in November 1997 and entered into force in May 2002. A Euro-Mediterranean Association Agreement with Egypt (which has been a major beneficiary of EU financial co-operation since the 1970s) was signed in June 2001 and was fully ratified in June 2004. In May 2001 Egypt, together with Jordan, Tunisia and Morocco, issued the Agadir Declaration, in which they determined to establish an Arab Mediterranean Free Trade Zone. The so-called Agadir Agreement on the establishment of a Free Trade Zone between the Arabic Mediterranean Nations was signed in February 2004 and came into force in

March 2007. An interim EU Association Agreement with Lebanon was signed in June 2002, and entered into force in April 2006. Protracted negotiations on an Association Agreement with Syria were concluded in October 2004, and a revised version of the Agreement was initialled in December 2008. In May 2011 the EU announced that co-operation with Syria was to be suspended, owing to the violent suppression of anti-Government protests there from March (see below); no further progress was to be made with regard to the EU-Syria Association Agreement. In December 2011 the Council agreed that negotiations could commence towards Deep and Comprehensive Free Trade Agreements (DCFTAs) with Egypt, Jordan, Morocco and Tunisia. The EU established an election observation mission (EOM) to monitor the legislative elections held in Jordan in January 2013. An EOM observed legislative elections in Algeria in May 2012, and subsequently emphasized the need for increased transparency and for political parties to be given systematic access to the national electoral list. In July 2013 a €10m. programme to support governance in Algeria was adopted by the European Commission.

In January 1989 the EC and Israel eliminated the last tariff barriers to full free trade for industrial products. A Euro-Mediterranean Association Agreement with Israel was signed in 1995, providing further trade concessions and establishing an institutional political dialogue between the two parties. The agreement entered into force in June 2000. In late 2004 an ENP Action Plan on further co-operation was agreed by the EU and Israel; it was adopted by the EU in February 2005 and by the Israeli authorities in April of that year.

Following the signing of the September 1993 Israeli-Palestine Liberation Organization (PLO) peace agreement, the EC committed substantial funds in humanitarian assistance for the Palestinians. A Euro-Mediterranean Interim Association Agreement on Trade and Co-operation was signed with the PLO in February 1997 and entered into force in July. In April 1998 the EU and the Palestinian (National) Authority (PA) signed a security co-operation agreement. The escalation of violence between Israel and the Palestinians from September 2000 resulted in a deterioration in EU-Israel relations. The EU formed part of the Quartet (alongside the UN, the USA and Russia), which was established in July 2002 to monitor and aid the implementation of Palestinian civil reforms, and to guide the international donor community in its support of the Palestinian reform agenda. In late 2004 the EU agreed an Action Plan with the PA; it was adopted by the EU in February 2005 and by the PA in May. In November, on the basis of an agreement reached by Israel and the PA following Israel's withdrawal from Gaza and the northern West Bank, the EU established an EU Border Assistance Mission (EU BAM Rafah), which monitored operations at the Rafah border crossing between Egypt and the Gaza Strip until June 2007. An EU Police Mission for the Palestinian Territories (EUPOL COPPS) commenced operations in January 2006, with an initial three-year mandate, subsequently repeatedly extended, to support the PA in establishing sustainable and effective policing arrangements. At July 2012 the mission comprised 41 international staff and 70 local personnel. In June 2006 EU member states and the European Commission established the Temporary International Mechanism (TIM), an emergency assistance mechanism to provide support directly to the Palestinian people. On 1 February 2008 the European Commission launched a new mechanism, known as PEGASE, with a wider remit than the TIM. PEGASE aimed to support activities in four principal areas: governance (including fiscal reform, security and the rule of law); social development (including social protection, health and education); economic and private-sector development; and development of public infrastructure (in areas such as water, the environment and energy). In May 2012 the EU urged progress in the implementation of the 'unity' agreement signed by representatives of 13 Palestinian groups in May 2011, which aimed to result in the formation of a joint administration for the West Bank and Gaza, predominantly comprising figures independent of the two main factions. In September 2012 the European Commission announced funding of €100m. for the Palestinian Autonomous Areas, to be primarily allocated to water and sanitation and support for refugees; total EU funding to Palestine consequently totalled €200m. in 2012. In November the EU Foreign Affairs Council condemned rocket attacks against Israel launched from the Gaza Strip, and urged Israel to seek to ensure the safety of civilians while protecting its population from such attacks. At the end of July 2013 the Quartet welcomed the resumption of direct negotiations between the Israeli and Palestinian sides, with preliminary talks taking place in Washington, DC, USA, in late July.

Talks were held with Iran in April 1992 on the establishment of a co-operation accord. In December the Council of Ministers recommended that a 'critical dialogue' be undertaken with Iran, owing to the country's significance to regional security. In April 1997 the 'critical dialogue' was suspended and ambassadors were recalled from Iran, after a German court found the Iranian authorities responsible for having ordered the murder of four Kurdish dissidents in Berlin in 1992. Later that month ministers of foreign affairs resolved to restore diplomatic relations with Iran, in order to protect the strong trading partnership. In November 2000 an EU-Iran Working Group on Trade and Investment met for the first time to discuss the possibility of increasing and diversifying trade and investment. During 2002 attempts were made to improve relations with Iran, as negotiations began in preparation for a Trade and Co-operation Agreement. An eventual trade deal was to be linked to progress in political issues, including human rights, weapons proliferation and counter-terrorism. In mid-2003 the EU (in conformity with US policy) warned Iran to accept stringent new nuclear inspections, and threatened the country with economic repercussions (including the abandonment of the proposed trade agreement) unless it restored international trust in its nuclear programme. A 'comprehensive dialogue' between the EU and Iran (which replaced the 'critical dialogue' in 1998) was suspended by Iran in December 2003. In January 2005 the EU resumed trade talks with Iran after the Iranian authorities agreed to suspend uranium enrichment. However, these talks were halted by the Commission in August, following Iran's resumption of uranium conversion to gas (the stage before enrichment). Following Iran's removal of international seals from a nuclear research facility in January 2006, the EU supported moves to refer Iran to the UN Security Council. In mid-2006, during a visit to Tehran, Javier Solana presented to the Iranian authorities new proposals by the international community on how negotiations on Iran's nuclear programme could be initiated. In December, in a declaration on Iran, the Council criticized the country's failure to implement measures required by both the International Atomic Energy Agency (IAEA) and the UN Security Council in respect of its nuclear programme, and warned that this failure would be to the detriment of EU-Iran relations. EU trade sanctions against Iran were strengthened in August 2008, after Iran failed to halt its uranium-enrichment programme. In July 2010 EU ministers of foreign affairs adopted a new set of sanctions, prohibiting investment, technical assistance and technology transfers to Iran's energy sector, and also targeting the country's financial services, insurance and transport sectors. Sanctions were strengthened in May 2011. In late 2011 a report published by the IAEA indicated that Iran's ongoing nuclear programme may involve a military component. EU sanctions were further strengthened in January 2012, when a ban on imports of Iranian crude oil was imposed and the assets of the Iranian central bank within the EU were frozen. The EU also has strong concerns over the human rights situation in Iran. As a consequence, the EU imposed sanctions on 61 people believed to be responsible for significant human rights abuses; in March 2012 EU ministers of foreign affairs expanded these sanctions to cover a further 17 individuals. In October 2012 ongoing concern about Iran's nuclear programme, together with Iran's unwillingness to co-operate with the so-called E3+3 grouping (comprising the People's Republic of China, France, Germany, Russia, the United Kingdom and the USA, and led by the EU's High Representative for Foreign Affairs and Security Policy, Catherine Ashton), prompted the EU further to extend its sanctions regime.

A co-operation agreement between the EC and the countries of the Gulf Cooperation Council (GCC), which entered into force in January 1990, provided for co-operation in industry, energy, technology and other fields. Negotiations on a full free trade pact began in October, but it was expected that any agreement would involve transition periods of some 12 years for the reduction of European tariffs on 'sensitive products' (i.e. petrochemicals). In November 1999 the GCC Supreme Council agreed to establish a customs union (a precondition of the proposed EU-GCC free trade agreement); the union was established in January 2003. At the 20th EU-GCC Joint Council and Ministerial Meeting, held in Luxembourg in June 2010, an EU-GCC Joint Action Programme for 2010–13 was adopted, with the aim of strengthening co-operation in a number of areas, principally economic and financial co-operation; trade and industry; energy and the environment; transport, telecommunications and information technology; education and research; and culture.

The increased tension in the Middle East prior to the US-led military action in Iraq in March 2003 placed considerable strain on relations between member states of the EU, and exposed the lack of a common EU policy on Iraq. In February 2003 the European Council held an extraordinary meeting to discuss the crisis in Iraq, and issued a statement reiterating its commitment to the UN. In April, however, the EU leaders reluctantly accepted a dominant role for the USA and the United Kingdom in post-war Iraq, and Denmark, Spain and the Netherlands announced plans to send peace-keeping troops to Iraq. At the Madrid Donors' Conference in October the EU and its accession states pledged more than €1,250m. (mainly in grants) for Iraq's reconstruction. In March 2004 the Commission adopted a programme setting three priorities for reconstruction assistance to Iraq in that year: restoring the delivery of principal public services; increasing employment and reducing poverty; and strengthening governance, civil society and human rights. The EU welcomed the handover of power by the Coalition Provisional Authority to the Iraqi Interim Government in June 2004 and supported the holding of elections to the Transitional National Assembly in Iraq in January 2005. An EU integrated rule-of-law mission for Iraq, to provide training in management and criminal investigation to staff and senior officials from the judiciary, the police and the penitentiary, commenced operations in July, with an initial mandate of 12 months. In December 2006 an agreement was signed on the establishment of a European Commission delegation office in the Iraqi capital, Baghdad. In June of that year, in response to the formation of a new Iraqi Government, the Commission set forth its proposals for an EU-wide strategy to govern EU relations with Iraq. The strategy comprised five objectives: overcoming divisions within Iraq and building democracy; promoting the rule of law and human rights; supporting the Iraqi authorities in the delivery of basic services; supporting the reform of public administration; and promoting economic reform. In November negotiations commenced on a trade and co-operation agreement with Iraq; at a round of negotiations on the agreement held in February 2009, participants agreed to upgrade the draft accord to a more comprehensive draft partnership agreement, which would provide for annual ministerial meetings and the establishment of a joint co-operation council. In November the EU and Iraq completed negotiations on the partnership and co-operation agreement, which had still to be signed. A memorandum of understanding on a strategic energy partnership between the EU and the Iraqi Government was signed in January 2010. Between 2003 and the end of 2008 the EU provided €933m. in reconstruction and humanitarian assistance to Iraq. The EU allocated €66m. towards development co-operation with Iraq during 2009–10 (€42m. for 2009 and €24m. for 2010). In November 2010 the EU adopted a Joint Strategy Paper for Iraq for 2011–13, which aimed to assist Iraq in making optimum use of its resources through: capacity-building activities relating to good governance; promoting education in order to aid socio-economic recovery; building institutional capacity; water management and agriculture.

A series of large-scale demonstrations in Tunisia, prompted by the self-immolation of a young Tunisian man in protest at state restrictions in mid-December 2010, led President Zine al-Abidine Ben Ali to flee the country in mid-January 2011. An EU-Tunisia Task Force was established to ensure the improved co-ordination of support for Tunisia's political and economic transition, the first meeting of which took place in late September in the capital, Tunis. An Electoral Observation Mission was dispatched to monitor elections to the Constituent Assembly in October 2011. Overall EU financial support for Tunisia was increased to €390m. for 2011–12, focused on facilitating the Government's political and socioeconomic reforms.

Mass protests also took place in Egypt in early 2011, which resulted in the resignation of the Egyptian President Lt-Gen. Muhammad Hosni Mubarak on 11 February. The EU dispatched electoral experts to monitor the conduct of the presidential election held in May–June 2012, which concluded that the election took place peacefully and fairly. The EU allocated some €449m. to Egypt in 2011–13, in support of the transition. Further funds, totalling some €5,000m., were made available jointly with the European Investment Bank (EIB) and the European Bank for Reconstruction and Development (EBRD). In late August 2013, following the escalation of violence in Egypt in that month, EU ministers of foreign affairs agreed to suspend the sale of armaments to the country.

In mid-February 2011 a series of violent clashes broke out between anti-Government protesters in Libya and armed forces loyal to the Libyan leader, Col Muammar al-Qaddafi. By 22 February it was reported that protesters had taken control of Benghazi and large parts of eastern Libya. At the end of February the Council of the EU adopted a UN Security Council Resolution on Libya, prohibiting the sale to that country of arms and ammunition, and agreed to impose additional sanctions against those responsible for the violent repression of the civilian protests, halting trade in any equipment that could be utilized for such purposes. The Council also imposed a visa ban on several people, including al-Qaddafi and other members of his family, and froze the assets of al-Qaddafi and 25 other people. On 1 April 2011 the Council agreed, in principle, to establish an EU mission in response to the crisis situation in Libya, should its deployment be requested by the UN Office for the Coordination of Humanitarian Affairs. After al-Qaddafi went into hiding in late August, and forces in support of the opposition National Transitional Council (NTC) took control of the capital, Tripoli, the European Council agreed measures to support the Libyan economy and to assist the UN mission in Libya. A number of hitherto frozen assets were released in support of humanitarian and civilian needs, and a ban on the use of European air space by Libyan aircraft was removed. At the end of August the EU opened an office in Tripoli. At an international conference held in Paris, France, in early September, the EU agreed to initiate assessments of the needs of the NTC in the fields of security, communication, civil society, border management and procurement, and a further €50m. was to be made available for longer-term support programmes. On 20 October it was confirmed that Qaddafi had been captured and killed during fighting in his home city of Sirte; three days later the NTC declared 'national liberation'. In mid-November the EU's Tripoli office was formally upgraded, becoming the headquarters of the new EU delegation to Libya. EU support to Libya included humanitarian assistance, mobilization of EU civil protection teams, and wide-ranging support for the transitional authorities in, for example, democratic transition and security sector reform. In March 2012 the EU also deployed an expert mission to Libya to advise on border management issues. In January 2013 Libya announced its intention to seek observer status with the Union for the Mediterranean.

Unrest also developed in Yemen in early 2011, with escalating conflict between forces loyal to Saleh and tribal groups, and ongoing protests against Field Marshal Ali Abdullah Saleh's rule in several cities. In late November the EU expressed satisfaction at the signature in Riyadh, Saudi Arabia, of the agreement for political transition signed by President Saleh and senior Yemeni officials, under the auspices of the GCC. The EU provided some €20m. in additional humanitarian aid to Yemen in 2011, and welcomed the presidential election that took place in late February 2012, and the subsequent inauguration of President Field Marshal Abd al-Rabbuh Mansur al-Hadi, prior to legislative elections in 2014. In September 2012 an EU donor conference resulted in pledges worth €170m. in support of Yemen.

After demonstrations commenced in the capital of Bahrain, Manama, in early 2011, the EU urged restraint, and exhorted all parties to take part in negotiations. None the less, protests were violently repressed, and the EU's High Representative dispatched a senior EU envoy to Bahrain for talks. The EU welcomed the establishment, in June, of the Bahrain Independent Commission of Inquiry (BICI)—an independent, international commission of judicial and human rights experts—to investigate both the causes of the unrest and allegations of human rights violations.

Meanwhile, from mid-March 2011 anti-Government protests in Syria were forcibly quashed by the authorities. In response, the EU imposed a number of restrictive measures, including an arms embargo and targeted sanctions, comprising a travel ban and the freezing of assets, against those deemed to be responsible for, or involved with, the repression. The Syrian authorities continued to implement harsh measures in an attempt to quell demonstrations against the rule of President Bashar al-Assad; by mid-October the Office of the UN High Commissioner for Human Rights estimated that more than 3,000 people had been killed in Syria since protests began. By August 2012 the EU had imposed 17 sets of sanctions on the Syrian authorities. In mid-November the Council expressed its continued support for ongoing efforts to reach a political solution to the situation in Syria. The EU's arms embargo against Syria was repeatedly renewed in 2012 and 2013. The EU delegation to Syria closed in December 2012, owing to security concerns. In that month the EU Foreign Affairs Council recognized the National Coalition for Syrian Revolutionary and Opposition Forces as the legitimate representatives of the Syrian people. The EU allocated over €400m. in humanitarian aid, while the Commission provided some €100m. to address the long-term consequences of the conflict for the civilian population. In late August 2013 Ashton expressed deep concern at reports of the use of chemical weapons in Syria, and urged intensified diplomatic efforts to bring about a rapid resolution to the civil conflict there.

In late February 2011, at a Senior Officials' meeting to discuss the instability in the Middle East (the 'Arab Spring'), Ashton identified the need to respond in three ways: by helping to develop 'deep democracy', through a process of political reform, democratic elections, institution-building, measures to combat corruption, and support for the independent judiciary and civil society; through economic development; and by facilitating the movement of people and of communications, while avoiding mass migration. In June a new Task Force for the Southern Mediterranean was established, which aimed to combine expertise from the European External Action Service, the Commission, the European Investment Bank, the European Bank for Reconstruction and Development and other international financial institutions to act as a focal point for assistance to countries in North Africa experiencing political transformation. The Council appointed an EU Special Representative for the Southern Mediterranean in July, who sought to strengthen the EU's political role in North Africa and the Middle East, to ensure the coherence of EU actions in relation to the region and to support the transition to democracy in the EU's southern neighbourhood. In late September the European Commission agreed to new economic support for the Middle East. The Support for Partnership Reform and Inclusive Growth (SPRING) programme was allocated a budget of €350m. in additional funds for 2011–12, to provide support on a so-called more-for-more basis to those countries that demonstrated progress in implementing democratic reforms. A Civil Society Facility was established, with a budget of €26.4m., to strengthen the capacity of civil society to promote reform and increase public accountability.

AID TO DEVELOPING AND NON-EU COUNTRIES

The European Commission's Humanitarian Aid Office (ECHO) was established in 1991, with a mandate to co-ordinate the provision of emergency humanitarian assistance and food aid. ECHO, which became fully operational in 1993 and is based in Brussels, Belgium, finances operations conducted by NGOs and international agencies, with which it works in partnership.

In 2011 ECHO provided €156m. in humanitarian and food aid to support populations in the Middle East and the Mediterranean. This total comprised €60m. to those affected by the crisis in Libya; €46m. to the occupied Palestinian territories; €25m. to Yemen; €10m. to the Iraq crisis; €9m. to Western Sahara; and €6m. to Palestinian refugees in Jordan, Lebanon and Syria.

ISLAMIC DEVELOPMENT BANK

Address: POB 5925, Jeddah 21432, Saudi Arabia.

Telephone: (2) 6361400; **fax:** (2) 6366871; **e-mail:** idbarchives@isdb.org; **internet:** www.isdb.org.

The Bank was established following a conference of Ministers of Finance of member countries of the then Organization of the Islamic Conference (now Organization of Islamic Cooperation—OIC), held in Jeddah in December 1973. Its aim is to encourage the economic development and social progress of member countries and of Muslim communities in non-member countries, in accordance with the principles of the Islamic *Shari'a* (sacred law). The Bank formally opened in October 1975. The Bank and its associated entities—the Islamic Research and Training Institute, the Islamic Corporation for the Development of the Private Sector, the Islamic Corporation for the Insurance of Investment and Export Credit, and the International Islamic Trade Finance Corporation—constitute the Islamic Development Bank Group.

MEMBERS

There are 56 members.

Organization

(September 2013)

BOARD OF GOVERNORS

Each member country is represented by a governor, usually its Minister of Finance, and an alternate. The Board of Governors is the supreme authority of the Bank, and meets annually. The 38th meeting was convened in Dushanbe, Tajikistan, in May 2013.

BOARD OF EXECUTIVE DIRECTORS

The Board consists of 18 members, half of whom are appointed by the eight largest subscribers to the capital stock of the Bank; the remaining eight are elected by Governors representing the other subscribers. Members of the Board of Executive Directors are elected for three-year terms. The Board is responsible for the direction of the general operations of the Bank.

ADMINISTRATION

President of the Bank and Chairman of the Board of Executive Directors: Dr AHMAD MOHAMED ALI AL-MADANI (Saudi Arabia).

Vice-President Corporate Services and Acting Vice-President Co-operation and Capacity Development, Acting Chief Economist: Dr AHMET TIKTIK (Turkey).

Vice-President Finance: Dr ABDULAZIZ BIN MOHAMED BIN ZAHIR AL HINAI (Oman).

Vice-President Operations: BIRAMA BOUBACAR SIDIBE (Mali).

REGIONAL OFFICES

Kazakhstan: 050000 Almatı, Aiteki bi 67; tel. (727) 272-70-00; fax (727) 250-13-03; e-mail idbroa@isdb.org; Dir HISHAM TALEB MAAROUF.

Malaysia: Menara Bank, Pembangunan Bandar Wawasan, Level 13, Jalan Sultan Ismail, 508250 Kuala Lumpur; tel. (3) 26946627; fax (3) 26946626; e-mail ROKL@isdb.org.

Morocco: Km 6.4, Ave Imam Malik Route des Zaers, POB 5003, Rabat; tel. (3) 7757191; fax (3) 7757260; Dir ABDERRAHAM EL-GLAOUI.

Senegal: 18 blvd de la République, Dakar; tel. (33) 889-1144; fax (33) 823-3621; e-mail RODK@isdb.org; Dir SIDI MOHAMED OULD TALEB.

FINANCIAL STRUCTURE

The Bank's unit of account is the Islamic Dinar (ID), which is equivalent to the value of one Special Drawing Right (SDR) of the IMF (average value of the SDR in 2011 was US $1.57868). In May 2006 the Bank's Board of Governors approved an increase in the authorized capital from ID 15,000m. to ID 30,000m. An increase in the authorized capital, to ID 100,000m., was approved by the Board in May 2013. An increase in subscribed capital, from ID 15,000m. to ID 16,000m. was approved by the Board of Governors in June 2008. In June 2010 the Board of Governors approved a further increase in subscribed capital to ID 18,000m., and an increase to ID 50,000 was approved in May 2013. At 14 November 2012 total committed subscriptions amounted to ID 17,782.6m.

Subscriptions
(million Islamic Dinars, as at 14 November 2012)

Afghanistan	9.93	Maldives	9.23
Albania	9.23	Mali	18.19
Algeria	459.22	Mauritania	9.77
Azerbaijan	18.19	Morocco	91.69
Bahrain	25.88	Mozambique	9.23
Bangladesh	182.16	Niger	24.63
Benin	20.80	Nigeria	1,384.00
Brunei	45.85	Oman	50.92
Burkina Faso	24.63	Pakistan	459.22
Cameroon	45.85	Palestine	19.55
Chad	9.77	Qatar	1,297.50
Comoros	4.65	Saudi Arabia	4,249.60
Côte d'Ivoire	4.65	Senegal	52.80
Djibouti	4.96	Sierra Leone	4.96
Egypt	1,278.67	Somalia	4.96
Gabon	54.58	Sudan	83.21
The Gambia	9.23	Suriname	9.23
Guinea	45.85	Syria	18.49
Guinea-Bissau	4.96	Tajikistan	4.96
Indonesia	406.48	Togo	4.96
Iran	1,491.20	Tunisia	19.55
Iraq	48.24	Turkey	1,165.86
Jordan	78.50	Turkmenistan	4.96
Kazakhstan	19.29	Uganda	24.63
Kuwait	985.88	United Arab Emirates	1,357.20
Kyrgyzstan	9.23	Uzbekistan	4.80
Lebanon	9.77	Yemen	92.38
Libya	1,704.46		
Malaysia	294.01		

Activities

The Bank adheres to the Islamic principle forbidding usury, and does not grant loans or credits for interest. Instead, its methods of project financing are provision of interest-free loans, mainly for infrastructural projects which are expected to have a marked impact on long-term socio-economic development; provision of technical assistance (e.g. for feasibility studies); equity participation in industrial and agricultural projects; leasing operations, involving the leasing of equipment such as ships, and instalment sale financing; and profit-sharing operations. Funds not immediately needed for projects are used for foreign trade financing. Under the Bank's trade financing operations funds are used for importing commodities for development purposes (i.e. raw materials and intermediate industrial goods, rather than consumer goods), with priority given to the import of goods from other member countries. In 2005 the Bank initiated a consultation process, led by a commission of eminent persons, to develop a new long-term strategy for the Bank. A document on the AH 1440 (2020) Vision was published in March 2006. It recommended that the Bank redefine its mandate and incorporate a broad focus on comprehensive human development, with priority concerns to be the alleviation of poverty and improvements to health, education and governance. The new strategy also envisaged greater community involvement in Bank operations and more support given to local initiatives. In October 2008 the Bank organized a forum to consider the impact of the international economic and financial crisis on the

Islamic financial system. The meeting resolved to establish a Task Force for Islamic Finance and Global Financial Stability, which met for the first time in January 2009, in Kuala Lumpur, Malaysia. In May the Board of Executive Directors agreed to double ordinary capital resources operations over a three-year period in order to support economic recovery in member countries. In the following month the Board of Governors approved the measure, along with others in support of mitigating the effects of the global financial crisis. During that year the Bank resolved to accelerate implementation of a major reform programme to enhance its relevance and impact in member countries, in accordance with the AH 1440 (2020) Vision. The Bank also adopted a Thematic Strategy for Poverty Reduction and Comprehensive Human Development to focus efforts to achieve the Vision's objectives.

By 14 November 2012 the Bank had approved a total of ID 28,566.3m. (equivalent to some US $42,020.9m.) for project financing since operations began in 1976, including ID 287.1m. ($405.7m.) for technical assistance, in addition to ID 31,172.7m. (44,073.4m.) for foreign trade financing, and ID 556.4m. ($725.8m.) for special assistance operations, excluding amounts for cancelled operations. Total net approved operations amounted to ID 60,582.6m. ($87,225.6m.) at that time.

During the Islamic year 1433 (27 November 2011–14 November 2012) the Bank approved a net total of ID 6,415.0m., for 386 operations, compared with ID 6,973.0m. for 403 operations in the previous year. Of the total approved in AH 1433 ID 255.3m. was approved for 62 loans, supporting projects concerned with the education and health sectors, infrastructural improvements, and agricultural developments. The Bank approved 77 technical assistance operations during that year in the form of grants and loans, amounting to ID 13.4m. Trade financing approved amounted to ID 2,902.9m. for 57 operations. During AH 1433 the Bank's total disbursements totalled ID 3,672.8m., bringing the total cumulative disbursements since the Bank began operations to ID 40,299.0m.

During AH 1427 the Bank's export financing scheme was formally dissolved, although it continued to fund projects pending the commencement of operations of the International Islamic Trade Finance Corporation (ITFC). The Bank also finances other trade financing operations, including the Islamic Corporation for the Development of the Private Sector (ICD, see below), the Awqaf Properties Investment Fund and the Treasury Department. In addition, a Trade Co-operation and Promotion Programme supports efforts to enhance trade among member countries of the Organization of Islamic Cooperation (OIC). In June 2005 the Board of Governors approved the establishment of the ITFC as an autonomous trade promotion and financing institution within the Bank Group. The inaugural meeting of the ITFC was held in February 2007. In May 2006 the Board of Governors approved a new fund to reduce poverty and support efforts to achieve the UN Millennium Development Goals, in accordance with a proposal of the OIC. It was inaugurated, as the Islamic Solidarity Fund for Development, in May 2007, and became operational in early 2008. By the end of the Islamic year 1433 capital contributions to the Fund amounted to US $1,661m., of a total of $2,661m. that had been pledged by 42 countries.

In AH 1407 (1986/87) the Bank established an Islamic Bank's Portfolio for Investment and Development (IBP) in order to promote the development and diversification of Islamic financial markets and to mobilize the liquidity available to banks and financial institutions. During AH 1428 resources and activities of the IBP were transferred to the newly established ITFC. The Bank's Unit Investment Fund (UIF) became operational in 1990, with the aim of mobilizing additional resources and providing a profitable channel for investments conforming to *Shari'a*. The initial issue of the UIF was US $100m., which was subsequently increased to $325m. The Fund finances mainly private sector industrial projects in middle-income countries and also finances short-term trade operations. The Bank also mobilizes resources from the international financial markets through the issuance of the International Islamic Sukuk bond. In October 1998 the Bank announced the establishment of a new fund to invest in infrastructure projects in member states. The Bank committed $250m. to the fund, which was to comprise $1,000m. equity capital and a $500m. Islamic financing facility. In January 2009 the Bank launched a second phase of the infrastructure fund. In November 2001 the Bank signed an agreement with Malaysia, Bahrain, Indonesia and Sudan for the establishment of an Islamic financial market. In April 2002 the Bank, jointly with governors of central banks and the Accounting and Auditing Organization for Islamic Financial Institutions, concluded an agreement, under the auspices of the IMF, for the establishment of an Islamic Financial Services Board. The Board, to be located in Kuala Lumpur, Malaysia, was intended to elaborate and harmonize standards for best practices in the regulation and supervision of the Islamic financial services industry.

The Bank's Special Assistance Programme was initiated in AH 1400 to support the economic and social development of Muslim communities in non-member countries, in particular in the education and health sectors. It also aimed to provide emergency aid in times of natural disasters, and to assist Muslim refugees throughout the world. Operations undertaken by the Bank are financed by the Waqf Fund (formerly the Special Assistance Account). By the end of the Islamic year 1433 some ID 556.4m. (US $725.8m.) had been approved under the Waqf Fund Special Assistance Programme for 1,440 operations. Other assistance activities include scholarship programmes, technical co-operation projects and the sacrificial meat utilization project (see below). In addition the Bank supports recovery, rehabilitation and reconstruction efforts in member countries affected by natural disasters or conflict.

In October 2002 the Bank's Board of Governors, meeting in Burkina Faso, adopted the Ouagadougou Declaration on the co-operation between the Bank group and Africa, which identified priority areas for Bank activities, for example education and the private sector. The Bank pledged US $2,000m. to finance implementation of the Declaration over the five year period 2004–08. A successor initiative, the IDB Special Programme for the Development of Africa, was endorsed at a summit meeting of the OIC held in March 2008. The Bank committed $4,000m. to the Programme for the next five-year period, 2008–12. By the end of the Islamic year 1433 $5,000m. had been approved under the Programme. During the Islamic year 1431 the Bank initiated a Membership Country Partnership (MCP) Strategy to strengthen dialogue with individual member countries and to contribute more effectively to their medium- and long-term development plans. By the end of AH 1433 eight MCPs were being implemented, in Indonesia, Kazakhstan, Malaysia, Mali, Mauritania, Pakistan, Turkey, and Uganda.

In June 2008 the Board of Governors inaugurated the Jeddah Declaration Initiative, with an allocation of US $1,500m. in funds over a five-year period, to assist member countries to meet the escalating costs of food and to attain greater food security. In November 2009 the Bank concluded a co-financing agreement with the International Fund for Agricultural Development, with funds of up to $1,500m., to support priority projects concerned with food security and rural development in the poorest member countries in Africa and Asia. The agreement was signed by the presidents of the two organizations in February 2010. During 2011 the Bank contributed to the preparation of an Action Plan on Food Price Volatility and Agriculture, which was adopted by heads of state and government of the Group of 20 (G20) industrialized and emerging economies in November. The Bank also contributed, through participation in a working group and high-level panel, to the elaboration of a G20 Multilateral Development Bank Infrastructure Action Plan. In April the Bank collaborated with the World Bank Group to inaugurate an Arab Financing Facility for Infrastructure in roder to support national and cros-border infrastructure development, in particular through use of public–private partnerships. In September the Bank participated in a meeting of ministers of finance of the Group of Eight (G8) industrialized nations and high-level representatives of international financial institutions active in the Middle East and North Africa region to further support of the so-called Deauville Partnership, which had been established in May in order to assist countries in the region undergoing social and economic transformations. The Bank was a founding member of the new Co-ordination Platform to facilitate and promote collaboration among the institutions extending assistance under the Partnership.

In AH 1404 (1983/84) the Bank established a scholarship programme for Muslim communities in non-member countries to provide opportunities for students to pursue further education or other professional training. The programme also assists 12 member countries on an exceptional basis. By the end of the Islamic year 1433 7,652 people had graduated and 3,794 were undertaking studies under the scheme. The Merit Scholarship Programme, initiated in AH 1412 (1991/92), aims to develop scientific, technological and research capacities in member countries through advanced studies and/or research. A total of 860 scholarships had been awarded by the end of AH 1433. In AH 1419 (1998/99) a Scholarship Programme in Science and Technology for IDB Least Developed Member Countries became operational for students in 20 eligible countries. The Bank awards annual prizes for science and technology to promote excellence in research and development and in scientific education.

The Bank's Programme for Technical Co-operation aims to mobilize technical capabilities among member countries and to promote the exchange of expertise, experience and skills through expert missions, training, seminars and workshops. In December 1999 the Board of Executive Directors approved two technical assistance grants to support a programme for the eradication of illiteracy in the Islamic world, and one for self-sufficiency in human vaccine production. The Bank also undertakes the distribution of meat sacrificed by Muslim pilgrims. The Bank was the principal source of funding of the International Centre for Biosaline Agriculture, which was established in Dubai, United Arab Emirates, in September 1999.

BANK GROUP ENTITIES

International Islamic Trade Finance Corporation: POB 55335, Jeddah 21534, Saudia Arabia; tel. (2) 6361400; fax (2)

6371064; e-mail info@isdb.org; internet www.itfc-idb.org; f. 2007; commenced operations Jan. 2008; aims to promote trade and trade financing in Bank member countries, to facilitate access to public and private capital, and to promote investment opportunities; during the Islamic year 1432 the ITFC approved US $3,033m. for 66 trade financing operations; auth. cap. $3,000m.; subs. cap. $750m. (Nov. 2011); CEO Dr WALID AL-WOHAIB.

Islamic Corporation for the Development of the Private Sector (ICD): POB 54069, Jeddah 21514, Saudi Arabia; tel. (2) 6441644; fax (2) 6444427; e-mail icd@isdb.org; internet www.icd-idb.org; f. 1999; to identify opportunities in the private sector, provide financial products and services compatible with Islamic law, mobilize additional resources for the private sector in member countries, and encourage the development of Islamic financing and capital markets; approved 18 projects and eight capital increases, amounting to US $419m., in the Islamic year 1433; the Bank's share of the capital is 50%, member countries 30% and public financial institutions of member countries 20%; auth. cap. $2,000m., subs. cap. $1,000m. (April 2013); mems: 51 countries, the Bank, and five public financial institutions; CEO and Gen. Man. KHALID M. AL-ABOODI.

Islamic Corporation for the Insurance of Investment and Export Credit (ICIEC): POB 15722, Jeddah 21454, Saudi Arabia; tel. (2) 6445666; fax (2) 6379504; e-mail idb.iciec@isdb.org.sa; internet www.iciec.com; f. 1994; aims to promote trade and the flow of investments among member countries of the OIC through the provision of export credit and investment insurance services; a representative office was opened in Dubai, UAE, in May 2010; auth. cap. increased from ID 150m. to ID 400m. in July 2011; mems: 40 mem. states and the Islamic Development Bank (which contributes two-thirds of its capital); CEO Dr ABDEL RAHMAN A. TAHA.

Islamic Research and Training Institute: POB 9201, Jeddah 21413, Saudi Arabia; tel. (2) 6361400; fax (2) 6378927; e-mail irti@isdb.org; internet www.irti.org; f. 1982 to undertake research enabling economic, financial and banking activities to conform to Islamic law, and to provide training for staff involved in development activities in the Bank's member countries; the Institute also organizes seminars and workshops, and holds training courses aimed at furthering the expertise of government and financial officials in Islamic developing countries; Dir-Gen. Dr MOHD AZMI OMAR (Malaysia); publs *Annual Report*, *Islamic Economic Studies* (2 a year), various research studies, monographs, reports.

Publication

Annual Report.

Statistics

Operations approved, Islamic year 1433
(27 November 2011–14 November 2012)

Type of operation	Number of operations	Amount (million Islamic Dinars)
Total project financing	281	3,480.6
Project financing	204	3,467.1
Technical assistance	77	13.4
Trade financing operations*	57	2,902.9
Special assistance operations	39	5.3
Total†	386	6,415.0

* Including operations by the ITFC, the ICD, the UIF, Treasury operations, and the Awqaf Properties Investment Fund.
† Excluding cancelled operations.

Distribution of project financing and technical assistance by sector, Islamic year 1433
(27 November 2011–14 November 2012)

Sector	Number of operations	Amount (million Islamic Dinars)	%
Agriculture	67	476.6	16.9
Education	25	182.6	6.5
Energy	15	802.4	28.5
Finance	56	164.6	5.8
Health	26	306.2	10.9
Industry and mining	3	83.4	3.0
Information and communications	1	0.2	0.0
Public administration	1	0.2	0.0
Trade	1	0.1	0.0
Transportation	8	281.9	10.0
Water, sanitation and urban services	12	521.6	18.5
Total*	215	2,819.8	100.0

* Excluding cancelled operations.

Source: Islamic Development Bank, *Annual Report 1433 H.*

LEAGUE OF ARAB STATES

Address: POB 11642, Arab League Bldg, Tahrir Sq., Cairo, Egypt.
Telephone: (2) 575-0511; **fax:** (2) 574-0331; **internet:** www.lasportal.org.

The League of Arab States (more generally known as the Arab League) is a voluntary association of sovereign Arab states, designed to strengthen the close ties linking them and to co-ordinate their policies and activities and direct them towards the common good of all the Arab countries. It was founded in March 1945.

MEMBERS

Algeria	Lebanon	Somalia
Bahrain	Libya*	Sudan
Comoros	Mauritania	Syria*
Djibouti	Morocco	Tunisia
Egypt	Oman	United Arab Emirates
Iraq	Palestine†	Yemen
Jordan	Qatar	
Kuwait	Saudi Arabia	

* Libya was suspended from participation in meetings of the League in February 2011. It was readmitted in August following an agreement that the new Libyan Transitional Council would represent the country at the League. In November Syria was suspended from meetings of the League; in November 2012 the League formally recognized the National Coalition for Syrian Revolutionary and Opposition Forces as Syria's 'legitimate representative and main interlocutor with the Arab League'.
† Palestine is considered to be an independent state, and therefore a full member of the League.

Brazil, Eritrea, India and Venezuela have observer status at the League.

Organization

(September 2013)

COUNCIL

The supreme organ of the Arab League, the Council consists of representatives of the member states, each of which has one vote, and a representative for Palestine. The Council meets ordinarily every March, normally at the League headquarters in Cairo, Egypt, at the level of heads of state ('kings, heads of state and emirs'), and in March and September at the level of ministers of foreign affairs. The summit level meeting reviews all issues related to Arab national security strategies, co-ordinates supreme policies of the Arab states towards regional and international issues, reviews recommendations and reports submitted to it by meetings at foreign minister level, appoints the Secretary-General of the League, and is mandated to amend the League's Pact. Decisions of the Council at the level of heads of state are passed on a consensus basis. Meetings of ministers of foreign affairs assess the implementation of summit resolutions, prepare relevant reports, and make arrangements for subsequent summits. Committees comprising a smaller group of ministers of foreign affairs may be appointed to follow up closely summit resolutions. Extraordinary summit meetings may be held at the request of one member state or the Secretary-General, if approved by a two-thirds' majority of member states. Extraordinary sessions of ministers of foreign affairs may be held at the request of two member states or of the Secretary-General. The presidency of ordinary meetings is rotated in accordance with the alphabetical order of the League's member states. Unanimous decisions of the Council are binding upon all member states of the League; majority decisions are binding only on those states that have accepted them.

The Council is supported by technical and specialized committees advising on financial and administrative affairs, information affairs and legal affairs. In addition, specialized ministerial councils have been established to formulate common policies for the regulation and the advancement of co-operation in the following sectors: communications; electricity; environment; health; housing and construction; information; interior; justice; social affairs; tourism; transportation; and youth and sports.

GENERAL SECRETARIAT

The administrative and financial offices of the League. The Secretariat carries out the decisions of the Council, and provides financial and administrative services for the personnel of the League. General departments comprise the Bureau of the Secretary-General; Arab Affairs; Economic Affairs; Information Affairs; Legal Affairs; Palestine Affairs; Political International Affairs; Military Affairs; Social Affairs; Administrative and Financial Affairs; and Internal Audit. In addition, there is a Documentation and Information Centre; an Arab League Centre in Tunis, Tunisia; an Arab Fund for Technical Assistance in African States; a Higher Arab Institute for Translation in Algiers, Algeria; a Music Academy in Baghdad, Iraq; and a Central Boycott Office, based in Damascus, Syria. The following bodies have also been established: an administrative court; an investment arbitration board; and a higher auditing board.

The Secretary-General is appointed at summit meetings of the Council by a two-thirds' majority of the member states, for a five-year, renewable term. He appoints the Assistant Secretaries-General and principal officials, with the approval of the Council. He has the rank of ambassador, and the Assistant Secretaries-General have the rank of ministers plenipotentiary.

Secretary-General: NABIL AL-ARABI (Egypt).

Deputy Secretary-General: AHMED BEN HELLI (Algeria).

DEFENCE AND ECONOMIC CO-OPERATION

Groups established under the Treaty of Joint Defence and Economic Co-operation, concluded in 1950 to complement the Pact of the League.

Economic and Social Council: compares and co-ordinates the economic policies of the member states; supervises the activities of the Arab League's specialized agencies. The Council is composed of ministers of economic affairs or their deputies; decisions are taken by majority vote. The first meeting was held in 1953. In February 1997 the Economic and Social Council adopted the Executive Programme of the League's (1981) Agreement to Facilitate and Develop Trade Among Arab Countries, with a view to establishing a Greater Arab Free Trade Area (see below). The Council's 92nd session: September 2013, Cairo, Egypt.

Joint Defence Council: supervises implementation of those aspects of the treaty concerned with common defence. Composed of ministers of foreign affairs and of defence; decisions by a two-thirds' majority vote of members are binding on all.

Permanent Military Commission: f. 1950; composed of representatives of army general staffs; main purpose: to draw up plans of joint defence for submission to the Joint Defence Council.

An Arab Unified Military Command, established in 1964 to co-ordinate military policies for the liberation of Palestine, is inactive.

ARAB TRANSITIONAL PARLIAMENT

Inaugurated in December 2005, the Arab Transitional Parliament, based in Damascus, Syria, comprises 88 members (four delegates from each Arab state, including some representing non-elected bodies). The Transitional Parliament is eventually to be replaced by a Permanent Arab Parliament, a Statute for which remains under discussion. The interim body (which has no legislative function) aims to encourage dialogue between member states and to provide a focal point for joint Arab action.

OTHER INSTITUTIONS OF THE LEAGUE

Other bodies established by resolutions adopted by the Council of the League:

Administrative Tribunal of the Arab League: f. 1964; began operations 1966.

Anti-Human Trafficking Co-ordination Unit: f. 2009.

Arab Fund for Technical Assistance to African Countries: f. 1975 to provide technical assistance for development projects by providing African and Arab experts, grants for scholarships and training, and finance for technical studies.

Central Boycott Office: POB 437, Damascus, Syria; f. 1951 to prevent trade between Arab countries and Israel, and to enforce a boycott by Arab countries of companies outside the region that conduct trade with Israel.

Higher Auditing Board: comprises representatives of seven member states, elected every three years; undertakes financial and administrative auditing duties.

Investment Arbitration Board: examines disputes between member states relating to capital investments.

SPECIALIZED AGENCIES

All member states of the Arab League are also members of the Specialized Agencies, which constitute an integral part of the Arab League. (See also the Arab Fund for Economic and Social Development, the Arab Monetary Fund and the Organization of Arab Petroleum Exporting Countries.)

Arab Academy for Science, Technology and Maritime Transport (AASTMT): POB 1029, Alexandria, Egypt; tel. (3) 5622388; fax (3) 5622525; internet www.aast.edu; f. 1975 as Arab Maritime Transport Academy; provides specialized training in marine transport, engineering, technology and management; Pres. Prof. Dr ISMAIL ABDEL GHAFAR ISMAIL; publs *Maritime Research Bulletin* (monthly), *Journal of the Arab Academy for Science, Technology and Maritime Transport* (2 a year).

Arab Administrative Development Organization (ARADO): 2A El-Hegaz St, POB 2692 al-Horreia, Heliopolis, Cairo, Egypt; tel. (2) 22580006; fax (2) 22580077; e-mail arado@arado.org.eg; internet www.arado.org.eg; f. 1961 (as Arab Organization of Administrative Sciences), became operational in 1969; administration development, training, consultancy, research and studies, information, documentation; promotes Arab and international co-operation in administrative sciences; includes Arab Network of Administrative Information; maintains an extensive digital library; Dir-Gen. Prof. REFAT ABDELHALIM ALFAOURI; publs *Arab Journal of Administration* (biannual), *Management Newsletter* (quarterly), research series, training manuals.

Arab Atomic Energy Agency (AAEA): 7 rue de l'assistance, Cité, El Khadhra, 1003 Tunis, Tunisia; tel. (71) 808400; fax (71) 808450; e-mail aaea@aaea.org.tn; internet www.aaea.org.tn; f. 1988; Dir-Gen. Prof. Dr ABDELMAJID MAHJOUB (Tunisia); publs *The Atom and Development* (quarterly), other publs in the field of nuclear sciences and their applications in industry, biology, medicine, agriculture, food irradiation and seawater desalination.

Arab Bank for Economic Development in Africa (Banque Arabe pour le Développement Economique en Afrique—BADEA): Sayed Abd ar-Rahman el-Mahdi St, POB 2640, Khartoum 11111, Sudan; tel. (1) 83773646; fax (1) 83770600; e-mail badea@badea.org; internet www.badea.org; f. 1973 by Arab League; provides loans and grants to African countries to finance development projects; in 2012 the Bank approved loans and grants totalling $192m. for 23 development projects, and $8m. for 32 technical assistance operations; by March 2013, total net loan and grant commitments approved since funding activities began in 1975 amounted to $4,434.4m; during 2012 the Bank contributed $2.08m. to the heavily indebted poor countries initiative, bringing the cumulative total to $230.8m. since the scheme commenced in 1997; subscribing countries: all countries of the Arab League, except the Comoros, Djibouti, Somalia and Yemen; recipient countries: all countries of the African Union, except those belonging to the Arab League; Chair. YOUSEF IBRAHEM AL-BASSAM (Saudi Arabia); Dir-Gen. ABDELAZIZ KHELEF (Algeria); publs *Annual Report* *Co-operation for Development* (quarterly), studies on Afro-Arab co-operation, periodic brochures.

Arab Center for the Studies of Arid Zones and Dry Lands (ACSAD): POB 2440, Damascus, Syria; tel. (11) 5743039; fax (11) 5743063; e-mail email@acsad.org; internet www.acsad.org; f. 1968 to conduct regional research and development programmes related to land and water uses, plant and animal resources, agro-meteorology, and socio-economic studies of arid zones; maintains six research stations; holds conferences and training courses and encourages the exchange of information by Arab scientists; Dir-Gen. Dr RAFIK ALI SALEH.

Arab Industrial Development and Mining Organization: rue France, Zanagat al-Khatawat, POB 8019, Rabat, Morocco; tel. (37) 274500; fax (37) 772188; e-mail aidmo@aidmo.org; internet www.aidmo.org; f. 1990 by merger of Arab Industrial Development Organization, Arab Organization for Mineral Resources and Arab Organization for Standardization and Metrology; comprises a 13-member Executive Council, a High Consultative Committee of Standardization, a High Committee of Mineral Resources and a Co-ordination Committee for Arab Industrial Research Centres; a Council of ministers of member states responsible for industry meets every two years; in Sept. 2011 organized, jointly with ESCWA, a conference on 'The Role of Green Industries in Promoting Socio-Economic Development in the Arab Countries'; Dir-Gen. MOHAMED BIN YOUSEF; publs *Arab Industrial Development* (monthly and quarterly newsletters).

Arab Investment & Export Credit Guarantee Corporation: POB 23568, Safat 13096, Kuwait; tel. 4959000; fax 4959596; e-mail operations@dhaman.org; internet www.dhaman.org; f. 1974; insures Arab investors for non-commercial risks, and export credits for commercial and non-commercial risks; undertakes research and other activities to promote inter-Arab trade and investment; total assets US $354.5m. (Dec. 2010); mems: 21 Arab countries and four multilateral Arab financial institutions; Chair NASIR BEN MOHAMAD AL-QUHTANI; Dir-Gen. FAHAD RASHID AL-IBRAHIM; publs *News Bulletin* (quarterly), *Arab Investment Climate Report* (annually).

Arab Labour Organization: POB 814, Cairo, Egypt; tel. (2) 3362721; fax (2) 3484902; internet www.alolabor.org; f. 1965 for co-operation between member states in labour problems; unification of labour legislation and general conditions of work wherever possible; research; technical assistance; social insurance; training, etc; the organization has a tripartite structure: governments, employers and workers; Dir-Gen. AHMAD MUHAMMAD LUQMAN; publs *ALO Bulletin* (monthly), *Arab Labour Review* (quarterly), *Legislative Bulletin* (annually), series of research reports and studies concerned with economic and social development issues in the Arab world.

Arab League Educational, Cultural and Scientific Organization (ALECSO): ave Mohamed V, POB 1120, Tunis, Tunisia; tel. (71) 784-466; fax (71) 784-496; e-mail alecso@email.ati.tn; internet www.alecso.org.tn; f. 1970 to promote and co-ordinate educational, cultural and scientific activities in the Arab region; implementing a plan for education covering the period 2008–18; regional units: Arab Centre for Arabization, Translation, Authorship, and Publication—Damascus, Syria; Institute of Arab Manuscripts—Cairo, Egypt; Institute of Arab Research and Studies—Cairo, Egypt; Khartoum International Institute for Arabic Language—Khartoum, Sudan; and the Arabization Co-ordination Bureau—Rabat, Morocco; Dir-Gen. MOHAMED-EL AZIZ BEN ACHOUR; publs *Arab Journal of Culture* (2 a year), *Arab Journal of Education* (2 a year), *Arab Journal of Science and Information* (2 a year), *Arab Bulletin of Publications* (annually), *ALECSO Newsletter* (monthly).

Arab Organization for Agricultural Development (AOAD): 7 al-Amarat St, POB 474, Khartoum 11111, Sudan; tel. (1) 83472176; fax (1) 83471402; e-mail info@aoad.org; internet www.aoad.org; f. 1970; began operations in 1972 to contribute to co-operation in agricultural activities, and in the development of natural and human resources for agriculture; compiles data, conducts studies, training and food security programmes; includes Information and Documentation Centre, Arab Centre for Studies and Projects, and Arab Institute of Forestry and Biodiversity; Dir-Gen. Dr TARIQ MOOSA AL-ZADJALI; publs *Agricultural Statistics Yearbook, Annual Report on Agricultural Development, the State of Arab Food Security* (annually), *Agriculture and Development in the Arab World* (quarterly), *Accession Bulletin* (every 2 months), *AOAD Newsletter* (monthly), *Arab Agricultural Research Journal, Arab Journal for Irrigation Water Management* (2 a year).

Arab Satellite Communications Organization (ARABSAT): POB 1038, Diplomatic Quarter, Riyadh 11431, Saudi Arabia; tel. (1) 4820000; fax (1) 4887999; e-mail info@arabsat.com; internet www.arabsat.com; f. 1976; regional satellite telecommunications organization providing broadcast, telecommunications and broadband services to members and private users; operates six satellites, which cover Arab, European, Central Asian and northern African countries; suspended satellite broadcasts to Syria in June 2012, at the request of the League Council; Pres. and CEO KHALID AHMED BALKHEYOUR.

Arab States Broadcasting Union (ASBU): POB 250, 1080 Tunis Cedex; rue 8840, Centre Urbain Nord, Tunisia; tel. (71) 843505; fax (71) 843054; e-mail asbu@asbu.net; internet www.asbu.net; f. 1969 to promote and study broadcasting, and to exchange expertise and technical co-operation in broadcasting; conducts training and audience research; Multimedia Exchange Network over Satellite (MENOS) network launched in 2009; organizes the biennial Arab Festival for Radio and Television, and an Arab Song Festival every one or two years; 28 active member radio and television organizations, seven participating mems, 19 assoc. mems; Pres. of Exec. Council ISMAIL AL-SHISHTAWI (Egypt); publ. *Arab Broadcasters* (quarterly).

ASSOCIATED BODY

Council of Arab Economic Unity: 1113 Corniche el-Nil, 4th Floor, POB 1 Mohammed Fareed, 11518 Cairo, Egypt; tel. (2) 5755321; fax (2) 5754090; f. 1957 by the Economic and Social Council of the Arab League to co-ordinate measures leading to a customs union subject to a unified administration; conduct market and commodity studies; assist with the unification of statistical terminology and methods of data collection; conduct studies for the formation of new joint Arab companies and federations; and to formulate specific programmes for agricultural and industrial co-ordination and for improving road and railway networks; was to administer the 1962 Arab Economic Unity Agreement; inaugural meeting held in 1964; representatives of member states—usually ministers of economy, finance and trade—meet twice a year; meetings are chaired by the representative of each country for one year on a rotational basis; the Council Secretariat is entrusted with the implementation of the Council's decisions and with proposing work plans, including efforts to encourage participation by member states in the Arab Economic Unity Agreement; the Secretariat also compiles statistics, conducts research and publishes studies on Arab economic problems and on the effects of major world economic trends; has permanent committees on Customs issues; Monetary and finance; Economic; Permanent representatives; and Follow-up; mems: Egypt, Iraq, Jordan, Libya, Mauritania, Palestine, Somalia, Sudan, Syria and Yemen; Sec.-Gen. MOHAMMED AL-RABEE (Yemen).

Activities

The League was founded in 1945 with the signing of the Pact of the Arab League. A Cultural Treaty was signed in the following year. In 1952, agreements were concluded on extradition, writs, letters of request and the nationality of Arabs outside their country of origin. At an emergency summit meeting held in 1985, two commissions were established to mediate in disagreements between Arab states (between Jordan and Syria, Iraq and Syria, Iraq and Libya, and Libya and the Palestine Liberation Organization (PLO). The League's headquarters, which had been transferred from Cairo, Egypt, to Tunis, Tunisia, in 1979, were relocated back to Cairo in 1990. In July 2002 the Egyptian Government unveiled a series of measures aimed at strengthening the League, including the adoption of majority voting and the establishment of a body to resolve conflicts in the region (previously agreed at the 1996 summit and sanctioned by member states' foreign ministers in 2000). The 2004 summit meeting of Arab League heads of state, scheduled to be held in Tunis in late March, was postponed by the Tunisian Government two days in advance following disagreements among member states over a number of issues on the summit's agenda, including democratic reforms in Arab states and the proposed reforms to the League. The meeting, which was eventually held in May, approved a *Pledge of Accord and Solidarity* that committed the League heads of state to implementing in full decisions of the League, and adopted an Arab Charter on Human Rights (which entered into force in January 2008). In March 2007 the summit meeting of heads of state, held in Riyadh, Saudi Arabia, determined that in future Arab consultative summits should be convoked when deemed necessary to address specific issues. The 22nd Arab League summit meeting, held in Sirte, Libya, in March 2010, approved the formation of a committee comprising the Egyptian, Iraqi, Libyan, Qatari and Yemeni heads of state, and the League Secretary-General, with a mandate to oversee the development of a new structure for joint Arab action. The committee prepared documentation on proposed reforms for consideration by an extraordinary summit of the League that was held in early October, also in Sirte.

From February–August 2011 the League suspended Libya from participation in its meetings owing to the use of military force against opposition movements in that country (see below). In mid-November Syria was suspended from meetings of the League, on similar grounds. The emerging civil unrest in countries in the region, notably, in addition, in Egypt, Tunisia and Yemen, led to the 23rd summit meeting, initially scheduled to be held in March 2011, being postponed until March 2012.

In mid-May 2011 a meeting of League ministers of foreign affairs unanimously elected Nabil al-Arabi, hitherto the Egyptian minister of foreign affairs, as the new Secretary-General of the League.

The 23rd summit meeting of Arab League heads of state, convened in Baghdad, Iraq, in March 2012, endorsed, and called for the immediate implementation of, a six-point plan on resolving the Syrian crisis that had been recently proposed by the Arab League-UN Joint Special Envoy on the Syrian Crisis. The UN Secretary-General attended the summit, owing to the inclusion of the Syrian crisis on its agenda. Saudi Arabia, seeking the imposition of stronger measures against the Syrian regime, and having reportedly failed to secure the agreement of the Iraqi Government to invite Syrian opposition representatives to the summit meeting, was represented at the gathering at the level of Ambassador. Egypt and Qatar also sent delegates lower than the level of head of state. The Amir of Kuwait participated in the meeting, representing the first visit by a Kuwaiti leader to Baghdad since prior to the 1990 invasion Kuwait by Iraq. Regional water shortages and means of coping with natural disasters were also discussed by the summit.

In early 2012, the League's Secretary-General tasked Lakhdar Brahimi, the former Algerian Minister of Foreign Affairs and UN official (and from August of that year the Joint Special Representative of the League of Arab States and the UN on Syria), to give consideration to reforming the organic structure of the League, and to make a series of recommendations on enhancing the interaction between the League and non-governmental organizations (NGOs); Brahimi submitted his findings to the Secretary-General in January 2013.

In November 2012 the League formally recognized the National Coalition for Syrian Revolutionary and Opposition Forces as Syria's 'legitimate representative and main interlocutor with the Arab League'. Heads of state attending the 24th Arab League summit, convened in Doha, Qatar, in March 2013, addressed an agenda including the continuing conflict in Syria; Palestine; restructuring of the League; and a proposal to establish an Arab fund to finance agricultural development and the implementation of food security plans. Syria was formally represented at the 24th summit by representatives of the National Coalition.

In late August 2013, in view of the overthrow in early July of the elected Egyptian regime in a military coup, and of ongoing violent unrest, 35 Arab NGOs urged the League to place on its formal agenda the situation in Egypt as a priority matter of concern, and also to send a fact-finding mission to conduct an investigation into the crisis there.

HUMAN RIGHTS

A Permanent Arab Commission on Human Rights, established in September 1968, meets every six months, and is the League's principal political organ for the protection of human rights. The primary focus of the Commission has traditionally been the pursuit of a settlement to the Arab-Israeli conflict, with less emphasis on addressing human rights issues within League member states. In May 2004 the League summit of heads of state adopted the Arab Charter on Human Rights; this entered into force in January 2008 and provided for the election of an Arab Human Rights Committee, which was inaugurated in March 2009, with a membership comprising seven men. In March 2011 the League Council adopted a resolution that urged the General Secretariat to prepare a review of the role of the Permanent Commission. In November of that year the League Secretary-General appointed a committee of experts to consider the establishment of an Arab Court on Human Rights. In February 2013 representatives of the League, of human rights-focused NGOs active in the region, and human rights experts from the UN, African Union, Organization of American States, and Council of Europe, convened in Cairo a conference entitled 'The League of Arab States, human rights and civil society: challenges ahead'. The Conference approved a set of recommendations for perusal by the League's Secretary-General and member states, focusing on the promotion of an effective human rights protection legislative framework for the Arab region, to be consistent with international human rights standards, including through reforms to the Arab Charter on Human Rights to clarify the League's protection mandate and to ensure engagement with NGOS; strengthening the Arab Human Rights Committee; amending the League's Pact explicitly to mention respect for universal human rights standards; and promoting effective dialogue with independent national, regional and international civil society organizations. The delegates agreed that, were the proposed Arab Court on Human Rights to be created, it should function in accordance with international standards. The establishment of the Arab Court was approved in principle by the March 2013 League summit.

The Arab Human Rights Committee conducted its first reviews of national human rights situations in 2012, addressing Jordan in March, and Algeria in October. The situation in Bahrain was reviewed in February 2013.

The League established an Anti-Human Trafficking Co-ordination Unit in 2009. In March 2010 a regional conference convened in Doha initiated an initiative for building national capacities to combat human trafficking in the Arab countries; the League and the UN Office on Drugs and Crime have subsequently supported the implementation of the initiative. The development of an Arab treaty on combating human trafficking and of a database on trafficking are under consideration.

PROMOTING ARAB IDENTITY

In February 2008 Arab ministers of information adopted the Arab League Satellite Broadcasting Charter, establishing principles for the regulation of satellite broadcasting and providing for the withdrawal of permits from channels that broadcast in a manner that might 'damage social harmony, national unity, public order or traditional values', including broadcasting content deemed to be offensive towards Arab leaders or national or religious symbols; erotic content; or content that promotes alcohol or smoking tobacco. Qatar (base of the international satellite broadcaster al-Jazeera) did not sign the Charter at that time.

In early 2012 the League submitted the prospective domain name .arab for registration under the Internet Corporation for Assigned Names and Numbers (ICANN)'s expanded generic top-level domains (gTLD) programme; it was envisaged that approval would be granted in 2013.

SECURITY

In 1950 Arab League member states concluded a Joint Defence and Economic Cooperation Treaty. An Arab Deterrent Force was established by the Arab League Council in June 1976 to supervise attempts at that time to cease hostilities in Lebanon; the Force's mandate was terminated in 1983.

In April 1998 Arab League ministers of the interior and of justice adopted the Arab Convention for the Suppression of Terrorism, which incorporated security and judicial measures, such as extradition arrangements and the exchange of evidence. The agreement entered into effect in May 2000. In August 1998 the League denounced terrorist bomb attacks against the US embassies in Kenya and Tanzania. Nevertheless, it condemned US retaliatory military action, a few days later, against suspected terrorist targets in Afghanistan and Sudan, and endorsed a request by the Sudanese Government that the Security Council investigate the incident. An emergency meeting of the League's Council, convened in mid-September 2001 in response to major terrorist attacks on the USA, perpetrated by militant Islamist fundamentalists, condemned the atrocities, while urging respect for the rights of Arab and Muslim US citizens. The Secretary-General subsequently emphasized the need for co-ordinated global anti-terrorist action to have clearly defined goals and to be based on sufficient consultations and secure evidence. He also deplored anti-Islamic prejudice, and stated that US-led action against any Arab state would not be supported and that Israeli participation in an international anti-terrorism alliance would be unacceptable. A meeting of League ministers of foreign affairs in Doha, in October condemned international terrorism but did not express support for retaliatory military action by the USA and its allies. In December a further emergency meeting of League foreign affairs ministers was held to discuss the deepening Middle East crisis. In January 2002 the League appointed a commissioner responsible for promoting dialogue between civilizations. The commissioner was mandated to encourage understanding in Western countries of Arab and Muslim civilization and viewpoints, with the aim of redressing perceived negative stereotypes (especially in view of the Islamist fundamentalist connection to the September 2001 terrorist atrocities). In April 2003 the Secretary-General expressed his regret that the Arab states had failed to prevent the ongoing war in Iraq, and urged the development of a new regional security order. In November the UN Secretary-General appointed the Secretary-General of the League to serve as the Arab region's representative on the UN High-Level Panel on Threats, Challenges and Change. In March 2007 the League's summit meeting resolved to establish an expert-level task force to consider national security issues.

In December 2010 the Arab League and the UN Office on Drugs and Crime jointly launched a five-year Regional Programme on Drug Control, Crime Prevention and Criminal Justice Reform for the Arab States, covering the period 2011–15, and based on the following pillars: countering illicit trafficking, organized crime and terrorism; promoting justice and integrity; and drug prevention and improving health.

In March 2013 the Arab League, the UN Office for Disaster Risk Reduction, the UN Development Programme and other partners organized the First Arab Conference on Disaster Risk Reduction, with participation by 22 Arab states; the Conference launched a new Arab Regional Platform on Disaster Risk Reduction.

TRADE AND ECONOMIC CO-OPERATION

In 1953 Arab League member states formed an Economic and Social Council. In 1956 an agreement was concluded on the adoption of a Common Tariff Nomenclature. In 1962 an Arab Economic Unity Agreement was concluded. The first meeting of the Council of Arab Economic Unity, mandated to administer the Arab Economic Unity Agreement, took place in June 1964. An Arab Common Market Agreement was endorsed by the Council in August. Customs duties and other taxes on trade between the member countries were to be eliminated in stages prior to the adoption of a full customs union, and ultimately all restrictions on trade between the member countries, including quotas, and restrictions on residence, employment and transport, were to be abolished. In practice, however, little progress was achieved in the development of an Arab common market during 1964–2000. In 2001 the Council of Arab Economic Unity's efforts towards liberalizing intra-Arab trade were intensified. A meeting of Council ministers of economy and trade convened in Baghdad, Iraq, in June, approved an executive programme for developing the proposed common market, determined to establish a compensation fund to support the integration of the least developed Arab states into the regional economy, and agreed to provide technical assistance for Arab states aiming to join the World Trade Organization.

A number of multilateral organizations in industry and agriculture have been formed on the principle that faster development and economies of scale may be achieved by combining the efforts of member states. In industries that are new to the member countries Arab Joint Companies are formed, while existing industries are co-ordinated by the setting up of Arab Specialized Unions. The unions are for closer co-operation on problems of production and marketing, and to help companies deal as a group in international markets. The companies are intended to be self-supporting on a purely commercial basis; they may issue shares to citizens of the participating countries. Council of Arab Economic Unity agreements aimed at encouraging Arab investment include an accord on Non-Double Taxation and Income Tax Evasion (adopted in December 1998); an accord on Investment Promotion and Protection (June 2000); and an accord on Investment Dispute Settlement in Arab Countries (December 2000).

In February 1997 the Economic and Social Council adopted the Executive Programme of the (1981) Agreement to Facilitate and Develop Trade Among Arab Countries, with a view to creating a Greater Arab Free Trade Area (GAFTA) which aimed to facilitate and develop trade among participating countries through the reduction (by 10% per year) and eventual elimination of customs duties over a 10-year period, with effect from January 1998, alongside a parallel elimination of trade barriers. In February 2002 the Economic and Social Council agreed to bring forward the inauguration of GAFTA to 1 January 2005. Consequently, customs duties between most member states, which, according to schedule, had been reduced by 50% from January 1998–January 2002, were further reduced by 10% by January 2003, 20% by January 2004, and a final 20% by January 2005; Sudan and Yemen, as less developed economies, were to be subject to a parallel longer schedule of customs reductions. GAFTA (also known as the Pan-Arab Free Trade Area) entered into force, as planned, then with 17 participating countries (accounting for about 94% of the total volume of intra-Arab trade). (In 2009 Algeria became the 18th member of GAFTA.) The Council agreed to supervise the implementation of the free trade agenda and formally to review its progress twice a year. Nevertheless, the level of inter-Arab trade and inter-Arab investments subsequently remained lower than anticipated, reportedly owing to restrictive degrees of bureaucracy and regulation.

In May 2001 Egypt, Jordan, Morocco and Tunisia (all then participants in the Euro-Mediterranean Partnership, re-launched in 2008 as the Union for the Mediterranean—see European Union), while convened in Agadir, Morocco, issued the 'Agadir Declaration' in which they determined to establish an Arab Mediterranean Free Trade Zone. The so-called Agadir Agreement on the establishment of a Free Trade Zone between the Arabic Mediterranean Nations was signed in February 2004, came into force in July 2006, and entered its implementation phase in March 2007. The signatories to the Agadir Agreement are also members of GAFTA.

The inaugural Economic, Development and Social summit meeting of Arab leaders, held in January 2009, in Kuwait, under the auspices of the Arab League, considered means of accelerating progress towards the achievement of Arab economic integration; agreed to create by 2015 a fully functioning Arab Customs Union, and by 2020 a fully functioning Arab Common Market; decided to launch a regional power grid and rail network; and agreed to launch a fund to finance Arab small and medium-sized enterprises (SMEs). Under the Arab Customs Union goods exempt from taxes were to comprise at least 40% of components originating in GAFTA member states. The second Economic, Development and Social summit meeting was convened in January 2011, in Sharm el-Sheikh, Egypt. Participants in the third summit, held in Riyadh, Saudi Arabia, in January 2013, adopted the Riyadh Declaration, in which they determined to activate the fund for SMEs; to strengthen the capacity of joint Arab institutions, including increasing by at least one-half the capital of joint financial institutions; to promote inter-Arab investment; to implement the ongoing Pan-Arab Strategy for Promoting Renewable Energy; to promote the efforts of Arab agencies in pursuing the attainment by 2015 of the UN Millennium Development Goals; and to finalize by the end of 2013 the prerequisites for the full functioning of the Arab Customs Union by 2015, and consequent full implementation of GAFTA. An Arab Private Sector Forum was convened in January 2013, also in Riyadh.

Meeting in October 2012 League ministers responsible for tourism determined to implement a new Arab Tourism Strategy. The proposed establishment of an Arab Youth Centres Observatory and an Arab Youth Training Centre—aimed at monitoring the challenges encountered by young people and facilitating skills development—was on the agenda of the 90th meeting of the Economic and Social Council, held in September 2012.

WATER RESOURCES AND RENEWABLE ENERGY

In April 1993 the Council approved the creation of a committee to consider the political and security aspects of water supply in Arab countries. In March 1996, following protests by Syria and Iraq that extensive construction work in southern Turkey was restricting water supply in the region, the Council determined that the waters of the Euphrates and Tigris rivers be shared equitably between the three countries. In April an emergency meeting of the Council issued a further endorsement of Syria's position in the dispute with Turkey.

In January 2009 the Economic, Development and Social Arab summit meeting determined to launch a regional power grid. The inaugural session of an Arab Ministerial Water Council was convened in June of that year. The new Council gave consideration to the development of an Arab Water Strategy; this was launched in March 2011. In October 2010 Arab ministers responsible for electricity adopted a Pan-Arab Strategy for Promoting Renewable Energy, covering the period 2010–30.

ARAB–ISRAELI AFFAIRS

The League regards Palestine as an independent state and therefore as a full League member. In 1951 a Central Boycott Office was established, in Damascus, Syria, to oversee the prevention of trade between Arab countries and Israel, and to enforce a boycott by Arab countries of companies outside the region that conduct trade with Israel. The second summit conference of Arab heads of state, convened in 1964, welcomed the establishment of the PLO.

The fifth summit conference of Arab heads of state, held in 1969, issued a call for the mobilization of all Arab nations against Israel. In 1977, by the so-called Tripoli Declaration, Algeria, Iraq, Libya and the People's Democratic Republic of Yemen decided to boycott meetings of the Arab League held in Egypt in response to a visit by President Sadat of Egypt to Israel. In 1979 a meeting of the League's Council resolved to withdraw Arab ambassadors from Egypt; to recommend severance of political and diplomatic relations with Egypt; to suspend Egypt's membership of the League on the date of the signing of its formal peace treaty with Israel (26 March); to transfer the headquarters of the League to Tunis; to condemn US policy regarding its role in concluding the Camp David agreements (in September 1978) and the peace treaty; to halt all bank loans, deposits, guarantees or facilities, as well as all financial or technical contributions and aid to Egypt; and to prohibit trade exchanges with the Egyptian state and with private establishments dealing with Israel.

In November 1981 the 12th summit conference of the Arab League was suspended owing to disagreement over a Saudi Arabian proposal, known as the Fahd Plan, which included not only the Arab demands on behalf of the Palestinians, as approved by the UN General Assembly, but also an implied de facto recognition of Israel. In September 1982 the 12th summit conference was reconvened. It adopted a peace plan, which demanded Israel's withdrawal from territories occupied in 1967, and removal of Israeli settlements in these areas; freedom of worship for all religions in the sacred places; the right of the Palestinian people to self-determination, under the leadership of the PLO; temporary supervision for the West Bank and the Gaza Strip; the creation of an independent Palestinian state, with Jerusalem as its capital; and a guarantee of peace for the states of the region by the UN Security Council.

In 1983 a summit meeting of the League due to be held in November was postponed owing to members' differences of opinion concerning Syria's opposition to Yasser Arafat's chairmanship of the PLO, and Syrian support for Iran in the war against Iraq. In July 1986 King Hassan of Morocco announced that he was resigning as chairman of the next League summit conference, after criticism by several Arab leaders of his meeting with the Israeli Prime Minister earlier that month. A ministerial meeting held in October condemned any attempt at direct negotiation with Israel. In November 1987 an extraordinary summit conference stated, *inter alia*, that the resumption of diplomatic relations with Egypt was a matter to be decided by individual states. In June 1988 a summit conference agreed to provide finance for the PLO to continue the Palestinian uprising in Israeli-occupied territories. It reiterated a demand for a peaceful settlement in the Middle East (thereby implicitly rejecting recent proposals by the US Government for a conference that would exclude the PLO). At a summit conference held in May 1989 Egypt was readmitted to the League. The conference expressed support for the then chairman of the PLO, Yasser Arafat, in his recent peace proposals made before the UN General Assembly, and reiterated the League's support for proposals that an international conference should be convened to discuss the rights of Palestinians: in so doing, it accepted UN Security Council Resolutions 242 and 338 on a peaceful settlement in the Middle East and thus gave tacit recognition to the State of Israel.

In April 1993 the League pledged its commitment to the ongoing US-sponsored Middle East Peace Process. Following the signing of the Israeli-PLO Oslo peace accords in September the Council convened in emergency session, at which it approved the agreement. In November it was announced that the League's boycott of commercial activity with Israel was to be maintained. In 1994 the League condemned a decision of the Cooperation Council for the Arab States of the Gulf (GCC), announced in late September, to end the secondary and tertiary trade embargo against Israel, by which member states refuse to trade with international companies that have investments in Israel. A statement issued by the League insisted that the embargo could be removed only on the decision of the Council.

In March 1995 Arab ministers of foreign affairs approved a resolution urging Israel to renew the Nuclear Non-Proliferation Treaty. The resolution stipulated that failure by Israel to do so would cause Arab states to seek to protect legitimate Arab interests by alternative means. In May an extraordinary session of the Council condemned a decision by Israel to confiscate Arab-owned land in East Jerusalem for resettlement. The Israeli Government announced the suspension of its expropriation plans. In April 1996 an emergency meeting of the Council was convened at the request of Palestine, in order to attract international attention to the problem of radiation from an Israeli nuclear reactor. The Council requested an immediate technical inspection of the site by the UN, and further demanded that Israel be obliged to sign the NPT to ensure the eradication of its nuclear weaponry. The 2009 Arab League summit stated that the International Atomic Energy Agency (IAEA) should provide guarantees on Israel's nuclear facilities and activities.

In June 1996 an extraordinary summit conference of Arab League heads of state was convened, the first since 1990, in order to formulate a united Arab response to the election, in May 1996, of a new government in Israel. The conference (from which Iraq was excluded from the meeting in order to ensure the attendance of the Gulf member states) urged Israel to honour its undertaking to withdraw from the Occupied Territories, including Jerusalem, and to respect the establishment of an independent Palestinian state, in order to ensure the success of the peace process. A final communiqué of the meeting warned that Israeli co-operation was essential to prevent Arab states from reconsidering their participation in the peace process and the re-emergence of regional tensions. In September the League met in emergency session following an escalation of civil unrest in Jerusalem and the Occupied Territories. The League urged the UN Security Council to prevent further alleged Israeli aggression against the Palestinians. In November the League criticized Israel's settlement policy, and at the beginning of December it convened in emergency session to consider measures to end any expansion of the Jewish population in the West Bank and Gaza. In March 1997 the Council met in emergency session in response to the Israeli Government's decision to proceed with construction of a new settlement at Har Homa (Jabal Abu-Ghunaim) in East Jerusalem. At the end of March ministers of foreign affairs of Arab League states agreed to end all efforts to secure normal diplomatic relations with Israel (although binding agreements already in force with Egypt, Jordan and Palestine were exempt) and to close diplomatic offices and missions while construction work continued in East Jerusalem.

In March 1999 a meeting of the League's Council expressed support for a UN resolution convening an international conference to facilitate the implementation of agreements applying to Israel and the Occupied Territories, condemned Israel's refusal to withdraw from the Occupied Territories without a majority vote in favour from its legislature, as well as its refusal to resume peace negotiations with Lebanon and Syria that had ended in 1996, and advocated the publication of evidence of Israeli violence against Palestinians. The Council considered other issues, including the need to prevent further Israeli expansion in Jerusalem and the problem of Palestinian refugees, and reiterated demands for international support to secure Israel's withdrawal from the Golan Heights. In June 1999 the League condemned an Israeli aerial attack on Beirut and southern Lebanon. Mauritania, although a League member state, established full diplomatic relations with Israel in October, prompting protests in a number of Arab countries. In November the League demanded that Israel compensate Palestinians for alleged losses incurred by their enforced use of the Israeli currency.

In February 2000 the League strongly condemned an Israeli aerial attack on southern Lebanon; the League's Council changed the venue of its next meeting, in March, from the League's Cairo headquarters to Beirut as a gesture of solidarity with Lebanon. The League welcomed the withdrawal of Israeli forces from southern Lebanon in May, although it subsequently condemned continuing territorial violations by the Israeli military. At a meeting of the Council in early September resolutions were passed urging international bodies to avoid participating in conferences in Jerusalem, reiterating a threatened boycott of a US chain of restaurants that was accused of operating a franchise in an Israeli settlement in the West Bank, and opposing an Israeli initiative for a Jewish emblem to be included as a symbol of the International Red Cross and Red Crescent Movement. At an emergency summit meeting convened in late October in response to mounting insecurity in Jerusalem and the Occupied Territories, 15 Arab heads of state, senior officials from six countries and Yasser Arafat, the then Palestinian National Authority (PA) leader, strongly rebuked Israel, which was accused of inciting the ongoing violent disturbances by stalling the progress of the peace process. The summit determined to 'freeze' co-operation with Israel and requested the formation of an international committee to conduct an impartial assessment of the situation. The summit also endorsed the establishment of an 'al-Aqsa Fund', with a value of US $800m., which was to finance initiatives aimed at promoting the Arab and Islamic identity of Jerusalem, and a smaller 'Jerusalem Intifada Fund' to support the families of Palestinians killed in the unrest. A follow-up committee was subsequently established to implement the resolutions adopted by the emergency summit.

In January 2001 a meeting of Arab League ministers of foreign affairs reviewed a proposed framework agreement, presented by outgoing US President Clinton, which aimed to resolve the continuing extreme tension between the Israeli and Palestinian authorities. The meeting agreed that the issues dominating the stalled Middle East peace process should not be redefined, strongly objecting to a proposal that, in exchange for Palestinian assumption of control over Muslim holy sites in Jerusalem, Palestinians exiled at the time of the foundation of the Israeli state in 1948 should forgo their claimed right to return to their former homes. In March 2001 the League's first ordinary annual summit-level Council was convened, in Amman, Jordan. The summit issued the Amman Declaration, which emphasized the promotion of Arab unity, and demanded the reversal of Israel's 1967 occupation of Arab territories. Heads of state attending the summit requested that the League consider means of reactivating the now relaxed Arab economic boycott of Israel. In May 2001 League ministers of foreign affairs determined that all political contacts with Israel should be suspended in protest at aerial attacks by Israel on Palestinian targets in the West Bank. In July representatives of 13 member countries met in Damascus, under the auspices of the Central Boycott Office. The meeting declared unanimous support for reactivating trade measures against Israeli companies and foreign businesses dealing with Israel. In August an emergency meeting of ministers of foreign affairs of the member states was convened at the request of the Palestinian authorities to address the recent escalation of hostilities and Israel's seizure of institutions in East Jerusalem. The meeting, which was attended by the League's Secretary-General and the leader of the Palestinian Authority (PA), Yasser Arafat, aimed to formulate a unified Arab response to the situation.

In early March 2002 a meeting of League ministers of foreign affairs agreed to support an initiative proposed by Crown Prince Abdullah of Saudi Arabia aimed at brokering a peaceful settlement to the, by then, critical Palestinian–Israeli crisis. The Saudi-backed plan—entailing the restoration of 'normal' Arab relations with Israel and acceptance of its right to exist in peace and security, in exchange for a full Israeli withdrawal from the Occupied Territories, the establishment of an independent Palestinian state with East Jerusalem at its capital, and the return of refugees—was unanimously endorsed, as the first-ever pan-Arab Palestinian-Israeli peace initiative, by the summit-level Council held in Beirut in late March. The plan urged compliance with UN Security Council Resolution 194 concerning the return of Palestinian refugees to Israel, or appropriate compensation for their property; however, precise details of eligibility criteria for the proposed return, a contentious issue owing to the potentially huge numbers of refugees and descendants of refugees involved, were not elaborated. Conditions imposed by Israel on Yasser Arafat's freedom of movement deterred him from attending the summit. At the end of March the League's Secretary-General condemned the Israeli military's siege of Arafat's presidential compound in Ramallah (initiated in retaliation against a succession of Palestinian bomb attacks on Israeli civilians). In April an extraordinary Council meeting, held at the request of Palestine to consider the 'unprecedented deterioration' of the situation in the Palestinian territories, accused certain states (notably the USA) of implementing a pro-Israeli bias that enabled Israel to act outside the scope of international law and to ignore relevant UN resolutions, and accused Israel of undermining international co-operation in combating terrorism by attempting to equate its actions towards the Palestinian people with recent anti-terrorism activities conducted by the USA. A meeting organized by the Central Boycott Office at the end of April agreed to expand boycott measures and assessed the status of 17 companies believed to have interests in Israel. Israel's termination of its siege of Arafat's Ramallah compound in early May was welcomed by the Secretary-General. Following an aerial raid by the Israeli military on targets in Gaza in late July, the League urged a halt to the export of weaponry, particularly F-16 military aircraft, to Israel. A Council meeting held in early September agreed to intensify Arab efforts to expose Israeli atrocities against the Palestinians and urged the international community to provide protection and reparations for Palestinians. The Council authorized the establishment of a committee to address the welfare of imprisoned Palestinians and urged the USA and the United Kingdom to reconsider their policies on exporting weaponry to Israel, while issuing a resolution concerning the danger posed by Israel's possession of weapons of mass destruction.

In November 2003 the League welcomed the adoption by the UN Security Council of a resolution endorsing the adoption in April by the so-called Quartet, comprising envoys from the UN, the European Union (EU), Russia and the USA, of a 'performance-based roadmap to a permanent two-state solution to the Israeli–Palestinian conflict'.

In January 2004 the International Court of Justice (ICJ) authorized the participation of the League in proceedings relating to a request for an advisory opinion on the *Legal Consequences of the Construction of a Wall in the Occupied Palestinian Territory*, referred to the ICJ by the UN General Assembly in late 2003; the League welcomed the ICJ's conclusions on the case, published in July 2004. The 2004 summit meeting of Arab League heads of state, held in Tunis, in May, condemned contraventions of international law by the Israeli Government, in particular continuing settlement activities and the use of unjudicial killings and other violence, and focused on the humanitarian situation of Palestinians recently displaced by large-scale house demolitions in Rafah, Gaza. In January 2005 the League welcomed the election of Mahmud Abbas as the new Executive President of the PA, following the death in November 2004 of Yasser Arafat.

In March 2007 the annual summit meeting of the League reaffirmed the League's support for the 2002 peace initiative proposed by Crown Prince Abdullah of Saudi Arabia, and urged the Israeli authorities to resume direct negotiations based on the principles of the initiative. In July 2007 the ministers of foreign affairs of Egypt and Jordan, representing the League, visited Israel to promote the 2002 initiative. The March 2009 League summit meeting condemned the intensive military assault on Gaza perpetrated by Israeli forces (with the stated aim of ending rocket attacks launched by Hamas and other militant groups on Israeli targets) during late December 2008–mid-January 2009. The summit urged Israel to establish a time frame for committing to the peace process. In October an emergency meeting of the League condemned attacks by the Israeli armed forces on the al-Aqsa Mosque in Jerusalem.

The March 2010 summit meeting, held in Sirte, agreed, in its final declaration, all Israeli measures seeking to alter the features and demographic, humanitarian and historic situation of occupied Jerusalem to be invalid and unacceptable, while appealing to the international community (particularly the UN Security Council, the EU and UNESCO) to act to save East Jerusalem and maintain the al-Aqsa Mosque. The meeting's declaration urged that a special session of the UN General Assembly should be held with a view to halting Israeli measures that contravened international law, and mandated the formation of a League legal committee to follow up the issue of the 'judaization' of East Jerusalem and the confiscation of Arab property, and to take these issues before national and international courts with appropriate jurisdiction. In March 2013 the meeting of League heads of state, convened in Doha, approved the establishment of an Arab East Jerusalem Fund, to finance projects and programmes that would maintain the Arab and Islamic character of the city.

In June 2010, in response to an Israeli raid at the end of May on a flotilla of vessels carrying humanitarian aid through international waters towards the Gaza Strip, resulting in nine civilian fatalities and wounding at least 40 further people, the League Secretary-General visited Gaza in a gesture of solidarity towards the Palestinian people. During the visit he demanded the termination of the blockade imposed since 2006 by Israel against Gaza. The League was critical of a UN-commissioned report on the flotilla incident, released in September 2011, which, while concluding that the Israeli army had used 'excessive and unreasonable' force, also found the Israeli naval blockade of Gaza to have been imposed as a 'legitimate security measure' to prevent weapons from reaching Gaza by sea, and found that the flotilla had acted recklessly in attempting to breach the naval blockade.

In July 2011 the recently appointed League Secretary-General, Nabil al-Arabi, announced that the League would encourage the UN to grant full membership—and consequently recognition as an independent state—to Palestine. In September the Executive President of the Palestinian Authority submitted a formal application to the UN Secretary-General for Palestine's admission to the UN; this, however, was rejected by the UN Security Council. In July 2012 the League mandated an internal committee to prepare a petition to be presented to the UN in support of Palestine's proposed membership. The UN General Assembly granted observer status (and consequently recognition of de facto statehood) to Palestine in November of that year. Later in that month, having met with the Palestinian leadership, al-Arabi announced that the League would continue to pursue the objective of full accession by Palestine to the UN.

In April 2013 a delegation of the League met with the US Secretary of State, in Washington, DC, USA, to discuss the 2002 Saudi Arabia-proposed peace initiative; subsequently the League delegation indicated that—rather than conforming to the precise land borders in place prior to the 1967 Israeli occupation of Arab territories—the Palestinians might be prepared to consider mutually agreed minor trades in territory in order to resolve the situation with Israel. In mid-May representatives of the League, Jordan and Palestine requested the UN Security Council, without success, to declare itself as actively engaged in efforts to restart the peace process. In July delegates of the League met again with the US Secretary of State to consider a US initiative to restart the Palestinian-Israeli peace talks; subsequently the League delegation issued a statement endorsing the initiative, and asserting that any future agreement must be based on a two-state solution, through the establishment of an independent Palestinian state in accordance with boundaries as at 4 June 1967, but reiterating the possibility of limited exchanges of territory of equal value and size.

CONFLICT IN THE PERSIAN (ARABIAN) GULF

In March 1984 an emergency meeting established an Arab League committee to encourage international efforts to bring about a negotiated settlement of the Iran–Iraq War. In May ministers of foreign affairs adopted a resolution urging Iran to stop attacking non-belligerent ships and installations in the Gulf region; similar attacks by Iraq were not mentioned. An extraordinary summit conference was held in November 1987, mainly to discuss the war between Iran and Iraq. Contrary to expectations, the participants unanimously agreed on a statement expressing support for Iraq in its defence of its legitimate rights, and criticizing Iran for its procrastination in accepting UN Security Council Resolution 598 of July, which had recommended a cease-fire and negotiations on a settlement of the conflict. In March 2001 the League's Council accused Iran of threatening regional security by conducting military manoeuvres on the three disputed islands—Abu Musa and the Greater and Lesser Tunb—in the Persian (Arabian) Gulf that were also claimed by the United Arab Emirates (UAE). In September 1992 the League's Council issued a condemnation of Iran's alleged occupation of the three islands and decided to refer the issue to the UN.

In May 1990 a summit conference, held in Baghdad, Iraq (which was boycotted by Syria and Lebanon), criticized recent efforts by Western governments to prevent the development of advanced weapons technology in Iraq. In August an emergency summit conference was held to discuss the invasion and annexation of Kuwait by Iraq. Twelve members (Bahrain, Djibouti, Egypt, Kuwait, Lebanon, Morocco, Oman, Qatar, Saudi Arabia, Somalia, Syria and the UAE) approved a resolution condemning Iraq's action, and demanding the withdrawal of Iraqi forces from Kuwait and the reinstatement of the Government. The 12 states expressed support for the Saudi Arabian Government's invitation to the USA to send forces to defend Saudi Arabia; they also agreed to impose economic sanctions on Iraq, and to provide troops for an Arab defensive force in Saudi Arabia. The remaining member states, however, condemned the presence of foreign troops in Saudi Arabia, and their ministers of foreign affairs refused to attend a meeting, held at the end of August, to discuss possible solutions to the crisis. In November King Hassan of Morocco urged the convening of a summit conference, in an attempt to find an 'Arab solution' to Iraq's annexation of Kuwait. However, the divisions in the Arab world over the issue meant that conditions for such a meeting could not be agreed.

In September 1996 the League condemned US missile attacks against Iraq as an infringement of that country's sovereignty. In addition, it expressed concern at the impact on Iraqi territorial integrity of Turkish intervention in the north of Iraq. In June 1997 the League condemned Turkey's military incursion into northern Iraq and demanded a withdrawal of Turkish troops from Iraqi territory. In November 1997 the League expressed concern at the tensions arising from Iraq's decision not to co-operate fully with UN weapons inspectors, and held several meetings with representatives of the Iraqi administration in an effort to secure a peaceful conclusion to the impasse.

In early 1998 the Secretary-General of the League condemned the use or threat of force against Iraq and continued to undertake diplomatic efforts to secure Iraq's compliance with UN Security Council resolutions. The League endorsed the agreement concluded between the UN Secretary-General and the Iraqi authorities in late February, and reaffirmed its commitment to facilitating the eventual removal of the international embargo against Iraq. In November, following an escalation of tensions between the Iraqi authorities and UN weapons inspectors, the Secretary-General reiterated the League's opposition to the use of force against Iraq, but urged Iraq to maintain a flexible approach in its relations with the UN. The League condemned the subsequent bombing of strategic targets in Iraq, conducted by US and British military aircraft from mid-December, and offered immediate medical assistance to victims of the attacks. An emergency meeting of ministers of foreign affairs, held in late January 1999 to formulate a unified Arab response to the aerial attacks on targets in Iraq, expressed concern at the military response to the stand-off between Iraq and the UN, and agreed to establish a seven-member ad hoc committee to consider the removal of punitive measures against Iraq within the framework of UN resolutions. However, the Iraqi delegation withdrew from the meeting in protest at the final statement, which included a request that Iraq recognize Kuwait's territorial integrity. During March 2000 the Secretary-General of the League expressed regret over Iraq's failure to join the ad hoc committee established in early 1999 and also over Iraq's refusal to co-operate with the recently established UN Monitoring, Verification and Inspection Commission (UNMOVIC).

In March 2001 the League, convened at the level of heads of state in Amman, Jordan, demanded the removal of the UN sanctions against Iraq. At the summit-level Council, held in Beirut in March 2002, a rapprochement occurred between Iraq and Kuwait when the Iraqi envoy representing Saddam Hussain declared Iraq's respect for Kuwait's sovereignty and security. In August the Secretary-General expressed strong concern at US threats to attack Iraq in view of its failure to implement UN resolutions, stating that such action would seriously undermine regional stability. A Council meeting held in early September reiterated its complete opposition to the threat of aggression against any Arab country, including Iraq, and demanded the withdrawal of the sanctions against that country. In mid-September, following an ultimatum by the USA that military action against Iraq would ensue were the UN to fail within a short time limit to ensure the elimination of any Iraqi-held weapons of mass destruction, the League urged Iraq to negotiate the return of UN weapons inspectors with a view to avoiding confrontation. Soon afterwards, following tripartite consultations between the Secretary-General of the League, the UN Secretary-General and the Iraqi foreign minister concerning the implementation of UN resolutions and eventual withdrawal of UN sanctions, Iraq agreed to admit UNMOVIC personnel. An emergency meeting of the Council, convened in early November, reviewed the recent adoption by the UN Security Council of Resolution 1441, establishing a strict time frame for Iraqi compliance with UN demands and authorizing the use of force against Iraq in response to non-compliance. The Council urged Iraq to co-operate with UNMOVIC and IAEA inspection teams, requested the inclusion of Arab weapons inspectors in the teams, and urged that the resolution should not be used as a pretext to launch a war against Iraq, emphasizing the importance of a peaceful resolution of the situation.

In March 2003 a meeting of heads of state, convened in Sharm el-Sheikh, Egypt, issued a final communiqué rejecting threatened aggression against Iraq, reiterating that the Saddam Hussain regime should co-operate with UN weapons inspectors, urging that the inspectors be given enough time to complete their work, and declaring that the League would form a committee of diplomats to explain its position to concerned international parties. In March, following the initiation of US-led military action against the Saddam Hussain regime, the League participated in a joint meeting of Arab organizations convened to consider means of assisting the Iraqi people. In March 2006 the League determined to establish a mission in Iraq to contribute to that country's rehabilitation and national reconciliation.

LIBYA

In December 1991 the League expressed solidarity with Libya, which was under international pressure to extradite two government agents who were suspected of involvement in the explosion which destroyed a US passenger aircraft over Lockerbie, United Kingdom, in December 1988. In March 1992 the League appointed a committee to seek to resolve the disputes between Libya and the USA, the United Kingdom and France over the Lockerbie bomb and the explosion which destroyed a French passenger aircraft over Niger in September 1989. The League condemned the UN's decision, at the end of March, to impose sanctions against Libya, and appealed for a negotiated solution. In September 1997 Arab League ministers of foreign affairs advocated a gradual removal of international sanctions against Libya, and agreed that member countries should permit international flights to leave Libya for specific humanitarian and religious purposes and when used for the purpose of transporting foreign nationals. In August 1998 the USA and United Kingdom accepted a proposal of the Libyan Government, supported by the Arab League, that the suspects in the Lockerbie case be tried in The Hague, Netherlands, under Scottish law. In March 1999 the League's Council determined that member states would suspend sanctions imposed against Libya, once arrangements for the trial of the suspects in the Lockerbie case had been finalized. (The suspects were transferred to a detention centre in the Netherlands in early April, whereupon the UN Security Council suspended its sanctions against Libya.) At the end of January 2001, following the completion of the trial in The Hague of the two Libyans accused of complicity in the Lockerbie case (one of whom was found guilty and one of whom was acquitted), the Secretary-General of the League urged the UN Security Council fully to terminate the sanctions against Libya that had been suspended in 1999. Meeting in mid-March, the League's Council pledged that member states would not consider themselves bound by the (inactive) UN sanctions. In early September 2002 the Council deplored the USA's continuing active imposition of sanctions against Libya and endorsed Libya's right to claim compensation in respect of these.

In mid-February 2011, in protest against violent measures taken by the regime of the Libyan leader Col Muammar al-Qaddafi against opposition groupings, the Libyan delegate to the League resigned his representative position. An emergency session of the League convened soon afterwards suspended Libya from participation in meetings of the League. The League supported the adoption by the UN Security Council, in March, of Resolution 1973, which imposed a no-fly zone in Libya's airspace, strengthened sanctions against the Qaddafi regime, demanded an immediate cease-fire, and authorized member states to take 'all necessary measures to protect civilians and civilian populated areas under threat of attack' by forces loyal to Qaddafi, 'while excluding a foreign occupation force of any form on any part of Libyan territory'. Following the instigation of the UN-mandated military action in Libya, the League Secretary-General reportedly emphasized that the focus of the military intervention ought to be on the protection of civilians and ought not to exceed the mandate to impose a no-fly zone. In August, as opposition forces captured the Libyan capital, Tripoli, the League Secretary-General offered full solidarity to the new Libyan National Transitional Council, as the legitimate representative of the Libyan people. Libya was readmitted to full League membership at the end of that month. The League at that time urged the international community to release all assets and property of the Libyan state, previously blocked by economic sanctions. Following the death of al-Qaddafi in October the Secretary-General urged unity and extended the League's full support for the country's transition.

In September 2012 the Secretary-General of the League condemned an armed attack on the US Consulate in Benghazi, Libya, in which the US Ambassador to Libya and three Consulate personnel were killed. The Secretary-General urged the US Government to denounce a US-produced film deemed to be deeply offensive to Islam, which initially was thought to have been the provocation for the attack.

SYRIA

By August 2011 it was estimated that around 2,200 anti-government street protesters had been killed by security forces—deploying tanks and snipers—during several months of unrest in Syria. A meeting of Arab League ministers responsible for foreign affairs convened in that month issued a statement urging the Syrian regime to act reasonably, stop the ongoing bloodshed, and respect the 'legitimate demands' of the Syrian people. The meeting also determined that the League Secretary-General, Nabil al-Arabi, would visit the Syrian authorities with a peace initiative aimed at resolving the situation through dialogue. Accordingly, talks were held between the Secretary-General and President Bashar al-Assad in the Syrian capital, Damascus, in early September. It was reported that al-Arabi and al-Assad discussed measures aimed at accelerating political reforms in Syria, and that the League Secretary-General stated his rejection of foreign intervention in the Syrian situation. The League's peace initiative was, however, reportedly rejected by both the Syrian authorities and protesters. In October al-Arabi led a further delegation to the country, amid an escalation of attacks by the security forces. In mid-November the League, meeting in emergency session, voted to suspend Syria from participation in meetings of the League, and to impose economic and diplomatic sanctions in protest at the violent repression of political opponents and civilian demonstrators by the government, and its failure to implement a peace initiative. The resolution was endorsed by 18 members; Syria, Lebanon and Yemen voted against the suspension (Iraq abstained). The measures came into effect four days later, when no concessions had been made by the Syrian authorities. On 19 December the Syrian authorities reportedly agreed to the League's peace plan to withdraw security forces and heavy weapons from civilian areas, to initiate negotiations with the opposition movement and to release political prisoners. The Arab League was to send an observer mission to the country, with an initial mandate of one month, in order to monitor compliance with the measures. However, within days of the arrival of the first 50 observers, on 26 December, the mission was strongly criticized for its ineffectiveness in preventing further government attacks and its inability to act independently of the authorities to assess accurately the level of violence. In early January 2012 Arab League ministers of foreign affairs met to consider the mission's initial findings and to discuss demands for its withdrawal. The meeting agreed to maintain and to reinforce the mission and demanded that the Syrian authorities co-operate fully. On 22 January Arab League ministers agreed on a plan of action to end the conflict, requiring President Assad to transfer his authority to an interim government within two months, and democratic parliamentary and presidential elections to be conducted within six months. The proposals were to be submitted for approval by the UN Security Council. They were rejected, the following day, by the Syrian authorities. The ministerial meeting agreed to extend the monitoring mission. Saudi Arabia, however, decided to withdraw from the operation. On 24 January members of the Gulf Cooperation Council also resolved to withdraw their monitors. A few days later the League announced that it was suspending the mission owing to a sharp deterioration in the security situation in Syria. In early February Russia and the People's Republic of China vetoed a draft resolution at the UN Security Council to endorse the League's peace plan for Syria. In mid-February League ministers adopted a resolution providing for the termination of the suspended monitoring mission; ending diplomatic co-operation with the Syrian regime; and proposing the creation of a joint Arab-UN peace-keeping mission to Syria. Later in that month the Secretaries-General of the League and of the UN appointed Kofi Annan—formerly the UN Secretary-General (until 2006)—as their Joint Special Envoy on the Syrian Crisis; in March Nasser al-Kidwa, a former minister of foreign affairs in the Palestine National Authority, and Jean-Marie Guéhenno, a former UN Under-Secretary-General for Peace-keeping Operations, were appointed as Deputy Joint Special Envoys. Towards the end of February an international conference on the situation in Syria, which had escalated significantly, was convened in Tunis, Tunisia, by the 'Friends of Syria', a coalition initiated by France and the USA, with League support (specifically, with endorsement from Qatar and Saudi Arabia), following China and Russia's veto of the Security Council's draft resolution on Syria. The conference urged the UN to consider establishing a peace-keeping mission for Syria. In late March the Syrian Government announced its acceptance of a six-point peace plan proposed earlier in that month by Annan. The plan envisaged: (i) a commitment to working with the Joint Envoy in an inclusive Syrian-led political process aimed at addressing the legitimate aspirations and concerns of the Syrian people; (ii) a UN-monitored cease-fire by all parties, including a commitment by the Syrian regime to withdraw troops and heavy weaponry from population centres; (iii) a commitment to enabling the timely provision of humanitarian assistance to all areas affected by the fighting, and the immediate implementation of a daily two-hour humanitarian pause; (iv) the expedited release of arbitrarily arrested detainees; (v) free access and movement for journalists; and (vi) freedom of association and the right to demonstrate peacefully for all. The plan did not demand explicitly the resignation of Syrian President Assad. Shortly afterwards Arab League heads of state, gathered at a summit meeting in Baghdad, Iraq, endorsed the plan, and called for its immediate and full implementation. In mid-April the UN Security Council—taking note of an assessment by the League-UN Joint Special Envoy that the parties to the Syrian violence appeared to be observing a cessation of fire, and that the Syrian Government had begun to implement its commitments under the plan—authorized an advance team of up to 30 unarmed military observers to monitor the cease-fire, pending the deployment of a full cease-fire supervision mission. Soon afterwards, as violence had escalated since the attempt to impose a cease-fire, and Syrian forces had not withdrawn from urban areas, the UN Secretary-General requested that a full team of 300 unarmed observers should be promptly deployed. Consequently, on 21 April, the UN Security Council unanimously authorized the establishment of the UN Supervision Mission in Syria (UNSMIS), initially for a period of 90 days, with a mandate to monitor the cessation of violence and to observe and support the full implementation of the six-point peace plan. Repeated violations of the terms of the peace plan continued, however, to be reported. In late May the UN Security Council issued a statement unanimously condemning—as an 'outrageous use of force against the civilian population' constituting a violation of applicable international law—the indiscriminate massacre (confirmed by UNSMIS observers), of an estimated 108 men, women and children, and the wounding of many more, resulting from the shelling of a residential neighbourhood—the rebel-controlled village of El-Houleh, near Homs—allegedly by Syrian government forces. The Council also condemned the killing of civilians in El-Houleh by shooting at close range and by severe physical abuse. Reiterating its full support to the efforts of the Arab League-UN Joint Special Envoy for the implementation of his six-point plan, the Council demanded that the Syrian Government immediately cease the use of heavy weapons in population centres, and immediately return its troops to their barracks. In early June the 'Free Syrian Army' group of anti-government militants announced that it was no longer committed to the six-point peace plan. Shortly afterwards at least an estimated further 78 people, again including women and children, were reported to have been killed in the western village of Qbeir, by pro-government militants, following the shelling of the area by government forces. A meeting of the Security Council held soon afterwards, with participation by the Arab League and UN Secretaries-General and the Joint Special Envoy, requested the UN Secretary-General to put forward a range of options for resolving the Syrian crisis. On 16 June, in view of the escalating insecurity, UNSMIS suspended its patrols in Syria, while remaining committed to ending the violence. In June an extraordinary ministerial-level meeting of the League Council requested the Arab Satellite Communications Organization and the Egyptian company Nilesat to suspend broadcasts via Arab Satellites of official and private Syrian television channels. In mid-July, by which time the violence in Syria had further intensified, and the situation was deemed to be a 'civil war', China and Russia vetoed a draft UN Security Council resolution that would have imposed sanctions on the Syrian regime. On 22 July 2012 an emergency meeting of Arab ministers of foreign affairs agreed that President Assad should resign and leave the country, and that opposition parties should form a government of national unity. At the beginning of August, in view of the failure of the parties to the Syrian conflict to adhere to the six-point peace plan, and of the divisions within the UN Security Council over Syria, Annan announced that he would step down as Joint Special Envoy at the end of that month; in mid-August the League and UN appointed a Joint Special Representative on Syria, Lakhdar Brahimi, to take office at the beginning of September, and appointed Nasser al-Kidwa (Deputy to Annan) as Deputy Joint Special Representative. The Security Council determined in mid-August not to extend the mandate of UNSMIS beyond 19 August, and the mission was terminated accordingly. In mid-September the new Joint Special Representative visited Damascus to discuss the ongoing, and worsening, crisis with the Syrian President and opposition representatives. In October, in view of mounting tensions between Syria and Turkey (including an incident at the two countries' border at the beginning of the month in which five Turkish civilians were killed, and others injured, by cross-border mortar fire from the Syrian military), the Joint Special Representative engaged in discussions with the Syrian and Turkish authorities. Following a bomb attack in Beirut, on 19 October, that resulted in eight fatalities, including the death of a senior commander in the Lebanese military, potentially destabilizing that country, it was feared that the conflict in Syria might ignite wider regional tensions. On the following day Brahimi entered into negotiations with parties to the Syrian conflict aimed at initiating a temporary cease-fire during the upcoming Muslim festival of Id al-Adha; it was announced on 24 October that this had been agreed. However, the truce, declared on 26 October, was almost immediately broken by a car bomb explosion in Damascus, and within 48 hours at least 100 further violent deaths had been reported.

In November 2012 the League formally recognized the National Coalition for Syrian Revolutionary and Opposition Forces, then under the leadership of Ahmed Moaz al-Khatib, as Syria's 'legitimate representative and main interlocutor with the Arab League'. In February 2013 the participants—including delegates from Arab NGOs—in a conference on human rights challenges to the League urged League member states to sign a letter issued in January by more than 50 UN member states, led by Switzerland, that urged the UN Security Council to refer the situation in Syria to the International Criminal Court. In early March the League Secretary-General, stated that, as the likelihood of achieving a political solution to Syria's internal conflict had receded, the onwards objective of the League/UN Joint Special Representative should be to support the formation of a Syrian transitional government. At that time League foreign ministers, meeting in Cairo, adopted a resolution urging the National Coalition to nominate an executive body to represent Syria at the impending 24th summit meeting of League heads of state, and thereafter to retain Syria's seat, pending the staging of elections leading to the establishment in that country of a government with a democratic mandate. Lebanon reportedly refused to support the resolution, while reservations were also expressed by Algeria and Iraq. Syria's seat at the 24th League summit of heads of state, convened in March, in Doha, was, consequently, taken by a delegation from the National Coalition, headed by al-Khatib (who shortly before the summit had resigned as the Coalition's leader).

In March 2013 the UN Secretary-General announced that a mission comprising UN weapons experts, in co-operation with specialists from the World Health Organization and the Organisation for the Prohibition of Chemical Weapons, would initiate an investigation into the alleged use of chemical weapons in the Syrian conflict; at the end of that month a Swedish scientist, Åke Sellström, was appointed by the UN Secretary-General to head the mission. Addressing the UN Security Council in mid-April the UN-Arab League Joint Special Representative emphasised his continuing pursuit of a political solution to the conflict. On 18 August the Sellström-led mission arrived in Syria to investigate three previously reported chemical attacks. The alleged use on 21 August of chemical weapons against unarmed civilians in the rebel-held area of Ghouta, Damascus, prompted widespread international condemnation. In the immediate aftermath of the incident several thousand patients were treated for apparently neurotoxic symptoms, and up to around 1,400 fatalities were reported. The UN Secretary-General initiated an impartial and thorough investigation into the situation, and from 26–30 August the UN mission visited the site of the attack, to examine the scene and to take relevant soil and biological samples. A meeting of League foreign ministers convened in early September, in Cairo, urged the UN Security Council and the international community to take 'deterrent' measures against the Syrian regime, which it accused of responsibility for the alleged Damascus chemical attack. A meeting held shortly afterwards, in Paris, France, between the US Secretary of State and the leaders of Bahrain, Egypt, Jordan, Kuwait, Morocco, the Palestinian Authority, Qatar and Saudi Arabia, also accused the al-Assad regime of using chemical weapons, and stated that the regime had thereby transgressed an international 'red line'; however, the League member states participating in the meeting did not commit to endorsing a US proposal that punitive military action should be launched against the Syrian regime. It was reported at that time that the participating League states had declared their readiness to sign a statement recently released by 11 G20 member states urging a strong international response in view of the atrocity of 21 August. In early September 2013 the Russian minister of foreign affairs, US Secretary of State and Joint Arab League-UN Special Representative on Syria gave consideration to a proposal by Russia that Syria should surrender its chemical stockpiles to international control. Soon afterwards the Syrian regime notified the UN Secretary-General that it was taking measures to accede to the 1992 Convention on the Prohibition of the Development, Production, Stockpiling and Use of Chemical Weapons and on their Destruction, and would observe the obligations imposed by the Convention prior to its national entry into force. By September 2013 the number of civilians killed in the conflict since March 2011 was estimated to have exceeded 100,000, and more than 2m. Syrians had fled their country.

Joint Special Representative of the League of Arab States and the UN on Syria: LAKHDAR BRAHIMI (Algeria).

LATIN AMERICA

The first summit of heads of state and government of the South American-Arab Countries (ASPA) was convened in May 2005, in Brasília, Brazil, and a second ASPA summit was organized in March 2009, in Doha, Qatar. The third ASPA summit was convened in Lima, Peru, in October 2012, and ASPA IV was to take place in Riyadh, Saudi Arabia, during 2015. ASPA also meets at the level of foreign ministers (every two years, on the sidelines of the UN General Assembly), senior officials (every six months), and in the format of a number of sectoral committees, covering co-operation in the following areas: cultural, economic, environmental, scientific and technological, and social. An Arab-South American Library is being developed in Algiers, Algeria, under the ASPA co-operation initiative. In January 2013 the first ASPA ministerial meeting on energy, held in Abu Dhabi, adopted the Abu Dhabi Declaration on enhanced co-operation.

SUB-SAHARAN AFRICA

In 1992 the League attempted to mediate between the warring factions in Somalia. In early June 2002 the League appointed a special representative to Somalia to assist with the ongoing reconciliation efforts in that country.

In early September 2002 the Council established a committee to encourage peace efforts in Sudan. In May 2004 representatives of the League participated in an African Union (AU) fact-finding mission to assess the ongoing humanitarian crisis in Darfur, Sudan. In August an emergency meeting of League ministers of foreign affairs, convened to address the situation in Darfur, declared support for the Sudanese Government's measures to disarm Arab militias and punish human rights violations there. In November the League was asked to join a panel appointed to monitor the cease-fire agreement that had been adopted in April by the parties to the Darfur conflict. In March 2006 the meeting of heads of state agreed to offer financial support to the AU Mission in Sudan, then deployed to the Darfur region of that country. The summit meeting in March 2007 expressed continued support for all peace accords signed between conflicting parties in Sudan. In March 2009 the summit of heads of state expressed full support and solidarity with Sudan in rejecting the legitimacy of the arrest warrant that had been issued earlier in that month by the International Criminal Court against President Omar Al-Bashir of Sudan.

In October 2010 the League and the AU jointly organized an Afro-Arab summit, held in Sirte; leaders attending the summit endorsed a new Strategic Plan of the Afro-Arab Co-operation, covering the period 2011–15. The next Afro-Arab summit was scheduled to be held in Kuwait, in November 2013.

Finance

The League budgets around US $60m. annually to fund the Secretariat, including a small allocation to the Arab Fund for Technical Assistance in African States. Member states' contributions are determined by a scale of assessments, under which Kuwait and Saudi Arabia each contribute 14% to the total budget (the largest national contributions).

Publications

Arab Perspectives—Sh'oun Arabiyya (monthly).

Journal of Arab Affairs (monthly).

Bulletins of treaties and agreements concluded among the member states, essays, regular publications circulated by regional offices.

ORGANIZATION OF ARAB PETROLEUM EXPORTING COUNTRIES—OAPEC

Address: POB 20501, Safat 13066, Kuwait.

Telephone: 24959000; **fax:** 24959755; **e-mail:** oapec@oapecorg.org; **internet:** www.oapecorg.org.

OAPEC was established in 1968 to safeguard the interests of members and to determine ways and means for their co-operation in various forms of economic activity in the petroleum industry. In 2011 OAPEC member states contributed around 31% of total world petroleum production and an estimated 14.5% of total global marketed natural gas. In that year OAPEC member states accounted for nearly 58% of total global oil reserves and almost 28% of total global reserves of natural gas.

MEMBERS

Algeria	Kuwait	Saudi Arabia
Bahrain	Libya	Syria
Egypt	Qatar	United Arab Emirates
Iraq		

Organization

(September 2013)

MINISTERIAL COUNCIL

The Council consists normally of the ministers of petroleum of the member states, and forms the supreme authority of the Organization, responsible for drawing up its general policy, directing its activities and laying down its governing rules. It meets twice yearly, and may hold extraordinary sessions. Chairmanship is on an annual rotating basis.

EXECUTIVE BUREAU

Assists the Council to direct the management of the Organization, approves staff regulations, reviews the budget, and refers it to the Council, considers matters relating to the Organization's agreements and activities and draws up the agenda for the Council. The Bureau comprises one senior official from each member state. Chairmanship is by rotation on an annual basis, following the same order as the Ministerial Council chairmanship. The Bureau convenes at least three times a year.

GENERAL SECRETARIAT

The General Secretariat is composed of the Secretary-General's Office; the Arab Centre for Energy Studies (established in 1983), which comprises units of Technical Affairs, and Economics; the Information and Library Department; and the Finance and Administrative Affairs Department.

Secretary-General: ABBAS ALI NAQI (Kuwait).

JUDICIAL TRIBUNAL

The Tribunal comprises seven judges from Arab countries. Its task is to settle differences in interpretation and application of the OAPEC Agreement, arising between members and also between OAPEC and its affiliates; disputes among member countries on petroleum activities falling within OAPEC's jurisdiction and not under the sovereignty of member countries; and disputes that the Ministerial Council decides to submit to the Tribunal.

Activities

OAPEC co-ordinates different aspects of the Arab petroleum industry through the joint undertakings described below. It co-operates with the League of Arab States and other Arab organizations, and attempts to link petroleum research institutes in the Arab states. It organizes or participates in conferences and seminars, many of which are held jointly with non-Arab organizations in order to enhance Arab and international co-operation. OAPEC collaborates with the Arab Fund for Economic and Social Development (AFESD), the Arab Monetary Fund and the League of Arab States in compiling the annual *Joint Arab Economic Report*, which is issued by the Arab Monetary Fund.

OAPEC provides training in technical matters and in documentation and information. The General Secretariat also conducts technical and feasibility studies and carries out market reviews. It provides information through a library, databank and the publications listed below.

In association with AFESD, OAPEC organizes the Arab Energy Conference every four years. The conference is attended by OAPEC ministers of petroleum and energy, senior officials from other Arab states, and representatives of invited institutions and organizations concerned with energy issues. The ninth Arab Energy Conference, focusing on the theme 'Energy and Arab Co-operation', was held in Doha, Qatar, in May 2010. The 10th was scheduled to take place in mid-2014, in Beirut, Lebanon. OAPEC, with other Arab organizations, participates in the Higher Co-ordination Committee for Higher Arab Action. In June 2012 OAPEC organized a conference, in Abu Dhabi, United Arab Emirates, on 'The development of production capacities of oil in the Arab countries and the current and future role in meeting the global energy demand'.

Finance

The combined General Secretariat and Judicial Tribunal proposed budget for 2013, approved by the Ministerial Council in December 2012, was 2.1m. Kuwaiti dinars.

Publications

Annual Statistical Report.
Energy Resources Monitor (quarterly, Arabic).
OAPEC Monthly Bulletin (Arabic and English editions).
Oil and Arab Co-operation (quarterly, Arabic).
Secretary-General's Annual Report (Arabic and English editions).
Papers, studies, conference proceedings.

OAPEC-Sponsored Ventures

Arab Maritime Petroleum Transport Company (AMPTC): POB 22525, Safat 13086, Kuwait; tel. 24959400; fax 24842996; e-mail amptc.kuwait@amptc.net; internet www.amptc.net; f. 1973 to undertake transport of crude petroleum, gas, refined products and petro-chemicals, and thus to increase Arab participation in the tanker transport industry; owns and operates a fleet of oil tankers and other carriers; also maintains an operations office in Giza, Egypt; auth. cap. US $200m.; Gen. Man. SULAYMAN AL-BASSAM.

Arab Petroleum Investments Corporation (APICORP): POB 9599, Dammam 31423, Saudi Arabia; tel. (3) 847-0444; fax (3) 847-0022; e-mail apicorp@apicorp-arabia.com; internet www.apicorp-arabia.com; f. 1975 to finance investments in petroleum and petrochemicals projects and related industries in the Arab world and in developing countries, with priority being given to Arab joint ventures; projects financed include gas liquefaction plants, petro-chemicals, tankers, oil refineries, pipelines, exploration, detergents, fertilizers and process control instrumentation; in Feb. 2013 launched the *Shari'a*-compliant US $150m. APICORP Petroleum Shipping Fund; auth. cap. $2,400m.; paid-up cap. $750m.; shareholders: Kuwait, Saudi Arabia and United Arab Emirates (17% each), Libya (15%), Iraq and Qatar (10% each), Algeria (5%), Bahrain, Egypt and Syria (3% each); CEO and Gen. Man. AHMAD BIN HAMAD AL-NUAIMI.

Arab Detergent Chemicals Company (ARADET): POB 27064, el-Mansour, Baghdad, Iraq; tel. (1) 541-9893; fax (1) 543-0265; e-mail info@aradetco.com; internet www.aradetco.com; f. 1981; produces and markets linear alkyl benzene; construction of a sodium multiphosphate plant is under way; APICORP holds 32% of shares in the co; auth. cap. 72m. Iraqi dinars; subs. cap. 60m. Iraqi dinars.

Arab Petroleum Services Company (APSCO): POB 12925, Tripoli, Libya; tel. (21) 3409921; fax (21) 3409923; e-mail info@apsco.com.ly; internet apsco.com.ly; f. 1977 to provide petroleum services through the establishment of companies specializing in various activities, and to train specialized personnel; auth. cap. 100m. Libyan dinars; subs. cap. 44m. Libyan dinars.

Arab Drilling and Workover Company: POB 680, Ring Rd, Wadi Rabee, Beir Ettota, Gasir bin Ghisher, Tripoli, Libya; tel. (21) 5635927; fax (21) 5635926; e-mail info@adwoc.com; internet www.adwoc.com; f. 1980; 40% owned by APSCO; auth. cap. 12m. Libyan dinars; Gen. Man. OMRAN ABUKRAA.

Arab Geophysical Exploration Services Company (AGESCO): POB 84224, Tripoli, Libya; tel. (21) 7155770; fax (21) 7155780; e-mail agesco@agesco-ly.com; internet agesco-ly.com; f. 1985; 40% owned by APSCO; auth. cap. 12m. Libyan dinars; subs. cap. 4m. Libyan dinars; Gen. Man. AHMED ESSED.

Arab Well Logging Company (AWLCO): POB 18528/14 JULY, Baghdad, Iraq; tel. (1) 541-8259; e-mail info@awlco.net; internet www.awlco.net; f. 1983 to provide well-logging services and data interpretation; wholly owned subsidiary of APSCO; auth. cap. 7m. Iraqi dinars.

Arab Petroleum Training Institute (APTI): POB 6037, Al-Tajeyat, Baghdad, Iraq; tel. (1) 523-4100; fax (1) 521-0526; f. 1978 to provide instruction in many technical and managerial aspects of the oil industry.

Arab Shipbuilding and Repair Yard Company (ASRY): POB 50110, Hidd, Bahrain; tel. 17671111; fax 17670236; e-mail asryco@batelco.com.bh; internet www.asry.net; f. 1974 to undertake repairs and servicing of vessels; operates a 500,000-dwt dry dock in Bahrain; two floating docks operational since 1992, and two slipways became operational in 2008; has recently diversified its activities, e.g. into building specialized service boats and upgrading oil rigs; cap. (auth. and subsidized) US $170m.; CEO CHRIS POTTER (United Kingdom).

ORGANIZATION OF ISLAMIC COOPERATION—OIC

Address: Medina Rd, Sary St, POB 178, Jeddah 21411, Saudi Arabia.

Telephone: (2) 690-0001; **fax:** (2) 275-1953; **e-mail:** info@oic-oci.org; **internet:** www.oic-oci.org.

The OIC was formally established, as the Organization of the Islamic Conference, at the first conference of Muslim heads of state convened in Rabat, Morocco, in September 1969; the first conference of Muslim foreign ministers, held in Jeddah in March 1970, established the General Secretariat; the latter became operational in May 1971. In June 2011 the 38th ministerial conference agreed to change the name of the organization, with immediate effect, to the Organization of Islamic Cooperation (abbreviated, as hitherto, to OIC).

MEMBERS

Afghanistan	Indonesia	Qatar
Albania	Iran	Saudi Arabia
Algeria	Iraq	Senegal
Azerbaijan	Jordan	Sierra Leone
Bahrain	Kazakhstan	Somalia
Bangladesh	Kuwait	Sudan
Benin	Kyrgyzstan	Suriname
Brunei	Lebanon	Syria*
Burkina Faso	Libya	Tajikistan
Cameroon	Malaysia	Togo
Chad	Maldives	Tunisia
Comoros	Mali	Turkey
Côte d'Ivoire	Mauritania	Turkmenistan
Djibouti	Morocco	Uganda
Egypt	Mozambique	United Arab Emirates
Gabon	Niger	Uzbekistan
The Gambia	Nigeria	Yemen
Guinea	Oman	
Guinea-Bissau	Pakistan	
Guyana	Palestine	

* In August 2012 Syria was suspended from participation in the activities of the OIC and also from all its subsidiary organs and specialized and affiliated institutions, in view of the Syrian Government's violent suppression of opposition elements and related acts of violence against civilian communities.

Note: Observer status has been granted to Bosnia and Herzegovina, the Central African Republic, Russia, Thailand, the Muslim community of the 'Turkish Republic of Northern Cyprus', the Moro National Liberation Front (MNLF) of the southern Philippines, the UN, the African Union, the Non-Aligned Movement, the League of Arab States, the Economic Cooperation Organization and the Cooperation Council for the Arab States of the Gulf. The revised OIC Charter, endorsed in March 2008, made future applications for OIC membership and observer status conditional upon Muslim demographic majority and membership of the UN.

Organization

(September 2013)

SUMMIT CONFERENCES

The supreme body of the organization is the Conference of Heads of State ('Islamic summit'), which met in 1969 in Rabat, Morocco, in 1974 in Lahore, Pakistan, and in January 1981 in Makkah (Mecca), Saudi Arabia, when it was decided that ordinary summit conferences would normally be held every three years in future. An extraordinary summit conference was convened in Doha, Qatar, in March 2003, to consider the situation in Iraq. A further extraordinary conference, held in December 2005, in Makkah, Saudi Arabia, determined to restructure the OIC, and, in August 2012, an extraordinary summit was convened, again in Makkah, with a focus on the ongoing civil war in Syria. The 12th ordinary Islamic summit was convened in Cairo, Egypt, in February 2013, and the 13th was to take place in Turkey, during 2016. The summit conference troika comprises member countries equally representing the OIC's African, Arab and Asian membership.

CONFERENCE OF MINISTERS OF FOREIGN AFFAIRS

Conferences take place annually, to consider the means of implementing the general policy of the OIC, although they may also be convened for extraordinary sessions. The ministerial conference troika comprises member countries equally representing the OIC's African, Arab and Asian membership.

SECRETARIAT

The executive organ of the organization, headed by a Secretary-General (who is elected by the Conference of Ministers of Foreign Affairs for a five-year term, renewable only once) and four Assistant Secretaries-General (similarly appointed).

In March 2013 a specialized Peace, Security and Mediation Unit was inaugurated at the Secretariat.

Secretary-General: Prof. Dr EKMELEDDIN IHSANOGLU (Turkey) (until 31 December 2013), IYAD BIN AMIN MADANI (Saudi Arabia) (designate).

At the summit conference in January 1981 it was decided that an International Islamic Court of Justice should be established to adjudicate in disputes between Muslim countries. Experts met in January 1983 to draw up a constitution for the court; however, by 2013 it was not yet in operation.

EXECUTIVE COMMITTEE

The third extraordinary conference of the OIC, convened in Mecca, Saudi Arabia, in December 2005, mandated the establishment of the Executive Committee, comprising the summit conference and ministerial conference troikas, the OIC host country, and the OIC Secretariat, as a mechanism for following up resolutions of the Conference.

STANDING COMMITTEES

Al-Quds Committee: f. 1975 to implement the resolutions of the Islamic Conference on the status of Jerusalem (Al-Quds); it meets at the level of ministers of foreign affairs; maintains the Al-Quds Fund; Chair. King MUHAMMAD VI OF MOROCCO.

Standing Committee for Economic and Commercial Co-operation (COMCEC): f. 1981; Chair. ABDULLAH GÜL (Pres. of Turkey).

Standing Committee for Information and Cultural Affairs (COMIAC): f. 1981; Chair. MACKY SALL (Pres. of Senegal).

Standing Committee for Scientific and Technological Co-operation (COMSTECH): f. 1981; Chair. ASIF ALI ZARDARI (Pres. of Pakistan).

Other committees include the Islamic Peace Committee, the Permanent Finance Committee, the Committee of Islamic Solidarity with the Peoples of the Sahel, the Eight-Member Committee on the Situation of Muslims in the Philippines, the Six-Member Committee on Palestine, the Committee on UN reform, and the ad hoc Committee on Afghanistan. In addition, there is an Islamic Commission for Economic, Cultural and Social Affairs, and there are OIC Contact Groups on Bosnia and Herzegovina, Iraq, Kosovo, Jammu and Kashmir, Mali (established in 2013), Myanmar (formed in 2012), Sierra Leone, and Somalia. A Commission of Eminent Persons was inaugurated in 2005.

OIC Independent Human Rights Commission (IPHRC): f. 2012 to promote the civil, political, social and economic rights enshrined in the covenants and declarations of the OIC, and in universally agreed human rights instruments, in conformity with Islamic values; inaugural session convened in Jakarta, Indonesia (Feb. 2012); second session convened (in Aug.) in Ankara, Turkey, with a focus on the human rights situations in Mali, Myanmar (with regard to the Rohingya Muslim minority), Palestine, and Syria; in Oct. 2012 issued a statement strongly condemning an assassination attempt made earlier in that month against the Pakistani schoolgirl Malala Yousufzai, who had campaigned for the recognition of the right to education for girls; the Commission emphasized that access to education remained a fundamental human right and identified the right to education and the rights of women and children as priority areas of activity; OIC human rights instruments include: the *Shari'a*-based Cairo Declaration on Human Rights in Islam (1990) and Covenant on the Rights of the Child in Islam (2005); IPHRC comprises 18 commissioners, equally representing Africa, Asia and the Middle East.

Activities

The Organization's aims, as proclaimed in the Charter (adopted in 1972, with revisions endorsed in 1990 and 2008), are:

(i) To promote Islamic solidarity among member states;

(ii) To consolidate co-operation among member states in the economic, social, cultural, scientific and other vital fields, and to arrange consultations among member states belonging to international organizations;

(iii) To endeavour to eliminate racial segregation and discrimination and to eradicate colonialism in all its forms;

(iv) To take necessary measures to support international peace and security founded on justice;

(v) To co-ordinate all efforts for the safeguard of the Holy Places and support of the struggle of the people of Palestine, and help them to regain their rights and liberate their land;

(vi) To strengthen the struggle of all Muslim people with a view to safeguarding their dignity, independence and national rights;

(vii) To create a suitable atmosphere for the promotion of co-operation and understanding among member states and other countries.

The first summit conference of Islamic leaders (representing 24 states) took place in 1969 following the burning of the al-Aqsa Mosque in Jerusalem. At this conference it was decided that Islamic governments should 'consult together with a view to promoting close co-operation and mutual assistance in the economic, scientific, cultural and spiritual fields, inspired by the immortal teachings of Islam'. Thereafter the ministers responsible for foreign affairs of the countries concerned met annually, and adopted the Charter of the Organization of the Islamic Conference in 1972.

At the second Islamic summit conference (Lahore, Pakistan, 1974), the Islamic Solidarity Fund was established, together with a committee of representatives that later evolved into the Islamic Commission for Economic, Cultural and Social Affairs. Subsequently, numerous other subsidiary bodies have been set up (see below).

ECONOMIC CO-OPERATION

A general agreement on economic, technical and commercial co-operation came into force in 1981, providing for the establishment of joint investment projects and trade co-ordination. A plan of action to strengthen economic co-operation was adopted at the third Islamic summit conference in 1981, aiming to promote collective self-reliance and the development of joint ventures in all sectors. The fifth summit conference, held in 1987, approved proposals for joint development of modern technology, and for improving scientific and technical skills in the less developed Islamic countries. In 1994 the 1981 plan of action was revised to place greater emphasis on private sector participation in its implementation. In October 2003 a meeting of COMCEC endorsed measures aimed at accelerating the hitherto slow implementation of the plan of action. A 10-year plan of action for fostering member states' development and strengthening economic and trade co-operation was launched in December 2005.

In 1991 22 OIC member states signed a Framework Agreement on a Trade Preferential System among the OIC Member States (TPS-OIC); this entered into force in 2003, following the requisite ratification by more than 10 member states, and was envisaged as representing the first step towards the eventual establishment of an Islamic common market. A Trade Negotiating Committee was established following the entry into force of the Framework Agreement. The first round of trade negotiations on the establishment of the TPS-OIC, concerning finalizing tariff reduction modalities and an implementation schedule for the Agreement, was held during April 2004–April 2005, and resulted in the conclusion of a Protocol on the Preferential Tariff Scheme for TPS-OIC (PRETAS). In November 2006, at the launch of the second round of negotiations, ministers adopted a roadmap towards establishing the TPS-OIC; the second round of negotiations ended in September 2007 with the adoption of rules of origin for the TPS-OIC. PRETAS entered into force in February 2010. By September 2013 the Framework Agreement had been ratified by 29 OIC member states, and PRETAS had 15 ratifications. In 2013 efforts were under way to enhance the role of the private sector through the promotion of intra-OIC small and medium-sized enterprise clusters, in sectors including agro-food processing, and transportation and logistics.

In March 2008 the summit adopted a five-year Special Programme for the Development of Africa, covering the period 2008–12, which aimed to promote the economic development of OIC African member states and to support these countries in achieving the UN Millennium Development Goals.

The first OIC Anti-Corruption and Enhancing Integrity Forum was convened in August 2006 in Kuala Lumpur, Malaysia. The seventh World Islamic Economic Forum was convened in Astana, Kazakhstan, in June 2011. In November 2009 a COMCEC Business Forum was held, in Istanbul, Turkey. An International Islamic Business and Finance Summit has been organized annually since 2009, in Kazan, Russia, by the OIC and the Russian Government; 'KAZANSUMMIT 2013' was to be convened in October 2013. The 14th Trade Fair of the OIC member states was to be staged in Tehran, Iran, in October–November of that year.

In March 2012 OIC ministers responsible for water approved the OIC Water Vision 2025, providing a framework for co-operation in maximizing the productive use of, and minimizing the destructive impact of, members' water resources. In May 2012 the fifth Islamic Conference of Environment Ministers, convened in Astana, adopted an Islamic Declaration on Sustainable Development. An OIC Green Technology Blue Print was under development in 2013.

CULTURAL AND TECHNICAL CO-OPERATION

The Organization supports education in Muslim communities throughout the world, and was instrumental in the establishment of Islamic universities in Niger and Uganda. It organizes seminars on various aspects of Islam, and encourages dialogue with the other monotheistic religions. Support is given to publications on Islam both in Muslim and Western countries. In June 1999 an OIC Parliamentary Union was inaugurated; its founding conference was convened in Tehran.

The OIC organizes meetings at ministerial level to consider aspects of information policy and new technologies. An OIC Digital Solidarity Fund was inaugurated in May 2005. Participation by OIC member states in the Fund was promoted at the 11th OIC summit meeting in March 2008, and the meeting also requested each member state to establish a board to monitor national implementation of the Tunis Declaration on the Information Society, adopted by the November 2005 second phase of the World Summit on the Information Society. In August 2011 the OIC organized a Decorative Arts and Calligraphy Exhibition, at its headquarters in Jeddah, Saudi Arabia.

HUMANITARIAN ASSISTANCE

Assistance is given to Muslim communities affected by violent conflict and natural disasters. It was announced in August 2010 that an OIC Emergency Fund for Natural Disasters would be established, to assist survivors of any natural disaster occurring in future in a Muslim country; the modalities of the establishment of the Fund were under consideration in 2013. The first conference of Islamic humanitarian organizations was convened by the OIC in March 2008, and a second conference, bringing together 32 organizations, took place in April 2009. The third conference of Islamic humanitarian organizations, held in March 2010, established a working group to draft a plan aimed at strengthening co-operation between the OIC and other humanitarian organizations active in Afghanistan, Gaza, Darfur, Iraq, Niger, Somalia and Sudan; and also approved the formation of a joint commission which was to study the structure and mechanism of co-operation and co-ordination between humanitarian organizations. The fourth conference was convened in June 2011, on the theme 'Civil Society Organizations in the Muslim World: Responsibilities and Roles'. In May 2012 the first Conference on Refugees in the Muslim World was convened by the OIC, UNHCR and the Turkmen Government, in Aşgabat, Turkmenistan. In November OIC ministers of foreign affairs agreed to grant non-governmental humanitarian relief agencies headquartered in member states consultative status in the Organization. In 2013 OIC was working to enhance co-operation and co-ordination of activities with the UN Office for Humanitarian Affairs (OCHA), with a view to achieving more efficient delivery of humanitarian assistance.

In mid-March 2012 a joint OIC-UN team of technical experts was dispatched to Syria to assess the humanitarian impact of the ongoing unrest there and to prepare an evaluation of the level of humanitarian aid required; in April, having considered the findings of the assessment team, the OIC Secretary-General stated that US $70m. in funding was required to assist at least 1m. Syrians at that time.

In March 2008 the OIC launched a humanitarian support operation for Palestinians in Gaza; an initial 'assistance caravan' transported medical supplies and equipment to the area. An expanded extraordinary meeting of the Executive Committee, convened, at the level of ministers of foreign affairs, in January 2009 to address the ongoing intensive bombardment of the Gaza Strip that was initiated by Israeli forces in late December 2008 with the stated aim of ending rocket attacks launched by Hamas and other militant groups on Israeli targets, requested the OIC Secretariat to co-ordinate with member states' civil society organizations to provide urgent humanitarian relief to the Palestinian people. OIC convoys of humanitarian aid, including medical supplies, food and clothing, were subsequently dispatched to Gaza.

POLITICAL CO-OPERATION

In June 2011 OIC ministers responsible for foreign affairs adopted the Astana Declaration on Peace, Co-operation and Development, in which they recognized emerging challenges presented by unfolding significant political developments in the Middle East and North Africa (the so-called Arab Spring) and appealed for engagement in constructive dialogue towards peaceful solutions. The Declaration expressed grave concern at the then ongoing conflict in Libya, and at the humanitarian consequences thereof. The foreign ministers also adopted the OIC Action Plan for Cooperation with Central Asia, which aimed to establish centres of excellence with a view to encouraging scientific innovation; and to promote job training and public-private partnership; to promote a reduction in the incidence of HIV/AIDS, polio, malaria and TB in the region; to build cultural understanding; and to combat trafficking in human beings and in illegal drugs. The OIC gives support to member countries in regaining or maintaining political stability.

In January 2009 the OIC and the League of Arab States signed an agreement providing for the strengthening of co-operation and co-ordination in the areas of politics, media, the economy, and in the social and scientific spheres.

The first OIC Conference on Women was held in November 2006, on the theme 'The role of women in the development of OIC member states'. An inaugural Conference of Muslim Women Parliamentarians was convened in January 2012, in Palembang, Indonesia. In December the statute of an OIC Women Development Organization (WDO) was opened for signature; upon entry into force the WDO was to become an OIC specialized agency, to be headquarterd in Cairo, Egypt, and focused on advancing the empowerment of women in member states.

Iraq: In August 1990 a majority of OIC member states' ministers of foreign affairs condemned Iraq's recent invasion of Kuwait, and demanded the withdrawal of Iraqi forces. In August 1991 the Conference of Ministers of Foreign Affairs obstructed Iraq's attempt to propose a resolution demanding the repeal of economic sanctions against the country. The sixth summit conference, held in Senegal in December, reflected the divisions in the Arab world that resulted from Iraq's invasion of Kuwait and the ensuing war. Twelve heads of state did not attend, reportedly to register protest at the presence of Jordan and the Palestine Liberation Organization (PLO) at the conference, both of which had given support to Iraq. In December 1994 OIC heads of state supported the decision by Iraq to recognize Kuwait. In December 1996 OIC ministers of foreign affairs demanded that Iraq fulfil its obligations for the establishment of security, peace and stability in the region. In December 1998 the OIC appealed for a diplomatic solution to the tensions arising from Iraq's withdrawal of co-operation with UN weapons inspectors, and criticized subsequent military air-strikes, led by the USA, as having been conducted without renewed UN authority. An extraordinary summit conference of Islamic leaders convened in Doha, Qatar, in early March 2003, to consider the ongoing Iraq crisis, welcomed the Saddam Hussain regime's acceptance of UN Security Council Resolution 1441 and consequent co-operation with UN weapons inspectors, and emphatically rejected military action against Iraq or threats to the security of any other Islamic state. The conference also urged progress towards the elimination of all weapons of mass destruction in the Middle East, including those held by Israel. In mid-May 2004 the OIC Secretary-General urged combat forces in Iraq to respect the inviolability of that country's holy places. In December 2005 he appealed to the people of Iraq to participate peacefully in the legislative elections that took place later in that month. In October 2006, under OIC auspices, Iraqi representatives, meeting in Jeddah, Saudi Arabia, signed the Mecca Agreement, a 10-point plan aimed at ending ongoing sectarian violence and at safeguarding Iraq's holy places territorial integrity. During 2008–13 the OIC Secretary-General repeatedly appealed for an end to sectarian strife in Iraq, and in October 2008 he condemned the persecution of Christians in northern Iraq. In April 2012 the OIC Secretary-General announced that a comprehensive plan was being developed to revive the 2006 Mecca Agreement.

Israel/Palestine: Since its inception the OIC has called for the vacation of Arab territories by Israel, recognition of the rights of Palestinians and of the PLO as their sole legitimate representative, and the restoration of Jerusalem to Arab rule. The 1981 summit conference called for a *jihad* (holy war—though not necessarily in a military sense) 'for the liberation of Jerusalem and the occupied territories'; this was to include an Islamic economic boycott of Israel. In 1982 Islamic ministers of foreign affairs decided to establish Islamic offices for boycotting Israel and for military co-operation with the PLO. The 1984 summit conference agreed to reinstate Egypt (suspended following the peace treaty signed with Israel in 1979) as a member of the OIC, although the resolution was opposed by seven states. In December 1991, at the sixth summit conference, disagreement arose between the PLO and the majority of other OIC members when a proposal was adopted to cease the OIC's support for the PLO's *jihad* in the Arab territories occupied by Israel, in an attempt to further the Middle East peace negotiations. In June the OIC condemned the decision by the US House of Representatives to recognize Jerusalem as the Israeli capital. The Secretary-General of the OIC issued a statement rejecting the US decision as counter to the role of the USA as sponsor of the Middle East peace plan. In view of the significant deterioration in relations between Israel and the Palestinian (National) Authority (PA) during late 2000, in December of that year the ninth summit conference of heads of state and of government, held in Doha, Qatar, issued a Declaration pledging solidarity with the Palestinian cause and accusing the Israeli authorities of implementing large-scale systematic violations of human rights against Palestinians. In May 2001 the OIC convened an emergency meeting, following an escalation of Israeli–Palestinian violence. The meeting resolved to halt all diplomatic and political contacts with the Israeli Government, while restrictions remained in force against Palestinian-controlled territories. In August the Secretary-General of the OIC condemned Israel's seizure of several Palestinian institutions in East Jerusalem and aerial attacks against Palestinian settlements. In June 2002 OIC ministers of foreign affairs endorsed the peace plan for the region that had been adopted by the summit meeting of the League of Arab States in March. In May 2004 the Secretary-General of the OIC condemned the ongoing destruction of Palestinian homes by Israeli forces, and consequent population displacement, particularly in Rafah, Gaza. He urged international organizations to condemn Israel's actions and appealed to the UN Security Council to intervene promptly in the situation and to compel Israel to respect international law. An observer mission dispatched by the OIC to monitor presidential elections held in the Palestinian territories in early January 2005, at the request of the PA, was rejected by Israel. In August 2006 the OIC convened a meeting of humanitarian bodies in Istanbul, Turkey, to address means of collecting donations for and delivering assistance to victims of the ongoing crises in Lebanon and the Palestinian territories. Shortly afterwards a meeting of the newly formed Executive Committee, held in Kuala Lumpur, Malaysia, agreed to form a Contact Group for Lebanon, to be co-ordinated by Malaysia. The summit meeting held in March 2008 welcomed recent contacts between the Israeli and Palestinian leaders. In early January 2009 an expanded extraordinary meeting of the Executive Committee, at the level of ministers of foreign affairs, convened to address the ongoing intensive bombardment of the Gaza Strip that was initiated by Israeli forces in late December 2008 with the stated aim of ending rocket attacks launched by Hamas and other militant groups on Israeli targets. The meeting strongly condemned the Israeli attacks and ensuing destruction and loss of civilian life, and requested the OIC Secretariat to co-ordinate with member states' civil society organizations to provide urgent humanitarian relief to the Palestinian people. In March 2009, while visiting the affected area, the OIC Secretary-General urged the reconciliation of the different Palestinian political factions. In October the OIC Secretary-General strongly condemned recent raids by Israeli special forces on the al-Aqsa Mosque in Jerusalem. An extraordinary meeting of the Executive Committee held at the beginning of November issued a final communiqué condemning Israeli violations of al-Aqsa and rejecting Israeli attempts to change the status of Jerusalem (Al-Quds) and consider it the united capital of Israel. The meeting urged the UN Security Council to address the Israeli actions.

In June 2010 an expanded extraordinary ministerial meeting of the Executive Committee condemned the attack by Israeli security forces, at the end of May, against a flotilla of vessels carrying humanitarian aid to Gaza, which had resulted in nine civilian deaths and caused injuries to at least 40 people. The OIC rejected a UN-commissioned report on the flotilla incident, released in September 2011, which—while concluding that the Israeli army had used 'excessive and unreasonable' force—also found the Israeli naval blockade of Gaza to have been imposed as a 'legitimate security measure' to prevent weapons from reaching Gaza by sea, and found that the flotilla had acted recklessly in attempting to breach the naval blockade. The OIC Secretary-General supported efforts to bring the issue of the blockade of Gaza before competent international legal authorities. In late September the OIC Secretary-General condemned a decision by Israel to build 1,100 new housing units in occupied East Jerusalem. During that month the OIC expressed support for the formal request by the Executive President of the Palestinian Authority for Palestine's admission to the UN, and recognition of its independent statehood. In early September 2012 it was announced that, later in that month, the OIC Palestine Committee would convene on the sidelines of the 67th General Assembly, to encourage support from the UN membership for Palestine's admission request.

In June 2012 the OIC Secretary-General welcomed the granting of World Heritage Site status to the Church of the Nativity in Bethlehem. Meeting in August the newly established OIC Independent Human Rights Commission addressed the human rights situation in Palestine and strongly condemned alleged continuing human rights violations by Israel. In September the OIC Secretary-General strongly objected to the Israeli authorities about a reported plan to stage a wine festival in the courtyard of a mosque in Beersheba, in southern Israel, describing this as a deliberate provocation of Muslims and as part of a series of Israeli attacks on Islamic sanctuaries and antiquities. The festival was eventually held outside the mosque boundaries.

In February 2013 the 12th OIC summit issued a declaration on Palestine which, *inter alia*, welcomed the decision, in November 2012, of the UN General Assembly to grant Palestine observer status at the UN.

In July 2013 the OIC Secretary-General commended a decision by the European Union to exclude Israeli settlements situated in Palestinian and Arab territories occupied since 1967 from any future agreements made with its member states.

Syria: In December 2011 the OIC Executive Committee convened a ministerial open-ended meeting to address the violent unrest that had prevailed since March in Syria. The OIC Secretary-General strongly condemned mass killings of civilians perpetrated by Syrian security forces in May, June and July 2012. In July the Secretary-General urged the Syrian authorities to place the interests of Syria and the Syrian people above all other considerations. An emergency summit of OIC heads of state and government, convened in Makkah (Mecca), Saudi Arabia, in August, determined to suspend Syria from participation in the activities of the Organization and from all its subsidiary organs and specialized and affiliated institutions. The summit demanded the immediate implementation of a UN-Arab League peace plan that had been agreed in March by the Syrian authorities and opposition, but was not being observed, and urged the development of a mechanism to facilitate the creation of a Syrian state based on pluralism and democratic values. The summit also urged the UN Security Council to take measures to end the ongoing violence and to pursue a peaceful and lasting solution to the Syrian crisis. Syria's suspension from the OIC was opposed by Iran. In November the OIC welcomed an agreement by the Syrian opposition to establish the Syrian National Coalition of Revolutionary and Opposition Forces. In February 2013 the 12th OIC summit urged a Syrian-led negotiated solution to the ongoing conflict, and reaffirmed support to the UN-Arab League Joint Special Representative on Syria. In mid-September the OIC Secretary-General welcomed the release of the report by a UN weapons inspection team into the deployment, on 21 August, of chemical weapons against civilians in Damascus, Syria, that had caused up to around 1,400 fatalities. Condemning the Damascus atrocity as a war crime and crime against humanity, he emphasized the need to hold to account any party involved in the production, transfer, development, and use of chemical weapons in Syria.

Combating Terrorism: In December 1994 OIC heads of state adopted a Code of Conduct for Combating International Terrorism, in an attempt to control Muslim extremist groups. The code commits states to ensuring that militant groups do not use their territory for planning or executing terrorist activity against other states, in addition to states refraining from direct support or participation in acts of terrorism. An OIC Convention on Combating International Terrorism was adopted in 1998. In September 2001 the OIC Secretary-General strongly condemned major terrorist attacks perpetrated against targets in the USA. Soon afterwards the US authorities rejected a proposal by the Taliban regime that an OIC observer mission be deployed to monitor the activities of the Saudi Arabian-born exiled militant Islamist fundamentalist leader Osama bin Laden, who was accused by the US Government of having co-ordinated the attacks from alleged terrorist bases in the Taliban-administered area of Afghanistan. An extraordinary meeting of OIC ministers of foreign affairs, convened in early October, in Doha, to consider the implications of the terrorist atrocities, condemned the attacks and declared its support for combating all manifestations of terrorism within the framework of a proposed collective initiative co-ordinated under the auspices of the UN. The meeting, which did not pronounce directly on the recently initiated US-led military retaliation against targets in Afghanistan, urged that no Arab or Muslim state should be targeted under the pretext of eliminating terrorism. In February 2002 the Secretary-General expressed concern at statements of the US Administration describing Iran and Iraq (as well as the Democratic People's Republic of Korea) as belonging to an 'axis of evil' involved in international terrorism and the development of weapons of mass destruction. In April OIC ministers of foreign affairs convened an extraordinary session on terrorism, in Kuala Lumpur, Malaysia. The meeting issued the Kuala Lumpur Declaration, which reiterated member states' collective resolve to combat terrorism, recalling the organization's 1994 code of conduct and 1998 convention to this effect; condemned attempts to associate terrorist activities with Islam or any other particular creed, civilization or nationality, and rejected attempts to associate Islamic states or the Palestinian struggle with terrorism; rejected the implementation of international action against any Muslim state on the pretext of combating terrorism; urged the organization of a global conference on international terrorism; and urged an examination of the root causes of international terrorism. The meeting adopted a plan of action on addressing the issues raised in the declaration. Its implementation was to be co-ordinated by a 13-member committee on international terrorism. Member states were encouraged to sign and ratify the Convention on Combating International Terrorism in order to accelerate its implementation. In May 2003 the 30th session of the Conference of Ministers of Foreign Affairs, entitled 'Unity and Dignity', issued the Tehran Declaration, in which it resolved to combat terrorism and to contribute to preserving peace and security in Islamic countries. The Declaration also pledged its full support for the Palestinian cause and rejected the labelling as 'terrorist' of those Muslim states deemed to be resisting foreign aggression and occupation. In April 2009 the heads of law enforcement agencies in OIC member states, gathered in Baku, Azerbaijan, adopted the Baku Declaration on co-operation in combating transnational organized crime, including international terrorism, extremism, aggressive separatism, and human trafficking. The OIC has repeatedly urged the world-wide adoption of a clear definition of terrorism; in September 2013 the OIC Secretary-General stated that an unambiguous definition should be incorporated into UN counter-terrorism planning.

Supporting Muslim Minorities and Combating Anti-Islamic Feeling: In December 1995 OIC ministers of foreign affairs determined that an intergovernmental group of experts should be established to address the situation of minority Muslim communities residing in non-OIC states. The OIC committee of experts responsible for formulating a plan of action for safeguarding the rights of Muslim communities and minorities met for the first time in 1998. In June 2001 the OIC condemned attacks and ongoing discrimination against the Muslim community in Myanmar. In October 2005 the OIC Secretary-General expressed concern at the treatment of Muslims in the southern provinces of Thailand. The first tripartite meeting between the OIC, the Government of the Philippines and Muslim separatists based in the southern Philippines took place in November 2007, and in April 2009 the OIC Secretary-General announced the appointment of an OIC special envoy to assist in negotiating a peaceful solution to the conflict in the southern Philippines.

In December 2007 the OIC organized the first International Conference on Islamophobia, aimed at addressing concerns that alleged instances of defamation of Islam appeared to be increasing worldwide (particularly in Europe). Responding to a reported rise in anti-Islamic attacks on Western nations, OIC leaders denounced stereotyping and discrimination, and urged the promotion of Islam by Islamic states as a 'moderate, peaceful and tolerant religion'. In June 2011 the OIC Secretary-General issued a statement strongly condemning 'attacks on Islam and insult and vilification of the Prophet Muhummad and his wives' by the right-wing Dutch politician Geert Wilders. The Secretary-General stated in June 2012 that Islamophobia was being exploited in electoral campaigns in Europe, citing the campaigns for the French presidential election held in April–May. An Islamic Observatory on Islamophobia, established in September 2006, has released periodic reports on intolerance against Muslims; the fifth, released in November 2012, and covering the period May 2011–September 2012, claimed that during the period under review symbols and personalities held sacred by Islam continued to be violated, and that levels of intolerance had reached unprecedented levels.

In March 2011 the UN Human Rights Council adopted by consensus a resolution (A/HRC/Res/16/18), that had been presented on behalf of the OIC, on 'Combating intolerance, negative stereotyping, and stigmatization of, and discrimination, incitement to violence and violence against, persons based on religion or belief'. Resolution 16/18 called on UN member states to ensure, *inter alia*, that public officials avoid discriminating against individuals on the basis of religion or belief; that citizens might manifest their religion; that religious profiling be avoided; and that places of worship be protected. Previous related draft resolutions proposed by the OIC had focused on combating 'defamation of religions', and had been rejected by human rights organizations and by some UN member states on grounds related to the right to freedom of expression. In July 2011 the OIC and the USA jointly launched the Istanbul Process for Combating Intolerance and Discrimination Based on Religion or Belief, and, in December, a joint OIC-USA Conference on Addressing the Istanbul Process was convened in Washington, DC, USA. In June 2013 the inaugural meeting of an OIC Media Forum—tasked with advancing the co-ordination of media oulets in Islamic countries—was held in Ankara, Turkey. An International Conference on Islamophobia: Law and Media, held in Istanbul in September, endorsed the establishment of an Advisory Media Committee to meet under the auspices of the Media Forum.

Reform of the OIC: In November 2000 OIC heads of state attended the ninth summit conference, held in Doha, Qatar, and issued the Doha Declaration, which reaffirmed commitment to the OIC Charter and undertook to modernize the organization. The 10th OIC summit meeting, held in October 2003, in Putrajaya, Malaysia, issued the Putrajaya Declaration, in which Islamic leaders resolved to enhance Islamic states' role and influence in international affairs. The leaders adopted a plan of action that entailed: reviewing and strengthening OIC positions on international issues; enhancing dialogue among Muslim thinkers and policy-makers through relevant OIC insitutions; promoting constructive dialogue with other cultures and civilizations; completing an ongoing review of the structure and efficacy of the OIC Secretariat; establishing a working group to address means of enhancing the role of Islamic education; promoting among member states the development of science and technology, discussion of ecological issues, and the role of information communication technology in development; improving mechanisms to assist member states in post-conflict situations; and advancing trade and investment through data-sharing and encouraging access to markets for products from poorer member states. In January 2005 the inaugural meeting of an OIC Commission of Eminent Persons was convened in Putrajaya. The Commission was mandated to make recommendations in the following areas: the preparation of a strategy and plan of action enabling the Islamic community to meet the challenges of the 21st century; the preparation of a comprehensive plan for promoting enlightened moderation, both within Islamic societies and universally; and the preparation of proposals for the future reform and restructuring of the OIC system. In December the third extraordinary OIC summit, convened in Makkah, adopted a Ten-Year Programme of Action to Meet the Challenges Facing the Ummah (the Islamic world) in the 21st Century, a related Declaration and a report by the Commission of Eminent Persons. The summit determined to restructure the OIC, and mandated the establishment of an Executive Committee, comprising the summit conference and ministerial conference troikas (equally reflecting the African, Arab and Asian member states), the OIC host country, and the OIC Secretariat, to implement Conference resolutions.

The 11th OIC heads of state summit meeting, held in Dakar, Senegal, in March 2008, endorsed a revised OIC Charter.

Finance

The OIC's activities are financed by mandatory contributions from member states.

Subsidiary Organs

Islamic Centre for the Development of Trade: Complexe Commercial des Habous, ave des FAR, BP 13545, Casablanca, Morocco; tel. (522) 314974; fax (522) 310110; e-mail icdt@icdt-oic.org; internet www.icdt-oic.org; f. 1983 to encourage regular commercial contacts, harmonize policies and promote investments among OIC mems; Dir-Gen. Dr EL HASSANE HZAINE; publs *Tijaris: International and Inter-Islamic Trade Magazine* (every two months), *Inter-Islamic Trade Report* (annually).

Islamic Jurisprudence (Fiqh) Academy: POB 13917, Jeddah, Saudi Arabia; tel. (2) 667-1664; fax (2) 667-0873; internet www.fiqhacademy.org.sa; f. 1982; Gen. Sec. MAULANA KHALID SAIFULLAH RAHMANI.

Islamic Solidarity Fund: c/o OIC Secretariat, POB 1997, Jeddah 21411, Saudi Arabia; tel. (2) 698-1296; fax (2) 256-8185; e-mail info@isf-fsi.org; internet www.isf-fsi.org; f. 1974 to meet the needs of Islamic communities by providing emergency aid and the finance to build mosques, Islamic centres, hospitals, schools and universities; Exec. Dir IBRAHIM BIN ABDALLAH AL-KHOZAIM.

Islamic University in Uganda: POB 2555, Mbale, Uganda; tel. (35) 2512100; fax (45) 433502; e-mail info@iuiu.ac.ug; internet www.iuiu.ac.ug; f. 1988 to meet the educational needs of Muslim populations in English-speaking African countries; second campus in Kampala; mainly financed by the OIC; Rector Dr AHMAD KAWEESA SSENGENDO.

Islamic University of Niger: BP 11507, Niamey, Niger; tel. 20-72-39-03; fax 20-73-37-96; e-mail unislam@intnet.ne; internet www.universite_say.ne/; f. 1984; provides courses of study in *Shari'a* (Islamic law) and Arabic language and literature; also offers courses in pedagogy and teacher training; receives grants from Islamic Solidarity Fund and contributions from OIC member states; Rector Prof. ABDELJAOUAD SEKKAT.

Islamic University of Technology (IUT): Board Bazar, Gazipur 1704, Dhaka, Bangladesh; tel. (2) 9291254; fax (2) 9291260; e-mail vc@iut-dhaka.edu; internet www.iutoic-dhaka.edu; f. 1981 as the Islamic Centre for Technical and Vocational Training and Resources, named changed to Islamic Institute of Technology in 1994, current name adopted in 2001; aims to develop human resources in OIC mem. states, with special reference to engineering, technology, and technical education; 145 staff and 800 students; library of 30,450 vols; Vice-Chancellor Prof. Dr M. IMTIAZ HOSSAIN; publs *Journal of Engineering and Technology* (2 a year), *News Bulletin* (annually), *News Letter* (6 a year), annual calendar and announcement for admission, reports, human resources development series.

Research Centre for Islamic History, Art and Culture (IRCICA): POB 24, Beşiktaş 34354, İstanbul, Turkey; tel. (212) 2591742; fax (212) 2584365; e-mail ircica@ircica.org; internet www.ircica.org; f. 1980; library of 60,000 vols; Dir-Gen. Prof. Dr HALIT EREN; publs *Newsletter* (3 a year), monographical studies.

Statistical, Economic and Social Research and Training Centre for Islamic Countries (SESRIC): Kudüs Cad. No. 9, Diplomatik Site, 06450, Ankara, Turkey; tel. (312) 4686172; fax (312) 4673458; e-mail oicankara@sesric.org; internet www.sesric.org; became operational in 1978; has a three-fold mandate: to collate, process and disseminate socio-economic statistics and information on, and for the utilization of, its member countries; to study and assess economic and social developments in member countries with the aim of helping to generate proposals for advancing co-operation; and to organize training programmes in selected areas; the Centre also acts as a focal point for technical co-operation activities between the OIC system and related UN agencies; and prepares economic and social reports and background documentation for OIC meetings; Dir-Gen. Dr SAVAŞ ALPAY (Turkey); publs *Annual Economic Report on the OIC Countries*, *Journal of Economic Cooperation and Development* (quarterly), *Economic Cooperation and Development Review* (semi-annually), *InfoReport* (quarterly), *Statistical Yearbook* (annually), *Basic Facts and Figures on OIC Member Countries* (annually).

Specialized Institutions

International Islamic News Agency (IINA): King Khalid Palace, Madinah Rd, POB 5054, Jeddah 21422, Saudi Arabia; tel. (2) 665-8561; fax (2) 665-9358; e-mail iina@islamicnews.org; internet www.iinanews.com; f. 1972; distributes news and reports daily on events in the Islamic world, in Arabic, English and French; Dir-Gen. ALI BIN AHMED AL-GHAMDI (acting).

Islamic Educational, Scientific and Cultural Organization (ISESCO): BP 2275 Rabat 10104, Morocco; tel. (37) 566052; fax (37) 566012; e-mail cid@isesco.org.ma; internet www.isesco.org.ma; f. 1982; Dir-Gen. Dr ABDULAZIZ BIN OTHMAN ALTWAIJRI; publs *ISESCO Newsletter* (quarterly), *Islam Today* (2 a year), *ISESCO Triennial*.

Islamic Broadcasting Union (IBU): POB 6351, Jeddah 21442, Saudi Arabia; tel. (2) 672-1121; fax (2) 672-2600; e-mail ibu@ibuj.org; internet www.ibuj.org; f. 1975; Dir-Gen. MOHAMED SALEM WALAD BOAKE.

Affiliated Institutions

International Association of Islamic Banks (IAIB): King Abdulaziz St, Queen's Bldg, 23rd Floor, Al-Balad Dist, POB 9707, Jeddah 21423, Saudi Arabia; tel. (2) 651-6900; fax (2) 651-6552; f. 1977 to link financial institutions operating on Islamic banking principles; activities include training and research; mems: 192 banks and other financial institutions in 34 countries.

Islamic Chamber of Commerce and Industry: POB 3831, Clifton, Karachi 75600, Pakistan; tel. (21) 5874910; fax (21) 5870765; e-mail icci@icci-oic.org; internet www.iccionline.net/en/icci-en/index.aspx; f. 1979 to promote trade and industry among member states; comprises nat. chambers or feds of chambers of commerce and industry; Pres. SALEH ABDULLAH KAMEL; Sec.-Gen. Dr BASSEM AWADALLAH.

Islamic Committee for the International Crescent: POB 17434, Benghazi, Libya; tel. (61) 9095824; fax (61) 9095823; e-mail info@icic-oic.org; internet www.icic-oic.org; f. 1979 to attempt to alleviate the suffering caused by natural disasters and war; Pres. ALI MAHMOUD BUHEDMA.

Islamic Solidarity Sports Federation: POB 5844, Riyadh 11442, Saudi Arabia; tel. (1) 480-9253; fax (1) 482-2145; e-mail issf@awalnet.net.sa; f. 1981; organizes the Islamic Solidarity Games (2005: Jeddah, Saudi Arabia, in April; 2013: Jakarta, Indonesia, in Sept.–Oct.); Sec.-Gen. Dr MOHAMMAD SALEH QAZDAR.

Organization of Islamic Capitals and Cities (OICC): POB 13621, Jeddah 21414, Saudi Arabia; tel. (2) 698-1953; fax (2) 698-1053; e-mail oiccmak@oicc.org; internet www.oicc.org; f. 1980; aims to preserve the identity and the heritage of Islamic capitals and cities; to achieve and enhance sustainable development in member capitals and cities; to establish and develop comprehensive urban norms, systems and plans to serve the growth and prosperity of Islamic capitals and cities and to enhance their cultural, environmental, urban, economic and social conditions; to advance municipal services and facilities in the member capitals and cities; to support member cities' capacity-building programmes; and to consolidate fellowship and co-ordinate the scope of co-operation between members; comprises 157 capitals and cities as active members, eight observer members and 18 associate members, in Asia, Africa, Europe and South America; Sec.-Gen. OMAR ABDULLAH KADI.

Organization of the Islamic Shipowners' Association: POB 14900, Jeddah 21434, Saudi Arabia; tel. (2) 663-7882; fax (2) 660-4920; e-mail mail@oisaonline.com; internet www.oisaonline.com; f. 1981 to promote co-operation among maritime cos in Islamic countries; in 1998 mems approved the establishment of a new commercial venture, the Bakkah Shipping Company, to enhance sea transport in the region; Sec.-Gen. Dr ABDULLATIF A. SULTAN.

World Federation of Arab-Islamic Schools: 2 Wadi el-Nile St, Maadi, Cairo, Egypt; tel. (2) 358-3278; internet www.wfais.org; f. 1976; supports Arab-Islamic schools world-wide and encourages co-operation between the institutions; promotes the dissemination of the Arabic language and Islamic culture; supports the training of personnel.

The statute of a new OIC Women Development Organization was opened for signature in December 2012.

ORGANIZATION OF THE PETROLEUM EXPORTING COUNTRIES—OPEC

Address: Helferstorferstrasse 17, 1010 Vienna, Austria.

Telephone: (1) 211-12-3303; **fax:** (1) 216-43-20; **e-mail:** prid@opec.org; **internet:** www.opec.org.

OPEC was established in 1960 to link countries whose main source of export earnings is petroleum; it aims to unify and co-ordinate members' petroleum policies and to safeguard their interests generally. In 1976 OPEC member states established the OPEC Fund for International Development.

OPEC's share of world petroleum production was 43% in 2011 (compared with 54.7% in 1974). OPEC members were estimated to possess 81% of the world's known reserves of crude petroleum in 2011. OPEC members also possessed 48% of known reserves of natural gas, and accounted for 19% of total production of marketed natural gas.

MEMBERS

Algeria	Iraq	Qatar
Angola	Kuwait	Saudi Arabia
Ecuador	Libya	United Arab Emirates
Iran	Nigeria	Venezuela

Organization

(September 2013)

CONFERENCE

The Conference is the supreme authority of the organization, responsible for the formulation of its general policy. It consists of representatives of member countries, who examine reports and recommendations submitted by the Board of Governors. It approves the appointment of Governors from each country and elects the Chairman of the Board of Governors. It works on the unanimity principle, and meets at least twice a year. In September 2000 the Conference agreed that regular meetings of heads of state or government should be convened every five years.

BOARD OF GOVERNORS

The Board directs the management of OPEC; it implements resolutions of the Conference and draws up an annual budget. It consists of one governor for each member country, and meets at least twice a year.

MINISTERIAL MONITORING COMMITTEE

The Committee is responsible for monitoring price evolution and ensuring the stability of the world petroleum market. As such, it is charged with the preparation of long-term strategies, including the allocation of quotas to be presented to the Conference. The Committee consists of all national representatives, and is normally convened four times a year. A Ministerial Monitoring Sub-committee, reporting to the Committee on production and supply figures, was established in 1993.

ECONOMIC COMMISSION

A specialized body operating within the framework of the Secretariat, with a view to promoting stability in international prices for petroleum at equitable levels; consists of a Board, national representatives and a commission staff; meets at least twice a year.

SECRETARIAT

Secretary-General: ABDALLA SALEM EL-BADRI (Libya).

Legal Office: Provides legal advice, supervises the Secretariat's legal commitments, evaluates legal issues of concern to the organization and member countries, and recommends appropriate action; General Legal Counsel ASMA MUTTAWA.

Office of the Secretary-General: provides the Secretary-General with executive assistance in maintaining contacts with governments, organizations and delegations, in matters of protocol and in the preparation for and co-ordination of meetings; Head ABDULLAH AL-SHAMERI.

Research Division: comprises the Data Services Department; the Energy Studies Department; and the Petroleum Market Analysis Department; Dir Dr OMAR S. ABDUL-HAMID.

Support Services Division: responsible for providing the required infrastructure and services to the whole Secretariat, in support of its programmes; has three departments: Administration and IT Services; Finance and Human Resources; and Public Relations and Information; Dir. (vacant).

Activities

OPEC's principal objectives, according to its Statute, are to co-ordinate and unify the petroleum policies of member countries and to determine the best means for safeguarding their individual and collective interests; to seek ways and means of ensuring the stabilization of prices in international oil markets, with a view to eliminating harmful and unnecessary fluctuations, and to provide a steady income to the producing countries, an efficient, economic and regular supply of petroleum to consuming nations, and a fair return on capital to those investing in the petroleum industry.

The first OPEC conference was held in Baghdad, Iraq, in September 1960. It was attended by representatives from Iran, Iraq, Kuwait, Saudi Arabia and Venezuela, the founder members. These were joined by Qatar in the following year, when a Board of Governors was formed and statutes agreed. Indonesia and Libya were admitted to membership in 1962, Abu Dhabi in 1967, Algeria in 1969, Nigeria in 1971, Ecuador in 1973 and Gabon in 1975; Abu Dhabi's membership was transferred to the United Arab Emirates (UAE) in 1974. Ecuador resigned from OPEC in 1992 and Gabon did so in 1996. Angola became a member in 2007, and Ecuador rejoined the organization in the same year. Indonesia withdrew from OPEC in 2009.

PRICES AND PRODUCTION

OPEC's five original members first met following the imposition of price reductions by petroleum companies in the previous month (August 1960). During the 1960s members sought to assert their rights in an international petroleum market that was dominated by multinational companies. Between 1965 and 1967 a two-year joint production programme limited annual growth in output so as to secure adequate prices. During the 1970s member states increased their control over their domestic petroleum industries, and over the pricing of crude petroleum on world markets. In 1971 the five-year Tehran Agreement on pricing was concluded between the six producing countries from the Arabian Gulf region and 23 petroleum companies. In January 1972 petroleum companies agreed to adjust the petroleum revenues of the largest producers after changes in currency exchange rates (Geneva Agreement), and in 1973 OPEC and the petroleum companies agreed to raise posted prices of crude petroleum by 11.9% and installed a mechanism to make monthly adjustments to prices in future (Second Geneva Agreement). In October of that year a pricing crisis occurred when Arab member states refused to supply petroleum to nations that had supported Israel in its conflict with Egypt and Syria earlier in that month. Negotiations on the revision of the Tehran Agreement failed in the same month, and the Gulf states unilaterally declared increases of 70% in posted prices, from US $3.01 to $5.11 per barrel. In December the OPEC Conference decided to increase the price to $11.65 per barrel (despite Saudi Arabian opposition). OPEC's first summit meeting of heads of state or government was held in March 1975, and in September a ministerial meeting agreed to increase prices by 10% for the period to June 1976. During 1976 and 1977 disagreements between 'moderate' members (principally Saudi Arabia and Iran) and 'radical' members (led by Algeria, Iraq and Libya) caused discrepancies in pricing: a 10% increase was agreed by 11 member states as of 1 January 1977, but Saudi Arabia and the UAE decided to limit their increase to 5%. A further increase of 5% by Saudi Arabia and the UAE in July restored a single level of pricing, but in December the Conference was unable to agree on a new increase, and prices remained stable until the end of 1978, when it was agreed that during 1979 prices should increase by an average of 10% in four instalments over the year, to compensate for the effects of the depreciation of the US dollar. The overthrow of the Iranian Government in early 1979, however, led to a new steep increase in petroleum prices.

In June 1980 the Conference decided to set the price for a 'marker' crude at US $32 per barrel. Prices continued to vary, however, and in May 1981 Saudi Arabia refused to increase its price of $32 per barrel unless the higher prices charged by other members were lowered. Members agreed to reduce surplus production during the year, and in October the marker price was increased to $34 per barrel. In March 1982 an emergency meeting of ministers of petroleum agreed (for the first time in OPEC's history) to defend the organization's price structure by imposing an overall production 'ceiling' of 18m. barrels per day (b/d), reducing this to 17.5m. b/d at the beginning of 1983, although ministers initially failed to agree on production quotas for individual members, or on price differentials for the different quality of crude petroleum produced. In February 1983 Nigeria reduced its price to $30 per barrel, and to avoid a 'price war' OPEC set the official price of marker crude at $29 per barrel. Quotas were allocated for each member country except Saudi Arabia, which was to act as a 'swing producer' to supply the balancing quantities to meet market requirements. In October 1984 the production ceiling was lowered to 16m. b/d, and in December price differentials for light (more expensive) and heavy (cheaper) crudes were altered in an attempt to counteract price-cutting by non-OPEC producers, particularly Norway and the United Kingdom. During 1985, however, most members effectively abandoned the marker price system, and production in excess of quotas, unofficial discounts and barter deals by members, and price cuts by non-members (such as Mexico, which had hitherto kept its prices in line with those of OPEC) contributed to a weakening of the market. In August 1986 all members except Iraq agreed upon a return to production quotas (Iraq declined to co-operate after its request to be allocated the same quota as Iran had been refused): total production was to be limited to 14.8m. b/d (16.8m. b/d including Iraq). This measure resulted in an increase in prices to about $15 per barrel. In December members (except Iraq) agreed to return to a fixed pricing system, at a level of $18 per barrel as the OPEC Reference Basket (ORB) price (based on a 'basket' of seven crudes, not, as hitherto, on a 'marker' crude, Arabian Light) with effect from 1 February 1987, setting a total production limit of 15.8m. b/d. OPEC's role of setting crude oil prices had come to an end, however, and from the late 1980s prices were determined by movements in the international markets, with OPEC's role being to increase or restrain production in order to prevent harmful fluctuations in prices. In June 1987, with prices having stabilized, the Conference decided to limit production to 16.6m. b/d (including Iraq's output) for the rest of the year. The production limit was increased to 18.5m. b/d for the first half of 1989 and, after prices had recovered to about $18 per barrel, to 19.5m. b/d for the second half of 1989, and to 22m. b/d for the first half of 1990.

In May 1990 members resolved to adhere more strictly to the agreed production quotas, in response to a decline in prices, which stood at about US $14 per barrel in June. In August Iraq invaded Kuwait (which it had accused, among other grievances, of violating production quotas). Petroleum exports by the two countries were halted by an international embargo, and petroleum prices immediately increased to exceed $25 per barrel. OPEC ministers promptly allowed a temporary increase in production by other members, of between 3m. and 3.5m. b/d (mostly by Saudi Arabia, the UAE and Venezuela), to stabilize prices, and notwithstanding some fluctuations later in the year, this was achieved. During 1991 and 1992 ministers attempted to reach a minimum ORB price of $21 per barrel by imposing production limits that varied between 22.3m. b/d and 24.2m. b/d. Kuwait, which resumed production in 1992 after extensive damage had been inflicted on its oil wells during the conflict with Iraq, was granted a special dispensation to produce without a fixed quota until the following year. Ecuador withdrew from OPEC in November 1992, citing the high cost of membership and the organization's refusal to increase Ecuador's production quota. In 1993 a Ministerial Monitoring Sub-committee was established to supervise compliance with quotas, because of members' persistent over-production. In July of that year discussions between Iraq and the UN on the possible supervised resumption of Iraqi petroleum exports depressed petroleum prices to below $16 per barrel, and at the end of the year prices fell below $14, after the Conference rejected any further reduction in the current limit of 24.5m. b/d, which remained in force during 1994 and 1995, although actual output continued to be well in excess of quotas. In May 1996 the UN and Iraq concluded an agreement allowing Iraq to resume exports of petroleum in order to fund humanitarian relief efforts within Iraq, and OPEC's overall production ceiling was accordingly raised to 25.0m. b/d from June. Gabon withdrew from OPEC in June, citing difficulties in meeting its budgetary contribution. Prices declined during the first half of 1997, falling to a low point of $16.7 per barrel in April, owing to the resumption of Iraqi exports, depressed world demand and continuing over-production: an escalation in political tension in the Gulf region, however, and in particular Iraq's reluctance to co-operate with UN weapons inspectors, prompted a price increase to about $21.2 per barrel in October. The overall production ceiling was raised by about 10%, to 27.5m. b/d, with effect from the beginning of 1998, but during that year prices declined, decreasing to below $12 per barrel from August (demand having been affected by the current economic difficulties in South-East Asia), and OPEC imposed a succession of reductions in output, down to 24.4m. b/d from 1 July. Non-member countries (chiefly Mexico) also concluded agreements with OPEC to limit their production in that year, and in March 1999 Mexico, Norway, Oman and Russia agreed to decrease production by a total of 388,000 b/d, while OPEC's own production limit was reduced to 22.97m. b/d. Evidence of almost 90% compliance with the new production quotas contributed to market confidence that stockpiles of petroleum would be reduced, and resulted in sustained price increases during the second half of the year.

By March 2000 petroleum prices had reached their highest level since 1990, briefly exceeding US $34 per barrel. In that month OPEC ministers agreed to raise output by 1.45m. b/d, in order to ease supply shortages, and introduced an informal price band mechanism that was to signal the need for adjustments in production should prices deviate for more than 20 days from an average bracket of $22–$28 per barrel. Further increases in production took effect in the second half of the year (with five non-OPEC members, Angola, Mexico, Norway, Oman and Russia, also agreeing to raise their output), but prices remained high and there was intense international pressure on OPEC to resolve the situation: in September both the Group of Seven industrialized countries (G7) and the IMF issued warnings about the potential economic and social consequences of sustained high petroleum prices. In that month OPEC heads of state and government, convened in their first summit meeting since 1975, responded by issuing the Caracas Declaration, in which they resolved to promote market stability through their policies on pricing and production, to increase co-operation with other petroleum exporters, and to improve communication with consumer countries. During the first half of 2001, with a view to stabilizing prices that by January had fallen back to around $25 per barrel, the Conference agreed to implement reductions in output totalling 2.5m. b/d, thereby limiting overall production to 24.2m. b/d, with a further reduction of 1m. b/d from 1 September. Terrorist attacks on targets in the USA in September gave rise to market uncertainty, and prices declined further, averaging $17–$18 per barrel in November and December. In September the Conference announced the establishment of a working group of experts from OPEC and non-OPEC petroleum-producing countries, to evaluate future market developments and advance dialogue and co-operation. In December the Conference announced a further reduction in output by 1.5m. b/d (to 21.7m. b/d) from 1 January 2002, provided that non-OPEC producers also reduced their output, which they agreed to do by 462,500 b/d. This output limit was maintained throughout 2002, and the ORB price averaged $24.4 per barrel during the year, with temporary increases caused partly by a one-month suspension of Iraq's exports in April (in protest at Israeli military intervention in Palestinian-controlled areas), and by a strike in the Venezuelan petroleum industry. From 1 January 2003 the production ceiling was raised to 23m. b/d, but stricter compliance with individual quotas meant a reduction in actual output, and prices rose above the target range, with the ORB price reaching $32 per barrel in February, as a result of the continued interruption of the Venezuelan supply, together with the market's reaction to the likelihood of US-led military action against Iraq. In January the Conference agreed to raise the production ceiling to 24.5m. b/d from 1 February, and in March (when Venezuelan production had resumed) members agreed to make up from their available excess capacities any shortfall that might result following military action against Iraq. In the event, the war on Iraq that commenced later in that month led to such a rapid overthrow of Saddam Hussain's regime that there were fears that a petroleum surplus, driving down prices, would result, and a production ceiling of 25.4m. b/d was set with effect from the beginning of June: although higher than the previous limit, it represented a 2m. b/d reduction in actual output at that time. The production ceiling of 24.5m. b/d was reinstated from 1 November, in view of the gradual revival of Iraqi exports. The ORB price averaged $28.1 per barrel in 2003. In 2004, however, petroleum prices increased considerably, with the ORB price averaging $36 per barrel over the year, despite OPEC's raising its production ceiling (excluding Iraq's output), in several stages, from the 23.5m. b/d limit imposed from 1 April to 27m. b/d with effect from 1 November. In January 2005 the Conference suspended the $22–$28 price band mechanism, acknowledging this to be unrealistic at the present time. The production ceiling was increased to 27.5m. b/d in March and to 28m. b/d in June; nevertheless the ORB price averaged $50.6 per barrel over the year. The

March Conference attributed the continuing rise in prices to expectations of strong demand, speculation on the futures markets, and geopolitical tensions; it expressed particular concern that a shortage of effective global refining capacity was also contributing to higher prices by causing 'bottlenecks' in the downstream sector, and announced that members had accelerated the implementation of existing capacity expansion plans. In September the Conference adopted a first Long-Term Strategy for OPEC, setting objectives concerning members' long-term petroleum revenues, fair and stable prices, the role of petroleum in meeting future energy demand, the stability of the world oil market, and the security of regular supplies to consumers. During 2006 petroleum prices continued to rise, with the ORB price averaging $61.1 per barrel for the year. The rise was partly attributable to uncertainty about Iran's future output (since there was speculation that international sanctions might be imposed on that country as a penalty for continuing its nuclear development programme), and to a reduction in Nigeria's production as a result of internal unrest. Existing production targets were maintained until November, when the production ceiling was lowered to 26.3m. b/d, and a further reduction of 500,000 b/d was announced in December. In March 2007 the Conference agreed to maintain the current level of production. Concern over fuel supplies and distribution contributed to steadily rising prices, in spite of OPEC's statements estimating that there were sufficient stock levels to meet demand. In October OPEC's Secretary-General reiterated that the market was well supplied, and attributed the rising prices chiefly to market speculators, with persistent refinery bottlenecks, seasonal maintenance work, ongoing geopolitical problems in the Middle East and fluctuations in the US dollar also continuing to play a role in driving oil prices higher. In November the third OPEC summit meeting of heads of state and government agreed on principles concerning the stability of global energy markets, the role of energy in sustainable development, and the relationship between energy and environmental concerns.

Meeting in March 2008, the Conference again determined to maintain the current production ceiling and in September, once again, the Conference resolved to maintain the production allocations agreed in September 2007 (with an adjustment to include the admission to the organization in late 2007 of both Angola and Ecuador while excluding Indonesia, whose membership was being terminated, resulting in an overall production ceiling of 28.8m. b/d). At 11 July 2008 the ORB price reached a record high of US $147.27 per barrel, although by late October it had decreased to below $60 per barrel. An extraordinary meeting of the Conference, convened at that time, observed that the ongoing global financial crisis was suppressing demand for petroleum. The Conference determined to decrease the production ceiling by 1.5m. b/d, with effect from 1 November. A subsequent extraordinary Conference meeting, held in mid-December, agreed to reduce production further, by 4.7m. b/d from the actual total production in September (29.0m. b/d), with effect from 1 January 2009. By 24 December 2008 the ORB price had fallen to $33.36 per barrel.

The ORB price stabilized in early 2009, fluctuating at around US $40 per barrel during January–mid-March (when a meeting of the Conference determined to maintain current production levels, but urged member states' full compliance with them: this had stood at 79% in February), and rising to around $50 per barrel during mid-March–early May. By mid-June the ORB price had risen to $70.9 per barrel. Meeting in late May the Conference noted that the impact of the ongoing global economic crisis had resulted in a reduction in the global demand for petroleum, this having declined during the second half of 2008 for the first time since the early 1980s. The Conference welcomed the positive effect of recent production decisions in redressing the balance of supply and demand, and decided to maintain current production levels. Reviewing the situation at the next meeting, convened in early September 2009, the Conference observed that the global economic situation continued to be very fragile and that the petroleum market remained over-supplied, and determined once more to maintain existing production levels. When convened again, in December, the Conference expressed concern at the gravity of the global economic contraction, noting that the worldwide demand for petroleum had now declined for two successive years. The March 2010 Conference observed some improvement in the global economy, and projected marginal improvements in global demand for petroleum, but observed, also, that serious threats remained to the economic situation, and that, owing to a forecast increase in petroleum supplies from non-OPEC sources, a third successive year of declining demand for the organization's crude oil was envisaged. The next ordinary meeting of the Conference, held in October, adopted a second Long-Term Strategy for the organization, setting objectives relating to member countries' long-term petroleum revenues; fair and stable prices; future energy demand and OPEC's share in world oil supply; stability of the global oil market; security of regular supply to consumers, and of global demand; and enhancing the collective interests of member states in global negotiations and future multilateral agreements. An extraordinary meeting of the Conference, convened in December, observed that the global economic outlook remained fragile, and, on that basis, agreed to maintain current oil production levels. The next ordinary meeting of the Conference, held in June 2011—following, in the first half of that year, the unforeseen eruption of unrest and uncertainty in several Middle Eastern and North African countries, including Libya (where a significant decline in production was recorded), and a sharp increase in petroleum prices—failed to reach consensus on a proposed agreement to raise output. In December OPEC ministers agreed to maintain the production ceiling at current output levels (some 30m. b/d). Ministers attending the ordinary Conference in mid-June 2012 agreed to maintain the production ceiling, despite marked over-production by some member states and a decline in prices from $122.97 per barrel in mid-March, to $96.02 (on 15 June). Meeting in December the Conference took note of continuing price volatility—reflecting increased speculation in the commodities markets and continuing pessimism concerning the global economy—while deciding further to maintain the 30m. b/d production ceiling. At the end of May 2013 the Conference resolved to maintain the existing production ceiling. At 16 September the ORB price stood at $109.04.

ENERGY DIALOGUES

Annual joint 'workshops' are convened jointly by OPEC, the International Energy Agency (IEA) and the International Energy Forum (IEF), bringing together experts, analysts and government officials to discuss aspects of energy supply and demand; the 2013 joint workshop took place in April, in Vienna, Austria, on the theme 'Interactions between Physical and Financial Energy Markets'. In October 2012 OPEC, the IEA and the IEF organized the First Joint Symposium on Gas and Coal Market Outlooks.

The first annual formal ministerial meeting of the European Union (EU)-OPEC Energy Dialogue took place in June 2005, with the aim of exchanging views on energy issues of common interest, including petroleum market developments, and thus contributing to stability, transparency and predictability in the market. The fifth EU-OPEC Energy Dialogue ministerial meeting, convened in June 2008, agreed to hold a round table on carbon capture and storage (this took place in October); to finalize a joint study on the impacts of financial markets on oil prices and market volatility, to be followed by an international workshop; to undertake a feasibility study on the establishment of an EU-OPEC Energy Technology Centre; and to prepare terms of reference for a joint study on the impacts of biofuels on oil refining. The sixth ministerial Dialogue, convened in June 2009, agreed to implement the joint study on the impacts of biofuels on oil refining and to conduct a workshop to review the findings of the study; to organize a round table on the impacts on the petroleum sector of the ongoing financial crisis; and to finalize the planned feasibility study on the proposed EU-OPEC Energy Technology Centre. In June 2010 a summary of the conclusions of the feasibility study was presented to the seventh ministerial Dialogue. The June 2010 Dialogue meeting determined to commission, in 2011, a study to explore the potential of technological advances in transportation, and to assess their impact on demand for petroleum; and also to arrange a round table to examine the causes of an ongoing shortage of skilled labour shortage in the energy and oil industries. The June 2011 Dialogue decided to organize, during 2011–12, a joint workshop to discuss the findings of the study on technological advances in the road transportation sector; to complete preparations for the proposed Energy Technology Centre; and to hold a roundtable on the key challenges confronting oil and gas exploration and production activities. In June 2012 the ninth ministerial Dialogue agreed the following objectives for the period 2012–13: organizing, in November 2012, an international roundtable meeting on offshore safety in oil and gas exploration/production; undertaking a study and organizing in 2013 a round table on possible human resource demand bottlenecks in the petroleum sector; and conducting a study on energy efficiency and its potential impact on demand.

Russia (a major producer of petroleum) was given OPEC observer status in 1992, and was subsequently represented at a number of ministerial and other meetings. A formal Energy Dialogue was established in December 2005, providing for annual ministerial meetings, together with technical exchanges, seminars and joint research, on such subjects as petroleum market developments and prospects, data flow, investments across the supply chain, and energy policies. The OPEC-Russia ministerial meeting held in September 2012 addressed broadening the scope of co-operation and considered establishing a joint working group on information exchange and analysis of the petroleum sector.

In March 2005 the Chinese Government proposed the creation of an official dialogue between OPEC and the People's Republic of China (a major customer of OPEC members) and this was formally established in December, with the aim of exchanging views on energy issues, particularly security of supply and demand, through annual ministerial meetings, technical exchanges and energy round-tables.

ENVIRONMENTAL CONCERNS

OPEC has frequently expressed its concern that any measures adopted to avert climate change by reducing the emission of carbon dioxide caused by the consumption of fossil fuels would seriously affect its members' income. In 1998, for example, OPEC representatives attending a conference of the parties to the UN Framework Convention on Climate Change warned that OPEC would claim compensation for any lost revenue resulting from initiatives to limit petroleum consumption, and at subsequent sessions, while expressing support for the fundamental principles of the Convention, OPEC urged that developing countries whose economies were dependent on the export of fossil fuels should not be unfairly treated. In June 2007 OPEC's Secretary-General criticized the industrialized nations' efforts to increase production of biofuel (derived from agricultural commodities) in order to reduce consumption of fossil fuels: he warned that OPEC might reduce its future investment in petroleum production accordingly. In November the third summit meeting of OPEC heads of state and government acknowledged the long-term challenge of climate change, but emphasized the continuing need for stable petroleum supplies to support global economic growth and development, and urged that policies aimed at combating climate change should be balanced, taking into account their impact on developing countries, including countries heavily dependent on the production and export of fossil fuels. The meeting stressed the importance of cleaner and more efficient petroleum technologies, and the development of technologies such as carbon capture and storage.

Finance

OPEC has an annual budget of about €25m.

Publications

Annual Report.
Annual Statistical Bulletin.
Environmental Newsletter (quarterly).
Monthly Oil Market Report.
OPEC Bulletin (10 a year).
OPEC Review (quarterly).
World Oil Outlook (annually).
Reports, information papers, press releases.

OPEC FUND FOR INTERNATIONAL DEVELOPMENT

Address: POB 995, 1011 Vienna, Austria.
Telephone: (1) 515-64-0; **fax:** (1) 513-92-38; **e-mail:** info@ofid.org; **internet:** www.ofid.org.

The OPEC Fund for International Development (initially referred to as 'the Fund', more recently as 'OFID') was established 1976 by OPEC member countries, in order to assist developing countries and to promote South-South co-operation. A revised agreement to establish the Fund as a permanent international agency was signed in May 1980.

MEMBERS

Algeria	Iraq	Qatar
Gabon	Kuwait	Saudi Arabia
Indonesia	Libya	United Arab Emirates
Iran	Nigeria	Venezuela

Organization

(September 2013)

ADMINISTRATION

OFID is administered by a Ministerial Council and a Governing Board. Each member country is represented on the Council by its minister of finance. The Board consists of one representative and one alternate for each member country.

Chairman, Ministerial Council: YOUSEF HUSSAIN KAMAL (Qatar).

Chairman, Governing Board: JAMAL NASSER LOOTAH (UAE).

Director-General of the Fund: SULEIMAN JASIR AL-HERBISH (Saudi Arabia).

FINANCIAL STRUCTURE

The resources of OFID, whose unit of account is the US dollar, consist of contributions by OPEC member countries, and income received from operations or otherwise accruing to the Fund.

The initial endowment of OFID amounted to US $800m. Its resources have been replenished four times—the Fourth Replenishment, totalling $1,000m., was approved by the Ministerial Council in June 2011; member states were to issue their respective letters of undertaking in this respect by mid-2012. OFID's resources have also been increased by the profits accruing to seven OPEC member countries through the sales of gold held by the International Monetary Fund (IMF). At the end of 2011 the total pledged contributions by member countries amounted to $3,435.0m., and paid-in contributions totalled some $3,079.1m.

Activities

The OPEC Fund for International Development (OFID) is a multilateral agency for financial co-operation and assistance. Its objective is to reinforce financial co-operation between OPEC member countries and other developing countries through the provision of financial support to the latter on appropriate terms, to assist them in their economic and social development. OFID was conceived as a collective financial facility which would consolidate the assistance extended by its member countries; its resources are additional to those already made available through other bilateral and multilateral aid agencies of OPEC members. It is empowered to:

(i) Provide concessional loans for balance of payments support;

(ii) Provide concessional loans for the implementation of development projects and programmes;

(iii) Contribute to the resources of other international development agencies;

(iv) Finance technical assistance, research, food aid and humanitarian emergency relief through grants; and

(v) Participate in the financing of private sector activities in developing countries.

The eligible beneficiaries of OFID's assistance are the governments of developing countries other than OPEC member countries, and international development agencies whose beneficiaries are developing countries. OFID gives priority to the countries with the lowest income.

OFID may undertake technical, economic and financial appraisal of a project submitted to it, or entrust such an appraisal to an appropriate international development agency, the executing national agency of a member country, or any other qualified agency. Most projects financed by the organization have been co-financed by other development finance agencies. In each such case, one of the co-financing agencies may be appointed to administer the loan in association with its own. This practice has enabled OFID to extend its lending activities to more than 100 countries and in a simple way, with the aim of avoiding duplication and complications. As its experience grew, OFID increasingly resorted to parallel, rather than joint financing, taking up separate project components to be financed according to its rules and policies. In addition, it started to finance some projects on its own. The loans are not tied to procurement from OFID member countries or from any other countries. The margin of preference for goods and services obtainable in developing countries is allowed on the request of the borrower and within defined limits. OFID assistance in the form of programme loans has a broader coverage than project lending. Programme loans are used to stimulate an economic sector or sub-sector, and assist recipient countries in obtaining inputs, equipment and spare parts. In 2004 a supplementary lending mechanism, a Blend Facility, was established to make available additional resources at higher rates than the standard concessional lending terms. Besides extending loans for project and programme financing and balance of payments support, OFID also undertakes other operations, including grants in support of technical assistance and other activities (mainly research), emergency relief and humanitarian aid, and financial contributions to other international institutions. In 1998 the Fund began to extend lines of credit to support private sector activities in beneficiary countries. The so-called Private Sector Facility aims to encourage the growth of private enterprises, in particular small and medium-sized enterprises (SMEs), and to support the development of local capital markets. A new Trade Finance Facility, to provide loans, lines of credit and guarantees in support of international trade operations in developing countries, was launched in December 2006.

OFID has contributed to the development of an 'Energy for the Poor' initiative launched in June 2008 by a meeting of energy consumers and producers held in Jeddah, Saudi Arabia. In March 2009 OFID participated in a meeting of international finance institutions and development banks to discuss closer co-operation in order to respond more effectively to the global financial and economic crisis. OFID agreed to provide US $30m. to an African sub-fund of the International Finance Corporation's Recapitalization Fund, which aimed to support banks in developing countries. It also participated in a Microfinance Enhancement Facility and, though its Trade Finance Facility, in the World Bank's Global Trade Liquidity Programme. In October 2010 OFID signed a Memorandum of Understanding (MOU) with the World Bank Group in order to strengthen their joint efforts to meet new development challenges, with a particular focus on the need to counter energy poverty (since 2007 a strategic priority of OFID), to improve the management of natural resources, to facilitate trade and to strengthen financial institutions. In May 2011 OFID signed an MOU with the Asian Development Bank, in order to enhance co-operation between the two organizations, and in July signed an MOU with the Arab Bank for Economic Development in Africa. In December of that year OFID's Director-General, addressing the 20th World Petroleum Congress, convened in Doha, Qatar, recommended that the Fund might act as a hub for efforts by the petroleum sector to promote the global 'Sustainable Energy for All by 2030' initiative that had been launched by the UN Secretary-General in September 2011. In June 2012 the Ministerial Council issued a landmark Ministerial Declaration on Energy Poverty, reaffirming member states' commitment to eradicating global energy poverty, and determining to commit a minimum of US $1,000m. to finance the ongoing 'Energy for the Poor Initiative'.

By the end of 2012 OFID had approved a total of US $15,116.3m. since operations began in 1976, of which $10,264.0m. was for public sector loans. Included in the public sector lending is the Fund's contribution to the Heavily Indebted Poor Countries (HIPC) initiative (see World Bank), which by the end of 2012 amounted to $269.8m. Private sector financing totalled $1,759.9m. committed in the same period, while loans committed under the Trade Finance Facility, amounted to $1,522.4m. At that time cumulative disbursements of all loans and operations amounted to $9,582.4m.

Direct loans are supplemented by grants to support technical assistance, food aid and research. By the end of December 2012 grants amounting to US $548.2m., had been committed since operations commenced, including $20m. as a special contribution to the International Fund for Agricultural Development (IFAD) and a further $20m. approved under a Food Aid Special Grant Account, which was established in 2003 to combat famine in Africa. In addition, OFID had committed $1,021.8m. to the resources of IFAD, an IMF Trust Fund and the IMF's Poverty Reduction and Growth Facility (PRGF) Trust.

During the year ending 31 December 2012 the Fund's total commitments amounted to US $1,301.9m. (compared with $758.5m. in the previous year). These commitments included public sector loans, amounting to $676.7m., supporting 39 projects in 32 countries. The largest proportion of loans (41% of the total) was for transportation projects, including the construction or rehabilitation of roads in Bangladesh, Bolivia, Chad, Democratic Republic of the Congo (DRC), Granada, Madagascar, Sierra Leone, Sri Lanka, Suriname, Tajikistan, Uganda and Viet Nam. The energy sector accounted for 32% of the total, for projects including the improvement of electricity generation, transmission and distributions in Cambodia, The Gambia, Kenya, Mauritania, Morocco, Pakistan, Rwanda, Tunisia and Yemen. Projects in the agriculture sector received 12% of the total, including irrigation development projects in the DRC and Egypt, and a project to strengthen farmers' linkages to value chains through the establishment of more efficient production, transport, storage, processing and marketing systems. Public sector loans for the education sector, amounting to 7% of the total, financed projects in the People's Republic of China, Madagascar, Sierra Leone and Zambia. Projects aimed at improving water supply and sanitation were approved for Cuba, Lesotho and Tanzania. A multi-sectoral project was approved for Djibouti, to assist the start-up and expansion of SMEs.

Private sector operations approved during 2012 amounted to US $165.0m., which funded projects in the energy and transportation sectors, and in support of micro-, small- and medium-sized enterprises. Approvals under the Trade Financing Facility amounted to $441.6m. in 2012 (compared with $117.0m. in 2011). A global risk-sharing guarantee programme amounting to $50.0m. was also concluded during 2012 in cooperation with the United Arab Emirates-based Banque du Commerce et du Placement.

During 2012 OFID approved US $18.5m. in grants. Of the total, $4.5m. was committed from the Special Grant Account for Palestine to support the provision of safe drinking water, to support civil society organizations, and to foster youth employment. Some $4.0m. was approved under OFID's Grant Account for Energy Poverty Operations (approved in 2011 by the Ministerial Council) for projects including several hydro and solar power schemes. A further $2.5m. was approved from the HIV/AIDS Special Account to assist participation by representatives of least developed countries at the 19th International AIDS Conference, held in June 2012 in Washington, DC, USA, and to advance HIV prevention, treatment and patient care activities. Some $4.5m. was approved for technical assistance projects in the agriculture, education, health and sanitation and water supply sectors.

Publications

Annual Report (in Arabic, English, French and Spanish).

OFID Quarterly.

Pamphlet series, author papers, books and other documents.

Statistics

Total approvals in 2012, by Sector and Region
(US $ million)

	Financing approved	%
Sector:		
Agriculture	91.2	7.0
Education and knowledge transfer	46.1	3.5
Emergency activities	1.5	0.1
Energy	382.6	29.4
Finance	181.6	13.9
Health	26.1	2.0
Industry	25.0	1.9
Multi-sector	207.3	15.9
Transportation	275.0	21.1
Water supply and sanitation	35.5	2.7
Telecommunications	30.1	2.3
Total	1,301.9	100.0
Region:		
Africa	558.0	42.9
Asia	438.6	33.7
Latin America and the Caribbean	101.3	7.8
Europe and multi-regional	204.1	15.7

Source: OFID, *Annual Report 2012*.

OTHER REGIONAL ORGANIZATIONS

Agriculture, Food, Forestry and Fisheries

(for organizations concerned with agricultural commodities, see Commodities)

Arab Authority for Agricultural Investment and Development (AAAID): POB 2102, Khartoum, Sudan; tel. (18) 7096100; fax (18) 7096295; e-mail info@aaaid.org; internet www.aaaid.org; f. 1976 to accelerate agricultural development in the Arab world and to ensure food security; acts principally by equity participation in agricultural projects in mem. countries; AAAID has adopted new programmes to help raise productivity of food agricultural products and introduced zero-tillage farming technology for developing the rain-fed sector, which achieved a substantial increase in the yields of grown crops, including sorghum, cotton, sesame, and sunflower; mems: 20 countries; Pres. and Chair. MOHAMED BIN OBAID ALMAZROOEI (UAE); publs *Journal of Agricultural Investment* (English and Arabic), *Extension and Investment Bulletins*, *Annual Report* (Arabic and English), *AAAID Newsletter* (quarterly).

Association of Agricultural Research Institutions in the Near East and North Africa: POB 950764, 11195 Amman, Jordan; tel. (6) 5525750; fax (6) 5525930; e-mail icarda-jordan@cgiar.org; internet www.aarinena.org; f. 1985; aims to strengthen co-operation among national, regional and international research institutions; operates the internet-based Near East and North Africa Rural and Agricultural Knowledge and Information Network (NERAKIN); Exec. Sec. MOHAMMAD MAHMOUD AJLOUNI (Jordan).

Indian Ocean Tuna Commission (IOTC): POB 1011, Victoria, Mahé, Seychelles; tel. 4225494; fax 4224364; e-mail secretariat@iotc.org; internet www.iotc.org; f. 1996 as a regional fisheries org. with a mandate for the conservation and management of tuna and tuna-like species in the Indian Ocean; mems: Australia, Belize, People's Republic of China, the Comoros, European Union, Eritrea, France, Guinea, India, Indonesia, Iran, Japan, Kenya, Republic of Korea, Madagascar, Malaysia, Maldives, Mauritius, Mozambique, Oman, Pakistan, Philippines, Seychelles, Sierra Leone, Sudan, Sri Lanka, Tanzania, Thailand, United Kingdom, Vanuatu, Yemen; co-operating non-contracting parties: Senegal, South Africa; Exec. Sec. RONDOLPH PAYET (Seychelles).

International Centre for Agricultural Research in the Dry Areas (ICARDA): POB 114, 5055 Beirut, Lebanon; tel. (1) 843472; fax (1) 804071; e-mail icarda@cgiar.org; internet www.icarda.org; f. 1977; aims to improve the production of lentils, barley and fava beans throughout the developing world; supports the improvement of on-farm water-use efficiency, rangeland and small-ruminant production in all dry-area developing countries; within the West and Central Asia and North Africa region promotes the improvement of bread and durum wheat and chickpea production and of farming systems; undertakes research, training and dissemination of information, in co-operation with national, regional and international research institutes, universities and ministries of agriculture, in order to enhance production, alleviate poverty and promote sustainable natural resource management practices; mem. of the network of 15 agricultural research centres supported by the Consultative Group on International Agricultural Research (CGIAR); Dir-Gen. Dr MAHMOUD MOHAMED BASHIR EL-SOLH; publs *Annual Report*, *Caravan Newsletter* (2 a year).

International Food Policy Research Institute (IFPRI): 2033 K St, NW, Washington, DC 20006, USA; tel. (202) 862-5600; fax (202) 467-4439; e-mail ifpri@cgiar.org; internet www.ifpri.org; f. 1975; co-operates with academic and other institutions in further research; develops policies for cutting hunger and malnutrition; committed to increasing public awareness of food policies; participates in the Agricultural Market Information System (f. 2011); Dir-Gen. SHENGGEN FAN (People's Republic of China).

Arts and Culture

Afro-Asian Writers' Association: 18 Ismail Abou el-Fotouh St, Veiny Sq., in front of Misr International Hospital, Dokki, Cairo, Egypt; tel. (2) 37600549; fax (2) 37600548; f. 1958; mems: writers' orgs in 51 countries; Chair. MOHAMED MAGDY MORGAN; publs *Lotus Magazine of Afro-Asian Writings* (quarterly in English, French and Arabic), *Afro-Asian Literature Series* (in English, French and Arabic).

Organization of World Heritage Cities: 15 rue Saint-Nicolas, Québec, QC G1K 1M8, Canada; tel. (418) 692-0000; fax (418) 692-5558; e-mail secretariat@ovpm.org; internet www.ovpm.org; f. 1993 to assist cities inscribed on the UNESCO World Heritage List to implement the Convention concerning the Protection of the World Cultural and Natural Heritage (1972); promotes co-operation between city authorities, in particular in the management and sustainable development of historic sites; holds an annual General Assembly, comprising the mayors of member cities; mems: 250 cities world-wide; Sec.-Gen. DENIS RICARD; publ. *OWHC Newsletter* (2 a year, in English, French and Spanish).

Commodities

African Petroleum Producers' Association (APPA): POB 1097, Brazzaville, Republic of the Congo; tel. 665-38-57; fax 669-99-13; e-mail appa@appa.int; internet appa.int; f. 1987 by African petroleum-producing countries to reinforce co-operation among regional producers and to stabilize prices; council of ministers responsible for the hydrocarbons sector meets twice a year; holds regular African Petroleum Congress and Exhibition (CAPE): fifth CAPE held in Libreville, Gabon, in March 2013; mems: Algeria, Angola, Benin, Cameroon, Democratic Republic of the Congo, Republic of the Congo, Côte d'Ivoire, Egypt, Equatorial Guinea, Gabon, Libya, Nigeria; Exec. Sec. GABRIEL DANSOU LOKOSSOU; publ. *APPA Bulletin* (2 a year).

Gas Exporting Countries Forum: POB 23753, Tornado Tower, 47-48th Floors, West Bay, Doha, Qatar; tel. 44048400; fax 44048415; e-mail gecfsg@gmail.com; internet www.gecf.org; f. 2001 to represent and promote the mutual interests of gas exporting countries; aims to increase the level of co-ordination among mem. countries and to promote dialogue between gas producers and consumers; a ministerial meeting is convened annually; the seventh ministerial meeting, convened in Moscow, Russia, in Dec. 2008, agreed on a charter and a permanent structure for the grouping; first meeting of heads of state convened in Doha, in 2011; second summit meeting held in Moscow, Russia, in July 2013; mems: Algeria, Bolivia, Egypt, Equatorial Guinea, Iran, Libya, Nigeria, Oman, Qatar, Russia, Trinidad and Tobago, UAE, Venezuela; observers: Iraq, Kazakhstan, Netherlands, Norway; Sec.-Gen. LEONID BOKHANOVSKIY.

International Energy Forum (IEF): POB 94736, Diplomatic Quarter, Riyadh 11614, Saudi Arabia; tel. (1) 4810022; fax (1) 4810055; e-mail info@ief.org; internet www.ief.org; f. 1991; the IEF is an intergovernmental arrangement aimed at promoting dialogue on global energy matters among its membership; ministers responsible for energy affairs from states accounting for about 90% of global oil and gas supply and demand convene every two years; the gathering in recent years has been preceded by a meeting of the International Business Energy Forum (IEBF), comprising energy ministers and CEOs of leading energy companies; 13th IEF and fifth IEBF: March 2012, Kuwait; mems: 89 states, including the mems of OPEC and the International Energy Agency; Sec.-Gen. ALDO FLORES-QUIROGA.

International Grains Council (IGC): 1 Canada Sq., Canary Wharf, London, E14 5AE, United Kingdom; tel. (20) 7513-1122; fax (20) 7513-0630; e-mail igc@igc.int; internet www.igc.int; f. 1949 as International Wheat Council, present name adopted in 1995; responsible for the administration of the International Grains Agreement, 1995, comprising the Grains Trade Convention (GTC) and the Food Aid Convention (FAC, under which donors pledge specified minimum annual amounts of food aid for developing countries in the form of grain and other eligible products); aims to further international co-operation in all aspects of trade in grains, to promote international trade in grains, and to achieve a free flow of this trade, particularly in developing mem. countries; seeks to contribute to the stability of the international grain market; acts as a forum for consultations between mems; provides comprehensive information on the international grain market (with effect from 1 July 2009 the definition of 'grain' was extended to include rice, and from 1 July 2013 it was expanded further, to include oilseeds); mems: 25 countries and the European Union; Exec. Dir ETSUO KITAHARA; publs *World Grain Statistics* (annually), *Grain Shipments* (annually), *Fiscal Year Reports* (annually), *Grain Market Report* (monthly), *IGC Grain Market Indicators* (weekly), *Rice Market Bulletin* (weekly).

International Olive Council: Príncipe de Vergara 154, 28002 Madrid, Spain; tel. (91) 5903638; fax (91) 5631263; e-mail iooc@internationaloliveoil.org; internet www.internationaloliveoil.org; f. 1959 to administer the International Agreement on Olive Oil and Table Olives, which aims to promote international co-operation in connection with problems of the world economy for olive products; works to prevent unfair competition, to encourage the production and consumption of olive products, and their international trade, and to reduce the disadvantages caused by fluctuations of supplies on the market; also takes action to foster a better understanding of the nutritional, therapeutic and other properties of olive products, to foster international co-operation for the integrated, sustainable development of world olive growing, to encourage research and development, to foster the transfer of technology and training activities in the olive products sector, and to improve the interaction between olive growing and the environment; mems: of the International Agreement on Olive Oil and Table Olives, 2005 (fifth Agreement, in force until 31 Dec. 2014): 14 countries, and the European Union; Exec. Dir JEAN-LOUIS BARJOL; publ. *OLIVAE* (2 a year, in Arabic, English, French, Italian and Spanish).

International Organisation of Vine and Wine (Organisation Internationale de la Vigne et du Vin—OIV): 18 rue d'Aguesseau, 75008 Paris, France; tel. 1-44-94-80-80; fax 1-42-66-90-63; e-mail contact@oiv.int; internet www.oiv.int; f. 2001 (agreement establishing an International Wine Office signed Nov. 1924, name changed to International Vine and Wine Office in 1958); researches vine and vine product issues in the scientific, technical, economic and social areas, disseminates knowledge, and facilitates contacts between researchers; mems: 45 countries; 10 orgs and 2 territories have observer status; Dir-Gen. FEDERICO CASTELLUCCI (Italy); publs *Bulletin de l'OIV* (every 2 months), *Lexique de la Vigne et du Vin*, *Recueil des méthodes internationales d'analyse des vins*, *Code international des Pratiques oenologiques*, *Codex oenologique international*, numerous scientific publications.

Development and Economic Co-operation

African Training and Research Centre in Administration for Development (Centre Africain de Formation et de Recherche Administratives pour le Développement—CAFRAD): POB 1796, Tangier, 90001 Morocco; tel. (661) 307269; fax (539) 325785; e-mail cafrad@cafrad.org; internet www.cafrad.org; f. 1964 by agreement between Morocco and UNESCO; undertakes research into administrative problems in Africa and documents results; provides a consultation service for govts and orgs; holds workshops to train senior civil servants; prepares the Biennial Pan-African Conference of Ministers of the Civil Service; mems: 37 African countries; Chair. ABDELAÂDIM GUERROUJ; Dir-Gen. Dr SIMON MAMOSI LELO; publs *African Administrative Studies* (2 a year), *Research Studies*, *Newsletter* (internet), *Collection: Etudes et Documents*, *Répertoires des Consultants et des institutions de formation en Afrique*.

Afro-Asian Rural Development Organization (AARDO): No. 2, State Guest Houses Complex, Chanakyapuri, New Delhi 110 021, India; tel. (11) 24100475; fax (11) 24672045; e-mail aardohq@nde.vsnl.net.in; internet www.aardo.org; f. 1962 to act as a catalyst for the co-operative restructuring of rural life in Africa and Asia and to explore opportunities for the co-ordination of efforts to promote rural welfare and to eradicate hunger, thirst, disease, illiteracy and poverty; carries out collaborative research on development issues; organizes training; encourages the exchange of information; holds international conferences and seminars; awards more than 300 individual training fellowships at 12 institutes in Bangladesh, Egypt, India, Republic of Korea, Malaysia, Nigeria, Pakistan, Taiwan and Zambia; mems: 15 African countries, 14 Asian countries, 1 African associate; Sec.-Gen. WASSFI HASSAN EL-SREIHIN (Jordan); publs *Afro-Asian Journal of Rural Development* (2 a year), *Annual Report*, *AARDO Newsletter* (2 a year).

Agadir Agreement: Fifth Circle, Hanna Qa'war St, Bldg 3, POB 830487, 11183 Amman, Jordan; tel. (6) 5935305; fax (6) 5935306; e-mail atu@agadiragreement.org; internet www.agadiragreement.org; a Declaration made in Agadir, in May 2001, by the govts of Egypt, Jordan, Morocco and Tunisia on the establishment of a common free trade area was followed, in Feb. 2004, by the adoption of the Agadir Agreement on the establishment of a Free Trade Zone between the Arabic Mediterranean Nations, as a means of implementing the Agadir Declaration; the Agadir Agreement entered into force in July 2006 and its implementation commenced in March 2007; a Technical Unit to follow-up implementation of the Agreement was established in April 2007; mems: Egypt, Jordan, Morocco, Tunisia; Technical Unit Exec. Pres. WALID EL-NOZAHY.

Arab Gulf Programme for the United Nations Development Organizations (AGFUND): POB 18371, Riyadh 11415, Saudi Arabia; tel. (1) 4418888; fax (1) 4412962; e-mail info@agfund.org; internet www.agfund.org; f. 1981 to provide grants for projects in mother and child care carried out by UN orgs, Arab non-governmental orgs and other international bodies, and to co-ordinate assistance by the nations of the Gulf; financing comes mainly from mem. states, all of which are mems of OPEC; mems: Bahrain, Kuwait, Oman, Qatar, Saudi Arabia, UAE; Pres. HRH Prince TALAL BIN ABDAL-AZIZ.

Community of Sahel-Saharan States (Communauté des états Sahelo-Sahariens—CEN-SAD): Pl. d'Algeria, POB 4041, Tripoli, Libya; tel. (21) 361-4832; fax (21) 334-3670; e-mail info@cen-sad.bj; internet www.cen-sad.bj; f. 1998; fmrly known as COMESSA; aims to strengthen co-operation between signatory states in order to promote their economic, social and cultural integration and to facilitate conflict resolution and poverty alleviation; partnership agreements concluded with many orgs, including the AU, UN and ECOWAS; extraordinary summit convened in Feb. 2013, in N'Djamena, Chad, to discuss regional security, with a particular focus on the ongoing situation in Mali; mems: Benin, Burkina Faso, Central African Republic, Chad, Côte d'Ivoire, Djibouti, Egypt, Eritrea, The Gambia, Ghana, Guinea-Bissau, Liberia, Libya, Mali, Morocco, Niger, Nigeria, Senegal, Sierra Leone, Somalia, Sudan, Togo, Tunisia; Sec.-Gen. Dr MOHAMMED AL-MADANI AL-AZHARI (Libya).

Developing Eight (D-8): Maya Aka Center, Kat 12 D, 50 Esentepe, 34390, Istanbul, Turkey; tel. (212) 3561823; fax (212) 3561829; e-mail secretariat@developing8.org; internet www.developing8.org; inaugurated at a meeting of heads of state in June 1997; aims to foster economic co-operation between mem. states and to strengthen the role of developing countries in the global economy; project areas include trade (with Egypt as the co-ordinating mem. state), agriculture (Pakistan), human resources (Indonesia), communication and information (Iran), rural development (Bangladesh), finance and banking (Malaysia), energy (Nigeria), and industry, and health (Turkey); a roadmap of co-operation for the period 2008–18 envisaged the implementation of preferential trade agreement; eighth summit held in Islamabad, Pakistan, in Nov. 2012; mems: Bangladesh, Egypt, Indonesia, Iran, Malaysia, Nigeria, Pakistan, Turkey; Sec.-Gen. Dr SEYED ALI MOHAMMAD MOUSAVI (Iran).

Economic Research Forum: POB 12311, 21 al-Sad al-Aaly St, Dokki, Cairo, Egypt; tel. (2) 33318600; fax (2) 33318604; e-mail erf@erf.org.eg; internet www.erf.org.eg; f. 1993 to conduct in-depth economic research, compile an economic database for the Arab countries, Iran and Turkey, and to provide training to contribute to sustainable development in the region; Man. Dir AHMED GALAL; publ. *ERF Newsletter* (quarterly).

Group of 15 (G15): G15 Technical Support Facility, 1 route des Morillons, CP 2100, 1218 Grand Saconnex, Geneva, Switzerland; tel. 227916701; fax 227916169; e-mail tsf@g15.org; internet www.g15.org; f. 1989 by 15 developing nations during the ninth summit of the Non-Aligned Movement; retains its original name although current membership totals 17; convenes biennial summits to address the global economic and political situation and to promote economic development through South-South co-operation and North-South dialogue; mems: Algeria, Argentina, Brazil, Chile, Egypt, India, Indonesia, Iran, Jamaica, Kenya, Malaysia, Mexico, Nigeria, Senegal, Sri Lanka, Venezuela, Zimbabwe; Head of Office SAURABH BHANDARI.

Group of 77 (G77): c/o UN Headquarters, Rm NL-2077, New York, NY 10017, USA; tel. (212) 963-0192; fax (212) 963-1753; e-mail secretariat@g77.org; internet www.g77.org; f. 1964 by the 77 signatory states of the Joint Declaration of the Seventy-Seven Countries (the G77 retains its original name, owing to its historic significance, although its membership has expanded since inception); first ministerial meeting, held in Algiers, Algeria, in Oct. 1967, adopted the Charter of Algiers as a basis for G77 co-operation; subsequently G77 Chapters were established with liaison offices in Geneva (UNCTAD), Nairobi (UNEP), Paris (UNESCO), Rome (FAO/IFAD), Vienna (UNIDO), and the Group of 24 (G24) in Washington, DC (IMF and World Bank); as the largest intergovernmental organization of developing states in the UN the G77 aims to enable developing nations to articulate and promote their collective economic interests and to improve their negotiating capacity with regard to global economic issues within the UN system; in Sept. 2006 G77 ministers of foreign affairs, and the People's Republic of China, endorsed the establishment of a new Consortium on Science, Technology and Innovation for the South (COSTIS); a chairperson, who also acts as spokesperson, co-ordinates the G77's activities in each Chapter; the chairmanship rotates on a regional basis between Africa, Asia, and Latin America and the Caribbean; the supreme decision-making body of the G77 is the South Summit, normally convened at five-yearly intervals (2005: Doha, Qatar; it is envisaged that the third Summit will be held in Africa); the annual meeting of G77 ministers of foreign affairs is convened at the start (in Sept.) of the regular session of the UN General Assembly; periodic sectoral ministerial meetings are organized in preparation for UNCTAD sessions and prior to the UNIDO and UNESCO General Conferences, and with the aim of promoting South-South co-operation; other special ministerial meetings are also convened from time to time; the first G77 Ministerial Forum on Water Resources was convened in February 2009, in Muscat, Oman; mems: 132 developing countries.

Indian Ocean Rim Association for Regional Co-operation (IOR–ARC): Nexteracom Tower 1, 3rd Floor, Ebene, Mauritius; tel. 454-1717; fax 468-1161; e-mail iorarcsec@iorarc.org; internet www.iorarc.org; the first intergovernmental meeting of countries in the region to promote an Indian Ocean Rim initiative was convened in March 1995; charter to establish the Asscn was signed at a ministerial meeting in March 1997; aims to promote the sustained growth and balanced devt of the region and of its mem. states and to create common ground for regional economic co-operation, *inter alia* through trade, investment, infrastructure, tourism, and science and technology; 13th meeting of the Working Group of Heads of Missions held in April 2012 (Pretoria, South Africa); mems: Australia, Bangladesh, Comoros, India, Indonesia, Iran, Kenya, Madagascar, Malaysia, Mauritius, Mozambique, Oman, Seychelles, Singapore, South Africa, Sri Lanka, Tanzania, Thailand, United Arab Emirates and Yemen. Dialogue Partner countries: People's Republic of China, Egypt, France, Japan, United Kingdom, USA. Observers: Indian Ocean Research Group (IORG) Inc., Indian Ocean Tourism Org; Sec.-Gen. K. V. BHAGIRATH.

Nile Basin Initiative: POB 192, Entebbe, Uganda; tel. (41) 321424; fax (41) 320971; e-mail nbisec@nilebasin.org; internet www.nilebasin.org; f. 1999; aims to achieve sustainable socio-economic development through the equitable use and benefits of the Nile Basin water resources and to create an enabling environment for the implementation of programmes with a shared vision. Highest authority is the Nile Basin Council of Ministers (Nile-COM); other activities undertaken by a Nile Basin Technical Advisory Committee (Nile-TAC); mems: Burundi, Democratic Republic of the Congo, Egypt, Eritrea, Ethiopia, Kenya, Rwanda, South Sudan, Sudan, Tanzania, Uganda; Chair. PAUL MAYOM AKEC (South Sudan).

Organization of the Black Sea Economic Cooperation (BSEC): Sakıp Sabancı Caddesi, Müşir Fuad Paşa Yalısı, Eski Tersane 34460 İstanbul, Turkey; tel. (212) 229-63-30; fax (212) 229-63-36; e-mail info@bsec-organization.org; internet www.bsec-organization.org; f. 1992 as the Black Sea Economic Cooperation (name changed on entry into force of BSEC Charter on 1 May 1999); aims to strengthen regional co-operation, particularly in the field of economic development; the following institutions have been established within the framework of BSEC: a Parliamentary Assembly (established in 1993), a Business Council (1992), a Black Sea Trade and Development Bank (inaugurated in 1998), a BSEC Co-ordination Centre, and a Black Sea International Studies Centre (opened in 1998); mems: Albania, Armenia, Azerbaijan, Bulgaria, Georgia, Greece, Moldova, Romania, Russia, Serbia, Turkey, Ukraine; Sec.-Gen. VICTOR TVIRCUN (Moldova).

Partners in Population and Development (PPD): IPH Bldg, 2nd Floor, Mohakhali, Dhaka 1212, Bangladesh; tel. (2) 988-1882; fax (2) 882-9387; e-mail partners@ppdsec.org; internet www.partners-popdev.org; f. 1994; aims to implement the decisions of the International Conference on Population and Development, held in Cairo, Egypt in 1994, in order to expand and improve South-South collaboration in the fields of family planning and reproductive health; administers a Visionary Leadership Programme, a Global Leadership Programme, and other training and technical advisory services; mems: 25 developing countries; Treas. Prof. MAJED ZEMINI.

Union of the Arab Maghreb (Union du Maghreb arabe—UMA): 73 rue Tensift, Agdal, Rabat, Morocco; tel. (53) 7681371; fax (53) 7681377; e-mail sg.uma@maghrebarabe.org; internet www.maghrebarabe.org; f. 1989; aims to encourage joint ventures and to create a single market; structure comprises a council of heads of state (meeting annually), a council of ministers of foreign affairs, a follow-up committee, a consultative council of 30 delegates from each country, a UMA judicial court, and four specialized ministerial commissions. Chairmanship rotates annually between heads of state. A Maghreb Investment and Foreign Trade Bank, funding joint agricultural and industrial projects, has been established and a customs union created; mems: Algeria, Libya, Mauritania, Morocco, Tunisia; Sec.-Gen. HABIB BEN YAHIA (Tunisia).

World Economic Forum: 91–93 route de la Capite, 1223 Cologny/Geneva, Switzerland; tel. 228691212; fax 227862744; e-mail contact@weforum.org; internet www.weforum.org; f. 1971; the Forum comprises commercial interests gathered on a non-partisan basis, under the stewardship of the Swiss Government, with the aim of improving society through economic development; convenes an annual meeting in Davos, Switzerland; organizes the following programmes: Technology Pioneers; Women Leaders; and Young Global Leaders; and aims to mobilize the resources of the global business community in the implementation of the following initiatives: the Global Health Initiative; the Disaster Relief Network; the West-Islamic World Dialogue; and the G20/International Monetary Reform Project; the Forum is governed by a guiding Foundation Board; an advisory International Business Council; and an administrative Managing Board; regular mems: representatives of 1,000 leading commercial cos in 56 countries world-wide; selected mem. cos taking a leading role in the movement's activities are known as 'partners'; Exec. Chair. KLAUS MARTIN SCHWAB.

Economics and Finance

Accounting and Auditing Organization for Islamic Financial Institutions (AAOIFI): POB 1176, Manama, Bahrain; tel. 244496; fax 250194; e-mail aaoifi@batelco.com.bh; internet www.aaoifi.com; f. 1990; aims to develop accounting, auditing and banking practices and to harmonize standards among mem. institutions; Sec.-Gen. Dr KHALED AL-FAKIH.

Arab Society of Certified Accountants (ASCA): POB 921100, Amman 11192, Jordan; tel. (6) 5100900; fax (6) 5100901; e-mail info@ascasociety.org; internet www.ascasociety.org; f. 1984 as a professional body to supervise qualifications for Arab accountants and to maintain standards; mems in 21 countries; Chair. TALAL ABU-GHAZALEH (Jordan); Gen. Sec. SAMAR AL-LABBAD (Egypt); publs *Arab Certified Accountant* (monthly), *ASCA Bulletin* (monthly), *International Accountancy Standards*, *International Audit Standards*, *Abu-Ghazaleh Dictionary of Accountancy*.

Equator Principles Association: tel. (1621) 853-900; fax (1621) 731-483; e-mail secretariat@equator-principles.com; internet www.equator-principles.com; f. July 2010; aims to administer and develop further the Equator Principles, first adopted in 2003, with the support of the International Finance Corporation, as a set of industry standards for the management of environmental and social risk in project financing; a Strategic Review conference was convened in Beijing, People's Republic of China, in Dec. 2010; 77 signed-up Equator Principles Financial Institutions (EPFIs) and two assoc. mems; Administrators JOANNA CLARK, SAMANTHA HOSKINS.

European Bank for Reconstruction and Development: One Exchange Square, London, EC2A 2JN, United Kingdom; tel. (20) 7338-6000; fax (20) 7338-6100; e-mail generalenquiries@ebrd.com; internet www.ebrd.com; f. f. 1990; aimed to contribute to the progress and the economic reconstruction of the countries of Central and Eastern Europe; since 2012 the bank has invested in four countries in the southern and eastern Mediterranean region: Egypt, Lebanon, Morocco and Tunisia (where a permanent office opened in June 2013); mems: 66 countries; Pres. Sir SUMA CHAKRABARTI (United Kingdom); publs *Annual Report*, *Donor Report* (annually), *Transition Report* (annually), *Economics of Transition* (quarterly), other reports, newsletters, economic reviews.

Financial Stability Board: c/o BIS, Centralbahnplatz 2, 4002 Basel, Switzerland; tel. 612808298; fax 612809100; e-mail fsb@bis.org; internet www.financialstabilityboard.org; f. 1999 as the Financial Stability Forum, name changed in April 2009; brings together senior representatives of national financial authorities, international financial institutions, international regulatory and supervisory groupings and cttees of central bank experts and the European Central Bank; aims to promote international financial stability and strengthen the functioning of the financial markets; in March 2009 agreed to expand its membership to include all Group of 20 (G20) economies, as well as Spain and the European Commission; in April 2009 the meeting of G20 heads of state and government determined to re-establish the then Forum as the Financial Stability Board, strengthen its institutional structure (to include a plenary body, a steering cttee and three standing cttees concerned with Vulnerabilities Assessment; Supervisory and Regulatory Co-operation; and Standards Implementation) and expand its mandate to enhance its effectiveness as an international mechanism to promote financial stability; the Board was to strengthen its collaboration with the IMF, and conduct joint 'early warning exercises'; in Dec. 2009 the Board initiated a peer review of implementation of the Principles and Standards for Sound Compensation Practices; in Nov. 2010 determined to establish six FSB regional consultative groups; Chair. MARK CARNEY (Canada).

Group of 20 (G20): internet www.g20.org; f. Sept. 1999 as an informal deliberative forum of finance ministers and central bank governors representing both industrialized and 'systemically important' emerging market nations; aims to strengthen the international financial architecture and to foster sustainable economic growth and development; in 2004 participating countries adopted the G20 Accord for Sustained Growth and stated a commitment to high standards of transparency and fiscal governance; the IMF Managing Director and IBRD President participate in G20 annual meetings; an extraordinary Summit on Financial Markets and the World Economy was convened in Washington, DC, USA, in Nov. 2008, attended by heads of state or govt of G20 mem. economies; a second summit meeting, held in London, United Kingdom, in April 2009, issued as its final communiqué a *Global Plan for Recovery and Reform* outlining commitments to restore economic confidence, growth and jobs, to strengthen financial supervision and regulation, to reform and strengthen global financial institutions, to promote global trade and investment and to ensure a fair and sustainable economic recovery; detailed declarations were also issued on measures agreed to deliver substantial resources (of some US $850,000m.) through international financial institutions and on reforms to be implemented in order to strengthen the financial system; as a follow-up to the London summit, G20 heads of state met in Pittsburgh, USA, in Sept. 2009; the meeting adopted a *Framework for Strong, Sustainable, and Balanced Growth* and resolved to expand the role of the G20 to be at the centre of future international economic policymaking; summit meetings were held in June 2010, in Canada (at the G8 summit), and in Seoul, Republic of Korea, in Nov; the sixth G20 summit, held in Cannes, France, in Nov. 2011, concluded an *Action Plan for Growth and Jobs* but was dominated by discussion of measures to secure financial stability in the euro area countries; the seventh summit, convened in Los Cabos, Baja California Sur, Mexico, in June 2012, further considered means of stabilizing the euro area, with a particular focus on reducing the borrowing costs of highly indebted mem. countries; the ongoing crisis in Syria was on the agenda of the eighth G20 summit of heads of state, which took place in Sept. 2013 in St Petersburg, Russia; 11 heads of state participating in the summit issued a statement condemning an alleged chemical attack perpetrated against civilians in Ghouta, Damascus, Syria, on 21 August, and urging a strong international response; the heads of state also adopted a new Base Erosion and Profit Shifting Action Plan, developed by OECD with the aim of combating corporate tax avoidance globally; a parallel Business 20 summit, facilitating dialogue between prominent business associations, is convened annually (2013: St Petersburg, in June); mems: Argentina, Australia, Brazil, Canada, People's Republic of China, France, Germany, India, Indonesia, Italy, Japan, Republic of Korea, Mexico, Russia, Saudi Arabia, South Africa, Turkey, United Kingdom, USA and the European Union; observers: Netherlands, Spain; the presidency rotates among the participating states on an annual basis (2013: Russia; 2014: Australia).

Intergovernmental Group of 24 (G24) on International Monetary Affairs and Development: 700 19th St, NW, Rm 3-600 Washington, DC 20431, USA; tel. (202) 623-6101; fax (202) 623-6000; e-mail g24@g24.org; internet www.g24.org; f. 1971; aims to co-ordinate the position of developing countries on monetary and development finance issues; operates at the political level of ministers of finance and governors of central banks, and also at the level of government officials; mems (Africa): Algeria, Côte d'Ivoire, DRC, Egypt, Ethiopia, Gabon, Ghana, Nigeria, South Africa; (Latin America and the Caribbean): Argentina, Brazil, Colombia, Guatemala, Mexico, Peru, Trinidad and Tobago and Venezuela; (Asia and the Middle East): India, Iran, Lebanon, Pakistan, Philippines, Sri Lanka and Syrian Arab Republic; the People's Republic of China has the status of special invitee at G24 meetings; G77 participant states may attend G24 meetings as observers.

Islamic Financial Services Board: Sasana Kijang, Level 5, Bank Negara Malaysia, 2 Jalan Dato Onn, 50840 Kuala Lumpur, Malaysia; tel. (3) 91951400; fax (3) 91951405; e-mail ifsb_sec@ifsb.org; internet www.ifsb.org; f. 2002; aims to formulate standards and guiding principles for regulatory and supervisory agencies working within the Islamic financial services industry; mems: 184, incl. 55 regulatory and supervisory authorities, 8 orgs (including the World Bank, IMF, Bank for International Settlements, Islamic Development Bank, Asian Development Bank) and 121 firms and industry asscns; Sec.-Gen. Jaseem Ahmed.

Union of Arab Banks (UAB): POB 11-2416, Riad El-Solh 1107 2210, Beirut, Lebanon; tel. (1) 377800; fax (1) 364927; e-mail uab@uabonline.org; internet www.uabonline.org; f. 1974; aims to foster co-operation between Arab banks and to increase their efficiency; prepares feasibility studies for projects; organizes an annual International Arab Banking Summit (2013: Vienna, Austria, in June); mems: more than 330 Arab banks and financial institutions; Chair. Mohammed Kamel Eddine Barakat (Egypt); Sec.-Gen. Wissam Hassan Fattouh (Lebanon).

Union of Arab Stock Exchanges and Securities Commissions: POB 22235, Safat 13083, Kuwait; tel. 22412991; fax 22420778; f. 1982 to develop capital markets in the Arab world.

Education

Alliance israélite universelle: 45 rue La Bruyère, 75009 Paris Cedex 09, France; tel. 1-53-32-88-55; fax 1-48-74-51-33; e-mail info@aiu.org; internet www.aiu.org; f. 1860 to work for the emancipation and moral progress of the Jews; maintains 40 schools in France, theMediterranean area and Canada; library of 150,000 vols; mems: 8,000 in 16 countries; Pres. Marc Eisenberg; Dir-Gen. Jo Tolédano; publs *Les Cahiers du Judaïsme* (quarterly), *Les Éditions du Nadir*.

Arab Bureau of Education for the Gulf States: POB 94693, Riyadh 11614, Saudi Arabia; tel. (1) 480-0555; fax (1) 480-2839; e-mail abegs@abegs.org; internet www.abegs.org; f. 1975; co-ordinates and promotes co-operation and integration among mem. countries in the fields of education, culture and science; aims to unify the educational systems of all Gulf Arab states; specialized organs: Gulf Arab States' Educational Research Center (POB 25566, Safat, Kuwait), Council of Higher Education, Arabian Gulf University (opened in Bahrain in 1982); mems: Governments of Bahrain, Kuwait, Oman, Qatar, Saudi Arabia, United Arab Emirates and Yemen; Dir-Gen. Dr Ali al-Karni; publs *Risalat Ul-Khaleej al-Arabi* (quarterly), *Arab Gulf Journal of Scientific Research* (2 a year).

Association of Arab Universities: POB 2000, Amman, Jordan 13110; tel. (6) 5345131; fax (6) 5332994; e-mail secgen@aaru.edu.jo; internet www.aaru.edu.jo; f. 1964; a scientific conference is held every three years; council meetings held annually; mems: 240 univs; Sec.-Gen. Prof. Dr Saleh Hashem; publ. *AARU Bulletin* (annually and quarterly, in Arabic).

European Union of Arabic and Islamic Scholars (Union Européenne des Arabisants et Islamisants—UEAI): c/o Bernadette Martel-Thoumian, Université de Grenoble, BP 47, 38040 Grenoble, Cedex 9, France; e-mail info@ueai.eu; internet www.ueai.eu; f. 1962 to organize congresses of Arabic and Islamic Studies; holds congress every two years; mems: 300 in 28 countries; Pres. Sebastian Günther (Germany); Sec.-Gen. Prof. Bernadette Martel-Thoumian (France).

Islamic World Academy of Sciences: POB 830036 Zahran, Amman 11183, Jordan; tel. (6) 5522104; fax (6) 5511803; e-mail ias@go.com.jo; internet www.iasworld.org; f. 1986; serves as a consultative organization of the Islamic *Ummah* in the field of science and technology; convenes international scientific conferences; organizes and supports capacity building workshops in basic sciences in developing countries; provides experts and consultants in science and technology to developing countries upon request; Sec.-Gen. Mohamed H A Hassan; publs *IAS Newsletter* (quarterly), science journals, conference proceedings.

Union of Arab Historians: POB 6387, al-Naqabat St, Tarablus Quarter, Baghdad, Iraq; tel. (1) 537-8691; fax (1) 537-2516; f. 1974; mems: historians in 22 countries of the region; Sec.-Gen. Dr Muhammad Jassim al-Mashhadani; publ. *Arab Historian*.

Environmental Conservation

Framework Convention for the Protection of the Marine Environment of the Caspian Sea: Interim Secretariat, c/o UNEP Regional Office for Europe, 11 chemin des Anémones, 1219 Châtelaine, Geneva, Switzerland; tel. 229178696; e-mail tehranconvention@unep.ch; internet www.tehranconvention.org; the Framework Convention for the Protection of the Marine Environment of the Caspian Sea (Tehran Convention) was adopted in November 2003 by the Governments of Azerbaijan, Iran, Kazakhstan, Russia and Turkmenistan; the Aktau Protocol Concerning Regional Preparedness, Response and Co-operation in Combating Oil Pollution Incidents was adopted in Aug. 2011; the fourth Conference of the Parties, convened in Moscow, Russia, in Dec. 2012, adopted a Protocol for the Protection of the Caspian Sea against Pollution from Land-based Sources and Activities; the Tehran Convention process is funded by the Global Environment Facility, the European Union and UNEP.

Global Coral Reef Monitoring Network: c/o IUCN Conservation Centre, 28 Rue Mauverney, 1196 Gland, Switzerland; tel. 229990217; fax 229990025; e-mail coordintor@gcrmn.org; internet www.gcrmn.org; f. 1994, as an operating unit of the International Coral Reef Initiative; active in more than 80 countries; aims include improving the management and sustainable conservation of coral reefs, strengthening links between regional organizations and ecological and socio-economic monitoring networks, and disseminating information to assist the formulation of conservation plans; publ. *Status of Coral Reefs of the World*.

International Coral Reef Initiative: c/o Australia/Great Barrier Reef Marine Park Authority (GBRMPA), 2–68 Flinders St, POB 1379, Townsville, QLD 4810, Australia; e-mail icri@gbrmpa.gov.au; internet www.icriforum.org; f. 1994 at the first Conference of the Parties of the Convention on Biological Diversity; a partnership of govts, int. orgs and non-governmental orgs; aims to raise awareness at all levels on the degradation of coral reefs around the world; promotes sustainable management practices and supports the conservation of reefs and related marine ecosystems; the Secretariat is co-chaired by a developed and a developing country, on a rotational basis among mem. states (2012–13, Australia and Belize); mems: 60

govts, int. and regional orgs; Co-Chair. MARGARET JOHNSON (Australia), BEVERLEY WADE (Belize).

International Renewable Energy Agency: C67 Office Bldg, Khalidiyah (32nd) St, POB 236, Abu Dhabi, United Arab Emirates; tel. (2) 4179000; internet www.irena.org; f. 2009 at a conference held in Bonn, Germany; aims to promote the development and application of renewable sources of energy; to act as a forum for the exchange of information and technology transfer; and to organize training seminars and other educational activities; inaugural Assembly convened in April 2011; mems: 116 mems (incl. the European Union); at July 2013 a further 45 countries had signed but not yet ratified the founding agreement or had applied to become full mems; Dir-Gen. ADNAN Z. AMIN (Kenya).

IUCN—International Union for Conservation of Nature: 28 rue Mauverney, 1196 Gland, Switzerland; tel. 229990000; fax 229990002; e-mail mail@iucn.org; internet www.iucn.org; f. 1948, as the International Union for Conservation of Nature and Natural Resources; supports partnerships and practical field activities to promote the conservation of natural resources, to secure the conservation of biological diversity as an essential foundation for the future; to ensure the equitable and sustainable use of the Earth's natural resources; and to guide the development of human communities towards ways of life in enduring harmony with other components of the biosphere, developing programmes to protect and sustain the most important and threatened species and ecosystems and assisting govts to devise and carry out national conservation strategies; incorporates the Species Survival Commission, a science-based network of volunteer experts aiming to ensure conservation of present levels of biodiversity; compiles annually updated Red List of Threatened Species (www.iucnredlist.org); the 2013 list, released in July of that year, comprised some 70,294 species, of which 20,934 were threatened with extinction; maintains a conservation library and documentation centre and units for monitoring traffic in wildlife; mems: more than 1,000 states, govt agencies, non-governmental orgs and affiliates in some 140 countries; Pres. ZHANG XINSHENG (People's Republic of China); publs *World Conservation Strategy*, *Caring for the Earth*, *Red List of Threatened Plants*, *Red List of Threatened Species*, *United Nations List of National Parks and Protected Areas*, *World Conservation* (quarterly), *IUCN Today*.

Wetlands International: POB 471, 6700 AL Wageningen, Netherlands; tel. (318) 660910; fax (318) 660950; e-mail post@wetlands.org; internet www.wetlands.org; f. 1995 by merger of several regional wetlands orgs; aims to protect and restore wetlands, their resources and biodiversity through research, information exchange and conservation activities; promotes implementation of the 1971 Ramsar Convention on Wetlands; Chair. JAN ERNST DE GROOT (Netherlands); CEO JANE MADGWICK.

WWF International: 27 ave du Mont-Blanc, 1196 Gland, Switzerland; tel. 223649111; fax 223648836; e-mail info@wwfint.org; internet www.wwf.panda.org; f. 1961 (as World Wildlife Fund), name changed to World Wide Fund for Nature in 1986, current nomenclature adopted 2001; aims to stop the degradation of natural environments, conserve biodiversity, ensure the sustainable use of renewable resources, and promote the reduction of both pollution and wasteful consumption; addresses six priority issues: forests, freshwater, marine, species, climate change, and toxics; has identified, and focuses its activities in, 200 'ecoregions' (the 'Global 200'), believed to contain the best part of the world's remaining biological diversity; global initiatives being implemented in 2013 focused on climate and energy, forest and climate, smart fishing, tigers, and, geographically, on the Amazon, the Arctic, 'China for a Global Shift' (relating to the growing global influence of the People's Republic of China), Coastal East Africa, the Coral Triangle (a marine area in the Western Pacific), the Green Heart of Africa, the Heart of Borneo, and Living Himalayas; actively supports and operates conservation programmes in more than 90 countries; mems: 54 offices, 5 assoc. orgs, c. 5m. individual mems world-wide; Pres. YOLANDA KAKABADSE (Ecuador); Dir-Gen. JAMES P. LEAPE; publs *Annual Report*, *Living Planet Report*.

Government and Politics

African Parliamentary Union: BP V314, Abidjan, Côte d'Ivoire; tel. 20-30-39-70; fax 20-30-44-05; e-mail upa1@aviso.ci; internet www.africanpu.org; f. 1976 (as Union of African Parliaments); holds annual conference (2013: Libreville, Gabon, in Nov.); mems: 40 parliaments; Chair. ROSE MUKANTABANA (Rwanda); Sec.-Gen. N'ZI KOFFI.

Afro-Asian Peoples' Solidarity Organization (AAPSO): 89 Abdel Aziz Al-Saoud St, POB 11559-61 Manial El-Roda, Cairo, Egypt; tel. (2) 3636081; fax (2) 3637361; e-mail aapso@idsc.net.eg; internet www.aapsorg.org; f. 1958; acts among and for the peoples of Africa and Asia in their struggle for genuine independence, sovereignty, socio-economic development, peace and disarmament; mems: nat. cttees and affiliated orgs in 66 countries and territories, assoc. mems in 15 European countries; Sec.-Gen. NOURI ABDEL RAZZAK HUSSEIN (Iraq); publs *Solidarity Bulletin* (monthly), *Socio-Economic Development* (3 a year).

Arab Inter-Parliamentary Union (Union Interparlementaire Arabe): POB 4130, AIPU Headquarters, Damascus, Syria; tel. (11) 6130042; fax (11) 6130224; e-mail info@arab-ipu.org; internet www.arab-ipu.org; f. 1974; aims to strengthen contacts and promote dialogue between Arab parliamentarians, to co-ordinate activities at international forums, to enhance democratic concepts and values in the Arab countries, to co-ordinate and unify Arab legislations, and to strengthen Arab solidarity; mems from 22 countries; Pres. JASEEM EL-KHURAFI; Sec.-Gen. NOUREDDINE BOUCHKOUJ.

Club of Madrid: Carrera de San Jerónimo 15, 3A planta, 28014 Madrid, Spain; tel. (91) 1548230; fax (91) 1548240; e-mail clubmadrid@clubmadrid.org; internet www.clubmadrid.org; f. 2001, following Conference on Democratic Transition and Consolidation; forum of former Presidents and Prime Ministers; aims to strengthen democratic values and leadership; maintains office in Brussels, Belgium; mems: 87 from 60 countries; Pres. WIM KOK (Netherlands); Sec.-Gen. CARLOS WESTENDORP (Spain).

Conference on Interaction and Confidence-building Measures in Asia: 050000, Almatı, Aiteke Bi 65, Kazakhstan; tel. (727) 390-11-00; fax (727) 390-12-00; e-mail s-cica@s-cica.kz; internet www.s-cica.org; f. 1999 at first meeting of 16 Asian ministers for foreign affairs, convened in Almatı; aims to provide a structure to enhance co-operation, with the objectives of promoting peace, security and stability throughout the region; first meeting of heads of state held in June 2002, adopted the Almatı Act; activities focused on a catalogue of confidence-building measures grouped into five areas: economic dimension; environmental dimension; human dimension; fight against new challenges and threats (such as drugs trafficking, terrorism, and money laundering); and military-political dimension; mems: Afghanistan, Azerbaijan, People's Republic of China, Egypt, India, Iran, Israel, Jordan, Kazakhstan, Republic of Korea, Kyrgyzstan, Mongolia, Pakistan, Palestine, Russia, Tajikistan, Thailand, Turkey, United Arab Emirates, Uzbekistan; observers: Indonesia, Japan, Malaysia, Qatar, Viet Nam, Ukraine, USA, and the UN, the OSCE and the League of Arab States; Exec. Dir ÇINAR ALDEMIR (Turkey).

Group of Eight (G8): an informal meeting of developed nations, originally comprising France, Germany, Italy, Japan, United Kingdom and the USA, first convened in Nov. 1975, at Rambouillet, France, at the level of heads of state and govt; Canada became a permanent participant in 1976, forming the Group of Seven major industrialized countries—G7; from 1991 Russia was invited to participate in the then G7 summit outside the formal framework of co-operation; from 1994 Russia contributed more fully to the G7 political dialogue and from 1997 Russia became a participant in nearly all of the summit process scheduled meetings, excepting those related to finance and the global economy; from 1998 the name of the co-operation framework was changed to Group of Eight—G8, and since 2003 Russia has participated fully in all scheduled summit meetings, including those on the global economy; the European Union (EU) is also represented at G8 meetings, although it may not chair fora; G8 heads of govt and the President of the European Commission and President of the European Council convene an annual summit meeting, the chairmanship and venue of which are rotated in the following order: France, USA, United Kingdom, Russia, Germany, Japan, Italy, Canada; G8 summit meetings address and seek consensus, published in a final declaration, on social and economic issues confronting the international community; heads of state or government of non-mem. countries, and representatives of selected intergovernmental organizations, have been invited to participate in meetings; dialogue commenced in 2005 in the 'G8+5' format, including the leaders of the five largest emerging economies: Brazil, the People's Republic of China, India, Mexico and South Africa; G8 sectoral ministerial meetings (covering areas such as energy, environment, finance and foreign affairs) are held on the fringes of the annual summit, and further G8 sectoral ministerial meetings are convened through the year; the 2011 G8 summit meeting, convened in May, in Deauville, France, established the Deauville Partnership, aimed at supporting political and economic reforms being undertaken by several countries in North Africa and the Middle East; the 2012 summit meeting, held in May, at Camp David, Maryland, USA, without participation by the Russian President, reaffirmed the imperative of creating global growth and jobs, and—in response to the protracted euro area sovereign debt crisis, exacerbated by recent inconclusive legislative elections in Greece amid a climate of popular resistance to the social impact of economic austerity measures—agreed on the relevance for global stability of promoting a strong eurozone, and welcomed ongoing discussion within the EU on means of stimulating economic growth while continuing to implement policies aimed at achieving fiscal consolidation; the participating

G8 leaders also gave consideration to, *inter alia*, energy and climate change, Afghanistan's economic transition, food security, and the ongoing Deauville Partnership; and indicated readiness to request the International Energy Agency to release emergency petroleum stocks should international sanctions imposed on Iran result in disruption to global supply; meeting in April 2013, in London, United Kingdom, G8 foreign ministers issued a Declaration on the Prevention of Sexual Violence in Conflict; the ministers at that time also considered an agenda that included security matters relating to the Democratic People's Republic of Korea and Syria; the 2013 summit, convened in June, in Lough Erne, Northern Ireland, agreed a 10-point plan to tighten regulations and transparency with regard to global corporate taxation; mems: Canada, France, Germany, Italy, Japan, Russia, United Kingdom and the USA; EU representation.

International Institute for Democracy and Electoral Assistance (IDEA): Strömsborg, 103 34 Stockholm, Sweden; tel. (8) 698-3700; fax (8) 20-2422; e-mail info@idea.int; internet www.idea.int; f. 1995; aims to promote sustainable democracy in new and established democracies; works with practitioners and institutions promoting democracy in Africa, Asia, Arab states and Latin America; mems: 28 mem. states and 1 observer; Sec.-Gen. VIDAR HELGESEN (Norway).

Inter-Parliamentary Union (IPU): 5 chemin du Pommier, CP 330, 1218 Le Grand-Saconnex/Geneva, Switzerland; tel. 229194150; fax 229194160; e-mail postbox@mail.ipu.org; internet www.ipu.org; f. 1889 to promote peace, co-operation and representative democracy by providing a forum for multilateral political debate between representatives of national parliaments; mems: nat. parliaments of 162 sovereign states; 10 assoc. mems; Pres. ABDELWAHAD RADI (Morocco); Sec.-Gen. ANDERS B. JOHNSSON (Sweden); publs *Chronicle of Parliamentary Elections* (annually), *The World of Parliaments* (quarterly), *World Directory of Parliaments* (annually).

North Atlantic Treaty Organization (NATO): blvd Léopold III, 1110 Brussels, Belgium; tel. (2) 707-41-11; fax (2) 707-45-79; e-mail natodoc@hq.nato.int; internet www.nato.int; NATO implements the objectives of the Atlantic Alliance, which was established on the basis of the 1949 North Atlantic Treaty and aims to provide common security for its mems through co-operation and consultation in political, military and economic fields, as well as scientific, environmental, and other non-military aspects; the highest authority of the Alliance is the North Atlantic Council (NAC), which meets at the level of permanent representatives of mem. countries, ministers of foreign affairs, defence ministers, or heads of state or government; in July 2004 a NATO Training Implementation Mission was initiated to assist the newly-inaugurated Iraqi Interim Government with the training of its security forces; in Dec. 2004 the NAC authorized an expansion of the Mission, to be known as the NATO Training Mission–Iraq (NTM-I); in July 2009 NATO and the Iraqi Government signed a long-term agreement regarding the training of Iraqi Security Forces; NTM-I expanded its remit in 2010 to include training of border personnel; in Dec. 2011 NTM-1 was terminated; Iraq was granted NATO partner status in April 2011; in early 2012 a NATO Transition Cell was established in Iraq to support the development of the partnership; in March 2011 NATO initiated Operation Unified Protector, using ships and aircraft operating in the Central Mediterranean, in order to monitor and enforce an arms embargo against the Libyan authorities, which had been imposed by the UN Security Council (Resolution 1973, adopted 17 March) in response to the violent oppression of an opposition movement in that country; later in that month NATO mems determined to enforce the UN sanctioned no-fly zone over Libya, alongside a military operation to prevent further attacks on civilians and civilian-populated areas, undertaken by a multinational coalition under British, France and US command; on 27 March, NATO mem. states agreed to assume full command of the operation to protect civilians in Libya (formal transfer of command took place on 31 March); the Operation was extended for 90 days from 27 June, and for a further 90 days in late Sept; in late Oct., following the capture by opposition forces of the last remaining government-controlled city, Sirte, and the arrest (and subsequent death) of the Libyan leader, Col Muammar al-Qaddafi, the NAC authorized the conclusion of the Operation with effect from the end of that month; in June 2012 the NAC met, at the request of Turkey, in accordance with Article 4 of the North Atlantic Treaty—invoked when the territorial integrity, political independence or security of any of the parties is threatened—following the shooting down by Syrian forces of a Turkish military jet; in December NATO ministers of foreign affairs agreed to strengthen Turkey's air defence capabilities along its border with Syria; meeting in late August the NAC strongly condemned the apparent use on 21 August of chemical weapons against civilians in Ghouta, Damascus, Syria; mems: 28 states; Sec.-Gen. ANDERS FOGH RASMUSSEN (Denmark).

Organisation for the Prohibition of Chemical Weapons (OPCW): Johan de Wittlaan 32, 2517 JR The Hague, Netherlands; tel. (70) 4163300; fax (70) 3063535; e-mail media@opcw.org; internet www.opcw.org; f. April 1997, on the entry into force of the Chemical Weapons Convention (CWC)—an international, multilateral disarmament treaty banning the development, production, stockpiling, transfer and use of chemical weapons—to oversee its implementation; verifies the irreversible destruction of declared chemical weapons stockpiles, as well as the elimination of all declared chemical weapons production facilities; OPCW mem. states undertake to provide protection and assistance if chemical weapons have been used against a state party, or if such weapons threaten a state party, and, together with OPCW inspectors, monitor the non-diversion of chemicals for activities prohibited under the CWC and verify the consistency of industrial chemical declarations; CWC states parties are obligated to declare any chemical weapons-related activities, to secure and destroy any stockpiles of chemical weapons within the stipulated deadlines, as well as to inactivate and eliminate any chemical weapons production capacity within their jurisdiction; the OPCW is a lead partner in the UN Counter-Terrorism Implementation Task Force's working group concerned with preventing and responding to weapons of mass destruction; in March 2013 the UN Secretary-General invited the OPCW to assist a UN fact-finding mission which was appointed at that time to investigate allegations relating to the use of chemical weapons by combatants in the ongoing conflict in Syria (which was not a signatory of the CWC); in Aug. the investigation team refocused its activities on the alleged use of chemical weapons in an attack in the Syrian capital Damascus; in mid-Sept. the mission's report confirmed that chemical weapons had been used in Syria; at that time the Syrian regime deposited its instrument of accession to the CWC (to enter into effect after 30 days) in accordance with a Russian–US agreement on a framework for the safeguarding and destruction of Syria's chemical weapons stockpiles; mems: states parties to the Convention (190 at Oct. 2013); 2013 budget: €69.8m.; Dir-Gen. AHMET ÜZÜMCÜ (Turkey).

Parliamentary Association for Euro-Arab Co-operation (PAEAC) (Institut européen de recherche sur la coopération euro-arabe): 24 Sq. de Meeus, 5th Floor, 1000 Brussels, Belgium; tel. (2) 231-13-00; fax (2) 231-06-46; e-mail secretariat@medeainstitute.org; internet www.medea.be; f. 1974 as an assen of 650 parliamentarians of all parties from the national parliaments of the Council of Europe countries and from the European Parliament, to promote friendship and co-operation between Europe and the Arab world; Executive Committee holds annual joint meetings with Arab Inter-Parliamentary Union; represented in Council of Europe and European Parliament; works for the progress of the Euro-Arab Dialogue and a settlement in the Middle East that takes into account the national rights of the Palestinian people; Pres. PIERRE COLOT; publs *Information Bulletin* (quarterly), *Euro-Arab and Mediterranean Political Fact Sheets* (2 a year), conference notes.

Union for the Mediterranean Secretariat (UfMS): Palacio de Pedralbes, Pere Duran Farell, 11, 08034 Barcelona, Spain; tel. (93) 5214100; fax (93) 5214102; e-mail info@ufmsecretariat.org; internet www.ufmsecretariat.org; f. 2008 as a continuation of the Euro-Mediterranean Partnership ('Barcelona Process'), which had been launched in 1995; the statutes of the UfMS were adopted in March 2010; the UfMS's mandate is defined by the July 2008 Paris Declaration of the Euro-Mediterranean summit, and by the subsequent Marseilles Declaration, adopted in Nov. of that year; the Union was established as a framework for advancing relations (political, economic and social) between the European Union and countries of the Southern and Eastern Mediterranean, in accordance with the goals detailed in the 1995 Barcelona Declaration: i.e. working to create an area of stability and shared economic prosperity, underpinned by full respect for democratic principles, human rights and fundamental freedoms; mems: 28 European Union mem. states, the European Commission and 15 Mediterranean countries; Sec.-Gen. FATHALLAH SIJILMASSI (Morocco).

Industrial and Professional Relations

African Regional Organization of ITUC (ITUC-Africa): route Internationale d'Atakpamé, POB 44101, Lomé, Togo; tel. and fax 225-07-10; fax 225-61-13; e-mail info@ituc-africa.org; internet www.ituc-africa.org; f. 2007; mems: 13m. workers in 44 countries; Pres. MODY GUIRO; Gen. Sec. KWASI ADU-AMANKWAH.

International Confederation of Arab Trade Unions (ICATU): POB 3225, Samat at-Tahir, Damascus, Syria; tel. (11) 4459544; fax (11) 4420323; e-mail icatu@net.sy; f. 1956; holds General Congress every five years (12th Congress: Khartoum, Sudan, Feb. 2010); mems: trade unions in 18 countries, and 11 affiliate int. feds; Sec.-Gen. RAJAB MAATOUK; publ. *Al-Oummal al-Arab* (every 2 months).

World Federation of Trade Unions (WFTU): 40 Zan Moreas St, 11745 Athens, Greece; tel. (210) 09236700; fax (210) 09214517; e-mail info@wftucentral.org; internet www.wftucentral.org; f. 1945 on a world-wide basis; mems: 135m. in 126 countries; Gen. Sec.

George Mavrikos (Greece); publ. *Flashes from the Trade Unions* (every 2 weeks).

Law

Arab Organization for Human Rights: 91 al-Marghany St, Heliopolis, Cairo, Egypt; tel. (2) 4181396; fax (2) 4185346; e-mail aohrarab@gmail.com; internet www.aohr.net; f. 1983 to defend fundamental freedoms of citizens of the Arab states; assists political prisoners and their families; has consultative status with UN Economic and Social Council; General Assembly convened every three years; mems in 31 countries; Sec.-Gen. Mohsen Awad; publs *Newsletter* (monthly), *Annual Report*, *The State of Human Rights in the Arab World*, *Nadwat Fikria* (series).

Asian-African Legal Consultative Organization (AALCO): 29-C, Rizal Marg, Diplomatic Enclave, Chanakyapuri, New Delhi 110057, India; tel. (11) 24197000; fax (11) 26117640; e-mail mail@aalco.int; internet www.aalco.int; f. 1956 to consider legal problems referred to it by mem. countries and to serve as a forum for Afro-Asian co-operation in international law, including international trade law, and economic relations; provides background material for conferences, prepares standard/model contract forms suited to the needs of the region; promotes arbitration as a means of settling international commercial disputes; trains officers of mem. states; has permanent UN observer status; has established four International Commercial Arbitration Centres in Kuala Lumpur, Malaysia; Cairo, Egypt; Lagos, Nigeria; and Tehran, Iran; mems: 47 countries; Sec.-Gen. Prof. Dr Rahmat bin Mohamad (Malaysia).

International Association of Jewish Lawyers and Jurists: 10 Daniel Frisch St, Tel Aviv 64731, Israel; tel. (3) 691-0673; fax (3) 695-3855; e-mail iajlj@goldmail.net.il; internet www.intjewishlawyers.org; f. 1969; promotes human rights and international co-operation based on the rule of law; works to combat anti-Semitism and Holocaust denial; holds international congresses; Pres. Irit Kohn; Exec. Dir. Ronit Gidron-Zemach; publ. *Justice*.

International Criminal Court (ICC): Maanweg 174, 2516 AB The Hague, Netherlands; tel. (70) 5158515; fax (70) 5158555; e-mail otp.informationdesk@icc-cpi.int; internet www.icc-cpi.int; f. 2002, upon the entry into force of the Rome Statute of the ICC, adopted by 120 states participating in a UN Diplomatic Conference in July 1998; by September 2013 18 cases in eight situations had been brought before the Court, including the 'Situation in Libya since February 2011', referred to the Court in February 2011 by the UN Security Council; in March the ICC Prosecutor agreed to open an investigation into the Situation in Libya; in late June the Court issued arrest warrants against the Libyan leader Col Muammar al-Qaddafi, Saif al-Islam (his son), and Abdullah al-Senussi (his former Head of Military Intelligence), regarding crimes against humanity (murder and persecution) committed in Libya—through the state apparatus and security forces—from 15 February until at least 28 February; in September the ICC Prosecutor requested INTERPOL to issue a Red Notice for the arrest of the three Libyan indictees; Col Qaddafi was killed during fighting with opposition forces on 20 October; in late November Saif al-Islam was detained in southern Libya; al-Senussi was detained by Mauritanian security forces in mid-March 2012 and was extradited to Libya in September; despite the ICC indictments the Libyan authorities have expressed their intention of bringing al-Islam and al-Senussi to trial within Libya on charges relating to their conduct under the al-Qaddafi regime, and in May 2012 the Libyan National Transitional Council presented a formal challenge to the ICC concerning the admissibility of the Court's case against the two men, on the grounds that the Libyan national judicial system was itself actively investigating their alleged crimes; in May 2013 the ICC rejected Libya's challenge to the admissibility of the case against Saif al-Islam, stressing Libya's obligation to transfer him to the Court; in January 2013 more than 50 UN member states, led by Switzerland, signed a letter urging the UN Security Council to refer the situation ongoing in Syria to the Court; Chief Prosecutor Fatou B. Bensouda (The Gambia); Registrar Silvana Arbia (Italy).

International Criminal Police Organization (INTERPOL): 200 quai Charles de Gaulle, 69006 Lyon, France; tel. 4-72-44-70-00; fax 4-72-44-71-63; e-mail info@interpol.int; internet www.interpol.int; f. 1923, reconstituted 1946; aims to promote and ensure mutual assistance between police forces in different countries; co-ordinates activities of police authorities of mem. states in international affairs; works to establish and develop institutions with the aim of preventing transnational crimes; centralizes records and information on international criminals; operates a global police communications network linking all mem. countries; maintains a Global Database on Maritime Piracy; holds General Assembly annually; mems: 190 countries; Sec.-Gen. Ronald K. Noble (USA); publ. *Annual Report*.

Union of Arab Jurists (UAJ): POB 6026, Al-Mansour, Baghdad, Iraq; tel. (1) 537-2371; fax (1) 537-2369; f. 1975 to facilitate contacts between Arab lawyers, to safeguard the Arab legislative and judicial heritage, to encourage the study of Islamic jurisprudence; and to defend human rights; mems: nat. jurists asscns in 15 countries; Sec.-Gen. Shibib Lazim al-Maliki; publ. *Al-Hukuki al-Arabi* (Arab Jurist).

Medicine and Health

Arab Medical Association Against Cancer: e-mail drsamikhatib@gmail.com; internet amaac.org; f. 2001, successor to Arab Council Against Cancer (f. 1995); aims to raise the awareness of cancer prevention and control, to advance the level of knowledge of cancer professionals, and to improve the efficacy of cancer treatment in Arab countries; 13th Annual Pan Arab Cancer Congress was held in Amman, Jordan, in April 2013; Sec.-Gen. Sami Khatib; publ. *Pan Arab Journal of Oncoloy* (quarterly).

Federation of Arab Medical Associations: 8-2 Gulberg Complex, Jail Rd, Lahore, Pakistan; tel. (42) 35716231; fax (42) 35715855; e-mail tanveer.zubairi@gmail.com; internet fimaweb.net; f. 1981; aims to foster the unity and welfare of Muslim medical and health care professionals, to promote Islamic medical activities including health services, education and research through co-operation and co-ordination among member organizations, to promote the understanding and the application of Islamic principles in the field of medicine, to mobilize professional and economic resources in order to provide medical care and relief to affected areas and communities, and to promote the exchange of medical information and technical expertise among member organizations; mems: 26 asscns, 5 observers; Sec. Dr Tanveer Zubairi.

World Medical Association (WMA): 13 chemin du Levant, CIB-Bâtiment A, 01210 Ferney-Voltaire, France; tel. 4-50-40-75-75; fax 4-50-40-59-37; e-mail wma@wma.net; internet www.wma.net; f. 1947 to achieve the highest international standards in all aspects of medical education and practice, to promote closer ties among doctors and national medical asscns by personal contact and all other means, to study problems confronting the medical profession, and to present its views to appropriate bodies; holds an annual General Assembly; mems: 107 nat. medical asscns; Pres. Dr Cecil B. Wilson (Brazil); Sec.-Gen. Dr Otmar Kloiber (Germany); publ. *The World Medical Journal* (quarterly).

Posts and Telecommunications

Arab Permanent Postal Commission: c/o Arab League Bldg, Tahrir Sq., Cairo, Egypt; tel. (2) 5750511; fax (2) 5740331; f. 1952; aims to establish stricter postal relations between the Arab countries than those laid down by the Universal Postal Union, and to pursue the development and modernization of postal services in mem. countries; publs *APU Bulletin* (monthly), *APU Review* (quarterly), *APU News* (annually).

Internet Corporation for Assigned Names and Numbers (ICANN): 12025 Waterfront Dr., Suite 300, Los Angeles, CA 90094-2536, USA; tel. (310) 301-5800; fax (310) 823-8649; e-mail icann@icann.org; internet www.icann.org; f. 1998; non-profit, private sector body; aims to co-ordinate the technical management and policy development of the Internet in relation to addresses, domain names and protocol; supported by an At-Large Advisory Committee (representing individual users of the internet), a Country Code Names Supporting Organization (ccNSO), a Governmental Advisory Committee, a Generic Names Supporting Organization (GNSO), and a Security and Stability Advisory Committee; through its Internet Assigned Numbers Authority (IANA) department ICANN manages the global co-ordination of domain name system roots and internet protocol addressing; at 30 June 2011 there were 310 top-level domains (TLDs), 30 of which were in non-Latin scripts, and the most common of which were generic TLDs (gTLDs) (such as .org or .com) and country code TLDs (ccTLDs); in June 2011 ICANN adopted an expanded gTLD programme, under which, from 2012, applications were accepted from qualified orgs wishing to register domain names of their choosing; details of the first 1,930 filed applications were published in June 2012 ('app' being the most popular): the ensuing objections process was administered by the International Chamber of Commerce International Centre for Expertise; the expanded programme provides for Internationalized Domain Names (IDNs) incorporating non-Latin character sets (Arabic, Chinese and Cyrillic), with a view to making the internet more globally inclusive; launched in Oct. 2012, jointly with the African Regional Registry for Internet Number Resources, a three-year 'New Approach to Africa' initiative aimed at expanding activities in Africa; Pres. and CEO Fadi Chehadé (Lebanon).

Religion

Middle East Council of Churches: POB 5376, Beirut, Lebanon; tel. (1) 344896; fax (1) 344894; e-mail mecc@cyberia.net.lb; internet www.mec-churches.org; f. 1974; mems: 28 churches; Pres Catholicos ARAM I, Patriarch THEOPHILOS III, Archbishop BOULOS MATAR, Rev. Dr SAFWAT AL-BAYADI; Gen. Sec. GUIRGIS IBRAHIM SALEH; publs *MECC News Report* (monthly), *Al Montada News Bulletin* (quarterly, in Arabic), *Courrier oecuménique du Moyen-Orient* (quarterly), *MECC Perspectives* (3 a year).

Muslim World League (MWL) (Rabitat al-Alam al-Islami): POB 537, Makkah, Saudi Arabia; tel. (2) 5600919; fax (2) 5601319; e-mail info@themwl.org; internet www.themwl.org; f. 1962; aims to advance Islamic unity and solidarity, and to promote world peace and respect for human rights; provides financial assistance for education, medical care and relief work; has 45 offices throughout the world; Sec.-Gen. Prof. Dr ABDULLAH BIN ABDUL MOHSIN AL-TURKI; publs *Al-Aalam al Islami* (weekly, Arabic), *Dawat al-Haq* (monthly, Arabic), *Muslim World League Journal* (monthly, English), *Muslim World League Journal* (quarterly, Arabic).

World Council of Churches (WCC): 150 route de Ferney, Postfach 2100, 1211 Geneva 2, Switzerland; tel. 227916111; fax 227910361; e-mail info@wcc-coe.org; internet www.oikoumene.org; f. 1948 to promote co-operation between Christian Churches and to prepare for a clearer manifestation of the unity of the Church; activities are grouped under the following programmes: The WCC and the ecumenical movement in the 21st century; Unity, mission, evangelism and spirituality; Public witness: addressing power, affirming peace; Justice, *diakonia* and responsibility for creation; Education and ecumenical formation; and Inter-religious dialogue and co-operation; mems: 349 Churches in more than 110 countries; Gen. Sec. Dr OLAV FYKSE TVEIT (Norway); publs *Current Dialogue* (2 a year), *Ecumenical News International* (weekly), *Ecumenical Review* (quarterly), *International Review of Mission* (quarterly), *WCC News* (quarterly), *WCC Yearbook*.

World Jewish Congress: 501 Madison Ave, New York, NY 10022, USA; tel. (212) 755-5770; fax (212) 755-5883; e-mail info@worldjewishcongress.org; internet www.worldjewishcongress.org; f. 1936 as a voluntary asscn of representative Jewish communities and orgs throughout the world; aims to foster the unity of the Jewish people and ensure the continuity and development of their heritage; mems: Jewish communities in 100 countries; Pres. RONALD LAUDER (USA); publs *Dispatches*, *Jerusalem Review*, regular updates, policy studies.

Science

CIESM—The Mediterranean Science Commission (Commission internationale pour l'exploration scientifique de la mer Méditerranée): Villa Girasole, 16 blvd de Suisse, 98000 Monaco; tel. 93-30-38-79; fax 92-16-11-95; e-mail contact@ciesm.org; internet www.ciesm.org; f. 1919 for scientific exploration of the Mediterranean Sea; organizes multilateral research investigations, workshops, congresses; includes six permanent scientific cttees; mems: 22 countries, 4,300 scientists; Pres. HSH Prince ALBERT II of MONACO; Dir-Gen. Prof. FREDERIC BRIAND; publs White Papers, Congress reports.

European-Mediterranean Seismological Centre (EMSC): c/o CEA, Bt. Sâbles Centre DAM, Ile de France, Bruyères le Châtel, 91297 Arpajon Cedex, France; fax 1-69-26-70-00; e-mail contact@emsc-csem.org; internet www.emsc-csem.org; f. 1976 for rapid determination of seismic hypocentres in the region; maintains database; mems: institutions in 45 countries; Pres. CHRIS BROWITT (United Kingdom); Sec.-Gen. RÉMY BOSSU (France); publ. *Newsletter* (2 a year).

International Council for Science (ICSU): 5 rue Auguste Vacquerie, 75116 Paris, France; tel. 1-45-25-03-29; fax 1-42-88-94-31; e-mail secretariat@icsu.org; internet www.icsu.org; f. 1919 as International Research Council; present name adopted 1998; revised statutes adopted 2011; incorporates national scientific bodies and International Scientific Unions, as well as 19 Interdisciplinary Bodies (international scientific networks established to address specific areas of investigation); through its global network co-ordinates interdisciplinary research to address major issues of relevance to both science and society; advocates for freedom in the conduct of science, promotes equitable access to scientific data and information, and facilitates science education and capacity building; General Assembly of representatives of national and scientific mems meets every three years to formulate policy. Interdisciplinary Bodies and Joint Initiatives: Future Earth; Urban Health and Well-being; Committee on Space Research (COSPAR); Scientific Committee on Antarctic Research (SCAR); Scientific Committee on Oceanic Research (SCOR); Scientific Committee on Solar-Terrestrial Physics (SCOSTEP); Integrated Research on Disaster Risk (IRDR); Programme on Ecosystem Change and Society (PECS); DIVERSITAS; International Geosphere-Biosphere Programme (IGBP); International Human Dimensions Programme on Global Environmental Change (IHDP); World Climate Research Programme (WCRP); Global Climate Observing System (GCOS); Global Ocean Observing System (GOOS); Global Terrestrial Observing System (GTOS); Committee on Data for Science and Technology (CODATA); International Network for the Availability of Scientific Publications (INASP); Scientific Committee on Frequency Allocations for Radio Astronomy and Space Science (IUCAF); World Data System (WDS); mems: 120 national mems from 140 countries, 31 Int. Scientific Unions; Pres. LEE YUAN-TSEH (Taiwan); publs *Insight* (quarterly), *Annual Report*.

Social Sciences

African Centre for Applied Research and Training in Social Development (ACARTSOD): Africa Centre, Wahda Quarter, Zawia Rd, POB 80606, Tripoli, Libya; tel. (21) 4835103; fax (21) 4835066; e-mail fituri_acartsod@hotmail.com; f. 1977 under the joint auspices of the ECA and OAU (now AU) to promote and co-ordinate applied research and training in social devt, and to assist in formulating national development strategies; Exec. Dir Dr AHMED SAID FITURI.

Arab Towns Organization (ATO): POB 68160, Kaifan 71962, Kuwait; tel. 24849705; fax 24849319; e-mail ato@ato.net; internet www.ato.net; f. 1967; works to preserve the identity and heritage of Arab towns; to support the development and modernization of municipal and local authorities in mem. towns; to improve services and utilities in mem. towns; to support development schemes in mem. towns through the provision of loans and other assistance; to support planning and the co-ordination of development activities and services; to facilitate the exchange of service-related expertise among mem. towns; to co-ordinate efforts to modernize and standardize municipal regulations and codes among mem. towns; to promote co-operation in all matters related to Arab towns; manages the Arab Towns Development Fund, the Arab Institute for Urban Development, the Arab Towns Organization Award, the Arab Urban Environment Centre, the Arab Forum on Information Systems, and the Heritage and Arab Historic City Foundation; mems: 413 towns; Sec.-Gen. ABD AL-AZIZ Y. AL-ADASANI; publ. *Al-Madinah Al-Arabiyah* (every 2 months).

Council for the Development of Social Science Research in Africa (CODESRIA): Ave Cheikh, Anta Diop X Canal IV, BP 3304, CP 18524, Dakar, Senegal; tel. 825-98-22; fax 825-12-89; internet www.codesria.org; f. 1973; promotes research, organizes conferences, working groups and information services; mems: research institutes and university faculties and researchers in African countries; Exec. Sec. Dr EBRIMA SALL; publs *Africa Development* (quarterly), *CODESRIA Bulletin* (quarterly), *Index of African Social Science Periodical Articles* (annually), *African Journal of International Affairs* (2 a year), *African Sociological Review* (2 a year), *Afrika Zamani* (annually), *Identity, Culture and Politics* (2 a year), *Afro Arab Selections for Social Sciences* (annually), directories of research.

International African Institute (IAI): School of Oriental and African Studies, Thornhaugh St, Russell Sq., London, WC1H 0XG, United Kingdom; tel. (20) 7898-4420; fax (20) 7898-4419; e-mail iai@soas.ac.uk; internet www.internationalafricaninstitute.org; f. 1926 to promote the study of African peoples, their languages, cultures and social life in their traditional and modern settings; organizes an international seminar programme bringing together scholars from Africa and elsewhere; links scholars in order to facilitate research projects, especially in the social sciences; Chair. Prof. V. Y. MUDIMBE; Hon. Dir Prof. PHILIP BURNHAM; publs *Africa* (quarterly), *Africa Bibliography* (annually).

International Peace Institute: 777 United Nations Plaza, New York, NY 10017-3521, USA; tel. (212) 687-4300; fax (212) 983-8246; e-mail ipi@ipinst.org; internet www.ipinst.org; f. 1970 (as the International Peace Academy) to promote the prevention and settlement of armed conflicts between and within states through policy research and development; educates government officials in the procedures needed for conflict resolution, peace-keeping, mediation and negotiation, through international training seminars and publications; off-the-record meetings are also conducted to gain complete understanding of a specific conflict; Chair. RITA E. HAUSER; Pres. TERJE ROD-LARSEN.

International Union for Oriental and Asian Studies: f. 1951 by the 22nd International Congress of Orientalists (now the International Congress of Asian and North African Studies) under the auspices of UNESCO, to promote contacts between orientalists throughout the world, and to organize congresses, research and publications; mems: in 24 countries; publs *Philologiae Turcicae Fundamenta*, *Materalien zum Sumerischen Lexikon*, *Sanskrit Dictionary*, *Corpus Inscriptionum Iranicarum*, *Linguistic Atlas of Iran*, *Matériels des parlers iraniens*, *Turcology Annual*, *Bibliographie egyptologique*.

Social Welfare and Human Rights

Arab Women's Solidarity Association United: Cairo, Egypt; tel. (20) 7324-2500; internet awsa.net; f. 1982 to promote the active participation of Arab women in social, economic, cultural, and political life; works to develop income-generating projects for economically underprivileged women and to raise awareness of the impact of political and social inequality on the lives of Arab women; granted consultative status with the United Nations Economic and Social Council in 1985; Pres. Dr NAWAL EL-SAADAWI.

Global Migration Group: 17 Route des Morillons, 1211, 19 Geneva, Switzerland; tel. 227179111; fax 227986150; internet www.globalmigrationgroup.org; f. 2003, as the Geneva Migration Group; renamed as above in 2006; mems: the ILO, IOM, UNCTAD, UNDP, United Nations Department of Economic and Social Affairs (UNDESA), UNESCO, UNICEF, UNFPA, UNITAR, OHCHR, UNHCR, UNODC, UN Women, the UN Regional Commissions, WHO and the World Bank; holds regular meetings to discuss issues relating to international migration, chaired by mem. orgs on a six-month rotational basis.

International Federation of Red Cross and Red Crescent Societies (IFRC): 17 chemin des Crêts, Petit-Saconnex, CP 372, 1211 Geneva 19, Switzerland; tel. 227304222; fax 227330395; e-mail secretariat@ifrc.org; internet www.ifrc.org; f. 1919 to prevent and alleviate human suffering and to promote humanitarian activities by national Red Cross and Red Crescent societies; conducts relief operations for refugees and victims of disasters, co-ordinates relief supplies and assists in disaster prevention; in July 2012 the IFRC launched an emergency appeal to raise 27.5m. Swiss francs in funding for the Syrian Arab Red Crescent (SARC), to enable SARC to assist, through the provision of emergency relief items, health care, and livelihoods support, some 200,000 conflict-affected Syrians; an appeal for 3.7m. Swiss francs was announced in August to support Red Crescent societies in neighbouring Iraq, Jordan and Lebanon in providing humanitarian assistance to an influx of Syrian refugees; Pres. TADATERU KONOÉ (Japan); Sec.-Gen. BEKELE GELETA (Canada/Ethiopia); publs *Annual Report*, *Red Cross Red Crescent* (quarterly), *Weekly News*, *World Disasters Report*, *Emergency Appeal*.

Médecins sans frontières (MSF): 78 rue de Lausanne, CP 116, 1211 Geneva 21, Switzerland; tel. 228498400; fax 228498404; internet www.msf.org; f. 1971; independent medical humanitarian org. composed of physicians and other mems of the medical profession; aims to provide medical assistance to victims of war and natural disasters; operates longer-term programmes of nutrition, immunization, sanitation, public health, and rehabilitation of hospitals and dispensaries; awarded the Nobel Peace Prize in 1999; mems: 23 asscns in more than 60 countries world-wide; Pres. Dr UNNI KARUNAKARA; Sec.-Gen. JEROME OBERREIT; publ. *Activity Report* (annually).

Union Africaine de la Mutualité (African Union of Mutuals): Rue Aram, Lot 14, Secteur 7, Hay Riad, Rabat, Morocco; tel. and fax (5) 37570988; internet www.am.org.ma; f. 2007; promotes co-operation among African companies concerned with health care and social insurance; mems: in 18 African countries; Pres. ABDELMOULA ABDELMOUMNI.

Sport and Recreations

Confederation of African Football (Confédération africaine de football—CFA): 3 Abdel Khalek Sarwat St, El Hay El Motamayez, POB 23, 6th October City, Egypt; tel. (2) 38371000; fax (2) 38370006; e-mail info@cafonline.com; internet www.cafonline.com; f. 1957; promotes football in Africa; organizes inter-club competitions and Cup of Nations (2013: held in South Africa, in Jan.–Feb.); General Assembly held every two years; mems: nat. asscns in 54 countries; Pres. ISSA HAYATOU (Cameroon); Sec.-Gen. HICHAM EL AMRANI (Morocco); publ. *CAF News* (quarterly).

International Olympic Committee (IOC): Château de Vidy, 1007 Lausanne, Switzerland; tel. 216216111; fax 216216216; internet www.olympic.org; f. 1894 to ensure the regular celebration of the Olympic Games; the IOC is the supreme authority on all questions concerning the Olympic Games and the Olympic movement; established the independent World Anti-Doping Agency in 1999; Olympic Games held every four years (summer games 2016: Rio de Janeiro, Brazil; winter games 2014: Sochi, Russia; youth games 2014: Nanjing, People's Republic of China); mems: 115 representatives; Pres. THOMAS BACH (Germany); publs *Newsletter* (weekly), *Olympic Review* (quarterly).

Union of Arab Olympic Committees: POB 62997, Riyadh 11595, Saudi Arabia; tel. (1) 482-4927; fax (1) 482-1944; e-mail olympiccommittees@gmail.com; f. 1976 as Arab Sports Confederation to encourage regional co-operation in sport; mems: 22 Arab nat. Olympic Committees, 53 Arab sports feds; Sec.-Gen. SAUD ABD AL-AZIZ; publ. *Annual Report*.

Technology

African Organization of Cartography and Remote Sensing: 5 route de Bedjarah, BP 102, Hussein Dey, Algiers, Algeria; tel. (21) 23-17-17; fax (21) 23-33-39; e-mail sg2@oact.dz; f. 1988 by amalgamation of African Association of Cartography and African Council for Remote Sensing; aims to encourage the development of cartography and of remote sensing by satellites; organizes conferences and other meetings, promotes establishment of training institutions; maintains four regional training centres (in Burkina Faso, Kenya, Nigeria and Tunisia); mems: national cartographic institutions of 24 African countries; Sec.-Gen. ANWER SIALA.

Federation of Arab Engineers: 30 Sharia Ramses, Cairo, Egypt; tel. (2) 25775744; fax (2) 25749404; e-mail arabengs@hotmail.com; internet www.arabfedeng.org; f. 1963 as Arab Engineering Union; a regional body of the World Federation of Engineering Organizations; co-operates with the Arab League, UNESCO and other regional engineering feds; holds a Pan-Arab conference on engineering studies every three years and annual symposia and seminars in different Arab countries; mems: engineering asscns in 15 Arab countries; Sec.-Gen. ADEL AL-HADITHI.

Union of Arab Information and Communication Technology Associations: Fouad Farrah Bldg, 1st Floor, cross rd of Masaref St and Wegan St, Beirut Central District, Beirut, Lebanon; tel. (1) 985440; internet www.ijma3.org; also has an office in Baghdad, Iraq; mems: Arab national associations; Sec.-Gen. and CEO NIZAR ZAKKA.

World Federation of Engineering Organizations (WFEO): Maison de l'UNESCO, 1 rue Miollis, 75732 Paris, Cedex 15, France; tel. 1-45-68-48-47; fax 1-45-68-48-65; e-mail info@wfeo.net; internet www.wfeo.net; f. 1968 to advance engineering as a profession; fosters co-operation between engineering organizations throughout the world; undertakes special projects in co-operation with other international bodies; hosts a World Engineering Forum (Sept. 2012: Ljubljana, Slovenia); mems: 90 nat. mems, 9 int. mems; Pres. MARWAN ABDELHAMID (Kuwait); Exec. Dir TAHANI YOUSSEF (France); publ. *WFEO Newsletter* (2 a year).

Trade and Industry

General Arab Insurance Federation: 8 Kasr en-Nil St, POB 611, 11511 Cairo, Egypt; tel. (2) 5743177; fax (2) 5762310; e-mail gaif@tedata.net.eg; internet www.gaif-1.org; f. 1964; Sec.-Gen. ABD AL-KHALIQ R. KHALIL (Iraq).

General Union of Chambers of Commerce, Industry and Agriculture for Arab Countries (GUCCIAAC): POB 11-2837, Beirut, Lebanon; tel. (1) 826020; fax (1) 826021; e-mail uac@uac.org.lb; internet www.uac.org.lb; f. 1951 to enhance Arab economic development, integration and security through the co-ordination of industrial, agricultural and trade policies and legislation; mems: Chambers of Commerce, Industry and Agriculture in 22 Arab countries; Pres. ADNAN KASSAR; Sec.-Gen. Dr IMAD SHIHAB; publs *Arab Economic Report*, *Al-Omran Al-Arabi* (every 2 months), economic papers, proceedings.

Gulf Organization for Industrial Consulting (GOIC): POB 5114, Doha, Qatar; tel. 4858888; fax 4831465; e-mail goic@goic.org.qa; internet www.goic.org.qa; f. 1976 by the Gulf Arab states to encourage industrial co-operation among Gulf Arab states, to pool industrial expertise and to encourage joint development of projects; undertakes feasibility studies, market diagnosis, assistance in policy-making, legal consultancies, project promotion, promotion of small and medium industrial investment profiles and technical training; maintains industrial data bank; mems: mem. states of the Cooperation Council for the Arab States of the Gulf; Sec.-Gen. ABDULAZIZ BIN HAMAD AL-AGEEL; publs *GOIC Monthly Bulletin* (in Arabic), *Al Ta'awon al Sina'e* (quarterly, in Arabic and English).

World Trade Organization: Centre William Rappard, 154 rue de Lausanne, 1211 Geneva 21, Switzerland; tel. 227395111; fax 227314206; e-mail enquiries@wto.org; internet www.wto.org;

f. Jan. 1995 as the successor to the General Agreement on Tariffs and Trade (GATT); aims to encourage development and economic reform among developing countries and countries with economies in transition participating in the international trading system; monitors trade policies and handles trade disputes; mems: 159 countries, incl. Bahrain, Cyprus, Egypt, Jordan, Kuwait, Oman, Qatar and the United Arab Emirates, with 26 countries and territories, incl. Algeria, Iran, Iraq, Lebanon, Libya and Yemen, as Observers; Dir-Gen. ROBERTO CARVALHO DE AZEVÊDO (Brazil); publs *Annual Report* (2 volumes), *World Trade Report*, *International Trade Statistics*.

Transport

African Airlines Association: POB 20116, Nairobi 00200, Kenya; tel. (20) 2320144; fax (20) 6001173; e-mail afraa@afraa.org; internet www.afraa.org; f. 1968 to give African air companies expert advice in technical, financial, juridical and market matters; to improve air transport in Africa through inter-carrier co-operation; and to develop manpower resources; mems: 34 nat. carriers, representing 80% of African airlines; Pres. SIZA MZIMELA; Sec.-Gen. ELIJAH CHINGOSHO; publs *Newsletter*, reports.

Arab Air Carriers' Organization (AACO): POB 13-5468, Beirut, Lebanon; tel. (1) 861297; fax (1) 863168; e-mail info@aaco.org; internet www.aaco.org; f. 1965 to promote co-operation in the activities of Arab airline cos; mems: 27 Arab air carriers; Chair. GHAIDA ABDULLATIF; Sec.-Gen. ABDUL WAHAB TEFFAHA; publs bulletins, reports and research documents.

Intergovernmental Organization for International Carriage by Rail (OTIF): Gryphenhübeliweg 30, 3006 Bern, Switzerland; tel. 313591010; fax 313591011; e-mail info@otif.org; internet www.otif.org; f. 1893 as Central Office for International Carriage by Rail, present name adopted 1985; aims to establish and develop a uniform system of law governing the international carriage of passengers and goods by rail in mem. states, and to facilitate its application and development; composed of a General Assembly, an Administrative Committee, a Revision Committee, a Committee of Experts on the Transport of Dangerous Goods, a Committee of Technical Experts and a Rail Facilitation Committee; mems: 47 states in Europe, the Middle East and North Africa, and 1 assoc. mem (Jordan); Sec.-Gen. FRANÇOIS DAVENNE; publ. *Bulletin des Transports Internationaux ferroviaires* (quarterly, in English, French and German).

Youth and Students

Pan-African Youth Union (Union pan-africaine de la jeunesse): Khartoum, Sudan; tel. 8037038097 (mobile); internet panafricanyouthunion.org; f. 1962; aims to encourage the participation of African youth in socio-economic and political development and democratization; organizes conferences and seminars, youth exchanges and youth festivals; 2011 Congress: Khartoum, Sudan, in Dec; mems: youth groups in 53 African countries and liberation movements; Pres. ANDILE LUNGISA (South Africa) (2012–14); publ. *MPJ News* (quarterly).

WFUNA Youth Network: c/o WFUNA, 1 United Nations Plaza, Room DC1-1177, New York, NY 10017, USA; tel. (212) 963-5610; fax (212) 963-0447; e-mail youth@wfuna.org; internet www.wfuna.org/youth; f. 1946 by the World Federation of United Nations Associations (WFUNA) as the International Youth and Student Movement for the United Nations, independent since 1949; an international non-governmental org. of students and young people dedicated especially to supporting the principles embodied in the United Nations Charter and Universal Declaration of Human Rights; encourages constructive action in building economic, social and cultural equality and in working for national independence, social justice and human rights on a world-wide scale; organizes periodic regional WFUNA International Model United Nations (WIMUN) conferences; maintains regional offices in Switzerland and the USA; mems: assens in over 100 mem. states of the UN.

CALENDARS IN THE MIDDLE EAST AND NORTH AFRICA

The Islamic Calendar

The Islamic era dates from 16 July 622, which was the beginning of the Arab year in which the *Hijra* ('flight' or migration) of the Prophet Muhammad (the founder of Islam), from Mecca to Medina (in modern Saudi Arabia), took place. The Islamic or *Hijri* Calendar is lunar, each year having 354 or 355 days, the extra day being intercalated 11 times every 30 years. Accordingly, the beginning of the *Hijri* year occurs earlier in the Gregorian Calendar by a few days each year. Dates are reckoned in terms of the *anno Hegirae* (AH) or year of the Hegira (*Hijra*). The Islamic year AH 1434 began on 14 November 2012.

The year is divided into the following months:

1. Muharram	30 days	7. Rajab	30 days
2. Safar	29 days	8. Shaaban	29 days
3. Rabia I	30 days	9. Ramadan	30 days
4. Rabia II	29 days	10. Shawwal	29 days
5. Jumada I	30 days	11. Dhu'l-Qa'da	30 days
6. Jumada II	29 days	12. Dhu'l-Hijja	29 or 30 days

The *Hijri* Calendar is used for religious purposes throughout the Islamic world and is the official calendar in Saudi Arabia. In most Arab countries it is used in conjunction with the Gregorian Calendar for official purposes, but in Turkey and Egypt the Gregorian Calendar has replaced it.

PRINCIPAL ISLAMIC FESTIVALS

New Year: 1st Muharram. The first 10 days of the year are regarded as holy, especially the 10th.

Ashoura: 10th Muharram. Celebrates the first meeting of Adam and Eve after leaving Paradise, also the ending of the Flood and the death of Husain, grandson of the Prophet Muhammad. The feast is celebrated with fairs and processions.

Mouloud or Yum al-Nabi (Birth of Muhammad): Celebrated by Sunni Muslims on 12th Rabia I. Shi'a Muslims celebrate the Birth of Muhammad on 17th Rabia I.

Leilat al-Meiraj (Ascension of Muhammad): 27th Rajab.

Ramadan (Month of Fasting).

'Id al-Fitr or 'Id al-Saghir or Küçük Bayram (The Small Feast): Three days beginning 1st Shawwal. This celebration follows the constraint of the Ramadan fast.

'Id al-Adha or 'Id al-Kabir or Büyük Bayram (The Great Feast, Feast of the Sacrifice): Four days beginning on 10th Dhu'l-Hijja. The principal Islamic festival, commemorating Abraham's sacrifice and coinciding with the pilgrimage to Mecca. Celebrated by the sacrifice of a sheep, by feasting and by donations to the poor.

Islamic Year	1433	1434	1435
New Year	26 Nov. 2011	14 Nov. 2012	4 Nov. 2013
Ashoura	5 Dec. 2011	23 Nov. 2012	13 Nov. 2013
Mouloud	4 Feb. 2012	23 Jan. 2013	13 Jan. 2014
Leilat al-Meiraj	16 June 2012	5 June 2013	26 May 2014
Ramadan begins	19 July 2012	8 July 2013	28 June 2014
'Id al-Fitr	18 Aug. 2012	7 Aug. 2013	28 July 2014
'Id al-Adha	25 Oct. 2012	14 Oct. 2013	4 Oct. 2014

Note: Local determinations may vary by one day from those given here.

The Iranian Calendar

The Iranian Calendar, introduced in 1925, was based on the Islamic Calendar, adapted to the solar year. Iranian New Year (*Now Ruz* or *Norouz*) occurs at the vernal equinox, which usually falls on 21 March in the Gregorian Calendar. In Iran it was decided to base the calendar on the coronation of Cyrus the Great, in place of the *Hijra*, from 1976, and the year beginning 21 March 1976 became 2535. During 1978, however, it was decided to revert to the former system of dating. The year 1392 began on 21 March 2013.

The Iranian year is divided into the following months:

1. Favardine	31 days	7. Mehr	30 days
2. Ordibehecht	31 days	8. Aban	30 days
3. Khordad	31 days	9. Azar	30 days
4. Tir	31 days	10. Dey	30 days
5. Mordad	31 days	11. Bahman	30 days
6. Chariver	31 days	12. Esfand	29 or 30 days

The Iranian Calendar is used for all purposes in Iran, except the determining of Islamic religious festivals, for which the lunar Islamic Calendar is used.

The Hebrew Calendar

The Hebrew Calendar is solar with respect to the year but lunar with respect to the months. The normal year has 353–355 days in 12 lunar months, but seven times in each 19 years an extra month of 30 days (*Adar II*) is intercalated after the normal month of Adar to adjust the calendar to the solar year. New Year (*Rosh Hashanah*) usually falls in September of the Gregorian calendar, but the day varies considerably. The year 5774 began on 5 September 2013.

The months are as follows:

1. Tishri	30 days	7. Nisan	30 days
2. Marcheshvan	29 or 30 days	8. Iyyar	29 days
3. Kislev	29 or 30 days	9. Sivan	30 days
4. Tebeth	29 days	10. Tammuz	29 days
5. Shebat	30 days	11. Av	30 days
6. Adar	29 days	12. Ellul	29 days
(Adar II)	30 days		

The Hebrew Calendar is used to determine the dates of Jewish religious festivals only. The civil year begins with the month Tishri, while the ecclesiastical year commences on the first day of Nisan.

RESEARCH INSTITUTES

ASSOCIATIONS AND INSTITUTES STUDYING THE MIDDLE EAST AND NORTH AFRICA*

ARGENTINA

Sección Interdisciplinaria de Estudios de Asia y Africa: Facultad de Filosofía y Letras, Universidad de Buenos Aires, Moreno 350, 1091 Buenos Aires; tel. and fax (11) 4345-8196; e-mail africayasia@yahoo.com.ar; internet www.museoetnografico.filo.uba.ar; f. 1982; research and lectures; Dir Prof. MARISA PINEAU; publ. *Temas de Africa y Asia* (2 a year).

ARMENIA

Institute of Oriental Studies of the National Academy of Sciences of Armenia: 24/4 Marshal Bagramyan Ave, 0019 Yerevan; tel. (1) 58-33-82; e-mail info@orient.sci.am; internet orient.sci.am; f. 1971; specializes in the history and philology of the Near and Middle East; Dir Dr RUBEN A. SAFRASTYAN; publ. *The Countries and Peoples of the Near and Middle East*.

AUSTRALIA

Centre for Arab and Islamic Studies: Bldg 127, Ellery Cres., The Australian National University, Canberra, ACT 0200; tel. (2) 6125-4982; fax (2) 6125-5410; e-mail cais@anu.edu.au; internet cais.anu.edu.au; research into the politics, history, political economy, international relations, strategic and defence issues and religion of the Middle East and Central Asia; Dir Prof. AMIN SAIKAL; publ. *Bulletin* (bi-annual journal), conference proceedings, occasional papers and monographs.

Centre for Middle East and North African Studies: Macquarie University, North Ryde, NSW 2109; tel. (2) 9850-8869; fax (2) 9850-6064; e-mail mecentre@mq.edu.au; internet www.mq.edu.au/mec; f. 1993; Dir Dr GENNARO GERVASIO; publ. *Newsletter* (annually).

Programme in Middle East Studies: Business School, University of Western Australia, Nedlands WA 6009; tel. (8) 6488-2926; fax (8) 6488-1016; e-mail rony.gabbay@uwa.edu.au; internet www.uwa.edu.au; f. 1975 to promote, encourage and facilitate teaching, research and the dissemination of information on the Middle East; Dir Dr RONY GABBAY.

AUSTRIA

Afro-Asiatisches Institut in Wien: Türkenstrasse 3, A-1090 Vienna; tel. (1) 310-51-45-311; fax (1) 310-51-45-312; e-mail office@aai-wien.at; internet www.aai-wien.at; f. 1959 by the Roman Catholic Church in Vienna; seminars, scholarship programmes and other religious and cultural exchange between Africans and Asians in Vienna; Rector Dr RAINER PORSTNER.

Institut für Orientalistik der Universität Wien: Spitalgasse 2, Hof 4, 1090 Vienna; tel. (1) 427-74-34-01; fax (1) 427-79-434; e-mail orientalistik@univie.ac.at; internet orientalistik.univie.ac.at; library of 26,200 vols; Dir Prof. Dr CLAUDIA RÖMER; publ. *Wiener Zeitschrift für die Kunde des Morgenlandes* (annually), *Turkologischer Anzeiger* (annually), *Archiv für Orientforschung* (annually).

AZERBAIJAN

Institute of Oriental Studies: Academy of Sciences, Pr. Husain Javid 31, 370143 Baku; tel. and fax (12) 439-23-51; e-mail sharq@lan.ab.az; internet www.science.gov.az/en/oriental; f. 1958; research into social, political, economic and cultural development of Oriental countries and their relations with Azerbaijan; history of Islam; philology; Dir GOVKHAR BAKHSHALI BAKHSHALIYEVA.

BELGIUM

Association Egyptologique Reine Elisabeth: Parc du Cinquantenaire, 10, 1000 Brussels; tel. (2) 741-73-64; fax (2) 733-77-35; e-mail aere.egke@kmkg-mrah.be; internet www.aere-egke.be; f. 1923 to encourage Egyptian studies; fmrly Fondation Égyptologique Reine Élisabeth; 480 mems; library of 90,000 vols; Chair. Compte ARNOUL D'ARSCHOT SCHOONHOVEN; Dirs HERMAN DE MEULENAERE, ALAIN MARTIN; publ. *Chronique d'Egypte*, *Bibliotheca Aegyptiaca*, *Papyrologica Bruxellensia*, *Bibliographie Papyrologique sur fiches*, *Monumenta Aegyptiaca*, *Rites égyptiens*, *Papyri Bruxellenses Graecae*, *Monographies Reine Elisabeth*, *Médecine égyptienne*.

Departement Oosterse en Slavische Studies: Faculteit Letteren, Katholieke Universiteit te Leuven, Blijde Inkomststraat 21, 3000 Leuven; tel. (16) 32-49-31; fax (16) 32-49-32; e-mail oriental.studies@arts.kuleuven.be; internet www.kuleuven.be; f. 1936; Pres. Prof. KAREL VAN LERBERGHE; 80 mems; publ. *Orientalia Lovaniensia Analecta*, *Orientalia Lovaniensia Periodica*, *Bibliothèque du Muséon* (1929–68), *Orientalia et Biblica Lovaniensia* (1957–68), *Inforient-Reeks*.

Middle East and North Africa Research Group (MENARG): University of Ghent, Universiteitsstraat 8, 9000 Gent; tel. (9) 264-69-15; fax (9) 264-69-97; e-mail menarg@ugent.be; internet www.menarg.ugent.be; dedicated to production of new knowledge about and critical insight into politics, society and economy in contemporary Middle East and North Africa; Co-ordinator SAMI ZEMNI.

Nederlands-Vlaams Instituut in Cairo (see under Egypt).

CUBA

Centro de Estudios de Africa y del Medio Oriente (Centre for African and Middle Eastern Studies): Avda 3ra, 1805, entre 18 y 20, Miramar, Playa, Havana; tel. and fax (7) 22-1222; e-mail ceamo@ceniai.inf.cu; internet www.nodo50.org/ceamo; f. 1979; scientific non-governmental assen; aims to expand the study of Africa and the Middle East and the impact of their cultures in Cuba, as well as Cuban policy towards these regions; organizes postgraduate courses, seminars, lectures and workshops; library includes 5,000 books, 4,000 documents and 450 periodicals; publ. journal *Revista de Africa y Medio Oriente* (2 a year, in English and Spanish), bulletins, research papers and books.

CYPRUS

Cyprus American Archaeological Research Institute (CAARI): 11 Andreas Demitriou St, Nicosia 1066; tel. (2) 456414; fax (2) 671147; e-mail admin@caari.org.cy; internet www.caari.org; f. 1978 to promote the study of Cypriot archaeology, as well as the history and culture of the Eastern Mediterranean; affiliated to the American Schools of Oriental Research (see under USA); hosts lectures, seminars and symposia; Dir Dr ANDREW MCCARTHY; publ. *CAARI News* (2 a year), newsletter on events around the world relevant to Cypriot archaeology and related history and art.

CZECH REPUBLIC

Orientální ústav AV ČR (Oriental Institute of the Academy of Sciences of the Czech Republic): Pod Vodárenskou věží 4, 182 08 Prague 8; tel. (2) 66053111; fax (2) 86581897; e-mail orient@orient.cas.cz; internet www.orient.cas.cz; f. 1922; research in Asian studies; Dir JAROSLAV HEŘMÁNEK; publ. *Archiv orientální* (3 a year), *Nový Orient* (quarterly).

DENMARK

Center for Mellemøst-Studier (Centre for Contemporary Middle East Studies): University of Southern Denmark, Main Campus, Odense University, Campusvej 55, 5230 Odense M; tel. 65-50-21-83; fax 65-50-21-61; e-mail middle-east@sdu.dk; internet www.sdu.dk/middle-east; f. 1983; national centre for interdisciplinary research in cultures and societies of the contemporary Middle East; 15-mem. research team; library of 3,000 vols and 90 periodicals; Head of Dept DIETRICH JUNG.

EGYPT

Academy of the Arabic Language: 15 Aziz Abaza St, Cairo 11211 (Zamalek); tel. (2) 7355983; fax (2) 7362002; e-mail acc@idsc.net.eg; f. 1932; library of 60,000 vols and periodicals; Pres. (vacant); publ. *Review* (2 a year), books on reviving Arabic heritage, council and conference proceedings, biographies of mems of Academy, lexicons and directories of scientific and technical terms.

Al-Ahram Center for Political and Strategic Studies (ACPSS): Al-Ahram Foundation, al-Galaa St, Cairo; tel. (2) 25786037; fax (2) 27703229; e-mail acpss@ahram.org.eg; internet acpss.ahram.org.eg; f. 1968; research into international relations, politics and economics; particular emphasis on Arab–Israeli relations; 35-mem. research team; library of 10,000 vols and 130 periodicals; Dir Dr ABD AL-MONEM SAID; publs incl. *The Arab Strategic Report* (annually), *Strategic Economic Directions* (annually), *The State of Religion in Egypt Report* (annually), *Strategic Papers* (monthly), *Al-Ahram*

*See also Regional Organizations—Education; Arts and Culture

Strategic File (monthly), *Israeli Digest* (monthly), *Strategic Readings* (monthly), *Egyptian Affairs* (quarterly), *Iran Digest* (monthly).

American Research Center in Egypt: 2 Midan Simón Bolívar, Cairo 11461 (Garden City); tel. (2) 27948239; fax (2) 27953052; e-mail cairo@arce.org; internet www.arce.org; and 8700 Crownhill Blvd, Suite 507, San Antonio, TX 78209-1130, USA; tel. (210) 821-7000; fax (210) 821-7007; e-mail info@arce.org; f. 1948 by American universities to promote research by US and Canadian scholars in all phases of Egyptian civilization, incl. archaeology, art history, humanities and social sciences; grants and fellowships available; 31 institutional mems and 1,250 individual mems; Pres. SAMEH ISKANDER; publ. *Journal* (annually), *Bulletin* (2 a year).

Institut Dominicain d'Etudes Orientales (Dominican Institute for Oriental Studies): Priory of the Dominican Fathers, 1 Sharia Masna al-Tarabish, BP 18 Abbasiyah, Cairo 11381; tel. (2) 24825509; fax (2) 26820682; e-mail info@ideo-cairo.org; internet www.ideo-cairo.org; f. 1953; library of 125,000 vols; Dir (vacant); publ. *Mélanges de L'Institut Dominicain d'Etudes Orientales—Midéo* (every 18 months), *Les Cahiers du Midéo* (series).

Institut d'Egypte: 13 Sharia Sheikh Rihane, Cairo; f. 1798; studies literary, artistic and scientific questions relating to Egypt and neighbouring countries; 120 mems, 50 assoc. mems, 50 corresponding mems; library of 160,000 vols; Pres. Prof. M. HAFEZ; publ. *Bulletin* (annually), *Mémoires* (irregular).

Institut Français d'Archéologie Orientale (French Institute of Oriental Archaeology): 37 rue Sheikh Ali Youssef, BP Qasr al-Aïny 11562, 11441 Cairo; tel. (2) 27971600; fax (2) 27944635; e-mail direction@ifao.egnet.net; internet www.ifao.egnet.net; f. 1880; excavations, research and publications; library of 85,000 vols; Dir Prof. BEATRIX MIDANT-REYNES; publ. *Bulletin de l'Institut Français d'Archéologie Orientale*, *Annales Islamologiques*, etc.

Institute of Arab Research and Studies: POB 229, 1 Arab Advocates Union St (fmrly Tolombat St), Cairo (Garden City); tel. (2) 7951648; fax (2) 7962543; e-mail iars@iarsecs.org; internet www.iars.net; f. 1953; research and studies into contemporary Arab affairs; international relations; library service; affiliated to the Arab League Educational, Cultural and Scientific Org.; Dir Prof. AHMAD YOUSUF AHMAD; publ. *Bulletin of Arab Research and Studies* (annually).

Middle East Research Centre: el-Khalifa el-Mahmoun St, Ain Shams University, Cairo 11566; tel. (2) 6847837; fax (2) 4854139; e-mail middleerc@asunet.shams.edu.eg; f. 1967; organizes conferences, symposia, lectures and training courses; Dir Prof. Dr MUHAMMAD REDA EL-EDET; publs include *Middle East Affairs* (quarterly) and *Middle East Research Periodical* (bi-annual).

National Centre for Middle East Studies: POB 18, 1 Sharia Qasr el-Nil, Bab el-Louk, Cairo 11513; tel. (2) 770041; fax (2) 770063; f. 1989; research into peace process, arms control and conflict resolution; Dir TAREK FAHMI; publ. *Middle East Papers* (3 a year).

Nederlands-Vlaams Instituut in Cairo (NVIC) (Netherlands-Flemish Institute in Cairo): POB 50, 1 Dr Mahmoud Azmi St, Cairo 11211 (Zamalek); tel. (2) 27382520; fax (2) 27382523; e-mail info@nvic.leidenuniv.nl; internet www.nvic.leidenuniv.nl; f. 1971; fmrly Netherlands Institute for Archaeology and Arabic Studies in Cairo; Dir Dr RUDOLF DE JONG; library and publs in the field of Arabic Studies, Egyptology, archaeology and Coptology.

Société Archéologique d'Alexandrie (Archaeological Society of Alexandria): POB 815, 6 Mahmoud Moukhtar St, Alexandria 21111; tel. and fax (3) 4860650; e-mail mona.haggag@asalex.org; internet asalex.org/index.html; f. 1893; 248 mems; Pres. Prof. MUSTAFA EL-ABBADI; publ. *Bulletins*, *Mémoires*, *Monuments de l'Egypte Gréco-Romaine*, *Cahiers*, *Publications Spéciales*, *Archaeological and Historical Studies*.

Société Egyptienne d'Economie Politique, de Statistique et de Législation: BP 732, 16 ave Ramses, Cairo; tel. (2) 5750797; fax (2) 5743491; e-mail espesl@hotmail.com; f. 1909; 1,550 mems; library of 50,000 vols; Pres. Prof. Dr AHMAD F. SURUR; Sec.-Gen. Prof. Dr MOUSTAFA K. EL-SAID; Library Dir SALEM S. ZAID; publ. *Revue L'Egypte Contemporaine* (quarterly in Arabic, French and English).

Society for Coptic Archaeology: 222 ave Ramses, Cairo; tel. (2) 4824252; f. 1934; 360 mems; library of 15,000 vols; Pres. WASSIF BOUTROS GHALI; Sec.-Gen. Dr A. KHATER; publ. *Bulletin* (annually), *Fouilles*, *Bibliothèque d'Art et d'Archéologie*, *Textes et Documents*, etc.

FINLAND

Suomen Itämainen Seura (Finnish Oriental Society): c/o Dept of World Cultures, University of Helsinki, POB 59, 00014 Helsinki; tel. (9) 19122224; fax (9) 19122094; e-mail saana.svard@helsinki.fi; internet www.suomenitamainenseura.org; f. 1917; Pres. SAANA SVÄRD; publ. *Studia Orientalia*.

FRANCE

Centre des Etudes Arabes (CEA): Orient et Monde arabe, Université de la Sorbonne Nouvelle (Paris III), 13 rue de Santeuil, 75005 Paris; tel. 1-45-87-41-38; e-mail Burhan.Ghalioun@univ-paris3.fr; internet www.univ-paris3.fr/cea; Dirs BURHAN GHALIOUN, SAADANE BENBABAALI.

Centre d'Etudes Euro-Arabe: 116 ave des Champs-Elysées, 75008 Paris; tel. 1-53-57-43-30; fax 1-53-57-43-31; e-mail paris@ceea.com; internet www.ceea.com; f. 1992; research into politics, history, security and economics of the Middle East; promotes European-Arab relationships in various fields; rep. office in Beirut, Lebanon; Pres. Dr SALEH BIN BAKR AL-TAYAR; Dir Dr MEHDI CHEHADE; publ. various research papers and a periodic newsletter in French, Arabic and English.

Fondation Nationale des Sciences Politiques: 27 rue Saint-Guillaume, 75337 Paris Cedex 07; tel. 1-45-49-50-50; fax 1-42-22-31-26; e-mail webmestre@sciences-po.fr; internet www.sciences-po.fr; f. 1945; eight research centres; library incl. 650,000 books and 4,500 periodicals; Pres. JEAN-CLAUDE CASANOVA; publs incl. *Maghreb-Machrek* (quarterly).

Institut d'Etudes Iraniennes (Institute of Iranian Studies): Université de la Sorbonne Nouvelle (Paris III), 13 rue Santeuil, 75231 Paris; tel. 1-45-87-42-61; fax 1-45-87-42-63; e-mail institut-etudes-iraniennes@univ-paris3.fr; internet www.univ-paris3.fr/etudes-iraniennes; f. 1947; library of c. 18,000 monographs and 110 periodicals; Dir YANN RICHARD; publ. *Travaux*, *Travaux et Mémoires* (series), *Studia Iranica* (journal), *Abstracta Iranica* (annual bibliography).

Institut d'Etudes Sémitiques (Institute of Semitic Studies): Institut d'Etudes Sémitiques, Collège de France, 52 rue du Cardinal Lemoine, 75231 Paris Cedex 05; tel. (1) 1-44-27-10-51; fax (1) 1-44-27-16-03; e-mail etudes.semitiques@college-de-france.fr; f. 1930; Pres. CHRISTIAN J. ROBIN; publ. *Semitica*.

Institut du Monde Arabe (Institute of the Arab World): 1 rue des Fossés Saint Bernard, pl. Mohammed V, 75236 Paris Cedex 05; tel. 1-40-51-38-38; fax 1-43-54-76-45; e-mail rap@imarabe.org; internet www.imarabe.org; f. 1980; Pres. RENAUD MUSELIER; Dir-Gen. MOKHTAR TALEB-BENDIAB; publ. *Al-Moukhtarat* and *Qantara* (both quarterly).

Institut National des Langues et Civilisations Orientales (National Institute of Oriental Languages and Civilizations): 65 rue des Grands Moulins, CS21351, 75214 Paris Cedex 13; tel. 1-81-70-10-00; e-mail secretariat.general@inalco.fr; internet www.inalco.fr; f. 1795; faculties of languages and world civilizations; c. 9,200 students, 250 teachers and lecturers (2007); library of 550,000 vols and 9,600 periodicals; Pres. JACQUES LEGRAND; High International Studies (DHEI), Dept of International Business (CPEI), Automatic Languages Treatment (TAL), Multilingual Engineering (IM); publ. *Livret de l'Etudiant* (annually), various Oriental studies and periodicals.

Institut de Papyrologie de la Sorbonne: Université de Paris-Sorbonne, IUFM de Paris, 10 rue Molitor, 75016 Paris; tel. and fax 1-40-50-25-88; e-mail institut-papyrologie@paris-sorbonne.fr; internet www.papyrologie.paris4.sorbonne.fr; f. 1920; library of 7,000 vols and 25 periodicals; Dir JEAN GASCOU.

Institut de Recherches et d'Etudes sur le Monde Arabe et Musulman (Institute of Research and Studies on the Arab and Muslim World): Université d'Aix-Marseille I et III, Maison Méditerranéenne des Sciences de l'Homme, 5 rue du Château de l'Horloge, BP 647, 13094 Aix-en-Provence Cedex 2; tel. 4-42-52-41-62; fax 4-42-52-49-80; e-mail secretariat.iremam@mmsh.univ-aix.fr; internet www.mmsh.univ-aix.fr/iremam; library of 65,000 vols and 250 periodicals (60 in Arabic); Dir GHISLAINE ALLEAUME; publ. *Série Iremam-Karthala*.

Société Asiatique: Palais de l'Institut, 23 quai Conti, 75006 Paris; tel. and fax 1-44-41-43-1; e-mail societeasiatique@yahoo.fr; internet www.aibl.fr/us/asie/home.html; f. 1822; more than 700 mems; library of 90,000 vols and 200 periodicals; Pres. JEAN-PIERRE MAHÉ; publ. *Journal Asiatique* (2 a year), *Cahiers de la Société Asiatique*.

GEORGIA

Tsereteli Institute of Oriental Studies of the Georgian Academy of Sciences: Acad. G. Tsereteli 3, 62, 380062 Tbilisi; tel. (32) 23-23-72; fax (32) 23-30-08; e-mail root@orient.acnet.ge; internet www.acnet.ge/orient.htm; f. 1960; researches languages, history and culture of Near, Middle and Far East; Dir Prof. TAMAZ V. GAMKRELIDZE.

GERMANY

Abteilung für Orientalische und Asiatische Sprachen (AOAS): Nassestr. 2, D-53113 Bonn; tel. (228) 738415; fax (228) 738446; e-mail aoas@uni-bonn.de; internet www.ioa.uni-bonn.de/abteilungen/orientalische-und-asiatische-sprachen; f. 1959 (1887

Berlin); part of Institute of Oriental and Asian Studies, University of Bonn; Dir of Institute Prof. Dr KONRAD KLAUS.

Deutsche Arbeitsgemeinschaft Vorderer Orient (DAVO): Centre for Research on the Arab World (CERAW), Institute of Geography, University of Mainz, 55099 Mainz; tel. (6131) 3922701; fax (6131) 3924736; e-mail davo@geo.uni-mainz.de; internet www.davo1.de/index.html; f. 1993; interdisciplinary asscn of more than 1,500 scholars, students and others interested in contemporary research on the Middle East and North Africa; Pres. Prof. Dr GÜNTER MEYER; publ. journal *DAVO-Nachrichten* (bi-annual) and weekly e-mail list with latest news on international Middle Eastern studies.

Deutsche Morgenländische Gesellschaft: Institut für Turkologie, Freie Universität Berlin, Schwendenerstr. 33, 14195 Berlin; tel. (30) 83853955; fax (30) 83853823; e-mail clcs@gmx.de; internet www.dmg-web.de; f. 1845; Sec. Dr CLAUS SCHÖNIG; publ. *Zeitschrift* (2 a year) and *Abhandlungen für die Kunde des Morgenlandes*.

GIGA Institut für Nahost-Studien (GIGA Institute of Middle East Studies): Neuer Jungfernstieg 21, 20354 Hamburg; tel. (40) 42825523; fax (40) 42825511; e-mail imes@giga-hamburg.de; internet www.giga-hamburg.de/imes; f. 2007; affiliated to Leibniz-Institut für Globale und Regionale Studien (German Institute of Global and Area Studies); devoted to research in politics, social sciences and economics of the Near and Middle East and North Africa; library of c. 33,000 books and 230 periodicals; Dir Prof. Dr HENNER FÜRTIG; publ. *Focus Nahost* (monthly).

Institut für Altorientalistik (Institute for Ancient Near Eastern Studies): Freie Universität Berlin, Hüttenweg 7, 14195 Berlin; tel. (30) 83853347; fax (30) 83853600; e-mail altorsek@zedat.fu-berlin.de; internet web.fu-berlin.de/altorientalistik; f. 1950; Dir Prof. Dr EVA CANCIK-KIRSCHBAUM.

Nah- und Mittelost Verein e.V. (German Near and Middle East Association): Jägerstr. 63D, 10117 Berlin; tel. (30) 2064100; fax (30) 20641010; e-mail numov@numov.de; internet www.numov.de; f. 1934; 600 mems; Hon. Chair. Dr GERHARD SCHRÖDER; Chair. Dr RAINER SEELE; publ.*WirtschaftsForum Nah-und Mittelost* (bi-monthly), *Qatar-German-Business-Forum* (bi-monthly).

Stiftung Zentrum für Türkeistudien (Centre for Studies on Turkey): Universität Duisburg-Essen, Altendorferstr. 3, 45127 Essen; tel. (201) 31980; fax (201) 3198333; e-mail zft@zft-online.de; internet www.zft-online.de; f. 1985; aims to promote German-Turkish relations and improve knowledge about Turkey and Turkish migrants in Europe; Dir Prof. Dr HACI HALIL USLUCAN; Man. Dir Dr ANDREAS GOLDBERG; publ. periodicals and working papers.

INDIA

Asiatic Society of Mumbai: Town Hall, Shahid Bhagat Singh Rd, Mumbai 400 023; tel. (22) 22660956; e-mail asml@mtnl.net.in; internet www.asiaticsocietymumbai.org/as/; f. 1804 as Bombay Literary Society; in 1973 established the Dr P. V. Kane Research Institute for Oriental Studies (later renamed the Dr P. V. Kane Institute for Post Graduate Studies and Research—affiliated to the University of Bombay); promotes and publ. research in culture, art and literature of Asia (both general and specifically Indian); offers scholarships and fellowships; holds seminars and lectures on current, historical and cultural affairs; 2,816 mems; 248,101 vols (2007), 2,493 MSS and 11,830 old coins; Pres. Dr AROON TIKEKAR; publs include *Journal* (annually), reports, critical annotated texts of rare Sanskrit and Pali MSS.

IRAN

British Institute of Persian Studies: 1553 Dr Shariati St, Gholhak, POB 11155-844, Tehran 19396-13661; tel. (21) 22601937; fax (21) 22604901; e-mail bips@parsonline.net; internet www.bips.ac.uk; f. 1961; cultural institute, with emphasis on history and archaeology; 400 mems; library of c. 14,000 vols; Pres. Prof. ROBERT GLEAVE; publ. *Iran* (annually).

Institute for Political and International Studies (IPIS): Shahid Bahonar Ave, Shahid Aghaii St, Tajrish, Tehran; POB 19395-1793, Tehran; tel. (21) 22802641; fax (21) 22802649; e-mail cominfo@ipis.ir; internet www.ipis.ir; f. 1983; research and information on Iran's foreign policy and international relations; emphasis on Middle East, Persian (Arabian) Gulf, Europe, South-east Asia and Central Asia; affiliated to the Ministry of Foreign Affairs; Dir-Gen. Dr MOSTAFA DOLATYAR; publ. *Central Asia and the Caucasus* (quarterly), *Iranian Journal of International Affairs* (quarterly), *Iranian Journal of Foreign Policy* (quarterly).

IRAQ

Centre for Arabian Gulf Studies: University of Basra, POB 49, Basra; tel. (40) 314637; fax (40) 213235; e-mail arabgulfcenter20042000@yahoo.com; internet www.albasrahuniv.com/gulfstudiescenter.htm; f. 1974; research into economics, politics, strategic issues, geography, history, anthropology and culture of the Persian (Arabian) Gulf region; seriously damaged and much of its collection looted during the US-led military campaign to oust the regime of Saddam Hussain in early 2003; Dir Dr JASIM G. AL-MALIKI; publ. *Arab Gulf Journal* (quarterly) and *The Gulf Economist* (quarterly).

Deutsches Archäologisches Institut (German Archaelogical Institute): POB 2105, Alwiya, Baghdad; tel. (1) 553-0793; e-mail sekretariat.istanbul@dainst.de; internet www.dainst.org; f. 1955; Baghdad branch of institution installed within the German Federal Foreign Office to undertake archaeological excavations and scientific research; organizes academic congresses, colloquia and tours; library with c. 500 vols and 15 periodicals; collection of photographs; currently closed and directed from Berlin, Germany; Pres. Prof. FRIEDRIKE FLESS.

Iraqi Academy of Sciences: Iraqi Academy of Sciences, POB 4023, Waziriya, Baghdad; tel. (1) 422-4202; fax (1) 422-2066; e-mail info@iraqacademy.org; internet www.iraqacademy.org; f. 1947 to maintain the Arabic language, to undertake research into Arabic history, Islamic heritage and the history of Iraq, and to encourage research in the modern arts and sciences; some of collection looted or destroyed during or after the US-led military intervention to oust the regime of Saddam Hussain in early 2003; Pres. Prof. Dr AHMAD MATLOUB; publ. *Journal of the Academy of Sciences* (quarterly, in Arabic; 2 a year, in Kurdish).

ISRAEL

The Academy of the Hebrew Language: Giv'at Ram Campus, Jerusalem 91904; tel. (2) 6493555; fax (2) 5617065; e-mail acad@vms.huji.ac.il; internet hebrew-academy.huji.ac.il; f. 1953; study and development of the Hebrew language and compilation of a historical dictionary; Pres. Prof. MOSHE BAR-ASHER; publ. *Zikhronot*, *Leshonenu* (quarterly), *Leshonenu La'am*, monographs and dictionaries.

W. F. Albright Institute of Archaeological Research (AIAR): POB 19096, 26 Salah el-Din St, Jerusalem 91190; tel. (2) 6288956; fax (2) 6264424; e-mail manager@albright.org.il; internet www.aiar.org; f. 1900 by the American Schools of Oriental Research; research in Syro-Palestinian archaeology, Biblical studies, Near Eastern history and languages; sponsors excavations; library with c. 30,000 vols and 650 journal titles relating to all aspects of ancient Near Eastern studies, with a concentration on Syro-Palestinian archaeology and Semitic languages and literature; Chair. VIVIAN BULL; Pres. Prof. J. EDWARD WRIGHT.

Arab Studies Society: Orient House Bldg, POB 20479, 10 Abu Obeidah ibn el-Jarah St, Jerusalem; tel. (2) 6273330; fax (2) 6274020; e-mail arabstudies@arabs.arabstudies; internet www.orienthouse.org/arabstudies; f. 1980 to promote Arabic culture, in particular Palestinian thought and culture; works undertaken by 8 centres with 14 depts; library of c. 14,000 vols on Palestine and the Middle East; Dir NABIH AWEIDAH; publ. more than 100 books on culture and history of Jerusalem and Palestine.

Begin-Sadat Center for Strategic Studies: Bar-Ilan University, Ramat-Gan 52900; tel. (3) 5318959; fax (3) 5359198; e-mail besa.center@mail.biu.ac.il; internet www.besacenter.org; f. 1993; research on Middle Eastern security; organizes conferences and workshops; Dir Prof. EFRAIM INBAR; publ. *BESA Bulletin*, *BESA Colloquia on Strategy and Diplomacy*, *BESA Middle East Security and Policy Studies*, *BESA Studies in International Security*, *BESA Perspectives Papers*.

The Ben-Zvi Institute for the Study of Jewish Communities in the East: POB 7660, 12 Abravanel St, Jerusalem 91076; tel. (2) 5398888; fax (2) 5638310; e-mail ybz@ybz.org.il; internet www.ybz.org.il; f. 1947; sponsors research in the history and culture of Jewish communities in the East; owned by Yad Izhak Ben-Zvi and the Hebrew University of Jerusalem; library of MSS and printed books; Dir JACOB YANIV; publ. *Pe'amim—Studies in Oriental Jewry*, *Pe'amim* (quarterly) and monographs.

Couvent Saint Etienne des Pères Dominicains, Ecole Biblique et Archéologique Française: POB 19053, 6 Nablus Rd, Jerusalem 91190; tel. (2) 6264468; fax (2) 6282567; e-mail directeur@ebaf.edu; internet www.ebaf.info; f. 1890; research, Biblical and Oriental studies, exploration and excavation in Israel, Palestine and Jordan; Dir Frère MARCEL SIGRIST; library of 140,000 vols; publ. *Revue Biblique*, *Etudes Bibliques*, *Cahiers de la Revue Biblique*, *Bible de Jérusalem* .

The Global Research in International Affairs (GLORIA) Center: POB 167, Interdisciplinary Center, Herzliya 46150; tel. and fax (9) 9602736; e-mail info@gloriacenter.org; internet www.gloria-center.org; f. 2002; private; organizes projects concerned with international affairs, especially relating to the modern Middle East; has established Turkish Studies Institute; Dir Prof. BARRY RUBIN; publ. *Middle East Review of International Affairs (MERIA) Journal* (quarterly).

The Harry S. Truman Research Institute for the Advancement of Peace: Hebrew University of Jerusalem, Mount Scopus, Jerusalem 91905; tel. (2) 5882300; fax (2) 5828076; e-mail truman@savion.huji.ac.il; internet truman.huji.ac.il; f. 1965; fosters peace and advances co-operation in the Middle East and the peoples of the world through research; library of more than 1,500 periodicals; Chair. MOSHE ARAD; Academic Dir MENAHEM BLONDHEIM; Exec. Dir NAAMA SHPETER; publ. works on the Middle East, Africa, Asia and Latin America.

Historical Society of Israel: POB 4179, 2 Betar St, Jerusalem 91041; tel. (2) 5650444; fax (2) 6712388; e-mail shazar@shazar.org.il; internet www.shazar.org.il; f. 1925 to promote the study of Jewish history and general history; 1,000 mems; Chair. EPHRAIM HALEVY; publishing arm, The Zalman Shazar Center for Jewish History, publ. *Zion* (quarterly), *Historia* (2 a year).

Institute of Asian and African Studies: Hebrew University, Mount Scopus, Jerusalem 91905; tel. (2) 5883516; fax (2) 5883659; e-mail asiaafrica@mscc.huji.ac.il; internet asiafrica.huji.ac.il; f. 1926 as the Institute of Oriental Studies; incorporates Max Schloessinger Memorial Foundation; studies of medieval and modern languages, culture and history of Middle East, Asia and Africa; Dir Prof. AMIKAM ELAD; publs incl. *Max Schloessinger Memorial Series*, *Collected Studies in Arabic and Islam Series*, *Jerusalem Studies in Arabic and Islam*, translation series and studies in classical Islam and Arabic language and literature, *Hebrew University Armenian Series*.

Institute for National Security Studies (INSS): Tel-Aviv University, POB 39950, 40 Haim Levanon St, Tel-Aviv 61398; tel. (3) 6400400; fax (3) 7447590; e-mail info@inss.org.il; internet www.inss.org.il; f. 2006; incorporates the fmr Jaffee Center for Strategic Studies (f. 1977); research into Middle Eastern strategic affairs; library of c. 6,000 vols; Dir Maj.-Gen. (retd) AMOS YADLIN; publ. *Strategic Survey for Israel* (annually), *Strategic Assessment* (quarterly), *Military and Strategic Affairs* (quarterly), *INSS Insight* (weekly).

Israel Exploration Society: POB 7041, 5 Avida St, Jerusalem 91070; tel. (2) 6257991; fax (2) 6247772; e-mail ies@vms.huji.ac.il; internet israelexplorationsociety.huji.ac.il; f. 1914; archaeological excavations and historical research, congresses and lectures; 4,000 mems; Chair. Prof. E. STERN; Dir H. GEVA; publ. *Eretz-Israel* (Hebrew and English, commemorative series), *Qadmoniot* (Hebrew, bi-annual), *Israel Exploration Journal* (English, bi-annual), various books on archaeology (in Hebrew and English).

Israel/Palestine Center for Research and Information (IPCRI): POB 11091, Tantur, Jerusalem 91110; tel. (2) 6769460; fax (2) 6768011; e-mail ipcri@ipcri.org; internet www.ipcri.org; f. 1988; jt Palestinian-Israeli organization; research into all aspects of the Israeli–Palestinian conflict; CEOs DAN GOLDENBLATT, RIMAN BARAKAT.

Jerusalem University College: POB 1276, Mt Zion, Jerusalem 91012; tel. (2) 6718628; fax (2) 6732717; e-mail admissions@juc.edu; internet webmaster@juc.edu; f. 1957 as Institute of Holy Land Studies; Christian study centre, graduate and undergraduate studies in the history, languages, religions and cultures of Israel in the Middle Eastern context; Chair. Dr HERBERT JACOBSEN.

The Jewish-Arab Center (JAC): University of Haifa, Mount Carmel, Haifa 31905; tel. (4) 8240156; fax (4) 8340231; e-mail jewrab@univ.haifa.ac.il; internet jac.haifa.ac.il; f. 1972; promotes studies and research that contribute to mutual understanding between Jews and Arabs, and aims to influence conflict resolution in the Middle East; organizes conferences, symposia, lectures and seminars; Chair. BASHA'ER FAHOUM-JAYOUSSI; Dir Prof. ITZCHAK WEISMANN; publ. *Al-Karmil* (annually).

The Kenyon Institute: POB 19283, Jerusalem 91192; tel. (2) 5828101; fax (2) 5323844; e-mail info@kenyon-institute.org.uk; internet www.kenyon-institute.org.uk; f. 1919; Council for British Research in the Levant (CBRL); fmrly British School of Archaeology in Jerusalem and British Institute at Amman for Archaeology and History; promotes study of arts and social sciences relevant to the Levant; library of c. 10,000 vols and more than 100 periodicals; Dir Dr MANDY TURNER; publ. *Levant* (2 a year), *Bulletin* (annually), *Monographs*.

The Middle East & Islamic Studies Association of Israel (MEISAI): Hebrew University, Mt Scopus, Jerusalem 91905; tel. (2) 5883633; e-mail orient@mscc.huji.ac.il; internet www.meisai.org.il; f. 1949 as the Israel Oriental Society; lectures and symposia to study all aspects of contemporary Middle Eastern, Asian and African affairs; Pres. Prof. MICHAEL LASKER; publ. *Hamizrah Hehadash (The New East)* (Hebrew—with English summary—annually), *Ruach Mizrahit (East Wind)* (Hebrew, electronic).

Moshe Dayan Center for Middle Eastern and African Studies/Shiloah Institute: Tel-Aviv University, Ramat Aviv, Tel-Aviv 69978; tel. (3) 6409100; fax (3) 6415802; e-mail dayancen@post.tau.ac.il; internet www.dayan.org; f. 1959; Dir Prof. UZI RABI; publ. *Bulletin* (2 a year).

Pontifical Biblical Institute: POB 497, 3 Paul Emile Botta St, Jerusalem 91004; tel. (2) 6252843; fax (2) 6241203; e-mail admipib@gmail.com; internet www.biblico.it/jerusalem.html; f. 1927; study of Biblical languages and Biblical archaeology, history, topography; in conjunction with Hebrew University of Jerusalem; seminar for postgraduate students, student tours; Dir Rev. JOSEPH DOAN CÔNG NGUYÊN.

Wilfrid Israel Museum: Kibbutz Hazorea 30060; tel. (4) 9899566; fax (4) 9590860; e-mail wilfrid@hazorea.org.il; internet www.wilfrid.org.il; f. 1947; opened 1951 in memory of late Wilfrid Israel; a cultural centre for reference, study and art exhibitions; houses Wilfrid Israel collection of Near and Far Eastern art and cultural materials; local archaeological exhibits from neolithic to Byzantine times; science and art library; Dir ELISSA DVIR; Curator for Far and Middle Eastern Art ORNA MERON; Curator for Archaeology RUTH GOSHEN.

ITALY

Istituto Italiano per l'Africa e l'Oriente (Italian Institute for Africa and the Orient—IsIAO): Via Ulisse Aldrovandi 16, 00197 Rome; tel. (06) 328551; fax (06) 3225348; e-mail info@isiao.it; internet www.isiao.it; f. 1906; absorbed Istituto Italiano per il Medio ed Estremo Oriente 1995; Pres. Prof. GHERARDO GNOLI; Dir-Gen. Dott. UMBERTO SINATTI.

Istituto per l'Oriente C. A. Nallino: Via A. Caroncini 19, 00197 Rome; tel. (06) 8084106; fax (06) 8079395; e-mail ipocan@ipocan.it; internet www.ipocan.it; f. 1921 as L'Istituto per l'Oriente; adopted current name in 1982 in honour of one of its founders, Carlo Alfonso Nallino; research into all aspects of bilateral and multilateral relations between Italy and the countries of the Near and Middle East; with particular emphasis on law, society and immigration; organizes courses on Arabic, Turkish and Persian languages and Arab-Islamic culture; library of c. 35,000 vols and 300 periodicals; Pres. Prof. CLAUDIO LO JACONO; publ. *Oriente Moderno* (monographic essays, catalogues and bibliographical reviews), *Eurasian Studies* (in collaboration with the Skilliter Centre for Ottoman Studies, Newnham College, University of Cambridge, United Kingdom), *Rassegna di Studi Etiopici* (in collaboration with University of Naples Orientale, Italy), *Quaderni di Studi Arabi*.

Istituto per le relazioni tra l'Italia e i paesi dell'Africa, America Latina e Medio Oriente (Institute for Relations between Italy and Africa, Latin America and the Middle and Far East): Via degli Scipioni 147, 00192 Rome; tel. (06) 32699701; fax (06) 32699750; e-mail ipalmo@ipalmo.com; internet www.ipalmo.com; f. 1971; Pres. GIANNI DE MICHELIS; publ. *Politica Internazionale* (6 a year, Italian edn).

JAPAN

Ajia Keizai Kenkyusho (Institute of Developing Economies/Japan External Trade Organization): 3-2-2 Wakaba, Mihama-ku, Chiba-shi, Chiba 261-8545; tel. (43) 299-9500; fax (43) 299-9724; e-mail info@ide.go.jp; internet www.ide.go.jp; f. 1958; 250 mems; Pres. TAKASHI SHIRAISHI; library of 572,409 vols (2006); publ. *Ajia Keizai* (Japanese, monthly), *The Developing Economies* (English, quarterly), occasional papers in English.

Chuto Chosakai (The Middle East Research Institute of Japan): Sanko Park Bldg 5F, 7-3-1 Nishi-Shinjuku Shinjuku-ku, Tokyo 160-0023; tel. (3) 3371-5798; fax (3) 3371-5799; e-mail mideastij@hotmail.com; internet www.meij.or.jp; f. 1960; Chair. MIKIO SASAKI; Pres. Dr TATSUO ARIMA; publ. *Chuto Kenkyu* (Journal of Middle Eastern Studies, quarterly), *Chuto Nenkan* (Yearbook of Middle East and North Africa), *Newsletter*.

JIME Center (Japanese Institute of Middle Eastern Economies): The Institute of Energy Economics, Inui Bldg, Kachidoki, 10th Floor, 13-1, Kachidoki 1-chome Chuo-ku, Tokyo 104-0054; tel. (3) 5547-0230; fax (3) 5547-0229; e-mail webmaster@jime.ieej.or.jp; internet jime.ieej.or.jp; f. 2005; provides in-depth analysis of the political, economic, social and cultural developments in the Middle East, as the leading supplier of global energy resources; Dir KOICHIRO TANAKA; publ. *Chuto Dokobunseki* (Middle Eastern and Energy Bulletin, Japanese, monthly), *Gendai Chuto Kenkyu* (Contemporary Middle Eastern Studies, Japanese, quarterly) and news and research reports, *Chutoken Kenkyu Hokoku* (report of JIME research achievements, Japanese, monthly), *Kunibetsu Teiki Hokoku* (Japanese, quarterly).

Nihon Islam Kyokai (Association for Islamic Studies in Japan): Dept of South and West Asian Studies, Tokyo University for Foreign Studies, Asahimachi, Fuchu-shi, Tokyo 183-8534; tel. and fax (42) 330-5343; e-mail mhachi@tufs.ac.jp; internet www.soc.nii.ac.jp/aisj; f. 1963; scientific and educational society founded to promote the research of Islamic studies and to have academic contacts with institutions in the Islamic world; publ. *The World of Islam* (Japanese, with summary in a European language, bi-annual).

Nippon Oriento Gakkai (The Society for Near Eastern Studies in Japan): Tokyo Tenrikyokan 9, 1-chome, Kanda Nishiki-cho,

Chiyoda-ku, Tokyo 101-0054; tel. and fax (3) 3291-7519; e-mail office@j-orient.com; internet www.j-orient.com; f. 1954; about 800 mems; Pres. AKIO TSUKIMOTO; publ. *Oriento* (Japanese, 2 a year), *Orient* (European languages, annually).

JORDAN

Centre for Strategic Studies: University of Jordan, Amman 11942; tel. (6) 5300100; fax (6) 5355515; e-mail css@css-jordan.org; internet www.css-jordan.org; f. 1984; research on strategic, political, economic and social issues concerning Jordan and the Middle East; since the 1990s has also been concerned with democracy, political pluralism, the economy and the environment; has specialist units concerned with Iranian, Euro-Mediterranean and economic studies; organizes conferences, seminars and workshops; also conducts opinion polls; Dir Dr MUSA SHTEIWI.

Institut Français du Proche Orient (IFPO): POB 830413, Zahran, Amman 11183; tel. (6) 4611171; fax (6) 4611170; e-mail contact.amman@ifporient.org; internet www.ifporient.org; f. 2003 by merger of Institut Français d'Archéologie du Proche Orient, Institut Français d'Etudes Arabes de Damas and Centre d'Etudes et de Recherches sur le Moyen-Orient Contemporain; university research and documentation institution with sections also in Beirut, Lebanon, and Damascus, Syria; library of c. 13,000 vols and 90 periodicals; Dir-Gen. BRUNO PAOLI (acting).

Al Urdun Al Jadid Research Centre (UJRC): POB 940631, Amman 11194; tel. (6) 5533112; fax (6) 5533118; e-mail ujrc@ujrc-jordan.org; internet www.ujrc-jordan.net; f. 1990; independent research centre seeking to consolidate role of civil society as an effective partner in promoting a sustainable democracy in Jordan and the Arab world, and in upholding the values of human rights, citizenship and equality, through scientific research, dialogue, conferences and workshops; also publ. proceedings (incl. research papers) and organizes training; Dir-Gen. HANI HOURANI; Exec. Dir HUSSEIN ABU RUMMAN; publ.*Civil Society Issues Magazine* (Arabic, monthly), *The Economic Policy Dialogue Newsletter* (English and Arabic, quarterly).

LEBANON

Centre for Arab Unity Studies: BP 113-6001 Hamra, Beirut 2034-2407; tel. (1) 750084; fax (1) 750088; e-mail info@caus.org.lb; internet www.caus.org.lb; f. 1975; fosters research into all aspects of Arab society with particular emphasis on pan-Arab projects; Gen. Dir KHAIREDDIN HASEEB; publ. *Arab Journal of Political Science* (Arabic, quarterly), *Al-Mustaqbal al-Arabi* (Arabic, monthly), *Contemporary Arab Affairs* (English, quarterly).

Institut Français du Proche Orient (IFPO): BP 11-1424, rue de Damas, Beirut; tel. (1) 420291; fax (1) 420295; e-mail adm.contemporaines@ifporient.org; internet www.ifporient.org; f. 2003 by merger of Institut Français d'Archéologie du Proche Orient, Institut Français d'Etudes Arabes de Damas and Centre d'Etudes et de Recherches sur le Moyen-Orient Contemporain; university research and documentation institution with sections also in Amman, Jordan, and Damascus, Syria; contemporary library of 16,000 vols and 120 periodicals, archaeological library and collection of 4,000 maps; Dir Prof. Dr FRANÇOIS BURGAT.

Institute for Palestine Studies (IPS): BP 11-7164, Anis Nsouli St, Verdun, Beirut 1107 2230; tel. (1) 868387; fax (1) 814193; e-mail ipsbrt@palestine-studies.org; internet www.palestine-studies.org; 3501 M St, NW, Washington, DC 20007; tel. (202) 342-3990; fax (202) 342-3927; e-mail ipsdc@palestine-studies.org; f. 1963; independent non-profit Arab research organization; aims to promote better understanding of the Palestine problem and the Arab–Israeli conflict; affiliated with the Institute of Jerusalem Studies, East Jerusalem; library of more than 70,000 vols, microfilm collection, private papers, archives and photographs; Gen. Dir MAHMOUD SOUEID (Beirut); Dirs MONA NSOULI (Beirut), MICHELE ESPOSITO (Washington, DC); publ. *Journal of Palestine Studies* (English, quarterly), *Jerusalem Quarterly* (English), *Majallat al-Dirasat al-Filistiniyah* (Arabic, quarterly) and documentary series, reprints, research papers, etc.

Lebanese Center for Policy Studies (LCPS): BP 55-215, 10th Floor, Sadat Tower, Leon St,, Beirut; tel. (1) 799301; fax (1) 799302; e-mail info@lcps-lebanon.org; internet www.lcps-lebanon.org; f. 1989; research into political, social and economic development; library facilities; Exec. Dir SAMI ATALLAH; publ. *Abaad*, *The Beirut Review*, *The Lebanon Report*.

MAURITANIA

Centre for Strategies on Security in the Sahel-Sahara (Centre 4s): Tevragh Zeina, Nouakchott; e-mail contact@centre4s.org; internet www.centre4s.org; research into issues related to defence, security, terrorism, impact of competition for hydrocarbons and uranium, migration, illegal trafficking of goods and people in the Sahel-Sahara region; principal countries of interest include Algeria, Burkina Faso, Cape Verde, Chad, Cameroon, The Gambia, Guinea, Guinea-Bissau, Mali, Mauritania, Niger, Nigeria and Senegal; Pres. AHMEDOU OULD-ABDALLAH.

THE NETHERLANDS

Middle East Research Associates (MERA): POB 10765, 1001 ET Amsterdam; tel. (20) 6201579; fax (20) 6264479; e-mail mera@xs4all.nl; internet mera.home.xs4all.nl/; independent information and research centre covering the Middle East, North Africa and Central Asia; Dir ROBERT E. SOETERIK; publ. journal and occasional papers.

Nederlands-Vlaams Instituut in Cairo (NVIC) (Netherlands-Flemish Institute in Cairo): POB 12200, 2500 DD The Hague (see under Egypt).

Netherlands Council for Trade Promotion (Nederlands Centrum voor Handelsbevordering): JPrinses Beatrixlaan 712, POB 10, 2501 CA The Hague; tel. (70) 3441590; fax (70) 3853531; e-mail info@nchnl.nl; internet www.handelsbevordering.nl; f. 1946; Area Man., Middle East MARIAN REIJNEN; Dir JAN SIEMONS.

Netherlands Institute for the Near East (Nederlands Instituut voor het Nabije Oosten—NINO): Witte Singel 25, POB 9515, 2300 RA Leiden; tel. (71) 5272036; fax (71) 5272038; e-mail c.van.zoest@hum.leidenuniv.nl; internet www.nino-leiden.nl; f. 1939; Dir Dr JESPER EIDEM; library of c. 50,000 vols and 300 periodicals; publ. *Uitgaven van het Nederlands Instituut voor het Nabije Oosten (PIHANS)*, *Egyptologische Uitgaven (EU)*, *Achaemenid History (AchHist)* (monographs), *Bibliotheca Orientalis (BiOr)*, *Anatolica*.

Opleiding Talen en Culturen van het Midden-Oosten (Institute for Languages and Cultures of the Middle East): Rijksuniversiteit Leiden, POB 9515, 2300 RA Leiden; tel. (71) 5272034; fax (71) 5272042; e-mail secrTCMO@let.leidenuniv.nl; internet www.tcmo.leidenuniv.nl; Head of Dept Prof. Dr OLAF KAPER; publ. *Altbabylonische Briefe in Umschrift und Übersetzung* (14 vols, continuing series), *Collection*, *Liagre Böhl Collection* (c. 3,000 cuneiform tablets) published in conjunction with the Netherlands Institute for the Near East, Leiden.

NORWAY

Centre for Middle Eastern and Islamic Studies (SMI): University of Bergen, POB 7800, Bergen; tel. 55-58-00-00; fax 55-58-96-43; e-mail post@uib.no; internet www.uib.no/smi; f. 1988; Chair. Prof. ANDERS BJØRKELO; publ. *Bergen Studies on the Middle East and Africa* (monographs).

PAKISTAN

Institute of Islamic Culture: 2 Club Rd, Lahore 3; tel. (42) 6363127; f. 1950; Dir QAZI JAVED; publ. *Al-Ma'arif* (quarterly) and about 200 publications on Islamic subjects in English and Urdu.

Islamic Research Institute: International Islamic University, Faisal Masjid, POB 1035, Islamabad; tel. (51) 2281289; fax (51) 2250821; e-mail dgiri@iiu.edu.pk; internet iri.iiu.edu.pk; f. 1960; conducts research in Islamic studies; organizes seminars and conferences on various aspects of Islam; library of 120,000 books and periodicals, 610 microfilms, 260 MSS, 1,035 photostats, 220 audio cassettes; Dir-Gen. Dr MUHAMMAD KHALID MASUD; publ. *Al-Dirasat al-Islamiyah* (Arabic, quarterly), *Islamic Studies* (English, quarterly), *Fikr O-Nazar* (Urdu, quarterly), also monographs, reports, etc.

PALESTINIAN TERRITORIES

Palestine Economic Policy Research Institute (MAS): Muin Bseiso St, al-Masyoun, POB 242, Ramallah; tel. (2) 2987053; fax (2) 2987055; e-mail info@mas.ps; internet www.mas.ps; f. 1994; independent, not-for-profit institute; Dir-Gen. SAMIR ABDULLAH; publ. *Economic and Social Monitor* (Arabic and English, quarterly), in conjunction with the Palestinian Central Bureau of Statistics and the Palestinian Monetary Authority, and various studies and pamphlets on economic and social development in the Palestinian territories.

Palestinian Research Centre: Ramallah; f. 1965; fmrly in Beirut, Lebanon, and then Nicosia, Cyprus; studies Palestine question; Dir SABRI JIRYIS; publ. *Shu'un Filastiniya* (Palestine Affairs, monthly) and various books and pamphlets on aspects of the Palestine problem.

POLAND

Zakład Archeologii Śródziemnomorskiej (Research Centre for Mediterranean Archaeology): Pałac Staszica, Room 33, Nowy Świat 72, 00-330 Warsaw; tel. (22) 6572791; fax (22) 8266560; e-mail zaspan@zaspan.waw.pl; internet www.zaspan.waw.pl; f. 1956; research institute of Polish Academy of Sciences; documentation and publication of Polish excavations in the Middle East and antiquities in Polish museums; Dir Prof. KAROL MYŚLIWIEC; publ. *Travaux du Centre d'Archéologie Méditerranéenne*, *Palmyre*, *Nubia*, *Faras*, *Deir el-Bahari*, *Nea Paphos*, *Alexandrie*, *Corpus Vasorum Antiquorum*, *Corpus Signorum Imperii Romani*, *Tell Atrib*, *Etudes et Travaux*, *Saqqara*.

PORTUGAL

Instituto de Estudos Árabes e Islâmicos (Institute of Arab and Islamic Studies): Faculdade de Letras da Universidade de Lisboa, Alameda da Universidade, Cidade Universitária, 1600-214 Lisbon; tel. (21) 7920000; fax (21) 7960063; e-mail inst.cultarabe@fl.ul.pt; internet www.fl.ul.pt/unidades/institutos/instituto_arabe.htm; f. 1966; specializes in Arabic and Islamic studies; library of c. 3,000 vols and 26 periodicals; Dir Prof. Dr ANTÓNIO DIAS FARINHA.

RUSSIA

Institute of Asian and African Studies: ul. Mokhovaya 11, 125009 Moscow; tel. (495) 629-43-49; fax (495) 629-74-91; e-mail office@iaas.msu.ru; internet www.iaas.msu.ru; f. 1956 as Institute for Oriental Languages, renamed as above 1972; comprises three sections: philology, history, and social and economic studies, and research centres, incl. Centre for Arabic and Islamic Studies and Centre of Judaica; 250 mems; Pres. Prof. MIKHAIL S. MEYER.

Russian Centre for Strategic and International Studies: ul. Rozhdestvenka 12, 103753 Moscow; tel. (495) 924-51-50; fax (495) 425-62-37; f. 1991; research and training in international relations; Islamic studies, strategic and military studies, the Middle East and North Africa; Pres. VITALII VIACHESLAVOVICH NAUMKIN; Exec. Dir ALEKSANDR FILONIK.

SAUDI ARABIA

Arab Urban Development Institute: POB 6892, Riyadh 11452; tel. (1) 480-2555; fax (1) 480-2666; e-mail info@araburban.org; internet www.araburban.org; f. 1980; affiliated to the Arab Towns Org. (ATO); provides training, research, consultancy and documentation services to Arab cities and municipalities and mems of ATO for improving the Arab city and preserving its original character and Islamic cultural heritage; membership comprises more than 400 Arab cities and towns, representing 22 Arab states; library of 78,630 vols and 630 periodicals; Chair. ABDULLAH AL-ALI AL-NUAIM; publ. books and research papers.

Gulf Research Center: 19 Rayat al-Etihad St, POB 10501, Jeddah 21443; tel. (2) 651-8888; fax (2) 653-0953; e-mail info@grc.net; internet www.grc.net; f. 2000; conducts research into political, economic, social and security issues affecting the countries of the Cooperation Council for the Arab States of the Gulf (Gulf Cooperation Council) and the wider region of the Persian (Arabian) Gulf; organizes conferences and workshops; Chair. ABD AL-AZIZ SAGER; publ. *Gulf Yearbook, Gulf Monitor* (bi-monthly), books, research papers, policy analysis, studies, newsletters and bulletins; Chair. ABD AL-AZIZ SAGER.

Islamic Economics Research Centre: King Abd al-Aziz University, POB 80214, Jeddah 21589; tel. (2) 695-2751; fax (2) 640-3458; e-mail cn-crie@kaau.edu.sa; internet islamiccenter.kau.edu.sa; f. 1977; research into all aspects of Islamic economics; library of 35,000 vols and 400 periodicals; Dir Dr ABDULLAH QURBAN TURKISTANI.

King Faisal Center for Research and Islamic Studies: POB 51049, Riyadh 11543; tel. (1) 465-2255; fax (1) 465-9993; e-mail KFCRISInfo@kff.com; internet www.kfcris.com; f. 1983; part of King Faisal Foundation; seeks to preserve and promote Islamic heritage and to contribute to the advancement of Islamic societies by encouraging research and issue-related studies; library of c. 1m. vols, 3,500 periodicals, 25,000 MSS and 40,000 microfilms; Chair. Prince TURKI AL-FAISAL; publ. *Journal of Linguistic Studies, Islam and Contemporary World, Issues* (English) and books.

SINGAPORE

Middle East Institute: National University of Singapore, 469A Bukit Timah Rd, Tower Blk, Level 2, Singapore 259770; tel. 65162380; fax 64678714; e-mail contact.mei@nus.edu.sg; internet www.mei.nus.edu.sg; an autonomous research unit within the National University of Singapore; specializes in the study of the contemporary affairs of the Middle East; publishes commentaries, analytical articles and research papers; Chair. LEE TZU-YANG; Dir. Prof. MICHAEL C. HUDSON.

SLOVAKIA

Institute of Oriental Studies: Slovak Academy of Sciences, Klemensova 19, 813 64 Bratislava; tel. and fax (2) 5292-6326; e-mail kaoreast@savba.sk; internet www.orient.sav.sk; f. 1960; library of 15,837 vols and 55 periodicals; Dir Dr DUŠAN MAGDOLEN; publ. *Asian and African Studies* (2 a year).

SPAIN

Asociación Española de Orientalistas (Spanish Association of Orientalists): Universidad Autónoma de Madrid, Edificio E-VI, 28049 Madrid; tel. (91) 3974112; fax (91) 3974123; e-mail asociacion.orientalistas@uam.es; f. 1963; Pres. ALEJANDRO LORCA CORRONS; Co-ordinator JESUS GIL; publs include *Boletín* (annually).

Instituto Egipcio de Estudios Islámicos (Egyptian Institute of Islamic Studies): Francisco de Asís Méndez Casariego 1, 28002 Madrid; tel. (91) 5639468; fax (91) 5638640; e-mail secretaria@institutoegipcio.com; internet www.institutoegipcio.com; f. 1950; works on both academic and cultural levels in the field of Arabic, Mediterranean and Hispanic cultures through its publications (incl. journals and books on Hispano-Arabic studies), courses, lectures, conferences, art gallery and library; Dir Dr EL-SAYED IBRAHIM SOHEIM; publ. *Revista del Instituto Egipcio de Estudios Islámicos* (annually) and *Crónicas Azahar* (bi-annual).

Instituto de Lenguas y Culturas del Mediterráneo y Oriente Próximo (Institute of Languages and Cultures of the Mediterranean and Middle East): Albasanz 26–28, 28037 Madrid; tel. (91) 6022300; fax (91) 6022971; e-mail maite.ortega@cchs.csic.es; internet www.ilc.csic.es; f. 1985 as Instituto de Filología, following the amalgamation of four existing institutes (the Benito Arias Montano, Miguel Asin, Miguel de Cervantes and Antonio de Nebrija); renamed as above 2007; research groups incl. Medieval Jewish Culture, Arab Studies, Biblical Philology, Languages and Culture of the Ancient Near East; ; Dir JOSÉ ANTONIO BERENGUER; publ. *Sefarad* (review of Hebrew, Sephardic and Near Eastern Studies, 2 a year), *Al-Qantara* (review of Arab Studies, 2 a year), *Emerita* (review of Linguistics and Classical Philology, 2 a year) and books.

SWEDEN

Nordiska Afrikainstitutet (Nordic Africa Institute): POB 1703, 75147, Uppsala; tel. (18) 471 52 00; fax (18) 56-22-90; e-mail nai@nai.uu.se; internet www.nai.uu.se; f. 1962; research and documentation centre for contemporary African affairs, organizes seminars and publ. wide range of books and reports; library of 70,000 vols and 400 periodicals; Dir INA SOIRI; publ. *NAI Policy Notes, Africa Now, NAI Policy Dialogue, Discussion Papers, Annual Report, Current African Issues* and monographs.

SWITZERLAND

Centre d'Etudes et de Recherche sur le Monde Arabe et Méditerranéen (CERMAM) (Study and Research Centre for the Arab and Mediterranean World): CP 1342, 1211 Geneva 1; tel. (22) 7000470; fax (22) 7410822; e-mail info@cermam.org; internet www.cermam.org; f. 2000; Dir HASNI ABIDI.

Schweizerische Asiengesellschaft (Swiss Asia Society): Ostasiatisches Seminar der Universität Zürich, Zürichbergstr. 4, 8032 Zürich; tel. (1) 6343181; fax (1) 6344921; e-mail asiengesellschaft@oas.uzh.ch; internet www.sagw.ch; f. 1939; 175 mems; Pres. Prof. Dr ULRICH RUDOLPH; publ. *Asiatische Studien/Etudes Asiatiques* (4 a year), *Schweizer Asiatische Studien/Etudes Asiatiques Suisses* (Monographien und Studienhefte).

SYRIA

Institut Français du Proche Orient (IFPO): BP 344, Abou Roumaneh, Damascus; BP 3694, Jisr al-Abyad, Damascus; tel. (11) 3330214; fax (11) 3327887; e-mail secretariat@ifporient.org; e-mail f.khouryfehde@ifporient.org; internet www.ifporient.org; f. 2003 by merger of Institut Français d'Archéologie du Proche Orient, Institut Français d'Etudes Arabes de Damas and Centre d'Etudes et de Recherches sur le Moyen-Orient Contemporain; university research and documentation institution with sections also in Amman, Jordan, and Beirut, Lebanon; medieval and modern library of 80,000 vols, 500 periodicals and 400 microfilms; archaeological library of 45,500 vols and 100 periodicals; collection of 7,000 maps and 50,000 photographs; Dir FRANÇOIS BURGAT.

TAJIKISTAN

Institute of Oriental Studies of Tajikistan: Tajik Academy of Sciences, Parvin 8, Dushanbe; tel. (31) 24-30-10; internet www.ant.tj; Dir AKBAR TURSONOV.

TUNISIA

Institut des Belles Lettres Arabes: 12 rue Jamâa el-Haoua, 1008 Tunis BM; tel. (71) 560133; fax (71) 572683; e-mail ibla@gnet.tn; internet www.iblatunis.org; f. 1926; cultural centre; Dir JOHN MACWILLIAM; publ. *IBLA* (2 a year) and special studies.

Institut de Recherche sur le Maghreb Contemporain: 20 rue Muhammad Ali Tahar, Mutuelleville, 1002 Tunis; tel. (71) 796722; fax (71) 797376; e-mail direction@irmcmaghreb.org; internet www.irmcmaghreb.org; f. 1992; library of c. 21,000 vols and 87 periodicals (2006); Dir PIERRE-NOËL DENIEUIL.

TURKEY

British Institute of Archaeology at Ankara: Tahran Cad. 24, Kavaklidere, 06700 Ankara; tel. (312) 4275487; fax (312) 4280159; e-mail ggirdivan@biaatr.org; internet www.biaa.ac.uk; f. 1948; archaeological research and excavation; library of c. 42,000 vols; Dir Dr LUTGARDE VANDEPUT; publ. *Anatolian Studies* and *Anatolian Archaeology* (annually), *Occasional Publications* and *BIAA Monographs*.

Deutsches Archäologisches Institut (German Archaeological Institute): İnönü Cad. 10, 34437 İstanbul; tel. (212) 3937600; fax (212) 3937614; e-mail sekretariat@istanbul.dainst.org; internet www.dainst.org/abteilung.php?id=266; f. 1929; library of c. 52,000 vols and 270 periodicals; archive of photographs; Dirs Dr FELIX PIRSON, MARTIN BACHMANN; publs incl. *Istanbuler Mitteilungen* (annually) and *Istanbuler Forschungen* (annually).

Institut Français d'Etudes Anatoliennes (French Institute of Anatolian Studies): Palais de France, Nuru Ziya Sok. 22, PK 54, Beyoğlu, 80072 İstanbul; tel. (212) 2443327; fax (212) 2528091; e-mail ifea@ifea-istanbul.net; internet www.ifea-istanbul.net; f. 1930; 15 scientific mems; library of c. 30,000 vols and 800 periodicals; Dir Prof. Dr NORA ŞENI; publ. *Collection IFEA*, *Collection Varia Turcica*, *Collection Varia Anatolica*, *Anatolia Antiqua*, *Anatolia Moderna*.

Institute for Research on Economic Relations in Turkey, Europe and the Middle East: Faculty of Economics, University of İstanbul, 34452 Beyazit, İstanbul; tel. (212) 4400000; internet www.istanbul.edu.tr/iktisat; Dir Prof. Dr EROL MANISALI.

Nederlands Instituut in Turkije/Hollanda Araştırma Enstitüsü (Netherlands Institute in Turkey—NIT): PK 132, İstiklal Caddesi, Nur-i Ziya Sok. 5, Beyoğlu 34431, İstanbul; tel. (212) 2939283; fax (212) 2513846; e-mail nit@nit-istanbul.org; internet www.nit-istanbul.org; f. 1958; administered by the Netherlands Institute for the Near East, Leiden (see under The Netherlands); library of 15,000 vols; Dir Dr FOKKE A. GERRITSEN; publ. *Publications de l'Institut Historique et Archéologique Néerlandais de Stamboul (PIHANS)*, *Anatolica* (annually).

Österreichisches Kulturforum Istanbul: Köybaşi Cad. 44, 34464 Yeniköy, İstanbul; tel. (212) 2237843; fax (212) 2233469; e-mail istanbul-kf@bmeia.gv.at; internet www.austriakult.org.tr; Dir Consul CHRISTIAN BRUNMAYR.

Türk Dil Kurumu (Turkish Language Institute): Atatürk Bul. 217, 06680 Kavaklidere, Ankara; tel. (312) 4575200; fax (312) 4680783; e-mail bilgi@tdk.org.tr; internet www.tdk.gov.tr; f. 1932 as Türk Dili Tetkik Cemiyeti (Society for the Investigation of the Turkish Language), an independent body to carry out linguistic research and contribute to the natural development of the language; brought under govt control in 1983; 40 mems; library of 45,272 vols; Pres. Prof. Dr MUSTAFA S. KAÇALIN; publ. *Türk Dili* (monthly), *Türk Dili Araştirmalari Yilliği-Belleten* (annually).

Türk Kültürünü Araştirma Enstitüsü (Institute for the Study of Turkish Culture): 17 Sok. 38, Bahçelievler, 06490 Ankara; tel. (312) 2133100; fax (312) 2134135; e-mail bilgi@turkkulturu.org.tr; internet www.turkkulturu.org.tr; f. 1961; scholarly research into all aspects of Turkish culture; Dir Prof. Dr DURSUN YILDIRM; publ. *Türk Kültürü* (monthly), *Cultura Turcica* (annually), *Türk Kültürü Araştirmalari* (annually).

Türk Tarih Kurumu (Turkish Historical Society): Kizilay Sok. 1, 06100 Ankara; tel. (312) 3102368; fax (312) 3101698; e-mail bilgi@ttk.org.tr; internet www.ttk.org.tr; f. 1931; 40 mems; library of 228,685 vols; Pres. Prof. Dr MEHMET METIN HÜLAGÜ; publ. *Belleten* (3 a year), *Belgeler* (annually).

UNITED ARAB EMIRATES

Centre for Documentation and Research: Presidential Court, POB 5884, Abu Dhabi; tel. (2) 4183333; fax (2) 4445811; internet www.cdr.gov.ae; f. 1968; attached to UAE Presidential Court; research, data collection and analysis on aspects of the Persian (Arabian) Gulf region; Pres. Sheikh MANSOUR BIN ZAYED AL NAHYAN; Dir-Gen. ABDULLA EL-REYES; publ. *Liwa* (academic journal).

UNITED KINGDOM

British Institute for the Study of Iraq (Gertrude Bell Memorial): 10 Carlton House Terrace, London, SW1Y 5AH; tel. (20) 7969-5274; fax (20) 7969-5401; e-mail bisi@britac.ac.uk; internet www.britac.ac.uk/institutes/iraq; f. 1932 to promote, support and undertake research in Iraq and neighbouring countries; charitable trust, funded in part by the British Academy and also from its own endowment; covers archaeology, history, anthropology, geography, language and other related domains from the earliest times until the present; has mems in 40 countries; Pres. Dr JOHN CURTIS; publ. journal *Iraq* (journal, annually; circ. c. 700), as well as occasional monographs.

British Society for Middle Eastern Studies (BRISMES): Administrative Office, c/o Institute for Middle Eastern and Islamic Studies, University of Durham, Elvet Hill Rd, Durham, DH1 3TU; tel. (191) 334-5179; fax (191) 334-5661; e-mail a.l.haysey@lamp.ac.uk; internet www.brismes.ac.uk; f. 1973; Pres. ALASTAIR NEWTON; Exec. Dir Dr JAMES DICKINS; publs include *British Journal of Middle Eastern Studies* (3 a year).

Centre for the Advanced Study of the Arab World (CASAW): University of Edinburgh, 16–19 George Sq., Edinburgh, EH8 9LD; tel. (131) 650-6814; fax (131) 650-6804; e-mail admin@casaw.ac.uk; internet www.casaw.ed.ac.uk; f. 2006; govt-funded org.; established to advance national expertise on Arabic-speaking countries, in order to serve national strategic interests and provide knowledge to the public and private sectors; collaboration between the Universities of Edinburgh, Durham and Manchester; Jt Dirs Prof. ANOUSH EHTESHAMI, Prof. MARILYN BOOTH.

Centre of Islamic Studies (CIS): University of Cambridge, Faculty of Asian and Middle Eastern Studies, Sidgwick Ave, Cambridge, CB3 9DA; tel. (1223) 335103; fax (1223) 335110; e-mail cis@cis.cam.ac.uk; internet www.cis.cam.ac.uk; f. 1960; conducts research to develop critical awareness of the role of Islam in wider society; research and outreach programmes; Dir Prof. YASIR SULEIMAN.

Council for Arab-British Understanding (CAABU): Arab-British Centre, 1 Gough Sq., London, EC4A 3DE; tel. (20) 7832-1321; fax (20) 7832-1329; e-mail info@caabu.org; internet www.caabu.org; f. 1967; aims to promote understanding between Arab nations and the United Kingdom through four principal programmes: parliamentary, educational, working with the media and organizing events; nearly 1,000 mems; Dir CHRIS DOYLE.

Egypt Exploration Society: 3 Doughty Mews, London, WC1N 2PG; tel. (20) 7242-1880; fax (20) 7404-6118; e-mail contact@ees.ac.uk; internet www.ees.ac.uk; f. 1882; library of 22,000 vols; c. 2,500 mems; Dir Dr CHRIS NAUNTON; publs include *Bulletin of the Egypt Exploration Society*, *Excavation Memoirs*, *Archaeological Survey*, *Graeco-Roman Memoirs*, *Journal of Egyptian Archaeology*, *Texts from Excavations*, *Egyptian Archaeology*.

Institute of Arab and Islamic Studies: University of Exeter, Stocker Rd, Exeter, EX4 4ND; tel. (1392) 725250; fax (1392) 264035; e-mail iais-info@ex.ac.uk; internet www.ex.ac.uk/iais; f. 1999 by amalgamation of Centre for Arab Gulf Studies, Dept of Middle Eastern Studies and Centre for Mediterranean Studies; multidisciplinary centre for Arab and Islamic studies; incorporates the Centre for Gulf Studies, the Centre for Kurdish Studies, the European Centre for Palestine Studies and the Centre for Persian and Iranian Studies; extensive library and documentation unit; Dir Prof. GARETH STANSFIELD; publ. *Journal of Arabian Studies: Arabia, the Gulf, and the Red Sea* (2 a year).

Institute for Iranian Studies: School of History, University of St Andrews, St Katharine's Lodge, The Scores, St Andrews, KY16 9AL; tel. (1334) 463027; fax (1334) 462927; e-mail iran@st-andrews.ac.uk; internet www.st-andrews.ac.uk/~iranian; f. 2006 to promote research and teaching in all aspects of Iranian civilization and culture; library of 12,000 Persian-language books; Dir Prof. ALI M. ANSARI.

Institute of Ismaili Studies: 210 Euston Rd, London, NW1 2DA; tel. (20) 7756-2700; fax (20) 7756-2740; e-mail info@iis.ac.uk; internet www.iis.ac.uk; f. 1977 by HH the Aga Khan; promotes scholarship and learning on Islam, with an emphasis on Shi'ism in general and its Ismaili *tariqah* in particular, and a better understanding of their relationship with other faiths and societies; it also encourages an interdisciplinary approach to the study of Islamic history and thought; library of printed and audiovisual materials and MSS; Dir Dr FARHAD DAFTARY.

Institute for Middle Eastern and Islamic Studies: School of Government and International Affairs, University of Durham, The Al-Qasimi Bldg, Elvet Hill Rd, Durham, DH1 3TU; tel. (191) 334-5656; fax (191) 334-5661; e-mail james.piscatori@durham.ac.uk; internet www.dur.ac.uk/sgia/imeis; f. 1962; teaches postgraduate programmes in political economy and international relations of the Middle East and North Africa, Middle Eastern and Islamic studies; organizes seminars, lectures and conferences; incorporates the Centre for Iranian Studies (f. 1999 to promote research and debate on Iran in the UK); documentation unit (f. 1970; now part of main university library) monitors economic, social and political devts in the region with some 200,000 documents; publ. programme of research monographs, occasional papers and bibliographies; Head of School Prof. JAMES PISCATORI; publ. *Middle East Papers* (annually).

The Islamic Cultural Centre and The London Central Mosque: 146 Park Rd, London, NW8 7RG; tel. (20) 7724-3363; fax (20) 7724-0493; e-mail info@iccuk.org; internet www.iccuk.org; f. 1944 to provide information and guidance on Islam and Islamic culture and to provide facilities for Muslims residing in Great Britain; library of 20,000 vols in Arabic, English, Urdu and Persian; Dir-Gen. Dr AHMAD AL-DUBAYAN.

Islamic and Middle Eastern Studies (IMES): University of Edinburgh, 19 George Sq., Edinburgh, EH8 9LD; tel. (131) 650-4182; fax (131) 650-6804; e-mail imes@ed.ac.uk; internet www.imes.ed.ac.uk; incorporates the Prince Alwaleed bin Talal Centre for the Study of Islam in the Contemporary World (Dir Prof. HUGH GODDARD); Iraq Chair. of Arabic and Islamic Studies Prof. MARILYN BOOTH.

London School of Jewish Studies (LSJS): Schaller House, 44A Albert Rd, London, NW4 2SJ; tel. (20) 8203-6427; fax (20) 8203-6420; e-mail info@lsjs.ac.uk; internet www.lsjs.ac.uk; Chief Exec. JASON MARANTZ.

Maghreb Studies Association: c/o The Executive Secretary, MOHAMED BEN-MADANI, 45 Burton St, London, WC1H 9AL; tel. and fax (20) 7388-1840; fax (20) 73881840; e-mail ben-madani@maghreb-studies-association.co.uk; internet www.maghreb-studies-association.co.uk; f. 1981 to promote the study of and interest in the Maghreb; independent; organizes lectures and conferences; Chair. Prof. HÉDI BOURAOUÏ; issues quarterly journal.

Middle East Association: Bury House, 33 Bury St, London, SW1Y 6AX; tel. (20) 7839-2137; fax (20) 7839-6121; e-mail info@the-mea.co.uk; internet www.the-mea.co.uk; f. 1961; independent non-profit asscn for firms actively promoting British trade with, and investment in, 20 Arab countries, as well as Iran, Turkey and Afghanistan; 400 mems; Dir-Gen. RANALD SPIERS; publ. *Opportunity Middle East* (quarterly), *MEA Digest*.

Middle East Centre: St Antony's College, 68 Woodstock Rd, Oxford, OX2 6JF; tel. (1865) 284780; fax (1865) 274529; e-mail mec@sant.ox.ac.uk; internet www.sant.ox.ac.uk/mec; f. 1957; Dir Dr WALTER ARMBRUST; library of 34,000 vols and archive of private papers and photographs; publ. St Antony's Middle East monographs.

The Muslim Institute: 109 Fulham Palace Rd, London, W6 8JA; tel. (20) 8563-1995; fax (20) 8563-1993; e-mail info@musliminstitute.com; internet www.musliminstitute.com; f. 1974; research and teaching programmes, academic and current affairs seminars; library of 6,000 vols; 800 mems; supplies publs of the Muslim Parliament of Great Britain; Dir MERRYL WYN DAVIES.

Oxford Centre for Hebrew and Jewish Studies: Yarnton Manor, Yarnton, Kidlington, Oxford, OX5 1PY; tel. (1865) 377946; fax (1865) 375079; e-mail enquiries@ochjs.ac.uk; internet www.ochjs.ac.uk; f. 1972; Pres. DAVID ARIEL; publ. *Journal of Jewish Studies*.

Oxford Centre for Islamic Studies: George St, Oxford, OX1 2AR; tel. (1865) 278730; fax (1865) 248942; e-mail islamic.studies@oxcis.ac.uk; internet www.oxcis.ac.uk; f. 1985; Dir Dr FARHAN AHMAD NIZAMI; publ. *Journal of Islamic Studies* (3 a year).

Palestine Exploration Fund: 2 Hinde Mews, Marylebone Lane, London, W1U 2AA; tel. (20) 7935-5379; fax (20) 7486-7438; e-mail execsec@pef.org.uk; internet www.pef.org.uk; f. 1865; the oldest organization in the world for the study of the archaeology, ancient history and geography of the southern Levant; extensive library; collections incl. archaeological, archival and photographic items; holds regular free public lectures at the British Museum; 926 subscribers; Chair. JOHN R. BARTLETT; Pres. JONATHAN N. TUBB; publ. *PEQ: The Palestine Exploration Quarterly* (3 a year), as well as annuals, monographs and photographic books.

Royal Asiatic Society of Great Britain and Ireland: 14 Stephenson Way, London, NW1 2HD; tel. (20) 7388-4539; fax (20) 7391-9429; e-mail info@royalasiaticsociety.org; internet www.royalasiaticsociety.org; f. 1823 for the study of the history, sociology, institutions, customs, languages and art of Asia; c. 700 mems; c. 700 subscribing libraries; library of 80,000 vols, as well as MSS, paintings, prints, drawings, photographs, maps and coins; affiliated societies in various Asian cities; Pres. Prof. P. ROBB; Dir ALISON OHTA; publ. *Journal*, *Storey Bibliography of Persian Literature* and monographs.

Royal Society for Asian Affairs: 25 Eccleston Place, London, SW1W 9NF; tel. (20) 7235-5122; e-mail info@rsaa.org.uk; internet www.rsaa.org.uk; f. 1901; 1,200 mems with knowledge of the past or present Near, Middle and Far East and Central Asia; library of c. 5,500 vols; Pres. Lord DAVIES; Chair. of Council Sir DAVID JOHN; publ. journal *Asian Affairs* (3 a year).

The Saudi-British Society: The Saudi-British Society, 1 Gough Sq., London, EC4A 3DE; tel. (20) 7373-8414; fax (20) 7835-2088; e-mail secretary@saudibritishsociety.org.uk; internet www.saudibritishsociety.org.uk; f. 1987; non-political; Chair. Sir SHERARD COWPER-COLES.

School of Oriental and African Studies, University of London: Thornhaugh St, Russell Sq., London, WC1H 0XG; tel. (20) 7637-2388; fax (20) 7436-3844; e-mail postmaster@soas.ac.uk; internet www.soas.ac.uk; f. 1916; library of c. 1.2m. vols and 2,750 MSS; Dir and Principal Prof. PAUL WEBLEY; publ. *Bulletin of the School of Oriental and African Studies* (3 a year), *The Journal of African Law* (2 a year).

Society for Libyan Studies: c/o The Institute of Archaeology, 31–34 Gordon Sq., London, WC1H 0PY; e-mail GenSec@societyforlibyanstudies.org; internet www.societyforlibyanstudies.org; f. 1969; promotes research into Libyan archaeology, history and linguistics; Chair. ROBERT MORKOT; Pres. S. E. C. WALKER; publ. journal *Libyan Studies* (annually).

UNITED STATES OF AMERICA

American Institute for Maghrib Studies (AIMS): Center for Middle Eastern Studies, 845 N. Park Ave, Marshall Bldg, Room 470, POB 210158-B Tucson, AZ 85721-0158; tel. (520) 626-6498; fax (520) 621-9257; e-mail aims@aimsnorthafrica.org; internet aimsnorthafrica.org; f. 1984; promotes systematic study of North Africa among interested scholars, specialists, students and others concerned with the region; Pres. JOHN ENTELIS; Exec. Dir KERRY ADAMS; publ. *The Journal of North African Studies* (quarterly), *Newsletter* (2 a year).

America-Mideast Educational and Training Services, Inc (AMIDEAST): Suite 1100, 1730 M St, NW, Washington, DC 20036-4505; tel. (202) 776-9600; fax (202) 776-7000; e-mail inquiries@amideast.org; internet www.amideast.org; f. 1951; private, non-profit org. that strengthens mutual understanding and co-operation between Americans and the peoples of the Middle East and North Africa through programmes of education, development and information, language training and academic exchange; headquarters in Washington, DC, with field offices in Egypt, Iraq, Jordan, Kuwait, Lebanon, Morocco, Oman, the Palestinian territories, Qatar, Syria, Tunisia, the United Arab Emirates and Yemen; Pres. and CEO THEODORE H. KATTOUF; publs include *Advising Quarterly* and *AMIDEAST News* (both quarterly).

American Oriental Society: Harlan Hatcher Graduate Library, University of Michigan, Ann Arbor, MI 48109-1205; tel. (734) 647-4760; e-mail jrodgers@umich.edu; internet www.umich.edu/~aos; f. 1842; research into Oriental civilizations and Asian languages and literature; 1,350 mems; library of 23,500 vols; Pres. ROBERT JOE CUTTER; publ. *Journal of the American Oriental Society* (quarterly), monograph series, essay series and offprint series.

American Schools of Oriental Research: Boston University, 656 Beacon St, 5th Floor, Boston, MA 02215-2010; tel. (617) 353-6570; fax (617) 353-6575; e-mail asor@bu.edu; internet www.asor.org; f. 1900; 1,500 mems; supports activities of independent archaeological institutions abroad: The Albright Institute of Archaeological Research, Jerusalem, Israel, the American Center of Oriental Research in Amman, Jordan, and the Cyprus American Archaeological Research Institute in Nicosia, Cyprus; Pres. TIMOTHY P. HARRISON; Exec. Dir ANDREW G. VAUGHN; publ. *Newsletter* (quarterly), *Near Eastern Archaeology* (quarterly), *Bulletin* (biannually), *Journal of Cuneiform Studies* (annually), *Annual*.

Center for Contemporary Arab Studies: 241 Intercultural Center, Georgetown University, 37th & O Sts, NW, Washington, DC 20057-1020; tel. (202) 687-5793; fax (202) 687-7001; e-mail ccasinfo@georgetown.edu; internet ccas.georgetown.edu; f. 1975; active in postgraduate education, public affairs, outreach to pre-college educators; Dir OSAMA ABI-MERSHED; publs on social, economic, political, cultural and development aspects of Arab world, newsletter (tri-annual) and occasional papers.

Center for Middle Eastern and North African Studies: University of Michigan, 1080 S University Ave, Suite 3603, Ann Arbor, MI 48109-1106; tel. (734) 764-0350; fax (734) 936-0996; e-mail cmenas@umich.edu; internet www.ii.umich.edu; f. 1961; research into the ancient, medieval and modern cultures of the modern Middle East and North Africa, Near Eastern languages and literature; library includes 340,000 vols on Middle East and North Africa; Dir GOTTFRIED HAGEN; publ. *Newsletter* (quarterly).

Center for Middle Eastern Studies: University of Chicago, 5828 S University Ave, Chicago, IL 60637; tel. (773) 702-8297; fax (773) 702-2587; e-mail cmes@uchicago.edu; internet www.cmes.uchicago.edu; f. 1965; research into medieval and modern cultures of North Africa and Western and Central Asia; Dir FRED M. DONNER.

Center for Middle Eastern Studies (CMES): Harvard University, 38 Kirkland St, Cambridge, MA 02138; tel. (617) 495-4055; fax (617) 496-8584; e-mail cmes@fas.harvard.edu; internet cmes.hmdc.harvard.edu; f. 1954; research on Middle Eastern subjects and Islamic studies; Dir BABER JOHANSEN; publ. *Middle East Monograph Series*, *Harvard Middle Eastern and Islamic Review*.

Center for Middle Eastern Studies: The University of Texas at Austin, West Mall Bldg 6/102 (F9400), Austin, TX 78712-0527; tel. (512) 471-3881; fax (512) 471-7834; e-mail dmes@uts.cc.utexas.edu; internet www.utexas.edu/cola/depts/mes/center/cmes.php; f. 1960; comprehensive interdisciplinary programme in area studies and languages of the Middle East, with some 50 affiliated faculties; offers graduate and undergraduate degrees in Middle Eastern studies, incl. jt degree programmes with Business, Public Affairs, Communications, the School of Information, and Law; publ. books on the modern

Middle East and translations of contemporary fiction and memoirs; Dir Dr KAMRAN AGHAIE.

Department of Near Eastern Languages and Cultures: Indiana University, Goodbody Hall 219, 1011 E Third St, Bloomington, IN 47405-7005; tel. (812) 855-5993; fax (812) 855-7841; e-mail nelc@indiana.edu; internet www.indiana.edu/~nelc; graduate and undergraduate courses in Islamic studies, Middle Eastern literatures, religions, and cultures and civilizations, Byzantine studies, and Arabic, Turkish and Persian language and linguistics; Chair. Prof. ASMA AFSARUDDIN.

Gustave E. von Grunebaum Center for Near Eastern Studies: University of California, 10286 Bunche Hall, Los Angeles, CA 90095-1480; tel. (310) 825-1181; fax (310) 206-2406; e-mail cnes@international.ucla.edu; internet www.isop.ucla.edu/cnes; f. 1957; social sciences, culture and language studies of the Near East since the rise of Islam; library of more than 500,000 vols and 10,000 MSS in Arabic, Armenian, Hebrew, Persian and Turkish; annual publication of series of colloquia and of Giorgio Levi Della Vida Award Conference in Islamic Studies vols; 100 associated faculty mems; Dir SUSAN SLYOMOVICS; publ. monographs, conference papers, working papers, etc.

Hoover Institution on War, Revolution and Peace: Stanford University, Stanford, CA 94305-6010; tel. (650) 723-1454; fax (650) 723-1687; e-mail lmaune@hoover.stanford.edu; internet www.hoover.org; f. 1919; extensive library and archives on 20th century history, incl. important collection of the Middle East and North Africa; Chair. HERBERT M. DWIGHT; publ. *Hoover Digest*, *Policy Review* monographs, books, etc.

Institute for the Transregional Study of the Contemporary Middle East, North Africa and Central Asia (TRI): Princeton University, 104 Jones Hall, Princeton, NJ 08544; tel. (609) 258-2178; fax (609) 258-0204; e-mail tri@princeton.edu; internet www.princeton.edu/transregional; f. 1994; comparative study and research focused on development, economic, social and political issues, democratization and human rights in the Middle East, North Africa and Central Asia regions; Dir Prof. BERNARD HAYKEL.

Middle East Center: University of Utah, Orson Spencer Hall, 260 South Central Campus Dr., Rm 153, Salt Lake City, UT 84112; tel. (801) 581-6181; fax (801) 581-6183; e-mail kellie.parker@utah.edu; internet www.mec.utah.edu; f. 1960; co-ordinates programme in Middle East languages and area studies in 12 academic depts; focuses on study of Arabic, Hebrew, Persian, Turkish, anthropology, history and political science; annual summer programme for Utah educators in the Middle East; library of 150,000 vols; Dirs ROBERT GOLDBERG, KIRK JOWERS.

Middle East Forum: Suite 1050, 1500 Walnut St, Philadelphia, PA 19102; tel. (215) 546-5406; fax (215) 546-5409; e-mail info@meforum.org; internet www.meforum.org; f. 1994; Dir DANIEL PIPES; Dir EFRAIM KARSH; publ. *Middle East Quarterly*.

Middle East Institute: 1761 N St, NW, Washington, DC 20036-2882; tel. (202) 785-1141; fax (202) 331-8861; e-mail information@mei.edu; internet www.mideasti.org; f. 1946; non-profit org. that promotes understanding of the Middle East, North Africa, Central Asia and the Caucasus; sponsors classes in Arabic, Hebrew, Persian and Turkish; convenes political and economic programmes and an annual conference; houses scholars and experts in a public policy centre; George Camp Keiser Library houses 25,000 vols and more than 300 periodicals; 1,300 mems; Pres. WENDY J. CHAMBERLIN; publ. *Middle East Journal* (quarterly).

The Middle East Institute: Columbia University, 606 W 122th St, Knox Hall, 3rd Floor, MC 9640, New York, NY 10027; tel. (212) 854-2584; fax (212) 854-1413; e-mail mei@columbia.edu; internet www.mei.columbia.edu; f. 1954; graduate training programme on the modern Middle East for students seeking professional careers as regional specialists, research into problems of economics, govt, law and international relations of the Middle East countries, and their languages and history; library of more than 150,000 vols in Middle East vernaculars and equally rich in Western languages, incl. Russian; Dir Prof. PETER J. AWN.

Middle East Policy Council: Suite 512, 1730 M St, NW, Washington, DC 20036; tel. (202) 296-6767; fax (202) 296-5791; e-mail info@mepc.org; internet mepc.org; f. 1981 to expand public discussion and understanding of issues affecting US policy in the Middle East; Chair. Dr OMAR KADER; publ. *Middle East Policy* (quarterly).

Middle East Studies Association of North America: University of Arizona, 1219 N Santa Rita Ave, Tucson, AZ 85721; tel. (520) 621-5850; fax (520) 626-9095; e-mail SBS-MESA@email.arizona.edu; internet www.mesana.org; f. 1966 to promote high standards of scholarship and instruction in Middle East studies, to facilitate communication among scholars through meetings and publications, and to foster co-operation among persons and organizations concerned with the scholarly study of the Middle East since the rise of Islam; more than 2,700 mems; Pres. FRED M. DONNER; publ. *International Journal of Middle East Studies* (quarterly), *Bulletin* (bi-annual), *Newsletter* (quarterly)*The Review of Middle East Studies* (2 a year).

Middle East Studies Center: East Hall 322, Portland State University, POB 751, Portland, OR 97207; tel. (503) 725-4074; fax (503) 725-5320; e-mail damisj@pdx.edu; internet oia.pdx.edu/mesc; f. 1959; Middle East language and area studies, Arabic, Hebrew, Persian and Turkish languages and literatures; contemporary Turkish studies and Islamic studies programme; area classes in history, political science, geography, anthropology and sociology; Dir JIM GREHAN.

Near East Foundation: 430–432 Crouse Hinds Hall, 900 S. Crouse Ave, Syracuse, NY 13244-2130; tel. (315) 428-8670; e-mail info@neareast.org; internet www.neareast.org; f. 1915; provides and promotes environment and natural resource management; agriculture and rural development; food security; urban development and rehabilitation; microfinance; community-based and bank-guaranteed lending; employment and job creation; population-, health- and family-planning; adult literacy and education; women's participation; in Jordan, Lebanon, the West Bank and Gaza, Egypt, Sudan, Ethiopia, Djibouti, Morocco and Mali; Chair. SHANT MARDIROSSIAN; Pres. Dr CHARLES BENJAMIN; publ. annual report online, printed brochures periodically.

Oriental Institute: University of Chicago, 1155 E 58th St, Chicago, IL 60637; tel. (773) 702-9514; fax (773) 702-9853; e-mail oi-administration@uchicago.edu; internet oi.uchicago.edu; f. 1919; principally concerned with cultures and languages of the ancient Near East; extensive museum; Dir GIL STEIN; extensive publication programme, incl. scholarly monographs, museum catalogues; also publ. *News and Notes* (bi-monthly).

Prince Alwaleed Bin Talal Center for Muslim-Christian Understanding (ACMCU): Georgetown University, Intercultural Center (ICC), Suite 260, 3700 O St, NW, Washington, DC 20057; tel. (202) 687-8375; fax (202) 687-8376; e-mail cmcu@georgetown.edu; internet cmcu.georgetown.edu; f. 1933 to improve relations between the Muslim world and the West, as well as between Islam and Christianity; renamed as above in 2005, following a substantial investment by HRH Prince Alwaleed bin Talal; organizes academic programmes and publ. books and articles; Dir Prof. JOHN L. ESPOSITO; Assoc. Dir JONATHAN A. C. BROWN.

Program in Near Eastern Studies: Princeton University, 110 Jones Hall, Princeton, NJ 08544-1008; tel. (609) 258-4272; fax (609) 258-9055; e-mail nep@princeton.edu; internet www.princeton.edu/nep; f. 1947; research into all aspects of the modern Near East and North Africa; library of 340,000 vols; Dir M. ŞÜKRÜ HANIOĞLU; publ. *Princeton Studies on the Near East* (irregular), *Princeton Papers: Inter-disciplinary Journal of Middle Eastern Studies* (semi-annual).

Semitic Museum of Harvard University: 6 Divinity Ave, Cambridge, MA 02138; tel. (617) 495-4631; fax (617) 496-8904; e-mail semiticm@fas.harvard.edu; internet www.fas.harvard.edu/~semitic; f. 1889; sponsors exploration and research in Western Asia; archaeological and ethnographic collections from ancient Near East; research collections open by appointment, museum open free to general public; Dir LAWRENCE E. STAGER.

Washington Institute for Near East Policy: Suite 1050, 1828 L St, NW, Washington, DC 20036; tel. (202) 452-0650; fax (202) 223-5364; e-mail info@washingtoninstitute.org; internet www.washingtoninstitute.org; f. 1985; promotes scholarly research and informed debate on the Middle East; Exec. Dir ROBERT SATLOFF; publs include *Analytical Reports Series*, *Conference Proceedings*, *Policy Focus Series*, *Policy Paper Series*, also monographs.

VATICAN CITY

Pontificio Istituto Orientale (Pontifical Oriental Institute): 7 Piazza Santa Maria Maggiore, 00185 Rome; tel. (06) 44741-7122; fax (06) 44741-7175; e-mail biblioteca@pio.urbe.it; internet www.pio.urbe.it; f. 1917; library of 181,000 vols; Rector Rev. SUNNY THOMAS KOKKARAVALAYIL; publ. *Orientalia Christiana Periodica*, *Orientalia Christiana Analecta*, *Concilium Florentinum (Documenta et Scriptores)*, *Anaphorae Syriacae*, *Kanonika*.

SELECT BIBLIOGRAPHY (BOOKS)

Books on the Middle East

(See also bibliographies at end of relevant chapters in Part Two.)

Abir, Mordechai. *Oil, Power and Politics: Conflict in Arabia, The Red Sea and The Gulf*. London, Frank Cass, 1974.

Abu-Rabi, Ibrahim M. *Contemporary Arab Thought: Studies in Post-1967 Arab Intellectual History*. London, Pluto Press, 2003.

Acharya, Amitar. *US Military Strategy in the Gulf*. London, Routledge, 1989.

Addas, Claude. *Quest for the Red Sulphur: The Life of Ibn 'Arabi*. Cambridge, Islamic Texts Society, 1995.

Adelson, Roger. *London and the Invention of the Middle East: Money, Power and War 1902–1922*. New Haven, CT, Yale University Press, 1995.

Adib-Moghaddam, Arshin. *The International Politics of the Persian Gulf: A Cultural Genealogy*. Abingdon, Routledge, 2006.

On the Arab Revolts and the Iranian Revolution: Power and Resistance Today. New York, Bloomsbury, 2013.

Afkhami, Mahnaz. *Faith and Freedom: Women's Human Rights in the Muslim World*. London, I. B. Tauris, 1996.

Ahmadi, Koroush. *Islands and International Politics in the Persian Gulf: Abu Musa and Tunbs in Strategic Context*. Abingdon, Routledge, 2008.

Ahmed, Akbar S. *Discovering Islam: Making Sense of Muslim History and Society*. London, Routledge, 1989.

Journey into Islam: The Crisis of Globalization. Washington, DC, Brookings Institution Press, 2007.

Ahmed, Akbar S., and Donnan, Hastings (Eds). *Islam, Globalization and Postmodernity*. London, Routledge, 1994.

Ajami, Fouad. *The Arab Predicament: Arab Political Thought and Practice since 1967*. Cambridge, Cambridge University Press, 2nd edn, 1992.

Akbarzadeh, Shahram, and MacQueen, Benjamin (Eds). *Islam and Human Rights in Practice: Perspectives Across the Ummah*. Abingdon, Routledge, 2008.

Akbarzadeh, Shahram, *et al* (Eds). *American Democracy Promotion in the Changing Middle East: From Bush to Obama*. Abingdon, Routledge, 2013.

Ali, Tariq. *The Clash of Fundamentalisms: Crusades, Jihads and Modernity*. London, Verso, 2002.

Allain, Jean. *International Law in the Middle East: Closer to Power Than Justice*. Aldershot, Ashgate, 2004.

Allan, Tony. *The Middle East Water Question: Hydropolitics and the Global Economy*. London, I. B. Tauris, 2001.

Allin, Dana H., and Simon, Steven. *The Sixth Crisis: Iran, Israel, America and the Rumors of War*. New York, Oxford University Press, 2010.

Alsharek, A., Springborg, R., and Stewart, S. (Eds). *Popular Culture and Political Identity in the Arab Gulf States*. London, Saqi Books, 2008.

Amir-Moezzi, Ali. *Spirituality and Islam: Belief and Practice in Shi'ism*. London, I. B. Tauris, 2008.

Andersen, Roy R., Seibert, Robert F., and Wagner, Jon G. *Politics and Change in the Middle East: Sources of Conflict and Accommodation*. Upper Saddle River, NJ, Prentice Hall, 2007.

Angrist, Michele Penner. *Party Building in the Modern Middle East*. Seattle, WA, University of Washington Press, 2006.

Aruri, Naseer Hasan, and Shuraydi, Mohammad A. (Eds). *Revising Culture, Reinventing Peace: The Influence of Edward W. Said*. Interlink Publishing Group, 2000.

Aruru, Naseer Hasan (Ed.). *Palestinian Refugees: The Right of Return*. London, Pluto Press, 2001.

Aslan, Reza. *No God but God: The Origins, Evolution and Future of Islam*. London, Arrow Books, revised edn, 2006.

Atwan, Abdel Bari. *The Secret History of al Qaeda*. Berkeley, CA, University of California Press, revised edn, 2008.

Ayoob, M. (Ed.). *The Middle East in World Politics*. London, Croom Helm, 1981.

Ayubi, Nazih N. *Over-Stating the Arab State: Politics and Society in the Middle East*. London, I. B. Tauris, 1995.

Azzam, Salem (Ed.). *Islam and Contemporary Society: Islamic Council of Europe*. London, Longman, 1982.

Bahgat, Gawdat. *Proliferation of Nuclear Weapons in the Middle East*. Gainsville, FL, University Press of Florida, 2009.

Bailey, Sydney. *Four Arab–Israeli Wars and the Peace Process*. London, Macmillan, 1990.

al-Barghouti, Tamim. *The Umma and the Dawla: The Nation State and the Arab Middle East*. London, Pluto Press, 2008.

Barkey, Henri. *The Politics of Economic Reform in the Middle East*. London, Macmillan, 1993.

Barnaby, Frank. *The Invisible Bomb: The Nuclear Arms Race in the Middle East*. London, I. B. Tauris, 1989.

Bauer, Alain, and Raufer, Xavier. *L'énigme Al-Qaida*. Paris, Éditions Jean-Claude Lattès, 2005.

Bazoobandi, Sara. *Political Economy of the Gulf Sovereign Wealth Funds: A Case Study of Iran, Kuwait, Saudi Arabia and the United Arab Emirates*. Abingdon, Routledge, 2013.

Beinin, Joel. *Workers and Peasants in the Modern Middle East*. Cambridge University Press, 2001.

Beinin, Joel, and Stork, Joe (Eds). *Political Islam: Essays from Middle East Report*. Berkeley, CA, University of California Press, 1996.

Bell, J. Bowyer. *The Long War, Israel and the Arabs since 1946*. Englewood Cliffs, NJ, 1969.

Ben-Ami, Shlomo. *Scars of War, Wounds of Peace: The Israeli–Arab Tragedy*. London, Phoenix Press, revised edn, 2006.

Ben-Porat, Guy (Ed.). *The Failure of the Middle East Peace Process?* London, Macmillan, 2008.

Ben-Zvi, Abraham. *Decade of Transition: Eisenhower, Kennedy, and the Origins of the American-Israeli Alliance*. New York, Columbia University Press, 1999.

Berberoglu, Berch (Ed.). *Power and Stability in the Middle East*. London, Zed Books, 1989.

Bergen, Peter, and Tiedemann, Katherine (Eds). *Negotiating the Borders Between Terror, Politics and Religion*. New York, Oxford University Press, 2013.

Berry, Mike, and Philo, Greg. *Israel and Palestine: Competing Histories*. London, Pluto Press, 2006.

Bianquis, Th., Bosworth, C. E., Donzel, E. van, and Heinrichs, W. P. (Eds). *Encyclopaedia of Islam*. 10 vols. Leiden, Brill Academic Publishers, 2000.

Bidwell, Robin (Ed.). *Dictionary of Modern Arab History*. London, Kegan Paul International, 1998.

Bill, J., and Springborg, R. *Politics in the Middle East*. London, HarperCollins, 5th edn, 2000.

Bin Huwaidin, Mohamed. *China's Relations with Arabia and the Gulf, 1949–1999*. London, Routledge, 2002.

Binder, Leonard. *The Ideological Revolution in the Middle East*. Melbourne, FL, Krieger Publishing, 1979.

Islamic Liberalism: A Critique of Development Ideologies. Chicago, IL, Chicago University Press, 1988.

Biswas, Asit K. *et al*. *Core and Periphery: A Comprehensive Approach to Middle Eastern Water*. Oxford University Press, 1998.

Bonine, Michael E. (Ed.). *Population, Poverty and Politics in Middle Eastern Cities*. Gainesville, FL, University Press of Florida, 1997.

Bonner, Michael. *Jihad in Islamic History: Doctrines and Practice*. Princeton, NJ, Princeton University Press, 2006.

Brachman, Jarret M. *Global Jihadism: Theory and Practice*. Abingdon, Routledge, 2008.

Bradley, John R. *After the Arab Spring: How Islamists Hijacked the Middle East Revolts*. Basingstoke, Palgrave Macmillan, 2012.

Brandell, Inga. (Ed.). *State Frontiers: Borders and Boundaries in the Middle East*. London, I. B. Tauris, 2006.

Bregman, Ahron (Ed.). *Warfare in the Middle East since 1945*. Aldershot, Ashgate, 2008.

Bregman, Ahron, and El-Tahri, Jihan. *The Fifty Years' War: Israel and the Arabs*. London, Penguin and BBC Books, 1998.

Brenchley, Frank. *Britain and the Middle East: An Economic History, 1945–1987*. London, Lester Crook Academic Publishing, 1989.

Breslauer, George W. (Ed.). *Soviet Strategy in the Middle East*. London, Routledge, 1989.

Browers, Michaelle L. *Political Ideology in the Arab World: Accommodation and Transformation*. Cambridge University Press, 2009.

Brown, Daniel. *Rethinking Tradition in Modern Islamic Thought*. Cambridge University Press, 1996.

Brown, L. Carl. *Religion and State: The Muslim Approach to Politics*. New York, Columbia University Press, 2000.

Diplomacy in the Middle East. London, I. B. Tauris, 2001.

Brown, Nathan, and Shahin, Emad el-Din. (Eds). *The Struggle over Democracy in the Middle East: Regional Politics and External Policies*. Abingdon, Routledge, 2009.

Buchanan, Andrew S. *Peace with Justice: A History of the Israeli-Palestinian Declaration of Principles on Interim Self-Government Arrangements*. Basingstoke, St Martin's Press, 2000.

Bulloch, John. *The Making of a War: The Middle East from 1967–1973*. London, Longman, 1974.

Bulloch, John, and Morris, Harvey. *The Gulf War*. London, Methuen, 1990.

Saddam's War. London, Faber and Faber, 1991.

Burgat, François. *Face to Face with Political Islam*. London, I. B. Tauris, 1997.

Islamism in the Shadow of al-Qaeda. Austin, TX, University of Texas Press, 2008.

Burke, Edmond. *Struggle for Survival in the Modern Middle East*. London, I. B. Tauris, 1994.

Burke, Jason. *Al-Qaeda: The True Story of Radical Islam*. London, Penguin, 2004.

Butt, Gerald. *A Rock and a Hard Place: Origins of Arab-Western Conflict in the Middle East*. London, HarperCollins, 1994.

The Arabs: Myth and Reality. London, I. B. Tauris, 1998.

Butterworth, Charles E., and Zartman, I. William (Eds). *Between the State and Islam*. Cambridge, Cambridge University Press, 2001.

Calabrese, John. *China's Changing Relations with the Middle East*. London, Pinter, 1990.

Carter, Hannah, and Ehteshami, Anoushiravan (Eds). *The Middle East's Relations with Asia and Russia*. London, Routledge, 2004.

Castellino, Joshua, and Cavanaugh, Kathleen A. *Minority Rights in the Middle East*. New York, Oxford University Press, 2013.

Cattan, Henry. *Palestine and International Law: The Legal Aspects of the Arab–Israeli Conflict*. London, Longman, 1973.

Cattan, J. *Evolution of Oil Concessions in the Middle East and North Africa*. Dobbs Ferry, NY, Oceana, 1967.

Celasun, Merih (Ed.). *State-Owned Enterprises in the Middle East and North Africa: Privatization, Performance and Reform*. London, Routledge, 2000.

Chamlou, Nadereh. *Gender and Development in the Middle East and North Africa: Women in the Public Sphere*. Washington, DC, The World Bank, 2004.

Choudhury, Masudul Alam. *Reforming the Muslim World*. London, Kegan Paul International, 1998.

Choueiri, Youssef M. *Arab History and the Nation-State: A Study in Modern Arab Historiography 1820–1980*. London, Routledge, 1980.

Arab Nationalism: A History. Oxford, Blackwell, 2001.

Islamic Fundamentalism. London, Continuum, 2002.

Modern Arab Historiography: Historical Discourse and the Nation-State. London, RoutledgeCurzon, 2002.

A Companion to the History of the Middle East. Oxford, Blackwell, 2005.

Clarke, Duncan. *Empires of Oil: Corporate Oil in Barbarian Worlds*. London, Profile, 2007.

Cleveland, William L. *A History of the Modern Middle East*. Oxford, Westview Press, 1994.

Coates Ulrichsen, Kristian. *Insecure Gulf: The End of Certainty and the Transition to the Post-Oil Era*. New York, Columbia University Press, 2011.

Cobham, David, and Dibeh, Ghassan (Eds). *Monetary Policy and Central Banking in the Middle East and North Africa*. Abingdon, Routledge, 2012.

Cohen, Michael J. *Palestine: Retreat from the Mandate*. London, Elek Books, 1978.

Commins, David. *The Gulf States: A Modern History*. London, I. B. Tauris, 2012.

Conrad, Lawrence J. (Ed.). *The Formation and Perception of the Modern Arab World, Studies by Marwan R. Buheiry*. Princeton, NJ, The Darwin Press, 1989.

Cook, David. *Understanding Jihad*. Berkeley, CA, University of California Press, 2005.

Cook, Stephen A. *Ruling But Not Governing: The Military and Political Development in Egypt, Algeria and Turkey*. Baltimore, MD, Johns Hopkins University Press, 2007.

Cooley, John K. *Green March, Black September: The Story of the Palestinian Arabs*. London, Frank Cass, 1973.

Payback: America's Long War in the Middle East. London, Brassey's UK, 1992.

Coon, C. S. *Caravan: The Story of the Middle East*. New York, 1951, and London, 1952.

The Impact of the West on Social Institutions. New York, 1952.

Corbin, Henry. *History of Islamic Philosophy*. London, Kegan Paul International, 1992.

Cordesman, Anthony H. *Weapons of Mass Destruction in the Middle East*. London, Brasseys, 1991.

Cordesman, Anthony H., and al-Rodhan, Khalid R. *The Changing Dynamics of Energy in the Middle East*. 2 vols. Westport, CT, Praeger Security International, 2006.

Courbage, Youssef, and Fargues, Philippe. *Christians and Jews under Islam*. London, I. B. Tauris, 1997.

Covarrubias, Jack, and Lansford, Tom (Eds). *Strategic Interests in the Middle East*. Aldershot, Ashgate, 2008.

Craig, Sir James Shemlan. *A History of the Middle East Centre for Arab Studies*. London, Macmillan, 1998.

Crone, Patricia. *Meccan Trade and the Rise of Islam*. Oxford, Basil Blackwell, 1987.

Cronin, Stephanie (Ed.). *Subalterns and Social Protest: History from Below in the Middle East and North Africa*. Abingdon, Routledge, 2007.

Cudsi, Alexander, and Dessouki, Ali E. Hillal (Eds). *Islam and Power*. London, Croom Helm, 1981.

Dabashi, Hamid. *The Arab Spring: The End of Postcolonialism*. London, Zed Books, 2012.

Daftary, Farhad. *A Short History of the Isma'ilis: Traditions of a Muslim Community*. Edinburgh University Press, 1999.

Danahar, Paul. *The New Middle East: The World After the Arab Spring*. London, Bloomsbury, 2013.

Daniel, Norman. *Islam, Europe and Empire*. Edinburgh University Press, 1964.

Islam and the West: The Making of an Image. Oneworld Publications, revised edn, 1993.

Dazi-Héni, Fatiha. *Monarchies et Sociétés d'Arabie, Le Temps des Confrontations*. Paris, Presses de la Fondation Nationale des Sciences Politiques, 2006.

de Châtel, Francesca. *Water Sheikhs and Dam Builders: Stories of People and Water in the Middle East*. Edison, NJ, Transaction Publishing, 2008.

Decobert, Christian. *Le mendiant et le combattant: l'institution de l'islam*. Paris, Editions du Seuil, 1991.

Dekmejian, R. H. *Islam in Revolution: Fundamentalism in the Arab World*. Syracuse, NY, Syracuse University Press, 1995.

DeLong-Bas, Natana J. *Wahhabi Islam: From Revival and Reform to Global Jihad*. London, I. B. Tauris, 2004.

Destani, Bejtullah D. *Minorities in the Middle East: Kurdish Communities 1918–1974*. 4 vols. Slough, Archive Editions, 2006.

Devji, Faisal. *Landscapes of the Jihad: Militancy, Morality, Modernity*. Ithaca, NY, Cornell University Press, 2005.

DeVore, Ronald M. (Ed.). *The Arab–Israeli Conflict: A Historical, Political, Social and Military Bibliography*. Oxford, Clio Press, 1977.

Dombroski, Kenneth R. *Peacekeeping in the Middle East as an International Regime*. Abingdon, Routledge, 2007.

Doumato, Eleanor A., and Posusney, Marsha P. (Eds). *Women and Globalization in the Arab Middle East: Gender, Economy and Society*. Boulder, CO, Lynne Rienner Publishers, 2003.

Dowek, Ephraim. *Israeli-Egyptian Relations, 1980–2000*. London, Frank Cass, 2001.

Dupuy, Trevor N. *Elusive Victory: The Arab–Israeli Wars 1947–1974*. London, MacDonald and Jane's, 1979.

Efrat, Moshe, and Bercovitch, Jacob. *Superpowers and Client States in the Middle East: The Imbalance of Influence*. London, Routledge, 1991.

Ehteshami, Anoushiravan. *Globalization and Geopolitics in the Middle East: Old Games, New Rules*. Abingdon, Routledge, 2007.

Dynamics of Change in the Persian Gulf: Political Economy, War and Revolution. Abingdon, Routledge, 2013.

Ehteshami, Anoushiravan, and Nonneman, Gerd. *War and Peace in the Gulf: Domestic Politics and Regional Relations into the 1990s*. Reading, Ithaca Press, 1991.

Eickelman, Dale F., and Piscatori, James. *Muslim Politics*. Princeton, NJ, Princeton University Press, 1996.

Elbadawi, Ibrahim, and Makdisi, Samir. (Eds). *Democracy in the Arab World: Explaining the Deficit*. Abingdon, Routledge, 2010.

Elkhafif, Mahmoud, Taghdisi-Rad, Sahar, and Elagraa, Mutasim. (Eds). *Economic and Trade Policies in the Arab World: Employment, Poverty Reduction and Integration*. Abingdon, Routledge, 2012.

Elon, Amos. *A Blood-Dimmed Tide: Dispatches from the Middle East*. London, Allen Lane, 2000.

Elsheshtawy, Yasser. *The Evolving Arab City: Tradition, Modernity and Urban Development*. Abingdon, Routledge, 2008.

Enayat, Hamid. *Modern Islamic Political Thought: The Response of the Shi'i and Sunni Muslims to the Twentieth Century*. London, Macmillan, 1982.

Enderlin, Charles. *Le Rêve brisé: Histoire de l'échec du processus de paix au Proche-Orient (1995–2002)*. Paris, Fayard, 2002.

Paix ou guerres. Les secrets des négociations israélo-arabes 1917–1995. Paris, Fayard, 2003.

Engert, Stefan. *EU Enlargement and Socialization: Turkey and Cyprus*. Abingdon, Routledge, 2010.

Ennaji, Moha, and Sadiqi, Fatima. (Eds). *Gender and Violence in the Middle East*. Abingdon, Routledge, 2011.

Esposito, John L. (Ed.). *Voices of Resurgent Islam*. New York, Oxford University Press, 1983.

The Oxford Encyclopaedia of the Modern Islamic World. New York, Oxford University Press, Inc, 1995.

The Islamic Threat, Myth or Reality? New York, Oxford University Press, Inc, 1992.

The Oxford History of Islam. New York, Oxford University Press, Inc, 2000.

Unholy War: Terror in the Name of Islam. New York, Oxford University Press, Inc, 2002.

Faath, Sigrid (Ed.). *Anti-Americanism in the Islamic World*. London, C. Hurst & Co, 2006.

Fain, W. Taylor. *American Ascendance and British Retreat in the Persian Gulf Region*. New York, Palgrave Macmillan, 2008.

Fawcett, Louise. *International Relations of the Middle East*. Oxford, Oxford University Press, 2nd edn, 2009.

Feldman, Noah. *After Jihad: America and the Struggle for Islamic Democracy*. New York, Farrar, Straus and Giroux, 2004.

The Fall and Rise of the Islamic State. Princeton, NJ, Princeton University Press, 2008.

Field, Michael. *Inside the Arab World*. Cambridge, MA, Harvard University Press, revised edn, 1998.

Findlay, Allan M. *The Arab World*. London, Routledge, 1996.

Fisher, S. N. *Social Forces in the Middle East*. Ithaca, NY, Cornell University Press, 3rd edn, 1977.

The Middle East: A History. New York, McGraw-Hill, 4th edn, 1990.

Fisher, W. B. *The Middle East—A Physical, Social and Regional Geography*. London, 7th edn, 1978.

Fisk, Robert. *The Great War for Civilisation: The Conquest of the Middle East*. London, HarperCollins, 2006.

Fox, J. W., Mourtada-Sabbah, N., and al-Mutawa, M. (Eds). *Globalization and the Gulf*. Abingdon, Routledge, 2006.

Frangi, Abdallah. *The PLO and Palestine*. London, Zed Press, 1984.

Freedman, Robert O. *The Middle East Enters the Twenty-first Century*. Gainesville, FL, University Press of Florida, 2002.

Fuller, Graham E., and Lesser, Jan O. *A Sense of Siege: The Geopolitics of Islam and the West*. Boulder, CO, Westview Press, 1995.

Galal, Ahmed, and Hoekman, Bernard. *Arab Economic Integration: Between Hope and Reality*. Washington, DC, Brookings Institution Press, 2003.

Gallagher, Nancy Elizabeth (Ed.). *Approaches to the History of the Middle East: Interviews with Leading Middle East Historians*. Reading, Garnet, 1995.

Garon, Lise. *Dangerous Alliances: Civil Society, the Media and Democratic Transition in North Africa*. London, Zed Books, 2003.

Gasiorowski, M., Long, D. E., and Reich, B. *The Government and Politics of the Middle East and North Africa*. Boulder, CO, Westview Press, 2007.

Gause, F. Gregory. *The International Relations of the Persian Gulf*. Cambridge, Cambridge University Press, 2009.

Gelber, Yoav. *Palestine 1948: War, Escape and the Emergence of the Palestinian Refugee Problem*. Brighton, Sussex Academic Press, 2001.

Gelvin, James L. *The Israeli–Palestinian Conflict: One Hundred Years of War*. Cambridge, Cambridge University Press, 2005.

Gerges, Fawaz A. *The Far Enemy: Why Jihad Went Global*. Cambridge University Press, 2005.

Gerner, Deborah J. *Understanding the Contemporary Middle East*. Boulder, CO, Lynne Rienner Publishers, 2000.

Gershoni, Israel, Erdem, Hakan, and Woköck, Ursula (Eds). *Histories of the Modern Middle East: New Directions*. Boulder, CO, Lynne Rienner Publishers, 2002.

Gershoni, Israel, and Jankowski, James (Eds). *Rethinking Nationalism in the Arab Middle East*. New York, Columbia University Press, 1998.

Ghareeb, Edmund, and Khadduri, Majid. *War in the Gulf, 1990–91: The Iraq–Kuwait Conflict and its Implications*. Oxford University Press, 1997.

Giacaman, George, and Jrund Lonning, Dag. *After Oslo: New Realities, Old Problems*. London, Pluto Press, 1998.

Gibb, H. A. R. *Modern Trends in Islam*. Chicago, 1947.

Studies on the Civilisation of Islam. London, 1962.

Gibb, H. A. R., and Bowen, Harold. *Islamic Society and the West*. London, 2 vols, 1950, 1957.

Gilbert, Martin. *The Routledge Atlas of the Arab–Israeli Conflict*. Abingdon, Routledge, 2005.

Gilsenan, Michael. *Recognizing Islam: Religion and Society in the Modern Middle East*. London, I. B. Tauris, 1990.

Gittings, John (Ed.). *Beyond the Gulf War: The Middle East and the New World Order*. London, Catholic Institute for International Relations, 1991.

Glassé, Cyril. *The Concise Encyclopedia of Islam*. London, revised edn, Stacey International, 2001.

Glubb, Lt-Gen. Sir John. *A Short History of the Arab Peoples*. London, Hodder and Stoughton, 1969.

Gomaa, Ahmed M. *The Foundation of the League of Arab States*. London, Longman, 1977.

al-Gosaibi, Ghazi. *The Gulf Crisis—An Attempt to Understand*. London, Kegan Paul International, 1993.

Gowers, Andrew, and Walter, Tony. *Behind the Myth: Yasir Arafat and the Palestinian Revolution*. London, W. H. Allen, 1990.

Graz, Liesl. *The Turbulent Gulf*. London, I. B. Tauris, 1990.

Gresh, Alain, and Vidal, Dominique. *The New A–Z of the Middle East*. London, I. B. Tauris, 2004.

Grinberg, Lev Luis. *Politics and Violence in Israel / Palestine: Democracy versus Military Rule*. Abingdon, Routledge, 2011.

Grossman, Mark. *Encyclopaedia of the Persian Gulf War*. Santa Barbara, California, ABC-Clio, 1996.

Grunebaum, Gustave E. von (Ed.). *Unity and Variety in Muslim Civilisation*. Chicago, 1955.

Islam: Essays on the Nature and Growth of a Cultural Tradition. London, Routledge and Kegan Paul, 1961.

Modern Islam: the Search for Cultural Identity. London, 1962.

Guazzone, Laura. *The Islamist Dilemma*. Reading, Ithaca Press, 1995.

Guazzone, Laura, and Pioppi, Daniela (Eds). *The Arab State and Neo-liberal Globalization: The Restructuring of State Power in the Middle East*. Reading, Ithaca Press, 2009.

Guyatt, Nicholas. *The Absence of Peace: Understanding The Israeli–Palestinian Conflict*. London, Zed Press, 1998.

Habeck, Mary. *Knowing the Enemy: Jihadist Ideology and the War on Terror*. New Haven, CT, Yale University Press, 2007.

Hafez, Mohammed M. *Why Muslims Rebel: Repression and Resistance in the Islamic World*. Boulder, CO, Lynne Rienner Publishers, revised edn, 2004.

Hakimian, Hassan, and Moshaver, Ziba (Eds). *The State and Global Change: The Political Economy of Change in the Middle East and North Africa*. Richmond, Curzon Press, 2001.

Halabi, Yakub. *US Foreign Policy in the Middle East: From Crises to Change*. Aldershot, Ashgate, 2009.

Halliday, Fred. *Nation and Religion in the Middle East*. Boulder, CO, Lynne Rienner Publishers, 2000.

Islam and the Myth of Confrontation: Religion and Politics in the Middle East. London, I. B. Tauris, revised edn, 2002.

The Middle East in International Politics: Power, Politics and Ideology. Cambridge University Press, 2005.

100 Myths about the Middle East. London, Saqi Books, 2005.

Halm, Heinz. *The Fatimids and their Traditions of Learning*. London, I. B. Tauris, 1997.

Halpern, Manfred. *The Politics of Social Change in the Middle East and North Africa*. Princeton, NJ, Princeton University Press, 1963.

Hanieh, Adam. *Capitalism and Class in the Gulf Arab States*. Basingstoke, Palgrave Macmillan, 2011.

Harders, Cilja, and Legrenzi, Matteo (Eds). *Beyond Regionalism?* Aldershot, Ashgate, 2008.

Hardy, Roger. *Arabia after the Storm: Internal Stability of the Gulf Arab States*. London, Royal Institute of International Affairs, 1992.

Hare, William. *The Struggle for the Holy Land*. London, Madison Publishing, 1998.

Harris, Lillian Craig. *China Considers the Middle East*. London, I. B. Tauris, 1994.

Hart, Alan. *Arafat—Terrorist or Peacemaker?* London, Sidgwick and Jackson, 2nd edn, 1994.

Hartshorn, J. E. *Oil Companies and Governments*. London, Faber, 1962.

Christianity in the Arab World. Norwich, SCM Press, revised edn, 1998.

Haugbolle, Sune, and Hastrup, Anders (Eds). *The Politics of Violence, Truth and Reconciliation in the Arab Middle East*. Abingdon, Routledge, 2008.

Hayes, J. R. (Ed.). *The Genius of Arab Civilisation: Source of Renaissance*. New York University Press, 3rd edn, 1992.

Heikal, Mohammed. *Illusions of Triumph: An Arab View of the Gulf War*. London, HarperCollins, 1992.

Held, David, and Ulrichsen, Kristian (Eds). *The Transformation of the Gulf: Politics, Economics and the Global Order*. Abingdon, Routledge, 2011.

Heradstvelt, Daniel, and Hveem, Helge. *Oil in the Gulf: Obstacles to Democracy and Development*. Aldershot, Ashgate, 2004.

Hertog, Steffen, Luciani, Giacomo, and Valeri, Marc (Eds). *Business Politics in the Middle East*. London, C. Hurst & Co, 2013.

Herzog, Maj.-Gen. Chaim. *The War of Atonement*. London, Weidenfeld and Nicolson, 1975.

The Arab–Israeli Wars. London, Arms and Armour Press, 1982.

Hewedy, Amin. *Militarisation and Security in the Middle East*. London, Pinter, 1989.

Higgins, Rosalyn. *United Nations Peacekeeping 1946–67: Documents and Commentary*, Vol. I, *The Middle East*. Oxford University Press, 1969.

Hiro, Dilip. *Inside the Middle East*. London, Routledge and Kegan Paul, 1981.

Islamic Fundamentalism. London, Paladin, 1988.

The Longest War. London, Grafton Books, 1990.

Dictionary of the Middle East. London, Macmillan, 1996.

Sharing the Promised Land. An Interwoven Tale of Israelis and Palestinians. London, Hodder & Stoughton, 1996.

War Without End: The Rise Of Islamist Terrorism And Global Response. London, Routledge, 2002.

The Essential Middle East: A Comprehensive Guide. New York, Carroll & Graf Publishers, 2003.

Hirst, David. *Oil and Public Opinion in the Middle East*. New York, Praeger, 1966.

The Gun and the Olive Branch: The Roots of Violence in the Middle East. London, Faber, 1977.

Hirszowicz, Lukasz. *The Third Reich and the Arab East*. London, Routledge and Kegan Paul, 1966.

A Short History of the Near East. New York, 1966.

Makers of Arab History. London, Macmillan, 1968.

Islam. A Way of Life. London, Oxford University Press, 1971.

Hitti, Philip K. *The Origins of the Druze People and Religion*. London, Saqi Books, 2007.

Hodgkin, E. C. *The Arabs*. Modern World Series, Oxford University Press, 1966.

(Ed.). *Two Kings in Arabia: Sir Reader Bullard's Letters from Jeddah*. Reading, Ithaca Press, 1999.

Holt, P. M., Lambton, A. K. S., and Lewis, B. (Eds). *The Cambridge History of Islam*. Vol. I, *The Central Islamic Lands*. Cambridge University Press, 1970; Vol. II, *The Further Islamic Lands, Islamic Society and Civilization*. Cambridge University Press, 1971.

Hopwood, Derek (Ed.). *Studies in Arab History*. London, Macmillan, 1990.

Hourani, A. H. *Minorities in the Arab World*. London, 1947.

Europe and the Middle East. London, Macmillan, 1980.

The Emergence of the Modern Middle East. London, Macmillan, 1981.

A History of the Arab Peoples. London, Faber and Faber, revised edn, 2005.

Islam in European Thought. Cambridge University Press, 1991.

Hourani, Albert, Khoury, Philip, and Wilson, Mary C. (Eds). *The Modern Middle East*. London, I. B. Tauris, 2004.

Hoveyda, Fereydoun. *Que veulent les arabes?* Paris, Editions First, 1991.

Hroub, Khaled (Ed.). *Political Islam: Ideology and Practice*. London, Saqi Books, 2009.

Hudson, Michael C. *Arab Politics: The Search for Legitimacy*. New Haven, CT, and London, Yale University Press, 1977/78.

Hurewitz, J. C. *Unity and Disunity in the Middle East*. New York, Carnegie Endowment for International Peace, 1952.

Middle East Dilemmas. New York, 1953.

Diplomacy in the Near and Middle East. Vol. I, *1535–1914*; Vol. II, *1914–1956*. Van Nostrand, 1956.

(Ed.). *Soviet-American Rivalry in the Middle East*. London, Pall Mall Press, and New York, Praeger, 1969.

Middle East Politics: The Military Dimension. London, Pall Mall Press, 1969.

Ibrahim, Badr el-Din A. *Economic Co-operation in the Gulf: Issues in the Economies of the Arab Gulf Cooperation Council States*. Abingdon, Routledge, 2012.

Inbar, Efraim, and Frisch, Hillel (Eds). *Radical Islam and National Society: Challenges and Responses*. Abingdon, Routledge, 2007.

International Institute for Strategic Studies. *Sources of Conflict in the Middle East*. London, Adelphi Papers, International Institute for Strategic Studies, 1966.

Domestic Politics and Regional Security: Jordan, Syria and Israel. London, Gower, International Institute for Strategic Studies, 1989.

Ionides, Michael. *Divide and Lose: The Arab Revolt 1955–58*. London, Bles, 1960.

Irwin, Robert. *For Lust of Knowing: The Orientalists and their Enemies*. London, Penguin, 2007.

Isaak, David T., and Fesharaki, F. *OPEC, the Gulf and the World Petroleum Market*. London, Croom Helm, 1983.

Ismail, Salwa. *Rethinking Islamist Politics: Culture, the State and Islamism*. London, I. B. Tauris, 2006.

Israeli, Raphael. *War, Peace and Terror in the Middle East*. London, Frank Cass, 2003.

Issawi, Charles. *An Economic History of the Middle East and North Africa*. London, Methuen, 1982.

Jaber, Faleh A. (Ed.). *Post-Marxism and the Middle East*. London, Saqi Books, 1997.

Jaber, Faleh A., and Dawod, Hosham (Eds). *The Kurds: Nationalism and Politics*. London, Saqi Books, 2006.

Jansen, Johannes J. G. *The Dual Nature of Islamic Fundamentalism*. Ithaca, NY, Cornell University Press, 1997.

Jawad, Haifaa A. *The Middle East in the New World Order*. London, Macmillan, 1996.

Jerichow, A. and Simonsen, J. B. (Eds). *Islam in a Changing World and the Middle East*. Richmond, Curzon Press, 1997.

Joffé, George (Ed.). *Islamic Radicalisation in Europe and the Middle East: Reassessing the Causes of Terrorism*. London, I.B. Tauris, 2012.

Johnson, Nels. *Islam and the Politics of Meaning in Palestinian Nationalism*. Henley-on-Thames, Kegan Paul International, 1983.

Jones, Jeremy. *Negotiating Change: The New Politics of the Middle East*. London, I. B. Tauris, 2006.

Kaim, Markus. *Great Powers and Regional Orders: The United States and the Persian Gulf*. Aldershot, Ashgate, 2008.

Kamrava, Mehran. *The New Voices of Islam: Rethinking Politics and Modernity—A Reader*. Berkeley, CA, University of California Press, 2006.

Kapiszewski, Andrzej. *Nationals and Expatriates: Population and Labour Dilemmas of the Gulf Cooperation Council States*. Reading, Ithaca Press, 2000.

Karsh, Efraim. *Rethinking the Middle East*. London, Frank Cass, 2003.

Islamic Imperialism: A History. New Haven, CT, Yale University Press, revised edn, 2007.

Karsh, Efraim, and Kumaraswamy, P. R. *Israel, the Hashemites and the Palestinians: The Fateful Triangle*. London, Frank Cass, 2003.

Katz, Mark N. *Russia and Arabia: Soviet Foreign Policy toward the Arabian Peninsula*. Baltimore, MD, and London, Johns Hopkins University Press, 1986.

Kayal, Alawi D. *The Control of Oil: East–West Rivalry in the Persian Gulf*. London, Kegan Paul, 2002.

Kaye, Dalia Dassa. *Beyond the Handshake: Multilateral Cooperation in the Arab-Israeli Peace Process, 1991–96*. New York, Columbia University Press, 2001.

Keating, Aileen. *Power, Politics and the Hidden History of Arabian Oil*. London, Saqi Books, 2006.

Keay, John. *The Arabs: A Living History*. London, Harvill, 1983.

Sowing the Wind: The Seeds of Conflict in the Middle East. London, John Murray, 2003.

Kéchichian, Joseph A. *Power and Succession in Arab Monarchies*. Boulder, CO, Lynne Rienner Publishers, 2008.

Keddie, Nikki R. *Women in the Middle East: Past and Present*. Princeton, NJ, Princeton University Press, 2006.

Kedourie, Elie. *England and the Middle East*. London, 1956.

The Chatham House Version and other Middle-Eastern Studies. London, Weidenfeld and Nicolson, 1970.

Arabic Political Memoirs and Other Studies. London, Frank Cass, 1974.

In the Anglo-Arab Labyrinth. 1976.

Islam in the Modern World and Other Studies. London, Mansell, 1980.

Towards a Modern Iran. 1980.

Kelly, J. B. *Eastern Arabian Frontiers*. London, Faber, 1963.

Arabia, the Gulf and the West: A Critical View of the Arabs and their Oil Policy. London, Weidenfeld and Nicolson, 1980.

Kemp, Geoffrey, and Harkavy, Robert. *The Strategic Geography of the Changing Middle East*. Washington, DC, Brookings Institution Press, 1996.

Kemp, Geoffrey, and Pressman, Jeremy. *Point of No Return: The Deadly Struggle for Middle East Peace*. Washington, DC, Brookings Institution Press, 1997.

Kepel, Gilles (trans. Jon Rothschild). *The Prophet and Pharaoh: Muslim Extremism in Egypt*. London, Saqi Books, 1985.

(trans. Antony Roberts). *Jihad: The Trail of Political Islam*. London, I. B. Tauris, 2002.

(trans. Pascale Ghazaleh). *The War for Muslim Minds: Islam and the West*. Cambridge, MA, Harvard University Press, 2004.

The Roots of Radical Islam. London, Saqi Books, revised edn, 2005.

Beyond Terror and Martyrdom: The Future of the Middle East. Cambridge, MA, Harvard University Press, 2008.

Kepel, Gilles, and Milelli, Jean-Pierre (Eds). *Al Qaeda in its Own Words*. Cambridge, MA, Harvard University Press, 2008.

Kerr, Malcolm. *The Arab Cold War 1958–1964*. Oxford University Press, 1965.

Khalaf, Abdulhadi and Luciani, Giacomo (Eds). *Constitutional Reform and Political Participation in the Gulf*. Dubai, Gulf Research Centre, 2007.

Khalidi, Rashid. *Resurrecting Empire: Western Footprints and America's Perilous Path in the Middle East*. London, I. B. Tauris, 2005.

Khalil, Muhammad. *The Arab States and the Arab League* (historical documents). Beirut, Khayats.

Khalili, Laleh. *Politics of the Modern Arab World*. Abingdon, Routledge, 2008.

Khan, Muhammad Akram. *Islamic Economics and Finance: A Glossary*. Abingdon, Routledge, 2007.

Khatab, Sayed, and Bouma, Gary D. *Democracy in Islam*. Abingdon, Routledge, 2007.

Khouri, Fred J. *The Arab–Israeli Dilemma*. Syracuse/New York, 1968.

Khuri, Fuad I. *Imams and Emirs: State, Religion and Sects in Islam*. London, Saqi Books, 1990.

Kingston, Paul W. T. *Britain and the Politics of Modernization in the Middle East, 1945–1958*. Cambridge University Press, 1996.

Kirk, George E. *The Middle East in the War*. London, 1953.

A Short History of the Middle East: From the Rise of Islam to Modern Times. New York, 1955.

Klein, Menachem. *Jerusalem: The Contested City*. New York University Press, 2001.

Kliot, Norit. *Water Resources and Conflict in the Middle East*. London, Routledge, 1994.

Koch, Christopher. *Gulf Security in the Twenty-First Century*. London, I. B. Tauris, 1997.

Korany, Bahgat, and Dessouki, Ali E. Hillal. *The Foreign Policies of Arab States: The Challenge of Globalization*. Cairo, American University in Cairo Press, revised edn, 2009.

Kraetzschmar, Hendrik Jan (Ed.). *The Dynamics of Opposition Cooperation in the Arab World: Contentious Politics in Times of Change*. Abingdon, Routledge, 2013.

Kreutz, Andrej. *Vatican Policy on the Palestinian–Israeli Conflict: The Struggle for the Holy Land*. London, Greenwood Press, 1990.

Russia in the Middle East: Friend or Foe? Westport, CT, and London, Praeger Security International, 2006.

Kubbig, Bernd, and Fikenscher, Sven-Eric (Eds). *Arms Control and Missile Proliferation in the Middle East*. Abingdon, Routledge, 2011.

Kumar, Ravinder. *India and the Persian Gulf Region*. London, 1965.

Kurzman, Dan. *Genesis 1948: The First Arab–Israeli War*. London, Vallentine Mitchell, 1972.

La Guardia, Anton. *Holy Land, Unholy War: Israelis and Palestinians*. London, John Murray, 2001.

Lahoud, Nelly, and Johns, Anthony H. (Eds). *Islam in World Politics*. Abingdon, Routledge, 2005.

Lall, Arthur. *The UN and the Middle East Crisis*. New York and London, 1968.

Landau, Emily B. *Arms Control in the Middle East: Cooperative Security Dialogue and Regional Constraints*. Brighton, Sussex Academic Press, 2006.

Lapidus, Ira M. *A History of Islamic Societies*. Cambridge University Press, 1989.

Laqueur, W. Z. *Communism and Nationalism in the Middle East*. London and New York, 1957.

(Ed.). *The Middle East in Transition*. London, Routledge and Kegan Paul, 1958.

The Struggle for the Middle East: The Soviet Union and the Middle East 1958–68. London, Routledge and Kegan Paul, 1969.

Confrontation: The Middle-East War and World Politics. London, Wildwood, 1974.

(Ed.). *The Israel-Arab Reader*. New York and London, Penguin, 4th edn, 1984.

Laskier, M. M., Reguer, S., and Simon, R. S. *The Jews of the Middle East and North Africa in Modern Times*. Irvington, NY, Columbia University Press, 2003.

Lawrence, Quil. *Invisible Nation: How the Kurds' Quest for Statehood is Shaping Iraq and the Middle East*. New York, Walker & Company, 2008.

Lee, Robert D. *Religion and Politics in the Middle East: Identity, Ideology, Institutions, and Attitudes*. Boulder, CO, Westview Press, 2009.

Legrenzi, Matteo, and Momani, Bessma. (Eds). *Shifting Geo-Economic Power of the Gulf: Oil, Finance and Institutions*. Farnham, Ashgate, 2011.

Lenczowski, George. *The Middle East in World Affairs*. Ithaca, NY, Cornell University Press, 4th edn, 1980.

Oil and State in the Middle East. Cornell University Press, 1960.

Lennon, A. T. J. (Ed.). *The Epicenter of Crisis: The New Middle East*. Washington, DC, Washington Quarterly Readers, 2008.

Lesch, David W. (Ed.). *The Middle East and the United States: A Historical and Political Reassessment*. Boulder, CO, Westview Press, 4th edn, 2007.

Lewis, Bernard. *The Arabs in History*. Oxford University Press, 6th edn, 1993.

Shaping of the Modern Middle East. New York, Oxford University Press, 1994.

The Middle East: 2000 Years of History from the Rise of Christianity to the Present Day. London, Phoenix Press, revised edn, 2000.

What Went Wrong?: Western Impact and Middle Eastern Response. New York, Oxford University Press, 2001.

The Crisis of Islam: Holy War and Unholy Terror. London, Weidenfeld and Nicolson, 2004.

Logan, William S., and White, Paul J. (Eds). *Remaking the Middle East*. Oxford, Berg, 1997.

Longrigg, S. H. *Oil in the Middle East*. London, 3rd edn, 1968.

The Middle East: A Social Geography. London, 2nd revised edn, 1970.

Longrigg, S. H., and Jankowski, J. P. *The Geography of the Middle East*. Piscataway, NJ, Aldine Transaction, 2nd revised edn, 2009.

Louër, Laurence. *Transnational Shia Politics: Religious and Political Networks in the Gulf*. New York, Columbia University Press, 2008.

Louis, William Roger. *The British Empire in the Middle East 1945–51*. Oxford University Press, 1984.

Lust-Okar, E., and Zerhouni, S. (Eds). *Political Participation in the Middle East*. Boulder, CO, Lynne Rienner Publishers, 2008.

Lynch, Marc. *Voices of the New Arab Public: Iraq, al-Jazeera, and Middle East Politics Today*. New York, Columbia University Press, 2006.

The Arab Uprising: The Unfinished Revolutions of the New Middle East. New York, PublicAffairs, 2012.

Maalouf, Amin. *The Crusades Through Arab Eyes*. London, Saqi Books, 1984.

McCarthy, Justin. *The Population of Palestine*. New York, Columbia University Press, 1991.

Maddy-Weitzmann, Bruce, and Inbar, Efraim (Eds). *Religious Radicalism in the Greater Middle East*. London, Frank Cass, 1997.

Mahler, Gregory S., and Mahler, Alden R. W. *The Arab–Israeli Conflict: An Introduction and Documentary Reader*. Abingdon, Routledge, 2009.

Makris, G. P. *Islam in the Middle East: A Living Tradition*. Oxford, Blackwell, 2006.

Mallat, Chibli. *The Middle East into the Twenty-First Century: The Japan Lectures and Other Studies on the Arab–Israeli Conflict, the Gulf Crisis and Political Islam*. Reading, Ithaca Press, 1996.

Mandaville, Peter. *Global Political Islam*. Abingdon, Routledge, 2008.

Mansfield, Peter. *The Ottoman Empire and Its Successors*. London, Macmillan, 1973.

(Ed.). *The Middle East: A Political and Economic Survey*. London, Oxford University Press, 5th edn, 1980.

The Arabs. Penguin, 5th edn, 1992.

A History of the Middle East. Harmondsworth, Penguin, 2003.

Mansouri, Fethi (Ed.). *Australia and the Middle East: A Front-line Relationship*. London, I. B. Tauris, 2006.

Ma'oz, Moshe, and Sheffer, Gabriel. *Middle Eastern Minorities and Diasporas*. Brighton, Sussex Academic Press, 2002.

Marcel, Valerie. *Oil Titans: National Oil Companies in the Middle East*. Washington, DC, The Brookings Institution, 2005.

Martin Muqoz, Gema (Ed.). *Islam, Modernism and the West: Cultural and Political Relations at the end of the Millennium*. London, I. B. Tauris, 1997.

Mattar, Philip (Ed.). *Encyclopedia of the Palestinians*. London, Fitzroy Dearborn, 2000.

Meijer, Roel (Ed.). *Cosmopolitanism, Identity and Authenticity in the Middle East*. Richmond, Curzon Press, 1999.

Menashiri, David (Ed.). *Central Asia Meets the Middle East*. London, Frank Cass, 1998.

Mendelsohn, Everett. *A Compassionate Peace: A Future for Israel, Palestine and the Middle East*. New York, The Noonday Press, 1989.

Meri, Josef W. *Medieval Islamic Civilization: An Encyclopedia*. Abingdon, Routledge, 2006.

Mernissi, Fatima. *Islam and Democracy—Fear of the Modern World*. London, Virago, 1993.

Meskell, Lynn. *Archaeology Under Fire: Nationalism, Politics and Heritage in the Eastern Mediterranean and Middle East*. London, Routledge, 1998.

Miles, Hugh. *Al-Jazeera: How Arab TV News Challenged America*. New York, Grove Press, 2005.

Milton-Edwards, Beverley. *Contemporary Politics in the Middle East*. Cambridge, Polity, 3rd edn, 2011.

Milton-Edwards, Beverley, and Hinchliffe, Peter. *Conflicts in the Middle East since 1945*. London, Routledge, 2001.

Mohs, Polly A. *Military Intelligence and the Arab Revolt*. Abingdon, Routledge, 2007.

Mojtahedzadeh, Pirouz. *Security and Territoriality in the Persian Gulf: A Maritime Political Geography*. Richmond, Curzon Press, 1999.

Moller, Bjorn (Ed.). *Oil and Water: Co-operative Security in the Persian Gulf*. London, I. B. Tauris, 2001.

Momen, Moojan. *An Introduction to Shi'i Islam*. New Haven, CT, Yale University Press, revised edn, 1987.

Mommer, Bernard. *Global Oil and the Nation State*. New York, Oxford University Press, Inc, 2002.

Monroe, Elizabeth. *Britain's Moment in the Middle East 1914–71*. London, Chatto and Windus, new edn, 1981.

Philby of Arabia. Reading, Ithaca Press, 1998.

Moore Henry, Clement, and Springborg, Robert. *Globalization and the Politics of Development in the Middle East*. Cambridge, Cambridge University Press, 2nd edn, 2010.

Morris, Claud. *The Last Inch: A Middle East Odyssey*. London, Kegan Paul International, 1996.

Mortimer, Edward. *Faith and Power: The Politics of Islam*. London, Faber, 1982.

Mosley, Leonard. *Power Play: The Tumultuous World of Middle East Oil 1890–1973*. London, Weidenfeld and Nicolson, 1973.

Mostyn, T. *Major Political Events in Iran, Iraq and the Arabian Peninsula 1945–1990*. Oxford and New York, Facts on File, 1991.

Censorship in Islamic Societies. London, Saqi Books, 2002.

Muasher, Marwan. *The Arab Center: The Promise of Moderation*. New Haven, CT, Yale University Press, 2008.

Munson, Henry, Jr. *Islam and Revolution in the Middle East*. New Haven, CT, and London, Yale University Press, 1988.

Murakami, Masahiro. *Managing Water for Peace in the Middle East: Alternative Strategies*. Tokyo, United Nations University Press, 1996.

Murden, Simon W. *Islam, the Middle East, and the New Global Hegemony*. Boulder, CO, Lynne Rienner Publishers, 2002.

Nafi, Basheer M and Taji-Farouki, Suha (Eds). *Islamic Thought in the Twentieth Century*. New York, Palgrave Macmillan, 2004.

Al-Na'im, Abdullahi Ahmed. *Islam and the Secular State: Negotiating the Future of Shari'a*. Cambridge, MA, Harvard University Press, 2008.

Nakash, Yitzhak. *Reaching for Power: The Shi'a in the Modern Arab World*. Princeton, NJ, Princeton University Press, 2007.

al-Naqeeb, Khaldoun. *Society and State in the Gulf and Arab Peninsula: A Different Perspective* (Routledge Library Editions: The Arab Nation). Abingdon, Routledge, 2012.

Nasr, Seyyed Hossein. *Science and Civilization in Islam*. Cambridge, MA, Harvard University Press, revised edn, 1987.

Nasr, Vali. *The Shia Revival: How Conflicts within Islam will Shape the Future*. New York, W. W. Norton and Co, 2007.

Meccanomics: The March of the New Muslim Middle Class. Oxford, Oneworld Publications, 2010.

Natali, Denise. *The Kurds and the State: Evolving National Identity in Iraq, Turkey and Iran*. Syracuse, NY, Syracuse University Press, 2005.

Navias, Martin. *Going Ballistic: The Build-up of Missiles in the Middle East*. London, Brassey's, 1993.

Nevakivi, Jukka *Britain, France and the Arab Middle East 1914–20*. Athlone Press, University of London, 1969.

Niblock, Tim. *'Pariah' States and Sanctions in the Middle East: Iraq, Libya, Sudan*. Boulder, CO, Lynne Rienner Publishers, 2001.

Niblock, Tim, and Murphy, Emma. *Economic and Political Liberalism in the Middle East*. London, British Academic Press, 1993.

Nizameddin, Talal. *Russia and the Middle East*. London, C. Hurst & Co, 1999.

Noland, Marcus, and Pack, Howard. *The Arab Economies in a Changing World*. Washington, DC, Peterson Institute for International Economics, 2007.

Nonneman, Gerd. *Development, Administration and Aid in the Middle East*. London, Routledge, 1988.

(Ed.). *The Middle East and Europe: The Search for Stability and Integration*. London, Federal Trust, 1993.

(Ed.). *Analyzing Middle East Foreign Policies, and the Relationship with Europe*. Abingdon, Routledge, 2005.

Noorani, A. G. *Islam and Jihad: Prejudice and Reality*. London, Zed Books, 2002.

Nydell, Margaret K. *Understanding Arabs: A Guide for Westerners*. Yarmouth, ME, Intercultural Press, 1992.

O'Ballance, Edgar. *The Third Arab–Israeli War*. London, Faber and Faber, 1972.

Oren, Michael B. *Six Days of War: June 1967 and the Making of the Modern Middle East*. London and New York, Oxford University Press, 2002.

Owen, Roger. *The Middle East in the World Economy 1800–1914*. London, I. B. Tauris (1972), revised edn, 1993.

A History of Middle East Economies in the 20th Century. London, I. B. Tauris, 1998.

State, Power and Politics in the Making of the Modern Middle East. London, Routledge, 3rd edn, 2004.

Palmer, Alan. *The Decline and Fall of the Ottoman Empire*. London, John Murray, 1992.

Pantelides, Veronica S. *Arab Education 1956–1978: A Bibliography*. London, Mansell, 1982.

Pappé, Ilan. *The Modern Middle East*. Abingdon, Routledge, 2005.

Pargeter, Alison. *The Muslim Brotherhood: From Opposition to Power*. London, Saqi Books, 2013.

Parker, Richard B. *The October War—A Retrospective*. Gainesville, FL, University Press of Florida, 2001.

Parra, Francisco. *Oil Politics: A Modern History of Petroleum*. London, I. B. Tauris, 2003.

Paya, Ali, and Esposito, John L. (Eds). *Iraq, Democracy and the Future of the Muslim World*. Abingdon, Routledge, 2010.

Pennar, Jaan. *The USSR and the Arabs: The Ideological Dimension*. London, C. Hurst & Co, 1973.

Persson, Magnus. *Great Britain, the United States and the Security of the Middle East: The Formation of the Baghdad Pact*. Lund, Lund University Press, 1998.

Peters, F. E. *The Hajj: The Muslim Pilgrimage to Mecca and the Holy Places*. Princeton, NJ, Princeton University Press, 1995.

Phares, Walid. *The War of Ideas: Jihadism Against Democracy*. New York, Palgrave Macmillan, 2007.

Pipes, Daniel. *In the Path of God: Islam and Political Power*. New York, Basic Books, 1983.

Piscatori, James P. (Ed.). *Islam in the Political Process*. Cambridge University Press, 1983.

Islam in a World of Nation-States. Cambridge University Press, 1986.

Playfair, Ian S. O. *The Mediterranean and the Middle East*. London, History of the Second World War, HMSO, 1966.

Poliak, A. N. *Feudalism in Egypt, Syria, Palestine and the Lebanon, 1250–1900*. London, Luzac, for the Royal Asiatic Society, 1939.

Polk, W. R. *The Arab World Today*. Cambridge, MA, Harvard University Press, 1991.

(Ed. with Chambers, R. L.) *Beginnings of Modernization in the Middle East: The Nineteenth Century*. Chicago, IL, University of Chicago Press, 1969.

The Elusive Peace: The Middle East in the Twentieth Century. London, Frank Cass, 1980.

Porath, Y. *The Emergence of the Palestinian Arab National Movement 1918–1929*. London, Frank Cass, 1974.

Pratt, N. *Democracy and Authoritarianism in the Arab World*. Boulder, CO, Lynne Rienner Publishers, 2006.

Quandt, William B. *Peace Process: American Diplomacy and the Arab–Israeli Conflict since 1967*. Berkeley, CA, University of California Press, 2001.

Qumsiyeh, Mazin B. *Sharing the Land of Canaan: Human Rights and the Israel–Palestinian Struggle*. London, Pluto Press, 2004.

Rabinovich, Itamar. *Waging Peace: Israel and the Arabs, 1948–2003*. Princeton, NJ, Princeton University Press, 2004.

Raufer, Xavier. *Atlas Mondial de l'Islam Activiste*. Paris, Editions de la Table Ronde, 1991.

Richards, A., and Waterbury, J. *A Political Economy of the Middle East*. Boulder, CO, Westview Press (1990 and 1996), 3rd edn (revised), 2007.

Rikhye, Maj.-Gen. I. J. *The Sinai Blunder*. London, Frank Cass, 1980.

Rivlin, B., and Szyliowicz, J. S. (Eds). *The Contemporary Middle East—Tradition and Innovation*. New York, Random House, 1965.

Rivlin, Paul. *Arab Economies in the Twenty-First Century*. Cambridge University Press, 2009.

Roded, Ruth (Ed.). *Women in Islam and the Modern Middle East: A Reader*. London, I. B. Tauris, 2007.

Rodinson, Maxime. *Islam and capitalisme*. Paris, Editions de Seuil, 1966.

Muhammad. London, Penguin, 1974.

La fascination de l'Islam. Paris, Maspero, 1980.

The Arabs. Chicago, IL, University of Chicago Press (1981), revised edn, 1989.

Israel and the Arabs. London, Penguin, 1982.

Rogan, Eugene. *The Arabs: A History*. London, Allen Lane, 2009.

Rogan, Eugene L., and Shlaim, Avi (Eds). *The War for Palestine: Rewriting the History of 1948*. Cambridge University Press, 2001.

Rogerson, Barnaby. *The Prophet Muhammad: A Biography*. Boston, MA, Little Brown & Co, 2003.

Romano, David. *The Kurdish Nationalist Movement: Opportunity, Mobilization and Identity*. Cambridge University Press, 2006.

Ronart, Stephan and Ronart, Nandy. *Concise Encyclopaedia of Arabic Civilization*. Amsterdam, 1966.

Rondot, Pierre. *The Destiny of the Middle East*. London, Chatto & Windus, 1960.

L'Islam. Paris, Prismes, 1965.

Rosen, Lawrence. *Varieties of Muslim Experience: Encounters with Arab Political and Cultural Life*. Chicago, IL, Chicago University Press, 2008.

Rouhani, Fuad. *A History of OPEC*. London, Pall Mall Press, 1972.

Roy, Olivier. *The Failure of Political Islam*. London, I. B. Tauris, 1995.

Globalized Islam: The Search for a New Ummah. New York, Columbia University Press, 2004.

The New Central Asia: Geopolitics and the Birth of Nations. London, I. B. Tauris, 2007.

The Politics of Chaos in the Middle East. London, C. Hurst & Co, 2008.

Rubin, Barry M. *The Arab States and the Palestine Conflict*. Syracuse, NY, Syracuse University Press, 1981.

(Ed.). *Conflict and Insurgency in the Contemporary Middle East*. Abingdon, Routledge, 2009.

(Ed.). *Security and Stability in the Middle East*. Abingdon, Routledge, 2011.

Russell, James A. *Critical Issues Facing the Middle East*. London, Macmillan, 2006.

Ruthven, Malise. *Islam in the World*. Harmondsworth, Penguin (1984), 2nd revised edn, 2000.

A Fury for God: The Islamist Attack on America. London, Granta Books, 2002.

Fundamentalism: The Search for Meaning. Oxford, Oxford University Press, 2005.

Islam in the World. London, Granta Books, revised edn, 2006.

Saba Yared, Nazik. *Secularism and the Arab World*. London, Saqi Books, 2008.

Sabet, Amr G. E. *Islam and the Political: Theory, Governance and International Relations*. London, Pluto Press, 2008.

Sachar, Howard M. *Europe Leaves the Middle East 1936–1954*. London, Allen Lane, 1973.

Sadiki, Larbi. *The Search for Arab Democracy: Discourses and Counter Discourses*. New York, Columbia University Press, 2004.

Islamist Democracy: (Re)Visions of Polity and Society in the Arab Middle East. London, C. Hurst & Co, revised edn, 2007.

Rethinking Arab Democratization: Elections without Democracy. Oxford University Press, 2009.

Said, Edward W. *The Question of Palestine*. London, Routledge, 1979 (reissued, Vintage, 1992).

Covering Islam. London, Routledge, 1982 (reissued, Vintage, 1997).

The End of the Peace Process: Oslo and After. New York, Pantheon Books, 2000.

Sajoo, Amyn B. (Ed.). *Civil Society in the Muslim World*. London, I. B. Tauris, 2004.

Sakr, Naomi (Ed.) *Women and Media in the Middle East: Power through Self-expression*. London, I. B. Tauris, 2004.

Salame, G. *Democracy without Democrats? The Renewal of Politics in the Muslim World*. London and New York, I. B. Tauris, 1994.

Salem, Paul (Ed.). *Conflict Resolution in the Arab World: Selected Essays*. Beirut, American University of Beirut Press, 1997.

Salhi, Zahi Smail, and Netton, Ian Richard. *The Arab Diaspora*. Abingdon, Routledge, 2005.

Salzman, Philip C., and Robinson Divine, Donna (Eds). *Postcolonial Theory and the Arab–Israel Conflict*. Abingdon, Routledge, 2008.

Sauvaget, J. *Introduction à l'histoire de l'orient musulman*. Paris, 1943. 2nd edn recast by C. Cahen, Berkeley, CA, University of California Press, 1965.

Sayan, Serdar. *Economic Performance in the Middle East and North Africa: Institutions, Corruption and Reform*. Abingdon, Routledge, 2009.

Sayigh, Fatallah. *Le Désert et la Gloire*. Paris, Editions Gallimard, 1993.

Sayigh, Yusif A. *The Determinants of Arab Economic Development*. London, Croom Helm, 1977.

The Economies of the Arab World. London, Croom Helm, 1978.

Arab Oil Policies in the 1970s. London, Croom Helm, 1983.

Elusive Development: From Dependence to Self-Reliance in the Arab Region. London, Routledge, 1991.

Scott Appleby, R. (Ed.). *Spokesmen for the Despised: Fundamentalist Leaders of the Middle East*. Chicago, IL, University of Chicago Press, 1997.

Seale, Patrick. *The Struggle for Arab Independence: Riad el-Solh and the Makers of the Modern Middle East*. Cambridge, Cambridge University Press, 2010.

Searight, Sarah. *The British in the Middle East*. London, Weidenfeld and Nicolson, 1969.

Sedgwick, Mark. *Islam and Muslims: A Guide to Diverse Experience in a Modern World*. Boston, MA, Intercultural Press, 2006.

Selby, Jan. *Water, Power & Politics in the Middle East. The Other Palestinian–Israeli Conflict*. London, I. B. Tauris, 2003.

Shaban, M. A. *The Abbasid Revolution*. Cambridge University Press, 1970.

Islamic History: A New Interpretation. 2 vols. Cambridge University Press, 1976–78.

Shadid, Muhammad K. *The United States and the Palestinians*. London, Croom Helm, 1981.

Shafik, Nemat. *Prospects for Middle East and North African Economies*. Basingstoke, Macmillan Press, 1997.

Shapland, Gregory. *Rivers of Discord: International Water Disputes in the Middle East*. London, C. Hurst & Co, 1997.

Sharabi, H. B. *Governments and Politics of the Middle East in the Twentieth Century*. London, Greenwood Press (1962), revised edn, 1987.

Nationalism and Revolution in the Arab World. New York, Van Nostrand, 1966.

Palestine and Israel: The Lethal Dilemma. New York, Pegasus Press, 1969.

Shay, Shaul. *The Shahids: Islam and Suicide Attacks*. Edison, NJ, Transaction Publishers, 2004.

Shehata, Samer. (Ed.). *Islamist Politics in the Middle East: Movements and Change*. Abingdon, Routledge, 2012.

Sheikh, Naveed Shahzad. *The New Politics of Islam*. Abingdon, Routledge, 2007.

Shlaim, Avi. *War and Peace in the Middle East*. New York and London, Penguin, 1995.

Israel and Palestine: Reappraisals, Revisions, Refutations. London, Verso, 2009.

Shlaim, Avi, and Sayigh, Y. (Eds). *The Cold War and The Middle East*. Oxford University Press, 1998.

Shulze, Reinhard. *A Modern History of the Islamic World*. London, I. B. Tauris, 2002.

Sid-Ahmad, Abd al-Salam, and Ehteshami, Anoushiravan (Eds). *Islamic Fundamentalism*. Boulder, CO, Westview Press, 1996.

Sid-Ahmad, Muhammad. *After the Guns Fell Silent*. London, Croom Helm, 1976.

Sivan, Emmanuel. *Radical Islam: Medieval Theology and Modern Politics*. New Haven, CT, Yale University Press, 1985.

Skaine, Rosemarie. *Female Suicide Bombers*. Jefferson, NC, McFarland, 2006.

Smith, Dan. *The State of the Middle East: An Atlas of Conflict and Resolution*. Berkeley, CA, University of California Press, 2006.

Sowell, Kirk H. *The Arab World. An Illustrated History*. New York, Hippocrene Books, 2004.

Stark, Freya. *Dust in the Lion's Paw*. London and New York, 1961.

Stewart, Dona J. *The Middle East Today: Political, Geographical and Cultural Perspectives*. Abingdon, Routledge, 2012.

Stewart, P. J. *Unfolding Islam*. Reading, Ithaca Press, 1995.

Stickley, Thomas (Ed.). *Man, Food and Agriculture in the Middle East*. Beirut, American University of Beirut Press, 1969.

Stocking, G. W. *Middle East Oil. A Study in Political and Economic Controversy*. Nashville, TN, Vanderbilt University Press, 1979.

Sultan, Nabil A., Weir, David, and Karake-Shalhoub, Zeinab (Eds). *The New Post-Oil Arab Gulf: Managing People and Wealth*. London, Saqi Books, 2011.

Sumner, B. H. *Tsardom and Imperialism in the Far East and Middle East*. London, Oxford University Press, 1940.

Susser, Asher, and Shmuelevitz, Aryeh (Eds). *The Hashemites in the Modern Arab World: Essays in Honour of the Late Professor Uriel Dann*. London, Frank Cass, 1995.

el-Tamimi, Abdul Malek Khalaf. *Water in The Arab World: The Politics and Economics of Access to Water Resources*. London, I. B. Tauris, 2010.

Tamimi, Azzam (Ed.). *Islam and Secularism in the Middle East*. London, C. Hurst & Co, 2000.

Taylor, Alan R. *The Arab Balance of Power*. Syracuse, NY, Syracuse University Press, 1982.

Taylor, Trevor. *The Middle East in the International System: Lessons from Europe and Implications for Europe*. London, Royal Institute of International Affairs, 1997.

Tempest, Paul (Ed.). *An Enduring Friendship: 400 Years of Anglo-Gulf Relations*. London, Stacey International, 2006.

Tétreault, Mary Ann, Okruhlik, Gwenn, and Kapiszewski, Andrzej (Eds). *Political Change in the Arab Gulf States: Stuck in Transition*. Boulder, CO, Lynne Rienner Publishers, 2011.

Thayer, P. W. (Ed.). *Tensions in the Middle East*. Baltimore, 1958.

Thomas, L. V., and Frye, R. N. *The United States and Turkey and Iran*. Cambridge, MA, 1951.

Tillman, Seth P. *The United States in the Middle East*. Bloomington, IN, Indiana University Press, 1982.

Toaldo, Mattia. *The Origins of the US War on Terror: Lebanon, Libya and American Intervention in the Middle East*. Abingdon, Routledge, 2012.

Trevelyan, Lord Humphrey. *The Middle East in Revolution*. London, Macmillan, 1970

Trimingham, J. Spencer. *The Sufi Orders in Islam*. Oxford, Clarendon Press, 1971.

Tripp, Charles. *The Power and the People: Paths of Resistance in the Middle East*. New York, Cambridge University Press, 2013.

Tschirgi, Dan. *The American Search for Mideast Peace*. New York, Praeger, 1989.

Usher, Graham. *Dispatches from Palestine*. London, Pluto Press, 1999.

Vaner, S., Heradstveit, D., and Kazancigil, A. (Eds). *Sécularisation et Démocratisation dans les Sociétés Musulmanes*. Bern, Peter Lang, 2008.

Vassiliev, Alexei. *Russian Policy in the Middle East: From Messianism to Pragmatism*. Reading, Ithaca Press, 1993.

Vatikiotis, P. J. *Conflict in the Middle East*. London, George Allen and Unwin, 1971.

Islam and the State. London, Routledge, 1991.

Viorst, Milton. *Reaching for the Olive Branch: UNRWA and Peace in the Middle East*. Washington, DC, Middle East Institute, 1989.

Volpi, Frédéric. *Transnational Islam and Regional Security*. Abingdon, Routledge, 2007.

(Ed.). *Political Civility in the Middle East*. Abingdon, Routledge, 2011.

Volpi, Frédéric, and Cavatorta, Francesco (Eds). *Democratization in the Muslim World: Changing Patterns of Authority and Power*. Abingdon, Routledge, 2007.

Waines, David. *The Unholy War*. Wilmette, Medina Press, 1971.

An Introduction to Islam. Cambridge University Press, 1995.

Warriner, Doreen. *Land and Poverty in the Middle East*. London, 1948.

Land Reform and Development in the Middle East: Study of Egypt, Syria and Iraq. London, 1962.

Wasserstein, Bernard. *Divided Jerusalem: The Struggle for the Holy City*. London, Profile, 2001.

Watkins, Eric (Ed.). *The Middle East Environment: Selected Papers of the 1995 Conference of the British Society for Middle Eastern Studies*. Cambridge, St Malo Press, 1995.

Islamic Political Thought: The Basic Concepts. Edinburgh University Press (1968), revised edn, 1987.

Wilson, Rodney. *Trade and Investment in the Middle East*. Macmillan Press, 1977.

Economic Development in the Middle East. Abingdon, Routledge, 2nd edn, 2012.

Winckler, Onn. *Arab Political Demography: Population Growth, Labour Migration, and Natalist Policies*. Brighton, Sussex Academic Press, 2009.

Wolf, Aaron T. *Hydropolitics Along the Jordan River: Scarce Water and its Impact on the Arab–Israeli Conflict*. Tokyo, United Nations University Press, 1996.

Wright, Clifford A. *Facts and Fables: The Arab–Israeli conflict*. London, Kegan Paul International, 1989.

Wright, J. W., Jr (Ed.). *The Political Economy of Middle East Peace: The Impact of Competing Arab and Israeli Trade*. London, Routledge, 1999.

Wright, J. W., Jr, and Drake, Laura (Eds). *Economic and Political Impediments to Middle East Peace: Critical Questions and Alternative Scenarios*. New York, St Martin's Press, 1999.

Yamani, Mai (Ed.). *Cradle of Islam: The Hijaz and the Quest for an Arabian Identity*. London, I. B. Tauris, 2005.

Yergin, Daniel. *The Prize: The Epic Quest for Oil, Money and Power*. New York, Simon and Schuster (1990), revised edn, 1993.

Youngs, Richard. *Europe and the Middle East: In the Shadow of September 11*. Boulder, CO, Lynne Rienner Publishers, 2006.

Zahlan, Rosemarie Said. *The Making of the Modern Gulf States*. Reading, Ithaca Press, revised edn, 1999.

Palestine and the Gulf States: The Presence at the Table. Abingdon, Routledge, 2009.

Zeitoun, Mark. *Power and Water in the Middle East: The Hidden Politics of the Palestinian–Israeli Water Conflict*. London, I. B. Tauris, 2008.

Zubaida, Sami. *Law and Power in the Islamic World*. London, I. B. Tauris, 2005.

Books on North Africa

(See also bibliographies at end of relevant chapters in Part Two.)

Abun-Nasr, Jamil M. *A History of the Maghreb*. Cambridge University Press, 1972.

Aghrout, Ahmed. *From Preferential Status to Partnership: The Euro-Maghreb Relationship*. Aldershot, Ashgate, 2000.

Ahmida, Ali A. *Beyond Colonialism and Nationalism in North Africa*. London, Macmillan, 2001.

Amin, Samir. *L'Economie du Maghreb*. 2 vols, Paris, Editions du Minuit, 1966.

The Maghreb in the Modern World. London, Penguin, 1971.

Amirah-Fernández, H., and Zoubir, Y. H. *North Africa: Politics, Regions, and the Limits of Transformation*. Abingdon, Routledge, 2008.

Balta, Paul. *Le Grand Maghreb*. Paris, Editions La Découverte, 1990.

Benichou Gottreich, Emily, and Schroeter, Daniel J. (Eds). *Jewish Culture and Society in North Africa*. Bloomington, IN, Indiana University Press, 2011.

Berque, Jacques. *Le Maghreb entre deux guerres*. Paris, Editions du Seuil, 2nd edn, 1967.

Bonnefous, Marc. *Le Maghreb: repères et rappels*. Paris, Editions du Centre des Hautes Etudes sur l'Afrique et l'Asie modernes de Paris, 1991.

Brown, Leon Carl (Ed.). *State and Society in Independent North Africa*. Washington, DC, Middle East Institute, 1966.

Brunel, Claire, and Hufbauer, Gary Clyde. *Maghreb Regional and Global Integration: A Dream to Be Fulfilled*. Washington, DC, Peterson Institute, 2008.

Burgat, François. *The Islamic Movement in North Africa*. Austin, TX, University of Texas Press, 1993.

Cammett, Melani C. *Globalization and Business Politics in Arab North Africa*. New York, Cambridge University Press, 2007.

Capot-Rey, R. *Le Sahara français*. Paris, 1953.

Centre d'Etudes des Relations Internationales. *Le Maghreb et la communauté économique européenne*. Paris, Editions FNSP, 1965.

Clancy-Smith, Julia. *North Africa, Islam and the Mediterranean World*. London, Frank Cass, 2001.

Collinson, Sarah. *Shore to Shore: The Politics of Migration in Euro-Maghreb Relations*. London, Royal Institute of International Affairs, 1997.

Cordesman, Anthony H. *A Tragedy of Arms: Military and Security Developments in the Maghreb*. Westport, CT, Praeger, 2002.

Damis, John. *Conflict in Northwest Africa: The Western Sahara Dispute*. Stanford, CA, Hoover Institution Press, 1983.

Duclos, J., Leca, J., and Duvignaud, J. *Les nationalismes maghrébins*. Paris, Centre d'Etudes des Relations Internationales, 1966.

Durand, Gwendal. *L'Organisation d'al-Qaïda au Maghreb islamique: réalité ou manipulations*. Paris, L'Harmattan, 2011.

Economic Commission for Africa. *Main Problems of Economic Co-operation in North Africa*. Tangier, 1966.

Entelis, John P. *Islam, Democracy and the State in North Africa*. Bloomington, IN, Indiana University Press, 1997.

Evers Rasander, E., and Westerlund, David (Eds). *African Islam and Islam in Africa: Encounters Between Sufis and Islamists*. London, C. Hurst & Co, 1997.

el-Fassi, Allal. (trans. H. Z. Nuseibeh). *The Independence Movements in Arab North Africa*. Washington, DC, 1954.

Furlonge, Sir Geoffrey. *The Lands of Barbary*. London, John Murray, 1966.

García, Alejandro. *Historias del Sáhara. El mejor y el peor de los mundos*. Madrid, Los Libros de la Catarata, 2002.

Historia del Sáhara y su conflicto. Madrid, Los Libros de la Catarata, 2010.

Garon, Lise. *Dangerous Alliances: Civil Society, The Media and Democratic Transition in North Africa*. London, Zed Books, 2003.

Gautier, E. F. *Le Passé de l'Afrique du Nord*. Paris, 1937.

Germidis, Dimitri, with the help of Delapierre, Michel. *Le Maghreb, la France et l'enjeu technologique*. Paris, Editions Cujas, 1976.

Ghazi, Mahmud Ahmad. *The Sansusiyyah Movement of North Africa*. Islamabad, Shariah Academy, International Islamic University, 2001.

Gordon, D. C. *North Africa's French Legacy 1954–62*. Cambridge, MA, Harvard University Press, 1962.

Hahn, Lorna. *North Africa: From Nationalism to Nationhood*. Washington, DC, 1960.

Hermassi, Elbaki. *Leadership and National Development in North Africa*. Berkeley, CA, University of California Press, 1973.

Heseltine, N. *From Libyan Sands to Chad*. Leiden, 1960.

Joffé, E. G. H. (Ed.). *North Africa: Nation, State and Region*. London, Routledge and University of London, 1993.

Joffé, George. (Ed.). *Islamist Radicalisation in North Africa: Politics and Process*. Abingdon, Routledge, 2011.

Julien, Ch.-A. *Histoire de l'Afrique du nord*. 2 vols, Paris, 2nd edn, 1951–52.

History of North Africa: From the Arab Conquest to 1830. Revised by R. Le Tourneau. Ed. C. C. Stewart. London, Routledge and Kegan Paul, 1970.

Khaldoun, Ibn. *History of the Berbers*. Translated into French by Slane. 4 vols, Algiers, 1852–56.

Knapp, Wilfrid. *North West Africa: A Political and Economic Survey*. Oxford University Press, 3rd edn, 1977.

La Guérivière, Jean de. *Amère Méditerranée: Le Maghreb et Nous*. Paris, Editions du Seuil, 2004.

Laskier, Michael M. *Israel and the Maghreb: From Statehood to Oslo*. Gainesville, FL, University Press of Florida; London, Eurospan, 2004.

Layachi, Azzedine. *The United States and North Africa: A Cognitive Approach to Foreign Policy*. New York and London, Praeger, 1990.

(Ed.). *Economic Crisis and Political Change in North Africa*. New York and London, Praeger, 1998.

Le Tourneau, Roger. *Evolution politique de l'Afrique du nord musulman*. Paris, 1962.

Liska, G. *The Greater Maghreb: From Independence to Unity?* Washington, DC, Center of Foreign Policy Research, 1963.

Maddy-Weitzman, Bruce. *The Berber Identity Movement and the Challenge to North African States*. Austin, TX, University of Texas Press, 2011.

Maddy-Weitzman, B., and Zisenwine, D. (Eds). *The Maghrib in the New Century: Identity, Religion and Politics*. Gainesville, FL, University of Florida Press, 2008.

McDougall, James. (Ed.). *Nation, Society and Culture in North Africa*. London, Frank Cass, 2003.

Marçais, G. *La Berberie musulmane et l'Orient au moyen age*. Paris, 1946.

Mezran, Karim K. *Negotiating National Identity: The Case of the Arab States of North Africa*. Rome, Antonio Pelicani, 2002.

Moore, C. H. *Politics in North Africa*. Boston, MA, Little, Brown, 1970.

Mortimer, Edward. *France and the Africans, 1944–1960*. London, Faber, 1969.

Naylor, Phillip C. *North Africa: A History from Antiquity to the Present*. Austin, TX, University of Texas Press, 2009.

Nickerson, Jane S. *Short History of North Africa*. New York, 1961.

Parrinder, Geoffrey. *Religion in Africa*. London, Pall Mall Press, 1970.

Pazzanita, Anthony G. *Historical Dictionary of Western Sahara*. Lanham, MA, Scarecrow Press, 3rd edn, 2006.

Polk, William R. (Ed.). *Developmental Revolution: North Africa, Middle East, South Asia*. Washington, DC, Middle East Institute, 1963.

Robana, Abderrahman. *The Prospects for an Economic Community in North Africa*. London, Pall Mall, 1973.

Rouis, Mustapha, and Tabor, Steven R. *Regional Economic Integration in the Middle East and North Africa: Beyond Trade Reform*. Washington, DC, The World Bank, 2013.

Rousseaux, Vanessa. *L'urbanisation au Maghreb: le langage des cartes*. Aix en Provence, Presses Universitaires d'Aix-Marseille, 2004.

Sahli, Mohamed Chérif. *Décoloniser l'histoire; introduction à l'histoire du Maghreb*. Paris, Maspero, 1965.

Sayeh, Ismail. *Les Sahraouis*. Paris, L'Harmattan, 1998.

Schramm, Josef. *Die Westsahara*. Freilassing, Paunonia Verlag, 1969.

Segura i Mas, Antoni. *El Magreb, del colonialismo al islamismo*. Barcelona, Universidad de Barcelona, 1994.

Shahin, Emad. *Political Ascent: Contemporary Islamic Movements in North Africa*. Boulder, CO, Westview Press, 1996.

Steel, R. (Ed.). *North Africa*. New York, Wilson, 1967.

Toynbee, Sir Arnold. *Between Niger and Nile*. Oxford University Press, 1965.

Trimingham, J. S. *The Influence of Islam upon Africa*. London, Longmans, and Beirut, Libraire du Liban, 1968.

Tvedt, Terje (Ed.). *The River Nile in the Post-Colonial Age*. Cairo, American University of Cairo Press, 2010.

Vermeren, Pierre. *Maghreb: la démocratie impossible?* Paris, Fayard, 2004.

White, Gregory. *A Comparative Political Economy of Tunisia and Morocco: On the Outside of Europe Looking in*. Albany, NY, State University of New York Press, 2001.

Willis, Michael. *Politics and Power in the Maghreb: Algeria, Tunisia and Morocco from Independence to the Arab Spring*. London, C. Hurst & Co, 2012.

Wippel, Steffen. *Wirtschaft, Politik und Raum: Territoriale und regionale Prozesse in der westlichen Sahara*. Berlin, Verlag Hans Schiler, 2012.

Zartman, I. William. *Government and Politics in North Africa*. London, Greenwood Press, revised edn, 1978.

(Ed.). *Man, State and Society in the Contemporary Maghreb*. London, Pall Mall, 1973.

Zoubir, Yahia H. *North Africa in Transition: State, Society and Economic Transformation in the 1990s*. Gainesville, FL, University Press of Florida, 1999.

Zoubir, Yahia H., and Dris-Aït-Hamadouche, Louisa. *Global Security Watch—The Maghreb: Algeria, Libya, Morocco and Tunisia*. Santa Barbara, CA, Praeger, 2013.

Zunes, Stephen, and Mundy, Jacob. *Western Sahara: War, Nationalism, and Conflict Irresolution*. Syracuse, NY, Syracuse University Press, 2010.

SELECT BIBLIOGRAPHY (PERIODICALS)

Al-Abhath: Publ. by American University of Beirut Press, POB 11-0236, Riad el-Solh, Beirut 1107 2020, Lebanon; tel. (1) 340460; fax (1) 744461; e-mail aubpress@aub.edu.lb; internet www.aub.edu.lb/php/aubpress/site/; f. 1948; annual specializing in Arab and Middle East studies; English and Arabic; Man. Editor Dr Amélie Beyhum; Editor Prof. Assad Khairallah; circ. c. 250.

Acta Orientalia: c/o Institutt for kulturstudier og orientalske språk, Universitetet i Oslo, POB 1010 Blindern, 0315 Oslo, Norway; tel. 22-85-55-86; fax 22-85-48-28; e-mail r.l.schmidt@ikos.uio.no; internet www.hf.uio.no/ikos/forskning/tidskrifter/html; f. 1922; publ. under auspices of the Oriental Societies of Denmark, Finland, Norway and Sweden; history, language, archaeology and religions of the Near and Far East and South Asia; Editor Prof. Ruth Laila Schmidt; annually; circ. c.171.

Acta Orientalia Academiae Scientiarum Hungaricae: Institute of Oriental Studies, Eötvös Loránd University, H-1088 Budapest, Múzeum krt. 4D, Hungary; tel. (1) 485-5202; fax (1) 464-8221; e-mail vasaryi@gmail.com; internet www.akademiai.com; f. 1950; English, French, German and Russian; Editor-in-Chief István Vásáry; quarterly.

Africa Contemporary Record: Africana Publishing Co, Holmes & Meier Publishers, Inc, POB 943, Teaneck, NJ 07666, USA; tel. (201) 833-2270; fax (201) 833-2272; e-mail info@holmesandmeier.com; internet www.holmesandmeier.com; annual surveys, special essays and indices.

Africa Quarterly: Indian Council for Cultural Relations, Azad Bhavan, Indraprastha Estate, New Delhi 110 002, India; tel. (11) 23370229; fax (11) 23378647; e-mail pdpub@iccrindia.org; f. 1961; Editor Manish Chand; circ. 1,000.

Africa Research Bulletin: Wiley-Blackwell, 9600 Garsington Rd, Oxford, OX4 2DQ, United Kingdom; tel. (1865) 776868; fax (1865) 714591; e-mail editors@africaresearch.co.uk; internet eu.wiley.com/WileyCDA/WileyTitle/productCd-ARBP.html?amp;site=1; f. 1964; monthly bulletins divided into Economic, Financial and Technical Series and Political, Social and Cultural Series; Editors Virginia Baily, Veronica Hoskins.

Africa Review: World of Information, 11 Clarendon St, Cambridge, CB1 1JU, United Kingdom; tel. and fax (1223) 312393; fax (1223) 351584; e-mail queries@worldinformation.com; internet www.worldinformation.com; f. 1977; political and economic analysis; Editor Tony Axon; annually.

Akhbar al-Alam al-Islami: Press and Publications Dept, Muslim World League, POB 537, Mecca al-Mukarramah 21955, Saudi Arabia; tel. (2) 560-0919; fax (2) 560-1319; e-mail info@themwl.org; internet www.themwl.org; Arabic; weekly.

Alam Attijarat (The World of Business): Keller International Publishing, 150 Great Neck Rd, Great Neck, New York, NY 11021, USA; tel. (516) 829-9210; fax (516) 829-5414; e-mail bdeluca@kellerpubs.com; internet www.kellerpubs.com/mp_media.htm; f. 1966; business and industry, incl. oil and gas, construction, banking, finance and manufacturing; Arabic; Editor Bryan DeLuca; 10 a year; circ. c. 42,000.

Anatolian Studies: BIAA, 10 Carlton House Terrace, London, SW1Y 5AH, United Kingdom; tel. (20) 7969-5204; fax (20) 7969-5401; e-mail biaa@britac.ac.uk; internet www.biaa.ac.uk; f. 1948; annual of the British Institute at Ankara; covers the arts, humanities, social sciences and environmental sciences in Turkey; Exec. Editor Gina Coulthard; Academic Editor Prof. Roger Matthews.

Anatolica: Nederlands Instituut in Turkije/Hollanda Araştırma Enstitüsü, PK 132, İstiklal Cad., Nur-i Ziya Sok. 5, Beyoğlu 34431, İstanbul; tel. (212) 2939283; fax (212) 2513846; e-mail nit@nit-istanbul.org; internet www.nit-istanbul.org/nitpublications.htm; f. 1967; publ. by the Netherlands Institute in Turkey in co-operation with the Netherlands Institute for the Near East (Nederlands Instituut voor het Nabije Oosten—NINO); Editors J. J. Roodenberg, G. Algaze, F. A. Gerritsen, A. H. DeGroot, M. Özdoğan, Th. van den Hout; annually.

Annales archéologiques Arabes Syriennes: Direction Générale des Antiquités et des Musées, University St, Damascus, Syria; tel. (11) 2214854; f. 1951; archaeological and historical review; Dir-Gen. Dr Sultan Moheisen; annually.

L'Année du Maghreb: Edited by the Institut de recherches et d'études sur le Monde Arabe et Musulman (IREMAM), 5 rue du Château de l'Horloge, BP 647, 13094 Aix-en-Provence Cedex 2, France; tel. 4-42-52-41-62; fax 4-42-52-49-80; e-mail anneemaghreb@mmsh.univ-aix.fr; internet anneemaghreb.revues.org; publ. by the Centre National de la Recherche Scientifique, CNRS Editions, 15 rue Malebranche, 75005 Paris, France; f. 1962 as Annuaire de l'Afrique du Nord; present name adopted 2005; year book contains special studies on current affairs and political science, report on a collective programme of social sciences research on North Africa, chronologies, chronicles, documentation and book reviews; Man. Editor Ghislaine Alleaume; Editor Frédéric Abécassis.

Arab Oil and Gas Directory: The Arab Petroleum Research Centre, 7 ave Ingrès, 75016 Paris, France; tel. 1-45-24-33-10; fax 1-45-20-16-85; e-mail aprc@arab-oil-gas.com; internet www.arab-oil-gas.com; f. 1971; petroleum and gas; in English and French; Editor Dr Nicolas Sarkis; fortnightly.

Arab Studies Quarterly: Center for Islamic and Middle Eastern Studies (CIMES), California State University, 5500 University Parkway, San Bernardino CA 92407-2318, USA; e-mail aoude@hawaii.edu; internet arabstudiesquarterly.plutojournals.org; f. 1979; Editor Ibrahim G. Aoudé.

Arabica (Revue d'Etudes Arabes et Islamiques): Université Paris III, 13 rue de Santeuil, 75231 Paris Cedex 05, France; e-mail secretariat.arabica@free.fr; internet www.brill.nl/arab; f. 1954; publ. by Brill Academic Publishers, POB 9000, 2300 PA, Leiden, Netherlands; Editor A. Cheikh-Moussa; quarterly.

Archiv für Orientforschung: c/o Institut für Orientalistik der Universität Wien, Spitalgasse 2, Hof 4, 1090 Vienna, Austria; tel. (1) 427-74-34-01; fax (1) 427-79-434; e-mail michaela.weszeli@univie.ac.at; internet orientalistik.univie.ac.at/forschung/publikationen/archiv-fuer-orientforschung; f. 1923; articles in English, German, French and Italian; Editors Prof. Dr Hermann Hunger, Prof. Dr Michael Jursa, Prof. Dr Gebhard J. Selz; bi-annually.

Asian Affairs: Royal Society for Asian Affairs, 2 Belgrave Sq., London, SW1X 8PJ, United Kingdom; tel. (20) 7235-5122; fax (20) 7259-6771; e-mail editor@rsaa.org.uk; internet www.rsaa.org.uk/page/journal; Editor Barney Smith; 3 a year.

Awal: Cahier d'Etudes Berbères: Editions de la Maison des sciences de l'homme, 54 blvd Raspail, 75006 Paris, France; tel. 1-49-54-22-00; e-mail yacine@msh-paris.fr; internet www.revues.msh-paris.fr/modele2/perbook2.asp?id_perio=31; f. 1985; Editorial Dir Tassadit Yacine; 2 a year.

Belleten: Türk Tarih Kurumu (Turkish Historical Society), Kizilay Sok. 1, 06100 Ankara, Turkey; tel. (312) 3102368; fax (312) 3101698; e-mail bilgi@ttk.org.tr; internet www.ttk.org.tr; f. 1937; history and archaeology of Turkey; Editor Prof. Dr Mehmet Metin Hülagü; 3 a year.

Bibliotheca Orientalis: Netherlands Institute for the Near East (Nederlands Instituut voor het Nabije Oosten—NINO), Witte Singel 25, POB 9515, 2300 RA Leiden, Netherlands; tel. (71) 5272036; fax (71) 5272038; e-mail bior@hum.leidenuniv.nl; internet www.nino-leiden.nl; f. 1943; Editors R. E. Kon, A. van der Kooij, L. Limme, D. J. W. Meijer, J. Eidem, J. de Roos, M. Stol; 3 double issues a year.

British Journal of Middle Eastern Studies: BRISMES Administrative Office, Institute for Middle Eastern and Islamic Studies, University of Durham, Elvet Hill Rd, Durham, DH1 3TU, United Kingdom; tel. (191) 334-5179; fax (191) 334-5661; e-mail a.l.haysey@durham.ac.uk; internet www.brismes.ac.uk/publications; f. 1974 as British Society of Middle Eastern Studies Bulletin; publ. by Taylor & Francis for BRISMES; Editor Prof. Ian Netton; 4 a year.

Bulletin d'études orientales: Institut Français du Proche Orient, BP 344, Abou Roumaneh, Damascus, Syria; tel. (11) 3330214; fax (11) 3327887; e-mail diffusion@ifporient.org; internet www.ifporient.org; f. 1922; annually.

Bulletin of the School of Oriental and African Studies: School of Oriental and African Studies, University of London, Thornhaugh St, Russell Sq., London, WC1H 0XG, United Kingdom; tel. (20) 7898-4064; fax (20) 7898-4849; e-mail bulletin@soas.ac.uk; internet journals.cambridge.org/jid_BSO; f. 1917; publ. by Cambridge University Press; publishes scholarly articles and book reviews on the history, languages and literatures, religions, arts and music of Asia, the Middle East and Africa; Editor Dr Ulrich Pagel; 3 a year.

Les Cahiers de l'Orient: 36 rue de la Convention, 75015 Paris, France; e-mail cahiersdelorient@wanadoo.fr; internet www.ser-sa.com/

boutique/LesCahiersdelOrient/2; f. 1986; publ. by CERPO (Centre of Near East Studies); review of Islamic and Arab affairs; Editor ANTOINE SFEIR; quarterly.

Les Cahiers de Tunisie: Publ. by Faculté des sciences humaines et sociales, Université de Tunis, 94 blvd de 9 Avril 1938, 1007 Tunis, Tunisia; tel. (71) 560-840; fax (71) 567-551; internet www.fshst.rnu.tn; f. 1953; research in humanities; Dir HÉDI CHÉRIF; Editor-in-Chief HASSAN ANNABI; quarterly.

The Cairo Review of Global Affairs: School of Global Affairs and Public Policy, American University in Cairo, AUC Ave, POB 74, New Cairo, 11835 Egypt; e-mail info@thecairoreview.com; internet www.aucegypt.edu/GAPP/CairoReview; Man. Editor SCOTT MACLEOD; quarterly.

Chuto Kenkyu (Journal of Middle Eastern Studies): The Middle East Research Institute of Japan, Sanko Park Bldg 5F, 7-3-1 Nishi-Shinjuku Shinjuku-ku, Tokyo 160-0023, Japan; tel. (3) 3371-5798; fax (3) 3371-5799; e-mail webmaster@meij.or.jp; internet www.meij.or.jp/chutokenkyu/index.html; f. 1960; Japanese; Editor TATSUO ARIMA; quarterly.

Le Commerce du Levant: PB 45-332, 3e étage, Immeuble l'Orient-Le Jour, route de Damas, Baabda, Hazmié, Lebanon; tel. (5) 952259; fax (5) 453644; e-mail redaction@lecommercedulevant.com; internet www.lecommercedulevant.com; economic; Editor-in-Chief SIBYLLE RIZK; monthly.

Contemporary Arab Affairs: Routledge, Taylor & Francis, 4 Park Sq., Milton Park, Abingdon, Oxon, OX14 4RN, United Kingdom; tel. (20) 7017-6000; fax (20) 7017-6336; e-mail tf.enquiries@tandf.co.uk; internet www.tandf.co.uk/journals/rcaa; f. 2008; journal of the Centre for Arab Unity Studies; modern Arab scholarship in the English language; Editors-in-Chief KHAIR EL-DIN HASEEB, ROSEMARY HOLLIS; quarterly.

Dawat al-Haq: Press and Publications Dept, Muslim World League, POB 537, Mecca al-Mukarramah 21955, Saudi Arabia; tel. (2) 560-0919; fax (2) 560-1319; e-mail info@themwl.org; internet www.themwl.org; Arabic; monthly.

Estudios de Asia y Africa: Centro de Estudios de Asia y Africa, Colegio de México, Camino al Ajusco 20, Pedregal de Santa Teresa, Tlalpan, 10740 México, DF; tel. (55) 5449-3022; fax (55) 5645-0464; e-mail reaa@colmex.mx; internet ceaa.colmex.mx/revista/INDEX.html; f. 1966; history, politics, anthropology and current affairs in Asia and Africa; Dir GILBERTO CONDE; 3 a year.

Hamizrah Hehadash (The New East): The Middle East & Islamic Studies Association of Israel (MEISAI), The Hebrew University, Jerusalem, Israel; e-mail meisai1949@gmail.com; internet www.meisai.org.il; f. 1949; Middle Eastern, Asian and African affairs; Hebrew, with English summary; Editors Dr RONEN YITZHAK, Dr MUSTAFA KABHA; annually.

Hesperis-Tamuda: Faculté des Lettres et des Sciences Humaines, Université Muhammad V, 3 ave Ibn Battouta, BP 1040, Rabat, Morocco; tel. (3) 7771873; fax (3) 7772068; f. 1921; history, anthropology, civilization of Maghreb and Western Islam, special reference to bibliography; Chief Editor BRAHIM BOUTALEB; annually; circ. 2,000.

Ibla: Institut des Belles Lettres Arabes, 12 bis, rue Jamâa el-Haoua, 1008 Tunis (Bab Menara), Tunisia; tel. (71) 560133; fax (71) 572683; e-mail ibla@gnet.tn; internet www.iblatunis.org; f. 1937; Dir JOHN MCWILLIAM; 2 a year.

Indo-Iranian Journal: Brill, POB 9000, 2300 PA Leiden, Netherlands; tel. (71) 5353500; fax (71) 5317532; e-mail paalvast@brill.com; internet www.brill.nl/iij; f. 1957; English, occasionally French and German; publishes papers on ancient and medieval Indian languages, literature, philosophy and religion, ancient and medieval Iran, and Tibet; Editors-in-Chief PETER BISSCHOP, JONATHAN SILK; quarterly.

Indo-Iranica: 12 Dr M. Ishaque Rd, Kolkata 700016, India; tel. and fax 2269899; f. 1944; publ. by Iran Society since 1946; promotion of Persian studies and Indo-Iranian cultural relations; English and Farsi; Gen. Sec. of Iran Society and Man. Editor M. A. MAJID; quarterly.

International Journal of Contemporary Iraqi Studies: Intellect Books Ltd, The Mill, Parnall Rd, Fishponds, Bristol, BS16 3JG, United Kingdom; tel. (117) 958-9910; fax (117) 958-9911; e-mail ijcis@intellectbooks.com; f. 2007; journal of the Int. Asscn of Contemporary Iraqi Studies; studies of modern Iraqi politics and society; Editors WILLIAM HADDAD (California State University), IBRAHIM AOUDE (University of Hawai'i); 3 a year.

International Journal of Middle East Studies: Cambridge University Press, 32 Ave of the Americas, New York, NY 10013-2473, USA; tel. (212) 924-3900; fax (212) 691-3239; e-mail ijmes@gc.cuny.edu; internet journals.cambridge.org/jid_mes; f. 1970; Journal of the Middle East Studies Asscn of North America; Editor BETH BARON; quarterly.

Iranian Studies: Routledge, Taylor & Francis, 4 Park Sq., Milton Park, Abingdon, Oxon, OX14 4RN, United Kingdom; tel. (20) 7017-6000; fax (20) 7017-6336; e-mail tf.enquiries@tandf.co.uk; internet www.tandf.co.uk/journals/cist; f. 1967; journal of the Int. Society for Iranian Studies; Iranian and Persian history, literature and society; Editor HOMA KATOUZIAN (University of Oxford, United Kingdom); quarterly.

Iraq: British Institute for the Study of Iraq (Gertrude Bell Memorial), 10 Carlton House Terrace, London, SW1Y 5AH, United Kingdom; tel. (20) 7969-5274; fax (20) 7969-5401; e-mail bisi@britac.ac.uk; internet www.britac.ac.uk/institutes/iraq; f. 1934 by the then British School of Archaeology in Iraq; Editors Dr MICHAEL SEYMOUR, Dr JON TAYLOR; annually; circ. c. 700.

Der Islam: Universität Hamburg, Edmund-Siemers-Allee 1-Ost, 20146 Hamburg, Germany; tel. (40) 428380; fax (40) 428386594; e-mail der_islam@uni-hamburg.de; internet www.uni-hamburg.de; 2 a year.

Islamic Quarterly: The Islamic Cultural Centre and the London Central Mosque, 146 Park Rd, London, NW8 7RG, United Kingdom; tel. (20) 7724-3363; fax (20) 7724-0493; e-mail iq@iccuk.org; internet www.iccuk.org; f. 1954; Editor Dr AHMAD AL-DUBAYAN; quarterly.

Israel Affairs: Routledge, Taylor & Francis, 4 Park Sq., Milton Park, Abingdon, Oxon, OX14 4RN, United Kingdom; tel. (20) 7017-6000; fax (20) 7017-6336; e-mail tf.enquiries@tandf.co.uk; internet www.tandf.co.uk/journals/fisa; f. 1994; Israeli history, politics, economics, art and literature; Editor EFRAIM KARSH (King's College London, United Kingdom); quarterly.

Jeune Afrique/L'Intelligent: Groupe Jeune Afrique, 57 bis, rue d'Auteuil, 75016 Paris, France; tel. 1-44-30-19-60; fax 1-44-30-19-30; e-mail serviceclient@laboutiquejeuneafrique.com; internet www.jeuneafrique.com; f. 1960; Pres. and Dir-Gen. BÉCHIR BEN YAHMED; weekly.

Journal of the American Oriental Society: American Oriental Society, Harlan Hatcher Graduate Library, University of Michigan, Ann Arbor, MI 48109-1190, USA; tel. (313) 747-4760; e-mail jrodgers@umich.edu; internet www.umich.edu/~aos; f. 1842; Oriental civilizations and Asian languages and literature; Editor-in-Chief STEPHANIE JAMISON; quarterly.

Journal of Arabian Studies: Routledge, Taylor & Francis, 4 Park Sq., Milton Park, Abingdon, Oxon, OX14 4RN, United Kingdom; tel. (20) 7017-6000; fax (20) 7017-6336; e-mail tf.enquiries@tandf.co.uk; internet www.tandf.co.uk/journals/rjab; f. 2011; history, politics, economics, art, literature of the Arabian peninsula; edited by the Centre for Gulf Studies, University of Exeter, United Kingdom; Editor JAMES ONLEY (University of Exeter, United Kingdom); 2 a year.

Journal Asiatique: Société Asiatique, Palais de l'Institut, 23 quai Conti, 75006 Paris, France; tel. and fax 1-44-41-44-93; e-mail poj@peeters-leuven.be; internet www.aibl.fr/us/asie/home.html; Publr Peeters, Bondgenotenlaan 153, 3000 Leuven, Belgium; f. 1822; covers all phases of Oriental research; Dir JEAN-MARIE DURAND; 2 a year.

Journal for Islamic Studies: Centre for Contemporary Islam, University of Cape Town, Dept of Religious Studies, Private Bag, Rondebosch 7701, South Africa; tel. (21) 6503889; fax (21) 6897575; e-mail shamiemah.jassiem@uct.ac.za; internet www.cci.uct.ac.za/publications/jis/overview; publishes original research on Islam as a world culture and civilization; covers religion, theology, law, history, culture, art, ethics, politics, international relations, philosophy, anthropology and sociology; Chief Editor MUNEER FAREED; annually.

Journal of Modern Jewish Studies: Routledge, Taylor & Francis, 4 Park Sq., Milton Park, Abingdon, Oxon, OX14 4RN, United Kingdom; tel. (20) 7017-6000; fax (20) 7017-6336; e-mail tf.enquiries@tandf.co.uk; internet www.tandf.co.uk/journals/cmjs; literature, history, religion and social studies; Editor GLENDA ABRAMSON (University of Oxford, United Kingdom); 3 a year.

Journal of Muslim Minority Affairs: Institute of Muslim Minority Affairs, 46 Goodge St, London, W1T 4LU, United Kingdom; tel. and fax (20) 7636-6740; e-mail editor@imma.org.uk; internet www.imma.org.uk/jmma.htm; f. 1979; publ. by Routledge; Chief Editor Dr SALEHA S MAHMOOD; 4 a year.

Journal of Near Eastern Studies: Oriental Institute, University of Chicago, 1155 E 58th St, Chicago, IL 60637, USA; tel. (773) 702-7700; fax (773) 702-9756; e-mail jnes@uchicago.edu; internet www.journals.uchicago.edu/JNES/home.html; f. 1884; owned by University of Chicago Press; devoted to the ancient, medieval and pre-modern Near and Middle East, archaeology, languages, history, Islam; Editor CHRISTOPHER WOODS; 2 a year.

The Journal of North African Studies: Routledge, Taylor & Francis, 4 Park Sq., Milton Park, Abingdon, Oxon, OX14 4RN, United Kingdom; tel. (20) 7017-6000; fax (20) 7017-6336; e-mail tf.enquiries@tandf.co.uk; internet www.tandf.co.uk/journals/fnas; f. 1996; history, sociology, anthropology, economics and diplomacy; Editors JOHN P. ENTELIS (Middle East Studies Program, Fordham University,

USA), GEORGE JOFFÉ (Centre for International Studies, University of Cambridge, United Kingdom); quarterly.

Journal of Palestine Studies: 3501 M St, NW, Washington, DC 20007, USA; tel. (202) 342-3990; fax (202) 342-3927; e-mail jps@palestine-studies.org; internet www.palestine-studies.org; f. 1971; publ. by the University of California Press for the Institute for Palestine Studies, Washington, DC; Palestinian affairs and the Arab–Israeli conflict; Editor RASHID I. KHALIDI; Man. Editor GEOFFREY D. SCHAD; quarterly; circ. 3,600.

Maghreb-Machrek: Institut Choiseul, 28 rue Etienne Marcel, 75002 Paris, France; tel. 1-53-34-09-93; fax 1-53-34-09-94; e-mail editions@choiseul.info; internet www.choiseul-editions.com/revues-geopolitique-Maghreb-Machrek-15.html; f. 1964; publ. with the assistance of the Institut du monde arabe and the Centre national du livre; Chief Editor JEAN-YVES MOISSERON; quarterly.

The Maghreb Review: 45 Burton St, London, WC1H 9AL, United Kingdom; tel. and fax (20) 7388-1840; e-mail maghreb@maghrebreview.com; internet www.maghrebreview.com; f. 1976; covers the Maghreb, the Middle East, Africa and Islamic studies; Editor MUHAMMAD BEN MADANI; quarterly.

Maghreb-Sélection: IC Publications, 10 rue Vineuse, 75784 Paris Cedex 16, France; tel. 1-44-30-81-05; fax 6-87-19-38-85; e-mail info@icpublications.com; internet www.icpublications.com; f. 1979; economic information about North Africa; weekly.

Majallat a-Rabita: Press and Publications Dept, Muslim World League, POB 537, Mecca al-Mukarramah 21955, Saudi Arabia; tel. (2) 560-0919; fax (2) 560-1319; e-mail info@themwl.org; internet www.themwl.org; Editor Dr OSMAN ABUZAID; Arabic; monthly.

Marchés Arabes: IC Publications, 10 rue Vineuse, 75784 Paris Cedex 16, France; tel. 1-44-30-81-05; fax 6-87-19-38-85; e-mail info@icpublications.com; internet www.icpublications.com; f. 1978; economic information about the Middle East; fortnightly.

MEN: Middle East News Agency, POB 1165, 17 Sharia Hoda Sharawi, Cairo, Egypt; tel. (2) 3933000; fax (2) 3935055; e-mail webmaster@mena.org.eg; internet www.mena.org.eg; f. 1962; weekly economic news bulletin in English; Chair. ADEL ABD AL-AZIZ.

Le Message de l'Islam: Islamic Thought Foundation, BP 14155-3899, Tehran, Iran; tel. (21) 88897662; fax (21) 88902725; e-mail info@itf.org.ir; internet www.itf.org.ir; theoretical review of Iranian Islam; monthly.

The Middle East: TME Media 21 Ltd, 46 Cleveland Rd, London, E18 2AL, United Kingdom; tel. (20) 8989-9551; e-mail tmemedia21@gmail.com; internet www.themiddleeastmagazine.com; f. 1974; political, economic and cultural; Editor-in-Chief PAT LANCASTER; circ. 22,141; monthly.

Middle East Contemporary Survey: Moshe Dayan Centre for Middle Eastern and African Studies, c/o Westview Press, 2465 Central Ave, Boulder, CO 80301, USA; tel. (303) 444-3541; fax (303) 449-3356; internet www.perseusbooksgroup.com/westview/home.jsp; 12 Hid's Copse Rd, Cumnor Hill, Oxford, OX2 9JJ, United Kingdom; tel. (1865) 865466; fax (1865) 862763; annual record of political developments, country surveys, special essays, maps, tables, notes, indices; Editors AMI AYALON, BRUCE MADDY-WEITZMAN.

Middle East Critique: Routledge, Taylor & Francis, 4 Park Sq., Milton Park, Abingdon, Oxon, OX14 4RN, United Kingdom; tel. (20) 7017-6000; fax (20) 7017-6336; e-mail tf.enquiries@tandf.co.uk; internet www.tandf.co.uk/journals/ccri; f. 1992 as Critique: Critical Middle Eastern Studies; renamed as above 2009; promotes an academic and critical examination of the history and contemporary political, social, economic and cultural affairs of Middle Eastern countries; Editor ERIC J. HOOGLUND; 3 a year.

Middle East Economic Digest (MEED): Greater London House, Hampstead Rd, London, NW1 7EJ, United Kingdom; tel. (20) 7728-5000; fax (20) 7728-4800; e-mail richard.thompson@meed.com; internet www.meed.com; f. 1957; weekly report on economic, business and political developments; Editorial Dir RICHARD THOMPSON; Editor COLIN FOREMAN.

Middle East Economic Survey: Middle East Petroleum and Economic Publications (Cyprus), POB 24940, 1355 Nicosia, Cyprus; tel. (22) 665431; fax (22) 671988; e-mail info@mees.com; internet www.mees.com; f. 1957 (in Beirut); weekly review and analysis of energy, finance and banking, and political developments; Publr SALEH S. JALLAD; Editor-in-Chief DAVID KNOTT.

The Middle East in London: London Middle East Institute, School of Oriental and African Studies—SOAS, University of London, Thornhaugh St, Russell Sq., London, WC1H 0XG, United Kingdom; tel. (20) 7898-4330; fax (20) 7898-4329; e-mail lmei@soas.ac.uk; internet www.lmei.soas.ac.uk; Co-ordinating Editor SARAH JOHNSON; monthly.

The Middle East Journal: Middle East Institute, 1761 N St, NW, Washington, DC 20036-2882, USA; tel. (202) 785-1141; fax (202) 331-8861; e-mail man-ed@mei.edu; internet www.mei.edu/middle-east-journal; journal devoted to the study of the modern-era Middle East; f. 1947; Editor MICHAEL COLLINS DUNN; Man. Editor JACOB PASSEL; quarterly; circ. 4,000.

Middle East and Africa Monitor: Business Monitor International, Senator House, 85 Queen Victoria St, London, EC4V 4AB, United Kingdom; tel. (20) 7248-0468; fax (20) 7248-0467; e-mail enquiries@meamonitor.com; internet www.meamonitor.com; f. 1984; monthly; economic and political brief, incl. macroeconomic forecasts, covering the Persian (Arabian) Gulf, East Mediterranean and North Africa; Editor (Middle East/East Med.) MARKUS SCHNEIDER; Editor (Middle East/Gulf) MATT CLANCY; Editor (North Africa) LISA LEWIN.

The Middle East Observer: 41 Sherif St, Cairo, Egypt; tel. (2) 3926919; fax (2) 3939732; e-mail journal@meobserver.org; internet www.meobserver.org; f. 1954; economics; Chief Editor HESHAM ABD AL-RAOUF; Publr AHMAD FODA; weekly.

Middle East Policy: Middle East Policy Council, 1730 M St, NW, Suite 512, Washington, DC 20036, USA; tel. (202) 296-6767; fax (202) 296-5791; e-mail info@mepc.org; internet www.mepc.org; policy analysis; Editor ANNE JOYCE; quarterly.

Middle East Quarterly: Middle East Forum, Suite 1050, 1500 Walnut St, Philadelphia, PA 19102, USA; tel. (215) 546-5406; fax (215) 546-5409; e-mail meq@meforum.org; internet www.mequarterly.org; f. 1994; politics, economics and culture; Publr DANIEL PIPES; Editor EFRAIM KARSH; quarterly.

Middle East Report: Middle East Research and Information Project, 1344 T St, NW 1, Washington, DC 20009, USA; tel. (202) 223-3677; fax (202) 223-3604; e-mail ctoensing@merip.org; internet www.merip.org; f. 1971; publishing, education and research; Editor CHRIS TOENSING; quarterly; circ. 7,500.

Middle East Review: World of Information, 11 Clarendon St, Cambridge CB1 1JU, United Kingdom; tel. and fax (1223) 312393; fax (1799) 524805; e-mail queries@worldinformation.com; internet www.worldinformation.com; f. 1974; political and economic analysis; Man. Editor TONY AXON.

Middle East Studies Association Bulletin: Dept of Anthropology, University of North Carolina at Charlotte, 9201 University City Blvd, Charlotte, NC 28223-0001, USA; tel. (704) 687-3203; fax (704) 687-3209; e-mail mesabulletin@uncc.edu; internet www.anthropology.uncc.edu; f. 1966; Editor GREGORY STARRETT; 2 a year.

Middle Eastern Literatures: Routledge, Taylor & Francis, 4 Park Sq., Milton Park, Abingdon, Oxon, OX14 4RN, United Kingdom; tel. (20) 7017-6000; fax (20) 7017-6336; e-mail tf.enquiries@tandf.co.uk; internet www.tandf.co.uk/journals/came; f. 1998; Editors Prof ROGER ALLEN, Prof MICHAEL BEARD, GEERT JAN VAN GELDER; 3 a year.

Middle Eastern Studies: Routledge, Taylor & Francis, 4 Park Sq., Milton Park, Abingdon, Oxon, OX14 4RN, United Kingdom; tel. (20) 7017-6000; fax (20) 7017-6336; e-mail tf.enquiries@tandf.co.uk; internet www.tandf.co.uk/journals/fmes; f. 1964; Editor SYLVIA KEDOURIE; 6 a year.

Miscellanea Arabica: Facoltà di Studi Orientali, Sapienza Università di Roma, via Principe Amedeo 182b, 00185 Rome, Italy; tel. (06) 49383289; fax (06) 49385915; e-mail arioliwebmaster@uniroma1.it; internet w3.uniroma1.it/studiorientali/pubblicazioni/publ.htm; f. 2007; publ. by Editore Nuova Cultura for La Sapienza Orientale; Arab studies incl. history, politics, literature and linguistics; Editor Prof. ANGELO ARIOLI.

The Muslim World: Macdonald Center, Hartford Seminary, 77 Sherman St, Hartford, CT 06105, USA; tel. (860) 509-9500; fax (860) 509-9509; e-mail info@hartsem.edu; internet www.hartsem.edu/macdonald/muslim-world-journal; f. 1911; Islamic studies in general and Muslim-Christian relations in past and present; Editor YAHYA MICHOT; quarterly.

The Muslim World League Journal: Press and Publications Dept, Muslim World League, POB 537, Mecca al-Mukarramah 21955, Saudi Arabia; tel. (2) 560-0919; fax (2) 560-1319; e-mail info@themwl.org; internet www.themwl.org; Chief Editor HAMID HASSAN AL-RADDADI; monthly.

Near East Report: The American Israel Public Affairs Committee, 251 H St, NW, Washington, DC 20001, USA; tel. (202) 639-5200; fax (202) 638-6349; e-mail ner@aipac.org; internet www.aipac.org/ner; f. 1957; analyses US policy in the Middle East; Editor-in-Chief Dr RAPHAEL DANZIGER; bi-weekly (except when Congress is out of session); circ. 55,000.

Oil & Gas Journal: 1455 West Loop South, Suite 400, Houston, TX 77027, USA; tel. (713) 621-9720; fax (713) 623-6285; e-mail bobt@ogjonline.com; internet www.ogj.com; f. 1902; publ. by PennWell Corpn; petroleum industry and business weekly; Editor BOB TIPPEE; circ. 106,000.

Oriente Moderno: Istituto per l'Oriente C. A. Nallino, via A. Caroncini 19, 00197 Rome, Italy; tel. (06) 8084106; fax (06) 8079395; e-mail ipocan@ipocan.it; internet www.ipocan.it; f. 1921; articles, book reviews; Pres. Prof. CLAUDIO LO JACONO.

Palestine Affairs (Shu'un Filastiniya): Ramallah, West Bank, Palestinian Territories; f. 1971; Arabic; journal of the Palestinian Research Centre; Editor BILAL EL-HASSAN; monthly.

Palestine-Israel: Middle East Publications, POB 19839, Jerusalem 91197, Israel; tel. (2) 6282159; fax (2) 6273388; e-mail pij@pij.org; internet www.pij.org; f. 1994; independent journal publ. as a joint venture between Israelis and Palestinians; promotes dialogue between the two sides and offers critical analysis of regional issues; Editors ZIAD ABU ZAYYAD, HILLEL SCHENKER; quarterly.

Persica: Dutch-Iranian Society, University of Leiden, Dept of Persian Studies, Witte Singel 24, POB 9515, 2300 RA Leiden, Netherlands; e-mail Persica@Let.Leidenuniv.nl; internet poj .peeters-leuven.be/content.php?journal_code=PERS&url=journal; f. 1963; publ. by Peeters; Editors Dr A. A. SEYED-GOHRAB, G. R. VAN DER BERG; annually.

Petroleum Economist: Nestor House, Playhouse Yard, London, EC4V 5EX, United Kingdom; tel. (20) 7779-8800; fax (20) 7779-8899; e-mail editorial@petroleum-economist.com; internet www .petroleum-economist.com; f. 1934; Editor DEREK BROWER; Exec. Editor ANTHEA PITT; monthly; circ. 5,500.

Pour la Palestine: Association France Palestine Solidarité, 21 rue Voltaire, 75011 Paris, France; tel. 1-43-72-15-79; fax 1-43-72-07-25; e-mail afps@france-palestine.org; internet www.france-palestine .org; quarterly.

Revue d'assyriologie et d'archéologie orientale: c/o Dominique Charpin, 14 rue des Sources, 92160 Antony, France; tel. 1-42-37-27-97; fax 1-48-87-82-58; e-mail charpin@msh-paris.fr; internet www.puf.com; f. 1884; Dir DOMINIQUE CHARPIN; 2 a year.

Revue des études islamiques: Librairie Orientaliste Paul Geuthner SA, 16 rue de la Grande Chaumière, 75006 Paris, France; tel. 1-43-29-75-64; fax 1-46-34-71-30; e-mail geuthner@geuthner.com; internet www.geuthner.com; f. 1927.

Rivista degli Studi Orientali: Dipartimento di Studi Orientali, Facoltà di Lettere, Università Degli Studi, 'La Sapienza', P. le Aldo Moro 5, 00185 Rome, Italy; tel. (06) 49913802; fax (06) 4451209; internet w3.uniroma1.it/dso/?m=Pubblicazioni; publ. by Istituti Editoriali e Poligrafici Internazionali; quarterly.

Rocznik Orientalistyczny: Instytut Orientalistyczny, Uniwersytet Warszawski, Krakowskie Przedmieście 26/28, 00-927 Warszawa, Poland; tel. (22) 5520343; e-mail rorient@pan.pl; internet www .kno.pan.pl; f. 1915; Editor-in-Chief MAREK M. DZIEKAN; 2 a year.

Royal Asiatic Society of Great Britain and Ireland Journal: 14 Stephenson Way, London, NW1 2HD, United Kingdom; tel. (20) 7388-4539; fax (20) 7391-9429; e-mail info@royalasiaticsociety.org; internet www.royalasiaticsociety.org; f. 1823; covers all aspects of Oriental research; Pres. PETER ROBB; Hon. Editor Dr SARAH ANSARI; Exec. Editor CHARLOTTE DE BLOIS; 4 a year.

Saudi Aramco World: Aramco Services Co, 9009 West Loop South, Houston, TX 77096, USA; tel. (713) 432-4000; fax (713) 432-5536; e-mail SAWorld@aramcoservices.com; internet www .saudiaramcoworld.com; f. 1949; non-political information—culture, history, natural history, economics, etc.—of the Middle East; Editor ROBERT ARNDT; Man. Editor DICK DOUGHTY; bi-monthly.

Studia Arabistyczne i Islamistyczne: Katedra Arabistyki i Islamistyki, Instytut Orientalistyczny, Uniwersytet Warszawski, Krakowskie Przedmieście 26/28, 00-927 Warszawa, Poland; tel. (022) 8263683; fax (022) 5524053; e-mail janusz.danecki@uw.edu.pl; internet www.orient.uw.edu.pl; f. 1993; Editor-in-Chief JANUSZ DANECKI; annually.

Studia Islamica: G. P. Maisonneuve et Larose, 15 rue Victor-Cousin, 75005 Paris, France; tel. 1-44-41-49-30; fax 1-43-25-77-41; e-mail contact@studiaislamica.com; internet www.studiaislamica.com; f. 1953; Editors A. L. UDOVITCH, H. TOUATI; 2 a year.

Studia Orientalia: Finnish Oriental Society, c/o Dept of World Cultures, POB 59, 00014 University of Helsinki; tel. (9) 19122224; fax (9) 19122094; e-mail saana.svard@helsinki.fi; internet www .suomenitamainenseura.org; Editor LOTTA AUNIO.

Sumer: State Board of Antiquities and Heritage, Karkh, Salihiya, Jamal Abd al-Nasr St, Baghdad, Iraq; tel. 537-6121; f. 1945; archaeological and historical; Chair., Editorial Bd Dr M. SAID; annually.

Turcica: Publ. by Université Marc Bloch, Strasbourg, and Association pour le développement des études turques, L'Ecole des Hautes Etudes en Sciences Sociale, 54 blvd Raspail, 75006 Paris, France; tel. 1-49-54-23-01; fax 1-49-54-26-72; e-mail etudes-turques@ehess.fr; internet chdt.ehess.fr; f. 1969; all aspects of Turkish and Turkic culture; Editors PAUL DUMONT, Prof. GILLES VEINSTEIN; annually.

Turkish Studies: Routledge, Taylor & Francis, 4 Park Sq., Milton Park, Abingdon, Oxon, OX14 4RN, United Kingdom; tel. (20) 7017-6000; fax (20) 7017-6336; e-mail tf.enquiries@tandf.co.uk; internet www.tandf.co.uk/journals/ftur; f. 2000; Turkish history, politics, government, international relations, foreign policy; economic, religious, social, and all other issues; Editor BARRY RUBIN; quarterly.

Turkologischer Anzeiger (Turkology Annual): Institut für Orientalistik der Universität Wien, Spitalgasse 2, Hof 4, 1090 Vienna, Austria; tel. (1) 427-74-34-01; fax (1) 427-79-434; e-mail ingeborg .brunner@univie ac.at; internet orientalistik.univie.ac.at/ publikationen/turkologischer-anzeiger; Editors GYÖRGY HAZAI, BARBARA KELLNER-HEINKELE; annually.

Vostok/Oriens (The East): Russian Academy of Sciences, 107031 Moscow, ul. Rozhdestvenka 12, Russia; tel. (495) 625-51-46; fax (495) 938-18-44; e-mail vostok.o@yandex.ru; internet www.vostokoriens .ru; f. 1955; fmrly Sovetskoye Vostokovedeniye (Soviet Oriental Studies); publ. by the History and Contemporaneity Asian-African Society, the Institute of Oriental Studies and Institute of Africa of the Russian Academy of Sciences; in Russian, with English summaries; Editor-in-Chief Dr VITALII V. NAUMKIN; 6 a year.

The Washington Report on Middle East Affairs: American Educational Trust, POB 53062, Washington, DC 20009, USA; tel. (202) 939-6050; fax (202) 265-4574; e-mail info@wrmea.org; internet www .wrmea.org; f. 1982; Exec. Editor RICHARD H. CURTISS; Man. Editor JANET MCMAHON; 9 a year.

Die Welt des Islams (International Journal for the Study of Modern Islam): Brill Academic Publishers, POB 9000, 2300 PA, Leiden, Netherlands; tel (71) 5353500; fax (71) 5317532; internet www .brill.nl; Seminar für Orientalistik der Ruhr-Universität Bochum, 44780 Bochum, Germany; fax (234) 3214671; e-mail stefan .reichmuth@ruhr-uni-bochum.de; f. 1951; contains articles in German, English and French on the contemporary Muslim world with special reference to history, society and culture; Editor STEFAN REICHMUTH (University of Bochum).

Wiener Zeitschrift für die Kunde des Morgenlandes: Institut für Orientalistik der Universität Wien, Spitalgasse 2, Hof 4, 1090 Vienna, Austria; tel. (1) 427-74-34-31; fax (1) 427-79-434; e-mail wzkmredaktion.orientalistik@univie.ac.at; internet orientalistik .univie.ac.at; Editor CLAUDIA RÖMER; annually.

Zeitschrift der Deutschen Morgenländischen Gesellschaft: Seminar für Sinologie, Humboldt University, Unter den Linden 6, 10099 Berlin, Germany; tel. (30) 20936611; e-mail florian.c.reiter@rz .hu-berlin.de; internet www.dmg-web.de; f. 1847; covers the history, languages and literature of the Orient; Editor Prof. Dr FLORIAN C. REITER; 2 a year.

INDEX OF REGIONAL ORGANIZATIONS

(Main reference only)

G

H

I

J

K

L

M

W

W